Early Childhood Education

AN ERIC BIBLIOGRAPHY

ERIC Clearinghouse on Early Childhood Education.

Early Childhood Education

AN ERIC BIBLIOGRAPHY

Foreword
by
Lilian G. Katz, Ph.D.
Director, ERIC Clearinghouse on Early Childhood Education
University of Illinois

Macmillan Information

New York 1973

Library of Congress Catalog Card Number 72-82742

International Standard Book Number 0-02-468500-3

Manufactured in the United States of America

Macmillan Information
866 Third Avenue
New York, N.Y. 10022

CONTENTS

Foreword	vii
Organization	xv
How to Order ERIC Documents	xvii
ERIC Documents	1
ERIC Journal Articles	233
Subject Index	321
Author Index	501

FOREWORD

EARLY CHILDHOOD EDUCATION: TOWARD A DEFINITION

Lilian G. Katz, Ph.D.
Director, ERIC Clearinghouse on
Early Childhood Education
University of Illinois

The bibliography which follows this foreword gives readers access to all the documents processed by the ERIC Clearinghouse on Early Childhood Education at the University of Illinois. ERIC/ECE, as we call it, is one of 18 clearinghouses in the national ERIC network, each focused on collecting, storing and disseminating information in its own field. Organizing and analyzing the information gathered at ERIC/ECE has raised some interesting questions concerning the scope and definition of what is encompassed by the term *early childhood education.* In the following discussion, a tentative definition of the discipline of early childhood education is presented, and some suggestions of how it can be used are offered.

Definition of Early Childhood Education

It is common to speak of early education as an interdisciplinary field encompassing the interests of specialists in developmental psychology, pediatrics, social work, anthropology, elementary education, nutrition and other fields. Specialists from these many fields have strong scientific interests in the young child. While young children have been the subjects of disciplined inquiry for more than a half century, their *education* has not. A distinct disciplinary approach to their education has been neglected in favor of problem-oriented investigations designed to discover the most powerful way to offset the ill effects of poverty. For the purposes of discussion, it is proposed that the referent for the term *early childhood education* be stated as follows:

> Group settings which are deliberately intended to effect developmental changes in children in the age range from birth up to the age of entering the first grade.

With this definition, education rather than child development or child rearing becomes the point of entry into the field, thus giving early childhood education disciplinary status in its own right. From this definition, the parameters of the field can be derived, and can then provide a basis for the development of the branch of knowledge called *early childhood education.*

Reprinted with permission from *Young Children,* Vol. XXVI, No. 2, December 1970, under the title "Early Childhood Education as a Discipline." Copyright © 1970, National Association for the Education of Young Children, 1834 Connecticut Ave., N.W., Washington, D.C. 20009.

Before we explore the parameters of the field, some comments on the definition are in order. First, the cutoff point at the age of entrance into the first grade seems to draw an undesirable division between preschool and primary education, a division that the profession has been striving to reduce. However, the definition proposed here can be used for synthesis of research related to the primary grades. The complex and crucial issues surrounding the problem of continuity of experience, learning and education, into the primary grades cannot be taken up here. Thorough analysis and discussion of those issues is greatly needed. A second point is that there are a number of projects and programs in early childhood education which are not in fact "group settings," but which properly fall into our domain. Included here are programs in which mothers in their homes are given assistance with the stimulation of their infants' learning and development.

Parameters of Early Childhood Education

The term *parameter* is used broadly here to indicate a superordinate category of variables which applies to *all* early educational settings, and which typically remains constant during a given study or a given event which we might call an *early childhood program.* That is to say, a parameter describes a class of phenomena in which every early childhood education program must have an entry, even though the entries of different programs vary. For example, every program must have clients (i.e., children), but the children of different programs may vary in age or in socioeconomic status; every program must have a physical location, but these locations may vary from quonset huts in a downtown area to elegant university laboratory settings in a comparatively rural setting.

The set of parameters presented here is suggested by two major research projects reported during the 1960s. John Pierce-Jones and his associates at the University of Texas conducted a large study of Project Head Start Centers in Texas in 1965 (Pierce-Jones, 1966, p. 6). The Texas group identified teacher and child antecedent variables which interacted, producing a variety of classroom "inputs," which in turn resulted in differential changes in the Head Start children. In 1967, Prescott and Jones (1967) reported a study of group day care in the Los Angeles area using a similar but more comprehensive framework. Prescott and Jones studied all of the same variables the Pierce-Jones group had examined, such as characteristics of children, teachers, classroom "input," and in addition examined variables of physical space, size of center, types of sponsorship, and other administrative factors.

The present state of the art does not permit us to look at the parameters of early childhood education, and ascertain the extent to which they are either independent of, or compounded with each other. The following descriptive outlines of the parameters are not intended to be exhaustive, but merely to suggest some of the variables within each parameter which have been or could be used to form guidelines for review and future research.

Parameter Descriptions

A. *Characteristics of clients.* Within this parameter are included variable characteristics of both the children and parents served by any given early childhood program. Examples of these variables are age, socioeconomic background and status, ethnicity, sex, physical and mental health, mother tongue, second language, urban/rural background, the goal orientation of parents, father absence, age and number of siblings, and other child rearing variables.

B. *Characteristics of teachers and other assisting adults.* This parameter includes variations in teacher characteristics such as teacher behavior, teacher role prescriptions, teacher performance, teaching styles, teacher attributes such as age, experience, sex, attitudes and beliefs, teacher self-concept, teachers' goals, ethnicity, training, satisfaction; teacher recruitment, occupational status, relationship with assistants, and credentialing patterns.

C. *Program organization.* Included in this parameter are such variables as the variety and quantity of stimulation in a program, the temporal organization of classroom activities, the lessons "taught" and not "taught," the materials available, the control of activity selection, the inclusion of rest time, storyreading, formal group instruction organized by ability groups, autotelic materials, etc. This group of variables is commonly referred to as the *curriculum.*

D. *Philosophical orientation and historical factors.* This parameter refers to the school of thought adhered to in any given early childhood program representing a range of values, goals and objectives; it includes also the learning theory "used." The philosophical orientation may be explicit or implicit, or it may vary on these two levels. Examples of programs with diverse philosophical orientation are Montessori Schools, and models such as Bank Street, the Behavior Analysis program, or the British Infant School. Historical factors may include remote or immediate antecedents of contemporary program operation.

E. *Parent power.* This parameter refers to variations in the extent to which parents participate in central or peripheral decision-making concerning the operation of early childhood education programs for their children. There are, for instance, parent cooperatives, where parents participate fully in program operations, and there are also university laboratory schools where parent participation and decision-making is minimal or peripheral. There are Head Start programs where parents select curriculum and staff, Head Start programs where parents are only consulted, and others where they are passive recipients of services. The extent to which parents pay for services rendered for a preschool program also represents a variation in their power.

F. *Administrative factors and sponsorship.* This parameter refers to variables associated with program administration such as size of program, distribution of authority, division of labor (maintenance, personnel, curriculum, etc.), staff morale, staff leadership, staff coordination, and staff cooperation versus staff friction. Also included in this parameter are the variety of public and private sponsoring agencies such as public school systems, community centers, churches, Office of Child Development, university laboratory schools, mental health departments, franchise entrepreneurs, parent cooperatives, and one-shot demonstration projects.

G. *Length of program.* Variables within this parameter include the length of the school day, and the number of school days. Examples are all-day daily care; two and one-half hours per day, morning or afternoon sessions; two, three, or four days per week and eight-week Head Start programs.

H. *Physical plant and climate.* This parameter includes variables in the amount of space, the type of space, outdoor/indoor facilities and their accessibility, neighborhood location, the number of classrooms per site, and regional climate (Head Start in Alaska as compared to Head Start in Hawaii).

A Matrix for Early Childhood Education

Figure 1 is a schematic representation showing how a matrix can be generated from the parameters of early childhood education proposed above. First, let us look in turn at each cell falling into the diagonal of the matrix and marked A, B, C, etc. In reviewing research on early childhood education each of these diagonal cells requires comprehensive analysis of all of the knowledge within itself. The within-parameter knowledge indicated by the diagonal cells focuses on those studies in which the cell's variables constitute both the dependent and independent variables. For example, in cell A, comprehensive analysis is needed of all of the literature related to child development and child rearing. Such a complete analysis would represent an encyclopedia of the developmental literature with special emphasis, of course, on the young child. In the cell marked B, where Parameter B intersects with itself, we need a comprehensive analysis of all of the knowledge related to these within-parameter variables, namely to teachers. The use of the matrix for analyzing problems of early childhood education and for reviewing research can be illustrated by looking at Parameter B (Characteristics of teachers) and moving down the column (we will speak of horizontal *rows* and vertical *columns*). Beginning with the first cell in Column B (marked A → B), it can be seen that one set of questions concerns the effect of A variables on B variables. Examples of the type of question which might be asked in this cell are: What characteristics of children influence the teacher behavior in what ways? What effect does the age range of the children in a given class have on the teacher's behavior? If a teacher has 15 or 20 three-year-olds in her class, then she is likely to be working with a smaller range of social and intellectual maturity than if the age range were from three to five years old. How does this age range composition affect the teacher's definition of her role? Or we could ask: What are the effects of the sex distribution of the class membership upon the teacher? Compare, for example, a class consisting of two-thirds boys with one consisting of two-thirds girls, or with classes of one sex only.

Figure 1: Schematic Representation of Parameters of Early Education

Parameters	A. Clients	B. Teachers	C. Program	D. Philosophy	E. Parents	F. Administration	G. Length	H. Physical
A. Characteristics of clients (children and parents)	A	A → B						
B. Characteristics of teachers and other assisting adults	B → A	B	B → C					
C. Program organization (curriculum)		C → B	C					
D. Philosophical orientation and historical factors		D → B		D				
E. Parent power		E → B			E			
F. Administrative factors and sponsorship		F → B				F		
G. Length of program		G → B					G	
H. Physical plant and climate		H → B						H

It is important to note, at this point, that questions concerning "effects" reflect an idealized conception of research on teaching. In general, research findings suggest relationships between co-occurring events. For example, returning to the effects of child variables on teachers (A → B), Dorothy Haupt reported (1966) differences between boys and girls in the content of the questions they asked their nursery school teachers. Haupt also found differences in the way teachers responded to the questions of boys and girls. These findings represent co-occurring events. It is difficult at our present stage of knowledge to separate cause from effect.

As already indicated, the cell marked B in Column B reflects the need for within-parameter knowledge and reviews. Moving down to the cell where Row C intersects with Column B (C → B), we can ask questions concerning the effects of program organization variables upon teachers, although again these are more likely to be co-occurring events than causes and effects. For example, let us suppose that a program is organized in such a way that children are obliged to attend to a group storyreading activity and that no alternative behavior is permitted during this activity. One might ask: How does such a programmatic constraint affect teachers? Or, which teachers are affected or troubled by such a program variable? Let us suppose, for example, that a particular curriculum model specifies that children should have water play regularly. Undoubtedly some teachers welcome this activity, and others do not. In a Behavior

Modification approach to preschool programs, teachers are expected to ignore children when they cry. How does this program specification affect teachers? We may be wise to ask which programs are congenial to which kind of teachers, and how we can facilitate matching program design with variation among teachers.

In Row D (D → B), information is sought pertaining to the relationships between and effects of philosophies (values, goals, and objectives, etc.) upon teacher performance and attitudes. Let us take for example the observation reported by Sears and Dowley (1963, p. 857) that there are teachers who have "child-centered *theory* and authoritarian practice." One could ask, at least theoretically: Can the reverse be true? That is, it may be that some teachers who describe themselves and their classrooms as traditional are really flexible and warm. Perhaps one of the most important questions to be answered in early childhood education is: What are the elements which account for the gap between rhetoric and performance? It is commonly assumed, for example, that when teachers can embrace the "philosophy" of the British Infant School, their classrooms will become open. However, it may be that embracing the philosophy is a necessary step but an insufficient one. Because of the way the British Infant School curriculum is organized, a teacher probably must also have the capacity for fluency and for flexibility in generating ideas about extending and elaborating children's spontaneously expressed interests.

Historical factors, namely a program's past experiences, may be causally related to teacher variables. Let us suppose, for example, that a Head Start program has had a history of threats of nonrefunding. In what ways might such a history affect teachers' commitment or their optimism about the future and their work?

In Row E (E → B), questions can be asked about the relationships between variables of parent power and teacher variables. For example, when parents pay high fees for an early childhood program, are teachers likely to experience pressure to interact with children in ways that they would otherwise not choose? How do teachers feel about being hired (or fired) by parents? One of the fundamental tenets of Head Start is that parents be involved in every part of Head Start operation. Parent involvement in Head Start includes making policy decisions that affect their children's growth and learning and participating in the development of the program (Office of Economic Opportunity, 1969). Among the questions raised here is: To what extent is there consensus between parents and teachers in Head Start on how their programs should be organized and implemented? And how are teachers affected by this high level of parent power?

In Row F (F → B), we pose questions concerning administrative factors and their impact or relationship to variables in Parameter B. For instance, Alexanian (1967, p. 1) reported that "in some instances, the administrative problems of Head Start centers were so overwhelming that the very survival of the program was the all-important focus." Almost anyone with Head Start experience can verify the observation that administrative factors can have a consuming effect on the energy of teachers and other staff members. Questions about the uncertainties associated with year-to-year funding belong in this cell. Similarly, questions concerning the way equipment and supplies are secured belong here.

It has also been observed in some Head Start programs that giving equal pay to teachers with widely different training and experience contributes to staff friction and unrest. It would be interesting to know to what extent administrative factors contribute to the total impact of a preschool program on children's development.

In Row G (G → B), questions concerning the relationship between the length of the program and teacher variables can be posed. One can ask, at least theoretically, whether teaching a whole day is characterized by twice as much of whatever characterizes a half-day? Obviously factors like fatigue should be considered. The management of naptimes in all-day programs frequently induces stresses and strains in teachers as well as children. In an interesting study comparing long- vs. short-day preschool programs, Handler (1970) proposed several important differences between the long- and short-day relating to teachers. For example, she stated that children are more dependent upon teachers in long- than in short-day schools (p. 38) and the teachers are more emotionally involved with children in the long- than in the short-day schools (p. 38). In what other ways do these length-of-day variables affect teachers?

In Row H, physical plant and climate (H → B), we pose questions concerning the relationship between the physical plant variables and the teacher variables. For example, in some physical facilities children can move freely from indoors to outdoors without encountering potential physical danger. In other places, all children must be visible and accounted for because the plant borders on a major highway, or because there are stairways or long corridors to consider. Similarly, in some geographical climates weather is congenial for outdoor activity only half of the school year—the proverbial rainy days affect the teachers as well as children.

The intersections between Column B variables, characteristics of teachers, and each of the parameters in the rows have been examined, and some questions have been raised concerning what effect the row variables have on column variables, namely on teachers and teaching. The use of the matrix can also be illustrated by taking Parameter B in the row (characteristics of teachers and other teaching adults), and examining the intersection of the row with each of the columns. Beginning with Row B, and going to the first column (B → A), questions concerning the effect of given teacher characteristics on child variables can be raised. Questions like the effect of the teacher's ethnic group on children's self-concepts, or the impact of teacher praise on children's motivation for learning, are examples of types of questions which belong in the cell marked B → A.

At the intersection of Row B with Column C (B → C), questions can be raised concerning the "effects" of teacher variables on program organization. For example, the organization of the Montessori classroom requires teachers to be fairly unobtrusive. One might ask: What personal attributes of teachers make the Montessori requirement for unobtrusiveness a more or less congenial one?

Continuing across the rows, questions concerning the relationships between characteristics of teachers and philosophy, parent power, administrative factors, length of program, physical plant and climate variables can be raised and the relevant research summarized. In addition to the information available or needed for each of these cells, a wide range of combinations of cells can be studied. For example, an important question for early childhood education is: What is the role of charismatic leaders (historically and contemporaneously) in program development? Or to what extent are effective programs, even though of widely different types, associated with leader evangelism? These questions fall into the intersection of cells B and C and D and F. Similarly, other groups of cells can be taken for inspection.

Summary

In summary, the parameters of early childhood education have been proposed and outlined above. Some ways in which the matrix generated from these parameters can be used have been illustrated. The major purpose of setting out the matrix is to emphasize that early childhood education is a complex domain which deserves extensive analysis which takes the complexities into full account. A major portion of the activity in early childhood education today is focused on either characteristics of clients (parameter A) or program organization (parameter C). (See also Scott et al., 1969.) There appears to be an assumption that it is possible to transport a carefully derived and "packaged" early childhood education program from one context to another, and to expect positive outcomes. The point here is not to deny the centrality of questions in these two parameters, but rather to emphasize that knowledge of the complex events in any given context, the gap between our rhetoric and our practice, and knowledge of the relative influence of all of the other parameters may enhance our power to predict and replicate the findings of current research and development, and deepen our understanding of the complex issues in the discipline of early childhood education.

References

Alexanian, Sandra. *Teacher Seminar.* Head Start Evaluation and Research Center, Office of Economic Opportunity. Available as ED 022567 from ERIC Document Reproduction Service. 1967.

Handler, Ellen O. *The professional self-image and the attributes of a profession: An exploratory study of the preschool teacher.* Unpublished paper. Urbana: University of Illinois, 1970a.

——*Preschools and their graduates.* Unpublished paper. Urbana: University of Illinois. Available as PS 003800 from ERIC/ECE. 1970b.

Haupt, Dorothy. *Children's questions: Teacher response.* Unpublished doctoral dissertation. Detroit: Wayne State University, 1966.

Office of Economic Opportunity. *Parent involvement: A Workbook of Training Tips for Head Start Staff* (Rainbow Series Packet No. 10A) Washington, D.C. 1969.

Pierce-Jones, John. *Outcomes of Individual and Programmatic Variations Among Project Head Start Centers. Final Report, Office of Economic Opportunity.* Austin: University of Texas. Available as ED 014325 from ERIC Document Reproduction Service, 1966.

Prescott, E. & Jones, E. *Group Day Care as a Child Rearing Environment: An Observation Study of Day Care Programs.* Pasadena: Pacific Oaks College. Available as ED 024453 from ERIC Document Reproduction Service, 1967.

Scott, M., Eklund, S.J. & Miller, J.O. *Analysis of Early Childhood Education Research and Development.* National Laboratory on Early Childhood Education, 1969.

Sears, Pauline S. & Dowley, Edith M. Research on teaching in the nursery school. In Gage, N.L. (ed.), *Handbook on Research on Teaching.* Chicago: Rand McNally, 1968, pp. 814-864.

ORGANIZATION

COVERAGE

Early Childhood Education, an ERIC Bibliography includes only those acquisitions of the ERIC Clearinghouse on Early Childhood Education at the University of Illinois. The documents cited were announced in *Research in Education* from November 1966 through December 1971. Journal articles indexed in *Current Index to Journals in Education* during 1969 through 1972 are also included. All material is organized into four sections: ERIC Documents, ERIC Journal Articles, Subject Index, and an Author Index.

ERIC DOCUMENTS

The sample entry below illustrates the information regarding each document included in this bibliography. Entries are arranged in ED accession number sequence, but these numbers are not consecutive. Most of the documents listed are available in either microfiche (MF) or hard copy (HC) form. For ordering information, see the section on **HOW TO ORDER ERIC DOCUMENTS.**

ED022561 PS001254
HEAD START EVALUATION AND RESEARCH CENTER, BOSTON UNIVERSITY. REPORT C-I, PERCEPTION OF EMOTION AMONG CHILDREN: RACE AND SEX DIFFERENCES. GITTER, A. GEORGE, 67 14P.
EDRS PRICE MF-$0.65 HC-$3.29

PERCEPTION OF EMOTION IS ONE EXAMPLE OF NONVERBAL COMMUNICATION AND IS THE SUBJECT OF THIS STUDY OF THE ACCURACY OF PERCEPTION OF VARIOUS EMOTIONS. SEVEN EMOTIONS WERE CHOSEN FOR THIS INVESTIGATION. EACH EMOTION WAS ACTED OUT BY ACTORS,.WHOSE PERFORMANCE WAS FILMED. FROM THE FILMS, STILLS WERE SELECTED WHICH BEST REPRESENTED THE EMOTION BEING EXPRESSED. THE PURPOSE OF THE STUDY WAS TO DETERMINE THE EFFECTS OF RACE AND SEX ON PERCEPTION OF EMOTION. THEREFORE, BOTH EXPRESSORS AND PERCEIVERS WERE DIVIDED BETWEEN NEGRO AND WHITE, MALE AND FEMALE. ALTHOUGH THE TEST WAS DESIGNED FOR CHILDREN, THE PERCEIVERS FOR THIS STUDY WERE 80 UNDERGRADUATE STUDENTS. EACH SUBJECT VIEWED 21 PHOTOGRAPHS OF THREE EXPRESSORS AND CHOSE FROM A LIST THE EMOTION HE THOUGHT THE EXPRESSOR WAS DEMONSTRATING. THE RESULTS INDICATED THAT (1) OVERALL ACCURACY OF PERCEPTION OF EMOTIONS WAS NOT INFLUENCED BY SEX OR RACE OF THE PERCIEVER OR SEX OF THE EXPRESSOR; (2) RACE OF EXPRESSOR DID AFFECT THE ACCURACY OF PERCEPTION OF EMOTION, WHITE EXPRESSORS LEADING TO GREATER ACCURACY OF PERCEPTION; AND (3) SOME PATTERNS OF ERRONEOUSLY PERCEIVED EMOTIONS WERE RELATED TO SEX OF EXPRESSOR AND RACE OF PERCEIVER. (WD)

ERIC JOURNAL ARTICLES

The complete journal citation is given for each entry. An annotation reflecting the content of the article is given when available.

EJ 017 903 PS 500 343
STAGES OF THE DREAM CONCEPT AMONG HASIDIC CHILDREN KAHANA, BOAZ, *J GENET PSYCHOL*, V116 N1, PP3-9, 70 MAR

ADMINISTERING OF KOHLBERG'S ADAPTATION OF PINARD AND LAURENDEAU'S DREAM INTERVIEW TO 24 HASIDIC BOYS AGED 4 TO 16

YIELDED DATA THAT FAILED TO SUPPORT THE INVARIANCE OF THE PROCESS OF EMERGING COGNITIVE STRUCTURES IN THE DEVELOPMENT OF THE DREAM CONCEPT AND UNDERSCORED THE IMPORTANCE OF CULTURAL INFLUENCES IN AFFECTING THE SEQUENCE OF COGNITIVE DEVELOPMENT. (DR)

Reprints of ERIC journal articles are available from the journal publishers only. For information regarding specific journals, contact Macmillan Information.

SUBJECT INDEX

References to both ED accession numbers and EJ accession numbers are given in the subject index. A title and ED number are included for each document listed under a subject heading. The ED number refers to a main entry in the ERIC Documents section where complete bibliographic information, price, and abstract can be found.

Listings in the subject index for ERIC journal articles include the title of the article and EJ number. The EJ number refers to a main entry in the ERIC Journal Articles section where complete bibliographic data as well as all subject headings used to describe the article can be found.

EMOTIONAL EXPERIENCE

HEAD START EVALUATION AND RESEARCH CENTER, BOSTON UNIVERSITY. REPORT C-I, PERCEPTION OF EMOTION AMONG CHILDREN: RACE AND SEX DIFFERENCES. ED022561
ON SEPARATION AND SCHOOL ENTRANCE EJ 017 902
WHEN WORDS FAIL...DANCE EJ 019 507
DEVELOPMENTAL CHARACTERISTICS OF EMOTIONAL EXPERIENCE EJ 043 860
AN EXPERIENCE WITH FEAR IN THE LIVES OF CHILDREN EJ 045 389
THE DEVELOPMENT OF THE LANGUAGE OF EMOTIONS: I. THEORETICAL AND METHODOLOGICAL INTRODUCTION EJ 061 059
THE DEVELOPMENT OF THE LANGUAGE OF EMOTIONS: II. INTENTIONALITY IN THE EXPERIENCE OF AFFECT EJ 061 064
THE DEVELOPMENT OF THE LANGUAGE OF EMOTIONS: III. TYPE OF ANXIETY IN THE EXPERIENCE OF AFFECT EJ 061 065

AUTHOR INDEX

References to both ED accession numbers and EJ accession numbers are included in the Author Index. These numbers refer to the appropriate main entry section where complete information relating to the entry can be found.

GITTER, A. G.

COLOR AND PHYSIOGNOMY AS VARIABLES IN RACIAL MISIDENTIFICATION AMONG CHILDREN. ED034584

HOW TO ORDER
ERIC DOCUMENT REPRODUCTIONS

The full text of documents cited in *Early Childhood Education*, except as noted, can be obtained from the ERIC Document Reproduction Service (EDRS). Copies of ERIC Documents are available in two forms:

- Microfiche (MF) – 4″ X 6″ sheet of microfilm on which up to 70 pages of text are reproduced
- Hard Copy (HC) – reproduction of the document on paper

Individual documents may be ordered at 65 cents per title for fiche and $3.29 for each 100 page increment (101-200 pages, $6.58; 201-300 pages, $9.87; etc.) for orders of hard copy titles. Orders must include the accession number (ED number), type of reproduction (MF or HC), and the number of copies desired. Payment must accompany orders under $10.00.

All prices quoted above include shipment by Book or Library Rate postage. The difference between that rate and First Class or Foreign postage (outside the continental United States) will be billed at cost. There is no handling charge for any order.

Orders for ERIC Documents should be sent to:

ERIC Document Reproduction Service
Post Office Drawer O
Bethesda, Maryland 20014

ERIC DOCUMENTS

ED013116 PS000020
THE CHILDREN'S CENTER--A MICROCOSMIC HEALTH, EDUCATION, AND WELFARE UNIT. PROGRESS REPORT. CALDWELL, BETTYE M.; RICHMOND, JULIUS B., 01MAR67 46P.
EDRS PRICE MF-$0.65 HC-$3.29

FOUNDED TWO YEARS AGO AS A RESEARCH AND DEMONSTRATION DAY CARE CENTER FOR VERY YOUNG CHILDREN, THE CHILDREN'S CENTER HAS UNDERGONE CHANGES, (1) FROM INVOLVING 25 CHILDREN AGED SIX MONTHS TO THREE YEARS OF AGE TO INVOLVING 85 CHILDREN AGED SIX MONTHS TO FIVE YEARS OF AGE, (2) FROM INCLUDING ONLY LOW INCOME HOMES IN WHICH THE MOTHER WORKS, TO INCLUDING MIDDLE-CLASS HOMES IN WHICH THE MOTHER DOES NOT WORK, (3) FROM FULL DAY CARE TO ALLOWING HALF-DAY ATTENDANCE. THE CENTER IS ORGANIZED AROUND THREE ON-GOING PROGRAMS. THE HEALTH PROGRAM HAS TWO PARTS (1) A LONGITUDINAL STUDY WITH EMPHASIS ON THE PROMOTION OF THE IDEAL WELL-CHILD CARE PROGRAM AND (2) A NURSERY SCHOOL HEALTH PROGRAM WITH EMPHASIS ON FAMILY EDUCATIONAL ACTIVITIES. THE EDUCATION PROGRAM IS INVOLVED WITH DEVELOPING A LOGICAL AND SYSTEMATIC INSTRUCTIONAL PROGRAM FOR CHILDREN WITHIN THE CENTER'S AGE RANGE--EVEN AS YOUNG AS SIX MONTHS. THE WELFARE PROGRAM PROVIDES INDIVIDUALIZED SERVICES TO THE FAMILIES OF THE CHILDREN'S CENTER, WITH HOME VISITS, PERSONAL INTERVIEWS, AND GROUP PARENT ACTIVITIES. (INCLUDED ARE CHARTS FOR THE TYPICAL DAY IN EACH OF THE CENTER'S SUBGROUPS AND A MODEL FOR STRUCTURING THE EDUCATIONAL ACTIVITIES FOR A DEVELOPMENT-FOSTERING ENVIRONMENT.) (EF)

ED013117 PS000088
OPERATION HEAD START--AN EVALUATION. FINAL REPORT. VAN EGMOND, ELMER; AND OTHERS, 01MAR66 100P.
EDRS PRICE MF-$0.65 HC-$3.29

DESCRIPTIONS OF PHYSICAL FACILITIES, A VERBAL AND NON-VERBAL INTERACTION ANALYSIS MEASURED ON A (1) TASK-ORIENTING, (2) MAINTAINING SOCIAL ORDER, AND (3) FACILITATING SCALE, TEACHER INTERVIEWS, AND OBSERVER VERBAL REPORTS ASSESS A SELECTED SAMPLE OF CLASSROOMS WITHIN THE 1965 CAMBRIDGE SUMMER HEAD START PROGRAM. PERFORMANCE OF HEAD START AND NON-HEAD START PUPILS ENROLLED IN PUBLIC SCHOOL KINDERGARTENS THE FOLLOWING FALL IS COMPARED AND ANALYSED IN TERMS OF NORMS, EXPECTATIONS, AND LIMITS OF THE CLASSROOM, I.E. IN TERMS OF "THE CLASSROOM GAME." PUPIL BEHAVIOR IS CODED AS "WITH IT" OR "NOT WITH IT." OTHER COMPARATIVE PROCEDURES ARE TEACHER INTERVIEWS, TEACHER RATINGS OF CHILDREN, AND A READING READINESS TEST. INTERPRETATION OF THE DATA CHARACTERIZES THE SUMMER HEAD START PROGRAM AS LARGELY A SOCIAL LEARNING PERIOD WITH LITTLE ATTENTION TO COGNITIVE DEVELOPMENT. ACTIVITIES WERE JUDGED AS NOT CAREFULLY PLANNED, NOT DIFFERENTIATING NEEDS, AND NOT GOAL ORIENTED. A MAJORITY OF TEACHERS INDICATED THE PRIMARY ADVANTAGE OF THE PROGRAM TO BE IN TERMS OF HELPING CHILDREN MEET THE EXPECTATIONS AND DEMANDS OF THE FORMAL SCHOOL SYSTEM. NEITHER THE READINESS TEST NOR "GAME" ANALYSIS SHOW A SIGNIFICANT STATISTICAL DIFFERENCE BETWEEN GROUPS. TEACHERS PERCEIVED THE BEHAVIOR OF HEAD START AND NON-HEAD START CHILDREN TO BE ESSENTIALLY SIMILAR. THE INITIAL BEHAVIOR OF THE HEAD START CHILDREN TENDED TO BE MORE ACTIVE AND EXPLORATORY. (BH)

ED013118 PS000092
PRESCHOOL PREDICTION AND PREVENTION OF LEARNING DISABILITIES. BEERY, KEITH E., MAR67 60P.
EDRS PRICE MF-$0.65 HC-$3.29

THE OBJECTIVES OF THIS INITIAL REPORT OF A FOUR-YEAR PROJECT WERE (1) TO DEMONSTRATE A METHOD FOR THE PREDICTION AND PREVENTION OF LEARNING DISABILITIES, (2) TO FOSTER UNDERSTANDING OF CHILD DEVELOPMENT AMONG TEACHERS, PARENTS, AND PHYSICIANS. SUBJECTS WERE THE 3 1/2 TO 5 1/2 YEAR OLD CHILDREN OF AN ENTIRE SCHOOL DISTRICT. RESEARCHERS WERE ASSISTED BY PARENTS AND TEACHERS. FIVE TESTS (NAMED AND EVALUATED IN THE REPORT) WERE ADMINISTERED DURING THE SUMMER OF 1966 TO 365 CHILDREN RANDOMLY ASSIGNED TO CONTROL AND EXPERIMENTAL GROUPS. THESE GROUPS WERE FURTHER DESIGNATED WITHIN THEMSELVES ACCORDING TO SEX, AGE, AND SCHOOL EXPERIENCE. TEST RESULTS INDICATED INITIAL SCREENING FOR VISION, HEARING, AND PERCEPTION TO BE HELPFUL IN PREDICTION AND PREVENTION OF LEARNING DISORDERS. ANNUAL RESCREENING WILL BE CONDUCTED FOR 3 YEARS. SUCCEEDING REPORTS WILL FOLLOW. (LG)

ED013119 PS000093
A READING READINESS TRAINING PROGRAM FOR PERCEPTUALLY HANDICAPPED KINDERGARTEN PUPILS OF NORMAL VISION. FINAL REPORT. MEYERSON, DANIEL W., MAY67 114P.
EDRS PRICE MF-$0.65 HC-$6.58

BASED ON THE HYPOTHESIS THAT KEPHART PERCEPTUAL TRAINING WOULD SHARPEN VISUAL PERCEPTION IN PERCEPTUALLY HANDICAPPED KINDERGARTENERS, THIS PROGRAM STUDIED 58 SUCH CHILDREN ACCORDING TO THREE CATEGORIES (1) THE FROSTIG DEVELOPMENTAL TEST OF VISUAL PERCEPTION, (2) SOCIO ECONOMIC STATUS, AND (3) VISUAL ACUITY (KEENNESS). THE CHILDREN WERE DIVIDED INTO TWO GROUPS (1) KEPHART-TRAINED, 15 MINUTES PER DAY AND (2) NO SPECIAL TRAINING. AT THE END OF 8 WEEKS, GINN PRE-READING AND LEE-CLARK READING READINESS TESTS WERE ADMINISTERED. THE 3 CATEGORIES WERE EXAMINED BY ANALYSIS OF VARIANCE. RESULTS SHOWED NO SIGNIFICANT DIFFERENCES AS THE RESULT OF KEPHART TRAINING. THE CHILDREN OF HIGH SOCIO-ECONOMIC STATUS WERE BETTER PREPARED FOR READING, REGARDLESS OF TRAINING OR VISUAL ADEQUACY. SOCIO-ECONOMIC FACTORS NOT CONTROLLED FOR IN THIS STUDY MAY AFFECT READING READINESS MORE THAN DO EITHER KEPHART TRAINING OR VISUAL ACUITY. (LG)

ED013120 PS000154
THE DEVELOPMENT OF AN ELEMENTARY SCHOOL MATHEMATICS CURRICULUM FOR INDIVIDUALIZED INSTRUCTION. LIPSON, JOSEPH I.; AND OTHERS, 66 31P.
EDRS PRICE MF-$0.65 HC-$3.29

INDIVIDUALIZED PRESCRIBED INSTRUCTION (IPI), DESIGNED FOR GRADES 1-6, IS A SEQUENTIAL MATHEMATICS CURRICULUM IN WHICH EACH OBJECTIVE IS A DESCRIPTION OF SOMETHING A STUDENT SHOULD BE ABLE TO DO. EACH OBJECTIVE IS A PREREQUISITE TO THE LEARNING OF A LATER OBJECTIVE. STUDENTS ARE TESTED FOR MASTERY OF OBJECTIVES AND THEN PLACED SO THAT THEY ARE STUDYING SOMETHING NOT YET LEARNED BUT SOMETHING FOR WHICH THEY HAVE ALL THE PREREQUISITES. CONSIDERATIONS WHICH SHAPED THE SEQUENCE OF OBJECTIVES DISCUSSED ARE (1) THE COMMITMENT TO THE NEW MATHEMATICS, (2) THE NEED FOR AND THE STRENGTH OF OBJECTIVES, (3) THE EFFECT OF INDIVIDUALIZED INSTRUCTION UPON CURRICULUM PREPARATION, (4) SUBJECT MATTER ACCURACY AND LOGICAL PROGRESSION, (5) THE USE OF MEMORIZATION AND MASTERY IN THE MATH CURRICULUM, (6) LEARNING THEORY AND EDUCATIONAL EXPERIMENTS, (7) TESTING REQUIREMENTS, (8) INTERACTION BETWEEN LESSON WRITERS AND THE NEW CURRICULUM, (9) THE EFFECT OF A DEVICE (A LANGUAGE MASTER) FOR COMMUNICATING WITH NON READERS. SOME CHILDREN MAY NOT BE ABLE TO LEARN AS WELL BY INDIVIDUALIZED INSTRUCTION AS IN A CONVENTIONAL CLASSROOM. ONE-DAY-A-WEEK, CLASS ACTIVITIES IN A MATHEMATICS SEMINAR WAS THE APPROACH USED TO OFFSET THIS POTENTIAL PROBLEM. ACHIEVEMENT RESULTS FOR THE SCHOOL YEAR 1964-1965 SHOW WIDE RANGES OF ACHIEVEMENT FOR INDIVIDUAL PUPILS. THE FIRST GRADE CLASS SEEMS TO HAVE MADE DOUBLE THE NORMALLY EXPECTED GROWTH. A SUGGESTION THAT HAS MANY POTENTIALS IS THE USE OF COMPUTER ASSISTED INSTRUCTION WITH INDIVIDUALIZED INSTRUCTION. (HH)

ED013121 PS000173
PSYCHOLOGICAL BASES FOR INSTRUCTIONAL DESIGN. GLASER, ROBERT, 66
DOCUMENT NOT AVAILABLE FROM EDRS.

THE PROCESS OF INSTRUCTION WOULD BENEFIT FROM BEING ORGANIZED IN TERMS OF BEHAVIORAL PSYCHOLOGY. FIRST, THE PROCESS OF TASK ANALYSIS SHOULD DIVIDE THE FINAL OBJECTIVE INTO A SERIES OF SUBTOPICS OR RELATED TASKS. PERHAPS DIFFERENT TEACHING PROCEDURES WILL BE NEEDED TO MASTER DIFFERENT SUBTOPICS OF THE FINAL OBJECTIVE. SECOND, AN ASSESSMENT SHOULD BE MADE OF THE PRESENT KNOWLEDGE OF THE LEARNER AND OF HIS ABILITY TO PROFIT FROM THE INSTRUCTION. THIRD, IN HIS PRESENTATION OF SUBJECT MATTER THE INSTRUCTOR SHOULD BE AWARE OF A NUMBER OF ISSUES, INCLUDING (1) THE NEED TO CONTROL THE PRESENTATION OF SUBTASKS TO ACHIEVE A MAXIMUM OF TRANSFER OF TRAINING, (2) VARYING THE MEANS OF THE LEARNER'S CONTACT WITH THE SUBJECT MATTER, (3) THE AMOUNT OF PRACTICE AND REVIEW CONSIDERED APPROPRIATE TO GIVEN SUBJECT MATTER, (4) THE BENEFIT OF

MINIMIZING ERRORS WHILE STILL RECOGNIZING THE USE WHICH CAN BE MADE OF ERRORS IN POINTING OUT THE SPECIFIC NEEDS OF INDIVIDUALS, AND (5) HOW TO PROVIDE EFFECTIVE REINFORCEMENT TO ENCOURAGE CONTINUED EFFORT. FOURTH, THE NATURE AND EXTENT OF TESTING PROCEDURES SHOULD BE VARIED ACCORDING TO THE EXPECTED OUTCOMES OF INSTRUCTION AND SHOULD BE USED TO EVALUATE THE INSTRUCTIONAL PROCESS ITSELF AS WELL AS THE LEARNER'S PERFORMANCE. THIS DOCUMENT APPEARED IN AV COMMUNICATION REVIEW, VOL. 14, NO. 4, WINTER 1966. (GW)

ED013122 PS000183
CURRICULUM DEVELOPMENT PROGRAM FOR PRESCHOOL TEACHER AIDES. FINAL REPORT. NAYLOR, NAOMI L., APR67 122P.
EDRS PRICE MF-$0.65 HC-$6.58

SHORTAGES IN TRAINED PERSONNEL FOR PRESCHOOL CHILD CARE AND HEAD START LED TO THIS PILOT PROGRAM THE PURPOSES OF WHICH WERE (1) TO DEVELOP A TRAINING MODEL FOR NON-PROFESSIONAL PRESCHOOL AIDES, (2) TO DETERMINE THE VALUE OF SELECTION CRITERIA IN TRAINEE SUCCESS, (3) TO EVALUATE THE TRAINEES' UNDERSTANDING, (4) TO DEVELOP MATERIALS SUITABLE FOR NON-PROFESSIONALS. TWO TRAINING SESSIONS WERE HELD IN AN EAST ST. LOUIS, ILLINOIS CHURCH BEGINNING IN NOVEMBER, 1965. PRELIMINARY TESTING OF 257 APPLICANTS ACCEPTED 24 FOR SESSION 1 AND 25 FOR SESSION 2. A FOUR WEEK OBSERVATION PERIOD USING ROLE-PLAYING AUDIO-VISUAL AIDS, DISCUSSION GROUPS, CREATIVE ARTS, AND LECTURE-DEMONSTRATIONS WAS FOLLOWED BY A TWELVE-WEEK PRACTICE TEACHING PERIOD WHICH INCLUDED WEEKLY ONE-DAY STAFF MEETINGS. THE TRAINING PERIOD WAS ON A 5 HOUR PER DAY BASIS FOR 16 WEEKS. WRITTEN REPORTS WERE REQUIRED OF THE TRAINEES TO FOCUS THEIR ATTENTION UPON BEHAVIOR DEVELOPMENT. EVALUATION OF THE TRAINEES OCCURRED DURING THE PRACTICE TEACHING PERIOD. EXPERIENCE WITH THE CHILDREN AND DISCUSSION RELATED TO THAT EXPERIENCE WERE FOUND TO HAVE GREATER LONG TERM EFFECTIVENESS THAN FILMS, LECTURES, AND SELF-SELECTED READING. A RESOURCE HANDBOOK USEFUL TO THE TRAINEES WAS DEVELOPED. THE TRAINEES WERE MOST INTERESTED IN INFORMAL PRESENTATIONS IN WHICH THEY WERE DIRECTLY INVOLVED. POST-TESTING OF THE TRAINEES SHOWED SIGNIFICANT CHANGES IN PUNITIVE, AUTHORITARIAN, AND RESTRICTIVE ATTITUDES. IT IS RECOMMENDED THAT NON-PROFESSIONAL TRAINING PROGRAMS BE CONTINUED AND THAT OPPORTUNITIES FOR ADDITIONAL EDUCATION AND IN-SERVICE TRAINING BE PROVIDED. (DETAILED APPENDICES INCLUDED.) (LG)

ED013662 PS000051
YOUNG CHILDREN'S THINKING, STUDIES OF SOME ASPECTS OF PIAGET'S THEORY. ALMY, MILLIE; AND OTHERS, 66
DOCUMENT NOT AVAILABLE FROM EDRS.

TWO STUDIES DEAL WITH THE THOUGHT PROCESSES CHILDREN DISPLAY WHEN FACED WITH PROBLEMS INVOLVING THE CONCEPTS OF QUANTITY AND NUMBER. INVOLVING CHILDREN IN KINDERGARTEN, FIRST GRADE AND SECOND GRADE, THE STUDIES USE PIAGET'S THEORIES IN BOTH A CROSS-SECTIONAL AND A LONGITUDINAL APPROACH TO STUDY CHILDREN'S THINKING IN AN EDUCATIONAL SETTING. TO DETERMINE THE VALIDITY OF THE STAGES OF THOUGHT AS DESCRIBED BY PIAGET, THE STUDIES DEAL WITH ONE ASPECT OF A CHILD'S THINKING, HIS ABILITY TO CONSERVE NUMBER AND QUANTITY AS REVEALED IN THREE TASKS. STUDIED ALSO ARE HOW THAT ABILITY RELATES ITSELF TO OTHER INTELLECTUAL ABILITIES AND TO SCHOOL READINESS AND ACHIEVEMENT, AND HOW THAT ABILITY CHANGES AND DEVELOPS OVER TIME. RESULTS OF THE CROSS-SECTIONAL STUDY CONFIRMED THE RELEVANCE OF PIAGET'S THEORY TO THE STUDY OF YOUNG CHILDREN. RESULTS OF THE LONGITUDINAL STUDY CONFIRMED CROSS-SECTIONAL RESULTS AND UNDERLINED THE RELEVANCE OF THE CHILD'S PROGRESS IN CONSERVATION OF NUMBER AND QUANTITY TO HIS PERFORMANCE IN THE CLASSROOM. THE DOCUMENT INCLUDES A BIBLIOGRAPHY AND TABLES. THIS DOCUMENT IS AVAILABLE FROM TEACHER'S COLLEGE PRESS, TEACHER'S COLLEGE, COLUMBIA UNIVERSITY, NEW YORK 10027. (EF)

ED013663 PS000072
THE EFFECTS OF ASSESSMENT AND PERSONALIZED PROGRAMMING ON SUBSEQUENT INTELLECTUAL DEVELOPMENT OF PREKINDERGARTEN AND KINDERGARTEN CHILDREN. COFFMAN, ALICE O.; DUNLAP, JAMES M., JUL67 106P.
EDRS PRICE MF-$0.65 HC-$6.58

THE OBJECTIVE FOR THIS STUDY WAS TO FOSTER PREKINDERGARTEN CHILDREN'S DEVELOPMENT THROUGH A PERSONALIZED PROGRAM BASED ON ASSESSMENTS OF EACH CHILD'S DEVELOPMENTAL SKILLS, USING NEW TESTS AND INSTRUCTIONAL MATERIALS ADAPTED TO INDIVIDUAL NEEDS. OF FOUR EXPERIMENTAL CLASSES, THREE FOCUSED ON AN AREA OF WEAKNESS (MOTOR, AUDITORY-LANGUAGE, OR VISUAL,) FOR 20 MINUTES DAILY, WITHIN A FRAMEWORK OF A NURSERY SCHOOL PROGRAM. CHILDREN WITH NO WEAKNESS IN THESE AREAS WERE PLACED IN THE FOURTH GROUP WHICH FOCUSED ON COGNITIVE SKILL DEVELOPMENT. PRE-TEST AND POST-TEST DATA AND GROWTH DIFFERENCES WERE ANALYZED FOR THE SIGNIFICANCE OF DIFFERENCES AMONG THE FOUR EXPERIMENTAL CLASSES, THE COMBINED EXPERIMENTAL GROUPS, AND CONTROL GROUPS WITH AND CONTROL GROUPS WITHOUT NURSERY SCHOOL EXPERIENCE. THE DATA WERE ANALYZED SEPARATELY FOR GIRLS AND BOYS. SIGNIFICANT GAINS RESULTED FROM PROGRAMS GIVEN TO HELP OVERCOME WEAKNESSES IN THE EXPERIMENTAL CHILDREN. THE EXPERIMENTAL GROUP GREW SIGNIFICANTLY IN MORE SKILLS DEVELOPMENT AREAS THAN DID THE CONTROL GROUP. THEY ALSO GREW SIGNIFICANTLY IN SKILL AREAS NOT SPECIFICALLY PROGRAMMED. THE CONTROL CHILDREN WITH PREVIOUS NURSERY SCHOOL EXPERIENCE GAINED IN MORE SKILLS DEVELOPMENT AREAS THAN THOSE CHILDREN WITHOUT SCHOOL EXPERIENCE. IN GENERAL, GIRLS SEEMED TO BENEFIT MORE THAN BOYS FROM NURSERY SCHOOL EXPERIENCE. (LG)

ED013664 PS000171
AN INDIVIDUALIZED SCIENCE LABORATORY. LIPSON, JOSEPH I., DEC66
DOCUMENT NOT AVAILABLE FROM EDRS.

THE LEARNING RESEARCH AND DEVELOPMENT CENTER AT THE UNIVERSITY OF PITTSBURGH IS WORKING ON AN EXPERIMENTAL PROJECT TO EXAMINE METHODS OF INDIVIDUALIZED INSTRUCTION IN SCIENCE AT THE ELEMENTARY SCHOOL LEVEL. AT THIS TIME, THE EXPERIMENT IS FOCUSED UPON NON-READERS IN GRADES K-3. EACH STUDENT RECEIVES A TAPE CARTRIDGE AND A PLASTIC BOX CONTAINING MATERIALS FOR HIS LESSON. TESTS PUT ON TAPE ARE USED FOR THE PURPOSE OF DIAGNOSIS SO THAT WORK CAN BE PROPERLY ASSIGNED. AS FEW AS THREE SETS OF EQUIPMENT FOR EACH EXPERIMENT ARE USED. A COMPARISON TEST WAS MADE BETWEEN UPPER ELEMENTARY CHILDREN AND SOME COLLEGE FRESHMAN ENGLISH STUDENTS WITH THE RESULTS THAT THE ELEMENTARY CHILDREN LEARNING THROUGH DIRECT EXPERIENCE PERFORMED AS WELL AS OR BETTER THAN COLLEGE STUDENTS WHO LEARNED THROUGH TEXT BOOKS. THIS DOCUMENT APPEARED IN "SCIENCE AND CHILDREN," VOLUME 4, NO. 4, DECEMBER 1966. (COD)

ED013665 PS000177
CONCEPT FORMATION BY KINDERGARTEN CHILDREN IN A CARD-SORTING TASK. PSYCHOLOGY SERIES. ROSENTHAL-HILL, IRENE; SUPPES, PATRICK, 27FEB67 40P.
EDRS PRICE MF-$0.65 HC-$3.29

CONCEPT FORMATION IN 50 KINDERGARTENERS WAS STUDIED BY REQUIRING THE CHILDREN TO SORT CARDS ACCORDING TO ONE OF FOUR ATTRIBUTES OF THREE DIFFERENT DIMENSIONS. THE OBJECTIVE WAS TO EXPLORE THE VALIDITY AND LIMITATIONS OF AN ALL-OR-NONE LEARNING MODEL FOR COMPLEX CLASSIFYING RESPONSES. INFORMATION WAS PRESENTED TO THE SUBJECT BY TWO POSITIVE EXAMPLES IN ONE PROBLEM SET AND BY A POSITIVE AND A NEGATIVE EXAMPLE IN THE OTHER SET. POSITIVE PROGRAM SETS WERE GIVEN FIRST. HALF OF THE CHILDREN BEGAN WITH GEOMETRICAL PROBLEM CARDS AND, AFTER REACHING CRITERION ON THESE, TRANSFERRED TO MORE DIFFICULT "PEOPLE" CARDS. THE OTHER HALF RECEIVED PROBLEMS IN REVERSE ORDER. WHEN POSITIVE EXAMPLES WERE GIVEN, POSITIVE TRANSFER EFFECTS WERE EVIDENCED. WHEN POSITIVE AND NEGATIVE EXAMPLES WERE GIVEN, CRITERION WAS REACHED RAPIDLY. GENERALLY, SUBJECTS ACHIEVED FEW CORRECT SOLUTIONS BEFORE REACHING CRITERION, AND BACKWARD AND FORWARD LEARNING CURVES SHOWED NO INCREASE IN PROPORTION OF CORRECT RESPONSE JUST BEFORE REACHING CRITERION. AN ALL-OR-NONE MODEL WAS REJECTED ON THE BASIS OF TESTS FOR INDEPENDENCE ON PAIRS OF ADJACENT RESPONSES AND FOR NUMBERS OF SUCCESSES IN BLOCKS OF THREE PROBLEMS. SUBJECTS LEARNED MEDIATING CONCEPTS, BUT REQUIRED ADDITIONAL SESSIONS TO APPLY CONCEPTS TO SPECIFIC PROBLEMS. (LB)

ED013666 PS000192
CHILDREN AND TV, TELEVISION'S IMPACT ON THE CHILD. GRAY, NAN; SUNDERLIN, SYLVIA, 67
DOCUMENT NOT AVAILABLE FROM EDRS.

VARIOUS POINTS OF VIEW ARE PRESENTED ON THE EFFECT OF TELEVISION UPON CHILDREN. CONTENTS--(1) TELEVISION, TIGER BY THE TAIL--ERNA CHRISTENSEN. (2) TELEVISION'S IMPACT ON THE CHILD--RALPH GARRY. (3) SOME RESEARCH ON TV--PAUL A. WITTY. (4) THE CURRICULUM CONTENT OF CHILDREN'S TELEVISION PROGRAMS AND COMMERCIALS--MARIE TOWNSEND MOORE AND JULIANA TOWNSEND GENSLEY. (5) TEACHERS AND TV--ELINOR RICHARDSON. EDUCATIONAL TELEVISION AND CHILDREN--FREDERICK BREITENFELD, JR. (7) TEACHING CHILDREN TO ANALYZE TELEVISION ADVERTISING--LEE BENNETT HOPKINS. (8) THE UNGUARDED HOURS--BETTY LONGSTREET AND FRANK ORME. PARENTS, THEIR CHILDREN AND TELEVISION--PATRICIA L. SWENSON. (10) A PARENT'S VIEW OF TV--LYN DAY. (11) PARENTS SAY... (12) OUR CHILDREN LEARN FROM TV--ARTHUR D. MCINTIRE. (13) PUBLIC TELEVISION, A CULTURAL OVERKILL--RICHARD SCHICKELL. THIS DOCUMENT IS AVAILABLE AS BULLETIN 21-A FOR $1.25 FROM THE ASSOCIATION FOR CHILDHOOD EDUCATION INTERNATIONAL, 3615 WISCONSIN AVENUE, N.W., WASHINGTON, D.C. 20016. (LG)

ED013667 PS000199
AN EVALUATION OF OPERATION HEAD START BILINGUAL CHILDREN, SUMMER, 1965. MONTEZ, PHILIP; AND OTHERS, AUG66 168P.
EDRS PRICE MF-$0.65 HC-$6.58

IN CALIFORNIA, THE MEXICAN-AMERICAN STUDENT IS TWO YEARS BEHIND THE NEGRO STUDENT AND THREE AND A HALF YEARS BEHIND THE ANGLO-AMERICAN IN SCHOLASTIC ACHIEVEMENT. SINCE HE REPRESENTS TWO DISTINCT AND OFTEN DIVERGENT CULTURES, ENGLISH-SPEAKING, MIDDLE-CLASS ORIENTED SCHOOLS MAKE ASSIMILATION VIRTUALLY IMPOSSIBLE. A HEAD START AND A FOLLOW THROUGH PROJECT IN THE SPANISH-SPEAKING COMMUNITY ARE EVALUATED IN TERMS OF SOCIAL ATTITUDES TOWARD THE LEARNING TASKS AND

EXPERIENCES OF THE MEXICAN-AMERICAN CHILD. THE PRE-SCHOOL PROGRAM IS DISCUSSED BY EACH OF THESE REPORTING GROUPS (1) TEACHERS, (2) PARENTS, (3) TEACHER AIDES, AND (4) "FOLLOW-UP" TEACHERS. (CD)

ED013668 PS000203
EVALUATION OF HEADSTART EDUCATIONAL PROGRAM IN CAMBRIDGE, MASSACHUSETTS. FINAL REPORT. PORTER, PHILIP J.; AND OTHERS, DEC65 43P.
EDRS PRICE MF-$0.65 HC-$3.29

BEGINNING WITH A REVIEW OF THE NURSERY SCHOOL MOVEMENT (FROEBEL, MONTESSORI, AND MCMILLAN,) THIS EVALUATION RELATES THE HISTORICAL MATERIAL TO HEAD START, SPECIFICALLY IN CAMBRIDGE MASS. DURING THE SUMMER OF 1965, MATCHED GROUPS OF 33 HEAD START CHILDREN AND 33 NON-HEAD START CHILDREN (CONTROL GROUP) WERE STUDIED. SCHOOL PRE-REGISTRATION LISTS PROVIDED NAMES AND SOCIO-ECONOMIC INFORMATION FOR BOTH THE HEAD START CHILDREN AND THE CONTROL GROUP CHILDREN. BOTH GROUPS WERE TESTED DURING THE TWO WEEKS BETWEEN THE CLOSE OF HEAD START SESSIONS AND THE FIRST DAY OF PUBLIC SCHOOL. SCORES ON MEASUREMENT INSTRUMENTS WERE ANALYZED ON THE BASIS OF (1) SEX, (2) MOTHER'S EDUCATIONAL LEVEL, AND (3) FAMILY INCOME LEVEL. THE MEASURE OF LEARNING RATE AS DETERMINED BY THE SEGUIN FORM BOARD WAS THE MOST CONSISTENT IN SHOWING DIFFERENCES RESULTING FROM HEAD START INTERVENTION. THE CHIEF DIFFERENCE SEEMS TO BE THAT HEAD START EXPERIENCE AIDED A CHILD IN ATTACKING LEARNING TASKS. FOLLOW-UP RESEARCH IS NEEDED INTO HEALTH, SOCIAL CASE WORK, EFFECTS ON FORMAL SCHOOLING, AND EVALUATION AND REFINEMENT OF THE PROGRAM. (LG)

ED013669 PS000209
PROJECT HEAD START AND THE CULTURALLY DEPRIVED IN ROCHESTER, NEW YORK, A STUDY OF PARTICIPATING AND NON-PARTICIPATING FAMILIES IN AREAS SERVED BY PROJECT HEAD START IN ROCHESTER, FINAL REPORT. CHANDLER, MARVIN; AND OTHERS, JAN66 114P.
EDRS PRICE MF-$0.65 HC-$6.58

A COMMUNITY PROFILE OF ROCHESTER, N.Y. CITES HISTORY, PRESENT COMMUNITY CHARACTERISTICS, AND CURRENT IMPROVEMENT PROGRAMS AS THEY RELATE TO CULTURAL DEPRIVATION AND AN ANTI-POVERTY PROGRAM. TO DETERMINE WHAT EFFECTS HISTORICAL, ECONOMIC, POLITICAL, ECOLOGICAL, AND SOCIAL FORCES HAVE UPON HEAD START CHILDREN, MATCHED GROUPS OF EIGHT HEAD START FAMILIES AND EIGHT NON-HEAD START FAMILIES WERE INTERVIEWED CONCERNING ATTITUDES TOWARD POLITICAL PARTIES, POLICE, CHURCH, AND HEAD START AND CONCERNING EXPECTATIONS FOR THEIR CHILDREN'S HEAD START PARTICIPATION, FOR THE ANTI-POVERTY PROGRAM, AND FOR THE FUTURE. OTHER FACTORS INCLUDING EDUCATIONAL LEVELS, SPEECH CLARITY, SOCIALIZATION, FAMILY RELATIONSHIPS, HOME CONDITIONS, FINANCIAL STATUS, AND MOBILITY WERE ALSO ASKED ABOUT. CONCLUSIONS WERE THAT HEAD START DID NOT REACH THE MORE SEVERELY CULTURALLY DEPRIVED. RECOMMENDATIONS WERE THAT AN ANTI-POVERTY PROGRAM STRESS INCREASE IN INCOME, THAT INCREASED USE BE MADE OF INDIGENOUS PERSONS, THAT HEAD START FAMILIES BE COMPENSATED FOR PARTICIPATION, AND THAT REALISTIC EVALUATION BE MADE OF CURRENT PROGRAMS. (LG)

ED013670 PS000236
SUMMARY AND OBSERVATIONS IN THE DAKOTAS AND MINNESOTA. INDIAN COMMUNITIES AND PROJECT HEAD START. WAX, MURRAY L.; WAX, ROSALIE H., 15SEP65 45P.
EDRS PRICE MF-$0.65 HC-$3.29

THE PROBLEMS OF GAINING COMMUNITY PARTICIPATION IS A MAJOR ONE IN MANY OF THE PROGRAMS AIMED AT ASSISTING THE AMERICAN INDIAN. THIS PROBLEM IS USUALLY INTENSIFIED WHEN WHITE PERSONS, ASSUMING THAT THEY CAN DO MORE THAN THE COMMUNITY ITSELF, INTERVENE TO THE PARTIAL EXCLUSION OF THE INDIANS. IN SPITE OF THIS PROBLEM, THE HEAD START PROGRAMS FOR INDIANS WERE JUDGED, WITH FEW EXCEPTIONS, TO BE HIGHLY SUCCESSFUL. THIS IS PART OF THE TOTAL REPORT "INDIAN COMMUNITIES AND PROJECT HEAD START--SUMMARY AND OBSERVATIONS IN THE DAKOTAS AND MINNESOTA." (COD)

ED013671 PS000237
AN APPRAISAL OF POSSIBILITIES FOR A HEAD START PROGRAM AMONG THE POTAWATOMI INDIANS OF KANSAS. INDIAN COMMUNITIES AND PROJECT HEAD START. BEE, ROBERT L., 15SEP65 24P.
EDRS PRICE MF-$0.65 HC-$3.29

AT THE TIME OF THIS REPORT, TO THE AUTHOR'S KNOWLEDGE, NO ACTION EITHER BY THE POTOWATOMI OR INTERESTED WHITES HAD BEEN TAKEN TOWARD SETTING UP A HEAD START PROGRAM FOR THE POTOWATOMI OF KANSAS. THE AUTHOR STATES WHY, IN THIS OPINION, THE POTOWATOMI DO NOT NEED A HEAD START PROGRAM. IN SPITE OF THE BELIEF, THE REPORT ATTEMPTS TO GIVE BASIC INFORMATION TO AID IN PLANNING FOR SUCH A PROGRAM FOR THOSE NOT SHARING THE SAME BELIEF. THIS IS PART OF THE TOTAL REPORT "INDIAN COMMUNITIES AND PROJECT HEAD START--SUMMARY AND OBSERVATIONS IN THE DAKOTAS AND MINNESOTA." (COD)

ED014317 PS000174
A QUANTITATIVE MEASURE FOR PROGRAMMED INSTRUCTION. HOLLAND, JAMES G., MAR67
DOCUMENT NOT AVAILABLE FROM EDRS.

IN AN ATTEMPT TO PROVIDE AN OBJECTIVE MEANS FOR IDENTIFYING THE DEGREE TO WHICH MATERIAL CAN BE TECHNICALLY TERMED "PROGRAMMED", THE SO-CALLED "BLACKOUT" TECHNIQUE HAS BEEN DEVELOPED. ALL WORDS IN A PROGRAM WHICH ARE NOT DIRECTLY NEEDED IN ORDER TO PROVIDE THE REQUIRED ANSWERS ARE COVERED WITH BLACK CRAYON, AND THIS EDITED VERSION IS TESTED AGAINST THE ORIGINAL. IF THE NUMBER OF ERRORS MADE ON THE PROGRAM HAS NOT INCREASED WITH THE NEW VERSION, THEN THE TOTAL NUMBER OF WORDS BLACKED OUT INDICATES THE PROPORTION OF THE MATERIAL WHICH HAS NO RELATION TO THE ANSWERS REQUIRED. THE MORE WORDS BLACKED OUT, THE LESS PROGRAMMED IS THE MATERIAL. WHEN APPLIED TO ONE PROGRAM DESIGNED FOR USE BY BANK PERSONNEL THIS TECHNIQUE REVEALED THAT 69 PERCENT OF THE WORDS COULD BE COVERED WITHOUT CAUSING ANY INCREASE IN ERRORS. FOR THIS PROGRAM ONLY 31 PERCENT OF THE MATERIAL COULD TECHNICALLY BE CALLED PROGRAMMED. A SIMILAR STUDY OF 12 OTHER PROGRAMS SHOWED THAT THE AMOUNT OF MATERIAL WHICH WAS ACTUALLY PROGRAMMED VARIED FROM APPROXIMATELY 90 PERCENT DOWN TO 10 PERCENT. SOME INDIRECT EVIDENCE SUGGESTS THAT BOTH INITIAL LEARNING AND LATER RECALL WILL BE HIGHER ON PROGRAMS WITH A LOW BLACKOUT RATIO. THIS ARTICLE IS PUBLISHED IN "AMERICAN EDUCATIONAL RESEARCH JOURNAL," VOLUME 4, NUMBER 2, MARCH 1967. (GW)

ED014318 PS000197
EVALUATION OF TWO ASSOCIATED YM-YWHA HEADSTART PROGRAMS. FINAL REPORT. HOLMES, DOUGLAS; HOLMES, MONICA B., 30DEC65 59P.
EDRS PRICE MF-$0.65 HC-$3.29

TWO SUMMER 1965 HEAD START PROGRAMS, ONE IN BRONX RIVER AND ONE IN EAST TREMONT, NEW YORK, WERE SELECTED IN ORDER TO MEASURE THE CHANGES PRODUCED IN THE 36 PARTICIPANTS AS A RESULT OF THEIR HEAD START EXPERIENCE. AREAS MEASURED WERE (1) COGNITIVE FUNCTIONING, (2) PATTERNS OF PLAY AND USE OF PLAY MATERIALS, AND (3) CHILDREN'S FANTASIES ABOUT THEIR PEERS AND ADULTS. A CONTROL POPULATION OF 60 CHILDREN WAS MATCHED WITH THE HEAD START CHILDREN ALONG THE DIMENSIONS OF AGE, SEX, ETHNIC BACKGROUND, PREVIOUS SCHOOL EXPERIENCE, NUMBER OF SIBLINGS LIVING AT HOME, PRESENCE OR ABSENCE OF FATHER AND MOTHER, AND EDUCATION AND OCCUPATION OF MAJOR WAGE EARNER. BOTH GROUPS HAD A MEAN AGE OF FIVE YEARS, FIVE MONTHS. BOTH THE HEAD START PARTICIPANTS AND THE CONTROLS WERE TESTED FOR COGNITIVE FUNCTIONING, PLAY BEHAVIOR, AND PICTURE INTERPRETATION DURING THE LAST TWO WEEKS IN AUGUST. THEY WERE RETESTED IN NOVEMBER, TWO MONTHS AFTER THE BEGINNING OF PUBLIC SCHOOL. RESULTS OF THE TESTING SHOW SIGNIFICANT DIFFERENCES BETWEEN THE TWO GROUPS AT THE TIME OF THEIR FIRST TESTING BUT NOT AT THE SECOND TESTING. (CO'D)

ED014319 PS000201
EVALUATION OF PROJECT HEAD START READING READINESS IN ISSAQUENA AND SHARKEY COUNTIES, MISSISSIPPI, SUMMER, 1965. FINAL REPORT. GORDON, SOL, 26AUG66 28P.
EDRS PRICE MF-$0.65 HC-$3.29

THE SUBSTANCE OF THIS FINAL REPORT ON THE HEAD START PROJECT OF 1965 IN MISSISSIPPI IS A DEEP CONCERN WITH THE EFFECT OF THE SOCIAL MILIEU IN WHICH THE PROJECT STRUGGLED RATHER THAN WITH THE USUAL VARIETY OF STATISTICS AND RESEARCH CONCLUSIONS. THIS IS DUE, IN PART, TO THE PAUCITY OF SIGNIFICANT RESULTS AND, MORE IMPORTANTLY, TO THE SHOCKINGLY DISRUPTIVE CHARACTER OF THE SOCIAL ATTITUDES IN THE AREA. FOR EXAMPLE, ALTHOUGH THE HEAD START STAFF WAS SUFFICIENTLY BUSY RECRUITING PUPILS AND PREPARING LESSONS AND CLASSROOM FACILITIES, IT BECAME ALSO NECESSARY THAT THEY GUARD THESE FACILITIES FROM VANDALISM AND ARSON. ALSO, THE STAFF WAS MADE AWARE OF THE THREAT TO NEGRO PARENTS THAT THEY WOULD LOSE THEIR JOBS IF THEIR CHILDREN WERE ENROLLED IN THE PROGRAM. IN SHORT THE GENERAL WHITE ATTITUDE WAS UNCOOPERATIVE AND HOSTILE, AND THE NEGRO ATTITUDE WAS FEARFUL. NEVERTHELESS, THE READING-READINESS PROGRAM WAS CARRIED THROUGH, AND SOME RESULTS WERE OBTAINED. IT WAS DETERMINED THAT BOTH THE ALLYN AND BACON AND THE ASHTON-WARNER METHODS OF TEACHING READING WERE MORE EFFECTIVE THAN THE PHONETIC METHOD. ALSO, THE USE OF RECORDS AND RECORD PLAYERS, DISTRIBUTED TO THE PUPILS' HOMES, WAS VERY SUCCESSFUL IN STIMULATING A DESIRE TO LEARN. (WD)

ED014320 PS000202

TEACHERS BELIEF SYSTEMS AND PRESCHOOL ATMOSPHERES. HARVEY, O.J.; AND OTHERS, 65 24P.

EDRS PRICE MF-$0.65 HC-$3.29

THIS STUDY INVESTIGATES THE EFFECT OF A TEACHER'S BELIEF OR CONCEPTUAL SYSTEM ON HIS TEACHING METHOD AND ON THE CLASSROOM ATMOSPHERE CREATED BY THAT TEACHING METHOD. A BELIEF SYSTEM WAS CHARACTERIZED AS EITHER CONCRETE OR ABSTRACT. A CONCRETE SYSTEM WAS REPRESENTED BY A TENDENCY FOR THE TEACHER'S INSTRUCTIONAL APPROACH TO BE MORE STRUCTURED, MORE INVARIANT, AND LESS FLEXIBLE THAN THE APPROACH OF A TEACHER MANIFESTING AN ABSTRACT SYSTEM. TEACHERS WERE GIVEN THE "THIS I BELIEVE" TEST (TIB) AND THE "CONCEPTUAL SYSTEMS TEST" (CST) TO INDICATE WHICH BELIEF SYSTEM THEY WOULD BE PLACED INTO, NAMELY, (1) CONCRETENESS-ORIENTED, (2) ABSTRACTNESS-ORIENTED, AND (3) IN-BETWEEN. TEN TEACHERS WERE SELECTED FOR EACH CATEGORY. THESE 30 FEMALE HEAD START TEACHERS WERE OBSERVED WHILE CONDUCTING THEIR CLASSES OF PRESCHOOL CHILDREN AND WERE RATED ON A 26 DIMENSION CHART. EACH DIMENSION REPRESENTED EITHER A DESIRABLE OR AN UNDESIRABLE TEACHER TRAIT. IT WAS HYPOTHESIZED THAT TEACHERS IN CATEGORY (1), CONCRETENESS-ORIENTED, WOULD SCORE LOWEST ON DESIRABLE TRAITS AND HIGHEST ON UNDESIRABLE TRAITS, THAT ABSTRACTNESS-ORIENTED TEACHERS WOULD SCORE HIGHEST ON DESIRABLE TRAITS AND LOWEST ON UNDESIRABLE TRAITS, AND THAT THE IN-BETWEEN GROUP WOULD SCORE IN THE MIDDLE. THE RESULTS SUBSTANTIALLY SUPPORTED THIS HYPOTHESIS. (WD)

ED014321 PS000204

REPORT ON THE ARTICULATORY AND INTELLIGIBILITY STATUS OF SOCIALLY DISADVANTAGED PRE-SCHOOL CHILDREN. FRIEDLANDER, GEORGE H., DEC65 63P.

EDRS PRICE MF-$0.65 HC-$3.29

THIS STUDY OF THE ARTICULATORY AND INTELLIGIBILITY LEVEL OF A SOCIALLY DISADVANTAGED GROUP OF CHILDREN IN THE HEAD START PROGRAM INVOLVED 150 CHILDREN, 4 1/2 - 6 YEARS OF AGE, WITH EQUAL NUMBERS OF BOYS AND GIRLS. THIS GROUP WAS COMPOSED OF CHILDREN OF FAMILIES WITH SPANISH LANGUAGE BACKGROUND, OF CHILDREN OF NATIVE NEGRO FAMILIES, AND OF CHILDREN OF NATIVE WHITE FAMILIES. ALL CHILDREN WERE TESTED WITH THE TEMPLIN-DARLEY DIAGNOSTIC TEST OF ARTICULATION. A TAPED CONVERSATION WITH EACH CHILD WAS USED FOR EVALUATION BY AN INDEPENDENT GROUP OF EXAMINERS IN THE AREAS OF INTELLIGIBILITY, VERBAL PROFICIENCY, FOREIGN ACCENT, REGIONAL ACCENT, AND ARTICULATORY DEFECTS. FAMILY DATA ON OCCUPATION, INCOME, FAMILY SIZE, AND LANGUAGES SPOKEN AND A SAMPLING OF PARENT ARTICULATORY LEVEL WAS OBTAINED. THIS DATA WAS CORRELATED AS VARIABLES WITH THE ARTICULATORY AND INTELLIGIBILITY LEVEL OF THE CHILDREN TESTED. DATA INDICATED THAT ALL GROUPS WERE MINIMALLY PROFICIENT IN INTELLIGIBILITY AND VERBAL PERFORMANCE. WHITE CHILDREN SHOWED GREATER ARTICULATORY MATURITY THAN THE NEGRO AND SPANISH-LANGUAGE CHILDREN. FACTORS SHOWN TO BE OF NO INFLUENCE WERE SEX OF CHILD, OCCUPATION AND INCOME OF FATHER, AND FOREIGN LANGUAGE BACKGROUND. POOR ARTICULATORY PERFORMANCE, THEREFORE, REFLECTS A DEVELOPMENTAL LAG IN ARTICULATORY GROWTH. NEW TESTING INSTRUMENTS WHICH ALLOW FOR ETHNIC DIFFERENCES IN ARTICULATION SHOULD BE DEVELOPED FOR FUTURE STUDY. (LG)

ED014322 PS000207

THE HOUSING ENVIRONMENT AS A FACTOR IN CHILD DEVELOPMENT. FINAL REPORT. RICE, ROBERT R., 1DEC66 33P.

EDRS PRICE MF-$0.65 HC-$3.29

IN KANSAS CITY, MO., 208 NEGRO FIVE YEAR OLDS WERE STUDIED TO EXAMINE THE INFLUENCE OF HOUSING UPON CHILD DEVELOPMENT AND TO COMPARE THE RELATIVE INFLUENCE OF HOUSING ON HEAD START AND NON-HEAD START CHILDREN. FOUR GROUPS OF 52 CHILDREN EACH INCLUDED (1) HEAD START, PUBLIC HOUSING, (2) HEAD START, SLUM HOUSING, (3) NON-HEAD START, PUBLIC HOUSING, (4) NON-HEAD START, SLUM HOUSING. INSTRUMENTS USED WERE "MOTHER INTERVIEWS" AND CALDWELL'S "THE PRESCHOOL INVENTORY" WHICH WAS A POST-TEST. THREE HYPOTHESES WERE STATED (1) HEAD START CHILDREN FROM BETTER HOUSING (GROUP 1) WILL SURPASS THE OTHER GROUPS IN GROWTH AND DEVELOPMENT, (2) NON-HEAD START CHILDREN FROM SLUM HOUSING (GROUP 4) WILL SHOW LEAST GROWTH AND DEVELOPMENT, AND (3) GROUPS 2 AND 3 WILL SHOW THE RELATIVE IMPORTANCE OF HOUSING VERSUS AN ENRICHMENT PROGRAM IN FACILITATING DEVELOPMENT. RESULTS SUPPORTED THE THREE HYPOTHESES, BUT SOME UNCERTAINTY REMAINED BECAUSE PRE-TESTING HAD NOT OCCURRED. (LG)

ED014323 PS000212

AN ASSESSMENT OF INTELLIGENCE, PSYCHOLINGUISTIC ABILITIES AND LEARNING APTITUDES AMONG PRESCHOOL CHILDREN. CAWLEY, JOHN F., 66 71P.

EDRS PRICE MF-$0.65 HC-$3.29

RESEARCH IN PRESCHOOL EDUCATION HAS PRODUCED VARIED RESULTS, BUT IT IS FELT THAT THE EARLIER THERE IS INTERVENTION INTO UNSATISFACTORY EDUCATIONAL DEVELOPMENT, THE MORE EFFECTIVE WILL BE THE EFFORT TO REDUCE EDUCATIONAL DISABILITIES. THIS STUDY WAS DESIGNED TO INVESTIGATE THE NATURE AND DEGREE OF CHANGE IN THE PERFORMANCE OF FOUR-YEAR OLD CHILDREN BEFORE AND AFTER A PRESCHOOL TRAINING PROGRAM. THE SUBJECTS WERE APPROXIMATLEY 150 FOUR-YEAR OLD CHILDREN FROM THREE HEAD START CENTERS IN A LARGE EASTERN CITY. EACH SUBJECT WAS ENROLLED IN A YEAR-LONG PRESCHOOL PROGRAM AND WAS GIVEN A BATTERY OF TESTS AT THE BEGINNING AND END OF THE TERM. THE TESTS USED WERE (1) THE STANFORD-BINET, L-M, 1960 REVISION, (2) THE ILLINOIS TEST OF PSYCHOLINGUISTIC ABILITIES, AND (3) THE DETROIT TESTS OF LEARNING APTITUDE. THE OBJECTIVE OF THE PRESCHOOL PROGRAM WAS TO IMPROVE THE CHILD'S SELF-IMAGE, LINGUISTIC ABILITIES, SOCIAL-EMOTIONAL DEVELOPMENT, AND PRE-ACADEMIC CONCEPTS. THE TEST RESULTS INDICATED THAT THE CHILDREN'S IQ SCORES, PSYCHOLINGUISTIC ABILITIES, AND LEARNING APTITUDES IMPROVED. THERE WAS NO CONTROL GROUP USED, THEREFORE, NO CONCLUSION COULD BE EXPRESSED AS TO THE VALUE TO SUBJECTS OF SUCH A PROGRAM COMPARED WITH NO PROGRAM AT ALL. BUT IT WAS CONCLUDED THAT HEAD START DOES HELP THOSE CHILDREN IN NEED OF A HEAD START. (WD)

ED014324 PS000213

A SURVEY AND EVALUATION OF PROJECT HEAD START AS ESTABLISHED AND OPERATED IN COMMUNITIES OF THE COMMONWEALTH OF MASSACHUSETTS DURING THE SUMMER OF 1965. CURWOOD, SARAH T., 30OCT65 275P.

EDRS PRICE MF-$0.65 HC-$9.87

THIS DESCRIPTIVE SURVEY AND EVALUATION WAS UNDERTAKEN PRIMARILY TO PROVIDE A MORE COMPLETE PICTURE OF NATIONAL AND STATE NEEDS FOR FUTURE PLANNING. A BRIEF BACKGROUND OF THE PURPOSES FOR HEAD START PROGRAMS IS GIVEN. FIFTY-SIX PROGRAMS WERE OPERATED IN MASSACHUSETTS DURING THE SUMMER OF 1965. CENSUS DATA IS GIVEN ON THE PARTICIPATING COMMUNITIES AND SPONSORS OF THE CENTERS. THREE TRAINING PROGRAMS WERE HELD IN BOSTON FOR JOB PREPARATION WITH HEAD START. THE TRAINING SESSION AT WHEELOCK COLLEGE IS DESCRIBED. TWO OTHER TRAINING PROGRAMS ARE TOUCHED UPON. A REUNION IN SEPTEMBER OF WHEELOCK TRAINEES BROUGHT OUT MANY WEAKNESSES AND DISAPPOINTMENTS IN THE PROGRAMS. TWO RESEARCH ASSOCIATES WERE CHOSEN TO HELP MAKE A FIELD STUDY OF 23 HEAD START PROGRAMS INVOLVING 30 MASSACHUSETTS COMMUNITIES. COMMENTS ON EACH CITY, INCLUDING NARRATIONS OF SPECIFIC EXPERIENCES, ARE GIVEN. ALTOGETHER, 289 PERSONS WERE INTERVIEWED. ANALYSES OF DATA COLLECTED ARE INCLUDED IN MANY TABLES. AFTER CONSIDERATION OF THE RESULTS OF THE SURVEY, SEVEN RECOMMENDATIONS MADE WERE (1) HAVE MORE CONSULTATION WITH POTENTIAL USERS, (2) EXAMINE THOROUGHLY THE HOURS AT WHICH PROGRAMS OPERATE, (3) USE NEIGHBORHOOD SCHOOLS FOR NON-PROFESSIONAL ACTIVITIES, ESPECIALLY THOSE INVOLVING PARENTS, (4) EXPLORE DAY CARE SERVICES FURTHER, (5) SECURE INTEREST AND PARTICIPATION OF BUSINESS CONCERNS, (6) PROVIDE MORE PREPARATION FOR KEY PERSONNEL TO GAIN UNDERSTANDING OF NEEDS OF CHILDREN AND FAMILIES, AND (7) GIVE MORE TRAINING FOR NON-PROFESSIONAL PERSONNEL. (APPENDICES GIVING RELATED INFORMATION ARE INCLUDED.) (EF)

ED014325 PS000216

OUTCOMES OF INDIVIDUAL AND PROGRAMMATIC VARIATIONS AMONG PROJECT HEAD START CENTERS, SUMMER, 1965. FINAL REPORT. PIERCE-JONES, JOHN; AND OTHERS, 30SEP66 265P.

EDRS PRICE MF-$0.65 HC-$9.87

A 15-MONTH EVALUATION RESEARCH STUDY OF THE 1965 SUMMER HEAD START PROGRAMS WAS CONDUCTED THROUGHOUT THE STATE OF TEXAS. A SCHEMATIC MODEL OF INTERACTING FACTORS OPERATING THROUGH HEAD START PROGRAMS TO PRODUCE AND PREDICT CHANGES IN EDUCATIONAL DEVELOPMENT AND IN OUT-OF-SCHOOL ENVIRONMENT WAS DEVELOPED. THIS MODEL GENERATED THE EMPIRICAL EVALUATION RESEARCH. IT WAS THOUGHT THAT VARIATIONS IN TEACHING BEHAVIOR PATTERNS WOULD HAVE AN EFFECT ON VARIOUS KINDS OF BEHAVIORAL CHANGES IN THE PUPILS. SEVENTY HEAD START CENTERS IN 40 COMMUNITIES WERE CHOSEN AND PRESUMED TO BE ADEQUATELY REPRESENTATIVE. A NEW RATING-SCALES DEVICE, THE OBSERVOR'S RATING FORM WAS DEVELOPED TO MEASURE THE CLASSROOM BEHAVIOR OF THE 1256 TEACHERS. TRAINED OBSERVER TEAMS MADE OBSERVATION VISITS TO THE CLASSROOMS. CHILDREN, RANDOMLY CHOSEN FROM THE CLASSROOMS, WERE TESTED BY QUALIFIED PSYCHOMETRISTS EARLY IN THE EIGHT-WEEK PROGRAM AND AGAIN LATE IN THE PROGRAM. TESTS ADMINISTERED WERE THE PEABODY PICTURE VOCABULARY TEST, THE SEQUIN FORM BOARD, HUBBARD'S GROUP ADAPTATION OF BENDER'S VISUAL MOTOR GESTALT TEST, AND CALDWELL'S PRESCHOOL ACHIEVEMENT INVENTORY. THE ONE SALIENT CONCLUSION DRAWN FROM THE REPORT IS THAT THE 1965 SUMMER HEAD START PROGRAM IN TEXAS

CHANGED THE CHILDREN IN VARIABLE YET GENERALLY SIGNIFICANTLY PREDICTABLE WAYS SUCH AS IN SCHOOL READINESS. (MANY TABLES AND FORMS ARE INCLUDED.) (EF)

ED014326 PS000217
ANALYSIS OF STORY RETELLING AS A MEASURE OF THE EFFECTS OF ETHNIC CONTENT IN STORIES. FINAL REPORT. BERNEY, TOMI D.; JOHN, VERA P., MAR67 90P.
EDRS PRICE MF-$0.65 HC-$3.29

THE PURPOSE OF THE STUDY WAS TO EXAMINE THE PSYCHOLOGICAL IMPACT OF STORIES AND STORY BOOKS ON 142 PRESCHOOL CHILDREN INCLUDING 46 NEGROES (N.Y. AND CALIF.), 22 PUERTO RICANS (N.Y.), 10 MEXICANS (CALIF.), 16 SIOUX (S. DAKOTA) AND 48 NAVAJO (ARIZ. - N. MEXICO) BY MEANS OF STANDARDIZED RETELLING OF STORIES. A FURTHER AIM WAS TO DISCOVER PATTERNS OF LANGUAGE PERFORMANCE AMONG THE FIVE DIFFERING ETHNIC GROUPS. THE INVESTIGATORS RECRUITED AND TRAINED TWELVE RESEARCH ASSISTANTS OR LIBRARIANS WHO WERE COLLEGE STUDENTS. EACH LIBRARIAN WAS PROVIDED WITH A STANDARD KIT OF TEN BOOKS OF THREE TYPES (1) BOOKS OF ETHNIC IDENTIFICATION, (2) NON-VERBAL BOOKS, AND (3) CLASSIC CHILDREN'S BOOKS. DURING THE LAST PART OF THE PROGRAM, THE LIBRARIANS READ ABBREVIATED VERSIONS OF TWO SELECTED STORIES TO THE CHILDREN AND HAD EACH CHILD RETELL BOTH STORIES. IT SEEMED THAT THE INCLUSION OF ETHNIC BOOKS IS USEFUL IN A PROGRAM AIMED AT NON-WHITE CHILDREN. (COD)

ED014327 PS000218
AN EVALUATION OF THE EFFECTS OF A SUMMER HEAD START PROGRAM. CHOROST, SHERWOOD B.; AND OTHERS, JUN67 82P.
EDRS PRICE MF-$0.65 HC-$3.29

THIS PROJECT WAS CONDUCTED TO INVESTIGATE THE EFFECT UPON DISADVANTAGED CHILDREN OF A HEAD START PROGRAM AND THE AFTER-EFFECT OF THAT PROGRAM ON THE SUBJECTS' SUBSEQUENT PERFORMANCE IN KINDERGARTEN AND FIRST GRADE. MEASURES OF APTITUDE AND ACHIEVEMENT WERE TAKEN DURING THE FIRST TWO WEEKS AND LAST TWO WEEKS OF THE EIGHT WEEK HEAD START PROGRAM, DURING THE THIRD MONTH OF THE SUBJECTS' FIRST YEAR OF FORMAL SCHOOL, AT THE COMPLETION OF THAT FIRST YEAR, AND DURING THE FIRST SIX MONTHS OF THEIR SECOND YEAR OF SCHOOL. RESULTS OF TESTING DURING THE HEAD START PROGRAM SHOWED SUBSTANTIAL GAIN IN ALL PERFORMANCE AREAS BETWEEN THE TWO TESTING PERIODS. NO CONTROL GROUP WAS USED. THEREFORE, NO EXPERIMENTALLY BASED CONCLUSION COULD BE MADE AS TO WHETHER THE GAIN WAS DUE TO THE HEAD START EXPERIENCE OR TO A SIMPLE PASSAGE OF TIME AND RESULTING GENERAL DEVELOPMENT. MEASURES OF PERFORMANCE AFTER THE SUBJECTS ENTERED SCHOOL SHOWED NO SIGNIFICANT GAINS BY HEAD START PUPILS OVER NON-HEAD START PUPILS. THE ONLY REAL DISTINCTION WAS IN SCHOOL ATTENDANCE, IN WHICH HEAD START PUPILS DID BETTER. THE FACT THAT THE EXPERIMENTAL SUBJECTS SHOWED HIGH GAINS DURING THE HEAD START PROGRAM BUT FAILED TO EVIDENCE SUCH GAINS IN THE FORMAL SCHOOL SITUATION WAS EXPLAINED IN PART AS DUE TO THE FACT THAT THE CHILDREN WERE EMOTIONALLY UNREADY AT THE BEGINNING OF THE HEAD START PROGRAM TO BE TESTED BY RELATIVE STRANGERS IN UNFAMILIAR SURROUNDINGS. IT IS HYPOTHESIZED, THEREFORE, THAT THE CHILDREN SCORED UNCHARACTERISTICALLY LOW. (WD)

ED014328 PS000220
SUMMARY REPORT OF A STUDY OF THE FULL-YEAR 1966 HEAD START PROGRAMS. , 22SEP67 27P.
EDRS PRICE MF-$0.65 HC-$3.29

THIS SUMMARY OF SELECTED HIGHLIGHTS IS FROM A MAJOR REPORT TITLED "A STUDY OF THE FULL-YEAR 1966 HEAD START PROGRAMS." THE STUDY WAS DONE TO DETERMINE WHETHER THE PERFORMANCE OF CHILDREN ON FIVE TESTS AND RATING SCALES IS RELATED TO THE LENGTH OF THE 1966 FULL-YEAR PROGRAM WHICH THEY ATTENDED. FULL-YEAR PROGRAMS WERE CLASSED AS SHORT TERM FOR 15 WEEKS, OR LESS, MEDIUM TERM FOR 17 TO 23 WEEKS, AND LONG TERM FOR 25 WEEKS OR MORE. NINETEEN TESTERS WHO FULFILLED SPECIAL REQUIREMENTS WERE CHOSEN TO ADMINISTER THE TESTS. IN ALL, 964 CHILDREN IN 72 CENTERS WERE TESTED. TESTS AND SCALES USED AND BRIEFLY DISCUSSED WERE THE PEABODY PICTURE VOCABULARY TEST, THE REVISED PRE-SCHOOL INVENTORY, THE BEHAVIOR INVENTORY, THE VINELAND SOCIAL MATURITY SCALE, AND THE DRAW-A-PERSON TEST. RECOMMENDATIONS ARE MADE REGARDING THE USE OF THESE TESTS. FROM ANALYSIS OF TEST SCORES IT WAS DETERMINED THAT THERE WAS NO RELIABLE EVIDENCE OF AN AVERAGE DIFFERENCE IN PERFORMANCE RELATED TO LENGTH OF PROGRAM ATTENDANCE. SOME UNRESOLVED QUESTIONS RAISED BY THE STUDY ARE GIVEN. EVIDENCE INDICATES A NEED FOR THE SPELLING OUT OF SPECIFIC GOALS AND OBJECTIVES FOR HEAD START PROGRAMS. (INCLUDES A COMMENTARY ON THIS REPORT BY JOHN MCDAVID.) (EF)

ED014329 PS000225
PROJECT HEAD START IN AN INDIAN COMMUNITY. ORTIZ, ALFONSO, OCT65 70P.
EDRS PRICE MF-$0.65 HC-$3.29

THE INFLUENCE OF HISTORICAL, SOCIAL, AND CULTURAL FACTORS UPON THE EARLY LEARNING PROCESS OF SAN JUAN INDIAN CHILDREN WAS RELATED TO THE CONDUCT OF HEAD START PROGRAMS. FOUR TYPES OF DATA WERE USED, (1) PERSONAL RESEARCH INTO THE PUEBLO'S HISTORY, (2) TESTS AND OBSERVATIONS OF 50 INDIAN CHILDREN OF ALL AGES, (3) INFORMATION ABOUT SPECIFIC HEAD START FAMILIES, AND (4) INTERVIEWS WITH SAN JUAN RESIDENTS. SPANISH INFLUENCE UPON INDIAN LIFE DATING FROM THE 16TH CENTURY IS RELATED TO CURRENT AGRICULTURAL, MORAL, ECONOMIC, HEALTH, GOVERNMENTAL, RELIGIOUS, AND EDUCATIONAL CONDITIONS. FORMAL EDUCATION IS REGARDED AS DESIRABLE BY THE INDIANS, BUT TEN PERCENT OF ALL SCHOOL-AGE CHILDREN ARE NOT IN SCHOOL, AND THE DROP-OUT RATE IS HIGH. BECAUSE OF ILLITERACY, RESIGNATION TO THE STATE OF THINGS AS THEY ARE, POOR COMMUNICATION, AND APATHY WITHIN THE PUEBLO, THE TYPICAL INDIAN CHILD WAS NOT REACHED BY THE 1965 ESPANOLA VALLEY SUMMER HEAD START PROGRAM. FUNDS ACCOMMODATED 45 CHILDREN, SEVEN OF WHOM WERE FROM SAN JUAN. HOWEVER, THEY WERE CHILDREN TO WHOM LOCAL ADVANTAGES WERE ALREADY ACCESSIBLE. PARALLEL TO THE HEAD START PROGRAM, THE AUTHOR CONDUCTED A TWO-WEEK EXPERIMENTAL PROGRAM IN HIS HOME, ASCERTAINING THAT THE COMMUNITY THINKS THAT HEAD START IS A POTENTIAL SOLUTION TO ALL EDUCATIONAL PROBLEMS. RECOMMENDATIONS BASED ON INTERVIEWS WITH TRIBAL LEADERS, PARENTS, TEACHERS, AND A CLERGYMAN INCLUDE EMPHASIS UPON TRIBAL SPONSORSHIP, LONGER DURATION OF PROGRAMS, TEACHERS TRAINED IN UNDERSTANDING INDIANS, INDIAN MATERIALS AND AUDIO-VISUAL AIDS, MODERN MEDICAL PRACTICES, ENGLISH, PROVISION FOR SLOW LEARNERS, EXTRA-TRIBAL SOCIAL ACTIVITIES, AND UNANIMOUS PARTICIPATION OF TRIBAL CHILDREN. FUTURE STUDIES SHOULD BE BASED UPON THE INFORMATION ON CULTURAL BACKGROUND CONTAINED IN THIS REPORT. (LG)

ED014330 PS000230
AN ASSESSMENT AND COMPARISON OF SELECTED CHARACTERISTICS AMONG CULTURALLY DISADVANTAGED HEADSTART CHILDREN (SUMMER PROGRAM 1965), CULTURALLY DISADVANTAGED NON-HEADSTART CHILDREN, AND NON-CULTURALLY DISADVANTAGED CHILDREN. (TITLE SUPPLIED). HODES, MARION R., AUG66 55P.
EDRS PRICE MF-$0.65 HC-$3.29

THIS STUDY IS AN ATTEMPT TO DETERMINE AND COMPARE THE STATUS AND DEGREE OF CHANGE IN SELECTED EDUCATIONAL CHARACTERISTICS AMONG THREE GROUPS OF CHILDREN WHO ENTERED CAMDEN, NEW JERSEY KINDERGARTEN IN SEPTEMBER 1965. THERE WERE 300 CHILDREN DIVIDED INTO THREE MAJOR GROUPS (1) 102 CHILDREN WHO PARTICIPATED IN THE SUMMER HEAD START PROGRAM, (2) 100 CHILDREN WHO DID NOT PARTICIPATE IN THE HEAD START PROGRAM AND WERE CULTURALLY DISADVANTAGED, AND (3) 98 CHILDREN WHO WERE NON-CULTURALLY DISADVANTAGED. THE AUTHOR CONCLUDES THAT PARTICIPATION IN HEAD START IS RELATED TO IMPROVEMENT IN CONCEPTUAL MATURITY, BUT NOT TO THE DEGREE THAT THE EFFECTS OF POVERTY ARE OVERCOME. TAKING THE RESULTS OF THE TESTS GIVEN THE CHILDREN IN NOVEMBER AND MAY OF THEIR KINDERGARTEN YEAR INTO CONSIDERATION, THE AUTHOR SUGGESTS THAT IT MIGHT BE CONSIDERED JUSTIFIABLE TO GROUP HEAD START CHILDREN INTO SEPARATE KINDERGARTEN CLASSES IN WHICH IT IS POSSIBLE TO TAKE FULLEST ADVANTAGE OF POSSIBLE LEARNING GAINS. (COD)

ED014331 PS000234
A STUDY OF SOME ECOLOGICAL, ECONOMIC AND SOCIAL FACTORS INFLUENCING PARENTAL PARTICIPATION IN PROJECT HEAD START. JOHNSON, HENRY S.; PALOMARES, UVALDO H., AUG65 77P.
EDRS PRICE MF-$0.65 HC-$3.29

THE MAJOR PURPOSE OF THIS STUDY WAS TO DETERMINE IF THERE WERE SIGNIFICANTLY DIFFERENT RESPONSES TO CERTAIN ECOLOGICAL, ECONOMIC, SOCIAL AND CIVIC RESPONSIBILITY FACTORS BETWEEN PARENTS WHOSE CHILDREN PARTICIPATED IN THE HEAD START PROJECT AND THOSE WHOSE CHILDREN WERE ELIGIBLE BUT DID NOT PARTICIPATE. ALL PARENTS OF PRE-SCHOOL CHILDREN, 2 1/2 TO 6 YEARS OF AGE, WHO RESIDED IN 3 DESIGNATED SCHOOL DISTRICTS, WERE INCLUDED IN A HOUSE-TO-HOUSE SURVEY. IN ALL 256 PARENTS WERE SURVEYED BY MEANS OF A 50 QUESTION FORM WRITTEN IN BOTH ENGLISH AND SPANISH. FINDINGS GENERALLY SHOW NO SIGNIFICANT DIFFERENCES IN RESPONSES. THE MAIN DIFFERENCE IS A MATTER OF COMMUNICATION. PARTICIPANTS WERE INFORMED OF THE HEAD START PROGRAM, NON-PARTICIPANTS WERE NOT. BROUGHT OUT IS THE FACT OF A DEFINITE NEED TO STEP UP COMMUNICATION IN ORDER THAT LOW INCOME FAMILIES CAN BE MADE AWARE OF AVAILABLE EDUCATION OPPORTUNITIES FOR THEIR CHILDREN AS WELL AS THE EXISTENT NEED FOR PRE-SCHOOL EDUCATION PROGRAMS THROUGHOUT THE SCHOOL YEAR. ENGLISH AND SPANISH QUESTIONNAIRES ARE INCLUDED. THERE ARE MANY TABLES OF ACCRUED DATA. (EF)

ED014332 PS000240
ACCELERATION OF INTELLECTUAL DEVELOPMENT IN EARLY CHILDHOOD. FINAL REPORT. BEREITER, CARL, JUN67 210P.
EDRS PRICE MF-$0.65 HC-$9.87

THE CHILD'S CAPACITY FOR SELF-ACTUATED INTELLECTUAL GROWTH AND THE POSSIBILITY OF SPEEDING UP INTELLECTUAL GROWTH THROUGH IMPROVED OPPORTUNITIES AND INCREASED STIMULATION WERE STUDIED. SIX EXPLORATORY STUDIES CARRIED OUT DURING THE FIRST TWO YEARS OF THIS PROJECT WERE REPORTED. THE THREE MAIN AREAS OF LEARNING WHICH WERE INVESTIGATED WITH THE IDEA OF LOCATING PROMISING APPROACHES WERE READING, CREATIVITY, AND LOGICAL OPERATIONS. THESE STUDIES CONCERNED (1) EXPLORING THE TEACHING OF READING TO VERY YOUNG CHILDREN, (2) A TEACHING MACHINE APPROACH WHICH SHOWED SOME PROMISE IN THE FIRST STUDY, (3) PREFERENCES FOR HIGH-FREQUENCY VERSUS LOW-FREQUENCY WORD USE OCCURRING IN CHILDREN'S SPEECH, (4) CONSTRUCTION ACTIVITIES INVOLVING INDEPENDENT PROBLEM-SOLVING, AND GUIDED CONSTRUCTION, (5) A METHOD OF INDUCING CONSERVATION OF SUBSTANCE IN KINDERGARTEN CHILDREN, AND (6) TEACHING FORMAL LOGICAL OPERATION TO PRESCHOOL CHILDREN. TWO OTHER STUDIES WERE DISCUSSED, INCLUDING (1) INSTRUCTION OF DIRECT VERBAL INSTRUCTION IN LANGUAGE, ARITHMETIC, AND READING TO FOUR-YEAR OLD DISADVANTAGED CHILDREN, AND (2) COMPARISON OF A DIRECT VERBAL INSTRUCTION WITH A MONTESSORI PROGRAM FOR FOUR-YEAR OLDS. RESULTS AND CONCLUSIONS WERE MANY AND VARIED. (EF)

ED014333 PS000241
THE 1965 HEAD START PSYCHOLOGICAL SCREENING PROGRAM. FINAL REPORT ON THE DATA ANALYSIS. SCHAIE, K. WARNER, MAR67 70P.
EDRS PRICE MF-$0.65 HC-$3.29

THE SCREENING PROGRAM HAD TWO PURPOSES. (1) IT WAS TO BE USED TO DETECT CHILDREN WITH UNUSUALLY SEVERE EMOTIONAL PROBLEMS AND CHILDREN WHO, BECAUSE OF THEIR SUSPECTED RETARDATION IN INTELLECTUAL DEVELOPMENT, MIGHT NEED SPECIAL EDUCATION FACILITIES. THE DATA FOUND WERE TO BE USED TO IMPLEMENT EARLY DETECTION AND REMEDIAL PROGRAMS. (2) IT WAS TO PROVIDE SOME MEASURES OF COGNITIVE AND PERSONALITY CHANGES WHICH MIGHT BE ATTRIBUTED TO THE EFFECT OF THE ENRICHMENT PROCEDURES USED AS PART OF THE 1965 HEAD START PROGRAM. THE CHOSEN TESTS WERE LIMITED TO THOSE WHICH COULD BE SCORED OBJECTIVELY, WERE SIMPLE TO ADMINISTER, AND WERE SCORED, TABULATED, ANALYZED, AND INTERPRETED BY SOME AUTOMATED MEANS, BECAUSE FEW EXAMINERS HAD PREVIOUS EXPERIENCE IN ADMINISTERING PSYCHOLOGICAL TESTS. EXAMINATIONS WERE CONDUCTED IN APPROXIMATELY 1300 HEAD START CLASSES. SEVEN TO EIGHT WEEKS LATER, ALL TESTS WERE REPEATED WITH APPROXIMATELY ONE-THIRD OF THE CHILDREN. THE CULTURE FAIR INTELLIGENCE TEST INDICATES AN AVERAGE IQ OF 104.9 FOR THE WHOLE STATE OF WEST VIRGINIA. HEAD START CHILDREN AT AGE SIX SEEMED TO BE AT AN AVERAGE INTELLECTUAL LEVEL WHICH WAS NOT SIGNIFICANTLY BELOW THEIR MIDDLE-CLASS PEERS. THE COLOR PYRAMID TEST SUGGESTS HIGH INCIDENCE IN THE HEAD START GROUP OF SUSPECTED AUTISTIC THINKING, DEPRESSION AND ASOCIAL BEHAVIOR, CURRENT EMOTIONAL DISTURBANCE, EMOTIONAL RETARDATION, AND EXTREME ACTING-OUT BEHAVIOR. ASSESSMENT OF CHANGE PRODUCED BY THE 1965 HEAD START PROGRAM IS RELATIVELY INCONCLUSIVE. (MANY TABLES ARE INCLUDED.) (EF)

ED014334 PS000242
THE PRESCHOOL INVENTORY. CALDWELL, BETTYE M.; SOULE, DONALD, 65 45P.
EDRS PRICE MF-$0.65 HC-$3.29

THE PRESCHOOL INVENTORY BEGAN AS AN ANSWER TO THE NEED FOR SOME TYPE OF INSTRUMENT THAT WOULD PROVIDE AN INDICATION OF HOW MUCH A DISADVANTAGED CHILD, PRIOR TO HIS INTRODUCTION TO HEAD START, HAD ACHIEVED IN AREAS REGARDED AS NECESSARY FOUNDATIONS FOR SUBSEQUENT SUCCESS IN SCHOOL. MEASURING BASIC INTELLIGENCE WAS NOT THE GOAL. RATHER, THE INVENTORY WAS AN ATTEMPT TO DEMONSTRATE THE FACT THAT THE DISADVANTAGED CHILD WAS FUNCTIONING AT A DEFICIT AT THE TIME HE BEGAN SCHOOL. IT WAS ALSO TO BE USED ON A BEFORE-AFTER BASIS AND TO BE AVAILABLE AS AN INDEX OF EDUCATIONAL ACHIEVEMENT ASSOCIATED WITH HEAD START. THE AUTHOR CONCLUDES THAT THE INVENTORY SHOULD BE MORE SYSTEMATICALLY STANDARDIZED BEFORE BEING MADE AVAILABLE FOR PUBLICATION. (APPENDIXES INCLUDE THE INSTRUMENT AND AN ADMINISTRATION AND SCORING MANUAL.) (COD)

ED015005 PS000021
CODING MANUAL FOR APPROACH (A PROCEDURE FOR PATTERNING RESPONSES OF ADULTS AND CHILDREN). CALDWELL, BETTYE; AND OTHERS, 118P.
EDRS PRICE MF-$0.65 HC-$6.58

DESCRIBED AND EXEMPLIFIED IS A CODING SYSTEM FOR TRANSLATING ON-GOING BEHAVIOR OF CHILDREN AND ADULTS INTO A NUMERICAL LANGUAGE, THUS PERMITTING THE DATA TO BE SUMMARIZED AND ANALYZED BY COMPUTER. APPROACH IS BASED ON OBSERVATION. THE OBSERVER, WHO BECOMES PART OF THE ENVIRONMENT, REPORTS INTO A TAPE RECORDER THE RESPONSES OF THE MAIN FIGURE BEING OBSERVED. THE REPORT MUST CONTAIN FOUR COMPONENTS WHICH ARE THE SUBJECT (WHO OR WHAT DOES THE ACT), THE PREDICATE (WHAT IS DONE), THE OBJECT (TOWARD WHOM OR WHAT THE ACT IS DIRECTED), AND ANY NECESSARY SUPPLEMENTARY INFORMATION (QUALIFIERS OF THE ACTION). THESE COMPONENTS ARE TRANSLATED ACCORDING TO THE CODING SYSTEM INTO THE NUMERICAL LANGUAGE. A CHART SUMMARIZES THE MAJOR APPROACH BEHAVIOR CATEGORIES AND NUMBERS ASSIGNED TO THEM. (EF)

ED015006 PS000205
DEVELOPMENT OF APPROPRIATE EVALUATION TECHNIQUES FOR SCREENING CHILDREN IN A HEAD START PROGRAM. A PILOT PROJECT. BERGER, STANLEY I., 13P.
EDRS PRICE MF-$0.65 HC-$3.29

THE PURPOSES OF THIS PILOT PROJECT WERE (1) TO ATTEMPT TO EVALUATE THE EFFECT OF THE LOCAL PROGRAM ON BOTH INDIVIDUAL CHILDREN AND THE GROUP AND (2) TO INVESTIGATE THE SENSITIVITY OF THE TEST INSTRUMENTS EMPLOYED IN EVALUATING SUCH A PROGRAM. SIXTY-ONE CHILDREN WERE ENROLLED IN THE LOCAL HEADSTART PROGRAM AND WERE ADMINISTERED THE STANFORD-BINET, LEITER INTERNATIONAL, RAVEN PROGRESSIVE MATRICES, AND PEABODY PICTURE VOCABULARY TESTS. IN ADDITION, 20 CHILDREN, SELECTED AT RANDOM FROM THE GROUP WERE TESTED BOTH BEFORE AND AFTER THE PROGRAM. RESULTS INDICATE (1) STATISTICALLY SIGNIFICANT IMPROVEMENT IN PERFORMANCE FOR THE 20 CHILDREN, (2) SIGNIFICANT CORRELATIONS AMONG THE VARIOUS TEST SCORES OF THE TOTAL GROUP, AND (3) PARTICULAR SENSITIVITY OF THE LEITER AND PEABODY TESTS IN REFLECTING CHANGES IN FUNCTIONING. IMPLICATIONS OF THE STUDY FOR FUTURE HEADSTART PROGRAMS AND ALSO FOR FURTHER RESEARCH WITH CULTURALLY DEPRIVED CHILDREN WERE DISCUSSED. (CO'D)

ED015007 PS000208
LANGUAGE RESEARCH STUDY--PROJECT HEAD START. DEVELOPMENT OF METHODOLOGY FOR OBTAINING AND ANALYZING SPONTANEOUS VERBALIZATIONS USED BY PRE-KINDERGARTEN CHILDREN IN SELECTED HEAD START PROGRAMS--A PILOT STUDY. RAPH, JANE BEASLEY, 18OCT65 30P.
EDRS PRICE MF-$0.65 HC-$3.29

THIS STUDY WAS DESIGNED TO DEVELOP METHODOLOGICAL APPROACHES FOR OBTAINING AND ANALYZING CONTINUOUS EXPRESSIVE LANGUAGE SAMPLES USED BY PRE-KINDERGARTEN CHILDREN WHEN THEY COMMUNICATE WITH EACH OTHER. IT ALSO WAS TO CONSIDER MEANS FOR ANALYZING THESE SAMPLES THAT WOULD YIELD CERTAIN QUALITATIVE AND QUANTITATIVE METHODS. FOUR INVESTIGATORS WERE ASSIGNED TO A DIFFERENT HEAD START CLASSROOM TO GENERALLY ENCOURAGE THE CHILDREN TO TALK AND KEPT CONTINUOUS, DETAILED, NARRATIVE DESCRIPTIONS OF FUNCTIONAL LANGUAGE USED BY THE CHILDREN. DURING THE LAST HALF OF THE PROGRAM, CHILDREN'S LANGUAGE RESPONSE TO SPECIFIC STIMULUS SITUATIONS WERE TAPE RECORDED, WITH THE ATTEMPT TO DETERMINE A REPRESENTATIVE RANGE FROM MOST TO LEAST VERBAL CHILDREN. (CO'D)

ED015008 PS000210
THE DEVELOPMENT OF SELF-OTHER RELATIONSHIPS DURING PROJECT HEAD START. LAMB, HOWARD E.; AND OTHERS, 65 181P.
EDRS PRICE MF-$0.65 HC-$6.58

PROJECT HEAD START WAS CONCEIVED IN PART, TO INCREASE THE ORDINARILY REDUCED NUMBER OF CONNECTIONS BETWEEN THE CHILD AND OTHER PEOPLE. FOUR QUESTIONS WERE ASKED. (1) WOULD THE DEVELOPMENT OF SELF-SOCIAL CONSTRUCTS OF HEAD START CHILDREN DIFFER FROM THE DEVELOPMENT OF CHILDREN IN A CONTROL GROUP. (2) WOULD HEAD START CHILDREN DEVELOP APPROPRIATE SOCIAL TRUST. (3) WOULD THE TEACHERS' COGNITIVE STYLES AFFECT THE DEVELOPMENT OF SELF-SOCIAL CONSTRUCTS. (4) WOULD THE TEACHERS' PERCEPTIONS OF HEAD START CHILDREN AFFECT THE DEVELOPMENT OF SELF-SOCIAL CONSTRUCTS. TWO-THIRDS OF THE STUDENTS, OR 978 CHILDREN IN THE DELAWARE SUMMER 1965 HEAD START PROGRAMS WERE GIVEN A PRE-TEST ON ELEVEN TASKS FROM THE SELF-SOCIAL SYMBOLS TASKS, AND 945 OF THE CHILDREN WERE POST-TESTED, 100 NON-HEAD START CHILDREN OF A COMPARABLE BACKGROUND WERE USED AS A CONTROL GROUP AND TESTED IN THEIR HOMES AT THE SAME TIME AS THE HEAD START STUDENTS. EIGHTY PAIRS OF CHILDREN WERE PRE-TESTED ON A SHARING TASK MEASURING SOCIAL TRUST, AND 20 PAIRS WERE POST-TESTED. RESULTS OF THE TESTS SHOWED THAT THE HEAD START EXPERIENCE PRODUCED POSITIVE CHANGES IN SELF AND SELF-OTHER RELATIONSHIPS. HEAD START CHILDREN GAINED A PERCEPTION OF SELF AS BEING SIMILAR TO OTHERS AND TENDED TO MAINTAIN SELF AS CENTRAL. CONTROLS SHOWED A SHIFT TOWARD LOWER SELF-ESTEEM AND A LACK OF CHANGE FROM A SELF-DIFFERENT TO A SELF-SAME RESPONSE. (CO'D)

ED015009 PS000211
THE EFFECTS OF MONTESSORI EDUCATIONAL TECHNIQUES ON CULTURALLY DISADVANTAGED HEAD START CHILDREN. JOHNSON, HENRY SIOUX, SEP65 77P.
EDRS PRICE MF-$0.65 HC-$3.29

TO DETERMINE WHETHER SIGNIFICANT DIFFERENCES EXIST IN SKILL PERFORMANCE AS A RESULT OF HEAD START EXPERIENCE AND TO DETERMINE WHETHER THESE DIFFERENCES EXIST BETWEEN TWO ETHNIC GROUPS, 17 ANGLO-AMERICAN AND 62 MEXICAN-AMERICAN CULTURALLY DISADVANTAGED CHILDREN WERE PRE-TESTED AND POST-TESTED DURING THE SUMMER OF 1965 IN CONNECTION WITH SIX-WEEK HEAD START PROGRAMS IN COSTA MESA AND FULLERTON, CALIFORNIA. FIVE TEACHERS USING MODIFIED MONTESSORI MATERIALS STRESSED THREE DEVELOPMENTAL AREAS, (1) PERCEPTUAL-MOTOR, (2) SOCIAL-EMOTIONAL, AND (3) INTELLECTUAL-ACADEMIC. SEVEN INSTRUMENTS WERE USED TO TEST THE PROGRAM'S EFFECTIVENESS--GESELL MATURATION INDEX, MATEER INVERSION TEST, TESTS OF DOMINANCE, TEACHER RATING SCALE, GOODENOUGH-HARRIS D-A-P, PEABODY PICTURE VOCABULARY TEST, AND WIDE RANGE ACHIEVEMENT TEST. RESULTS SHOWED THAT CERTAIN HANDICAPS DO EXIST AMONG CULTURALLY DISADVANTAGED CHILDREN PRIOR TO SCHOOL EXPERIENCE AND THAT POSITIVE GAINS OCCURRED WHEN ENRICHMENT EXPERIENCES WERE PROVIDED. GREATEST GAINS WERE IN THE AREAS OF INTELLECTUAL-ACADEMIC AND SOCIAL-EMOTIONAL SKILLS. ETHNIC DIFFERENCES APPEARED IN THE LINGUISTIC SKILLS LIMITATIONS OF THE MEXICAN-AMERICAN CHILDREN. NEED FOR MEDICAL AND DENTAL ATTENTION WAS APPARENT IN BOTH GROUPS. FUTURE PROVISION SHOULD BE MADE FOR CONTINUED PRESCHOOL EDUCATION AND WIDER DISSEMINATION OF HEALTH SERVICES. (LG)

ED015010 PS000219
A STUDY OF THE FULL-YEAR 1966 HEAD START PROGRAMS. CORT, H. RUSSELL, JR.; AND OTHERS, 31JUL67 269P.
EDRS PRICE MF-$0.65 HC-$9.87

AS PART OF THE EVALUATION OF EFFECTIVENESS OF FULL-YEAR HEAD START PROGRAMS, CHILDREN FROM A NATIONWIDE SAMPLE OF CENTERS WERE TESTED WITH FIVE INSTRUMENTS (PEABODY PICTURE VOCABULARY TEST, PRE-SCHOOL INVENTORY, VINELAND SOCIAL MATURITY SCALE, DRAW-A-PERSON, AND BEHAVIOR INVENTORY). CENTERS WERE SELECTED TO BE REPRESENTATIVE OF PROGRAMS OF DIFFERENT LENGTHS. POST-TESTS WERE USED TO EXAMINE THE QUESTION OF WHETHER THE LENGTH OF THE PROGRAM AFFECTS THE PERFORMANCE OF THE CHILDREN. THERE WAS NO RELIABLE EVIDENCE OF A SYSTEMATIC RELATIONSHIP BETWEEN LENGTH OF PARTICIPATION IN A PROGRAM AND LEVEL OF PERFORMANCE OR DEVELOPMENT. FACTORS AFFECTING THE INTERPRETATION OF RESULTS ARE DISCUSSED IN THIS REPORT. (DESCRIPTIVE STATISTICS ON THE TEST SCORES, CHARACTERISTICS OF PARENTS, FAMILIES, AND STAFF MEMBERS ARE PRESENTED. INTER-TEST CORRELATIONAL DATA ARE REPORTED.) A SUMMARY OF THIS REPORT IS ALSO AVAILABLE AS A SEPARATE DOCUMENT. (LG)

ED015011 PS000221
AN EVALUATION OF HEAD START PRESCHOOL ENRICHMENT PROGRAMS AS THEY AFFECT THE INTELLECTUAL ABILITY, THE SOCIAL ADJUSTMENT, AND THE ACHIEVEMENT LEVEL OF FIVE-YEAR-OLD CHILDREN ENROLLED IN LINCOLN, NEBRASKA. KRIDER, MARY A.; PETSCHE, MARY, 67 101P.
EDRS PRICE MF-$0.65 HC-$6.58

THREE GROUPS OF DISADVANTAGED CHILDREN WERE ESTABLISHED IN ORDER TO INVESTIGATE THE EFFECT ON ACHIEVEMENT OF PROVIDING SOME CHILDREN WITH A PRESCHOOL PROGRAM AND SOME CHILDREN WITH NO SUCH PROGRAM. AN EXPERIMENTAL GROUP OF HEAD START CHILDREN WERE MATCHED ACCORDING TO SEX, RACE, GENERAL LEVEL OF INTELLIGENCE, AND PARENT'S OCCUPATIONAL LEVEL WITH A CONTROL GROUP OF NON-HEAD START CHILDREN. THE SUBJECTS INVOLVED WERE APPROXIMATELY FOUR TO FIVE YEARS OLD AND ABOUT 200 IN NUMBER. A THIRD NON-MATCHED GROUP OF 41 CHILDREN CONSISTED OF 24 HEAD START SUBJECTS AND 17 NON-HEAD START SUBJECTS. THE TEST RESULTS SHOWED NO SIGNIFICANT DIFFERENCES BETWEEN THE MATCHED GROUPS ON THE VARIABLES OF INCREASE OF INTELLECTUAL ABILITY AND OF LEVEL OF ACHIEVEMENT. ON THE VARIABLE OF SOCIAL ADJUSTMENT, THE HEAD START MATCHED GROUP DID SIGNIFICANTLY BETTER THAN ITS MATCHED NON-HEAD START COUNTERPART ON THE BASIS OF A T-TEST BUT NOT ON THE BASIS OF AN ANALYSIS OF COVARIANCE. THE NON-MATCHED NON-HEAD START GROUP DID SIGNIFICANTLY BETTER ON INCREASE OF INTELLECTUAL ABILITY AND ON LEVEL OF ACHIEVEMENT THAN THE NON-MATCHED HEAD START GROUP, BUT NO OTHER DIFFERENCES WERE FOUND. ALL GROUPS DEMONSTRATED HIGHLY SIGNIFICANT GAINS ON THE VARIABLES ON THE BASIS OF THE WITHIN-GROUP SCORES. (WD)

ED015012 PS000229
AN EVALUATION OF DIFFERENCES AMONG DIFFERENT CLASSES OF HEAD START PARTICIPANTS. FINAL REPORT. HOLMES, DOUGLAS; HOLMES, MONICA BYCHOWSKI, 31AUG66 106P.
EDRS PRICE MF-$0.65 HC-$6.58

THREE HEAD START PROGRAMS WERE ESTABLISHED TO INVESTIGATE THE DIFFERENCES BETWEEN FOUR GROUPS OF CHILDREN IN THE AREAS OF INTELLIGENCE, COGNITION AND ACHIEVEMENT, ENVIRONMENT, AND PARENTAL EXPECTATIONS. THE FOUR GROUPS WERE (1) THE SR GROUP IN WHICH THE CHILDRENS' PARENTS SOUGHT OUT ENTRY FOR THEIR CHILDREN IN THE HEAD START PROGRAM, (2) THE SAP GROUP IN WHICH THE CHILDREN'S ENTRY INTO THE PROGRAM WAS SOUGHT OUT BY THE HEAD START PERSONNEL, (3) THE SANP GROUP WHO WERE LIKEWISE SOUGHT OUT BY PROGRAM PERSONNEL BUT DID NOT PARTICIPATE, AND (4) THE MC GROUP WHO WERE NON-PARTICIPATING MIDDLE CLASS CHILDREN AVERAGING A YEAR YOUNGER IN AGE THAN THE OTHER THREE GROUPS. GROUPS 1 AND 2 PARTICIPATED IN THE HEAD START PROGRAM ONLY. GROUP 1, 2, AND 3 WERE CHILDREN OF LOWER-INCOME FAMILIES. THE HEAD START PROGRAM LASTED SIX MONTHS. TESTING WAS CARRIED ON IN ALL FOUR GROUPS. ONE BATTERY OF TESTS WAS GIVEN ALL CHILDREN NEAR THE TIME GROUPS 1 AND 2 BEGAN THE PROGRAM. GROUPS 1 AND 2 WERE GIVEN THE BATTERY AGAIN AT THE CONCLUSION OF THE PROGRAM. THE RESULTS SHOWED THAT THE MC GROUP SCORED CONSISTENTLY HIGHEST ON ALL TESTS. THE SR GROUP WAS GENERALLY SECOND HIGHEST. THE ENVIRONMENT OF GROUPS 1 AND 4 APPEARED MORE FAVORABLE TO A STIMULATION OF EFFECTIVE LEARNING THAN THE VERY DEPRIVED ENVIRONMENTS OF GROUPS 2 AND 3. ALSO, THE PARENTS OF GROUP 1 AND 4 CHILDREN APPEARED MORE ENCOURAGING TOWARD AND INTERESTED IN THEIR CHILD'S DEVELOPMENT. (WD)

ED015013 PS000233
COMPARATIVE STUDIES OF A GROUP OF HEAD START AND A GROUP OF NON-HEAD START PRESCHOOL CHILDREN. FINAL REPORT. HOROWITZ, FRANCES DEGEN; RESENFELD, HOWARD M., JAN66 43P.
EDRS PRICE MF-$0.65 HC-$3.29

TWO GROUPS OF CHILDREN ATTENDED THE UNIVERSITY OF KANSAS NURSERY SCHOOL FOR EIGHT WEEKS. THE MORNING CLASS WAS HELD FOR 20 FOUR-YEAR-OLD CHILDREN OF MIDDLE-CLASS FAMILIES. THE AFTERNOON CLASS WAS FOR 24 FIVE-YEAR-OLD CHILDREN OF LOW-INCOME FAMILIES. THREE COMPARATIVE STUDIES WERE MADE. IN STUDY I NO CHANGE WAS FOUND ON THE PEABODY PICTURE VOCABULARY TEST IN THE MIDDLE-CLASS GROUP, WHEREAS AND INCREASE IN SCORES WAS FOUND FOR THE HEAD START GROUP. THE PRESCHOOL INVENTORY SHOWED THE MIDDLE-CLASS PRESCHOOL GROUP TO BE SIGNIFICANTLY HIGHER IN PERFORMANCE, BUT SOME CHANGES DID OCCUR OVER THE SUMMER FOR THE HEAD START GROUP. IN STUDY II NO OVERALL DIFFERENCES WERE FOUND BETWEEN THE GROUPS ON TWO DISCRIMINATION LEARNING TASKS, BUT AN INTERACTION OF GROUP AND SEX WAS INDICATED. IN STUDY III CHILDREN JUDGED TO BE LOW IN SOCIAL RESPONSIVENESS WERE SELECTED FROM THE TWO GROUPS, AND THEIR PERFORMANCE IN A LABORATORY SETTING WAS ASSESSED. THE MAJOR DIFFERENCES BETWEEN THE HEAD START AND MIDDLE-CLASS GROUP IN A BASELINE ASSESSMENT APPEARED TO BE IN VOCALIZATIONS. A FINAL IMPLICATION OF THIS STUDY IS THAT THE PERSISTENT BEHAVIORAL DEFICIENCES OF THE HEAD START CHILDREN REVEALED IN THE BASELINE SESSIONS APPEAR TO BE REVERSIBLE. (CO'D)

ED015014 PS000243
REPORT OF A RESEARCH AND DEMONSTRATION PROJECT FOR CULTURALLY DISADVANTAGED CHILDREN IN THE ANCONA MONTESSORI SCHOOL. JENSEN, JUDITH; KOHLBERG, LAWRENCE, 66 164P.
EDRS PRICE MF-$0.65 HC-$6.58

A PRESCHOOL EXPERIENCE WAS PROVIDED FOR LOWER-INCOME NEGRO CHILDREN, AND THEN THEIR GAINS OR LOSSES IN IQ AND SOCIAL INTEGRATION WERE EVALUATED IN TERMS OF THE TYPE OF THE TEACHING METHOD USED. THIRTY LOWER-INCOME NEGRO CHILDREN AND 17 MIDDLE-INCOME NEGRO AND WHITE CHILDREN WERE SEPARATED INTO THREE GROUPS AND EXPOSED TO THREE TEACHING METHODS. CLASS ONE WAS UNINTEGRATED (ALL LOWER-INCOME NEGRO CHILDREN) AND NON-MONTESSORIAL IN METHODOLOGY. IT WAS THE MOST UNRESTRICTED IN TERMS OF TEACHER CONTROL. CLASS TWO AS INTEGRATED AND NON-MONTESSORIAL, BUT TEACHER CONTROL AND RESTRICTION WAS MORE EVIDENT. CLASS THREE WAS INTEGRATED AND MONTESSORIAL. THE PUPILS HERE WERE THE MOST DISCIPLINED AND CONTROLLED. A THOROUGH STUDY WAS MADE OF THESE CLASSROOM PROCEDURES, TEACHING TECHNIQUES, AND PUPIL ACTIVITIES. THE RESULTS OF THE STANFORD-BINET INTELLIGENCE TESTS SHOWED NO SIGNIFICANT IQ GAIN AMONG THE GROUPS OR WITHIN A GROUP FROM TEST ONE AT THE BEGINNING OF THE EIGHT WEEK SUMMER SESSION TO TEST TWO AT THE END OF THE SESSION. BUT INDIVIDUAL GAINS APPEARED. THESE WERE FOUND TO BE AN INVERSE FUNCTION OF DISTRACTIBILITY. A WINTER PRE-SCHOOL SESSION, WITH NEW PUPILS AND USING ONLY THE MONTESSORI METHOD, RESULTED IN IQ GAINS. THIS WAS ATTRIBUTED TO AN IMPROVED CLASSROOM ATMOSPHERE. IN GENERAL, THE SESSIONS DID INCREASE THE CHILDREN'S READINESS TO BEGIN SCHOOL WORK AND HELPED THEM TO GAIN SOCIAL CONFIDENCE.

ENCOURAGING PARENTAL INTEREST AND PARTICIPATION WAS A COLLATERAL ASPECT OF THE PROGRAMS. (WD)

ED015015 PS000256
THE FORMATION OF ADDITION AND SUBTRACTION CONCEPTS BY PUPILS IN GRADES ONE AND TWO. FINAL REPORT. PAYNE, JOSEPH N., 1MAY67 24P.
EDRS PRICE MF-$0.65 HC-$3.29

TO DETERMINE THE EFFECT OF INSTRUCTIONAL APPROACHES FOR SUBTRACTION AND/OR TIME OF SYMBOLIZATION UPON (1) ACHIEVEMENT IN ARITHMETIC, (2) ATTAINMENT OF NUMBER CONCEPTS, (3) ATTITUDES TOWARD ARITHMETIC IN GRADES ONE AND TWO, THIS REPORT ASSESSES FOUR EXPERIMENTAL CLASSES, THERE WERE TWO FIRST GRADE CLASSES OF 20 PUPILS EACH AND TWO SECOND GRADE CLASSES OF 17 PUPILS EACH. THE INSTRUCTIONAL APPROACH USED FOUR TREATMENTS (1) PPW-E (PART-PART-WHOLE WITH EARLY SYMBOLIZATION), (2) PPW-L (LATE SYMBOLIZATION), (3) TA-E (TAKE-AWAY WITH EARLY SYMBOLIZATION), (4) TA-L (LATE SYMBOLIZATION). A CONCEPT ATTAINMENT TEST WAS DESIGNED FOR USE AT THE BEGINNING AND END OF GRADE ONE. OTHER TESTS WERE ALSO ADMINISTERED BEFORE, DURING, AND AFTER GRADES ONE AND TWO. THE TESTS USED WERE THE CONCEPT ATTAINMENT TEST (BEGINNING AND END OF GRADE ONE), THE STANFORD ACHIEVEMENT TEST (END OF GRADE TWO), A SUBTRACTION APPLICATIONS AND TRANSFER TEST (END OF GRADES ONE AND TWO), LORGE-THORNDIKE INTELLIGENCE TEST (BEGINNING OF GRADE ONE), AN ARITHMETIC ATTITUDE SCALE (THREE TIMES IN EACH GRADE), SUBTRACTION FACTS TEST (END OF GRADE TWO), AND A LOGIC TEST (END OF THE STUDY). THERE WERE NINE CONCLUSIONS. (1) GRADES ONE AND TWO CAN LEARN USING PPW. (2) TA WAS MORE EFFECTIVE FOR TEACHING SUBTRACTION SKILLS AFTER GRADE ONE BUT, AFTER GRADE TWO, THE EFFECT OF TA AND PPW EQUALIZED. (3) AFTER GRADE TWO, PPW WAS SUPERIOR IN TEACHING APPLICATIONS OF SUBTRACTION. (4) AFTER GRADE TWO, PPW WAS SUPERIOR IN PROBLEMS REQUIRING TRANSFER. (5) PPW WAS SUPERIOR IN RELATING ADDITION AND SUBTRACTION. PPW FOSTERED PARTITIONING. (6) TA WAS INITIALLY EASIER TO TEACH. (7) HIGHER ACHIEVEMENT FOLLOWED EARLY SYMBOLIZATION. (8) CHANGES IN ATTITUDE WERE NOT PRODUCED BY ANY OF THE FOUR TREATMENTS. (9) NO DIFFERENCES WERE ATTRIBUTABLE TO SEX. FUTURE RESEARCH USING HIGHER GRADES, LARGER NUMBERS OF STUDENTS, AND OTHER MATHEMATICAL TOPICS SHOULD BE DONE. (LG)

ED015016 PS000261
BEHAVIOR PATTERNS OF NORMAL CHILDREN. PINNEAU, SAMUEL R.; AND OTHERS, 67 268P.
EDRS PRICE MF-$0.65 HC-$9.87

DURING THE PERIOD 1930 TO 1938, THE PATTERNS OF BEHAVIOR OF A BASIC SAMPLE OF 138 THREE TO FOUR AND ONE-HALF YEAR-OLD CHILDREN WERE OBTAINED BY TEACHER RATINGS. THE TEACHERS USED A RATING CHART OF 61 BEHAVIOR VARIABLES. TEN BEHAVIOR PATTERNS WERE ISOLATED FROM THIS GROUP. EACH PATTERN, FOR EXAMPLE, EMOTIONAL REACTIVITY, WAS COMPRISED OF SEVERAL BEHAVIOR MANIFESTATIONS, FOR EXAMPLE, (1) DISPLAYS TEMPER, (2) CRIES, AND (3) AROUSED BY THWARTING FROM ADULTS. THE SEVERAL BEHAVIOR MANIFESTATIONS HAD THE COMMON FACTOR DESIGNATED BY THE NAME OF THE PATTERN. MOST OF THE TEN PATTERNS WERE FOUND TO BE CONSISTENT IN FORM FOR DIFFERENT SAMPLES OF CHILDREN. THERE WERE NO QUALITATIVE DIFFERENCES IN BEHAVIOR PATTERNS ON THE BASIS OF SEX. COMPARISONS OF A SUBGROUP OF THE BASIS SAMPLE AT TWO TIME PERIODS, ONE 18 MONTHS AFTER THE OTHER, SHOWED SOME QUALITATIVE AND QUANTITATIVE CHANGES IN BEHAVIOR PATTERNS WITH GROWTH OF THE CHILD. SIMILARLY, COMPARISONS OF BEHAVIOR PATTERNS OF THE SAME SAMPLE OF CHILDREN IN FIRST, THIRD, AND FIFTH GRADES INDICATED SOME SHIFTING IN BOTH THE TYPE AND IMPORTANCE OF BEHAVIOR PATTERN DIMENSIONS. THIS STUDY INVESTIGATED BEHAVIOR CHARACTERISTICS OF CHILDREN BY CROSS-SECTIONAL AND LONGITUDINAL APPROACHES. IN GENERAL, THE STUDY FOUND A RELATIVE CONSISTENCY IN THE BEHAVIOR PATTERN FORMS THEMSELVES AND IN THE PATTERNS OF A PARTICULAR CHILD OVER THE TIME PERIOD INVOLVED. (WD)

ED015017 PS000262
A SOCIAL PSYCHOLOGICAL ANALYSIS OF THE TRANSITION FROM HOME TO SCHOOL. FINAL REPORT. SECORD, PAUL F., AUG67 67P.
EDRS PRICE MF-$0.65 HC-$3.29

THE TRADITIONAL VIEW THAT A CHILD'S INTELLECTUAL ACHIEVEMENTS DEPEND PRIMARILY UPON GENETIC PREDISPOSITIONS IS NOW BEING SUPERSEDED BY THE IDEA, SUPPORTED BY MANY RECENT STUDIES, THAT THE FACTORS OF ENVIRONMENT AND EXPERIENCE PROFOUNDLY AFFECT PERFORMANCE ON MENTAL TASKS AND SUCCESS IN THE EDUCATIONAL SYSTEM. THE SOCIOECONOMIC LEVEL OF THE PUPIL IS AN IMPORTANT INFLUENCE ON A CHILD'S INTELLECTUAL DEVELOPMENT BECAUSE IT DETERMINES, FOR THE MOST PART, THE ENVIRONMENT AND TYPES OF EXPERIENCES A PUPIL WILL HAVE. TWO TYPES WHICH ARE OF PARTICULAR IMPORT ARE (1) THE QUALITY OF PRESCHOOL EXPERIENCE AND (2) THE QUALITY OF EARLY EXPERIENCE IN THE PRIMARY GRADES. IN OTHER WORDS, THE TYPE OF FAMILY A CHILD IS A PART OF (ITS ATTITUDES AND AMBITIONS) AND THE TYPE OF SCHOOL HE FIRST ATTENDS MAY SIGNIFICANTLY INFLUENCE HIS LATER LEARNING ACHIEVEMENTS. BOTH THE TYPE OF FAMILY LIFE AND TYPE OF EARLY SCHOOLING A LOWER CLASS CHILD EXPERIENCES CAUSES HIM TO BE BEHIND HIS UPPER CLASS PEERS IN INTELLECTUAL DEVELOPMENT AND TO REMAIN BEHIND THEM. THE MODERN TREND OF SCHOOLS TOWARD ABILITY GROUPING, THAT IS, SEPARATING THE GOOD STUDENTS FROM THE POOR STUDENTS, MAY ALSO CONTRIBUTE TO HALTING OR DISCOURAGING THE MENTAL DEVELOPMENT OF STUDENTS WHO ARE BEHIND THE OTHERS. ABILITY GROUPING MAY ADVERSELY AFFECT TEACHER ATTITUDES TOWARD LOWER-ABILITY GROUPS AND MAY DEPRESS THE MORALE OF SUCH GROUPS. (WD)

ED015018 PS000267
HANDBOOK FOR PROJECT HEAD START. GRAHAM, JORY, 23P.
EDRS PRICE MF-$0.65 HC-$3.29

THIS BOOKLET WAS DESIGNED TO MEET SOME IMMEDIATE NEEDS FOR THE FIRST SUMMER SESSION OF PROJECT HEAD START. IT CONTAINS SOME OF THE MOST WORKABLE AND PROMISING TEACHING METHODS IN THE ENTIRE FIELD OF COMPENSATORY EDUCATIONS, METHODS THAT HAVE BEEN USED IN PRIVATELY SPONSORED CENTERS AND HAVE PROVED VALUABLE IN COPING WITH PROBLEMS ENCOUNTERED IN THOSE CENTERS. (1) EACH CHILD SHOULD BE SPOKEN WITH EVERY DAY, IN ORDER TO OVERCOME HIS SILENCE. (2) HELPING CHILDREN BECOME SKILLFUL AT OBSERVATION BY CLASSIFYING OBJECTS AND READING PICTURES WILL ALSO INCREASE THEIR CURIOSITY. (3) DEMONSTRATIONS SUCH AS ZIPPING A ZIPPER ARE EFFECTIVE IN TEACHING PRACTICAL SKILLS. (4) THERE ARE MANY WAYS TO BUILD SELF IMAGE OR SELF RESPECT IN CHILDREN. ONE WAY IS TO LEARN RESPECT FOR OTHERS BY GIVING EACH CHILD SOME PERSONAL POSSESSION. (5) CHILDREN ALSO NEED TO USE PHYSICAL AND EMOTIONAL ACTIVITIES SUCH AS RUNNING AND PAINTING EXPRESS THEIR FEELINGS. (6) FOR CHILDREN TO DEVELOP CURIOSITY THROUGH SCIENCE THEY CAN HAVE PETS AND PLANTS IN THE CLASSROOM. MANY CONCRETE SUGGESTIONS FOR WORKING WITH BOTH INDIVIDUAL CHILDREN AND GROUPS OF CHILDREN ARE GIVEN. THIS DOCUMENT IS AVAILABLE FROM THE ANTI-DEFAMATION LEAGUE OF B'NAI B'RITH, 315 LEXINGTON AVE., N.Y., N.Y., 10016, FOR $0.50. (COD)

ED015019 PS000268
THE INTERNATIONAL WALDORF SCHOOL MOVEMENT. VON BARAVALLE, HERMANN, 63
DOCUMENT NOT AVAILABLE FROM EDRS.

AN HISTORICAL REVIEW OF THE WALDORF SCHOOL PLAN TRACES THE MOVEMENT FROM ITS FOUNDING IN STUTTGART, GERMANY IN 1919, BY THE WALDORF ASTORIA COMPANY AND UNDER THE DIRECTION OF RUDOLF STEINER, TO ITS INTRODUCTION INTO SWITZERLAND, OTHER EUROPEAN COUNTRIES, THE AMERICAS, AUSTRALIA, NEW ZEALAND, AND SOUTH AFRICA, A TOTAL OF 175 SCHOOLS AS OF 1963. THE MOVEMENT SEEKS NEW WAYS OF SOCIAL CONSOLIDATION THROUGH EDUCATING THE YOUNG ACCORDING TO SPECIFIC METHODS AND DEMOCRATIC PRINCIPLES. A CLASS TEACHER FOLLOWS ONE GROUP FROM FIRST THRO GH EIGHTH GRADES, TEACHING ALL SUBJECTS. EACH SCHOOL DAY BALANCES INTELLECTUAL ACTIVITIES WITH MOTOR ACTIVITIES, BEGINNING WITH ONE MAJOR SUBJECT AND ENDING WITH RECREATION. SUBJECTS ARE CHANGED EVERY TWO OR THREE WEEKS, ALLOWING CONCENTRATED STUDY ON SINGLE SUBJECTS. LOVE OF LEARNING IS THE MOTIVATION PREFERRED TO COERCION OR COMPETITION. METHODS OF INSTRUCTION INCLUDE WRITING BEFORE READING, TEACHING MATHEMATICS WITH RHYTHMIC MOVEMENT, RELATING ACADEMIC WITH ARTISTIC WORK, SYMTOMATOLOGICAL AND PHENOMENOLOGICAL APPROACH, AND RELATING BASIC LIFE FUNCTIONS TO FARM EXPERIENCE. CHILDREN'S TEMPERAMENTS ARE CONSIDERED IN DEVELOPING THEIR POTENTIAL. THE EUROPEAN SCHOOLS ARE FINANCED PARTIALLY WITH GOVERNMENT FUNDS. AMERICAN SCHOOLS OPERATE BY TUITION AND DONATION. ADDITIONAL FUNDING IS NEEDED TO REMAIN ACCESSIBLE TO THE GENERAL PUBLIC. THIS DOCUMENT IS AVAILABLE FROM WALDORF SCHOOL MONOGRAPHS, 25 PERSHING ROAD, ENGLEWOOD, N.J. (LG)

ED015020 PS000271
TEACHING READING TO CHILDREN WITH LOW MA'S. ENGELMANN, SIEGFRIED, 20P.
EDRS PRICE MF-$0.65 HC-$3.29

ONE OF THE PROBLEMS OF TEACHING READING TO CHILDREN WITH LOW MENTAL AGES, FOR EXAMPLE, OF FOUR TO FIVE, IS THAT MOST READING PROGRAMS ARE GEARED TO THE CHILDREN WITH A MENTAL AGE OF ABOUT SIX AND ONE-HALF. A CHILD WITH THIS HIGHER MENTAL DEVELOPMENT WILL OFTEN HAVE MANY OF THE BASIC READING SKILLS ALREADY ACCOMPLISHED, OR HE CAN LEARN THEM QUICKLY AND WITHOUT THE BENEFIT OF THE MOST EFFICIENT INSTRUCTION. A CHILD WITH A LOW MENTAL-AGE MIGHT STRUGGLE TO LEARN TO READ UNDER SUCH A PROGRAM FOR AN INORDINATE AMOUNT OF TIME. RETARDED, HANDICAPPED, AND DEPRIVED CHILDREN MUST GENERALLY BE INSTRUCTED IN THE MOST BASIC READING SKILLS. THEY MUST BE SHOWN THAT EACH LETTER REPRESENTS A SOUND. THEY MUST THEN BE TAUGHT THAT THESE SOUNDS ARE SEQUENCED IN A WORD IN TIME. THAT IS, THEY MUST LEARN HOW TO BLEND. RHYMING AND ALLITERATION TASKS ARE USEFUL IN TEACHING BLENDING SKILLS. IN DEVELOPING THIS SOUND-SEQUENCE SKILL, CONTINUOUS-SOUND WORDS LIKE "FAN" AND "RAN" SHOULD BE INTRODUCED BEFORE STOP-SOUND WORDS LIKE "CAT" AND "RAT." WORDS WHOSE PRONUNCIATION DOES NOT FIT THE FUNDAMENTAL SOUND-SEQUENCE APPROACH, FOR EXAMPLE, "HAVE," IN WHICH THE "E" IS NOT PRONOUNCED, AND "SHE," WHICH CONTAINS A DOUBLE LETTER SOUND, ARE CALLED IRREGULAR WORDS AND ARE TO BE

INTRODUCED LAST. INSTRUCTION SHOULD BE UNIFORM FOR ALL PUPILS. (WO)

ED015021 PS000272
TEACHING A TEACHING LANGUAGE TO DISADVANTAGED CHILDREN. OSBORN, JEAN, 23P.
EDRS PRICE MF-$0.65 HC-$3.29

THE GOAL OF THE BEREITER-ENGELMANN PRESCHOOL PROGRAM IS TO GET DISADVANTAGED CHILDREN READY FOR THE LEARNING TASKS OF PUBLIC SCHOOL BY TEACHING A TEACHING LANGUAGE. THIS IS DONE BY MEANS OF A HIGHLY ORGANIZED AND STRUCTURED DIRECT LANGUAGE INSTRUCTION DESIGNED TO TEACH THAT A SENTENCE IS A SEQUENCE OF MEANINGFUL PARTS. THE CHILDREN BEGIN WITH LEARNING THE BASIC POINTING-OUT, OR IDENTIFYING, STATEMENT. WHEN THE CHILDREN ARE ABLE TO MAKE A REASONABLE RENDITION OF THE IDENTIFYING STATEMENT, THEY ARE TAUGHT THE NEGATIVE STATEMENT. CATEGORIZATIONS, SUCH AS FARM ANIMALS AND WILD ANIMALS, ARE THEN INTRODUCED. THE CHILDREN LEARN THE VARIOUS AND PRECISE USES OF "AND," "OR," "ONLY," AND "SOME." THEY ARE NEXT GIVEN A SERIES OF TASKS THAT DEAL WITH VERB TENSES, VERB EXPANSIONS, AND PERSONAL PRONOUNS. WHEN THE CHILDREN HAVE BEEN DIRECTED THROUGH THIS COURSE IN BASIC LOGICAL USAGE, THEIR LANGUAGE ABILITY THEN PERMITS SOME PROBLEM SOLVING. RESULTS OF THE STANFORD-BINET AT THE END OF TWO YEARS OF INSTRUCTION INDICATE THAT THE CHILDREN'S IQ'S HAVE RISEN AND ALSO THAT THEY HAVE BEEN ABLE TO USE THE LANGUAGE OF INSTRUCTION TO ACQUIRE READING AND ARITHMETIC SKILLS. (CO'D)

ED015022 PS000274
THE DIRECT INSTRUCTION PROGRAM FOR TEACHING READING. BRUNER, ELAINE C., AUG67 14P.
EDRS PRICE MF-$0.65 HC-$3.29

UNTIL SUBSTANTIAL MASTERY HAS BEEN ACHIEVED BY THE SLOWER READERS, THE SUB-SKILLS TO LEARNING THE MECHANICS OF READING SHOULD BE MADE THE OBJECTIVES OF INSTRUCTION. FOCUSING ON WORDS, BLENDING, AND HANDLING IRREGULARS ARE THREE OF THE SUB-SKILLS NEEDED. TO TEACH THE CHILD TO FOCUS ON WORDS, THE TEACHER INTRODUCES VERBAL RHYMING AND ALLITERATION TASKS. THE FIVE MAJOR BLENDING STAGES ARE (1) (ORAL) THE CHILD BLENDS TOGETHER TWO PARTS OF A FAMILIAR WORD, (2) (ORAL-VISUAL) THE CHILD BLENDS THE LETTERS IN WRITTEN WORDS BEFORE HE CAN IDENTIFY ALL THE LETTERS IN THESE WORDS, (3) (VISUAL) THE CHILD IDENTIFIES AND BLENDS ALL THE LETTERS IN WRITTEN WORDS, (4) (ORAL) THE CHILD UNBLENDS (SPELLS) A WORD INTO ITS SEPARATE LETTERS, (5) (VISUAL) THE CHILD LEARNS THE WRITTEN EXTENSION OF ORAL SPELLING. THE FINAL STEP IN THE BEGINNING READING PROGRAM IS THE INTRODUCTION OF IRREGULARLY SPELLED WORDS. THE PROGRAM HAS HAD GOOD RESULTS (ONE GROUP OF CULTURALLY DEPRIVED FOUR YEAR OLDS TESTED AT THE 2.6 GRADE LEVEL IN READING AFTER ABOUT 100 HOURS OF INSTRUCTION). THIS PAPER WAS PRESENTED AT AND PUBLISHED BY THE FOURTH INTERNATIONAL I.T.A. CONFERENCE, MCGILL UNIVERSITY, MONTREAL, CANADA, AUGUST, 1967. (COD)

ED015023 PS000275
MEMORANDUM ON--FACILITIES FOR EARLY CHILDHOOD EDUCATION. DEUTSCH, MARTIN; AND OTHERS, 40P.
EDRS PRICE MF-$0.65 HC-$3.29

BECAUSE LEARNING ENVIRONMENT HAS SIGNIFICANCE FOR THE DISADVANTAGED CHILD, INSTRUCTIONAL SPACE SHOULD BE PROVIDED THAT WILL FACILITATE INTELLECTUAL DEVELOPMENT. GUIDELINES ARE GIVEN FOR GENERAL AREA, BLOCK ALCOVE, MANIPULATIVE TOY AREA, READING AND LISTENING AREA, DOLL AND HOUSEKEEPING AREA, ART AREA, TUTORING BOOTH, CUBICLES, TOILETS, STORAGE, OUTDOOR PLAY AREA, AND OBSERVATION SPACE. THE SQUARE FOOTAGE, CONTENTS, PURPOSES, AND ADAPTABILITY OF THESE ELEMENTS ARE GIVEN IN DETAIL. THE AIM IS TO ACHIEVE AN ENVIRONMENT THAT FOSTERS THE EDUCATIONAL OBJECTIVES OF THE PROGRAM CONTAINED WITHIN THE SPACE. THREE EXAMPLES OF EXISTING FACILITIES ARE DESCRIBED TO ILLUSTRATE THE GUIDELINES' APPLICATION TO RENOVATING A HOUSE, REMODELING A PUBLIC SCHOOL CLASSROOM, AND DESIGNING A NEW EARLY CHILDHOOD EDUCATION CENTER. (FLOOR PLANS AND BIBLIOGRAPHY ARE INCLUDED.) (LG)

ED015024 PS000280
A BIBLIOGRAPHY (WITH SELECTED ANNOTATIONS) ON NONGRADED ELEMENTARY SCHOOLS. SHINN, BYRON M., JR., FEB67 21P.
EDRS PRICE MF-$0.65 HC-$3.29

THIS DOCUMENT IS A BIBLIOGRAPHY OF BOOKS AND ARTICLES ON THE SUBJECT OF NONGRADED ELEMENTARY SCHOOL SYSTEMS. THE BASIC BIBLIOGRAPHY IS TAKEN FROM A BIBLIOGRAPHICAL WORK BY VOGEL AND WEINGARTEN DONE AT NORTHWESTERN UNIVERSITY. THE PRESENT BIBLIOGRAPHY IS DIVIDED INTO THREE PARTS, (1) RESEARCH STUDIES EVALUATING THE RESULTS OF NONGRADED ELEMENTARY SCHOOLS, (2) ANNOTATED ARTICLES DESCRIBING VARIOUS FACETS OF NONGRADED ELEMENTARY SCHOOLS, AND (3) BOOKS AND ADDITIONAL ARTICLES DESCRIBING NONGRADED ORGANIZATION. SECTIONS (1) AND (2) INCLUDE A BRIEF DESCRIPTIVE PARAGRAPH OR TWO OF THE NATURE OR FINDINGS OF THE DOCUMENT LISTED, WHILE SECTION (3) IS MERELY A LISTING OF BOOKS AND ARTICLES WITH THEIR USUAL BIBLIOGRAPHICAL INFORMATION. (WD)

ED015025 PS000281
SIX MONTHS LATER--A COMPARISON OF CHILDREN WHO HAD HEAD START, SUMMER, 1965, WITH THEIR CLASSMATES IN KINDERGARTEN, A CASE STUDY OF THE KINDERGARTENS IN FOUR PUBLIC ELEMENTARY SCHOOLS, NEW YORK CITY. STUDY I. STEIN, ANNIE; WOLFF, MAX, 18AUG66 98P.
EDRS PRICE MF-$0.65 HC-$3.29

KINDERGARTENS IN FOUR PUBLIC ELEMENTARY SCHOOLS (ONE NEGRO, TWO PUERTO RICAN, AND ONE MIXED) IN NEW YORK CITY WERE STUDIED TO DETERMINE WHETHER A POSITIVE DEVELOPMENTAL EFFECT HAD RESULTED FROM A SUMMER HEAD START PROGRAM. THE PERFORMANCE OF 179 FORMER HEAD START CHILDREN WAS MEASURED AGAINST 388 OF THEIR NON-HEAD START CLASSMATES. SEVEN INSTRUMENTS, INCLUDING SIX DEVELOPED FOR THIS STUDY (RANKING ARRAY, COOPERATIVE RATING SCHEDULES, CALDWELL PRE-SCHOOL INVENTORY, TEACHER INTERVIEWS, CLASS OBSERVATIONS, PARENT INTERVIEWS, AND CHILD INTERVIEWS), MEASURED THE EFFECT OF HEAD START ON READINESS TO ENTER FIRST GRADE, ON OVERALL READINESS, ON SOCIAL ADJUSTMENT TO KINDERGARTEN ROUTINES, AND ON EDUCATIONAL ACHIEVEMENT. IMPACT OF THE KINDERGARTEN TEACHER WAS STUDIED, AS WAS THE IMPACT OF HEAD START ON THE KINDERGARTEN CLASS AND ON THE HOME. TEACHER AND PARENT RECOMMENDATIONS FOR HEAD START IMPROVEMENT WERE RECORDED. RESULTS INDICATED THAT ALTHOUGH NO EDUCATIONAL GAINS HAD BEEN MADE, HEAD START CHILDREN SHOW GREATER LEARNING READINESS AND EAGERNESS TO LEARN THAN NON-HEAD START CHILDREN SIX MONTHS LATER. (SEE ALSO PS 000 282, PS 000 293, PS 000 284, PS 000 285, AND PS 000 286.) (LG)

ED015026 PS000282
FACTORS INFLUENCING THE RECRUITMENT OF CHILDREN INTO THE HEAD START PROGRAM, SUMMER 1965--A CASE STUDY OF SIX CENTERS IN NEW YORK CITY. STUDY II. STEIN, ANNIE; WOLFF, MAX, 18AUG66 31P.
EDRS PRICE MF-$0.65 HC-$3.29

TO RESOLVE THE QUESTION OF WHY SOME PARENTS SENT ELIGIBLE CHILDREN TO HEAD START AND SOME DID NOT, A STUDY WAS MADE OF SIX HEAD START CENTERS IN NEW YORK CITY. THE STUDY SAMPLE WAS COMPOSED OF THE THREE CENTERS HAVING THE BEST RECRUITMENT RECORD AND THE THREE HAVING THE POOREST. EACH GROUP HAD ONE NEGRO, ONE PUERTO RICAN, AND ONE MIXED SCHOOL. MATCHED SETS OF 150 HEAD START AND 150 NON-HEAD START CHILDREN FROM THESE SCHOOLS WERE CHOSEN. THEIR PARENTS WERE INTERVIEWED BY INTERVIEWERS OF THE MATCHING ETHNIC GROUP. FINDINGS WERE THAT SOME ELIGIBLE FAMILIES HAD THE MEANS TO PROVIDE OTHER SUMMER PROGRAMS AS ALTERNATES AND SO DID NOT ENROLL THEIR CHILDREN. SOME LOW INCOME PARENTS HELD HIGH EDUCATIONAL ASPIRATIONS FOR THEIR CHILDREN AND ENROLLED THEM TO HELP REALIZE THEIR GOALS. INTERVIEWS BY INDIGENOUS PERSONNEL WERE FOUND TO BE MOST EFFECTIVE IN RECRUITING. ETHNIC BACKGROUND AFFECTED PARENTAL REASONS FOR ENROLLMENT. FOR INSTANCE, PUERTO RICAN MOTHERS WANTED THEIR CHILDREN TO BE EXPOSED TO SITUATIONS OUTSIDE THEIR OWN CULTURAL EXPERIENCE. THE MOST COMMON REASON FOR ENROLLMENT WAS THAT HEAD START WOULD HELP CHILDREN ADJUST SOCIALLY TO SCHOOL. SOME PARENTS GAVE EDUCATION, RECREATION, AND CHILD CARE AS REASONS FOR ENROLLMENT. THE MOST COMMON REASON FOR NOT ENROLLING CHILDREN WAS THE LACK OF ENROLLMENT INFORMATION. INTERVIEWS REVEALED ENTHUSIASM FOR HEAD START AND A NEED FOR MORE EFFECTIVE RECRUITMENT. (SEE ALSO PS 000 281, PS 000 283, PS 000 284, PS 000 285, PS 000 286.) (LG)

ED015027 PS000283
LONG-RANGE EFFECT OF PRE-SCHOOLING ON READING ACHIEVEMENT. STUDY III. STEIN, ANNIE; WOLFF, MAX, 18AUG66 17P.
EDRS PRICE MF-$0.65 HC-$3.29

SIX NEW YORK CITY DAY CARE CENTERS WITH PROGRAMS SIMILAR TO HEAD START WERE SELECTED AS STUDY SAMPLES TO DETERMINE WHETHER THERE IS A MEASURABLE LONG-RANGE EFFECT OF PRE-SCHOOLING UPON READING ACHIEVEMENT. EACH CENTER WAS CONSIDERED TO HAVE A GOOD PROGRAM, HAD BEEN OPERATING FOR AT LEAST SIX YEARS, AND HAD RACIALLY MIXED POPULATIONS. DAY CARE CENTER RECORDS WERE USED TO TRACE CHILDREN ORIGINALLY IN THE CENTERS TO PUBLIC ELEMENTARY SCHOOLS WHERE THEY WOULD BE IN THIRD, FOURTH, AND FIFTH GRADES. GRADE-EQUIVALENT SCORES FROM METROPOLITAN ACHIEVEMENT TEST I WERE RECORDED FOR ALL TESTED CHILDREN, INCLUDING DAY CARE CENTER GRADUATES. UNCONTROLLED INFLUENCES AND ERROR INTRODUCED BY THE METHOD USED CREATED DIFFICULTIES IN ISOLATING AND MEASURING THE INFLUENCE OF PRE-SCHOOLING. A GREATER NUMBER OF DAY CARE CENTER GRADUATES SCORED AT OR ABOVE GRADE LEVEL THAN THEIR CLASSMATES, ALTHOUGH THIS NUMBER DECLINES AS GRADE LEVEL RISES. THE EVIDENCE IS INSUFFICIENT TO SUPPORT THE HYPOTHESIS THAT DAY CARE CENTERS WERE THE ONLY OR EVEN THE MAJOR FACTOR IN ACADEMIC SUCCESS, BUT IT IS SUFFICIENT TO WARRANT FURTHER STUDY. (SEE ALSO PS 000 281, PS 000 282, PS 000 284, PS 000 285, PS 000 286.) (LG)

ED015028 PS000284
APPENDIX, STUDIES I, II AND III. ORIGINAL INSTRUMENTS USED AND BIBLIOGRAPHY. WOLFF, MAX, 23P.
EDRS PRICE MF-$0.65 HC-$3.29

SEVEN INSTRUMENTS WERE USED TO TEST HEAD START CHILDREN'S PROGRESS IN KINDERGARTENS IN NEW YORK CITY IN 1965. ONE OF THESE INSTRUMENTS WAS THE CALDWELL PRE-SCHOOL INVENTORY. THE REMAINING SIX, DEVELOPED SPECIFICALLY FOR THIS STUDY, APPEAR IN THIS APPENDIX. (THE THREE-PART STUDY CAN BE FOUND UNDER THE FOLLOWING TITLES (PS 000 281) SIX MONTHS LATER. STUDY I, A COMPARISON OF CHILDREN WHO HAD HEAD START, SUMMER, 1965, WITH THEIR CLASSMATES IN KINDERGARTEN, A CASE STUDY OF THE KINDERGARTENS IN FOUR PUBLIC ELEMENTARY SCHOOLS, NEW YORK CITY. (PS 000 282) SIX MONTHS LATER. STUDY II, FACTORS INFLUENCING THE RECRUITMENT OF CHILDREN INTO THE HEAD START PROGRAM, SUMMER 1965, A CASE STUDY OF SIX CENTERS IN NEW YORK CITY. (PS 000 283) SIX MONTHS LATER. STUDY III, LONG-RANGE EFFECT OF PRE-SCHOOLING ON READING ACHIEVEMENT.) (LIST OF REFERENCES INCLUDED) (LG)

ED015029 PS000285
MEMO--COMMENTS ON THE WOLFF AND STEIN STUDY. BRONFENBRENNER, URIE, JAN67 4P.
EDRS PRICE MF-$0.65 HC-$3.29

THE VALIDITY OF THE WOLFF AND STEIN CONCLUSIONS (SIX MONTHS LATER. STUDY I. PS 000 281) IS CHALLENGED ON THE BASIS OF ONE MAJOR AND FOUR MINOR METHODOLOGICAL DEFICIENCIES. THE STUDY'S MAJOR CONCLUSION WAS THAT FORMER HEAD START CHILDREN HAVE GREATER LEARNING READINESS THAN THEIR CLASSMATES HAVE SIX MONTHS LATER BUT THAT NO EDUCATIONAL GAINS HAD BEEN MADE. THE MAJOR CRITICISM IS THAT, ALTHOUGH ECONOMIC AND SOCIAL ADVANTAGES GREATLY FAVORED NON-HEAD START CHILDREN, WOLFF AND STEIN CONSIDERED THE ADVANTAGE TO BE "SLIGHT." THE ALTERNATIVE TO WOLFF'S CONCLUSION IS THAT CHILDREN FROM DEPRIVED HOMES ARE ABLE TO HOLD THEIR OWN WITH CLASSMATES FROM BETTER ADVANTAGED FAMILIES AS A RESULT OF HEAD START ENRICHMENT. (LG)

ED015030 PS000286
REMARKS ON THE MAX WOLFF REPORT. GORDON, EDMUND W., 5P.
EDRS PRICE MF-$0.65 HC-$3.29

STRENGTHS AND WEAKNESSES OF THE WOLFE REPORT (SIX MONTHS LATER. STUDY I. PS 000 281) ARE NOTED. WEAKNESSES ARE JUDGED TO BE THAT WOLFF DID NOT CONTROL VARIATIONS IN TEACHER EFFECTIVENESS, CURRICULUM, OR STUDENT CHARACTERISTICS. STRENGTHS ARE (1) PARENT INTERVIEWS, (2) ASSESSMENT OF HEAD START-KINDERGARTEN TRANSITION, (3) RECOGNITION OF THREE FACTORS AS INTERRELATED (A) PERCENTAGE OF HEAD START CHILDREN IN CLASS, (B) THE KINDERGARTEN TEACHER'S KNOWLEDGE OF HEAD START ATTENDANCE AND (C) TEACHER ATTITUDES TOWARD VARIOUS LEARNING STYLES, AND (4) THE POSITION THAT GAINS CAN EVEN OUT IF PRIMARY SCHOOL EXPERIENCE FAILS TO DEVELOP THEM. (SEE ALSO PS 000 281.) (LG)

ED015770 PS000084
FROM THEORY TO THE CLASSROOM, BACKGROUND INFORMATION ON THE FIRST GRADE PROJECT IN NEW YORK CITY SCHOOLS. BUSSIS, ANNE M.; AND OTHERS, 65 28P.
EDRS PRICE MF-$0.65 HC-$3.29

BECAUSE TEACHERS NEED RESOURCES BOTH TO ASSESS AND TO DEVELOP INTELLECTUAL SKILLS IN YOUNG CHILDREN, THE NEW YORK CITY BOARD OF EDUCATION AND THE EDUCATIONAL TESTING SERVICE UNDERTOOK A PROJECT IN THE FIRST GRADES OF 25 ELEMENTARY SCHOOLS DURING THE 1964-1965 SCHOOL YEAR. FOUR ASSUMPTIONS FORMED THE THEORETICAL BASE OF THE PROJECT--(1) INTELLIGENCE IS A SET OF DEVELOPED SKILLS, NOT AN INHERITED CHARACTERISTIC, (2) INTELLECTUAL SKILLS DEVELOP AS A RESULT OF INTERACTION WITH ENVIRONMENT, (3) LEARNING MOTIVATION IS INHERENT IN CHILDREN, AND (4) INTELLECTUAL DEVELOPMENT IS SEQUENTIAL AND PRODUCES QUALITATIVE CHANGE IN THOUGHT PROCESSES. THESE ASSUMPTIONS WERE APPLIED TO CLASSROOM SITUATIONS THROUGH THE DEVELOPMENT OF (1) A GUIDE FOR TEACHERS, "LET'S LOOK AT FIRST GRADERS," (2) BOTH TESTING AND INSTRUCTIONAL MATERIALS FOR CLASSROOM USE, AND (3) WRITTEN EXERCISES, ALL OF WHICH RELATED TO INTELLECTUAL RATHER THAN TO EMOTIONAL, SOCIAL, OR MOTOR SKILLS. THESE INITIAL TRYOUT MATERIALS WERE USED AND APPRAISED BY PARTICIPATING EDUCATORS AND REVISED FOR USE IN A LARGER NUMBER OF SCHOOLS IN 1965-66. FUTURE RESEARCH WAS TO DETERMINE THE LONG-RANGE EFFECTS OF THE PROJECT. (LG)

ED015771 PS000214
FOLLOW-UP OF OPERATION HEAD START PARTICIPANTS IN THE STATE OF IOWA. FINAL REPORT. FOLEY, WALTER J., 67 23P.
EDRS PRICE MF-$0.65 HC-$3.29

A STEP BY STEP OUTLINE OF THE SYSTEM DEVELOPED TO MAKE AND KEEP RECORDS FOR A 2-YEAR FOLLOWUP STUDY OF IOWA HEADSTART PARTICIPANTS (SUMMER 1965), SUPPLIES DETAILED INFORMATION FOR THE ESTABLISHMENT OF A SIMILAR SYSTEM. THE IOWA EDUCATION INFORMATION CENTER OF THE UNIVERSITY OF IOWA AND THE OFFICE OF ECONOMIC OPPORTUNITY COOPERATED TO DEVELOP AN INFORMATION RETRIEVAL SYSTEM INCLUDING PUPIL IDENTIFICATION AND CONTINUOUS FILE MAINTENANCE. INCLUDED IN THIS FINAL REPORT OF THE PROJECT ARE COPIES OF THE TAPE LAYOUTS RELEVANT TO THE FILES, AND RETRIEVAL FORMATS NEEDED TO EXTRACT INFORMATION ABOUT THE HEADSTART POPULATION. A LONGITUDINAL FILE HAS BEEN SUCCESSFULLY MAINTAINED ON 79.4 PER CENT OF THE ORIGINAL HEADSTART PARTICIPANTS, A VERY GOOD RECORD CONSIDERING THE NUMBER OF PUPILS ENROLLED IN PAROCHIAL SCHOOL IN IOWA. (MS)

ED015772 PS000222
TECHNIQUES FOR ASSESSING COGNITIVE AND SOCIAL ABILITIES OF CHILDREN AND PARENTS IN PROJECT HEAD START. HESS, ROBERT D.; AND OTHERS, JUL66 139P.
EDRS PRICE MF-$0.65 HC-$6.58

IN ORDER TO DEVELOP AND EVALUATE MEASURING INSTRUMENTS FOR ASSESSING THE COGNITIVE CAPACITIES OF DISADVANTAGED CHILDREN, EXTENSIVE TESTING OF PRESCHOOL PUPILS AT 4 HEADSTART CENTERS IN CHICAGO WAS CONDUCTED. ACHIEVEMENT AND BEHAVIOR TESTS WERE ADMINISTERED DIRECTLY TO THE PUPILS. PUPILS' MOTHERS WERE INTERVIEWED AND TESTED TO OBTAIN INFORMATION ABOUT THE PUPILS' HOME ENVIRONMENT. OBSERVATION AND RATING EXERCISES BY TEACHERS AND OTHERS INDICATED SOME CHARACTERISTICS OF PUPIL ACHIEVEMENT AND BEHAVIOR. IT WAS HOPED THAT AS A RESULT OF THIS COMPREHENSIVE TESTING AND TEST-INSTRUMENT EVALUATION, A BATTERY OF EFFECTIVE INSTRUMENTS COULD BE IDENTIFIED THAT WOULD RELIABLY PREDICT PRESCHOOL CHILDREN'S SUBSEQUENT SCHOOL ACHIEVEMENT, EVALUATE THEIR SCHOOL READINESS, AND POINT OUT AREAS OF SPECIAL DISABILITY. IT WAS FOUND THAT INFORMATION ON THESE 3 AREAS COULD BE OBTAINED MOST RELIABLY BY MEASURING INTELLIGENCE AND ACHIEVEMENT BY (1) THE STANFORD-BINET, (2) THE PRESCHOOL INVENTORY, AND (3) THE DRAW-A-PERSON AND BY MEASURING BEHAVIOR AND ADJUSTMENT TO SCHOOL BY (1) CERTAIN ITEMS OF THE READINESS CHECKLIST, (2) CERTAIN ITEMS OF THE FACE SHEET OF THE STANFORD-BINET, AND (3) THE BEHAVIOR INVENTORY. IN A SUBSEQUENT STUDY COMPARING THE SCORES ON VARIOUS TESTS OF THESE HEADSTART CHILDREN WITH NON-HEADSTART CHILDREN WHEN IN KINDERGARTEN, NO DIFFERENCE WAS FOUND BETWEEN GROUPS IN ACADEMIC ACHIEVEMENT. (WD)

ED015773 PS000227
IMPACT OF SUMMER 1965 HEAD START ON CHILDREN'S CONCEPT ATTAINMENT DURING KINDERGARTEN. FINAL REPORT. ALLERHAND, MELVIN E., 65 100P.
EDRS PRICE MF-$0.65 HC-$3.29

THIS STUDY EXAMINES THE PROGRESS OF 125 CHILDREN IN THE CLEVELAND PUBLIC SCHOOL KINDERGARTENS WHO ATTENDED HEADSTART DURING THE SUMMER AND 125 CHILDREN IN THE SAME SCHOOLS WHO DID NOT ATTEND THE HEADSTART PROGRAM. SOME INDICATIONS IN THIS STUDY SUGGEST THAT A HEADSTART CHILD SHOWS MUCH GREATER VARIABILITY IN HIS CONCEPTUAL DEVELOPMENT THAN A NON-HEADSTART CHILD. HE ALSO TENDS TO PERFORM BETTER IN THE AREAS OF COLOR AND FORM DISCRIMINATION AND POSSIBLY GROUPING WHEN HE IS IN A NON-HEADSTART TEACHER'S CLASS. IN A HEADSTART TEACHER'S CLASS, THE HEADSTART CHILD SEEMS TO ACHIEVE IN THE MORE ORGANIZATIONAL AREAS, AS BEST REFLECTED IN INCREASED VERBAL FACILITY IN THE TIME SEQUENCE AND ORDERING CONCEPTS. THE RESULTS OF THIS STUDY RAISE THE QUESTION OF WHETHER THE IMPACT OF A STIMULATION EXPERIENCE CAN BE MAINTAINED. FOLLOWUP STUDIES AND EVALUATION OF DEMONSTRATION PROJECTS REPORT THE PHENOMENON OF THE DECREASING DIFFERENCE OF SUCCESS BETWEEN THE EXPERIMENTAL AND CONTROL GROUPS. (CO)

ED015774 PS000244
HEADSTART OPERATIONAL FIELD ANALYSIS. PROGRESS REPORT I. ALLERHAND, MELVIN E., 01OCT65 5P.
EDRS PRICE MF-$0.65 HC-$3.29

DURING THE SUMMER OF 1965, 5 AGENCIES SPONSORED A HEADSTART PROJECT FOR 4500 CHILDREN FROM THE GREATER CLEVELAND OHIO AREA. EFFORTS WERE CONCENTRATED ON ORGANIZING 5 ENDEAVORS. (1) THE DIRECTORS OF THE 5 AGENCIES WORKED TOGETHER TO ESTABLISH STANDARDS FOR PSYCHOLOGICAL EVALUATION PROCEDURES. (2) FROM 8 CENTERS, 125 HEADSTART CHILDREN AND 125 NON-HEADSTART CHILDREN WERE CHOSEN AT RANDOM AS SAMPLES IN A PROGRAM TO DEVELOP CLASSROOM OBSERVATION METHODS. (3) THE SAME GROUPS OF CHILDREN WERE TESTED ON THE PRE-SCHOOL INVENTORY AND PEABODY PICTURE VOCABULARY TEST BY PARENTS AND PSYCHOLOGY GRADUATE STUDENTS TO STUDY THE EFFECTIVENESS OF HEADSTART PARENTS AS ADMINISTRATORS OF PSYCHOLGICAL TESTS. (4) ALL 250 CHILDREN WERE TESTED DURING THE THIRD WEEK OF THE PROGRAM AND BEFORE THE END OF SCHOOL. DATA CONCERNING 50 SELECTED CHILDREN WERE GIVEN SPECIAL EXAMINATION AS A FOLLOWUP STUDY. (5) TWO SERVICE AND RESEARCH POSSIBILITIES DISCUSSED WERE A JOINT PROGRAM OF CLEVELAND AREA PEDIATRICIANS AND PSYCHOLOGISTS IN THE DETECTION AND SERVICING OF THE DEVIATING CHILD AND THE TRAINING OF PARENTS TO WORK WITH TEACHERS IN THE CLASSROOM. (CO)

ED015775 PS000245
HEADSTART OPERATIONAL FIELD ANALYSIS. PROGRESS REPORT II. ALLERHAND, MELVIN E., 01JAN66 30P.
EDRS PRICE MF-$0.65 HC-$3.29

DURING THE PERIOD OF OCTOBER 1, 1965 TO JANUARY 1, 1966 AT THE HEADSTART OPERATIONAL FIELD ANALYSIS IN CLEVELAND, OHIO THE FOLLOWING ACTIVITIES TOOK PLACE. (1) THE METHODOLOGY FOR CLASSROOM OBSERVATION OF HEADSTART (HS) AND NON-HEADSTART (NHS) CHILDREN AND INTERVIEWS WITH THEIR CLASSROOM TEACHERS WAS REVISED. THE HS GROUP OF 125 WAS SELECTED FROM 8 SAMPLE CENTERS. AN INTENSIVE SAMPLE OF 50 CHILDREN WAS USED FOR A DETAILED EXAMINATION OF HOW THIS GROUP MOVED FROM ONE LEVEL OF A CONCEPT TO ANOTHER. THE EXTENSIVE SAMPLE SHOWED HOW THE CHILD REACTED TO ACADEMICALLY RELATED MATERIAL AS MEASURED BY THESE CONCEPTS. TEACHER INTERVIEWS AND EVENT SAMPLING IN THE CLASSROOM WERE THE 2 RATING APPROACHES. (2) PRELIMINARY RESULTS PERTAINING TO THE HS AND NHS CHILDREN WERE FOUND. AN ANALYSIS SUGGESTED THAT HS CHILDREN WERE EXCEEDING THE NHS CHILDREN IN CONCEPT ATTAINMENT EVEN IN THOSE AREAS IN WHICH SIGNIFICANCE WAS NOT ACHIEVED. (3) A FULL REPORT OF THE EFFECTIVENESS OF HS PARENTS AS ADMINISTRATORS OF PSYCHOLOGICAL TESTS WAS MADE. SEVEN PARENTS (4 NEGRO AND 3 WHITE), WITH FROM NINTH TO TWELFTH GRADE EDUCATIONS WERE RANDOMLY SELECTED FROM AMONG 30 VOLUNTEERS. CLINICAL PSYCHOLOGY GRADUATE STUDENTS WHO SERVED AS CONTROL TEST ADMINISTRATORS WERE ALL WHITE AND WERE GENERALLY EXPERIENCED IN TESTING PROCEDURES. FOUR TABLES WERE USED TO COMPARE RESULTS OF PARENT TESTERS AND GRADUATE STUDENT TESTERS. THE MOST SIGNIFICANT DIFFERENCE RESULTED NOT FROM THE TESTER, BUT FROM THE TIME OR ORDER THE PRE-SCHOOL INVENTORY TEST WAS GIVEN. THIS STUDY SHOWS THAT UNTRAINED PEOPLE MAY BE UTILIZED FOR TESTING IF THEY ARE HIGHLY MOTIVATED. (4) OTHER DEVELOPMENTS INCLUDED DISCUSSING SECOND AND THIRD YEAR FOLLOWUP STUDIES, DEVELOPING SERVICE JOB OPPORTUNITIES FOR THE POOR, AND PRESENTATIONS OF PAPERS DEALING WITH A BROADENING OF THE FIELD OF PSYCHOLOGY TO INCLUDE COMMUNITY AND GROUP PROBLEMS. (CO)

ED015776 PS000246
HEADSTART OPERATIONAL FIELD ANALYSIS. PROGRESS REPORT III. ALLERHAND, MELVIN E., 15APR66 68P.
EDRS PRICE MF-$0.65 HC-$3.29

FROM JANUARY 1, 1966 TO APRIL 15, 1966 THE HEADSTART OPERATIONAL FIELD ANALYSIS IN CLEVELAND, OHIO PERFORMED 5 STUDIES. (1) SAMPLES OF HEADSTART (HS) AND NON-HEADSTART (NHS) CHILDREN WERE COMPARED AFTER 6 MONTHS OF KINDERGARTEN. FOUR OBSERVATIONS WERE MADE, USING 2 TEACHER RATINGS AND 2 OBSERVER RATINGS. THERE WERE 191 CHILDREN AT THE TIME OF THE LAST RATING. A REDUCTION IN SIGNIFICANT DIFFERENCES BETWEEN THE SAMPLES OCCURRED. (TABLES WITH RESULTS OF THE 4 RATING PERIODS ARE SHOWN.) (2) THE RELATIONSHIP BETWEEN HS AND NHS TEACHERS AND CHILDREN'S CONCEPT ATTAINMENT WAS STUDIED. THE SAMPLES WERE DIVIDED INTO 25 CLASSROOMS, OF WHICH 12 OF THEM WERE TAUGHT BY A HS TEACHER. THE POSSIBLE VARIABLES INCLUDED STIMULATION EVENTS, TOOLS OF LEARNING, AND TEACHER DIFFERENCES. THERE WERE SOME SIGNIFICANT VARIABLES IN FAVOR OF THE NHS TEACHERS' CLASSROOMS. (3) THE RESULTS OF THE ANALYSES OF THE RELATIONSHIP BETWEEN SEX AND CONCEPT ATTAINMENT INDICATED THAT BOYS ARE MORE EFFECTIVE IN VISUAL DISCRIMINATION AND THAT GIRLS ARE MORE EFFECTIVE IN HANDLING PERFORMANCE DEMANDS. (4) EXAMINATION OF THE CONCEPT ATTAINMENT OF THE TOTAL SAMPLE THROUGH THE 4 PERIODS OF MEASUREMENT INCLUDES 6 CHARTS REPRESENTING THE STEPS TAKEN BY THE EXTENSIVE SAMPLE. THE STEPS TAKEN INCLUDED COLOR CONCEPT, FORM-SPACE CONCEPT USAGE, GROUPING, ORDERING, TIME SEQUENCE, AND TIME DURATION. (5) FOUR CASE STUDIES, 2 HS AND 2 NHS, WERE MADE TO PRESENT A CONTRAST OF PATTERNS OF DEVELOPMENT. (CO)

ED015777 PS000247
HEADSTART OPERATIONAL FIELD ANALYSIS. PROGRESS REPORT IV. ALLERHAND, MELVIN E., 01AUG66 21P.
EDRS PRICE MF-$0.65 HC-$3.29

THIS REPORT IS THE FOURTH PROGRESS REPORT OF A STUDY OF HOW A PUPIL'S ACADEMIC ACHIEVEMENT IS AFFECTED BY PARTICIPATING IN A PRESCHOOL HEADSTART PROGRAM. THE ACHIEVEMENT OF THE HEADSTART GROUP IS BEING COMPARED WITH THE ACHIEVEMENT OF PUPILS WHO RECEIVED NO PRESCHOOL PROGRAM. THE PRESCHOOL INVENTORY TEST WAS USED TO MEASURE PUPIL ACHIEVEMENT IN 5 CONCEPT AREAS, (1) COLOR, (2) FORM, (3) GROUPING, (4) ORDERING, AND (5) TIME. IT WAS GIVEN AS A PRE-TEST AT THE BEGINNING OF KINDERGARTEN AND AS A POST-TEST AT THE END OF KINDERGARTEN. THE RESULTS SHOWED THAT BOTH HEADSTART AND NON-HEADSTART GROUPS ACHIEVED SIGNIFICANT ACADEMIC PROGRESS DURING KINDERGARTEN. THE HEADSTART GROUP SHOWED A GREATER GAIN WHICH, HOWEVER, WAS NOT SIGNIFICANT. IN ADDITION TO THE INVENTORY, A TEACHER AND AN OBSERVER RATED THE PUPILS AS TO GAIN, LOSS, OR NO-CHANGE IN DEMONSTRATED CONCEPT ABILITY DURING THE YEAR. NO SIGNIFICANT DIFFERENCES IN ATTAINMENT BETWEEN THE 2 GROUPS WERE FOUND WITH THE EXCEPTION THAT THE TEACHER FOUND A SIGNIFICANTLY HIGHER GAIN IN GROUPING CONCEPT ABILITY BY THE HEADSTART GROUP. THE OBSERVER DID NOT FIND A SIGNIFICANT DIFFERENCE. (WD)

ED015778 PS000258
THE EFFECTS OF SEVERAL VERBAL PRETRAINING CONDITIONS ON PRESCHOOL CHILDREN'S TRANSFER IN PROBLEM SOLVING. FINAL REPORT. BERNHEIM, GLORIA D., JUN67 117P.
EDRS PRICE MF-$0.65 HC-$6.58

THREE- AND 4-YEAR-OLDS WERE GIVEN VERBAL LEARNING PRETRAINING TO DETERMINE ITS EFFECT UPON THE PERFORMANCE OF REVERSAL AND NONREVERSAL SHIFT DISCRIMINATION TASKS. THE EXPERIMENTAL TASK WAS THE CLASSICAL REVERSAL-NONREVERSAL SHIFT PARADIGM. THE 96 PRE-SCHOOLERS, PRIMARILY FROM THE PENNSYLVANIA STATE UNIVERSITY NURSERY SCHOOL, WERE DIVIDED INTO 4 GROUPS, 3 OF WHICH RECEIVED PRETRAINING AND 1 OF WHICH DID NOT. THE DATA COLLECTED WERE TREATED BY ANALYSIS OF VARIANCE. RESULTS SHOWED THAT THE REVERSAL SHIFT WAS QUICKER AND EASIER FOR THE CHILDREN THAN THE NONREVERSAL. A SECOND EXPERIMENT USING 48 CHILDREN CONFIRMED THESE FINDINGS ALTHOUGH PREVIOUS EXPERIMENTAL RESULTS AND VERBAL MEDIATION THEORY HAD INDICATED THAT THE NONREVERSAL SHIFT WAS EASIER FOR THE CHILDREN. OTHER VARIABLES SUCH AS THE CHILDREN'S PROFICIENCY IN VERBAL MEDIATING RESPONSES MAY HAVE CAUSED THE PRESENT STUDY RESULTS, BUT THE RELATIONSHIP BETWEEN VERBAL LABELING PRETRAINING AND TYPE OF SHIFT REMAINS INCONCLUSIVE. FURTHER STUDIES SHOULD DETERMINE WAYS TO IDENTIFY AND ISOLATE VARIABLES WHICH AFFECT THE ABILITY OF YOUNGSTERS TO PERFORM EXPERIMENTAL TASKS. THIS DOCUMENT WAS SUBMITTED IN PARTIAL FULFILLMENT OF THE REQUIREMENTS FOR THE DEGREE OF DOCTOR OF PHILOSOPHY AT PENNSYLVANIA STATE UNIVERSITY. (MS)

ED015779 PS000260
CONCEPT FORMATION AS A FUNCTION OF METHOD OF PRESENTATION AND RATIO OF POSITIVE TO NEGATIVE INSTANCES. SMUCKLER, NANCY SIDON, JAN67 30P.
EDRS PRICE MF-$0.65 HC-$3.29

TO STUDY WHICH OF SEVERAL CONDITIONS PROMOTES EFFICIENT CONCEPT LEARNING, AN EXPERIMENT INVOLVING 2 CONDITIONS, METHOD OF PRESENTATION OF STIMULI AND RATIO OF POSITIVE TO NEGATIVE STIMULI, WAS ADMINISTERED TO 80 SECOND-GRADE CHILDREN. THE CHILDREN WERE DIVIDED INTO 8 TREATMENT GROUPS. THESE 8 GROUPS WERE FORMED BY VARYING THE 2 METHODS OF PRESENTATION, SIMULTANEOUS AND SUCCESSIVE, WITH THE 4 RATIOS OF POSITIVE TO NEGATIVE INSTANCES, P100 (POSITIVE INSTANCES ON ALL TRIALS), P75, P50, AND P25. AN INSTANCE WAS THE SHOWING OF A SPECIFIC GEOMETRIC SHAPE TO THE SUBJECT. IF THE SHAPE WAS A TRAPEZOID, THAT WAS THE POSITIVE INSTANCE. ANY OTHER SHAPE WAS A NEGATIVE INSTANCE. CHILDREN RECEIVED ACQUISITION, TRANSFER, AND RETENTION TASKS. THE SCORES ON THE ACQUISITION PHASE SHOWED THAT THE SUCCESSIVE METHOD OF PRESENTATION RESULTED IN SIGNIFICANTLY MORE CORRECT RESPONSES THAN THE SIMULTANEOUS METHOD. THERE WAS NO SIGNIFICANT DIFFERENCE BETWEEN THE 2 METHODS ON EITHER THE TRANSFER OR RETENTION TASKS. THE RATIO VARIABLE DEMONSTRATED A POSITIVE RELATIONSHIP WITH PERCENTAGE OF CORRECT RESPONSES ON THE ACQUISITION TASK. ON THIS TASK, THE P25 GROUP DID SIGNIFICANTLY WORSE THAN THE OTHER 3 GROUPS. ON THE ACQUISITION TASK, THE RATIO RANKING IN TERMS OF MOST CORRECT RESPONSES WAS (1) P100, (2) P75, (3) P50, AND (4) P25. ON THE TRANSFER AND RETENTION TASKS, THE RANKINGS WERE (1) P100, (2) P50, (3) P25, AND (4) P75. THIS DOCUMENT IS BASED ON A MASTER'S THESIS DONE AT THE UNIVERSITY OF WISCONSIN. (WD)

ED015780 PS000273
OPTIMIZING EDUCATIONAL INVESTMENT STRATEGIES. WEBER, ROBERT E., 20P.
EDRS PRICE MF-$0.65 HC-$3.29

THE DETERMINATION OF THE OPTIMUM DISTRIBUTION OF EDUCATIONAL INVESTMENTS IS A CURRENT AND ACUTE PROBLEM. EXAMINATION OF SEVERAL INTERRELATED PROBLEMS OF UNDERDEVELOPMENT IN ORDER TO CONSIDER THEIR PROGRAMMATIC IMPLICATIONS LEADS TO THE IDENTIFICATION OF GENERAL AREAS FOR EDUCATIONAL INVESTMENT EXPENDITURES. THE AREA OF MOST PERVASIVE NEED IS THE LANGUAGE ARTS, IN WHICH A NATIONAL PROGRAM WITH A SYSTEM OF SUPPLEMENTARY LEARNING CENTERS IS NEEDED TO OVERCOME BASIC DEVELOPMENTAL PROBLEMS. OTHER AREAS FOR WHICH SPECIFIC RECOMMENDATIONS ARE MADE ARE (1) AREAS OF UNDERINVESTMENT, (2) AREAS OF PREVIOUS PROGRAM FAILURES, (3) AREAS OF GREATEST POSSIBLE COST REDUCTION, AND (4) AREAS OF CRITICAL MANPOWER SHORTAGES. (DR)

ED015781 PS000277
KICKAPOO - NORTH CANADIAN PROJECT, 1966-67. FINAL REPORT. KEELY, SUZANN, 15JUN67 134P.
EDRS PRICE MF-$0.65 HC-$6.58

SEVENTY-ONE CHILDREN WERE ENROLLED IN THE KICKAPOO-NORTH CANADIAN PROJECT FOR A PERIOD OF 2 MONTHS OR LONGER. THIS REPORT IS DIVIDED INTO 7 SECTIONS AND 2 APPENDICES. PART I CONTAINS A DESCRIPTION OF THE PROGRESS OF EACH CHILD DURING THE PROJECT. PART II CONTAINS BIOGRAPHICAL DESCRIPTIONS OF THE STAFF. PART III CONTAINS A LIST OF SPECIAL ACTIVITIES INCLUDED IN THE DAILY PROGRAM. (A COPY OF THE PLAN OF DAILY ACTIVITIES IS INCLUDED IN THE APPENDIX.) PART IV DESCRIBES THE HEALTH PROGRAM.

PART V DESCRIBES AND ILLUSTRATES EQUIPMENT AND SUPPLIES. PART VI LISTS VISITORS (OTHER THAN PARENTS AND COMMUNITY RESIDENTS) TO THE PROJECT. PART VII DESCRIBES THE TRAINING PROGRAM WHICH INCLUDES TEACHER AIDE TRAINING AND THE INTERNSHIP TRAINING PROGRAM. APPENDIX I SHOWS COPIES OF ALL THE MATERIALS PROVIDED TO INTERNS. APPENDIX II CONTAINS ALL OF THE INTERNS' REPORTS, PURPOSES OF THE INTERNSHIP TRAINING PROGRAM, AND BIOGRAPHICAL DATA ON THE INTERNS. (CO)

ED015782 PS000289
PROGRAMED INSTRUCTION AS A STRATEGY FOR DEVELOPING CURRICULA FOR CHILDREN FROM DISADVANTAGED BACKGROUNDS. GOTKIN, LASSAR G., 67 29P.
EDRS PRICE MF-$0.65 HC-$3.29

MATRIX GAMES IS A MODIFIED PROGRAMED-INSTRUCTION APPROACH TO TEACHING AND DEVELOPING LANGUAGE SKILLS. IN THIS STUDY, A BOARD DISPLAYING 16 PICTURES IN A 4 X 4 MATRIX WAS PLACED IN FRONT OF SEVERAL 4- OR 5-YEAR-OLDS. THE PICTURES COMPOSING A ROW CONTAINED A COMMON ITEM, FOR EXAMPLE, A BOY. THE PICTURES OF A COLUMN ALSO CONTAINED A COMMON ITEM, FOR EXAMPLE, DRINKING MILK. THE GAME BEGAN WHEN THE TEACHER COVERED 1 OF THE 16 PICTURES AND ASKED THE CHILDREN TO DESCRIBE THE CONTENTS OF THAT PICTURE. BY SCANNING BOTH THE ROW AND COLUMN OF WHICH THE COVERED PICTURE WAS A PART, THE CHILD COULD DETERMINE, BY ABSTRACTING OUT THE COMMON ITEMS OF THE PICTURES IN THAT ROW AND COLUMN, THAT THE COVERED PICTURE WAS, SAY, 2 BOYS WEARING A HAT. THIS PROCEDURE INDICATES THE CHILD'S COGNITIVE AND ARTICULATION ABILITIES SO THAT DIFFICULTIES IN THESE 2 AREAS CAN BE DISCOVERED AND CORRECTED. MATRIX GAMES INCLUDES WITHIN ITS INSTRUCTIONAL FRAMEWORK THE IMPORTANT PRINCIPLES OF TEXTBOOK AND MACHINE-TYPE PROGRAMING, NAMELY (1) CLEAR SPECIFICATION OF INSTRUCTIONAL OBJECTIVES, (2) CAREFUL SEQUENCING OF STEPS, (3) USE OF SMALL SEQUENCING STEPS, (4) SUBSTANTIAL ACTIVE PARTICIPATION BY THE STUDENT, AND (5) CONFIRMATION OF THE CORRECTNESS OF THE STUDENT'S RESPONSE. THE ADVANTAGE OF PROGRAMED-INSTRUCTION ORIENTED CURRICULA, LIKE MATRIX GAMES, IS THEIR FLEXIBILITY. THEY RESPOND TO INDIVIDUAL DIFFERENCES AND RATES OF LEARNING. (WD)

ED015783 PS000332
A COMPARISON OF THE DEVELOPMENTAL DRAWING CHARACTERISTICS OF CULTURALLY ADVANTAGED AND CULTURALLY DISADVANTAGED CHILDREN. FINAL REPORT. EISNER, ELLIOTT W., SEP67 139P.
EDRS PRICE MF-$0.65 HC-$6.58

THE DEVELOPMENTAL STAGES IN THE ART OF CHILDREN HAVE BEEN THE SUBJECT OF MUCH CHILD DEVELOPMENT THEORY AND RESEARCH. MUCH OF THIS WORK, EXAMPLES OF WHICH ARE PRESENTED IN THE INTRODUCTORY PORTION OF THIS DOCUMENT, HAS BEEN MERELY ANECDOTAL. OF CONCERN IN THIS STUDY ARE (1) THE FORMULATION OF OBJECTIVE PROCEDURES TO ASSESS THE DEVELOPMENTAL DRAWING CHARACTERISTICS FOUND IN CHILDREN'S ART, (2) A COMPARISON OF THE DRAWINGS OF ADVANTAGED AND DISADVANTAGED CHILDREN, AND (3) A DETERMINATION OF THE RELATIONSHIP BETWEEN PERCEPTION AS MANIFESTED IN DRAWING AND LANGUAGE AS ASSESSED BY A TEST OF READING VOCABULARY. THE SUBJECTS OF THIS STUDY WERE 1093 FIRST, THIRD, FIFTH, AND SEVENTH GRADE CHILDREN OF NEGRO OR WHITE RACES AND MIDDLE OR LOW INCOME LEVELS. THESE CHILDREN WERE INSTRUCTED DURING A CLASS PERIOD TO DRAW A PLAYGROUND SCENE. A DAY LATER, THE FIFTH AND SEVENTH GRADE PUPILS WERE ADMINISTERED THE GATES READING TEST. ON THE BASIS OF THE PLAYGROUND DRAWINGS, A 14-CATEGORY SCALE OF DRAWING DEVELOPMENTAL LEVEL WAS CONSTRUCTED, THE CRITERION BEING PERCEPTION OF SPACIAL RELATIONSHIPS. THE MORE SOPHISTICATED THE CHILD'S PRESENTATION OF SPACIAL RELATIONSHIPS, THE HIGHER HIS DEVELOPMENT. THE SCALE WAS VALIDATED BY HAVING 2 JUDGES INDEPENDENTLY CLASSIFY EXTRA PLAYGROUND DRAWINGS ACCORDING TO THE 14 CATEGORIES COMPOSING THE SCALE. THE CORRELATION WAS ABOUT .72. THE RESULTS OF CATEGORIZING THE EXPERIMENTAL DRAWINGS SHOWED THAT ADVANTAGED CHILDREN HAD A HIGHER DEVELOPMENT THAN THE DISADVANTAGED CHILDREN IN ALL 4 GRADES, ALTHOUGH THE GAP APPEARED TO DIMINISH FROM GRADE 1 TO GRADE 7. THERE ALSO APPEARED TO BE A SIGNIFICANT POSITIVE CORRELATION BETWEEN DRAWING SCORES AND READING VOCABULARY SCORES. (WD)

ED015784 PS000335
THRESHOLD BY IDENTIFICATION OF PICTURES (TIP) TEST AND DISCRIMINATION BY IDENTIFICATION OF PICTURES (DIP) TEST. HASPIEL, GEORGE S.; SIEGENTHALER, BRUCE M., 82P.
EDRS PRICE MF-$0.65 HC-$3.29

THIS DOCUMENT COMPRISES 2 HEARING ABILITY TESTS FOR 3- TO 8-YEAR-OLD CHILDREN. THEIR ADMINISTRATION REQUIRES A SPEECH AUDIOMETER. TEST NORMS WERE ESTABLISHED FOR RECORDED MATERIALS IN A SOUND FIELD. BOTH TESTS USE COLORED PICTURE CARDS, AND IT IS ESSENTIAL THAT THE CHILD BE ABLE TO IDENTIFY ALL ITEMS SHOWN. THE THRESHOLD BY IDENTIFICATION OF PICTURES (TIP) TEST DETERMINES THE SPEECH RECEPTION THRESHOLD WITH AN ERROR OF 3 DB. THE DISCRIMINATION BY IDENTIFICATION OF PICTURES (DIP) TEST USED 48 PAIRED ITEMS DIFFERING IN INITIAL CONSONANTS AND MAY BE USED TO DETERMINE SPEECH DISCRIMINATION AT LEVELS FROM 0 TO 10 DB ABOVE THE SPEECH RECEPTION THRESHOLD. INSTRUCTIONS FOR THE ADMINISTRATION, SCORING, AND INTERPRETATION OF THE TESTS ARE GIVEN. THE PICTURE CARDS ARE INCLUDED, AND SCORING SHEETS FOR BOTH TESTS ACCOMPANY THE DOCUMENT. (DR)

ED015785 PS000336
FACTORS ASSOCIATED WITH A PROGRAM FOR ENCOURAGING SELF-INITIATED ACTIVITIES BY FIFTH AND SIXTH GRADE STUDENTS IN A SELECTED ELEMENTARY SCHOOL EMPHASIZING INDIVIDUALIZED INSTRUCTION. SCANLON, ROBERT G., 66 99P.
EDRS PRICE MF-$0.65 HC-$3.29

RECENT RESEARCH ON INDIVIDUALIZED INSTRUCTION AND ITS EFFECT ON SELF-INITIATED LEARNING BEHAVIOR SUGGESTS THAT A CLASSROOM ATMOSPHERE OF GUIDED SELF-DEVELOPMENT AND AN EDUCATIONAL SYSTEM ADAPTABLE TO INDIVIDUAL DIFFERENCES ARE MOST EFFECTIVE IN PROMOTING THE GROWTH OF THE PUPIL'S FULL TALENTS, CREATIVITY, AND INTEREST. THIS STUDY ATTEMPTED AN ANALYSIS OF THE RELATIONSHIP BETWEEN INDIVIDUALIZED INSTRUCTION AND SELF-INITIATION. DURING A 4-MONTH PERIOD, 28 FIFTH GRADE PUPILS AND 22 SIXTH GRADE PUPILS RECEIVED 3 EXPERIMENTAL TREATMENTS INTENDED TO ENCOURAGE SELF-INITIATED LEARNING BEHAVIOR. THESE INCLUDED (1) DEVELOPMENT OF A MATHEMATICS MATERIAL CENTER BY THE CHILDREN, (2) SELECTION OF OPTIONAL WORK IN MATHEMATICS, AND (3) REINFORCEMENT OF PUPILS BY THE TEACHER DURING MATHEMATICS CLASS. THE 3 TREATMENTS WERE INTRODUCED IN A STAGGERED ORDER, NOT ALL AT ONE TIME. STUDENTS WERE OBSERVED DURING MATHEMATICS, SCIENCE, AND SOCIAL STUDIES CLASSES BUT ONLY THE MATHEMATICS CLASS HAD AN INDIVIDUALIZED INSTRUCTION ORIENTATION. MEASURING INSTRUMENTS WERE DESIGNED TO QUANTIFY PUPIL BEHAVIOR. NINE HYPOTHESES WERE TESTED. FOUR WERE REJECTED, 5 WERE NOT. THE RESULTS INDICATED THAT MORE SELF-INITIATED BEHAVIOR WAS ENCOURAGED BY THE INDIVIDUALIZED MATHEMATICS CLASS THAN BY THE TEACHER-DOMINATED SCIENCE AND SOCIAL STUDIES CLASSES. THE GENERAL FINDING WAS THAT A HIGHLY-INDIVIDUALIZED CLASSROOM ENVIRONMENT ENCOURAGES SELF-INITIATED LEARNING BEHAVIOR. (WD)

ED015786 PS000337
COGNITIVE DEVELOPMENT IN INFANTS OF DIFFERENT AGE LEVELS AND FROM DIFFERENT ENVIRONMENTAL BACKGROUNDS. WACHS, THEODORE D.; AND OTHERS, 67 12P.
EDRS PRICE MF-$0.65 HC-$3.29

DO CHILDREN RAISED IN ENVIRONMENTS ASSOCIATED WITH LATER DEFICITS IN PSYCHOMETRIC INTELLIGENCE SHOW ANY DEFICITS DURING INFANCY AND, IF SO, WHEN DO SUCH DEFICITS APPEAR AND WHAT ABILITIES ARE AFFECTED. ARE THE ENVIRONMENTAL FACTORS ASSOCIATED WITH EARLY DEVELOPMENT OF INTELLIGENCE. FIFTY-ONE SLUM INFANTS AND A CONTROL GROUP OF 51 NON-SLUM INFANTS IN CHAMPAIGN-URBANA, ILLINOIS WERE TESTED IN THEIR 7TH, 11TH, 15TH, 18TH, AND 22ND MONTHS BY 3 SUB-SCALES OF THE INFANT PSYCHOLOGICAL DEVELOPMENT SCALE, AND 3 OTHER MEASURES OF DEVELOPMENT. IN ADDITION, EACH INFANT WAS HOME TESTED BY AN EXAMINER WHOSE NOTES WERE LATER TRANSLATED INTO A 4-POINT SCORING SYSTEM AND ADDED TO INFORMATION SUPPLIED BY THE INFANT'S MOTHER. DATA WERE ANALYZED USING THE SIGN TEST, AND THE RELATIONSHIP BETWEEN HOME STIMULATION AND DEVELOPMENTAL ITEMS WAS ANALYZED THROUGH POINT-BISERIAL CORRELATIONS. RESULTS INDICATED THAT SLUM INFANTS SHOW SLOWER DEVELOPMENT AT A MUCH EARLIER AGE THAN PREVIOUSLY SUSPECTED, SUGGESTING THAT COMPENSATORY PROGRAMS SHOULD START EARLIER THAN 3 YEARS OF AGE. IT ALSO APPEARS THAT, CONTRARY TO ACCEPTED HYPOTHESES, OVER-STIMULATION DURING INFANCY MAY BE MORE DETRIMENTAL THAN UNDER-STIMULATION AS AN ENVIRONMENTAL FACTOR. THIS PAPER WAS DELIVERED TO THE BIENNIAL MEETING OF THE SOCIETY FOR RESEARCH IN CHILD DEVELOPMENT IN NEW YORK, MARCH 29 - APRIL 1, 1967. (MS)

ED015787 PS000338
THE RELATIONSHIPS BETWEEN CERTAIN TEACHER CHARACTERISTICS AND ACHIEVEMENT AND CREATIVITY OF GIFTED ELEMENTARY SCHOOL STUDENTS. FINAL REPORT SUMMARY. MCNARY, SHIRLEY R., 30APR67 3P.
EDRS PRICE MF-$0.65 HC-$3.29

THE RELATIONSHIP BETWEEN TEACHER CHARACTERISTICS AND THE DEGREE OF CHANGE SHOWN BY GIFTED ELEMENTARY PUPILS IN CONVERGENT AND DIVERGENT THINKING AREAS WAS INVESTIGATED. CHARACTERISTICS WERE ASSESSED BY MEASURES OF INTELLIGENCE, PERSONALITY FACTORS, AND A PERSONAL INFORMATION QUESTIONNAIRE. SIX PRE- AND POST-TESTS OF CONVERGENT AND 4 TESTS OF DIVERGENT PRODUCTION MEASURED THE GROWTH OF THE GIFTED CHILDREN OVER 1 ACADEMIC YEAR. A SERIES OF MULTIPLE REGRESSION EQUATIONS WAS CALCULATED TO ASSESS THE RELATIONSHIP BETWEEN THE CHANGES IN THE 23 CLASSES IN THE TEST SCORES AND THE 34 TEACHER, CLASS, AND STUDENT VARIABLES. FOR EACH MEASURE OF CHANGE, ITEMS SIGNIFICANT AT THE 1 PERCENT LEVEL WERE GROUPED FOR THE DEVELOPMENT OF A FINAL REGRESSION ANALYSIS LEADING TO AN INFLUENCE PROFILE. IT WAS FOUND THAT TEACHER PERSONALITY TRAITS WERE THE MOST EFFECTIVE OF THE CHANGE-PRODUCING VARIABLES AND THAT DIFFERENT TYPES OF TEACHERS INFLUENCED DIFFERENT AREAS OF GROWTH. THE CHILDREN'S READING GROWTH RELATED SIGNIFICANTLY TO A TEACHER'S VERBAL I.Q., AND GROWTH IN WRITING RELATED SIGNIFI-

CANTLY TO A TEACHER'S ANNUAL INCOME AND THE NUMBER OF COURSE-WORK HOURS IN THE EDUCATION OF GIFTED CHILDREN. THE NUMBER OF STUDENTS PER CLASS SIGNIFICANTLY AFFECTED GROWTH IN MATH. STUDY IMPLICATIONS ARE THAT GIFTED CHILDREN SHOULD BE EXPOSED BOTH TO TEACHERS WHOSE PERSONALITY TRAITS ARE BEST SUITED TO TEACH THE DIVERGENT AREA AND TO THOSE BEST SUITED TO TEACH THE CONVERGENT AREA, WITH TEACHER SELECTION BASED ACCORDINGLY. (MS)

ED015788 PS000339
A NATIONAL DEMONSTRATION PROJECT UTILIZING TELEVISED MATERIALS FOR THE FORMAL EDUCATION OF CULTURALLY DISADVANTAGED PRESCHOOL CHILDREN. FINAL REPORT. MUKERJI, ROSE; AND OTHERS, JUL66 124P.
EDRS PRICE MF-$0.65 HC-$6.58

TO SUPPLY DISADVANTAGED PRESCHOOL CHILDREN WITH CULTURALLY STIMULATING EXPERIENCES, A TV SERIES, "ROUNDABOUT," WAS DESIGNED TO BE USED IN WASHINGTON, D.C. INNER-CITY PRESCHOOL AND DAY CARE CENTERS. THE 15-MINUTE PROGRAMS WERE TO INTRODUCE NEW EXPERIENCES AND SUPPLEMENT REGULAR ACTIVITIES. IT WAS HOPED THAT THE CHILDREN WOULD IDENTIFY WITH A POSITIVE MODEL, THE MALE NEGRO STAR. TWICE WEEKLY FOR 28 WEEKS THE PROGRAMS WERE SHOWN, AND THE REACTIONS OF 60 3- AND 4-YEAR-OLDS IN 3 SELECTED SCHOOLS WERE OBSERVED. TEACHERS HAD A WEEKLY, INSERVICE TRAINING SESSION. BOTH TEACHERS' AND OBSERVERS' ANECDOTAL RECORDS WERE CODED INTO 13 CATEGORIES AND STATISTICALLY DESCRIBED. IT WAS FOUND THAT THE PRESCHOOLERS IDENTIFIED ONLY SLIGHTLY WITH THE TV PERFORMER, THE TEACHERS MADE INSUFFICIENT USE OF THE SERIES, AND THE CHILDREN HAD TOO LITTLE SPACE TO PARTICIPATE IN THE SUGGESTED MOTOR ACTIVITIES. FURTHER RESEARCH MIGHT TEST THE HYPOTHESES THAT SCHOOL ACTIVITIES REINFORCED AT HOME PROVIDE MORE LEARNING, LOW AND MIDDLE INCOME CHILDREN REACT SIMILARLY TO A TV CURRICULUM IF TEACHING ABILITIES ARE HELD CONSTANT, AND THE MORE CREATIVE THE TEACHER AND THE MORE "UNREALISTIC" THE TV CHARACTERS, THE MORE THE CHILDREN RESPOND TO TV. APPENDICES INCLUDED IN THIS REPORT ARE, (1) DEMOGRAPHIC DESCRIPTION OF THE POPULATION, (2) IN-SERVICE TRAINING QUESTIONNAIRE, (3) MONITORS FORM, (4) FREQUENCY OF RESPONSES FOR SCHOOLS, (5) CODING CATEGORIES, AND (6) ANECDOTES. (MS)

ED015789 PS000340
SOCIAL AND EMOTIONAL BEHAVIOR IN INFANCY--SOME DEVELOPMENTAL ISSUES AND PROBLEMS. RICCIUTI, HENRY N., JAN68 29P.
EDRS PRICE MF-$0.65 HC-$3.29

INVESTIGATIONS INTO THE NATURE AND DEVELOPMENT OF SOCIAL AND EMOTIONAL BEHAVIOR IN HUMAN INFANCY HAVE RAISED MANY RESEARCH ISSUES AND HAVE INDICATED MANY ADDITIONAL AREAS OF INQUIRY. EARLY AND CONTEMPORARY STUDIES HAVE BOTH BEEN CONCERNED WITH PROVIDING MORE PRECISE ANALYSES OF STIMULUS AND SITUATIONAL DETERMINANTS OF SOCIAL AND EMOTIONAL BEHAVIOR, ALTHOUGH THE EARLY STUDIES WERE PRIMARILY DESCRIPTIVE WHEREAS THE EMPHASIS TODAY IS ON ANALYTIC STUDIES. TWO IMPORTANT ASPECTS OF STIMULUS-AND-SITUATIONAL-DETERMINANTS RESEARCH ARE (1) THE DEVELOPMENT OF ATTACHMENT BEHAVIOR IN INFANTS (ESPECIALLY TO THE MOTHER) AND (2) THE ROLE OF VARIOUS STIMULUS CUES AS ELICITORS OR REINFORCERS OF BEHAVIOR. INVESTIGATIONS OF APPROACH AND WITHDRAWAL PROCESSES INVOLVE A SECOND MAJOR RESEARCH AREA. ASPECTS OF APPROACH AND WITHDRAWAL THAT DEAL ESSENTIALLY WITH THE DIRECTIONAL AND AROUSAL CHARACTERISTICS OF INFANT RESPONSES ARE (1) EXPLORATORY BEHAVIOR, (2) CURIOSITY, AND (3) INTRINSIC MOTIVATION. PRESENT RESEARCH PROBLEMS INVOLVE (1) ADEQUATE CONCEPTUALIZATION OF EMOTIONAL PROCESSES EARLY IN LIFE, (2) IDENTIFICATION OF THE BEHAVIORAL INDICATORS OF EMOTIONAL RESPONSES IN INFANTS, AND (3) DETERMINATION OF THE INFLUENCE OF OTHER BASIC PSYCHOLOGICAL PROCESSES ON SOCIAL AND EMOTIONAL BEHAVIOR. THIS PAPER WAS PRESENTED AT THE MERRILL-PALMER INSTITUTE CONFERENCE ON RESEARCH AND TEACHING OF INFANT DEVELOPMENT (FEBRUARY 9-11, 1967). IT IS TO BE PUBLISHED IN THE MERRILL-PALMER QUARTERLY, VOLUME 14, 1968. (WD)

ED015790 PS000346
THE DEVELOPMENT OF A TEST TO ASSESS THE OCCURRENCE OF SELECTED FEATURES OF NON-STANDARD ENGLISH IN THE SPEECH OF DISADVANTAGED PRIMARY CHILDREN. TAFT, JEROME; TENNIS, MELVIN, 68 22P.
EDRS PRICE MF-$0.65 HC-$3.29

THE INSTRUCTIONAL RESEARCH, DEVELOPMENT, AND EVALUATION UNIT OF THE DADE COUNTY (FLORIDA) PUBLIC SCHOOLS CONSTRUCTED SEVERAL INSTRUMENTS TO MEASURE CHILDREN'S LANGUAGE DEVELOPMENT. FOUR OF THESE INSTRUMENTS WERE USED BY THE SPECIAL LANGUAGE TEACHER PROJECT IN A STUDY CONDUCTED FROM FEBRUARY TO MAY, 1967 IN DADE COUNTY SCHOOLS. THE OBJECTIVES OF THIS STUDY WERE (1) TO GAIN INFORMATION ON THE VALUE OF THE TESTING DEVICES, AND (2) TO ASCERTAIN THE LANGUAGE DEVELOPMENT PROBLEMS OF FIRST AND SECOND GRADE DISADVANTAGED CHILDREN, SOME OF WHOM ATTENDED PROJECT SCHOOLS AND SOME OF WHOM DID NOT. THE 4 TESTS USED WERE (1) THE AURAL COMPREHENSION TEST, (2) THE ORAL USAGE TEST, (3) AN EVALUATION FORM, AND (4) AN ORAL LANGUAGE RATING FORM. TO TEST THE RELIABILITY OF INSTRUMENTS (3) AND (4), TEACHERS AND SPECIAL JUDGES INDEPENDENTLY EVALUATED THE CHILDREN'S LANGUAGE CHARACTERISTICS. THESE INDEPENDENT EVALUATIONS WERE THEN CORRELATED TO OBTAIN A MEASURE OF THE RELIABILITY OF THE INSTRUMENTS. THE CORRELATIONS WERE FOUND TO BE GENERALLY HIGH. DATA ON THE CHILDREN'S LANGUAGE DEVELOPMENT IN THE PROJECT SCHOOLS VERSUS SUCH DEVELOPMENT IN NONPROJECT SCHOOLS DURING THIS STUDY IS INCOMPLETE. IT WAS FOUND, HOWEVER, THAT THE SCORES OF A MATCHED SAMPLE OF PROJECT AND NONPROJECT CHILDREN ON INSTRUMENT (1) INDICATE NO SIGNIFICANT DIFFERENCE IN GAIN IN LANGUAGE DEVELOPMENT BETWEEN THE 2 GROUPS FROM FEBRUARY TO MAY. (WD)

ED015791 PS000361
EFFECTS OF A STRUCTURED PROGRAM OF PRESCHOOL MATHEMATICS ON COGNITIVE BEHAVIOR. DEAL, THERRY N., 69P.
EDRS PRICE MF-$0.65 HC-$3.29

AN EXPERIMENTAL TRAINING PROGRAM DESIGNED TO TEACH 1 TO 1 CORRESPONDENCE TO PRESCHOOL CHILDREN WAS TESTED TO SEE WHAT EFFECT IT MIGHT HAVE ON THEIR UNDERSTANDING OF NUMBER CONSERVATION. THIRTY-FIVE CHILDREN OF AGES 3, 4, AND 5 WERE RANDOMLY DIVIDED INTO 3 EXPERIMENTAL AND 3 CONTROL GROUPS. THE EXPERIMENTAL GROUPS WERE TRAINED TO PERFORM 1 TO 1 CORRESPONDENCE TASKS IN 8 DAILY HALF-HOUR SESSIONS. THE CONTROL GROUP RECEIVED A GENERAL PRESCHOOL PROGRAM INTENDED TO FACILITATE MATHEMATICAL UNDERSTANDING. A PRETEST INDICATED THAT THERE WAS NO SIGNIFICANT DIFFERENCE BETWEEN THE EXPERIMENTAL AND CONTROL GROUPS. POSTTESTS INDICATED THAT THE EXPERIMENTAL GROUP PERFORMED BETTER ON SPECIFICALLY 1 TO 1 TEST ITEMS, BUT WERE NO BETTER ABLE TO UNDERSTAND NUMBER CONSERVATION THAN BEFORE. AS WAS EXPECTED, THE OLDER CHILDREN PERFORMED SIGNIFICANTLY BETTER THAN THE YOUNGER CHILDREN, BUT THE INCREASE IN MEAN SCORES WAS APPROXIMATELY EQUAL FOR EACH AGE GROUP, INDICATING THAT EVEN THE 3-YEAR-OLDS HAD PROFITED FROM THE TRAINING. TWO EXTENSIVE APPENDICES CONTAIN A DETAILED DESCRIPTION OF THE TRAINING PROGRAM AND THE TEST USED TO EVALUATE CONCEPT UNDERSTANDING. (DR)

ED015792 PS000362
THE EVALUATION OF PROJECT HEAD START--A CONCEPTUAL STATEMENT. MCDAVID, JOHN W., 16P.
EDRS PRICE MF-$0.65 HC-$3.29

EVALUATION OF HEADSTART HAS AS ITS GENERAL CRITERION OF EFFECTIVENESS THE RATIO BETWEEN COST AND BENEFIT. IF THE LATTER CAN BE DEMONSTRATED TO JUSTIFY THE FORMER, THE INTERVENTION PROJECT IS A GOOD INVESTMENT IN TERMS OF IMMEDIATE HELP FOR THE DISADVANTAGED PRESCHOOLER AND IN LONG RANGE BENEFITS FOR HIS FAMILY, COMMUNITY, AND SOCIETY. IN TERMS OF A MODEL, INPUT (POPULATION) PLUS OPERATIONS (PROGRAM ATTRIBUTES) MUST YIELD OUTPUT (CHANGES IN POPULATION ATTRIBUTES). IT IS DIFFICULT TO ASSESS AN OVERALL PROGRAM WHICH HAS SUCH A LARGE NUMBER OF VARIABLES, BUT HEADSTART GOALS CAN BE TRANSLATED INTO OPERATIONAL DIMENSIONS. THUS, THE PHYSICAL AND MENTAL HEALTH, SOCIAL ATTITUDES AND BEHAVIOR, AND COMMUNICATION SKILLS OF THE CHILDREN BECOME SOME OF THE OUTPUT VARIABLES WHICH CAN BE MEASURED BY PRE- AND POST-TESTING. METHODS OF ASSESSMENT OF THESE VARIABLES INCLUDE THE USE OF STANDARDIZED TESTS, NEW TESTS DEVELOPED SPECIFICALLY TO MEASURE DISADVANTAGED POPULATIONS, FILES ACCUMULATED AT HEADSTART CENTERS, AND CLASSROOM OBSERVATIONAL PROCEDURES. APPLIED RESEARCH WILL BE EMPHASIZED IN THE 13 EVALUATION AND RESEARCH CENTERS THROUGHOUT THE COUNTRY WHICH WILL IMPLEMENT THE ONGOING EVALUATION. BOTH CROSS-SECTIONAL AND LONGITUDINAL EVALUATION DESIGNS WILL BE NEEDED TO MEASURE HEADSTART'S SHORT AND LONG RANGE EFFECTS. (MS)

ED015793 PS000363
PROBLEMS OF EDUCATIONAL EVALUATION IN PROJECT HEAD START--SAMPLING, DESIGN, AND CONTROL GROUPS. MCDAVID, JOHN W., 10FEB68 15P.
EDRS PRICE MF-$0.65 HC-$3.29

CONTRARY TO THE OPINION OF MANY PEOPLE, PROJECT HEADSTART (HS) IS NOT A STABLE AND UNIFORM PROGRAM WHICH DEALS WITH AN EASILY DEFINABLE POPULATION. THERE ARE, THEREFORE, SEVERAL PROBLEMS WHICH EXIST IN CONNECTION WITH EVALUATIVE RESEARCH CONCERNED WITH HS. IN ORDER TO PROVIDE GUIDANCE IN PROGRAM PLANNING, THIS RESEARCH SEEKS TO DESCRIBE POTENTIAL RECIPIENTS OF HS ATTENTION AND POTENTIALLY USEFUL PROGRAMS, TO ESTABLISH SPECIFIC RELATIONSHIPS BETWEEN PROGRAM ELEMENTS AND POPULATION CHARACTERISTICS, AND TO EVALUATE SPECIFIC HYPOTHESES IN TERMS OF USEFULNESS. DUE TO (1) THE COMPREHENSIVE MULTIDIMENSIONAL NATURE OF HS, (2) THE SIMULTANEOUS PURSUIT OF BOTH IMMEDIATE AND ULTIMATE IMPACT, AND (3) THE PAUCITY OF INFORMATION ABOUT THE DISADVANTAGED POPULATION AND ABOUT PRESCHOOL EDUCATION PROGRAM ELEMENTS, THE GREATEST INITIAL PROBLEM CONCERNED WITH HS EVALUATIVE RESEARCH IS A CONCEPTUAL ONE, THE FORMULATION OF QUESTIONS WHICH ARE PROPERLY "RESEARCHABLE." THE SECOND PROBLEM IS THAT OF METHODOLOGY, HOW TO SAMPLE AND TO DEVELOP MEASUREMENT INSTRUMENTS. SAMPLING PROBLEMS ARE ENCOUNTERED BECAUSE OF THE NON-RANDOM VARIA-

TIONS IN HS POPULATIONS AND THE INACCESSIBILITY OF SUITABLE CONTROL GROUPS. THE THIRD PROBLEM IS THAT OF LOGISTIC DIFFICULTIES. IT IS NECESSARY FOR EVALUATIVE PROCEDURES TO BE UNOBTRUSIVE. TYPICAL CIRCUMSTANCES OF THE DISADVANTAGED HOME, LOW LITERACY LEVELS, AND THE PROBLEM OF RAPPORT BETWEEN DISADVANTAGED ADULTS AND MIDDLE-CLASS SCIENTISTS CONTRIBUTE TO THE LOGISTIC DIFFICULTIES ENCOUNTERED IN GATHERING RESEARCH DATA. THE FOURTH PROBLEM IS THE INTERPRETATION OF DATA IN HS EVALUATIVE RESEARCH. THIS PAPER WAS PRESENTED IN A SYMPOSIUM AT THE AMERICAN EDUCATIONAL RESEARCH ASSOCIATION MEETINGS, CHICAGO, ILLINOIS, FEBRUARY 10, 1968. (JS)

ED015794 PS000364
FACTORS AFFECTING COGNITIVE GROWTH IN PROJECT HEAD START CHILDREN--WHAT KINDS OF CHANGES OCCUR IN WHAT KINDS OF CHILDREN UNDER WHAT KINDS OF PROGRAMS. MCDAVID, JOHN W., 10FEB68 10P.
EDRS PRICE MF-$0.65 HC-$3.29

THE HEADSTART PROGRAM, NOW 3 YEARS OLD, IS AN ATTEMPT TO BREAK INTO THE SELF-PERPETUATING "CULTURES OF POVERTY." THE EVALUATION WHICH HAS ACCOMPANIED THIS SOCIAL EXPERIMENT HAS BEEN DIRECTED TOWARDS IDENTIFYING EFFECTIVE AND PROFITABLE KINDS OF INTERVENTION. THE OBJECTIVES OF HEADSTART ARE NOT SOLELY ACADEMIC BUT SEEK BROAD IMPROVEMENTS IN THE CHILD'S SOCIAL SKILLS AND HEALTH. HEADSTART OPERATES 6 TO 8 WEEK SUMMER PROGRAMS AND LONGER PROGRAMS WITHIN THE SCHOOL YEAR. DESCRIPTIVE DATA COME FROM A NATIONAL SAMPLE OF 2200 CHILDREN. FUTURE EVALUATION WILL BE BASED ON A SMALLER SAMPLE OBSERVED BY TRAINED EXPERIMENTERS. ALTHOUGH THE POPULATION SERVED BY HEADSTART HAS BEEN FAIRLY STABLE, THE SEVERELY DISADVANTAGED HAVE REMAINED HARD TO REACH. RECRUITING PROFESSIONAL PERSONNEL HAS BEEN EASIER THAN ANTICIPATED, BUT FINDING SUB-PROFESSIONAL WORKERS HAS IN SOME AREAS BEEN DIFFICULT. ABOUT 500,000 CHILDREN HAVE BEEN ENROLLED IN EACH SUMMER HEADSTART PROGRAM. THE NUMBER IN THE FULL-YEAR PROGRAMS HAS REACHED A BUDGET-LIMITED 200,000. ABOUT HALF OF THE CHILDREN ARE NEGRO, AND THE SEXES ARE EQUALLY REPRESENTED. THE CHILDREN SHOW THE EFFECTS OF ECONOMIC POVERTY. AS THE STAFF HAS BECOME EXPERIENCED, THE PROGRAMS HAVE BECOME BETTER DIRECTED. ALTHOUGH THE SUCCESS OF HEADSTART CANNOT BE CALLED TOTAL, IT HAS BEEN ENCOURAGING TO ITS INITIAL PROPONENTS. THIS PAPER WAS PRESENTED IN A SYMPOSIUM AT THE AMERICAN EDUCATIONAL RESEARCH ASSOCIATION MEETINGS, CHICAGO, ILLINOIS, FEBRUARY 10, 1968. (DR)

ED016510 PS000235
INDIAN COMMUNITIES AND PROJECT HEAD START. SUMMARY AND OBSERVATIONS IN THE DAKOTAS AND MINNESOTA, TOGETHER WITH AN APPRAISAL OF POSSIBILITIES FOR A HEAD START PROGRAM AMONG THE POTAWATOMI INDIANS OF KANSAS. WAX, MURRAY L.; AND OTHERS, 15SEP67 65P.
EDRS PRICE MF-$0.65 HC-$3.29

THE HOMOGENOUS AND HARMONIOUS INDIAN BAND HAS VANISHED, IF IT EVER EXISTED. THE CONTEMPORARY INDIAN COMMUNITY IS AS HETEROGENEOUS AND DIVIDED AS ANY MORE ORDINARY COMMUNITY. OEO PROGRAMS ARE SOMETIMES MISDIRECTED BECAUSE THEY ARE ORGANIZED FROM THE ASSUMPTION THAT ONE INDIAN CAN SPEAK FOR THE TOTAL COMMUNITY. TWO REPORTS CONCERNING HEAD START PROGRAMS AMONG INDIANS WERE MADE. ONE REPORT CONCLUDES THAT, JUDGED BY ORDINARY SCHOLASTIC STANDARDS, THE HEAD START PROGRAMS OBSERVED AMONG THE INDIANS OF MINNESOTA AND THE DAKOTAS WERE HIGHLY SUCCESSFUL, WITH FEW EXCEPTIONS. IN THE SECOND REPORT, INVESTIGATING THE POSSIBILITIES AND PROBLEMS OF INITIATING A HEAD START PROGRAM, THE AUTHOR CONCLUDES THAT SUCH A PROGRAM WOULD NOT BE SUCCESSFUL WITH THE POTAWATOMI INDIANS OF KANSAS. (C.O'D)

ED016511 PS000248
THE INITIAL COORDINATION OF SENSORIMOTOR SCHEMAS IN HUMAN INFANTS - PIAGET'S IDEAS AND THE ROLE OF EXPERIENCE. WHITE, BURTON L., 24P.
EDRS PRICE MF-$0.65 HC-$3.29

THE PURPOSE OF THIS STUDY WAS TO FIND OUT IF INFANTS WOULD EXHIBIT BEHAVIORS CONSISTENT WITH PIAGET'S OBSERVATIONS ON THE DEVELOPMENT OF RECIPROCAL COORDINATIONS AMONG THE LOOKING, SUCKING AND GRASPING SCHEMAS. A SECOND PURPOSE WAS TO SEE IF INCREASED LOOKING AT AND TOUCHING OF NEARBY OBJECTS BY INFANTS WOULD RESULT IN ACCELERATION OF THE COORDINATING PROCESS. EXPERIMENTAL SUBJECTS WERE A GROUP OF NORMAL BUT INSTITUTION-REARED INFANTS (1 1/2 TO 5 MONTHS OLD) WITH A CONTROL GROUP OF 43 WHO HAD BEEN SPECIALLY TRAINED. ONCE A WEEK EACH BABY WAS BROUGHT TO THE TESTING ROOM AND GIVEN 3 OPPORTUNITIES TO RESPOND TO THE PRESENTATION OF THE TEST OBJECT. EACH WAS THEN GIVEN THE OBJECT-IN-HAND TEST. SOME OF THE INFANTS HAD BEEN REARED UNDER CONDITIONS DESIGNED TO ACCELERATE SENSORIMOTOR DEVELOPMENT. THESE SUBJECTS SHOWED PRECOCIOUS VISUALLY-DIRECTED REACHING AND HEIGHTENED VISUAL ATTENTIVENESS DEMONSTRATING A FUNCTIONAL RELATIONSHIP BETWEEN REARING CONDITIONS AND DEVELOPMENTAL PROCESSES. THE RESULTS OF THE STUDY SUPPORT PIAGET'S THEORY OF SEQUENTIAL DEVELOPMENT AND RECIPROCAL COORDINATION BUT SUGGEST THAT (1) MANY MORE INFANT RESPONSES ARE IDENTIFIABLE AND (2) THAT ENVIRONMENT CAN AFFECT THE RATE OF SENSORIMOTOR DEVELOPMENT. (MS)

ED016512 PS000249
A CREATIVE GUIDE FOR PRESCHOOL TEACHERS. GOALS, ACTIVITIES, AND SUGGESTED MATERIALS FOR AN ORGANIZED PROGRAM. WYLIE, JOANNE, ED., 66
DOCUMENT NOT AVAILABLE FROM EDRS.

THIS DOCUMENT IS A COMPREHENSIVE MANUAL FOR THE IMPLEMENTATION OF A NURSERY OR PRESCHOOL PROGRAM. EMPHASIZING THE PHYSICAL, INTELLECTUAL, AND EMOTIONAL NEEDS OF THE 4-YEAR-OLD, THIS MANUAL DELINEATES THE GOALS OF A PRESCHOOL PROGRAM AND SUGGESTS THE MEANS OF ACHIEVING THEM. IT CONSIDERS IN SOME DEPTH SPECIFIC AREAS OF THE PRESCHOOL CURRICULUM, NAMELY, (1) PLAY IN THE CLASSROOM AND ON THE PLAYGROUND, (2) LANGUAGE ARTS, (3) ARTS AND CRAFTS, (4) MUSIC, (5) MATHEMATICS, (6) SCIENCE, AND (7) HEALTH. BESIDES A WELL-DEVELOPED, MEANINGFUL CURRICULUM, THE TEACHER IS A MOST IMPORTANT ELEMENT OF THE PRESCHOOL PROGRAM. SHE IS EXPECTED TO DEMONSTRATE A GREAT INSIGHT AND UNDERSTANDING IN DEALING WITH HER 4-YEAR-OLDS AND THEIR WIDE RANGE OF PERSONALITIES AND FEELINGS. MUCH OF THE SUCCESS OF IMPLEMENTING THE CURRICULUM WILL DEPEND ON HER FEELING FOR WHEN AND HOW THE VARIOUS ACTIVITIES ARE TO BE PRESENTED. THE PRESCHOOL PROGRAM IS ESSENTIALLY A SOCIAL STUDIES PROGRAM, NOT AN INTENSE ACADEMIC EXPERIENCE. IT MUST BE DESIGNED AND ADMINISTERED TO DEVELOP EFFICIENTLY AND POSITIVELY THE PUPIL'S INDIVIDUAL AND SOCIAL PERSONALITY. THIS DOCUMENT IS AVAILABLE FROM WESTERN PUBLISHING EDUCATION, RACINE, WISCONSIN. (WD)

ED016513 PS000266
AN INFANT RATING SCALE, ITS VALIDATION AND USEFULNESS. HOOPES, JANET L., JAN67
DOCUMENT NOT AVAILABLE FROM EDRS.

IT IS GENERALLY RECOGNIZED THAT COMPATIBILITY IN ADOPTION DEPENDS ON A SOUND EVALUATION OF THE ADOPTIVE PARENTS AND OF THE INFANT AND THAT THE BEST INTERESTS OF THE CHILD ARE SERVED BY EARLY PLACEMENT IN A PERMANENT HOME. EARLY ASSESSMENT OF THE INFANT, ON WHICH PROPER PLACEMENT IS DEPENDENT, MUST BE PRIMARILY PREDICTIVE. HOWEVER, EXISTING INFANT TESTS HAVE BEEN FOUND TO BE UNSATISFACTORY PREDICTORS OF SUBSEQUENT DEVELOPMENT. THEREFORE, THE INFANT RATING SCALE, FOR USE WITH INFANTS UNDER 3 MONTHS OF AGE, WAS DEVISED IN ORDER TO FACILITATE THE ACCELERATION OF ADOPTION PROCEDURES. THIS INSTRUMENT SCALES (1) INTELLIGENCE OF THE NATURAL PARENTS, (2) PRENATAL MEDICAL INFORMATION ON THE MOTHER, (3) INFORMATION CONCERNED WITH BIRTH AND DELIVERY, (4) EARLY BEHAVIOR OF THE INFANT, AND (5) MEDICAL CONDITION AND PROGRESS OF THE INFANT. THE INFANT RATING SCALE WAS ADMINISTERED TO 114 INFANTS, AND ITS EFFECTIVENESS AS A PREDICTOR OF SUBSEQUENT DEVELOPMENT WAS EXPLORED IN A LONGITUDINAL FOLLOW-UP STUDY OF 73 OF THESE CHILDREN AT APPROXIMATELY 4.5 YEARS OF AGE. THE RESULTS OF THIS STUDY ESTABLISHED THE RELIABILITY AND VALIDITY OF THE INFANT RATING SCALE AND ITS USEFULNESS AS A SCREENING MEASURE FOR PURPOSES OF EARLY PLACEMENT FOR ADOPTION. DETAILED STATISTICS ARE PRESENTED IN 40 TABLES, AND AN APPENDIX CONTAINS THE FORMS USED IN THE ADMINISTRATION OF THE SCALE. THIS DOCUMENT IS AVAILABLE FROM CHILD WELFARE LEAGUE OF AMERICAN, INC., 44 EAST 23RD STREET, NEW YORK, N. Y. 10010 FOR $3.00. (JS)

ED016514 PS000299
THE EARLY TRAINING PROJECT FOR DISADVANTAGED CHILDREN--A REPORT AFTER FIVE YEARS. GRAY, SUSAN W.; KLAUS, RUPERT A., SEP67 68P.
EDRS PRICE MF-$0.65 HC-$3.29

THE EARLY TRAINING PROJECT IS A FIELD RESEARCH STUDY WHICH IS CONCERNED WITH THE PROBLEM OF THE PROGRESSIVE RETARDATION OF THE CULTURALLY DEPRIVED IN THE PUBLIC SCHOOLS. THE CHILDREN INVOLVED IN THE STUDY WERE ALL NEGRO. FROM A GROUP OF 61 CULTURALLY DEPRIVED NEGRO PRESCHOOL CHILDREN, 3 GROUPS WERE CONSTITUTED BY RANDOMIZATION. THE FIRST OF THESE ATTENDED A 10-WEEK PRESCHOOL OVER A PERIOD OF 3 SUMMERS. IN ADDITON THIS GROUP HAD 3 YEARS OF WEEKLY CONTACTS IN THE HOME WITH A CERTIFIED ELEMENTARY SCHOOL TEACHER. THE SECOND GROUP RECEIVED 2 SUMMERS OF SPECIAL EXPERIENCE PLUS 2 YEARS OF CONTACTS WITH AN ELEMENTARY TEACHER IN THE HOME. A THIRD GROUP BECAME THE LOCAL CONTROL GROUP. ANOTHER CONTROL GROUP WAS FROM A CITY 60 MILES DISTANT. THE GENERAL PROGRAM CENTERED AROUND ACHIEVEMENT MOTIVATION AND APTITUDE FOR ACHIEVEMENT. TEST RESULTS SHOWED THAT GAINS TENDED TO BE MAINTAINED AT A SIGNIFICANT LEVEL FOR 4 YEARS. IN SPITE OF THE FACT THAT PUBLIC SCHOOLS HAVE NOT BEEN ABLE TO SUSTAIN ADEQUATELY THE GAINS WHICH MAY HAVE BEEN MADE IN THE EARLY INTERVENTION PROGRAM, IT SEEMS POSSIBLE THAT A PROGRAM PLANNED WITH THESE CHILDREN'S DEFICITS IN MIND COULD HAVE A LASTING EFFECT. (CO)

ED016515 PS000319
POSITIVE SOCIAL REINFORCEMENT IN THE NURSERY SCHOOL PEER GROUP. CHARLESWORTH, ROSALIND; HARTUP, WILLARD W., 6P.
EDRS PRICE MF-$0.65 HC-$3.29

FOR 5 WEEKS, 2 OBSERVERS MADE DAILY VISITS TO A LABORATORY PRESCHOOL TO COLLECT INFORMATION ON THE AMOUNT AND KINDS OF POSITIVE SOCIAL REINFORCEMENT CHILDREN GIVE TO EACH OTHER IN NURSERY SCHOOL. SEVENTY CHILDREN (AGED 3 YEARS 4 MONTHS TO 4 YEARS 9 MONTHS) WERE GROUPED INTO 2 OLDER AND 2 YOUNGER CLASSES. EACH CHILD WAS OBSERVED IN RANDOM ORDER FOR 3-MINUTE PERIODS AT 12 DIFFERENT TIMES. OBSERVATIONS WERE RECORDED IN PRESET PROTOCOLS CODED IN 4 CATEGORIES ACCORDING TO KINDS OF REINFORCEMENT, (1) GIVING POSITIVE ATTENTION AND APPROVAL, (2) GIVING AFFECTION AND PERSONAL ACCEPTANCE, (3) SUBMISSION, AND (4) TOKEN GIVING. ANALYSIS OF VARIANCE OF THE DATA SHOWED THAT 4-YEAR-OLDS HAD A SIGNIFICANTLY HIGHER RATE OF POSITIVE SOCIAL REINFORCEMENT IN A WIDER DISTRIBUTION THAN DID 3-YEAR-OLDS. REINFORCEMENT OVERTURES OCCURRED MOST FREQUENTLY DURING SUCH DRAMATIC PLAY ACTIVITIES AS PLAYING HOUSE OR PLAYING WITH BLOCKS, TRUCKS, AND PUPPETS. SUPPORT GIVEN RELATED POSITIVELY TO THE AMOUNT RECEIVED AND USUALLY SUSTAINED ONGOING BEHAVIOR. INVESTIGATORS CONCLUDED THAT THERE IS A MARKED INCREASE IN A CHILD'S USE OF GENERALIZED SOCIAL REINFORCERS DURING PRESCHOOL YEARS AND THAT A WIDE VARIETY OF POSITIVE RESPONSES ARE USED. THIS ARTICLE IS PUBLISHED IN "CHILD DEVELOPMENT," VOLUME 38, NUMBER 4, DECEMBER, 1967. (MS)

ED016516 PS000328
DEVELOPMENT OF CHILDREN'S ABILITY TO COORDINATE PERSPECTIVES. MILLER, JACK W., 09FEB68 10P.
EDRS PRICE MF-$0.65 HC-$3.29

THE PERSPECTIVE ABILITY TEST INVOLVED 285 CHILDREN BETWEEN 66 AND 155 MONTHS OF AGE. TO MEASURE ABILITY TO COORDINATE PERSPECTIVE, THE RESEARCHER BUILT A CIRCULAR TABLE WITH AN ISLAND DISC MODELED AND PAINTED TO REPRESENT WATERS AND MOUNTAINOUS LAND. TWENTY COLOR PHOTOGRAPHS WERE TAKEN FROM DIFFERENT EQUALLY SPACED VANTAGE POINTS. THE SUBJECTS WERE ASKED TO STAND IN ONE PLACE AND INDICATE WHERE THE CAMERA HAD TO HAVE BEEN WHEN A PARTICULAR PICTURE WAS TAKEN. THE DATA INDICATE THAT THERE WAS A PROGRESSION FROM HIGHER TO LOWER ERROR SCORES AS THE AGE OF THE CHILDREN INVOLVED INCREASED. THE TEST APPEARED TO BE A REASONABLY RELIABLE AND PRECISE INSTRUMENT FOR ASSESSING CHANGE IN ABILITY TO COORDINATE PERSPECTIVES AS THE CULMINATION OF DEVELOPMENTAL PROCESSES. AT THE TIME OF THE STUDY RESEARCH WAS UNDERWAY FOR FURTHER INVESTIGATION OF NORMAL TRENDS AND VARIABILITY IN TIME REQUIRED FOR ACQUISITIONS OF SPATIAL ABILITY AND DETERMINING THE FEASIBILITY OF SPECIAL TRAINING TO ACCELERATE OR MAKE MORE PRECISE THE ABILITY TO COORDINATE PERSPECTIVES. (CO)

ED016517 PS000330
DEVELOPMENT OF A TECHNIQUE FOR IDENTIFYING ELEMENTARY SCHOOL CHILDREN'S MUSICAL CONCEPTS. FINAL REPORT. ANDREWS, FRANCES M.; DEIHL, NED C., SEP67 193P.
EDRS PRICE MF-$0.65 HC-$6.58

CURRENT LITERATURE RELEVANT TO MUSIC EDUCATION OF CHILDREN STRESSES THE IMPORTANCE OF CURRICULUM DEVELOPMENT BASED ON A CONCEPTUAL APPROACH TO MUSIC LEARNING. THERE BEING LITTLE UNDERSTANDING OF CHILDREN'S CONCEPTS OF BASIC MUSICAL ELEMENTS ON WHICH TO FOUND SUCH CURRICULUM DEVELOPMENT, AN INSTRUMENT WAS DEVELOPED TO IDENTIFY THE IDEAS REGARDING PITCH, DURATION, AND LOUDNESS WHICH ARE POSSESSED BY CHILDREN. TWO GROUP MEASURES ELICITING WRITTEN RESPONSES TO (1) WRITTEN STIMULI AND (2) MULTIDIMENSIONAL MUSICAL STIMULI WERE DEVISED. IN ADDITION, 2 INDIVIDUAL MEASURES REQUIRING (1) THE MANIPULATION OF ELEMENTARY SOUND PRODUCING INSTRUMENTS AND (2) OVERT MOVEMENT IN RESPONSE TO MUSICAL STIMULI WERE FORMULATED. AFTER PILOT TESTING AND DEVELOPMENT, THIS INSTRUMENT WAS EMPLOYED IN A STUDY OF FOURTH-GRADE CHILDREN. THE GROUP MEASURES WERE ADMINISTERED TO 429 SUBJECTS AND THE INDIVIDUAL MEASURES TO 214 SUBJECTS. DERIVED SCORES, STATISTICAL EVALUATIONS, AND CORRELATIONS WITH IQ AND READING SCORES (REPORTED IN 61 TABLES) DEMONSTRATE THAT, ALTHOUGH FURTHER REFINEMENT IS NEEDED BEFORE IT WILL BE USEABLE FOR PRACTICAL PURPOSES, THE INSTRUMENT IS ADEQUATE FOR RESEARCH PURPOSES. THE DEVELOPMENT OF THIS MEASURE HAS SUGGESTED SEVERAL AREAS IN WHICH THE NEED FOR FURTHER RESEARCH IS INDICATED. (JS)

ED016518 PS000331
DISCRIMINATION LEARNING, PROBLEM SOLVING, AND CHOICE PATTERNING BY CHILDREN AS A FUNCTION OF INCENTIVE VALUE, MOTIVATION, AND SEQUENTIAL DEPENDENCIES. FINAL REPORT. WITRYOL, SAM L., 30JUN67 90P.
EDRS PRICE MF-$0.65 HC-$3.29

THE EXTENT TO WHICH INCENTIVES INFLUENCE CHILDREN'S LEARNING WAS STUDIED BY INVESTIGATORS AT THE UNIVERSITY OF CONNECTICUT. BOTH VERBAL AND MATERIAL REWARDS WERE OFFERED TO SELECTED GROUPS OF CHILDREN WHICH VARIED IN NUMBER FROM 48 TO 80 CHILDREN. A DIFFERENTIAL METHOD PERMITTED THE CHILDREN TO EXPLORE THE RANGE OF REWARDS SO THAT THE COMPARATIVE VALUE OF DIFFERENT INCENTIVES COULD BE DETERMINED. RESULTS SHOWED THAT INCENTIVES AFFECTED LEARNING POSITIVELY AND THAT CHILDREN WOULD PREFER VERBAL TO MATERIAL REWARDS WHEN GIVEN RELEVANT MOTIVATIONAL INSTRUCTIONS AND A FAVORABLE INCENTIVE SCHEDULE. THE NOVELTY OF UNEXPECTED REWARDS PROVIDED GREATER LEARNING INCENTIVE. HOWEVER, A DELAY IN RECEIVING REWARDS GENERALLY IMPAIRED LEARNING. ADDITIONAL STUDIES, USING THE SAME DIFFERENTIAL METHOD, SHOULD FURTHER CONSIDER THE SPECIFIC RELATIONSHIP OF REWARD TIMING AND TASK-RELEVANT INSTRUCTIONS TO MOTIVATION. DOCUMENT ED 010 530 WAS AN INTERIM REPORT OF THIS PROJECT. (MS)

ED016519 PS000333
INCREASING THE AWARENESS OF ART IDEAS OF CULTURALLY DEPRIVED KINDERGARTEN CHILDREN THROUGH EXPERIENCES WITH CERAMICS. FINAL REPORT. DOUGLAS, NANCY J.; SCHWARTZ, JULIA B., JUN67 40P.
EDRS PRICE MF-$0.65 HC-$3.29

THIS STUDY COVERED A PERIOD OF 8 WEEKS AND 14 SESSIONS. AN EXPERIMENTAL GROUP OF 29 5-YEAR-OLDS WAS TAUGHT BY AN EXPERIENCED EARLY CHILDHOOD AND ART EDUCATION TEACHER. A CONTROL GROUP OF 26 5-YEAR-OLDS WAS USED ONLY FOR MEASUREMENT OF NORMAL GROWTH DURING A BEGINNING AND A FINAL SESSION. THE PURPOSE OF THE STUDY WAS TO INCREASE MEANINGFUL LANGUAGE DEVELOPMENT AND AWARENESS OF CULTURALLY DEPRIVED CHILDREN TO SELECTED ART IDEAS THROUGH GUIDED PARTICIPATION. A NEW CERAMIC ART PIECE WAS SHARED WITH THE EXPERIMENTAL GROUP AT EACH OF THE 14 SESSIONS. THESE WORKS REPRESENTED A VARIETY OF IDEAS, FROM THE SIMPLE PIECES BY COLLEGE STUDENTS TO WORKS BY PROFESSIONALS AND INCLUDING 2 PIECES FROM OTHER CULTURES. CLAY FOR MODELING WAS PLACED ON THE WORK AREA IN THE BACK OF THE ROOM. QUESTIONS POSED AND DISCUSSED WERE BASED ON 4 BASIC ART IEDEAS, (1) WHAT IS IT, (2) WHO DID IT, (3) HOW DID HE DO IT, AND (4) COULD HE DO IT WITH AN ALTERNATE MATERIAL. TAPE RECORDINGS WERE MADE OF EACH SESSION. THE CHILDREN WERE RATED ON VERBALIZATION AND CLAY PRODUCTS. ON THE POST-TEST THERE WAS A SIGNIFICANT GAIN IN FAVOR OF THE CONTROL GROUP ON VERBALIZATION SCORES AND THE ABILITY TO USE CLAY. (CO)

ED016520 PS000341
PROJECT TOBI, THE DEVELOPMENT OF A PRE-SCHOOL ACHIEVEMENT TEST. FINAL REPORT. MOSS, MARGARET H., 31OCT67 23P.
EDRS PRICE MF-$0.65 HC-$3.29

THE TEST OF BASIC INFORMATION (TOBI) IS A 54-ITEM, MULTIPLE-CHOICE PICTURE TEST DEVELOPED TO MEASURE PREACADEMIC, SCHOOL-RELEVANT KNOWLEDGE. IT CAN BE USED TO ASSESS PROGRAM EFFECTIVENESS BY GIVING IT AS A PRE- AND POSTTEST. IT CAN BE ADMINISTERED INDIVIDUALLY, OR TO GROUPS OF UP TO 15 IF THERE IS 1 ADULT FOR 3 OR 4 CHILDREN, AND TAKES FROM 15 TO 30 MINUTES TO ADMINISTER. THE TEST ITEMS ARE URBAN-ORIENTED AND WERE SELECTED FROM A POOL OF 500. THE FINAL TEST STANDARDIZATION WAS BASED ON STAFF-ADMINISTERED TESTS OF A SAMPLE OF 539 DISADVANTAGED CHILDREN SELECTED FROM URBAN AREAS ACROSS THE COUNTRY. A KUDER-RICHARDSON 20 (KR 20) RELIABILITY OF .90 WAS OBTAINED, TOGETHER WITH A TEST-RETEST RELIABILITY OF .87. THE LAST IS QUITE UNUSUAL FOR A GROUP TEST OF 4-YEAR OLDS. THE TEST IS NOW AVAILABLE ONLY ON AN EXPERIMENTAL BASIS, BUT PUBLICATION IS BEING CONSIDERED. (DR)

ED016521 PS000343
DEVELOPMENT OF AN ENLARGED MUSIC REPERTORY FOR KINDERGARTEN THROUGH GRADE SIX (JUILLIARD REPERTORY PROJECT). FINAL REPORT. DICKEY, GEORGE, DEC67 89P.
EDRS PRICE MF-$0.65 HC-$3.29

PERFORMANCE MATERIALS CURRENTLY AVAILABLE FOR USE IN ELEMENTARY SCHOOL MUSIC PROGRAMS DO NOT ADEQUATELY REPRESENT THE BODY OF SIGNIFICANT MUSIC WHICH IS A PART OF OUR CULTURAL HERITAGE. THE JUILLIARD REPERTORY PROJECT WAS ESTABLISHED TO FIND NEW MATERIALS, IN THE FORM OF GOOD MUSIC IN ITS ORIGINALLY COMPOSED STATE, SUITABLE FOR USE IN THE ELEMENTARY GRADES. EXPERT CONSULTANTS WERE ENGAGED TO COLLECT AND EVALUATE A GREAT QUANTITY OF INSTRUMENTAL AND VOCAL MUSIC FROM THE VARIOUS PERIODS OF MUSIC HISTORY (PRE-RENAISSANCE, RENAISSANCE, BAROQUE, CLASSICAL, ROMANTIC AND CONTEMPORARY) AND FROM THE INTERNATIONAL FOLK MUSIC REPERTORY OF ALL PERIODS. A PANEL OF MUSIC EDUCATORS REVIEWED THE SELECTIONS SUBMITTED BY THE CONSULTANTS AND RECOMMENDED CERTAIN ONES OF THEM FOR CLASSROOM TESTING. SEVEN DIVERSE PUBLIC SCHOOL SYSTEMS, EACH RECOGNIZED AS MAINTAINING A HIGH QUALITY OF MUSICAL INSTRUCTION, PARTICIPATED IN THE TESTING PROGRAM. EVALUATIONS OF TEACHER AND STUDENT RESPONSES TO THE TEST MATERIALS WERE SUBMITTED TO THE PROJECT STAFF. AN ANTHOLOGY OF WORKS SELECTED FROM THOSE TESTED IS TO BE PUBLISHED. INCLUDED IN THE PROJECT REPORT ARE (1) ACCOUNTS OF THE PROCEDURES EMPLOYED IN THE SELECTION OF SUITABLE WORKS FOR TESTING, (2) DESCRIPTIONS OF THE TESTING ENVIRONMENTS AND PROCEDURES, (3) EVALUATIVE REPORTS FROM PROJECT CONSULTANTS

AND TESTERS, AND (4) A LIST OF THE MATERIALS PRODUCED BY THIS PROJECT. (JS)

ED016522 PS000345
THE EFFECTS OF DIFFERENT LANGUAGE INSTRUCTION ON THE USE OF ATTRIBUTES OF PRE-KINDERGARTEN DISADVANTAGED CHILDREN. DAY, DAVID E., 09FEB68
DOCUMENT NOT AVAILABLE FROM EDRS.

THIS 10-MONTH STUDY WAS CONDUCTED TO COMPARE THE EFFECTIVENESS OF (1) A HIGHLY STRUCTURED TEACHING PLAN FOR LANGUAGE INSTRUCTION AND (2) A DEVELOPMENTAL, FLEXIBLE INSTRUCTIONAL APPROACH IN CORRECTING LANGUAGE DEFICIENCIES. THE EXPERIMENTAL CONDITIONS WERE ESTABLISHED CONSISTENT WITH THE RECOGNITION OF THE NEED TO INTERVENE EARLY IN THE DISADVANTAGED CHILD'S LANGUAGE DEVELOPMENT. NEAR THE END OF THE 10-MONTH LANGUAGE INSTRUCTION PROGRAM, THE CHILDREN OF BOTH GROUPS WERE ASKED TO DESCRIBE SEVERAL OBJECTS. THESE DESCRIPTIONS MAKE UP THE DATA THAT WAS SUBMITTED TO AN ANALYSIS BY 2 JUDGES USING A MODIFICATION OF SIEGEL'S SYSTEM FOR ORGANIZING LANGUAGE GROUPING PREFERENCE BEHAVIOR. THE JUDGES INDEPENDENTLY GROUPED THE CHILDREN'S DESCRIPTIONS INTO 4 CATEGORIES. (THERE WAS 90 PERCENT AGREEMENT BETWEEN THE JUDGES ON THE CLASSIFICATIONS.) THE CHILDREN'S DESCRIPTIONS PLACED IN CATEGORY 1, TOTAL LANGUAGE PRODUCTION, SHOWED NO SIGNIFICANT DIFFERENCE BETWEEN THE 2 GROUPS. CATEGORY 2, USE OF RELATIONAL-CONTEXTUAL WORDS, SHOWED THAT THE DEVELOPMENTAL GROUP DESCRIBED OBJECTS BY FUNCTION MORE THAN DID THE STRUCTURED GROUP. CATEGORY 3, CONCEPTUAL RESPONSES, INDICATED NO SIGNIFICANT DIFFERENCE BETWEEN GROUPS. CATEGORY 4, USE OF DESCRIPTIVE PART-WHOLE WORDS, SHOWED THAT THE STRUCTURED GROUP USED COLOR AND FORM DESCRIPTIONS MORE THAN DID THE DEVELOPMENTAL GROUP. IT WAS CONCLUDED THAT OVERALL THE STRUCTURED GROUP WAS MORE ADEPT AT USING LANGUAGE WITH CLARITY AND SPECIFICITY. THIS PAPER WAS PRESENTED AT THE ANNUAL MEETING OF THE AMERICAN EDUCATIONAL RESEARCH ASSOCIATION, CHICAGO, ILLINOIS, FEBRUARY 9, 1968. (WD)

ED016523 PS000348
SECOND-YEAR REPORT ON AN EVALUATIVE STUDY OF PREKINDERGARTEN PROGRAMS FOR EDUCATIONALLY DISADVANTAGED CHILDREN. DI LORENZO, LOUIS T.; SALTER, RUTH, 14NOV67 40P.
EDRS PRICE MF-$0.65 HC-$3.29

PREKINDERGARTENS IN 8 NEW YORK STATE SCHOOL SYSTEMS WERE EVALUATED TO FIND OUT IF THE CHILDREN INVOLVED SHOWED INCREASED CAPACITY TO LEARN, AND IMPROVEMENT IN LANGUAGE AND COGNITIVE SKILLS. 1010 DISADVANTAGED AND 225 NONDISADVANTAGED SUBJECTS WERE RANDOMLY ASSIGNED TO EXPERIMENTAL AND CONTROL GROUPS AND PRE- AND POST-TESTED WITH THE STANFORD-BINET AND THE PEABODY PICTURE VOCABULARY TEST. AT THE END OF THE PREKINDERGARTEN YEARS THE ILLINOIS TEST OF PSYCHOLINGUISTIC ABILITIES WAS GIVEN, AND LATE IN THE KINDERGARTEN YEAR THE METROPOLITAN READINESS TESTS WERE USED TO SEE IF GAINS OBTAINED DURING PREKINDERGARTEN WERE SUSTAINED OR INCREASED. THE GENERAL CURRICULUM IN ALL PROGRAMS WAS THE SAME, BUT CERTAIN ACTIVITIES WERE ADDED TO SELECTED CLASSES. CHILDREN WHO WERE GIVEN READING READINESS INSTRUCTION OR LANGUAGE TRAINING SHOWED THE GREATEST GAINS. IMPLICATIONS ARE THAT THE MOST EFFECTIVE PREKINDERGARTEN PROGRAMS ARE THOSE WHOSE CONTENT IS DESIGNED TO DEVELOP COGNITIVE ACTIVITIES EFFECTIVE IN INCREASING LEARNING CAPACITIES. IT ALSO APPEARS THAT PREKINDERGARTEN EFFECTS WILL BE MOST LASTING IF SPECIAL PROGRAMMING FOR THE DISADVANTAGED IS CONTINUED INTO THE PRIMARY GRADES. THIS PAPER WAS PRESENTED AT THE 1967 ANNUAL CONVOCATION OF THE EDUCATIONAL RESEARCH ASSOCIATION OF NEW YORK STATE, NOVEMBER 14, 1967. (MS)

ED016524 PS000349
A COMPARATIVE STUDY OF TWO PRESCHOOL PROGRAMS FOR CULTURALLY DISADVANTAGED CHILDREN--A HIGHLY STRUCTURED AND A TRADITIONAL PROGRAM. KARNES, MERLE B.; AND OTHERS, AUG66 111P.
EDRS PRICE MF-$0.65 HC-$6.58

THIS STUDY REPORTS THE FIRST PHASE OF A 5-YEAR LONGITUDINAL INVESTIGATION OF THE COMPARATIVE EFFECTIVENESS OF A HIGHLY STRUCTURED PRESCHOOL PROGRAM AND A TRADITIONAL NURSERY SCHOOL PROGRAM IN AMELIORATING THE LEARNING DEFECTS OF CULTURALLY DISADVANTAGED CHILDREN. THE HIGHLY STRUCTURED PROGRAM IS INTENDED TO OVERCOME PARTICULAR WEAKNESSES OF DISADVANTAGED CHILDREN, WITH PARTICULAR STRESS PLACED ON LANGUAGE SKILLS. THE 55 SUBJECTS WHO TOOK PART IN THE 2-MONTH STUDY WERE SELECTED FROM LOW SOCIOECONOMIC HOMES AND WERE ASSIGNED TO CLASSES IN SUCH A WAY THAT EXPERIMENTAL AND CONTROL GROUPS WERE MATCHED IN IQ, SEX, RACE, AND SOCIOECONOMIC STATUS. THE SUBJECTS WERE PRE- AND POSTTESTED WITH THE STANFORD-BINET INTELLIGENCE SCALE, THE ILLINOIS TEST OF PSYCHOLINGUISTIC ABILITIES, THE PEABODY PICTURE VOCABULARY TEST, AND THE FROSTIG DEVELOPMENTAL TEST OF VISUAL PERCEPTION, AND WERE POSTTESTED WITH THE METROPOLITAN READINESS TESTS. COMPARISONS INDICATED THAT (1) EXPERIMENTAL SUBJECTS SHOWED SIGNIFICANTLY GREATER PROGRESS IN MEASURED IQ, (2) OVERALL PROGRESS IN PSYCHOLINGUISTIC ABILITIES WAS ESSENTIALLY THE SAME FOR BOTH GROUPS, (3) THE CONTROL GROUP SHOWED SLIGHTLY HIGHER VOCABULARY GAINS, ALTHOUGH THE GROUPS DID NOT DIFFER SIGNIFICANTLY, (4) THE EXPERIMENTAL GROUP SHOWED GREATER GAINS IN VISUAL PERCEPTUAL DEVELOPMENT, AND (5) THE EXPERIMENTAL GROUP SCORED SIGNIFICANTLY HIGHER IN EACH AREA OF THE READINESS TESTS. THESE RESULTS SUGGEST THAT THE HIGHLY STRUCTURED PROGRAM IS MORE EFFECTIVE, BUT FINAL EVALUATION MUST AWAIT THE EVALUATION OF THE PERFORMANCE OF THE SUBJECTS IN SCHOOL. (DR)

ED016525 PS000353
"PRE-SCHOOL" EDUCATION, PROS AND CONS. A SURVEY OF "PRE-SCHOOL" EDUCATION WITH EMPHASIS ON RESEARCH PAST, PRESENT, AND FUTURE. PALMER, JUDITH A., APR66 27P.
EDRS PRICE MF-$0.65 HC-$3.29

THIS REPORT WAS A SURVEY OF THE PROS AND CONS CONCERNING PRESCHOOL EDUCATION. THE INTRODUCTION WAS A DISCUSSION OF SOME OF THE HISTORY BEHIND THE PRESCHOOL PROGRAMS OF TODAY. IN THE NEXT PART OF THE REPORT IT WAS SUGGESTED THAT THE MOST IMPORTANT YEARS OF LEARNING ARE BETWEEN THE AGES OF 4 AND 6. JUNIOR KINDERGARTENS COULD THEREFORE HAVE GREAT IMPLICATIONS FOR THE CHILD'S FUTURE LEARNING PATTERN. YET, SOME EDUCATORS FEEL THAT PRESCHOOL IS NOT NECESSARY FOR THE MIDDLE-CLASS CHILD AND THAT KINDERGARTEN IS ADEQUATE. STILL OTHER EDUCATORS FEEL THAT IT IS THEIR RESPONSIBILITY TO PROVIDE STIMULATION AND GUIDANCE TO ALL PRESCHOOL-AGE CHILDREN. THERE HAVE BEEN CONFLICTING RESULTS IN STUDIES MADE. THESE COULD BE DUE TO THE VARIOUS TYPES OF CHILDREN, TEACHER-CHILD INTERACTION AND THE NATURE OF THE PROGRAM. DUE TO THE LACK OF CONCLUSIVE RESULTS, FURTHER RESEARCH TO DETERMINE THE VALUE OF HAVING A JUNIOR KINDERGARTEN WAS JUDGED TO BE NECESSARY. (CO)

ED016526 PS000357
THE EFFECTS OF JUNIOR KINDERGARTEN ON ACHIEVEMENT--THE FIRST FIVE YEARS. PALMER, JUDITH A., 66 46P.
EDRS PRICE MF-$0.65 HC-$3.29

IN 1960 AT TORONTO, CANADA, A LONGITUDINAL STUDY OF ACHIEVEMENT WAS BEGUN IN JUNIOR KINDERGARTEN WITH 8,695 CHILDREN. THE OBJECTIVES OF THE STUDY WERE (1) TO EVALUATE THE EFFECT OF JUNIOR KINDERGARTEN ATTENDANCE ON THE ACHIEVEMENT AND DEVELOPMENT OF CHILDREN, AND (2) TO EXAMINE THE NATURE OF THE WORLD OF JUNIOR AND SENIOR KINDERGARTEN CHILDREN. THE DATA COLLECTED CONSISTED OF INFORMATION AND SCORES FROM (1) THE DRAW-A-CLASSROOM TEST, (2) THE PUPIL PROFILE FOLDER, (3) THE RATING QUESTIONNAIRE, (4) THE METROPOLITAN ACHIEVEMENT TEST, AND (5) THE OTIS QUICK-SCORING MENTAL ABILITY TEST. FOUR TABLES WERE MADE TO COMPARE JUNIOR KINDERGARTEN CHILDREN WITH SENIOR KINDERGARTEN CHILDREN WHO HAD NOT ATTENDED JUNIOR KINDERGARTEN. OF THOSE WHO DID NOT GO TO JUNIOR KINDERGARTEN, MATCH 1 INCLUDES CHILDREN WHOSE PARENTS CHOSE NOT TO SEND THEM TO JUNIOR KINDERGARTEN. MATCH 2 INCLUDES CHILDREN LIVING WHERE JUNIOR KINDERGARTEN WAS NOT AVAILABLE. STATISTICALLY, MATCH 1 SHOWED JUNIOR KINDERGARTEN TO BE A GREAT ADVANTAGE. MATCH 2 SHOWED LITTLE DIFFERENCE, AND IN SOME CASES THE JUNIOR KINDERGARTEN GROUP WAS ACTUALLY SURPASSED BY THE SENIOR KINDERGARTEN GROUP. A POSSIBLE EXPLANATION FOR THE INSIGNIFICANT DIFFERENCE SHOWN IN MATCH 2 IS THAT PARENTS OF THOSE SENIOR KINDERGARTEN CHILDREN HAD JUST ENOUGH SCHOOLING TO PLACE A HIGH VALUE ON EDUCATION. THE EFFECTS OF JUNIOR KINDERGARTEN DISAPPEAR IN ABOUT 4 YEARS. IF JUNIOR KINDERGARTEN IS TO HAVE A LASTING EFFECT, THEN THE ENTIRE SCHOOL PROGRAM SHOULD BUILD ON THIS EXPERIENCE. THE APPENDIX TO THIS DOCUMENT IS PS 000 358. (CO)

ED016527 PS000358
THE EFFECTS OF JUNIOR KINDERGARTEN ON ACHIEVEMENT--THE FIRST FIVE YEARS. APPENDIX. PALMER, JUDITH A., JUN66 64P.
EDRS PRICE MF-$0.65 HC-$3.29

TEN TABLES, EACH WITH SEVERAL SUBDIVISIONS, WERE USED TO PRESENT THE VALUES OF "T" REPRESENTING THE DIFFERENCES BETWEEN MEANS FOR JUNIOR AND SENIOR KINDERGARTEN GROUPS (1) IN MATCH 1, (2) IN MATCH 2, (3) IN MATCH 1, ISOLATED FOR LANGUAGE, (4) IN MATCH 2, ISOLATED FOR LANGUAGE, (5) IN MATCH 1, ISOLATED FOR FATHERS' EDUCATIONS, (6) IN MATCH 2, ISOLATED FOR FATHERS' EDUCATIONS, (7) IN MATCH 1, ISOLATED FOR MOTHERS' EDUCATIONS, (8) IN MATCH 2, ISOLATED FOR MOTHERS' EDUCATIONS, (9) IN MATCH 1, ISOLATED FOR FATHERS' OCCUPATIONS, (10) IN MATCH 2, ISOLATED FOR FATHERS' OCCUPATIONS. THIS DOCUMENT IS THE APPENDIX TO PS 000 257 AND CONTAINS ONLY TABLES. (CO)

ED016528 PS000360
DEVELOPMENTAL LEVEL AND CONCEPT-LEARNING--A REPLICATION AND EXTENSION. FRIEDMAN, STANLEY R., 24P.
EDRS PRICE MF-$0.65 HC-$3.29

TO VERIFY A PREVIOUSLY OBSERVED DEVELOPMENTAL INVERSION IN PROBLEM-SOLVING ABILITY AND TO EXPLORE PROBLEM-SOLVING STRATEGIES, RESEARCHERS GAVE A SET OF SEQUENTIAL-PATTERN RECOGNITION TESTS TO 316 CHILDREN, REPRESENTING NURSERY SCHOOL THROUGH SIXTH GRADE. EACH TEST CONSISTED OF FINDING TOKENS PLACED BEHIND 5 DOORS IN A PREDETERMINED PATTERN. THE CHILDREN WERE ALLOWED 50 TRIALS TO DISCOVER THE PATTERN. THE PERCENTAGE OF CHILDREN LEARNING EACH PATTERN SHOWS AN INCREASE FROM GRADE LEVEL TO GRADE LEVEL, EXCEPT FOR AN INVERSION AT GRADE 4. THIS INVERSION, WHICH WAS NOTED IN EARLIER WORK AND HAS BEEN SEEN BY SOME OTHER EXPERIMENTERS, MAY BE DUE TO INCOMPATIBLE RATES OF DEVELOPMENT OF INFORMATION-PROCESSING AND HYPOTHESIS-GENERATING ABILITIES USED IN PROBLEM SOLVING. THE STRATEGIES WHICH THE CHILDREN WERE USING WERE INFERRED FROM THE SEQUENCES OF THEIR CHOICES. YOUNG CHILDREN TENDED TO LOOK FOR THE PREVIOUS PATTERN IN A NEW TEST. AT ABOUT THE FIRST GRADE LEVEL THEY BEGIN TO ASSUME IT WILL BE DIFFERENT. IN GENERAL, YOUNGER CHILDREN TENDED TO USE SEQUENTIAL SEARCH PATTERNS. RANDOM SEARCHING APPEARS TO BE A LATER DEVELOPMENT. THE PATTERN 1, 3, 5 WAS EASIER TO IDENTIFY THAN THE PATTERN 3, 3, 5, BECAUSE THE CHILDREN SHOWED A PREFERENCE FOR HYPOTHESES LIKE 3, 3, 5, 5 OR 3, 5, 3, 5 AND WERE VERY RELUCTANT TO ABONDON THEM. FURTHER, WHEN THEY DID ABANDON THEM, THEY TENDED TO BEGIN SEARCHING RANDOMLY RATHER THAN TO MODIFY THE HYPOTHESIS. (DR)

ED016529 PS000367
THE WARRIOR DROPOUTS. WAX, ROSALIE H., MAY67 8P.
EDRS PRICE MF-$0.65 HC-$3.29

THE AMERICAN INDIAN SUBCULTURE, AS REPRESENTED IN THIS STUDY BY THE SIOUX OF THE PINE RIDGE RESERVATION IN SOUTH DAKOTA, EXPERIENCES PROBLEMS WITH ITS YOUTHS' BECOMING HIGH SCHOOL DROPOUTS. MANY OF THE REASONS FOR THIS PROBLEM PARALLEL THE PROBLEMS OF OTHER AMERICAN MINORITIES, NAMELY, (1) DISSIMILARITY BETWEEN THE VALUES OF THE MINORITY SUBCULTURE AND THAT OF THE MIDDLE-CLASS WHITE-CITIZEN ORIENTED SCHOOLS, AND (2) A SEEMING INABILITY OF THE SCHOOL SYSTEM TO BE CAPABLE OF THE FLEXIBILITY AND INSIGHT TO ADAPT THE INSTRUCTION AND THE FACILITIES TO THE NEEDS OF THE PUPILS. FOR EXAMPLE, THE SIOUX CULTURE INCULCATES IN ITS YOUTH THE VALUES OF INDEPENDENCE, VITALITY, PHYSICAL COURAGE, AND INTENSE LOYALTY TO PEERS, AMONG OTHERS. WHEN THE SIOUX YOUTH GOES OFF TO HIGH SCHOOL, WHICH IS GENERALLY A BOARDING SCHOOL, CONFLICTS DEVELOP. THE HIGH SCHOOL EXPECTS FROM STUDENTS OBEDIENCE, NARROW AND ABSOLUTE RESPECT FOR PROPERTY, AND ROUTINE AND DISCIPLINED CONDUCT. IN THE CLASH OF VALUES THAT FOLLOWS, THE SIOUX YOUTH BECOMES DISCONCERTED. HIS ADJUSTMENT PROBLEMS ARE ADDED TO BY RACIAL OR CULTURAL MISUNDERSTANDINGS AND BY LONELINESS. THE END RESULT FOR TOO MANY OF THE YOUTH IS THAT THEY DROP-OUT OF SCHOOL. THE QUESTION IS TO WHAT EXTENT WAS THE DECISION VOLUNTARY AND SELF-DETERMINED, AND TO WHAT EXTENT WAS IT FORCED UPON HIM BY AN INSENSITIVE SYSTEM. THIS ARTICLE IS A REPRINT FROM TRANS-ACTION, VOLUME 4, NUMBER 6, MAY, 1967. (WD)

ED016530 PS000371
WHERE IS DAY CARE HEADING. REED, MILDRED A., 08FEB68 12P.
EDRS PRICE MF-$0.65 HC-$3.29

IN SEATTLE AND IN THE NATION, GOOD DAY CARE SERVICES MUST BE MADE MORE COMPREHENSIVE. A NARRATIVE OF THE EXPERIENCES OF THE SEATTLE DAY NURSERY ASSOCIATION SUGGESTS WAYS TO INITIATE AND SUSTAIN NEEDED CHILD CARE SERVICES. THESE SERVICES SHOULD BE AVAILABLE TO FAMILIES WITH VARYING INCOMES WHO PAY FEES ON A SLIDING SCALE. EMERGENCY HELP FOR FAMILIES IN A CRISIS SHOULD INCLUDE HOME CARE GIVEN AT NIGHT AS WELL AS DURING PARENT OR CHILD ILLNESS. A CHILD CARE REGISTRY MIGHT RETAIN SUCH TRAINED EMPLOYEES AS RETIRED COUPLES TO HELP CARE FOR CHILDREN FROM 3 P.M. TO 11 P.M., TEEN-AGERS TO CARE FOR YOUNGSTERS AFTER SCHOOL, AND MATURE WOMEN TO PROVIDE HOME NURSING. IT HAS PROVED SUCCESSFUL TO RECRUIT MOTHERS FROM HOUSING PROJECTS TO BE TRAINED IN DAY CARE FOR THE CHILDREN OF FAMILIES IN THE IMMEDIATE NEIGHBORHOOD. CONGRESSIONAL LEGISLATION MUST BE CHANGED SO THAT IT FACILITATES, BUT DOES NOT COMPEL, THE USE OF DAY CARE CENTERS BY POVERTY PROGRAM PARTICIPANTS. DAY CARE PROGRAMS MUST BE CAREFULLY PLANNED IF THEY ARE TO AVOID BEING MERELY CUSTODIAL. CASE HISTORIES RECORDED BY THE SEATTLE DAY NURSERY ASSOCIATION ARE INCLUDED. THIS PAPER WAS DELIVERED AT THE ANNUAL MEETING OF THE SEATTLE DAY NURSERY ASSOCIATION (SEATTLE, FEBRUARY 8, 1968). (MS)

ED016531 PS000372
SUMMARY OF BEHAVIOR PATTERNS OF NORMAL CHILDREN. PINNEAU, SAMUEL R.; AND OTHERS, 66 9P.
EDRS PRICE MF-$0.65 HC-$3.29

THE INTENT OF THIS STUDY WAS TO DETERMINE THE PATTERNS OF BEHAVIOR OF NURSERY SCHOOL CHILDREN, AND TO DETERMINE HOW THESE ARE RELATED TO BEHAVIOR PATTERNS AND ACHIEVEMENT IN ELEMENTARY SCHOOL. IN 1930-1938, THE BEHAVIORS OF 138 NURSERY SCHOOL CHILDREN WERE CHARACTERIZED BY THEIR TEACHERS IN TERMS OF 61 MOLAR VARIABLES. SUB-SAMPLES OF THIS GROUP WERE LATER RATED IN ELEMENTARY SCHOOL ON A SUBSET OF 20 BEHAVIORAL VARIABLES AND ON 6 ACHIEVEMENT MEASURES. PRINCIPLE COMPONENT FACTOR ANALYSIS WITH VARIMAX ROTATIONS WAS USED TO DETERMINE BEHAVIOR PATTERN FACTORS. TEN FACTORS, CONSISTING OF COMBINATIONS OF FROM 5 TO 12 OF THE BEHAVIORAL VARIABLES, WERE FOUND IN THE NURSERY SCHOOL SAMPLE. THESE COULD BE CHARACTERIZED BY SUCH TERMS AS EMOTIONAL REACTIVITY, SOCIABILITY, AND SOCIALIZATION. THE CONSISTENCY OF THE FACTORS WAS DEMONSTRATED BY PERFORMING INDEPENDENT ANALYSES ON HALVES OF THE BASIC SAMPLE. SEPARATE ANALYSES ON BOYS AND GIRLS FOUND SIMILAR FACTORS, BUT THEIR RELATIVE IMPORTANCE IN ACCOUNTING FOR BEHAVIOR VARIANCE DIFFERED. LONGITUDINAL STUDIES COMPARING 69 OF THE CHILDREN AT AGES 3 AND 4 1/2, AND SAMPLES OF 78, 61, AND 32 OF THE CHILDREN IN GRADES 1, 3, AND 5 FOUND SIMILAR BEHAVIOR PATTERNS. BUT SOME NEW FACTORS APPEARED IN THE OLDER CHILDREN. A COMPARISON OF THE NURSERY SCHOOL AND ELEMENTARY SCHOOL FACTORS INDICATED THAT ALTHOUGH THE FACTOR PATTERNS WERE MODERATELY CONSISTENT, THE RELATIVE RANKINGS OF THE INDIVIDUAL CHILDREN ON THE FACTORS EXHIBITED LITTLE CONSISTENCY. (THE FULL REPORT OF THIS STUDY IS PS 000 261.) (DR)

ED016532 PS000378
A TECHNIQUE FOR GATHERING CHILDREN'S LANGUAGE SAMPLES FROM NATURALISTIC SETTINGS. HORNER, VIVIAN M.; SHER, ABIGAIL B., MAR67 13P.
EDRS PRICE MF-$0.65 HC-$3.29

A MAIN CONCERN OF THE 2 STUDIES DESCRIBED IN THIS PAPER WAS TO DEVELOP A METHOD OF COLLECTING LANGUAGE SAMPLES OF CHILDREN. IN THE BELIEF THAT LANGUAGE SHOULD BE STUDIED AS A PART OF SOCIAL INTERACTION, THE CHILDREN'S SPEECH WAS RECORDED AS IT WAS BEING USED IN FAMILAR HOME AND SCHOOL SETTINGS. IN THE FIRST STUDY (TO AVOID INTRODUCING ALIEN ELEMENTS WHICH MIGHT HAVE MODIFIED NORMAL LANGUAGE) A TRANSMITTER WITH AN INTERNAL MICROPHONE WAS CONCEALED INSIDE A 3-YEAR-OLD CHILD'S CLOTHING. HE COULD MOVE ABOUT FREELY AS HIS CONVERSATIONS WERE BROADCAST TO A BATTERY-OPERATED RADIO AND RECORDED ON A TAPE RECORDER. IN THE SECOND STUDY, NURSERY SCHOOL SUBJECTS (AGED 4), EACH WORE A SMALL POCKETBOOK CONTAINING A TRANSMITTER. A MICROPHONE WAS CLIPPED TO THE POCKETBOOK'S SHOULDER STRAP, ABOUT 6 INCHES FROM THE CHILD'S MOUTH. FIVE MINUTE SPEECH SAMPLES WERE RECORDED EVERY 20 MINUTES OVER 2 MORNINGS FOR EACH CHILD. SOUNDS WERE TRANSMITTED TO A TUNER AND TAPED. AN ADVANTAGE OF THE METHODS OF COLLECTING LANGUAGE SAMPLES USED IN THESE STUDIES IS THAT THE RECORDINGS HAVE A POINT OF VIEW, WITH THE CHILD'S SPEECH RELATED TO ANOTHER PERSON'S. TRANSCRIPTS OF THE LANGUAGE SAMPLES ARE INCLUDED. THIS PAPER WAS PRESENTED AT THE BIENNIAL MEETINGS OF THE SOCIETY FOR RESEARCH IN CHILD DEVELOPMENT (NEW YORK CITY, MARCH, 1967). (MS)

ED016533 PS000383
TRAINING EFFECTS AND CONCEPT DEVELOPMENT--A STUDY OF THE CONSERVATION OF CONTINUOUS QUANTITY IN CHILDREN. TOWLER, J.O., 68 11P.
EDRS PRICE MF-$0.65 HC-$3.29

A STUDY WAS CONDUCTED TO FIND OUT WHAT MENTAL PROCESSES ARE INVOLVED IN THE DEVELOPMENT OF THE CONCEPT OF CONSERVATION OF CONTINUOUS QUANTITY, AT WHAT AGES THESE PROCESSES ARE DEVELOPED IN CHILDREN, AND WHETHER THEY ARE ADEQUATELY EXPLAINED BY PIAGET'S THEORY. ONE HUNDRED 5.75 TO 7-YEAR-OLDS WITH A MEAN I.Q. OF 105 WERE PRETESTED AND CLASSIFIED AS CONSERVERS, NON-CONSERVERS, OR PARTIAL CONSERVERS. HALF OF THE NON-CONSERVERS AND HALF OF THE PARTIAL CONSERVERS WERE GIVEN 1 15-MINUTE TRAINING SESSION (USING CONTAINERS OF LIQUID) BASED ON THE THEORY THAT THE MENTAL PROCESSES NEEDED FOR CONSERVATION WERE (1) RECOGNITION OF IDENTITY (QUALITY OF QUANTITY REMAINS UNCHANGED EVEN IF TRANSFORMED, (2) A LOGICAL MULTIPLICATIVE OPERATION (ALTERATION IN HEIGHT OR WIDTH MIGHT BE COMPENSATED FOR BY THE OTHER), AND (3) OPERATIONAL REVERSIBILITY (QUANTITIES ARE UNCHANGED IN RECIPROCAL OPERATION). A MATCHED CONTROL GROUP HAD NO TRAINING. POSTTEST I (THE PRETEST) RESULTS SHOWED THAT ALL BUT 4 OF THE CHILDREN TRAINED WERE RECLASSIFIED AS CONSERVERS. A DIFFERENT POSTTEST GIVEN TO ALL 100 SUBJECTS SHOWED THAT CONSERVER LEARNING WAS RETAINED AND TRANSFERRED, SUGGESTING THAT 1 OR ALL OF THE SUGGESTED MENTAL PROCESSES MUST BE NEEDED AS PIAGET'S THEORY CLAIMS. HOWEVER, THEY MAY EXIST IN CHILDREN AT AGES EARLIER THAN PIAGET PREDICTED. (MS)

ED016534 PS000384
AN OBJECTIVE MEASURE OF STRUCTURAL COMPLEXITY IN CHILDREN'S WRITING. O'DONNELL, ROY C., 03JAN68 8P.
EDRS PRICE MF-$0.65 HC-$3.29

AN INSTRUMENT FOR MEASURING LANGUAGE MATURITY SHOULD BE EASILY ADMINISTRABLE AND SCOREABLE AND SHOULD BE BASED ON VALID INDICES OF LANGUAGE MATURITY. A RECENT STUDY BY KELLOG W. HUNT SUGGESTED THAT THESE INDICES BE BASED ON A NEW SYNTACTIC UNIT, THE T-UNIT, CONSISTING OF 1 MAIN CLAUSE TOGETHER WITH ANY CLAUSES SUBORDINATED TO IT. COORDINATED MAIN CLAUSES, WHICH ARE USUALLY A SIGN OF IMMATURITY, WILL THUS HAVE NO EFFECT ON THE INDEX. HUNT'S STUDIES, BASED ON 1000-WORD SAMPLES, INDICATED THAT T-UNIT LENGTH, CLAUSE LENGTH, AND NUMBER OF CLAUSES PER T-UNIT INCREASED FROM GRADES 4 TO 12. TO SEE IF THE INDICES COULD BE RELIABLY COMPUTED FROM SHORTER SAMPLES, 80 CHILDREN IN GRADES 4, 6, AND 8 WERE ASKED TO REWRITE A NARRATIVE COMPOSED OF SIMPLE DECLARATIVE SENTENCES, COMBINING THESE INTO LONGER UNITS. ALSO, 69 CHILDREN IN GRADES 4, 8, AND 12 WERE ASKED TO REWRITE A STRUCTURALLY SIMPLIFIED EXPOSITORY ESSAY USING LONGER SENTENCES. OBSERVED INCREASES WITH GRADE IN THE CLAUSE LENGTH, T-UNIT LENGTH, AND NUMBER OF CLAUSES PER T-UNIT WERE STATISTICALLY SIGNIFICANT. BECAUSE OF THE INTERRELATION OF THE INDICES, T-UNIT LENGTH APPEARS TO BE THE MOST USEFUL INDEX. FURTHER REFINEMENT OF THE NARRATIVE AND THE ESSAY IS NECESSARY, TOGETHER WITH STUDIES TO DETERMINE THEIR GENERAL VALIDITY AND RELIABILITY. THE PAPER WAS PRESENTED AT THE ANNUAL MEETING OF AMERICAN EDUCATIONAL RESEARCH ASSOCIATION, FEBRUARY 9, 1968. (DR)

ED016535 PS000451
THE PERFORMANCE OF FIRST GRADE CHILDREN IN FOUR LEVELS OF CONSERVATION OF NUMEROUSNESS AND THREE IQ GROUPS WHEN SOLVING ARITHMETIC ADDITION PROBLEMS. STEFFE, LESLIE P., DEC66 67P.
EDRS PRICE MF-$0.65 HC-$3.29

ACCORDING TO PIAGET, THE CONCEPT OF CONSERVATION IS A PREREQUISITE TO MATHEMATICAL UNDERSTANDING. THIS STUDY SOUGHT TO DETERMINE WHETHER THE ABILITY OF FIRST GRADE CHILDREN TO SOLVE ADDITION PROBLEMS WAS DEPENDENT ON THEIR MASTERY OF CONSERVATION OF NUMEROUSNESS. SECONDARY PURPOSES WERE TO INVESTIGATE THE EFFECT IN PROBLEM STATEMENTS OF (1) PHYSICAL OR PICTORIAL AIDS, AND (2) THE PRESENCE OR ABSENCE OF TRANSFORMATIONS. A TEST OF CONSERVATION OF NUMEROUSNESS THAT DIVIDED CHILDREN INTO 4 LEVELS WAS DEVELOPED IN A PILOT STUDY. THE POPULATION FOR THE MAIN STUDY WAS 2,166 FIRST GRADE CHILDREN WHO HAD PROGRESSED THROUGH ABOUT 3/4 OF AN ARITHMETIC CURRICULUM. ALL WERE GIVEN AN IQ TEST, WHICH WAS USED TO DEFINE 3 IQ LEVELS, AND THEN 341 CHILDREN WERE RANDOMLY SELECTED AND GIVEN (1) THE CONSERVATION OF NUMEROUSNESS TEST, (2) A TEST WITH 18 ADDITION PROBLEMS, EACH HAVING EITHER (A) PHYSICAL, (B) PICTORIAL, OR (C) NO AIDS, AND EITHER HAVING OR LACKING A TRANSFORMATION, AND (3) A TEST OF ADDITION FACTS. AN ANALYSIS OF VARIANCE EVALUATIONS BASED ON A SUBSAMPLE OF 121 CHILDREN INDICATED THAT BOTH THOSE AT THE LOWEST LEVEL OF CONSERVATION MASTERY AND THOSE AT THE LOWEST IQ LEVEL PERFORMED SIGNIFICANTLY LESS WELL ON TESTS (2) AND (3) ABOVE. FOR THE PROBLEM-SOLVING TEST, PROBLEMS HAVING A TRANSFORMATION WERE SIGNIFICANTLY EASIER THAN THOSE WITHOUT, AND PROBLEMS HAVING NO AIDS WERE SIGNIFICANTLY HARDER THAN THOSE WITH PHYSICAL OR PICTORIAL AIDS. CORRELATION OF .49 WAS FOUND BETWEEN THE PROBLEM-SOLVING AND ADDITION FACTS TESTS, WHICH WAS FELT TO INDICATE THAT ACTUAL PROBLEM-SOLVING RATHER THAN SIMPLE DRILL WAS NECESSARY TO LEARNING ADDITION FACTS. (DR)

ED017316 PS000200
EVALUATION OF CHANGES OCCURRING IN CHILDREN WHO PARTICIPATED IN PROJECT HEAD START. MORRIS, BERNIECE E.; MORRIS, GEORGE L., SEP66 123P.
EDRS PRICE MF-$0.65 HC-$6.58

THE ENVIRONMENT OF CHILDREN FROM LOW SOCIO-ECONOMIC LEVELS MILITATES STRONGLY AGAINST THEIR SUCCESS IN SCHOOL. TO HELP THWART OR REVERSE THE DEFICIENCES OF DISADVANTAGED YOUTH, THE PRESCHOOL ENRICHMENT PROGRAM WAS CREATED. THIS DOCUMENT IS AN EVALUATION OF A 1965 SUMMER HEADSTART PROGRAM FOR 4- AND 5-YEAR-OLDS IN KEARNEY, NEBRASKA. TESTS WERE ADMINISTERED TO HEADSTART CHILDREN AT THE BEGINNING OF THAT PROGRAM AND AGAIN NEAR THE END OF KINDERGARTEN. THE RESULTS WERE COMPARED WITH TEST SCORES OF A MATCHED GROUP OF NON-HEADSTART CHILDREN TESTED AT THE BEGINNING AND END OF KINDERGARTEN. THE PRIMARY PURPOSE OF THIS COMPARISON WAS TO SEE IF THE ENRICHMENT PROGRAM PLUS KINDERGARTEN RESULTED IN GREATER ACHIEVEMENT THAN KINDERGARTEN, ALONE, WOULD HAVE PRODUCED. THE GENERAL CONCLUSION FROM THE RESULTS OF THE TESTS OF (1) INTELLECTUAL ABILITY, (2) VISUAL-MOTOR PERCEPTION, (3) ACHIEVEMENT, AND (4) SOCIAL GROWTH AND ADJUSTMENT WAS THAT THE FORMER COMBINATION PRODUCED GREATER GAINS. STATISTICALLY SIGNIFICANT DIFFERENCES IN FAVOR OF THE EXPERIMENTAL GROUP WERE ACTUALLY OBTAINED ONLY WITH RESPECT TO THE TEST OF INTELLECTUAL ABILITY, BUT FAVORABLE TRENDS WERE OBSERVED GENERALLY. A SECONDARY PURPOSE OF THIS STUDY WAS TO INVESTIGATE THE EFFECT ON DISADVANTAGED CHILDREN'S RESPONSES OF USING LOW FIDELITY STIMULI OR HIGH FIDELITY STIMULI IN VARIOUS PERCEPTUAL-MOTOR EXERCISES. THE RESULTS WERE INCONCLUSIVE. THE DOCUMENT ALSO INCLUDES A BREIF REVIEW OF THE LITERATURE ON ACHIEVEMENT BY THE CULTURALLY DEPRIVED, AND SEVERAL CASE STUDIES OF CHILDREN WHO PARTICIPATED IN THE HEADSTART PROGRAM. (WD)

ED017317 PS000224
THE EFFECTS OF NEUROLOGICAL AND ENVIRONMENTAL FACTORS ON THE LANGUAGE DEVELOPMENT OF HEAD START CHILDREN--A EVALUATION OF THE HEAD START PROGRAM. MILGRAM, NORMAN A.; OZER, MARK N., 60P.
EDRS PRICE MF-$0.65 HC-$3.29

THIS HEADSTART STUDY WAS CONDUCTED TO DETERMINE THE INFLUENCE OF NEUROLOGICAL FACTORS AND HOME ENVIRONMENT ON THE LANGUAGE AND COGNITIVE DEVELOPMENT OF THE DISADVANTAGED CHILD. TWO DISTRICT OF COLUMBIA CENTERS WERE USED. THE SUBJECTS WERE ABOUT 70 NEGRO PRESCHOOL CHILDREN FROM LOW-INCOME FAMILIES. THESE CHILDREN WERE GIVEN SEVERAL BATTERIES OF TESTS DURING THE 8-WEEK SUMMER HEADSTART SESSION. NEUROLOGICAL TESTS OF BOTH VERBAL AND MOTOR TYPES WERE ADMINISTERED INITIALLY TO OBTAIN AN INDICATION OF THE MATURITY OR IMMATURITY OF THE DEVELOPMENT OF THE CHILD'S NERVOUS SYSTEM. THESE RESULTS, INDICATING WHICH CHILDREN NEEDED THE MOST HELP, WERE LATER COMPARED WITH THE RESULTS OF THE SCHOOL READINESS EVALUATION TESTS. THE SRE MEASURES THE LEVEL OF LINGUISTIC AND COGNITIVE ABILITY OF THE CHILD AND IS ESPECIALLY CONSTRUCTED TO REFLECT A DEFICIT OR ABUNDANCE OF THOSE ATTRIBUTES A CHILD WILL NEED IN THE FORMAL SCHOOL SITUATION. THE RESULTS OF THE SRE TEST SHOWED A GENERAL PERFORMANCE GAIN BETWEEN THE 2 TESTING PERIODS, GAINS CONSIDERED TO BE A FUNCTION, IN PART, OF THE CHILD'S MENTAL AGE. IN ORDER IN SHOW THE RELATION BETWEEN THE CHILD'S PERFORMANCE AND HIS HOME ENVIRONMENT, A SOCIAL WORKER VISITED EACH PUPIL'S HOME AND TALKED WITH THE MOTHER. THE WORKER FILLED OUT A QUESTIONNAIRE DURING THIS VISIT AND LATER GAVE HIS IMPRESSION OF THE QUALITY OF THE VERBAL ENVIRONMENT IN THE HOME. (WD)

ED017318 PS000334
A PRELIMINARY INVESTIGATION TO ESTABLISH A REGIONAL CENTER FOR EDUCATIONAL DEVELOPMENTAL STUDIES OF DISADVANTAGED PRESCHOOL CHILDREN. FINAL REPORT. LEVINE, LOUIS S., 15JAN67 39P.
EDRS PRICE MF-$0.65 HC-$3.29

THIS REPORT DESCRIBES SEVERAL STEPS UNDERTAKEN BY A RESEARCH GROUP FROM SAN FRANCISCO STATE COLLEGE PRELIMINARY TO THE PROPOSED CREATION OF A RESEARCH CENTER FOR STUDIES OF DISADVANTAGED PRESCHOOL CHILDREN. THE PLANS ANTICIPATE FORMATION OF A COMPREHENSIVE SERVICE, RESEARCH, AND TRAINING CENTER FOR DISADVANTAGED CHILDREN AND THEIR FAMILIES. THE COMMUNITY SELECTED FOR PLACEMENT OF THE CENTER WAS HAYES VALLEY IN SAN FRANCISCO. IT HAS A LONG HISTORY OF POVERTY, IS OVERCROWDED, AND HAS VERY POOR FACILITIES FOR THE POSITIVE DEVELOPMENT OF ITS YOUTH. THE RESEARCH GROUP CONTACTED SEVERAL COMMUNITY GROUPS ALREADY ORGANIZED IN HAYES VALLEY TO DISCUSS THE CENTER AND THE POSSIBILITIES OF COOPERATION BETWEEN THEM. A SPECIFIC SITE FOR THE CENTER WAS LOCATED. THE SPECIFIC SERVICES THE CENTER IS TO PROVIDE INCLUDE PROGRAMS FOR THE PRESCHOOL CHILDREN IN THE FORM OF NURSERY SCHOOL AND OTHER DAY AND NIGHT CARE FACILITIES, PROGRAMS FOR THE OLDER YOUTH, A PROGRAMS BENEFICIAL TO THE PARENTS OR FAMILY AS A WHOLE. A SECONDARY PURPOSE OF THE CENTER IS TO BE A TRAINING FACILITY, NONPROFESSIONAL IN SCOPE FOR LOCAL CITIZENS INTERESTED IN SOCIAL AND EDUCATIONAL WORK AND PROFESSIONAL IN SCOPE FOR COLLEGE STUDENTS. THE MANIFEST BREADTH OF THE CENTER'S CONTRIBUTION TO THIS DISADVANTAGED COMMUNITY REFLECTS THE GROWING NEED TO MEET NOT ONLY THE EDUCATIONAL NEEDS OF DISADVANTAGED CITIZENS BUT THE SOCIAL AND CULTURAL NEEDS ALSO. INCREASED RESEARCH INTO WHO THE DEPRIVED ARE AND WHAT SUCH DEPRIVATION DOES TO THE GROWTH AND DEVELOPMENT OF THE DEPRIVED CHILD IS NEEDED. (WD)

ED017319 PS000347
A RESEARCH PROGRAM TO DETERMINE THE EFFECTS OF VARIOUS PRESCHOOL INTERVENTION PROGRAMS ON THE DEVELOPMENT OF DISADVANTAGED CHILDREN AND THE STRATEGIC AGE FOR SUCH INTERVENTION. KARNES, MERLE B., 10FEB68 38P.
EDRS PRICE MF-$0.65 HC-$3.29

THIS DOCUMENT EXAMINES 3 METHODS OF PRESCHOOL INTERVENTION, (1) HOME TUTORING SERVICES, (2) HOME TRAINING OF THE INFANT BY THE MOTHER, AND (3) CLASSROOM (NURSERY SCHOOL) INTERVENTION. THE RESULTS OF PROVIDING 1 YEAR OF TUTORING IN THE HOME OF DISADVANTAGED CHILDREN WAS ENCOURAGING. THE TUTORED AND NONTUTORED CHILDREN WERE COMPARABLE ON THE CATTELL AS A PRETEST, BUT THE TUTORED CHILDREN PERFORMED HIGHER THAN THE NONTUTORED ON 31 OF 33 VARIABLES OF THE STANFORD-BINET AS A POSTTEST. THE SECOND METHOD OF INTERVENTION FOCUSED ON INSTRUCTING MOTHERS IN WAYS OF STIMULATING THE INTELLECTUAL AND LANGUAGE DEVELOPMENT OF THEIR CHILDREN. THESE CHILDREN

SCORED GAINS ON BOTH THE STANFORD-BINET AND ITPA OVER THOSE OF THE CONTROL CHILDREN WHOSE MOTHERS DID NOT PARTICIPATE IN THE PROGRAM. THE THIRD METHOD INVOLVED COMPARING 5 TYPES OF 1-YEAR PRESCHOOL INTERNVENTION PROGRAMS. THE RESULTS OF MEASURES OF PERFORMANCE OF CHILDREN IN THESE 5 PROGRAMS INDICATED THAT THE MORE HIGHLY STRUCTURED PROGRAMS WERE MORE EFFECTIVE AS SHOWN BY SCORES ON THE STANFORD-BINET AND ITPA. PART OF THIS STUDY WAS EXTENDED INTO A SECOND YEAR IN WHICH CHILDREN FROM 2 OF THE 3 MOST EFFECTIVE PROGRAMS OF THE 5 PROGRAM STUDY WENT ON TO KINDERGARTEN AND THE CHILDREN OF THE THIRD EFFECTIVE PROGRAM REMAINED IN THAT INTERVENTION PROGRAM. THE RESULTS OF SCORES OF THESE 3 GROUPS INDICATE THAT PERHAPS GAINS MADE DURING A YEAR OF NURSERY SCHOOL ARE NOT MAINTAINED WITHOUT FURTHER SPECIAL INTERVENTION. THIS PAPER WAS PRESENTED AT THE AMERICAN EDUCATIONAL RESEARCH ASSOCIATION (CHICAGO, FEBRUARY 10, 1968). (WD)

ED017320 PS000350
MONTESSORI PRE-SCHOOL EDUCATION. FINAL REPORT. FLEEGE, URBAN H.; AND OTHERS, JUN67 112P.
EDRS PRICE MF-$0.65 HC-$6.58

IN ORDER TO INVESTIGATE THE EFFECTIVENESS OF MONTESSORI PRESCHOOL EDUCATION AS COMPARED WITH NON-MONTESSORI PRESCHOOL EDUCATION, PHASE I OF THIS STUDY MATCHED 2 GROUPS, EACH OF 21 PRESCHOOL CHILDREN, ON INTELLIGENCE QUOTIENT AND CERTAIN SOCIO-ECONOMIC FACTORS. ONE GROUP ATTENDED A MONTESSORI PRESCHOOL AND THE OTHER A NON-MONTESSORI PRESCHOOL. THE CHILDREN WERE ADMINISTERED TESTS NEAR THE BEGINNING AND END OF THE PRESCHOOL YEAR TO DETERMINE ANY DIFFERENCES IN ACHIEVEMENT DUE TO THE PRESCHOOL TRAINING. IN PHASE II A TRAINED RESARCHER INTERVIEWED THE PRIMARY GRADE TEACHERS WHO BY THEN HAD SOME OF THE PRESCHOOL CHILDREN OF PHASE I IN THEIR CLASSROOMS. RATINGS OF THESE TEACHERS PROVIDED INFORMATION ON THE PERSONALITY AND ABILITY OF 3 GROUPS OF CHILDREN, (1) FORMER MONTESSORI PRESCHOOL CHILDREN, (2) FORMER NON-MONTESSORI PRESCHOOL CHILDREN, AND (3) NON-PRESCHOOL CHILDREN. THE CHILDREN WERE RATED ON 8 MAJOR TRAITS WHICH CONTAINED 27 STIMULUS VARIABLES. PHASE I DATA INDICATED THAT MONTESSORI PRESCHOOL CHILDREN GAINED SIGNIFICANTLY MORE IN VERBAL ABILITY THAN NON-MONTESSORI PRESCHOOL CHILDREN. PHASE II DATA INDICATED THAT MONTESSORI CHILDREN WERE SUPERIOR TO THE CHILDREN OF THE OTHER 2 GROUPS IN READING READINESS, INTEREST IN LEARNING, INDEPENDENCE, INTERPERSONAL RELATIONS, LEADERSHIP, AND LEARNING ABILITY. NO DIFFERENCES WERE FOUND IN CREATIVITY OR ABILITY TO ADJUST TO THE TRADITIONAL-TYPE SCHOOL. (WD)

ED017321 PS000354
STUDY OF ACHIEVEMENT--REPORT POPULATION STUDY OF JUNIOR AND SENIOR KINDERGARTEN PUPILS, 1960-61 AND 1961-62. , APR65 83P.
EDRS PRICE MF-$0.65 HC-$3.29

THIS DOCUMENT IS A POPULATION STUDY OF JUNIOR (JKP) AND SENIOR (SKP) KINDERGARTEN PUPILS IN TORONTO, CANADA. IT IS TO BE USED IN CONJUNCTION WITH A LONGITUDINAL "STUDY OF ACHIEVEMENT" (PS 000 355) THAT WILL ATTEMPT TO ASCERTAIN WHETHER THE EFFECTS OF JUNIOR KINDERGARTEN ON PUPILS' SCHOOL ACHIEVEMENT TEND TO DIMINISH FROM GRADE TO GRADE OR TEND TO PERSIST OVER TIME. IN ORDER TO ASCERTAIN THE INFLUENCE OF THIS SINGLE VARIABLE OF JUNIOR KINDERGARTEN ON LATER ACHIEVEMENT IN SENIOR KINDERGARTEN, ALL OTHER VARIABLES THAT MIGHT EFFECT ACHIEVEMENT MUST BE CONTROLLED. THE POPULATION STUDY PRESENTED IN THIS DOCUMENT INVOLVED GATHERING PUPIL PROFILE INFORMATION ON JKP AND SKP AND ORGANIZING THIS INFORMATION TO SEE IF THE PUPIL PROFILES DIFFER FOR THE 2 GROUPS. SUCH DIFFERENCES MIGHT REPRESENT VARIABLES, BESIDES JUNIOR KINDERGARTEN PARTICIPATION, THAT CAN INFLUENCE ACHIEVEMENT. CONSEQUENTLY, THEY WOULD HAVE TO BE CONTROLLED. AFTER GATHERING INFORMATION ON THE PUPIL HIMSELF AND ON HIS FAMILIAL, SOCIOECONOMIC, AND CULTURAL CHARACTERISTICS FROM 1486 JKP IN 1960-61 AND FROM 7209 SKP IN 1961-62, THE PERCENTAGE OF EACH PUPIL-GROUP THAT PLACED IN THE VARIOUS CATEGORIES WAS DETERMINED. THESE PERCENTAGES INDICATED CHARACTERISTICS OF THE PUPIL OR HIS ENVIRONMENT THAT DIFFERED BETWEEN JKP AND SKP. FOUR OF THESE AREAS OF DIFFERENCE, WHICH POSSBILY EFFECT ACHIEVEMENT AND MUST THEREFORE BE CONTROLLED IN THE MAJOR STUDY MENTIONED ABOVE, ARE (1) PUPIL AGE, (2) PRESENCE OR ABSENCE OF OLDER SIBLINGS, (3) FATHER'S EDUCATIONAL AND OCCUPATIONAL LEVEL, AND (4) THE LANGUAGE OF THE FAMILY AND PUPIL. (WD)

ED017322 PS000355
STUDY OF ACHIEVEMENT--JUNIOR KINDERGARTEN, WHO IS SERVED AND WHO GOES. , APR65 35P.
EDRS PRICE MF-$0.65 HC-$3.29

IN THE TORONTO SCHOOL SYSTEM IN 1961-1962 THERE WERE 8,684 CHILDREN IN SENIOR KINDERGARTEN. NINETY-EIGHT OF THE STUDENTS WERE NOT TORONTO RESIDENTS AND SO WERE NOT INCLUDED IN THE ANALYSIS. THERE WERE 3,839 OF THESE CHILDREN ATTENDING SCHOOLS WHICH PROVIDED JUNIOR KINDERGARTENS, BUT OF THIS NUMBER ONLY SLIGHTLY OVER 1/3 ACTUALLY ATTENDED JUNIOR KINDERGARTEN. TWO QUESTIONS POSED WERE, (1) WHAT SORT OF PARENTS (BY POPULATION CHARACTERISTICS) HAD JUNIOR KINDERGARTEN AVAILABLE FOR THEIR CHILDREN, AND (2) WHAT WERE THE CHARACTERISTICS OF THE PARENTS WHO WERE ACTUALLY SENDING THEIR CHILDREN TO JUNIOR KINDERGARTEN. THE 3 TYPES OF POPULATION CHARACTERISTICS STUDIED WERE CULTURAL, SOCIO-ECONOMIC AND FAMILIAL. IT WAS FOUND THAT MORE JUNIOR KINDERGARTENS WERE AVAILABLE IN AREAS WHERE THE CHILD SPOKE A FOREIGN LANGUAGE EITHER WITH OR WITHOUT ENGLISH. HOWEVER, IN COMPARING WHO ENROLLED AND WHO DID NOT, A CHILD FROM AN ENGLISH SPEAKING HOME WAS TWICE AS LIKELY TO BE ENROLLED. IT WAS FOUND THAT THE CHARACTERISTICS OF THE CHILDREN ACTUALLY ENROLLED IN JUNIOR KINDERGARTEN CLOSELY PARALLELED THOSE TO WHOM IT WAS NOT AVAILABLE. THE AUTHOR CONCLUDED THAT IN SPITE OF THE FACT THAT JUNIOR KINDERGARTENS WERE LOCATED WHERE THEY WERE MOST NEEDED, THE STUDENTS WHO WOULD BENEFIT MOST FROM THE EXPERIENCE WERE NOT BEING SENT. (CO)

ED017323 PS000356
STUDY OF ACHIEVEMENT, TORONTO INFORMATION BULLETIN NO. 1. , JUN63 9P.
EDRS PRICE MF-$0.65 HC-$3.29

FIVE SCHOOLS TOOK PART IN A SAMPLE STUDY TO SET SCORING PROCEDURES IN A LONGITUDINAL STUDY IN PROGRESS TO DETERMINE THE EFFECTS OF JUNIOR KINDERGARTEN ATTENDANCE ON THE CHILDREN'S LATER ACHIEVEMENT AND DEVELOPMENT. PUPIL CHARACTERISTIC DATA ARE BEING COLLECTED ON PROFILE CARDS AND A TEACHER-RATED QUESTIONNAIRE WHICH WAS DESIGNED TO PROVIDE INFORMATION ON A CHILD'S SOCIAL, EMOTIONAL, MENTAL, PHYSICAL, AND LANGUAGE DEVELOPMENT. KINDERGARTEN DRAWINGS WILL ALSO BE EXAMINED TO FIND OUT THE CHILDREN'S PERCEPTIONS OF THE WORLD. HALF OF THE CHILDREN INVOLVED IN THE SAMPLE HAD HAD JUNIOR KINDERGARTEN AND HALF HAD NOT. RESULTS SHOWED THAT THE FORMER HAD HIGHER QUESTIONNAIRE RATINGS IN ALL 5 CATEGORIES, THAT CHILDREN WITH POOR ENGLISH BACKGROUNDS RATED LOWER, AND THAT CHILDREN WHO HAD REPEATED SENIOR KINDERGARTEN HAD CAUGHT UP WITH THEIR CLASSMATES BEFORE ENTERING GRADE I. THE STUDY IS BEING CONTINUED AT GRADE I LEVEL USING THE DOMINION READING READINESS AND METROPOLITAN ACHIEVEMENT TESTS. (MS)

ED017324 PS000359
A NEW THEORY OF SCRIBBLING AND DRAWING IN CHILDREN. GIBSON, JAMES J.; YONAS, PATRICIA M., JUN67 16P.
EDRS PRICE MF-$0.65 HC-$3.29

INFANT SCRIBBLING ACTIVITY IS NOT SIMPLY PLAY. IT CONTRIBUTES TO THE DEVELOPMENT OF VISUAL ATTENTION AND PERCEPTION. YET, SCRIBBLING, UNLIKE WRITING IN THE COMMUNICATION SENSE, IS NOT MOTIVATED BY THE DESIRE TO INFORM, NOR TO SET DOWN THOUGHTS AND FEELINGS. THE EXPERIMENTAL HYPOTHESIS OF THIS STUDY WAS THAT THE MOTIVATIONS FOR SCRIBBLING ARE (1) MAKING A MARK OR TRACE ON THE PAPER, (2) CONTROLLING THE VISUALLY PERCEIVED TRACE, AND (3) SIMPLY PERCEIVING THE TRACE, NOT THE MOTOR STIMULATION INVOLVED IN THE ACT OF SCRIBBING. TO TEST THIS HYPOTHESIS, 14 INFANTS, 15 TO 38 MONTHS OF WRITE AND THE OTHER WOULD NOT. THE ORDER OF USE OF THE 2 INSTRUMENTS WAS VARIED SO THAT SOME INFANTS SCRIBBLED FIRST WITH THE TRACING AND SOME INFANTS FIRST WITH THE NONTRACING, INSTRUMENT. THE SCRIBBLING ACTIVITY WITH BOTH INSTRUMENTS WAS TIMED. IN THE CASE OF ALL 14 CHILDREN, USE OF THE NONTRACING INSTRUMENT REDUCED SCRIBBLING TIME AN AVERAGE OF 2/3. IN A SECOND, RELATED EXPERIMENT, 4 3-YEAR-OLDS WERE ASKED TO DRAW IN THE AIR. AGAIN, THE HYPOTHESIS TESTED WAS THAT REINFORCEMENT AND MOTIVATION FOR SCRIBBLING ACTIVITY WAS THE TRACE, AND NOT THE KINESTHETIC STIMULI. NONE OF THE CHILDREN WOULD DRAW IN THE AIR, ALTHOUGH THEY DID ASK FOR PAPER ON WHICH TO DRAW SOMETHING THEY COULD SEE. (WD)

ED017325 PS000380
EQUIPMENT AND SUPPLIES TESTED AND APPROVED FOR PRESCHOOL/SCHOOL/ HOME. , 68
DOCUMENT NOT AVAILABLE FROM EDRS.

THIS CATALOG LISTS EQUIPMENT THAT HAS BEEN TESTED AND APPROVED FOR USE WITH PRESCHOOL AND SCHOOL-AGE CHILDREN. THE FIRST SECTION OF THE CATALOG GIVES SUGGESTIONS FOR EQUIPMENT THAT WOULD BE SUITABLE FOR NURSERY SCHOOL, KINDERGARTEN, PRIMARY, OR INTERMEDIATE GROUPS. EQUIPMENT LISTS IN THE BODY OF THE CATALOG ARE BROKEN INTO THE CLASSIFICATIONS, ART AND CRAFT, AUDIOVISUAL, BASIC CLASSROOM, COMPUTING AND MEASURING, MUSIC, PLAY, AND SCIENCE. EACH LISTING GIVES THE MANUFACTURER'S DESIGNATION, THE MANUFACTURER, DISTRIBUTORS FROM WHICH THE ITEM IS AVAILABLE, AND THE AGE RANGE FOR WHICH THE ITEM IS CONSIDERED SUITABLE. A DIRECTORY OF MANUFACTURERS AND DISTRIBUTORS IS INCLUDED. THIS DOCUMENT IS AVAILABLE FROM THE ASSOCIATION FOR CHILDHOOD EDUCATION INTERNATIONAL, 3615 WISCONSIN AVENUE, N.W., WASHINGTON, D.C., 20016, FOR $1.50. (DR)

ED017326 PS000385

INTERIM PROGRESS REPORT OF A REMOTE TEACHER TRAINING INSTITUTE FOR EARLY CHILDHOOD EDUCATORS (FUNDED BY NDEA TITLE XI). BRUDENELL, GERALD A.; MEIER, JOHN H., FEB68 18P.
EDRS PRICE MF-$0.65 HC-$3.29

IN AN EFFORT TO TRAIN TEACHERS TOO GEORGRAPHICALLY SEPARATED TO MEET REGULARLY FOR COURSE WORK, AN INSTITUTE WAS PLANNED AT COLORADO STATE COLLEGE IN GREELEY, COLORADO, ONE HUNDRED TEACHERS ATTENDED 2- TO 5-DAY ORIENTATION SESSIONS CONCERNING THE USE OF MICROTEACHING TECHNIQUES AND SPECIFICALLY DEVELOPED MATERIALS IN WORKING WITH DISADVANTAGED NURSERY SCHOOL CHILDREN. UPON RETURNING TO THEIR OWN PRESCHOOLS, THE TEACHERS WERE INSTRUCTED TO VIEW A FILMED DEMONSTRATION TEACHING EXAMPLE, TO TEACH 4 PREWRITTEN LEARNING EPISODES TO SEVERAL OF THEIR CHILDREN, AND TO VIDEOTAPE 1 OF THE LESSONS IN A NEARBY RECORDING CENTER. THE TEACHER WAS THEN TO COMPARE THE RESULTS WITH THE FILMED SAMPLE, FILL OUT EVALUATION FORMS AND MAIL THESE WITH THE TAPE TO THE INSTITUTE FOR CHILD STUDY IN GREELEY WHERE THE LESSON WOULD BE CRITICIZED AND LATER RETURNED TO THE TEACHER. PROJECT DATA WILL BE ANALYZED AND FINDINGS REPORTED BY JULY 1968. IF THIS TYPE OF REMOTE TEACHER TRAINING PROVES TO BE SUCCESSFUL, IT COULD PROFITABLY BE USED FOR TEACHER SELF-EVALUATION OR TRAINING IN AREAS REMOTE FROM EDUCATIONAL INSTITUTIONS. THIS PAPER WAS PRESENTED AT THE AMERICAN EDUCATIONAL RESEARCH ASSOCIATION (CHICAGO, FEBRUARY, 1968). (MS)

ED017327 PS000387

A STUDY OF THE KINDERGARTEN PROGRAM, FULL-DAY OR HALF-DAY. GORTON, HARRY B.; ROBINSON, RICHARD L., 24JAN68 23P.
EDRS PRICE MF-$0.65 HC-$3.29

THE ROLE OF KINDERGARTEN IN THE FUTURE EDUCATIONAL STRUCTURE IS PRESENTLY UNDERGOING REEVALUATION, ESPECIALLY IN THE PENN-TRAFFORD SCHOOL DISTRICT OF HARRISON CITY, PENNSYLVANIA. THE POSSIBILITY OF EXTENDING KINDERGARTEN FROM A HALF-DAY TO A FULL-DAY PROGRAM IS A PRIME AREA OF DEBATE. IT IS SUGGESTED THAT MODERN SOCIETY WILL SOON, IF NOT IMMEDIATELY, DEMAND A KINDERGARTEN PROGRAM THAT PROVIDES A MORE CREATIVE, MORE SUBSTANTIAL CURRICULUM, WITH IMPROVED FACILITIES AND A TEACHER-ATTITUDE FOCUSING MORE ON INSTRUCTION THAN ON BABY-SITTING. A SAMPLE SCHEDULE FOR A FULL-DAY KINDERGARTEN AND A DELINEATION OF ITS GOALS IS PRESENTED IN THIS DOCUMENT. THESE ITEMS ARE BASED ON A PLAN DEVISED BY THE FORT MYER ELEMENTARY SCHOOL OF ARLINGTON, VIRGINIA. THE ESTIMATED COSTS OF IMPLEMENTING SUCH A PROGRAM IN THE PENN-TRAFFORD SCHOOL DISTRICT ARE DISCUSSED. A STUDY DONE IN HAWAII, WHERE FULL-DAY KINDERGARTENS ARE THE RULE, COMPARES THE VALUE OF HALF-DAY SESSIONS TO FULL-DAY SESSIONS AND IS REPRODUCED IN THIS BROCHURE BECAUSE IT DISCUSSES MANY OF THE PROS AND CONS OF THE 2 TYPES OF KINDERGARTEN SESSIONS OF INTEREST TO THE PENN-TRAFFORD EDUCATORS. (WD)

ED017328 PS000388

THE STUDY OF MUSIC IN THE ELEMENTARY SCHOOL--A CONCEPTUAL APPROACH. GARY, CHARLES L., ED., 67 197P.
EDRS PRICE MF-$0.65 HC NOT AVAILABLE FROM EDRS.

THIS GUIDE TO THE STUDY OF MUSIC IN THE ELEMENTARY SCHOOL EMPHASIZES THE CENTRALITY OF INTELLECTUAL APPREHENSION IN THE MUSIC EDUCATION PROGRAM. THE IMPORTANCE OF DEVELOPING A GENUINE UNDERSTANDING OF THE ART OF MUSIC IS EMPHASIZED. AN INTRODUCTORY CHAPTER PROVIDES A DISCUSSION OF A CONCEPTUAL APPROACH TO MUSIC LEARNING AND NAMES AND DEFINES THE CONSTITUENT ELEMENTS OF MUSIC. THE CENTRAL PORTION OF THE VOLUME SUGGESTS APPROPRIATE ACTIVITIES AND MATERIALS TO BE EMPLOYED IN THE DEVELOPMENT OF CONCEPTS ABOUT THE CONSTITUENT ELEMENTS OF (1) RHYTHM, (2) MELODY, (3) HARMONY, (4) FORM IN MUSIC, (5) FORMS OF MUSIC, (6) TEMPO, (7) DYNAMICS, AND (8) TONE COLOR. ALTHOUGH THE CONCEPTS TO BE LEARNED ABOUT EACH OF THESE ELEMENTS ARE PRESENTED IN INDEPENDENT SECTIONS OF THE TEXT, FREQUENT CROSS REFERENCES ARE INCLUDED AND ARE DESIGNED TO CLARIFY THE INTERRELATIONSHIPS WHICH EXIST AMONG THEM. ADDITIONAL CHAPTERS ARE CONCERNED WITH (1) THE IMPORTANCE OF PERCEPTIONS (LISTENING EXPERIENCES) IN THE DEVELOPMENT OF MUSICAL CONCEPTS, (2) THE ROLE OF THE ELEMENTARY CHORUS, (3) THE STUDY OF INSTRUMENTAL MUSIC IN THE ELEMENTARY SCHOOL, AND (4) MUSICAL EDUCATION OF GIFTED AND OF HANDICAPPED CHILDREN. GUIDELINES FOR THE PURCHASE OF MUSICAL INSTRUMENTS, A GUIDE TO THE EVALUATION OF BASIC SONG BOOKS, AND LISTS OF SELECTED FILMS, FILMSTRIPS, BOOKS, AND REQUISITE CLASSROOM EQUIPMENT AND SUPPLIES ARE APPENDED. THIS DOCUMENT IS AVAILABLE FROM THE MUSIC EDUACTORS NATIONAL CONFERENCE, NEA CENTER, 1201 SIXTEENTH STREET, N.W., WASHINGTON, D.C. 20036 FOR $3.50. (JS)

ED017329 PS000389

DEPARTMENTALIZATION IN ELEMENTARY SCHOOLS. OCT65 24P.
EDRS PRICE MF-$0.65 HC NOT AVAILABLE FROM EDRS.

THE RESULTS OF A SURVEY CONCERNED WITH DEPARTMENTALIZATION IN ELEMENTARY SCHOOLS ARE REPORTED IN STATISTICAL TABLES WHICH ARE ACCOMPANIED BY DESCRIPTIVE COMMENTARY. FOR THE PURPOSE OF THE SURVEY, THE DEFINITION OF DEPARTMENTALIZATION IS RESTRICTED TO INCLUDE ONLY THOSE SITUATIONS IN WHICH STUDENTS RECEIVE INSTRUCTION IN THE VARIOUS ACADEMIC SUBJECTS FROM MORE THAN 1 TEACHER. OF THE 400 SCHOOL SYSTEMS RESPONDING TO AN INITIAL INQUIRY, 97 WERE FOUND TO BE PRACTICING DEPARTMENTALIZATION. INFORMATION ELICITED BY MEANS OF A QUESTIONNAIRE IS REPORTED CONCERNING THE EXTENT OF DEPARTMENTALIZATION (ACCORDING TO GRADE LEVELS) WITHIN EACH OF THE 97 SCHOOL SYSTEMS. VARIOUS ORGANIZATIONAL PATTERNS OF THE DEPARTMENTALIZED PROGRAMS ARE ENUMERATED AND THE FREQUENCY WITH WHICH THEY ARE EMPLOYED IS REPORTED. INFORMATION IS GIVEN CONCERNING THE FLEXIBILITY OF THE PROGRAMS IN ALLOWING STUDENTS TO MOVE BETWEEN GRADE LEVELS AND FROM ABILITY GROUP TO ABILITY GROUP WITHIN GRADE LEVELS. MISCELLANEOUS EVALUATIVE COMMENTS OF MANY OF THE REPORTING SCHOOL SYSTEMS ARE PRESENTED. THE SURVEY QUESTIONNAIRE IS REPRODUCED AND A SELECTED BIBLIOGRAPHY IS APPENDED. THIS CIRCULAR IS AVAILABLE FROM EDUCATIONAL RESEARCH SERVICE, NATIONAL EDUCATION ASSOCIATION, 1201 SIXTEENTH, N.W., WASHINGTON, D.C. 20036, FOR $1.00. (JS)

ED017330 PS000390

SEQUENCE IN LEARNING--FACT OR FICTION. MIEL, ALICE, 6P.
EDRS PRICE MF-$0.65 HC NOT AVAILABLE FROM EDRS.

SEQUENCE IN LEARNING IS USEFUL ONLY AS IT CONTRIBUTES TO THE CONTINUITY OF A CHILD'S OVERALL DEVELOPMENT. CHILDREN MAY NOT GO THROUGH THE SAME SEQUENCE TO ARRIVE AT A SIMILAR POINT OF UNDERSTANDING. EDUCATIONAL PROGRESS IS INDICATED BY A CHILD'S GROWTH IN THE DEVELOPMENT OF STRATEGIC CONCEPTS, IN WAYS OF PROCESSING INFORMATION, AND IN WAYS OF RELATING TO PEOPLE. A COMBINATION OF THE POOLED JUDGMENT OF ADULTS, HELP FROM RESEARCH ON CHILDREN, AND HELP FROM THE CHILDREN THEMSELVES IN PLANNING THE USE OF THE SCHOOL DAY TOGETHER WITH AN OPEN CURRICULUM DESIGN WILL FOSTER CONTINUITY IN LEARNING. IF LEARNING IS TO BE MEANINGFUL, THE TEACHER MUST BE FREE TO SELECT EVENTS AND PROBLEMS OF IMMEDIATE INTEREST TO THE CHILDREN, AS SHE ENCOURAGES CONCERN FOR OTHER PEOPLE AND PROVIDES FOR INTELLECTUAL DEVELOPMENT. ONE EXAMPLE OF A CONTINUITY THREAD WHICH COULD COVER TRADITIONAL TOPICS AND NEWER GOALS MIGHT BE "CHANGE," A MODERN CONDITION TO WHICH INDIVIDUALS ARE EXPECTED TO ADAPT. THE COGNITIVE TASKS OF GROUPING AND LABELING, INTERPRETING AND MAKING INFERENCES, AND PREDICTING CONSEQUENCES CAN USEFULLY BE APPLIED TO SUCH A BROAD TOPIC. THE CHILDREN CAN BEGIN WITH SPECIFICS AND THEN EXPAND INTO MORE GENERAL SUBJECTS. THIS DOCUMENT IS AVAILABLE FROM THE DEPARTMENT OF ELEMENTARY-KINDERGARTEN-NURSERY EDUCATION, NATIONAL EDUCATION ASSOCIATION, 1201 SIXTEENTH STREET, N.W., WASHINGTON, D.C. 20036. (MS)

ED017331 PS000391

WHEN THE CHILD IS ANGRY. SOLTYS, JOHN J., JR., 6P.
EDRS PRICE MF-$0.65 HC NOT AVAILABLE FROM EDRS.

THE ABILITY TO HAVE AND EXPRESS FEELINGS IN THE YOUNG CHILD IS CLOSELY LINKED TO BODILY FUNCTIONS AND MOVEMENTS. AS HE GROWS, HUMAN RELATIONSHIPS GIVE MEANING AND DIRECTION TO THE EXPRESSION OF FEELINGS. AGGRESSION AND ANGER ARE EXPRESSION OF FEELINGS THAT ARE RELATED BUT NOT IDENTICAL. AGGRESSION MAY BE ROOTED IN ANGER, BUT IT POSITIVE SENSE, IT ENABLES THE CHILD TO USE HIS ENVIRONMENT FOR SATISFACTION OF ESSENTIAL NEEDS. THE CHILD DEVELOPS A CAPACITY FOR CONSTRUCTIVE OR DESTRUCTIVE AGGRESSIVE ACTION AND FEELINGS FROM THE EXPERIENCE OF INTERACTING WITH OTHERS. THIS INTERACTION WITH OTHERS IS ALWAYS ASSOCIATED WITH SOME DEGREE OF FRUSTRATION. FRUSTRATION IS A CONTROL IMPOSED ON AN INDIVIDUAL THAT BLOCKS SATISFACTION OF A PHYSICAL OR PSYCHOLOGICAL NEED. UNLESS THIS FRUSTRATION IS OVERLY SEVERE, IT BECOMES A CONSTRUCTIVE FACTOR, TEACHING THE CHILD TO ASSERT HIMSELF. A CHILD'S CAPACITY TO TOLERATE FRUSTRATION CAN BE GREATLY REDUCED BY HUNGER, INSECURITY, PHYSICAL ILLNESS OR FEAR. ANGER CAN BE AGGRESSIVE, BUT IT CAN ALSO BE PASSIVE. A CHILD STRIKING ANOTHER CHILD MAY BE NOT MORE ANGRY THAN A CHILD REFUSING TO LEARN HIS LESSON. IT MAY TAKE ALL A TEACHER'S TOLERANCE AND UNDERSTANDING TO WORK WITH AN ANGRY CHILD. THIS DOCUMENT IS AVAILABLE FROM THE DEPARTMENT OF ELEMENTARY-KINDERGARTEN-NURSERY EDUCATION, NATIONAL EDUCATION ASSOCIATION, 1201 SIXTEENTH STREET, N.W., WASHINGTON, D.C. 20036. (CO)

ED017332 PS000392
INDEPENDENT AND GROUP LEARNING. DICKINSON, MARIE B., 6P.
EDRS PRICE MF-$0.65 HC NOT AVAILABLE FROM EDRS.

IN CONTRAST TO THE TRADITIONAL EMPHASES ON ROTE LEARNING AND FACT ACCUMULATION, RECENT TRENDS EMERGING FROM EDUCATIONAL RESEARCH STRESS THE DEVELOPMENT OF THINKING PROCESSES SUCH AS THE ABILITY TO REASON ABSTRACTLY AND TO SYNTHESIZE. CHILDREN WORKING INDEPENDENTLY OR IN GROUPS MOVE THROUGH A DISCOVERY LEARNING CURRICULUM IN WHICH THE TEACHER PROVIDES OPPORTUNITIES FOR SENSORY EXPLORATION AND MANIPULATION OF CONCRETE MATERIALS. THE CHILDREN ARE EXPECTED TO TRANSFER THIS LEARNING TO MORE COMPLEX LEVELS. THE CHILDREN THEMSELVES ARE RECOGNIZED AS BEING COMPLEX ORGANISMS, WHOSE LEARNING DEPENDS UPON THE INTERRELATIONSHIP OF EMOTIONAL, SOCIAL AND INTELLECTUAL PROCESSES. THEREFORE, THE CHILD'S IMAGE OF HIMSELF ASSUMES NEW IMPORTANCE SINCE IT AFFECTS HIS ABILITY TO LEARN THROUGH HIS SCHOOL CAREER. TECHNOLOGICAL AIDS SUCH AS TELEVISED AND COMPUTER ASSISTED INSTRUCTION WHICH ALLOW A CHILD TO PROGRESS AT HIS OWN RATE HELP HIM TO DEVELOP AND PRESERVE A POSITIVE SELF-IMAGE. SIMILARLY, GROUP INTERACTION, GUIDED BY AN UNDERSTANDING TEACHER, CAN PROVIDE FOR MOTIVATION AND SUPPORT BY CLASSMATES. THIS DOCUMENT IS AVAILABLE FROM THE DEPARTMENT OF ELEMENTARY-KINDERGARTEN-NURSURY EDUCATION, NATIONAL EDUCATION ASSOCIATION, 1201 SIXTEENTH STREET, N.W, WASHINGTON, D.C 20036. (MS)

ED017333 PS000429
A REPLICATIVE INVESTIGATION OF THE BUCKINGHAM-DOLCH FREE-ASSOCIATION WORD STUDY. FINAL REPORT. JACOBS, HUGH DONALD, AUG67 200P.
EDRS PRICE MF-$0.65 HC-$6.58

PUBLISHED CHILDREN'S VOCABULARY LISTS BASED ON ACTUAL USAGE ARE ALL DRAWN FROM RESEARCH DONE PRIOR TO 1930. THE PRESENT STUDY REPLICATED THE 1926 BUCKINGHAM-DOLCH STUDY TO DETERMINE ANY VOCABULARY CHANGES. THE 2 HYPOTHESES TESTED WERE (1) THERE IS NO SIGNIFICANT VOCABULARY SHIFT, AND (2) COMMON WORDS DID NOT DIFFER IN GRADE-PLACEMENT (THE EARLIEST GRADE IN WHICH THE WORD APPEARS FREQUENTLY). THE EARLY VOCABULARY STUDIES WERE EXTENSIVELY REVIEWED AND THEIR LIMITATIONS DISCUSSED. THE STUDY SAMPLE WAS DRAWN FROM SCHOOLS IN THE WILLAMETTE VALLEY PLAIN, OREGON, AND CONSISTED OF 8,506 CHILDREN IN GRADES 2 THROUGH 6. INITIAL WORD LISTS WERE OBTAINED BY HAVING THE CHILDREN WRITE DOWN "ALL THE WORDS THAT CAME TO MIND" IN 15 MINUTES. COMPUTER PROCESSING WAS USED TO OBTAIN FINAL WORKD LISTS AND TO COMPARE THE 1926 AND 1966 LISTS. ALTOGETHER, 9,045 DIFFERENT WORDS WERE OBTAINED, OF WHICH 1,715 ON THE INTERNATIONAL KINDERGARTEN UNION LIST AND 2,820 WHICH COULD NOT BE GRADE-PLACED WERE REMOVED, GIVING 4,510 GRADE-PLACED WORDS. THE 1926 STUDY REPORTED 4,924 GRADE-PLACED WORDS. THERE WERE 2,969 COMMON TO BOTH LISTS, 1,955 UNIQUE TO THE 1926 LIST, AND 1,541 UNIQUE TO THE 1966 LIST. GRADE-PLACING IN 1926 REQUIRED THAT 2 STUDENTS OUT OF THE 16,813 IN THAT STUDY HAD WRITTEN THE WORD. THE 1966 STUDY REQUIRED 3 STUDENTS OUT OF 8,506 FOR GRADE-PLACING. THE GRADE-PLACEMENT OF 1,999 WORDS CHANGED, 1,395 MOVING TO A HIGHER GRADE IN THE 1966 LIST. IT WAS CONCLUDED THAT BOTH HYPOTHESES SHOULD BE REJECTED, THAT THE 1966 STUDENTS KNEW FEWER WORDS, AND THAT THE VOCABULARY ACHIEVEMENT OF THE 1966 STUDENTS CAME LATER. THE DATA OF THIS STUDY WILL BE AVAILABLE FOR ADDITIONAL RESEARCH. (DR)

ED017334 PS000450
A TRAINING PROGRAM FOR MOTHERS. HORTON, DELLA M., 5P.
EDRS PRICE MF-$0.65 HC-$3.29

FOUR OBJECTIVES WERE DESCRIBED AS PART OF THE TRAINING PROGRAM FOR MOTHERS. STEP 1 WAS TO ESTABLISH PARENTAL COOPERATION EXPLAINING THE NEED FOR INTERACTION BETWEEN MOTHER AND CHILD. STEP 2 WAS TO ERASE SOME OF THE TENSION, FEAR, AND FRUSTRATION THAT WAS AROUSED WHEN MOTHERS KNEW THEY WOULD BE TESTED BEFORE THE PROGRAM WAS UNDER WAY. STEP 3 WAS TO GIVE MOTHERS AN OVERALL VIEW OF THE VARIABLES PERCEPTUAL AND CONCEPTUAL, AS WELL AS ATTITUDINAL DEVELOPMENT IN PERSISTENCE, TOLERANCE AND DELAY OF GRATIFICATION. STEP 4 WAS TO HELP MOTHERS UNDERSTAND THE DEVELOPMENT OF THEIR CHILDREN AS THE PROCESS OF A SERIES OF SYSTEMATIC EXPERIENCES BEING LINKED TOGETHER TO FORM A COMPLETE PATTERN OF SKILLS AND UNDERSTANDING. PHASE 1 OF THE PROGRAM IN THE CLASSROOM CONSISTED OF ORIENTATION AND DIRECTED OBSERVATION. PHASE 2 CONSISTED OF DEMONSTRATION AND ROLE PLAY. PHASE 3 CONSISTED OF CLASSROOM PARTICIPATION WITH MINIMAL STRUCTURE. PHASE 4 CONSISTED OF INSTRUCTIONAL PARTICIPATION IN THE CLASSROOM. THESE 4 PHASES OF INVOLVEMENT BEGAN TO YIELD IMMEDIATE RESULTS. THE MOTHERS BEGAN TO BE CURIOUS AND TO ASK QUESTIONS. THE DATA FROM THE RESEARCH INDICATED THAT SUCH A PROGRAM CAN HAVE A MARKED EFFECT UPON THE MOTHERS FROM DISADVANTAGED BACKGROUNDS. FOR EXAMPLE, SEVERAL MOTHERS RETURNED TO SCHOOL. ALSO, SEVERAL FAMILIES PLANNED TO LEAVE FEDERAL HOUSING TO BUY THEIR OWN HOMES. (CO)

ED017335 PS000454
AN APPROACH FOR WORKING WITH MOTHERS OF DISADVANTAGED PRESCHOOL CHILDREN. KARNES, MERLE B.; AND OTHERS, 18P.
EDRS PRICE MF-$0.65 HC-$3.29

A PRESCHOOL EDUCATIONAL PROGRAM WAS DEVELOPED IN WHICH THE ONLY TEACHER FOR THE CHILD IS HIS MOTHER. IT WAS HYPOTHESIZED THAT MOTHERS OF LOW SOCIOECONOMIC AND EDUCATIONAL LEVEL CAN CONTRIBUTE MATERIALLY, WITH MINIMAL BUT PROPER TRAINING, TO THE INTELLECTUAL AND LINGUISTIC DEVELOPMENT OF THEIR CHILDREN. THE TRAINING PROGRAM FOR THE MOTHERS CONSISTED OF 11 WEEKLY 2-HOUR SESSIONS IN WHICH EXPERIENCED PRESCHOOL TEACHERS WORKED WITH THE MOTHERS IN PREPARING SIMPLE, INEXPENSIVE PROJECTS AND MATERIALS TO BE USED WITH THE CHILD, AND INSTRUCTED THE MOTHERS IN HOW TO USE THE MATERIALS. THESE MOTHERS WERE PAID $3.00 PER SESSION. THIRTY CHILDREN WERE INVOLVED, RANGING IN AGE FROM 39 MONTHS TO 51 MONTHS AT THE TIME THE 12-WEEK PROGRAM BEGAN. THE CHILDREN, HALF OF WHOM WERE TO BE INSTRUCTED BY THEIR MOTHERS AND HALF OF WHOM WERE TO RECEIVE NO COMPENSATORY INSTRUCTION, WERE INITIALLY MATCHED ON SEX AND INTELLIGENCE QUOTIENT. ALL OF THE CHILDREN RECEIVED PRE- AND POSTTESTS ON THE STANFORD-BINET, WHICH MEASURES INTELLIGENCE LEVEL, AND ON THE ITPA, WHICH MEASURES LANGUAGE ABILITY. THE TEST RESULTS SHOWED THAT THE INSTRUCTED CHILDREN GAINED SIGNIFICANTLY MORE IN INTELLIGENCE LEVEL OVER THE 12 WEEKS THAN DID THE CONTROL CHILDREN AND ALSO IMPROVED IN LINGUISTIC FUNCTIONING MORE THAN DID THE CONTROL GROUP. THE HYPOTHESIS WAS DEMONSTRATED TO BE ACCURATE, BUT IS CANNOT YET BE CONCLUDED WHETHER OR NOT THE GAINS CAN BE SUSTAINED OVER THE FUTURE. (WD)

ED017336 PS000459
EFFECTS OF DIFFERENTIAL PRIOR EXPOSURE ON YOUNG CHILDREN'S SUBSEQUENT OBSERVING AND CHOICE OF NOVEL STIMULI. ENDSLEY, RICHARD C.; KESSEL, LESLEY D., 14P.
EDRS PRICE MF-$0.65 HC-$3.29

TWO EXPERIMENTS WERE PERFORMED TO INVESTIGATE THE EFFECT OF RELATIVE NOVELTY ON CHOICE BEHAVIOR. IN THE FIRST, 48 CHILDREN OF MEAN AGE 4.4 YEARS WERE PREEXPOSED TO 1 OF 2 SETS OF TOYS FOR 0, 1, 3, OR 5 MINUTES. EACH WAS THEN GIVEN 10 OPPORTUNITIES TO PLAY WITH 1 SET FOR 30 SECONDS. THE MEAN NUMBER OF CHOICES OF THE NOVEL SET INCREASED WITH THE PREEXPOSURE TIME FROM 5.1 TO 7.7. THE NUMBER OF ALTERNATIONS OF CHOICE IN THE 10 TRAILS TENDED TO FALL WITH INCREASED EXPOSURE TIME. IN THE SECOND EXPERIMENT, 80 KINDERGARTEN CHILDREN OF MEAN AGE 6 YEARS WERE PREEXPOSED TO 1 OF THE 2 TOY SETS FOR 1/2, 1-1/2, 3, OR 5 MUNUTES. THEY WERE THEN GIVEN 16 OPPORTUNITIES TO LOOK AT BOTH SETS AND CHOOSE 1 TO PLAY WITH FOR EITHER 5 OR 30 SECONDS. THE TIME SPENT OBSERVING EACH SET PRIOR TO CHOOSING WAS RECORDED. IN THIS EXPERIMENT THE AMOUNT OF PRIOR EXPOSURE TIME DID NOT AFFECT THE CHOICES. THE AMOUNT OF TIME SPENT LOOKING AT THE SETS BEFORE CHOOSING DECREASED EXPONENTIALLY WITH TRIALS. THE MEAN NUMBER OF CHOICE ALTERNATIONS WAS 11.1, SIGNIFICANTLY HIGHER THAN THE EXPECTED VALUE OF 7.5. IT IS FELT THAT THIS MAY BE DUE TO A "TAKING TURNS" PROPENSITY NOTED IN CHILDREN OF THIS AGE, AND THAT THIS ACCOUNTS FOR THE LACK OF AGREEMENT WITH EXPERIMENT I. (DR)

ED017337 PS000461
THE ROLE OF SOCIALIZATION AND SOCIAL INFLUENCE IN A COMPENSATORY PRESCHOOL PROGRAM. RADIN, NORMA, 25NOV67 18P.
EDRS PRICE MF-$0.65 HC-$3.29

COMPENSATORY PRESCHOOL PROGRAMS, REPRESENTED IN THIS STUDY BY THE EARLY EDUCATION PROGRAM OF YPSILANTI, MICHIGAN, ARE THOUGHT TO BE MOST EFFECTIVE IF BOTH THE MOTHER AND THE CHILD ARE INVOLVED. THEREFORE, THE YPSILANTI PROGRAM INCLUDES, BESIDES 4 HALF-DAY SCHOOL SESSIONS, A 1/1/2 HOUR TUTORIAL SESSION EVERY OTHER WEEK IN THE CHILD'S HOME BY THE SCHOOL TEACHER. AT THIS SESSION, THE MOTHER IS TO BE PRESENT AND, HOPEFULLY, PARTICIPATING. THERE ARE 100 4-YEAR-OLD LOW-INCOME CHILDREN IN THE YPSILANTI PROGRAM. THE MOTHERS ARE ENCOURAGED TO ATTEND AN 18-WEEK GROUP SESSION IN WHICH THEY ARE INSTRUCTED IN THE FUNDAMENTAL CONCEPTS OF CHILD REARING, INCLUDING CHILD EDUCATION. THE EFFECT OF THE YPSILANTI PROGRAM ON THE MOTHERS OF THE PARTICIPATING CHILDREN IS INTENDED TO BE SOCIAL INFLUENCE, A GRADUAL BUT RELATIVELY SUPERFICIAL CHANGE IN THE MOTHERS' ATTITUDES AND PERSPECTIVIES TOWARDS MIDDLE-CLASS EDUCATIONAL VALUES. IT IS HOPED THE CHANGE WILL BE POSITIVE, THAT IS, THAT THE MOTHERS WILL ACCEPT THESE VALUES AND SUPPORT THEM. THE PROCESS WHICH THE CHILDREN ARE EXPERIENCING BY PARTICIPATION IN THE PROGRAM IS INTENDED TO BE SOMETHING MORE THAN SOCIAL INFLUENCE. IT IS INTENDED TO BE A SOCIALIZATION PROCESS, THE INTERNALIZATION OF THE VALUES AND BEHAVIOR PATTERNS OF THE SCHOOL ENVIRONMENT. THE YPSILANTI PROGRAM IS INTENDED TO INTERVENE IN THE DEVELOPMENT IN LOWER SOCIOECONOMIC CLASS CHILDREN OF ATTITUDES AND BASIC SKILLS INCOMPATIBLE WITH MIDDLE-CLASS EDUCATIONAL VAUES NECESSARY FOR GENERAL ACADEMIC ACHIEVEMENT. EQUALLY IMPORTANT IS THE PROGRAM'S HOPE

OF SUBSTITUTING MIDDLE-CLASS EDUCATIONAL VALUES AND MOTIVATIONS FOR THE LOWER-CLASS CHILD'S ATTITUDE TOWARD SCHOOL. (WD)

ED017338 PS000462
HEAD START, WEST VIRGINIA, SUMMER 1966--A SEVEN-COUNTY OVERVIEW, A SPECIAL ASSIGNMENT OF THE WEST VIRGINIA DEPARTMENT OF MENTAL HEALTH. MITCHELL-BATEMAN, M.; AND OTHERS, 66 34P.
EDRS PRICE MF-$0.65 HC-$3.29

PROJECT HEAD START (HS), FEDERALLY-SUPPORTED AND OPERATING UNDER FEDERAL REGULATIONS WHICH PERMITTED NO MORE THAN 10 PERCENT OF ENROLLED CHILDREN TO BE FROM FAMILIES WITH INCOMES ABOVE THE PRESCRIBED POVERTY LEVEL, WAS CONDUCTED DURING THE SUMMER OF 1966 IN ALL 55 WEST VIRGINIA COUNTIES. IN 7 OF THESE COUNTIES, SUPPLEMENTARY STATE FUNDS WERE ALLOCATED IN ORDER TO PERMIT ENROLLMENT OF CHILDREN WHO, BECAUSE OF FAMILY INCOME IN EXCESS OF THE POVERTY LEVEL, WERE NOT OTHERWISE ELIGIBLE FOR HS PARTICIPATION. A PROGRAM OF EVALUATIVE RESEARCH WAS CONDUCTED TO COMPARE THE BENEFITS DERIVED FROM HS BY ECONOMICALLY DEPRIVED CHILDREN AND BY THOSE FROM MORE AFFLUENT HOMES. THE CALDWELL ACHIEVEMENT TEST AND THE DRAW-A-PERSON TEST, SELECTED AS MEETING THE BASIC CRITERIA OF ECONOMY, BREVITY, AND EASE OF ADMINISTRATION, WERE ADMINISTERED TO 675 CHILDREN. TEST RESULTS ARE REPORTED IN A PSYCHOLOGICAL EVALUATION WHICH CONCLUDES THAT ECONOMICALLY DEPRIVED CHILDREN ARE CLEARLY DEFICIENT IN ACHIEVEMENT AND INTELLECTUAL FUNCTIONING WHEN COMPARED WITH CHILDREN FROM FAMILIES WITH INCOMES ABOVE THE POVERTY LEVEL. THE PROJECT REPORT CITES THE NEED FOR MORE EXTENSIVE PRESCHOOL EDUCATION PROGRAMS AS A MEANS OF PROVIDING COMPENSATORY PREPARATION FOR ECONOMICALLY DEPRIVED CHILDREN. (JS)

ED017339 PS000463
A PARENT EDUCATION APPROACH TO PROVISION OF EARLY STIMULATION FOR THE CULTURALLY DISADVANTAGED. FINAL REPORT. GORDON, IRA J., 30NOV67 118P.
EDRS PRICE MF-$0.65 HC-$6.58

AN INTERVENTION PILOT PROGRAM WAS DEVELOPED TO PROVIDE DISADVANTAGED INFANTS WITH STIMULATING EXPERIENCES TO HLEP THEM ACHIEVE HIGHER LEVELS OF INTELLECTUAL DEVELOPMENT THAN MIGHT NORMALLY BE EXPECTED IN CHILDREN FROM DEPRIVED HOMES. FIFTEEN DISADVANTAGED WOMEN TRAINED AS "PARENT EDUCATORS" WENT INTO 100 HOMES ONCE A WEEK FOR 40 WEEKS AND TAUGHT MOTHERS A SERIES OF PERCEPTUAL, MOTOR, AUDITORY, TACTILE, AND KINESTHETIC EXERCISES WHICH THE MOTHER WAS TO INTRODUCE TO HER INFANT. IT WAS ALSO HOPED THAT PARTICIPATION IN THE PROJECT WOULD INCREASE THE MOTHER'S FEELINGS OF COMPETENCE AND SELF-WORTH. THE EXPERIMENTAL INFANTS WERE TESTED AT 6 MONTHS ON DIFFERENT DEVELOPMENTAL TESTS AS WERE 25 INFANTS IN A MATCHED CONTROL GROUP. A SECOND CONTROL GROUP OF 25 INFANTS WAS TESTED AS THEY REACHED 1 YEAR OF AGE. RESULTS OF THE GROUPS WERE COMPARED TO MEASURE THE EFFECTIVENESS OF THE INTERVENTION PROGRAM. IN MOST INSTANCES, THE EXPERIMENTAL GROUP SHOWED GREATER DEVELOPMENT SUGGESTING THE VALUE OF EARLY STIMULATION FOR THE CULTURALLY DISADVANTAGED. PARENT EDUCATORS EXHIBITED SELF-GROWTH AND RESPONSIBLY FILLED THEIR ASSIGNMENTS. MEASUREMENT OF THE MOTHERS' FEELINGS PROVED TO BE A DIFFICULT TASK, WITH MEASURES STILL BEING DEVELOPED. CONTINUED RESEARCH IS BEING DONE ON AN EXPANDED PARENT EDUCATION PROJECT NOW IN OPERATION. (MS)

ED017340 PS000493
KINDERGARTEN OVERSEAS, A STUDY OF THE REQUIREMENTS FOR ESTABLISHING KINDERGARTEN AS PART OF THE DEPARTMENT OF DEFENSE OVERSEAS DEPENDENTS SCHOOLS. FINAL REPORT. DUNWORTH, JOHN, SEP67 358P.
EDRS PRICE MF-$0.65 HC-$13.16

THIS REPORT PRESENTS THE RESULTS OF A STUDY MADE TO DETERMINE THE REQUIREMENTS FOR EXPANDING OVERSEAS DEPENDENT SCHOOLS TO INCLUDE KINDERGARTEN. THE SPECIFIC OBJECTIVES OF THE STUDY WERE (1) TO DETERMINE PERSONNEL REQUIREMENTS, (2) TO DETERMINE FACILITY REQUIREMENTS, (3) TO DETERMINE EQUIPMENT AND EDUCATIONAL MATERIAL REQUIREMENTS, (4) TO DEVELOP A CURRICULUM GUIDE, (5) TO ESTIMATE COSTS. CHAPTERS II AND III DISCUSS THE RATIONALE FOR ESTABLISHING KINDERGARTENS AND THE METHODOLOGY USED IN THE STUDY. CHAPTER IV PRESENTS THE CURRICULUM GUIDE THAT WAS DEVELOPED, AND INCLUDES A SECTION COVERING THE INSTRUCTIONAL MATERIALS REQUIREMENTS. CHAPTER V CONSIDERS THE PERSONNEL REQUIREMENTS, BOTH PROFESSIONAL AND PARAPROFESSIONAL. CHAPTER VI PRESENTS THE COST ESTIMATES, BROKEN DOWN BY MILITARY OVERSEAS DISTRICTS. INDIVIDUAL SCHOOL SITE REPORTS AND OVERALL MONETARY REQUIREMENTS ARE GIVEN FOR EACH DISTRICT. THERE ARE 7 APPENDICES. (DR)

ED017341 PS000497
THE NEW ELEMENTARY SCHOOL. FRAZIER, ALEXANDER, ED., 68 157P.
EDRS PRICE MF-$0.65 HC NOT AVAILABLE FROM EDRS.

THE 8 PAPERS OF THIS BOOKLET DEAL WITH VARIOUS ASPECTS OF THE NEW ELEMENTARY SCHOOLS. THE INTRODUCTION SINGLES OUT, AS MAJOR AREAS OF CONCERN, (1) THE NEW STRESS ON THE EDUCATION OF YOUNGER CHILDREN, (2) NEW EVALUATIONS OF ADULT-CHILD RATIOS FOR SCHOOLS, (3) NEW ORGANIZATIONAL PATTERNS FOR SCHOOLS, (4) CHANGES IN TEACHER FUNCTIONS, AND (5) CURRICULUM REDEVELOPMENT. THE FIRST 3 PAPERS DEAL WITH NEW KNOWLEDGE ABOUT CHILDREN, THE FIRST WITH THE PSYCHOLOGY OF UNDERSTANDING, THE SECOND WITH THE EFFECTS OF HOME AND FAMILY ON CONCEPTUAL DEVELOPMENT, AND THE THIRD WITH THE ACQUISITION OF LANGUAGE. THE SECOND GROUP OF 3 PAPERS IS CONCERNED WITH NEW APPROACHES TO ORGANIZATION AND STAFFING. THE FIRST DISCUSSES NEW ORGANIZATIONAL PATTERNS, WITH PARTICULAR ATTENTION TO THE "MIDDLE SCHOOL" PROPOSAL. THE SECOND SURVEYS THE STATUS OF IN-SERVICE EDUCATION FOR ELEMENTARY TEACHERS. THE THIRD SUGGESTS NEW MODELS FOR THE ELEMENTARY TEACHER AND CONSIDERS THE KNOWLEDGE NECESSARY FOR EACH. THE LAST 2 PAPERS COVER CURRICULUM CONTENT AND CURRICULUM DESIGN. THE FIRST REVIEWS AN EXAMPLE OF SOCIAL STUDIES IN THE ELEMENTARY SCHOOL, AND THE SECOND DISCUSSES THE BASIC ASSUMPTIONS AND CONTENT PRIORITIES OF THE NEW CURRICULUM DESIGNS. THIS DOCUMENT IS AVAILABLE FROM ASSOCIATION FOR SUPERVISION AND CURRICULUM DEVELOPMENT, NATIONAL EDUCATION ASSOCIATION, 1201 SIXTEENTH STREET, N.W., WASHINGTON, D.C 20036 FOR $2.50. (DR)

ED017342 PS000746
HOW TO HELP YOUR CHILD LEARN, A HANDBOOK FOR PARENTS OF CHILDREN IN KINDERGARTEN THROUGH GRADE 6. , 60 42P.
EDRS PRICE MF-$0.65 HC NOT AVAILABLE FROM EDRS.

THIS HANDBOOK PROVIDES INFORMATION AND ADVICE FOR PARENTS OF CHILDREN IN KINDERGARTEN THROUGH GRADE 6. INDIVIDUAL CHAPTERS OF THE HANDBOOK ARE DEVOTED TO THE VARIOUS AREAS OF THE ELEMENTARY CURRICULUM--(1) READING, (2) SPELLING, (3) HANDWRITING, (4) ARITHMETIC, (5) SCIENCE, (6) SOCIAL STUDIES, (7) ART AND MUSIC, (8) FOREIGN LANGUAGES, AND (9) HEALTH AND PHYSICAL EDUCATION. ADDITIONAL CHAPTERS ARE CONCERNED WITH THE SUBJECTS OF HOMEWORK AND REPORT CARDS. IN EACH CHAPTER, AN INFORMATIVE INTRODUCTORY SECTION CONSISTS OF A GENERAL DESCRIPTION OF CURRENT PROCEDURES IN ELEMENTARY EDUCATION AND OF THE CURRICULAR ACTIVITIES AND GOALS APPROPRIATE TO THE VARIOUS AGE AND GRADE LEVELS. THE INFORMATIVE SECTION OF EACH CHAPTER IS FOLLOWED BY AN ENUMERATION OF WAYS IN WHICH PARENTS CAN ASSIST PROFESSIONAL EDUCATORS IN MOTIVATING, STIMULATING, AND ENCOURAGING CHILDREN TO REALIZE MAXIMUM BENEFITS FROM THE ELEMENTARY SCHOLASTIC EXPERIENCE. THE SUGGESTIONS FOR PARENTS, BOTH GENERAL AND SPECIFIC, INCLUDE RECOMMENDATIONS CONCERNING (1) APPROPRIATE MATERIALS AND ACTIVITIES TO SUPPLEMENT AND ENRICH CURRICULAR EXPERIENCES AND (2) MEANS BY WHICH AN ENVIRONMENT CONDUCIVE TO ACADEMIC EXCELLENCE CAN BE FOSTERED IN THE HOME. THIS DOCUMENT IS AVAILABLE FROM EITHER THE DEPARTMENT OF ELEMENTARY SCHOOL PRINCIPALS OR THE NATIONAL SCHOOL PUBLIC RELATIONS ASSOCIATION, 1201 SIXTEENTH STREET, N.W., WASHINGTON, D.C. 20036 FOR $0.75. (JS)

ED017343 PS000747
MULTI-AGE GROUPING--ENRICHING THE LEARNING ENVIRONMENT. , 68 39P.
EDRS PRICE MF-$0.65 HC NOT AVAILABLE FROM EDRS.

HETEROGENEOUS MIXTURES OF CHILDREN OCCUR NATURALLY IN PLAY AND IN MANY SCHOOL ACTIVITIES, FOR EXAMPLE, STUDENT COUNCIL MEETINGS, CLUBS, AND SOCIAL AFFAIRS. THESE ACTIVITIES DEMAND THE VARIETY OF AGES, TALENTS, INTERESTS, AND EXPERIENCES REPRESENTED BY THE WHOLE RANGE OF STUDENTS IN A SCHOOL. IT IS QUESTIONED WHETHER ACADEMIC ACTIVITIES WOULD NOT ALSO BE GREATLY ENHANCED BY THE CONTRIBUTIONS OF, AND COOPERATION AMONG, A HETEROGENEOUS GROUP OF STUDENTS LEARNING TOGETHER. THE AMERICAN SCHOOL SYSTEM AT PRESENT GENERALLY ORGANIZES STUDENTS INTO CLASSES ACCORDING TO AGE. BECAUSE OF THE ABUNDANT RESEARCH DEMONSTRATING THE VAST DIFFERENCES IN ABILITY AND RATE OF DEVELOPMENT WITHIN ANY ONE AGE GROUP, IT IS ARGUED IN THIS PAMPHLET THAT IT IS PERHAPS HIGHLY ARTIFICIAL TO ORGANIZE CLASSROOMS BY AGE ALONE. THE STUDY COMMITTEE RESPONSIBLE FOR THE CONTENT OF THIS PAMPHLET INVESTIGATED BOTH THE THEORY AND PRACTICE OF MULTI-AGE GROUPING. IN MULTI-AGE GROUPING, CHILDREN ARE GROUPED RANDOMLY WITH NO PARTICULAR CONSIDERATION OF AGE OR ABILITY, ALTHOUGH IT IS RECOGNIZED THAT NOT ALL AREAS OF STUDY ARE AMENABLE TO SUCH GROUPING. BUT FOR THOSE SUBJECTS LIKE ART, CREATIVE WRITING, AND DISCUSSION PERIODS, IN WHICH VARIED LEVELS OF MATURITY, PERSPECTIVE, AND EXPERIENCE CAN CONTRIBUTE MORE TO THE LEARNING PROCESS, THE LEARNING PROCESS WILL BE MORE LIKELY ENRICHED BY A GREATER HETEROGENEITY OF PUPILS. HETEROGENEOUS INTERACTION OF AGE GROUPS CONTRIBUTES TO SOCIAL GROWTH AND UNDERSTANDING AS WELL AS TO ACADEMIC GROWTH. THIS DOCUMENT IS AVAILABLE FROM

THE NATIONAL EDUCATION ASSOCIATION, 1201 SIXTEENTH STREET, N.W., WASHINGTON, D.C. 20036 FOR $1.00. (WD)

ED017344 PS000763
THE CREATIVE-AESTHETIC APPROACH TO SCHOOL READINESS AND MEASURED CREATIVE GROWTH. TORRANCE, E. PAUL; AND OTHERS, JUL67 17P.
EDRS PRICE MF-$0.65 HC-$3.29

IN RESPONSE TO THE OBSERVATION THAT CHILDREN LOSE MUCH OF THEIR IMAGINATIVENESS AND CREATIVENESS AT ABOUT AGE 5 OR DURING THEIR KINDERGARTEN YEAR, A PROGRAM CALLED THE "CREATIVE-AESTHETIC APPROACH TO SCHOOL READINESS" WAS EMPLOYED TO SEE IF IT WOULD PREVENT SUCH A LOSS. THE PROGRAM IS NORMALLY USED WITH PRESCHOOL CHILDREN TO DEVELOP THE BEGINNINGS OF INTELLECTUAL SKILLS WHICH WILL BE OF FUTURE VALUE. IN THE PRESENT STUDY, THIS PROGRAM WAS USED WITH 24 5-YEAR-OLDS IN AN EXPERIMENTAL KINDERGARTEN. AN ORTHODOX KINDERGARTEN CLASS OF 39 CHILDREN WAS THE CONTROL GROUP. ALTHOUGH BOTH KINDERGARTEN PROGRAMS BEGAN IN SEPTEMBER, 1966, A PRETEST WAS NOT ADMINISTERED TO THE EXPERIMENTAL GROUP UNTIL JANUARY, 1967. THE POSTTEST FOR THE EXPERIMENTAL GROUP WAS GIVEN IN MAY, 1967. THE CONTROL GROUP WAS ADMINISTERED ONLY 1 TEST, THE MAY POSTTEST. THE JANUARY AND MAY TESTS CONSISTED OF (1) TORRANCE TESTS OF CREATIVE THINKING, (2) MOTHER GOOSE PROBLEMS TESTS, AND (3) THE STARKWEATHER TEST OF ORIGINALITY. THE RESULTS WERE FIRST ANALYZED TO COMPARE THE SCORES OF THE EXPERIMENTAL GROUP ALONE ON THEIR PRE- AND POSTTESTS. THE CHILDREN IMPROVED ON ALL 9 TESTS, WITH SIGNIFICANT IMPROVEMENT ON 6 OF THEM. A COMPARISON OF THE MAY SCORES OF BOTH THE EXPERIMENTAL AND CONTROL GROUPS SHOWED THAT THE EXPERIMENTAL GROUP SIGNIFICANTLY OUT-PERFORMED THE CONTROLS ON 6 OF THE 8 TESTS ADMINISTERED TO BOTH GROUPS, AND SCORED HIGHER ON THE REMAINING 2 TESTS. IT WAS CONCLUDED THAT THE KINDERGARTEN EXPERIENCE OR THE REACHING OF 5 YEARS OF AGE NEED NOT RESULTS IN SERIOUS DIMINUTION OF A CHILD'S CREATIVITY. (WD)

ED018245 PS000198
NORTHFIELD, VERMONT--A COMMUNITY DEPTH STUDY. SOULE, ALLEN, 1DEC65 141P.
EDRS PRICE MF-$0.65 HC-$6.58

THIS REPORT IS A STUDY IN DEPTH OF NORTHFIELD, VERMONT. IT WAS UNDERTAKEN IN ORDER TO UNDERSTAND THE PLACE OF HEAD START CHILDREN AND THEIR FAMILIES IN THEIR CULTURAL CONTEXT AND TO EXAMINE THESE CHILDREN'S INTERACTIONS WITH SOCIETY AND WITH EDUCATIONAL OPPORTUNITIES. THREE MAJOR SECTIONS DESCRIBE (1) THE HISTORICAL DEVELOPMENT OF THE SOCIOECONOMIC FORCES WHICH HAVE SHAPED PRESENT-DAY COMMUNITY LIFE, (2) THE FAMILIES OF THE HEAD START CHILDREN, THEIR EDUCATIONAL LEVELS, THEIR ECONOMIC STATUS, THEIR ATTITUDES TOWARD HEAD START, AND THE ATTITUDES OF FAMILY MEMBERS TOWARD EACH OTHER, AND (3) THE NORTHFIELD SCHOOL SYSTEM, ITS INTERACTION WITH HEAD START FAMILIES, AND THE WRITER'S REFLECTIONS ON THE ROLE OF THE SCHOOL SYSTEM IN SATISFYING THE NEEDS OF THE DEPRIVED CHILD. SECTION (4) IS COMPOSED OF 10 TABLES DETAILING INFORMATION ON POPULATION, INCOME TAX, AGES AND GRADE LEVELS OF THE CHILDREN OF HEAD START FAMILIES, NUMBERS OF CHILDREN IN HEAD START FAMILIES AND IN SCHOOL, SCHOOL SYSTEM ENROLLMENT, NUMBER OF CHILDREN GOING ON TO HIGHER EDUCATION, AND NUMBER OF CHILDREN REPEATING GRADES. SECTION (5) IS COMPOSED OF APPENDICES A, B, C, AND D. "A" IS A REPORT ON THE HEAD START PROGRAM. "B" IS A REPORT BY THE BOARD OF DEACONS OF NORTHFIELD'S UNITED CHURCH. "C" IS A SAMPLE FAMILY QUESTIONNAIRE. "D" IS THE 80-PAGE ANNUAL REPORT OF THE TOWN OF NORTHFIELD FOR 1964. (LG)

ED018246 PS000263
PROJECT HEAD START--SUMMER 1966. FINAL REPORT. SECTION ONE, SOME CHARACTERISTICS OF CHILDREN IN THE HEAD START PROGRAM. STEWART, E. ELIZABETH; WILLIAMS, RICHARD H., MAY67 94P.
EDRS PRICE MF-$0.65 HC-$3.29

THIS DOCUMENT IS SECTION 1 OF A 3-PART REPORT BY THE EDUCATIONAL TESTING SERVICE. THIS SECTION DESCRIBES, IN EXTENSIVE STATISTICAL TERMS, A SAMPLE OF 445 HEAD START CHILDREN IN TERMS OF THEIR SCORES ON (1) THE STANFORD-BINET L-M, (2) THE CALDWELL PRESCHOOL INVENTORY, AND (3) THE PROJECT HEAD START BEHAVIOR INVENTORY. THE SAMPLING PROCEDURES USED INCLUDED BOTH RANDOM AND SYSTEMATIC PROCEDURES AND WERE USED TO CHOOSE BOTH THE PUPILS AND THE HEAD START CENTERS FROM WHICH THE PUPILS WERE TO COME. THE HEAD START PROGRAMS THAT THESE PUPILS ATTENDED LASTED FROM 5 TO 9 WEEKS. THE TESTING WAS BEGUN AFTER THE FOURTH WEEK. THE PUPILS' SCORES WERE ORGANIZED ON THE DIMENSIONS OF GEOGRAPHICAL REGION (SOUTH, WEST, MIDWEST, AND NORTHEAST), CITY SIZE (URBAN AND NONURBAN), SEX, RACE, AGE, AND COMBINATIONS THEREOF. (WD)

ED018247 PS000264
PROJECT HEAD START--SUMMER 1966. FINAL REPORT. SECTION TWO, FACILITIES AND RESOURCES OF HEAD START CENTERS. BOYD, JOSEPH L., MAY67 63P.
EDRS PRICE MF-$0.65 HC-$3.29

THIS DOCUMENT IS SECTION 2 OF A 3-PART REPORT BY THE EDUCATIONAL TESTING SERVICE. THE "CENTER FACILITIES AND RESOURCES INVENTORY" WAS SENT TO THE DIRECTORS OF 630 HEAD START CENTERS. THE INVENTORIES WERE TO BE COMPLETED AND RETURNED TO THE SERVICE SO THAT INFORMATION DESCRIBING THE GENERAL PHYSICAL FACILITIES AND HUMAN AND PROGRAM RESOURCES OF HEAD START CENTERS WOULD BE AVAILABLE IN AN ORGANIZED AND INTELLIGIBLE FORM. INVENTORIES FROM 350 CENTERS WERE ULTIMATELY RECEIVED. THE INFORMATION IN THESE INVENTORIES WAS REORGANIZED SO THAT ON ANY ONE CHARACTERISTIC, SUCH AS "NUMBER OF WORKERS," A FREQUENCY DISTRIBUTION WAS DETERMINED WHICH REFLECTED THE NUMBERS OF WORKERS IN THE VARIOUS CENTERS. THIS DOCUMENT IS COMPOSED OF MANY SUCH FREQUENCY DISTRIBUTION TABLES COVERING THE GENERAL TOPICAL AREAS OF (1) HEAD START CENTER PHYSICAL FACILITIES, (2) HEAD START CENTER HUMAN RESOURCES, AND (3) THE NATURE, ORIENTATION, AND GOALS OF HEAD START PROGRAMS. PRESENTED WITH THE TABLES IS A BRIEF DISCUSSION AND EXPLANATION OF THE DATA. (WD)

ED018248 PS000265
PROJECT HEAD START--SUMMER 1966. FINAL REPORT. SECTION THREE, PUPILS AND PROGRAMS. ANDERSON, SCARVIA B.; TEMP, GEORGE, MAY67 86P.
EDRS PRICE MF-$0.65 HC-$3.29

THIS DOCUMENT IS SECTION 3 OF A 3-PART REPORT BY THE EDUCATIONAL TESTING SERVICE. THE DATA USED IN THIS SECTION WERE COMPILED FROM 79 CLASSES CONTAINING ABOUT 1,000 PUPILS. THE CLASSES WERE PART OF THE 1966 SUMMER HEAD START PROGRAM. THE PURPOSE OF THIS DOCUMENT IS TO NOTE GENERAL PERFORMANCE CHANGES IN THE PUPILS AS MEASURED BY TESTS ADMINISTERED AT THE BEGINNING OF THE PROGRAM AND AGAIN AT THE END. THE RESULTS WERE INTERPRETED AS SHOWING THAT, ALTHOUGH THE PUPILS' SCORES WERE BELOW THE DESIRED INTELLIGENCE LEVEL NORMS OF THEIR AGE-GROUP AT BOTH THE BEGINNING AND END OF THE PROGRAM, SOME POSITIVE IMPROVEMENT DID OCCUR. BECAUSE OF THE EXPERIMENTAL DESIGN, IT WAS NOT POSSIBLE TO DEFINITELY ASSESS THE EXTENT, OR EVEN THE VERY EXISTENCE, OF CONTRIBUTIONS BY 4 POSSIBLE CAUSES OF THE IMPROVEMENT IN PERFORMANCE. THE 4 POSSIBLE CAUSES WERE (1) THE HEAD START PROGRAM, (2) MATURATION, (3) OUTSIDE EXPERIENCES, AND (4) TESTING EFFECTS. A SECOND ASPECT OF THE STUDY, CLASSROOM OBSERVATION, PRODUCED AN ADDITIONAL SET OF POSSIBLE INFLUENCES ON PUPIL PERFORMANCE, NAMELY, (1) TEACHER CHARACTERISTICS, (2) PUPIL CHARACTERISTICS, (3) PUPIL EXPERIENCES IN THE CLASSROOM, AND (4) SCHOOL-COMMUNITY-PARENTAL FACTORS. (WD)

ED018249 PS000276
TEACHERS' BELIEFS, CLASSROOM ATMOSPHERE AND STUDENT BEHAVIOR. FINAL REPORT. HARVEY, O.J.; AND OTHERS, 28JUL67 74P.
EDRS PRICE MF-$0.65 HC-$3.29

THIS FINAL REPORT CONSISTS OF 3 SECTIONS. ITS CONCERN IS WITH THE INTERACTION OF HOME AND CLASSROOM ENVIRONMENTS ON THE ACHIEVEMENT OF LOWER SOCIOECONOMIC LEVEL CHILDREN WHO ATTENDED OR WERE ELIGIBLE TO ATTEND THE 1965 COLORADO HEAD START PROGRAM. SECTION 1 REPLICATES AND ELABORATES A STUDY ON THE EXISTENCE OF CONCRETE AND ABSTRACT BELIEF SYSTEMS IN TEACHERS AND ON HOW SUCH BELIEF SYSTEMS EFFECT CLASSROOM ATMOSPHERE. THE SAME ELEMENTS WERE INVESTIGATED IN THIS STUDY IN ADDITION TO THE PRIMARY OBJECTIVE OF OBSERVING THE EFFECT OF THE 2 BELIEF SYSTEMS ON STUDENT PERFORMANCE. THE HYPOTHESIS THAT THE GREATER THE ABSTRACTNESS OF THE TEACHER'S BELIEF SYSTEM, THE GREATER WOULD BE HER RESOURCEFULNESS, THE LESS HER DICTATORIALNESS AND PUNITIVENESS, AND THE BETTER THE ACADEMIC PERFORMANCE OF THE PUPILS WAS DEMONSTRATED. SECTION 2 IS A FAMILY SURVEY USED TO DETERMINE FAMILY ATTITUDES AND VALUES WHICH WERE THEN ANALYZED TO SEE IF AND HOW SUCH ATTITUDES RELATED TO THE CHILD'S PERFORMANCE IN HEAD START AND IN PUBLIC SCHOOL. SECTION 3 PRESENTS THE CHILDREN'S PERFORMANCE SCORES OBTAINED DURING THEIR ATTENDANCE IN PUBLIC SCHOOL AT THE PRIMARY LEVEL. THE TEST MATERIALS WERE MOVIE FILMS OF 13 BRIEF SITUATIONS RELEVANT TO SOME ASPECT OF THE CHILD'S BEHAVIOR AND ON WHICH HE WAS ASKED TO COMMENT. THE SCORES OF THESE TESTS WERE THEN COMBINED WITH THE INFORMATION FROM SECTIONS 1 AND 2 TO SHOW THE RESULTS OF THE INTERACTION OF THE 3 VARIABLES OF TEACHER, PUPIL, AND PARENT ON PUPIL PERFORMANCE. (WD)

ED018250 PS000278
RESULTS OF THE SUMMER 1965 PROJECT HEAD START. VOLUMES I AND II. CORT, H. RUSSELL, JR.; AND OTHERS, 9MAY66 561P.
EDRS PRICE MF-$0.65 HC-$19.74

AN OVERALL SURVEY AND ANALYSIS OF THE SUMMER 1965 PROJECT HEAD START IS PRESENTED IN THIS REPORT. THE FIRST SECTION DISCUSSES THE INCEPTION, IMPLEMENTATION, AND FORMAL ORGANIZATION OF THE PROJECT. THE SECOND SECTION PRESENTS DETAILED INFORMATION ON THE COMMUNITIES, CHILDREN, PARENTS, STAFF, AND WORKERS INVOLVED IN THE PROJECT. THE THIRD SECTION DISCUSSES AND EVALUATES SPECIFIC HEAD START PROGRAMS. THE FOURTH SECTION CONSIDERS THE IMPACT OF THE HEAD START PROGRAM ON THE PARTICIPATING COMMUNITIES, ON THE HEALTH, MENTAL DEVELOPMENT, AND SOCIAL DEVELOPMENT OF THE CHILDREN, ON THE PARENTS, AND ON THE STAFF OF THE CHILD DEVELOPMENT CENTERS. THE FINAL SECTION SUMMARIZES THE RESULTS AND PRESENTS SEVERAL SPECIFIC RECOMMENDATIONS. VOLUME II OF THE REPORT CONTAINS THE APPENDIXES. (DR)

ED018251 PS000304
PRESCHOOL INTERVENTION--A PRELIMINARY REPORT OF THE PERRY PRESCHOOL PROJECT. WEIKART, DAVID P., ED., 12APR67
DOCUMENT NOT AVAILABLE FROM EDRS.

THE PERRY PRESCHOOL PROJECT IS AN EXPERIMENT WITH REPLICATIONS DESIGNED TO ASSESS THE LONGITUDINAL EFFECTS OF A 2-YEAR, COGNITIVELY ORIENTED, COMPENSATORY EDUCATION PROGRAM. SELECTED FROM A POPULATION WHICH IS NEGRO, FUNCTIONALLY RETARDED, AND CULTURALLY DEPRIVED, CONTROL AND EXPERIMENTAL GROUPS ARE EQUATED FOR MEAN CULTURAL-DEPRIVATION RATING AND MEAN STANFORD-BINET IQ. THE EDUCATIONAL PROGRAM CONSISTS OF (1) DAILY MORNING CLASSROOM SESSIONS, (2) WEEKLY AFTERNOON HOME TUTORIAL SESSIONS DIRECTED TOWARD THE STIMULATION OF MATERNAL INVOLVEMENT IN THE EDUCATIVE PROCESS, AND (3) PARENTAL GROUP MEETINGS. CONCOMITANT EVALUATIVE RESEARCH CONSISTS OF THE ADMINISTRATION, AT ENTRANCE INTO THE PROGRAM AND YEARLY THEREAFTER INCLUDING LONGITUDINAL FOLLOW-UP THROUGH THE FIRST FEW YEARS OF SCHOOL, OF VARIOUS MEASURES INCLUDING (1) STANFORD BINET, (2) LEITER INTERNATIONAL PERFORMANCE SCALE, (3) PEABODY PICTURE VOCABULARY TEST, AND (4) ILLINOIS TEST OF PSYCHOLINGUISTIC ABILITY. ALTHOUGH THE PROJECT IS IN PROGRESS, DATA ARE CURRENTLY AVAILABLE ON 4 WAVES OF PARTICIPANTS. THESE DATA REVEAL STATISTICALLY SIGNIFICANT DIFFERENCES BETWEEN CONTROL AND EXPERIMENTAL GROUPS WHICH TENTATIVELY ESTABLISH (1) THE VALUE OF THIS PROJECT AS A REMEDIAL PROGRAM AND (2) THE SUPERIORITY OF COGNITIVELY ORIENTED PROGRAMS IN CONTRAST TO TRADITIONAL NURSERY SCHOOL PROGRAMS. DETAILED RESEARCH STATISTICS ARE TABULARLY PRESENTED THROUGHOUT THE REPORT AND APPENDED MATERIAL INCLUDES ILLUSTRATIONS OF PROJECT SESSIONS AND PREVIOUSLY PUBLISHED REVIEWS AND ARTICLES CONCERNED WITH THE PROJECT. THIS DOCUMENT IS AVAILABLE FROM CAMPUS PUBLISHERS, 711 NORTH UNIVERSITY AVENUE, ANN ARBOR, MICHIGAN 48108. (JS)

ED018252 PS000442
THE STATUS OF BEHAVIORAL MEASUREMENT AND ASSESSMENT IN CHILDREN. JENKINS, W.O.; AND OTHERS, 6JUN66 114P.
EDRS PRICE MF-$0.65 HC-$6.58

THIS PAPER PRESENTS INDEFINITIVE APPROACHES FOR THE BEHAVIORAL ASSESSMENT OF PRESCHOOL CHILDREN. IT REVIEWS THE STATE OF THE ART OF BEHAVIOR MEASUREMENT OF PRESCHOOL CHILDREN AND SUGGESTS SOME NEW OR MODIFIED MEASURES. AN INTRODUCTORY OVERVIEW DISCUSSES REASONS FOR BEHAVIOR ASSESSMENT AND FACTORS WHICH AFFECT ANY BEHAVIORAL APPROACH. SOME PROCEDURAL CONSIDERATIONS AFFECTING ANY RESEARCH WITH PRESCHOOL CHILDREN ARE GIVEN. THESE CONSIDERATIONS DEAL PRIMARILY WITH DIFFICULTIES THAT CAN ARISE WITH THE PHYSICAL SETTING AND WITH INTERPERSONAL RELATIONSHIPS. MAJOR AREAS FOR BEHAVIOR ASSESSMENT ARE SURVEYED--(1) OBTAINING BACKGROUND AND ENVIRONMENTAL INFORMATION, (2) LEARNING, (3) SENSORI- AND PERCEPTUAL-MOTOR ACTIVITY, (4) LANGUAGE AND VERBAL BEHAVIOR, (5) ATTENTION AND MOTIVATION, (6) EMOTIONAL BEHAVIOR, AND (7) SOCIAL BEHAVIOR. IN EACH OF THESE 7 AREAS, THE BASIC CONCEPTS INVOLVED ARE EXPLICATED, CURRENT EXPERIMENTAL WORK OR THEORIES ARE SURVEYED, AND SPECIFIC PROPOSALS FOR APPLYING EACH TYPE OF ASSESSMENT TO PRESCHOOL CHILDREN ARE GIVEN. (DR)

ED018253 PS000475
THE COGNITIVE ENVIRONMENTS OF URBAN PRE-SCHOOL CHILDREN. MANUAL OF INSTRUCTIONS FOR ADMINISTERING AND SCORING THE HOME INTERVIEW. HESS, ROBERT D.; AND OTHERS, 67 38P.
EDRS PRICE MF-$0.65 HC-$3.29

THIS MANUAL DESCRIBES MEASURES USED IN "THE COGNITIVE ENVIRONMENTS OF URBAN PRE-SCHOOL CHILDREN" PROJECT AT THE UNIVERSITY OF CHICAGO. THE SAMPLE FOR THE STUDY CONSISTED OF 163 NEGRO MOTHER-CHILD PAIRS SELECTED FROM 3 SOCIOECONOMIC CLASSES BASED ON THE FATHER'S OCCUPATION AND THE PARENTS' EDUCATION. A FOURTH GROUP INCLUDED FATHER-ABSENT FAMILIES. THE MOTHERS WERE INTERVIEWED AT HOME AND THE MOTHERS AND CHILDREN WERE TESTED AT THE UNIVERSITY OF CHICAGO WHEN THE CHILDREN WERE 4 YEARS OLD. FOLLOW-UP DATA WERE OBTAINED WHEN THE CHILDREN WERE 6 AND AGAIN WHEN THEY WERE 7. THE HOME INTERVIEW WAS AN EXTENSIVE SET OF QUESTIONS DIRECTED TO THE MOTHER. IT WAS ADMINISTERED IN 2 SESSIONS, EACH LASTING ABOUT 1-1/2 HOURS. THE RESPONSES WERE RATED ON NUMERICAL SCALES FOR COMPUTER CODING. THE GENERAL AREAS COVERED BY THE INTERVIEW WERE (1) OPEN END-- INTERVIEWER'S RATINGS, (2) DEMOGRAPHIC MATERIAL, (3) INFORMATION ON THE CHILD, (4) MOTHER'S ATTITUDES TO SCHOOL AND JOB, AND (5) FAMILY ACTIVITIES AND LIVING PATTERNS. ALL QUESTIONS ARE GIVEN AND THE SCORING SCALES FOR THE RESPONSES ARE DESCRIBED. ADDITIONAL INFORMATION ON SPECIFIC PARTS OF THE INTERVIEW IS CONTAINED IN MANUALS PS 000 476 THROUGH PS 000 482. THE COMPLETE SET OF PROJECT MANUALS COMPRISES PS 000 475 THROUGH PS 000 492. (DR)

ED018254 PS000476
THE COGNITIVE ENVIRONMENTS OF URBAN PRE-SCHOOL CHILDREN. MANUAL OF INSTRUCTIONS FOR ADMINISTERING AND SCORING "SCHOOLS" QUESTION. HESS, ROBERT D.; AND OTHERS, 67 4P.
EDRS PRICE MF-$0.65 HC-$3.29

THIS MANUAL DESCRIBES MEASURES USED IN "THE COGNITIVE ENVIRONMENTS OF URBAN PRE-SCHOOL CHILDREN" PROJECT AT THE UNIVERSITY OF CHICAGO. THE SAMPLE FOR THE STUDY CONSISTED OF 163 NEGRO MOTHER-CHILD PAIRS SELECTED FROM 3 SOCIOECONOMIC CLASSES BASED ON THE FATHER'S OCCUPATION AND THE PARENTS' EDUCATION. A FOURTH GROUP INCLUDED FATHER-ABSENT FAMILIES. THE MOTHERS WERE INTERVIEWED AT HOME AND THE MOTHERS AND CHILDREN WERE TESTED AT THE UNIVERSITY OF CHICAGO WHEN THE CHILDREN WERE 4 YEARS OLD. FOLLOW-UP DATA WERE OBTAINED WHEN THE CHILDREN WERE 6 AND AGAIN WHEN THEY WERE 7. THE "SCHOOLS" QUESTION ASKED OF THE MOTHER WAS WHAT SHE WOULD DO ABOUT THE SCHOOLS IF SHE COULD DO AS SHE WISHED. RESPONSES WERE TAPE RECORDED AND TRANSCRIBED AND WERE SCORED BY THE PRESENCE OR ABSENCE OF SUGGESTIONS IN EACH OF 9 CATEGORIES GROUPED ROUGHLY AS (1) CONVENTIONAL, (2) SOCIAL OR POLITICAL, OR (3) ESSENTIALLY NO SUGGESTIONS. THIS IS A PART OF THE HOME INTERVIEW DESCRIBED IN PS 000 475. (DR)

ED018255 PS000477
THE COGNITIVE ENVIRONMENTS OF URBAN PRE-SCHOOL CHILDREN. MANUAL OF INSTRUCTIONS FOR ADMINISTERING AND SCORING EDUCATIONAL ATTITUDE SURVEY. HESS, ROBERT D.; AND OTHERS, 67 8P.
EDRS PRICE MF-$0.65 HC-$3.29

THIS MANUAL DESCRIBES MEASURES USED IN "THE COGNITIVE ENVIRONMENTS OF URBAN PRE-SCHOOL CHILDREN" PROJECT AT THE UNIVERSITY OF CHICAGO. THE SAMPLE FOR THE STUDY CONSISTED OF 163 NEGRO MOTHER-CHILD PAIRS SELECTED FROM 3 SOCIOECONOMIC CLASSES BASED ON THE FATHER'S OCCUPATION AND THE PARENTS' EDUCATION. A FOURTH GROUP INCLUDED FATHER-ABSENT FAMILIES. THE MOTHERS WERE INTERVIEWED AT HOME AND THE MOTHERS AND CHILDREN WERE TESTED AT THE UNIVERSITY OF CHICAGO WHEN THE CHILDREN WERE 4 YEARS OLD. FOLLOW-UP DATA WERE OBTAINED WHEN THE CHILDREN WERE 6 AND AGAIN WHEN THEY WERE 7. THE EDUCATIONAL ATTITUDE SURVEY IS A SET OF 27 STATEMENTS TO WHICH THE MOTHERS WERE ASKED TO RESPOND ON A 5-POINT AGREEMENT-DISAGREEMENT SCALE. THE SPECIFIC INSTRUCTIONS FOR THE MOTHERS ARE GIVEN IN THE MANUAL, AS ARE THE 27 STATEMENTS. PRINCIPAL COMPONENT FACTOR ANALYSIS OF THE 27 STATEMENTS GAVE 6 FACTORS WHICH WERE LABELED FOR THE MAIN THEME EXPRESSED BY THE FACTORS--(1) FUTILITY, (2) CONSERVATISM, (3) RESIGNATION, (4) IMPORTANCE OF EDUCATION, (5) DE-EMPHASIS OF EDUCATION, AND (6) GRIPES. THE SCORING ON THE FACTORS WAS ADJUSTED SO THAT A LOW SCORE INDICATED AGREEMENT WITH THE THEME OF THE FACTOR CLUSTER. THIS IS PART OF THE HOME INTERVIEW DESCRIBED IN PS 000 475. (DR)

ED018256 PS000478
THE COGNITIVE ENVIRONMENTS OF URBAN PRE-SCHOOL CHILDREN. MANUAL OF INSTRUCTIONS FOR ADMINISTERING AND SCORING MOTHER'S ATTITUDES TOWARD CHILD'S BEHAVIOR LEADING TO MASTERY. HESS, ROBERT D.; AND OTHERS, 67 7P.
EDRS PRICE MF-$0.65 HC-$3.29

THIS MANUAL DESCRIBES MEASURES USED IN "THE COGNITIVE ENVIRONMENTS OF URBAN PRE-SCHOOL CHILDREN" PROJECT AT THE UNIVERSITY OF CHICAGO. THE SAMPLE FOR THE STUDY CONSISTED OF 163 NEGRO MOTHER-CHILD PAIRS SELECTED FROM 3 SOCIOECONOMIC CLASSES BASED ON THE FATHER'S OCCUPATION AND THE PARENTS' EDUCATION. A FOURTH GROUP INCLUDED FATHER-ABSENT FAMILIES. THE MOTHERS WERE INTERVIEWED AT HOME AND THE MOTHERS AND CHILDREN WERE TESTED AT THE UNIVERSITY OF CHICAGO WHEN THE CHILDREN WERE 4 YEARS OLD. FOLLOW-UP DATA WERE OBTAINED WHEN THE CHILDREN WERE 6 AND AGAIN WHEN THEY WERE 7. TO DETERMINE HER ATTITUDES TOWARDS HER CHILD'S MASTERY BEHAVIOR, EACH MOTHER WAS GIVEN HYPOTHETICAL SITUATIONS IN WHICH HER CHILD'S BEHAVIOR IN MASTERING SKILLS CONFLICTED WITH OTHER PEOPLE OR DAMAGED OBJECTS. APPEALS USED TO CHANGE THE CHILD'S BEHAVIOR

WERE SCORED ACCORDING TO 3 BASIC TYPES--(1) THE STATUS-NORMATIVE, (2) THE PERSON-SUBJECTIVE, AND (3) THE COGNITIVE-RATIONAL. AN ADDITIONAL CATEGORY, UNSCORABLE, WAS USED FOR VAGUE OR INAPPROPRIATE RESPONSES. THE SITUATION DESCRIPTIONS AND THE CRITERIA USED FOR SCORING ARE GIVEN, AND THE BASIC SCORING CATEGORIES ARE DISCUSSED. THIS IS A PART OF THE HOME INTERVIEW DESCRIBED IN PS 000 475. (DR)

ED018257 PS000479
THE COGNITIVE ENVIRONMENTS OF URBAN PRE-SCHOOL CHILDREN. MANUAL OF INSTRUCTIONS FOR ADMINISTERING AND SCORING MOTHER'S ROLE IN TEACHER/CHILD AND CHILD/PEER SCHOOL SITUATIONS. HESS, ROBERT D.; AND OTHERS, 67 10P.
EDRS PRICE MF-$0.65 HC-$3.29

THIS MANUAL DESCRIBES MEASURES USED IN "THE COGNITIVE ENVIRONMENTS OF URBAN PRE-SCHOOL CHILDREN" PROJECT AT THE UNIVERSITY OF CHICAGO. THE SAMPLE FOR THE STUDY CONSISTED OF 163 NEGRO MOTHER-CHILD PAIRS SELECTED FROM 3 SOCIOECONOMIC CLASSES BASED ON THE FATHER'S OCCUPATION AND THE PARENTS' EDUCATION. A FOURTH GROUP INCLUDED FATHER-ABSENT FAMILIES. THE MOTHERS WERE INTERVIEWED AT HOME AND THE MOTHERS AND CHILDREN WERE TESTED AT THE UNIVERSITY OF CHICAGO WHEN THE CHILDREN WERE 4 YEARS OLD. FOLLOW-UP DATA WERE OBTAINED WHEN THE CHILDREN WERE 6 AND AGAIN WHEN THEY WERE 7. TO ASSESS THE MOTHER'S VIEW OF HER ROLE IN SCHOOL SITUATIONS, EACH MOTHER WAS GIVEN 8 HYPOTHETICAL SCHOOL SITUATIONS IN WHICH A CONFLICT OCCURRED BETWEEN HER CHILD AND THE TEACHER, A PEER, OR THE INSTITUTIONAL DEMANDS OF THE SCHOOL. IN HALF OF THE CASES THE CHILD WAS IN THE WRONG, AND IN THE OTHER HALF HE WAS THE INNOCENT VICTIM OF ANOTHER'S MISBEHAVIOR. RESPONSES WERE SCORED BY 2 SCHEMES. (1) THE TYPE OF THE MAJOR APPEAL USED IN THE MOTHER'S STATEMENT OF WHAT SHE WOULD DO WAS CLASSIFIED AS STATUS-NORMATIVE, PERSON-SUBJECTIVE, OR COGNITIVE-RATIONAL. (2) EACH RESPONSE UNIT, WHICH WAS BASICALLY A SUBJECT-PREDICATE PAIR, WAS SCORED IN THE SAME CATEGORIES, AND PERCENTAGES WERE COMPUTED FOR ALL 8 SITUATIONS. THE SITUATION DESCRIPTIONS AND THE CODING CRITERIA ARE GIVEN, AND THE SCORING CATEGORIES ARE DISCUSSED. THIS IS A PART OF THE HOME INTERVIEW DESCRIBED IN PS 000 475. (DR)

ED018258 PS000480
THE COGNITIVE ENVIRONMENTS OF URBAN PRE-SCHOOL CHILDREN. MANUAL OF INSTRUCTIONS FOR ADMINISTERING AND SCORING FIRST DAY. HESS, ROBERT D.; AND OTHERS, 67 16P.
EDRS PRICE MF-$0.65 HC-$3.29

THIS MANUAL DESCRIBES MEASURES USED IN "THE COGNITIVE ENVIRONMENTS OF URBAN PRE-SCHOOL CHILDREN" PROJECT AT THE UNIVERSITY OF CHICAGO. THE SAMPLE FOR THE STUDY CONSISTED OF 163 NEGRO MOTHER-CHILD PAIRS SELECTED FROM 3 SOCIOECONOMIC CLASSES BASED ON THE FATHER'S OCCUPATION AND THE PARENTS' EDUCATION. A FOURTH GROUP INCLUDED FATHER-ABSENT FAMILIES. THE MOTHERS WERE INTERVIEWED AT HOME AND THE MOTHERS AND CHILDREN WERE TESTED AT THE UNIVERSITY OF CHICAGO WHEN THE CHILDREN WERE 4 YEARS OLD. FOLLOW-UP DATA WERE OBTAINED WHEN THE CHILDREN WERE 6 AND AGAIN WHEN THEY WERE 7. EACH MOTHER WAS ASKED HOW SHE WOULD PREPARE HER CHILD FOR THE FIRST DAY OF SCHOOL. THE RESPONSES WERE TAPE RECORDED AND TRANSCRIBED AND WERE SCORED FOR CONTENT AND METHOD OF COMMUNICATION. SUBJECT-PREDICATE PAIRS WERE USED AS THE BASIC SCORING UNITS WITH EXCEPTIONS BEING MADE FOR OBVIOUSLY DEPENDENT CLAUSES. IMPLIED SUBJECTS AND VERBS WERE SUPPLIED WHEN CLEARLY INDICATED. THE NUMBER OF THESE UNITS WAS TALLIED AND THEN SCORED FOR CONTENT ACCORDING TO THE CATEGORIES (1) OBEDIENCE, (2) ACHIEVEMENT, (3) AFFECTIVE ELEMENTS, AND (4) PREPARATION. THE METHODS OF COMMUNICATION WERE CLASSED AS IMPERATIVE OR INSTRUCTIVE. THIS IS A PART OF THE HOME INTERVIEW DESCRIBED IN PS 000 475. (DR)

ED018259 PS000481
THE COGNITIVE ENVIRONMENTS OF URBAN PRE-SCHOOL CHILDREN. MANUAL OF INSTRUCTIONS FOR ADMINISTERING AND SCORING MOTHER-TEACHER PICTURE. HESS, ROBERT D.; AND OTHERS, 67 5P.
EDRS PRICE MF-$0.65 HC-$3.29

THIS MANUAL DESCRIBES MEASURES USED IN "THE COGNITIVE ENVIRONMENTS OF URBAN PRE-SCHOOL CHILDREN" PROJECT AT THE UNIVERSITY OF CHICAGO. THE SAMPLE FOR THE STUDY CONSISTED OF 163 NEGRO MOTHER-CHILD PAIRS SELECTED FROM 3 SOCIOECONOMIC CLASSES BASED ON THE FATHER'S OCCUPATION AND THE PARENTS' EDUCATION. A FOURTH GROUP INCLUDED FATHER-ABSENT FAMILIES. THE MOTHERS WERE INTERVIEWED AT HOME AND THE MOTHERS AND CHILDREN WERE TESTED AT THE UNIVERSITY OF CHICAGO WHEN THE CHILDREN WERE 4 YEARS OLD. FOLLOW-UP DATA WERE OBTAINED WHEN THE CHILDREN WERE 6 AND AGAIN WHEN THEY WERE 7. A PICTURE OF 2 NEGRO WOMEN SEATED AT A DESK WAS SHOWN TO THE MOTHER, AND SHE WAS TOLD IT WAS A PICTURE OF A TEACHER AND A MOTHER IN THE CLASSROOM. THE MOTHER WAS ASKED TO TELL A STORY ABOUT WHY THE MOTHER HAD COME TO THE SCHOOL AND WHAT THE MOTHER AND TEACHER WERE TALKING ABOUT. THE RESULT OF THE MOTHER-TEACHER CONVERSATION WAS ASKED FOR IF NOT VOLUNTEERED IN THE STORY. THE RESPONSES WERE TAPE RECORDED, AND THE TRANSCRIPTS WERE SCORED ACCORDING TO 3 CATEGORIES--(1) INITIATOR OF MEETING, (2) PURPOSE OR CONTENT OF MEETING, AND (3) MOTHER-TEACHER RELATIONSHIP. THIS IS A PART OF THE HOME INTERVIEW DESCRIBED IN PS 000 475 AND IS ONE OF THE SAMPLE SOURCES FOR THE LANGUAGE-STYLE ANALYSIS DESCRIBED IN PS 000 492. (DR)

ED018260 PS000482
THE COGNITIVE ENVIRONMENTS OF URBAN PRE-SCHOOL CHILDREN. MANUAL OF INSTRUCTIONS FOR ADMINISTERING AND SCORING HOME RESOURCES PATTERNS. HESS, ROBERT D.; AND OTHERS, 67 24P.
EDRS PRICE MF-$0.65 HC-$3.29

THIS MANUAL DESCRIBES MEASURES USED IN "THE COGNITIVE ENVIRONMENTS OF URBAN PRE-SCHOOL CHILDREN" PROJECT AT THE UNIVERSITY OF CHICAGO. THE SAMPLE FOR THE STUDY CONSISTED OF 163 NEGRO MOTHER-CHILD PAIRS SELECTED FROM 3 SOCIOECONOMIC CLASSES BASED ON THE FATHER'S OCCUPATION AND THE PARENTS' EDUCATION. A FOURTH GROUP INCLUDED FATHER-ABSENT FAMILIES. THE MOTHERS WERE INTERVIEWED AT HOME AND THE MOTHERS AND CHILDREN WERE TESTED AT THE UNIVERSITY OF CHICAGO WHEN THE CHILDREN WERE 4 YEARS OLD. FOLLOW-UP DATA WERE OBTAINED WHEN THE CHILDREN WERE 6 AND AGAIN WHEN THEY WERE 7. THE INFORMATION OBTAINED IN THIS PORTION OF THE HOME INTERVIEW WAS USED TO ASSESS THE DEGREE TO WHICH OBJECTS, EXPERIENCES, AND ATTITUDES IN THE HOME AID THE CHILD'S READINESS FOR SCHOOL. THE DATA WERE OBTAINED FROM THE MOTHER'S RESPONSES TO AN EXTENSIVE SERIES OF QUESTIONS SUPPLEMENTED BY THE INTERVIEWER'S OBSERVATIONS. THE RATING, ON A 5-POINT SCALE, WAS MADE FROM AN ASSESSMENT OF THE AVAILABILITY AND UTILIZATION OF THE RESOURCES WHICH WERE CLASSIFIED INTO 9 PATTERNS. INTERPRETATIONS OF THE RATINGS FOR EACH PATTERN ARE GIVEN. PRINCIPAL COMPONENT FACTOR ANALYSIS SHOWED THAT ALL 9 SCALES LOADED HEAVILY ON THE FIRST UNROTATED FACTOR. THE SCORE ON THIS FACTOR WAS USED AS THE BASIC HOME RESOURCES MEASURE. THIS IS A PART OF THE HOME INTERVIEW DESCRIBED IN PS 000 475 AND IS ONE OF THE SAMPLE SOURCES FOR THE LANGUAGE-STYLE ANALYSIS DESCRIBED IN PS 000 492. (DR)

ED018261 PS000483
THE COGNITIVE ENVIRONMENTS OF URBAN PRE-SCHOOL CHILDREN. MANUAL OF INSTRUCTIONS FOR ADMINISTERING AND SCORING THE TWENTY QUESTIONS TASK. HESS, ROBERT D.; AND OTHERS, 67 5P.
EDRS PRICE MF-$0.65 HC-$3.29

THIS MANUAL DESCRIBES MEASURES USED IN "THE COGNITIVE ENVIRONMENTS OF URBAN PRE-SCHOOL CHILDREN" PROJECT AT THE UNIVERSITY OF CHICAGO. THE SAMPLE FOR THE STUDY CONSISTED OF 163 NEGRO MOTHER-CHILD PAIRS SELECTED FROM 3 SOCIOECONOMIC CLASSES BASED ON THE FATHER'S OCCUPATION AND THE PARENTS' EDUCATION. A FOURTH GROUP INCLUDED FATHER-ABSENT FAMILIES. THE MOTHERS WERE INTERVIEWED AT HOME AND THE MOTHERS AND CHILDREN WERE TESTED AT THE UNIVERSITY OF CHICAGO WHEN THE CHILDREN WERE 4 YEARS OLD. FOLLOW-UP DATA WERE OBTAINED WHEN THE CHILDREN WERE 6 AND AGAIN WHEN THEY WERE 7. THE TWENTY QUESTIONS TASK WAS GIVEN AT THE FIRST TESTING SESSION AT THE UNIVERSITY. THE MOTHERS WERE GIVEN A TERSE DESCRIPTION OF AN AUTO ACCIDENT AND WERE REQUESTED TO ASK QUESTIONS ANSWERABLE BY "YES" OR "NO" TO DISCOVER WHY IT HAPPENED. THE RESPONSES WERE RECORDED VERBATIM AND THE SUBJECTS WERE SCORED ACCORDING TO SUCCESS IN SOLVING THE PROBLEM AND THE STRATEGY USED IN QUESTIONING. IN SCORING STRATEGIES, EACH QUESTION WAS CLASSED ACCORDING TO 4 CATEGORIES--(1) BROAD FOCUSING, (2) NARROW FOCUSING, (3) TRIAL AND ERROR, OR (4) IRRELEVANT. THE PERCENTAGE OF QUESTIONS FALLING IN EACH CATEGORY WAS COMPUTED. THE COMPLETE SET OF PROJECT MANUALS COMPRISES PS 000 475 THROUGH PS 000 492. (DR)

ED018262 PS000484
THE COGNITIVE ENVIRONMENTS OF URBAN PRE-SCHOOL CHILDREN. MANUAL OF INSTRUCTIONS FOR ADMINISTERING AND SCORING PLUTCHIK EXPLORATORY-INTEREST QUESTIONNAIRE. HESS, ROBERT D.; AND OTHERS, 67 4P.
EDRS PRICE MF-$0.65 HC-$3.29

THIS MANUAL DESCRIBES MEASURES USED IN "THE COGNITIVE ENVIRONMENTS OF URBAN PRE-SCHOOL CHILDREN" PROJECT AT THE UNIVERSITY OF CHICAGO. THE SAMPLE FOR THE STUDY CONSISTED OF 163 NEGRO MOTHER-CHILD PAIRS SELECTED FROM 3 SOCIOECONOMIC CLASSES BASED ON THE FATHER'S OCCUPATION AND THE PARENTS' EDUCATION. A FOURTH GROUP INCLUDED FATHER-ABSENT FAMILIES. THE MOTHERS WERE INTERVIEWED AT HOME AND THE MOTHERS AND CHILDREN WERE TESTED AT THE UNIVERSITY OF CHICAGO WHEN THE CHILDREN WERE 4 YEARS OLD. FOLLOW-UP DATA WERE OBTAINED WHEN THE CHILDREN WERE 6 AND AGAIN WHEN THEY WERE 7. IN ORDER TO MEASURE CURIOSITY MOTIVATION, THE PLUTCHIK EXPLORATORY-INTEREST QUESTIONNAIRE WAS ADMINISTERED DURING ONE OF THE UNIVERSITY TESTING SESSIONS. THE QUESTIONNAIRE CONSISTS OF 58 ITEMS DESCRIBING ACTIVITIES, HALF OF WHICH ARE CLASSED AS EXPLORATORY AND HALF OF WHICH ARE CLASSED AS NONEXPLORATORY. THE MOTHER WAS READ EACH ITEM AND WAS ASKED IF SHE LIKED OR DISLIKED THE

ACTIVITY. THE SUBJECTS WERE SCORED BY THE TOTAL NUMBER OF ACTIVITIES LIKED AND BY THE TOTAL NUMBER OF EXPLORATORY ACTIVITIES LIKED. THE COMPLETE SET OF PROJECT MANUALS COMPRISES PS 000 475 THROUGH PS 000 492. (DR)

ED018263 PS000485
THE COGNITIVE ENVIRONMENTS OF URBAN PRE-SCHOOL CHILDREN. MANUAL OF INSTRUCTIONS FOR ADMINISTERING AND SCORING SIGEL CONCEPTUAL STYLE SORTING TASKS. HESS, ROBERT D.; AND OTHERS, 67 15P.
EDRS PRICE MF-$0.65 HC-$3.29

THIS MANUAL DESCRIBES MEASURES USED IN "THE COGNITIVE ENVIRONMENTS OF URBAN PRE-SCHOOL CHILDREN" PROJECT AT THE UNIVERSITY OF CHICAGO. THE SAMPLE FOR THE STUDY CONSISTED OF 163 NEGRO MOTHER-CHILD PAIRS SELECTED FROM 3 SOCIOECONOMIC CLASSES BASED ON THE FATHER'S OCCUPATION AND THE PARENTS' EDUCATION. A FOURTH GROUP INCLUDED FATHER-ABSENT FAMILIES. THE MOTHERS WERE INTERVIEWED AT HOME AND THE MOTHERS AND CHILDREN WERE TESTED AT THE UNIVERSITY OF CHICAGO WHEN THE CHILDREN WERE 4 YEARS OLD. FOLLOW-UP DATA WERE OBTAINED WHEN THE CHILDREN WERE 6 AND AGAIN WHEN THEY WERE 7. THE SIGEL CONCEPTUAL STYLE SORTING TASK WAS ADMINISTERED AT THE FIRST UNIVERSITY TESTING SESSION. THE MOTHERS WERE SHOWN BLACK-AND-WHITE PAPER CUTOUTS OF HUMAN FIGURES WHICH HAD BEEN PLACED RANDOMLY ON A TABLETOP, AND THEY WERE ASKED TO PICK OUT ONE GROUP OF FIGURES HAVING A COMMON CHARACTERISTIC. THE REACTION TIME TAKEN BEFORE THE SUBJECT PICKED UP THE FIRST FIGURE WAS RECORDED, AND THE REASON OFFERED FOR THE GROUPING WAS RECORDED VERBATIM. THE MOTHER WAS ASKED TO MAKE 11 ADDITIONAL SORTS USING A DIFFERENT REASON FOR EACH GROUPING. THE CHILDREN WERE TESTED WITH 15 SETS OF BLACK-AND-WHITE PICTURES AND 5 SETS OF BLACK-AND-WHITE CUTOUTS. EACH SET HAD 4 ITEMS WHICH THE CHILD WAS SHOWN. ONE ITEM WAS SELECTED BY THE TESTER AS THE PRESENTATION PICTURE. THE CHILD WAS ASKED TO IDENTIFY THE 3 REMAINING ITEMS AND TO PICK THE ONE THAT BELONGED WITH THE PRESENTATION PICTURE. THE CHILDREN WERE ASKED TO GIVE REASONS FOR THEIR SELECTIONS. THE SCORING CATEGORIES WERE THE SAME FOR THE MOTHERS AND CHILDREN, AND FOLLOW DR. IRVING E. SIGEL'S CATEGORIES OF DESCRIPTIVE, FUNCTIONAL, AND CATEGORICAL CRITERIA. THE SUBJECTS WERE SCORED FOR BOTH THEIR SORTING AND THEIR VERBAL RESPONSES. THE COMPLETE SET OF PROJECT MANUALS COMPRISES PS 000 475 THROUGH PS 000 492. (DR)

ED018264 PS000486
THE COGNITIVE ENVIRONMENTS OF URBAN PRE-SCHOOL CHILDREN. MANUAL OF INSTRUCTIONS FOR ADMINISTERING AND SCORING TOY SORTING TASK. HESS, ROBERT D.; AND OTHERS, 67 6P.
EDRS PRICE MF-$0.65 HC-$3.29

THIS MANUAL DESCRIBES MEASURES USED IN "THE COGNITIVE ENVIRONMENTS OF URBAN PRE-SCHOOL CHILDREN" PROJECT AT THE UNIVERSITY OF CHICAGO. THE SAMPLE FOR THE STUDY CONSISTED OF 163 NEGRO MOTHER-CHILD PAIRS SELECTED FROM 3 SOCIOECONOMIC CLASSES BASED ON THE FATHER'S OCCUPATION AND THE PARENTS' EDUCATION. A FOURTH GROUP INCLUDED FATHER-ABSENT FAMILIES. THE MOTHERS WERE INTERVIEWED AT HOME AND THE MOTHERS AND CHILDREN WERE TESTED AT THE UNIVERSITY OF CHICAGO WHEN THE CHILDREN WERE 4 YEARS OLD. FOLLOW-UP DATA WERE OBTAINED WHEN THE CHILDREN WERE 6 AND AGAIN WHEN THEY WERE 7. THE TOY SORTING TASK WAS THE FIRST OF 3 MOTHER-CHILD INTERACTION TASKS GIVEN DURING THE SECOND UNIVERSITY TESTING SESSION. THE OTHER 2 ARE DESCRIBED IN MANUALS PS 000 487 AND PS 000 489. THE TASK CONSISTED OF GROUPING 9 TOYS INTO 3 CLASSES BASED ON EITHER THE KIND OF TOY OR ITS COLOR. THE MOTHER WAS SHOWN THE 2 POSSIBLE SORTING METHODS AND WAS THEN ASKED TO TEACH HER CHILD HOW TO SORT THE TOYS BOTH WAYS. THE MOTHER WAS GIVEN FREEDOM OF TIME AND METHOD FOR TEACHING HER CHILD. THE TECHNIQUES USED TO OBSERVE HER TEACHING ARE DESCRIBED IN PS 000 491. THE CHILD WAS THEN ASKED TO SORT THE TOYS THE WAY HIS MOTHER TAUGHT HIM AND TO TELL THE REASON FOR EACH SORT. THE SCORING WAS ON A 6-POINT SCALE, A POINT BEING GIVEN FOR EACH CORRECT SORT, FOR A PARTIAL EXPLANATION OF EACH SORT, AND FOR A FULL EXPLANATION OF EACH SORT. THE COMPLETE SET OF PROJECT MANUALS COMPRISES PS 000 475 THROUGH PS 000 492. (DR)

ED018265 PS000487
THE COGNITIVE ENVIRONMENTS OF URBAN PRE-SCHOOL CHILDREN. MANUAL OF INSTRUCTIONS FOR ADMINISTERING AND SCORING THE EIGHT-BLOCK SORTING TASK. HESS, ROBERT D.; AND OTHERS, 67 9P.
EDRS PRICE MF-$0.65 HC-$3.29

THIS MANUAL DESCRIBES MEASURES USED IN "THE COGNITIVE ENVIRONMENTS OF URBAN PRE-SCHOOL CHILDREN" PROJECT AT THE UNIVERSITY OF CHICAGO. THE SAMPLE FOR THE STUDY CONSISTED OF 163 NEGRO MOTHER-CHILD PAIRS SELECTED FROM 3 SOCIOECONOMIC CLASSES BASED ON THE FATHER'S OCCUPATION AND THE PARENTS' EDUCATION. A FOURTH GROUP INCLUDED FATHER-ABSENT FAMILIES. THE MOTHERS WERE INTERVIEWED AT HOME AND THE MOTHERS AND CHILDREN WERE TESTED AT THE UNIVERSITY OF CHICAGO WHEN THE CHILDREN WERE 4 YEARS OLD. FOLLOW-UP DATA WERE OBTAINED WHEN THE CHILDREN WERE 6 AND AGAIN WHEN THEY WERE 7. THE BLOCK SORTING TASK WAS THE SECOND OF 3 MOTHER-CHILD INTERACTION TASKS GIVEN DURING THE SECOND UNIVERSITY TESTING SESSION. THE OTHER 2 ARE DESCRIBED IN PS 000 486 AND PS 000 489. EIGHT BLOCKS HAVING 4 DISTINGUISHABLE ATTRIBUTES--HEIGHT, SHAPE, COLOR, AND A MARK--WERE SORTED INTO 4 GROUPS USING PAIRS OF ATTRIBUTES. EACH MOTHER WAS SHOWN THE BASIS OF THE GROUPINGS SO THAT ADDITIONAL BLOCKS COULD BE CORRECTLY ADDED. SHE WAS THEN ASKED TO TEACH HER CHILD HOW TO ADD EXTRA BLOCKS TO THE GROUPS. HER INSTRUCTION WAS OBSERVED AS DESCRIBED IN PS 000 491 AND SCORED AS DESCRIBED IN PS 000 488. THE CHILD WAS TESTED WITH 2 NEW BLOCKS. SCORING WAS ON A 6-POINT SCALE, A POINT BEING GIVEN FOR EACH CORRECT PLACEMENT AND FOR EACH ATTRIBUTE MENTIONED AS A REASON FOR PLACEMENT. THE COMPLETE SET OF PROJECT MANUALS COMPRISES PS 000 475 THROUGH PS 000 492. (DR)

ED018266 PS000488
THE COGNITIVE ENVIRONMENTS OF URBAN PRE-SCHOOL CHILDREN. MANUAL FOR CODING MOTHER-CHILD INTERACTION ON THE EIGHT-BLOCK SORTING TASK. HESS, ROBERT D.; AND OTHERS, 67 75P.
EDRS PRICE MF-$0.65 HC-$3.29

THIS MANUAL DESCRIBES MEASURES USED IN "THE COGNITIVE ENVIRONMENTS OF URBAN PRE-SCHOOL CHILDREN" PROJECT AT THE UNIVERSITY OF CHICAGO. THE SAMPLE FOR THE STUDY CONSISTED OF 163 NEGRO MOTHER-CHILD PAIRS SELECTED FROM 3 SOCIOECONOMIC CLASSES BASED ON THE FATHER'S OCCUPATION AND THE PARENTS' EDUCATION. A FOURTH GROUP INCLUDED FATHER-ABSENT FAMILIES. THE MOTHERS WERE INTERVIEWED AT HOME AND THE MOTHERS AND CHILDREN WERE TESTED AT THE UNIVERSITY OF CHICAGO WHEN THE CHILDREN WERE 4 YEARS OLD. FOLLOW-UP DATA WERE OBTAINED WHEN THE CHILDREN WERE 6 AND AGAIN WHEN THEY WERE 7. THE MOTHER-CHILD INTERACTION OBSERVED IN THE 8-BLOCK SORTING TASK (PS 000 487) WAS ANALYZED ACCORDING TO 2 SCHEMES. THE FIRST SCHEME DIVIDES THE INTERACTION INTO MESSAGE UNITS, AND THE SECOND SCHEME CONCENTRATES ON QUALITATIVE ASPECTS OF BEHAVIOR. THE MESSAGE UNITS WERE CATEGORIZED AND CODED ACCORDING TO SUCH SCHEMA AS VERBAL MESSAGE TYPE, PHYSICAL MESSAGE TYPE, AND FEEDBACK FROM CHILD. FROM THESE MESSAGE UNITS, 15 MATERNAL AND 16 CHILD MEASURES WERE CALCULATED. THE BEHAVIORAL ANALYSIS WAS USED TO CALCULATE 13 MATERNAL AND 2 CHILD MEASURES. PRINCIPAL COMPONENT FACTOR ANALYSIS OF THESE MEASURES FOUND 6 MATERNAL AND 4 CHILD FACTORS. THE FACTORS FOR THE MOTHER WERE DESIGNATED (1) REWARD-ORIENTED MOTIVATION TECHNIQUES, (2) PUNISHMENT-ORIENTED MOTIVATION TECHNIQUES, (3) ORIENTATION, (4) SPECIFICITY IN PRERESPONSE INSTRUCTIONS, (5) SPECIFICITY IN POSTRESPONSE FEEDBACK, AND (6) GENERAL SATURATION OF TASK-SPECIFIC INFORMATION. THOSE FOR THE CHILD WERE LABELED (7) RESISTANCE, (8) BLOCK PLACEMENT ERRORS, (9) VERBALIZATION OF LABELS, AND (10) VERBAL PARTICIPATION. FACTOR SCORES WERE BASED ON UNROTATED, NONORTHOGANAL FACTORS SO THAT SOME CORRELATIONS ARE PRESENT. THE COMPLETE SET OF PROJECT MANUALS COMPRISES PS 000 475 THROUGH PS 000 492. (DR)

ED018267 PS000489
THE COGNITIVE ENVIRONMENTS OF URBAN PRE-SCHOOL CHILDREN. MANUAL OF INSTRUCTIONS FOR ADMINISTERING AND SCORING "ETCH-A-SKETCH" TASK. HESS, ROBERT D.; AND OTHERS, 67 16P.
EDRS PRICE MF-$0.65 HC-$3.29

THIS MANUAL DESCRIBES MEASURES USED IN "THE COGNITIVE ENVIRONMENTS OF URBAN PRE-SCHOOL CHILDREN" PROJECT AT THE UNIVERSITY OF CHICAGO. THE SAMPLE FOR THE STUDY CONSISTED OF 163 NEGRO MOTHER-CHILD PAIRS SELECTED FROM 3 SOCIOECONOMIC CLASSES BASED ON THE FATHER'S OCCUPATION AND THE PARENTS' EDUCATION. A FOURTH GROUP INCLUDED FATHER-ABSENT FAMILIES. THE MOTHERS WERE INTERVIEWED AT HOME AND THE MOTHERS AND CHILDREN WERE TESTED AT THE UNIVERSITY OF CHICAGO WHEN THE CHILDREN WERE 4 YEARS OLD. FOLLOW-UP DATA WERE OBTAINED WHEN THE CHILDREN WERE 6 AND AGAIN WHEN THEY WERE 7. THE "ETCH-A-SKETCH" TASK WAS THE LAST OF 3 MOTHER-CHILD INTERACTION TASKS GIVEN DURING THE SECOND UNIVERSITY TESTING SESSION. THE OTHER 2 ARE DESCRIBED IN MANUALS PS 000 486 AND PS 000 487. THE "ETCH-A-SKETCH" TOY USED HAS 2 KNOBS WHICH CONTROL THE VERTICAL AND HORIZONTAL MOTIONS OF AN ERASABLE LINE TRACE. THE MOTHER WAS SHOWN HOW TO USE THE TOY FIRST AND WAS ALLOWED TO BECOME FAMILIAR WITH IT. SHE WAS THEN GIVEN AN OPPORTUNITY TO SHOW IT TO HER CHILD. THE TESTER THEN ASKED THEM TO COPY 5 FIGURES OF INCREASING COMPLEXITY DRAWN ON CARDS, WITH THE MOTHER WORKING ONE KNOB AND THE CHILD THE OTHER. THE FIGURES PRODUCED WERE TRACED BY THE TESTER FOR SCORING. FOUR PERFORMANCE MEASURES, BASED ON THE DRAWN FIGURE AND THE TIME TAKEN TO COMPLETE IT, WERE OBTAINED. IN ADDITION, THE MOTHER WAS SCORED ON 3 TEACHING MEASURES BASED ON (1) PRACTICE PERIOD BEHAVIOR, (2) SPECIFICITY OF DIRECTIONS, AND (3) USE OF THE CARDS AS MODELS. THE COMPLETE SET OF PROJECT MANUALS COMPRISES PS 000 475 THROUGH PS 000 492. (DR)

ED018268 PS000490
THE COGNITIVE ENVIRONMENTS OF URBAN PRE-SCHOOL CHILDREN. MANUAL OF INSTRUCTIONS FOR ADMINISTERING AND SCORING THE CURIOSITY TASK. HESS, ROBERT D.; AND OTHERS, 67 6P.
EDRS PRICE MF-$0.65 HC-$3.29

THIS MANUAL DESCRIBES MEASURES USED IN "THE COGNITIVE ENVIRONMENTS OF URBAN PRE-SCHOOL CHILDREN" PROJECT AT THE UNIVERSITY OF CHICAGO. THE SAMPLE FOR THE STUDY CONSISTED OF 163 NEGRO MOTHER-CHILD PAIRS SELECTED FROM 3 SOCIOECONOMIC CLASSES BASED ON THE FATHER'S OCCUPATION AND THE PARENTS' EDUCATION. A FOURTH GROUP INCLUDED FATHER-ABSENT FAMILIES. THE MOTHERS WERE INTERVIEWED AT HOME AND THE MOTHERS AND CHILDREN WERE TESTED AT THE UNIVERSITY OF CHICAGO WHEN THE CHILDREN WERE 4 YEARS OLD. FOLLOW-UP DATA WERE OBTAINED WHEN THE CHILDREN WERE 6 AND AGAIN WHEN THEY WERE 7. THE CURIOSITY TASK WAS GIVEN TO THE CHILD DURING THE SECOND UNIVERSITY TESTING SESSION. SIXTEEN PICTURES, DIVIDED INTO 8 COMPLEX/SIMPLE PAIRS OF SIMILAR STIMULUS TYPES, WERE SHOWN TO THE CHILD IN A BOX WHICH LIT WHEN THE CHILD'S HEAD WAS PUSHED AGAINST A BAR. THE VIEWING TIME WAS AUTOMATICALLY RECORDED. SCORING WAS BASED ON (1) THE TOTAL VIEWING TIME IN SECONDS, (2) THE TOTAL COMPLEX-PICTURE VIEWING TIME, AND (3) THE TOTAL SIMPLE-PICTURE VIEWING TIME. IN ADDITION, "CURIOSITY PROPORTIONS," DEFINED AS THE RATIO OF COMPLEX TO COMPLEX PLUS SIMPLE VIEWING TIME, WERE CALCULATED FOR EACH PAIR, FOR EACH TYPE OF STIMULUS COMPLEXITY, AND FOR THE OVERALL TASK. THE COMPLETE SET OF PROJECT MANUALS COMPRISES PS 000 475 THROUGH PS 000 492. (DR)

ED018269 PS000491
THE COGNITIVE ENVIRONMENTS OF URBAN PRE-SCHOOL CHILDREN. MANUAL OF RECORDING AND OBSERVATION TECHNIQUES FOR MOTHER-CHILD INTERACTION. HESS, ROBERT D.; AND OTHERS, 67 6P.
EDRS PRICE MF-$0.65 HC-$3.29

THIS MANUAL DESCRIBES MEASURES USED IN "THE COGNITIVE ENVIRONMENTS OF URBAN PRE-SCHOOL CHILDREN" PROJECT AT THE UNIVERSITY OF CHICAGO. THE SAMPLE FOR THE STUDY CONSISTED OF 163 NEGRO MOTHER-CHILD PAIRS SELECTED FROM 3 SOCIOECONOMIC CLASSES BASED ON THE FATHER'S OCCUPATION AND THE PARENTS' EDUCATION. A FOURTH GROUP INCLUDED FATHER-ABSENT FAMILIES. THE MOTHERS WERE INTERVIEWED AT HOME AND THE MOTHERS AND CHILDREN WERE TESTED AT THE UNIVERSITY OF CHICAGO WHEN THE CHILDREN WERE 4 YEARS OLD. FOLLOW-UP DATA WERE OBTAINED WHEN THE CHILDREN WERE 6 AND AGAIN WHEN THEY WERE 7. THE INTERACTIONS OF THE MOTHER AND CHILD DURING THE TOY SORTING (PS 000 486) AND BLOCK SORTING (PS 000 487) TASKS WERE OBSERVED AND TAPE RECORDED. THE OBSERVER WAS IN AN ADJACENT ROOM WITH A ONE-WAY OBSERVATION WINDOW AND RECORDED A RUNNING DESCRIPTION. THE DESCRIPTION TAPE AND THE TAPE OF THE MOTHER'S AND CHILD'S VOICES WERE COORDINATED BY SUPERIMPOSED TIME SIGNALS. THE DESCRIPTIONS WERE MADE AT THE LEVEL OF THE MOLAR BEHAVIORAL ACT, WITH THE CONTEXT OF THE ACT GIVEN EXPLICITLY. INITIAL TESTING WITH 2 OBSERVERS INDICATED THAT ONLY 1 OBSERVATION TAPE WAS NECESSARY. AN ADVANTAGE OF THE OBSERVATION TAPE TECHNIQUE IS THAT IT PRESERVES RAW DATA FOR ANY LATER, MORE REFINED ANALYSES. THE COMPLETE SET OF PROJECT MANUALS COMPRISES PS 000 475 THROUGH PS 000 492. (DR)

ED018270 PS000492
THE COGNITIVE ENVIRONMENTS OF URBAN PRE-SCHOOL CHILDREN. MANUAL OF INSTRUCTIONS FOR ADMINISTERING AND SCORING MATERNAL LANGUAGE STYLES. HESS, ROBERT D.; AND OTHERS, 67 30P.
EDRS PRICE MF-$0.65 HC-$3.29

THIS MANUAL DESCRIBES MEASURES USED IN "THE COGNITIVE ENVIRONMENTS OF URBAN PRE-SCHOOL CHILDREN" PROJECT AT THE UNIVERSITY OF CHICAGO. THE SAMPLE FOR THE STUDY CONSISTED OF 163 NEGRO MOTHER-CHILD PAIRS SELECTED FROM 3 SOCIOECONOMIC CLASSES BASED ON THE FATHER'S OCCUPATION AND THE PARENTS' EDUCATION. A FOURTH GROUP INCLUDED FATHER-ABSENT FAMILIES. THE MOTHERS WERE INTERVIEWED AT HOME AND THE MOTHERS AND CHILDREN WERE TESTED AT THE UNIVERSITY OF CHICAGO WHEN THE CHILDREN WERE 4 YEARS OLD. FOLLOW-UP DATA WERE OBTAINED WHEN THE CHILDREN WERE 6 AND AGAIN WHEN THEY WERE 7. IN ORDER TO DETERMINE MATERNAL LANGUAGE STYLES, LANGUAGE SAMPLES WERE OBTAINED FROM VERBATIM TRANSCRIPTS OF TAPE-RECORDED RESPONSES TO (1) THE TYPICAL-DAY QUESTION (DESCRIBED IN PS 000 482), (2) THE MOTHER-TEACHER PICTURE (DESCRIBED IN PS 000 481), AND (3) THE CHILDREN'S APPERCEPTION TEST CARD NO. 3. LANGUAGE SAMPLES WERE ANALYZED AND SCORED, USING THE CRITERIA DESCRIBED IN THE MANUAL, FOR (1) MEAN SENTENCE LENGTH, (2) MEAN PRE-VERB LENGTH, (3) UNCOMMON ADJECTIVES, (4) UNCOMMON ADVERBS, (5) VERB ELABORATION, (6) ABSTRACTION, (7) STRUCTURE ELABORATION, AND (8) CONTENT ELABORATION. THE PRINCIPAL COMPONENT FACTOR ANALYSIS DISCLOSED A SINGLE FACTOR INVOLVING (1), (2), (5), AND (7) ABOVE. SCORES ON THESE FACTORS WERE CONVERTED TO Z-SCORES, AND A MEAN Z-SCORE WAS COMPUTED FOR EACH LANGUAGE SAMPLE. THESE WERE THEN AVERAGED FOR EACH SUBJECT TO OBTAIN THE AVERAGE LANGUAGE ELABORATION T-SCORE. THE COMPLETE SET OF PROJECT MANUALS COMPRISES PS 000 475 THROUGH PS 000 492. (DR)

ED018271 PS000745
THE HUMAN CONNECTION--LANGUAGE AND LITERATURE. MARTIN, BILL, JR., 67 52P.
EDRS PRICE MF-$0.65 HC NOT AVAILABLE FROM EDRS.

THE AUTHOR CHARACTERIZES THIS BULLETIN AS A MESSAGE ON LANGUAGE. THE MESSAGE IS FACILITATED BY (1) A FLUID AND IMAGINATIVE USE OF TYPESETTING, (2) A NARRATIVE-FORM STORY, AND (3) A STORY-PLOT THAT INVOLVES SEVERAL LANGUAGE PROBLEMS AND SOLUTIONS. ALTHOUGH THE STORY COMPRISES THE ENTIRE BULLETIN, THE PURPOSE OF THE BULLETIN IS NOT JUST TO TELL A STORY. ITS PURPOSE, IN PART, IS TO ILLUSTRATE THE DIFFICULTIES LANGUAGE CAN CREATE AND THE BETTER UNDERSTANDING OF YOURSELF AND OTHERS THAT THE PROPER USE OF LANGUAGE CAN PROVIDE. LANGUAGE, AS COMMUNICATION BETWEEN PEOPLE, CAN BE EITHER A SOURCE OF UNDERSTANDING OR OF ALIENATION. THE KINDERGARTEN TEACHER IN THE STORY STRUGGLES WITH TURNING HER INITIAL ALIENATION FROM A STRONG-WILLED LITTLE BOY INTO UNDERSTANDING OF HIS INDIVIDUAL PERSONALITY. BY DISCUSSING THE PROBLEM WITH THE PRINCIPAL, WITH OTHER TEACHERS AT A TEACHERS' MEETING, AND WITH HERSELF, SHE COMES TO UNDERSTAND AND APPRECIATE THE BOY'S ABILITIES AND, AT THE SAME TIME, HER OWN LACK OF INSIGHT. SOON SHE IS ABLE TO CHANNEL THE BOY'S INDIVIDUAL STRENGTHS TO THE BENEFIT OF ALL. THE STORY POINTS OUT THAT LANGUAGE AS A MEDIUM OF COMMUNICATION IS ONLY EFFECTIVE WHEN THE LISTENER LISTENS CAREFULLY. THE IMPORT OF THE COMMUNICATION OFTEN GOES BEYOND THE SPOKEN WORD. ANOTHER LESSON THE STORY INTRODUCES IS THE GREAT NEED FOR FLEXIBLE, CREATIVE, AND IMAGINATIVE INSTRUCTION IN GUIDING CHILDREN'S LANGUAGE DEVELOPMENT. THE VERBAL CHARACTERISTICS OF CHILDREN ARE AS DIFFERENT AS THEIR SOCIAL PERSONALITIES. INTERACTION BETWEEN LANGUAGE AND EXPERIENCE IS AN AREA OF LANGUAGE INSTRUCTION THAT NEEDS MORE EFFECTIVE IMPLEMENTATION IN ALL ASPECTS OF TEACHING. THIS DOCUMENT IS AVAILABLE FROM THE NATIONAL EDUCATION ASSOCIATION, 1201 SIXTEENTH STREET, N.W., WASHINGTON, D.C. 20036 FOR $1.50. (WD)

ED018272 PS000777
IN-SERVICE EDUCATION IN ELEMENTARY SCHOOL MATHEMATICS. , 67 60P.
EDRS PRICE MF-$0.65 HC NOT AVAILABLE FROM EDRS.

A BULLETIN WHICH EMPHASIZES THE NEED FOR EFFECTIVE INSERVICE EDUCATION IN ELEMENTARY SCHOOL MATHEMATICS BEGINS WITH AN INTRODUCTORY SECTION WHICH (1) DESCRIBES TYPICAL ELEMENTARY SCHOOL ORGANIZATIONAL PATTERNS AND MATHEMATICS PROGRAMS, (2) LISTS FACTORS WHICH INFLUENCE TEACHERS' ATTITUDES TOWARDS MATHEMATICS TEACHING, AND (3) CITES IMPLICATIONS OF (1) AND (2) FOR INSERVICE EDUCATION PROGRAMS. THE CENTRAL PORTION OF THE BULLETIN DESCRIBES 3 TYPES OF EXISTING INSERVICE EDUCATION PROGRAMS. THE FIRST TYPE IS SELF-DIRECTED STUDY. PUBLICATIONS AND MATERIALS SUITABLE FOR USE IN PROGRAMS OF INDEPENDENT STUDY ARE ENUMERATED. THE SECOND TYPE CONSISTS OF DIRECTED SHORT-TERM STUDIES WHICH ARE CLASSIFIED AS ORIENTATION CONFERENCES AND AS WORKSHOPS AND INSTITUTES. REPRESENTATIVE PROGRAMS OF THIS TYPE ARE DESCRIBED. THE THIRD TYPE IS DIRECTED LONG-TERM STUDY. DESCRIPTIONS ARE PRESENTED OF PROGRAMS OF THIS TYPE WHICH ARE CURRENTLY IN OPERATION UNDER (1) LOCAL SPONSORSHIP, (2) JOINT STATE AND LOCAL SPONSORSHIP, AND (3) JOINT NATIONAL, STATE, AND LOCAL SPONSORSHIP. THE THIRD PRINCIPAL SECTION OF THE BULLETIN DISCUSSES THE ESTABLISHMENT OF GOALS, STANDARDS, AND EVALUATION CRITERIA FOR INSERVICE EDUCATION PROGRAMS AND SUGGESTS WAYS IN WHICH SCHOOL SYSTEMS CAN ENCOURAGE CONTINUING EDUCATION FOR TEACHERS. APPENDIXES INCLUDE A BIBLIOGRAPHY AND SOURCES OF MATHEMATICS INFORMATION. THIS DOCUMENT IS AVAILABLE FROM THE NATIONAL COUNCIL OF TEACHERS OF MATHEMATICS, 1201 SIXTEENTH STREET, N.W., WASHINGTON, D.C. 20036. (JS)

ED018273 PS000778
UNDERSTANDING THE FOURTH GRADE SLUMP IN CREATIVE THINKING. FINAL REPORT. TORRANCE, E. PAUL, DEC67 443P.
EDRS PRICE MF-$0.65 HC-$16.45

STUDIES OF CREATIVITY AND OF PSYCHOLOGICAL DISTURBANCES IN CHILDREN HAVE SUGGESTED THE PRESENCE OF SLUMPS (OR INVERSIONS) WHICH MAY BE CORRELATED WITH DEVELOPMENTAL TRANSITIONS. THE MOST NOTABLE OF THESE OCCURS AT ABOUT THE FOURTH GRADE AND IS THE OBJECT OF THIS STUDY. THREE SETS OF INVESTIGATIONS WERE UNDERTAKEN--(1) A STUDY OF CREATIVE DEVELOPMENT IN 7 CULTURES, (2) A STUDY OF THE DEVELOPMENT OF CONFORMITY TENDENCIES, AND (3) LONGITUDINAL STUDIES OF CREATIVE DEVELOPMENT. THE 7 CULTURES SELECTED WERE (1) UNITED STATES, DOMINANT, ADVANTAGED, (2) UNITED STATES, SEGREGATED, NEGRO, (3) WESTERN AUSTRALIA, (4) WESTERN SAMOA, (5) WEST GERMANY, (6) NORWAY, AND (7) INDIA. THE BASIC DATA WERE OBTAINED FROM A BATTERY OF VERBAL AND NONVERBAL TESTS GIVEN TO THE CHILDREN AND WERE SUPPLEMENTED WITH INFORMATION FROM TEACHERS ABOUT THEIR TEACHING PRACTICES AND THEIR CONCEPTS OF AN "IDEAL PUPIL." SAMPLE SIZES FOR EACH CULTURE RANGED FROM 500 TO 1000

CHILDREN COVERING GRADES 1 THROUGH 6. THE CONFORMITY TENDENCIES WERE EXPLORED IN A SERIES OF 6 STUDIES, EACH INVOLVING FROM 150 TO 500 U.S. ADVANTAGED-CULTURE CHILDREN IN GRADES 2 THROUGH 6. THE LONGITUDINAL STUDY WAS BASED ON A SAMPLE OF 100 U.S. ADVANTAGED-CULTURE CHILDREN WHOSE PERFORMANCES IN THE THIRD, FOURTH, AND FIFTH GRADES WERE COMPARED. THE INTERCULTURAL STUDY FOUND THAT DISCONTINUITIES IN DEVELOPMENT OCCUR IN MOST CULTURES AND CONCLUDED THAT THERE IS EVIDENCE TO SUGGEST THAT THEY ARE ASSOCIATED WITH THE IMPOSITION OF ADDITIONAL SOCIAL DEMANDS. THE TEACHERS' RESPONSES ON AN IDEAL PUPIL CHECKLIST PROVED ABLE, WHEN COMPARED WITH THOSE OF AN EXPERT PANEL ASKED TO DETERMINE THE CHARACTERISTICS OF A CREATIVE CHILD, TO PREDICT THE RELATIVE ACHIEVEMENTS OF THE DIFFERENT CULTURES' CHILDREN IN CREATIVITY. THE CONFORMITY STUDIES REVEALED AN INCREASED TENDENCY FOR CHILDREN TO CONSULT WITH THEIR PEERS AT ABOUT THE FOURTH GRADE, AND THE LONGITUDINAL STUDY CONFIRMED THE EXISTENCE OF THE SLUMP IN INDIVIDUALS. (DR)

ED018274 PS000844
ART EDUCATION IN THE ELEMENTARY SCHOOL. PACKWOOD, MARY M., ED., 67
DOCUMENT NOT AVAILABLE FROM EDRS.

ART EDUCATION IN THE ELEMENTARY SCHOOL IS THE SUBJECT OF THIS MULTIPLE-AUTHOR DOCUMENT WHICH BEGINS WITH A CHAPTER ON THE ROLE OF ART IN CONTEMPORARY SOCIETY. THE BASIC PRINCIPLES WHICH SERVE AS THE FOUNDATION FOR THE DEVELOPMENT OF AN EFFECTIVE PROGRAM OF ART INSTRUCTION AND THE FACTORS TO BE CONSIDERED IN PLANNING FOR THE TEACHING OF ART ARE PRESENTED IN THE SECOND CHAPTER. CITING DEVELOPMENTAL STAGES WHICH ARE TYPICAL OF ELEMENTARY SCHOOL STUDENTS, A CHAPTER CONCERNED WITH THE SELECTION OF ART EXPERIENCES SUITABLE TO THESE VARIOUS LEVELS OF DEVELOPMENT ENUMERATES (1) THE CHARACTERISTICS OF THE CHILD AND HIS VISUAL EXPRESSION, (2) GROWTH EXPECTATIONS AND THEIR IMPLICATIONS FOR MOTIVATION AND GUIDANCE, (3) SUGGESTED LEARNINGS, (4) EXPERIENCES EMPHASIZING DIFFERENT ASPECTS OF LEARNING, AND (5) TEACHING APPROACHES. THE FORMULATION OF OBJECTIVES AND THE EVALUATION OF STUDENT PROGRESS, TEACHER EFFECTIVENESS, AND CURRICULUM EFFECTIVENESS ARE THE SUBJECTS OF THE SUBSEQUENT CHAPTER. CONCERNED WITH THE RELATIONSHIP AND INTERACTION OF THE SCHOOL ART PROGRAM AND THE COMMUNITY, THE CONCLUDING CHAPTER EMPHASIZES THE NEED FOR THE CULTIVATION OF AN INFORMED AND COOPERATIVE CITIZENRY. AN ANNOTATED BIBLIOGRAPHY AND LISTS OF SUITABLE VISUAL AIDS AND REQUISITE FACILITIES, EQUIPMENT, AND SUPPLIES ARE APPENDED. THIS DOCUMENT IS AVAILABLE FROM THE NATIONAL ART EDUCATION ASSOCIATION, 1201 16TH STREET, N.W., WASHINGTON, D.C. 20036. (JS)

ED018275 PS000845
SOCIAL STUDIES IN ELEMENTARY SCHOOLS (THIRTY-SECOND YEARBOOK). MICHAELIS, JOHN U., ED., 62 343P.
EDRS PRICE MF-$0.65 HC NOT AVAILABLE FROM EDRS.

THIS YEARBOOK IS INTENDED TO PRESENT AN OVERVIEW OF RECENT TRENDS, ISSUES, AND PROBLEMS IN ELEMENTARY SCHOOL SOCIAL STUDIES. CHAPTER I EXAMINES THE CURRENT CHALLENGE TO SOCIAL STUDIES, DISCUSSES THE CHARACTERISTICS AND PURPOSES OF AN EFFECTIVE SOCIAL STUDIES PROGRAM, AND PROVIDES A SUMMARY OF THE YEARBOOK'S CONTENTS. CHAPTER II EXAMINES ISSUES INVOLVING THE SOCIAL AND PSYCHOLOGICAL FOUNDATIONS OF THE SOCIAL SCIENCES IN 4 ARTICLES DEALING WITH (1) SOCIAL DEMANDS AND PROBLEMS, (2) CHILDREN'S SOCIAL PERCEPTION, (3) PRINCIPLES FROM STUDIES OF CHILD DEVELOPMENT, AND (4) LEARNING, PROBLEM SOLVING, AND DECISION MAKING IN THE CLASSROOM. CHAPTER III CONTAINS 2 ARTICLES WHICH DEAL WITH CONTENT IN THE SOCIAL SCIENCES--ONE PRESENTS A COLLECTION OF GENERALIZATIONS, THE OTHER AN OVERVIEW OF CONTENT, TRENDS, AND TOPICS. CHAPTER IV COVERS TRENDS IN THE ORGANIZATION OF SOCIAL STUDIES. CHAPTER V DISCUSSES CURRENT AFFAIRS, SPECIAL EVENTS, AND CIVIC PARTICIPATION. CHAPTER VI SURVEYS THE SKILLS AND PROCESSES INVOLVED IN SOCIAL STUDIES IN 6 ARTICLES DEALING WITH (1) CRITICAL THINKING AND PROBLEM SOLVING, (2) COMMUNICATION SKILLS, (3) MAP READING, (4) GROUP WORK SKILLS, (5) DRAMATIC PLAY, AND (6) INDUSTRIAL ARTS. THE 3 ARTICLES OF CHAPTER VII COVER (1) INSTRUCTIONAL RESOURCES, (2) THE USE OF TELEVISION, AND (3) THE VALUE OF BIOGRAPHIC MATERIALS. CHAPTER VIII DEALS WITH INSTRUCTIONAL PLANNING IN 4 ARTICLES ON (1) THE PHILOSOPHER-TEACHER, (2) DESIGNS FOR RESOURCE UNITS, (3) CLASS PLANNING, AND (4) THE INTRODUCTION OF NEW CONTENT. CHAPTER IX TREATS THE PROBLEM OF PLANNING FOR CHILDREN OF VARYING ABILITY, AND CHAPTER X CONCLUDES THE YEARBOOK WITH A DISCUSSION OF LEARNING EVALUATION TECHNIQUES. THE AUTHORS OF THE ARTICLES INCLUDED IN THE YEARBOOK ARE IDENTIFIED IN A CONTRIBUTORS' WHO'S WHO AT THE BACK OF THE BOOK. THIS DOCUMENT IS AVAILABLE FOR $4.00 FROM THE NATIONAL COUNCIL FOR THE SOCIAL STUDIES, 1201 SIXTEENTH STREET, N.W., WASHINGTON, D.C. 20036. (DR)

ED018276 PS000846
MATHEMATICS FOR ELEMENTARY SCHOOL TEACHERS. , 66 219P.
EDRS PRICE MF-$0.65 HC NOT AVAILABLE FROM EDRS.

PRODUCED AS PART OF A PROJECT FOR THE IMPROVEMENT OF CLASSROOM TEACHING, THIS BOOK DISCUSSES THE BASIC CONCEPTS AND OPERATIONS OF ARITHMETIC WHICH ARE TAUGHT TO ELEMENTARY SCHOOL STUDENTS. THE CONCEPT OF A SET IS USED THROUGHOUT AS A BASIS FOR EXPLANATION, AND THE DISCUSSION STRESSES WAYS BY WHICH STUDENTS CAN BE BROUGHT TO UNDERSTAND THE CONCEPTS. THE FIRST CHAPTER COVERS BEGINNING NUMBER CONCEPTS--SETS, PAIRING, COUNTING. SUCCEEDING CHAPTERS COVER THE DECIMAL NUMERATION SYSTEM, ADDITION, MULTIPLICATION, SUBTRACTION, DIVISION, ALGORITHMS FOR ARITHMETIC COMPUTATIONS, AND THE WHOLE NUMBER SYSTEM. THE FINAL SECTIONS OF THE BOOK INCLUDE ANSWERS TO THE EXERCISES GIVEN IN THE CHAPTERS AND DESCRIPTIVE DEFINITIONS OF TERMS USED. THIS DOCUMENT IS AVAILABLE FROM THE NATIONAL COUNCIL OF TEACHERS OF MATHEMATICS, 1201 SIXTEENTH STREET, N.W., WASHINGTON, D.C. 20036. (DR)

ED018277 PS000871
TEACHING GENERAL MUSIC, A RESOURCE HANDBOOK FOR GRADES 7 AND 8. SAETVEIT, JOSEPH G.; AND OTHERS, 66 186P.
EDRS PRICE MF-$0.65 HC-$6.58

THIS HANDBOOK PRESENTS SPECIFIC SUGGESTIONS CONCERNING CONTENT, METHODS, AND MATERIALS APPROPRIATE FOR USE IN THE IMPLEMENTATION OF AN INSTRUCTIONAL PROGRAM IN GENERAL MUSIC FOR GRADES 7 AND 8. TWENTY-FIVE TEACHING UNITS ARE PROVIDED AND ARE RECOMMENDED FOR ADAPTATION TO MEET SITUATIONAL CONDITIONS. THE TEACHING UNITS ARE GROUPED UNDER THE GENERAL TOPIC HEADINGS OF (1) ELEMENTS OF MUSIC, (2) THE SCIENCE OF SOUND, (3) MUSICAL INSTRUMENTS, (4) AMERICAN FOLK MUSIC, (5) MUSIC IN NEW YORK STATE, (6) MUSIC OF THE THEATER, (7) MUSIC FOR INSTRUMENTAL GROUPS, (8) OPERA, (9) MUSIC OF OTHER CULTURES, AND (10) HISTORICAL PERIODS IN MUSIC. THE PRESENTATION OF EACH UNIT CONSISTS OF SUGGESTIONS FOR (1) SETTING THE STAGE, (2) INTRODUCTORY DISCUSSION, (3) INITIAL MUSICAL EXPERIENCES, (4) DISCUSSION AND DEMONSTRATION, (5) APPLICATION OF SKILLS AND UNDERSTANDINGS, (6) RELATED PUPIL ACTIVITIES, AND (7) CULMINATING CLASS ACTIVITY (WHERE APPROPRIATE). SUITABLE PERFORMANCE LITERATURE, RECORDINGS, AND FILMS ARE CITED FOR USE WITH EACH OF THE UNITS. SEVEN EXTENSIVE BIBLIOGRAPHIES ARE INCLUDED, AND SOURCES OF BIBLIOGRAPHICAL ENTRIES, RECORDINGS, AND FILMS ARE LISTED. (JS)

ED018278 PS000872
ON RESPONSIVE ENVIRONMENTS. MOORE, OMAR KHAYYAM, APR67 12P.
EDRS PRICE MF-$0.65 HC-$3.29

EDUCATIONAL TECHNOLOGY IS OF GREAT IMPORTANCE NOW BECAUSE THE ENORMOUS INCREASE IN THE RATE OF TECHNOLOGICAL CHANGE WHICH TOOK PLACE DURING THE 1940'S HAS ALTERED OUR SOCIETY FROM A PERFORMANCE TO A LEARNING SOCIETY. IN A PERFORMANCE SOCIETY, LEARNING IS A PRELUDE TO THE PRACTICE OF A FIXED SET OF SKILLS. HOWEVER, IN A LEARNING SOCIETY THE REQUIRED SKILLS CHANGE TOO RAPIDLY FOR THIS TO BE POSSIBLE. LEARNING MUST CONTINUE INTO ADULTHOOD, AND MAKING THIS POSSIBLE REQUIRES A THOROUGHGOING REFORM OF EDUCATIONAL INSTITUTIONS. THESE MUST NOW INCULCATE FUNDAMENTAL CONCEPTS AND ABSTRACT SYMBOLIC SKILLS RATHER THAN TECHNICAL VIRTUOSITY. THROUGH THE USE OF COMPUTERS AS TEACHING MACHINES, TECHNOLOGY CAN BE TURNED BACK ON ITSELF TO SOLVE THE PROBLEMS IT POSES. THIS USAGE IS NOW BEGINNING TO BE REALIZED THROUGH THE INTERVENTION OF "BIG BUSINESS" AND GOVERNMENT. ONE EXAMPLE OF THIS USAGE IS THE DEVELOPMENT OF THE EDISON RESPONSIVE ENVIRONMENT MACHINE OR "TALKING TYPEWRITER." HERETOFORE, THE BEHAVIORAL SCIENCES HAVE NOT CONTRIBUTED TO EDUCATIONAL TECHNOLOGY, BUT THIS MACHINE IS BASED ON A SOCIOLOGICAL CONCEPTUALIZATION OF THE LEARNER AND HIS ENVIRONMENT. THIS HAS LED TO STARTLING RESULTS. IT ALSO HAS OFFERED A POSSIBLE SOLUTION TO THE PROBLEM OF MATCHING HARDWARE AND SOFTWARE AVAILABILITIES BY USING THE LEARNER AS A SOURCE OF MATERIAL FOR HIS OWN EDUCATION. SOME EXAMPLES OF THE CAPABILITIES OF LEARNERS, IN THIS CASE CHILDREN FROM 3 TO 6 YEARS OF AGE, ARE ILLUSTRATED BY 5 FILM CLIPS (REFERRED TO AND DESCRIBED BUT NOT INCLUDED IN THE DOCUMENT). THIS PAPER WAS PRESENTED AT THE ABINGTON CONFERENCE '67, "NEW DIRECTIONS IN INDIVIDUALIZED LEARNING," APRIL 23-27, 1967. (DR)

ED018279 PS000902
ORAL OR WRITTEN LANGUAGE--THE CONSEQUENCES FOR COGNITIVE DEVELOPMENT IN AFRICA AND THE UNITED STATES. GREENFIELD, PATRICIA M., 9FEB68 16P.
EDRS PRICE MF-$0.65 HC-$3.29

SPEAKING AN ORAL LANGUAGE AND SPEAKING A WRITTEN LANGUAGE INVOLVE DIFFERENT PATTERNS OF LANGUAGE USE WHICH ARE IN TURN RELATED TO DIFFERENT EDUCATIONAL METHODS AND DIFFERENT COURSES OF COGNITIVE DEVELOPMENT. BECAUSE ORAL SPEECH RELIES ON CONTEXT FOR COMMUNICATION, A COMMON CONTEXT AND POINT OF VIEW IS ASSUMED BY THE SPEAKER TO EXIST BETWEEN THE LISTENER AND HIMSELF, AND HIS SPEECH IS ATTACHED TO CONTEXT-DEPENDENT THOUGHT. IN ORAL CULTURES, EDUCATION IS ACCOMPLISHED BY THE

CHILD'S LEARNING TO IMITATE, USING CONCRETE OBJECTS IN CONCRETE ACTIVITIES. IN A WRITTEN LANGUAGE CULTURE, WHERE KNOWLEDGE EXCEEDS THE AMOUNT WHICH ANY 1 INDIVIDUAL CAN KNOW, ABSTRACT THINKING IS ENCOURAGED, WITH EMPHASIS ON THE ABILITY TO GENERALIZE AND TO MANIPULATE SYMBOLS. IN EXPERIMENTS CONDUCTED WITH THE WOLOF CHILDREN IN SENEGAL IT WAS DEMONSTRATED THAT LANGUAGE USE RATHER THAN LANGUAGE STRUCTURE DETERMINES COGNITIVE DEVELOPMENT. IT WAS FOUND THAT WOLOF SCHOOL CHILDREN TAUGHT IN FRENCH NONETHELESS CHANGED THEIR USE OF WOLOF IN A CONCEPT-FORMATION SITUATION SO THAT IN FUNCTIONAL TERMS WOLOF BECAME MORE "WRITTEN." UNITED STATES NEGRO LOWER CLASS CHILDREN HAVE BEEN FOUND TO HAVE THE SAME OBJECT-CONTEXT ORIENTATION FOUND IN ORAL CULTURES AND HAVE SIMILARLY IMPROVED IN ABSTRACT THINKING ABILITY WHEN GIVEN TRAINING. INCREASED STUDY OF AFRICAN SUBCULTURES MAY LEND DIRECTION TO AMERICAN SUBCULTURAL DEVELOPMENT. THIS PAPER WAS PRESENTED AT THE SYMPOSIUM ON CROSS-CULTURAL COGNITIVE STUDIES, AMERICAN EDUCATIONAL RESEARCH ASSOCIATION (CHICAGO, FEBRUARY 9, 1968). (MS)

ED019107 PS000001
CHILDREN WHO READ EARLY, TWO LONGITUDINAL STUDIES. DURKIN, DOLORES, 66
DOCUMENT NOT AVAILABLE FROM EDRS.

THE EXTENSION OF THE CONCEPT OF READINESS INTO EDUCATION EARLIER IN THIS CENTURY RESULTED IN STUDIES WHICH CONCLUDED THAT CHILDREN ARE NOT READY TO READ UNTIL A MENTAL AGE OF 6.5. BUT ACTUAL RESEARCH ON PRESCHOOL READING WAS, AS OF 1957, EXTREMELY LIMITED. TWO LONGITUDINAL STUDIES WERE UNDERTAKEN TO REMEDY THIS LACK. BOTH STUDIES SOUGHT TO DETERMINE THE PERCENTAGE OF PRESCHOOL READERS ENTERING THE FIRST GRADE, THE EFFECT OF THIS ABILITY ON LATER READING ACHIEVEMENT, AND FACTORS WHICH PROMOTED THIS ABILITY. THE FIRST STUDY, BEGUN IN SEPTEMBER 1958, WAS BASED ON A SAMPLE DRAWN FROM 5,103 FIRST GRADERS IN OAKLAND, CALIFORNIA. IN THIS GROUP WERE FOUND 49 PREREADERS, OR LESS THAN 1 PERCENT. THESE 49 WERE GIVEN IQ TESTS AND WERE TESTED FOR READING ACHIEVEMENT EACH YEAR UNTIL 1964. THE FAMILIES WERE INTERVIEWED TO DETERMINE THEIR SOCIOECONOMIC BACKGROUND, THE PERSONALITY CHARACTERISTICS OF THE EARLY READERS, AND THE WAY IN WHICH THE EARLY READING ABILITY DEVELOPED. THE SECOND STUDY, STARTED IN SEPTEMBER 1961, TESTED 4,465 NEW YORK CITY FIRST GRADERS AND FOUND 156 EARLY READERS, OR ABOUT 3-1/2 PERCENT. A SPECIAL GROUP OF 30 NONEARLY READERS WAS MATCHED ON SEX AND IQ WITH A GROUP OF 30 PREREADERS. MUCH THE SAME KINDS OF DATA WERE GATHERED IN THIS STUDY AS IN THE FIRST. SOME GENERAL CONCLUSIONS DRAWN FROM THESE STUDIES WERE (1) THAT PESSIMISTIC OPINIONS ABOUT THE EFFECTS OF EARLY READING WERE NOT CORROBORATED, AND (2) THAT THE EARLY AND NONEARLY READING CHILDREN WERE NOT MARKEDLY DISSIMILAR. HOWEVER, EARLY READERS TENDED TO COME FROM FAMILIES THAT WERE MORE WILLING TO HELP CHILDREN LEARN TO READ. THE FINDINGS OF THESE STUDIES ALSO SUGGEST THAT KINDERGARTEN PROGRAMS SHOULD ASSIST AND ENCOURAGE THOSE CHILDREN WHO WISH TO LEARN TO READ. CASE STUDIES OF SOME PREREADERS IN BOTH STUDIES AND SOME NONEARLY READERS OF THE NEW YORK STUDY ARE INCLUDED. THIS DOCUMENT IS AVAILABLE FOR $4.25 FROM TEACHERS COLLEGE PRESS, TEACHERS COLLEGE, COLUMBIA UNIVERSITY, NEW YORK 10027. (DR)

ED019108 PS000181
THE INITIAL TEACHING ALPHABET AND THE WORLD OF ENGLISH. (PROCEEDINGS OF THE SECOND ANNUAL INTERNATIONAL CONFERENCE ON THE INITIAL TEACHING ALPHABET, AUGUST 18-20, 1965). MAZURKIEWICZ, ALBERT J., 66
DOCUMENT NOT AVAILABLE FROM EDRS.

COMPLETE TRANSCRIPTIONS OF 60 PAPERS CONCERNED WITH THE INITIAL TEACHING ALPHABET (ITA) ARE PRESENTED IN THIS REPORT, THE INITIAL SECTION OF WHICH IS DEVOTED TO A DESCRIPTION OF ITA AND A SURVEY OF ITS GENESIS AND DEVELOPMENT. SUBSEQUENT SECTIONS DEAL WITH THE ROLE OF ITA IN (1) THE DEVELOPMENT OF ENGLISH AS A UNIVERSAL LANGUAGE AND THE TEACHING OF ENGLISH AS A SECOND LANGUAGE, (2) PRESCHOOL READING PROGRAMS, (3) REMEDIAL READING PROGRAMS, (4) READING PROGRAMS FOR PHYSICALLY AND EMOTIONALLY HANDICAPPED CHILDREN, AND (5) PROGRAMS FOR THE DEVELOPMENT OF LITERACY IN ADULT POPULATIONS. THE FINDINGS OF ITA RESEARCH STUDIES ARE PRESENTED AS ARE INTERIM REPORTS OF U.S. OFFICE OF EDUCATION STUDIES OF FIRST GRADE READING PROGRAMS. NEEDED FUTURE RESEARCH IN ITA IS DISCUSSED. THE USE OF ITA IN CANADA, BRITAIN, AND THE UNITED STATES IS REPORTED, AND SPECIFIC ATTENTION IS GIVEN TO THE PROGRESS OF INSTRUCTIONAL PROGRAMS IN ENGLAND AND THE UNITED STATES. THE DEVELOPMENT OF EFFECTIVE TEACHER USE, THE VIEWS OF AUTHORS AND PUBLISHERS REGARDING INSTRUCTIONAL MATERIALS, AND DEVELOPMENTAL USES OF ITA ARE REPORTED. A CONCLUDING SECTION DISCUSSES THE PROBABLE EFFECT OF ITA ON THE ELEMENTARY CURRICULUM. THIS DOCUMENT IS AVAILABLE FROM THE INITIAL TEACHING ALPHABET FOUNDATION, HOFSTRA UNIVERSITY, HEMPSTEAD, NEW YORK. (JS)

ED019109 PS000418
THE IMPACT OF COGNITIVE MATURITY ON THE DEVELOPMENT OF SEX-ROLE ATTITUDES IN THE YEARS 4 TO 8. KOHLBERG, LAWRENCE; ZIGLER, EDWARD, 67
DOCUMENT NOT AVAILABLE FROM EDRS.

A SERIES OF STUDIES WAS CONDUCTED TO CLARIFY THE ROLE OF INTELLIGENCE IN PERSONALITY ORGANIZATION AND TO ASSESS A COGNITIVE-DEVELOPMENTAL INTERPRETATION OF IQ-PERSONALITY CORRELATIONS. THE SPECIFIC FOCUS OF THE STUDY WAS THE RELATIONSHIP OF INTELLECTUAL MATURITY TO THE DEVELOPMENT OF SEX-ROLE ATTITUDES. AGE-DEVELOPMENTAL TRENDS IN SEX-ROLE ATTITUDES WERE EMPIRICALLY ESTABLISHED, AND TESTING WAS UNDERTAKEN TO EVALUATE THE HYPOTHESIS THAT THESE TRENDS OCCUR EARLIER IN BRIGHT CHILDREN THAN IN AVERAGE CHILDREN. MEASURES OF (1) TOTAL AND SEX-TYPED DEPENDENCY, (2) TOTAL AND SEX-TYPED IMITATION OF ADULTS, (3) DOLL-PLAY ATTACHMENT AND IMITATION OF MOTHER AND FATHER, (4) SEX-TYPED INTERESTS, AND (5) SEX-TYPED PEER PREFERENCES WERE ADMINISTERED TO A CORE GROUP OF 64 MIDDLE CLASS CHILDREN AGED 4 TO 8. A FOLLOW-UP STUDY, CONDUCTED 1 YEAR AFTER THE FIRST STUDY, CONFIRMED THE VALIDITY OF THE INITIAL TESTING, AND AN ADDITIONAL GROUP OF 10-YEAR-OLDS WERE TESTED ON 1 OF THE MEASURES FOR PURPOSES OF COMPARISON. ACCORDING TO THE RESULTS OF TESTING WITH THE STANFORD-BINET TEST AND THE GESELL DEVELOPMENTAL EXAMINATION, THE SUBJECTS WERE DIVIDED INTO GROUPS OF BRIGHT AND AVERAGE CHILDREN. SIGNIFICANT DIFFERENCES WERE FOUND TO EXIST BETWEEN THE 2 GROUPS IN PERFORMANCE ON THE SEX-ROLE MEASUREMENTS. BRIGHT CHILDREN WERE FOUND TO BE MORE ADVANCED IN AGE TRENDS OF SEX-ROLE ATTITUDE DEVELOPMENT. THE FINDINGS OF THE STUDY WERE COMPATIBLE WITH A COGNITIVE-DEVELOPMENTAL THEORY OF THE FORMATION OF SEX-ROLE ATTITUDES. THIS DOCUMENT APPEARED IN GENETIC PSYCHOLOGY MONOGRAPHS, VOLUME 75, PAGES 89-165, 1967, PUBLISHED BY THE JOURNAL PRESS, 2 COMMERCIAL STREET, PROVINCETOWN, MASSACHUSETTS 02657. (JS)

ED019110 PS000437
THE NATIONAL TEACHER CORPS PROGRAM, 1966-67 EVALUATION REPORT. DZIUBAN, CHARLES; AND OTHERS, 67 56P.
EDRS PRICE MF-$0.65 HC-$3.29

A PROJECT TO DETERMINE THE EFFECTIVENESS OF NATIONAL TEACHER CORPS (NTC) INTERNS IN THE ATLANTA, GEORGIA SCHOOL SYSTEM WAS DESIGNED TO FIND OUT IF THE INTERNS HAD HELPED THE DISADVANTAGED PUPILS IN THEIR CLASSES TO RAISE ACHIEVEMENT LEVELS AND IMPROVE SELF-CONCEPTS. SPECIFIC RESEARCH OBJECTIVES WERE (1) TO ASSESS THE PROGRESS IN VERBAL MENTAL AGE ATTAINED BY NTC PUPILS AS MEASURED BY A PRE- AND POSTTEST ON THE PEABODY PICTURE VOCABULARY TEST AND THE GOODENOUGH DRAW-A-MAN TEST, (2) TO COMPARE THE SELF-CONCEPTS OF THE NTC PUPILS WITH THOSE OF A SIMILAR GROUP OF PUPILS BY USING A TEACHER CHECK LIST DEVELOPED BY THE EVALUATION COMMITTEE, (3) TO COMPARE PUPIL READINESS FOR FIRST GRADE WITH THAT OF KINDERGARTEN PUPILS A YEAR EARLIER (WHO HAD NOT HAD INTERNS) BY USING THE METROPOLITAN READING READINESS TEST, FORM A, AND (4) TO COMPARE TEACHER ATTITUDES OF NTC INTERNS WITH THOSE OF OTHER BEGINNING TEACHERS OF TITLE I AND NON-TITLE I SCHOOLS BY MEANS OF THE MINNESOTA ATTITUDE INVENTORY. STATISTICAL TREATMENT OF THE DATA COLLECTED ON A VARIETY OF MEASURES SHOWED THAT THE NTC INTERNS POSITIVELY AFFECTED THE CHILDREN'S LANGUAGE AND SELF-CONCEPT DEVELOPMENT AND IMPROVED THEIR READINESS FOR FIRST GRADE. THE NTC INTERNS EXHIBITED ATTITUDES ASSOCIATED WITH EFFECTIVE TEACHING MORE OFTEN AND TO A GREATER EXTENT THAN DID REGULAR TEACHERS. (MS)

ED019111 PS000456
SOCIAL CLASS AND COGNITIVE DEVELOPMENT IN INFANCY. BIRNS, BEVERLY; GOLDEN, MARK, 30MAR67 10P.
EDRS PRICE MF-$0.65 HC-$3.29

THE PURPOSE OF THIS STUDY WAS TO FIND OUT WHETHER SOCIAL CLASS DIFFERENCES IN INTELLECTUAL DEVELOPMENT ARE PRESENT IF (1) CHILDREN FROM SOCIALLY DISORGANIZED SLUM FAMILIES ARE COMPARED WITH CHILDREN FROM STABLE, LOW INCOME AND MIDDLE INCOME FAMILIES, (2) THE PIAGET OBJECT SCALE, A NEW MEASURE OF COGNITIVE DEVELOPMENT BASED ON PIAGET'S SENSORIMOTOR OBSERVATIONS, IS EMPLOYED, AND (3) EFFORT IS MADE TO OVERCOME ANY MOTIVATIONAL FACTORS ABLE TO INTERFERE WITH TEST PERFORMANCE. IN A CROSS-SECTIONAL APPROACH, 184 NEGRO CHILDREN, OF 12, 18, AND 24 MONTHS OF AGE REPRESENTING 3 SOCIOECONOMIC STATUS GROUPS, WERE COMPARED ON THE PIAGET OBJECT SCALE AND THE CATTELL INFANT INTELLIGENCE SCALE. RESULTS SHOWED NO DIFFERENCES AMONG THE 3 GROUPS ON EITHER SCALE. HOWEVER, INFANTS WERE RATED ON SUCCESS OR FAILURE ON A GIVEN ITEM WITHOUT REGARD TO THE NUMBER OF TRIALS OR TIME REQUIRED, SO SOCIAL CLASS DIFFERENCES MAY HAVE BEEN HIDDEN. PREVIOUS RESEARCH FINDINGS WHICH INDICATED THAT SOCIAL CLASS DIFFERENCES IN INTELLECTUAL DEVELOPMENT DO NOT APPEAR DURING THE FIRST 2 YEARS WERE CONFIRMED. AFTER 2 YEARS LANGUAGE BECOMES IMPORTANT FOR LEARNING, AND DIFFERENCES ARE NOTED. DIFFERENCES IN PATTERNS OF MOTIVATION AND COGNITIVE STYLE OCCUR EARLY BUT SHOW UP IN LATER LEARNING. THEREFORE, COMPENSATORY EDUCATION

PROGRAMS SHOULD FOSTER THE KINDS OF MOTIVATIONS AND COGNITIVE SKILLS WHICH WILL BE NEEDED FOR ABSTRACT THINKING AND ACADEMIC SUCCESS. THIS PAPER WAS PRESENTED AT THE MEETING OF THE SOCIETY FOR RESEARCH IN CHILD DEVELOPMENT, (NEW YORK CITY, MARCH 30, 1967). (MS)

ED019112 PS000735
A REPORT OF THE SOUTHERN REGIONAL CONFERENCE ON EARLY CHILDHOOD EDUCATION. CARTER, BARBARA, OCT67 45P.
EDRS PRICE MF-$0.65 HC-$3.29

ONE HUNDRED EDUCATORS FROM 13 SOUTHERN STATES MET FOR A 3-DAY CONFERENCE IN WHICH POSSIBLE DIRECTIONS FOR EARLY CHILDHOOD EDUCATION WERE EXPLORED WITH SPECIFIC EMPHASIS ON STATE-FUNDED PRESCHOOL EDUCATION FOR THE DISADVANTAGED CHILD. REPORTS WERE GIVEN ON THE FOLLOWING ONGOING PROJECTS--(1) DEMONSTRATION AND RESEARCH CENTER FOR EARLY EDUCATION (DARCEE), GEORGE PEABODY COLLEGE FOR TEACHERS, (2) THE LEARNING TO LEARN SCHOOL, JACKSONVILLE, FLORIDA, (3) RESEARCH AND DEVELOPMENT CENTER IN EDUCATIONAL STIMULATION, UNIVERSITY OF GEORGIA, (4) DURHAM EDUCATION IMPROVEMENT PROGRAM, DUKE UNIVERSITY AND NORTH CAROLINA COLLEGE, (5) FRANK PORTER GRAHAM INSTITUTE ON EARLY CHILDHOOD EDUCATION, UNIVERSITY OF NORTH CAROLINA, (6) PARENT EDUCATION PROJECT, INSTITUTE FOR DEVELOPMENT OF HUMAN RESOURCES, UNIVERSITY OF FLORIDA, (7) SUMTER CHILD STUDY PROJECT, SOUTH CAROLINA, (8) NATIONAL TEACHER CORPS, UNIVERSITY OF GEORGIA, (9) HEAD START. INCLUDED ARE A LIST OF CONFERENCE PARTICIPANTS AND A BIBLIOGRAPHY ON EARLY CHILDHOOD STUDIES. THIS DOCUMENT IS ALSO AVAILABLE FROM THE SOUTHERN EDUCATION FOUNDATION, 811 CYPRESS STREET, N.E., ATLANTA, GEORGIA 30308. (MS)

ED019113 PS000757
THE EFFECTS OF TWO VARIABLES ON THE PROBLEM-SOLVING ABILITIES OF FIRST-GRADE CHILDREN. STEFFE, LESLIE P., MAR67 23P.
EDRS PRICE MF-$0.65 HC-$3.29

NINETY FIRST GRADE CHILDREN WERE RANDOMLY SELECTED FROM 3 SCHOOLS (WHICH EACH USED A DIFFERENT ARITHMETIC PROGRAM) TO PARTICIPATE IN A STUDY TO INVESTIGATE THE EFFECTS OF 2 VARIABLES ON THE CHILDREN'S ABILITY TO SOLVE ADDITION PROBLEMS. THE VARIABLES WERE (1) THE PRESENCE OR ABSENCE OF AN EXISTENTIAL QUANTIFIER PRECEDING THE START OF THE PROBLEM, AND (2) EITHER THE PRESENCE OF 3 DIFFERENT NAMES FOR THE 3 SETS IN ANY PROBLEM OR THE PRESENCE OF COMMON NAMES FOR THE 3 SETS. THE CHILDREN WERE INDIVIDUALLY TESTED ON 20 PROBLEMS WHICH WERE READ TO THEM BY 1 EXPERIMENTER. FORTY-FIVE CHILDREN RECEIVED PROBLEMS WHICH INVOLVED AN EXISTENTIAL QUANTIFIER, AND 45 HAD PROBLEMS WHICH DID NOT. TEN OF THE PROBLEMS GIVEN TO EACH CHILD HAD DIFFERENT NAMES WITHIN THE PROBLEM SETS, AND 10 PROBLEMS HAD THE SAME SET NAMES. ANALYSIS OF VARIANCE OF THE DATA SHOWED THAT THE ONLY SIGNIFICANT DIFFERENCE OCCURRED BETWEEN THE PROBLEMS INVOLVING SET NAMES. ALTHOUGH THE STUDY SCOPE IS LIMITED, RESULTS SUGGEST THAT CHILDREN SHOULD BE GIVEN MORE CHANCES TO INTERPRET PROBLEMS PRESENTED VERBALLY AND THAT PICTORIAL REPRESENTATIONS OF SETS IN EXERCISE BOOKS SHOULD BE DESCRIBED BY DIFFERENT WORDS RATHER THAN BY 1 COMMON TERM. (MS)

ED019114 PS000776
EARLY CHILDHOOD EDUCATION AND THE WALDORF SCHOOL PLAN. GRUNELIUS, ELIZABETH M., 66
DOCUMENT NOT AVAILABLE FROM EDRS.

THE WALDORF SCHOOL NURSERY-KINDERGARTEN PLAN PROPOSES AN UNSTRUCTURED ENVIRONMENT IN WHICH THE YOUNG CHILD IS PERMITTED TO DEVELOP AT HIS NATURAL RATE THROUGHOUT THE DISCOVERY PERIOD OF CHILDHOOD. BECAUSE THE CHILD LEARNS BEST THROUGH IMITATION, ADULT MODELS WHO PROVIDE APPROPRIATE EXPERIENCES FOR SENSORY PERCEPTION AND IMITATION LEARNING OFFER THE BEST TEACHING. A PHYSICAL ENVIRONMENT WHICH HAS OPPORTUNITIES FOR EXPLORATION AND ADEQUATE LIGHT, SPACE, AND MATERIALS ABLE TO BE MANIPULATED IN VARIOUS WAYS PROVIDE THE CHILD WITH CHANCES TO LEARN MEANINGFUL CONCEPTS. THE HOME AND SCHOOL ENVIRONMENT WORK TOGETHER TO ENCOURAGE THE CHILD'S NATURAL DEVELOPMENT, ALLOWING HIM TO PROCEED AT HIS OWN RATE, ACCORDING TO HIS OWN NEEDS. THIS DOCUMENT IS AVAILABLE FOR $1.25 FROM WALDORF SCHOOL MONOGRAPHS, 25 PERSHING ROAD, ENGLEWOOD, NEW JERSEY. (MS)

ED019115 PS000779
EXPANDED PREKINDERGARTEN PROGRAM, EVALUATION OF NEW YORK CITY TITLE I EDUCATIONAL PROJECTS 1966-67. SCHWARTZ, SYDNEY L., SEP67 132P.
EDRS PRICE MF-$0.65 HC-$6.58

A STRATIFIED RANDOM SAMPLE OF 20 SCHOOLS WITH 35 PREKINDERGARTEN ROOMS SERVING 500 CHILDREN WAS USED IN AN EVALUATION OF AN EXPANDED PREKINDERGARTEN PROGRAM OF COMPENSATORY EDUCATION FOR DISADVANTAGED 4-YEAR-OLDS. THE EVALUATIVE EMPHASIS CENTERED ON ONGOING CLASSROOM PROGRAMS, ADMINISTRATIVE AND SUPERVISORY PERSONNEL, AND A FAMILY-COMMUNITY COMPONENT WHICH INVOLVED A LUNCH PROGRAM AND HOME VISITS BY A FAMILY ASSISTANT. EVALUATION TEAM MEMBERS USED THEIR OWN OBSERVATIONAL RECORDINGS AND PERSONAL REPORTS, TEACHERS' PERSONAL REPORTS, AND INFORMATION COLLECTED ON IDENTIFYING DATA FORMS CONCERNED WITH STAFF MEMBERS, PHYSICAL FACILITIES, AND ATTENDANCE. SUMMARIES OF THE DATA INDICATED THAT TEACHERS FELT THEY WOULD BENEFIT FROM INTENSIVE INSERVICE TRAINING WITH SUBJECT MATTER SPECIALISTS TO LEARN TO STIMULATE GROWTH IN LINGUISTIC AND PERCEPTUAL-COGNITIVE SKILLS. BOTH ADMINISTRATORS AND SUPERVISORS REPORTED THAT A WORK OVERLOAD CAUSED THEM TO DEAL MAINLY WITH CRISIS SITUATIONS RATHER THAN WITH THE DEVELOPMENT OF INSTRUCTIONAL PROGRAMS. CONFLICT BETWEEN PROFESSIONALS AND NONPROFESSIONALS WAS TIME-CONSUMING AND DISRUPTIVE. A WELL-DELINEATED OUTLINE OF GOALS AND RESPONSIBILITIES OF PARTICIPANTS IS NEEDED AS WELL AS REGULAR MEETINGS TO PROVIDE FOR SKILL DEVELOPMENT AND TEAM COOPERATION ON ALL LEVELS. HALF OF THE REPORT CONTAINS EVALUATIVE INSTRUMENT SAMPLES AND TABLES OF DATA COLLECTED. (MS)

ED019116 PS000780
THE EFFECTS OF A HIGHLY STRUCTURED PRESCHOOL PROGRAM ON THE MEASURED INTELLIGENCE OF CULTURALLY DISADVANTAGED FOUR-YEAR-OLD CHILDREN. INTERIM REPORT. HODGINS, AUDREY; KARNES, MERLE B., 10P.
EDRS PRICE MF-$0.65 HC-$3.29

TWENTY-SEVEN DISADVANTAGED 4-YEAR-OLDS PARTICIPATED IN A STRUCTURED PRESCHOOL PROGRAM WHICH STRESSED LANGUAGE AND COGNITIVE DEVELOPMENT. THE CHILDREN WERE PLACED IN EITHER A MORNING OR AN AFTERNOON CLASS. THESE CLASSES WERE SUBDIVIDED INTO 3 ABILITY GROUPS, EACH WITH ITS OWN TEACHER WHO STAYED WITH HER CHILDREN. CONTENT AREA MATERIALS USED IN TEACHING MATH CONCEPTS, LANGUAGE ARTS AND READING READINESS, SOCIAL STUDIES AND SCIENCE WERE KEPT IN DIFFERENT ROOMS. THE TEACHER MOVED FROM ROOM TO ROOM WITH HER CLASS. LEARNING PERIODS WERE 25 MINUTES LONG AND EMPHASIZED A GAME FORMAT APPROACH. A TEACHER TO CHILD RATIO OF 1 TO 5 PROVIDED A CHANCE TO BUILD A MOTIVATIVE RELATIONSHIP AND OPPORTUNITY FOR TRANSFER AND REINFORCEMENT LEARNING. ALL CHILDREN WERE PRE- AND POSTTESTED ON THE 1960 STANFORD-BINET INDIVIDUAL INTELLIGENCE SCALE, FORM L-M. AT THE END OF THE 7-MONTH PROGRAM, THE CHILDREN SHOWED IQ TEST GAINS OF FROM 4 TO 29 POINTS SUGGESTING THAT SUCH A PROGRAM IS EFFECTIVE IN PREPARING PRESCHOOLERS FOR LATER ACADEMIC WORK. (THE FULL REPORT OF THIS LONGITUDINAL STUDY IS PS 000 349). (MS)

ED019117 PS000810
A FRESH APPROACH TO EARLY CHILDHOOD EDUCATION AND A STUDY OF ITS EFFECTIVENESS. LEARNING TO LEARN PROGRAM. SPRIGLE, HERBERT; AND OTHERS, 29P.
EDRS PRICE MF-$0.65 HC-$3.29

AN EXPERIMENTAL PRESCHOOL PROGRAM HAS BEEN DEVELOPED, THE PRIMARY OBJECTIVE OF WHICH IS TO HELP THE CHILD TO LEARN THE PROCESS OF LEARNING. ORGANIZED ON THE ASSUMPTION THAT COGNITIVE GROWTH PROCEEDS FROM MOTOR TO PERCEPTUAL TO SYMBOLIC FUNCTIONING, THE PROGRAM EMPHASIZES THE IMPORTANCE OF LANGUAGE AS A TOOL FOR THINKING AND REASONING. AN EVALUATIVE STUDY OF THE PROGRAM WAS CONDUCTED IN WHICH 23 LOWER-MIDDLE CLASS PARTICIPANTS WERE COMPARED WITH A CONTROL GROUP OF SIMILAR CHILDREN ENROLLED IN A TRADITIONAL KINDERGARTEN PROGRAM. PRETESTS OF SCHOOL READINESS SKILLS, VOCABULARY DEVELOPMENT, MOTOR COORDINATION, AND INTELLIGENCE WERE ADMINISTERED. INDIVIDUALS WERE MATCHED ACCORDING TO PRETEST SCORES, AGE, SEX, AND SOCIOECONOMIC LEVEL. ON 21 OF 25 DEVELOPMENTAL MEASURES ADMINISTERED AS POSTTESTS, THE EXPERIMENTAL GROUP EXCELLED SIGNIFICANTLY. THE SUPERIOR PERFORMANCE OF THE EXPERIMENTAL GROUP WAS MOST APPARENT IN THE AREA OF LANGUAGE SKILLS DEVELOPMENT. ANALYSIS OF THE DATA INDICATES THAT THE EXPERIMENTAL PROGRAM IS OF MOST BENEFIT TO THOSE CHILDREN WITH PRETEST SCORES IN THE LOWER RANGE OF INTELLIGENCE. A COMPARISON OF THE DATA ACCUMULATED IN THIS STUDY WITH THAT OF A PREVIOUS STUDY OF CULTURALLY DEPRIVED CHILDREN SUGGESTS THAT THE EXPERIMENTAL PROGRAM IS PARTICULARLY EFFICACIOUS FOR CHILDREN FROM LOWER SOCIOECONOMIC BACKGROUNDS. (JS)

ED019118 PS000826
FINAL REPORT ON HEAD START EVALUATION AND RESEARCH--1966-67 TO THE INSTITUTE FOR EDUCATIONAL DEVELOPMENT. SECTION II, ON THE INTERPRETATION OF MULTIVARIATE SYSTEMS. LAND, KENNETH C., 31AUG67 82P.
EDRS PRICE MF-$0.65 HC-$3.29

THIS REPORT PRESENTS A DISCUSSION OF 2 TECHNIQUES WHICH CAN BE USED TO REPRESENT AND INTERPRET MULTIVARIATE STATISTICAL SYSTEMS WHEN IT IS FELT THAT THERE ARE CAUSAL RELATIONS BETWEEN SOME OF THE VARIABLES. THE BASIC TECHNIQUE IS PATH ANALYSIS AND THE OTHER IS ITS EXTENSION THROUGH THE USE OF RECURSIVE SYSTEMS OF EQUATIONS. THE ANALYSIS IS RESTRICTED IN APPLICATION TO RELATIONSHIPS BETWEEN INTERVAL-MEASURABLE VARIABLES THAT ARE LINEAR, ADDITIVE, AND ASYMMETRIC. TO MAKE A PATH ANALYSIS, THE VARIABLES IN THE SYSTEM ARE CLASSIFIED AS EITHER EXOGENOUS, THAT IS, HAVING THEIR VALUES DETERMINED BY FACTORS OUTSIDE THE SYSTEM, OR ENDOGENOUS, THAT IS, HAVING THEIR VALUES

DETERMINED BY FACTORS REPRESENTED BY VARIABLES WITHIN THE SYSTEM. BASED ON THIS ANALYSIS, A SET OF REGRESSION EQUATIONS REPRESENTING THESE RELATIONS IS FORMED. THIS SET IS TERMED THE PATH MODEL, AND GRAPHIC CONVENTIONS ARE GIVEN FOR DIAGRAMING IT. THE COEFFICIENTS IN THE EQUATIONS ARE SIMILAR TO THE CORRELATION COEFFICIENTS OCCURRING IN ORDINARY LEAST-SQUARES REGRESSION EQUATIONS. THE ADVANTAGE OF THE PATH ANALYSIS APPROACH IS THAT IT ENABLES THE EXPERIMENTER TO UTILIZE ALL THE INFORMATION AT HIS DISPOSAL, PARTICULARLY THAT CONCERNING CAUSAL RELATIONS BETWEEN VARIABLES. THE TECHNIQUE IS ILLUSTRATED WITH APPLICATIONS TO BIVARIATE AND MULTIVARIATE SYSTEMS HAVING SINGLE AND MULTIPLE STAGES OF CAUSAL INFLUENCE. SOME EXAMPLES DRAWN FROM ACTUAL RESEARCH PROJECTS ARE INCLUDED. (DR)

ED019119 PS000827
FINAL REPORT ON HEAD START EVALUATION AND RESEARCH--1966-67 TO THE INSTITUTE FOR EDUCATIONAL DEVELOPMENT. SECTION III, INFLUENCING ATTITUDES OF PARENTS AND TEACHERS THROUGH REWARDING CHILDREN. MANDEL, DAVID MARC, 31AUG67 130P.
EDRS PRICE MF-$0.65 HC-$6.58

SIXTY-NINE MEXICAN AND NEGRO PRESCHOOL CHILDREN RANGING IN AGE FROM 5 TO 7 YEARS TOOK PART IN A STUDY TO FIND OUT IF MATERIAL REWARDS GIVEN TO HEAD START CHILDREN WOULD AFFECT THE ATTITUDES OF MOTHERS AND TEACHERS TOWARDS THE CHILDREN. BOTH MOTHERS AND TEACHERS RATED THE CHILDREN ON THE HEAD START SOCIAL BEHAVIOR INVENTORY, AND MOTHERS ALSO ESTIMATED THEIR CHILDREN'S ABILITIES TO DO TASKS ADAPTED FROM THE CALDWELL PRESCHOOL INVENTORY (PSI). THE CHILDREN WERE PRETESTED ON THE PSI AND THE PEABODY PICTURE VOCABULARY TEST, THEN GROUPED INTO EXPERIMENTAL AND CONTROL CLASSES. TWICE A WEEK FOR THE NEXT 5 WEEKS EACH CHILD IN THE REWARDED CLASSES WAS GIVEN A TOY AND A BAG OF FRUIT WITH A NOTE FROM THE TEACHER STATING THAT THESE WERE REWARDS FOR THE CHILD'S PERFORMANCE IN SCHOOL THAT DAY. NONREWARDED CHILDREN TOOK HOME ITEMS MADE IN SCHOOL THAT DAY SUCH AS SCHOOL VALENTINES AND CUT-OUTS. AFTER 5 WEEKS, MOTHERS AND TEACHERS AGAIN RATED CHILDREN'S BEHAVIOR, AND MOTHERS AGAIN ESTIMATED TASK ABILITY. ALL CHILDREN WERE GIVEN A POSTTEST OF TASKS AND A PARALLEL FORM OF THE PRETEST ACHIEVEMENT MEASURE. ANALYSES OF VARIANCE OF THE DATA SHOWED THAT MOTHERS' ATTITUDES DID NOT CHANGE AS A RESULT OF REWARDS BUT THAT TEACHERS' ATTITUDES WERE POSITIVELY AFFECTED. AN APPENDIX INCLUDES FACSIMILES OF TESTS AND SCALES USED. THIS STUDY WAS DONE IN PARTIAL FULFILLMENT FOR DOCTORAL DEGREE REQUIREMENTS. (MS)

ED019120 PS000828
FINAL REPORT ON HEAD START EVALUATION AND RESEARCH--1966-67 TO THE INSTITUTE FOR EDUCATIONAL DEVELOPMENT. SECTION IV, AN EXPLORATORY STUDY OF ORAL LANGUAGE DEVELOPMENT AMONG CULTURALLY DIFFERENT CHILDREN. HUBBARD, JAMES L.; ZARATE, LEONORE T., 31AUG67 105P.
EDRS PRICE MF-$0.65 HC-$6.58

THE CULTURALLY DISADVANTAGED CHILD, ALTHOUGH VERY VERBAL IN HIS LOCAL ENVIRONMENT, IS USUALLY VERBALLY DEFICIENT WITH RESPECT TO SOCIETY AS A WHOLE. PART OF THE ANSWER TO PROVIDING A MORE EFFECTIVE LANGUAGE EDUCATION TO THE CULTURALLY DEPRIVED YOUTH IS ENRICHMENT OR COMPENSATORY PROGRAMS LIKE HEAD START. TO INVESTIGATE THE EFFECT OF THE AUSTIN HEAD START PROGRAM ON THE LANGUAGE DEVELOPMENT AND ABILITY OF PRIMARY GRADE PUPILS, A 15-ITEM ORAL LANGUAGE DEVELOPMENT SCALE WAS CREATED TO EVALUATE THE LANGUAGE ABILITY OF 49 HEAD START AND 105 NON-HEAD START DISADVANTAGED PUPILS IN THE FIRST AND SECOND GRADES. THE CHILDREN WERE ASKED QUESTIONS BY A TEACHER, AND THEIR SPONTANEOUS EXPRESSIONS WERE TAPED. THESE TAPED EXPRESSIONS WERE THEN INDEPENDENTLY EVALUATED BY 2 TEACHERS ON THE RATING SCALE, AND THE SCORES WERE RECORDED. THE SCORES WERE DIVIDED INTO 12 GROUPS REFLECTING THE DIFFERENCES IN CHARACTERISTICS OF THE PARTICIPATING PUPILS ON 3 DIMENSIONS, NAMELY, (1) HEAD START OR NON-HEAD START, (2) FIRST OR SECOND GRADE, AND (3) HIGH, MIDDLE, OR LOW READING ABILITY. AN EXAMPLE OF A GROUP DENOMINATION WOULD BE "HEAD START FIRST GRADERS OF MIDDLE READING ABILITY." SCORES FOR EACH GROUP WERE OBTAINED IN THE FALL OF 1966 AND AGAIN IN THE SPRING OF 1967. THE DATA SHOWED NO REAL SIGNIFICANT DIFFERENCES BETWEEN THE HEAD START AND NON-HEAD START GROUPS OVER THE OTHER 2 DIMENSIONS. A COMPARISON OF THE FALL AND SPRING SCORES SHOWED THAT ONLY MIDDLE ABILITY FIRST GRADE HEAD START PUPILS AND LOW ABILITY FIRST GRADE NON-HEAD START PUPILS MADE CONSIDERABLE IMPROVEMENT IN LANGUAGE DEVELOPMENT FROM THE FALL TO SPRING SESSION. THE INCONCLUSIVENESS OF THE RESULTS, A MATTER FOR FUTURE IMPROVEMENT, WAS MOST LIKELY DUE TO THE TYPE OF MEASURING PROCEDURE USED. (WD)

ED019121 PS000830
FINAL REPORT ON HEAD START EVALUATION AND RESEARCH--1966-67 TO THE INSTITUTE FOR EDUCATIONAL DEVELOPMENT. SECTION V, THE ROLE OF DIALECT IN THE SCHOOL-SOCIALIZATION OF LOWER CLASS CHILDREN. STOLZ, WALTER S.; AND OTHERS, 31AUG67 96P.
EDRS PRICE MF-$0.65 HC-$3.29

IT HAS BEEN HYPOTHESIZED THAT THE ADOPTION OF THE LINGUISTIC CHARACTERISTICS OF A SUBCULTURE OTHER THAN A CHILD'S OWN IS A VALID INDICATION OF THE DEGREE TO WHICH THE CHILD HAS BECOME SOCIALIZED INTO THAT SUBCULTURE. TO EXAMINE THIS HYPOTHESIS, RESEARCH WAS CONDUCTED (1) TO EXPLORE THE RELATIONSHIP BETWEEN LINGUISTIC HABITS AND ATTITUDE SOCIALIZATION IN UNDERPRIVILEGED CHILDREN AND (2) TO COMPARE THE LANGUAGE BEHAVIOR AND ATTITUDES TOWARD HOME AND SCHOOL OF LOWER AND MIDDLE CLASS CHILDREN. AN EXPERIMENTAL POPULATION OF 54 FIRST THROUGH THIRD GRADE STUDENTS FROM AN ISOLATED RURAL AREA WAS COMPARED WITH A CONTROL POPULATION FROM THE SAME 3 GRADES OF AN UPPER-MIDDLE CLASS SUBURBAN ELEMENTARY SCHOOL. COLLECTION OF DIALECT SAMPLES PROVIDED INDICES OF PHONOLOGICAL, LEXICAL, AND SYNTACTICAL VARIANTS WHICH DIFFERENTIATED THE LINGUISTIC BEHAVIORS OF THE 2 POPULATIONS. THREE SOCIALIZATION MEASURES, DESIGNED TO ASSESS THE CHILD'S ACCEPTANCE OF MIDDLE CLASS VALUES, WERE DEVELOPED. AFTER PRETESTING WITH POPULATION SAMPLES SIMILAR TO THE CONTROL AND EXPERIMENTAL GROUPS, THE SOCIALIZATION MEASURES WERE ADMINISTERED TO THE TEST GROUPS AND SPEECH SAMPLES ELICITED FROM THEM. ALTHOUGH ANALYSIS OF THE DATA IS IN PROGRESS, THE COMPUTATION OF CORRELATION COEFFICIENTS FOR SOCIALIZATION AND LINGUISTIC VARIABLES HAS, THUS FAR, FAILED TO SUPPORT THE ORIGINAL HYPOTHESIS REGARDING THE RELATIONSHIPS BETWEEN ATTITUDE SOCIALIZATION AND LINGUISTIC BEHAVIOR. (JS)

ED019122 PS000830
FINAL REPORT ON HEAD START EVALUATION AND RESEARCH--1966-67 TO THE INSTITUTE FOR EDUCATIONAL DEVELOPMENT. SECTION VI, THE MEASUREMENT OF BILINGUALISM AND BICULTURAL SOCIALIZATION OF THE CHILD IN THE SCHOOL SETTING--THE DEVELOPMENT OF INSTRUMENTS. CERVENKA, EDWARD J., 31AUG67 238P.
EDRS PRICE MF-$0.65 HC-$9.87

A STUDY TO DEVELOP INSTRUMENTS TO MEASURE CHILD BILINGUALISM AND BICULTURAL SOCIALIZATION WAS CONDUCTED IN DEL RIO, TEXAS, A MEXICAN-AMERICAN COMMUNITY IN WHICH SCHOOL IS TAUGHT IN BOTH SPANISH AND ENGLISH. THREE INSTRUMENTS WERE DEVELOPED--(1) A SERIES OF 6 TESTS FOR MEASURING LINGUISTIC COMPETENCE IN ENGLISH, (2) A SIMILAR SERIES OF 6 TESTS FOR SPANISH, AND (3) A SERIES OF 3 INSTRUMENTS FOR MEASURING SOCIALIZATION. TEST BATTERIES FOCUSED ON THE ORAL-AURAL USE OF LANGUAGE IN REALISTIC SCHOOL SITUATIONS. A RANDOM SAMPLE OF 97 FIRST GRADERS WAS GROUPED INTO 4 EXPERIMENTAL SECTIONS TAUGHT BILINGUALLY BY MEXICAN-AMERICAN TEACHERS AND INTO 4 CONTROL SECTIONS TAUGHT IN ENGLISH BY ENGLISH TEACHERS. THE CONTROL GROUP CHILDREN WERE GIVEN THE ENGLISH SERIES AND INVENTORY OF SOCIALIZATION WHILE THE EXPERIMENTAL CHILDREN WERE GIVEN BOTH THE ENGLISH AND SPANISH SERIES AND THE INVENTORY. ANALYSIS OF TEST RESULTS SHOWED THAT THE EXPERIMENTAL SUBJECTS WERE AS COMPETENT IN ENGLISH AS THOSE LEARNING ONLY IN ENGLISH AND ALSO BETTER ADJUSTED SOCIALLY. TEST INSTRUMENT VALIDITY AND RELIABILITY WAS DETERMINED AND AN ITEM ANALYSIS CARRIED OUT. APPENDIXES WHICH INCLUDE FACSIMILES OF TEST INSTRUMENTS AND ANALYSES OF EXPERIMENTAL DATA COMPRISE MORE THAN HALF OF THE REPORT. (MS)

ED019123 PS000831
FINAL REPORT ON HEAD START EVALUATION AND RESEARCH--1966-67 TO THE INSTITUTE FOR EDUCATIONAL DEVELOPMENT. SECTION VII, SENSORY AND PERCEPTUAL STUDIES. HOLMES, DAVID S.; AND OTHERS, 31AUG67 54P.
EDRS PRICE MF-$0.65 HC-$3.29

THREE STUDIES OF PRESCHOOL CHILDREN ARE INCLUDED IN THIS EVALUATION REPORT. (1) "'NEURAL CONDUCTIVITY' AND ACHIEVEMENT IN CULTURALLY DEPRIVED STUDENTS." NEURAL CONDUCTIVITY WAS INFERRED FROM A CORRELATION BETWEEN PUPILLARY RESPONSE AND CHILDREN'S PRESCHOOL PERFORMANCE. COMPLICATIONS IN ACQUIRING AND USING THE NECESSARY EQUIPMENT RESULTED IN THE AVAILABILITY OF ONLY 7 SUBJECTS AND INSUFFICIENT DATA FOR ANALYSIS. (2) "STIMULUS PREFERENCE AMONG CHILDREN OF DIFFERENT ETHNIC BACKGROUNDS." PREFERENCE FOR COLOR OR FORM, SYMMETRICAL OR ASYMMETRICAL DIMENSIONS WAS TESTED WITH CHILDREN OF NEGRO, INDIAN, AND ANGLO BACKGROUNDS. SUBJECTS WERE SHOWN 40 1-FOOT-SQUARE CARDS, EACH WITH 3 STIMULI ARRANGED IN A TRIANGLE, AND ASKED TO MAKE SELECTIONS. RESULTS SHOWED THAT PERSONALITY VARIABLES AND SOCIALIZATION INFLUENCES AFFECTED STIMULUS PREFERENCE, WITH CHILDREN FROM A CERTAIN CULTURAL BACKGROUND GENERALLY PREFERRING THE SAME STIMULI. (3) "A PERCEPTUAL COMPONENT OF VISUAL-ANALYTIC SKILLS." A TACHISTOSCOPE WAS USED FOR CHILDREN TO VIEW DRAWINGS OF CLASSROOM OBJECTS AND TO INDICATE RECOGNITION BY IDENTIFYING THE ACTUAL OBJECTS. A VISUAL-ANALYTIC SKILLS TEST, DEVELOPED FOR THE EXPERIMENT, WAS USED AS

A CRITERION INSTRUMENT OF FORM PERCEPTION ACCURACY. THE EXPERIMENTAL TREATMENT WAS INEFFECTIVE IN PRODUCING VISUAL DISCRIMINATION ACCURACY GAINS OVER AN 8- TO 10-WEEK PERIOD. (MS)

ED019124 PS000832
FINAL REPORT ON HEAD START EVALUATION AND RESEARCH--1966-67 TO THE INSTITUTE FOR EDUCATIONAL DEVELOPMENT. SECTION VIII, RELATIONSHIPS BETWEEN SELF-CONCEPT AND SPECIFIC VARIABLES IN A LOW-INCOME CULTURALLY DIFFERENT POPULATION. MCDANIEL, ELIZABETH LOGAN, 31AUG67 163P.
EDRS PRICE MF-$0.65 HC-$6.58

ANGLO, NEGRO, AND MEXICAN-AMERICAN CHILDREN WERE STUDIED TO INVESTIGATE FUNCTIONAL RELATIONSHIPS WHICH EXIST BETWEEN THE SELF-CONCEPT OF THE LOW-INCOME, CULTURALLY DIFFERENT CHILD AND CERTAIN ORGANISMIC (RACE, SEX, FAMILY SIZE, BIRTH ORDER, GRADE LEVEL) AND BEHAVIORAL (ACHIEVEMENT AND INTELLIGENCE TEST RESULTS) VARIABLES. ONE HUNDRED AND EIGHTY CHILDREN (30 EACH IN GRADES 1 THROUGH 6) WERE RATED ON A 30-ITEM, 5-POINT, INFERRED SELF-CONCEPT SCALE DEVELOPED FOR THE STUDY. RATINGS MADE BY THE CHILD'S TEACHER AND THE SCHOOL COUNSELOR WERE USED TO TEST SCALE RELIABILITY AND VALIDITY, BUT ONLY THE TEACHERS' RATINGS WERE USED IN THE ANALYSES OF HYPOTHESES. CORRELATION OF SELF-CONCEPT RATINGS WITH THE ABOVE VARIABLES SHOWED THAT THE CHILDREN VIEWED THEMSELVES POSITIVELY. AFTER 6 MONTHS OF SCHOOL, THE CHILDREN WERE AGAIN RATED BY TEACHERS AND ANALYSIS OF THE DATA SHOWED (1) THAT SELF-CONCEPTS OF ALL THE EXPERIMENTAL CHILDREN HAD DECLINED SIGNIFICANTLY, (2) THAT INADEQUATE VERBAL SKILLS (FOUND IN THE MEXICAN-AMERICAN CHILDREN) WERE RELATED TO LOW SELF-CONCEPTS, AND (3) THAT IT CANNOT BE ASSUMED THAT ALL MEMBERS OF ONE SPECIFIC RACE OR ECONOMIC CLASS HAVE LOW SELF-CONCEPTS. SINCE THIS EXPERIMENT WAS BASED ON THE THEORY THAT SOCIAL PRESSURE FORMS SELF-CONCEPT, ONE CONCLUSION IS THAT CHILDREN MUST FEEL THAT THERE IS PERSONAL VALUE IN ACHIEVING MIDDLE CLASS GOALS IF THEY ARE TO ACHIEVE IN SCHOOL. THEREFORE, ACHIEVEMENT MUST BE POSITIVELY RELATED TO THE VALUE SYSTEM OF A SPECIFIC POPULATION. (MS)

ED019125 PS000835
LANGUAGE DEVELOPMENT EXPERIENCES FOR YOUNG CHILDREN. ENGEL, ROSE C.; AND OTHERS, 66 300P.
EDRS PRICE MF-$0.65 HC-$9.87

ALTHOUGH ORIGINALLY DESIGNED TO AID THE TEACHERS OF MENTALLY HANDICAPPED CHILDREN, THIS COMPREHENSIVE HANDBOOK OF LANGUAGE DEVELOPMENT EXPERIENCES IS USEFUL FOR ALL TEACHERS OF PRESCHOOLERS, INCLUDING THOSE CHILDREN WHO ARE DISADVANTAGED, PHYSICALLY HANDICAPPED, OR LEARNING ENGLISH AS A SECOND LANGUAGE. AN INITIAL DISCUSSION OF LANGUAGE DEVELOPMENT AND PROGRAM PLANNING IS FOLLOWED BY EXPLICIT LANGUAGE EXPERIENCE ACTIVITIES IN ART, COOKING, DRAMATIC PLAY, MUSIC, SCIENCE, WATER PLAY, AND DURING STORY TIME AND COMMUNITY TRIPS. EACH EXPERIENCE IS PRESENTED ON A SINGLE PAGE OF THE MANUAL WITH LISTS OF MATERIAL NEEDED, THINGS TO DO, THINGS TO TALK ABOUT, AND VARIATIONS OF THE EXPERIENCES SUGGESTED TO DO ON ANOTHER DAY. ALSO INCLUDED ARE LISTS OF BOOKS FOR TEACHERS AND BOOKS FOR CHILDREN TO FURTHER EXPAND LANGUAGE GROWTH. FORMS FOR EVALUATION OF A CHILD'S LANGUAGE DEVELOPMENT AND PROGRESS AS WELL AS A CROSS- INDEX OF RECEPTIVE AND EXPRESSIVE LANGUAGE EXPERIENCES DISCUSSED ARE ALSO CONTAINED IN THE HANDBOOK. (MS)

ED019126 PS000837
GUIDE FOR TEACHING PHYSICAL EDUCATION, GRADES 1-6. ANDERSON, JESSIE T., 66 306P.
EDRS PRICE MF-$0.65 HC-$13.16

THE INTRODUCTORY CHAPTER OF THIS GUIDE CONSISTS OF A DISCUSSION OF THE HISTORICAL DEVELOPMENT OF PHYSICAL EDUCATION AND OF THE BASIC PRINCIPLES WHICH SERVE AS THE FOUNDATION FOR PHYSICAL EDUCATION IN THE PUBLIC SCHOOLS. THE SUCCEEDING CHAPTER IS CONCERNED WITH (1) THE AIMS OF PHYSICAL EDUCATION, (2) THE IMPORTANCE OF INITIAL AND ONGOING HEALTH APPRAISAL OF STUDENTS, (3) THE PSYCHOLOGICAL AND PHYSIOLOGICAL GROWTH AND DEVELOPMENTAL CHARACTERISTICS OF CHILDREN, (4) METHODS OF ASSISTING CHILDREN WITH WEIGHT CONTROL PROBLEMS, AND (5) THE CARDIAC-RESPIRATORY ENDURANCE OF ELEMENTARY SCHOOL STUDENTS. SUGGESTIONS FOR PLANNING, SCHEDULING, CONDUCTING, AND EVALUATING AN ACCEPTABLE PROGRAM ARE PRESENTED IN CHAPTER 3. THE TEACHING OF BODY MOVEMENT SKILLS, POSTURE, AND SAFETY IN PHYSICAL ACTIVITIES ARE THE SUBJECTS OF CHAPTER 4. INDIVIDUAL CHAPTERS ARE DEVOTED TO EACH OF THE ELEMENTARY GRADE LEVELS (GRADES 1 TO 6) AND INCLUDE SPECIFIC DESCRIPTIONS OF (1) THE CHARACTERISTICS OF THE CHILD, (2) THE OBJECTIVES OF THE PROGRAM, (3) SUGGESTED ACTIVITIES, AND (4) CRITERIA AND TOOLS FOR THE EVALUATION OF STUDENT PERFORMANCE. APPENDIXES INCLUDE SUGGESTIONS FOR (1) REFERENCE MATERIALS, (2) ORGANIZATION OF PLAYGROUND AREAS, (3) EQUIPMENT AND SUPPLIES, (4) SELF-MADE, INEXPENSIVE MATERIALS, (5) TOURNAMENT DESIGN, AND (6) CUMULATIVE RECORDS. (JS)

ED019127 PS000838
EARLY LEARNING IN THE HOME. BLOOM, BENJAMIN S., 18JUL65 30P.
EDRS PRICE MF-$0.65 HC-$3.29

RECOGNITION OF THE EDUCATIONAL PROBLEMS OF CULTURALLY AND SOCIALLY DEPRIVED CHILDREN TOGETHER WITH THE GROWING EVIDENCE OF THE EFFECTS OF EARLY CHILDHOOD DEVELOPMENT ON LATER EDUCATIONAL ACHIEVEMENT HAS LED TO THE PROPOSING OF LARGE-SCALE PROGRAMS TO ATTACK THESE PROBLEMS. IT SEEMS THAT SPECIAL NURSERY SCHOOL AND KINDERGARTEN PROGRAMS OFFER THE HIGHEST POTENTIAL PAYOFF. SUCH PROGRAMS ARE BEING DEVELOPED FIRST FOR DISADVANTAGED CHILDREN BUT WILL EVENTUALLY BE EXTENDED TO ALL. AN IMPORTANT QUESTION WHICH IS RAISED IS WHAT THE GOALS OF SUCH PROGRAMS SHOULD BE. SOME ANSWERS TO THE QUESTION POSED ARE AVAILABLE FROM VARIOUS TYPES OF RESEARCH INCLUDING LONGITUDINAL STUDIES, OTHER THEORETICAL AND EMPIRICAL STUDIES OF DEVELOPMENT, RESEARCH IN THE HOME ENVIRONMENT, AND RESEARCH ON PROCESSES IN INTELLECTUAL DEVELOPMENT. A GENERAL CONCLUSION FROM THIS RESEARCH IS THAT VERY EARLY DEVELOPMENT IS QUITE CRITICAL. THE LIKELIHOOD THAT THE PARENTS, PARTICULARLY THOSE OF CULTURALLY DEPRIVED CHILDREN, ARE ABLE TO ADEQUATELY SUPPLY THIS DEVELOPMENT SEEMS SLIGHT. THUS, THERE IS AN IMPORTANT TASK FOR THE SCHOOLS BOTH IN HELPING THE PARENTS AND IN SUPPLEMENTING THEIR EFFORTS. SOME MAJOR PROGRAM OBJECTIVES SUGGESTED BY THE RESEARCH ON CHILD DEVELOPMENT ARE (1) INCREASING THE RANGE OF THE CHILD'S PERCEPTIONS AND EXPERIENCES, (2) DEVELOPING AN EXTENDED AND ACCURATE USE OF LANGUAGE, (3) CREATING AN ENTHUSIASM FOR LEARNING THROUGH THE CHILD'S ABILITY TO MASTER LEARNING TASKS, (4) DEVELOPING THE CHILD'S THINKING AND REASONING SKILLS, AND (5) DEVELOPING PURPOSIVE LEARNING ACTIVITY IN THE CHILD. THIS PAPER WAS GIVEN AT THE FIRST B. J. PALEY LECTURE, UNIVERSITY OF CALIFORNIA AT LOS ANGELES, JULY 18, 1965. (DR)

ED019128 PS000853
A POSITION PAPER ON EARLY CHILDHOOD EDUCATION. , 67 9P.
EDRS PRICE MF-$0.65 HC-$3.29

THIS POSITION PAPER ON EARLY CHILDHOOD EDUCATION BEGINS BY SUGGESTING 4 GENERAL GOALS FOR THE EXPERIENCES WHICH THE EARLY CHILDHOOD CURRICULUM SHOULD PROVIDE FOR CHILDREN. THESE EXPERIENCES SHOULD BE DESIGNED TO PROMOTE PHYSICAL AND MENTAL HEALTH, TO PRODUCE SOME UNDERSTANDING OF THE SOCIAL AND SCIENTIFIC ASPECTS OF OUR WORLD, TO DEVELOP COMPETENCE IN COMMUNICATION, AND TO LEAD TO UNDERSTANDING, APPRECIATION, AND EXPRESSIVE ABILITY IN THE ARTS. WAYS IN WHICH TEACHERS AND ADMINISTRATORS CAN HELP PROVIDE THESE ARE SUGGESTED, AND RECOMMENDATIONS FOR IMPROVING EARLY CHILDHOOD EDUCATION ARE MADE. AN OUTLINE OF A DAILY PRIMARY PROGRAM IS GIVEN. A SUMMARY STATEMENT OF THE KINDS OF EXPERIENCES CHILDREN SHOULD RECEIVE IS INCLUDED AS IS A STATEMENT OF SOME BASIC HUMAN VALUES WHICH SHOULD BE DEVELOPED IN CHILDREN. THIS PAPER WAS PREPARED BY THE EARLY CHILDHOOD WORKSHOP PARTICIPANTS, KIRKSVILLE, MISSOURI. (DR)

ED019129 PS000857
ABSTRACTS OF RESEARCH PERTAINING TO--UNGRADED VS SELF-CONTAINED CLASSROOM ORGANIZATION IN THE ELEMENTARY SCHOOL (GRADES 1-7). , 21FEB67 25P.
EDRS PRICE MF-$0.65 HC-$3.29

THIS BULLETIN CONSISTS OF 32 ABSTRACTS WHICH ARE CONCERNED WITH THE RELATIVE MERITS OF UNGRADED AND SELF-CONTAINED CLASSROOM ORGANIZATION IN THE ELEMENTARY SCHOOL. ABSTRACTED DOCUMENTS INCLUDE THOSE WHICH ARE (1) STATEMENTS OF PROFESSIONAL OPINION, (2) SURVEYS OF PROFESSIONAL OPINION, (3) REVIEWS OF GENERAL TRENDS OR OF SPECIFIC PROGRAMS, AND (4) REPORTS OF EVALUATIVE RESEARCH. THREE FORMATS ARE EMPLOYED. ABSTRACTS OF LITERATURE CONSISTING OF GENERAL PROGRAM REVIEWS, SUMMARIES OF RESEARCH, OR STATEMENTS OF OPINION (15 ENTRIES) ARE PRESENTED IN A FORMAT WHICH CONSISTS OF (1) CITATION, (2) PURPOSE, AND (3) AUTHOR'S COMMENTS. ELEVEN REPORTS OF RESEARCH PROJECTS ARE ABSTRACTED IN A FORMAT WHICH CONSISTS OF (1) CITATION, (2) PURPOSE AND/OR OBJECTIVE, (3) PROCEDURE, (4) RESULTS, AND (5) AUTHOR'S GENERALIZATIONS. SIX ENTRIES ARE BASED ON PREVIOUS ABSTRACT OF RESEARCH PROJECTS AND ARE PRESENTED IN A FORMAT WHICH CONSISTS OF (1) CITATION, (2) PURPOSE, (3) SOURCES OF CITED EVIDENCE, (4) SUMMAR OF CITED EVIDENCE, AND (5) AUTHOR'S GENERALIZATIONS. ADDITIONAL COPIES OF THIS BULLETIN ARE AVAILABLE FREE FROM DOYNE M. SMITH, RESEARCH AND DEVELOPMENT CENTER IN EDUCATIONAL STIMULATION, 103 BALDWIN HALL, UNIVERSITY OF GEORGIA, ATHENS, GEORGIA. (JS)

ED019130 PS000858
GROUP WORK WITH PARENTS OF CHILDREN WITH LEARNING DISORDERS. BARMAN, ALICEROSE S., 17P.
EDRS PRICE MF-$0.65 HC-$3.29

SINCE THE PARENTS OF CHILDREN WITH LEARNING DISORDERS FELT ISOLATED FROM THEIR CHILDREN, THE PSYCHIATRIST IN CHARGE OF THE NORTH SHORE MENTAL HEALTH ASSOCIATION DECIDED GROUP WORK WITH THESE PARENTS WAS NEEDED. FROM THE EXPERIENCES OF WORKING WITH SEVERAL SUCH GROUPS IT HAS BEEN DECIDED THAT (1) A GROUP SHOULD BE COMPOSED ONLY OF PARENTS WHOSE CHILDREN HAVE BEEN PROFESSIONALLY DIAGNOSED AS HAVING A PERCEPTUAL PROBLEM, (2) THE GROUP SHOULD MEET EVERY OTHER WEEK FOR 8 SESSIONS FOR A PERIOD OF 1-1/2 HOURS, (3) A FEE OF $10 SHOULD BE CHARGED, ALTHOUGH NO ONE WOULD BE DENIED ADMISSION BECAUSE OF INABILITY TO PAY, (4) GROUP SIZE SHOULD BE FROM 10 TO 12, (5) THE CHILDREN REPRESENTED SHOULD RANGE NO MORE THAN 4 YEARS IN GRADE LEVEL, AND (6) A GROUP SHOULD BE COMPOSED OF PARENTS AT THE SAME LEVEL OF KNOWLEDGE OR LACK OF IT CONCERNING PERCEPTUAL HANDICAPPING. THE GOALS OF THESE GROUPS HAVE BEEN (1) TO GIVE FACTUAL KNOWLEDGE ABOUT A KIND OF DIFFICULTY WHICH IS LITTLE UNDERSTOOD, (2) TO PROVIDE A PLACE FOR DISCUSSION OF FEELINGS CONCERNING THE CHILD, AND (3) TO PROVIDE A CLEARINGHOUSE WHERE USEFUL TECHNIQUES OF MANAGEMENT CAN BE SHARED. EVALUATIONS MADE BY MOST OF THE MEMBERS OF THE GROUPS HAVE INDICATED THAT THESE GOALS HAVE BEEN MET WITH SOME DEGREE OF SUCCESS IN ALL AREAS. ALSO, IN SPITE OF THE FACT THAT NO PATTERN OF PERCEPTUAL DIFFICULTY IS LIKE THE NEXT, CERTAIN GUIDEPOSTS TO HELP PARENTS HAVE BEEN FORMED BY THESE GROUPS. INCLUDED ALSO ARE QUOTATIONS TAKEN FROM A PARENT'S EVALUATION SHEET TELLING WHY THE GROUP WAS BENEFICIAL. (CO)

ED019131 PS000859
REPORT OF THE EFFECTIVENESS OF PROJECT HEAD START, LUBBOCK, TEXAS. PARTS I, II, AND APPENDICES. CARTWRIGHT, WALTER J.; STEGLICH, W.G., 65 75P.
EDRS PRICE MF-$0.65 HC-$3.29

WITH THE COMPLETION OF THE FIRST GRADE BY THE FIRST HEAD START CLASS IN LUBBOCK, TEXAS, THIS STUDY WAS UNDERTAKEN TO PRESENT DATA ON THE EFFECTIVENESS OF THE HEAD START PROGRAM IN IMPROVING DISADVANTAGED CHILDREN'S CHANCES FOR SCHOOL SUCCESS. TWO HUNDRED AND NINETY-FIVE URBAN AREA HEAD START CHILDREN FROM NEGRO, ANGLO-AMERICAN, AND MEXICAN-AMERICAN FAMILIES WERE COMPARED WITH A CONTROL GROUP MATCHED ON SEX, ETHNIC GROUP, AND ECONOMIC LEVEL. WHENEVER POSSIBLE, THE MATCHED PAIRS OF CHILDREN WERE IN THE SAME SCHOOL CLASSROOM SO THAT THE TEACHER COULD OBSERVE AND MAKE SUBJECTIVE EVALUATIONS OF HEAD START AND CONTROL CHILDREN ON 8 FACTORS SUCH AS PARTICIPATION, ATTENDANCE, AND EDUCATIONAL ACCOMPLISHMENT. A SOCIOLOGICAL RATHER THAN AN INDIVIDUAL APPROACH WAS USED IN MAKING THIS EVALUATION. TO MEASURE SCHOOL SUCCESS, GRADES WERE OBTAINED AND COMPARED FOR ALL CHILDREN INVOLVED. RESULTS SHOWED THAT THE CONTROL GROUP WAS SUPERIOR TO THE HEAD START GROUP BOTH AT THE END OF THE FIRST YEAR OF SCHOOL AND ALSO AT THE END OF THE SECOND SCHOOL YEAR WHEN ADDITIONAL EXAMINATIONS AND STANDARDIZED TESTS COMPARED THE 140 MATCHED PAIRS STILL AVAILABLE OUT OF THE ORIGINAL GROUP OF 295. APPENDIXES RELATED TO 1966 DATA (END OF FIRST YEAR) AND 1967 DATA (END OF SECOND YEAR) ARE INCLUDED IN THE REPORT. (MS)

ED019132 PS000861
CHILDREN LEARN AND GROW THROUGH ART EXPERIENCES. ILLINOIS CURRICULUM PROGRAM, THE SUBJECT FIELD SERIES. PAGE, RAY, 58
DOCUMENT NOT AVAILABLE FROM EDRS.

THIS BULLETIN IS A GUIDE FOR THE CREATION OR IMPLEMENTATION OF AN ART CURRICULUM FOR THE SCHOOL. BECAUSE OF THE RECOGNIZED VARIETY OF TALENTS AND INTERESTS IN ANY ONE CLASSROOM OR GRADE, THE IDEAS AND PROCEDURES PRESENTED IN THE BULLETIN ARE NOT MEANT TO FOLLOW ANY AGE-GRADE ORGANIZATION. INSTEAD, THE TEACHER IS URGED TO PERUSE THE ENTIRE GUIDE AND USE THE SUGGESTIONS TO HIS OR HER PARTICULAR ADVANTAGE. TO EFFECT AN IMAGINATIVE, MOTIVATIVE, ART PROGRAM, THE SCHOOL ADMINISTRATOR CAN FULFILL HIS ROLE BY HIRING CAPABLE TEACHERS AND BY SUPPORTING THEIR REQUESTS FOR FACILITIES AND MATERIALS. THE TEACHER MUST BE KEENLY INTERESTED IN ART EDUCATION AND CONSTANTLY SEARCHING FOR CREATIVE NEW WAYS TO INVOLVE HER PUPILS IN ARTISTIC EXPRESSION. NOT ALL CHILDREN CAN DRAW A HORSE WELL, BUT THEY ALL HAVE SOME URGE TO CREATIVITY THAT CAN BE TAPPED IN VARIOUS WAYS. THIS BULLETIN ENUMERATES AND ILLUSTRATES THE MANY WAYS TO MANIPULATE AND EXPERIMENT WITH MATERIALS AND IDEAS IN ORDER TO EXPLORE AND DISCOVER THE ALMOST INFINITE VISUAL AND TACTILE FORMS AND FEELINGS THAT EXIST IN THE WORLD OF ARTISTIC EXPRESSION AND CREATIVITY. IT IS IMPORTANT THAT THE CHILD BE INTRODUCED TO AS MANY OF THESE FORMS, IDEAS, AND STIMULI AS POSSIBLE, FOR THE CREATIVE PROCESS IS NOT JUST A MEANS OF PERSONAL ENJOYMENT FOR THE INDIVIDUAL PUPIL, IT IS AN EXERCISE IN DISCOVERY AND UNDERSTANDING OF HIMSELF AND OF THE WORLD ABOUT HIM. THIS DOCUMENT IS AVAILABLE FROM THE ILLINOIS CURRICULUM PROGRAM, OFFICE OF THE SUPERINTENDENT OF PUBLIC INSTRUCTION, SPRINGFIELD, ILLINOIS, AS BULLETIN NO. C-FOUR OF THE SUBJECT FIELD SERIES. (WD)

ED019133 PS000862
DESIGN FOR A PLAYROOM. L'ABATE, LUCIANO, 14P.
EDRS PRICE MF-$0.65 HC-$3.29

ALTHOUGH IT IS ASSUMED THAT PLAY THERAPY IS BENEFICIAL TO CHILDREN, LITTLE RELEVANT RESEARCH DATA IS AVAILABLE CONCERNING THE NATURE AND EXTENT OF ITS EFFECTIVENESS. THE EXISTING PAUCITY OF RESEARCH INFORMATION CONCERNED WITH PLAYROOM BEHAVIOR IS ATTRIBUTABLE TO (1) THE INADEQUATE CONCEPTUALIZATION OF RELEVANT THEORY AND OF THE SITUATIONAL VARIABLES, (2) AN INSUFFICIENT CONCERN WITH THE PHYSICAL CHARACTERISTICS OF THE PLAYROOM ENVIRONMENT, (3) THE ECONOMIC WASTE TRADITIONALLY ASSOCIATED WITH PLAYROOM RESEARCH, AND (4) THE DIFFICULTIES ENCOUNTERED IN ATTEMPTING TO CATEGORIZE PLAY BEHAVIOR. IN ORDER TO ACCOUNT FOR THESE SHORTCOMINGS, PLAY THERAPY FACILITIES CONSISTING OF 2 ADJACENT BUT INTERCONNECTED ROOMS SHOULD BE CONSTRUCTED. THE 2 ROOMS SHOULD CONTAIN, RESPECTIVELY, TOYS WHICH PERMIT THE EXPRESSION OF CONSTRUCTIVE AND AGGRESSIVE BEHAVIOR. TIMERS AND/OR COUNTERS CONNECTED TO EACH OF THE TOYS SHOULD BE TAPE-PUNCHED TO ALLOW DIRECT COMPUTER ANALYSIS OF TIME SPENT IN EACH OF THE ROOMS AND WITH EACH OF THE TOYS. A MASTER CONTROL BOOTH EQUIPPED WITH A ONE-WAY MIRROR AND CONTAINING THE METERING EQUIPMENT WOULD PERMIT THE USE OF TRADITIONAL OBSERVATION AND TAPE-RECORDING PROCEDURES. A PLAYROOM AREA CONSTRUCTED IN THIS MANNER WOULD NOT INTERFERE WITH CLINICAL PRACTICE AND WOULD PERMIT THE GATHERING OF RESEARCH DATA CONCERNED WITH THE EFFECTIVENESS OF PLAY THERAPY. (JS)

ED019134 PS000864
LINGUISTICS IN THE ELEMENTARY SCHOOL. DOLIVE, EARLINE, MAY67 94P.
EDRS PRICE MF-$0.65 HC-$3.29

THIS GUIDE WAS PREPARED FOR THE ELEMENTARY SCHOOL TEACHER WHO HAS HAD LITTLE OR NO TRAINING IN LINGUISTICS. OPPORTUNITIES FOR CALLING ATTENTION TO THE LINGUISTIC ASPECTS OF LANGUAGE OCCUR FREQUENTLY IN THE CLASSROOM, AND THIS GUIDE PROVIDES SUGGESTIONS FOR MAKING USE OF THEM. FOUR INITIAL CHAPTERS DISCUSS THE USAGE OF LINGUISTICS, PROVIDE A GLOSSARY OF LINGUISTIC TERMS, SUGGEST GUIDING PRINCIPLES FOR TEACHERS, AND DESCRIBE THE LINGUISTIC CONCEPTION OF LANGUAGE. SIX SUCCEEDING CHAPTERS PRESENT INDIVIDUAL LINGUISTIC CONCEPTS-- PHONOLOGY, MORPHOLOGY, FORM CLASSES, SYNTAX, DIALECT, AND USAGE. EACH CHAPTER HAS AN INTRODUCTORY SECTION THAT DEFINES AND ILLUSTRATES THE CONCEPT, AND A SECTION WITH ACTIVITIES FOR DEMONSTRATING THE CONCEPT TO THE STUDENTS. A CONCLUDING CHAPTER PRESENTS A BIBLIOGRAPHY OF ABOUT 50 TITLES. (DR)

ED019135 PS000866
AN EVALUATION OF A PRESCHOOL TRAINING PROGRAM FOR CULTURALLY DEPRIVED CHILDREN. FINAL REPORT. TAMMINEN, ARMAS W.; AND OTHERS, OCT67 42P.
EDRS PRICE MF-$0.65 HC-$3.29

TO FIND OUT IF CULTURALLY DEPRIVED CHILDREN SHOW CHANGE IN ACADEMIC READINESS AS A RESULT OF SPECIAL PRESCHOOL PROGRAMS, 3 GROUPS OF CHILDREN (14 TO 17 IN EACH) IN 3 DULUTH SCHOOL AREAS WERE PRE- AND POSTTESTED WITH THE STANFORD-BINET AND SRA PRIMARY MENTAL ABILITIES TESTS. A CONTROL GROUP OF 30 CHILDREN FROM THE SAME 3 SCHOOL AREAS WERE GIVEN THE TESTS BUT DID NOT ATTEND PRESCHOOL. THE REGULAR HEAD START CURRICULUM WAS USED IN 1 PRESCHOOL GROUP WHILE A SECOND GROUP WAS GIVEN SPECIAL CREATIVE MONTESSORI PLAY EQUIPMENT IN ADDITION TO THE HEAD START CURRICULUM. A THIRD GROUP OF CHILDREN HAD THE SAME EQUIPMENT AND EXPERIENCES PLUS A PARENT COORDINATOR WHO VISITED EACH CHILD'S PARENTS 3 TIMES DURING THE SUMMER PROGRAM IN AN EFFORT TO INCREASE FAMILY INVOLVEMENT. ALL CHILDREN WERE RETESTED AT THE END OF THE KINDERGARTEN YEAR TO SEE HOW THE EXPERIMENTAL AND CONTROL GROUPS COMPARED WITH EACH OTHER AND WITH KINDERGARTEN PUPILS IN PREVIOUS YEARS. ANALYSIS OF VARIANCE OF THE DATA SHOWED THAT THE ACADEMIC POTENTIAL OF DISADVANTAGED CHILDREN CAN BE INCREASED BY PRESCHOOL TRAINING INASMUCH AS THE CONTROL GROUP CHILDREN DID NOT SHOW IQ INCREASES WHILE THE IQ'S OF THE EXPERIMENTAL GROUPS INCREASED. THIS INCREASE WAS RETAINED DURING THE KINDERGARTEN YEAR. THERE WAS NO SIGNIFICANT DIFFERENCE IN THE EFFECTIVENESS OF 1 PROGRAM OVER ANOTHER ALTHOUGH TOO LITTLE TIME MAY HAVE ELAPSED FOR POSITIVE MONTESSORI AND PARENTAL INVOLVEMENT EFFECTS TO APPEAR. (MS)

ED019136 PS000867
DEVELOPMENT OF A GROUP MEASURE TO ASSESS THE EXTENT OF PRE-LOGICAL AND PRE-CAUSAL THINKING IN PRIMARY SCHOOL AGE CHILDREN. DE AVILA, EDWARD; STRUTHERS, JOSEPH A., MAR67 8P.
EDRS PRICE MF-$0.65 HC-$3.29

A GROUP MEASUREMENT INSTRUMENT WAS CONSTRUCTED TO TEST THE DEVELOPMENT OF CRITICAL THINKING IN YOUNG CHILDREN. DESIGNED TO ELICIT CHOICES OF THE MOST SATISFACTORY OF 3 ALTERNATIVE CONCLUSIONS FOR EACH OF 26 INCOMPLETE STORIES PRESENTED IN CARTOON PANEL FORMAT, THE INSTRUMENT MEASURES

THE DEVELOPMENT OF THE 4 PIAGETIAN CONCEPTS OF CONSERVATION, CAUSALITY, RELATIONS, AND LOGIC. THE TEST WAS INITIALLY ADMINISTERED TO 1,972 CHILDREN IN THE BOULDER (COLORADO) SCHOOL DISTRICT. HOMOGENEITY RATIOS, RELIABILITY COEFFICIENTS, AND INTERITEM CONSISTENCIES WERE COMPUTED FOR EACH OF THE CONCEPTUAL SCALES. THE LOGIC AND RELATIONS SCALES APPEARED TO CONTAIN ITEMS WHICH WERE TOO DISSIMILAR AND, AS A RESULT, FAILED TO CLUSTER SATISFACTORILY. THE CONSERVATION AND CAUSALITY SCALES, HOWEVER, EXHIBITED STATISTICALLY SIGNIFICANT INTERITEM CONSISTENCIES. MEAN SCORES ON THE CONSERVATION AND CAUSALITY SCALES WERE COMPUTED AS A FUNCTION OF CHRONOLOGICAL AGE, AND AGE-RELATED TRENDS WERE FOUND TO EXIST IN THESE AREAS. THE RESULTS THUS FAR SUGGEST THAT THIS GROUP MEASUREMENT INSTRUMENT IS A PROMISING MEANS FOR OBTAINING INFORMATION WHICH HAS HERETOFORE BEEN OBTAINED ONLY IN CLINICAL TESTING WHICH INVOLVES THE EXTENSIVE INTERVIEWING OF EACH SUBJECT. THIS PAPER WAS PRESENTED AT THE 1967 ANNUAL CONVENTION OF THE NATIONAL SCIENCE TEACHERS ASSOCIATION. (JS)

ED019137 PS000868
COVERT PROJECT, YEAR 1. KLEIN, GENEVIEVE; AND OTHERS, 67 27P.
EDRS PRICE MF-$0.65 HC-$3.29

A TUCSON EDUCATIONAL PROJECT, CALLED COVERT (CHILDREN OFFERED VITAL EDUCATIONAL RETRAINING AND THERAPY), HAS BEEN PROPOSED TO IMPROVE THE EDUCATIONAL OPPORTUNITY OF EMOTIONALLY DISTURBED CHILDREN. SURVEYS INDICATE THAT FROM 5 TO 14 PERCENT OF TUCSON'S SCHOOL CHILDREN HAVE EMOTIONAL-BEHAVIORAL PROBLEMS WHICH INTERFERE WITH THEIR LEARNING ACHIEVEMENT IN REGULAR SCHOOL SURROUNDINGS. THIS PROJECT INTENDS TO PLACE THESE DISTURBED CHILDREN IN A SEPARATE, MORE THERAPEUTIC SCHOOL ENVIRONMENT IN WHICH EDUCATORS AND CLINICIANS CAN WORK TOGETHER TO HELP CORRECT THE DISTURBED CHILDREN'S SPECIAL PROBLEMS. THE EDUCATIONAL PHILOSOPHY OF THIS SPECIAL SCHOOL WILL NOT VARY ESSENTIALLY FROM THAT OF REGULAR SCHOOLS, EXCEPT THAT THERE WILL BE MORE INDIVIDUAL ATTENTION AND MORE FLEXIBILITY IN THE CURRICULUM. MOST OF THE CHILDREN QUALIFYING FOR THE COVERT SCHOOL WILL BE IDENTIFIED IN AND TRANSFERRED FROM THE REGULAR SCHOOL SYSTEM. THE TEACHING STRUCTURE OF THE COVERT SCHOOL WILL BE TEAM-ORIENTED SO THAT INTERACTION AND CONSULTATION BETWEEN THE ENTIRE STAFF CAN BEST BE USED TO EFFECT THE PURPOSE OF THE PROJECT, NAMELY, TO DIAGNOSE AND TREAT EACH CHILD'S EMOTIONAL- BEHAVIORAL PROBLEMS. THIS DOCUMENT DESCRIBES IN DETAIL THE ANTICIPATED ORGANIZATIONAL SCHEME OF THE WHOLE COVERT PROJECT, INCLUDING (1) THE TEACHER'S ROLE, OBJECTIVES, AND PURPOSES, (2) THE TYPE OF PERSONNEL TO BE USED, (3) THE 6 EDUCATIONAL APPROACHES TO BE IMPLEMENTED, INCLUDING A RESIDENT SCHOOL AND A DAY SCHOOL, AND (4) SUGGESTIONS FOR GOOD CLASSROOM MANAGEMENT. (WD)

ED019138 PS000873
DIFFERENTIATION BETWEEN NORMAL AND DISORDERED CHILDREN BY A COMPUTER ANALYSIS OF EMOTIONAL AND VERBAL BEHAVIOR. ALEXANDER, THERON; LEAVERTON, PAUL, 16P.
EDRS PRICE MF-$0.65 HC-$3.29

IT HAS BEEN SUGGESTED THAT THE EMOTIONAL CHARACTERISTICS OF PEOPLE CAN BE INVESTIGATED BY STUDYING THEIR VERBAL BEHAVIOR. THIS STUDY INVESTIGATED THE USE OF EMOTIONAL WORDS, BOTH POSITIVE AND NEGATIVE, AND THE TOTAL VERBAL OUTPUT OF NORMAL AND DISORDERED CHILDREN TO DETERMINE IF SIGNIFICANT DIFFERENCES IN VERBAL EXPRESSION OCCUR. TWO GROUPS OF CHILDREN, 7 TO 12 YEARS OF AGE, WERE RECRUITED. FORTY OF THEM WERE DIAGNOSED AS NORMAL CHILDREN, AND 38 AS HAVING BEHAVIOR DISORDERS. EACH CHILD WAS SHOWN 5 STIMULUS CARDS PORTRAYING A NEUTRAL SCENE CONTAINING 1 OR 2 PEOPLE AND WAS ASKED TO DESCRIBE INTERACTION AND EMOTION. THESE IMPRESSIONS WERE RECORDED AND THEN ANALYZED TO SEE IF THEY CONTAINED ANY OF 5 POSITIVE OR 5 NEGATIVE WORDS SELECTED TO INDICATE WHETHER THE CHILD'S REACTION TO THE STIMULUS CARD WAS POSITIVE OR NEGATIVE. ALL OF THE DATA ANALYSIS WAS DONE BY COMPUTER. THE COMPUTER WAS PROGRAMMED TO ANALYZE THE RECORDINGS FOR THE USE OF THE 10 EMOTION-DETERMINATION WORDS AND WAS ALSO PROGRAMMED TO DETERMINE TOTAL WORDS USED. THE SCORE FOR EACH CHILD WAS DERIVED BY THE COMPUTER ON THE BASIS OF A PREPROGRAMMED FORMULA. THE RESULTS SHOWED THAT THE NORMAL CHILDREN USED SIGNIFICANTLY MORE POSITIVE WORDS TO DESCRIBE THE PICTURES AND ALSO USED SIGNIFICANTLY MORE TOTAL WORDS THAN THE CHILDREN WITH BEHAVIOR DISORDERS. IT IS CONCLUDED THAT THIS COMPUTER PROCEDURE FOR ANALYSIS OF THE EXISTENCE OF EMOTIONAL DISORDERS MEANINGFULLY DIFFERENTIATES BETWEEN EMOTIONALLY NORMAL AND EMOTIONALLY DISTURBED CHILDREN. THEREFORE, IT SHOULD HAVE GENERAL VALUE IN ANALYZING GROUPS OF CHILDREN THAT HAVE NOT BEEN PREVIOUSLY DIAGNOSED FOR THE EXISTENCE OF EMOTIONAL DISORDERS. (WD)

ED019139 PS000874
EXTINCTION IN DISCRIMINATION LEARNING--PRESENTATION AND CONTINGENCY VARIABLES AND ASSOCIATED SIDE EFFECTS. COHEN, MIRIAM; AND OTHERS, FEB68 36P.
EDRS PRICE MF-$0.65 HC-$3.29

STUDIES HAVE SHOWN THAT IT IS POSSIBLE TO ESTABLISH DISCRIMINATORY RESPONSES TO PAIRS OF STIMULI WITHOUT ERROR RESPONSES TO THE UNREINFORCED (S-) STIMULUS. THE PURPOSE OF THIS STUDY WAS TO DETERMINE THE EFFECTS OF 2 METHODS OF INTRODUCING S- (FADING AND CONSTANT) AND 2 RESPONSE CONTINGENCIES (DELAY AND NO DELAY) ON THE OCCURRENCE OF S- RESPONSES. THE SUBJECTS WERE 27 KINDERGARTEN CHILDREN WHO WERE DIVIDED INTO 3 GROUPS WHICH RECEIVED 1 OF 3 TRAINING PROCEDURES--(1) FADING-NO DELAY, (2) CONSTANT-NO DELAY, AND (3) CONSTANT-DELAY. THE STIMULI WERE A HORIZONTAL AND A VERTICAL LINE PROJECTED ONTO A PLEXIGLASS SCREEN. THE RESPONSE CONSISTED OF PUSHING ON THE SCREEN, AND THE S+ STIMULUS WAS REINFORCED WITH CANDY. IN THE INITIAL SESSION THE S+ STIMULUS WAS PROJECTED 5 TIMES TO ESTABLISH THE RESPONSE, AND THEN THE S- STIMULUS WAS INTRODUCED IN A RANDOM FASHION. IN THE FADING PROCEDURE, ITS INTENSITY AND DURATION WERE GRADUALLY INCREASED UNTIL IT MATCHED THAT OF THE S+ STIMULUS. IN THE CONSTANT PROCEDURE IT WAS KEPT AT THE SAME INTENSITY AS S+. IF THERE WAS NO RESPONSE TO S-, IT TERMINATED IN 5 SECONDS. IN THE DELAY CONTINGENCY, 5 SECONDS HAD TO ELAPSE WITHOUT A RESPONSE BEFORE IT WOULD TERMINATE. IN THE NO-DELAY CONTINGENCY A RESPONSE IMMEDIATELY TERMINATED IT, AND IT WAS THEN REPROJECTED. THE SUBJECTS WERE TRAINED UNTIL THEY WENT THROUGH ONE SESSION OF 20 PRESENTATIONS OF EACH STIMULUS WITH NO S- RESPONSES. SUBJECTS TRAINED WITH THE FADING PROCEDURE MADE SIGNIFICANTLY FEWER RESPONSES IN THE COURSE OF TRAINING THAN SUBJECTS TRAINED WITH THE CONSTANT PROCEDURE. SUBJECTS TRAINED WITH THE CONSTANT-DELAY PROCEDURE MADE SIGNIFICANTLY FEWER RESPONSES THAN THE SUBJECTS TRAINED WITH THE CONSTANT-NO DELAY PROCEDURE. IN THE LATTER, IT WAS FELT THAT THE OFFSET OF THE S- STIMULUS WITH A RESPONSE WAS ACTING AS A REINFORCEMENT. (DR)

ED019141 PS000911
EVALUATING THE CHILD'S LANGUAGE COMPETENCE. KLIMA, URSULA BELLUGI, 68 21P.
EDRS PRICE MF-$0.65 HC-$3.29

LANGUAGE ABILITY IS ESSENTIAL TO A CHILD'S SUCCESS IN SCHOOL, AND THE MOST IMPORTANT PART OF COMMUNICATION IS THE CHILD'S ABILITY TO PUT WORDS TOGETHER IN MEANINGFUL PATTERNS. THE ABILITY OF ADULTS TO GIVE AN INTERPRETATION TO NONSENSE LIKE "JABBERWOCKY" DEPENDS ON THE SYNTACTIC CUES GIVEN BY RELATIONAL WORDS AND WORD ORDER. IN ORDER TO FIND OUT IF CHILDREN UNDERSTAND THESE CUES, IT IS NECESSARY TO DEVISE TESTS OF SYNTACTIC UNDERSTANDING. THE TESTS MUST BE POSED IN SUCH A WAY THAT THE SITUATIONAL CUES ARE MINIMIZED. THEY MUST USE WORDS THAT ARE KNOWN TO BE IN THE CHILD'S VOCABULARY AND MUST BE CONSTRUCTED SO THAT THE ABILITY TO GIVE A CORRECT ANSWER DEPENDS ON COMPREHENSION OF A PARTICULAR SYNTACTIC CONSTRUCTION. SEVERAL COMPREHENSION TESTS ARE INCLUDED. IN EACH TEST THE CHILD IS ASKED TO DISCRIMINATE BETWEEN 2 SENTENCES WHOSE ONLY DIFFERENCE IS IN SYNTACTIC CONSTRUCTION. THE TESTS ARE ARRANGED ACCORDING TO LEVELS OF DIFFICULTY WHICH ARE BASED ON THE ORDER IN WHICH CONSTRUCTS HAVE BEEN FOUND TO APPEAR IN CHILDREN'S SPEECH. (DR)

ED019142 PS000912
CRITICAL OVERVIEW OF EARLY CHILDHOOD EDUCATION PROGRAMS. LAVATELLI, C.B., 3APR68 18P.
EDRS PRICE MF-$0.65 HC-$3.29

PRESENT PRESCHOOL PROGRAMS FOR DISADVANTAGED CHILDREN ARE OF 3 KINDS--(1) AN INVENTORY TYPE WHICH ATTEMPTS TO IDENTIFY DEFICITS WHICH WILL AFFECT SCHOOL LEARNING AND TO OVERCOME THESE THROUGH EDUCATIONAL ACTIVITIES, (2) A PLAN BASED ON A RECAPITULATION THEORY WHICH ATTEMPTS TO DESCRIBE DEVELOPMENTAL STAGES AND TO COMPENSATE FOR THOSE WHICH A PARTICULAR CHILD HAS MISSED, AND (3) A COMPUTER MODEL IN WHICH THE CURRICULUM DOES NOT TAKE INTO CONSIDERATION SUCH PERSONAL FACTORS AS A CHILD'S ATTITUDE OR PERSONALITY BUT CONCENTRATES ON THE MECHANISTIC FUNCTION OF THE BRAIN TO RECEIVE, PROCESS, AND STORE DATA. PRESCHOOL PROGRAMS FOR THE DISADVANTAGED HAVE CONCENTRATED ON LANGUAGE AND COGNITIVE DEVELOPMENT AS THE CHILDREN HAVE DEMONSTRATED LACKS IN THESE AREAS. SOME OF THE DEVELOPMENTAL PRINCIPLES THAT APPLY TO LANGUAGE TRAINING ALSO APPLY TO INTELLECTIVE PROCESSES. THEREFORE, APPLICATION OF THESE TRAINING PRINCIPLES SHOULD RESULT IN A HIGHER LEVEL OF INTELLECTUAL FUNCTIONING. A FIRST PRINCIPLE OF LANGUAGE TRAINING IS THAT A CHILD SHOULD HEAR GOOD SAMPLES OF LANGUAGE USAGE SO THAT HE CAN LEARN TO DECODE MEANING AND TO CONSTRUCT HIS OWN RESPONSES. A MOTHER OR TEACHER WHO EXPANDS OR EXTENDS THE CHILD'S SENTENCES IMPROVES HIS LANGUAGE ENVIRONMENT. WHEN THE TEACHER IS AWARE OF SENTENCE STRUCTURE SHE CAN RECOGNIZE LANGUAGE AREAS IN WHICH A CHILD IS WEAK. THESE AREAS CAN THEN BE STRENGTHENED BY OFFERING PRESCHOOL ACTIVITIES DESIGNED TO ELICIT DESCRIPTIVE AND COMPARATIVE RESPONSES, THUS

STIMULATING VERBAL EXPRESSION. POSITIVE REINFORCEMENT BY THE TEACHER HELPS TO IMPROVE THE CHILD'S MEANINGFUL COMMUNICATION. THIS PAPER WAS PREPARED FOR THE HEAD START CONFERENCE (BERKELEY, APRIL 3, 1968). (MS)

ED019143 PS000916
SENSORIMOTOR EXPERIENCE AND CONCEPT FORMATION IN EARLY CHILDHOOD. FINAL REPORT. MELCER, DONALD; PECK, ROBERT F., FEB67 90P.
EDRS PRICE MF-$0.65 HC-$3.29

IN ORDER TO INVESTIGATE THE RELATIONSHIP BETWEEN SENSORIMOTOR EXPERIENCE AND THE FORMATION OF CONCEPTS IN CHILDHOOD, 2 GROUPS OF CHILDREN--1 MOTORICALLY NORMAL, THE OTHER COMPOSED OF CEREBRAL PALSIED CHILDREN--WERE COMPARED FOR ACQUISITION OF SIMPLE ACTION AND OBJECT CONCEPTS. THREE HYPOTHESES WERE TESTED. IT WAS PREDICTED (1) THAT CEREBRAL PALSIED CHILDREN WOULD IDENTIFY FEWER ACTION CONCEPTS THAN NONHANDICAPPED CHILDREN, (2) THAT PREVIOUS SENSORIMOTOR EXPERIENCE WOULD DETERMINE WHETHER CHILDREN WOULD UTILIZE A MOTORIC OR NONMOTORIC MODE OF PROBLEM SOLVING, AND (3) THAT CEREBRAL PALSIED CHILDREN WOULD HAVE POORER WEIGHT DISCRIMINATION THAN NORMAL CHILDREN. THE EXPERIMENT WAS A SIMPLE EX POST FACTO COMPARISON OF 2 GROUPS AND HAD THE DISADVANTAGE THAT THE INDEPENDENT VARIABLE-- SENSORIMOTOR EXPERIENCE--WAS NOT CONTROLLED. TWO GROUPS OF 40 CHILDREN RANGING IN AGE FROM 42 TO 66 MONTHS MADE UP THE SAMPLE. THE MAJOR CRITERION FOR INCLUSION WAS THE ABILITY TO RESPOND TO THE EXAMPLE PLATES OF THE PEABODY PICTURE VOCABULARY TEST (PPVT). THE CHILDREN WERE GIVEN 4 TESTS--(1) THE PPVT, FORM A, (2) A MODIFIED PPVT DESIGNED TO ALLOW AN ACTION OR CONCEPT PICTORIAL IDENTIFICATION IN RESPONSE TO A WORD, (3) A TEST OF WEIGHT DISCRIMINATION, AND (4) A TEST OF ADAPTIVE MODE. CHI-SQUARE ANALYSIS OF THE TEST SCORES OF THE 2 GROUPS STRONGLY SUPPORTED THE ACCEPTANCE OF ALL 3 HYPOTHESES. THE MAJOR CONCLUSION THAT CAN BE DRAWN IS THAT CONSIDERABLE SUPPORT IS GIVEN TO CURRENT THEORIES THAT SENSORIMOTOR EXPERIENCE IN INFANCY IS AN IMPORTANT FACTOR IN CONCEPT FORMATION. ONE EDUCATIONAL IMPLICATION IS THAT SEVERELY CEREBRAL PALSIED CHILDREN MIGHT PROFIT FROM SPECIALLY DESIGNED EDUCATIONAL PROGRAMS. (DR)

ED019144 PS000931
A COMPARISON BETWEEN THE ORAL AND WRITTEN RESPONSES OF FIRST-GRADE CHILDREN IN I.T.A. AND T.O. CLASSES. SANDEL, LENORE, 67 17P.
EDRS PRICE MF-$0.65 HC-$3.29

TWO FIRST GRADE CLASSES, ONE USING THE INITIAL TEACHING ALPHABET (ITA) AND ONE USING TRADITIONAL ORTHOGRAPHY (TO), WERE RANDOMLY SELECTED FROM A SCHOOL IN EACH OF 4 SCHOOL DISTRICTS. THE TOTAL SAMPLE CONSISTED OF 100 CHILDREN IN ITA CLASSES AND 100 CHILDREN IN TO CLASSES. THE CLASSES WERE GROUPED HETEROGENEOUSLY. THE PINTNER- CUNNINGHAM PRIMARY TEST, FORM A, WAS ADMINISTERED TO DETERMINE THE INTELLIGENCE RATING FOR EACH SUBJECT. THE DATA GATHERED INCLUDED 1 ORAL RESPONSE AND 1 WRITTEN RESPONSE FOR EACH PUPIL IN THE STUDY FOR EACH OF 3 STIMULI. THE RESULTS SUGGEST THAT THE WRITTEN LANGUAGE OF CHILDREN INSTRUCTED IN ITA, WHEN COMPARED WITH CHILDREN INSTRUCTED IN TO, SHOWED (1) AN INCREASED QUANTITY OF WRITING, (2) A GREATER VARIETY OF VOCABULARY EMPLOYED IN THE COMPOSITION, AND (3) AN INCREASED NUMBER OF THOUGHT UNITS WHEN EVALUATED BY CATEGORY OF INTELLIGENCE AND ORAL LANGUAGE COMPETENCY. THE RESULTS ALSO SUGGEST THAT A BROADER SAMPLE BE EVALUATED TO INCLUDE SUCH DISCRIMINATING FACTORS AS CLASSROOM PROCEDURE, INSTRUCTIONAL MATERIAL, AND CORRELATION WITH RELATED LANGUAGE ARTS ACTIVITIES. THE LONGITUDINAL EFFECT ON THE WRITTEN LANGUAGE COMPETENCY OF THE FIRST GRADE CHILDREN IN THE PILOT STUDY WAS TO BE DETERMINED WHEN THET PROCEEDED TO SECOND GRADE. (CO)

ED019987 PS000206
A COMPARATIVE STUDY OF VARIOUS PROJECT HEAD START PROGRAMS. HARDING, JOHN, 30JUN66 40P.
EDRS PRICE MF-$0.65 HC-$3.29

A FULL-DAY, YEAR-LONG, EXPERIMENTAL NURSERY SCHOOL PROGRAM FOR POOR CHILDREN FROM THE ITHACA, N.Y. AREA WAS CONDUCTED TO OBTAIN INFORMATION ON THE OPERATION OF THIS TYPE OF PRESCHOOL EXPERIENCE FOR THREE- AND FOUR-YEAR-OLD CHILDREN OF POOR FAMILIES AND TO DETERMINE SOME OF THE EFFECTS OF THE PROGRAM ON THE CHILDREN. THE CHILDREN WERE TESTED WITH THE PEABODY PICTURE VOCABULARY TEST AND THE STANFORD-BINET IN OCTOBER OF 1965 AND IN APRIL OF 1966. THE RESULTS SHOWED A SIGNIFICANT INCREASE IN THE IQ SCORES OF THE CHILDREN BETWEEN THE TWO TESTING PERIODS. SUMMER HEAD START PROGRAMS WERE CONDUCTED IN THE DRYDEN, NEWFIELD, AND ITHACA, N.Y. AREAS IN 1965. A FOLLOWUP STUDY ON 74 OF THE 77 HEAD START CHILDREN WAS DONE DURING THEIR KINDERGARTEN YEAR. DURING THE SECOND AND SEVENTH WEEK OF EACH OF THE THREE SUMMER PROGRAMS, THE CHILDREN WERE TESTED FOR COGNITIVE AND SOCIAL DEVELOPMENT. IT WAS DETERMINED THAT COGNITIVE DEVELOPMENT DID NOT SIGNIFICANTLY CHANGE FOR CHILDREN IN ANY OF THE GROUPS BUT SOCIAL DEVELOPMENT IMPROVED SLIGHTLY. THE CHILDREN IN THE FOLLOWUP STUDY WERE TESTED TWICE DURING THEIR KINDERGARTEN YEAR. ALSO, A CONTROL GROUP OF 67 NON-HEAD START CHILDREN IN KINDERGARTEN WAS SO TESTED. BOTH GROUPS DEMONSTRATED SIGNIFICANT INCREASES IN IQ, BUT THERE WAS NO DIFFERENCE FOUND BETWEEN THE SCORES OF THE HEAD START AND NON-HEAD START CHILDREN. THE MOTHERS OF CHILDREN IN BOTH GROUPS WERE INTERVIEWED TO OBTAIN THEIR OPINIONS OF THE PROGRAMS IN WHICH THEIR CHILDREN PARTICIPATED. THEIR OPINIONS ABOUT HEAD START WERE GENERALLY ENTHUSIASTIC AND POSITIVE. IT WAS CONCLUDED THAT THE SUCCESS OF THESE HEAD START PROGRAMS COULD BE MEASURED MORE IN TERMS OF PUPIL ENJOYMENT AND PARENTAL SATISFACTION THAN OF COGNITIVE DEVELOPMENT. (WD)

ED019988 PS000238
NUMBER TRAINING TECHNIQUES AND THEIR EFFECTS ON DIFFERENT POPULATIONS. FINAL REPORT. MERMELSTEIN, EGON; MEYER, EDWINA, AUG67 37P.
EDRS PRICE MF-$0.65 HC-$3.29

PIAGET HAS PROPOSED THAT THE CONCEPT OF NUMBER IS PREDICATED ON THE CONCEPT OF CONSERVATION OF SUBSTANCE--THAT IS, THE CONCEPT THAT THE AMOUNT OR NUMBER REMAINS THE SAME DESPITE SPATIAL REARRANGEMENTS. BECAUSE OF THE CURRENT EMPHASIS ON REVISION OF MATHEMATICS CURRICULUM AND OF THE APPARENT VALUE OF NUMBER TRAINING TO PRESCHOOL DISADVANTAGED CHILDREN, THIS STUDY WAS CREATED TO INVESTIGATE (1) WHETHER TRAINING PROGRAMS CAN EFFECTIVELY TEACH 3- TO 6-YEAR-OLD CHILDREN THE CONCEPT OF CONSERVATION OF SUBSTANCE, AND (2) IF SO, WHETHER SOME TRAINING PROCEDURES ARE MORE EFFECTIVE WITH CERTAIN POPULATIONS THAN OTHER PROCEDURES. ACCORDING TO PIAGET, TRAINING PROGRAMS ALONE ARE NOT SUFFICIENT TO TEACH CHILDREN THE CONSERVATION CONCEPT. ALL OF THE ACTIVITIES OF A CHILD, HIS GRADUAL INTELLECTUAL DEVELOPMENT, LEAD TO THE ACQUISITION OF THE CONCEPT. TO INVESTIGATE PIAGET'S IDEAS ON THE FORMATION OF THE CONCEPT OF CONSERVATION OF SUBSTANCE, 416 CHILDREN OF AGES THREE TO SIX AND OF VARIED SOCIOECONOMIC LEVELS WERE ADMINISTERED ONE OF FOUR TRAINING PROCEDURES AFTER A PRETEST. THE FOUR TRAINING PROCEDURES USED WERE (1) SMEDSLUND'S COGNITIVE CONFLICT METHOD, (2) SIGEL'S MULTIPLE CLASSIFICATION METHOD, (3) BEILIN'S VERBAL RULE INSTRUCTION METHOD, AND (4) BRUNER'S LANGUAGE ACTIVATION METHOD. AT THREE TIME INTERVALS AFTER THIS TRAINING PERIOD, POSTTESTS WERE ADMINISTERED TO ASCERTAIN THE QUALITY AND EXTENT OF THE CHILD'S LEARNING OF THE CONCEPT. THE CONCLUSION REACHED FROM COMPARING THE TEST RESULTS FOR THE FOUR TRAINING GROUPS TO THE RESULTS FROM A CONTROL GROUP WAS THAT THE TRAINING PROCEDURES, ALONE, WERE INEFFECTIVE, REGARDLESS OF THE POPULATION TYPE, IN TEACHING THE CHILDREN THE CONSERVATION-OF-SUBSTANCE CONCEPT. (WD)

ED019989 PS000254
THE EFFECT OF PRESCHOOL GROUP EXPERIENCE ON VARIOUS LANGUAGE AND SOCIAL SKILLS IN DISADVANTAGED CHILDREN. FINAL REPORT. VANCE, BARBARA J., AUG67 217P.
EDRS PRICE MF-$0.65 HC-$9.87

FIFTY DISADVANTAGED CHILDREN, RANGING IN AGE FROM 33 TO 56 MONTHS, PARTICIPATED IN A 7-MONTH PRESCHOOL EDUCATIONAL PROGRAM DESIGNED TO IMPROVE THEIR LANGUAGE AND SOCIAL SKILLS. THE ILLINOIS TEST OF PSYCHOLINGUISTIC ABILITIES, THE PEABODY PICTURE VOCABULARY TEST (FORM A), AND THE VANCE LANGUAGE SKILLS TEST MEASURED THE CHILDREN'S DEVELOPMENT IN LANGUAGE SKILLS, AND THE CAIN-LEVINE SOCIAL COMPETENCY SCALE MEASURED PREEXPERIMENTAL AND POSTEXPERIMENTAL SOCIAL COMPETENCY. RESULTS WERE ANALYZED BY T-TEST AND ANALYSIS OF VARIANCE AND WERE MATCHED AGAINST THOSE OF A COMPARABLE GROUP OF PRESCHOOLERS WHO HAD REMAINED AT HOME. IT WAS CONCLUDED THAT THE PRESCHOOL PROGRAM IN THIS STUDY WAS NOT EFFECTIVE IN INCREASING THE LANGUAGE SKILLS SCORES AND SOCIAL COMPETENCY SCORES OF 3-YEAR-OLD AND 4-YEAR-OLD DISADVANTAGED CHILDREN AS MEASURED BY TESTS ADMINISTERED AT THE END OF THE PROGRAM. CONTRARY TO PRESENT EDUCATIONAL THEORY, THE HOME AND NEIGHBORHOOD ENVIRONMENT APPEARS TO BE AS USEFUL AS A CAREFULLY PLANNED PRESCHOOL SITUATION IN DEVELOPING NECESSARY LANGUAGE AND SOCIAL SKILLS. FUTURE STUDIES MIGHT FOLLOW UP THE TWO GROUPS OF CHILDREN WHEN THEY REACH KINDERGARTEN TO SEE IF LATENT LEARNING TOOK PLACE DURING THE EXPERIMENTAL PERIOD. APPENDIXES INCLUDE COPIES OF THE TESTS USED IN THE STUDY. TABLES SHOW STATISTICAL METHODS. (MS)

ED019990 PS000279
TEACHING FORMAL OPERATIONS TO PRESCHOOL ADVANTAGED AND DISADVANTAGED CHILDREN. ENGELMANN, SIEGFRIED, 67
DOCUMENT NOT AVAILABLE FROM EDRS.

TO DETERMINE HOW TRAINING WOULD AFFECT CHILDREN FROM DIFFERENT LEVELS OF DEVELOPMENT, FIVE DISADVANTAGED AND FIVE ADVANTAGED PRESCHOOLERS WERE GIVEN SPECIFIC PROBLEM SOLVING TRAINING TO PREPARE TO SOLVE A CRITERION PROBLEM. THIS STUDY WAS AN ATTEMPT TO DISPROVE PIAGET'S THEORY THAT CHILDREN MUST HAVE REACHED A CERTAIN STAGE OF CONCRETE-OPERATIONAL THOUGHT BEFORE THEY CAN SOLVE FORMAL-OPERATIONAL PROBLEMS. A LARGE NUMBER OF CHILDREN WERE NOT NEEDED SINCE PIAGET ASSUMED THAT

ALL CHILDREN PROCEED THROUGH FIXED STEPS IN COGNITIVE GROWTH SO THAT ANY VARIANCE WOULD BE SIGNIFICANT. THE INVESTIGATOR TAUGHT THE COMPONENT SKILLS NECESSARY TO SOLVE THE CRITERION PROBLEM BY PRESENTING SIMILAR DIAGRAMMED PROBLEMS ON THE CHALKBOARD WITH PRACTICE IN THE LOGICAL STEPS NECESSARY TO LEAD TO THE CORRECT CONCLUSIONS. THE CULTURALLY ADVANTAGED GROUP QUICKLY GRASPED THE SIMILARITY OF PROBLEM COMPONENTS, WHEREAS THE DISADVANTAGED GROUP NEVER DISCOVERED THE PATTERN AT ALL. WHEN THE CRITERION PROBLEM WAS PRESENTED, SEVEN CHILDREN SOLVED IT. YET, ALL BUT ONE OF THESE CHILDREN HAD NOT REACHED THE STAGE OF CONCRETE OPERATIONS, ACCORDING TO THEIR PERFORMANCE ON THE SMEDSLUND TEST OF LIQUID AMOUNT. THE INVESTIGATOR CONCLUDED THAT THE ABILITY TO HANDLE FORMAL OPERATIONAL PROBLEMS IS A FUNCTION OF SPECIFIC INSTRUCTION RATHER THAN A FUNCTION OF DEVELOPMENT. THIS ARTICLE WAS PUBLISHED IN THE ONTARIO JOURNAL OF EDUCATIONAL RESEARCH, 9, 3, SPRING, 1967. (MS)

ED019991 PS000530
TEACHING MUSICAL CONCEPTS RELATED TO MELODY, RHYTHM, FORM, AND HARMONY, TEACHER RESOURCE MATERIAL KINDERGARTEN, GRADES 1 AND 2. PURDY, ROBERT J.; CHAFFEE, EVERETT, 66
DOCUMENT NOT AVAILABLE FROM EDRS.

THIS RESOURCE GUIDE TO THE TEACHING OF MUSICAL CONCEPTS IN KINDERGARTEN AND GRADES ONE AND TWO IS PREFACED BY A GENERAL ENUMERATION OF OBJECTIVES AND OF THE TECHNIQUES TO BE EMPLOYED IN THE DEVELOPMENT OF A BACKGROUND OF AUDITORY PERCEPTION THROUGH (1) SINGING, (2) KINESTHETIC RHYTHMIC EXPERIENCES, (3) PLAYING INSTRUMENTS, AND (4) LISTENING. THE PRINCIPAL SECTION OF THE GUIDE IS IN TABULAR FORMAT AND LISTS (1) CONCEPTS OF MELODY, RHYTHM, FORM, AND HARMONY TO BE DEVELOPED, (2) ACTIVITIES WHICH MAY LEAD TO THE DEVELOPMENT OF THE CONCEPTS, AND (3) SUGGESTED SONG MATERIALS WHICH EXEMPLIFY THE CONCEPTS. THE FINAL SECTION OF THE GUIDE CONSISTS OF REPRODUCTIONS OF 11 SONGS SELECTED FROM AMONG THOSE SUGGESTED IN THE PRECEDING MATERIAL. THIS DOCUMENT IS PUBLISHED BY LOS ANGELES CITY SCHOOLS, DIVISION OF INSTRUCTIONAL SERVICES, CURRICULUM BRANCH, LOS ANGELES, CALIFORNIA. (JS)

ED019992 PS000737
SEX AND RACE DIFFERENCES IN THE DEVELOPMENT OF UNDERPRIVILEGED PRESCHOOL CHILDREN. KOHLWES, GARY F., APR66 194P.
EDRS PRICE MF-$0.65 HC-$6.58

THIS STUDY WAS UNDERTAKEN TO DETERMINE IF THERE ARE ANY DIFFERENCES IN THE DEVELOPMENTAL CHARACTERISTICS OF UNDERPRIVILEGED PRESCHOOL CHILDREN THAT CAN BE TRACED TO DIFFERENCES IN RACE OR SEX. THE STUDY SAMPLE WAS DRAWN FROM A GROUP OF 368 CAUCASIAN AND NEGRO CHILDREN ENROLLED IN THE SUMMER 1965 PORTLAND, OREGON HEAD START PROGRAM. THE CHILDREN WERE RATED ON SIX INSTRUMENTS, THE BEHAVIOR INVENTORY, PRESCHOOL INVENTORY, AND PSYCHOLOGICAL SCREENING PROCEDURE SUPPLIED BY THE OEO, THE STANFORD-BINET INTELLIGENCE TEST, AND PERCEPTUAL DRAWING AND DEVELOPMENTAL CHART TESTS DEVISED BY THE AUTHOR. A MULTIVARIATE ANALYSIS OF INDIVIDUAL TEST ITEMS WAS MADE TO DETERMINE THE EXISTENCE OF DIFFERENCES BASED ON SEX, RACE, OR SEX-BY-RACE CLASSIFICATIONS. THERE WERE FEW GENERALIZED DIFFERENCES FOUND FOR EITHER SEX OR RACE GROUPINGS. FEMALES SHOWED SOME SUPERIORITY IN CONCEPT DEVELOPMENT, IN APPROPRIATENESS OF SOCIAL BEHAVIOR, AND IN MEAN IQ. NEGROES WERE FOUND TO BE MORE SKILLFUL PHYSICALLY AND TO HAVE BETTER SENSORY PERCEPTION. SOME STATISTICALLY SIGNIFICANT DIFFERENCES ON SPECIFIC ITEMS WERE FOUND FOR SEX-BY-RACE CLASSIFICATION. THE RESULTS OF THE ANALYSES OF INDIVIDUAL TESTS ARE CONTAINED IN EXTENSIVE APPENDIXES. (DR)

ED019993 PS000812
ANALYSES OF STORIES DICTATED IN CLASSES OF THE COOPERATIVE PROJECT. HUGHES, MARIE M.; TAYLOR, JEWELL C., SEP67 40P.
EDRS PRICE MF-$0.65 HC-$3.29

STORIES DICTATED BY STUDENTS FROM GRADES 1 AND 2 OF SCHOOLS IN A POVERTY AREA OF TUCSON, ARIZONA WERE TRANSCRIBED BY CLASSROOM TEACHERS AND ARE REPRODUCED WITH ACCOMPANYING SEMANTIC ANALYSES. ANALYZED FOR BASIC PREDICATION FORMS AND MAJOR FORM-CLASS CONCEPTS WHICH ARE CONTAINED IN THEM, THE STORIES ARE PRESENTED TO SHOW (1) DIFFERENCES IN THE DEGREE OF LANGUAGE CONTROL DEMONSTRATED AMONG INDIVIDUAL CHILDREN, (2) VARYING SKILLS IN LABELING, (3) INDIVIDUAL DIFFERENCES IN THE ABILITY TO ORGANIZE AN EXPERIENCE INTELLECTUALLY AND TO MAKE VERBAL ASSOCIATION WITH OTHER SIMILAR EXPERIENCES, (4) RANGE IN LANGUAGE CONTROL DENOTING INTELLECTUAL ORGANIZATION, (5) GROWTH FROM CONCRETE TO ABSTRACT EXPRESSION, AND (6) INDICATION OF DEGREE OF INDIVIDUAL AFFECTIVE INVOLVEMENT. THE EIGHT GROUPS OF STORIES WHICH ARE PRESENTED ARE SELECTED FROM AUTUMN AND SPRING STORIES DICTATED BY STUDENTS FROM FIRST AND SECOND GRADE CLASSROOMS OF SCHOOLS IN (1) A LESS PRIVILEGED NEIGHBORHOOD OF A GENERAL POVERTY AREA AND (2) A RELATIVELY MORE PRIVILEGED NEIGHBORHOOD OF A GENERAL POVERTY AREA. SUMMARY COMMENTS BASED ON THE INDIVIDUAL ANALYSES ARE PRESENTED AT THE CONCLUSION OF EACH GROUP OF STORIES. (JS)

ED019994 PS000836
AN EVALUATION OF THE EFFECTS OF A UNIQUE SEQUENTIAL LEARNING PROGRAM ON CULTURALLY DEPRIVED PRESCHOOL CHILDREN. FINAL REPORT. VAN DE RIET, VERNON; VAN DE RIET, HANI, OCT67 69P.
EDRS PRICE MF-$0.65 HC-$3.29

TO IMPROVE THE DEVELOPMENTAL RATE OF CULTURALLY DEPRIVED CHILDREN, A PRESCHOOL PROGRAM WAS OFFERED WHICH CONSISTED OF A PLANNED SEQUENCE OF ENVIRONMENTAL STIMULATION BASED ON THE THEORY THAT COGNITIVE DEVELOPMENT PROCEEDS THROUGH MOTOR-PERCEPTUAL-SYMBOLIC PHASES. SEVENTY-TWO DISADVANTAGED CHILDREN WERE DIVIDED INTO THREE MATCHED GROUPS. GROUP A WAS EXPOSED TO AN EXPERIMENTAL "LEARNING TO LEARN" PROGRAM DEVELOPED BY HERBERT SPRIGLE WHICH CONCENTRATED ON MANIPULATING, ORGANIZING, CLASSIFYING, AND ORDERING MATERIALS DESIGNED TO LEAD TO INTERNALIZED THOUGHT AND EFFECTIVE VERBAL EXPRESSION. GROUP B ATTENDED TRADITIONAL PRESCHOOL. GROUP C HAD NO PRESCHOOL EXPERIENCE. NINETEEN DEVELOPMENTAL MEASURES WERE TAKEN FOR EACH CHILD AT THE END OF THE 9-MONTH EXPERIMENTAL PERIOD. RESULTS SHOWED THAT GROUP A CHILDREN WERE SUPERIOR ON ALL MEASURES. GROUP B WAS SUPERIOR TO GROUP C ON ONE-HALF OF THE MEASURES. IN A FOLLOWUP STUDY AT THE END OF THE FIRST GRADE, THE CHILDREN WERE GIVEN ADDITIONAL STANDARDIZED TESTS WHICH WERE SUPPLEMENTED BY TEACHERS' RATINGS. ANALYSIS OF THE DATA INDICATED THAT THE EXPERIMENTAL PRESCHOOL PROGRAM HAD BEEN EFFECTIVE, SINCE GROUP A CHILDREN WERE STILL SUPERIOR IN MEASURES OF INTELLECTUAL FUNCTIONING EVEN THOUGH DIFFERENCES BETWEEN THE THREE GROUPS HAD BEGUN TO DISAPPEAR BECAUSE THE NONPRESCHOOL GROUP HAD IMPROVED. ONE-HALF OF THIS REPORT IS A DETAILED ACCOUNT OF SPRIGLE'S PROGRAM PLUS FOLLOWUP STUDY DATA. (MS)

ED019995 PS000840
PHYSICAL EDUCATION ACTIVITIES FOR THE ELEMENTARY SCHOOL. SMALLEY, JEANNETTE, 56
DOCUMENT NOT AVAILABLE FROM EDRS.

PHYSICAL EDUCATION ACTIVITIES FOR USE IN GRADES ONE THROUGH SIX ARE ENUMERATED AND DESCRIBED IN THIS MANUAL. UNITS OF THE MANUAL WHICH ARE CONCERNED WITH SIDEWALK GAMES, SCHOOLROOM GAMES, BALL GAMES FOR GRADES ONE AND TWO, STUNTS AND STUNT GAMES, AND GAMES OF LOW ORGANIZATION ARE PRESENTED IN A FORMAT WHICH CONSISTS OF (1) A LISTING OF CRITERIA BY WHICH THE APPROPRIATENESS OF A GIVEN GAME MAY BE EVALUATED, (2) SUGGESTIONS FOR CLASS ORGANIZATION, (3) SUGGESTIONS FOR CHOOSING, PRESENTING, AND SUPERVISING GAMES, AND (4) DESCRIPTIONS OF SPECIFIC GAMES CATEGORIZED ACCORDING TO THEIR SUITABILITY FOR THE VARIOUS GRADE LEVELS, THE DEGREE OF ACTIVITY INVOLVED, AND THE NECESSARY NUMBER OF PLAYERS. THE TEAM GAMES OF SOCCER AND SPEEDBALL, SOFTBALL, VOLLEYBALL, AND BASKETBALL ARE PRESENTED IN UNITS WHICH INCLUDE THE GAME RULES AND SUGGESTED PRELIMINARY ACTIVITIES FOR THE DEVELOPMENT OF PLAYING SKILLS. ADDITIONAL UNITS ARE DEVOTED TO (1) RELAYS AND (2) RHYTHMS, SINGING GAMES, AND FOLK DANCES. THE CONCLUDING UNIT IS PRESENTED IN WORKBOOK FORMAT AND CONSISTS OF QUESTIONS AND EXERCISES CONCERNED WITH THE ORGANIZATION OF AN ELEMENTARY SCHOOL PHYSICAL EDUCATION PROGRAM. BLANK PAGES ARE PROVIDED AT THE END OF EACH UNIT FOR THE ACCUMULATION OF SUPPLEMENTARY MATERIALS. THIS BOOK IS PUBLISHED BY THE NATIONAL PRESS, 850 HANSEN WAY, PALO ALTO, CALIFORNIA. (JS)

ED019996 PS000841
SKILL DEVELOPMENT THROUGH GAMES AND RHYTHMIC ACTIVITIES. NAGEL, CHARLES; MOORE, FREDRICKA, 66
DOCUMENT NOT AVAILABLE FROM EDRS.

A DISCUSSION OF THE OVERALL OBJECTIVES OF PHYSICAL ACTIVITIES IN THE ELEMENTARY SCHOOL, THE PURPOSES OF DEVELOPING MOVEMENT SKILLS IN GAMES AND RHYTHMS, AND THE ROLE OF THE TEACHER IN PHYSICAL EDUCATION COMPRISES THE INTRODUCTORY CHAPTER OF THIS TEXTBOOK FOR BEGINNING PHYSICAL EDUCATION TEACHERS. SUCCEEDING CHAPTERS ARE CONCERNED WITH FIVE SUBJECTS. (1) "PLANNING THE PROGRAM" IS A DESCRIPTION OF METHODS IN CLASS ORGANIZATION, FORMATIONS FOR SKILL PRACTICE AND RELAYS, SAMPLE LESSON PLANS, AND EVALUATION TECHNIQUES. (2) "FUNDAMENTAL BALL SKILLS AND RELATED GAMES" ILLUSTRATES HOW SKILLS ENABLE CHILDREN TO PLAY GAMES EFFECTIVELY. (3) "FUNDAMENTAL RHYTHM SKILLS AND RELATED ACTIVITIES" OFFERS A VISUAL, DESCRIPTIVE, AND RHYTHMIC ANALYSIS OF THE BASIC SKILLS OF MOTION. (4) "BALL SKILLS AND RELATED TEAM GAMES" IS A DISCUSSION OF ADVANCED BALL SKILLS USED IN BASKETBALL, SOCCER, FOOTBALL, VOLLEYBALL AND SOFTBALL. (5) "DANCE SKILLS FOR FOLK AND SOCIAL DANCE" PRESENTS TECHNIQUES FOR TEACHING TRADITIONAL AND CURRENT FOLK DANCES TO HELP CHILDREN ENJOY PARTICIPATION IN THIS KIND OF RHYTHMIC ACTIVITY. DRAWINGS AND DIAGRAMS ILLUSTRATE PLAYING POSITIONS AND FORM IN EACH CHAPTER. BOOK AND RECORD REFERENCES ARE ALSO INCLUDED. THIS BOOK WAS PUBLISHED BY THE NATIONAL PRESS, 850 HANSEN WAY, PALO ALTO, CALIFORNIA. (MS)

ED019997 PS000842
EFFECTS OF ADULT SOCIAL REINFORCEMENT ON CHILD BEHAVIOR. HARRIS, FLORENCE R.; AND OTHERS, OCT64
DOCUMENT NOT AVAILABLE FROM EDRS.

IN AN ATTEMPT TO MODIFY OR SUBSTANTIALLY REDUCE UNDESIRABLE BEHAVIOR IN NURSERY SCHOOL CHILDREN, A TEACHING TECHNIQUE WAS INTRODUCED WHEREIN THE TEACHER WOULD ATTEND TO THE CHILD ONLY WHEN THE CHILD WAS MANIFESTING ACCEPTABLE BEHAVIOR AND WOULD IGNORE THE CHILD WHEN HE WAS MANIFESTING UNDESIRABLE BEHAVIOR. IT WOULD THEN BE POSSIBLE TO DETERMINE THE EFFECT ON CHILDREN'S BEHAVIOR OF TEACHER ATTENTION, REPRESENTING POSITIVE REINFORCEMENT. WHEN THE PARTICULAR CHILD CONSISTENTLY MANIFESTED THE DESIRED BEHAVIOR TO THE EXCLUSION OF THE UNDESIRED BEHAVIOR, THE TEACHER TECHNIQUE OF ATTENDING TO THE ACCEPTABLE BEHAVIOR OF CHILDREN AND IGNORING UNDESIRED BEHAVIOR WAS REVERSED. IF THE CHILD THEN REVERTED TO THE UNDESIRABLE BEHAVIOR, THE TEACHER REESTABLISHED THE DESIRED BEHAVIOR. THESE MANIPULATIONS DEMONSTRATED THE VALIDITY OF THE INDEPENDENT VARIABLE, TEACHER ATTENTION, AS A SIGNIFICANT INFLUENCE UPON CHILD BEHAVIOR. FIVE CASE STUDIES OF NURSERY SCHOOL CHILDREN WITH PARTICULAR BEHAVIOR PROBLEMS INDICATED THAT THE TEACHER TECHNIQUE SUCCESSFULLY ALTERED THE UNDESIRED BEHAVIOR, WHICH INCLUDED CRYING SPELLS, ISOLATE PLAY, AND EXCESSIVE PASSIVITY. IN EACH CASE, BY IGNORING THE UNDESIRED BEHAVIOR AND REINFORCING THE DESIRED BEHAVIOR, THE LATTER BEHAVIOR CHANGED FROM SUBORDINATE TO DOMINANT. IT MUST BE UNDERSTOOD, HOWEVER, THAT TO ACHIEVE SUCCESS WITH THIS TECHNIQUE, THE ATTENTION OF THE TEACHER MUST BE POSITIVELY REINFORCING TO THE CHILD. THIS ARTICLE IS A REPRINT FROM YOUNG CHILDREN, VOLUME 20, NUMBER 1, OCTOBER, 1964. (WD)

ED019998 PS000843
GUIDELINES FOR ELEMENTARY SOCIAL STUDIES. JAROLIMEK, JOHN, 67 41P.
EDRS PRICE MF-$0.65 HC NOT AVAILABLE FROM EDRS.

PRECEDED BY SUMMARIES OF THE RATIONALE AND CURRENT STATUS OF ELEMENTARY SOCIAL STUDIES EDUCATION, 12 GUIDELINES FOR ASSESSING EXISTING CURRICULUMS ARE PRESENTED AND DISCUSSED IN THIS BOOKLET. THE GIVEN GUIDELINES CONSTITUTE A CANON OF CRITERIA FOR THE EVALUATION OF AN INSTRUCTIONAL PROGRAM AND ARE CONCERNED WITH (1) THE EXISTENCE OF CLEAR AND SPECIFIC STATEMENTS OF AIMS, PURPOSES, AND OBJECTIVES, (2) THE PSYCHOLOGICAL SOUNDNESS OF THE PROGRAM, (3) THE PROVISION FOR BALANCE IN ATTENTION TO COGNITIVE, AFFECTIVE, AND SKILLS OBJECTIVES, (4) THE PROVISION FOR SEQUENTIAL AND SYSTEMATIC DEVELOPMENT OF CONCEPTS AND SKILLS, (5) THE CLEAR SPECIFICATION OF CRITERIA FOR THE SELECTION OF SUBSTANTIVE CONTENT, (6) THE RELEVANCE OF THE TOTAL PROGRAM, (7) THE EXTENT TO WHICH THE SCOPE OF THE PROGRAM IS REALISTICALLY ORIENTED TO CONTEMPORARY CONDITIONS, (8) THE DEGREE OF CONSISTENCY AMONG ACTIVITIES, RESOURCES, AND STATED PURPOSES, (9) THE ADEQUACY OF PROVISION FOR DIFFERENTIATED INSTRUCTION, (10) THE EXTENT TO WHICH COGNIZANCE IS TAKEN OF THE NEED FOR TEACHER UNDERSTANDING AND SUPPORT, (11) THE FORMULATION OF CURRICULUM DOCUMENTS WHICH ARE SIMULTANEOUSLY STRUCTURED AND FLEXIBLE, AND (12) THE PROVISION FOR PROGRAM EVALUATION IN TERMS OF STATED OBJECTIVES. PROCEDURES FOR CURRICULUM REVISION AND DEVELOPMENT ARE DISCUSSED IN THE CONCLUDING SECTION OF THE BOOKLET, AND SELECTED REFERENCES ARE APPENDED. THIS DOCUMENT IS ALSO AVAILABLE FROM ASSOCIATION FOR SUPERVISION AND CURRICULUM DEVELOPMENT, NEA, 1201 SIXTEENTH STREET, N.W., WASHINGTON, D.C. 20036 FOR $1.50. (JS)

ED019999 PS000855
THE CHILD WHO DISLIKES GOING TO SCHOOL. MITCHELL, SHEILA; SHEPHERD, MICHAEL, FEB67
DOCUMENT NOT AVAILABLE FROM EDRS.

THIS INVESTIGATION, WHICH TOOK PLACE IN ENGLAND, COMPARES THE ATTITUDES TOWARD SCHOOL OF A RANDOM SAMPLING OF 6,100 5- TO 15-YEAR-OLD PUPILS WITH THEIR PERFORMANCE AND BEHAVIOR AT SCHOOL. PARENTS OF EACH PUPIL WERE SENT A QUESTIONNAIRE WHICH REQUIRED AN ASSESSMENT OF THEIR CHILD'S ATTITUDE TOWARD SCHOOL. IN ADDITION, INFORMATION WAS REQUESTED ON THE CHILD'S HOME BEHAVIOR AND ON THE FAMILY'S SOCIOECONOMIC STATUS. THE TEACHERS OF THESE PUPILS WERE ASKED TO SUPPLY INFORMATION ABOUT EACH PUPIL'S ACADEMIC ATTAINMENT LEVEL, ATTENDANCE RECORD, AND IN-SCHOOL BEHAVIOR. THE DATA, UPON ANALYSIS, LED TO SEVERAL CONCLUSIONS. (1) GIRLS, GENERALLY, HAVE A MORE POSITIVE ATTITUDE TOWARDS SCHOOL. FOR BOTH SEXES, THERE IS A TENDENCY FOR ENTHUSIASM FOR SCHOOL TO DECLINE WITH AN INCREASE IN AGE. (2) CHILDREN WHO ARE JUDGED BY THEIR PARENTS TO DISLIKE SCHOOL ARE GENERALLY LESS SUCCESSFUL ACADEMICALLY. (3) THE RELATIONSHIP BETWEEN ATTITUDE TOWARD SCHOOL AND ATTENDANCE VARIES ACCORDING TO THE AGE OF THE PUPIL. PUPILS AGED 5 TO 10 DEMONSTRATE FAIRLY CONSISTENT ATTENDANCE NO MATTER WHAT THEIR ATTITUDE TOWARD SCHOOL. PUPILS FROM 11 TO 15 TEND TO BE ABSENT MORE, THE MORE THEY DISLIKE SCHOOL. (4) THERE EXISTS A HIGHLY SIGNIFICANT RELATIONSHIP, AMONG BOYS, BETWEEN BEHAVIOR AND ATTITUDE. THE BOYS WHO ARE JUDGED TO DISLIKE SCHOOL HAVE MORE BEHAVIOR PROBLEMS, ACCORDING TO THEIR TEACHERS, (5) THE SOCIOECONOMIC INFORMATION OBTAINED FROM THE PARENTS INDICATES THAT PUPILS WHO DISLIKE SCHOOL ARE MORE ANXIOUS AND MORE PRONE TO PHYSICAL AILMENTS. A HIGHER PROPORTION OF PUPILS WHO LIKE SCHOOL HAVE FATHERS IN NONMANUAL OCCUPATIONS. THIS DOCUMENT IS A REPRINT FROM THE BRITISH JOURNAL OF EDUCATIONAL PSYCHOLOGY, VOLUME 37, PART I, FEBRUARY, 1967. (WD)

ED020000 PS000856
EVALUATION OF THE CLEVELAND CHILD DEVELOPMENT PROGRAM. A LONGITUDINAL STUDY (FIRST YEAR REPORT). CORTES, CARLOS F.; AND OTHERS, 66 101P.
EDRS PRICE MF-$0.65 HC-$6.58

IN ORDER TO EVALUATE THE EFFECT OF A STRUCTURED PRESCHOOL ACADEMIC PROGRAM UPON THE COGNITIVE GROWTH OF CULTURALLY DEPRIVED CHILDREN, A LONGITUDINAL STUDY WAS BEGUN ON 107 FOUR-YEAR-OLDS IN CLEVELAND, OHIO. RELEVANT RESEARCH LITERATURE WAS REVIEWED IN DESIGNING THE STUDY. THE FIRST PHASE, RECOUNTED IN THIS REPORT, EXPLORED PSYCHO-LINGUISTIC, PERCEPTUAL, AND INTELLECTUAL FUNCTIONING. THE CHILDREN WERE DIVIDED INTO ONE CONTROL GROUP RECEIVING CUSTODIAL CARE AND TWO EXPERIMENTAL GROUPS, ONE WHITE AND ONE NEGRO, BOTH BELONGING TO THE PUBLIC SCHOOL CHILD DEVELOPMENT PROGRAM. PRE- AND POSTTESTING OCCURRED AT A 10-WEEK INTERVAL, USING THE STANFORD-BINET INTELLIGENCE SCALE (S-B) AND THE ILLINOIS TEST OF PSYCHOLINGUISTIC ABILITY (ITPA). A SECONDARY RESEARCH PROJECT USED THE FROSTIG TESTS TO MEASURE 45 CHILDREN, RANDOMLY SELECTED FROM THE THREE GROUPS, WHO HAD BEEN GIVEN ADDITIONAL PERCEPTUAL TRAINING. DATA WERE ANALYZED IN TERMS OF PRESCHOOL OR NONPRESCHOOL AND BOYS OR GIRLS. RESULTS SHOWED THAT (1) S-B AND ITPA ARE MORE STABLE MEASURES THAN FROSTIG AT THIS AGE, (2) GAINS WERE GREATER IN BRIGHTER CHILDREN, (3) EXERCISE IS NEEDED IN VOCALIZING EXPERIENCE, (4) GIRLS SURPASS BOYS IN LANGUAGE DEVELOPMENT, AND (5) VISUAL PERCEPTION IMPROVED AFTER USING THE FROSTIG PROGRAM. A FAIRLY EXTENSIVE BIBLIOGRAPHY IS INCLUDED. (LG)

ED020001 PS000860
GUIDEBOOK FOR TEACHERS. FRYE, KENNETH, MAR65 40P.
EDRS PRICE MF-$0.65 HC-$3.29

THIS DOCUMENT IS A GUIDEBOOK FOR PRESCHOOL TEACHERS. PREPARED BY STAFF MEMBERS OF THE HARDY COUNTY, WEST VIRGINIA SCHOOL SYSTEM, IT DELINEATES THE OBJECTIVES AND BASIC FORMAT OF A PRESCHOOL ENRICHMENT PROGRAM. THE PROGRAM IS DESIGNED AS A PREPARATORY ENRICHMENT EXPERIENCE FOR CULTURALLY AND ECONOMICALLY DEPRIVED CHILDREN WHO, WITHOUT SUCH A PROGRAM, WILL BEGIN FORMAL SCHOOLING WITH A MENTAL AND SOCIAL PERFORMANCE LEVEL SIGNIFICANTLY BELOW THAT OF CHILDREN FROM MIDDLE AND HIGH INCOME FAMILIES. A DETAILED BLUEPRINT OF THE PROGRAM PLAN IS PRESENTED. INCLUDED IN THE PRESENTATION IS INFORMATION REGARDING (1) THE PROJECT PERSONNEL, (2) A SUGGESTED DAILY SCHEDULE FOR THE THREE HOUR PRESCHOOL SESSION, (3) A SUGGESTED LIST OF MATERIALS AND SUPPLIES, AND (4) A SUGGESTED CURRICULUM. THE SUGGESTED CURRICULUM ITEM IS TAKEN UP IN SOME DETAIL AND INCLUDES A DISCUSSION OF SUCH ASPECTS AS (1) THOSE CLASSROOM EXPERIENCES NECESSARY IN ESTABLISHING THE BASIC MENTAL, PHYSICAL, AND SOCIAL PATTERNS THAT WILL BE REQUIRED IN REGULAR SCHOOL, (2) THE TEACHING OF SOUND HEALTH PRACTICES, (3) FIELD TRIPS, (4) A NUTRITIONAL LUNCH PROGRAM, AND (5) MONTHLY PARENT DISCUSSION GROUPS. THE GREATEST EMPHASIS OF THE SUGGESTED CURRICULUM IS WITH ITEMS ONE AND TWO, THE DEVELOPMENT OF A COMPREHENSIVE, ALTHOUGH NOT EXHAUSTIVE, OUTLINE OF POSSIBLE CLASSROOM EXPERIENCES OR ACTIVITIES. TWENTY-FIVE SUCH CLASSROOM EXPERIENCES ARE TREATED IN THE DOCUMENT, WITH MENTION OF SEVERAL SUBPOINTS UNDER EACH. (WD)

ED020002 PS000863
LANGUAGE LEARNING ACTIVITIES FOR THE DISADVANTAGED CHILD. BEREITER, CARL; ENGELMANN, SIEGFRIED, 34P.
EDRS PRICE MF-$0.65 HC-$3.29

THIS BOOKLET DESCRIBES SEVERAL GAMELIKE ACTIVITIES WHICH ARE DESIGNED TO FACILITATE LANGUAGE LEARNING AMONG DISADVANTAGED CHILDREN. THE INTRODUCTORY DISCUSSION EMPHASIZES (1) THE IMPORTANT ROLE OF LANGUAGE IN COGNITIVE DEVELOPMENT AND (2) THE NEED FOR A STRUCTURED PROGRAM OF LANGUAGE LEARNING ACTIVITIES FOR YOUNG CHILDREN. FOURTEEN ACTIVITIES (FOR EXAMPLE, THE FOOLER GAME, THE PREPOSITION GAME, AND THE QUESTION-ASKING GAME) ARE DESCRIBED. THE ACTIVITIES FOCUS ON THE MOST CRUCIAL LANGUAGE DEFICITS OF DISADVANTAGED CHILDREN, AND EACH OF THEM IS DESIGNED TO ELICIT MAXIMUM STUDENT PARTICIPATION IN THE LEARNING PROCESS. EXPLICIT DIRECTIONS FOR USING THE ACTIVITIES ARE PROVIDED, AND LARGE AMOUNTS OF SAMPLE DIALOG ARE INCLUDED. THE CONCLUDING SECTION OF THE BOOKLET CONSISTS OF SIX METHODOLOGICAL SUGGESTIONS WHICH ARE APPLICABLE TO ALL OF THE DESCRIBED ACTIVITIES. THIS DOCUMENT IS ALSO AVAILABLE FOR $0.60 FROM THE ANTI-DEFAMATION LEAGUE OF B'NAI B'RITH, 315 LEXINGTON AVENUE, NEW YORK, N.Y. 10016. (JS)

ED020003 PS000914
EFFECT OF TRIMESTER SCHOOL OPERATION ON THE ACHIEVEMENT AND ADJUSTMENT OF KINDERGARTEN AND FIRST THROUGH THIRD GRADE CHILDREN. FINAL REPORT. WITHERSPOON, RALPH L., FEB68 37P.
EDRS PRICE MF-$0.65 HC-$3.29

AT THE FLORIDA STATE UNIVERSITY SCHOOL, A LONGITUDINAL STUDY ATTEMPTED TO FIND OUT IF KINDERGARTEN THROUGH THIRD GRADE CHILDREN WHO ATTENDED THE EXTENDED SCHOOL YEAR OF THE TRIMESTER SYSTEM SHOWED SIGNIFICANT DIFFERENCES IN ACHIEVEMENT AND ADJUSTMENT AS COMPARED WITH CHILDREN OF A SIMILAR MEAN IQ WHO ATTENDED ONLY DURING THE REGULAR SCHOOL YEAR. THE URBAN AREA SUBJECTS HAD THESE ATTENDANCE PATTERNS, (1) 38 CHILDREN ATTENDED FOR THREE SUMMERS, (2) 38 FOR NO SUMMERS, (3) 44 FOR ONE SUMMER, AND (4) 43 FOR TWO SUMMERS. FIRST, SECOND, AND THIRD GRADE ACHIEVEMENT WAS DETERMINED BY THE METROPOLITAN ACHIEVEMENT TEST AND THE DEVELOPMENTAL READING TEST. ADJUSTMENT WAS EVALUATED BY THE HAGGERTY-OLSON-WICKMAN BEHAVIOR RATING SCHEDULES, WHICH USED TEACHERS' RATINGS, AND THE CALIFORNIA TEST OF PERSONALITY. ALL TESTS WERE GIVEN EACH OCTOBER AND MAY FOR A THREE-YEAR PERIOD. THE SCIENCE RESEARCH ASSOCIATES MENTAL ABILITIES TEST WAS GIVEN TO ALL SUBJECTS BEFORE MID-OCTOBER OF THE FIRST YEAR. ANALYSIS OF VARIANCE OF THE DATA PERMITTED RESULTS TO BE ADJUSTED IN TERMS OF VARIATION DUE TO INTELLIGENCE. ALTHOUGH THE EVIDENCE IS INCONCLUSIVE, FINDINGS INDICATE THAT EXTENDING THE LENGTH OF THE SCHOOL YEAR HAS A NEGATIVE EFFECT ON CHILDREN'S ACHIEVEMENT AND ADJUSTMENT. FURTHER TREND ANALYSES OF THE DATA COLLECTED WILL DETERMINE THE MOST CRITICAL AGE LEVELS IN RELATION TO SCHOOL YEAR LENGTH. A STUDY WILL ALSO BE MADE TO FIND OUT WHY CHILDREN DO OR DO NOT ATTEND SUMMER SCHOOL. AN EXTENSIVE BIBLIOGRAPHY IS INCLUDED IN THIS REPORT. (MS)

ED020004 PS000915
DEVELOPMENT OF A SOCIAL COMPETENCY SCALE FOR PRESCHOOL CHILDREN. FINAL REPORT. LEVINE, SAMUEL; ELZEY, FREEMAN F., FEB68 53P.
EDRS PRICE MF-$0.65 HC-$3.29

A SOCIAL COMPETENCY SCALE DESIGNED TO RATE PRESCHOOL CHILDREN AGED TWO YEARS, SIX MONTHS THROUGH FIVE YEARS, SIX MONTHS WITHIN A NURSERY SCHOOL CONTEXT WAS DEVELOPED AND STANDARDIZED. AFTER EXTENSIVE OBSERVATIONS OF PRESCHOOLERS, DISCUSSIONS WITH PRESCHOOL PERSONNEL, AND REVIEWS OF AVAILABLE MATERIAL THE FIRST FORM OF THE SCALE WAS WRITTEN, BASED ON CERTAIN PREDETERMINED CRITERIA. THE SCALE ITEMS WERE INITIALLY JUDGED BY GROUPS OF PRESCHOOL TEACHERS AND TEACHER EDUCATORS WHO RANKED ITEMS IN TERMS OF THEIR IMPORTANCE IN REGARD TO CHILDREN'S SOCIAL COMPETENCE. AN INITIAL SAMPLE OF 1165 CALIFORNIA CHILDREN WERE RATED, AND 30 ITEMS WERE SELECTED FOR THE FINAL SCALE FORM. A REPRESENTATIVE SAMPLE OF CHILDREN IN NURSERY SCHOOLS THROUGHOUT THE UNITED STATES PROVIDED THE NORMING POPULATION. TEACHER RATINGS WERE OBTAINED FOR 800 CHILDREN, EQUALLY DISTRIBUTED BY AGE (2, 3, 4, AND 5), SEX, AND OCCUPATIONAL LEVEL (LOW AND HIGH). STATISTICAL TREATMENT OF THE DATA BY A THREE-WAY ANALYSIS OF VARIANCE INDICATED THAT THE SCALE RELIABLY DISCRIMINATED BETWEEN VARIOUS AGE GROUPS. F RATIOS FOR THE MAIN EFFECTS WERE SIGNIFICANT BEYOND THE .01 LEVEL. NONE OF THE INTERACTIONS WAS SIGNIFICANT. SEPARATE NORMS WERE MADE FOR EACH OF THE FOUR AGE GROUPS BY SEX AND OCCUPATIONAL LEVEL. APPENDICES INCLUDE THE RATING SCALE WITH ITEM RATING PERCENTILES AND NORMING PERCENTILES. (MS)

ED020005 PS000917
THE INTERPLAY OF SOME EGO FUNCTIONS IN SIX YEAR OLD CHILDREN. LOVINGER, SOPHIE L., 14MAR67 113P.
EDRS PRICE MF-$0.65 HC-$6.58

IN A PROGRAM DESIGNED TO INVESTIGATE THE RELATIONSHIPS AMONG SELF-CONCEPT, SENSE-OF-COMPETENCE, READING ACHIEVEMENT, AND DEPENDENCE IN KINDERGARTEN AND FIRST GRADE CHILDREN, 110 MIDDLE CLASS, WHITE KINDERGARTEN CHILDREN FROM THE NEW YORK CITY AREA WERE TESTED AND RATED DURING THEIR KINDERGARTEN AND FIRST GRADE YEARS. THE TESTS AND RATING SCALES USED WERE (1) THE BELLER DEPENDENCY SCALE, (2) THE MORIARTY SENSE-OF-COMPETENCE SCALE, (3) THE CREELMAN SELF-CONCEPT TEST, (4) THE STANFORD-BINET SHORTFORM L-M, AND (5) THE METROPOLITAN ACHIEVEMENT TEST. NINE HYPOTHESES INVOLVING THE INTERRELATIONSHIPS OF THE FOUR ABOVE-MENTIONED FACTORS WERE TESTED, AND ON THE BASIS OF THE RESULTS FROM THE FIVE MEASURING DEVICES, IT WAS GENERALLY FOUND THAT (1) A NEGATIVE RELATIONSHIP BETWEEN DEPENDENCY AND SELF-CONCEPT DID NOT EXIST (IN FACT, THE RELATIONSHIP FOR THE CHILDREN INVOLVED APPEARED CLOSER TO POSITIVE), (2) THERE WAS NO NEGATIVE RELATIONSHIP BETWEEN DEPENDENCY AND SENSE-OF-COMPETENCE, (3) THERE WAS A POSITIVE RELATIONSHIP BETWEEN SELF-CONCEPT AND SENSE-OF-COMPETENCE IN THE KINDERGARTEN BUT NOT IN THE FIRST GRADE, (4) THERE WAS NOT A NEGATIVE RELATIONSHIP BETWEEN DEPENDENCY AND READING ABILITY, (5) THERE WAS A POSITIVE RELATIONSHIP BETWEEN SELF-CONCEPT AND READING ABILITY, (6) THERE WAS NOT CLEARLY AN EXISTENCE OF A POSITIVE RELATIONSHIP BETWEEN SENSE-OF-COMPETENCE AND READING, (7) THERE WAS NOT AN INCREASE IN SENSE-OF-COMPETENCE WITH THE DEVELOPMENT OF READING SKILLS, (8) THERE WAS A DECREASE IN DEPENDENCY BEHAVIOR WITH THE DEVELOPMENT OF READING SKILLS ONLY FOR SOME OF THE BOYS, AND (9) THERE WAS NO INCREASE IN SELF-CONCEPT WITH THE DEVELOPMENT OF READING SKILLS. DEVELOPMENTAL FACTORS, SOCIAL OR SEX ROLE FACTORS, AND INDEPENDENCE RATHER THAN DEPENDENCE WERE NOT SPECIFICALLY PART OF THE ORIGINAL INVESTIGATIVE DESIGN BUT HAD IMPORTANT EFFECTS AND SHOULD BE FURTHER CONSIDERED. (WD)

ED020006 PS000918
IDENTIFICATION AND EVALUATION OF CHARACTERISTICS OF KINDERGARTEN CHILDREN THAT FORETELL EARLY LEARNING PROBLEMS. FINAL REPORT. REECE, WILLIAM K., NOV66 253P.
EDRS PRICE MF-$0.65 HC-$9.87

TO EVALUATE THE EFFECTIVENESS OF A KINDERGARTEN PROGRAM OF SPECIFIC TRAINING RELATED TO MOTOR, SENSORY, AND PERCEPTUAL (M-S-P) PERFORMANCE, AN INSTRUMENT WAS DEVISED TO MEASURE THE M-S-P NEEDS AND STRENGTHS OF INDIVIDUAL PUPILS. RESEARCH WAS CONDUCTED TO TEST THE DIAGNOSTIC AND PREDICTIVE POTENTIALS OF THE M-S-P INSTRUMENT AND TO ASCERTAIN THE DEGREE OF INDEPENDENCE AND SPECIFICITY AMONG ITS VARIOUS DIMENSIONS. THE M-S-P TEST, THE METROPOLITAN READINESS TEST, THE PINTNER-CUNNINGHAM ABILITY TEST, AND A 52-ITEM TEACHER RATING SCALE WERE ADMINISTERED IN PRE- AND POSTTESTING TO 412 STUDENTS IN SEVEN EXPERIMENTAL AND SEVEN CONTROL CLASSES. SPECIFIC TRAINING IN MOTOR, KINESTHETIC, TACTILE, AUDITORY, VISUAL, AND GRAPHIC ACTIVITIES WAS PROVIDED FOR THE EXPERIMENTAL CHILDREN DURING A 24-WEEK PERIOD BETWEEN PRE- AND POSTTESTING. ANALYSIS OF PRE- AND POSTTEST DATA DEMONSTRATED THE LIMITED EFFECTIVENESS OF THE EXPERIMENTAL TRAINING PROGRAM. THE VARIOUS DIMENSIONS OF THE M-S-P TEST EXHIBITED ONLY PARTIAL SPECIFICITY AND THE PREDICTION OF YEARLY PROGRESS IN INDIVIDUAL M-S-P PERFORMANCE WAS NOT FOUND TO BE FEASIBLE WITH THE PRETRAINING MEASURES EMPLOYED IN THIS STUDY. THE M-S-P TEST WAS, HOWEVER, DEMONSTRATED TO BE A USEFUL INSTRUMENT FOR THE IDENTIFICATION OF PUPILS EXHIBITING DISABILITIES AND/OR DEVELOPMENTAL DELAYS INDICATIVE OF A LACK OF READINESS FOR ACADEMIC ACHIEVEMENT. STATISTICAL DATA ARE REPORTED IN 16 TABLES. THREE APPENDIXES CONTAIN INSTRUCTIONS FOR THE ADMINISTRATION OF THE M-S-P TEST, DESCRIPTIONS OF SPECIFIC TRAINING ACTIVITIES, AND THE FORM EMPLOYED IN TEACHER EVALUATION OF THE SUBJECTS. (JS)

ED020007 PS000919
IDENTIFICATION AND EVALUATION OF CHARACTERISTICS OF KINDERGARTEN CHILDREN THAT FORETELL EARLY LEARNING PROBLEMS. SUMMARY REPORT. REECE, WILLIAM K., NOV66 10P.
EDRS PRICE MF-$0.65 HC-$3.29

THIS DOCUMENT CONSISTS OF THE SUMMARY REPORT CONTAINED IN "IDENTIFICATION AND EVALUATION OF CHARACTERISTICS OF KINDERGARTEN CHILDREN THAT FORETELL EARLY LEARNING PROBLEMS." SEE ABSTRACT UNDER PS 000 918. (JS)

ED020008 PS000924
KINDERGARTEN GUIDEBOOK. HILL, IONE A., 67 128P.
EDRS PRICE MF-$0.65 HC-$6.58

PREPARED BY THE LOUISIANA STATE DEPARTMENT OF PUBLIC EDUCATION, THIS KINDERGARTEN GUIDEBOOK IS INTENDED TO PROVIDE DIRECTION AND ASSISTANCE IN THE IMPROVEMENT OF EXISTING PROGRAMS AND IN THE ESTABLISHMENT AND DEVELOPMENT OF OTHERS. THE FIRST OF FOUR PRINCIPAL SECTIONS INCLUDES (1) A SUMMARY OF THE RATIONALE, HISTORY, AND STATUS OF KINDERGARTEN EDUCATION IN THE UNITED STATES AND IN LOUISIANA, (2) LOUISIANA ACCREDITATION STANDARDS AND TEACHER CERTIFICATION REQUIREMENTS, (3) ENUMERATIONS OF THE CHARACTERISTICS OF KINDERGARTEN CHILDREN AND OF THE PROFESSIONAL AND PERSONAL QUALIFICATIONS OF TEACHERS, (4) GENERAL DISCUSSIONS OF KINDERGARTEN READINESS, THE HOME-SCHOOL RELATIONSHIP, THE ATTRIBUTES OF A SUITABLE HEALTH PROGRAM, AND THE KEEPING OF RECORDS AND REPORTS, AND (5) DESCRIPTIONS OF TYPICAL FULL- AND HALF-DAY PROGRAMS. THE SECOND SECTION, CONCERNED WITH THE CONTENTS OF A PROGRAM OF CONCEPT DEVELOPMENT, ENUMERATES APPROPRIATE PROGRAM ELEMENTS IN (1) THE LANGUAGE ARTS, (2) SOCIAL STUDIES, (3) SCIENCE, (4) MATHEMATICS, (5) ART, (6) MUSIC, AND (7) PHYSICAL EDUCATION. REQUISITE AND DESIRABLE PHYSICAL FACILITIES AND EQUIPMENT ARE THE SUBJECT OF THE THIRD SECTION. THE LOCATION, SIZE, AND ARRANGEMENT OF THE CLASSROOM ARE DISCUSSED. SUGGESTED MATERIALS, FURNISHINGS, EQUIPMENT, AND SUPPLIES ARE LISTED. THE CONCLUDING SECTION OF THE GUIDEBOOK CONSISTS OF A BIBLIOGRAPHY AND LISTS OF SOURCES OF INFORMATION AND SUPPLIES. (JS)

ED020009 PS000927
THE DEUTSCH MODEL--INSTITUTE FOR DEVELOPMENTAL STUDIES. , 68 20P.
EDRS PRICE MF-$0.65 HC-$3.29

THE DEUTSCH INTERVENTION MODEL IS BASED ON THE THEORY THAT ENVIRONMENT PLAYS A MAJOR ROLE IN THE DEVELOPMENT OF COGNITIVE SKILLS AND OF FUNCTIONAL USE OF INTELLECTUAL CAPABILITIES. DISADVANTAGED CHILDREN HAVE INTELLECTUAL DEFICITS WHICH MAY BE OVERCOME BY USE OF MATCHED REMEDIAL MEASURES. LANGUAGE SKILLS AND MOTIVATION CAN BE IMPROVED BY TEACHING STANDARD ENGLISH AS IF IT WERE A SECOND LANGUAGE. NAMING AND LABELING OBJECTS AND DIALOGUE PRACTICE ARE STEPS TAKEN TO INCREASE LANGUAGE ABILITY WHICH HOPEFULLY LEAD TO MORE COMPLEX LANGUAGE USAGE AND MINIMAL DIFFICULTY IN LEARNING TO READ. IMMEDIATE INDIVIDUALIZED FEEDBACK, EITHER CORRECTIVE OR CONFIRMING, IMPROVES LEARNING. A SECOND INTERVENTION AIM, PERCEPTUAL AND CONCEPTUAL DEVELOPMENT, INVOLVES STIMULUS RECOGNITION, DISCRIMINATION AND DIFFERENTIATION. CHILDREN ARE THEREFORE TRAINED TO FOCUS ON RELEVANT STIMULI AND TO RECOGNIZE, DISCRIMINATE AND CATEGORIZE THROUGH CONCRETE OBJECT MANIPULATION. TIME ORIENTATION IN ACTIVITIES GIVES A DISADVANTAGED CHILD, WHO MAY HAVE HAD LITTLE ORDER OR ROUTINE AT HOME, A SENSE OF SEQUENCE OF EVENTS, EACH OF WHICH HAS A BEGINNING, A MIDDLE, AND A CONCLUSION. TO ACHIEVE THE GOAL OF FOSTERING A CHILD'S DEVELOPMENT OF SELF-RELIANCE, ACHIEVEMENT MOTIVATION, AND A POSITIVE SELF-CONCEPT, TEACHERS VISIT CHILDREN'S HOMES BEFORE THE OPENING OF SCHOOL AND ENCOURAGE PERSONAL NAME USE FOR IDENTIFICATION. IN THE CLASSROOM, A FULL-LENGTH MIRROR AND POLAROID CAMERA PHOTOS, CREATIVE DRAMATICS, AND OPPORTUNITIES FOR VERBAL EXPRESSION HELP CHILDREN CREATE POSITIVE SELF-CONCEPTS. (MS)

ED020010 PS000930
LOGICAL OPERATIONS AND CONCEPTS OF CONSERVATION IN CHILDREN, A TRAINING STUDY. FINAL REPORT. SHANTZ, CAROLYN UHLINGER; SIGEL, IRVING E., JUN67 79P.
EDRS PRICE MF-$0.65 HC-$3.29

PIAGET HAS BEEN CONCERNED WITH THE ASSESSMENT OF THE PRESENCE OR ABSENCE OF CONSERVATION AND RELATED PROCESSES, BUT HE HAS NOT FOCUSED EXPERIMENTALLY ON THE FACTORS WHICH CAN ACCOUNT FOR THE LEARNING OF CONSERVATION. TO INVESTIGATE SUCH FACTORS, RESEARCH WAS CONDUCTED (1) TO DETERMINE THE RELATIVE EFFECTIVENESS OF TWO PARTICULAR GROUP TRAINING PROCEDURES DESIGNED TO INDUCE CONSERVATION AND (2) TO ASSESS THE RELATIONSHIP BETWEEN CONSERVATION AND THE LOGICAL OPERATIONS OF CLASSIFICATION, SERIATION, AND REVERSIBILITY. AFTER PRETESTING WITH CONSERVATION TASKS, 36 KINDERGARTEN CHILDREN WERE SELECTED AS SUBJECTS BECAUSE THEY WERE ABLE TO CORRECTLY USE THE COMPARATIVE TERMS "MORE," "SAME," AND "LESS" BUT UNABLE TO CONSERVE QUANTITY, NUMBER, AND AREA. ADDITIONAL PRETESTING WITH LOGICAL OPERATIONS TASKS WAS ADMINISTERED TO THE SUBJECTS WHO WERE THEN EQUALLY DISTRIBUTED AMONG SIX TRAINING GROUPS. FOUR GROUPS RECEIVED TRAINING IN LABELING AND CLASSIFICATION SKILLS. DISCRIMINATION-MEMORY TRAINING WAS PROVIDED FOR TWO GROUPS. EACH GROUP HAD NINE 20-MINUTE TRAINING SESSIONS, AND ALL SUBJECTS WERE SUBSEQUENTLY RETESTED WITH BOTH THE CONSERVATION AND THE LOGICAL OPERATIONS TASKS TO DETERMINE IF CONSERVATION LEARNING HAD TAKEN PLACE. BASED ON ANALYSIS OF THE DATA, IT IS CONCLUDED THAT (1) BOTH TRAINING METHODS WERE SUCCESSFUL IN INDUCING CONSERVATION, (2) NEITHER METHOD WAS SIGNIFICANTLY MORE EFFECTIVE, AND (3) ONLY LIMITED RELATIONSHIPS WERE FOUND BETWEEN CONSERVATION AND LOGICAL OPERATIONS. DETAILED RESULTS, SUBSIDIARY FINDINGS, EDUCATIONAL IMPLICATIONS, AND SUGGESTIONS FOR FURTHER RESEARCH ARE INCLUDED IN THE TEXT OF THE PROJECT REPORT. FIVE APPENDIXES CONTAIN (1) TEST FORMATS AND PROTOCOLS, (2) DESCRIPTIONS OF TRAINING PROCEDURES, AND (3) RAW STATISTICAL DATA. (JS)

ED020011 PS000937
BLOCKBUILDING. STARKS, ESTHER B., 60 31P.
EDRS PRICE MF-$0.65 HC NOT AVAILABLE FROM EDRS.

ALTHOUGH BLOCKS ARE THE MOST IMPORTANT TYPE OF EQUIPMENT IN A SCHOOLROOM FOR YOUNG CHILDREN, INADEQUATE EMPHASIS HAS BEEN PLACED ON THE EDUCATIVE VALUES THEY PROVIDE. THEY ARE ADAPTABLE MATERIALS WHICH PROVIDE OPPORTUNITIES FOR GROWTH ACCORDING TO INDIVIDUAL RATES OF DEVELOPMENT. THEIR USE ENCOURAGES THE DEVELOPMENT OF COOPERATION, RESPONSIBILITY IN AND TO THE GROUP, DESIRABLE SOCIAL ATTITUDES, AND EFFECTIVE WORK HABITS. BLOCKBUILDING STIMULATES ACCURATE OBSERVATION AND FUNCTIONS AS AN AID IN THE TEACHING OF ARITHMETIC, GEOGRAPHY, AND SCIENCE. THROUGH BUILDING WITH BLOCKS CONCEPTS ARE CLARIFIED, PHYSICAL SKILLS ARE DEVELOPED, AND CREATIVITY IS STIMULATED. THE TEACHER PLAYS A KEY ROLE IN REALIZING THE POTENTIAL EDUCATIONAL BENEFITS OF BLOCKBUILDING. SHE MUST (1) PROVIDE MATERIALS, ADEQUATE FLOOR SPACE, TIME FOR BUILDING, AND HER OWN SYMPATHETIC, ALERT INTEREST, (2) DIRECT THE CHILDREN TO COOPERATIVE AND CONSTRUCTIVE ACTIVITY, (3) ENCOURAGE THE DEVELOPMENT OF SAFETY AND PERFORMANCE STANDARDS, (4) PROVIDE OPPORTUNITIES FOR CONCEPT DEVELOPMENT, AND (5) OFFER APPRECIATIVE RECOGNITION OF GOOD EFFORTS AND WORK WELL DONE. BLOCKS ARE AVAILABLE IN A VARIETY OF SIZES, SHAPES, AND MATERIALS. SMOOTH WOODEN BLOCKS ARE OF MAXIMUM VALUE AND WILL, IF CAREFULLY LACQUERED AND PROPERLY STORED ON SHELVING CONSTRUCTED FOR THAT PURPOSE, ENDURE FROM 10 TO 20 YEARS OF CONSTANT USE. THIS DOCUMENT IS AVAILABLE FOR $0.75 FROM NEA, 1201 SIXTEENTH STREET, N.W., WASHINGTON, D.C. 20036. (JS)

ED020012 PS000940
THINKING, FEELING, EXPERIENCING--TOWARD REALIZATION OF FULL POTENTIAL. WOODS, MARGARET S., 62 44P.
EDRS PRICE MF-$0.65 HC NOT AVAILABLE FROM EDRS.

THE EDUCATIONAL PROCESS CONDUCTED BY ANY SCHOOL SYSTEM INVOLVES MUCH MORE THAN THE PRESENTATION OF FACTS TO BE LEARNED OR THE DISCIPLINING OF UNDESIRABLE BEHAVIOR. THE TEACHER SHOULD INSPIRE THE PUPIL TO WANT TO LEARN AND TO UNDERSTAND AND SHOULD SEEK THE PROGRAM OR CURRICULUM MOST CONDUCIVE TO REALIZING THE FULL POTENTIAL OF THE PUPIL'S ABILITIES, PARTICULARLY HIS CREATIVE POTENTIAL. THE EFFORTS OF THE TEACHER TO ARRANGE PUPIL ACTIVITIES INVOLVING THINKING, FEELING, AND EXPERIENCING ARE MOST NECESSARY AND ARE MOST FLEXIBLE IN THE FIRST YEARS OF SCHOOL. AT THIS TIME THE ACADEMIC CURRICULUM IS NOT VERY INTENSE, AND THE EMPHASIS IS MORE ON THE GENERAL DEVELOPMENT OF BASIC SKILLS AND ABILITIES. INCLUDED AMONG THE BASIC SKILLS AND EXPERIENCES NEEDING SENSITIVE ATTENTION AND GUIDANCE BY THE TEACHER ARE (1) SELF-EXPRESSION, (2) THE CAPACITY TO THINK, IMAGINE, AND REFLECT, (3) SELF-CONFIDENCE AND THE EXPERIENCE OF SUCCESS, (4) A SENSE OF SOCIAL BEING AND RESPONSIBILITY, AND (5) THE GROWTH OF THE CHILD'S MIND AND PERSONALITY FROM ENCOUNTERING NEW IDEAS, OBJECTS, AND SITUATIONS. NOT ONLY MUST THE PUPIL BE INTRODUCED TO AN EXPANSIVE, CREATIVE, AND IMAGINATIVE ENVIRONMENT AT SCHOOL, BUT ALSO THE TEACHER MUST BE CAPABLE OF MENTAL GROWTH AND CONTINUED SELF-ACTUALIZATION. A TEACHER COGNIZANT OF HER OWN NEED FOR CONTINUAL INTELLECTUAL GROWTH WILL BE MORE LIKELY TO APPRECIATE AND TO BE ABLE TO PROVIDE FOR THE EDUCATIONAL NEEDS OF HER PUPILS. A CREATIVE, CHALLENGING ENVIRONMENT CAN AND MUST EXIST IN NURSERY SCHOOL, KINDERGARTEN, PRIMARY, AND UPPER ELEMENTARY CLASSROOMS. TO SOME DEGREE, THAT ENVIRONMENT SHOULD BE PRESENT THROUGHOUT THE WHOLE FORMAL EDUCATIVE PROCESS, INCLUDING TEACHER EDUCATION. IT IS IMPERATIVE THAT THE TEACHER GAIN THE INSIGHT INTO THE NATURE OF SUCH AN ENVIRONMENT FOR IT IS HER RESPONSIBILITY TO PROVIDE SUCH FOR HER PUPILS. THIS DOCUMENT IS AVAILABLE FOR $0.75 FROM NEA, 1201 SIXTEENTH STREET, N.W., WASHINGTON, D.C. 20036. (WD)

ED020013 PS000941
THE USE OF CONTEMPORARY MATERIALS IN THE CLASSROOM. KNOX, LOIS; AND OTHERS, 63 34P.
EDRS PRICE MF-$0.65 HC NOT AVAILABLE FROM EDRS.

THE INTRODUCTORY CHAPTER OF THIS PAMPHLET EMPHASIZES THE IMPORTANCE OF SUPPLEMENTARY INSTRUCTIONAL MATERIALS AND PROVIDES GUIDELINES FOR THE EVALUATION OF THE SPECIFIC USEFULNESS OF VARIOUS TEACHING AIDS. SUBSEQUENT CHAPTERS ARE DEVOTED TO EACH OF THE AREAS OF THE ELEMENTARY CURRICULUM, INCLUDING (1) SOCIAL STUDIES, (2) LANGUAGE ARTS, (3) SCIENCE, (4) MATHEMATICS, (5) MUSIC, (6) ART, AND (7) HEALTH, SAFETY, AND PHYSICAL EDUCATION. EACH CHAPTER CONSISTS OF (1) A BRIEF STATEMENT OF PROGRAM SCOPE AND OBJECTIVES, (2) A SUMMARY OF THE UNDERSTANDINGS, FEELINGS, ATTITUDES, AND PERCEPTIONS CONTRIBUTED TO THE EDUCATIONAL ENVIRONMENT BY THE INDIVIDUAL STUDENTS, (3) A DISCUSSION OF THE TEACHER'S ROLE IN ORGANIZING AND PRESENTING INSTRUCTIONAL AIDS, AND (4) AN ENUMERATION OF THE MATERIALS AND RESOURCES FURNISHED BY THE SCHOOL FOR THE ENRICHMENT OF THE EDUCATIONAL PROGRAM. AMONG THOSE THINGS LISTED AS MATERIALS AND RESOURCES ARE STUDY TRIPS, RESOURCE CLASSROOM VISITORS, GUIDANCE PERSONNEL TO HELP TEACHERS, MOVABLE FURNITURE, AMPLE PINBOARD SPACE, WALL PICTURES AND CHARTS, MAPS, GLOBES, FILM AND FILMSTRIP PROJECTORS, TELEVISION SETS, RADIOS, TAPE RECORDERS, MUSICAL INSTRUMENTS, AND ART SUPPLIES. A BIBLIOGRAPHY IS PROVIDED WHICH INCLUDES GENERAL ENTRIES AND ENTRIES PERTINENT TO EACH OF THE INDIVIDUAL CHAPTERS OF THE PAMPHLET. THIS DOCUMENT IS AVAILABLE FOR $0.75 FROM NEA, 1201 SIXTEENTH STREET, N.W., WASHINGTON, D.C. 20036. (JS)

ED020014 PS000942
TEACHING MUSIC IN THE ELEMENTARY SCHOOL, OPINION AND COMMENT. HARTSELL, O.M., 63 63P.
EDRS PRICE MF-$0.65 HC NOT AVAILABLE FROM EDRS.

CONCERNED WITH THE ELEMENTARY SCHOOL MUSIC EDUCATION PROGRAM, THIS BOOKLET CONSISTS OF TWO PRINCIPAL SECTIONS. PART ONE CONTAINS (1) A STATEMENT OF THE BASIC ELEMENTS REQUISITE TO AN EFFECTIVE PROGRAM, (2) A DISCUSSION OF THE ROLES AND RESPONSIBILITIES OF TEACHERS, SCHOOL ADMINISTRATORS, AND MUSIC SUPERVISORS IN THE PLANNING AND IMPLEMENTING OF SUCH A PROGRAM, AND (3) SUGGESTIONS FOR COOPERATIVE ACTION BY ADMINISTRATORS AND TEACHERS IN FORMULATING AND EVALUATING AN INSTRUCTIONAL PROGRAM DESIGNED TO MEET THE SPECIFIC NEEDS OF INDIVIDUAL SCHOOLS. PART TWO CONSISTS OF ANSWERS TO QUESTIONS WHICH ARE FREQUENTLY ASKED BY TEACHERS AND INCLUDES INFORMA-

TION CONCERNED WITH (1) THE RATIONALE FOR INCLUDING SINGING, MOVEMENT-TO-MUSIC, LISTENING, AND INSTRUMENTAL ACTIVITIES IN A SCHOOL MUSIC PROGRAM, (2) THE SCOPE OF THE MUSIC EDUCATION CURRICULUM, (3) SCHEDULING AND SEQUENCING OF ACTIVITIES, (4) APPROPRIATE METHODS, AND (5) NECESSARY EQUIPMENT AND MATERIALS. THE DEVELOPMENT OF MUSIC READING SKILLS, THE PROVISION OF ACTIVITIES FOR EXCEPTIONAL CHILDREN, AND THE PROPER TIME FOR BEGINNING PRIVATE MUSIC STUDY ARE ALSO CONSIDERED. A BIBLIOGRAPHY OF PERTINENT LITERATURE IS APPENDED. THIS DOCUMENT IS AVAILABLE FROM THE ASSOCIATION FOR SUPERVISION AND CURRICULUM DEVELOPMENT, NEA, 1201 SIXTEENTH STREET, N.W., WASHINGTON, D.C. 20036. (JS)

ED020015 PS000947
MAKING PRIMARY ARITHMETIC MEANINGFUL TO CHILDREN. SWENSON, ESTHER J., 61 35P.
EDRS PRICE MF-$0.65 HC NOT AVAILABLE FROM EDRS.

MATHEMATICS EDUCATION IN THE PRIMARY GRADES HAS TRADITIONALLY CONSISTED OF THE ROUTINE AND REPETITIVE SOLVING OF GREAT QUANTITIES OF NUMERICAL PROBLEMS AND THE ROTE LEARNING OF THE NUMBER COUNTING SEQUENCE, OR LATER, THE ADDITION OR MULTIPLICATION TABLES. THIS EMPHASIS IS CHANGING, HOWEVER, FOR IT IS BECOMING EVIDENT THAT FOR SUBJECT MATTER TO BE LEARNED WELL, IT MUST BE PRESENTED TO THE STUDENT IN A MEANINGFUL WAY. PROBLEM SOLVING MUST ACCOMPANY NUMBER-CONCEPT COMPREHENSION, AND THE ROTE LEARNING OF NUMBER SEQUENCES OR TABLES MUST BE ACCOMPANIED BY AN UNDERSTANDING OF THE RELATIONSHIPS BETWEEN NUMBERS. AN UNDERSTANDING OF MATHEMATICAL CONCEPTS AND PROCESSES IS VERY IMPORTANT FOR THE PUPIL'S YEAR-BY-YEAR SUCCESS IN MATHEMATICS COURSES. THE DEVELOPMENT OF THIS UNDERSTANDING SHOULD BEGIN IN THE PRIMARY GRADES. TO ACCOMPLISH THIS UNDERSTANDING, A MEANINGFUL MATHEMATICS EDUCATION MUST BE OFFERED THE PUPIL. IT SHOULD INCLUDE (1) VARIED EXPERIENCES IN DEALING WITH NUMBERS AND THEIR MANY USES, (2) THE USE OF MATHEMATICAL CONCEPTS AND PROCESSES IN PROBLEM CONTEXTS THAT ARE FAMILIAR AND RELEVANT TO PRIMARY-AGE PUPILS, (3) DEMONSTRATION OF THE PURPOSES AND INTENT OF MATHEMATICS, THAT IS, THE AIMS OF ALL THE NUMBER MANIPULATIONS CHILDREN ARE REQUIRED TO DO BEYOND JUST THE AIM OF OBTAINING ANSWERS, AND (4) ORGANIZING THE PRESENTATION OF THE MATHEMATICAL CONCEPTS AND PROCESSES IN A LOGICAL SEQUENCE, IN AN EFFICIENT BUILDING-BLOCK FASHION. THIS DOCUMENT IS AVAILABLE FOR $0.75 FROM NEA, 1201 SIXTEENTH STREET, N.W., WASHINGTON, D.C. 20036. (WD)

ED020016 PS000959
REPORT ON ACTIVITIES, 1964-1966. FROIMSON, MARCIA; MAX, DAVID, JUN67 105P.
EDRS PRICE MF-$0.65 HC-$6.58

A REPORT ISSUED BY THE ISRAELI NATIONAL INSTITUTE FOR RESEARCH IN THE BEHAVIORAL SCIENCES INDICATES THAT MANY OF THEIR CURRENT PROJECTS ARE INVESTIGATING CULTURALLY DEPRIVED ISRAELI CHILDREN. TOPICS INCLUDE THE GROWTH AND DEVELOPMENT, LEARNING PSYCHOLOGY, AND FAMILY AND KINDERGARTEN BACKGROUNDS OF THESE CHILDREN AS WELL AS THE PREPARATION OF SPECIAL PROGRAMED LEARNING MATERIALS, THE EFFECT OF THE DEVELOPMENT OF REGIONAL ENRICHMENT CENTERS, AND THE STRUCTURING OF SPECIFIC INSTRUCTIONAL MATERIALS IN ARITHMETIC AND GEOGRAPHY FOR DISADVANTAGED CHILDREN. SELECTION OF GIFTED CHILDREN FROM DEPRIVED GROUPS, A STUDY OF THEIR ATTITUDES AND VALUES, EVALUATION AND FOLLOW-UP STUDIES OF THESE STUDENTS AS THEY PROGRESS THROUGH SCHOOL ARE ALSO AREAS OF INTEREST. OTHER EVALUATIVE RESEARCH EFFORTS EXAMINE THE EFFECTS OF AN EXTENDED SCHOOL DAY, ABILITY GROUPING, USE OF ACHIEVEMENT TESTS AND ASSESSMENT INSTRUMENTS, INDEXES FOR SELECTION OF PROGRAMS IN SECONDARY EDUCATION, VOCATIONAL TRAINING, AND RELIGIOUS STANDARDS OF GIRLS. INFORMAL EDUCATION STUDIES ARE INVESTIGATING ASPECTS OF THE ISRAELI YOUTH CORPS PROGRAM, URBAN YOUTH CULTURE, DROPOUTS, CRIMINAL BEHAVIOR IN CHILDREN, JUVENILE DELINQUENCY PREDICTION, AND MENTAL RETARDATION. HALF OF THE DOCUMENT IS A LIST OF PUBLICATIONS ISSUED BY THE INSTITUTE WITH A SUBJECT INDEX AND A VOLUME INDEX OF "MEGAMOT," THE ISRAELI JOURNAL OF EDUCATION, PSYCHOLOGY, AND SOCIOLOGY. (MS)

ED020017 PS000960
MOTIVATIONAL FACTORS AND IQ-CHANGES IN CULTURALLY DEPRIVED CHILDREN ATTENDING NURSERY SCHOOL. ZIGLER, EDWARD; BUTTERFIELD, EARL C., 25P.
EDRS PRICE MF-$0.65 HC-$3.29

RECENT STUDIES HAVE INDICATED THAT (1) COGNITIVE ABILITY, (2) AMOUNT AND KIND OF INFORMATION LEARNED TO DATE, AND (3) MOTIVATIONAL FACTORS ALL CONTRIBUTE TO THE INTELLECTUAL FUNCTIONING OF CULTURALLY DEPRIVED CHILDREN. THE PURPOSE OF THIS STUDY WAS TO TEST THE EFFECT OF COGNITIVE ACHIEVEMENT AND MOTIVATIONAL FACTORS ON INTELLIGENCE TEST SCORES. STANFORD-BINET TESTS, FORM LM, WERE ADMINISTERED TO 40 NURSERY SCHOOL CHILDREN AND 12 NONNURSERY SCHOOL CHILDREN. AT THE BEGINNING OF THE NURSERY SCHOOL PROGRAM, THE NURSERY AND NONNURSERY CHILDREN RECEIVED INTELLIGENCE TESTS BY BOTH THE STANDARD AND OPTIMALLY-MOTIVATING PROCEDURES. THIS PROCESS WAS REPEATED ABOUT 7 MONTHS LATER, NEAR THE END OF THE NURSERY PROGRAM. IT WAS HYPOTHESIZED THAT (1) STANDARD TESTING PROCEDURES UNDERESTIMATE THE CULTURALLY DEPRIVED CHILD'S INTELLIGENCE, SO THAT INITIAL OPTIMAL TEST SCORES SHOULD BE HIGHER THAN INITIAL STANDARD TEST SCORES, (2) INCREASES IN STANDARD IQ SCORES SHOULD BE GREATER FOR THE NURSERY THAN FOR THE NONNURSERY CHILDREN, AND (3) THE CHILD'S MOTIVATIONAL STRUCTURE SIGNIFICANTLY AFFECTS TEST SCORES. THE EXPERIMENTAL RESULTS REQUIRED THE ACCEPTANCE OF ALL THREE HYPOTHESES. IT WAS CONCLUDED THAT THE NURSERY SCHOOL CHILDREN DID NOT INCREASE THEIR INTELLECTUAL ABILITY DURING THE NURSERY SCHOOL PROGRAM BUT BECAME BETTER ABLE TO USE THE INTELLECTUAL CAPACITY THAT THEY ALREADY HAD. (WD)

ED020018 PS000963
A DEVELOPMENTAL STUDY OF THE RELATIONSHIP BETWEEN REACTION-TIME AND PROBLEM-SOLVING EFFICIENCY. FINAL REPORT. FRIEDMAN, STANLEY R., 30APR68 32P.
EDRS PRICE MF-$0.65 HC-$3.29

MANY STUDIES HAVE INDICATED THE PRESENCE OF A SLUMP OR INVERSION IN THE PROBLEM-SOLVING EFFICIENCY OF CHILDREN AT THE FOURTH GRADE LEVEL. IT HAS BEEN SUGGESTED THAT THIS MAY BE DUE TO THE INTERFERING EFFECT OF THE FORMATION OF COMPLEX HYPOTHESES BY THE CHILDREN. SINCE A TENDENCY TO RESPOND RAPIDLY WOULD PRESUMABLY INHIBIT THE FORMATION OF COMPLEX HYPOTHESES, IT WAS HYPOTHESIZED THAT IF CHILDREN WERE DICHOTOMIZED INTO FAST AND SLOW RESPONDERS, THE FAST GROUP WOULD FAIL TO SHOW THE SLUMP. A TOTAL OF 168 STUDENTS, 42 IN EACH OF GRADES TWO THROUGH FIVE, WERE GIVEN A SET OF FOUR SEQUENCE-DETERMINATION PROBLEMS. THE AMOUNT OF TIME THE STUDENTS TOOK TO COMPLETE A SERIES OF 50 TRIALS ON EACH PROBLEM WAS USED TO DIVIDE EACH GRADE INTO FAST AND SLOW RESPONDERS. FOR THE COMPLETE SAMPLE, THE PERCENTAGES OF CHILDREN SUCCESSFULLY DETERMINING EACH SEQUENCE SHOWED THE EXPECTED INVERSION FOR THREE OF THE FOUR PROBLEMS. HOWEVER, WHEN THE SAMPLE WAS DIVIDED, THE SLOW RESPONDERS SHOWED AN INVERSION FOR ALL PROBLEMS. BUT THE FAST RESPONDERS SHOWED AN INVERSION ON ONLY ONE PROBLEM. ALTHOUGH THE PREDICTION OF THE HYPOTHESIS WAS CONFIRMED, THE FACT THAT, AFTER THE SECOND GRADE, THE FAST RESPONDERS ALWAYS DID BETTER THAN THE SLOW RESPONDERS CLOUDS THE INTERPRETATION OF THE RESULTS. IT IS FELT THAT THE COMPLEX HYPOTHESIS ASSUMPTION IS INSUFFICIENT TO ACCOUNT FOR THE IMPORTANCE OF THE REACTION TIME VARIABLE. (DR)

ED020019 PS000964
A LONGITUDINAL ASSESSMENT OF PRESCHOOL CHILDREN IN HAPTIC LEARNING. FINAL REPORT. COYLE, SISTER JOHN VIANNEY; CONCANNON, SISTER JOSEPHINA, FEB68 123P.
EDRS PRICE MF-$0.65 HC-$6.58

RECENTLY MUCH ATTENTION HAS BEEN FOCUSED ON THE SUBJECT OF CONCEPT FORMATION IN CHILDREN. THE DEVELOPMENT OF SPATIAL PERCEPTION IS AN IMPORTANT ASPECT OF THIS, AND ONE IMPORTANT PART OF SPATIAL PERCEPTION IS HAPTIC PERCEPTION--THE RECOGNITION OF OBJECTS BY TOUCH. THIS STUDY IS A LONGITUDINAL INVESTIGATION OF THE RETENTION OF HAPTIC ABILITIES DEVELOPED IN THE COURSE OF A 3-MONTH TRAINING EXPERIMENT, REPORTED IN ED 010 126. THE FINAL TEST OF THAT STUDY WAS USED AS THE PRETEST FOR THE LONGITUDINAL STUDY. TESTS WERE GIVEN TO THE PARTICIPANTS OF THE EARLIER STUDY 6 MONTHS AND 12 MONTHS AFTER ITS COMPLETION. OF THE 144 SUBJECTS OF THE EARLIER STUDY, 131 COMPLETED RETESTING. THE AGES OF THESE SUBJECTS RANGED, AT THE BEGINNING OF THE EARLIER STUDY, FROM 36 TO 71 MONTHS. THE SUBJECTS CAME FROM MONTESSORI AND NON-MONTESSORI PRESCHOOL PROGRAMS AND HAD BEEN DIVIDED INTO EXPERIMENTAL AND CONTROL GROUPS WHICH RECEIVED EITHER INDIVIDUAL OR GROUP INSTRUCTION. FIVE TESTS OF HAPTIC PERCEPTION WERE USED. IN EACH TEST THE SUBJECT HANDLED PLYWOOD FORMS THROUGH AN OPENING IN A SCREEN AND WAS THEN ASKED TO DO SUCH THINGS AS NAME THE OBJECT, DESCRIBE IT, OR DRAW IT. ANALYSES IN WHICH THE PRETEST SCORES WERE CONTROLLED INDICATED THAT RETENTION WAS NOT STRONGLY AFFECTED BY THE TYPE OF PRESCHOOL, THE TYPE OF INSTRUCTION, CHRONOLOGICAL OR MENTAL AGE, OR SEX. EXAMINATION OF THE SCORES OVER THE 12-MONTH PERIOD SHOWED THAT ALTHOUGH THE EXPERIMENTAL SUBJECTS SCORED CONSISTENTLY HIGHER, THE CONTROL SUBJECTS HAD HIGHER CHANGE SCORES. THIS SEEMS TO HAVE RESULTED FROM A LOSS OF PROFICIENCY IN HAPTIC ABILITIES BY THE EXPERIMENTAL SUBJECTS, COUPLED WITH SOME DEVELOPMENT OF HAPTIC ABILITIES BY THE CONTROL GROUP AS A RESULT OF MATURATION. (DR)

ED020020 PS000965
FAMILY BACKGROUND EFFECTS ON PERSONALITY DEVELOPMENT AND SOCIAL ACCEPTANCE. COX, SAMUEL H., AUG66 252P.
EDRS PRICE MF-$0.65 HC-$9.87

IT WAS HYPOTHESIZED THAT FOUR PRIMARY FACTORS SIGNIFICANTLY INTERACT TO AFFECT THE PERSONALITY DEVELOPMENT OF CHILDREN. THESE FACTORS WERE (1) FAMILY BACKGROUND VARIABLES, (2) PARENTAL CHILD-REARING PRACTICE AND ATTITUDE VARIABLES, (3) CHILD PERSONALITY AND SELF-CONCEPT VARIABLES, AND (4) CHILD-PEER RELATIONSHIP VARIABLES. THE PURPOSE OF THIS STUDY WAS TO INVESTIGATE THE PRESENCE OF THE INTERRELATIONSHIPS BETWEEN THE FOUR CATEGORIES OF VARIABLES. STUDENTS OF THE CASTLEBERRY

SCHOOL DISTRICT NEAR FORT WORTH, TEXAS HAD PARTICIPATED FOR FOUR YEARS IN THE DISTRICT'S PEER RELATIONS PROGRAM. SOCIOMETRIC RATING SCORES WERE THUS AVAILABLE FOR A LARGE GROUP OF STUDENTS. THESE SCORES REPRESENTED A CHILD'S RATING ACCORDING TO HIS PEERS AND TEACHERS. BOYS AND GIRLS IN GRADES SIX, SEVEN, AND EIGHT WHO PLACED HIGH OR LOW ON THE SOCIOMETRIC RATING SCORE WERE THE SAMPLE POOL. THE PARENTS OF THESE CHILDREN WERE SOLICITED FOR PARTICIPATION IN THE STUDY AND WHEN 100 FAMILIES AGREED TO PARTICIPATE, THE SAMPLE WAS CLOSED. THE PARENTS AND CHILDREN WERE SUBSEQUENTLY ADMINISTERED A BATTERY OF INTERVIEWS, QUESTIONNAIRES, TESTS, AND RATING FORMS CONCERNING VARIABLE-CATEGORIES (1), (2), AND (3). THE RESULTS OF THESE DATA, PLUS THE SOCIOMETRIC RATING DATA USED IN SELECTING THE SAMPLE, WERE ANALYZED TO OBTAIN THE EXISTENCE OF THE INTERRELATIONSHIPS, IF ANY. SIGNIFICANT INTERRELATIONSHIPS BETWEEN THE FOUR GROUPS OF VARIABLES WERE FOUND TO EXIST. FAMILY BACKGROUND FACTORS WERE ASSOCIATED WITH VARIABLES AT EACH OF THE OTHER THREE LEVELS. FAMILY TENSION, A VARIABLE UNDER CATEGORY (2), HAD A DISRUPTING INFLUENCE ON CHILD-REARING PRACTICES, THE CHILD'S PERSONALITY DEVELOPMENT, AND SOCIAL ACCEPTANCE OF THE CHILD BY PEERS. ANOTHER CATEGORY (2) VARIABLE, PARENTAL LOVE OR REJECTION, ALSO INFLUENCED THE CHILD'S CHARACTER AND SOCIAL ACCEPTANCE. (WD)

ED020021 PS000966
PRELIMINARY FINDINGS FROM A LONGITUDINAL EDUCATIONAL IMPROVEMENT PROJECT BEING CONDUCTED FOR INSTRUCTIONALLY IMPOVERISHED PUPILS IN INTACT SCHOOLS IN THE URBAN SOUTH. PLATTOR, STANTON D., 9FEB68 15P.
EDRS PRICE MF-$0.65 HC-$3.29

A STUDY WAS CONDUCTED TO FIND OUT WHETHER OR NOT A SIGNIFICANT CHANGE IN PUPILS' ACADEMIC POTENTIAL (AS MEASURED BY A STANDARDIZED GROUP TEST OF INTELLIGENCE) COULD BE MADE AS A RESULT OF APPROPRIATE MODIFICATIONS OF THE TEACHING-LEARNING ENVIRONMENT TO MEET THE SPECIFIC NEEDS OF DISADVANTAGED PUPILS. DEPRIVED NEGRO PUPILS AND THEIR TEACHERS IN TWO NEW ORLEANS URBAN ELEMENTARY SCHOOLS TOOK PART IN AN EDUCATIONAL IMPROVEMENT PROJECT, INVOLVING A SPECIAL INSTRUCTIONAL PROGRAM. PRELIMINARY TESTING SUPPLIED DEMOGRAPHIC DATA ON BOTH TEACHERS AND PUPILS, NONCOGNITIVE DATA ON TEACHER VARIABLES, AND COGNITIVE DATA ON PUPILS. AT THE PROJECT'S INCEPTION, PUPILS HAD SUCH LEARNER BEHAVIOR CHARACTERISTICS AS DEPRESSED LEARNING POTENTIAL, LOW READINESS LEVELS, INADEQUATE READING SKILLS AND POOR IN-SCHOOL ACHIEVEMENT. THE LONG FORM OF THE CALIFORNIA TEST OF MENTAL MATURITY WAS GIVEN TO ALL (APPROXIMATELY 2,200) PUPILS IN THE FALL OF 1966, PRIOR TO THE INTERVENTION PROGRAM. INTERIM POSTTESTS WERE GIVEN IN THE SPRING OF 1967, AND POSTTESTS WILL BE GIVEN ANNUALLY IN GRADES ONE, THREE, AND FIVE. THERE WERE 305 GRADE ONE, 205 GRADE THREE, AND 250 GRADE FIVE PUPILS PARTICIPATING. ALL GAINS BETWEEN THE PRETESTS AND POSTTESTS IN GRADES ONE, THREE, AND FIVE WERE STATISTICALLY SIGNIFICANT AT OR BEYOND THE .001 LEVEL EXCEPT THE GRADE FIVE NONLANGUAGE GAIN, WHICH WAS SIGNIFICANT AT THE .05 LEVEL. LANGUAGE GAINS WERE HIGHER IN ALL CASES THAN NONLANGUAGE GAINS. THESE PRELIMINARY RESULTS APPEAR TO INDICATE THAT IQ SCORES, AS AN INDEX OF ACADEMIC POTENTIAL, CAN BE IMPROVED SIGNIFICANTLY WHEN GENERAL LEARNING ENVIRONMENT MODIFICATIONS ARE COUPLED WITH INSTRUCTIONAL INTERVENTION PROGRAMS. A DISTINCTION NEEDS TO BE MADE BETWEEN STATISTICAL AND EDUCATIONAL SIGNIFICANCE IN USING DATA TO PLAN OR EVALUATE PROGRAMS. (MS)

ED020022 PS000973
CO-OPERATIVE NURSERY SCHOOLS--A HANDBOOK FOR PARENTS. A GUIDE FOR ORGANIZATION AND ADMINISTRATION. REVISED EDITION. , SEP67
DOCUMENT NOT AVAILABLE FROM EDRS.

THIS HANDBOOK IS DESIGNED TO HELP PARENTS WHO MIGHT WISH TO ORGANIZE A COOPERATIVE NURSERY SCHOOL. IT IS BASED ON AND DESCRIBES THE OPERATION OF THE COOPERATIVE NURSERY SCHOOLS OF THE MONTGOMERY COUNTY, MARYLAND, COUNCIL. THE HANDBOOK FOCUSES ON ADMINISTRATIVE, RATHER THAN EDUCATIONAL, PROBLEMS. INDIVIDUAL CHAPTERS TREAT SPECIFIC TOPICS THAT WOULD FALL WITHIN THE SCOPE OF A SINGLE COMMITTEE. THE DESCRIPTIONS AND RECOMMENDATIONS ARE IN GENERAL QUITE SPECIFIC. THE TOPICS COVERED ARE (1) PROGRAM, (2) ORGANIZATION, (3) MEMBERSHIP, (4) STAFF, (5) FINANCES, (6) PARENT EDUCATION, (7) HEALTH, (8) EQUIPMENT, (9) CALENDAR, (10) TRIPS, AND (11) LIBRARY. THIS DOCUMENT IS AVAILABLE FOR $2.00 FROM THE MONTGOMERY COUNTY COUNCIL OF COOPERATIVE NURSERY SCHOOLS, P.O. BOX 624, GLEN ECHO, MARYLAND 20768. (DR)

ED020023 PS000977
SOCIOECONOMIC STATUS AND LEARNING PROFICIENCY IN YOUNG CHILDREN. ROHWER, WILLIAM D., JR.; AND OTHERS, 13P.
EDRS PRICE MF-$0.65 HC-$3.29

THIS STUDY WAS INITIATED TO DETERMINE WHY CHILDREN OF LOWER SOCIOECONOMIC STATUS, WHO DO INFERIOR WORK ON SCHOOL-RELATED LEARNING TASKS WHEN COMPARED TO UPPER SOCIOECONOMIC STATUS CHILDREN, LEARN AS EFFICIENTLY AS UPPER LEVEL CHILDREN ON PAIRED-ASSOCIATE TASKS. THE SAMPLE CONSISTED OF 120 LOWER STATUS CHILDREN AND 120 UPPER STATUS CHILDREN, EQUALLY DISTRIBUTED AMONG THE KINDERGARTEN, FIRST GRADE AND THIRD GRADE, WHO WERE ADMINISTERED PAIRED-ASSOCIATE TASKS. FOUR METHODS OF PRESENTATION OF THE 20 PAIRED ASSOCIATES WERE USED--(1) PROVIDED-PHRASE (PP), (2) PROVIDED-SENTENCE (PS), (3) GENERATED-STILL (GS), AND (4) GENERATED-ACTION (GA). THE PRIMARY DIFFERENCE BETWEEN THE PP-PS METHODS AND THE GA-GS METHODS WAS THAT IN THE LATTER, THE CHILDREN HAD TO CONSTRUCT THEIR OWN SENTENCES, USING THE PAIR NAMES. IN THE PP AND PS METHODS, THE CHILDREN JUST REPEATED A PHRASE (PP) OR SENTENCE (PS) GIVEN BY THE EXPERIMENTER. A PROJECTOR AND SCREEN APPARATUS WERE USED TO PRESENT THE PAIRED OBJECTS. THE PICTURES USED IN THE PP, PS, AND GS METHODS WERE STILL PICTURES. THE GA METHOD USED ACTION PICTURES IN WHICH THE DISPLAYED OBJECTS WERE PART OF AN ACTION CONTEXT. TWO TEST TRIALS WERE SUBSEQUENTLY CONDUCTED. THE TEST TRIALS INVOLVED DISPLAYING ONE OF THE PAIR ON THE SCREEN AND REQUIRING THE PUPIL TO NAME THE OTHER ITEM OF THE PAIR. THE RESULTS OF THE TEST TRIALS INDICATED THAT THE LOWER LEVEL CHILDREN DID NOT HAVE THE LANGUAGE DEFICIENCY ANTICIPATED ALTHOUGH THEY LEARNED LESS EFFICIENTLY THAN THE UPPER STATUS CHILDREN AT THE KINDERGARTEN AND FIRST GRADE LEVEL. A POSSIBLE REASON FOR THIS LOWER PERFORMANCE BY THE LOWER STATUS CHILDREN IS THAT UPPER STATUS CHILDREN BENEFITED MORE FROM LARGER NUMBERS OF PAIRING-TRIAL REPETITIONS. (WD)

ED020024 PS000979
THE INTERACTION OF FATHER-ABSENCE AND SIBLING-PRESENCE ON COGNITIVE ABILITIES. SUTTON-SMITH, B.; AND OTHERS, 13P.
EDRS PRICE MF-$0.65 HC-$3.29

THE PURPOSE OF THIS STUDY WAS TO INVESTIGATE THE INFLUENCE UPON A CHILD'S COGNITIVE DEVELOPMENT OF THE FATHER'S PRESENCE IN (FP) OR ABSENCE FROM (FA) THE FAMILY IN A ONE-, TWO-, OR THREE-CHILD FAMILY. THE EFFECT OF THE SEX AND ORDINAL POSITION OF A SIBLING UPON COGNITIVE DEVELOPMENT WAS ALSO CONSIDERED. DATA FOR THIS ANALYSIS WERE OBTAINED FROM SOPHOMORE STUDENTS IN AN ELEMENTARY PSYCHOLOGY COURSE AT BOWLING GREEN STATE UNIVERSITY SAMPLED OVER A FIVE-YEAR PERIOD. FA SUBJECTS NUMBERED 295 AND FP SUBJECTS NUMBERED 760. ALL SUBJECTS HAD TAKEN THE ACE PSYCHOLOGICAL EXAM AS FRESHMEN. A COMPARISON WAS MADE BETWEEN THE SCORES OF FA SUBJECTS AND FB SUBJECTS ON THE ACE TEST, WITH SPECIAL FOCUS ON WHEN IN THE LIFE OF THE SUBJECT THE FATHER'S ABSENCE OCCURRED AND THE LENGTH THEREOF. IN ADDITION, SCORES OF ALL SUBJECTS ON THE ACE TEST WERE COMPARED ON THE BASIS OF THE SIBLING INFORMATION OBTAINED. THE RESULTS OF THE ANALYSES SHOWED (1) THAT FA SUBJECTS SCORED CONSISTENTLY LOWER ON THE ACE TEST THAN FP SUBJECTS, (2) THAT THE EFFECT OF FATHER-ABSENCE IS MORE DELETERIOUS TO MALES THAN FEMALES EXCEPT WHERE THE MALE IS AN ONLY CHILD, (3) THAT FIRST BORN BOYS FROM FP FAMILIES, WHO HAVE A YOUNGER SISTER, SHOW HIGHER SCORES THAN BOYS WITH YOUNGER BROTHERS, (4) THAT RESULTS ARE SIMILAR FOR FIRST BORN GIRLS, (5) THAT HAVING AN OLDER SIBLING APPEARS SOMEWHAT TO OFFSET THE NEGATIVE EFFECT ON COGNITIVE DEVELOPMENT OF FATHER-ABSENCE, AND (6) THAT THE TOTAL NUMBER OF YEARS THE FATHER WAS ABSENT APPEARS TO HAVE NO PARTICULAR EFFECT, IN AND OF ITSELF, ON EITHER MALES OR FEMALES. (WD)

ED020025 PS000982
AN ANNOTATED BIBLIOGRAPHY OF BEHAVIOR MODIFICATION WITH CHILDREN AND RETARDATES. L'ABATE, LUCIANO; WHITAKER, DANIEL L., 15AUG67 38P.
EDRS PRICE MF-$0.65 HC-$3.29

PAPERS OR STUDIES CONCERNED WITH THE APPLICATION OF BEHAVIOR MODIFICATION PRINCIPLES TO CHILDREN AND RETARDATES ARE INCLUDED IN THIS ANNOTATED BIBLIOGRAPHY. AUTHORS ARE LISTED ALPHABETICALLY. A SHORT PARAGRAPH DESCRIBES THE GENERAL NATURE OF EACH STUDY CITED, AND BIBLIOGRAPHIC REFERENCES ARE GIVEN. THERE ARE 130 ENTRIES IN THIS BIBLIOGRAPHY. (MS)

ED020026 PS000983
THE EFFECT OF HEADSTART ON DEVELOPMENTAL PROCESSES. EISENBERG, LEON; CONNERS, C. KEITH, 11APR66 15P.
EDRS PRICE MF-$0.65 HC-$3.29

AS PART OF AN EFFORT TO ASSESS THE EFFECT OF THE BALTIMORE HEAD START PROGRAM ON COGNITIVE DEVELOPMENT, CHILDREN ENROLLED IN THIS PROGRAM WERE GIVEN THE PEABODY PICTURE VOCABULARY TEST (PPVT) AND THE DRAW-A-PERSON (DAP) TEST AT THE START OF THE PROGRAM, AT ITS TERMINATION, AND WHEN THEY ENROLLED IN KINDERGARTEN. A CONTROL GROUP, DRAWN FROM THE SAME NEIGHBORHOODS, WAS TESTED AT KINDERGARTEN ENROLLMENT. THE NUMBER OF CHILDREN TESTED IN EACH GROUP WAS SLIGHTLY OVER

400. DATA ON THE FAMILIES OF THE HEAD START CHILDREN INDICATED THAT THEY WERE SEVERELY DISADVANTAGED. RESULTS OF THE PPVT SHOWED SIGNIFICANT GAINS DURING THE PROGRAM AND BETWEEN THE END OF THE PROGRAM AND KINDERGARTEN ENROLLMENT. THE CONTROL GROUP SCORED AT THE SAME LEVEL THAT THE HEAD START CHILDREN HAD SCORED AT THE BEGINNING OF THE PROGRAM. RESULTS OF THE DAP TEST SHOWED A SIMILAR PATTERN OF GAINS, BUT WITH THE CONTROL GROUP SCORING AT THE SAME LEVEL THAT THE HEAD START CHILDREN HAD SCORED AT THE END OF THE PROGRAM. CLASSROOM EVALUATIONS OF TEACHER BEHAVIOR WERE MADE, AND PRELIMINARY ANALYSES INDICATE THAT TEACHERS WHO WERE RATED AS WARM, VARIED, AND FLEXIBLE AND WHO SPENT A RELATIVELY HIGH PROPORTION OF TIME TEACHING PRODUCED THE HIGHEST GAINS. (DR)

ED020770 PS000098
AN EXPLORATION OF THE USES OF RHYTHMIC MOVEMENT TO DEVELOP AESTHETIC CONCEPTS IN THE PRIMARY GRADES. ROWEN, BETTY J.R., 66 247P.
EDRS PRICE MF-$0.65 HC-$9.87

ON THE BASIS OF THE ASSUMPTIONS THAT EDUCATION NEEDS TO DEVELOP CHILDREN'S FEELINGS AS MUCH AS THEIR ABILITIES TO RETAIN FACTS AND UNDERSTAND CONCEPTS AND THAT INSTRUCTION IN THE AREA OF AESTHETICS IS POSSIBLE, THIS STUDY DESCRIBES AND EVALUATES A PROGRAM FOR PRIMARY CHILDREN IN WHICH MOVEMENT EXPLORATION IS EMPLOYED TO DEVELOP AESTHETIC CONCEPTS. A 16-WEEK PROGRAM WAS ADMINISTERED TO SOME 20 SECOND GRADE CHILDREN. THE MAIN FOCUS OF EACH OF THE SESSIONS WAS ON ONE OF FIVE PREDETERMINED COMPONENTS OF AESTHETIC EXPERIENCE--(1) THEME, (2) QUALITY OF SENSORY PERCEPTION, (3) PATTERN, (4) RHYTHM, AND (5) DOMINANCE. THE DATA WERE THE CHILDREN'S BEHAVIOR RESPONSES DURING THE PROGRAM SESSIONS, AS COLLECTED FROM TAPE-RECORDINGS, FILMS, RECORDED OBSERVATIONS, ARTWORK, AND WRITINGS. THE FINDINGS INDICATE THAT THE CHILDREN ALL RESPONDED WITH A HIGH DEGREE OF INVOLVEMENT AND GAINED IN ORIGINALITY WHILE REDUCING THEIR SELF-CONSCIOUSNESS. EACH CHILD DISPLAYED AN AREA OF PARTICULAR SENSITIVITY WHICH DEVELOPED TO A GREATER DEGREE THAN OTHER AREAS. THE STRONGEST AREA OF AESTHETIC COMPONENT RESPONSE BY THE CHILDREN WAS TO THE ACTIVITIES DEALING WITH RHYTHM. IT WAS CONCLUDED THAT THE PROGRAM DID PROVIDE AN OPPORTUNITY FOR THE CHILDREN'S INNATE SENSITIVITY TO FIND EXPRESSION AND ENCOURAGEMENT. (WD)

ED020771 PS000195
EFFECTIVENESS OF THE HEAD START PROGRAM IN ENHANCING SCHOOL READINESS OF CULTURALLY DEPRIVED CHILDREN. CHESTEEN, HILLIARD E., JR.; AND OTHERS, JUN66 170P.
EDRS PRICE MF-$0.65 HC-$6.58

TO STUDY THE EFFECT OF A 6-WEEK HEAD START PROGRAM ON THE SCHOOL READINESS OF 81 CULTURALLY DEPRIVED CHILDREN IN EAST BATON ROUGE PARISH, LOUISIANA, COMPARISONS WERE MADE BETWEEN HEAD START AND NONCULTURALLY DEPRIVED CHILDREN. IQ SCORES AND CULTURAL-SOCIOLOGICAL-ECONOMICAL STATUS INFLUENCE UPON SCHOOL READINESS WERE STUDIED. ALL CHILDREN INVOLVED WERE GIVEN THE PRIMARY MENTAL ABILITIES TEST (PMA), WHICH MEASURES VERBAL MEANING, NUMBER FACILITY, PERCEPTUAL SPEED, AND SPATIAL RELATIONS. PRETESTS AND POSTTESTS WERE GIVEN TO HEAD START CHILDREN. BOTH HEAD START AND CONTROL GROUPS WERE TESTED AT THE BEGINNING, MIDDLE, AND END OF THE FIRST SCHOOL YEAR. CONTROL GROUP I (28 MIDDLE AND UPPER CLASS WHITE AND NEGRO CHILDREN, MATCHED WITH THE HEAD START GROUP BY AGE AND GEOGRAPHICAL LOCALE) WAS USED TO SEE HOW WELL HEAD START CHILDREN COULD APPROXIMATE THE SCHOOL CAPACITY OR IQ OF THE NONCULTURALLY DEPRIVED. CONTROL GROUP II WAS MADE UP OF 126 CLASSROOM PEERS. HEAD START CHILDREN SHOWED AN INCREASE IN IQ MEAN SCORES (86.56 TO 99.53) FROM THE BEGINNING OF THE PROGRAM TO THE END OF THE FIRST SCHOOL YEAR. THE GREATEST GAINS, AS MEASURED BY PMA SUBTESTS, WERE IN THE AREAS OF PERCEPTUAL SPEED AND NUMBER FACILITY. DURING THEIR FIRST TERM IN SCHOOL, GAINS WERE IN THESE SAME AREAS. THEREFORE, HEAD START HAD A POSITIVE INFLUENCE ON SCHOOL READINESS, ALTHOUGH IT DID NOT ENABLE THE CULTURALLY DEPRIVED CHILDREN TO REACH THE SCHOOL READINESS LEVEL OF THE NONCULTURALLY DEPRIVED. ABOUT 100 PAGES OF THIS THESIS ARE DEVOTED TO A DISCUSSION OF CULTURAL DEPRIVATION AND PERTINENT EDUCATIONAL LITERATURE AND THEORIES. (MS)

ED020772 PS000223
THE IMPACT OF OPERATION HEAD START ON GREENE COUNTY, OHIO, AN EVALUATION REPORT. COHNSTAEDT, MARTIN L.; IRONS, PETER H., FEB66 296P.
EDRS PRICE MF-$0.65 HC-$9.87

THIS REPORT PRESENTS A DESCRIPTION OF THE IMPACT OF THE SUMMER 1965 HEAD START PROGRAM IN GREENE COUNTY, OHIO ON GROUPS OF PERSONS HAVING SOME CONTACT WITH IT. THE REPORT DOES NOT ATTEMPT TO ASSESS THE EFFECT THE PROGRAM HAD ON THE CHILDREN PARTICIPATING IN IT. INITIAL SECTIONS OF THE REPORT PROVIDE AN INTRODUCTION, DESCRIBE THE PLANNING OF THE PROGRAM, AND DESCRIBE THE PROGRAM ITSELF. SUBSEQUENT SECTIONS ASSESS THE REACTIONS OF THE FAMILIES OF PARTICIPATING CHILDREN, PERSONNEL IN AGENCIES PROVIDING SERVICES TO THE CHILDREN, PERSONNEL IN THE MEDICAL AND DENTAL PROGRAM, PARTICIPATING AND NONPARTICIPATING TEACHERS, ELEMENTARY SCHOOL PRINCIPALS, SCHOOL SUPERINTENDENTS, AND SCHOOL BOARD MEMBERS. A FINAL SECTION ASSESSES THE COUNTYWIDE IMPACT OF THE PROGRAM. SIX APPENDIXES PRESENT ADDITIONAL INFORMATION ON THE TEACHERS, QUESTIONNAIRES USED IN THE STUDY, A SUMMARY REPORT OF THE MEDICAL AND DENTAL EVALUATIONS, AND PROGRAM PLANNING MATERIALS. (DR)

ED020773 PS000228
BIBLIOGRAPHY OF PAPERS COVERING WORK UNDER OEO CONTRACT NUMBER 510. FINAL REPORT. (TITLE SUPPLIED). EISENBERG, LEON; AND OTHERS, 24OCT66 2P.
EDRS PRICE MF-$0.65 HC-$3.29

THIS DOCUMENT IS A BIBLIOGRAPHY OF PAPERS COVERING WORK DONE UNDER OEO CONTRACT 510. THE PAPERS ARE INDIVIDUALLY ABSTRACTED UNDER THE FOLLOWING ACCESSION NUMBERS. PS 000 983, "THE EFFECT OF HEADSTART ON DEVELOPMENTAL PROCESSES." PS 000 984, "THE EFFECT OF TEACHER BEHAVIOR ON VERBAL INTELLIGENCE IN OPERATION HEADSTART CHILDREN." PS 000 985, "A FOLLOW-UP STUDY OF INTELLIGENCE CHANGES IN CHILDREN WHO PARTICIPATED IN PROJECT HEADSTART." PS 000 986, "THE LIMITATIONS OF BRIEF INTELLIGENCE TESTING WITH YOUNG CHILDREN." PS 000 987, "THE JOHNS HOPKINS PERCEPTUAL TEST, THE DEVELOPMENT OF A RAPID INTELLIGENCE TEST FOR THE PRE-SCHOOL CHILD." PS 000 988, "THE SYNTACTIC STRUCTURES OF 5 YEAR OLD CULTURALLY DEPRIVED CHILDREN." PS 000 989, "LANGUAGE CONTROL IN A GROUP OF HEADSTART CHILDREN." ADDITIONAL PAPERS NOT AVAILABLE FOR ABSTRACTING ARE "CLINICAL CONSIDERATIONS IN THE PSYCHIATRIC EVALUATION OF INTELLIGENCE," "SOCIAL CLASS AND INDIVIDUAL DEVELOPMENT," "THE DEVELOPMENT OF INTELLIGENCE," "DEVELOPMENT PATTERNS OF YOUNG CHILDREN," AND "THE ROLE OF LINGUISTIC PRE-TRAINING IN CONCEPT ATTAINMENT IN YOUNG CHILDREN." (DR)

ED020774 PS000563
THE LIMITATIONS OF BRIEF INTELLIGENCE TESTING WITH YOUNG CHILDREN. ROSENBERG, LEON A.; STROUD, MICHAEL, 13P.
EDRS PRICE MF-$0.65 HC-$3.29

A STUDY EXAMINED THE VALIDITY OF TWO BRIEF INTELLIGENCE SCALES, THE PEABODY PICTURE VOCABULARY TEST (PPVT) AND THE COLUMBIA MENTAL MATURITY SCALE (CMMS), TO SEE IF THESE TESTS OVERESTIMATED THE INCIDENCE OF INTELLECTUAL RETARDATION AMONG POVERTY AREA CHILDREN. THESE TWO TESTS AND AN EXPERIMENTAL MEASURE OF INTELLIGENCE, THE JOHNS HOPKINS PERCEPTUAL TEST (JHPT), HAD BEEN GIVEN TO 28 KINDERGARTEN CHILDREN. A SIGNIFICANTLY LESS RETARDATION INCIDENCE WAS FOUND WITH THE JHPT. ACTUAL PERCENTAGES WERE 69.56 ON THE PPVT, 17.86 ON THE CMMS, AND 3.57 ON THE JHPT. THEREFORE, AS A CRITERION MEASURE, THE STANFORD-BINET WAS ADMINISTERED TO EACH CHILD. IT WAS FOUND THAT THE CHILDREN TESTED ON A MUCH HIGHER LEVEL OF INTELLIGENCE THAN REPORTED ON THE PPVT AND CMMS, ALTHOUGH THE CMMS EXAGGERATED LESS THE DEGREE OF RETARDATION. IN THE SAME SCHOOL, A SAMPLE OF FIRST GRADE CHILDREN REPRESENTING AN ENTIRE KINDERGARTEN CLASS OF THE PREVIOUS YEAR WAS GIVEN THE PPVT, CCMS, AND THE STANDFORD-BINET. TWENTY-NINE CHILDREN PARTICIPATED. IT WAS FOUND THAT THE PPVT STILL UNDERESTIMATED INTELLIGENCE TO A STATISTICALLY SIGNIFICANT DEGREE. THE MEAN IQ SCORE INCREASED 18.86 POINTS ON PPVT PERFORMANCE, INDICATING THE INFLUENCE OF EDUCATIONAL EXPERIENCE. ALTHOUGH THE STANFORD-BINET STILL PLACED ALL CHILDREN IN THE NONRETARDED CATEGORY, THE PPVT RATED 24.14 PER CENT AND THE CMMS SCALE, 10.34 PER CENT AS RETARDED. A BRIEF CULTURE-FAIR SCREENING MEASURE IS NEEDED. (MS)

ED020775 PS000854
COMMUNICATIVE COMPETENCE OF LOW-INCOME CHILDREN--ASSUMPTIONS AND PROGRAMS. JOHN, VERA, 30MAR67 16P.
EDRS PRICE MF-$0.65 HC-$3.29

TO NARROW THE LANGUAGE SKILLS GAP BETWEEN DISADVANTAGED AND MIDDLE CLASS CHILDREN IS A PRIMARY AIM OF MOST INTERVENTION PROGRAMS, ACTING ON THE THEORY THAT INCREASED LANGUAGE COMMAND LEADS TO INCREASED ABILITY IN ABSTRACT THINKING. HOWEVER, THERE IS A DIFFERENCE BETWEEN LANGUAGE AS A COMMUNICATIVE PROCESS AND LANGUAGE AS AN INTELLECTIVE PROCESS. RECOMMENDATIONS ARE THAT THE ROLE OF LANGUAGE IN THOUGHT NEEDS PRAGMATIC EXAMINATION, A SOCIOLINGUISTIC APPROACH TO LANGUAGE DEVELOPMENT SHOULD BE ATTEMPTED, AND EDUCATIONAL IDEOLOGY SHOULD BE DEVELOPED WITH A FOCUS UPON THE EDUCATION OF THE DISADVANTAGED. INTERVENTION PROGRAMS SHOULD BE REGULARLY EVALUATED AND IMPROVED AS MORE INFORMATION IS LEARNED ABOUT LANGUAGE AND COGNITIVE DEVELOPMENT. FILLING THE GAP IN LANGUAGE LEARNING IS NOT SOLELY A QUANTITATIVE MATTER. (MS)

ED020776 PS000928

AN ANALYSIS OF A CLASS OF PROBLEM SOLVING BEHAVIOR. FINAL REPORT. ANDERSON, RICHARD C., JAN68 188P.

EDRS PRICE MF-$0.65 HC-$6.58

A CONCEPT ATTAINMENT TASK IN WHICH CHILDREN ARE ASKED TO IDENTIFY A CONCEPT THROUGH DETERMINING WHICH OF A SET OF OBJECTS ARE OR ARE NOT INSTANCES OF IT WAS USED TO INVESTIGATE THEIR PROBLEM-SOLVING BEHAVIOR. OF PARTICULAR INTEREST WAS THE QUESTION OF TO WHAT EXTENT THEY USED OR LEARNED THE STRATEGY OF VARYING ONE FACTOR WHILE HOLDING ALL OTHERS CONSTANT. IN THE FIRST OF THREE EXPERIMENTS A SAMPLE OF 144 FOURTH GRADERS WERE GIVEN 24 APTITUDE TESTS AND NINE CONCEPT ATTAINMENT TASKS. OF SEVEN APTITUDE FACTORS FOUND, ONLY TWO, CALLED SPATIAL ORIENTATION AND FIGURAL ADAPTIVE FLEXIBILITY, SHOWED SIGNIFICANT CORRELATIONS WITH PROBLEM-SOLVING PERFORMANCE. THE SECOND EXPERIMENT INVESTIGATED THE EFFECT OF THE PRESENCE OR ABSENCE OF ACTUAL OBJECTS ON CHILDREN'S PERFORMANCE. A SAMPLE OF 24 THIRD OR FOURTH GRADERS WERE EACH GIVEN THREE PROBLEMS TO SOLVE. OF FOUR GROUPS, ONLY THE ONE NEVER SHOWN ANY OBJECTS PERFORMED SIGNIFICANTLY MORE POORLY. THE THIRD EXPERIMENT WAS INTENDED TO COMPARE TWO METHODS OF TEACHING THE DESIRED PROBLEM-SOLVING STRATEGY, A PART-TASK METHOD WHICH ATTEMPTED TO TEACH COMPONENT SKILLS AND A WHOLE-TASK METHOD WHICH ATTEMPTED TO TEACH THE TOTAL SKILL. TWO GROUPS OF 18 FIRST GRADERS RECEIVED ONE OR THE OTHER FORM OF TRAINING, AFTER WHICH THEIR PERFORMANCE WAS COMPARED WITH A GROUP OF UNTRAINED FIRST GRADERS. ON RETENTION PROBLEMS THE PART-TASK GROUP WAS SIGNIFICANTLY BETTER THAN THE WHOLE-TASK GROUP, WHICH WAS IN TURN BETTER THAN THE UNTRAINED GROUP. (DR)

ED020777 PS000939

PREVENTION OF FAILURE. , 65 96P.

EDRS PRICE MF-$0.65 HC NOT AVAILABLE FROM EDRS.

THE IMPORTANCE OF THE PREVENTION OF FAILURE IN SCHOOL IS THE MAIN THEME OF THIS PAMPHLET. THE DIFFERENT FORCES WHICH INFLUENCE THE SELF-IMAGES OF CHILDREN, THEIR SCHOOL PERFORMANCE, ACCEPTANCE OR REJECTION BY OTHER CHILDREN, AND, MOST IMPORTANT, ACCEPTANCE OR REJECTION BY THE TEACHER HERSELF, ARE DISCUSSED IN A GROUP OF PAPERS UNDER ELEVEN TITLES--(1) "WHAT MAY WE NOW BELIEVE," A PLEA FOR INNER-DIRECTED TEACHING WHICH STRESSES THE IMPORTANCE OF EACH INDIVIDUAL CHILD, (2) "REFLECTIONS ON CHILDHOOD IDENTITY AND THE SCHOOL," WHICH ASSERTS THAT THE CHILD'S SENSE OF IDENTITY IS BASED ON HIS POSITIVE OR NEGATIVE IDENTITY WITH HIS TEACHER, (3) "FACILITATING DEVELOPMENT IN THE PRESCHOOL CHILD--SOCIAL AND PSYCHOLOGICAL PERSPECTIVES," (4) "GROUPING AS A FACTOR IN FAILURE," (5) "EVALUATING CHILDREN'S GROWTH," WHICH URGES EVALUATION OF CHILDREN'S ATTITUDINAL CHANGES AS WELL AS ACADEMIC PROGRESS, (6) "THE EDUCATION OF TEACHERS," WHICH INCLUDES THE SUB-TOPICS OF TEACHER PLACEMENT, IN-SERVICE EDUCATION, AND ADMINISTRATIVE PLANNING, (7) "WHAT HARVEST WILL WE REAP," WHICH SUGGESTS THAT A POSITIVE CLIMATE AND INTELLECTUAL STIMULATION PROMOTE INDIVIDUAL DEVELOPMENT, (8) "PARENTS CAN HELP PREVENT SCHOOL FAILURE," (9) "IMPLICATIONS FOR PARENT EDUCATION," WHICH STRESSES PARENT CONFERENCES AND PARENT SUPPORT FOR CHILDREN'S LEARNING, (10) "THE SCHOOL WITHIN THE COMMUNITY," AND (11) "TOWARD A PROGRAM TO PREVENT FAILURE," A CHECKLIST OF QUESTIONS TO BE ANSWERED IN EVALUATING ANY PARTICULAR SCHOOL. A BIBLIOGRAPHY IS ALSO INCLUDED. THIS DOCUMENT IS AVAILABLE FOR $1 FROM NEA, 1201 SIXTEENTH STREET, N.W., WASHINGTON, D.C. 20036. (MS)

ED020778 PS000948

FREEDOM TO MOVE. CARPENTER, ETHELOUISE; SHIPLEY, FERNE, 62 34P.

EDRS PRICE MF-$0.65 HC NOT AVAILABLE FROM EDRS.

PLAY WHICH INVOLVES NATURAL MOVEMENT HELPS THE CHILD TO LEARN ABOUT THE PROPERTIES OF MATTER AND ABOUT HIMSELF. AN EXPANSIVE AND VERSATILE USE OF SPACE FOR LIVING INCREASES WITH EXPLORATION. FREEDOM TO MOVE IS INTELLECTUAL AND EMOTIONAL, AS WELL AS PHYSICAL. NEW EXPERIENCES ARISING OUT OF CURIOSITY AND INTERACTION WITH HIS OWN FAMILY AND OTHER CHILDREN HELP THE CHILD TO SORT OUT HIS FEELINGS AND RESPONSES. THEREFORE, THE CHILD NEEDS TO LEARN ABOUT THE POTENTIAL USES OF DIFFERENT PARTS OF HIS BODY THROUGH IMITATIVE MOVEMENT (OF TRAINS MOVING, BIRDS FLYING, ETC.) AND DRAMATIC PLAY. IT IS IMPORTANT TO RECOGNIZE THAT CHILDREN WILL PACE THEMSELVES IN ALTERNATING PERIODS OF MOVEMENT AND REST, IF THEIR ENVIRONMENT IS NOT TOO STRUCTURED. IN A SCHOOLROOM SITUATION CHILDREN CAN CONTROL SOME PHYSICAL MOTION WHEN THEY FEEL COMFORTABLE SOCIALLY AND ARE EXPERIENCING REWARDING MENTAL ACTIVITY. TOO RIGID A SCHEDULE OR TOO MUCH TIME PRESSURE CAN INHIBIT A CHILD'S REACTIONS AND ACTUALLY HOLD UP LEARNING. THIS DOCUMENT IS AVAILABLE FOR $0.85 FROM NEA, 1201 SIXTEENTH STREET, N.W., WASHINGTON, D.C. 20036. (MS)

ED020779 PS000968

SEMO PROJECT HEAD START, PSYCHOLOGICAL SERVICES REPORT, SUMMER 1967. PHASE THREE FINAL REPORT. THORNTON, SAM M., JAN68 37P.

EDRS PRICE MF-$0.65 HC-$3.29

A THIRD AND FINAL PHASE OF A THREE-PHASE PSYCHOLOGICAL SERVICE PROGRAM WAS COMPLETED DURING THE SUMMER OF 1967. THIS "CHILD STUDY" SERVICE WAS CARRIED OUT IN THE HEAD START CENTERS OF THE DELTA REGION OF SOUTHEAST MISSOURI. THE CHILDREN ATTENDING THE HEAD START PROGRAM WERE ABOUT EQUALLY REPRESENTED BY CAUCASIANS AND NEGROES. AN AVERAGE OF 5 YEARS OLD, THE CHILDREN CAME FROM FAMILIES OF A QUITE LOW SOCIOECONOMIC LEVEL. THE PSYCHOLOGICAL SERVICE PROGRAM WAS SUPPLEMENTARY TO THE HEAD START PROGRAM. ITS PURPOSE WAS TO MAKE COMPREHENSIVE PSYCHOLOGICAL STUDIES OF CHILDREN REFERRED TO IT BY THE HEAD START PROGRAM PERSONNEL. THE SERVICE ALSO PROVIDED AN IN-SERVICE TRAINING OPPORTUNITY FOR TEACHERS AND OTHER HEAD START PEOPLE. THE PSYCHOLOGICAL SERVICE STAFF WAS COMPOSED OF VARIOUS SPECIALISTS WHO WERE COMPETENT TO CONTRIBUTE TO THE ANALYSIS AND RESOLUTION OF THE REFERRED CHILD'S PROBLEMS. THE STAFF VISITED 23 HEAD START CENTERS AND EXAMINED 45 CHILDREN. THE EXAMINATION OR EVALUATION OF THE CHILD INVOLVED OBSERVATION, TESTING, AND DISCUSSION OF THE RESULTING DATA. ALL THOSE PROFESSIONALLY INTERESTED IN THE CHILD, THAT IS, TEACHERS, SOCIAL WORKERS, AND DOCTORS, COULD PARTICIPATE IN THE DISCUSSION SESSIONS. THESE SESSIONS PLUS NUMEROUS CASE PRESENTATION DAY SESSIONS PROVIDED THE PARTICIPANTS WITH INSIGHT AND UNDERSTANDING OF THE CHILD'S NEEDS AND WITH WAYS OF MEETING THOSE NEEDS. MOST OF THE 45 CHILDREN WERE REFERRED AS BEHAVIOR PROBLEM CHILDREN, BUT, UPON EXAMINATION, MOST OF THEM WERE FOUND TO SUFFER FROM CENTRAL NERVOUS SYSTEM PROBLEMS. (THE APPENDIX OF THIS STUDY CONTAINS A REPRESENTATIVE CHILD STUDY REPORT AND SPEECH-AND-HEARING REPORT.) (WD)

ED020780 PS000969

SEMO PROJECT HEAD START, PSYCHOLOGICAL SERVICES REPORT, 1966-67 YEAR PROGRAM. THORNTON, SAM M., NOV67 20P.

EDRS PRICE MF-$0.65 HC-$3.29

THIS FOUR-PHASE TRANSITIONAL PSYCHOLOGICAL SERVICES PROGRAM IS PART TWO OF A THREE-PART STUDY DESIGNED TO EXAMINE AND EVALUATE CHILDREN IN HEAD START PROGRAMS IN SIX SOUTHEAST MISSOURI COUNTIES. THESE FOUR PHASES, USING 428 CHILDREN IN A 1966-1967 ACADEMIC YEAR HEAD START PROGRAM, WERE (1) CHILD OBSERVATION BY A PSYCHOLOGICAL COUNSELOR, (2) SCREENING OF CHILDREN THROUGH PSYCHOLOGICAL TESTING, (3) INDIVIDUAL EXAMINATION OF CHILDREN, AND (4) COMPLETION OF A SMALL RESEARCH PROJECT. THE SERVICE PERSONNEL VISITED TWELVE HEAD START CENTERS, WHERE THEY CONDUCTED THEIR OBSERVATION AND TESTING. THE DATA FROM THIS TESTING SHOWED THAT THE CHILDREN'S INTELLIGENCE QUOTIENT INCREASED SIGNIFICANTLY OVER THE HEAD START PROGRAM PERIOD AND THAT DISADVANTAGED CHILDREN WHO ARE INITIALLY BEHIND IN HAND-EYE MOTOR DEVELOPMENT CONTINUE TO BECOME FARTHER BEHIND. THE RESEARCH PROJECT WAS CREATED TO TEST THE EFFECT OF FROSTIG REMEDIAL MATERIALS. AN EXPERIMENTAL GROUP WAS TAUGHT BY THE FROSTIG METHOD, A METHOD KEYED TO VISUAL PERCEPTION DEVELOPMENT. A CONTROL GROUP RECEIVED THE REGULAR HEAD START PROGRAM. UPON ANALYSIS OF PRETESTS AND POSTTESTS, A SIGNIFICANT DIFFERENCE WAS FOUND BETWEEN THE TWO GROUPS, WITH THE FROSTIG GROUP PROGRESSING AN AVERAGE OF 18 1/2 MONTHS DURING THE FIRST SEMESTER AND THE CONTROL GROUP PROGRESSING LESS THAN 1 MONTH. (WD)

ED020781 PS000970

HEAD START EVALUATION AND RESEARCH CENTER, TEACHERS COLLEGE, COLUMBIA UNIVERSITY. ANNUAL REPORT (1ST), SEPTEMBER 1966-AUGUST 1967. (TITLE SUPPLIED). THORNDIKE, ROBERT L., 30NOV67 32P.

EDRS PRICE MF-$0.65 HC-$3.29

COMPLETE EVALUATION DATA WERE GATHERED ON 162 CHILDREN IN 23 CLASSES IN NINE HEAD START CENTERS. FIVE AREAS EXPLORED WERE--(1) ITEM ANALYSIS OF EVALUATION TESTS--STANFORD-BINET AND THE CALDWELL-SOULE PRESCHOOL INVENTORY, (2) COMPARISON OF AGE-MATCHED GROUPS--43 MATCHED PAIRS WITHIN THE HEAD START POPULATION (THERE WERE NO SIGNIFICANT DIFFERENCES ON THE ZIGLER BEHAVIOR INVENTORY EXCEPT THAT THE CONTROL GROUP RECEIVED MORE FAVORABLE RATINGS IN THE AREA OF JEALOUSY), (3) FOLLOWUP OF CHILDREN FORMERLY ENROLLED IN A PREKINDERGARTEN PROGRAM--20 MATCHED PAIRS OF SECOND GRADERS (DATA COLLECTED FROM SCHOOL RECORDS OF ACHIEVEMENT IN READING, WRITING, AND ARITHMETIC SHOWED NO SIGNIFICANT DIFFERENCES BETWEEN CONTROL CHILDREN AND CHILDREN WHO HAD ATTENDED PREKINDERGARTEN), (4) CHILDREN'S CONCEPTUAL DEVELOPMENT AND LANGUAGE COMPREHENSION (RESULTS INDICATED THAT WHEN VERBAL INSTRUCTIONS ARE TO BE FOLLOWED, SYNTAX, TEMPORAL ORDER OF ELEMENTS, AND SEMANTICS GUIDE CHILDREN'S ACTIONS), AND (5) EXPLORATORY WORK ON BLOCKBUILDING AS A COGNITIVE INDICATOR (PROTOCOLS WERE COLLECTED ON THE MANIPULATIVE AND VERBAL BEHAVIOR OF 100 CHILDREN). SEVEN TABLES RELEVANT TO THE ABOVE FIVE AREAS ARE INCLUDED IN

THE REPORT, ALTHOUGH PORTIONS OF THE REPORT ARE NOT AVAILABLE FROM EDRS. (MS)

ED020782 PS000971
HEAD START EVALUATION AND RESEARCH CENTER, TULANE UNIVERSITY. FINAL REPORT. (TITLE SUPPLIED). JONES, SHUELL H., 31AUG67 152P.
EDRS PRICE MF-$0.65 HC-$6.58

IN PROJECT I, A FREE ASSOCIATION TECHNIQUE WAS USED TO ANALYZE CHILDREN'S VOCABULARIES IN TERMS OF DERIVATIONS OF WORDS USED, THE RELATION OF WORD DERIVATIONS TO THE CHILD'S LANGUAGE LEARNING, AND THE EFFECTS OF DERIVATIONAL STRUCTURE ON COGNITION. IT WAS FOUND THAT "FREE" ASSOCIATIONS TEND TO OCCUR WITHIN "SETS" DEFINED BY WORD SOURCES. PROJECT II INVESTIGATORS USED A 50-ITEM FREE ASSOCIATION RESPONSE TEST TO TRY TO SCALE THE DEGREE OF COGNITIVE DIFFERENCE BETWEEN DIFFERENT SUBGROUPS (COLLEGE STUDENTS AND INSTITUTIONALIZED SCHIZOPHRENICS) IN TERMS OF RESPONSE OVERLAP. HOWEVER, RESPONSE DIFFERENCES DEFIED RATIONAL SYSTEMIZATION. IN PROJECT III, SIXTY 7-YEAR-OLDS AND THEIR FAMILIES (WHITES AND NEGROES WITH LOW INCOMES) TOOK PART IN A PILOT STUDY OF TEACHER-STUDENT INTERACTION AND ITS ROLE IN LEARNING. TWENTY-SIX OF THE CHILDREN WERE DIVIDED INTO THREE EXPERIMENTAL GROUPS AND ATTENDED SCHOOL FOR 6 WEEKS. THROUGH CLINICAL INTERVIEWS, THE TEACHERS' PERSONALITIES WERE EVALUATED. DURING READING CLASSES CHILDREN WERE OBSERVED AND TEACHER INTERACTION NOTED. THE 34 CONTROL CHILDREN HAD NO CLASSES. INITIALLY ALL CHILDREN WERE GIVEN A READING TEST, INTELLIGENCE TEST AND VINELAND SOCIAL MATURITY TEST. THEY WERE ALSO GIVEN POSTTESTS IN READING. THERE WAS NO STATISTICAL SIGNIFICANCE BETWEEN EXPERIMENTAL AND CONTROL GROUPS REGARDING GAIN ON READING TESTS. TEACHER INTERACTION FINDINGS SUGGEST THAT A FIRM, UNDERSTANDING TEACHER AIDS THE LEARNING PROCESS MORE THAN AN OVERLY PERMISSIVE, PERSONAL ONE. THE FIRST 48 PAGES OF THIS DOCUMENT ARE NOT AVAILABLE FROM EDRS. (MS)

ED020783 PS000974
CHILD REARING IN CALIFORNIA, A STUDY OF MOTHERS WITH YOUNG CHILDREN. HEINSTEIN, MARTIN, OCT65 101P.
EDRS PRICE MF-$0.65 HC-$6.58

A STUDY CONCERNED WITH THE CHILD REARING PRACTICES OF MOTHERS WITH YOUNG CHILDREN UNDER SIX WAS UNDERTAKEN TO PROVIDE NORMATIVE DATA ON BREAST-FEEDING, BOWEL TRAINING, AND DISCIPLINE AND TO RELATE THE DATA TO FAMILY SOCIOECONOMIC STATUS. FACTORS CONSIDERED WERE OCCUPATION OF THE HEAD OF THE HOUSE, LEVEL OF INCOME, AND EDUCATION OF THE MOTHER. DATA WAS COLLECTED FROM CLUSTER SAMPLES FROM TWO AREAS, THE STATE OF CALIFORNIA AND THE METROPOLITAN COUNTY OF CONTRA COSTA IN CALIFORNIA. EIGHT HUNDRED AND NINE INTERVIEWS WITH MOTHERS IN THE STATE AND 812 IN CONTRA COSTA COUNTY WERE CONDUCTED, USING A QUESTIONNAIRE WITH OPEN-ENDED QUESTIONS ON CHILD REARING PRACTICES. RESULTS OF STATISTICAL ANALYSIS OF THE DATA SHOWED THAT WOMEN WITH SOME COLLEGE EDUCATION HAD A HIGHER RATE OF STARTING TO BREAST-FEED, BEGAN BOWEL TRAINING LATER AND WITH LESS SEVERE METHODS, AND DID NOT USE PHYSICAL PUNISHMENT AS MUCH AS OTHER MOTHERS. THE LEAST EDUCATED GROUP OF MOTHERS (LESS THAN EIGHT YEARS OF SCHOOLING) SHOWED THE SAME CHARACTERISTICS. THE AMOUNT OF EDUCATION OF MOTHERS HAD THE GREATEST INFLUENCE ON CHILD REARING PRACTICES. FAMILY INCOME WAS THE LEAST IMPORTANT SOCIOECONOMIC FACTOR. FOUR APPENDIXES INCLUDE COMPARISONS OF STATEWIDE AND CONTRA COSTA COUNTY SAMPLES, SAMPLING ERRORS, A FACSIMILE OF THE QUESTIONNAIRE, AND A BIBLIOGRAPHY. (MS)

ED020784 PS000976
COGNITIVE PROCESSES IN THE DEVELOPMENT OF CHILDREN'S APPRECIATION OF HUMOR. ZIGLER, EDWARD; AND OTHERS, 23P.
EDRS PRICE MF-$0.65 HC-$3.29

THIS STUDY INVESTIGATED THE RELATIONSHIP BETWEEN CHILDREN'S HUMOR RESPONSE AND COGNITIVE DEVELOPMENT. BY USING CHILDREN OF DIFFERENT GRADE LEVELS AS SUBJECTS, IT WAS ASSUMED THAT THE STUDY WOULD INCLUDE SEVERAL LEVELS OF COGNITIVE DEVELOPMENT. TWENTY-FIVE CARTOONS WERE SHOWN TO 64 TEST CHILDREN. THE TEST CHILDREN WERE CHOSEN FROM GRADES TWO, THREE, FOUR, AND FIVE ON THE BASIS OF HAVING AVERAGE INTELLIGENCE AND ABILITY. EACH CHILD WAS SHOWN THE CARTOONS TWICE, ONCE TO OBTAIN THE CHILD'S SPONTANEOUS MIRTH RESPONSE AND HIS OPINION OF THE HUMOROUSNESS OF THE CARTOON AND AGAIN TO OBTAIN AN IDEA OF HIS COMPREHENSION OF THE JOKE INVOLVED. AN ANALYSIS OF THE THREE TYPES OF SCORES OBTAINED, (1) THE CHILD'S STATEMENT OF WHETHER THE CARTOON WAS FUNNY OR NOT, (2) THE CHILD'S FACIAL MIRTH RESPONSE, AND (3) THE CHILD'S COMPREHENSION SCORE, SHOWED THE EXISTENCE OF A POSITIVE RELATIONSHIP BETWEEN MIRTH RESPONSE AND DEGREE OF COMPREHENSION. AS THE COMPREHENSION OF THE CARTOONS BECAME EASIER FOR THE CHILDREN, HOWEVER, MIRTH RESPONSE DECLINED. THE MIRTH RESPONSE INCREASED FROM GRADES TWO TO FOUR BUT DECREASED FOR ALL LEVELS OF COMPREHENSION IN GRADE FIVE. THESE FINDINGS INDICATE THAT PERHAPS THE NATURE OF THE RELATIONSHIP BETWEEN HUMOR APPRECIATION AND COGNITIVE DEVELOPMENT IS SUCH THAT CARTOONS WHICH REQUIRE GREATER COGNITIVE ABILITY TO UNDERSTAND ELICIT A GREATER HUMOR RESPONSE. (WD)

ED020785 PS000981
PRE-SCHOOL EDUCATION. GETZELS, J.W., 10P.
EDRS PRICE MF-$0.65 HC-$3.29

THESE ISSUES SHOULD BE DISCUSSED AND RESOLVED BEFORE A LARGE-SCALE INTRODUCTION OF PRESCHOOL PROGRAMS FOR CULTURALLY DISADVANTAGED CHILDREN--(1) THE EFFECT OF ENVIRONMENT ON THE DEVELOPMENT OF SCHOOL-RELATED ABILITIES. NUMEROUS STUDIES ATTEST TO THE SIGNIFICANCE OF THE PRESCHOOL YEARS IN ESTABLISHING THE BASIC SKILLS ESSENTIAL TO SUCCESS IN SCHOOL. (2) AT WHAT AGE THE OPPORTUNITY FOR SCHOOL-RELATED EXPERIENCES MUST BE AVAILABLE IN THE ENVIRONMENT. STUDIES WITH ANIMALS AND CONGENITALLY BLIND PEOPLE GIVEN SIGHT BY OPERATION INDICATE THAT BASIC SKILLS ARE DEVELOPED QUITE EARLY. (3) THE DIFFERENCES IN THE CONTINUITY OR DISCONTINUITY OF PRESCHOOL EXPERIENCES AND SCHOOL EXPECTATIONS BETWEEN CULTURALLY DEPRIVED AND NONDEPRIVED CHILDREN. THE LANGUAGE OF THE DEPRIVED CHILD TENDS TO BE RESTRICTED IN DEVELOPMENT AND SIMPLE IN STRUCTURE. THE LANGUAGE REQUIRED BY THE SCHOOL IS RICH AND COMPLEX. THE SCHOOL REQUIRES AN ACHIEVEMENT ETHIC, WITH HIGH VALUATION ON DEFERRED GRATIFICATION AND SYMBOLIC COMMITMENT. THE LOWER CLASS CHILD HAS A SET OF VALUES BASED ON IMMEDIATE GRATIFICATION AND CONCRETE COMMITMENT. (4) THE NATURE OF COMPENSATORY PRESCHOOL EDUCATION AND SOME OF THE CURRENT PROCEDURAL ISSUES. THE PRESENT VARIETY OF TYPES OF PRESCHOOL PROGRAMS REPRESENT THREE APPROACHES--(A) SUPPLEMENTARY, (B) ACADEMIC-PREPARATORY, AND (C) COMPENSATORY. (5) SOME OF THE LONG-RANGE UNDERLYING ISSUES. SO-CALLED DISADVANTAGED CHILDREN MAY HAVE CERTAIN ASSETS AND ABILITIES WHICH MIDDLE CLASS CHILDREN DO NOT POSSESS. THESE ASSETS MAY HAVE SIGNIFICANT INTRINSIC VALUE FOR SOCIETY AS A WHOLE, BUT THEY MAY BE WIPED OUT IF IMPOSED UPON BY THE MIDDLE CLASS ORIENTED SCHOOLS. THERE ARE NUMEROUS CRITICS WHO CLAIM THAT THE SCHOOLS TODAY ARE EDUCATIONALLY DEFECTIVE. THIS ARTICLE IS A REPRINT FROM "FOCUS," (N.D.), MASSACHUSETTS COUNCIL FOR PUBLIC SCHOOLS, INC., 16 ARLINGTON ST., BOSTON, MASS., 02116. (WD)

ED020786 PS000985
A FOLLOW-UP STUDY OF INTELLIGENCE CHANGES IN CHILDREN WHO PARTICIPATED IN PROJECT HEADSTART. CONNERS, C. KEITH; WALLER, DAVID A., 66 21P.
EDRS PRICE MF-$0.65 HC-$3.29

IN A STUDY TO ASSESS THE VALUE OF A 1965 SUMMER HEAD START PROGRAM IN BALTIMORE, 83 PARTICIPATING CHILDREN WERE TESTED ON THE PEABODY PICTURE VOCABULARY TEST (PPVT) AND THE DRAW-A-PERSON (DAP), AND THEIR SCORES WERE COMPARED WITH THOSE OF A MATCHED GROUP OF CONTROL NON-HEAD START CHILDREN. ALL WERE TESTED IN SEPTEMBER 1965 (AT THE BEGINNING OF THE KINDERGARTEN YEAR) AND IN MAY 1966. THE SEPTEMBER SCORES OF THE HEAD START PUPILS WERE HIGHER THAN THOSE OF THE CONTROL PUPILS ON BOTH THE PPVT AND DAP. THE MAY SCORES SHOWED SIGNIFICANT GAINS BY BOTH GROUPS ON BOTH TESTS, AND ON THE BASIS OF THE SEPTEMBER AND MAY SCORES, IT WAS CONCLUDED THAT THE HEAD START PROGRAM DID EFFECTIVELY INCREASE THE ACADEMIC ABILITY OF THE ATTENDING CHILDREN. HOWEVER, THE MAY SCORES SHOW A NARROWING OF THE DIFFERENCE ON THE PPVT AND A WASHING-OUT OF THE DIFFERENCE ON THE DAP. IT APPEARS THAT SPECIFIC INSTRUCTIONAL ATTEMPTS MUST BE MADE IN FORMAL SCHOOLING TO MAINTAIN THE ACHIEVEMENT INCREASE REALIZED FROM THE HEAD START PROGRAM. (WD)

ED020787 PS000987
THE JOHNS HOPKINS PERCEPTUAL TEST, THE DEVELOPMENT OF A RAPID INTELLIGENCE TEST FOR THE PRESCHOOL CHILD. ROSENBERG, LEON A.; AND OTHERS, APR66 17P.
EDRS PRICE MF-$0.65 HC-$3.29

IN ORDER TO DEVELOP AN INTELLIGENCE TEST FOR PRESCHOOL-AGE CHILDREN THAT WOULD OVERCOME SOME OF THE LIMITATIONS OF AVAILABLE TESTS, A PERCEPTUAL DISCRIMINATION TEST USING POLYGONAL FORMS HAS BEEN DESIGNED AND TESTED. THE CHILD POINTS TO ONE OF TWO, THREE, OR FIVE FORMS MATCHING A STIMULUS FORM. INITIAL TESTING WITH 44 CHILDREN RANGING IN AGE FROM 3 YEARS TO 5 YEARS 10 MONTHS SHOWED GOOD CORRELATION OF THE TEST SCORES WITH AGE AND THE RAW SCORES OF THE PEABODY PICTURE VOCABULARY TEST (PPVT). A SHORTENED TEST HAVING 30 CHOICES WAS DEVELOPED AND GIVEN TO TWENTY-TWO 4- TO 5-YEAR-OLD NURSERY SCHOOL CHILDREN. AGAIN, GOOD CORRELATIONS WITH AGE, THE PPVT, AND THE DRAW-A-PICTURE (DAP) TEST WERE OBTAINED. VALIDITY STUDIES OF THIS TEST, DESIGNATED THE JOHNS HOPKINS PERCEPTION TEST (JHPT), HAVE SO FAR INVOLVED SOME 340 CHILDREN. STATISTICALLY SIGNIFICANT CORRELATIONS OF THE SCORES ON THE JHPT WITH SCORES ON THE PPVT, THE DAP, AND THE COLUMBIA MENTAL MATURITY SCALE (CMMS) HAVE BEEN OBTAINED. A COMPARISON WAS MADE OF THE PERFORMANCE OF 37 UPPER AND 52 LOWER SOCIOECONOMIC STATUS CHILDREN ON THE JHPT, THE PPVT, AND THE DAP. THE DIFFERENCES IN MEAN SCORES BETWEEN GROUPS WAS HIGHEST FOR THE PPVT, LESS MARKED FOR THE DAP, AND STATISTICALLY INSIGNIFICANT FOR THE JHPT, SUGGESTING THAT IT MAY BE A CULTURE-FREE INSTRUMENT. THIS

PAPER WAS PRESENTED AT THE EASTERN PSYCHOLOGICAL ASSOCIATION ANNUAL MEETING (NEW YORK, APRIL, 1966). (DR)

ED020788 PS000988
THE SYNTACTIC STRUCTURES OF 5-YEAR-OLD CULTURALLY DEPRIVED CHILDREN. OSSER, HARRY, 15APR66 5P.
EDRS PRICE MF-$0.65 HC-$3.29

THIS STUDY WAS MADE IN AN ATTEMPT TO DISCOVER HOW MUCH ENVIRONMENTAL STIMULATION IS NECESSARY FOR NORMAL LANGUAGE DEVELOPMENT IN CHILDREN. THROUGH ANALYSIS OF TRANSFORMATIONAL GRAMMER, THE SYNTACTIC STRUCTURES OF TWENTY 5-YEAR-OLD CULTURALLY DEPRIVED NEGRO CHILDREN IN BALTIMORE WERE COMPARED TO THOSE OF A GROUP OF MIDDLE CLASS WHITE NURSERY SCHOOL CHILDREN IN BOSTON WHO WERE SUBJECTS OF A STUDY BY PAULA MENYUK. DIALECT DIFFERENCES WERE MINIMIZED BY A CONCEPT OF FUNCTIONAL EQUIVALENCE WHICH EQUATED STATEMENTS HAVING DIFFERENT WORDS BUT THE SAME MEANING. THE TOTAL NUMBER OF SENTENCES WHICH THE CHILDREN PRODUCED IN THE EXPERIMENTAL SESSION, THE TOTAL NUMBER OF DIFFERENT SYNTACTIC STRUCTURES USED, AND AN AVERAGE SENTENCE COMPLEXITY SCORE WERE TAKEN AS INDICES OF LINGUISTIC PERFORMANCE. A SUBSTANTIAL DIFFERENCE IN STRUCTURE USE WAS FOUND BETWEEN THE TWO GROUPS, WITH THE BOSTON GROUP USING MANY MORE SYNTACTIC STRUCTURES. THE NEGRO GROUP WAS NOT HOMOGENEOUS IN PERFORMANCE BUT HAD A WIDE RANGE OF DIFFERENCE IN COMPLEXITY AND NUMBER OF SYNTACTIC STRUCTURES USED. LARGE DIFFERENCES WITHIN THE NEGRO GROUP WOULD SUGGEST THAT ENVIRONMENT PLAYS A MAJOR ROLE IN LANGUAGE DEVELOPMENT. IF LANGUAGE IS IMPLICATED IN THINKING BEHAVIOR, THEN IT IS POSSIBLE THAT THE DEGREE OF IMMATURITY IN LANGUAGE DEVELOPMENT IN EARLY CHILDHOOD IS SIGNIFICANT IN THE CHILD'S GENERAL COGNITIVE DEVELOPMENT. EXPLORATION IN THIS AREA IS CONTINUING. THE NEGRO SPEECH SAMPLE IS BEING INCREASED, AND A TABLE OF STRUCTURAL EQUIVALENTS BETWEEN STANDARD ENGLISH AND THE NONSTANDARD ENGLISH OF NEGRO CHILDREN IS BEING DEVELOPED. (MS)

ED020789 PS000989
LANGUAGE CONTROL IN A GROUP OF HEAD START CHILDREN. OSSER, HARRY, 5P.
EDRS PRICE MF-$0.65 HC-$3.29

TWENTY HEAD START PRESCHOOL CHILDREN WERE GIVEN THREE LANGUAGE TASKS DESIGNED TO MEASURE THEIR LANGUAGE DEVELOPMENT--(1) A PRODUCTION TASK REQUIRED THE CHILDREN TO ENGAGE IN FREE SPEECH. THE CHILDREN WERE ASKED TO ANSWER A QUESTION, TO DESCRIBE A SERIES OF PICTURES, AND TO RETELL A STORY. THE FREE SPEECH OF THE CHILDREN IN RESPONSE TO THESE SUB-TASKS WAS ANALYZED IN TERMS OF THE RANGE AND FREQUENCY OF SYNTACTIC STRUCTURES USED, THE NUMBER OF KERNEL AND TRANSFORMED SENTENCES USED, AND THE COMPLEXITY OF THE SYNTAX. THE DATA FROM THIS TASK IS NOT YET AVAILABLE. (2) AN IMITATION TASK REQUIRED THE CHILDREN TO REPEAT 20 SENTENCES USING 10 DIFFERENT SYNTACTIC STRUCTURES. EACH STRUCTURE WAS USED IN TWO SENTENCES. OF A POSSIBLE 400 CORRECT RESPONSES, 281 CORRECT RESPONSES WERE MADE. THE LENGTH OF THE SENTENCE WAS FOUND TO BE NEGATIVELY RELATED TO NUMBER OF CORRECT RESPONSES FOR ONE SET OF THE STRUCTURES. THERE WAS EVIDENCE OF MODIFICATION OF SENTENCES BY THE CHILDREN TO CONFORM THEM TO THEIR OWN LINGUISTIC SYSTEM. (3) THE SAME SENTENCES USED IN TASK NUMBER 2 WERE USED IN A COMPREHENSION TASK THAT REQUIRED THE CHILDREN, AFTER HEARING A SENTENCE, TO POINT TO THE PICTURE CORRESPONDING TO THAT SENTENCE FROM A THREE-PICTURE DISPLAY. CORRECT RESPONSES NUMBERED 266 OUT OF A POSSIBLE 400. LENGTH OF SENTENCE WAS NOT FOUND TO BE RELATED SIGNIFICANTLY TO THIS TASK. A RECOGNIZED PROBLEM IN INTERPRETING THE DATA FROM THESE TASKS IS CHOOSING CRITERIA THAT WILL RELIABLY INDICATE WHEN THE CHILD REALLY HAS CONTROL OF A PARTICULAR SYNTACTIC STRUCTURE. TOTAL CORRECT-RESPONSES, AS A CRITERION, DOES NOT INDICATE WHETHER THE CHILD CONSISTENTLY RESPONDED CORRECTLY ON A PARTICULAR SYNTACTIC STRUCTURE IN TASKS NUMBER 2 AND NUMBER 3. IF THE CONSISTENCY OF CORRECT RESPONSE CRITERION WERE USED ON THE DATA, THE TOTAL SCORE OF THE CHILDREN WOULD BE 64. (WD)

ED020790 PS000991
A STUDY OF A MEASUREMENT RESOURCE IN CHILD RESEARCH, PROJECT HEAD START. BOMMARITO, JAMES; JOHNSON, ORVAL G., 152P.
EDRS PRICE MF-$0.65 HC-$6.58

MEASURES OF CHILD BEHAVIOR AND CHARACTERISTICS, NOT YET PUBLISHED AS SEPARATE ENTITIES, WERE COLLECTED THROUGH A PAGE-BY-PAGE SEARCH OF ISSUES OF 46 JOURNALS (LISTED IN APPENDIX A) PUBLISHED DURING THE PERIOD OF JANUARY 1956 TO DECEMBER 1965 AND 50 RELEVANT BOOKS. CORRESPONDENCE WITH RESEARCHERS AND AUTHORS OF MEASURES YIELDED ADDITIONAL MEASUREMENT RESOURCES. AS PRESENTED IN THE REPORT, THE MEASURES WERE GROUPED INTO SIX KINDS, (1) DEVELOPMENT, ACADEMIC APTITUDE, AND ACHIEVEMENT, (2) PERSONALITY, (3) ATTITUDES, (4) SOCIAL INTERACTION AND SKILLS, (5) PERCEPTUAL SKILLS, AND (6) MISCELLANEOUS. THE LISTING FOR EACH TEST INCLUDED ITS NAME, THE AUTHOR, THE AGE OF THE POPULATION FOR WHOM IT WAS DESIGNED, THE GENERAL AREA OF INTEREST, THE TYPE OF MEASURE, AND THE SOURCE FROM WHICH A COPY OF THE MEASURE MIGHT BE OBTAINED. A DESCRIPTION OF THE MEASURE (OFTEN QUOTING ITS AUTHOR) INCLUDED SAMPLE ITEMS AND AN OUTLINE OF THE ADMINISTRATIVE AND SCORING PROCEDURES. WHEN AVAILABLE, RELIABILITY AND VALIDITY DATA WERE BRIEFLY SUMMARIZED. A BIBLIOGRAPHICAL REFERENCE WAS PROVIDED FOR EACH MEASURE. (MS)

ED020791 PS000999
REGIONAL EVALUATION AND RESEARCH CENTER FOR PROJECT HEAD START, SUPPLEMENTARY RESEARCH REPORT, SEPTEMBER 1, 1967-DECEMBER 31, 1967. FRIEDMAN, MYLES I., 60P.
EDRS PRICE MF-$0.65 HC-$3.29

IN PHASE I (OF THREE) OF A RESEARCH PROJECT, 475 SOUTHERN DISADVANTAGED CHILDREN (RANGING IN AGE FROM 3 TO 6) WERE TESTED IN AN INVESTIGATION INTO THE DESCRIPTION, DEVELOPMENT, AND SEQUENCING OF COGNITIVE ABILITIES DESIGNED TO YIELD INFORMATION ON CHILDREN'S LEARNING WITH IMPLICATIONS FOR TEACHING AND CURRICULUMS. COGNITIVE TASKS WERE SELECTED FROM MORE THAN 50 PUBLISHED MEASURING INSTRUMENTS. TESTERS WERE TRAINED TO AIM FOR A CHILD'S MAXIMUM PERFORMANCE AS THE INVESTIGATORS' OBJECT WAS TO MAKE A CONTINUUM OF PROBLEM SOLVING ABILITIES. DATA WILL BE FACTOR ANALYZED AND A MATRIX OF TETRACHORIC CORRELATION COEFFICIENTS USED. THE RELATIONSHIP OF INDIVIDUAL ITEMS TO THE FACTORS IDENTIFIED WILL BE DETERMINED. IT IS HOPED THAT ITEM SEQUENCING MAY INDICATE A PATTERN OF COGNITIVE DEVELOPMENT WHICH CAN PROVIDE A NATURAL ORDER FOR TEACHING COGNITIVE TRAITS. SEVEN APPENDIXES ARE INCLUDED WHICH GIVE DETAILED INFORMATION ABOUT TESTS AND PROCEDURES. THREE OTHER SUBPOPULATIONS OF CHILDREN WILL BE STUDIED AS PART OF THIS PROJECT. (MS)

ED020792 PS001000
REGIONAL EVALUATION AND RESEARCH CENTER FOR HEAD START, SOUTHERN UNIVERSITY. ANNUAL REPORT. JOHNSON, EDWARD E.; AND OTHERS, 27NOV67 32P.
EDRS PRICE MF-$0.65 HC-$3.29

A STUDY, IN PROGRESS, IS ATTEMPTING TO DETERMINE THE INTERACTION OF VARIOUS REWARD CONDITIONS AND VARIOUS TYPES OF PRESCHOOL EXPERIENCE WITH DISCRIMINATION LEARNING. THE SUBJECTS ARE 240 4- AND 5-YEAR-OLD CHILDREN WITH THREE TYPES OF PRESCHOOL EXPERIENCE--1 TO 3 MONTHS OF HEAD START, 10 TO 12 MONTHS OF HEAD START, AND NO ATTENDANCE IN A PRESCHOOL PROGRAM. THE STUDY IS ATTEMPTING TO ASCERTAIN WHETHER OR NOT THE CULTURALLY DISADVANTAGED CHILD, SUPPOSEDLY IMMEDIATE-GRATIFICATION ORIENTED, WILL, AS A FUNCTION OF PARTICIPATION IN HEAD START, ADOPT A MORE FUTURE-RELATED PERSPECTIVE. FOUR REWARD CONDITIONS ARE BEING USED WHEN THE CHILD MAKES A CORRECT CHOICE IN THE ASSIGNED TASK--(1) A LIGHT GOES ON, (2) A PROMISE OF CANDY UPON COMPLETION OF THE EXPERIMENT, (3) AN IMMEDIATE REWARD OF CANDY, AND (4) AN IMMEDIATE REWARD OF A TOKEN WHICH CAN BE EXCHANGED LATER FOR CANDY. THE TENTATIVE RESULTS SHOW THAT THE HEAD START GROUPS LEARN THE CORRECT RESPONSE SOONER THAN THE NON-HEAD START GROUP ON CONDITIONS ONE AND TWO BUT NOT NECESSARILY ON CONDITIONS THREE AND FOUR. PART TWO OF THIS DOCUMENT PROPOSES EIGHT STUDIES TO OBTAIN INFORMATION ON WHETHER OR NOT CHILDREN OF DIFFERENT RACES PERCEIVE SIMILAR STIMULI DIFFERENTLY BECAUSE SUCH STIMULI HAVE RACIALLY RELATED ASPECTS. (WD)

ED020793 PS001002
HEAD START RESEARCH AND EVALUATION OFFICE, UNIVERSITY OF CALIFORNIA AT LOS ANGELES. APPENDIX I TO THE ANNUAL REPORT, NOVEMBER 1967. LOMBARD, AVIMA; STERN, CAROLYN, NOV67 42P.
EDRS PRICE MF-$0.65 HC-$3.29

THE LITERATURE ON LANGUAGE ABILITY AND ITS RELATIONSHIP TO ACADEMIC SUCCESS INCREASINGLY VOICES ALARM THAT THE CULTURALLY DISADVANTAGED ARE SERIOUSLY DEFICIENT IN LANGUAGE ABILITY. INTERVENTION PROGRAMS CREATED TO CORRECT THIS PROBLEM ALL RECOGNIZE THE IMPORTANCE OF LANGUAGE TOOLS FOR INTELLECTUAL FUNCTIONING. ESSENTIAL TO SUCH PROGRAMS, AND FREQUENTLY ABSENT FROM THEM, ARE RELIABLE MEASUREMENT TECHNIQUES FOR EVALUATING THE INTERACTION OF THE PROGRAM WITH THE CHILD'S COGNITIVE PROCESSES. THE PRESCHOOL LANGUAGE PROJECT AT THE UNIVERSITY OF CALIFORNIA AT LOS ANGELES IS CONSTRUCTING AND USING NEW MEASURING DEVICES--FOR EXAMPLE, THE VISUAL DISCRIMINATION INVENTORY (VDI). THE VDI WAS ADMINISTERED TO 291 PRESCHOOL CHILDREN TO OBTAIN DATA ON THE VISUAL DISCRIMINATION ABILITY OF THE 199 NEGRO AND 92 CAUCASIAN CHILDREN. THE CHILDREN REPRESENTED TWO LEVELS OF ECONOMIC STATUS AND RANGED IN AGE FROM 3 TO ALMOST 6. ADMINISTRATION OF THE VDI INVOLVED PRESENTING THE CHILD WITH A MODEL FIGURE AND THREE CHOICE FIGURES FROM WHICH TO SELECT THE ONE THAT MATCHED THE MODEL. AGE AND RACE APPEAR TO BE RELATED TO DISCRIMINATION ABILITY. THE VDI WAS FOUND TO HAVE BOTH RELIABILITY AND VALIDITY. THIS DOCUMENT IS COMPOSED OF TWO REPORTS. ONE WAS PRESENTED AT THE BIENNIAL MEETING OF THE SOCIETY FOR RESEARCH IN CHILD DEVELOPMENT (NEW YORK, APRIL, 1967) AND THE OTHER, AT THE AMERICAN PSYCHOLOGICAL ASSOCIATION ANNUAL MEETING (WASHINGTON, SEPTEMBER, 1967). (WD)

ED020794 PS001003
AN EVALUATION AND FOLLOW-UP STUDY OF SUMMER 1966 HEAD START CHILDREN IN WASHINGTON, D.C. CLINE, MARVIN; DICKEY, MARGUERITE, 68 81P.
EDRS PRICE MF-$0.65 HC-$3.29

THE EXPERIMENTAL GROUP IN THIS STUDY WAS 112 KINDERGARTEN CHILDREN FROM 11 HEAD START CENTERS. IN ORDER TO ASSESS THE VALUE OF THE HEAD START PROGRAM, THE MEASUREMENT OF THE EXPERIMENTAL GROUP TAKEN DURING THE FALL WAS COMPARED TO A MEASUREMENT OF NON-HEAD START KINDERGARTEN CHILDREN TESTED ABOUT THE SAME TIME. AT LEAST FOUR MONTHS AFTER THE PRETESTING, POSTTESTS WERE ADMINISTERED. THE PRETEST BATTERY CONSISTED OF THE STANFORD-BINET (S-B) AND TWO FORMS OF THE PEABODY PICTURE VOCABULARY TEST (PPVT). THE POSTTEST BATTERY CONSISTED OF (1) S-B, (2) PPVT, BOTH FORMS, (3) THE BEHAVIOR INVENTORY, AND (4) THE METROPOLITAN READING READINESS TEST. THE MOST SIGNIFICANT RESULTS WERE (1) NO DIFFERENCES WERE FOUND BETWEEN THE SCORES OF THE EXPERIMENTAL GROUP AND THE SCORES OF THE CONTROL GROUP, (2) THE CHILDREN SHOWED SIGNIFICANT IMPROVEMENT BETWEEN PRETEST AND POSTTEST PERIODS ONLY ON THE RECEPTIVE FORM OF THE PPVT, (3) THE CHILDREN CONSISTENTLY DEMONSTRATED HIGHER SCORES ON THE S-B THAN ON THE RECEPTIVE PPVT, AND (4) THE PERFORMANCE OF THE KINDERGARTEN CHILDREN APPEARED TO BE AFFECTED BY WHICH SCHOOL THEY ATTENDED AND WHICH TEACHER PRESIDED IN THE CLASSROOM. ALSO 160 HEAD START CHILDREN, WHO WERE TOO YOUNG TO START KINDERGARTEN, WERE TESTED IN THEIR HOMES AND WILL BE USED FOR A FOLLOWUP STUDY. (WD)

ED020795 PS001004
EDUCATION FOR INITIATIVE AND RESPONSIBILITY, COMMENTS ON A VISIT TO THE SCHOOLS OF LEICESTERSHIRE COUNTY, APRIL 1967. SECOND EDITION. YEOMANS, EDWARD, FEB68
DOCUMENT NOT AVAILABLE FROM EDRS.

THE LEICESTERSHIRE COUNTY (ENGLAND) EDUCATIONAL PROGRAM PROVIDES A LEARNING ATMOSPHERE IN WHICH EACH PUPIL CHOOSES HIS OWN ACTIVITIES AND WORKS IN A GIVEN SUBJECT AREA UNTIL HE IS READY TO CHANGE ACTIVITIES. THE SCHOOL SYSTEM HAS DROPPED THE TRADITIONAL ELEVEN-PLUS EXAMINATION, DESIGNED TO SELECT HIGHLY ABLE STUDENTS (ABOUT 1/5) FOR ACADEMIC PROGRAMS. INSTEAD, PUPIL MOTIVATION IS BASED ON INDIVIDUAL INVOLVEMENT. THE TEACHER SEES THAT CHILDREN HAVE OPPORTUNITIES TO TRY A VARIETY OF ACTIVITIES, HAS PROGRAMMED LESSONS READY TO SATISFY THE NEEDS OF THE MOST ADVANCED PUPILS, AND OBSERVES AND NOTES WORK PERFORMANCE. SHE SELECTS MATERIALS AND APPROACHES TO LEARNING WHICH SHE FEELS ARE RELEVANT. THERE IS NO ESTABLISHED FORMULA FOR THE SCHOOLS, HOWEVER. THERE ARE DIFFERENCES FROM SCHOOL TO SCHOOL AND EVEN FROM ROOM TO ROOM. EXPONENTS OF THE LEICESTERSHIRE PROGRAM SUGGEST THAT A MAJOR BENEFIT IS THE STUDENT'S MORE POSITIVE ATTITUDE TOWARDS SECONDARY SCHOOL. SIMILAR METHODS OF INDIVIDUALIZED TEACHING MAY BE EFFECTIVE IN DEVELOPING COUNTRIES AS WELL AS IN AMERICA. FIVE APPENDIXES INCLUDE TEACHER DISCUSSIONS OF THE INTEGRATED DAY, VERTICAL GROUPING, OBSERVATIONS OF AN INFANT SCHOOL DIRECTOR, SUGGESTED READING ON THE LEICESTERSHIRE PROJECT, AND RECOMMENDED EQUIPMENT. THIS MONOGRAPH IS NO. 13 IN A SERIES OF STUDIES INITIATED BY THE COMMITTEE ON EDUCATIONAL PRACTICES OF THE NATIONL ASSOCIATION OF INDEPENDENT SCHOOLS. IT IS AVAILABLE FOR $1.00 FROM NATIONAL ASSOCIATION OF INDEPENDENT SCHOOLS, 4 LIBERTY SQUARE, BOSTON, MASSACHUSETTS 02109. (MS)

ED020796 PS001007
INFLUENCES OF CULTURAL PATTERNS ON THE THINKING OF CHILDREN IN CERTAIN ETHNIC GROUPS, A STUDY OF THE EFFECT OF JEWISH SUB-CULTURE ON THE FIELD-DEPENDENCE-INDEPENDENCE DIMENSION OF COGNITION. DERSHOWITZ, ZACHARY, 66
DOCUMENT NOT AVAILABLE FROM EDRS.

THIS PAPER IS CONCERNED WITH THE RELATIONSHIP BETWEEN ETHNIC OR OTHER SUBGROUP MEMBERSHIP AND THE INDIVIDUAL'S COGNITIVE STYLE. THE COGNITIVE STYLE CHOSEN FOR INVESTIGATION HERE IS THAT OF FIELD-DEPENDENCE OR INDEPENDENCE. THE TWO ETHNIC-RELIGIOUS SUBCULTURES INVESTIGATED WERE JEWISH AND WHITE ANGLO-SAXON PROTESTANT. IT WAS HYPOTHESIZED THAT JEWISH CHILDREN, BECAUSE OF THE VALUES AND FAMILY STRUCTURE OF THEIR CULTURE, WOULD BE MORE FIELD-DEPENDENT. APPROXIMATELY 50 JEWISH CHILDREN OF AN AVERAGE AGE OF 10.9 YEARS FROM A BACKGROUND OF HIGH JEWISH ACCULTURATION AND 30 WHITE PROTESTANT CHILDREN OF AN AVERAGE AGE OF 10.2 YEARS WERE ADMINISTERED FOUR TESTS, WHICH INVOLVED (1) PERCEPTUAL, (2) INTELLECTUAL, (3) FIGURE DRAWING, AND (4) VERBAL DISEMBEDDING TASKS. THE SCORES OF THE TWO GROUPS WERE COMPARED WITH EACH OTHER AND WITH SCORES OF OTHER CHILDREN OF ANOTHER STUDY. THE DATA ANALYSIS REVEALED THAT THE JEWISH GROUP WAS THE MOST FIELD-DEPENDENT, AS HYPOTHESIZED. IT DOES NOT APPEAR, HOWEVER, THAT FIELD-DEPENDENCE EXTENDS TO VERBAL MATTERS FOR THE JEWISH GROUP. IT IS CONCLUDED THAT DIFFERENCES AMONG THESE GROUPS ARE NOT LIMITED TO CONTENT, BUT EXTEND TO THE WAY IN WHICH THE ENVIRONMENT IS PERCEIVED. THE DIFFERENCE DIMINISHES AS ETHNICITY DIMINISHES. THIS DOCUMENT IS AVAILABLE IN MICROFILM FOR $3.05 AND IN XEROX COPY FOR $10.60 (234P.), ORDER NUMBER 67-109, FROM UNIVERSITY MICROFILMS, ANN ARBOR, MICHIGAN 48103. (WD)

ED020797 PS001009
VARIABLES AFFECTING THE PERFORMANCE OF YOUNG CHILDREN ON A LETTER DISCRIMINATION TASK. HALL, VERNON C.; AND OTHERS, DEC67 11P.
EDRS PRICE MF-$0.65 HC-$3.29

THE PURPOSE OF THIS STUDY WAS TO DETERMINE THE RELATIVE INFLUENCE OF FIVE VARIABLES (INITIAL INSTRUCTIONS, REWARD, LETTER SIZE, TYPE OF WARM-UP, AND FEEDBACK) ON KINDERGARTEN CHILDREN'S PERFORMANCE OF A LETTER DISCRIMINATION TASK. IT HAS BEEN ARGUED THAT ATTENTION IS THE KEY FACTOR IN LETTER DISCRIMINATION. THE PRESENT STUDY PROPOSES THAT A PRECONDITION TO SUCCESS BY CHILDREN IN LETTER DISCRIMINATION IS HAVING AN ADEQUATE CONCEPT OF "SAMENESS." THAT IS, IF THE CHILD IS NOT AWARE OF WHAT THE EXPERIMENTER MEANS BY THE WORDS "SAME" AND "DIFFERENT" IN A DISCRIMINATION TASK, ATTENTION IS ALMOST IRRELEVANT. EIGHTY KINDERGARTEN PUPILS WERE DIVIDED INTO FIVE TEST CONDITIONS TO PERFORM THE DISCRIMINATION TASK. THE TASK METHODOLOGY CONSISTED OF PRESENTING A SINGLE LETTER ON THE LEFT SIDE OF A PIECE OF PAPER AND FOUR ROWS OF TEN LETTERS ON THE RIGHT SIDE. AMONG THESE 40 LETTERS WERE FIVE LETTERS IDENTICAL TO THE SINGLE LETTER, FIVE MOST LIKELY TO BE CONFUSED WITH THE SINGLE LETTER, AND 30 ADDITIONAL LETTERS. THE CHILD WAS ASKED TO IDENTIFY THE LETTERS IN THE FOUR ROWS THAT MATCHED THE SINGLE LETTER. THIS METHOD REPRESENTED TEST CONDITION ONE. THE REMAINING FOUR CONDITIONS WERE ESSENTIALLY THE SAME AS CONDITION ONE EXCEPT FOR VARIATIONS IN SCORING INSTRUCTION GIVEN (CONDITION TWO), USE OF REWARD (CONDITIONS THREE AND FIVE), AND TYPE OF WARM-UP (CONDITION FOUR). THE RESULTS SHOWED THAT NEITHER VARIATION OF LETTER SIZE NOR SCORING INSTRUCTIONS HAD AN EFFECT ON PUPIL PERFORMANCE. THE FEEDBACK WAS EFFECTIVE, FOR IT HELPED THE PUPIL DEVELOP THE CONCEPT OF "SAMENESS" NECESSARY TO MAKE THE DISCRIMINATION. (WD)

ED020798 PS001010
GRADE EQUIVALENT COMPARISONS BETWEEN DISADVANTAGED NEGRO URBAN CHILDREN WITH AND WITHOUT KINDERGARTEN EXPERIENCE WHEN TAUGHT TO READ BY SEVERAL METHODS. HARRIS, ALBERT J.; MORRISON, COLEMAN, 4P.
EDRS PRICE MF-$0.65 HC-$3.29

THIS STUDY IS PART OF THE CRAFT READING PROJECT OF THE NEW YORK PUBLIC SCHOOL SYSTEM WHICH IS INVESTIGATING THE READING PROGRESS OF DISADVANTAGED URBAN NEGRO CHILDREN. IN THE PRESENT STUDY, CHILDREN IN GRADES ONE, TWO, AND THREE, WITH AND WITHOUT PREVIOUS KINDERGARTEN EXPERIENCE, WERE TAUGHT READING BY TWO BASIC METHODS, EACH DIVIDED INTO TWO SUBMETHODS. ONE BASIC METHOD WAS THE SKILLS-CENTERED METHOD, DIVIDED INTO (1) A BASAL READER METHOD, WHICH USED CONVENTIONAL BASAL READERS, AND (2) A PHONOVISUAL METHOD, WHICH COMBINED USE OF BASAL READERS WITH A PHONOVISUAL SYSTEM OF TEACHING. THE SECOND BASIC METHOD WAS THE LANGUAGE-EXPERIENCE METHOD, WHICH DEVELOPED READING MATERIALS FROM THE EXPERIENCES AND VERBALIZATIONS OF THE CHILDREN, GRADUALLY MOVING INTO INDIVIDUALIZED READING. THE RESULTS OF THIS STUDY ARE BASED ON METROPOLITAN ACHIEVEMENT TEST SCORES OF THE PUPILS OBTAINED IN GRADES TWO AND THREE OF THE ORIGINAL CRAFT PROJECT AND IN GRADE TWO OF A REPLICATION STUDY. THE PUPILS WITH KINDERGARTEN EXPERIENCE GENERALLY SCORED HIGHER THAN NONKINDERGARTEN PUPILS, ALTHOUGH SIGNIFICANT RESULTS, ON AN INDIVIDUAL TEACHING METHOD BASIS, OCCURRED CONSISTENTLY ONLY FOR THE REGULAR LANGUAGE-EXPERIENCE METHOD. ON THE BASIS OF THE TWO BASIC METHODS OF TEACHING READING, AGAIN, ONLY THE LANGUAGE-EXPERIENCE METHOD SCORES WERE CONSISTENTLY SIGNIFICANT. (WD)

ED020799 PS001011
AN OVERVIEW OF RESEARCH IN LEARNING, MOTIVATION, AND PERCEPTION. ZIGLER, EDWARD, MAY62 9P.
EDRS PRICE MF-$0.65 HC-$3.29

RESEARCH IN THE LEARNING, MOTIVATION, AND PERCEPTION OF MENTAL RETARDATES IS ESSENTIAL TO AN UNDERSTANDING OF THEIR BEHAVIOR AND OF THEIR ABILITIES. MANY INVESTIGATORS HAVE USED THE PROBLEMS AND DESIGNS OF RESEARCH WITH LOWER ANIMALS IN STUDYING THE BEHAVIOR OF HUMAN RETARDATES. IT IS QUESTIONABLE THAT SUCH ORIENTATION WILL REALLY ADD TO THE UNDERSTANDING OF MENTAL RETARDATION. ALSO, RESEARCH WITH THE MENTALLY RETARDED HAS TENDED TO TREAT THE PROCESSES OF LEARNING, MOTIVATION, AND PERCEPTION AS UNRELATED. THIS CAUSES THE RESULTS OF SUCH INVESTIGATIONS TO BE DIFFICULT TO INTERPRET AND RESTRICTED IN VALUE FOR GENERALIZATION. THERE HAVE APPEARED, HOWEVER, ENCOURAGING EXAMPLES OF NEW RESEARCH ON RETARDATION THAT ARE NOT SO NARROW, FRAGMENTARY, AND UNIMAGINATIVE. EXAMPLES OF THIS RESEARCH INCLUDE (1) A SERIES OF STUDIES INVESTIGATING THE RELATIVE SIGNIFICANCE OF CHRONOLOGICAL AGE, MENTAL AGE, AND INTELLIGENCE QUOTIENT FOR LEARNING IN RETARDED INDIVIDUALS, (2) STUDIES REEVALUATING BEHAVIORAL DIFFERENCES IN LEARNING AND PERCEPTION BETWEEN FAMILIAL AND ORGANIC RETARDATES, (3) WORK

ON COMPARING THE PERFORMANCE OF INSTITUTIONALIZED AND NON-INSTITUTIONALIZED RETARDATES, (4) INVESTIGATIONS OF THE RELATIONSHIP BETWEEN ABILITY TO PERFORM COMPLEX LEARNING TASKS AND ABILITY TO UTILIZE VERBAL CUES, AND (5) STUDIES ON THE EFFECT OF STIMULI FROM THE PHYSICAL ENVIRONMENT ON THE BEHAVIOR OF RETARDED CHILDREN. THIS ARTICLE WAS PUBLISHED IN "EXCEPTIONAL CHILDREN," VOLUME 28, MAY 1962. IT IS A SHORTENED VERSION OF A LONGER PRESENTATION PREPARED BY HAROLD STEVENSON AND EDWARD ZIGLER UNDER THE SPONSORSHIP OF THE COOPERATIVE RESEARCH PROGRAM OF THE OFFICE OF EDUCATION, U.S. DEPARTMENT OF HEALTH, EDUCATION, AND WELFARE. (WD)

ED020800 PS001012
TEAM TEACHING IN ELEMENTARY GRADES. , DEC65 20P.
EDRS PRICE MF-$0.65 HC NOT AVAILABLE FROM EDRS.

INFORMATION ON THE PRACTICE OF TEAM TEACHING IN THE ELEMENTARY GRADES DRAWN FROM A SURVEY OF SCHOOL SYSTEMS HAVING SUCH PROBLEMS IS PRESENTED IN THIS CIRCULAR. OVER 400 SCHOOL SYSTEMS WITH ENROLLMENTS OF 12,000 AND ABOVE WERE INITIALLY SURVEYED, AND THE 169 WHICH INDICATED THEY USED SOME TEAM TEACHING WERE SENT QUESTIONNAIRES. THE PROGRAMS OF 76 OF THESE SYSTEMS WERE FELT TO MEET THE DEFINITION OF TEAM TEACHING GIVEN ON THE QUESTIONNAIRE. THE NUMBER OF STUDENTS INVOLVED WAS USUALLY A SMALL FRACTION (LESS THAN 20 PERCENT) OF THE TOTAL ENROLLMENT, AND THE PRACTICE WAS MOST FREQUENTLY USED IN THE UPPER GRADES (FIVE THROUGH EIGHT). THE MOST COMMON TEAM COMPOSITION WAS TEACHERS OF DIFFERENT SUBJECTS AT THE SAME GRADE LEVEL. THE SIZE OF CLASSES WAS OFTEN ADJUSTED ACCORDING TO THE SUBJECT TAUGHT, AND MOST OF THE SCHOOLS HAD SPECIAL BUILDING FACILITIES AVAILABLE. A LIST OF ADVANTAGES AND DISADVANTAGES CLAIMED FOR TEAM TEACHING IS QUOTED FROM A RECENT ANTHOLOGY ON ELEMENTARY SCHOOL ORGANIZATION. A SUMMARY OF THE QUESTIONNAIRE DATA IS GIVEN FOR EACH OF THE 76 SYSTEMS, TOGETHER WITH SOME OF THE COMMENTS MADE BY THE RESPONDENTS. A SELECTED BIBLIOGRAPHY OF 31 ITEMS IS INCLUDED, AS IS A COPY OF THE QUESTIONNAIRE USED IN THE SURVEY. THIS DOCUMENT IS AVAILABLE FOR $1.00 FROM EDUCATIONAL RESEARCH SERVICE, 1201 SIXTEENTH STREET, N.W., WASHINGTON, D.C. 20036. ORDER CIRCULAR NO. 9, 1965. (DR)

ED020801 PS001014
AGE OF ENTRANCE INTO THE FIRST GRADE AS RELATED TO ARITHMETIC ACHIEVEMENT. ILIKA, JOSEPH, 7FEB68 16P.
EDRS PRICE MF-$0.65 HC-$3.29

THIS INVESTIGATION WAS DESIGNED TO ASSESS THE INFLUENCE OF AGE OF ENTRANCE INTO THE FIRST GRADE ON ARITHMETIC ACHIEVEMENT. THE SCORES ON ARITHMETIC ACHIEVEMENT TESTS WERE COMPARED FOR 378 LATE AND EARLY ENTRANT BOYS AND GIRLS IN THE FIRST TO SIXTH GRADES. THE LATE ENTRANTS WERE BETWEEN 8 AND 9 MONTHS OLDER THAN THE EARLY ENTRANTS. THEORETICALLY, AN EARLY START SHOULD NOT RESULT IN SIGNIFICANT GAINS OF LONG TERM DURATION. IN TESTING THIS CONCLUSION, THE ARITHMETIC ACHIEVEMENT SCORES WERE COMPARED ON THE BASIS OF BOTH GRADE AND AGE. FOR BOTH BOYS AND GIRLS, THE RESULTS SHOWED THAT, MEASURED ON THE BASIS OF GRADE, THE ARITHMETIC ACHIEVEMENT SCORES WERE HIGHER FOR THE LATE ENTRANTS, BUT, MEASURED ON THE BASIS OF EQUATED AGE, THE EARLY ENTRANTS SCORED HIGHER. THESE RESULTS SUPPORT OTHER FINDINGS IN THE AREA AND LEAD TO THE CONCLUSIONS THAT (1) PUPILS IN THE AMERICAN GRADE SCHOOLS CAN LEARN EARLIER IN LIFE THAN NOW THOUGHT, (2) THEY CAN LEARN MORE COMPLEX ARITHMETIC, AND (3) SUCH LEARNING MAY HAVE AN ENDURING CUMULATIVE EFFECT AT AGE 11. PERHAPS, AS A SUGGESTION, THE PRESENT ARITHMETIC CURRICULUM SHOULD BE REEVALUATED, FOR IT HAS TOO FREQUENTLY BEEN FOUND INSUFFICIENTLY STIMULATING TO THE PUPILS. THIS PAPER WAS PRESENTED TO THE AMERICAN EDUCATIONAL RESEARCH ASSOCIATION, (CHICAGO, FEBRUARY 7, 1968). (WD)

ED020802 PS001015
MAKING WAVES, DENVER HEAD START. , 7MAR68 21P.
EDRS PRICE MF-$0.65 HC-$3.29

THIS DOCUMENT PROVIDES A DESCRIPTIVE SURVEY OF PROJECT HEAD START ACTIVITIES IN DENVER, COLORADO. THE PRIMARY EDUCATIONAL OBJECTIVES OF THE PROGRAM ARE CITED AS (1) CONCEPT DEVELOPMENT THROUGH EXPERIENCES IN AN ENLARGED ENVIRONMENT, (2) SELF-CONCEPT DEVELOPMENT THROUGH SUCCESSFUL INTERACTION WITH TEACHERS AND WITH PEERS, AND (3) THE DEVELOPMENT OF LANGUAGE FACILITY. THE ROLES OF TEACHERS AND TEACHER AIDES AND THE OPPORTUNITIES FOR STAFF SELF-EVALUATION AND SELF-IMPROVEMENT ARE DESCRIBED. SUPPLEMENTARY SERVICES AVAILABLE TO PROGRAM PARTICIPANTS ARE ENUMERATED AS (1) SPEECH THERAPY, (2) MEDICAL AND DENTAL SERVICES, (3) PSYCHOLOGICAL SERVICES, AND (4) SOCIAL SERVICES. A DESCRIPTION IS PROVIDED OF THE NUTRITION PROGRAM WHICH IS OPERATED IN THE 41 DENVER HEAD START CENTERS. THE RECRUITMENT OF VOLUNTEER WORKERS AND THE IMPORTANT FUNCTION OF VOLUNTEERS IN THE OVERALL PROGRAM ARE CONSIDERED. THE ACHIEVEMENTS OF THE DENVER PROGRAM OF PARENTAL INVOLVEMENT ARE ENUMERATED, AND A UNIQUE CAMPING PROGRAM FOR PARENTS IS DESCRIBED. THE FINAL SECTION OF THIS DOCUMENT IS CONCERNED WITH THE FUTURE OF HEAD START IN DENVER. THREE APPENDIXES CONTAIN ELIGIBILITY GUIDELINES FOR HEAD START PARTICIPATION AND LISTINGS OF COORDINATING STAFF MEMBERS AND OF DENVER DELEGATE AGENCIES AND PROGRAM CENTERS. (JS)

ED020803 PS001045
RESPONSE TO VARYING LEVELS OF CONDITIONING REWARDS. FINAL REPORT. SILVERMAN, ROBERT E.; AND OTHERS, 30JUN68 54P.
EDRS PRICE MF-$0.65 HC-$3.29

TWO EXPERIMENTS WERE CONDUCTED TO CLASSIFY AND TO CONDITION REWARD RESPONSIVENESS IN KINDERGARTEN CHILDREN. IN THE FIRST EXPERIMENT, 207 CHILDREN WITH A MEDIAN AGE OF 6.0 WERE CLASSIFIED ACCORDING TO THEIR RESPONSIVENESS TO A HIERARCHY OF REWARDS. AFTER TWO SESSIONS INVOLVING TWO-CHOICE INSTRUMENTAL CONDITIONING TASKS, 60 PERCENT OF THE CHILDREN WERE CLASSIFIED AS RESPONSIVE TO TANGIBLE REWARDS, 30 PERCENT AS RESPONSIVE TO SOCIAL APPROVAL (HALF OF WHICH WERE ALSO RESPONSIVE TO CONFIRMATION OF CORRECT RESPONSE), AND 10 PERCENT AS UNRESPONSIVE TO ANY OF THE THREE REWARDS. IN A THIRD SESSION, STIMULI WERE PAIRED TO CONDITION THE CHILDREN TO BECOME RESPONSIVE TO PREVIOUSLY NONREWARDING STIMULI. A FINAL SESSION WAS DEVOTED TO EVALUATION OF THE EFFECTIVENESS OF THE NEWLY ESTABLISHED REWARDS. DATA FROM THIS EXPERIMENT SHOWED THAT TANGIBLE REWARDS WERE MORE EFFECTIVE FOR KINDERGARTEN CHILDREN THAN WERE APPROVAL REWARDS AND THAT APPROVAL REWARDS AND CONFIRMATION OF CORRECT RESPONSES WERE EQUALLY EFFECTIVE AND POSITIVELY CORRELATED. IN THE SECOND EXPERIMENT, INVOLVING 90 KINDERGARTEN CHILDREN, IT WAS FOUND THAT A NEUTRAL WORD CAN BE CONDITIONED TO BECOME A REWARD STIMULUS AND THAT CONDITIONING IS STRENGTHENED BY A PERIOD OF REWARD DEPRIVATION. EVIDENCE WAS ALSO OBTAINED SHOWING THAT CHILDREN WHO ARE UNDERACHIEVERS TEND TO BE LOWER IN APPROVAL RESPONSIVENESS. THESE FINDINGS SUGGEST CERTAIN PROCEDURES TO BE EMPLOYED IN ESTABLISHING ACHIEVEMENT MOTIVATION AMONG KINDERGARTEN CHILDREN. DETAILED STATISTICS ARE REPORTED IN 24 TABLES. (JS)

ED020804 PS001046
STUDY TO DETERMINE THE FEASIBILITY OF ADAPTING THE CARL ORFF APPROACH TO ELEMENTARY SCHOOLS IN AMERICA. FINAL REPORT. GLASGOW, ROBERT B.; HAMREUS, DALE G., 27MAY68 72P.
EDRS PRICE MF-$0.65 HC-$3.29

A STUDY WAS CONDUCTED TO DETERMINE THE FEASIBILITY OF ADAPTING FOR USE IN THE ELEMENTARY SCHOOLS OF AMERICA THE MUSIC TEACHING TECHNIQUES DEVELOPED BY THE GERMAN COMPOSER AND TEACHER, CARL ORFF. THE POPULATION OF AN ELEMENTARY SCHOOL WAS EMPLOYED IN THE STUDY. FIFTEEN STUDENTS FROM EACH CLASSROOM (TOTALING 180 STUDENTS) WERE RANDOMLY SELECTED FOR TESTING. FOLLOWING PRETESTING OF CERTAIN MUSIC SKILLS AND OF STUDENT ATTITUDES TOWARD MUSIC, A YEARLONG TEACHING PROGRAM INVOLVING THE SEQUENTIAL STEPS OF THE ORFF APPROACH WAS CONDUCTED DURING TWO 30-MINUTE PERIODS PER WEEK IN EACH OF THE CLASSES. AMERICAN VERBAL AND MUSICAL MATERIALS SUITABLE FOR USE WITH THE ORFF APPROACH WERE SUBJECTIVELY SELECTED AND WERE FOUND TO BE SUFFICIENTLY ABUNDANT. AT THE CONCLUSION OF THE SCHOOL YEAR, POSTTESTING WAS ADMINISTERED TO DETERMINE THE EFFECTS OF THE PROGRAM ON MUSIC SKILLS AND ATTITUDES. COMPARISON OF PRETEST AND POSTTEST SCORES INDICATED GAINS IN TWO OF THE FOUR BASIC MUSIC SKILLS WHICH WERE TESTED. POSITIVE GROWTH IN ATTITUDES TOWARD MUSIC DID NOT OCCUR. IT WAS GENERALLY CONCLUDED THAT THE ORFF APPROACH IS ADAPTABLE TO ELEMENTARY SCHOOL MUSIC IN AMERICA. STATISTICS ARE REPORTED IN FOUR TABLES, AND THREE APPENDIXES CONTAIN (1) MUSIC SKILLS TESTING MATERIALS, (2) ATTITUDE SCALES, AND (3) A LISTING OF SUITABLE TEACHING MATERIALS. (JS)

ED020805 PS001047
THE TEACHING OF INQUIRY SKILLS TO ELEMENTARY SCHOOL CHILDREN. FINAL REPORT. ALLENDER, JEROME S., 31MAY68 177P.
EDRS PRICE MF-$0.65 HC-$6.58

A SERIES OF EXPERIMENTS HAVE BEEN CARRIED OUT OVER A PERIOD OF 3 YEARS TO FIND MEANS FOR DESCRIBING INQUIRY BEHAVIOR IN GRADE SCHOOL STUDENTS AND TO TEST THE EFFECT OF TEACHING METHODS AND ENVIRONMENT ON THIS BEHAVIOR. INQUIRY ACTIVITY WAS TESTED BY HAVING CHILDREN PLAY THE ROLE OF A SMALL CITY MAYOR USING SPECIALLY DEVELOPED MATERIALS. THREE SEPARATE STUDIES WERE CONDUCTED. IN THE FIRST, 51 FROM THE MATERIALS. ALL WERE ABLE TO SUSTAIN INDEPENDENT ACTIVITY, BUT WIDE DIFFERENCES IN THE LEVEL OF ACTIVITY WERE OBSERVED. IN THE SECOND STUDY, 177 ADDITIONAL STUDENTS IN THE THIRD THROUGH SEVENTH GRADES WERE GIVEN ONE UNIT OF WORK. COMBINING THEIR SCORES WITH THE FIRST UNIT SCORES OF THE PREVIOUS STUDY, IT WAS FOUND THAT THERE WAS A GENERAL TENDENCY FOR INQUIRY ACTIVITY TO INCREASE WITH GRADE LEVEL, BUT THERE WERE NO SIGNIFICANT EFFECTS ATTRIBUTABLE TO SEX, INTELLIGENCE, OR READING LEVEL. IN THE THIRD STUDY, TWO EXPERIMENTS WERE CONDUCTED TO SEE IF INQUIRY BEHAVIOR COULD BE TAUGHT. THREE MEANS OF TEACHING WERE TRIED WITH 20 FIFTH GRADE CHILDREN IN THE FIRST EXPERIMENT, BUT NO EFFECT ON INQUIRY ACTIVITY WAS NOTED. A SECOND EXPERIMENT, USING A SPECIAL TRAINING CENTER, WAS CONDUCTED WITH 54 FIFTH GRADE CHILDREN,

WHO WERE DIVIDED INTO THE CENTER SHOWED INCREASING INQUIRY ACTIVITY, BUT NO DIFFERENCE WAS NOTED BETWEEN TEACHER-DIRECTION OR STUDENT-DIRECTION, LEADING TO THE CONCLUSION THAT THE SPECIAL ENVIRONMENT WAS THE CRITICAL FACTOR. (DR)

ED020806 PS001068
PARENTS' EVALUATION OF THE HEAD START PROGRAM IN THE MILWAUKEE PUBLIC SCHOOLS. BELTON, JOHN; GOLDBERG, SIDNEY, 66 9P.
EDRS PRICE MF-$0.65 HC-$3.29

A QUESTIONNAIRE WAS ADMINISTERED TO A REPRESENTATIVE SAMPLE COMPOSED OF PARENTS OF 50 CHILDREN (TWO PUPILS RANDOMLY SELECTED FROM EACH OF 25 HEAD START CLASSES). COMPILED FROM THE QUESTIONNAIRE, STATISTICS ARE REPORTED CONCERNING (1) REASONS FOR ENROLLMENT OF CHILDREN, (2) DEGREE OF PARENT INVOLVEMENT, (3) PARENTS' PERCEPTION OF THE HELP GIVEN THEIR CHILD AND FAMILY, AND (4) PARENTS' SUGGESTIONS FOR IMPROVING THE PROGRAM. BASED ON THE REPORTED STATISTICS, IT IS CONCLUDED THAT (1) MANY PARENTS DID NOT SEEK TO INFORM THEMSELVES ABOUT THE GOALS OF THE PROGRAM, (2) PARENTAL INVOLVEMENT IN CENTER ACTIVITIES TENDED TO BE MINIMAL AND MODERATE, AND (3) PARENTS' EVALUATION OF THE PROGRAM WAS VERY POSITIVE. ALTHOUGH IT IS APPARENT THAT THE HEAD START CENTERS HAVE ESTABLISHED GOOD RAPPORT WITH THE PARENTS OF THE COMMUNITY, THE RESULTS OF THIS SURVEY SUGGEST THE NEED FOR MORE THOROUGH AND EFFECTIVE TECHNIQUES OF INFORMATION DISSEMINATION AND OF SECURING PARENTAL INVOLVEMENT IN THE PROGRAM ACTIVITIES. (JS)

ED021608 PS000146
MODIFICATION OF CLASSIFICATORY COMPETENCE AND LEVEL OF REPRESENTATION AMONG LOWER-CLASS NEGRO KINDERGARTEN CHILDREN. SIGEL, IRVING E.; OLMSTED, PATRICIA, JUN 67 72P.
EDRS PRICE MF-$0.65 HC-$3.29

THE BASIC HYPOTHESES WERE (1) CHILDREN WITH DETAILED EXPOSURE TO OBJECTS WOULD INCREASE IN KNOWLEDGE OF THE COMPLEXITY OF OBJECTS BUT WOULD ALSO EXHIBIT A CORRESPONDING INCREASE IN OBJECT-PICTURE DISCREPANCY, (2) CHILDREN EXPOSED ONLY TO PICTURES WOULD SHOW MINIMAL OBJECT-PICTURE DISCREPANCY BUT WOULD EXHIBIT A LOWER RESPONSE REPERTOIRE, AND (3) CHILDREN USING OBJECTS FOLLOWED BY PICTURES WOULD SHOW MOST INCREASE IN CLASSIFICATION SKILLS, EXHIBITING LESS OBJECT-PICTURE DISCREPANCY. THE SAMPLE CONSISTED OF 117 CHILDREN OF LOWER SOCIOECONOMIC CLASS FROM KINDERGARTENS OF REPRESENTATIVE INNER-CITY, LOWER CLASS SCHOOLS. TESTS ADMINISTERED WERE THE OBJECT-PICTURE CATEGORIZATION TEST, A HAPTIC TEST, AND THE MOTOR ENCODING TEST. RESULTS INDICATE THAT CLASSIFICATION TRAINING DOES ENHANCE THE CHILD'S ABILITY TO EMPLOY GROUPING AND SCORABLE RESPONSES, AS WELL AS INCREASE THE VARIETY OF CRITERIA BY WHICH TO CLASSIFY. DETAILED RESULTS, TABLES, AND APPENDIXES ARE INCLUDED. THIS PAPER WAS PRESENTED AT THE SIXTH WORK CONFERENCE ON CURRICULUM AND TEACHING IN DEPRESSED AREAS, TEACHERS COLLEGE, COLUMBIA UNIVERSITY, JUNE 1967. (EF)

ED021609 PS000616
AN EARLY INTERVENTION PROGRAM THAT FAILED. TANNENBAUM, ABRAHAM J., 26 JAN 66 12P.
EDRS PRICE MF-$0.65 HC-$3.29

TWENTY-FOUR MATCHED PAIRS OF CULTURALLY DEPRIVED FIRST GRADE CHILDREN WERE DIVIDED INTO AN EXPERIMENTAL AND CONTROL GROUP TO INVESTIGATE THE EFFECT OF SPECIAL READING INSTRUCTION ON THE READING ABILITY OF THESE CHILDREN. THE TEACHER WHO ADMINISTERED THIS SPECIAL INSTRUCTION WAS CONSIDERED VERY COMPETENT, AND THE INSTRUCTIONAL CONTENT, ALTHOUGH NOT NEW, WAS WELL ORGANIZED. THE EXPERIMENTAL GROUP RECEIVED THE ADDITIONAL INSTRUCTION THREE TIMES A WEEK FOR 40-MINUTE PERIODS FROM OCTOBER 1964 TO JUNE 1965. POSTTESTS INDICATED NO EXISTENCE OF SIGNIFICANT DIFFERENCES IN READING ABILITY BETWEEN THE TWO GROUPS. IT WAS CONCLUDED THAT THE FAILURE OF THIS INTERVENTION PROGRAM MIGHT BE DUE TO THE INADEQUACY OF USING ADDITIONAL CONVENTIONAL READING READINESS INSTRUCTION INSTEAD OF INTRODUCING INSTRUCTIONAL INNOVATIONS. THE FIVE AREAS STRESSED BY THE INTERVENTION PROGRAM WERE (1) VISUAL DISCRIMINATION, (2) AUDITORY DISCRIMINATION, (3) LANGUAGE DEVELOPMENT, (4) COGNITIVE LEARNINGS, AND (5) DEVELOPING BODY IMAGE SENSE. PERHAPS THE ELABORATION OF THESE CURRICULUM-CONTENT AREAS HEREIN WILL SUGGEST POSSIBLE FRESH APPROACHES TO TEACHING READING READINESS TO THE EDUCATIONALLY DISADVANTAGED. (WD)

ED021610 PS000723
CULTURAL ENVIRONMENTAL ACHIEVEMENT PROJECT, A SUMMARIZATION AND EVALUATION OF AN EXPERIMENTAL PRE-SCHOOL PROGRAM. , JUL 64 124P.
EDRS PRICE MF-$0.65 HC-$6.58

A 4-WEEK PRESCHOOL ENRICHMENT PROGRAM WAS CONDUCTED IN THE BETHLEHEM, PENNSYLVANIA AREA DURING THE SUMMER OF L964 TO COUNTERACT THE EDUCATIONAL DEFICIENCIES OF THE CULTURALLY DISADVANTAGED. FOUR- AND FIVE-YEAR-OLD NEGRO, PUERTO RICAN, AND CAUCASIAN CHILDREN ATTENDED SIX CLASSROOMS STAFFED BY THREE MASTER TEACHERS AND 22 STUDENT TEACHERS. ABOUT LL5 CHILDREN PARTICIPATED. THE PROGRAM SCHEDULE WAS OF A TYPICAL NURSERY SCHOOL OR KINDERGARTEN PATTERN. WEEKLY MEETINGS OF THE PARENTS OF THE PUPILS WERE HELD IN ORDER TO IMPROVE THEIR UNDERSTANDING OF THE OBJECTIVES OF THE PROGRAM AND TO INCREASE THEIR SENSE OF RESPONSIBILITY IN PREPARING THEIR CHILDREN FOR THE SCHOOL EXPERIENCE. THE PUPILS WERE TESTED AT THE BEGINNING AND END OF THE PROGRAM. THIS DATA SHOWED THE EXISTENCE OF ENCOURAGING IMPROVEMENT IN TERMS OF THE PUPILS' READINESS TO ENTER KINDERGARTEN. NOT ONLY DID IT APPEAR THAT THE PROGRAM ENRICHED THE EDUCATIONAL SKILLS OF THE PUPILS, BUT IT PROVIDED A SIGNIFICANT STUDENT-TEACHING EXPERIENCE FOR THE 22 COLLEGE STUDENTS. THIS DOCUMENT CONSISTS PRIMARILY OF (1) A DETAILED ACCOUNT OF THE SUBSTANCE OF THE PRESCHOOL PROGRAM, (2) SELECTED STUDENT PROFILES AS RECORDED BY THE STUDENT-TEACHERS, AND (3) DAY-TO-DAY REPORTS OF CLASSROOM EXPERIENCES BY THREE OF THE STUDENT TEACHERS. (WD)

ED021611 PS000725
PROJECT HEAD START, REPORT ON THE PREKINDERGARTEN PROGRAM, 1965. , 65
DOCUMENT NOT AVAILABLE FROM EDRS.
AVAILABLE FROM: BENJAMIN C. WILLIS, GENERAL SUPERINTENDENT OF SCHOOLS, BOARD OF EDUCATION, CITY OF CHICAGO, CHICAGO, ILLINOIS.

THIS REPORT LISTS THE GOALS OF THE HEAD START PROJECT AND DESCRIBES ITS ORGANIZATION AND PROCEDURES. A BRIEF INTRODUCTION DESCRIBES THE NEED FOR PRESCHOOL EDUCATION IN CHICAGO AND PAST AND PRESENT PROGRAMS WHICH HAVE ATTEMPTED TO MEET THE NEED. THE REPORT DESCRIBES THE CHILDREN'S SOCIAL AND ECONOMIC DEPRIVATION. MORE ATTENTION, HOWEVER, IS GIVEN TO PERSONNEL, SUCH AS STAFF SELECTION AND TRAINING, VARIOUS COMPONENTS OF A TEAM OF TEACHING AIDES, AND THE IDENTIFICATION AND SERVICES OF VOLUNTEERS. THE DOCUMENT DESCRIBES THE SCHOOL ROOM, THE PATTERN OF DAILY ACTIVITIES, AND THE PURPOSE AND STRUCTURE OF CURRICULUM AND OF SPECIAL FIELD TRIPS. IN ADDITION, THE REPORT GIVES A DESCRIPTION OF THE PROGRAM'S HEALTH SERVICES. A SECTION ON THE EVALUATION PROGRAM DISCUSSES RESULTS BASED ON PRETESTS AND POSTTESTS, OBSERVATIONS OF MANY PERSONNEL INVOLVED, AND HEALTH REPORTS. THE REPORT CONTAINS NUMEROUS ILLUSTRATIONS OF CHILDREN, TOYS, AND EQUIPMENT. (JS)

ED021612 PS000990
HEAD START EVALUATION AND RESEARCH CENTER. PROGRESS REPORT OF RESEARCH STUDIES, 1966-1967. ZIMILES, HERBERT; HORTON, DONALD, DEC 67 228P.
EDRS PRICE MF-$0.65 HC-$9.87

THE STUDIES WHICH COMPRISE THIS REPORT ARE AS FOLLOWS: (A) DOCUMENT 1, DEVELOPMENT OF THE MATRIX TEST BY HERBERT ZIMILES AND HARVERY ASCH (PS 001 072); (B) DOCUMENT 2, STUDIES OF THE SOCIAL ORGANIZATION OF HEAD START CENTERS BY DONALD HORTON AND OTHERS (PS 001 073); (C) DOCUMENT 3, AN EXPERIMENTAL APPROACH TO STUDYING NON-VERBAL REPRESENTATION IN YOUNG CHILDREN BY MARGERY FRANKLIN AND JUDITH COBB (PS 001 074); (D) DOCUMENT 4, DEVELOPMENT OF OBSERVATION PROCEDURES FOR ASSESSING PRESCHOOL CLASSROOM ENVIRONMENT BY VIRGINIA STERN AND ANNE GORDON (PS 001 075); (E) DOCUMENT 5, COMPARATIVE ITEM-CONTENT ANALYSIS OF ACHIEVEMENT TEST PERFORMANCE IN YOUNG CHILDREN BY HERBERT ZIMILES AND STEPHEN SILK (PS 001 076); (F) DOCUMENT 6, INDIVIDUAL INSTRUCTION PROJECT 1 BY RENEE REENS AND OTHERS (PS 001 077). (BO)

ED021613 PS001001
HEAD START RESEARCH AND EVALUATION OFFICE, UNIVERSITY OF CALIFORNIA AT LOS ANGELES. ANNUAL REPORT, NOVEMBER 1967. SECTION II. STERN, CAROLYN, NOV 67 134P.
EDRS PRICE MF-$0.65 HC-$6.58

A HEAD START RESEARCH REPORT ON WAYS TO IMPROVE ACADEMIC ACHIEVEMENT OF DISADVANTAGED CHILDREN DESCRIBES FIVE PROJECTS: (1) A STUDY OF SOCIOLINGUISTIC VARIABLES IN SCHOOL LEARNING AND PROBLEM SOLVING WHEN CLASSES ARE TAUGHT IN DIALECT VERSUS STANDARD ENGLISH; (2) SUBCULTURAL DETERMINANTS OF COOPERATIVE AND COMPETITIVE BEHAVIOR IN PRESCHOOL CHILDREN AS A FUNCTION OF REWARD CONDTION, SEX, AND ETHNIC BACKGROUND, AND GROUP VERSUS INDIVIDUAL REWARD CONTINGENCIES AS A MEASURE OF DIFFERENCES IN COOPERATION AND COMPETITION (A CROSS-CULTURAL COMPARISON WAS ALSO MADE OF SUCH BEHAVIOR IN KIBBUTZ AND URBAN CHILDREN IN ISRAEL); (3) MEASUREMENT OF CHANGE IN SOCIAL AND PERSONAL ATTITUDES OF PARENTS WHICH INVESTIGATED THE EFFECT OF THEIR PARTICIPATION IN HEAD START ON SUBSEQUENT USE OF COMMUNITY RESOURCES, THE MEASUREMENT OF CHANGES IN PARENTAL FEELINGS OF ALIENATION AS A RESULT OF PARTICIPATION, AND THE EVALUATION OF SPECIAL INSTRUCTION IN IMPROVING THE HOME TEACHING OF PARENTS OF DISADVANTAGED CHILDREN; (4) DEVELOPMENT OF EVALUATION INSTRUMENTS TO STUDY THE ECHOIC RESPONDING OF DISADVANTAGED PRESCHOOLERS AS A FUNCTION OF THE TYPE OF SPEECH MODELED; AND (5) AN EXPERIMENTAL STUDY OF VARIABLES IN TEACHING MATHEMATICAL CONCEPTS TO INVESTIGATE THE EFFECTIVENESS OF INSTRUCTION IN PUZZLE-ASSEMBLY SKILLS. (MS)

ED021614 PS001006
HEAD START EVALUATION AND RESEARCH CENTER, UNIVERSITY OF KANSAS. FINAL REPORT ON RESEARCH ACTIVITIES. ETZEL, BARBARA C.; AND OTHERS, 30 NOV 67 293P.
EDRS PRICE MF-$0.65 HC-$9.87

THIS DOCUMENT IS THE FINAL REPORT TO THE INSTITUTE OF EDUCATIONAL DEVELOPMENT FOR HEAD START RESEARCH EVALUATION ACTIVITIES AT THE UNIVERSITY OF KANSAS FOR 1966-67. IT CONTAINS 16 SEPARATE REPORTS OF STUDIES COMPLETED OR IN THE PROCESS OF COMPLETION. THE SUBJECT MATTER OF THE REPORTS CONTAINS 15 DISTINCT TOPICS AND WARRANTS INDIVIDUAL ABSTRACTS. THE 15 ABSTRACT NUMBERS AND TOPICS ARE AS FOLLOWS: PS 001 218 (REINFORCEMENT BEHAVIOR OF TEACHERS); PS 001 219 (AUDITORY DISCRIMINATION); PS 001 220 (VERBAL IMITATION); PS 001 221 (LANGUAGE PROGRAM); PS 001 222 (BRIE ORAL RESPONSES); PS 001 223 (PEER GROUP INFLUENCE); PS 001 224 (REINFORCEMENT OF INTELLIGENCE); PS 001 225 (DIFFERENTIATED SPEECH RESPONSE); PS 001 226 (COLOR LABELING); PS 001 227 (ERRORLESS DISCRIMINATION OF DELAY OF REINFORCEMENT); PS 001 228 (GROSS MOTOR RESPONSES); PS 001 229 (PHYSICAL DEVELOPMENT); PS 001 230 (MATCHING ABSTRACTIONS); PS 001 231 (SOCIAL REINFORCEMENT); AND PS 001 232 (VERBAL RECALL). (WD)

ED021615 PS001008
SELF-SOCIAL CONSTRUCTS OF CHILDREN. ZILLER, ROBERT C., ED.; LONG, BARBARA H., ED., 67 103P.
EDRS PRICE MF-$0.65 HC-$6.58

BASED ON A THEORY OF PERSONALITY IN WHICH THE SELF, CONSIDERED AS A PERCEPTUAL AGENT, IS DEFINED IN TERMS OF INTERPERSONAL ORIENTATION, SEVEN COMPONENTS OF SELF-OTHER ORIENTATION ARE PROPOSED: (1) MAJORITY IDENTIFICATION, (2) COMPLEXITY, (3) POWER, (4) SELF-ESTEEM, (5) SELF-CENTRALITY, (6) IDENTIFICATION, AND (7) SOCIAL DEPENDENCE. THE SELF-SOCIAL SYMBOLS TASKS DEVELOPED TO MEASURE THESE COMPONENTS REQUIRE THE SUBJECT TO RELATE HIMSELF TO THE SOCIAL ENVIRONMENT AND ARE PRIMARILY NONVERBAL IN CHARACTER. FOUR STUDIES WERE CONDUCTED WITHIN THIS THEORETICAL FRAMEWORK. STUDY I INVESTIGATED THE RELATION BETWEEN SELF-CONCEPT AND SOCIAL DESIRABILITY IN 50 SIXTH GRADE WHITE CHILDREN. STUDY II CONSIDERED THE RELATION BETWEEN SELF-CONCEPT AND GEOGRAPHIC MOBILITY IN 219 EIGHTH GRADE STUDENTS. STUDY III INVESTIGATED DEVELOPMENTAL CHANGES IN SELF-CONCEPTS DURING ADOLESCENCE BASED ON A SAMPLE OF 420 SIXTH THROUGH TWELFTH GRADE STUDENTS. STUDY IV COMPARED THE SELF-OTHER ORIENTATIONS OF 100 INDIAN CHILDREN FROM 10 TO 14 YEARS OF AGE WITH 100 AMERICAN CHILDREN IN THE SIXTH THROUGH EIGHTH GRADES. AN APPENDIX CONTAINS THE SEVEN SELF-SOCIAL SYMBOLS TASKS. (DR)

ED021616 PS001064
THE RELATION BETWEEN TEST ANXIETY AND NEED FOR MEMORY SUPPORT IN PROBLEM SOLVING. REVISED RESEARCH MEMORANDUM NO. 11. SIEBER, JOAN E.; KAMEYA, LAWRENCE I., MAY 68 24P.
EDRS PRICE MF-$0.65 HC-$3.29

FORTY FIFTH AND SIXTH GRADERS, MATCHED ON SEX AND MEASURES OF TEST ANXIETY, DEFENSIVENESS, AND IQ, WERE DIVIDED INTO TWO GROUPS, EACH OF WHICH SOLVED PORTEUS MAZE TASKS AND A MARBLE PUZZLE, WITH AND WITHOUT MEMORY SUPPORT, RESPECTIVELY. AN ANXIETY-BY-MEMORY SUPPORT INTERACTION OCCURRED IN THE NUMBER OF ERRORS MADE PRIOR TO SOLVING THE MARBLE PUZZLE, AS PREDICTED, BUT DID NOT OCCUR IN THE PORTEUS MAZE TASK. IT WAS SUGGESTED THAT ANXIETY'S INTERFERENCE WITH SHORT-TERM MEMORY COULD BE OFFSET BY A VARIETY OF EXTERNAL AIDS, SUCH AS DIAGRAMS OR NOTATIONAL SYSTEMS, WHICH PROBLEM SOLVERS COULD BE TAUGHT TO USE. (AUTHOR)

ED021617 PS001065
MEASUREMENT OF MOTIVATION TO ACHIEVE IN PRESCHOOL CHILDREN. FINAL REPORT. ADKINS, DOROTHY; AND OTHERS, 68 37P.
EDRS PRICE MF-$0.65 HC-$3.29

A PREVIOUS STUDY WAS SUCCESSFUL IN DESIGNING AN INSTRUMENT TO MEASURE MOTIVATION WHICH CAN BE USED WITH PRESCHOOL CHILDREN. THE PURPOSE OF THE PRESENT RESEARCH WAS (1) TO DEVELOP FURTHER THE NEW INSTRUMENT BY GIVING IT AN INITIAL TRIAL ON A SUBSTANTIAL NUMBER OF SUBJECTS, (2) TO SELECT AND REVISE THE TEST ITEMS ON THE BASIS OF ITEM ANALYSIS, AND (3) TO IDENTIFY THE FACTORIAL STRUCTURE UNDERLYING THE PRESCHOOL CHILDRENS' RESPONSES. THIS STUDY WAS CONDUCTED IN HAWAII AND INVOLVED 4- AND 5-YEAR -OLD CHILDREN. OF THE 182 SUBJECTS, 114 ATTENDED HEAD START CLASSES AND 68 ATTENDED PRIVATE PRESCHOOLS. THE TEST INSTRUMENT CONSISTED OF 200 ITEMS, EACH COMPOSED OF A PAIR OF FIGURES AND A SHORT SITUATIONAL SETTING. THE TWO FIGURES IN THE ITEM REPRESENTED DIFFERENT RESPONSES TO THE SITUATION. THE CHILD WAS TOLD THE SITUATION AND ASKED TO CHOOSE THE RESPONSE HE WOULD MAKE. EACH RESPONSE HAD A DIFFERENT MOTIVATIONAL OVERTONE. THUS, AN EVALUATION OF ALL OF THE CHILD'S RESPONSES PROVIDED AN INDICATION OF HIS MOTIVATIONAL STRUCTURE. THE ITEM ANALYSIS OF THE DATA LED TO THE ELIMINATION OF 100 UNNECESSARY ITEMS. THE FACTORIAL STRUCTURE WAS TENTATIVELY MAPPED, AND DATA WILL BE GATHERED TO EXPLORE THE VALIDITY OF THE INSTRUMENT. RESEARCH IS BEING PLANNED TO USE THIS INSTRUMENT TO TEACH MOTIVATION TO PRESCHOOLERS. (WD)

ED021618 PS001066
PRELIMINARY EVALUATION OF A LANGUAGE CURRICULUM FOR PRESCHOOL CHILDREN. FINAL REPORT. ADKINS, DOROTHY C.; AND OTHERS, 67 23P.
EDRS PRICE MF-$0.65 HC-$3.29

DURING THE SUMMER OF 1967, A 1-WEEK TRAINING PROGRAM WAS CONDUCTED AT THE UNIVERSITY OF HAWAII IN WHICH SEVEN TEACHERS AND SIX AIDES WERE INSTRUCTED IN THE USE OF THE BEREITER-EGNELMANN TEACHING STRATEGY FOR LANGUAGE PROGRAMS. THE BEREITER-ENGELMANN APPROACH INVOLVES CONCENTRATION UPON THE DEVELOPMENT OF LANGUAGE SKILLS AND FACILITY WITH BASIC SENTENCE USAGE. THE TEACHERS WHO PARTICIPATED IN THE SUMMER TRAINING PROGRAM WERE EACH THEN ASSIGNED A SUMMER HEAD START CLASS. THE 49 EXPERIMENTAL PUPILS WERE ADMINISTERED AN EXPERIMENTAL LANGUAGE CURRICULUM. A CONTROL GROUP OF 20 CHILDREN RECEIVED A MORE EXTENSIVE BUT LESS INTENSIVE BEREITER-ENGELMANN LANGUAGE CURRICULUM. A GROUP OF ANALOG TASKS WAS DEVELOPED TO COMPLEMENT THE BASIC LEARNING TASKS OF THE EXPERIMENTAL PROGRAM. THE ANALOG TASKS, AS DISTINGUISHED FROM THE BASIC TASKS, INVOLVED ONLY NONVERBAL RESPONSES. THE PUPILS OF BOTH CONDITIONS WERE ADMINISTERED THE SCHOOL READINESS TASKS AS POSTTESTS. THE RESULTS SHOWED THAT ON MOST TASKS THERE WAS NO SIGNIFICANT DIFFERENCE BETWEEN THE PERFORMANCE OF THE EXPERIMENTAL AND CONTROL GROUPS. (WD)

ED021619 PS001067
THE EXTENSION OF CONTROL IN VERBAL BEHAVIOR. FINAL REPORT. REEBACK, ROBERT T., 10 MAY 68 21P.
EDRS PRICE MF-$0.65 HC-$3.29

SEVEN 18- TO 32-MONTH-OLD CHILDREN RECEIVED FROM SEVEN TO 26 EXPERIMENTAL SESSIONS EACH BETWEEN OCTOBER 1966 AND APRIL 1967. A SESSION LASTED FROM 5 TO 15 MINUTES AND CONCERNED CONTROL OVER THE VERBAL RESPONSES OF THE CHILDREN WITH TOKEN-OPERATED REINFORCEMENT DEVICES. IN ORDER TO MAKE THE RESULTS OF THE EXPERIMENTAL SESSIONS MEANINGFUL, AN ATTEMPT WAS MADE TO DESCRIBE THE ENTERING VERBAL REPERTOIRES OF THE CHILDREN BY OBSERVING VOCALIZATIONS OUTSIDE AND WITHIN THE SESSIONS. THE OBJECTIVES OF THE EXPERIMENT WERE DIFFERENT FOR CHILDREN OF DIFFERENT AGES. THE FOUR CHILDREN UNDER 22 MONTHS OF AGE AT THE BEGINNING OF THE PROJECT WERE INVOLVED IN THE ELICITATION OF ECHOIC RESPONSES ONLY. IT WAS FOUND THAT IT WAS POSSIBLE TO ELICIT COMPLEX OR MULTICOMPONENT ECHOIC RESPONSES BY STRENGTHENING EACH OF THE COMPONENTS SEPARATELY. FOR THE THREE OLDER CHILDREN, 30 MONTHS OF AGE OR MORE, THE GOAL WAS TO EXPAND THE VERBAL CAPACITY OF THE CHILD BEYOND ACQUISITION OF MERE ARBITRARY ECHOIC RESPONSES TO THE ACQUISITION OF MORE MEANINGFUL UTTERANCES. THE RESULTS WERE ENCOURAGING THAT SUCH A GOAL IS PRACTICABLE. TEACHERS AND PARENTS CAN AND SHOULD BE TRAINED IN THE STRATEGIES OF ELICITING VOCAL VERBAL RESPONSES FROM YOUNG CHILDREN. (WD)

ED021620 PS001069
THE EFFECT OF SUBJECT-DETERMINED VERBALIZATION ON DISCRIMINATION LEARNING IN PRESCHOOLERS. WOLFF, JOSEPH L., 67 18P.
EDRS PRICE MF-$0.65 HC-$3.29

PREVIOUS EXPERIMENTS WITH NURSERY SCHOOL CHILDREN HAVE SUGGESTED THAT (1) SUBJECTS OF PRESCHOOL AGE DO NOT VERBALIZE DURING TRANSFER LEARNING OR THAT (2) FOR THESE SUBJECTS, SELF-PRODUCED VERBAL CUES HAVE LITTLE INFLUENCE ON THE LEARNING PROCESS. TO INVESTIGATE THE RELATIVE MERITS OF THESE ALTERNATIVE POSITIONS, RESEARCH WAS CONDUCTED AMONG 80 NURSERY SCHOOL CHILDREN IN CHAMPAIGN AND URBANA, ILLINOIS. THE SUBJECTS WERE ASSIGNED DISCRIMINATION TASKS WITH STIMULI VARYING IN EITHER BRIGHTNESS OR SIZE. HALF OF THE SUBJECTS WERE REQUIRED TO VERBALIZE THEIR CHOICES. THE OTHERS RESPONDED THROUGHOUT THE EXPERIMENT WITHOUT SPEAKING. CONFIRMATION WAS FOUND FOR THE PRELIMINARY POSTULATES THAT VERBALIZATION WOULD CAUSE MOST SUBJECTS TO USE BRIGHTNESS LABELS TO DESCRIBE THE STIMULUS REGARDLESS OF THE DIMENSION AND THAT VERBALIZATION WOULD SIGNIFICANTLY FACILITATE PERFORMANCE ON THE BRIGHTNESS DIMENSION. CONTRARY TO PREDICTION, HOWEVER, VERBALIZATION DID NOT INTERFERE WITH PERFORMANCE ON THE SIZE DIMENSION. THE RESULTS OF THIS RESEARCH SUGGEST THAT, FOR NURSERY SCHOOL CHILDREN, SIZE DISCRIMINATION IS DETERMINED BY PROPRIOCEPTIVE FEEDBACK AND IS NOT, THEREFORE, GREATLY INFLUENCED BY VERBALIZATION. DETAILED METHODOLOGICAL AND THEORETICAL DISCUSSIONS ARE INCLUDED IN THIS RESEARCH REPORT AND STATISTICS ARE REPORTED IN FIVE TABLES. (JS)

ED021621 PS001070
EVALUATION OF THE PRESCHOOL CHILD AND PARENT EDUCATION PROJECT AS EXPANDED THROUGH THE USE OF ELEMENTARY AND SECONDARY EDUCATION ACT, TITLE I, FUNDS. O'PIELA, JOAN, FEB 68 47P.
EDRS PRICE MF-$0.65 HC-$3.29

A PROJECT TO EVALUATE THE EFFECTIVENESS OF 14 PRESCHOOL CENTERS IN COMBINING THE SERVICES OF FAMILY, COMMUNITY, AND PROFESSIONAL RESOURCES IN A PROGRAM TO INCREASE CHILDREN'S SCHOOL READINESS AND POTENTIAL FOR ACADEMIC SUCCESS INVOLVED EIGHT HUNDRED 3- AND 4-YEAR-OLDS AND THEIR PARENTS. MEETINGS WERE HELD TO TEACH PARENTS TO REINFORCE CHILDREN'S SCHOOL EXPERIENCE AND TO STRENGTHEN THE ADULTS' OWN SELF-CONCEPTS. INSERVICE TEACHER WORKSHOPS WERE ALSO HELD. A LANGUAGE PROGRAM PILOT STUDY WAS CONDUCTED IN EIGHT OF THE CENTERS. DATA WERE COLLECTED BY MEANS OF A QUESTIONNAIRE FILLED OUT BY PRESCHOOL STAFF PERSONNEL, AN EXPERIMENTAL TEST BATTERY ADMINISTERED TO A SAMPLE OF THE PRESCHOOLERS, TEACHER REPORTS ON PARENT MEETINGS, THE CHILDREN'S MEDICAL SERVICE RECORDS, AND OTHER TEST RESULTS. A SIGNIFICANT RESULT WAS THAT AT ALMOST ALL AGE LEVELS, THE PRESCHOOL SAMPLE EXCEEDED THE NORMS MEANS GAINS OF A FORMER PILOT STUDY GROUP IN LANGUAGE ACHIEVEMENT. THE RESULTS SUGGEST THAT THE PRESCHOOL CENTER PROGRAM BE CONTINUED WITH EMPHASIS ON A MULTISENSORY APPROACH TO CURRICULUM AND LANGUAGE FUNCTIONING, THAT STAFF INSERVICE WORKSHOPS BE CONTINUED, AND THAT PARENT EDUCATION MEETINGS STRESS CURRICULUM AND PROGRAM ACTIVITIES WHICH THE CHILDREN WERE EXPERIENCING. AN INDEPTH STUDY TO DEVELOP THE BEST MODE OF PRESENTATION FOR SPECIAL LANGUAGE CLASSES SHOULD BE SUPPORTED. TEN TABLES ARE INCLUDED. (MS)

ED021622 PS001071
PILOT STUDY OF FIVE METHODS OF PRESENTING THE SUMMER HEAD START CURRICULAR PROGRAM. O'PIELA, JOAN M., MAR 68 20P.
EDRS PRICE MF-$0.65 HC-$3.29

A PILOT STUDY WAS CONDUCTED TO ASSESS THE EFFECTIVENESS OF FIVE CURRICULAR METHODS USED IN A SUMMER HEAD START PROGRAM DESIGNED TO DEVELOP PERCEPTUAL-MOTOR SKILLS. THREE HUNDRED AND SEVENTY-THREE INNER-CITY CHILDREN IN 15 HEAD START CENTERS WERE GIVEN THE PEABODY PICTURE VOCABULARY TEST AND THE BRENNER DEVELOPMENTAL GESTALT TEST OF SCHOOL READINESS AT THE BEGINNING AND END OF THE PROGRAM. CHILDREN IN THE FROSTIG EXPERIMENTAL AND CONTROL CENTERS WERE PRETESTED AND POST-TESTED WITH THE MARIANNE FROSTIG DEVELOPMENTAL TEST OF VISUAL PERCEPTION. CHILDREN IN THE DOMAN DELACATO EXPERIMENTAL AND CONTROL CENTERS WERE PRETESTED AND POSTTESTED FOR LATERAL AND VISUAL DOMINANCE IN THREE AREAS: HANDEDNESS, FOOTEDNESS, AND EYEDNESS. THE METHODS USED IN THE BEREITER EXPERIMENTAL CENTER WERE PRESCRIBED BY THE BEREITER CURRICULUM. TEACHERS AND AIDES FILLED OUT EVALUATIVE QUESTIONNAIRES. TEST GAINS OF HEAD START CENTER PUPILS WERE COMPARED TO GAINS OF CHILDREN IN CENTERS USING CURRICULAR MODIFICATIONS. THE TOTAL POPULATION SHOWED IMPROVEMENT AT THE .01 LEVEL OF SIGNIFICANCE ON THESE VARIABLES: VOCABULARY, TOTAL SCHOOL READINESS, ACHIEVEMENT-ABILITY ASSESSMENT, AND SOCIAL-EMOTIONAL BEHAVIOR. NONE OF THE EXPERIMENTAL TEACHING METHODS WAS FOUND TO BE STRIKINGLY SUPERIOR TO THE MULTISENSORY PROGRAM PRESCRIBED BY THE BASIC DETROIT HEAD START AND KINDERGARTEN PROGRAM. (MS)

ED021623 PS001072
HEAD START EVALUATION AND RESEARCH CENTER. PROGRESS REPORT OF RESEARCH STUDIES 1966 TO 1967. DOCUMENT 1, DEVELOPMENT OF THE MATRIX TEST. ZIMILES, HERBERT; ASCH, HARVEY, DEC 67 28P.
EDRS PRICE MF-$0.65 HC-$3.29

A MATRIX TEST WAS DEVISED TO ASSESS COGNITIVE SKILLS ASSOCIATED WITH INFERENTIAL REASONING. THE FORMAT OF THE TEST REQUIRES THE SUBJECT TO CHOOSE, FROM AMONG FOUR ALTERNATIVES, A FIGURE WHICH IS RELATED TO OTHER GIVEN FIGURES ON THE BASIS OF APPEARANCE, CONTENT, OR SPATIAL POSITION IN THE MATRIX. THE TEST CONSISTS OF THREE PERCEPTUAL MATCHING ITEMS, 18 CLASS MEMBERSHIP ITEMS, 11 ONE- WAY CLASSIFICATION ITEMS, AND 12 TWO-WAY CLASSIFICATION ITEMS. ONLY MINIMALLY DEPENDENT UPON THE COMMUNICATION OF VERBAL INSTRUCTIONS AND REQUIRING NO VERBAL RESPONS S FROM THE SUBJECT, THE TEST IS SUITABLE FOR USE WITH YOUNG AND DISADVANTAGED CHILDREN. TO IDENTIFY THE FACTORS THAT INFLUENCE PERFORMANCE ON THE MATRIX TEST, COMPARATIVE STUDIES HAVE BEEN CONDUCTED WITH (1) LOWER AND MIDDLE CLASS URBAN POPULATIONS FROM KINDERGARTEN AND GRADES ONE, TWO, AND THREE, (2) 4-YEAR-OLD CHILDREN FROM VARIOUS HEAD START PROGRAMS AND FROM A MIDDLE CLASS NURSERY SCHOOL PROGRAM, AND (3) 5-YEAR-OLD CHILDREN FROM MOUNT OLIVE, NORTH CAROLINA AND FROM ROME, GEORGIA. THESE STUDIES HAVE SHOWN THAT THE MATRIX TEST IS A USEFUL TOOL FOR OBTAINING DATA RELEVANT TO THE EARLY EDUCATION OF DISADVANTAGED CHILDREN. REFINEMENT OF THE INSTRUMENT AND FURTHER ANALYSIS OF THE AVAILABLE DATA ARE PROJECTED. THE PROJECT REPORT CONTAINS DETAILED RESULTS OF THE VARIOUS STUDIES AND INCLUDES FIVE STATISTICAL TABLES. (JS)

ED021624 PS001073
HEAD START EVALUATION AND RESEARCH CENTER. PROGRESS REPORT OF RESEARCH STUDIES 1966 TO 1967. DOCUMENT 2, STUDIES OF THE SOCIAL ORGANIZATION OF HEAD START CENTERS. HORTON, DONALD; AND OTHERS, DEC 67 113P.
EDRS PRICE MF-$0.65 HC-$6.58

AN EXPLORATORY, QUALITATIVE, AND COMPARATIVE RESEARCH STUDY CONCERNING SOCIOLOGICALLY RELEVANT ASPECTS OF PROJECT HEAD START (HS) WAS CONDUCTED IN TWO NEW YORK CITY HS CENTERS. THE STUDY INVESTIGATED (L) THE INTERNAL ORGANIZATIONAL DEVELOPMENT OF THE HS CENTERS, (2) TEACHER-PARENT RELATIONS IN HS, (3) HS IN RELATION TO THE FAMILY LIFE OF THE PARTICIPANTS, (4) THE HS PROGRAM OF ORGANIZING PARENTS FOR GROUP ACTION, (5) ORGANIZATIONAL RELATIONS BETWEEN HS AND THE PUBLIC SCHOOLS, AND (6) THE CHARACTERISTICS OF THE SPONSORING AGENCY AND THE PARTICIPATING POPULATION. AN INDUCTIVE METHOD WAS EMPLOYED IN THE STUDY. THEORETICAL FORMULATIONS WERE DEVELOPED AS THE PROJECT PROCEEDED AND WERE REFINED AS NEW DATA WERE OBTAINED. DATA WERE COLLECTED CHIEFLY THROUGH OBSERVATION AND INFORMAL INTERVIEWING. AN OVERVIEW OF THE FIRST YEAR OF THE RESEARCH STUDY IS PRESENTED IN THIS PROJECT REPORT, WHICH INCLUDES INFORMATION CONCERNED WITH (1) THE CHRONOLOGY OF ACTIVITIES AND OF PROGRAM DEVELOPMENT, (2) THE FORMULATION OF RESEARCH PROBLEMS, (3) RESEARCH METHODS, (4) FIELD PROCEDURES, (5) SPECIAL PROBLEMS OF FIELD WORK, (6) ANALYTIC PROCEDURES, (7) A REVIEW OF FINDINGS ON TWO SELECTED PROBLEMS (INTERNAL ORGANIZATIONAL DEVELOPMENT AND THE HS PROGRAM OF ORGANIZING PARENTS FOR GROUP ACTION), AND (8) FUTURE DIRECTIONS OF THE PROJECT. (JS)

ED021625 PS001074
HEAD START EVALUATION AND RESEARCH CENTER. PROGRESS REPORT OF RESEARCH STUDIES 1966 TO 1967. DOCUMENT 3, AN EXPERIMENTAL APPROACH TO STUDYING NON-VERBAL REPRESENTATION IN YOUNG CHILDREN. FRANKLIN, MARGERY; COBB, JUDITH, DEC 67 14P.
EDRS PRICE MF-$0.65 HC-$3.29

A CURRENT EXPLORATORY RESEARCH PROJECT IS DIRECTED TOWARD DEVELOPING MEANS FOR GATHERING SYSTEMATIC DATA ON NONVERBAL REPRESENTATION IN YOUNG CHILDREN. TASKS INVOLVING NONVERBAL REPRESENTATIONAL FUNCTIONING HAVE BEEN DEVELOPED, EVALUATED IN PRELIMINARY WORK WITH FIFTEEN 4-YEAR-OLD SUBJECTS, AND REVISED. THE REVISED SERIES OF TASKS CONSISTS OF FOUR GROUPS, DESIGNATED AS (1) PLAY SITUATIONS, (2) IMITATIONS, (3) SPATIAL ARRANGEMENTS, AND (4) PICTURE-OBJECT MATCHING. THIS REVISED INSTRUMENT WILL BE EMPLOYED IN A STUDY OF WHICH THE OBJECTIVES ARE (1) THE INVESTIGATION OF ASPECTS OF NONVERBAL REPRESENTATION IN DISADVANTAGED, AS COMPARED WITH MIDDLE CLASS, PRESCHOOL CHILDREN, (2) THE INVESTIGATION OF RELATIONSHIPS BETWEEN NONVERBAL SYMBOLIZING ABILITY AND LINGUISTIC COMPETENCE, AND (3) THE DEVELOPMENT OF A MORE REFINED SERIES OF EVALUATIVE TASKS. IN ADDITION TO THE EXPERIMENTAL INSTRUMENT, THREE TESTS OF LANGUAGE USAGE WILL BE ADMINISTERED, AND ADDITIONAL DATA WILL BE ACCUMULATED CONCERNING SUBJECT'S TEST PERFORMANCE, BACKGROUND, AND CLASSROOM BEHAVIOR. FOR THE COMPARATIVE TESTING, 30 DISADVANTAGED AND 30 ADVANTAGED 4- AND 5-YEAR-OLDS WILL BE MATCHED FOR AGE AND SEX. ATTACHMENTS TO THIS REPORT INCLUDE THE LIST OF TASKS AND THE INVENTORY FORM FOR RECORDING FACTORS AFFECTING TEST PERFORMANCE. (JS)

ED021626 PS001075
HEAD START EVALUATION AND RESEARCH CENTER. PROGRESS REPORT OF RESEARCH STUDIES 1966 TO 1967. DOCUMENT 4, DEVELOPMENT OF OBSERVATION PROCEDURES FOR ASSESSING PRESCHOOL CLASSROOM ENVIRONMENT. STERN, VIRGINIA; GORDON, ANNE, DEC 67 39P.
EDRS PRICE MF-$0.65 HC-$3.29

A PRESCHOOL ENVIRONMENT INVENTORY WAS DEVELOPED TO PROVIDE A METHOD FOR CHARACTERIZING THE SCHOOL ENVIRONMENT OF CHILDREN IN HEAD START AND OTHER PRESCHOOL PROGRAMS. THE INVENTORY SUMMARIZES THE MOST SALIENT FEATURES OF A PRESCHOOL ENVIRONMENT AND DESCRIBES THESE DIMENSIONS FOR MEASUREMENT WITH ORDINAL SCALES. CONSISTEING OF 44 SCALES AND 23 CHECK LISTS, THE INSTRUMENT REQUIRES ADMINISTRATION BY OBSERVERS FAMILIAR WITH BASIC CONCEPTS IN EARLY CHILDHOOD EDUCATION. THE INVENTORY WILL BE SUBJECTED TO SYSTEMATIC CLASSROOM USE AND, AFTER EVALUATION, WILL BE REFINED, CLARIFIED, AND TRIMMED. UPON COMPLETION OF THE FINAL REVISION, DETERMINATION WILL BE MADE OF THE DEGREE OF TRAINING REQUIRED TO ACHIEVE SATISFACTORY LEVELS OF INTERSCORER AGREEMENT. THIS PROGRESS REPORT INCLUDES A COMPLETE REPRODUCTION OF THE INVENTORY FORM. CHECK LISTS AND SCALES ARE GROUPED UNDER THE HEADINGS OF (1) PHYSICAL SET-UP, MATERIALS, AND EQUIPMENT, (2) PLAY ACTIVITIES, (3) STRUCTURE, BALANCE, AND ORGANIZATION OF PROGRAM, (4) MODE OF TEACHING, (5) TEACHER'S ROLE REGARDING LANGUAGE, COMMUNICATION, AND ARTICULATION OF IDEAS AND FEELINGS, (6) CONTROL AND MANAGEMENT, (7) ASPECTS OF TEACHER'S RELATIONSHIP WITH THE CHILDREN, (8) TEACHER'S ROLE REGARDING PEER RELATIONS, (9) STYLE AND TONE OF TEACHER, AND (10) CLASSROOM ATMOSPHERE. (JS)

ED021627 PS001076
HEAD START EVALUATION AND RESEARCH CENTER. PROGRESS REPORT OF RESEARCH STUDIES 1966 TO 1967. DOCUMENT 5, COMPARATIVE ITEM-CONTENT ANALYSIS OF ACHIEVEMENT TEST PERFORMANCE IN YOUNG CHILDREN. ZIMILES, HERBERT; SILK, STEPHEN, DEC 67 15P.
EDRS PRICE MF-$0.65 HC-$3.29

TO CONTRIBUTE TO A MORE DIFFERENTIATED DESCRIPTION OF THE COGNITIVE STATUS OF YOUNG DISADVANTAGED CHILDREN, A COMPARATIVE STUDY WAS MADE OF ACHIEVEMENT TEST PERFORMANCE OF DISADVANTAGED AND MIDDLE CLASS GROUPS OF CHILDREN. ON THE BASIS OF PUBLISHED READING TEST SCORES, TEST DATA WERE GATHERED FROM NINE PUBLIC SCHOOLS, FOUR OF WHICH WERE SELECTED FROM AMONG THE HIGHEST SCORING IN EACH OF FOUR SCHOOL DISTRICTS. THE REMAINING FIVE WERE SELECTED AS REPRESENTATIVE OF CONSPICUOUSLY LOW SCORING SCHOOLS. THE CHILDREN FROM THE HIGH SCORING SCHOOLS WERE PREDOMINANTLY FROM WHITE MIDDLE CLASS FAMILIES. THE CHILDREN FROM THE LOW SCORING SCHOOLS WERE PREDOMINANTLY FROM LOWER CLASS NEGRO OR PUERTO RICAN FAMILIES. DATA ANALYSIS CONSISTED OF AN ITEM-BY-ITEM COMPARISON OF THE PERFORMANCES OF THE TWO GROUPS ON EACH OF THE SIX SUBTESTS OF THE NEW YORK STATE READINESS TEST. THE SMALLEST DIFFERENCES IN THE HIGH AND LOW SCORING GROUPS OCCURRED ON THE LISTENING , MATCHING, AND COPYING SUBTESTS. THE GREATEST DIFFERENCES OCCURRED ON THE NUMBERS SUBTEST. THE PERVASIVE DIFFERENCES FOUND TO EXIST IN EVERY AREA OF INTELLECTUAL FUNCTIONING SUGGEST THE NEED FOR A PROGRAM DESIGNED TO PROMOTE GENERAL INTELLECTUAL GROWTH AT A BASIC AND INTEGRATIVE LEVEL. STATISTICAL DATA ARE PRESENTED IN TWO TABLES, AND A SUMMARY OF FUTURE RESEARCH TO BE CONDUCTED IS INCLUDED IN THE TEXT OF THIS PROGRESS REPORT. (JS)

ED021628 PS001077
HEAD START EVALUATION AND RESEARCH CENTER. PROGRESS REPORT OF RESEARCH STUDIES 1966 TO 1967. DOCUMENT 6, INDIVIDUAL INSTRUCTION PROJECT I. REENS, RENEE; AND OTHERS, DEC 67 16P.
EDRS PRICE MF-$0.65 HC-$3.29

RESEARCH WAS CONDUCTED TO EVALUATE THE EFFECTIVENESS OF A 12-WEEK INTERVENTION PROGRAM OF INDIVIDUAL INSTRUCTION FOR DISADVANTAGED PRESCHOOL CHILDREN. BASED ON THIS PRETEST, 17 CHILDREN WITH IQ SCORES OF 107 OR LESS WERE SELECTED AND PLACED INTO EXPERIMENTAL AND CONTROL GROUPS. THE EXPERIMENTAL GROUP WAS EXPOSED TO INDIVIDUAL COGNITIVE AND LANGUAGE DEVELOPMENT INSTRUCTION DESIGNED TO OFFSET LAGS IN INTELLECTUAL GROWTH COMMONLY IDENTIFIED AS EFFECTS OF SOCIOECONOMIC DISADVANTAGE. TUTORIAL SESSIONS FOR EACH MEMBER OF THE EXPERIMENTAL GROUP WERE SCHEDULED FOR FOUR 15- TO 20-MINUTE PERIODS PER WEEK, BUT ONLY 56 PERCENT OF AVAILABLE SESSIONS WERE UTILIZED. CONTENT OF THE SESSIONS FOCUSED ON CLASSIFICATION AND DIFFERENTIATION. POSTTESTS SHOWED GAINS FOR THE EXPERIMENTAL AND CONTROL GROUPS OF 4.7 AND 5.9, RESPECTIVELY. DISCUSSION OF THESE RESULTS INCLUDES SUGGESTIONS CONCERNING THE SELECTION OF CHILDREN FOR PARTICIPATION IN INDIVIDUAL INSTRUCTIONAL PROGRAMS, COUNTERINDICATIONS OF THE PRESENT STUDY, AND RECOMMENDATIONS REGARDING PATTERNS OF INDIVIDUAL TEACHING ASSIGNMENTS. STATISTICS ARE REPORTED IN TWO TABLES, AND AN APPENDIX CONTAINS AN ENUMERATION OF THE CONTENT OF THE TUTORIAL SESSIONS.(JS)

ED021629 PS001079
A BIBLIOGRAPHY OF RESEARCH ON FOREIGN STUDENT AFFAIRS. SPENCER, RICHARD E.; AWE, RUTH, AUG 68 370P.
EDRS PRICE MF-$0.65 HC-$13.16
AVAILABLE FROM: INSTITUTE OF INTERNATIONAL EDUCATION, 809 UNITED NATIONS PLAZA, NEW YORK, N.Y. 10017

THIS BIBLIOGRAPHY WAS ORGANIZED FOR THE PRUPOSES OF (1) ENHANCING THE CAPABILITY OF INTERESTED SCHOLARS TO PURSUE RESEARCH IN THE FOREIGN STUDENT FIELD; (2) INDICATING TO FOREIGN STUDENT RESEARCHERS THE WEALTH OF DATA AND INFORMATION AVAILABLE FROM AREAS OF PSYCHOLOGY, SOCIOLOGY, AND ANTHROPOLOGY; (3) EMPHASIZING THE NEED FOR MORE LONGITUDINAL AND LARGE SCALE RESEARCH EFFECTS ACROSS INSTITUTIONS AND NATIONAL BOUNDARIES; (4) INFORMING THOSE WHO ARE INTERESTED IN WHAT HAS BEEN ACCOMPLISHED IN ORDER TO BRING CLOSER THE CONGRUENCE BETWEEN RESEARCH AND PRACTICE; AND (5) ENABLING THOSE WHO PURSUE RESEARCH TO LEAD INTO NEW AREAS OF INVESTIGATION, AND NOT TO REPORT WHAT ALREADY HAS BEEN DONE. THE BIBLIOGRAPHY IS DIVIDED INTO FOUR MAJOR HEADINGS AND 17 SUBHEADINGS AND HAS ABOUT 4000 ENTRIES. MAJOR HEADINGS ARE (1) INTERNATIONAL EXCHANGE, (2) EDUCATIONAL CURRICULUM, (3) WORLD COOPERATION IN EDUCATION, AND (4) SURVEY REPORTS, CONFERENCES, AND EVALUATIONS. DESCRIPTIONS OF ALL THE BIBLIOGRAPHICAL DIVISIONS PRECEDE THE BIBLIOGRAPHY. SOME BIBLIOGRAPHIC ENTRIES ARE CROSS-REFERENCED WHEN THE CONTENT APPLIES TO MORE THAN ONE BIBLIOGRAPHICAL DIVISION. AN AUTHOR INDEX FOLLOWS THE BIBLIOGRAPHY. (WD)

ED021630 PS001120
CHILD'S PLAY, A CREATIVE APPROACH TO PLAYSPACES FOR TODAY'S CHILDREN. AARON, DAVID; WINAWER, BONNIE P., 65
DOCUMENT NOT AVAILABLE FROM EDRS.
AVAILABLE FROM: HARPER & ROW, PUBLISHERS, 49 E. 33RD ST., NEW YORK, N.Y. 10016 ($4.95)

THIS BOOK DISCUSSES THE PROBLEM OF PROVIDING APPROPRIATE PLAYSPACES FOR CHILDREN TODAY. IT IS INTENDED TO GIVE CURRENCY TO A PRACTICAL FRAMEWORK FOR SOLUTIONS TO THIS PROBLEM. CHAPTER ONE DISCUSSES THE PROBLEM, POINTING OUT OUR SOCIETY'S NEED FOR CREATED PLAYSPACES. CHAPTER TWO CONSIDERS THE USE CHILDREN MAKE OF PLAY AND OUTLINES WHAT THEY WANT AND NEED IN PLAY AREAS. CHAPTER THREE CRITICIZES TRADITIONAL PLAYGROUNDS, ARGUING THAT THEY ARE BOTH UNSUITABLE AND DANGEROUS. CHAPTER FOUR TAKES UP THE PROBLEM OF FINDING SPACE FOR PLAY AREAS. SMALLER AREAS EQUIPPED WITH MULTIPURPOSE "PLAY SCULPTURES" ARE RECOMMENDED AS A SOLUTION. CHAPTER FIVE DISCUSSES THE PROBLEMS OF PLAYSPACE IN SUBURBIA. CHAPTER SIX CONSIDERS THE DESIGN OF PLAYSPACE FOR HANDICAPPED CHILDREN AND USES AS AN EXAMPLE A CAMP DESIGNED FOR CEREBRAL PALSIED CHILDREN. CHAPTER SEVEN CONCLUDES THE BOOK WITH AN ASSESSMENT OF THE PROSPECTS FOR SOLVING THE PROBLEM OF PLAYSPACES. THE BOOK IS HEAVILY ILLUSTRATED WITH PHOTOGRAPHS OF CHILDREN AT PLAY. (DR)

ED021631 PS001133
EARLY CHILDHOOD EDUCATION TODAY. FRAZIER, ALEXANDER, ED.; AND OTHERS, 68 50P.
EDRS PRICE MF-$0.65 HC NOT AVAILABLE FROM EDRS.
AVAILABLE FROM: ASSOCIATION FOR SUPERVISION AND CURRICULUM DEVELOPMENT, NEA, 1201 16TH ST., N. W., WASHINGTON, D. C. 20036 ($2.00).

THIS BOOKLET DELINEATES MANY ELEMENTS FOR ORGANIZING AND DEVELOPING EDUCATIONAL PROGRAMS FOR PRESCHOOL AND KINDERGARTEN CHILDREN. THE PRIMARY GOALS OF SUCH PROGRAMS ARE GIVEN AS (1) SOCIALIZATION, (2) DEVELOPMENT OF BASIC LEARNING AND LANGUAGE SKILLS, (3) PREPARATION FOR THE REGULAR SCHOOL EXPERIENCE, (4) ESTABLISHMENT OF MOTIVATIONAL SYSTEMS, AND (5) STIMULATION OF SELF-EXPRESSION. A SAMPLE DAILY SCHEDULE OF ACTIVITIES IS PRESENTED IN THE BOOKLET. ALSO ENUMERATED ARE POSSIBLE CENTERS OF INTEREST INTO WHICH THE CLASSROOM CAN BE DIVIDED. ONE IS REMINDED THAT CHILDREN WITH SPECIAL NEEDS WILL REQUIRE SPECIAL PROGRAMS. BECAUSE OF THE NEW EMPHASES ON PARENT INVOLVEMENT IN THE EDUCATION OF THEIR CHILDREN, PROGRAMS TO IMPROVE COMMUNICATION BETWEEN SCHOOL AND HOME ARE DISCUSSED. ALSO DISCUSSED IS THE INCREASING INTEREST IN IMPROVING THE QUALITY AND QUANTITY OF PROGRAM PERSONNEL. THE BOOKLET PRESENTS SOME IDEAS ON THE NATURE OF THE PROBLEM AND POSSIBLE RESOLUTIONS. IN CONCLUSION, GUIDELINES FOR THE EVALUATION OF EARLY CHILDHOOD EDUCATION PROGRAMS ARE SUGGESTED. (WD)

ED021632 PS001159
ADAPTATIONAL TASKS IN CHILDHOOD IN OUR CULTURE. MURPHY, LOIS B., NOV 64 11P.
EDRS PRICE MF-$0.65 HC-$3.29

DURING THE FIRST MONTHS AFTER BIRTH, A CHILD'S FUNCTIONS BEGIN TO EMERGE. BY AGE THREE A CHILD IS EXPECTED TO HAVE MASTERED THE BASIC TASKS OF (1) GOOD VEGETATIVE FUNCTIONING (MANAGEMENT OF DRIVES AND IMPULSES INVOLVED IN EATING AND ELIMINATION), (2) PERCEPTUAL ORGANIZATION AND FAMILIARIZATION WITH THE HOME ENVIRONMENT AND SKILLS TO ORIENT TO A NEW ENVIRONMENT, (3) MOTOR SKILLS, (4) COMMUNICATION SKILLS, (5) EMOTIONAL ORGANIZATION, INCLUDING THE CAPACITY TO ATTACH AND RESPOND TO OTHER ADULTS AND CHILDREN AND THE CAPACITY FOR LOVE AND ANGER, (6) SPHINCTER CONTROL, AND (7) BEGINNING TO UNDERSTAND TIME, NUMBER, AND SPACE WHICH HELP TO ORGANIZE THE PRESENT, RECENT PAST AND NEAR FUTURE. AS THE PRESCHOOLER NEARS SCHOOL AGE HE LEARNS HOW TO ADAPT TO SEPARATION FROM HIS MOTHER AND HOME, TO RELATE TO PEERS AND A NEUTRAL TEACHER, AND TO ACCEPT RULES OF BEHAVIOR REQUIRED BY A STRUCTURED SCHOOL ATMOSPHERE. THROUGHOUT A CHILD'S DEVELOPMENT, LEARNING PROCESSES INCLUDING PAVLOVIAN CONDITIONING, TRIAL AND ERROR LEARNING, AND OPERANT CONDITIONING TAKE PLACE. INDIVIDUAL DIFFERENCES AFFECT THE COMPLEX ADAPTATIONAL STYLE WHICH EVOLVES AS THE CHILD ATTEMPTS TO DEAL WITH HIS ENVIRONMENT. A BIBLIOGRAPHY IS INCLUDED. (MS)

ED021633 PS001218
HEAD START EVALUATION AND RESEARCH CENTER, UNIVERSITY OF KANSAS. REPORT NO. I, THE OBSERVATION OF REINFORCEMENT BEHAVIOR OF TEACHERS IN HEAD START CLASSROOMS AND THE MODIFICATION OF A TEACHER'S ATTENDING BEHAVIOR. COOPER, MARGARET; THOMSON, CAROLYN, 30 NOV 67 31P.
EDRS PRICE MF-$0.65 HC-$3.29

TWO TEACHERS WERE SUBJECTS OF THIS INVESTIGATION INTO THE EFFECT OF VARIOUS FORMS OF FEEDBACK ON THE FREQUENCY OF A TEACHER'S ATTENDING TO DESIRABLE CHILD BEHAVIOR. THE FEEDBACK TOOK THREE FORMS: (1) A REPORT OF THE FREQUENCY OF THE TEACHER'S ATTENDING TO APPROPRIATE PUPIL RESPONSES, (2) A

REPORT OF THE FREQUENCY OF ATTENDED AND UNATTENDED APPROPRIATE PUPIL RESPONSES, AND (3) "IRRELEVANT" FEEDBACK IN THE FORM OF OBSERVER QUESTIONS OR COMMENTS. TEACHER A, WHO MANIFESTED THE LOWER INITIAL ATTENDING BEHAVIOR DURING THE BASELINE OBSERVATION PERIOD, WAS GIVEN A TRAINING PROGRAM WHILE TEACHER B WAS GIVEN A CONTROL CONDITION. SUBSEQUENTLY, TEACHER B ALSO RECEIVED THE TRAINING PROGRAM. THE STUDY WAS CONDUCTED IN TWO SCHOOLS SERVING LOW INCOME FAMILIES IN A LARGE MIDWESTERN CITY. THE RESULTS INDICATED THAT (1) BOTH TEACHERS INCREASED IN TOTAL ATTENTION TO APPROPRIATE CHILD RESPONSES DURING THE TRAINING PERIODS, TEACHER A INCREASING MORE THAN TEACHER B, (2) THE CHILDREN DID NOT SHOW A NOTICEABLE INCREASE IN AVERAGE OUTPUT OF APPROPRIATE RESPONSES, (3) SOCIAL ATTENTION BY THE OBSERVER DID NOT, BY ITSELF, PRODUCE MODIFICATION OF TEACHER ATTENDING BEHAVIOR, AND (4) THE INCREASE IN TEACHER ATTENDING BEHAVIOR INVOLVED ONLY APPROPRIATE CHILD RESPONSES RATHER THAN ALL CHILD RESPONSES. (WD)

ED021634 PS001219
HEAD START EVALUATION AND RESEARCH CENTER, UNIVERSITY OF KANSAS. REPORT NO. IIA, A STUDY OF AUDITORY DISCRIMINATION AND VERBAL RESPONDING. BRIGHAM, THOMAS A., 30 NOV 67 13P.
EDRS PRICE MF-$0.65 HC-$3.29

AN AUDITORY DISCRIMINATION PROCEDURE WAS USED IN THIS STUDY TO ATTEMPT TO CORRECT THE SPEECH PROBLEM OF A 4-YEAR-OLD GIRL. THE MAJOR CHARACTERISTIC OF THAT SPEECH PROBLEM WAS THE CONSISTENT USE OF INAPPROPRIATE FIRST CONSONANT SOUNDS IN SOME WORDS, LIKE "GOG" FOR "DOG." THE CHILD WAS GIVEN 25 TRAINING SESSIONS AND TWO POSTTRAINING SESSIONS. THE FIRST THREE TRAINING SESSIONS INVOLVED ASCERTAINING WHICH OF 45 STIMULUS WORDS THE SUBJECT MISPRONOUNCED. THE 13 WORDS SO ASCERTAINED WERE USED LATER IN THE STUDY. SESSIONS FOUR AND FIVE INVOLVED A VISUAL MATCH EXERCISE. SESSIONS 12 THROUGH 15 PAIRED THE VISUAL STIMULI OF THE PREVIOUS EXERCISES WITH THE SOUNDS THEY REPRESENTED. SESSIONS 16 THROUGH 25 INTRODUCED A FADING TECHNIQUE TO ELIMINATE THE VISUAL STIMULI AND TRANSFER CONTROL OF THE DISCRIMINATION TO THE AUDITORY STIMULI. BEGINNING AT THE END OF SESSIONS EIGHT THROUGH 11, THE L3 MISPRONOUNCED WORDS OBTAINED IN THE FIRST THREE SESSIONS WERE INTRODUCED AS STIMULUS ITEMS. IT WAS FOUND THAT THE CHILD'S ABILITY TO DISCRIMINATE "AUDITORIALLY" BETWEEN HER RESPONSE AND THE CORRECT RESPONSE IMPROVED OVER THE SESSIONS BUT THAT THIS DISCRIMINATIVE ABILITY DID NOT APPEAR TO AFFECT HER VERBAL INABILITY TO CORRECTLY PRONOUNCE THE STIMULUS WORDS. (WD)

ED021635 PS001220
HEAD START EVALUATION AND RESEARCH CENTER, UNIVERSITY OF KANSAS. REPORT NO. IIB, AN EXPERIMENTAL ANALYSIS OF VERBAL IMITATION IN PRESCHOOL CHILDREN. BRIGHAM, THOMAS A., 30 NOV 67 18P.
EDRS PRICE MF-$0.65 HC-$3.29

THREE 4-YEAR-OLD BOYS WERE SUBJECTS OF AN EXPERIMENT INVOLVING REINFORCEMENT OF VERBAL IMITATION. INTENDED TO PROVIDE INSIGHTS INTO LANGUAGE LEARNING AND SPEECH THERAPY, THIS INVESTIGATION BEGAN BY INTRODUCING TO THE SUBJECTS THE IDEA OF IMITATION OF THE EXPERIMENTER'S WORDS. EACH TIME THE CHILD CORRECTLY REPRODUCED THE STIMULUS WORD, HE WAS GIVEN CANDY AND PRAISE. THE NEXT PART OF THE STUDY WAS SIMILAR IN PROCEDURE EXCEPT THAT RUSSIAN WORDS WERE ADDED BUT WERE NEVER REINFORCED. IN THE THIRD PHASE, SUBJECTS WERE NOT REINFORCED FOR IMITATING EITHER ENGLISH OR RUSSIAN WORDS. LATER REINFORCEMENT OF ENGLISH WORD IMITATION WAS REINSTATED. THE RESULTS, BASED ON THE NUMBER OF CORRECT IMITATIONS, SHOWED THAT DURING EXPERIMENTAL PHASES WHEN REINFORCEMENT WAS TIED TO CORRECT IMITATIVE RESPONSES, THE CORRECT IMITATION OF ENGLISH AND RUSSIAN WORDS INCREASED, EVEN THOUGH THE RUSSIAN WORDS WERE NEVER REINFORCED. WHEN REINFORCEMENT WAS NOT TIED TO CORRECT IMITATION OF THE ENGLISH WORDS, CORRECT IMITATION OF BOTH ENGLISH AND RUSSIAN WORDS DECREASED. (WD)

ED021636 PS001221
HEAD START EVALUATION AND RESEARCH CENTER, UNIVERSITY OF KANSAS. REPORT NO. III, EFFECTS OF A LANGUAGE PROGRAM ON CHILDREN IN A HEAD START NURSERY. BYRNE, MARGARET C., 30 NOV 67 33P.
EDRS PRICE MF-$0.65 HC-$3.29

A COMPENSATORY LANGUAGE PROGRAM WAS ADMINISTERED TO 13 CHILDREN, CONSIDERED, FOR THE MOST PART, AS CULTURALLY DISADVANTAGED AND LINGUISTICALLY DEFICIENT. THESE 13 CHILDREN COMPRISED THE EXPERIMENTAL GROUP, WHILE 12 OTHER CHILDREN WERE USED AS A CONTROL GROUP. THE AGES OF THE CHILDREN RANGED FROM 3 YEARS, 3 MONTHS TO 5 YEARS, 10 MONTHS. THE AVERAGE AGE OF THE EXPERIMENTAL GROUP WAS LESS THAN THAT OF THE CONTROL GROUP. THE EXPERIMENTAL GROUP WAS DIVIDED INTO THREE GROUPS ON THE BASIS OF LANGUAGE ABILITY. THE LANGUAGE PROGRAM REQUIRED THE CHILDREN TO DESCRIBE THINGS, LISTEN TO THE LANGUAGE MODELS OF THE TEACHER, AND IMITATE THOSE MODELS. PRETESTS ADMINISTERED AT THE BEGINNING OF THE 5-MONTH PROGRAM WERE (1) THE ILLINOIS TEST OF PSYCHOLINGUISTIC ABILITIES (ITPA), (2) THE PEABODY PICTURE VOCABULARY TEST (PPVT), AND (3) THE IRWIN ARTICULATION TEST. ONLY THE ITPA AND PPVT WERE GIVEN AS POSTTESTS. THE SCORES OF THE EXPERIMENTAL AND CONTROL GROUPS ON THE ITPA AND PPVT DID NOT DIFFER SIGNIFICANTLY EXCEPT ON TWO SUBTESTS OF THE ITPA, BOTH OF WHICH TESTED GRAMMAR SKILLS. THUS, IT WAS CONCLUDED THAT THE LANGUAGE PROGRA DID PRODUCE SOME GAIN IN THE LANGUAGE ABILITY OF THE EXPERIMENTAL GROUP. IT WAS ALSO FOUND THAT THE MOST ABLE CHILDREN AT THE BEGINNING OF THE PROGRAM BENEFITED THE MOST FROM THE PROGRAM. (WD)

ED021637 PS001222
HEAD START EVALUATION AND RESEARCH CENTER, UNIVERSITY OF KANSAS. REPORT NO. IV, A COMPARISON OF FOUR MODES OF ELICITING BRIEF ORAL RESPONSES FROM CHILDREN. IRWIN, JOHN V., 30 NOV 67 14P.
EDRS PRICE MF-$0.65 HC-$3.29

A 112-ITEM MULTI-MODAL ARTICULATION ANALYSIS TEST WAS ADMINISTERED TO 116 HEAD START CHILDREN RANGING IN AGE FROM 4 YEARS, 6 MONTHS TO 5 YEARS, 5 MONTHS. THE TEST INVOLVES PRESENTING TO THE SUBJECT AN OBJECT, OR REPRESENTATION THEREOF, REQUIRING A ONE-WORD RESPONSE. FOUR MODES OF STIMULUS PRESENTATION WERE USED: (1) ACTUAL OBJECTS, (2) BLACK AND WHITE PRINTS, (3) COLOR PRINTS, AND (4) COLOR TRANSPARENCIES. THE CHILDREN'S RESPONSES TO THE 112 TEST STIMULI WERE STUDIED IN TERMS OF ITEM RECOGNITION, RESPONSE LATENCY, ARTICULATORY ACCURACY, AND SUBJECT PREFERENCE FOR ONE OF THE FOUR MODES OF STIMULUS PRESENTATION. THE RESULTS SHOWED THAT (1) ITEM RECOGNITION IMPROVED WITH INCREASING AGE OF THE SUBJECTS AND WAS NOT SIGNIFICANTLY AFFECTED BY THE MODE OF STIMULUS PRESENTATION, (2) RESPONSE LATENCY DID NOT APPEAR TO BE AFFECTED EITHER BY MODE OF STIMULUS PRESENTATION OR AGE OR SEX OF SUBJECT, (3) ARTICULATORY ABILITY TENDS TO INCREASE WITH AGE, AND (4) THE SUBJECT PREFERENCE WAS HIGHEST FOR THE ACTUAL OBJECTS, LOWEST FOR THE BLACK AND WHITE PRINTS. THE DATA SHOWED NO SIGNIFICANT DIFFERENCES IN SUBJECT RESPONDING ON THE BASIS OF SEX. (WD)

ED021638 PS001223
HEAD START EVALUATION AND RESEARCH CENTER, UNIVERSITY OF KANSAS. REPORT NO. V, A COMPARATIVE BEHAVIORAL ANALYSIS OF PEER-GROUP INFLUENCE TECHNIQUES IN HEAD START AND MIDDLE CLASS POPULATIONS. ROSENFELD, HOWARD M.; RUSSELL, RICHARD L., 30 NOV 67 37P.
EDRS PRICE MF-$0.65 HC-$3.29

THIRTY-EIGHT PRESCHOOL CHILDREN WERE SUBJECTS IN THIS INVESTIGATION. THEY WERE PAIRED ON THE BASIS OF SIMILARITY OF SEX AND DISSIMILARITY OF SOCIOECONOMIC LEVEL. REWARD FOR COMPLETION OF SIX PUZZLES WAS BASED ON COOPERATION BETWEEN THE PARTNERS AND, FOR ANOTHER SIX, ON COMPETITION BETWEEN THEM. THE DATA OF THIS STUDY CONSISTED OF (A) THE CONTENT OF THE INTERACTION BETWEEN PARTNERS, (B) THE LOCUS OF THEIR VISUAL ORIENTATION, AND (C) THE AMOUNT OF TIME EACH SUBJECT TOOK TO COMPLETE A PUZZLE. THE RESULTS INDICATED THAT INTERACTION WAS PRIMARILY THROUGH (1) VERBAL DEMANDS, (2) PHYSICAL TAKINGS, (3) COMPLYING, AND (4) OFFERS. MIDDLE CLASS (MC) SUBJECTS TENDED TO TAKE MORE WHILE LOWER CLASS (LC) SUBJECTS COMPLIED LESS THAN THEIR OPPOSITES. LC GIRLS MANIFESTED THE MOST TOTAL ACTS. IN TERMS OF VISUAL ORIENTATION, THERE APPEARED NO SIGNIFICANT DIFFERENCE BETWEEN THE TWO SOCIOECONOMIC GROUPS. THE MC SUBJECTS WON THE MOST PUZZLE COMPLETION CONTESTS AND THEIR SUCCESS WAS DUE TO SPEED. THE SUCCESS OF THE LC SUBJECTS WAS RELATED TO TOTAL FREQUENCY OF TASK-RELEVANT ACTS. THE REWARD CONDITION SEQUENCE, COOPERATION FOR THE FIRST SIX PUZZLES AND COMPETITION FOR THE SECOND SIX PUZZLES, OR VICE VERSA, HAD AN EFFECT ON ALL THREE VARIABLES, (A), (B), AND (C), MENTIONED ABOVE. (WD)

ED021639 PS001224
HEAD START EVALUATION AND RESEARCH CENTER, UNIVERSITY OF KANSAS. REPORT NO. VI, A FAILURE TO SHOW AND INVOLVEMENT OF CURRENT MOTIVATIONAL VARIABLES IN THE RESPONSE OF HEAD START CHILDREN IN THE ASSESSMENT OF INTELLIGENCE BY MEANS OF THE STANFORD BINET TEST. BAER, DONALD M., 30 NOV 67 4P.
EDRS PRICE MF-$0.65 HC-$3.29

IN ORDER TO INVESTIGATE THE EFFECT OF REINFORCING SUBJECT RESPONSES TO STANFORD-BINET TEST ITEMS, REGARDLESS OF WHETHER SUCH RESPONSES WERE CORRECT OR NOT, ONE-HALF OF A SAMPLE OF HEAD START CHILDREN WERE ADMINISTERED A STANDARD STANFORD-BINET TEST AND THE OTHER HALF WERE ADMINISTERED THE SAME TEST WITH THE MODIFICATION THAT RESPONSES WERE OCCASIONALLY REWARDED WITH M&M CANDIES. SIX MONTHS LATER THE CHILDREN WERE TESTED AGAIN UNDER THE TWO CONDITONS. THE AVERAGE INTELLIGENCE QUOTIENTS FOR THE TWO GROUPS ON THE FIRST TESTING WERE FOUND NOT TO BE SIGNIFICANTLY DIFFERENT. THIS SAME RESUTL WAS FOUND FOR THE SECOND TESTING. THUS, IT APPEARS THAT RESULTS FROM THE STANFORD-BINET TEST ARE INSENSITIVE TO INFLUENCES OF POSSIBLE INTERACTION BETWEEN SUBJECT RESPONSES

AND REINFORCEMENT OR NONREINFORCEMENT OF THOSE RESPONSES. (WD)

ED021640 PS001225
HEAD START EVALUATION AND RESEARCH CENTER, UNIVERSITY OF KANSAS. REPORT NO. VIIA, A CASE STUDY IN ESTABLISHING A DIFFERENTIATED SPEECH RESPONSE THROUGH GENERALIZATION PROCEDURES. JACOBSON, JOAN M.; ETZEL, BARBARA C., 30 NOV 67 14P.
EDRS PRICE MF-$0.65 HC-$3.29

A 2-YEAR, 8-MONTH OLD BOY WITH A LANGUAGE HANDICAP WAS THE SUBJECT OF A 5-MONTH TRAINING PROGRAM WHICH INVESTIGATED THE GENERALIZATION OF ARTICULATORY ABILITY DURING AND AFTER A SERIES OF SESSIONS AIMED AT CORRECTING THE BOY'S MISARTICULATION OF THE LETTER "T." BEFORE TRAINING BEGAN, THREE MATTERS NECESSITATED ATTENTION: (1) THE ESTABLISHMENT OF INSTRUCTIONAL CONTROL, (2) THE ASSESSMENT OF THE BOY'S LANGUAGE BEHAVIOR, AND (3) THE ADMINISTRATION OF A 26-WORD PROBE TEST. THE TRAINING CONDITION CONSISTED OF FIVE PHASES INTERSPERSED WITH SIX PROBE TESTS. THE TRAINING PROCEDURES WERE TO CORRECT THE SUBJECT'S MISARTICULATION OF THE LETTER T. THE PROBE TESTS WERE TO MEASURE THE IMPROVEMENT AND GENERALIZATION OF THE SUBJECT'S ABILITY TO ARTICULATE. TRAINING PHASE FIVE AND PROBE TESTS FIVE AND SIX INVOLVED A CHANGE IN PROCEDURE FROM AUDITORY STIMULI TO VISUAL STIMULI. THE RESULTS INDICATED THAT PROPER ARTICULATION OF TRAINING AND NONTRAINING WORDS ENDING IN T INCREASED, WITH SOME FLUCTUATION, DURING THE PROGRAM AND LED TO THE CONCLUSION THAT GENERALIZATION OF ARTICULATORY ABILITY WAS DEMONSTRATED. (WD)

ED021641 PS001226
HEAD START EVALUATION AND RESEARCH CENTER, UNIVERSITY OF KANSAS. REPORT NO. VIIB, ESTABLISHMENT OF NONVERBAL COLOR DISCRIMINATION RESPONSES TO AUDITORY COLOR-LABELING STIMULI AND SUBSEQUENT EFFECTS ON COLOR-LABELING RESPONSES. WROBEL, PATRICIA A.; AND OTHERS, 30 NOV 67 12P.
EDRS PRICE MF-$0.65 HC-$3.29

SEVENTEEN PRESCHOOL CHILDREN WERE ADMINISTERED TWO COLOR-DISCRIMINATION PRETESTS, VERBAL AND NONVERBAL. THE FIVE CHILDREN WHO SCORED LOWEST WERE CHOSEN TO RECIEVE THE COLOR PROGRAM. FOUR SCORED ELOW 85 PERCENT ON THE NONVERBAL PRETEST, WHEREAS THE OTHER 12 CHILDREN SCORED ABOVE 85 PERCENT. ON THE VERBAL PRETEST, ALL FIVE EXPERIMENTAL SUBJECTS SCORED BELOW 80 PERCENT, WHILE THE 12 REMAINING CHILDREN SCORED ABOVE 80 PERCENT. THE COLOR PROGRAM ADMINISTERED TO THE FIVE CHILDREN WAS DESIGNED TO TEACH EIGHT COLORS. THREE TEACHING PROCEDURES USING COLOR-STIMULUS CARDS WERE USED. EACH WAS NONVERBAL IN CHARACTER, REQUIRING THE CHILD TO POINT TO THE CORRECT STIMULUS. THE EXPERIMENTER DID PRESENT THE VERBAL STIMULUS INCIDENTALLY, HOWEVER, WHEN ASKING THAT THE SUBJECT POINT TO THE PARTICULAR COLOR. RESPONSE REINFORCEMENT WAS GIVEN THROUGHOUT THE PROGRAM. EXCEPT FOR ONE CHILD ON THE VERBAL TEST, ALL SUBJECTS SCORED 90 PERCENT OR MORE ON THE NONVERBAL AND VERBAL POSTTESTS. IT WAS CONCLUDED THAT THE COLOR PROGRAM NOT ONLY TAUGHT THE CHILDREN THE INTENDED VISUAL-STIMULUS DISCRIMINATIONS, BUT ALSO NONPROGRAMED VERBAL-STIMULUS INFORMATION. (WD)

ED021642 PS001227
HEAD START EVALUATION AND RESEARCH CENTER, UNIVERSITY OF KANSAS. REPORT NO. VIIC, ERRORLESS DISCRIMINATION IN PRESCHOOL CHILDREN: A PROGRAM FOR ESTABLISHING A ONE-MINUTE DELAY OF REINFORCEMENT. KOLB, DORIS H.; ETZEL, BARBARA C., 30 NOV 67 22P.
EDRS PRICE MF-$0.65 HC-$3.29

SEVERAL 3- TO 5-YEAR-OLD CHILDREN PARTICIPATED IN THIS STUDY DESIGNED TO DISCOVER THE NECESSARY PROCEDURES TO ESTABLISH NONRESPONDING IN PRESCHOOL CHILDREN DURING DELAY OF REINFORCEMENT. THE CHILDREN WERE DIVIDED INTO TWO GROUPS: (1) THE PROGRAMED GROUP (PG), TO WHICH A 60-SECOND DELAY PERIOD WAS INTRODUCED GRADUALLY AND (2) THE BASELINE GROUP (BG), TO WHICH THE 60-SECOND DELAY WAS INTRODUCED ABRUPTLY. THEY WERE TOLD TO PUSH A BUTTON, WHICH SOMETIMES RESULTED IN THE CHILD'S RECEIVING POKER CHIPS WHICH COULD LATER BE EXCHANGED FOR A TOY. DURING THE TEST SESSIONS THE BG WAS REINFORCED ON A VARIABLE INTERVAL (VI) SCHEDULE OF TWO TO NINE SECONDS. THE ABRUPT DELAY CONDITION WAS INTRODUCED ON THE FIRST RESPONSE AFTER A VI, AND NO REINFORCEMENT OCCURRED FOR RESPONSES UNTIL 60 SECONDS HAD ELAPSED. THE PG RECEIVED THE GRADUAL 60-SECOND DELAY CONDITION, IN WHICH THE DURATION OF THE DELAY WAS INCREASED IN 2-SECOND INCRE ENTS. IN BOTH GROUPS, SUPPORTIVE STIMULI (A TONE AND A LIGHT) WERE USED TO INDICATE THE DELAY PERIOD. RESULTS OF SUBJECT RESPONSE DATA INDICATED THAT CHILDREN OF THIS AGE CAN LEARN THE DISCRIMINATION INVOLVED, BUT AT LEAST ONE PG SUBJECT DID NOT LEARN IT. THE BG SUBJECTS DID NOT APPEAR TO LEARN TO DISCRIMINATE BETWEEN RESPONDING DURING THE VI SCHEDULE AND DURING THE DELAY CONDITION. (WD)

ED021643 PS001228
HEAD START EVALUATION AND RESEARCH CENTER, UNIVERSITY OF KANSAS. REPORT NO. VIID, A CASE STUDY ILLUSTRATING AN EXPERIMENTAL DESIGN FOR EVALUATING THE EFFECTS OF SHAPING GROSS MOTOR COORDINATION IN A 31 MONTH OLD CHILD. MICHEALIS, MARY LOU; ETZEL, BARBARA C., 30 NOV 67 29P.
EDRS PRICE MF-$0.65 HC-$3.29

A MULTIPLE BASELINE DESIGN FOR MODIFYING THE GROSS MOTOR COORDINATION OF A 31-MONTH-OLD BOY SUSPECTED OF SUFFERING FROM CONGENITAL BRAIN DAMAGE WAS CONDUCTED AT THE UNIVERSITY OF KANSAS INFANT STUDY LABORATORY. THE PRIMARY PURPOSE OF THE STUDY WAS TO ESTABLISH, BY EXPERIMENTAL PROCEDURES, THE DESIRED, BUT ABSENT, BEHAVIOR OF WALKING, GETTING UP, AND CLIMBING STAIRS, AT THE EXPENSE OF THE EXISTING BEHAVIOR OF SCOOTING, PULLING UP WITH SUPPORT, AND NOT CLIMBING STAIRS. IT WAS HYPOTHESIZED THAT, INCIDENTAL TO ESTABLISHING THE THREE DESIRED BEHAVIORS, THE BEHAVIOR OF STANDING WITHOUT SUPPORT WOULD REPLACE THE SUBJECT'S NEED TO STAND WITH SUPPORT. THE TRAINING SESSIONS FOR EACH OF HE THREE DESIRED BEHAVIORS WERE BASED ON THE GRADUAL MODIFICATION OF UNDESIRABLE INTO DESIRABLE BEHAVIOR THROUGH SELECTIVE REINFORCEMENT. THE THREE DESIRED BEHAVIORS WERE INITIALLY OF ZERO INCIDENCE BUT WERE ULTIMATELY ESTABLISHED AS PART OF THE CHILD'S RESPONSE REPERTOIRE, ALTHOUGH NOT TO THE COMPLETE DISPLACEMENT OF THE UNDESIRABLE BEHAVIORS. (WD)

ED021644 PS001229
HEAD START EVALUATION AND RESEARCH CENTER, UNIVERSITY OF KANSAS. REPORT NO. VIII, PHYSICAL DEVELOPMENT OF CHILDREN IN THE HEAD START PROGRAM IN THE CENTRAL UNITED STATES. BASS, WILLIAM; AND OTHERS, 30 NOV 67 15P.
EDRS PRICE MF-$0.65 HC-$3.29

INFORMATION ON THE NUTRITIONAL HABITS OF 154 HEAD START CHILDREN FROM RURAL, SMALL CITY, AND METROPOL TAN AREAS IN THE CENTRAL UNITED STATES WAS OBTAINED FROM QUESTIONNAIRES ANSWERED BY THE CHILDREN'S MOTHERS. THE INFORMATION WAS RESTRICTED TO WHAT FOODS THE CHILDREN LIKED AND DISLIKED, EXCEPT THAT A DETERMINATION OF THE QUANTITY OF MILK CONSUMED PER DAY BY EACH CHILD WAS ATTEMPTED. IN ADDITION, A 1-WEEK MENU FROM EACH HEAD START CENTER INVOLVED WAS ANALYZED TO CHECK ITS NUTRIENT SUFFICIENCY. THE DATA INDICATED THAT OVER 80 PERCENT OF ALL CHILDREN WERE REPORTED AS RECEIVING THREE OR MORE GLASSES OF MILK PER DAY. THERE WAS NO SIGNIFICANT DIFFERENCES IN PREFERENCES OF FOODS BETWEEN THE THREE GROUPS OF CHILDREN, NOR WERE THERE SIGNIFICANT DIFFERENCES IN THE MENUS OF HEAD START CENTERS IN THE THREE AREAS. THE MENUS WERE ALL SATISFACTORY. IT WAS CONCLUDED THAT IF THE CHILDREN RECEIVED THEIR PREFERRED FOOD FREQUENTLY, THEIR NUTRITIONAL NEEDS WOULD BE MET QUITE WELL, ALTHOUGH NO SUCH INDICATIONS OF CONSUMPTION QUANTITIES, OTHER THAN FOR MILK, WERE OBTAINED. A SHORT REPORT ON THE ANTHROPOMETRIC MEASUREMENTS OF HEAD START CHILDREN IS ALSO INCLUDED. (WD)

ED021645 PS001230
HEAD START EVALUATION AND RESEARCH CENTER, UNIVERSITY OF KANSAS. REPORT NO. IX, DEVELOPMENT OF "MATCHING" ABSTRACTIONS IN YOUNG CHILDREN. SHERMAN, JAMES A., 30 NOV 67 10P.
EDRS PRICE MF-$0.65 HC-$3.29

TWO 4-YEAR-OLD CHILDREN WERE SHOWN THE USE OF AN APPARATUS WHEREBY THEY COULD OBTAIN TOYS AND CANDY BY MAKING CERTAIN RESPONSES. THE APPARATUS WAS A MATCHING-TO-SAMPLE DEVICE ON WHICH WERE ARRANGED FIVE RESPONSE BUTTONS IN A CIRCLE AND ONE IN THE MIDDLE. EACH RESPONSE BUTTON HAD A DISPLAY WINDOW FOR THE STIMULUS. FOUR OF THE FIVE WINDOWS ON THE CIRCLE WERE LIGHTED, AND ONE CONTAINED A STIMULUS MATCHING THE CENTER STIMULUS. THE FIFTH WINDOW ON THE CIRCLE REMAINED DARK. DURING TRAINING, A MATCHING AND NONMATCHING CONDITION WAS ALTERNATELY REINFORCED. ONE STIMULUS WAS NEVER REINFORCED AND REPRESENTED A NEUTRAL STIMULUS. IT WAS FOUND THAT DURING REINFORCEMENT OF NOT MATCHING, NONMATCHING RESPONSES TO THE STIMULI INCREASED, EVEN FOR THE NEUTRAL STIMULUS. WHEN MATCHING WAS REINFORCED, MATCHING BEHAVIOR INCREASED FOR ALL FOUR STIMULI. ON THE BASIS OF THESE RESULTS, IT WAS CONCLUDED THAT RESPONSE GENERALIZATION WAS DEMONSTRATED. (WD)

ED021646 PS001231
HEAD START EVALUATION AND RESEARCH CENTER, UNIVERSITY OF KANSAS. REPORT NO. X, ENHANCEMENT OF THE SOCIAL REINFORCING VALUE OF A PRESCHOOL TEACHER. PADEN, LUCILE Y., 30 NOV 67 17P.
EDRS PRICE MF-$0.65 HC-$3.29

A TEACHER OF YOUNG CHILDREN MAY BE ABLE TO XERCISE CONTROL OVER HER PUPILS' BEHAVIOR BY TEMPORARILY ASSOCIATING HERSELF WITH TANGIBLE MEANS OF REINFORCEMENT. THIS STUDY INVESTIGATES WHETHER CONTINGENT (C) OR NONCONTINGENT (NC) TANGIBLE REINFORCEMENT IS MORE EFFECTIVE. FOUR HEAD START AND FOUR MIDDLE CLASS CHILDREN WERE USED AS SUBJECTS. THEIR TASK

WAS TO NAME PICTURE CARDS OF ANIMALS. A FIRST THE SUBJECTS RECEIVED ONLY SOCIAL REINFORCEMENT. IN THE C CONDITION THE CHILD WAS GIVEN THE CARD IF HE NAMED IT, AND UNDER THE NC CONDITION HE WAS JUST GIVEN SOME CARDS AT THE BEGINNING OF THE TASK. ON THE BASIS OF THE QUANTITY OF NONATTENDING BEHAVIOR DURING EACH CONDITION, IT WAS DETERMINED THAT THERE WAS NO SIGNIFICANT DIFFERENCE IN THE RESPONSES OF THE TWO GROUPS OF CHILDREN, THOUGH THE MIDDLE CLASS GROUP CONSISTENTLY RESPONDED LESS. THE C CONDITION APPEARED TO BE THE MOST EFFECTIVE OF THE THREE IN MINIMIZING PUPIL INATTENTION. BOTH FORMS OF TANGIBLE REINFORCEMENT ENHANCED THE TEACHER'S CONTROL. (WD)

ED021647 PS001232
HEAD START EVALUATION AND RESEARCH CENTER, UNIVERSITY OF KANSAS. REPORT NO. XI, VERBAL RECALL RESEARCH. HOROWITZ, FRANCES DEGEN; HOROWITZ, FLOYD R., 30 NOV 67 19P.
EDRS PRICE MF-$0.65 HC-$3.29

APPROXIMATELY 60 3-, 4-, AND 5-YEAR-OLD CHILDREN WERE ADMINISTERED A LANGUAGE TEST CONSTRUCTED TO DETERMINE THEIRLANGUAGE USAGE LEVELS AND LIMITATIONS. HALF OF THE CHILDREN WERE CLASSIFIED AS HEAD START AND HALF AS MIDDLE CLASS. THE LANGUAGE TEST INVOLVED THE PRESENTATION OF STRINGS OF THREE TO SEVEN PHONEMES ORGANIZED ON FIVE LEVELS OF INTELLIGIBILITY: (1) NONSENSE WORDS, (2) NONSENSE WORDS WITH A VERB IN THE MIDDLE OF THE STRING, (3) RECOGNIZABLE WORDS IN NONGRAMMATICAL FORM, (4) SIMPLE SENTENCES, AND (5) TRANSFORM SENTENCES; THAT IS, SENTENCES IN INTELLIGIBLE FORM BUT WHICH NECESSITATE TRANSFORMATION OF A WORD OR TWO TO BE GRAMATICALLY CORRECT, WHICH THE CHILD WAS THEN ASKED TO REPEAT BACK TO THE EXPERIMENTER. THE DATA FROM THIS STUDY HAS NOT YET BEEN COMPLETELY ANALYZED, BUT SOME TRENDS HAVE APPEARED. THE FIVE TYPES OF WORD FORMATIONS APPEAR TO REPRESENT A HIERARCHY, RELATED, IN TERMS OF THE CHILD'S ABILITY TO RECALL THEM, TO AGE. THAT IS, THE OLDER THE CHILD, THE MORE COMPLETE IS HIS RECALL OF WORDS IN HIGHER ORDER WORD FORMATIONS. FOR STRINGS OF NONSENSE WORDS, HOWEVER, THE 5-YEAR-OLDS DID NOT DO ANY BETTER THAN THE 3- AND 4-YEAR-OLDS. IT APPEARS THAT THE LANGUAGE ABILITY OF THE HEAD START CHILD ON THE EXPERIMENTAL TASK IS ABOUT ONE YEAR BEHIND THAT OF THE MIDDLE CLASS CHILD. (WD)

ED022526 PS001078
A COMPARISON OF WISC AND OSA IN ASSESSING THE INTELLIGENCE OF IMMIGRANT CHILDREN OF NON-ENGLISH SPEAKING BACKGROUND. A PILOT PROJECT. , [64] 16P.
EDRS PRICE MF-$0.65 HC-$3.29

TWENTY-FIVE ENGLISH SPEAKING AND TWENTY-FIVE NON-ENGLISH SPEAKING CANADIAN CHILDREN EQUATED ON SEX AND CHRONOLOGICAL AGE WERE GIVEN THE ONTARIO SCHOOL ABILITY (OSA) TEST AND THE PERFORMANCE SECTION OF THE WECHSLER INTELLIGENCE SCALE FOR CHILDREN (WISC). THE PILOT STUDY WAS CONDUCTED TO COMPARE THE ABILITY OF THE TWO TESTS TO ASSESS THE INTELLIGENCE LEVEL OF ENGLISH SPEAKING AND NON-ENGLISH SPEAKING CHILDREN. THE ONTARIO TEST HAD BEEN DEVELOPED ORIGINALLY TO DECIDE THE ELIGIBILITY OF CANDIDATES FOR ADMISSION TO THE ONTARIO SCHOOL FOR DEAF. BOTH GROUPS SCORED HIGHER ON THE OSA THAN ON WISC. RESULTS SHOWED THAT THE TWO TESTS DO NOT TAP THE SAME AREAS OF INTELLIGENCE; THEREFORE, SCORES ON THESE TESTS SHOULD NOT BE USED INTERCHANGEABLY. THE AGE AND BACKGROUND OF EACH CHILD SHOULD BE TAKEN INTO CONSIDERATION ALONG WITH TEST RESULTS. BECAUSE RESULTS OF THIS PILOT STUDY WERE INCONCLUSIVE, ADDITIONAL RESEARCH WITH A LARGER GROUP OF CHILDREN IS RECOMMENDED. (MS)

ED022527 PS001080
PROJECT HEAD START, THE URBAN AND RURAL CHALLENGE. FINAL REPORT. CHERTOW, DORIS S., APR 68 303P.
EDRS PRICE MF-$0.65 HC-$13.16

AN ANALYSIS OF TWO RURAL AND TWO URBAN HEAD START CENTERS IN THE STATE OF NEW YORK DURING THE SCHOOL YEAR 1966-67 ATTEMPTED TO FIND OUT IF RURAL-URBAN VARIABLES AFFECT THE ADMINISTRATION OF HEAD START PROGRAMS. THE FOUR PROGRAMS WERE COMPARED IN TERMS OF (1) COMMUNITY SOCIOECONOMIC CHARACTERISTICS, (2) ADMINISTRATIVE ORGANIZATION, (3) PUPIL RECRUITMENT, (4) STAFF, (5) PARENT INVOLVEMENT, AND, (6) FOLLOW THROUGH. DATA WERE COLLECTED DURING FIELD TRIP INTERVIEWS AND FROM EXAMINATIONS OF PROPOSALS AND OFFICE FILES AT THE CENTERS. ALL HEAD START PROGRAMS WERE NURSERY-SCHOOL, RATHER THAN ACADEMICALLY, ORIENTED. RESULTS INDICATED THAT URBAN BUREAUCRACY CAUSED DEPERSONALIZATION OF THE STAFF AND REQUIRED MORE WRITTEN REPORTS THAN SMALL RURAL ADMINISTRATIVE UNITS. HOWEVER, URBAN CENTERS HAD BETTER FACILITIES, A WIDER RANGE OF PERSONNEL FROM WHICH TO CHOOSE TEACHERS AND AIDES, AND A MORE HETEROGENEOUS POPULATION FROM WHICH TO RECRUIT CHILDREN THAN RURAL COUNTERPARTS. RURAL CENTERS SUFFERED FROM TRANSPORTATION PROBLEMS AND FROM UNAVAILABILITY OF SOCIAL, HEALTH, AND PSYCHOLOGICAL SERVICES. THE ADVANTAGES AND DISADVANTAGES OF HEAD START CENTERS BEING ATTACHED TO A PUBLIC SCHOOL SYSTEM ARE ALSO DISCUSSED IN THE REPORT. APPENDIX A IS AN INTERVIEW GUIDE USED IN THE STUDY. A BIBLIOGRAPHY IS INCLUDED. (MS)

ED022528 PS001081
SAN ANTONIO LANGUAGE RESEARCH PROJECT, 1965-66 (YEAR TWO) FINDINGS. ARNOLD, RICHARD D., JAN 68 100P.
EDRS PRICE MF-$0.65 HC-$3.29

A STUDY TO DETERMINE THE EFFECTS OF ORAL-AURAL TEACHING (INTENSIVE LANGUAGE INSTRUCTION) TECHNIQUES ON PUPILS' GAINS IN READING PROFICIENCY INVOLVED 1418 PUPILS. A SAMPLE OF FIRST GRADERS AND A SAMPLE OF SECOND GRADERS WERE EACH SUBDIVIDED INTO FOUR GROUPS. GROUP ONE WAS EXPOSED TO ORAL-AURAL TEACHING METHODS IN ENGLISH FOR THE PRESENTATION OF SCIENCE MATERIALS. GROUP TWO WAS TAUGHT THE SAME CONTENT IN ORAL-AURAL SPANISH. GROUP THREE RECEIVED THE SCIENCE CONTENT WITHOUT ORAL-AURAL METHODS, AND THE CONTROL GROUP, REPRESENTING A CROSS SECTION OF SOCIOECONOMIC LEVELS IN CONTRAST TO THE THREE DISADVANTAGED GROUPS, HAD NEITHER THE EXPERIMENTAL SCIENCE MATERIALS NOR THE ORAL-AURAL INSTRUCTION. PRETEST AND POSTTEST SCORES ON READING ACHIEVEMENT AND INTELLIGENCE FOR ALL GROUPS PROVIDED DATA TREATED BY ANALYSIS OF COVARIANCE. FINDINGS INDICATED NO SIGNIFICANT DIFFERENCE IN THE ORAL-AURAL METHOD IN THE SECOND GRADE. RESULTS FROM THE FIRST GRADE RATED THE ORAL-AURAL ENGLISH TREATMENT AS THE MOST SUCCESSFUL OF ALL. A POSSIBLE EXPLANATION OF THE DIFFERENCE IN SAMPLE RESULTS MAY BE THAT THE FIRST GRADE TEACHERS HAD HAD A YEAR'S EXPERIENCE WITH THE EXPERIMENTAL METHODS AND MATERIALS. THE DEVELOPMENT OF MORE APPROPRIATE EVALUATION INSTRUMENTS AND ADDITIONAL STUDY OF THE TEACHER VARIABLE ARE NEEDED. FOURTEEN TABLES AND A BIBLIOGRAPHY ARE INCLUDED. APPENDIX A SUMMARIZES THE STATISTICAL PROCEDURE, AND APPENDIX B GIVES THE STUDY'S STATISTICAL RESULTS. (MS)

ED022529 PS001082
HEAD START EVALUATION AND RESEARCH CENTER, BOSTON UNIVERSITY. REPORT OF RESEARCH, SEPTEMBER, 1966-AUGUST, 1967. GARFUNKEL, FRANK; AND OTHERS, 67 156P.
EDRS PRICE MF-$0.65 HC-$6.58

THIS DOCUMENT IS A REPORT OF RESEARCH CONDUCTED FROM SEPTEMBER 1966 TO AUGUST 1967 BY THE HEAD START EVALUATION AND RESEARCH CENTER OF BOSTON UNIVERSITY. ELEVEN STUDIES AND PROJECTS ARE REPORTED, MANY OF THEM IN PRELIMINARY OR INCOMPLETE FORM BECAUSE EITHER THEY ARE ONGOING STUDIES OR THE DATA ANALYSIS IS NOT FINISHED. THE 11 STUDIES CONTAIN SIX TOPICS. THESE TOPICS AND THE ACCESSION NUMBERS OF THE INDIVIDUAL ABSTRACTS ARE AS FOLLOWS: OBSERVATION OF TEACHING AND CURRICULUM (PA 001 250, PS 001 251, AND PS 001 252); EMOTIONAL DISTURBANCE OF HEAD START AND MIDDLE CLASS PRESCHOOL CHILDREN (PS 001 253); PERCEPTION AND SOCIAL VALUES (PS 001 254 AND PS 001 255); TEACHING PROGRAMS AND LEARNING (PS 001 256, PS 001 257, AND PS 001 258); NONPROFESSIONAL INTERVIEWS (PS 001 259); AND THE TEACHER SEMINAR (PS 001 260). (WD)

ED022530 PS001085
CHILDREARING ANTECEDENTS OF FLEXIBLE THINKING. BUSSE, THOMAS V., [67] 29P.
EDRS PRICE MF-$0.65 HC-$3.29

THE BEHAVIOR, ATTITUDES, AND SOCIAL CLASS OF 48 NEGRO MOTHERS AND 48 NEGRO FATHERS WERE RELATED TO THE DEVELOPMENT OF THEIR FIFTH GRADE BOYS' FLEXIBLE THINKING, DEFINED AS THE ABILITY TO CONSIDER ALTERNATIVE MEANS TO A GIVEN END. THE PARENTS WERE INTERVIEWED AT HOME AND ASKED TO TEACH THEIR SONS FOUR TASKS. LINEAR RELATIONSHIPS WERE FOUND LINKING FLEXIBLE THINKING WITH MOTHER COMMANDS, FATHER LOVE, FATHER TOTAL WORDS, SOCIAL CLASS, AND TWO FATHER FACTORS, "POWERLESSNESS VERSUS POWERFULNESS" AND "RIGID, ABSOLUTE VERSUS WARM, SYMPATHETIC STANDARDS." QUADRATIC RELATIONSHIPS WERE FOUND LINKING FLEXIBLE THINKING WITH MOTHER MANIPULATION, MOTHER COMMANDS, MOTHER POINTING, FATHER MANIPULATION, AND THREE FATHER FACTORS, "ACTIVE VERSUS IGNORING ROLE WITH CHILDREN," "DISCOURAGING VERSUS TOLERATING PHYSICAL AGGRESSION IN CHILDREN," AND "POWERLESSNESS VERSUS POWERFULNESS." (AUTHOR/JS)

ED022531 PS001102
THE YPSILANTI EARLY EDUCATION PROGRAM. KAMII, CONSTANCE; RADIN, NORMA, NOV 67 35P.
EDRS PRICE MF-$0.65 HC-$3.29

THIS 3-YEAR PROGRAM HAS THREE GOALS: (1) TO DEVISE A CURRICULUM FOR DISADVANTAGED 4-YEAR-OLDS, (2) TO DEVELOP A MODEL FOR INTRODUCING NEW CURRICULUMS INTO A SCHOOL SETTING, AND (3) TO DEVELOP PARENT GROUP-WORK PROGRAMS TO FOSTER ACHIEVEMENT, INNER CONTROL, AND COGNITIVE DEVELOPMENT IN THE CHILD. THE SAMPLE CONSISTS OF 50 NEGRO AND 50 WHITE (INCLUDING 50 BOYS AND 50 GIRLS) EACH YEAR. THE CURRICULUM INCLUDES WORK IN INNER CONTROL, IS BASED ON PIAGET'S OPERATIVE AND FIGURATIVE ASPECTS OF KNOWLEDGE, AND USES A MODIFIED BEREITER METHOD FOR LANGUAGE PATTERNING. THE SECOND GOAL WAS ACHIEVED BY INVOLVING THE TEACHERS IN CURRICULUM DEVELOPMENT AND USING A SUPERVISORY TEAM TO HELP TEACHERS EFFECTIVELY PRACTICE THE CURRICULUM THEORIES THROUGH AN ORIENTATION AND INSERVICE

TRAINING PROGRAM. IN THE PARENT GROUP-WORK PROGRAM, TWO EXPERIMENTAL GROUPS MET IN THREE SESSIONS STUDYING BEHAVIOR MODIFICATION, INNER CONTROL, AND COGNITIVE DEVELOPMENT. A CONTROL GROUP WENT TO P.T.A. MEETINGS ONLY. THE PROGRAM'S GOALS WILL BE EVALUATED ON ITS SHORT AND LONG TERM EFFECTS ON THE CHILDREN AND ITS GENERAL EFFECTS ON PARENTS. DISSEMINATION INCLUDES OBSERVATIONS, REPORTS, AND CONFERENCES. TABLES AND A BIBLIOGRAPHY ARE INCLUDED. (JS)

ED022532 PS001121

EARLY CHILDHOOD SELECTED BIBLIOGRAPHIES SERIES. NUMBER 1, PHYSICAL. , 68 25P.

EDRS PRICE MF-$0.65 HC-$3.29

THIS IS THE FIRST IN A SERIES OF SIX ANNOTATED BIBLIOGRAPHIES. IT HAS AS ITS GENERAL SUBJECT THE PHYSICAL ASPECTS OF EARLY CHILDHOOD EDUCATION AND INCLUDES THREE SUBDIVISIONS: GENETICS, SENSORY-MOTOR PROCESSES, AND GROWTH. EACH OF THE 15 ABSTRACTS INCLUDED HAS BEEN CLASSIFIED BY GENERAL AND SPECIFIC SUBJECT, BY FOCUS OF STUDY, AND ALPHABETICALLY BY AUTHOR. FOCUS OF STUDY CATEGORIES ARE NORMATIVE, ENVIRONMENTAL, MEASUREMENT AND TECHNIQUES, INTERVENTION, PATHOLOGY, PHYSIOLOGY, ANIMALS, AND GENERAL. STUDIES ARE DESCRIBED IN TERMS OF PROBLEM OR PURPOSE, METHOD, AND FINDINGS. THE GENERAL SUBJECTS OF OTHER BIBLIOGRAPHIES IN THE SERIES ARE LANGUAGE, EDUCATION, COGNITION, PERSONALITY, AND SOCIAL ASPECTS OF EARLY CHILDHOOD EDUCATION. (MS)

ED022533 PS001123

AN EXPERIMENTAL STUDY OF FORMAL READING INSTRUCTION AT THE KINDERGARTEN LEVEL. KELLEY, MARJORIE L.; CHEN, MARTIN K., [62] 6P.

EDRS PRICE MF-$0.65 HC-$3.29

FOR 4 MONTHS, 221 KINDERGARTEN CHILDREN TOOK PART IN A CONTROLLED EXPERIMENT ON THE EFFECTS OF TEACHING FORMAL READING AT THE KINDERGARTEN LEVEL. TEACHERS INVOLVED IN THE STUDY WERE JUDGED COMPARABLE IN EFFICIENCY AND ATTITUDES TOWARDS THE CHILDREN. THE CALIFORNIA TEST OF MENTAL MATURITY PRE-PRIMARY KINDERGARTEN 1 WAS ADMINISTERED TO HALF OF THE CHILDREN AND THE LEE CLARK READING READINESS TEST WAS GIVEN TO THE OTHER HALF. HIGH IQ, LOW IQ, HIGH READINESS, AND LOW READINESS GROUPS EMERGED. CHILDREN WERE RANDOMLY ASSIGNED TO FORMAL READING OR READINESS PROGRAMS. AT THE END OF THE SCHOOL YEAR THE CHILDREN WERE GIVEN THE CALIFORNIA READING TEST AND THE SCHOOL ATTITUDE INVENTORY. THE TEACHERS FILLED OUT RATING SCALES ON EACH CHILD'S ATTITUDE TOWARDS SCHOOL. RESULTS OF ANALYSIS OF VARIANCE OF THE DATA IMPLY THAT THE TWO TYPES OF INSTRUCTION OPERATED UNIFORMLY ON ALL FOUR CATEGORIES OF SUBJECTS. CHILDREN IN THE FORMAL READING PROGRAM SURPASSED CHILDREN IN THE READINESS INSTRUCTION PROGRAM IN READING SKILLS. ACCORDING TO TEACHERS' RATINGS, ATTITUDES TOWARDS SCHOOL AND READING WERE A FUNCTION OF INTELLIGENCE AND READING READINESS. HOWEVER, ON THE PUPIL SELF-REPORTING SCALE, CHILDREN IN THE READINESS GROUP HAD MORE FAVORABLE ATTITUDES TOWARDS SCHOOL. (MS)

ED022534 PS001124

THE HIERARCHICAL ORGANIZATION OF INTELLECTUAL STRUCTURES. WHITE, SHELDON H., DEC 66 13P.

EDRS PRICE MF-$0.65 HC-$3.29

A DISCUSSION OF THE ASSUMPTIONS ABOUT THE COMPOSITION OF INTELLIGENCE WHICH UNDERLIE PRESCHOOL INTERVENTION EFFORTS TODAY OFFERS THEORETICAL EVIDENCE OF A HIERARCHICAL ARRANGEMENT OF LEARNING PROCESSES. INTERNATIONAL STUDIES ON COGNITIVE DEVELOPMENT HAVE CONCLUDED THAT THE EMERGENCE OF SYMBOLIC OR CONCEPTUAL THOUGHT OCCURS AT A TRANSITIONAL AGE BETWEEN 5 AND 7 YEARS, WHEN THE CHILD NORMATIVELY SHOWS "READINESS" TO LEARN READING BY THE USUAL SCHOOL METHODS. COGNITIVE AND PSYCHOANALYTICAL THEORISTS APPEAR TO AGREE THAT A MORE MATURE LEVEL OF COGNITIVE AND EMOTIONAL ORGANIZATION IS SUPERIMPOSED UPON A MORE JUVENILE LEVEL, THE LATTER BEING INHIBITED AT THIS TIME. A CONCISE REVIEW OF THE BEHAVIORAL DEVELOPMENT LITERATURE SUPPORTS THIS GENERAL THEORY. IN ADDITION, THE RANGE AND DIVERSITY OF BEHAVIORAL CHANGES BETWEEN 5 AND 7 SEEM TO REFLECT THE IMPACT OF SCHOOLING. THE FOLLOWING QUESTION NEEDS INVESTIGATION: IF THE NECESSARY MATURATION CAN BE ADVANCED OR RETARDED BY ENVIRONMENTAL STIMULATION, SHOULD A PRESCHOOL GOAL BE TO ADVANCE THE TIME OF TRANSITION? THE IMPLICATIONS FOR EDUCATIONAL PROGRAMS ARE APPARENT. ONE EXAMPLE IS THE NEED FOR SOME MEASUREMENT OTHER THAN IQ CHANGES IN EVALUATING PRESCHOOL PROGRAM OUTCOMES. (MS)

ED022535 PS001125

THE EFFECT OF EARLY STIMULATION: THE PROBLEM OF FOCUS IN DEVELOPMENTAL STIMULATION. FOWLER, WILLIAM, 16 FEB 67 19P.

EDRS PRICE MF-$0.65 HC-$3.29

STUDIES OF THE EFFECT OF ENVIRONMENTAL STIMULATION ON AN INDIVIDUAL'S DEVELOPMENT IN EITHER GENERAL OR SPECIFIC ABILITY CONCLUDE THAT SOME SPECIFIC STIMULATION SHOULD BE INTRODUCED AT AN EARLY AGE WHILE A CHILD IS STILL MALLEABLE. AN INTENSE, PERSISTENT, AND REGULAR TUTORIAL APPROACH WITHIN THE FAMILY ENCOURAGES THE DEVELOPMENT OF A SPECIAL TALENT OR ABILITY AND DEVELOPS LEARNING SETS USEFUL IN THE FUTURE. A CHILD MUST LEARN THE SPECIALIZED SYMBOLIC LANGUAGE OF THE AREA IN WHICH HE IS BEING TRAINED, SUCH AS IN MUSIC OR MATHEMATICS. STUDIES HAVE SHOWN THAT PERSONS WHO EXCEL IN ONE FIELD MAY SHOW VERY LITTLE COMPETENCE IN OTHERS. GENERAL ABILITY IS PRESENT BUT CONCENTRATION IN THE SYMBOLIC LANGUAGE AND WORK PRODUCTION IN ONE SPECIFIC AREA IS REFLECTED IN LESS LEARNING IN OTHER AREAS. SIMILARLY, IF A FAMILY OR SCHOOL ENVIRONMENT ENCOURAGES YOUNG CHILDREN TO RESPOND TO CERTAIN STIMULATION WHICH DIRECTS THEIR ENERGIES AND TIME IN A PARTICULAR WAY, THESE SAME CHILDREN MAY DO LESS WELL ON IQ TESTS MEASURING GENERAL ABILITY BUT VERY WELL ON TESTS OF SPECIFIC ABILITIES. HOW MUCH TRAINING IN CERTAIN SYMBOLIC LANGUAGES AND CONCEPTS IS TRANSFERRED TO GENERAL COGNITIVE FUNCTIONING IS AS YET UNKNOWN. ENVIRONMENTAL STIMULATION IS A MEANS OF DEVELOPING THE GREATEST POTENTIAL ABILITIES IN ANY INDIVIDUAL. (MS)

ED022536 PS001129

THE TWO YEAR OLD. BAYLEY, NANCY, [66] 65P.

EDRS PRICE MF-$0.65 HC-$3.29

THIS STUDY ATTEMPTED TO FIND WHICH FACTORS DETERMINE THE COURSE OF MENTAL GROWTH. THE HYPOTHESES WERE AS FOLLOWS: (1) EARLY GROWTH RATES ARE RAPID, CHAOTIC, AND UNEVEN; (2) INTELLECTUAL FUNCTIONS BECOME MORE COMPLEX AT AGE 2; (3) LANGUAGE IS OF OVERRIDING IMPORTANCE IN INTELLECTUAL GROWTH; (4) MORE DEVELOPED INDIVIDUALS HAVE A LONGER INFANCY PERIOD BUT ACCELERATE LATER; (5) EFFECTS OF ENVIRONMENT ARE MANIFEST AT AGE 2; AND (6) PARENTAL WARMTH IS IMPORTANT FOR HEALTHY DEVELOPMENT. A REVIEW OF THE BERKELEY GROWTH STUDIES AND RELATED STUDIES SHOWED THAT (1) EARLY MENTAL GROWTH RATES ARE UNEVEN BUT NOT CHAOTIC; (2) GENETIC FACTORS ARE IMPORTANT IN DETERMINING INTELLECTUAL CAPACITY, AND AROUND AGE 2 THE NATURE OF MENTAL FUNCTIONS BECOME MORE COMPLEX; (3) MATERNAL ATTITUDES AFFECT MENTAL SCORES DIFFERENTLY, BEFORE AND AFTER AGE 2; AND (4) WITH RETARDED CHILDREN, LACK OF LANGUAGE (AND, THEREFORE, COMMUNICATION) AND A NONSTIMULATING ENVIRONMENT CAN RETARD MENTAL GROWTH. IT WAS CONCLUDED THAT MANY FACTORS WHICH AFFECT MENTAL GROWTH CONVERGE AT AGE 2. FURTHER RESEARCH, HOWEVER, IS NEEDED TO IDENTIFY AND SPECIFY THE NATURE OF THE PROCESSES OF THESE FACTORS. NUMEROUS TABLES AND A BIBLIOGRAPHY ARE INCLUDED. (JS)

ED022537 PS001132

A COMPARISON OF THE PSYCHOLINGUISTIC FUNCTIONING OF "EDUCATIONALLY-DEPRIVED" AND "EDUCATIONALLY-ADVANTAGED" CHILDREN. BARRITT, LOREN S.; AND OTHERS, [65] 16P.

EDRS PRICE MF-$0.65 HC-$3.29

A STUDY WAS CONDUCTED TO DELINEATE THE QUALITATIVE DIFFERENCES IN THE LANGUAGE ABILITIES OF TWO DISADVANTAGED GROUPS AND ONE ADVANTAGED GROUP OF KINDERGARTEN AND FIRST GRADE CHILDREN WHO WERE TESTED ON THE ILLINOIS TEST OF PSYCHOLINGUISTIC ABILITIES. (AS PART OF A LARGER STUDY, THE PRESENT REPORT DEALS ONLY WITH A PART OF THE PRETEST PHASE.) SCORES WERE COMPARED, AND AN ANALYSIS OF PROFILE SIMILARITIES SHOWED THAT GROUPS WERE MOST SIMILAR ON SUBTESTS REQUIRING SEQUENTIAL HABITS. THE GREATEST PERFORMANCE DISCREPANCIES AMONG THE GROUPS OCCURRED ON THE ANALOGS, VOCABULARY, AND GRAMMAR SUBTESTS. RESULTS INDICATE THAT STRONG SYNTACTIC HABITS ARE CHARACTERISTIC OF HIGHER-LEVEL FUNCTIONING AND THAT SEQUENTIAL LANGUAGE HABITS ARE CHARACTERISTIC OF MORE PRIMITIVE LEVELS OF LANGUAGE ABILITY. TWO HYPOTHESES ARE PROPOSED IN EXPLANATION OF THE STUDY RESULTS: (1) PERFORMANCE ON SEQUENTIAL TESTS IS DEPENDENT ON THE RELATIVELY FIXED CAPACITY OF A SUBJECT'S SHORT-TERM MEMORY, WHILE OTHER SUBTESTS REQUIRE THE ABILITY TO "STRUCTURE" LEARNING WHICH IS RELATIVELY MORE DEPENDENT UPON EXPERIENCE; AND (2) SINCE THE EDUCATIONALLY-DEPRIVED CHILDREN HAVE NOT DEVELOPED THE HIGHER-LEVEL FACILITY WITH THEIR LANGUAGE, THEY ARE RELATIVELY FREE FROM HYPOTHESES ABOUT LEARNING TASKS. (MS)

ED022538 PS001134
EARLY CHILDHOOD SELECTED BIBLIOGRAPHIES SERIES. NUMBER 2, LANGUAGE. , 68 47P.
EDRS PRICE MF-$0.65 HC-$3.29

THIS IS THE SECOND IN A SERIES OF SIX ANNOTATED BIBLIOGRAPHIES. IT HAS AS ITS GENERAL SUBJECT THE LANGUAGE ASPECTS OF EARLY CHILDHOOD EDUCATION AND INCLUDES SIX SUBDIVISIONS: PHONOLOGY AND SPEECH, GRAMMAR, VOCABULARY, FUNCTIONS OF LANGUAGE, VERBAL LEARNING, AND "ALL." EACH OF THE 38 ABSTRACTS INCLUDED HAS BEEN CLASSIFIED BY GENERAL AND SPECIFIC SUBJECT, BY FOCUS OF STUDY, AND ALPHABETICALLY BY AUTHOR. FOCUS OF STUDY CATEGORIES ARE NORMATIVE, ENVIRONMENTAL, MEASUREMENT AND TECHNIQUES, INTERVENTION, PATHOLOGY, PHYSIOLOGY, ANIMALS, AND GENERAL. THE GENERAL SUBJECTS OF OTHER BIBLIOGRAPHIES IN THE SERIES ARE PHYSICAL, EDUCATION, COGNITION, PERSONALITY AND SOCIAL ASPECTS OF EARLY CHILDHOOD EDUCATION. (MS)

ED022539 PS001152
A STUDY OF LANGUAGE DEVELOPMENT FROM INFANCY TO AGE 5. MCGEE, DONALD, MAR 68 18P.
EDRS PRICE MF-$0.65 HC-$3.29

CONCEPTUAL MODELS OF LANGUAGE LEARNING AND LANGUAGE USE WERE MADE BY A COMMITTEE OF SCHOOL PERSONNEL INTERESTED IN INVESTIGATING LEARNING DIFFERENCES IN PRESCHOOL LANGUAGE DEVELOPMENT, EVEN THOUGH PUBLIC SCHOOL SYSTEMS DO NOT AS YET INCLUDE PRESCHOOL CLASSES. NORMATIVE INFORMATION WAS COLLECTED FROM VARIOUS RESEARCH SOURCES AND CLASSIFIED. DISCUSSIONS OF MODEL FORMATION CONSIDERED THE RELATIONSHIP OF LANGUAGE TO COGNITIVE DEVELOPMENT, THE RELATIONSHIP OF CRITICAL LEARNING TIMES TO SENSORY AND LANGUAGE DEVELOPMENT, LINGUISTICS, AND THE SPECIFICATION OF LISTENING BEHAVIORS CRUCIAL TO LANGUAGE DEVELOPMENT. LINGUISTIC INVESTIGATIONS BECAME A MAJOR FOCUS. SINCE THE SENSORY, PSYCHOMOTOR, AFFECTIVE AND COGNITIVE AREAS OF HUMAN DEVELOPMENT AFFECT LANGUAGE ACQUISITION, THESE AREAS WERE INCLUDED IN THE LANGUAGE ANALYSIS. A BIBLIOGRAPHY IS INCLUDED, AND APPENDIXES ILLUSTRATE THE MODELS AND SHOW THE CLASSIFICATIONS OF THE DATA. (MS)

ED022540 PS001155
SOME EFFECTS OF SOCIAL CLASS AND RACE ON CHILDREN'S LANGUAGE AND INTELLECTUAL ABILITIES. WHITEMAN, MARTIN; AND OTHERS, 65 31P.
EDRS PRICE MF-$0.65 HC-$3.29

A CROSS-SECTIONAL STUDY OF 292 FIRST AND FIFTH GRADE NEGRO AND WHITE CHILDREN EXAMINED THE RELATIONSHIP BETWEEN ENVIRONMENTAL FACTORS AND PERFORMANCE TEST SCORES OF VERBAL AND COGNITIVE ABILITY. THE SOCIOECONOMIC STATUS (SES) OF EACH SUBJECT WAS DETERMINED AND INCLUDED IN A DEPRIVATION INDEX FORMED BY OBTAINING A COMPOSITE SCORE FOR EACH SUBJECT ACROSS SIX BACKGROUND VARIABLES: HOUSING DILAPIDATION, PARENTAL EDUCATIONAL ASPIRATIONS, NUMBER OF CHILDREN UNDER 18, DINNER CONVERSATION, WEEKEND CULTURAL EXPERIENCES, AND ATTENDANCE OF CHILD IN KINDERGARTEN. THE TWO DEPENDENT VARIABLES WERE A NONLANGUAGE TEST OF GENERAL INTELLECTUAL ABILITY, THE LORGE-THORNDIKE INTELLIGENCE TEST, AND THE VOCABULARY SUBTEST OF WECHSLER'S INTELLIGENCE SCALE FOR CHILDREN. DATA WAS TREATED BY A THREE WAY ANALYSIS OF VARIANCE. RESULTS INDICATED THAT THE DEPRIVATION INDEX ACTED AS A FACTOR INDEPENDENT OF SES AND RACE IN CONTRIBUTING TO VARIATION IN TEST PERFORMANCE. OLDER CHILDREN SCORED LOWER THAN YOUNGER ONES, INDICATING THAT DEFICIT IS PROGRESSIVE. ENVIRONMENT, HOWEVER, CAN OFFSET DEFICITS. NEGRO STATUS AND LOWER SES ARE ASSOCIATED , SO THE NEGRO CHILD IS TWICE DISADVANTAGED. PRESCHOOL INTERVENTION MAY BE ABLE TO PREVENT ACCUMULATION OF DEFICITS EARLY IN THE CHILD'S LIFE. (MS)

ED022541 PS001160
PRE-SCHOOL RESEARCH AND EVALUATION PROJECT. STARKWEATHER, ELIZABETH KEZIA, NOV 66 58P.
EDRS PRICE MF-$0.65 HC-$3.29

A RESEARCH PROJECT WAS CONDUCTED TO STUDY THE EFFECTS OF AN 8-WEEK PREKINDERGARTEN ENRICHMENT PROGRAM AND OF TWO 15-MONTH PRESCHOOL ENRICHMENT PROGRAMS. PRETEST AND POSTTEST SCORES OF EXPERIMENTAL AND CONTROL KINDERGARTEN CHILDREN (A SAMPLE OF 100 OUT OF 1,000 SUBJECTS) SHOWED THAT BOTH GROUPS MADE SIGNIFICANT GAINS IN ALL ABILITY CATEGORIES O F THE CALDWELL PRESCHOOL INVENTORY (CPI). THE EXPERIMENTAL GROUP MADE SIGNIFICANTLY GREATER GAINS IN NUMERICAL CONCEPT ACTIVATION. IN THE PRESCHOOL STUDY (100 CHILDREN), SUBJECTS IN BOTH EXPERIMENTAL GROUPS MADE GREATER GAINS IN VERBAL ABILITY (PEABODY PICTURE VOCABULARY TEST) THAN THE CONTROL GROUP. ON THE CPI, CHILDREN IN ONE PROGRAM GAINED IN AREAS OF PERSONAL SOCIAL RESPONSIVENESS AND SENSORY CONCEPT ACTIVATION, WHILE CHILDREN IN THE SECOND PROGRAM GAINED IN BOTH AREAS OF CONCEPT ACTIVATION, SENSORY AND NUMERICAL. PRESCHOOL CHILDREN IN BOTH PROGRAMS MADE GREATER ACHIEVEMENT GAINS THAN DID CONTROL CHILDREN. IT IS POSSIBLE THAT GREATER MOTIVATION TO LEARN WAS FOSTERED BY THE ENRICHMENT PROGRAM. ABOUT 2/3 OF THIS REPORT IS MADE UP OF APPENDIXES OF TABLES AND OF FORMS USED IN THE STUDY. (MS)

ED022542 PS001163
PROBLEMS AND PROSPECTS OF EDUCATION IN THE BIG CITIES AS EXEMPLIFIED BY PITTSBURGH, PENNSYLVANIA. MARLAND, SIDNEY P., 68 15P.
EDRS PRICE MF-$0.65 HC-$3.29
AVAILABLE FROM: UNIVERSITY OF ILLINOIS PRESS, URBANA, ILL. 61801 ($0.35)

RACIAL INTEGRATION AND COMPENSATORY EDUCATION MUST BE USED TO SOLVE THE PROBLEMS IN THE BIG CITIES. A LITTLE BOY OR A LITTLE GIRL WHO GROWS UP FEELING DIFFERENT FROM OTHER PEOPLE AND IS UNABLE TO HAVE ACCESS TO SOLUTIONS THAT WOULD LIFT HIM OUT OF HIS EXCLUDED AND ISOLATED WAY OF LIFE HAS EVERY REASON TO BE SICK, TO BE DESPERATE, TO BE INCOMPLETE AS A HUMAN BEING. COMPENSATORY PROGRAMS SUCH AS TEAM TEACHING, TRANSITION ROOMS, PREPRIMARY EDUCATION (INCLUDING PARENTAL PREPRIMARY COUNSELING), AND EXPECTANT UNWED MOTHERS' PROGRAMS CAN GIVE AID TO THE MEMBERS OF SOCIETY WHO NEED THE EXTRA HELP. FURTHERMORE, IT WILL TAKE ONE GENERATION BEFORE REHABILITATIVE RESULTS CAN BE SEEN. (JS)

ED022543 PS001164
USING MUSIC WITH HEAD START CHILDREN. GRIFFIN, LOUISE, 68 25P.
EDRS PRICE MF-$0.65 HC-$3.29

THIS PAMPHLET DESCRIBES THE FUNCTION OF MUSIC IN HEAD START PROGRAMS. SUGGESTIONS ARE MADE TO HELP CHILDREN SENSE MOTION AND DEVELOP THEIR SELF-CONCEPTS AND MOTOR COORDINATION SKILLS THROUGH RHYTHMIC SONGS AND ACTIVITIES. THE CONSTRUCTION AND USE OF RHYTHM INSTRUMENTS ARE SUGGESTED AS A MEANS OF INVOLVING MOTHERS IN HEAD START PROGRAMS. CERTAIN TYPES OF SONGS ARE DESCRIBED AS AIDS IN TEACHING LANGUAGE DEVELOPMENT. LISTENING TO MUSIC IS SUGGESTED AS A STIMULUS TO DEVELOP AUDITORY DISCRIMINATION. A FEW POSITIVE AND NEGATIVE SUGGESTIONS ARE GIVEN TO TEACHERS, AND A SHORT SECTION EMPHASIZES THAT A TEACHER'S LACK OF APPLIED MUSIC TRAINING DOES NOT PREVENT SUCCESSFUL TEACHING. ALONG WITH AN EXTENSIVE BIBLIOGRAPHY OF RECORDINGS, BACKGROUND READING, AND RESOURCE AND SONG BOOKS, A LIST OF MUSIC PUBLISHERS AND SUPPLIERS AND THEIR ADDRESSES IS APPENDED. (JS)

ED022544 PS001165
BIBLIOGRAPHY, EARLY CHILDHOOD EDUCATION. , AUG 68 11P.
EDRS PRICE MF-$0.65 HC-$3.29

THE 124 PROFESSIONAL BOOKS LISTED IN THIS BIBLIOGRAPHY WERE SELECTED BY A COMMITTEE OF U. S. OMEP NATIONAL COMMITTEE MEMBERS FROM BALTIMORE, MARYLAND. IT WAS THE INTENTION OF THE COMMITTEE TO PRESENT A REPRESENTATIVE SAMPLING OF DIFFERENT POINTS OF VIEW AS WELL AS A SAMPLING OF THE WIDE VARIETY OF PROFESSIONAL MATERIALS AVAILABLE IN THE UNITED STATES TO THOSE WHO ARE CONCERNED WITH THE EDUCATION AND WELFARE OF YOUNG CHILDREN. (JS)

ED022545 PS001166
PLAY BEHAVIOR IN THE YEAR-OLD INFANT: EARLY SEX DIFFERENCES. GOLDBERG, SUSAN; AND OTHERS, 67 8P.
EDRS PRICE MF-$0.65 HC-$3.29

THE PURPOSE OF THIS STUDY WAS TO DETERMINE IF SEX DIFFERENCES WERE OBSERVABLE IN 1-YEAR-OLDS IN RESPONSE TO THEIR MOTHER AND IN CHOICE AND STYLE OF PLAY WITH TOYS. THIRTY-TWO BOYS AND THIRTY-TWO GIRLS WERE PUT IN SEPARATE ROOMS WITH SEVERAL TOYS, SEVERAL NONTOYS (DOOR KNOBS, TAPED SOCKETS, ETC.) AND THEIR MOTHERS. THE INFANT'S MOTHER WAS TO OBSERVE THE CHILD IN PLAY AND RESPOND AS SHE DESIRED. OBSERVATION WAS CONDUCTED FROM ANOTHER ROOM. EARLIER IN THE STUDY, THE MOTHER'S TOUCHING BEHAVIOR OF THE 6-MONTH-OLD INFANT WAS OBSERVED. THE RESULTS SHOWED THAT AT 1 YEAR, BOYS WERE MORE INDEPENDENT OF THEIR MOTHERS THAN WERE THE GIRLS, WHO TOUCHED THEIR MOTHERS AND VOCALIZED MORE FREQUENTLY. BOYS DEMONSTRATED MORE EXPLORATORY PLAY AND BANGING OF TOYS THAN THE SEDATE AND QUIET PLAYING GIRLS. IT WAS SHOWN THAT THE BOYS' DEPENDENCE WAS DIRECTLY PROPORTIONATE TO THE AMOUNT OF TOUCHING AT 6 MONTH'S OLD GIVEN BY THE MOTHER. FOR GIRLS, A CURVILINEAR SCALE RESULTED. GIRLS WHO WERE TOUCHED MODERATELY WERE MORE INDEPENDENT THAN THOSE TOUCHED GREATLY OR VERY LITTLE. IT WAS CONCLUDED THAT THE CHILD'S INDEPENDENCE WAS INFLUENCED BY THE MOTHER'S BEHAVIOR TOWARD THE CHILD AT AN EARLIER AGE. FROM THE RESULTS OF TOY PLAY BEHAVIOR, IT WAS CONCLUDED THAT PARENTS REINFORCED SEX ROLE BEHAVIOR IN THE 1-YEAR-OLD AND LATER THE CHILD INTERNALIZED SUCH ROLES. (JS)

ED022546 PS001172
EARLY CHILDHOOD SELECTED BIBLIOGRAPHIES SERIES. NUMBER 3, EDUCATION. , 68 29P.
EDRS PRICE MF-$0.65 HC-$3.29

THIS IS THE THIRD IN A SERIES OF SIX ANNOTATED BIBLIOGRAPHIES. IT HAS AS ITS GENERAL SUBJECT THE EDUCATIONAL ASPECTS OF EARLY CHILDHOOD AND INCLUDES THREE SUBDIVISIONS: CHILD-REARING PRACTICES, SCHOOL PERFORMANCE, AND EFFECTS OF NURSERY SCHOOL AND DAY CARE. EACH OF THE 11 ABSTRACTS INCLUDED HAS BEEN CLASSIFIED BY GENERAL AND SPECIFIC SUBJECT, BY FOCUS OF STUDY, AND ALPHABETICALLY BY AUTHOR. FOCUS OF STUDY CATEGORIES ARE NORMATIVE, ENVIRONMENTAL, MEASUREMENT AND TECHNIQUES, INTERVENTION, PATHOLOGY, PHYSIOLOGY, ANIMALS, AND GENERAL. THE GENERAL SUBJECTS OF OTHER BIBLIOGRAPHIES IN THE SERIES ARE PHYSICAL, LANGUAGE, COGNITION, PERSONALITY, AND SOCIAL ASPECTS OF EARLY CHILDHOOD EDUCATION. (MS)

ED022547 PS001187
EDUCATIONAL SPECIFICATIONS FOR PIEDMONT ELEMENTARY SCHOOL. , 68 60P.
EDRS PRICE MF-$0.65 HC-$3.29

A REPORT WAS MADE ON THE DESIGN, GOALS, FACILITIES, AND PERSONNEL OF AN INNOVATIVE ELEMENTARY SCHOOL PLANNED TO SERVE AS A DEMONSTRATION MODEL. THE EDUCATION PROGRAM IS DESCRIBED IN TERMS OF OBJECTIVES, PROGRAM ELEMENTS, PERSONNEL, ORGANIZATION, CONTENT, MATERIALS AND EQUIPMENT, METHODS, ACTIVITIES, AND EVALUATION. ADDITIONAL TOPICS CONSIDERED ARE: THE STUDENTS AND AREA TO BE SERVED, THE NATURE OF THE SCHOOL SITE, THE COST OF THE PROJECT, INSTRUCTIONAL SPACES, ADMINISTRATIVE AND SERVICE FACILITIES, FOOD SERVICE FACILITIES, CUSTODIAL AND ENGINEERING ROOMS, THE FACULTY LOUNGE, AND SITE DEVELOPMENT. (MS)

ED022548 PS001188
SKILL GAMES FOR MATHEMATICS. CORLE, CLYDE G., 68 49P.
DOCUMENT NOT AVAILABLE FROM EDRS.
AVAILABLE FROM: INSTRUCTOR HANDBOOK SERIES #372, F. A. OWEN PUBLISHING CO., DANSVILLE, N.Y., 14437

THIS GUIDE IS TO ASSIST TEACHERS WITH MOTIVATIONAL IDEAS FOR TEACHING ELEMENTARY SCHOOL MATHEMATICS. THE ITEMS INCLUDED ARE A WIDE VARIETY OF GAMES (PAPER AND PENCIL, VERBAL, AND PHYSICAL), JINGLES, CONTESTS, TEACHING DEVICES, AND THOUGHT PROVOKING EXERCISES. SUGGESTIONS FOR SELECTION OF MATHEMATICAL GAMES ARE OFFERED. THE DEVICES ARE USED TO EXPLAIN THEORY OF SETS, COUNTING AND NUMERATION, COMPUTATION, THE NUMBER LINE, FRACTIONS, MEASUREMENTS, AND GEOMETRY. INCLUDED IN THE GUIDE IS A BRIEF INDEX. (JS)

ED022549 PS001235
THE DEVELOPMENT OF FORMS OF THE NEGATIVE. LAVATELLI, CELIA B., ED., [67] 7P.
EDRS PRICE MF-$0.65 HC-$3.29

TO MEASURE THE EFFECTIVENESS OF AN INTERVENTION PROGRAM OF LANGUAGE DEVELOPMENT, IT IS NECESSARY TO UNDERSTAND CHILDRENS' KNOWLEDGE AND USE OF GRAMMATICAL STRUCTURES. IN BOTH STANDARD AND DIALECTAL ENGLISH, GRAMMAR RULES ARE LEARNED WITHOUT FORMAL INSTRUCTION FOR FORMING THE NEGATIVE, INTERROGATIVE, AND OTHER PARTS OF SPEECH. A MENTAL TRANSFORMATION TAKES PLACE WHEN A STATEMENT IS CONVERTED TO A QUESTION. SINCE THE RELATIONSHIP BETWEEN THOUGHT AND LANGUAGE IS REFLECTED BY CHANGES IN GRAMMAR, THESE ARE OF PSYCHOLOGICAL IMPORTANCE TO LEARNING AND INTELLECTUAL ABILITY. A RECENT DOCTORAL STUDY IS CITED WHICH DESCRIBES THE DEVELOPMENT OF FORMS OF THE NEGATIVE IN THE LANGUAGE OF THREE CHILDREN. (MS)

ED022550 PS001238
HEAD START EVALUATION AND RESEARCH CENTER, THE UNIVERSITY OF CHICAGO. REPORT A, MATERNAL INFLUENCES UPON DEVELOPMENT OF COGNITION. HESS, ROBERT D.; SHIPMAN, VIRGINIA C., 30 NOV 67 68P.
EDRS PRICE MF-$0.65 HC-$3.29

THIS PROJECT WAS DESIGNED TO FOLLOW UP A GROUP OF 163 MOTHERS AND THEIR 4-YEAR-OLD CHILDREN, WHO WERE SUBJECTS IN A STUDY OF THE DIFFERENTIAL EFFECTS OF MIDDLE CLASS AND LOWER CLASS COGNITIVE ENVIRONMENTS ON NEGRO URBAN PRESCHOOL CHILDREN. THE OBJECTIVES OF THE FOLLOWUP PROJECT WERE: (1) THE EXPANSION OF THE INVESTIGATION OF COGNITIVE INPUT FEATURES OF THE HOME, (2) THE PREDICTION OF THE CHILD'S COGNITIVE DEVELOPMENT AND SCHOOL ACHIEVEMENT DURING HIS FIRST 3 YEARS OF SCHOOL FROM PRESCHOOL DATA, AND (3) THE LONGITUDINAL ANALYSIS OF THE GROWTH OF COGNITIVE ABILITIES OVER THESE YEARS. THE DATA OF THIS PROJECT WAS OBTAINED BY PRESENTING TO THE CHILD TESTS MEASURING COGNITIVE ABILITIES, IMPULSIVITY, AND READING READINESS; AND, TO THE MOTHER, TESTS MEASURING HER ATTITUDES ABOUT SCHOOL, HER INTELLIGENCE LEVEL, AND HER FLEXIBILITY OF THOUGHT. BECAUSE OF THE LONGITUDINAL NATURE OF THE FOLLOWUP PROJECT, THE DATA ANALYSIS IS NOT YET COMPLETE. AVAILABLE RESULTS INDICATE THAT SOME OF THE TESTS, LIKE KAGAN'S MEASURE OF REFLECTIVENESS, DISCRIMINATE BETWEEN MOTHERS ACCORDING TO SOCIAL CLASS, WHILE SOME OF THE OTHER TESTS DO NOT. THE SAME EFFECT HAS BEEN FOUND FOR THE TESTS ADMINISTERED TO THE CHILDREN. DATA ANALYSIS OF THE RELATIONSHIP BETWEEN HOME ENVIRONMENT AND CHILD PERFORMANCE IN SCHOOL WAS NOT YET COMPLETE. AN APPENDIX CONTAINING DESCRIPTIONS OF TESTS USED IN THE PROJECT FOLLOWS THE REPORT. (WD)

ED022551 PS001239
HEAD START EVALUATION AND RESEARCH CENTER, THE UNIVERSITY OF CHICAGO. REPORT B, MATERNAL ANTECEDENTS OF INTELLECTUAL ACHIEVEMENT BEHAVIORS IN LOWER CLASS PRESCHOOL CHILDREN. HESS, ROBERT D.; SHIPMAN, VIRGINIA C., 30 NOV 67 27P.
EDRS PRICE MF-$0.65 HC-$3.29

THE PURPOSE OF THIS RESEARCH WAS TO DETERMINE TO WHAT EXTENT YOUNG LOWER CLASS NEGRO CHILDREN'S ACTUAL ACHIEVEMENTS IN THE MIDDLE CLASS SCHOOL SETTING ARE INFLUENCED BY MATERNAL BEHAVIOR AND ATTITUDES. NINETY NEGRO CHILDREN, FROM 53 TO 66 MONTHS OF AGE, PLUS THEIR MOTHERS, WERE SELECTED AS THE RESEARCH SAMPLE. INTERVIEWS WERE CONDUCTED WITH THE MOTHERS TO DISCOVER AND ASSESS THEIR BEHAVIORS CONSIDERED RELEVANT IN INFLUENCING THE SCHOOL PERFORMANCE OF THEIR CHILDREN. THE MIDDLE CLASS SCHOOL SETTING IN WHICH THE CHILDREN WERE PLACED WAS A SUMMER PRESCHOOL PROGRAM. DURING THIS PROGRAM THE ABILITY OF THE CHILDREN WAS TESTED AND RATED. THESE MEASURES OF THE CHILDREN'S ACHIEVEMENT WERE INTERRELATED TO THE MATERNAL BEHAVIOR DATA. IT WAS FOUND THAT MOTHERS WITH HIGH MATERNAL INDIVIDUATION (THAT IS, MOTHERS HIGH IN ACTIVE AND ANALYTICAL BEHAVIOR) HAD A MORE SIGNIFICANT POSITIVE INFLUENCE ON THE ACHIEVEMENT OF THEIR CHILDREN. TWO OTHER MATERNAL BEHAVIORS THAT APPEARED TO CONTRIBUTE SIGNIFICANTLY TO THEIR CHILDREN'S ACHIEVEMENT IN SCHOOL WERE (1) OPEN COMMUNICATION BETWEEN MOTHER AND CHILD AND (2) DEGREE OF SOCIAL ISOLATION OF THE MOTHER. (WD)

ED022552 PS001240
HEAD START EVALUATION AND RESEARCH CENTER, THE UNIVERSITY OF CHICAGO. REPORT C, COGNITIVE INTERACTION BETWEEN TEACHER AND PUPIL IN A PRESCHOOL SETTING. HESS, ROBERT D.; SHIPMAN, VIRGINIA C., 30 NOV 67 15P.
EDRS PRICE MF-$0.65 HC-$3.29

THIS PROGRESS REPORT DESCRIBES THE METHOD USED IN ACQUIRING THE VERBAL BEHAVIOR OF TEACHERS DURING CLASS TIME. THE METHOD OF ACQUIRING THIS DATA IS AN IMPORTANT PART OF THE LARGER STUDY CONCERNED WITH THE EVALUATION AND STANDARDIZATION OF CODING CATEGORIES FOR USE AS AN OBSERVATION AND RESEARCH TOOL IN ANALYZING TEACHER BEHAVIOR. IN FACT, THE CATEGORIES WERE DERIVED FROM RESEARCH ON MATERNAL TEACHING STYLES BUT WERE ADAPTED TO TEACHERS' CLASSROOM BEHAVIOR IN PRESCHOOL SITUATIONS. THE EMPHASIS OF THIS RESEARCH IS ON THE COGNITIVE INTERCHANGE BETWEEN TEACHER AND PUPIL. THE CODING CATEGORIES ALLOW TABULATION OF THE DIFFERENT TYPES OF COMMUNICATION USED IN THE CLASSROOM. DURING THE INITIAL DEVELOPMENT OF THE TEACHER BEHAVIOR CODING SCHEME, TEACHER OBSERVATION WAS CONDUCTED AT TWO NURSERY SCHOOLS, ONE FOR LOW INCOME CHILDREN AND ONE FOR HIGH INCOME CHILDREN. A SECOND OBSERVATION PHASE WAS CONDUCTED IN THREE DIFFERENT TYPES OF CLASSROOMS: (1) A SETTLEMENT HOUSE CLASS, (2) A MONTESSORI CLASS, AND (3) TWO HEAD START CLASSES. EACH OBSERVATION SESSION WAS TAPED AND CODED BY AN OBSERVER. THE TEACHER INVOLVED WORE A CORDLESS MICROPHONE AND THE OBSERVER RECEIVED THE BROADCAST, FOR PURPOSES OF CONSISTENT PICK UP, BY EARPHONES. THE 17 TRANSCRIPTS TAKEN ARE BEING CODED AND ANALYZED. TWO APPENDIXES AT THE END OF THE REPORT ENUMERATE THE CODING CATEGORIES. (WD)

ED022553 PS001241
HEAD START EVALUATION AND RESEARCH CENTER, THE UNIVERSITY OF CHICAGO. REPORT D, THE INTERACTION OF INTELLIGENCE AND BEHAVIOR AS ONE PREDICTOR OF EARLY SCHOOL ACHIEVEMENT IN WORKING CLASS AND CULTURALLY DISADVANTAGED HEAD START CHILDREN. HESS, ROBERT D.; SHIPMAN, VIRGINIA C., 30 NOV 67 50P.
EDRS PRICE MF-$0.65 HC-$3.29

THIS STUDY SEEKS TO DETERMINE THE DEGREE TO WHICH CERTAIN BEHAVIORAL MEASURES INTERACT WITH INTELLIGENCE, WHETHER IN A LINEAR OR CURVILINEAR FASHION, TO HELP ONE PREDICT ACADEMIC ACHIEVEMENT IN HEAD START CHILDREN TO A GREATER DEGREE THAN WOULD BE POSSIBLE WERE INTELLIGENCE TEST PERFORMANCE ALONE USED AS THE PREDICTOR VARIABLE. CHILDREN WERE TESTED DURING A SUMMER HEAD START PROGRAM AND RETESTED IN THE FALL IN A FOLLOWUP STUDY. OF THE TESTS OF ABILITY USED WITH THE CHILDREN, THE TWO BEST PREDICTORS OF SUCCESS IN THE ACADEMIC TASKS IN KINDERGARTEN WAS THE PRESCHOOL INVENTORY AND THE STANFORD-BINET. THE BEST PREDICTOR OF SOCIALLY CONFORMING BEHAVIOR WAS THE PROBABLE ADAPTATION RATING MADE BY TEACHERS. THE BEHAVIOR AND POSSIBILITIES FOR FUTURE PROGRESS OF THE CHILDREN WERE RATED AT THE END OF THE SUMMER SESSION AND DURING THE FOLLOWUP. AN INITIAL HYPOTHESIS, THAT DIFFERENCES IN BEHAVIOR LEVEL WOULD AFFECT SUCCESS CRITERIA SCORES IN LOW IQ CHILDREN MORE THAN IT WOULD IN HIGH IQ CHILDREN, WAS GENERALLY NOT

SUPPORTED. IN ADDITION, NO STRIKING CURVILINEAR INTERACTION WAS FOUND BETWEEN BEHAVIOR LEVEL AND INTELLIGENCE, BUT THE MAJORITY OF SUCCESS CRITERIA APPEAR TO INTERACT IN A LINEAR FASHION ACROSS BEHAVIOR AREAS. (WD)

ED022554 PS001242
HEAD START EVALUATION AND RESEARCH CENTER, THE UNIVERSITY OF CHICAGO. REPORT E, COMPARATIVE USE OF ALTERNATIVE MODES FOR ASSESSING COGNITIVE DEVELOPMENT IN BILINGUAL OR NON-ENGLISH SPEAKING CHILDREN. SHIPMAN, VIRGINIA C., 30 NOV 67
EDRS PRICE MF-$0.65 HC-INQUIRE EDRS

IN ORDER TO ASSESS THE FEASIBILITY OF ALTERNATIVE METHODS FOR DETERMINING THE COGNITIVE DEVELOPMENT OF BILINGUAL OR NON-ENGLISH SPEAKING CHILDREN FROM A DISPARATE CULTURAL BACKGROUND, 28 SEMINOLE INDIAN CHILDREN FROM TWO HEAD START CENTERS WERE ADMINISTERED A SERIES OF INTELLIGENCE TESTS, SOME BASED ON VERBAL ABILITY, SOME NOT. THE TESTS USED WERE (1) THE RAVENS COLORED MATRICES, (2) THREE PIAGETIAN MEASURES DESIGNED TO ASSESS THE CHILD'S STAGE OF CONCRETE OPERATIONS, (3) TWO MEASURES OF CLASSIFICATORY BEHAVIOR (CLASS INCLUSION AND OBJECT SORTING), AND (4) THE STANFORD-BINET. THE RAVENS TEST PURPORTS TO ASSESS A PERSON'S PRESENT CAPACITY FOR INTELLECTUAL ACTIVITY AND HAS A MINUMUM OF VERBAL REQUIREMENTS. THIS TEST SHOWED THE LEAST DEFICIT FOR THE INDIAN CHILDREN AND WAS A GOOD PREDICTOR OF THE CHILD'S FUNCTIONING ON OTHER TASKS. THE STANFORD-BINET SHOWED THE CHILDREN TO BE VERY DEFICIENT IN INTELLECTUAL ABILITY. THE CHILDREN DID POORLY ON THE PIAGETIAN MEASURES, CONSIDERABLY BELOW NORMATIVE LEVELS. ON THE SORTING TASKS, THE INDIAN CHILDREN SCORED BELOW URBAN NEGRO CHILDREN WHO HAD TAKEN THE SAME TEST. AN APPENDIX CONTAINING TASK DESCRIPTIONS FOLLOWS THIS REPORT. (WD)

ED022555 PS001244
GAMES AND OTHER ACTIVITIES FOR DEVELOPING LANGUAGE SKILLS. GOTKIN, LASSAR G., 16P.
EDRS PRICE MF-$0.65 HC-$3.29

DR. GOTKIN HAS DEVELOPED SEVERAL WAYS TO USE EFFECTIVELY GAMES AND MECHANICAL DEVICES TO TEACH LANGUAGE SKILLS TO PRESCHOOL AND KINDERGARTEN CHILDREN. THE MATRIX GAME, A SET OF PICTURES IN COLUMNS AND ROWS, WHICH FUNCTIONS ON THE PRINCIPLES AND METHODS OF PROGRAMED INSTRUCTION, REQUIRES THE CHILD TO DISCRIMINATE SYMBOLS, PICTURES, AND COLORS AND TO VERBALIZE HIS ANSWER. THE TELEPHONE INTERVIEW IS USED TO INDUCE THE INDIVIDUAL CHILD TO STRUCTURE CONVERSATIONS AS THE TEACHER GIVES HIM THEMATIC PROMPTS OVER THE TELEPHONE. A THIRD METHOD USES THE LANGUAGE MASTER (A TAPE RECORDER AND A MOVING CARD HOLDER) TO MAKE THE CHILD VERBALIZE AFTER HE HAS BEEN AURALLY AND VISUALLY STIMULATED. ALSO, IT PROVIDES THE CHILD WITH IMMEDIATE FEEDBACK. THE ALPHABET BOARD IS A BOARD GROOVED WITH THE SHAPE OF THE LETTERS OF THE ALPHABET INTO WHICH THE LETTERS ARE PLACED, MUCH AS IN A PUZZLE. THIS DEVICE HELPS DISADVANTAGED CHILDREN, ESPECIALLY, TO LEARN TO DISCRIMINATE THE SHAPES AND NAMES OF LETTERS AND TO REALIZE THAT LETTERS ARE A CODE FOR THE SPOKEN LANGUAGE. ALL OF THESE METHODS ARE DESIGNED FOR SUPPLEMENTARY TOOLS FOR TEACHERS. (JS)

ED022556 PS001249
LET'S TRY THIS IN NURSERY SCHOOL AND KINDERGARTEN. STANT, MARGARET ADAMS, 63 32P.
DOCUMENT NOT AVAILABLE FROM EDRS.
AVAILABLE FROM: SANMAR PUBLISHING, BOX 174, COLLEGE PARK, MARYLAND.

IN THIS PAMPHLET ON NURSERY SCHOOL AND KINDERGARTEN EXPERIENCES, SUGGESTIONS ARE MADE TO ENRICH AND VARY ACTIVITIES IN SCIENCE AND THE CREATIVE ARTS. INCLUDED ARE INSTRUCTIONS FOR MAKING SIMPLE EQUIPMENT FOR USE IN SCIENCE AND SUGGESTIONS FOR CURRICULUM-RELATED ACTIVITIES WHICH COULD EXTEND OR SUPPLEMENT REGULAR NURSERY SCHOOL AND KINDERGARTEN PROGRAM PLANS. (MS)

ED022557 PS001250
HEAD START EVALUATION AND RESEARCH CENTER, BOSTON UNIVERSITY. REPORT A-I, TEACHING STYLE: THE DEVELOPMENT OF TEACHING TASKS. GARFUNKEL, FRANK, 67 15P.
EDRS PRICE MF-$0.65 HC-$3.29

SIX TEACHERS WERE GIVEN INSTRUCTIONS AND MATERIALS WITH WHICH TO CONDUCT A 20-MINUTE TEACHING SESSION. THE SESSIONS WERE FILMED. THE FILMS WILL BE SCRUTINIZED TO OBTAIN COMPARISONS OF TEACHING STYLES, TASKS (THE INSTRUCTIONS AND MATERIALS PROVIDED EACH TEACHER), AND TEACHER-TASK INTERACTIONS. THE FILMS HAVE NOT BEEN COMPLETELY PROCESSED YET AND SO NO DATA IS AVAILABLE. SEVERAL SCALES HAVE BEEN DETERMINED WHICH WILL BE USED TO CLASSIFY TEACHING STYLES: (1) CONTROL, (2) APPROACH TO CHILD ACTIVITIES, (3) VALUE, OR ORIENTATION OF CLASSROOM ACTIVITIES, (4) WARMTH, (5) HUMOR, (6) FLEXIBILITY, (7) DIRECTION, AND (8) DIFFERENTIATION. AN APPENDIX DESCRIBES THE FOUR TASKS GIVEN EACH TEACHER; (1) MASKS, (2) BALLOONS, (3) HOMES AND FAMILIES, AND (4) GAMES. (WD)

ED022558 PS001251
HEAD START EVALUATION AND RESEARCH CENTER, BOSTON UNIVERSITY. REPORT A-II, OBSERVATION OF TEACHERS AND TEACHING: STRATEGIES AND APPLICATIONS. GARFUNKEL, FRANK, 67 32P.
EDRS PRICE MF-$0.65 HC-$3.29

THERE ARE REASONS WHY TEACHING BEHAVIOR SHOULD BE ASSESSED, INCLUDING (1) UPGRADING TEACHER EDUCATION, (2) GAINING INSIGHTS INTO THE LEARNING OF BOTH TEACHERS AND CHILDREN, AND (3) STUDYING SOCIAL INTERACTIONS. TWO MEANS OF ASSESSING TEACHER ABILITY ARE QUANTIFICATION OF TEACHER BEHAVIOR BY THE USE OF RATING SCALES, BEHAVIORAL CATEGORIES, ETC., AND PARTICIPANT OBSERVATION (PO). THE FIRST, ASSESSMENT BY INSTRUMENT, CONFOUNDS THE EFFECTS OF TOO MANY INTERACTING VARIABLES FOR THE INSTRUMENT TO RELIABLY REPRESENT THE EFFECTS OF TEACHER BEHAVIOR. IN THE PO METHOD, VERY WELL QUALIFIED AND TRAINED PEOPLE ARE THE ASSESSING INSTRUMENT. OBSERVER JUDGMENT AND OBSERVER INFLUENCE UPON THE CLASSROOM SITUATION ARE PRESENT, BUT IF THE OBSERVER IS WELL QUALIFIED AND WELL TRAINED, AS HE MUST BE FOR THE SUCCESS OF THE METHOD, THE DATA OBTAINED SHOULD BE MORE RELIABLE AND MORE RELEVANT. FILMING THE CLASSROOM SITUATION CAN ALSO BE USED AND ADDS MUCH TO THE ASSESSMENT PROCESS. THE PO APPROACH WAS TESTED ON SELECTED HEAD START AND ELEMENTARY SCHOOL CLASSES. THE DATA ANALYSIS FROM THIS TESTING IS INCOMPLETE. IT HAS BEEN FOUND, HOWEVER, FROM A COMBINED PO AND FILMING OF SUBURBAN AND INNER-CITY (HARTFORD, CONNECTICUT) ELEMENTARY CLASSES, THAT SUBURBAN CLASSES ARE UNIFORMLY SUPERIOR TO INNER-CITY CLASSES. (WD)

ED022559 PS001252
HEAD START EVALUATION AND RESEARCH CENTER, BOSTON UNIVERSITY. REPORT A-III, OBSERVATIONAL STRATEGIES FOR OBTAINING DATA ON CHILDREN AND TEACHERS IN HEAD START CLASSES. (OSOD). GARFUNKEL, FRANK, 1 SEP 67 30P.
EDRS PRICE MF-$0.65 HC-$3.29

WITH THE PURPOSE OF OBTAINING RELEVANT DATA ABOUT THE CURRICULUM, CLASSROOM, TEACHER, AND PEER EFFECTS ON INDIVIDUAL HEAD START CHILDREN, THIS PROJECT PLANS TO HAVE TRAINED OBSERVERS SPEND SEVERAL HOURS IN THE CLASSROOM (1) ATTENDING TO AND RECORDING THE TOTAL FUNCTIONS OF THE CLASS AND (2) ATTENDING TO AND RECORDING THE BEHAVIOR OF INDIVIDUAL CHILDREN. A COMPREHENSIVE, SOMEWHAT COMPLEX, SYSTEM OF RATING TEACHER-CHILD BEHAVIOR AND CLASSROOM ACTIVITIES HAS BEEN DEVISED TO RECORD THE DATA. EXPLORATORY OBSERVATION AND TRAINING OF OBSERVERS WILL PRECEDE THE PRIMARY DATA GATHERING PROJECT. THERE ARE PLANS TO FILM THE CLASSROOMS BEING OBSERVED IN ORDER TO RECONSIDER AS A WHOLE WHAT THE OBSERVERS, BY THEIR RATING SCALES, PULVERIZE INTO MANY PIECES OF DATA. THE ANALYSIS OF THE DATA WILL BE DIRECTED TOWARDS DEVELOPING SPECIFIC PREDICTIONS FOR INDIVIDUAL CHILDREN, CLASSES, AND CLUSTERS OF CLASSES REGARDING EFFECTS OF VARIOUS KINDS OF PROGRAMS ON CHILDREN. (WD)

ED022560 PS001253
HEAD START EVALUATION AND RESEARCH CENTER, BOSTON UNIVERSITY. REPORT B-I, PRIMARY AND SECONDARY PREVENTION STUDYING CLINICAL PROCESS AND DISTURBANCE WITH PRESCHOOL CHILDREN. FISH, CAROLINE; AND OTHERS, 67 15P.
EDRS PRICE MF-$0.65 HC-$3.29

TWO GROUPS OF PRESCHOOL CHILDREN FROM THE BOSTON AREA WERE SELECTED TO PARTICIPATE IN A STUDY OF MARGINAL EMOTIONAL DISORDERS, THEIR DIAGNOSIS BY AN INTERDISCIPLINARY TEAM, AND THEIR EFFECT UPON A CHILD'S FUNCTIONING IN THE PRESCHOOL SETTING. THE TWO GROUPS OF CHILDREN WHO ATTENDED THE DIAGNOSTIC SESSIONS CONSISTED OF 19 LOWER CLASS HEAD START PUPILS FROM THE INNER-CITY AND EIGHT MIDDLE CLASS CHILDREN FROM A SUBURB PRESCHOOL PROGRAM. THE INTERDISCIPLINARY TEAM INCLUDED MASTER TEACHERS, CHILD PSYCHIATRISTS, PSYCHOLOGISTS, SOCIAL WORKERS, AND A SPEECH-HEARING SPECIALIST. GRADUATE STUDENTS RECORDED THE BEHAVIOR OF THE CHILDREN. THE 27 CHILDREN ATTENDED THE DIAGNOSTIC SESSIONS 3 DAYS A WEEK AND WERE OBSERVED, BY MEANS OF ONE-WAY MIRRORS, BY THE INTERDISCIPLINARY TEAM. STAFF MEETINGS WERE HELD AFTER THE SESSIONS TO DISCUSS WHAT HAD BEEN OBSERVED AND WHAT ASSISTANCE COULD BE RENDERED TO EMOTIONALLY DISTURBED CHILDREN AND THEIR TEACHERS. THE PROJECT RAISED MORE QUESTIONS THAN IT ANSWERED, BUT AMONG ITS FINDINGS WERE (1) THAT SOCIAL CLASS DIFFERENCES IN PATHOLOGY WERE NOT STRIKING, (2) THAT THE DATA GATHERING PROCESS WAS NOT EXTENSIVE ENOUGH, (3) THAT PROJECT COMMUNICATION WITH THE LOWER CLASS COMMUNITY WAS INSUFFICIENT, AND (4) THAT THE USE OF AN INTERDISCIPLINARY TEAM DID PROVIDE A WELCOME DEPTH TO THE INFORMATIONAL ANALYSIS. (WD)

ED022561 PS001254

HEAD START EVALUATION AND RESEARCH CENTER, BOSTON UNIVERSITY. REPORT C-I, PERCEPTION OF EMOTION AMONG CHILDREN: RACE AND SEX DIFFERENCES. GITTER, A. GEORGE, 67 14P.

EDRS PRICE MF-$0.65 HC-$3.29

PERCEPTION OF EMOTION IS ONE EXAMPLE OF NONVERBAL COMMUNICATION AND IS THE SUBJECT OF THIS STUDY OF THE ACCURACY OF PERCEPTION OF VARIOUS EMOTIONS. SEVEN EMOTIONS WERE CHOSEN FOR THIS INVESTIGATION. EACH EMOTION WAS ACTED OUT BY ACTORS, WHOSE PERFORMANCE WAS FILMED. FROM THE FILMS, STILLS WERE SELECTED WHICH BEST REPRESENTED THE EMOTION BEING EXPRESSED. THE PURPOSE OF THE STUDY WAS TO DETERMINE THE EFFECTS OF RACE AND SEX ON PERCEPTION OF EMOTION. THEREFORE, BOTH EXPRESSORS AND PERCEIVERS WERE DIVIDED BETWEEN NEGRO AND WHITE, MALE AND FEMALE. ALTHOUGH THE TEST WAS DESIGNED FOR CHILDREN, THE PERCEIVERS FOR THIS STUDY WERE 80 UNDERGRADUATE STUDENTS. EACH SUBJECT VIEWED 21 PHOTOGRAPHS OF THREE EXPRESSORS AND CHOSE FROM A LIST THE EMOTION HE THOUGHT THE EXPRESSOR WAS DEMONSTRATING. THE RESULTS INDICATED THAT (1) OVERALL ACCURACY OF PERCEPTION OF EMOTIONS WAS NOT INFLUENCED BY SEX OR RACE OF THE PERCIEVER OR SEX OF THE EXPRESSOR; (2) RACE OF EXPRESSOR DID AFFECT THE ACCURACY OF PERCEPTION OF EMOTION, WHITE EXPRESSORS LEADING TO GREATER ACCURACY OF PERCEPTION; AND (3) SOME PATTERNS OF ERRONEOUSLY PERCEIVED EMOTIONS WERE RELATED TO SEX OF EXPRESSOR AND RACE OF PERCEIVER. (WD)

ED022562 PS001255

HEAD START EVALUATION AND RESEARCH CENTER, BOSTON UNIVERSITY. REPORT C-II, THE EXPRESSION OF AGGRESSION IN PRE-SCHOOL CHILDREN. DORMAN, LYNN M., 67 7P.

EDRS PRICE MF-$0.65 HC-$3.29

TEN BOYS AND 16 GIRLS FROM TWO HEAD START SCHOOLS IN MASSACHUSETTS WERE ADMINISTERED TWO PROJECTIVE MEASURES OF AGGRESSION. A THIRD MEASURE WAS OBTAINED FROM TEACHER RANKINGS OF BEHAVIOR BASED ON CLASSROOM CONDUCT. FOR THE PROJECTIVE MEASURES, EACH CHILD WAS ASKED TO RESPOND TO THREE SOCIAL SITUATIONS AS DEPICTED BY DOLLS AND DRAWINGS. THE CHILD WAS TO COMMENT UPON WHAT HE WOULD DO IF PLACED INTO EACH SITUATION. THE SITUATIONS COULD ELICIT AN AGGRESSIVE OR NONAGGRESSIVE RESPONSE. THE THREE SOCIAL SITUATIONS WERE (1) BLOCK PLAY AND SWINGING FOR BOYS, (2) DOLL PLAY AND PAINTING FOR GIRLS, AND (3) A BOOK SITUATION FOR BOTH SEXES. EACH RESPONSE BY A CHILD IN ONE OF THE SITUATIONS WAS CODED AS AGGRESSIVE OR NONAGGRESSIVE. THE RESULTS SHOWED THAT THE GIRLS IN ONE HEAD START SCHOOL MANIFESTED THE MOST AGGRESSIVE BEHAVIOR, WITH LITTLE DIFFERENCE BETWEEN THE SEXES IN THE SECOND SCHOOL. IT WAS ALSO FOUND THAT CHILDREN WHO EXPRESS MORE AGGRESSION ON PROJECTIVE TESTS ARE MORE VERBAL AND MORE COOPERATIVE. THE CORRELATIONS BETWEEN THE RATINGS OF AGGRESSION ON THE PROJECTIVE TESTS AND THE RANKINGS BY THE CLASSROOM TEACHER WERE LOW. (WD)

ED022563 PS001256

HEAD START EVALUATION AND RESEARCH CENTER, BOSTON UNIVERSITY. REPORT D-I, LANGUAGE PROJECT: THE EFFECTS OF A TEACHER DEVELOPED PRE-SCHOOL LANGUAGE TRAINING PROGRAM ON FIRST GRADE READING ACHIEVEMENT. ALEXANIAN, SANDRA, 67 7P.

EDRS PRICE MF-$0.65 HC-$3.29

THIRTY-FIVE HEAD START CHILDREN RECEIVED SPECIAL INSTRUCTION IN VARIOUS LANGUAGE SKILLS. A CONTROL GROUP CONSISTED OF 25 HEAD START CHILDREN. THE PURPOSE OF THIS STUDY WAS TO DETERMINE THE EFFECTS OF THIS SPECIAL TEACHER-DEVELOPED LANGUAGE READINESS CURRICULUM ON THE GRADE ONE READING ACHIEVEMENT WHEN COMPARED TO THE ACHIEVEMENT OF THE CONTROL GROUP, WHICH RECEIVED NO SPECIAL PROGRAM. THE THREE TEACHERS OF THE EXPERIMENTAL CLASSES ATTENDED WORKSHOP SESSIONS PROVIDED BY CURRICULUM EXPERTS AND RECEIVED SPECIAL CLASSROOM MATERIALS AND CLASSROOM VISITS FROM THE EXPERTS, WHO PRESENTED RELEVANT DEMONSTRATIONS. ALL CHILDREN WERE ADMINISTERED THE MURPHY DURRELL READING READINESS ANALYSIS DURING THE BEGINNING AND END OF THE SUMMER HEAD START SESSION. THEY ARE TO BE TESTED AGAIN AFTER ONE SEMESTER OF FIRST GRADE. AT THE TIME OF THE WRITING OF THIS REPORT, THAT FINAL TESTING HAD NOT BEEN GIVEN, BUT THE RESULTS OF THE PRETEST AND POSTTEST FROM THE HEAD START SESSION SHOWED THE EXPERIMENTAL CLASSES TO HAVE MADE GREATER GAINS IN LANGUAGE SKILLS THAN THE CONTROL GROUP. (WD).

ED022564 PS001257

HEAD START EVALUATION AND RESEARCH CENTER, BOSTON UNIVERSITY. REPORT D-II, TRAINING FOR NUMBER CONCEPT. BLUM, A. H., 67 9P.

EDRS PRICE MF-$0.65 HC-$3.29

IN A PROGRAM TO FACILITATE THE EMERGENCE OF NUMBER CONSERVATION IN PRESCHOOL CHILDREN, 45 MIDDLE CLASS CHILDREN AND 64 HEAD START AND TITLE I CHILDREN WERE TRAINED TO DEAL WITH PERCEPTUAL CONFUSIONS SO THAT THEY COULD UTILIZE THIS UNDERSTANDING TO DISREGARD IRRELEVANT CHANGES, SUCH AS SPATIAL REARRANGEMENT, AND THEREBY BECOME AWARE OF CONSERVATION OF QUANTITY. THE CHILDREN RANGED IN AGE FROM FOUR TO NINE. THE CHILDREN WERE TRAINED AND TESTED UNDER TWO EXPERIMENTAL TREATMENTS FOR EACH OF TWO CONDITIONS. IN EACH AGE GROUP, THE CHILDREN WERE CATEGORIZED, ON THE BASIS OF PRETESTING, AS (1) CONSERVERS (WHO WOULD RECEIVE NO TRAINING), (2) NONCONSERVERS AND TRANSITIONAL CONSERVERS (WHO WOULD RECEIVE TRAINING), AND (3) UNTESTABLE. INCOMPLETE DATA ANALYSIS INDICATED THAT MIDDLE CLASS 7- AND 8-YEAR-OLDS WERE MUCH BETTER CONSERVERS, BEFORE TRAINING, THAN THEIR HEAD START PEERS. BOTH GROUPS OF CHILDREN, HOWEVER, AT ALL AGES, APPEARED TO BENEFIT GREATLY FROM THE TRAINING SESSIONS AND WERE FACILITATED THEREBY IN LEARNING NUMBER CONSERVATION. (WD)

ED022565 PS001258

HEAD START EVALUATION AND RESEARCH CENTER, BOSTON UNIVERSITY. REPORT D-III, A STUDY OF PREFERENCES AMONG QUALITATIVELY DIFFERING UNCERTAINTIES. MOSTOFSKY, DAVID, 67 7P.

EDRS PRICE MF-$0.65 HC-$3.29

THE PURPOSE OF THIS STUDY WAS TO MEASURE NONVERBALLY THE PREFERENCE OF ALTERNATIVE RESPONSES WHEN THE NET PROBABILITY OF BEING REWARDED WAS THE SAME. A DEMONSTRATION OF PREFERENCE UNDER THESE CIRCUMSTANCES WOULD SUGGEST THE ABILITY TO CONTROL OR MAINTAIN BEHAVIOR WITHOUT EXPLICIT ADMINISTRATION OF A REINFORCING AGENT. HEAD START CHILDREN WERE USED AS SUBJECTS. THEY WERE PROVIDED, IN THE EXPERIMENTAL SITUATION, WITH A TWO-BUTTON CONSOLE. THE RIGHT BUTTON, WHEN PUSHED, RESULTED IN THE ILLUMINATION OF A YELLOW LIGHT AND THE DISPENSING OF A PENNY FOR EVERY SECOND ILLUMINATION (A CONSISTENT REWARD SCHEDULE). THE PUSHING OF THE LEFT BUTTON WOULD RESULT IN A 50 PERCENT CHANCE OF THE ILLUMINATION OF A RED LIGHT, WHICH WAS NEVER FOLLOWED BY REWARD, AND A 50 PERCENT CHANCE OF THE ILLUMINATION OF A GREEN LIGHT, WHICH WAS ALWAYS REWARDED. THUS, WHICHEVER BUTTON WAS PUSHED, THERE FOLLOWED A NET 50 PERCENT CHANCE OF REWARD. HOWEVER, ONLY THE RIGHT BUTTON PROVIDED A CONSISTENT 50 PERCENT REWARD. THE RESULTS INDICATE THAT CHILDREN PREFER A CONSISTENT REWARD SITUATION TO A REWARD UNCERTAINTY SITUATION. (WD)

ED022566 PS001259

HEAD START EVALUATION AND RESEARCH CENTER, BOSTON UNIVERSITY. REPORT E-I, THE UTILIZATION OF NONPROFESSIONAL INTERVIEWERS IN THE NEW ENGLAND AND MISSISSIPPI SAMPLES BY THE BOSTON UNIVERSITY HEAD START EVALUATION AND RESEARCH PROGRAM, 1966-1967. CLAY, SUZANNE, 67 10P.

EDRS PRICE MF-$0.65 HC-$3.29

TWENTY-FOUR MEMBERS OF TWO POVERTY AREAS WERE CHOSEN TO BE TRAINED AS NONPROFESSIONAL PARENT INTERVIEWERS. THEY WERE GIVEN THE TRAINING AND THEN SENT TO THEIR RESPECTIVE COMMUNITY AREAS TO OBTAIN INTERVIEWS WITH THE PARENTS OF HEAD START CHILDREN. THE GEOGRAPHICAL AREAS INVOLVED WERE THE NEW ENGLAND REGION AROUND BOSTON AND BOLIVAR COUNTY, MISSISSIPPI. THE PURPOSE OF THIS PROJECT WAS TWOFOLD: (1) TO OBTAIN PARENTS' ATTITUDES TOWARD THE HEAD START PROGRAM ATTENDED BY THEIR CHILDREN, AND (2) TO INVOLVE SOME OF THE PARENTS IN A MEANINGFUL AND PRODUCTIVE ROLE WITHIN THE HEAD START EVALUATION AND RESEARCH DESIGN. IT WAS NECESSARY, FOR THE SUCCESS OF THIS PROJECT, TO SUSTAIN CLOSE COOPERATION AND JOINT PLANNING BETWEEN THE PROFESSIONAL STAFF AND THE NONPROFESSIONAL INTERVIEWERS. HIRING OF THE INTERVIEWERS WAS BASED ON RECOMMENDATIONS OF NEW ENGLAND HEAD START DIRECTORS WHO HAD PRIOR EXPERIENCE WORKING IN SOME PHASE OF THE OVERALL RESEARCH PROGRAM. TWELVE INTERVIEWERS SAMPLED THE NEW ENGLAND REGION, AND 12 INTERVIEWED MISSISSIPPI PARENTS. THE RESULTING INTERVIEWS HAVE BEEN JUDGED TO BE , ON THE WHOLE, VERY SATISFACTORY. (WD)

ED022567 PS001260

HEAD START EVALUATION AND RESEARCH CENTER, BOSTON UNIVERSITY. REPORT E-II, TEACHER SEMINAR. ALEXANIAN, SANDRA, 67 5P.

EDRS PRICE MF-$0.65 HC-$3.29

EIGHT HEAD START TEACHERS WERE ASKED TO BE CONSULTANTS IN AN ASSESSMENT OF THE HEAD START PROGRAM AND THEIR ROLE IN IT. THE TEACHERS MET WITH A SEMINAR LEADER FROM THE EVALUATION AND RESEARCH CENTER AT BOSTON UNIVERSITY FOR SEVEN CONSECUTIVE 2-HOUR TAPED SESSIONS. THE TOPICS FOR DISCUSSION INCLUDED (1) THE ADMINISTRATIVE STRUCTURE OF THE AGENCY IN WHICH THEY WORKED, (2) TEACHER TRAINING PRIOR TO WORKING AND INSERVICE TRAINING, (3) SUPERVISION AND SUPPORT GIVEN TO TEACHERS, (4)

CONDITIONS UNDER WHICH TEACHERS WORK AND THE ANXIETIES GENERATED BY THEM, (5) THE GAP BETWEEN THE NEEDS OF THE CHILDREN AND THE TYPE OF PROGRAM OFFERED, AND (6) THE PUBLIC SCHOOLS AND THE LACK OF COMMUNICATION WITH THEM. SOME OF THE SPECIFIC POINTS MADE BY THE HEAD START TEACHERS IN THE SEMINAR WERE AS FOLLOWS: (1) THERE EXIST SERIOUS INADEQUACIES IN THE ADMINISTRATION OF HEAD START PROGRAMS, (2) JOB SECURITY IS UNSATISFACTORY, (3) MORE KNOWLEDGE OR TRAINING IS NECESSARY CONCERNING THE UNIQUE PROBLEMS OF HEAD START CHILDREN, AND (4) THE HEAD START CURRICULUM IS OFTEN VERY UNSATISFACTORY. (WD)

ED023444 PS000635
SPONTANEOUS PLAY: AN AVENUE FOR INTELLECTUAL DEVELOPMENT. ALMY, MILLIE, 66 15P.
DOCUMENT NOT AVAILABLE FROM EDRS.

IT IS GENERALLY CONCEDED THAT THERE IS MUCH FOR A CHILD TO LEARN WHILE ATTENDING NURSERY SCHOOL, BUT THE TEACHER IS OFTEN UNSURE AS TO WHAT TYPE OF CURRICULUM OR PROGRAM WILL BEST ASSURE SUCH LEARNING. SPECIFICALLY, ALTHOUGH PLAY HAS BEEN PART OF ALL NURSERY SCHOOL PROGRAMS, IT IS QUESTIONED WHETHER SPONTANEOUS PLAY (THAT IS, RELATIVELY UNSTRUCTURED PLAY) HAS BEEN USED TO ITS FULLEST ADVANTAGE. SPONTANEOUS PLAY IS NOT COMPLETELY UNSTRUCTURED, AS IT OCCURS IN THE NURSERY CLASSROOM, FOR IT MUST BE RESPONSIVE TO THE NATURE OF THE EQUIPMENT OR PLAY-OBJECTS AVAILABLE. IF IT IS UNDERSTOOD HOW IMPORTANT SPONTANEOUS PLAY IS IN THE INTELLECTUAL AND COGNITIVE DEVELOPMENT OF THE CHILD, IT WILL BE EASIER TO CHOOSE AND PROVIDE TOYS AND PLAY-OBJECTS THAT HAVE SIGNIFICANT TEACHING POTENTIAL; FOR EXAMPLE, BLOCKS OF VARIOUS COLORS OR SIZES CONTRIBUTE TO THE FUNDAMENTAL DISCRIMINATION AND CONCEPT LEARNING THAT OCCURS FROM THE THIRD TO THE FIFTH OR SIXTH YEAR OF LIFE. THE RANGE OF TOYS PROVIDED MUST REFLECT NOT ONLY THE NEEDS OF MANY INDIVIDUAL TASTES AND INTERESTS, BUT THE MANY LEVELS OF DEVELOPMENT REPRESENTED IN A NURSERY SCHOOL CLASS. BOTH THE PSYCHOANALYTIC AND THE PIAGET VIEW OF THE VALUE OF PLAY SUPPORT THE NEED OF SPONTANEOUS PLAY IN EARLY CHILDHOOD EDUCATION. THE PSYCHOANALYTIC VIEW IS THAT PLAY ALLOWS THE CHILD TO WORK OUT HIS EMOTIONS WHILE FORCING HIM TO USE HIS REASONING AND CREATIVE ABILITIES. PIAGET SEES PLAY AS A MEANS OF TRANSITION OF THE CHILD FROM EGOCENTRISM TO SOCIALIZATION AND OBJECTIVIZATION. (WD)

ED023445 PS001083
HEAD START EVALUATION AND RESEARCH CENTER, THE UNIVERSITY OF CHICAGO. ANNUAL REPORT, 1966-1967. SHIPMAN, VIRGINIA C.; AND OTHERS, 30 NOV 67 227P.
EDRS PRICE MF-$0.65 HC-$9.87

THIS DOCUMENT CONTAINS SIX STUDIES CONCERNED, PRIMARILY, WITH THE EFFECT OF MATERNAL INFLUENCES AND ATTITUDES ON PRESCHOOL CHILDREN. THE SUBJECTS WERE LOWER CLASS NEGROES, WHITES, AND SEMINOLE INDIANS. THE TITLES OF THE STUDIES AND THE ACCESSION NUMBERS OF THE INDIVIDUAL ABSTRACTS ARE AS FOLLOWS: (A) MATERNAL INFLUENCES UPON DEVELOPMENT OF COGNITION (PS 001 238), (B) MATERNAL ANTECEDENTS OF INTELLECTUAL ACHIEVEMENT BEHAVIORS IN LOWER CLASS PRESCHOOL CHILDREN (PS 001 239), (C) COGNITIVE INTERACTION BETWEEN TEACHER AND PUPIL IN A PRESCHOOL SETTING (PS 001 240), (D) THE INTERACTION OF INTELLIGENCE AND BEHAVIOR AS ONE PREDICTOR OF EARLY SCHOOL ACHIEVEMENT IN WORKING CLASS AND CULTURALLY DISADVANTAGED HEAD START CHILDREN (PS 001 241), (E) COMPARATIVE USE OF ALTERNATIVE MODES FOR ASSESSING COGNITIVE DEVELOPMENT IN BILINGUAL OR NON-ENGLISH SPEAKING CHILDREN (PS 001 242), AND (F) SOCIALIZATION INTO THE ROLE OF PUPIL (PS 001 243). (WD)

ED023446 PS001084
A DIGEST OF THE RESEARCH ACTIVITIES OF REGIONAL EVALUATION AND RESEARCH CENTERS FOR PROJECT HEAD START (SEPTEMBER 1, 1966 TO NOVEMBER 30, 1967). WILLERMAN, EMILY G.; AND OTHERS, 15 JAN 68 159P.
EDRS PRICE MF-$0.65 HC-$6.58

A SUMMARY OF THE RESEARCH ACTIVITIES OF 13 HEAD START REGIONAL EVALUATION CENTERS IS PRESENTED IN THREE SECTIONS: RESEARCH ON CHILDREN, RESEARCH ON PARENTS AND FAMILIES, AND RESEARCH ON CLASSROOMS, TEACHERS, AND SOCIAL ORGANIZATIONS OF HEAD START CENTERS. STUDIES ARE GROUPED UNDER APPROPRIATE SUBHEADINGS, SUCH AS "LANGUAGE" OR "LEARNING," AND SUMMARIZED. INVESTIGATORS' NAMES, THE UNIVERSITY AT WHICH THE WORK WAS DONE, AND THE PURPOSE, METHOD, AND RESULTS OF THE STUDY, AS WELL AS IMPLICATIONS FOR FURTHER RESEARCH, ARE INCLUDED FOR EACH PROJECT. AN APPENDIX SUPPLIES THE ADDRESS, DIRECTOR'S NAME, AND UNIVERSITY AFFILIATION OF EACH EVALUATION AND RESEARCH CENTER. A TABLE OF CONTENTS OF THE FINAL REPORTS OF THE UNIVERSITIES ARE SUPPLIED, AS WELL AS AN AUTHOR INDEX TO THE ACTUAL STUDIES WITHIN THIS DIGEST. (MS)

ED023447 PS001167
EXTRA-CURRICULAR PARENT-CHILD CONTACT AND CHILDREN'S SOCIALLY REINFORCED TASK BEHAVIOR. GROSSMAN, BRUCE D., [63] 12P.
EDRS PRICE MF-$0.65 HC-$3.29

THE PURPOSE OF THIS STUDY WAS TO DETERMINE IF CHILDREN WITH WARM SOCIAL CONTACT WITH THEIR PARENTS (NONCARETAKING FUNCTIONS) ARE MORE RESPONSIVE TO SOCIAL REINFORCEMENT THAN ARE CHILDREN WHO ARE DEPRIVED OF SUCH CONTACT. DATA WAS GATHERED FROM INTERVIEWS WITH MOTHERS, WHO DESCRIBED THE AMOUNT AND QUALITY OF BOTH PARENTS' CONTACT WITH THE CHILD. THE SAMPLE OF MIDDLE CLASS CHILDREN, 13 GIRLS AND 14 BOYS, PERFORMED A TASK TWICE. RESPONSES WERE MEASURED BEFORE AND AFTER SOCIAL REINFORCEMENT. FOR GIRLS, THE RESULTS SHOWED A POSITIVE DIRECT RELATIONSHIP BETWEEN WARM SOCIAL CONTACT AND INITIAL RESPONSE RATE BUT NOT BETWEEN PARENTAL CONTACT AND SOCIAL REINFORCEMENT. IN CONTRAST, BOYS WHO HAD LESS WARM SOCIAL CONTACT WERE HIGHER IN INITIAL RESPONSE RATE AND MORE RESPONSIVE TO SOCIAL REINFORCEMENT. THE RESULTS ARE DISCUSSED IN TERMS OF SEX DIFFERENCES AND DIFFERENT SCHOOLS OF THOUGHT CONCERNING AMOUNTS OF SOCIAL CONTACTS PARENTS GIVE TO CHILDREN. A BIBLIOGRAPHY IS INCLUDED. (JS)

ED023448 PS001168
PROMISING DIRECTIONS FOR RESEARCH AND DEVELOPMENT IN EARLY CHILDHOOD EDUCATION. ELLIOTT, DAVID L., 15 MAR 66 16P.
EDRS PRICE MF-$0.65 HC-$3.29

A SURVEY OF RESEARCH AND DEVELOPMENT STUDIES CURRENTLY NEEDED IN EARLY CHILDHOOD EDUCATION STRESSES CHILD DEVELOPMENT AND ITS RELATION TO INSTRUCTION. TOPICS WHICH HAVE BEEN DISCUSSED ARE PERCEPTION, ORAL LANGUAGE, CONCEPT FORMATION, LEARNING SET, MOTIVATION, AND THE PSYCHOLOGY OF LEARNING. UNIVERSITIES AND PUBLIC SCHOOL SYSTEMS WORKING TOGETHER IN LONGITUDINAL RESEARCH STUDIES OF TEACHER-PUPIL INTERACTION, CURRICULUM EFFECTIVENESS, AND INSTRUCTIONAL METHODS WILL PROVIDE INFORMATION TO BE BUILT INTO EDUCATIONAL ACTION PROGRAMS. SINCE CHILDREN DEVELOP BOTH THROUGH MATURATION AND INTERACTION WITH ENVIRONMENTAL STIMULATION, SPECIFIC INSTRUCTION FOR COGNITIVE, LANGUAGE, AND PERCEPTUAL DEVELOPMENT IS PRESENTLY BEING GIVEN IN COMPENSATORY PRESCHOOL PROGRAMS. FOLLOWUP-STUDY RESULTS FROM THESE PROGRAMS, AS WELL AS FROM RESEARCH PROJECTS, SHOULD BE USED TO REVISE AND IMPROVE FUTURE INSTRUCTIONAL SCHEMES. A REVIEW OF THE LITERATURE OF CURRICULUM DEVELOPMENT FOR KINDERGARTEN CHILDREN AND A BIBLIOGRAPHY OF EARLY CHILDHOOD STUDIES ARE PROVIDED. (MS)

ED023449 PS001169
SCHOOL READINESS, BEHAVIOR TESTS USED AT THE GESELL INSTITUTE. ILG, FRANCES L.; AMES, LOUISE BATES, 64 399P.
DOCUMENT NOT AVAILABLE FROM EDRS.
AVAILABLE FROM: HARPER AND ROW, PUBLISHERS, KEYSTONE INDUSTRIAL PARK, SCRANTON, PA. 18512 ($8.95).

THIS COMBINED TEXT AND MANUAL PRESENTS THE BASIC EDUCATIONAL VIEWPOINT OF THE GESELL INSTITUTE, THAT CHILDREN SHOULD BE ENTERED IN SCHOOL (AND CONSEQUENTLY GROUPED AND PROMOTED) ON THE BASIS OF THEIR DEVELOPMENTAL OR BEHAVIORAL AGE, NOT ON THE BASIS OF THEIR CHRONOLOGICAL AGE OR IQ. THE INTRODUCTION DESCRIBES THE RESEARCH IN WHICH THE INSTITUTE STUDIED ITS THEORY. THE MAIN PART OF THE BOOK DEPICTS THE VARIOUS ASPECTS OF THE INSTITUTE'S DEVELOPMENTAL TEST, DESCRIBING ITS ADMINISTRATION, EVALUATING THE RESULTS, AND DEFINING ITS USE IN DETERMINING SCHOOL READINESS. ALSO, THE RESULTS ARE USED TO DEMONSTRATE THE CONCEPT OF THE EXISTENCE OF A SPECIFIC AGE, SUCH AS 7-YEAR-OLDNESS. A SECTION IS DEVOTED TO PARENTS, TEACHERS, AND ADMINISTRATORS TO HELP THEM UNDERSTAND THE FUNCTION OF THE TESTING AND HOW IT CAN HELP THE CHILD. A BIBLIOGRAPHY AND SEVERAL APPENDIXES ARE INCLUDED. (JS)

ED023450 PS001176
CENTRAL AND INCIDENTAL LEARNING IN CHILDREN. HAGEN, JOHN W.; SABO, RUTH, 15 MAY 68 13P.
EDRS PRICE MF-$0.65 HC-$3.29

EARLIER STUDIES FOUND THAT RECALL SCORES OF INFORMATION CENTRAL TO THE TASK INCREASED WITH AGE WHILE INCIDENTAL INFORMATION RECALL SCORES REMAINED CONSTANT. THIS STUDY REPEATED THE EARLIER ONES MODIFYING PROCEDURES OF INSTRUCTIONS, TESTING, AND SCHEDULE OF RECALL. ALSO, IT TESTED THE EFFECT OF LABELING PICTORIAL STIMULI. THE SAMPLE OF 253 CHILDREN WERE TO LEARN TO DISCRIMINATE EITHER CONTENT OR POSITION OF PRESENTED PICTURES AS CENTRAL INFORMATION. THE SAMPLE WAS DIVIDED BY THREE AGE GROUPS, 7 TO 9, 10 TO 11, AND 12 TO 14. THESE GROUPS WERE FURTHER SUBDIVIDED INTO FOUR GROUPS. THE FIRST GROUP RECEIVED MORE AMBIGUOUS DIRECTIONS THAN DID THE OTHER GROUPS. THE SECOND GROUP WAS TESTED ON A BALANCED SCHEDULE OF RECALL. THE THIRD GROUP WAS SHOWN NAMES OF ANIMALS, WHILE THE FOURTH GROUP WAS SHOWN NUMBERS DESIGNATING POSITIONS OF PICTURES. THE RESULTS SHOWED THAT (1) AS BEFORE, CONTENT RECALL SCORES INCREASE WITH AGE, (2) MORE

AMBIGUOUS DIRECTIONS LED TO LESS SELECTIVITY AT ALL AGES, (3) A BALANCED SCHEDULE OF RECALL WAS EFFECTIVE AT AN OLDER AGE, (4) LABELING DEPRESSES INCIDENTAL INFORMATION SCORES AT ALL AGES, AND (5) NAME LABELING IS MORE EFFECTIVE THAN NUMERICAL LABELING, BUT NOT AT A SIGNIFICANT LEVEL. A BIBLIOGRAPHY AND TABLES ARE INCLUDED. (JS)

ED023451 PS001179
A STUDY OF VISUAL PERCEPTIONS IN EARLY CHILDHOOD. , [67] 95P.
EDRS PRICE MF-$0.65 HC-$3.29

OVER A PERIOD OF THREE YEARS A GROUP OF 510 RURAL CHILDREN PARTICIPATED IN A STUDY OF VISUAL PERCEPTIONS, INCLUDING EYE MOTOR COORDINATION, DISCERNMENT OF FIGURES IN A GROUND PATTERN, FORM CONSTANCY, POSITION IN SPACE, AND SPATIAL RELATIONS, AS MEASURED BY THE FROSTIG VISUAL PERCEPTIONS TEST. VISUAL PERCEPTIONS OF CHILDREN OF OTHER CULTURES WERE COMPARED TO THOSE OF CHILDREN OF THE DOMINANT ANGLO-SAXON CULTURE. THE RELATIONSHIP OF VISUAL PERCEPTIONS TO CULTURAL DEPRIVATION WAS ALSO STUDIED. THE DEVELOPMENT OF CHILDREN'S VISUAL PERCEPTIONS OVER A PERIOD OF 18 TO 25 MONTHS AND THE EFFECTIVENESS OF VARIOUS TYPES OF PROGRAMS IN IMPROVING A CHILD'S VISUAL PERCEPTIONS WERE INVESTIGATED. RESULTS OF TESTING SHOWED THAT ALL RURAL CHILDREN SCORED LOW IN FORM CONSTANCY. CULTURALLY DEPRIVED CHILDREN SCORED LOWER IN ALL PERCEPTIONS, BUT VISUAL PERCEPTION HANDICAPS WERE SOMETIMES AS GREAT AS EIGHT TIMES THAT O F CONTROL GROUP CHILDREN. THE VALUS OF THE FROSTIG DEVELOPMENTAL TRAINING PROGRAM WAS DEMONSTRATED. PUPIL PROGRESS WAS RETAINED FOR AT LEAST ONE ACADEMI C YEAR. THE STUDY CONCLUDES THAT VISUAL PERCEPTION HANDICAPS RESULT FROM CULTURAL DEPRIVATION RATHER THAN FROM PARTICIPATION IN A NONDOMINANT CULTURE. IMPLICATIONS ARE THAT RURAL CHILDREN WOULD BENEFIT FROM FORM CONSTANCY TRAINING DURING THEIR FIRST YEAR AT SCHOOL. (MS)

ED023452 PS001180
STIMULUS DIMENSIONALITY AND MANIPULABILITY IN VISUAL PERCEPTUAL LEARNING. KERPELMAN, LARRY C., JUN 67 10P.
DOCUMENT NOT AVAILABLE FROM EDRS.

FOUR-, FIVE-, AND SIX-YEAR-OLD CHILDREN WERE USED AS SUBJECTS IN THIS INVESTIGATION. THERE WERE 192 EXPERIMENTAL AND 96 CONTROL CHILDREN USED, DIVIDED EQUALLY BETWEEN THE THREE AGE GROUPS. THE EXPERIMENTAL CHILDREN RECEIVED A 1-MINUTE PRETEST EXPOSURE PROCEDURE IN WHICH 1/4 OF THE CHILDREN OBSERVED 4 TWO-DIMENSIONAL STIMULI (IRREGULAR PENTAGONS), 1/4 OBSERVED 4 THREE-DIMENSIONAL STIMULI, 1/4 MANIPULATED THE TWO-DIMENSIONAL STIMULI, AND 1/4 MANIPULATED THE THREE-DIMENSIONAL STIMULI. THE CONTROL GROUP RECEIVED NO PRETEST CONDITION. THE TEST CONDITION GIVEN TO ALL CHILDREN INVOLVED CHOOSING THE ONE OF FOUR COMPARISON STIMULI THAT MATCHED A STANDARD STIMULUS. FOR HALF OF EACH GROUP, EXPERIMENTAL AND CONTROL, THE STIMULI WERE TWO-DIMENSIONAL, AND FOR THE OTHER HALF, THREE-DIMENSIONAL. THE RESULTS INDICATED THAT THERE WAS A SIGNIFICANT AGE MAIN EFFECT; THAT IS, THE OLDER THEY WERE, THE FASTER THE CHILDREN LEARNED THE TEST TASK. ALSO, CHILDREN FOUND IT EASIER TO DISCRIMINATE AMONG TWO-DIMENSIONAL STIMULI THAN AMONG THREE-DIMENSIONAL STIMULI. THE ABSENCE OF A SIGNIFICANT MAIN EFFECT OF PRETEST EXPOSURE TO STIMULUS DIMENSIONALITY AND/OR OF EXPOSURE TO A MANIPULATION CONDITION WAS CONTRARY TO THE EXPERIMENTAL HYPOTHESIS. NO SIGNIFICANT DIFFERENCE WAS FOUND BETWEEN THE EXPERIMENTAL GROUP AND CONTROL GROUP IN DISCRIMINATION LEARNING ABILITY. (WD)

ED023453 PS001181
INTERACTION PATTERNS AS A SOURCE OF ERROR IN TEACHERS' EVALUATIONS OF HEAD START CHILDREN. FINAL REPORT. HOLMES, MONICA BYCHOWSKI; AND OTHERS, 5 AUG 68 67P.
EDRS PRICE MF-$0.65 HC-$3.29

IN AN EFFORT TO DETERMINE WHETHER INTELLIGENCE AND SCHOOL READINESS COULD BE ESTIMATED FROM OBSERVIN G BEHAVIOR AND IF MIDDLE CLASS HEAD START TEACHERS RANKED HIGHLY THOSE PUPILS WHOSE BEHAVIOR RESEMBLED MIDDLE CLASS BEHAVIOR, THE BEHAVIOR PATTERNS OF 36 HEAD START PUPILS WERE COMPARED WITH THEIR TEACHERS' RANKING OF PERCEIVED INTELLIGENCE AND SCHOOL READINESS AND WITH BEHAVIOR PATTERNS OF 32 MIDDLE CLASS AND 40 UPPER-MIDDLE CLASS CHILDREN, ALL APPROXIMATELY AGE 4. THE CHILDREN'S INTELLIGENCE AND SCHOOL READINESS WERE MEASURED BY STANDARDIZED TESTS. BEHAVIOR PATTERNS WERE OBSERVED ON TWO SCHEDULES: CONTINUOUS AND SUMMARY. THE RESULTS SHOWED THAT (1) INTELLIGENCE AND SCHOOL READINESS WERE NOT CORRECTLY PREDICTED FROM DIFFERENT TYPES OF BEHAVIOR PATTERNS, (2) WHILE THERE WAS NO DIFFERENCE IN BEHAVIOR AMONG THOSE HEAD START PUPILS WITH ACTUAL INTELLIGENCE DIFFERENCES, THE BEHAVIOR OF THOSE PERCEIVED TO BE BRIGHTER CLOSELY RESEMBLED MIDDLE CLASS BEHAVIOR, AND (3) BEHAVIOR PATTERNS OF ALL HEAD START PUPILS WERE SIMILAR, REGARDLESS OF ACTUAL SCHOOL READINESS. THE DATA WERE TABULATED, AND SUGGESTIONS WERE MADE FOR A REPLICA STUDY. A MANUAL FOR USING THE OBSERVATION SCHEDULE IS INCLUDED. (JS)

ED023454 PS001183
FINAL REPORT ON HEAD START EVALUATION AND RESEARCH: 1967-68 TO THE OFFICE OF ECONOMIC OPPORTUNITY. SECTION I: PART A, MIDDLE CLASS MOTHER-TEACHERS IN AN EXPERIMENTAL PRESCHOOL PROGRAM FOR SOCIALLY DISADVANTAGED CHILDREN. PIERCE-JONES, JOHN; AND OTHERS, JUN 68 59P.
EDRS PRICE MF-$0.65 HC-$3.29

A SHORT TERM PRESCHOOL READINESS PROGRAM WAS DESIGNED IN 1967 TO EMPLOY NONPEDAGOGICALLY TRAINED MIDDLE CLASS MOTHERS AS TEACHERS FOR PRESCHOOL DISADVANTAGED CHILDREN. THE CHILDREN CHOSEN FOR THIS STUDY WERE 43 MEXICAN-AMERICANS AND FIVE NEGROES FROM LOWER CLASS FAMILIES. THREE CLASSROOMS, CONSISTING OF 12 CHILDREN AND THREE MOTHERS EACH, WERE ESTABLISHED. THE REMAINING 12 CHILDREN BECAME PART OF A NOVEL "HOME ACCULTURATION" GROUP IN WHICH THE CHILDREN, IN GROUPS OF FOUR, WENT TO THE MOTHER-TEACHER'S HOME FOR THE WHOLE 6-WEEK SUMMER PROGRAM. ALL CHILDREN WERE ADMINISTERED INTELLIGENCE TESTS DURING THE FIRST AND SIXTH WEEKS OF THE PROGRAM. A CONTROL GROUP WAS TESTED AND THE RESULTS COMPARED TO THE EXPERIMENTAL GROUP, BUT IT WAS NOT POSSIBLE TO SAY THAT THE TWO GROUPS HAD SIMILAR ENTERING ABILITIES, AND THE TEST SCORES' ANALYSIS WAS INCONCLUSIVE. THE SCORES FROM THE TWO EXPERIMENTAL PROGRAMS SHOWED AN INCREASE FROM PRETESTING TO POSTTESTING BUT NO SIGNIFICANT DIFFERENCES BETWEEN PROGRAMS. AN OVERALL GAIN IN ACHIEVEMENT MOTIVATION WAS FOUND FOR ALL CHILDREN, ALTHOUGH THERE WAS A SIGNIFICANTLY GREATER GAIN FOR THOSE INITIALLY LOW IN MOTIVATION ON THE PRETESTS. NO SIGNIFICANT DIFFERENCES WERE FOUND BETWEEN THE EXPERIMENTAL AND CONTROL GROUPS. (WD)

ED023455 PS001184
FINAL REPORT ON HEAD START EVALUATION AND RESEARCH: 1967-68 TO THE OFFICE OF ECONOMIC OPPORTUNITY. SECTION I: PART B, ACCURACY OF SELF-PERCEPTION AMONG CULTURALLY DEPRIVED PRESCHOOLS. PIERCE-JONES, JOHN; JONES, JOANNA, JUN 68 17P.
EDRS PRICE MF-$0.65 HC-$3.29

SEVENTY CULTURALLY DEPRIVED PRESCHOOL CHILDREN, PRIMARILY OF MEXICAN-AMERICAN ETHNICITY, WERE CHOSEN TO PARTICIPATE IN THIS STUDY OF SELF-PERCEPTION. ONE OF THE MOST IMPORTANT ASPECTS OF A CHILD'S PERSONALITY DEVELOPMENT CONCERNS THE CONCEPTIONS HE HAS OF HIMSELF. IT IS POSITED THAT TWO IMPORTANT INFLUENCES UPON THESE CONCEPTIONS ARE (1) INTERPERSONAL RELATIONSHIPS AND (2) PHYSICAL ENVIRONMENT. TO TEST THESE POSTULATES, 39 OF THE SUBJECTS OF THIS STUDY WERE PLACED IN AN EXPERIMENTAL CLASS PRESIDED OVER BY MOTHERS WITH NO TEACHER TRAINING AND WITH A RATIO OF ONE ADULT TO FOUR CHILDREN. THE REMAINING PRESCHOOLERS ATTENDED A REGULAR HEAD START CLASS. IT WAS HYPOTHESIZED THAT ALL SUBJECTS WOULD DEMONSTRATE GREATER SENSITIVITY TO THEIR OWN SELVES AT THE CONCLUSION OF THE 6-WEEK SUMMER PROGRAM THAN THEY HAD AT THE BEGINNING AND THAT THE CHILDREN IN THE EXPERIMENTAL CLASS WOULD SHOW A MORE SIGNIFICANT CHANGE IN ACCURACY OF SELF-PERCEPTION THAN THE OTHERS BECAUSE OF THE LOW ADULT-CHILD RATIO. A DOLL-SELF POINT TASK AND A DRAW-A-PERSON TASK WERE USED AS PRETESTS AND POSTTESTS. THE RESULTS FROM THESE TASKS SUPPORTED THE FIRST PART OF THE HYPOTHESIS AND, WITH RESERVATIONS, THE SECOND PART. ALTHOUGH THE EXPERIMENTAL CLASS GROUP SHOWED SIGNIFICANTLY GREATER INCREASES IN SELF-DRAWING SCORES, THEY ALSO HAD HIGHER PRETEST SCORES. (WD)

ED023456 PS001243
HEAD START EVALUATION AND RESEARCH CENTER, THE UNIVERSITY OF CHICAGO. REPORT F, SOCIALIZATION INTO THE ROLE OF PUPIL. SHIPMAN, VIRGINIA C.; HESS, ROBERT D., 30 NOV 67 15P.
EDRS PRICE MF-$0.65 HC-$3.29

EARLY CHILDHOOD EXPERIENCE IS OFTEN CRUCIAL IN ESTABLISHING THE COGNITIVE AND AFFECTIVE STRUCTURES OF THE CHILD. IN PARTICULAR, THE PRESCHOOL EXPERIENCE OF THE LOWER CLASS CHILD ESTABLISHES PATTERNS OF RESPONSIVE BEHAVIOR AND WAYS OF RELATING TO THE AUTHORITY STRUCTURE OF THE SCHOOL WHICH ARE NOT CONDUCIVE TO ACADEMIC LEARNING AND PREVENT THE CHILD FROM TAKING FULL ADVANTAGE OF THE COGNITIVE EXPERIENCES AVAILABLE. THE INFLUENCE ON THE CHILD OF HIS MOTHER'S ATTITUDES IS THE SUBJECT OF THIS STUDY. MOTHERS HAVE BEEN GROUPED INTO TWO TYPES FOR THIS STUDY: (1) STATUS ORIENTED MOTHERS, WHO EMPHASIZE THE DIFFERENCE IN STATUS AND POWER BETWEEN THE CHILD AND THE TEACHER AND OFFER COMPLIANCE AND DOCILITY AS TECHNIQUES FOR THE CHILD TO DEAL WITH THE CLASSROOM SITUATION, AND (2) THE PERSON ORIENTED MOTHER, WHO SEES LESS DISTANCE BETWEEN HERSELF AND THE SCHOOL AND IS THUS LESS CONCERNED WITH OBEDIENCE AND MORE CONCERNED WITH COGNITIVE DEVELOPMENT. THE POPULATION INVESTIGATED IN THIS STUDY WAS URBAN AND RURAL NEGRO, WHITE, AND SEMINOLE INDIAN FAMILIES. EIGHT PREDICTIONS WERE MADE CONCERNING THE EFFECT OF THE MOTHER'S ATTITUDE ON THE CHILD'S PERFORMANCE ON VARIOUS COGNITIVE TESTS. THE DATA ANALYSIS IS NOT YET COMPLETE. AN APPENDIX FOLLOWING THE STUDY PRESENTS A PARENT ATTITUDE QUESTIONNAIRE. (WD)

ED023457 PS001246

FINAL REPORT ON HEAD START EVALUATION AND RESEARCH: 1967-68 TO THE OFFICE OF ECONOMIC OPPORTUNITY. SECTION I: PARTS A AND B. PIERCE-JONES, JOHN; AND OTHERS, JUN 68 81P.

EDRS PRICE MF-$0.65 HC-$3.29

THIS DOCUMENT IS SECTION ONE OF A FINAL REPORT ON HEAD START EVALUATION AND RESEARCH FOR 1967-68 BY THE CHILD DEVELOPMENT EVALUATION AND RESEARCH CENTER OF THE UNIVERSITY OF TEXAS AT AUSTIN. THIS SECTION IS COMPOSED OF TWO STUDIES: (A) MIDDLE CLASS MOTHER-TEACHERS IN AN EXPERIMENTAL PRESCHOOL PROGRAM FOR SOCIALLY DISADVANTAGED CHILDREN (PS 001 183) AND (B) ACCURACY OF SELF-PERCEPTION AMONG CULTURALLY DEPRIVED PRESCHOOLERS (PS 001 184). (WD)

ED023458 PS001247

FINAL REPORT ON HEAD START EVALUATION AND RESEARCH: 1967-68 TO THE OFFICE OF ECONOMIC OPPORTUNITY. SECTION II: ACHIEVEMENT MOTIVATION AND PATTERNS OF REINFORCEMENT IN HEAD START CHILDREN. ESPINOSA, RENATO, JUN 68 124P.

EDRS PRICE MF-$0.65 HC-$6.58

EIGHTY-SIX NEGRO AND MEXICAN-AMERICAN CHILDREN WERE DIVIDED INTO EXPERIMENTAL AND CONTROL GROUPS IN A STUDY DESIGNED TO LEARN THE EFFECTS OF AN 8-WEEK SUMMER HEAD START PROGRAM ON THE ACHIEVEMENT MOTIVE OF THESE CHILDREN. THE STUDY WAS BASED ON MCCLELLAND'S THEORY OF ACHIEVEMENT MOTIVE AND THE MODELS OF ATKINSON AND ARONSON. CHILDREN WERE PRETESTED AND POSTTESTED WITH THE ARONSON AND LEVEL OF ASPIRATION TESTS. DATA CONCERNING TEACHERS WAS COLLECTED ON THE OBSERVER'S RATING FORM. MOTHERS FILLED IN THE WINTERBOTTOM QUESTIONNAIRE. BOTH ETHNIC GROUPS OF CHILDREN MADE GAINS IN ACHIEVEMENT MOTIVE. THE TOTAL HEAD START EXPERIENCE WAS APPARENTLY RESPONSIBLE FOR THE CHANGE IN SUBJECTS TOWARDS MOTIVE TO AVOID FAILURE. HEAD START REINFORCEMENT PRACTICES WERE MORE STRUCTURED AND SYSTEMATIC THAN IS COMMON TO LOWER CLASS PARENTS' PRACTICES. TYPE OF REINFORCEMENT IS ASSOCIATED WITH THE DEVELOPMENT OF THE ACHIEVEMENT MOTIVE. BECAUSE TEACHER AIDES SPEND MUCH TIME WITH THE CHILDREN, A WORKSHOP ON THE NATURE AND EFFECTS OF REINFORCEMENT IS RECOMMENDED AS PART OF ANY FUTURE AIDE TRAINING PROGRAM. FACSIMILES OF THE SPANISH AND ENGLISH QUESTIONNAIRE FORMS AND THE RATING SCALE ARE IN THE APPENDIXES. (MS)

ED023459 PS001248

LEARNING AND TEACHING, GRADES N-9 (EMPHASIS ON EARLY CHILDHOOD). , [67] 62P.

EDRS PRICE MF-$0.65 HC-$3.29

A CURRICULUM UNIT WAS DEVELOPED TO TEACH APPRENTICE TEACHERS THE THEORIES UNDERLYING THE TEACHING-LEARNING PROCESS AND THEIR RELATIONSHIP TO CLASSROOM APPLICATION. THE UNIVERSITY SUPERVISING TEACHER, SUBJECT AREA SPECIALISTS, AND THE COOPERATING CLASSROOM TEACHER WOULD WORK WITH THE APPRENTICE TEACHER AS SHE LEARNED SPECIFIC TECHNIQUES OF TEACHING AND CLASSROOM MANAGEMENT AND PRACTICES. THE MODEL, RATIONALE, AND AN EXTENSIVE BIBLIOGRAPHY FOR THE COURSE ARE INCLUDED IN THIS SYLLABUS. ALTHOUGH MOST OF THE MATERIAL IS DIRECTED TOWARDS TEACHERS OF MIDDLE GRADES, GENERAL METHODS WHICH COULD BE USED BY TEACHERS WORKING IN ANY AGE GROUP ARE ALSO DESCRIBED. (MS)

ED023460 PS001261

NURSERIES IN CROSS-CULTURAL EDUCATION. PROGRESS REPORT. , JUN 68 121P.

EDRS PRICE MF-$0.65 HC-$6.58

A 5-YEAR PROJECT WHICH FOCUSES UPON THE PROCESSES NECESSARY FOR INITIATION AND IMPLEMENTATION OF A CROSS-CULTURAL NURSERY SCHOOL IS AT ITS MIDPOINT IN OPERATION, WITH PROJECT NURSERIES HAVING BEEN ESTABLISHED AND PRESENTLY OPERATING IN THE SAN FRANCISCO AREA. THE FAMILY DWELLINGS FROM WHICH CHILDREN ARE DRAWN CONSIST OF APPROXIMATELY EQUALLY DIVIDED MIDDLE-INCOME COOPERATIVELY OWNED HOUSING DEVELOPMENT UNITS, PUBLIC HOUSING UNITS, AND INDIVIDUAL DWELLINGS. THE RACIAL COMPOSITION OF THE INITIAL CHILD SAMPLE ENROLLED IN THE THREE NURSERY SCHOOLS INCLUDED 41 NEGRO CHILDREN, 15 CAUCASIAN CHILDREN, THREE ORIENTAL CHILDREN, AND SIX CHILDREN IDENTIFIED BY RACE AS "MIXED." ASSESSMENT OF THE TOTAL PROJECT IS BEING MADE BY IDENTIFYING BEHAVIORAL CHANGES, IN THE CHILDREN, OF FACTORS RELATED TO MENTAL HEALTH; IN THE FAMILIES OF THE CHILDREN, OF FACTORS RELATED TO MENTAL HEALTH; AND IN FAMILY UTILIZATION OF COMMUNITY RESOURCES. (EV)

ED023461 PS001262

MODIFICATION OF A DEVIANT SIBLING INTERACTION PATTERN IN THE HOME. O'LEARY, K. DANIEL; AND OTHERS, 14 DEC 66 9P.

DOCUMENT NOT AVAILABLE FROM EDRS.

EXPERIMENTAL MODIFICATION OF DESTRUCTIVE AND ASSAULTIVE SIBLING INTERACTION WAS CARRIED OUT WITHIN THE HOME ENVIRONMENT. TWO BROTHERS (6 AND 3 YEARS OLD) WERE TREATED THROUGH TOKEN POSITIVE REINFORCEMENT TECHNIQUES IN AN EFFORT TO IMPROVE THEIR BEHAVIOR TOWARDS EACH OTHER. A "TIME OUT" FROM REINFORCEMENT PROCEDURES INVOLVED AN ISOLATION PERIOD FOR THE SIBLING PRACTICING DESTRUCTIVE BEHAVIOR. AT FIRST THE PROGRAM WAS CARRIED ON BY THE EXPERIMENTER, WHO DEVISED TECHNIQUES TO MEET CLINICAL AND RESEARCH NEEDS AS THE STUDY PROGRESSED. WHEN THE BOYS HAD SHOWN SUFFICIENT IMPROVEMENT, THE MODIFICATION TECHNIQUES WERE TAKEN OVER BY THEIR MOTHER, UNDER THE EXPERIMENTER'S GUIDANCE. THE CHILDREN'S BEHAVIOR CHANGED MARKEDLY UNDER THE REINFORCEMENT SYSTEM AND WAS GENERALIZED TO OTHER TIMES AND SITUATIONS, ACCORDING TO PARENTAL AND TEACHER REPORTS. WHILE THE INVESTIGATORS RECOGNIZE THAT FACTORS OTHER THAN BEHAVIORAL THERAPY (SUCH AS THE 3-YEAR-OLD'S IMPROVED VERBAL FACILITY) CONTRIBUTED TO THE BEHAVIORAL IMPROVEMENT, THEY CONCLUDE THAT PARENTS CAN USE MODIFICATION PRINCIPLES TO CHANGE DEVIANT BEHAVIOR IN THEIR OWN CHILDREN. (MS)

ED023462 PS001263

BEHAVIOR MODIFICATION OF AN ADJUSTMENT CLASS: A TOKEN REINFORCEMENT PROGRAM. O'LEARY, K. DANIEL; BECKER, WESLEY C., 67 6P.

DOCUMENT NOT AVAILABLE FROM EDRS.

A BASE RATE OF DEVIANT BEHAVIOR WAS OBTAINED FOR THE EIGHT MOST DISRUPTIVE CHILDREN IN A THIRD GRADE ADJUSTMENT CLASS. IN A TOKEN REINFORCEMENT PROGRAM, THE CHILDREN RECEIVED TEACHER'S RATINGS, WHICH WERE EXCHANGEABLE FOR REINFORCERS SUCH AS CANDY AND TRINKETS. WITH THE INTRODUCTION OF THE TOKEN REINFORCEMENT PROGRAM, AN ABRUPT REDUCTION IN DEVIANT BEHAVIOR OCCURRED. DELAY OF REINFORCEMENT WAS GRADUALLY INCREASED TO 4 DAYS WITHOUT INCREASE IN DEVIANT BEHAVIOR. THE PROGRAM WAS EQUALLY SUCCESSFUL FOR ALL CHILDREN OBSERVED, AND ANECDOTAL EVIDENCE SUGGESTS THAT THE CHILDREN'S APPROPRIATE BEHAVIOR GENERALIZED TO OTHER SCHOOL SITUATIONS. (AUTHOR)

ED023463 PS001264

GUIDELINES FOR PLANNING PRESCHOOL PROGRAMS FOR EDUCATIONALLY DEPRIVED CHILDREN UNDER TITLE I OF THE ELEMENTARY AND SECONDARY EDUCATION ACT OF 1965. , 67 27P.

EDRS PRICE MF-$0.65 HC-$3.29

THIS GUIDELINE BULLETIN WAS PREPARED TO ASSIST LOCAL SCHOOLS IN PLANNING AND IMPLEMENTING PRESCHOOL PROGRAMS FOR EDUCATIONALLY DEPRIVED CHILDREN. PROGRAM OBJECTIVES AND ORGANIZATION (INCLUDING TOPICS SUCH AS PUPILS, PERSONNEL, EVALUATION, PARENTAL INVOLVEMENT, AND RECORDS) ARE INCLUDED. THE GENERAL CHARACTERISTICS OF 4- AND 5-YEAR-OLDS AND THE EDUCATIONAL PROGRAM BEST SUITED FOR CHILDREN IN THIS AGE GROUP ARE DISCUSSED. A DESCRIPTION OF NEEDED SCHOOL FACILITIES AND AN EQUIPMENT COST ESTIMATE ARE ALSO GIVEN. (MS)

ED023464 PS001267

BIBLIOGRAPHY OF RESEARCH STUDIES IN ELEMENTARY SCHOOL AND PRE-SCHOOL MATHEMATICS. PIKAART, LEN; AND OTHERS, JAN 66 55P.

EDRS PRICE MF-$0.65 HC-$3.29

THIS BIBLIOGRAPHY IS DIVIDED INTO SEVEN SECTIONS. THE FIRST INCLUDES STUDIES ON STUDENTS AT VARIOUS ELEMENTARY LEVELS, GROUPING PROCEDURES, PRACTICES AND IMPLICATIONS FOR TEACHING MATHEMATICS, AND ATTITUDE IMPROVEMENT BY EFFECTIVE TEACHING. STUDIES IN THE SECOND SECTION COVER TEACHER TRAINING, ATTITUDES, ABILITIES, AND LEVEL OF ACHIEVEMENT. ANOTHER SECTION PROVIDES RESEARCH INFORMATION ON TEXTBOOKS, TOPICS FOR PROGRAMS, AND PROGRAM COMPARISON (FOREIGN AND AMERICAN). WITHIN THIS SECTION, FEASIBILITY STUDIES ON SEPARATE ELEMENTARY LEVELS AND APPROPRIATENESS STUDIES ARE INCLUDED. A FOURTH SECTION DEALS WITH STUDIES ON DIFFERENT TEACHING METHODS AT SPECIFIC LEVELS AND IN ELEMENTARY SCHOOL IN GENERAL. REPORTS ON INSTRUCTIONAL AIDS ARE INCLUDED IN THIS SECTION. STUDIES ON CURRICULUM DEVELOPMENT ARE GROUPED ALONG WITH THOSE ON THE PHILOSOPHY, HISTORY, AND FUTURE OF TEACHING MATHEMATICS. EVALUATION LITERATURE IS IN THE SIXTH SECTION. A FINAL SECTION GIVES REVIEWS OF RESEARCH AND BIBLIOGRAPHIES. MOST ENTRIES ARE DATED IN THE LATE 1950'S AND EARLY 1960'S; SOME ARE LISTED MORE THAN ONCE, BUT NONE ARE ANNOTATED. (JS)

ED023465 PS001268
CHILD DEVELOPMENT AND SOCIAL SCIENCE EDUCATION. PART I: THE PROBLEM, PART II: CONFERENCE REPORT. SIGEL, IRVING, MAR 66 20P.
EDRS PRICE MF-$0.65 HC-$3.29

PARTS I AND II OF A FOUR-PART REPORT ON A STUDY OF THE RELEVANCE OF EXISTING KNOWLEDGE ABOUT CHILD DEVELOPMENT TO SOCIAL SCIENCE CURRICULUM DEVELOPMENT ARE COMBINED IN THIS DOCUMENT. PART I EXPLORES THE PROBLEM OF INADEQUATE COMMUNICATION BETWEEN THE DEVELOPMENTAL PSYCHOLOGISTS AND CURRICULUM WORKERS AND SUGGESTS SOME DIRECTIONS FOR COOPERATIVE EFFORTS INVOLVING THE TWO GROUPS. PART II IS AN ACCOUNT OF A TEST RUN OF SUCH A COOPERATIVE EFFORT IN WHICH THE FINDINGS OF DEVELOPMENTAL PSYCHOLOGISTS WERE APPLIED TO THE SPECIFIC PROBLEMS OF SOCIAL SCIENCE EDUCATORS. PART II PERTAINS TO AN AGE GROUP OF 10- AND 11-YEAR-OLDS. (MS)

ED023466 PS001269
CHILD DEVELOPMENT AND SOCIAL SCIENCE EDUCATION. PART III: ABSTRACTS OF RELEVANT LITERATURE. SIGEL, IRVING; WATERS, ELINOR, MAR 66 91P.
EDRS PRICE MF-$0.65 HC-$3.29

PART III OF A FOUR-PART REPORT CONTAINS OVER 60 ANNOTATED ABSTARCTS OF CHILD DEVELOPMENT SOURCE MATERIALS RELEVANT TO THE CONSTRUCTION OF SOCIAL STUDIES CURRICULUMS. FOR THIS COLLECTION, SOCIAL SCIENCES WERE DEFINED AS ANTHROPOLOGY, SOCIOLOGY, ECONOMICS, POLITICAL SCIENCE, AND PSYCHOLOGY. AN ACCEPTED OPERATIONAL DEFINITION WAS THAT A SOCIAL SCIENCE CONCEPT IS ANY TERM THAT IS INCLUSIVE OF A NUMBER OF THINGS, INSTANCES, OR EVENTS. ABSTRACTS WERE CULLED FROM MAJOR JOURNALS AND OTHER COLLECTIONS OF WRITINGS CONCERNING SOCIAL SCIENCE DISCIPLINES. ARTICLES ON THE CONTENT AND STRATEGY OF TEACHING SOCIAL SCIENCE WERE CHOSEN ON THE BASIS OF USE TO A PRACTITIONER, WHETHER CLASSROOM TEACHER OR CURRICULUM SPECIALIST. (MS)

ED023467 PS001270
CHILD DEVELOPMENT AND SOCIAL SCIENCE EDUCATION. PART IV: A TEACHING STRATEGY DERIVED FROM SOME PIAGETIAN CONCEPTS. SIGEL, IRVING, MAR 66 24P.
EDRS PRICE MF-$0.65 HC-$3.29

IN THIS FOURTH PART OF A STUDY OF THE RELEVANCE OF EXISTING KNOWLEDGE ABOUT CHILD DEVELOPMENT TO SOCIAL SCIENCE CURRICULUM DEVELOPMENT, SOME TENTATIVE SUGGESTIONS ARE MADE FOR INCORPORATING SOME OF THE FUNDAMENTAL IDEAS OF PIAGET INTO A TEACHING STRATEGY. THE ABILITY OF CHILDREN TO DEAL WITH CLASSIFICATIONS ON THE BASIS OF SINGLE DISCRETE ATTRIBUTES AND THEIR LATER ABILITY TO MAKE MULTIPLE CLASSIFICATIONS AND RELATIONSHIPS ARE DISCUSSED. REVERSIBILITY AND RECIPROCITY, AS INTELLECTUAL OPERATIONS WHICH ARE NECESSARY PRIOR TO MULTIPLE CLASSIFICATION AND CONSERVATION UNDERSTANDING ARE ALSO DISCUSSED. (MS)

ED023468 PS001271
THE DEVELOPMENT OF A BEHAVIOR CHECKLIST FOR BOYS. ROSS, ALAN O.; AND OTHERS, DEC 65 16P.
EDRS PRICE MF-$0.65 HC-$3.29

THE PITTSBURGH ADJUSTMENT SURVEY SCALES WERE DEVELOPED TO MEET THE NEED FOR THE OBJECTIVE EVALUATION OF THE SOCIAL BEHAVIOR OF ELEMENTARY SCHOOL-AGE BOYS USING THE OBSERVATIONS OF CLASSROOM TEACHERS. AN INITIAL ITEM POOL WAS REDUCED TO 94 ITEMS BY AN EXTREME-GROUP PROCEDURE (202 SUBJECTS). A FACTOR ANALYSIS (209 SUBJECTS) OF THE INVENTORY RESULTED IN THE ISOLATION OF FOUR FACTORS, LABELED AGGRESSIVE BEHAVIOR, WITHDRAWN BEHAVIOR, PASSIVE-AGGRESSIVE BEHAVIOR, AND PROSOCIAL BEHAVIOR. RESULTS FROM OTHER SAMPLES ARE PRESENTED CONCERNING TEST-RETEST RELIABILITY AND CONSTRUCT VALIDITY. THE SCALES DO NOT REVEAL AGE-RELATED CHANGE OVER THE GRADES SAMPLED. (AUTHOR)

ED023469 PS001274
SIX STRUCTURE-OF-INTELLECT HYPOTHESES IN SIX-YEAR-OLD CHILDREN. ORPET, R.E.; MEYERS, C.E., 66 7P.
DOCUMENT NOT AVAILABLE FROM EDRS.

THE STUDY OF ABILITY FACTORS IN YOUNG CHILDREN HAS PASSED THE STAGE OF DEMONSTRATING THAT SEPARATE FACTORS EXIST, THE EFFORT NOW BEING DEVOTED TO SYSTEMATIC IDENTIFICATION OF MEASURABLE ABILITIES. THIS STUDY WAS DESIGNED TO CONFIRM SOME OF THE TENTATIVE ABILITIES DEMONSTRATED IN OTHER STUDIES AND TO EXTEND THE EXPLORATION INTO MEMORY PROCESSES AND SYMBOLIC CONTENT. SIX ABILITIES WERE HYPOTHESIZED. THEY HAVE BEEN SHOWN TO BE WELL ESTABLISHED AT THE ADULT LEVEL BUT HAVE NOT BEEN SHOWN TO EXIST IN CHILDHOOD. IN AN ATTEMPT TO DEMONSTRATE THE EXISTENCE OF THESE SIX ABILITIES IN CHILDREN, 100 WHITE KINDERGARTEN CHILDREN, AGE 6, FROM MIDDLE CLASS HOMES WERE ADMINISTERED A BATTERY OF 20 TESTS GEARED TO MEASURE THE FOLLOWING HYPOTHESIZED ABILITIES: (1) VISUAL MEMORY FOR FIGURAL UNITS, (2) AUDITORY MEMORY FOR SYMBOLIC UNITS, (3) COVERGENT SEMANTIC PRODUCTION, (4) DIVERGENT PRODUCTION OF SEMANTIC UNITS--IDEATIONAL FLUENCY, (5) EVALUATION OF FIGURAL UNITS, AND (6) EVALUATION OF SYMBOLIC UNITS. THE TEST RESULTS SUPPORTED THE EXISTENCE OF ABILITIES (2), (3), (4), AND (5). THE REMAINING TWO ABILITY DOMAINS WERE NOT DEFINITELY DEMONSTRATED. (WD)

ED023470 PS001275
PROCESSES OF CURIOSITY AND EXPLORATION IN PRESCHOOL DISADVANTAGED CHILDREN. MINUCHIN, PATRICIA, JUN 68 59P.
EDRS PRICE MF-$0.65 HC-$3.29

THIS STUDY WAS CREATED PRIMARILY TO EXPLORE NEW TECHNIQUES AND TO GENERATE FRUITFUL NEW HYPOTHESES AND PROCEDURES FOR THE (1) DESCRIPTION OF VARIATIONS IN EXPRESSED CURIOSITY AND CONSTRUCTIVE EXPLORATION AMONG DISADVANTAGED PRESCHOOL CHILDREN AND (2) ASSESSMENT OF THE RELATIONSHIP BETWEEN SUCH CURIOSITY AND EXPLORATION AND OTHER ASPECTS OF THE CHILD'S DYNAMIC AND COGNITIVE DEVELOPMENT. THE STUDY WAS CONDUCTED AT TWO PHILADELPHIA GET SET (HEAD START) PRESCHOOL CENTERS WITH EIGHTEEN 4-YEAR-OLD NEGRO CHILDREN. DATA SOURCES WERE (1) OBSERVATIONS OF THE CHILDREN IN THE PRESCHOOL SETTING, (2) TEACHER RANKINGS, AND (3) FOUR SESSIONS WITH THE INDIVIDUAL CHILDREN. DURING THE DATA GATHERING, SPECIAL MEASURES WERE USED TO ASSESS THE CHILD'S CURIOSITY AND EXPLORATION, SELF-IMAGE, PERCEPTION OF ADULTS AND ENVIRONMENT, AND CONCEPT FORMATION. THE RESULTS SHOWED THAT ALTHOUGH THE SUBJECTS WERE NOT AS ADVANCED AS MIDDLE CLASS CHILDREN, THEY DID DIVIDE INTO HIGH AND LOW DEVELOPED GROUPS. THOSE SUBJECTS WITH MORE ACTIVE EXPLORATORY BEHAVIOR WERE MORE COHERENT, HAD MORE POSITIVE IMAGES, AND HAD A MORE ADEQUATE CONCEPT FORMATION. THESE CHILDREN SEEM TO HAVE A GOOD CHANCE TO SUCCEED IN SCHOOL, BUT THE LESS DEVELOPED CHILDREN, WHO APPEARED TO BE VERY DISADVANTAGED, WILL NEED SIGNIFICANT AMOUNTS OF ADDED HELP. (WD)

ED023471 PS001276
THERE IS A BETTER WAY. A PREMISE POINTS THE WAY, A PROFILE WITH PROMISE, A COMPOSITE OF THE SURVEY. , JUL 68 35P.
EDRS PRICE MF-$0.65 HC-$3.29

THIS DOCUMENT IS A BROCHURE PUBLISHED BY THE SOUTH ST. PAUL PUBLIC SCHOOLS DESCRIBING SOME OF THE RESULTS OF A QUESTIONNAIRE-SURVEY OF OVER 200 TEACHERS IN MINNESOTA USING SULLIVAN'S PROGRAMMED READING IN THE PRIMARY GRADES. THE BROCHURE IS COMPOSED OF (1) AN INTRODUCTORY SECTION WHICH DISCUSSES THE PREMISE OF PROGRAMMED READING; NAMELY, THE INDIVIDUALIZATION OF BASIC READING INSTRUCTION; (2) A PROFILE OF THE TYPICAL TEACHER WHO RESPONDED TO THE QUESTIONNAIRE-SURVEY; AND (3) A COMPOSITE OF 158 RESPONSES TO THE SURVEY, INCLUDING (A) A STATISTICAL DATA SHOWING HOW THE TEACHERS ANSWERED THE ITEMS OF THE QUESTIONNAIRE, (B) THE PHILOSOPHY AND PROCEDURES OF THE TEACHERS, (C) THE TEACHERS' PERSONAL OPINIONS ABOUT THE USE OF PROGRAMMED READING, AND (D) SOME GENERAL COMMENTS OFFERED BY THE TEACHERS. (WD)

ED023472 PS001277
AN EVALUATION OF THE PRESCHOOL READINESS CENTERS PROGRAM IN EAST ST. LOUIS, ILLINOIS, JULY 1, 1967-JUNE 30, 1968. FINAL REPORT. BITTNER, MARGUERITE L.; AND OTHERS, JUN 68 99P.
EDRS PRICE MF-$0.65 HC-$3.29

FIVE GROUPS OF CHILDREN WERE TESTED, AND THEIR TEST PERFORMANCES WERE COMPARED. EXPERIMENTAL GROUP ONE (X-1) CONSISTED OF 105 CHILDREN WHO HAD ATTENDED A YEARLONG PRESCHOOL READINESS CENTER PROGRAM. EXPERIMENTAL GROUP TWO (X-2) CONSISTED OF 93 CHILDREN WHO HAD ATTENDED A SUMMER HEAD START PROGRAM. CONTROL GROUPS ONE AND TWO (C-1 AND C-2) CONSISTED OF 79 LOW INCOME CHILDREN WITH NO PRESCHOOL TRAINING. CONTROL GROUP THREE (C-3) CONSISTED OF 59 MIDDLE INCOME CHILDREN WITH NO PRESCHOOL EXPERIENCE. ALL PRESCHOOL CHILDREN WERE TESTED UPON ENTRY INTO THEIR PARTICULAR PROGRAM BY MEANS OF THE PEABODY PICTURE VOCABULARY TEST, THE PRESCHOOL INVENTORY, AND THE CALIFORNIA TEST OF PERSONALITY. ALL CHILDREN WERE TESTED UPON ENTRY INTO THE FIRST GRADE BY MEANS OF THE ABOVE THREE MEASURES PLUS THE METROPOLITAN READINESS TEST. IN MAY 1968, DURING THE END OF THEIR FIRST-GRADE YEAR, ALL CHILDREN WERE ADMINISTERED THE METROPOLITAN ACHIEVEMENT TEST (MAT). A COMPARISON OF THESE RESULTS SHOWED THAT UPON ENTRY INTO THE FIRST GRADE, GROUP X-1 PERFORMED THE BEST OF ALL GROUPS ON THE FOUR MEASURES, WITH GROUP C-3 SECOND BEST. GROUP C-3 SCORED SIGNIFICANTLY BETTER THAN ALL OTHER GROUPS ON THE MAT, GROUP X-1 NOT PERFORMING SIGNIFICANTLY BETTER THAN X-2, C-1, AND C-2. THUS, GROUP X-1'S INITIAL SUPERIOR PERFORMANCE WAS NOT SUSTAINED OVER THE FIRST YEAR OF SCHOOL. IT WAS DISCOVERED THAT CHILDREN WHOSE PARENTS DID NOT PARTICIPATE IN THE PROGRAMS DEMONSTRATED THE POOREST TEST PERFORMANCES. (WD)

ED023473 PS001278
LEARNING OF INCENTIVE-VALUE BY CHILDREN. NUNNALLY, JUM C., JUN 68 21P.
EDRS PRICE MF-$0.65 HC-$3.29

THE RESEARCH CONCERNED THE ASSOCIATION OF NEUTRAL OBJECTS, SUCH AS NONSENSE SYLLABLES, WITH REWARDS, SUCH AS MONEY AND CANDY, IN CHILDREN. THIRTY-SIX SUBJECTS WERE OBTAINED FROM GRADES TWO THROUGH SIX OF LOCAL PUBLIC ELEMENTARY SCHOOLS IN NASHVILLE, TENNESSEE. ASSOCIATIONS BETWEEN NEUTRAL OBJECTS AND REWARDS WERE FORMED IN A TASK CONCERNING DISCRIMINATION LEARNING. SUBSEQUENTLY, MEASURES OF THE EFFECTS OF THE ASSOCIATIONS WERE OBTAINED WITH RESPECT TO VERBAL EVALUATION, EXPECTANCY OF OBTAINING NEW REWARDS, CHOICE BEHAVIOR, AND A VARIETY OF ASPECTS OF SELECTIVE ATTENTION. IN DIFFERENT EXPERIMENTS, PARAMETERS OF LEARNING, SUCH AS MAGNITUDE OF REWARD AND PER CENT OF REWARD, WERE INVESTIGATED. THE HYPOTHESIZED EFFECTS WERE OBTAINED WITH RESPECT TO THE DEPENDENT MEASURES. STUDIES OF SELECTIVE ATTENTION SUCH AS EYE MOVEMENTS, WERE MADE WITH RESPECT TO A WIDE VARIETY OF STIMULUS VARIABLES CONCERNING DIFFERENT ASPECTS OF INFORMATION, SUCH AS NOVELTY. WITH ALL TYPES OF MATERIALS, SELECTIVE ATTENTION WAS FOUND TO BE A MONOTONICALLY INCREASING FUNCTION OF AMOUNT OF INFORMATION IN THE DISPLAY. (AUTHOR/JS)

ED023474 PS001279
A COMPARISON OF PRE-KINDERGARTEN AND PRE-1ST GRADE BOYS AND GIRLS ON MEASURES OF SCHOOL READINESS AND LANGUAGE DEVELOPMENT. INTERIM REPORT. RUBIN, ROSALYN; BALOW, BRUCE, 29 AUG 68 19P.
EDRS PRICE MF-$0.65 HC-$3.29

ALTHOUGH NORMATIVE FIGURES OF THE PERFORMANCE OF LATE KINDERGARTEN AND ENTERING FIRST GRADE STUDENTS ON STANDARDIZED READINESS MEASURES ARE USUALLY AVAILABLE IN THE TEST MANUALS, NO SUCH DATA IS AVAILABLE FOR PUPILS ABOUT TO ENTER KINDERGARTEN. IN ORDER TO OBTAIN SUCH DATA, 638 KINDERGARTEN (P-K) CHILDREN IN MINNESOTA WERE TESTED ON THREE INSTRUMENTS: (1) THE METROPOLITAN READINESS TESTS (MRT), (2) THE ILLINOIS TEST OF PSYCHOLINGUISTIC ABILITIES (ITPA), AND (3) THE BEHAVIOR RATING SCALE. SOME 570 PREFIRST-GRADE (P-1) CHILDREN WERE ALSO TESTED, INCLUDING 300 OF THE CHILDREN TESTED AT THE P-K LEVEL. IT WAS FOUND THAT P-K GIRLS DID SIGNIFICANTLY BETTER ON THE MRT THAN P-K BOYS, AND GIRLS DID BETTER THAN BOYS AT THE P-1 LEVEL. COMPARED WITH NORMS AVAILABLE FOR P-1 CHILDREN, THE P-1 BOYS IN THIS STUDY FELL AT THE THIRTY-FIFTH PERCENTILE; THE GIRLS, AT THE FORTY-SECOND. ON THE ITPA, NEITHER AT THE P-K LEVEL NOR AT THE P-1 LEVEL DID THERE EXIST OVERALL DIFFERENCES IN PERFORMANCE ON THE BASIS OF SEX. IT APPEARS, THEREFORE, THAT THE KINDERGARTEN EXPERIENCE TENDS TO MODIFY INITIAL PERFORMANCE DIFFERENCES ON THE BASIS OF SEX TOWARDS UNIFORMITY RATHER THAN TOWARDS GREATER DIVERGENCE IN FAVOR OF THE GIRLS. P-K GIRLS RATED HIGHER THAN THE BOYS ON ALL ITEMS OF THE BEHAVIOR RATING SCALE, BUT AT THE P-1 LEVEL THERE WAS NO SIGNIFICANT DIFFERENCE. (WD)

ED023475 PS001280
A STANDARDIZED NEUROLOGICAL EXAMINATION: ITS VALIDITY IN PREDICTING SCHOOL ACHIEVEMENT IN HEAD START AND OTHER POPULATIONS. FINAL REPORT. OZER, MARK N.; DEEM, MICHAEL A., JUN 68 52P.
EDRS PRICE MF-$0.65 HC-$3.29

A NEUROLOGICAL EXAMINATION HAS BEEN DEVELOPED TO DISCOVER CHILDREN WITH PHYSIOLOGICALLY BASED LEARNING PROBLEMS WHO DO NOT MANIFEST ASYMMETRICAL FUNCTIONING. THIS STUDY ATTEMPTS TO DETERMINE THE VALIDITY OF THIS EXAMINATION BY ITS ACCURACY IN PREDICTING THE PERFORMANCE OF CHILDREN IN A SUMMER HEAD START PROGRAM. VALIDITY WAS DETERMINED BY COMPARING THE EXAMINATION RESULTS WITH RESULTS OF THE METROPOLITAN READINESS TEST (MRT) AND THEN TESTING BOTH GROUPS OF PREDICTIONS BY EXAMINING THE ACTUAL PERFORMANCE OF THE CHILDREN ON THE CRITERION MEASURES; THAT IS, THE ACHIEVEMENT TESTS. THE SUBJECTS OF THIS STUDY WERE 43 FIRST GRADE NEGRO CHILDREN, HALF OF WHICH HAD PARTICIPATED IN A SUMMER HEAD START PROGRAM AND ALL OF WHICH REPRESENTED A POPULATION MEETING THE CRITERIA FOR FUNDING BY THE OFFICE OF ECONOMIC OPPORTUNITY (OEO), AND 45 NEGRO FIRST GRADE CHILDREN WHO WERE FROM SCHOOLS NOT MEETING THE OEO CRITERIA. BOTH GROUPS WERE ADMINISTERED THE NEUROLOGICAL SCREENING TEST, THE MRT, CERTAIN TESTS FROM THE STANFORD ACHIEVEMENT BATTERY, AND VARIOUS PSYCHOLOGICAL TESTS. ALTHOUGH THE RESULTS OF THIS STUDY INDICATE THAT THE NEUROLOGICAL TEST WAS NOT CONSISTENTLY AS GOOD A PREDICTOR OF SCHOOL PERFORMANCE AS THE MRT, IT DID DEMONSTRATE IT HAD PREDICTIVE VALUE. IT SHOULD BE NOTED THAT THE NEUROLOGICAL TEST TAKES ABOUT 15 MINUTES TO ADMINISTER WHILE THE MRT TAKES ONE TO TWO HOURS. (WD)

ED023476 PS001282
PROCEEDINGS OF THE ANNUAL CONVENTION OF THE CHRISTIAN ASSOCIATION FOR PSYCHOLOGICAL STUDIES ON THE DYNAMICS OF LEARNING CHRISTIAN CONCEPTS (12TH, GRAND RAPIDS, MICHIGAN, MARCH 31-APRIL 1, 1965). BIJKERK, ROEL; AND OTHERS, 1 APR 65 106P.
EDRS PRICE MF-$0.65 HC-$6.58

TWO PAPERS IN THIS REPORT DEAL WITH EARLY CHILDHOOD. "DEVELOPMENTAL FACTORS--EARLY COGNITIVE GROWTH" DISCUSSES THE EXPERIMENTAL-ANALYTICAL AND EXISTENTIAL-EXPERIMENTAL APPROACHES TO RELIGIOUS COGNITIVE GROWTH. THE SECOND PAPER, "DEVELOPMENTAL FACTORS--EARLY EMOTIONAL-SOCIAL GROWTH" ASSERTS THAT EMOTIONAL AND SOCIAL INTEGRITY HAS TO BE ACHIEVED THROUGH PROGRESSIVE BUT GRADUAL MATURATION OF THE PERSONALITY FROM INFANCY ONWARD. (MS)

ED023477 PS001286
METHODOLOGICAL ISSUES IN THE STUDY OF AGE DIFFERENCES IN INFANTS' ATTENTION TO STIMULI VARYING IN MOVEMENT AND COMPLEXITY. AMES, ELINOR W.; SILFEN, CAROLE K., MAR 65 16P.
EDRS PRICE MF-$0.65 HC-$3.29

PIONEERING RESEARCH HAS SHOWN THAT INFANTS ARE CAPABLE OF PERCEPTUAL DISCRIMINATION AND HAS PROVIDED SOME INDICATION OF THE NATURE OF THE DISCRIMINATION; THAT IS, WHAT STIMULI ARE DIFFERENTIABLE. STUDIES HAVE DEMONSTRATED THAT SIGNIFICANT EFFECTS EXIST, IN STIMULUS-PAIR COMPARISONS, FOR AGE OF INFANT, SPEED OF MOVEMENT OF STIMULUS DURING PERCEPTION, AND FOR THE AGE-SPEED INTERACTION. THE STIMULUS INVOLVED WAS CHECKERBOARD DESIGNS. IT HAS BEEN DISCOVERED THAT THE LOOKING PATTERN OF INFANTS VARIES WITH AGE. THE YOUNGER INFANT TAKES FEWER BUT LONGER LOOKS, WHILE THE OLDER INFANT TAKES MORE BUT SHORTER LOOKS. IT HAS ALSO BEEN FOUND THAT YOUNGER INFANTS ARE MORE LIKELY, WHEN FINALLY SHIFTING THEIR GAZE, TO SHIFT IT BACK TO THE FIRST STIMULUS. THIS FACTOR CUTS INTO THE RELIABILITY OF USING PAIR-COMPARISONS FOR MEASURING INFANT STIMULUS PREFERENCE, ESPECIALLY BECAUSE TRIAL TIMES ARE OFTEN BRIEF (ABOUT 30 SECONDS). IT IS POSSIBLE TO MEASURE PREFERENCE BY JUST PRESENTING ONE STIMULUS AND RECORDING FIXATION TIME. IT WAS DISCOVERED THAT 10-WEEK-OLD CHILDREN LOOKED AT THE MOST COMPLEX OF THREE CHECKERBOARD STIMULI THE MOST AND THE LEAST COMPLEX STIMULUS THE LEAST. THIS WAS ALSO FOUND TRUE OF 20-WEEK-OLD CHILDREN. EIGHT-WEEK-OLD CHILDREN PREFERRED THE MEDIUM COMPLEXITY STIMULUS. A HYPOTHESIS NOW UNDER INVESTIGATION IS THAT YOUNGER THAN 8-WEEK-OLD CHILDREN WILL LOOK AT THE LEAST COMPLEX STIMULUS THE MOST. (WD)

ED023478 PS001292
SAN MATEO COUNTY HUMAN RESOURCES COMMISSION PROJECT HEAD START - SUMMER 1966. AN EVALUATIONAL REPORT. PETERS, DONALD L.; STEIN, NANCY L., 66 214P.
EDRS PRICE MF-$0.65 HC-$9.87

THIS HANDBOOK IS A RESPONSE TO THE INFORMATION PROBLEMS THAT MAY ARISE IN THE PLANNING OF A HEAD START PROGRAM. IT IS ESPECIALLY DESIGNED FOR USE IN SAN MATEO COUNTY, CALIFORNIA. IT PURPORTS TO BRING TOGETHER AN EXPLANATION OF THE REQUIREMENTS FOR HEAD START PROGRAMS AND SUGGESTS HOW THESE REQUIREMENTS MIGHT BEST BE MET WITH THE RESOURCES AVAILABLE. PART ONE OF THE HANDBOOK PROVIDES INFORMATION CONCERNING THE REQUIREMENTS OF THE OFFICE OF ECONOMIC OPPORTUNITY FOR THE CONDUCT OF HEAD START PROGRAMS AND A REVIEW OF SOME OF THE ACTIVITIES CARRIED ON IN BEHALF OF THE 1966 SUMMER PROGRAM IN SAN MATEO COUNTY. PART ONE IS SUBDIVIDED INTO FIVE CHAPTERS: (1) INTRODUCTION, (2) ADMINISTRATION, (3) THE PEOPLE OF THE PROGRAM, (4) OTHER ASPECTS OF HEAD START, AND (5) PARENT PARTICIPATION. PART TWO PRESENTS THE BACKGROUND AND RESULTS OF THE COMPARATIVE AND EVALUATIONAL STUDIES OF THE OVERALL SAN MATEO COUNTY HEAD START PROGRAM. SEVERAL DIFFERENT THEORIES OF PRESCHOOL EDUCATION WERE EXPERIMENTED WITH DURING THE PROGRAM. THE EVALUATION TELLS ABOUT THE GAINS OF THE PROGRAM. PART TWO IS DIVIDED INTO THREE CHAPTERS: (6) EVALUATION MEASURES, (7) EVALUATION, AND (8) COMPARATIVE STUDY. APPENDIX A PROVIDES A BIBLIOGRAPHY OF PRESCHOOL EDUCATION; APPENDIX B, SOME SAMPLE FORMS USED TO COLLECT INFORMATION ON THE HEAD START CHILDREN; AND APPENDIX C, SOME ADDITIONAL STATISTICAL TABLES. (WD)

ED023479 PS001295
REINFORCEMENT GROWS UP: THE EXPERIMENTAL ANALYSIS OF BEHAVIOR AS A SYSTEMATIC APPROACH TO THE TEACHING OF DEVELOPMENTAL PSYCHOLOGY. BAER, DONALD M., 66 12P.
EDRS PRICE MF-$0.65 HC-$3.29

AN IMPORTANT APPROACH TO UNDERSTANDING CHILD BEHAVIOR AND DEVELOPMENT IS THE EXPERIMENTAL ANALYSIS OF SUCH BEHAVIOR. THE EXPERIMENTAL ANALYSIS PROCEDURE MUST BE DISTINGUISHED FROM RELATED ANALYSES USED OCCASIONALLY. AN ANALYSIS BY ANECDOTE IS AN ANALYSIS BASED UPON THE ACCUMULATION OF RECURRING ASSOCIATIONS; FOR EXAMPLE, B FOLLOWED BY A. THIS DOES NOT ASSURE THE EXISTENCE OF A CAUSATIVE RELATIONSHIP. AN ANALYSIS BY CORRELATION IS A SURVEY OF TWO ANECDOTES, (1) IF B,

THEN A, AND (2) IF NO B, THEN NO A. BUT THIS ANALYSIS DOES NOT ASSURE THAT WHEN FACTORS 1 AND 2 EXIST, SOME FACTOR 3 EXISTS OR THAT BOTH A AND B ARE CONTROLLED BY C. THE EXPERIMENTAL METHOD REQUIRES THAT THE EXPERIMENTER MANIPULATE OR CONTROL A AND B IN AN ARBITRARY FASHION. THIS REASONABLY PRECLUDES CONTROL BY SOME UNKNOWN C AND REASONABLY ILLUSTRATES THE CAUSATIVE RELATIONSHIP. THE AGE OF A CHILD LIMITS THE APPLICATION OF THE EXPERIMENTAL ANALYSIS APPROACH; THAT IS, VERY YOUNG CHILDREN ARE GENERALLY NOT AVAILABLE FOR USE IN A COMPREHENSIVELY CONTROLLED ENVIRONMENT. THE OPERANT BEHAVIOR PROCEDURE DOES NOT REQUIRE CONTROL OVER A BROAD RANGE OF ENVIRONMENTAL FACTORS, HOWEVER, AND EVIDENCE FROM SUCH PROCEDURES INDICATES THE POSSIBILITY OF INVESTIGATING CHILD BEHAVIOR AND DEVELOPMENT THROUGH THE USE OF REINFORCEMENT, PUNISHMENT, AND EXTINCTION CONTINGENCIES. (WD)

ED023480 PS001296
LONG TERM EFFECT OF STRUCTURED TRAINING ON 3 YOUNG CHILDREN. WILSON, JOHN A.R., 11 MAR 66 8P.
EDRS PRICE MF-$0.65 HC-$3.29

THIS REPORT IS A BRIEF DISCUSSION OF THE CASE HISTORIES OF THREE PRESCHOOL CHILDREN WHO WERE PARTICIPANTS IN AN "EXPLORATORY STUDY OF THE EFFECTS OF INDIVIDUAL WORK ON THE FUNCTIONING OF MALADJUSTED PRE-SCHOOL CHILDREN." THIS EXPLORATORY STUDY WAS CONCERNED WITH EMOTIONAL-SOCIAL LEARNING AND DEVELOPED THE HYPOTHESIS THAT CERTAIN DESIRABLE ACTIVITIES CAN BE ASSOCIATED WITH PLEASURE SIMPLY BY LINKING THE MANIFESTATION OF THE ACTIVITY WITH PLEASURABLE REINFORCEMENT. WHEN THE LINKAGE IS SUFFICIENTLY WELL DEVELOPED, THE CHILD CAN BE HELPED TO SEE THE RELATIONSHIP BETWEEN HIS PLEASURE AND THOSE ACTIVITIES WHICH PROVIDE IT. TO ESTABLISH THE LINKAGE, PRESCHOOL CHILDREN WITH BEHAVIOR PROBLEMS WERE INTRODUCED INTO A PROGRAM IN WHICH ADULTS OBSERVED THE CHILD'S PERSONALITY PROBLEMS AND, THROUGH REINFORCEMENT, ATTEMPTED TO MODIFY THE UNDESIRABLE BEHAVIOR INTO DESIRABLE BEHAVIOR. THE PROGRAM WAS FOR AN HOUR TWO TIMES A WEEK FOR MOST OF A SCHOOL YEAR. THE THREE CASE HISTORIES OF THIS REPORT INCLUDE (1) A 3-YEAR-OLD GIRL WITH SERIOUS BEHAVIOR PROBLEMS AND POSSIBLE RETARDATION, (2) A 3 1/2-YEAR-OLD BOY WHO HAD SUFFERED PHYSICAL DEFORMITIES AND WAS BEHIND HIS PEERS SOCIALLY AND EDUCATIONALLY, AND (3) A 5-YEAR-OLD BOY WHO WAS OF NORMAL DEVELOPMENT PHYSICALLY BUT CAME FROM A POOR HOME ENVIRONMENT. INDIVIDUAL GOALS WERE SET FOR EACH CHILD OF THE STUDY, AND IT WAS FOUND THAT THE PROGRAM DID HELP EACH CHILD TO DEVELOP MORE DESIRABLE AND SELF-SATISFYING BEHAVIOR. (WD)

ED023481 PS001299
ON LEARNING TO TALK: ARE PRINCIPLES DERIVED FROM THE LEARNING LABORATORY APPLICABLE? PALERMO, DAVID S., FEB 66 40P.
EDRS PRICE MF-$0.65 HC-$3.29

WHILE STUDIES IN LEARNING AND VERBAL BEHAVIOR SHOW THAT LEARNING COMES THROUGH PAIRED-ASSOCIATE PROBLEMS, THEY DO NOT EXPLAIN THE ACQUISITION OF LANGUAGE. THREE PARADIGMS DEMONSTRATE MEDIATION EFFECT IN PAIRED-ASSOCIATE LEARNING: RESPONSE EQUIVALENCE, STIMULUS EQUIVALENCE, AND CHAINING MODEL. BY REVIEWING CHILDREN'S LANGUAGE ACQUISITION PATTERNS IN TERMS OF THE THREE PARADIGMS, SEVERAL CONCLUSIONS WERE REACHED. A CHILD UTTERS WORDS WHICH ARE RELATED TO HIS EXPERIENCE. HE ESTABLISHES RESPONSE AND STIMULUS EQUIVALENCE PARADIGMS SIMULTANEOUSLY. IN A RESPONSE EQUIVALENCE SITUATION, HE LEARNS ONE RESPONSE CAN APPLY TO SEVERAL STIMULI, AND IN A STIMULUS EQUIVALENCE SITUATION, ONE STIMULUS IS PAIRED WITH MANY RESPONSES. WHEN LEARNING COMPLEX UTTERANCES, THE CHILD CHAINS EQUIVALENCE PARADIGMS. THE SAME PATTERNS ARE APPLIED IN LEARNING PLURALS, TENSES, AND NEGATIVES. IN AN ADDENDUM, THE AUTHOR DISCUSSES THE POSITIONS OF A PSYCHOLOGIST AND A LINGUIST IN LANGUAGE ACQUISITION. THE PSYCHOLOGIST IGNORES THE COMPLEXITIES OF THE LANGUAGE, OVERSIMPLIFIES IMITATION, AND DISREGARDS THE RELATIONSHIP BETWEEN MEMORIZING AND MEANINGFUL LEARNING. THE LINGUIST ASSUMES HIERARCHICAL LEARNING BUT DOES NOT TEST IT, AND HE REJECTS MEDIATION LEARNING THEORIES. ALTHOUGH MAINTAINING SEPARATE GOALS, THE TWO SCHOOLS SHOULD ACT JOINTLY TO STIMULATE NEEDED FURTHER RESEARCH IN LANGUAGE ACQUISITION. (JS)

ED023482 PS001301
THE PRESCHOOL LANGUAGE PROJECT. A REPORT OF THE FIRST YEAR'S WORK. STERN, CAROLYN, AUG 66 23P.
EDRS PRICE MF-$0.65 HC-$3.29

THE EFFECT OF A FORMAL, STRUCTURED APPROACH TO LANGUAGE DEVELOPMENT ON PRESCHOOL CHILDREN IS THE SUBJECT OF THIS PROJECT STUDY. FROM AUGUST 1965 TO AUGUST 1966, 157 PROGRAMS ADMINISTERED TO 1,663 CHILDREN EXPLORED MENTAL ABILITY, AUDITORY AND VISUAL DISCRIMINATION, LANGUAGE USE, VOCABULARY, AND MOTIVATION. CHILDREN ATTENDING DAY CARE CENTERS, NURSERY SCHOOLS, AND HEAD START CLASSES WERE TESTED, AND THE FOLLOWING OBSERVATIONS WERE NOTED: (1) CHILDRE N FROM POOR HOMES HAVE INFERIOR ABILITY TO DISCRIMINATE SPOKEN WORD SOUNDS; (2) WHEN CHILDREN ARE GIVEN INTERESTING MATERIALS, THEIR VERBAL OUTPUT SHOWS NO DIFFERENTIATION; AND (3) MOTIVATION IS EQUAL IN ADVANTAGED AND DISADVANTAGED CHILDREN. NEW TESTS ARE NEEDED TO MEASURE VOCABULARY, AUDITORY AND VISUAL DISCRIMINATIONS. EXPERIMENTAL STUDIES PROVED THREE-DIMENSIONAL TOYS DO NOT PRODUCE SUPERIOR LEARNING, AND REPETITION OF GRAMMATICAL SENTENCES IS PREFERRED TO STORY-TELLING IN DEVELOPING VERBAL FLUENCY. AS A RESULT OF ASSESSMENTS AND EXPERIMENTS, THE PROJECT PROPOSES A 30-WEEK PROGRAM TO DEVELOP FAMILIARITY AND FACILITY WITH LANGUAGE IN SCIENCE, MATHEMATICS, SOCIAL STUDIES, LITERATURE, LANGUAGE USAGE, AND LOGICAL PROCESSES ON A PRESCHOOL LEVEL. THE PROGRAM WOULD OCCUPY ONLY 15 MINUETS OF THE SCHOOL DAY AND WOULD NOT MINIMIZE THE PRODUCTIVE VALUE OF PRESENT DAY CARE CENTER PROGRAMS. (DO)

ED023483 PS001306
NOVELTY AND FAMILIARITY AS DETERMINANTS OF INFANT ATTENTION WITHIN THE FIRST YEAR. LEWIS, MICHAEL; AND OTHERS, [66] 47P.
EDRS PRICE MF-$0.65 HC-$3.29

THREE RELATED EXPERIMENTS WERE CONDUCTED TO INVESTIGATE THE EFFECTS OF NOVEL AND FAMILIAR STIMULI ON INFANT ATTENTION. THE PROCEDURE IN EACH OF THE EXPERIMENTS WAS TO PLACE AN INFANT BEFORE A MATRIX PANEL COMPOSED OF SIX ROWS OF SIX LIGHTS. TWO PATTERNS OF LIGHTS WERE USED TO OBTAIN THE INFANTS' FIXATION TIME: (1) A POINT PATTERN, A SINGLE BLINKING LIGHT IN THE CENTER OF THE PANEL, AND (2) A HELIX PATTERN, A SINGLE BLINKING LIGHT WHICH MOVED ACROSS THE BOARD. IN EXPERIMENT ONE, 122 INFANTS OF APPROXIMATE AGES 12, 24, 36, 56, AND 68 WEEKS RECEIVED FOUR 30-SECOND POINT PATTERN TRIALS AND A FIFTH HELIX PATTERN TRIAL. HABITUATION (DECREASE IN FIXATION TIME) INCREASED WITH AGE OF THE CHILD. HOWEVER, NO RESPONSE INCREMENT WAS FOUND UPON THE CHANGE TO THE NOVEL STIMULUS (THE HELIX PATTERN). EXPERIMENT TWO USED 80 INFANTS OF 3, 6, 9, AND 13 MONTHS OF AGE. HERE, FOUR HELIX TRIALS WERE FOLLOWED BY ONE POINT PATTERN TRIAL. THE RESULTS WERE SIMILAR TO EXPERIMENT ONE. EXPERIMENT THREE REPEATED THE PROCEDURE OF EXPERIMENT ONE IN LONGITUDINAL-STUDY FORM; THAT IS, ALL OF THE INFANTS IN THE EXPERIMENT WERE TESTED AT 3, 6, 9, AND 13 MONTHS OF AGE. THE HABITUATION DATA WAS SIMILAR TO EXPERIMENTS ONE AND TWO IN THAT THE YOUNGER CHILDREN SHOWED LESS HABITUATION. (WD)

ED023484 PS001307
THE CONCEPT OF DEVELOPMENTAL LEARNING. FOWLER, WILLIAM, 30 DEC 66 20P.
EDRS PRICE MF-$0.65 HC-$3.29

COGNITIVE DEVELOPMENTAL LEARNING IS A CONCEPT EXPRESSING THE HYPOTHESIS THAT LEARNING HAS A CONTINUING, CUMULATIVE, AND TRANSFORMATIONAL FUNCTION IN THE DEVELOPMENT OF INTELLIGENCE. TWO IMPORTANT QUESTIONS ARE, "HOW MUCH DO WE KNOW ABOUT METHODS?" AND "WHAT CLASSES OF KNOWLEDGE AND ABILITIES SHOULD WE DEVELOP?" AN ANALYSIS OF PAST INVESTIGATIONS, INCLUDING ANIMAL RESEARCH, GROUP EDUCATIONAL PROJECTS, STUDIES OF SOCIOPSYCHOLOGICAL VARIABLES, IQ TESTS, STIMULATION AND MEASUREMENT EXPERIMENTS, AND METHODOLOGICAL STUDIES, INDICATES THEY ARE OF LIMITED USE IN EXPLORING THE SPHERE OF COGNITIVE DEVELOPMENTAL LEARNING. CURRENT RESEARCH IS AIDED BY THE ADVANCED STATE OF KNOWLEDGE, CONVERGENCE OF LEARNING AND DEVELOPMENTAL THEORIES, AND INTENSIVE STUDY OF COGNITIVE PROCESSES, BUT MUCH OF IT CONCENTRATES ON SOCIALLY DISADVANTAGED CHILDREN. A SYSTEMATIC RESEARCH UTILIZING DIMENSIONS FOR DESIGNING DEVELOPMENTAL STIMULATION PROGRAMS COULD CONCENTRATE ON THE GIFTED CHILD. EARLY AND INTENSIVE STIMULATION AND PERVASIVE ENVIRONMENTAL ARRANGEMENTS PROVIDED BY PARENTS ARE FACTORS OF THE GIFTED CHILD'S INTELLIGENCE. STIMULATION CONTROL OVER BRIGHT CHILDREN IS A COMPELLING ILLUSTRATION OF THE PROPOSITION OF THE DEVELOPMENTAL LEARNING HYPOTHESIS. FURTHER RESEARCH IS NEEDED. (DO)

ED023485 PS001310
FURTHER EVIDENCE ON THE STABILITY OF THE FACTOR STRUCTURE OF THE TEST ANXIETY SCALE FOR SCHILDREN. FELD, SHEILA; LEWIS, JUDITH, FEB 67 35P.
EDRS PRICE MF-$0.65 HC-$3.29

IN A 1963 EXPERIMENT, 3,867 BOYS AND 3,684 GIRLS IN THE SECOND GRADE WERE USED TO INVESTIGATE THE DIMENSIONALITY OF THE TEST ANXIETY SCALE FOR CHILDREN (TASC). FACTORS INCLUDED TEST ANXIETY, REMOTE SCHOOL CONCERN, POOR SELF-EVALUATION AND SOMATIC SIGNS OF ANXIETY. FACTOR ANALYSIS DEMONSTRATES A STABLE MULTIDIMENSIONAL STRUCTURE FOR TASC. RESULTS INDICATE INDEPENDENT DIMENSIONS ARE REQUIRED. WHILE THE QUESTIONS COMPRISING TASC ADMIT A FULL RANGE OF ANXIETY REACTIONS, THE TEST IS LIMITED TO ACADEMIC EVALUATION. ADDITIONAL ANALYSES OF ANXIETY COULD INCLUDE COMPARISONS TO SITUATIONS OCCURRING OUTSIDE OF SCHOOL. THE SECOND GRADE DATA INDICATE THAT THE STIMULUS CLASS IN TASC NEEDS DELIMITING BY DISTINGUISHING BETWEEN FORMAL TEST AND OTHER SCHOOL EVALUATION SITUATIONS AND THAT THERE IS MORE THAN ONE MODE OF ANXIETY RESPONSE TO SCHOOL EVALUATION SITUATIONS. TO UNDERSTAND THE NATURE OF COMPONENTS OF ANXIETY, MEASURES OF ANXIETY TO TEST AND AFFILIATIVE SITUATIONS COULD BE INCLUDED IN A SINGLE FACTOR ANALYSIS. A SAMPLING OF ALL STIMULI AND RESPONSES WOULD DEFINE

THEIR INDEPENDENT AND INTERACTIVE EFFECTS ON ANXIETY. WHILE TASC SCORES AND SCHOOL ACHIEVEMENT MEASURES DIFFER, LATER RESEARCH WILL DETERMINE IF THIS IS CAUSED BY ONLY SOME DIMENSIONS UNDERLYING RESPONSES TO TASC. AFTER EXPLORATIONS, TASC SHOULD BE EXPANDED SO THAT SEVERAL DIMENSIONS HAVE ADEQUATE ITEM COVERAGE. (DO)

ED023486 PS001311
THE ACQUISITION OF LINGUISTIC STRUCTURE. TECHNICAL REPORT VIII, A STUDY IN THE ACQUISITION OF LANGUAGE: FREE RESPONSES TO COMMANDS. SHIPLEY, ELIZABETH F.; AND OTHERS, [67] 60P.
EDRS PRICE MF-$0.65 HC-$3.29

TO DETERMINE WHETHER CHILDREN'S LANGUAGE PATTERNS ARE LEARNED RESPONSES OR INHERENTLY ORGANIZED, THIS STUDY OBSERVED CHILDREN'S RESPONSES TO COMMANDS. THE 13 SUBJECTS WERE MIDDLE CLASS CHILDREN AGED 18 TO 30 MONTHS. THE CHILDREN WERE RATED AS VERBALLY MATURE, INTERMEDIATE, OR IMMATURE; AND RESPONSES WERE CLASSIFIED AS ACTION, VERBAL, AND RELEVANT. THE CHILDREN'S MOTHERS GAVE SYNTACTICALLY VARIED COMMANDS (ADULTS' AND CHILDREN'S LANGUAGE PATTERNS) AND SEMANTICALLY VARIED COMMANDS (ENGLISH AND NONSENSE WORDS). THE RESULTS SHOWED THAT THE CHILDREN RESPONDED MORE TO THE WELL-FORMED COMMAND. THERE WAS A SIGNIFICANTLY POSITIVE RELATIONSHIP BETWEEN VERBAL MATURITY AND OBEDIENCE TO COMMAND. A SIGNIFICANT NUMBER OF CHILDREN RESPONDED LESS FREQUENTLY TO NONSENSE COMMANDS THAN ENGLISH WORDS EXCEPT TO REPEAT THE COMMAND. THE ONLY RELATIONSHIP BETWEEN RESPONSES AND VERBAL MATURITY OCCURRED WHERE THE VERBALLY MATURE CHILD REPEATED THE NONSENSE COMMAND. THREE CONCLUSIONS WERE REACHED: (1) THE CHILD DOES MAKE DISTINCTIONS AT SOME STAGE, ALTHOUGH IT MAY NOT BE EVIDENT IN SPEECH; (2) THE DISTINCTIONS VARY WITH VERBAL MATURITY; AND (3) THE CHILD HAS SOME MEANS OF ORGANIZING LANGUAGE TO CONTROL NEW INFORMATION. A NUMBER OF REFERENCES ARE CITED, AND DATA ARE INCLUDED IN APPENDIXES. (JS)

ED023487 PS001322
THE EFFECTS OF ASSESSMENT AND PERSONALIZED PROGRAMMING ON SUBSEQUENT INTELLECTUAL DEVELOPMENT OF PREKINDERGARTEN AND KINDERGARTEN CHILDREN. FINAL REPORT OF PHASE II. COFFMAN, ALICE O.; DUNLAP, JAMES M., JUL 68 88P.
EDRS PRICE MF-$0.65 HC-$3.29

THIS REPORT IS THE SECOND FROM A 3 1/2-YEAR PROJECT. THE PREKINDERGARTEN RESEARCH INVOLVED MATCHED GROUPS OF CHILDREN (91 EXPERIMENTAL, 115 CONTROL), REPRESENTATIVE OF THE LOCAL POPULATION, WHOSE DEVELOPMENTAL NEEDS (MOTOR, AUDITORY, LANGUAGE, VISUAL RETENTION) WERE IDENTIFIED BY A TEST BATTERY. HALF-DAY CLASSES FOCUSED ON SPECIFIC NEED FOR 20 MINUTES DAILY. ACTIVITIES WERE CONDUCTED WITHIN THE FRAMEWORK OF A WELL-BALANCED PREKINDERGARTEN PROGRAM. RESULTS INDICATED THAT THE EXPERIMENTAL GROUP EXCELLED THE CONTROL GROUP NOT PARTICIPATING IN THE PROGRAM AT A STATISTICALLY SIGNIFICANT LEVEL OF CONFIDENCE. THE KINDERGARTEN EXPERIMENT WAS A FOLLOWUP STUDY OF THE PREKINDERGARTEN CHILDREN OF THE PREVIOUS YEAR (80 EXPERIMENTAL, 124 CONTROL). THESE CHILDREN ATTENDED MANY DIFFERENT KINDERGARTEN PROGRAMS. RESULTS INDICATED THAT THE EXPERIMENTAL GROUP DID NOT MAINTAIN THE SUPERIORITY AT A STATISTICALLY SIGNIFICANT LEVEL FROM THE PREVIOUS YEAR. THE EFFECT OF PREKINDERGARTEN EXPERIENCE ON PRIMARY SCHOOL SUCCESS WILL BE MEASURED DURING THE THIRD YEAR OF THE PROJECT. (AUTHOR/JS)

ED023488 PS001326
EARLY CHILDHOOD SELECTED BIBLIOGRAPHIES SERIES. NUMBER 4, COGNITION. , 68 116P.
EDRS PRICE MF-$0.65 HC-$6.58

THIS DOCUMENT IS THE FOURTH IN A SERIES OF SIX ANNOTATED BIBLIOGRAPHIES RELEVANT TO EARLY CHILDHOOD EDUCATION. ITS GENERAL SUBJECT IS COGNITION, AND I T INCLUDES SEVEN SUBDIVISIONS: INTELLIGENCE, HIGHER MENTAL PROCESSES, COGNITIVE STYLE, EXPERIMENTAL STUDIES OF LEARNING, CONCEPT DEVELOPMENT, PERCEPTION AND RECOGNITION, AND MOTIVATION. EACH OF THE 72 ABSTRACTS INCLUDED HAS BEEN CLASSIFIED BY GENERAL AND SPECIFIC SUBJECT, BY FOCUS OF STUDY, AND ALPHABETICALLY BY AUTHOR. FOCUS OF STUDY CATEGORIES ARE NORMATIVE, ENVIRONMENTAL, MEASUREMENT AND TECHNIQUES, INTERVENTION, PATHOLOGY, PHYSIOLOGY, ANIMALS, AND GENERAL. THE GENERAL SUBJECTS OF OTHER BIBLIOGRAPHIES IN THE SERIES ARE LANGUAGE, EDUCATION, PERSONALITY, PHYSICAL, AND SOCIAL ASPECTS OF EARLY CHILDHOOD EDUCATION. (MS)

ED024437 PS001127
MEMORY AND "CONTINGENCY ANALYSIS" IN INFANT LEARNING. WATSON, JOHN S., 67 22P.
DOCUMENT NOT AVAILABLE FROM EDRS.

IN ORDER TO DETERMINE IF INFANTS POSSESSED CONTINGENCY AWARENESS AND IF IT WERE RELATED TO A TEMPORAL UNIT, TWO HYPOTHESES WERE CONSTRUCTED. (1) REINFORCEMENT OF A RESPONSE WOULD PROBABLY LEAD TO EMISSION OF THAT RESPONSE ONLY IF THE INFANT'S NEXT RESPONSE OCCURRED WITHIN A PERIOD OF TIME DURING WHICH HE COULD REMEMBER THE PRECEDING RESPONSE-REWARD CONTINGENCY. (2) AT BIRTH, HUMANS ARE STRUCTURED FOR CONTINGENCY AWARENESS, YET IT IS UNDEVELOPED IN INFANTS BECAUSE OF THE REDUCED NUMBER AND FREQUENCY OF RESPONSES THEY MAKE WHICH ELICIT REWARDING STIMULATION FROM THE PHYSICAL ENVIRONMENT. OF THIRTY-TWO 13- AND 14-WEEK-OLD INFANTS, 16 WERE GIVEN AUDIO AND 16 WERE GIVEN VISUAL STIMULATION CONTINGENT ON LOOKING AT ONE OF TWO CIRCLES ON THE CEILING OF A BASSINET HOOD DURING A 2-MINUTE LEARNING SESSION. OF TWENTY-FOUR 9- AND 10-WEEK-OLD INFANTS, EIGHT WERE GIVEN VISUAL, EIGHT WERE GIVEN AUDIO, AND EIGHT WERE GIVEN BOTH TYPES OF STIMULATION FOR 2 1/2 MINUTES. THE DATA SUPPORTED THE HYPOTHESES, AND RESULTS WERE DISCUSSED IN TERMS OF MEMORY AND LEARNING STUDIES. (JS)

ED024438 PS001128
AN ARTICULATION STUDY OF 15,255 SEATTLE FIRST GRADE CHILDREN WITH AND WITHOUT KINDERGARTEN. PENDERGAST, KATHLEEN; AND OTHERS, APR 66 7P.
DOCUMENT NOT AVAILABLE FROM EDRS.

IN ORDER TO INVESTIGATE THE EFFECT OF KINDERGARTEN UPON ARTICULATION OF FIRST GRADE CHILDREN, 15,255 FIRST GRADE CHILDREN WERE TESTED FOR ARTICULATION PROBLEMS. ONE-HALF WERE TESTED IN 1960 BECAUSE SEATTLE HAD HAD NO KINDERGARTEN PROGRAM IN 1959. THE OTHER HALF WERE TESTED IN 1961 BECAUSE SEATTLE REINSTITUTED A KINDERGARTEN PROGRAM IN 1960. CONSISTENCY OF ARTICULATION PATTERNS WAS ASSUMED TO EXIST FOR THE 2-YEAR PERIOD. ALL CHILDREN WERE FIRST TESTED WITH A SCREENING SENTENCE. IF THEY DEMONSTRATED ANY MISARTICULATED SOUNDS, THEY WERE GIVEN THE COMPLETE BRYNGELSON-GLASPEY TEST. TESTING WAS DONE IN SEPTEMBER AND MAY OF BOTH YEARS. THE RESULTS OF THIS TESTING SHOWED THAT (1) SLIGHTLY MORE THAN 1/4 OF THE FIRST GRADE CHILDREN MISARTICULATED ONE OR MORE SOUNDS, (2) CHILDREN WHO ATTENDED KINDERGARTEN DID NOT APPEAR TO HAVE FEWER SOUND ERRORS WHEN THEY ENTERED THE FIRST GRADE THAN CHILDREN WHO DID NOT ATTEND KINDERGARTEN, AND (3) OF THE 2/3 OF THE CHILDREN WITH SOME ARTICULATION PROBLEM WHO WERE NOT ENROLLED IN SPEECH THERAPY, KINDERGARTEN EXPERIENCE APPEARED TO HELP REDUCE SOUND ERRORS IN THE FIRST GRADE. THIS STUDY WAS COMPARED WITH THE ROE-MILISEN AND TEMPLIN STUDIES. (WD)

ED024439 PS001158
PERSONALITY DEVELOPMENT IN INFANCY FREEDMAN, D. G., [67] 46P.
EDRS PRICE MF-$0.65 HC-$3.29
AVAILABLE FROM: HOLT, RINEHARD & WINSTON, INC., 383 MADISON AVE., N.Y., N.Y. 10017 IN WASHBURN, S. L., ED. "PERSPECTIVES IN HUMAN EVOLUTION" (PAP. $3.95).

THIS COMPREHENSIVE PAPER PROPOSING THE USE OF EVOLUTIONARY THEORY AS A BASIS FOR STUDIES IN DEVELOPMENTAL PSYCHOLOGY INCLUDES THESE SPECIFIC SECTIONS: (1) DEVELOPMENTAL THEORIES--A BRIEF OVERVIEW, (2) INDIVIDUAL DIFFERENCES, (3) CULTURE AND INBREEDING, (4) SEXUAL DIMORPHISM, (5) CRITICAL PERIODS IN THE DEVELOPMENT OF ATTACHMENTS, (6) CONTINUITY VS. NON-CONTINUITY IN PERSONALITY, AND (7) AN EVOLUTIONARY VIEW OF EARLY ATTACHMENTS. AN EXTENSIVE SEVEN-PAGE BIBLIOGRAPHY IS INCLUDED. (MS)

ED024440 PS001170
COGNITIVE AND LINGUISTIC DEFICITS IN PSYCHOTIC CHILDREN. STUDY M: DEVELOPMENT OF SELECTIVE ATTENTION ABILITIES. HAGEN, JOHN W.; AND OTHERS, 25 OCT 67 25P.
EDRS PRICE MF-$0.65 HC-$3.29

TASKS INVOLVING SEVERAL AREAS OF COGNITIVE FUNCTIONING WERE GIVEN TO 10 PSYCHOTIC CHILDREN AND 30 NORMAL CHILDREN. COMPARISONS OF PERFORMANCE WERE MADE BETWEEN THE TWO GROUPS AND ALSO WITHIN THE PSYCHOTIC GROUP. THE DIMENSION FOR DIFFERENTIATION WAS THE PSYCHOTIC CHILDREN'S VARYING DEGREE OF LANGUAGE FACILITY. THE PSYCHOTIC CHILDREN WERE CLASSIFIED INTO THREE LANGUAGE FACILITY GROUPS: FUNCTIONAL, SEMIFUNCTIONAL, AND NONFUNCTIONAL. THE COGNITIVE ABILITIES TESTED FOR WERE SHORT TERM MEMORY, DISCRIMINATION, GENERALIZATION, TRANSPOSITION, AND DISCRIMINATION REVERSAL. THEY WERE CHOSEN BECAUSE THEY WERE SIGNIFICANTLY LANGUAGE-RELATED OR LANGUAGE-MEDIATED. THE RESULTS OF PERFORMANCE ON THE COGNITIVE FUNCTIONING TASKS SHOWED THAT (1) THE NORMAL CHILDREN PERFORMED CONSISTENTLY BETTER THAN THE PSYCHOTIC CHILDREN, (2) THE LANGUAGE FACILITY GROUPS OF THE PSYCHOTIC CHILDREN DIFFERENTIATED THEIR PERFORMANCE ON THE MEMORY TASK INVOLVING A VERBAL CUE, WITH THE FUNCTIONAL GROUP PERFORMING BEST, AND (3) CERTAIN TRENDS IN THE DATA SUGGEST A RELATIONSHIP BETWEEN LANGUAGE FUNCTIONING AND COGNITIVE PERFORMANCE ON THE TASKS INVESTIGATED. (WD)

ED024441 PS001171
AGE DIFFERENCES IN THE IDENTIFICATION OF CONCEPTS OF THE NATURAL LANGUAGE. STUDY B: DEVELOPMENTAL STUDIES IN SEMANTICS. QUARTERMAN, CAROLE J.; RIEGEL, KLAUS F., 20 JUN 67 14P.
EDRS PRICE MF-$0.65 HC-$3.29

TWENTY-FOUR CHILDREN EACH AT THE AGE LEVELS OF 6, 9, 12, AND 15 YEARS WERE TESTED ON FOUR TYPES OF EXPERIMENTALLY DETERMINED CONCEPTUAL CLUES IN A STUDY OF CONCEPT IDENTIFICATION AND, THEREFORE, LANGUAGE COMPREHENSION. SUPERORDINATES, SIMILARS, PARTS, AND LOCATIONS WERE SELECTED AS CLUE WORDS, AND THE FOUR CLUES WERE COMBINED INTO ALL POSSIBLE PAIRS. THE

TASK WAS TO RETRIEVE 16 STIMULI WHICH WERE ORIGINALLY USED IN A RESTRICTED ASSOCIATION STUDY. THE NUMBER OF CORRECT ANSWERS WAS FOUND TO INCREASE AS A FUNCTION OF AGE, CLUE TYPES, AND THE NUMBER OF CLUES GIVEN. SIMILARS PROVED TO BE THE MOST USEFUL SINGLE CLUES. THE RESULTS INDICATE THAT WHILE DIFFERENT EXPLANATORY TECHNIQUES FOR WORDS ARE NOT NECESSARY FOR DIFFERENT AGE LEVELS, THE TYPE OF RELATIONSHIP AND THE NUMBER OF CLUES GIVEN ARE IMPORTANT DETERMINANTS FOR CONCEPT IDENTIFICATION. (MS)

ED024442 PS001173
LINGUISTIC AND PSYCHOLOGICAL FACTORS IN THE SPEECH REGULATION OF BEHAVIOR IN VERY YOUNG CHILDREN. BEISWENGER, HUGO A., 12 JUL 68 120P.
EDRS PRICE MF-$0.65 HC-$6.58

THIS DISSERTATION EXAMINES THE THESIS THAT IT IS THE HUMAN LANGUAGE SYSTEM WHICH LARGELY MAKES POSSIBLE THE HUMAN CAPACITY FOR MODIFIABILITY OF RESPONSES CALLED "INTELLIGENT" AND "ADAPTIVE" MODES OF INTERACTION WITH THE ENVIRONMENT. CHAPTER TITLES ARE (1) A PROCESS VIEW OF HUMAN BEHAVIOR, (2) ASPECTS OF THE MULTI-DIMENSIONAL NATURE OF COGNITIVE PROCESSES IN THE VERY YOUNG CHILD, (3) LINGUISTIC THEORY AS A MODEL OF LANGUAGE PERCEPTION AND LEARNING, (4) THE STRUCTURE OF LINGUISTICALLY INITIATED BEHAVIORAL ACTS, (5) THE RELATIONSHIP OF THE COMPREHENSION OF SENTENCES TO THEIR COMPLEXITY, (6) AN EXPERIMENTAL STUDY OF LINGUISTIC AND OTHER PSYCHOLOGICAL FACTORS IN THE R-EGULATION OF BEHAVIOR IN VERY YOUNG CHILDREN, AND (7) DISCUSSION OF RESULTS. THE AUTHOR CONCLUDES THAT PERCEPTUAL OR ATTENTIONAL PROCESSES WHICH INVOLVE EXPRESSIONS OF ORIENTING ACTIVITY SHOULD BE STUDIED IN REGARD TO ONTOGENETIC DEVELOPMENT AND ITS RELATIONSHIP TO THE VERBAL SYSTEM OF PRESCHOOL CHILDREN. (MS)

ED024443 PS001177
LURIA'S MODEL OF THE VERBAL CONTROL OF BEHAVIOR. STUDY F: MOTIVATIONAL AND CONTROL IN THE DEVELOPMENT OF LANGUAGE FUNCTIONS, D. BIRCH. BEISWENGER, HUGO, 20 FEB 68 25P.
EDRS PRICE MF-$0.65 HC-$3.29

A. R. LURIA, IN HIS CONCEPTION OF THE VERBAL CONTROL OF BEHAVIOR, REGARDS FOUR FUNDAMENTAL AND DISTINCTIVE FUNCTIONAL ATTRIBUTES OF THE HUMAN SPEECH SYSTEM AS MAKING UP A SIGNALING SYSTEM THAT HUMANS ALONE POSSESS: (1) THE NOMINATIVE ROLE OF LANGUAGE, (2) THE GENERALIZING OR SEMANTIC ROLE, (3) THE COMMUNICATIVE ROLE, AND (4) THE ROLE OF REGULATING, DIRECTING, OR CONTROLLING SEQUENTIAL BEHAVIOR. PRIOR TO THE TIME A CHILD LEARNS TO SPEAK, HIS SIGNALING SYSTEM IS NONVERBAL AND IS GENERATED BY THE PHYSICAL ATTRIBUTES OF THE SURROUNDING ENVIRONMENT. LURIA CONTENDS THAT AS THE INDIVIDUAL MATURES, THE TWO SIGNALING SYSTEMS, VERBAL AND NONVERBAL, WORK MORE CLOSELY TOGETHER. HE STATES THAT THE VERBAL SYSTEM, BOTH IN ITS COMMUNICATIVE AND REGULATIVE ASPECTS, MAKES POSSIBLE NOVEL AND FLEXIBLE BEHAVIOR WITHOUT THE TEDIOUS CONDITIONING NECESSARY FOR ANIMAL LEARNING. LURIA VIEWS SPEECH AS BEING FORMED THROUGH A SERIES OF TRANSFORMATIONS (SUBSTAGES) RATHER THAN THROUGH QUANTITATIVE INCREASES IN SUCH THINGS AS VOCABULARY AND GRAMMATICAL RULES. IN ORDER TO TEST LURIA'S THEORY, AN EXPERIMENT INVOLVING DISCRIMINATION WAS ADMINISTERED TO 32 CHILDREN BETWEEN THE AGES OF 41 AND 78 MONTHS. THE RESULTS GENERALLY SUPPORTED THE HYPOTHESES. (WD)

ED024444 PS001182
INDUCED VERSUS SPONTANEOUS REHEARSAL IN SHORT-TERM MEMORY IN NURSERY SCHOOL CHILDREN. STUDY M: DEVELOPMENT OF SELECTIVE ATTENTION ABILITIES. KINGSLEY, PHILLIP R.; HAGEN, JOHN W., 3 JAN 68 19P.
EDRS PRICE MF-$0.65 HC-$3.29

EIGHTY NURSERY SCHOOL CHILDREN WERE RANDOMLY DIVIDED INTO FOUR GROUPS OF 20 AND GIVEN A SERIAL SHORT-TERM MEMORY TASK IN WHICH DIFFICULT-TO-LABEL STIMULI WERE USED. THREE EXPERIMENTAL GROUPS WERE PROVIDED WITH LABELS FOR THE STIMULI. OF THESE, ONE GROUP OVERTLY PRONOUNCED THE LABELS AND REHEARSED THEM DURING THE TASK, ONE GROUP MERELY PRONOUNCED THE LABELS OVERTLY, AND ONE GROUP WAS INSTRUCTED TO SAY THE LABELS COVERTLY. A CONTROL GROUP RECEIVED NO LABELS FOR THE STIMULI. REHEARSAL OF THE LABELS WAS FOUND TO FACILITATE RECALL PERFORMANCE ON EARLY SERIAL ITEMS, AND OVERT LABELING FACILITATED RECALL ON THE LAST SERIAL ITEM. COVERT LABELING DID NOT FACILITATE RECALL. THE RESULTS SUPPORTED THE HYPOTHESIS THAT QUALITATIVELY DIFFERENT PROCESSING STRATEGIES DETERMINE PRIMACY AND RECENCY EFFECTS. CURRENT THEORIES OF THE ROLE OF VERBALIZING IN CHILDREN'S MEMORY PERFORMANCE ARE DISCUSSED. (AUTHOR/MS)

ED024445 PS001186
SOME STUDIES OF THE MORAL DEVELOPMENT OF CHILDREN. EDWARDS, J.B., JUN 65 15P.
DOCUMENT NOT AVAILABLE FROM EDRS.

IMPRECISE CONCEPTS AND VAGUENESS IN THE FIELD OF MORAL DEVELOPMENT OF CHILDREN SHOULD BE COUNTERBALANCED BY FUTURE RESEARCH BY EDUCATIONALISTS AND PSYCHOLOGISTS. FROM A REVIEW OF THE SCANTY RESEARCH AVAILABLE IN MORAL DEVELOPMENT IT CAN BE CONCLUDED THAT (1) MORAL DEVELOPMENT IS MORE COMPLEX THAN HERETOFORE CONCEIVED; (2) INDIVIDUAL DIFFERENCES IN MORAL DEVELOPMENT MUST BE RECOGNIZED, NOT IGNORED; (3) EDUCATION MUST PRESENT CHILDREN WITH WORTHWHILE IDEAL PERSONS TO EMULATE; (4) BRIGHT CHILDREN GRASP COMPLEX MORAL ISSUES AND APPRECIATE THE MOTIVE BEHIND AN ACTION, AND HELP MUST BE GIVEN TO DULLER STUDENTS; (5) CAREFUL USE OF TERMS (FOR EXAMPLE, CHARACTER, HONESTY, AND CONSCIENCE) IS ACUTELY NECESSARY IN RESEARCH; AND (6) NO ONE THEORY OF MORAL DEVELOPMENT SEEMS ADEQUATE TO EXPLAIN THIS MANY-FACETED AREA. (DO)

ED024446 PS001190
LEARNING IN INFANTS. PAPOUSEK, HANUS, [66] 11P.
EDRS PRICE MF-$0.65 HC-$3.29

STUDIES ON LEARNING IN INFANTS SHOW THAT IN INFANCY EVERY MONTH OF LIFE REPRESENTS A NEW LEVEL OF LEARNING. THE FUNCTIONAL STATE OF THE CENTRAL NERVOUS SYSTEM CAN BE INFLUENCED BY PHYSIOLOGICAL FACTORS WHICH CAUSE FLUCTUATING CHANGES IN FUNCTIONS IMPORTANT FOR LEARNING. ONCE A STIMULUS BECOMES A CONDITIONED SIGNAL, IT ACQUIRES STRONG POWER IN INFLUENCING AN INFANT'S BEHAVIOR. MORE IS KNOWN ABOUT THE RELATIVE VALUE OF DIFFERENT REINFORCING UNCONDITIONED STIMULI THAN ABOUT THE RELATIVE VALUE OF CONDITIONING STIMULI. FURTHER RESEARCH IS NEEDED ON THE DEVELOPMENT OF CENTRAL MECHANISMS RESPONSIBLE FOR THE PROCESSING OF SENSORY INPUT AND FOR THE STRUCTURING AND INTEGRATION OF INFORMATION. IT IS LIKELY THAT PREVERBAL FORMS OF INFORMATION INTERACTION AND INTEGRATION WILL BECOME THE CENTER OF INCREASED RESEARCH ATTENTION. IN STUDIES OF POSTNATAL DEVELOPMENT, THE PHYSIOLOGICAL AND PSYCHOLOGICAL DISCIPLINES MERGE. (MS)

ED024447 PS001287
PARENTAL ANTECEDENTS OF CHILDREN'S BELIEFS IN INTERNAL-EXTERNAL CONTROL OF REINFORCEMENTS IN INTELLECTUAL ACHIEVEMENT SITUATIONS. KATKOVSKY, WALTER; AND OTHERS, 66 32P.
EDRS PRICE MF-$0.65 HC-$3.29

THIS REPORT SUMMARIZES TWO STUDIES ON THE INFLUENCE OF PARENT BEHAVIORS ON THE DEVELOPMENT OF THEIR CHILDREN'S BELIEFS THAT THEY (THE CHILDREN), RATHER THAN EXTERNAL AGENTS, CAUSE AND ARE RESPONSIBLE FOR THE REINFORCEMENTS THEY RECEIVE. CHILDREN'S BELIEFS IN INTERNAL CONTROL WERE CORRELATED WITH RATINGS OF THE MOTHER'S BEHAVIORS WHEN SHE WAS IN INTERACTION WITH THE CHILD (STUDY A, WITH 41 CHILDREN AND THEIR MOTHERS), INTERVIEW DATA FROM MOTHERS AND FATHERS ON THE PARENT-CHILD RELATIONSHIP (STUDY B, WITH 40 CHILDREN AND THEIR PARENTS), AND A QUESTIONNAIRE WHICH ASSESSED PARENTS' POSITIVE AND NEGATIVE REACTIONS TO THEIR CHILDREN'S ACHIEVEMENT BEHAVIOR. FINDINGS INDICATED THAT VARIOUS ASPECTS OF THE PARENT-CHILD RELATIONSHIP ARE SIGNIFICANT ANTECEDENTS, ESPECIALLY IN THE RELATIONSHIP BETWEEN MOTHER AND CHILD. THE MORE PROTECTIVE, NURTURAL AND LOVING THE MOTHER, THE GREATER WAS HER CHILD'S BELIEF IN INTERNAL CONTROL. PARENTAL DOMINANCE AND REJECTION APPEAR TO DISCOURAGE GIRLS' BELIEFS IN INTERNAL CONTROL. A TREND WAS ALSO FOUND FOR MOTHERS' ACCELERATIONAL ATTEMPTS TO RELATE POSITIVELY TO THEIR SONS' (BUT NOT THEIR DAUGHTERS') BELIEFS IN INTERNAL CONTROL. ON THE QUESTIONNAIRE MEASURE, PATERNAL PRAISE GENERALLY CORRELATED POSITIVELY WITH CHILDREN'S BELIEFS IN INTERNAL CONTROL, AND PATERNAL CRITICISM RELATED NEGATIVELY TO SUCH BELIEFS. (AUTHOR/MS)

ED024448 PS001289
ELEMENTARY EDUCATION RESPONDS TO A CHANGING SOCIETY CAZDEN, COURTNEY B., 20 MAY 66 16P.
EDRS PRICE MF-$0.65 HC-$3.29

PROJECTIONS INTO THE FUTURE OF SCHOOLS WHICH ARE DIVIDED INTO LITERARY PROGRAMS, LABORATORIES, AND COMMUNITY SEMINARS REFLECT MODERN TRENDS IN EDUCATION. SPECIALIZED BOOKS ARE BEING DEMANDED IN INDIVIDUAL INSTRUCTION, EITHER THROUGH HOMOGENEOUS GROUPING OR PROGRAMED INSTRUCTION (LITERACY PROGRAMS). IN GREATER DEMAND ARE LIBRARIES WITH INDEPENDENT STUDY PROGRAMS (LABORATORIES) AND WITH THE NEW IDEA OF A DUAL CURRICULUM OF CONTENT AND STRUCTURE. IN ADDITION, BOOKS WHICH REFLECT A CHANGING SOCIETY AND BUILD A "SENSE OF COMMUNITY" ARE NEEDED. FINALLY, NONPROFESSIONAL PERSONNEL ARE IN GREATER DEMAND TO HELP USE BOOKS AND SHARE THEIR EXPERIENCES WITH THE CHILDREN (COMMUNITY SEMINARS). BOOKS USED IN LANGUAGE ENRICHMENT PROGRAMS ARE OF THE WIDEST VARIETY TO PROVIDE STUDENTS WITH MANY STIMULI. WITH THE INCREASE IN PERSONNEL, TEACHER'S AIDES CAN GIVE CHILDREN THE EXPERIENCE OF BEING READ TO ON AN INDIVIDUAL BASIS, AND CHILDREN CAN ENJOY A WARM RELATIONSHIP BETWEEN BOOKS AND PEOPLE. ALSO TEACHER'S AIDES FREE THE

TEACHER TO CONCENTRATE ON SPECIFIC PROBLEMS. REFERENCES ARE INCLUDED. (JS)

ED024449 PS001293
AN EVALUATION OF THE LANGUAGE ARTS PROGRAM OF THE DISTRICT OF COLUMBIA. FINAL REPORT. DAILEY, JOHN T.; NEYMAN, CLINTON A., JR., NOV 65 8P.
EDRS PRICE MF-$0.65 HC-$3.29

IN AN EVALUATION OF A LANGUAGE ARTS PROGRAM FOR ORAL AND WRITTEN FACILITY AND COMPREHENSION AMONG CHILDREN OF AN URBAN CULTURE, 262 CHILDREN IN KINDERGARTEN COMPRISED THE EXPERIMENTAL GROUP, AND 369 STUDENTS SERVED AS CONTROLS. CHILDREN IN BOTH GROUPS WERE PRESENTED WITH THREE PICTURES AND INSTRUCTED TO TELL A STORY ABOUT EACH. OBSERVERS RATED SPEECH FACILITY AND OVERALL VERBALIZATION. PRETESTS AND POST-TESTS WERE GIVEN TO BOTH GROUPS. THE RESULTS SHOWED THAT STUDENTS IN EXPERIMENTAL SCHOOLS DO SIGNIFICANTLY BETTER IN WORD MEANING, LANGUAGE FACILITY, PICTURE VOCABULARY, AND THE MERRILL-PALMER SCALE AND RELATIVELY BETTER ON ENGLISH ERROR SCORE AND IN READING THAN THEIR READINESS SCORE PREDICTED. THEY MADE SIGNIFICANTLY FEWER ERRORS ON THE DAILEY LANGUAGE FACILITY TEST. SCHOOL CHARACTERISTICS AND SCHOOL SUCCESS WERE COMPARED WITH DATA FROM ANOTHER STUDY. IT WAS FOUND THAT TEACHERS' SALARIES, TEACHERS' EXPERIENCE, NUMBER OF BOOKS IN THE SCHOOL LIBRARY, AND PER-PUPIL EXPENDITURE ARE MORE CLOSELY RELATED TO SCHOOL SUCCESS THAN ARE SCHOOL SIZE, AVERAGE CLASS SIZE, AGE OF BUILDING AND SUBURBAN LOCATION. FAMILY INCOME WAS MOST CLOSELY RELATED. THE LANGUAGE ARTS PROGRAM WAS FOUND TO BE NEEDED AND SUCCESSFUL AND SHOULD BE EXTENDED TO THE PREKINDERGARTEN LEVEL. A REEVALUATION SHOULD BE MADE IN A FEW YEARS. (JS)

ED024450 PS001297
DIFFERENCES IN VOCABULARY INPUT-OUTPUT IN PSYCHODIAGNOSIS OF CHILDREN. L'ABATE, LUCIANO, 1 APR 66 9P.
EDRS PRICE MF-$0.65 HC-$3.29

THIS PAPER SUPPORTS THE HYPOTHESIS THAT PICTURE VOCABULARY TESTS SHOULD NOT BE USED AS INTERCHANGEABLE MEASURES OF INTELLIGENCE FOR COMPLEX, LENGTHY INTELLIGENCE TESTS (WISC AND STANFORD-BINET). IN PICTURE VOCABULARY TESTS ASSESSING RECEPTIVE FUNCTIONS (INPUT), THE CHILD RECOGNIZES A WORD BY POINTING TO OR STATING THE NUMBER STANDING FOR AN OBJECT. IN WISC AND STANFORD-BINET TESTS ASSESSING EXPRESSIVE FUNCTIONS (OUTPUT), THE CHILD ARTICULATES THE DEFINITION OF A WORD. SUBJECTS WERE DRAWN FROM THREE GROUPS: (1) 56 RETARDED CHILDREN FROM A PSYCHODIAGNOSTIC LABORATORY; (2) 41 CHILDREN FROM A CHILD GUIDANCE CLINIC; AND (3) 41 FROM MULTIPLY HANDICAPPED CHILDREN. THEY WERE TESTED TO SEE IF DIFFERENCES IN VOCABULARY INPUT AND OUTPUT SCORES WOULD VARY ACCORDING TO PHYSICAL SETTING, DIAGNOSIS, INTELLECTUAL FUNCTIONING, AND EDUCATIONAL ACHIEVEMENT. THE RESULTS SHOWED THAT INPUT-OUTPUT DIFFERENCES MAY BE PREDICTIVE OF EDUCATIONAL ACHIEVEMENT IN CHILDREN OF BORDERLINE MENTALITY BUT TEND TO BE INFLUENCED BY DIAGNOSIS, CEREBRAL DYSFUNCTION OR BEHAVIORAL DISTURBANCE IN CHILDREN OF AVERAGE INTELLIGENCE. CHILDREN'S INTELLECTUAL AND EDUCATIONAL POTENTIAL IS MORE PRECISELY EVALUATED BY JUDGING BOTH THE INPUT AND OUTPUT OF A CHILD'S VOCABULARY. CORRELATIONS BETWEEN PICTURE AND WISC VOCABULARY SCORES DO NOT JUSTIFY EQUIVALENCE OF MEASURE AND FUNCTIONS, ESPECIALLY WITH DEVIANT GROUPS OF CHILDREN. (DO)

ED024451 PS001305
TWO STUDIES OF THE SYNTACTIC KNOWLEDGE OF YOUNG CHILDREN. A PRELIMINARY REPORT. SMITH, CARLOTA S., 66 33P.
EDRS PRICE MF-$0.65 HC-$3.29

THIS PAPER DEALS WITH TWO EXPERIMENTS WHOSE PURPOSES ARE TO INVESTIGATE THE LINGUISTIC COMPETENCE OF YOUNG CHILDREN AND THEIR RECEPTIVITY TO ADULT SPEECH. IN THE FREE RESPONSE EXPERIMENT, IMPERATIVE SENTENCES WERE PRESENTED TO 1 1/2- TO 2 1/2-YEAR-OLDS. THE SENTENCES WERE MINIMAL (A SINGLE NOUN), TELEGRAPHIC, OR FULL ADULT SENTENCES. THE YOUNGEST CHILDREN WERE MOST RESPONSIVE TO MINIMAL OR TELEGRAPHIC FORM, WHILE THE OLDEST RESPONDED TO FULL SENTENCES. THE CONCLUSION IS THAT THERE IS A PERIOD WHEN LANGUAGE INPUT AND OUTPUT IS TELEGRAPHIC AND A SLIGHTLY LATER STAGE WHEN CHILDREN UNDERSTAND FULL ADULT SPEECH AS INPUT BUT WHEN THEIR OUTPUT IS STILL TELEGRAPHIC. THEY TEND NOT TO LISTEN TO ADULT SPEECH BEGINNING WITH UNFAMILIAR WORDS. IN THE REPITITION EXPERIMENT, GRAMMATICAL AND UNGRAMMATICAL SENTENCES WERE PRESENTED FOR IMMEDIATE REPETITION TO EIGHTEEN 3- AND 4-YEAR-OLDS. RESPONSES CONTAINED ERRORS IN RELATION TO THE COMPLEXITY OF SENTENCE STRUCTURE AND LESS ACCURATE IDENTIFICATION OF UNGRAMMATICAL SENTENCES. THE CHILD CORRECTS UNGRAMMATICAL SENTENCES IN RATIO TO HIS FAMILIARITY WITH THE STRUCTURE. WHEN HE CANNOT IDENTIFY A STRUCTURE, HE TENDS TO GIVE A SIMPLER STRUCTURE RATHER THAN A CONFUSED VERSION OF THE DIFFICULT ONE. IT IS SUGGESTED AS A RESULT OF THE TWO EXPERIMENTS THAT CHILDREN LISTEN SELECTIVELY TO ADULT SPEECH AND THAT REPETITION IS USEFUL IN INVESTIGATING LANGUAGE COMPETENCE. (DO)

ED024452 PS001314
INFORMAL EDUCATION DURING THE FIRST MONTHS OF LIFE. WHITE, BURTON L., 8 FEB 66 14P.
EDRS PRICE MF-$0.65 HC-$3.29

THE PURPOSE OF THIS STUDY WAS TO SEE IF A CHANGE IN ENVIRONMENT AFFECTED THE RATE OF SENSORIMOTOR DEVELOPMENT IN INFANTS. FIRST A CONTROL GROUP OF INSTITUTIONALLY-REARED INFANTS AGED 1 TO 6 MONTHS WAS OBSERVED TO DETERMINE AVERAGE AGE OF VISUALLY DIRECTED REACHING, VISUAL EXPLORATION, VISUAL ACCOMMODATION, AND THE BLINK RESPONSE. THEN THE ENVIRONMENT FOR THREE EXPERIMENTAL GROUPS WAS MODIFIED IN THREE WAYS. THE FIRST GROUP WAS HANDLED FOR AN EXTRA PERIOD OF TIME, THE SECOND GROUP WAS GIVEN AN ENRICHED VISUAL SURROUND IN ADDITION TO BEING PLACED ON THEIR BACKS AND HANDLED FOR EXTRA TIME, AND THE THIRD GROUP HAD PACIFIERS MOUNTED ON THEIR CRIBS IN ADDITION TO RECEIVING THE SAME ATTENTION AS THE SECOND GROUP. THE RESULTS SHOWED THAT THE RATE OF DEVELOPMENT OF VISUAL ATTENTIVENESS, HAND REGARD, AND VISUALLY DIRECTED REACHING WAS AFFECTED BY THE ENVIRONMENTAL MODIFICATIONS PRACTICED ON THE SECOND AND THIRD GROUPS. RESEARCH ON PLASTICITY IN OTHER AREAS OF SENSORIMOTOR DEVELOPMENT SHOULD BE CARRIED OUT. ENRICHMENT PROGRAMS AND EDUCATION ARE A CONTINUOUS PROCESS AND SHOULD BE TREATED AS SUCH. FURTHERMORE, INDUCTIVE THEORIZING SHOULD BE USED IN THE STUDY OF CHILD BEHAVIOR. (JS)

ED024453 PS001315
GROUP DAY CARE AS A CHILD-REARING ENVIRONMENT. AN OBSERVATIONAL STUDY OF DAY CARE PROGRAM. PRESCOTT, ELIZABETH; AND OTHERS, NOV 67 453P.
EDRS PRICE MF-$0.65 HC-$16.45

THE PURPOSE OF THIS STUDY WAS TO DESCRIBE FULLY DAY CARE PROGRAMS, TO FIND FACTORS PREDICTIVE OF DIFFERENCES IN PROGRAMS, AND TO EVALUATE THE EFFECTIVENESS OF DAY CARE CENTERS. TEACHERS IN 50 RANDOMLY SELECTED DAY CARE CENTERS IN LOS ANGELES WERE OBSERVED FOR FOUR 20-MINUTE PERIODS DAILY FOR 10 DAYS. THE RESULTS INDICATED THE FOLLOWING POINTS: TEACHERS VARY INDIVIDUALLY IN THE USE OF ENCOURAGEMENT AND RESTRICTION, AND PROGRAM FORMATS REFLECT (THROUGH TEACHING STYLES) THE THEORIES THAT THE ADULT EITHER IS A MODEL FOR SOCIALIZATION OR ENFORCES SOCIETY'S RULES. PREDICTORS OF PROGRAM DIFFERENCES ARE STRUCTURAL CHARACTERISTICS (SUCH AS ACTIVITY, TYPE OF SETTINGS, NUMBER OF ADULTS, AND AGE OF CHILDREN) WHICH DICTATE THE AMOUNT OF TEACHING INVOLVEMENT AND STAFF ATTITUDES WHICH REFLECT THE AMOUNT OF THEIR TRAINING. MOST CHILD-CENTERED STAFF MEMBERS WERE WELL TRAINED, ALTHOUGH SOME WELL TRAINED DIRECTORS WERE ADULT-CENTERED. THE SIZE AND SPACIAL LAYOUT OF THE CENTER REGULATE TEACHER PERFORMANCE. DAY CARE WAS MOST EFFECTIVE WHERE WARM, CHILD-CENTERED TEACHERS PROVIDED MANY STIMULATING ACTIVITIES, WHERE THE STAFF WAS FLEXIBLE, AND WHERE CHILDREN'S NEEDS WERE MET. STUDIES OF BROAD ENVIRONMENT FACTORS AND OF STAFF DECISION POLICIES ARE NEEDED. DATA ARE TABULATED AND A BIBLIOGRAPHY IS APPENDED. (JS)

ED024454 PS001316
CONCEPT LEARNING IN EARLY CHILDHOOD. FOWLER, WILLIAM, NOV 65 21P.
EDRS PRICE MF-$0.65 HC-$3.29

BECAUSE DISADVANTAGED CHILDREN HAVE USUALLY EXPERIENCED SENSORY-COGNITIVE DEPRIVATION OR DISTORTION, IT IS NECESSARY TO DISCOVER WAYS TO OFFSET THIS DEFICIT. A PROGRAM IS BEING CONDUCTED TO LEARN TO WHAT DEGREE THE INTRODUCTION OF SYSTEMATIC PROGRAMING, WHILE MOTIVATION TECHNIQUES ARE RETAINED, CAN REORIENT ESSENTIALLY NONCOGNITIVE LEARNING STYLES AND SETS IN YOUNG CHILDREN. SEQUENTIAL AND ORGANIZED PRESENTATION OF STIMULI, EMOTIONALLY SUPPORTIVE TEACHING ATTITUDES, AND FLEXIBLE TEACHING STYLES ARE IMPORTANT IF DISADVANTAGED CHILDREN ARE TO PROGRESS IN THEIR COGNITIVE DEVELOPMENT. ACCOMPLISHMENT OF THE BASIC FORMS OF LEARNING TASKS REQUIRES CHILDREN TO MASTER THREE PROCESSES: (1) DISCRIMINATION-IDENTIFICATION, (2) MATCHING-CONSTRUCTING, AND (3) SORTING-GROUPING ACTIVITIES. SMALL GROUPS (FOUR TO EIGHT CHILDREN) ARE TAUGHT BY TWO TYPES OF TEACHING TECHNIQUES: PLAY-GAME ACTIVITIES AND ATMOSPHERE OR A PROBLEM-SOLVING SITUATION. THE CHILD MOVES FROM SIMPLE TO MORE DIFFICULT LEVELS OF ACTIVITY AND FROM CONCRETE TO ABSTRACT REASONING. (MS)

ED024455 PS001319
INFANTS' RESPONSES TO FACIAL STIMULI DURING THE FIRST YEAR OF LIFE: EXPLORATORY STUDIES IN THE DEVELOPMENT OF A FACE SCHEMA. LEWIS, MICHAEL; AND OTHERS, [67] 35P.
EDRS PRICE MF-$0.65 HC-$3.29

FIXATION TIME, SMILING, VOCALIZATION, AND FRET/CRY WERE RECORDED TO OBTAIN A COMPLETE PICTURE OF INFANTS' RESPONSES TO FACIAL STIMULI OVER THE FIRST YEAR OF LIFE. FOUR STIMULI WERE PRESENTED TO 120 INFANTS. RESULTS OF FIXATION DATA INDICATE THAT (1) THERE IS A MARKED DECREASE IN FIXATION TOWARD FACIAL STIMULI WITHIN THE FIRST YEAR, (2) AT ALL AGES BOYS LOOK LONGER THAN GIRLS, AND (3) IN THE FIRST HALF YEAR REALISTIC STIMULI WERE PREFERRED, AND IN THE SECOND HALF YEAR NONREALISTIC STIMULI WERE PREFERRED. THE RESULTS OF SMILING AND VOCALIZATION WERE

PARALLEL: (1) BOTH INCREASED OVER THE FIRST YEAR, (2) GIRLS SMILED AND VOCALIZED MORE THAN BOYS, (3) REALISTIC FACIAL PATTERNS ELICITED MORE SMILING AND VOCALIZATION REGARDLESS OF AGE. FRET/CRY DATA WERE INCLUDED TO DETERMINE IF STIMULI WOULD ELICIT CONSISTENT FEAR OR UNPLEASANT RESPONSES. RESULTS INDICATE (1) A DECREASE IN FRET/CRY OVER AGE, (2) THAT BOYS SHOW MORE FRET/CRY THAN GIRLS, AND (3) THAT STIMULI FAIL TO ELICIT CONSISTENT OR OBSERVABLE FEAR RESPONSES. THE DIFFERENCE BETWEEN THE MEASURES SUGGESTS THAT THE RESPONSES ARE UNDER THE SERVICE OF TWO SYSTEMS, ONE AFFECTED BY FAMILIARITY AND NOVELTY; THE OTHER, BY INNATE RELEASING MECHANISMS OR SOCIAL LEARNING. (DO)

ED024456 PS001321
SOCIO-CULTURAL INFLUENCES ON ATTENTION IN ELEMENTARY SCHOOL CHILDREN. FINAL REPORT. KNOPF, IRWIN J., 1 JUN 68 21P.
EDRS PRICE MF-$0.65 HC-$3.29

FIVE EXPERIMENTS (CONDUCTED IN 1968 ON OBSERVING RESPONSES AND VIGILANCE, REWARD PREFERENCES, AND LEARNING STRATEGIES IN CONCEPT FORMATION) INDICATE THAT SOCIOECONOMIC LEVEL (SEL) HAS AN INFLUENCE ON INTELLECTUAL AND EDUCATIONAL FUNCTIONING OF ELEMENTARY SCHOOL CHILDREN. EXPECTATION OF REINFORCEMENT WAS TESTED IN EXPERIMENT 1, USING 60 KINDERGARTNERS. LOW SEL CHILDREN RAPIDLY STOPPED MAKING OBSERVING RESPONSES WHEN AN EXPECTED EVENT DID NOT OCCUR, WHILE HIGH SEL CHILDREN MAINTAINED A SIGNIFICANT RATE OF OBSERVING RESPONSES. IN EXPERIMENT 2, 32 SECOND GRADERS AND 24 FOURTH GRADERS WERE TESTED TO INVESTIGATE LEFT-RIGHT DIRECTIONAL PREFERENCE. FOURTH GRADERS AND HIGH SEL SECOND GRADERS PERFORMED WITH MORE DIRECTIONAL RESPONSES THAN DID LOW SEL SECOND GRADERS. REWARD PREFERENCES AND REINFORCEMENT WERE INVESTIGATED IN 60 KINDERGARTNERS IN EXPERIMENT 3. LOW SEL CHILDREN HAD SIGNIFICANTLY GREATER PREFERENCE FOR CONSISTENCY THAN HIGH SEL CHILDREN. EXPERIMENT 5 TESTED 60 FIRST GRADERS AND INDICATED THAT THE CHAOTIC REINFORCEMENT VARIABLE ALONE PRODUCES DETERIORATION OF PERFORMANCE. COMPARATIVELY, LOW SEL CHILDREN FAILED TO OBSERVE ENVIRONMENTAL STIMULI NOT PREVIOUSLY CONDITIONED TO LEARNED RESPONSES. FURTHER RESEARCH ON BEHAVIOR STRATEGIES IS RECOMMENDED. PRESENT ACADEMIC CURRICULUM IS INAPPROPRIATE FOR THE FACILITATION OF LEARNING IN LOW SEL CHILDREN. (DO)

ED024457 PS001323
COMPARISON OF AMERICAN AND NORWEGIAN NURSERY SCHOOL CHILDREN ON INDEPENDENCE BEHAVIOR AND TRAINING. HJERTHOLM, ELSE WERNO, SEP 68 95P.
EDRS PRICE MF-$0.65 HC-$3.29

TO COMPARE INDEPENDENCE TRAINING AND CULTURAL EXPECTATIONS OF INDEPENDENCE TRAINING AMONG AMERICAN AND NORWEGIAN NURSERY SCHOOL CHILDREN, THIS STUDY HYPOTHESIZED THAT (1) CULTURAL EXPECTATIONS OF INDEPENDENCE ARE GREATER FOR NORWEGIAN CHILDREN THAN AMERICAN, (2) SUCH EXPECTATIONS ARE GREATER FOR GIRLS, (3) CHILDREN'S INDEPENDENT BEHAVIOR AND PARENTAL EXPECTATIONS ARE POSITIVELY CORRELATED, AND THAT (4) NORWEGIAN CHILDREN WOULD BE MORE SELF-RELIANT. MOTHERS WERE GIVEN TWO QUESTIONNAIRES WHICH ASSESSED CULTURAL EXPECTATIONS AND CHILD REARING PRACTICES IN INDEPENDENCE TRAINING. THIRTY-FOUR NURSERY SCHOOL CHILDREN OF THE UPPER-MIDDLE CLASS (NORWEGIAN: NINE BOYS AND EIGHT GIRLS; AMERICAN: 10 BOYS AND SEVEN GIRLS) WERE INVOLVED IN TWO SIMPLE TASKS WITH THE MOTHER AND INVESTIGATOR AND TWO DIFFICULT TASKS WITH THE INVESTIGATOR. THE DATA WERE ANALYZED BY T-TESTS, ANALYSIS OF VARIANCE, AND INTERCORRELATION PROGRAMS. THE RESULTS SUPPORTED ALL HYPOTHESES BUT ONE. AMERICAN BOYS WERE FOUND TO BE SUBJECT TO GREATER CULTURAL EXPECTATIONS THAN WERE THE GIRLS. THE CONCLUSIONS SUGGESTED THE DIFFERENCES MIGHT BE DUE TO CULTURAL PRESSURE, NOT TRAINING. DATA ARE TABULATED AND AN EXTENSIVE BIBLIOGRAPHY IS APPENDED. (JS)

ED024458 PS001327
BIG QUESTIONS AND LITTLE CHILDREN: SCIENCE AND HEAD START. GRIFFIN, LOUISE, 68 38P.
EDRS PRICE MF-$0.65 HC-$3.29

THIS RESOURCE PAMPHLET IS INTENDED TO ACQUAINT THE HEAD START TEACHER WITH THE POSSIBILITIES OF TEACHING SCIENCE IN A PRESCHOOL PROGRAM FOR DISADVANTAGED CHILDREN. INTRODUCTORY SECTIONS STRESS THE IMPORTANCE OF INCLUDING SCIENCE IN A HEAD START PROGRAM, BRIEFLY INDICATE HOW TO USE THE PAMPHLET, AND SUGGEST SOME THINGS TO SEEK AND AVOID. A SECTION ENTITLED "SOME THINGS TO KEEP IN MIND" PRESENTS OBJECTIVES FOR A SCIENCE PROGRAM. THESE ARE (1) TO USE SCIENCE EXPERIENCES TO DEVELOP LANGUAGE SKILLS, (2) TO PROVIDE OPPORTUNITIES FOR CHILDREN TO RELATE TO ADULTS, (3) TO PROVIDE VARIETY IN THE CHILD'S EXPERIENCES, (4) TO ESTABLISH A SENSE OF THE ORDER IN THE WORLD, (5) TO DEVELOP COMPLETION EXPERIENCES, (6) TO GIVE THE CHILD A FEELING OF BEING ABLE TO SOLVE PROBLEMS, AND (7) TO DIFFUSE ELEMENTS ACQUIRED THROUGH SCIENCE INTO THE CHILD'S WHOLE LIFE. SUGGESTIONS FOR PLANNING SCIENCE ACTIVITIES ARE PRESENTED THROUGH THREE SAMPLE LESSON PLANS. A FINAL SECTION LISTS READINGS FOR ADULTS, BOOKS AND RECORDS TO USE WITH CHILDREN, AND SOURCES FOR FILMSTRIPS, FILMS, BOOKS, AND SCIENCE MATERIALS. (DR)

ED024459 PS001335
PRODUCTIVE THINKING IN EDUCATION. ASCHNER, MARY JANE, ED.; BISH, CHARLES E., ED., 65 321P.
DOCUMENT NOT AVAILABLE FROM EDRS.
AVAILABLE FROM: NATIONAL EDUCATION ASSOCIATION, 1201 SIXTEENTH ST., N.W., WASHINGTON, D.C. 20036 (CLOTH, $4.50, PAPER $3.00).

THIS PUBLICATION IS COMPOSED OF A COLLECTION OF ARTICLES BASED ON THE IDEAS PRODUCED AND PRESENTED AT TWO CONFERENCES ON PRODUCTIVE THINKING. INTENDED, OVERALL, TO INTRODUCE NEW CONCEPTS OF INTELLECTUAL ABILITIES, THE BOOK IS DIVIDED INTO FOUR PARTS: PART I DESCRIBES A CONSIDERABLE AMOUNT OF THE SIGNIFICANT RESEARCH IN "INTELLIGENCE AND ITS DEVELOPMENT" AND CONTAINS ARTICLES BY GUILFORD, AUSUBEL, AND OJEMANN. PART II (WITH ARTICLES BY ALPERT, CARON, AND MACKINNON) ATTEMPTS TO BRIDGE THE GAP BETWEEN CURRENT RESEARCH AND CLASSROOM TEACHING IN THIS AREA OF INTELLECTUAL DEVELOPMENT. PART III EXTENDS THE REVIEW OF RESEARCH OF PART I AND CONTAINS ARTICLES BY TORRANCE AND BARRON. PART IV PROVIDES AN OVERALL CONSIDERATION OF PRODUCTIVE THINKING IN THE EDUCATIONAL PROCESS AS VIEWED BY TAYLOR, PASSOW, AND GOLDBERG. (WD)

ED024460 PS001336
PROJECT HEAD START, PSYCHOLOGICAL SERVICES REPORT, RESEARCH, SUMMER 1968. THORNTON, SAM, SEP 68 17P.
EDRS PRICE MF-$0.65 HC-$3.29

IN A SUMMER PROGRAM, 351 HEAD START CHILDREN WERE ASSESSED. GOALS OF THE PROGRAM WERE (1) TO ASSESS THE EDUCABILITY OF THESE CHILDREN AS A GROUP, (2) TO IDENTIFY TO PUBLIC SCHOOLS THE CHILDREN IN NEED OF EARLY SPECIAL HELP, AND (3) TO OBTAIN INFORMATION GERMANE FOR FUTURE HEAD START PROGRAMS. CHILDREN WERE SCREENED WITH REFERENCE TO PROBABLE SUCCESS IN MEETING FIRST GRADE REQUIREMENTS ON THE BASIS OF A MEASURED PERFORMANCE AND TEACHER JUDGMENT. SCREENING FACTORS INCLUDED PHYSICAL DEVELOPMENT AND COORDINATION, MENTAL DEVELOPMENT, PERCEPTION (VISUAL AND AUDITORY), MOTIVATION, AND SOCIALIZATION. RECOMMENDATIONS INCLUDE ADDING VISUAL PERCEPTION, LANGUAGE, AND VISUAL MOTOR PROGRAMS TO THE CURRICULUM AND STRESSING THE IMPORTANCE OF FINDINGS IN CHILD DEVELOPMENT RESEARCH, PRESCHOOL METHODOLOGY, AND TEACHING MATERIALS FOR TEACHER ORIENTATION. (DO)

ED024461 PS001337
TEACHER AIDES: HANDBOOK FOR INSTRUCTORS AND ADMINISTRATORS. FERVER, JACK, ED.; COOK, DORIS M., ED., 68 95P.
DOCUMENT NOT AVAILABLE FROM EDRS.
AVAILABLE FROM: UPPER MIDWEST REGIONAL EDUCATIONAL LABORATORY, 2698 UNIVERSITY AVENUE, ST. PAUL, MINNESOTA 55114.

THIS HANDBOOK WAS PREPARED TO ASSIST ADMINISTRATORS AND INSTRUCTORS OF TEACHER-AIDE PERSONNEL TO DEAL WITH THE EXPANDING RECRUITMENT, TRAINING, AND UTILIZATION OF PARAPROFESSIONALS IN EDUCATION. SOME OF THE OBJECTIVES OF THE HANDBOOK ARE (1) TO DEFINE THE ROLE OF TEACHER-AIDE, (2) TO ESTABLISH GUIDELINES FOR THEIR PRESERVICE AND INSERVICE TRAINING, (3) TO HELP TEACHERS GAIN AN UNDERSTANDING OF THEIR ROLES AS LEADERS, (4) TO IDENTIFY METHODS OF TRAINING, (5) TO ESTABLISH CRITERIA FOR A JOB DESCRIPTION OF VARIOUS KINDS OF AIDES, AND (6) TO EVALUATE CRITERIA IN CERTIFYING AIDES. A FOUR-PAGE BIBLIOGRAPHY IS INCLUDED. (DO)

ED024462 PS001338
SUPPLEMENTARY MATERIALS FOR TEACHER AIDE TRAINING PROGRAMS, TO SUPPLEMENT THE PUBLICATION "TEACHER AIDES: HANDBOOK FOR INSTRUCTORS AND ADMINISTRATORS." FERVER, JACK C., ED.; COOK, DORIS M., ED., 68 134P.
EDRS PRICE MF-$0.65 HC-$6.58
AVAILABLE FROM: UNIVERSITY EXTENSION BOOKSTORE, THE UNIVERSITY OF WISCONSIN, 432 N. LAKE STREET, MADISON, WISCONSIN 53706 ($2.00).

IN PLANNING A PROGRAM, SCHOOL AND COMMUNITY NEEDS MUST BE RECOGNIZED; ADMINISTRATORS, SELECTED; AND A STEP-BY-STEP PROGRAM FOR TRAINEES, EVOLVED. OBJECTIVES ESTABLISHED SHOULD (1) DEVELOP AN UNDERSTANDING OF THE PHILOSOPHY OF THE ELEMENTARY SCHOOL, (2) ACQUAINT AIDES WITH THE ASSIGNED CLASSROOM SCHEDULE, AND (3) DEVELOP AN AWARENESS OF QUALIFICATIONS AND RESPONSIBILITIES RELEVANT TO PRACTICAL ASSISTANCE IN THE CLASSROOM. THIS MANUAL CONTAINS CHAPTERS DEVOTED TO CLASSROOM TECHNIQUES, TIPS ON BULLETIN BOARDS, A GUIDE TO OPERATING AUDIOVISUAL EQUIPMENT, A SECTION ON ACTIVITIES (GAMES, MUSIC, FINGER PLAY, AND PHYSICAL EDUCATION), AND CHAPTERS ON AIDES' ASSISTANCE IN THE LIBRARY AND IN ART, LANGUAGE ARTS, AND MATH PROGRAMS. (DO)

ED024463 PS001340
ACHIEVEMENT, CREATIVITY, AND SELF-CONCEPT CORRELATES OF TEACHER-PUPIL TRANSACTIONS IN ELEMENTARY SCHOOL CLASSROOMS. SPAULDING, ROBERT L., 65 230P.
EDRS PRICE MF-$0.65 HC-$9.87

THIS REPORT DESCRIBES THE SECOND PHASE OF A CONTINUING ANALYSIS OF THE RECORDED CLASSROOM BEHAVIOR OF SUPERIOR TEACHERS IN TRANSACTION WITH PUPILS. THE PROBLEM WAS TO DISCOVER HO W TEACHING METHOD AND STYLE AFFECTED PUPIL PERSONALITY DEVELOPMENT AND EDUCATIONAL PROGRESS. EIGHT HYPOTHESES WERE TESTED, USING 21 TEACHERS OF 507 FOURTH AND SIXTH GRADERS OF HIGH SOCIOECONOMIC BACKGROUND. THERE IS A SIGNIFICANT RELATIONSHIP BETWEEN THE PLACEMENT O F A CHILD IN A SUPERIOR CLASSROOM AND SUBSEQUENT SELF-ESTEEM, ACADEMIC ACHIEVEMENT, AND CREATIVE THINKING. HEIGHT OF SELF-CONCEPT WAS RELATED TO SOCIALLY INTEGRATIVE, LEARNER-SUPPORTIVE TEACHER BEHAVIORS. PREDICTIONS OF SUPERIOR READING AND MATHEMATICAL ACHIEVEMENT TAUGHT BY ACADEMICALLY ORIENTED TEACHERS AND HIGHER SELF-CONCEPTS IN CLASSROOMS WITH COUNSELOR-TYPE TEACHERS WERE UNSUPPORTED. SUPERIOR PUPIL ORIGINALITY WITH CREATIVE TEACHERS WAS UNSUPPORTED. HIGH DEGREE OF PRIVATE COMMUNICATION WITH PUPILS YIELDED HIGH SELF-ESTEEM. LITTLE SUPPORT WAS GIVEN TO THE PREDICTED RELATIONSHIPS WITH DEMOCRATIC TEACHER BEHAVIOR. SEQUENTIAL ANALYSES OF TEACHER TRANSACTIONS WITH DIFFERENT TYPES OF CHILDREN WERE RECOMMENDED. (DO)

ED024464 PS001341
MOTIVATIONAL AND SOCIAL COMPONENTS IN COMPENSATORY EDUCATION PROGRAMS: SUGGESTED PRINCIPLES, PRACTICES, AND RESEARCH DESIGNS. BRONFENBRENNER, URIE, 1 FEB 68 34P.
EDRS PRICE MF-$0.65 HC-$3.29

DEVELOPMENT OF COGNITIVE COMPETENCE AND CONSTRUCTIVE PATTERNS OF MOTIVATION AND BEHAVIOR IN THE DISADVANTAGED CHILD ARE THE TOPICS OF THIS PAPER. FIVE SUBJECTS ARE EXPLORED: (1) THE POTENCY OF MODELS, (2) SOCIAL REINFORCEMENT, (3) INTENSIVE RELATIONSHIPS, (4) GROUP FORCES, AND (5) SUPERORDINATE GOALS. THE FIRST TWO SUBJECTS COVER BASIC PROCESSES WHICH INFLUENCE THE BEHAVIOR AND DEVELOPMENT OF THE CHILD, WHILE THE LAST THREE SUBJECTS EXAMINE THE SOCIAL CONTEXT IN WHICH THESE PROCESSES CAN BE EFFECTIVELY EVOKED. THE AUTHOR PROPOSES CONCRETE EXAMPLES OF INNOVATIVE AND UNCONVENTIONALLY RESEARCH THAT COULD BE ATTEMPTED IN ALL ENVIRONMENTS AND WHICH WOULD SUBSTANTIALLY ADVANCE PROGRESS IN EDUCATION OF THE DISADVANTAGED. (DO)

ED024465 PS001342
MOTHER-CHILD RELATIONS AND CHILDREN'S ACHIEVEMENT. TERMINAL REPORT. CHANCE, JUNE ELIZABETH, MAY 68 41P.
EDRS PRICE MF-$0.65 HC-$3.29

THIS CROSS-SECTIONAL ANALYSIS EXPLORED (A) CHILDREN'S ACHIEVEMENT PERFORMANCE, ASSESSED BY ACADEMIC TESTS AND MEASURE OF INTELLIGENCE, (B) CHILDREN'S ATTITUDES TOWARD ACHIEVEMENT, AND (C) MATERNAL ATTITUDES TOWARD INDEPENDENCE TRAINING. FIFTY-NINE BOYS AND FIFTY-FIVE GIRLS OF HIGH IQ AND THEIR MOTHERS WERE SUBJECTS. EFFECTIVE ACHIEVEMENT PERFORMANCE WAS ASSOCIATED WITH PERMISSIVENESS TOWARD CONTROLLING CHILD BEHAVIOR, BUT IT DID NOT RELY ON EITHER EARLIER OR LATER INDEPENDENCE TRAINING. MOTHERS WHO FAVORED EARLY TRAINING REWARDED EFFORTS, DESPITE QUALITY OF PERFORMANCE, AND THE CHILDREN ASPIRED TO THE EXPECTED ROLE. THE CHILD'S ATTITUDE, PREDICTIVE OF EFFECTIVE ACHIEVEMENT, WAS THAT HIS EFFORTS DETERMINED THE OUTCOME HE RECEIVED. IN BOYS AND GIRLS, BELIEF IN PERSONAL CONTROL OF OUTCOME WAS ASSOCIATED WITH EARLY INDEPENDENCE TRAINING ATTITUDES IN A PERMISSIVE MOTHER. NEED ACHIEVEMENT IN BOYS WAS ASSOCIATED WITH EARLY TRAINING BY A MOTHER CONCERNED WITH CONTROLLING CHILD BEHAVIOR; AND IN GIRLS, IT WAS ASSOCIATED WITH LATER TRAINING. OVER 100 CHILDREN WERE SUBJECTS OF A LONGITUDINAL ANALYSIS, WHICH INDICATED ACHIEVEMENT AND MOTHER-AND-CHILD CORRELATES WERE SIMILAR TO THE CROSS-SECTIONAL ANALYSIS. ONE FINDING, HOWEVER, WAS THAT MATERNAL "CONTROLLINGNESS" WAS NEGATIVELY ASSOCIATED WITH BETWEEN-CHILD DIFFERENCES IN ACHIEVEMENT IN BOTH SEXES. THE TABLES AND APPENDIXES ARE NO T INCLUDED. (DO)

ED024466 PS001352
THE DISTANCING HYPOTHESIS: A HYPOTHESIS CRUCIAL TO THE DEVELOPMENT OF REPRESENTATIONAL COMPETENCE. SIGEL, IRVING, 68 15P.
EDRS PRICE MF-$0.65 HC-$3.29

REPRESENTATIONAL COMPETENCE REFERS TO THE INDIVIDUAL'S CAPABILITY TO RESPOND APPROPRIATELY TO EXTERNAL REPRESENTATIONS. FOR EXAMPLE, A CHILD ENGAGED IN A GROUPING TASK MAY COLLECT TOGETHER ALL LIKE OBJECTS EVEN IF THE GROUP CONTAINS VARYING REPRESENTATIONS OF THE OBJECT, INCLUDING (1) THE OBJECT ITSELF, (2) A THREE-DIMENSIONAL LIKENESS OF THE OBJECT, (3) A PICTURE OF THE OBJECT, AND (4) A WORD THAT SYMBOLIZES THE OBJECT. RESEARCH INDICATED THAT MIDDLE CLASS CHILDREN GENERALLY DEMONSTRATE MUCH GREATER REPRESENTATIONAL COMPETENCE THAN DISADVANTAGED BLACK CHILDREN. THE ACQUISITION OF REPRESENTATIONAL COMPETENCE IS IN PART OBTAINED FROM EXPERIENCES WHICH CREATE TEMPORAL, SPATIAL, OR PSYCHOLOGICAL DISTANCE BETWEEN SELF AND OBJECT. THIS PROCESS IS TERMED "DISTANCING," AND THE HYPOTHESIS OFFERED TO EXPLAIN IT IS CALLED THE "DISTANCING HYPOTHESIS." IN SHORT, REPRESENTATIONAL COMPETENCE IS THE RESULTANT OF EXPERIENCES CREATING AN AWARENESS OF THE DIFFERENCE BETWEEN OBJECTS AND THEIR SYMBOLS AND AN AWARENESS OF IDEAS FROM ACTIONS. ALTHOUGH SOME AUTHORITIES HAVE SAID THE CRUCIAL PERIOD FOR OBTAINING THESE DISTANCING EXPERIENCES IS THE FIRST 2 YEARS OF LIFE, RECENT DATA SUGGEST THAT THE CRUCIAL PERIOD IS BETWEEN 2 AND 4 YEARS OF AGE. (WD)

ED024467 PS001356
LEARNING AND TEACHING, GRADES N-9 (EMPHASIS ON MIDDLE GRADES). , [67] 83P.
EDRS PRICE MF-$0.65 HC-$3.29

A 1-YEAR COURSE FOR STUDENT TEACHERS SEEKING CERTIFICATION FOR THE NURSERY THROUGH THE SIXTH GRADE IS OUTLINED IN THIS DOCUMENT. THE CONTENT OF THE COURSE IS DIVIDED INTO FOUR AREAS: (1) DIRECTED OBSERVATION (WHAT CAN BE LEARNED FROM OBSERVATION OF THE CLASSROOM; (2) LEARNING AND TEACHING OF AN INDIVIDUAL CHILD (HOW WE KNOW THE INDIVIDUAL CHILD); (3) THE CURRICULUM OF GRADES THREE THROUGH SIX (HOW CURRICULUM CAN BE MADE MORE RELEVANT TO STUDENT CONCERNS); AND (4) CLASSROOM TEACHING AND LEARNING PROCEDURES (HOW TO STRUCTURE AND ORGANIZE THE CLASS). THE COURSE WOULD BE CONDUCTED PREDOMINANTLY AS A DISCUSSION GROUP, ALTHOUGH SUGGESTIONS ARE MADE FOR GUEST LECTURERS, MULTIMEDIA PRESENTATIONS, AND STUDENT FEEDBACK. AN EXTENSIVE LIST OF READINGS COVERING COURSE CONTENT IS INCLUDED AS PART OF THE CURRICULUM GUIDE. APPENDIXES INCLUDE AN EXTENSIVE BIBLIOGRAPHY, DIRECTIONS FOR WHAT STUDENT TEACHERS SHOULD OBSERVE, AND A DELINEATION OF READING SKILLS CHILDREN SHOULD HAVE AT DIFFERENT GRADE LEVELS. (JS)

ED024468 PS001358
THE POLITICAL SOCIALIZATION OF CHILDREN AND THE STRUCTURE OF THE ELEMENTARY SCHOOL. HALLER, EMIL J.; THORSON, SONDRA J., FEB 68 23P.
EDRS PRICE MF-$0.65 HC-$3.29

THE PURPOSE OF THIS PAPER WAS TO DETERMINE THE EFFECT OF THE SCHOOL'S STRUCTURE UPON THREE ASPECTS OF THE STUDENT'S POLITICAL SOCIALIZATION: COMMUNITY, REGIME, AND AUTHORITIES. AGE LEVEL DIVISIONS FOSTER A SENSE OF COMMUNITY IN AND OUT OF SCHOOL, AND PUPIL-TEACHER AUTHORITY RELATIONSHIPS ESTABLISH ATTITUDES TOWARD AUTHORITIES AND NORMS OF BEHAVIOR EXPECTED IN A SYSTEM (REGIME). SOCIAL-PSYCHOLOGICAL CONSEQUENCES ARE INFERRED FROM THESE STRUCTURAL ATTRIBUTES. FROM AGE COHORTS, CHILDREN ESTABLISH A RELATIONSHIP AMONG THEIR EQUALS AND A SOCIETY OF PEERS WHICH PERMIT EMPATHY. THROUGH THE PUPIL-TEACHER RELATIONSHIP, CHILDREN EXPECT NONFAMILY AUTHORITY FIGURES TO BEHAVE UNIVERSALISTICALLY AND BENEVOLENTLY. THE STRUCTURE ALSO PROMOTES THE CHILD TO DEVELOP A SENSE OF PERSONAL EFFICACY. THE IMPLICATIONS FOR THE MODERN POLITICAL SYSTEM ARE AS FOLLOWS: (1) A SENSE O F COMMUNITY AND ABILITY TO EMPATHIZE WITH PEERS ARE ESSENTIAL. (2) THE ABILITY TO ACT IN TERMS OF RELEVANT CATEGORIES AND UNIVERSALISM ARE CENTRAL TO NORMS IN A REGIME WHICH STRESSES EQUALITY BEFORE THE LAW AND THE RULE OF THE MAJORITY. (3) ATTITUDES TOWARD AUTHORITIES ARE IMPORTANT IN MAINTAINING STABILITY. (4) PERSONAL EFFICACY OF CITIZENS IS BASIC TO A POPULARLY CONTROLLED SYSTEM. RESEARCH IS CONCLUSIVE IN DEMONSTRATING THAT ELEMENTARY SCHOOL AGE CHILDREN ARE NOT APOLITICAL. (JS)

ED024469 PS001362
REACHING THE HARD-TO-REACH: THE USE OF PARTICIPANT GROUP METHODS WITH MOTHERS OF CULTURALLY DISADVANTAGED PRESCHOOL CHILDREN. WOHLFORD, PAUL; STERN, HARRIS W., MAR 68 7P.
EDRS PRICE MF-$0.65 HC-$3.29

THIRTEEN NEGRO MOTHERS OF PRESCHOOL CHILDREN WHO ATTENDED A DAY CARE PROGRAM PARTICIPATED IN A SERIES O F SIX WEEKLY MEETINGS LED BY AN EDUCATOR AND DEVOTED TO (1) DISCUSSION AND DEMONSTRATION O F WAYS THE MOTHERS COULD EXPAND THEIR CHILDREN'S LEARNING SKILLS AND (2) DISCUSSION OF ASPECTS OF THE MOTHER-CHILD RELATIONSHIP. THE REASON FOR THESE GROUP MEETINGS, CALLED THE PARTICIPANT SMALL GROUP METHOD, WAS TO ATTEMPT TO REDUCE THE CONFLICT BETWEEN THE HOME ENVIRONMENT AND SCHOOL ENVIRONMENT OF DISADVANTAGED CHILDREN. THIS REDUCTION IN CONFLICT WAS TO BE ACCOMPLISHED BY IMPROVING THE EMOTIONAL RELATIONS OF THE FAMILY AND THE COGNITIVE-INTELLECTUAL FUNCTIONING OF THE FAMILY. IN GENERAL, ALL OF THE MOTHERS SEEMED QUITE CONCERNED ABOUT THEIR COMPETENCY AS MOTHERS; BUT BECAUSE OF THE SMALL EXTENT OF THE PROGRAM'S IMPACT, IT SEEMS UNLIKELY THAT IT WAS VERY EFFECTIVE IN MODIFYING THE MOTHERS' BEHAVIOR. (WD)

ED024470 PS001365
PERCEPTUAL-COGNITIVE DEVELOPMENT IN INFANCY: A GENERALIZED EXPECTANCY MODEL AS A FUNCTION OF THE MOTHER-INFANT INTERACTION. LEWIS, MICHAEL; GOLDBERG, SUSAN, FEB 68 42P.
EDRS PRICE MF-$0.65 HC-$3.29

TWENTY INFANTS, 12 WEEKS OF AGE, WERE SUBJECTS IN AN EXPERIMENT TO TEST THE EFFECTS OF MATERNAL BEHAVIOR ON THEIR PERCEPTUAL-COGNITIVE DEVELOPMENT. EACH MOTHER AND CHILD WERE OBSERVED IN A CONTROLLED NATURALISTIC SETTING, EVERY 10 SECONDS THEIR VARIOUS BEHAVIORS WERE RECORDED, AND THEN THE MOTHER WAS INTERVIEWED. DURING AN EXPERIMENTAL SESSION THE INFANT WAS PLACED IN A RECLINING SEAT WITH A MATRIX PANEL ON WHICH STIMULI WERE PRESENTED 18 INCHES IN FRONT OF HIM. THE MOTHER SAT TO THE REAR AND SIDE OF THE INFANT. RESPONSE DECREMENT WAS POSITIVELY CORRELATED WITH THE AMOUNT OF TOUCHING, LOOKING, HOLDING, AND SMILING THE MOTHER EXHIBITED AND NEGATIVELY CORRELATED WITH THE AMOUNT OF TIME THE MOTHER WAS READING. HIGHER FREQUENCIES OF MATERNAL RESPONSE WERE ASSOCIATED WITH GREATER RESPONSE DECREMENT. DATA CONSISTENTLY INDICATE THERE IS POSITIVE CORRELATION BETWEEN MATERNAL RESPONSE TO INFANT BEHAVIOR AND THE COGNITIVE DEVELOPMENT OF THE INFANT AS MEASURED BY RESPONSE DECREMENT. HELPLESSNESS OR CONTROL IS A LEARNED MOTIVE AND HAS IMPORTANT CONSEQUENCES FOR SUBSEQUENT PERCEPTUAL-COGNITIVE DEVELOPMENT. MATERNAL BEHAVIOR STIMULATES WITHIN THE INFANT THE EXPECTANCY THAT HIS BEHAVIOR CAN AFFECT HIS ENVIRONMENT AND MOTIVATES HIM TO PRODUCE AND UTILIZE BEHAVIORS AND SKILLS NOT REINFORCED IN HIS PAST EXPERIENCE. (DO)

ED024471 PS001366
A PRELIMINARY SEARCH FOR FORMAL OPERATIONS STRUCTURES. NEIMARK, EDITH D., AUG 68 20P.
EDRS PRICE MF-$0.65 HC-$3.29

IN A TEST THE PRESENCE OR ABSENCE OF A "STRUCTURE" IN THE INDIVIDUAL'S COGNITIVE PROCESSES OF FORMAL OPERATIONS THINKING, 61 FOURTH, FIFTH, AND SIXTH GRADE STUDENTS WERE ADMINISTERED THREE TASKS SUPPOSEDLY REQUIRING SUCH A METHOD OF THINKING. THE THREE TASKS WERE (1) A PROBLEM SOLVING TASK (PS), (2) A CHEMISTRY TASK REQUIRING A CERTAIN COMBINATION OF SUBSTANCES TO OBTAIN A CORRECT ANSWER(CH), AND (3) A CORRELATION TASK REQUIRING THE MATCHING OF CERTAIN ELEMENTS TO OBTAIN THE CORRECT ANSWER (CO). EACH SUBJECT WAS GIVEN ALL THREE TASKS DURING TWO SESSIONS WITH THE EXPERIMENTER. THE HIGHER THE CORRELATION BETWEEN THE PERFORMANCES OF THE STUDENTS ON ALL THREE TASKS, THE GREATER WAS THE POSSIBILITY OF THE EXISTENCE OF A FORMAL OPERATIONS THINKING STRUCTURE. THE RESULTS INDICATED THE PRESENCE OF A LOW BUT CONSISTENT AND SIGNIFICANT CORRELATION BETWEEN TASKS PS AND TASK CO. TASK CH DID NOT CORRELATE WITH EITHER PS OR CO. IT IS POSSIBLE THAT THE CH TASK CONTAINED PROPERTIES THAT MADE IT INAPPROPRIATE FOR USE WITH THIS AGE LEVEL OF SUBJECT. (WD)

ED024472 PS001367
EARLY CHILDHOOD SELECTED BIBLIOGRAPHIES SERIES. NUMBER 5, SOCIAL. , 68 66P.
EDRS PRICE MF-$0.65 HC-$3.29

THIS DOCUMENT IS THE FIFTH IN A SERIES OF SIX ANNOTATED BIBLIOGRAPHIES RELEVANT TO EARLY CHILDHOOD EDUCATION. ITS GENERAL SUBJECT IS SOCIAL, AND IT INCLUDES THREE SUBDIVISIONS: INTERPERSONAL RELATIONS, SEX-ROLE IDENTIFICATION, AND SOCIAL REINFORCEMENT. EACH OF THE 45 ABSTRACTS INCLUDED HAS BEEN CLASSIFIED BY GENERAL AND SPECIFIC SUBJECT, BY FOCUS OF STUDY, AND ALPHABETICALLY BY AUTHOR. FOCUS OF STUDY CATEGORIES ARE NORMATIVE, ENVIRONMENTAL, MEASUREMENT AND TECHNIQUES, INTERVENTION AND GENERAL. THE GENERAL SUBJECTS OF OTHER BIBLIOGRAPHIES IN THE SERIES ARE LANGUAGE, PERSONALITY, COGNITION, EDUCATION, AND PHYSICAL ASPECTS OF EARLY CHILDHOOD EDUCATION. (JS)

ED024473 PS001368
PRESCHOOL PROGRAMS AND THE INTELLECTUAL DEVELOPMENT OF DISADVANTAGED CHILDREN. O'BRIEN, ROSLYN A.; LOPATE, PHILLIP, 68 14P.
EDRS PRICE MF-$0.65 HC-$3.29

EVIDENCE INDICATES THAT DISADVANTAGED CHILDREN ARE INTELLECTUALLY INFERIOR TO MIDDLE CLASS CHILDREN AT THE TIME THEY ENTER SCHOOL; AND AS SCHOOL CONTINUES, THE GAP WIDENS. THE ENVIRONMENT OF THE DISADVANTAGED CHILD LACKS MUCH OF THE OPPORTUNITY AND STIMULATION FOR INTELLECTUAL GROWTH PRESENT IN THE MIDDLE AND UPPER CLASS ENVIRONMENTS AND GENERALLY NECESSARY FOR ACADEMIC SUCCESS IN SCHOOL. COMPENSATORY PRESCHOOL EDUCATION FOR THE DISADVANTAGED CHILD HAS BEEN CREATED TO ALLEVIATE THE GAP, AT LEAST PARTIALLY. PROJECT HEAD START WAS THE FIRST WIDE-SCALE ATTEMPT TO PROMOTE THE INTELLECTUAL GROWTH OF THE DISADVANTAGED PRESCHOOLER. SOME EARLY EVALUATIONS OF THE HEAD START PROGRAM INDICATED WHICH ASPECTS OF ANY SUCH PROGRAM CONTRIBUTE THE MOST TO SUBSTANTIAL INTELLECTUAL GROWTH; NAMELY, (1) A WARM, SUPPORTIVE, AND STIMULATING TEACHER; (2) A TASK-ORIENTED PROGRAM APPROACH; (3) AN ACADEMICALLY ORIENTED PROGRAM FORMAT; AND (4) AN EMPHASIS ON VERBAL DEVELOPMENT. (WD)

ED024474 PS001397
URBAN EDUCATION BIBLIOGRAPHY: AN ANNOTATED LISTING. RANDOLPH, H. HELEN, APR 68 110P.
EDRS PRICE MF-$0.65 HC-$6.58
AVAILABLE FROM: CENTER FOR URBAN EDUCATION, 105 MADISON AVENUE, NEW YORK, NEW YORK 10016 ($1.00).

THIS ANNOTATED REVIEW OF LITERATURE BRINGS TOGETHER RESEARCH REPORTS, ARTICLES, BOOKS, AND OTHER PUBLICATIONS CONCERNING URBAN EDUCATION. THE CONTENTS ARE DESIGNED FOR RESEARCHERS, TEACHERS, STUDENTS, ADMINISTRATORS, AND POLICYMAKERS. THE REFERENCES ARE PRIMARILY FROM MATERIAL PRODUCED FROM SEPTEMBER 1964 THROUGH DECEMBER 1965. THE BULK OF THE MATERIAL FOCUSES ON MINORITY GROUP INTEGRATION INTO THE EDUCATIONAL, SOCIAL, AND ECONOMIC INSTITUTIONS OF THE COUNTRY; THE CLASSROOM AND PROCEDURES OF INNER-CITY SCHOOLS; THE TEACHERS AND STUDENTS OF THESE SCHOOLS; THE CURRICULUMS AND TEACHING TECHNIQUES; THE INVOLVEMENT OF COMMUNITY AND PARENTS; AND THE ROLE OF SCHOOL BOARDS, POLITICS, AND BUREAUCRATIZATION AS THEY AFFECT THESE SCHOOLS. REVIEW NOTES INDICATE WHERE DATA ARE LACKING AND LIST OTHER BIBLIOGRAPHIES. APPROXIMATELY 1,000 ANNOTATIONS ARE ARRANGED UNDER SUBJECT HEADINGS. BOTH A SUBJECT LISTING AND LIBRARY OF CONGRESS LISTING ARE INCLUDED. AN UNANNOTATED LIST OF SOME 350 ENTRIES IS ALSO INCLUDED. AN AUTHOR INDEX IS PROVIDED FOR CROSS REFERENCE. (JS)

ED024475 PS001409
EARLY CHILDHOOD SELECTED BIBLIOGRAPHIES SERIES. NUMBER 6, PERSONALITY. , 68 29P.
EDRS PRICE MF-$0.65 HC-$3.29

THIS DOCUMENT IS THE SIXTH IN A SERIES OF SIX ANNOTATED BIBLIOGRAPHIES RELEVANT TO EARLY CHILDHOOD EDUCATION. ITS GENERAL SUBJECT IS PERSONALITY, AND IT INCLUDES THREE SUBDIVISIONS: BASIC TEMPERAMENTAL AND MOTIVATIONAL TRAITS, ATTITUDE, AND EGO FUNCTIONING. EACH OF THE 15 ABSTRACTS INCLUDED HAS BEEN CLASSIFIED BY GENERAL AND SPECIFIC SUBJECT, BY FOCUS OF STUDY, AND ALPHABETICALLY BY AUTHOR. FOCUS OF STUDY CATEGORIES ARE NORMATIVE, ENVIRONMENTAL, MEASUREMENT AND TECHNIQUES, INTERVENTION, PATHOLOGY, PHYSIOLOGY, ANIMALS, AND GENERAL. THE GENERAL SUBJECTS OF OTHER BIBLIOGRAPHIES IN THE SERIES ARE LANGUAGE, EDUCATION, COGNITION, PHYSICAL, AND SOCIAL ASPECTS OF EARLY CHILDHOOD EDUCATION. (DO)

ED024476 PS001469
COMPARISON OF AMERICAN AND NORWEGIAN NURSERY SCHOOL CHILDREN OF INDEPENDENCE BEHAVIOR AND TRAINING. SUMMARY REPORT. HJERTHOLM, ELSE WERNO, SEP 68 9P.
EDRS PRICE MF-$0.65 HC-$3.29

THIS DOCUMENT IS A SUMMARY REPORT OF A STUDY WHICH COMPARED INDEPENDENCE TRAINING OF UPPER MIDDLE CLASS NORWEGIAN AND AMERICAN NURSERY SCHOOL CHILDREN (SEE PS 001 323). SIX TASKS OF INCREASING DIFFICULTY WERE PRESENTED TO THE CHILDREN, AND THEIR RESPONDING BEHAVIOR WAS RATED ON A BEHAVIOR RATING LIST. AFTER OBTAINING A MEASURE OF VALIDITY, THE DATA WERE ANALYZED. ALL BUT ONE OF THE HYPOTHESES WERE SUPPORTED. (JS)

ED025298 PS001126
ROLE OF MOTHERS' LANGUAGE STYLES IN MEDIATING THEIR PRESCHOOL CHILDREN'S COGNITIVE DEVELOPMENT. OLIM, ELLIS G.; AND OTHERS, 67 12P.
DOCUMENT NOT AVAILABLE FROM EDRS.

A STUDY RELATING MOTHERS' LANGUAGE STYLES AND TECHNIQUES OF FAMILY CONTROL TO CHILDREN'S COGNITIVE DEVELOPMENT WAS CONDUCTED WITH 163 URBAN NEGRO MOTHERS FROM THE LOWER AND MIDDLE CLASSES AND THEIR 4-YEAR-OLD CHILDREN. THE FOLLOWING CONCLUSIONS WERE DRAWN: (1) THERE WAS A SIGNIFICANT NEGATIVE CORRELATION BETWEEN RESPONSES OF STATUS-ORIENTED MOTHERS AND PERSONAL- OR COGNITIVE-ORIENTED MOTHERS. (2) THERE WAS A SIGNIFICANT NEGATIVE CORRELATION BETWEEN RESPONSES OF MOTHERS USING IMPERATIVES AND THOSE USING INSTRUCTIONS. (3) STATUS-NORMATIVE ORIENTATION AND IMPREATIVE LANGUAGE WERE SIGNIFICANTLY AND POSITIVELY RELATED, WHILE PERSONAL-SUBJECTIVE AND COGNITIVE-RATIONAL ORIENTATION AND INSTRUCTIVE LANGUAGE TENDED TO BE POSITIVELY RELATED. (4) STATUS-NORMATIVE ORIENTED MOTHERS HAD LIMITED LANGUAGE, WHEREAS ELABORATE LANGUAGE WAS USED BY PERSONAL-SUBJECTIVE AND COGNITIVE-RATIONAL ORIENTED MOTHERS. (5) CHILDREN OF STATUS-NORMATIVE ORIENTED MOTHERS DID NOT PERFORM AS WELL AS CHILDREN OF PERSONAL-SUBJECTIVE AND COGNITIVE-RATIONAL ORIENTED MOTHERS. (6) MOTHERS LANGUAGE STYLES WERE SIGNIFICANTLY CORRELATED WITH THEIR CHILDREN'S PERFORMANCE ON VARIOUS COGNITIVE MEASURES. (7) LOWER CLASS MOTHERS USED IMPERATIVE LANGUAGE AND WERE STATUS-NORMATIVE ORIENTED, WHEREAS MIDDLE CLASS MOTHERS USED INSTRUCTIVE LANGUAGE AND WERE PERSONAL-SUBJECTIVE AND COGNITIVE-RATIONAL ORIENTED. IMPLICATIONS INDICATE THAT BECAUSE OF SOCIAL-STATUS DIFFERENCES, EFFECTIVE INTERVENTION MUST INVOLVE SOCIAL REFORM. (JS)

ED025299 PS001131

LANGUAGE ABILITY AND READINESS FOR SCHOOL OF CHILDREN WHO PARTICIPATED IN HEAD START PROGRAMS. A DISSERTATION ABSTRACT. COWLING, DOROTHY N. C., 67 12P.

EDRS PRICE MF-$0.65 HC-$3.29

AVAILABLE FROM: UNIVERSITY MICROFILMS, 300 ZEEB RD., ANN ARBOR, MICHIGAN 48106 (ORDER NO. 67-14,931, MF-$3.00. XEROGRAPHY, $6.00, 123P. FOR COMPLETE DISSERTATION).

IN ORDER TO TEST LANGUAGE ABILITY AND SCHOOL READINESS IN CHILDREN WITH HEAD START EXPERIENCE, 168 DISADVANTAGED CHILDREN WERE RANDOMLY SELECTED. ONLY HALF OF THE CHILDREN HAD PREVIOUS HEAD START EXPERIENCE. ALL CHILDREN RECEIVED THE METROPOLITAN READINESS TEST AND WERE OBSERVED BY THEIR TEACHER AND EXAMINER. THE RESULTS SHOWED THAT IN LANGUAGE ABILITY, THE HEAD START CHILDREN WERE SIGNIFICANTLY BETTER ABLE TO BE UNDERSTOOD BY THEIR TEACHER AND THE EXAMINER, TO RESPOND TO THEIR PEERS' QUESTIONS, ALTHOUGH NOT THE TEACHER'S, AND TO RETELL A SIMPLE STORY. IN SCHOOL READINESS HEAD START CHILDREN WERE SIGNIFICANTLY MORE READY FOR SCHOOL AS MEASURED BY THE METROPOLITAN READINESS TEST, AND THEY WERE SIGNIFICANTLY BETTER ABLE TO GIVE THEIR FULL NAME AND FOLLOW DIRECTIONS. IN REACTION TO SCHOOL ENVIRONMENT, HEAD START CHILDREN RANKED SIGNIFICANTLY HIGHER IN PARTICIPATING IN VOLUNTARY DISCUSSIONS, SHOWING RESPECT FOR EACH OTHER, FEELING AT EASE WITH THEIR PEERS, FEELING SELF-CONFIDENT IN SCHOOL, ASKING QUESTIONS ABOUT UNCLEAR DIRECTIONS, ANSWERING THE EXAMINER'S QUESTIONS, AND TELLING PERSONAL EXPERIENCES TO THE EXAMINER. HEAD START CHILDREN SHOWED ONLY A TENDENCY TO FEEL THE NEED TO CONFORM TO REGULATIONS. FUTURE RESEARCH SHOULD PRODUCE A FOLLOWUP STUDY AND AN INSTRUMENT TO MEASURE LANGUAGE DEVELOPMENT IN DISADVANTAGED CHILDREN. A BIBLIOGRAPHY IS INCLUDED. (JS)

ED025300 PS001234

PROBLEMS OF DIALECT. LAVATELLI, CELIA B., ED., [67] 7P.

EDRS PRICE MF-$0.65 HC-$3.29

CHILDREN WHO LEARN A DIALECT DIFFER IN PRONUNCIATION, SYNTAX, OR BOTH FROM CHILDREN WHO LEARN STANDARD ENGLISH. IT HAS BEEN ASSUMED THAT DIALECTAL DIFFERENCES CONTRIBUTE TO DIFFICULTIES IN LEARNING TO READ. ANOTHER QUESTION IS WHETHER A DISADVANTAGED CHILD WHO SPEAKS A DIALECT IS EXPOSED TO A LANGUAGE ENVIRONMENT RICH ENOUGH FOR HIM TO MAKE NORMAL PROGRESS WITHIN THAT DIALECT. PRESCHOOL LANGUAGE PROGRAMS HAVE BEEN TRYING TO ELIMINATE DIALECTUAL PRONUNCIATION DIFFERENCE SO THAT CHILDREN WILL BE BETTER PREPARED FOR THE FIRST GRADE. ALTHOUGH IT IS AGREED THAT A SOCIAL CLASS PREJUDICE AGAINST DIALECT EXISTS, THERE IS NO AGREEMENT AS TO WHETHER DIALECTS REFLECTING SUBSTANDARD GRAMMAR ARE A HINDRANCE TO THINKING PROCESSES. EUROPEAN CHILDREN WHO SPEAK REGIONAL DIALECTS USE STANDARD LANGUAGE AT SCHOOL WITHOUT RESULTING LEARNING DEFICITS. EXPERIMENTAL WORK IS NEEDED TO IDENTIFY AND PLAN FOR THE USE OF CERTAIN SYNTACTICAL SYSTEMS IN REMEDIAL WORK WITH PRESCHOOL CHILDREN. (MS)

ED025301 PS001236

PARENTS AS TEACHERS, HOW LOWER-CLASS AND MIDDLE-CLASS MOTHERS TEACH. HESS, ROBERT; SHIPMAN, VIRGINIA, [67] 29P.

EDRS PRICE MF-$0.65 HC-$3.29

IN AN INVESTIGATION OF MATERNAL TEACHING STYLES, 162 MOTHERS TAUGHT THEIR CHILDREN TWO COGNITIVE SORTING TASKS. MATERNAL TEACHING VARIABLES EXAMINED INCLUDED LANGUAGE, MOTIVATION TECHNIQUES, ABILITY TO INTERPRET CHILD'S RESPONSES, AND SUCCESS IN GIVING APPROPRIATE FEEDBACK IN RETURN. THE EFFECTS OF TEACHING STYLES ON CHILDREN WERE ALSO ANALYZED. ONCE THE MOTHERS UNDERSTOOD THE SORTING TASKS, THEY WERE GIVEN UNLIMITED TIME TO TEACH THEM TO THEIR CHILDREN, ALTHOUGH THEY WERE NOT SUPPLIED WITH METHODS. TASK 1 REQUIRED CHILDREN TO SORT A GROUP OF TOYS BY COLOR AND KIND. TASK 2 REQUIRED BLOCK SORTING BY HEIGHT, COLOR AND MARKING. ONLY 10 OF THE 162 CHILDREN MADE PERFECT SCORES ON THE POSTTEST. RESULTS INDICATED THAT MATERNAL VARIABLES OF EDUCATION, GENERAL INTELLIGENCE, COERCIVE OR ENCOURAGING TEACHING STYLES, AND ABILITY TO MOTIVATE AFFECTED THE CHILD'S PERFORMANCE, AS DID HIS OWN INTELLIGENCE, INTEREST IN THE TASKS, AND ATTITUDE TOWARD THE MOTHER. THE MOST SUCCESSFUL TEACHING STYLES SHOWED SPECIFICITY OF LANGUAGE AND ORGANIZATION AND SEQUENTIAL PRESENTATION OF MATERIAL TO BE LEARNED. THE PAPER CONTAINS EXAMPLES OF POSITIVE AND NEGATIVE WAYS OF MOTIVATING CHILDREN AND DEVELOPING CONSTRUCTIVE OR DESTRUCTIVE ATTITUDES TOWARD LEARNING. THE RESEARCH WAS CONDUCTED AT THE UNIVERSITY OF CHICAGO EARLY EDUCATION RESEARCH CENTER, ONE OF THE COMPONENTS OF THE NATIONAL LABORATORY FOR EARLY CHILDHOOD EDUCATION. (MS)

ED025302 PS001285

THE PREPARED ENVIRONMENT AND ITS RELATIONSHIP TO LEARNING. LOEFFLER, MARGARET HOWARD, 67 34P.

DOCUMENT NOT AVAILABLE FROM EDRS.

AVAILABLE FROM: TRUSTEES OF CASADY SCHOOL, OKLAHOMA CITY, OKLAHOMA.

A "PREPARED ENVIRONMENT" IS A PLANNED LEARNING FACILITY FOR YOUNG CHILDREN WHICH OFFERS A SUPPORTIVE AND STIMULATING ENVIRONMENT. CURRENT THINKING ON EARLY LEARNING AND THE RESULTANT IMPLICATIONS FOR THE DESIGN OF A PHYSICAL ENVIRONMENT WHICH WOULD ENCOURAGE CONCEPTUAL DEVELOPMENT ARE EXAMINED IN THIS BOOK. EACH SECTION CONSIDERS A PARTICULAR CONCEPT: (1) DEPENDENCE, INDEPENDENCE, INTERDEPENDENCE, (2) EARLY STIMULATION AND LEARNING, (3) MANAGEABLE COMPLEXITY, (4) THE PLAY OF YOUNG CHILDREN, AND (5) THE ROLE OF THE TEACHER. THE EDUCATIONAL RATIONALE AND ARCHITECTURAL INTERPRETATIONS IN TERMS OF EQUIPMENT AND PHYSICAL SURROUNDINGS ARE GIVEN FOR EACH SECTION. DRAWINGS SUPPLEMENT THE DISCUSSIONS. (MS)

ED025303 PS001390

INKSTER PUBLIC SCHOOLS IMPLEMENT CHILD DEVELOPMENT CENTER. , [68] 12P.

EDRS PRICE MF-$0.65 HC-$3.29

AN INNOVATIVE KINDERGARTEN PROGRAM WAS ESTABLISHED AS A FEDERALLY FUNDED PROJECT TO PURSUE THE FOLLOWING OBJECTIVES: (1) TO DISCOVER AND DEVELOP THE POTENTIAL ABILITY OF EACH CHILD, (2) TO DEVELOP FEELINGS OF AUTONOMY AND SELF-WORTH, (3) TO PROVIDE EXPERIENCES FOR DEVELOPING INQUIRING ATTITUDES AND FOR DEVELOPMENT OF SELF-CONFIDENCE AND POSITIVE SELF-CONCEPTS, (4) TO PROVIDE AN ACCEPTING CLIMATE, (5) TO DEVELOP A MULTISENSORY APPROACH IN TERMS OF ACTIVITIES AND MATERIALS, AND (6) TO INVOLVE CHILDREN AND PARENTS IN MEANINGFUL ACTIVITIES. APPROXIMATELY 500 CHILDREN WHO WOULD HAVE BEEN ASSIGNED TO SEVEN LOCAL ELEMENTARY SCHOOLS WERE BROUGHT TO THIS CHILD DEVELOPMENT CENTER FOR KINDERGARTEN. AN EARLY CHILDHOOD EDUCATION CONSULTANT WAS ASSIGNED TO COORDINATE THE PROGRAM AND ACT AS A LIAISON BETWEEN THE CENTER AND PARENTS. AN ORAL COMMUNICATION SPECIALIST, A LEARNING AND MATERIALS SPECIALIST, PARAPROFESSIONALS, AND A PSYCHOLOGIST WERE ASSIGNED TO THE PROJECT. UNIQUE FEATURES INCLUDED A READING PROGRAM, A BOYS' CENTER EMPHASIZING GROSS MOTOR ACTIVITY, A LANGUAGE LABORATORY, AND AN INSTRUCTIONAL MATERIALS CENTER. THE CURRICULUM WAS FOCUSED ON PERCEPTUAL SKILLS (MOTOR AND VISUAL), COGNITIVE, LANGUAGE, AND SOCIAL SKILLS, AND ON COMMUNICATION OF ATTITUDES AND FEELINGS. THE STAFF COMMITTED THEMSELVES TO THE THESIS THAT EXCELLENCE IN EDUCATION MUST BEGIN BEFORE CHILDREN REACH GRADED EDUCATION. (DO)

ED025304 PS001392

INDEX AND DESCRIPTION OF TESTS. , MAY 65 106P.

EDRS PRICE MF-$0.65 HC-$6.58

THE TESTS DESCRIBED IN THIS INDEX ARE USED BY THE INSTITUTE FOR DEVELOPMENTAL STUDIES IN ITS PRINCIPAL AREAS OF RESEARCH AND DO NOT INCLUDE RECENTLY DEVELOPED TESTS. THE RESEARCH AT THE INSTITUTE IS CONCERNED WITH (1) THE RELATIONSHIP OF DIFFERING ENVIRONMENTS TO LANGUAGE DEVELOPMENT, (2) CLASSROOM COMMUNICATION BETWEEN TEACHERS AND CHILDREN OF VARIOUS SOCIOECONOMIC LEVELS, (3) THE EFFECT OF PSYCHOPHARMACOLOGICAL AGENTS ON CHILDREN'S LEARNING, AND (4) RELATIONSHIPS AMONG SENSORY MODALITY PREFERENCE AND EFFICIENCY, LATERAL DOMINANCE, AND PSYCHOLOGICAL DEVELOPMENT AND FUNCTIONING. DESCRIBED, TOO, ARE INTERVIEWS, QUESTIONNAIRES, A VARIETY OF TOOLS USED TO STUDY PERCEPTION AND COGNITION, AND STANDARDIZED INSTRUMENTS FOR ASSESSING INTELLIGENCE, ACADEMIC ACHIEVEMENT, AND PERSONALITY FACTORS. THIS INDEX PROVIDES A BRIEF DESCRIPTION OF MEASUREMENT AND EVALUATION TECHNIQUES IN THE FORM OF A SUMMARY OF THE PURPOSES FOR WHICH EACH TEST WAS DEVISED, THE METHOD OF ADMINISTRATION, THE WAY IT HAS BEE N USED TO DATE, AND PLANS FOR ITS FUTURE USE. (DO)

ED025305 PS001396

THE MARIE HUGHES LANGUAGE TRAINING MODEL. HOBSON, ARLINE, [68] 27P.

EDRS PRICE MF-$0.65 HC-$3.29

BECAUSE DISADVANTAGED SPANISH-AMERICAN CHILDREN WERE HANDICAPPED BY LIMITED LANGUAGE LEARNING AND INABILITY TO EXPRESS THEMSELVES FREELY, A MODEL FOR LANGUAGE TRAINING WAS DEVELOPED AND IS BEING USED IN THE PRIMARY GRADES OF THE TUCSON , ARIZONA, PUBLIC SCHOOLS. THE MODEL IS BASED ON JOHN CARROLL'S GRAMMATICAL ANALYSIS AND INVOLVES TEACHING CHILDREN THE SKILLS OF SENTENCE TRANSFORMATION, SEQUENCING, ASSOCIATING AND CATEGORIZING. SINCE THE CHILDREN TEND TO SPEAK IN BRIEF, TELEGRAPHIC LANGUAGE, INCREASED VARIETY AND CONTROL OF VERBAL EXPRESSION IS A PRIMARY AIM OF THE HUGHES DEVELOPMENT MODEL. INTERESTING CURRICULUM ACTIVITIES, INCLUDING TRIPS AND SENSORY EXPERIENCES, ARE OFFERED TO PROVIDE STIMULI TO GET CHILDREN TO TALK. VERBAL EXPRESSION IS ELICITED AND REINFORCED BY THE TEACHER AND HER TECHNICAL ASSISTANTS. THE TEACHER, HERSELF, GAINS UNDERSTANDING OF LANGUAGE STRUCTURE AND MODELS. THE CHILD'S OWN LANGUAGE OUTPUT, IN THE FORM OF STORIES OR CONVERSATION, IS TAPE RECORDED AND USED BOTH FOR ANALYSIS AND

TO PROVIDE FEEDBACK TO THE CHILD ON HIS PROGRESS. COMPARISONS OF LANGUAGE SAMPLES TAKEN IN THE AUTUMN AND IN THE SPRING PROVIDE SOME MEASURE OF GROWTH. THE TEACHER PRESCRIBES FOR AND TALKS TO A CHILD ON THE BASIS OF HIS DEMONSTRATED INDIVIDUAL NEEDS. SPECIFIC EXAMPLES OF TEACHING PROCEDURES ARE GIVEN. (MS)

ED025306 PS001398
BETTER FEEDING CAN MEAN BETTER SPEAKING. BLANCHARD, IRENE, NOV 63 3P.
DOCUMENT NOT AVAILABLE FROM EDRS.

MAN USES ESSENTIALLY THE SAME STRUCTURES FOR EATING AS HE DOES FOR SPEAKING. SPEECH, HOWEVER, IS ACCOMPLISHED BY ELABORATING UPON THE BASIC INGESTION FUNCTIONS OF THESE STRUCTURES. IT IS THEORIZED THAT THE APPROPRIATE AND EFFICIENT USE OF THESE MOTILE ORGANS IN EATING SHOULD LEAD EVENTUALLY TO MORE APPROPRIATE AND EFFICIENT PATTERNS OF SPEECH. FOR EXAMPLE, IT IS A REASONABLE ASSUMPTION THAT THE NATURAL EXERCISE OF THE TONGUE AND LIPS WHILE EATING IS NECESSARY TO PREPARE THESE STRUCTURES FOR LATER USE IN TALKING. A ROUTINE FOR THE PROPER PRESENTATION OF FOOD ESPECIALLY IN THE CASE OF THE MENTALLY RETARDED, WHO OFTEN HAVE SUBSTANTIAL SPEECH HANDICAPS, INCLUDES (1) A SIGNIFICANT AMOUNT OF COMMUNICATION WITH THE CHILD DURING FEEDING, (2) POSITIONING THE CHILD TO FACE THE FEEDER, (3) PRESENTING JUST A TASTE OF FOOD FIRST, NOT A WHOLE SPOONFUL, (4) ENCOURAGING PROPER MASTICATION, (5) REMOVING THE SPOON FROM THE LIP AREA AT ONCE, AND (6) NOT PRESENTING A DIFFERENT TASTE UNTIL OVERT SWALLOWING OF THE LAST TASTE HAS BEEN OBSERVED. (WD)

ED025307 PS001399
PARENT-CHILD INTERACTION AND THE CHILD'S APPROACH TO TASK SITUATIONS. HEINICKE, CHRISTOPH M., 68 14P.
EDRS PRICE MF-$0.65 HC-$3.29

TEN NORMAL 3-YEAR-OLD CHILDREN AND THEIR PARENTS SERVED AS SUBJECTS FOR THIS LONGITUDINAL STUDY OF THE INTERACTION BETWEEN PARENT-CHILD RELATIONSHIPS AND THE CHILD'S APPROACH TO TASK SITUATIONS WHILE ATTENDING NURSERY SCHOOL. TO ILLUSTRATE THE NATURE OF THE DATA GATHERED AND OBSERVATIONS MADE IN THIS STUDY, THREE OF THE 10 CHILDREN WERE CONSIDERED IN SOME DETAIL. THE EMPHASIS WAS ON COMPARING THE CHILD'S TASK BEHAVIOR DURING NURSERY SCHOOL TO HIS RELATIONSHIP WITH HIS MOTHER. THESE COMPARISONS WERE MADE AT THE END OF THE FIRST YEAR OF NURSERY SCHOOL AND AGAIN AT THE END OF THE SECOND YEAR OF NURSERY SCHOOL. THE RESULTS INDICATED THAT IT WAS IMPORTANT TO LOOK BEYOND THE AFFECTION DISPLAYED BY THE MOTHER TOWARDS HER CHILD TO THE WHOLE CONTEXT OF THE HOME ENVIRONMENT IN WHICH THE MOTHER-CHILD RELATIONSHIP TOOK PLACE. THAT IS, MOTHERS WHO RATE ABOUT THE SAME IN TERMS OF PROVIDING ADEQUATE AFFECTION FOR THEIR CHILD MAY, BECAUSE OF OTHER FACTORS OF THE RELATIONSHIP OR OF THE HOME CONTEXT, ESTABLISH DIFFERENT POSITIVE OR NEGATIVE BEHAVIORAL CHARACTERISTICS IN THEIR CHILD THAT WOULD NOT BE UNDERSTANDABLE WITHOUT A MORE COMPREHENSIVE AWARENESS OF THE TOTAL MOTHER-CHILD RELATIONSHIP. WHERE MOTHER TO CHILD WARMTH WAS ADEQUATE, WHERE MOTHER AVAILABILITY WAS WELL DEFINED, WHERE NEW RELATIONSHIPS FOR THE CHILD WERE ENCOURAGED, WHERE LIMITS ON BEHAVIOR WERE SET, AND WHERE ACHIEVEMENT WAS ENCOURAGED, THE CHILD DEMONSTRATED A MORE STABLE PERSONALITY AND A SUPERIOR APPROACH TO TASK BEHAVIOR. (WD)

ED025308 PS001400
ENGINEERING VERBAL BEHAVIOR. SAPON, STANLEY M., MAR 68 35P.
EDRS PRICE MF-$0.65 HC-$3.29

AT THE CHILD LANGUAGE DEVELOPMENT CENTER AT THE UNIVERSITY OF ROCHESTER, BASIC RESEARCH IN CHILDREN'S VERBAL BEHAVIOR AND THE EXPLORATION OF PROCEDURES FOR EXTENDING SUCCESSFUL LABORATORY TECHNIQUES TO THE TYPICAL PRESCHOOL SETTING ARE BEING CONTINUED. EXPERIMENTS IN CONTINGENCY MANAGEMENT AND THE ESTABLISHMENT OF REQUISITE ANTECEDENT BEHAVIORS SUCH AS SITTING, LISTENING, ETC. NECESSARY FOR PRESCHOOL ACTIVITIES ARE BEING CONDUCTED. THE CENTER'S OPERATION IS BASED ON THE THEORY THAT VERBAL BEHAVIOR AS WELL AS OTHER BEHAVIORS CAN BE ENGINEERED WHEN SUPPORTIVE CONSEQUENCES ARE CONTINGENT UPON PRODUCTION OF DESIRED BEHAVIOR. A BEHAVIOR IS INTRODUCED TO AN INDIVIDUAL CHILD IN A SPECIAL SETTING BY A TEACHER. ONCE THE DESIRED BEHAVIOR HAS BEEN LEARNED, THE CHILD IS RETURNED TO THE "NATURAL" PLAYROOM SETTING WHERE IT HAS BEEN DEMONSTRATED THAT HE WILL AGAIN REPEAT THE LEARNED BEHAVIOR WITHOUT ADDITIONAL INSTRUCTION. (MS)

ED025309 PS001401
A STUDY OF FAMILY INFLUENCES ON THE EDUCATION OF NEGRO LOWER-CLASS CHILDREN. PROJECT I. BELL, ROBERT R., 31 AUG 67 37P.
EDRS PRICE MF-$0.65 HC-$3.29

THIS STUDY ENCOMPASSES FAMILY INFLUENCES ON EDUCATION AND, PARTICULARLY, VALUES HELD BY MOTHERS TOWARD THE HEAD START PROGRAM. IN INTERVIEWS, 200 NEGRO MOTHERS INDICATED SATISFACTION WITH THE EDUCATIONAL EXPERIENCES IN HEAD START, ESPECIALLY SOCIALIZATION OF CHILDREN. INTERVIEWEES FELT THAT THE MOTHER ROLE WAS IMPORTANT. THEY EXPRESSED THE MOST COMMON PROBLEMS AT HOME AS EITHER DISCIPLINARY OR ECONOMIC. MOTHERS PERCEIVED THEMSELVES AS THE MOST IMPORTANT INFLUENCE ON THEIR CHILDREN; TEACHERS WERE A CLOSE SECOND. FORMAL LEARNING TOOK PLACE IN SCHOOL, AND MOTHERS DEPENDED ON NO SIGNIFICANT COMMUNITY AGENCIES FOR HELP IN THE EDUCATION OF THEIR CHILDREN. ALTHOUGH 73 PERCENT ASPIRED TO A COLLEGE EDUCATION FOR THEIR CHILDREN, ONLY 23 PERCENT THOUGHT IT WOULD BE A REALITY. CHOOSING WELL-KNOWN MEN AS MODELS FOR EMULATION FOR THEIR SONS, MOTHERS SELECTED CIVIL RIGHTS WORKERS OF HIGH STANDARDS, MORALS, AND COURAGE; AND FOR DAUGHTERS, MOTHERS SELECTED WOMEN OF TALENT, ACHIEVEMENT, AND POSITIVE PERSONALITY. WHEN ASKED ABOUT MODELS THEY HAD ACTUALLY KNOWN, THE RESPONDENTS STRESSED POSITIVE VALUES OF ECONOMICALLY RESPONSIBLE MALE ROLES AND MATERNALLY RESPONSIBLE FEMALE ROLES. FOURTEEN TABLES ARE INCLUDED IN THIS DOCUMENT. (DO)

ED025310 PS001408
A STUDY OF COGNITIVE AND SOCIAL FUNCTIONING. PROJECT II BELLER, E. KUNO, 31 AUG 67 61P.
EDRS PRICE MF-$0.65 HC-$3.29

THIS PROJECT DEALS WITH CHARACTERISTIC FUNCTIONING OF LOWER CLASS EDUCATIONALLY DISADVANTAGED PRESCHOOL CHILDREN, THE IMPACT OF THE PRESCHOOL EXPERIENCE, AND THE PERSONALITY OF THE CHILD AND HIS READINESS TO GAIN FROM THE EDUCATIONAL PROCESS. THE DISADVANTAGED PRESCHOOL CHILDREN FUNCTIONED INTELLECTUALLY AND VERBALLY BELOW THEIR MIDDLE CLASS PEERS AND WERE 8 MONTHS BEHIND THEM IN LANGUAGE DEVELOPMENT. LONGITUDINAL DATA INDICATE THAT CHILDREN WHO HAVE HAD PRESCHOOL TRAINING SCORED HIGHER ON TEST BATTERIES IN THE FIRST GRADE, THAT THEIR LANGUAGE DEVELOPMENT IS SUPERIOR, AND THAT THEIR ACADEMIC ACHIEVEMENT AND ATTITUDES TOWARD LEARNING ARE SIGNIFICANTLY HIGHER. EARLY EDUCATION INTERVENTION IS VALUABLE TO THE DEVELOPMENT OF SELF-CONFIDENCE AND GREATER TRUST IN THEIR ENVIRONMENT. THESE CHILDREN SCORED HIGHER ON DEPENDENCY ON TEACHERS, ON AGGRESSION, AND ON ACHIEVEMENT STRIVING THAN DID CHILDREN WITHOUT PRESCHOOL TRAINING. A STUDY OF MOTHER-CHILD INTERACTION WILL CONTINUE, AND A STUDY OF GAINERS, NONGAINERS, AND LOSERS IS UNDERWAY. TWENTY-EIGHT TABLES AND A LIST OF OTHER ARTICLES BY THE AUTHOR ARE GIVEN. (DO)

ED025311 PS001412
INVESTMENTS IN PREVENTION, AN ACTIVITY GROUP PROGRAM FOR YOUNG CHILDREN, SUMMER - 1967. , 67 48P.
EDRS PRICE MF-$0.65 HC-$3.29

NINETY-EIGHT YOUNG CHILDREN WITH LEARNING OR BEHAVIOR PROBLEMS PARTICIPATED IN A 5-WEEK SUMMER PROGRAM. THE OBJECTIVE OF THE PROGRAM WAS TO PROVIDE (1) AN ACTIVITY-ORIENTED GROUP EXPERIENCE, (2) CONTINUITY OF EXPERIENCE BETWEEN JUNE AND SEPTEMBER, AND (3) A CLOSER RELATIONSHIP WITH AN ADULT THAN IS POSSIBLE DURING THE SCHOOL TERM. ALL PACERS, AS THESE CHILDREN ARE CALLED, SHOWED GAINS IN INDEPENDENCE, RECOVERY AND COPING STRENGTH, AND POSITIVE SELF-CONCEPT, EVEN THOUGH THEY SHOWED MORE DISTURBED BEHAVIOR THAN HAD BEEN ANTICIPATED. WITHDRAWN, FEARFUL, OR MOODY CHILDREN GAINED MOST IN SELF-CONCEPT, RELATEDNESS TO ENVIRONMENT, AND INDEPENDENCE. AGGRESSIVE CHILDREN SHOWED MOST GAIN IN RELATEDNESS TO PEOPLE AND RECOVERY AND COPING STRENGTH. THE ACTIVITY GROUP SUMMER PROGRAM WAS AN EFFECTIVE INTERVENTION TECHNIQUE. (DO)

ED025312 PS001414
HELPS FOR PARENTS IN HOUSING PEET, ANNE, 67 33P.
DOCUMENT NOT AVAILABLE FROM EDRS.
AVAILABLE FROM: PLAY SCHOOLS ASSOCIATION, 120 WEST 57TH ST., NEW YORK, N.Y. 10019.

THIS DOCUMENT IS COMPOSED OF SEVEN LEAFLETS TO AID PARENTS IN HOUSING PROJECTS TO DEVELOP PLAY PROGRAMS FOR THEIR CHILDREN. "BOARD STRUCTURE AND LEADERSHIP" DESCRIBES THE CONSTITUTION OF A BOARD OF DIRECTORS, THE PLANNING OF A PROGRAM BY COMMITTEES, AND THE DEVELOPMENT OF LEADERSHIP. "PUBLICITY AND FUND RAISING" RELATES THE VALUE AND OUTLINES ACTION FOR SUCCESS OF BOTH. "ADMINISTRATION" COVERS LICENSING, INSURANCE, TAXES, BOOKKEEPING, EQUIPMENT, FEES, REGISTRATION, AND CONTRACTS. "STAFF" LISTS QUALIFICATIONS OF TEACHING PERSONNEL AND TELLS HOW TO FIND STAFF. INCORPORATION AND BYLAWS ARE COVERED IN THE FIFTH LEAFLET. RELATIONSHIPS WITH OTHER PARENTS, NEIGHBORS, THE COMMUNITY, AND OTHER GROUPS ARE DISCUSSED IN THE SIXTH LEAFLET. THE SEVENTH LEAFLET COVERS BUDGETS FOR PLAY PROGRAMS. (DO)

ED025313 PS001415
THE ASSESSMENT OF ACHIEVEMENT ANXIETIES IN CHILDREN: HOW IMPORTANT IS RESPONSE SET AND MULTIDIMENSIONALITY IN THE TEST ANXIETY SCALE FOR CHILDREN? FELD, SHEILA; LEWIS, JUDITH, 20 OCT 67 81P.
EDRS PRICE MF-$0.65 HC-$3.29

THIS IS A PROGRESS REPORT ON RESEARCH CONDUCTED (1) TO CONSIDER THE METHODOLOGICAL ISSUES OF RESPONSE SET AND MULTIDIMENSIONALITY, WHICH MIGHT LEAD TO A REFINEMENT OF THE TEST ANXIETY SCALE FOR CHILDREN (TASC) AND THE DEFENSIVENESS SCALE FOR CHILDREN AND (2) TO INVESTIGATE SOCIAL BACKGROUND AND SCHOOL ACHIEVEMENT CORRELATES OF TEST ANXIETY AND DEFENSIVENESS IN A MORE HETEROGENEOUS GROUP THAN HAD PREVIOUSLY BEEN DONE. THE SCALES WERE EXPANDED SO THAT 7,551 SECOND GRADERS WERE RANDOMLY ASSIGNED TO ONE OF SIX POSSIBLE TEST SITUATIONS . FACTOR ANALYSIS OF THE ORIGINAL TASC FOR EACH SEX REVEALED FOUR FACTORS, THREE OF WHICH WERE REPLICATED ON A FACTOR ANALYSIS OF THE EXPANDED TASC. NONE OF THE FACTORS WERE INTERPRETED AS CLEARLY DEFINING RESPONSE SET. THE FOUR FACTORS WERE USED AS SUBSCALES IN A TWO-WAY MULTIVARIATE ANALYSIS TO TEST THE RACE AND SEX EFFECT. ALL FOUR SUBSCALES CONTRIBUTED TO THE RACE EFFECT, WHILE THE OVERALL SEX EFFECT WAS DUE TO THE WHITE SAMPLE ONLY. WHEN RESULTS WERE COMPARED TO TOTAL TASC SCORES, THE EFFECTS PROVED SIGNIFICANT. THE FOLLOWING CONCLUSIONS AND DIRECTIONS WERE MADE: (1) ACQUIESCENT RESPONSE SET IS NOT A MAJOR SOURCE OF VARIANCE IN TASC, (2) MULTIDIMENSIONALITY OF THE SCALE ORIENTS RESEARCHERS TO FOCUS ON CHILDRENS' ANXIETY RESPONSES TO SCHOOL SITUATIONS, AND (3) IT WOULD BE DIFFICULT TO USE THE INTERDEPENDENT SUBSCALES AS DIFFERENTIATING CORRELATES OF TASC. (JS)

ED025314 PS001416
COMPARATIVE EFFECTIVENESS OF ECHOIC AND MODELING PROCEDURES IN LANGUAGE INSTRUCTION WITH CULTURALLY DISADVANTAGED CHILDREN. STERN, CAROLYN; KEISLAR, EVAN, AUG 68 14P.
EDRS PRICE MF-$0.65 HC-$3.29

IN AN ATTEMPT TO EXPLORE A SYSTEMATIC APPROACH TO LANGUAGE EXPANSION AND IMPROVED SENTENCE STRUCTURE, ECHOIC AND MODELING PROCEDURES FOR LANGUAGE INSTRUCTION WERE COMPARED. FOUR HYPOTHESES WERE FORMULATED: (1) CHILDREN WHO USE MODELING PROCEDURES WILL PRODUCE BETTER STRUCTURED SENTENCES THAN CHILDREN WHO USE ECHOIC PROMPTING, (2) BOTH ECHOIC AND MODELING PROCEDURES WILL BE MORE EFFECTIVE IN VERBAL BEHAVIOR THAN LISTENING TO STORIES AND REMAINING SILENT, (3) ALL THREE PROCEDURE WILL BE MORE EFFECTIVE THAN THOSE OF THE CONTROL GROUP, WHO RECEIVE NO SPECIAL INSTRUCTION, AND (4) GIRLS WILL BE SUPERIOR TO BOYS IN PARALLEL SENTENCE PRODUCTION. FORTY-EIGHT HEAD START CHILDREN, DIVIDED INTO FOUR GROUPS, WERE RANDOMLY ASSIGNED TO ONE OF THE FOLLOWING TREATMENTS: ECHOIC PROMPTING (CHILDREN LISTENED TO AND ECHOED EACH SENTENCE IN EVERY LESSON); PARALLEL PROMPTING (CHILDREN LISTENED TO A SENTENCE FOR THE FIRST PICTURE AND, USING THIS AS A MODEL, PRODUCED THE SENTENCE FOR THE SECOND PICTURE); LISTENING ONLY (NO OVERT RESPONSE); AND CONTROL (PRETESTS AND POSTTESTS WITH NO SPECIAL INSTRUCTION). THE RESULTS SUPPORTED ONLY THE FIRST HYPOTHESIS SIGNIFICANTLY. EVIDENCE SHOWS, HOWEVER, THAT CHILDREN WHO LISTEN TO, ECHO OR MODEL WELL FORMED SENTENCES HAVE A FACILITY TO PRODUCE APPROPRIATE SENTENCES WHEN COMPARED TO CHILDREN WHO ARE NOT SO EXPOSED. (JS)

ED025315 PS001420
KINDERGARTEN, 1967-68. AN EVALUATION REPORT. VALOTTO, EVELYN; DEARDEN, RONALD A., 68 155P.
EDRS PRICE MF-$0.65 HC-$6.58

IN 1967, SEVEN DEMONSTRATION KINDERGARTEN CLASSES WERE SET UP IN ORDER TO OBSERVE CHILDREN'S CHARACTERISTICS; TO DETERMINE ACTIVITIES, INDIVIDUALIZED INSTRUCTION, AND TEACHER AIDE FUNCTIONS AND TRAINING; TO DEVELOP CURRICULUM AND PLANS FOR EVALUATION AND MANAGEMENT ROUTINES; TO EXAMINE INSTRUCTIONAL MATERIALS AND CLASS SIZE; AND TO HELP PARENTS UNDERSTAND THE FUNCTIONS OF KINDERGARTEN. THE POPULATION INCLUDED 320 CHILDREN, SEVEN TEACHERS, SEVEN TEACHER AIDES, AND SEVEN PRINCIPALS. RECORD DATA WERE COLLECTED, AND INSTRUMENTS WHICH COULD BE CROSS-CHECKED WERE USED. RELIABILITY WAS ACHIEVED BY PRETESTING AND POSTTESTING WITH STANDARDIZED TESTS. TEACHERS AND AIDES WERE ORIENTED TOPROCEDURES BEFORE EVALUATION, AND HIGHLY COMPETENT PERSONNEL WERE EMPLOYED. CONCLUSIONS REACHED WERE AS FOLLOWS: (1) KINDERGARTEN PROGRAMS SHOULD BE FLEXIBLE TO MEET VARYING COGNITIVE, SOCIAL, EMOTIONAL, AND PHYSICAL NEEDS OF THE CHILDREN; (2) EVALUATIVE INSTRUMENT" SHOULD BE DEVELOPED AND GIV"N PRIORITY TO ASSESS PROGRAMS; (3) DEMONSTRATION CENTERS SHOULD BE ORGANIZED AND INSERVICE TRAINING SHOULD BE ESTABLISHED FOR PROSPECTIVE TEACHERS; (4) TEACHING STRATEGIES AND CURRICULUM SHOULD BE STUDIED IN DEPTH; AND (5) HOME-SCHOOL RELATIONS AND ROLE OF ALL PERSONNEL SHOULD BE DELINEATED. FOLLOWUP STUDIES ON ALL PHASES OF THE PROGRAM WERE RECOMMENDED. (DO)

ED025316 PS001476
THE IDENTIFICATION AND ASSESSMENT OF THINKING ABILITY IN YOUNG CHILDREN. FINAL REPORT. STOTT, LELAND H.; BALL, RACHEL S., JUN 68 66P.
EDRS PRICE MF-$0.65 HC-$3.29

A STUDY WAS CONDUCTED TO IDENTIFY TYPES OF MENTAL OPERATIONS OF 4- AND 5-YEAR-OLDS AND TO RELATE THEM TO THE CHILD'S AGE AND THE EDUCATIONAL LEVEL OF THE MOTHER. THE SAMPLE CONSISTED OF 423 WHITE ENGLISH-SPEAKING CHILDREN OF AMERICAN PARENTAGE, EVENLY DIVIDED BY SEX AND AS EVENLY DISTRIBUTED AS POSSIBLE OVER THE 12-MONTH-AGE RANGE OF 4 TO 5 YEARS. THEIR MOTHERS' EDUCATION CONSISTED OF ELEMENTARY, SECONDARY, OR COLLEGE LEVEL ACHIEVEMENT. ITEMS FROM THE MERRILL-PALMER SCALE AND THE GUILFORD MODEL WERE SELECTED AND TESTED FOR ABILITY TO IDENTIFY THINKING ACTIVITIES. A FACTOR ANALYSIS IDENTIFIED SIX SPECIFIC TYPES OF THINKING: TWO CONVERGENT, TWO DIVERGENT, ONE COGNITIVE, AND ONE MATURATIONAL. FOR 4- TO 5-YEAR-OLDS, SEX DIFFERENCES WERE RELATIVELY INSIGNIFICANT. AGE DIFFERENCES WERE SIGNIFICANTLY RELATED TO THE CONVERGENT, COGNITIVE, AND MATURATIONAL ABILITIES, BUT NOT TO THE DIVERGENT TYPE. THE MOTHERS' EDUCATION WAS RELATED TO FOUR OF THE SIX ABILITIES, AND THE AREA OF RESIDENCE WAS RELATED TO THREE OF THE SIX ABILITIES. A "Q" ANALYSIS INDICATED THAT CHILDREN COULD BE CLASSIFIED BY "TYPES." THUS, ENVIRONMENTAL FACTORS ARE IMPORTANT IN COGNITIVE DEVELOPMENT. APPENDIXES CONTAIN TABULATED DATA AND DIRECTIONS FOR ADMINISTERING THE TESTS. (JS)

ED025317 PS001477
CHILDREN AND THE ARTS. PRESENTATIONS FROM A WRITING CONFERENCE. DEVERS, DIANA DEE, ED., 67 160P.
EDRS PRICE MF-$0.65 HC-$6.58

THIS DOCUMENT IS A PUBLICATION OF THE MAJOR PRESENTATIONS FROM CAREL'S (CENTRAL ATLANTIC REGIONAL EDUCATIONAL LABORATORY) FIRST WRITING CONFERENCE HELD DURING JULY AND AUGUST 1967. THE FOCUS OF CAREL IS THE IMPROVEMENT OF EDUCATIONAL OPPORTUNITIES FOR CHILDREN IN THE EARLY YEARS OF SCHOOLING. IT HAS BEGUN THE DEVELOPMENT OF CURRICULUM PLANS IN FIVE AREAS OF THE ARTS AND HUMANITIES, AND IT HELD THIS WRITING CONFERENCE (1) TO DETERMINE THE EDUCATIONAL OBJECTIVES OF CURRICULA IN FIVE AREAS OF THE ARTS, (2) TO SPECIFY, IN BEHAVIORAL TERMS, THOSE OBJECTIVES WHICH CHILDREN MIGHT ACHIEVE THROUGH THE ARTS, AND (3) TO DEVELOP INSTRUCTIONAL STRATEGIES DESIGNED TO REACH THE OBJECTIVES. AN INTRODUCTORY ARTICLE AND 10 TOPICAL ARTICLES BASED UPON CONFERENCE DISCUSSIONS CONSTITUTE THE TEXT OF THIS PUBLICATION. (WD)

ED025318 PS001479
HEAD START CRIB. CHILDHOOD RESEARCH INFORMATION BULLETIN: SELECTED RESUMES OF EARLY CHILDHOOD RESEARCH REPORTS. BULLETIN NO. 1. O'DONNELL, CAROLYN, COMP., 69 55P.
EDRS PRICE MF-$0.65 HC-$3.29
AVAILABLE FROM: HEAD START CRIB, ERIC CLEARINGHOUSE ON EARLY CHILDHOOD EDUCATION, 805 WEST PENNSYLVANIA AVENUE, URBANA, ILL. 61801 ($0.60).

THIS COMPILATION OF 57 ABSTRACTS IS DIRECTED TO THE EDUCATIONAL COMMUNITY INTERESTED IN RESEARCH ACTIVITIES RELATED TO HEAD START. THE PURPOSE OF VOLUME I IS TO PUBLISH RESUMES OF CURRENT RESEARCH REPORTS INVOLVING HEAD START CHILDREN. THE RESEARCH PROJECTS ARE CONCERNED WITH ETHNIC FACTORS, EVALUATION OF HEAD START PROGRAMS, COMMUNITY INFLUENCE, TEACHER EFFECTIVENESS, BILINGUAL CONCENTRATION, AUDIOVISUAL EQUIPMENT, PHYSICAL FACILITIES, PARENT INVOLVEMENT, AND FOLLOWUP STUDIES. CRIB WILL BE PUBLISHED BIANNUALLY. (DO) CH

ED025319 PS001480
METHODOLIGICAL CONSIDERATIONS IN DEVISING HEAD START PROGRAM EVALUATIONS. ALPERN, GERALD D.; LEVITT, EUGENE E., APR 67 13P.
EDRS PRICE MF-$0.65 HC-$3.29

IN AN ATTEMPT TO IMPROVE HEAD START EVALUATIONS, SEVERAL METHODOLOGICAL TECHNIQUES ARE PROPOSED. SINCE PROGRAMS VARY IN APPROACH, EVALUATIONS MUST BE MADE ON THE SUCCESS OF THE INDIVIDUAL PROGRAMS. FORMULATION OF RESEARCH QUESTIONS SHOULD PROVIDE INFORMATION AS TO THE PROCESS AND OUTCOME OF THE PROGRAM. TO AVOID EXPERIMENTER BIAS, EXPERIMENTERS SHOULD BE SELECTED ON THE BASIS OF THEIR DISENGAGEMENT FROM HEAD START. A BASELINE GROUP (EITHER A CONTROL GROUP OR THE EXPERIMENTAL GROUP ASSESSED ON PRETREATMENT PERFORMANCE SHOULD BE USED, AND VARIABLES AFFECTING THEIR BEHAVIOR SHOULD BE NOTED. SOME OF THE PROBLEMS DUE TO THE LACK OF MEASURING INSTRUMENTS COULD BE AVOIDED IF EXPERIMENTERS WOULD NOT MEASURE SPECIFIC BEHAVIOR AS INDICATIVE OF GENERAL ABILITY. TO AVOID THE PROBLEM OF PUBLISHING ONLY POSITIVE HEAD START REPORTS, THE OFFICE OF ECONOMIC OPPORTUNITY SHOULD PUBLISH ANNUALLY ALL HEAD START EVALUATIONS. SEVERAL REFERENCES ARE INCLUDED. (JS)

ED025320 PS001481
ANNUAL RESEARCH REPORT OF COMPLETED AND INCOMPLETE INVESTIGATIONS FOR NATIONAL HEAD START EVALUATION. PIERCE-JONES, JOHN, AUG 68 18P.
EDRS PRICE MF-$0.65 HC-$3.29

A LIST OF NINE COMPLETED INVESTIGATIONS AND TWO PROGRESS REPORTS OF INCOMPLETE INVESTIGATIONS MAKES UP THIS ANNUAL RESEARCH REPORT. ONE INCOMPLETE PROJECT IS CONCERNED WITH BILINGUAL INSTRUCTION AND OTHER COMPENSATORY EDUCATION PROGRAMS FOR MEXICAN-AMERICAN CHILDREN IN THE SOUTHWEST. THE OBJECTIVE OF THE OTHER INCOMPLETE PROJECT IS TO EXAMINE RELATIONSHIPS BETWEEN MOTIVATIONAL VARIABLES AND RETENTION PROCESSES. A BIBLIOGRAPHY IS ALSO INCLUDED. (MS)

ED025321 PS001482
THE SHIFT FROM COLOR TO FORM PREFERENCE IN YOUNG CHILDRE N OF DIFFERENT ETHNIC BACKGROUNDS. PART OF THE FINAL REPORT. SPELLMANN, CHARLES MAC, AUG 68 92P.
EDRS PRICE MF-$0.65 HC-$3.29

YOUNG CHILDREN PREFER TO MATCH IN TERMS OF COLOR RATHER THAN FORM, AND BETWEEN THE AGES OF 4 AND 7 YEARS THEY SHIFT TO A PREFERENCE FOR FORM. A CURRENT EXPLANATION POSITS THAT THE SHIFT IS AN ADAPTIVE RESPONSE BY THE YOUNG CHILD TO CLASSROOM STIMULI, WHICH STRESSES ATTENTION TO FORM. IN ORDER TO TEST THIS HYPOTHESIS, 120 CHILDREN (5- AND 6-YEAR-OLDS) OF LOWER SOCIOECONOMIC STATUS WERE GIVEN A STIMULUS PREFERENCE TEXT. SIXTY OF THESE CHILDREN WERE ENROLLED IN HEAD START CLASSES; THE OTHERS WERE ELIGIBLE BUT WERE NOT ENROLLED IN SCHOOL. TWENTY OF THE HEAD START SUBJECTS WERF ANGLO, 20 WERE NEGRO, AND 20 WERE INDIAN. THE SAME WAS TRUE FOR THE NONSCHOOL GROUP. THE TEST WAS GIVEN AT SEVERAL POINTS DURING THE SCHOOL YEAR, AND IT WAS EXPECTED THAT AT THE FIRST TESTING OF EACH GROUP THERE WOULD BE NO DIFFERENCE IN THE NUMBER OF FORM RESPONSES GIVEN. ON THE FINAL TESTING, HOWEVER, IT WAS EXPECTED THAT THE SCHOOL GROUP WOULD RESPOND TO FORM SIGNIFICANTLY MORE OFTEN THAN THE NONSCHOOL GROUP. THE RESULTS CONFIRMED THE HYPOTHESIS: SCHOOL CHILDREN SHOWED A STEADY INCREASE IN FORM RESPONSES ACROSS THE SCHOOL YEAR, WHILE THE NONSCHOOL CHILDREN DID NOT. ANALYSIS OF RACE SHOWED THAT NEGRO SCHOOL CHILDREN SHIFTED FROM COLOR TO FORM MUCH SLOWER THAN DID ANGLO AND INDIAN SCHOOL CHILDREN. TWENTY-SEVEN TABLES OR GRAPHS AND A BIBLIOGRAPHY ARE INCLUDED. (AUTHOR/DO)

ED025322 PS001483
COOPERATIVE, TRUSTING BEHAVIOR AS A FUNCTION OF ETHNIC GROUP SIMILARITY-DISSIMILARITY AND OF IMMEDIATE AND DELAYED REWARD IN A TWO-PERSON GAME. PART OF THE FINAL REPORT. MANNING, BRAD A.; AND OTHERS, AUG 68 40P.
EDRS PRICE MF-$0.65 HC-$3.29

ONE HUNDRED AND THIRTY-SIX 5- AND 6-YEAR-OLDS PARTICIPATED IN THIS STUDY, WHICH INVESTIGATED THE EXTENT TO WHICH COOPERATIVE, TRUSTING BEHAVIOR COULD BE DEMONSTRATED BETWEEN MEXICAN-AMERICAN, NEGRO, AND ANGLO-AMERICAN CHILDREN. ALSO CONSIDERED WERE SOME OF THE BASIC VARIABLES WHICH WERE IMPORTANT IN THE DEVELOPMENT OF SUCH BEHAVIOR. SIMILAR AND DISSIMILAR ETHNIC-GROUP PAIRS WERE PLACED INTO IMMEDIATE OR DELAYED REWARD GROUPS. EACH CHILD WAS GIVEN A CHOICE OF EITHER COMPETITIVE OR COOPERATIVE BEHAVIOR IN RELATION TO AN UNSEEN PARTNER'S BEHAVIOR. MALE SUBJECTS SHOWED NO SIGNIFICANT DIFFERENCES IN BEHAVIOR. FEMALE SIMILAR ETHNIC PAIRS WERE MORE COOPERATIVE THAN WERE DISSIMILAR ETHNIC PAIRS, WITH THE EXCEPTION OF MEXICAN-AMERICAN AND NEGRO PAIRS. ANGLO-AMERICAN FEMALES COMPETED THE MOST. TYPE OF REINFORCEMENT AND NUMBER OF TRIALS DID NOT AFFECT COOPERATIVE BEHAVIOR. GREATER MATURITY AND UNDERSTANDING OF ETHNIC MORES MIGHT HAVE BEEN RESPONSIBLE FOR FEMALE BEHAVIORAL DIFFERENCES. A BIBLIOGRAPHY IS INCLUDED. (MS)

ED025323 PS001484
THE RELATIONSHIP BETWEEN SPECIFIC AND GENERAL TEACHING EXPERIENCE AND TEACHER ATTITUDES TOWARD PROJECT HEAD START. PART OF THE FINAL REPORT. HELGE, SWEN; PIERCE-JONES, JOHN, AUG 68 43P.
EDRS PRICE MF-$0.65 HC-$3.29

ONE HUNDRED AND FORTY-FIVE HEAD START TEACHERS, FROM LOWER-MIDDLE CLASS FAMILIES, ATTENDED A WORKSHOP IN 1965 BEFORE WORKING IN THE HEAD START PROGRAM. DURING THE WORKSHOP AND AGAIN IN 1967 THEY FILLED OUT AUTOBIOGRAPHICAL AND EXPERIENCE FORMS. THE FORMS WERE USED TO TEST THREE HYPOTHESES REGARDING DIFFERENCES ASSOCIATED WITH DIFFERENTIAL TEACHING EXPERIENCES. TEACHERS WERE GROUPED ACCORDING TO THEIR YEARS OF TEACHING EXPERIENCE AND TYPE OF EXPERIENCE; I.E., GENERAL OR WITH THE CULTURALLY DEPRIVED. RESULTS BY ANALYSIS OF VARIANCE INDICATED SIGNIFICANT DIFFERENCES BETWEEN GROUPS OF TEACHERS ON VARIABLES MEASURING TEACHERS' PERCEPTIONS OF THE EFFECTIVENESS AND ACCEPTANCE OF HEAD START, THEIR AWARENESS OF THE EFFECTS OF CULTURAL DEPRIVATION, THEIR PERCEPTIONS OF THEIR SUCCESS AS HEAD START TEACHERS, AND A COMPARISON OF HEAD START AND NON-HEAD START CHILDREN FROM SIMILAR ENVIRONMENTS. GENERALLY, THE MORE GENERAL THE EXPERIENCE, THE MORE STABLE AND POSITIVE WERE THE TEACHER ATTITUDES. THE SAME WAS TRUE WITH TEACHERS WITH NO EXPERIENCE OR SIX OR MORE YEARS OF SPECIFIC EXPERIENCE. DUE TO COGNITIVE TRACES FROM PREVIOUS EXPERIENCE, EXPERIENCED TEACHERS HAD GREATER INSIGHT INTO PROBLEM AREAS AND COULD MORE EASILY INCORPORATE NEW EXPERIENCES WITH THE CULTURALLY DEPRIVED. ALL ATTITUDES OF ALL GROUPS WERE POSITIVE. AREAS FOR ADDITIONAL RESEARCH IN THIS SUBJECT ARE SUGGESTED. TEN TABLES AND SEVERAL GRAPHS ARE GIVEN. (DO)

ED025324 PS001485
EARLY INTELLECTIVE TRAINING AND SCHOOL PERFORMANCE. SUMMARY OF NIH GRANT NUMBER HD-02253. PALMER, FRANCIS H., AUG 68 5P.
EDRS PRICE MF-$0.65 HC-$3.29

A 7-YEAR STUDY IS BEING CONDUCTED TO DETERMINE IF AN 8-MONTH INTELLECTIVE TRAINING PROGRAM AT AGES TWO AND THREE WILL IMPROVE A CHILD'S PERFORMANCE AND IF THE EFFECTS WILL LAST THROUGH THE FIRST GRADE. THE SUBJECTS CONSIST OF 240 NEGRO MALES FROM ALL SOCIAL LEVELS IN MANHATTAN. HALF OF THEM ARE 2 YEARS OLD AND HALF ARE 3 YEARS OLD. SUBJECTS WERE ASSIGNED TO AN INDIVIDUAL INSTRUCTOR IN EITHER A TRAINING GROUP (WHERE THEY WERE TAUGHT CONCEPTS) OR A DISCOVERY GROUP (WHERE THEY HAD FREE PLAY) FOR 2 HOURS A WEEK. IN ADDITION, A CONTROL GROUP OF 70 CHILDREN ARE BEING SEEN FOR ASSESSMENT PURPOSES ONLY. ALL CHILDREN WERE PRETESTED AND ARE MEASURED ANNUALLY. AFTER 2 YEARS OF THE PROGRAM, THE RESULTS INDICATED THAT UP TO AGE THREE SOCIAL CLASS IS NOT A FUNCTION OF PERFORMANCE; FROM AGES THREE TO EIGHT DIFFERENCES ARF PRESENT BUT INSIGNIFICANT; THE EXPERIMENTAL CHILDREN PERFORM BETTER THAN THE CONTROL CHILDREN; THE EFFECT S OF THE PROGRAM RECEIVED AT AGE TWO LAST AT LEAST 1 YEAR; AND BOTH EXPERIMENTAL GROUPS PRODUCE EQUALLY WELL. THE RESULTS IMPLY THAT EARLY TRAINING MAY BE BENEFICIAL, PROVIDED IT IS SYSTEMATIC, IS UNINTERRUPTED, AND OCCURS AT LEAST 2 HOURS A WEEK WITH A ONE-TO-ONE TEACHER-PUPIL RATIO. (JS)

ED025325 PS001486
THE DEVELOPMENT OF LANGUAGE FUNCTIONS. REPORT NUMBER 8, DEVELOPMENT OF LANGUAGE FUNCTIONS: A RESEARCH PROGRAM PROJECT. RIEGEL, KLAUS F., ED., 30 NOV 65 193P.
EDRS PRICE MF-$0.65 HC-$6.58

THIS DOCUMENT INCLUDES 10 ARTICLES DEALING WITH FIVE SPECIFIC AREAS OF LANGUAGE DEVELOPMENT. TWO ARTICLES AND A COMMENTARY COVER EACH AREA. RESUMES OF THE ARTICLES HAVE BEEN ASSIGNED THE FOLLOWING NUMBERS: MEMORY FUNCTIONS (PS 001 487 AND PS 001 488), ASSOCIATIONS AND VERBAL HABITS (PS 001 489 AND PS 001 490), LANGUAGE PERCEPTION AND DISCRIMINATION (PS 001 491 AND PS 001 492), VERBAL STRUCTURES (PS 001 493 AND PS 001 494), AND VERBAL CONTROL PS 001 495 AND PS 001 496). (WD)

ED025326 PS001487
EXTENSION OF A THEORY OF PREDICTIVE BEHAVIOR TO IMMEDIATE RECALL BY PRESCHOOL CHILDREN. BOGARTZ, RICHARD S., 30 NOV 65 14P.
EDRS PRICE MF-$0.65 HC-$3.29

THIS PAPER IS CONCERNED WITH MEMORY FUNCTIONS IN SEQUENTIALLY STRUCTURED BEHAVIOR. TWENTY-FIVE 4- AND 5-YEAR-OLD PRESCHOOL CHILDREN PARTICIPATED IN A PREDICTION EXPERIMENT IN WHICH A STACK OF CARDS (EACH CARD ALTERNATELY HAVING A PATCH OF RED OR GREEN TAPE ON IT) WAS DISPLAYED TO THE CHILD. THE CHILD WAS PRESENTED WITH A CARD AND ASKED TO PREDICT THE COLOR ON THE NEXT CARD. TWO INTERVAL LENGTHS, A LONG AND A SHORT, WERE USED BETWEEN PRESENTATION AND PREDICTION. THE SUBJECT'S PERFORMANCE, IT WAS THOUGHT, WAS AFFECTED BY (1) MEMORY OF EACH TRIAL, (2) EFFECTS OF THE PREVIOUS RESPONSE, (3) LAGGING OF ATTENTION, (4) GUESSING, AND (5) THE VARIATION IN INTERVAL LENGTH. THE RESULTS FROM 100 TRIALS INDICATED THAT THE PROBABILITY OF AN ERROR, GIVEN A CORRECT RESPONSE ON THE PREVIOUS TRIAL, IS GREATER FOLLOWING THE LONG INTERVAL THAN FOLLOWING THE SHORT. IT WAS ALSO FOUND THAT THE PROBABILITY OF AN ERROR, GIVEN A CORRECT RESPONSE, IS LESS THAN OR EQUAL TO BOTH THE PROBABILITY OF A CORRECT RESPONSE, GIVEN AN ERROR, AND THE PROBABILITY OF AN ERROR, GIVEN AN ERROR. THE THEORETICAL BASIS OF THIS TASK IS BEING USED TO DEVELOP A RECALL TASK SIMILAR IN FORM TO THE PREDICTION TASK. (WD)

ED025327 PS001488
AGE AND MEMORY AS FACTORS IN PROBLEM SOLVING. WEIR, MORTON W., 30 NOV 65 19P.
EDRS PRICE MF-$0.65 HC-$3.29

IN A 1964 INVESTIGATION OF THE EFFECTS OF AGE AND MEMORY ON PROBLEM SOLVING, USING SUBJECTS FROM AGE THREE TO AGE NINETEEN, IT WAS FOUND THAT THE YOUNGEST AND OLDEST SUBJECTS PERFORMED A THREE-CHOICE PROBABILISTIC TASK SIGNIFICANTLY DIFFERENT FROM THE "MIDDLE-AGE" CHILDREN (7 TO 9 YEARS OLD). THE THREE-CHOICE TASK WAS AN APPARATUS WITH A SIGNAL LIGHT, THREE BUTTONS, AND A CONTAINER INTO WHICH MARBLES WERE DISPENSED FOR "CORRECT" RESPONSES. ONLY ONE BUTTON WAS SET UP TO

RELEASE A MARBLE, AND EVEN IT WAS ON A PARTIAL REINFORCEMENT SCHEDULE. THE YOUNGER AND OLDER SUBJECTS TENDED TO MAXIMIZE THEIR CHOICE OF THE "PAY-OFF" BUTTON. THE MIDDLE-AGE CHILDREN TENDED TO RESPOND IN SIMPLE PATTERNS REGARDLESS OF THE FACT THAT SUCH PATTERNS DID NOT INCREASE THE PAY-OFF. IT WAS THOUGHT THAT THIS RESULT INTERFERED WITH THEIR MEMORY IN REGARD TO WHICH BUTTON WAS PAYING OFF. A LATER STUDY, IN WHICH A MEMORY AID WAS USED FOR HALF OF THE SUBJECTS, WAS CONDUCTED. IT WAS FOUND THAT THE YOUNGER AND OLDER SUBJECTS PERFORMED ABOUT THE SAME AS BEFORE, REGARDLESS OF THE EXISTENCE OF THE MEMORY AID. THE 7- AND 9-YEAR-OLDS WHO USED THE AID PERFORMED SIGNIFICANTLY BETTER THAN THOSE WHO DID NOT. A THIRD STUDY, SIMILAR TO THE PREVIOUS STUDIES EXCEPT THAT FOUR DIFFERENT REINFORCEMENT SCHEDULES WERE USED, INDICATED THAT RESPONSES BECOME MORE COMPLEX WITH AGE. (WD)

ED025328 PS001489
FREE-ASSOCIATION NORMS AND ASSOCIATIVE STRUCTURE. BILODEAU, EDWARD A., 30 NOV 65 14P.
EDRS PRICE MF-$0.65 HC-$3.29

THIS PAPER DISCUSSES THE THEORY AND PRESENTS EXAMPLES OF FREE-ASSOCIATION NORMS. EXAMPLES FROM SEVERAL CATEGORIES OF FREE-ASSOCIATION DATA ARE GIVEN. THEIR USE IN EXPERIMENTS ON CULTURAL CHARACTERISTICS OF THE ASSOCIATIVE STRUCTURES OF WORDS ARE ALSO EXPLAINED. A GRAPH OF THE RELATIONSHIP BETWEEN PRIMARY AND SECONDARY ASSOCIATIONS AND TABLES OF ASSOCIATIONS AND PROBABILITY HIERARCHIES ARE INCLUDED. THESE TABLES ARE EXPLAINED IN THE TEXT OF THE PAPER AND ILLUSTRATED IN THE APPENDIX. A BIBLIOGRAPHY IS ALSO INCLUDED. (WD)

ED025329 PS001490
WORD ASSOCIATIONS AS RELATED TO CHILDREN'S VERBAL HABITS. PALERMO, DAVID S., 30 NOV 65 12P.
EDRS PRICE MF-$0.65 HC-$3.29

FREE-ASSOCIATION NORMS FOR 200 WORDS WERE OBTAINED IN 1964 FROM THE RESPONSES OF 500 SUBJECTS IN EACH OF GRADES FOUR THROUGH EIGHT, 10, AND 12 AND FROM 1,000 COLLEGE STUDENTS. AN ANALYSIS OF THIS NORMATIVE DATA REVEALED THAT (1) THE FREQUENCY OF OCCURRENCE OF THE MOST POPULAR ASSOCIATIVE RESPONSES TO STIMULUS WORDS INCREASES WITH THE AGE OF THE SUBJECT, (2) THE NUMBER OF DIFFERENT RESPONSES TO A WORD DECREASES WITH THE AGE OF THE SUBJECT, (3) THE RESPONSE WORDS THEMSELVES UNDERGO ABOUT A 50 PERCENT CHANGE FROM THE FOURTH GRADE TO COLLEGE, (4) CONTRAST OR OPPOSITE RESPONSES INCREASE WITH AGE, AND (5) PARADIGMATIC RESPONSES ALSO INCREASE WITH THE AGE OF THE SUBJECT. THUS, WORD-ASSOCIATION CHARACTERISTICS VARY IMPORTANTLY BETWEEN CHILDREN AND ADULTS. THE INFLUENCE OF THE ASSOCIATIVE STRENGTH OF WORDS ON DIFFERENT VERBAL LEARNING TASKS HAS BEEN INVESTIGATED. SUCH AN INFLUENCE HAS BEEN DEMONSTRATED FOR PAIRED-ASSOCIATE LEARNING, CLUSTERING IN FREE RECALL, ASSOCIATIVE GENERALIZATION, AND MEDIATED GENERALIZATION. NORMATIVE WORD ASSOCIATION DATA HAVE ALSO BEEN COLLECTED FOR CHILDREN IN GRADES ONE THROUGH FOUR. ANALYSIS OF THESE DATA SHOWS THE SAME TRENDS AS OBSERVED IN THE NORMS DISCUSSED FOR THE LARGER POPULATION. (WD)

ED025330 PS001491
A DISTINCTIVE FEATURES ANALYSIS OF PRE-LINGUISTIC INFANT VOCALIZATIONS. RINGWALL, EGAN A.; AND OTHERS, 30 NOV 65 10P.
EDRS PRICE MF-$0.65 HC-$3.29

A RESEARCH PROJECT WAS AIMED AT MEASURING THE RELATIONSHIP BETWEEN INFANT VOCALIZATIONS AND LINGUISTIC DEVELOPMENT AND DETERMINING THE FEASIBILITY OF USING INFANT VOCALIZATIONS AS A PREDICTOR OF LATER PSYCHOLOGICAL AND INTELLECTUAL STATUS. HOWEVER, A METHOD WAS NEEDED TO ANALYZE THE VOCALIZATIONS OF INFANTS. THIS REPORT DESCRIBES A METHOD USED TO ANALYZE THE VOCAL BEHAVIOR OF INFANTS IN THEIR PRELINGUISTIC STAGE, FROM BIRTH TO 4 MONTHS. THE METHOD WAS BASED ON THE "DISTINCTIVE FEATURES" CONCEPT. EIGHT DISTINCTIVE FEATURES OF INFANT VOCALIZATION WERE CODED BY OBSERVERS. THIS DATA YIELDED INFORMATION ON THE QUALITY AND FREQUENCY OF INFANT VOCAL BEHAVIOR AND PROVIDED A MEASURE OF INDIVIDUAL DIFFERENCES BETWEEN PRELINGUISTIC INFANTS. DATA HAVE BEEN COLLECTED ON FORTY 3-DAY-OLD INFANTS. THIS EIGHT-FEATURE CODING SCHEME HAS PROVEN TO BE RELIABLE. (WD)

ED025331 PS001492
DEVELOPMENT OF THE PROSODIC FEATURES OF INFANTS' VOCALIZING. LANE, HARLAN; SHEPPARD, WILLIAM, 30 NOV 65 12P.
EDRS PRICE MF-$0.65 HC-$3.29

TRADITIONAL RESEARCH METHODS OF RECORDING INFANT VERBAL BEHAVIOR, NAMELY, DESCRIPTIONS BY A SINGLE OBSERVER TRANSCRIBING THE UTTERANCES OF A SINGLE INFANT IN A NATURALISTIC SETTING, HAVE BEEN INADEQUATE TO PROVIDE DATA NECESSARY FOR MODERN LINGUISTIC ANALYSES. THE CENTER FOR RESEARCH ON LANGUAGE AND LANGUAGE BEHAVIOR HAS UNDERTAKEN TO CORRECT THIS INADEQUACY. THE CENTER COLLECTED PERMANENT, COMPLETE, AND CONTINUOUS RECORDS OF ALL VOCALIZATIONS OF TWO INFANTS DURING THEIR FIRST FIVE MONTHS OF LIFE. THIS DATA WAS THEN PROCESSED BY NEW ELECTRO-ACOUSTIC TECHNIQUES. IN PROCESSING ONE HUNDRED AND EIGHT 95-SECOND VOCAL BEHAVIOR SAMPLES, THE COMPUTER DETERMINED (1) THE NUMBER OF UTTERANCES, (2) THE DURATION OF EACH UTTERANCE, AND (3) THE MEAN AND STANDARD DEVIATION OF THE FUNDAMENTAL FREQUENCY AND AMPLITUDE OF EACH UTTERANCE. FURTHER STATISTICAL ANALYSES ARE NOW IN PROGRESS. (WD)

ED025332 PS001493
GRAMMATICAL DEVELOPMENT IN RUSSIAN-SPEAKING CHILDREN. SLOBIN, DAN I., 30 NOV 65 9P.
EDRS PRICE MF-$0.65 HC-$3.29

A CONTRIBUTION TO THE DEBATE ON INNATE FACTORS IN CHILDREN'S LANGUAGE ACQUISITION IS RENDERED BY CROSS-LINGUISTIC COMPARISONS OF CHILDREN'S LANGUAGES. RUSSIAN, FOR EXAMPLE, IS SUFFICIENTLY DIFFERENT FROM ENGLISH TO SERVE AS A USEFUL CONTRAST. EARLY SYNTACTIC DEVELOPMENT IS VERY MUCH THE SAME IN BOTH LANGUAGES. A SMALL CLASS OF "PIVOT WORDS" AND A LARGER OPEN CLASS OF WORDS ARE USED FIRST. WORD ORDER IS QUITE INFLEXIBLE AT EACH OF THE EARLY STAGES OF SYNTACTIC DEVELOPMENT. TWO-WORD SENTENCES APPEAR AT ABOUT 1:8 (1 YEAR, 8 MONTHS); THREE- OR FOUR-WORD SENTENCES APPEAR AT ABOUT 1:10. MORPHOLOGICAL MARKERS ENTER WITH THE THREE- AND FOUR-WORD SENTENCES. THE LEARNING OF MORPHOLOGY GOES ON LONGER THAN THE LEARNING OF SYNTACTIC PATTERNS. A MAJOR RUSSIAN WORK ON LANGUAGE DEVELOPMENT CONTENDS THAT THE RUSSIAN CHILD DOES NOT MASTER HIS MORPHOLOGY UNTIL SEVERAL YEARS BEYOND THE AGE AT WHICH THE AMERICAN CHILD COMPLETES HIS PRIMARY GRAMMATICAL LEARNING. THIS FACTOR SUGGESTS THAT IT MAY BE MORE DIFFICULT TO LEARN TO SPEAK ONE LANGUAGE NATIVELY THAN ANOTHER, ALTHOUGH IN BOTH, BASIC LEARNING IS ACCOMPLISHED RAPIDLY. (WD)

ED025333 PS001494
THE DEVELOPMENT OF INTERROGATIVE STRUCTURES IN CHILDREN'S SPEECH. BELLUGI, URSULA, 30 NOV 65 35P.
EDRS PRICE MF-$0.65 HC-$3.29

THE VERBAL BEHAVIOR OF THREE CHILDREN WAS SAMPLED. THE SAMPLES WERE ANALYZED TO OBTAIN A PICTURE OF THREE STAGES OF THE CHILDREN'S LANGUAGE DEVELOPMENT, SPECIFICALLY THE INTERROGATIVE STRUCTURES. EACH STAGE WAS ABOUT 4- OR 5-MONTHS LONG, STARTING AT THE 18TH TO 28TH MONTH, DEPENDING UPON THE CHILD'S LEVEL OF LINGUISTIC ABILITY. THE INTERROGATIVE STRUCTURES OF PRIMARY INTEREST WERE (1) INTONATION PATTERNS, (2) AUXILIARY INVERSION, (3) NEGATION, (4) WH WORD (WHAT, WHO, WHY, ETC.) PLACEMENT, AND (5) TAG QUESTIONS. AT STAGE ONE, INFLECTIONS, AUXILIARIES, ARTICLES, AND MOST PRONOUNS WERE ABSENT. THE CHILD USED INTONATION TO MARK A QUESTION. THERE WERE NO YES-OR-NO QUESTIONS AND ONLY A FEW WH QUESTIONS. THERE WERE NO TAG QUESTIONS. THE CHILD AT THIS STAGE DID NOT APPEAR TO UNDERSTAND THE INTERROGATORY STRUCTURE WHEN HE HEARD IT. AT STAGE TWO, ARTICLES, PRONOUNS, AND NEGATIVE PREVERB FORMS APPEARED. AUXILIARIES WERE STILL NOT PRESENT, NOR WERE TAG QUESTIONS. STAGE THREE INCLUDED THE EMERGENCE OF THE USE OF AUXILIARIES, AUXILIARY INVERSION, AND THE DO TRANSFORMATION. INVERSION AND TRANSFORMATION WERE FOUND IN YES-OR-NO QUESTIONS BUT WERE ABSENT IN WH QUESTIONS. TAG QUESTIONS WERE STILL ABSENT, BUT THE CHILDREN UNDERSTOOD AND RESPONDED WELL TO QUESTIONS. AN APPENDIX OF SAMPLE QUESTIONS OBTAINED FROM THE SUBJECTS AT EACH STAGE IS INCLUDED. (WD)

ED025334 PS001495
TANGENT TO EXPERIMENTAL TECHNIQUES OF VERBAL CONTROL. BILODEAU, INA MCD., 30 NOV 65 7P.
EDRS PRICE MF-$0.65 HC-$3.29

THIS PAPER IS A CRITICAL COMMENT AND REACTION TO A 1965 ARTICLE BY G. A. MILLER ENTITLED "SOME PRELIMINARIES TO PSYCHOLINGUISTICS." THE SUBJECT MATTER IS VERBAL CONTROL OF BEHAVIOR. SEVEN SPECIFIC ASPECTS OF THE MILLER ADDRESS ARE DISCUSSED. (WD)

ED025335 PS001496
SUBJECTS' HYPOTHESES, EXPERIMENTAL INSTRUCTIONS AND AUTONOMIC "CONDITIONING". ERIKSEN, CHARLES W., 30 NOV 65 15P.
EDRS PRICE MF-$0.65 HC-$3.29

RESEARCH ON LEARNING AND CONDITIONING SUGGESTS THAT VERBAL RESPONSE MODIFICATION DOES NOT OCCUR IN THE ABSENCE OF THE SUBJECT'S ABILITY TO DEFINE VERBALLY (1) THE RESPONSE-REINFORCEMENT RELATIONSHIPS AND (2) HIS INTENTION TO CHANGE HIS BEHAVIOR IN THE DIRECTION OF REINFORCEMENT. THIS SEEMS TO BE TRUE FOR OPERANT CONDITIONING OF VERBAL BEHAVIOR, OPERANT CONDITIONING OF SKELETAL NONVERBAL RESPONSES, AND PERCEPTUAL LEARNING OF CORRELATED CUES. RESEARCH IN THE AREA OF CONDITIONING OF AUTONOMIC RESPONSES SHOWS CONSISTENTLY THAT SUBJECTS WHO ARE AWARE OF THE STIMULUS-NEGATIVE REINFORCEMENT CONDITION MANIFEST GREATER AUTONOMIC RESPONSE CONDITIONING THAN SUBJECTS WHO ARE NOT AWARE OF THE EXPERIMENTAL CONDITIONS. (WD)

ED025336 PS001497
AUDITORY COMPONENTS OF NEONATAL EXPERIENCE: A PRELIMINARY REPORT. JOHNSON, VIRGINIA, 66 5P.
EDRS PRICE MF-$0.65 HC-$3.29

THE NATURE AND SIGNIFICANCE OF THE CONDITIONING OF FETAL AND NEONATAL RESPONSE SYSTEMS FOR LATER LEARNING WAS NOT CLEARLY UNDERSTOOD. THEREFORE, SUBJECTS CHOSEN FOR THIS RESEARCH PROJECT WERE PEOPLE WHO HAD BEEN TRAINED IN EXPERIENTIAL RECALL. DURING RECALL THE SUBJECTS SPONTANEOUSLY REPORTED WHAT APPEARED TO BE AUDITORY COMPONENTS OF A COMPLEX CONDITIONING SITUATION RELATED TO BIRTH OR SPEECH AND NEONATAL ENVIRONMENT. THESE AUDITORY COMPONENTS WERE THEN CORRELATED WITH THE SPEECH AND SOMATIC SYMPTOMATOLOGY OBSERVED IN THE SUBJECTS. IT WAS CONCLUDED THAT PRENATAL OR NEONATAL TRAUMA MAY CONTRIBUTE TO LATER NEURAL DISORGANIZATION AND FUNCTIONAL PSYCHOPATHOLOGY. THIS RESULT SUPPORTS THE HYPOTHESIS THAT WHEN THE BIRTH EXPERIENCE IS TRAUMATIC, THERE IS A TENDENCY TO ESTABLISH POTENTIALLY PATHOGENETIC RESPONSES. IF SUBSEQUENT EXPERIENCES REINFORCE THE TENDENCY BY APPROXIMATING THE TRAUMATIC VARIABLES, SUCH CONDITIONING MAY LEAD TO VARIOUS FORMS OF PSYCHOPATHOLOGY. ALSO, WORDS HEARD BY AN INFANT BEFORE HE UNDERSTANDS SPEECH MAY AFFECT HIS LEARNING LATER. (WD)

ED026109 PS000729
INFANT AND PRESCHOOL MENTAL TESTS: REVIEW AND EVALUATION. STOTT, LELAND H.; BALL, RACHELL S., 65 159P.
DOCUMENT NOT AVAILABLE FROM EDRS.
AVAILABLE FROM: THE UNIVERSITY OF CHICAGO PRESS, 5750 ELLIS AVENUE, CHICAGO, ILL. 60637 ($3.00).

A COMPREHENSIVE EVALUATION OF THE PRESENT STATE OF INFANT AND PRESCHOOL MENTAL TESTING IN THE UNITED STATES IS THE CONCERN OF THIS MONOGRAPH BY THE SOCIETY FOR RESEARCH IN CHILD DEVELOPMENT. LITERATURE, TECHNICAL AND PROFESSIONAL, COVERING THE CONCEPT OF INTELLIGENCE AND ITS MEASUREMENT, WAS REVIEWED, ORGANIZED, AND SUMMARIZED (CHAPTERS II AND III). A QUESTIONNAIRE SURVEY (CHAPTER IV) WAS MADE OF PRACTICES IN CURRENT TESTING OF INFANTS' AND PRESCHOOLERS' INTELLIGENCE. ANALYSES WERE MADE OF FIVE OF THE MOST WIDELY USED TEST SCALES IN TERMS OF ACTUAL PERFORMANCES ON EACH TEST ITEM (CHAPTER V). CONCLUSIONS INDICATE THE NEED FOR MORE ADEQUATE MEANS OF APPRAISING THE MENTALITY OF YOUNG CHILDREN. THE ANALYSES OF SCALE CONTENT DEMONSTRATED A LACK OF CONSISTENCY IN THE SCALES NOW USED. MORE CONSISTENT AND ADEQUATE TEST SCALES WERE RECOMMENDED. (DO)

ED026110 PS000967
THE EFFECT OF A STRUCTURED TUTORIAL PROGRAM ON THE COGNITIVE AND LANGUAGE DEVELOPMENT OF CULTURALLY DISADVANTAGED INFANTS. PAINTER, GENEVIEVE, [67] 29P.
EDRS PRICE MF-$0.65 HC-$3.29

BASED ON THE BELIEF THAT STRUCTURED PRESCHOOL ACTIVITIES AID IN THE DEVELOPMENT OF DISADVANTAGED CHILDREN, THIS STUDY ATTEMPTED (1) TO EVOLVE A TUTORIAL PROGRAM TO ACCELERATE SPONTANEOUS DEVELOPMENT IN DISADVANTAGED CHILDREN AND PREVENT COGNITIVE AND LANGUAGE DEFICITS, AND (2) TO ASSESS GROWTH OF THE INFANT'S COGNITIVE AND LANGUAGE DEVELOPMENT AFTER 1 YEAR OF INDIVIDUAL TUTORING. TEN CHILDREN (MALE AND FEMALE, NEGRO AND CAUCASIAN, 8 TO 24 MONTHS OLD) RECEIVED INTELLECTUAL STIMULATION FOR 1 HOUR A DAY, 5 DAYS A WEEK, FOR 1 YEAR. A MATCHED CONTROL GROUP RECEIVED NO STIMULATION. PRETESTS AND POSTTESTS WERE ADMINISTERED. THE TRAINING PROGRAM EMPHASIZED LANGUAGE DEVELOPMENT, SYMBOLIC REPRESENTATION, AND CONCEPT FORMATION. THE RESULTS SHOWED THAT SAMPLE VALUES OF THE EXPERIMENTAL GROUP WERE SUPERIOR TO THOSE OF THE CONTROL GROUP IN 25 OF 26 VARIABLES TESTED, EIGHT BEING SIGNIFICANT AT THE .05 LEVEL. IQ SCORES OF THE EXPERIMENTAL GROUP WERE GREATER THAN THOSE OF THE CONTROL GROUP, AND THE DIFFERENCE WAS SIGNIFICANT AT THE .05 LEVEL. SAMPLE VALUES OF THE EXPERIMENTAL GROUP EXCEEDED THOSE OF THE CONTROL GROUP ON 14 OF 15 LANGUAGE SUBTESTS, TWO BEING SIGNIFICANT AT THE .05 LEVEL. ON TESTS ADMINISTERED TO ASSESS CONCEPTUAL DEVELOPMENT, THE EXPERIMENTAL GROUP WAS CONSISTENTLY SUPERIOR TO THE CONTROL GROUP. FOLLOWUP STUDIES SHOULD BE DONE TO DETERMINE LONG TERM EFFECTIVENESS OF THE PROGRAM. REFERENCES AND TABULATED DATA ARE INCLUDED. (JS)

ED026111 PS001041
KINDERGARTEN RESEARCH STUDY: LEVEL OF SKILLS DEVELOPMENT RELATED TO GROWTH IN SKILLS AND TO READINESS FOR THE FIRST PRIMARY YEAR. , DEC 67 27P.
EDRS PRICE MF-$0.65 HC-$3.29

TWO HYPOTHESES WERE EXAMINED IN THIS RESEARCH PROJECT: (1) CHILDREN WITH HIGH LEVEL PERCEPTUAL SKILLS IN THE INITIAL ASSESSMENT WILL RETAIN THEIR ADVANTAGE BUT WILL GROW LESS IN SKILLS THAN CHILDREN WITH LOW LEVEL SKILLS DEVELOPMENT AT THE OUTSET; AND (2) AFTER A PERIOD OF SKILLS DEVELOPMENT, CHILDREN WITH HIGH LEVEL SKILLS DEVELOPMENT WILL SHOW GREATER READINESS FOR THE FIRST GRADE THAN CHILDREN WITH LOWER LEVELS OF SKILLS DEVELOPMENT. SUBJECTS WERE 132 KINDERGARTEN CHILDREN, DIVIDED INTO SIX CLASSES BY ABILITY, WHO WERE ASSESSED INDIVIDUALLY PRIOR TO AND AFTER 6 MONTHS OF THE PROGRAM. TO MEASURE GROWTH, THE ILLINOIS TEST OF PSYCHOLINGUISTIC ABILITIES AND THE METROPOLITAN READINESS TESTS WERE EMPLOYED. THE FIRST PART OF THE FIRST HYPOTHESIS WAS SUPPORTED, BUT THE SECOND PART WAS NOT. THE SECOND HYPOTHESIS WAS SUPPORTED. IN GENERAL, THE SKILLS DEVELOPMENT PROGRAM MARKEDLY CONTRIBUTED BOTH TO HIGHER SCORES IN SKILLS DEVELOPMENT AFTER 6 OR 8 MONTHS AND TO GREATER THAN NORMAL GROWTH OF THE CHILDREN. (DO)

ED026112 PS001059
A RATIONALE FOR A STRUCTURED EDUCATIONAL PROGRAM AND SUGGESTED ACTIVITIES FOR CULTURALLY DISADVANTAGED INFANTS. PAINTER, GENEVIEVE, APR 68 15P.
EDRS PRICE MF-$0.65 HC-$3.29

SINCE EDUCATIONAL DEFICIENCIES DO EXIST IN DISADVANTAGED CHILDREN, THE EMPHASIS SHOULD BE ON PREVENTION SO THAT COMPENSATION NEED NOT PLAY THE MAJOR ROLE IT DOES TODAY. PRESCHOOL PROGRAMS ARE BEING EFFECTED IN PRIMARY SCHOOLS, NURSERY SCHOOLS, COMMUNITY CENTERS, AND EVEN PRIVATE HOMES. THE CONTROVERSY IS NO LONGER WHETHER OR NOT SUCH PROGRAMS CAN HELP PRECLUDE DEVELOPMENTAL DEFICITS. IT IS WHETHER THE PROGRAMS SHOULD BE CHILD-CENTERED OR HAVE A UNIFORM, STRUCTURED CURRICULUM. THIS PAPER IS INTENDED TO PRESENT A RATIONALE FOR THE STRUCTURE OF INFANT EDUCATION TO BE USED BY TEACHERS, PARAPROFESSIONALS, AND PARENTS. EMPHASIS SHOULD BE ON LANGUAGE AND CONCEPTUAL DEVELOPMENT, BECAUSE DISADVANTAGED CHILDREN APPEAR PARTICULARLY DEFICIENT IN THESE AREAS. THE CHILD SHOULD BE 10 TO 12 MONTHS OLD WHEN THE PROGRAM IS INITIATED. SUGGESTIONS FOR THE TRAINING OF THE INFANT IN LANGUAGE AND CONCEPTUAL TASKS AND ACTIVITIES ARE PRESENTED AFTER A BRIEF DISCUSSION OF THE RATIONALE FOR THE USE OF SUCH ACTIVITIES. (WD)

ED026113 PS001151
HELPING THE CHILD DEVELOP HIS CREATIVE POTENTIAL. WILLIAMS, FRANK E., FEB 68 21P.
EDRS PRICE MF-$0.65 HC-$3.29

IN ORDER TO HELP THE CHILD DEVELOP HIS CREATIVE POTENTIAL, IT IS NECESSARY TO UNDERSTAND (1) WHAT PERSONALITY CHARACTERISTICS DISTINGUISH THE POTENTIALLY CREATIVE CHILD FROM THE AVERAGE CHILD AND (2) WHAT ENVIRONMENTAL CONDITIONS, IF ANY, FACILITATE THE DEVELOPMENT OF CREATIVE BEHAVIOR. RESEARCH ON THE CONTRIBUTION OF ATTITUDE, TEMPERAMENT, AND ENVIRONMENTAL CLIMATE IN NURTURING THE CREATIVE POTENTIAL OF THE YOUNG CHILD IS SMALL. SOME TRENDS, HOWEVER, DO APPEAR IN THE EXISTING STUDIES, ESPECIALLY ADULT STUDIES IN WHICH NOT ONLY THE PERSONALITY OF THE CREATIVE INDIVIDUAL IS EXPLORED, BUT HIS CHILDHOOD IS REEXAMINED. ALTHOUGH THE RELATIONSHIPS BETWEEN CHILDHOOD EXPERIENCE, PERSONAL ATTITUDES, AND CREATIVITY OFTEN APPEAR INCONSISTENT AND EVEN CONTRADICTORY ACROSS INDIVIDUALS, IT HAS BEEN SHOWN THAT CREATIVE PEOPLE OFTEN (1) HAVE GREAT CONFIDENCE IN THEMSELVES, (2) ARE INTROVERTED AND WITHDRAWN, (3) ARE VERY INTELLECTUALLY CURIOUS, (4) ARE NONCONFORMING AND INDEPENDENT, (5) HAD A PLEASANT BUT NOT NECESSARILY CLOSE RELATIONSHIP WITH THEIR PARENTS, (6) DID RECEIVE SUPPORT, RESPECT, AND RELATIVE AUTONOMY FROM THEIR PARENTS, AND (7) WERE ALLOWED EARLY TO EXERCISE THEIR OWN JUDGMENT WITHIN LIMITS OF CONSISTENT DISCIPLINE. (WD)

ED026114 PS001157
AN EVALUATION OF A SIX-WEEK HEADSTART PROGRAM USING AN ACADEMICALLY ORIENTED CURRICULUM: CANTON, 1967. RUSK, BRUCE A., APR 68 49P.
EDRS PRICE MF-$0.65 HC-$3.29
AVAILABLE FROM: DR. GEORGE P. YOUNG, SUPERINTENDENT OF SCHOOLS, 618 HIGH AVE., N.W., CANTON, OHIO 44703 ($1.00).

A STUDY WAS CONDUCTED TO SEE IF CHILDREN IN A 6-WEEK HEAD START PROGRAM IN CANTON, OHIO WOULD MAKE GREATER COGNITIVE GAINS IN AN ACADEMICALLY STRUCTURED CURRICULUM THAN IN A LESS STRUCTURED ONE. WITH THE EXCEPTION OF THE EDUCATIONAL PROGRAM, ALL OTHER ASPECTS OF THE TRADITIONAL HEAD START PROGRAM REMAINED THE SAME FOR ALL CHILDREN. INSERVICE TRAINING PROGRAMS FOR TEACHERS AND AIDES WERE CONDUCTED AND PARENT-TEACHER MEETINGS WERE ENCOURAGED. FIFTEEN CHILDREN IN EACH OF EIGHT BEREITER-ENGELMANN PROGRAM CENTERS AND 15 IN EACH OF EIGHT CONTROL CENTERS WERE PRETESTED AND POSTTESTED ON THE CALDWELL PRESCHOOL INVENTORY AND THE ENGELMANN CONCEPT INVENTORY. RESULTS OF STATISTICAL ANALYSIS OF THE DATA BY MATCHED PAIRS SHOWED THAT, OVER A SHORT TERM, CHILDREN IN THE STRUCTURED CURRICULUM MADE GREATER GAINS THAN THOSE IN THE UNSTRUCTURED PROGRAM. A FOLLOWUP STUDY WAS NOT ATTEMPTED SO THAT IT WAS NOT LEARNED WHETHER GAINS WOULD BE SUSTAINED AFTER A YEAR OR MORE IN SCHOOL. OTHER STUDY FINDINGS SUGGEST THAT ELEMENTARY SCHOOL TEACHERS, RATHER THAN THOSE TRAINED FOR KINDERGARTEN, MOST EASILY ADAPT TO STRUCTURED PRESCHOOL PROGRAMS AND THAT NEIGHBORHOOD WOMEN MAY PROFITABLY BE RECRUITED AND TRAINED TO BE TEACHER AIDES. FURTHER INVESTIGA-

TION INTO THE NATURE OF THE OPTIMAL TYPE OF HEAD START CURRICULUM IS URGED. (MS)

ED026115 PS001162
HEAD START PROGRAMS OPERATED BY PUBLIC SCHOOL SYSTEMS, 1966-67. , 68 43P.
DOCUMENT NOT AVAILABLE FROM EDRS.
AVAILABLE FROM: NATIONAL EDUCATION ASSOCIATION, 1201 SIXTEENTH STREET, N.W., WASHINGTON, D.C. 20036 ($1.00).

THE NATIONAL EDUCATION ASSOCIATION SPONSORED THIS STUDY OF PUBLIC SCHOOL SYSTEMS' HEAD START PROGRAMS. DATA ANALYSES BASED ON QUESTIONNAIRES REVEALED THAT IN 1966-67 (INCLUDING SUMMER, 1966) ONE-THIRD OF FULL-YEAR HEAD START PROGRAMS AND TWO-THIRDS OF HEAD START SUMMER PROGRAMS WERE OPERATED BY PUBLIC SCHOOL SYSTEMS. A SECTION ON ORGANIZATION DEALS WITH DAILY ORGANIZATION, LENGTH OF SESSIONS, FOLLOW THROUGH, PERIOD OF OPERATION, AND SPECIAL SERVICES. TWO SECTIONS ARE ENTITLED "PUPILS, TEACHERS, AND PARENTAL PARTICIPATION," AND "FINANCES AND FACILITIES," AND ALL SECTIONS ARE DOCUMENTED BY TABLES OF STATISTICS. (DO)

ED026116 PS001320
DEVELOPMENT AND IMPLEMENTATION OF A COMPREHENSIVE EVALUATION AND REPORTING SYSTEM FOR KINDERGARTEN AND PRIMARY GRADE SCHOOLS. FINAL REPORT. HEDGES, WILLIAM D.; KANE, ELMER R., JUN 68 79P.
EDRS PRICE MF-$0.65 HC NOT AVAILABLE FROM EDRS.

THE PROJECT DISCUSSED IN THIS REPORT ATTEMPTS TO ESTABLISH, WITHIN A REAL SCHOOL SETTING, A COMPREHENSIVE AND VIABLE WAY OF DETERMINING AND REPORTING THE GROWTH AND DEVELOPMENT OF KINDERGARTEN AND PRIMARY GRADE CHILDREN IN THE PUBLIC SCHOOL. THE PROJECT WAS DEVELOPED BY A STEERING COMMITTEE OF FACULTY MEMBERS FROM THE CLAYTON SCHOOL DISTRICT OF CLAYTON, MISSOURI. ONE OF THE CLAYTON SCHOOLS WAS CHOSEN TO IMPLEMENT THE BITS AND PIECES OF THE PROGRAM AS IT WAS DEVELOPED. FULL-SCALE IMPLEMENTATION OF THE SYSTEM IS TO OCCUR IN THAT PILOT SCHOOL IN THE 1968-69 ACADEMIC YEAR. THE COMPREHENSIVE EVALUATION AND REPORTING SYSTEM CONSISTS OF TWO MAJOR PARTS: (1) A COMPREHENSIVE STUDENT FOLDER TO FOLLOW THE STUDENT FROM KINDERGARTEN THROUGH GRADE SIX AND (2) REPORTS TO PARENTS, INCLUDING (A) TWO WRITTEN REPORTS PER YEAR AND (B) TWO PARENT CONFERENCES PER YEAR. THE SPECIFIC TYPES OF INFORMATION TO BE KEPT IN THE STUDENT FOLDER ARE INDICATED IN APPENDIXES A THROUGH I OF THIS REPORT. ALSO SKETCHED IN THIS REPORT ARE EIGHT RECOMMENDATIONS AND 22 IDEAS CONSIDERED IN DEVELOPING THE EVALUATION AND REPORTING SYSTEM AND NINE AREAS OF INFORMATION ABOUT EACH CHILD TO BE INVESTIGATED AND REPORTED IN THE FOLDER. (WD)

ED026117 PS001410
SEX DIFFERENCES IN MENTAL AND BEHAVIORAL TRAITS. GARAI, JOSEF E.; SCHEINFELD, AMRAM, 68 132P.
DOCUMENT NOT AVAILABLE FROM EDRS.

THIS REVIEW OF RESEARCH CONDUCTED ON SEX DIFFERENCES ATTEMPTS TO ANSWER THE FOLLOWING QUESTIONS: (1) DO THE SEXES DIFFER IN THEIR BASIC CAPACITIES FOR SPECIFIC TYPES OF MENTAL PERFORMANCE AND OCCUPATIONAL ACHIEVEMENT? (2) IF SUCH DIFFERENCES EXIST, TO WHAT EXTENT ARE THEY GENETICALLY DETERMINED? (3) ARE SEX DIFFERENCES IN ABILITIES, INTERESTS, AND PSYCHOLOGICAL TRAITS DETERMINED BY GENETICS, ENVIRONMENT, OR A COMBINATION OF BOTH FACTORS? (4) DO THEY APPEAR IN EARLY LIFE, DEVELOP, AND INTERACT WITH OTHER FACTORS, AND CAN THEY BE MEASURED AND DETECTED AT SUCCESSIVE AGES? (5) WHAT SIGNIFICANCE DO THE SEX DIFFERENCES POSSESS WITH REGARD TO THE SCHOOL CURRICULA, THE EDUCATIONAL PROGRAMS, AND THE POSSIBILITIES FOR THE INCREASED UTILIZATION OF WOMEN IN BUSINESS, INDUSTRY, THE PROFESSIONS, AND PUBLIC LIFE? THE REVIEW OF LITERATURE CENTERS AREOUND THE FOLLOWING TOPICS: INSUFFICIENT CONSIDERATION OF SEX DIFFERENCES IN RESEARCH, EARLY STUDIES OF SEX DIFFERENCES, BIOLOGICAL SEX DIFFERENCES, MANIFESTATIONS OF SEX DIFFERENCES IN THE FIRST YEAR OF LIFE, SENSORY DISCRIMINATION, AND SEX DIFFERENCES IN ABILITIES, INTERESTS, AND INTELLECTUAL PERFORMANCE. CONCLUSIONS ARE DISCUSSED IN TERMS OF SCHOLASTIC AND OCCUPATIONAL ACHIEVEMENT, PRACTICES WHICH DISADVANTAGE ONE SEX OR THE OTHER, AND SEX-RELATED VARIABLES WHICH REQUIRE A BETTER UNDERSTANDING ON THE BASIS OF APPROPRIATE RESEARCH. AN EXTENSIVE BIBLIOGRAPHY IS INCLUDED. (JS)

ED026118 PS001411
PRESCHOOL PARENT EDUCATION PROGRAM: A CURRICULUM GUIDE FOR USE BY TEACHERS CONDUCTING PARENT EDUCATION PROGRAMS AS A PART OF OVER-ALL COMPENSATORY PRESCHOOL PROJECTS. EXPERIMENTAL EDITION. , SEP 66 24P.
EDRS PRICE MF-$0.65 HC-$3.29

THE PURPOSE OF THIS DOCUMENT IS TWOFOLD: (1) TO DESCRIBE AN EXPERIMENTAL PARENT EDUCATION PROGRAM AND (2) TO DESCRIBE HOW SUCH A PROGRAM WILL BE EVALUATED. PARENTS CAN POSITIVELY INFLUENCE PRESCHOOL CHILDREN'S PERCEPTUAL, LANGUAGE, AND COGNITIVE DEVELOPMENT WITH DIRECTION. IN THIS PROJECT TEACHERS ARE RELEASED IN THE AFTERNOON TO TEACH PARENTS HOW TO REMEDY SOME OF THE SERIOUS DEFICIENCIES IN THEIR CHILDREN. TEACHERS ASSUME DIAGNOSTIC ROLES. SPECIFIC CURRICULA INSURE THE PROGRAM'S SUCCESS. STUDENTS' COMMON DISABILITIES ARE TREATED IN GROUPS USING COMMON CURRICULA. DEMONSTRATION SESSIONS ARE CONDUCTED WITH PARENTS OBSERVING AND UTILIZING TECHNIQUES AT HOME. THE IMPACT OF THIS PROGRAM ON ACADEMIC READINESS OF CHILDREN WILL BE ASSESSED. AN EXPERIMENTAL SUBSTUDY WILL BE EVALUATED AND CHANGES IN THE INTELLECTUAL HOME ENVIRONMENT WILL BE ASSESSED. A TABLE OF SAMPLE DIAGNOSTIC GROUPING AND A TYPICAL SCHEDULE OF DAILY ACTIVITIES ARE GIVEN. THE ROLE OF THE SOCIAL WORKER IN MAINTAINING PARENT ATTENDANCE AND ESTABLISHING HOME VISITS IS OUTLINED. ANOTHER TABLE SHOWS HOW THE DEMONSTRATIONS MAY BE FOLLOWED THROUGH AT HOME. (DO)

ED026119 PS001417
PARENTAL BEHAVIOR TOWARD BOYS AND GIRLS OF PRESCHOOL AGE. ECKHOFF, EVA; AND OTHERS, 61 17P.
DOCUMENT NOT AVAILABLE FROM EDRS.

RESEARCH ON THE ACQUISITION OF SEX ROLES IN THE UNITED STATES HAS INDICATED A TENDENCY FOR PARENTS TO TREAT GIRLS LESS HARSHLY THAN BOYS AND FOR FATHERS TO TREAT GIRLS WITH MORE SPECIAL WARMTH THAN THEY DO BOYS. EIGHTEEN CHILDREN AND THEIR PARENTS WERE INTERVIEWED AND OBSERVED IN OSLO, NORWAY, AS PART OF A LONGITUDINAL STUDY OF PARENTAL INFLUENCE ON CHILD DEVELOPMENT. PARENTS WERE SELECTED BEFORE THE CHILD WAS BORN, AND DATA WERE GATHERED UNTIL THE CHILD WAS 6 YEARS OF AGE. THE DATA FROM THIS STUDY WERE LOOKED AT IN TERMS OF PROVIDING INFORMATION ON DIFFERENTIAL TREATMENT OF BOYS AND GIRLS BY PARENTS. IT WAS FOUND THAT MOTHERS TREATED SONS WITH MORE WARMTH AND PERMISSIVENESS THAN THEY DID DAUGHTERS. THIS FINDING WAS CONFOUNDED BY WHETHER THE CHILD WAS THE FIRST OR SECOND CHILD AND THE FACTOR THAT THE MORE MALADJUSTED FAMILIES HAPPENED TO HAVE THE GIRLS. THIS LATTER FACTOR, ESPECIALLY, MAY EXPLAIN THE FINDING OF BETTER TREATMENT OF BOYS THAN GIRLS BY THE MOTHERS. A SECOND SAMPLE OF FAMILIES FROM A DIFFERENT STUDY IN NORWAY TENDED TO DUPLICATE THE OSLO FINDINGS. IT IS UNCLEAR, BUT DOUBTFUL, THAT THE CONFLICTING RESULTS IN THE UNITED STATES AND NORWAY ARE INDICATIVE OF REAL NATIONAL DIFFERENCES IN ATTITUDES TOWARD AND THE CHILD REARING OF BOYS AND GIRLS. (WD)

ED026120 PS001421
LISTENING. WHAT RESEARCH SAYS TO THE TEACHER, NO. 29. TAYLOR, STANFORD E., APR 64 36P.
EDRS PRICE MF-$0.65 HC NOT AVAILABLE FROM EDRS.
AVAILABLE FROM: NATIONAL EDUCATION ASSOCIATION, 1201 SIXTEENTH STREET, N.W., WASHINGTON, D.C. 20036 ($0.25).

IN THIS PAMPHLET, THE ROLE OF LISTENING IN CHILDREN'S LEARNING EXPERIENCES IS DESCRIBED. DISCUSSED ARE FACTORS WHICH INFLUENCE HEARING (SOUND RECEPTION AND MODIFICATION), LISTENING (THE PROCESS OF BECOMING AWARE OF SOUND SEQUENCES), AND AUDING (THE TRANSLATION OF SPEECH SOUNDS INTO MEANING). A PRACTICAL TEACHING PROGRAM IS SUGGESTED TO IMPROVE CHILDREN'S LISTENING ABILITY THROUGH DEVELOPMENT OF SPECIFIC SKILLS, SUCH AS PAYING ATTENTION, FOLLOWING DIRECTIONS, AND LISTENING TO LANGUAGE SOUNDS. IT IS SUGGESTED THAT IMPROVED LISTENING WILL PROMOTE IMPROVEMENT IN THE OTHER COMMUNICATION SKILLS. (MS)

ED026121 PS001422
CONCEPT GROWTH AND THE EDUCATION OF THE CHILD: A SURVEY OF RESEARCH ON CONCEPTUALIZATION. NATIONAL FOUNDATION FOR EDUCATIONAL RESEARCH IN ENGLAND AND WALES OCCASIONAL PUBLICATION SERIES NO. 12. WALLACE, J. G., 65 273P.
DOCUMENT NOT AVAILABLE FROM EDRS.
AVAILABLE FROM: NEW YORK UNIVERSITY PRESS, WASHINGTON SQUARE, NEW YORK, NEW YORK 10003 ($6.00).

TWO SECTIONS IN THIS SURVEY OF RESEARCH ON CONCEPTUALIZATION ARE DEVOTED TO "RECENT CONCEPTUAL STUDIES IN THE BEHAVIOURIST MOULD" AND "MAIN STREAM OF ONTOGENETIC STUDIES OF CONCEPTUALIZATION." UNDER SECTION I, TOPICS INVESTIGATED ARE BEHAVIOURIST APPROACHES TO THE CONCEPTUAL PROCESS, CONCEPTUAL PROBLEMS, AND DEVELOPMENTAL STUDIES. IN SECTION II, SUBJECTS INCLUDE INTRODUCTION TO PIAGET'S WORK, MATHEMATICAL AND SCIENTIFIC CONCEPTS (NUMBER, QUANTITY, WEIGHT, AREA, VOLUME, SPACE, TIME, VELOCITY, CAUSALITY, AND LOGICAL THINKING), CONCEPTUALIZATION IN THE MENTALLY AND PHYSICALLY HANDICAPPED, EDUCATIONAL ASPECTS, AND SOCIAL, SELF, AND CLASS CONCEPTS. A CONCLUDING CHAPTER DEALS WITH GENERAL ASPECTS OF CONCEPTUALIZATION. A LENGTHY BIBLIOGRAPHY IS ALSO INCLUDED. (DO)

ED026122 PS001424
ERROR, RESPONSE TIME AND IQ: SEX DIFFERENCES IN COGNITIVE STYLE OF PRESCHOOL CHILDREN. LEWIS, MICHAEL; AND OTHERS, 68 6P.
DOCUMENT NOT AVAILABLE FROM EDRS.

IN A STUDY ON COGNITIVE STYLE, REFLECTIVITY-IMPULSIVITY IN RESPONSE TO TASK UNCERTAINTY WAS INVESTIGAGED. AT 44 MONTHS OF AGE, 23 BOYS AND 25 GIRLS WERE TESTED ON A MATCHING-FIGURES TEST. CORRELATIONS WERE MADE BETWEEN NUMBER OF ERRORS, RESPONSE TIME, INTELLIGENCE, AND SEX. RESULTS INDICATED THAT THERE WERE SIGNIFICANT SEX DIFFERENCES IN PRESCHOOL CHILDREN'S COGNITIVE STYLE. BOYS' ERRORS WERE SIGNIFICANTLY CORRELATED WITH RESPONSE TIME BUT NOT WITH IQ. GIRLS' ERRORS AND RESPONSE TIME WERE SIGNIFICANTLY CORRELATED WITH INTELLIGENCE, BUT THEIR ERRORS AND RESPONSE TIME WERE NOT SIGNIFICANTLY CORRELATED WITH EACH OTHER. SIMILAR SEX DIFFERENCES HAVE BEEN FOUND IN STUDIES USING OLDER CHILDREN. FINDINGS INDICATE THAT DATA BY SEX SHOULD NOT BE POOLED AND THAT A MORE CAREFUL EXPLORATION OF SEX DIFFERENCES IN COGNITIVE STYLE SHOULD BE MADE. (MS)

ED026123 PS001425
ELEMENTARY SCHOOL MATHEMATICS: A GUIDE TO CURRENT RESEARCH. THIRD EDITION. GLENNON, VINCENT J.; CALLAHAN, LEROY G., 68 137P.
EDRS PRICE MF-$0.65 HC NOT AVAILABLE FROM EDRS.
AVAILABLE FROM: ASSOCIATION FOR SUPERVISION AND CURRICULUM DEVELOPMENT, NATIONAL EDUCATION ASSOCIATION, 1201 SIXTEENTH ST., N.W., WASHINGTON, D.C. 20036 ($2.75).

STUDIES CONCERNING THE CURRICULUM, THE CHILD, THE LEARNING ENVIRONMENT, AND TEACHING METHODS ARE COVERED IN THE FOUR PARTS OF THIS GUIDE TO CURRENT RESEARCH IN THE ELEMENTARY SCHOOL MATHEMATICS. SUBJECTS OF THE FIRST PART INCLUDE THE SOURCES OF THE CURRICULUM, THE RELATIONSHIP OF PIAGET'S WORK IN CHILD DEVELOPMENT TO ACHIEVEMENT IN MATHEMATICS, CUISENAIRE MATERIALS, INNOVATIVE PROGRAMS, KINDERGARTEN PROGRAMS, AND COMPARISON OF U.S. AND FOREIGN PROGRAMS. READINESS, CONCEPTUALIZATION, AND ACHIEVEMENT OF NORMAL, GIFTED, MENTALLY RETARDED, AND CULTURALLY DEPRIVED CHILDREN ARE DISCUSSED IN PART II. THEIR ATTITUDE, ANXIETY, EMOTIONAL DISTURBANCE, PERSONALITY, AND SELF-CONCEPT IN RELATION TO MATHEMATICAL LEARNING ARE ALSO CONSIDERED IN PART II. PART III EXPLORES CLASS SIZE, GROUPS, TIME ALLOTMENT, TEXTBOOKS, TEACHER TRAINING, AND INSERVICE EDUCATION. APPROACHES TO INSTRUCTION, MOTIVATION, DIAGNOSIS, MENTAL GROWTH, PROGRAMED INSTRUCTION, AND METHODS OF TEACHING SEGMENTS OF MATHEMATICS ARE THE SUBJECTS CONSIDERED IN PART IV. (DO)

ED026124 PS001426
A PREKINDERGARTEN PROGRAM FOR FOUR-YEAR-OLDS, WITH A REVIEW OF THE LITERATURE ON PRESCHOOL EDUCATION. AN OCCASIONAL PAPER. BOUCHARD, RUTH A.; MACKLER, BERNARD, NOV 67 54P.
EDRS PRICE MF-$0.65 HC-$3.29
AVAILABLE FROM: CENTER FOR URBAN EDUCATION, 33 WEST 42 STREET, NEW YORK, N.Y. 10038 ($0.25).

IN A PREKINDERGARTEN PROGRAM IN THE ECONOMICALLY DISADVANTAGED AREA OF HARLEM, THE TEACHER, CURRICULUM, DAILY ACTIVITIES, BEHAVIOR, SCHOOL, AND PARENTS OF THE 15 ENROLLED CHILDREN WERE STUDIED. EVALUATIONS EMPHASIZED THE OUTCOMES OF LEARNING RATHER THAN THE SOCIAL, EMOTIONAL, AND INTELLECTUAL PROCESSES OF LEARNING. THE FOLLOWING CONCLUSIONS WERE REACHED: (1) NURSERY SCHOOL ATTENDANCE SEEMS TO MAKE ITS GREATEST CONTRIBUTION IN THE DEVELOPMENT OF SOCIAL SKILLS, (2) NURSERY SCHOOL SEEMS TO HELP CHILDREN BECOME MORE INDEPENDENT AND ACHIEVE GREATER EMOTIONAL MATURITY, (3) WHETHER OR NOT IT ACCELERATES INTELLECTUAL GROWTH IS UNCLEAR, AND (4) THERE IS SOME QUESTION AS TO WHETHER DEVELOPMENT OF DISADVANTAGED CHILDREN IS ENHANCED BY NURSERY SCHOOL. A REVIEW OF LITERATURE ON NURSERY SCHOOL, PRESCHOOL, AND PROJECT HEAD START IS INCLUDED WITH DATA COVERING THE SUBJECTS OF SOCIAL, EMOTIONAL, AND COGNITIVE DEVELOPMENT OF CHILDREN. (DO)

ED026125 PS001432
THE EFFECTIVENESS OF THE PEABODY LANGUAGE DEVELOPMENT KITS AND THE INITIAL TEACHING ALPHABET WITH DISADVANTAGED CHILDREN IN THE PRIMARY GRADES: AFTER TWO YEARS. DUNN, LLOYD M.; AND OTHERS, AUG 67 140P.
EDRS PRICE MF-$0.65 HC-$6.58

THIS COOPERATIVE LANGUAGE DEVELOPMENT PROJECT HAD TWO OBJECTIVES: (1) TO PROVIDE A MODIFIED LANGUAGE PROGRAM FOR CULTURALLY DISADVANTAGED FIRST GRADERS AND (2) TO EVALUATE THE EFFECTIVENESS OF THE PROGRAM IN TERMS OF ACADEMIC, INTELLECTUAL, AND LINGUISTIC GROWTH. IN A 2-YEAR INTERVENTION PROGRAM EXPERIMENTAL VERSIONS OF THE PEABODY LANGUAGE DEVELOPMENT KIT (PLDK) AND THE EARLY-TO-READ INITIAL TEACHING ALPHABET (ITA) WERE USED FOR AN EXPERIMENTAL GROUP. THERE WERE 630 SUBJECTS THE FIRST YEAR AND 343 THE SECOND YEAR. A CONVENTIONAL BASAL READING PROGRAM WITH NO LANGUAGE STIMULATION WAS USED FOR A CONTROL GROUP WITH 102 SUBJECTS THE FIRST YEAR AND 41 THE SECOND YEAR. THE COMBINATION OF ITA AND 2 YEARS OF PLDK PRODUCED THE MOST EFFECTIVE RESULTS. READING ACHIEVEMENT AFTER 2 YEARS WAS EQUAL FOR BOTH GROUPS. THE EFFECTS OF PLDK ON INTELLECTUAL FUNCTIONING ARE QUESTIONABLE. THESE FINDINGS MUST BE VIEWED CAUTIOUSLY SINCE (1) INCREMENTS FAVORING THE ITA AND PLDK MAY NOT LAST THROUGH THE THIRD GRADE, AND (2) PRESENT RESEARCH DOES NOT SUGGEST THE SAME SUPERIORITY OF ITA AS DEMONSTRATED IN THIS PROJECT. HOWEVER, ITA AND PLDK HOLD PROMISE FOR INNER-CITY SLUM CHILDREN WITH REDUCED VERBAL ABILITY, RESTRICTED AND NONSTANDARD ENGLISH, AND INABILITY TO ARTICULATE SPEECH SOUNDS CLEARLY. (DO)

ED026126 PS001438
LEARNING READINESS IN TWO JEWISH GROUPS: A STUDY IN "CULTURAL DEPRIVATION." AN OCCASIONAL PAPER. GROSS, MORRIS, DEC 67 45P.
EDRS PRICE MF-$0.65 HC-$3.29
AVAILABLE FROM: CENTER FOR URBAN EDUCATION, 33 WEST 42 STREET, NEW YORK, N.Y. 10036 ($0.25).

IN A STUDY OF SCHOOL READINESS, 90 AMERICAN BORN, MIDDLE CLASS JEWISH CHILDREN WERE TESTED BEFORE ENTERING THE FIRST GRADE AND DIVIDED INTO TWO GROUPS. THE GROUPS WERE WELL-MATCHED WITH ONE DIFFERENCE: CHILDREN WERE EITHER ASHKENAZIC (OF EUROPEAN DESCENT) OR SEPHARDIC (OF SYRIAN DESCENT). FAMILIES OF BOTH OF THESE GROUPS, HOWEVER, HAD BEEN IN THE UNITED STATES FOR AT LEAST 25 YEARS. COGNITIVE MEASURES SUCH AS THE STANFORD-BINET, COLUMBIA MENTAL MATURITY SCALE, PEABODY PICTURE VOCABULARY TEST, AND THE BENDER VISUAL MOTOR GESTALT TEST WERE GIVEN TO THE CHILDREN; PARENT ATTITUDE SCALES WERE GIVEN TO THE MOTHERS. ADDITIONAL DATA WERE COLLECTED ON THE EDUCATIONAL AND FINANCIAL ASPIRATIONS OF THE MOTHERS FOR THEIR CHILDREN. ANALYSIS OF THE DATA SHOWED SIGNIFICANT SCHOOL READINESS DIFFERENCES. THE ASHKENAZIC CHILDREN, WHOSE CULTURAL BACKGROUND POSSIBLY SUPPORTED ACADEMIC ACHIEVEMENT, WERE MORE PREPARED THAN THE SEPHARDIC CHILDREN, WHOSE TRAINING SEEMED TO STRESS FINANCIAL SUCCESS. STUDY FINDINGS SUGGEST THAT IMPLICIT CULTURAL FACTORS, ASPIRATIONS, AND MORES AFFECT CHILDREN'S SCHOOL READINESS, EVEN WHEN POVERTY AND OTHER DISADVANTAGES ARE ABSENT. (MS)

ED026127 PS001478
DIFFUSION OF INTERVENTION EFFECTS IN DISADVANTAGED FAMILIES. MILLER, JAMES O., 68 29P.
EDRS PRICE MF-$0.65 HC-$3.29

THIS PAPER ASSUMES THAT ENVIRONMENTAL INADEQUACY IS THE PRIMARY FACTOR LEADING TO PROGRESSIVE INTELLECTUAL RETARDATION AND INABILITY TO COPE IN A COMPLEX SOCIETY. AN INTERVENTION PROJECT BEGUN IN 1966 WAS DESIGNED TO DEVELOP COGNITIVE, MOTIVATIONAL, PERSONAL STYLE, AND PHYSICAL VARIABLES, WHICH ARE FUNCTIONAL CATEGORIES RELATED TO COMPETENCE. SUBJECTS INCLUDED 60 DISADVANTAGED PRESCHOOLERS (THE "TARGET" CHILDREN), THEIR YOUNGER SIBLINGS (THE EXPERIMENTAL GROUPS), AND THEIR MOTHERS. GROUP I (THE MAXIMUM IMPACT GROUP) INVOLVED THE MOTHER AND THE TARGET CHILD AT THE EARLY TRAINING CENTER. THE MOTHER'S SEQUENTIAL PROGRAM CONSISTED OF SKILL DEVELOPMENT, OBSERVATION, AND PARTICIPATION AS A TEACHER. APTITUDES OF SKILLS FOR ENVIRONMENTAL MASTERY AND SUSTAINING ATTITUDES FOR CONTINUED GROWTH WERE DEVELOPED IN TARGET CHILDREN. IN GROUP II, THE TARGET CHILD WAS THE ONLY MEMBER OF THE FAMILY ENROLLED IN THE PROGRAM. FAMILIES IN GROUP III (THE HOME VISITOR GROUP) HAD NO CONTACT WITH THE CENTER, BUT A HOME-VISITING TEACHER DESCRIBED PROCEDURES. A NATURAL ENVIRONMENTAL GROUP WAS CHOSEN TO MATCH DEMOGRAPHIC CHARACTERISTICS OF TREATMENT FAMILIES. IN 2 1/2 YEARS, YOUNGER SIBLINGS WHOSE MOTHERS PARTICIPATED WERE SUPERIOR IN ALL COMPARISONS. ANALYSIS OF PSYCHOMETRIC DATA ON TARGET CHILDREN WAS SIGNIFICANTLY GREATER THAN THOSE WHERE NO PARENTAL CONTACT WAS MAINTAINED. (DO)

ED026128 PS001498
A HEAD START CONTROL GROUP. PART OF THE FINAL REPORT. CUNNINGHAM, GROVER, AUG 68 14P.
EDRS PRICE MF-$0.65 HC-$3.29

A STUDY WAS CONDUCTED TO DETERMINE IF THE OBSERVED CHANGES IN HEAD START CHILDREN WERE RELATED TO THE PRACTICE EFFECTS INHERENT IN A TEST-RETEST SITUATION. THE "CONTROL" GROUP CONSISTED OF 64 CHILDREN WHO HAD BEEN ELIGIBLE FOR A HEAD START PROGRAM. THEY ROUGHLY MATCHED A GROUP OF HEAD START (HS) CHILDREN IN IQ SCORES, AGE, AND SOCIOECONOMIC LEVEL. ON TWO OCCASIONS, WITH ABOUT 83 DAYS BETWEEN TESTINGS, THE STANFORD-BINET AND PRESCHOOL INVENTORY TESTS WERE ADMINISTERED TO THE CONTROL GROUP. THE SAME TESTS HAD BEEN ADMINISTERED TO THE HS GROUP IN A STUDY BY TEMP AND ANDERSON IN 1967. THE CONTROL GROUP DID NOT HAVE A STATISTICAL GAIN IN STANFORD-BINET IQ SCORES, WHEREAS THE HS GROUP DID HAVE. ON THE PRESCHOOL INVENTORY BOTH GROUPS SHOWED STATISTICALLY SIGNIFICANT GAINS IN MOST INSTANCES. THE RESULTS SUPPORT THE POSITION THAT THE GAINS IN THE STANFORD-BINET IQ SCORES WERE ATRRIBUTABLE TO HEAD START PRACTICES AND THAT THE INCREASES IN THE PRESCHOOL INVENTORY SCORES WERE ATTRIBUTABLE TO MATURA-

TION. THE PRESCHOOL INVENTORY SHOULD BE SCORED TO ALLOW FOR MATURATIONAL DIFFERENCES. TABULATED DATA ARE INCLUDED. (JS)

ED026129 PS001499
DEPENDENCY AND SOCIAL PERFORMANCE: THE DEVELOPMENT OF A SCALE TO MEASURE LEVEL OF INDEPENDENCE IN SMALL CHILDREN. PART OF THE FINAL REPORT. SOTO-PADIN, JOSE L., AUG 68 114P.
EDRS PRICE MF-$0.65 HC-$6.58

INFORMATION ON SOCIAL BEHAVIOR INDEPENDENCE, AND INTELLIGENCE WAS GATHERED ON 74 HEAD START SUBJECTS (ANGLO, NEGRO, AND MEXICAN-AMERICAN) AGED 5 TO 7 YEARS, FOR THE DEVELOPMENT OF A SCALE TO MEASURE THE LEVEL OF INDEPENDENCE IN SMALL CHILDREN. THE FOLLOWING HYPOTHESES WERE TESTED: (1) LEVEL OF INDEPENDENCE WILL DIFFERENTIATE ETHNIC GROUPS. RANKING ORDER WILL BE NEGRO, ANGLO, MEXICAN. (2) LEVEL OF INDEPENDENCE WILL CORRELATE POSITIVELY WITH THE FOLLOWING MEASURES OF SOCIAL BEHAVIOR: (A) TEACHER'S ESTIMATED RANK OF CHILD'S SOCIAL COMPETENCE; (B) TEACHER'S ESTIMATED RANK OF CHILD'S POPULARITY; (C) INTERPERSONAL AND COMMUNICATIVE SCORE; (D) STATUS AMONG PEERS; AND (E) SCHOOL ADJUSTMENT. (3) STATUS AMONG PEERS WILL BE LOWER FOR HIGH DEPENDENT GIRLS THAN FOR HIGH DEPENDENT BOYS. (4) INTELLIGENCE WILL CORRELATE POSITIVELY WITH LEVEL OF INDEPENDENCE. (5) ACHIEVEMENT WILL CORRELATE POSITIVELY WITH LEVEL OF INDEPENDENCE. (6) AGE WILL CORRELATE POSITIVELY WITH LEVEL OF INDEPENDENCE. THE RESULTS SUPPORTED ONLY THE SECOND AND SIXTH HYPOTHESES WITH LOW CORRELATIONS. RESULTS WERE NOT CONCLUSIVE FOR THE FIFTH HYPOTHESIS. EXTREMES IN DEPENDENCE AND INDEPENDENCE FOR EACH SEX AND AGE LEVEL MUST BE ESTABLISHED BEFORE STUDIES RELATING LEVEL OF INDEPENDENCE WITH OTHER VARIABLES CAN BE FRUITFUL. REFERENCES AND TABULATED DATA ARE INCLUDED. (JS)

ED026130 PS001503
AN INVESTIGATION OF THE STANDARD-NONSTANDARD DIMENSION OF CENTRAL TEXAN ENGLISH. PART OF THE FINAL REPORT. STOLZ, WALTER; BILLS, GARLAND, AUG 68 51P.
EDRS PRICE MF-$0.65 HC-$3.29

THE SPEECH OF 23 PEOPLE IN A RURAL TEXAS COMMUNITY WAS STUDIED. THE POPULATION OF THE AREA WAS OVER 90 PERCENT WHITE ANGLO-PROTESTANT. THE SUBJECTS VARIED FROM ILLITERATE TO COLLEGE EDUCATED AND RANGED IN AGE FROM 17 TO 60 YEARS. SEVENTEEN DIALECT FEATURES WERE CHOSEN AS ILLUSTRATIVE OF THE VARIATIONS IN THE USE OF LINGUISTIC FORMS FOR PEOPLE OF THIS GEOGRAPHICAL AREA. IT WAS ASSUMED PRIOR TO THE STUDY THAT THERE EXISTED A CONTINUUM ON WHICH BOTH THE SPEAKER AND THE DIALECT FEATURES COULD BE LOCATED. TWELVE OF THE 17 DIALECT FEATURES WERE ANALYZED. A CORRELATION WAS FOUND BETWEEN DIALECT SCORE (DS) AND AMOUNT OF EDUCATION OF THE SUBJECT; THE HIGHER THE EDUCATION, THE CLOSER THE SPEAKER WAS TO THE STANDARD ENGLISH END OF THE CONTINUUM. A SIMILAR RESULT WAS FOUND BETWEEN DS AND SOCIOECONOMIC LEVEL. IN ANOTHER PART OF THE STUDY, ONE OF THE DIALECT FEATURES WAS INTENSIVELY ANALYZED FOR THE SPEECH OF 12 SUBJECTS. A CORRELATION WAS FOUND BETWEEN SOCIOECONOMIC CLASS AND THE USE OF "HAVE" OR "HAVE GOT," WITH THE LOWER CLASSES USING "HAVE GOT." (WD)

ED026131 PS001506
A METHODOLOGY FOR FOSTERING ABSTRACT THINKING IN DEPRIVED CHILDREN. BLANK, MARION, MAR 68 21P.
EDRS PRICE MF-$0.65 HC-$3.29

RESEARCH HAS INDICATED THAT ONE SIGNIFICANT DEFICIENCY IN THE INTELLECTUAL CAPABILITIES OF DISADVANTAGED CHILDREN IS A DISABILITY IN ABSTRACT THINKING. ALTHOUGH ALL VERY YOUNG CHILDREN LACK THIS ABILITY, THE ENVIRONMENT OF THE MIDDLE CLASS CHILD PROVIDES AN OPPORTUNITY SO THAT AS THIS CHILD MATURES, THE ABILITY TO THINK IN ABSTRACT TERMS NATURALLY DEVELOPS. THE ENVIRONMENT OF THE DISADVANTAGED CHILD DOES NOT PROVIDE ADEQUATE OPPORTUNITIES FOR THE DEVELOPMENT OF THIS ABILITY. IN RESPONSE TO THIS NEED OF DISADVANTAGED CHILDREN, A TUTORIAL PROGRAM WAS CREATED WITH THE GOAL OF FOSTERING ABSTRACT THINKING. THE PROGRAM OCCUPIES ONLY SOME 15 TO 20 MINUTES OF A NURSERY SCHOOL DAY; BUT, AS IT IS TUTORIAL, IT IS EFFECTIVE BECAUSE OF THE ONE-TO-ONE TEACHER-PUPIL RATIO. THE TEACHING TECHNIQUES TO BE USED IN THIS PROGRAM INCLUDE (1) TECHNIQUES FOR THE DEVELOPMENT OF COGNITIVELY DIRECTED PERCEPTION, (2) TECHNIQUES TO FACILITATE THE CHILD'S USE AND UNDERSTANDING OF LANGUAGE, AND (3) TECHNIQUES TO FOCUS THE CHILD ON DEVELOPING PROBLEM SOLVING SKILLS. THE SEVERAL SPECIFIC TECHNIQUES WITHIN EACH OF THE ABOVE THREE BROAD TOPICAL AREAS ARE ALSO DELINEATED IN THE TEXT OF THE PAPER. (WD)

ED026132 PS001508
PERCEPTUAL MODE DOMINANCE: AN APPROACH TO ASSESSMENT OF FIRST GRADE READING AND SPELLING. BUKTENICA, NORMAN A., [67] 26P.
EDRS PRICE MF-$0.65 HC-$3.29

THIS STUDY INVESTIGATES THE RELATIONSHIP BETWEEN AUDITORY AND VISUAL ACUITY AND THE LEARNING OF FIRST GRADE READING AND SPELLING. IT WAS THE AIM OF THIS STUDY (1) TO CLARIFY THE RELATIONSHIP BETWEEN AUDITORY AND VISUAL PERCEPTION; (2) TO INVESTIGATE THE ABILITY OF SUBJECTS TO READ AND SPELL WHEN, AND IF, DIFFERENCES EXIST IN THE PERCEPTUAL MODALITIES; AND (3) TO SEE IF THERE EXISTS A RELATIONSHIP BETWEEN PERCEPTUAL ABILITY AND SOCIOECONOMIC STATUS. THE SUBJECTS, 342 FIRST GRADE CHILDREN FROM THREE TYPES OF SOCIOECONOMIC GROUPS, WERE ADMINISTERED AN INTELLIGENCE TEST, THEN AUDITORY AND VISUAL TESTS, AND, AT THE END OF THE SCHOOL YEAR, READING AND SPELLING TESTS. THE RESULTS SHOWED THAT (1) THERE WAS NO SUBSTANTIAL RELATIONSHIP BETWEEN VISUAL AND AUDITORY PERCEPTUAL MODALITIES; (2) THE COMPOSITE USE OF BOTH MODALITIES AS PREDICTORS OF ACHIEVEMENT WAS MORE EFFECTIVE THAN THE USE OF EACH ALONE; (3) NONVERBAL AUDITORY AND VISUAL PERCEPTUAL VARIABLES WERE BETTER PREDICTORS THAN PERCEPTUAL VARIABLES WITH VERBAL COMPONENTS; (4) AUDITORY DISCRIMINATION WAS MORE IMPORTANT IN MIDDLE CLASS CHILDREN AND VISUAL PERCEPTION WAS MORE IMPORTANT IN LOWER CLASS SUBJECTS FOR PREDICTION OF FIRST GRADE ACHIEVEMENT; AND (5) MIDDLE CLASS CHILDREN WERE MORE ABLE ON PERCEPTUAL VARIABLES HAVING VERBAL COMPONENTS THAN LOWER CLASS CHILDREN. (WD)

ED026133 PS001510
A DISTANCE MEASURE OF RACIAL ATTITUDES IN PRIMARY GRADE CHILDREN: AN EXPLORATORY STUDY. KOSLIN, SANDRA COHEN; AND OTHERS, SEP 68 10P.
EDRS PRICE MF-$0.65 HC-$3.29

THE PURPOSE OF THIS STUDY WAS TO DESIGN AN INSTRUMENT TO MEASURE INTERPERSONAL RACIAL ATTITUDES AMONG PRIMARY CHILDREN IN SEGREGATED AND NONSEGREGATED SCHOOL SETTINGS. SUBJECTS WERE 129 FIRST AND SECOND GRADERS ENROLLED IN A LOWER-MIDDLE CLASS ALL WHITE SCHOOL, AN ALL NEGRO SLUM SCHOOL, AND AN INTEGRATED LOWER-MIDDLE CLASS SCHOOL. ALL RECEIVED TEST BOOKLETS WITH DECALS OF A TARGET FIGURE (NEGRO TEACHER, WHITE TEACHER, PEER, OR SCHOOL) ON EACH PAGE, AND A PACKAGE OF STICKERS ON WHICH SELF-FIGURES WERE PRINTED. THEY WERE DIRECTED TO PASTE THE SELF-FIGURES IN WHATEVER POSITION AND AT WHATEVER DISTANCE FROM THE TARGET FIGURE THEY CHOSE. WHITE SUBJECTS PLACED THE SELF FIGURES FARTHER AWAY FROM NEGRO TARGETS THAN FROM WHITE TARGETS. NEGRO SUBJECTS PLACED THEMSELVES EQUALLY CLOSE TO WHITE AND NEGRO TARGETS. INTEGRATED NEGROES PLACED THEMSELVES SIGNIFICANTLY CLOSER TO WHITE-CHILDREN TARGETS THAN DID SEGREGATED NEGRO SUBJECTS. FIGURE PLACEMENT INDICATED INTEGRATION ACCELERATED A TENDENCY FOR WHITE SUBJECTS TO MOVE CLOSER TO NEGRO CHILDREN TARGETS AS GRADE INCREASED. REGARDLESS OF RACE, INTEGRATED SUBJECTS PLACED THEMSELVES CLOSER TO SCHOOL THAN DID SEGREGATED SUBJECTS. BECAUSE THIS STUDY WAS PRELIMINARY AND SMALL, MANY INTERPRETATIONS EXIST AND CANNOT BE RESOLVED FOR SOME FINDINGS. FURTHER RESEARCH IS NEEDED TO COMPARE THE VALIDITY OF ALTERNATIVE INTERPRETATIONS. (DO)

ED026134 PS001513
SEX ROLE TYPING IN THE PRESCHOOL YEARS: AN OVERVIEW. VROEGH, KAREN; HANDRICH, MILLICENT, 66 36P.
EDRS PRICE MF-$0.65 HC-$3.29
AVAILABLE FROM: INSTITUTE FOR JUVENILE RESEARCH, 907 SOUTH WOLCOTT AVENUE, CHICAGO, ILLINOIS 60"12.

SEX ROLE TYPING IN THE PRESCHOOL CHILD IS THE SUBJECT OF THIS RESEARCH REPORT. SPECIFIC TOPICS CONSIDERED ARE SEX DIFFERENCES, AWARENESS OF SEX DIFFERENCES, SEX ROLE PREFERENCES, PARENT PREFERENCES, SEX ROLE IDENTIFICATION, AND FAMILY VARIABLES RELATED TO SEX ROLE TYPING. THIS SUMMARY OF RESEARCH STUDIES IN THE FIELD REPORTS EXPERIMENTAL AND OBSERVATIONAL FINDINGS ABOUT BEHAVIOR AND CHARACTERISTICS TYPICAL OF WHITE MIDDLE CLASS BOYS AND GIRLS BETWEEN THE AGES OF THREE AND FIVE. HOWEVER, CONFLICTING RESULTS OF THE RESEARCH MAKE FIRM GENERALIZATIONS IMPOSSIBLE. IT IS SUGGESTED THAT STANDARD TESTS OF SEX ROLE PREFERENCE AND IDENTIFICATION ARE OF LITTLE VALUE AND MAY NOT BE VALID INSTRUMENTS. ALTHOUGH CHILDREN WERE AWARE OF AND SHOWED SEX-APPROPRIATE BEHAVIOR, THE FACTORS RESPONSIBLE FOR THIS SEX ROLE TYPING HAVE NOT BEEN IDENTIFIED. FURTHER RESEARCH IS SUGGESTED TO INVESTIGATE THE GROWTH OF SEX ROLE IDENTITY IN CHILDREN. A THEORY OF SEX ROLE DEVELOPMENT IS ALSO CALLED FOR. A NINE-PAGE BIBLIOGRAPHY IS INCLUDED IN THE REPORT. (MS)

ED026135 PS001518
GROUPING. HEATHERS, GLEN, FEB 67 33P.
EDRS PRICE MF-$0.65 HC NOT AVAILABLE FROM EDRS.

THE IDEA OF "GROUPING" IN SCHOOLS RANGES FROM GROUP TEACHING TO GROUPING OF PUPILS, WITH MANY VARIATIONS ON THESE TWO THEMES. THE SELF-CONTAINED CLASSROOM, FOUND USUALLY IN THE ELEMENTARY GRADES, CONSISTS OF ONE TEACHER WITH ONE GRADE-LEVEL CLASS FOR THE FULL DAY AND FOR ALL SUBJECTS. THE DEPARTMENTAL APPROACH, FOUND AT ALL LEVELS, EMPLOYS TEACHERS TO TEACH A PARTICULAR SUBJECT OR TWO ONLY, AND THE PUPILS, DURING A SCHOOL DAY, MOVE FROM CLASS TO CLASS. TEAM TEACHING OCCURS WHEN TWO OR MORE TEACHERS SHARE IN TEACHING ONE PARTICULAR GROUP OF STUDENTS, USUALLY IN JUST ONE CURRICULAR AREA. NONGRADED INSTRUCTION ENABLES STUDENTS TO ADVANCE IN THE CURRICULUM ACCORDING TO THEIR INDIVIDUAL CAPACITIES. PERHAPS MOST RESEARCH IN THE GROUPING AREA HAS INVOLVED ABILITY GROUPING, IN WHICH STUDENTS OF A GIVEN GRADE ARE DIVIDED UP ACCORDING TO DEGREE OF ABILITY OR ACHIEVEMENT. OTHER WITHIN-GRADE ORGANIZATION HAS BEEN ATTEMPTED; FOR EXAMPLE, PLANNED HETEROGENEOUS GROUPING AND TEACHABILITY GROUPING. THE RESEARCH IN MANY OF THESE AREAS IS INCONCLUSIVE AND INCOMPLETE AND FAILS TO DETERMINE THE CONTRIBUTION OF THE ORGANIZATIONAL PLAN BEING EXAMINED. (WD)

ED026136 PS001524
ARITHMETIC AND MATHEMATICS. DIMENSIONS IN EARLY LEARNING SERIES. BEREITER, CARL, 68 95P.
DOCUMENT NOT AVAILABLE FROM EDRS.
AVAILABLE FROM: DIMENSIONS PUBLISHING CO., SAN RAFAEL, CALIFORNIA 94903 ($2.50).

THIS BOOK DEALS WITH TEACHING MATHEMATICS TO CHILDREN DURING THE YEARS OF THREE TO NINE. ACCORDING TO THE AUTHOR, THE BOOK ESPOUSES "THE PEDAGOGICAL PRINCIPLE THAT THE CHILD OUGHT TO HAVE SOME IDEA OF WHAT IS GOING ON." THE CONTENT OF THE BOOK IS DIVIDED INTO ELEVEN CHAPTERS: (1) AN INTRODUCTION, (2) COUNTING, (3) MEASUREMENT AND QUANTITATIVE PROBLEMS, (4) MATHEMATICAL NOTATION, (5) NUMERICAL OPERATIONS, (6) DETECTING NUMERICAL RELATIONSHIPS, (7) PLACE VALUE AND NUMBER BASES, (8) ONE-TO-ONE CORRESPONDENCE, (9) RELATING GEOMETRY TO NUMBER, (10) NOTES ON TEACHING METHODS, AND (11) PARENTS AND PRIMARY MATHEMATICS. (WD)

ED026137 PS001530
PROJECT HEAD START RESEARCH AND EVALUATION CENTER, SYRACUSE UNIVERSITY RESEARCH INSTITUTE. FINAL REPORT, NOVEMBER 1, 1967. HALL, VERNON; AND OTHERS, 1 NOV 67 148P.
EDRS PRICE MF-$0.65 HC-$6.58

THIS DOCUMENT DESCRIBES THE RESEARCH ACTIVITIES OF THE SYRACUSE UNIVERSITY EVALUATION AND RESEARCH CENTER FOR THE YEAR SEPTEMBER 1, 1966 THROUGH AUGUST 31, 1967. THIS FINAL REPORT IS ORGANIZED ON THE BASIS OF SIX RESEARCH PROJECTS, WHICH HAVE BEEN ABSTRACTED UNDER THE FOLLOWING TITLES AND NUMBERS: (1) EXPERIMENTS IN GRAMMATICAL PROCESSING IN CHILDREN (PS 001 531); (2) ACQUISITION AND TRANSFER DIFFERENCES BETWEEN KINDERGARTENERS AND SECOND-GRADERS ON AURALLY AND VISUALLY PRESENTED PAIRED-ASSOCIATES USING AN A-B, A-C DESIGN (PS 001 532); (3) CONCEPT IDENTIFICATION STRATEGIES (PS 001 533); (4) FEAR AND ATTACHMENT IN YOUNG CHILDREN (PS 001 534); (5) EVALUATING BEHAVIORAL CHANGE DURING A SIX-WEEK PRE-KINDERGARTEN INTERVENTION EXPERIENCE (PS 001 535); AND (6) VARIABLES AFFECTING THE PERFORMANCE OF YOUNG CHILDREN ON A LETTER DESCRIMINATION TASK (PS 001 009 OR ED 020 797). (WD)

ED026138 PS001531
EXPERIMENTS IN GRAMMATICAL PROCESSING IN CHILDREN. RESEARCH PROJECT NUMBER 1 OF PROJECT HEAD START RESEARCH AND EVALUATION CENTER, SYRACUSE UNIVERSITY RESEARCH INSTITUTE. FINAL REPORT, NOVEMBER 1, 1967. MIRON, MURRAY S.; AND OTHERS, 1 NOV 67 33P.
EDRS PRICE MF-$0.65 HC-$3.29

IN PERCEIVING SPEECH, A HEARER MAY DIVIDE THE UTTERANCE INTO PREDICTABLE UNITS. IN THE PRESENT INVESTIGATION OF THESE UNITS, AN ALLEGED PHENOMENON (THE RESISTANCE OF THE HEARER TO PERCEIVE EXTRANEOUS AUDITORY STIMULI) WAS EMPLOYED. IT WAS ARGUED THAT THIS RESISTANCE CAUSED THE HEARER TO PERCEIVE THE IRRELEVANT STIMULUS, IF AT ALL, PRIMARILY AT THE JUNCTURE OF MAJOR UNITS. ALSO INVESTIGATED WAS THE INTERACTION BETWEEN THE VERBAL MATERIALS USED AND THE PERCEPTION OF THE EXTRANEOUS STIMULUS (A CLICK). THE SUBJECTS WERE EIGHT KINDERGARTEN AND EIGHT SECOND GRADE CHILDREN. THE VERBAL MATERIALS, SPOKEN TO THE CHILDREN BY AN ADULT, WERE SENTENCES AND NONSENTENCE STRINGS OF WORDS. ALSO CLICKING SOUNDS WERE MADE. THE CHILDREN WERE ASKED TO TELL WHERE IN THE SENTENCE OR STRING OF WORDS THE CLICK OCCURRED. THE RESULTS INDICATED THAT A GREATER MAGNITUDE OF DISPLACEMENT OF THE CLICK FROM ITS ACTUAL POSITION OCCURRED FOR THE SENTENCES THAN FOR THE NONSENTENCE MATERIAL. THE YOUNGER CHILDREN TENDED TO PREPOSITION THE CLICK. IN BOTH AGE GROUPS, THERE WAS A TENDENCY FOR CLICK LOCATION TO BE PREPOSITIONED IN NONSENTENCES AND POSTPOSITIONED IN SENTENCES. ALSO, AS HAS BEEN OBSERVED WITH ADULTS, THE PRECEPTION OF THE CLICK TENDED TO MIGRATE TOWARDS MAJOR UNIT BOUNDARIES IN THE SENTENCE MATERIAL. THESE BOUNDARIES WERE DETERMINED BY RULON WELLS' IMMEDIATE CONSTITUENT ANALYSIS. (WD)

ED026139 PS001532
ACQUISTION AND TRANSFER DIFFERENCES BETWEEN KINDERGARTENERS AND SECOND-GRADERS ON AURALLY AND VISUALLY PRESENTED PAIRED-ASSOCIATES USING AN A-B, A-C DESIGN RESEARCH PROJECT NUMBER 2 OF PROJECT HEAD START RESEARCH AND EVALUATION CENTER, SYRACUSE UNIVERSITY RESEARCH INSTITUTE. FINAL REPORT, NOVEMBER 1, 1967. HALL, VERNON C., 1 NOV 67 12P.
EDRS PRICE MF-$0.65 HC-$3.29

SIXTY KINDERGARTEN AND SIXTY SECOND GRADE CHILDREN WERE ADMINISTERED A PAIRED-ASSOCIATE (P-A) TASK. THE SUBJECTS IN EACH AGE GROUP WERE RANDOMLY ASSIGNED TO ONE OF FOUR GROUPS: (1) EXPERIMENTAL WITH AURAL PRESENTATION OF THE P-A'S, (2) EXPERIMENTAL WITH VISUAL PRESENTATION OF THE P-A'S, (3) CONTROL WITH AURAL PRESENTATION OF THE P-A'S AND (4) CONTROL WITH VISUAL PRESENTATION OF THE P-A'S. AN AB-AC PARADIGM WAS USED. EACH OF THE TWO P-A LISTS OF THIS STUDY WAS COMPOSED OF FIVE WORD-PAIRS OR FIVE PICTURE-PAIRS. THE FIRST LIST PRESENTED TO THE SUBJECT WAS REPEATED UNTIL ONE PERFECT ANTICIPATION TRIAL WAS PERFORMED, AND THEN THE SECOND LIST WAS PRESENTED FOR NINE TRIALS. THE RESULTS SHOWED THAT CHILDREN REACHED CRITERION SIGNIFICANTLY FASTER IN THE VISUAL PRESENTATION GROUPS. IT WAS ALSO FOUND THAT THE YOUNGER CHILDREN SHOWED LESS NEGATIVE TRANSFER IN THE AB-AC DESIGN THAN THE OLDER CHILDREN. (WD)

ED026140 PS001533
CONCEPT IDENTIFICATION STRATEGIES. RESEARCH PROJECT NUMBER 3 OF PROJECT HEAD START RESEARCH AND EVALUATION CENTER, SYRACUSE UNIVERSITY RESEARCH INSTITUTE, NOVEMBER 1, 1967. MEYER, WILLIAM J.; HULTSCH, DAVID, 1 NOV 67 24P.
EDRS PRICE MF-$0.65 HC-$3.29

THE PURPOSE OF THIS STUDY WAS TO DETERMINE THE EFFECTS OF AGE DIFFERENCES AND DIFFERENCES IN MEMORY LOAD ON CONCEPT IDENTIFICATION (CI) TASKS OF VARYING LEVELS OF COMPLEXITY. PREVIOUS STUDIES WITH YOUNG CHILDREN FOUND INCREASINGLY BETTER PERFORMANCE ON CI TASKS WITH INCREASING AGE. THIS WAS IN PART DUE TO THE FACT THAT OLDER SUBJECTS CATEGORIZE STIMULUS INFORMATION TO A GREATER EXTENT THAN YOUNGER SUBJECTS. PERHAPS A REDUCTION OF THE MEMORY LOAD REQUIRED IN THE TASK WOULD BENEFIT THE YOUNGER CHILDREN MORE THAN THE OLDER CHILDREN, BECAUSE IT WOULD REDUCE THE IRRELEVANT STIMULUS DIMENSIONS OF THE TASK WHICH BOTHER YOUNGER CHILDREN. THE SUBJECTS FOR THIS STUDY WERE 54 KINDERGARTEN AND 54 SECOND GRADE CHILDREN. THEY WERE ADMINISTERED CI TASKS OF THREE LEVELS OF COMPLEXITY AND THREE LEVELS OF MEMORY LOAD. THE RESULTS FROM THE SUBJECTS' PERFORMANCES ON THESE TASKS INDICATED THAT THE YOUNGER CHILDREN WERE MORE ADVERSELY AFFECTED BY INCREASED CONCEPT COMPLEXITY THAN THE OLDER CHILDREN. NO SIGNIFICANT AGE-MEMORY LOAD INTERACTION OCCURRED. (WD)

ED026141 PS001534
FEAR AND ATTACHMENT IN YOUNG CHILDREN. RESEARCH PROJECT NUMBER 4 OF PROJECT HEAD START RESEARCH AND EVALUATION CENTER, SYRACUSE UNIVERSITY RESEARCH INSTITUTE. FINAL REPORT, NOVEMBER 1, 1967. SCHWARZ, J. CONRAD, 1 NOV 67 18P.
EDRS PRICE MF-$0.65 HC-$3.29

THE OBJECTIVE OF THIS PROJECT WAS TO TEST THE EFFECT OF THE PRESENCE OF A MOTHER, COMPARED WITH THE PRESENCE OF AN ADULT FEMALE STRANGER, UPON THE APPREHENSIVENESS OF CHILDREN CONFRONTED WITH NOVEL STIMULI. SUBJECTS WERE 10 CHILDREN, 3 1/2 TO 5 1/2 YEARS OLD, WHO WERE INDIVIDUALLY PLACED IN A ROOM CONTAINING A TOY CASH REGISTER, A MARBLE-RACE TOY, AND A HIDDEN MECHANICAL TOY GORILLA. EACH CHILD WAS ACCOMPANIED EITHER BY A MOTHER OR BY AN ASSISTANT EXPERIMENTER. RATINGS WERE MADE OF FACIAL EXPRESSION, MOVEMENT ABOUT THE ROOM, AND VISUAL ORIENTATION OVER A 5-MINUTE PERIOD WHEN THE GORILLA WAS ANIMATED. IT WAS PREDICTED THAT BEHAVIOR WOULD DIFFER BETWEEN THE SUBJECTS IN A MANNER SUGGESTING LESS INITIAL FEAR AND RAPID DISSIPATION OF FEAR BY THOSE ACCOMPANIED BY A MOTHER. RESULTS WERE OPPOSITE TO PREDICTIONS. THE DIFFERENCE IN THE EFFECTS OF THE PRESENCE OF AN ATTACHED INDIVIDUAL AND AN UNATTACHED INDIVIDUAL ARE NOT AS MARKED FOR CHILDREN 3 1/2 TO 5 1/2 YEARS OLD AS THEY ARE FOR CHILDREN 9 MONTHS TO 2 1/2 YEARS OLD. SINCE THIS STUDY IS INCONCLUSIVE, OTHER STUDIES WITH ADDITIONAL EXPERIMENTAL AND CONTROL GROUPS ARE PLANNED. (DO)

ED026142 PS001535
EVALUATING BEHAVIORAL CHANGE DURING A SIX-WEEK PRE-KINDERGARTEN INTERVENTION EXPERIENCE. RESEARCH PROJECT NUMBER 5 OF PROJECT HEAD START RESEARCH AND EVALUATION CENTER, SYRACUSE UNIVERSITY RESEARCH INSTITUTE. FINAL REPORT, NOVEMBER 1, 1967. HAYWEISER, LOIS; AND OTHERS, 1 NOV 67 43P.
EDRS PRICE MF-$0.65 HC-$3.29

THE OBJECTIVE OF THIS STUDY WAS THE DEVELOPMENT OF EVALUATION TECHNIQUES AND THE ASSESSMENT OF THESE TECHNIQUES WHEN COMPARED WITH STANDARD PROCEDURES OF THE NATIONAL HEAD START PROGRAM. ASSESSMENTS OF COGNITIVE BEHAVIOR, SOCIAL BEHAVIOR, AND TEACHERS' PERCEPTIONS--AS OPPOSED TO AIDES' PERCEPTIONS--OF CHILDREN WERE MADE. THE SUBJECTS WERE 33 CHILDREN OF BROAD SOCIOECONOMIC LEVELS. THE FOLLOWING CONCLUSIONS WERE DRAWN FROM THE COMPARATIVE AND INTERCORRELATIONAL ANALYSES: (1) A MEANINGFUL PROPORTION OF THE VARIANCE IN STANFORD-BINET PERFORMANCE IS RELATED TO PERFORMANCE ON THE "IMPULSIVITY MEASURES" AND SUGGESTS THAT IMPULSIVITY HAS DELETERIOUS EFFECTS ON CHILDREN DESPITE THE DEGREE OF THEIR COGNITIVE ABILITY; (2) FINDINGS WITH DRAW-A-LINE AND WALK-A-LINE INDICATE NO RELATIONSHIP BETWEEN "FAST" CONDITION AND THE STANFORD-BINET SCORE; (3) INCREASES IN PERCENT WORK RESPONSES ARE NOT ESPECIALLY RELATED TO INCREASES IN STANFORD-BINET SCORES; AND (4) TEACHERS' PERCEPTIONS OF CHILDREN'S SOCIAL ADAPTIVENESS IS POSITIVELY CORRELATED WITH INTELLIGENCE. FURTHER ANALYSES WILL BE REPORTED LATER. FUTURE RESEARCH SHOULD CONCENTRATE ON IDENTIFYING DIMENSIONS OF VARIABILITY AND THEN CONCENTRATE ON VARIATIONS IN PROGRAMING FOR INDIVIDUAL CHILDREN. (DO)

ED026143 PS001536
EVALUATION OF THE PRESCHOOL PROGRAM, 1966-67, FUNDED UNDER ESEA TITLE I, P.L. 89-10. IRELAND, VERA M.; COX, FRANCES M., FEB 68 28P.
EDRS PRICE MF-$0.65 HC-$3.29

THIS PROJECT WAS FUNDED UNDER TITLE I OF THE ELEMENTARY AND SECONDARY EDUCATION ACT. THE PROJECT'S OBJECTIVES INCLUDED (1) PROVIDING EXPERIENCES FOR 4-YEAR-OLD CHILDREN FROM FAMILIES IN LOW SOCIOECONOMIC AREAS THAT WOULD PREPARE THE CHILDREN TO COPE ADEQUATELY WITH THE REGULAR SCHOOL PROGRAM; (2) DEVELOPING A "FRAMEWORK AND CURRICULUM OBJECTIVES OUTLINE FOR PREKINDERGARTEN"; AND (3) PROVIDING TRAINING AND CONSULTATIVE ASSISTANCE TO PRESCHOOL TEACHERS. FOR THE PURPOSES OF THIS PROJECT, THE 4-YEAR-OLDS WERE ORGANIZED INTO UNITS OF 20, EACH UNIT HAVING A LEAD TEACHER, A TEACHER ASSISTANT, AND A TEACHER AID. PRESCHOOL SPECIALISTS WORKED WITH THESE TEACHERS. IN ORDER TO MEASURE THE EFFECTIVENESS OF THE PRESCHOOL PROGRAM, THE PERFORMANCES OF THE PREKINDERGARTEN CHILDREN ON VARIOUS TESTS WERE COMPARED TO THE PERFORMANCE OF TITLE I AND NON-TITLE I KINDERGARTEN CHILDREN. THE RESULTS OF THE TESTING AND COMPARISON SHOWED THAT THE PREKINDERGARTEN CHILDREN IMPROVED SIGNIFICANTLY IN COGNITIVE AREAS AND LANGUAGE PERFORMANCE, AND EVEN FREQUENTLY THEY COMPARED FAVORABLY IN PERFORMANCE TO THE KINDERGARTEN CHILDREN. (WD)

ED026144 PS001537
A CURRICULUM OF TRAINING FOR PARENT PARTICIPATION IN PROJECT HEAD START. , 67 132P.
EDRS PRICE MF-$0.65 HC-$6.58

THIS DOCUMENT IS BASED ON THE THEORY THAT THE ULTIMATE SUCCESS OF THE HEAD START PROGRAM IN SIGNIFICANTLY CORRECTING THE EDUCATIONAL DISABILITIES OF CULTURALLY DEPRIVED CHILDREN DEPENDS ON INVOLVING AND EDUCATING THE PARENTS. THIS METHOD WOULD AT LEAST IMPROVE THE IMMEDIATE FAMILY ENVIRONMENT OF THE DEPRIVED CHILD. THIS DOCUMENT THEREFORE SETS OUT A CURRICULUM OF TRAINING FOR THOSE WHO INTEND TO TRAIN PARENTS TO PARTICIPATE IN HEAD START. THE CURRICULUM EMBODIES THE CONTENT AREAS, METHODOLOGY, TECHNIQUES, AND SKILLS THE TRAINER WILL NEED AND USE IN SUBSEQUENT PARENT INVOLVEMENT SESSIONS. NINE MAJOR TOPICAL AREAS ARE DISCUSSED IN THIS CURRICULUM GUIDE: (1) THE IMPACT OF POVERTY ON FAMILY LIFE, (2) TEAMWORK FOR EFFECTIVE PARENT PARTICIPATION, (3) SUPERVISION, (4) RECRUITMENT OF PARENTS, (5) WORK WITH GROUPS, (6) INVOLVEMENT OF THE INDIVIDUAL PARENT, (7) COMMUNITY ASSESSMENT, (8) COMMUNITY ACTION, AND (9) DEVELOPMENT AND IMPLEMENTATION OF TRAINING PROGRAMS FOR PARENT PARTICIPATION. (WD)

ED026145 PS001539
FEDERAL INTERAGENCY DAY CARE REQUIREMENTS, PURSUANT TO SEC. 522 (D) OF THE ECONOMIC OPPORTUNITY ACT. , 23 SEP 68 25P.
EDRS PRICE MF-$0.65 HC-$3.29

THIS DOCUMENT DEFINES FEDERAL INTERAGENCY REQUIREMENTS WHICH DAY CARE PROGRAMS MUST MEET IF THEY ARE RECEIVING FUNDS UNDER ANY OF THE FOLLOWING PROGRAMS: TITLE IV (PARTS A AND B) OF THE SOCIAL SECURITY ACT; TITLE I, TITLE II, TITLE III (PART B), AND TITLE V (PART B) OF THE ECONOMIC OPPORTUNITY ACT; THE MANPOWER DEVELOPMENT AND TRAINING ACT; AND TITLE I OF THE ELEMENTARY AND SECONDARY EDUCATION ACT. COMPREHENSIVE AND COORDINATED SERVICES, WHOSE REQUIREMENTS ARE CLARIFIED, ARE DIVIDED INTO NINE SECTIONS: (1) DAY CARE FACILITIES, (2) ENVIRONMENTAL STANDARDS, (3) EDUCATIONAL SERVICES, (4) SOCIAL SERVICES, (5) HEALTH AND NUTRITION SERVICES, (6) TRAINING OF STAFF, (7) PARENT INVOLVEMENT, (8) ADMINISTRATION AND COORDINATION, AND (9) EVALUATION. (DO)

ED026146 PS001541
SCIENCE ADVENTURES IN CHILDREN'S PLAY. RIEGER, EDYTHE, 68 50P.
DOCUMENT NOT AVAILABLE FROM EDRS.
AVAILABLE FROM: THE PLAY SCHOOLS ASSOCIATION, INC., 120 WEST 57 STREET, NEW YORK, N.Y. 10019.

THE STATED PURPOSE OF THIS PAMPHLET IS TO SUGGEST SIMPLE, NATURAL, INTERESTING EXPERIENCES IN CHILDREN'S PLAY THAT HAVE SCIENCE IMPLICATIONS. IT TELLS HOW THE TEACHER MAY CAPITALIZE ON THE INNATE CURIOSITY OF CHILDREN BY INCORPORATING SCIENCE DISCOVERY IN DAILY CLASSROOM EXPERIENCES. THIS HOW-TO-DO-IT MANUAL DIRECTS MAP-MAKING AND ACTIVITIES FOR DEVELOPING KNOWLEDGE OF TREES, BIRDS, ROCKS, MINERALS, AND SOIL. A CHAPTER ON SHADOWS AND WEATHER CONTAINS SEVEN ACTIVITIES TO STIMULATE LEARNING. OTHER CHAPTERS DEAL WITH INSECTS, FISH, PLANTS, AND ANIMALS. THEY INCLUDE NOT ONLY SUGGESTIONS FOR RELATED ACTIVITIES, BUT INSTRUCTIONS FOR THEIR FRUITION. THE PAMPHLET IS ADDRESSED TO ELEMENTARY TEACHERS AND CONTAINS A BIBLIOGRAPHY. (DO)

ED026147 PS001553
TEACHING SAFETY IN THE ELEMENTARY SCHOOL. YOST, CHARLES PETER, 62 35P.
EDRS PRICE MF-$0.65 HC NOT AVAILABLE FROM EDRS.
AVAILABLE FROM: NATIONAL EDUCATION ASSOCIATION, 1201 SIXTEENTH ST., N.W., WASHINGTON, D.C. 20036 ($0.75).

THIS TEACHING MANUAL IS DIVIDED INTO FOUR SECTIONS: (1) GENERAL SAFETY INFORMATION FOR TEACHERS, (2) SPECIAL PROBLEMS IN TEACHING SAFETY, (3) LEARNING EXPERIENCES FOR FIRST THROUGH THIRD GRADES AND FOURTH THROUGH SIXTH GRADES AND (4) SELECTED SOURCES OF INFORMATION AND SAFETY TEACHING AIDS. SUBJECTS INCLUDE DEFINITION AND CAUSES OF ACCIDENTS, ACCIDENT PREVENTION, SAFETY TASKS OF THE TEACHER, ACCIDENT REPORTING, METHODS FOR TEACHING SAFETY, WHAT TO TEACH AND WHEN, AND SPECIAL PROBLEMS. (DO)

ED026148 PS001554
TEACHING NUTRITION IN THE ELEMENTARY SCHOOL. BANKS, MARY ALICE; DUNHAM, MARGARET A., 59 35P.
EDRS PRICE MF-$0.65 HC NOT AVAILABLE FROM EDRS.
AVAILABLE FROM: NATIONAL EDUCATION ASSOCIATION, 1201 SIXTEENTH STREET, N.W., WASHINGTON, D.C. 20036 ($0.75).

THIS TEACHING MANUAL IS DIVIDED INTO THREE SECTIONS: (1) BASIC INFORMATION ON NUTRITION FOR TEACHERS, (2) ACTIVITIES FOR LEARNING ABOUT NUTRITION, SUITABLE FOR FIRST THROUGH THIRD GRADES AND FOURTH THROUGH SIXTH, AND (3) SOURCES OF TEACHING AIDS AND INFORMATION ON NUTRITION. SUBJECTS INCLUDE THE FOUR FOOD GROUPS, NUTRIENTS AND PRINCIPAL FOOD SOURCES, PLANNING MEALS, SNACKS, GOOD EATING HABITS, AND THE IMPORTANT FOOD NEEDS OF CHILDREN. (DO)

ED026149 PS001578
A LONGITUDINAL INVESTIGATION OF CHANGE IN THE FACTORIAL COMPOSITION OF INTELLIGENCE WITH AGE IN YOUNG SCHOOL CHILDREN. OSBORNE, R. TRAVIS; LINDSEY, JAMES M., 2 APR 65 7P.
EDRS PRICE MF-$0.65 HC-$3.29

A TOTAL OF 125 WHITE CHILDREN FROM THREE COUNTIES IN GEORGIA (SELECTED AS REPRESENTATIVE OF SMALL RURAL AND MEDIUM AND LARGE INDUSTRIAL URBAN POPULATIONS) WERE ADMINISTERED A BATTERY OF TESTS IN THREE PHASES OF THEIR SCHOOLING: (1) DURING THE SUMMER PRECEDING THEIR ADMISSION TO THE FIRST GRADE, (2) NEAR THE END OF THE FIRST GRADE, AND (3) NEAR THE END OF THE THIRD GRADE. THE TWO OBJECTIVES OF THIS LONGITUDINAL TESTING WERE TO DESCRIBE THE FACTORIAL ORGANIZATION OF INTELLIGENCE AT THE AGE LEVELS TESTED AND TO OBSERVE CHANGES IN THIS ORGANIZATION AS THEY OCCURRED WHEN THE SAME SUBJECTS WERE MEASURED REPEATEDLY. THE TEST BATTERY INCLUDED THE WECHSLER INTELLIGENCE SCALE FOR CHILDREN, THE PEABODY PICTURE VOCABULARY TEST, AND THE AMMONS FULL RANGE PICTURE VOCABULARY TEST. TWELVE FACTORS WERE DISCOVERED, OVERALL. THE OVERLAPPING APPEARANCE OF SOME FACTORS IN TWO OR MORE PHASES CONFIRMED THE IDEA OF THE EXISTENCE OF STABLE MENTAL FACTORS AT THE PRESCHOOL LEVEL. IDENTIFICATION OF TWO EMERGENT FACTORS SUPPORTED THE IDEA THAT INTELLIGENCE TENDS TO DIFFERENTIATE WITH INCREASING AGE AND EXPERIENCE. (WD)

ED027057 PS001361
COGNITIVE GROWTH IN PRESCHOOL CHILDREN. MELTON, RICHARD S.; AND OTHERS, JUN 68 115P.
EDRS PRICE MF-$0.65 HC-$6.58

THE PAPERS IN THIS DOCUMENT REPRESENT PRELIMINARY RESULTS OF A STUDY WHICH IS PART OF A 3-YEAR PROJECT BEING CONDUCTED BY THE EDUCATIONAL TESTING SERVICE IN COOPERATION WITH THE NEW YORK CITY BOARD OF EDUCATION, WITH SUPPORT FROM THE CARNEGIE CORPORATION OF NEW YORK. THIS DOCUMENT IS DIVIDED INTO SEVEN SECTIONS: (1) INTRODUCTION, (2) CLASSIFICATION SKILLS, (3) TIME SEQUENCE TASK, (4) PRESCHOOL CHILDREN'S UNDERSTANDING OF THE COORDINATED CONCEPTS OF DISTANCE, MOVEMENT, NUMBER, AND TIME, (5) A STUDY OF NUMBER CONSERVATION IN YOUNG CHILDREN, UNDER TWO MATERIALS CONDITIONS, (6) CHILDREN'S UNDERSTANDING OF BASIC LANGUAGE STRUCTURE, AND (7) DISCUSSION: COGNITIVE GROWTH IN PRESCHOOL CHILDREN. A BIBLIOGRAPHY IS INCLUDED AT THE END OF EACH SECTION. (WD)

ED027058 PS001371
FURTHER EVIDENCE ON THE RELATION BETWEEN AGE OF SEPARATION AND SIMILARITY IN IQ AMONG PAIRS OF SEPARATED IDENTICAL TWINS. VANDENBERG, STEVEN G.; JOHNSON, RONALD C., APR 66 10P.
EDRS PRICE MF-$0.65 HC-$3.29

RONALD C. JOHNSON ARGUED THAT IF EARLY ENVIRONMENTAL STIMULATION OR DEPRIVATION HAS A SIGNIFICANT EFFECT ON INTELLECTUAL ABILITY, THEN INDIVIDUALS WHO ARE GENETICALLY IDENTICAL AND WHO ARE EXPOSED TO A COMMON EARLY ENVIRONMENT SHOULD RESEMBLE ONE ANOTHER MORE CLOSELY IN IQ THAN SIMILAR INDIVIDUALS WHO HAVE NOT SHARED A COMMON ENVIRONMENT. JOHNSON COMPARED THE IQ'S OF 23 PAIRS OF TWINS SEPARATED AT DIFFERENT TIMES. HE FOUND THAT TWINS WHO WERE SEPARATED AFTER THEY WERE 1 YEAR OLD RESEMBLED ONE ANOTHER SIGNIFICANTLY LESS CLOSELY THAN EARLY SEPARATED TWINS. A DANISH STUDY OF 12 PAIRS OF JUEL-NIELSEN (1962) SUPPORTED THIS RESULT. A STUDY BY SHIELDS IN 1962 FOUND NO SIGNIFICANT DIFFERENCE IN THE SCORES OF 48 PAIRS OF TWINS ON (1) RAVEN'S DOMINOES INTELLIGENCE TEST AND (2) THE SYNONYMS PART OF THE MILL HILL VOCABULARY SCALE, REGARDLESS OF THE AGE OF THE PAIR OF SEPARATION. (WD)

ED027059 PS001376
HOW TO USE ERIC. REVISED EDITION. GRIFFIN, LOUISE, JAN 69 24P.
EDRS PRICE MF-$0.65 HC-$3.29
AVAILABLE FROM: ERIC CLEARINGHOUSE ON EARLY CHILDHOOD EDUCATION, 805 WEST PENNSYLVANIA AVENUE, URBANA, ILLINOIS 61801 ($0.25).

THIS BOOKLET DEFINES THE ERIC SYSTEM AND GIVES DIRECTIONS ON THE USE OF "RESEARCH IN EDUCATION." IT ALSO TELLS ABOUT THE ERIC DOCUMENT REPRODUCTION SERVICE (EDRS), ITS USE, AND ITS PRODUCTS. IN ADDITION, IT TELLS WHAT TYPES OF MATERIALS ERIC CLEARINGHOUSES PROCESS. A LIST OF THE 19 CLEARINGHOUSES, WITH A DESCRIPTION OF THEIR SPECIFIC INTERESTS AND SERVICES IS INCLUDED. A LIST OF ERIC AND U. S. OFFICE OF EDUCATION PRODUCTIONS IS APPENDED ALONG WITH DIRECTIONS AND FORMS FOR ORDERING THEM. (JS)

ED027060 PS001391
AN INVESTIGATION OF SIMILARITIES IN PARENT-CHILD TEST SCORES FOR EVIDENCE OF HEREDITARY COMPONENTS. STAFFORD, RICHARD E., APR 63 150P.
EDRS PRICE MF-$0.65 HC-$6.58

THIS STUDY ON PSYCHOLOGICAL TRAITS EXAMINES THREE HYPOTHESES: (1) THERE IS A SIMILARITY BETWEEN PARENTS AND THEIR CHILDREN UNEXPLAINED BY A SIMILARITY BETWEEN THE PARENTS, (2) THIS SIMILARITY MAY BE EXPLAINED BY HEREDITARY COMPONENTS, AND (3) THESE HEREDITARY COMPONENTS ARE OF THE DISCRETE OR SEGREGATED TYPE OF INHERITANCE. THERE WERE 104 FAMILIES SELECTED. INCLUDED IN THE STUDY WERE THE FATHERS, THE MOTHERS, AND 58 TEENAGE SONS, AND 72 TEENAGE DAUGHTERS. THEY WERE GIVEN EIGHT PSYCHOLOGICAL TESTS. IN THE 58 TESTS OF THE FIRST HYPOTHESIS, WORD ASSOCIATION WAS THE ONLY VARIABLE WHICH DID NOT SHOW SIGNIFICANT SIMILARITY BETWEEN PARENT AND CHILD. IN REGARD TO THE LAST PART OF THE HYPOTHESIS, ENGLISH VOCABULARY AND HEIGHT WERE THE ONLY FACTORS WHICH SHOWED A SIGNIFICANT CORRELATION BETWEEN FATHER AND MOTHER. THE SECOND HYPOTHESIS WAS ACCEPTED BECAUSE SPATIAL VISUALIZATION AND REASONING ABILITY SHOWED A UNIQUE FAMILY CORRELATION PATTERN. IN THE THIRD HYPOTHESIS, ONLY PERCEPTUAL SPEED AND MUSICAL APTITUDE CLEARLY FULFILLED THE REQUIREMENT THAT THE BEST FITS TO THE AUTOSOMAL GENETIC MODEL WERE APPROXIMATELY SAME PERCENTAGES FOR THE FATHER-SON DISTRIBUTION OF SCORES AS THEY WERE FOR THE MOTHER-DAUGHTER SCORES. INDUCTIVE REASONING SHOWED A POSSIBILITY OF HAVING AN UNDERLYING DICHOTOMY, BUT NONE OF THE REMAINING VARIABLES SHOWED ANY EVIDENCE OF UNDERLYING DICHOTOMY FOR BOTH FATHER-SON AND MOTHER-DAUGHTER DISTRIBUTION.S (DO)

ED027061 PS001393
SOCIAL STUDIES EDUCATION: THE ELEMENTARY SCHOOL. JAROLIMEK, JOHN, ED., 67 71P.
EDRS PRICE MF-$0.65 HC NOT AVAILABLE FROM EDRS.
AVAILABLE FROM: NATIONAL EDUCATION ASSOCIATION, 1201 SIXTEENTH STREET, N.W., WASHINGTON, D.C. 20036 ($1.50).

A COLLECTION OF REPRINTED ARTICLES, THIS DOCUMENT EXAMINES CONCEPTS, VALUES, SKILLS, AND INDIVIDUALIZING INSTRUCTION IN ELEMENTARY SOCIAL STUDIES EDUCATION. THE SUBJECTS OF THE ARTICLES AND THEIR AUTHORS ARE AS FOLLOWS: (1) CONCEPTUAL APPROACHES, JOHN JAROLIMEK, (2) INTRODUCING SOCIAL STUDIES CONCEPTS, MELVIN ARNOFF, (3) PROBLEMS IN DEVELOPING SOCIAL STUDIES CONCEPTS, AGNES M. S. INN, (4) USING LEARNING RESOURCES IN CONCEPT DEVELOPMENT, LLOYD KENDALL, (5) CONCEPT-BASED CURRICULA, FRANCIS PETER HUNKINS, (6) VALUES, WILLIAM R. FIELDER, (7) VALUES AND THE PRIMARY SCHOOL TEACHER, BERNICE J. WOLFSON, (8) VALUE TEACHING IN THE MIDDLE AND UPPER GRADES, MELVIN EZER, (9) USING LEARNING RESOURCES IN TEACHING VALUES, GERALD M. TORKELSON, (10) VALUES COMPONENT, NANCY W. BAUER, (11) THE ROLE OF SKILLS, HELEN MCCRACKEN CARPENTER, (12) SKILLS TEACHING, O. L. DAVIS, JR. (14) USING LEARNING RESOURCES, CLARENCE O. BERGESON, (15) SKILLS IN THE ELEMENTARY SCHOOL SOCIAL STUDIES CURRICULUM, CLIFFORD D. FOSTER, (16) THE INDIVIDUAL AND THE SOCIAL STUDIES, VINCENT R. ROGERS, (17) INDIVIDUALIZING INSTRUCTION, LORRAINE D. PETERSON, (18) PROVIDING FOR INDIVIDUAL DIFFERENCES, W. LINWOOD CHASE, (19) LEARNING RESOURCES FOR INDIVIDUALIZING INSTRUCTION, HUBER M. WALSH, (20) CURRICULUM PROVISIONS FOR INDIVIDUAL DIFFERENCES, ROBERT GROESCHELL. (JS)

ED027062 PS001500
ADMINISTRATION MANUAL FOR THE INVENTORY OF SOCIALIZATION OF BILINGUAL CHILDREN AGES THREE TO TEN. PART OF THE FINAL REPORT. CERVENKA, EDWARD JOHN, AUG 68 75P.
EDRS PRICE MF-$0.65 HC-$3.29

THIS BATTERY OF TEST INSTRUMENTS IS ONE OF A SET OF THREE DEVELOPED FOR USE IN THE STUDY OF BILINGUAL (ENGLISH-SPANISH) INSTRUCTION PROGRAMS AND OTHER COMPENSATORY PROGRAMS IN TEXAS. THE SOCIALIZATION INVENTORY HAS BEEN BASED ON A SOCIOLOGICAL VIEW OF PERSONALITY AS A DEVELOPING AND CHANGING ENTITY. FOUR SUBMEASURES OF SOCIALIZATION ARE INCLUDED IN THIS MANUAL: (1) A MEASURE OF SELF-CONCEPT INDIVIDUALLY ADMINISTERED FOR PRESCHOOLERS OR GROUP-ADMINISTERED FOR SCHOOL-AGE CHILDREN, (2) A BEHAVIOR RATING SCALE OF A CHILD'S INTERPERSONAL BEHAVIOR IN AN INTERVIEW WITH THE TEST ADMINISTRATOR, (3) A BEHAVIOR RATING SCALE OF A CHILD'S GENERAL SOCIAL BEHAVIOR IN THE CLASSROOM, AND (4) A QUESTIONNAIRE GIVEN TO PARENTS OF CHILDREN IN THE BILINGUAL PROGRAMS. DIRECTIONS FOR ADMINISTERING AND RATING EACH MEASURE ARE GIVEN. SAMPLES OF THE SOCIALIZATION MEASURES AND THEIR RATING SHEETS FORM THE BULK OF THIS REPORT. (MS)

ED027063 PS001501
ADMINISTRATION MANUAL FOR TESTS OF BASIC LANGUAGE COMPETENCE IN ENGLISH AND SPANISH. LEVEL I (PRESCHOOL) CERVENKA, EDWARD JOHN, AUG 68 146P.
EDRS PRICE MF-$0.65 HC-$6.58

THIS BATTERY OF TEST INSTRUMENTS IS ONE OF A SET OF THREE DEVELOPED FOR USE IN THE STUDY OF BILINGUAL (ENGLISH-SPANISH) INSTRUCTION PROGRAMS AND OTHER COMPENSATORY PROGRAMS IN TEXAS. THE TESTS ARE TO BE INDIVIDUALLY ADMINISTERED AND ARE DESIGNED TO MEASURE CHILDREN'S BASIC LANGUAGE COMPETENCE VIA THE PERCEPTUAL AND MOTOR SIDES OF LINGUISTIC AND COMMUNICATIVE PHENOMENA. IN THIS MANUAL, GUIDELINES FOR THE SELECTION AND TRAINING OF TEST ADMINISTRATORS SUGGEST DESIRABLE PROFESSIONAL AND PERSONALITY QUALIFICATIONS. THE IMPORTANCE OF A TRIAL TESTING PERIOD IS STRESSED. GENERAL DIRECTIONS ARE GIVEN FOR ESTABLISHING RAPPORT WITH THE CHILD TO BE TESTED AND FOR GIVING APPROPRIATE RESPONSES TO THE CHILD DURING TESTING. FORMS A AND B OF THE TESTS IN BOTH LANGUAGE VERSIONS ARE INCLUDED. SAMPLES IN THE APPENDIX INCLUDE PICTURES FOR THE ORAL VOCABULARY TESTS, THE SCORING SHEET FOR SUBTESTS, AND THE RATING SHEET OF THE CHILD'S INTERPERSONAL BEHAVIOR IN AN INTERVIEW WITH THE TEST ADMINISTRATOR. (MS)

ED027064 PS001502
ADMINISTRATION MANUAL FOR TESTS OF BASIC LANGUAGE COMPETENCE IN ENGLISH AND SPANISH. LEVEL II (PRIMARY GRADES): CHILDREN AGES SIX TO TEN, ENGLISH AND SPANISH VERSIONS, FORMS A AND B. PART OF THE FINAL REPORT. CERVENKA, EDWARD JOHN, AUG 68 112P.
EDRS PRICE MF-$0.65 HC-$6.58

THIS BATTERY OF TEST INSTRUMENTS IS ONE OF A SET OF THREE DEVELOPED FOR USE IN THE STUDY OF BILINGUAL (ENGLISH-SPANISH) INSTRUCTION AND OTHER COMPENSATORY EDUCATION PROGRAMS IN TEXAS. THESE TESTS ARE DESIGNED TO MEASURE CHILDREN'S BASIC COMPETENCE IN A LANGUAGE VIA THEIR PERCEPTION OF LINGUISTIC PHENOMENA. THE LEVEL II BATTERY IS GROUP-ADMINISTERED FOR CHILDREN AGED SIX TO TEN OR IN PRIMARY GRADES ONE TO FOUR. INCLUDED IN THIS MANUAL ARE GENERAL INSTRUCTIONS FOR THE TEST

ADMINISTRATOR. THEY WERE DESIGNED TO HELP DIMINISH THE INFLUENCE OF EXTRANEOUS FACTORS IN THE TESTING SITUATION AND TO OBTAIN COMPARABLE RESULTS FROM ONE SITUATION TO ANOTHER. THE TESTS AND SAMPLE ANSWER SHEETS FORM THE BULK OF THIS REPORT. (MS)

ED027065 PS001504
DAY CARE AS A SOCIAL INSTRUMENT: A POLICY PAPER. MAYER, ANNA B., JAN 65 182P.
EDRS PRICE MF-$0.65 HC-$6.58

THIS REPORT IS AN ANALYSIS OF THE PROBLEMS FACING URBAN AREAS IN RELATION TO THEIR PRESCHOOL PROGRAMS FOR THE DISADVANTAGED. THE MAIN FOCUS IS NEW YORK CITY DAY CARE CENTERS. SUBJECTS INCLUDE DAY CARE AND PRESCHOOL EDUCATION, HISTORY OF THE ORIGIN AND EXPANSION OF DAY CARE CENTERS, NEW YORK CITY'S DAY CARE, AND EDUCATIONAL ISSUES ENCOMPASSING LEGISLATIVE PROPOSALS, SECTARIANISM, AND RELIGIOUS ISSUES. CHAPTER VI RELATES TO NATIONAL PROBLEMS AND DISCUSSES VARIOUS STATES' SOLUTIONS. THE FOLLOWING SUBJECTS ARE ALSO DISCUSSED: THE INTERPRETATIONS OF DAY CARE'S RESPONSIBILITY, THE VALIDITY OF ITS SOLUTIONS, NEW AGENCIES WITH RELATED FUNCTIONS, NEW FEDERAL LEGISLATION, AND NEW THEORIES OF EDUCATION AND CHILD DEVELOPMENT. THE REPORT ENDS WITH A PROPOSAL FOR THE BEGINNERS' DAY SCHOOL. (DO)

ED027066 PS001525
THE EFFECTS OF TEACHER IN-SERVICE EDUCATION ON THE DEVELOPMENT OF ART IDEAS WITH SIX-YEAR OLD CULTURALLY DEPRIVED CHILDREN. FINAL REPORT. SCHWARTZ, JULIA B.; DOUGLAS, NANCY J., DEC 67 73P.
EDRS PRICE MF-$0.65 HC-$3.29

THE PURPOSE OF THIS STUDY WAS TO DETERMINE (1) WHAT EFFECTS A TEACHER WHO WAS HELPED TO UNDERSTAND BASIC ART IDEAS WOULD HAVE ON THE DEVELOPMENT OF THESE IDEAS IN CULTURALLY DEPRIVED 6-YEAR-OLDS, AS EXPRESSED IN THEIR VERBAL LANGUAGE AND IN THEIR ART PRODUCTS IN CLAY, AND (2) WHETHER OR NOT THERE WOULD BE A DIFFERENCE IN THE DEVELOPMENT OF THESE IDEAS IN NEGRO AND WHITE CHILDREN AND THEIR TEACHERS. SUBJECTS WERE 110 CHILDREN AND FOUR TEACHERS. THERE WERE FOUR GROUPS: WHITE CONTROL, WHITE EXPERIMENTAL, NEGRO CONTROL, AND NEGRO EXPERIMENTAL. EXPERIMENTAL TEACHERS WERE INSTRUCTED IN FOUR BASIC ART CRITERIA FOR VISUAL MATERIALS: (1) WHAT IT WAS, (2) WHO DID IT, (3) HOW HE DID IT, AND (4) WHETHER HE COULD DO IT WITH ANOTHER MATERIAL. SEVEN SHARING SESSIONS WERE TAPED AND RATED. THE EXPERIMENTAL GROUPS EXCEEDED THE CONTROL GROUPS IN VERBALIZATION ON ALL CRITERIA AND FOR ALL SESSIONS. THE WHITE GROUPS EXCEEDED THE NEGRO GROUPS ON ALL SESSIONS AND ON ALL CRITERIA. IN THE CLAY PRODUCTS CLASS, SIGNIFICANT DIFFERENCES AT THE .01 LEVEL IN FAVOR OF THE LAST SESSION OVER THE FIRST WERE FOUND FOR THE EXPERIMENTAL GROUPS AND FOR THE WHITE GROUPS; NO SIGNIFICANT DIFFERENCE AT THE .05 LEVEL WAS FOUND FOR THE CONTROL GROUPS OR THE NEGRO GROUPS. (DO)

ED027067 PS001526
LEARNING TO READ THROUGH EXPERIENCE. SECOND EDITION. LEE, DORRIS M.; ALLEN, R. V., 63 154P.
DOCUMENT NOT AVAILABLE FROM EDRS.
AVAILABLE FROM: MEREDITH PUBLISHING COMPANY, 440 PARK AVENUE SOUTH, NEW YORK, NEW YORK 10016 (PAPER $1.95).

THIS BOOK DISCUSSES A PLAN FOR "LEARNING TO READ THROUGH EXPERIENCE." IT IS A PLAN FOR DEVELOPING READING ABILITY AS AN INTEGRAL PART OF THE DEVELOPMENT OF ALL THE COMMUNICATION SKILLS. IT IS INTENDED TO BUILD ON AND TO CONTINUE TO PROVIDE INDIVIDUAL EXPERIENCES FOR EACH CHILD WHILE INCREASING THE COMMON GROUP EXPERIENCES. ALTHOUGH THE PLAN FOCUSES ON LEARNING TO READ THROUGH EXPERIENCE, THE BOOK DEALS WITH THE LANGUAGE ARTS, READING, LISTENING, SPEAKING, AND WRITING AS FACTORS WHICH CONTRIBUTE TO READING DEVELOPMENT. FIVE CHAPTERS COMPRISE THE TEXT OF THE BOOK: (1) READING AS COMMUNICATION, (2) GAUGING A CHILD'S DEVELOPMENT, (3) LANGUAGE EXPERIENCES IN READING DEVELOPMENT, (4) A GOOD LEARNING ENVIRONMENT, AND (5) GROUP AND INDIVIDUAL ACTIVITIES. APPENDIXES ARE AS FOLLOWS: (A) BASIC WORD LIST, (B) RELATIONSHIP OF COMMUNICATION SKILLS, (C) OBSERVATION CHART, AND (D) TESTS. (WD)

ED027068 PS001528
THE THOMAS SELF-CONCEPT VALUES TEST. THOMAS, WALTER L., JUN 67 44P.
DOCUMENT NOT AVAILABLE FROM EDRS.
AVAILABLE FROM: EDUCATIONAL SERVICE COMPANY, P. O. BOX 1882, GRAND RAPIDS, MICHIGAN 49501.

A TEST WAS DEVELOPED TO ASSESS PERSONAL SELF-CONCEPT VALUES OF PREPRIMARY AND PRIMARY AGED CHILDREN. IF LARGE SCALE PRESCHOOL PROGRAMS ARE TO BE JUSTIFIED, EFFECTS IN THE AREAS OF INTELLECTUAL GROWTH, ACHIEVEMENT PERFORMANCE, AND PERSONAL-SOCIAL GROWTH MUST BE OBSERVABLE IN CHILDREN SEVERAL YEARS AFTER PRESCHOOL EXPERIENCE AND MUST BE MEASURABLE BY STANDARDIZED METHODS. SINCE THE SELF-CONCEPT IS RELATED TO FUTURE ASPIRATIONS AND ACADEMIC ACHIEVEMENT, VALUE TRAINING APPEARS TO BE AN IMPORTANT OUTCOME OF PRESCHOOL EDUCATION. THE FOURTEEN VALUE FACTORS INCLUDED IN THIS INSTRUMENT ARE HAPPINESS, CLEANLINESS, SOCIABILITY, SHARING, ABILITY, MALE ACCEPTANCE, FEAR OF THINGS, FEAR OF PEOPLE, STRENGTH, SIZE, HEALTH, ATTRACTIVENESS, MATERIAL (DESIRE FOR THINGS), AND INDEPENDENCE. EACH CHILD TESTED IS ASKED TO RESPOND TO A SET OF ITEMS WHICH INDICATE HOW HE FEELS HIS MOTHER (OR TEACHER OR PEERS) VIEWS HIM. A FOURTH SET OF ITEMS ASKS HOW HE PERCEIVES HIMSELF. A POLAROID PRINT OF THE CHILD HELPS HIM TO GAIN OBJECTIVITY AS HE THINKS OF HIMSELF IN RELATION TO ANOTHER'S PERCEPTION OF HIM. ADMINISTRATION AND SCORING INSTRUCTIONS, NORMING DATA, AND CONVERSION TABLES, AS WELL AS A COMPREHENSIVE BIBLIOGRAPHY, ARE INCLUDED IN THIS REPORT. (MS)

ED027069 PS001540
COGNITIVE FACTORS IN SEMANTIC CONDITIONING. A THESIS IN EDUCATIONAL PSYCHOLOGY. WALLS, RICHARD T., DEC 68 143P.
EDRS PRICE MF-$0.65 HC-$6.58

ONE CONTROL GROUP AND EIGHT EXPERIMENTAL GROUPS, EACH COMPOSED OF 12 FIRST GRADE CHILDREN, PARTICIPATED IN THIS EXPERIMENT. IT WAS DESIGNED TO INVESTIGATE THE EFFECTS OF FREQUENCY OF REINFORCEMENT AND REPEATED EVALUATION OF STIMULI ON THE CONDITIONING OF PREFERENCES. EACH CHILD PARTICIPATED IN THE EXPERIMENT FOR SEVEN CONSECUTIVE SCHOOL DAYS. THE EXPERIMENTAL CHILDREN WERE DIVIDED INTO TWO STIMULUS CONDITION GROUPS; ONE RECEIVED THE SAME STIMULI EACH SESSION, AND ONE RECEIVED DIFFERENT STIMULI FROM ONE SESSION TO THE NEXT. EACH OF THESE TWO GROUPS WAS ALSO DIVIDED INTO FOUR RATING GROUPS. DURING A RATING SESSION, THE CHILD WAS ASKED TO CHOOSE FROM 14 ADJECTIVES THE ONE THAT HE THOUGHT BEST DESCRIBED A PARTICULAR GREEK LETTER. A CONDITIONING SESSION CONSISTED OF A TASK INVOLVING REINFORCEMENT OF PARTICULAR GREEK LETTERS. THE OVERALL PROCEDURE ALLOWED FOR THE DETERMINATION OF ANY SUBJECT'S CHANGE IN PREFERENCE FOR CERTAIN GREEK LETTERS AS A FUNCTION OF EITHER (1) NUMBER OF EVALUATION SESSIONS OR (2) FREQUENCY OF REINFORCEMENT. IT WAS FOUND THAT BOTH FACTORS AFFECTED PREFERENCE. (WD)

ED027070 PS001542
READING. DIMENSIONS IN EARLY LEARNING SERIES. STRANG, RUTH, 68 83P.
DOCUMENT NOT AVAILABLE FROM EDRS.
AVAILABLE FROM: DIMENSIONS PUBLISHING COMPANY, SAN FAFAEL, CALIFORNIA 94903 ($2.50).

A VOLUME OF "THE DIMENSIONS IN EARLY LEARNING SERIES," THIS MONOGRAPH EXPLORES BEGINNING READING. THE INTRODUCTION DEFINES READING, AND CHAPTERS I AND II REVIEW READING DEVELOPMENT AND DISCUSS THEORY AND HIERARCHY OF READING DEVELOPMENT. HOW TO EVALUATE READING ACHIEVEMENT, WAYS TO TEACH READING, AND WHAT PARENTS CAN DO TO HELP ARE SUBJECTS CONSIDERED. AN ANNOTATED BIBLIOGRAPHY AND A LIST OF INSTRUCTIONAL MATERIALS ARE INCLUDED. (DO)

ED027071 PS001546
THE INITIAL PHASE OF A PRESCHOOL CURRICULUM DEVELOPMENT PROJECT. FINAL REPORT. HOOPER, FRANK H.; MARSHALL, WILLIAM H., AUG 68 327P.
EDRS PRICE MF-$0.65 HC-$13.16

WHILE THE PURPOSE OF THIS PROJECT WAS CURRICULUM DEVELOPMENT, LONG RANGE BENEFITS ARE CONTINGENT UPON A RADICAL REORGANIZATION AND UPGRADING OF PUBLIC SCHOOL SYSTEMS THROUGHOUT APPALACHIA. SUBJECTS IN THE PILOT ASSESSMENT CONSISTED OF 80 CHILDREN (3 1/2 TO 6 1/2 YEARS OLD) AND THEIR MOTHERS FROM EACH OF MONONGALIA AND UPSHUR COUNTIES, WEST VIRGINIA. MOTHERS WERE GIVEN A DEMOGRAPHIC CHILD-REARING PRACTICES INTERVIEW-QUESTIONNAIRE. CHILDREN WERE DIVIDED INTO TWO GROUPS AND WERE GIVEN DIFFERENT BATTERIES OF TESTS. THEIR PERFORMANCE REVEALED CULTURAL DIVERSITY RATHER THAN UNIFORM COGNITIVE-INTELLECTUAL DEFICITS. CLEAREST DEFICITS CENTERED ON VERBAL TASKS OR PROBLEM SETTINGS WHICH DEMANDED SYMBOLIC REPRESENTATION, WHICH APPEARED TO INCREASE IN SEVERITY IN DISADVANTAGED CHILDREN. SPATIAL REASONING, MEMORY FUNCTIONS, AND CONSERVATION OR LOGICAL OPERATIONS SKILLS DID NOT APPEAR IMPAIRED. A SECTION ON BEHAVIORAL OBJECTIVES FOR A PRESCHOOL CURRICULUM IS OUTLINED IN THE DOCUMENT, AND A SECTION IS DEVOTED TO A SURVEY OF REPRESENTATIVE PRESCHOOL INTERVENTION RESEARCH. AN EXTENSIVE BIBLIOGRAPHY IS APPENDED. (DO)

ED027072 PS001548
PREPRIMARY PROGRAM. 1968 REPORT. , 68 50P.
EDRS PRICE MF-$0.65 HC-$3.29

AN EVALUATION OF THE PITTSBURGH PUBLIC SCHOOLS PREPRIMARY PROGRAM FOR 2,000 DISADVANTAGED CHILDREN CONCLUDED THAT THE PROGRAM CONTRIBUTED TO THE SOCIOEMOTIONAL MATURATION OF THE CHILDREN INVOLVED BUT DID NOT AFFECT THEIR READING READINESS OR FIRST GRADE READING TEST SCORES. THIS FINDING MAY BE EXPLAINED IN PART BY A LACK OF SPECIFIC ACADEMIC ACHIEVEMENT OBJECTIVES IN THE PROGRAM DESIGN. THE EVALUATION PROCESSES ALSO SHOWED A NEED FOR A MORE DETAILED DEFINITION OF DESIRED TEACHER BEHAVIOR. EACH TEACHER WAS OBSERVED FOR 1 HOUR ON TWO SEPARATE OCCASIONS IN ACCORDANCE WITH AN OBSERVATION SCHEDULE, TO FIND OUT THE NUMBER AND KIND OF ADULT-CHILD INTERACTIONS IN HER CLASSROOM. EACH CHILD WAS RATED BY HIS TEACHER ON THE

CHILDREN'S RATING SCALE DEVELOPED IN THE PITTSBURGH PROJECT. ANALYSIS OF THE DATA LED TO THE RECOMMENDATION THAT MORE SPECIFIC GUIDELINES BE ESTABLISHED FOR CLASSROOM PERSONNEL CONCERNING THEIR DUTIES, WAYS OF REINFORCING LEARNING BEHAVIOR, USE OF INDIVIDUALIZED INSTRUCTION, AND ACADEMIC SKILL DEVELOPMENT. OVER HALF OF THIS REPORT IS MADE UP OF APPENDIXES, WHICH INCLUDE A DETAILED DESCRIPTION OF THE PRIMARY PROGRAM AND FACSIMILES OF THE RATING SCALE AND OBSERVATION SCHEDULE. (MS)

ED027073 PS001549
NATURALISTIC OBSERVATION IN THE STUDY OF PARENT-CHILD INTERACTION. BAUMRIND, DIANA, 68 20P.
EDRS PRICE MF-$0.65 HC-$3.29

THIS PROJECT INVESTIGATED PATTERNS OF PARENTAL AUTHORITY AMONG BERKELEY PRESCHOOL CHILDREN AND THE PROCESSES BY WHICH THESE PARENTS CONTRIBUTED TO THE DEVELOPMENT OF CHILDREN'S SOCIAL RESPONSIBILITY AND INDIVIDUALITY. SUBJECTS WERE 140 FAMILIES FROM CITY-SPONSORED, PRIVATE COOPERATIVE, AND UNIVERSITY-OPERATED NURSERY SCHOOLS. EIGHT CONSTRUCTS WERE DEVISED: (1) HIGH VS. LOW STRESS TOLERANCE, (2) SELF-CONFIDENT VS. FEARFUL, (3) ACHIEVEMENT-ORIENTED VS. NONACHIEVEMENT-ORIENTED, (4) APPROACH-ORIENTED VS. WITHDRAWN, (5) AUTONOMOUS VS. SUGGESTIBLE, (6) REBELLIOUS VS. DEPENDABLE, (7) DESTRUCTIVE VS. CONSTRUCTIVE, AND (8) ALIENATED VS. TRUSTING. OBSERVATION DATA ON PARENT BEHAVIOR WERE RATED ON SCALES APPROXIMATING CHILD SCALES AND SELF-REPORT PARENTAL ATTITUDES WERE COLLECTED. RESEARCH IS INCOMPLETE, BUT LABORATORY EXPERIMENTAL AND NATURALISTIC OBSERVATIONS WERE ASSESSED AND THE LATTER WAS FAVORED. IT WAS CONCLUDED THAT OBSERVATIONAL STUDIES WHICH FOCUS ON THE HUMAN PSYCHE AND HUMAN BEHAVIOR SELDOM CAN ACHIEVE SITUATIONAL CONTROL, RELIABILITY OF MEASUREMENT, OR PRECISE FORMULATION OF PROCESS VARIABLES. THEY CAN, HOWEVER, PROCEED SELF-CRITICALLY, USING STATISTICAL TESTS OF SIGNIFICANCE ON WELL-FORMULATED HYPOTHESES WHICH ARE WELL DEFINED CONCEPTUALLY AND OPERATIONALLY. (DO)

ED027074 PS001551
ANXIETY AS A FACTOR IN THE CHILD'S RESPONSIVENESS TO SOCIAL REINFORCEMENT. GROSSMAN, BRUCE D., [64] 17P.
EDRS PRICE MF-$0.65 HC-$3.29

IT HAS BEEN OBSERVED THAT FOLLOWING A BRIEF PERIOD OF ISOLATION, CHILDREN TEND TO SHOW A GREATER INCREASE IN RESPONSIVENESS ON A SIMPLE MOTOR TASK THAN NONISOLATED CHILDREN DO WHEN VERBAL REINFORCEMENT IS GIVEN PERIODICALLY DURING A TASK. ONE EXPLANATION IS THAT THE SOCIAL DEPRIVATION OF THE BRIEF ISOLATION HEIGHTENS THE MOTIVATION TO RECEIVE SOCIAL REINFORCEMENT. ANOTHER EXPLANATION IS THAT THE PHENOMENON IS ATTRIBUTABLE TO THE GENERALIZED MOTIVATIONAL PROPERTIES OF THE ANXIETY WHICH THE CONDITION OF ISOLATION AROUSES. FORTY FIRST-GRADE CHILDREN WERE GIVEN A SIMPLE MOTOR (MARBLE DROP) TASK AFTER THEIR ANXIETY LEVEL HAD BEEN MEASURED. AFTER THE CHILD BECAME FAMILIAR WITH THE TASK, PERIODIC VERBAL REINFORCEMENT WAS GIVEN AS THE CHILD PERFORMED THE TASK. AN ANALYSIS OF THE DATA SHOWED THAT RESPONSE-RATE INCREASE OVER THE TASK PERIOD (4 MINUTES) DID NOT DISTINGUISH BETWEEN HIGH AND LOW ANXIETY CHILDREN. IT WAS CONCLUDED FROM THE OVERALL FINDINGS THAT ANXIETY IN YOUNG CHILDREN IS MORE LIKELY TO OBSTRUCT THAN FACILITATE PERFORMANCE ON A SIMPLE MOTOR TASK INVOLVING PERIODIC SOCIAL REINFORCEMENT. (WD)

ED027075 PS001552
A GUIDE FOR PERCEPTUAL-MOTOR TRAINING ACTIVITIES. , 68 79P.
EDRS PRICE MF-$0.65 HC-$3.29

THIS DOCUMENT HAS BEEN PREPARED AS PART OF A KINDERGARTEN PERCEPTUAL-TRAINING PROGRAM OF THE SOUTH EUCLID-LYNDHURST CITY SCHOOL DISTRICT NEAR CLEVELAND, OHIO. THE GUIDE CONTAINS INFORMATION ON TRAINING AND PROCEDURES RELATED TO PERCEPTUAL-MOTOR LEARNING. THIS INFORMATION IS STRUCTURED PRIMARILY INTO 150 LESSON PLANS, DEVISED AS 30-MINUTE SESSIONS FOR GROUPS OF EIGHT CHILDREN. A THREE-PAGE LIST OF EQUIPMENT FOR GROSS MOTOR SKILLS IS PROVIDED, INCLUDING A DESCRIPTION OF THE EQUIPMENT ITEM, ITS SOURCE, AND ITS PRICE. PICTORIAL REPRESENTATIONS OF THE FORM PERCEPTION PATTERNS USED IN THE LESSONS ARE ALSO PRESENTED. A LIST OF ADDRESSES OF SOURCES OF EQUIPMENT AND MANUALS IS INCLUDED. (WD)

ED027076 PS001555
RESEARCH ON THE NEW NURSERY SCHOOL. PART I, A SUMMARY OF THE EVALUATION OF THE EXPERIMENTAL PROGRAM FOR DEPRIVED CHILDREN AT THE NEW NURSERY SCHOOL USING SOME EXPERIMENTAL MEASURES. INTERIM REPORT. NIMNICHT, GLEN; AND OTHERS, DEC 67 46P.
EDRS PRICE MF-$0.65 HC-$3.29

THE NEW NURSERY SCHOOL (NNS) PROGRAM WAS SET UP TO HELP 3- AND 4-YEAR-OLD, SPANISH-SURNAMED, ENVIRONMENTALLY DEPRIVED CHILDREN. THE OBJECTIVES SET WERE (1) TO IMPROVE SELF-IMAGE, (2) TO INCREASE PERCEPTUAL ACUITY, (3) TO IMPROVE LANGUAGE ABILITY, AND (4) TO IMPROVE PROBLEM-SOLVING AND CONCEPT-FORMATION SKILLS. THE SCHOOL IS ORGANIZED AS AN AUTOTELIC RESPONSIVE ENVIRONMENT WHICH THE CHILDREN ATTEND FOR 3 HOURS A DAY. THE PROGRAM HAS BEEN OPERATING FOR 3 YEARS, WITH THE NUMBER OF CHILDREN PARTICIPATING EACH YEAR BEING 30, 30, AND 50. EVALUATIONS HAVE BEEN BASED ON PRETESTS AND POSTTESTS OF NNS CHILDREN, ON COMPARISONS WITH MIDDLE CLASS CHILDREN WHO ALSO USE THE SCHOOL, AND ON COMPARISON IN KINDERGARTEN AND FIRST GRADE WITH CHILDREN FROM SIMILAR BACKGROUNDS. TESTS HAVE BEEN SELECTED OR DEVELOPED TO MEASURE PROGRAM EFFECTS. DUE TO THE SMALL SAMPLE SIZES, THE RESULTS ARE QUITE TENTATIVE. BUT THE FOLLOWING CONCLUSIONS ARE SUPPORTED FOR GRADUATES OF THE PROGRAM: (1) THE SCHOOL SEEMS TO IMPROVE THEIR SELF-IMAGE AND (2) THEIR LANGUAGE AND PERCEPTUAL DEVELOPMENT IS AHEAD OF WHAT WOULD BE EXPECTED HAD THEY NOT HAD THE PROGRAM. ONE NEGATIVE DATUM IS THAT FIRST GRADE TEACHERS DO NOT SEE ANY DIFFERENCE BETWEEN NNS AND OTHER DEPRIVED CHILDREN WHICH SUGGEST THAT THE PROGRAM EFFECTS MAY WASH OUT BY THE MIDDLE OF THE FIRST GRADE. (DR)

ED027077 PS001556
RESEARCH ON THE NEW NURSERY SCHOOL. PART II: A REPORT ON THE USE OF TYPEWRITERS AND RELATED EQUIPMENT WITH THREE- AND FOUR-YEAR-OLD CHILDREN AT THE NEW NURSERY SCHOOL. INTERIM REPORT. NIMNICHT, GLEN; AND OTHERS, DEC 67 23P.
EDRS PRICE MF-$0.65 HC-$3.29

IN AN ATTEMPT TO IMPROVE THE READINESS OF 3- AND 4-YEAR-OLD DISADVANTAGED MEXICAN-AMERICAN CHILDREN, THE NEW NURSERY SCHOOL WAS DEVELOPED IN GREELEY, COLORADO. THE ACTIVITIES ARE AUTOTELIC; THAT IS, THE CHILD DOES SOMETHING FOR ITS OWN SAKE RATHER THAN FOR THE SAKE OF OBTAINING REWARDS OR AVOIDING PUNISHMENTS THAT HAVE NO INHERENT CONNECTION WITH THE ACTIVITY ITSELF. ONE OF THE ACTIVITIES AVAILABLE IS THE TYPING BOOTH. IF THE CHILD WISHES, HE CAN PLAY WITH AN ELECTRIC TYPEWRITER. THIS ACTIVITY IS STRUCTURED TO SUBTLY LEAD THE PARTICIPANT THROUGH SEVERAL LEVELS OF ACHIEVEMENT WITH RESPECT TO LANGUAGE DEVELOPMENT: (1) FREE EXPLORATION, (2) MATCHING UPPER CASE LETTERS ON A CARD AND ON THE TYPEWRITER, (3) MATCHING UPPER AND LOWER CASE LETTERS, (4) TYPING WORDS, AND (5) DICTATING STORIES. THE CHILDREN'S PERFORMANCE ON THE TYPEWRITER AND ON SUBSEQUENT ACHIEVEMENT TESTS INDICATES THAT (1) THERE IS A RELATIONSHIP BETWEEN THE NUMBER OF TIMES THE CHILD GOES INTO THE BOOTH, THE AMOUNT OF TIME SPENT THEREIN, AND ACHIEVEMENT ON THE BOOTH ACTIVITIES, (2) THE BOOTH EXPERIENCE IS OF LITTLE VALUE TO THE 3-YEAR-OLDS, (3) CHILDREN WITH LOW IQ SCORES ARE LEAST LIKELY TO BE HIGH ACHIEVERS IN THE BOOTH, AND (4) THE CHILDREN WITH HIGH BOOTH ACHIEVEMENT WERE THE MOST BENEFITED IN LANGUAGE DEVELOPMENT. (WD)

ED027078 PS001558
CURRICULUM GUIDE FOR CHILDREN'S ACTIVITIES, PARENT PRESCHOOL PROGRAM. DEFRANCO, ELLEN, 68 58P.
EDRS PRICE MF-$0.65 HC-$3.29

THIS CURRICULUM GUIDE FOR TEACHERS WAS DEVELOPED FOR PRESCHOOL EDUCATION IN THE CHILD OBSERVATION AND PARENT-PRESCHOOL CHILD CLASSES CONDUCTED THROUGH THE PARENT EDUCATION PROGRAM, DIVISION OF ADULT EDUCATION OF LOS ANGELES CITY SCHOOLS. THE CLASSES FOR WHICH THIS CURRICULUM GUIDE IS INTENDED ARE ATTENDED BY PARENTS AND THEIR CHILDREN, AGES TWO TO FIVE. THE CONTENTS OF THE GUIDE ARE DIVIDED INTO SEVERAL SECTIONS, INCLUDING (1) SOCIAL AND EMOTIONAL OBJECTIVES, (2) EDUCATIONAL OBJECTIVES, (3) PROGRAM ORGANIZATION, (4) PRESENTATION OF MATERIALS, AND (5) THE ROLE OF MOTHERS. (WD)

ED027079 PS001559
A STUDY OF THE EFFECTS OF TEACHER ATTITUDE AND CURRICULUM STRUCTURE ON PRESCHOOL DISADVANTAGED CHILDREN. ANNUAL PROGRESS REPORT I. ERICKSON, EDSEL L.; AND OTHERS, AUG 68 62P.
EDRS PRICE MF-$0.65 HC-$3.29

THIS DOCUMENT IS THE FIRST YEAR'S REPORT OF A CONTINUING STUDY OF THE EFFECTS OF TWO HEAD START PRESCHOOL EXPERIMENTAL PROGRAMS. SUBJECTS WERE CHILDREN FROM POVERTY AREAS IN GRAND RAPIDS, MICHIGAN. SEVEN TEACHERS WHO WERE MOST OPPOSED TO A BEREITER-ENGELMANN TYPE HIGHLY ACADEMIC STRUCTURED PROGRAM WERE ASSIGNED TO GROUP I; AND SEVEN TEACHERS LEAST OPPOSED, TO GROUP II FOR TEACHER TRAINING. THREE TEACHERS FROM GROUP II AND FOUR TEACHERS FROM GROUP I WERE ASSIGNED TO CLASSES IN EXPERIMENT A (BEREITER-ENGELMANN), AND FOUR TEACHERS FROM GROUP II AND THREE FROM GROUP I TAUGHT IN EXPERIMENT B. OBSERVATION REVEALED THAT WHILE THERE WAS MORE VARIATION AMONG B CLASSES THAN AMONG A CLASSES, NO CLASSES IN B WERE SIMILAR TO CLASSES IN A, EITHER IN TERMS OF CONTENT EMPHASIS OR PREDOMINANT METHOD OF INSTRUCTION. AT THE END OF THE PROGRAM TESTS WERE ADMINISTERED TO THE CHILDREN, AND TEACHERS AND PARENTS WERE INVENTORIED. EXPERIMENT A APPEARED TO OVERCOME INITIALLY NEGATIVE TEACHER ATTITUDES. STUDENTS IN EXPERIMENT A (WITH A MEAN IQ OF 108.1) AND EXPERIMENT B (WITH A MEAN IQ OF 105.7) HAD A HIGHER MEASURED INTELLIGENCE THAN THE CONTROL GROUP (WITH A MEAN IQ OF 94.8). RESULTS WERE REPORTED AS A STATEMENT OF PROGRESS. RESEARCH ANALYSES AND KINDERGARTEN-FIRST GRADE FOLLOWTHROUGH STUDIES WILL BE MADE. (DO)

ED027080 PS001560
EVALUATION OF THE PRESCHOOL PROGRAM, 1967-68, FUNDED UNDER ESEA TITLE I, P.L. 89-10. IRELAND, VERA M.; AND OTHERS, OCT 68 38P.
EDRS PRICE MF-$0.65 HC-$3.29

A BATTERY OF COGNITIVE, PERSONAL, AND DEMOGRAPHIC TESTS WERE GIVEN TO 216 CHILDREN FROM TITLE I (OF THE ELEMENTARY AND SECONDARY EDUCATION ACT) SCHOOLS, WITH AND WITHOUT PREVIOUS SCHOOL EXPERIENCE, AND TO 31 CHILDREN FROM NON-TITLE I SCHOOLS. THE EFFECTS OF PREKINDERGARTEN EXPERIENCE UPON SUBSEQUENT SCHOOL EXPERIENCE WERE EVALUATED. THE TITLE-I SAMPLE INCLUDED 122 PREKINDERGARTNERS, 52 KINDERGARTNERS WITH PREVIOUS SCHOOL EXPERIENCE, AND 42 KINDERGARTNERS WITH NO PREVIOUS SCHOOL EXPERIENCE. PREKINDERGARTNERS IMPROVED ON THREE SUBSCALES OF THE ILLINOIS TEST OF PSYCHOLINGUISTIC ABILITIES (ITPA) AND ON COLOR AND SHAPE NAMING. THE GROUP HAVING PREKINDERGARTEN EXPERIENCE SURPASSED THE OTHERS ONLY ON THE VOCAL ENCODING SCALE OF ITPA. TITLE I CHILDREN SURPASSED NON-TITLE I CHILDREN ONLY ON THE VERBAL SHAPE NAME INVENTORY. NON-TITLE I CHILDREN EXCELLED IN THE AUDITORY VOCAL ASSOCIATION AND THE AUDITORY VOCAL AUTOMATIC SUBTESTS. NO SIGNIFICANT DIFFERENCES WERE FOUND ON TEACHER-RATED PUPIL BEHAVIOR. IT WAS CONCLUDED THAT PREKINDERGARTEN EXPERIENCE IS RELATED TO VERBAL BEHAVIOR. ADDITIONAL RESEARCH IS SUGGESTED AS NECESSARY TO EVALUATE READINESS IN DISADVANTAGED CHILDREN. (DO)

ED027081 PS001561
THE SPIRIT OF THE TIMES IN CHILDHOOD EDUCATION. THE FIRST EVANGELINE BURGESS MEMORIAL LECTURE. SENN, MILTON J. E., 3 APR 68 22P.
EDRS PRICE MF-$0.65 HC NOT AVAILABLE FROM EDRS.
AVAILABLE FROM: PACIFIC OAKS COLLEGE, 714 W. CALIFORNIA BLVD., PASADENA, CALIFORNIA 91105 ($1.00).

EDUCATION OF THE CHILD, INCLUDING PRESCHOOL EDUCATION, HAS BEEN AND STILL IS A TOPIC OF GREAT CONCERN TO MANY PEOPLE. TRANSLATION OF THIS CONCERN INTO CONSTRUCTIVE PROGRAMS FOR EARLY CHILDHOOD EDUCATION IS A PROFOUND PROBLEM, ONE THAT IS DEBATED OFTEN AND EMOTIONALLY. THERE IS A DICHOTOMY BETWEEN THOSE WHO FAVOR EDUCATIONAL PRACTICES BASED ON CONCEPTS OF THE CHILD IN TERMS OF HIS WHOLE EMOTIONAL-COGNITIVE DEVELOPMENT AND THOSE WHO FAVOR A NARROWER APPROACH AIMED SPECIFICALLY AT DEVELOPING CERTAIN SKILLS MEASURABLE BY INTELLIGENCE TESTS. EVANGELINE BURGESS AND THE PACIFIC OAKS COLLEGE AND CHILDREN'S SCHOOL FALL CLOSE TO THE FORMER CLASS; THE BEREITER-ENGELMANN PROGRAM, CLOSE TO THE LATTER. THERE ARE ALSO DEBATES ON THE MERIT OF PIAGET'S IDEAS ON THE RELATIONSHIP OF EARLY EXPERIENCE AND COGNITIVE DEVELOPMENT. THERE IS CONCERN FOR THE NEED TO UNDERSTAND THE QUALITY AND QUANTITY OF STIMULATION MOST BENEFICIAL TO INTELLECTUAL DEVELOPMENT. THIS INCLUDES THE DEBATE OVER THE VALUE OF SUCH PROJECTS AS HEAD START AND THE IMPORTANCE OF EMPLOYING TEACHERS WHO CAN DO THE JOB INTENDED BY THE EDUCATIONAL PROGRAM INVOLVED. OFTEN NEGLECTED BY EDUCATIONAL PROGRAM PLANNERS IS THE CLEAR DEFINITION OF THEIR EDUCATIONAL GOALS--WHETHER THEY WOULD OR SHOULD EMPHASIZE INTELLIGENCE AND NARROW SKILLS OR INTELLECT AND UNDERSTANDING. (WD)

ED027082 PS001562
THE DEVELOPMENT OF ROLE-TAKING AND COMMUNICATION SKILLS IN CHILDREN. FLAVELL, JOHN H.; AND OTHERS, 68 247P.
DOCUMENT NOT AVAILABLE FROM EDRS.
AVAILABLE FROM: JOHN WILEY AND SONS, INC., 605 THIRD AVENUE, NEW YORK, NEW YORK 10016.

THE PURPOSE OF THIS BOOK IS TO REPORT AND INTERPRET A GROUP OF RESEARCH STUDIES RELATING TO SOCIAL-COGNITIVE DEVELOPMENT IN EARLY CHILDHOOD THROUGH ADOLESCENCE. ADULTS INTERPRET THE COVERT PSYCHOLOGICAL PROPERTIES OF OTHER PEOPLE, THEIR ABILITIES, KNOWLEDGE, MOTIVES, ATTITUDES, PERCEPTIONS, AND INTENTIONS RELEVANT TO CONCRETE SITUATIONS. AN INFANT IS UNABLE TO DO THIS; THEREFORE, BOTH DISPOSITION AND ABILITY MUST EVOLVE DURING INTERVENING CHILDHOOD. THIS COGNITIVE PROCESS IS LABELED "ROLE TAKING." THIS BOOK INCLUDES THE SUBJECTS OF ROLE TAKING AND COMMUNICATION IN MIDDLE CHILDHOOD AND ADOLESCENCE, ROLE TAKING IN EARLY CHILDHOOD, THE MODIFICATION OF COMMUNICATIVE BEHAVIOR, AND RETROSPECT AND PROSPECT. (DO)

ED027083 PS001564
TEAM TEACHING. A DESCRIPTIVE AND EVALUATIVE STUDY OF A PROGRAM FOR THE PRIMARY GRADES. WALL, HARVEY R.; REASONER, ROBERT W., FEB 62 140P.
EDRS PRICE MF-$0.65 HC-$6.58

TEAM TEACHING WAS INTRODUCED IN A SUMMER ACADEMIC PROGRAM FOR GRADES ONE THROUGH THREE IN CONCORD, CALIFORNIA. EACH TEAM WAS COMPOSED OF THREE OR FOUR TEACHERS AND A TEACHER AIDE. A TOTAL OF 410 CHILDREN WERE ASSIGNED TO FOUR TEAMS, AND CURRICULUM WAS BASICALLY ENRICHMENT ORIENTED WITH ASSISTANCE FOR THOSE WITH REMEDIAL PROBLEMS. THE CURRICULUM INCLUDED READING, MATHEMATICS, MUSIC, SPANISH, SOCIAL STUDIES, ART, PHYSICAL EDUCATION, AND FOLK DANCING. AFTER A PERIOD OF EXPERIMENTING WITH ORGANIZATION, TEAMS DEVELOPED CREATIVITY, FLEXIBILITY, AND PRODUCTIVITY BY ADAPTING CURRICULUM TO EMERGING NEEDS OF THE CHILDREN. THE PRINCIPAL'S ROLE OF COORDINATOR STRENGTHENED INTERPERSONAL RELATIONSHIPS WITHIN TEAMS. THIS DOCUMENT DESCRIBES AND EVALUATES THE PROGRAM. (DO)

ED027084 PS001566
CHILD DEVELOPMENT AND MATERIAL SURVEY. PART I, TECHNICAL REPORT. FINAL REPORT. , [68] 341P.
EDRS PRICE MF-$0.65 HC-$13.16

THIS DOCUMENT IS PART I OF A TWO-PART PROJECT WHOSE GOAL WAS TO IDENTIFY THE SEQUENTIAL DEVELOPMENT OF CHILD BEHAVIOR FROM BIRTH THROUGH AGE SEVEN AND TO IDENTIFY THE MATERIALS WHICH COULD BE USED TO STRENGTHEN OR INITIATE A BEHAVIORAL FACET. RESEARCH ON CHILD DEVELOPMENT WAS COLLECTED, ORGANIZED, AND ANALYZED FOR CORRELATIVE EVENTS PERTINENT TO THE DEVELOPMENTAL TAXONOMY. A SURVEY OF MATERIALS PRODUCED BY AMERICAN MANUFACTURERS WAS MADE. SECTION I OF THE DOCUMENT IS THE INTRODUCTION, AND SECTION II REFLECTS PHYSIOLOGICAL DEVELOPMENT EMPHASIZING MOTOR DEVELOPMENT, SENSATION, PERCEPTION, AND LEARNED RESPONSES. SECTION III COVERS COGNITIVE DEVELOPMENT, SECTION IV INVESTIGATES COMMUNICATION SKILLS, AND SECTION V REFLECTS SOCIAL AND PERSONALITY DEVELOPMENT. SECTION VI IS COMPOSED OF SUMMARY GRAPHS INDICATING THE INFORMATION GAINED IN THE DEVELOPMENTAL STUDY, AND SECTION VII CONTAINS AN EXTENSIVE BIBLIOGRAPHY AND A SUBJECT INDEX TO THE BIBLIOGRAPHY. (DO)

ED027085 PS001567
CHILD DEVELOPMENT AND MATERIAL SURVEY. PART II, MATERIAL SURVEY. FINAL REPORT. , [68] 120P.
EDRS PRICE MF-$0.65 HC-$6.58

THIS DOCUMENT IS PART II OF A TWO-PART PROJECT WHOSE OBJECT WAS TO IDENTIFY CHILDREN'S SEQUENTIAL DEVELOPMENT FROM BIRTH THROUGH AGE SEVEN AND TO IDENTIFY THE MATERIALS WHICH WOULD BE USED TO STRENGTHEN OR INITIATE A BEHAVIORAL FACET. THE MATERIALS SURVEYED FOR POTENTIAL USE WITH PRESCHOOL CHILDREN ARE DESCRIBED AS RANGING FROM STANDARD TOYS THROUGH MATERIALS UTILIZED IN SECONDARY SCHOOL SYSTEMS FOR EDUCATIONAL PURPOSES. THE MATERIALS ARE EVALUATED FOR APPLICATION IN THE DEVELOPMENTAL SEQUENCE. THE REPORT IS DIVIDED INTO THREE SECTIONS: (1) MATERIAL SURVEY AND APPLICATION, (2) MANUFACTURERS' MATERIALS SURVEY, AND (3) MATERIALS AND TECHNIQUES USED IN CHILD DEVELOPMENT CENTERS, APPENDIXES INCLUDE (A) SUMMARY OF MANUFACTURERS' REPORTS, (B) LIST OF MANUFACTURERS SUPPLYING PRODUCT DATA, AND (C) DIRECTIONS FOR ABSTRACT CARD SORTING. (DO)

ED027086 PS001572
DESIRABLE ATHLETIC COMPETITION FOR CHILDREN OF ELEMENTARY SCHOOL AGE. , 68 37P.
EDRS PRICE MF-$0.65 HC NOT AVAILABLE FROM EDRS.
AVAILABLE FROM: NATIONAL EDUCATION ASSOCIATION PUBLICATIONS-SALES, 1201 16TH STREET, N.W., WASHINGTON, D.C. 20036 ($1.00).

A COMMITTEE WAS FORMED TO EXAMINE THE KINDS OF ATHLETIC PROGRAMS PROVIDED FOR ELEMENTARY CHILDREN AND THE CONDITIONS UNDER WHICH THEY ARE CONDUCTED AND TO PREPARE RECOMMENDATIONS. A QUESTIONNAIRE WAS PREPARED FOR A SAMPLE OF 786 ELEMENTARY SCHOOL PRINCIPALS IN ORDER TO DETERMINE THE NATURE AND EXTENT OF SCHOOL SPONSORED AND AGENCY SPONSORED COMPETITIVE ATHLETIC PROGRAMS FOR BOYS. SCHOOLS IN 528 DISTRICTS FILED USABLE RETURNS. THE RETURNS SUPPLIED THE FOLLOWING STATISTICS: AGENCY SPONSORED COMPETITION OCCURRED IN ALMOST TWICE THE NUMBER OF COMMUNITIES (64 PERCENT) AS SCHOOL SPONSORED INTERSCHOOL ATHLETICS (37 PERCENT); 81 PERCENT OF THE SCHOOLS UTILIZED A TEACHER TRAINED OR EXPERIENCED IN SPORTS, WHILE ONLY 28 PERCENT OF THE AGENCIES EMPLOYED ADULTS WITH TRAINING; MANY SCHOOLS AND A VAST MAJORITY OF AGENCIES DID NOT PROVIDE ADEQUATE MEDICAL SCREENING FOR BOYS JOINING TEAMS; AND LESS THAN HALF OF THE PRINCIPALS EXPRESSED APPROVAL OF SCHOOL SPONSORED ATHLETICS, AND 13 PERCENT RESERVED OPINION. RESEARCH DOES NOT PROVE THAT SPORTS ADVERSELY AFFECT PHYSICAL GROWTH, AND THERE ARE NO DATA CONCERNING LONG-RANGE PHYSIOLOGICAL EFFECTS OF COMPETITIVE ATHLETICS ON YOUTH. ON THE BASIS OF THESE FINDINGS, THE COMMITTEE ISSUED A POLICY STATEMENT CONTAINING GUIDELINES FOR A SOUND PHYSICAL EDUCATION PROGRAM. THE STATEMENT AND A BIBLIOGRAPHY ARE INCLUDED IN THIS DOCUMENT. (DO)

ED027087 PS001577
MENTAL HEALTH. WHAT RESEARCH SAYS TO THE TEACHER SERIES NUMBER 24. PECK, ROBERT F.; MITCHELL, JAMES V., JR., 67 36P.
EDRS PRICE MF-$0.65 HC NOT AVAILABLE FROM EDRS.
AVAILABLE FROM: NATIONAL EDUCATION ASSOCIATION PUBLICATIONS-SALES, 1201 16TH STREET, N.W., WASHINGTON, D.C. 20036 ($0.25).

REASONABLY GOOD MENTAL HEALTH IS A NECESSARY PRECONDITION TO ORDERLY THOUGHT AND RESPONSIBLE ACTION. IN HUMAN RELATIONSHIPS, THE MENTAL HEALTH STATUS OF TEACHER AND CHILD INTERACT TO PRODUCE A POSITIVE OR NEGATIVE CLASSROOM ENVIRONMENT. MENTAL HEALTH CONSISTS OF (1) OBJECTIVE JUDGMENT, (2)

AUTONOMY, (3) EMOTIONAL MATURITY, (4) SELF-REALIZING DRIVE, (5) SELF-ACCEPTANCE, AND (6) RESPECT FOR OTHERS. BASIC NEEDS OF AN INDIVIDUAL CAN BE DIVIDED INTO FIVE CATEGORIES: PHYSIOLOGICAL NEEDS, SAFETY NEEDS, LOVE NEEDS, ESTEEM NEEDS, AND THE NEED FOR SELF-ACTUALIZATION. THE HOME AND SCHOOL SHOULD FULFILL THESE NEEDS AS A MINIMAL REQUIREMENT FOR GOOD MENTAL HEALTH. NEUROTIC ANXIETY EXISTS WHEN A NEED IS UNFULFILLED, AND TEACHERS CAN DO THINGS TO COPE WITH PUPILS' ANXIETIES. MENTAL HEALTH AIDS FOR TEACHERS ARE IMPORTANT, AND SCHOOLS SHOULD HAVE COUNSELING SERVICES. (DO)

ED027088 PS001587
THE PROGRAM OF RESEARCH OF THE MERRILL-PALMER INSTITUTE IN CONJUNCTION WITH THE HEAD START EVALUATION AND RESEARCH CENTER, MICHIGAN STATE UNIVERSITY. ANNUAL REPORT. VOLUME II: RESEARCH. SIGEL, IRVING E.; AND OTHERS, 31 AUG 67 195P.
EDRS PRICE MF-$0.65 HC-$6.58

THIS DOCUMENT IS AN ANNUAL REPORT FOR THE ACADEMIC YEAR 1966-67 DEALING WITH RESEARCH OF THE MERRILL-PALMER INSTITUTE CONDUCTED IN CONJUNCTION WITH THE HEAD START EVALUATION AND RESEARCH CENTER OF MICHIGAN STATE UNIVERSITY. SECTION ONE OF THE REPORT CONSISTS OF FIVE RESEARCH STUDIES ON LEARNING AND COGNITION: (1) MODIFICATION OF CLASSIFICATORY COMPETENCE AND LEVEL OF REPRESENTATION AMONG LOWER-CLASS NEGRO KINDERGARTEN CHILDREN (SEE ABSTRACT NUMBER ED 021 608); (2) DEVELOPMENTAL STUDIES IN EGOCENTRICISM: I. VIOLATION OF EXPECTANCIES; (3) BIDIMENSIONAL ATTENTION IN LOWER- AND MIDDLE-CLASS PRESCHOOL CHILDREN: A DEVELOPMENTAL STUDY; (4) A TRAINING STUDY OF OBJECT RELATED FLUENCY; AND (5) EXPLORATORY STUDIES IN CREATIVITY. SECTION TWO REPORTS THE CURRENT STATUS OF FOUR PROJECTS IN FAMILY STUDIES: (1) FAMILY ASPIRATIONS AND EXPECTATION; (2) THE DYNAMICS OF THE HUSBAND-WIFE RELATIONSHIP; (3) PARENT-CHILD INTERACTIONS, ATTITUDES AND FOCUS OF CONTROL; AND (4) EARLY ENVIRONMENTAL STIMULATION. AN APPENDIX SETS OUT A COMPREHENSIVE PARENT INTERVIEW FORM USED IN THE HEAD START PROJECT. (WD)

ED027089 PS001589
VISUAL LEARNING. DIMENSIONS IN EARLY LEARNING SERIES. BUKTENICA, NORMAN A., 68 99P.
DOCUMENT NOT AVAILABLE FROM EDRS.
AVAILABLE FROM: DIMENSIONS PUBLISHING COMPANY, SAN RAFAEL, CALIFORNIA 94903 ($2.50).

A VOLUME IN THE "DIMENSIONS IN EARLY LEARNING SERIES" THIS MONOGRAPH PROPOSES SUGGESTIONS FOR PARENTS AND TEACHERS TO SUPPLEMENT NORMAL CLASSROOM PROCEDURES IN THE AREA OF VISUAL LEARNING. CHAPTER I CONCLUDES THAT A CHILD'S DEVELOPMENT OF VISUAL SKILLS IS DIRECTLY INFLUENCED BY INBORN TENDENCIES, PHYSICAL CHARACTERISTICS, AND ENVIRONMENTAL FACTORS. IT URGES SCHOOLS TO ASSESS SKILLS EARLY AND DEVELOP APPROPRIATE VISUAL INSTRUCTION. IN CHAPTER II, SUGGESTIONS ARE OFFERED TO TEACHERS FOR EVALUATING VISUAL PERCEPTUAL PERFORMANCE. A FINAL CHAPTER ON TEACHING METHODS CONCLUDES THAT FACTORS FAVORABLY INFLUENCING PERCEPTION ARE STABILITY, REGULARITY, PREDICTABILITY, AND ADEQUATE VISUAL STIMULATION. AN ANNOTATED BIBLIOGRAPHY, A GENERAL BIBLIOGRAPHY, AND AN ADDITIONAL REFERENCES LIST ARE INCLUDED. (DO)

ED027090 PS001600
AIDES TO TEACHERS AND CHILDREN. , 68 68P.
DOCUMENT NOT AVAILABLE FROM EDRS.
AVAILABLE FROM: ASSOCIATION FOR CHILDHOOD EDUCATION INTERNATIONAL, 3615 WISCONSIN AVENUE, N.W., WASHINGTON, D.C. 20016 ($1.50).

THIS BOOKLET CONTAINS 12 ARTICLES ON TEACHER AIDES WRITTEN BY EDUCATORS. SUBJECTS OF THE ARTICLES ARE "MORE HELP FOR TEACHERS," "FINDING AND SCREENING AIDES," "FINDING AND USING AIDES," "PARENTS TO THE RESCUE," "SIXTH-GRADE AIDES FOR THE KINDERGARTEN," "TEEN-AGE AIDES," "CURRICULUM RESOURCES IN THE COMMUNITY," "PARAPROFESSIONALS DEVELOP PROFESSIONAL SKILLS," "THE TEACHER AND THE PARAPROFESSIONAL," "STAFF DEVELOPMENT ACTIVITIES FOR AIDES," "EDUCATION OF AIDES," AND "HELPING PARENTS BECOME BETTER TEACHERS." A BIBLIOGRAPHY IS INCLUDED. (DO)

ED027091 PS001611
REVIEW OF SELECTED INTERVENTION RESEARCH WITH YOUNG CHILDREN. MILLER, JAMES O., 69 24P.
EDRS PRICE MF-$0.65 HC-$3.29

REVIEWING OF LONG TERM AND SHORT TERM INTERVENTION RESEARCH UNDERTAKEN BY SKEELS AND DYE (1939), DAWE (1942), BRAZZIEL AND TERRELL (1962), CARTER (1966), SIGEL, ROEPER, AND HOOPER (1966), WEIKART (1967), KLAUS AND GRAY (1967), KARNES AND OTHERS (1966), BEREITER AND ENGELMANN (1966), BLATT AND GARFUNKEL (1965), NIMNICHT (1966), AND SMILANSKY (1964 AND 1966) SUGGESTS THAT FUTURE RESEARCH SHOULD BE APPROACHED CAUTIOUSLY BUT WITH OPTIMISM. SHORT TERM INTERVENTION RESEARCH HAS MADE GAINS WHEN DIRECTED TO SPECIFIC BEHAVIORS, BUT ITS EFFECTS ON COMPLEX BEHAVIORS HAVE NOT BEEN ESTABLISHED. MASSIVE ENVIRONMENTAL CHANGE PRODUCES GREAT IMPROVEMENT IN ABILITIES ASSOCIATED WITH ADULT SOCIAL COMPETENCE AND AFFECTS INTELLECTUAL FUNCTIONING, EDUCATIONAL ATTAINMENT, ECONOMIC PRODUCTIVITY, AND FAMILY STABILITY. INTERVENTION EFFORT WHICH LIES BETWEEN THESE EXTREMES IS TOO NEW TO BE ADEQUATELY ASSESSED. WHILE PHYSICAL ENVIRONMENT HAS RECEIVED MUCH ATTENTION, PRIORITY SHOULD BE GIVEN TO THE BEHAVIOR OF THE INTERPERSONAL ENVIRONMENTAL AGENT INTERACTING WITH THE CHILD AND MEDIATING BETWEEN THE CHILD AND PHYSICAL ENVIRONMENT. BEHAVIORAL REQUIREMENTS OF AN EFFECTIVE ENVIRONMENTAL AGENT ARE OUTLINED. LONGITUDINAL INTERVENTION RESEARCH IS NEEDED AND SHOULD BE ENCOURAGED. (DO)

ED027092 PS001663
THE AUDITORY MEMORY OF CHILDREN FROM DIFFERENT SOCIO-ECONOMIC BACKGROUNDS. BARRITT, LOREN S., 1 SEP 68 16P.
EDRS PRICE MF-$0.65 HC-$3.29

A TOTAL OF 102 CHILDREN (17 FROM EACH OF THE KINDERGARTEN, FIRST, AND SECOND GRADES AND OF TWO DISPARATE SOCIOECONOMIC BACKGROUNDS) WERE ADMINISTERED A SERIES OF TASKS INVOLVING VERBAL RECALL. THE PURPOSE OF THIS TESTING WAS TO COMPARE THE VERBAL RECALL ABILITY OF CHILDREN OF DIFFERENT AGES AND SOCIOECONOMIC STATUS. THE VERBAL MATERIAL WAS READ TO THE CHILD. AT THE COMPLETION OF EACH ITEM, THE CHILD WAS ASKED TO RECALL THE VERBAL MATERIAL IN THE ORDER GIVEN. TASK I CONSISTED OF CVC TRIGRAMS. TASK 2 CONSISTED OF NOUNS. TASKS 3 AND 4 CONSISTED OF SENTENCES, MEANINGLESS AND MEANINGFUL, RESPECTIVELY. THE LANGUAGE SKILLS NECESSARY TO PERFORM THE TASKS INCREASED, THEORETICALLY, FROM TASK 1 TO TASK 4. THE HYPOTHESES THAT CHILDREN REMEMBER MORE VERBAL UNITS AS LANGUAGE HABITS CAN BE MORE FULLY UTILIZED AND THAT OLDER CHILDREN REMEMBER MORE UNITS THAN YOUNGER CHILDREN ON THE HIGHER LEVEL TASKS AND THAT THERE IS AN INTERACTION BETWEEN SOCIOECONOMIC STATUS AND PERFORMANCE ON THE TASKS WERE NOT CONFIRMED. A PREDICTION OF A CUMULATIVE DEFICIT BETWEEN SOCIOECONOMIC GROUPS WITH INCREASING AGE WAS REJECTED. (WD)

ED027093 PS001689
EVALUATION OF INKSTER PRESCHOOL PROJECT. FINAL REPORT. RYCKMAN, DAVID B.; VAN EVERY, PHILLIP, 1 SEP 68 12P.
EDRS PRICE MF-$0.65 HC-$3.29

AN EXPERIMENTAL GROUP OF 22 PRESCHOOL CHILDREN FROM INKSTER, MICHIGAN, PARTICIPATED IN AN APRIL 1967 TO AUGUST 1967 PREKINDERGARTEN ENRICHMENT PROGRAM FOR LOW SOCIOECONOMIC CHILDREN. THE PROGRAM CLASSES WERE UNSTRUCTURED AND PERMISSIVE. A CONTRAST GROUP OF 33 CHILDREN WAS ALSO CHOSEN. BOTH GROUPS OF CHILDREN PARTICIPATED IN A PRESCHOOL PROGRAM WHICH BEGAN IN SEPTEMBER 1967. THE CONTRAST GROUP WOULD ALSO BE READY TO ENTER KINDERGARTEN IN THE FALL OF 1968, BUT THEY HAD NOT PARTICIPATED IN A PRESCHOOL PROGRAM PRIOR TO SEPTEMBER 1967. THE CHILDREN IN BOTH GROUPS WERE ADMINISTERED THE ILLINOIS TEST OF PSYCHOLINGUISTIC ABILITIES (ITPA) IN NOVEMBER 1967. THE TEST RESULTS INDICATED THAT BOTH GROUPS WERE FUNCTIONING BELOW AGE NORMS. ANOTHER FINDING WAS THAT THE CONTRAST GROUP PERFORMED SIGNIFICANTLY BETTER THAN THE EXPERIMENTAL GROUP ON THE TOTAL ITPA. THE CONTRAST GROUP DID SIGNIFICANTLY BETTER ON TWO OF THE SUBTESTS: VISUAL DECODING AND VISUAL-MOTOR-SEQUENTIAL. THE EXPLANATION FOR THIS RESULT WOULD SEEM TO BE THE EXISTENCE OF SYSTEMATIC SAMPLE BIAS. THE BOYS SCORED CONSISTENTLY HIGHER THAN THE GIRLS ON THE SUBTESTS, AN UNUSUAL FINDING EXPLAINED PERHAPS IN PART BY THE FACT THAT A MALE TEACHER WAS PRESENT IN THE PROGRAM. STATISTICAL TABLES AND A BIBLIOGRAPHY ARE INCLUDED. (WD)

ED027094 PS001694
PREPRIMARY ENROLLMENT OF CHILDREN UNDER SIX: OCTOBER 1967. GERTLER, DIANE B., OCT 67 28P.
EDRS PRICE MF-$0.65 HC NOT AVAILABLE FROM EDRS.
AVAILABLE FROM: SUPERINTENDENT OF DOCUMENTS, U. S. GOVERNMENT PRINTING OFFICE, WASHINGTON, D.C. 20402 ($0.30).

DATA USED IN THIS STUDY ARE BASED ON INFORMATION COLLECTED BY THE BUREAU OF CENSUS, WHICH CANVASSED 52,000 HOUSEHOLDS. ABOUT 273,000 THREE-YEAR-OLDS, 872,000 FOUR-YEAR-OLDS, AND 2,724,000 FIVE-YEAR-OLDS WERE ENROLLED IN PREPRIMARY PROGRAMS IN 1967. ABOUT 5.4 PERCENT OF THE 3-YEAR-OLDS, 15.6 PERCENT OF THE 4-YEAR-OLDS, AND 45 PERCENT OF THE 5-YEAR-OLDS WERE FROM FAMILIES WITH ANNUAL INCOMES UNDER $3,000. THREE- TO 5-YEAR-OLDS MOST LIKELY TO BE ENROLLED IN PREPRIMARY PROGRAMS WERE THOSE IN FAMILIES WITH ANNUAL INCOMES OF $10,000 OR MORE, IN HOUSEHOLDS WITH WHITE-COLLAR HEADS, IN URBAN AREAS, AND IN THE WEST. (DO)

ED027095 PS001710
A PILOT STUDY INTEGRATING VISUAL FORM AND ANTHROPOLOGICAL CONTENT FOR TEACHING CHILDREN AGES 6 TO 11 ABOUT CULTURES AND PEOPLES OF THE WORLD PRIMUS, PEARL E., FEB 68 100P.
EDRS PRICE MF-$0.65 HC-$3.29

A PILOT STUDY WAS CONDUCTED TO DEMONSTRATE THE USE OF DANCE AS A METHOD FOR IMPROVING AND EXTENDING CURRICULUM CONTENT OF WORLD CULTURES IN ELEMENTARY SCHOOLS. THE SECONDARY OBJECTIVES EMPHASIZED NONVERBAL EXPERIENCE AS A MEANS OF INTERPRETING THE PATTERNS OF CULTURAL VALUES IN WEST

AND CENTRAL AFRICA. MOST OF THE 41 PRESENTATIONS OF THE DANCE PROGRAM WERE PERFORMED BEFORE A VARIETY OF ELEMENTARY SCHOOL AUDIENCES, BUT SOME PRESENTATIONS WERE SHOWN TO THE PUBLIC. THE EVALUATION CONSISTED OF ANALYZING 666 LETTERS AND 691 DRAWINGS FROM CHILDREN, PHOTOGRAPHS, TAPED INTERVIEWS USING QUESTIONNAIRES, AND LETTERS FROM EDUCATORS AND PROFESSIONAL ADVISORS. THE RESULTS SHOWED THAT AN EDUCATIONAL PROGRAM USING DANCE, MUSIC, AND SCULPTURE TO INTEGRATE VISUAL FORM AND ANTHROPOLOGICAL CONTENT COULD BE USED SUCCESSFULLY TO TEACH CHILDREN OF AGES SIX TO ELEVEN ABOUT VARIOUS CULTURES. THE DIRECTOR URGED THE USE OF SUCH PROGRAMS AS "CULTURAL BRIDGES" TO ESTABLISH BETTER UNDERSTANDING AMONG PEOPLES OF THE WORLD. (JS)

ED027096 PS001711
EFFECTS OF PARENTAL EXPECTATIONS OF EDUCATIONAL PLANS OF WHITE AND NONWHITE ADOLESCENTS. FINAL REPORT. RHODES, ALBERT LEWIS, SEP 68 254P.
EDRS PRICE MF-$0.65 HC-$9.87

THIS STUDY WAS DESIGNED TO EXAMINE THE RELATIONSHIP BETWEEN AN ADOLESCENT'S EDUCATIONAL PLANS AS REPORTED BY THE ADOLESCENT HIMSELF AND HIS MOTHER'S EDUCATIONAL EXPECTATIONS FOR HIM AS REPORTED BY HER. THE DATA WERE OBTAINED IN A PREVIOUS STUDY, A SURVEY INCLUDING A MULTISTAGE, CLUSTER SAMPLE OF SOME 7,000 CASES REPRESENTING 13,484,000 PUBLIC AND PRIVATE SCHOOL STUDENTS. THE DATA HAD BEEN GATHERED THROUGH QUESTIONNAIRES. TESTS FOR INTERACTION WERE USED TO DETERMINE IF THE EFFECTS OF THE MOTHER'S ASPIRATION, RACE, AND OTHER CHARACTERISTICS INFLUENCED COLLEGE PLANS. FINDINGS INDICATED THAT A SUBJECT'S PLAN TO ATTEND COLLEGE WAS CLOSELY ASSOCIATED WITH HIS MOTHER'S EDUCATIONAL EXPECTATION FOR HIM. THIS EXPECTATION WAS RELATED TO THE MOTHER'S EDUCATIONAL ATTAINMENT AND RELIGION BUT WAS RELATIVELY INDEPENDENT OF SUCH CHARACTERISTICS AS THE SUBJECT'S IQ AND THE SOCIOECONOMIC STATUS OF THE FAMILY. NEGROES HAD THE SAME LEVEL OF EDUCATIONAL ASPIRATION AS WHITES, BUT THE MOTHERS WERE LESS LIKELY TO EXPECT THAT THEIR CHILDREN WOULD GO TO COLLEGE, PRIMARILY BECAUSE OF THE COST INVOLVED. NEGROES WERE ALSO LESS LIKELY TO BE ENROLLED IN A COLLEGE PREPARATORY CURRICULUM. EDUCATIONAL GOALS APPEARED TO BE FORMED AT HOME AND IN THE PEER GROUP, RATHER THAN IN THE SCHOOL ENVIRONMENT. (MS)

ED027936 PS001529
PRESCHOOL AND PRIMARY EDUCATION PROJECT. 1967-68 ANNUAL PROGRESS REPORT TO THE FORD FOUNDATION. MCINERNEY, BEATRICE L.; AND OTHERS, [68] 127P.
EDRS PRICE MF-$0.65 HC-$6.58

AFTER 5 YEARS, THE PROJECTS' THREE PROGRAMS WERE REVIEWED. THE EDUCATIONAL PROGRAM, CONDUCTED IN THREE SCHOOLS, WAS DEVISED TO COMPENSATE FOR BEHAVIORAL DEFICITS AND TO REWARD POSITIVE BEHAVIOR IN CULTURALLY DEPRIVED CHILDREN, AGES 3 TO 9. CHILDREN WERE INDIVIDUALLY ASSESSED AND RATED BY STAGES OF ACHIEVEMENT. AS A RESULT, ALL CHILDREN MADE SIGNIFICANT GAINS ON STANDARDIZED TESTS AND PERFORMED AT NORMS FOR THE POPULATION. TEACHERS NOTED POSITIVE DIFFERENCES IN THE SUBJECTS' BEHAVIOR. THE THREE PARENT EDUCATION PROGRAMS, AIMED AT CHANGING PARENTAL ATTITUDES AND BEHAVIOR TO POSITIVELY INFLUENCE THEIR CHILDREN'S EDUCATIONAL DEVELOPMENT, VARIED IN PRACTICE. ALTHOUGH NO INSTRUMENTS WERE USED TO TEST RESULTS, SOCIAL WORKERS AND TEACHERS REPORTED INCREASED INVOLVEMENT BY PARENTS. THROUGH WORKSHOPS, TEAM MEETINGS, AND CONSULTANT SERVICES, A TEACHER INSERVICE PROGRAM ATTEMPTED TO HELP TEACHERS BE MORE EFFECTIVE IN WORKING WITH CULTURALLY DISADVANTAGED CHILDREN. THE TEACHERS AND PROGRAM DIRECTOR NOTED CHANGES IN THE TEACHERS' BEHAVIOR AND FEELINGS. FOR THE NEXT YEAR, TEACHERS WOULD ASSESS NEW STUDENTS. THERE WAS STILL A NEED FOR ACCURATE INSTRUMENTS TO ASSESS INDIVIDUAL BEHAVIOR. (JS)

ED027937 PS001557
THE ELEMENTARY MATHEMATICS STUDY: AN INTERIM REPORT ON KINDERGARTEN YEAR RESULTS. LEIDERMAN, GLORIA F.; ROSENTHAL-HILL, IRENE, MAY 68 23P.
EDRS PRICE MF-$0.65 HC-$3.29

THE SCHOOL MATHEMATICS STUDY GROUP OF STANFORD UNIVERSITY IS CONDUCTING A 4-YEAR LONGITUDINAL STUDY OF MATHEMATICAL LEARNING IN THE PRIMARY GRADES. THE PURPOSE OF THIS PAPER IS TO PRESENT THE RESULTS OF THIS STUDY FOR THE KINDERGARTEN YEAR. APPROXIMATELY 2,000 KINDERGARTEN CHILDREN FROM TWO LARGE CITIES WERE DIVIDED INTO LOWER AND MIDDLE INCOME GROUPS. ONE GROUP FROM EACH INCOME LEVEL USED THE SCHOOL MATHEMATICS STUDY GROUP CURRICULUM, AND ONE GROUP FROM EACH USED THE SCIENCE RESEARCH ASSOCIATES PROGRAM. A BATTERY OF TESTS (K01) WAS ADMINISTERED TO THE CHILDREN IN SEPTEMBER TO EVALUATE THEIR ABILITY UPON ENTERING KINDERGARTEN, AND A SECOND BATTERY (K02) WAS ADMINISTERED IN MAY TO MEASURE GAIN. THE TESTS MEASURED COGNITIVE PROCESSES AND MATHEMATICAL ACHIEVEMENT. THE LOWER SOCIOECONOMIC GROUP PERFORMED CONSISTENTLY LESS WELL THAN THE MIDDLE INCOME GROUP ON ALL K01 TESTS EXCEPT THE TEST OF VISUAL MEMORY. THIS SAME PATTERN PERSISTED IN K02 TESTS, EVEN THOUGH THE ENTIRE SAMPLE SHOWED SIGNIFICANT MEAN SCORE INCREASES FROM K01 TO K02. DIFFERENTIAL GAINS WERE FOUND, HOWEVER, BETWEEN THE TWO INCOME GROUPS, THE LOWER GROUP SHOWING A GREATER GAIN ON FIVE TESTS, THE MIDDLE GROUP SHOWING A GREATER GAIN ON THREE TESTS, AND NO DIFFERENCE EXISTING ON FIVE TESTS. (WD)

ED027938 PS001565
A METHOD TO INVESTIGATE THE MOVEMENT PATTERNS OF CHILDREN. WUELLNER, LANCE H.; AND OTHERS, [68] 17P.
EDRS PRICE MF-$0.65 HC-$3.29

A NEW METHOD FOR INVESTIGATING THE MOVEMENT PATTERNS OF CHILDREN HAS BEEN DEVELOPED. IT USES A COMPUTER ANALYSIS AND DISPLAY PROCEDURE FOR REDUCING CARTESIAN COORDINATE POSITION DATA TO NUMERICAL AND GRAPHICAL STATEMENTS ABOUT MOVEMENT PATTERNS. A TIME-LAPSE PHOTOGRAPHIC SYSTEM IS USED TO OBTAIN THE POSITION DATA FOR CHILDREN DURING PLAY. THIS STUDY EXPLORED (1) THE POTENTIALITIES AND LIMITATIONS OF THIS NEW METHOD AND (2) THE DIFFERENCE IN MOVEMENT PATTERNS OF PRESCHOOL CHILDREN WITH SUCCEEDING PLAY SESSIONS. FOUR GROUPS OF PRESCHOOL CHILDREN WERE FILMED WHILE ENGAGING IN A 15-MINUTE PLAY SESSION DURING NURSERY SCHOOL. EACH GROUP WAS FILMED FOR NINE SESSIONS. THE PLAYROOM WAS ARRANGED THE SAME WAY FOR THE FIRST SIX SESSIONS. ON THE SEVENTH, A NOVEL APPARATUS WAS INTRODUCED. THE DATA ANALYSIS INDICATED THAT AS A GROUP THE CHILDREN SHOWED LESS MOVEMENT OVER SUCCEEDING SESSIONS. THE INTRODUCTION OF THE NOVEL OBJECT WAS ACCOMPANIED BY A SUBSTANTIAL DECREASE IN MOVEMENT, WITH PLAY GRAVITATING TO THAT OBJECT. TEACHER PRESENCE WAS FOUND TO INFLUENCE MOVEMENT ALSO. THE FINDINGS OF THIS STUDY, COUPLED WITH SUGGESTED REVISIONS OF THE METHOD, INDICATE THAT THE TECHNIQUE CAN BE USED SUCCESSFULLY TO COLLECT AND ANALYZE CHILDREN'S MOVEMENT PATTERNS IN A CLOSED ENVIRONMENT. (WD)

ED027939 PS001568
AN APPRAISAL OF HEAD START PARTICIPANTS AND NON-PARTICIPANTS: EXPANDED CONSIDERATIONS ON LEARNING DISABILITIES AMONG DISADVANTAGED CHILDREN. CAWLEY, JOHN F.; AND OTHERS, 68 115P.
EDRS PRICE MF-$0.65 HC-$6.58

FIRST GRADE CHILDREN FROM TWO HEAD START (HS) GROUPS AND ONE NON-HEAD START (NHS) GROUP WERE ADMINISTERED A BATTERY OF TESTS FOR THE PURPOSES OF (1) COMPARING THE DEVELOPMENTAL STATUS OF HS AND NHS SUBJECTS, (2) EXAMING PATTERNS OF SPECIFIC LEARNING DISABILITIES AMONG HS AND NHS CHILDREN, (3) DETERMINING THE STABILITY COEFFICIENTS OF SELECTED INSTRUMENTS, AND (4) ANALYZING THE PREDICTIVE CAPABILITIES AND FACTORAL STRUCTURE OF SELECTED EVALUATIVE INSTRUMENTS. GROUP ONE, THE PRIMARY HEAD START SAMPLE, WAS COMPOSED OF 54 DISADVANTAGED CHILDREN WHO HAD ATTENDED A YEAR-LONG PRESCHOOL PROGRAM AND HAD BEEN TESTED DURING THAT TIME. GROUP TWO, A SECONDARY HEAD START SAMPLE, CONSISTED OF 77 DISADVANTAGED CHILDREN WHO HAD ALSO ATTENDED A YEAR-LONG PROGRAM BUT HAD NOT HAD TESTING EXPERIENCE. THE COMPARISON GROUP CONSISTED OF 78 NON-HEAD START DISADVANTAGED CHILDREN. AVAILABLE DATA INDICATED THAT HS AND NHS CHILDREN DEMONSTRATED NO SIGNIFICANT DIFFERENCES IN DEVELOPMENTAL CHARACTERISTICS IN KINDERGARTEN. THE COMPREHENSIVE TESTING IN THE FIRST GRADE SHOWED THE SAME TREND: THERE WERE NO SIGNIFICANT DIFFERENCES BETWEEN CHILDREN HAVING PARTICIPATED IN HS AND NOT HAVING PARTICIPATED IN HS IN LEARNING ABILITY. THE FIRST GRADE DATA ALSO SHOWED THAT ALL OF THE SUBJECTS IN THIS STUDY LABORED UNDER SERIOUS LEARNING DISABILITIES. (WD)

ED027940 PS001569
CURRICULUM GUIDE FOR EARLY CHILDHOOD EDUCATION. BEHAVIORAL GOALS - PRE-K THROUGH ONE. , 1 SEP 68 60P.
EDRS PRICE MF-$0.65 HC-$3.29

ASSUMING THE PREMISE THAT "A CHILD HAS GONE FIFTY PERCENT OF THE WAY IN ORGANIZING THE THINKING PATTERNS THAT WE CALL HIS INTELLIGENCE BY THE TIME HE HAS REACHED THE AGE OF FOUR, AND THE NEXT THIRTY PERCENT BY THE TIME HE IS EIGHT," 50 SCHENECTADY KINDERGARTEN-THROUGH-FIRST-GRADE TEACHERS AND ADMINISTRATORS FORMULATED A CHART OF BEHAVIORAL EXPECTATIONS WHICH THEY CONSIDERED ESSENTIAL TO THE FOUNDATION AND DEVELOPMENT OF THE CHILD'S EDUCATION. THE CHART CONTAINS EIGHT MAJOR GOAL AREAS: (1) SCHOOL READINESS AND SKILLS FOUNDATION, (2) MOTIVATIONAL SKILLS, (3) BASIC LEARNING SKILLS, (4) DEVELOPMENT OF LANGUAGE SYSTEM, (5) SOCIALIZATION, (6) MEANS OF SELF EXPRESSION, (7) PHYSICAL DEVELOPMENT, AND (8) ESTHETIC APPRECIATION. THE DESIRED BEHAVIORS WERE LISTED UNDER APPROPRIATE CATEGORIES. THE CHART WAS DESIGNED WITH THE INTENT THAT THE TEACHER COULD QUICKLY DETERMINE THE DESIRED SCOPE OF EMPHASIS BY EVALUATING HER CLASS IN ACCORDANCE WITH THE CHART AND COULD BRING HER PROFESSIONAL SKILLS TO BEAR IN DETERMINING, SELECTING, OR CREATING ACTIVITIES TO DEVELOP DESIRED BEHAVIORS. THIS DOCUMENT INCLUDES A COMPLETE CHART. (DO)

ED027941 PS001570

SUPERMARKET DISCOVERY CENTER, PILOT STUDY, MAY - SEPTEMBER, 1968. INITIAL REPORT. FILEP, ROBERT T., 15 SEP 68 49P.

EDRS PRICE MF-$0.65 HC-$3.29

THE OBJECTIVES OF THIS RESEARCH PILOT PROJECT WERE (1) TO TRAIN 3- AND 4-YEAR-OLDS IN COGNITIVE AND TACTILE DISCOVERY TASKS; (2) TO PROVIDE GUIDANCE FOR PARENTS, ENABLING THEM TO REINFORCE AND REVIEW THE CONCEPTS TAUGHT; AND (3) TO ESTABLISH TRAINING AND EMPLOYMENT, AS TUTORS, FOR CENTRAL CITY HIGH SCHOOL AND JUNIOR COLLEGE STUDENTS. A "DISCOVERY CENTER" WAS ESTABLISHED IN A LOS ANGELES SUPERMARKET, WHERE CHILDREN WERE TUTORED 45 MINUTES TO 1 HOUR ONCE OR TWICE A WEEK WHILE PARENTS SHOPPED. TUTORS INSTRUCTED ON A ONE-TO-ONE BASIS, USING INSTRUCTIONAL SEQUENCES ESPECIALLY DESIGNED TO TEACH BASIC CONCEPTS. THE POPULATION CONSISTED OF 58 PARENTS AND 68 PRESCHOOLERS, PREDOMINANTLY NEGRO, WITH FIVE PERCENT MEXICAN-AMERICAN. THREE JUNIOR COLLEGE STUDENTS WERE HIRED AS TUTORS. THE LIMITED PILOT STUDY GENERATED PARENTAL ACCEPTANCE AND COMMUNITY ENTHUSIASM AND INDICATED THAT THE PROGRAM WAS VIABLE ON A LARGE SCALE. PROCEDURES AND MINOR MODIFICATIONS WERE SUGGESTED FOR A FULL SCALE DISCOVERY CENTER DEMONSTRATION AND EVALUATION. (DO)

ED027942 PS001576

CHANGING PARENT ATTITUDES AND IMPROVING LANGUAGE AND INTELLECTUAL ABILITIES OF CULTURALLY DISADVANTAGED FOUR-YEAR-OLD CHILDREN THROUGH PARENT INVOLVEMENT. MCCARTHY, JANET LEE GORRELL, JUN 68 115P.

EDRS PRICE MF-$0.65 HC-$6.58

THE PURPOSES OF THIS STUDY WERE TO ANALYZE PARENT INVOLVEMENT AS IT RELATED TO (1) THE DEVELOPMENT OF LANGUAGE ABILITIES OF CULTURALLY DISADVANTAGED PRESCHOOL CHILDREN AND (2) THE INTELLIGENCE TEST SCORES OF THESE CHILDREN AND TO ANALYZE PARENT ATTITUDES RESULTING FROM INVOLVEMENT. NINE HYPOTHESES WERE TESTED. FORTY-ONE 4-YEAR-OLD HEAD STARTERS IN TERRE HAUTE, INDIANA, PARTICIPATED. IN GROUP I, NO PARENTAL INVOLVEMENT WAS ATTEMPTED. IN GROUP II, PARENTS PARTICIPATED IN GENERAL MEETINGS. HOME VISITING WAS THE TECHNIQUE USED WITH GROUP III. ANALYSIS OF DATA SUGGESTED THESE CONCLUSIONS: (1) CONTRARY TO OPINION, THESE PARENTS ARE CONCERNED ABOUT THEIR CHILDREN AND ARE WILLING TO COOPERATE WITH SCHOOL PERSONNEL WITHIN THE REALM OF THEIR CAPABILITIES: (2) HOME EXPERIENCES INFLUENCE A CHILD'S LANGUAGE ABILITIES; (3) THE CHILD HAS MORE CAPACITY TO PERFORM WHEN HIS VISUAL PROCESSES ARE UTILIZED, AS OPPOSED TO HIS AUDIOTYPE PROCESSES; (4) HE IS VERY INADEQUATE IN HIS ABILITY TO COMPREHEND THE SPOKEN WORD AND TO EXPRESS IDEAS ORALLY; (5) DISADVANTAGED PARENTS TEND TO SHOW LITTLE TRUST IN THEIR CHILDREN. IMPLICATIONS OF THE CONCLUSIONS WERE DISCUSSED, AND SUGGESTIONS FOR FUTURE RESEARCH WERE PROPOSED. (DO)

ED027943 PS001580

LANGUAGE STYLE OF THE LOWER CLASS MOTHER: A PRELIMINARY STUDY OF A THERAPEUTIC TECHNIQUE. SWIFT, MARSHALL, [68] 58P.

EDRS PRICE MF-$0.65 HC-$3.29

WHILE THE CONCEPT OF PARENT INVOLVEMENT IS STRESSED BY ALMOST ALL PROGRAMS FOR PRESCHOOL CHILDREN, THERE IS LITTLE EVIDENCE OF PARENT-FOCUSED PROGRAMS SPECIFICALLY DESIGNED TO OVERCOME THE DEFICITS OF THE LOWER CLASS PARENT. IT WAS THE PURPOSE OF THE PRESENT STUDY TO DEVELOP A PROGRAM TO ENHANCE THE FUNCTIONING OF THE LOWER CLASS MOTHER IN LANGUAGE STYLE. THE LOWER CLASS MOTHER NEEDS ACTIVITIES DESIGNED SPECIFICALLY TO INCREASE HER CONFIDENCE AND HER ABILITY TO AFFECT THE GROWTH AND LEARNING OF HER CHILD IN A SOCIALLY VALUED MANNER. SEVEN LOWER CLASS MOTHERS OF NORTH PHILADELPHIA WERE INTRODUCED TO A PROGRAM IN WHICH THEY LEARNED TO TELL STORIES TO THEIR CHILDREN. IN COOPERATION WITH THE GET SET PROGRAM, MOTHERS AND THEIR PRESCHOOL CHILDREN ATTENDED SESSIONS IN WHICH AN ATTEMPT WAS MADE (BY ENGAGING THE PARTICIPATION OF THE MOTHERS IN READING AND STORYTELLING) TO INCREASE THE QUANTITY AND QUALITY OF THE MOTHERS' VERBALIZATIONS AND TO HELP THE MOTHERS TO ENCOURAGE THEIR CHILDREN TO DO SO. HIGH-INTEREST PRESCHOOL-LEVEL BOOKS WERE USED. THE LANGAUGE ABILITIES OF THE MOTHERS AND CHILDREN WERE MEASURED BY A BATTERY OF TESTS. THE MOTHERS SHOWED A GOOD DEAL OF INTEREST IN THE PROGRAM; AND ALTHOUGH THEY WERE QUITE LIMITED IN EDUCATION, THEY CLEARLY INCREASED THEIR LANGUAGE ABILITIES IN SEVERAL RESPECTS. (WD)

ED027944 PS001588

A SOURCE REPORT FOR DEVELOPING PARENT-CHILD EDUCATIONAL CENTERS. MOORE, HAROLD E.; STOUT, IRVING W., JUN 68 340P.

EDRS PRICE MF-$0.65 HC-$13.16

THIS "SOURCE REPORT" PRESENTS THE RESEARCH, PROCESS, AND FINDINGS INVOLVED IN DEVELOPING A PROGRAM FOR A PARENT-CHILD EDUCATIONAL CENTER FOR THE NEW CITY OF LITCHFIELD PARK, ARIZONA. THE CENTER IS INTENDED TO BE A BASIC NEIGHBORHOOD UNIT OF THE PUBLIC SCHOOL SYSTEM AND WILL SERVE BOTH PARENTS AND CHILDREN; THE LATTER, FROM INFANCY THROUGH 7 YEARS OLD. THE ACTIVITIES OF THE CENTER ARE TO BE CARRIED ON THROUGH THE MUTUAL INITIATIVE AND INVOLVEMENT OF PARENTS AND PROFESSIONAL STAFF FOR THE PURPOSES OF (1) PROVIDING FOR THE DEVELOPMENTAL WELL-BEING OF THE INFANTS AND YOUNG CHILDREN OF THE CITY, AND (2) ACHIEVING AN EVER INCREASING EFFECTIVENESS OF PARENTAL SKILLS. THE REPORT IS DIVIDED INTO SIX MAJOR SECTIONS: (1) INTRODUCTION AND ORIENTATION, (2) REVIEW OF RESEARCH RELATING TO PARENT-CHILD EDUCATIONAL CENTERS, (3) THE RATIONALE FOR PARENT-CHILD EDUCATIONAL CENTERS, (4) THE CENTER PROGRAM: WORKING PAPER NO. 2, (5) A PLAN FOR PROGRAM FUNCTIONING: WORKING PAPER NO. 3, AND (6) A PLAN OF ACTION FOR PARENT-CHILD EDUCATIONAL CENTERS. "A PLAN OF ACTION FOR PARENT-CHILD EDUCATIONAL CENTERS" (PS 001 609) ALSO CONCERNS THIS STUDY. (WD)

ED027945 PS001590

SOCIAL STUDIES UNIT: FIRST GRADE. BOSTON-NORTHAMPTON LANGUAGE ARTS PROGRAM, ESEA - 1965, PROJECTS TO ADVANCE CREATIVITY IN EDUCATION. HERR, BLODWEN, SEP 68 18P.

EDRS PRICE MF-$0.65 HC-$3.29

THIS DOCUMENT DESCRIBES A SOCIAL STUDIES UNIT, PRIMARILY COMPOSED OF VARIOUS FIELD TRIPS AND SUBSEQUENT CLASSWORK RELATED THERETO, FOR THE FIRST GRADE CHILD. IT IS DIVIDED INTO FOUR SECTIONS: (1) COMMUNITY HELPERS, (2) THE TRIP TO THE ZOO, (3) THE TRAIN TRIP, AND (4) A TRIP TO A DAIRY FARM. THE DOCUMENT ILLUSTRATES SEVERAL TRIPS THE CHILDREN OF A FIRST GRADE CLASS PARTICIPATED IN AND THE DISCUSSIONS BETWEEN TEACHER AND PUPILS THAT FOLLOWED. IN THE FIRST SECTION THERE IS A DISCUSSION OF FATHERS AND THEIR VOCATIONS AND OF TRIPS TO THE POST OFFICE, PUBLIC LIBRARY, POLICE STATION, FIRE STATION, AND A SERVICE STATION. IN THE OTHER THREE SECTIONS SIMILAR ILLUSTRATIONS ARE GIVEN OF OTHER FIELD TRIPS AND THE RANGE OF RELATED CLASSROOM ACTIVITIES THAT CAN BE ARRANGED. (WD)

ED027946 PS001591

INTEGRATED, INDEPENDENT AND INDIVIDUAL LEARNING ACTIVITIES, FIRST AND SECOND GRADES. SUMMER LEARNING ACTIVITIES, SECOND AND THIRD GRADES. BOSTON-NORTHAMPTON LANGUAGE ARTS PROGRAM, ESEA - 1965, PROJECTS TO ADVANCE CREATIVITY IN EDUCATION. BALDWIN, VIRGINIA, SEP 68 27P.

EDRS PRICE MF-$0.65 HC-$3.29

THE PURPOSE OF THIS DOCUMENT IS TO HELP TEACHERS STIMULATE CHILDREN AND PROVIDE SUCCESSFUL LEARNING EXPERIENCES IN ORDER TO DEVELOP POSITIVE SELF-CONCEPTS. PART I CONTAINS LISTS OF SUGGESTIONS OF ACTIVITIES FOR UNSUPERVISED WORK AT THE FOLLOWING CENTERS: (1) LANGUAGE, (2) CHALK, (3) MATH, (4) MEASURING, (5) MUSIC, (6) GAMES, TOYS, AND PUZZLES, (7) LIBRARY, (8) PAINTING, (9) SEWING, (10) CUTTING AND PASTING AND CLAY, AND (11) SCIENCE. PART II CONTAINS SUMMER LEARNING ACTIVITIES FOR SECOND AND THIRD GRADERS CONCERNING READING, WRITING, MATH, SCIENCE, SOCIAL STUDIES, TOPICS TO TALK ABOUT, AND THINGS TO MAKE AND DO. (DO)

ED027947 PS001592

[THE JUNIPER GARDENS CHILDREN'S PROJECT.] FINAL PROGRESS REPORT FOR OEO GRANT CG-8180. , 31 AUG 68 31P.

EDRS PRICE MF-$0.65 HC-$3.29

RESEARCH AND DEMONSTRATION ACTIVITIES AT THE JUNIPER GARDENS CHILDREN'S PROJECT AT THE UNIVERSITY OF KANSAS INVOLVED STUDIES IN THESE AREAS: (1) AN AFTER SCHOOL REMEDIAL CLASSROOM PROGRAM, (2) INAPPROPRIATE STUDY BEHAVIOR IN CLASS, AND (3) DEMONSTRATION ACTIVITIES WHICH INVOLVED TEACHER AND PARENT TRAINING. THE EFFECTS OF REINFORCEMENT CONTINGENCIES ARRANGED FOR INCREASING ACCURACY AND RATE OF ACADEMIC PERFORMANCE AND FOR APPROPRIATE CLASSROOM BEHAVIOR WERE ANALYZED IN FOUR EXPERIMENTS IN THE ABOVE AREAS. STUDY FINDINGS INDICATED THAT (1) TOKEN REINFORCEMENT INCREASED ACCURACY IN PUPILS WHO WERE GIVEN AFTER-SCHOOL REMEDIAL WORK IN READING AND ARITHMETIC; (2) TEACHER ATTENTION WHICH REWARDED GOOD STUDY HABITS INCREASED THE FREQUENCY OF THIS BEHAVIOR IN STUDENTS WHILE PUNISHMENT DECREASED GOOD PERFORMANCE; (3) PEER CONTROL WAS A POSSIBILITY IN IMPROVING THE SOCIAL AND ACADEMIC BEHAVIOR OF STUDENTS WHO FREQUENTLY LEFT THEIR SEATS IN CLASS; (4) AUDITORY REINFORCEMENT DURING READING INSTRUCTION ASSISTED READING PERFORMANCE; (5) THE EFFECT OF PEER COMPETITION IN ARITHMETIC PROBLEM SOLVING WAS INCONCLUSIVE, ALTHOUGH SOME IMPROVEMENT WAS NOTED IN ACCURACY; AND (6) IN A HOME

STUDY PROGRAM INVOLVING MOTHERS WHO TUTORED THEIR OWN CHILDREN IN READING, THE READING SKILL INCREASED WHEN MOTHERS WERE TAUGHT TO USE REINFORCEMENT RATHER THAN PUNITIVE PRACTICES. (MS)

ED027948 PS001595
GUIDELINES: PRE-SCHOOL PROJECTS, HEAD START: EARLY CHILDHOOD EDUCATION. REVISED EDITION. POPE, JANE F.; AND OTHERS, SEP 68 44P.
EDRS PRICE MF-$0.65 HC-$3.29

THIS DOCUMENT MENTIONS THAT THE CINCINNATI PRESCHOOL PROGRAM IS FUNDED THROUGH THE ECONOMIC OPPORTUNITY ACT AND THE ELEMENTARY AND SECONDARY EDUCATION ACT AND THAT THE PROGRAM'S PURPOSE IS TO PROVIDE AN ENVIRONMENT TO STIMULATE AND AID THE INTELLECTUAL, PHYSICAL, EMOTIONAL, AND SOCIAL DEVELOPMENT OF 4- AND 5-YEAR OLDS. THE GUIDELINES IN THIS REPORT STATE OBJECTIVES CONCERNING CLASSROOM ORGANIZATION, CHILD SELECTION, AND CURRICULUM. INSTRUCTIONAL ACTIVITIES ARE OUTLINED IN A DAILY TIMETABLE. CLASSROOM LEARNING AREAS, A LANGUAGE PROGRAM, HEALTH, SPECIAL SERVICES, DISCIPLINE, MATERIALS, AND FIELD TRIPS ARE ALSO DISCUSSED. UNDER THE PROGRAM STAFF SECTION, THE QUALIFICATIONS, RESPONSIBILITIES, AND INSERVICE TRAINING PROGRAM ARE DISCUSSED. THE ROLES OF PARENTS AND VOLUNTEERS ARE DELINEATED IN ANOTHER SECTION. AN APPENDIX CONTAINS FORMS FOR BUSINESS CONDUCTED BY THE PROGRAM AND A LIST OF EQUIPMENT FOR EACH CLASSROOM. (DO)

ED027949 PS001596
THE CHANGE PROCESS IN ACTION: KINDERGARTEN DEARDEN, RONALD A.; VALOTTO, EVELYN, OCT 68 51P.
EDRS PRICE MF-$0.65 HC-$3.29

THIS MONOGRAPH DESCRIBES A PILOT KINDERGARTEN PROGRAM CONDUCTED IN FAIRFAX COUNTY (VIRGINIA) SCHOOLS IN 1967-68 AND SUPERVISED BY THE CENTER FOR EFFECTING EDUCATIONAL CHANGE. THE STATED PURPOSE OF THE PILOT KINDERGARTEN PROGRAM WAS TO DEVELOP DEMONSTRATION KINDERGARTEN CLASSES AT SEVEN SELECTED FAIRFAX COUNTY SCHOOLS IN ORDER TO OBTAIN INFORMATION AND MAKE RECOMMENDATIONS FOR IMPLEMENTING THE PROGRAM ON A COUNTRYWIDE BASIS DURING 1968-69. THIS MONOGRAPH IS A RESULT OF THE ACQUISITION OF SUCH INFORMATION AND THE MAKING OF SUCH RECOMMENDATIONS. THE CONTENTS OF THE MONOGRAPH ARE DIVIDED INTO TWO SECTIONS: (1) THE PROGRAM AND (2) THE EVALUATION. ELEVEN SPECIFIC OBJECTIVES OF THE PROGRAM ARE DELINEATED. EVALUATION OF THE PROGRAM TOOK THE FORM OF MEASURING THE DEGREE OF ATTAINMENT OF THESE OBJECTIVES AS REFLECTED IN THE TESTS, INVENTORIES, SURVEYS, AND QUESTIONNAIRES ADMINISTERED TO THE PUPILS AND TEACHERS. THE EVALUATION SECTION TREATS, IN BRIEF, EACH OF THE ELEVEN PROGRAM OBJECTIVES. INCLUDED IN THE DOCUMENT ARE STATISTICAL CHARTS OF PUPIL PERFORMANCE RESULTS ON THE METROPOLITAN READINESS TEST AND THE WIDE RANGE ACHIEVEMENT TEST. (WD)

ED027950 PS001598
THE PSYCHOEDUCATIONAL APPROACH TO LEARNING DISABILITIES. BLOM, GASTON E., 6 DEC 67 27P.
EDRS PRICE MF-$0.65 HC-$3.29

CHILDREN WHO HAVE LEARNING DISABILITIES WHICH PREVENT ACHIEVEMENT IN SKILL SUBJECTS OR BEHAVIORAL DIFFICULTIES WHICH INTERFERE WITH LEARNING CAN BE HELPED TO LEARN TO SUBSTITUTE MORE ADAPTIVE PATTERNS FOR MADADAPTIVE ONES. BECAUSE LEARNING DISABILITIES ARE ONLY PART OF A DISORDERED DEVELOPMENTAL PROCESS IN A CHILD, BOTH CLINICAL AND COMPETENCE THEORY AND PRACTICE ARE INTEGRATED IN THE PSYCHOEDUCATIONAL APPROACH TO EVALUATION AND MODIFICATION OF THE DEVELOPMENTAL DISORDER. SOME DILUTION AND FRAGMENTATION OF EFFORT MAY OCCUR IN CERTAIN SETTINGS, BUT THE BASIC PRINCIPLES AND SPECIFIC TECHNIQUES OF THE PSYCHOEDUCATIONAL APPROACH ARE GENERALLY APPLICABLE. THESE BASIC PRINCIPLES ARE CONCERNED WITH STRUCTURE, PREDICTABILITY, AND CLARITY; MANAGEMENT OF ENVIRONMENTAL AND INTRAPSYCHIC STIMULATION; THE SUCCESS-FAILURE DIMENSION; THE STUDENT-TEACHER REALTIONSHIP; THE UTILIZATION OF THERAPY FOR A CHILD AND HIS PARENTS; AND BIOLOGICAL FACTORS. A DISCUSSION OF INSTRUCTION FOR REMEDIAL EFFORTS INCLUDES THESE TOPICS: THE BASIC SKILL SUBJECTS, COGNITIVE TRAINING, MOTOR SKILL TRAINING, AND THE USE OF SPECIAL MEDIA, CONTENT, SKILL PROGRAMS, AND METHODS. A BIBLIOGRAPHY IS ALSO INCLUDED. (MS)

ED027951 PS001601
CHILD PSYCHIATRY: THE PAST QUARTER CENTURY. EISENBERG, LEON, 3 OCT 68 29P.
EDRS PRICE MF-$0.65 HC-$3.29

THE DEVELOPMENTS IN CHILD PSYCHIATRY IN THE PAST 25 YEARS HAVE BEEN ENCOURAGING BUT REPRESENT ONLY A PRELUDE TO THE SIGNIFICANT WORK THAT MUST BE DONE RELATIVELY SOON TO MEET THE NEEDS OF THE CONTEMPORARY CHILD. BEFORE 1940, THE DESIRABILITY OF MULTIDISCIPLINARY STUDY OF THE CHILD HAD BEEN WELL ESTABLISHED, AND CHILD GUIDANCE CLINICS HAD APPEARED. UNTIL THE 1960'S, HOWEVER, THE FOCUS WAS ON THE CLINICAL STUDY OF INDIVIDUAL PATIENTS AND FAMILIES, RATHER THAN POPULATION STUDIES, AND GENERALIZATIONS WERE MADE FROM THE FORMER TO THE LATTER. CONCERN FOR THE POOR AND THE BLACK WAS DORMANT FOR TOO LONG IN THE PAST QUARTER CENTURY; IT IS IN SUCH AREAS AS POVERTY AND RACISM THAT SERIOUS PSYCHOLOGICAL AND ORGANIC PROBLEMS IN CHILDREN OCCUR. SPECIFICALLY, RESEARCH IN CHILD DEVELOPMENT MUST BE CONCERNED WITH MANY IMPORTANT FACTORS, INCLUDING (1) THE "TEST BIAS" IN INTERPRETING RESULTS OF ACHIEVEMENT TESTS; (2) THE PRENATAL AND PARANATAL FACTORS THAT INFLUENCE BRAIN DEVELOPMENT; (3) NUTRITIONAL FACTORS, BEFORE AND AFTER BIRTH; (4) THE PSYCHOSOCIAL ENVIRONMENT OF THE CHILD, ESPECIALLY THE FAMILY ENVIRONMENT; (5) THE INFLUENCE AND ROLE OF SCHOOL; AND (6) THE EFFECTS OF RACISM. (WD)

ED027952 PS001602
FUN WHILE LEARNING AND EARNING. A LOOK INTO CHATTANOOGA PUBLIC SCHOOLS' TOKEN REINFORCEMENT PROGRAM. SMITH, WILLIAM F.; SANDERS, FRANK J., 68 13P.
EDRS PRICE MF-$0.65 HC-$3.29
AVAILABLE FROM: CHATTANOOGA PUBLIC SCHOOLS', DIVISION OF RESEARCH AND DEVELOPMENT, 1161 WEST FORTIETH STREET, CHATTANOOGA, TENNESSEE 37409

A TOKEN REINFORCEMENT PROGRAM WAS USED BY THE PINEY WOODS RESEARCH AND DEMONSTRATION CENTER IN CHATTANOOGA, TENNESSEE. CHILDREN WHO WERE FROM ECONOMICALLY DEPRIVED HOMES RECEIVED TOKENS FOR POSITIVE BEHAVIOR. THE TOKENS WERE REDEEMABLE FOR RECESS PRIVILEGES, ICE CREAM, CANDY, AND OTHER SUCH REINFORCERS. ALL TOKENS WERE SPENT ON THE DAY EARNED SO THAT THERE WOULD BE NO SAVING UP FOR A RAINY DAY. THE RESULTS SHOWED THAT MINOR AS WELL AS EXTREME NEGATIVE BEHAVIOR WAS MODIFIED. FOR EXAMPLE, ONE BOY WOULD THROW HIS LUNCH AND SHOES INTO A WASTE BASKET UPON ARRIVING AT SCHOOL. HE WOULD ALSO THROW TEMPER TANTRUMS. AFTER THE TEACHER CONTINUALLY REWARDED THE CHILDREN AROUND HIM FOR THEIR POSITIVE BEHAVIOR, THE BOY JOINED CLASS ACTIVITIES MORE READILY AND HAD FEWER OUTBURSTS OF TEMPER. TO MEASURE MORE EFFECTIVELY THE RESULTS OF THE PROGRAM, A PRETEST AND POSTTEST RESEARCH DESIGN HAS BEEN DEVELOPED AND IS BEING TESTED WITH MORE TRADITIONAL FIRST GRADES. (JS)

ED027953 PS001603
PUERTO RICAN CHILDREN IN MAINLAND SCHOOLS. A SOURCE BOOK FOR TEACHERS. CORDASCO, FRANCESCO, ED.; BUCCHIONI, EUGENE, ED., 68 465P.
DOCUMENT NOT AVAILABLE FROM EDRS.
AVAILABLE FROM: THE SCARECROW PRESS, INC., 52 LIBERTY STREET, P.O. BOX 656, METUCHEN, NEW JERSEY 08840

AS AN ATTEMPT TO PROVIDE A SOURCE BOOK FOR TEACHERS ON THE PUERTO RICAN CHILD, THIS TEXT OF COLLECTED READINGS FOCUSES ON SOCIOCULTURAL ASPECTS. PART I DEALS WITH PUERTO RICAN CULTURE; PART II, THE FAMILY; PART III, EXPERIENCE ON THE MAINLAND (CONFLICT AND ACCULTURATION), AND PART IV, PUERTO RICAN CHILDREN IN NORTH AMERICAN SCHOOLS. APPENDIXES INCLUDE PUERTO RICAN STATISTICS AND AN EXTENSIVE BIBLIOGRAPHY. (DO)

ED027954 PS001604
[ACHIEVEMENT TEST CORRELATION STUDY: SURVEY OF 40 CHILDREN.] SMITH, WILLIAM F., DEC 68 30P.
EDRS PRICE MF-$0.65 HC-$3.29

A COMPREHENSIVE PROFILE OF 40 TITLE I CHILDREN FROM A CHATTANOOGA SCHOOL WAS OBTAINED BY PARENT AND CHILD INTERVIEWS. THE PROFILE WAS PART OF A CLINICAL EVALUATION IN THE "EAST FIFTH STREET MIDDLE SCHOOL SPECIAL STUDY." ALTHOUGH SOME FINDINGS WERE UNIQUE FOR EACH CHILD, SOME OCCURRED IN THE HISTORY OF SEVERAL CHILDREN. GENERALLY, THE TITLE I CHILDREN LACKED PREVIOUS GROUP EXPERIENCES; THAT IS, AT THE TIME THEY ENTERED PUBLIC SCHOOL, THEY HAD NOT PARTICIPATED IN KINDERGARTEN, NURSERY SCHOOL, OR ANY OTHER PRESCHOOL PROGRAM. MANY OF THE CHILDREN HAD PHYSICAL OR EMOTIONAL PROBLEMS. THE CHILDREN TENDED TO LIVE IN MARGINAL OR SUBSTANDARD HOUSING IN RAPIDLY DETERIORATING NEIGHBORHOODS. THE MEASURED INTELLIGENCE OF THE CHILDREN WAS BELOW AVERAGE, AND THEIR SCHOOL PERFORMANCE WAS POOR. THE FAMILY RELATIONSHIPS OF THE CHILDREN WERE DISRUPTED BY POVERTY, LACK OF EDUCATION OF PARENTS, AND BROKEN-HOME SITUATIONS. IT WAS CONCLUDED, HOWEVER, THAT SUCH PUPILS CAN BE MARGINAL ACHIEVERS IF GIVEN ADEQUATE COUNSELING, EXPERIENCES, AND TRAINING. AN APPENDIX REPORTS THE RESULTS OF A TITLE I SURVEY, AN ACHIEVEMENT TEST CORRELATION STUDY. (WD)

ED027955 PS001605
MEDIATIONAL STYLES: AN INDIVIDUAL DIFFERENCE VARIABLE IN CHILDREN'S VERBAL LEARNING ABILITY. HOHN, ROBERT L.; MARTIN, CLESSEN J., [68] 17P.
EDRS PRICE MF-$0.65 HC-$3.29

SEVEN MEDIATIONAL STRATEGIES FOR USE IN VERBAL ASSOCIATIVE LEARNING HAVE BEEN DISCOVERED. THEY RANGE FROM THE SIMPLE TO THE INTERMEDIATE TO THE COMPLEX. THE SUBJECTS OF THIS STUDY WERE 173 FIFTH GRADERS, WHO WERE ADMINISTERED A PAIRED-ASSOCIATE (PA) TASK AND ASKED TO IDENTIFY THE STRATEGIES THEY USED. ON THE BASIS OF THIS DATA, THEY WERE THEN PLACED INTO ONE OF THE THREE CLASSES OF STRATEGIES AND ADMINISTERED A CRITERION PA TASK. THEN THE SUBJECTS WERE AGAIN ASKED TO IDENTIFY THE STRATEGIES THEY USED. ONE WEEK LATER THE SUBJECTS WERE GIVEN A RETENTION PA TASK AND ASKED UPON THE COMPLETION THEREOF TO STATE THE STRATEGIES USED. DURING THE CRITERION TASK, THREE TYPES OF EXPERIMENTER-SUPPLIED MEDIATORS (SIMPLE, COMPLEX, AND

NONE) WERE DISTRIBUTED AMONG THE THREE SUBJECT GROUPS. IT WAS DISCOVERED THAT COMPLEX-STRATEGY CHILDREN LEARNED PA'S AT A SIGNIFICANTLY FASTER RATE THAN SIMPLE-STRATEGY CHILDREN, WITH THE INTERMEDIATE GROUP FALLING IN-BETWEEN. THE COMPLEX EXPERIMENTER-SUPPLIED MEDIATOR CONDITION WAS THE MOST EFFECTIVE FOR LEARNING, REGARDLESS OF SUBJECT-STRATEGY STYLE. ON THE RETENTION TEST, THE COMPLEX-STRATEGY CHILDREN AGAIN PERFORMED SIGNIFICANTLY BETTER THAN SIMPLE-STRATEGY CHILDREN. THUS, MEDIATIONAL STYLE WAS SHOWN TO BE AN IMPORTANT VARIABLE IN ACCOUNTING FOR INDIVIDUAL DIFFERENCES IN RATE OF LEARNING AND AMOUNT OF RETENTION. (WD)

ED027956 PS001606
THE NEED FOR A MULTI-DIMENSIONAL APPROACH TO LEARNING DISABILITIES. A MULTI-DISCIPLINARY SYMPOSIUM ON DYSLEXIS AND ASSOCIATED LEARNING DISABILITIES. BLOM, GASTON E., 25 MAY 68 16P.
EDRS PRICE MF-$0.65 HC-$3.29

LEARNING DISABILITIES ARE GENERALLY DUE TO A VARIETY OF DISORDERS, FROM THE BIOLOGICAL TO THE ENVIRONMENTAL. UNFORTUNATELY, TODAY, THE TENDENCY EXISTS TO SEIZE UPON ONE SUCH DISORDER AND TO INVESTIGATE THE LEARNING DISABILITY CONCEPT IN THAT NARROW VIEW ONLY. EVIDENCE, HOWEVER, SUGGESTS THAT A MULTIFACTOR APPROACH SHOULD BE USED AND THAT SYSTEM CONCEPTS AND MODELS SHOULD BE DEVELOPED TO UNDERSTAND LEARNING DISABILITY AS A MULTIDIMENSIONAL DISORDER. ONE PROBLEM WITH SUCH AN APPROACH IS THE DIFFICULTY IN EFFECTING A COMMONALITY OF EFFORT AMONG THE MANY PROFESSIONAL DISCIPLINES INVOLVED IN THE SUBJECT OF LEARNING DISABILITY. IN SHORT, IT MIGHT BE SAID THAT THERE ARE DIFFICULTIES IN (1) CONCEPTUALIZING MULTIDIMENSIONALITY: (2) DECIDING ON THE APPROACH TO USE; AND (3) APPLYING THE MULTIDIMENSIONAL APPROACH, ONCE IT IS DECIDED UPON. ON THE BASIS OF KNOWLEDGE GAINED FROM AN INTEGRATED SYSTEMS APPROACH USED AT THE DAY CARE CENTER AT THE UNIVERSITY OF COLORADO MEDICAL CENTER IN DENVER, IT MAY BE POSSIBLE TO CREATE A COORDINATED PLAN TO UTILIZE THE EFFORTS OF THE VARIOUS PROFESSIONAL GROUPS AND TO INSTITUTE CROSS-COMMUNICATION BETWEEN THEM, IN ORDER TO ESTABLISH THE INTEGRATED APPROACH NECESSARY TO THE INVESTIGATION AND TREATMENT OF MULTIDIMENSIONAL LEARNING DISABILITIES. (WD)

ED027957 PS001607
PROGRAM FOR EARLY CHILDHOOD EDUCATION. , 68 438P.
DOCUMENT NOT AVAILABLE FROM EDRS.
AVAILABLE FROM: SOUTHWEST EDUCATIONAL DEVELOPMENT LABORATORY, SUITE 550, COMMODORE PERRY HOTEL, AUSTIN, TEXAS

THIS HANDBOOK SETS OUT A PROGRAM FOR EARLY CHILDHOOD EDUCATION. IT WAS PREPARED TO BE USED AS A GUIDE FOR THE TESTING, REVISION, REFINEMENT, AND EXPANSION OF MATERIALS AND TEACHING STRATEGIES. THE CONTENT OF THE HANDBOOK IS DIVIDED INTO NINE SECTIONS: (1) RESEARCH ESTABLISHING NEED FOR THE EARLY CHILDHOOD EDUCATION PROGRAM, (2) MODIFYING BEHAVIOR IN EARLY CHILDHOOD EDUCATION, (3) THE STRUCTURE-PROCESS APPROACH TO EARLY CHILDHOOD EDUCATION, (4) OBJECTIVES OF THE STRUCTURE-PROCESS MODEL IN EARLY CHILDHOOD EDUCATION, (5) EARLY CHILDHOOD EDUCATION PROGRAM ACTIVITIES, (6) PARENTAL-SCHOOL-COMMUNITY INVOLVEMENT, (7) EVALUATION, (8) ORGANIZATION AND MANAGEMENT, AND (9) INSTRUCTIONAL MATERIALS AND EQUIPMENT. SECTION 5 IS DIVIDED INTO SIX SPECIFIC TOPICAL AREAS: (A) COMMUNICATIONS, (B) MATHEMATICS, (C) SCIENCE, (D) ART, (E) MUSIC, AND (F) WORK-PLAY. (WD)

ED027958 PS001608
A STUDY OF LANGUAGE DEVIATIONS AND COGNITIVE PROCESSES. PROGRESS REPORT NO. 3. BRENT, SANDOR B.; KATZ, EVELYN W., 1 MAR 67 64P.
EDRS PRICE MF-$0.65 HC-$3.29

THIS REPORT SUMMARIZES THE WORK COMPLETED AND OUTLINES THE PLANS FOR FUTURE RESEARCH OF AN ONGOING RESEARCH PROGRAM OF THE DEPARTMENT OF PSYCHOLOGY AT WAYNE STATE UNIVERSITY. THE PROGRAM IS CONCERNED WITH THE IDENTIFICATION AND DESCRIPTION OF CROSS-CULTURAL AND DEVELOPMENTAL DIFFERENCES IN THE CONCEPTUALIZATION AND LINGUISTIC EXPRESSION OF SPATIAL, TEMPORAL, CAUSAL, AND LOGICAL RELATIONSHIPS. SEVERAL SPECIFIC AREAS OF CONCENTRATION WITHIN THIS BROAD TOPIC HAVE EMERGED: (1) INVESTIGATIONS OF CULTURAL, DEVELOPMENTAL, CONTEXTUAL, AND SITUATIONAL FACTORS WHICH INFLUENCE THE CONNECTEDNESS AND COHERENCE OF SPONTANEOUS DISCOURSE; (2) DEVELOPMENTAL AND NORMATIVE INVESTIGATIONS OF THE PRINCIPLES UNDERLYING THE USAGE AND COMPREHENSION OF LINGUISTIC CLAUSE CONNECTORS (GRAMMATICAL CONJUNCTIONS); AND (3) INVESTIGATIONS OF CROSS-CULTURAL AND DEVELOPMENTAL DIFFERENCES IN THE PRINCIPLES UNDERLYING THE CONCEPTUALIZATION AND LINGUISTIC REPRESENTATION OF SIMPLE GEOMETRIC FORMS AND CONCRETE SPATIAL RELATIONSHIPS. (WD)

ED027959 PS001609
A PLAN OF ACTION FOR PARENT-CHILD EDUCATIONAL CENTERS. MOORE, HAROLD E.; STOUT, IRVING W., JUN 68 30P.
EDRS PRICE MF-$0.65 HC-$3.29

AFFECTED SCHOOL DISTRICTS AND THE LITCHFIELD PARK LAND AND DEVELOPMENT COMPANY REQUESTED THIS STUDY FOR A MASTER PLAN FOR AN EDUCATIONAL AND FACILITY PROGRAM COVERING EARLY CHILDHOOD THROUGH COLLEGE FOR A NEW CITY OF 100,000 IN ARIZONA. THE PURPOSE OF THE CENTER IS TO BE OF SERVICE TO PARENTS (1) IN PROVIDING FOR THE DEVELOPMENTAL WELL-BEING OF THEIR CHILDREN AND (2) IN ACHIEVING INCREASING EFFECTIVENESS IN THEIR PARENTAL SKILLS. CHILDREN (FROM INFANCY THROUGH 7 YEARS) WILL BE GROUPED ON A CONTINUOUS PROGRESS BASIS, THE DETERMINING FACTORS BEING THE INDIVIDUAL'S DEVELOPMENTAL CHARACTERISTICS, NEEDS, AND STAGE OF LEARNING. A PLAN FOR STAFFING, AN INSERVICE TRAINING PROGRAM, AND CATEGORIES OF FUTURE RESEARCH RELATING TO PARENTS, CHILDREN, AND STAFF ARE OUTLINED. "A SOURCE REPORT FOR DEVELOPING PARENT-CHILD EDUCATIONAL CENTERS" (PS 001 588) ALSO CONCERNS THIS STUDY. (DO)

ED027960 PS001610
THE CONCEPT, "PERCEPTUALLY HANDICAPPED," ITS ASSETS AND LIMITATIONS. BLOM, GASTON E., 27 APR 68 16P.
EDRS PRICE MF-$0.65 HC-$3.29

PERCEPTION IS A PROCESS BY WHICH SIMPLE AND COMPLEX INFORMATION (STIMULI) IS EXPERIENCED. WE GAIN INFORMATION ABOUT HOW SUCH STIMULUS INPUTS ARE EXPERIENCED BY A CHILD, FOR EXAMPLE, BY HIS RESPONSES OR OUTPUTS. OUTPUTS ARE IN THE FORM OF VOCALIZATIONS AND MOTOR ACTS. THUS, THE PERCEPTUAL PROCESS IS FREQUENTLY CALLED PERCEPTUAL-MOTOR. BUT THE CONCERN IS NOT ONLY WITH INPUTS AND OUTPUTS, BUT WITH WHAT GOES ON IN BETWEEN. THIS PROCESS IS COGNITION; THAT IS, COGNITION IS THE PROCESS OF THE INPUT BEING ORGANIZED AND PROCESSED WITHIN THE MIND FOR A RESPONSE. THEREFORE, A PERCEPTUAL-COGNITIVE-MOTOR (PCM) PROCESS IS INVOLVED. THE TERM "PERCEPTUAL HANDICAPS" REFERS TO DEVIATIONS IN THIS PROCESS FROM THE EXPECTED NORMS AT A GIVEN AGE. LEARNING DISABILITIES CONSTITUTE THE WHOLE OF WHICH PERCEPTUAL HANDICAPS ARE A PART. PERCEPTUAL HANDICAPS DO NOT NECESSARILY INDICATE CENTRAL NERVOUS SYSTEM DAMAGE; A DEPRIVED ENVIRONMENT CAN AFFECT THE DEVELOPMENT OF A CHILD'S PERCEPTION, LANGUAGE, AND COGNITION. IMPORTANT TO REMEDIAL PCM TRAINING PROCEDURES IS THE EFFECTIVE USE OF MOTIVATION TO LEARN. PERFORMANCE ON TESTS AND GENERAL BEHAVIOR INDEXES SHOULD BE CONSIDERED IN EVALUATION A CHILD'S PCM SKILLS. (WD)

ED027961 PS001612
JDC GUIDE FOR DAY CARE CENTERS, A HANDBOOK TO AID COMMUNITIES IN DEVELOPING DAY CARE CENTER PROGRAMS FOR PRE-SCHOOL CHILDREN. , JUL 62 67P.
EDRS PRICE MF-$0.65 HC-$3.29

THIS BROCHURE SUGGESTS STANDARDS AND PROCEDURES FOR ESTABLISHING DAY CARE CENTER PROGRAMS FOR PRESCHOOL CHILDREN. IT INCLUDES CHAPTERS WHICH (1) DESCRIBE DAY CARE CENTERS AND THE ROLE THEY PLAY FOR THE PUPIL, (2) TELL HOW TO START A DAY CARE CENTER IN A COMMUNITY, (3) EXPLAIN STANDARDS OR RULES OF OPERATION FOR DAY CARE CENTERS, AND (4) DISCUSS QUALIFICATIONS AND RESPONSIBILITIES REQUIRED OF THE STAFF. SEVERAL APPENDIXES PROVIDE ADDITIONAL INFORMATION SUCH AS (1) A LIST OF EQUIPMENT GENERALLY NEEDED FOR A CENTER, (2) THE TYPES OF RECORDS AND REPORTS THAT MUST BE KEPT OR MADE, (3) A COURSE OUTLINE FOR A TEACHER TRAINING PROGRAM, (4) A LIST OF AGENCIES WHICH CAN HELP IN THE ESTABLISHMENT OF A DAY CARE CENTER, AND (5) A LIST OF THE RIGHTS OF THE CHILD. THE INFORMATION CONTAINED IN THIS DOCUMENT IS INTENDED FOR USE IN THE CREATION OF DAY CARE CENTERS IN ANY COUNTRY OF THE WORLD. (WD)

ED027962 PS001613
JDC HANDBOOK FOR TEACHERS IN DAY CARE CENTERS. , 67 156P.
EDRS PRICE MF-$0.65 HC-$6.58

THIS GUIDE FOR TEACHERS IN DAY CARE CENTERS OFFERS DISCUSSIONS (BOTH PHILOSOPHICAL AND PRACTICAL) ABOUT THE NEEDS AND BEHAVIORS OF PRESCHOOL CHILDREN, MAKES SUGGESTIONS FOR TEACHER GUIDANCE THROUGHOUT THE DAILY PROGRAM ACTIVITIES AND ROUTINES, AND DEFINES A SUITABLE NURTURING AND EDUCATIONAL DAY CARE CENTER ENVIRONMENT. DIRECTED TO THE TEACHER, THE HANDBOOK COVERS ASPECTS OF TEACHER-CHILD AND TEACHER-CENTER RELATIONSHIPS. A LENGTHY SECTION ON ART, MUSIC, LANGUAGE, AND INDOOR-AND-OUTDOOR PLAY ACTIVITIES GIVES SPECIFIC PROGRAM INFORMATION. INCLUDED IS A SECTION ON JEWISH HOLIDAY CELEBRATIONS AND FOOD PREPARATION, WHICH COULD BE INCORPORATED INTO THE CENTER'S ACTIVITIES, IF APPROPRIATE. ONE OF THE ORIGINAL PURPOSES OF THIS HANDBOOK WAS TO ASSIST TEACHERS OF DISADVANTAGED CHILDREN IN MOROCCO, TUNISIA, AND IRAN. APPENDIXES INCLUDE DESCRIPTIONS OF GAMES, ART ACTIVITIES, AND HEBREW SONGS AND PRAYERS. (MS)

ED027963 PS001615
A LONDON INFANT SCHOOL. AN INTERVIEW. CAZDEN, COURTNEY B., 3 SEP 67 19P.
EDRS PRICE MF-$0.65 HC-$3.29

THIS DOCUMENT IS THE TRANSCRIPT OF AN INTERVIEW WITH SUSAN WILLIAMS, DIRECTOR OF GORDONBROCK INFANT SCHOOL IN BROCKLEY, LONDON, ENGLAND. HER SCHOOL IS THE SUBJECT OF A FILM BY LILLIAN WEBER. THE INTERVIEW WAS CONDUCTED BY COURTNEY CAZDEN OF THE HARVARD GRADUATE SCHOOL OF EDUCATION. THE SUBSTANCE OF SOME OF HER REMARKS FOLLOW: (1) THE MAJOR DIFFERENCES BETWEEN THE TRADITIONAL GRADE SCHOOL CLASSROOM AND THE NEW FORM USED AT GORDONBROCK ARE (A) THE FORMER WAS TEACHER-DIRECTED; THE LATTER IS CHILD-DIRECTED; AND (B) THE NEW FORM INVOLVES MORE CONCERN FOR TEACHING SOMETHING TO THE CHILD WHEN THE CHILD IS READY, AND THIS NECESSITATES A GOOD DEAL OF INDIVIDUAL OR SMALL-GROUP INSTRUCTION. (2) THE TEACHERS' DAILY LESSONS, ALTHOUGH PREPLANNED, ARE NOT RIGID, BUT FLUID, DEPENDING UPON HOW THE TEACHER-PUPIL INTERACTION DEVELOPS DURING THE CLASS PERIOD. (3) MUCH OF THE INSTRUCTION IS DONE, NOT WITH THE WHOLE CLASS OF PUPILS, BUT WITH SMALLER GROUPS WHO HAVE DEMONSTRATED THE NEED FOR A PARTICULAR TYPE OF INSTRUCTION. (4) THE CLASSROOMS ARE COMPOSED OF ABOUT 40 CHILDREN FROM AGES FIVE TO SEVEN. (5) THE TEACHERS KEEP INFORMAL RECORDS ON EACH CHILD'S PROGRESS AND ABILITIES SO AS TO BE AWARE AT ALL TIMES OF WHAT TYPE OF INSTRUCTION IS RELEVANT OR NECESSARY FOR HIM. (WD)

ED027964 PS001616
LEICESTERSHIRE REPORT: THE CLASSROOM ENVIRONMENT. SCHLESINGER, JOY, 66 15P.
EDRS PRICE MF-$0.65 HC-$3.29

IN THE INDUSTRIAL MIDLANDS OF ENGLAND, THE COUNTY EDUCATION AUTHORITY IN LEICESTERSHIRE COUNTY HAS JURISDICTION OVER APPROXIMATELY 250 PRIMARY SCHOOLS AND 50 SECONDARY SCHOOLS. A CHILD ATTENDING AN INFANT OR JUNIOR SCHOOL WORKS AT HIS OWN PACE, IS CREATIVE AND SPONTANEOUS, AND LEARNS ON HIS OWN TERMS. PRINCIPALS ARE GIVEN COMPLETE AUTONOMY AND MAY INNOVATE OR EXPERIMENT WITHOUT INTERFERENCE. WITHIN THIS NONRESTRICTIVE SYSTEM, EDUCATIONAL ISSUES ARE DISCUSSED WITH THE ADVISORY CENTER, WHICH IS COMPOSED OF EDUCATORS WHO ARE AVAILABLE TO CONSULT WITH TEACHERS. A PROBLEM EXISTS BECAUSE SOME OF THE SCHOOLS IN THE COUNTY, PARTICULARLY SECONDARY SCHOOLS, DO NOT SUBSCRIBE TO THIS SYSTEM OF EDUCATION. UNIVERSITY ADMISSION IS BASED ALMOST ENTIRELY ON DIFFICULT, STANDARDIZED EXAMINATIONS, WHICH CHILDREN TAKE AT THE END OF SECONDARY SCHOOL. THIS REPORT DESCRIBES THE CLASSROOM ENVIRONMENT OF TWO INFANT SCHOOLS (FOR AGES 5 TO 7), TWO JUNIOR SCHOOLS (FOR AGES 7 TO 11), ONE PRIMARY (INFANT AND JUNIOR) SCHOOL, AND TWO HIGH SCHOOLS (FOR AGES 11 TO 15). (DO)

ED027965 PS001618
IDENTIFICATION AND DEVELOPMENT OF CREATIVE ABILITIES. MACKINNON, DONALD W., 14 MAR 64 20P.
EDRS PRICE MF-$0.65 HC-$3.29

AT BERKELEY, AN ASSESSMENT WAS MADE OF REPRESENTATIVES OF ARTISTIC CREATIVITY (POETS, NOVELISTS, AND ESSAYISTS), REPRESENTATIVES OF SCIENTIFIC CREATIVITY (ENGINEERS, RESEARCH SCIENTISTS, AND INVENTORS) AND REPRESENTATIVES OF CREATIVITY WHICH IS BOTH SCIENTIFIC AND ARTISTIC (MATHEMATICIANS AND ARCHITECTS). CHARACTERISTICS OF ALL GROUPS EMPHASIZED THAT (1) A CERTAIN AMOUNT OF INTELLIGENCE IS REQUIRED FOR CREATIVITY, BUT BEYOND THAT POINT, BEING MORE OR LESS INTELLIGENT DOES NOT DETERMINE CREATIVITY, (2) CREATIVE PERSONS ARE ORIGINAL, (3) THEY ARE INDEPENDENT IN THOUGHT AND ACTION, (4) THEY ARE ESPECIALLY OPEN TO EXPERIENCE BOTH OF THE INNER SELF AND OF THE OUTER WORLD, (5) CREATIVE PERSONS ARE INTUITIVE, (6) THEY HAVE STRONG THEORETICAL AND AESTHETIC INTERESTS, AND (7) THEY HAVE A STRONG SENSE OF DESTINY WHICH INCLUDES A DEGREE OF RESOLUTENESS AND ALMOST INEVITABLY A MEASURE OF EGOTISM. IT WAS CONCLUDED THAT IT IS IMPORTANT FOR PARENTS AND TEACHERS TO RECOGNIZE, STIMULATE, AND DEVELOP CREATIVITY IN CHILDREN. (DO)

ED027966 PS001619
PIAGET, SKINNER, AND AN INTENSIVE PRESCHOOL PROGRAM FOR LOWER CLASS CHILDREN AND THEIR MOTHERS. RADIN, NORMA, 28 FEB 68 18P.
EDRS PRICE MF-$0.65 HC-$3.29

IN AN EARLY EDUCATION PROGRAM, 100 DISADVANTAGED 4-YEAR-OLDS (50 NEGROES AND 50 WHITES) ATTEND CLASSES ONE-HALF DAY, FOUR DAYS A WEEK, FROM OCTOBER THROUGH JUNE. A TEACHER VISITS EACH CHILD'S HOME EVERY OTHER WEEK TO CONDUCT A TUTORIAL SESSION LASTING 1 1/2 HOURS. THREE OBJECTIVES OF THE PROGRAM ARE (1) TO DEVELOP A PRESCHOOL CURRICULUM BASED ON PIAGET'S THEORY OF SEQUENTIAL DEVELOPMENT OF INTELLIGENCE, (2) TO DEVELOP A MODEL OF CURRICULUM INNOVATION IN A SCHOOL SYSTEM UTILIZING A THEORIST, A DIFFUSER, AND A TEACHER, AND (3) TO DEVELOP A GROUP PARENT EDUCATION PROGRAM. GOALS OF THE PRESCHOOL CURRICULUM ARE (1) TO FACILITATE THE MOVEMENT OF THE CHILDREN FROM THE SENSORY-MOTOR PERIOD TO THE PREOPERATIONAL PERIOD AND (2) TO HELP CHILDREN MOVE FROM THE CONCRETE TO THE SYMBOLIC LEVEL. THE THEORIST DERIVES SPECIFIC GOALS FROM THE ABSTRACT THEORY, WHICH SERVES AS THE FOUNDATION FOR THE PROGRAM. THE MASTER TEACHER (DIFFUSER) TRANSLATES THESE GOALS INTO SPECIFIC TEACHING ACTIVITIES AND WORKS WITH THE CLASSROOM TEACHER (CHOSEN FOR HER INTEREST IN A NEW CURRICULUM AND HER WILLINGNESS TO TRY UNORTHODOX APPROACHES), WHO PROVIDES FEEDBACK RELEVANT TO THE EFFECTIVENESS OF THE CURRICULUM. IN A PILOT PROGRAM IN 1968, INVOLVING 20 CHILDREN, THE MEAN GAIN ON THE STANFORD-BINET INTELLIGENCE SCALE WAS 13.7 POINTS. (DO)

ED027967 PS001648
CONCEPT AND LANGUAGE DEVELOPMENT IN A KINDERGARTEN OF DISADVANTAGED CHILDREN. ROBISON, HELEN F.; MUKERJI, ROSE, MAY 66 228P.
EDRS PRICE MF-$0.65 HC-$9.87

THIS DOCUMENT PROPOSES A KINDERGARTEN CURRICULUM DESIGNED TO CONTRIBUTE TO A SUBSTANTIAL REDUCTION OF THE CULTURAL AND CONCEPTUAL GAPS IN THE DEVELOPMENT OF DISADVANTAGED CHILDREN. THE STUDY OF AN URBAN KINDERGARTEN CLASS OF 25 FOCUSES ON A CURRICULUM EMPHASIZING SOCIAL STUDIES, MATHEMATICS, AND LANGUAGE AND ON TEACHING METHODOLOGY WITH EMPHASIS ON PARENT INVOLVEMENT. A DESCRIPTION OF THE PROJECT IS FOLLOWED BY CHAPTERS ON STRUCTURAL PROGRAMS IN SOCIAL SCIENCE, MATHEMATICS, AND LANGUAGE AND A CHAPTER DEVOTED TO THE TEACHER AND TEACHING STRATEGIES. ACCORDING TO THIS DOCUMENT, A MAJOR FINDING OF THE STUDY WAS THAT THE SINGLE MOST PRODUCTIVE TEACHING STRATEGY FOR DISADVANTAGED KINDERGARTEN CHILDREN WAS THE SELECTION OF VERY SPECIFIC GOALS TOWARD WHICH TO PLAN. CONCLUSIONS ON CURRICULUM SUCCESS ARE OUTLINED. (DO)

ED027968 PS001649
THE READABILITY OF SELECTED SECOND GRADE SOCIAL STUDIES TEXTBOOKS. TURNER, DEVONNE GAE, [68] 65P.
EDRS PRICE MF-$0.65 HC-$3.29

THE AIMS OF THE SOCIAL STUDIES CURRICULUMS INCLUDE GROWTH OF THE PUPIL IN SOCIAL COMPETENCE AND AWARENESS. IN ORDER TO PERMIT THE TEACHER KNOWLEDGE AS TO WHAT SOCIAL STUDIES MATERIALS BEST CONTRIBUTE TO THE DEVELOPMENT OF THOSE AIMS, THIS STUDY EVALUATED THE READABILITY LEVEL OF THREE SECOND GRADE SOCIAL STUDIES TEXTBOOKS. (1) "WE HAVE FRIENDS," (2) "YOU AND THE NEIGHBORHOOD," AND (3) "LEARNING ABOUT OUR NEIGHBORS." TWO READABILITY FORMULAS (ONE DEVELOPED BY SPACHE; THE OTHER, BY YOAKAM) WERE USED TO OBTAIN THE READABILITY LEVELS. THE FIRST BOOK WAS FOUND TO BE ON THE SECOND GRADE LEVEL, BUT THE OTHER TWO YIELDED HIGHER GRADE LEVELS OF READABILITY. THE YOAKAM FORMULA RATED THE BOOKS HIGHER THAN THE SPACHE FORMULA BUT NOT SIGNIFICANTLY SO. SOME VARIATION IN READABILITY LEVEL WAS FOUND TO EXIST WITHIN A SINGLE BOOK, THE RESULT BEING THAT SOME SECTIONS WERE READILY COMPREHENSIBLE TO THE STUDENT WHILE OTHERS WERE RELATIVELY MORE DIFFICULT. (WD)

ED027969 PS001651
GOOD REFERENCES ON DAY CARE. , JUL 68 27P.
EDRS PRICE MF-$0.65 HC-$3.29

THIS ANNOTATED BIBLIOGRAPHY, WITH ABOUT 70 ENTRIES, DEALS WITH MANY FACETS OF DAY CARE PROGRAMS. CITATIONS ARE DIVIDED BY THE FOLLOWING SUBJECTS: DAY CARE GUIDES AND STANDARDS, ENVIRONMENTAL STANDARDS, EDUCATION AND CHILD DEVELOPMENT, SOCIAL SERVICES, HEALTH AND NUTRITION, TRAINING OF STAFF, PARENT INVOLVEMENT, ADMINISTRATION AND COORDINATION, AND EVALUATION. COPIES OF THE PUBLICATIONS LISTED CAN BE OBTAINED BY WRITING DIRECTLY TO THE PUBLISHERS OF THESE MATERIALS. THE MAILING ADDRESS IS INCLUDED IN THE BIBLIOGRAPHIC REFERENCE. FREE COPIES ARE INDICATED IN SOME ENTRIES. SOME PRICES ARE ALSO LISTED. (JS)

ED027970 PS001655
RESEARCH ISSUES IN THE HEALTH AND NUTRITION IN EARLY CHILDHOOD. NORTH, A. FREDERICK, JR., 1 NOV 68 31P.
EDRS PRICE MF-$0.65 HC-$3.29

ILL HEALTH AND ITS CAUSES, SUCH AS POOR NUTRITION, CAN KEEP A CHILD FROM FULLY EXPLOITING HIS ENVIRONMENT. IMPORTANT ISSUES TO BE CONSIDERED ARE AS FOLLOWS: (1) FUNCTIONALLY IMPORTANT HEALTH PROBLEMS FREQUENTLY FOUND IN CHILDREN, (2) TECHNIQUES WHICH IDENTIFY THE CHILDREN WHO HAVE PROBLEMS, (3) TREATMENT MOST EFFECTIVE TO REMEDY THE PROBLEMS, AND (4) RESOURCES (FINANCIAL, MANPOWER, ADMINISTRATIVE, ORGANIZATIONAL), TO IDENTIFY, REMEDY, AND PREVENT THE PROBLEMS. GAPS IN BASIC DATA GOVERNING THESE ISSUES INDICATE THE NEED FOR DECISIONS CONCERNING THE CONTENT AND ORGANIZATION OF HEALTH PROGRAMS. DIVERSE SYSTEMS SHOULD BE SELF-CRITICAL WITH BUILT-IN EVALUATION AND MONITORING TO INSURE DEFINITE KNOWLEDGE ABOUT THE EFFECTIVENESS OF THEIR TREATMENT TECHNIQUE AND ORGANIZATIONAL PLANS. (DO)

ED027971 PS001665
PERCEPTUAL TESTING AND TRAINING METHODS USED IN THE PRIMARY GRADES. SOLAN, HAROLD A., MAY 68 4P.
DOCUMENT NOT AVAILABLE FROM EDRS.

AS A CHILD MATURES FROM INFANCY TO EARLY CHILDHOOD, A SHIFT OCCURS IN HIS SENSORY HIERARCHY FROM TACTILE TO AUDITORY TO VISUAL. THE TRANSITION BETWEEN THE PREDOMINANCE OF THE AUDITORY SENSE AND VISUAL SENSE TAKES PLACE IN ABOUT GRADES FOUR AND FIVE. ALTHOUGH THE SENSORY SYSTEMS DO NOT FUNCTION SINGULARLY (BUT ARE INTEGRATED IN THE TOTAL ACTION SYSTEM OF THE CHILD), THE CHILD'S GENERAL ACADEMIC DEVELOPMENT IS SIGNIFICANTLY LINKED TO HIS PERCEPTUAL DEVELOPMENT. THUS, IT IS IMPORTANT THAT A CHILD'S PERCEPTUAL DEVELOPMENT BE ADEQUATELY MEASURED. SUCH MEASUREMENT CAN BE ACCOMPLISHED THROUGH THE USE OF MANY TYPES OF GEOMETRIC-FORM TESTS. HIS VISUAL PERCEPTUAL SPAN CAN BE MEASURED WITH A TACHISTOSCOPE. NOT ONLY IS IT IMPORTANT TO DETERMINE THE CHILD'S SENSORY AND INTERSENSORY DEVELOPMENT IN ORDER TO BE ABLE TO RESPOND TO HIS ACADEMIC NEEDS, BUT PERCEPTUAL ORGANIZATION IS IMPORTANT IN THE DEVELOPMENT OF A POSITIVE SELF-IMAGE. (WD)

ED027972 PS001823
HEAD START ON HEALTH. THOMPSON, NANCY, 69 47P.
EDRS PRICE MF-$0.65 HC-$3.29

THIS BOOKLET PRESENTS HINTS, TIPS, AND SUPPLEMENTARY SUGGESTIONS (IN THE AREAS OF HEALTH AND SAFETY) FOR THE LESS EXPERIENCED PRESCHOOL TEACHER. IN THE SECTION "LIVING IN HEALTH," MEANS FOR MAINTAINING HEALTH AND DAILY ROUTINES ARE DISCUSSED. "PRACTICING SAFETY" INCLUDES SECTIONS ON RESPONSIBILITY AND PREVENTION. "GROWING BIG AND STRONG" COVERS PHYSICAL DEVELOPMENT AND NUTRITION, WHILE "DISCOVERING SELF" DISCUSSES SELF-IDENTITY AND ANSWERING QUESTIONS. IN THE SECTION "USING COMMUNITY RESOURCES," WAYS IN WHICH PARENTS AND COMMUNITY WORKERS CAN BE HELPFUL ARE CITED. ALSO GIVEN ARE SUGGESTIONS ABOUT VISITORS, FIELD TRIPS, AND FOLLOWUP ACTIVITIES. AN EXTENSIVE APPENDIX INCLUDES BOOKS TO READ WITH PRESCHOOL CHILDREN, BOOKS FOR ADULTS TO READ, RECORDS, FILMS, POSTERS, OTHER SOURCES OF INFORMATION, AND A LIST OF PUBLISHERS AND BOOK WHOLESALERS. (JS)

ED027973 PS001897
THE VALUE OF THE SPOKEN RESPONSE IN TEACHING LISTENING SKILLS TO YOUNG CHILDREN THROUGH PROGRAMMED INSTRUCTION. FINAL REPORT. KEISLAR, EVAN R.; STERN, CAROLYN, JAN 69 164P.
EDRS PRICE MF-$0.65 HC-$6.58

THE MAIN FOCUS OF THIS PROJECT WAS THE IMPROVEMENT OF THE UNDERSTANDING OF SPOKEN LANGUAGE BY LOWER CLASS KINDERGARTEN CHILDREN. THUS, THE PROJECT WAS CONCERNED WITH (1) IDENTIFYING AREAS IN WHICH YOUNG CHILDREN ARE DEFICIENT IN LISTENING SKILLS, (2) PREPARING AND EVALUATING INSTRUCTIONAL PROGRAMS FOR THE IMPROVEMENT OF THESE SKILLS, AND (3) TESTING UNDER CLASSROOM CONDITIONS A HYPOTHESIS REGARDING THE VALUE OF HAVING CHILDREN SPEAK ALOUD IN DEVELOPING LISTENING AND COMPREHENSION SKILLS. SIX STUDIES WERE CONDUCTED TO OBTAIN INFORMATION ON THE PUPILS' DEFICIENCIES, TO USE THE PROGRAMS CONSTRUCTED TO IMPROVE THE DEFICIENCIES, AND TO INVESTIGATE THE HYPOTHESIS. SEVERAL OF THE SIX STUDIES USED SUBJECTS OTHER THAN LOWER CLASS KINDERGARTEN PUPILS FOR CONTROL OR COMPARISON PURPOSES. THE RESULTS OF THE STUDIES INDICATED THAT (1) LOWER CLASS CHILDREN USE A RESTRICTED LANGUAGE CODE, ESPECIALLY WITH REGARD TO FUNCTION WORDS, AND (2) INSTRUCTIONS TO VERBALIZE AND THE SUBSEQUENT OVERT RESPONSES HAVE MEASURABLE VALUE WHERE THERE IS A DIRECT CORRESPONDENCE BETWEEN THE STIMULUS AND THE VERBAL RESPONSE. HOWEVER, THE EFFECT OF ORAL RESPONDING WAS MUCH LESS CLEAR WHEN THE MATERIAL WAS MORE COMPLEX. AN IMPORTANT CONTRIBUTION OF THIS PROJECT TO EDUCATION WAS THE DEVELOPMENT AND EVALUATION OF A NUMBER OF REPLICABLE INSTRUCTIONAL PROGRAMS ACCOMPANIED BY CRITERION TEST ITEMS. (WD)

ED027974 PS001901
EARLY CHILDHOOD PROJECT, NEW YORK CITY , 69 28P.
EDRS PRICE MF-$0.65 HC NOT AVAILABLE FROM EDRS.
AVAILABLE FROM: SUP. OF DOCUMENTS, U.S. GOVERNMENT PRINTING OFFICE, WASHINGTON, D.C. 20402 ($0.35)

THIS PRESCHOOL PROGRAM CONCENTRATED ON LANGUAGE DEVELOPMENT, SELF-CONCEPT, PERCEPTION, AND CONCEPT FORMATION. ALSO, A VERTICALLY ORGANIZED PROGRAM OF READING, MATH, SCIENCE, AND CREATIVE DRAMATICS, ALONG WITH PARENT ACTIVITY, INSERVICE TRAINING, AND DISSEMINATION, COVERED PREKINDERGARTEN THROUGH THE THIRD GRADE. INDIVIDUAL AND SMALL GROUP WORK ALLOWED CHILDREN TO PROCEED AT THEIR OWN RATE. THE SUBJECTS, MOSTLY NEGROES FROM NONINTACT LOWER CLASS FAMILIES, ORIGINALLY VARIED IN NUMBER FROM 120 TO 200 (INCLUDING CONTROLS) IN EACH OF SIX GROUPS (WAVES) STUDIES. PRETESTS WERE ADMINISTERED BEFORE PREKINDERGARTEN. TWO POSTTESTS WERE GIVEN, ONE AFTER PREKINDERGARTEN AND THE OTHER AFTER KINDERGARTEN. EVALUATION WAS HAMPERED BY A LOSS OF SUBJECTS, BY AN ARRANGEMENT IN WHICH ONLY SUBSAMPLES WERE TESTED, AND BY THE USE OF VARIOUS TESTS. THE RESULTS ON THE COLUMBIA MENTAL MATURITY SCALE SHOWED THAT FOR THE SUBSAMPLES DRAWN FROM THE FIRST EXPERIMENTAL WAVE AND THE BASIC CONTROL GROUP, THE DIFFERENCE IN THE MEANS WERE NOT STATISTICALLY SIGNIFICANT ON PRETESTS, YET THEY WERE SIGNIFICANT ON THE FIRST POSTTEST BUT NOT ON THE SECOND POSTTEST. FOR SUBSAMPLES DRAWN FROM WAVES TWO THROUGH FOUR, RESULTS ON THE STANFORD-BINET SHOWED THAT THE EXPERIMENTAL GROUPS PERFORMED SIGNIFICANTLY BETTER ON BOTH POSTTESTS BUT NOT ON PRETESTS. (JS)

ED027975 PS001902
PERRY PRESCHOOL PROJECT, YPSILANTI, MICHIGAN , 69 22P.
EDRS PRICE MF-$0.65 HC NOT AVAILABLE FROM EDRS.
AVAILABLE FROM: SUPT. OF DOCUMENTS, U.S. GOVERNMENT PRINTING OFFICE, WASHINGTON, D.C. 20402 ($0.35)

THE PERRY PRESCHOOL PROJECT ASSESSED LONGITUDINAL EFFECTS OF A 2-YEAR PROGRAM CONSISTING OF A DAILY 3-HOUR COGNITIVELY ORIENTED NURSERY, A WEEKLY 90-MINUTE HOME VISIT, AND LESS FREQUENT GROUP MEETINGS OF THE PUPILS' PARENTS. SUBJECTS CONSISTED OF 3- AND 4-YEAR-OLD NEGRO DISADVANTAGED AND FUNCTIONALLY RETARDED CHILDREN, WHOSE PRETEST SCORES ON THE STANFORD BINET INTELLIGENCE SCALE WERE NOT ABOVE 85. THE PROGRAM OPERATED FROM SEPTEMBER 1962 UNTIL JUNE 1966. ABOUT 24 CHILDREN TOOK PART EACH YEAR. UPON ENTERING, THE CHILDREN WERE PRETESTED ON THE STANFORD-BINET, THE PEABODY PICTURE VOCABULARY TEST, AND THE LEITER INTERNATIONAL PERFORMANCE SCALE. THESE AND OTHER TESTS WERE USED LATER IN THE PROGRAM. FEW SIGNIFICANT DIFFERENCES BETWEEN EXPERIMENTALS AND CONTROLS WERE NOTED ON THE PRETESTS. THE CALIFORNIA ACHIEVEMENT TESTS IN READING, LANGUAGE, AND MATHEMATICS WERE GIVEN AT THE END OF THE FIRST GRADE AND AGAIN AT THE END OF THE SECOND GRADE. THE RESULTS SHOWED SIGNIFICANT GAINS FOR THE EXPERIMENTALS OVER THE CONTROLS. (JS)

ED027976 PS001903
INFANT EDUCATION RESEARCH PROJECT, WASHINGTON, D.C. , 69 26P.
EDRS PRICE MF-$0.65 HC NOT AVAILABLE FROM EDRS.
AVAILABLE FROM: SUPT. OF DOCUMENTS, U.S. GOVERNMENT PRINTING OFFICE, WASHINGTON, D.C. 20402 ($0.35)

IN A STUDY TO DETERMINE WHETHER OR NOT CULTURALLY DEPRIVED CHILDREN DEVELOP AT PROGRESSIVELY GREATER DEFICITS IN INTELLECTUAL FUNCTIONING DURING THE AGES OF 15 MONTHS TO 3 YEARS, TUTORS PROVIDED 15-MONTH-OLD INFANTS WITH INTELLECTUAL AND VERBAL STIMULATION ONE HOUR DAILY, FIVE TIMES A WEEK UNTIL THEY WERE 36 MONTHS OLD. THE SUBJECTS CONSISTED OF NEGRO MALES FROM HOMES THAT MET TWO OF THE FOLLOWING THREE CRITERIA: (1) FAMILY INCOME WAS $5,000 OR LESS, (2) MOTHER'S FORMAL EDUCATION WAS LESS THAN 12 YEARS, AND (3) MOTHER HAD BEEN AN UNSKILLED OR SEMISKILLED WORKER. THE EXPERIMENTAL GROUP CONTAINED 28 CHILDREN AND THE CONTROL GROUP NUMBERED 30. PRETESTS ON THE BAYLEY INFANT SCALES SHOWED THE CONTROLS SLIGHTLY SUPERIOR (BUT NOT SIGNIFICANTLY) TO THE EXPERIMENTALS AT 14 MONTHS. AT 21 MONTHS, THE EXPERIMENTALS HAD GAINED SIGNIFICANTLY (.05 LEVEL). POSTTESTING ON THE STANFORD-BINET AT AGES 27 AND 36 MONTHS SHOWED EXPERIMENTALS WERE SIGNIFICANTLY SUPERIOR TO CONTROLS AT THE .01 LEVEL. WHEN THE SUBJECTS WERE 36 MONTHS OLD, THE PEABODY PICTURE VOCABULARY TEST AND JOHNS HOPKINS PERCEPTUAL TEST SHOWED THAT THE EXPERIMENTALS WERE SIGNIFICANTLY SUPERIOR AT THE .01 LEVEL; THE AARONSON-SCHAEFER PREPOSITION TEST ALSO SHOWED GAINS BUT NOT AT A SIGNIFICANT LEVEL. (JS)

ED027977 PS001904
PRESCHOOL PROGRAM, FRESNO, CALIFORNIA , 69 19P.
EDRS PRICE MF-$0.65 HC NOT AVAILABLE FROM EDRS.
AVAILABLE FROM: SUPT. OF DOCUMENTS, U.S. GOVERNMENT PRINTING OFFICE, WASHINGTON, D.C. 20402 ($0.25)

FOR EACH OF 4 YEARS VARYING NUMBERS (FROM 45 TO 750) OF 3-TO 5-YEAR-OLD CHILDREN, MOSTLY MEXICAN-AMERICAN, SPANISH SPEAKING, PARTICIPATED IN A PROGRAM AIMED AT LANGUAGE DEVELOPMENT. CLASSES MET 3 HOURS DAILY, FIVE TIMES A WEEK, IN SMALL DISCUSSION-AND-ACTIVITY GROUPS THAT INCLUDED FIVE CHILDREN AND ONE ADULT. THE PEABODY PICTURE VOCABULARY TEST WAS USED AS A PRETEST AND POSTTEST MEASURE. ON THE PILOT PROJECT NEARLY EVERY CHILD RAISED HIS IQ BY 10 TO 20 POINTS. FOR THE SECOND YEAR, THERE WERE NEGLIGIBLE GAINS, POSSIBLY DUE TO THE BREVITY OF THE PROGRAM (2 TO 5 MONTHS) AND THE TEACHERS' LACK OF NURSERY EXPERIENCE. THE THIRD YEAR'S TEST RESULTS, WHICH WERE DIVIDED INTO THREE ETHNIC GROUPS (CAUCASIAN, NEGRO, AND MEXICAN-AMERICAN), WERE COMPARED. THE GROUPS DIFFERED SIGNIFICANTLY ON THE PRETEST BUT NOT ON THE POSTTEST. ALL GROUPS GAINED SIGNIFICANTLY. THE SAME PROCEDURE WAS FOLLOWED THE FOURTH YEAR, AND ALL GROUPS GAINED SIGNIFICANTLY. (JS)

ED027978 PS001905
DIAGNOSTICALLY BASED CURRICULUM, BLOOMINGTON, INDIANA , 69 40P.
EDRS PRICE MF-$0.65 HC NOT AVAILABLE FROM EDRS.
AVAILABLE FROM: SUPT. OF DOCUMENTS, U.S. GOVERNMENT PRINTING OFFICE, WASHINGTON, D.C. 20402 ($0.45)

THE PURPOSE OF THIS STUDY WAS TO DEVELOP AND EVALUATE A DIAGNOSTICALLY BASED CURRICULUM FOR DISADVANTAGED PRESCHOOL CHILDREN. FOR EACH OF 3 YEARS, 45 LOWER CLASS APPALACHIAN WHITE 5-YEAR-OLDS WERE EQUALLY DIVIDED INTO THREE GROUPS. THE EXPERIMENTAL PRESCHOOL GROUP (EPS) RECEIVED A STRUCTURAL CURRICULUM DESIGNED TO REMEDY SPECIFIC, DIAGNOSED DEFICITS IN LANGUAGE DEVELOPMENT, FINE MOTOR COORDINATION, CONCEPT DEVELOPMENT, AND SOCIALIZATION. TWO CONTRAST GROUPS WERE USED. THE KINDERGARTEN CONTRAST GROUP (KC) RECEIVED A TRADITIONAL KINDERGARTEN PROGRAM, WHILE THE "AT HOME" CONTRAST GROUP (AHC) RECEIVED ONLY THE PRETESTING AND POSTTESTING GIVEN TO ALL GROUPS. THE EXPERIMENTAL CURRICULUM WAS ANNUALLY REVISED TO BENEFIT FROM THE PAST EXPERIENCES. WHEN THE DATA FROM THE POPULATIONS OF 3 YEARS WERE COMBINED, THEY REVEALED THAT IN THE INTELLIGENCE CATEGORY, THE EPS MEAN WAS SIGNIFICANTLY GREATER THAN EITHER THE KC OR AHC MEAN, AND THE KC MEAN WAS SIGNIFICANTLY GREATER THAN THE AHC MEAN. TESTING DURING THE FIRST GRADE, HOWEVER, SHOWED THAT THE EPS AND KC HAD STABILIZED IN IQ BY THE END OF THEIR PRESCHOOL YEAR, BUT THE AHC GROUP GAINED ENOUGH IN THE FIRST GRADE TO CANCEL THE IQ DIFFERENCES THAT FORMERLY EXISTED. STATISTICS FOR THE OTHER CATEGORIES ARE ALSO LISTED. (JS)

ED027979 PS001906
ACADEMIC PRESCHOOL, CHAMPAIGN, ILLINOIS , 69 27P.
EDRS PRICE MF-$0.65 HC NOT AVAILABLE FROM EDRS.
AVAILABLE FROM: SUPT. OF DOCUMENTS, U.S. GOVERNMENT PRINTING OFFICE, WASHINGTON, D.C. 20402 ($0.35)

A STUDY WAS CONDUCTED TO TEST THE EFFECTIVENESS OF A PRESCHOOL PROGRAM WHICH EMPHASIZED RAPID ATTAINMENT OF BASIC ACADEMIC CONCEPTS. THE EXPERIMENTALS WERE 4- TO 5-YEAR-OLD LOWER CLASS, PREDOMINANTLY NEGRO, CHILDREN. FOR 2 YEARS THEY RECEIVED INSTRUCTION 2 HOURS DAILY, 5 TIMES A WEEK, IN A GROUP WHERE THE PUPIL-TEACHER RATIO WAS FIVE TO ONE. TO INDUCE LEARNING AT AN ABOVE-AVERAGE RATE, POSITIVE AND NEGATIVE REINFORCERS WERE USED. A COMPARISON GROUP WAS PRETESTED AND POSTTESTED. AFTER THE FIRST YEAR OF INSTRUCTION, RESULTS FROM THE STANFORD-BINET SHOWED A GAIN OF 17.14 POINTS FOR THE EXPERIMENTAL GROUP; THE COMPARISON GROUP SHOWED A GAIN OF 8.07 POINTS. AFTER THE SECOND YEAR OF INSTRUCTION, THE EXPERIMENTAL GROUP GAINED AN ADDITIONAL 8.61 POINTS; THE COMPARISON GROUP LOST 2.96 POINTS. INTERVIEWS WITH PARENTS AND OBSERVATIONS OF THE PARTICIPATING CHILDREN REVEALED NO BEHAVIORAL PROBLEMS AFTER THE SECOND WEEK OF INSTRUCTION AND NO REGRESSIVE BEHAVIOR IN GENERAL. (JS)

ED028812 PS000178
TOWARD THE PREVENTION OF INCOMPETENCE. HUNT, J. MCVICKER, 2 FEB 67 20P.
EDRS PRICE MF-$0.65 HC-$3.29

THE MENTAL HEALTH OF THE CITIZENS OF A COMMUNITY IS IN PART DEPENDENT UPON THEIR ABILITY TO JOIN IN AND OBTAIN THE REWARDS OF THE FULFILLED LIFE OF A COMPETENT MEMBER OF SOCIETY. THIS HAS BEEN VERY DIFFICULT FOR THE DISADVANTAGED TO ACCOMPLISH BECAUSE THEIR BACKGROUNDS HAVE BEEN ONE OF DEPRIVATION AND THEIR OPPORTUNITIES HAVE BEEN LIMITED. BUT THE INCOMPETENCE OF THE DISADVANTAGED IS NOT SIGNIFICANTLY ATTRIBUTABLE TO GENETIC DEFICIENCIES; RATHER IT IS MOSTLY ATTRIBUTABLE TO THEIR DEPRIVED BACKGROUNDS. HEAD START AND SIMILAR COMPENSATORY EDUCATION PROGRAMS HAVE BEEN CREATED TO ALLEVIATE THE INTELLECTUAL AND COGNITIVE DEFICIENCIES OF DISADVANTAGED CHILDREN. SUCH PROGRAMS HAVE MET WITH VARIED SUCCESS. INTERVENTION EARLIER THAN AGE FOUR OR FIVE WOULD BE GOOD, HOWEVER, BECAUSE OF THE IMPORTANCE OF EARLY DEVELOPMENT. THIS INTERVENTION SHOULD BE COUPLED WITH SOME FORM OF PARENT EDUCATION OR PARENT PARTICIPATION. SUCH A TOTAL PROGRAM (CALLED "CENTERS FOR CHILDREN AND PARENTS)" HAS BEEN SUGGESTED. NOT ONLY WOULD YOUNG DEPRIVED CHILDREN BE GIVEN A COMPENSATORY EDUCATION AT SUCH A CENTER, BUT PROFESSIONAL PERSONNEL THERE WOULD ESTABLISH RELATIONS WITH THE PARENTS AND COUNSEL THEM AS TO PROPER CHILD REARING PRACTICES. (WD)

ED028813 PS001650
CURRENT ISSUES IN RESEARCH ON EARLY DEVELOPMENT. SIEGEL, ALBERTA E., 31 AUG 68 9P.
EDRS PRICE MF-$0.65 HC-$3.29

RESEARCH ON EARLY DEVELOPMENT IS MOVING APACE. DEVELOPMENTAL PSYCHOLOGY IS AGAIN GIVING SERIOUS ATTENTION TO AGES AND STAGES. THIS ATTENTION IS DUE, IN GREAT PART, TO THE FORMULATIONS ABOUT COGNITIVE DEVELOPMENT BY PIAGET. EARLIER IN THE CENTURY, THE EXPERIMENTAL APPROACH TO CHILD STUDY CAME TO REFLECT PSYCHOLOGY'S GENERALLY HEAVY COMMITMENT TO PHYSICS AND CHEMISTRY. LATELY, HOWEVER, THE INFLUENCE OF BIOLOGY ON DEVELOPMENTAL PSYCHOLOGY HAS BECOME PREDOMINANT. EXAMPLES OF THIS INTERACTION INCLUDE (1) THE STUDY OF ETHOLOGY (PARTICULARLY OF THE CHILD'S EARLY TIES TO OTHER HUMAN BEINGS, ESPECIALLY TO THE CARETAKING PERSON); (2) THE INVESTIGATIONS IN EVOLUTIONARY BIOLOGY (THE EFFECT THAT THE NATURALISTIC FIELD STUDIES OF NONHUMAN PRIMATES HAVE ON THE NATURALISTIC STUDY OF HUMAN PRIMATES); (3) THE NEW USES OF KARYOTYPING, (LOOKING AT THE GENETIC CHARACTERISTICS OF THE NEWBORN); (4) THE LINK BETWEEN PSYCHOLOGY AND PHYSIOLOGY; AND (5) THE USE OF ELECTROENCEPHALOGRAPHIC DATA TO STUDY BRAIN BEHAVIOR RELATIONSHIPS. (WD)

ED028814 PS001652
PSYCHOLOBIOLOGICAL REFERENTS FOR THE TREATMENT OF AUTISM. SCHOPLER, ERIC; REICHLER, ROBERT J., APR 68 25P.
EDRS PRICE MF-$0.65 HC-$3.29

IN STUDIES OF PRESCHOOL CHILDREN, FOUR CLUSTERS OF SYMPTOMS SEEM MOST USEFUL IN CHARACTERIZING THOSE CHILDREN WHO MANIFEST AUTISM: (1) FAILURE TO ESTABLISH HUMAN RELATEDNESS AND MEANINGFUL SOCIAL ATTACHMENTS; (2) IMPAIRMENT OF MOTIVATION TO BECOME COMPETENT; (3) DISTURBANCES OF PERCEPTUAL INTEGRATION; AND (4) IMPAIRMENT OF THE DEVELOPMENT OF COGNITIVE FUNCTIONS. ONE OF THE MOST IMPORTANT IMPAIRMENTS OF AUTISTIC CHILDREN IS PERCEPTUAL INCONSTANCY (IRREGULARITY IN THE PROCESSING OF SENSORY DATA BY THE VARIOUS RECEPTOR SYSTEMS). THE LIKELIHOOD OF PHYSIOLOGICAL AND BIOCHEMICAL CHANGES UNDER AUTISTIC CONDITIONS OF SENSORY DEPRIVATION REQUIRE THAT PERCEPTUAL PATTERNS BE PROMOTED IN THE CHILD AS EARLY AS POSSIBLE. A PROGRAM OF TREATMENT FOR THE AUTISTIC CHILD SHOULD INCLUDE PARENT PARTICIPATION AND PARENT EDUCATION, WITH THE GOAL OF REDUCING DISTORTIONS IN THE PARENT-CHILD RELATIONSHIP. OTHERWISE, TREATMENT OF THE PRESCHOOL AUTISTIC CHILD SHOULD BE CONCERNED WITH ESTABLISHING PERCEPTUAL ORGANIZATION AND CORTICAL CONTROL OVER HIS SENSORY EXPERIENCES. FURTHER RESEARCH IS NEEDED ON THE RELATIONSHIP BETWEEN PARENTAL ATTITUDES OR CHILD REARING PRACTICES AND THE EXISTENCE OF AN AUTISTIC CHILD. (WD)

ED028815 PS001653
A THEORY OF PARENT EFFECTIVENESS. GORDON, THOMAS, [67] 28P.
EDRS PRICE MF-$0.65 HC-$3.29

IN ORDER TO HELP PARENTS IN REARING CHILDREN, A THEORY OF PARENT EFFECTIVENESS WAS DEVELOPED. BASED ON THE IDEA THAT PARENTS SHOULD BE HONEST WITH THEIR CHILDREN ABOUT THE CHILD'S BEHAVIOR, THE THEORY IDENTIFIED OWNERSHIP OF PROBLEMS AND CONFLICT RESOLUTION. CHILDREN'S BEHAVIOR WAS DEFINED AS BEING ACCEPTABLE AND NONACCEPTABLE TO THE PARENT, DEPENDING ON THE THE INDIVIDUAL PARENT AND CHILD AND ON CHANGES WITHIN THE PARENT, CHILD, OR ENVIRONMENT. CONFLICTS AROSE WHEN THE CHILD OR THE PARENT "OWNED" A PROBLEM; THAT IS, WHEN THEIR INDIVIDUAL NEEDS WERE NOT MET BECAUSE OF THE CHILD'S BEHAVIOR. THE CONFLICTS COULD BE RESOLVED BY THE PARENT IN BOTH CASES. WHEN THE CHILD OWNED A PROBLEM, THE PARENT COULD LISTEN TO THE CHILD EXPRESS HIS FEELINGS. WHEN THE PARENT OWNED A PROBLEM, HE COULD HONESTLY EXPRESS HIS OWN FEELINGS TO THE CHILD. IF CONFLICT AROSE WHEN NEITHER PARTY'S NEEDS WERE MET, THE PARENT AND CHILD COULD SEEK A MUTUALLY ACCEPTABLE SOLUTION. RESOLUTIONS WHERE EITHER THE PARENT OR CHILD "WON ALL" WERE NOT CONSIDERED SATISFACTORY, BECAUSE RESENTMENT BUILT UP IN THE LOSING PARTY. BY RESOLVING CONFLICT SITUATIONS THROUGH COMPROMISE, PARENTS COULD INCREASE THEIR CHILDREN'S ACCEPTABLE BEHAVIOR. FURTHERMORE, COMPROMISE, AS A TECHNIQUE FOR CONFLICT RESOLUTION, WAS CONSIDERED APPLICABLE TO ALL HUMAN RELATIONSHIPS. (JS)

ED028816 PS001657
AN EVALUATIVE STUDY OF COLOR-VISION TESTS FOR KINDERGARTEN AND FIRST GRADE PUPILS. LAMPE, JOHN M., 9 NOV 68 9P.
EDRS PRICE MF-$0.65 HC-$3.29

BECAUSE OF THE INCREASING USE OF COLOR IN INSTRUCTIONAL MATERIALS AT THE LEVEL OF THE PRIMARY GRADES, THE HEALTH SERVICE DEPARTMENT OF THE DENVER PUBLIC SCHOOLS BECAME INTERESTED IN INVESTIGATING THE COLOR VISION OF 5- AND 6-YEAR-OLDS. A PROJECT WAS ESTABLISHED TO CREATE COLOR-VISION TESTING METHODS AND TO USE THOSE METHODS TO ASCERTAIN INCIDENCE AND TO IDENTIFY COLOR-DEFICIENT PUPILS. THE TWO BASIC TYPES OF TESTS USED WERE (1) COLOR MATCHING AND (2) RECOGNITION OF COLORED SYMBOLS DIFFERENTIATED FROM SURROUNDINGS OF OTHER COLORS. SOME 3,400 CHILDREN WERE TESTED DURING THE 1967-68 SCHOOL YEAR. IT WAS FOUND THAT THE TESTS USED WERE PRACTICAL FOR THEIR AGE GROUP. THE TESTS PRODUCED HIGH INTEREST AND SHOULD BE USED EITHER IN THE LATTER PART OF KINDERGARTEN OR IN THE FIRST GRADE. THE INCIDENCE OF SOME DEGREE OF COLOR DEFICIENCY WAS 0.5 PERCENT FOR GIRLS AND 3.0 TO 3.5 PERCENT FOR BOYS. THE COLOR-SYMBOL TESTS WERE SIGNIFICANTLY MORE DEFINITE THAN THE COLOR-MATCHING TEST. (WD)

ED028817 PS001664
THE SOCIAL DEVELOPMENT OF HUMAN INTELLIGENCE. EISENBERG, LEON, AUG 68 21P.
EDRS PRICE MF-$0.65 HC-$3.29

INTELLIGENCE MAKES MAN UNIQUE. TO DATE MAN'S USE OF THIS INTELLIGENCE HAS BEEN DEFICIENT. THE DEFICIT LIES IN THE ONE-SIDED DEVELOPMENT OF HIS PROBLEM-SOLVING CAPACITY; THAT IS, AN ENORMOUS GROWTH HAS OCCURRED IN TECHNOLOGICAL CAPABILITIES WITHOUT A CORRESPONDING GAIN IN SOLUTIONS TO SOCIAL PROBLEMS. THIS DEFICIT IS PARTICULARLY SIGNIFICANT BECAUSE INTELLIGENCE IS, TO A GREAT DEGREE, A PRODUCT OF THE SOCIAL ENVIRONMENT. IMPORTANT TO THE DEVELOPMENT OF THE BRAIN IS PROPER NUTRITION, A CLEAN ENVIRONMENT TO REDUCE THE EFFECTS OF DISEASE, ADEQUATE AND VARIED SENSORY STIMULATION, AND RICH ADULT-INFANT SOCIAL INTERACTIONS. YET, GIVEN THE SATISFACTORY DEVELOPMENT OF THE BRAIN, THE CONTRAST BETWEEN OUR INTELLECTUAL PROWESS IN UNDERSTANDING AND MANIPULATING THE PHYSICAL WORLD AND OUR INSENSITIVITY TO (IF NOT DEBASED JUDGMENTS OF) THE SOCIAL PURPOSES OF THAT MANIPULATION POINTS UP THE PERVERSION OF INTELLIGENCE. TODAY THE PROBLEMS FOR MENTAL HEALTH AND HUMAN DEVELOPMENT ARE (1) THE VIET NAM WAR, (2) RACISM, AND (3) THE GROSS INEQUALITIES IN ACCESS TO RESOURCES BETWEEN AND WITHIN NATIONS. (WD)

ED028818 PS001673
SOME DIMENSIONS OF CREATIVE THINKING ABILITY ACHIEVEMENT, AND INTELLIGENCE IN FIRST GRADE. ALIOTTI, NICHOLAS C.; BLANTON, WILLIAM E., FEB 69 10P.
EDRS PRICE MF-$0.65 HC-$3.29

THE PICTURE INTERPRETATION TEST (TORRANCE AND GROSSMAN, 1967) WAS USED IN A BATTERY OF CREATIVE TESTS AS PART OF A CONSTRUCT VALIDITY TEST. THE TEST WAS ADMINISTERED TO 46 BOYS AND 37 GIRLS IN FIVE FIRST GRADE CLASSROOMS IN A CLAYTON COUNTY, GEORGIA, ELEMENTARY SCHOOL. THE PURPOSE OF THE TEST WAS TO MEASURE THE CHILD'S ABILITY TO "READ A PICTURE." A SUBJECT WAS PRESENTED A NOVEL STIMULUS AND ASKED TO AGREE OR DISAGREE WITH STATEMENTS CONCERNING THE PICTURE. WHEN A FACTOR ANALYSIS WAS PERFORMED ON THE DATA, FOUR FACTORS EMERGED: (1) SOME MEASURE OF GENERAL INTELLIGENCE, (2) A GENERAL INDEX OF ACADEMIC ACHIEVEMENT, (3) FIGURAL MEASURES OF CREATIVE THINKING, AND (4) VERBAL CREATIVITY MEASURES. THE FACTORS WERE THEN CORRELATED WITH THE FOLLOWING RESULTS: (1) VERBAL CREATIVE THINKING WAS INDEPENDENT OF GENERAL INTELLIGENCE, ACADEMIC ACHIEVEMENT, AND FIGURAL CREATIVITY; AND (2) FIGURAL CREATIVITY SHARED COMMON VARIANCE WITH GENERAL INTELLIGENCE AND ACADEMIC ACHIEVEMENT. THE INDEPENDENCE OF THE VERBAL CREATIVE THINKING FACTOR WAS INCONGRUOUS, SINCE MANY OTHER STUDIES REPORTED AT LEAST A LOW CORRELATION BETWEEN VERBAL CREATIVE THINKING AND ACADEMIC ACHIEVEMENT OR GENERAL INTELLIGENCE. THE RESULTS SUGGEST THAT A REPLICATION BE CONDUCTED WITH PARTICULAR ATTENTION TO PERCEPTUAL SENSITIVITY TASKS. (JS)

ED028819 PS001677
TEACHING MOTHERS TO TEACH: A HOME COUNSELING PROGRAM FOR LOW-INCOME PARENTS. ORHAN, SHIJE; RADIN, NORMA, NOV 68 17P.
EDRS PRICE MF-$0.65 HC-$3.29

TWENTY-FOUR CHILDREN ATTENDED A SPECIAL HALF-DAY CLASS WHEN NOT ATTENDING REGULAR KINDERGARTEN, AND 12 OF THEIR MOTHERS PARTICIPATED IN A HOME COUNSELING PROGRAM. CHILDREN WHOSE MOTHERS WERE COUNSELED ACHIEVED SIGNIFICANTLY HIGHER ON THE METROPOLITAN READING TEST, AND THEIR MOTHERS SHOWED A SIGNIFICANTLY GREATER GAIN ON THE COGNITIVE HOME ENVIRONMENT SCALE. IN BIWEEKLY HOME VISITS, PARENTS WERE SHOWN HOW TO TEACH SPECIFIC COGNITIVE CONCEPTS TO SUPPORT SCHOOL CURRICULUM, TO EVALUATE CHILDREN'S PROGRESS, AND TO MOTIVATE THE CHILDREN TO BECOME INVOLVED IN THE HOME EDUCATION PROGRAM. APPROACHES AND TECHNIQUES EMPLOYED TO ABET PARENTS' TEACHING SKILLS ARE DELINEATED IN THE REPORT, AND AN EVALUATION OF THE PROGRAM WITH RECOMMENDATIONS FOR MODIFICATIONS ARE INCLUDED. (DO)

ED028820 PS001680
AN EVALUATION OF THE INTERIM CLASS: AN EXTENDED READINESS PROGRAM. BERNABEI, RAYMOND, [68] 10P.
EDRS PRICE MF-$0.65 HC-$3.29

THIS 3-YEAR LONGITUDINAL STUDY IS EXPLORING READINESS SKILLS OF CHILDREN BETWEEN 5 AND 8 YEARS OF AGE AND PROPOSES A DESIGN FOR CURRICULUM DEVELOPMENT. IN THIS STUDY, GENERALIZED CONCEPTS, VISUAL-MOTOR TRIORDINATION, VISUAL AND AUDITORY DISCRIMINATION, VISUAL AND AUDITORY MEMORY (IMAGERY), AND ORAL LANGUAGE USAGE, ARE IDENTIFIED IN ORDER TO CATEGORIZE LEARNING BEHAVIORS. BEHAVIORAL INDICATORS FOR READINESS SKILLS ARE MATCHED TO SKILLS FOR READING ACHIEVEMENT, PERCEPTION, RECALL, WORD ANALYSIS, COMPREHENSION, AND TRANSFERENCE. COMMERCIAL MATERIALS AND SPECIALLY PREPARED MATERIALS ARE DEVELOPED INTO A CONCEPTUAL DESIGN FOR CURRICULUM DEVELOPMENT. A CHILD IS GUIDED INTO A PERSONALIZED LEARNING PROGRAM, HIS PROGRESS IS ASSESSED, AND HE IS PLACED FOR THE COMING YEAR ACCORDING TO HIS READINESS TO LEARN. EVALUATION OF THE PROGRAM AFTER 1 YEAR INDICATES SIGNIFICANT DIFFERENCES IN READINESS SKILLS BETWEEN THE INTERIM CLASS AND NORMAL CLASSES. (DO)

ED028821 PS001684
A COMPARATIVE STUDY OF THE SELF-IMAGES OF DISADVANTAGED CHILDREN. SOARES, ANTHONY T.; SOARES, LOUISE M., [FEB 69] 15P.
EDRS PRICE MF-$0.65 HC-$3.29

ON THE BASIS OF PREVIOUS RESEARCH, WHICH REVEALED DIFFERENCE IN SELF-PERCEPTION OF DISADVANTAGED AND ADVANTAGED CHILDREN, THIS PROJECT INVESTIGATED WHETHER DIFFERENCES IN PERSONALITY TRAITS EXISTED AND WHAT THESE DIFFERENCES MIGHT BE AS REVEALED BY THEIR SELF-PERCEPTIONS. FOURTH THROUGH EIGHTH GRADERS IN AN URBAN SCHOOL SYSTEM WERE SUBJECTS. ABOUT 200 SUBJECTS WERE DISADVANTAGED, AND ABOUT 300 SUBJECTS WERE FROM AN ADVANTAGED AREA OF THE SAME CITY. FORTY BIPOLAR TRAITS WERE EXPRESSED IN SENTENCE FORM, AND CHILDREN RATED THEMSELVES ON THE INVENTORY, INDICATING THEIR SELF-CONCEPTS. RESULTS SHOWED HIGHER PERCENTAGES ON THE POSITIVE PERSONALITY TRAITS FOR THE DISADVANTAGED AND REVEALED GREATER DIFFERENCES BETWEEN BOYS THAN BETWEEN GIRLS. THE DISADVANTAGED, MORE THAN THE ADVANTAGED, TENDED TO SEE THEMSELVES AS INDEPENDENT, COMPETENT, PATIENT, AND DELIBERATE; WHILE THE ADVANTAGED PERCEIVED THEMSELVES AS HAPPY, SELF-CONFIDENT, TRUSTING, FEARLESS, AND WORTHY. DESPITE DIFFERENCES, BOTH GROUPS HAD HIGHER PERCENTAGES OF RESPONSES IN THE POSITIVE END OF THE CONTINUUM, INDICATING THAT DISADVANTAGED CHILDREN DO NOT NECESSARILY REVEAL NEGATIVE PERSONALITY TRAITS IN THEIR SELF-PERCEPTIONS. DATA ALSO INDICATED THAT THESE DIFFERENCES DID NOT NECESSARILY MEAN THAT ONE GROUP HAD NEGATIVE PERSONALITY TRAITS AND THE OTHER HAD POSITIVE PERSONALITY TRAITS. (DO)

ED028822 PS001688
INDUCING CONSERVATION OF NUMBER, WEIGHT, VOLUME, AREA, AND MASS IN PRE-SCHOOL CHILDREN. YOUNG, BEVERLY S., 9 FEB 69 11P.
EDRS PRICE MF-$0.65 HC-$3.29

THE MAJOR QUESTION THIS STUDY ATTEMPTED TO ANSWER WAS, "CAN CONSERVATION OF NUMBER, AREA, WEIGHT, MASS, AND VOLUME TO BE INDUCED AND RETAINED BY 3- AND 4-YEAR-OLD CHILDREN BY STRUCTURED INSTRUCTION WITH A MULTIVARIATE APPROACH? THREE NURSERY SCHOOLS IN IOWA CITY SUPPLIED SUBJECTS FOR THIS STUDY. THE INSTITUTE OF CHILD BEHAVIOR AND DEVELOPMENT CONTRIBUTED 80 CHILDREN; THE UNIVERSITY PARENTS COOPERATIVE PRE-SCHOOL CONTRIBUTED 52; AND IOWA CITY MONTESSORI NURSERY SCHOOL FURNISHED 53. THE INSTITUTE WAS SELECTED AS THE CONTROL GROUP; THE UNIVERSITY PARENTS COOPERATIVE PRE-SCHOOL COMPRISED THE EXPERIMENTAL GROUP, AND THE MONTESSORI NURSERY SCHOOL CHILDREN WERE USED FOR THE PILOT STUDY. AN INDIVIDUAL STANFORD-BINET INTELLIGENCE TEST, A CRITERION PRETEST, AND A POSTTEST WERE ADMINISTERED. CRITERION SCORES WERE BASED ON ONE OF TWO EQUIVALENT FORMS, EACH CONTAINING A 57-ITEM CONSERVATION TEST, ONE TEST OF ROTE COUNTING, ONE TEST OF RATIONAL COUNTING, AND A RATING OF ATTENTIVENESS. THE EXPERIMENTAL GROUP SHOWED A SIGNIFICANT GAIN OVER THEIR OWN PRETEST SCORES IN EVERY SUBTEST EXCEPT ONE. THE ANALYSIS INDICATED THAT GAINS BY THE EXPERIMENTAL GROUP IN 16 OF THE 17 SUBTESTS WERE SIGNIFICANTLY GREATER THAN GAINS BY THE CONTROL GROUP. THE RESULTS SHOWED CONCLUSIVELY THAT THE CONCEPTS COULD BE LEARNED BY 3- AND 4-YEAR-OLD CHILDREN. (DO)

ED028823 PS001690
THE USE OF COLOURED RODS IN TEACHING PRIMARY NUMBERWORK. , MAY 64 40P.
EDRS PRICE MF-$0.65 HC-$3.29

A REVIEW OF RESEARCH LITERATURE REVEALED THAT SOME RESEARCHERS FELT THAT THE USE OF COLORED RODS, SUCH AS THE CUISENAIRE MATERIALS, IN TEACHING NUMBER WORK GAVE PERCEPTUAL SUPPORT TO MANY RELATIONSHIPS. EXPERIMENTS CONDUCTED OVER 3 YEARS ATTEMPTED TO TEST SOME OF THESE RELATIONSHIPS. DURING EACH YEAR, EXPERIMENTAL CLASSES IN GRADE ONE WERE RECEIVING CUISENAIRE INSTRUCTION WHILE CONTROL GROUPS WERE NOT. EACH ENSUING YEAR, CLASSES IN GRADE TWO AND THEN GRADE THREE WERE INCLUDED IN THE EXPERIMENTS. THE RESULTS FROM STANDARDIZED TESTS AND TEACHERS' QUESTIONNAIRES LED TO THE FOLLOWING CONCLUSIONS: (1) CHILDREN TAUGHT WITH CUISENAIRE MATERIALS GAINED FACILITY IN MANIPULATING WHOLE NUMBERS AND FRACTIONS AS SHOWN ON A CUISENAIRE TEST; (2) CUISENAIRE MATERIALS WERE MORE EFFECTIVE WITH BRIGHT CHILDREN; (3) CHILDREN WHO USED CUISENAIRE MATERIALS FOR 2 YEARS SCORED HIGHER THAN THOSE USING THEM FOR 1 YEAR, AND THEY IN TURN SCORED HIGHER THAN THE CONTROL GROUPS; (4) FIRST GRADE CLASSES BENEFITED MORE FROM THE MATERIALS THAN SECOND GRADE CLASS; AND (5) TEACHERS AND CONSULTANTS WERE ENTHUSIASTIC ABOUT THE VALUE OF THE MATERIALS. AN EXTENSIVE BIBLIOGRAPHY IS APPENDED. (JS)

ED028824 PS001713
EARLY EDUCATION: THE CREATION OF CAPACITY. TUMIN, MELVIN, 8 FEB 68 13P.
EDRS PRICE MF-$0.65 HC-$3.29

EVERY HUMAN BEING IS ALWAYS OPEN TO SOME DEGREE; FOR EXAMPLE, OPEN FOR LEARNING, EXPERIENCE, CHANGE, IMPROVEMENT, OR FURTHER DEGRADATION BY HIS OWN STANDARDS OR THOSE OF OTHERS. EVERY EXPERIENCE ALTERS AN INDIVIDUAL'S LEARNING CAPACITY. THEREFORE, TO SAY A CHILD IS NATURALLY OF HIGH OR LOW INTELLIGENCE WITH UNLIMITED OR LIMITED LEARNING POWER IS UNJUST. EDUCATORS MUST EXPLORE INTERVENTIONS THAT MAKE MORE EFFECTIVE DIFFERENCES IN THE CREATION OF NEW CAPACITIES THAN DO THE TRADITIONAL INTERVENTIONS THAT CHARACTERIZE OUR EDUCATIONAL SYSTEM. OUR EMPHASIS ON COMPETITIVE GRADES PRECLUDES THE POSSIBILITY OF MULTIFACETED CHILDREN WITH MANY DIMENSIONS OF SKILLS. MEASURING SUCCESS OR FAILURE ON THE BASIS OF COGNITIVE SKILL ALONE IS WIDESPREAD IN OUR SYSTEM, WHICH VALUES AND REWARDS THAT SKILL. AN ALTERNATIVE IS THE MOTIVATION OF INDIVIDUALS. MOTIVATION INVOLVES GETTING THE CHILD TO PERCEIVE GOALS, GIVING HIM A SENSE OF POSSIBLY ACHIEVING THEM, PROVIDING RESOURCES HE WILL NEED FOR ACHIEVEMENT, AND ELICITING HIS WILLINGNESS TO PAY FOR GAINS THAT WILL ACCRUE TO HIM. OUR SCHOOLS MUST BE DIVERSE. WE NEED RANGES OF EXPERIENCE; VARIABILITY OF METHODS AND CONTENT; AND TEMPO, PLACE, AND PROGRAM TO ACCOMMODATE THE DIVERSITY IN CHILDREN. (DO)

ED028825 PS001716
POINTERS FOR PARTICIPATING PARENTS. , 68 268P.
DOCUMENT NOT AVAILABLE FROM EDRS.
AVAILABLE FROM: CALIFORNIA COUNCIL OF PARENT PARTICIPATION NURSERY SCHOOLS, INC., 998 EDDY ST., SAN FRANCISCO, CALIFORNIA 94601 ($5.40)

THIS HANDBOOK IS A COMPILATION OF INFORMATION AND SOURCE MATERIAL USED BY THE CALIFORNIA COUNCIL OF PARENT PARTICIPATION NURSERY SCHOOLS IN ORGANIZAING AND CONSTRUCTING THEIR SYSTEM OF NURSERY SCHOOLS, IN WHICH THE PARENTS PARTICIPATE IN THE EDUCATION OF THE CHILDREN. THE HANDBOOK IS DESIGNED TO HELP NEW SCHOOLS GET STARTED OR TO ANTICIPATE OR CORRECT PROBLEMS IN EXISTING SCHOOLS. THE TEXT OF THIS HANDBOOK IS DIVIDED INTO FOUR MAJOR SECTIONS: (1) GETTING STARTED, (2) OPERATING A SCHOOL, (3) SCHOOL ADMINISTRATION, AND (4) THE COUNCILS. THERE ARE 17 SUBSECTIONS, RANGING FROM A LIST OF THE ARTICLES OF INCORPORATION OF THE ORGANIZATION TO TIPS ON HOW TO CONDUCT PUBLIC RELATIONS. (WD)

ED028826 PS001717
PROJECT HEAD START: EVALUATION AND RESEARCH SUMMARY 1965-1967. , 67 16P.
EDRS PRICE MF-$0.65 HC-$3.29

PROJECT HEAD START HAS AS ITS GOAL THE IMPROVEMENT OF THE CHILD'S PHYSICAL HEALTH, INTELLECTUAL PERFORMANCE, SOCIAL ATTITUDES, AND SENSE OF SELF. THE PROJECT INVOLVES OVER HALF A MILLION CHILDREN EACH YEAR, INCLUDING CHILDREN IN BOTH SUMMER AND YEARLONG PROGRAMS. ABOUT 40 PERCENT OF HEAD START PUPILS ARE NEGRO, ABOUT 30 PERCENT ARE WHITE, AND THE OTHERS COME FROM OTHER RACIAL BACKGROUNDS. THESE CHILDREN COME FROM ECONOMICALLY OR CULTURALLY DISADVANTAGED HOMES. HEAD START CHILDREN (ALTHOUGH THEY PERFORM MORE POORLY ON ACADEMIC TASKS AND TESTS THAN THEIR MIDDLE CLASS PEERS) PERFORM SIGNIFICANTLY BETTER THAN LOW INCOME CHILDREN WHO DO NOT PARTICIPATE IN HEAD START. THIS IMPROVEMENT IN PERFORMANCE BY HEAD START PUPILS HAS BEEN ATTRIBUTED TO (1) PARTIAL MIDDLE CLASS ACCULTURATION, (2) THE HIGHER QUALITY OF THE EDUCATIONAL PROGRAM, (3) THE WARMTH AND COMPETENCY OF TEACHERS, AND (4) INCREASED PARENTAL INTEREST IN THE CHILD'S DEVELOPMENT. THERE REMAIN QUESTIONS ABOUT THE ENDURANCE OF THE GAINS MADE BY HEAD START CHILDREN AND ABOUT THE RELATIVE MERITS OF THE SHORT SUMMER PROGRAM COMPARED TO THE YEARLONG PROGRAM. (WD)

ED028827 PS001719
POSITIVE EFFECTS OF A BICULTURAL PRESCHOOL PROGRAM ON THE INTELLECTUAL PERFORMANCE OF MEXICAN-AMERICAN CHILDREN. HENDERSON, RONALD W.; AND OTHERS, 8 FEB 69 10P.
EDRS PRICE MF-$0.65 HC-$3.29

IN A STUDY OF THE EFFECTS OF MIXING CHILDREN OF DIFFERENT BACKGROUNDS, 18 DISADVANTAGED MEXICAN-AMERICAN CHILDREN WERE INTEGRATED INTO CLASSES WITH 36 ADVANTAGED ANGLO PEERS TO SEE IF THE INTELLECTUAL PERFORMANCE OF THE MEXICAN-AMERICANS WOULD BE FAVORABLY AFFECTED. COMPARISONS WERE ALSO MADE BETWEEN 18 CHILDREN OF THE SAME ETHNIC GROUP WHO WERE IN HEAD START AND ANOTHER GROUP OF 18 CHILDREN WHO WERE NOT IN A PRESCHOOL PROGRAM. ALL CHILDREN WERE PRETESTED AND POSTTESTED ON THE WECHSLER PRE-PRIMARY SCALE OF INTELLIGENCE. AS EXPECTED, CHILDREN IN THE EXPERIMENTAL INTEGRATED GROUP MADE GREATER GAINS THAN CHILDREN EITHER IN NO PROGRAM OR IN HEAD START; HOWEVER, HEAD START SUBJECTS DID NOT MAKE GREATER GAINS THAN THE CHILDREN IN NO PRESCHOOL PROGRAM. ON THE BASIS OF THIS STUDY, IT SEEMS POSSIBLE THAT IMPROVED INTELLECTUAL PERFORMANCE WOULD BE MAINTAINED IF CHILDREN WERE ACTIVE FOR A LONGER PERIOD OF TIME IN AN ENVIRONMENT SUPPORTIVE OF NEWLY ACQUIRED SKILLS. TOO OFTEN "TRACKING" OR "ABILITY GROUPING" RESULTS IN EFFECT, IN A SEGREGATED SCHOOL ENVIRONMENT. FURTHER INVESTIGATION IS NEEDED TO OBTAIN MORE SPECIFIC DATA ON THE ROLE OF IMITATION IN CLASSROOM SETTINGS. (MS)

ED028828 PS001720
LITERATURE AND THE YOUNG CHILD. FOSTER, FLORENCE P., MAR 67 13P.
EDRS PRICE MF-$0.65 HC-$3.29

THE VALUES, SELECTION, AND PRESENTATION OF LITERATURE FOR YOUNG CHILDREN ARE DESCRIBED IN THIS PAMPHLET. THE VALUES DISCUSSED ARE EDUCATIONAL IMPORTANCE AND SELF-CONCEPT AND INTERPERSONAL RELATIONSHIP DEVELOPMENT. THE SELECTION CRITERIA INCLUDE DEFINING A GOOD BOOK, IDENTIFYING TYPES OF LITERATURE WHICH APPEAL TO CHILDREN, AND NOTING THE LEVEL, CONTENT, LANGUAGE, AND REALITY OF A BOOK. A NOTE IS MADE OF WHAT ASSISTANCE IS AVAILABLE IN SELECTING CHILDREN'S LITERATURE. IN THE SECTION DESCRIBING PRESENTATION, TECHNIQUES ARE LISTED FOR BOTH TELLING AND READING A STORY. SUGGESTIONS ARE MADE FOR DESIGNING A READING CENTER. ADDITIONAL WAYS OF STIMULATING INTEREST IN LITERATURE ARE LISTED. FINALLY, MANY SUGGESTIONS ARE GIVEN FOR HELPING CHILDREN TO CREATE THEIR OWN STORIES. A SHORT BIBLIOGRAPHY IS INCLUDED. (JS)

ED028829 PS001721
A STUDY OF FOOD AND POVERTY AMONG 113 HEAD START CHILDREN IN MISSOULA, MONTANA. MUNRO, NANCY, [68] 113P.
EDRS PRICE MF-$0.65 HC-$6.58

A STUDY OF THE EFFECTS OF INADEQUATE NUTRITION UPON DISADVANTAGED CHILDREN INVOLVED 113 HEAD START CHILDREN AND THEIR FAMILIES. INFORMATION WAS COLLECTED ON HOME DIET, SOCIOECONOMIC DATA, PERFORMANCE ON INTELLIGENCE TESTS, HEMOGLOBIN LEVELS, CLASS ATTENDANCE, HEIGHT, AND WEIGHT TO FIND OUT WHETHER OR NOT THERE WAS A RELATIONSHIP BETWEEN NUTRITION AND BEHAVIOR. SINCE ADEQUATE NUTRITION ENABLES ONE TO COPE BETTER WITH STRESSES, IT IS PROBABLE THAT A SATISFACTORY DIET CAN POSITIVELY INFLUENCE BEHAVIOR. RESULTS INDICATE THAT HIGH AMOUNTS OF REFINED CARBOHYDRATES AND LOW AMOUNTS OF MEAT ARE ASSOCIATED WITH LOW PLAYGROUND ACTIVITY, HYPERACTIVITY AND SHORT ATTENTION SPANS. CHILDREN WITH SMALL AMOUNTS OF VITAMIN A HAD LOWER PLAYGROUND ACTIVITY, LESS HYPERACTIVITY, AND LONGER ATTENTION SPANS. SPECIFIC MEASURES NEED TO BE DESIGNED TO TEST THE RELATIONSHIPS BETWEEN DIET AND BEHAVIOR. "THE RELATIONSHIP BETWEEN HEMOGLOBIN LEVEL AND INTELLECTUAL FUNCTION" (PS 001 723), BY THE SAME AUTHOR, IS A SHORTER REPORT ON THE SAME SUBJECT. (MS)

ED028830 PS001723
THE RELATIONSHIP BETWEEN HEMOGLOBIN LEVEL AND INTELLECTUAL FUNCTION. MUNRO, NANCY, [67] 22P.
EDRS PRICE MF-$0.65 HC-$3.29

IN A STUDY TO LEARN WHETHER OR NOT POOR NUTRITION, AS INDICATED BY LOW HEMOGLOBIN LEVELS, AFFECTS INTELLIGENCE AND BEHAVIOR, 113 HEAD START CHILDREN IN MISSOULA, MONTANA TOOK PART. GROUP TESTING WITH THE LORGE THORNDIKE INTELLIGENCE TEST AND INDIVIDUAL TESTING WITH THE WECHSLER AND PRIMARY SCALE OF INTELLIGENCE OR WECHSLER INTELLIGENCE SCALE FOR CHILDREN PROVIDED IQ INFORMATION. AN EXPERIMENTAL GROUP OF THE HEAD START CHILDREN WAS GIVEN IRON TABLETS DAILY AT SCHOOL, AND A CONTROL GROUP WAS GIVEN PLACEBOS. BLOOD TESTS WERE TAKEN AT INTERVALS IN THE SCHOOL YEAR, AND TEACHERS RATED THE BEHAVIOR OF ALL THE CHILDREN. RESULTS OF DATA ANALYSIS INDICATED THAT THE IRON PILLS DID NOT SIGNIFICANTLY AFFECT HOMEGLOBIN LEVELS. HOWEVER, FOR THOSE WITH LOW HEMOGLOBIN LEVELS, INCREASES IN THE LEVELS WERE ASSOCIATED WITH INCREASES IN INTELLIGENCE SCORES. "A STUDY OF FOOD AND POVERTY" (PS 001 721), BY THE SAME AUTHOR, IS A LONGER REPORT ON THE SAME SUBJECT. (MS)

ED028831 PS001729
COORDINATED HELPS IN LANGUAGE DEVELOPMENT (CHILD). NORTHWEST REGIONAL EDUCATIONAL LABORATORY STUDY. SECOND EXPERIMENTAL EDITION. , 68 85P.
EDRS PRICE MF-$0.65 HC-$3.29

THIS GUIDE TO A TOTAL DEVELOPMENTAL LANGUAGE PROGRAM FOR KINDERGARTEN IS DIVIDED INTO THREE SECTIONS: (1) HELPFUL HINTS TO THE TEACHER, (2) EXPANDING VERBAL POWER, AND (3) LINKING LANGUAGE AND THOUGHT. SUBJECTS IN SECTION 2 INCLUDE HEARING AND SPEAKING CLEARLY, INCREASING VOCABULARY, EXTENDING MEANING, EXPANDING LANGUAGE PATTERNS, CONVEYING IDEAS, AND EXPRESSING FEELINGS. SECTION 3 INVOLVES CLASSIFYING THINGS, CONVEYING IMAGINATION, SOLVING PROBLEMS, AND EXPRESSING ABSTRACT REASONING. EACH TOPIC IS DIVIDED INTO A LISTING OF ACTIVITIES, OBJECTIVES, MATERIALS, PROCEDURES, OBSERVATIONS, AND CONCOMITANT LEARNINGS. (DO)

ED028832 PS001737
EVALUATION OF THE EFFECTS OF HEAD START EXPERIENCE IN THE AREA OF SELF-CONCEPT, SOCIAL SKILLS, AND LANGUAGE SKILLS. PRE-PUBLICATION DRAFT. MCNAMARA, J. REGIS; AND OTHERS, JUL 68 54P.
EDRS PRICE MF-$0.65 HC-$3.29

ABOUT 180 NEGRO HEAD START CHILDREN IN DADE COUNTY, FLORIDA, WERE TESTED (1) TO DISCOVER IF THE COUNTY'S PROGRAM CONTRIBUTED SIGNIFICANTLY TO LANGUAGE SKILLS, SOCIAL SKILLS, AND SELF-CONCEPT DEVELOPMENT AND (2) TO DETERMINE IF AN EFFICIENT INSTRUMENT COULD BE DEVELOPED TO MEASURE SELF-CONCEPT IN THE DISADVANTAGED CHILD. PRETESTS AND POSTTESTS USED WERE THE CHILDREN'S PROJECTIVE PICTURES OF SELF-CONCEPT, THE PRESCHOOL ATTAINMENT RECORD, THE SELF-CONCEPT RATING SCALE, AND AN ANXIETY SCALE. IN THE POSTTEST PHASE, 20 SUBJECTS IN A PROPORTIONAL RANDOM SELECTION WERE COMPARED WITH 20 CONTROL CHILDREN (FROM THE SAME DISTRICTS) WITH NO PRESCHOOL EXPERIENCE. THE HEAD START SAMPLE PERFORMED SIGNIFICANTLY BETTER ON TESTS MEASURING SOCIAL SKILLS, LANGUAGE SKILLS, AND SELF-CONCEPT. THE MEANING OF THE SIGNIFICANCE WAS UNCLEAR BECAUSE OF THE POSSIBILITY OF AN INTERACTION EFFECT BETWEEN THE PRETEST AND THE EXPERIMENTAL VARIABLE; NAMELY, EXPOSURE TO THE HEAD START PROGRAM. IT WAS SUGGESTED THAT HEAD STARTERS ENTERING THE FIRST GRADE THE FOLLOWING FALL BE TESTED AND THAT THEIR PERFORMANCE BE COMPARED WITH THE PERFORMANCE OF A CONTROL GROUP WITH NO PRESCHOOL EXPERIENCE. (DO)

ED028833 PS001739
AFFECTIVE DIMENSIONS OF TEACHERS OF DISADVANTAGED CHILDREN IN SIX MAJORITY NEGRO SCHOOL DISTRICTS. WHITE, WILLIAM F., [69] 8P.
EDRS PRICE MF-$0.65 HC-$3.29

DURING A SUMMER INSTITUTE AT THE UNIVERSITY OF GEORGIA, 10 CONCEPTS OF 144 TEACHERS (120 FEMALES AND 24 MALES) WERE ASSESSED. THIS STUDY EXAMINED THE STRUCTURE OF THE AFFECT THAT TEACHERS IN SIX MAJORITY NEGRO SCHOOL DISTRICTS HAD ON THE TEACHER LEARNING PROCESS. TWELVE ADJECTIVE PAIRS WERE USED TO MEASURE EACH OF THE FOLLOWING TEN CONCEPTS: (1) THIS SUMMER'S INSTITUTE, (2) THE ECONOMICALLY DEPRIVED CHILD, (3) MYSELF, (4) A NEGRO TEACHER, (5) A WHITE TEACHER, (6) NEGRO PRINCIPALS, (7) WHITE PRINCIPALS, (8) OTHER TEACHERS, (9) A NEGRO CHILD, AND (10) A WHITE CHILD. TEACHERS' PERCEPTIONS OF FOUR CONCEPTS SHIFTED SIGNIFICANTLY OVER THE TENURE OF THE INSTITUTE: (1) PERCEIVED INITIALLY AS NEGATIVE AND WORTHLESS, THE NEGRO TEACHER APPEARED TO BECOME MORE VALUABLE, WITH A HIGHER MEASURE OF PERSONAL WORTH; (2) ATTITUDE TOWARD THE SUMMER INSTITUTE IMPROVED; (3) TEACHERS DEVELOPED MORE INDEPENDENCE IN THEIR ATTITUDES AND POSSESSED MORE EGO STRENGTH IN RESOLVING FEELINGS ABOUT TEACHING IN DISADVANTAGED AREAS; AND (4) AT THE CONCLUSION OF THE INSTITUTE, THE CONCEPTS OF THE WHITE CHILD AND THE NEGRO CHILD REFLECTED THE CONCERN OF FEDERAL PROGRAMS FOR DEPRIVED CHILDREN, REGARDLESS OF RACE. (DO)

ED028834 PS001790
A THEORETICAL APPROACH FOR SELECTING ELEMENTARY SCHOOL ENVIRONMENTAL VARIABLES. SINCLAIR, ROBERT L., [69] 13P.
EDRS PRICE MF-$0.65 HC-$3.29

TO DETERMINE SPECIFIC ENVIRONMENTAL VARIABLES OF THE ELEMENTARY SCHOOL IS THE PURPOSE OF THIS STUDY. STABLE CHARACTERISTICS OF INTELLIGENCE AND ACHIEVEMENT WERE SELECTED BECAUSE THEY WERE CONSIDERED USEFUL FOR GENERATING SALIENT ENVIRONMENTAL COUNTERPARTS LIKELY TO EXIST IN ELEMENTARY INSTITUTIONS. ACHIEVEMENT MOTIVATION, LANGUAGE DEVELOPMENT, AND GENERAL LEARNING WERE THREE ENVIRONMENTAL VARIABLES CONSIDERED TO BE COUNTERPARTS OF INTELLIGENCE. COUNTERPARTS OF ACHIEVEMENT WERE ACHIEVEMENT PRESS, LANGUAGE MODELS, ACADEMIC GUIDANCE, ACTIVENESS OF THE SCHOOL, INTELLECTUALITY IN THE SCHOOL, AND WORK HABITS IN THE SCHOOL. C. ROBERT PACE'S VARIABLES (PRACTICALITY, COMMUNITY, AWARENESS, PROPRIETY, AND SCHOLARSHIP) ARE DIMENSIONS WHICH DESCRIBE THE ELEMENTARY ENVIRONMENT AND THEY WERE INCLUDED WITH THE SEVEN ENVIRONMENTAL COUNTERPARTS (FOR DEVELOPING INTELLIGENCE AND ACHIEVEMENT) WHICH WERE CONSIDERED IN THIS INVESTIGATION. (DO)

ED028835 PS001796
A RATIONALE FOR DEVELOPMENTAL TESTING AND TRAINING. ARNER, ROBERT S., 13 DEC 65 17P.
EDRS PRICE MF-$0.65 HC-$3.29

MAN'S PHYLOGENETIC DEVELOPMENT HAS RESULTED IN A POTENTIAL FOR ENVIRONMENTAL INTERACTION IN A SYMBOLIC AND CONCEPTUAL MANNER. THERE ARE ONTOGENETIC REQUIREMENTS TO DEVELOP SUCH POTENTIAL. THE PROCESS BY WHICH MAN LEARNS IS SEQUENTIAL AND INVOLVES PERCEPTUAL-MOTOR-COGNITIVE ABILITIES. THERE IS AN OPTIMUM RESPECTIVITY PERIOD AT EACH DEVELOPMENTAL LEVEL; AND IF THIS PERIOD IS PASSED WITHOUT LEARNING TAKING PLACE, GUIDANCE SHOULD BE PROVIDED TO AVOID PERFORMANCE DIFFICULTIES. PHYSICAL MOVEMENT IS THE BASIS FOR PERCEPTION. A GOAL OF DEVELOPMENTAL EFFICIENCY IS THE REDUCTION OF MOVEMENT THROUGH SYMBOLIC MANIPULATION AND VISUALIZATION. DEVELOPMENTAL GUIDANCE MUST RECAPITUATE ONTOGENY. THE IMPLICATIONS OF DEVELOPMENTAL INADEQUACIES IN PERCEPTUAL MOTOR SKILLS IN ADULTS, EMOTIONALLY DISTURBED, AND MENTALLY HANDICAPPED CHILDREN ARE DISCUSSED, AND MANY CITATIONS ARE INCLUDED IN THIS MASTER'S THESIS. (MS)

ED028836 PS001797
PERSPECTIVES ON TEACHER-AIDES. A TEACHING TEXT. GODGART, MARTIN, ED., JUN 68 190P.
DOCUMENT NOT AVAILABLE FROM EDRS.
AVAILABLE FROM: EDUCATIONAL CONSULTING CENTER, 2279 MT. VERNON RD., SOUTHINGTON, CONNECTICUT 06489

FIVE STAFF MEMBERS OF THE EDUCATIONAL CONSULTING CENTER CONTRIBUTED SEVEN PAPERS TO THIS TEXT FOR TRAINING TEACHER-AIDES. "TEACHER-AIDES; AN OVERVIEW" CONCERNS QUALIFICATIONS, TRAINING, DUTIES, PLACEMENT, A CODE OF ETHICS, AND EMPLOYMENT PRACTICES. "THE DISADVANTAGED CHILD" DISCUSSES SELF-CONCEPT, ITS DEVELOPMENT, AND ITS IMPROVEMENT. "THE CLIMATE FOR TEACHING THE DISADVANTAGED" DISCUSSES EDUCATIONALLY DISADVANTAGED STUDENTS, THE LEARNING PROCESS, EDUCATIONAL AND FUNDAMENTAL GOALS, SUBURBAN YOUTH, SOCIAL CLASS INFLUENCES, UNDERACHIEVERS, NONACHIEVERS, AND TEACHER-STUDENT RELATIONSHIPS. "DISCIPLINE IN THE INNER-CITY CLASSROOM" ENUMERATES 16 GUIDELINES FOR MINIMIZING DISCIPLINE PROBLEMS, AND "THE TEACHER-AIDE AND THE AUDIO-VISUAL PROGRAM" OUTLINES DUTIES FOR PRESENTATIONS AND DESCRIBES THE FUNCTIONS OF THE EQUIPMENT. "GUIDELINES FOR THE TEACHER-AIDE" DEALS WITH PERSONAL QUALITIES, FILING AN APPLICATION, THE INTERVIEW, ORIENTATION, AND ACADEMIC INVOLVEMENT. "LEGAL RESPONSIBILITIES OF THE TEACHER-AIDE" IS THE TITLE OF THE FINAL CHAPTER. SUPPLEMENTARY ACTIVITIES ARE LISTED AT THE END OF EACH CHAPTER. (DO)

ED028837 PS001801
A STUDY OF PUBLIC AND PRIVATE KINDERGARTEN AND NON-KINDERGARTEN CHILDREN IN THE PRIMARY GRADES. CONWAY, C. B.; AND OTHERS, JAN 68 54P.
EDRS PRICE MF-$0.65 HC-$3.29
AVAILABLE FROM: THE EDUCATIONAL RESEARCH INST. OF B.C., BOARD OF TRADE TOWER, 1177 WEST HASTINGS STREET, VANCOUVER 1, BRITISH COLUMBIA

A SHORT HISTORY OF THE ESTABLISHMENT OF KINDERGARTENS IN BRITISH COLUMBIA PREFACES THIS STUDY OF 22,000 PUBLIC SCHOOL CHILDREN IN GRADES ONE, TWO, AND THREE (WHO HAD OR HAD NOT ATTENDED KINDERGARTEN) IN SCHOOL DISTRICT 39 OF VANCOUVER AND DISTRICT 61 OF VICTORIA. THE EFFECT OF KINDERGARTEN ATTENDANCE WAS EVALUATED AS IT RELATED TO (1) REPORT CARD RATINGS, (2) ADAPTATION TO SCHOOL, (3) INTELLIGENCE, (4) ACADEMIC ACHIEVEMENT IN GRADE 2 (VICTORIA ONLY), AND (5) RETARDATION AND ACCELERATION IN GRADES ONE, TWO, AND THREE. SOMEWHAT LESS THAN HALF THE PUPILS HAD ATTENDED KINDERGARTEN. A "BLIND STUDY" WAS CONDUCTED, WHICH OBTAINED TEACHER RATINGS ON INDIVIDUALS ON A DESCENDING SCALE FROM OUTSTANDING TO UNSATISFACTORY ON THE FIVE EFFECTS UNDER INVESTIGATION. RESULTS REVEALED THAT (1) REPORT CARD RATINGS (FOR WORK AND HEALTH HABITS AND BEHAVIOR) WERE GENERALLY HIGHER FOR CHILDREN WHO ATTENDED PRIVATE KINDERGARTENS; (2) SCHOOL ADAPTATION SEEMED TO BE RELATED TO KINDERGARTEN ATTENDANCE; (3) IQ'S WERE HIGHEST FOR THOSE WHO HAD ATTENDED PRIVATE KINDERGARTENS, AND NONKINDERGARTNERS RANKED LOWEST; (4) KINDERGARTEN ATTENDANCE WAS RELATED TO HIGHER ACHIEVEMENT SCORES IN READING COMPREHENSION, WORD MEANING, SPELLING, AND ARITHMETIC FOR GRADE TWO; AND (5) VERY LITTLE ACCELERATION WAS FOUND, BUT THAT IN EVIDENCE WAS RELATED TO PRIVATE KINDERGARTEN ATTENDANCE. (DO)

ED028838 PS001803
INSTRUCTIONAL AND EXPRESSIVE EDUCATIONAL OBJECTIVES: THEIR FORMULATION AND USE IN CURRICULUM. EISNER, ELLIOT W., [67] 21P.
EDRS PRICE MF-$0.65 HC-$3.29

BECAUSE DIFFERENT EDUCATIONAL GOALS ARE BASED ON INDIVIDUAL SETS OF VALUES, RESEARCH FINDINGS CONSIDERED HIGHLY SIGNIFICANT BY ONE GROUP OF EDUCATORS WILL SEEM IRRELEVANT TO OTHERS. EMPIRICAL STUDIES OF EDUCATIONAL OBJECTIVES ARE NEEDED TO INVESTIGATE (1) THE RELATIONSHIP BETWEEN THE WAY OBJECTIVES ARE FORMULATED AND THEIR QUALITY, (2) THE EXTENT TO WHICH TEACHERS HAVE EDUCATIONAL OBJECTIVES, (3) THE EFFECT OBJECTIVES HAVE ON CURRICULUM PLANNING AND INSTRUCTION, AND (4) THE USEFULNESS OF EDUCATIONAL OBJECTIVES IN FACILITATING LEARNING. EDUCATIONAL OBJECTIVES MAY BE DIVIDED INTO TWO DIVISIONS: INSTRUCTIONAL OBJECTIVES, WHICH EMPHASIZE THE ACQUISITION OF THE KNOWN (SKILLS DEFINED IN A PREDICTIVE MODEL OF CURRICULUM DEVELOPMENT), AND EXPRESSIVE OBJECTIVES, WHICH ELABORATE AND MODIFY EXISTING KNOWLEDGE. EXPRESSIVE OBJECTIVES MAY PRODUCE NEW KNOWLEDGE AS A RESULT OF AN EDUCATIONAL ENCOUNTER IN WHICH THE CHILD IS FREE TO EXPLORE. WHEN EXPRESSIVE OBJECTIVES ARE USED BY TEACHERS, DIVERSITY (RATHER THAN HOMOGENEITY OF RESPONSE) IS SOUGHT. RESEARCH NEEDS TO BE UNDERTAKEN ON THE CONSEQUENCES OF THE USE OF EACH KIND OF OBJECTIVE. (MS)

ED028839 PS001805
ECONOMICS IN THE ELEMENTARY SCHOOL , 67 23P.
EDRS PRICE MF-$0.65 HC-$3.29

ECONOMIC EDUCATION IS NEEDED. ELEMENTARY SCHOOL CHILDREN SHOULD BE TAUGHT THE FOLLOWING CONCEPTS OF ECONOMICS: THAT ECONOMICS IS CONCERNED WITH THE PROBLEM OF DECIDING HOW TO MAKE THE BEST USE OF RESOURCES TO SATISFY HUMAN WANTS; THAT PRODUCTION AND CONSUMPTION ARE FUNCTIONS OF ANY ECONOMIC SYSTEM; THAT IN AMERICA COMPETITION IN A MARKET IS THE SYSTEM WHEREBY CONSUMER AND PRODUCER GOODS AND SERVICES ARE ALLOCATED; THAT THE FEDERAL GOVERNMENT HELPS TO REGULATE THE SYSTEM AND PARTICIPATES IN THE ALLOCATION OF GOODS AND SERVICES THROUGH ITS SPENDING; THAT ECONOMIC GROWTH DEPENDS ON THE QUALITY AND QUANTITY OF PRODUCTIVE RESOURCES; THAT MONEY IS A MEDIUM OF EXCHANGE, A MEASURE FOR COMPARING ALL ECONOMIC GOODS, AND A STORE OF VALUE; THAT SPECIALIZATION LEADS TO INTERDEPENDENCY LOCALLY AND INTERNATIONALLY; AND THAT OTHER NATIONS HAVE THE SAME BASIC ECONOMIC CONSIDERATIONS. THE KINDERGARTEN SHOULD BE CONCERNED WITH THE HOME AND SCHOOL; THE FIRST GRADE, WITH THE HOME AND NEIGHBORHOOD; THE SECOND GRADE, WITH THE NEIGHBORHOOD; THE THIRD GRADE, WITH THE CITY--PAST AND PRESENT; THE FOURTH GRADE, WITH THE STATE; THE FIFTH GRADE, WITH THE NATION; AND THE SIXTH GRADE, WITH THE WESTERN HEMISPHERE. (JS)

ED028840 PS001807
FEDERAL PROGRAMS ASSISTING CHILDREN AND YOUTH. , DEC 67 106P.
EDRS PRICE MF-$0.65 HC-$6.58

DATA ON THE AMOUNT OF UNITED STATES FEDERAL FUNDS USED FOR PROGRAMS ASSISTING CHILDREN AND YOUTH UNDER 21 BOTH DIRECTLY AND INDIRECTLY ARE COLLECTED IN THIS REPORT. A LIST OF THE SIX CABINET DEPARTMENTS AND FIVE OTHER AGENCIES WHICH SUPPORT OR ADMINISTER THE EDUCATIONAL, MEDICAL, AND WELFARE PROGRAMS IS SUPPLIED. SUMMARIES OF FEDERAL EXPENDITURES ARE CLASSIFIED BY AGENCY AS WELL AS BY CATEGORY. THE FUNDS ARE ALSO ANALYZED IN PER CAPITA TERMS. DEMOGRAPHIC AND SOCIAL DATA ON CHILDREN AND YOUTH ARE PRESENTED. DESCRIPTIONS ARE GIVEN OF THE EDUCATION AND TRAINING PROGRAMS; HEALTH PROGRAMS; NUTRITION PROGRAMS; CASH BENEFITS; SOCIAL, WELFARE, AND REHABILITATION PROGRAMS; EMPLOYMENT SERVICES AND LABOR STANDARDS; AND HOUSING AND OTHER PROGRAMS. (NT)

ED028841 PS001810
AN EXPLORATORY INVESTIGATION OF THE CARROLL LEARNING MODEL AND THE BLOOM STRATEGY FOR MASTERY LEARNING. WANG, MARGARET; LINDVALL, C. M., 8 FEB 69 15P.
EDRS PRICE MF-$0.65 HC-$3.29

A GROUP OF STUDENTS NORMALLY DISTRIBUTED IN APTITUDE AND GIVEN THE SAME INSTRUCTION WILL PRODUCE A NORMAL DISTRIBUTION OF STUDENT ACHIEVEMENT. IT HAS BEEN CONTENDED THAT IF EACH OF FIVE PRIMARY VARIABLES IN LEARNING ARE OPTIMIZED FOR EACH STUDENT, ALL STUDENTS SHOULD BE EXPECTED TO ACHIEVE MASTERY OF THE MATERIAL. THESE VARIABLES ARE (1) APTITUDE OF STUDENT, (2) QUALITY OF INSTRUCTION, (3) ABILITY TO UNDERSTAND INSTRUCTION, (4) PERSERVERANCE, AND (5) TIME ALLOWED FOR LEARNING. THIS STUDY INVESTIGATED THIS HYPOTHESIS WITH AN INDIVIDUALIZED LEARNING PROGRAM (ILP), IN WHICH ALL STUDENTS WERE SUPPOSED TO ATTAIN MASTERY ON EACH LESSON BEFORE GOING ON IN THE PROGRAM. STUDENTS IN GRADES TWO THROUGH SIX WERE GIVEN APTITUDE TESTS, AND THEIR PERFORMANCE IN THE ILP WAS COMPARED WITH THE TEST RESULTS. LITTLE RELATIONSHIP BETWEEN RATE OF LEARNING AND APTITUDE WAS FOUND WHEN VARIABLES NUMBER TWO, THREE, AND FOUR WERE IGNORED OR WERE ASSUMED TO BE OPERATING AT AN OPTIMUM LEVEL FOR ALL. THUS, EITHER THE VARIABLES SHOULD NOT HAVE BEEN IGNORED OR THE EXPERIMENTAL DESIGN IN THIS STUDY WAS FAULTY. APTITUDE MAY STILL BE FOUND TO BE THE MOST IMPORTANT FACTOR IN RATE OF LEARNING. (WD)

ED028842 PS001813
VISION TRAINING - A NEW DEVELOPMENTAL CONCEPT IN CHILD VISION. SCHAFFEL, ADRIENNE, 68 37P.
DOCUMENT NOT AVAILABLE FROM EDRS.
AVAILABLE FROM: OPTOMETRIC EXTENSION PROGRAM FOUNDATION, INC., DUNCAN, OKLAHOMA 73553

THE PURPOSE OF THIS PAPER IS TO ILLUSTRATE THE PARENTS' ROLE IN THEIR CHILD'S VISUAL GUIDANCE PROGRAM, THE PHILOSOPHIES BEHIND THE PROGRAM, AND THE TEACHER'S RESPONSIBILITY TO CHILD VISION. THE FIRST CHAPTER, ON PARENT INVOLVEMENT, INSTRUCTS THEM TO PROVIDE AN ENVIRONMENT TO STIMULATE INTELLECTUAL GROWTH AND STRESSES THE IMPORTANCE OF THE DEVELOPMENT OF EYE-HAND COORDINATION AND MANUAL AND VISUAL EXPLORATION OF THE INFANT. IT ALSO STATES THAT VISUAL TRAINING DURING PRESCHOOL YEARS IS ENHANCED BY LOCOMOTION, LOCATION, LABELING, AND LANGUAGE. IN CHAPTER II, DEVELOPMENT THEORIES OF DR. CARL H. DELACATO, DR. RAY BARSCH, AND DR. G. N. GETMAN ARE MENTIONED, AND DR. A. M. SKEFFINTON'S DIAGRAM OF VISUAL PROCESSES AND AN EXPLANATION OF IT ARE GIVEN. A CONCLUDING CHAPTER STATES THAT POTENTIAL DROPOUTS AND LOW ACHIEVERS MAY BE DETECTED BY OBSERVANT TEACHERS WHO ARE INFORMED ON CHILD VISION. ALSO INCLUDED IS A CHART SHOWING EXPECTED PROGRESS IN VARIOUS PHASES OF GROWTH AND DEVELOPMENT FOR CHILDREN IN EIGHT DIFFERENT AGE GROUPS (FROM 4 YEARS OLD THROUGH AGE 13). (DO)

ED028843 PS001817
AGE OF ENTRANCE INTO THE FIRST GRADE AS RELATED TO RATE OF SCHOLASTIC ACHIEVEMENT. ILIKA, JOSEPH, 8 FEB 69 20P.
EDRS PRICE MF-$0.65 HC-$3.29

THE INFLUENCE OF AGE OF ENTRANCE TO FIRST GRADE ON SUBSEQUENT RATE OF SCHOLASTIC DEVELOPMENT WAS TESTED IN THIS LONGITUDINAL INVESTIGATION. FORTY-ONE PAIRS OF BOYS AND FORTY-NINE PAIRS OF GIRLS, MATCHED ACCORDING TO SEX, INTELLIGENCE, AND SOCIOECONOMIC STATUS, WERE SUBJECTS. THE MEAN CHRONOLOGICAL AGE OF LATE ENTRANTS WAS 81 MONTHS, OPPOSED TO 72 MONTHS FOR EARLY ENTRANTS. READING, SPELLING, ARITHMETIC, TOTAL LANGUAGE, AND TOTAL ACHIEVEMENT SCORES WERE OBTAINED. RESULTS OF BOYS' RATE OF ACHIEVEMENT REVEALED NO SIGNIFICANT DIFFERENCES. LATE-ENTRANT BOYS' RATES TENDED TO BE FASTER THAN EARLY-ENTRANT BOYS' RATES IN ALL MEASURES EXCEPT ARITHMETIC DEVELOPMENT. LEG'S LATE-ENTRANT GIRLS' RATES REFLECTED FASTER SCHOLASTIC DEVELOPMENT THAN THE EARLY-ENTRANT GIRLS' RATES. THE RESULTS UPHELD WILLARD C. OLSON'S STATEMENT OF THE PRINCIPLE OF RESISTANCE TO DISPLACEMENT OF RATE OF DEVELOPMENT IN THAT INITIALLY FASTER RATES OF THE EARLY ENTRANTS DECLINED AND DID NOT EXCEED THE RATES OF DEVELOPMENT BY THE LATE ENTRANTS. (DO)

ED028844 PS001900
EFFECT OF MATERNAL ATTITUDES, TEACHER ATTITUDES, AND TYPE OF NURSERY SCHOOL TRAINING ON THE ABILITIES OF PRESCHOOL CHILDREN. FINAL REPORT. COX, HELEN R., DEC 68 94P.
EDRS PRICE MF-$0.65 HC-$3.29

THE PURPOSE OF THIS STUDY WAS TO ASSESS THE IMPORTANCE OF TEACHER ATTITUDES, MATERNAL ATTITUDES, AND TRADITIONAL VERSUS MONTESSORI NURSERY SCHOOL TRAINING ON THE LEARNING AND ACHIEVEMENT OF THE PRESCHOOL CHILD. EIGHTY-TWO MIDDLE CLASS CHILDREN AND THIRTY-EIGHT DISADVANTAGED CHILDREN WHO ATTENDED EITHER MONTESSORI OR TRADITIONAL PRESCHOOLS COMPRISED THE SAMPLE. THE CHILDREN WERE TESTED IN THE FALL ON THE STANFORD-BINET AND PEABODY PICTURE VOCABULARY TEST AND RETESTED IN THE SPRING WITH THE CALDWELL PRESCHOOL INVENTORY AND THE STANFORD-BINET. TEACHERS OF NURSERY SCHOOL CLASSES COMPLETED THE MINNESOTA TEACHER ATTITUDE INVENTORY, AND MOTHERS OF THE CHILDREN COMPLETED THE MARYLAND PARENT ATTITUDE SURVEY. RESULTS OF THE STUDY SHOWED THAT MIDDLE CLASS MONTESSORI CHILDREN SCORED SIGNIFICANTLY HIGHER ON PERSONAL-SOCIAL RESPONSIVENESS, ASSOCIATIVE VOCABULARY, AND TOTAL TEST SCORES THAN MIDDLE CLASS CHILDREN IN A TRADITIONAL NURSERY SCHOOL PROGRAM. DISADVANTAGED MONTESSORI CHILDREN ALSO OBTAINED SIGNIFICANTLY HIGHER SCORES THAN DID THEIR COUNTERPARTS IN A TRADITIONAL PROGRAM. FURTHER FINDINGS INDICATED THAT DEMOCRATIC TEACHER ATTITUDES WERE NOT HIGHLY RELATED TO PRESCHOOL CHILDREN'S ACHIEVEMENT AND THAT MATERNAL ATTITUDES HAD NO SIGNIFICANT EFFECT ON THE ACHIEVEMENT OF THESE CHILDREN. (MS)

ED028845 PS001907
DEVELOPMENT OF A PRESCHOOL LANGUAGE-ORIENTED CURRICULUM WITH A STRUCTURED PARENT EDUCATION PROGRAM. FINAL REPORT. ADKINS, DOROTHY C.; AND OTHERS, [68] 34P.
EDRS PRICE MF-$0.65 HC-$3.29

THE OBJECTIVES OF THIS PROJECT WERE TO TEST (1) A STRUCTURED LANGUAGE-ORIENTED CURRICULUM, USED FOR AN ACADEMIC YEAR IN HAWAIIAN HEAD START CLASSES, AND (2) A PARENT EDUCATION PROGRAM. TEACHERS IN EIGHT EXPERIMENTAL CLASSES USED SEMISTRUCTURED LANGUAGE-STRENGTHENING ACTIVITIES ALONG WITH STRUCTURED LESSONS AND WERE GUIDED BY SUPERVISORS. EIGHT CONTROL CLASSES USED OTHER METHODS OF LANGUAGE INSTRUCTION. AUDIO AND VIDEO TAPES STIMULATED PERIODIC TEACHER DISCUSSIONS, WHICH LED TO CONTINUAL REVISIONS OF THE PROGRAM. THE PARENT PROGRAM TAUGHT PARENTS TO WORK AS AIDES THROUGH STAFF-PARENT MEETINGS. THE ILLINOIS TEST OF PSYCHOLINGUISTIC ABILITIES, THE PEABODY PICTURE VOCABULARY TEST, AND THE SCHOOL READINESS TASKS WERE USED AS PRETESTS AND POSTTESTS. ALTHOUGH THE TEST RESULTS DID NOT SHOW IMPRESSIVE RELATIONSHIPS, THE ENTHUSIASTIC REPORTS BY TEACHERS AND PARENTS REGARDING THE INCREASED VERBAL ABILITY OF THE CHILDREN INDICATED A LACK OF APPROPRIATE INSTRUMENTS TO MEASURE VERBAL COMMUNICATION SKILLS. A CURRICULUM OUTLINE IS INCLUDED. (JS)

ED028846 PS001908
[REGIONAL RESEARCH AND RESOURCE CENTER IN EARLY CHILDHOOD.] FINAL REPORT. , 68 91P.
EDRS PRICE MF-$0.65 HC-$3.29

QUALITATIVE AND QUANTITATIVE EVALUATIONS WERE MADE OF THE 1967-68 ACADEMIC PERIOD, THE SIXTH YEAR OF DEMONSTRATION CLASSES, CONDUCTED BY THE INSTITUTE FOR DEVELOPMENTAL STUDIES AT NEW YORK UNIVERSITY. QUALITATIVE EVALUATIONS WERE OBTAINED FOR READING, MATHEMATICS, CLASSROOM BEHAVIOR, SCIENCE, CREATIVE DRAMATICS, AND USE OF THE LANGUAGE MASTER THROUGH A CURRICULUM INDEX QUESTIONNAIRE, EXAMINATION OF TEACHERS' DAILY

LOGS, AND INTERVIEWS WITH ADMINISTRATORS, SUPERVISORS, TEACHERS, PARENTS, AND OBSERVERS. SUBJECTS WERE CULTURALLY DEPRIVED CHILDREN ATTENDING PREKINDERGARTEN THROUGH GRADE THREE. CONCLUSIONS WERE AS FOLLOWS: (1) ONGOING INSERVICE TRAINING IS NECESSARY, (2) PURPOSES AND LIMITATIONS OF THE PROGRAM MUST BE CONTINUOUSLY ARTICULATED, (3) EDUCATORS SHOULD BE REORIENTED TO INNOVATIVE TEACHING METHODS, AND (4) PARENTAL FEEDBACK ON CHILDREN'S RELATIVE GROWTH SHOULD BE USED. QUANTITATIVE FOLLOWUP PSYCHOLOGICAL EVALUATIONS OF EXPERIMENTAL, FILLER, AND CONTROL SUBJECTS WERE MADE. A PARENT PROGRAM WAS INITIATED TO HELP WITH PERSONAL AND ENVIRONMENTAL PROBLEMS. (DO)

ED028847 PS001918
PERFORMANCE OF KINDERGARTEN CHILDREN FROM LOW INCOME FAMILIES ON SELECTED CONCEPT CATEGORIES. LOCATIS, CRAIG; SMITH, FRANK A., 15 MAR 69 7P.
EDRS PRICE MF-$0.65 HC-$3.29

SOME 180 KINDERGARTEN CHILDREN FROM LOW INCOME FAMILIES WERE TESTED MIDWAY THROUGH THE SCHOOL YEAR ON AN INSTRUCTIONAL CONCEPTS INVENTORY CREATED BY THE SOUTHWEST REGIONAL LABORATORY FOR EDUCATIONAL RESEARCH AND DEVELOPMENT (SRL). THE INVENTORY WAS DESIGNED TO MEASURE THE BASIC CONCEPTS KNOWN BY A CHILD. IT IS SPECIFICALLY GEARED TO TEST KINDERGARTEN PUPILS FOR THEIR SKILL WITH CONCEPTS NECESSARY FOR SUCCESSFUL ACHIEVEMENT IN THE FIRST GRADE. THE INVENTORY DRAWS FROM A LIST OF 86 CONCEPTS GROUPED INTO SEVEN CATEGORIES: COLOR, SIZE, SHAPE, POSITION, AMOUNT, TIME, AND EQUIVALENCE. THE INVENTORY, AS USED IN THIS STUDY, HAD 36 ITEMS INVOLVING THE SEVEN CATEGORIES. EACH ITEM CONSISTED OF A PICTURE ILLUSTRATION OF A CONCEPT AND TWO DISTRACTORS. EACH CHILD TESTED WAS ASKED TO POINT TO THE ILLUSTRATION OF THE CONCEPT NAMED BY THE EXAMINER. THE TEST RESULTS SHOWED THAT, ON AN AVERAGE, THE SUBJECTS KNEW ABOUT 23 OF THE 36 CONCEPTS. THE RESULTS INDICATED THAT KINDERGARTEN CHILDREN FROM LOW INCOME FAMILIES NEEDED INSTRUCTION IN THE BASIC CONCEPTS. SRL IS DEVELOPING A PROGRAM TO TEACH THE BASIC CONCEPTS MEASURED BY THIS INVENTORY. (WD)

ED028848 PS001933
IMPLICIT VERBAL BEHAVIOR IN ELEMENTARY SCHOOL CHILDREN, (INTERNAL VERBAL RESPONSES OF ELEMENTARY SCHOOL CHILDREN ELICITED BY THE ASSOCIATION OF WORDS). FINAL REPORT. HALL, JAMES W., 19 AUG 68 35P.
EDRS PRICE MF-$0.65 HC-$3.29

THE FOUR EXPERIMENTS OF THIS STUDY REPRESENT THE FIRST STAGE ON A PROGRAM OF RESEARCH DESIGNED TO CLARIFY THE NATURE AND DEVELOPMENT OF CERTAIN IMPLICIT VERBAL BEHAVIOR AND TO MOVE TOWARD APPLICATION OF THIS KNOWLEDGE TO SCHOOL LEARNING SITUATIONS AND PROBLEMS. SPECIFICALLY, THE EXPERIMENTS WERE CREATED TO INVESTIGATE SOME ASPECT OF THE IMPLICIT ASSOCIATIVE RESPONSE (IAR). THE SUBJECTS WERE PRESENTED WITH ONE LIST OF WORDS, THEN WERE PRESENTED WITH A PARTIALLY DIFFERENT LIST, AND THEN WERE ASKED TO IDENTIFY THOSE WORDS WHICH ALSO APPEARED ON THE FIRST LIST. ON THE SECOND LIST WERE ALSO NEW WORDS WITH AND WITHOUT AN ASSOCIATIONAL VALUE TO THE FIRST-LIST WORDS. THE SUBJECTS MISTAKENLY RECOGNIZED MORE NONFIRST-LIST ASSOCIATED WORDS THAN NONFIRST-LIST NONASSOCIATED WORDS. SUCH A MISTAKE IS CONSIDERED TO BE THE EFFECT OF IAR. THE RESULTS OF THE FOUR EXPERIMENTS INDICATED THAT (1) WHEN CHILDREN WERE ASKED TO USE THE STRATEGY OF ASSOCIATION IN LEARNING THE FIRST-LIST WORDS, IAR WAS FACILITATED; (2) WHEN CHILDREN WERE ASKED TO PRONOUNCE EACH WORD IN THE FIRST LIST AS THEY LEARNED IT, THE IAR EFFECT WAS REDUCED; AND (3) THE IAR EFFECT WAS REDUCED WITH THE AGE OF THE CHILD. (WD)

ED029680 PS000671
AN EXPERIMENTAL PROGRAM DESIGNED TO INCREASE AUDITORY DISCRIMINATION WITH HEAD START CHILDREN. BRICKNER, C. ANN, [67] 16P.
EDRS PRICE MF-$0.65 HC-$3.29

THE PURPOSE OF THIS STUDY WAS TO TEST THE EFFECTIVENESS OT TWO TRAINING SEQUENCES DESIGNED TO INCREASE AUDITORY DISCRIMINATION IN PRESCHOOL EDUCATIONALLY DISADVANTAGED CHILDREN. AUDITORY DISCRIMINATION IS IMPORTANT BECAUSE, AMONG OTHER REASONS, STUDIES HAVE SHOWN THE EXISTENCE OF A HIGH POSITIVE CORRELATION BETWEEN A CHILD'S ABILITY TO LISTEN AND HIS ABILITY TO READ. IT WAS HYPOTHESIZED THAT THE ENVIRONMENT OF DISADVANTAGED YOUTH PRODUCES SO MUCH NOISE THAT A BLOCKING OF INDIVIDUAL SOUNDS OCCURS. ONE HUNDRED AND SIX HEAD START CHILDREN TOOK PART IN THIS STUDY. THE FIRST TRAINING GROUP LISTENED TO TAPES CONTAINING 12 CATEGORIES OF SOUNDS FAMILIAR TO CHILDREN. THE SECOND TRAINING GROUP LISTENED TO NARRATIVE MATERIALS PLAYED ON TAPE RECORDERS. POSTTRAINING TEST SCORES SHOWED THAT GROUP ONE CHILDREN PERFORMED BETTER THAN GROUP TWO CHILDREN FOR BOTH VERBAL DISCRIMINATION AND FOLLOWING DIRECTIONS. BOTH TRAINING GROUPS PERFORMED BETTER THAN THE CONTROL GROUP, AND GIRLS GENERALLY PERFORMED BETTER THAN BOYS. (WD)

ED029681 PS001470
KINDERGARTEN: THE CHILD IN HIS HOME AND SCHOOL ENVIRONMENTS. COURSE OF STUDY AND RELATED LEARNING ACTIVITIES. (CURRICULUM BULLETIN, 1967-68 SERIES, NO. 2A.) , 15 SEP 67 118P.
EDRS PRICE MF-$0.65 HC NOT AVAILABLE FROM EDRS.
AVAILABLE FROM: BOARD OF EDUCATION OF THE CITY OF NEW YORK, PUBLICATIONS SALES OFFICE, 110 LIVINGSTON STREET, BROOKLYN, NEW YORK 11201 ($2.00)

THIS PUBLICATION IS A PRELIMINARY BULLETIN, GIVING THE BASIC COURSE OF STUDY AND RELATED LEARNING ACTIVITIES IN HISTORY AND THE SOCIAL SCIENCES FOR KINDERGARTEN IN THE CITY OF NEW YORK. THIS BULLETIN IS ONE OF A SERIES DESIGNED TO PROVIDE STUDENTS FROM PREKINDERGARTEN THROUGH THE 12TH GRADE WITH A REVITALIZED CURRICULUM IN HISTORY AND THE SOCIAL SCIENCES. THE PHILOSOPHY OF THE PROGRAM IS SUMMARIZED INTO SIX BASIC EMPHASES: (1) THE TEACHING OF CONCEPTS RATHER THAN THE ACCUMULATION OF DATA; (2) PROVIDING ALL STUDENTS WITH THE VALUES, SKILLS, UNDERSTANDING, AND KNOWLEDGE NEEDED TO COPE WITH THE PRESSING SOCIAL PROBLEMS OF OUR AGE; (3) THE ATTEMPT TO INCORPORATE INTO THE CURRICULUM BASIC CONCEPTS DRAWN FROM THE DISCIPLINES OF HISTORY AND THE SOCIAL SCIENCES; (4) THE ATTEMPT TO DEVELOP SKILLS AND RESEARCH TECHNIQUES SEQUENTIALLY; (5) THE ATTEMPT TO PROVIDE LEARNING ACTIVITIES THAT AIM AT CONCEPTUALIZATION THROUGH TECHNIQUES OF INQUIRY AND DISCOVERY; AND (6) THE USE OF MULTIMEDIA RESOURCES RATHER THAN THE TRADITIONAL TEXTBOOK. THE BULLETIN FOR GRADE ONE IS ABSTRACTED UNDER NUMBER PS 001 473, AND THE BULLETIN FOR GRADE TWO IS ABSTRACTED UNDER NUMBER PS 001 788. (WD)

ED029682 PS001473
GRADE 1: LIVING AND WORKING TOGETHER IN THE COMMUNITY. COURSE OF STUDY AND RELATED LEARNING ACTIVITIES. (CURRICULUM BULLETIN, 1967-68 SERIES, NO. 2B.) , 15 SEP 67 147P.
EDRS PRICE MF-$0.65 HC NOT AVAILABLE FROM EDRS.
AVAILABLE FROM: BOARD OF EDUCATION OF THE CITY OF NEW YORK, PUBLICATION SALES OFFICE, 110 LIVINGSTON STREET, BROOKLYN, N.Y. 11201 ($3.00)

THIS PUBLICATION IS A PRELIMINARY BULLETIN, GIVING THE BASIC COURSE OF STUDY AND RELATED LEARNING ACTIVITIES IN HISTORY AND THE SOCIAL SCIENCES FOR GRADE ONE IN THE CITY OF NEW YORK. THIS BULLETIN IS ONE OF A SERIES DESIGNED TO PROVIDE STUDENTS FROM PREKINDERGARTEN THROUGH THE 12TH GRADE WITH A REVITALIZED CURRICULUM IN HISTORY AND THE SOCIAL SCIENCES. THE PHILOSOPHY OF THE PROGRAM IS SUMMARIZED INTO SIX BASIC EMPHASES: (1) THE TEACHING OF CONCEPTS RATHER THAN THE ACCUMULATION OF DATA; (2) PROVIDING ALL STUDENTS WITH THE VALUES, SKILLS, UNDERSTANDINGS, AND KNOWLEDGE NEEDED TO COPE WITH THE PRESSING SOCIAL PROBLEMS OF OUR AGE; (3) THE ATTEMPT TO INCORPORATE INTO THE CURRICULUM BASIC CONCEPTS DRAWN FROM THE DISCIPLINES OF HISTORY AND THE SOCIAL SCIENCES; (4) THE ATTEMPT TO DEVELOP SKILLS AND RESEARCH TECHNIQUES SEQUENTIALLY; (5) THE ATTEMPT TO PROVIDE LEARNING ACTIVITIES THAT AIM AT CONCEPTUALIZATION THROUGH TECHNIQUES OF INQUIRY AND DISCOVERY; AND (6) THE USE OF MULTIMEDIA RESOURCES RATHER THAN THE TRADITIONAL TEXTBOOK. THE BULLETIN FOR THE KINDERGARTEN IS ABSTRACTED UNDER NUMBER PS 001 470, AND THE BULLETIN FOR GRADE TWO IS ABSTRACTED UNDER NUMBER PS 001 788. (WD)

ED029683 PS001617
LEICESTERSHIRE REVISITED. HULL, WILLIAM P.; ARMINGTON, DAVID, 17P.
EDRS PRICE MF-$0.65 HC-$3.29

IT IS BELIEVED THAT THE BEST OF THE NEW PROGRESSIVE INFANT AND JUNIOR SCHOOLS IN LEICESTERSHIRE COUNTY, ENGLAND, ARE SUPERIOR TO THOSE IN THE UNITED STATES. PRIMARILY FOUND IN THE INFANT SCHOOLS, THIS NEW CONCEPT IN EDUCATION EMPHASIZES AN ENVIRONMENT IN WHICH A CHILD IS ENCOURAGED TO LEARN BUT IS GIVEN THE FREEDOM TO DO SO IN HIS OWN STYLE AT HIS OWN PACE. THE CHILDREN ARE REGARDED AS INDIVIDUALS CAPABLE OF TAKING AN ACTIVE PART IN THEIR OWN LEARNING INSTEAD OF DISRUPTIVE CREATURES WHO NEED TO BE MANAGED AND GUIDED THROUGH SERIES OF DETAILED TASKS. THE PUPILS IN THESE ENGLISH SCHOOLS, ALTHOUGH ALLOWED GREAT FREEDOM OF MOVEMENT, DISPLAY A REMARKABLE SELF-RESTRAINT, INTEGRITY, AND LEARNING LEVEL. SEVERAL OF THE LEICESTERSHIRE INFANT SCHOOLS HAVE DONE AWAY WITH CLASSES ORGANIZED ON THE BASIS OF AGE AND HAVE REPLACED THEM WITH VERTICAL GROUPING. LEICESTERSHIRE HAS ALSO DONE AWAY WITH THE ELEVEN-PLUS EXAMINATION (USED IN ENGLAND TO QUALIFY HIGH SCORERS FOR HIGH STATUS GRAMMAR SCHOOLS) BECAUSE OF ITS HARSH EFFECT. MANY CLASSES NO LONGER NEED TO MAKE A DISTINCTION BETWEEN ONE SUBJECT AND ANOTHER OR BETWEEN WORK AND PLAY. (WD)

ED029684 PS001654
PSYCHOMOTOR EDUCATION - THEORY AND PRACTICE. NAVILLE, SUZANNE; BLOM, GASTON E., [68] 40P.
EDRS PRICE MF-$0.65 HC-$3.29

THIS PRESENTATION INTRODUCED THE THEORY AND PRACTICE OF PSYCHOMOTOR EDUCATION AS DEVELOPED BY DE AJURIAGUERRA AND NAVILLE AT THE UNIVERSITY OF GENEVA. SOME OVERLAP OF THEIR CONCEPTS AND PRINCIPLES WITH PERCEPTUAL MOTOR TRAINING METHODS OCCURRED IN THE UNITED STATES, ACCORDING TO THE AUTHORS. THE FOCUS OF THE THEORETICAL DISCUSSION INTEGRATED DEVELOPMENTAL AND PERSONALITY CONCEPTS FROM PSYCHOANALYTIC THEORY AND PIAGET COGNITIVE THEORY. FOUR "PRACTICAL" ASPECTS OF PSYCHOMOTOR EDUCATION WERE ALSO DISCUSSED: (1) ITS STRUCTURE, WHICH INCLUDED BASIC ELEMENTS OF MOTORICITY, BODY EGO, ORGANIZATION IN TIME AND SPACE, AND EDUCATION THROUGH MOVEMENT; (2) ITS INDICATIONS IN PSYCHOMOTOR DISORDERS, WHICH INCLUDED MOTOR DEBILITY, INHIBITION, AND HYPERACTIVITY; (3) ITS APPLICATION IN PRACTICE; AND (4) SOME PEDAGOGICAL CONSIDERATIONS. IT WAS NOTED THAT TRAINING PROCEDURES MODIFY BODY MOTOR SYMPTOMS AND SIGNS AND MAKE POSSIBLE THE USE OF THE BODY IN EMOTIONAL EXPRESSION, SOCIAL RELATIONSHIPS, AND THE DEVELOPMENT OF BODY SKILLS. FURTHER RESEARCH WAS SUGGESTED TO ESTABLISH MORE CLEARLY THE RELATIONSHIP BETWEEN MENTAL AND MOTOR DEVELOPMENT. (JS)

ED029685 PS001692
PROBLEM SOLVING AND CONCEPT FORMATION: ANNOTATED LISTING OF NATIONAL AND INTERNATIONAL CURRICULAR PROJECTS AT THE EARLY CHILDHOOD LEVEL. , 1 JUN 68 17P.
EDRS PRICE MF-$0.65 HC-$3.29
AVAILABLE FROM: SOUTHWEST REGIONAL LABORATORY FOR EDUCATIONAL RESEARCH AND DEVELOPMENT, 11300 LA CIENEGA BLVD., INGLEWOOD, CALIFORNIA 90304

THIS DOCUMENT IS AN ANNOTATED LISTING OF NATIONAL AND INTERNATIONAL CURRICULAR PROJECTS CONCERNED WITH PROBLEM SOLVING AND CONCEPT FORMATION AT THE EARLY CHILDHOOD LEVEL. IT CONTAINS 50 CITATIONS. (WD)

ED029686 PS001700
A TWO-YEAR LANGUAGE ARTS PROGRAM FOR PRE-FIRST GRADE CHILDREN: FIRST YEAR REPORT. DURKIN, DOLORES, [68] 19P.
EDRS PRICE MF-$0.65 HC-$3.29

IN THE SPRING OF 1967, TWO GROUPS OF ABOUT TWENTY 4-YEAR-OLDS FROM VARYING SOCIOECONOMIC BACKGROUNDS OF A SMALL MIDWESTERN COMMUNITY WERE SUBJECTS IN A STUDY TO DESIGN A PRESCHOOL CURRICULUM. AFTER AN IQ TEST, INDIVIDUAL IDENTIFICATION TESTS (WORD, LETTER, AND NUMERAL) WERE ADMINISTERED TO DETERMINE THE CHILDREN'S KNOWLEDGE. HOME INTERVIEWS AND CLASSROOM VISITATIONS BY PARENTS WERE CONDUCTED. THE PROGRAM HAD A LANGUAGE ARTS FOCUS RATHER THAN A READING FOCUS, USED ALL PHASES OF LANGUAGE ARTS APPEALING TO CHILDREN'S INTERESTS, AND DEVELOPED READING VOCABULARIES THROUGH THE WHOLE WORD APPROACH. LETTER, WORD, AND NUMERAL IDENTIFICATION WAS STRESSED. READING AND CONVERSATION PERIODS WERE HELD AT LEAST ONCE A DAY. AFTER 8 MONTHS, TESTS WERE READMINISTERED. WHILE ACHIEVEMENT IN SOME GOALS WAS NOT ASSESSED QUANTITATIVELY, IT WAS ASSUMED THAT SUCH ACHIEVEMENT WOULD HAVE A POSITIVE EFFECT ON LATER SCHOOL PERFORMANCE. BECAUSE THIS STUDY CONCERNS ONLY THE FIRST OF A TWO YEAR PROJECT, OVERALL RESULTS WILL BE REPORTED LATER. (DO)

ED029687 PS001715
COMPETENCE VS. PERFORMANCE IN YOUNG CHILDREN'S USE OF COMPLEX LINGUISTIC STRUCTURES. BRYSON, JUANITA; STERN, CAROLYN, FEB 69 9P.
EDRS PRICE MF-$0.65 HC-$3.29

SIXTEEN MEXICAN-AMERICAN 4-YEAR-OLDS, CLASSIFIED AS CULTURALLY DISADVANTAGED, WERE ADMINISTERED A SPECIAL PROGRAM IN AN ATTEMPT TO TEACH THEM THE CONCEPT OF ADJECTIVAL COMPARATIVES IN A SHORT TIME. THE CHILDREN WERE DIVIDED INTO TWO TREATMENT GROUPS. ONE, THE INDUCTIVE OR "DISCOVERY" GROUP, WAS SHOWN A PICTURE OF AN OBJECT (FOR EXAMPLE, A PIG) AND A COMPARATIVE PICTURE (PERHAPS A FATTER PIG) AND ASKED TO ECHO THE INSTRUCTOR'S STATEMENTS AS HE POINTED TO THE APPROPRIATE PICTURE. THE SECOND GROUP, THE DEDUCTIVE GROUP, WERE PROVIDED WITH A RULE FOR FORMING THE COMPARATIVE AND WERE ALSO SHOWN THE PICTURES. TEN COMPARATIVES WERE TAUGHT TO THE CHILDREN OVER A 3-DAY PERIOD. EACH CHILD RECEIVED A PRETEST AND POSTTEST INVOLVING SOME OF THE SAME 10 COMPARATIVES USED IN THE PROGRAM. THE TESTS WERE THE SAME, REQUIRING THE CHILD TO SELECT THE PICTURE OF THE COMPARATIVE OBJECT AND STATE THE COMPARATIVE. THE CHILDREN WERE ALSO ADMINISTERED A TRANSFER TEST, SIMILAR TO THE OTHER TESTS, BUT USING FIVE UNTAUGHT COMPARATIVES. THE CHILDREN WERE RETESTED 6 MONTHS LATER. THE TEST RESULTS INDICATED THAT LANGUAGE-HANDICAPPED CHILDREN CAN LEARN THIS PARTICULAR TASK QUICKLY. NO SIGNIFICANT DIFFERENCES WERE FOUND BETWEEN THE PERFORMANCE OF THE TWO TREATMENT GROUPS. (WD)

ED029688 PS001722
CONDITIONS FOSTERING THE USE OF INFORMATIVE FEEDBACK BY YOUNG CHILDREN. TEAGER, JOYCE; STERN, CAROLYN, FEB 69 13P.
EDRS PRICE MF-$0.65 HC-$3.29

IN ORDER TO INVESTIGATE THE EFFECT OF REINFORCEMENT ON LEARNING, 21 DISADVANTAGED BLACK CHILDREN, 4 TO 5 YEARS OF AGE, WERE DIVIDED AMONG THREE TREATMENT GROUPS. GROUP I CHILDREN RECEIVED ONLY FEEDBACK (INFORMATION) AS TO THE CORRECTNESS OR INCORRECTNESS OF THEIR RESPONSES. GROUP II CHILDREN RECEIVED A RAISIN FOR EACH CORRECT RESPONSE, AND GROUP III CHILDREN RECEIVED ONLY SOME FORM OF VERBAL REINFORCEMENT. THE TASK INVOLVED ANSWERING QUESTIONS RELATING TO A STORY BY TOUCHING A DOT LOCATED UNDER EACH RESPONSE CHOICE WITH A WATER PEN. THE DOT WAS CHEMICALLY TREATED TO TURN EITHER GREEN (CORRECT ANSWER) OR RED (INCORRECT ANSWER). EACH CHILD WAS ADMINISTERED A PRETEST AND A POSTTEST (IDENTICAL TESTS) OVER THE VOCABULARY INTRODUCED IN THE STORY. EACH CHILD WAS SUBSEQUENTLY GIVEN A NEW LEARNING SITUATION IN WHICH THE SAME TYPE OF RESPONSE WAS REQUIRED, BUT TO A SLIGHTLY DIFFERENT TASK. THE DATA INDICATED THAT ALTHOUGH THE RAISIN REWARD APPEARED TO BE A MORE POTENT REINFORCER, THE CHILDREN LEARNED TO USE FEEDBACK TO CORRECT ERRONEOUS RESPONSES AND USED IT IN NEW LEARNING SITUATIONS. IN FACT, TANGIBLE AND VERBAL REWARDS MA Y PRODUCE EMOTIONAL SIDE EFFECTS DISRUPTIVE TO LEARNING. (WD)

ED029689 PS001724
COMPARATIVE EFFECTIVENESS OF SPEAKING VERSUS LISTENING IN IMPROVING THE SPOKEN LANGUAGE OF DISADVANTAGED YOUNG CHILDREN. GUPTA, WILLA; STERN, CAROLYN, FEB 69 11P.
EDRS PRICE MF-$0.65 HC-$3.29

FORTY PRESCHOOL NEGRO CHILDREN TOOK PART IN A STUDY TO TEST THE EFFECT OF ORAL RESPONSE VERSUS LISTENING IN IMPROVING THE SPOKEN LANGUAGE OF DISADVANTAGED CHILDREN. IT WAS HYPOTHESIZED THAT CHILDREN WHO ECHO AND PRODUCE SENTENCES IN RESPONSE TO AN INSTRUCTION TO SELECT THE APPROPRIATE PICTURE TO MATCH A SPOKEN SENTENCE WOULD SHOW GREATER VERBAL SKILL THAN THOSE CHILDREN WHO ONLY LISTENED TO THE CORRECT RESPONSE. TRANSFER AND RETENTION OF THIS VERBAL LEARNING PATTERN (AS WELL AS THE EFFECT OF STRUCTURED TEACHING) WAS ALSO TESTED IN THE STUDY. A PRETEST-POSTTEST DESIGN WAS USED. AS PREDICTED, THE 20 SUBJECTS IN THE VERBAL GROUP SCORED HIGHER ON THE POSTTEST THAN THE CHILDREN IN THE LISTENING GROUP. TRANSFER OF LEARNING AND RENTENTION (AS TESTED 5 WEEKS LATER) WAS ALSO HIGHER IN THE VERBAL GROUP. IQ, MEASURED BY THE PEABODY PICTURE VOCABULARY TEST, ALSO SHOWED GAINS IN THIS GROUP. THE STRUCTURED PROGRAM APPEARED TO BE A SUCCESSFUL MODE OF INSTRUCTION IN INCREASING VERBAL LEARNING. (MS)

ED029690 PS001725
EFFECT OF VARIETY ON THE LEARNING OF A SOCIAL STUDIES CONCEPT BY PRESCHOOL CHILDREN. SCHWAB, LYNNE; STERN, CAROLYN, FEB 69 11P.
EDRS PRICE MF-$0.65 HC-$3.29

FIFTY-FOUR 5-YEAR-OLD HEAD START CHILDREN PARTICIPATED IN A STUDY OF THE EFFECT OF VARIED VERSUS REPEATED TRAINING ON THE DEVELOPMENT OF THE ABILITY TO CATEGORIZE AND TRANSFER LEARNING. THE CHILDREN WERE GROUPED ACCORDING TO CHRONOLOGICAL AGE AND RESULTS OF A MASTERY TEST AND THE PEABODY PICTURE VOCABULARY TEST. WORK CATEGORIES TRANSLATED INTO SINGLE VERBS, SUCH AS "SELL" OR "CLEAN," WERE USED IN AN INSTRUCTIONAL PATTERN INVOLVING TWO FRAMES. THE FIRST FRAME CONTAINED A SINGLE STIMULUS PICTURE OF A SPECIFIC KIND OF WORKER, AND THE SECOND FRAME CONTAINED THREE PICTURES OF DIFFERENT KINDS OF WORKERS. AFTER COMMENTARY, THE CHILDREN WERE ASKED TO MATCH THE WORKER IN FRAME ONE WITH THE WORKER WHO WAS DOING THE SAME KIND OF WORK IN FRAME TWO. DIFFERENT INSTRUCTIONAL TREATMENTS INVOLVED NUMBER AND VARIETY OF INSTANCES PRESENTED IN THESE MATCHING-TO-SAMPLE TESTS. WHEN THE CHILDREN'S RESULTS ON MASTERY, NEAR-TRANSFER, AND FAR-TRANSFER TESTS WERE COMPARED, IT WAS FOUND THAT IF THE NUMBER OF CATEGORIES WERE HELD CONSTANT AND IF THE INSTANCES WERE EITHER VARIED OR REPEATED, THE CHILDREN TRAINED WITH GREATER VARIETY RATHER THAN GREATER REPETITION WERE SUPERIOR ON THE TRANSFER TO NEW INSTANCES TEST. THERE WERE NO SIGNIFICANT DIFFERENCES AMONG GROUPS ON THE OTHER MEASURES. (MS)

ED029691 PS001726
YOUNG CHILDREN'S USE OF LANGUAGE IN INFERENTIAL BEHAVIOR. STERN, CAROLYN; KEISLAR, EVAN R., FEB 69 25P.
EDRS PRICE MF-$0.65 HC-$3.29

THIS EXPERIMENT WAS DESIGNED TO STUDY THE VALUE OF ORAL RESPONSE AS OPPOSED TO NONORAL RESPONSE IN LEARNING BY KINDERGARTEN CHILDREN. APPROXIMATELY 108 KINDERGARTEN CHILDREN WERE USED. ABOUT 80 OF THEM WERE PLACED IN THE TWO EXPERIMENTAL GROUPS (THAT IS, THE ORAL AND NONORAL GROUPS), AND THE OTHERS WERE PLACED IN A CONTROL GROUP. PHASE I INVOLVED TEACHING THE CHILDREN TO DRAW SIMPLE INFERENCES FROM

INFORMATION PRESENTED TO THEM. PHASE II EMPHASIZED LISTENING COMPREHENSION IN ANSWERING QUESTIONS. PHASE III, LIKE PHASE I, FOCUSED UPON CONCEPT FORMATION AND APPLICATION. THE DIFFERENCE IN TREATMENT OF THE ORAL AND NONORAL GROUP WAS THAT THE FORMER SAID ALOUD CRITICAL WORDS WHILE THE LATTER JUST LISTENED TO THE INSTRUCTION. ONLY ON PHASE II TESTS DID THE ORAL GROUP PERFORM SIGNIFICANTLY BETTER THAN THE NONORAL GROUP. THE CONTROL GROUP PERFORMED MORE POORLY THAN THE EXPERIMENTAL GROUPS. THIS STUDY DEMONSTRATED THE VALUE OF INSTRUCTING CHILDREN TO TRY TO UNDERSTAND AND RESPOND TO CERTAIN LINGUISTIC FORMS INVOLVED IN THE COMMUNICATION OF RELATIONSHIPS. (WD)

ED029692 PS001728
INDIVIDUALIZED MOTOR-PERCEPTUAL STUDY. , [68] 117P.
EDRS PRICE MF-$0.65 HC-$6.58

THIS GUIDE IS BEING USED IN THE INDIVIDUALIZED MOTOR-PERCEPTUAL STUDY TO DETERMINE WHETHER WORKING DIRECTLY WITH KINDERGARTEN CHILDREN TO IMPROVE PERFORMANCE ON MOTOR-PERCEPTUAL TASKS WILL AFFECT READING ABILITY AT THE END OF GRADES ONE, TWO, AND THREE. THE 5-YEAR PROJECT INVOLVES SIX SCHOOLS. IN THIS GUIDE, THERE ARE TIPS FOR TEACHING, SUGGESTED BEGINNING ACTIVITIES, AN APPENDIX DEFINING TERMS USED IN THE PROGRAM, A BIBLIOGRAPHY, TEACHER CHECKLISTS, AND SUGGESTED TAPE RECORDINGS TO BE USED DURING THE PROGRAM. THERE ARE ACTIVITIES TO DEVELOP GENERAL COORDINATION, BALANCE, BODY IMAGE, EYE-HAND COORDINATION, EYE MOVEMENTS, AND SENSORY PERCEPTION. EACH ACTIVITY IS DIVIDED INTO OBJECTIVE, GENERAL PURPOSE, MATERIALS, DIRECTIONS FOR TEACHERS, SUGGESTED DIRECTIONS TO THE CHILDREN, AND VARIATIONS OF THE ACTIVITY. (DO)

ED029693 PS001730
THE EFFECT OF DIRECT INSTRUCTION IN LISTENING ON THE LISTENING AND READING COMPREHENSION OF FIRST GRADE CHILDREN. DISSERTATION ABSTRACT. THORN, ELIZABETH A., [68] 14P.
EDRS PRICE MF-$0.65 HC-$3.29

TO EXPLORE THE EFFECTS OF LISTENING INSTRUCTION ON FIRST GRADERS' ACHIEVEMENT AND, SPECIFICALLY, TO ASSESS IMPROVEMENT IN LISTENING COMPREHENSION AND DETERMINE THE EFFECT OF LISTENING INSTRUCTION ON ACHIEVEMENT IN READING COMPREHENSION ARE THE PURPOSES OF THIS STUDY. SIX FIRST GRADE CLASSES WERE RANDOMLY ASSIGNED TO THREE GROUPS. A PROGRAM OF LISTENING INSTRUCTION WAS DEVELOPED, AND SYSTEMATIC LESSONS WERE TAUGHT TO THE EXPERIMENTAL GROUP. ONE OF THE CONTROL GROUPS FOLLOWED THE USUAL LANGUAGE PROGRAM, WHILE THE OTHER HAD SPECIAL LESSONS IN ORAL LANGUAGE. CONTROLS DID NOT RECEIVE DIRECT LISTENING INSTRUCTION. ACHIEVEMENT IN LISTENING, VOCABULARY, AND READING WERE MEASURED AT THE BEGINNING AND END OF THE STUDY. ANY GENERALIZATIONS BASED ON THE FINDINGS CAN BE APPLICABLE ONLY TO LIKE SUBJECTS AND TEACHERS AND TO SIMILAR CONDITIONS. IT WAS CONCLUDED THAT (1) LISTENING COMPREHENSION OF THE EXPERIMENTAL GROUP WAS SIGNIFICANTLY IMPROVED; (2) INSTRUCTION USED IN BASAL READING PROGRAMS IMPROVED LISTENING COMPREHENSION WHEN ADAPTED FOR USE WITH AURALLY PRESENTED MATERIAL; AND (3) LISTENING INSTRUCTION HAD A STRONG POSITIVE EFFECT ON READING ACHIEVEMENT, ALTHOUGH IT DID NOT PRODUCE HIGHLY SIGNIFICANT IMPROVEMENT IN READING COMPREHENSION. IMPLICATIONS OF THE FINDINGS AND SUGGESTIONS FOR FURTHER RESEARCH ARE DELINEATED. (DO)

ED029694 PS001788
GRADE 2: HOW PEOPLE LIVE IN CITY COMMUNITIES AROUND THE WORLD. COURSE OF STUDY AND RELATED LEARNING ACTIVITIES. (CURRICULUM BULLETIN, 1968-69 SERIES, NO. 2.) , 4 SEP 68 225P.
EDRS PRICE MF-$0.65 HC NOT AVAILABLE FROM EDRS.
AVAILABLE FROM: BOARD OF EDUCATION OF THE CITY OF NEW YORK, PUBLICATIONS SALES OFFICE, 110 LIVINGSTON STREET, BROOKLYN, N.Y. 11201 ($4.00)

THIS PUBLICATION IS A PRELIMINARY BULLETIN, GIVING THE BASIC COURSE OF STUDY AND RELATED LEARNING ACTIVITIES IN HISTORY AND THE SOCIAL SCIENCES FOR GRADE TWO IN THE CITY OF NEW YORK. THIS BULLETIN IS ONE OF A SERIES DESIGNED TO PROVIDE STUDENTS FROM PREKINDERGARTEN THROUGH THE 12TH GRADE WITH A REVITALIZED CURRICULUM IN HISTORY AND THE SOCIAL SCIENCES. THE PHILOSOPHY OF THE PROGRAM IS SUMMARIZED INTO SIX BASIC EMPHASES: (1) THE TEACHING OF CONCEPTS RATHER THAN THE ACCUMULATION OF DATA; (2) PROVIDING ALL STUDENTS WITH THE VALUES, SKILLS, UNDERSTANDINGS AND KNOWLEDGE NEEDED TO COPE WITH THE PRESSING SOCIAL PROBLEMS OF OUR AGE; (3) THE ATTEMPT TO INCORPORATE INTO THE CURRICULUM BASIC CONCEPTS DRAWN FROM THE DISCIPLINES OF HISTORY AND THE SOCIAL SCIENCES; (4) THE ATTEMPT TO DEVELOP SKILLS AND RESEARCH TECHNIQUES SEQUENTIALLY; (5) THE ATTEMPT TO PROVIDE LEARNING ACTIVITIES THAT AIM AT CONCEPTUALIZATION THROUGH TECHNIQUES OF INQUIRY AND DISCOVERY; AND (6) THE USE OF MULTIMEDIA RESOURCES RATHER THAN THE TRADITIONAL TEXTBOOK. THE BULLETIN FOR THE KINDERGARTEN IS ABSTRACTED UNDER NUMBER PS 001 470, AND THE BULLETIN FOR GRADE ONE IS ABSTRACTED UNDER NUMBER PS 001 473. (WD)

ED029695 PS001791
THE USE OF THE GOODENOUGH DRAW-A-MAN TEST AS A PREDICTOR OF ACADEMIC ACHIEVEMENT. SCHROEDER, GLENN B.; BEMIS, KATHERINE A., [FEB 69] 12P.
EDRS PRICE MF-$0.65 HC-$3.29

IN AN ATTEMPT TO FIND A TEST WHICH MINIMIZED CULTURAL BIAS, THREE TESTS WERE ADMINISTERED TO 335 FIRST GRADE PUPILS. THE SUBJECTS COMPRISED 2 GROUPS (123 ANGLO CHILDREN AND 212 SPANISH SURNAMED CHILDREN). THE GOODENOUGH DRAW-A-MAN TEST (GDAM) AND THE LORGE-THORNDIKE INTELLIGENCE TEST (LT), FORM A, WERE ADMINISTERED AS MEASURES OF INTELLIGENCE. THE CALIFORNIA ACHIEVEMENT TEST (CAT), FORM W, 1957 EDITION, WAS USED AS A MEASURE OF ACHIEVEMENT. RESULTS SHOWED A MEAN IQ DIFFERENCE BETWEEN THE TWO GROUPS OF 4.39 ON THE LT AND OF 2.63 ON THE GDAM, WITH THE ANGLO GROUP SCORING HIGHER ON BOTH TESTS. WHEN THE CAT SCORES WERE COVARIED WITH THE LT IQ SCORES THE ONLY SIGNIFICANT DIFFERENCE FOUND BETWEEN THE TWO GROUPS AT THE .01 LEVEL WAS IN THE "MEANING OF OPPOSITES" SUBTEST. WHEN THE CAT SCORES WERE COVARIED WITH THE GDAM IQ SCORES, DIFFERENCES IN SIX CATEGORIES WERE REVEALED AT THE .01 LEVEL: (1) MEANING OF OPPOSITES, (2) TOTAL READING VOCABULARY, (3) TOTAL READING, (4) ARITHMETIC PROBLEMS, (5) TOTAL ARITHMETIC REASONING, AND (6) TOTAL BATTERY. WITH THIS PARTICULAR POPULATION, THE GDAM AND LT WERE NEARLY IDENTICAL IN PREDICTING THE CAT. THE GDAM TENDS TO BRING THESE TWO DIVERGENT POPULATIONS CLOSER TOGETHER AS FAR AS IQ SCORES ARE CONCERNED. A BIBLIOGRAPHY AND TABLES ARE ATTACHED. (NT)

ED029696 PS001792
A STUDY OF COMPOSITION ABILITY AS ASSESSED WITH A STANDARDIZED INSTRUMENT FOR SECOND AND THIRD GRADE CHILDREN. BIESBROCK, EDIEANN, 69 12P.
EDRS PRICE MF-$0.65 HC-$3.29

WRITTEN COMPOSITIONS OF 200 SECOND AND THIRD GRADE CHILDREN WERE COMPARED FOUR TIMES OVER A 2-YEAR PERIOD TO DETERMINE RELATIONSHIPS OF COMPOSITION ABILITY WITH INTELLIGENCE AND READING LEVEL. A GLOBAL ESSAY INSTRUMENT DEVELOPED AT THE UNIVERSITY OF GEORGIA WAS USED FOR THE COMPARISONS TO FIND OUT WHETHER OR NOT THE INSTRUMENT REVEALED ANY IMPROVEMENT IN THE ESSAYS. FOUR RATERS SCORED EACH ESSAY INDEPENDENTLY AND WITHOUT KNOWLEDGE OF THE OTHER THREE RATINGS BY FOLLOWING STANDARDIZED PROCEDURES. FOUR MEAN TEST SCORES FOR EACH STUDENT FORMED A CHRONOLOGICAL SEQUENCE FROM THE FALL OF 1966 THROUGH THE SPRING OF 1968. THERE WAS A STEADY INCREASE IN THE GLOBAL ESSAY MEANS OF BOTH BOYS AND GIRLS OVER 2 YEARS. CORRELATIONS BETWEEN READING LEVEL, VOCABULARY, INTELLIGENCE, AND GLOBAL ESSAY SCORES SHOWED POSITIVE RELATIONSHIPS. THERE WAS NOT A SIGNIFICANT CORRELATION BETWEEN GLOBAL ESSAY SCORES AND SEX OR GRADE LEVEL. THE STUDY CONFIRMED THE SENSITIVITY OF THE GLOBAL ESSAY INSTRUMENT IN MEASURING THE GROWTH TREND OF SECOND AND THIRD GRADE CHILDREN. (DO)

ED029697 PS001793
A STUDY COMPARING GLOBAL QUALITY AND SYNTACTIC MATURITY IN THE WRITING COMPOSITION OF SECOND AND THIRD GRADE STUDENTS. BIESBROCK, EDIEANN F.; VEAL, L. RAMON, 69 10P.
EDRS PRICE MF-$0.65 HC-$3.29

SHORT ESSAYS WRITTEN BY 60 SECON D AND THIRD GRADE CHILDREN WERE ANALYZED IN ORDER TO COMPARE THE GLOBAL QUALITY WITH THE SYNTACTIC MATURITY CONTAINED THEREIN. GLOBAL QUALITY IS A BROAD MEASURE OF THE LEVEL OF ABILITY AND DEVELOPMENT EVIDENCED BY THE PUPIL IN HIS PARTICULAR WRITING. SYNTACTIC MATURITY IS A MEASURE BASED ON THE EXISTENCE OF VARIOUS SYNTACTICAL STRUCTURES IN THE WRITING. CONSIDERED IN THIS STUDY WERE (1) THE NUMBER OF T-UNITS (MINIMAL TERMINABLE SYNTACTIC UNITS), (2) THE MEAN T-UNIT LENGTH, (3) THE NUMBER OF SUBORDINATE CLAUSES, AND (4) THE NUMBER OF ALL CLAUSES. HIGH CORRELATIONS WERE FOUND BETWEEN GLOBAL QUALITY MEASURES AND THE NUMBER OF T-UNITS, THE RATIO OF THE CLAUSES PER T-UNIT, THE NUMBER OF SUBORDINATE CLAUSES, AND THE NUMBER OF ALL CLAUSES. THESE RESULTS INDICATE THAT FLUENCY AND COMPLEXITY ARE RELATED TO QUALITY IN THE WRITTEN COMPOSITIONS OF THESE STUDENTS. FURTHER RESEARCH IS NEEDED. A BIBLIOGRAPHY AND STATISTICAL TABLES ARE INCLUDED. (WD)

ED029698 PS001799
EXEL BEHRMANN, POLLY; MILLMAN, JOAN, 68 55P.
DOCUMENT NOT AVAILABLE FROM EDRS.
AVAILABLE FROM: EDUCATORS PUBLISHING SERVICE, INC., 75 MOULTON STREET, CAMBRIDGE, MASSACHUSETTS 02138 ($2.00)

THE ACTIVITIES COLLECTED IN THIS HANDBOOK ARE PLANNED FOR PARENTS TO USE WITH THEIR CHILDREN IN A LEARNING EXPERIENCE. THEY CAN ALSO BE USED IN THE CLASSROOM. SECTIONS CONTAIN GAMES DESIGNED TO DEVELOP VISUAL DISCRIMINATION, AUDITORY DISCRIMINATION, MOTOR COORDINATION AND ORAL EXPRESSION. AN OBJECTIVE IS GIVEN FOR EACH GAME, AND DIRECTIONS FOR PLAYING ARE INCLUDED. A GLOSSARY DEFINES THE TERMS USED THROUGHOUT THE TEXT. ACTIVITIES ARE RATED FOR DEGREE OF DIFFICULTY. (NT)

ED029699 PS001819
MATCHED-PAIR SCORING TECHNIQUE USED ON A FIRST-GRADE YES-NO TYPE ECONOMICS ACHIEVEMENT TEST. LARKINS, A. GUY; SHAVER, JAMES P., 21 APR 67 17P.
EDRS PRICE MF-$0.65 HC-$3.29

THERE EXIST SPECIAL PROBLEMS IN TESTING FIRST-GRADE CHILDREN. ORALLY ADMINISTERED YES-NO TESTS REDUCE THE PROBLEMS FOUND IN THE OTHER TYPES, BUT THEY HAVE THEIR OWN DRAWBACKS. A SOLUTION TO SOME OF THESE DRAWBACKS IS THE USE OF THE MATCHED-PAIR SCORING TECHNIQUE. FOR EACH "YES" ITEM ON THE TEST THERE IS INCLUDED A "REVERSED" OR "NO" ITEM ON THE SAME CONCEPT BEING TESTED, AND VICE VERSA. THE PUPIL MUST RESPOND CORRECTLY TO BOTH IN ORDER TO BE GIVEN CREDIT FOR EITHER ONE. HOWEVER, THE DRAWBACK THEN BECOMES THE NECESSITY OF DOUBLING THE SIZE OF THE TEST. A 30-ITEM TEST, BASED ON "FAMILIES AT WORK" ECONOMICS, WAS ADMINISTERED TO SIX FIRST GRADE CLASSES; THREE HAD BEE N STUDYING THE MATERIAL, AND THREE HAD NOT. THE TEST RESULTS SHOWED THAT (1) THE MATCHED-PAIR SCORING TECHNIQUE INCREASED THE RELIABILITY OF THE YES-NO TEST AND ALSO INCREASED AND GENERAL DISCRIMINATORY POWER OF THE TEST AND (2) THE STUDENTS WHO WERE STUDYING THE ECONOMICS MATERIAL SCORED HIGHER THAN STUDENTS WHO WERE NOT, INDICATING THAT THE PROGRAM WAS RESULTING IN DEMONSTRABLE LEARNING. ANOTHER ARTICLE BY THE SAME AUTHORS (SEE PS 001 822) ALSO DEALS WITH THIS SUBJECT. (WD)

ED029700 PS001821
SRA ECONOMICS MATERIALS IN GRADES ONE AND TWO. EVALUATION REPORTS. SHAVER, JAMES P.; LARKINS, A. GUY, 1 JUL 66 25P.
EDRS PRICE MF-$0.65 HC-$3.29

A CLASS OF FIRST GRADERS AND A CLASS OF SECOND GRADERS IN FOUR SALT LAKE CITY SCHOOLS COMPRISED THE EXPERIMENTAL SAMPLE IN A STUDY WHOSE OBJECTIVES WERE (1) TO DEVELOP A TEST FOR ASSESSING LEARNING WITH "OUR WORKING WORLD" MATERIALS, PUBLISHED BY SCIENCE RESEARCH ASSOCIATE (SRA), AND (2) TO DETERMINE IF STUDENTS USING THE MATERIALS MADE GREATER LEARNING GAINS THAN STUDENTS NOT USING THEM. FOUR CLASSES AT EACH GRADE LEVEL WERE RANDOMLY SELECTED FROM TWO SCHOOLS AND SERVED AS CONTROLS IN THE INVESTIGATION. APPROXIMATELY 400 CHILDREN TOOK PART IN THE STUDY. BOTH THE EXPERIMENTALS AND THE CONTROLS WERE GIVEN THE SRA TEST OF GENERAL ABILITY. THE PRIMARY ECONOMIC TEST--FIRST GRADE (PET-1) OF 64 ITEMS (DEVISED FOR THIS PROJECT) WAS ADMINISTERED TO THE CHILDREN AFTER THE MATERIALS HAD BEEN USED FOR 3 MONTHS. ANALYSIS OF COVARIANCE WAS USED TO ADJUST GROUP MEANS FOR DIFFERENCES OF SCHOLASTIC APTITUDE. IT WAS CONCLUDED THAT (1) THE ASSESSMENT INSTRUMENT (PET-1) WAS VALUABLE IN TESTING STUDENT PROGRESS AND (2) THE EXPERIMENTAL FIRST GRADERS SCORED SIGNIFICANTLY HIGHER ON THE TEST THAN DID THE CONTROL STUDENTS. ATTACHMENT A OF THIS DOCUMENT IS THE PET-1, ATTACHMENT B CONTAINS INSTRUCTIONS FOR ADMINISTERING THE TEST, AND ATTACHMENT C IS A CHART OF SELECTED PERCENTILES AND THE RANGES FOR THE EXPERIMENTAL AND CONTROL GROUPS. (DO)

ED029701 PS001822
COMPARISON OF YES-NO, MATCHED-PAIRS, AND ALL-NO SCORING OF A FIRST-GRADE ECONOMICS ACHIEVEMENT TEST. LARKINS, A. GUY; SHAVER, JAMES P., 12 APR 68 12P.
EDRS PRICE MF-$0.65 HC-$3.29

DEVELOPING PRACTICAL ACHIEVEMENT TESTS FOR USE AT THE PRIMARY-GRADE LEVEL IS A DIFFICULT TASK. SOME PROBLEMS ENCOUNTERED APPEAR TO BE RESOLVED BY USING VERBALLY ADMINISTERED YES-NO TESTS. BUT SUCH TESTS ARE CRITICIZED AS HAVING A LOW RELIABILITY BECAUSE THEY OFFER ONLY TWO CHOICES. TWO MODIFICATIONS OF THE YES-NO TEST HAVE BEEN PROPOSED TO INCREASE RELIABILITY. ONE IS THE "MATCHED-PAIRS" TECHNIQUE, IN WHICH EVERY "YES" ITEM HAS A MATCHING ITEM TO BE ANSWERED "NO". BOTH ITEMS MUST BE ANSWERED CORRECTLY FOR EITHER TO BE COUNTED. THE SECOND TECHNIQUE OF THE ALL-NO TEST, AN ATTEMPT TO COUNTER THE CHILDREN'S PROCLIVITY TO ANSWER "YES" EVEN WHEN THE ANSWER IS NOT KNOWN. SOME 200 FIRST GRADE CHILDREN WERE ADMINISTERED AN ECONOMICS TEST, IN WHICH ALL THREE TECHNIQUES WERE USED. THE TEST SCORES INDICATED THAT THE ALL-NO TEST HAD THE GREATEST RELIABILITY, BUT IT WAS LESS VALID THAN THE MATCHED-PAIRS TEST. THUS, THE MATCHED-PAIRS TEST WOULD BE THE BEST WAY TO CONSTRUCT THE YES-NO TYPE OF ACHIEVEMENT TESTS. ANOTHER ARTICLE BY THE SAME AUTHORS (SEE PS 001 819) ALSO DEALS WITH THE SUBJECT. (WD)

ED029702 PS001899
USE OF NON-PROFESSIONAL PERSONNEL FOR HEALTH SCREENING OF HEAD START CHILDREN. FINAL REPORT. CONNOR, ANGIE; AND OTHERS, NOV 68 29P.
EDRS PRICE MF-$0.65 HC-$3.29

THIS STUDY INVESTIGATED THE EXTENT TO WHICH TRAINED NONPROFESSIONAL PERSONNEL UNDER NURSING SUPERVISION COULD EFFECTIVELY CONDUCT HEALTH SCREENING OF HEAD START CHILDREN. RESULTS OF SCREENING BY NONPROFESSIONALS WERE COMPARED WITH RESULTS OF THE TRADITIONAL PEDIATRIC EXAMINATIONS. THE NONPROFESSIONALS WERE TRAINED BY A PEDIATRICIAN AND A PSYCHOLOGIST AND USED THE FOLLOWING INSTRUMENTS TO FACILITATE SCREENING: PARENT INTERVIEWS, PHYSICAL OBSERVATION FORMS, A REVISED DENVER DEVELOPMENTAL SCREENING TEST, THE AMMONS QUICK TEST, AND A REVISED WILLOUGHBY-HAGGERTY BEHAVIOR RATING SCALE. THERE WAS A POSITIVE CORRELATION BETWEEN THE RESULTS OF PEDIATRIC EXAMINATIONS AND THOSE OF THE NONPROFESSIONALS. THEIR REFERRALS FOR INTELLECTUAL AND DEVELOPMENTAL PROBLEMS ALSO REFLECTED A LOW BUT POSITIVE CORRELATION WITH THOSE OF PSYCHOLOGISTS. THE CORRELATION BETWEEN PEDIATRICIANS' AND PSYCHOLOGISTS' REFERRALS WAS EVEN LOWER. THESE RESULTS SUGGEST THAT WITH MORE TRAINING, NONPROFESSIONALS COULD BE USEFUL IN HEALTH SCREENING UNDER PROPER SUPERVISION AND THUS PROVIDE A VALUABLE SERVICE TO AREAS SHORT OF MEDICAL AND NURSING PERSONNEL. (AUTHOR/WD)

ED029703 PS001931
THE ROLE OF THE TEACHER IN THE INFANT AND NURSERY SCHOOL. GARDNER, DOROTHY E.M.; CASS, JOAN E., 65 181P.
DOCUMENT NOT AVAILABLE FROM EDRS.
AVAILABLE FROM: PERGAMON PRESS INC., 122 EAST 55TH STREET, NEW YORK, NEW YORK 10022 ($4.50)

THIS PUBLICATION IS INTENDED TO HELP TEACHERS OF YOUNG CHILDREN IN THE INFORMAL PRESCHOOL SETTING, PARTICULARLY INFANT SCHOOL TEACHERS IN ENGLAND. DETAILS OF WHAT 48 SELECTED NURSERY AND INFANT SCHOOL TEACHERS DID AND SAID DURING CLASSROOM "FREE TIME" PERIODS WERE RECORDED BY TRAINED OBSERVERS. THIS DATA IS INCLUDED IN THIS BOOK TO PROVIDE SOME CLARIFICATION OF WHAT CONSTITUTES GOOD AND SUCCESSFUL TEACHING AT THAT LEVEL. ALSO DISCUSSED IN THIS BOOK ARE DEVELOPMENTS IN ENGLISH INFANT AND NURSERY SCHOOLS AND TEACHERS' FUNCTIONS THEREIN. A BIBLIOGRAPHY IS INCLUDED. (WD)

ED029704 PS001937
THE INTERGROUP RELATIONS CURRICULUM: A PROGRAM FOR ELEMENTARY SCHOOL EDUCATION. VOLUMES I AND II. GIBSON, JOHN S., 69 784P.
DOCUMENT NOT AVAILABLE FROM EDRS.
AVAILABLE FROM: LINCOLN CENTER FOR CITIZENSHIP AND PUBLIC AFFAIRS, TUFTS UNIVERSITY, MEDFORD, MASS. 02155 ($5.00)

VOLUME I OF THIS STUDY DESCRIBES THE BACKGROUND OF THE LINCOLN FILENE CENTER'S RESEARCH AND DEVELOPMENT ON THE INTERGROUP RELATIONS CURRICULUM AND PROPOSITIONS, CRITIQUES, AND RECOMMENDATIONS RELEVANT TO INTERGROUP RELATIONS EDUCATION IN THE UNITED STATES. IT CONTAINS A REPORT ON INSERVICE TEACHER PROGRAMS, EVALUATION INSTRUMENTS, AND PROCEDURES FOR DISSEMINATING INFORMATION AND FINDINGS CONCERNING THE CURRICULUM. VOLUME II PRESENTS AN INTRODUCTION TO THE CURRICULUM, THE CONCEPTUAL FRAMEWORK, THE METHODOLOGICAL TOOLS, RECOMMENDATIONS FOR TEACHING, LEARNING ACTIVITIES AND UNITS, AND RECOMMENDED INSTRUCTIONAL RESOURCES FOR TEACHERS AND STUDENTS. (DO)

ED029705 PS001939
HEAD START EVALUATION AND RESEARCH CENTER, TULANE UNIVERSITY. ANNUAL REPORT. , 31 AUG 68 83P.
EDRS PRICE MF-$0.65 HC-$3.29

TO MEASURE THE EFFECTS OF GROUP PROGRAMED INSTRUCTION ON ASPECTS OF READING IN HEAD START CHILDREN, THE SULLIVAN ASSOCIATES READINESS IN LANGUAGE ARTS SERIES WAS USED WITH APPROXIMATELY 15 CHILDREN IN EACH OF FIVE HEAD START CLASSES. AN EQUAL NUMBER SERVED AS CONTROLS. PRETESTS AND POSTTEST WERE LEE-CLARK READINESS TEST, MURPHY-DURRELL ANALYSIS, AND GATES READING READINESS TESTS. DATA PROVIDED EVIDENCE THAT THE EXPERIMENTAL GROUPS HAD GREATER ACHIEVEMENT IN (1) RECOGNITION OF LETTER SYMBOLS, (2) IDENTIFYING NAMES OF LETTERS, AND (3) FAMILIARITY WITH NUMBERS AND PRINTED LETTERS OF THE ALPHABET. THE CONTROL GROUPS MADE GREATER ADVANCES IN (1) BOTH SIMILLARITIES AND DIFFERENCES IN WORD FORMATION, (2) LEARNING MORE WORDS IN ONE DAY UNDER STANDARD CONDITIONS OF PRESENTATION, AND (3) BEING ABLE TO UNDERSTAND ORAL INSTRUCTIONS AND SENSITIVITY TO SOUNDS OF WORDS. STUDIES ARE UNDERWAY IN THREE MORE AREAS: MORAL JUDGEMENT IN YOUNG CHILDREN AS A FUNCTION OF SELECTED ABILITIES, BEHAVIORAL CORRELATES OF NUTRITIONAL STATES IN YOUNG CHILDREN, AND CONDITIONS UNDER WHICH HEAD START'S BENEFITS TO CHILDREN AND FAMILIES ARE MAXIMIZED. PROCEDURES ARE OUTLINED FOR THESE PROJECTS. (NT)

ED029706 PS001953
EFFECTS OF KINDERGARTEN ATTENDANCE ON DEVELOPMENT OF SCHOOL READINESS AND LANGUAGE SKILLS. INTERIM REPORT. RUBIN, ROSALYN, 30 JAN 69 21P.
EDRS PRICE MF-$0.65 HC-$3.29

THIS STUDY WAS MADE TO FIND OUT TO WHAT EXTENT KINDERGARTENS CONTRIBUTE TO SCHOOL READINESS. NINETY CHILDREN WITH A MEAN CHRONOLOGICAL AGE OF 4.9 WERE TESTED WITH THE METROPOLITAN READINESS TEST (MRT), THE ILLINOIS TEST OF PSYCHOLINGUISTIC ABILITIES (ITPA), AND A BEHAVIOR RATING SCALE AND WERE RETESTED ONE YEAR LATER. DURING THE INTERVENING YEAR, 36 OF THE CHILDREN ATTENDED KINDERGARTEN, WHILE 54 DID NOT. THE DATA WERE ANALYZED BY SEX. ON THE PRETEST SCORES, THERE WERE NO

DIFFERENCES BETWEEN KINDERGARTEN (K) AND NONKINDERGARTEN (N-K) BOYS. K GIRLS, HOWEVER, DID SCORE SIGNIFICANTL Y HIGHER THAN N-K GIRLS ON TOTAL MRT AND ITPA SCORES AND ON PARTS OF THE BEHAVIOR RATING SCALE., GIRLS SCORED CONSISTENTLY HIGHER THAN BOYS IN OVERALL PRETESTING. THE RESULTS OF THE STUDY SUPPORT THE PREVAILING VIEW THAT AS CHILDREN REACH KINDERGARTEN AGE, SCHOOL READINESS AND LANGUAGE SKILLS OF GIRLS ARE FURTHER DEVELOPED THAN ARE THOSE OF BOYS AND THAT GROWTH IN THESE AREAS CANNOT BE ATTRIBUTED TO ANY SPECIAL INFLUENCE OF THE NORMAL TYPE OF KINDERGARTEN PROGRAM IN THIS STUDY. (JS)

ED029707 PS001961
EIDETIC IMAGERY IN CHILDREN. FINAL REPORT. HABER, RALPH NORMAN, 1 FEB 69 74P.
EDRS PRICE MF-$0.65 HC-$3.29

TWO GROUPS OF CHILDREN TOOK PART IN THIS LONGITUDINAL STUDY OF EIDETIC IMAGERY (EI). THE NEW HAVEN SAMPLE CONSISTED OF 12 ELEMENTARY SCHOOL CHILDREN, AND THE ROCHESTER SAMPLE CONSISTED OF 23 CHILDREN (AGED 7 TO 11 YEARS AT THE BEGINNING OF THE STUDY). THE STUDY WAS DESIGNED TO FIND OUT SOME OF THE QUALITIES OF EI AND ITS RELATIONSHIP TO MEMORY. AN EIDETIC IMAGE WAS DEFINED AS A LONG-LASTING VISUAL IMAGE OF A FIGURE LOCALIZED IN SPACE IN FRONT OF THE SUBJECT, POSITIVE IN COLOR, AND USUALLY ON THE PLACE WHERE THE ORIGINAL FIGURE WAS SHOWN. THE IMAGE PERSISTS AFTER THE STIMULUS IS GONE. SUBJECTS WERE SHOWN PICTURES ONE AT A TIME FOR A BRIEF PERIOD AND ASKED TO COMMENT ON EACH PICTURE ONCE IT HAD BEEN REMOVED. STUDY RESULTS SUGGEST THAT EIDETIC IMAGERY IS A STABLE PERCEPTUAL ABILITY, WITHOUT DEVELOPMENTAL TRENDS AS THE SUBJECT GROWS OLDER. THE AMOUNT OF INFORMATION REPORTED ON A PICTURE IN EIDETIC IMAGERY DIFFERED LITTLE FROM THAT OF NORMAL MEMORY. STUDY CONCLUSIONS INDICATE THAT EI I S A VISUAL PHENOMENA, NOT MERELY A REPORT OF VIVID MEMORY. ADDITIONAL RESEARCH IS NEEDED TO RELATE EI TO PERCEPTUAL AND DEVELOPMENTAL THEORIES. (MS)

ED029708 PS001962
REPLICATION OF THE "MOTIVATED LEARNING" COGNITIVE TRAINING PROCEDURES WITH CULTURALLY DEPRIVED PRESCHOOLERS. REPORT FROM PROJECT MOTIVATED LEARNING. STAATS, ARTHUR W., AUG 68 22P.
EDRS PRICE MF-$0.65 HC-$3.29

TWELVE CULTURALLY DISADVANTAGED 4-YEAR-OLDS OF BORDERLINE NORMAL INTELLIGENCE WERE SUBJECTS OF THIS STUDY. ITS PRIMARY PURPOSE WAS TO TEST FURTHER THE COGNITIVE LEARNING THEORY PREVIOUSLY DEVELOPED, AS WELL AS THE REINFORCEMENT SYSTEM, THE FACILITIES, AND THE EXPERIMENTAL-LONGITUDINAL METHODS OF RESEARCH. THE STUDY DID NOT INCLUDE A CONTROL GROUP AND WAS CONDUCTED IN PART TO ASSESS THE POSSIBILITY THAT THE EFFECTS OF TRAINING ON SPECIFIC INTELLECTUAL SKILLS WOULD BE REFLECTED ON STANDARDIZED TESTS. THESE NURSERY SCHOOL CHILDREN PARTICIPATED IN 13-MINUTE EXPERIMENTAL SESSIONS THREE TIMES A DAY IN THE STUDY OF WRITING, READING LETTERS, AND NUMBER CONCEPT LEARNING WITH TOKEN-REINFORCERS (ACCUMULATED TOKENS WHICH COULD BE EXCHANGED FOR TOYS, ETC.) USED TO STIMULATE ACHIEVEMENT. DATA WAS COLLECTED ON THE CHILD'S RESPONSES, THE REINFORCERS, AND THE STIMULI THAT ELICITED RESPONSES. RESULTS OF THE STANFORD BINET AND METROPOLITAN READINESS TESTS, ADMINISTERED FOUR TIMES DURING THE STUDY, SHOWED CONSIDERABLE GAIN IN THE INTELLIGENCE MEASURES AND IN THE COGNITIVE SKILLS INVOLVED IN READINESS FOR SCHOOL. THE FINDINGS INDICATE THE NEED FOR FURTHER RESEARCH. (DO)

ED029709 PS001963
A COMPARISON OF THE READING READINESS OF KINDERGARTEN PUPILS EXPOSED TO CONCEPTUAL-LANGUAGE AND BASAL READER PREREADING PROGRAMS. A PILOT STUDY. FINAL REPORT. O'DONNELL, C. MICHAEL P., 3 AUG 68 98P.
EDRS PRICE MF-$0.65 HC-$3.29

SEVENTY-EIGHT KINDERGARTEN CHILDREN WERE RANDOMLY PLACED IN FOUR EXPERIMENTAL CLASSROOMS. TWO OF THE CLASSES WERE TAUGHT WITH THE BASAL READER APPROACH TO READING READINESS, AND TWO WERE TAUGHT WITH THE CONCEPTUAL-LANGUAGE PROGRAM APPROACH. AN EXTENSIVE PRETEST BATTERY WAS GIVEN TO THESE CHILDREN IN OCTOBER 1967. INSTRUCTION IN THE TWO APPROACHES WAS GIVEN FROM NOVEMBER 1967 TO MAY 1968. AT THE END OF THE INSTRUCTIONAL PERIOD AN EXTENSIVE POSTTEST BATTERY WAS GIVEN TO THE CHILDREN. THIS INVESTIGATION WAS DESIGNED TO TEST THE EFFECTIVENESS OF THE TWO METHODS OF INSTRUCTION IN DEVELOPING READING READINESS IN KINDERGARTEN. THE CONCEPTUAL-LANGUAGE PROGRAM WAS FOUND TO BE SUPERIOR TO THE BASAL-CENTERED PROGRAM IN PROMOTING GENERAL READINESS FOR READING. (WD)

ED029710 PS001964
IDENTIFICATION IN THE KINDERGARTEN OF FACTORS THAT MAKE FOR FUTURE SUCCESS IN READING AND IDENTIFICATION AND DIAGNOSIS IN THE KINDERGARTEN OF POTENTIAL READING DISABILITY CASES. FINAL REPORT. HIRST, WILMA E.; AND OTHERS, 28 FEB 69 108P.
EDRS PRICE MF-$0.65 HC-$6.58

IN A 3-YEAR LONGITUDINAL STUDY, APPROXIMATELY 300 KINDERGARTEN CHILDREN WERE SELECTED FOR TESTING IN THE KINDERGARTEN AND FIRST AND SECOND GRADES TO DETERMINE PREDICTOR VARIABLES OF FUTURE SUCCESS IN READING AND ARITHMETIC. RESULTS OF THE RESEARCH TENDED TO INDICATE THAT AGE AND INTELLIGENCE TEST SCORES WERE NOT GOOD PREDICTORS OF FIRST AND SECOND GRADE READING ACHIEVEMENT. IT WAS CONCLUDED THAT THE MOST SIGNIFICANT PREDICTORS FOUND WERE AS FOLLOWS: (1) THE NUMBERS SUBTEST OF THE METROPOLITAN READINESS TEST, (2) THE DIGIT SPAN OF THE WECHSLER INTELLIGENCE SCALE FOR CHILDREN, (3) THE VISUAL 3 AND COMPLETE-A-MAN OF THE GESELL DEVELOPMENT TEST, (4) TITLES FROM THE MINNESOTA NONVERBAL TEST OF CREATIVITY, (5) SEX (FOR FIRST GRADE READING SUCCESS), (6) SOCIOECONOMIC STATUS (FOR SECOND GRADE READING AND ARITHMETIC ACHIEVEMENT), (7) EDUCATION OF THE MOTHER, (8) KINDERGARTEN TEACHER'S PREDICTION OF THE SUBJECT'S READING ABILITY, (9) KINDERGARTEN TEACHER'S RATING OF THE PUPIL'S SOCIOEMOTIONAL GROWTH, AND (10) SOCIOMETRIC EVALUATION OF "NUMBER OF TIMES CHILD IS SEEN IN A POSITIVE ROLE." TABULATED DATA AND A BIBLIOGRAPHY WITH 79 REFERENCES ARE APPENDED. (JS)

ED029711 PS001975
THE NURSERY YEARS: THE MIND OF THE CHILD FROM BIRTH TO SIX YEARS. ISAACS, SUSAN, 68 155P.
DOCUMENT NOT AVAILABLE FROM EDRS.
AVAILABLE FROM: SCHOCKEN BOOKS, INC., 67 PARK AVENUE, NEW YORK, NEW YORK 10016 ($4.50)

THIS IS THE 1968 EDITION OF A BOOK THAT WAS FIRST PUBLISHED IN 1929. SUBTITLED "THE MIND OF THE CHILD FROM BIRTH TO SIX YEARS," IT IS PRIMARILY AN EXPLANATION OF PRINCIPLES OF CHILD GUIDANCE, BASED ON THE FACTORS OF PHYSICAL AND MENTAL GROWTH DURING THE PRESCHOOL YEARS. THE POINTS OF VIEW OF BOTH THE PARENT AND THE CHILD ARE EXAMINED. A LIST OF "DONT'S" FOR PARENTS, A BIBLIOGRAPHY, AND AN INDEX ARE ALSO INCLUDED. (WD)

ED029712 PS001984
THE MAGIC YEARS: UNDERSTANDING AND HANDLING THE PROBLEMS OF EARLY CHILDHOOD. FRAIBERG, SELMA H., 59 317P.
DOCUMENT NOT AVAILABLE FROM EDRS.
AVAILABLE FROM: CHARLES SCRIBNER'S SONS, 597 FIFTH AVENUE, NEW YORK, NEW YORK 10017 ($4.50, PAPER $2.45)

THE PERSONALITY DEVELOPMENT DURING THE FIRST 5 YEARS OF LIFE CONSISTS OF SEVERAL STAGES, AND EACH DEVELOPMENTAL PHASE BRINGS WITH IT CHARACTERISTIC PROBLEMS. TRAINING OF THE INTELLECT MUST BE INCLUDED IN THE EDUCATION OF A CHILD. REASON AND JUDGMENT SHOULD BE REMOVED AS FAR AS POSSIBLE FROM MAGIC, SELF-GRATIFICATION AND EGOCENTRIC MOTIVES. THE PARENTS' METHODS OF HELPING THE CHILD'S MENTAL DEVELOPMENT, SELF-CONTROL, AND INTELLECTUAL GROWTH MUST TAKE INTO ACCOUNT THE CHILD'S OWN STAGE OF DEVELOPMENT AND HIS MENTAL EQUIPMENT AT THAT STAGE. PARENTS MAY BE INEXPERIENCED AND MAY SOMETIMES EMPLOY A WRONG METHOD; BUT IF THE BONDS BETWEEN PARENTS AND CHILD ARE STRONG AND PROVIDE THE INCENTIVES FOR GROWTH AND DEVELOPMENT, THEY HAVE AN EXCELLENT CHANCE OF REARING A HEALTHY CHILD. (NT)

ED029713 PS001991
A REPORT ON THE 1967-68 PROGRAM FOR PRESCHOOL CHILDREN AND THEIR PARENTS. RESEARCH REPORT SERIES 1968-69, NO. 4. , 1 AUG 68 38P.
EDRS PRICE MF-$0.65 HC-$3.29

SOME OF THE GENERAL OBJECTIVES OF THIS COMPENSATOR Y PROGRAM WERE TO PROVIDE EDUCATIONAL EXPERIENCES AND TO ASSESS THE NEEDS OF THE CHILDREN AND THEIR PARENTS. DURING THE 1967-1968 SCHOOL YEAR IT COMPRISED 23 CLASSES SITUATED IN 14 SCHOOLS AND WAS DESIGNED TO SERVE UP TO 405 PUPILS AND 345 PARENTS. THE CLASSES WERE FINANCED BY CALIFORNIA STATE AND U.S. GOVERNMENT FUNDS. THE PROGRAMS FOR THE CHILDREN WERE BASIC PRESCHOOL PROGRAMS STRESSING LANGUAGE DEVELOPMENT, EXPERIENCE BUILDING, AND READINESS ACTIVITIES. THE PROGRAMS FOR THE PARENTS STRESSED CHILD GROWTH AND DEVELOPMENT, NUTRITION, HEALTH, PRESCHOOL EDUCATION, AND THE NATURE, AVAILABILITY, AND USE OF COMMUNITY RESOURCES. EACH CLASS EMPLOYED A WORK EXPERIENCE AIDE AND A TEACHER AIDE FROM THE NEIGHBORHOOD. DATA WERE COLLECTED FROM A KINDERGARTEN TEACHER ASSESSMENT OF PUPIL READINESS AND THE EFFECTS OF COMPENSATORY PROGRAMS ON INCOMING KINDERGARTEN PUPILS. THE CALDWELL PRESCHOOL INVENTORY AND THE SLOSSON INTELLIGENCE TEST WERE ADMINISTERED TO 100 PUPILS IN THE FALL AND TO 77 AVAILABLE FOR RETESTING IN THE SPRING. A FIELD TRIP PROGRAM REPORT, PARENT QUESTIONNAIRE, TEACHER QUESTIONNAIRE, AND REPORTS FROM THE STAFF MEMBERS COMPLETED THE DATA AVAILABLE. ABOUT HALF OF THIS REPORT IS A

DETAILED ACCOUNT OF THE "FINDINGS," BUT NO GENERAL CONCLUSIONS ARE LISTED. (NT)

ED029714 PS001997
THE MIDDLE SCHOOL: A SELECTED BIBLIOGRAPHY WITH INTRODUCTION. PANSINO, LOUIS P., COMP., APR 69 8P.
EDRS PRICE MF-$0.65 HC-$3.29

THE INTRODUCTION TO THIS BIBLIOGRAPHY GIVES A DEFINITION OF THE MIDDLE SCHOOL AND INDICATES THAT IN 1966 THE NUMBER OF SUCH SCHOOLS IN THE UNITED STATES WAS 499. THE COMPILER POINTS OUT THE DISADVANTAGES OF THE JUNIOR HIGH IN CONTRAST TO THE ADVANTAGES OF THE MIDDLE SCHOOL. IN ADDITION, HE INCLUDES A BRIEF REVIEW OF TWO BOOKS WHICH SUPPORT OPPOSITE SIDES OF THE CONTROVERSY. THE SELECTED UNANNOTATED BIBLIOGRAPHY, COMPILED FROM "EDUCATION INDEX" AND "RESEARCH IN EDUCATION," CONTAINS CITATIONS FOR FIVE BOOKS, 43 JOURNAL ARTICLES, AND THREE REPORTS. (JS)

ED029715 PS002000
CHILDREN'S ABILITY TO OPERATE WITHIN A MATRIX: A DEVELOPMENTAL STUDY. SIEGEL, ALEXANDER W.; KRESH, ESTHER, DEC 68 24P.
EDRS PRICE MF-$0.65 HC-$3.29

EIGHT CHILDREN FROM EACH OF FIVE AGE GROUPS, 4, 5, 6, 7, AND 8 YEARS, WERE ADMINISTERED MATRIX TASKS INVOLVING TWO NOMINAL DIMENSIONS, COLOR AND SHAPE. NINE STIMULUS CELLS AND SIX ATTRIBUTE CELLS MADE UP THE APPARATUS. THE ATTRIBUTE CELLS CONSISTED OF THREE COLORS AND THREE GEOMETRIC SHAPES; THE STIMULUS CELLS MADE UP A MATRIX CONSISTING OF THE NINE POSSIBLE COMBINATIONS OF THE TWO BASIC ATTRIBUTES. THE SUBJECTS WERE ASKED TO PERFORM THREE OPERATIONS ON THE MATRIX: (1) TO DEFINE THE COVERED CONTENTS OF THE STIMULUS CELLS BY LOOKING AT THE ATTRIBUTE CELLS, (2) TO PLACE THE STIMULI IN THEIR CORRECT CELLS WHILE BEING GUIDED BY THE ATTRIBUTE CELLS, AND (3) TO DEFINE AND FILL THE ATTRIBUTE CELLS BY VIEWING THE STIMULUS CELLS. THE RESULTS SHOWED THAT ON ALL THREE TASKS THE PERFORMANCE OF THE 4-YEAR-OLDS WAS CLOSE TO CHANCE, THE PERFORMANCE OF THE 8-YEAR-OLDS WAS NEAR MAXIMUM, AND THERE WAS GRADUAL IMPROVEMENT OF PERFORMANCE FOR THE AGES IN BETWEEN. FOR SUBJECTS 4 TO 7 YEARS OF AGE, TASKS (1) AND (2) WERE POSITIVELY RELATED BUT WERE INDEPENDENT OF TASK (3). FOR THE 8-YEAR-OLDS, TASKS (1) AND (3) WERE POSITIVELY RELATED AND TASKS (1) AND (2) WERE INDEPENDENT. THIS DIFFERENCE IN TASK RELATIONSHIPS IS PROBABLY DUE, IN PART, TO DIFFERENCES IN THE TYPES OF VERBAL MEDIATORS INVOLVED. (WD)

ED029716 PS002001
BIBLIOGRAPHY: TEACHER CHARACTERISTICS. SPENCER, MIMA, COMP., 69 51P.
EDRS PRICE MF-$0.65 HC-$3.29
AVAILABLE FROM: ERIC CLEARINGHOUSE ON EARLY CHILDHOOD EDUCATION, 805 WEST PENNSYLVANIA AVENUE, URBANA, ILLINOIS 61801 ($1.00)

THIS TEACHER CHARACTERISTICS BIBLIOGRAPHY, PUBLISHED BY THE ERIC CLEARINGHOUSE ON EARLY CHILDHOOD EDUCATION, PRESENTS THE RESUMES OF 82 DOCUMENTS RELEVANT TO THE TEACHER HERSELF OR WHICH CONCERN HER RELATIONSHIP TO PUPILS OR COLLEAGUES. MOST OF THE DOCUMENTS DEAL WITH TEACHERS OF PRESCHOOL OR PRIMARY AGE CHILDREN, BUT A FEW REPORT ON TEACHERS OF OLDER STUDENTS OR ADULTS. THE MAJORITY OF THE DOCUMENTS SELECTED FOR THIS BIBLIOGRAPHY ARE AVAILABLE THROUGH THE ERIC SYSTEM. FOR THE REMAINDER, A SOURCE IS PROVIDED AT THE END OF THE RESUME. DIRECTIONS FOR ORDERING DOCUMENTS AND AN ORDER BLANK ARE INCLUDED. (WD)

ED029717 PS002006
THE EFFECTS OF STANDARD DIALECT TRAINING ON NEGRO FIRST-GRADERS LEARNING TO READ. FINAL REPORT. RYSTROM, RICHARD, 30 SEP 68 123P.
EDRS PRICE MF-$0.65 HC-$6.58

THIS STUDY WAS CONDUCTED TO EXPLORE THE IDEA THAT THE NEGRO DIALECT OPERATES AS A SOURCE OF INTERFERENCE IN THE ACQUISITION OF READING SKILLS BY NEGRO CHILDREN. TWO FIRST GRADE CLASSES FROM AN OAKLAND, CALIFORNIA, INNER CITY SCHOOL WERE CHOSEN TO PARTICIPATE IN THIS EXPERIMENT. THE PUPILS WERE ALL PRETESTED. HALF OF THEM WERE THEN RANDOMLY CHOSEN TO BE THE EXPERIMENTAL GROUP AND SUBSEQUENTLY RECEIVED SPECIAL DIALECT LESSONS IN CERTAIN FEATURES OF STANDARD ENGLISH. THE CONTROL PUPILS RECEIVED NO SPECIAL LESSONS. IT WAS HYPOTHESIZED THAT (1) IN 8 WEEKS, NEGRO CHILDREN COULD BE TAUGHT TO USE ELEMENTS OF STANDARD ENGLISH DIALECT WHICH DID NOT OCCUR IN THEIR NATIVE DIALECT; (2) THIS KNOWLEDGE WOULD HAVE A POSITIVE AND SIGNIFICANT INFLUENCE ON THEIR WORD READING SCORES; AND (3) DIALECT LESSONS WOULD HAVE A POSITIVE AND SIGNIFICANT INFLUENCE ON SCORES OF WORD READING TESTS IN WHICH THE RELATIONSHIP BETWEEN LETTERS AND SOUNDS WAS CONTROLLED. POSTTESTS WERE ADMINISTERED TO ALL THE PUPILS AT THE CONCLUSION OF THE PROGRAM. ON THE BASIS OF THIS TESTING, ALL THREE HYPOTHESES WERE REJECTED. (WD)

ED029718 PS002008
LANGUAGE. , [66] 8P.
EDRS PRICE MF-$0.65 HC-$3.29

THIS DOCUMENT DISCUSSES, BRIEFLY, THE IMPORTANCE OF PRESCHOOL LANGUAGE LEARNING AND HOW SUCH LEARNING CAN BE FACILITATED. IN THE MAIN, THE DOCUMENT SETS OUT THREE LISTS FOR TEACHERS CONCERNING LANGUAGE INSTRUCTION TO PRESCHOOLERS. LIST ONE PRESENTS THE "AGE OF ARTICULATORY EFFICIENCY OF 23 CONSONANT SOUNDS." FIVE AGES, FROM 3" TO 7" YEARS, ARE GIVEN ALONG WITH THE SOUNDS THAT SHOULD BE MASTERED BY THOSE AGES. LIST TWO DELINEATES 17 SOUNDS WHICH SPANISH SPEAKING CHILDREN OFTEN HAVE DIFFICULTY PRODUCING. LIST THREE GIVES 58 FINGERPLAYS FOR PRESCHOOL CHILDREN. (WD)

ED029719 PS002019
SIX SCHOOL READINESS SCREENING DEVICES USED IN PEDIATRIC OFFICES: CONCURRENT VALIDITY. FINAL REPORT. BEERY, KEITH E., SEP 67 51P.
EDRS PRICE MF-$0.65 HC-$3.29

THIS STUDY IS PHASE ONE OF A 4-YEAR PROJECT. IT WAS AIMED AT EXAMINING THE PREDICTIVE VALIDITY OF SIX PRESCHOOL SCREENING INSTRUMENTS ON LATER ACADEMIC ACHIEVEMENT. THE SIX INSTRUMENTS WERE (1) THE STANFORD-BINET INTELLIGENCE TEST, (2) THE SPRIGLE SCHOOL READINESS SCREENING TEST, (3) THE ANTON BRENNER DEVELOPMENTAL GESTALT TEST OF SCHOOL READINESS, (4) THE SCHOOL READINESS CHECK LIST (THE "READY OR NOT" TEST), (5) THE SCHOOL READINESS SURVEY, AND (6) THE CHILD STUDY UNIT SCREENING SCALES. INFORMAL RATINGS WERE ALSO MADE BY PEDIATRICIANS. THIS PHASE OF THE PROJECT INVOLVED THE INITIAL SCREENING OF 100 PRESCHOOLERS ON THE SIX TESTS. THE TESTS WERE ADMINISTERED AT TWO PEDIATRIC OFFICES. THE TEST RESULTS INDICATED THAT THE INSTRUMENTS HAD A MODERATE TO HIGH RELATIONSHIP WITH THE CHRONOLOGICAL AGE AND MENTAL AGE OF THE CHILDREN AND ALSO A HIGH CORRELATION AMONG THEMSELVES. HOWEVER, SOME OF THE TESTS HAVE A LIMITED AGE RANGE. SUBSEQUENT PHASES OF THE PROJECT WILL FOLLOW THESE SUBJECTS AND COMPARE THEIR ACADEMIC ACHIEVEMENT TO THEIR SCREENING TEST RESULTS. (WD)

ED029720 PS002021
SPOTLIGHT ON FOLLOW THROUGH. PLUNKETT, VIRGINIA R. L., 69 28P.
EDRS PRICE MF-$0.65 HC-$3.29
AVAILABLE FROM: COLORADO DEPARTMENT OF EDUCATION, DENVER, COLORADO ($0.50)

THIS PUBLICATION DESCRIBES (1) THE ORIGIN OF THE FOLLOW THROUGH PROGRAM, (2) THE PRESENT STATUS OF THE COLORADO FOLLOW THROUGH PROGRAM, AND (3) CRITERIA FOR ESTABLISHING OTHER SUCH PROGRAMS. IT CONTAINS A DOZEN PHOTOGRAPHS OF CHILDREN PARTICIPATING IN FOLLOW THROUGH PROGRAMS. (WD)

ED030471 PS001423
HEAD START IN ACTION. RILEY, CLARA M. D.; EPPS, FRANCES M. J., 67 271P.
DOCUMENT NOT AVAILABLE FROM EDRS.
AVAILABLE FROM: PARKER PUBLISHING COMPANY, INC., 1 VILLAGE SQUARE, WEST NYACK, NEW YORK 10994

RECORDS AND OBSERVATIONS FROM A SUMMER HEAD START PROGRAM, CONDUCTED IN LOS ANGELES BY DELTA SIGMA THETA, ARE DELINEATED IN THIS BOOK. IT RELATES FIRSTHAND EXPERIENCES OF THE PARTICIPATING PERSONNEL AS THEY DEVELOPED AND IMPLEMENTED A HEAD START PROGRAM FOR SOME 300 CHILDREN. THE BOOK IS DIVIDED INTO THREE SECTIONS. SECTION I, "PROCEDURES," DETAILS THE LEGAL, PHYSICAL, AND PERSONNEL REQUISITES FOR ESTABLISHING THE PROGRAM. SECTION II, "PROGRAM," DISCUSSES THE OPENING AND OPERATION OF THE HEAD START SESSIONS. SECTION III, "PROMISE," SETS OUT THE RESEARCH RESULTS OF THE PROGRAM AND SUGGESTS A DESIGN FOR A FOLLOWUP STUDY. THE BOOK PRESENTS AN OVERVIEW OF WHAT HEAD START IS AND A DETAILED ACCOUNT OF THE SETTING UP OF THE PROGRAM, HOW THE PROGRAM WORKED IN ACTUAL PRACTICE, AND WHAT PROMISE HEAD START PROGRAMS OFFER FOR THE FUTURE AS INDICATED BY THE RESEARCH DATA. A BIBLIOGRAPHY IS INCLUDED. (WD)

ED030472 PS001621
CONCEPT AND LANGUAGE DEVELOPMENT. A RESOURCE GUIDE FOR TEACHING YOUNG CHILDREN. , MAR 68 94P.
EDRS PRICE MF-$0.65 HC-$3.29

IN RESPONSE TO THE RESEARCH FINDINGS OF HEAD START PROGRAMS, IN PARTICULAR, AND OF RESEARCH IN EARLY CHILDHOOD EDUCATION, IN GENERAL, THIS MANUAL WAS CREATED BY THE KINDERGARTEN STUDY GROUP OF THE CINCINNATI PUBLIC SCHOOLS TO EXAMINE THE KINDERGARTEN PROGRAM. THE PURPOSE OF THIS MANUAL IS TO HELP TEACHERS BROADEN AND EXTEND THE LEARNING OF THE PUPILS, ESPECIALLY IN THE LANGUAGE ARTS. WAYS ARE SUGGESTED FOR WORKING WITH CHILDREN TO PROVIDE FOR INDIVIDUAL, SMALL GROUP, AND TOTAL CLASS INSTRUCTION. THE MANUAL SETS OUT ACTIVITIES FOR DEVELOPING PUPILS' SKILLS IN VOCABULARY, ORGANIZATION OF IDEAS, AUDITORY AND VISUAL PERCEPTION, AND SPEECH. ALSO, APPROACHES TO BUILDING READING READINESS ARE DESCRIBED. (WD)

ED030473 PS001789
THE COMPARATIVE EFFICACIES OF SPANISH, ENGLISH AND BILINGUAL COGNITIVE VERBAL INSTRUCTION WITH MEXICAN-AMERICAN HEAD START CHILDREN. FINAL REPORT. BARCLAY, LISA FRANCES KURCZ, JAN 69 304P.
EDRS PRICE MF-$0.65 HC-$13.16

SIXTY-SEVEN MEXICAN-AMERICAN CHILDREN WERE ADMINISTERED A SPECIAL 7-WEEK HEAD START LANGUAGE TRAINING PROGRAM DURING THE SUMMER OF 1967. THREE BASIC TREATMENTS WERE USED, AND THERE WAS A CONTROL GROUP. TWO TEACHERS WERE USED, THUS RAISING THE NUMBER OF GROUPS TO EIGHT. THE THREE BASIC TREATMENTS INVOLVED A STRUCTURED ENGLISH LANGUAGE TRAINING PROGRAM; IN ONE GROUP, SPANISH WAS THE LANGUAGE OF INSTRUCTION; IN A SECOND GROUP, ENGLISH WAS THE INSTRUCTIONAL LANGUAGE; AND IN THE THIRD, BOTH LANGUAGES WERE USED. THE CONTROL GROUPS RECEIVED THE USUAL PRESCHOOL ART AND MUSIC ACTIVITIES. TESTS WERE ADMINISTERED AT THE BEGINNING OF THE PROGRAM, AT THE END, AND THE NEXT SPRING. IT WAS FOUND THAT (1) SINCE THE GROUPS WERE INITIALLY OF VARYING ABILITY, FINAL DIFFERENCES IN PERFORMANCE COULD HAVE BEEN DUE TO THIS INITIAL DIFFERENCE; (2) THE TEACHER FACTOR, SEX FACTOR, AND AGE FACTOR CONTRIBUTED NOTHING TO THE RESULTS; (3) THE STRUCTURED LANGUAGE TREATMENTS DID NOT PRODUCE BETTER SCORES THAN THE CONTROL TREATMENT; AND (4) THE BILINGUAL TREATMENT WAS NOT SIGNIFICANTLY SUPERIOR TO THE SPANISH OR ENGLISH TREATMENT. (WD)

ED030474 PS001848
THE RELATIONSHIP BETWEEN INSTRUMENTAL ASSERTION AND THE STANFORD-BINET. DORMAN, LYNN; REBELSKY, FREDA, MAR 69 15P.
EDRS PRICE MF-$0.65 HC-$3.29

ASSERTIVE BEHAVIOR IN CHILDREN IS CHARACTERIZED AS MANIPULATION AND EXPLORATION OF THE ENVIRONMENT. ASSERTIVE BEHAVIOR CAN BE NONDESTRUCTIVE OR DESTRUCTIVE. IT HAS BEEN SUGGESTED THAT LEARNING IS DEPENDENT ON ASSERTION AND THAT DISTORTION OR INHIBITION OF ASSERTIVE BEHAVIOR MAY RESTRICT OR DISTORT THE LEARNING PROCESS. FIFTY HEAD START CHILDREN WERE TESTED FOR THE EXISTENCE OF ASSERTIVE BEHAVIOR BY TEACHER AND OBSERVER RATINGS, AND THAT DATA WAS COMPARED WITH THE CHILDRENS' SCORES ON THE STANFORD-BINET. AN ASSERTIVE BEHAVIOR TASK, THE BELLER TASK, WAS ALSO ADMINISTERED TO THE CHILDREN. COMPARISON OF THE TEACHER AND OBSERVER RATINGS RESULTED IN A SIGNIFICANTLY HIGH CORRELATION. BOTH KINDS OF RATINGS WERE ALSO CORRELATED WITH THE BELLER TASK DATA, AND THE RESULTS INDICATED THAT THE LATTER WAS A VALID MEASURE OF ASSERTION. OF THE 35 ITEMS ON THE BINET, THE "ASSERTIVE" CHILDREN SCORED BETTER ON 29 ITEMS THAN THE LESS ASSERTIVE CHILDREN, WITH SIGNIFICANT DIFFERENCES OCCURRING ON EIGHT OF THE 29. THUS, ASSERTIVE BEHAVIOR AND COGNITIVE PERFORMANCE APPEARED TO BE POSITIVELY RELATED. (WD)

ED030475 PS001909
ATTITUDES, EXPECTATIONS, AND BEHAVIOR OF PARENTS OF HEAD START AND NON-HEAD START CHILDREN. REPORT NUMBER 1. HERVEY, SARAH D., AUG 68 24P.
EDRS PRICE MF-$0.65 HC-$3.29

HEAD START WAS CONCEIVED NOT ONLY AS AN INTERVENTION PROGRAM WITH CHILDREN, BUT AS A TOTAL EFFORT OF INTERVENTION IN THE DISADVANTAGED FAMILY. HEAD START SEEKS TO INFLUENCE THE CHILD NOT ONLY DIRECTLY THROUGH THE CLASSROOM PROGRAM, BUT INDIRECTLY THROUGH THE PARENTS. IT IS, THEREFORE, IMPORTANT TO DETERMINE IF PARENT PARTICIPATION IN HEAD START MODIFIES THEIR ATTITUDES AND BEHAVIOR IN A WAY RELEVANT TO THE POSITIVE DEVELOPMENT OF THEIR CHILDREN. IN ORDER TO ASCERTAIN IF SUCH A CHANGE TAKES PLACE, HEAD START PARENTS WERE COMPARED WITH NON-HEAD START PARENTS AS TO EDUCATIONAL AND CHILD REARING PRACTICES. THE DATA WAS OBTAINED BY ADMINISTERING THE MERRILL-PALMER HEAD START QUESTIONNAIRE TO 103 HEAD START PARENTS AND 77 NON-HEAD START PARENTS. BOTH SAMPLES WERE NEGRO AND COMPARABLE ON INCOME LEVEL AND FAMILY SIZE. VERY FEW BEHAVIOR AND ATTITUDINAL DIFFERENCES BETWEEN THE TWO GROUPS OF PARENTS WERE FOUND. THOSE FEW DIFFERENCES WERE MEANINGFUL ONLY INDIVIDUALLY AND DID NOT FOLLOW ANY PATTERN. THESE FINDINGS FAIL TO SUPPORT THE ASSUMPTION THAT HEAD START EXPERIENCE WILL CHANGE THE PARENTS AND THEREBY INFLUENCE THE CHILD. (WD)

ED030476 PS001910
SOCIAL ANTECEDENTS OF PRESCHOOL CHILDREN'S BEHAVIORS. REPORT NUMBER 2. WEBER, JAMES, AUG 68 51P.
EDRS PRICE MF-$0.65 HC-$3.29

THIS STUDY WAS MADE TO IDENTIFY AND MEASURE SOCIAL-ENVIRONMENTAL CHARACTERISTICS OF LOW INCOME CHILDREN AND TO ANALYZE THE RELATIONSHIP OF THESE VARIABLES TO COGNITIVE AND SOCIOEMOTIONAL MEASURES TAKEN SHORTLY AFTER ENTRANCE INTO HEAD START. IT WAS FELT THAT SUCH INFORMATION WOULD BE USEFUL TO TEACHERS AND CURRICULUM PLANNERS WHO WISHED TO DEVISE EXPERIENCES FOR HEAD START CHILDREN BASED ON DEFINED AREAS OF DEPRIVATION. DATA WAS OBTAINED FROM HEAD START CHILDREN AND THEIR MOTHERS. THESE LOW AND MIDDLE INCOME MOTHERS WERE ADMINISTERED THE SOCIAL-SYSTEM INTERVIEW, BASED ON THE OPEN-SYSTEMS THEORY. ONLY THE VARIABLE OF HIERARCHICAL ORDER WAS INVESTIGATED. BECAUSE OF THE SMALL SAMPLE (45 CHILDREN AND 45 MOTHERS) AND THE LARGE ERROR VARIANCES, NO DEFINITE CONCLUSIONS WERE REACHED ABOUT THE RELATIONSHIP BETWEEN THE MOTHERS' ATTITUDES AND THE PERFORMANCE OF THE CHILDREN. IT WAS FOUND THAT THE LOW INCOME GROUP WAS QUITE HETEROGENEOUS IN ATTITUDE. (WD)

ED030477 PS001911
A NOTE ON PUNISHMENT PATTERNS IN PARENTS OF PRESCHOOL CHILDREN. REPORT NUMBER 3. HERVEY, SARAH D., AUG 68 13P.
EDRS PRICE MF-$0.65 HC-$3.29

THIS STUDY WAS PART OF A LARGER HEAD START RESEARCH PROJECT. THE PARENTS (251 WOMEN AND 185 MEN) OF HEAD START CHILDREN WERE ASKED WHETHER OR NOT THEY WOULD PUNISH THEIR CHILDREN FOR CERTAIN BEHAVIOR; FOR EXAMPLE, LYING, STEALING, OR HITTING A SISTER. EIGHTEEN SITUATIONS WERE HYPOTHESIZED IN THE QUESTIONS. PARENTS WERE ALSO ASKED HOW SEVERE SUCH PUNISHMENT WOULD BE. THE PARENTS OF THIS GROUP OF CHILDREN WERE PRIMARILY NEGRO AND PRIMARILY OF THE LOWER SOCIOECONOMIC LEVEL. THE DATA INDICATED THAT MEN OF LOWER SOCIOECONOMIC LEVELS PUNISHED ANTISOCIAL AND ANNOYING BEHAVIOR MORE SEVERELY THAN MIDDLE LEVEL MEN. THERE WAS NO SUCH DIFFERENCE, HOWEVER, IN THE MEN'S PUNISHMENT OF BEHAVIOR CONSIDERED MORALLY WRONG BY MIDDLE-CLASS STANDARDS. THE WOMEN WERE FOUND TO PUNISH LESS SEVERELY, BUT THERE WERE NO CLEAR DIFFERENCES IN THE TYPES OF PUNISHMENT. (WD)

ED030478 PS001912
FAMILY SOCIOLOGY OR WIVES' FAMILY SOCIOLOGY? A COMPARISON OF HUSBANDS' AND WIVES' ANSWERS ABOUT DECISION MAKING IN THE GREEK AND AMERICAN CULTURE. REPORT NUMBER 4. SAFILIOS-ROTHSCHILD, CONSTANTINA, AUG 68 36P.
EDRS PRICE MF-$0.65 HC-$3.29

THIS STUDY COMPARED THE RESPONSES OF HUSBANDS AND WIVES REGARDING DECISION-MAKING IN TWO CULTURES, GREEK AND AMERICAN, AS OBTAINED BY TWO DIFFERENT SAMPLING TECHNIQUES. THE AMERICAN DATA WERE OBTAINED FROM 160 COUPLES WHO LIVED IN THE DETROIT AREA AND WHO HAD A CHILD UNDER 6 YEARS OLD. THE GREEK SAMPLE WAS 133 WIVES AND 117 HUSBANDS, NONE OF WHOM WAS A SPOUSE OF ANOTHER MEMBER OF THE SAMPLE. THESE 250 ADULTS WERE FROM ATHENS, GREECE. THE DETROIT COUPLES WERE ASKED IF THE HUSBAND, THE WIFE, OR BOTH WERE RESPONSIBLE FOR THE MAKING OF 14 SPECIFIC DECISIONS. THE GREEK SUBJECTS WERE ASKED WHOSE OPINION USUALLY PREVAILED IN EIGHT DECISIONAL AREAS. OF THE RESPONSES MADE BY THE DETROIT COUPLES, CLEAR DISAGREEMENT OCCURRED BETWEEN SPOUSES IN 55 PERCENT; SLIGHT DISAGREEMENT, IN 21 PERCENT; AND COMPLETE AGREEMENT, IN ONLY 24 PERCENT. IN COMPARING THE RESPONSES OF THE GREEK PARTICIPANTS, SIGNIFICANT DIFFERENCES IN PERSPECTIVE WERE DISCOVERED BETWEEN THE MEN AND WOMEN. THE OVERALL FINDINGS DEMONSTRATED THE UNRELIABILITY OF GENERALIZING THE OPINIONS OF WIVES, WHICH COMPRISED A GOOD DEAL OF FAMILY SURVEY DATA, TO THE HUSBANDS. A NUMBER OF METHODOLOGICAL PROCEDURES ARE SUGGESTED WITH A VIEW TO REFINING THE STUDY OF FAMILIAL DECISION-MAKING. (WD)

ED030479 PS001913
INTERRELATIONS BETWEEN SOCIAL-EMOTIONAL BEHAVIOR AND INFORMATION ACHIEVEMENT OF HEAD START CHILDREN. REPORT NUMBER 5. NOBLE, MARJORIE; HERVEY, SARAH D., AUG 68 46P.
EDRS PRICE MF-$0.65 HC-$3.29

THE PURPOSES OF THIS STUDY WERE (1) TO IDENTIFY THE SOCIAL-EMOTIONAL AND INFORMATION-ACHIEVEMENT CHARACTERISTICS OF 133 CHILDREN ENROLLED IN HEAD START AND (2) TO EXPLORE THE INTERRELATIONSHIPS FOUND TO EXIST BETWEEN SOCIAL-EMOTIONAL BEHAVIOR, AS ASSESSED BY THE TEACHER AT THE OUTSET OF THE PROGRAM, AND THE GAINS EXHIBITED OVER THE YEAR IN INFORMATION ACHIEVEMENT, AS ASSESSED BY THE PRESCHOOL INVENTORY (PI) AND THE OPERATION HEAD START BEHAVIOR INVENTORY (BI). THE PI WAS ADMINISTERED DURING THE FIRST AND LAST MONTHS OF THE YEAR-LONG HEAD START PROGRAM; THE BI WAS GIVEN ONLY DURING THE BEGINNING OF THE PROGRAM. THE GENERAL HYPOTHESIS WAS THAT THERE EXISTED POSITIVE RELATIONSHIPS BETWEEN POSITIVE ASPECTS OF TEACHERS' RATINGS OF SOCIAL-EMOTIONAL BEHAVIOR AND GAINS IN INFORMATION ACHIEVEMENT AND NEGATIVE RELATIONSHIPS BETWEEN NEGATIVE ASPECTS OF TEACHERS' RATINGS OF SOCIAL-EMOTIONAL BEHAVIOR AND GAINS IN INFORMATION-ACHIEVEMENT OF CHILDREN ENROLLED IN HEAD START. THE DATA FAILED TO DEMONSTRATE ANY SUCH SIGNIFICANT RELATIONSHIPS. (WD)

ED030480 PS001914
MODIFICATION OF COGNITIVE SKILLS AMONG LOWER-CLASS NEGRO CHILDREN: A FOLLOW-UP TRAINING STUDY. REPORT NUMBER 6. SIGEL, IRVING E.; OLMSTED, PATRICIA, AUG 68 126P.
EDRS PRICE MF-$0.65 HC-$6.58

THE FOUR PURPOSES OF THIS STUDY WERE (1) TO TEST THE LONG-RANGE EFFECTS OF CLASSIFICATION TRAINING (CT) ON DISADVANTAGED BLACK CHILDREN, (2) TO EVALUATE THE EFFECTS OF REINTRODUCING CT TO THOSE PREVIOUSLY TRAINED, (3) TO COMPARE CT AT TWO AGE PERIODS (5 AND 6 YEARS OLD), AND (4) TO COMPARE CT WITH ATTENTION TRAINING (AT). OF THE 69 CHILDREN USED IN THIS STUDY, 30 HAD RECEIVED CT THE YEAR BEFORE, AND 39 HAD RECEIVED NO TRAINING (NT). CT FOCUSES ON THE MANY ATTRIBUTES OF OBJECTS THAT MAY BE USED AS A BASIS FOR GROUPING. AT TEACHES THE CHILD TO FOCUS ON OBSERVABLE ATTRIBUTES AND TO DISCRIMINATE AMONG THEM. THE CHILDREN WERE PRETESTED, AND 59 OF THEM WERE DIVIDED INTO SIX GROUPS: (1) CT-CT (THE SYMBOLS SIGNIFYING THAT THE GROUP RECEIVED CT THE PREVIOUS YEAR AND THE CURRENT YEAR), (2) NT-CT, (3) CT-AT, (4) NT-AT, (5) CT-NT, AND (6) NT-NT. PRETRAINING SCORES ON A BATTERY OF GROUPING TASKS INDICATED THAT THE PREVIOUS YEAR'S TRAINING HAD HAD A LASTING EFFECT, AT LEAST IN FACILITATING A MORE FLEXIBLE APPROACH TO CLASSIFICATION IN THE CURRENT YEAR. CT-CT, NT-AT, AND NT-CT CHILDREN SHOWED A SIGNIFICANT INCREASE IN GROUPING RESPONSES ON POSTTESTS. (WD)

ED030481 PS001915
RELATION OF SPATIAL EGOCENTRISM AND SPATIAL ABILITIES OF THE YOUNG CHILD. REPORT NUMBER 7. SHANTZ, CAROLYN A.; WATSON, JOHN S., AUG 68 25P.
EDRS PRICE MF-$0.65 HC-$3.29

IN ORDER TO INVESTIGATE WHAT CONCEPTS YOUNG CHILDREN ACQUIRE THAT BREAK DOWN THEIR INABILITY TO VIEW SPATIAL SITUATIONS OBJECTIVELY, THREE GROUPS OF 16 CHILDREN EACH WERE ADMINISTERED TWO TASKS: (1) A BOX TASK, IN WHICH THE CHILD WAS ASKED TO PREDICT THE LOCATION OF OBJECTS UPON A CHANGE IN HIS LOCATION; AND (2) A PIAGETIAN TASK, IN WHICH THE CHILD WAS ASKED TO IDENTIFY THE ARRANGEMENT OF OBJECTS FROM ANOTHER'S POSITION. THE CHILDREN WERE GROUPED ON THE BASIS OF AGE, 44 TO 60 MONTHS, 61 TO 71 MONTHS, AND 72 TO 78 MONTHS. THE MAJOR HYPOTHESIS WAS THAT A HIGH POSITIVE RELATIONSHIP EXISTED BETWEEN A YOUNG CHILD'S ACCURACY IN PREDICTING OBJECT LOCATIONS WHEN (1) THE CHILD WAS MOVED TO VARIOUS POSITIONS AND (2) WHEN ANOTHER (IN THIS CASE, A DOLL) WAS MOVED TO VARIOUS POSITIONS WHILE THE CHILD REMAINED IN THE SAME POSITION. THIS HYPOTHESIS WAS NOT SUPPORTED, BUT THE BOX TASK WAS MUCH EASIER THAN THE PIAGETIAN TASK. THE PIAGETIAN FINDING THAT CHILDREN BELOW 7 YEARS OF AGE USUALLY CANNOT TAKE THE VIEWPOINT OF ANOTHER WAS CORROBORATED IN THIS STUDY. (WD)

ED030482 PS001916
SOCIAL CLASS AND PARENT'S ASPIRATIONS FOR THEIR CHILDREN. REPORT NUMBER 8. RODMAN, HYMAN; VOYDANOFF, PATRICIA, AUG 68 18P.
EDRS PRICE MF-$0.65 HC-$3.29

THIS IS A STUDY OF EDUCATIONAL, OCCUPATIONAL, AND INCOME ASPIRATIONS AS THEY ARE RELATED TO SOCIAL CLASS. IT WAS ASSUMED THAT INDIVIDUALS HAVE A RANGE OF ASPIRATIONS RATHER THAN A SINGLE LEVEL OF ASPIRATION. RESEARCH HAS INDICATED THAT LOWER CLASS INDIVIDUALS HAVE A LOWER LEVEL OF ASPIRATION THAN MIDDLE CLASS INDIVIDUALS. IT MAY BE, HOWEVER, THAT ALTHOUGH THE LOWER CLASS HAS THE SAME PEAK OF ASPIRATIONS, THEY ALSO HAVE A LARGER RANGE OF ASPIRATIONS, INCLUDING A LOWER BASE. THUS, ON SINGLE RESPONSE QUESTIONNAIRES, THEY MAY APPEAR TO HAVE A LOWER LEVEL OF ASPIRATION. PARENTS OF NEGRO CHILDREN ENROLLED IN HEAD START WERE INTERVIEWED WITH REGARD TO THEIR ASPIRATIONS FOR THE EDUCATION, OCCUPATION, AND INCOME OF THEIR CHILDREN. IT WAS FOUND THAT THE SOCIAL CLASS OF THE PARENTS WAS INVERSELY RELATED TO THE WIDTH OF THE RANGE OF ASPIRATIONS BUT THAT THE PEAK OF THE LOWER CLASS WAS THE SAME AS THAT OF THE MIDDLE CLASS. (WD)

ED030483 PS001925
THE RELATIONSHIP BETWEEN RACE AND PERCEPTION OF RACIALLY-RELATED STIMULI IN PRESCHOOL CHILDREN. STABLER, JOHN R.; AND OTHERS, [67] 12P.
EDRS PRICE MF-$0.65 HC-$3.29

RESEARCH EVIDENCE INDICATES THAT RACIAL AWARENESS, INCLUDING DIFFERENTIAL PREFERENCE BASED ON SUCH AN AWARENESS, IS QUITE PERVASIVE AND DEVELOPS VERY EARLY IN LIFE. IN AN EFFORT TO INVESTIGATE THE EXISTENCE OF RACIAL AWARENESS AS MANIFESTED IN DIFFERENTIAL PREFERENCE IN PRESCHOOL CHILDREN, THIS TWO-PART STUDY WAS CONDUCTED. IN PART ONE, 40 OBJECTS CONSIDERED TO HAVE DIFFERENTIAL AFFECTIVE QUALITIES, ON THE BASIS OF RACE, WERE EVALUATED AS GOOD OR BAD BY 37 NEGRO HEAD START CHILDREN AND 30 PRESCHOOL WHITE CHILDREN. NO SIGNIFICANT DIFFERENCES IN EVALUATION OF THE OBJECTS BETWEEN THE TWO RACES WERE FOUND. IN PART TWO, 15 OF THE CHILDREN OF EACH RACE WERE ASKED TO GUESS IN WHICH OF TWO CLOSED BOXES, WHITE AND BLACK, EACH OF THE 22 MOST CLEARLY EVALUATED OBJECTS OF THE ORIGINAL 40 WERE TO BE FOUND. IT WAS HYPOTHESIZED THAT THE CHILDREN'S RACIAL ATTITUDES WOULD BE INDIRECTLY INDICATED BY A FINDING THAT THE CHILDREN PUT NEGATIVELY EVALUATED OBJECTS IN THE BLACK BOX AND POSITIVE OBJECTS IN THE WHITE BOX. THIS HYPOTHESIS WAS SUPPORTED, ONLY MORE SO FOR THE WHITE CHILDREN THAN THE BLACK CHILDREN. THE COMMENTS OF THE CHILDREN SUPPORTED THE HYPOTHESIS THAT RACIAL ATTITUDES DETERMINED THE GUESSING OF CERTAIN OBJECTS AS BEING IN A CERTAIN BOX. (WD)

ED030484 PS001926
THE EFFECT OF VERBALIZATION OF RELEVANT AND IRRELEVANT DIMENSIONS ON CONCEPT FORMATION. DEMBO, MYRON H.; AND OTHERS, FEB 69 11P.
EDRS PRICE MF-$0.65 HC-$3.29

THE PURPOSE OF THIS STUDY WAS TO INVESTIGATE BOTH THE RELATIONSHIP BETWEEN VERBALIZATION AND SHIFT-LEARNING AND THE POSSIBLE PREPOTENT STIMULUS DIMENSIONS OF THE EIGHTY-FOUR 7-YEAR-OLDS USED AS SUBJECTS. FOUR PAIRS OF TWO-DIMENSIONAL STIMULI WERE PRESENTED TO THE CHILDREN, FOR THE DISCRIMINATION LEARNING TASK, IN THE FOLLOWING ORDER: LARGE BLACK, SMALL WHITE; LARGE WHITE, SMALL BLACK; SMALL BLACK, LARGE WHITE; AND SMALL WHITE, LARGE BLACK. THE TWO TYPES OF INITIAL DISCRIMINATION DIMENSIONS WERE SIZE (S) AND BRIGHTNESS (B). TWO TYPES OF SHIFTS, REVERSAL (R) AND NONREVERSAL (NR), AND THREE TYPES OF VERBALIZATION (NO VERBALIZATION, ONE-DIMENSION VERBALIZATION, AND TWO-DIMENSION VERBALIZATION) WERE ALSO USED. THIS CREATED 12 TREATMENT GROUPS INTO WHICH THE 84 CHILDREN WERE DIVIDED. THE SCORES FROM DISCRIMINATION LEARNING UNDER THE 12 CONDITIONS INDICATED THAT (1) THE R GROUP PERFORMED SUPERIOR TO THE NR GROUP, (2) THE S GROUP LEARNED MORE EASILY THAN THE B GROUP, AND (3) NO EFFECT WAS DUE TO VERBALIZATION CONDITIONS OR TO INTERACTIONS. (WD)

ED030485 PS001934
DISTURBANCE AND DISSONANCE - COMMUNITY UNIVERSITY COLLABORATION IN DIAGNOSIS AND TREATMENT OF DISTURBANCES. FISH, CAROLINE C.; AND OTHERS, 31 AUG 68 21P.
EDRS PRICE MF-$0.65 HC-$3.29

IN 1967 THE HEAD START EVALUATION AND RESEARCH CENTER AT BOSTON UNIVERSITY INITIATED A PROJECT AIMED AT DEVISING AND ASSESSING NEW CLINICAL APPROACHES TO PRIMARY AND SECONDARY PREVENTION OF EMOTIONAL DISTURBANCE IN PRESCHOOL CHILDREN. THE GROWTH OF "BLACK POWER" PLUS A YEAR OF EXPERIENCE RESULTED IN THE MAKING OF SEVERAL CHANGES IN THE PROGRAM IN 1968: (1) THE CLINICAL ACTIVITIES WERE MOVED FROM THE IMPOSING OFFICES AT BOSTON UNIVERSITY TO SUITABLE QUARTERS IN THE HEART OF THE BLACK COMMUNITY BEING SERVED; (2) THE PERSONNEL INVOLVED WERE EXPANDED TO INCLUDE NOT ONLY PARENTS, BUT KEY PERSONS FROM THE COMMUNITY INVOLVED; (3) ALL PARTICIPANTS WERE CONVERTED TO A FRESH CONCEPTION OF WHAT COULD BE ACHIEVED IN A GIVEN COMMUNITY BY A MORE INCLUSIVE AND COORDINATED EFFORT. THUS, THE PROJECT, AS NOW STRUCTURED, PROVIDES COMMUNITIES WITH THE KNOWLEDGE OF HOW TO HANDLE EMOTIONAL DISTURBANCES OF YOUNG CHILDREN WITHIN THEIR OWN INDIGENOUS SOCIAL SYSTEM. (WD)

ED030486 PS001938
PROJECT HEAD START RESEARCH AND EVALUATION CENTER, SYRACUSE UNIVERSITY, RESEARCH INSTITUTE. FINAL REPORT. MEYER, WILLIAM J.; AND OTHERS, 31 AUG 68 114P.
EDRS PRICE MF-$0.65 HC-$6.58

THE FOLLOWING RESEARCH PROJECTS ARE DESCRIBED IN THIS ANNUAL REPORT: (1) "CONCEPT LEARNING IN DISCRIMINATION TASKS," WHICH INDICATES THAT KINDERGARTEN CHILDREN ARE ABLE TO DISCRIMINATE THE LETTERS "B," "D," "P," AND "Q"; (2) "DISCRIMINATION OF LETTER-LIKE FORMS," INDICATING THAT NURSERY SCHOOL CHILDREN DISCRIMINATE AS WELL AS SECOND GRADERS IN BRIEF BUT APPROPRIATE EXPERIENCES; (3) "PRESENCE OF AN ATTACHED PEER AND SECURITY IN A NOVEL ENVIRONMENT," WHICH SUPPORTS THE HYPOTHESIS THAT PROXIMITY OF A PEER FRIEND HAS A DISTRESS INHIBITING OR SECURITY INDUCING EFFECT ON CHILDREN WHICH IS GREATER THAN THAT AFFORDED BY PROXIMITY TO A STRANGE PEER; (4) "KINDERGARTEN 'LEARNING TO LEARN' PROGRAM EVALUATION," A STUDY OF ALTERNATIVE LEARNING SITUATIONS FOR EFFECTS ON YOUNG CHILDREN'S DEVELOPMENT; (5) "CHANGES IN STANFORD-BINET IQ PERFORMANCE VS. COMPETENCE," WHICH CONTENDS THAT INSTEAD OF CONCENTRATING ON IQ GAINS IN EVALUATING PRESCHOOL PROGRAMS, INVESTIGATORS SHOULD STUDY CHARACTERISTICS OF CHILDREN AS THEY INTERACT WITH CHARACTERISTICS OF THE PROGRAM; (6) "THE ADAPTIVE BEHAVIOR RATING SCALE," INDICATING THAT CRUCIAL ADAPTIVE BEHAVIORS, AS DEFINED BY PRESCHOOL TEACHERS, INVOLVE SOCIAL COMPETENCY AND COMPLIANCE; AND (7) "DISSEMINATION ACTIVITIES." (MS)

ED030487 PS001940
CHILD DEVELOPMENT RESEARCH AND EVALUATION CENTER FOR HEAD START, TEMPLE UNIVERSITY. ANNUAL REPORT. , 31 AUG 68 257P.
EDRS PRICE MF-$0.65 HC-$9.87

THIS ANNUAL REPORT DESCRIBES THE RESULTS OF THE SECOND YEAR (ACADEMIC YEAR 1967-68) OF RESEARCH WORK DONE IN THE CHILD DEVELOPMENT RESEARCH AND EVALUATION CENTER FOR HEAD START AT TEMPLE UNIVERSITY. PART ONE OF THIS REPORT DISCUSSES THE CENTER'S NATIONAL DATA PROGRAM AND SETS OUT IN TABULAR FORM DEMOGRAPHIC AND COGNITIVE DATA OBTAINED ON 86 URBAN CHILDREN (MOSTLY NEGROES) FROM PHILADELPHIA AND 41 APPALACHIAN CHILDREN (MOSTLY WHITES) FROM WEST VIRGINIA, KENTUCKY, AND TENNESSEE. A SECOND PART OF THE REPORT PRESENTS DESCRIPTIONS AND DISCUSSIONS OF SEVERAL FACULTY STUDIES. DESCRIBED THEREIN ARE THREE PROJECTS AND NINE STUDIES. THIS RESEARCH DEALS PRIMARILY WITH THE DEVELOPMENTAL PROBLEMS OF DISADVANTAGED LOWER CLASS CHILDREN. (WD)

ED030488 PS001941
A STUDY OF EARLY ELEMENTARY TEACHER EVALUATION OF SELECTED EYE-HAND COORDINATION SKILLS OF KINDERGARTEN CHILDREN. INGHAM INTERMEDIATE COOPERATIVE RESEARCH PROJECT, 1967-68: SUMMARY REPORT. , [68] 11P.
EDRS PRICE MF-$0.65 HC-$3.29

IT WAS THE PURPOSE OF THIS STUDY TO INVESTIGATE AND COMPARE THE EXPECTATIONS OF THE SCHOOL FOR THE CHILD AND THE EXPECTATIONS BASED ON RESEARCH FINDINGS FROM THE FIELD OF CHILD GROWTH AND DEVELOPMENT AND TO DISCOVER THE NATURE OF THE DISCREPANCY, IF ANY, BETWEEN THESE TWO EXPECTATIONS. DATA WAS GATHERED FOR COMPARING THE EVALUATIONS OF EARLY ELEMENTARY EDUCATION TEACHERS AND CHILD GROWTH AND DEVELOPMENT SPECIALISTS ON THE EYE-HAND COORDINATION SKILL OF 104 KINDERGARTEN CHILDREN. IT WAS FOUND THAT THE EXPECTATIONS OF THE TEACHERS WERE HIGHER THAN THOSE OF THE SPECIALISTS. THE NUMBER OF YEARS OF THE TEACHERS' FORMAL EDUCATION OR TEACHING EXPERIENCE WERE NOT SIGNIFICANT FACTORS IN DETERMINING THIS HIGH EXPECTATION. PERHAPS THE DISCREPANCY BETWEEN THE TWO GROUPS CAN BE PARTIALLY EXPLAINED BY THE SURRENDERING OF TEACHERS TO THE PRESSURES OF ACADEMIC ACCELERATION. THE TEACHERS IN THIS STUDY, ALTHOUGH REPRESENTING THREE GRADE LEVELS (KINDERGARTEN, FIRST, AND SECOND), AGREED CONSISTENTLY AMONG THEMSELVES ON THE PROPER LEVEL OF THE CHILDREN'S PERFORMANCE, BUT ALL TENDED TO RATE THAT PERFORMANCE NEGATIVELY. (WD)

ED030489 PS001977
THE MONTESSORI RESEARCH PROJECT. FOUR PROGRESS REPORTS. BANTA, THOMAS J., 69 16P.
DOCUMENT NOT AVAILABLE FROM EDRS.
AVAILABLE FROM: AMERICAN MONTESSORI SOCIETY, 175 FIFTH AVENUE, NEW YORK, NEW YORK 10010 ($0.25)

THIS DOCUMENT DESCRIBES, IN FOUR PROGRESS REPORTS, THE DEVELOPMENT AND INITIAL PROJECTS OF A 6-YEAR STUDY, THE MONTESSORI RESEARCH PROJECT, WHICH IS SEEKING TO DETERMINE THE BENEFITS TO PRESCHOOL CHILDREN OF VARIOUS EDUCATIONAL PROGRAMS, SPECIFICALLY, MONTESSORI PROGRAMS VERSUS NON-MONTESSORI PROGRAMS. THE STUDY IS BEING CONDUCTED BY THE UNIVERSITY OF CINCINNATI. (WD)

ED030490 PS002013
PRELIMINARY RESULTS FROM A LONGITUDINAL STUDY OF DISADVANTAGED PRESCHOOL CHILDREN. WEIKART, DAVID P., 67 19P.
EDRS PRICE MF-$0.65 HC-$3.29

THE PERRY PRESCHOOL PROJECT IN YPSILANTI, MICHIGAN, IS STRUCTURED SO THAT A GROUP OF DISADVANTAGED 3-YEAR-OLD NEGRO CHILDREN BEGIN A 2-YEAR PRESCHOOL PROGRAM EACH YEAR. THE PROGRAM WAS ORIGINALLY VERY VERBAL-LEARNING ORIENTED BUT HAS RECENTLY BEEN MODIFIED TO MAKE USE OF PIAGET'S COGNITIVE DEVELOPMENT THEORIES. FROM THE BEGINNING OF THE PROGRAM THROUGH FORMAL SCHOOL, THE PARTICIPANTS ARE TESTED EACH YEAR. THESE TESTS PROVIDE LONGITUDINAL DATA. EACH GROUP OF PARTICIPANTS IS MATCHED BY A CONTROL GROUP OF CHILDREN WHO RECEIVE NO PRESCHOOL PROGRAM. THE FIRST EXPERIMENTAL GROUP STARTED IN 1962. TEST RESULTS AND TEACHER RATINGS OF THIS FIRST GROUP OVER THE SUCCEEDING YEARS SHOW THAT (1) NO DIFFERENCES IN MEASURED INTELLECTUAL GROWTH BETWEEN THE EXPERIMENTAL AND CONTROL GROUP HAS ENDURED BY THE THIRD GRADE; (2) THE EXPERIMENTAL CHILDREN HAVE DEMONSTRATED SUPERIOR ACADEMIC ACHIEVEMENT AND SOCIAL BEHAVIOR; AND (3) THE EXPERIMENTAL GROUP CAN BE DIVIDED INTO TWO GROUPS, ACHIEVERS AND NONACHIEVERS. THE LAST FINDING MEANS THAT SOME CHILDREN SIGNIFICANTLY BENEFIT FROM THE PRESCHOOL PROGRAM WHILE SOME DO NOT, A RESULT NOT EXPLICABLE AT THIS TIME. (WD)

ED030491 PS002014
EFFECT OF A KINDERGARTEN PROGRAM OF PERCEPTUAL TRAINING UPON THE LATER DEVELOPMENT OF READING SKILLS. FINAL REPORT. ROY, IRVING; ROY, MURIEL L., 18 OCT 68 21P.
EDRS PRICE MF-$0.65 HC-$3.29

FIFTEEN CHILDREN FROM EACH OF THREE KINDERGARTEN CLASSES WERE RANDOMLY CHOSEN TO PARTICIPATE IN THIS STUDY AND WERE RANDOMLY ASSIGNED TO ONE OF THREE TREATMENT GROUPS: (1) A GROUP THAT RECEIVED A PERCEPTUAL TRAINING PROGRAM; (2) A GROUP THAT RECEIVED AUGMENTED ATTENTION BUT NO PROGRAM; AND (3) A CONTROL GROUP THAT RECEIVED NO SPECIAL PROGRAM NOR ATTENTION. THE PROGRAM AND ATTENTION SESSIONS OCCURRED ONCE A WEEK FOR 25 MINUTES. THE PURPOSE OF THIS STUDY WAS TO DISCOVER IF KINDERGARTEN CAN FACILITATE LATER READING SKILL DEVELOPMENT AND, SPECIFICALLY, IF A PERCEPTUAL TRAINING PROGRAM INCREASES THE LIKELIHOOD THAT CHILDREN WILL SUCCEED IN LEARNING TO READ. ALL THE CHILDREN IN THE STUDY WERE PRETESTED ON A PERCEPTUAL MOTOR DEVELOPMENT TEST AND POSTTESTED ON A READING READINESS TEST. THE STUDY RAN FROM SEPTEMBER 1967 TO MAY 1968. CHILDREN IN GROUP ONE SCORED HIGHER THAN THOSE IN GROUP TWO, WHO, IN TURN, SCORED HIGHER THAN CHILDREN IN THE CONTROL GROUP. THESE DIFFERENCES, HOWEVER, WERE NOT SIGNIFICANT. ALSO, ALTHOUGH CHRONOLOGICAL AGE WAS NOT FOUND TO CORRELATE WITH READING READINESS SCORES, THE SCORES ON THE PERCEPTUAL MOTOR DEVELOPMENT TEST DID CORRELATE WITH THE READINESS SCORES. NO PERFORMANCE DIFFERENCES WERE ATTRIBUTED TO VARIATIONS IN TEACHING STYLE OR CLASSROOM. (WD)

ED030492 PS002015
AN EXPERIMENTAL STUDY OF SYNTACTICAL FACTORS INFLUENCING CHILDREN'S COMPREHENSION OF CERTAIN COMPLEX RELATIONSHIPS. FINAL REPORT. OLDS, HENRY F., JR., 68 132P.
EDRS PRICE MF-$0.65 HC-$6.58
AVAILABLE FROM: CENTER FOR RESEARCH AND DEVELOPMENT ON EDUCATIONAL DIFFERENCES, HARVARD UNIVERSITY PUBLICATIONS OFFICE, LONGFELLOW HALL, APPIAN WAY, CAMBRIDGE, MASSACHUSETTS 02138

THIS STUDY WAS CONDUCTED TO EXPLORE THE ABILITY OF CHILDREN (6 TO 12 YEARS OF AGE) TO UNDERSTAND CERTAIN RELATIVELY COMPLEX RELATIONSHIPS AS THEY ARE COMMONLY SIGNALED SYNTACTICALLY IN OUR LANGUAGE. IT WAS HYPOTHESIZED THAT DEVELOPMENT IN LANGUAGE PERFORMANCE DURING THIS AGE RANGE WAS, IN SOME MEASURE, A FUNCTION OF A GROWING ABILITY TO COMPREHEND THE PRECISE MEANING OF A VARIETY OF STRUCTURAL SIGNALS AND TO PRODUCE THEM IN APPROPRIATE SITUATIONS. FOUR SUCH SIGNALS AND THE ABILITY OF 20 BOYS (AGES 7, 9, AND 11 YEARS) TO UNDERSTAND THEM WERE STUDIED: (1) SIMPLE ACTIVE-DECLARATIVE UTTERANCES, (2) UTTERANCES INVOLVING COMPLEX LOGICAL RELATIONS, (3) SPECIAL VERB-INDIRECT OBJECT RELATION UTTERANCES, AND (4) UTTERANCES INVOLVING COMPLEX SUBJECT-VERB-OBJECT RELATIONS. LITTLE DIFFICULTY WAS EXPERIENCED BY ANY AGE GROUP WITH SIMPLE STATEMENTS, AFFIRMATIVE CONDITIONALS, AND EMBEDDED SENTENCES. LIMITING CONTINGENCIES WITH "ALTHOUGH" AND "BUT" AND NEGATIVE CONDITIONALS WITH "IF" AND "NOT" WERE MORE DIFFICULT, WITH PERFORMANCE IMPROVING WITH AGE. "ASK-TELL" COMBINATION UTTERANCES AND NEGATIVE CONDITIONALS WITH "UNLESS" WERE VERY DIFFICULT, ESPECIALLY FOR THE 7- AND 9-YEAR-OLDS. GAME INSTRUCTIONS AND A BIBLIOGRAPHY ARE INCLUDED IN THE DOCUMENT. (WD)

ED030493 PS002016
DISCRIMINATION OF RECENCY IN CHILDREN. FINAL REPORT. MATHEWS, MARY ELIZABETH, 28 FEB 69 46P.
EDRS PRICE MF-$0.65 HC-$3.29

TWO EXPERIMENTS COMPRISED THIS STUDY COMPARING THE ABILITY OF CHILDREN FROM AGES 4 TO 12 YEARS TO DISCRIMINATE THE ORDER IN WHICH ITEMS FROM A PREVIOUSLY PRESENTED SEQUENCE OF STIMULI HAD BEEN PRESENTED. THE HYPOTHESES WERE THAT THE DISCRIMINATION OF RECENCY (DR) IMPROVES WITH AGE, THAT BROADER SEPARATIONS OF TEST ITEMS ARE EASIER TO DISCRIMINATE THAN NARROWER ONES, AND THAT LENGTH OF THE STIMULUS LIST INFLUENCES DR. IN EXPERIMENT ONE, 76 CHILDREN WERE GIVEN SIX TEST LISTS OF PICTORIAL STIMULI. AFTER EACH LIST WAS PRESENTED, THE SUBJECT WAS SHOWN TWO OF THE PICTURES AGAIN AND ASKED TO STATE WHICH ONE HE HAD SEEN MORE RECENTLY. THE LISTS CONSISTED OF SEVEN OR 12 ITEMS; EITHER TWO OR FOUR ITEMS SEPARATED THE PICTURES IN QUESTION. EXPERIMENT TWO WAS SIMILAR TO THE FIRST BUT INVOLVED 52 CHILDREN AND INCREASED THE SEPARATION BETWEEN ITEMS ON THE TESTING PHASE TO FOUR AND SEVEN. EXPERIMENT TWO WAS CONDUCTED BECAUSE PERFORMANCES ON THE FIRST WERE GENERALLY POOR. THE RESULTS FROM THE TWO EXPERIMENTS SHOWED THAT DR IMPROVED WITH AGE AND THAT PERFORMANCE IMPROVED WHEN SHORTER LISTS AND WIDER SEPARATIONS WERE USED. (WD)

ED030494 PS002017
THE EFFECTS OF A LEARNING PROGRAM IN PERCEPTUAL-MOTOR ACTIVITY UPON THE VISUAL PERCEPTION OF SHAPE. FINAL REPORT. KANNEGIETER, RUTHAN BRINKER-HOFF, JUN 68 175P.
EDRS PRICE MF-$0.65 HC-$6.58

THIS STUDY INVOLVED FIFTY-EIGHT 3-YEAR-OLDS. IT SOUGHT TO DETERMINE WHETHER THE PRESCHOOLERS COULD LEARN TO DISCRIMINATE VISUALLY THE CRITICAL ELEMENTS OF SHAPE THROUGH A PROGRAM OF PERCEPTUAL-MOTOR TRAINING, TRANSFER SUCH KNOWLEDGE TO SIMILAR BUT DIFFERENT SHAPES, AND THEN RESIST THE PROCESS OF FORGETTING THE CRITICAL ELEMENTS. THE CHILDREN WERE RANDOMLY ASSIGNED TO AN EXPERIMENTAL GROUP AND A CONTROL GROUP. THE EXPERIMENTAL GROUP TOOK PART IN A 14-SESSION PROGRAM DESIGNED TO TEACH THE CRITICAL ELEMENTS OF SHAPE THROUGH PERCEPTUAL-MOTOR ACTIVITY. THE CONTROL GROUP RECEIVED INDIRECT PERCEPTUAL TRAINING THROUGH PUZZLES AND MATCHING GAMES, NONE OF WHICH CONTAINED THE SHAPES USED IN THE EXPERIMENTAL PROGRAM. A PRETEST, A POSTTEST, AND A POST-POSTTEST, INVOLVING GEOMETRIC LINE DRAWINGS, WERE ADMINISTERED TO THE TWO GROUPS. IT WAS FOUND THAT THE EXPERIMENTAL GROUP DID NOT PERFORM SIGNIFICANTLY BETTER THAN THE CONTROL GROUP ON THE POSTTEST AND POST-POSTTEST IN COPYING THE GEOMETRIC FIGURES USED IN THE EXPERIMENTAL PROGRAM; AND ON THE POSTTEST, IN COPYING CRITERION FIGURES (FIGURES NOT USED IN THE EXPERIMENTAL PROGRAM). THE EXPERIMENTAL GROUP, HOWEVER, DID BETTER IN COPYING THE CRITERION FIGURES ON THE POST-POSTTEST. (WD)

ED030495 PS002018
A PREVENTIVE SUMMER PROGRAM FOR KINDERGARTEN CHILDREN LIKELY TO FAIL IN FIRST GRADE READING. FINAL REPORT. GEIS, ROBLEY, JUL 68 42P.
EDRS PRICE MF-$0.65 HC-$3.29

IN AN ATTEMPT TO LESSEN ACADEMIC FAILURE DURING THE EARLY YEARS OF SCHOOLING, 23 MIDDLE CLASS KINDERGARTEN CHILDREN WHO SCORED LOW ON TESTS OF COGNITIVE DEVELOPMENT WERE GIVEN A SPECIAL 6-WEEK SUMMER ENRICHMENT PROGRAM. A CONTROL GROUP OF 23 LOW SCORERS RECEIVED NO ENRICHMENT PROGRAM. PARENTS OF THE EXPERIMENTAL SUBJECTS WERE INVITED TO VISIT THE 2-HOUR SESSIONS TO OBSERVE THE PROGRAM AND WERE SUBSEQUENTLY GIVEN ADVICE ON HOW THEY COULD HELP THEIR CHILDREN AT HOME. PRIOR TO THE SUMMER PROGRAM, THE EXPERIMENTAL GROUP'S MEAN SCORE ON THE METROPOLITAN READINESS TEST (FORM R) WAS 54.2; FOR THE CONTROL GROUP, IT WAS 58.8; AND FOR THE DISTRICT KINDERGARTEN POPULATION, IT WAS 77.5. AFTER THE PROGRAM, IN AUGUST 1967, THE EXPERIMENTAL GROUP HAD RAISED ITS SCORE TO 73. IN SEPTEMBER 1967, THE EXPERIMENTAL GROUP SCORED 53.1 ON FORM A, AND THE CONTROL GROUP SCORED 45.3. THIS DIFFERENCE WAS NOT SIGNIFICANT. IN MAY 1968, ALL FIRST GRADERS WERE ADMINISTERED THE STANFORD ACHIEVEMENT TEST OF READING. THE EXPERIMENTAL CHILDREN SCORED 30; THE CONTROL CHILDREN, 25; AND THE OVERALL FIRST GRADE POPULATION, 44. THESE DIFFERENCES WERE SIGNIFICANT. IT SEEMED THAT THE METROPOLITAN READINESS TEST SUCCESSFULLY PREDICTED WHICH CHILDREN WOULD BE LOW READING ACHIEVERS, AND IT APPEARED THAT THE SUMMER PROGRAM DID AID THE EXPERIMENTAL CHILDREN. (WD)

ED030496 PS002020
EFFECTIVENESS OF DIRECT VERBAL INSTRUCTION ON IQ PERFORMANCE AND ACHIEVEMENT IN READING AND ARITHMETIC. BEREITER, CARL; ENGELMANN, SIEGFRIED, [66] 32P.
EDRS PRICE MF-$0.65 HC-$3.29

THIS EXPERIMENT WAS BASED ON THE ASSUMPTION THAT THE ACADEMIC FAILURE OF THE DISADVANTAGED OR MIDDLE CLASS CHILD IS DUE TO A FAILURE OF INSTRUCTION AND THAT IF ABOVE-NORMAL LEARNING SCHEDULES WERE MAINTAINED, THE SECOND YEAR OF AN ENRICHMENT PROGRAM WOULD NOT SHOW THE CUSTOMARY DROP IN GAINS FROM THE FIRST YEAR. THE SUBJECTS OF THIS STUDY WERE 43 DISADVANTAGED NEGRO AND WHITE 4-YEAR-OLDS OF HIGH, MIDDLE, AND LOW INTELLIGENCE. FIFTEEN OF THE CHILDREN WERE PLACED IN AN EXPERIMENTAL GROUP (I) AND 28 IN A CONTROL GROUP (II). A 2-YEAR PROGRAM INVOLVING A GROUP (III) OF MIDDLE CLASS 4-YEAR-OLDS WAS ALSO CONDUCTED, WITH A CONTROL GROUP (IV) CONSISTING OF MIDDLE CLASS 4-YEAR-OLDS IN A MONTESSORI PRESCHOOL. GROUPS I AND III RECEIVED A 2-YEAR EXPERIMENTAL PROGRAM IN WHICH RAPID ATTAINMENT OF BASIC ACADEMIC CONCEPTS WAS EMPHASIZED. GROUP II RECEIVED A 2-YEAR TRADITIONAL PRESCHOOL EDUCATION. GROUP I ACHIEVED SIGNIFICANTLY GREATER STANFORD-BINET IQ GAINS THAN GROUP II AND MAINTAINED THEM OVER THE 2-YEAR PROGRAM. GROUP III CHILDREN ALSO BENEFITED MEASUREABLY FROM THE PROGRAM AND DEMONSTRATED GREATER ACHIEVEMENT IN MANY AREAS THAN GROUP IV. (WD)

ED030497 PS002022
COMPETENCE AND DEPENDENCE IN CHILDREN: PARENTAL TREATMENT OF FOUR-YEAR-OLD GIRLS. FINAL REPORT. CLAPP, WILLIAM FORD, 13 OCT 68 57P.
EDRS PRICE MF-$0.65 HC-$3.29

THIS STUDY INVESTIGATED THE RELATIONSHIPS BETWEEN PARENTAL TREATMENT OF THIRTY-TWO 4-YEAR-OLD GIRLS AND THE GIRLS' RELATIVE COMPETENCE AND DEPENDENCE. THE CONDUCT OF THE GIRLS AND THEIR PARENTS WAS OBSERVED. THE PARENTS' CHILD-REARING ATTITUDES WERE ASSESSED FROM QUESTIONNAIRES. THE FOLLOWING CLASSIFICATION SCHEME WAS CREATED: PARENTS WHO TREATED THEIR CHILD AS AN ADULT WOULD BE TYPE I; THOSE WHO TREATED THEIR CHILD AS AN INFANT, TYPE II; AND THOSE WHO TREATED THEIR CHILD AS A 4-YEAR-OLD, TYPE III. IT WAS HYPOTHESIZED THAT (1) PARENTS OF DEPENDENT CHILDREN WOULD BE RATED HIGHER ON BOTH THE TYPE I AND TYPE II VARIABLES THAN PARENTS OF COMPETENT CHILDREN, (2) PARENTS OF COMPETENT CHILDREN WOULD BE RATED HIGHER ON THE TYPE III VARIABLE THAN PARENTS OF DEPENDENT CHILDREN, AND (3) DISCREPANCY BETWEEN CHILD-REARING PRACTICES AND CHILD REARING PHILOSOPHY WOULD BE MORE EVIDENT IN PARENTS OF DEPENDENT CHILDREN. HYPOTHESIS (1) WAS SUPPORTED BY THE DATA ON FATHERS, BUT NO SIGNIFICANT DIFFERENCES WERE FOUND BETWEEN THE MOTHERS. HYPOTHESIS (2) WAS SUPPORTED FOR MOTHERS, BUT NO SIGNIFICANT DIFFERENCES WERE FOUND BETWEEN THE FATHERS. THE DATA FOR HYPOTHESIS (3) INDICATED THAT NO SIGNIFICANT DIFFERENCES FOR EITHER MOTHERS OR FATHERS EXISTED. (WD)

ED030498 PS002023
INVESTIGATION OF CONCEPT LEARNING IN YOUNG CHILDREN. FINAL REPORT. GINSBERG, ROSE, [69] 16P.
EDRS PRICE MF-$0.65 HC-$3.29

THREE EXPERIMENTS WERE CONDUCTED TO INVESTIGATE THE LEARNING OF THE CONCEPT "MORE THAN" BY PRESCHOOL CHILDREN. IN THE FIRST EXPERIMENT, 48 NURSERY SCHOOL CHILDREN, AGES 4 1/2 TO 5 1/2 YEARS, WERE DIVIDED INTO THREE GROUPS. ALL WERE REQUIRED TO SAY WHICH OF TWO PICTURES CONTAINED THE GREATER NUMBER OF OBJECTS. IN GROUP ONE, CIRCLES WERE USED AS THE OBJECTS IN THE PICTURE; FOR GROUP TWO, LIKE OBJECTS WERE USED IN EACH PAIR, BUT THE TYPES OF OBJECTS VARIED BETWEEN PAIRS; AND IN GROUP THREE, UNLIKE OBJECTS WERE USED IN THE PICTURES. FOR EACH GROUP, 42 TRIALS WERE CONDUCTED PER DAY FOR 3 DAYS OR TO A CRITERION OF EIGHT CONSECUTIVE CORRECT RESPONSES. SUBJECTS IN GROUPS ONE AND TWO WHO REACHED CRITERION WERE GIVEN THE SAME PROCEDURE AGAIN, EXCEPT WITH UNLIKE OBJECTS (A TRANSFER CONDITION). THE RESULTS SHOWED THAT SUBJECTS WHO INITIALLY LEARNED THE CONCEPT WITH THE SIMPLEST STIMULI (GROUP ONE) LEARNED MOST EFFICIENTLY. EXPERIMENT TWO SUBSTANTIALLY REPLICATED THE RESULTS OF EXPERIMENT ONE, USING CHILDREN 41 TO 51 MONTHS OF AGE. EXPERIMENT THREE DID LIKEWISE, USING CHILDREN WITH A MEAN AGE OF 38 MONTHS. THE OVERALL RESULTS INDICATED THAT CONCEPT LEARNING IN YOUNG CHILDREN WAS MOST EFFICIENT WHEN THE CONCEPT WAS INTRODUCED IN THE SIMPLEST CONTEXT. (WD)

ED030499 PS002024
A GUIDE FOR PRESCHOOLS: A HANDBOOK ABOUT THE OPERATION AND FUNCTION OF PRESCHOOLS IN THE FRESNO CITY UNIFIED SCHOOL DISTRICT. GILLEN, WILLIAM; AND OTHERS, DEC 66 48P.
EDRS PRICE MF-$0.65 HC-$3.29

THIS HANDBOOK IS A DESCRIPTION OF THE PRESCHOOL PROGRAM OF FRESNO CITY, CALIFORNIA, UNIFIED SCHOOL DISTRICT AND WAS EXPRESSLY DESIGNED (1) TO PROVIDE SPECIFIC DIRECTION TO THE PRESCHOOL PROGRAM, (2) TO PROVIDE A READY SOURCE OF INFORMATION ABOUT THE PRESCHOOLS, (3) TO ESTABLISH UNIFORM PRACTICES WHERE REQUIRED OR NECESSARY, AND (5) TO PROVIDE WRITTEN MATERIALS REGARDING THE PROGRAM TO WHICH OTHERS MAY REACT CRITICALLY AND MAY MAKE SUGGESTIONS FOR IMPROVEMENT. (WD)

ED031289 PS001921
DEVELOPMENTAL LEARNING AS A CONCEPT IN EARLY READING. FOWLER, WILLIAM, 30 MAR 67 7P.
EDRS PRICE MF-$0.65 HC-$3.29

IN THIS STUDY, ONE HUNDRED 3- TO 5-YEAR-OLDS WERE SELECTED FOR READING INSTRUCTION DURING REGULAR 12- TO 30-MINUTE PERIODS FOR 4 TO 6 MONTHS. THE PROGRAM WAS ORDERED TO ESTABLISH A HIGH LEVEL OF SUSTAINED DAILY CONTROL OVER THE ATTENTIONAL AND MOTIVATIONAL PROCESSES OF THE CHILDREN. LEARNING TASKS WERE DESIGNED TO FACILITATE THE CHILD'S GRASP OF CONCEPTS CRITICAL TO MASTERY OF THE PERCEPTUAL-COGNITIVE DIMENSIONS OF BEGINNING READING. THE TASKS WERE ALSO DESIGNED TO GENERATE BOTH ANALYTIC AND SYNTHESIZING PERCEPTUAL-COGNITIVE STYLES TO ACQUIRE BASIC STRUCTURAL DIMENSIONS. CHILDREN WERE PRETESTED AND POSTTESTED ON WORD RECOGNITION, WORD GENERALIZATION, AND COMPREHENSION IN SENTENCE AND PARAGRAPH READING. OF 63 CHILDREN WHO COMPLETED THE PROGRAM, 46 LEARNERS SCORED 96 PERCENT ON THE UNIT RECOGNITION TEST OF READING COMPETENCE. ON WORD RECOGNITION, THE TOTAL GROUP RECOGNIZED A MEAN OF 95 PERCENT OF ALL WORDS USED. ON WORD GENERALIZATION, THE TOTAL GROUP SCORED A MEAN OF 84 PERCENT. A MEAN OF 93 PERCENT WAS OBTAINED ON SENTENCE READING; AND IN PARAGRAPH READING, MEANS OF 92 PERCENT AND 81

PERCENT WERE SCORED ON WORD RECOGNITION AND COMPREHENSION, RESPECTIVELY. THE HIGH WORD GENERALIZING AND COMPREHENSION LEVELS SUGGEST THE EFFECTIVE INVOLVEMENT OF COGNITIVE PROCESSES THROUGH THE ANALYTIC-STRUCTURAL APPROACH. (DO)

ED031290 PS001942
THE ROLE OF INCENTIVES IN DISCRIMINATION LEARNING OF CHILDREN WITH VARYING PRE-SCHOOL EXPERIENCE. BERKE, MELVYN; JOHNSON, EDWARD E., [67] 16P.
EDRS PRICE MF-$0.65 HC-$3.29

IT WAS THE PURPOSE OF THIS STUDY TO ASCERTAIN WHETHER THE CULTURALLY DISADVANTAGED CHILD, WHO APPEARED TO ADHERE TO THE PRINCIPLE OF IMMEDIATE GRATIFICATION, HAD LEARNED, AS A FUNCTION OF HIS PARTICIPATION IN HEAD START, A MORE FUTURE-RELATED ORIENTATION WHEN COMPARED TO HIS NON-HEAD START COUNTERPARTS. ONE HUNDRED AND EIGHTY-SEVEN 4- AND 5-YEAR-OLDS, DIVIDED AMONG THREE EDUCATIONAL CONDITIONS, WERE GIVEN A SIMPLE LEARNING TASK WITH FOUR CONDITIONS OF REINFORCEMENT. THE EDUCATIONAL CONDITIONS WERE CHILDREN WITH 1 TO 3 MONTHS OF HEAD START (I), CHILDREN WITH 10 TO 12 MONTHS OF HEAD START (II), AND CHILDREN WITH NO HEAD START (III). THE REINFORCEMENT CONDITIONS WERE A LIGHT FLASH, A PROMISE OF FUTURE REWARD, AN IMMEDIATE REWARD (CANDY), AND A TOKEN THAT COULD BE CASHED IN LATER. IN OVERALL PERFORMANCE, GROUPS I AND II WERE SIGNIFICANTLY SUPERIOR TO III. SPECIFICALLY, THEY WERE SUPERIOR UNDER THE "PROMISE OF A FUTURE REWARD" CONDITION. NO SIGNIFICANT DIFFERENCES WERE FOUND BETWEEN THE PERFORMANCES OF GROUPS I AND II. GROUP III, HOWEVER, DISPLAYED A SIGNIFICANT DIFFERENCE IN PERFORMANCE UNDER THE "PROMISE" AND "IMMEDIATE REWARD" CONDITIONS, IN FAVOR OF THE LATTER. (WD)

ED031291 PS001943
THE DEVELOPMENT OF EARLY SOCIAL INTERACTION--AN ETHOLOGICAL APPROACH. OMARK, DONALD R.; EDELMAN, MURRAY S., JAN 69 11P.
EDRS PRICE MF-$0.65 HC-$3.29

THE ETHOLOGICAL APPROACH MAY BECOME AN IMPORTANT METHODOLOGY IN THE DEVELOPMENTAL STUDIES OF CHILDREN. THE ETHOLOGICAL APPROACH TAKES INTO CONSIDERATION THE TOTAL WORLD OF THE CHILD, SOCIAL AND COGNITIVE, WHEN THE CHILD'S DEVELOPMENT IN THAT WORLD IS ANALYZED. INFORMATION CAN BE OBTAINED BOTH FROM STUDIES OF OTHER PRIMATES (FOR EXAMPLE, THE STUDY OF THE SOCIAL BEHAVIOR OF MONKEYS) AND FROM THE STUDY OF THE BEHAVIOR OF CHILDREN. EXAMPLES OF THE LATTER INCLUDE (1) A STUDY OF HIERARCHIZATION IN FIRST GRADE BOYS, IN WHICH IT WAS FOUND THAT THE BOYS COULD STRUCTURE SOCIAL RELATIONS EARLIER THAN PHYSICAL RELATIONS; (2) A STUDY OF THE STARING ENCOUNTER IN NURSERY SCHOOL AND FIRST GRADE BOYS, WHICH SHOWED THAT THE NURSERY SCHOOL BOYS DID NOT HAVE A CONCEPT OF A DOMINANCE HIERARCHY BUT THAT THE FIRST GRADE BOYS DID; AND (3) A STUDY IN COOPERATIVE PICTURE DRAWING, WHICH DEMONSTRATED THAT BOYS IN THE FIRST GRADE WOULD MORE OFTEN INTEGRATE THEIR EFFORTS WHILE GIRLS AT THAT AGE WOULD EITHER IMITATE EACH OTHER OR DRAW INDEPENDENTLY. IN THIS LAST STUDY, THERE APPEARED NO SEX DIFFERENCES IN THE WAY THE DRAWINGS WERE DONE BY NURSERY SCHOOL CHILDREN; ALL WERE PRIMARILY INDIVIDUAL EFFORTS. (WD)

ED031292 PS001944
A STUDY IN VISUAL-MOTOR-PERCEPTUAL TRAINING IN FIRST GRADE. , [65] 36P.
EDRS PRICE MF-$0.65 HC-$3.29

RESEARCH INDICATES THE EXISTENCE OF A RELATIONSHIP BETWEEN THE LEVEL OF VISUAL PERCEPTUAL SKILLS IN THE FIRST GRADE AND ACADEMIC SUCCESS IN LATER GRADES. SPECIAL VISUAL-MOTOR TRAINING WAS GIVEN TO SOME 275 PRIMARY SCHOOL CHILDREN WITH A LIKE NUMBER OF CHILDREN ACTING AS A CONTROL GROUP. THE CONTROL GROUP WAS ONE GRADE AHEAD OF THE EXPERIMENTAL GROUP. TESTING AT THE END OF THE FIRST YEAR OF THIS STUDY SHOWED THE CONTROL GROUP SCORING SIGNIFICANTLY HIGHER ON ACADEMIC TESTS THAN THE EXPERIMENTAL GROUP, THIS RESULT BEING EXPECTED BECAUSE OF THE EXTRA YEAR OF FORMAL EDUCATION RECEIVED BY THE CONTROL GROUP. TEST RESULTS AFTER THE SECOND YEAR SHOWED NO SIGNIFICANT DIFFERENCES BETWEEN THE TWO GROUPS, BUT THE EXPERIMENTAL GROUP CHILDREN APPEARED TO HAVE THE FASTER GROWTH RATE. AT THE END OF 3 YEARS, TESTING AGAIN RESULTED IN NO SIGNIFICANT DIFFERENCES BETWEEN THE TWO GROUPS. SLOWER CHILDREN SEEMED TO HAVE BENEFITED FROM THE SPECIAL TRAINING, WHEREAS THE OTHER CHILDREN GENERALLY HAD NOT. (WD)

ED031293 PS001967
TECHNOLOGY AND THE EDUCATION OF THE DISADVANTAGED. MARTIN, JOHN HENRY, NOV 68 23P.
EDRS PRICE MF-$0.65 HC-$3.29

EDUCATIONAL INTERVENTION PROGRAMS INVOLVING DISADVANTAGED CHILDREN HAVE NOT SUFFICIENTLY SUCCEEDED IN THE REMEDIATION OF THEIR ACADEMIC DEFICIENCIES. GAINS MADE APPEAR TO BE VERY SHORT TERM AND GENERALLY UNIMPRESSIVE. ACCEPTING THE ASSUMPTION THAT THE DEFICIENCIES ARE NOT GENETIC, ONE IS LED TO SUSPECT THE ADEQUACY OF THE EDUCATIONAL SYSTEM. EDUCATIONAL TECHNOLOGY SUGGESTS THE FOLLOWING CHANGES: (1) THE ABANDONMENT OF THE LOCK-STEP PROCEDURE FOR GROUP LEARNING IN FAVOR OF INDIVIDUAL LEARNING AND SELF-PACING, (2) CHANGE OF THE STUDENT ROLE FROM PASSIVE TO ACTIVE, (3) THE STRESSING OF LANGUAGE LEARNING (THAT IS, TALKING, READING, AND WRITING), (4) RAPID FEEDBACK TO THE STUDENTS, AND (5) CHANGE OF THE MOTIVATION FOR LEARNING FROM AN EXERCISE IN COMPETITION TO A JOY IN SELF-ENLIGHTENMENT AND DISCOVERY. THESE CHANGES SHOULD BE MADE THROUGH EMPHASIS ON MULTISENSORY LEARNING AND LEARNER MANIPULATION OF THE LEARNING ENVIRONMENT. (WD)

ED031294 PS001979
MOTHERS AS TEACHERS OF THEIR OWN PRESCHOOL CHILDREN: THE INFLUENCE OF SOCIO-ECONOMIC STATUS AND TASK STRUCTURE ON TEACHING SPECIFICITY. BROPHY, JERE EDWARD, FEB 69 26P.
EDRS PRICE MF-$0.65 HC-$3.29

THIS STUDY INVESTIGATED THE DEGREE TO WHICH MOTHERS OF 4-YEAR-OLD CHILDREN PLACED SPECIFIC BEHAVIOR OF THEIR CHILDREN IN A MEANINGFUL CONTEXT AND WHETHER SUCH DEGREE WAS A FUNCTION OF THE SOCIOECONOMIC STATUS (SES) OF THE MOTHER AND/OR OF THE PARTICULAR SITUATION INVOLVED. THE SUBJECTS WERE 137 MOTHER-CHILD PAIRS OF NEGROES, WHO RANGED IN SES FROM MIDDLE CLASS TO LOWER-LOWER CLASS. THE MOTHER WAS OBSERVED DURING A STRUCTURED INTERACTION (WITH HER CHILD), IN WHICH THE MOTHER ATTEMPTED TO TEACH HER CHILD A BLOCK SORTING TASK. FOR PURPOSES OF DATA COLLECTION, THE TASK WAS DIVIDED INTO SECTIONS OR "SITUATIONS." IT WAS FOUND THAT THE DEGREE OF INFORMATIONAL SPECIFICITY IN THE MOTHERS' COMMUNICATIONS VARIED BOTH WITH SOCIAL STATUS AND WITH THE SECTIONS OF THE TASK. THE MIDDLE CLASS MOTHERS GENERALLY SCORED HIGHEST ON SPECIFICITY. SHARP DIFFERENCES IN THE AMOUNT OF MEANINGFUL ACTIVITY BETWEEN MOTHER AND CHILD WERE FOUND FOR (1) STIMULATING OR ENRICHING ACTIVITY, (2) COMPLEX OR ABSTRACT ACTIVITY, AND (3) TEACHING DESIRED BEHAVIOR, RATHER THAN JUST ELIMINATING UNDESIRED BEHAVIOR. THE DATA FAVORED THE HIGHER SES MOTHERS. (WD)

ED031295 PS001981
EVALUATION OF AN INTERDISCIPLINARY APPROACH TO PREVENTION OF EARLY SCHOOL FAILURE. FOLLOW-UP STUDY, FINAL REPORT. FARGO, GEORGE A.; AND OTHERS, AUG 68 51P.
EDRS PRICE MF-$0.65 HC-$3.29

FORTY-TWO PRESCHOOL CHILDREN PARTICIPATED IN THIS 2-YEAR HEAD START RESEARCH PROJECT CONDUCTED AT THE UNIVERSITY OF HAWAII. THE OBJECTIVES OF THE OVERALL PROJECT WERE (1) TO FOCUS INTEREST ON THE NEED FOR EARLY INTERVENTION WITH POORLY-FUNCTIONING PRESCHOOL CHILDREN WITH THE INTENT TO OFFER SERVICES OF A PREVENTIVE RATHER THAN REMEDIAL FUNCTION; (2) TO DEMONSTRATE THE NEED FOR AND VALUE OF AN INTERDISCIPLINARY APPROACH TO DIAGNOSIS AND EDUCATIONAL PLANNING; AND (3) TO SERVE AS A TRAINING FUNCTION FOR PROSPECTIVE TEACHERS AND PEDIATRIC RESIDENTS. TWO OTHER OBJECTIVES WERE ADDED FOR THE SECOND, OR FOLLOWUP, YEAR OF THE PROJECT: (1) ASSESSMENT OF THE ABILITY OF THE MEMBERS OF THE ORIGINAL DISCIPLINARY TEAM TO PREDICT SUCCESS IN SCHOOL AT THE PRESCHOOL LEVEL AND (2) ASSESSMENT OF THE PROGRESS OF PROBLEM CHILDREN WHO RECEIVED THE SPECIAL EDUCATION INTERVENTION. THE OBJECTIVES WERE SUCCESSFULLY REALIZED, AND IT WAS FOUND THAT THERE WAS A NEED FOR MORE INTERDISCIPLINARY SERVICES FOR CHILDREN IN HAWAII AND A NEED FOR EARLY IDENTIFICATION OF AND EDUCATIONAL AND MEDICAL INTERVENTION WITH HIGH-RISK CHILDREN. (WD)

ED031296 PS001982
INFANCY IN HOLLAND: THE FIRST THREE MONTHS. REBELSKY, FREDA; ABELES, GINA, 1 NOV 68 23P.
EDRS PRICE MF-$0.65 HC-$3.29

TEN NORMAL WHITE BABIES OF MIDDLE CLASS PARENTS FROM THE UNITED STATES AND 11 FROM HOLLAND WERE OBSERVED FOR ONE 3-HOUR PERIOD EVERY 2 WEEKS FOR THE FIRST 3 MONTHS OF LIFE. THE OBSERVATION FORM CALLED FOR AN OBSERVATION ABOUT EVERY 5 MINUTES, ABOUT 36 OBSERVATIONS PER VISIT. ALTHOUGH ALL THE DATA ON THE AMERICAN BABIES HAVE NOT BEEN COMPLETELY ANALYZED, SOME RESULTS ARE AVAILABLE. THE EARLY ENVIRONMENTS OF THE DUTCH AND AMERICAN BABIES WERE DIFFERENT. THE DUTCH BABIES WERE KEPT IN A COOL ROOM AND DRESSED MORE HEAVILY THAN THE AMERICAN BABIES, WHO WERE KEPT IN WARMER ROOMS. THE DUTCH MOTHERS SPENT LESS TIME RESPONDING TO THEIR BABIES THAN AMERICAN MOTHERS BUT DID TEND TO RESPOND TO BOYS MORE THAN GIRLS. THE FEEDING SCHEDULE FOR DUTCH BABIES WAS MORE RIGIDLY STRUCTURED AND THE FEEDING TIME WAS SHORTER THAN FOR THE AMERICAN BABIES. IT WAS FOUND THAT THOSE BABIES IN THE DUTCH SAMPLE WHOSE MOTHERS PERFORMED THE MOST ACTIONS TOWARDS THEM TENDED TO DO LESS NEGATIVE VOCALIZING. U.S. BABIES TENDED TO MAKE MORE PLEASANT VOCALIZATIONS THAN DUTCH BABIES. THE DUTCH BABIES SUCKED THEIR THUMBS MORE THAN U.S. BABIES. THE RELATIVELY INFREQUENT INTERACTION OF DUTCH MOTHERS WITH THEIR BABIES AND THE LACK OF VISUAL STIMULATION IN THE BABIES' ENVIRONMENTS DO NOT APPEAR TO PRODUCE ANY DAMAGE IN THE DUTCH CHILDREN, HOWEVER, CONTRARY TO THE PREDICTIONS OF SOME THEORISTS. (WD)

ED031297 PS001985
SUCCESSFUL NUMBER CONSERVATION TRAINING. BLUM, ABRAHAM H.; ADCOCK, CAROLYN, FEB 69 6P.
EDRS PRICE MF-$0.65 HC-$3.29

TO INVESTIGATE THE EFFICACY OF A TRAINING PROCEDURE DESIGNED TO FACILITATE THE ATTAINMENT OF THE MATHEMATICAL CONCEPT OF NUMBER CONSERVATION, 43 CHILDREN FROM GRADES 1 AND 2 WERE TESTED FOR THEIR ABILITY TO CONSERVE. SOME OF THE PUPILS WERE FOUND TO BE NONCONSERVERS; SOME, TRANSITIONAL CONSERVERS; AND SOME, CONSERVERS. PUPILS OF THE FIRST TWO GROUPS WERE DIVIDED INTO A TRAINING AND CONTROL GROUP. THE TRAINING GROUP RECEIVED SPECIAL SESSIONS DEALING WITH NUMBER CONSERVATION; THE CONTROL GROUP DID NOT. IT WAS FOUND THAT ALTHOUGH THE OLDER CHILDREN HAD MORE INITIAL CONSERVERS, BOTH THE YOUNGER AND OLDER CHILDREN RESPONDED SIMILARLY TO THE TRAINING PROGRAM. THE TRAINING GROUP CHILDREN ALL LEARNED HOW TO CONSERVE. THE CONTROL GROUP REMAINED GENERALLY UNABLE TO PERFORM CONSERVATION TASKS. RETESTING INDICATED THAT THE ABILITIES GAINED FROM THE TRAINING SESSIONS WERE SURPRISINGLY PERMANENT. (WD)

ED031298 PS001989
CHILDREN'S UNDERSTANDING OF SOCIAL INTERACTION. FLAPAN, DOROTHY, 68 93P.
DOCUMENT NOT AVAILABLE FROM EDRS.
AVAILABLE FROM: TEACHERS COLLEGE PRESS, TEACHERS COLLEGE, COLUMBIA UNIVERSITY, 525 WEST 120TH ST., NEW YORK, NEW YORK 10027 ($3.95)

TO INVESTIGATE CHILDREN'S ABILITY TO DESCRIBE AND MAKE INFERENCES ABOUT FEELINGS, THOUGHTS, AND INTENTIONS THAT OCCUR IN INTERPERSONAL RELATIONSHIPS, 60 MIDDLE CLASS GIRLS WERE DIVIDED INTO THREE AGE GROUPS: 6, 9, AND 12 YEARS. EACH GROUP VIEWED TWO SECTIONS OF A MOVIE PORTRAYING EPISODES OF SOCIAL INTERACTION. AFTER EACH SECTION, THE CHILDREN GAVE AN ACCOUNT OF THE EPISODES IN THEIR OWN WORDS AND THEN ANSWERED SPECIFIC QUESTIONS. DEVELOPMENTAL TRENDS OF DESCRIPTIONS APPEARED IN THE CHILDREN'S ACCOUNTS. WHEREVER THERE WERE STATISTICAL DIFFERENCES BETWEEN 6- AND 12-YEAR-OLDS, THERE WERE STATISTICAL DIFFERENCES BETWEEN 6- AND 9-YEAR-OLDS. OLDER CHILDREN GAVE MORE CAUSAL EXPLANATIONS. BETWEEN AGES 6 AND 9, SHIFTS OCCURRED IN THE KINDS OF EXPLANATIONS OFFERED AND INFERENCES OF FEELINGS MADE. WHEN RESPONSES TO SPECIFIC QUESTIONS WERE SCORED ON A THREE-POINT SCALE OF COMPLEXITY, DEVELOPMENTAL TRENDS OCCURRED IN RESPONSES EXPLAINING BEHAVIOR AND NAMING FEELINGS. A CONTENT ANALYSIS OF THE CHILDREN'S ACCOUNTS AND RESPONSES TO SPECIFIC QUESTIONS REVEALED THAT 6-YEAR-OLDS TENDED TO MENTION ACTIONS AND DESCRIBE SCENES, WHEREAS THE OLDER GROUPS REPORTED ADULT COMMUNICATIONS AND FEELINGS AND WERE BETTER ABLE TO ANSWER SPECIFIC QUESTIONS ON ADULT MOTIVATIONS. THE STUDY SUGGESTED THAT AN IMPORTANT TRANSITIONAL PHASE IN UNDERSTANDING SOCIAL INTERACTION OCCURS BETWEEN THE AGES OF 6 AND 9. (JS)

ED031299 PS001995
THE RELATIONSHIP OF INDIVIDUAL DIFFERENCES IN THE ORIENTING RESPONSE TO COMPLEX LEARNING IN KINDERGARTNERS. FARLEY, FRANK H.; MANSKE, MARY E., 9 FEB 69 12P.
EDRS PRICE MF-$0.65 HC-$3.29

HEART RATE CHANGE WAS USED AS THE INDEX OF THE ORIENTING RESPONSE (OR) OF 102 KINDERGARTEN CHILDREN. HEART RATE CHANGE WAS MEASURED BY RECORDING HEART RATE UPON THE PRESENTATION OF TONES. 15 SIMILAR TONES FOLLOWED BY A DIFFERENT, 16TH TONE, WERE USED. FROM THIS DATA THE CHILDREN WERE DIVIDED INTO HIGH, MEDIUM, OR LOW ORIENTORS. FOLLOWING THE "OR" TESTING SESSION, 96 SUBJECTS RECEIVED TWO PICTORIAL ANALOGUES OF VERBAL DISCRIMINATION TASKS. SUBSEQUENTLY, 65 SUBJECTS RECEIVED A PAIRED-ASSOCIATE (P-A) TASK. LEARNING ON THESE TASKS, WHEN RELATED TO "OR" CLASSIFICATION, SHOWED THAT LOW "OR" MALES AND MEDIUM "OR" FEMALES PERFORMED BEST, WHILE MEDIUM "OR" MALES AND LOW "OR" FEMALES PERFORMED WORST. THIS FINDING WAS SIGNIFICANT FOR THE P-A TASK, INDICATING A RELATIONSHIP BETWEEN "OR" CLASSIFICATION AND LEARNING PERFORMANCE ON THIS PARTICULAR P-A TASK. IT IS DIFFICULT TO EXPLAIN THE FACT THAT PERFORMANCE WAS REVERSED BETWEEN THE SEXES. (WD)

ED031300 PS002002
THE EFFECT OF TEACHERS' INFERRED SELF CONCEPT UPON STUDENT ACHIEVEMENT. ASPY, DAVID N., [69] 20P.
EDRS PRICE MF-$0.65 HC-$3.29

A STUDY WAS CONDUCTED TO DETERMINE IF STUDENTS WITH TEACHERS OF HIGH SELF-CONCEPTS ACHIEVED GREATER GAINS THAN STUDENTS WITH TEACHERS OF LOW SELF-CONCEPTS. SIX THIRD-GRADE TEACHERS WERE OBSERVED ONE HOUR IN SEPTEMBER AND ANOTHER HOUR IN MARCH DURING A READING LESSON, BY THREE RATERS WHO COMPLETED A CHECKLIST DESIGNED TO ASSESS SELF-CONCEPT. TWENTY STUDENTS FROM EACH CLASS WERE SELECTED BY IQ AND SEX. FIVE SUBTESTS OF THE STANFORD ACHIEVEMENT TEST WERE ADMINISTERED AS PRETESTS AND POSTTESTS. A POSITIVE RELATIONSHIP BETWEEN TEACHER SELF-CONCEPT AND STUDENT ACHIEVEMENT GAINS WAS OBSERVED ON SUBTESTS OF PARAGRAPH MEANING, LANGUAGE, WORD MEANING, AND WORD STUDY SKILLS, AND WAS STATISTICALLY SIGNIFICANT AT OR ABOVE THE .05 LEVEL. ON THE SPELLING SUBTEST, TEACHER SELF-CONCEPT WAS RELATED NEGATIVELY TO THE TEST SCORE GAINS, BUT THE RELATIONSHIP WAS NOT STATISTICALLY SIGNIFICANT AT OR ABOVE THE .05 LEVEL. ON THE SPELLING SUBTEST, TEACHER SELF-CONCEPT WAS RELATED NEGATIVELY TO THE TEST SCORE GAINS, BUT THE RELATIONSHIP WAS NOT STATISTICALLY SIGNIFICANT AT THE .05 LEVEL. FURTHER STUDIES SHOULD BE CONDUCTED. REFERENCES AND BEHAVIOR RATING SCALES ARE INCLUDED. (JS)

ED031301 PS002003
ENCOURAGING STUDENTS' RESEARCH ON COGNITIVE DEVELOPMENT. FORMANEK, RUTH, FEB 69 10P.
EDRS PRICE MF-$0.65 HC-$3.29

THE EXPERIENCED TEACHER FELLOWSHIP PROGRAM AT HOFSTRA UNIVERSITY INVOLVES THE PARTICIPANTS IN INVESTIGATING THE STRUCTURE, CLAIMS, AND METHODOLOGIES OF THE NATURAL SCIENCES, MATHEMATICS, SOCIAL SCIENCES, AND THE PSYCHOLOGICAL FINDINGS OF PIAGETIAN-ORIENTED COGNITIVE DEVELOPMENT STUDIES. THE FELLOWS IN THE PROGRAM FORM GROUPS TO DECIDE ON RESEARCH TOPICS, SOME OF WHICH HAVE RESULTED IN STUDIES OF (1) CONSERVATION OF QUANTITY IN FIRST GRADE CHILDREN, (2) THE LEVEL OF MORAL JUDGMENTS OF CHILDREN ENROLLED OR NOT ENROLLED, IN A SCHOOL OF THE ETHICAL CULTURE SOCIETY, AND (3) THE ATTITUDES OF LOWER-CLASS CHILDREN AND MIDDLE-CLASS CHILDREN TOWARD POLICEMEN, FATHERS, MOTHERS, AND TEACHERS. (WD)

ED031302 PS002009
THE FACTORIAL STRUCTURE OF REASONING, MORAL JUDGMENT, AND MORAL CONDUCT. STEPHENS, BETH; AND OTHERS, [68] 20P.
EDRS PRICE MF-$0.65 HC-$3.29

TWO FACTOR ANALYSES WERE CONDUCTED ON DATA OBTAINED FROM MEASUREMENTS OF THE REASONING, MORAL JUDGMENT, AND MORAL CONDUCT OF 75 RETARDED AND 75 NORMAL SUBJECTS RANGING IN AGE FROM 6 TO 18 YEARS. ONE FACTOR ANALYSIS SOUGHT TO DETERMINE RELATIONSHIPS BETWEEN THE REASONING VARIABLES AND STANDARD MEASURES OF INTELLIGENCE AND ACHIEVEMENT. A SECOND FACTOR ANALYSIS WAS PERFORMED TO DETERMINE THE RELATIONSHIPS AMONG MORAL CONDUCT, MORAL JUDGMENT, AND REASONING VARIABLES. RESULTS OF THE FIRST FACTOR ANALYSIS INDICATED THAT PIAGETIAN OPERATIVITY, AS DETERMINED BY MEASURES OF CONSERVATION, DOES MEASURE PERFORMANCE DISTINCT FROM THAT MEASURED BY THE WECHSLER SCALES AND WIDE RANGE ACHIEVEMENT TEST. THE SECOND FACTOR ANALYSIS REVEALED THAT IN MOST INSTANCES SKILL IN COGNITIVE AREAS WAS NOT HIGHLY CORRELATED WITH ACTS OF MORAL CONDUCT OR WITH MORAL JUDGMENT. NOR WERE TEACHER RATINGS ON MORAL CHARACTER HIGHLY CORRELATED WITH OBSERVED CONDUCT OR EXPRESSED VIEWS ON MORALITY. (WD)

ED031303 PS002012
A STUDY OF THE INTERRELATIONSHIPS OF CONSERVATION OF LENGTH RELATIONS, CONSERVATIONS OF LENGTH, AND TRANSITIVITY OF LENGTH RELATIONS OF THE AGE OF FOUR AND FIVE YEARS. CAREY, RUSSEL L.; STEFFE, LESLIE P., 69 14P.
EDRS PRICE MF-$0.65 HC-$3.29

THREE UNITS OF INSTRUCTION WERE GIVEN TO 20 FOUR-YEAR-OLD CHILDREN AND 34 FIVE-YEAR-OLD CHILDREN. UNIT I WAS DESIGNED TO DEVELOP THE CHILDREN'S ABILITY TO ESTABLISH A LENGTH RELATION BETWEEN CURVED LINES; UNIT II, TO DEVELOP ABILITY TO CONSERVE LENGTH; AND UNIT III, TO DEVELOP ABILITY TO CONSERVE LENGTH RELATIONS. TESTING OF THE CHILDREN OCCURRED BETWEEN UNITS I AND II, AND AFTER UNIT III. THREE TESTS WERE ADMINISTERED DURING THE TESTING SESSION: (1) A SIX-ITEM TEST DESIGNED TO MEASURE THE CHILDREN'S ABILITY TO CONSERVE LENGTH; (2) AN 18-ITEM TEST TO MEASURE THE CHILDREN'S ABILITY TO CONSERVE LENGTH RELATIONS; AND (3) A SIX-ITEM TEST TO MEASURE THE CHILDREN'S ABILITY TO DEAL WITH TRANSITIVITY OF LENGTH. THE TEST RESULTS INDICATED THAT (1) THE ABILITY TO CONSERVE LENGTH AS MEASURED IN THIS STUDY IS NOT A NECESSARY OR SUFFICIENT CONDITION FOR THE ABILITY TO USE TRANSITIVITY OF LENGTH; (2) ABILITY TO CONSERVE LENGTH RELATIONS MAY BE NECESSARY FOR TRANSITIVITY; AND (3) ABILITY TO CONSERVE LENGTH IS NOT A NECESSARY OR SUFFICIENT CONDITION FOR CONSERVATION OF LENGTH RELATIONS. (WD)

ED031304 PS002027
INTELLIGENCE QUOTIENT VERSUS LEARNING QUOTIENT: IMPLICATIONS FOR ELEMENTARY CURRICULA. ROHWER, WILLIAM D., JR., [69] 19P.
EDRS PRICE MF-$0.65 HC-$3.29

RESEARCH DATA CONSISTENTLY DEMONSTRATES THAT WHITE SCHOOL CHILDREN SCORE HIGHER ON TESTS OF ACADEMIC ABILITY THAN NEGRO CHILDREN OF THE SAME AGE AND GRADE LEVEL, AND THAT THIS DISCREPANCY INCREASES WITH TIME. IS THIS DISCREPANCY DUE TO A LACK OF LEARNING PROFICIENCY ON THE PART OF NEGRO CHILDREN OR TO A LACK OF LEARNING OPPORTUNITY? IN AN ATTEMPT TO ANSWER THIS QUESTION, 48 LOWER CLASS NEGRO CHILDREN AND 48 UPPER-MIDDLE CLASS WHITE CHILDREN FROM KINDERGARTEN, FIRST, AND THIRD GRADE WERE GIVEN (1) A PAIRED-ASSOCIATE (P-A) TASK, (2) THE PEABODY PICTURE VOCABULARY TEST, AND (3) THE RAVEN PROGRESSIVE MATRICES TEST. THE LATTER TWO TESTS ARE USED TO MEASURE

INTELLIGENCE, WHILE THE P-A TASK MEASURES LEARNING PROFICIENCY. THE TEST RESULTS SHOWED THAT THE WHITE CHILDREN PERFORMED SIGNIFICANTLY BETTER THAN THE NEGRO CHILDREN ON TESTS (2) AND (3). THE P-A DATA SHOWED A SMALL DISCREPANCY BETWEEN THE TWO GROUPS (DIMINISHING IN MAGNITUDE WITH INCREASING GRADE LEVEL) WHICH SUGGESTED THAT THE TESTED NEGRO CHILDREN SHOULD HAVE LEARNED AS WELL AS THE WHITE GROUP. LACK OF SKILL IN LEARNING TACTICS APPEARS TO BE THE MAIN HANDICAP OF THESE CHILDREN AS THEY CONTINUED TO IMPROVE ON P-A TASKS WITH PRACTICE WHILE THE OTHER GROUP DID NOT. INSTRUCTIONAL PROGRAMS THAT ARE CONCRETE, EXPLICIT, AND SPECIFIC OFFER THE MOST TO LOWER CLASS CHILDREN WHO NEED SKILL MASTERY. TESTS TO MEASURE LEARNING PROFICIENCY MUST ALSO BE DEVELOPED. (WD)

ED031305 PS002034
INDEPENDENT AND SMALL GROUP ACTIVITIES FOR SOCIAL STUDIES IN THE PRIMARY GRADES. BALL, BARBARA; AND OTHERS, 68 113P.
EDRS PRICE MF-$0.65 HC-$6.58

A TEACHERS' GUIDE FOR SOCIAL STUDIES, THIS MANUAL STRESSES GEOGRAPHY CURRICULUM AND ACTIVITIES FOR THE PRIMARY GRADES. IT IS SUGGESTED THAT A TEACHER WORK WITH ONE GROUP WHILE THE OTHER CHILDREN WORK INDIVIDUALLY. CHILDREN FIRST WORK INDEPENDENTLY FOR A TEAM, AND THEN PROGRESS TO LESS STRUCTURED SMALL GROUP ACTIVITIES. POSITIVE REINFORCEMENT BY THE TEACHER IS ENCOURAGED. THE REGIONS OF SANTA MONICA, CALIFORNIA, INCLUDING RESIDENTIAL AND COMMERCIAL AREAS, INDUSTRIAL AREAS, HARBORS, AND HISTORICAL SITES ARE THE OBJECTS OF STUDY. THIS MANUAL, HOWEVER, IS NOT LIMITED TO ANY REGION; ITS UNITS ARE APPLICABLE UNIVERSALLY. SPECIFIC TEACHING INSTRUCTIONS FOR EACH UNIT ON A SPECIFIC GEOGRAPHIC AREA ARE GIVEN. PUPILS, AFTER OBSERVING PICTURES AND AERIAL PHOTOGRAPHS, CONSTRUCT MAPS WHICH THEY MAY LATER RE-DESIGN. MAPS ARE LABELED USING SYMBOLS TO INDICATE DISTRICTS, OCCUPATIONS, LANDFORMS, STREETS, AND SIGNS. MULTI-TEXT READINGS, STORIES, TAPES, FIELD TRIPS, GAMES, WRITTEN AND ORAL REPORTS, AND GUEST SPEAKERS ARE FREQUENTLY UTILIZED. ART, SCIENCE, LANGUAGE ARTS, AND GEOLOGY ACTIVITIES, IF THEY RELATE TO THE GEOGRAPHY STUDIED, ARE SUGGESTED IN EACH UNIT. (DR)

ED031306 PS002056
CONCEPT FORMATION IN CHILDREN: A STUDY USING NONSENSE STIMULI AND A FREE-SORT TASK. FELDMAN, CAROL FLEISHER, [69] 15P.
EDRS PRICE MF-$0.65 HC-$3.29

TO INVESTIGATE HOW A CHILD ORGANIZES NEW OBJECTS AND HOW CATEGORIES FUNCTION FOR A CHID, TWELVE 6- AND TWELVE 8-YEAR-OLDS WERE INDIVIDUALLY GIVEN SEVERAL SORTING TASKS INVOLVING 21 THREE-DIMENSIONAL NONSENSE OBJECTS. THE CHILD WAS EXPOSED TO ALL THE OBJECTS; THREE OBJECTS WERE POINTED OUT AND WITHDRAWN; AND THEN THE CHILD WAS ASKED TO DESCRIBE THEM. THE CHILD GROUPED ALL 21 OBJECTS AS HE THOUGHT THEY SHOULD GO TOGETHER. AFTER GROUPING, THE ITEMS WERE MIXED AND THE CHILD WAS SHOWN ONE OF THE THREE OBJECTS HE DESCRIBED EARLIER. HE STATED TO WHICH GROUP IT BELONGED, AND WHY. AGAIN THE OBJECT WAS WITHDRAWN AND THE CHILD DESCRIBED IT AND FINALLY HE REGROUPED THE OBJECTS AS THEY HAD PREVIOUSLY BEEN ARRANGED. PART II OF THE STUDY WAS DIVIDED INTO TWO CONDITIONS: (1) THE CHILD NAMED FIVE OBJECTS, AND (2) NO NAMES WERE GIVEN. EIGHT NEW OBJECTS WERE ADDED TO THE FIVE AND THE CHILD WAS ASKED TO FIND THE ORIGINAL FIVE. THE RESULTS INDICATED THAT (1) THE SORTING PROCESSES OF THE 8-YEAR-OLDS WERE MORE HOMOGENEOUS THAN THOSE OF THE 6-YEAR-OLDS, (2) THE OLDER CHILDREN USED MORE GROUPS AND RECALLED SORTING BETTER, (3) NAMING OBJECTS IMPROVED RECALL OF THE OBJECTS FOR 6-YEAR-OLDS, BUT DID NOT SPECIFICALLY HELP THE 8-YEAR-OLDS, AND (4) CATEGORIZATION INDUCED THE 6-YEAR-OLDS TO NOTICE NEW ASPECTS OF AN OBJECT BUT TO IGNORE PREVIOUSLY NOTICED ATTRIBUTES OF THE OBJECTS, WHILE 8-YEAR-OLDS SIMPLY IGNORED THE ATTRIBUTES OF THE OBJECTS. (WD)

ED031307 PS002057
SOME LANGUAGE-RELATED COGNITIVE ADVANTAGES OF BILINGUAL FIVE YEAR OLDS. FELDMAN, CAROL; SHEN, MICHAEL, [69] 21P.
EDRS PRICE MF-$0.65 HC-$3.29

FIFTEEN BILINGUAL AND 15 MONOLINGUAL HEAD START CHILDREN, RANGING IN AGE FROM 4 TO 6, WERE ADMINISTERED THREE TYPES OF TASKS: (1) OBJECT CONSTANCY TASK: SUBJECT WAS SHOWN A COMMON OBJECT, A TRANSFORMATION WAS DONE ON THE OBJECT, E.G., CRUSHING A PAPER CUP, AND THEN THAT OBJECT PLUS AN IDENTICAL PRE-TRANSFORMED OBJECT, WERE SHOWN TO THE SUBJECT AND HE WAS ASKED TO PICK OUT THE FIRST OBJECT; (2) NAMING TASK: SUBJECT WAS ASKED TO USE OBJECT LABELS UNDER THREE CONDITIONS: USE OF THE COMMON NAME, USE OF A NONSENSE NAME, AND USE OF SWITCHED COMMON NAMES; AND (3) A SENTENCE TASK: SUBJECT WAS REQUIRED TO USE THE THREE LABEL CONDITIONS (2) IN SIMPLE RELATIONAL SENTENCES. IT WAS HYPOTHESIZED THAT (I) BILINGUALS WOULD PERFORM BETTER THAN MONOLINGUALS ON ALL THREE TASKS, AND (II), THAT FOR ALL SUBJECTS, TASK (1) WOULD BE EASIER THAN (2) WHICH WOULD BE EASIER THAN (3). BOTH HYPOTHESES WERE SUPPORTED BY THE GROSS DATA. IT WAS FOUND THAT BILINGUALS, ALTHOUGH BETTER AT USING NAMES IN RELATIONAL STATEMENTS, WERE NOT BETTER THAN MONOLINGUALS IN THE USE OF COMMON NAMES ALONE NOR NONSENSE NAMES ALONE. ALSO, BILINGUALS PERFORMED CONSISTENTLY BETTER THAN MONOLINGUALS WHERE NONVERBAL POINTING RESPONSES WERE REQUIRED, BUT NOT WHERE SPOKEN RESPONSES WERE REQUIRED. IT WAS SUGGESTED THAT HAVING A NOTION OF MEANING AS A FUNCTION OF USE FACILITATES ACQUISITION OF THE ABILITY OF YOUNG CHILDREN TO USE LABELS IN SENTENCES. (WD)

ED031308 PS002058
HELP FOR TEACHERS IN PRESCHOOLS: A PROPOSAL. KATZ, LILIAN G.; WEIR, MARY K., MAY 69 10P.
EDRS PRICE MF-$0.65 HC-$3.29

AN EDUCATIONAL ISSUE TODAY CONCERNS THE QUALITY OF TEACHING IN PRESCHOOLS. MANY ADDITIONAL PRESCHOOL TEACHERS WILL BE REQUIRED IN THE NEXT FEW YEARS TO MEET THE INCREASED ENROLLMENTS IN PRESCHOOL PROGRAMS. NOT ONLY MUST PROPER TRAINING PROGRAMS FOR FUTURE TEACHERS BE DESIGNED, BUT IT HAS BEEN NOTED THAT MOST PEOPLE NOW TEACHING PRESCHOOL CHILDREN HAVE NOT HAD PROPER TRAINING FOR THE JOB. PERSONNEL AND TRAINING CRISES ARE CURRENTLY RELIEVED BY: (1) FEDERALLY FUNDED INSTITUTES AND FELLOWSHIP PROGRAMS, (2) THE REGIONAL TRAINING OFFICE FOR HEAD START PROGRAMS, (3) TECHNICAL CONSULTANTS WHO VISIT CLASSROOMS, AND (4) ITINERANT TRAINERS WHO ARE EXPERIENCED PRESCHOOL EDUCATORS TRAVELING THROUGH REMOTE COMMUNITIES DEMONSTRATING TECHNIQUES AND SKILLS. HOWEVER, PROGRAMS THAT PROVIDE INSERVICE EDUCATION UNFORTUNATELY PROVIDE ONLY MINIMAL CONTACT WITH CLASSROOMS. EVIDENCE REVEALS THAT NEW TEACHERS NEED HELP IN THEIR CLASSROOMS FROM TRAINERS WHO CAN ANSWER CONCRETE "HOW TO" QUESTIONS. EMPHASIS SHOULD BE TRANSPOSED FROM INSERVICE TRAINING TO INSERVICE HELPING. COLLEGES, UNIVERSITIES, PROFESSIONAL ASSOCIATIONS OF PRESCHOOL TEACHERS, ETC., SHOULD EXPLORE AND REFINE INSERVICE HELPING STRATEGIES. EXPANSION AND STRENGTHENING OF THE REGIONAL TRAINING OFFICE OF HEAD START WOULD INCREASE THE INSERVICE HELPING RESOURCES ALREADY AVAILABLE. (WD)

ED031309 PS002059
MATERNAL BEHAVIOR AND THE DEVELOPMENT OF READING READINESS IN URBAN NEGRO CHILDREN. HESS, ROBERT D., [69] 28P.
EDRS PRICE MF-$0.65 HC-$3.29

IN THIS PAPER THE EFFECTS OF ENVIRONMENTAL INFLUENCES UPON THE DEVELOPMENT OF READING READINESS IN YOUNG CHILDREN WERE DISCUSSED. IT WAS ASSUMED THAT THE EFFECTS OF SOCIAL, CULTURAL, AND ECONOMIC FACTORS ON A PRESCHOOL CHILD ARE MEDIATED IN A LARGE PART THROUGH ADULTS CLOSELY INVOLVED WITH THE CHILD'S LIFE. ONE HUNDRED SIXTY NEGRO MOTHERS AND THEIR 4-YEAR-OLD CHILDREN, REPRESENTING FOUR SOCIAL STATUS LEVELS, WERE SELECTED AS SUBJECTS. OBSERVATIONS OF THE SUBJECTS AND QUESTIONNAIRE DATA SHOWED THAT MATERNAL BEHAVIOR AND PHYSICAL ENVIRONMENT DO INFLUENCE THE CHILD'S EARLY COGNITIVE AND ACADEMIC DEVELOPMENT. CHILDREN WERE AFFECTED BY (1) DEGREE OF CROWDING IN THE LIVING QUARTERS, (2) USE OF HOME RESOURCES BY THE MOTHER TO AID THE CHILD'S COGNITIVE GROWTH, (3) AMOUNT OF TIME A MOTHER READS TO A CHILD, (4) MOTHER'S PARTICIPATION IN OUTSIDE ACTIVITIES, (5) MOTHER'S FEELINGS OF EFFECTIVENESS IN DEALING WITH LIFE, (6) REGULATION OF BEHAVIOR STRATEGIES USED BY THE MOTHER, (7) MATERNAL TEACHING STYLE WHEN ATTEMPTING TO SHOW THE CHILD HOW TO DO SOMETHING, (8) MOTHER'S AFFECTIVE BEHAVIOR, AND (9) TO SOME EXTENT, THE MOTHER'S OWN LANGUAGE FACILITY. TO THE EXTENT THAT THESE FACTORS AFFECT THE CHILD'S COGNITIVE DEVELOPMENT, THEY APPEAR TO INCLUDE THE MOTIVATIONAL AND OTHER ABILITIES INVOLVED IN LEARNING TO READ. (WD)

ED031310 PS002067
PERSONALITY DEVELOPMENT IN DISADVANTAGED FOUR-YEAR-OLD BOYS: OBSERVATIONS WITH PLAY TECHNIQUES. HIRSCH, JAY G.; BOROWITZ, GENE H., 67 10P.
EDRS PRICE MF-$0.65 HC-$3.29

THIRTY-ONE 4-YEAR-OLD NEGRO BOYS ATTENDING A RESEARCH PRESCHOOL IN CHICAGO WERE OBSERVED DURING A PLAY SESSION. PRELIMINARY EVALUATION OF THE DATA FROM THE OBSERVATIONS INDICATED A MARKED HETEROGENEITY IN THE SUBJECTS WITH REGARD TO VERBAL FACILITY, COGNITIVE DEVELOPMENT, AND QUALITY AND NATURE OF OBJECT RELATIONSHIPS. POOR CORRELATION WAS FOUND BETWEEN DEGREE OF VERBAL FACILITY AND LEVEL OF COGNITIVE DEVELOPMENT. THE CHILDREN FELL INTO THREE GROUPS: (1) PROBABLE FUTURE ACADEMIC ACHIEVERS, (2) PROBABLE NON-ACHIEVERS, AND (3) DIFFICULT-TO-PREDICT. GROUP (1) SHOWED CONCERN OVER STATE-APPROPRIATE DEVELOPMENTAL ISSUES, A MINIMUM OF CONFLICT REGARDING EARLIER STAGES, AND A CAPACITY TO MOVE TOWARD AN INTEGRATIVE RESOLUTION, AND SHOWED SUPERIOR COGNITIVE DIFFERENTIATION. GROUP (2) MANIFESTED MINIMAL CONCERN OVER DEVELOPMENT, SUBSTANTIAL CONFLICTS REGARDING EARLIER STAGES, AND DISINTERGRATION. GROUP (3) SHOWED VARYING DEGREES TO BOTH GOOD AND BAD CHARACTERISTICS. THERE IS WIDE VARIATION IN THE INDIVIDUAL PERSONALITY DEVELOPMENT OF THE DISADVANTAGED. EXPLANATIONS OF UNDERACHIEVEMENT, MEASURED ONLY BY COGNITIVE AND/OR LANGUAGE FACTORS, IS ADEQUATE. THERE IS A GREAT NEED

FOR STUDY ON THE RELATIONSHIP OF THE SOCIALIZATION PROCESS DURING THE FIRST FOUR YEARS OF LIFE TO LATER ACADEMIC ACHIEVEMENT. (WD)

ED031311 PS002068
INFORMATION VALUE OF FEEDBACK WITH PRESCHOOL CHILDREN. STERN, CAROLYN; TEAGER, JOYCE, MAR 68 8P.
EDRS PRICE MF-$0.65 HC-$3.29

NINETEEN NEGRO CHILDREN, AGES 5 TO 5 1/2, WERE DIVIDED INTO FOUR TREATMENT GROUPS TO STUDY THE VALUE OF FEEDBACK TO LEARNING. GROUP I RECEIVED FEEDBACK ON CORRECT AND INCORRECT RESPONSES ON A SIMPLE CONCEPT IDENTIFICATION TASK. GROUP II RECEIVED INFORMATION ONLY ON CORRECT ANSWERS. GROUP III WERE GIVEN THE SAME TASK AS I AND II, BUT RECEIVED NO FEEDBACK. GROUP IV DID NOT HAVE ANY TASK PRACTICE BETWEEN TESTING SESSIONS. ALL CHILDREN WERE PRE- AND POSTTESTED WITH THE PEABODY PICTURE VOCABULARY TEST, AND GIVEN A TRANSFER TEST, THE EDWARDS MULTIPLE CATEGORIZATION TEST, AFTER THE TRAINING PERIOD. THE RESULTS SHOWED THAT ALTHOUGH GROUP II HAPPENED TO HAVE A HIGHER MENTAL AGE THAN GROUP I, THE PERFORMANCE OF THE TWO GROUPS ON THE CONCEPT IDENTIFICATION TASK WAS NOT SIGNIFICANTLY DIFFERENT. THE PERFORMANCE OF GROUP I ON THE TRANSFER TEST WAS SUPERIOR TO THAT OF ALL OTHER GROUPS. ALTHOUGH THE POPULATION WAS SMALL, AND THE PROGRAM CONTENT WAS INSUFFICIENTLY CHALLENGING TO PROVIDE DEFINITIVE RESULTS, IT APPEARS THAT PRESCHOOL CHILDREN ARE ABLE TO LOOK AT FEEDBACK AS INFORMATION AND TO PROFIT FROM SUCH GUIDANCE IN CONCEPT IDENTIFICATION. FURTHER STUDY IS INDICATED. (WD)

ED031312 PS002095
MULTI-ETHNIC BOOKS FOR HEAD START CHILDREN. PART I: BLACK AND INTEGRATED LITERATURE. WHITE, DORIS, COMP., 69 38P.
EDRS PRICE MF-$0.65 HC-$3.29

THE PURPOSE OF THIS ANNOTATED BIBLIOGRAPHY IS TO DIRECT ADULTS TOWARD THE SELECTION OF "BLACK" AND "INTEGRATED" LITERATURE FOR ALL CHILDREN. THE CHILDREN'S BOOKS WHICH ARE INCLUDED ARE DESIGNED FOR AN INDEPENDENT READING LEVEL OF KINDERGARTEN THROUGH ABOUT THE SECOND GRADE. HOWEVER, THESE BOOKS CAN BE READ TO NURSERY-SCHOOL CHILDREN. THE BOOKLET ALSO CONTAINS SECTIONS ON ADULT BACKGROUND READING, ADDRESSES OF PUBLISHERS, AND RECORDS AND FILMS. (WD)

ED031313 PS002102
VERBAL REINFORCEMENT AS AN ADJUSTMENT PREDICTOR WITH KINDERGARTEN CHILDREN. FINAL REPORT. BOMMARITO, JAMES W., DEC 68 136P.
EDRS PRICE MF-$0.65 HC-$6.58

IN AN ATTEMPT TO DEVELOP AN INSTRUMENT TO SCREEN EMOTIONALLY DISTURBED CHILDREN, A STUDY WAS DESIGNED TO VERIFY AND EXTEND PREVIOUS RESEARCH FINDINGS. THESE FINDINGS INDICATED THAT ADJUSTED CHILDREN IN KINDERGARTEN EXHIBITED GREATER CONDITIONALITY ON A SIMPLE DISCRIMINATION LEARNING TASK THAN MALADJUSTED PUPILS UNDER A PROCESS OF CONTINUOUS MILD VERBAL PUNISHMENT FOR EVERY UNDESIRABLE RESPONSE. OF THE 224 CHILDREN RANDOMLY SELECTED WITH STRATIFICATION FOR SEX, 30 WERE CHOSEN FOR EACH GROUP (ADJUSTED AND MALADJUSTED) ON THE BASIS OF EXTREME SCORES ON THREE PERSONALITY SCALES, THE PROBLEM CHECKLIST, THE BEHAVIOR CHECKLIST, AND THE MINNESOTA SCALE. THE EXPERIMENTAL TASK ITSELF INVOLVED A CHOICE BETWEEN A PICTURE OF A HUMAN AND A PICTURE OF A TOY WITH A VERBAL "THAT'S BAD" FROM THE EXAMINER CONTINGENT ON EACH TOY CHOICE. A SUBJECT'S SCORE WAS HIS INCREASE IN HUMAN CHOICES FROM HIS FIRST TO HIS FOURTH BLOCK OF 25 TRIALS. THE INFLUENCE OF SEVERAL INTERVENING VARIABLES WAS EVALUATED: VERBAL REINFORCEMENT AS AN EFFECTIVE PUNISHMENT (SIGNIFICANT AND CUMMULATIVE IN EFFECT); CORRELATION OF MENTAL AGE, AS REASURED BY THE PEABODY PICTURE VOCABULARY TEST, TO TASK SCORE (INSIGNIFICANT); EXAMINER EFFECTS (INSIGIFICANT); AND CORRELATION OF TASK SCORE TO SOCIOECONOMIC STATUS (INSIGNIFICANT). A REEVALUATION OF THE DATA AFTER THE STUDY PARTIALLY SUPPORTED THE MAIN HYPOTHESIS. (MH)

ED031314 PS002103
A DESCRIPTIVE STUDY OF COGNITIVE AND AFFECTIVE TRENDS DIFFERENTIATING SELECTED GROUPS OF PRESCHOOL CHILDREN. HILLERY, MILTON C.; AND OTHERS, 69 169P.
EDRS PRICE MF-$0.65 HC-$6.58

THE PURPOSE OF THE STUDY WAS TO DESCRIBE WAYS IN WHICH DISADVANTAGED CHILDREN DIFFER FROM THEIR MORE ADVANTAGED PEERS IN THE AREAS OF COGNITIVE AND AFFECTIVE DEVELOPMENTAL PATTERNS, AND TO USE THIS DESCRIPTION TO RESTRUCTURE CURRICULAR EXPERIENCES FOR DISADVANTAGED CHILDREN. FIVE GROUPS OF APPROXIMATELY 30 PRESCHOOL CHILDREN EACH WERE TESTED THREE TIMES WITH A BATTERY OF INSTRUMENTS. THE INSTRUMENT PACKAGE, BROKEN DOWN INTO SEVEN SUBSETS, WAS DESIGNED TO TEST A VARIETY OF DEVELOPMENTAL TASKS. THE APPENDIXES DESCRIBE THE INSTRUMENTS USED. DISADVANTAGED GROUPS OF CHILDREN PERFORMED AT LOWER LEVELS IN ALL MEASURED AREAS OF COGNITIVE FUNCTIONING, CONTRARY TO THE INVESTIGATORS' EXPECTATIONS. THEREFORE, AREAS OF SERIOUS DEFICIT MUST BE IDENTIFIED AND TASKS DESIGNED TO BUILD AND IMPROVE THESE AREAS. THE EFFECTS ATTRIBUTABLE TO HEAD START SEEM TO BE THOSE CHANGES WHICH OCCUR DURING THE FIRST WEEKS OF ANY FORMAL SCHOOL PROGRAM. IMPROVEMENT IN SELF-CONCEPT OCCURRED IN TWO OF THE FIVE GROUPS, WHICH MAY BE ATTRIBUTED TO THE INTEGRATION OF DISADVANTAGED WITH ADVANTAGED CHILDREN IN THOSE GROUPS. ADVANTAGED CHILDREN ARE CURRENTLY EXCLUDED FROM NEEDED PROGRAMS. ECONOMIC CRITERIA PROVIDE AN INACCURATE BASIS FOR THE ALLOCATION OF FUNDS TO EQUALIZE EDUCATIONAL OPPORTUNITY, THUS FUNDING SHOULD BE ALLOCATED ACCORDING TO THE NEEDS OF DIVERSE GROUPS. (DR)

ED031315 PS002110
A STUDY OF THE EFFECTS OF A GROUP LANGUAGE DEVELOPMENT PROGRAM UPON THE PSYCHOLINGUISTIC ABILITIES AND LATER BEGINNING READING SUCCESS OF KINDERGARTEN CHILDREN. MILLIGAN, JERRY L., [65] 9P.
EDRS PRICE MF-$0.65 HC-$3.29

IN THIS STUDY, THE PEABODY LANGUAGE DEVELOPMENT KIT, ORIGINALLY DESIGNED FOR CULTURALLY DEPRIVED AND MENTALLY RETARDED CHILDREN, WAS TESTED TO SEE HOW IT AFFECTED THE PSYCHOLINGUISTIC ABILITIES AND BEGINNING READING DEVELOPMENT OF NORMAL CHILDREN. NINETY-SEVEN KINDERGARTNERS WERE RANDOMLY DIVIDED INTO AN EXPERIMENTAL GROUP WHO USED THE PEABODY KIT AND A CONTROL GROUP TAUGHT LANGUAGE SKILLS BY CONVENTIONAL METHODS. THE EXPERIMENTAL TREATMENT EMPHASIZED (1) ORAL EXPRESSION, (2) DIVERGENT THINKING, (3) USE OF SPOKEN ANALOGY, (4) AUTOMATIC USE OF INFLECTIONAL ENDINGS, (5) AUDITORY MEMORY, AND (6) VISUAL MEMORY. THE CONTROL TREATMENT STRESSED CONVERGENT THINKING AND TASKS REQUIRING PAPER AND PENCIL RESPONSES ON THE PART OF THE CHILD. AT THE END OF THE 24-WEEK TREATMENT PERIOD A RANDOM SAMPLE OF 30 SUBJECTS FROM EACH GROUP WAS GIVEN THE ILLINOIS TEST OF PSYCHOLINGUISTIC ABILITIES. THE EXPERIMENTAL GROUP PERFORMED SIGNIFICANTLY BETTER THAN THE CONTROL GROUP, ESPECIALLY IN THE AUDITORY-VOCAL ASSOCIATION AND THE VOCAL ENCODING SUBTESTS. THE SUBJECTS WERE RANDOMLY DISTRIBUTED (CONTROL AND EXPERIMENTAL GROUPS TOGETHER) INTO FIRST GRADE CLASSES FOR TRAINING IN THE GINN BASIC READER. AT THE END OF THE YEAR, THE SAME SAMPLE OF 30 SUBJECTS FROM EACH GROUP WAS GIVEN THE GATES-MACGINITIE READING TEST. THERE WAS NO SIGNIFICANT DIFFERENCE BETWEEN GROUPS. (MH)

ED032111 PS001736
OPTOMETRIC CHILD VISION CARE AND GUIDANCE. A SERIES OF PAPERS RELEASED BY THE OPTOMETRIC EXTENSION PROGRAM TO ITS MEMBERSHIP 1966-1967. , 67 114P.
DOCUMENT NOT AVAILABLE FROM EDRS.
AVAILABLE FROM: OPTOMETRIC EXTENSION PROGRAM FOUNDATION, INC., DUNCAN, OKLAHOMA 73533

THE DIAGNOSIS AND TREATMENT OF EARLY LEARNING PROBLEMS AND THEIR RELATION TO VISUAL DEVELOPMENT IS THE SUBJECT OF A SERIES OF 12 ARTICLES. THE OPTOMETRIC VIEWPOINT EXPRESSED IS THAT VISION IS LEARNED. A CHILD'S METHOD OF ORGANIZING HIS WORLD, AND MANIFESTATIONS OF HIS DISORGANIZED BEHAVIOR, INCLUDING POOR EARLY ACADEMIC ACHIEVEMENT, PROBABLY RESULT IN LEARNING TO SEE. VISION IS VIEWED AS AN EMERGENT FROM FOUR UNDERLYING SUBSYSTEMS: (1) ANTI-GRAVITY (WHERE AM I IN SPACE?), (2) CENTERING (WHERE IS IT IN SPACE?), (3) IDENTIFICATION (WHAT IS IT?), AND (4) SPEECH-AUDITORY (COMMUNICATES HIS VISUAL IMPRESSIONS). POOR DEVELOPMENT IN ANY OF THESE SUBSYSTEMS HAS DISRUPTIVE EFFECTS ON THE REMAINING SUBSYSTEMS AND ON THE CHILD'S BEHAVIOR AS A WHOLE, PARTICULARLY ON HIS PERFORMANCE IN EARLY EDUCATION. PROPER DEVELOPMENT, ON THE OTHER HAND, WHETHER ACHIEVED NORMALLY OR THROUGH THE METHODS OF REMEDIAL THERAPY OUTLINED IN THE SERIES, LEADS TO INTEGRAL FUNCTIONING OF THE SUBSYSTEMS AND ULTIMATELY TO VISUALIZATION, WHICH IS DESCRIBED AS THE SUPREME PROCESS OF UNCONSCIOUSLY USING THE SENSING MODES THAT BRING INFORMATION TO THE CHILD FOR SYNTHESIS. (MH)

ED032112 PS001988
THE UTILIZATIONS OF CONCRETE, FUNCTIONAL, AND DESIGNATIVE CONCEPTS IN MULTIPLE CLASSIFICATION. PARKER, RONALD K.; HALBROOK, MARY CAROL, 69 62P.
EDRS PRICE MF-$0.65 HC NOT AVAILABLE FROM EDRS.

IN ORDER TO INVESTIGATE DEVELOPMENTAL CHANGES IN MULTIPLE CLASSIFICATION, A MATRIX TASK WAS ADMINISTERED TO 80 KINDERGARTEN FIRST, SECOND, AND THIRD GRADE CHILDREN. CORRECT SOLUTION OF THE INCOMPLETE MATRICES, COMPRISED OF THREE PICTURES IN A ROW AND THREE PICTURES IN A COLUMN MEETING AT A BLANK INTERSECTION, REQUIRED IDENTIFICATION AND COMBINATION OF THE COMMON ATTRIBUTES OF THE ROW AND THE COLUMN. CONCRETE, FUNCTIONAL, AND DESIGNATIVE CONCEPTS WERE USED IN CONSTRUCTION OF THE MATRICES. RESULTS INDICATED PERFORMANCE IMPROVEMENT WITH GRADE LEVEL AND A SIGNIFICANT INTERACTION BETWEEN GRADE AND TYPE OF MATRIX. THIS INTERACTION MEANS THAT DEVELOPMENT OF THE ABILITY TO CLASSIFY THE THREE TYPES OF CONCEPTS OCCURS IN CHRONOLOGICAL ORDER: FIRST, CONCRETE, THEN FUNCATIONAL, AND FINALLY, DESIGNATIVE. IN GENERAL, WHEN ERRORS WERE MADE, CHILDREN SEEMED TO CHOOSE THE PICTURE REPRESENT-

ING THE TYPE OF CONCEPT (CONCRETE, FUNCTIONAL, OR DESIGNATIVE) SHOWN BY OBJECT-SORTING STUDIES TO BE THE MOST FREQUENT MODE OF CATEGORIZATION. THE TIME REQUIRED TO RESPOND DECREASED WITH PRACTICE AND WAS NEGATIVELY CORRELATED WITH CORRECT MATRIX SOLUTION. FURTHER RESEARCH SHOULD FOCUS ON DEVELOPING A TRAINING PROGRAM FOR THE PREREQUISITE SKILLS NECESSARY TO SOLVE THE MATRICES. [NOT AVAILABLE IN HARD COPY DUE TO MARGINAL LEGIBILITY OF ORIGINAL DOCUMENT]. (MH)

ED032113 PS001993
MOTIVATIONAL EFFECTS OF INDIVIDUAL CONFERENCES AND GOAL SETTING ON PERFORMANCE AND ATTITUDES IN ARITHMETIC. REPORT FROM THE PROJECT ON SITUATIONAL VARIABLES AND EFFICIENCY OF CONCEPT LEARNING. KENNEDY, BARBARA J., JUL 68 24P.
EDRS PRICE MF-$0.65 HC-$3.29

THIS EXPERIMENT COMPARED THE MOTIVATIONAL EFFECTS OF COGNITIVE INCENTIVES (GOAL SETTING TECHNIQUES) AND INVESTIGATED THESE EFFECTS COMBINED WITH SOCIAL INTERACTION (INDIVIDUAL PUPIL-TEACHER CONFERENCES). SUBJECTS WERE 48 PREDOMINANTLY NEGRO, LOW-SOCIOECONOMIC STATUS, THIRD AND FOURTH GRADERS FROM THREE ARITHMETIC CLASSES, REPRESENTING HIGH, MEDIUM, AND LOW ACHIEVEMENT. THE CHILDREN WERE RANDOMLY ASSIGNED TO A CONTROL GROUP OR TO ONE OF THREE EXPERIMENTAL GROUPS: (1) DO BEST SUBJECTS SIMPLY WERE TOLD TO DO THEIR BEST, (2) SELF-SET CHILDREN STATED THEIR GOAL EACH WEEK, AND (3) TEACHER-SET CHILDREN'S WEEKLY GOALS WERE SET BY THE TEACHER. EXPERIMENTAL GROUPS MET WITH THE TEACHER ONCE A WEEK FOR 6 WEEKS. TESTS AND RECORDS MEASURED PERFORMANCE, RETENTION, AND ATTITUDE CHANGE. SIGNIFICANT EFFECTS DUE TO ACHIEVEMENT LEVEL WERE FOUND FOR ACQUISITION AND RETENTION SCORES. CHILDREN ATTENDING CONFERENCES PERFORMED BETTER THAN THOSE WHO HAD NOT, AND CHILDREN WITH SPECIFIC GOALS PERFORMED BETTER THAN THOSE WITH GENERAL GOALS. HIGH ACHIEVEMENT STUDENTS REFLECTED POSITIVE ATTITUDE CHANGE, WHILE LOW ACHIEVERS REFLECTED NEGATIVE ATTITUDE CHANGE. THE EFFECTS OF SOCIAL AND COGNITIVE MOTIVES ON ATTITUDE CHANGE WERE INCONCLUSIVE. (DR)

ED032114 PS002010
EARLY CHILDHOOD EDUCATION IN AMERICAN SAMOA, 1968. JOHNSTON, BETTY, 68 11P.
EDRS PRICE MF-$0.65 HC-$3.29

IN 1968, A NEW PHASE OF THE TOTAL EDUCATIONAL PLAY FOR AMERICAN SAMOA AIMED AT INCREASING POWER IN LANGUAGE AND THINKING. AN IN-SCHOOL PROGRAM, INCLUDING A TELEVISED COMPONENT WAS DESIGNED FOR ALL THE 5-YEAR-OLDS ENTERING SCHOOL IN SEPTEMBER. A CURRICULUM WAS DEVISED TO ENCOURAGE THE USE OF THE SAMOAN LANGUAGE. MATERIALS WERE IMPORTED WHEN COMMERCIALLY AVAILABLE PRODUCTS WERE TOO EXPENSIVE OR DID NOT REFLECT SAMOAN CULTURE. A PILOT PROJECT WITH 15 SAMOAN 5-YEAR-OLDS WAS CONDUCTED TO DETERMINE THE APPROPRIATENESS OF THE CURRICULUM MATERIALS, TO OBSERVE THE RESPONSE OF THE CHILDREN AND THEIR PARENTS TO THE PROGRAM, AND TO BEGIN TO TRAIN SAMOANS WHO WOULD BE TEACHING. THE PROGRAM WAS REPEATED USING TWO GROUPS OF CHILDREN WHO WERE OBSERVED BY 111 SAMOAN TEACHERS AND ASSISTANT PRINCIPALS PARTICIPATING IN THE 5-WEEK WORKSHOP. DURING AUGUST AND PART OF SEPTEMBER, 800 SAMOAN CHILDREN WHO WOULD BE ENTERING SCHOOL, PARTICIPATED IN THE EARLY CHILDHOOD PROGRAM. THE GROUPS AVERAGED 15 IN NUMBER AND WERE TAUGHT BY THE TEACHERS ATTENDING THE WORKSHOP. CLASSROOM ACTIVITIES WERE SIMILAR TO THE EXPERIMENTAL PROGRAMS. EARLY CHILDHOOD PERSONNEL GUIDED TEACHERS IN CONDUCTING THE SUCCESSFUL PROGRAM. IT WAS FELT THAT THE MAJORITY OF THE TEACHERS DID A BETTER THAN AVERAGE JOB. THE CHILDREN RESPONDED WELL TO THE ACTIVITIES, CURRICULUM MATERIALS, AND THE TELECAST. (JS)

ED032115 PS002025
EVAULATION OF THE DEMONSTRATION PHASE OF THE TEEN TUTORIAL PROGRAM: A MODEL OF INTERRELATIONSHIP OF SEVENTH GRADERS, KINDERGARTEN PUPILS AND PARENTS TO MEET THE DEVELOPMENTAL NEEDS OF DISADVANTAGED CHILDREN. O'BRYAN, SHARLEEN; AND OTHERS, 31 AUG 68 254P.
EDRS PRICE MF-$0.65 HC NOT AVAILABLE FROM EDRS.

THIS DOCUMENT DESCRIBES AND EVALUATES A TEEN TUTORIAL PROGRAM CONDUCTED IN GROVE CITY, OHIO. FORTY SEVENTH GRADE PUPILS, TWO KINDERGARTEN CLASSES, AND PARENTS OF BOTH GROUPS WERE SUBJECTS OF THIS PROJECT TO CREATE AND DEMONSTRATE A STRATEGY TO HELP YOUNG DISADVANTAGED TEENAGERS DEVELOP AN UNDERSTANDING OF PERSONAL AND FAMILY RELATIONSHIPS BEFORE THEY THEMSELVES BECAME ADULTS OR PARENTS. IN THE FUTURE THEY MIGHT THEN BE BETTER EQUIPPED TO PROVIDE AN ENVIRONMENT FOR THEIR CHILDREN THAT WOULD PRECLUDE A CONTINUATION OF THE DEFICIT THAT USUALLY ACCOMPANIES EARLY CHILDHHOD IN LOWER INCOME GROUPS. THE PROJECT PROPOSED TO (1) PROVIDE THE SEVENTH GRADERS WITH A COURSE IN HUMAN RELATIONS AND FAMILY LIVING, (2) OFFER THE TEENAGERS A CHANCE TO TUTOR KINDERGARTEN CHILDREN, AND (3) EDUCATE THE PARENTS OF THE CHILDREN INVOLVED. THE PROGRAM REPORT HAS NINE APPENDIXES WHICH CONTAIN (1) EVALUATION PROCEDURES, (2) COMMENTS BY ADMINISTRATORS, (3) COMMENTS ABOUT TEAM TEACHING, (4) COMMENTS ON CHANGE IN TEEN TUTORS, (5) COMMENTS ON CHANGE IN KINDERGARTNERS, (6) COMMENTS BY OBSERVERS, (7) GENERAL END OF YEAR COMMENTS, (8) OUTLINE OF EDUCATION PROGRAM FOR PARENTS, AND (9) EVALUATION FORM FOR SELECTION OF TEEN TUTORS. [NOT AVAILABLE IN HARD COPY DUE TO MARGINAL LEGIBILITY OF ORIGINAL DOCUMENT.] (WD)

ED032116 PS002046
FAMILY LIFE AROUND THE WORLD, LEVEL I. , AUG 68 181P.
EDRS PRICE MF-$0.65 HC-$6.58

THIS DOCUMENT, INTENDED FOR USE WITH FIRST GRADERS, IS ONE OF A SERIES OF SOCIAL STUDIES CURRICULUM GUIDES. LESSONS INCLUDE (1) FAMILIES IN OUR COMMUNITY, (2) FAMILIES IN HIGH RISE APARTMENTS, (3) FAMILIES IN OLD HOMES OF THE CITY, (4) FAMILIES IN ALASKA, (5) FAMILIES IN MEXICO, AND (6) FAMILIES IN JAPAN. THE PROGRAM IS STRUCTURED SO THAT (1) THE COURSE CONTENT IS TAUGHT WITHIN A CONCEPTUAL FRAMEWORK, I.E., THE STUDENT IS TAUGHT TO UNDERSTAND BASIC CONCEPTS RATHER THAN A MASS OF ISOLATED FACTS, (2) THE USE OF THE DISCOVERY OR INQUIRY METHOD OF STUDY IS EMPHASIZED, (3) MANY DISCIPLINES OF THE SOCIAL SCIENCES (ECONOMICS, GEOGRAPHY, HISTORY, ANTHROPOLOGY, AND POLITICAL SCIENCE) ARE INTEGRATED INTO THE MATERIAL, (4) THE CHILD IS PLACED IN A WORLD WIDE COMMUNITY, (5) BASIC SKILLS AND RESEARCH TECHNIQUES ARE ENCOURAGED, (6) MULTI-MEDIA RESOURCES ARE USED, AND (7) PROGRAM OBJECTIVES ARE STATED IN TERMS OF CHILDREN'S BEHAVIOR. AN INSTRUCTIONAL KIT CONTAINING SLIDES, FILMS, TAPES, AND TRANSPARENCIES TO ACCOMPANY THE GUIDE IS AVAILABLE. BIBLIOGRAPHIES SUGGEST ADDITIONAL MATERIALS. (WD)

ED032117 PS002100
UNDERSTANDING READINESS: AN OCCASIONAL PAPER. JENSEN, ARTHUR R., 69 19P.
EDRS PRICE MF-$0.65 HC-$3.29

READINESS TO LEARN OCCURS WHEN A CHILD HAS ACHIEVED CUMULATIVE LEARNING OF COMPONENT SUBSKILLS AND THE DEVELOPMENTAL MATURITY NECESSARY TO INTEGRATE THESE SUBSKILLS INTO THE DESIRED SKILL. READINESS IS RELATIVE, HOWEVER, NOT ONLY TO THE SKILL, BUT ALSO TO THE TECHNIQUE OF INSTRUCTION. THUS, READINESS FOR LEARNING A PARTICULAR SKILL BY DIFFERENT TECHNIQUES MAY COME AT DIFFERENT TIMES. ATTEMPTING TO FORCE INSTRUCTION ON A CHILD WHO IS NOT READY CAN CAUSE THE CHILD EITHER TO LEARN THE SKILL BY A MORE PRIMITIVE TECHNIQUE (ONE WHICH HAS LITTLE TRANSFER VALUE TO OTHER LEARNING) OR TO "TURN OFF" TO LEARNING ALTOGETHER. "TURNING OFF" MEANS EXTINCTION OR INHIBITION OF BEHAVIORS NECESSARY TO LEARNING, SUCH AS ATTENTION AND ACTIVE INVOLVEMENT. MANY SCHOOL LEARNING PROBLEMS, PARTICULARLY THOSE OF DISADVANTAGED CHILDREN, MIGHT BE AVOIDED IF MORE ATTENTION WERE PAID TO READINESS IN THE PRIMARY GRADES, WHEN THE DANGER OF "TURNING OFF" BECAUSE OF LACK OF READINESS IS GREATEST. EXPERIMENTAL PROGRAMS ARE NEEDED THAT WOULD ACTUALLY DELAY FORMAL INSTRUCTION (WHILE FILLING IN NECESSARY EXPERIENTIAL FACTORS) UNTIL READINESS IS APPARENT. (MH)

ED032118 PS002101
PREPRIMARY ENROLLMENT OF CHILDREN UNDER SIX: OCTOBER 1968. NEHRT, ROY C.; HURD, GORDON E., JUN 69 23P.
EDRS PRICE MF-$0.65 HC-$3.29
AVAILABLE FROM: SUPERINTENDENT OF DOCUMENTS, U.S. GOVERNMENT PRINTING OFFICE, WASHINGTON, D.C. 20402 ($0.30)

THIS STUDY, BASED ON INFORMATION COLLECTED BY THE U.S. BUREAU OF THE CENSUS IN ITS CURRENT POPULATION SURVEY, SHOWS THE NUMBER OF CHILDREN 3 TO 5 YEARS OLD IN THE UNITED STATES AND THE EXTENT OF THEIR ENROLLMENT IN PUBLIC AND NONPUBLIC PREPRIMARY PROGRAMS. IN 1968 THE GAP CONTINUED TO CLOSE BETWEEN WHITE AND NONWHITE CHILDREN ENROLLED IN PREPRIMARY PROGRAMS, REFLECTING THE INFLUENCE OF STATE AND FEDERAL PRESCHOOL PROJECTS IN POORER AREAS. AS AGE INCREASED, ENROLLMENT RATES INCREASED, BUT THE PROPORTION ENROLLED IN PRIVATE SCHOOLS DECREASED. AS FAMILY INCOME ROSE, ENROLLMENT INCREASED, WITH THE HIGHEST PERCENTAGE IN THE "$10,000 AND OVER" GROUP. A HIGHER PERCENTAGE OF NONWHITE CHILDREN THAN WHITE CHILDREN FROM THE LOWER INCOME GROUPS WAS ENROLLED, AND FOR ALL REGIONS OF THE COUNTRY, NONWHITE ENROLLMENT WAS HIGHER. ENROLLMENT RATES FOR NONWHITES WERE HIGHER THAN FOR WHITES IN WHITE-COLLAR AND MANUAL SERVICE OCCUPATIONS. CHILDREN IN FARM FAMILIES HAD THE LOWEST ENROLLMENT RATES, WHILE CHILDREN IN WHITE-COLLAR FAMILIES HAD THE HIGHEST ENROLLMENT. THE ENROLLMENT RATE OF NONMETROPOLITAN RESIDENTS CONTINUED TO BE LOWER THAN THAT OF CENTRAL CITY OR SUBURBAN RESIDENTS. THE PERCENTAGE OF 3- TO 5-YEAR-OLDS ENROLLED IN PREPRIMARY PROGRAMS CONTINUED TO INCREASE, FROM 25.5 PERCENT IN OCTOBER 1964 TO 33.0 PERCENT IN OCTOBER 1968. (DR)

ED032119 PS002108
A STUDY OF THE COMMUNICATIVE ABILITIES OF DISADVANTAGED CHILDREN. FINAL REPORT. OSSER, HARRY; AND OTHERS, 30 JAN 68 45P.
EDRS PRICE MF-$0.65 HC-$3.29

THE PURPOSE OF THIS SERIES OF FOUR STUDIES WAS TO PRECISELY DESCRIBE THE CODE AND DIALECT FEATURES OF THE SPEECH OF BOTH LOWER CLASS NEGRO CHILDREN AND MIDDLE CLASS WHITE CHILDREN. IN THE FIRST STUDY, 16 WHITE MIDDLE CLASS (WMC) CHILDREN WERE COMPARED TO 16 NEGRO LOWER CLASS (NLC) CHILDREN ON BOTH AN IMITATION AND A COMPREHENSION TASK. THE WMC SUBJECTS SCORED SIGNIFICANTLY HIGHER ON BOTH TASKS, EVEN AFTER THE SCORES OF THE NLC SUBJECTS ON THE IMITATION TASKS WERE IMPROVED BY ADJUSTING THEM FOR DIFFERENCES OF DIALECT IN THE CHILDREN'S RESPONSES. NO ADJUSTMENT, HOWEVER, WAS MADE FOR THE ADMINISTERING OF BOTH TASKS IN STANDARD ENGLISH. THE SECOND STUDY TOOK FREE SPEECH SAMPLES FROM 20 NLC AND 20 WMC 5-YEAR-OLDS TO DISCOVER ANY POSSIBLE LINGUISTIC CODE VARIATIONS BETWEEN GROUPS. THE WMC SUBJECTS SHOWED A SIGNIFICANTLY SUPERIOR RANGE OF SYNTACTIC STRUCTURES, BUT THERE WAS NO SIGNIFICANT DIFFERENCE BETWEEN GROUPS IN THE USE OF SPECIFIC TYPES OF COMPLEX SENTENCES. THE SAME FREE SPEECH SAMPLES WERE THEN ANALYZED IN THE THIRD STUDY TO FIND AND LIST EXAMPLES OF NONSTANDARD DIALECT VARIATIONS OF NLC. THE FOURTH STUDY DEVELOPED A PSYCHOLINGUISTIC MODEL FOR MEASURING SYNTACTIC COMPLEXITY IN BOT H QUANTITATIVE AND QUALITATIVE TERMS. (MH)

ED032120 PS002109
CATEGORIES AND UNDERLYING PROCESSES, OR REPRESENTATIVE BEHAVIOR SAMPLES AND S-R ANALYSIS: OPPOSING STRATEGIES. STAATS, ARTHUR W., [68] 13P.
EDRS PRICE MF-$0.65 HC-$3.29

PSYCHOLOGICAL RESEARCHERS SHOULD DEAL WITH THE CONCRETE STIMULUS-RESPONSE PRINCIPLES OF LEARNING ON WHICH BEHAVIOR IS BASED, AND STUDY BEHAVIORS THAT ARE REPRESENTATIVE OF REAL LIFE BEHAVIORS. THE PRESENT RESEARCH STRATEGY HAS COME FROM TWO FAULTY IDEAS: FIRST, A CONCERN WITH UNDERLYING, INFERRED MENTAL PROCESSES, RATHER THAN WITH ACTUAL TASKS OR BEHAVIORS; AND SECOND, A BELIEF THAT BEHAVIOR AND PROBLEM SOLVING CAN BE FUNCTIONALLY DIVIDED INTO PERCEPTION AND PERFORMANCE. THESE IDEAS LEAD (1) TO THE USE OF TASKS THAT ARE NOT REPRESENTATIVE OF THE UNIVERSE OF BEHAVIORS OF EVERYDAY LIVING (E.G. THE ANAGRAM PROBLEM, THE WATER JAR PROBLEM), (2) TO A LUMPING TOGETHER OF BEHAVIORS THAT ARE DIFFERENT IN NATURE (E.G. CLASSICAL CONDITIONING OF A CAT TO "NO!" AND INSTRUMENTAL CONDITIONING OF A CAT TO HIS NAME), AND (3) TO THE SEPARATION OF BEHAVIORS THAT ARE SIMILAR IN NATURE (E.G. LEARNING TO READ LETTERS AND LEARNING TO WRITE LETTERS). ONLY BY A SHIFT OF EMPHASIS TO CONCRETE FUNCTIONAL ANALYSIS CAN THE ARTIFICIAL PERCEPTION-PERFORMANCE DICHOTOMY BE DISCARDED AND A GREAT DEAL ABOUT BEHAVIOR AND ACQUISITION OF SKILLS BE DISCOVERED. (MH)

ED032121 PS002113
INVESTIGATION OF METHODS TO ASSESS THE EFFECTS OF CULTURAL DEPRIVATION. FINAL REPORT. MOELLENBERG, WAYNE P., SEP 67 94P.
EDRS PRICE MF-$0.65 HC-$3.29

THIS STUDY INVESTIGATED METHODS OF ASSESSING THE EFFECTS OF CULTURAL DEPRIVATION IN RELATION TO SCHOOL ADJUSTMENT. THE INVESTIGATORS DEVELOPED NEW METHODS OF ASSESSMENT IN AREAS OF SELF-CONCEPT, (SAMPLE OF 49 CHILDREN) CONCEPT FORMATION, (314 CHILDREN) AND VALUE ORIENTATION, (45 CHILDREN) THE PEABODY PICTURE VOCABULARY TEST (SAMPLE OF 60 CHILDREN) AND THE LEE-CLARK READING READINESS TEST (50 HEAD START CHILDREN) WERE ALSO ADMINISTERED. THE FOLLOWING CONCLUSIONS WERE REACHED: (1) DIFFERENCES IN SELF-CONCEPT WERE DETECTED WHEN PICTORIAL REPRESENTATIONS WERE USED. (2) PICTORIAL REPRESENTATIONS OF VERBAL CONCEPTS PROVIDED MEANINGFUL ASSESSMENTS OF ESSENTIAL CONCEPTS WITHOUT RELYING ON READING ABILITY. (3) THE PRESENTATION OF VALUE DISTINCTIONS BY OVERHEAD PROJECTOR RESULTED IN DIFFERENT PATTERNS OF RESPONSE BY CONTRASTED GROUPS OF CHILDREN. (4) PEABODY PICTURE VOCABULARY TEST SCORES WERE SIGNIFICANTLY DIFFERENT FOR MIDDLE CLASS CHILDREN THAN FOR LOWER CLASS CHILDREN. (5) RESPONSES ON THE LEE-CLARK READING READINESS TEST INDICATED DIFFICULTY FOR UNDERPRIVILEGED CHILDREN TO RECOGNIZE AND CATEGORIZE SYMBOLS. THESE ABILITIES WERE IMPROVED THROUGH HEAD START EXPERIENCES. IT IS RECOMMENDED THAT ADDITIONAL TRIAL FORMS OF THE PICTORIAL INSTRUMENTS BE DEVISED, AND THAT ALL OF THE INSTRUMENTS BE USED ON DIFFERENT GROUPS OF CHILDREN. LONGITUDINAL STUDIES SHOULD FOLLOW. (DR)

ED032122 PS002114
INFANT MORTALITY: A CHALLENGE TO THE NATION. , 66 15P.
EDRS PRICE MF-$0.65 HC-$3.29

FROM 1956-1960 AN ESTIMATED 34,000 INFANTS ANNUALLY FAILED TO SURVIVE IN MANY PARTS OF THE UNITED STATES DUE TO RISKS FAR IN EXCESS OF THOSE FOR SOME AREAS OF THE COUNTRY. THERE IS A GROWING GAP BETWEEN DEATH RATES FOR WHITE AND NONWHITE INFANTS IN THE UNITED STATES, WITH THE EXCESS MORTALITY RATE OF NONWHITE INFANTS CONTINUING TO RISE. ONLY 15 STATES LOWERED INFANT MORTALITY RATES FROM 1960-62 TO 1964. LARGE CITIES HAD AN INFANT MORTALITY RATE OF 27.9 IN 1964, COMPARED TO THE NATIONAL AVERAGE OF 24.8. THIS WAS A RESULT OF A DECREASE IN THE DEATH RATE FOR WHITE INFANTS OFFSET BY AN INCREASE IN THE NONWHITE INFANT MORTALITY RATE. MOST U.S. COUNTIES WHICH SHOWED EXCESS INFANT MORTALITY HAD CITIES OF 50,000 OR MORE. URBAN AREAS HAD NEARLY THREE OUT OF FOUR EXCESS NEONATAL DEATHS (UNDER 28 DAYS) IN 1964. TWENTY-TWO PERCENT OF THE ANNUAL EXCESS INFANT DEATHS OCCURRED IN THE 21 LARGEST CITIES, IN AREAS WITH A LOW STANDARD OF LIVING CHARACTERIZED BY HIGH MATERNAL AND INFANT DEATH RISKS. EXCESS NEONATAL MORTALITY IN RURAL AREAS WAS CONCENTRATED IN NON-METROPOLITAN COUNTIES. EXCESS WHITE POSTNEONATAL DEATHS (1-11 MONTHS) WERE MOST FREQUENT IN RURAL AND SMALL URBAN AREAS, WHILE EXCESS POSTNEONATAL DEATHS OF NONWHITES WAS CONFINED TO URBAN AREAS. (DR)

ED032123 PS002116
A COMPARATIVE STUDY OF CURRENT EDUCATIONAL TELEVISION PROGRAMS FOR PRESCHOOL CHILDREN. FINAL REPORT. PALMER, EDWARD L.; AND OTHERS, 30 JUN 68 100P.
EDRS PRICE MF-$0.65 HC-$3.29

THE PURPOSE OF THIS STUDY WAS TO IDENTIFY THE FACTORS IN PRESCHOOL EDUCATIONAL TELEVISION THAT ENGAGE AND SUSTAIN CHILDREN'S ATTENTION. THE METHOD USED TO MEASURE THE CHILDREN'S ATTENTION WAS DECIDED ON IN A PILOT STUDY OF THREE MEASUREMENT TECHNIQUES, AND CONSISTED OF AN OBSERVER RATING SCALE WITH THE PERIODIC INTRODUCTION OF A KALEIDOSCOPIC DISTRACTOR. THERE WERE THREE GROUPS OF CHILDREN OBSERVED: 2- AND 3-YEAR-OLD MIDDLE CLASS CHILDREN, 4- AND 5-YEAR-OLD MIDDLE CLASS CHILDREN, AND 4- AND 5-YEAR-OLD MEXICAN-AMERICAN CHILDREN FROM LOWER INCOME FAMILIES. FIVE TELEVISION PROGRAMS FOR PRESCHOOL CHILDREN AND ONE SET OF ANIMATED CARTOONS WERE VIEWED. TO CHECK FOR ANY POSSIBLE CORRELATION BETWEE N LANGUAGE DEVELOPMENT AND ATTENTIVENESS, THE CHILDREN WERE GIVEN THE PEABODY PICTURE VOCABULARY TEST. THE RESULTS OF THE BETWEE N GROUPS ANALYSES REVEALED A VERY HIGH DEGREE OF GENERALITY IN TERMS OF THE TYPE OF PROGRAM CONTENT THAT APPEALED TO THE AGE, SEX, AND SOCIAL GROUPS STUDIED. FURTHER, THERE WAS NO CORRELATION BETWEEN PEABODY SCORES AND ATTENTION LEVELS, ONCE AGE WAS PARTIALLED OUT. ATTENTION LEVEL WAS VERY LOW; ANALYSIS OF THE PROGRAM CONTENT SHOWED THAT CHILDREN PAID GREATER ATTENTION TO ANIMATED CARTOONS, INTRODUCTION TO NOVEL OBJECTS, AND INITIATION OF NOVEL ACTION BY THE TEACHER-PERFORMER. (MH)

ED032124 PS002117
[COMPETENCE IN YOUNG CHILDREN.] WHITE, BURTON L., MAR 69 55P.
EDRS PRICE MF-$0.65 HC-$3.29

FOUR PAPERS DISCUSS THE HARVARD PRESCHOOL PROJECT WHOSE GOAL IS TO LEARN HOW TO STRUCTURE THE EXPERIENCES OF THE FIRST SIX YEARS OF LIFE TO ENCOURAGE MAXIMAL DEVELOPMENT OF HUMAN COMPETENCE. TO DETERMINE WHAT COMPETENCE AT AGE 6 IS, A GROUP OF 13 HIGHLY COMPETENT 6-YEAR-OLDS OF MIXED RESIDENCE, CLASS, AND ETHNICITY WERE COMPARED TO A LIKE GROUP OF 13 LOW COMPETENCE 6-YEAR-OLDS AND THE RESULTANT INFORMATION WAS COLLECTED IN PROTOCOLS. FROM THIS MATERIAL, A LIST OF DIFFERENTIATING ABILITIES, SOME SOCIAL AND SOME NONSOCIAL, WAS COMPILED. HIGHLY COMPETENT 3-YEAR-OLDS WERE FOUND TO BE MORE ADVANCED IN THESE ABILITIES THAN 6-YEAR-OLDS WHO WERE DOING POORLY. AS THERE WAS LITTLE COMPETENCE DIVERGENCE AT AGE ONE, IT WAS CLEAR THAT AN INVESTIGATION OF THE INTERACTION OF EXPERIENCE AND THE DEVELOPMENT OF COMPETENCE SHOULD BE FOCUSED ON THE SECOND AND THIRD YEARS OF LIFE, (MOSTLY FAMILIAL EXPERIENCES). TO MEASURE COMPARATIVE EXPERIENTIAL HISTORIES, AN INSTRUMENT WAS DEVELOPED FOR CODIFICATION OF MOMENT-TO-MOMENT BEHAVIOR ON THE BASIS OF INFERRED PURPOSE. THE NEXT STEP WILL BE THE COLLECTION AND ANALYSIS OF DATA FROM FAMILIES THAT HAVE SUCCEEDED OR FAILED TO DEVELOP CHILDREN OF HIGH COMPETENCE. ALSO PLANNED ARE LONGITUDINAL STUDIES IN WHICH CHILDREN WILL FOLLOW TASK SEQUENCES DESIGNED FOR OPTIMAL DEVELOPMENT. (MH)

ED032125 PS002120

DEVELOPMENT OF THE UNDERSTANDING OF LOGICAL CONNECTIVES. NEIMARK, EDITH D.; SLOTNICK, NAN S., JUL 69 24P.

EDRS PRICE MF-$0.65 HC-$3.29

IN AN EFFORT TO CROSS-VALIDATE A JAPANESE STUDY, A 16 ITEM TEST OF LOGICAL CONNECTIVES WAS ADMINISTERED TO 223 BOYS AND GIRLS AT EACH GRADE LEVEL (THIRD THROUGH NINTH GRADES) AND TWO GROUPS OF COLLEGE SOPHOMORE GIRLS. THE PURPOSE OF THE TEST WAS TO ASSESS THEIR UNDERSTANDING OF CLASS INCLUSION AND EXCLUSION, CLASS INTERSECTION, AND CLASS UNION. HALF OF THE GROUPS RECEIVED A TEST IN WHICH SET ELEMENTS WERE PICTURES; THE OTHER HALF HAD WORDS AS SET ELEMENTS. ALTHOUGH THERE WERE SIGNIFICANT DIFFERENCES BETWEE N GRADES FOR ALL THREE TYPES OF QUESTIONS, (A) INCLUSION AND EXCLUSION ARE UNDERSTOOD BY A MAJORITY OF EVEN THE YOUNGEST CHILDREN, (B) INTERSECT IS UNDERSTOOD BY A MAJORITY OF ALL BU T THE YOUNGEST CHILDREN, AND (C) UNION IS NOT UNDERSTOOD BY THE MAJORITY OF SUBJECTS EXCEPT AT THE COLLEGE LEVEL. THOSE TAKING THE TEST, IN WHICH SET ELEMENTS WERE PICTURES, PERFORMED BETTER THAN THOSE TAKING THE TEST IN WHICH SET ELEMENTS WERE WORDS. THESE RESULTS, IN GENERAL, SUPPORT THE FINDINGS OF THE JAPANESE STUDY, ALTHOUGH JAPANESE CHILDREN AS A GROUP SCORED HIGHER THAN AMERICAN CHILDREN. THE MOST COMPLETE EXPLANATION OF THE PRESENT DATA SEEMS TO BE AN ANALYSIS OF PERFORMANCE IN TERMS OF COMPONENT OPERATIONS FOR PROCESSING AND STORING INFORMATION. (MH)

ED032126 PS002121

ENVIRONMENT INFLUENCES ON THE DEVELOPMENT OF ABILITIES. LITMAN, FRANCES, MAR 69 11P.

EDRS PRICE MF-$0.65 HC-$3.29

OBSERVATIONAL RESEARCH WAS CONDUCTED IN HOMES WITH A WIDE SOCIOECONOMIC RANGE TO IDENTIFY THE MAJOR FACTORS OF EXPERIENCE THAT AFFECT THE DEVELOPMENT OF A CHILD'S ABILITIES. THIRTY CHILDREN, AGED 12 TO 36 MONTHS, WERE OBSERVED IN THREE ASPECTS OF THEIR ENVIRONMENT: HUMAN (FAMILY AND PEERS), STATIC PHYSICAL (HOME AND NEIGHBORHOOD), AND RANGE OF EXPERIENCE (SITUATIONS AND ACTIVITIES IN CHILD'S REGULAR LIFE PATTERN). ON STANDARDIZED SCALES OR SCALES DEVISED FOR THIS STUDY, CHILDREN WERE RATED AS VERY WELL DEVELOPED OR VERY POORLY DEVELOPED WITH RESPECT TO SOCIAL AND NONSOCIAL COMPETENCY. RATING SCALES WHICH ASSESSED PATTERNS AND EFFECTS OF MATERNAL BEHAVIOR SHOWED THAT WELL-DEVELOPED CHILDREN CAN COME FROM CROWDED OR SPACIOUS HOMES AND THAT LIMITED USE OF RESOURCES CAN BE FOUND IN BOTH LOWER CLASS AND MIDDLE CLASS HOMES. THE QUALITY RATHER THAN QUANTITY OF MOTHER-CHILD INTERACTION WAS SIGNIFICANT. AFTER RATING MOTHERS ON INTERACTION, MOTIVATIONAL FACTORS IMPLICIT IN THE MOTHER'S BEHAVIOR, AND MATERIAL RESOURCES AVAILABLE TO AND USED BY THE CHILD, FIVE PATTERNS OF MATERNAL BEHAVIOR WERE DESCRIBED. THESE FIVE PROTOTYPES WERE (1) THE COMPETENT MOTHER, (2) THE "ALMOST" MOTHER, (3) THE MOTHER WHO IS OVERWHELMED BY LIFE'S CIRCUMSTANCES, (4) THE RIGID, CONTROLLING MOTHER, AND (5) THE SMOTHERING MOTHER. (DR)

ED032127 PS002122

PRIMARY INFLUENCES ON THE DEVELOPMENT OF COMPETENCE: THE DEVELOPMENT OF A MATERNAL BEHAVIOR SCALE. PROGRESS REPORT. LACROSSE, E. ROBERT, JR., MAR 69 10P.

EDRS PRICE MF-$0.65 HC-$3.29

THIS IS A PROGRESS REPORT ON THE DEVELOPMENT OF A MATERNAL BEHAVIOR SCALE, ONE WHICH WOULD REFLECT BOTH THE ACTUAL BEHAVIOR OF A MOTHER WHEN CONFRONTED BY HER CHILD'S ACTIVITIES AND ALSO SHOW THE BEHAVIORS INSTIGATED BY THE MOTHER IN THE CHILD'S PRESENCE. THE ULTIMATE GOAL OF THE RESEARCH IS TO PRODUCE A HUMAN BEHAVIOR SCALE WHICH WILL RECORD THE BEHAVIOR OF THE MOTHER, FATHER, OTHER ADULTS, PEERS, AND SIBLINGS. IN FOCUSING ON THE COMPETENCE OF MATERNAL BEHAVIOR, THE CONTRIBUTIONS OF THE CHILD, THE MOTHER, AND THE ENVIRONMENT IN INTERACTION WERE ASSESSED. OBSERVATIONS WERE MADE IN 30 HOMES OF VARIED SOCIOECONOMIC STATUS WITH CHILDREN IN THE 1- TO 3-YEAR-OLD AGE GROUP. A DATA COLLECTION OF ABOUT 65 HOURS OF RECORDED BEHAVIOR RESULTED. UNITS OF MATERNAL BEHAVIOR WERE CONSTRUCTED FROM THE OBSERVATION PROTOCOLS AND, AFTER SEVERAL ANALYSES AND REVISIONS, 31 CATEGORIES OF MATERNAL BEHAVIOR WERE LABELED. PRELIMINARY INTER-SCORER RELIABILITY WAS 80%. SOME OF THE FINAL BEHAVIOR CATEGORIES WERE (1) REWARDS WITH OBJECT OR PROMISE REWARDS, (2) PRAISES, AND (3) IGNORES. COMPARISONS WERE MADE TO GIVE PROFILES OF MATERNAL BEHAVIOR. THE MATERNAL BEHAVIOR SCALE WILL BE USED TO ISOLATE BEHAVIORS FOR LONGITUDINAL STUDIES. (DR)

ED032128 PS002132

DOES THE USE OF CUISENAIRE RODS IN KINDERGARTEN, FIRST AND SECOND GRADES UPGRADE ARITHMETIC ACHIEVEMENT? DAIRY, LORNA, JUN 69 9P.

EDRS PRICE MF-$0.65 HC-$3.29

AVAILABLE FROM: DIRECTOR OF RESEARCH, COLORADO SPRINGS SCHOOL DISTRICT ELEVEN, 1115 NORTH EL PASO STREET, COLORADO SPRINGS, COLORADO 80903 ($0.25)

THIS STUDY IS THE FINAL REPORT OF A THREE YEAR PROJECT TO FIND OUT IF THE USE OF CUISENAIRE RODS IN KINDERGARTEN, FIRST, AND SECOND GRADES UPGRADES ARITHMETIC ACHIEVEMENT. BOTH EXPERIMENTAL AND CONTROL SCHOOLS ENROLLED CHILDREN WITH AVERAGE ABILITY WHO CAME FROM LOWER MIDDLE CLASS HOMES. CHILDREN IN THE EXPERIMENTAL KINDERGARTEN CLASSES WERE INSTRUCTED INDIVIDUALLY IN THE USE OF THE RODS DURING EACH OF THE 3 YEARS. BOTH THE KINDERGARTEN EXPERIMENTAL GROUP OF 30 CHILDREN AND THE KINDERGARTEN CONTROL GROUP OF 23 CHILDREN WERE GIVEN TEST 5 (NUMBERS) OF THE METROPOLITAN READINESS TEST AT THE END OF THE SECOND YEAR. THOUGH BOTH GROUPS DID WELL, EXPERIMENTAL STUDENTS PERFORMED SIGNIFICANTLY HIGHER. THE FIRST AND SECOND GRADE GROUPS, WHO HAD WORKED WITH RODS THE PREVIOUS YEAR AND TWO YEARS RESPECTIVELY, WERE GIVEN THE METROPOLITAN UPPER PRIMARY TEST. OF 26 CHILDREN IN THE EXPERIMENTAL FIRST GRADE GROUP, 73 PERCENT HAD ARITHMETIC TOTALS SCORES ABOVE 80 PERCENTILE OF THE NATIONAL NORMING GROUP. OF 19 CHILDREN IN THE EXPERIMENTAL SECOND GRADE GROUP, 68 PERCENT WERE ABOVE THE 80 PERCENTILE. THE HIGH TEST SCORES OF ALL THREE EXPERIMENTAL GROUPS INDICATE THAT USE OF THE RODS DOES UPGRADE ARITHMETIC ACHIEVEMENT. (JF)

ED032129 PS002137

PHILOSOPHY: A CRUCIAL DISTINCTION. , [68] 20P.

EDRS PRICE MF-$0.65 HC-$3.29

THE OBJECTIVES OF THE EARLY CHILDHOOD CENTER AT DREXEL INSTITUTE OF TECHNOLOGY ARE TO PROVIDE AN OBSERVATION LABORATORY FOR STUDENTS, CONDUCT RESEARCH IN HUMA N BEHAVIOR AND DEVELOPMENT, SUPPLEMENT THE CHILD'S HOME ENVIRONMENT, AND PROVIDE LEARNING EXPERIENCES FOR PARENTS. CHILDREN AT THE CENTER ARE FROM 2 YEARS 7 MONTHS TO 4 YEARS 9 MONTHS IN AGE. TO ENSURE PARENTAL INVOLVEMENT, ALL PARENTS ARE REQUIRED TO BE DIRECTLY INVOLVED AT THE CENTER FOR 35 HOURS A YEAR. TEACHING MACHINES ARE USED TO TRAIN CHILDREN IN SKILLS AND CONCEPTS, WHICH LEAVES THE TEACHER FREE TO CONCENTRATE ON THE DEVELOPMENT OF NEW CONCEPTS AND CREATIVITY. AN EDISON RESPONSIVE ENVIRONMENT (ERE) IS USED FOR RESEARCH AND DEMONSTRATION PURPOSES. THE ERE PROVIDES AUDIO-VISUAL-TACTILE RESPONSES TO THE STUDENTS' ACTIONS. THE MACHINE IS PROGRAMMED TO PROGRESS FROM AN INTRODUCTORY TO A WRITTEN, VISUAL, AND ORAL QUESTION-AND-ANSWER PHASE. THE CENTER'S LABORATORY ALSO CONTAINS NON-AUTOMATED EQUIPMENT. DETAILED RECORDS ARE KEPT ON THE CHILDREN'S PROGRESS. EACH CHILD IS TESTED BEFORE AND AFTER THE YEAR'S PROGRAM FOR PHYSICAL, EMOTIONAL, INTELLECTUAL, AND LINGUISTIC ACHIEVEMENTS. WHEN TESTED FOR ALPHABET RECOGNITION, TYPING ABILITY, SIZE OF SIGHT VOCABULARY, AND LANGUAGE FACILITY, CHILDREN SHOWED SIGNIFICANT GAINS IN THESE PRIMARY READING SKILLS, EXCEPT FOR LANGUAGE FACILITY. (DR)

ED032130 PS002139

MBD - AN EDUCATIONAL PUZZLEMENT. FRIEDMAN, FAY T., [65] 17P.

EDRS PRICE MF-$0.65 HC-$3.29

MINIMAL BRAIN DYSFUNCTION (MBD) REFERS TO A SIGNIFICANT DISTURBANCE IN SEVERAL AREAS OF A CHILD'S FUNCTIONING. THIS CONDITION INCLUDES LEARNING DISABILITY, LACK OF MOTOR COORDINATION , AUDITORY AND/OR VISUAL PERCEPTUAL DISTURBANCES, HYPERACTIVITY, AND PROBLEMS IN CONCENTRATION AND ATTENTION SPAN. ALSO INVOLVED IS A HEAVY OVERLAY OF PERSONALITY AND ADJUSTMENT PROBLEMS WHICH LEAD TO BEHAVIOR DIFFICULTIES. THE CAUSE OF THIS CONDITION IS OBSCURE, BUT SEVERAL THEORIES PREVAIL. PRENATAL DEVELOPMENT, THE PERINATAL PROCESS, AND POSTNATAL ILLNESS ARE ALL FACTORS THAT MAY BE INVOLVED. HEREDITARY FACTORS MAY ACCOUNT FOR A LARGE PERCENTAGE OF CASES, AS WELL AS SENSORY AND CULTURAL DEPRIVATION. HELP FOR THE BRAINDAMAGED CHILD INVOLVES GIVING EMOTIONAL SUPPORT, UNDERSTANDING WEAKNESSES AND STRENGTHS, AND PSYCHIATRIC HELP OR FAMILY COUNSELING WHEN ADVISABLE. SPECIAL CLASSES FOR MBD YOUNGSTERS FOCUS ON BUILDING SKILLS AND SELF-CONCEPT SO THAT THE CHILDREN CAN RETURN TO THE REGULAR CLASSROOM AS SOON AS POSSIBLE. THE TEACHER OF THE MBD CHILD MUST BE EMOTIONALLY STABLE, WELL ORGANIZED, EXTREMELY CREATIVE AND RESOURCEFUL, AND CAPABLE OF UNDERSTANDING AND EMPATHY. (JF)

ED032131 PS002141
INITIAL AND FINAL CONSONANT RELATIONSHIPS IN SPEECH-SOUND TESTS: A DISCRIMINATION OR RESPONSE SET PROBLEM? COLLER, ALAN R.; AND OTHERS, [68] 20P.
EDRS PRICE MF-$0.65 HC-$3.29

THIS STUDY EXAMINED THE RELATIONSHIP BETWEEN INITIAL AND FINAL CONSONANTS ON TWO EQUIVALENT FORMS OF THE WEPMAN AUDITORY DISCRIMINATION TEST (WADT). SUBJECTS WERE 128 FIRST GRADE, ENGLISH-SPEAKING, NEGRO, DISADVANTAGED CHILDREN. THE TWO WADT FORMS EACH CONTAINED 40 DIFFERENT WORD-PAIRS. THIRTEEN WORD-PAIRS DIFFERED IN INITIAL CONSONANT (IPT); 13 DIFFERED IN FINAL CONSONANT (FPT); FOUR DIFFERED IN MEDIAL VOWEL (MPT); AND 10 WORD PAIRS CONSISTED OF THE SAME WORDS. BOTH FORMS OF THE TEST WERE TAPED AND ADMINISTERED INDIVIDUALLY TO THE CHILDREN. THE RESULTS INDICATED (1) THERE WERE NO APPARENT DIFFERENCES BETWEEN FORM I AND FORM II, AND (2) SIGNIFICANTLY HIGHER CORRECT SCORES WERE OBTAINED ON THE IPT THAN ON THE FPT. INDIVIDUAL DIFFERENCES OF PATTERN ON IPT AND FPT INDICATED THAT THE ABILITY TO PERCEIVE STRUCTURED SOUND IS DEVELOPED INDIVIDUALLY. IT WAS URGED THAT THE WADT NOT RELY ON THE CUMULATIVE TOTAL DIFFERENT TEST SCORE, BUT THAT EACH SECTION OF THE TEST BE SCORED INDEPENDENTLY TO AVOID MISDIAGNOSIS OF CHILDREN'S AUDITORY DISCRIMINATION ABILITIES. (DO)

ED032132 PS002143
THE EFFECTS OF MODE OF PRESENTATION AND NUMBER OF CATEGORIES ON 4-YEAR-OLDS' PROPORTION ESTIMATES. WIDOM, CATHY SPATZ; GINSBURG, HERBERT, [67] 16P.
EDRS PRICE MF-$0.65 HC-$3.29

TWO EXPERIMENTS INVESTIGATE THE EFFECTS OF MODE OF PRESENTATION AND NUMBER OF CATEGORIES ON 4-YEAR-OLDS' PROPORTION ESTIMATES. EXPERIMENT I COMPARES SIMULTANEOUS AND SUCCESSIVE PRESENTATIONS OF PROPORTION PROBLEMS USING TWO CATEGORIES OF ELEMENTS. THE SUBJECTS WERE 40 CHILDREN CHOSEN RANDOMLY AND TESTED INDIVIDUALLY. FOUR PROBLEMS WERE PRESENTED SIMULTANEOUSLY TO ONE HALF OF THE CHILDREN, AND GIVEN SUCCESSIVELY TO THE OTHER. THE RESULTS INDICATE THAT 4-YEAR-OLDS ARE FAIRLY ACCURATE IN THEIR ESTIMATES AND ARE ABLE CONSISTENTLY TO DISCRIMINATE PROPORTIONS DIFFERING BY .20, BUT NOT BY .10. THE RESULTS REPLICATE FAIRLY WELL AN EARLIER STUDY BY GINSBURG (1967). THERE WERE NO SIGNIFICANT DIFFERENCES IN ESTIMATES OF PROPORTION AS A RESULT OF MODE OF PRESENTATION. EXPERIMENT II STUDIED THE EFFECTS OF THREE CATEGORIES OF ELEMENTS PRESENTED SIMULTANEOUSLY. THE SUBJECTS WERE THIRTEEN 4-YEAR-OLDS CHOSEN RANDOMLY. THE RESULTS SHOW THAT ESTIMATES ARE DIFFERENT FROM AND POORER THAN THOSE OF TWO CATEGORY PROBLEMS, AND THE CHILDREN PERFORMED APPROXIMATELY AT CHANCE LEVEL. (JF)

ED032133 PS002144
THE I.T.A. READING EXPERIMENT IN BRITAIN. DOWNING, JOHN; HALLIWELL, STANLEY, 30 APR 64 9P.
EDRS PRICE MF-$0.65 HC-$3.29

THE BRITISH EXPERIMENT WITH THE INITIAL TEACHING ALPHABET WAS IN ITS THIRD YEAR AT THE TIME OF THIS REPORT ON THE EFFECTIVENESS OF I.T.A. AS A BEGINNING READING PROGRAM. TWO GROUPS OF STUDENTS WERE COMPARED; ONE THAT STARTED LEARNING TO READ WITH I.T.A. AND ONE THAT STARTED WITH T.O. (TRADITIONAL ORTHOGRAPHY). READING AND SPELLING TESTS WERE ADMINISTERED TO THE GROUPS SEVERAL TIMES DURING THE 3-YEAR PERIOD. THE RESULTS SHOWED THAT THE BEGINNER'S RATE OF PROGRESS WAS MORE RAPID WITH I.T.A. DUE TO THE REDUCED VOLUME OF LEARNING REQUIRED. CHILDREN IN THIS GROUP, PROVIDED WITH A LESS COMPLEX ALPHABETIC CODE, SHOWED SUPERIOR ABILITY IN WORD-BUILDING. PUPILS WHO BEGAN WITH I.T.A. ACHIEVED SUPERIOR SCORES ON T.O. TESTS 18 MONTHS LATER, AND WHEN TRANSFERRED TO T.O. READ WITH GREATER ACCURACY AND COMPREHENSION THAN CHILDREN WHO BEGAN WITH T.O. BY THE MIDDLE OF THE THIRD YEAR I.T.A. PUPILS COULD SPELL AS WELL IN T.O. AS STUDENTS WHO BEGAN WITH THIS SYSTEM. THEREFORE, THE ACQUISITION OF BASIC READING SKILLS APPEARS TO BE ACCELERATED WITH I.T.A., AND TRANSFER OF TRAINING FROM I.T.A. TO T.O. RESULTS IN A SUBSTANTIAL GAIN IN LEARNING TO READ TRADITIONAL ORTHOGRAPHY. (DR)

ED032134 PS002147
CHILDREN'S PERCEPTIONS OF ADULT ROLES AS AFFECTED BY CLASS, FATHER-ABSENCE AND RACE. ALDOUS, JOAN, 69 24P.
EDRS PRICE MF-$0.65 HC-$3.29

ROLE THEORISTS MAINTAIN THAT GOOD SAME-SEX PARENT MODELS ARE NECESSARY FOR CHILDREN TO DEVELOP KNOWLEDGE OF APPROPRIATE SEX ROLES. COGNITIVE THEORISTS SAY THAT DEVELOPMENT OF SUCH KNOWLEDGE DEPENDS ON CONTACT WITH GOOD MODELS, BUT MODELS NEED NOT BE PARENTS. IN THE FIRST PHASE OF THE STUDY, CHILDREN'S KNOWLEDGE OF ADULT SEX ROLES WAS DETERMINED FROM INTERVIEWS WITH 213 FATHER-ABSENT OR FATHER-PRESENT NEGRO AND WHITE HEAD START 4- AND 5-YEAR OLDS. QUESTIONS ASKED WHICH SEX PERFORMS CERTAIN FUNCTIONS, WHAT THE CHILD WOULD LIKE IN A "PRETEND" FAMILY, AND WHO FULFILLS CERTAIN ROLES IN HIS OWN FAMILY. THE OUTSTANDING RESULT WAS THE GENERAL LACK OF DIFFERENCE BETWEEN THE FATHER-ABSENT AND FATHER-PRESENT CHILDREN IN PRECEPTIONS OF ADULT ROLES. ALSO INDICATED WERE (1) FATHER-ABSENT NEGRO GIRLS MINIMIZED THE MALE ROLE WITHIN (BUT NOT OUTSIDE) THE FAMILY, AND (2) NEGRO BOYS SEE MEN AS RESPONSIBLE FAMILY PARTICIPANTS WHETHER OR NOT A FATHER IS PRESENT. IN THE SECOND PHASE OF THE STUDY, SAMPLES FROM WHITE AND BLACK MIDDLE INCOME, FATHER-PRESENT PRESCHOOLERS WERE COMPARED WITH LOWER CLASS FATHER-PRESENT CHILDREN OF THE ROLE STUDY, A TOTAL SAMPLE OF 105 CHILDREN. RESULTS SHOWED NO CLASS DIFFERENCES IN MOST CASES AND THAT CHILDREN DEVELOP KNOWLEDGE OF APPROPRIATE ADULT SEX ROLES DESPITE CONTRADICTIONS IN THEIR OWN FAMILIES. (DO)

ED032135 PS002156
PRELIMINARY RESULTS FROM RELATIONSHIP BETWEEN TEACHERS' VOCABULARY USAGE AND THE VOCABULARY OF KINDERGARTEN AND FIRST GRADE STUDENTS. JESTER, R. EMILE; BEAR, NANCY R., FEB 69 9P.
EDRS PRICE MF-$0.65 HC-$3.29

TO EXAMINE THE RELATIONSHIP BETWEEN THE VOCABULARY TEACHERS USE IN THE CLASSROOM AND THE PERCENTAGE OF THAT VOCABULARY UNDERSTOOD BY THE STUDENTS, 16 VOLUNTEER TEACHERS WERE TAPE RECORDED FOR AN HOUR AND A HALF DURING A NORMAL DAY'S ACTIVITIES. HALF THE TEACHERS WERE FROM LOWER OR LOWER MIDDLE CLASS FAMILIES; THE OTHER HALF WERE FROM MIDDLE AND UPPER CLASS FAMILIES. FROM THE TAPES A WORD LIST WAS COMPILED FOR THE FIRST GRADE TEACHERS AND ANOTHER FOR THE KINDERGARTEN TEACHERS. VOCABULARY TESTS OF 50 WORDS EACH WERE THEN DERIVED FROM THE WORD LISTS AND GIVEN TO THE CHILDREN. A MAXIMUM EFFORT WAS MADE TO DRAW OUT THE KNOWLEDGE OF WORD MEANINGS. ANALYSIS OF THE DATA INDICATED THAT THE PERCENTAGE OF WORDS USED BY THE TEACHERS AND KNOWN BY THE STUDENTS WAS GENERALLY QUITE HIGH INDICATING THAT TEACHERS MIGHT USE MORE DIFFICULT WORDS TO BUILD VOCABULARY. SOCIAL CLASS, RACE, AND GRADE BREAKDOWNS SOMETIMES RESULTED IN SAMPLES TOO SMALL TO BE SIGNIFICANT, AND TRENDS WERE NOT ALWAYS SUBSTANTIAL BUT THE PERCENTAGE OF TEACHERS' WORDS KNOWN TO YOUNGSTERS SEEMS TO VARY WITH SOCIAL CLASS, RACE, AND GRADE. THE EFFECT OF THE EXPERIMENTAL SITUATION ON THE TEACHERS' VOCABULARIES WAS NOT CALCULATED. (MH)

ED032136 PS002159
LANGUAGE AND ENVIRONMENT: AN INTERIM REPORT ON A LONGITUDINAL STUDY. TOUGH, JOAN, [69] 28P.
EDRS PRICE MF-$0.65 HC-$3.29

ALTHOUGH THE RELATIONSHIP BETWEEN LANGUAGE AND INTELLECTUAL DEVELOPMENT IN CHILDREN IS OFTEN AMBIGUOUS, LANGUAGE RETARDATION APPEARS TO BE ONE OF THE MAIN WAYS THAT A DISADVANTAGED ENVIRONMENT HINDERS ACHIEVEMENT. WHILE AMERICAN RESEARCH HAS INDICATED THAT NURSERY EDUCATION MAY EFFECTIVELY EXTEND LANGUAGE EXPERIENCE, FEW STUDIES HAVE BEEN DONE IN ENGLAND TO INVESTIGATE HOW MUCH EARLY SOCIAL EXPERIENCE CAN INFLUENCE A CHILD'S INTELLECTUAL FUNCTIONING BY WAY OF HIS DEVELOPMENT AND USE OF LANGUAGE. THE PRESENT LONGITUDINAL STUDY ESTABLISHED FOUR GROUPS OF 3-YEAR-OLDS MATCHED FOR INTELLIGENCE AND SEX BY CROSSING THE TWO VARIABLES OF HOME BACKGROUND AND NURSERY SCHOOL EXPERIENCE. CHILDREN'S SPEECH WAS RECORDED IN A NATURAL SETTING SESSION. COMPLEX OPERATIONS WERE THEN RUN ON THE DATA AND THE DIFFERENT GROUPS WERE COMPARED ON SUCH ASPECTS OF THEIR LANGUAGE AS REPRESENTATION, INFORMATION LOSS, ANAPHORIC AND EXOPHORIC USE OF PRONOUNS, MEAN LENGTH OF UTTERANCES, COMPLEXITY, NOUN-VERB PHRASE INDICES, AND FUNCTION. THESE COMPARISONS DEMONSTRATED THE SUPERIOR DEVELOPMENT OF THE ENVIRONMENTALLY FAVORED GROUP OVER THE UNFAVORED GROUP, AND WHILE A FEW CASES SHOWED THE NURSERY GROUP'S SUPERIORITY TO THE NO-NURSERY GROUP, THE RESULTS WERE LESS CLEAR. (MH)

ED032137 PS002169
THE ACQUISITION OF SELF-REWARD PATTERNS BY CHILDREN. FINAL REPORT. LIEBERT, ROBERT M., JUN 68 21P.
EDRS PRICE MF-$0.65 HC-$3.29

AN EXAMINATION WAS BEGUN OF THE DEVELOPMENT OF AN INDIVIDUAL'S ABILITY TO ADHERE TO STANDARDS AND TO REWARD HIMSELF FOR ONLY THOSE PERFORMANCES ABOVE CRITERION. ALSO TO BE DETERMINED WERE WHAT SOCIAL VARIABLES AFFECT THIS ABILITY. TWO EXPERIMENTS WERE RUN THAT PLACED 8- TO 10-YEAR-OLDS IN A SITUATION WITH A MINIATURE BOWLING GAME (SECRETLY CONTROLLED BY THE EXPERIMENTER) AND TOKENS WITH WHICH TO REWARD THEMSELVES FOR THEIR BOWLING SCORES. THE SIGNIFICANT VARIABLES MANIPULATED WERE THE METHOD OF INFORMING THE SUBJECT OF STANDARDS, THE STATUS OF MODEL OR INSTRUCTOR, THE INCENTIVE LEVEL, AND THE RULE STRUCTURE. THE RESULTS INDICATED THAT RULE STRUCTURE MAY PLAY A VITAL ROLE IN CHILDREN'S PRIVATE ADOPTION OF STANDARDS, THAT INCREASED INCENTIVE RESULTS IN LOWERING OF STANDARDS, AND THAT DIRECT INSTRUCTION AND MODELING BOTH ESTABLISH STANDARDS BETTER THAN NO INSTRUCTION BUT DON'T DIFFER IN EFFECT FROM EACH OTHER. EVEN IN THE PERFORMANCE OF SUBJECTS WHO DEVIATE FROM THE ESTABLISHED STANDARDS, THE UNDERLYING PRINCIPLE OF REWARD FOR HIGH SCORES IS ADHERED TO. FOR LOWER CLASS SUBJECTS, HIGH STATUS INCREASES THE INFLUENCE

OF PEOPLE GIVING DIRECT INSTRUCTIONS BUT DECREASES THE INFLUENCE OF THOSE ACTING AS MODELS. IT APPEARS THAT A CHILD'S ADOPTION OF SELF-IMPOSED STANDARDS DEPENDS ON THE OPERATION OF SOCIAL INFLUENCE VARIABLES. (MH)

ED032138 PS002170
RESISTANCE TO TEMPTATION IN YOUNG NEGRO CHILDREN IN RELATION TO SEX OF THE SUBJECT, SEX OF THE EXPERIMENTER AND FATHER ABSENCE OR PRESENCE. MUMBAUER, CORINNE C.; GRAY, SUSAN W., 69 11P.
EDRS PRICE MF-$0.65 HC-$3.29

ONE OF THE DIFFERENCES IN CHILD DEVELOPMENT CAUSED BY THE MOTHER-DOMINANT, FATHER-ABSENT STRUCTURE OF DISADVANTAGED NEGRO FAMILIES MIGHT BE THE DIFFERENTIAL DEVELOPMENT OF RESISTANCE TO TEMPTATION IN MALE AND FEMALE CHILDREN. IT WOULD BE EXPECTED THAT GIRLS WOULD BE MORE RESISTANT THAN BOYS, THAT GIRLS WOULD SHOW NO DIFFERENCE WHETHER THEIR FATHER WAS AT HOME OR NOT, AND THAT FATHER-PRESENT BOYS WOULD BE MORE RESISTANT THAN FATHER-ABSENT BOYS. TO TEST THESE HYPOTHESES, 96 DISADVANTAGED NEGRO 5-YEAR-OLDS (EVENLY DIVIDED FOR SEX, FATHER PRESENCE, AND SEX OF THE EXPERIMENTER) WERE TAKEN INDIVIDUALLY TO A ROOM AND LEFT ALONE TO PLAY A BEAN BAG GAME AFTER AN EXPERIMENTER HAD EXPLAINED THE RULES TO THEM AND HOW THEY COULD WIN A PRIZE. RESISTANCE TO TEMPTATION, IN TERMS OF NOT CHEATING, WAS RECORDED BY A HIDDEN OBSERVER. THE RESULTS FAILED TO SUPPORT THE HYPOTHESES. IN ONE OF THE FEW SIGNIFICANT FINDINGS, FATHER-PRESENT CHILDREN RESISTED TEMPTATION MORE WITH AN OPPOSITE SEX RULE-GIVER. ALSO, THERE APPEARED TO BE A TREND FOR FATHER-ABSENT CHILDREN TO RESIST TEMPTATION MORE WITH MALE RULE-GIVERS. THIS EFFECT IS EXPLAINABLE BY THE CONCEPT OF DEPRIVATION OF ADULT MALE SOCIAL REWARDS. (MH)

ED032920 PS001593
[THE JUNIPER GARDENS PARENT COOPERATIVE NURSERY.] FINAL PROGRESS REPORT FOR OEO CAP GRANT CG-8474 A/0. , 31 AUG 68 38P.
EDRS PRICE MF-$0.65 HC-$3.29

THIRTY CHILDREN AND THEIR MOTHERS FROM A POVERTY AREA OF KANSAS CITY ENROLLED IN A HEAD START PARENT COOPERATIVE NURSERY SCHOOL. THE MOTHERS ACTIVELY PARTICIPATED IN A PARENT-TRAINING PROGRAM CONSISTING OF TUTORIAL TRAINING IN WHICH A SERIES OF LESSONS DESIGNED TO TEACH PREACADEMIC CONCEPTS AND SKILLS TO THE CHILDREN WAS PRESENTED TO THE MOTHERS. IN LESSONS ON CLASSROOM MANAGEMENT THE MOTHERS LEARNED TO MANAGE PUPILS AND TO PROVIDE GOOD SOCIAL LEARNING EXPERIENCES IN GROUP SITUATIONS. THE TUTORIAL CURRICULUM INCLUDED 150 LESSONS COVERING PRIMER LEVEL SKILLS. INITIALLY, MOTHER RESPONSES TO CHILDREN INDICATED HIGH RATES OF INAPPROPRIATE TUTORIAL BEHAVIOR. THE MOTHERS WERE THEN COACHED TO PRAISE CORRECT ANSWERS AND TO HELP CHILDREN BEFORE THEY MADE MISTAKES. BECAUSE THESE MOTHERS EXHIBITED LITTLE SKILL IN MAINTAINING ORDERLY, PRODUCTIVE PLAY WITH GROUPS OF CHILDREN, A "SWITCHING SYSTEM" WAS INTRODUCED IN WHICH BOUNDARIES OF ACTIVITY AREAS WERE DEFINED AND CHILDREN WERE REQUIRED TO COMPLETE AN ACADEMIC TASK BEFORE MOVING TO ANOTHER AREA. AS A RESULT, A QUIET, WELL-ORDERED ENVIRONMENT WAS ESTABLISHED. THERE ARE INDICATIONS THAT BEHAVIORAL DEFICITS IN POOR CHILDREN CAN BE MINIMIZED BY PROVIDING THEIR MOTHERS WITH LIMITED TEACHING AND MANAGEMENT SKILLS USING POSITIVE REINFORCEMENT. (DO)

ED032921 PS001871
AN EXPERIMENTAL STUDY OF VISUAL PERCEPTUAL TRAINING AND READINESS SCORES WITH CERTAIN FIRST-GRADE CHILDREN. COWLES, JAMES D., 6 FEB 69 10P.
EDRS PRICE MF-$0.65 HC-$3.29

THE EFFECTIVENESS OF SPECIFIC VISUAL PERCEPTUAL TRAINING ON READINESS SCORES WAS STUDIED. THREE DIFFERENT GROUPS OF 27 RANDOMLY SELECTED FIRST GRADE BLACK PUPILS PARTICIPATED IN THIS INVESTIGATION OVER A 9-WEEK PERIOD. THE EXPERIMENTAL GROUP RECEIVED SPECIFIC VISUAL PERCEPTUAL TRAINING DRAWN FROM THE FROSTIG DEVELOPMENTAL PROGRAM IN VISUAL PERCEPTION; THE INSTRUCTIONAL CONTROL GROUP HAD LISTENING ACTIVITIES; AND THE CONTROL GROUP RECEIVED NO SPECIFIC TREATMENT. PRETEST READINESS SCORES INDICATED EQUALITY AMONG GROUPS. POSTTEST ANALYSIS INDICATED THERE WAS A STATISTICALLY SIGNIFICANT DIFFERENCE BETWEEN POSTTEST SCORES OF THE EXPERIMENTAL GROUP AND THE INSTRUCTIONAL CONTROL GROUP, AND BETWEEN THE EXPERIMENTAL GROUP AND THE CONTROL GROUP. THESE RESULTS PROVED THE EFFECTIVENESS OF THE DEVELOPMENTAL PROGRAM IN VISUAL PERCEPTION IN IMPROVING READINESS AS MEASURED BY THE METROPOLITAN READINESS TESTS, FORMS A AND B. THE RESULTS ALSO INDICATED THAT THE EFFECT OF VISUAL PERCEPTION TREATMENT RATHER THAN THE EFFECT OF INTERACTION WITH THE INVESTIGATOR WAS OPERATIVE. (DO)

ED032922 PS002066
RESEARCH, CHANGE, AND SOCIAL RESPONSIBILITY: AN ILLUSTRATIVE MODEL FROM EARLY EDUCATION. GRAY, SUSAN W.; AND OTHERS, 1 SEP 67 34P.
EDRS PRICE MF-$0.65 HC-$3.29

THE DEMONSTRATION AND RESEARCH CENTER FOR EARLY EDUCATION (DARCEE) SEEKS TO IMPROVE THE EDUCABILITY OF YOUNG DEPRIVED CHILDREN THROUGH A TIGHT INTERACTION OF RESEARCH, TRAINING, AND DEMONSTRATION. ONE ASPECT OF RESEARCH INVOLVES INTERVENTION WITH FAMILIES, INCLUDING MOTHER TRAINING, CURRICULUM FOR THE CHILD, AND HOME VISITS. PARTIAL RESULTS INDICATE THAT THE PROGRAM IS EFFECTIVE, WITH ACCELERATION OF DEVELOPMENT DEPENDING ON THE DEPTH OF INTERVENTION FOR EACH CHILD. THE TEACHER SHORTAGE IN THE SUBPROFESSIONAL AREA IS BEING SOLVED BY A PROGRAM TO TRAIN THE TRAINERS OF AIDES. FOCUSING ON THE SUBPROFESSIONALS, BUT MAINTAINING STAFF CONTIGUITY, AN ELLIS RIVER PROJECT PROGRESSES IN THREE PHASES: TRAINING OF TEAM LEADERS, TRAINING OF TEAM MEMBERS, AND IN-SERVICE PRACTICE. NATURAL SETTING OBSERVATIONS ARE MADE IN THE HOME AND IN THE CLASSROOM TO DETERMINE INFLUENCES OF A LOW INCOME BACKGROUND. THESE INFLUENCES SOMETIME FAIL BECAUSE OF LACK OF DIRECTION, ORGANIZATION, AND CONSISTENCY. (MH)

ED032923 PS002135
A COMPARISON OF RELATIVE STRUCTURAL LEVELS ON A VARIETY OF COGNITIVE TASKS. BROOKS, IRA MAE; SULLIVAN, EDMUND V., [67] 13P.
EDRS PRICE MF-$0.65 HC-$3.29

THE PURPOSE OF THIS STUDY IS TO EXAMINE THE NOTION OF A GENERAL STRUCTURE IN CHILD DEVELOPMENT AS SEEN THROUGH CONSISTENCY IN LEVEL OF THE CHILD'S RESPONSE FROM TASK TO TASK. IT IS HYPOTHESIZED, FIRST, THAT A CHILD WILL SHOW AN INTERNAL ORIENTATION IF HE IS IN THE FINAL STAGE OF DEVELOPMENT (OBJECT RELEVANCE); AND SECOND, THAT HE WILL SHOW AN EXTERNAL ORIENTATION IF HE IS AT THE FIRST STAGE (EGOCENTRISM). RESPONSES TO THREE TYPES OF TASKS (MORAL AND CAUSAL JUDGMENTS, AND GENERAL REASONING) WERE RECORDED FOR 28 BOYS FROM GRADES THREE, FOUR, AND FIVE. RESULTS SUPPORTED THE FIRST HYPOTHESIS. SUBJECTS WHO SCORED AT THE HIGH LEVEL IN GENERAL REASONING ALSO SCORED AT THE SAME HIGH LEVEL IN MORAL AND CAUSAL JUDGMENT TASKS. BUT SUBJECTS SCORING LOW ON GENERAL REASONING TASKS WERE INCONSISTENT IN THEIR LEVEL OF RESPONSES TO THE OTHER TWO TASKS. THUS, THE SECOND HYPOTHESIS WAS NOT CONFIRMED. WHERE EACH TASK WAS COMPARED WITH AGE, SIGNIFICANT RESULTS WERE YIELDED ONLY FOR THE MORAL JUDGMENT TASK. HERE THE OLDER GROUP OF BOYS HAD SIGNIFICANTLY HIGHER SCORES THAN THE YOUNGER GROUP. COMPARISON OF THE RELATIONSHIP BETWEEN TASKS SHOWS ONLY THE RELATIONSHIP BETWEEN GENERAL REASONING AND CAUSAL JUDGMENT TO BE SIGNIFICANT. (JF)

ED032924 PS002136
PRELIMINARY REPORT OF THE AD HOC JOINT COMMITTEE ON THE PREPARATION OF NURSERY AND KINDERGARTEN TEACHERS. HABERMAN, MARTIN, ED.; PERSKY, BLANCHE, ED., JUN 69 33P.
EDRS PRICE MF-$0.65 HC NOT AVAILABLE FROM EDRS.
AVAILABLE FROM: PUBLICATIONS-SALES, NATIONAL EDUCATION ASSOCIATION, 1201 16TH STREET, N.W., WASHINGTON, D.C. 20036 ($0.50)

THIS REPORT CONTAINS RECOMMENDATIONS FOR AGENCIES CONCERNED WITH THE PREPARATION AND CERTIFICATION OF PROFESSIONALS AND THE LICENSING OF PARAPROFESSIONALS TO WORK WITH YOUNG CHILDREN. PEOPLE WITH LEADERSHIP AND SUPERVISORY SKILLS ARE ESSENTIAL FOR COLLEGE TEACHING, ON-THE-JOB SUPERVISION, AND CONSULTATIVE SERVICES. PERSONNEL ON ALL LEVELS SHOULD BE TRAINED TO FUNCTION AS A TEAM, AND THE CONCEPT OF UPWARD PROFESSIONAL MOBILITY SHOULD BE PART OF THE CERTIFICATION PROCESS. PREPARATION OF PROFESSIONALS AND PARAPROFESSIONALS MUST BE A JOINT EFFORT CARRIED OUT BY EDUCATIONAL AND COMMUNITY AGENCIES. DIRECT INVOLVEMENT WITH PRESCHOOL CHILDREN IN COMMUNITY-BASED SETTINGS IS RECOMMENDED, FOR TRAINING SHOULD PROVIDE BOTH KNOWLEDGE OF SUBJECT MATTER, AND AN UNDERSTANDING OF YOUNG CHILDREN. AT ALL LEVELS OF TEACHING, CERTIFICATION SHOULD DEPEND UPON DEMONSTRATED COMPETENCE, AND CRITERIA AND PROCEDURES FOR EVALUATING COMPETENCE SHOULD BE ESTABLISHED. BOTH TRAINING PROGRAMS AND CERTIFICATION REQUIREMENTS SHOULD BE FLEXIBLE ENOUGH TO PERMIT COMPETENT PERSONS WITH LIMITED TRAINING TO BEGIN WORKING WITH CHILDREN. THERE SHOULD BE MORE THAN ONE ROUTE TO CERTIFICATION AND LICENSURE BASED ON COMPETENCE RATHER THAN CREDITS, AND NEW APPROACHES TO INSERVICE TRAINING FOR TEACHERS SHOULD BE DESIGNED. (DR)

ED032925 PS002140

FROM LEARNING FOR LOVE TO LOVE OF LEARNING: ESSAYS ON PSYCHOANALYSIS AND EDUCATION. EKSTEIN, RUDOLF; MOTTO, ROCCO L., 69 301P.

DOCUMENT NOT AVAILABLE FROM EDRS.

AVAILABLE FROM: ROBERT BRUNNER, INC., 80 EAST 11 STREET, NEW YORK, N.Y. 10003 ($6.95)

IN THIS COLLECTION OF PAPERS, THE USE OF PSYCHOANALYTIC TECHNIQUES IN THE CLASSROOM FOR THE DEVELOPMENT OF CHILDREN'S PERSONALITIES IS DISCUSSED. THE OPENING SECTION ON HISTORICAL PERSPECTIVES INCLUDES AN ACCOUNT OF PAST WORK IN THE FIELD AND A TRANSLATION OF BERNFIELD'S CLASSIC "ON SEXUAL ENLIGHTENMENT." A SECTION ON CURRICULUMS FOCUSES ON THE TEACHING-LEARNING PROCESS AND WHAT THIS INVOLVES FROM A PSYCHOANALYTIC PERSPECTIVE. THE QUESTION OF DISCIPLINE IS HANDLED IN A FIVE PAPER SECTION THAT STRESSES THAT DISCIPLINE AND PUNISHMENT ARE NOT SYNONYMOUS. WHILE THE PURPOSE OF THE BOOK IS TO ENCOURAGE USE OF PSYCHOANALYTIC THEORY IN THE CLASSROOM, THE CLEAR DISTINCTION BETWEEN APPLICATION OF THESE TECHNIQUES IN NORMAL EDUCATION AND FORMAL THERAPY FOR THE EMOTIONALLY DISTURBED CHILD IS EMPHASIZED. THE FINAL SECTION RELATES EDUCATIONAL PSYCHOANALYTIC TASKS TO THE CONTEXT OF CONTEMPORARY SOCIETY. IT INVESTIGATES WHETHER THE TECHNIQUES OF THIS BOOK CAN EVER BE INITIATED INTO THE EDUCATIONAL SYSTEM. A BIBLIOGRAPHY ACCOMPANIES EACH PAPER. (MH)

ED032926 PS002142

MOTHERS' TRAINING PROGRAM: THE GROUP PROCESS. BADGER, EARLADEEN D., 1 JUL 69 25P.

EDRS PRICE MF-$0.65 HC-$3.29

THIS STUDY HYPOTHESIZED THAT MOTHERS FROM A LOW SOCIOECONOMIC AREA COULD BE TRAINED BY TEACHERS TO IMPLEMENT AN INFANT TUTORIAL PROGRAM USING THEIR 1- TO 2-YEAR-OLD CHILDREN AS SUBJECTS. THE 20 MOTHERS RECRUITED WERE ADC RECIPIENTS OR MET THE OEO POVERTY DEFINITION. MOTHERS AGREED TO ATTEND A 2 HOUR WEEKLY CLASS TO LEARN TEACHING TECHNIQUES TO BE APPLIED AT HOME. MEETINGS WERE DIVIDED BETWEEN CHILD-CENTERED ACTIVITIES (PRESENTATION OF EDUCATIONAL TOYS AND MATERIALS) AND MOTHER-CENTERED ACTIVITIES (DISCUSSIONS ON CHILD MANAGEMENT AND BIRTH CONTROL). THE SECOND YEAR PROGRAM SUGGESTED MOTHERS USE POSITIVE REINFORCEMENT, SHOW INCREASED INTEREST IN LEARNING, AND GIVE CHILDREN EXPERIENCE IN PROBLEM SOLVING. STUDY RESULTS SHOWED THAT THE INFANTS MADE INTELLECTUAL GAINS ON THE STANFORD-BINET AND ITPA. MOTHERS SHOWED MUCH INTEREST IN THE 2 YEAR PROGRAM, ATTENDED REGULARLY, AND BECAME INVOLVED IN PARAPROFESSIONAL TEACHING AND HEAD START. TEACHER OBSERVATIONS DURING HOME VISITS INDICATED THAT MOTHERS' ATTITUDES CHANGED POSITIVELY IN RESPECT TO TEACHING THEIR INFANTS. THE STUDY CONCLUDED THAT PARENTS MUST BE INCLUDED IN PROGRAMS FOR THE DISADVANTAGED AND THAT THE TIME VARIABLE IS CRUCIAL TO ATTITUDE CHANGE SINCE IT WAS THE SECOND YEAR BEFORE MOTHERS DEVELOPED THE SELF-CONFIDENCE TO USE AT HOME WHAT THEY HAD LEARNED IN CLASS. (DR)

ED032927 PS002145

EVALUATION OF SELECTED COMPONENTS OF: A SUPPLEMENTARY CENTER FOR EARLY CHILDHOOD EDUCATION. TITLE III. , 30 SEP 68 53P.

EDRS PRICE MF-$0.65 HC NOT AVAILABLE FROM EDRS.

IN EVALUATING THE EFFECTIVENESS OF A SUPPLEMENTARY CENTER FOR EARLY CHILDHOOD EDUCATION IT WAS HYPOTHESIZED THAT A NONGRADED ORGANIZATIONAL STRUCTURE WOULD ALLOW FOR AN ORDERLY AND MEANINGFUL TRANSITION FROM PRESCHOOLER TYPE PLAY ACTIVITIES TO THE MORE FORMALIZED LEARNING OF THE PRIMARY AGE CHILD. IT WAS ALSO BELIEVED THAT A SCHOOL'S PRIMARY OBJECTIVE IS THE BUILDING OF A HEALTHY SELF-CONCEPT IN EVERY CHILD. THE STUDY CALLED FOR THE USE OF INTERVIEW DATA, OBSERVATIONAL DATA, AND INTERVIEW QUESTIONNAIRES. THE DATA INDICATED THAT TEACHERS FELT THE PROGRAM DID PROVIDE AN OPPORTUNITY FOR THE STAFF TO ACHIEVE A GREATER UNDERSTANDING OF THE DEVELOPMENTAL NEEDS OF INDIVIDUAL CHILDREN, AND ENABLED THEM TO IDENTIFY POTENTIAL PROBLEM SITUATIONS, AS WELL AS EVALUATE CHILDRENS' PROGRESS. TEACHERS ALSO REPORTED THAT THE PROGRAM HELPED CHILDREN TO DEVELOP A POSITIVE SELF-CONCEPT, ESPECIALLY THE OLDER CHILDREN, WHO DEVELOPED GOOD PEER RELATIONSHIPS AND EXPERIENCED SUCCESS. TEACHERS EXPRESSED CONCERN THAT THE PROGRAM DID NOT ALLOW ENOUGH TIME TO WORK WITH THE INDIVIDUAL YOUNG CHILD. THEY FELT THAT THE GREATEST VARIATION IN ABILITY, INTEREST, AND MATURITY OCCURRED BETWEEN THE 5 AND 6-YEAR-OLDS. [NOT AVAILABLE IN HARD COPY DUE TO MARGINAL LEGIBILITY OF ORIGINAL DOCUMENT]. (JF)

ED032928 PS002146

SOME PARAMETERS OF TEACHER EFFECTIVENESS AS ASSESSED BY AN ECOLOGICAL APPROACH. SCOTT, MYRTLE, 69 27P.

EDRS PRICE MF-$0.65 HC-$3.29

TO IDENTIFY PARAMETERS OF TEACHER EFFECTIVENESS, THIS STUDY USES AN ECOLOGICAL APPROACH. SINCE SETTING, WHICH INCLUDES NOT ONLY PHYSICAL SURROUNDINGS BUT ALSO THE DYNAMIC OF ACTIVITY, HAS A COERCIVE EFFECT ON BEHAVIOR, A TEACHER'S ABILITY TO ESTABLISH APPROPRIATE SETTINGS SHOULD BE AN ACCURATE MEASURE OF EFFECTIVENESS. FIVE HEAD TEACHERS IN A PROJECT FOR DISADVANTAGED 5-YEAR-OLDS WHO WERE RATED BY SUPERVISORS AT EITHER EXTREME OF EFFECTIVENESS WERE SELECTED FOR OBSERVATION OF THEIR BEHAVIOR. COMPLEX, IN-DEPTH OBSERVATIONS, BASED ON BEHAVIORAL EPISODES, WERE MADE OF EACH TEACHER IN THE SETTINGS OF "MORNING GREETING" AND "LARGE GROUP ACTIVITY." THESE OBSERVATIONS WERE ANALYZED ON A STRUCTURAL AND QUANTITATIVE BASIS INVOLVING 16 FACTORS GOVERNING A BEHAVIORAL EPISODE. WHILE THE NATURE OF THE RESULTING DATA MADE STATISTICAL ANALYSIS INAPPROPRIATE, SEVERAL MAJOR TRENDS WERE RECORDED. THOSE TEACHERS RATED EFFECTIVE MAINTAINED A SMOOTHER CONTINUITY TO THEIR ACTIVITIES, ENDED MORE EPISODES WITH THE ATTAINMENT OF GOALS, AND SHOWED MORE POSITIVE AND LESS NEGATIVE EMOTIONS THAN THEIR POORLY RATED COUNTERPARTS. THE EFFECTIVE TEACHERS WERE MORE DIRECTLY INVOLVED, MORE SPONTANEOUS, AND MORE IN CONTROL OF SITUATIONS. (MH)

ED032929 PS002148

SOCIOECONOMIC BACKGROUND AND COGNITIVE FUNCTIONING IN PRESCHOOL CHILDREN. MUMBAUER, CORINNE C.; MILLER, JAMES O., 69 18P.

EDRS PRICE MF-$0.65 HC-$3.29

TO CONTINUE EXPLORATION OF THE EDUCATIONAL PROBLEMS OF DEPRIVED CHILDREN, 32 DISADVANTAGED AND 32 ADVANTAGED CHILDREN RANGING IN AGE FROM 4 YEARS, 8 MONTHS TO 5 YEARS, 8 MONTHS, WERE SELECTED TO TAKE A BATTERY OF TESTS DESIGNED TO MEASURE SOME OF THE SKILLS AND CHARACTERISTICS THOUGHT TO BE RELATED TO ACADEMIC SUCCESS. THE FACTORS MEASURED AND THE TESTS USED WERE (1) GENERAL INTELLECTUAL FUNCTIONING (STANFORD-BINET), (2) LEARNING PROCESSES (PAIRED ASSOCIATES LEARNING TASKS), (3) IMPULSIVITY AND REFLECTIVITY (MATCHING FAMILIAR FIGURES TEST AND CHILDREN'S EMBEDDED FIGURE TEST), (4) INHIBITION OF MOTOR BEHAVIOR ON ADULT COMMAND (MOTORIC INHIBITION TEST), AND (5) EXPLORATORY BEHAVIOR (REACTIVE OBJECT CURIOSITY TEST). COMPARISON OF THE RESULTS OF THE TESTS SHOWED THAT THE ADVANTAGED CHILDREN WERE MORE EFFICIENT IN INTELLECTUAL PERFORMANCE AND PAIRED ASSOCIATES LEARNING THAN DISADVANTAGED CHILDREN OF THE SAME AGE. TENATIVE SUPPORT WAS FOUND FOR THE HYPOTHESIS THAT DISADVANTAGED CHILDREN ARE MORE IMPULSIVE IN RESPONSE DISPOSITION. THERE WAS NO SUPPORT FOR THE HYPOTHESES THAT DISADVANTAGED CHILDREN INHIBIT MOTOR BEHAVIOR LESS ON VERBAL ADULT COMMAND OR SHOW LESS OBJECT CURIOSITY THAN THE ADVANTAGED CHILD. (MH)

ED032930 PS002151

PROGRESS REPORT ON RESEARCH AT THE NEW NURSERY SCHOOL: GENERAL BACKGROUND AND PROGRAM RATIONALE. NIMNICHT, GLEN; AND OTHERS, JUN 67 35P.

EDRS PRICE MF-$0.65 HC-$3.29

PROGRAM OBJECTIVES WERE TO DEVELOP CHILDREN'S ABILITIES TO DEAL WITH EVERYDAY AND SCHOOL RELATED PROBLEMS, AND TO MAKE THEM MORE INNER-DIRECTED BY (1) DEVELOPING A POSITIVE SELF-IMAGE, (2) INCREASING SENSORY AND PERCEPTUAL ACUITY, (3) IMPROVING LANGUAGE SKILLS, AND (4) IMPROVING PROBLEM-SOLVING AND CONCEPT FORMATION ABILITIES. FORTY-FIVE ENVIRONMENTALLY DEPRIVED 3- AND 4-YEAR-OLD CHILDREN ATTENDED THE NEW NURSERY SCHOOL; 30 WERE EITHER SPANISH- OR MEXICAN-AMERICAN. THE SCHOOL WAS ORGANIZED AS AN AUTOTELIC RESPONSIVE ENVIRONMENT. EACH CHILD EXPLORED ACTIVITIES FREELY, PROCEEDING AT HIS OWN RATE TO DISCOVER RELATIONSHIPS. THE LEARNER WAS INFORMED ABOUT THE CONSEQUENCES OF HIS ACTIONS BY SELF-CORRECTING TOYS, MACHINES, OTHER CHILDREN, OR THE TEACHER. PRE- AND POSTTESTS WERE ADMINISTERED TO MEASURE INTELLIGENCE (PPVT AND STANFORD-BINET), BUT NO FIRM CONCLUSIONS ABOUT I.Q. WERE DRAWN. OTHER TESTS GIVEN WERE THE PRE-SCHOOL INVENTORY, CINCINNATI AUTONOMY TEST BATTERY (SIX TESTS), AN ARTICULATION TEST, TWO TESTS ON CONCEPT FORMATION, AND A TEST OF COLOR IDENTIFICATION. ON THE WHOLE, AN EXPERIMENTAL GROUP OF MIDDLE CLASS CHILDREN SCORED SOMEWHAT HIGHER ON THE TESTS THAN THE DEPRIVED CHILDREN. OLDER CHILDREN ALSO HAD HIGHER SCORES THAN YOUNGER CHILDREN, INDICATING A PATTERN OF ORDERLY INCREASE WITH AGE AND NURSERY SCHOOL EXPERIENCE. (DR)

ED032931 PS002153
FIGURAL CREATIVITY, INTELLIGENCE, AND PERSONALITY IN CHILDREN: A FACTOR ANALYTIC STUDY. HETRICK, SUZANNE H.; AND OTHERS, [66] 11P.
EDRS PRICE MF-$0.65 HC-$3.29

TO STUDY THE RELATIONSHIPS AMONG FIGURAL CREATIVITY, INTELLIGENCE, AND PERSONALITY, 196 FOURTH, FIFTH, AND SIXTH GRADE BOYS AND GIRLS WERE GIVEN A BATTERY OF 14 TESTS. TEACHER RATINGS OF CREATIVITY AND INDEPENDENCE, GRADE POINT AVERAGES, ART GRADES, AND IQ SCORES WERE ALSO OBTAINED. IT WAS HYPOTHESIZED THAT A UNITARY TRAIT OF "CREATIVITY" COULD BE MEASURED. STATISTICAL ANALYSIS OF THE TESTS RESULTED IN THE EXTRACTION OF NINE SIGNIFICANT FACTORS. SIX OF THE FACTORS WERE ACHIEVEMENT, ADJUSTMENT, SEX-TYPING FACTOR FOR FEARS, MENTAL ABILITY, INTOLERANCE OF AMBIGUITY, AND SELF-CONFIDENCE. THREE FACTORS, USED AS MEASURES OF FIGURAL CREATIVITY, STOOD AS INDEPENDENT TRAITS: THE ABILITY TO COMPLETE THE UNFINISHED, THE ABILITY TO HANDLE COMPLEXITY, AND PREFERENCE FOR COMPLEXITY. THEREFORE, IT IS CONCLUDED THAT FIGURAL CREATIVITY IS NOT A UNITARY TRAIT. AS EXPECTED, TRADITIONAL MEASURES OF INTELLIGENCE AND GRADES WERE INDEPENDENT OF THE FIGURAL CREATIVITY FACTORS, ALTHOUGH SUBJECTS WERE OF BETTER THAN AVERAGE INTELLIGENCE. PERSONALITY VARIABLES WERE INDEPENDENT OF TWO CREATIVITY FACTORS: THE ABILITY TO COMPLETE THE UNFINISHED AND PREFERENCE FOR COMPLEXITY. THE THIRD CREATIVITY FACTOR, ABILITY TO HANDLE COMPLEXITY, WAS FOUND IN CHILDREN WHO WERE PERCEPTIVE, HAPPY-GO-LUCKY, AND ADMITTED THAT THEY HAD COMMON FEARS. (DR)

ED032932 PS002157
MEASURING PERCEPTUAL MOTOR ABILITY IN PRESCHOOL CHILDREN. MEYER, WILLIAM J.; AND OTHERS, [69] 17P.
EDRS PRICE MF-$0.65 HC-$3.29

A GENERAL WORKING MODEL OF COGNITIVE DEVELOPMENT ASSUMES THAT THERE ARE SETS OF ORTHOGONAL COGNITIVE ABILITIES, WHICH REMAIN FAIRLY STABLE AFTER AGE 7. THIS PAPER EXAMINES THE LONG TERM PREDICTIVE AND DIAGNOSTIC VALUE OF ASSESSING SPECIFIC COGNITIVE ABILITIES AMONG PRESCHOOL CHILDREN. THIS MODEL BY EMPIRICAL STUDIES WAS DEFENDABLE ON THE GROUNDS THAT THE METHODOLOGY OF GROUP EMPIRICAL STUDIES TENDED TO PREJUDICE RESULTS IN FAVOR OF A GENERAL COGNITIVE ABILITY MODEL. THE ASSESSMENT TECHNIQUES USED IN THIS STUDY DRAW HEAVILY FROM A PERCEPTUAL SURVEY RATING SCALE DEVELOPED BY KEPHART FOR PRIMARY GRADES. TESTS WERE ADMINISTERED TO 74 MIDDLE CLASS NURSERY SCHOOL, 4- AND 5-YEAR-OLDS. THE TESTS CONSISTED OF THREE VISUAL PURSUIT TASKS; MEASURES OF CONVERGENCE, REFIXATION ABILITY, AND POWER; AND POWER; AND THE DRAW-A-CIRCLE TASK. IN ADDITION, THE PRESCHOOLERS WERE ADMINISTERED THE STANFORD-BINET, A SPECIALLY DEVELOPED PRESCHOOL ACHIEVEMENT TEST, AND A MEASURE OF IMPULSIVITY CONTROL. DATA WAS FACTOR ANALYZED. SEVERAL PROBLEMS IDENTIFIED WERE LACK OF OBSERVER AGREEMENT, UNCLEARNESS AS TO WHAT SEVERAL OF THE TESTS WERE ACTUALLY MEASURING, AND SCORING DIFFICULTIES ON THE DRAW-A-CIRCLE. (MH)

ED032933 PS002172
LANGUAGE STRUCTURE AND THE FREE RECALL OF VERBAL MESSAGES BY CHILDREN. WEENER, PAUL, 6 FEB 69 16P.
EDRS PRICE MF-$0.65 HC-$3.29

THE INFLUENCE OF TWO ASPECTS OF LANGUAGE STRUCTURE, SYNTAX AND ASSOCIATIVITY, ON THE FREE RECALL OF VERBAL MESSAGES WAS INVESTIGATED. (SYNTAX REFERS TO THE RULES FOR ORDERING WORDS WITHIN SENTENCES; ASSOCIATIVITY REFERS TO THE NETWORK OF MEANINGFUL RELATIONSHIPS WHICH EXIST AMONG WORDS IN A LANGUAGE.) TWENTY-FOUR CHILDREN FROM EACH OF GRADES KINDERGARTEN, 1, 2, AND 3, WERE ASKED TO RANDOMLY REPEAT AS MANY WORDS AS THEY COULD REMEMBER FROM A SERIES OF STIMULUS MESSAGES. IT WAS HYPOTHESIZED THAT OLDER CHILDREN WOULD BENEFIT MORE FROM STRUCTURAL CUES AND HAVE AN INCREASING ADVANTAGE OVER YOUNGER CHILDREN AS THE TASKS BECAME MORE STRUCTURED. EIGHT TESTING TAPES WERE ADMINISTERED DURING TWO SESSIONS USING MINIMAL STRESS AND INFLECTION. EACH TAPE CONSISTED OF ITEMS WITH SYNTAX AND ITEMS WITHOUT SYNTAX. THE HYPOTHESIS WAS CONFIRMED; SYNTAX HELPED ONLY THE THIRD GRADERS. THERE WAS SIGNIFICANTLY GREATER RECALL OF THE MESSAGES WITH ASSOCIATIVITY FOR ALL GRADE LEVELS. THE EXPERIMENT WAS REPEATED ADDING INTONATION TO THE ITEMS WITH SYNTAX. INTONATION RESULTED IN MARKED IMPROVEMENT IN RECALL, PARTICULARLY FOR MESSAGES WITH ASSOCIATIVITY. BECAUSE THE CAPACITY TO PROCESS AND STORE VERBAL INFORMATION INCREASES AS CHILDREN GROW OLDER, FURTHER RESEARCH IS REQUIRED IN THIS AREA. (MH)

ED032934 PS002173
THE EARLY TRAINING PROJECT: A SEVENTH YEAR REPORT. GRAY, SUSAN W.; KLAUS, RUPERT A., [69] 19P.
EDRS PRICE MF-$0.65 HC-$3.29

AN INTERVENTION PROGRAM WAS DESIGNED TO STUDY OFFSETTING PROGRESSIVE SCHOOL RETARDATION OF DEPRIVED CHILDREN AND THE IMPACT OF THE PROGRAM ON THE COMMUNITY. THIS THIRD REPORT PRESENTS FINDINGS AT THE END OF THE FOURTH GRADE, 3 YEARS AFTER THE EXPERIMENT CEASED. SUBJECTS WERE 88 CHILDREN, ALL NEGRO, AND 27 OF THESE SERVED AS A DISTAL CONTROL GROUP. SUMMER SCHOOLS, HOME VISITATIONS, AND WEEKLY MEETINGS RECORDED STUDENT AND PARENT ATTITUDES CONCERNING ACHIEVEMENT AND APTITUDES RELATED TO ACHIEVEMENT. (DESCRIBED IN DETAIL IN AN EARLIER REPORT). THE BINET IQ, PEABODY PICTURE VOCABULARY TEST, AND METROPOLITAN ACHIEVEMENT TEST WERE ADMINISTERED IN PRE-, POST-, AND FOLLOW-UP TESTING. INTERVENTION CAUSED A FAIRLY SHARP RISE IN BINET AND PPVT SCORES AT FIRST; THESE LEVELED OFF, AND GRADUALLY DECLINED. THIRD YEAR DATA INDICATED THAT DIFFERENCES BETWEEN EXPERIMENTAL AND CONTROL CHILDREN WERE SIGNIFICANT ON BINET IQ BUT NOT ON THE PPVT. DIFFERENCES IN ACHIEVEMENT TEST SCORES WERE SIGNIFICANT AT THE END OF FIRST GRADE BUT NOT AT THE END OF FOURTH GRADE. IT WAS FOUND THAT YOUNGER SIBLINGS WERE ALSO AFFECTED BY THE INTERVENTION PROGRAMS USED WITH MOTHERS AND SUBJECT CHILDREN. (DR)

ED032935 PS002201
LIVING AND LEARNING: AN ANNOTATED BIBLIOGRAPHY FOR THOSE WHO LIVE AND LEARN WITH YOUNG CHILDREN. BOGGAN, LUCILLE B.; ACKERMAN, SATOKO I., MAY 69 38P.
EDRS PRICE MF-$0.65 HC-$3.29

THIS ANNOTATED BIBLIOGRAPHY REPORTS ON 52 ESSAYS, BOOKS, COMPILATIONS, REPORTS, SPEECHES, HANDBOOKS, AND MAGAZINE ARTICLES ON THE EDUCATION OF YOUNG CHILDREN. EDUCATION, AS USED HERE, COVERS THE ENTIRE SPECTRUM OF A CHILD'S EXPERIENCE. THE VIEWPOINTS TAKEN ARE PSYCHOLOGICAL, EDUCATIONAL, AND SOCIOLOGICAL AND DEAL WITH ISSUES OF DEPRIVED YOUTH AND OTHER SPECIAL PROBLEMS. THE BOOKLET CONCLUDES WITH A SUBJECT INDEX. (MH)

ED032936 PS002202
DEVELOPMENT OF A DANCE CURRICULUM FOR YOUNG CHILDREN. CAREL ARTS AND HUMANITIES CURRICULUM DEVELOPMENT PROGRAM FOR YOUNG CHILDREN. DIMONDSTEIN, GERALDINE; PREVOTS, NAIMA, JUN 69 72P.
EDRS PRICE MF-$0.65 HC-$3.29

THE LONG-RANGE OBJECTIVE OF THE CENTRAL ATLANTIC REGIONAL EDUCATIONAL LABORATORY (CAREL) DANCE PROGRAM WAS TO DEVELOP CHILDREN'S ABILITY TO SOLVE PROBLEMS IN MOVEMENT TERMS AND TO EXPRESS EMOTIONAL INVOLVEMENT AND CREATIVE IDEAS THROUGH DANCE. WORKSHOPS WERE CONDUCTED FOR 15 NON-SPECIALIST TEACHERS TO EXPLORE THE CONCEPTS OF SPACE, TIME, AND FORCE, AND TO INCORPORATE THESE CONCEPTS INTO A DANCE CURRICULUM. PROTOTYPE LESSONS WERE DEVELOPED FOR 3- TO 8-YEAR-OLDS. CLASSROOM ACTIVITIES FOCUSED ON SOLVING PROBLEMS THROUGH MOVEMENT; DISCOVERING THE CONCEPTS OF SPACE (SHAPES, SIZES, AND RELATIONSHIPS); TIME (BOTH CLOCK AND CALENDAR INTERVALS); AND FORCE (WEIGHT, GRAVITY, ENERGIES IN MOTION, AND RELATIONSHIPS BETWEEN OBJECTS IN SPACE). EVALUATIONS CONSISTED OF TEACHER AND CLASSROOM OBSERVATIONS. THESE EVALUATIONS INDICATED POSITIVE OUTCOMES OF BEHAVIORAL OBJECTIVES. RECOMMENDATIONS WERE MADE FOR THE IMPROVEMENT OF TEACHER SELECTION AND PREPARATION AND DEVELOPMENT OF A PROCESS-MODEL CURRICULUM. (DR)

ED032937 PS002203
DEVELOPMENT OF A THEATRE ARTS CURRICULUM FOR YOUNG CHILDREN. CAREL ARTS AND HUMANITIES CURRICULUM DEVELOPMENT PROGRAM FOR YOUNG CHILDREN. ALEXANDER, ROBERT; AND OTHERS, JUN 69 57P.
EDRS PRICE MF-$0.65 HC-$3.29

A CURRICULUM ON THEATER IS PRESENTED IN THIS VOLUME PREPARED BY THE CENTRAL ATLANTIC REGIONAL EDUCATIONAL LABORATORY (CAREL) ARTS AND HUMANITIES CURRICULUM DEVELOPMENT PROGRAM FOR YOUNG CHILDREN. TOPICS IN THE 23 PAGE RATIONALE SECTION RANGE FROM THEORIES OF COGNITIVE DEVELOPMENT TO AN EXTENSIVE EXPLANATION OF THE WORKSHOP CONCEPT WHICH IS RECOMMENDED AS THE BASIS OF THE THEATER CURRICULUM. THE WORKSHOP SHOULD EMPHASIZE CREATIVE PROBLEM SOLVING IN AN ATMOSPHERE OF HUMAN INTERACTION WITHOUT AUTHORITY-IMPOSED DISCIPLINE OR INSTRUCTOR APPROVAL-DISAPPROVAL. THE WORKSHOP EXPERIENCE SHOULD BE CHILD-ORIENTED TO PERMIT EACH CHILD TO PROCEED AT HIS OWN RATE, AND SHOULD TEACH PROCESSES AND METHODS OF WORKING RATHER THAN FACTS. THE AUTHORS OUTLINE THEIR PROPOSED PROGRAM OF TEACHER PREPARATION, INVOLVING SUMMER SESSIONS AND AN ACADEMIC YEAR APPRENTICESHIP. THEATRICAL LIGHTING, PROPS, STUDENT-TEACHER RATIO, COACHING, AND EVALUATION ARE EXPLORED. SPECIFIC SUGGESTIONS FOR WORKSHOP ACTIVITY AND IMPROVISATIONS ARE MADE. FINALLY, ALTHOUGH THE PILOT PROJECT WAS UNABLE TO SECURE MANY OF THE CONDITIONS CONSIDERED ESSENTIAL TO AN EFFECTIVE THEATER PROGRAM, THE ORIGINAL RECOMMENDATIONS WERE CONFIRMED. (MH)

ED032938 PS002204
DEVELOPMENT OF A MUSIC CURRICULUM FOR YOUNG CHILDREN. CAREL ARTS AND HUMANITIES CURRICULUM DEVELOPMENT PROGRAM FOR YOUNG CHILDREN. BIASINI, AMERICOLE; POGONOWSKI, LEE, JUN 69 107P.
EDRS PRICE MF-$0.65 HC-$6.58

OBJECTIVES OF THIS PROGRAM WERE (1) TO DEVELOP AURAL SENSITIVITY, (2) TO DISCOVER BASIC CONCEPTS OF MUSICAL ELEMENTS AND STRUCTURE, (3) TO ACQUIRE SIMPLE MUSICAL SKILLS, AND (4) TO DEVELOP POSITIVE ATTITUDES TOWARD MUSIC AND SELF. PARTICIPANTS WERE 689 STUDENTS FROM ALL SOCIOECONOMIC LEVELS, RANGING

FROM 2 TO 13 YEARS IN AGE. FOLLOWING A WORKSHOP AND PLANNING CONFERENCE, THE CENTRAL ATLANTIC REGIONAL EDUCATIONAL LABORATORY (CAREL) STAFF, CLASSROOM TEACHERS, AND MUSIC SPECIALISTS INSTIGATED THE DEVELOPMENTAL PHASES OF MUSICAL EXPLORATION. THE SIX PHASES WERE FREE EXPLORATION, GUIDED EXPLORATION, FREE IMPROVISATION, PLANNED IMPROVISATION, REINFORCEMENT, AND EVALUATION. THE PROGRAM, USING A TEAM TEACHING APPROACH, UTILIZED A MUSIC LABORATORY, AUDIO EQUIPMENT, AND ELECTRONIC MUSIC. TEACHERS WERE EVALUATED THROUGH QUESTIONNAIRES, CLASSROOM VISITS, INDIVIDUAL TEACHER CONSULTATIONS, AND EXPERIENCE REPORTS. STUDENTS WERE EVALUATED BY A PRE- AND POSTTEST, CLASSROOM OBSERVATIONS, AND TAPES OF MUSICAL EXPERIENCES. RESULTS INDICATED HIGH TEACHER AND STUDENT INVOLVEMENT AND STUDENTS' DEVELOPMENT OF MUSICAL CREATIVITY AND POSITIVE ATTITUDES TOWARD MUSIC. AURAL TESTS REQUIRE FURTHER ANALYSIS. REFINEMENT OF THE PROGRAM INTO A PILOT PROCESS-MODEL CURRICULUM AND INCORPORATION OF MUSIC INTO A MULTI-ARTS CORE CURRICULUM WERE RECOMMENDED. (DR)

ED032939 PS002205
DEVELOPMENT OF A VISUAL ARTS CURRICULUM FOR YOUNG CHILDREN. CAREL ARTS AND HUMANITIES CURRICULUM DEVELOPMENT PROGRAM FOR YOUNG CHILDREN. GRAYSON, MARY; AND OTHERS, JUN 69 166P.
EDRS PRICE MF-$0.65 HC-$6.58

THE OBJECTIVE OF THE CENTRAL ATLANTIC REGIONAL EDUCATIONAL LABORATORY (CAREL) VISUAL ARTS PROGRAM WAS TO DEVELOP A CURRICULUM THAT WOULD INCREASE CHILDREN'S VISUAL KNOWLEDGE OF ARTISTS AND ART WORK, DEVELOP THEIR VISUAL SENSITIVITY AND PERCEPTUAL ABILITY, AND ENCOURAGE CREATIVE PRODUCTION AND PERCEPTION OF ART WORK. WORKSHOPS WERE CONDUCTED TO COMBINE CURRICULUM THEORY WITH TEACHING PRACTICE AND TO PRESENT A CONCEPTUAL ART FRAMEWORK TO TEACHERS. THE CURRICULUM WAS PRESENTED TO 190 CHILDREN, GRADES KINDERGARTEN THROUGH 3, FROM ALL SOCIOECONOMIC LEVELS. FOCAL POINTS WERE DEFINITION OF THE ARTIST, ARTISTIC EXPRESSIVENESS, SPATIAL AWARENESS AND SPATIAL RELATIONSHIPS, VISUAL RHYTHM (RECOGNIZED PATTERN OF PARTS TO PARTS AND PARTS TO WHOLE), AND VISITS TO AN ART MUSEUM. TEACHER PREPARATION AND CURRICULUM CONTENT WERE EVALUATED THROUGH CLASSROOM OBSERVATION BY THE CAREL STAFF, TEACHERS' RESPONSES TO WORKSHOPS AND QUESTIONNAIRES, AND ANECODOTAL RECORDS. RESULTS INDICATED A NEED FOR BETTER TEACHER PREPARATION AND CURRICULUM DESIGN PLANNING. CHILDREN SHOWED DEVELOPMENT OF VISUAL RHYTHM, AND IMPROVEMENT IN THEIR PERCEPTION OF AESTHETIC QUALITIES. CURRICULUM UNITS AND SAMPLE EVALUATIONS ARE ARE INCLUDED. (DR)

ED032940 PS002206
DEVELOPMENT OF A LITERATURE CURRICULUM FOR YOUNG CHILDREN. CAREL ARTS AND HUMANITIES CURRICULUM DEVELOPMENT PROGRAM FOR YOUNG CHILDREN. AMIDON, JEANETTE; AND OTHERS, JUN 69 113P.
EDRS PRICE MF-$0.65 HC-$6.58

THE PURPOSE OF THE CENTRAL ATLANTIC REGIONAL EDUCATIONAL LABORATORY (CAREL) LITERATURE PROGRAM WAS TO ENCOURAGE PUPILS' IMAGINATIVE AND EXPRESSIVE POWER AND TO IMPROVE THEIR ABILITY TO USE LANGUAGE EFFECTIVELY. THE CURRICULUM WAS DESIGNED FOR 3- TO 8-YEAR-OLDS WHO REPRESENTED A WIDE SOCIOECONOMIC BACKGROUND. SPECIALISTS TRAINED TEACHERS TO RELATE LITERATURE TO CHILDREN'S EXPERIENCES AND TO USE STUDENTS' EXPERIENCES AS LITERARY MATERIAL. IN WORKSHOPS AND CLASSROOMS, TEACHERS USED STORIES, PICTURES, POEMS, AND CLASS DISCUSSION TO ENCOURAGE STUDENT RESPONSE AND EXPRESSION, BOTH ORAL AND WRITTEN. TO ENCOURAGE CREATIVITY, CORRECTION OF GRAMMATICAL AND SPELLING ERRORS WAS DE-EMPHASIZED. EVALUATIONS WERE MADE OF TAPED CLASSROOM AND WORKSHOP SESSIONS, ORAL AND WRITTEN REPORTS PREPARED BY THE TEACHERS AND CAREL STAFF, AND CHILDREN'S WRITTEN WORK. RESULTS INDICATED IMPROVEMENT IN CHILDREN'S SELF-EXPRESSION AND WRITING ABILITY. TEACHERS ACCEPTED STUDENTS AND RESPONDED TO THEM MORE READILY THAN BEFORE TRAINING AND USED LESS STRUCTURED TEACHING STRATEGIES. IT IS RECOMMENDED THAT FUTURE PROGRAMS SEEK STAFF MEMBERS REPRESENTING DIFFERENT BACKGROUNDS AND LIFE STYLES. APPENDIXES DESCRIBE PARTICIPANTS, EVALUATIONS, AND CURRICULUM CONTENT. (DR)

ED032941 PS002302
ANNUAL PROGRESS IN CHILD PSYCHIATRY AND CHILD DEVELOPMENT 1969. CHESS, STELLA, ED.; THOMAS, ALEXANDER, ED., 69 710P.
DOCUMENT NOT AVAILABLE FROM EDRS.
AVAILABLE FROM: BRUNNER/MAZEL, INC., 80 EAST 11 STREET, NEW YORK, NEW YORK 10003 ($15.00)

THIS BOOK, THE SECOND IN AN ANNUAL SERIES, CONTAINS 38 ARTICLES PUBLISHED DURING THE PAST YEAR IN THE FIELD OF CHILD PSYCHIATRY AND CHILD DEVELOPMENT. THE EDITORS ATTEMPTED TO COMPILE ARTICLES "OF MOST VALUE TO WORKERS IN THIS FIELD BOTH FOR IMMEDIATE INFORMATION AND FOR LONG-TERM REFERENCE." ACCORDINGLY, THE ARTICLES ARE OF TWO TYPES: (1) ORIGINAL WORK THAT SHOULD AID PROGRESS IN THE STUDY OF THE CHILD, AND (2) REVIEWS AND DISCUSSIONS OF PRESENT KNOWLEDGE AND ISSUES. ARTICLES OF BOTH TYPES FALL UNDER ONE OF THE NINE MAJOR AREAS OF INTEREST COVERED BY THE BOOK: INFANCY STUDIES, THE LEARNING PROCESS, LANGUAGE STUDIES, THE IMPACT OF SOCIAL PATHOLOGY, MENTAL RETARDATION, CHILDHOOD PSYCHOSIS, CLINICAL PSYCHIATRY, PROBLEMS OF ADOLESCENCE, AND TREATMENT. THE ISSUES EXAMINED ARE CONTEMPORARY AND IMMEDIATE, AS IN THE NEW SECTION ON THE IMPACT OF SOCIAL PATHOLOGY, WHICH REFLECTS EVER-GROWING CONCERN WITH THE PSYCHOLOGICAL PROBLEMS OF THE CHILD WHO LIVES IN AN ENVIRONMENT OF RACISM AND POVERTY. (MH)

ED032942 PS002304
TEACHING IN PRESCHOOLS: ROLES AND GOALS. KATZ, LILIAN G., APR 69 18P.
EDRS PRICE MF-$0.65 HC-$3.29

TWO ASPECTS OF PRESCHOOL TEACHING, TEACHER ROLE AND TEACHER STYLE, ARE DISCUSSED IN THIS PAPER. TEACHER ROLE REFERS TO A TEACHER'S BEHAVIOR CONCERNING THE DUTIES, RESPONSIBILITIES, AND FUNCTIONS EXPECTED OF THE TEACHER BY HER CLIENTS AND HERSELF. TEACHER STYLE REFERS TO THE WAY IN WHICH INDIVIDUAL TEACHERS PERFORM THEIR ROLES. TEACHERS HAVE HAD THREE BASIC ROLE MODELS: (1) MATERNAL: KEEP CHILDREN SAFE AND BUSY, (2) THERAPEUTIC: HELP CHILDREN EXPRESS FEELINGS AND REDUCE TENSIONS, AND (3) INSTRUCTIONAL: TRANSMIT KNOWLEDGE. THE AUTHOR PREDICTS THE INSTRUCTIONAL MODEL IS "IN", BUT WILL MEET RESISTANCE BECAUSE OF THESE LIMITATIONS: (1) ACADEMIC AND INTELLECTUAL GOALS ARE CONFUSED, (2) IMPORTANT TEACHING STYLE ELEMENTS (FLEXIBILITY, WARMTH, ENJOYMENT, AND ENCOURAGEMENT) HAVE BEEN NEGLECTED, AND (3) THE RELATIONSHIPS BETWEEN TEACHERS AND CLIENTS, PARTICULARLY PARENTS, HAVE NOT BEEN STRESSED. A NEW DEFINITION OF THE INSTRUCTIONAL ROLE IS NEEDED. CURRENT LIMITED KNOWLEDGE SUGGESTS ROLE MODELS MAY NOT BE AS IMPORTANT AS INDIVIDUAL TEACHING STYLES. (DO)

ED032943 PS002307
A COMPARISON OF THE ORAL LANGUAGE PATTERNS OF THREE LOW SOCIOECONOMIC GROUPS OF PUPILS ENTERING FIRST GRADE. SILVAROLI, NICHOLAS J.; WHITCOMB, MARY WAKEFIELD, [67] 15P.
EDRS PRICE MF-$0.65 HC-$3.29

THE LANGUAGE PATTERNS OF LOW SOCIOECONOMIC NEGRO, SPANISH-SURNAME, AND ANGLO CHILDREN ARE SUFFICIENTLY DIFFERENT FROM THE MIDDLE CLASS LANGUAGE PATTERNS USED IN SCHOOLS TO PUT THESE CHILDREN AT A DISTINCT EDUCATIONAL DISADVANTAGE. BY COMPARING THE SPEECH PATTERNS OF THESE CHILDREN, THIS STUDY SOUGHT TO DETERMINE WHETHER THEIR LANGUAGE DEVELOPMENT IS LIMITED BY THEIR ECONOMIC STATUS OR BY THEIR ETHNIC GROUP STATUS. TWENTY RANDOMLY SELECTED BEGINNING FIRST GRADERS FROM EACH OF THE THREE ETHNIC GROUPS WERE INTERVIEWED AND RECORDED AT LENGTH AS THEY TOLD STORIES ABOUT PICTURES THEY WERE SHOWN. THE RECORDINGS WERE ANALYZED FOR BOTH PATTERNS AND MAZES (HESITATIONS, FALSE STARTS, ETC.) ON THE BASIS OF A SIMPLIFIED FORM OF THE INDIANA CONFERENCE SCHEME OF ANALYSIS ON THE FIRST LEVEL. THE THREE GROUPS RESPONDED APPROXIMATELY THE SAME ON TOTAL SENTENCE PATTERNS AND ALL SPECIFIC SENTENCE PATTERNS EXCEPT ONE. THEY ALSO RESPONDED APPROXIMATELY THE SAME FOR TOTAL MAZES (TANGLES OF LANGUAGE NOT EFFECTIVE FOR COMMUNICATION) AND ALL SPECIFIC MAZES. THESE RESULTS IMPLY THAT LOW SOCIOECONOMIC NEGRO, SPANISH-SURNAME, AND ANGLO CHILDREN BEGINNING FIRST GRADE ARE AWARE OF AND USE BASIC ENGLISH SYNTAX PATTERNS IN APPROXIMATELY THE SAME MANNER. DIFFERENTIATED MATERIALS ARE NOT NEEDED IN CLASS AS MUCH AS EXPOSURE TO TOTAL LANGUAGE DEVELOPING EXPERIENCES. (MH)

ED032944 PS002371
THE SOCIOLOGY OF EARLY CHILDHOOD EDUCATION: A REVIEW OF LITERATURE. TECHNICAL REPORT NO. 1. TURKNETT, CAROLYN NORRIS; AND OTHERS, JUN 69 120P.
EDRS PRICE MF-$0.65 HC-$6.58

THE PRINCIPAL PUBLISHED RESEARCH FINDINGS AND OTHER RELEVANT LITERATURE IN THE SOCIOLOGY OF EARLY CHILDHOOD EDUCATION ARE REVIEWED AND SUMMARIZED IN THIS PAPER. PART I EXAMINES THE SHAPING OF A CHILD'S ABILITIES AND ACHIEVEMENT BY THE NORMS, ROLES, AND PRACTICES OF HIS PARENTS. THE INFLUENCE OF PARENTAL SEX ROLES ON THE PARENT-CHILD RELATIONSHIP IS DISCUSSED. PART II DISCUSSES FAMILY INFLUENCES ON ACHIEVEMENT. THE FAMILY STRUCTURE, NOW UNDERGOING IMPORTANT CHANGES, AFFECTS THE EDUCABILITY OF THE CHILD. IN TODAY'S SMALLER FAMILY, THE CHILD IS DEPENDENT ON THE IMMEDIATE FAMILY GROUP RATHER THAN A KINSHIP GROUP. MEMBERSHIP IN A SOCIAL CLASS OR ETHNIC GROUP INFLUENCES VALUES, CHILD-REARING APPROACHES, FAMILY ORGANIZATION, AND CHARACTERISTICS OF THE CHILD. LANGUAGE, SOCIAL BEHAVIOR, AND SOCIAL CLASS ARE ALSO RELATED. ALTHOUGH MOST OF THE YOUNG CHILD'S EXPERIENCE IS WITHIN THE FAMILY, THERE ARE IMPORTANT EXTRAFAMILIAL INFLUENCES, WHICH ARE DISCUSSED IN PART III AS ARE STUDIES ON MASS MEDIA DEALING WITH SOCIALIZING AND LEARNING EFFECTS. ADDITIONAL RESEARCH ON THE EFFECTS OF PEER GROUPS AND SCHOOL ENVIRONMENT IS RECOMMENDED. (DR)

ED032945 PS002390
ARTS AND HUMANITIES FOR YOUNG SCHOOL CHILDREN. DISHART, MARTIN,, JUN 69 50P.
EDRS PRICE MF-$0.65 HC-$3.29

THIS FIRST VOLUME OF A PROPOSED SERIES IS AN OVERVIEW OF PHASE ONE OF THE CENTRAL ATLANTIC REGIONAL EDUCATIONAL LABORATORY (CAREL) ARTS AND HUMANITIES CURRICULUM DEVELOPMENT PROGRAM FOR YOUNG CHILDREN. GOALS OF CAREL WERE TO DEVELOP (1) FIVE COMPONENTS OF THE ARTS AND HUMANITIES: VISUAL ARTS, DANCE, LITERATURE, MUSIC, AND THEATRE FOR KINDERGARTEN THROUGH GRADE 3, (2) A PROGRAM TO PREPARE CLASSROOM TEACHERS TO TEACH THE ARTS AND HUMANITIES, AND (3) A CONCEPTUAL APPROACH TO SHOW THE GOALS AND KINDS OF RESOURCES THAT CAN MEET PUPIL NEEDS IN THE ARTS AND HUMANITIES. THE CHILDREN WERE ENCOURAGED TO EXPLORE FREELY WITHIN EACH ART FORM. PROBLEM FORMULATING AND PROBLEM SOLVING ABILITIES WERE DEVELOPED THROUGH TEACHER AND STUDENT FEEDBACK. ALTHOUGH STUDENTS WERE INITIALLY INHIBITED, IT WAS FOUND THAT WITHIN MINUTES PUPILS COULD BE "TURNED ON" AS THEY BEGAN TO IMPROVISE AND COMMUNICATE. AN ATTEMPT TO ESTABLISH BEHAVIORAL OBJECTIVES IN THE INITIAL STAGES FAILED, AND IT WAS CONCLUDED THAT CHILDREN'S NEEDS MUST FIRST BE DETERMINED. A SUMMER WORKSHOP PREPARED TEACHERS, AND CURRICULUM DEVELOPMENT WORKSHOPS WERE CONDUCTED THROUGHOUT THE YEAR. APPENDIXES INCLUDE A SUMMARY OF FIELD SCHOOL PARTICIPANTS AND A PROPOSAL FOR THE CONTINUATION OF THE PROGRAM. HOWEVER, BECAUSE OF LACK OF FUNDS, THE PROGRAM WAS DISCONTINUED. (DR)

ED032946 PS002391
FUNCTIONAL PRINCIPLES OF LEARNING. HUMPHREYS, LLOYD G., [69] 9P.
EDRS PRICE MF-$0.65 HC-$3.29

IN ORDER OF IMPORTANCE, CURRICULUM, MOTIVATION, ACADEMIC ABILITY, AND TEACHING METHODS ARE DESCRIBED IN THIS PAPER AS PRINCIPLES AFFECTING CLASSROOM LEARNING THAT CAN LEAD TO MORE EFFECTIVE INSTRUCTION. CURRICULUM SIMPLY EXPOSES STUDENTS TO APPROPRIATE CONTENT AND SUBJECT MATTER. EDUCATIONAL RESEARCH SHOULD CONCENTRATE ON THE EVALUATION OF CURRICULUM INNOVATION, INCLUDING RECOMMENDATIONS TO SCRAP IRRELEVANT SUBJECTS IN HIGH SCHOOL CURRICULUMS. THE SECOND PRINCIPLE IS MOTIVATION (WHETHER EXTRINSIC OR INTRINSIC) WHICH IS ESSENTIAL FOR CLASSROOM LEARNING EVEN WHEN THERE IS A GOOD CURRICULUM. THE THIRD PRINCIPLE OF LEARNING IS ACADEMIC ABILITY. INTELLIGENCE IS NOT HIGHLY CHANGEABLE BUT NEITHER IS IT FIXED. THE TEACHER SHOULD ASSUME A POSITIVE ATTITUDE TOWARD LEARNING PROBLEMS AS SHE ATTEMPTS TO BE EFFECTIVE. LESS IMPORTANT THAN THE OTHERS IS THE FOURTH PRINCIPLE, TEACHING METHODS, WHICH ONLY SLIGHTLY AFFECTS SUBJECT MATTER PROFICIENCY. RESEARCH SHOULD BE DIRECTED TOWARD FINDING TEACHING TECHNIQUES THAT MINIMIZE TIME AND MONEY EXPENDITURE, WITHOUT REGARD FOR EFFECTIVENESS. SELECTIVE USE OF APPROPRIATE REINFORCEMENTS TO SHAPE LEARNING BEHAVIOR IS RECOMMENDED. (MH)

ED032947 PS002392
DETERMINANTS OF INFANT BEHAVIOUR IV. FOSS, B. M., ED., 69 317P.
DOCUMENT NOT AVAILABLE FROM EDRS.
AVAILABLE FROM: BARNES AND NOBLE, INC., 105 FIFTH AVENUE, NEW YORK, NEW YORK 10003

THIS VOLUME CONSISTS OF REPORTS OF INDIVIDUAL STUDIES AND SURVEYS OF RESEARCH WORK ON MOTHER-INFANT INTERACTIONS. IT IS DIVIDED INTO TWO PARTS. THE FIRST SECTION PRESENTS A WIDE RANGE OF STUDIES ON MOTHER-INFANT RELATIONS AS EXHIBITED IN THE BEHAVIOR OF ANIMALS. THE SECOND PART, CONCERNING HUMAN BEHAVIOR, INCLUDES STUDIES ON THE NATURAL HISTORY OF CRYING, THE EFFECTS OF STRANGE ENVIRONMENT, THE MENTAL AND EMOTIONAL DEVELOPMENT OF THE THALIDOMIDE CHILD, AND SEVERAL STUDIES OF BABIES' REACTIONS TO STRANGERS. THE WORK PRESENTED REPRESENTS A POOLING OF SEVERAL DISCIPLINES AND DEMONSTRATES A VARIETY OF METHODS AND THEORETICAL BACKGROUNDS INCLUDING PSYCHOANALYSIS, PSYCHOLOGY, ETHOLOGY, AND ZOOLOGY. (JF)

ED032948 PS002507
CHILDHOOD RESOURCES INFORMATION BULLETIN. VOLUME 1, NUMBER 2, FALL 1969. , 69 60P.
EDRS PRICE MF-$0.65 HC-$3.29

THE FALL 1969 EDITION OF THIS BIANNUAL PUBLICATION CONTAINS CURRENT INFORMATION ON EARLY CHILDHOOD EDUCATION. ARTICLES REVIEWING 53 PUBLICATIONS ARE ADDRESSED TO RESEARCHERS, EDUCATORS, HEAD START PERSONNEL, PARAPROFESSIONALS, AND PARENTS. REPORTS ON RESEARCH PROJECTS, BOOKLETS ON ACTIVITIES FOR CHILDREN, PRESCHOOL PROGRAMS, AND CURRICULUM GUIDES ARE PRESENTED. IN A QUESTION-ANSWER FORMAT, THE FOLLOWING QUESTIONS, AMONG OTHERS, ARE POSED AND ANSWERED IN 200-400 WORD ARTICLES: "WHAT IS THE BEREITER-ENGELMANN APPROACH TO LANGUAGE LEARNING?" "HOW DO YOU TEST A BILINGUAL CHILD?" "HOW CAN A TEACHER DECIDE WHICH ARE THE BEST EDUCATIONAL MATERIALS TO USE IN HER CLASS?" "WHAT KIND OF RESEARCH STUDIES ARE CARRIED OUT IN HEAD START REGIONAL EVALUATION CENTERS?" "WHAT CURRICULAR METHODS ARE CURRENTLY USED TO FOSTER PERCEPTUAL MOTOR DEVELOPMENT IN PRESCHOOL CHILDREN?" AN AUTHOR-TITLE INDEX IS COMPREHENSIVE AND CONTAINS THE SOURCE AND PRICE FOR EACH PUBLICATION REVIEWED. (DO)

ED033741 PS001550
FEDERAL FUNDS FOR DAY CARE PROJECTS. (REVISED EDITION). ROSENBERG, BEATRICE, FEB 69 79P.
EDRS PRICE MF-$0.65 HC-$3.29
AVAILABLE FROM: U.S. DEPARTMENT OF LABOR, WAGE AND LABOR STANDARDS ADMINISTRATION, WOMEN'S BUREAU, WASHINGTON, D.C. 20210

THIS PUBLICATION, A REVISION OF THE WOMEN'S BUREAU PUBLICATION ISSUED IN APRIL 1967, LISTS SEVERAL FEDERAL AGENCIES WHICH PROVIDE FUNDING FOR DAY CARE PROJECTS. THESE AGENCIES ARE THE DEPARTMENT OF HEALTH, EDUCATION, AND WELFARE, THE OFFICE OF ECONOMIC OPPORTUNITY, THE DEPARTMENT OF HOUSING AND URBAN DEVELOPMENT, THE DEPARTMENT OF LABOR, THE SMALL BUSINESS ADMINISTRATION, AND THE DEPARTMENT OF AGRICULTURE. SEVERAL PROGRAMS ARE LISTED FOR EACH AGENCY. THE PUBLICATION SUMMARIZES EACH PROGRAM UNDER FOUR HEADINGS: AUTHORIZATION, ELIGIBILITY, FUNDS, AND REVIEW. ADDRESSES FOR FURTHER INFORMATION ARE ALSO LISTED. THE PROGRAMS FOR WHICH FUNDS MAY BE USED INCLUDE PROVIDING DIRECT CARE OF CHILDREN IN DAY CARE FACILITIES, OTHER DAY CARE SERVICES SUCH AS THE TRAINING OF PERSONNEL, RESEARCH, AND DEMONSTRATION PROJECTS RELATING TO VARIOUS ASPECTS OF DAY CARE. GRANTS ARE AWARDED EITHER BY MATCHING FORMULAS OR BY FULL FUNDING. THOUGH MOST OF THE PROGRAMS AWARD FUNDS OR LOANS TO STATE OR LOCAL PUBLIC AGENCIES, PRIVATE ORGANIZATIONS, AND SCHOOLS, A FEW PROGRAMS GRANT FUNDS TO INDIVIDUALS. (JF)

ED033742 PS001949
IMPLICATIONS OF STUDIES ON SELF-ESTEEM FOR EDUCATIONAL RESEARCH AND PRACTICE. COOPERSMITH, STANLEY, 6 FEB 69 25P.
EDRS PRICE MF-$0.65 HC NOT AVAILABLE FROM EDRS.

THE RESEARCH OF THIS AUTHOR INDICATES THAT THE DEVELOPMENT OF HIGH SELF-ESTEEM (DEFINED AS THE GOOD-BAD DIMENSION OF SELF-CONCEPT) IS ASSOCIATED WITH (1) ACCEPTANCE, (2) CLEARLY DEFINED LIMITS AND MODERATELY HIGH GOALS, AND (3) RESPECTFUL TREATMENT. SUCH FACTORS AS STATUS, INCOME, AND EDUCATION ARE ONLY RELATED TO HIGH SELF-ESTEEM IF THEY ARE A PART OF AN INDIVIDUAL'S PERSONAL DEFINITION OF SUCCESS. SINCE HIGH SELF-ESTEEM IS CORRELATED WITH NEED-ACHIEVEMENT, WHICH PROVES TO BE A SELF-FULFILLING PROPHECY FOR SUCCESS, AND LOW SELF-ESTEEM IS CORRELATED WITH FEAR OF FAILURE, WHICH PROVES TO BE A SELF-FULFILLING PROPHECY FOR FAILURE, IT IS CLEAR THAT OUR EDUCATIONAL TECHNIQUES SHOULD FOSTER HIGH SELF-ESTEEM. FURTHER, IT HAS BEEN SHOWN THAT (1) SELF-MOTIVATION DERIVES FROM SEEING ONESELF DEVELOP COMPETENCY (THROUGH INTERNAL FEEDBACK, NOT SOCIAL APPROVAL), (2), STRINGENT BUT REASONABLE EARLY CHALLENGES FACILITATE DEVELOPMENT, AND (3) THE SCHOOL SITUATION CAN EITHER HURT A STUDENT'S SELF-ESTEEM OR EQUIP HIM WITH THE MECHANISMS TO MAINTAIN IT AT A HIGH LEVEL. OUR PRESENT EDUCATIONAL SYSTEM HINGES ON THE ANXIETY-PROVOKING, SELF-ESTEEM LOWERING RELIANCE OF THE STUDENT ON THE TEACHER'S APPROVAL, GRADES, AND ATTENTION. A PREFERABLE ALTERNATIVE WOULD SHIFT EMPHASIS TO SELF-MOTIVATION, BASED ON HIGH SELF-ESTEEM. [NOT AVAILABLE IN HARD COPY DUE TO MARGINAL LEGIBILITY OF ORIGINAL DOCUMENT.] (MH)

ED033743 PS002060
A STRUCTURE-PROCESS APPROACH TO COGNITIVE DEVELOPMENT OF PRESCHOOL NEGRO CHILDREN: RATIONALE AND EFFECTS. FROST, JOE L., FEB 69 23P.
EDRS PRICE MF-$0.65 HC-$3.29

THIS REPORT PRESENTS A DESCRIPTION OF THE STRUCTURE-PROCESS APPROACH TO COGNITION AND LITERACY, SUGGESTS TECHNIQUES FOR IMPLEMENTATION OF THE MODEL, AND ASSESSES THE EFFECTS OF THE MODEL ON A SPECIFIC POPULATION. THE STRUCTURE-PROCESS APPROACH ASSUMES THAT INTELLIGENCE DEVELOPS CUMULATIVELY. THE MODEL WAS USED FOR CURRICULUM DEVELOPMENT IN FOUR RURAL AND URBAN EARLY CHILDHOOD CENTERS ENROLLING 290 3- TO 7-YEAR-OLD DISADVANTAGED NEGRO CHILDREN. A CHECKLIST WAS FILLED OUT BY THE TEACHER THREE TIMES DURING THE YEAR TO ASSESS EACH CHILD'S PROGRESS IN COMMUNICATION, FINE ARTS, AND PHYSICAL ACTIVITIES. ANALYSIS OF VARIANCE RESULTS SHOWED SIGNIFICANTLY HIGHER GAINS FOR GIRLS COMPARED TO BOYS, PERHAPS REFLECTING MATURATIONAL SUPERIORITY AND/OR TEACHER FAVORITISM. PRE- AND POSTADMINISTRATION OF THE PRESCHOOL ATTAINMENT RECORD PRODUCED SIGNIFICANT GAINS ON MEASURES OF CREATIVITY, AND PHYSICAL, SOCIAL, AND INTELLECTUAL DEVELOPMENT. ACCORDING TO PRE- AND POSTTEST SCORES ON THE SLOSSON INTELLIGENCE TEST, THE PROGRAM HAD MAXIMUM EFFECT ON YOUNGER CHILDREN. CROSS-TEST COMPARISONS USING THE WECHSLER PRESCHOOL AND PRIMARY SCALE OF INTELLIGENCE AND VARIATIONS IN ADMINISTRATION OF INSTRUMENTS INDICATE THAT PRETEST SCORES MAY HAVE BEEN INFLATED, THUS REDUCING PRETEST-POSTTEST DIFFERENCES. (JF)

ED033744 PS002106
SOCIAL-EMOTIONAL TASK FORCE. FINAL REPORT. BOGER, ROBERT P.; KNIGHT, SARAH S., 31 MAY 69 176P.
EDRS PRICE MF-$0.65 HC-$6.58

TO DEVELOP AND FIELD TEST NEW ASSESSMENT PROCEDURES FOR THE 1969-70 HEAD START NATIONAL EVALUATION, A LIST OF EXISTING TESTS MEASURING SELECTED SOCIAL AND EMOTIONAL VARIABLES WAS COMPILED. TESTS WERE SELECTED ON THESE CRITERIA: (1) CONCEPTUAL SOUNDNESS, (2) RELEVANCE FOR PRESCHOOL CHILDREN, (3) WHETHER DISADVANTAGED CHILDREN MIGHT BE EXPECTED TO SHOW A DEFICIT COMPARED TO THEIR ADVANTAGED PEERS, AND (4) THE DEGREE OF OVERLAP WITH THE COGNITIVE DOMAIN. THE VARIABLES AND RESPECTIVE TESTS FINALLY SELECTED WERE (1) CURIOSITY: CURIOSITY BOX SUBTEST OF THE CINCINNATI AUTONOMY TEST BATTERY (CATB), (2) FRUSTRATION: MICHIGAN STATE UNIVERSITY PUZZLE BOX TASK BASED ON THE KEISTER-FUNICH TASK, (3) SOCIOMETRIC STATUS: PLAY SITUATION-PICTURE BOARD SOCIOMETRIC TECHNIQUE, (4) SELF-CONCEPT: BROWN IDS SELF-CONCEPT REFERENTS TEST, THE SELF-SOCIAL CONSTRUCTS TEST, PRESCHOOL SELF-CONCEPT TEST, AND EXPERIMENTAL PHOTOGRAPHIC SELF-CONCEPT TEST, (5) DELAY OF GRATIFICATION: THE MISCHEL TECHNIQUE, (6) TASK PERSISTENCE: PERSISTENCE SUBTEST OF THE CATB, AND (7) IMPULSIVITY: MOTOR IMPULSIVITY SUBTEST OF THE CATB. OTHER VARIABLES IDENTIFIED BUT NOT EXAMINED IN DEPTH WERE SEX-IDENTIFICATION, DEPENDENCY, ANXIETY, AND AGGRESSION. THE AUTHORS DISCUSS EACH OF THE ASSESSMENT INSTRUMENTS AND GIVE FIELD TESTING RESULTS. (MH)

ED033745 PS002134
A COMPARISON OF READING READINESS ACHIEVEMENT OF KINDERGARTEN CHILDREN OF DISPARATE ENTRANCE AGES. ROSENTHAL, MURIEL, MAY 69 52P.
EDRS PRICE MF-$0.65 HC-$3.29

THIS STUDY INVESTIGATED (1) THE DIFFERENCE, IF ANY, BETWEEN THE ACHIEVEMENT IN READING READINESS OF YOUNGER KINDERGARTEN CHILDREN (4 YEARS 9 MONTHS TO 5 YEARS 1 MONTH UPON SCHOOL ENTRANCE) AND OLDER CHILDREN (5 YEARS 5 MONTHS TO 5 YEARS 8 MONTHS AT ENTRANCE), (2) WHETHER KINDERGARTEN POSITIVELY AFFECTS THE READING READINESS ACHIEVEMENT OF CHILDREN REGARDLESS OF AGE, AND (3) WHETHER YOUNGER KINDERGARTEN CHILDREN WITH TRAINING EQUAL THE LEVEL OF READING READINESS ATTAINED BY THE OLDER KINDERGARTEN CHILDREN WITH TRAINING. THE 39 MIDDLE CLASS CHILDREN WERE MEASURED WITH THE LEE-CLARK READING READINESS TEST AFTER 5 WEEKS OF SCHOOL AND AGAIN AFTER 90 DAYS. RESULTS INDICATED (1) THAT THERE WAS A POSITIVE RELATIONSHIP BETWEEN READING READINESS ACHIEVEMENT AND KINDERGARTEN TRAINING IN YOUNGER CHILDREN, AND (2) THAT WITHOUT KINDERGARTEN TRAINING, MATURATION PLAYS A LARGE PART IN AFFECTING CHILDREN'S READING READINESS ACHIEVEMENT. IT WAS CONCLUDED THAT EARLY EXPOSURE TO FORMAL SCHOOL TRAINING IS DESIRABLE FOR ALL CHILDREN, AND A REEVALUATION AND REVISION OF AVAILABLE READING READINESS TESTS WAS SUGGESTED. (DR)

ED033746 PS002207
SOURCE BOOK OF SELECTED MATERIALS FOR EARLY CHILDHOOD EDUCATION IN THE ARTS. MCINTYRE, BARBARA M., MAY 69 265P.
EDRS PRICE MF-$0.65 HC-$9.87

THE CENTRAL ATLANTIC REGIONAL EDUCATIONAL LABORATORY'S PROGRAM IN EARLY CHILDHOOD EDUCATION INCLUDED THE DEVELOPMENT OF CURRICULUMS IN THE ARTS. THESE CURRICULUMS, INTENDED TO PROMOTE ESTHETIC SENSITIVITY IN YOUNG CHILDREN THROUGH ENCOUNTERS WITH THE ARTS, INVOLVED EXPERIENCED TEACHER-ARTISTS AND THE TRAINING OF CLASSROOM TEACHERS. THIS SOURCE BOOK WAS DEVELOPED FOR INTERESTED TEACHERS WHO COULD NOT PARTICIPATE IN WORKSHOP CLASSROOM TRAINING PROJECTS SPONSORED BY CAREL. PART A DESCRIBES WRITTEN MATERIALS: BOOKS, ARTICLES, MANUALS, AND WORKBOOKS. THE ITEMS IN PART A ARE DIVIDED INTO SEVEN SECTIONS: PHILOSOPHY, CURRICULUM DEVELOPMENT, ART, DANCE, LITERATURE, MUSIC, AND THEATRE ARTS. PART B DISCUSSES MULTIMEDIA MATERIALS: FILMS, FILMSTRIPS, RECORDS, AND TRANSPARENCIES. EACH ITEM SELECTED IS CONSIDERED RELEVANT, ACCESSIBLE, AND RECENT, AND IS RECOMMENDED BY AN ARTS SUPERVISOR OR ACTIVE ARTS TEACHER. ANALYSIS OF ITEMS IS COMPREHENSIVE, INCLUDES DIRECT QUOTES WHEN POSSIBLE AND RECOMMENDS ADDITIONAL RECOMMENDED SOURCES. (MH)

ED033747 PS002301
LOGICAL THINKING IN SECOND GRADE. FINAL REPORT. ALMY, MILLIE; AND OTHERS, JUN 69 227P.
EDRS PRICE MF-$0.65 HC-$9.87

A 3-YEAR STUDY BASED ON PIAGETIAN THEORY CONSIDERED THIS QUESTION: DO CHILDREN WHO RECEIVE SYSTEMATIC INSTRUCTION IN THE BASIC CONCEPTS OF MATHEMATICS AND SCIENCE WHEN THEY ARE IN KINDERGARTEN THINK MORE LOGICALLY WHEN THEY REACH SECOND GRADE THAN DO CHILDREN WHO DID NOT HAVE SUCH EARLY INSTRUCTION? THE GROUPS HAVING PRESCRIBED LESSONS IN KINDERGARTEN WERE ALSO COMPARED WITH GROUPS WHOSE PRESCRIBED LESSONS BEGAN ONLY IN THE FIRST GRADE. KINDERGARTENERS WERE ASSESSED IN THE FALL OF 1965, 1966, AND 1967, AND FIRST GRADERS IN THE FALL OF 1966 AND 1967. THE CHILDREN WERE PRE- AND POSTTESTED ON A SERIES OF TASKS DERIVED FROM PIAGET'S WORK. THE RESULTS IN LOGICAL THINKING ABILITY SEEM TO POSE A PARADOX. THE SECOND GRADE GROUP WHO HAD NO PRESCRIBED LESSONS IN EITHER KINDERGARTEN OR FIRST GRADE PERFORMED ABOUT AS WELL AS THE GROUP WHO HAD PRESCRIBED LESSONS IN KINDERGARTEN. BUT THE LATTER GROUP PERFORMED BETTER THAN THE GROUP WHOSE PRESCRIBED LESSONS BEGAN IN THE FIRST GRADE. THESE AMBIGUOUS RESULTS SUGGEST THAT THE COMPARABILITY OF THE GROUPS OF CHILDREN, AND THE COMPARABILITY OF THEIR SCHOOL EXPERIENCE, APART FROM THE PRESCRIBED PROGRAMS, NEEDS FURTHER EXAMINATION. (JF)

ED033748 PS002303
ESOL-SESD GUIDE: KINDERGARTEN. PETRINI, ALMA MARIA, 69 143P.
EDRS PRICE MF-$0.65 HC-$6.58

THIS GUIDE CONSISTS OF 135 LESSONS DESIGNED TO TEACH ENGLISH TO SPEAKERS OF OTHER LANGUAGES, OR TO TEACH STANDARD ENGLISH AS A SECOND DIALECT. EACH LESSON GUIDES THE KINDERGARTEN TEACHER THROUGH A DAY'S ACTIVITIES. EACH ACTIVITY IS IDENTIFIED WITH A HEADING, A BRIEF DESCRIPTIVE PARAGRAPH, AND AN EXAMPLE OF SUGGESTED DIALOGUE. LESSONS ALSO LIST VARIOUS MATERIALS SUCH AS PICTURES, TOYS, AND PUPPETS TO BE USED DURING THE ACTIVITIES. THE PROGRAM, PRESENTED IN A LINGUISTIC SEQUENCE, EMPHASIZES ORAL SPEECH DEVELOPMENT. CHILDREN HEAR THE LANGUAGE PATTERNS MODELED BY THE TEACHER AND THEN REPEAT WHAT HAS BEEN SAID. DIRECTIONS LIKE "GUIDE," "HELP," AND "WITH THE TEACHER'S HELP" INDICATE WHEN THE TEACHER SHOULD MODEL THE PATTERN FOR THE CHILDREN. ONCE THE CHILDREN ARE ABLE TO CONTROL A PATTERN AUTOMATICALLY THROUGH SEVERAL ORAL REPETITIONS, THEY CAN USE THE LANGUAGE IN MEANINGFUL SITUATIONS. THOUGH THE GUIDE HAS BEEN PLANNED TO COVER 1 YEAR, THE TIME REQUIRED TO COMPLETE IT MAY VARY, DEPENDING ON THE MATURATIONAL LEVEL OF THE CHILDREN AND THE AMOUNT OF TIME DEVOTED TO THE LESSONS. (JF)

ED033749 PS002393
AN INTEGRATIVE APPROACH TO CLASSROOM LEARNING. SOAR, ROBERT S., 66 343P.
EDRS PRICE MF-$0.65 HC-$13.16

BY MAKING DETAILED OBSERVATIONS OF THE ENTIRE CLASSROOM PROCESS AND BY ADMINISTERING RELEVANT TESTS AND INDICES TO TEACHERS AND STUDENTS, THIS 2-YEAR STUDY ATTEMPTED TO DETERMINE WHAT FACTORS AFFECT EDUCATIONAL EFFECTIVENESS. THE THEORETICAL BASIS WAS THAT THE WAYS TO ACHIEVE THE VARIED GOALS OF EDUCATION (KNOWLEDGE OF SUBJECT MATTER AND DEVELOPMENT OF ALL ASPECTS OF THE INDIVIDUAL) ARE COMPATIBLE. THE STUDY HAD TWO PHASES. IN THE MAJOR PHASE, THE CAUSES OF STUDENT PROGRESS WERE SOUGHT BY RELATING SUCH PROGRESS TO MEASURES OF CLASSROOM PROCESS AND TO MEASURES OF A TEACHER'S PERSONALITY AND BEHAVIOR. IN THE MINOR PHASE, THE EFFECTS OF SENSITIVITY TRAINING FOR TEACHERS WERE MEASURED IN A CLASSIC CONTROL-EXPERIMENTAL GROUP PROCEDURE. THE SUBJECTS WERE THE TEACHERS AND STUDENTS IN 57 CLASSROOMS, GRADES 3 THROUGH 6, IN FOUR METROPOLITAN ELEMENTARY SCHOOLS. PRETESTING, POSTTESTING, PERSONALITY MEASURES AND OBSERVATIONS OF CLASSROOM PROCESS WERE EXTENSIVE AND DETAILED. RESULTS OF THE MINOR PHASE ARE NOT CLEAR, BUT TEND TO SUPPORT PREVIOUS FINDINGS THAT EFFECTIVENESS OF SENSITIVITY TRAINING TENDS TO CORRELATE HIGHLY WITH THE TEACHER'S LEVEL OF PSYCHIC RESOURCES. RESULTS OF THE MAJOR PHASE IN GENERAL SUPPORT THE THEORY OF COMPATIBILITY OF THE VARIED GOALS OF EDUCATION. BENEFITS OF SENSITIVITY TRAINING CAN BE MEASURED, ALTHOUGH NOT EVERYONE IS BENEFITED. (MH)

ED033750 PS002430
PRELUDE TO SCHOOL: AN EVALUATION OF AN INNER-CITY PRESCHOOL PROGRAM. KRAFT, IVOR; AND OTHERS, 68 96P.
EDRS PRICE MF-$0.65 HC NOT AVAILABLE FROM EDRS.
AVAILABLE FROM: SUPERINTENDENT OF DOCUMENTS, U.S. GOVERNMENT PRINTING OFFICE, WASHINGTON, D.C. 20402 ($1.00)

THE PURPOSE OF HOWARD UNIVERSITY'S PRE-"WAR ON POVERTY" EXPERIMENT, OPERATING A 2 YEAR, FULL DAY NURSERY SCHOOL FOR DISADVANTAGED 3-YEAR-OLDS, WAS TO DETERMINE WHETHER AND TO WHAT EXTENT A STANDARD NURSERY SCHOOL PROGRAM IN WHICH PARENTS ARE INVOLVED COULD HELP CHILDREN IN THEIR LATER SCHOOLING. THIS BOOKLET GIVES AN OVERALL VIEW OF THE PROJECT, EXPLAINING ITS EXPERIMENTAL-CONTROL GROUP DESIGN, THE RECRUITING AND SCREENING OF SUBJECTS FOR BOTH GROUPS AND THE DETAILED CHARACTERISTICS OF CHILDREN SELECTED AND THEIR FAMILIES. THE SCHOOL DESCRIPTION INCLUDES PERSONNEL, PHYSICAL SETTING, CURRICULUM, AND HEALTH MAINTENANCE MEASURES. THE ADULT ACTIVITIES PROGRAM IS ALSO DISCUSSED. THE RESULTS OF THE PRE-POSTTESTING PROGRAM (STANFORD-BINET, PEABODY PICTURE VOCABULARY TEST, MERRILL-PALMER SCALE, AND THE ILLINOIS TEST OF PSYCHOLINGUISTIC ABILITIES) ARE GIVEN. THE LOWER A CHILD'S INITIAL IQ WAS, THE MORE LIKELY HE WAS TO MAKE LARGE GAINS AFTER NURSERY SCHOOL EXPERIENCE INDICATING THAT THE DIVERSITY OF INTELLECTUAL CAPACITY WAS NOT AS GREAT AS THE ORIGINAL IQS SHOWED. THE CHILDREN OF LOW SOCIOECONOMIC STATUS WHO SCORED LOW ON THE INITIAL IQ TEST MADE THE MOST GAINS DURING THE

SECOND YEAR OF THE PROGRAM. LANGUAGE ABILITY, HOWEVER, REMAINED BELOW AVERAGE EVEN AFTER THE SECOND YEAR. CHILDREN IN THE HIGHER SES MADE GAINS DURING THE FIRST YEAR. (MH)

ED033751 PS002460
GROUP SCREENING OF AUDITORY AND VISUAL PERCEPTUAL ABILITIES: AN APPROACH TO PERCEPTUAL ASPECTS OF BEGINNING READING. BUKTENICA, NORMAN A., SEP 69 11P.
EDRS PRICE MF-$0.65 HC-$3.29

A 3-YEAR STUDY ATTEMPTED (1) TO PREDICT READING ACHIEVEMENT THROUGH THIRD GRADE, (2) TO ESTABLISH DATA FOR A NONVERBAL DISCRIMINATION TEST, (3) TO DEVISE SUPPLEMENTARY PERCEPTUAL INSTRUCTIONAL PROGRAMS, AND (4) TO DEVELOP SCREENING DEVICES TO ASSESS PERCEPTUAL ABILITIES AND IDENTIFY POTENTIAL LEARNING DISABILITIES. IN FIRST, SECOND, AND THIRD GRADES 140 NEGRO AND WHITE CHILDREN OF LOWER AND MIDDLE CLASS BACKGROUNDS WERE ADMINISTERED A BATTERY OF AUDITORY AND VISUAL PERCEPTUAL TESTS. THE CHILDREN HAD THE SAME READING PROGRAM AND TOOK A READING ACHIEVEMENT TEST IN FIRST GRADE AND AT THE END OF THIRD GRADE. CORRELATIONS BETWEEN TESTS OF NONVERBAL AUDITORY AND VISUAL PERCEPTION AND READING ACHIEVEMENT REMAINED SIGNIFICANTLY HIGH AND RATHER CONSTANT OVER THE 3-YEAR PERIOD. THE BEST PREDICTOR OF READING ABILITY WAS THE TEST OF NON-VERBAL AUDITORY DISCRIMINATION, BUT ALL PERCEPTUAL TESTS WERE MORE EFFECTIVE THAN IQ MEASURES. BY USING GROUP-ADMINISTERED, NONVERBAL AUDITORY AND VISUAL PERCEPTION TESTS, IT IS POSSIBLE TO IDENTIFY CHILDREN'S POTENTIAL IN READING ACHIEVEMENT AT THE BEGINNING OF FIRST GRADE, AND TO DEVELOP SPECIAL INSTRUCTIONAL METHODS FOR CHILDREN WITH PERCEPTUAL PROBLEMS. (MH)

ED033752 PS002474
MODIFICATION OF THE PEABODY PICTURE VOCABULARY TEST. FAIZUNISA, ALI; COSTELLO, JOAN, 69 18P.
EDRS PRICE MF-$0.65 HC-$3.29

THIS STUDY REPORTS AN ATTEMPT TO IMPROVE THE ADMINISTRATION OF THE PEABODY PICTURE VOCABULARY TEST (PPVT) BY IDENTIFYING AND MODIFYING ASPECTS OF THE TEST WHICH ADVERSELY AFFECT DISADVANTAGED PRESCHOOLERS' PERFORMANCE. THE RESULTANT TEST WAS CALLED THE MODIFIED PEABODY PICTURE VOCABULARY TEST (M-PPVT). TWO SAMPLES FROM THE SAME LOWER CLASS POPULATION WERE COMPARED ON THE STANDARD AND MODIFIED TEST VERSIONS. THE M-PPVT REQUIRED THE EXAMINER TO PROVIDE ENCOURAGEMENT AND APPROVAL, TO FOLLOW A SCHEDULE OF HIGH REINFORCEMENT, AND TO GIVE SPECIFIC INSTRUCTIONS BEFORE EACH STIMULUS WORD. A MODIFIED RECORD SHEET FACILITATED ADMINISTRATION AND RECORDING OF RESPONSES. IN STUDY I BOTH TEST FORMS WERE ADMINISTERED TWICE TO 36 NEGRO CHILDREN. THERE WAS SLIGHTLY INCREASED SCORE STABILITY UNDER THE M-PPVT, BUT PRACTICE EFFECTS WERE NOT SIGNIFICANT. BOYS SCORED SIGNIFICANTLY HIGHER THAN GIRLS. IN STUDY II, 19 BLACK CHILDREN TOOK THE PPVT AND 19 TOOK THE M-PPVT. RESULTS SUGGESTED THAT THE M-PPVT OFFERED A SLIGHT ADVANTAGE TO LOW-SCORING SUBJECTS POSSIBLY DUE TO EXAMINER CONTROLS. SELECTION AND EVALUATION OF TEST INSTRUMENTS FOR DISADVANTAGED PRESCHOOLERS SHOULD CONSIDER PSYCHOMETRIC PROPERTIES, AND THE INFLUENCES OF EXAMINER STYLES AND TEST ADMINISTRATION CONTROLS ON PERFORMANCE. (DR)

ED033753 PS002485
THE TUCSON EARLY EDUCATION MODEL. HUGHES, MARIE M.; AND OTHERS, [68] 12P.
EDRS PRICE MF-$0.65 HC-$3.29

THE OBJECTIVES OF THIS MODEL PROGRAM ARE (1) TO DEVELOP LANGUAGE COMPETENCE, (2) TO ACQUIRE SKILLS NECESSARY IN THE PROCESS OF LEARNING, (3) TO ACQUIRE ATTITUDES AND BEHAVIORAL CHARACTERISTICS RELATED TO PRODUCTIVE SOCIAL INVOLVEMENT, AND (4) TO LEARN ARTS AND SKILLS ASSOCIATED WITH SOCIAL INTERACTION, TRANSMISSION OF INFORMATION, AND SCIENTIFIC ADVANCE. PARTICIPANTS ARE MEXICAN-AMERICAN CHILDREN, GRADES 1 TO 3. THE PROGRAM RECOGNIZES THE INDIVIDUALISM OF EACH CHILD, ENCOURAGES IMITATION OF MODEL BEHAVIORS, AND PROVIDES VERBAL REWARDS AND REINFORCING EXPERIENCES. SKILLS ARE TAUGHT SIMULTANEOUSLY IN FUNCTIONAL SETTINGS TO ENCOURAGE GENERALIZATION OF LEARNING. INTERACTION OF THE CHILD WITH HIS ENVIRONMENT AND OTHER PEOPLE IS FACILITATED BY ROOM ORGANIZATION, THE VARIETY OF BEHAVIORS ENGAGED IN, AND SMALL GROUP LESSONS. TEACHERS USE THE EXPERIENCES AND BACKGROUNDS OF THE CHILDREN AS INSTRUCTIONAL RESOURCES, ALTHOUGH THE STAFF STRUCTURES AND DIRECTS LESSONS. MODELS FOR PARENT INVOLVEMENT AND PSYCHOLOGICAL SERVICES ARE BEING DEVELOPED. TO INTRODUCE AND MAINTAIN THE PROGRAM'S INNOVATIVE PRACTICES, PROGRAM ASSISTANTS ARE TRAINED TO SERVE AS TECHNICAL CONSULTANTS TO CLASSROOM TEACHERS SEVERAL HOURS EACH WEEK. (DR)

ED033754 PS002508
SOCIAL CLASS DIFFERENTIATION IN COGNITIVE DEVELOPMENT: A LONGITUDINAL STUDY. GOLDEN, MARK; AND OTHERS, 69 24P.
EDRS PRICE MF-$0.65 HC-$3.29

IN AN EFFORT TO ISOLATE THE EMERGENCE AND CAUSES OF SOCIAL CLASS DIFFERENCES IN INTELLECTUAL PERFORMANCE, THIS LONGITUDINAL STUDY WAS UNDERTAKEN AS A FOLLOW-UP ON A CROSS-SECTIONAL STUDY THAT YIELDED NO SOCIAL CLASS DIFFERENCES ON THE CATTELL INFANT INTELLIGENCE SCALE FOR 12-, 18-, AND 24-MONTH-OLD BLACK CHILDREN. IN THE PRESENT STUDY, 89 CHILDREN FROM THE 18 AND 24 MONTH SAMPLES OF THE PREVIOUS STUDY WERE TESTED ON THE STANFORD-BINET AT 3 YEARS OF AGE, AND THEIR MOTHERS WERE GIVEN THE PEABODY PICTURE VOCABULARY TEST. THERE WERE HIGHLY SIGNIFICANT DIFFERENCES ON THE STANFORD-BINET BETWEEN GROUPS BASED ON DIFFERENT SOCIOECONOMIC STATUS. CORRELATIONS BETWEEN CHILD'S SCORE AND MOTHER'S SCORE TEND TO INCREASE WITH THE CHILD'S AGE. THESE FINDINGS MATCH THOSE PREVIOUSLY REPORTED FOR WHITE CHILDREN. INTERPRETATION OF THE DATA SEEMS TO INDICATE THAT SOCIAL CLASS INFLUENCES ON INTELLECTUAL PERFORMANCE ARE OPERATING BUT STATISTICALLY INSIGNIFICANT AT 18 AND 24 MONTHS, FINALLY BECOMING SIGNIFICANT DURING THE THIRD YEAR OF LIFE. RATHER THAN BEING CAUSED BY EITHER MALNUTRITION OR HEREDITARY FACTORS, SOCIAL CLASS DIFFERENCES IN INTELLECTUAL DEVELOPMENT MAY BE DUE TO DIFFERENCES IN THE ACQUISITION OF ABSTRACT KNOWLEDGE, THE PATTERN OF VERBAL INTERACTION BETWEEN PARENTS AND CHILD, AND DIFFERENCES IN SYMBOLIC THINKING ABILITY. (MH)

ED033755 PS002510
INFANT DAY CARE AND ATTACHMENT. CALDWELL, BETTYE M.; AND OTHERS, 1 APR 69 30P.
EDRS PRICE MF-$0.65 HC-$3.29

IN A LONGITUDINAL STUDY, A GROUP OF 41 CHILDREN FROM LOWER CLASS FAMILIES WERE EXAMINED FOR DIFFERENCES IN CHILD-MOTHER AND MOTHER-CHILD ATTACHMENT PATTERNS AT 30 MONTHS OF AGE. TWENTY-THREE CHILDREN HAD BEEN CARED FOR BY THEIR MOTHERS FROM BIRTH UNTIL 30 MONTHS OF AGE, AND 18 HAD BEEN ENROLLED IN A DAY CARE CENTER FOR AT LEAST 1 YEAR. DATA SOURCES WERE AN INTENSIVE SEMISTRUCTURED INTERVIEW TO RATE MOTHER-CHILD INTERACTION, A HOME STIMULATION INVENTORY SCORED ON THE BASIS OF A HOME VISIT, AND DEVELOPMENTAL TESTING USING THE STANFORD-BINET OR CATTELL INFANT INTELLIGENCE SCALE. NO SIGNIFICANT DIFFERENCES IN CHILD-MOTHER OR MOTHER-CHILD ATTACHMENT WERE FOUND BETWEEN CHILDREN REARED AT HOME AND DAY CARE CHILDREN. IN RESPECT TO CHILD-MOTHER ATTACHMENT, BETTER DEVELOPED INFANTS TENDED TO BE MORE POSITIVELY RELATED TO THEIR MOTHERS AND CAME FROM HOMES WHERE A HIGH QUANTITY AND QUALITY OF STIMULATION WAS AVAILABLE. IT WAS CONCLUDED THAT INFANT DAY CARE PROGRAMS CAN CONTRIBUTE POSITIVELY TO THE COGNITIVE, SOCIAL, AND EMOTIONAL DEVELOPMENT OF THE CHILD WITHOUT HARMING THE CHILD'S EMOTIONAL ATTACHMENT TO THE MOTHER. (DR)

ED033756 PS002511
YOUNG CHILDREN'S COMPREHENSION OF LOGICAL CONNECTIVES. SUPPES, PATRICK; FELDMAN, SHIRLEY, 15 OCT 69 33P.
EDRS PRICE MF-$0.65 HC-$3.29

TO DETERMINE TO WHAT EXTENT CHILDREN OF PRESCHOOL AGE COMPREHEND THE MEANING OF LOGICAL CONNECTIVES, 64 5- AND 6-YEAR-OLDS WERE TOLD TO HAND DIFFERENTLY COLORED AND SHAPED WOODEN BLOCKS TO AN EXPERIMENTER. THE COMMANDS INVOLVED VARIOUS ENGLISH IDIOMS USED FOR CONJUNCTION (E.G. BOTH BLACK AND ROUND), DISJUNCTION (EITHER BLACK OR ROUND), AND NEGATION (NOT ROUND). ANALYSIS OF THE RESULTS INDICATED THAT SOCIOECONOMIC STATUS WAS THE MOST TELLING FACTOR, WITH DISADVANTAGED CHILDREN PERFORMING POOREST. IN ADDITION, THE OLDER CHILDREN PERFORMED BETTER THAN THE YOUNGER ONES, BUT SEX DIFFERENCES WERE NOT SIGNIFICANT. THE DATA FURTHER SHOWED THAT DISJUNCTION WAS BY FAR THE MOST DIFFICULT OPERATION FOR CHILDREN AND THAT THE IDIOM IN WHICH THE CONCEPT WAS EXPRESSED WAS A SIGNIFICANT FACTOR. A PREDICTIVE REGRESSION MODEL WAS DEVELOPED FROM THE DATA. A SECOND EXPERIMENT WAS PERFORMED WITH 112 4- TO 6-YEAR-OLDS. THIS EXPERIMENT WAS MODELED AFTER THE FIRST EXCEPT THAT TYPE OF CONNECTIVE, TYPE OF IDIOM, AND ORDER OF COMMANDS WERE VARIED. THE TYPE OF CONNECTIVE HAD THE GREATEST EFFECT BUT NEGATION WAS ALSO AN IMPORTANT VARIABLE. (MH)

ED033757 PS002512
EFFECT OF SENSORIMOTOR ACTIVITY ON PERCEPTION AND LEARNING IN THE NEUROLOGICALLY HANDICAPPED CHILD. FINAL PROGRESS REPORT. AYRES, A. JEAN, SEP 68 21P.
EDRS PRICE MF-$0.65 HC-$3.29

BECAUSE SOME LEARNING DISORDERS IN CHILDREN MAY BE ASSOCIATED WITH PERCEPTUAL-MOTOR DYSFUNCTION, THIS STUDY TESTED THE EFFECTS OF SENSORIMOTOR TREATMENT ON LEARNING DISORDERS AND EXPLORED THE NATURE OF NEURODEVELOPMENTAL DISORDERS. IN PART ONE, 64 NEUROMUSCULAR, PERCEPTUAL, AND COGNITIVE MEASUREMENTS MADE ON 36 EDUCATIONALLY HANDICAPPED CHILDREN WITH NORMAL IQ'S WERE SUBJECTED TO Q-TECHNIQUE FACTOR ANALYSIS. THE TWO MAJOR PATTERNS OF DEFICITS ASSOCIATED

WITH LOW ACADEMIC ACHIEVEMENT WERE (1) AUDITORY, LANGUAGE, AND SEQUENCING, AND (2) POSTURAL AND BILATERAL INTEGRATION. PART TWO SOUGHT SYNDROMES OF DYSFUNCTION FROM AN R-TECHNIQUE FACTOR ANALYSIS OF PERCEPTUAL-MOTOR TEST SCORES. Q-ANALYSIS SUBJECTS AND ADDITIONAL CHILDREN WITH ACADEMIC PROBLEMS WERE TESTED. EMERGING FACTORS REPRESENTED TYPES OF STATISTICAL ASSOCIATIONS AMONG BEHAVIORAL PARAMETERS APT TO BE AFFECTED BY NEURODEVELOPMENTAL DISORDERS. PART THREE HYPOTHESIZED THAT EDUCATIONALLY HANDICAPPED CHILDREN IN SPECIAL CLASSES RECEIVING SENSORIMOTOR TRAINING SHOW A GREATER CHANGE IN PERCEPTUAL-MOTOR, LANGUAGE, AND ACADEMIC ACHIEVEMENT SCORES THAN CHILDREN RECEIVING THE EQUIVALENT AMOUNT OF ADDITIONAL CLASSROOM INSTRUCTION. TEST SCORES FAILED TO SUPPORT THIS HYPOTHESIS. THE MAJOR CONTRIBUTION OF THE ENTIRE PROJECT WAS THE IDENTIFICATION OF POSTURAL AND BILATERAL INTEGRATION DEFICIT WHICH INTERFERED WITH LEARNING. (JF)

ED033758 PS002513
FOCUS ON PARENT EDUCATION AS A MEANS OF ALTERING THE CHILD'S ENVIRONMENT. JESTER, R. EMILE, [69] 11P.
EDRS PRICE MF-$0.65 HC-$3.29

THE FLORIDA PARENT EDUCATION MODEL, WORKING WITH 5- TO 7-YEAR-OLDS ENROLLED IN FOLLOW THROUGH PROGRAMS, IS BASED ON THE PREMISE THAT A CHILD'S HOME ENVIRONMENT HAS THE MOST LASTING INFLUENCE ON HIS ADAPTATION TO SCHOOL AND TO THE WORLD AROUND HIM. THE PROGRAM WORKS WITH THE MOTHER, WHO, AS EDUCATORS ARE DISCOVERING, HAS MORE INFLUENCE ON THE CHILD THAN ANYONE ELSE. THE PROGRAM RECRUITS PARENT EDUCATORS FROM ENVIRONMENTS SIMILAR TO THOSE OF MOTHERS WITH WHOM THEY WILL WORK. THE PARENT EDUCATORS VISIT PARENTS IN THEIR HOMES AND PROVIDE THEM WITH SPECIFIC TASKS TO WORK ON WITH THEIR CHILDREN. THE PARENT EDUCATOR IS ALSO EXPECTED TO BE A PART OF THE CLASSROOM INSTRUCTIONAL SYSTEM SO SHE AND THE TEACHER COLLABORATE ON HOME TASKS TO PROVIDE BOTH SCHOOL-RELEVANT AND HOME-RELEVANT BEHAVIOR IN THE CHILD. THE PROGRAM AT THIS POINT APPEARS TO BE MODERATELY SUCCESSFUL. ALTHOUGH, THE ONLY INFORMATION AVAILABLE IS SUBJECTIVE, IT INDICATES THAT PARENT INTEREST IS INCREASED, THAT PARENTS ARE WORKING MORE WITH CHILDREN, AND THAT THERE IS MORE INDIVIDUAL AND SMALL GROUP INSTRUCTION IN THE CLASSROOM THAN EVER BEFORE. (JF)

ED033759 PS002525
PENNSYLVANIA PRESCHOOL AND PRIMARY EDUCATION PROJECT: 1968-1969 FINAL REPORT TO THE FORD FOUNDATION. KERSHNER, KEITH M., OCT 69 161P.
EDRS PRICE MF-$0.65 HC-$6.58

TO IMPROVE THE EDUCATION OF CULTURALLY DISADVANTAGED CHILDREN, THIS PROJECT FOCUSED ON CHILDREN'S SPECIFIC BEHAVIORAL DEFICITS, TEACHER PREPARATION, PARENT ATTITUDES, HEALTH AND SERVICE AGENCIES, AND LOCAL SCHOOL DISTRICTS. THE PROJECT WAS CARRIED OUT IN A RURAL APPALACHIAN SCHOOL WITH 122 CHILDREN, 30 PERCENT NEGRO AND 70 PERCENT WHITE, AND IN AN URBAN SCHOOL WITH 350 CHILDREN, 95 PERCENT WHITE AND 5 PERCENT NONWHITE. BOTH SCHOOLS WERE IN LOW INCOME AREAS. AN EMPHASIS ON INDIVIDUALIZATION AND AN UNGRADED TEACHING APPROACH WAS USED IN THE RURAL SCHOOL FOR CHILDREN IN KINDERGARTEN THROUGH THIRD GRADE. TEACHERS MET WITH TESTING AND CURRICULUM CONSULTANTS; PARENTS ATTENDED GROUP MEETINGS; AND FUTURE PROGRAM PLANS WERE MADE BY THE LOCAL SCHOOL DISTRICT. THE URBAN SCHOOL PROGRAM WAS SIMILAR BUT HAD A MORE ACTIVE AND SUCCESSFUL PARENT EDUCATION PROGRAM AND BETTER COORDINATION OF AGENCIES. TO EVALUATE THE PROGRAM, ALL CHILDREN WERE PRE- AND POSTTESTED, USING THE ORAL LANGUAGE SCALE, THE SCIENCE AND MATH STUDY GROUP INDIVIDUAL MATH INVENTORY, THE METROPOLITAN ACHIEVEMENT TEST, AND THE CALIFORNIA TEST OF MENTAL MATURITY. THERE WERE NO CONTROL GROUPS. BOTH GROUPS OF CHILDREN SHOWED SIGNIFICANT COGNITIVE GAINS AND TEACHERS IN BOTH SCHOOLS IMPROVED IN KNOWLEDGE OF EDUCATION FOR THE CULTURALLY DEPRIVED. (DR)

ED033760 PS002527
INFANT EDUCATION. PAINTER, GENEVIEVE, 68 164P.
DOCUMENT NOT AVAILABLE FROM EDRS.
AVAILABLE FROM: DIMENSIONS PUBLISHING CO., BOX 4221, SAN RAFAEL, CALIFORNIA 94903 ($3.50)

THIS INVESTIGATION EVALUATED A GROUP OF 20 8-MONTH TO 2-YEAR-OLD CULTURALLY DISADVANTAGED CHILDREN WHO WERE GIVEN A 1-YEAR STRUCTURED EDUCATIONAL PROGRAM AS A MEANS OF ENVIRONMENTAL INTERVENTION. THE PROGRAM INVOLVED LANGUAGE TRAINING, CONCEPTUAL TRAINING, AND SENSORY-MOTOR TRAINING. THE STUDY IS THE FIRST PHASE OF A LONGITUDINAL STUDY TO DETERMINE HOW EARLY INTERVENTION SHOULD BEGIN. SUBJECTS WERE THE YOUNGER SIBLINGS OF 4-YEAR-OLDS IN AN EXPERIMENTAL NURSERY SCHOOL. TEN OF THEM, THE EXPERIMENTAL GROUP, WERE GIVEN THE TUTORIAL PROGRAM IN THEIR HOMES 1 HOUR DAILY 5 DAYS A WEEK. THE OTHER 10, THE CONTROL GROUP, PROGRESSED NORMALLY IN THEIR OWN ENVIRONMENTS. WHEN THE TWO GROUPS WERE COMPARED AT THE END OF A YEAR, THE EXPERIMENTAL GROUP RATED SIGNIFICANTLY HIGHER IN GENERAL IQ AND IN AREAS OF LANGUAGE AND CONCEPTUAL DEVELOPMENT, SUGGESTING THAT THE TUTORIAL PROGRAM WAS EFFECTIVE. HOWEVER, TO DETERMINE OPTIMAL AGE FOR INTERVENTION, THESE SUBJECTS AT AGE 4 WILL HAVE TO BE COMPARED WITH THE PRENURSERY SCHOOL RECORDS OF THEIR OLDER SIBLINGS NOW IN NURSERY SCHOOL. (JF)

ED033761 PS002528
THE EFFECTS OF SOCIODRAMATIC PLAY ON DISADVANTAGED PRESCHOOL CHILDREN. SMILANSKY, SARA, 68 171P.
DOCUMENT NOT AVAILABLE FROM EDRS.
AVAILABLE FROM: JOHN WILEY AND SONS, INC., 605 THIRD AVENUE, NEW YORK, NEW YORK 10016 ($7.50)

THIS BOOK EXPLORES SOCIODRAMATIC PLAY AS A POTENTIAL COMPENSATORY TOOL FOR EDUCATIONALLY DISADVANTAGED CHILDREN. THE AUTHOR EXAMINES THE ANTECEDENTS OF EDUCATIONAL DISADVANTAGEMENT AND DEVELOPS A RATIONALE FOR THE USE OF SOCIODRAMATIC PLAY. SHE PLACES SOCIODRAMATIC PLAY IN PERSPECTIVE AS A PARTICULAR STAGE OF PLAY BEHAVIOR AND FURTHER INVESTIGATES THE PHENOMENON IN THIS LIGHT. USING OBSERVATIONS OF ADVANTAGED AND DISADVANTAGED CHILDREN, SHE STUDIES PARTICULAR DIFFERENCES AND SIMILARITIES BETWEEN THE TWO GROUPS, WITH SPECIAL ATTENTION ON FACTORS RELATED TO SOCIODRAMATIC PLAY. AFTER PLACING THE OBSERVATIONS ON A CONCEPTUAL FRAMEWORK, THE AUTHOR DISCUSSES IDENTIFICATION AND THE ROLE OF PARENTS IN DEVELOPING THE REQUIREMENTS FOR SOCIODRAMATIC PLAY. GROUP DIFFERENCES ARE THEN ISOLATED AS CAUSES FOR DIFFERENCES IN SOCIODRAMATIC PLAY, AND AN EXPERIMENT IS DESIGNED AND PERFORMED TO TEST THE EFFECTIVENESS OF THESE FACTORS IN ELICITING SOCIODRAMATIC PLAY AMONG DISADVANTAGED CHILDREN. THE RESULTS ARE PRESENTED AND INTERPRETED, AND, FINALLY, VARIOUS FINDINGS AND IMPRESSIONS COLLECTED DURING THE EXPERIMENT AND CONSIDERED OF SIGNIFICANCE ARE REPORTED AND DISCUSSED. (MH)

ED033762 PS002529
SELECTED LONGITUDINAL STUDIES OF COMPENSATORY EDUCATION--A LOOK FROM THE INSIDE. GRAY, SUSAN W., 69 13P.
EDRS PRICE MF-$0.65 HC-$3.29

THIS DOCUMENT, PREPARED FOR A SYMPOSIUM ON PRESCHOOL COMPENSATORY PROGRAMS, MAKES PRELIMINARY COMMENTS ON THE DIFFICULTY OF PROGRAM ASSESSMENT AND TIGHT EXPERIMENTAL DESIGN, ON THE NECESSITY OF IN-DEPTH INVOLVEMENT, AND ON THE NEED FOR VIGILANCE IN MAINTAINING AN EXPERIMENTAL CONDITION. A NUMBER OF STUDIES IN PRESCHOOL INTERVENTION ARE REVIEWED AND EVALUATED. AMONG THESE ARE THE SKEELS (1966) 21-YEAR FOLLOWUP STUDY ON INSTITUTIONALIZED, RETARDED CHILDREN, THE KLAUS AND GRAY STUDY (1968-69) INVOLVING LOW INCOME NEGROES IN THE UPPER SOUTH IN A SUMMER AND HOME-VISIT FOLLOWUP PROGRAM, AND WEIKART'S STUDY (1967) UTILIZING 2-1/2 HOUR MORNING SESSIONS AND AFTERNOON HOME VISITS. TWO CURRICULUM COMPARISON STUDIES (WEIKART, 1969 AND KARNES, 1969) AND A STUDY OF COMPARATIVE KINDERGARTEN CONDITIONS FOR RURAL CHILDREN ARE ALSO DISCUSSED. (MH)

ED033763 PS002530
CHILDREN LEARNING: SAMPLES OF EVERYDAY LIFE OF CHILDREN AT HOME. SHAW, JEAN W.; SCHOGGEN, MAXINE, 69 81P.
EDRS PRICE MF-$0.65 HC NOT AVAILABLE FROM EDRS.
AVAILABLE FROM: MRS. JEAN SHAW OR MRS. MAXINE SCHOGGEN, DARCEE, BOX 151, GEORGE PEABODY COLLEGE FOR TEACHERS, NASHVILLE, TENNESSEE 37203

THIS HANDBOOK DESCRIBES YOUNG CHILDREN'S INTERACTION WITH PEOPLE, PARTICULARLY THEIR MOTHERS. CHILDREN FROM CONTRASTING SOCIOECONOMIC CONDITIONS WERE USED AS SUBJECTS, AND DESCRIPTIONS OF THESE SIX 3-YEAR-OLDS IN THEIR HOMES ARE RELATED IN DETAIL. THE HOME OBSERVATION EXCERPTS DEAL WITH THE EFFECT OF MOTHERS' INSTRUCTIONS AND DEMONSTRATIONS ON THEIR CHILDREN, THE EXPERIENCES MOTHERS PROVIDE FOR THEIR CHILDREN IN THE HOME, CHILDREN'S SUBSEQUENT LEARNING, AND MOTHERS' INFLUENCES ON CHILDREN'S LANGUAGE DEVELOPMENT. AN APPENDIX GIVES POSSIBLE ANSWERS TO THE STUDY SUGGESTIONS. EACH DESCRIPTION IS FOLLOWED BY SUGGESTIONS FOR STUDY AND COMMENTS. A SECTION ON PLAY IS IN PREPARATION. THE HANDBOOK IS INTENDED TO BE USED AS SUPPLEMENTARY MATERIAL FOR TRAINING ADULTS WHO WORK WITH YOUNG CHILDREN. (DR)

ED033764 PS002541
THE DESIGN OF A PRE-SCHOOL "LEARNING LABORATORY" IN A REHABILITATION CENTER. GORDON, RONNIE, 69 66P.
DOCUMENT NOT AVAILABLE FROM EDRS.
AVAILABLE FROM: PUBLICATION OFFICE, INSTITUTE OF REHABILITATION MEDICINE, 400 EAST 34 STREET, NEW YORK, NEW YORK 10016 ($3.00, CHECKS PAYABLE TO N.Y. UNIVERSITY MEDICAL CENTER)

THE EDUCATIONAL PHILOSOPHY AND MEDICAL SETTING OF A PRESCHOOL PROGRAM IN A REHABILITATION CENTER FOR HANDICAPPED CHILDREN ARE PRESENTED IN THIS MONOGRAPH. CHILDREN WITH DIVERSE PHYSICAL, MENTAL, AND BEHAVIORAL PROBLEMS ARE SERVED BY THE CENTER, WHICH EMPHASIZES DEVELOPMENT OF EACH CHILD'S POTENTIAL WITHIN THE LIMITS OF HIS DISABILITIES. THE BASIC PHYSICAL DESIGN IS DESCRIBED AND ILLUSTRATED, SHOWING UNITS FOR ADULT USE, INCLUDING AN OBSERVATION ROOM FOR PARENTS AND STAFF, AND

CHILDREN'S FEATURES SUCH AS A WINDOW UNIT, HANDRAIL, AND HOUSEKEEPING UNIT. THERE ARE PHOTOGRAPHS OF THE CHILDREN USING SPECIALLY DESIGNED EQUIPMENT CONSISTING OF CIRCULAR WORK TABLES, A CARPENTRY TABLE, AND SAND AND WATER TABLES USED BY WHEELCHAIR-BOUND CHILDREN. THERE ARE ADJUSTABLE EASELS THAT ALLOW SMALL CHILDREN AND CHILDREN WITHOUT ARMS TO PAINT. A CHILD CAN WORK ALONE OR BE TUTORED AT THE "ISOLATION TABLE". EMPHASIS IS PLACED ON THE QUALITY OF THE STAFF AND A HIGH TEACHER-CHILD RATIO. IT IS CONCLUDED THAT TEACHERS MUST HAVE THEORETICAL AND PRACTICAL KNOWLEDGE OF NORMAL CHILDREN'S LEARNING AND BEHAVIOR BEFORE EVALUATING AND EDUCATING HANDICAPPED CHILDREN. (DR)

ED033765 PS002542
THE SATURDAY SCHOOL: AN INSTALLATION MANUAL. PARRISH, VALINDA E.; WILSON, WINSTON T., 69 147P.
EDRS PRICE MF-$0.65 HC-$6.58

THIS MANUAL DESCRIBES THE MECHANICS AND MAJOR FEATURES OF A SATURDAY SCHOOL PROJECT FOR 40 NEGRO PRESCHOOL CHILDREN IMPLEMENTED BY THE SOUTH CENTRAL REGION EDUCATIONAL LABORATORY IN THE 1968-69 SCHOOL YEAR IN CADDO PARISH, LOUISIANA. THE MANUAL HAS TWO GOALS: (1) TO INFORM THE READER ABOUT HOW THE PROJECT WAS SUCCESSFULLY IMPLEMENTED, AND (2) TO OFFER RECOMMENDATIONS ON WAYS TO IMPROVE SPECIFIC ASPECTS ON FUTURE PROJECTS. THE SATURDAY SCHOOL CONCEPT WAS DEVELOPED WITH THE CULTURALLY DISADVANTAGED CHILD AND THE EDUCATIONALLY RETARDED PARENT IN MIND, AND IS USEFUL WHEN FINANCIAL AND PROFESSIONAL RESOURCES ARE NOT AVAILABLE TO SUPPORT WEEKDAY KINDERGARTENS. THE REPORT IS DIVIDED INTO EIGHT SECTIONS. SECTIONS COVER DESCRIPTION OF POPULATION, PHYSICAL SETTING AND LOGISTICS, EDUCATIONAL OBJECTIVES, MEANS OF ACHIEVING OBJECTIVES, STAFFING, AND A BUDGET-COST ITEMIZATION. ALSO INCLUDED IS A THREE-PAGE EVALUATION OF THE PROJECT. THE APPENDICES (3/4 OF THE MANUAL) CONTAIN DETAILED INFORMATION, INCLUDING LESSON PLANS OUTLINING THE OBJECTIVES AND ACTIVITIES FOR 29 SEPARATE SCHOOL DAYS, AND 29 CORRESPONDING PARENT SCHEDULES. ALSO INCLUDED ARE EQUIPMENT/SUPPLY LISTS, RELATED LITERATURE, A COPY OF AN ANNOTATED TAPE OF PARENTS COMMENT, AND DIRECTIONS FOR MAKING EQUIPMENT AND MATERIALS. (JF)

ED033766 PS002557
THE INFLUENCE OF THEORETICAL CONCEPTIONS OF HUMAN DEVELOPMENT ON THE PRACTICE OF EARLY CHILDHOOD EDUCATION. GARDNER, D. BRUCE, 14 NOV 69 37P.
EDRS PRICE MF-$0.65 HC NOT AVAILABLE FROM EDRS.

COMMUNICATION IS URGED BETWEEN THEORISTS OF HUMAN DEVELOPMENT AND PRACTITIONERS IN EARLY CHILDHOOD EDUCATION. MAJOR PSYCHOLOGICAL THEORIES ON MATURATION, CHILD DEVELOPMENT, CHILD BEHAVIOR, PERSONALITY FORMATION, AND AFFECTIVE AND INTELLECTUAL DEVELOPMENT ARE SUMMARIZED AND THEIR EFFECTS ON NURSERY SCHOOL PRACTICES FROM THE 1920'S TO THE PRESENT ARE DESCRIBED. THREE MODELS OF EARLY CHILDHOOD EDUCATION ARE CHOSEN TO ILLUSTRATE THE DIVERSE TYPES OF PROGRAMS AVAILABLE FOR YOUNG CHILDREN TODAY. THE KEY FEATURES OF THE BANK STREET MODEL, THE KANSAS MODEL, AND THE YPSILANTI MODEL ARE DESCRIBED, COMPARED, AND CONTRASTED. EACH PROGRAM'S THEORETICAL CONCEPTIONS OF HUMAN NATURE ARE ANALYZED TO ILLUSTRATE THE MODELS' FUNDAMENTAL DIFFERENCES ABOUT THE SOURCES OF HUMAN DEVELOPMENT. CONCLUSIONS ARE THAT (1) TEACHERS SHOULD BE AWARE OF PHILOSOPHICAL ASSUMPTIONS AND PSYCHOLOGICAL THEORIES IN EARLY CHILDHOOD EDUCATION MODELS AND (2) THE ABSENCE OF CONSENSUS ON THE "RIGHT" WAY TO EDUCATE YOUNG CHILDREN SHOULD LEAD TO CONTINUED EXPERIMENTATION AND RECEPTIVITY TO PSYCHOLOGICAL THEORIES AND EDUCATIONAL STRATEGIES. [NOT AVAILABLE IN HARD COPY DUE TO MARGINAL LEGIBILITY OF ORIGINAL DOCUMENT.] (DR)

ED033767 PS002558
EFFECTS OF SOCIAL REINFORCEMENT ON SELF-ESTEEM OF MEXICAN-AMERICAN CHILDREN. LONG ABSTRACT. FIRMA, THEREZA PENNA, [67] 6P.
EDRS PRICE MF-$0.65 HC-$3.29

MEXICAN-AMERICAN SCHOOL CHILDREN ARE HANDICAPPED BY POOR ACADEMIC PERFORMANCE AND LOW SELF-ESTEEM. THIS STUDY HYPOTHESIZED THAT REINFORCEMENT AND REWARD TECHNIQUES USED TO PROMOTE SELF-ESTEEM SHOULD INCLUDE ACTIVITIES RELEVANT TO BOTH MEXICAN AND AMERICAN CULTURES. SPECIFIC PREDICTIONS WERE THAT (1) THE MOST EFFECTIVE TREATMENT WOULD BE REINFORCEMENT OF ACHIEVEMENT BEHAVIOR USING REWARDS ACCEPTABLE TO THE MEXICAN COMMUNITY, (2) THE SECOND MOST EFFECTIVE TREATMENT WOULD BE REINFORCEMENT OF SOCIOEMOTIONAL BEHAVIOR USING NON-MEXICAN REWARDS, AND (3) THE LEAST EFFECTIVE TREATMENT WOULD BE REINFORCEMENT OF SOCIOEMOTIONAL BEHAVIOR USING MEXICAN REWARDS AND REINFORCEMENT OF ACHIEVEMENT BEHAVIOR USING NON-MEXICAN REWARDS. SUBJECTS WERE 56 LOW ACHIEVING MEXICAN-AMERICAN CHILDREN, GRADES 1 TO 4. CHILDREN WERE RANDOMLY ASSIGNED TO TREATMENT GROUPS THAT STRESSED SIMPLE ACADEMIC TASKS, AND REWARDS FOR SELECTED BEHAVIORS. RESULTS FROM PRE- AND POSTTESTING ON A VARIETY OF TESTS DID NOT CONFIRM SPECIFIC PREDICTIONS, BUT DID SUPPORT THE GENERAL HYPOTHESIS OF A BICULTURAL APPROACH TO IMPROVE MEXICAN-AMERICAN CHILDREN'S SELF-ESTEEM. (DR)

ED033768 PS002559
DESIGNING A PROGRAM FOR BROADCAST TELEVISION. LESSER, GERALD S., 69 6P.
EDRS PRICE MF-$0.65 HC-$3.29

FUNDED BY BOTH PUBLIC AND PRIVATE AGENCIES, SESAME STREET, PRODUCED BY THE CHILDREN'S TELEVISION WORKSHOP, IS AN EXPERIMENTAL SERIES OF TELEVISION PROGRAMS FOR 3- TO 5-YEAR-OLDS. THE PROGRAM IS CONSIDERED A COMPLEMENT AND SUPPLEMENT TO EARLY EDUCATION SINCE 4/5 OF THE NATION'S YOUNG CHILDREN DO NOT ATTEND PRESCHOOL, BUT DO HAVE TELEVISION SETS AT HOME. DESIGN AND CONSTRUCTION OF THE PROGRAMS ARE GUIDED BY A RESEARCH STAFF RESPONSIBLE FOR CHILD-WATCHING TO DETERMINE WHAT THE CHILD ACTUALLY SEES, HEARS, AND LEARNS WHEN WATCHING SESAME STREET. THE INFORMATION RESULTING FROM THIS FORMATIVE EVALUATION IS USED BY PRODUCERS TO IMPROVE PROGRAMS. CITED FOR EXAMPLES OF TEACHING APPROACHES ALTERED BECAUSE CHILD-WATCHING INFORMATION INDICATED CHANGES WERE NEEDED. (MS)

ED034568 PS002183
A BILINGUAL ORAL LANGUAGE AND CONCEPTUAL DEVELOPMENT PROGRAM FOR SPANISH-SPEAKING PRE-SCHOOL CHILDREN. MIRANDA, CONSUELO; AND OTHERS, AUG 68 356P.
EDRS PRICE MF-$0.65 HC-$13.16
AVAILABLE FROM: FOREIGN LANGUAGE CONSULTANT, CURRICULUM DIVISION, MICHIGAN DEPT. OF EDUCATION, LANSING, MICHIGAN

THIS PAPERBOUND EDITION CONSISTS OF A SERIES OF LESSONS TO BE USED IN AN ENGLISH LANGUAGE AND CONCEPTUAL DEVELOPMENT PROGRAM FOR 4 TO 5-YEAR-OLD SPANISH-SPEAKING CHILDREN. THE OVERALL GOAL OF THE LESSONS, DESIGNED FOR USE WITH MIGRANT CHILDREN, IS TO PROVIDE THE CHILD WITH THE LANGUAGE AND CONCEPTUAL SKILLS HE NEEDS TO BENEFIT FROM A STANDARD SCHOOL SETTING. LESSONS ARE BUILT AROUND STRUCTURED ORAL LANGUAGE CIRCLES AND TAKE ABOUT 15 MINUTES EACH. THERE ARE 59 ENGLISH CIRCLES AND 61 SPANISH CIRCLES TO BE USED IN SEQUENCE AT A RATE OF THREE PER DAY FOR 8 WEEKS. THE SPANISH LESSONS PREPARE THE CHILD IN HIS FIRST LANGUAGE FOR THE CONTENT OF ENGLISH, WHILE AT THE SAME TIME HELPING HIM TO ACQUIRE STANDARD ALTERNATES FOR CERTAIN NONSTANDARD FEATURES OF HIS OWN DIALECT. THE VOLUME IS DIVIDED INTO FOUR PARTS. PART ONE INCLUDES A DESCRIPTION OF THE PROGRAM, ANSWERS TO COMMON QUESTIONS, AND A GENERAL LISTING OF A PRESCHOOL CLASSROOM'S PERMANENT EQUIPMENT. PART TWO CONSISTS OF THE LESSONS. PART THREE CONTAINS AN ART MATERIALS SUPPLEMENT PROVIDING PATTERNS FOR ANY ART WORK OR DEMONSTRATION OBJECTS NOT EASILY OBTAINABLE WITHIN THE SCHOOL. PART FOUR IS AN ORAL LANGUAGE TEST OF PRODUCTIVE ENGLISH WHICH CAN BE USED TO GAUGE A CHILD'S PROGRESS. (JF)

ED034569 PS002291
HEAD START PROGRAMS AND PARTICIPANTS 1965-1967. , [67] 209P.
EDRS PRICE MF-$0.65 HC-$9.87

THIS REPORT DESCRIBES THE CHILDREN, THEIR FAMILIES, AND STAFF MEMBERS WHO HAVE PARTICIPATED IN PROJECT HEAD START FROM ITS INCEPTION IN THE SUMMER OF 1965 THROUGH 1967. THE INFORMATION HAS BEEN COMPILED FROM TABULATIONS OF DATA PREPARED BY THE BUREAU OF CENSUS AND OFFERS A GENERAL PICTURE OF THE POPULATIONS SERVED TO DATE AND WHERE POSSIBLE INCLUDES PROGRAM INFORMATION. THE REPORT IS DIVIDED INTO SIX SECTIONS AND INCLUDES BOTH AN INTRODUCTION AND AN OVERVIEW. THESE SECTIONS REPRESENT A DESCRIPTION OF THE HEAD START CHILDREN AND THEIR FAMILIES, THE MEDICAL STATUS OF THE CHILDREN, CENTER INFORMATION WHERE AVAILABLE, STAFF MEMBER CHARACTERISTICS, EVALUATION OF THE PROGRAM, AND PARENT ACTIVITIES. TABLES INCLUDED WITH EACH SECTION CONSIST OF ITEM FREQUENCY DISTRIBUTIONS OF THE DATA COLLECTED TO DATE. THE DATA DEPICT SELECTED TRENDS IN THE COMPOSITION AND CHARACTERISTICS OF THE HEAD START PARTICIPANTS BY COMPARING THEM FROM ONE PROGRAM TERM TO THE NEXT. THE OVERVIEW PROVIDES A CONTEXT FOR INTERPRETING THE DATA. THE PAPER IS PLANNED TO BE SUGGESTIVE OF LEADS FOR ADDITIONAL AND MORE REFINED ANALYSIS OF DATA, AND SHOULD BE USEFUL IN BOTH PROGRAM PLANNING AND THE DESIGN OF RESEARCH AND EVALUATIVE STUDIES RELATED TO HEAD START. (AUTHOR/JF)

ED034570 PS002300
REDUCING BEHAVIOR PROBLEMS: AN OPERANT CONDITIONING GUIDE FOR TEACHERS. BECKER, WESLEY C.; AND OTHERS, NOV 69 20P.
EDRS PRICE MF-$0.65 HC-$3.29

CLASSROOM MANAGEMENT AND WHAT TEACHERS CAN DO TO MAKE IT POSSIBLE FOR CHILDREN TO BEHAVE BETTER, WHICH PERMITS LEARNING TO OCCUR, ARE THE SUBJECTS OF THIS HANDBOOK. THE AUTHORS HYPOTHESIZE THAT THE FIRST STEP TOWARD BETTER CLASSROOM MANAGEMENT IS A TEACHER'S RECOGNITION THAT HOW CHILDREN BEHAVE IS LARGELY DETERMINED BY THE TEACHER'S BEHAVIOR. WHEN TEACHERS EMPLOY OPERANT CONDITIONING THEY SYSTEMATICALLY USE REWARDING PRINCIPLES TO STRENGTHEN CHILDREN'S SUITABLE BEHAVIOR. IGNORING UNSUITABLE BEHAVIOR WILL

DISCOURAGE ITS CONTINUANCE. BEHAVIOR CAN BE CHANGED BY THREE METHODS: (1) REWARD APPROPRIATE BEHAVIOR AND WITHDRAW REWARDS FOLLOWING INAPPROPRIAGE BEHAVIOR, (2) STRENGTHEN THE REWARDS IF THE FIRST METHOD IS UNSUCCESSFUL, AND (3) PUNISH INAPPROPRIATE BEHAVIOR WHILE REWARDING APPROPRIATE BEHAVIOR IF METHODS (1) AND (2) FAIL. THE BOOKLET EXPLAINS EACH METHOD AND OFFERS SUPPORTING RESEARCH AND EVALUATIONS OF THE USE OF DIFFERENT METHODS. IT OUTLINES STEP-BY-STEP PROCEDURES AND HAS APPEAL FOR PARENTS, TEACHERS, AND ANYONE INVOLVED IN TRAINING CHILDREN. (DO)

ED034571 PS002375
LANGUAGE EXPERIENCES WHICH PROMOTE READING. VAN ALLEN, ROACH, 29 SEP 69 16P.
EDRS PRICE MF-$0.65 HC NOT AVAILABLE FROM EDRS.

IN THE LANGUAGE-EXPERIENCE APPROACH TO READING INSTRUCTION, COMMUNICATIVE SKILLS ARE VIEWED WITHOUT DISTINCTION AMONG LISTENING, SPEAKING, SPELLING, AND WRITING. THE CHILDREN LEARN TO CONCEIVE OF EXPRESSION AND RECEPTION OF EXPRESSION AS NATURAL PARTS OF EXPERIENCE, RATHER THAN AS SEPARATE TASKS THAT OCCUR DURING A BREAK IN REGULAR ACTIVITY. THE SKILLFUL LANGUAGE-EXPERIENCE TEACHER WEAVES OPPORTUNITIES FOR COMMUNICATION PRACTICE (LISTENING, SPEAKING, WRITING, READING, AND DICTATING) UNOBTRUSIVELY INTO THE FABRIC OF DAILY EXPERIENCE. THROUGH THIS PRACTICE, THE CHILD COMES TO FEEL THAT HE CAN TALK ABOUT WHAT HE THINKS, THAT HE CAN TALK ABOUT WHAT HE CAN COMMUNICATE IN OTHER WAYS, AND THAT HE CAN RECALL WHAT HE OR OTHERS DICTATE AND WHAT HE OR OTHERS WRITE THROUGH READING. THE CHILD COMES TO RECOGNIZE LETTERS AND THEIR FUNCTION, AND LEARNS LITTLE BY LITTLE THE DETAILS OF LANGUAGE USE, BECAUSE HE WANTS TO. NEW SKILLS ARE PUT TO IMMEDIATE USE AND RECEIVE IMMEDIATE POSITIVE FEEDBACK. THROUGH THIS METHOD, CHILDREN NOT ONLY LEARN TO READ BETTER, BUT THEY ALSO DEVELOP MATURE CONCEPTS ABOUT THE VALUE AND USE OF READING AND OTHER COMMUNICATIVE SKILLS. [NOT AVAILABLE IN HARD COPY DUE TO MARGINAL LEGIBILITY OF ORIGINAL DOCUMENT]. (MH)

ED034572 PS002385
INDIVIDUAL DIFFERENCES IN GHETTO FOUR-YEAR-OLDS. HIRSCH, JAY G.; AND OTHERS, 69 23P.
EDRS PRICE MF-$0.65 HC-$3.29

THIRTY-FIVE DISADVANTAGED NEGRO 4-YEAR-OLDS WERE OBSERVED BY ONE OR THE OTHER OF TWO WHITE MALE CHILD PSYCHIATRISTS DURING A 30-MINUTE PLAY SESSION. AFTER THE SESSION, THE OBSERVER DICTATED A DESCRIPTIVE SUMMARY OF THE SESSION. HE FILLED OUT A RATING SCALE ON ASPECTS OF THE CHILD'S BEHAVIOR, INCLUDING SPEECH AND PLAY BEHAVIOR, NATURE OF SOCIAL INTERACTION, INTEREST IN PLAY MATERIALS, ABILITY TO FOCUS ATTENTION, INFERENCES ABOUT HIS PREVIOUS EXPERIENCE WITH CARETAKERS, AND GENERAL DEVELOPMENTAL ASSESSMENT RATING. EIGHTEEN MONTHS LATER TYPED COPIES OF THE DICTATED SUMMARIES WERE DISTRIBUTED TO THE TWO OBSERVERS AND TO FIVE INDEPENDENT JUDGES, ALL OF WHOM WERE PSYCHOANALYTICALLY ORIENTED. ANALYSIS OF THE RATINGS SUGGESTS THAT PRE-ENTRANCE RATINGS DO PROVIDE INFORMATION FOR READINESS GROUPINGS AND CAN BE MADE ON THE BASIS OF THE CHILD'S RESPONSE TO A NEW ADULT AND HIS INTERACTION WITH PRESCHOOL MATERIALS. THE STABILITY OF THE OBSERVERS' TWO SETS OF RATINGS WAS HIGH, AS WAS AGREEMENT BETWEEN OBSERVERS, AGREEMENT AMONG THE FIVE INDEPENDENT JUDGES, AND AGREEMENT BETWEEN OBSERVERS AND JUDGES. FINALLY, IT IS SUGGESTED THAT GROUPING CHILDREN INTO COMPETENCE GROUPS, BASED ON RATINGS BY EXPERIENCED OBSERVERS, WILL FACILITATE PRESCHOOL PROGRAM PLANNING AND MAKE CHILDREN MORE ACCESSIBLE TO GROWTH THROUGH PRESCHOOL EXPERIENCE. (MH)

ED034573 PS002482
TRAINING THE INTELLECT VERSUS DEVELOPMENT OF THE CHILD. ZIGLER, EDWARD, [68] 29P.
EDRS PRICE MF-$0.65 HC-$3.29

IN A SPEECH BEFORE THE AMERICAN EDUCATIONAL RESEARCH ASSOCIATION, THE AUTHOR ASSERTS THAT CHILDHOOD EDUCATION THEORY IS GOING THROUGH ONE OF ITS PERIODIC OVER-REACTIONS TO NEW FINDINGS. THE RESULT IS THE PRESENT OVEREMPHASIS ON ENVIRONMENTALLY CAUSED COGNITIVE DEVELOPMENT. YET A VERY BASIC BIOLOGICAL LAW IS THE LAW OF HUMAN VARIABILITY. THE OVEREMPHASIS ON THE INTELLECTUAL ASPECT OF CHILD DEVELOPMENT IS HARMFUL IF OTHER CRUCIAL PERSONAL DEVELOPMENT AREAS INVOLVING EMOTION, MOTIVATION, AND SOCIAL COMPETENCE ARE IGNORED. IF THE GENERAL ASPECTS OF A CHILD'S DEVELOPMENT ARE ATTENDED TO AND APPROPRIATE CONDITIONS ESTABLISHED, THE CHILD WILL LEARN BECAUSE LEARNING IS AN INHERENT FEATURE OF BEING A HUMAN BEING. THE CHILD'S HISTORY OF DEPRIVATION OR FAILURE, HIS MOTIVATION FOR ATTENTION AND AFFECTION, HIS FEELINGS TOWARDS ADULTS AND HIS SELF-CONCEPT ARE AS IMPORTANT DETERMINANTS OF HOW HE FUNCTIONS AS IS HIS FORMAL COGNITION. (MS)

ED034574 PS002509
THE EFFECTS OF PSYCHOSOCIAL DEPRIVATION ON HUMAN DEVELOPMENT IN INFANCY. CALDWELL, BETTYE M., [68] 35P.
EDRS PRICE MF-$0.65 HC-$3.29

THE CONCEPT OF DEPRIVATION HAS BECOME VERY APPEALING TO SPECIALISTS OF MANY DISCIPLINES AS AN EXPLANATION FOR DEVIATIONS IN HUMAN DEVELOPMENT. THIS IS UNDERSTANDABLE, SINCE THE PHENOMENON DOES SEEM TO BE A KEY FACTOR IN DEVELOPMENT, BUT SEVERAL TECHNICAL AND METHODOLOGICAL CONSIDERATIONS HINDER IMMEDIATE EFFORTS AT UNDERSTANDING AND ALLEVIATING IT. AMBIGUITIES IN DEFINITIONS OF THE CONCEPT OF DEPRIVATION AND THE NECESSITY TO RELY ON FIELD STUDY RESEARCH DESIGNS CONSTITUTE MAJOR DETERRENTS TO THE ACQUISITION OF DEFINITIVE DATA. TO DETERMINE MORE CLEARLY THE EFFECTS OF PSYCHOSOCIAL DEPRIVATION ON HUMAN DEVELOPMENT THERE HAVE TO BE IMPROVED TECHNIQUES FOR ASSESSING THE PSYCHOSOCIAL ENVIRONMENT AND FOR STANDARDIZING CHANGE-SENSITIVE MEASURES OF EARLY DEVELOPMENT. ALSO, MORE ATTENTION NEEDS TO BE GIVEN TO CLARIFYING THE RELATIONSHIP BETWEEN CONSTITUTIONAL FACTORS AND SUSCEPTIBILITY TO DEPRIVATION. THE SINGLE CASE MODEL DESERVES MORE USE IN ATTEMPTS TO DEMONSTRATE THE EFFECTS OF THE OPERATION AND REMOVAL OF PSYCHOSOCIAL DEPRIVATION. FINALLY, PSYCHOSOCIAL ENRICHMENT MIGHT HAVE AN OPTIMUM LEVEL WHICH SHOULD BE TAKEN INTO CONSIDERATION. (AUTHOR/MH)

ED034575 PS002515
KINDERGARTEN CURRICULUM GUIDE: EARLY CHILDHOOD EDUCATION. , [69] 46P.
EDRS PRICE MF-$0.65 HC-$3.29

THIS BOOKLET IS INTENDED AS A RESOURCE GUIDE FOR ADMINISTRATORS, TEACHERS, AND CURRICULUM PLANNERS. ITS PROGRAM IS BASED ON CHARACTERISTICS AND GOALS RELATED TO 5-YEAR-OLD CHILDREN. GENERAL PROGRAM OBJECTIVES ARE EXPLAINED, AS ARE GOALS FOR LANGUAGE ARTS, NUMBER EXPERIENCES, SOCIAL STUDIES, SCIENCE, MUSIC, ART, HEALTH AND SAFETY, AND PHYSICAL EDUCATION. AN INFORMAL APPROACH THROUGH INDIVIDUAL, GROUP, AND COMMUNITY ACTIVITIES IS ENCOURAGED. SUGGESTIONS FOR ORGANIZING THE KINDERGARTEN RELATE TO CLASS SIZE, SCHEDULE, AND WORKING WITH PARENTS. A PLAN FOR MAINTAINING PUPIL RECORDS, MATERIALS AND EQUIPMENT FOR CURRICULUMS IS RECOMMENDED. ALSO INCLUDED IS A BIBLIOGRAPHY ON EARLY CHILDHOOD EDUCATION. (DR)

ED034576 PS002537
DAY CARE AND CHILD DEVELOPMENT IN YOUR COMMUNITY. , 69 33P.
DOCUMENT NOT AVAILABLE FROM EDRS.
AVAILABLE FROM: DAY CARE AND CHILD DEVELOPMENT COUNCIL OF AMERICA, INC., ROOM 712, NEW POST OFFICE BUILDING, 433 WEST VAN BUREN STREET, CHICAGO, ILLINOIS 60607 ($1.00)

UNCOORDINATED COMMUNITY DAY CARE EFFORTS OFTEN RESULT IN AN UNBALANCED AVAILABILITY OF KINDS OF NURSERY SCHOOL PROGRAMS. TOO MUCH MONEY IS WASTED ON UNNECESSARY ADMINISTRATIVE SERVICES, AND TRAINING OF PERSONNEL IS NOT CONSISTENT IN QUALITY OR QUANTITY. COMMUNITY COORDINATED CHILD CARE (4-C) PROGRAM TRIES TO ALLEVIATE THIS CONFUSION. THIS HANDBOOK IS TO HELP CITIZENS WHO WANT TO IMPLEMENT A 4-C PROGRAM IN THEIR COMMUNITY. IT EXPLAINS HOW THE 4-C PROGRAM CAN BE EFFECTIVE IN PLANNING AND COORDINATING THE PRESCHOOL AND DAY CARE EFFORTS OF LOCAL GROUPS. 4-C CONSULTING PERSONNEL PROVIDE CITIZENS WITH THE RESOURCES AND STRUCTURE TO USE IN THEIR OWN COMMUNITY PROJECTS. THE HANDBOOK OUTLINES 4-C STRUCTURE FROM THE FEDERAL LEVEL DOWN TO THE COMMUNITY LEVEL ADVISING THAT FEDERAL AND STATE BODIES ACT ONLY AS ADMINISTRATIVE SERVICES TO THE LOCAL PEOPLE WHO HOLD ALL THE POLICY-MAKING POWER. THE NECESSARY FIRST STEPS FOR ORGANIZING A LOCAL 4-C PROGRAM ARE DETAILED AND POTENTIAL SOURCES OF FUNDING ARE OUTLINES IN THIS HANDBOOK. (REFER TO PS 002 545 FOR ADDITIONAL INFORMATION ON THE 4-C PROGRAM). (MH)

ED034577 PS002540
VERBAL BEHAVIOR OF PRESCHOOL TEACHERS. A VERY PRELIMINARY REPORT. KATZ, LILIAN G., NOV 69 9P.
EDRS PRICE MF-$0.65 HC-$3.29

THIS PAPER IS A PRELIMINARY REPORT OF A SMALL RESEARCH PROJECT UNDERTAKEN TO FOLLOW UP SOME OBSERVATIONS OF HEAD START CLASSES. THE PROJECT, WHICH IS IN THE EARLY STAGES OF DEVELOPING PROCEDURES AND TECHNIQUES, HOPES TO INVESTIGATE THE PRELIMINARY OBSERVATION THAT TEACHERS' VERBAL RESPONSES TO CHILDREN HAVE THE FUNCTION OF ENDING A CHILD'S THINKING RATHER THAN EXTENDING IT. SOME OF THE RESEARCH RELATED TO CHILDREN'S INTELLECTUAL DEVELOPMENT WHICH HAS COME FROM STUDIES OF MOTHER-CHILD INTERACTION WILL BE APPLIED TO THE CLASSROOM PROCESS. IF RESEARCH INDICATES A NEED FOR IMPROVEMENT OF TEACHER'S VERBAL RESPONSES, IT IS HOPED THAT TECHNIQUES WILL BE DEVELOPED TO MAKE THIS POSSIBLE. RELATED RESEARCH CONFIRMS HYPOTHESES THAT CERTAIN CHARACTERISTICS OF ADULT VERBAL BEHAVIOR ARE CRUCIAL ASPECTS OF THE CHILD'S ENVIRONMENT AND THAT TEACHERS DO DIFFER IN THEIR SPEECH STYLES. PROJECT PLANS ARE TO ANALYZE TRANSCRIPTS OF TEACHERS' CLASSROOM

SPEECH IN TERMS OF FUNCTION (EFFECT IT WILL LEAVE ON THE CHILD) AND MESSAGE (ACTUAL INFORMATION CARRIED). THE METHODS FOR CLASSIFYING FUNCTIONS AND MESSAGES ARE NOT YET PERFECTED. THE PROJECT HOPES TO DETERMINE AN OPTIMUM LEVEL FOR DIFFERENT TYPES OF VERBAL BEHAVIOR BY TEACHERS AND TO STUDY SITUATIONAL DETERMINANTS OF TEACHERS' SPEECH. (MH)

ED034578 PS002544
A SOCIALLY INTEGRATED KINDERGARTEN. MOSELEY, DOLLY; AND OTHERS, [69] 37P.
EDRS PRICE MF-$0.65 HC-$3.29

THE OBJECT OF THIS STUDY WAS TO DETERMINE THE EXTENT TO WHICH DISADVANTAGED KINDERGARTEN PUPILS WOULD BENEFIT FROM ASSOCIATION WITH ADVANTAGED PUPILS AND TEACHERS IN THE IMPROVEMENT OF BASIC SKILLS AND SELF-CONCEPT. THE SAMPLE FOR 1967-68 WAS COMPOSED OF 20 DISADVANTAGED RURAL NEGRO AND CAUCASION 5-YEAR-OLD CHILDREN RANDOMLY SELECTED. THE SAMPLE FOR 1968-69 WAS REDUCED TO 16 CHILDREN. IN EACH INSTANCE THESE CHILDREN WERE INTEGRATED WITH APPROXIMATELY 30 FOREIGN AND CAUCASIAN MIDDLE CLASS CHILDREN. IN 1967-68 ONLY THE DISADVANTAGED CHILDREN WERE ADMINISTERED PRE- AND POSTTESTS APPROXIMATELY 7 MONTHS APART. COMPARISON OF RESULTS SHOWED SIGNIFICANT GAINS IN TOTAL PERFORMANCE, LANGUAGE SKILLS, AND SELF-CONCEPT, WHILE IQ SCORES YIELDED NONSIGNIFICANT RESULTS. IN 1968-69, EVALUATION FOCUSED ON COMPARISONS OF EXPERIMENTAL (DEPRIVED) AND CONTROL (UNDERPRIVED) MEANS FOR PRETESTS, POSTTESTS, AND MEAN GAINS FROM PRE- TO POST FOR EACH GROUP. THE RESULTS MUST BE VIEWED WITH CAUTION, FOR ALTHOUGH SCORES DID NOT SHOW THAT THE DISADVANTAGED GAINED MORE, THEY DID GAIN AS MUCH AS THE ADVANTAGED. MORE STATISTICALLY SIGNIFICANT DIVERGENCE IN FAVOR OF THE CONTROL GROUP WAS FOUND BETWEEN PRETEST RESULTS THAN POSTTEST RESULTS. THIS REDUCTION OF DIFFERENCE COULD HAVE BEEN DUE TO A COMBINATION OF SOCIALIZATION AND CURRICULUM. (JF)

ED034579 PS002545
COMMUNITY COORDINATED CHILD CARE: 1. INTERIM POLICY GUIDANCE FOR THE 4-C PROGRAM , 69 26P.
EDRS PRICE MF-$0.65 HC-$3.29

THE COMMUNITY COORDINATED CHILD CARE (4-C) PROGRAM IS A SYSTEM UNDER WHICH LOCAL PUBLIC AND PRIVATE AGENCIES INTERESTED IN DAY CARE AND PRESCHOOL PROGRAMS DEVELOP PROCEDURES FOR COOPERATING WITH ONE ANOTHER ON PROGRAM SERVICES, STAFF DEVELOPMENT, AND ADMINISTRATIVE ACTIVITIES. THIS PUBLICATION SERIES (3 PAPERS) EXPLAINS HOW TO ORGANIZE LOCAL CHILD CARE RESOURCES INTO A 4-C PROGRAM. AN INTERIM POLICY GUIDE CONTAINS A DISCUSSION OF KINDS OF COORDINATION, FUNDING SOURCES AVAILABLE, AND SUGGESTED STEPS FOR ORGANIZING. ORGANIZATION OF STATE CHILD CARE RESOURCES INCLUDES ESTABLISHMENT, COMPOSITION, AND FUNCTIONS OF STATE 4-C COMMITTEES. FEDERAL RELATIONSHIPS WITH STATE AND LOCAL 4-C PROGRAMS ARE DISCUSSED. A FACT SHEET ANSWERS INQUIRIES ABOUT THE 4-C PROGRAM, AND A STATUS REPORT EXPLAINS DEVELOPMENTS AND CURRENT POSITION OF THE PROGRAM IN THE NINE HEW REGIONAL AREAS. A LIST OF SELECTED REFERENCE SOURCES PROVIDES INFORMATION ON 4-C, DAY CARE, AND CHILD DEVELOPMENT. (REFER TO PS 002 537 FOR ADDITIONAL INFORMATION). (DR)

ED034580 PS002560
A CHANGE OF POSSIBLE NEUROLOGICAL AND PSYCHOLOGICAL SIGNIFICANCE WITHIN THE FIRST WEEK OF NEONATE LIFE: SLEEPING REM RATE. MINARD, JAMES; AND OTHERS, 69 2P.
DOCUMENT NOT AVAILABLE FROM EDRS.
AVAILABLE FROM: AMERICAN PSYCHOLOGICAL ASSOCIATION, 1200 17TH STREET, N.W., WASHINGTON, D.C. 20036 (DIVISION 7, $1.50)

THE PERCENTAGE OF RAPID EYE MOVEMENT (REM) DURING SLEEP IS SUBSTANTIALLY GREATER IN NEONATES (INFANTS IN FIRST MONTH AFTER BIRTH) THAN IN OTHER CHILDREN OR ADULTS. IT WAS HYPOTHESIZED THAT REM RATE MAY DECLINE AS RATES OF MANY RESPONSE SEQUENCES DO WHEN REPEATEDLY ELICITED. ELECTRICAL RECORDINGS OF EYE MOVEMENTS WERE OBTAINED FROM A 3-DAY-OLD MALE AND FOLLOWED THROUGH HIS SEVENTH DAY, FROM 25 FEMALES AGED 3, 4, OR 5 DAYS, AND A KITTEN OBSERVED 8 HOURS AFTER BIRTH AND FOR THE NEXT 5 DAYS. THE REM RATE WAS OBTAINED UNDER NOISE CONDITIONS AND QUIET CONDITIONS. THE CRITICAL STATISTIC WAS THE EYES-CLOSED REM RATE, AND RESULTS SUPPORTED THE HYPOTHESIS. THE RATE FOR 5-DAY-OLD INFANTS WAS SIGNIFICANTLY LOWER THAN FOR 3-DAY-OLD INFANTS. DIFFERENCES OVER SHORT TIME PERIODS AND RECORDS OF INDIVIDUAL REM RATES FOR INFANTS AND THE KITTEN WERE IN THE EXPECTED DIRECTION. NEUROLOGICAL AND PSYCHOLOGICAL SIGNIFICANCE CAN BE ATTRIBUTED TO THE DEVELOPMENTAL CHANGE IN REM SLEEP, OF WHICH SLEEPING REM RATE IS A PARTICULARLY PROMISING INDICATOR. (DR)

ED034581 PS002566
RATE AND UNIQUENESS IN CHILDREN'S CREATIVE RESPONDING. WARD, WILLIAM C., 69 2P.
DOCUMENT NOT AVAILABLE FROM EDRS.
AVAILABLE FROM: AMERICAN PSYCHOLOGICAL ASSOCIATION, 1201 17TH STREET, N.W., WASHINGTON, D.C. 20036 (DIVISION 7, $1.50)

BASED ON PREVIOUS STUDIES WITH COLLEGE STUDENTS, THIS STUDY INVESTIGATED THE HIERARCHY AND CREATIVITY OF RESPONSES IN YOUNG CHILDREN. ACCORDING TO THE THEORY OF HIERARCHIES, THE UNCREATIVE PERSON INITIALLY PRODUCES STEREOTYPED RESPONSES AND SOON RUNS OUT OF ALTERNATIVES, WHILE THE CREATIVE PERSON INITIALLY HAS COMMON IDEAS BUT SUBSEQUENT IDEAS ARE MORE UNIQUE. THIRTY-FOUR 7- AND 8-YEAR-OLDS, PREDOMINANTLY MIDDLE CLASS, WITH A MEAN IQ OF 115 WERE THE SUBJECTS. THREE CREATIVITY MEASURES, ADAPTED FROM WALLACH AND KOGAN, WERE ADMINISTERED AND EACH CHILD'S TESTS WERE SCORED FOR THE TOTAL NUMBER OF APPROPRIATE IDEAS GIVEN. THERE WERE NO CONSISTENT DIFFERENCES BETWEEN CREATIVE AND UNCREATIVE CHILDREN IN RESPONSE RATE OR OVERALL PROBABILITY OF UNIQUE RESPONSES. RESULTS INDICATED THAT (1) RESPONSE RATE DECREASED WITH TIME, (2) UNCOMMONNESS OF RESPONSES INCREASED OVER SUCCESSIVE RESPONSE POSITIONS, AND (3) SUBJECTS WHO EVENTUALLY PRODUCED MORE IDEAS GAVE THEM AT A GREATER RATE THROUGHOUT THE TASK. IT IS SUGGESTED THAT RESPONSE HIERARCHIES FOR CREATIVE AND UNCREATIVE CHILDREN ARE IDENTICAL, BUT CREATIVE CHILDREN CONTINUE TO GENERATE RESPONSES, MANY OF THEM UNIQUE, AFTER UNCREATIVE CHILDREN CEASE RESPONDING. IT IS ALSO SUGGESTED THAT PERSONALITY AND MOTIVATIONAL VARIABLES MAY AFFECT RESPONSES. (DR)

ED034582 PS002567
PRESCHOOL INTELLIGENCE OF OVERSIZED NEWBORNS. BABSON, S. GORHAM; AND OTHERS, 69 2P.
DOCUMENT NOT AVAILABLE FROM EDRS.
AVAILABLE FROM: AMERICAN PSYCHOLOGICAL ASSOCIATION, 1201 17TH STREET, N.W., WASHINGTON, D.C. 20036 (DIVISION 7, $1.50)

THIS STUDY INVESTIGATED WHETHER CHILDREN OVERSIZED AT BIRTH, LIKE THOSE UNDERSIZED AT BIRTH, HAVE AN INCREASED CHANCE OF MENTAL SUBNORMALITY. SUBJECTS WERE 4-YEAR-OLDS BORN OF URBAN DISADVANTAGED WHITE MOTHERS WHOSE AVERAGE EDUCATION WAS 10.8 YEARS. STANFORD-BINET INTELLIGENCE SCORES OF THE SUBJECTS WERE COMPARED TO THEIR BIRTH WEIGHTS. BETWEEN MID-1959 AND SEPTEMBER 1964, 1,126 CHILDREN, 564 BOYS AND 562 GIRLS, WERE FOLLOWED AND GIVEN INTELLIGENCE TESTS. THESE CHILDREN WERE DIVIDED INTO A LOW (BELOW 2,501 GM.), A HIGH (OVER 4,250 GM.), AND A STANDARD BIRTH WEIGHT GROUP (ALL OTHERS). THE HEAVIEST 5 PERCENT OF NEWBORNS WAS SELECTED FROM THE HIGH GROUP. THE REPORT INDICATES THAT OF THE HEAVIEST 5 PERCENT THERE WAS A SIGNIFICANTLY LARGER PERCENTAGE WITH INTELLIGENCE SCORES BELOW 80 (SUBNORMAL) AT 4 YEARS OF AGE. THIS PERCENTAGE (23 PERCENT) IS MORE THAN DOUBLE THAT OF ALL OTHER CHILDREN TESTED WHO WEIGHED OVER 2,500 GM, AND IS COMPARABLE TO THAT FOUND IN CHILDREN OF LOW BIRTH WEIGHT. A GREATER VARIABILITY AND LOWER MEAN IQ IS ALSO FOUND IN THE OVERSIZED GROUP THAN IN THOSE OF USUAL SIZE AT BIRTH. THESE RESULTS ARE SUFFICIENTLY CHALLENGING TO WARRANT INVESTIGATION OF FETAL, MATERNAL, AND ENVIRONMENTAL FACTORS WHICH MIGHT HAVE AFFECTED THE RESULTS. (JF)

ED034583 PS002570
TRAINING ELEMENTARY READING SKILLS THROUGH REINFORCEMENT AND FADING TECHNIQUES. HAUSERMAN, NORMA; MCINTIRE, ROGER, 69 2P.
DOCUMENT NOT AVAILABLE FROM EDRS.
AVAILABLE FROM: AMERICAN PSYCHOLOGICAL ASSOCIATION, 1201 17TH STREET, N.W., WASHINGTON, D.C. 20036 (DIVISION 15, $2.50)

THIS RESEARCH PROJECT WAS DESIGNED TO EXPLORE SUITABLE OPERANT METHODS TO ASSURE SUCCESSFUL ACQUISITION OF SOME INITIAL FORMAL READING SKILLS BY FIRST AND SECOND GRADERS. THE SUBJECTS WERE 12 PUPILS DIAGNOSED AS PREDICTED READING FAILURES BY FAILING SCORES ON FOUR OR MORE SUBTESTS OF A 10 TEST BATTERY SUGGESTED BY DEHIRSCH, JANSKY, AND LANGFORD (1966). FADING AND REINFORCEMENT TECHNIQUES WERE EMPLOYED TO BRING ABOUT THE DESIRED TERMINAL READING BEHAVIOR OF CORRECTLY IDENTIFYING ANY OF 80 STIMULUS WORDS, PRINTED EITHER ON CARDS OR WITHIN STORY CONTEXT. COMMON PREPRIMERS WERE USED TO MEASURE TERMINAL READING BEHAVIOR. IT WAS HYPOTHESIZED THAT NEAR ERRORLESS READING OF THESE WORDS IN A VARIETY OF STORY CONTEXTS WOULD DEMONSTRATE SUCCESSFUL EARLY READING BEHAVIOR. RESULTS SHOWED THAT BOTH CONCRETE REINFORCEMENTS AND FADING TECHNIQUES WERE EFFECTIVE IN REDUCING HIGH ERROR RATES EMITTED DURING EARLY READING ATTEMPTS. FADING TECHNIQUES WERE CRUCIAL IN ENABLING THE STUDENT TO CONTINUE TO RESPOND CORRECTLY DURING THE TRANSITION FROM LARGE PRINT WITH PICTORIAL CUES TO SMALL TYPE UNACCOMPANIED BY SUCH CUES. CONCRETE REINFORCEMENT, WITH SOCIAL REINFORCEMENT, COMPARED TO SOCIAL REINFORCEMENT ONLY, WAS MOST EFFECTIVE WHEN COMBINED WITH FADING PROCEDURES. (JF)

ED034584 PS002571

COLOR AND PHYSIOGNOMY AS VARIABLES IN RACIAL MISIDENTIFICATION AMONG CHILDREN. GITTER, A. G.; SATOW, YOICHI, 69 2P.

DOCUMENT NOT AVAILABLE FROM EDRS.

AVAILABLE FROM: AMERICAN PSYCHOLOGICAL ASSOCIATION, 1201 17TH STREET, N.W., WASHINGTON, D.C. 20036 (DIVISION 16, $0.50)

THIS STUDY INVESTIGATED RACIAL MISIDENTIFICATION AMONG CHILDREN THROUGH THE MANIPULATION OF TWO INDEPENDENT VARIABLES: SKIN COLOR AND PHYSIOGNOMY. EIGHTY 4- TO 6-YEAR-OLD CHILDREN ENROLLED IN HEAD START CENTERS MADE UP THE SAMPLE. COLOR SLIDES OF THREE DOLLS EACH, WITH EACH SET IDENTICAL EXCEPT FOR COLOR AND PHYSIOGNOMY, WERE USED AS STIMULI MATERIAL. MALE DOLLS WERE USED WITH MALE SUBJECTS AND FEMALE DOLLS WITH FEMALE SUBJECTS. A SERIES OF FACTORIAL ANALYSES OF VARIANCE WAS PERFORMED ON THE DATA. USING RACE AS THE INDEPENDENT VARIABLE, BLACKS MISIDENTIFIED SIGNIFICANTLY MORE THAN WHITES ON COLOR DISCREPANCY, PHYSIOGNOMIC DISCREPANCY, AND VERBAL RACIAL SELF-IDENTIFICATION. SEX WAS ALSO SIGNIFICANT, WITH MALES MISIDENTIFYING MORE THAN FEMALES IN TERMS OF COLOR DISCREPANCY SCORES. AGE AS WELL AS FIRST- AND SECOND-ORDER INTERACTION BETWEEN ALL OF THE INDEPENDENT VARIABLES WERE NONSIGNIFICANT. THE FINDINGS CLEARLY SUPPORT THE EXISTENCE OF RACIAL MISIDENTIFICATION AMONG BLACK CHILDREN, AND REVEAL THAT IT OCCURS NOT ONLY IN TERMS OF COLOR, BUT ALSO IN TERMS OF PHYSIOGNOMY. IN FACT, PHYSIOGNOMY MAY BE A MORE POTENT VARIABLE THAN COLOR. (JF)

ED034585 PS002572

AN EVALUATION OF THE PRESCHOOL READINESS CENTERS PROGRAM IN EAST ST. LOUIS, ILLINOIS, JULY 1, 1968 - JUNE 30, 1969. FINAL REPORT. BITTNER, MARGUERITE L.; AND OTHERS, SEP 69 115P.

EDRS PRICE MF-$0.65 HC-$6.58

OBJECTIVES OF THIS STUDY WERE (1) TO DETERMINE THE EFFECT OF PRESCHOOL EXPERIENCE ON THE PERSONAL AND SOCIAL ADJUSTMENT AND SCHOOL READINESS AND ACHIEVEMENT OF THE DEPRIVED CHILD, (2) TO DETERMINE WHAT COMBINATION OF AGE AT INTERVENTION AND TREATMENT INTENSITY WAS MOST EFFECTIVE, AND (3) TO ASSESS THE EFFECTS OF PARENT INVOLVEMENT ON THE CHILD'S ACADEMIC PERFORMANCE. PHASE I TESTED CHILDREN IN THE PRESCHOOL READINESS PROGRAM, SUMMER HEAD START CHILDREN, LOW INCOME CHILDREN WITHOUT PRESCHOOL EXPERIENCE, AND MIDDLE INCOME CHILDREN WHO ENTERED FIRST GRADE IN SEPTEMBER, 1967. PHASE II CONSISTED OF EXPERIMENTAL AND CONTROL GROUPS WHO ENTERED FIRST GRADE IN SEPTEMBER, 1968. RESULTS OF THE METROPOLITAN READINESS TEST AND THE PEABODY PICTURE VOCABULARY TEST SHOWED THAT DISADVANTAGED CHILDREN WHO PARTICIPATED IN THE PRESCHOOL READINESS PROGRAM WERE BETTER PREPARED TO COMPETE WITH CHILDREN WITHOUT SUCH EXPERIENCE. THIS WAS CONFIRMED FOR BOTH PHASE I AND PHASE II, AND BOTH PHASES MADE SIGNIFICANT GAINS ON THE PPVT. PHASE I CHILDREN MADE SIGNIFICANT GAINS ON THE MRT, BUT MIDDLE INCOME CHILDREN SCORED HIGHEST IN PHASE II. THERE WAS NO SIGNIFICANT CHANGE IN PERSONAL ADJUSTMENT. CHILDREN WHOSE PARENTS WERE ACTIVELY INVOLVED SHOWED GREATER ACHIEVEMENT. (DR)

ED034586 PS002573

ARIZONA CENTER FOR EARLY CHILDHOOD EDUCATION ANNUAL REPORT, JUNE 1968 - JUNE 1969. , 1 JUN 69 76P.

EDRS PRICE MF-$0.65 HC-$3.29

THIS 71-PAGE ANNUAL REPORT, JUNE 1968-JUNE 1969, FOCUSES ON THE PURPOSE, DEVELOPMENT, AND WORK OF THE ARIZONA CENTER FOR EARLY CHILDHOOD EDUCATION ADMINISTERED THROUGH THE UNIVERSITY OF ARIZONA'S COLLEGE OF EDUCATION. THE CENTER IS COMMITTED TO THE SYSTEMATIC ANALYSIS, CONTINUED DEVELOPMENT, VALIDATION AND MODIFICATION OF A NEW AND EXISTING EDUCATIONAL PROGRAM. THE PURPOSE OF THE CENTER IS TO EVALUATE INNOVATIONS AND TO EVOLVE A RESEARCH BASE TO GUIDE FUTURE DEVELOPMENT OF THE EARLY EDUCATION PROGRAM. THE REPORT INCLUDES A DISCUSSION OF THE ADVANTAGES AND DISADVANTAGES OF THE CENTER, A DESCRIPTION OF THE HISTORY, INSTRUCTIONAL GOALS, AND PRINCIPLES OF INSTRUCTION BEHIND THE TUCSON EARLY EDUCATION MODEL, AND A PROGRESS REPORT ON RESEARCH AND DEVELOPMENT AT THE ARIZONA CENTER. THE PROGRESS REPORT INCLUDES SEVERAL ABSTRACTS OF PERTINENT LITERATURE WHICH INVOLVE BEHAVIORAL RESEARCH, CASE STUDIES, AND TRAINING TECHNIQUES. APPENDIXES INCLUDE THE CENTER'S PERSONNEL ROSTER, A CASE STUDY OF THE PROGRAM'S IMPLEMENTATION AT THE FOURTH GRADE LEVEL, AND A LIST OF SELECTED PAPERS CONTAINED IN THE PROGRESS REPORT. (AUTHOR/JF)

ED034587 PS002575

PEDAGOGICAL ATTITUDES OF CONVENTIONAL AND SPECIALLY-TRAINED TEACHERS. ROSENTHAL, TED L.; AND OTHERS, [69] 27P.

EDRS PRICE MF-$0.65 HC-$3.29

IN TUCSON, THE ARIZONA CENTER FOR EARLY CHILDHOOD EDUCATION HAS DEVELOPED AN EXPERIMENTAL PROGRAM (EP) OF TEACHER REEDUCATION AIMED AT MODIFICATION OF CURRICULUM EMPHASES, CLASSROOM PRACTICES, AND PEDAGOGICAL ORIENTATION OF TEACHERS. THIS STUDY OF INCENTIVE PRACTICES IN BOTH EP AND NP (NONPROGRAM) CLASSROOMS INDICATED THE SUPERIORITY OF THE EP PRACTICES. TWO STUDIES COMPARED PEDAGOGICAL ATTITUDES OF EP AND NP TEACHERS REGARDING CLASSROOM APPLICATION OF CONTEMPORARY PRINCIPLES AND THE NEEDS AND NATURE OF DISADVANTAGED YOUNGSTERS. IN THE FIRST STUDY, INCULCATION OF EP ATTITUDES WAS EFFECTED INDIRECTLY THROUGH CLASSROOM INTERACTION WITH SPECIALLY TRAINED EP PERSONNEL. ATTITUDES WERE MEASURED BY A 75-ITEM SURVEY OF EDUCATIONAL ATTITUDES (SEA). THE SECOND STUDY EXAMINED A 6-WEEK INTENSIVE WORKSHOP TRAINING PROJECT, ALSO EVALUATED BY SEA. IN BOTH STUDIES THE EP TEACHERS HAD SUBSTANTIALLY AND CONSISTENTLY ACQUIRED THE DESIRED EP VIEWPOINT. LONG-TERM DIFFUSE AND SHORT-TERM INTENSIVE TRAINING PRODUCED SIGNIFICANT MODIFICATION OF TEACHER'S PEDAGOGICAL CONVICTIONS. (MH)

ED034588 PS002576

A LONGITUDINAL INVESTIGATION OF MONTESSORI AND TRADITIONAL PREKINDERGARTEN TRAINING WITH INNER CITY CHILDREN: A COMPARATIVE ASSESSMENT OF LEARNING OUTCOMES. THREE PART STUDY. BERGER, BARBARA, SEP 69 164P.

EDRS PRICE MF-$0.65 HC-$6.58

THIS RESEARCH INVESTIGATES THE LEARNING IMPACT OF MONTESSORI PREKINDERGARTEN TRAINING AS COMPARED TO TRADITIONAL APPROACHES WITH ECONOMICALLY DEPRIVED PUERTO RICAN AND NEGRO CHILDREN. THE THREE-PART, 156-PAGE MONOGRAPH INCLUDES A 22-PAGE INTRODUCTION TO PARTS I AND II, AND A 37-PAGE APPENDIX TO PART I. PARTS I AND II ASSESS TRAINING EFFECTS OF THE FIRST YEAR OF SCHOOLING, FOCUSING ON CHILDREN BEGINNING PREKINDERGARTEN AT APPROXIMATELY 4 TO 4 1/2 YEARS OF AGE. THE BASIC RESEARCH DESIGN ALSO INCLUDES AN EVALUATION OF TRAINING FOR CHILDREN BEGINNING SCHOOL AT 3 TO 3 1/2 YEARS. PART I CONTAINS AN EVALUATION OF PERCEPTUAL AND COGNITIVE ABILITIES. PART II INVESTIGATES PUPIL PREFERENCE FOR COGNITIVE STYLES TYPIFYING EGO STRENGTH IN THE YOUNG CHILD AND RELEVANT FOR AUTONOMOUS PROBLEM-SOLVING STRATEGIES. PART III INCLUDES A FOLLOW-UP ASSESSMENT CONDUCTED AT THE END OF KINDERGARTEN IN ORDER TO INVESTIGATE THE CUMULATIVE EFFECTS OF TRAINING OVER A LONGER PERIOD OF SCHOOLING. THE APPENDIX TO PART I CONTAINS AGE, SEX, AND ETHNICITY TRENDS FOR THE POPULATION INVESTIGATED, A 25-PAGE DESCRIPTION OF THE TEST BATTERY, A SAMPLE TEACHING LOG MONTHLY CHECKLIST, AND A LIST OF SAMPLE QUESTIONS FOR TEACHER INTERVIEWS. THE MONOGRAPH ALSO INCLUDES A LIST OF 54 REFERENCES USED FOR PARTS I, II, AND III. (JF)

ED034589 PS002598

STAFFING PRESCHOOLS: BACKGROUND INFORMATION. KATZ, LILIAN G.; WEIR, MARY K., MAR 69 8P.

EDRS PRICE MF-$0.65 HC-$3.29

THIS REPORT EXPLORES BACKGROUND VARIABLES RELATED TO PRESCHOOL TEACHING, AND EMPHASIZES THAT STATISTICS FLUCTUATE IN EARLY CHILDHOOD EDUCATION. THE INCREASE FOR PREPRIMARY ENROLLMENT OF 3- AND 4-YEAR-OLDS WAS 26 PERCENT FROM 1966 TO 1967. ACCURATE FIGURES ON PRESCHOOL TEACHING PERSONNEL ARE NOT AVAILABLE, BUT A LARGE PROPORTION OF HEAD START TEACHERS HAD LESS THAN 6 MONTHS EXPERIENCE WITH YOUNG CHILDREN BEFORE EMPLOYMENT. HOWEVER, ONE THIRD OF HEAD START PROFESSIONAL STAFF AND ALMOST TWO THIRDS OF PROGRAM ASSISTANTS WERE DRAWN FROM MINORITY GROUPS. CERTIFICATION AND CREDENTIALING VARY WIDELY FROM STATE TO STATE. NURSERY SCHOOL TEACHERS ARE REQUIRED TO HOLD CERTIFICATES IN ONLY 19 STATES, ALTHOUGH PRESCHOOL PROGRAMS RECEIVING FEDERAL FUNDS MUST HIRE TEACHERS WITH TRAINING OR ABILITY IN CHILD CARE. TEACHER TRAINING PROGRAMS IN COLLEGES REFLECT INADEQUATE CREDENTIALING REGULATIONS. THE PRESENT GROWTH RATE SUGGESTS DOUBLE ENROLLMENT OF PRESCHOOL CHILDREN BY 1972. IT IS CONCLUDED THAT THE CRITICAL SHORTAGE OF TRAINED PRESCHOOL PERSONNEL WILL CONTINUE TO GROW. (DR)

ED034590 PS002599

AN EDUCATIONAL IMPERATIVE AND ITS FALLOUT IMPLICATIONS. MILLER, JAMES O., 3 JUL 69 29P.

EDRS PRICE MF-$0.65 HC-$3.29

THIS PAPER DISCUSSES THE IMPACT OF SOCIETAL CHANGE ON THE EDUCATIONAL SYSTEM. BECAUSE OF TECHNOLOGICAL AND ECONOMIC DEVELOPMENTS, IT IS IMPERATIVE THAT THE EDUCATIONAL SYSTEM ACCOMMODATE AND UTILIZE CHANGE TO BENEFIT ALL SECTORS OF THE POPULATION. EARLY CHILDHOOD EDUCATION PROGRAMS HAVE BEEN CONCEIVED AS AGENTS OF CHANGE, PARTICULARLY FOR DISADVANTAGED GROUPS. A MAJOR PROBLEM NOW FACING THE FIELD IS A SHORTAGE OF TRAINED PERSONNEL, BECAUSE INCREASING NUMBERS OF

CHILDREN ARE ENROLLED IN PRESCHOOL PROGRAMS EACH YEAR. MOST PRESCHOOL STAFF MEMBERS HAVE LITTLE EXPERIENCE OR TRAINING IN EARLY CHILDHOOD EDUCATION, AND PRESENT TRAINING PROGRAMS ARE INADEQUATE, PARTICULARLY FOR INNER CITY PERSONNEL. RESOURCES AVAILABLE FOR DEVELOPING TRAINING PROGRAMS ARE BASED ON INAPPROPRIATE CRITERIA. TO MEET THE CONTINUED GROWTH IN PRESCHOOL PROGRAMS, IT IS PROPOSED THAT (1) INSERVICE TRAINING PROGRAMS BE DEVELOPED, (2) A MINIMUM OF SIX REGIONAL TEACHER-DEMONSTRATION CENTERS BE CREATED, (3) PRESERVICE TRAINING BE OFFERED BY COMMUNITY COLLEGES, (4) NATIONAL CERTIFICATION STANDARDS BE ESTABLISHED, WITH PROFESSIONAL ORGANIZATIONS ACTING AS THE LEGAL REGULATORY AGENCIES OF THE LOCAL AND STATE LEVELS, AND (5) A NATIONAL INSTITUTE ON EARLY CHILDHOOD BE ESTABLISHED TO INTEGRATE AND INNOVATE PRACTICES IN EARLY CHILDHOOD EDUCATION. (DR)

ED034591 PS002654
THE SIMULTANEOUS REHABILITATION OF MOTHERS AND THEIR CHILDREN. BUSHELL, DON, JR.; JACOBSON, JOAN M., 30 AUG 68 11P.
EDRS PRICE MF-$0.65 HC-$3.29

THE JUNIPER GARDENS COOPERATIVE PRESCHOOL IS A HEAD START PROJECT STAFFED BY THE MOTHERS OF 30 4- AND 5-YEAR-OLDS WHO ATTEND THE PRESCHOOL. THIS PAPER REPORTS ON TWO STUDIES THAT ATTEMPTED TO UPGRADE PRACTICES IN TWO TEACHING SKILLS; CLASSROOM MANAGEMENT AND INDIVIDUAL TUTORING. THE CLASSROOM WAS DIVIDED INTO FIVE ACTIVITY AREAS WHICH THE CHILDREN COULD USE FREELY. HOWEVER, CHILDREN SWITCHED AREAS SO FREQUENTLY THAT THERE WASN'T ENOUGH TIME TO OFFER INSTRUCTION IN ANY ONE AREA. FURTHERMORE, WHEN AN ACADEMIC ACTIVITY (ANAGRAMS) WAS INITIATED IN ONE OF THE AREAS, THE CHILDREN TENDED TO AVOID IT. TO SOLVE THESE PROBLEMS, A RULE CHANGE WAS MADE. CHILDREN HAD TO COMPLETE A TASK (SIMILAR TO THE ANAGRAM ACTIVITY) BEFORE THEY COULD SWITCH AREAS. OBSERVATIONS SHOWED THAT, AS A RESULT, CHILDREN SWITCHED AREAS LESS OFTEN AND PLAYED THE ANAGRAM GAME MORE OFTEN. THE MOTHERS WERE DEFICIENT IN INDIVIDUAL TUTORING BECAUSE THEY TOO OFTEN MADE NEGATIVE OR IRRELEVANT COMMENTS AND TOO SELDOM MADE REINFORCING OR HELPING COMMENTS. WRITTEN INSTRUCTIONS DID LITTLE TO RECTIFY THIS SITUATION, BUT "TELE-COACHING" OVER EARPHONES QUICKLY INCREASED THE MOTHERS' USE OF SOUND LEARNING PRINCIPLES AND DECREASED THEIR USE OF UNDESIRABLE TUTORING BEHAVIOR. (MH)

ED034592 PS002686
A TRANSFORMATIONAL ANALYSIS OF THE LANGUAGE OF KINDERGARTEN AND ELEMENTARY SCHOOL CHILDREN. GRIFFIN, WILLIAM J., 19 FEB 66 20P.
EDRS PRICE MF-$0.65 HC-$3.29

THE TWO PURPOSES OF THIS STUDY WERE (1) TO EXPLORE THE VALIDITY OF CERTAIN INDEXES USED TO MEASURE CHILDREN'S DEVELOPMENT TOWARD MATURITY IN THE CONTROL OF ENGLISH SYNTAX, AND (2) TO EXAMINE THE CHARACTERISTIC EXPLOITATION OF SYNTACTIC RESOURCES (A) BY BOYS AND GIRLS, (B) AT VARIOUS AGE-GRADE LEVELS, AND (C) IN SPEECH AND WRITING. THE NORMATIVE DATA WAS COLLECTED FROM TAPED ORAL RESPONSES OR WRITTEN LANGUAGE SAMPLES OF 180 WHITE MIDDLE CLASS CHILDREN, 30 EACH FROM KINDERGARTEN AND GRADES 1, 2, 3, 5, AND 7. ANALYSIS WAS BASED ON THE MEAN LENGTH OF THE T-UNIT (A SINGLE, INDEPENDENT PREDICATION WITH ALL ITS COMPLEMENTS AND MODIFIERS), WHICH KELLOGG HUNT (1964) CLAIMED TO BE A DISCRIMINATING INDICATOR OF THE DEGREE OF SYNTACTIC MASTERY IN CHILDREN'S LANGUAGE PRODUCTION. THIS STUDY SUPPORTED HUNT'S FINDING. T-UNITS WERE FURTHER ANALYZED FOR CHOMSKY'S "SENTENCE COMBINING TRANSFORMATIONS." RESULTS INDICATED THAT MEAN WORD LENGTH OF TOTAL LANGUAGE PRODUCTION INCREASES WITH EVERY ADVANCE IN GRADE LEVEL. THE MOST SIGNIFICANT INCREASES IN SPEECH MASTERY WERE FOUND IN GRADES 1 AND 7, AND IN WRITING MASTERY IN GRADE 5. IN GRADE 3 SPEECH WAS BETTER THAN WRITING, BUT THIS REVERSED IN GRADES 5 AND 7. BOYS WERE BETTER SPEAKERS THAN GIRLS IN ALL BUT GRADE 5. GIRLS WROTE BETTER THAN BOYS IN THE MIDDLE BUT BOYS SURPASSED THEM IN SEVENTH GRADE. (MH)

ED034593 PS002699
ORCHESTRATED INSTRUCTION: A COOKING EXPERIENCE. NELSON, VIOLET; AND OTHERS, 1 AUG 69 27P.
EDRS PRICE MF-$0.65 HC-$3.29

THE TUCSON EARLY EDUCATION PROGRAM IS WORKING WITH "ORCHESTRATED INSTRUCTION," A COOKING EXPERIENCE WHICH IS AN EXPERIMENTAL ATTEMPT TO PULL TOGETHER THE VARIOUS COMPONENTS OF EARLY EDUCATION. INDIVIDUAL SUBSKILLS SUCH AS ARITHMETIC AND LANGUAGE ARTS ARE LEARNED FOR A LARGER PROJECT THAT THE CHILDREN ARE INTERESTED IN, AND SKILLS ARE DEVELOPED AS THE NEED ARISES. THE PROJECT DISCUSSED HERE IS COOKING STEW IN A THIRD GRADE CLASSROOM. PREPARATORY DISCUSSION AND A COLORFUL, ILLUSTRATED STORYBOOK PREPARED BY TEACHERS HEIGHTENED THE INTEREST THE CHILDREN HAD IN THE PROJECT, AND THEY CHEERFULLY TOOK ON THE VARIOUS TASKS INVOLVED IN MAKING STEW, FROM BUYING THE INGREDIENTS AND COLLECTING THE UTENSILS TO FOLLOWING THE RECIPE AND TASTING THE FRUITS OF THEIR EFFORTS (GRATIFICATION). POST-STEW EXERCISES PRESENTED THE OPPORTUNITY FOR FURTHER LEARNING AS CHILDREN WROTE BRIEF STORIES ABOUT THE COOKING EXPERIENCE USING NEW "STEW" VOCABULARY WORDS. SKILLFUL INTERACTION BY THE HEAD TEACHER AND HER AIDES WEAVES THE SUBSTANTIVE CONTENT OF ACADEMIC SUBJECTS INTO THE TURNED-ON GROUP ACTIVITY, AND THE CHILDREN RECEIVE IMMEDIATE AND GRATIFYING FEEDBACK FOR THEIR NEW SKILLS. (MH)

ED034594 PS002700
STANDARDIZED TESTS AND THE DISADVANTAGED. RANKIN, RICHARD J.; HENDERSON, RONALD W., NOV 69 13P.
EDRS PRICE MF-$0.65 HC-$3.29

THE PURPOSE OF THIS PAPER IS TO EVALUATE THE RELIABILITY OF THE WECHSLER PRESCHOOL AND PRIMARY SCALE OF INTELLIGENCE AND TO MEASURE WHETHER THIS RELIABILITY IS AFFECTED WHEN SUBJECTS ARE FROM A DISADVANTAGED GROUP. THE SUBJECTS WERE 25 MALE AND 24 FEMALE 5 1/2-YEAR-OLD POOR MEXICAN-AMERICANS. GENERALLY, THE WECHSLER PRESCHOOL SCALE SHOWED HIGH RELIABILITY WITH THIS SAMPLE, FULL SCALE RELIABILITY BEING .95. THE IMPACT OF DISADVANTAGE CAN BE SEEN BY COMPARING THE SCALE SCORES OF THIS GROUP WITH THE RESULTS REPORTED FOR AN ANGLO-AMERICAN STANDARDIZATION GROUP. THE MEXICAN-AMERICAN GROUP FALLS BELOW THE GENERAL MEAN IN ALL SUBTESTS, NOTICEABLY IN THE VERBAL SECTION AND MOST NOTABLY IN THE INFORMATION AND SIMILARITIES SECTIONS OF THE WECHSLER SCALE. THE HIGH RELIABILITY OF THE SCALE SUGGESTS IMPLICATIONS FOR TESTING CHILDREN FROM ETHNIC MINORITIES. SINCE MOST OF THE CHILDREN HAD LIMITED FACILITY WITH ENGLISH, STUDY RESULTS WILL ENCOURAGE RESEARCHERS WHO WANT AN ACCURATE MEASURE OF INTELLECTUAL SKILLS REQUIRED FOR SUCCESSFUL PERFORMANCE IN TECHNICAL CULTURES. MEASUREMENT WITHIN A DISADVANTAGED GROUP MAY NOT REQUIRE NEW TESTS TO PREDICT SKILLS BUT MAY DEPEND UPON THE USE OF TESTS SAMPLING EXISTING KNOWN FACTORS AND UTILIZING THEM TO PREDICT WITHIN GROUPS. NORMS SHOULD BE ESTABLISHED FOR THE SPECIFIC GROUP TESTED. (JF)

ED034595 PS002701
AN EVALUATION OF A PILOT PROJECT TO ASSESS THE INTRODUCTION OF THE MODERN ENGLISH INFANT SCHOOL APPROACH TO LEARNING WITH SECOND AND THIRD YEAR DISADVANTAGED CHILDREN. SCHEINER, LOUIS, OCT 69 20P.
EDRS PRICE MF-$0.65 HC-$3.29

THIS STUDY TESTED THE MODERN ENGLISH INFANT SCHOOL APPROACH TO TEACHING AS A PARTIAL SOLUTION TO THE PROBLEM OF PROPERLY EDUCATING THE GHETTO CHILD. IT WAS HOPED THAT THE APPROACH COULD (1) IMPROVE ACHIEVEMENT IN READING AND ARITHMETIC, (2) IMPROVE ABILITY IN WRITTEN COMPOSITION, (3) IMPROVE STUDENTS' ATTITUDES TOWARD SELF, THE SCHOOL, THE TEACHER, AND PEERS, AND (4) INCREASE STUDENTS' ABILITY TO THINK CREATIVELY. TO ASSESS THIS APPROACH, A COMPARISON WAS MADE BETWEEN THREE THIRD GRADE CLASSROOMS (N62) IN WHICH THE ENGLISH SCHOOL APPROACH WAS USED AND THREE OTHER THIRD GRADE CLASSROOMS (N58) IN WHICH A TRADITIONAL APPROACH WAS USED. AT THE END OF THE YEAR, ALL THE CHILDREN TOOK THE IOWA TESTS OF BASIC SKILLS, THE WAY I FEEL ABOUT MYSELF, AND THE PUPIL ATTITUDE TOWARD SCHOOL INVENTORY. TEACHERS' SUBJECTIVE EVALUATIONS WERE ALSO COLLECTED. STUDENTS IN THE NEW APPROACH GROUP SHOWED NEITHER SIGNIFICANTLY GREATER ACHIEVEMENT GAINS NOR SIGNIFICANT ADVANTAGE OVER THE CONTROL GROUP IN ATTITUDE TOWARD SELF, SCHOOL, TEACHER, OR PEERS. TEACHERS' OPINIONS POINTED TO IMPROVED COOPERATION, PARTICIPATION, AND STUDENT-TEACHER RELATIONSHIP. RECOMMENDATIONS INCLUDE SECURING TEACHER AIDES, PARENT PARTICIPATION, AN ON-GOING STAFF DEVELOPMENT PROGRAM, AND CAREFUL PLANNING, MONITORING, AND EVALUATION OF THE PROJECT. (AUTHOR/MH)

ED034596 PS002704
THE EFFECTS OF MOTHERS' PRESENCE AND PREVISITS ON CHILDREN'S EMOTIONAL REACTIONS TO STARTING NURSERY SCHOOL. SCHWARTZ, CONRAD, NOV 69 36P.
EDRS PRICE MF-$0.65 HC-$3.29

THIS STUDY INVESTIGATED THE EMOTIONAL EFFECTS OF VARIOUS TREATMENT CONDITIONS ON CHILDREN STARTING NURSERY SCHOOL. SUBJECTS WERE 108 CHILDREN, PREDOMINANTLY MIDDLE CLASS, 3 1/2 TO 5 YEARS OLD. TREATMENT CONDITIONS WERE ANALYZED ACCORDING TO (1) PREVISIT TO SCHOOL VS. NO PREVISIT, (2) MOTHER PRESENT VS. MOTHER ABSENT, (3) PEER GROUP EXPERIENCES VS. NO EXPERIENCE, AND (4) MALE VS. FEMALE. CHILDREN'S EMOTIONAL REACTIONS WERE RATED ACCORDING TO (1) REACTION TO SEPARATION FROM MOTHER, (2) POSITION AND ACTIVITY RELATIVE TO OTHERS IN THE LAST 20 MINUTES OF EACH SESSION, (3) MOTILITY (LOCOMOTION IN THE ENVIRONMENT), (4) FEELING TOWARD SCHOOL, AND (5) COMFORT IN CLASS. ALL EMOTIONAL REACTIONS, EXCEPT MOTILITY, WERE MUTUALLY INTERCORRELATED. THE TEACHERS' RATING OF COMFORT HAD THE HIGHEST CORRELATION WITH THE OTHER INDICES OF EMOTIONAL REACTION. THE FOUR EXPERIMENTAL TREATMENT VARIABLES HAD NO SIGNIFICANT EFFECT ON A CHILD BY THE LAST 20 MINUTES OF THE FIRST SESSION, AND FOLLOW-UP STUDIES SUPPORTED THIS FINDING. IT IS CONCLUDED THAT MOST MIDDLE CLASS CHILDREN READILY ADAPT TO A NURSERY SCHOOL SITUATION, REGARDLESS OF TREATMENT CONDITIONS AT TIME OF ENTRANCE. (DR)

ED034597 PS002717
LANGUAGE TEACHING: PREPOSITIONS AND CONJUNCTIVES. HOBSON, ARLINE B., JUL 69 18P.
EDRS PRICE MF-$0.65 HC-$3.29

THIS BULLETIN IS THE FIRST OF THREE DESIGNED TO GIVE DETAILED HELP ON FOSTERING LANGUAGE COMPETENCE IN 4- TO 6-YEAR-OLD SCHOOL CHILDREN. THE BULLETIN INTRODUCES THE TEACHER TO A GROUP OF PREPOSITIONS AND CONJUNCTIONS (CHOSEN FROM THE DOLCH BASIC SIGHT VOCABULARY LIST OF 220 WORDS) WHICH ARE IMPORTANT TO THE MEANING OF SENTENCES. THE LIST WAS COMPILED FROM THOSE WORDS OCCURRING MOST FREQUENTLY IN ORDINARY WRITTEN COMMUNICATION. THE WORDS OCCUR WITH HIGH FREQUENCY IN PRIMERS AND FIRST GRADE MATERIALS. THREE-FOURTHS OF THE DOCUMENT IS DEVOTED TO DESCRIBING THE POTENTIAL FUNCTION OF THESE CONJUNCTIVES AND PREPOSITIONS IN THE LANGUAGE, AND MAKING SUGGESTIONS TO THE TEACHER AND THE READER, ALERTING THEM TO THE PRIMARY POSITION OF SUCH WORDS IN LANGUAGE LEARNING. (AUTHOR/JF)

ED034598 PS002740
THE EFFECTS OF MANIPULATION OF TEACHER COMMUNICATION STYLE IN THE PRESCHOOL. SMOTHERGILL, NANCY L.; AND OTHERS, MAR 69 9P.
EDRS PRICE MF-$0.65 HC-$3.29

THIS STUDY ASSESSES THE INFLUENCE OF AN ELABORATIVE VS. NON-ELABORATIVE TEACHING STYLE ON CHILDREN'S NURSERY SCHOOL BEHAVIOR. (ELABORATIVE TEACHERS ELICIT MORE COMMENTS FROM THE CHILD, AND OFFER MORE OPTIONS FOR SOLVING PROBLEMS THAN NON-ELABORATIVE TEACHERS). SUBJECTS, 24 WHITE CHILDREN OF WELFARE MOTHERS, WERE ASSIGNED TO AN ELABORATIVE (EXPERIMENTAL) OR NON-ELABORATIVE (CONTROL) GROUP. EXPERIENCED TEACHERS CONDUCTED FOUR 20-MINUTE SESSIONS EACH DAY FOR 17 DAYS, MODIFYING THEIR TEACHING STYLE DEPENDING ON THE GROUP BEING TAUGHT. RECORDINGS AND OBSERVATIONS OF TEACHING STYLE AND CHILD VERBALIZATIONS WERE MADE. RESULTS INDICATED RELIABILITY OF TEACHING STYLES OVER TIME AND GREATER FREQUENCY OF ELABORATIVE STATEMENTS IN RESPONSE TO TEACHER ELICITATION FOR THE EXPERIMENTAL GROUP. A POSSIBLE MODELING EFFECT OF TEACHERS ON CHILDREN WAS SUGGESTED FOR BOTH GROUPS. RESULTS ON PRE- AND POSTTESTS DESIGNED TO MEASURE PROBLEM SOLVING ABILITIES SHOWED FEW DIFFERENCES BETWEEN THE TWO GROUPS. GREATEST DIFFERENCES APPEARED ON VERBAL TASKS. IT WAS CONCLUDED THAT NURSERY SCHOOL TEACHERS WHO TEACH ELABORATIVELY AND GIVE POSITIVE AND INDIVIDUALIZED RESPONSES TO CHILDREN'S VERBALIZATIONS HAVE CHILDREN WHO EXHIBIT ELABORATIVE BEHAVIOR IN CLASS. (DR)

ED034599 PS002768
INFORMATION EXCHANGE IN MOTHER-CHILD INTERACTIONS. BALDWIN, CLARA P., MAR 69 15P.
EDRS PRICE MF-$0.65 HC-$3.29

TO ASSESS MOTHER-CHILD INTERACTION, 23 MOTHER-CHILD PAIRS FROM THE WEST HARLEM GHETTO (HALF LOWER CLASS AND HALF MIDDLE CLASS NEGROES) AND FROM WASHINGTON SQUARE (WHITE MIDDLE CLASS) WERE OBSERVED. CHILDREN WERE 3-YEAR-OLD BOYS. EACH PAIR SPENT 30 MINUTES IN A LABORATORY PLAYROOM AND WERE OBSERVED AND TAPE-RECORDED. CHILDREN'S NONVERBAL EXPLORATORY BEHAVIOR WAS ASSIGNED TO A PRECODED CATEGORY SYSTEM. VERBAL BEHAVIOR WAS GROUPED FOR FREQUENCY, FORM, MODE, RESPONSE, AND MANNER. ALTHOUGH THERE WAS WIDE VARIATION IN VERBAL INTERACTION, RESULTS INDICATED THAT THE TWO GROUPS DID NOT DIFFER IN (1) MEAN NUMBER OF TOTAL UTTERANCES, (2) RATIO BETWEEN THE MOTHERS' UTTERANCES AND THE CHILDREN'S (3) PERCENTAGE OF TIMES MOTHERS INITIATED A CHANGE IN TOPIC, (4) TYPES OF INFORMATION CONTAINED IN MOTHERS' VERBALIZATIONS, AND (5) PERCENTAGE OF TIMES THEY RESPONDED TO OR IGNORED THEIR CHILDREN'S STATEMENTS. SIGNIFICANT DIFFERENCES BETWEEN THE TWO GROUPS WERE: (1) WEST HARLEM MOTHERS ASKED MORE QUESTIONS, (2) W.H. INTERACTIONS CONTAINED MORE REQUESTS FOR CLARIFICATION, AND (3) UTTERANCES OF W.H. CHILDREN CONTAINED MORE PERMANENT INFORMATION AND W.S. CHILDREN MORE FANTASY. WASHINGTON SQUARE MOTHERS WHO IGNORED CHILDREN WERE IGNORED BY THEM, BUT CHILDREN IN HARLEM DEMANDED MORE ATTENTION WHEN IGNORED. (DR)

ED035434 PS001620
FOUR YEARS ON. A FOLLOW-UP STUDY AT SCHOOL LEAVING AGE OF CHILDREN FORMERLY ATTENDING A TRADITIONAL AND A PROGRESSIVE JUNIOR SCHOOL. GOOCH, S.; PRINGLE, M. L. KELLMER, DEC 65 222P.
EDRS PRICE MF-$0.65 HC NOT AVAILABLE FROM EDRS.

BEGINNING IN 1956 ABOUT 250 STUDENTS IN TWO LONDON, ENGLAND JUNIOR SCHOOLS WERE INTENSIVELY STUDIED OVER A 4-YEAR PERIOD FOR INTELLECTUAL, EDUCATIONAL, EMOTIONAL, AND SOCIAL DEVELOPMENT. THE SCHOOLS APPROACHED INSTRUCTION DIFFERENTLY; ONE WAS CHILD-ORIENTED; THE OTHER WAS SUBJECT-ORIENTED. IN 1964 THIS FOLLOWUP STUDY WAS CONDUCTED WITH SOME OF THE SAME STUDENTS IN THE 1956 STUDY WHO HAD GONE INTO FOUR SECONDARY MODERN SCHOOLS. THE STUDENTS SELECTED FOR RESTUDY HAD BEEN OF AVERAGE OR BELOW-AVERAGE READING ABILITY IN THEIR JUNIOR SCHOOL. STANDARDIZED TESTS AND PROJECTIVE TASKS WERE ADMINISTERED TO THESE STUDENTS. THE MEASURES WERE SIMILAR TO THOSE USED IN THE 1956 STUDY. SEVERAL QUESTIONNAIRES WERE COMPLETED. THE STUDENT HIMSELF, AN INTERVIEWER, A TEACHER, AND HIS PARENTS WERE INFORMANTS. THE FOLLOWUP DATA AND THE DATA FROM THE 1956 STUDY SUGGEST THAT QUESTIONS SUCH AS WHETHER A CHILD-CENTERED OR SUBJECT-CENTERED APPROACH ACHIEVE BETTER RESULTS ARE SO BROAD THEY ARE ALMOST MEANINGLESS. THE BACKGROUND AND PERSONALITY OF THE INDIVIDUAL CHILD ARE VERY IMPORTANT DETERMINANTS OF SCHOOL ACHIEVEMENT. THE DATA ALSO INDICATE THAT THE PROJECTIVE TASKS USED IN ASSESSING THE STUDENT'S DEVELOPMENT ARE ACCURATE. [NOT AVAILABLE IN HARD COPY DUE TO MARGINAL LEGIBILITY OF ORIGINAL DOCUMENT.] (WD)

ED035435 PS002158
MONTESSORI INDEX. THIRD EDITION. FLEEGE, VIRGINIA B.; AND OTHERS, 69 43P.
EDRS PRICE MF-$0.65 HC-$3.29
AVAILABLE FROM: VIRGINIA FLEEGE, 831 FAIR OAKS, OAK PARK, ILLINOIS ($7.00)

THIS VOLUME, THE RESULT OF 2 YEARS OF WORK, IS AN INDEX TO 24 VOLUMES ON MONTESSORI THEORY AND PRACTICE. THE BOOKS WERE READ AND ANALYZED A MINIMUM OF SIX TIMES. SIXTEEN OF THE VOLUMES ARE AUTHORED BY MARIA MONTESSORI. (DR)

ED035436 PS002325
THE ADVANTAGED: A PRESCHOOL PROGRAM FOR THE DISADVANTAGED. , 69 84P.
EDRS PRICE MF-$0.65 HC-$3.29

OBJECTIVES OF THIS PROGRAM ARE TO PROVIDE HEALTH SERVICES, FOSTER EMOTIONAL DEVELOPMENT, PLAN FOR EDUCATIONAL GROWTH AS A DEVELOPMENTAL AND PURPOSEFUL PROCESS, AND ENCOURAGE PARENT PARTICIPATION. CHILDREN RECEIVE MEDICAL AND DENTAL EXAMINATIONS AND CARE. SOCIAL WORKERS SERVE AS LIAISONS BETWEEN SCHOOL, HOME, AND COMMUNITY FOR RECRUITMENT AND FOLLOW-UP PARENT PARTICIPATION. A PARENT PROGRAM INCLUDES A RECRUITMENT MEETING, FOLLOWED BY SEMI-MONTHLY MEETINGS TO EXPLAIN AND SHOW VIDEO TAPES OF THEIR CHILDREN IN THE PROGRAM. PARENTS ARE ENCOURAGED TO REINFORCE LEARNED SKILLS AT HOME. THE PHYSICAL ACTIVITY PROGRAM STRESSES BASIC SKILLS AT HOME. THE PHYSICAL ACTIVITY PROGRAM STRESSES BASIC MOTOR SKILLS AND PHYSICAL GROWTH THROUGH STRUCTURED ACTIVITIES. MEDICAL EXAMINATIONS AND SPEECH SCREENING IDENTIFY SPEECH PROBLEMS AND ARE A BASIS FOR DETERMINING A PROGRAM SUITABLE FOR EACH CHILD. THE SCHOOL'S RESOURCE CENTER CONTAINS MANIPULATIVE TOYS, PLAY EQUIPMENT, BOOKS, A PROFESSIONAL LIBRARY, AND FACILITIES FOR PLANNING AND TRAINING PURPOSES. A NUTRITIONIST PLANS MENUS FOR BREAKFAST, SNACK, AND LUNCH AT THE CENTER, AND MEALTIME IS CONSIDERED LEARNING EXPERIENCE. APPENDIXES INCLUDE PROGRAM GOALS, A TEACHING GUIDE, EVALUATION RECORDS, A FACULTY SCHEDULE, AND ASSISTANT TEACHERS' DUTIES. (DR)

ED035437 PS002539
ON COGNIZING COGNITIVE PROCESSES. RIMOLDI, H. J. A., 4 OCT 69 31P.
EDRS PRICE MF-$0.65 HC-$3.29

IN THIS REPORT ON COGNITIVE PROCESSES, A DISCUSSION OF THE RATIONALE AND ASSUMPTIONS USED BY INVESTIGATORS EXPLAINS THE EXPERIMENTAL PROCEDURES. TO DETERMINE ACTUAL COGNITIVE PROBLEM-SOLVING PROCESSES, (RATHER THAN INFERRING THEM FROM RESULTS), SUBJECTS IN THESE STUDIES WERE PRESENTED WITH A PROBLEM AND ALLOWED TO ASK A SEQUENCE OF QUESTIONS WHICH THE EXPERIMENTER ANSWERED AND RECORDED. THE SEQUENCE OF QUESTIONS IS CALLED THE SUBJECT'S TACTIC AND IS IDENTIFIED BY THE NUMBER OF QUESTIONS, TYPE OF QUESTIONS, AND THE TEMPORAL ORDER OF THE QUESTIONS. IT IS RECOGNIZED THAT PROBLEMS ARE BUILT WITH A CERTAIN LOGICAL STRUCTURE (INTRINSIC DIFFICULTY) AND A CERTAIN LANGUAGE STRUCTURE (EXTRINSIC DIFFICULTY). AN IDEAL TACTIC APPROXIMATES THE LOGICAL STRUCTURE OF THE PROBLEM, HAS NO ORDER REVERSALS, AND IS NOT REDUNDANT. GOOD TACTICS ARE THOSE WHICH PROVIDE ENOUGH INFORMATION TO SOLVE THE PROBLEM. A SYSTEM OF NUMERICAL INDICES WAS DEVELOPED FOR SCORING TACTICS. PREVIOUS RESEARCH USING THESE INSTRUMENTS TO INVESTIGATE INDIVIDUAL COGNITIVE PROCESSES AND THE EFFECTS OF LANGUAGE ON THESE PROCESSES HAS REVEALED THAT CONCRETE AND VERBAL LANGUAGES RUN THROUGH A LARGER VARIETY OF LOGICAL STRUCTURES THAN DO ABSTRACT SYMBOLIC LANGUAGES. (MH)

ED035438 PS002561
"CONSERVATION" BELOW AGE THREE: FACT OR ARTIFACT? ACHENBACH, THOMAS M., 69 2P.
DOCUMENT NOT AVAILABLE FROM EDRS.
AVAILABLE FROM: AMERICAN PSYCHOLOGICAL ASSOCIATION, 1200 17TH STREET, N.W., WASHINGTON, D.C. 20036 (DIVISION 7, $1.50)

THIS STUDY REPLICATED A STUDY BY MEHLER AND BEVER (1967) WHICH HAD REPORTED CONSERVATION OBSERVED IN VERY YOUNG CHILDREN BETWEEN 2 YEARS 4 MONTHS AND 2 YEARS 7 MONTHS OLD. BOTH PIAGET (1968) AND BIELEN (1968) CRITICIZED THE MEHLER-BEVER FINDING, CLAIMING THAT TRUE CONSERVATION HAD NOT BEEN DEMONSTRATED. THE INVESTIGATOR IN THE PRESENT STUDY SOUGHT TO DETERMINE WHETHER THE ORIGINAL STUDY ACTUALLY SHOWED CONSERVATION OR WHETHER THE RESULTS WERE ARTIFACTS OF ORDER AND

POSITION FACTORS SUPERIMPOSED ON THE CHANCE LEVEL OF 50% FOR THE BINARY CHOICE OFFERED SUBJECTS. IT WAS FOUND THAT WHEN THE ORDER AND POSITION EFFECTS IN THE MEHLER-BEVER STUDY WERE REDUCED, THE RESULTS WERE AS WOULD BE EXPECTED FROM RANDOM RESPONSES TO A BINARY CHOICE. THUS, THE REPORTED CONSERVATION BEHAVIOR IN CHILDREN UNDER 3 APPEARS TO HAVE BEEN AN ARTIFACT OF EXPERIMENTAL PROCEDURE. (MH)

ED035439 PS002562
VISUAL SCANNING BY HUMAN NEWBORNS: RESPONSES TO COMPLETE TRIANGLE, TO SIDES ONLY, AND TO CORNERS ONLY. NELSON, KEITH; KESSEN, WILLIAM, 69 2P.
DOCUMENT NOT AVAILABLE FROM EDRS.
AVAILABLE FROM: AMERICAN PSYCHOLOGICAL ASSOCIATION, 1200 17TH STREET, N.W., WASHINGTON, D.C. 20036 (DIVISION 7, $1.50)

THIS STUDY TESTED THE HYPOTHESIS THAT NEWBORNS SELECTIVELY ORIENT TOWARD ANGULAR ELEMENTS IN THEIR VISUAL FIELD. SUBJECTS WERE 36 AWAKE AND ALERT INFANTS UNDER 6 DAYS OF AGE. FOR EACH NEWBORN, THE STUDY COMPARED VISUAL ATTENTION TO THREE SEPARATELY PRESENTED STIMULUS PATTERNS: A COMPLETE OUTLINE TRIANGLE, ONLY THE SIDES OF THIS TRIANGLE, AND ONLY THE ANGLES. NEWBORNS WERE INITIALLY SHOWN A CIRCULAR PANEL CONSISTING OF A HOMOGENEOUS BLACK FIELD. AT LEAST 15 FRAMES AT THE RATE OF ONE PER SECOND WERE OBTAINED WITH ONE OF THE INFANT'S EYES COVERED. FIFTEEN FRAMES WERE THEN OBTAINED FOR EACH OF THE EXPERIMENTAL STIMULUS PATTERNS. ANALYSIS OF DEPENDENT MEANS REVEALED THAT REGIONAL CONTOUR SCORES DID NOT SIGNIFICANTLY DIFFER FOR CONTROL AND SIDES-ONLY STIMULI. HOWEVER, BOTH ANGLES-ONLY AND COMPLETE TRIANGLE PATTERNS ATTRACTED SIGNIFICANTLY MORE OCULAR ORIENTATIONS THAN THE HOMOGENEOUS CONTROL STIMULUS. THESE RESULTS REAFFIRM THE CONCLUSION OF SALAPATEK AND KESSEN (1966) THAT ANGULAR ELEMENTS OF A TRIANGLE ARE ELEMENTS WHICH ATTRACT THE INFANT'S GAZE INDEPENDENTLY OF THE PRESENCE OR ABSENCE OF SIDE CONTOURS. SCANNING RECORDS REVEALED THAT INFANTS LOOKED ONLY TOWARD A SINGLE ANGULAR COMPONENT. MORE DETAILED ANALYSES OF ORIENTATION ARE PLANNED. (JF)

ED035440 PS002563
QUASI-DISGUISED AND STRUCTURED MEASURE OF SCHOOL-CHILDREN'S RACIAL PREFERENCES. KOSLIN, SANDRA COHEN; AND OTHERS, 69 2P.
DOCUMENT NOT AVAILABLE FROM EDRS.
AVAILABLE FROM: AMERICAN PSYCHOLOGICAL ASSOCIATION, 1200 17TH STREET, N.W., WASHINGTON, D.C. 20036 (DIVISION 15, $2.50)

A QUASI-DISGUISED NONVERBAL ATTITUDE MEASURE FOR YOUNG CHILDREN WAS USED TO MEASURE RACIAL AWARENESS AND PREFERENCE. SUBJECTS WERE 429 FIRST AND THIRD GRADE WHITE AND NEGRO PUBLIC SCHOOL CHILDREN. VARIED CLASS ACTIVITIES WERE PRESENTED IN 18 PEN AND INK SKETCHES WITH DIFFERENT RACIAL COMBINATION OF TEACHERS AND CHILDREN. THESE SKETCHES WERE ARRANGED IN BOOKLET FORM SO THAT ON ANY GIVEN PAGE, THREE OF THE SIX RACIAL COMPOSITIONS APPEARED, ONE IN EACH OF THE THREE CLASS ACTIVITIES. CHILDREN MARKED WHICH CLASS THEY WOULD MOST PREFER AND WHICH CLASS THEY WOULD LIKE LEAST. CHOICES THAT WERE RANDOM OR BASED ONLY ON ACTIVITIES WERE ELIMINATED. ANALYSES OF VARIANCE NESTED HIERARCHICAL DESIGNS, WITH RACE, GRADE AND SEX AS MAIN FACTORS AND TYPE OF SCHOOL ATTENDED (SEGREGATED OR DESEGREGATED) AS A NESTED FACTOR WITHIN RACE. RESULTS SUGGESTED THAT WHITE SUBJECTS GENERALLY BEGAN THE FIRST GRADE WITH A CLEAR PREFERENCE FOR AN ALL-WHITE SOCIAL SURROUNDING IN SCHOOL AND MAINTAINED THAT PREFERENCE INTO THE THIRD GRADE. NEGROES STARTED THE FIRST GRADE WITH A SLIGHT PREFERENCE FOR AN ALL-WHITE CLASS, BUT BY THIRD GRADE CLEARLY PREFERRED NEGRO TEACHERS AND PEERS. WHITE SUBJECTS' RACIAL PREFERENCES WERE MORE PRONOUNCED THAN NEGROES', AND THIRD GRADERS SHOWED CLEARER RACIAL AWARENESS THAN FIRST GRADERS. INTEGRATION HAD NO MEASURABLE EFFECT ON RACIAL PREFERENCES IN THE SCHOOLS STUDIED. (DR)

ED035441 PS002564
STIMULUS ABSTRACTNESS AND THE CONSERVATION OF WEIGHT. MURRAY, FRANK B., 69 2P.
DOCUMENT NOT AVAILABLE FROM EDRS.
AVAILABLE FROM: AMERICAN PSYCHOLOGICAL ASSOCIATION, 1200 17TH STREET, N.W., WASHINGTON, D.C. 20036 (DIVISION, 15, $2.50)

IT WAS HYPOTHESIZED THAT THE ACQUISITION OF CONSERVATION BEHAVIOR WOULD BE FACILITATED WHEN STIMULI WERE MORE CONCRETE THAN ABSTRACT. EIGHTY WHITE SECOND GRADERS WERE RANDOMLY ASSIGNED TO FOUR GROUPS AND PRESENTED WITH THREE CONSERVATION-OF-WEIGHT PROBLEMS. CLAY BALLS AND THE CONSERVATION TRANSFORMATIONS WERE EITHER SHOWN, DEMONSTRATED, AND DESCRIBED (GROUP I); SHOWN IN PHOTOGRAPHS AND DESCRIBED (GROUP II); SHOWN IN LINE DRAWINGS AND DESCRIBED (GROUP III); OR SIMPLY VERBALLY DESCRIBED (GROUP IV). THE TRANSFORMING PROBLEMS WERE (1) CHANGING THE SHAPE OF THE BALL, (2) DIVIDING THE BALL INTO THREE PIECES, AND (3) PLACING THE BALL NEXT TO LARGER AND SMALLER CLAY BALLS. CONSERVERS WERE THOSE WHO SAID THE BALL'S WEIGHT WAS UNCHANGED BY THE TRANSFORMATION, WHILE NONCONSERVERS SAID WEIGHT HAD CHANGED. SEVENTY-THREE PERCENT OF THE SUBJECTS CONSERVED PROBLEM 1, 72 PERCENT CONSERVED PROBLEM 2, AND 26 PERCENT CONSERVED PROBLEM 3. THERE WERE SIGNIFICANTLY MORE CONSERVERS IN THE GROUP ABOVE THE SAMPLE'S MEDIAN AGE, BUT PERFORMANCE WAS INSENSITIVE TO DIFFERENCES IN STIMULUS ABSTRACTNESS. (DR)

ED035442 PS002565
PAPER-AND-PENCIL VERSUS CONCRETE PERFORMANCE OF NORMALS AND RETARDATES ON THE ETS WRITTEN EXERCISES. STEPHENS, WILL BETH; KOWATRAKUL, SURANG, 69 2P.
DOCUMENT NOT AVAILABLE FROM EDRS.
AVAILABLE FROM: AMERICAN PSYCHOLOGICAL ASSOCIATION, 1201 17TH STREET, N.W., WASHINGTON, D.C. 20036 (DIVISION 15, $2.50)

PIAGET'S CONCEPTION OF COGNITIVE DEVELOPMENT AS THE DEVELOPMENT OF A SET OF SKILLS RESULTING FROM INTERACTION WITH THE ENVIRONMENT HAS HAD A GREAT EFFECT ON CONTEMPORARY EDUCATIONAL THEORY AND SPURRED THE EDUCATIONAL TESTING SERVICE (ETS) TO DEVELOP A SET OF WRITTEN EXERCISES BASED ON THIS CONCEPT. PIAGET'S EMPHASIS, HOWEVER, WAS ON CONCRETE MANIPULATION AND THE ETS EXERCISES ARE IN WRITTEN PAPER-AND-PENCIL FORM. THIS STUDY SOUGHT TO TEST CONCRETE FORMS AS OPPOSED TO THE FORMS ETS OFFERED. THE SUBJECTS WERE 48 RETARDED AND 40 NORMAL CHILDREN ALL MATCHED FOR MENTAL AGE AT 5 TO 7 YEARS. THE AVERAGE CHRONOLOGICAL AGE OF THE RETARDATES WAS 10 YEARS 2 MONTHS. CONCRETE FORMS OF THE WRITTEN EXERCISES WERE DEVISED AND ADMINISTERED TO A RANDOM HALF OF EACH GROUP. THE REMAINING SUBJECTS TOOK THE REGULAR WRITTEN FORM. THE RESULTS SHOWED THAT BOTH RETARDATES AND NORMALS PERFORMED SIGNIFICANTLY BETTER ON THE CONCRETE FORM IN EVERY SUB-AREA. THIS FINDING SUPPORTED PIAGET'S THEORY THAT, AS FAR AS POSSIBLE, CHILDREN SHOULD FIRST BE TAUGHT THROUGH DIRECT MANIPULATION OF THEIR ENVIRONMENT AND LATER PROGRESS TO SYMBOLIC FORMS OF INSTRUCTION. FINDINGS ALSO INDICATED THAT THE RETARDATES WERE INFERIOR TO NORMALS ON ETS COMMUNICATION SKILLS. (MH)

ED035443 PS002568
NURTURANCE, DEPENDENCE, AND EXPLORATORY BEHAVIOR IN PREKINDERGARTENERS. STARR, R. H., JR., 69 2P.
DOCUMENT NOT AVAILABLE FROM EDRS.
AVAILABLE FROM: AMERICAN PSYCHOLOGICAL ASSOCIATION, 1201 17TH STREET, N.W., WASHINGTON, D.C. 20036 (DIVISION 7, $1.50)

THIS STUDY EXAMINED THE RELATION BETWEEN EXPLORATORY BEHAVIOR AND (1) THE EXPERIMENTER-CHILD RELATIONSHIP, AND (2) TEACHER RATINGS OF DEPENDENCY AND AUTONOMOUS ACHIEVEMENT STRIVING. SUBJECTS WERE 34 GIRLS AND 38 BOYS RANDOMLY SELECTED FROM TWO PREKINDERGARTENS. EXPERIMENTAL CONDITIONS CONSISTED OF TWO LEVELS OF PRE-EXPERIMENTAL SOCIAL INTERACTION WITH THE EXPERIMENTER (NURTURANT AND NON-NURTURANT), THREE SETS OF INSTRUCTIONS, AND THREE MATERIALS DESIGNED TO ELICIT EXPLORATION. EACH SUBJECT WAS GIVEN THREE TRIALS, EACH TIME USING A DIFFERENT MATERIAL AND INSTRUCTION. SUBJECTS WERE SCORED FOR PRESENCE OR ABSENCE OF CERTAIN BEHAVIORS DURING THEIR TRIALS. TEACHERS RATED SUBJECTS DEPENDENCY AND AUTONOMUOUS ACHIEVEMENT STRIVING ON BELLER'S (1955) RATING SCALES. RESULTS SHOWED THAT SOCIAL INTERACTION INFLUENCED ORIENTATION AND VERBALIZATION MORE THAN TOTAL EXPLORATION OR RESIDUAL RESPONDING. WHILE SOCIAL ORIENTATION (TO EXPERIMENTER) DECREASED OVER TRIALS, NONSOCIAL RESPONDING WAS CONSTANT ACROSS TRIALS. INSTRUCTIONS INFLUENCED MATERIAL EXPLORATION AND RESIDUAL RESPONDING, BUT NOT SOCIAL ORIENTATION. THE NURTURANT INTERACTION FOSTERED DEPENDENT BEHAVIOR. INDEPENDENCE, AS MEASURED BY AUTONOMOUS ACHIEVEMENT STRIVING, IS UNRELATED TO EXPLORATORY BEHAVIOR. (MH)

ED035444 PS002569
SEX DIFFERENCES IN GENERALITY AND CONTINUITY OF VERBAL RESPONSIVITY. MINTON, CHERYL, 69 2P.
DOCUMENT NOT AVAILABLE FROM EDRS.
AVAILABLE FROM: AMERICAN PSYCHOLOGICAL ASSOCIATION, 1201 17TH STREET, N.W., WASHINGTON, D.C. 20036 (DIVISION 7, $1.50)

THIS REPORT EXAMINES THE INTERRELATIONS AMONG SEVERAL VERBALIZATION INDEXES ON A SAMPLE OF 27-MONTH-OLD CHILDREN AND THE RELATION OF THIS DATA TO VOCALIZATION SCORES OBTAINED IN THE FIRST YEAR. SUBJECTS, 67 GIRLS AND 75 BOYS, WERE FIRSTBORN CAUCASIAN CHILDREN OBSERVED AT 4, 8, 13, AND 27 MONTHS. PARENT EDUCATION VARIED FROM INCOMPLETE HIGH SCHOOL TO GRADUATE DEGREES. THE EVALUATION AT 27 MONTHS INCLUDED A 2 HOUR LABORATORY VISIT WHERE CHILDREN RECEIVED VERBALIZATION SCORES ON FREE PLAY, NARRATED VISUAL SCENES, HUMAN FORMS, AND CLAY FACES. WITHIN TWO WEEKS, THROUGH 6-8 HOURS OF HOME OBSERVATION, SPEECH QUALITY AND QUANTITY WERE RATED. AT 4 AND 8 MONTHS OF AGE, SUBJECTS WERE SHOWN SLIDES OF FOUR MALE FACES, AND THE CLAY FACES USED AT 27 MONTHS. AT 13 MONTHS THEY SAW THE HUMAN FORMS AND CLAY FACES USED AT 27 MONTHS. TOTAL TIME

VOCALIZING WAS THE VARIABLE OF INTEREST. THE MAJOR RESULTS SUGGEST (A) GREATER INTEREPISODE CONSISTENCY FOR SPONTANEOUS VERBALIZATION AT 27 MONTHS FOR GIRLS THAN FOR BOYS, (B) A STRONGER COVARIATION BETWEEN PARENTAL EDUCATIONAL LEVEL AND VOCABULARY SCORE AMONG GIRLS THAN BOYS, AND (C) GREATER PREDICTIVE STABILITY OF SPONTANEOUS VOCALIZATION AT 1 YEAR TO SPONTANEOUS VERBALIZATION AT 27 MONTHS FOR GIRLS THAN FOR BOYS. THESE DATA SUGGEST THAT THE TENDENCY TO VOCALIZE IS A MORE STABLE RESPONSE TENDENCY FOR GIRLS THAN FOR BOYS. (AUTHOR/JF)

ED035445 PS002646
ELEMENTARY PHYSICAL EDUCATION: TOPEKA PUBLIC SCHOOLS. , [69] 476P.
EDRS PRICE MF-$0.65 HC-$16.45

THAT PHYSICAL EDUCATION SHOULD BE AN INTEGRAL AND UNIFIED ASPECT OF EARLY EDUCATION IS THE BASIC TENET OF THIS GUIDEBOOK FOR KINDERGARTEN THROUGH SIXTH GRADE. PHYSICAL EDUCATION SHOULD NOT BE THOUGHT OF AS PLAY, SPORTS, OR JUST EXERCISE; IT SHOULD BE A SCIENTIFIC PROGRAM WHOSE EVERY ACTIVITY HAS SPECIFIC GOALS AND SOLID PRINCIPLES FOR ACHIEVING THOSE GOALS. THE GUIDEBOOK OUTLINES BASIC PRINCIPLES AS A BASIS TO DETERMINE THE CONTENT AND SCOPE OF A PHYSICAL EDUCATION PROGRAM. TIPS ON ORGANIZATION, AND SUGGESTIONS FOR TEACHING ARE INCLUDED. THERE IS A GRADE-BY-GRADE BREAKDOWN OF PHYSICAL CHARACTERISTICS, NEEDS, AND ACTIVITIES, TIPS ON FIRST AID, ACCIDENT PREVENTION, AND INTEGRATION OF PHYSICAL EDUCATION WITH CLASSROOM SUBJECTS. THE BULK OF THE GUIDEBOOK IS TAKEN UP BY DESCRIPTIONS OF SPECIFIC GAMES, CALISTHENICS, RHYTHMS, ACTIVITIES, TUMBLING STUNTS, SPORTS, FITNESS PROJECTS AND INTRAMURALS. THE LAST SECTION SHOWS SAMPLE LESSON PLANS FOR THE VARIOUS GRADES. AN INDEX OF ACTIVITIES IS INCLUDED. (MH)

ED035446 PS002678
CLASSIFICATION AND INFERENTIAL THINKING IN CHILDREN OF VARYING AGE AND SOCIAL CLASS. ZIMILES, HERBERT, SEP 68 19P.
EDRS PRICE MF-$0.65 HC-$3.29

THE CONSISTENTLY INFERIOR PERFORMANCE OF ECONOMICALLY DISADVANTAGED CHILDREN LED TO THIS STUDY DESIGNED TO INVESTIGATE HOW COGNITIVE DEVELOPMENT CHANGES WITH AGE AND HOW IT IS AFFECTED BY PREVIOUS LIFE EXPERIENCE. CLASSIFICATION BEHAVIOR AND INFERENTIAL THINKING WERE THE MAIN CONCERNS OF THE STUDY. THE MEASUREMENT INSTRUMENT WAS THE MATRIX TEST, A DEVICE THAT REQUIRES THE CHILD TO SELECT A PICTURE TO COMPLETE A ROW OF PICTURES ON THE BASIS OF THE RELATIONSHIP ESTABLISHED BY THE OTHER PICTURES. THE 44 ITEMS ON THE TEST CAN BE SEEN AS FALLING INTO ONE OF FOUR CLASSES: PERCEPTUAL MATCHING, CLASS MEMBERSHIP, ONE-WAY CLASSIFICATION, OR TWO-WAY CLASSIFICATION. THE SUBJECTS WERE 160 BLACK LOWER CLASS CHILDREN (40 EACH FROM KINDERGARTEN AND GRADES 1 THROUGH 3) AND A SIMILAR GROUP OF WHITE MIDDLE CLASS CHILDREN FOR COMPARISON. ONLY A CHILD'S SELECTION RESPONSES WERE RECORDED; NO MEASURE WAS MADE OF THE THOUGHT PROCESSES BEHIND THEM. THE MEASURABLE RESULTS SHOWED NO DIFFERENCES BASED ON SEX OR THE ABSTRACT-REPRESENTATIONAL CHARACTER OF THE STIMULI. HOWEVER, CONSISTENT DIFFERENCES BETWEEN ADVANTAGED AND DISADVANTAGED CHILDREN WERE FOUND TO BE SIGNIFICANT FOR ALL FOUR CLASSES OF ITEMS. (MH)

ED035447 PS002682
EFFECT OF VERBALIZATION ON YOUNG CHILDREN'S LEARNING OF A MANIPULATIVE SKILL. LOMBARD, AVIMA; STERN, CAROLYN, SEP 68 15P.
EDRS PRICE MF-$0.65 HC-$3.29

TO DETERMINE THE EFFECT OF VERBALIZATION ON THE ACQUISITION OF MANIPULATIVE SKILLS IN YOUNG CHILDREN, A PUZZLE-ASSEMBLY EXPERIMENT WAS DESIGNED. EACH OF 65 HEAD START CHILDREN BETWEEN THE AGES OF 47 AND 58 MONTHS WAS RANDOMLY ASSIGNED TO ONE OF THE FOUR TREATMENT GROUPS: PRACTICE WITH VERBALIZATION (PV); PRACTICE WITH NO VERBALIZATION (PNV); VERBALIZATION WITH NO PRACTICE (VNP); AND A CONTROL GROUP. ALL CHILDREN WERE PRETESTED ON THE PEABODY PICTURE VOCABULARY TEST, GOODENOUGH DRAW-A-MAN TEST, A SIMPLE PUZZLE ASSEMBLY, THE SPECIFIC VOCABULARY FROM THE TASK, AND PROGRESSIVELY MORE DIFFICULT PUZZLES. THE PV GROUP WAS TAUGHT PUZZLE ASSEMBLY WITH A CAREFULLY SEQUENCED PROGRAM OF PUZZLES AND RELATED VOCABULARY. THE PNV GROUP SPENT EQUAL TIME WITH THE SAME PUZZLES, BUT WERE NOT TAUGHT VOCABULARY. THE VNP GROUP READ BOOKS THAT EMPHASIZED THE SPECIAL VOCABULARY BUT WERE NOT GIVEN PUZZLES. THE CONTROL GROUP SPENT AN EQUAL AMOUNT OF TIME ON A NEUTRAL TASK. PV AND PNV GROUPS SHOWED HIGH INTEREST AND SIMILAR, SIGNIFICANT GAINS IN PUZZLE-ASSEMBLY SKILLS. THE VNP GROUPS, HOWEVER, REGRESSED IN PERFORMANCE AND SHOWED LITTLE INTEREST. VERBALIZATION AND PRACTICE MANIPULATION SEEMED TO BE IMPORTANT ELEMENTS IN IMPROVING PUZZLE-ASSEMBLY SKILLS. (MH)

ED035448 PS002687
A COMPARATIVE STUDY OF THREE FORMS OF THE METROPOLITAN READINESS TEST AT TWO SOCIO-ECONOMIC LEVELS. GLASNAPP, DOUGLAS R., AUG 67 31P.
EDRS PRICE MF-$0.65 HC-$3.29

THE METROPOLITAN READINESS TESTS, FIRST PUBLISHED IN 1948 (FORMS R AND S), WERE REVISED IN 1966 (FORMS A AND B). THIS STUDY WAS INSTIGATED AS A RESULT OF THE CHARGE THAT THE REVISIONS OF THE TESTS MADE THEM MORE DIFFICULT AND MORE UNFAIR TO DEPRIVED CHILDREN. THIRTY-SIX CAUCASIAN BEGINNING FIRST GRADERS (DIVIDED EVENLY BY HIGH AND LOW SOCIOECONOMIC STATUS) WERE GIVEN THREE FORMS (S, A, AND B) OF THE METROPOLITAN READINESS TEST. THE FOLLOWING SPRING, THE CHILDREN TOOK PRIMARY I BATTERY OF THE SAME TEST. THE SCORES WERE CONVERTED TO PERCENTILE RANKS AND ANALYZED. HIGH SES CHILDREN SCORED SIGNIFICANTLY HIGHER THAN LOW SES CHILDREN. THE REVISED FORMS WERE EQUAL IN DIFFICULTY AND HARDER THAN THE OLD FORM. A SIGNIFICANT PRACTICE EFFECT WAS MANIFEST WITH MEAN PERCENTILE RANKINGS PROGRESSIVELY INCREASING WITH EACH SUBSEQUENT ADMINISTRATION OF THE TESTS. THERE WAS NO RELIABLE SUPPORT THAT THE NEW FORMS DISCRIMINATED AGAINST DISADVANTAGED CHILDREN MORE THAN DID THE OLD FORM. THERE WAS HIGHER VARIABILITY FOR THE HIGHER SES CHILDREN, BUT THE DIFFERENCE WAS SIGNIFICANT ONLY FOR THE NEW FORMS. THE NEW FORMS ARE PREDICTIVE OF MATURITY AND LIMITATIONS OF ABILITY FOR HIGH SES CHILDREN, BUT ARE QUESTIONABLE WHEN APPLIED TO LOW SES CHILDREN. FORMS A AND B ARE RELIABLE OVER THE TOTAL RANGE OF POPULATION, BUT NOT FOR A RESTRICTED SUBGROUP POPULATION. (MH)

ED035449 PS002703
THE ROLE OF UNDERDETERMINACY AND REFERENCE IN THE SENTENCE RECALL OF YOUNG CHILDREN. FELDMAN, CAROL FLEISHER, DEC 69 21P.
EDRS PRICE MF-$0.65 HC-$3.29

IT WAS HYPOTHESIZED THAT BY AGE 8 CHILDREN WOULD MANIFEST AN ADULT MEANING SYSTEM, AND THAT 5-YEAR-OLD CHILDREN WOULD NOT. AN ADULT MEANING SYSTEM ALLOWS AN ADULT TO TRANSCEND COMPONENT WORD MEANINGS AND INTEGRATE, IN THE PRESENCE OF A SPEAKER, THE UNDERDETERMINED AND THE FACTUAL PROPOSITION INTO A MEANINGFUL WHOLE. SUBJECTS WERE 60 5- AND 8-YEAR-OLD MIDDLE CLASS, RACIALLY MIXED CHILDREN. SUBJECTS WERE ASKED TO REPEAT SENTENCES HEARD IN CONVERSATION AND ON TAPE. SENTENCES INCLUDED: (1) THOSE WITH REFERENTIAL NOUNS, (2) THOSE WITH "MODALS," AND (3) CONTROL SENTENCES CONTAINING NEITHER. A THREE-WAY ANALYSIS OF VARIANCE WAS COMPUTED ON AGE BY CONDITION BY SENTENCE TYPE, USING THE TWO AGES, THE TWO CONDITIONS, AND THE MODAL AND CONTROL SENTENCES. RESULTS INDICATE THAT RECALL OF THE MODAL SENTENCES IS BETTER THAN THE CONTROL SENTENCES HEARD IN CONVERSATION BUT NOT HEARD ON TAPE. THE INTERACTION OF SENTENCE BY AGE SHOWS THAT THE OLDER, BUT NOT THE YOUNGER, SUBJECTS PERCEIVE THE DIFFERENCE BETWEEN THE MODAL AND CONTROL SENTENCES. THIS SUPPORTS THE HYPOTHESIS. ALL SUBJECTS, HOWEVER, MASTER SENTENCES CONTAINING REFERENTIAL NOUNS. BOTH THE MODAL AND THE REFERENTIAL SYSTEMS SEEM TO BE NECESSARY TO UNDERSTAND SENTENCE MEANING. (JF)

ED035450 PS002742
A STUDY OF THE INFLUENCE OF CERTAIN PRESCHOOL EDUCATIONAL MOVEMENTS ON CONTEMPORARY PRESCHOOL PRACTICES. SCHMIDT, VELMA E., JUL 68 179P.
EDRS PRICE MF-$0.65 HC-$6.58

IDENTIFIED IN THIS DISSERTATION ARE THE MAJOR INFLUENCES ON AMERICAN PRESCHOOL EDUCATION: (1) THE FROEBEL KINDERGARTEN, (2) THE MONTESSORI MOVEMENT, (3) THE CHILD STUDY MOVEMENT, AND (4) PROJECT HEAD START. EACH MOVEMENT IS DESCRIBED ACCORDING TO HISTORY, AIM, CURRICULUM, MATERIALS, AND METHODS. CRITERIA FOR EACH SECTION OF THE CONTEMPORARY PRESCHOOL WERE IDENTIFIED BY ANALYSIS AND SYNTHESIS OF OPINIONS OF FOUR CURRENT AUTHORITATIVE SOURCES IN PRESCHOOL EDUCATION. THE CRITERIA WERE THEN COMPARED TO THE DESCRIPTION OF EACH PRESCHOOL MOVEMENT TO IDENTIFY ITS INFLUENCE. THE FROEBEL KINDERGARTEN CONTRIBUTED THE VIEW THAT EDUCATION IS A PROCESS OF GROWTH AND ADVOCATED USING THE METHOD OF SELF-ACTIVITY THROUGH PLAY. THE MONTESSORI MOVEMENT PUT EMPHASIS ON RESPONSIBILITY TO BE GIVEN TO CHILDREN FOR CARE OF SELF AND ENVIRONMENT. THE CHILD STUDY MOVEMENT RESULTED IN INCREASED ATTENTION TO THE PHYSICAL, SOCIAL, AND MENTAL DEVELOPMENTAL NEEDS OF CHILDREN. HEAD START INFLUENCE CAN ONLY BE PREDICTED, BUT EFFECTIVE FACTORS MAY BE INCREASED ATTENTION TO SOCIAL SERVICES, HEALTH SERVICES, PARENT AND VOLUNTEER INVOLVEMENT, AND THE EFFORT TO ADAPT A PROGRAM TO THE NEEDS OF A SPECIFIC GROUP OF CHILDREN. A BIBLIOGRAPHY AND CHRONOLOGY TABLES OF SIGNIFICANT DEVELOPMENTS IN PRESCHOOL MOVEMENTS ARE INCLUDED. (DR.)

ED035451 PS002743
WORKTABLE ON WHEELS. GLOCKNER, MARY, OCT 69 2P.
EDRS PRICE MF-$0.65 HC-$3.29

THIS ARTICLE BRIEFLY DESCRIBES THE FUNCTION AND FEATURES OF THE SMITH CIRCULAR LEARNING STATION USED IN CHATTANOOGA, TENNESSEE'S HEAD START AND FOLLOW THROUGH PROGRAM. THE STATIONS ARE USED IN PLACE OF TRADITIONAL ROWS OF CLASSROOM DESKS. EACH STATION CONSISTS OF A MOBILE WORKTABLE AND A SET OF STACKABLE CHAIRS. CHILDREN ARE ALLOWED TO MOVE ABOUT FREELY, AND TO PARTICIPATE IN A NUMBER OF LEARNING ACTIVITIES. THE WORKTABLES ALLOW GREATER FLEXIBILITY IN THE CLASSROOM, ARE INEXPENSIVE TO BUILD, ARE EQUIPPED WITH A SELF-CONTAINED EXTENSION CORD AND JACK, ARE EASY TO FOLD, AND SAVE SPACE. THE ARTICLE ALSO INCLUDES A LIST OF BUILDING MATERIALS FOR THE WORKTABLE, AND CONSTRUCTION PLAN AND DIMENSIONS. (JF)

ED035452 PS002744
MAKING A CHILD'S OWN BOOK. , NOV 69 2P.
EDRS PRICE MF-$0.65 HC-$3.29

THIS PAPER DESCRIBES A CLASSROOM ACTIVITY IN WHICH CHILDREN MAKE THEIR OWN BOOKS, AN ACTIVITY WHICH MAY INCREASE CHILDREN'S LANGUAGE ABILITIES AND CONFIDENCE. FOUR POSSIBILITIES FOR CLASSROOM-PRODUCED BOOKS ARE MENTIONED: (1) THE DICTATED STORY, WITH THE TEACHER TAKING DOWN THE CHILD'S EXACT WORDS, (2) THE PICTURE-STORY BOOK WITH THE CHILD MAKING UP A STORY TO GO ALONG WITH A PICTURE HE HAS DRAWN, (3) THE PICTURE DICTIONARY, WITH THE CHILD TELLING WHAT CERTAIN PICTURES REPRESENT, AND (4) THE LANGUAGE EXPERIENCE BOOK, WITH THE EXERCISE CENTERED AROUND SOME PARTICULAR USE OF WORDS. USE OF A FELT-TIPPED PEN AND LARGE DISTINCT LETTERS HELP TO FAMILIARIZE THE CHILDREN WITH THE WRITTEN WORD. THE BOOKS SHOULD BE ON STANDARD SIZE PAPER AND CAN BE STAPLED OR THREADED TOGETHER ON THE LEFT SIDE. THE CHILD CAN PUT HIS NAME ON HIS BOOK AND DECORATE ITS COVER. ALL BOOKS CAN BECOME PART OF THE CLASSROOM LIBRARY. (MH)

ED035453 PS002766
ASSESSING PROCESS AND PRODUCT WITH YOUNG CHILDREN IN SCHOOL SETTINGS. STERN, CAROLYN, MAR 69 7P.
EDRS PRICE MF-$0.65 HC-$3.29

WHAT NEEDS TO BE DONE WITH PRESCHOOL PROGRAMS IS TO DEFINE SPECIFICALLY THEIR DESIRED PRODUCT (THE BEHAVIORS WE WANT IN THE CHILDREN) AND TO DETERMINE THE OPTIMAL PROCESS BY WHICH THIS PRODUCT CAN BE BROUGHT ABOUT. USING AN INSTRUMENT CALLED THE OBSERVATION OF SUBSTANTIVE CURRICULAR INPUT IN 1967-68, A CODING SYSTEM BASED ON A SERIES OF 3-MINUTE SCANS OF CLASSROOM ACTIVITY, DATA WERE COMPILED FOR 151 HEAD START CLASSES. ANALYSIS OF THE DATA INDICATED THAT WHILE HEAD START CLASSES DIFFERED AMONG THEMSELVES, CERTAIN GENERALIZATIONS COULD BE DRAWN. COMPARATIVELY LITTLE TIME WAS SPENT ON CARETAKING ACTIVITIES, AIMLESS WANDERING, AND TEACHING OF PRE-ACADEMIC SKILLS. A CONSIDERABLE AMOUNT OF TIME WAS SPENT ON STRUCTURED WAITING FOR THE TEACHER, LANGUAGE DEVELOPMENT, DRAMATIC PLAY, AND SOCIAL INTERACTION. GROUP VS INDIVIDUAL ACTIVITY DIFFERENTIATED CLASSES AND SEEMED DEPENDENT ON TEACHER CONTROL. THE NEXT STEP WILL BE TO RELATE THE OBTAINED CLASSROOM CHARACTERISTICS TO SPECIFIC CHANGES IN CHILDREN. WITH THE CAUSAL RELATIONSHIPS BETWEEN PROCESS AND PRODUCT MORE CLEARLY UNDERSTOOD, MORE EFFECTIVE PROGRAMS CAN BE DEVISED BASED ON DATA RATHER THAN INTUITION. (MH)

ED035454 PS002767
SYNTACTIC COMPLEXITY IN MOTHER-CHILD INTERACTIONS. BALDWIN, A. L.; FRANK, S. M., MAR 69 16P.
EDRS PRICE MF-$0.65 HC-$3.29

TO FIND OUT WHAT FACTORS ARE INVOLVED IN A CHILD'S LEARNING OF SYNTAX, INVESTIGATORS STUDIED THE SYNTACTIC COMPLEXITY OF THE LANGUAGE A MOTHER AND CHILD USE WHEN TALKING TO EACH OTHER. THE COMPLEXITY MEASURE USED WAS ONE DEVELOPED BY DR. SHELDON FRANK AND DR. HARRY OSSER, AND IS BASED ON THE CONCEPTS OF GENERATIVE GRAMMAR AND TRANSFORMATIONS. LANGUAGE SAMPLES WERE COLLECTED FROM MOTHERS ALONE IN AN INTERVIEW AND MOTHERS AND CHILDREN TOGETHER IN A PLAY SESSION. THERE WERE TWO GROUPS OF MOTHER-CHILD PAIRS: ONE FROM HARLEM (BLACK LOWER CLASS) AND ONE FROM WASHINGTON SQUARE (WHITE MIDDLE CLASS). ANALYSIS OF THE LANGUAGE SAMPLES INDICATED THAT ALL THE MOTHERS GREATLY REDUCED THEIR SYNTACTIC COMPLEXITY WHEN TALKING TO THEIR CHILDREN, BUT EACH MOTHER'S LANGUAGE WAS STILL MORE COMPLEX THAN THAT OF HER CHILD. THERE WAS NO DIFFERENCE BETWEEN THE HARLEM MOTHERS AND THE WASHINGTON SQUARE MOTHERS IN THEIR SYNTACTIC COMPLEXITY IN THE INTERVIEW, BUT THE HARLEM MOTHER-CHILD INTERACTIONS WERE LESS COMPLEX AND MORE DIDACTIC THAN THOSE OF THE WASHINGTON SQUARE GROUP. FINALLY, THE HARLEM CHILDREN SEEMED TO ARTICULATE LESS CLEARLY THAN THE WASHINGTON SQUARE CHILDREN AND THEIR MOTHERS HAD MORE DIFFICULTY IN UNDERSTANDING THEM. THERE WERE MORE REQUESTS FOR CLARIFICATION IN THE HARLEM INTERACTIONS. (MH)

ED035455 PS002769
POSTDOCTORAL RESEARCH TRAINING PROGRAM IN EDUCATIONAL STIMULATION. FINAL REPORT. FINDLEY, WARREN G.; AND OTHERS, 27 FEB 69 40P.
EDRS PRICE MF-$0.65 HC-$3.29

A 1-YEAR POSTDOCTORAL RESEARCH TRAINING PROGRAM PREPARED ONE TRAINEE IN EARLY CHILDHOOD EDUCATION DURING 1966-67. FLEXIBLE ARRANGEMENTS ALLOWED THIS MATURE TRAINEE TO PLAN AND FOLLOW HIS OWN PROGRAM IN CONSULTATION WITH THE STAFF OF THE RESEARCH AND DEVELOPMENT CENTER IN EDUCATIONAL STIMULATION AT THE UNIVERSITY OF GEORGIA. EXPERIMENTATION IN ONGOING SCHOOL PROGRAMS ENABLED THE TRAINEE TO DEVELOP AN INVENTORY OF EARLY MATHEMATICS ACCOMPLISHMENTS FOR 5-YEAR-OLDS, WHICH WAS THEN USED SYSTEMATICALLY BY HIM IN NEW YORK STATE AS WELL AS BY OTHERS IN FOLLOW THROUGH PROGRAMS. DEVELOPMENT OF THIS GROUP TEST OF MATHEMATICS ACHIEVEMENT IS DESCRIBED, INCLUDING THE SPECIFICATION OF DETAILED ADMINISTRATIVE PROCEDURES NECESSARY WITH YOUNG CHILDREN. THE POSTDOCTORAL RESEARCH TRAINING PROGRAM WAS JUDGED EFFECTIVE FOR ITS PURPOSE, FOLLOWING THE ORIGINAL PROPOSAL TO PROVIDE A HIGH LEVEL PROFESSIONAL APPRENTICESHIP. SUGGESTIONS ARE MADE FOR IMPROVEMENT OF THE USOE RESEARCH TRAINING PROGRAM BY EXPANDING ITS SCOPE TO INCLUDE ESTABLISHMENT AND SUPPORT OF ADVANCED TRAINING CENTERS TO MEET CURRENT RETOOLING DEMANDS FOR HIGH LEVEL EDUCATIONAL PERSONNEL. (AUTHOR/DR)

ED035456 PS002781
EXEMPLARY AND INNOVATIVE PRESCHOOL CHILD DEVELOPMENT DEMONSTRATION CENTERS, 1966-1969. THREE YEAR EVALUATION AND NARRATIVE REPORT. , 22 AUG 69 75P.
EDRS PRICE MF-$0.65 HC-$3.29

THIS DOCUMENT EVALUATES THE FIRST THREE YEARS OF A PRESCHOOL PROJECT IN KALAMAZOO SCHOOL DISTRICT WHICH WAS FUNDED BY TITLE III OF THE ELEMENTARY AND SECONDARY EDUCATION ACT. THE PROGRAM AIMS TO MAXIMIZE THE POTENTIAL OF EACH PRESCHOOL CHILD AND TO INVOLVE PARENTS AND COMMUNITY AGENCIES IN THE PROJECT. THIS REPORT DESCRIBES THE OBJECTIVES OF THE PROGRAM AND THE AREAS IN WHICH OBJECTIVES ARE BEING MET. A COMPARISON OF DISADVANTAGED KINDERGARTEN CHILDREN AND A CONTROL GROUP IS MADE, AND A FOLLOW-UP STUDY OF FIRST GRADE PERFORMANCE OF THE TWO GROUPS IS ANALYZED. NO SIGNIFICANT DIFFERENCES ARE REPORTED BETWEEN EITHER THE EXPERIMENTAL AND CONTROL GROUPS OR BETWEEN O.E.O. AND TITLE III CHILDREN. FOR THE FINAL EVALUATION, PRINCIPALS, TEACHERS, AND PARENTS ASSESS THE PROJECT'S STRENGTHS AND WEAKNESSES THROUGH INTERVIEWS. THE FORMAT OF THE INTERVIEWS AND INDIVIDUAL RESPONSES COMPRISE MORE THAN HALF THE REPORT. SELECTED CASE HISTORIES ILLUSTRATE THE COOPERATION OF STAFF MEMBERS AND COMMUNITY AGENCIES. AN EVALUATION OF THE PERFORMANCE OF VOLUNTEERS IS INCLUDED AND A HEALTH SERVICES REPORT STATES THE NUMBER OF TYPES OF SERVICES COMPLETED. FINAL RECOMMENDATIONS FOR THE 1969-70 PRESCHOOL PROGRAM COMPLETE THE EVALUATION. (DR)

ED035457 PS002783
SEX EDUCATION: RESOURCE UNIT , 69 26P.
EDRS PRICE MF-$0.65 HC NOT AVAILABLE FROM EDRS.
AVAILABLE FROM: AMERICAN ASSOCIATION FOR HEALTH, PHYSICAL EDUCATION, AND RECREATION, 1201 SIXTEENTH STREET, N.W., WASHINGTON, D.C. 20036

THIS BOOKLET IS PART OF A SERIES ON HEALTH INSTRUCTION DEVELOPED BY THE PUBLICATIONS COMMISSION OF THE SCHOOL HEALTH DIVISION OF THE AMERICAN ASSOCIATION FOR HEALTH, PHYSICAL EDUCATION, AND RECREATION. AN AID TO TEACHERS, IT DESCRIBES THE PROPER ROLE OF SEX EDUCATION IN THE CLASSROOM. THE SPECIFIC AIMS AND OBJECTIVE OF SEX EDUCATION FOR GRADE LEVELS FROM KINDERGARTEN TO FOURTH GRADE ARE INCLUDED, AS ARE CLASSROOM METHODS AND TECHNIQUES FOR ACHIEVING THESE GOALS. RELEVANT VOCABULARY WORDS ARE LISTED. THERE ARE TWO LISTS OF REFERENCES; ONE FOR STUDENTS, AND ONE FOR TEACHERS. SOME SUPPLEMENTARY TEACHING AIDS, INCLUDING SOUND FILMS AND FILM STRIPS, ARE DESCRIBED AND THEIR SOURCES LISTED. FINALLY, SOME SELECTED SOURCES FOR ADDITIONAL INFORMATION ARE MENTIONED. (MH)

ED035458 PS002786
ANALYSIS OF HOME ENVIRONMENT AND DEVELOPMENT OF PARENT INTERVENTION. BAYER, HELEN; RAY, MARGARET, [69] 2P.
EDRS PRICE MF-$0.65 HC-$3.29

THE 5-YEAR PROJECT REPORTED IN THIS PAPER SOUGHT INITIALLY TO EXAMINE THE HOME ENVIRONMENTS BOTH OF ISOLATED, INTACT RURAL WHITE FAMILIES AND OF SINGLE PARENT AFDC NEGRO FAMILIES. THE INFORMATION THUS GATHERED WAS TO BE COMPARED TO WHAT IS KNOWN ABOUT MIDDLE CLASS WHITE FAMILIES IN HOPES OF ISOLATING THE DIFFERENCES THAT RESULT IN THE POORER ACADEMIC PERFORMANCE OF POOR CHILDREN AND DEVELOPING PROGRAMS OF PARENT INTERVENTION TO ALLEVIATE THIS PROBLEM. THE INTERVENTION PROJECT IS PRESENTLY BEING CARRIED ON THROUGH WEEKLY HOME VISITS. THESE VISITS HAVE FOUR OBJECTIVES: (1) TO INCREASE THE QUANTITY AND QUALITY OF MOTHER-CHILD VERBAL INTERACTION, (2) TO

INSTILL THE IDEA IN BOTH THE MOTHER AND THE CHILD THAT ADULTS ARE HELPFUL, RESOURCE-CONTROLLING PERSONS, (3) TO SHIFT THE BEHAVIOR CONTROL TECHNIQUES FROM DIFFUSE NONVERBAL REINFORCEMENT TO VERBAL REINFORCEMENT WITH SPECIFIC EXPLANATIONS, AND (4) TO HAVE THE MOTHER ENCOURAGE INCREASED COMPLEXITY IN THE CHILD'S LANGUAGE. THIS HOME TEACHING PROGRAM LASTS 12 WEEKS; 9 FOR THE PROGRAM, 1 FOR MAKE-UP, AND 2 FOR EVALUATION. FIELD TRIPS, SINGING, READING, AND A WIDE VARIETY OF GAMES WERE AMONG THE PROGRAM ACTIVITIES. (MH)

ED035459 PS002787
INDUSTRIAL ARTS FOR THE PRIMARY GRADES. HALL, RONALD B., 69 12P.
EDRS PRICE MF-$0.65 HC-$3.29

THIS ARTICLE, PART OF A SERIES COMPILED BY THE DIVISION OF EARLY CHILDHOOD EDUCATION, IS INTENDED TO HELP ELEMENTARY TEACHERS DEVELOP THE PROPER TEACHING METHODS, PROCEDURES, AND KNOWLEDGE OF AVAILABLE MATERIALS FOR THE IMPLEMENTATION OF INDUSTRIAL ARTS ACTIVITIES. THE ARTICLE INCLUDES SECTIONS ON THE THEORY OF INDUSTRIAL ARTS IN THE ELEMENTARY SCHOOL, THE OBJECTIVES OF ELEMENTARY INDUSTRIAL ARTS, THE USE OF INDUSTRIAL ARTS TO IMPROVE THE LEARNING EXPERIENCE, AND CLASSROOM APPROACHES TO EMPLOYING ELEMENTARY INDUSTRIAL ARTS. A BIBLIOGRAPHY IS INCLUDED. (AUTHOR/JF)

ED035460 PS002788
SOCIAL STUDIES IN THE PRIMARY GRADES. SCHLAPPICH, LEON, 69 16P.
EDRS PRICE MF-$0.65 HC-$3.29

THIS ARTICLE SEEKS TO PROVIDE BASIC INFORMATION AND GUIDELINES FOR THE TEACHING OF SOCIAL STUDIES IN KINDERGARTEN AND GRADES 1 THROUGH 3. IT EMPHASIZES THE IMPORTANCE OF MOLDING YOUTH TO FIT INTO A DEMOCRATIC SOCIETY AND POINTS OUT THE USEFULNESS OF SOCIAL STUDIES TO ACHIEVE THIS END. AN INTERDISCIPLINARY APPROACH IS ADVOCATED, WHICH WOULD INCLUDE ANTHROPOLOGY, SOCIOLOGY, ECONOMICS, AND SOCIAL PSYCHOLOGY AS WELL AS THE TRADITIONAL SUBJECTS OF GEOGRAPHY, HISTORY, AND POLITICAL SCIENCE. A GRADE-BY-GRADE OUTLINE OF THE CONTENT, SCOPE, AND SEQUENCE OF THE SOCIAL STUDIES IS INCLUDED, WITH A SPECIFIC LIST OF GOALS AND SUBCOMMUNITIES TO BE INVESTIGATED. THERE IS A DISCUSSION OF TEACHING METHODS THAT FAVORS A MULTI-TEXT APPROACH AND CONCERN FOR THE INDIVIDUAL NEEDS OF THE STUDENTS AND THE COMMUNITY. THE UNIT APPROACH TO THE SUBJECT MATTER OF SOCIAL STUDIES IS ALSO ADVOCATED. THE PAPER SUGGESTS THAT THE SOCIAL STUDIES CLASSROOM BE WELL-EQUIPPED WITH MAPS, AUDIO-VISUAL MATERIAL, AND REFERENCE MATERIALS. (MH)

ED035461 PS002789
SCIENCE FOR THE PRIMARY GRADES: QUESTIONS AND ANSWERS. EDGAR, IRVIN T., 69 14P.
EDRS PRICE MF-$0.65 HC-$3.29

THIS ARTICLE, WHICH PROVIDES ANSWERS TO COMMONLY ASKED QUESTIONS ABOUT TEACHING SCIENCE IN THE PRIMARY GRADES, IS PART OF A SERIES INCLUDED IN THE PRIMARY PACKET OF MATERIALS COMPILED BY THE DIVISION OF EARLY CHILDHOOD EDUCATION OF THE PENNSYLVANIA DEPARTMENT OF PUBLIC INSTRUCTION. QUESTIONS CONSIDERED ARE: WHAT IS SCIENCE? WHAT SHOULD STUDENTS BE TAUGHT IN SCIENCE? WHICH TEXTBOOK IS BEST, OR IS A MULTI-TEXT APPROACH BEST? HOW DOES ONE FIND TIME TO TEACH SCIENCE? HOW ARE STUDENT DIFFERENCES PROVIDED FOR? ARE THERE NATIONAL PROGRAMS FOR SCIENCE AS THERE ARE FOR MATHEMATICS? THE ARTICLE ALSO INCLUDES A LIST OF DESIRABLE CHARACTERISTICS FOR A SCHOOL SCIENCE PROGRAM AND A 2-PAGE BIBLIOGRAPHY. (JF)

ED035462 PS002806
A PILOT STUDY TO ASSESS THE ACADEMIC PROGRESS OF DISADVANTAGED FIRST GRADERS ASSIGNED TO CLASS BY SEX AND TAUGHT BY A TEACHER OF THE SAME SEX. SCHEINER, LOUIS, NOV 69 17P.
EDRS PRICE MF-$0.65 HC-$3.29

FIRST GRADE DISADVANTAGED CHILDREN WERE SEPARATED INTO CLASSES BY SEX AND TAUGHT BY A TEACHER OF THE SAME SEX. IT WAS HYPOTHESIZED THAT (1) SINGLE SEX CLASSES WOULD SCORE HIGHER ON READING AND ARITHMETIC TESTS AND SHOW A MORE POSITIVE ATTITUDE TOWARD SCHOOL, TEACHER, AND PEERS THAN COEDUCATIONAL CLASSES, AND (2) THE ONE ALL-GIRLS CLASS WOULD SCORE HIGHER ON READING AND ARITHMETIC THAN THE TWO ALL-BOYS CLASSES. BOTH EXPERIMENTAL AND CONTROL GROUPS WERE GIVEN THE PHILADELPHIA READING TEST AND THE PHILADELPHIA TEST IN FUNDAMENTALS IN ARITHMETIC. ATTITUDE MEASURES WERE THE PUPIL ATTITUDE TOWARD SCHOOL INVENTORY AND THE WAY I FEEL ABOUT MYSELF INSTRUMENTS. THE SINGLE SEX CLASSES SCORED SIGNIFICANTLY HIGHER IN READING THAN THE CONTROL GROUP, BUT THERE WERE NO SIGNIFICANT DIFFERENCES BETWEEN THE ALL-BOYS CLASSES AND THE ALL-GIRLS CLASS IN READING AND ARITHMETIC. ALL-BOYS CLASSES WERE MORE POSITIVE TOWARD SCHOOL, LEARNING, TEACHERS, PEERS, AND SELF THAN THE OTHER GROUPS. THE CONTROL GROUP WAS MORE POSITIVE IN THESE ATTITUDES THAN THE ALL-GIRLS CLASS. IT WAS RECOMMENDED THAT TEACHER PERSONALITY AND COMPETENCY VARIABLES BE CONSIDERED IN A CONTROLLED LONGITUDINAL STUDY AND THAT DIFFERENT MATERIALS AND TEACHING TECHNIQUES BE STRESSED FOR TRAINING TEACHERS TO WORK WITH ALL MALE CLASSES. (DR)

ED035463 PS002830
THE TEACHER, TEACHER STYLE, AND CLASSROOM MANAGEMENT. PROCEEDINGS OF THE HEAD START RESEARCH SEMINARS: SEMINAR NO. 2, THE TEACHER AND CLASSROOM MANAGEMENT (1ST, WASHINGTON, D.C., JULY 22, 1968). RASHID, MARTHA; AND OTHERS, 22 JUL 68 70P.
EDRS PRICE MF-$0.65 HC-$3.29

ONE OF A SERIES OF SEMINARS ON HEAD START RESEARCH, THIS PAPER DEALS WITH THE POTENTIAL CONTRIBUTION OF TEACHER STYLE TO CLASSROOM MANAGEMENT. IT IS SUGGESTED THAT STUDIES BE DESIGNED TO (1) COMPARE AND DESCRIBE PRESCHOOL AND PRIMARY PROGRAMS, (2) DEVELOP A STANDARD SYSTEM OF NOTATION FOR RECORDING BEHAVIOR IN CLASSROOMS, (3) DETERMINE THE EFFECT OF THE CLASSROOM SETTING ON TEACHER BEHAVIOR, AND (4) PROVIDE INSERVICE EDUCATION FOR PRESCHOOL TEACHERS TO TEACH THEM PRACTICAL PROCEDURES FOR GETTING SYSTEMATIC FEEDBACK ABOUT THEIR OWN BEHAVIOR. FURTHER STUDIES ARE NEEDED TO EXAMINE BOTH TEACHER AND PUPIL STYLE, AS WELL AS THE DEVELOPMENT OF SEX ROLE AND MOTIVATION IN YOUNG CHILDREN. THE EFFECT OF THE TEACHER'S STYLE ON CHILDREN'S COGNITIVE AND SOCIAL DEVELOPMENT DESERVES FURTHER ATTENTION. RESPONSES TO THIS PAPER ARE MADE BY IRA GORDON, MARTIN HABERMAN, AND HELEN RICHARDS. A BIBLIOGRAPHY ON THE TEACHER AND CLASSROOM MANAGEMENT IS INCLUDED. (DOCUMENT ED 034 088 HAS THE FULL TEXT OF THE PROCEEDINGS OF ALL SIX HEAD START SEMINARS IN THIS SERIES.) (DR)

ED035464 PS002861
THE STORY OF AN AFTER - SCHOOL PROGRAM. STREET, VIRGINIA, [69] 11P.
EDRS PRICE MF-$0.65 HC-$3.29

IN WASHINGTON, D.C. IN SEPTEMBER 1968, BECAUSE THERE WERE NO AFTER-SCHOOL PROGRAMS WHERE THE STAFF TOOK RESPONSIBILITY FOR THE CHILDREN, THE NATIONAL CAPITAL AREA CHILD DAY CARE ASSOCIATION SET UP A DEMONSTRATION PROGRAM. THIS REPORT PROVIDES AN ANECDOTAL RECORD OF THE PROGRAM'S DEVELOPMENT. TWO ROOMS WERE SECURED IN THE BASEMENT OF A SCHOOL, 50 BLACK, UNDERPRIVILEGED FIRST AND SECOND GRADERS WERE SELECTED, AND A SMALL STAFF WAS HIRED. THE STAFF INCLUDED A TEACHER-IN-CHARGE, TWO ASSISTANT TEACHERS, TWO AIDES, AND A CLERK. THE INITIAL GOALS WERE TO KEEP THE CHILD SAFE, TO IMPROVE HIS SELF-IMAGE, TO DEVELOP HIS EXPRESSIVE AND CREATIVE ABILITIES, TO WORK ON REMEDIAL ACADEMIC WORK, AND TO OFFER SUPPLEMENTARY NOURISHMENT IN THE FORM OF DAILY SNACKS. THE TEACHER-IN-CHARGE INVOLVED THE CHILDREN IN PROJECTS AND TRIPS AND ENCOURAGED THEM TO LEARN THROUGH DOING. HOWEVER, THE PROBLEMS WERE MANY: STAFFING, INEXPERIENCE, LACK OF INTRA-STAFF COMMUNICATION, DISTURBED CHILDREN, VANDALISM, AND INABILITY TO LOSE THE FEELING OF BEING INTRUDERS IN THE BASEMENT ROOMS. THE PROGRAM IS STILL IN THE TESTING PHASE BUT SOME PROGRESS HAS BEEN MADE IN SOLVING THESE PROBLEMS. (MH)

ED036311 PS000290
PROJECT HEAD START AT WORK. REPORT OF A SURVEY STUDY OF 335 PROJECT HEAD START CENTERS, SUMMER, 1965. , APR 66 56P.
EDRS PRICE MF-$0.65 HC-$3.29

A NATIONAL OBSERVER TEAM SURVEYED 335 HEAD START CENTERS DURING AN 8-WEEK SUMMER PERIOD TO LOCATE USEFUL INNOVATIONS AND DEVELOPMENTS IN PRESCHOOL EDUCATION METHODS WHICH MIGHT HAVE FUTURE IMPLICATIONS FOR THE WHOLE EDUCATIONAL SYSTEM. TEAM REPORTS AGREED THAT THE PROGRAMS HAD BEEN MORE SUCCESSFUL IN BOLSTERING THE SOCIAL AND EMOTIONAL NEEDS OF THE CHILDREN THAN IN THE ADVANCEMENT OF THEIR INTELLECTUAL SKILLS. THE INTERACTION OF THE PRESCHOOLERS WITH THEIR TEACHERS AND TEACHER AIDES, WHETHER THESE WERE TEENAGERS OR ADULTS, WAS CRITICALLY IMPORTANT IN ESTABLISHING AN ACCEPTABLE LEARNING ENVIRONMENT. CONTACT WITH OLDER PERSONS ABLE TO RESPOND QUICKLY TO CHILDREN'S QUESTIONS AND NEEDS FOR ATTENTION ENCOURAGED AND REINFORCED DEVELOPMENT. MALE TEENAGE AIDES WERE ESPECIALLY VALUABLE AS MANY OF THE CHILDREN DID NOT HAVE SATISFACTORY FATHER CONTACTS AT HOME. IT WAS GENERALLY AGREED THAT THE ESSENTIAL TRAINING AND EXPERIENCE IN PRESCHOOL EDUCATION COULD BE GIVEN IN INSERVICE PROGRAMS OR IN SHORT INSTITUTE SESSIONS. LEARNING BY DOING WAS STRESSED BY ALL CENTERS, AND ADOLESCENT, PARENT, AND COMMUNITY INVOLVEMENT IN THE EDUCATIVE PROCESS WAS SUGGESTED BY THE SURVEY REPORT. (MS)

ED036312 PS001538
INSTITUTE FOR DEVELOPMENTAL STUDIES INTERIM PROGRESS REPORT. PART II: RESEARCH AND EVALUATION. DEUTSCH, MARTIN; AND OTHERS, NOV 68 239P.
EDRS PRICE MF-$0.65 HC-$9.87

THE INSTITUTE FOR DEVELOPMENTAL STUDIES (IDS) IS ENGAGED IN RESEARCH AIMED AT SPECIFYING WHAT THE ACADEMIC HANDICAPS OF DEPRIVED CHILDREN ARE, WHAT CAUSES THESE HANDICAPS, AND WHAT CAN BE DONE TO OVERCOME THEM. THIS IDS REPORT ON THEIR RESEARCH AND EVALUATION PROGRAM IS DIVIDED INTO TWO SECTIONS. THE FIRST, "SUMMARIES OF BASIC RESEARCH, APPLIED RESEARCH AND EVALUATION," OFFERS A CONDENSED OVERVIEW OF THE WORK OF THE INSTITUTE FOR DEVELOPMENTAL STUDIES. THE SECOND, AN APPENDIX,

INCLUDES SUCH DETAILED MATERIAL AS A SELECTION OF COMPLETE REPORTS AND A COMPLETE "BIBLIOGRAPHY OF THE INSTITUTE FOR DEVELOPMENTAL STUDIES." THE ACTUAL WORK REPORTS COVER A WIDE VARIETY OF SUBJECTS RELATED TO POVERTY AND EARLY CHILDHOOD EDUCATION: LANGUAGE DEVELOPMENT, AUDITORY DISCRIMINATION, PHONEMIC DISCRIMINATION, CONSERVATION, COGNITIVE DIFFERENTIATION, KINDERGARTEN CURRICULUM, BEGINNING READING, VISUAL DISCRIMINATION OF ALPHABET LETTERS, AND DEVELOPMENT OF PRESCHOOL OBSERVATION TECHNIQUES. OTHER AREAS EXPLORED ARE SELF-CONCEPT, CLASSROOM INTEGRATION, AND USE OF EARLY CHILDHOOD INVENTORIES. ONE CONSISTENT FINDING IS THAT LASTING CHANGES CAN'T BE EXPECTED UNLESS INTERVENTION EXTENDS AT LEAST THROUGH THE THIRD GRADE. (MH)

ED036313 PS001675
AN INVESTIGATION OF THE MANNER IN WHICH YOUNG CHILDREN PROCESS INTELLECTUAL INFORMATION. FINAL REPORT. LAUGHLIN, PATRICK R., AUG 68 11P.
EDRS PRICE MF-$0.65 HC NOT AVAILABLE FROM EDRS.

IN ORDER TO STUDY THE INFLUENCE OF THE INFORMATION-PROCESSING STRATEGY OF AN ADULT MODEL ON THE SUBSEQUENT STRATEGY OF CHILDREN, 216 GRADE SCHOOL CHILDREN SOLVED MODIFIED TWENTY-QUESTIONS PROBLEMS. A REPEATED-MEASURES FACTORIAL DESIGN WAS USED WITH THE FOLLOWING VARIABLES: (1) INFORMATION-PROCESSING OF MODEL (HYPOTHESIS SCANNING, CONSTRAINT SEEKING, OR CONTROL), (2) STIMULUS DISPLAY (PICTORIAL OR VERBAL), (3) SCHOOL GRADE (THREE, FIVE, OR SEVEN), (4) SEX (MALE OR FEMALE), (5) PROBLEMS (2 PER SUBJECT). MAJOR RESULTS WERE: (1) FEWER QUESTIONS TO SOLUTION WITH THE CONSTRAINT-SEEKING MODEL THAN THE HYPOTHESIS-TESTING MODEL OR CONTROL, WHO DID NOT DIFFER, (2) BOTH A HIGHER PERCENTAGE OF CONSTRAINTS, AND HIGHER AVERAGE NUMBER OF ITEMS PER QUESTION WITH THE CONSTRAINT-SEEKING MODEL THAN THE CONTROL OF HYPOTHESIS-TESTING MODEL, AND WITH THE CONTROL THAN WITH THE HYPOTHESIS-TESTING MODEL, (3) BOTH A HIGHER PERCENTAGE OF CONSTRAINTS, AND HIGHER NUMBER OF ITEMS PER QUESTION, FOR SEVENTH THAN FIFTH AND THIRD GRADERS, AND FOR FIFTH THAN THIRD, (4) SIGNIFICANT MODEL BY GRADE INTERACTIONS FOR BOTH PERCENTAGE OF CONSTRAINTS AND ITEMS PER QUESTION, (5) NO EFFECTS FOR STIMULUS DISPLAY, SEX, OR SUCCESSIVE PROBLEMS ON ANY MEASURE. [NOT AVAILABLE IN HARD COPY DUE TO MARGINAL LEGIBILITY OF ORIGINAL DOCUMENT]. (AUTHOR)

ED036314 PS001696
LOGICAL INFERENCE IN DISCRIMINATION LEARNING OF YOUNG CHILDREN. REPORT FROM THE RULE LEARNING PROJECT. FLETCHER, HAROLD J.; GARSKE, JOHN P., APR 68 12P.
EDRS PRICE MF-$0.65 HC-$3.29

TEN KINDERGARTEN AND 46 FIRST GRADE CHILDREN WERE GIVEN TWO-CHOICE OBJECT DISCRIMINATION PROBLEMS, DURING WHICH A PROMPT INDICATED THE POSITIVE (REWARDED) OBJECT, P. GUIDED BY THE PROMPT, ALL SS SUBJECTS DISPLACED P AND THEREFORE OBSERVED ONLY ITS REWARD VALUE; NO DIRECT OBSERVATION WAS MADE OF THE REWARD VALUE OF THE NEGATIVE (NONREWARDED) OBJECT, N. ON TEST TRIALS, A NEW OBJECT, X, WAS SUBSTITUTED FOR P AND PAIRED WITH N. THE PERFORMANCE OF BOTH GROUPS WAS SIGNIFICANTLY ABOVE CHANCE ON THESE X + N TEST TRIALS. CONTROL CONDITIONS AND CONFIRMING VERBAL DATA ALLOWED THE CONCLUSION THAT THESE SS SUBJECTS HAD LOGICALLY INFERRED THE NEGATIVE VALUE OF N WHILE DISPLACING ONLY P DURING PROMPTED TRIALS AND WERE THEREFORE APPROPRIATELY AVOIDING N ON THE TEST TRIAL. (AUTHOR)

ED036315 PS001697
INVESTIGATIONS OF THE ROLE OF SELECTED CUES IN CHILDREN'S PAIRED-ASSOCIATE LEARNING. REPORT FROM THE READING PROJECT. OTTO, WAYNE; COOPER, CARIN, MAY 68 24P.
EDRS PRICE MF-$0.65 HC-$3.29

THESE FOUR STUDIES IN A SERIES DEAL WITH GOOD AND POOR READERS' UTILIZATION OF SELECTED CUES IN PAIRED-ASSOCIATE LEARNING. SPECIFIC CUES CONSIDERED WERE COLOR, ORDER OF PRESENTATION, AND VERBAL MEDIATORS. ANSWERS TO TWO BASIC QUESTIONS WERE SOUGHT: (1) DO THE SELECTED CUES HAVE A FACILITATIVE EFFECT UPON CHILDREN'S PAIRED-ASSOCIATE LEARNING? (2) IS THE LEARNING OF GOOD AND POOR READERS AFFECTED DIFFERENTLY BY THE ADDITIONAL CUES? FOR THE 72 ELEMENTARY SCHOOL SUBJECTS IN THE STUDY, COLOR WAS SHOWN TO HAVE A POSITIVE EFFECT UPON LEARNING WHEN INTRALIST SIMILARITY WAS HIGH, BUT THERE WAS NO RELIABLE DIFFERENTIAL EFFECT FOR GOOD AND POOR READERS. SERIAL (AS OPPOSED TO SCRAMBLED) ORDER OF PRESENTATION WAS SHOWN TO ENHANCE BOTH INITIAL LEARNING AND RECALL. INSTRUCTIONS TO USE VERBAL MEDIATORS ALSO ENHANCED LEARNING; BUT AGAIN THERE WAS NO DIFFERENTIAL EFFECT FOR GOOD AND POOR READERS. INTERACTIONS AMONG THE SELECTED CUES AND OTHER RELEVANT FACTORS AND IMPLICATIONS WERE CONSIDERED IN TERMS OF CONSTRUCTING A PROGRAM FOR THE TEACHING OF READING. (AUTHOR/JS)

ED036316 PS001990
PRESCHOOL INTERVENTION THROUGH SOCIAL LEARNING. VAN DEN DAELE, LELAND D., [69] 27P.
EDRS PRICE MF-$0.65 HC-$3.29

THIS SUMMARY ON STUDIES ON PRESCHOOL INTERVENTION THROUGH SOCIAL LEARNING INDICATE THAT A CHILD'S MODE OF ORIENTATION AND HIS GENERAL LEVEL OF COMPETENCE AND MATURITY ARE, IN LARGE PART, DERIVED FROM HIS SOCIAL ENVIRONMENT. TO THE EXTENT THAT SPECIFIC ASPECTS OF THAT ENVIRONMENT CAN BE IDENTIFIED AS SIGNIFICANT ANTECEDENTS TO BEHAVIORAL INADEQUACIES, REMEDIAL EFFORTS SHOULD CONCERN THEMSELVES WITH THOSE ASPECTS. DISADVANTAGED BOYS FROM FATHER-ABSENT HOMES EXHIBIT A LOW LEVEL OF MATURITY IN THEIR COGNITIVE, AFFECTIVE, AND BEHAVIORAL PROCESSES. YET, WHILE THIS IMMATURITY SEEMS CLEARLY TO SPRING FROM SOCIAL FACTORS, PRESCHOOLS HAVE TRADITIONALLY STRESSED SCHOOL READINESS SKILLS. THE PROBLEMS EXPERIENCED BY DISADVANTAGED BOYS SEEMED TO BE CAUSED BY A COMBINATION OF (1) PATERNAL ABSENCE, (2) LACK OF APPROPRIATE MASCULINE MODEL, AND (3) LOW SOCIAL ESTEEM OF THE MALE AND MALE ROLE. REMEDIATION SEEMS TO REQUIRE AT LEAST (1) A COMPETENT MASCULINE MODEL, (2) VARIED CHILD-MODEL INTERACTION, AND (3) REINFORCEMENT OF THE BOY'S IMITATING BEHAVIOR. THE PRESENCE OF THESE CONDITIONS IN A COORDINATED SOCIAL-LEARNING PROGRAM YIELDED SIGNIFICANT INTELLECTUAL AND EMOTIONAL GAINS. SOCIAL-LEARNING TECHNIQUES CAN BE USED TO SUPPLEMENT PROGRAMS WITH SPECIFIC ENRICHMENT GOALS, AND MAY ALSO BE USED TO BROADEN THE RANGE OF THE ADVANTAGED AS WELL AS THE DISADVANTAGED. (MH)

ED036317 PS002089
BIOGENETICS OF RACE AND CLASS. GOTTESMAN, I. I., 68 41P.
DOCUMENT NOT AVAILABLE FROM EDRS.
AVAILABLE FROM: HOLT, RINEHART AND WINSTON, INC., 383 MADISON AVENUE, NEW YORK, N.Y. 10017 ($7.00)

THIS PAPER IS THE FIRST CHAPTER OF A BOOK AND IS DIVIDED INTO SIX SECTIONS. THE FIRST SECTION DISCUSSES RACE TAXONOMY, THE NEGRO AMERICAN'S ORIGINS FROM AFRICA, AND THE ORIGIN OF RACE DIFFERENCES. THE SECOND SECTION INVESTIGATES THE GENETIC ASPECTS OF RACE DIFFERENCES IN INTELLECTUAL PERFORMANCE, AND INCLUDES A LENGTHY INTRODUCTORY DISCUSSION ON THE DIALECTICS OF HEREDITY AND ENVIRONMENT. THE THIRD SECTION DEALS WITH THE GENETIC ASPECTS OF SOCIAL CLASS DIFFERENCES, WHILE SECTION FOUR COVERS BOTH RACE AND CLASS DIFFERENCES. THE FIFTH SECTION DEALS WITH THE RELATIONSHIP BETWEEN INTELLIGENCE AND FAMILY SIZE IN AN INTRODUCTORY FASHION, AND THE FINAL SECTION CONSISTS OF A ONE-PARAGRAPH SUMMARY OF THE MATERIAL COVERED IN THE CHAPTER. A LIST OF REFERENCES AND A GLOSSARY OF TERMS ARE APPENDED. (JF)

ED036318 PS002138
EARLY LEARNING AND COMPENSATORY EDUCATION: CONTRIBUTION OF BASIC RESEARCH. KESSEN, WILLIAM, 31 AUG 69 3P.
EDRS PRICE MF-$0.65 HC-$3.29

IN A PAPER GIVEN AT THE 1969 AMERICAN PSYCHOLOGICAL ASSOCIATION MEETING, THE AUTHOR POINTED OUT THAT THE APPARENT COMMITMENT OF OUR SOCIETY TO THE EDUCATION OF THE YOUNG WILL BE OF QUESTIONABLE VALUE UNTIL THE ENERGIES AND EFFORTS OF EDUCATORS FIND A MEANINGFUL DIRECTION. RIGHT NOW, THE FLURRY OF ACTIVITY IN EDUCATIONAL REFORM FOR THE VERY YOUNG IS MORE CONCERNED WITH ACTIVITY THAN RESULTS. FOR EXAMPLE, THE HEAD START PROGRAM IS RECEIVING MORE AND MORE AMPLIFICATION IN SPITE OF THE MIXED EVIDENCE CONCERNING ITS SUCCESS. ALSO, THE QUESTIONABLE TACTIC OF IMPOSING MIDDLE-CLASS LIFE ON THE ECONOMICALLY DEPRIVED TO ATTUNE THEM TO OUR MIDDLE-CLASS SCHOOLS CONTINUES AS ONE OF THE MOST WELL-ADVERTISED EFFORTS OF CONCERNED REFORMERS. PSYCHOLOGISTS CAN BE MOST USEFUL IF THEY WILL ASSUME ROLES AS SETTERS OF GOALS, SOURCES OF INNOVATIVE EDUCATIONAL IDEAS, REPOSITORIES OF KNOWLEDGE, AND GATHERERS OF INFORMATION. THE CURRENT STATE OF KNOWLEDGE OF BASIC PSYCHOLOGICAL PRINCIPLES FOR EDUCATIONAL REFORM IS INDEED SAD. IT IS IN RESEARCH THAT PSYCHOLOGISTS HAVE THE MOST TO CONTRIBUTE. THIS RESEARCH COULD BEST BE CARRIED OUT IN EXPERIMENTAL SCHOOLS WITH VARIOUS INNOVATIVE TECHNIQUES BEING MEASURED AGAINST EACH OTHER. (MH)

ED036319 PS002395
AN INSTITUTIONAL ANALYSIS OF DAY CARE PROGRAM. PART I, GROUP DAY CARE: A STUDY IN DIVERSITY. FINAL REPORT. MILICH, CYNTHIA; AND OTHERS, JUL 69 145P.
EDRS PRICE MF-$0.65 HC-$6.58

AT THE OUTSET OF THIS REPORT ON GROUP DAY CARE, TWO QUESTIONS OF PRIMARY CONCERN ARE POSED: HOW DOES A COMMUNITY GET GROUP DAY CARE? ANE ONCE IT IS OBTAINED, HOW CAN THE COMMUNITY REGULATE ITS QUALITY? WITH THESE QUESTIONS AS GENERAL GUIDELINES, THE REPORT EXAMINES MOST ASPECTS OF EVERY POSSIBLE KIND OF GROUP DAY CARE PROJECT RANGING FROM LOCAL CHURCH PROJECTS TO FEDERALLY FUNDED PROGRAMS. SPECIFIC EXAMPLES ARE TREATED ANECDOTALLY TO HELP THE READER UNDERSTAND THE SPECIFIC PROBLEMS OF ESTABLISHING AND MAINTAINING QUALITY DAY CARE. ANOTHER SECTION PLACES DAY CARE IN HISTORICAL

PERSPECTIVE. THE MAIN FACETS EXAMINED ARE THE PHYSICAL SITE, POPULATION CHARACTERISTICS, REGULATORY BODIES, ABILITY TO COMMAND STAFF RESOURCES, ADMINISTRATIVE CONSTRAINTS, AND LEADERSHIP ABILITIES. A DIRECTOR'S LEADERSHIP ABILITIES DEPEND ON FIVE FACTORS: (1) PROFESSIONAL SKILL, (2) BUSINESS COMPETENCE, (3) POLITICAL KNOWHOW, (4) CREATIVE INGENUITY, AND (5) COMMITMENT. IN AN EVALUATION OF EXISTING DAY CARE FACILITIES IN CALIFORNIA, THE REPORT STATES THAT THE STRONGEST POINT IS THE DIVERSITY OF AVAILABLE PROGRAMS. A BIBLIOGRAPHY IS INCLUDED. (MH)

ED036320 PS002524
NEW NURSERY SCHOOL RESEARCH PROJECT, OCTOBER 1, 1968 TO SEPTEMBER 30, 1969. ANNUAL PROGRESS REPORT. , 30 SEP 69 159P.
EDRS PRICE MF-$0.65 HC-$6.58

THIS REPORT DESCRIBES THE PRIMARY AND SECONDARY OBJECTIVES OF THE NURSERY SCHOOL PROJECT AND THE METHODS AND PROCEDURES USED IN THE PROGRAM. DEMOGRAPHIC INFORMATION IS SUPPLIED FOR THE 30 3- AND 4-YEAR-OLDS WHO WERE ENROLLED. THE SCHEDULE AND TENTATIVE LESSON PLANS EMPHASIZE FREE CHOICE ACTIVITIES, GROUP TIME, AND OUTDOOR PLAY. PLANNING AND IMPLEMENTATION OF THE PROGRAM ARE CONSIDERED. A SECTION ON THE DEVELOPMENT OF CURRICULUM MATERIALS GIVES SPECIFIC SUGGESTIONS FOR LEARNING ACTIVITIES DURING SNACK AND LUNCH TIME AND METHODS FOR LEARNING CONCEPTS SUCH AS "ROUND," UNDERSTANDING OPPOSITES LIKE FAST AND SLOW, USING CONJUNCTIONS, AND PLAYING WITH ALPHABET BLOCKS OR PICTURE LOTTO GAMES. TO ENRICH THE CHILDREN'S HOME ENVIRONMENTS, A MOBILE INSTRUCTIONAL LIBRARY IS USED FOR HOME VISITS. THE SCHOOL FUNCTIONS AS A DEMONSTRATION CENTER, AND METHODS OF OBSERVATION AND AVAILABLE INFORMATION MATERIALS ARE EXPLAINED. A RESUME OF THE TESTING AND DATA COLLECTION DESCRIBES IN DETAIL THE USE OF PRE- AND POSTTESTS, RATING SCALES, OBSERVATIONS, AND INVENTORIES. A LIST OF ALL PERSONNEL IN THE NURSERY SCHOOL CONCLUDES THE REPORT. (DR)

ED036321 PS002603
THE IMPACT OF HEAD START: AN EVALUATION OF THE EFFECTS OF HEAD START ON CHILDREN'S COGNITIVE AND AFFECTIVE DEVELOPMENT. (EXECUTIVE SUMMARY). , JUN 69 12P.
EDRS PRICE MF-$0.65 HC-$3.29
AVAILABLE FROM: CLEARINGHOUSE FOR FEDERAL SCIENTIFIC & TECHNICAL INFORMATION, SPRINGFIELD, VA. 22151 (VOL. 1, PB-184328, $6.00

THE WESTINGHOUSE LEARNING CORPORATION AND OHIO UNIVERSITY CARRIED OUT A STUDY ON THE IMPACT OF HEAD START FOR THE OFFICE OF ECONOMIC OPPORTUNITY. THE MAIN INQUIRY OF THE STUDY CONCERNED THE DIFFERENCE BETWEEN HEAD START FIRST, SECOND, AND THIRD GRADERS AND NON-HEAD START FIRST, SECOND, AND THIRD GRADERS IN INTELLECTUAL AND SOCIAL-PERSONAL DEVELOPMENT. DATA WERE COLLECTED FROM TESTS, INTERVIEWS, AND QUESTIONNAIRES OF STUDENTS, PARENTS, AND TEACHERS FROM 104 HEAD START CENTERS ACROSS THE COUNTRY, AND CONTROL AREAS. THE MAJOR CONCLUSIONS DRAWN FROM THESE DATA WERE: (1) SUMMER PROGRAMS ARE INEFFECTIVE IN PRODUCING LASTING GAINS IN AFFECTIVE AND COGNITIVE DEVELOPMENT, (2) FULL-YEAR PROGRAMS ARE INEFFECTIVE IN AIDING AFFECTIVE DEVELOPMENT AND ONLY MARGINALLY EFFECTIVE IN PRODUCING LASTING COGNITIVE GAINS, (3) ALL HEAD START CHILDREN ARE STILL CONSIDERABLY BELOW NATIONAL NORMS ON TESTS OF LANGUAGE DEVELOPMENT AND SCHOLASTIC ACHIEVEMENT, WHILE SCHOOL READINESS AT GRADE ONE APPROACHES THE NATIONAL NORM, AND (4) PARENTS OF HEAD START CHILDREN VOICED STRONG APPROVAL OF THE PROGRAM. THUS, WHILE FULL-YEAR HEAD START IS SOMEWHAT SUPERIOR TO SUMMER HEAD START, NEITHER COULD BE DESCRIBED AS SATISFACTORY. FURTHER RESEARCH AIMED AT THE DEVELOPMENT OF AN EFFECTIVE PRESCHOOL PROGRAM IS RECOMMENDED. (MH)

ED036322 PS002669
PLANNING PARENT-IMPLEMENTED PROGRAMS: A GUIDE FOR PARENTS, SCHOOLS AND COMMUNITIES. FOSTER, FLORENCE P., 6 FEB 69 53P.
EDRS PRICE MF-$0.65 HC-$3.29

THIS BOOKLET IS THE PRODUCT OF A SMALL BUT DIVERSE GROUP OF PARENTS AND PROFESSIONALS WHO CAME TOGETHER TO TRY TO ALLEVIATE THE PROBLEMS POSED BY THE ESCALATING STRUGGLE FOR POWER IN THE SCHOOLS. THEY HOPE THAT THROUGH PARENT-IMPLEMENTED FOLLOW THROUGH PROGRAMS, DISCONTENTED MEMBERS OF THE COMMUNITY CAN BE MADE TO FEEL THAT THEY HAVE A SIGNIFICANT ROLE IN THE SCHOOLS' DECISION MAKING PROCESSES. FOLLOW THROUGH IS EXPLAINED AS AN EXTENSION OF HEAD START AND THE BOOKLET RELATES SOME OF THE WORK OF THE NEW JERSEY WORK-STUDY CONFERENCE WHICH PROPOSED A PLAN FOR PARENT INVOLVEMENT. A TENTATIVE FRAMEWORK FOR EDUCATIONAL DECISION MAKING IS PROPOSED, WITH EMPHASIS ON MAKING PARENTS FEEL THAT THEY SHARE IN THE POLICY MAKING PROCESS AND ON CASTING PROFESSIONALS IN A LIAISON ROLE. A PHASE-BY-PHASE OUTLINE OF THE PLAN IS INCLUDED WHICH SHOWS HOW VARIOUS DETAILS CAN BE HANDLED, FROM BUDGET AND FACILITIES TO PERSONNEL AND COMMUNITY RELATIONS. (MH)

ED036323 PS002684
A TOKEN REINFORCEMENT SYSTEM IN THE PUBLIC SCHOOLS. O'LEARY, K. DANIEL, SEP 68 16P.
EDRS PRICE MF-$0.65 HC-$3.29

A TOKEN REINFORCEMENT SYSTEM WAS INTRODUCED INTO A SECOND GRADE CLASSROOM, AND SEVEN (OUT OF 21) CLASS MEMBERS AND THE TEACHER WERE OBSERVED FOR 8 MONTHS. EACH OF THE EIGHT PHASES OF THE STUDY LASTED FROM 2 TO 5 WEEKS. THE FIRST FOUR PHASES ESTABLISHED A BASE PERIOD AND DETERMINED THE SEPARATE EFFECTS OF CLASSROOM RULES, HALF HOUR ACADEMIC LESSONS, AND TEACHER PRAISE. IN THE TOKEN I PHASE EACH CHILD IN THE AFTERNOON CLASSES RECEIVED POINTS FOR DESIRABLE BEHAVIOR, WHICH WERE EXCHANGED FOR BACK-UP REINFORCERS INCLUDING COMIC BOOKS AND DOLLS. THE PERCENTAGE OF DISRUPTIVE BEHAVIOR SIGNIFICANTLY DECREASED. TOKENS AND BACK-UP REINFORCERS WERE THEN WITHDRAWN, AND DISRUPTIVE BEHAVIOR INCREASED, BUT NOT SIGNIFICANTLY. TOKENS AND BACK-UP REINFORCERS WERE AGAIN REINSTATED AND WITHDRAWN AND THEN REPLACED BY THE USE OF MORE USUAL CLASSROOM REINFORCERS BY THE TEACHER. AT THIS TIME DISRUPTIVE BEHAVIOR WAS 37% COMPARED TO 53% DURING THE BASE PERIOD. RESULTS INDICATED STUDENT GAINS ON THE CALIFORNIA ACHIEVEMENT TEST, HIGHER CLASS ATTENDANCE, AND THE TEACHER'S INCREASED USE OF PRAISE AND DECREASED USE OF CRITICISM AND THREATS. (DR)

ED036324 PS002741
CHILDREN AND TEACHERS IN TWO TYPES OF HEAD START CLASSES. KATZ, LILIAN G., 69 14P.
EDRS PRICE MF-$0.65 HC-$3.29

TO COMPARE THE EFFECTIVENESS OF THE TRADITIONAL AND THE EXPERIMENTAL APPROACHES TO HEAD START CLASSROOMS, 68 CHILDREN AND SIX TEACHERS IN SAN FRANCISCO PARTICIPATED IN AN EDUCATIONAL EXPERIMENT. THE TRADITIONAL APPROACH EMPHASIZES THE CHILDREN'S INTERNAL MOTIVATION RESULTING FROM SPONTANEOUS FREE PLAY AND WARM, ACCEPTING TEACHERS, WHILE THE EXPERIMENTAL APPROACH EMPHASIZES SOCIAL LEARNING THEORY IN THE FORM OF TEACHER-DIRECTED ACTIVITIES AND FREQUENT PRAISE OR REINFORCEMENT FOR APPROPRIATE BEHAVIORS. EACH OF THE SIX TEACHERS WAS GIVEN A CHOICE OF APPROACH. THREE CHOSE TRADITIONAL; THREE EXPERIMENTAL. THE CLASSROOMS WERE OBSERVED AND EVALUATED FOR STUDENT BEHAVIOR (CHILD BEHAVIOR SURVEY INSTRUMENT) AND TEACHER BEHAVIOR. THE THREE TEACHERS IN THE EXPERIMENTAL APPROACH DID NOT CARRY OUT THEIR ROLES AS PRAISE-DISPENSERS, THUS MAKING THE MORE DESIRABLE BEHAVIOR OF THE CHILDREN IN THE TRADITIONAL APPROACH CLASSES MEANINGLESS FOR ANY COMPARISON OF THE TWO APPROACHES. THE MAJOR IMPLICATION OF THIS RESEARCH IS THAT ACTUAL APPLICATION OF SOCIAL LEARNING THEORY REQUIRES MORE THAN AGREEMENT WITH ITS PRINCIPLES. OBSERVED INTRA-APPROACH DIFFERENCES SUGGEST THAT A STUDY OF INDIVIDUAL TEACHER STYLE IS NEEDED AS WELL AS A RECOGNITION THAT DIFFERENT CHILDREN THRIVE IN DIFFERENT KINDS OF CLASSROOMS. (MH)

ED036325 PS002765
OBSERVED COGNITIVE COMMUNICATION PATTERNS OF ADULTS AND CHILDREN IN FOUR PRE-SCHOOL AGE GROUPS. HONIG, ALICE S.; AND OTHERS, MAR 69 28P.
EDRS PRICE MF-$0.65 HC-$3.29

THE APPROACH (A PROCEDURE FOR PATTERNING RESPONSES OF ADULTS AND CHILDREN) TECHNIQUE WAS USED TO CODE OBSERVATIONS OF BEHAVIOR AND SETTING IN THIS ECOLOGICAL STUDY OF ADULT-CHILD COGNITIVE COMMUNICATION PATTERNS. THE SUBJECTS OBSERVED WERE 32 CHILDREN WHO PROPORTIONATELY REPRESENTED EACH OF FOUR AGE GROUPS (1 YEAR, 2 YEARS, 3 YEARS, AND 4 YEARS) AND WHO WERE STRATIFIED FOR SEX, RACE, AND SOCIOECONOMIC STATUS. THE DATA RESULTING FROM THE APPROACH CODING PROVIDED A QUANTIFIED, FINELY-DETAILED DESCRIPTION OF BEHAVIORAL EVENTS AND THEIR ENVIRONMENTAL FRAMEWORK. THE MAJOR FINDINGS WERE: (1) THERE IS A SIGNIFICANT SHIFT IN THE SOCIAL SETTING AT AGE 3 FROM ADULT AND CHILD ALONE TO ADULT TEACHING A GROUP OF CHILDREN, (2) THE OBJECT OF A CHILD'S COMMUNICATION VARIES WITH THE SOCIAL SETTING, (3) MORE THAN 2/3 OF ADULT BEHAVIOR PREDICATES EMITTED TO CHILDREN ARE VERBAL, (4) TOTAL FREQUENCY OF ADULT COGNITIVE INQUIRING AND INFORMING BEHAVIOR EMITTED TO A CHILD REMAINS HIGH AND CONSTANT TO CHILDREN IN ALL AGE GROUPS, (5) ADULTS SHIFT FROM MOSTLY INFORMING TO MOSTLY INQUIRING AS CHILDREN GROW OLDER AND (6) THE ADULT USES SHOWING ON DEMONSTRATION TO THE CHILD-ALONE LESS FREQUENTLY AS THE CHILD GROWS OLDER. (MH)

ED036326 PS002790
INDEPENDENT LEARNING IN THE ELEMENTARY SCHOOL CLASSROOM. WILLIAMS, LOIS E., NOV 69 45P.
EDRS PRICE MF-$0.65 HC NOT AVAILABLE FROM EDRS.
AVAILABLE FROM: E/K/N/E-NEA, 1201 SIXTEENTH STREET, N.W., WASHINGTON, D.C. 20036 ($1.25)

THIS ILLUSTRATED BOOK WAS WRITTEN TO ENCOURAGE AND SHARE WITH TEACHERS THE MEANS TO DEVELOP INDEPENDENT LEARNERS IN THEIR CLASSROOMS. IT IS SUGGESTED THAT TEACHERS START LEARNING ACTIVITIES BY SCHEDULING A DAILY PERIOD WHEN CHILDREN MAY FREELY USE MATERIALS AND INTERACT WITH OTHERS. ONE SECTION OF THE BOOK IS DEVOTED TO ORGANIZING AND HELPING CHILDREN TO USE

LEARNING CENTERS FOR LISTENING, READING, AND WRITING. TO ILLUSTRATE THE LEARNING POTENTIAL OF STUDENT CHOICE-MAKING, EXCERPTS FROM A STUDY GROUP'S EXPERIENCES AND A FIRST GRADE TEACHER'S LOG ARE PRESENTED. SUGGESTIONS ARE GIVEN FOR MAKING AND CARRYING OUT RULES AND GUIDELINES FOR INDIVIDUAL AS WELL AS GROUP ACTIVITIES. OBSERVATIONS AND INTERVIEWS INVOLVING CONSULTANTS, TEACHERS, AND CHILDREN CAN BE USED TO EVALUATE INDEPENDENT LEARNING FOR EACH CHILD AND THE CLASS. THE BOOK CONCLUDES BY OFFERING CRITERIA FOR THE TEACHER'S SELF-EVALUATION AND APPRAISAL OF THE SCHOOL'S PROGRAM. (DR)

ED036327 PS002803
PARENT HANDBOOK: DEVELOPING YOUR CHILD'S SKILLS AND ABILITIES AT HOME. AHR, A. EDWARD; SIMONS, BENITA, JUL 68 40P.
DOCUMENT NOT AVAILABLE FROM EDRS.
AVAILABLE FROM: PRIORITY INNOVATIONS, INC., P.O. BOX 792, SKOKIE, ILL. 60076 ($0.70)

THERE IS A GROWING BELIEF AMONG EDUCATORS THAT PARENTS CAN MAKE AN INFLUENTIAL CONTRIBUTION TO THEIR CHILDREN'S EDUCATIONAL OPPORTUNITIES BY WORKING WITH THEM ON THE DEVELOPMENT OF CERTAIN SKILLS IN THE YEARS BEFORE THE INITIATION OF FORMAL SCHOOLING. THIS PARENTS' HANDBOOK ATTEMPTS TO SUPPLY A MIXTURE OF GENERAL PRINCIPLES AND SPECIFIC PRACTICES FOR THE CONCERNED PARENT. IT IS SUGGESTED, THOUGH NOT NECESSARY, THAT THE HANDBOOK BE USED IN CONJUNCTION WITH THE PARENT READINESS EVALUATION OF PRESCHOOLERS (PREP) TEST, SO THAT PARENTS CAN HAVE AN OBJECTIVE MEASURE OF THEIR CHILD'S DEVELOPMENTAL STRENGTHS AND WEAKNESSES. LANGUAGE, ARITHMETIC, MOTOR COORDINATION, SPATIAL RELATIONSHIP, DISCRIMINATION, AND MEMORY ARE ALL MATTERS OF CONCERN AND THE HANDBOOK LISTS SPECIFIC PRACTICES TO FACILITATE THEIR DEVELOPMENT. (MH)

ED036328 PS002804
EARLY CHILDHOOD EDUCATION: AN INTRODUCTION TO THE PROFESSION. HYMES, JAMES L., JR., 68 48P.
DOCUMENT NOT AVAILABLE FROM EDRS.
AVAILABLE FROM: PUBLICATIONS DEPARTMENT, NATIONAL ASSOCIATION FOR THE EDUCATION OF YOUNG CHILDREN, 1834 CONNECTICUT AVENUE, N.W., WASHINGTON, D.C. 20009 ($1.25)

THIS MONOGRAPH DISCUSSES THE BACKGROUND AND CURRENT STATE OF EARLY CHILDHOOD EDUCATION, AND THE GOALS AND METHODS OF PROJECT HEAD START ARE EMPHASIZED. THE DEVELOPMENT OF FOLLOW THROUGH AND THE PRESENT STATUS OF TITLE I PROGRAMS, KINDERGARTENS, DAY CARE CENTERS, AND NURSERY SCHOOLS ARE BRIEFLY CONSIDERED. THE BOOKLET DISCUSSES 10 PROBLEMS FACING THE FIELD OF EARLY CHILDHOOD EDUCATION, INCLUDING TYPES OF PROGRAMS, CLASS SIZE AND STAFFING. (DR)

ED036329 PS002828
DO NEGRO CHILDREN PROJECT A SELF-IMAGE OF HELPLESSNESS AND INADEQUACY IN DRAWING A PERSON? HENDERSON, NORMAN B.; AND OTHERS, 69 2P.
DOCUMENT NOT AVAILABLE FROM EDRS.
AVAILABLE FROM: AMERICAN PSYCHOLOGICAL ASSOCIATION, 1200 17TH STREET, N.W., WASHINGTON, D.C. 20036 (DIVISION 8, $4.00)

IT WAS ASSUMED ON THE BASIS OF PROJECTION THEORY THAT A PICTURE OF A PERSON DRAWN BY A CHILD REFLECTS THAT CHILD'S SELF-IMAGE. SIX HUNDRED NINETY-EIGHT 7-YEAR-OLD ECONOMICALLY DISADVANTAGED CHILDREN (NEGRO N232, WHITE N466) WERE TOLD TO DRAW A PICTURE OF A PERSON. EACH PICTURE WAS THEN SCORED AS A DRAW-A-PERSON TEST. THERE WAS NO SIGNIFICANT DIFFERENCE BETWEEN THE BLACK GROUP AND THE WHITE GROUP ON THE TOTAL RAW SCORE. THE BLACK GROUP'S DRAWINGS WERE SIGNIFICANTLY MORE COMPLETE ON THE NINE FACIAL ITEMS AND THE WHITE GROUP'S DRAWINGS WERE SIGNIFICANTLY MORE COMPLETE ON THE FIVE ARM-HAND-FINGER ITEMS. THE DIFFERENCES BETWEEN BLACK AND WHITE GROUPS WERE SMALL ENOUGH TO DEMAND CAUTION IN DRAWING CONCLUSIONS FROM THEM ABOUT IMPORTANT SOCIALLY DETERMINED PERSONALITY DIFFERENCES BETWEEN THE RACES. (MH)

ED036330 PS002831
POPULATION CHARACTERISTICS OF DISADVANTAGED PRESCHOOL CHILDREN. PROCEEDINGS OF THE HEAD START RESEARCH SEMINARS: SEMINAR NO. 3, HEAD START POPULATIONS (1ST, WASHINGTON, D.C., OCTOBER 9, 1968). FRIEDMAN, MYLES I., ED.; AND OTHERS, 9 OCT 68 133P.
EDRS PRICE MF-$0.65 HC-$6.58

THIS DOCUMENT INCLUDES THREE PAPERS ON LONG-TERM INVESTIGATIONS OF THE POPULATION CHARACTERISTICS OF DISADVANTAGED PRESCHOOL CHILDREN. MYLES I. FRIEDMAN, ET.AL., APPROACHED THE PROBLEM OF CURRICULUM CONSTRUCTION BY DESCRIBING AND IDENTIFYING READINESS BEHAVIORS IN CHILDREN. TWENTY-TWO TESTS WERE ADMINISTERED TO 1600 4- TO 6-YEAR-OLD ADVANTAGED AND DISADVANTAGED CHILDREN. RESULTS WILL BE AVAILABLE SOON. CONSIDERING THE DISADVANTAGED A HETEROGENEOUS GROUP, ROBERT P. BOGER AND SUEANN R. AMBRON CONSTRUCTED A BEHAVIORAL MODEL INCLUDING SUBPOPULATIONS (RURAL OR URBAN, SOCIAL CLASS, ETC.), PSYCHO-EDUCATIONAL DIMENSIONS (INTELLIGENCE, LANGUAGE SKILL, ETC.), AND PROCESS VARIABLES (ENVIRONMENTAL FACTORS). THE INTERACTING VARIABLES OF THIS MODEL WILL BE USED TO IDENTIFY AND ASSESS DISADVANTAGEMENT. A BIBLIOGRAPHY IS INCLUDED. E. KUNO BELLER INVESTIGATED THE EFFECTS OF EARLY EDUCATIONAL INTERVENTION ON THE INTELLECTUAL DEVELOPMENT OF LOWER CLASS, DISADVANTAGED CHILDREN, MEASURING INTELLECTUAL FUNCTIONING BY STANDARDIZED TESTS AND CLASSROOM GRADES AND MOTIVATION BY RATINGS AND DIRECT OBSERVATION. MAJOR FINDINGS AND CONCLUSIONS WERE REPORTED. THESE FINDINGS INDICATE A NEED FOR PLANNING CURRICULUM DESIGNED TO HELP DISADVANTAGED CHILDREN EXPLORE THINGS ON THEIR OWN INITIATIVE AND CARRY ACTIVITIES TO COMPLETION, BY HELPING THEM DEVELOP GREATER TRUST IN THEIR ADULT ENVIRONMENT. (DR)

ED036331 PS002832
RESEARCH ISSUES IN CHILD HEALTH, I-IV. PROCEEDINGS OF THE HEAD START RESEARCH SEMINARS: SEMINAR NO. 4, HEALTH AND NUTRITION IN EARLY CHILDHOOD (1ST, WASHINGTON, D.C., NOVEMBER 1, 1968). NORTH, A. FREDERICK, JR.; AND OTHERS, 1 NOV 68 82P.
EDRS PRICE MF-$0.65 HC-$3.29

ONE OF A SERIES OF FOUR SYMPOSIUM PAPERS, THIS DOCUMENT DEALS WITH RESEARCH ISSUES IN EARLY CHILDHOOD HEALTH AND NUTRITION. DR. A. FREDERICK NORTH, JR., PRESENTS AN OVERVIEW OF RESEARCH AND EMPHASIZES THE IMPORTANCE OF IDENTIFYING CHILDREN'S HEALTH PROBLEMS, USING THE MOST EFFECTIVE TREATMENT AND INTERVENTION TECHNIQUES, AND UTILIZING RESOURCES TO IDENTIFY AND REMEDY PROBLEMS. THE MEDICAL AND ECONOMIC ISSUES OF PROVIDING BASIC MEDICAL CARE TO CHILDREN ARE DISCUSSED BY DR. ROBERT J. HAGGERTY, AND A MODEL FOR A HEALTH CARE SYSTEM WITHIN THE CONTEXT OF HEAD START IS PROPOSED. DR. MARSDEN G. WAGNER STRESSES THE CULTURAL AND SUBCULTURAL FACTORS AND ORGANIZATIONAL CONSIDERATIONS OF PROVIDING HEALTH SERVICES TO HEAD START CHILDREN. THE UNDERLYING PHILOSOPHY OF ESTABLISHING HEALTH CARE AND OTHER SERVICES FOR THE DISADVANTAGED IS GIVEN CONSIDERATION BY DR. HERBERT BIRCH. (DOCUMENT ED 034 088 HAS THE FULL TEXT OF THE PROCEEDINGS OF ALL SIX HEAD START SEMINARS IN THIS SERIES.) (DR)

ED036332 PS002833
PARENTAL BEHAVIOR AND CHILDREN'S SCHOOL ACHIEVEMENT: IMPLICATIONS FOR HEAD START. PROCEEDINGS OF THE HEAD START RESEARCH SEMINARS: SEMINAR NO. 5, INTERVENTION IN FAMILY LIFE (1ST, WASHINGTON, D.C., JANUARY 13, 1969). HESS, ROBERT D.; AND OTHERS, 13 JAN 69 119P.
EDRS PRICE MF-$0.65 HC-$6.58

THIS DOCUMENT CONTAINS THE THREE PAPERS THAT COMPRISED THE HEAD START RESEARCH SEMINAR NO. 5 ON INTERVENTION IN FAMILY LIFE. THE MAIN THRUST OF THIS SEMINAR IS THE INVESTIGATION OF FAMILY AND PARENT CHARACTERISTICS THAT INFLUENCE THE ACADEMIC PERFORMANCE OF YOUNG CHILDREN. ROBERT HESS, IN THE OPENING PAPER, SUMMARIZES THE INFORMATION AVAILABLE ON THE SUBJECT, REVIEWS THE EVIDENCE FOR SOCIAL CLASS AND ETHNIC DIFFERENCES IN PARENTAL BEHAVIOR, SKETCHES THE CONCEPTIONS OF ASSOCIATION BETWEEN FEATURES OF THE SOCIETY AND COGNITIVE DEVELOPMENT, AND SPECULATES ON THE IMPLICATIONS OF THE ABOVE FOR HEAD START. A SUMMARY OF STUDIES MADE FROM 1945 TO 1969 OF PARENTAL INFLUENCES ON CHILDREN'S ACADEMIC ACHIEVEMENT AND COGNITIVE BEHAVIOR IS INCLUDED, WITH BIBLIOGRAPHY. THE SECOND PAPER, BY IRA GORDON, COMMENTS ON HESS' PAPER AND EXPANDS ON IT. GORDON CLASSIFIES THE FACTORS INFLUENCING CHILD DEVELOPMENT AS EITHER DEMOGRAPHIC, PARENTAL-COGNITIVE, OR PARENTAL-EMOTIONAL AND DISCUSSES IN DETAIL SEVERAL FACTORS IN EACH CATEGORY. HIS INVESTIGATION OF THESE FACTORS LEADS HIM TO ENUNCIATE THE IDEA OF PARENT POWER IN PROGRAMS OF EDUCATION. IN THE FINAL PAPER, DANIEL SCHEINFELD DISCUSSES THE CHANGES THAT MUST BE MADE IN PARENTS AND HOME LIFE TO INSURE MORE ADVANTAGEOUS DEVELOPMENT FOR THE CHILDREN. IN ORDER FOR BASIC STRUCTURAL CHANGE TO TAKE PLACE IN THE LIVES OF DISADVANTAGED FAMILIES, THE PARENTS MUST BECOME ACTIVELY AND EFFECTIVELY ENGAGED WITH THE ENVIRONMENT. (MH)

ED036333 PS002834
THE ROLE OF THE TEACHER IN INTERVENTION PROGRAMS. PROCEEDINGS OF THE HEAD START RESEARCH SEMINARS: SEMINAR NO. 6, THE TEACHER IN INTERVENTION PROGRAMS (1ST, WASHINGTON, D.C., APRIL 18, 1969). SIGEL, IRVING E.; AND OTHERS, 18 APR 69 65P.
EDRS PRICE MF-$0.65 HC-$3.29

THIS SEMINAR ON THE ROLE OF TEACHERS IN INTERVENTION PROGRAMS CONSISTS OF FIVE PAPERS. THE FIRST SERVES AS AN INTRODUCTION AND STRESSES THE NECESSITY OF TEACHERS' ACCEPTANCE OF CHANGE FOR PROGRAM SUCCESS. IN THE SECOND PAPER, SIGEL AND JACKSON EXPAND ON ONE OF SIGEL'S INTRODUCTORY THEMES, THE CENTRAL ROLE OF THE TEACHER IN THE PROCESS OF CHANGE AND HER NEED TO HAVE THE RIGHT ATTITUDES. NEXT, SCHALOCK PRESENTS A DETAILED MODEL FOR TEACHER TRAINING PROGRAMS. THE BASIC ASSUMPTION OF THIS MODEL IS THAT PROSPECTIVE TEACHERS SHOULD, BEFORE CERTIFICATION, DEMONSTRATE BOTH THE PROPER ATTITUDE AND THE ABILITY TO CARRY ON THE FUNCTIONS

OF A MODERN TEACHER, INCLUDING PARTICIPATING IN INTERVENTION PROJECTS. IN THE FOURTH PAPER, MCDAVID DISCUSSES THE TEACHER AS A SOCIALIZATION AGENT, HELPING THE CHILD TO BE ABLE TO LIVE IN HIS OWN SOCIETY. FINALLY, DR. BELLER REPORTS ON AN EXPERIMENTAL STUDY OF AUTHORITARIAN AND DEMOCRATIC TEACHERS THAT SHOWS THE SIGNIFICANT EFFECT THE TEACHER HAS BOTH ON WHAT THE CHILD LEARNS, AND ON HIS APPROACH TO LEARNING. (DOCUMENT ED 034 088 HAS THE FULL TEXT OF THE PROCEEDINGS OF ALL SIX HEAD START SEMINARS IN THIS SERIES.) (MH)

ED036334 PS002835
THE EFFECT OF SELECTED TRAINING EXPERIENCES ON PERFORMANCE ON A TEST OF CONSERVATION OF NUMEROUSNESS. REPORT FROM PHASE 2 OF THE PROTOTYPIC INSTRUCTIONAL SYSTEMS IN ELEMENTARY MATHEMATICS PROJECT. SCOTT, JOSEPH A., JUL 69 73P.
EDRS PRICE MF-$0.65 HC-$3.29

THE CHILD'S ABILITY TO IDENTIFY NUMEROUSNESS AS A PROPERTY OF A SET, DISTINCT FROM ALL THE OTHER PROPERTIES OF THAT SET, MAY BE A PREREQUISITE TO CONSERVATION OF NUMEROUSNESS OF SETS. TO TEST THIS THEORY, 11 LESSONS DESIGNED TO DEVELOP THE ABILITY TO IDENTIFY PROPERTIES OF OBJECTS AND OF SETS OF OBJECTS AND TO REPRESENT LENGTH AND NUMEROUSNESS WERE PRESENTED TO KINDERGARTEN AND PRESCHOOL CHILDREN. IT WAS HYPOTHESIZED THAT THIS TRAINING WOULD HELP THE SUBJECTS SCORE HIGHER ON A TEST OF CONSERVATION OF NUMEROUSNESS. THE DIFFERENCE, HOWEVER, BETWEEN EXPERIMENTAL GROUPS, WHO RECEIVED THE TRAINING LESSONS, AND CONTROL GROUPS, WHO RECEIVED NO SPECIAL TRAINING, WAS NOT STATISTICALLY SIGNIFICANT. NEVERTHELESS, SINCE THERE WERE SOME NOTICEABLE DIFFERENCES BETWEEN THE AMOUNT OF IMPROVEMENT IN THE GROUPS, IT WAS CONCLUDED THAT KINDERGARTEN AND PRESCHOOL CHILDREN CAN BE TAUGHT WITH LITTLE DIFFICULTY TO RECOGNIZE, DISCRIMINATE AND LABEL PROPERTIES OF OBJECTS AND SETS, AND THAT THIS TRAINING CAN OFTEN BE ENOUGH TO INCREASE THE CHILDREN'S SCORES ON A TEST OF CONSERVATION OF NUMEROUSNESS. (AUTHOR/MH)

ED036335 PS002836
AN INTRODUCTION OF LENGTH CONCEPTS TO KINDERGARTEN CHILDREN. REPORT FROM THE PROJECT ON ANALYSIS OF MATHEMATICS INSTRUCTION. GILBERT, LYNN ELLEN, JUL 69 100P.
EDRS PRICE MF-$0.65 HC-$3.29

CONSERVATION OF A PROPERTY IS THE ABILITY TO RECOGNIZE THAT THE PROPERTY IN QUESTION HASN'T ALTERED, EVEN THOUGH OTHER PROPERTIES HAVE BEEN VARIED. IT IS PIAGET'S VIEW, CONFIRMED BY EMPIRICAL EVIDENCE THAT CHILDREN ARE NOT ABLE TO CONSERVE LENGTH UNTIL AGE 7 OR 8. RECENT CONCERN OVER CONFOUNDING VARIABLES LED TO THE PRESENT STUDY IN WHICH THE CHILDREN FROM THREE KINDERGARTEN CLASSES (N71) WERE TESTED FOR CONSERVATION OF LENGTH AFTER DIFFERENT TRAINING CONDITIONS. ONE CLASS RECEIVED A PRETEST, TRAINING, AND POSTTEST; ONE CLASS RECEIVED ONLY TRAINING AND POSTTEST; AND ONE CLASS RECEIVED BOTH TESTS BUT NO TRAINING. THE TRAINING WAS THREE 20-MINUTE SESSIONS AIMED AT AN UNDERSTANDING OF THE PROPERTY OF LENGTH. ANALYSES OF VARIANCE DETERMINED DIFFERENTIAL EFFECTS ON PERFORMANCE OF THE PRETEST, THE TRAINING PROGRAM, AGE AND SEX OF THE SUBJECT, AND TESTER BIAS. RESULTS SHOWED THE TRAINING PROGRAM TO BE A SIGNIFICANT VARIABLE, AND GIRLS MADE GREATER GAINS THAN DID BOYS. (AUTHOR/MH)

ED036336 PS002860
A STUDY OF NON-VERBAL REPRESENTATION IN YOUNG CHILDREN. FRANKLIN, MARGERY B., 14 NOV 69 17P.
EDRS PRICE MF-$0.65 HC-$3.29

IN THIS STUDY, REPRESENTATIONAL THOUGHT, WHICH INVOLVES THE CHILD'S ABILITY TO FUNCTION IN TERMS OF NONPRESENT REALITY, IS VIEWED WITHIN A COGNITIVE-DEVELOPMENTAL FRAMEWORK. TO SEE IF DISADVANTAGED CHILDREN WOULD FUNCTION IN THE SAME WAY AS ADVANTAGED CHILDREN ON TASKS WHICH REQUIRED REPRESENTATIONAL THOUGHT RATHER THAN VERBALIZATION, CHILDREN WERE TESTED ON PICTURE-OBJECT MATCHING TASKS, SPATIAL ARRANGEMENT TASKS AND IN STRUCTURED PLAY SITUATIONS. THERE WERE AN EQUAL NUMBER OF 4- TO 5-YEAR-OLD BOYS AND GIRLS IN EACH GROUP. SCORES INDICATED THAT THE DISADVANTAGED GROUP GENERALLY DID NOT PERFORM AS WELL AS THE ADVANTAGED CHILDREN ALTHOUGH THERE WAS MUCH VARIATION AMONG INDIVIDUALS TESTED. DISCUSSION OF STUDY FINDINGS INDICATE THAT PRESCHOOL PROGRAMMING SHOULD ENCOURAGE REPRESENTATIONAL FUNCTIONING BECAUSE IT IS AN IMPORTANT ASPECT OF THE CHILD'S COMPREHENSION AND USE OF LANGUAGE, AND BECAUSE IT PLAYS A CENTRAL ROLE IN THE CHILD'S OVERALL COGNITIVE DEVELOPMENT. (AUTHOR/NH)

ED036337 PS002883
THE SCHOOL SOCIAL WORKER IN THE NEW YORK STATE EXPERIMENTAL PREKINDERGARTEN PROGRAM. , [69] 5P.
EDRS PRICE MF-$0.65 HC-$3.29

THE NEW YORK STATE EXPERIMENTAL PREKINDERGARTEN PROGRAMS ARE INTERDISCIPLINARY ENDEAVORS WHOSE PURPOSE IS TO IMPROVE THE EDUCATIONAL OPPORTUNITIES OF DISADVANTAGED 3- AND 4-YEAR-OLDS. BECAUSE THE PUPIL SERVICES THEY OFFER ARE OF CENTRAL IMPORTANCE TO THESE PROGRAMS, THE SOCIAL WORKER IS AN INTEGRAL MEMBER OF THE PREKINDERGARTEN STAFF AND HAS MANY DIVERSE FUNCTIONS TO PERFORM. THE SOCIAL WORKER CAN BE ASSISTED IN THE SOCIAL SERVICES COMPONENT OF THE PROGRAM BY PUPIL SERVICES AIDES RECRUITED FROM LOCAL DISADVANTAGED NEIGHBORHOODS. RECENT EMPHASIS ON PARENT PARTICIPATION IN PRESCHOOL PROGRAMS HIGHLIGHTS THE IMPORTANCE OF THE SOCIAL WORKER'S MAIN FUNCTION: THE ESTABLISHMENT OF EFFECTIVE RELATIONSHIPS WITH PARENTS. SOME OTHER SUGGESTED FUNCTIONS FOR A SOCIAL WORKER ARE (1) TO ACT AS LIAISON BETWEEN THE PROGRAM AND COMMUNITY SOCIAL AGENCIES, (2) TO PARTICIPATE ACTIVELY IN THE SELECTION AND RECRUITMENT OF CHILDREN, (3) TO COORDINATE THE EFFORTS OF ALL INDIVIDUALS AND AGENCIES INVOLVED, AND (4) TO CONTRIBUTE INFORMATION TO CONFIDENTIAL PUPIL RECORDS. (MH)

ED036338 PS002884
A LONGITUDINAL STUDY OF DISADVANTAGED CHILDREN WHO PARTICIPATED IN THREE DIFFERENT PRESCHOOL PROGRAMS. KARNES, MERLE B.; AND OTHERS, [68] 26P.
EDRS PRICE MF-$0.65 HC-$3.29

THIS 3-YEAR STUDY MADE A LONGITUDINAL COMPARISON OF THREE TYPES OF PRESCHOOL INTERVENTION PROGRAMS. THE TRADITIONAL APPROACH (TWO CLASSES OF 15 STUDENTS AND THREE TEACHERS EACH) WORKED IN CONVENTIONAL WAYS TO IMPROVE PERSONAL, SOCIAL, MOTOR AND GENERAL LANGUAGE DEVELOPMENT; CHILDREN WERE PLACED IN A REGULAR PUBLIC SCHOOL KINDERGARTEN THE FOLLOWING YEAR. THE AMELIORATIVE APPROACH (TWO CLASSES OF 15 STUDENTS AND THREE TEACHERS EACH) EMPHASIZED LANGUAGE DEVELOPMENT THROUGH SMALL GROUP LESSONS USING VERBALIZATIONS AND CONCRETE MANIPULATION. THE NEXT YEAR CHILDREN ENTERED REGULAR KINDERGARTEN BUT CONTINUED ADDITIONAL 1-HOUR-A-DAY SUPPORTIVE WORK. THE DIRECT VERBAL APPROACH (ONE CLASS) UTILIZED INTENSIVE ORAL DRILL IN VERBAL AND LOGICAL PATTERNS AND MINIMIZED VISUAL AND MANIPULATIVE MATERIALS, CONTINUING THIS APPROACH THE FOLLOWING YEAR. DURING THE PRESCHOOL YEAR, CHILDREN IN THE AMELIORATIVE AND DIRECT VERBAL APPROACHES BOTH MADE MORE PROGRESS THAN THE TRADITIONAL GROUP. DURING THE KINDERGARTEN YEAR, ONLY THE DIRECT VERBAL APPROACH SHOWED CONTINUED PROGRESS. AT THE END OF THE THIRD YEAR, THE LOSSES EXPERIENCED BY THE DIRECT VERBAL AND AMELIORATIVE GROUPS RESULTED IN NONDIFFERENTIATED PERFORMANCE IN INTELLECTUAL AND LANGUAGE FUNCTIONING AMONG THE THREE GROUPS. AMELIORATIVE AND DIRECT VERBAL GROUPS WERE SUPERIOR TO THE TRADITIONAL IN SCHOOL ACHIEVEMENT. (MH)

ED036339 PS002885
A NEW ROLE FOR TEACHERS: INVOLVING THE ENTIRE FAMILY IN THE EDUCATION OF PRESCHOOL DISADVANTAGED CHILDREN. KARNES, MERLE B., [69] 21P.
EDRS PRICE MF-$0.65 HC-$3.29

THIS APPROACH TO PRESCHOOL EDUCATION OF THE DISADVANTAGED USES A TEACHER TRAINING PROGRAM WHICH WAS DEVELOPED ONLY AFTER EACH COMPONENT OF THE PROGRAM HAD BEEN EMPIRICALLY TESTED. TEACHERS WERE RETRAINED THROUGH COURSE WORK AND WORKSHOPS TO TEACH DISADVANTAGED PRESCHOOL CHILDREN. THESE TEACHERS THEN TAUGHT MOTHERS AND OLDER SIBLINGS OF DISADVANTAGED FAMILIES THE SKILLS AND KNOWLEDGE NECESSARY TO INSTRUCT THE PRESCHOOL CHILD BOTH IN THE HOME AND IN THE SCHOOL SETTING. PRE- AND POSTTEST SCORES ON STANDARDIZED TESTS INDICATED THAT PRESCHOOL CHILDREN WHO PARTICIPATED IN THE PROJECTS MADE GAINS COMPARABLE TO THOSE MADE BY CHILDREN TAUGHT BY A PROFESSIONAL STAFF. RESEARCH FINDINGS WERE INCORPORATED INTO ONGOING DEMONSTRATION CLASSES AT THE UNIVERSITY OF ILLINOIS. THE CLASSES PROVIDED (1) PRACTICUM EXPERIENCES FOR STUDENTS IN A LEADERSHIP TRAINING PROGRAM, (2) OBSERVATION FACILITIES FOR TEACHER-TRAINING STUDENTS IN ELEMENTARY AND SPECIAL EDUCATION, (3) THE BASIS FOR WORKSHOPS INVOLVING TEACHERS AND ADMINISTRATORS FROM LOCAL COMMUNITIES, AND (4) GUIDELINES FOR JUNIOR COLLEGE PERSONNEL INTERESTED IN DEVELOPING TRAINING PROGRAMS FOR PARAPROFESSIONALS. (AUTHOR/DR)

ED036340 PS002900
TEACHING STYLES IN FOUR-YEAR-OLDS. FESHBACH, NORMA D.; DEVOR, GERALDINE, MAR 69 8P.
DOCUMENT NOT AVAILABLE FROM EDRS.
AVAILABLE FROM: CENTER FOR THE STUDY OF EVALUATION, MOORE HALL 145, UNIVERSITY OF CALIFORNIA, LOS ANGELES, CALIFORNIA 90024 (REPRINT NO. 6)

THIS STUDY INVESTIGATES THE RELATIONSHIP BETWEEN SOCIAL-CLASS FACTORS AND PATTERNS OF REINFORCEMENT USED BY PRESCHOOL CHILDREN WHEN INSTRUCTING YOUNGER PEERS. IT WAS HYPOTHESIZED THAT MIDDLE CLASS CAUCASIAN CHILDREN WOULD

SPONTANEOUSLY USE MORE POSITIVE REINFORCEMENTS AND LOWER CLASS CHILDREN MORE NEGATIVE REINFORCEMENTS WHEN INTERACTING WITH PEERS. SUBJECTS WERE 204 3- AND 4-YEAR-OLDS. DATA WERE OBTAINED BY HAVING 4-YEAR-OLD BOYS AND GIRLS OF DIFFERENT RACE AND SOCIAL-CLASS BACKGROUNDS INSTRUCT 3-YEAR-OLDS OF THE SAME SOCIAL CLASS AND RACE. ALL COMMENTS WERE RECORDED AND CLASSIFIED AS EITHER POSITIVE OR NEGATIVE REINFORCEMENTS. THE PREDICTION FOR POSITIVE REINFORCEMENT WAS CONFIRMED FOR MIDDLE CLASS CAUCASIANS. WHILE LOWER-CLASS CHILDREN DID MAKE GREATER USE OF NEGATIVE REINFORCEMENT, FOR MOST OF THE SOCIAL-CLASS COMPARISONS THE DIFFERENCES WERE NOT STATISTICALLY SIGNIFICANT. MIDDLE-CLASS NEGRO CHILDREN DISPLAYED THE LEAST NUMBER OF REINFORCEMENTS, POSITIVE OR NEGATIVE, OF ALL THE GROUPS. FURTHER RESEARCH DIRECTLY LINKING SPECIFIC PARENTAL BEHAVIORS TO THE CHILD'S USE OF AND DIFFERENTIAL RESPONSIVENESS TO DIFFERENT CLASSES OF REINFORCEMENT IS NEEDED. (AUTHOR/DR)

ED036341 PS002904
NEGRO HERITAGE: A SELECTED BOOK LIST FOR ALL AGES. , [69] 18P.
EDRS PRICE MF-$0.65 HC-$3.29

THE DENVER PUBLIC LIBRARY HAS PUBLISHED THREE BOOKLETS THAT LIST ALL MATERIALS AVAILABLE THROUGH THE LIBRARY ON HISPANIC, NEGRO, AND INDIAN HERITAGE. THE BOOKLET ON NEGRO HERITAGE CONTAINS A BALANCED ASSORTMENT OF BOOKS, FILMS, AND RECORDS. ALTHOUGH THE RESOURCES ARE LISTED AS EITHER JUVENILE OR YOUNG ADULT, CONTENT IS OF GENERAL INTEREST. THE SUBJECT MATTER INCLUDES BLACK HISTORY, LITERATURE, AND THE ARTS AND A LIST OF FILMS AND RECORDS. THOUGH THE LIST IS COMPREHENSIVE, THE COMPILERS EMPHASIZE THAT IT IS NOT EXHAUSTIVE. IT IS INTENDED TO BE A POPULAR RESOURCE LIST, AND AS SUCH IT REFLECTS ONLY A PORTION OF AVAILABLE MATERIALS. (MH)

ED036342 PS002905
HISPANIC HERITAGE: A SELECTED BOOK LIST FOR ALL AGES. , [69] 14P.
EDRS PRICE MF-$0.65 HC-$3.29

A PAMPHLET ON HISPANIC HERITAGE, ONE OF A SERIES OF THREE ETHNIC BOOKLETS PUBLISHED BY THE DENVER PUBLIC LIBRARY, LISTS TOPICAL BOOKS AND SOME APPROPRIATE FILMS AND RECORDINGS. ALTHOUGH THE BOOKS ARE LISTED AS EITHER JUVENILE OR YOUNG ADULT, CONTENT IS OF GENERAL INTEREST. THE BOOKS RANGE OVER A WIDE VARIETY OF TOPICS, FROM OLD MEXICO AND FOLKLORE TO THE ARTS AND WORKS OF FICTION. THOUGH THE LIST IS COMPREHENSIVE, THE COMPILERS EMPHASIZE THAT IT IS NOT EXHAUSTIVE. IT IS INTENDED TO BE A POPULAR BOOK LIST, AND AS SUCH IT REFLECTS ONLY A PORTION OF AVAILABLE MATERIALS. (MH)

ED036343 PS002906
CHARACTERISTICS OF PRIMARY LEVEL CHILDREN. PECK, DONNA, [69] 21P.
EDRS PRICE MF-$0.65 HC-$3.29

WRITTEN FOR TEACHER AIDES, THIS PAMPHLET PROVIDES A HANDY, READABLE, AND HIGHLY USABLE GUIDE TO DAILY CLASSROOM INTERACTION WITH CHILDREN. USING EASILY UNDERSTOOD EXAMPLES, THE AUTHOR TAKES YOU THROUGH THE WORLD OF THE CHILD, POINTING OUT WHAT TO EXPECT IN VARIOUS SITUATIONS AND WHAT TO DO ABOUT IT. FOR INSTANCE, SHE NOTES THAT CHILDREN ARE BETTER ABLE TO RUN AND JUMP THAN THEY ARE TO DRAW OR CUT BECAUSE OF DIFFERENTIAL RATES OF DEVELOPMENT OF LARGE AND SMALL MUSCLES. SHE DISCUSSES THE PROBLEM OF THE DISPARITY IN MATURITY BETWEEN BOYS AND GIRLS. SHE WARNS OF CHILDREN WHO WILL COME TO SCHOOL WITH A GERMINATING SICKNESS AND PASS IT AROUND THE CLASSROOM. SHE MENTIONS THE PROBLEM OF VERBAL EXPRESSION FOR ALL CHILDREN, BUT ESPECIALLY FOR THOSE TO WHOM ENGLISH IS RELATIVELY UNFAMILIAR. HER ADVICE IN ALL SITUATIONS IS BASED ON LEARNING PRINCIPLES WHICH ADVOCATE GIVING THE CHILD A SECURE AND COMFORTABLE OPPORTUNITY TO RESPOND TO EXPERIENCES AND HAVING ADULTS REACT TO HIM IN A FRIENDLY, POSITIVE WAY. (MH)

ED036344 PS002908
CHILD REARING. AN INQUIRY INTO RESEARCH AND METHODS. YARROW, MARIAN RADKE; AND OTHERS, 68 215P.
DOCUMENT NOT AVAILABLE FROM EDRS.
AVAILABLE FROM: JOSSEY-BASS, INC., PUBLISHERS, 615 MONTGOMERY STREET, SAN FRANCISCO, CALIFORNIA 94111 ($8.50)

THE OBJECTIVE OF THIS BOOK IS TO EXAMINE THE METHODS USED IN BASIC RESEARCH ON CHILD DEVELOPMENT. STUDIES OF REPLICATIONS AND NEAR-REPLICATIONS OF COMMONLY EMPLOYED PROCEDURES OF DATA COLLECTION AND ANALYSIS ARE USED. EVIDENCE OF CONSISTENCY IN RESEARCH RESULTS IS SOUGHT, THEREBY ENABLING THE AUTHORS TO ASSESS THE METHODOLOGICAL ADEQUACY OF USING SUCH DATA AS BASIC EVIDENCE ON PARENT-CHILD RELATIONS AND PERSONALITY DEVELOPMENT. NINETEEN METHODS AND INSTRUMENTS TO MEASURE THE RELATION BETWEEN PARENTAL PRACTICES AND THREE AREAS OF CHILD BEHAVIOR ARE STUDIED. THE THREE AREAS CONSIDERED ARE CHILD DEPENDENCY, AGGRESSION, AND CONSCIENCE FORMATION. ALSO, OF CONCERN ARE THE MECHANICS OF DATA COLLECTION AND ANALYSIS, AS WELL AS THE COMMUNICATION OF RESEARCH RESULTS AND CHARACTERISTICS OF A GENERAL RESEARCH STRATEGY. (DR)

ED036345 PS002980
INDIAN HERITAGE: A SELECTED BOOK LIST FOR ALL AGES. , [69] 22P.
EDRS PRICE MF-$0.65 HC-$3.29

THIS BOOK LIST, A SAMPLING OF RESOURCES FROM THE DENVER PUBLIC LIBRARY, PERTAINS TO THE INDIANS OF NORTH AMERICA, ESPECIALLY THOSE WEST OF THE MISSISSIPPI RIVER. THE ANNOTATED LIST IS DIVIDED INTO TWO MAIN PARTS: "ADULT AND YOUNG ADULT BOOKS, FILMS, AND RECORDS" AND "CHILDREN'S BOOKS, FILMS, AND RECORDS." THE BULK OF THE LIST IS ADULT AND YOUNG ADULT BOOKS, AND CATEGORIES INCLUDE HISTORY AND CULTURE, MYTHOLOGY AND LEGENDS, RELIGION AND CEREMONIALS, AND ARTS AND CRAFTS. THERE ARE SPECIAL SECTIONS ON NORTH AMERICAN TRIBES AND SOUTHWEST PUEBLO INDIANS. BIOGRAPHIES AS WELL AS FICTION COMPLETE THE ADULT BOOK LIST. IN ANOTHER SECTION, BOOK, FILM, AND RECORD SELECTIONS FOR THE YOUNG AND VERY YOUNG ARE MAINLY HISTORICAL OR FICTIONAL. (DR)

ED037230 PS000800
CHILD BEHAVIOR SURVEY INSTRUMENT: MANUAL OF INSTRUCTIONS AND DEFINITIONS. KATZ, LILIAN G., 28 MAR 68 11P.
EDRS PRICE MF-$0.65 HC-$3.29

THIS DOCUMENT IS A MANUAL OF INSTRUCTION ON HOW TO ADMINISTER THE CHILD BEHAVIOR SURVEY INSTRUMENT (CBSI). THIS MANUAL ALSO PRESENTS DEFINITIONS OF THE CATEGORIES USED TO DEFINE THE NATURE OF THE OBSERVED CHILD'S BEHAVIOR. THE CBSI PROVIDES A SCHEME FOR OBSERVING THE CLASSROOM BEHAVIOR OF CHILDREN ALONG NINE MAJOR CATEGORIES: (1) ORIENTATION, (2) SUBJECTIVE MOOD, (3) MOTILITY, (4) MOTIVATION, (5) COGNITIVE BEHAVIOR, (6) SATISFACTION, (7) INTERACTION BETWEEN CHILD AND TEACHER, (8) INTERACTION BETWEEN CHILD AND CHILD, AND (9) VERBALIZATION. EACH OF THESE CATEGORIES HAS SUBCATEGORIES WITH WHICH THE CHILD'S BEHAVIOR CAN BE CHARACTERIZED. (WD)

ED037231 PS001714
TEACHING KINDERGARTEN CHILDREN TO APPLY CONCEPT-DEFINING RULES. KEISLAR, EVAN R.; SCHUTZ, SAMUEL R., FEB 69 20P.
EDRS PRICE MF-$0.65 HC-$3.29

THIS STUDY SOUGHT (1) TO DISCOVER WAYS TO TEACH KINDERGARTEN CHILDREN TO LISTEN TO A RULE THAT DEFINES A CONCEPT AND THEN TO APPLY IT, AND (2) TO LEARN IF RULE-LEARNING IS FACILITATED WHEN THE PUPIL IS REQUIRED TO VERBALIZE THE RULE WHILE USING IT. THE TASK USED IN THE STUDY (1) INVOLVES DEDUCTIVE REASONING, (2) REQUIRES RULE UTILIZATION RATHER THAN RULE VERIFICATION, (3) REQUIRES THE LEARNING OF FOUR RULES (NEGATION, CONJUNCTION, DISJUNCTION, AND JOINT DENIAL) THAT WERE FOUND TO BE APPROPRIATE FOR THIS POPULATION, (4) REQUIRES AN UNDERSTANDING OF CERTAIN FUNCTION WORDS, AND (5) WAS PRESENTED AT A LEVEL OF COMPLEXITY ABOVE THAT USED IN LABORATORY EXPERIMENTS. THE SUBJECTS, 5-YEAR-OLD NEGRO CHILDREN, WERE DIVIDED INTO THREE GROUPS: ONE GROUP WHO RECEIVED INSTRUCTION IN THE RULES THAT REQUIRED THEM TO VERBALIZE THE RULES THEMSELVES (N6), ONE WHICH RECEIVED NO INSTRUCTION (N6), AND ONE GROUP WHICH RECEIVED INSTRUCTION IN THE RULES BUT WHO WERE NOT REQUIRED TO VERBALIZE THE RULES THEMSELVES (N8). THE ORAL GROUP SCORED SIGNIFICANTLY HIGHER THAN THE CONTROL GROUP, BUT THERE WAS NO SIGNIFICANT DIFFERENCE BETWEEN THE ORAL EXPERIMENTAL GROUP AND THE NON-ORAL EXPERIMENTAL GROUP. THERE WAS NO RELIABLE EVIDENCE THAT SELF-VERBALIZATION IS SUPERIOR TO NORMAL INSTRUCTION. (MH)

ED037232 PS002038
THE ANALYSIS OF DATA GENERATED IN A RESEARCH DESIGNED TO SECURE BASELINE INFORMATION ON A HEAD START PROGRAM. A REPORT TO THE U.S. OFFICE OF ECONOMIC OPPORTUNITY FROM THE DEPARTMENT OF RESEARCH, MONTGOMERY COUNTY, MARYLAND PUBLIC SCHOOLS. , NOV 68 50P.
EDRS PRICE MF-$0.65 HC NOT AVAILABLE FROM EDRS.

THIS REPORT DESCRIBES HEAD START CLASSROOM ACTIVITY, CONTAINS DATA ON THE CHILDREN FROM A TESTING PROGRAM, AND INCLUDES TEACHER RATINGS OF PUPILS ON A CLASSROOM ADJUSTMENT CHECKLIST. (INDIVIDUAL DATA IS BEING PRESERVED FOR FOLLOW-UP STUDIES.) CLASSROOM OBSERVATIONS WERE MADE IN 13 OF 27 HEAD START CLASSROOMS, WHILE TESTING ACTIVITIES AND TEACHER RATINGS OF PUPIL GROWTH WENT ON IN ALL 27. CLASSROOM OBSERVATIONS WERE MADE ON THE BASIS OF THE GOODMAN TIME-SAMPLED OBSERVATION TECHNIQUE AND YIELDED INFORMATION ON SUCH ITEMS AS PUPIL ACTIVITIES, ADULT ACTIVITIES, USE OF INSTRUCTIONAL MATERIALS, AND PUPIL-ADULT RATIO. THE PUPIL TESTING PROGRAM CONSISTED OF THE PEABODY LANGUAGE DEVELOPMENT TEST, THE VOCABULARY, SENTENCES, AND GEOMETRIC DESIGN SUBTESTS OF THE WPPSI, THE DAILEY LANGUAGE FACILITY TEST, AND THE TEST OF BASIC INFORMATION. THE CLASSROOM ADJUSTMENT CHECKLIST, DEVELOPED FOR THIS REPORT, DESCRIBES SUCH VARIABLES AS SOCIAL INTERACTION, SELF-CONTROL, QUALITY AND FLUENCY OF SPEECH, INDEPENDENCE, AND RESPONSIBILITY. [NOT AVAILABLE IN HARD COPY DUE TO MARGINAL LEGIBILITY OF ORIGINAL DOCUMENT.] (MH)

ED037233 PS002115
INTRA-FAMILY DIFFUSION OF SELECTED COGNITIVE SKILLS AS A FUNCTION OF EDUCATIONAL STIMULATION. GILMER, BARBARA R., 69 29P.
EDRS PRICE MF-$0.65 HC-$3.29

IN ORDER TO INVESTIGATE DIFFUSION EFFECTS WITHIN FAMILIES INVOLVED IN AN INTERVENTION PROGRAM, 80 DISADVANTAGED CHILDREN WERE DIVIDED INTO FOUR GROUPS, THREE OF WHICH WERE MADE UP OF YOUNGER SIBLINGS OF PRESCHOOL CHILDREN IN THE INTERVENTION PROGRAM. IN TWO OF THESE THREE GROUPS, THE MOTHER WAS ALSO INVOLVED IN THE PROGRAM. THE FOURTH GROUP WAS FOR CONTROL. THE DIFFUSION EFFECTS STUDIED WERE THOSE THAT RELATED TO CONCEPTS (DEFINED AS KNOWLEDGE THAT CAN BE SHOWN BY MATCHING, RECOGNITION, OR IDENTIFICATION BEHAVIOR). THE MEASUREMENT INSTRUMENT WAS THE BASIC CONCEPT TEST, WHOSE CONTENT WAS DRAWN FROM THE CURRICULUM MATERIAL USED IN THE INTERVENTION PROGRAM. IT WAS HYPOTHESIZED THAT THE TWO GROUPS HAVING BOTH SIBLING AND MATERNAL INVOLVEMENT WOULD SHOW GREATER CONCEPTUAL DEVELOPMENT, AND THAT THESE GROUPS WOULD ALSO HAVE THE INFORMATION NECESSARY TO RECOGNIZE AND IDENTIFY THE TEST STIMULI. RESULTS FROM ORTHOGONAL COMPARISONS SUPPORTED BOTH THE HYPOTHESES. SUPERIOR PERFORMANCE BY THE MATERNAL INVOLVEMENT GROUPS WAS RECOGNIZED AS A MANIFESTATION OF A LEVEL OF CONCEPTUAL DEVELOPMENT DIRECTLY ASSOCIATED WITH INTRA-FAMILY DIFFUSION EFFECTS. MAXIMUM INTERVENTION EFFECTS APPEAR TO RESULT WHEN MOTHERS ARE INVOLVED IN A PROGRAM AND VERTICAL DIFFUSION AFFECTS THE YOUNGER SIBLINGS OF CHILDREN IN THE PROGRAM. (MH)

ED037234 PS002126
TEACHING MATHEMATICAL CONCEPTS TO TWO- AND THREE-YEAR-OLDS: SOME EXPERIMENTAL STUDIES. GREENFIELD, PATRICIA MARKS, [68] 53P.
EDRS PRICE MF-$0.65 HC-$3.29

EXPERIMENTS CONDUCTED TO FIND WAYS OF TEACHING TWO AND THREE YEAR OLDS MATHEMATICAL CONCEPTS WERE FOUND TO HAVE GENERAL IMPLICATIONS FOR CONCEPT LEARNING. THE FAILURE OF AN INITIAL ATTEMPT TO TEACH THE CONCEPTS "FAT" AND "SKINNY" LED TO A DESIGN OF INSTRUCTIONAL PROCEDURES THAT WOULD UTILIZE A CONCEPT'S NAME WHILE TRYING TO TEACH ITS SEMANTIC CONTENT. A STUDY OF VARIANT PROCEDURES USED TO TEACH THE CONCEPT "ROUND" EMPHASIZED THE IMPORTANCE OF VERBAL REPRESENTATION, AND A FINAL EXPERIMENT, DESIGNED TO TEACH "SQUARE," WAS PERFORMED TO DETERMINE WHETHER LINGUISTIC OR CONCRETE REFERENTIAL CONTEXTS WERE MORE IMPORTANT. THE RESULTS SUPPORTED THE LINGUISTIC APPROACH TO SEMANTICS RATHER THAN THE PSYCHOLOGICAL: THE RELATION OF WORDS TO OTHER WORDS APPEARS MORE CRUCIAL THAN THE RELATION OF WORDS TO THINGS. PRESCHOOL INSTRUCTIONAL APPROACHES SHOULD CONSIDER THE COMMUNICATIVE CONTEXT OF EXPERIENCES AS WELL AS CHILDREN'S DIRECT EXPERIENCE WITH MATERIALS. (DR)

ED037235 PS002662
THE MAKING OF A PUPIL: CHANGING CHILDREN INTO SCHOOL CHILDREN. ANDERSON, SCARVIA B., 17 JUL 68 18P.
EDRS PRICE MF-$0.65 HC-$3.29

EDUCATORS HAVE RATIONALIZED THE TRADITIONAL SCHOOL STARTING AGE OF 6 BY SAYING THAT CHILDREN HAVE BY THEN NORMALLY ACQUIRED SUFFICIENT MUSCULAR CONTROL AND LANGUAGE ABILITY TO BEGIN READING INSTRUCTION. WHEN IT BECAME APPARENT THAT MANY CHILDREN DID NOT BEGIN TO READ AT THE SUPPOSEDLY PROPER TIME, FURTHER RATIONALIZATIONS DEVELOPED CONCERNING READINESS AND TESTING FOR READINESS. THIS PAPER REPORTS AN EDUCATIONAL TESTING SERVICE STUDY OF ATTITUDES TOWARD READINESS. A NATIONAL SAMPLE OF 250 FIRST GRADE TEACHERS JUDGED THE READINESS OF 7000 PUPILS, AND INDICATED THAT ONLY 60% OF THE CHILDREN WERE READY FOR FIRST GRADE IN ALL OR MOST RESPECTS. TEACHERS CITED INTELLECTUAL FACTORS OVER NONINTELLECTUAL FACTORS 3 TO 2. A COMMITTEE OF CHILD DEVELOPMENT EXPERTS ASSESSED MAJOR DEVELOPMENTAL AREAS (SENSORY/MOTOR, COGNITIVE/INTELLECTUAL, AND SOCIAL/PERSONAL) IN TERMS OF READINESS AND JUDGED EACH AREA EQUALLY IMPORTANT. A SECOND COMMITTEE CONSIDERED PRESCHOOL OBJECTIVES AND ADDED MORAL JUDGMENT AND MORAL CONDUCT TO FACTORS THE OTHER GROUPS HAD FELT WERE IMPORTANT. A FRESH LOOK SHOULD BE TAKEN AT THE PURPOSES OF EARLY EDUCATION AND AT THE SCHOOL STARTING AGE. EMPHASIS SHOULD BE ON FITTING THE SCHOOL TO THE INDIVIDUAL CHILD, RATHER THAN THE CHILD TO THE SCHOOL. (NH)

ED037236 PS002702
AN ANALYSIS OF BEHAVIORAL MECHANISMS INVOLVED IN CONTROL OVER INFANT FEEDING BEHAVIOR KRON, REUBEN E.; AND OTHERS, [68] 30P.
EDRS PRICE MF-$0.65 HC-$3.29

TO DETERMINE THE ANTECEDENTS OF SUCKING IN INFANTS, THE BEHAVIOR OF 24 INFANTS FROM 48- TO 60-HOURS-OLD WAS OBSERVED IN RELATION TO A SUCKING DEVICE. THE DEVICE MEASURED PRESSURE AND RATE OF SUCKING AND DELIVERED A CONTROLLED FLOW OF NUTRIENT. THE INTERFEEDING INTERVAL WAS VARIED AMONG THE EXPERIMENTAL AND CONTROL GROUPS. LITTLE SUCKING BEHAVIOR WAS FOUND IN THE FIRST HALF HOUR AFTER ROUTINE FEEDING, BUT SUCKING PRESSURE QUICKLY RECOVERED IN THE FIRST HOUR AND SUCKING RATE GRADUALLY REACHED ITS HIGHEST LEVEL BY 3 HOURS AFTER THE MEAL. WHILE A PARTICULAR CHILD'S SUCKING PRESSURE DOESN'T EVER VARY MUCH, HIS SUCKING RATE, AND THUS VOLUME OF NUTRIENT CONSUMED, IS DEPENDENT ON A VARIETY OF ENVIRONMENTAL FACTORS, INCLUDING INTERFEEDING INTERVAL, OBSTETRIC SEDATION, LEVEL OF WAKEFULNESS, AND TYPE OF NUTRIENT. KNOWLEDGE CONCERNING THE FACTORS INFLUENCING SUCKING RATE SHOULD BE APPLIED TO THE PROBLEM OF INFANTS WHO FAIL TO THRIVE ON ROUTINE MANAGEMENT. (MH)

ED037237 PS002780
MATERIALS FOR KINDERGARTEN. , 69 57P.
EDRS PRICE MF-$0.65 HC-$3.29

IN RESPONSE TO INCREASED INTEREST IN EARLY CHILDHOOD PROGRAMS, THIS REPORT, PREPARED BY THE PENNSYLVANIA DEPARTMENT OF PUBLIC INSTRUCTION, PRESENTS THE GOALS OF KINDERGARTENS AND THE RATIONALE FOR THEIR EXISTENCE. BOTH SUPPORTIVE AND NONSUPPORTIVE STATEMENTS ON COMPULSORY KINDERGARTEN ARE INCLUDED. CHILD DEVELOPMENT CHARTS DESCRIBE THE PHYSICAL, EMOTIONAL, SOCIAL, INTELLECTUAL, AND LANGUAGE CHARACTERISTICS AND NEEDS OF 4-, 5-, AND 6-YEAR-OLDS, AND SUGGEST WAYS IN WHICH THE KINDERGARTEN TRIES TO MEET THESE NEEDS. INCLUDED IS A LIST OF DESIRABLE PERSONALITY CHARACTERISTICS OF KINDERGARTEN TEACHERS, A LIST OF SUGGESTED EQUIPMENT, AND A CHECKLIST OF CRITERIA FOR EVALUATING A GOOD KINDERGARTEN. (NH)

ED037238 PS002802
AN ECOLOGICAL STUDY OF THREE-YEAR-OLDS AT HOME. FINAL REPORT. SCHOGGEN, MAXINE, 69 81P.
EDRS PRICE MF-$0.65 HC-$3.29

THE PURPOSE OF THIS STUDY WAS TO GENERATE A LIBRARY OF 198 SPECIMEN RECORDS OF THE BEHAVIOR OF 24 3-YEAR-OLD CHILDREN IN DIFFERENT SOCIOECONOMIC ENVIRONMENTS: LOW INCOME URBAN, LOW INCOME RURAL, AND MIDDLE INCOME URBAN. (A SPECIMEN RECORD PROVIDES A CONTINUOUS NARRATIVE IN NATURAL LANGUAGE OF THE BEHAVIOR OF AN INDIVIDUAL TOGETHER WITH THE ENVIRONMENTAL CONTEXT OF THAT BEHAVIOR.) FOLLOWING A PERIOD OF ADAPTATION VISITS, EACH CHILD WAS OBSERVED AT HOME FOR 40-50 MINUTES FROM SEVEN TO 10 TIMES. THE SPECIMEN RECORDS FOR EACH OBSERVATION WERE DIVIDED INTO ENVIRONMENTAL FORCE UNITS, DEFINED AS A GOAL-DIRECTED ACTIVITY INITIATED BY ANOTHER PERSON (AGENT) IN THE CHILD'S ENVIRONMENT. (FOR EXAMPLE, ONE UNIT MIGHT CONSIST OF THE MOTHER, OR AGENT, TELLING THE CHILD TO PUT ON SHOES AND SOCKS.) THE RATE OF ENVIRONMENTAL FORCE UNITS PER MINUTE FOR EACH CHILD WAS FIGURED, AND ANALYSIS SHOWED THAT MIDDLE URBAN CHILDREN HAD THE HIGHEST MEAN RATES. THE PERCENT OF UNITS IN WHICH THE MOTHER ACTED AS AN AGENT WAS DETERMINED, AND MIDDLE URBAN MOTHERS HAD THE HIGHEST PERCENTAGE. APPENDIXES INCLUDE A TYPICAL OBSERVER'S LOG OF VISITS AND A SPECIMEN RECORD OF A LOW INCOME RURAL CHILD. (DR)

ED037239 PS002825
A REPORT ON EVALUATION STUDIES OF PROJECT HEAD START. DATTA, LOIS-ELLIN, 69 26P.
EDRS PRICE MF-$0.65 HC-$3.29

EVALUATION OF HEAD START HAS BEEN BASED ON FOUR SOURCES OF INFORMATION: (1) CENSUS SURVEYS OF CHILDREN AND FAMILIES SERVED AND PROGRAMS OFFERED, (2) SPECIAL RESEARCH, PROJECTS ON CHILD DEVELOPMENT AND EXPERIMENTAL PROGRAMS, (3) A LONGITUDINAL STUDY OF THE DEVELOPMENT OF LOW INCOME CHILDREN, AND (4) A SERIES OF NATIONAL EVALUATION STUDIES. AVAILABLE DATA APPEAR TO INDICATE THAT HEAD START AND OTHER PRESCHOOL PROGRAMS HAVE AN IMMEDIATE IMPACT, BUT LITTLE IS KNOWN ABOUT WHY, OR UNDER WHAT CIRCUMSTANCES OPTIMUM RESULTS MAY BE OBTAINED. SUSTAINED GAINS ARE STILL BEING SOUGHT. CHILDREN WHO HAVE NOT ATTENDED PRESCHOOL PROGRAMS TEND TO CATCH UP IN PRIMARY SCHOOL WITH ATTENDERS, BUT LITTLE IS KNOWN ABOUT WHY THIS HAPPENS. A PLANNED VARIATION STUDY IS IN PROGRESS COMPARING CHILDREN IN SPONSORED HEAD START AND SPONSORED FOLLOW-THROUGH CLASSES AND CHILDREN ATTENDING "REGULAR" HEAD START AND "REGULAR" PRIMARY SCHOOLS. HEAD START EVALUATIONS HAVE TRIED TO LOCATE PROGRAM VARIATIONS OTHER THAN ADMINISTRATIVE WHICH MAY AFFECT CHILD DEVELOPMENT. CONSIDERING THE EVIDENCE NOW AVAILABLE, THE ASSUMPTIONS ON WHICH HEAD START WAS BASED STILL SEEM TENABLE. RESEARCH IS NEEDED TO CLARIFY RELATIONSHIPS BETWEEN PROGRAM AND CHILD VARIATIONS, AND THE EFFECTS OF LONG-TERM INTERVENTIONS. (NH)

ED037240 PS002826
RESEARCH AND CONSULTATION IN THE NATURAL ENVIRONMENT. HENDERSON, RONALD W., DEC 69 15P.
EDRS PRICE MF-$0.65 HC-$3.29

THIS DESCRIPTION OF A FOLLOW THROUGH IMPLEMENTATION PROJECT SUMMARIZES RESEARCH RELATED TO ENVIRONMENTAL VARIABLES AND INTELLECTUAL PERFORMANCE, AND DESCRIBES AN ENVIRONMENTAL INTERVENTION PROGRAM THAT MANIPULATES THESE VARIABLES. ANALYSIS OF ENVIRONMENTAL DATA COLLECTED ON 33 DISADVANTAGED FAMILIES OF FIRST GRADE CHILDREN SUGGESTED THAT THEIR NATURAL ENVIRONMENT CONTRIBUTED HEAVILY TO LACK OF ACHIEVEMENT. THEREFORE, THE PARENT INVOLVEMENT PROGRAM, BASED ON TWO

CONCEPTUAL FRAMEWORKS, WAS DESIGNED TO MODIFY THE ENVIRONMENT. ONE FRAMEWORK ILLUSTRATED THE RELATIONSHIPS AMONG LEARNING OBJECTIVES, LEARNING VARIABLES, AND THE LEARNING ENVIRONMENTS OF HOME AND SCHOOL. THE SECOND FRAMEWORK ORGANIZED PARENT INVOLVEMENT ACTIVITIES AIMED AT A REDUCTION OF PARENTAL ALIENATION, AN INCREASE OF PARENT PARTICIPATION IN CLASS, AND AN APPLICATION OF CLASSROOM PRINCIPLES AT HOME. THE PROGRAM, WHICH INVOLVED DEMONSTRATION, OBSERVATION, AND GUIDED PARTICIPATION, WAS IMPLEMENTED BY PARENT INVOLVEMENT COORDINATORS WHO ATTENDED A 6-WEEK SUMMER TRAINING SESSION AND THEN RETURNED TO THEIR COMMUNITIES TO TRAIN FAMILY LIAISON WORKERS. FOLLOW UP VISITS TO COORDINATORS WERE MADE BY FIELD REPRESENTATIVES FROM THE ARIZONA CENTER. (DR)

ED037241 PS002912
PRESCHOOL CURRICULUM GUIDE FOR CHILDREN'S CENTERS IN CALIFORNIA. , 68 50P.
EDRS PRICE MF-$0.65 HC-$3.29

THIS BOOKLET EXPLAINS THE OBJECTIVES AND CURRICULUM OF THE PROGRAM USED IN THE CALIFORNIA CHILDREN'S CENTERS. THIS PROGRAM IS BASED UPON THE BELIEF THAT EACH CHILD SHOULD HAVE AN OPPORTUNITY TO FULFILL HIS TOTAL DEVELOPMENT AS AN INDIVIDUAL. THE CURRICULUM IS GEARED TO NINE OBJECTIVES: PROTECTING HEALTH AND GROWTH, FURTHERING PHYSICAL DEVELOPMENT, FOSTERING EMOTIONAL DEVELOPMENT, GUIDING SOCIAL DEVELOPMENT, DEVELOPING LANGUAGE SKILLS, BUILDING MATHEMATICAL CONCEPTS, EXPLORING SCIENCE CONCEPTS, EXPANDING AESTHETIC EXPERIENCES, AND ENRICHING THE ENVIRONMENT. LISTED (IN TABLE FORM) FOR EACH OF THE 9 CURRICULUM PHASES ARE INTRODUCTORY GOALS, TEACHING METHODS, MATERIALS, EQUIPMENT, AND FACILITIES FOR EACH AREA OF LEARNING. INCLUDED ARE APPENDIXES ON LANGUAGE AND SCIENCE OBJECTIVES, PARENT EDUCATION, AND STAFF TRAINING FOR THE PRESCHOOL PROGRAM. (DR)

ED037242 PS002991
THE EFFECT OF THE REINSTEIN REINFORCEMENT SCHEDULE ON LEARNING OF SPECIFIC CONCEPTS CONTAINED IN THE BUCHANAN LANGUAGE PROGRAM. PART OF THE FINAL REPORT ON HEAD START EVALUATION AND RESEARCH: 1968-69 TO THE OFFICE OF ECONOMIC OPPORTUNITY. ESPINOSA, RENATO; AND OTHERS, AUG 69 21P.
EDRS PRICE MF-$0.65 HC-$3.29

THE REINSTEIN REINFORCEMENT SCHEDULE, BASED ON A SIMPLE PROGRAM OF REINFORCEMENT FOR SUCCESS AND NONREINFORCEMENT FOR FAILURE, WAS ONE OF THE IMPORTANT VARIABLES INTRODUCED IN THE UNIVERSITY OF TEXAS 1968-69 HEAD START INTERVENTION STUDY. THE EFFECT OF THE SCHEDULE WAS ASSESSED AS PART OF AN EVALUATION OF THE BUCHANAN LANGUAGE PROGRAM. THREE GROUPS OF CHILDREN WERE COMPARED: A GROUP OF NEGRO ENGLISH-SPEAKING CHILDREN, A GROUP OF MEXICAN-AMERICAN CHILDREN WHOSE FIRST LANGUAGE WAS SPANISH (WHO WERE TESTED THROUGHOUT THE LANGUAGE PROGRAM WITH THE SCHEDULE), AND A SECOND MEXICAN-AMERICAN GROUP WHO DID NOT RECEIVE THE SCHEDULE. THE GROUPS WERE COMPARED FOR MASTERY OF CONCEPTS IN THE LANGUAGE PROGRAM AND ON THE METROPOLITAN READING READINESS TEST TO TEST FOR GENERALIZATION OF LEARNING EFFECTS. RESULTS CONTROLLED FOR ETHNIC GROUP SUPPORT THE HYPOTHESIS THAT IMPROVED LEARNING MAY RESULT FROM THE USE OF THE SCHEDULE. AN INVESTIGATION OF POSSIBLE EFFECTS OF NONREINFORCEMENT, USING A SPECIALLY DEVISED CRITERION, REVEALED NO EFFECTS. INFORMAL OBSERVATION SUGGESTED THAT THE POSITIVE EFFECTS OF THE SCHEDULE COULD WELL BE DUE TO THE ADDITIONAL PRACTICE THE CHILDREN RECEIVING IT OBTAINED. (DR)

ED037243 PS002992
THE INFLUENCE OF TWO COUNSELING METHODS ON THE PHYSICAL AND VERBAL AGGRESSION OF PRESCHOOL INDIAN CHILDREN. PART OF THE FINAL REPORT ON HEAD START EVALUATION AND RESEARCH: 1968-69 TO THE OFFICE OF ECONOMIC OPPORTUNITY. PRESTWICH, SHELDON, AUG 69 93P.
EDRS PRICE MF-$0.65 HC-$3.29

THE PURPOSES OF THIS STUDY WERE (1) TO INVESTIGATE THE INFLUENCE OF ANTHROPOMORPHIC MODELS AS A THERAPEUTIC VEHICLE TO HELP 5-YEAR-OLD INDIAN CHILDREN TO APPROPRIATELY HANDLE, AND THEREBY DECREASE, PHYSICAL AND VERBAL AGGRESSION, AND (2) TO INVESTIGATE THE INFLUENCE OF GROUP COUNSELING WITH INDIAN MOTHERS AS IT AFFECTS AGRESSION IN THEIR PRESCHOOL CHILDREN. SUBJECTS IN THE 8-WEEK STUDY WERE 30 CHILDREN RANDOMLY ASSIGNED TO THREE GROUPS. IN GROUP I, CHILDREN WERE PLACED IN A CONTROLLED ENVIRONMENT WITH HUMAN-FEATURE, LIFE-SIZE DOLLS. MOTHERS OF GROUP II MET FOR 90 MINUTES WEEKLY TO SEE A FILM AND PARTICIPATE IN GROUP COUNSELING. THE COUNSELING MODEL USED WAS PERCEPTUAL MODIFICATION THROUGH VERBAL REINFORCEMENT. GROUP III WAS THE CONTROL GROUP. PRE- AND POST-OBSERVATIONS AND RATINGS WERE MADE FOR THE SUBJECTS ON AN EXPERIMENTER-DESIGNED INSTRUMENT WHICH MEASURED QUANTITATIVE AGGRESSION RESPONSES. STUDY RESULTS REVEALED NO SIGNIFICANT DIFFERENCES IN PHYSICAL, VERBAL, OR TOTAL AGGRESSION BETWEEN EXPERIMENTAL AND CONTROL GROUPS BEFORE OR AFTER TREATMENT. INDIAN MOTHERS SIGNIFICANTLY INCREASED VERBAL OUTPUT DURING TREATMENT, BUT RESULTS INDICATED THAT THIS CHANGE BORE NO RELATIONSHIP TO CHILDREN'S AGGRESSIVE BEHAVIOR AT PRESCHOOL. (DR)

ED037244 PS002993
PARENT INVOLVEMENT IN PROJECT HEAD START. PART OF THE FINAL REPORT ON HEAD START EVALUATION AND RESEARCH: 1968-1969 TO THE OFFICE OF ECONOMIC OPPORTUNITY. JACOBS, SYLVIA H.; PIERCE-JONES, JOHN, OCT 69 101P.
EDRS PRICE MF-$0.65 HC-$6.58

THE PRESENT STUDY WAS AN ATTEMPT TO ASSESS THE IMPACT OF PROJECT HEAD START UPON THE PARENTS OF CHILDREN WHO PARTICIPATED IN A 6-MONTH HEAD START INTERVENTION PROGRAM IN AUSTIN, TEXAS. THE SAMPLE WAS COMPRISED OF 57 NEGRO AND 51 LATIN-AMERICAN PARENTS. FROM THE PARENT INTERVIEW, WHICH WAS ADMINISTERED TO THE FEMALE CARETAKER (USUALLY THE MOTHER) OF EACH CHILD ENROLLED IN THE HEAD START PROGRAM BOTH BEFORE AND AFTER THE INTERVENTION HAD TAKEN PLACE, SCALES WERE CONSTRUCTED TO MEASURE THE LEVEL OF GENERAL OPTIMISM REPORTED BY EACH PARENT, AND THE ASPIRATION LEVEL FOR THE PARTICIPATING CHILD REPORTED BY EACH PARENT. IT WAS HYPOTHESIZED THAT PRIOR PARENTAL EXPERIENCE WITH PROJECT HEAD START, CURRENT PARENTAL EXPERIENCE WITH THE PROGRAM, AND ACTIVE PARENTAL PARTICIPATION IN THE PROGRAM WOULD INCREASE PARENTAL SCORES ON THE TWO SCALES. NONE OF THESE HYPOTHESES WAS CONFIRMED. IT WAS FURTHER PREDICTED THAT CHILDREN OF PARENTS WHO SHOWED FAVORABLE CHANGES ON A SCALE WOULD GAIN MORE FROM THEIR OWN HEAD START EXPERIENCES, IN TERMS OF CHANGES IN THE SCORES ON THE TESTS ADMINISTERED TO THEM BOTH BEFORE AND AFTER THE PROGRAM, THAN CHILDREN OF PARENTS WHO SHOWED UNFAVORABLE CHANGES ON THAT SCALE. THIS PREDICTION WAS NOT CONFIRMED. IT WAS ALSO HYPOTHESIZED THAT LATIN-AMERICAN PARENTS WOULD SHOW MORE FAVORABLE CHANGE ON THE SCALES THAN NEGRO PARENTS; THIS HYPOTHESIS WAS NOT CONFIRMED. (AUTHOR)

ED037245 PS002995
A PILOT PROJECT USING A LANGUAGE DEVELOPMENT PROGRAM WITH PRESCHOOL DISADVANTAGED CHILDREN. PART OF THE FINAL REPORT ON HEAD START EVALUATION AND RESEARCH: 1968-69 TO THE OFFICE OF ECONOMIC OPPORTUNITY. CUNNINGHAM, GROVER; PIERCE-JONES, JOHN, AUG 69 13P.
EDRS PRICE MF-$0.65 HC-$3.29

A 3-MONTH PILOT PROJECT WAS UNDERTAKEN AT THE UNIVERSITY OF TEXAS TO GAIN EXPERIENCE IN ADMINISTERING THE CYNTHIA BUCHANAN LANGUAGE PROGRAM (BUCHANAN, 1967) AND TO TEST ITS EFFECTIVENESS IN MAKING MEANINGFUL CHANGES IN THE LANGUAGE DEVELOPMENT OF DISADVANTAGED MEXICAN-AMERICAN PRESCHOOLERS. A GROUP OF 114 MEXICAN-AMERICAN CHILDREN WERE CHOSEN AS EXPERIMENTAL SUBJECTS WHO WOULD RECEIVE INSTRUCTION FROM THE BUCHANAN PROGRAM, WHILE ANOTHER GROUP OF 101 SUBJECTS SERVED AS THE CONTROL. IT WAS HYPOTHESIZED THAT WHILE BOTH GROUPS WOULD MAKE SIGNIFICANT GAINS IN LANGUAGE DEVELOPMENT, THE RATE OF GAIN OF THE EXPERIMENTAL GROUP WOULD BE SIGNIFICANTLY GREATER THAN THAT OF THE CONTROL GROUP. BOTH GROUPS WERE PRE- AND POSTTESTED WITH THE METROPOLITAN READINGESS TEST, THE MURPHY-DURRELL READING READINESS ANALYSIS, THE GATES READING READINESS TEST, AND THE LEE-CLARK READING READINESS TEST. THE RESULTS SOLIDLY SUPPORTED THE HYPOTHESIS. NEXT, AN ANALYSIS OF COVARIANCE WAS RUN ON THE DATA TO DETERMINE WHETHER OR NOT THE RESULTS WERE GENERALIZABLE TO ALL LEVELS OF BEGINNING SCORES. THE RESULTS OF THE ANALYSIS INDICATED THAT THEY WERE NOT GENERALIZABLE. (MH)

ED037246 PS002996
VISUAL AND AUDITORY MEMORY IN CHILDREN. PART OF THE FINAL REPORT ON HEAD START EVALUATION AND RESEARCH: 1968-69 TO THE OFFICE OF ECONOMIC OPPORTUNITY. MULRY, RAY C.; DUNBAR, PHILIP W., AUG 69 20P.
EDRS PRICE MF-$0.65 HC-$3.29

A COMPARISON WAS MADE OF SHORT- AND LONG-TERM VISUAL AND AUDITORY MEMORY IN RELATION TO VISUAL AND AUDITORY INTERFERENCE. THE QUESTIONS INVESTIGATED WERE: (1) WILL INTERFERENCE BE GREATER WHEN IT OCCURS IN THE SAME MODALITY (AUDITORY OR VISUAL) IN WHICH IT WAS LEARNED (I.E., SIMILARITY HYPOTHESIS), OR (2) WILL INTERFERENCE BE GREATER WHEN IT OCCURS IN ONE SPECIFIC CHANNEL (AUDITORY OR VISUAL) REGARDLESS OF THE CHANNEL IN WHICH IT WAS LEARNED (I.E., CHANNEL SPECIFICITY HYPOTHESIS)? FIFTY BOYS AND 50 GIRLS, ALL 6 YEARS OLD, WERE RANDOMLY ASSIGNED TO ONE OF TWO CONTROL GROUPS OR ONE OF EIGHT EXPERIMENTAL GROUPS; EACH GROUP WITH THE SAME NUMBER OF BOYS AS GIRLS. EXPERIMENTAL GROUP SUBJECTS LEARNED AN ORIGINAL SEVEN-ITEM SERIAL TASK. FOUR OF THE GROUPS HAD THE ITEMS PRESENTED VISUALLY; FOUR, AUDITORIALLY. THESE GROUPS WERE FURTHER SUBDIVIDED ON THE BASIS OF THE NATURE OF THE INTERFERENCE TASK (I.E., EITHER AUDITORY OR VISUAL, AND EITHER FOUR ITEMS OR SEVEN ITEMS). CONTROL GROUPS HAD NO INTERFERENCE TASK. ALL GROUPS WERE TESTED FOR SHORT-TERM MEMORY AND 7 DAYS LATER, FOR LONG-TERM

MEMORY. RESULTS SUPPORTED NEITHER OF THE HYPOTHESES, BUT INDICATE THAT AUDITORY INTERFERENCE LEADS TO A SIGNIFICANTLY GREATER DECREMENT IN SERIAL ORDER RECALL THAN VISUAL INTERFERENCE. (MH)

ED037247 PS002997
A COMPARISON OF HEAD START CHILDREN WITH A GROUP OF HEAD START ELIGIBLES AFTER ONE YEAR IN ELEMENTARY SCHOOL. PART OF THE FINAL REPORT ON HEAD START EVALUATION AND RESEARCH: 1968-69 TO THE OFFICE OF ECONOMIC OPPORTUNITY. CUNNINGHAM, GROVER; PIERCE-JONES, JOHN, AUG 69 6P.
EDRS PRICE MF-$0.65 HC-$3.29

IN THIS STUDY, A GROUP OF FIRST GRADERS WHO HAD ATTENDED FULL-YEAR HEAD START WERE COMPARED COGNITIVELY TO A GROUP OF FIRST GRADERS WHO HAD BEEN ELIGIBLE FOR HEAD START BUT DID NOT ATTEND. RESULTS OF THE STUDY MAY BE SUSPECT BECAUSE THE CHILDREN WHO PARTICIPATED IN HEAD START WERE SELECTED FROM THE MOST DEPRIVED OF THOSE ELIGIBLE; THEREFORE STUDY GROUPS MAY NOT HAVE BEEN COMPARABLE. BOTH GROUPS WERE TESTED ON THE STANFORD-BINET AND THE PRESCHOOL INVENTORY BEFORE AND AFTER FIRST GRADE AND ON THE GATES-MACGINITIE READING TEST, PRIMARY A, AFTER FIRST GRADE. RESULTS INDICATED THAT AT THE BEGINNING OF THE YEAR THE GROUPS WERE THE SAME IN SOME AREAS AND DIFFERENT IN OTHERS. AT THE END OF THE FIRST GRADE THERE WERE NO SIGNIFICANT DIFFERENCES BETWEEN THE TWO GROUPS. THE EXPERIMENTAL GROUP SEEMED TO HAVE A HIGHER RATE OF GAIN THAN THE CONTROL, BUT THE DIFFERENCE WAS SELDOM SIGNIFICANT. IT IS CONCLUDED THAT THERE IS A TENUOUS CASE FOR SAYING THAT THE SIMILAR SCORES OF THE TWO GROUPS UPON COMPLETION OF FIRST GRADE INDICATE THE ACADEMIC EFFECTIVENESS OF HEAD START BECAUSE THE SELECTION PROCESS PLACED THE MORE DEPRIVED CHILDREN IN THE EXPERIMENTAL GROUP. (MH)

ED037248 PS002999
FAMILY FACTORS RELATED TO COMPETENCE IN YOUNG, DISADVANTAGED MEXICAN-AMERICAN CHILDREN. PART OF THE FINAL REPORT ON HEAD START EVALUATION AND RESEARCH: 1968-69 TO THE OFFICE OF ECONOMIC OPPORTUNITY. STEDMAN, JAMES M.; MCKENZIE, RICHARD E., AUG 69 24P.
EDRS PRICE MF-$0.65 HC-$3.29

AS PART OF THE CONTINUING SEARCH FOR THE ENVIRONMENTAL ANTECEDENTS OF COMPETENCE IN YOUNG CHILDREN, THIS STUDY INVESTIGATED SEVERAL PARAMETERS OF A POPULATION OF DISADVANTAGED MEXICAN-AMERICAN CHILDREN. THE FACTORS OF CHILD COMPETENCE ON WHICH THIS STUDY FOCUSED WERE BEHAVIORAL ADJUSTMENT AND LINGUISTIC ABILITY. THE ANTECEDENTS OF COMPETENCE WERE SOUGHT IN FAMILY VARIABLES, SPECIFICALLY IN OVERALL FAMILY CONSTELLATION, PARENTAL LANGUAGE PATTERNS, CHILD-REARING ATTITUDES, PARENTAL SELF-CONCEPT, PARENTAL AND OTHER ROLES WITHIN THE FAMILY, AND VARIOUS ATTITUDINAL CONCEPTS. THE SAMPLE OF DISADVANTAGED MEXICAN-AMERICAN CHILDREN CONSISTED OF 134 5-YEAR-OLD HEAD START ENROLLEES. AFTER THE SUBJECTS WERE RATED ON BEHAVIORAL ADJUSTMENT AND LANGUAGE ABILITY (BY TEACHER RATINGS AND LANGUAGE SCORES), 20 WERE SELECTED FOR A HIGH-ADJUSTMENT, HIGH-LANGUAGE (H-H) GROUP AND 20 OTHERS FOR A LOW-ADJUSTMENT, LOW-LANGUAGE (L-L) GROUP. FAMILIAL DATA WERE COLLECTED ON 15 CHILDREN IN EACH GROUP. ANALYSIS OF THE CHILD COMPETENCE DATA REVEALS A MODERATE RELATIONSHIP BETWEEN BEHAVIORAL ADJUSTMENT AND LINGUISTIC ABILITY. ANALYSIS OF FAMILIAL DATA AND THE CHILD COMPETENCE DATA SUGGESTS MORE ADEQUATE FAMILY ADJUSTMENT AND MORE FAVORABLE "SEMANTIC STRUCTURE" REGARDING SCHOOL-RELATED CONCEPTS IN THE H-H GROUP. (MH)

ED037249 PS003000
A REPLICATION AND EXTENSION STUDY ON N-LENGTH, INHIBITION AND COOPERATIVE BEHAVIOR WITH A MEXICAN-AMERICAN POPULATION. PART OF THE FINAL REPORT ON HEAD START EVALUATION AND RESEARCH: 1968-69 TO THE OFFICE OF ECONOMIC OPPORTUNITY. MANNING, BRAD A.; AND OTHERS, AUG 69 28P.
EDRS PRICE MF-$0.65 HC-$3.29

A STUDY OF COOPERATIVE BEHAVIOR (SOCIAL LEARNING) AND N-LENGTHS USING NEGRO SUBJECTS WAS REPLICATED AND EXTENDED. SUBJECTS WERE 100 MEXICAN-AMERICAN CHILDREN, 4 1/2 TO 6 YEARS OLD. N-LENGTH WAS DEFINED AS THE NUMBER OF NONREINFORCED TRIALS SPACED BETWEEN REINFORCED TRIALS AND INTERTRIAL REINFORCEMENT (ITR), INTRODUCED BETWEEN REGULARLY SCHEDULED TRIALS. THE EXPERIMENTAL SITUATION WAS A TWO-PERSON, TWO-CHOICE GAME IN WHICH EACH SUBJECT HAD CONTROL OVER THE OTHER PLAYER'S GAIN AND COULD CHOOSE EITHER TO COOPERATE OR NOT TO COOPERATE. THE EXPERIMENT CONSISTED OF TWO PHASES: THE ACQUISITION PHASE (DEFINED AS THE FIRST 30 COOPERATIVE RESPONSES), AND THE 30 TRIAL EXTINCTION PHASE. THE SUBJECTS WERE DIVIDED INTO FIVE GROUPS OF 20 EACH. THE FIRST FOUR GROUPS RECEIVED 50% PARTIAL REINFORCEMENT FOR THE FIRST 30 RESPONSES AND ITR IN N-LENGTHS OF 1, 2, 3, AND FOUR. THE FIFTH GROUP RECEIVED CONTINUOUS OR 100% REINFORCEMENT. THE FINDINGS MATCHED THOSE OF THE PREVIOUS STUDY IN THAT THE 100% GROUP WAS LEAST RESISTANT TO EXTINCTION AND THE N1-LENGTH GROUP WAS MOST RESISTANT TO EXTINCTION. HOWEVER, IN CONTRAST TO THE NEGRO STUDY, IN THE PRESENT STUDY N-LENGTH GROUPS DID NOT DIFFER IN ACQUISITION AND INCREASED THEIR COOPERATION AS A FUNCTION OF TRIALS. (MH)

ED037250 PS003031
A STUDY OF COMMUNICATION PATTERNS IN DISADVANTAGED CHILDREN. KOGAN, KATE L.; WIMBERGER, HERBERT C., 31 AUG 69 42P.
EDRS PRICE MF-$0.65 HC-$3.29

TO STUDY MOTHER-CHILD INTERACTION PATTERNS IN CULTURALLY DISADVANTAGED AND CULTURALLY ADVANTAGED FAMILIES, VERBAL AND NONVERBAL COMMUNICATIONS WERE OBSERVED, RECORDED, AND ANALYZED BOTH INDEPENDENTLY AND COLLECTIVELY. SUBJECTS WERE 10 HEAD START CHILDREN, 10 CULTURALLY ADVANTAGED CHILDREN, AND THE MOTHERS OF BOTH GROUPS. COMMUNICATIONS WERE ASSESSED ACCORDING TO THE INTERPERSONAL DIMENSIONS OF STATUS, AFFECTION, AND INVOLVEMENT. IN GENERAL, HEAD START MOTHERS PROVIDED LESS SOCIAL REINFORCEMENT FOR THEIR CHILDREN'S ACTIVITIES, AND MANY OF THEIR INVOLVEMENTS WERE HIGHLY AUTHORITATIVE INTERVENTIONS. HEAD START CHILDREN TOOK AND SOLICITED LEADERSHIP MORE OFTEN, AND THEY DISPLAYED BOTH MORE HOSTILITY AND MORE WARMTH THAN THE ADVANTAGED GROUP. THUS, HEAD START MOTHER-CHILD DYADS HAD FEWER AFFECTION-BASED INTERACTIONS AND MORE STATUS-BASED INTERACTIONS. THERE WERE EQUAL AMOUNTS OF CONVERSATIONAL INTERCHANGE IN THE TWO GROUPS. SIGNIFICANT DIFFERENCES BETWEEN THE TWO SAMPLES WERE FOUND IN THE FREQUENCIES WITH WHICH CERTAIN COMMUNICATION PATTERNS OCCURRED, AND THE CONTEXTS IN WHICH THEY OCCURRED. HOWEVER, WHEN THE SAME PATTERNS DID OCCUR, THE CONSEQUENCES WERE LIKELY TO BE THE SAME FOR BOTH POPULATION SAMPLES. (DR)

ED037251 PS003060
CHARACTERIZATION OF THE EFFECT OF SPACE, MATERIALS, AND TEACHER BEHAVIOR ON PRESCHOOL CHILDREN'S FREE PLAY ACTIVITY PATTERNS. RESEARCH REPORT NO. 1. HOLT, CAROL; BOGER, ROBERT P., NOV 69 22P.
EDRS PRICE MF-$0.65 HC-$3.29

THE OBJECT OF THIS STUDY WAS TO DETERMINE THE EXTENT TO WHICH CHILDREN DISPLAYED PREDICTABLE, RECURRING PATTERNS OF BEHAVIOR WHEN ENGAGED IN SELF-SELECTED ACTIVITIES. SUBJECTS WERE FOUR GIRLS AND THREE BOYS, 4 YEARS OF AGE, ALL FROM MIDDLE CLASS URBAN FAMILIES. THE CLASSROOM'S FREE PLAY SPACE WAS DIVIDED INTO FOUR EQUAL AREAS. TOYS WERE DIVIDED INTO FOUR GROUPS: ART MATERIALS, BLOCKS, DRAMATIC TOYS, AND MANIPULATIVE TOYS AND BOOKS. EACH DAY THE TOY GROUPS WERE RANDOMLY ASSIGNED TO THE FOUR AREAS, WITH EACH FREE PLAY SESSION BEING VIDEOTAPED SIMULTANEOUSLY FROM TWO DIRECTIONS. OBSERVER RECORDINGS OF EACH CHILD'S MOVEMENTS AND THE TOYS HE USED WERE SUMMARIZED, CODED, AND ANALYZED. SIGNIFICANT DIFFERENCES WERE FOUND IN THE TIME SPENT BY CHILDREN IN SPECIFIC PHYSICAL LOCATIONS. THESE DIFFERENCES WERE RELATED TO THE NATURE OF THE AREA AND THE PROXIMITY OF THE PLAY MATERIALS TO THE TEACHER. CHILDREN TENDED TO CHOOSE PLAY MATERIALS THAT COULD BE MOVED TO ANOTHER AREA OF THE ROOM. DIFFERENCES IN THE NATURE OF INDEPENDENT AND GROUP PLAY WERE RELATED TO MATERIALS AND LOCATION. (DR)

ED037252 PS003061
NUTRITION AND MENTAL DEVELOPMENT. RESEARCH REPORT NO. 5. WAGNER, MURIEL G., NOV 69 35P.
EDRS PRICE MF-$0.65 HC-$3.29

THIS STUDY INVESTIGATED (1) THE NUTRITIONAL STATUS OF URBAN AMERICAN DISADVANTAGED CHILDREN, (2) THE RELATIONSHIP OF NUTRITIONAL STATUS TO MENTAL GROWTH AND DEVELOPMENT, (3) THE RELATIONSHIP OF PHYSICAL MATURATION TO THE DEVELOPMENT OF PERCEPTUAL-MOTOR FACTORS OF INTELLIGENCE, AND (4) IF FOUND, THE EFFECTS OF UNDERNUTRITION ON INTELLECTUAL ACHIEVEMENT AND PHYSICAL DEVELOPMENT. SUBJECTS WERE 60 DETROIT 5-YEAR-OLDS, HALF OF WHOM WERE DISADVANTAGED. SEX AND RACE WERE ALSO CONTROLLED IN THE SAMPLE. RESULTS SHOWED FEW, IF ANY, NUTRITIONAL DEFICIENCIES. NEGRO CHILDREN APPEARED SLIGHTLY TALLER AND HEAVIER AS A GROUP WHEN COMPARED TO THE NORMS OF CAUCASIAN CHILDREN MEASURED OVER 3 DECADES AGO. WITH THE EXCEPTION OF A MARKED POSITIVE CORRELATION BETWEEN HEIGHT AND PSYCHOLOGICAL PERFORMANCE TEST SCORES IN BOYS, NO RELATIONSHIP BETWEEN PHYSICAL MEASURES AND INTELLIGENCE TEST SCORES WAS FOUND. IT WAS FELT THAT IF A NUTRITIONAL DEFICIENCY EXISTED IN THE CHILDREN, IT WAS AT A LEVEL THAT PERMITTED PHYSIOLOGICAL ADAPTATION BY THE CHILD SO THAT GROWTH WAS NOT APPRECIABLY AFFECTED. RE-EXAMINATION OF THE DATA IS SUGGESTED, SINCE RESULTS IMPLY THAT OTHER FACTORS EXERT A MORE PROFOUND INFLUENCE ON MENTAL DEVELOPMENT IN THE CHILDREN STUDIED THAN DO NUTRITIONAL AND PHYSICAL GROWTH VARIABLES, PER SE. (AUTHOR/DR)

ED037253 PS003091
DEVELOPMENT OF A READINESS TEST FOR DISADVANTAGED PRE-SCHOOL CHILDREN IN THE UNITED STATES. FINAL REPORT. WALKER, WANDA, 31 OCT 69 147P.
EDRS PRICE MF-$0.65 HC-$6.58

THE OBJECT OF THIS PROJECT WAS TO DEVELOP A CULTURE-FAIR, NONVERBAL INDIVIDUAL READINESS TEST FOR DISADVANTAGED PRESCHOOL CHILDREN. TWO EQUIVALENT FORMS OF THE TEST WERE DEVELOPED SO THAT TEACHERS COULD ADMINISTER THE FIRST FORM TO IDENTIFY NEEDS EARLY IN A PRESCHOOL PROGRAM, SET UP SPECIFIC REMEDIAL PROGRAMS FOR INDIVIDUALS, AND USE THE SECOND FORM OF THE TEST TO ASSESS THE EFFICIENCY OF THE PROGRAM AND INDIVIDUAL PROGRESS. A TOTAL OF 6662 CHILDREN IN 364 HEAD START AND DAY CARE CENTERS WERE TESTED TO REFINE AND STANDARDIZE FORM A OF THE TEST. ANALYSIS AND NORMING OF FORM B WAS CARRIED ON IN 301 CENTERS WITH 5271 CHILDREN PARTICIPATING. ITEM ANALYSES OF BOTH FORMS OF THE TEST WERE MADE. THE DATA INDICATE THAT BOTH FORMS OF THE TEST ARE SUFFICIENTLY VALID AND RELIABLE FOR USE IN AN EVALUATION PROGRAM FOR DISADVANTAGED PRESCHOOL CHILDREN. TWO-THIRDS OF THIS REPORT GIVES SUPPLEMENTARY AND APPENDIX MATERIALS WHICH INCLUDE STATISTICAL TABLES, DATA OF PARTICIPANTS IN THE RESEARCH PROJECT AND FACSIMILIES OF FORM A AND FORM B OF THE TEST DEVELOPED. (MS)

ED038161 PS002160
FEDERAL PROGRAMS ASSISTING CHILDREN AND YOUTH. REVISED EDITION. , 68 120P.
EDRS PRICE MF-$0.65 HC-$6.58

THIS REPORT INVENTORIES FEDERAL PROGRAMS WHICH ASSIST CHILDREN AND YOUTH AND PROVIDES INFORMATION ON THE AMOUNT OF FEDERAL FUNDS WHICH FINANCE THESE PROGRAMS. IT UPDATES AN EARLIER REPORT BY CONCENTRATING ON AN ANALYSIS OF THE FUNDS PROVIDED BY THE SEVERAL AGENCIES AND ON THE VARIOUS CATEGORIES OF BENEFITS AND SERVICES FOR CHILDREN AND YOUTH. DATA ON FUNDS FOR THE FISCAL YEARS 1960, 1963, 1966, 1967, 1968, AND 1969 ARE PROVIDED. ALSO INCLUDED ARE DATA ON APPROPRIATIONS AND EXPENDITURES FOR PROGRAMS. PER CAPITA EXPENDITURES FOR CHILDREN AND YOUTH ARE ANALYZED, AND DEMOGRAPHIC AND SOCIAL FACTS ON THIS PORTION OF THE POPULATION ARE PROVIDED. STATISTICS ARE GIVEN FOR EDUCATION AND TRAINING PROGRAMS, HEALTH PROGRAMS, AND NUTRITION PROGRAMS. CURRENT SERVICES AND OBJECTIVES FOR THESE PROGRAMS ARE DESCRIBED. OTHER FEDERAL PROGRAMS ARE EXPLAINED SUCH AS CASH BENEFITS FOR CHILDREN, SOCIAL WELFARE SERVICES, EMPLOYMENT SERVICES, AND HOUSING PROGRAMS. APPENDIXES GIVE TABULAR SUMMARIES OF PROGRAM FUNDING. (DR)

ED038162 PS002782
PLANNING ENVIRONMENTS FOR YOUNG CHILDREN: PHYSICAL SPACE. KRITCHEVSKY, SYBIL; AND OTHERS, 69 58P.
DOCUMENT NOT AVAILABLE FROM EDRS.
AVAILABLE FROM: PUBLICATIONS DEPARTMENT, NATIONAL ASSOCIATION FOR THE EDUCATION OF YOUNG CHILDREN, 1629 21ST STREET, N.W., WASHINGTON, D.C. 20009 ($1.50)

THIS MONOGRAPH, ILLUSTRATED WITH PHOTOGRAPHS AND DIAGRAMS, EXPLAINS HOW TO USE PHYSICAL SPACE TO ENCOURAGE CHILDREN TO INVOLVE THEMSELVES CONSTRUCTIVELY IN PARTICULAR PROGRAM ACTIVITIES. PROGRAM GOALS SHOULD BE STATED IN SPECIFIC AND CONCRETE TERMS TO ALLOW SELF-DIRECTION OF YOUNG CHILDREN AND TEACHER FLEXIBILITY. ANALYSIS IS MADE OF THE PARTS OF A PLAY SPACE AND HOW THESE PARTS FUNCTION AS A WHOLE. PLAY SPACE CONSISTS OF EMPTY SPACE UNITS SURROUNDED BY VISIBLE BOUNDARIES, AND UNITS CONTAINING SOMETHING TO PLAY WITH, CLASSIFIED ACCORDING TO COMPLEXITY. PLAY UNITS THAT PROVIDE VARIETY, COMPLEXITY, AND ADEQUATE AMOUNT OF ACTIVITY PER CHILD ARE CONSIDERED CONSISTENT WITH GOALS FOR YOUNG CHILDREN. GOOD ORGANIZATION OF PLAY SPACE REQUIRES CLEAR PATHS FOR MOVEMENT AND AN ADEQUATE AMOUNT OF EMPTY SPACE, AS THE EXAMPLE GIVEN DEMONSTRATES. COMMON PROBLEMS IN SPACE DEVELOPMENT AND USE ARE DISCUSSED AND SOLUTIONS SUGGESTED. EXAMPLES OF SUCCESSFUL DEVELOPMENT OF SPACE, ONE YARD AND TWO CHILDREN'S CENTERS, ARE FULLY DESCRIBED. AGAIN, EACH SPATIAL AREA DISCUSSED HAS BEEN DESIGNED OR ALTERED TO MEET STATED GOALS. A CASE STUDY, CHECKLISTS, AND APPROACHES ARE GIVEN TO HELP PEOPLE PLAN PLAY AREAS. (DR)

ED038163 PS002807
RECORDING INDIVIDUAL PUPIL EXPERIENCES IN THE CLASSROOM: A MANUAL FOR PROSE RECORDERS. MEDLEY, DONALD M.; AND OTHERS, DEC 68 31P.
EDRS PRICE MF-$0.65 HC-$3.29

THIS DOCUMENT IS A MANUAL FOR USERS OF THE PUPIL RECORD OF SCHOOL EXPERIENCE (PROSE) TECHNIQUE OF CLASSROOM OBSERVATION. PROSE IS A MARK-SENSING SHEET OF PAPER TESTING 148 CATEGORIES OF STUDENT BEHAVIOR, AND PROVIDING SPACES IN WHICH THE RECORDER CAN INDICATE WHICH OF THEM HE OBSERVES. A REPRODUCTION OF THE FORM IS GIVEN AND ITS USE IS CAREFULLY DETAILED. (MH)

ED038164 PS002827
PIAGET'S THEORY AND SPECIFIC INSTRUCTION: A RESPONSE TO BEREITER AND KOHLBERG. KAMII, CONSTANCE, JAN 70 21P.
EDRS PRICE MF-$0.65 HC NOT AVAILABLE FROM EDRS.

SPECIFIC INSTRUCTION REFERS TO THE TEACHER'S KNOWING (A) WHAT TO TEACH AND WHEN, (B) WHAT NOT TO TEACH AND WHY, AND (C) WHEN TO LET THE PREOPERATIONAL CHILD BE "WRONG." THIS PAPER IS IN AGREEMENT WITH BEREITER'S CRITICISM OF KOHLBERG'S CONCLUSION AGAINST SPECIFIC INSTRUCTION BUT SUGGESTS THAT BEREITER'S ARGUMENT SHOULD BE DEVELOPED INTO A GUIDE USEFUL FOR ACTUAL TEACHING. A DETAILED DISCUSSION FOLLOWS OF SPECIFIC INSTRUCTION AS IT IS RELATED TO PIAGET'S THREE AREAS OF KNOWLEDGE, (SOCIAL, PHYSICAL, AND LOGICO-MATHEMATICAL) TO DEVELOPMENT, AND TO THEORIES OF LEARNING. IT IS ARGUED THAT INSTRUCTION CAN BE MORE SPECIFIC IN SOME WAYS, AS IN THE TEACHING OF SOCIAL KNOWLEDGE, AND IN THE STRUCTURING OF COGNITIVE PROCESSES THAT WILL EVENTUALLY RESULT IN LOGICAL THINKING. PIAGETIAN PRINCIPLES OF LEARNING SEEM TO INDICATE THAT TEACHING MUST TAKE INTO ACCOUNT THE PREOPERATIONAL CHILD'S TOTAL COGNITIVE STRUCTURE EVEN WHEN THE CONTENT AND STRATEGY OF TEACHING ARE SPECIFIC. [NOT AVAILABLE IN HARD COPY DUE TO MARGINAL LEGIBILITY OF ORIGINAL DOCUMENT.] (AUTHOR/NH)

ED038165 PS002829
EVALUATION OF EDUCATIONAL PROGRAMS AS RESEARCH ON EDUCATIONAL PROCESS. MESSICK, SAMUEL, 69 11P.
EDRS PRICE MF-$0.65 HC-$3.29

BECAUSE OF THE PRESSURE TOWARDS IMMEDIATE IMPLEMENTATION OF INNOVATIVE EDUCATIONAL PROGRAMS, EVALUATION EMPHASIS HAS BEEN PUT ON THE OVERALL EFFECTIVENESS OF THESE PROGRAMS. THIS TYPE OF RESEARCH YIELDS ONLY YES-NO ANSWERS ABOUT GENERAL EFFECTIVENESS WITHOUT PROBING INTO THE PROCESS OF EDUCATION ITSELF. MORE RESEARCH IS NEEDED ON THE FACTORS THAT MAKE PROGRAMS EFFECTIVE; THIS RESEARCH CAN BE UNDERTAKEN WITHOUT SACRIFICING ACTION-ORIENTATION, BY CARRYING OUT THE RESEARCH AND THE PROGRAM SIMULTANEOUSLY. EVALUATIVE RESEARCH SHOULD INCLUDE ASSESSMENT OF BOTH POSSIBLE AND INTENDED OUTCOMES, MEASUREMENTS OF ANTECEDENT CONDITIONS AND CONSEQUENCES OF INTERVENTION. IF THIS ALTERATION IN RESEARCH ORIENTATION TAKES PLACE, IT COULD BE SEEN AS A SHIFT FROM THE ENGINEERING MODEL OF EVALUATION STUDIES (INPUT-OUTPUT DIFFERENCES RELATIVE TO COST) TO THE MEDICAL MODEL (CONCERN FOR SPECIFIC PROCESSES). A MAJOR ADVANTAGE OF THE MEDICAL MODEL IS THAT GOALS, SIDE EFFECTS AND PROGRAM BY-PRODUCTS RECEIVE INCREASED ATTENTION. FINALLY, THIS TYPE OF EVALUATIVE RESEARCH CAN SERVE TO ADVANCE SCIENCE AS WELL AS SOCIAL WELFARE. (MH)

ED038166 PS002839
EARLY CHILD STIMULATION THROUGH PARENT EDUCATION. GORDON, IRA J., SEP 69 20P.
EDRS PRICE MF-$0.65 HC-$3.29

STUDY OBJECTIVES WERE TO FIND OUT WHETHER THE USE OF DISADVANTAGED WOMEN AS PARENT EDUCATORS OF INDIGENT MOTHERS OF INFANTS AND YOUNG CHILDREN (1) ENHANCED THE DEVELOPMENT OF THE INFANTS AND CHILDREN, (2) INCREASED THE MOTHER'S COMPETENCE AND SENSE OF PERSONAL WORTH, AND (3) CONTRIBUTED TO THE KNOWLEDGE OF THE HOME LIFE OF INFANTS IN THE STUDY. IN WEEKLY HOME VISITS, PARENT EDUCATORS TAUGHT A SERIES OF EXERCISES THAT STIMULATED INFANTS' PERCEPTUAL, MOTOR, AND VERBAL ACTIVITIES. MATERNAL VERBAL CUES ELICITED THE SEQUENTIAL ARRANGEMENT OF TASKS. VARIABLES WERE TYPE, CONTENT, LENGTH, TIMING, AND PRESENCE OF INSTRUCTION. A TOTAL OF 124 BABIES (3 MONTHS - 2 YEARS) WERE OBSERVED AND TESTED. EXCEPT FOR A CONTROL GROUP OF 27, ALL INFANTS RECEIVED STIMULATION FOR AT LEAST 9 MONTHS. STUDY FINDINGS WERE THAT (1) PARAPROFESSIONALS CAN BE USED TO TEACH MOTHERS, (2) A PARENT EDUCATION PROGRAM SHOULD BE PART OF A COMPREHENSIVE SYSTEM OF SOCIAL CHANGE, (3) CONCRETE, SPECIFIC STIMULATION EXERCISES ARE A SOUND CURRICULUM APPROACH, (4) HOW A CHILD IS TAUGHT MAY BE MORE IMPORTANT THAN WHAT HE IS TAUGHT, AND (5) STANDARDIZED TECHNIQUES FOR MEASURING LEARNING AND DEVELOPMENT ARE NEEDED. (DR)

ED038167 PS002850
AN EARLY CHILDHOOD EDUCATION MODEL: A BILINGUAL APPROACH. NEDLER, SHARI, [67] 19P.
EDRS PRICE MF-$0.65 HC-$3.29

TO AID SCHOOL ADJUSTMENT OF CHILDREN FROM LOW INCOME FAMILIES OF MEXICAN DESCENT, THIS PROGRAM HAS DEVELOPED NEW METHODS FOR TEACHING ENGLISH AS A SECOND LANGUAGE WHILE PRESERVING AND REINFORCING CHILDREN'S USE OF SPANISH. THE CLASSROOM MODEL EMPHASIZES LEARNING COGNITIVE CONCEPTS AND EXPLORING THE CHILD'S ATTITUDES TOWARDS THESE CONCEPTS. SENSORY-PERCEPTUAL SKILLS AND LANGUAGE SKILLS ARE SYSTEMATICALLY PRESENTED TO DEVELOP CHILDREN'S THINKING PROCESSES. AN INSTRUCTIONAL PROGRAM, BASED ON THIS MODEL, CONSISTS OF A SEQUENCED SERIES OF LESSONS, INITIALLY PRESENTED IN SPANISH AND LATER IN ENGLISH. THIS DEVELOPMENTAL APPROACH INCLUDES TRAINING IN VISUAL, AUDITORY, AND MOTOR SKILLS. THE CHILD LEARNS A SEQUENTIAL PATTERN OF LANGUAGE AND SPEECH CONCEPTS IN BOTH SPANISH AND ENGLISH, WITH CONTENT SELECTED TO RELATE TO THE

CHILD AND HIS ENVIRONMENT. INSTRUCTION IS INDIVIDUALIZED WHEN APPROPRIATE. IT IS IMPORTANT THAT TEACHERS STRUCTURE AND SEQUENCE LEARNING ACTIVITIES WHICH MATCH INDIVIDUAL LEARNING ABILITIES SO THAT EACH CHILD MAY DEVELOP TO HIS POTENTIAL. (DR)

ED038168 PS002909
PRESCHOOL MATHEMATICS CURRICULUM PROJECT. FINAL REPORT. ADKINS, DOROTHY C.; AND OTHERS, NOV 69 28P.
EDRS PRICE MF-$0.65 HC-$3.29

THE PRESENT PROJECT PROVIDED FOR THE DEVELOPMENT OF A DETAILED QUANTITATIVE CURRICULUM APPROPRIATE FOR USE IN HEAD START CLASSES, TRIAL OF THE DEVELOPED MATERIALS WITH PRESCHOOL CHILDREN IN HAWAII, AND PRELIMINARY ASSESSMENT OF THE CURRICULUM IN COMPARISON WITH A MORE SPONTANEOUS, INFORMAL QUANTITATIVE CLASSROOM EXPERIENCE. DIRECTIONS FOR TASKS RELATED TO NUMBER AND COUNTING, GEOMETRY, DIMENSION, PREARITHMETIC OPERATIONS, AND SYMBOLS WERE PREPARED AND REVISED THROUGHOUT THE SCHOOL YEAR 1968-69 AND PRESENTED TO 55 CHILDREN IN THREE EXPERIMENTAL CLASSES DAILY IN 20-MINUTE LESSONS. THE TASKS WERE THEN COMPILED INTO A TEACHER'S MANUAL. THE GEOMETRIC DESIGN, ARITHMETIC, AND BLOCK DESIGN SUBTESTS OF THE WPPSI; AN EXPERIMENTAL FORM OF THE HEAD START ARITHMETIC TEST; AND TWO PIAGETIAN CONSERVATION TASKS WERE ADMINISTERED TO THE EXPERIMENTAL SUBJECTS AND 30 SUBJECTS IN TWO COMPARISON CLASSES TO MEASURE MATHEMATICAL KNOWLEDGE AND UNDERSTANDING. THE MEAN SCORES ON THE WPPSI SUBTESTS FOR THE EXPERIMENTAL CLASSES WERE ALL ABOVE THE STANDARDIZED NORMS AND CONSISTENTLY HIGHER THAN FOR THE COMPARISON CLASSES. THE DIFFERENCES WERE STATISTICALLY SIGNIFICANT ON THE GEOMETRIC DESIGN AND BLOCK DESIGN SUBTESTS. THE NET GAIN ON THE HEAD START ARITHMETIC TEST WERE ALSO SIGNIFICANTLY GREATER FOR THE EXPERIMENTAL GROUP THAN FOR THE COMPARISON GROUP. (AUTHOR)

ED038169 PS002948
CURRICULUM GUIDE FOR PHYSICAL EDUCATION: KINDERGARTEN AND UNGRADED PRIMARY. BALDWIN, WILLIAM O.; AND OTHERS, 69 87P.
EDRS PRICE MF-$0.65 HC-$3.29

THIS PHYSICAL EDUCATION PROGRAM CONSISTS OF TEACHING BASIC SKILLS AND THE USE OF THESE SKILLS IN IMPLEMENTING A PROGRESSIVE SEQUENCE FROM KINDERGARTEN THROUGH UNGRADED PRIMARY GRADES. A SECTION ON GAMES INCLUDES A DESCRIPTION OF THEIR GENERAL PURPOSE, DIRECTIONS FOR PLAYING EACH GAME, AND TEACHING SUGGESTIONS. INCLUDED ARE 11 GAMES TO BE INTRODUCED AT THE KINDERGARTEN LEVEL; 27 GROUP GAMES AND 11 CLASSROOM GAMES FOR THE NEXT LEVEL; 26 GROUP GAMES AND EIGHT CLASSROOM GAMES FOR A SUBSEQUENT LEVEL; AND 25 GROUP GAMES AND SIX CLASSROOM GAMES FOR THE FINAL LEVEL. THE RHYTHM PROGRAM IS DIVIDED INTO FUNDAMENTAL RHYTHMS AND SINGING GAMES AND DANCES. THIS SECTION INCLUDES A LIST OF RECORDS AS WELL AS RHYTHMIC ACTIVITIES FOR EACH LEVEL. A SECTION ON STUNTS DESCRIBES THEIR PURPOSE, GIVES TEACHING SUGGESTIONS AND RECOMMENDS SAFETY PRECAUTIONS. DIAGRAMS OF STUNTS AT ALL DEVELOPMENTAL LEVELS ARE ILLUSTRATED. THE FINAL SECTION CONTAINS A PHYSICAL FITNESS TEST. THE GUIDE WAS PLANNED TO BE USED IN CONJUNCTION WITH "ELEMENTARY SCHOOL PHYSICAL EDUCATION HANDBOOK." (DR)

ED038170 PS002967
HEAD START PLANNED VARIATION PROGRAM. KLEIN, JENNY, SEP 69 5P.
EDRS PRICE MF-$0.65 HC-$3.29

THERE IS LITTLE AGREEMENT CONCERNING WHICH METHODS OF PRESCHOOL INTERVENTION ARE MOST EFFECTIVE. IN ORDER TO EVALUATE SEVERAL APPROACHES TO EARLY CHILDHOOD EDUCATION, PROJECT HEAD START, IN CONJUNCTION WITH PROJECT FOLLOW THROUGH, HAS INITIATED THE PLANNED VARIATION PROGRAM. THIS YEAR ONLY A PILOT PROJECT IS UNDERWAY WITH EIGHT SCHOOLS PARTICIPATING. THESE ARE (1) UNIVERSITY OF KANSAS, WHERE BUSHELL USES A BEHAVIOR ANALYSIS APPROACH; (2) UNIVERSITY OF ILLINOIS, WHERE BECKER AND ENGELMANN USE A STRUCTURED, ACADEMIC APPROACH; (3) BANK STREET COLLEGE, WHERE GILKESON PRESENTS A DEVELOPMENTAL APPROACH WITH EMPHASIS ON SELF-DIRECTION; (4) UNIVERSITY OF ARIZONA, WHERE HENDERSON STRESSES BEHAVIORAL SKILLS AND ATTITUDES; (5) YPSILANTI, WHERE WEIKART RELIES ON PIAGET'S COGNITIVE THEORIES; (6) UNIVERSITY OF FLORIDA, WHERE GORDON USES THE CONCEPT OF THE PARENT-EDUCATOR; (7) FAR WEST LAB, WHERE NIMNICHT RELIES ON THE AUTOTELIC DISCOVERY APPROACH; AND (8) EDUCATION DEVELOPMENT CENTER, WHERE ARMINGTON FOLLOWS ON ACTION-ORIENTED APPROACH. EVALUATION WILL INVOLVE COMPARISON OF THE DEVELOPMENT OF CHILDREN PARTICIPATING IN THE ABOVE PROGRAMS WITH THAT OF CHILDREN ATTENDING REGULAR HEAD START PROGRAMS WITHIN THE SAME COMMUNITY OR IN A SIMILAR COMMUNITY. (MH)

ED038171 PS002990
AN EXPERIMENTAL GAME IN ORAL LANGUAGE COMPREHENSION. KEISLAR, EVAN R.; PHINNEY, JEAN, JAN 70 9P.
EDRS PRICE MF-$0.65 HC-$3.29

A PROJECT HAS BEEN INITIATED TO DEVELOP EDUCATIONAL GAMES FOR TEACHING COGNITIVE SKILLS TO HEAD START CHILDREN. IT IS HYPOTHESIZED THAT WHILE A GAME FORMAT MAY BE LESS EFFICIENT AND LESS EFFECTIVE THAN CONVENTIONAL METHODS FOR THE TEACHING OF SPECIFIC SKILLS, THE USE OF GAMES IN THE CURRICULUM WILL LEAD TO SIGNIFICANT IMPROVEMENT IN ATTITUDE TOWARD INTELLECTUAL TASKS AND WILL MINIMIZE THE NEED FOR CONSTANT SUPERVISION. THIS PAPER REPORTS ON A PILOT STUDY WHOSE GOAL WAS TO CREATE A GAME WHAT WOULD TEACH CHILDREN A LISTENING COMPREHENSION OF FOUR LINGUISTIC CONSTRUCTIONS: CONJUNCTION, NEGATION, JOINT DENIAL, AND EXCLUSION. IT WAS HYPOTHESIZED THAT AFTER PLAYING THE GAME, CHILDREN WOULD SHOW IMPROVEMENT IN THEIR COMPREHENSION OF SPOKEN SENTENCES USING THESE CONSTRUCTIONS. IN ADDITION, CHILDREN WERE EXPECTED TO FIND THE GAME ENJOYABLE. THE SUBJECTS, EIGHT HEAD START CHILDREN FROM 4 YEARS 3 MONTHS TO 5 YEARS OLD, WERE PRE- AND POSTTESTED WITH FOUR GAME SESSIONS INTERVENING. GAINS IN POSTTEST SCORES SUPPORTED BELIEF IN THE GENERAL EFFECTIVENESS OF THE GAME FOR TEACHING THE FOUR LINGUISTIC CONSTRUCTIONS. ALTHOUGH THERE WAS NO OBJECTIVE MEASURE OF THE CHILDREN'S ATTITUDES, THEY ENJOYED THE GAME AND ASKED TO PLAY AGAIN, WHICH SEEMS TO INDICATE THAT THE GAME APPROACH IS APPROPRIATE FOR TEACHING TASKS NOT INTRINSICALLY INTERESTING. (MH)

ED038172 PS002998
THE EFFECT OF N-LENGTH ON THE DEVELOPMENT OF COOPERATIVE AND NON-COOPERATIVE BEHAVIOR IN A TWO-PERSON GAME. PART OF THE FINAL REPORT ON HEAD START EVALUATION AND RESEARCH: 1968-69 TO THE OFFICE OF ECONOMIC OPPORTUNITY. MANNING, BRAD A.; PIERCE-JONES, JOHN, AUG 69 50P.
EDRS PRICE MF-$0.65 HC-$3.29

IN THIS STUDY OF COOPERATIVE BEHAVIOR AND ITS ANTECEDENTS, THE MAIN EXPERIMENTAL TOOL WAS A TWO-PERSON, TWO-CHOICE GAME. THE SUBJECTS, 80 NEGRO MALES RANGING IN AGE FROM 4 1/2 TO 6 YEARS, COULD CHOOSE EITHER TO COOPERATE BY GIVING A PIECE OF CANDY OR NOT TO COOPERATE BY REFUSING TO GIVE A PIECE OF CANDY TO THE OTHER CHILD DURING AN ACQUISITION PHASE (THE FIRST 30 COOPERATIVE RESPONSES MADE) AND AN EXTINCTION PHASE OF 30 TRIALS. N-LENGTH WAS DEFINED AS THE NUMBER OF NONREINFORCED TRIALS SPACED BETWEEN REINFORCED TRIALS AND INTERTRIAL REINFORCEMENT (ITR), INTRODUCED BETWEEN REGULARLY SCHEDULED TRIALS. THE SUBJECTS WERE DIVIDED INTO FOUR GROUPS OF 20 EACH. THE FIRST THREE GROUPS WERE GIVEN 50% REINFORCEMENT WITH THE NONREINFORCED TRIALS SPACED BETWEEN REINFORCED TRIALS AND ITR IN N-LENGTHS OF 1, 2, AND 3. THE FOURTH GROUP RECEIVED CONTINUOUS 100% REINFORCEMENT. THIS LAST GROUP WAS FOUND TO BE LEAST RESISTANT TO EXTINCTION. THE GROUP WITH N-LENGTH OF 1 WAS MOST RESISTANT TO EXTINCTION. IT WAS THEORIZED THAT N-LENGTHS BEYOND 1 INHIBIT COOPERATIVE RESPONSES SINCE THE SUBJECT MORE READILY REALIZES THAT HIS COOPERATION IS NOT BEING RECIPROCATED. (MH)

ED038173 PS003002
AN ATTRIBUTIONAL (COGNITIVE) MODEL OF MOTIVATION. WEINER, BERNARD; AND OTHERS, AUG 69 55P.
EDRS PRICE MF-$0.65 HC NOT AVAILABLE FROM EDRS.

A COGNITIVE MODEL OF MOTIVATION IS PROPOSED WHICH POSTULATES FOUR COMPONENTS AS THE DETERMINANTS OF THE ACTUAL AND ANTICIPATED OUTCOME OF AN ACHIEVEMENT-RELATED EVENT. THE FOUR DETERMINANTS ARE ABILITY, EFFORT, TASK DIFFICULTY, AND LUCK. THESE FACTORS MAY BE CLASSIFIED AS EITHER INTERNAL OR EXTERNAL SOURCES OF CONTROL, AND AS EITHER STABLE OR UNSTABLE ELEMENTS. FOUR EXPERIMENTS ARE REPORTED WHICH SUBSTANTIATE BELIEF THAT INDIVIDUALS ARE ABLE TO ATTRIBUTE THE BEHAVIOR OF OTHERS, AS WELL AS THEIR PERSONAL BEHAVIOR, TO THESE FOUR DIMENSIONS OF CAUSALITY. THE PERCEPTIONS ABOUT CAUSALITY ALSO ARE DEMONSTRATED TO INFLUENCE SUBJECTIVE EXPECTANCY OF SUCCESS, AND ARE RELATED TO RESISTANCE TO EXTINCTION. ACHIEVEMENT CONCERNS, FRUSTRATION AND CONFLICT, SELF VS. OTHER PERCEPTION, AND THE EDUCATIONAL IMPLICATIONS OF THIS MOTIVATIONAL APPROACH ARE DISCUSSED. [NOT AVAILABLE IN HARD COPY DUE TO MARGINAL LEGIBILITY OF ORIGINAL DOCUMENT.] (AUTHOR/DR)

ED038174 PS003059
ANALYSIS OF THE OBJECT CATEGORIZATION TEST AND THE PICTURE CATEGORIZATION TEST FOR PRESCHOOL CHILDREN. SIGEL, IRVING E.; OLMSTED, PATRICIA P., NOV 69 84P.
EDRS PRICE MF-$0.65 HC-$3.29

THIS STUDY ANALYZES THE OBJECT CATEGORIZATION TEST (OCT) AND THE PICTURE CATEGORIZATION TEST (PCT) TO PROVIDE (1) PSYCHOMETRIC ANALYSIS OF THE TESTS, (2) SUBSTANTIVE ANALYSIS DETAILING VARIATION IN PERFORMANCE LEVEL AS A FUNCTION OF AGE, RACE, CLASS, AND SEX, AND (3) NORMATIVE DATA YIELDING FREQUENCIES OF VARIOUS SCORE PATTERNS. DATA WAS TAKEN FROM TESTS GIVEN TO MORE THAN 500 BLACK AND WHITE CHILDREN FROM LOWER AND MIDDLE CLASS BACKGROUNDS. ITEM ANALYSIS REVEALED THAT THE

OCT AND PCT WERE SENSITIVE TO SEX, EDUCATION, AND TEST ORDER, AND PROVIDED A RANGE OF TYPES OF RESPONSES FOR 4- AND 5-YEAR-OLDS. THERE WERE GREATER DIFFERENCES BETWEEN AGES THAN WITHIN AN AGE GROUP. TEST-RETEST RELIABILITY WAS MODERATELY HIGH. TEST ORDER (OCT BEFORE PCT, OR VICE VERSA) HAD AN EFFECT, INTERACTING WITH SEX AND SOCIAL CLASS OF THE CHILD. MIDDLE CLASS CHILDREN TENDED TO PROVIDE MORE CONSISTENT RESPONSE PATTERNS ON THE OCT AND PCT THAN LOWER CLASS CHILDREN, ESPECIALLY LOWER CLASS BLACK CHILDREN. BOYS AND GIRLS SHOWED DIFFERENTIAL RESPONSE PATTERNS DEPENDENT ON TEST ORDER. DOMINANT STYLES OF RESPONDING TO TEST ITEMS WERE IDENTIFIED FOR LOWER CLASS BLACKS, INDICATING THAT STYLES VARIED WITH AGE, SEX, AND EDUCATIONAL STATUS. RECOMMENDATIONS ARE MADE REGARDING THE USE OF THE OCT AND PCT. (DR)

ED038175 PS003065
CURRICULAR INTERVENTION IN LANGUAGE ARTS READINESS FOR HEAD START CHILDREN. TULANE UNIVERSITY, HEAD START EVALUATION AND RESEARCH CENTER ANNUAL REPORT TO THE OFFICE OF ECONOMIC OPPORTUNITY. JONES, SHUELL H., 31 AUG 69 74P.
EDRS PRICE MF-$0.65 HC-$3.29

THE PURPOSE OF THE STUDY WAS TO DETERMINE THE EFFECTIVENESS OF A "PACKAGED" LANGUAGE DEVELOPMENT PROGRAM, ON THE GENERAL COGNITIVE, INTELLECTUAL, AND LANGUAGE DEVELOPMENT OF PRESCHOOL CHILDREN. A SELECTED BASIC LANGUAGE PROGRAM (BUCHANAN LANGUAGE READINESS PROGRAM) AND SUPPLEMENTARY MATERIALS (OTHER LANGUAGE PROGRAMS), WERE USED TO COLLECT DATA ON 13 HEAD START CLASSES IN MISSISSIPPI AND ALABAMA. DIFFERENT LEVELS OF TEACHER PREPARATION AND/OR VARIATIONS IN THE USE OF SUPPLEMENTARY MATERIALS AND REINFORCEMENT PROCEDURES WERE PART OF THE RESEARCH DESIGN. FOUR TRAINED CLASSROOM MONITORS, USING AN INTERVENTION CHECKLIST DESIGNED FOR THE STUDY, REPORTED OBSERVATIONS EACH WEEK FOR THE FIVE EXPERIMENTAL GROUPS AND TWICE MONTHLY FOR THE TWO CONTROL GROUPS. (A LENGTHY ANECDOTAL RECORD IS INCLUDED IN THIS REPORT.) CHILDREN WERE PRE- AND POSTTESTED ON SELECTED MEASURES OF LANGUAGE DEVELOPMENT. THE STANDARDIZED TESTS DID NOT YIELD SIGNIFICANT ACHIEVEMENT RESULTS, BUT BECAUSE OF A LATE START, THE PRESCRIBED LANGUAGE PROGRAM WAS NOT COMPLETED. IT IS RECOMMENDED THAT THE FOLLOWING AREAS RECEIVE EMPHASIS: TEACHER INSERVICE TRAINING AND SUPERVISION, ADEQUATE PREPARATION OF AIDES BEFORE THEY ARE PLACED IN THE CLASSROOM, PARENT INVOLVEMENT, AND LONGITUDINAL STUDIES OF CHILDREN IN CURRICULAR INTERVENTION STUDIES. (NH)

ED038176 PS003103
EFFECTS OF TRAINING YOUNG BLACK CHILDREN IN VOCABULARY VS. SENTENCE CONSTRUCTION. AMMON, PAUL R.; AMMON, MARY SUE, MAR 70 13P.
EDRS PRICE MF-$0.65 HC-$3.29

THIS EXPERIMENT COMPARED THE EFFECTS OF TRAINING YOUNG BLACK CHILDREN IN VOCABULARY VERSUS SENTENCE CONSTRUCTION TO SEE WHICH TYPE OF TRAINING WOULD RESULT IN GREATER TRANSFER TO OTHER AREAS OF LANGUAGE PERFORMANCE. A TOTAL OF 144 BLACK CHILDREN IN PRESCHOOL AND KINDERGARTEN WERE RANDOMLY ASSIGNED TO VOCABULARY TRAINING, SENTENCE TRAINING, OR CONTROL GROUPS. ALL CHILDREN WERE TESTED WITH THE PEABODY PICTURE VOCABULARY TEST (PPVT), A SENTENCE IMITATION TEST (SIT), AND A PICTURE INTERVIEW (PI), BEFORE AND AFTER THE 6-WEEK TRAINING PERIOD. VOCABULARY TRAINING INVOLVED PRACTICE IN RECOGNIZING AND APPLYING WORDS FROM THE PPVT AND THE PI. FOR SENTENCE TRAINING, THE CHILDREN IMITATED SENTENCES SIMILAR TO THOSE IN THE SIT AND CONSTRUCTED NEW INSTANCES OF THE SAME SENTENCE TYPES. ANALYSES OF VARIANCE SHOWED A POSITIVE EFFECT OF VOCABULARY TRAINING ON THE PPVT, BUT SENTENCE TRAINING DID NOT AFFECT PERFORMANCE ON THE SIT. THERE WAS NO EVIDENCE OF TRANSFER FROM VOCABULARY TO SENTENCE IMITATION. THE IMPLICATION OF THE RESULTS IS THAT TIME DEVOTED TO LANGUAGE TRAINING FOR YOUNG BLACK CHILDREN IS BETTER SPENT ON VOCABULARY THAN ON SENTENCE CONSTRUCTION. (AUTHOR/DR)

ED038177 PS003105
THE EFFECT OF MEDIATIONAL INSTRUCTIONS ON ASSOCIATIVE SKILLS OF FIRST GRADE INNERCITY CHILDREN. MONTAGUE, RUTH B., MAR 70 28P.
EDRS PRICE MF-$0.65 HC-$3.29

THE PURPOSE OF THIS STUDY WAS TO TEST ASSOCIATIVE SKILLS BY MEANS OF A PAIRED-ASSOCIATE TASK WITH VARIED MEDIATIONAL INSTRUCTIONS. SUBJECTS WERE 84 FIRST GRADE GHETTO CHILDREN, 25% OF WHOM WERE FROM SPANISH-SPEAKING HOMES; VIRTUALLY ALL THE OTHER SUBJECTS WERE BLACK. THE 3 X 2 X 4 FACTORIAL DESIGN INCLUDED: THREE MEDIATION SETS (IMAGERY, VERBALIZATION-SENTENCES, AND VERBALIZATION-NAMING), TWO ABILITY LEVELS (MEDIATIONAL ABILITY AND PRODUCTION ABILITY), AND FOUR TRIALS. A CONTROL GROUP WAS TESTED FOR SPONTANEOUS PRODUCTION. RESULTS INDICATE THAT PERFORMANCE WAS BETTER (A) UNDER THE SENTENTIAL AND IMAGERY SETS THAN UNDER THE NAMING SET, (B) WHEN MEDIATIONAL RATHER THAN PRODUCTION ABILITY WAS REQUIRED, AND (C) ON LATER TRIALS, ALTHOUGH RATE OF LEARNING VARIED BY CONDITION. AN INTERACTION OF MODE, ELABORATION, AND ABILITY WAS FOUND. RESULTS SUGGEST THE SAME PATTERNS OF MEDIATIONAL ABILITY OBTAIN FOR FIRST GRADERS FROM GHETTO AND WHITE MIDDLE CLASS BACKGROUNDS. THE INTERACTION OF MEDIATIONAL DEFICIENCY WITH MEDIATION SET REQUIRES THE REVISION OF THE STAGE MODEL OF MEDIATIONAL DEFICIENCY. (AUTHOR/NH)

ED038178 PS003128
BOOKS IN PRESCHOOL: A GUIDE TO SELECTING, PURCHASING, AND USING CHILDREN'S BOOKS. GRIFFIN, LOUISE, 70 68P.
EDRS PRICE MF-$0.65 HC-$3.29

THIS DOCUMENT IS A GUIDE TO THE SELECTION, PURCHASE, AND USE OF CHILDREN'S BOOKS. EMPHASIS IS PUT ON THE DEVELOPMENT OF STANDARDS OF EVALUATION THROUGH ATTENTION TO CERTAIN FEATURES, SUCH AS QUALITY OF ILLUSTRATIONS, LANGUAGE, AND WRITING STYLE. READING ALOUD AND TEACHING CHILDREN TO USE BOOKS ARE OTHER TOPICS DISCUSSED. THE PROJECT OF WRITING AND MAKING HIS OWN BOOK IS PROPOSED AS A REWARDING AND ENRICHING EXPERIENCE FOR A CHILD; INSTRUCTIONS ARE GIVEN FOR THIS ACTIVITY. A CHAPTER ON HOW TO FIND AND USE BOOKS IN OTHER LANGUAGES INCLUDES A SELECTION OF ERIC DOCUMENTS ON BILINGUAL EDUCATION. INTRODUCING CHILDREN AND PARENTS TO REGULAR USE OF THE PUBLIC LIBRARY IS EXPLORED. A BOOK BUYING DISCUSSION COVERS THE RELATIVE MERITS OF PAPERBOUND AND HARDBOUND BOOKS, AND PURCHASE FROM LOCAL BOOKSTORES, PUBLISHERS, AND WHOLESALERS. INTERCHAPTER SUPPLEMENTARY MATERIAL INCLUDES A SELECTED ANNOTATED BIBLIOGRAPHY OF CHILDREN'S BOOKS, A LIST OF RESOURCES TO AID SELECTION, AND A CHART OF INFORMATION ABOUT WHOLESALERS. (MH)

ED038179 PS003148
EARLY INFANT STIMULATION AND MOTOR DEVELOPMENT. FRICHTL, CHRIS; PETERSON, LINDA WHITNEY, DEC 69 16P.
EDRS PRICE MF-$0.65 HC-$3.29

PROFESSIONAL WORKERS CAN ASSIST PARENTS OF RETARDED INFANTS BY (1) HELPING THEM TO RECOGNIZE AND COPE WITH THEIR FEELINGS OF GUILT AND DESPAIR, AND (2) ESTABLISHING A HOME PROGRAM OF EXERCISES TO ALLAY THE INFANT'S INERTIA. SUCH EXERCISES HAVE BEEN DEMONSTRATED BY NUMEROUS INVESTIGATORS TO BE OF POSITIVE VALUE IN IMPROVEMENT OF MOTOR PERFORMANCE. THIS PAPER GIVES THE INTERVENTIONIST AND PARENT A TOOL FOR DETERMINING THE INFANT'S FUNCTIONAL LEVEL, USING THE PRINCIPLE THAT MATURATION PROCEEDS IN A CEPHALOCAUDAL DIRECTION. THE CHILD IS TO BE RATED ON A LIST OF MOTOR SKILLS RELATED TO HEAD CONTROL AND TO LOCOMOTION. USING THIS ASSESSMENT AS A BASIS, AND WITH THE PHYSICIAN'S APPROVAL, THE INTERVENTIONIST CAN SUGGEST STIMULATION EXERCISES FOR THE CHILD WHICH WILL HELP HIM TO LEARN TO PERFORM PHYSICAL TASKS, IN SEQUENCE AND OVER A PERIOD OF TIME. DETAILED INSTRUCTIONS AND DIAGRAMS ARE GIVEN FOR HELPING THE CHILD TO ATTAIN 18 MOTOR SKILLS, WHICH RANGE FROM RAISING THE HEAD TO WALKING UNAIDED. THE VERBAL RESPONSE OF THE PARENT, BOTH IN PROVIDING DIRECTION AND IN SHOWING PLEASURE AND PRAISE, IS OF CRUCIAL IMPORTANCE TO THE SUCCESS OF THE RETARDED CHILD IN PERFORMING THESE PROGRAMMED EXERCISES. (NH)

ED038180 PS003156
YOUNG BLACK AND WHITE LISTENERS. WALTERS, ELIZABETH, MAR 70 3P.
EDRS PRICE MF-$0.65 HC-$3.29

THE PURPOSES OF THIS STUDY WERE (1) TO DEVISE TWO FORMS OF AN INSTRUMENT FOR MEASURING THE LISTENING ABILITY OF FIRST, SECOND, AND THIRD GRADERS; (2) TO TEST THE INSTRUMENT ON STUDENTS AND TEACHERS; AND (3) TO MEASURE THE RELIABILITY OF THE INSTRUMENT. TO OBTAIN OBJECTIVE DATA CONCERNING THE LISTENING ABILITY OF YOUNG CHILDREN (6-9), FOUR SUBPROBLEMS WERE EXAMINED: (1) THE RELATIONSHIP OF LISTENING ABILITY TO INTELLIGENCE AND ACHIEVEMENT AND THE RELATIVE LISTENING ABILITIES OF (2) MALES AND FEMALES, (3) FIRST, SECOND, AND THIRD GRADERS, AND (4) BLACK AND WHITE STUDENTS. THE LISTENING SKILLS MEASURED (COMPREHENSION, INTERPRETATION, AND EVALUATION) WERE DERIVED FROM BLOOM'S TAXONOMY. THE LISTENING TEST WAS ADMINISTERED TO 453 WHITE AND 255 BLACK PRIMARY SCHOOL CHILDREN BY THEIR OWN TEACHERS. ACHIEVEMENT WAS MEASURED BY THE STANFORD ACHIEVEMENT TESTS AND INTELLIGENCE BY THE KUHLMAN-ANDERSON TEST. ANALYSIS OF THE DATA INDICATED THAT LISTENING ABILITY CORRELATED MORE HIGHLY WITH ACHIEVEMENT THAN WITH THE INTELLIGENCE MEASURE. THERE WAS NO DIFFERENCE IN THE LISTENING SCORES OF MALES AND FEMALES. THERE WAS A SIGNIFICANT, BUT NOT UNEXPECTED, DIFFERENCE IN SCORES OBTAINED BY STUDENTS IN EACH GRADE LEVEL. AN EXTREMELY SIGNIFICANT DIFFERENCE REVEALED THAT BLACK CHILDREN WERE ABOUT ONE STANDARD DEVIATION BELOW WHITE CHILDREN AS MEASURED BY THESE LISTENING ABILITY INSTRUMENTS. (MH)

ED038181 PS003158
DEVELOPMENT OF THE EARLY CHILDHOOD EDUCATION PROGRAM. BASIC PLAN. , 15 SEP 69 12P.
EDRS PRICE MF-$0.65 HC-$3.29

THE EARLY CHILDHOOD EDUCATION PROGRAM DESCRIBED IN THIS REPORT IS A 3-YEAR PROGRAM OF PRESCHOOL EDUCATION TO PREPARE 6-YEAR-OLD RURAL CHILDREN TO PERFORM TASKS AND ACQUIRE SKILLS EXPECTED OF THE AVERAGE CHILD AT THE FIRST GRADE LEVEL. LANGUAGE, COGNITION, MOTOR SKILLS, AND ORIENTING AND ATTENDING SKILLS ARE EMPHASIZED. THIS PROGRAM IS PROPOSED AS AN ALTERNATIVE TO CONVENTIONAL KINDERGARTEN IN APPALACHIA. THE PROGRAM WILL BE CONSIDERED SUCCESSFUL IF ALL CHILDREN WITH IQS OF 90 AND ABOVE, MASTER 90 PERCENT OF 250 BEHAVIORAL OBJECTIVES. THE STRATEGY IS TO DEVELOP A CHILD-CENTERED, HOME-ORIENTED PROGRAM FOR 3-, 4-, AND 5-YEAR-OLDS. TELEVISION BROADCASTS, BASED ON SPECIFIC BEHAVIORAL OBJECTIVES, WILL BE PRESENTED ON COMMERCIAL CHANNELS. WEEKLY HOME VISITS WILL BE MADE BY TRAINED PARAPROFESSIONALS DRAWN FROM THE FIELD TEST AREA, AND A MOBILE CLASSROOM WILL PROVIDE A SETTING FOR GROUP ACTIVITIES AND SOCIAL DEVELOPMENT OF CHILDREN. OVER A PERIOD OF 5 YEARS, THE PROGRAM'S WORK PLAN PROVIDES FOR 1 YEAR OF DESIGN, 3 YEARS OF FORMATIVE EVALUATION, AND 1 YEAR OF SUMMATIVE EVALUATION AND PROGRAM DESCRIPTION (JULY 1971 - JUNE 1972). ESTIMATED COSTS FOR THE TOTAL PROGRAM ARE PRESENTED. (DR)

ED038182 PS003160
EXTENDING OPEN EDUCATION IN THE UNITED STATES. SPODEK, BERNARD, 5 MAR 70 18P.
EDRS PRICE MF-$0.65 HC-$3.29

THE EDUCATIONAL IDEALOGY AND ADMINISTRATION OF THE PERSON-ORIENTED ENGLISH INFANT SCHOOL AND THE OBJECT-ORIENTED TRADITIONAL AMERICAN PRIMARY SCHOOL ARE CONTRASTED IN THIS PAPER. THE ENGLISH INFANT SCHOOL MOVEMENT IS A CONTEMPORARY MODEL OF OPEN EDUCATION. DEVELOPMENT OF OPERN EDUCATIONAL SYSTEMS IN AMERICA SHOULD EMPHASIZE TRANSFER OF THE SPIRIT OF THE ENGLISH INFANT SCHOOL, RATHER THAN ITS PHYSICAL ATTRIBUTES ALONE. DIRECT IMPORTATION IS QUESTIONABLE, FOR ENGLISH INFANT SCHOOLS HAVE DEVELOPED AS A UNIQUE REFLECTION OF ENGLISH SOCIETY AND CHILD WELFARE CONCERNS. ATTEMPTS TO DEVELOP OPEN EDUCATIONAL OPPORTUNITIES HERE SHOULD BE TEACHER-ORIENTED. RATHER THAN IMPOSING AN OUTSIDE MODEL ON TEACHERS, THE MODEL SHOULD BE PROVIDED AND TEACHERS HELPED TO UNDERSTAND IT. TEACHERS WHO ACCEPT THE MODEL SHOULD BE GIVEN SUPPORT AND RESOURCES TO HELP THEM DEVELOP OPEN CLASSROOMS. THIS SUPPORT INVOLVES NOT ONLY SPECIFIC TECHNIQUES, BUT REINFORCEMENT OF TEACHER'S BELIEF IN THE CHILD AND IN THE AUTONOMY OF THE CLASSROOM AS A LEGITIMATE GOAL. AN INCREASING POLARIZATION OF EDUCATIONAL SYSTEMS IN THIS COUNTRY TO SERVE DIFFERENT SEGMENTS OF SOCIETY IS SEEN AS A TREND IN THE FUTURE. (NH)

ED038183 PS003161
TEACHER EXPECTANCY OR MY FAIR LADY. FLEMING, ELYSE S.; ANTTONEN, RALPH C., 5 MAR 70 18P.
EDRS PRICE MF-$0.65 HC-$3.29

THIS STUDY EXAMINED THE EFFECTS OF TEACHER EXPECTANCY ON CHANGES IN INTELLIGENCE, KNOWN AS THE PHENOMENON OF THE SELF-FULFILLING PROPHECY. DIFFERENCES IN SEX, SOCIOECONOMIC STATUS, AND TEACHER OPINION ABOUT STANDARDIZED TESTS WERE CONTROL FACTORS. THE TEACHERS COMPLETED A QUESTIONNAIRE THAT PROVIDED THE BASIS FOR CLASSIFYING TEACHERS INTO HIGH, MIDDLE, AND LOW OPINION GROUPS WITH REGARD TO THE VALUE THEY PLACED UPON THE USEFULNESS OF INTELLIGENCE TESTS. A TOTAL OF 859 SECOND GRADE STUDENTS IN 39 CLASSES, WITH HIGH AND LOW POVERTY BACKGROUNDS, WERE RANDOMLY ASSIGNED TO ONE OF FOUR TREATMENT CONDITIONS. TEACHERS WERE PROVIDED WITH ONE OF FOUR KINDS OF TEST INFORMATION FOR EACH GROUP: (1) KUHLMANN-ANDERSON IQ REPORTED AS TESTED, (2) IQS INFLATED BY 16 POINTS, (3) PRIMARY MENTAL ABILITIES PERCENTILES, AND (4) INTELLIGENCE TEST INFORMATION WITHHELD ENTIRELY. FOLLOWING RE-TESTING SEVERAL MONTHS LATER, TEACHERS WERE ASKED TO ASSESS IQ ACCURACY FOR EACH CHILD. NO SIGNIFICANT IQ DIFFERENCES WERE FOUND AMONG THE FOUR TREATMENT GROUPS OR BETWEEN SEXES. THERE WERE SIGNIFICANT DIFFERENCES BETWEEN TEACHER OPINION, SOCIOECONOMIC STATUS, AND FOR THE INTERACTION OF TEACHER OPINION AND SOCIOECONOMIC STATUS. THE STUDY FAILED TO SUPPORT A GENERALIZED SELF-FULFILLING PROPHECY. (AUTHOR/DR)

ED038184 PS003164
THE DEVELOPMENT OF A COMPUTER TECHNIQUE FOR THE CONTENT ANALYSIS OF PSYCHO-SOCIAL FACTORS IN THE ORAL LANGUAGE OF KINDERGARTEN CHILDREN. SAUSE, EDWIN F.; CROWLEY, FRANCIS J., MAR 70 10P.
EDRS PRICE MF-$0.65 HC-$3.29

TO FIND OUT IF A COMPUTER COULD BE PROGRAMMED TO EFFICIENTLY ANALYZE THE PSYCHOSOCIAL FACTORS IN THE SPEECH OF CHILDREN, TAPED LANGUAGE SAMPLES WERE COLLECTED FROM STRUCTURED INTERVIEWS WITH 81 MALE AND 63 FEMALE KINDERGARTEN CHILDREN. THIRTY PSYCHOLOGICAL AND SOCIAL FACTORS RELEVANT TO CHILDREN'S SPEECH WERE DRAWN FROM THE WORDS IN THE SAMPLES. A GROUP OF SCHOOL PSYCHOLOGISTS THEN INDEPENDENTLY PLACED EACH SAMPLE WORD INTO ITS APPROPRIATE CATEGORY TO FORM A CONTENT ANALYSIS DICTIONARY. SUBSEQUENT COMPUTER CONTENT ANALYSIS OF DATA AGREED CLOSELY WITH THE CONTENT ANALYSIS PERFORMED BY A KINDERGARTEN TEACHER. COMPUTER CONTENT ANALYSIS OF SEX DIFFERENCES ALSO AGREED CLOSELY WITH RESEARCH AND OPINION ABOUT PERSONALITY DIFFERENCES IN BOYS AND GIRLS. IT WAS CONCLUDED THAT COMPUTER ANALYSIS OF PSYCHOSOCIAL FACTORS IN THE LANGUAGE OF YOUNG CHILDREN IS A QUICK, EFFICIENT WAY TO GATHER INFORMATION THAT WAS PREVIOUSLY EXPENSIVE AND TIME CONSUMING TO OBTAIN. THE SECOND PART OF THIS DOCUMENT IS A PAPER WHICH DESCRIBES THE DEVELOPMENT OF THE ANALYSIS TECHNIQUE USED IN THE LANGUAGE STUDY AND CONTAINS THE DATA AND IMPLICATIONS OF THE PROJECT. (MH)

ED038185 PS003165
PUPIL IMITATION OF A REWARDING TEACHER'S VERBAL BEHAVIOR. FRIEDMAN, PHILIP; BOWERS, NORMAN D., [69] 13P.
EDRS PRICE MF-$0.65 HC-$3.29

THIRTY CLASSROOMS (10 PRESCHOOL, 10 KINDERGARTEN, AND 10 FIRST GRADE) IN NEW YORK AND CHICAGO WERE OBSERVED IN THIS STUDY OF TEACHER AND STUDENT VERBAL BEHAVIOR. THE STUDY INVESTIGATED THE EXTENT TO WHICH PUPILS IMITATE A REWARDING TEACHER'S VERBAL STYLE WHEN TALKING AMONG THEMSELVES. FROM THE 10 CLASSES AT EACH GRADE LEVEL, THE SIX THAT SHOWED THE HIGHEST FREQUENCY OF TEACHER REINFORCING VERBAL BEHAVIOR WERE CHOSEN FOR FURTHER OBSERVATION AND DESIGNATED THE "REWARDING TEACHER" GROUP. THE FINAL SAMPLE OF 72 STUDENTS WAS DERIVED BY RANDOMLY SELECTING FOUR STUDENTS (TWO BOYS; TWO GIRLS) FROM EACH OF THE CLASSES. PUPIL VERBAL STATEMENTS WERE SCORED USING FIVE SCALES OF IMITATIVE BEHAVIOR DEVELOPED FROM THE OBSERVATION SCHEDULE AND RECORD 4V (OSCAR) PROTOCOLS. THE DATA WERE ANALYZED USING A 2X3 FACTORIAL DESIGN (SEX X GRADE LEVELS). THE RECORDS OF TEACHER AND PUPIL VERBAL CHARACTERISTICS WERE MADE NEAR THE END OF THE SCHOOL YEAR BY TRAINED OBSERVERS WHO HAD SPENT ADAPTIVE TIME IN THE CLASSROOMS BEFORE COLLECTING ANY DATA. THE MAJOR FINDINGS WERE THAT GIRLS IMITATED MORE THAN BOYS AND THAT IMITATION INCREASED WITH GRADE LEVEL. IT IS FELT THAT THESE FINDINGS ARE IMPORTANT IN DEMONSTRATING THE USEFULNESS OF THE OSCAR TECHNIQUE FOR MEASURING CONSTRUCTS SUCH AS IMITATION AND FOR MEASURING PUPIL AS WELL AS TEACHER BEHAVIOR. (MH)

ED038186 PS003166
CONDITIONAL LOGIC AND PRIMARY CHILDREN. ENNIS, ROBERT H., 6 MAR 70 13P.
EDRS PRICE MF-$0.65 HC-$3.29

CONDITIONAL LOGIC, AS INTERPRETED IN THIS PAPER, MEANS DEDUCTIVE LOGIC CHARACTERIZED BY "IF-THEN" STATEMENTS. THIS STUDY SOUGHT TO INVESTIGATE THE KNOWLEDGE OF CONDITIONAL LOGIC POSSESSED BY PRIMARY CHILDREN AND TO TEST THEIR READINESS TO LEARN SUCH CONCEPTS. NINETY STUDENTS WERE DESIGNATED THE EXPERIMENTAL GROUP AND PARTICIPATED IN A 15-WEEK PROGRAM OF WEEKLY AUDIO-TUTORIAL LESSONS IN CONDITIONAL LOGIC. 87 PUPILS WERE IN A CONTROL GROUP. A MEASURE OF VERBAL INTELLIGENCE, AND INFORMATION ABOUT SOCIOECONOMIC STATUS, AND RURAL, SUBURBAN, OR URBAN DWELLING AREAS WERE COLLECTED FROM BOTH GROUPS. AT THE END OF THE 15 WEEKS, THE SMITH-STURGEON CONDITIONAL REASONING TEST WAS ADMINISTERED TO BOTH GROUPS TO ASSESS THE EFFECTS OF THE LESSONS. THERE WAS NO SIGNIFICANT INTERGROUP DIFFERENCE. THEREFORE, ALTHOUGH THE EXPERIMENTAL METHOD DID NOT EFFECTIVELY TEACH CONDITIONAL LOGIC, MANY OF THE CHILDREN HAD ALREADY MASTERED IT EVEN THOUGH THEY WERE WELL BELOW THE AGE OF 11 TO 12 WHICH PIAGET CONSIDERED NECESSARY FOR MASTERY. CONDITIONAL LOGIC ABILITY WAS FOUND TO BE SIGNIFICANTLY RELATED TO VERBAL INTELLIGENCE AND SOCIOECONOMIC STATUS, BUT NOT TO SEX. (MH)

ED038187 PS003168
A DISCUSSION OF RESEARCH AIMS AND STRATEGIES FOR STUDYING EDUCATION IN THE INNER-CITY (A CRITIQUE OF NON-PARTICIPANT OBSERVATIONS). PRELIMINARY DRAFT. TALBERT, CAROL, 2 MAR 70 24P.
EDRS PRICE MF-$0.65 HC-$3.29

THE OBJECTIVE OF NATURALISTIC OBSERVATIONS CONDUCTED IN SCHOOLS AND HOMES IN THE INNER CITY WAS TO RELATE TEACHER EXPECTATION TO PUPIL BEHAVIOR. FOLLOWING KINDERGARTEN OBSERVATIONS, SELECTED BLACK CHILDREN PREDICTED AS POTENTIALLY SUCCESSFUL AND BLACK CHILDREN PREDICTED AS POOR ACHIEVERS WERE OBSERVED IN THEIR HOMES ALONG WITH THEIR MOTHERS. THIS REPORT IS A CRITIQUE OF THE RESEARCH METHODS EMPLOYED IN THE STUDY. IT SUGGESTS THAT NATURAL OBSERVATION IS PARTICULARLY SUITED TO WHITE MIDDLE CLASS PARTICIPANTS. FOR A MINORITY GROUP SUBCULTURE, HOWEVER, THE CONCEPT OF A "UNI-CULTURAL" VIEW OF AMERICAN FAMILIES DOES NOT APPLY. THE ALTERNATIVE OFFERED IS AN ANTHROPOLOGICAL APPROACH, IN WHICH THE OBSERVER ASSUMES AN ACTIVIST POSITION TO DEVELOP AN HONEST RECIPROCAL RELATIONSHIP WITH THE SUBJECTS. FOR THE PURPOSES OF CURRICULUM GUIDES AND TEACHER TRAINING, AN ATTEMPT SHOULD BE MADE TO ELIMINATE MIDDLE CLASS BIASES AND STEREOTYPES WHEN STUDYING BLACK CHILDREN'S LEARNING PATTERNS. THE BEHAVIORS OF POOR BLACK CHILDREN AT HOME AND IN SCHOOL DIFFER FROM THOSE OF MIDDLE

CLASS WHITE CHILDREN. THEIR EDUCATIONAL NEEDS ARE ALSO DIFFERENT. THE CONCEPTS OF AGE, STATUS, SEX, AND COMMUNICATION FACTORS ARE DISCUSSED AS THEY APPLY TO THESE DIFFERENCES. THE APPENDIX OFFERS A SELECTION OF TAPE-RECORDED DATA THAT ILLUSTRATE THE CONTENT OF BLACK CHILDREN'S VERBALIZATIONS AND THEMES. (DR)

ED038188 PS003213
SOUTHWESTERN COOPERATIVE EDUCATIONAL LABORATORY INTERACTION OBSERVATION SCHEDULE (SCIOS): A SYSTEM FOR ANALYZING TEACHER-PUPIL INTERACTION IN THE AFFECTIVE DOMAIN. BEMIS, KATHERINE A.; LIBERTY, PAUL G., 2 MAR 70 12P.
EDRS PRICE MF-$0.65 HC-$3.29

THE SOUTHWESTERN COOPERATIVE INTERACTION OBSERVATION SCHEDULE (SCIOS) IS A CLASSROOM OBSERVATION INSTRUMENT DESIGNED TO RECORD PUPIL-TEACHER INTERACTION. THE CLASSIFICATION OF PUPIL BEHAVIOR IS BASED ON KRATHWOHL'S (1964) THEORY OF THE THREE LOWEST LEVELS OF THE AFFECTIVE DOMAIN. THE LEVELS ARE (1) RECEIVING: THE LEARNER SHOULD BE SENSITIZED TO THE EXISTENCE OF CERTAIN PHENOMENA AND STIMULI, (2) RESPONDING: THE STUDENT'S RESPONSES GO BEYOND MERELY ATTENDING TO THE PHENOMENA, AND (3) VALUING: THE STUDENT'S BEHAVIOR IS CONSISTENT AND STABLE ENOUGH TO HAVE TAKEN ON THE CHARACTERISTICS OF A BELIEF OR ATTITUDE. CLASSIFICATION OF TEACHER BEHAVIOR WAS BASED ON SULLIVAN'S (1953) SOCIAL-PSYCHOLOGICAL THEORY OF PERSONALITY. THERE ARE TWO MAJOR CATEGORIES OF TEACHER BEHAVIOR: (1) BEHAVIOR THAT RESULTS IN TENSION-REDUCTION AND NEED SATISFACTION FOR THE STUDENT, AND (2) BEHAVIOR THAT INCREASES STUDENT TENSION OR ANXIETY. USE OF THE SCIOS IN THE CLASSROOM TAKES 16 MINUTES WITH AN ADDITIONAL 5 MINUTES FOR FORM INFORMATION, SUCH AS TEACHER'S CODE NUMBER AND THE DATE AND TIME OF THE CLASS. DURING THE FIRST 5 MINUTES IN THE CLASS, AN OBSERVER RECORDS SUBJECTIVE IMPRESSIONS OF VISUAL AIDS AND CLASSROOM ATMOSPHERE. THE OBSERVER THAN RECORDS TEACHER AND PUPIL BEHAVIORS IN EIGHT SECTIONS ON THE SCHEDULE, EACH REQUIRING A 2-MINUTE TIME SEGMENT. A COPY OF THE OBSERVATION SCHEDULE IS INCLUDED IN THIS REPORT. (MH)

ED038189 PS003216
RELATIONSHIPS BETWEEN TEACHER BEHAVIOR, PUPIL BEHAVIOR, AND PUPIL ACHIEVEMENT. BEMIS, KATHERINE A.; LUFT, MAX, 2 MAR 70 24P.
EDRS PRICE MF-$0.65 HC-$3.29

IN THIS STUDY, WHICH WAS DESIGNED TO EXAMINE THE RELATIONSHIPS AMONG TEACHER BEHAVIOR, STUDENT BEHAVIOR, AND STUDENT ACHIEVEMENT, THE SOUTHWESTERN COOPERATIVE EDUCATIONAL LABORATORY INTERACTION OBSERVATION SCHEDULE (SCIOS) WAS DEVELOPED. USING THIS INSTRUMENT, PUPIL BEHAVIORS WERE ISOLATED TO ASSESS THE DEGREE TO WHICH PUPILS (1) RECEIVE, (2) RESPOND TO, AND (3) VALUE A STIMULUS; IN THIS CASE, THE TEACHER. TEACHER BEHAVIORS WERE CATEGORIZED AS EITHER TENSION-REDUCING OR TENSION-INCREASING FOR PUPILS. THE SUBJECTS OF OBSERVATION WERE 15 TEACHERS AND 296 FIRST GRADERS IN TITLE I SCHOOLS. PUPILS WERE PRE- AND POSTTESTED ON THE LEE-CLARK READING READINESS TEST. STATISTICAL ANALYSES OF 18 TEACHER BEHAVIORS AND 20 PUPIL BEHAVIORS INCLUDED COMPUTATION OF CANONICAL CORRELATIONS, FACTOR ANALYSES, AND MULTIPLE REGRESSION ANALYSES. RESULTS INDICATED THAT THERE WAS A SIGNIFICANT RELATIONSHIP BETWEEN TEACHER AND PUPIL BEHAVIOR AND THERE IS A SIGNIFICANT RELATIONSHIP BETWEEN PUPIL CLASSROOM BEHAVIOR AND PUPIL COGNITIVE BEHAVIOR AS MEASURED BY A STANDARDIZED TEST. NO ATTEMPT WAS MADE TO VALIDATE THE OBSERVATION INSTRUMENT, THE SCIOS. (MH)

ED039011 PS002129
INTELLECTUAL OPERATIONS IN TEACHER-CHILD INTERACTION. ZIMMERMAN, BARRY J.; BERGAN, JOHN R., [68] 16P.
EDRS PRICE MF-$0.65 HC-$3.29

BECAUSE THE PRESSURE OF TECHNOLOGICAL ADVANCEMENT HAS MADE TEACHING FACTUAL KNOWLEDGE INCREASINGLY DIFFICULT, EDUCATORS HAVE BEEN DEVELOPING CURRICULUMS TO TRANSMIT INTELLECTUAL PROCESSES APPLICABLE TO MANY TASKS INSTEAD OF SUBJECT MATTER CONTENT. ONE OF THE 20 EDUCATIONAL FOLLOW THROUGH PROGRAMS, THE TUCSON EARLY EDUCATION MODEL, SURVEYED 42 TEEM-TRAINED TEACHERS (EP) AND 75 NON-TEEM TEACHERS IN IOWA, TEXAS, GEORGIA, AND LOUISIANA TO DETERMINE IF TEACHERS ASK QUESTIONS WHICH ELICIT INTELLECTUAL OPERATIONS IN CHILDREN. TEACHERS WERE AUDIO TAPED FOR 40 MINUTES IN CLASSROOMS. THEIR QUESTIONS WERE CLASSIFIED ACCORDING TO AN INTELLECTUAL OPERATIONS MODEL BASED ON GUILFORD'S STRUCTURE OF THE INTELLECT. THE SIX CLASSIFICATIONS WERE (1) PERCEPTION, (2) COGNITION, (3) MEMORY, (4) DIVERGENT PRODUCTION, (5) CONVERGENT PRODUCTION, AND (6) EVALUATION. ANALYSIS OF DATA REVEALED THAT EP AND NP TEACHERS DIFFERED IN TEACHING STYLE. ALTHOUGH BOTH GROUPS PLACED INORDINATE STRESS ON KNOWLEDGE AND MEMORY QUESTIONS WHICH PRECLUDED THE OPPORTUNITY TO TEACH OTHER INTELLECTUAL OPERATIONS, EP TEACHERS EXHIBITED A SIGNIFICANT SHIFT AWAY FROM THIS PRACTICE. THE TEEM PROCESS APPROACH ATTEMPTS TO PREVENT THE TEACHER'S IMPOSITION OF INTELLECTUAL DEMANDS FOR SKILLS NOT PRESENT IN THE CHILD'S REPERTOIRE AND CAPITALIZES ON THE MOTIVATION INHERENT IN HIS SUCCESS. THIS NEW EMPHASIS MAY HAVE GREAT IMPACT, ESPECIALLY WHEN EMPLOYED TO TEACH DISADVANTAGED CHILDREN. (MH)

ED039012 PS002670
[NATIONAL LABORATORY ON EARLY CHILDHOOD EDUCATION PROGRAM, [69] 399P.
EDRS PRICE MF-$0.65 HC-$13.16

THIS VOLUME EXPLAINS THE PURPOSES AND PROGRAMS OF THE NATIONAL LABORATORY ON EARLY CHILDHOOD EDUCATION. ITS OVERRIDING OBJECTIVE IS TO BROADEN THE BASE OF KNOWLEDGE CONCERNING EDUCATIONAL INTERVENTION AND TO DEVELOP COMPREHENSIVE EARLY CHILDHOOD EDUCATIONAL MODELS. A BRIEF DISCUSSION DEALS WITH THE PROBLEMS, STRATEGIES, AND CAPACITIES OF THE NATIONAL LAB, AND AN OVERVIEW OF ITS PROGRAM IS PRESENTED. THE DOCUMENT IS DEVOTED TO RESUMES OF THE PROGRAMS, PROJECTS, AND ACTIVITIES OF THE LAB NOW IN PROGRESS OR TO BE INITIATED. THESE INCLUDE A PROGRAM OF INTEGRATIVE CAPACITY AND THE DEVELOPMENT OF A RESEARCH CAPACITY. THE RESEARCH ACTIVITIES ARE ORGANIZED INTO THREE MAJOR CATEGORIES: (1) KNOWLEDGE BASE DEVELOPMENT, WHICH CONCERNS STUDIES OF DEVELOPMENTAL PROCESSES, INDIVIDUAL CHARACTERISTICS, AND ENVIRONMENTAL INFLUENCES; (2) APPLIED EXPERIMENTATION, WHICH CONCERNS STUDIES OF INSTRUCTIONAL CONTENT, INSTRUCTIONAL METHODS AND TECHNIQUES, AND INSTRUCTIONAL DELIVERY SYSTEMS; AND (3) THE SUPPORT OF RESEARCH TECHNOLOGY, WHICH INCLUDES INSTRUCTIONAL MATERIALS DESIGN AND TESTING, DESIGN AND VALIDATION OF ASSESSMENT INSTRUMENTS, AND STATISTICAL MODEL DEVELOPMENT. THE LAB IS ALSO CREATING A CENTRALIZED DEVELOPMENT AND DEMONSTRATION PROGRAM AND A RESOURCE PRODUCTION PROJECT. (DR)

ED039013 PS002709
A PIAGETIAN METHOD OF EVALUATING PRESCHOOL CHILDREN'S DEVELOPMENT IN CLASSIFICATION. KAMII, CONSTANCE; PEPER, ROBERT, JUL 69 35P.
EDRS PRICE MF-$0.65 HC-$3.29

A PRESCHOOL CURRICULUM FOR LOWER CLASS CHILDREN WAS DEVELOPED BASED ON PIAGET'S THEORY. EVALUATION PROCEDURES WERE DEVELOPED TO PARALLEL A PIAGETIAN CURRICULUM. ACCORDING TO PIAGETIAN THEORY, THE MECHANISM OF CLASSIFICATION IS THE COORDINATION OF THE INTENSIVE AND EXTENSIVE PROPERTIES OF A GROUP OF OBJECTS. THE ABILITY TO DICHOTOMOUSLY CLASSIFY ALL OBJECTS IN A GROUP OCCURS AT A RATHER HIGH DEVELOPMENTAL LEVEL, ATTAINED IN FOUR STAGES DELINEATED BY PIAGET, AND DISCUSSED AT LENGTH IN THIS REPORT IN RELATION TO THE DEVELOPMENT OF LOGIC. IN A NONNCONTROLLED EXPERIMENT, PRE- AND POSTTESTS WERE GIVEN TO 23 DISADVANTAGED WHITE AND BLACK NURSERY SCHOOL CHILDREN USING THREE SETS OF OBJECTS. THESE SCORES WERE COMPARED WITH SCORES OF 16 MIDDLE CLASS NURSERY SCHOOL CHILDREN. THE PIAGETIAN EXPLORATORY METHOD WAS USED, ALLOWING THE EXAMINER TO HELP THE CHILD TO UNDERSTAND THE QUESTIONS. IT WAS CONCLUDED THAT CURRICULUM SIGNIFICANTLY INCREASED THE CHILDREN'S ABILITY TO MAKE BOTH FIRST AND SECOND DICHOTOMIES AND TO SHIFT CRITERIA. THE MIDDLE CLASS CHILDREN'S CLASSIFICATORY ABILITY REMAINED AT THE SAME LEVEL. BOTH GROUPS PROGRESSED IN THEIR ABILITY TO GIVE VERBAL JUSTIFICATIONS. WITH SUGGESTED MODIFICATIONS, THE TESTING METHOD SEEMS VALUABLE BECAUSE IT EVALUATES THE ABILITY TO COORDINATE BOTH INTENSION AND EXTENSION. (NH)

ED039014 PS002721
STUDIES OF SUCKING BEHAVIOR IN THE HUMAN NEWBORN: THE DIAGNOSTIC AND PREDICTIVE VALUE OF MEASURES OF EARLIEST ORAL BEHAVIOR. KRON, REUBEN E., [68] 22P.
EDRS PRICE MF-$0.65 HC-$3.29

THIS PAPER OFFERS A CONCISE 3-PAGE SUMMARY OF THE RESULTS OF SOME INVESTIGATIONS OF SUCKING BEHAVIOR DURING THE NEONATAL PERIOD. THIS IS FOLLOWED BY A PAGE OF REFERENCES AND 16 PAGES OF PERTINENT DIAGRAMS AND THEIR DESCRIPTIONS. THE INVESTIGATIONS ARE THE RESULT OF AN OBJECTIVE TECHNIQUE DEVELOPED FOR MEASURING THE NUTRITIVE SUCKING BEHAVIOR OF THE NEWBORN. (JF)

ED039015 PS002785
CHILD STUDY-KINDERGARTEN, 1968-69: AN INFORMATION REPORT. VALOTTO, EVELYN; AND OTHERS, SEP 69 133P.
EDRS PRICE MF-$0.65 HC-$6.58

THIS DOCUMENT IS A PROGRESS REPORT ON EFFECTING EDUCATIONAL CHANGE IN A KINDERGARTEN PROGRAM AND ITS INTERIM RESEARCH FINDINGS. A GENERAL DESCRIPTION OF THE PROGRAM AND ITS BACKGROUND ARE GIVEN, FOLLOWED BY AN EXPLANATION OF THE DIAGNOSTIC-PRESCRIPTIVE APPROACH TAKEN IN THE PROGRAM. THIS EXPLANATION INCLUDES DESCRIPTIONS OF THE RATIONALE FOR INSTRUCTION, THE ROLE OF THE KINDERGARTEN TEACHER, STAFF DEVELOPMENT, AND INSTRUCTIONAL MATERIALS. THE REPORT GIVES THE STRATEGY DESIGN FOR EVALUATING THE PROGRAM, WHICH INCLUDES EXTENSIVE OBSERVATIONS MADE IN THE CLASSROOM. CERTAIN OBSTACLES WERE ENCOUNTERED IN CARRYING OUT THIS EVALUATIVE DESIGN; HOWEVER, AND THE REVISED OBJECTIVES OF THE PROJECT ARE STATED. THE LIST OF RECOMMENDATIONS EMPHASIZES EXPANDED USE OF THE DIAGNOSTIC-PRESCRIPTIVE APPROACH THROUGH CURRICULAR AND STAFF DEVELOPMENT, THE INVOLVEMENT OF THE DEPARTMENT OF CURRICULUM AND

INSTRUCTION, AND COMMITMENT OF TIME, PERSONNEL, AND FUNDS TOWARD THE USE OF A DIAGNOSTIC-PRESCRIPTIVE APPROACH IN INSTRUCTION. THE FINAL RECOMMENDATION IS FOR THE SCHOOL SYSTEM TO ESTABLISH PILOT CLASSROOMS TO STUDY ISSUES RELATED TO KINDERGARTEN EDUCATION. (MH)

ED039016 PS002858
COMMUNITY COORDINATED CHILD CARE (4-C) MANUAL. , JUL 69 421P.
DOCUMENT NOT AVAILABLE FROM EDRS.
AVAILABLE FROM: DAY CARE AND CHILD DEVELOPMENT COUNCIL OF AMERICA, INC., 1426 H STREET, N.W., WASHINGTON, D.C. 20005 ($13.00 PLUS $0.75 POSTAGE)

THIS MANUAL, WHICH WILL BE PERIODICALLY SUPPLEMENTED AND REVISED, CONTAINS REFERENCE MATERIALS AND INFORMATION RELATING TO THE COMMUNITY COORDINATED CHILD CARE (4-C) CONCEPT. THE 4-C PROGRAM IS A MECHANISM FOR COORDINATING FEDERAL, STATE, AND LOCAL RESOURCES TO DEVELOP DAY CARE SERVICES IN A COMMUNITY. THE MANUAL EXPLAINS THE STEPS FOR ESTABLISHING A CHILD CARE PROGRAM, INCLUDING ORGANIZATION, FEDERAL-STATE COOPERATION, AND FUNDING PROCEDURES. ONE SECTION DISCUSSES ORGANIZATION ON THE COMMUNITY LEVEL, RANGING FROM PROGRAM OBJECTIVES AND PLANNING TO FISCAL COORDINATION AND ANALYSIS OF RESOURCES. EACH FEDERAL AGENCY INVOLVED IN 4-C IS LISTED AND ITS STRUCTURE AND SERVICES ARE EXPLAINED. TO AID COMMUNITY ORGANIZERS IN WORKING WITH THE GOVERNMENT, A SECTION CONTAINS NAMES AND ADDRESSES OF PERSONS AVAILABLE TO GIVE INFORMATION, CONSULT, AND HELP IN MAKING DECISIONS AFFECTING DAY CARE. SELECTED REFERENCE SOURCES ARE PROVIDED FOR TOPICS SUCH AS PROGRAM PLANNING, CHILD DEVELOPMENT AND EARLY CHILDHOOD EDUCATION, PARENT INVOLVEMENT, AND RESEARCH. APPENDIXES CONTAIN 4-C FACT SHEETS, POLICY STATEMENTS, AND AMENDMENTS RELATING TO CHILD CARE. A BOOKLET ENTITLED "FEDERAL FUNDS FOR DAY CARE PROJECTS" IS INCLUDED. (DR)

ED039017 PS002862
MALNUTRITION, LEARNING AND INTELLECTUAL DEVELOPMENT: RESEARCH AND REMEDIATION. RICCIUTI, HENRY N., 2 SEP 69 33P.
EDRS PRICE MF-$0.65 HC-$3.29

AFTER A DISCUSSION OF THE PROBLEM OF MALNUTRITION AND ITS EFFECT ON INTELLECTUAL DEVELOPMENT, THIS PAPER CONCENTRATES ON THE STUDY OF PROTEIN-CALORIE MALNUTRITION IN INFANTS AND CHILDREN AS IT OCCURS IN POSTNATAL AND SUBSEQUENT DEVELOPMENT. AN OVERVIEW AND SUMMARY OF THE PRINCIPAL INVESTIGATIONS ON THE RELATIONSHIP OF MALNUTRITION TO INTELLECTUAL DEVELOPMENT IS PRESENTED. SOME STUDIES FOCUS ON INFANTS AND CHILDREN WHOSE MALNUTRITION REQUIRED HOSPITALIZATION AND OTHERS CONSIDER NONHOSPITALIZED CHILDREN SUFFERING FROM MALNUTRITION. THE DIFFICULTIES OF DEFINING AND ASSESSING PROTEIN-CALORIE MALNUTRITION AND SEPARATING ITS INFLUENCE FROM OTHER BIOLOGICAL, SOCIAL, AND ENVIRONMENTAL CONDITIONS ARE EMPHASIZED. EXAMPLES OF STUDIES INVOLVING ATTEMPTS TO IMPROVE CHILDREN'S NUTRITIONAL STATUS BY MEANS OF DIETARY INTERVENTION ARE ALSO GIVEN. A DISCUSSION FOLLOWS OF THE SUBSTANTIVE AND PRACTICAL IMPLICATIONS OF THE RESEARCH STUDIES. IT IS CONCLUDED THAT PSYCHOLOGISTS MUST CONTINUE TO DEVELOP EDUCATIONAL PROGRAMS THAT FACILITATE THE PHYSICAL AND PSYCHOLOGICAL DEVELOPMENT OF CHILDREN BOTH AT HOME AND IN SCHOOL. (DR)

ED039018 PS002863
A FOLLOWUP STUDY OF ADOPTIONS: POST-PLACEMENT FUNCTIONING OF ADOPTION FAMILIES. LAWDER, ELIZABETH A.; AND OTHERS, 69 236P.
DOCUMENT NOT AVAILABLE FROM EDRS.
AVAILABLE FROM: CHILD WELFARE LEAGUE OF AMERICA, INC., 44 EAST 23RD STREET, NEW YORK, N.Y. 10010 ($4.00)

THIS VOLUME REPORTS ON THE FINAL PHASE OF A RESEARCH PROJECT TO STUDY THE EFFECTS OF ADOPTION ON PARENTAL, CHILD, AND FAMILY FUNCTIONING. TO PROVIDE A BACKGROUND FOR THE STUDY, THE DEVELOPMENT OF ADOPTION IN THE UNITED STATES AND THE THEORY AND PRACTICE OF ADOPTION ARE DISCUSSED. THE STUDY ASKED THREE QUESTIONS: (1) HOW ADEQUATELY DO ADOPTIVE COUPLES ADJUST TO THE RESPONSIBILITIES OF PARENTHOOD FOLLOWING COMPLETION OF ADOPTION? (2) WHAT INFORMATION ABOUT THE ADOPTIVE PARENTS AND CHILDREN, THAT CAN BE OBTAINED BEFORE THE COMPLETION OF THE ADOPTION, IS PREDICTIVE OF HOW THE FAMILY WILL LATER FUNCTION? AND (3) WHAT ARE THE DEVELOPMENTAL PATTERNS OF ADOPTED CHILDREN? A QUESTIONNAIRE WAS COMPLETED BY 556 ADOPTIVE FAMILIES, AND 200 OF THE FAMILIES WERE LATER INTERVIEWED. ANALYSIS OF THE FINDINGS WAS MADE AND THESE ARE REPORTED IN DETAIL. CASE ILLUSTRATIONS OF ADOPTIVE FAMILIES LEND SUBSTANCE AND PERSPECTIVE TO THE REPORTED FINDINGS BY DESCRIBING BOTH SUPERIOR AND POOR FAMILY FUNCTIONING. A SECTION OF THE BOOK DISCUSSES THE IMPLICATIONS OF THE RESEARCH FINDINGS FOR ADOPTION PRACTICES. APPENDIXES INCLUDE THE QUESTIONNAIRE AND INTERVIEW SCHEDULES AND ANALYSIS OF THE DATA. (DR)

ED039019 PS002864
CHILD WELFARE LEAGUE OF AMERICA STANDARDS FOR DAY CARE SERVICE. REVISED EDITION. , 69 132P.
DOCUMENT NOT AVAILABLE FROM EDRS.
AVAILABLE FROM: CHILD WELFARE LEAGUE OF AMERICA, INC., 44 EAST 23RD STREET, NEW YORK, N.Y. 10010 ($2.50)

REVISED STANDARDS FOR DAY CARE SERVICE ARE GIVEN IN THIS DOCUMENT. THE STANDARDS ARE PRESENTED AS GOALS TO BE ATTAINED, AS DISTINGUISHED FROM MINIMUM REQUIREMENTS FOR LICENSING. STANDARDS APPLY TO ALL CHILDREN RECEIVING CARE OUTSIDE THEIR HOMES WHETHER OR NOT THEY ARE IN COMMUNITY DAY CARE PROGRAMS. CHAPTER TOPICS INCLUDE (1) DAY CARE AS A CHILD WELFARE SERVICE; (2) THE INTEGRATION OF SOCIAL WORK, HEALTH AND EDUCATION IN DAY CARE SERVICE; (3) PARENTAL ROLE; (4) EDUCATION AND CARE OF CHILDREN IN GROUP DAY CARE; (5) CARE OF CHILDREN IN FAMILY DAY CARE HOMES; (6) HEALTH PROGRAMS; (7) SOCIAL WORK IN DAY CARE SERVICE; (8) DAY CARE FOR SCHOOL-AGE CHILDREN; (9) BUILDING AND EQUIPMENT OF THE DAY CARE CENTER; (10) ORGANIZATION AND ADMINISTRATION OF AGENCIES PROVIDING DAY CARE SERVICE; AND (11) COMMUNITY PLANNING AND ORGANIZATION FOR DAY CARE SERVICE. A LIST OF REFERENCES IS INCLUDED. (NH)

ED039020 PS002866
ESTABLISHING TOKEN PROGRAMS IN SCHOOLS: ISSUES AND PROBLEMS. O'LEARY, K. DANIEL, 31 AUG 69 10P.
EDRS PRICE MF-$0.65 HC-$3.29

THIS PAPER SEEKS TO ANSWER SOME OF THE QUESTIONS ASKED BY TEACHERS AND PRINCIPALS WHEN A PROPOSAL FOR A TOKEN REINFORCEMENT SYSTEM IS INTRODUCED AT A PUBLIC SCHOOL. THE QUESTION OF COST SHOULD NOT BE A DETERRENT, SINCE A WELL-PLANNED TOKEN SYSTEM PUTS LITTLE FINANCIAL STRAIN ON A SCHOOL, AND THE TRANSITION FROM TOKENS TO SOCIAL REINFORCERS CAN TAKE PLACE WITHIN 3 TO 4 MONTHS WITHOUT LOSS OF APPROPRIATE BEHAVIOR. AT PRESENT, TOKEN SYSTEMS SHOULD BE UNDERTAKEN ON A PILOT STUDY BASIS IN ORDER TO GENERATE PROGRESS AND EVALUATION DATA ON THE CHILDREN INVOLVED. NECESSARY CONSULTATION TIME IS NOT EXCESSIVE WHEN COMPARED TO THERAPIST HOURS SPENT IN TRADITIONAL THERAPEUTIC CENTERS. TEACHERS NEED NOT WORRY ABOUT THE AMOUNT OF TIME SPENT IN THE ACTUAL DISPENSING OF TOKENS IN THE CLASSROOM, BECAUSE THE SMALL AMOUNT OF TIME IT TAKES IS MORE THAN MADE UP FOR BY TIME SAVED CORRECTING INAPPROPRIATE BEHAVIORS. A TOKEN REINFORCEMENT PROGRAM CAN IMPROVE CLASSROOM BEHAVIORS BUT CAN ONLY ENHANCE ACADEMIC BEHAVIOR WHEN ACADEMIC MATERIALS ARE ADEQUATELY PRESENTED. BOLSTERING THE STUDENTS' CONFIDENCE, INVOLVING THE PARENTS, AND PROVIDING REINFORCEMENT FOR TEACHERS AND ADMINISTRATORS ARE ALSO IMPORTANT ELEMENTS IN THE SUCCESS OF A TOKEN PROGRAM. RECOMMENDATIONS ARE GIVEN FOR THE ESTABLISHMENT OF AN EFFECTIVE TOKEN SYSTEM. (MH)

ED039021 PS002882
EDUCATION FOR SURVIVAL. ALLEN, JAMES E., JR., 23 JAN 70 17P.
EDRS PRICE MF-$0.65 HC-$3.29

IN THIS ADDRESS, JAMES E. ALLEN, JR., ASSISTANT SECRETARY FOR EDUCATION AND U.S. COMMISSIONER OF EDUCATION, DISCUSSES THE RELATIONSHIP OF EDUCATION TO THE PROBLEM OF ECOLOGICAL DESTRUCTION. HE STATES THAT THE SOLUTIONS TO THE PROBLEMS OF AIR, WATER, AND SOIL POLLUTION MAY BE FOUND IN REDIRECTED EDUCATION. THIS "EDUCATION FOR SURVIVAL" CAN SERVE TO REPLACE CONFUSION WITH KNOWLEDGE AND, THUS, BE THE KEY TO HUMAN SURVIVAL. HE MAINTAINS THAT EDUCATION IS MORE IMPORTANT THAN ENVIRONMENTAL LEGISLATION, BECAUSE IN A FREE SOCIETY IT IS ALWAYS THE CITIZENS WHO MUST BEAR ULTIMATE RESPONSIBILITY. HE ASKS HUMANISTS AND SOCIAL SCIENTISTS TO TAKE THE LEAD IN SOLVING OUR PRESENT ECOLOGICAL DILEMMA. THE SPECIFIC TASK OF THE NEW ENVIRONMENTAL/ECOLOGICAL EDUCATION IS TO INSTILL AWARENESS, CONCERN, MOTIVATION, AND TRAINING AT EVERY LEVEL OF LEARNING. (MH)

ED039022 PS002895
WAKULLA COUNTY PRESCHOOL. FINAL REPORT. PARKER, RONALD K., SEP 69 97P.
EDRS PRICE MF-$0.65 HC-$3.29

THIS STUDY'S PURPOSE WAS TO DEVELOP AND EVALUATE PROGRAMS BASED ON PSYCHOLINGUISTIC THEORY FOR RURAL BLACK DISADVANTAGED 4-YEAR-OLDS. THE TREATMENT CONDITIONS, ADMINISTERED IN MOBILE LABS, WERE (1) A 9-MONTH GENERAL ENRICHMENT CURRICULUM, GE (N8 COMPARATIVELY ADVANTAGED WHITE CHILDREN), (2) A 3-MONTH STRUCTURED PEABODY CURRICULUM, P3 (N8 DISADVANTAGED BLACK CHILDREN), AND (3) A 9-MONTH STRUCTURED PEABODY CURRICULUM P9 (N8 DISADVANTAGED BLACK CHILDREN). EACH CHILD WAS MATCHED BY AGE, RACE, SEX, AND SOCIOECONOMIC STATUS TO AN UNTREATED CONTROL CHILD. INTERNAL EVALUATION BY TWO OBSERVERS DOCUMENTED THE ATTAINMENT LEVEL OF EACH CHILD OVER A YEAR AND PROVIDED DIAGNOSTIC DATA FOR THE TEACHERS. EXTERNAL EVALUATION INVOLVED POST-PROGRAM TESTING ON THE STANFORD-BINET, ILLINOIS TEST OF PSYCHOLINGUISTIC ABILITIES, CALDWELL PRESCHOOL INVENTORY, ENGLEMANN CONCEPT INVENTORY SCALE, AND THE METROPOLITAN READINESS TESTS. TEST RESULTS INDICATED: (1) STANFORD-BINET: A TREATMENT EFFECT; FAVORED THE PEABODY

CURRICULUM, (2) ITPA: A TREATMENT EFFECT; FAVORED BOTH THE GE AND P9 CURRICULA, (3) CALDWELL: UNCOVERED ONLY A TREATMENT EFFECT, (4) ENGLEMANN: DID NOT DIFFERENTIATE BETWEEN GROUPS, AND (5) METROPOLITAN: FOUND ONLY A SURPRISING SUPERIORITY OF THE P3 CURRICULUM. MORE THAN ONE-THIRD OF THE DOCUMENT PRESENTS DATA IN TABULAR FORM. (MH)

ED039023 PS002898
DETERMINANTS OF CHILDREN'S ATTEMPTS TO HELP ANOTHER CHILD IN DISTRESS. STAUB, ERVIN, SEP 69 18P.
EDRS PRICE MF-$0.65 HC-$3.29

THIS PAPER REPORTS RESEARCH STUDIES ON THE DETERMINANTS OF CHILDREN'S HELPING OF ANOTHER CHILD IN DISTRESS. EFFECTS OF AGE AND VARIOUS ENVIRONMENTAL CONDITIONS WERE INVESTIGATED. EXPERIMENTS HAD A SIMILAR DESIGN: SUBJECTS WERE GIVEN A TASK AND MADE AWARE THAT A CHILD WAS ALONE IN AN ADJOINING ROOM. THE EXPERIMENTER THEN LEFT THE ROOM AND SUBJECTS HEARD THE CHILD'S DISTRESS SOUNDS; SOBBING AND/OR CALLS FOR HELP. IN ONE STUDY INVOLVING ELEMENTARY SCHOOL CHILDREN, AGE AND NUMBER OF CHILDREN IN THE GROUP WERE THE VARIABLES EXAMINED. A CURVILINEAR RELATIONSHIP WAS FOUND BETWEEN HELPING BEHAVIOR AND AGE. HELPING BEHAVIOR INCREASED FROM K TO GRADE 2, BUT DECREASED FROM GRADE 2 TO 6; SIXTH GRADERS HELPING ABOUT AS MUCH AS KINDERGARTENERS. UP TO SECOND GRADE, PAIRS OF CHILDREN TENDED TO HELP MORE THAN INDIVIDUAL CHILDREN. IN OTHER EXPERIMENTS, 7TH GRADERS WERE GIVEN VARIED INFORMATION ABOUT THE PERMISSIBILITY OF ENTERING AN ADJOINING ROOM FROM WHICH DISTRESS SOUNDS WOULD SUBSEQUENTLY BE HEARD. CHILDREN WHO RECEIVED PERMISSION HELPED SIGNIFICANTLY MORE OFTEN THAN OTHERS. THIS FINDING SUGGESTS THAT SOCIETY MAY OVEREMPHASIZE OBEDIENCE. AN EXPERIMENT ON LEARNING HELPING BEHAVIOR USED KINDERGARTEN SUBJECTS TO TEST VARIABLES OF ROLE PLAYING, INDUCTION, AND SEX. THE FINDINGS SUGGEST THAT TRAINING IN ROLE PLAYING MAY HELP CHILDREN TO LEARN PROSOCIAL HELPING BEHAVIOR. (NH)

ED039024 PS002910
THE KINDERGARTEN, A PLACE FOR LEARNING. BULLETIN TWO: OPERATIONAL GUIDELINES FOR ADMINISTRATORS. , 69 19P.
EDRS PRICE MF-$0.65 HC-$3.29

THIS BULLETIN (SECOND IN A SERIES OF THREE) PROVIDES CURRENT INFORMATION AND BASIC GUIDELINES FOR THE ESTABLISHMENT OR CONTINUATION OF KINDERGARTEN PROGRAMS. THE BULLETIN DISCUSSES PRE-6-YEAR-OLD PROGRAMS IN THEIR HISTORICAL PERSPECTIVE AND INCLUDES A SECTION ON THE CURRENT STATUS OF RESEARCH. THE LEGAL BASIS FOR KINDERGARTENS IS ALSO INVESTIGATED. TERMS SUCH AS EARLY CHILDHOOD EDUCATION, NURSERY SCHOOL, KINDERGARTEN, AND PRIMARY SCHOOL ARE LEGALLY DEFINED. FIVE GUIDELINES ARE GIVEN CONCERNING MANDATORY KINDERGARTENS, LENGTH OF SCHOOL YEAR, DEFINITION OF SCHOOL DAY, ELIGIBILITY FOR KINDERGARTEN ATTENDANCE, AND CONTROL OF COMMUNICABLE DISEASES. ANOTHER 10 GUIDELINES GOVERN OPERATION OF THE PROGRAM. THESE GUIDELINES RELATE TO COMMUNITY RESOURCES, PUPILS' SELF-CONCEPT, PUPIL-TEACHER RATION, STAFF SIZE, DAILY SCHEDULE, CURRICULUM, AND THE FIRST STEPS IN ESTABLISHMENT. INTER-RELATIONS, INTERACTION, AND INVOLVEMENT WITH TEACHERS, AUXILIARY PERSONNEL, PARENTS, ADMINISTRATORS, AND THE STATE DEPARTMENT OF EDUCATION ARE EXAMINED IN THE FINAL BULLETIN SECTION. (MH)

ED039025 PS002911
A SOCIAL LEARNING APPROACH TO EARLY CHILDHOOD EDUCATION. SPAULDING, ROBERT L., [68] 14P.
EDRS PRICE MF-$0.65 HC-$3.29

DURHAM EDUCATION IMPROVEMENT PROGRAM (EIP) SEEKS TO COUNTERACT EARLY STIMULATION DEPRIVATION WITH A CLASSROOM EXPERIENCE BASED ON THE REINFORCEMENT PRINCIPLES OF SOCIAL LEARNING THEORY. THE EIP CLASSROOM EMPHASIZES BOTH WARM, PERSONAL ATTENTION FROM THE TEACHER AND CAREFULLY STRUCTURED, CONCRETE ENVIRONMENTS THAT INVITE EXPLORATION, LANGUAGE, AND THOUGHT. DEVELOPMENT OF SELF CONTROL AND INTRINSIC REINFORCEMENT THROUGH INTELLECTUAL COMPETENCE ARE CLASSROOM GOALS. A PUNISHMENT IS AVOIDED EXCEPT IN CASES OF PERSONAL OR PROPERTY DAMAGE, AND EVEN THEN ONLY CONSISTS OF 3 TO 5 MINUTES OF ISOLATION. SINCE TEACHING IN AN EIP CLASSROOM REQUIRES CERTAIN SPECIALIZED SKILLS, EIP TEACHERS ARE TRAINED IN BEHAVIOR ANALYSIS (THROUGH USE OF THE COPING ANALYSIS SCHEDULE FOR EDUCATIONAL SETTINGS) AND REINFORCEMENT PROCEDURES. INITIAL PROGRAM DATA (OBTAINED THROUGH OBSERVATIONS OF BEHAVIOR) SHOW GAINS IN SOCIALIZATION AND READINESS FOR ACADEMIC INSTRUCTION. GAINS IN INTELLIGENCE HAVE BEEN NOTED FOR CHILDREN WHO HAVE BEEN EXPOSED TO EIP PROGRAMMING FOR THREE YEARS. INVESTIGATIONS WILL CONTINUE TO ASSESS THE STABILITY OF BEHAVIORAL CHANGES. (MH)

ED039026 PS002913
THE KINDERGARTEN, A PLACE FOR LEARNING. BULLETIN ONE: MATERIALS AND EQUIPMENT FOR THE FOURS AND FIVES. , 69 16P.
EDRS PRICE MF-$0.65 HC-$3.29

THIS BULLETIN, THE FIRST OF A SERIES, CONSIDERS THE IMPORTANCE OF A PHYSICAL ENVIRONMENT PLANNED ESPECIALLY FOR KINDERGARTEN CHILDREN. THE CREATIVE USE OF SPACE WITHIN THE CLASSROOM AND OUTDOORS IS DISCUSSED. SUGGESTIONS ARE GIVEN FOR FURNISHING INTEREST CENTERS SUCH AS A HOUSEKEEPING AREA, A SCIENCE COUNTER, AND A PAINTING AREA. GUIDELINES FOR SELECTING EQUIPMENT LIST SPECIFIC MATERIALS NEEDED FOR ACADEMIC ACTIVITIES, WATER AND SAND PLAY, AND SCIENCE EXPERIENCES. OUTDOOR EQUIPMENT, AUDIOVISUAL AIDS, AND STANDARD CLASSROOM MATERIALS ARE CONSIDERED. A BIBLIOGRAPHY OF ESSENTIAL BOOKS FOR THE TEACHER'S LIBRARY IS INCLUDED, AS WELL AS SUGGESTED VOLUMES FOR 4- TO 6-YEAR-OLDS. AN OVERALL COST ESTIMATE FOR EQUIPPING A KINDERGARTEN IS PROVIDED. (DR)

ED039027 PS002914
FOLLOW THROUGH PROJECT, WICHITA UNIFIED SCHOOL DISTRICT 259: INITIAL YEAR, SEPTEMBER 1968 - MAY 1969 EVALUATION REPORT. , OCT 69 156P.
EDRS PRICE MF-$0.65 HC-$6.58

THIS STUDY OBTAINED DATA TO COMPARE THE PROGRESS OF LOW INCOME FOLLOW THROUGH PUPILS WITH FULL-YEAR HEAD START PUPILS ATTENDING REGULAR KINDERGARTEN CLASSES. FIVE GROUPS OF CHILDREN WERE COMPARED ACCORDING TO CLASS CHARACTERISTICS, PARENT PARTICIPATION, TEACHER INTERVIEWS, AND PARENT INTERVIEWS. ALL GROUPS WERE ADMINISTERED THE METROPOLITAN READINESS TEST AND THE WICHITA GUIDANCE CENTER KINDERGARTEN CHECK LIST. ITPA WAS GIVEN AS A PRE- AND POSTTEST. THE HOME CONDITIONS OF THE TWO GROUPS OF PUPILS WHO HAD FULL-YEAR HEAD START WERE FOUND TO BE COMPARABLE. A HIGH LEVEL OF PARENT INVOLVEMENT IN SCHOOL AND SCHOOL-RELATED ACTIVITIES WAS INDICATED. INTERVIEW DATA SHOWED THAT TEACHERS WERE ENTHUSIASTIC ABOUT HAVING TEACHER AIDES AND NOTED IMPROVEMENT IN PUPILS IN THE AREAS OF AWARENESS AND SELF-ACCEPTANCE, DEVELOPMENT OF INTEREST LEVELS AND CURIOSITY, AND READINESS FOR MORE FORMAL INSTRUCTION. OF THE FIVE GROUPS, FOLLOW THROUGH PUPILS SHOWED THE GREATEST GAINS IN ADJUSTMENT TO SCHOOL. ON A TEST OF READINESS, FULL-YEAR HEAD START PUPILS NOT IN FOLLOW THROUGH WERE COMPARABLE TO FULL-YEAR HEAD START PUPILS IN FOLLOW THROUGH. IN LANGUAGE DEVELOPMENT, GREATER MEAN GAINS WERE MADE BY FOLLOW THROUGH PUPILS ON SIX OUT OF NINE SUBTESTS AND ON THE TOTAL SCORE. THE GROWTH OF FOLLOW THROUGH PUPILS WILL BE STUDIED AS THEY PROGRESS THROUGH THE VARIOUS GRADE LEVELS. (DR)

ED039028 PS002915
AN ANALYSIS OF EARLY CHILDHOOD EDUCATION RESEARCH AND DEVELOPMENT. SCOTT, MYRTLE; AND OTHERS, DEC 69 319P.
EDRS PRICE MF-$0.65 HC-$13.16

THIS VOLUME ORGANIZES INFORMATION ON RESEARCH AND DEVELOPMENT IN EARLY CHILDHOOD EDUCATION. GOALS AND OBJECTIVES OF THE 77 PROGRAMS REVIEWED ARE DESCRIBED, AND THE STRATEGIES FOR IMPLEMENTING THE PROGRAMS ARE DISCUSSED. ORGANIZATIONAL FACTORS AND THE PROBLEMS ENCOUNTERED IN THE PROGRAMS AND PROJECTS ARE CONSIDERED. THERE IS A SHORT DISCUSSION OF THE CONCLUSIONS AND IMPLICATIONS OF THE PRECEDING. THE VOLUME CONSISTS OF APPENDIXES, WHICH LIST PROGRAMS OF THE NATIONAL LABORATORY ON EARLY CHILDHOOD EDUCATION, RESEARCH AND DEVELOPMENT CENTERS, REGIONAL EDUCATIONAL LABORATORIES, AND COOPERATIVE RESEARCH PROJECTS. THE GOALS AND OBJECTIVES OF THESE PROGRAMS AND PROJECTS ARE LISTED, AND TAXONOMY SHEETS ARE PROVIDED. EACH PROGRAM IS SUMMARIZED ACCORDING TO TITLE, STAFF, GOALS, METHODS, AND CHARACTERISTICS OF THE USERS. ALSO LISTED FOR EACH OF THE 77 PROGRAMS ARE EXPECTED RESULTS, EVALUATION PROCEDURES, RELATIONSHIP TO OTHER CENTER PROGRAMS, AND CENTER FOCUS. TIME SCHEDULES AND ACTIVITIES WITHIN EACH PROGRAM ARE GIVEN. (DR)

ED039029 PS002916
SELECTED BOOKS ABOUT THE AFRO-AMERICAN FOR VERY YOUNG CHILDREN K-2. BRITTON, JEAN E., SEP 69 19P.
EDRS PRICE MF-$0.65 HC-$3.29
AVAILABLE FROM: BUREAU OF CURRICULUM INNOVATION, 182 TREMONT STREET, BOSTON, MASS. 02111

THE SEARCH FOR AFRO-AMERICAN BOOKS WAS LAUNCHED TO FIND BOOKS WHICH WOULD GIVE BLACK CHILDREN A SENSE OF DIGNITY AND SELF-RESPECT FOR THEIR HERITAGE AND WHICH WOULD HELP WHITE CHILDREN APPRECIATE THEIR FELLOW AMERICANS. THE SHORTAGE OF SUCH BOOKS IS DISCUSSED. CRITERIA IS GIVEN FOR SELECTING AND FOR EVALUATING CHILDREN'S BOOKS, ESPECIALLY IN REFERENCE TO THE BOOKS INCLUDED IN THIS BIBLIOGRAPHY. BOTH WHITE AND AFRO-AMERICAN AUTHORS ARE REPRESENTED WITH 44 BOOKS OF FICTION, AND 17 NONFICTION BOOKS ANNOTATED. EACH REFERENCE INCLUDES THE NAME AND ADDRESS OF THE PUBLISHER AND THE PRICE OF THE BOOK. FIFTEEN BIBLIOGRAPHIES OF CHILDREN'S BOOKS ABOUT AFRO-AMERICANS ARE LISTED. (DR)

ED039030 PS002917
THE EFFECT OF A PRESCHOOL EXPERIENCE UPON INTELLECTUAL FUNCTIONING AMONG FOUR-YEAR-OLD, WHITE CHILDREN IN RURAL MINNESOTA. LARSON, DARO E., 69 8P.
EDRS PRICE MF-$0.65 HC-$3.29

THE LANGUAGE, INTELLECTUAL, AND SOCIAL DEFICITS OF ECONOMICALLY DEPRIVED CHILDREN ARE THE TARGETS OF A 4-YEAR STUDY DESIGNED TO FOLLOW THE EDUCATIONAL PROGRESS OF A GROUP OF DEPRIVED CHILDREN FROM PRESCHOOL THROUGH GRADE 3. THIS DOCUMENT REPORTS ON THE PRESCHOOL YEAR, THE FIRST PHASE OF THE LONGITUDINAL STUDY, WHICH INVESTIGATED WHETHER OR NOT THERE IS A SIGNIFICANT INTELLIGENCE TEST SCORE DIFFERENCE BETWEEN (1) CHILDREN WHO ATTENDED A 9-MONTH HEAD START PROGRAM AND CHILDREN WHO WERE ELIGIBLE BUT DID NOT ATTEND, (2) CHILDREN WHO ATTENDED THE PROGRAM AND CHILDREN WHO WERE NOT ELIGIBLE, AND (3) CHILDREN BEFORE THEY ATTENDED THE PROGRAM AND THE SAME CHILDREN AFTER THE PROGRAM. THE SUBJECTS FOR THE 3 GROUPS IN THIS STUDY WERE 108 RURAL, 4-YEAR-OLD CHILDREN (48 MALE, 60 FEMALE). THE HEAD START INTERVENTION EMPHASIZED LANGUAGE DEVELOPMENT, CONCEPT LEARNING, SOCIALIZATION, AND PSYCHOMOTOR DEVELOPMENT. THE INTELLIGENCE TEST USED WAS THE 1960 STANFORD-BINET INTELLIGENCE SCALE. THE CHILDREN WHO ATTENDED THE PROGRAM SCORED SIGNIFICANTLY HIGHER AT POSTTEST THAN AT PRETEST AND SIGNIFICANTLY HIGHER THAN BOTH GROUPS WHO DID NOT ATTEND THE HEAD START PROGRAM. (MH)

ED039031 PS002918
AN APPROACH TO THE STUDY OF INFANT BEHAVIOR. STEDMAN, DONALD J., [66] 13P.
EDRS PRICE MF-$0.65 HC-$3.29

THIS PAPER ON INFANT BEHAVIOR OFFERS A PROGRAM TO POSITIVELY CHANGE DECELERATING MENTAL DEVELOPMENT CURVES IN INFANTS. IT ATTEMPTS TO (1) SUGGEST A THEORETICAL MODEL, (2) PRESENT A DEVELOPMENTAL MATRIX DERIVED FROM OBSERVATION USING THE MODEL, AND (3) NOTE SPECIFIC INSTRUMENTATION FOR INFANT OBSERVATION AND AN EXPERIMENTAL-STIMULATING RESPONSIVE ENVIRONMENT FOR INFANTS. THE THEORETICAL MODEL PROPOSED IS AN EXPANSION OF THE KIRK AND MCCARTHY (1961) PSYCHOLINGUISTIC MODEL. THE PROPOSED MODEL, WHICH IS DIAGRAMMED IN THE APPENDIX, CAN BE A USEFUL RESEARCH MODEL FROM WHICH RESEARCH HYPOTHESES MAY BE GENERATED FOR TEST. AS AN EXAMPLE OF THE CONCEPTUALIZATIONS CONCERNING INFANT BEHAVIOR THAT CAN BE DEVELOPED FROM THIS MODEL, A DEVELOPMENTAL MATRIX IS PRESENTED, ALONG WITH A HYPOTHESIS THAT MIGHT BE DERIVED FROM SUCH A MATRIX. THE HYPOTHESIS IS LIMITED TO THE INPUT PHASE OF INFANTS IN THEIR FIRST 6 MONTHS OF LIFE, BUT OTHER, BROADER HYPOTHESES CAN FOLLOW. FINALLY, AN EXPERIMENTAL-STIMULATING RESPONSIVE ENVIRONMENT IS SUGGESTED BOTH FOR OBSERVING INFANT BEHAVIOR AND FOR MODIFYING IT IN CASES OF DECELERATED GROWTH PATTERNS. (MH)

ED039032 PS002994
CURRICULAR INTERVENTION TO ENHANCE THE ENGLISH LANGUAGE COMPETENCE OF HEAD START CHILDREN. PART OF THE FINAL REPORT ON HEAD START EVALUATION AND RESEARCH: 1968-69 TO THE OFFICE OF ECONOMIC OPPORTUNITY. PIERCE-JONES, JOHN; CUNNINGHAM, GROVER, AUG 69 150P.
EDRS PRICE MF-$0.65 HC-$6.58

THIS RESEARCH WAS DESIGNED TO ASSESS THE EFFECTS OF VARIOUS CURRICULUM MATERIALS AND DIFFERENT LEVELS OF TEACHER TRAINING ON THE COGNITIVE, INTELLECTUAL, AND LANGUAGE DEVELOPMENT OF FULL-YEAR HEAD START CHILDREN WHO WERE GIVEN INTENSIVE LANGUAGE TRAINING. THE CURRICULUM MATERIALS USED WERE THE "SULLIVAN-BUCHANAN READINESS PROGRAM," THE "SULLIVAN ENRICHMENT SUPPLEMENT," THE "SWANSON SUPPLEMENT," AND THE "REINSTEIN REINFORCEMENT PROGRAM" WHICH ARE DESCRIBED IN DETAIL. THERE WERE THREE CONTROL GROUPS AND 10 EXPERIMENTAL GROUPS (FIVE EACH OF ENGLISH AND SPANISH SPEAKERS) GROUPED ACCORDING TO CURRICULUM MATERIALS AND LEVELS OF TEACHER TRAINING. CHILDREN WERE PRE- AND POSTTESTED ON A BATTERY OF LANGUAGE AND INTELLIGENCE TESTS TO DETERMINE THE EXTENT OF CHANGES IN THEIR LANGUAGE COMPETENCE. THERE WERE SIGNIFICANT PRETRIAL INTERGROUP DIFFERENCES ON THE DEPENDENT VARIABLES; HOWEVER, RESULTS MUST BE SEEN IN THE LIGHT OF DIFFERING SUBJECT POPULATIONS. THE EXPERIMENTAL GROUPS WHO RECEIVED A STRUCTURED LANGUAGE PROGRAM SHOWED MORE IMPROVEMENT THAN THE CONTROL GROUPS WHO DID NOT. MORE THAN ONE-HALF OF THIS DOCUMENT IS COMPRISED OF DATA IN TABULAR FORM. (MH)

ED039033 PS003001
A REPORT ON THE RESULTS OF THE ADMINISTRATION OF THE GUMPGOOKIES TEST TO THE TEXAS EVALUATION SAMPLE. PART OF THE FINAL REPORT ON HEAD START EVALUATION AND RESEARCH: 1968-69 TO THE OFFICE OF ECONOMIC OPPORTUNITY. ESPINOSA, RENATO; PIERCE-JONES, JOHN, AUG 69 33P.
EDRS PRICE MF-$0.65 HC-$3.29

AN EXPERIMENTAL TEST FOR ACHIEVEMENT MOTIVATION WHICH CONSISTS OF 100 PICTURES OF IMAGINARY FIGURES CALLED GUMPGOOKIES WAS TESTED ON HEAD START CHILDREN. ON EACH PICTURE, TWO GUMPGOOKIES ARE PRESENTED IN A SEMI-STRUCTURED SITUATION, EACH ENGAGED IN BEHAVIORS THAT REFLECT DIFFERENT DEGREES OF MOTIVATION TO ACHIEVE. THE CHILD BEING TESTED IS ASKED TO SELECT THE GUMPGOOKIE ON EACH PICTURE WHICH IS MOST LIKE HIMSELF, DOING WHAT HE WOULD DO. SUBJECTS WERE 179 NEGRO, MEXICAN-AMERICAN, AND ANGLO CHILDREN. PARENT INTERVIEW DATA WERE EXAMINED AND SUBSCALES WERE CONSTRUCTED TO ASSESS EDUCATIONAL OPPORTUNITIES, ASPIRATIONS AND ATTITUDES, PHYSICAL CONTROL, REJECTION, GUILT, AND REACTION TO INFRACTION. THE 100 ITEMS OF THE TEST WERE CLASSIFIED DEPENDING ON (1) VERBAL CLUES ALONE, (2) VISUAL CLUES ALONE, (3) BOTH VERBAL AND VISUAL CLUES; AND WERE ALSO CLASSIFIED AS EITHER SHORT OR LONG AND EASY OR HARD. AN ITEM ANALYSIS INDICATED THAT CERTAIN SUBJECTS RESPONDED POSITIONALLY THROUGHOUT THE TEST. SOME ITEMS WERE ELIMINATED BECAUSE OF LACK OF RESPONSE CONSISTENCY ON A RETEST. ALTHOUGH POSITIONAL PREFERENCE PROBLEMS WITH THE VERSION OF THE TEST USED IN THIS STUDY HAVE NECESSITATED MAJOR ALTERATIONS, A NEW VERSION OF THE TEST HAS BEEN DEVELOPED WHICH SHOULD SIGNIFICANTLY DECREASE THE POSITIONAL RESPONSE SET. (MH)

ED039034 PS003121
THE EFFECT OF THE MALE ELEMENTARY TEACHER ON CHILDREN'S SELF-CONCEPTS. SWEELY, H. D., 5 MAR 70 7P.
EDRS PRICE MF-$0.65 HC-$3.29

THE PURPOSE OF THIS STUDY WAS TO DETERMINE IF THERE WERE SIGNIFICANT DIFFERENCES BETWEEN SELF-CONCEPT SCORES OF CHILDREN WHO HAD FEMALE TEACHERS AND THOSE WHO HAD MALE TEACHERS IN THE FIFTH GRADE. FIFTEEN MALE AND 15 FEMALE ELEMENTARY SCHOOL TEACHERS' CLASSROOMS WERE RANDOMLY SELECTED FOR OBSERVATION. SUBJECTS WERE THOSE CHILDREN WHO HAD NEVER HAD A MALE TEACHER BEFORE FIFTH GRADE. TESTS USED WERE THE PERKINS SELF-CONCEPT Q-SORT TEST AND THE SRA JUNIOR INVENTORY. ANALYSIS OF THE DATA COLLECTED INDICATED THAT (1) MALE TEACHERS HAD NO DIFFERENTIAL EFFECT ON CHILDREN'S SELF-CONCEPT WHEN COMPARED TO FEMALE TEACHERS, (2) INTERACTION BETWEEN THE SEX OF THE TEACHER AND THE SEX OF THE STUDENTS ON STUDENTS' SELF-CONCEPT SCORES WAS NOT SIGNIFICANT, (3) FEMALE STUDENTS' SELF-CONCEPT SCORES WERE SIGNIFICANTLY HIGHER THAN THOSE OF MALE STUDENTS, (4) INTERACTION BETWEEN INDIVIDUAL TEACHERS AND CHILDREN'S SELF-CONCEPT SCORES WAS NOT SIGNIFICANT, AND (5) MEAN SELF-CONCEPT SCORES DIDN'T VARY FROM CLASSROOM TO CLASSROOM. THE CLAIM OF A NEED FOR MORE MALE TEACHERS IN THE ELEMENTARY CLASSROOM TO ENHANCE THE MALE STUDENT'S SELF-CONCEPT WAS NOT SUPPORTED BY THE FINDINGS. THE SEX DIFFERENCE FOUND BETWEEN STUDENTS' SELF-CONCEPTS HAS STRONG IMPLICATIONS FOR INNOVATORS IN ELEMENTARY SCHOOL CURRICULUMS AND RESEARCH. (MH)

ED039035 PS003273
RESEARCH IN A BLACK COMMUNITY: FOUR YEARS IN REVIEW. COSTELLO, JOAN, MAR 70 23P.
EDRS PRICE MF-$0.65 HC-$3.29

A PSYCHOLOGIST ON THE STAFF OF A RESEARCH PRESCHOOL IN CHICAGO FOUND THAT CONTACT WITH BLACK COMMUNITY LEADERS WAS ESSENTIAL TO THE SUCCESS OF THE PROJECT. SPECIFIC QUESTIONS DEALT WITH THE PROPER FOCUS OF RESEARCH AND THE USE OF RESEARCH FUNDS IN THE COMMUNITY. THIS ESSAY PRESENTS THE RESEARCH PSYCHOLOGIST'S VIEWS CONCERNING THE NEGROES' QUESTIONS ABOUT RESEARCH AND THE PUBLIC'S GROWING DISENCHANTMENT WITH RESEARCH. IT IS RECOGNIZED THAT THE RESEARCH ENTERPRISE ITSELF HAS ENGENDERED PROBLEMS, DERIVING FROM INTERVENTION-EVALUATION PROJECTS, BASIC RESEARCH STUDIES, AND RESEARCH "OVERSELL." INTERVENTION RESEARCH POSES PROBLEMS OF GOALS, METHODOLOGIES, VALIDITY OF FINDINGS, REPLICABILITY, AND THE CHANGE AND CONFUSION IN THE RESEARCHER'S ROLE AS THE PROGRAM PROGRESSES. THE DIFFICULTY OF EXPLAINING BASIC RESEARCH ISSUES TO THE PEOPLE INVOLVED IS DISCUSSED, AND PROFESSIONALS ARE ENCOURAGED TO RESIST THE TENDENCY TO OVERSELL THE PURPOSES AND PROBABLE OUTCOMES OF RESEARCH. CONSIDERING THE CONTEXT OF SOCIAL CHANGE IN WHICH THESE ISSUES ARE RAISED, RESEARCHERS ARE URGED TO BE AWARE OF THEIR VALUES AND GOALS FOR RESEARCH AND TO COMMUNICATE THESE HONESTLY TO BLACK PEOPLE. IN SUM, NEGOTIATIONS BETWEEN RESEARCHERS AND COMMUNITY ARE CONSIDERED A MEANS TO ACCEPTANCE IN THE HOST COMMUNITY AND SHOULD FORM THE BASIS OF VALID RESEARCH DESIGNS. (DR)

ED039036 PS003277
BEHAVIORAL RESEARCH RELEVANT TO THE CLASSROOM. MARTIN, MARIAN, APR 70 56P.
EDRS PRICE MF-$0.65 HC-$3.29

BEHAVIORAL RESEARCH PRESENTS AN ANALYSIS OF THE CLASSROOM IN WHICH SOURCES OF ACADEMIC SUCCESS OR FAILURE ARE SOUGHT IN CONTINGENCIES OF REINFORCEMENT FUNCTIONING IN THE CHILD'S LEARNING ENVIRONMENT. MOTIVATION IS ANALYZED IN BEHAVIORAL TERMS, AND BEHAVIOR PRINCIPLES ARE PROPOSED AS A POWERFUL TOOL FOR TEACHERS FOR THE AMELIORATION OF BEHAVIOR PROBLEMS AND THE INDIVIDUALIZATION OF CURRICULUMS AND EXPERIENCES. MUCH OF THE RESEARCH REPORTED IN THIS PAPER TOOK PLACE IN NATURAL ENVIRONMENTS OF CHILDREN AND INVOLVED COMPLEX BEHAVIORS AS DEPENDENT VARIABLES. NUMEROUS INVESTIGATIONS HAVE SHOWN THAT SOCIAL REINFORCEMENT DISPENSED BY ADULTS FUNCTIONS AS A

POSITIVE REINFORCER FOR MANY BEHAVIORS OF CHILDREN. OTHER STUDIES INDICATE THAT TOKEN REINFORCEMENT, AS PART OF WELL-DESIGNED PROGRAMS, IS EFFECTIVE IN BEHAVIOR MODIFICATION AND IN PROMOTING ACADEMIC ACHIEVEMENT. THE STUDIES REPORTED DEAL WITH HYPERACTIVITY, BEHAVIORAL AND LEARNING DISABILITIES, REMEDIAL PROGRAMS, AND PARENT INVOLVEMENT. THE BEHAVIORAL ANALYSIS OF COMPLEX ACADEMIC BEHAVIORS, SUCH AS SPEECH PATHOLOGY AND READING DIFFICULTIES, HAS ALSO SHOWN PROMISING RESULTS. THE PAPER CONCLUDES WITH A DISCUSSION OF METHODOLOGICAL CONSIDERATIONS, IMPLICATIONS FOR EDUCATION, AND THE VALUE JUDGMENTS INVOLVED IN BEHAVIORAL RESEARCH. (AUTHOR/DR)

ED039037 PS003290
PSYCHOLINGUISTIC BEHAVIORS OF BLACK, DISADVANTAGED RURAL CHILDREN. COWLES, MILLY; DANIEL, KATHRYN BARCHARD, 5 MAR 70 13P.
EDRS PRICE MF-$0.65 HC-$3.29

THIS STUDY WAS DESIGNED TO COMPARE THE PSYCHOLINGUISTIC ABILITIES OF A RANDOMLY SELECTED SAMPLE OF 32 KINDERGARTEN CHILDREN AND 32 FIRST GRADE CHILDREN (WITH NO KINDERGARTEN EXPERIENCE) AND TO ANALYZE ANY DISCREPANCY EXISTING BETWEEN PSYCHOLINGUISTIC AGE (PLA) AND CHRONOLOGICAL AGE (CA). EACH OF THE KINDERGARTEN CLASSROOMS FROM WHICH CHILDREN WERE SELECTED WAS STAFFED BY A TEACHER AND TEACHER ASSISTANT WHO HAD RECEIVED A 6-WEEK INTENSIVE TRAINING SESSION EMPHASIZING LANGUAGE DEVELOPMENT. INSTRUCTION WAS LARGELY INFORMAL, ALTHOUGH PERCEPTION, LANGUAGE, AND CONCEPT DEVELOPMENT WERE EMPHASIZED. A WIDE VARIETY OF MATERIALS WAS AVAILABLE FOR SELF-SELECTION BY CHILDREN. EACH OF THE EIGHT FIRST GRADE CLASSROOMS WAS STAFFED BY ONE TEACHER WHO HAD RECEIVED NO SPECIAL TRAINING. INSTRUCTION WAS HIGHLY STRUCTURED FOR TOTAL GROUP PARTICIPATION IN A TEACHER DOMINATED ATMOSPHERE. THE ROOMS WERE USUALLY VOID OF MATERIALS THAT COULD BE SELF-SELECTED BY STUDENTS. BOTH GROUPS WERE GIVEN THE ILLINOIS TEST OF PSYCHOLINGUISTIC ABILITIES (ITPA) AT THE END OF 5 MONTHS OF SCHOOL. ANALYSIS OF VARIANCE OF THE DATA INDICATED THAT THE KINDERGARTEN CHILDREN SCORED SIGNIFICANTLY HIGHER THAN THE FIRST GRADERS ON SEVEN OF THE 10 SUBTESTS OF THE ITPA AND THAT THE DISCREPANCY BETWEEN CA AND PLA WAS SIGNIFICANTLY LESS FOR KINDERGARTEN SUBJECTS THAN FIRST GRADE SUBJECTS. (MG)

ED039038 PS003300
A STUDY OF THE ABILITY OF PRIMARY SCHOOL CHILDREN TO GENERALIZE BEHAVIORAL COMPETENCIES SPECIFIED FOR "SCIENCE--A PROCESS APPROACH" TO OTHER CONTENT SETTINGS. CARTER, HEATHER L., 70 13P.
EDRS PRICE MF-$0.65 HC-$3.29

CURRICULUM DEVELOPMENT WOULD BE GREATLY AIDED IF IT COULD BE DEMONSTRATED THAT CERTAIN INSTRUCTIONAL TECHNIQUES HAVE A GENERALIZATION EFFECT THAT ENCOMPASSES SEVERAL CONTENT SETTINGS. THE EVIDENCE THAT TRANSFER DOES OCCUR WITHIN THE LEARNING PROCESS IS STRONG ENOUGH TO WARRANT THIS STUDY INTO THE GENERALIZATION OF SCIENCE INSTRUCTION. IT WAS HYPOTHESIZED THAT STUDENTS RECEIVING INSTRUCTION IN A CERTAIN SCIENCE PROGRAM WOULD DOMONSTRATE COMPETENCE IN SOCIAL STUDIES, LANGUAGE ARTS, AND FINE ARTS EQUAL TO OR GREATER THAN THEIR COMPETENCE IN SCIENCE. SUBJECTS WERE 64 STUDENTS RANDOMLY SELECTED FROM GRADES 1, 2, 3, AND 4 IN THE OSHKOSH, WISCONSIN PUBLIC SCHOOLS SYSTEM, WHICH USES SCIENCE - A PROCESS APPROACH. THE INSTRUMENTS USED TO OBTAIN THE OBJECTIVE MEASURES OF STUDENT COMPETENCE WERE THE OBSERVING PROCESS HIERARCHY AND THE SCIENCE PROCESS INSTRUMENT (AAAS, 1967). ANALYSIS OF THE DATA TENDED TO SUPPORT THE HYPOTHESES OF GENERALIZED COMPETENCE IN SOCIAL STUDIES, LANGUAGE ARTS, AND FINE ARTS. THERE WERE SOME RESERVATIONS IN THE RESULTS OF THE THIRD GRADERS WHICH MAY HAVE BEEN CAUSED BY UNCLEAR ITEMS OR ITEMS IN WHICH WORDING OR PROCEDURE WAS TOO COMPLEX. (MH)

ED039039 PS003301
SOCIAL CLASS DIFFERENTIATION IN COGNITIVE DEVELOPMENT AMONG BLACK PRESCHOOL CHILDREN. GOLDEN, MARK; AND OTHERS, 69 15P.
EDRS PRICE MF-$0.65 HC-$3.29

IN A LONGITUDINAL STUDY OF 89 BLACK CHILDREN FROM DIFFERENT SOCIAL CLASSES, WHILE THERE WERE NO SIGNIFICANT SES DIFFERENCES ON THE CATTELL INFANT INTELLIGENCE SCALE AT 18 AND 24 MONTHS OF AGE, THERE WAS A HIGHLY SIGNIFICANT 23 POINT MEAN IQ DIFFERENCE BETWEEN CHILDREN FROM WELFARE AND MIDDLE CLASS BLACK FAMILIES ON THE STANFORD-BINET AT 3 YEARS OF AGE. THE RANGE IN MEAN IQS OF THE BLACK CHILDREN IN THE EXTREME SES GROUPS (93-116) WAS ALMOST IDENTICAL TO THAT OBTAINED BY TERMAN AND MERRILL IN THEIR STANDARDIZATION SAMPLE OF 831 WHITE CHILDREN BETWEEN 2 1/2 AND 5 YEARS OF AGE. THE UNIQUE CONTRIBUTION OF THE PRESENT STUDY IS THAT THE SAME PATTERN OF SOCIAL CLASS DIFFERENTIATION IN COGNITIVE DEVELOPMENT, EMERGING DURING THE THIRD YEAR OF LIFE, PREVIOUSLY REPORTED FOR WHITE CHILDREN HAS NOW BEEN DEMONSTRATED FOR BLACK CHILDREN. (AUTHOR/MH)

ED039040 PS003395
THE PREVALENCE OF BEHAVIOR SYMPTOMS IN YOUNGER ELEMENTARY SCHOOL CHILDREN. WERRY, JOHN S.; QUAY, HERBERT C., 70 17P.
EDRS PRICE MF-$0.65 HC-$3.29

THE PURPOSE OF THIS EPIDEMIOLOGICAL STUDY OF PSYCHOPATHOLOGICAL DISORDERS WAS TO OBTAIN PREVALENCE DATA ON 55 BEHAVIOR SYMPTOMS AS THEY OCCUR IN KINDERGARTENERS AND FIRST AND SECOND GRADERS. THE BEHAVIOR SYMPTOMS ARE COMMONLY FOUND IN CHILD GUIDANCE CLINIC POPULATIONS. THE POPULATION RATED IN THIS STUDY WAS THE KINDERGARTEN AND FIRST AND SECOND GRADERS IN THE URBANA SCHOOL SYSTEM, WHICH INCLUDED 926 BOYS AND 827 GIRLS. THE CHILDREN WERE RATED BY THEIR TEACHERS WITH THE USE OF THE QUAY PETERSON PROBLEM CHECKLIST. THE UNIVERSALITY OF THE POPULATION AND THE DATA IS LIMITED BECAUSE URBANA IS A UNIVERSITY TOWN AND THE PER CAPITA INCOME, EDUCATION LEVEL, AND YOUTH OF THE TOWN IS HIGHER THAN USUAL. ANALYSIS OF THE DATA INDICATED THAT: (1) PREVALENCE OF MANY OF THE PSYCHOPATHOLOGICAL SYMPTOMS IS QUITE HIGH, (2) BOYS HAVE HIGHER RATES OF ACTING OUT OR DISRUPTIVE SYMPTOMS, WHILE GIRLS HAVE SLIGHT EXCESS OF NEUROTIC TYPE SYMPTOMS, (3) THERE IS A TENDENCY FOR MANY SYMPTOMS TO DECREASE AT AGE 5 WITH A SLIGHT INCREASE AGAIN AT 8 YEARS, (4) TOTAL NUMBER OF SYMPTOMS PER CHILD IS SIGNIFICANTLY HIGHER IN BOYS THAN IN GIRLS, AND (5) THERE IS LITTLE DOUBT THAT NOT ONLY DO BOYS HAVE MORE SYMPTOMS THAN GIRLS, BUT FEMALE TEACHERS CONSIDER BOYS MORE TROUBLE THAN GIRLS. (MH)

ED039041 PS003400
THE RELATION OF CERTAIN HOME ENVIRONMENT FACTORS TO THE THINKING ABILITIES OF THREE-YEAR-OLD CHILDREN. FINAL REPORT. BALL, RACHEL S., APR 70 51P.
EDRS PRICE MF-$0.65 HC-$3.29

THIS STUDY INVESTIGATED (1) THREE KINDS OF MENTAL OPERATION IN CHILDREN: DIVERGENT PRODUCTION, CONVERGENT PRODUCTION, AND COGNITIVE THINKING MANIFESTED IN 3- TO 4-YEAR-OLDS AND COMPARED THE RESULTS TO RESULTS OF A STUDY OF 4- TO 5-YEAR-OLDS, AND (2) THE RELATIONSHIP BETWEEN CHILDREN'S ABILITIES AND THEIR PARENTS' LEVEL OF EDUCATION, CHILDREN'S SEX AND AGE, PARENTS' OCCUPATIONS, THE AMOUNT OF TIME THE FATHER SPENDS IN THE HOME AND THE MOTHER SPENDS READING AND PLAYING WITH HER 3-YEAR-OLD, AND THE TYPE OF NURSERY SCHOOL ATTENDED. MOTHER INTERVIEWS AND TEST PROTOCOLS WERE OBTAINED FOR 416 CHILDREN BETWEEN THE AGES 3-0 AND 3-11. RESULTS INDICATED THE MOST STRIKING RELATIONSHIPS BETWEEN LEVEL OF EDUCATION, ENVIRONMENTAL EXPERIENCE, AND ASPECTS OF THINKING ABILITY. CHILDREN WITH MOTHERS AT HOME FULL-TIME WERE LESS ABLE IN VISUAL AND SPATIAL MANIPULATION. CHILDREN WITH PROFESSIONAL FATHERS SHOWED LESS ABILITY BUT SCORED HIGHER IN IDEATIONAL FLUENCY. CHILDREN OF FATHERS WHO ATTENDED COLLEGE WERE MORE ABLE IN CONVERGENT FIGURAL THINKING. MOTHERS' EDUCATION WAS RELATED TO VERBAL TASKS AS WELL AS FIGURAL. SOME GEOGRAPHIC DIFFERENCES WERE FOUND. IT WAS EVIDENT THAT 3- AND 4-YEAR-OLDS SHOWED "TYPES" OF THINKING ABILITY. (AUTHOR/DR)

ED039917 PS001955
ANGER IN CHILDREN: CAUSES, CHARACTERISTICS, AND CONSIDERATIONS. SHEVIAKOV, GEORGE, 69 27P.
EDRS PRICE MF-$0.65 HC NOT AVAILABLE FROM EDRS.
AVAILABLE FROM: PUBLICATIONS-SALES SECTION, NATIONAL EDUCATION ASSOCIATION, 1201 SIXTEENTH ST., N.W., WASHINGTON, D.C. 20036 ($0.75)

THE AUTHOR OF THIS BOOKLET DISCUSSES REASONS FOR ANGER AND WAYS OF COPING WITH IT. WHEN ANGER ERUPTS IN A CLASSROOM, IT MAY BE THE RESULT OF CULTURAL CONDITIONS THAT PRODUCE FRUSTRATION AND TENSION OR ADULT-CAUSED FRUSTRATIONS THAT COULD BE AVOIDED, SUCH AS RIGID RULES OR LACK OF RESPECT FOR THE CHILD. IN DISCUSSING THE CHARACTERISTICS OF ANGER, THE AUTHOR STRESSES THAT ANGER MAY NOT BE CONSCIOUSLY RECOGNIZED BY THE SUFFERER AND THAT ANGER IS CUMULATIVE AND MAY SUDDENLY "EXPLODE." THE DEGREES OF ANGER ARE DISCUSSED, AND DESCRIPTIONS OF ANGER'S PHYSIOLOGICAL EFFECTS ARE GIVEN. GUIDELINES ARE GIVEN FOR TEACHERS AND SCHOOLS TO FOLLOW IN WORKING WITH TROUBLED CHILDREN. INCLUDED ARE CASE DESCRIPTIONS OF TWO CHILDREN WHO WERE SEVERE CLASSROOM PROBLEMS. THE POINT OF VIEW EMPHASIZED IS THAT THE ORIGINS OF A CHILD'S ANGER MUST BE UNDERSTOOD INTELLECTUALLY TO EFFECTIVELY PLAN STRATEGY NEEDED TO HELP THE CHILD. A FLEXIBLE APPROACH TO TREATMENT, INVOLVING THE CHILD ON BOTH THE COGNITIVE AND EMOTIONAL LEVEL, IS URGED. A NONJUDGMENTAL, PATIENT, AND HUMANITARIAN APPROACH IS STRESSED IN HANDLING ANGER IN CHILDREN. (DR)

ED039918 PS002543
EDUCATIONAL DAY CARE: AN INSTALLATION MANUAL. , [69] 105P.
EDRS PRICE MF-$0.65 HC NOT AVAILABLE FROM EDRS.

THIS MANUAL EVALUATES AND DESCRIBES AN EDUCATIONAL DAY CARE MODEL AFTER 1 YEAR OF DEVELOPMENT. THE MODEL WAS DESIGNED FOR 3- AND 5-YEAR-OLD DISADVANTAGED YOUNGSTERS WHO EXHIBIT LOW SCORES ON INTELLIGENCE, LINGUISTIC, AND PERCEPTUAL TESTS. MODEL OBJECTIVES WERE BASED ON THE FOLLOWING CRITERIA: (1) EFFECTIVENESS OF THE CURRICULUM WITH CHILDREN, (2) MANAGEABILITY OF STAFF AND CURRICULUM DEVELOPMENT ACTIVITY, (3) FLEXIBILITY, AND (4) TRANSPORTABILITY OF THE MODEL. THE MANUAL INCLUDES A DESCRIPTION OF POPULATION, A LIST OF BEHAVIORAL OBJECTIVES FOR 3-, 4-, AND 5-YEAR-OLDS, AN ITEMIZED LIST OF EQUIPMENT AND MATERIALS, AND A DESCRIPTION OF STAFF FUNCTIONS. THE MANUAL ALSO INCLUDES A PRELIMINARY ANALYSIS OF TEST SCORES USED TO COMPARE EXPERIMENTAL AND CONTROL GROUPS AND MEASURE LANGUAGE AND PERCEPTUAL DEVELOPMENT. APPENDIX ONE CONTAINS AN OUTLINE OF A 5-YEAR PLAN FOR DAY CARE, AND APPENDIX TWO, WHICH TAKES UP 86 OF THE MANUAL'S 104 PAGES, CONTAINS EXAMPLES OF WEEKLY PLANNING SHEETS AND INSTRUCTIONAL THEMES. [NOT AVAILABLE IN HARD COPY DUE TO MARGINAL LEGIBILITY OF ORIGINAL DOCUMENT.] (JF)

ED039919 PS002896
A SUPPLEMENTARY REPORT ON EVALUATION OF THE NEW NURSERY SCHOOL PROGRAM AT COLORADO STATE COLLEGE. NIMNICHT, GLEN; AND OTHERS, [68] 42P.
EDRS PRICE MF-$0.65 HC-$3.29

THIS REPORT, AN EXPANSION ON "THE INTERIM REPORT: RESEARCH OF THE NEW NURSERY SCHOOL," IS PRESENTED IN THREE SECTIONS. THE FIRST SECTION EXAMINES THE TEST RESULTS OF 29 CHILDREN ENROLLED IN THE NEW NURSERY SCHOOL (NNS, FOR ACADEMICALLY HANDICAPPED, LOW INCOME MEXICAN-AMERICANS) AND THE REN SCHOOL (SIMILAR TO THE NNS BUT FOR CHILDREN WHOSE PARENTS CAN AFFORD TUITION). THE TESTS INCLUDED THE PEABODY, THE CALDWELL, THE "C" TEST, AND THE CATEGORIES TEST. THOUGH THE TESTS HAVE A VERY LIMITED VALUE FOR EVALUATING THE EFFECTIVENESS OF THE PROGRAM AT THIS TIME, THE RESULTS SEEM TO INDICATE THE NNS IS AFFECTING CHILDREN'S BEHAVIOR IN A DESIRED DIRECTION. SECTION TWO, A FOLLOW-UP STUDY OF CHILDREN WHO PREVIOUSLY ATTENDED THE SCHOOLS, USED STANDARD TESTS, SUCH AS THE STANFORD-BINET, AND TEACHER RATINGS. THE TESTS TEND TO SHOW THAT OLD NNS STUDENTS ARE PERFORMING AT LEAST SATISFACTORILY IN THEIR GRADE. THE TEACHER RATINGS, HOWEVER, CORRELATE POORLY WITH MORE OBJECTIVE MEASURES AND LEAD TO THE UNFORTUNATE CONCLUSION THAT TEACHERS ARE STILL PREJUDGING CHILDREN AS POOR-LEARNING STEREOTYPES. THE FINAL SECTION REPORTS ON THE USEFULNESS OF THE "TYPING BOOTH," A FACILITY AT THE NNS. (MH)

ED039920 PS002920
A REPORT ON THE EVALUATION OF THE STATE PRESCHOOL PROGRAM CONTRASTED WITH THE WESTINGHOUSE REPORT ON HEAD START. NOLAN, JEANEDA H., 12 JUN 69 10P.
EDRS PRICE MF-$0.65 HC-$3.29

THIS DOCUMENT IS AN EDITED TRANSCRIPT OF A PRESCHOOL EDUCATOR'S CRITICISM OF THE WESTINGHOUSE REPORT ON THE FEDERAL HEAD START PROGRAM. THE FOLLOWING POINTS ARE MADE: (1) EVALUATIONS SHOULD BE PLANNED AT THE TIME THE PROGRAM IS PLANNED AND THIS WAS NOT THE CASE WITH THE WESTINGHOUSE REPORT, AND (2) AN EVALUATION PROGRAM SHOULD MEASURE THE FACTORS THE EDUCATIONAL PROGRAM INTENDED TO IMPROVE. WHILE THE WESTINGHOUSE REPORT MEASURED SUCH FACTORS AS LANGUAGE DEVELOPMENT, LEARNING READINESS, AND ACHIEVEMENT, THE OBJECTIVES OF HEAD START ARE MUCH BROADER AND INVOLVE HEALTH, SOCIAL, AND EMOTIONAL NEEDS. FURTHER, THE REPORT DIDN'T TEST CHILDREN RIGHT AFTER THEY COMPLETED HEAD START, BUT WAITED TO SEE IF LEARNING GAINS WERE MAINTAINED A FULL YEAR LATER. SINCE HEAD START IS A COMMUNITY PROGRAM, IT DIFFERS FROM ONE TOWN TO ANOTHER IN GOALS AND METHODS AND THEREFORE CAN'T BE EVALUATED ON A NATIONAL BASIS. (MH)

ED039921 PS002921
LANGUAGE FOR LEARNING: ORAL LANGUAGE AND COGNITIVE DEVELOPMENT, PRE-K, K, GRADE 1. SECTION 1, TEACHER'S GUIDE. FLINTON, DORIS HOLT, 69 68P.
DOCUMENT NOT AVAILABLE FROM EDRS.
AVAILABLE FROM: FACULTY-STUDENT ASSOCIATION, STATE UNIVERSITY OF N.Y. AT ALBANY, INC., 135 WESTERN AVE., ALBANY, N.Y. 12203 ($10.95

THIS HANDBOOK FOR TEACHERS CONTAINS LANGUAGE LESSONS FOR YOUNG CHILDREN. THROUGH SEQUENCING AND FEEDBACK, THE PROGRAM USES A DIRECT METHOD OF TEACHING AND LEARNING STANDARD ENGLISH. IT IS AN EXPOSITORY APPROACH, IN WHICH PROGRESS IS BASED ON PERFORMANCE, RATHER THAN ON THE KNOWLEDGE OF RULES. EACH UNIT IS ORGANIZED SO THAT LANGUAGE DEVELOPMENT AND COGNITIVE DEVELOPMENT ADVANCE TOGETHER. THE ORDER OF PRESENTATION OF EACH OF THE 20 LESSONS INCLUDES (1) THE TEACHER'S DEMONSTRATION WITH OBJECTS, PERSONS OR PICTURES WHILE SHE USES THE SENTENCE PATTERNS UNDER THE LANGUAGE STRUCTURE AT THE TOP OF HER PAGE, (2) PUPIL'S RESPONSE WHILE DEMONSTRATING WITH OBJECTS, (3) PRESENTATION OF THE PICTURE IN THE BOOK, (4) PUPIL'S RESPONSE TO THE PICTURE, (5) APPLICATION OF PATTERNS LEARNED ORALLY TO A NEW SITUATION BY THE PUPILS, AND (6) WORKSHEET ACTIVITIES. DESIGNED FOR USE WITH SMALL HETEROGENEOUS GROUPS OF SIX TO EIGHT PUPILS, THE TEACHER IS URGED TO ENCOURAGE FLEXIBILITY AND INVENTIVENESS THROUGH DEMONSTRATION AND EXAMPLE. THIS ORAL LANGUAGE PROGRAM SERVES AS A READINESS PROGRAM FOR BEGINNING READING AND WRITING INSTRUCTION. (DR)

ED039922 PS002923
A COMPARISON OF PARENT AND TEACHER RATINGS ON THE PRESCHOOL ATTAINMENT RECORD OF SEVENTEEN FIVE-YEAR-OLD DISADVANTAGED CHILDREN. STEDMAN, DONALD J.; AND OTHERS, [67] 6P.
EDRS PRICE MF-$0.65 HC-$3.29

THIS PAPER REPORTS ON THE ADMINISTRATION OF THE PRESCHOOL ATTAINMENT RECORD (PAR), WHICH IS USED TO ESTIMATE DEVELOPMENTAL LEVELS IN CHILDREN FROM 6 MONTHS TO 8 YEARS OF AGE. THE PAR WAS GIVEN TO 17 5-YEAR-OLD DISADVANTAGED BOYS AND GIRLS OF AVERAGE INTELLIGENCE. TO REDUCE THE TENDENCY OF EVALUATORS TO INFLATE SCORES, THE TEST WAS ADMINISTERED BY BOTH THE MOTHER AND TEACHER OF EACH CHILD. ATTAINMENT AGES (AA) AND ATTAINMENT QUOTIENTS (AQ) WERE DETERMINED FOR EACH CHILD, AND THESE SCORES WERE COMPARED FOR SIMILARITY OF PARENT AND TEACHER EVALUATIONS. COMPARISON OF AQ SCORES SHOWED THAT PARENTS SCORED BOYS HIGHER THAN TEACHERS DID, BUT THERE WERE NO DIFFERENCES IN JUDGMENTS OF GIRLS' DEVELOPMENTAL LEVELS. IT IS SUGGESTED THAT THE REASONS FOR DISAGREEMENT BETWEEN PARENTS AND TEACHERS ON BOYS' ATTAINMENT BE PURSUED. (DR)

ED039923 PS002924
OSCAR GOES TO NURSERY SCHOOL: A NEW TECHNIQUE FOR RECORDING PUPIL BEHAVIOR. MEDLEY, DONALD M., MAY 69 17P.
EDRS PRICE MF-$0.65 HC-$3.29

A NEW INSTRUMENT FOR CLASSROOM OBSERVATION CALLED THE PERSONAL RECORD OF SCHOOL EXPERIENCE (PROSE), HAS BEEN DEVELOPED AT EDUCATIONAL TESTING SERVICE. WHILE PROSE WAS INVENTED FOR A SPECIFIC PROJECT INVOLVING 2000 4-YEAR-OLD GHETTO CHILDREN, ITS GENERAL APPLICABILITY HAS ALREADY BECOME APPARENT. PROSE REPRESENTS A PRIMITIVE METHOD OF CLASSROOM OBSERVATION SINCE IT DOES NOT PROVIDE AN OBSERVER RATING TYPE OF CLASSROOM RECORD. PROSE STRIVES TO ELIMINATE OBSERVER SUBJECTIVITY BY REQUIRING ONLY THE OBJECTIVE RECORDING OF OBSERVABLE EVENTS. THE RECORD IS ALSO PERSONAL SINCE THE OBSERVER ONLY WATCHES ONE CHILD AT A TIME AND RECORDS ALL HIS ACTIVITY. PROSE IS THUS SIMILAR TO ECOLOGICAL STUDIES, EXCEPT THAT THE CHILD'S RECORD IS CODED IN THE CLASSROOM RATHER THAN FROM A LATER REVIEW OF FILMS AND RECORDINGS TAKEN IN CLASS. THE IN-CLASS CODING IS MADE POSSIBLE BY THE PROSE "LANGUAGE," BASED ON 11 WORD STATEMENTS THAT CAN BE FED DIRECTLY TO THE COMPUTER. STATIC CONDITIONS, SUCH AS SUBJECT MATTER, CLASS ORGANIZATION, AND INSTRUCTIONAL MATERIALS ARE ALSO RECORDED. THE 11 WORD STATEMENTS USED BY THE OBSERVER CODE ALL ASPECTS OF THE PARTICULAR STUDENTS'S CURRENT ACTIVITY, INCLUDING LEVEL OF ATTENTION, PHYSICAL ACTIVITY, AND MANIFEST AFFECT. (MH)

ED039924 PS002929
COGNITIVE ASPECTS OF CHILDREN'S OCCUPATIONAL PRESTIGE RANKINGS. FISHER, VIRGINIA LEE, 29 OCT 69 22P.
EDRS PRICE MF-$0.65 HC-$3.29

SIXTY CHILDREN OF VARIED SOCIOECONOMIC BACKGROUNDS WHO RANGED IN AGE FROM FIRST THROUGH EIGHTH GRADE WERE SHOWN PHOTOGRAPHS OF WORKERS IN DIFFERENT OCCUPATIONS, ASKED TO RATE JOBS ACCORDING TO PRESTIGE AND TO GIVE REASONS FOR THEIR RANKINGS. THESE REASONS WERE THEN ANALYZED FOR LEVEL OF COGNITIVE FUNCTIONING MANIFESTED. REASONS WERE SEEN AS REPRESENTING ONE OF THREE LEVELS: (1) EXPLANATION, (2) COMPARISON-FUNCTIONAL DESCRIPTION, AND (3) LABELING, FIAT, OR "DON'T KNOW." THE CHILDREN'S ACTUAL RANKINGS WERE CHECKED FOR ACCURACY BY COMPARING THEM TO NORC OCCUPATIONAL PRESTIGE RANKINGS. ACCURACY TENDED TO INCREASE WITH AGE AND GIRLS WERE SOMEWHAT MORE ACCURATE THAN BOYS, BUT NEITHER OF THESE TRENDS WAS SIGNIFICANT. THE COGNITIVE LEVEL OF CHILDREN'S REASONS FOR RANKINGS IMPROVED WITH GRADE LEVEL. CHILDREN WERE MOST ACCURATE IN RANKING LOW-PRESTIGE OCCUPATIONS AND LEAST ACCURATE WITH MIDDLE-PRESTIGE OCCUPATIONS. YOUNG CHILDREN WERE VERY ACCURATE IN RANKING LOW-PRESTIGE JOBS, BUT THEY WERE USUALLY UNABLE TO GIVE ANY EXPLANATION FOR THEIR RANKING. THESE RESULTS SUGGEST THAT CHILDREN LEARN OCCUPATIONAL PRESTIGE DIRECTLY RATHER THAN DEVELOPING A RATIONAL SCHEMA FROM WHICH SUBJECTIVE PRESTIGE RANKINGS COULD BE DERIVED. THUS, PARENTS APPARENTLY TRANSMIT TO CHILDREN TRADITIONAL STATUS DISTINCTIONS BEFORE CHILDREN ARE EVEN OLD ENOUGH TO UNDERSTAND WHY. (MH)

ED039925 PS002946

KINDERGARTEN HANDBOOK: A GUIDE TO THOSE ACTIVELY INTERESTED IN KINDERGARTENS AND IN ESTABLISHING NEW CENTRES. THIRD EDITION. , 69 19P.

DOCUMENT NOT AVAILABLE FROM EDRS.

AVAILABLE FROM: THE KINDERGARTEN UNION OF SOUTH AUSTRALIA, INC., 95 PALMER PLACE, NORTH ADELAIDE, AUSTRALIA

THIS GUIDE TO THE FUNCTIONING OF KINDERGARTENS AND THE ESTABLISHING OF NEW CENTERS IS DIVIDED INTO THREE SECTIONS. THE FIRST SECTION IS CONCERNED PRIMARILY WITH THE BUREAUCRATIC STRUCTURE OF KINDERGARTEN AGENCIES IN AUSTRALIA. IT DESCRIBES THE KINDERGARTEN UNION, ITS COUNCILS AND COMMITTEES, THE BOARD OF MANAGEMENT, THE AUSTRALIAN PRE-SCHOOL ASSOCIATION, AND THE KINDERGARTEN TEACHERS COLLEGE. A BRIEF DESCRIPTION OF AVAILABLE SPECIAL SERVICES (PSYCHOLOGIST, SPEECH THERAPIST) IS GIVEN. SECTION II PROVIDES PRACTICAL INFORMATION ON BEGINNING A BRANCH KINDERGARTEN OF THE KINDERGARTEN UNION. CONDITIONS FOR MEMBERSHIP, PRINCIPLES OF PLANNING, FINANCE AND INSURANCE, AND THE MODEL RULES FOR K.U. BRANCH KINDERGARTENS ARE DISCUSSED. ALSO INVESTIGATED IN THIS SECTION ARE PARENT-TEACHER AND PARENT-COMMITTEE RELATIONSHIPS. THE THIRD SECTION ACKNOWLEDGES THE IMPORTANCE OF KINDERGARTEN AS THE CHILD'S FIRST AWAY-FROM-HOME EXPERIENCE AND EXAMINES WAYS THAT KINDERGARTENS CAN MAKE THIS EXPERIENCE AS PLEASANT AND MEANINGFUL AS POSSIBLE. THIS SECTION ALSO DISCUSSES DETERMINATION OF THE OPTIMUM NUMBER OF CHILDREN FOR A KINDERGARTEN AND TAKES A FINAL LOOK AT THE AUSTRALIAN PRE-SCHOOL ASSOCIATION. (MH)

ED039926 PS002962

IMPLEMENTING DIFFERENT AND BETTER SCHOOLS. GLINES, DON E., DEC 69 219P.

EDRS PRICE MF-$0.65 HC-$9.87

AVAILABLE FROM: CAMPUS PUBLISHERS, BOX 1005, MANKATO, MINNESOTA ($5.00)

THIS VOLUME PROVIDES GUIDELINES FOR IMPLEMENTING CHANGE IN SCHOOLS, GRADES K-12. AN EXAMPLE OF INNOVATIVE EDUCATION IS WILSON CAMPUS SCHOOL, THE LABORATORY SCHOOL OF MANKATO STATE COLLEGE, WHICH STRESSES PERSONALIZED PROGRAMS, CONCERN WITH HUMAN RELATIONS AND SELF-CONCEPT, NONGRADED CURRICULUM REFORM, AND TEAM PLANNING. THE AUTHOR CHALLENGES CURRENT SCHOOL PRACTICES THAT LEAD TO INEFFICIENCY AND STUDENT FAILURE. HE OFFERS A PHILOSOPHY FOR IMMEDIATE AND MASSIVE CHANGE AND URGES ONGOING INNOVATION FROM PRESCHOOL THROUGH COLLEGE. SUGGESTIONS ARE GIVEN FOR IMPROVING INSTRUCTION, LEARNING, AND STUDENT EVALUATION AND THE USE OF TECHNOLOGY. THE MECHANISMS FOR CHANGE ARE DESCRIBED AND THE ORGANIZATION OF NEW STRUCTURES ARE EXPLAINED. THESE CHANGES ARE TO BE IMPLEMENTED BY ADMINISTRATORS, TEACHERS, AND STUDENTS. SPECIFIC PROGRAMS ARE DISCUSSED FOR VARIABLE SCHEDULING, INDIVIDUALIZED INSTRUCTION, STUDENT FREEDOM, ETC. EVALUATION OF PRESENT PROGRESS AND FUTURE PLANNING NEEDS IS INCLUDED. APPENDIXES PROVIDE FURTHER INFORMATION ON STARTING NEW PROGRAMS AND LIST NAMES OF EDUCATORS, SCHOOLS, AND ORGANIZATIONS WHO ARE INVOLVED IN EDUCATIONAL REVISION. CURRICULUM PROJECT DESCRIPTIONS AND A BIBLIOGRAPHY ON CHANGE ARE PROVIDED. (DR)

ED039927 PS002964

THE ETS-OEO LONGITUDINAL STUDY OF DISADVANTAGED CHILDREN. , [68] 6P.

EDRS PRICE MF-$0.65 HC-$3.29

THE EDUCATIONAL TESTING SERVICE (ETS) IS BEGINNING A COMPREHENSIVE LONGITUDINAL STUDY OF THE COGNITIVE, PERSONAL, AND SOCIAL DEVELOPMENT OF DISADVANTAGED CHILDREN FROM AGE 3 TO GRADE 3. ETS HOPES TO IDENTIFY THE ANTECEDENTS OF FAVORABLE INTELLECTUAL AND SOCIAL DEVELOPMENT AND TO SUGGEST WHAT KINDS OF EDUCATIONAL PROGRAMS MIGHT HELP TO BRIDGE THE GAP BETWEEN THE DISADVANTAGED AND THE MORE AFFLUENT. THE STUDY WILL INVOLVE 9 GROUPS OF CHILDREN IN 23 ELEMENTARY SCHOOL DISTRICTS IN NEW JERSEY, ALABAMA, MISSOURI, AND OREGON. SOME OF THE PRINCIPAL FEATURES OF THE STUDY DESIGN ARE THAT: (1) THE GROUPS WILL BE "NATURAL" RATHER THAN "CONTRIVED," I.E. PARENTS WILL DECIDE ABOUT THEIR CHILDREN'S PARTICIPATION IN HEAD START OR KINDERGARTEN IN THE ORDINARY WAY; (2) THE SUBJECTS WILL BE ENGLISH-SPEAKING NEGRO AND WHITE CHILDREN; (3) WHERE POSSIBLE, ETS SELECTED DISTRICTS THAT WERE MIXED BY RACE AND SOCIOECONOMIC STATUS; AND (4) CROSS-SECTIONAL COMPARISON GROUPS WERE INCLUDED TO PROVIDE BASELINE DATA. DATA WILL BE COLLECTED FROM MEASURES OF THE FAMILY, MEASURES OF THE CHILD'S PHYSICAL, PERCEPTUAL, COGNITIVE, AND PERSONAL-SOCIAL DEVELOPMENT, AND MEASURES OF THE CLASSROOM, TEACHER, SCHOOL, AND COMMUNITY. INTERVIEWS, OBSERVATION TECHNIQUES, MEDICAL EXAMINATIONS, QUESTIONNAIRES, AND TESTS WILL BE USED TO COLLECT DATA. COOPERATION FROM PARENTS, SCHOOLS AND HEAD START PROGRAM PERSONNEL IS ACTIVELY BEING SOUGHT BY ETS. (MH)

ED039928 PS002966

TEACHER EFFECTIVENESS: A POSITION. SCOTT, MYRTLE, 69 15P.

EDRS PRICE MF-$0.65 HC-$3.29

THIS DOCUMENT SUMMARIZES THE HIGHLIGHTS OF RESEARCH ON TEACHER EFFECTIVENESS AND CONCLUDES WITH RECOMMENDATIONS BASED ON A SYNTHESIS OF THIS PAST WORK. THE VARIOUS METHODOLOGIES THAT HAVE BEEN USED ARE DISCUSSED, FROM RATING SCALES TO OBJECTIVE OBSERVATION TECHNIQUES, SUCH AS OSCAR AND THE ECOLOGICAL STUDIES. THE MAJOR PROBLEMS IN TEACHER EFFECTIVENESS RESEARCH ARE EXAMINED. RECOMMENDATIONS ARE THAT RESULTS OF: (1) RESEARCH ON PRESAGE VARIABLES ARE CONFLICTING SUGGESTING THAT SUCH RESEARCH MIGHT BE SUSPENDED FOR THE MOMENT: (2) CLEARER GUIDELINES REGARDING ULTIMACY OF PRODUCT CRITERIA ARE NEEDED; (3) OBSERVATIONAL TECHNIQUES SEEM TO BE MORE BEHAVIORALLY ORIENTED AND MORE OBJECTIVE THAN OTHER METHODOLOGIES; (4) AN ATTEMPT SHOULD BE MADE TO INTEGRATE, TRANSLATE, AND RELATE ALREADY AVAILABLE MATERIALS ON TEACHER EFFECTIVENESS; AND (5) THE SUB-SEGMENTS OF TEACHER EFFECTIVENESS SHOULD BE UNDERSTOOD AND QUANTIFIED BEFORE RESEARCHERS TRY TO UNIFY THE WHOLE. (MH)

ED039929 PS002983

KINDERGARTEN CURRICULUM GUIDE. , 69 70P.

EDRS PRICE MF-$0.65 HC-$3.29

THIS CURRICULUM GUIDE FOR KINDERGARTEN HAS A FORMAT THAT IS HIGHLY READABLE AND EASY FOR A TEACHER TO USE. FOR EACH AREA OF THE CURRICULUM (MATH, LANGUAGE ARTS, SCIENCE, SOCIAL SCIENCE, AND ART) SPECIFIC OBJECTIVES AND ACCOMPANYING ACTIVITIES ARE PROVIDED. DETAILED DIRECTIONS HELP THE TEACHER ENABLE CHILDREN TO GET THE MAXIMUM BENEFIT FROM EACH ACTIVITY. METHODS OF EVALUATING PUPIL PROGRESS, A LIST OF USEFUL MATERIALS AND EQUIPMENT, AND A BIBLIOGRAPHY ARE ALSO INCLUDED IN THE GUIDE. (DR)

ED039930 PS003003

AN EXAMINATION OF CHANGES IN ATTITUDES TO VISUAL COMPLEXITY WITH INCREASING AGE. DAY, H. I.; CRAWFORD, GAIL, JAN 69 19P.

EDRS PRICE MF-$0.65 HC-$3.29

IN MEASURING AFFECTIVE EVALUATIONS OF COMPLEXITY, TWO QUESTIONS HAVE BEEN GENERATED BY FINDINGS IN THE LITERATURE: (1) WHETHER THE RESPONSE INDICATORS, "INTERESTING," "PLEASING," AND "LIKING," REPRESENT INTERCHANGEABLE LABELS FOR THE SAME EVALUATIVE RESPONSES, AND (2) WHETHER THESE EVALUATIONS EVIDENCE A POSITIVE ATTITUDE TOWARDS COMPLEX STIMULATION BY YOUNG CHILDREN AND A LESS POSITIVE ATTITUDE WITH OLDER CHILDREN AND ADULTS. IN ATTEMPTING TO ANSWER THESE QUESTIONS, SUBJECTS FROM GRADE ONE THROUGH GRADE 13 WERE SHOWN 15 PAIRS OF RANDOM POLYGONS, THE ALTERNATIVES DIFFERING IN LEVEL OF COMPLEXITY, AND ASKED TO SELECT THE ALTERNATIVE THEY "LIKED," "FOUND MORE PLEASING," OR "FOUND MORE INTERESTING." ANALYSIS OF THE NUMBER OF "MORE COMPLEX" (DEFINED IN TERMS OF NUMBER OF SIDES) SELECTIONS MADE BY EACH GRADE AND RESPONSE GROUP SUGGESTED THAT COMPLEX STIMULI WERE CONSIDERED TO BE MORE INTERESTING THAN EITHER PLEASING OR LIKEABLE. THERE WAS ALSO A SIGNIFICANT DECREASE IN LIKING FOR MORE COMPLEX STIMULATION WITH AGE. RESULTS WERE INTERPRETED AS SUPPORTING RESEARCH WHICH HAS ARGUED THAT THE VERBAL EVALUATIONS OF "LIKE," "INTERESTING," AND "PLEASING" ARE NOT SYNONYMOUS ALTHOUGH RELATED, AND FINDINGS THAT POSITIVE EVALUATION OF COMPLEXITY DECREASES WITH AGE. (AUTHOR/DR)

ED039931 PS003004

ECHOIC RESPONSE INVENTORY FOR CHILDREN (ERIC). STERN, CAROLYN, JAN 69 19P.

EDRS PRICE MF-$0.65 HC-$3.29

THE ECHOIC RESPONSE INVENTORY FOR CHILDREN (ERIC) IS PART OF A TEST BATTERY WHICH INCLUDES THE EXPRESSIVE VOCABULARY INVENTORY (EVI) AND THE CHILDREN'S AUDITORY DISCRIMINATION INVENTORY (CADI), DESIGNED TO ASSESS LANGUAGE SKILLS OF DISADVANTAGED CHILDREN. THESE TESTS ALSO SEEK TO PROVIDE DATA THAT CAN HELP DETERMINE WHAT CHANGES IN LANGUAGE PERFORMANCE MAY BE ATTRIBUTED TO REPLICABLE TYPES OF INSTRUCTIONAL PROGRAMS. PERFORMANCE ON THE ERIC REPRESENTS A COMPOSITE MEASURE OF AUDITORY PERCEPTION, VERBAL OUTPUT, RANGE OF SENTENCE MEMORY, AND ACCURACY OF PHONEMIC REPRODUCTION. THUS, IT SHOULD PROVIDE A GOOD BASIS FOR DECIDING WHETHER A CHILD IS READY TO BEGIN READING. THE ERIC CONSISTS OF A SERIES OF 20 SENTENCES, ARRANGED IN ORDER OF INCREASING DIFFICULTY. CHILDREN HEAR THE SENTENCES ONE AT A TIME AND ARE ASKED TO REPEAT THEM. THEY RECEIVE A SCORE OF EITHER "CREDIT" (1 OR NO MISTAKES) OR "NO CREDIT" (2 OR MORE MISTAKES). THE ERIC WAS TESTED ON 450 PRESCHOOL CHILDREN OF VARYING SEX, AGE, RACE, AND SOCIOECONOMIC STATUS TO SEE IF ANY OF THESE VARIABLES AFFECTED TEST PERFORMANCE. ANALYSIS OF VARIANCE TREATMENT OF RESULTS SHOWED THAT MAIN EFFECTS WERE FOUND FOR AGE AND SES, BUT NOT FOR RACE OR SEX. THE INSTRUMENT WAS FOUND TO BE A USEFUL TOOL FOR ASSESSING A CHILD'S LEVEL OF READINESS FOR BEGINNING READING INSTRUCTION. (MH/AUTHOR)

ED039932 PS003006
THE EFFECTIVENESS OF A STANDARD LANGUAGE READINESS PROGRAM AS A FUNCTION OF TEACHER DIFFERENCES. STERN, CAROLYN, JUN 69 17P.
EDRS PRICE MF-$0.65 HC-$3.29

IN ORDER TO FOSTER SKILLS WHICH WOULD FACILITATE DISADVANTAGED CHILDREN'S ABILITY TO LEARN TO READ, BUCHANAN AND SULLIVAN DEVELOPED THE READINESS FOR LANGUAGE ARTS PROGRAM PUBLISHED BY THE BEHAVIORAL RESEARCH LABORATORIES (BRL). A PILOT STUDY WAS RUN (1) TO TEST THE EFFECTIVENESS OF THE BRL PROGRAMMED MATERIALS ON HEAD START CHILDREN AND (2) TO SEE IF POSTTEST DIFFERENCES BETWEEN SUBJECT AND CONTROL GROUPS WOULD BE DUE TO THE PROGRAM OR TEACHER DIFFERENCES. SEVEN HEAD START CLASSES WERE RANDOMLY DESIGNATED AS EXPERIMENTAL GROUPS AND 4 AS CONTROL GROUPS. ALL SUBJECTS WERE PRETESTED ON THE PEABODY, THE UCLA LANGUAGE CONCEPTS TEST, AND THE LEE-CLARK READING READINESS TEST. ALSO, THE EXPERIMENTAL CLASSES WERE GIVEN THE UCLA VISUAL DISCRIMINATION INVENTORY. THE 7 TEACHERS AND 7 TEACHER AIDES FROM THE EXPERIMENTAL CLASSES WERE TRAINED IN USE OF THE BRL PROGRAM BEFORE THEY ADMINISTERED IT TO THEIR STUDENTS. THE PROGRAM IS HIGHLY STRUCTURED AND TOOK 4 MONTHS TO CARRY OUT. THE CHILDREN WERE POSTTESTED ON THE UCLA LANGUAGE CONCEPTS TEST AND THE LEE-CLARK READING READINESS TEST, BUT NO SIGNIFICANT BETWEEN-GROUP DIFFERENCE WAS FOUND. TEACHER BEHAVIORS APPEARED TO BE RELATED TO PROGRAM EFFECTIVENESS. (MH)

ED039933 PS003007
SOCIAL INFLUENCES ON CHILDREN'S HUMOR RESPONSES. KOSSLYN, STEPHEN M.; HENKER, BARBARA A., 70 11P.
EDRS PRICE MF-$0.65 HC-$3.29

TWO EXPERIMENTS TO STUDY THE DEVELOPMENT OF THE MEANING OF LAUGHTER IN CHILDREN ARE REPORTED. A PILOT STUDY PRESENTED RECORDED AUDIO TAPES WITH BOTH HUMOROUS AND NONHUMOROUS EPISODES, SOME WITH ACCOMPANYING CANNED LAUGHTER, TO 24 BOYS BETWEEN THE AGES OF 4 AND 6 YEARS. OBSERVERS RECORDED DURATIONS OF LAUGHTER AND SMILING. RESULTS SHOWED THAT BOTH RESPONSES REFLECT SOCIAL CONTEXT, AND OCCUR MORE IN A GROUP SITUATION. FOUR-YEAR-OLDS SMILED MORE WHEN ALONE THAN 6-YEAR-OLDS WHO SMILED MOST WHEN IN THE GROUP SITUATION. THE TWO GROUPS GAVE DIFFERENT RESPONSES IN RATING STIMULI AS HUMOROUS. HUMOR RESPONSES AND RATINGS WERE NOT CORRELATED. IN THE SECOND STUDY, 48 4- AND 6-YEAR-OLD BOYS, IN GROUPS OF THREE, LISTENED TO TWO AUDIO TAPES WHICH CONTAINED ESSENTIALLY NONVERBAL HUMOROUS AND NONHUMOROUS STIMULI. ON ONE TAPE THE THIRD STIMULUS WAS FOLLOWED BY 10 SECONDS OF SILENCE, ON THE SECOND TAPE BY 5 SECONDS OF LAUGHTER AND 5 OF SILENCE. VIDEOTAPES SHOWED THAT 6-YEAR-OLDS LAUGHED AND SMILED WITH THE LAUGH TRACK MORE THAN 4-YEAR-OLDS. LAUGHTER AND SMILING WERE SIGNIFICANTLY RELATED AT AGE 4 BUT NOT AT AGE 6. THIS STUDY SUPPORTS THE HYPOTHESIS THAT THE SOCIAL MIRTH RESPONSE, IN TERMS OF BOTH LIVE GROUP AND RECORDED LAUGHTER, IS DEVELOPMENTAL IN NATURE. (DR)

ED039934 PS003008
A FACTOR ANALYSIS OF A THREE-YEAR LONGITUDINAL STUDY OF CONSERVATION OF NUMBER AND RELATED MATHEMATICAL CONCEPTS. DEAL, THERRY N., MAR 70 12P.
EDRS PRICE MF-$0.65 HC-$3.29

THIS STUDY REPORTS A FACTOR ANALYSIS OF THE DATA RESULTING FROM A 3-YEAR LONGITUDINAL INVESTIGATION INTO CONSERVATION OF NUMBER AND RELATED MATHEMATICAL TYPE CONCEPTS. CONSERVATION OF NUMBER, WHICH REPRESENTS A SUBSET WITHIN THE CONCEPT OF CONSERVATION, WAS MEASURED BY USE OF A 20-ITEM, CRITERION-REFERENCED TESTING DEVICE. THE SUBJECTS, WHO WERE TESTED 3 YEARS IN SUCCESSION DURING A 4-WEEK PERIOD EACH SPRING, WERE 5, 6, AND 7 YEARS OF AGE (AT THE TIME OF THE LAST DATA COLLECTION). THE FACTOR ANALYSIS OF THE TEST RESULTS REVEALED A PATTERN OF DEVELOPMENT THAT SHOWED AN INCREASING EMERGENCE OF THE CONSERVATION FACTOR. FURTHERMORE, SUCCESSIVE FACTOR ANALYSES INDICATED THAT THIS CONSERVATION FACTOR HAS ITS ROOTS IN RELATED SUBSKILLS, PARTICULARLY VOCABULARY DISCRIMINATION. THE OVERALL DEVELOPMENTAL PATTERN, AS SHOWN BY THIS ANALYSIS, MOVES FROM DIFFUSENESS TOWARD INCREASING ORGANIZATION AS THE SUBSKILLS DEVELOP AND CONSERVATION EMERGES. THESE RESULTS ARE SEEN AS SUPPORT FOR PIAGET'S THEORETICAL NOTION OF THE EMERGENCY OF CONSERVATION. (MH)

ED039935 PS003018
RESEARCH, CHANGE, AND SOCIAL RESPONSIBILITY: STUDIES OF THE IMPRINT OF THE LOW-INCOME HOME ON YOUNG CHILDREN. SCHOGGEN, MAXINE, [67] 4P.
EDRS PRICE MF-$0.65 HC-$3.29

BOTH MOTHER AND TEACHER ARE SOCIAL AGENTS IN THE CHILD'S ENVIRONMENT AND PROVIDE THE FOCI FOR THE TWO SEPARATE, BUT RELATED, ONGOING STUDIES ON REINFORCEMENT PATTERNS DESCRIBED IN THIS PAPER. THE SPECIMEN RECORD IS THE PRIMARY METHOD USED TO OBTAIN DATA. FOR THE STUDY OF CHILDREN AT HOME, THE SAMPLE INCLUDES 24 3-YEAR-OLD CHILDREN FROM LOWER INCOME URBAN, MIDDLE INCOME URBAN, AND LOWER INCOME RURAL FAMILIES. EIGHT HALF-HOUR OBSERVATIONS ARE PLANNED FOR EACH CHILD. MEALTIME WAS CHOSEN AS THE SITUATIONAL SETTING, BUT SAMPLING HAS BEEN DIFFICULT SINCE SOME LOWER INCOME FAMILIES DO NOT HAVE ORGANIZED MEALS. THIS GENERAL LACK OF SCHEDULING OR TEMPORAL PATTERNING IS ONE OF THE ENVIRONMENTAL FACTORS AFFECTING CHILDREN'S DEVELOPMENT; A SECOND ONE IS THE BEHAVIORAL INCONSISTENCY OF THE ADULTS AROUND CHILDREN. THE QUALITATIVE ASPECTS OF MOTHERS' BEHAVIOR AND THE FREQUENCY OF UNPREDICTABLE BEHAVIOR TOWARDS THE CHILD ARE TO BE EXAMINED IN THIS STUDY. THE PILOT STUDY OF FIVE TEACHERS OF CULTURALLY DEPRIVED 5-YEAR-OLDS, INVOLVES GATHERING HALF-HOUR SPECIMEN RECORDS OF TEACHER BEHAVIOR IN TWO CLASSROOM SETTINGS. TEACHER BEHAVIOR WILL THEN BE DIVIDED INTO EPISODES (IDENTIFIABLE GOAL-DIRECTED ACTIONS). THE LONG RANGE STUDY GOAL IS TO FIND CLUES ON HOW TO SELECT TEACHERS AND HELP THEM ACT AS CONSTRUCTIVE AGENTS IN THE CHILD'S ENVIRONMENT. (NH)

ED039936 PS003055
EMOTIONAL DEVELOPMENT IN THE FIRST TWO YEARS. RICCIUTI, HENRY N., DEC 69 25P.
EDRS PRICE MF-$0.65 HC NOT AVAILABLE FROM EDRS.
AVAILABLE FROM: CRM ASSOCIATES, 1330 CAMINO DEL MAR, DEL MAR, CALIFORNIA 92014

CONCERNING THE ISSUES OF EMOTIONAL DEVELOPMENT, GENERAL AGREEMENT CAN ONLY BE REACHED ON THE DEFINITION OF "EMOTIONAL" BEHAVIOR. BEHAVIOR IS EMOTIONAL WHEN IT VARIES FROM AN INDIVIDUAL'S BEHAVIORAL BASELINE BY THE ADDITION OF THREE COMPONENTS: (1) AN ACTION COMPONENT, (2) AN AROUSAL COMPONENT, AND (3) A SUBJECTIVE "FEELING" COMPONENT. IN ALL AREAS OF INFANTILE EMOTION RESEARCHERS HAVE ATTEMPTED TO DELINEATE SUCH BASIC GROUNDWORK AS "PRIMITIVE, UNLEARNED EMOTIONS," BUT SUBSEQUENT STUDY HAS INDICATED THAT THEIR CONCLUSIONS ARE MORE THE RESULT OF SITUATIONAL AND SUBJECTIVE FACTORS THAN OF MEASURABLE, OBJECTIVE DATA. INFANT EMOTIONS ARE DIVIDED INTO NEGATIVE AND POSITIVE CATEGORIES IN THIS PAPER. DISCUSSION OF SPECIFIC EMOTIONS INCLUDES FEAR OF STRANGERS AND MATERNAL ATTACHMENT, OTHER FEARS AND ANXIETY. A BROAD DEVELOPMENTAL OUTLINE OF RESPONSES TO FEAR-INDUCING STIMULI IS GIVEN. OTHER NEGATIVE EMOTIONS, SUCH AS ANGER, DEPRESSION, AND SHAME ARE DISCUSSED. THE PAPER ALSO OUTLINES SOME OF THE WORK THAT HAS BEEN DONE WITH POSITIVE EMOTIONS AND CONCLUDES WITH COMMENTS ON THE FUNCTIONAL SIGNIFICANCE OF EMOTIONS IN EARLY DEVELOPMENT. (MH)

ED039937 PS003069
ENVIRONMENTALLY DEPRIVED CHILDREN. NIMNICHT, GLEN, [JUL 69] 10P.
EDRS PRICE MF-$0.65 HC-$3.29

THIS PAPER DISCUSSES THE MEANING OF ENVIRONMENTAL DEPRIVATION, SPECIFICALLY THE EFFECTS OF RACIAL, ETHNIC, AND CULTURAL DIFFERENCES ON EDUCATION. OBJECTIVES ARE ALSO GIVEN FOR A HEAD START AND FOLLOW THROUGH PROGRAM. A CHILD IS ENVIRONMENTALLY DEPRIVED TO THE EXTENT THAT HE HAS NOT DEVELOPED HIS INTELLECTUAL ABILITY AND A POSITIVE SELF-IMAGE. ENVIRONMENTAL DEPRIVATION IS OFTEN CAUSED BY A LIMITED QUANTITY AND POOR QUALITY OF INTERACTION BETWEEN A CHILD AND ADULTS, PARTICULARLY HIS PARENTS. THE QUALITY AND THE AMOUNT OF INTERACTION ARE REDUCED BY CONDITIONS PREVALENT IN POOR HOMES: (1) PARENTS' LOW EDUCATIONAL ACHIEVEMENT, (2) ABSENCE OF THE FATHER IN THE HOME, (3) A LARGE FAMILY, (4) A CROWDED HOME, (5) A HIGH RATE OF PHYSICAL AND MENTAL ILLNESS, AND (6) A PARENTAL ATTITUDE OF PSYCHOLOGICAL DEFEAT. ALL OF THESE FACTORS CONTRIBUTE TO LIMITED INTELLECTUAL DEVELOPMENT AND A NEGATIVE SELF-CONCEPT. BECAUSE SCHOOLS ARE ORIENTED TO THE WHITE MIDDLE CLASS, THEY FAIL TO RESPOND TO THE LIFE STYLE, VALUES, AND CULTURE OF MINORITY GROUP CHILDREN. HEAD START AND FOLLOW THROUGH SHOULD RESPOND TO MINORITY GROUPS AND FOCUS ON DEVELOPING SENSORY AND PERCEPTUAL ACUITY, CONCEPT FORMATION AND PROBLEM SOLVING ABILITY, AND LANGUAGE COMPETENCE. HOME INVOLVEMENT IS ALSO NEEDED. PROGRAMS SHOULD RESPOND TO THE CHILD'S NEEDS AND INVOLVE THE FAMILY IN A MEANINGFUL WAY. (DR)

ED039938 PS003071
ATTENTIONAL PREFERENCE AND EXPERIENCE: II. AN EXPLORATORY LONGITUDINAL STUDY OF THE EFFECTS OF VISUAL FAMILIARITY AND RESPONSIVENESS. UZGIRIS, INA C.; HUNT, J. MCV., JAN 70 13P.
EDRS PRICE MF-$0.65 HC-$3.29

THE HUMAN INFANT IS NOW CONSIDERED CAPABLE OF ACTIVE INFORMATIONAL INTERACTION WITH THE ENVIRONMENT. THIS STUDY TESTED CERTAIN HYPOTHESES CONCERNING THE NATURE OF THAT INTERACTION. THESE HYPOTHESES, DEVELOPED PARTLY FROM PIAGET'S WORK, ARE (1) THAT REPEATED VISUAL ENCOUNTERS WITH A STIMULUS PATTERN LEADS FIRST TO ATTENTIONAL PREFERENCE FOR THAT PATTERN, BEFORE LEADING TO PREFERENCE FOR AN UNFAMILIAR PATTERN AND (2) THAT PATTERNS RESPONSIVE TO AN INFANT'S OWN ACTS WILL ACQUIRE AN EXTRA ATTRACTIVENESS. STUDY SUBJECTS, 15 INFANTS, APPROXIMATELY 1 MONTH OLD, HAD 2 PATTERNS (COLORFUL MOBILES OF YARN, MATCH BOXES OR PAPER UMBRELLAS) INTRODUCED ABOVE THEIR CRIBS WHEN THEY WERE 4-5 WEEKS OF AGE. ONE OF THESE PATTERNS WAS STABLE AND ONE WAS SET UP TO BE RESPONSIVE

TO THE INFANTS' MOVEMENTS, BUT VARIATION IN SIZE AND MOBILITY OF CRIBS IN THE VARIOUS HOMES MADE DATA RELATING TO THE SECOND HYPOTHESIS INVALID. AFTER THE INFANTS HAD HAD 4 WEEKS OF FAMILIARIZATION WITH THE PATTERNS, OBSERVERS TESTED THEM TWICE FOR ATTENTIONAL PREFERENCE, WITH A THIRD, UNFAMILIAR PATTERN ADDED ABOVE THE CRIB. ANOTHER PERIOD OF 4 WEEKS WAS FOLLOWED BY A FINAL TEST. RESULTS INDICATED INITIAL ATTENTIONAL PREFERENCE FOR FAMILIAR PATTERNS, FOLLOWED BY PREFERENCE FOR UNFAMILIAR PATTERNS AFTER THE ADDITIONAL PERIOD. (MH)

ED039939 PS003072
ATTENTIONAL PREFERENCE AND EXPERIENCE: III. VISUAL FAMILIARITY AND LOOKING TIME. GREENBERG, DAVID; AND OTHERS, JAN 70 13P.
EDRS PRICE MF-$0.65 HC-$3.29

THIS STUDY IS THE THIRD OF THREE INVESTIGATING ATTENTIONAL PREFERENCE IN INFANTS. IN THE SECOND STUDY (PS 003 071), INFANTS GAVE INITIAL ATTENTIONAL PREFERENCE TO FAMILIAR PATTERNS OF VISUAL STIMULI, AND LATER SWITCHED THEIR PREFERENCE TO THE UNFAMILIAR, NOVEL STIMULI. THE PURPOSE OF THE PRESENT STUDY WAS TO DUPLICATE THESE RESULTS WITH IMPROVED EXPERIMENTAL TECHNIQUES, INCLUDING ADDITIONAL CONTROLS. EACH OF A GROUP OF 24 INFANTS AND A CONTROL GROUP OF 10 INFANTS RECEIVED A BASSINET AND A STIMULUS PATTERN (MOBILES OF YARN TASSELS, STREAMERS, PAPER BALLS) AT ABOUT ONE MONTH OF AGE. ATTENTIONAL PREFERENCE WAS DETERMINED BY A RUSTRAK EVENT-RECORDER INSTEAD OF THE STOPWATCH USED IN THE PREVIOUS STUDY. RELIABILITY WAS ALSO ASSURED IN THIS STUDY BY HAVING TWO EXPERIENCED EXAMINERS RECORD LOOKING TIMES INDEPENDENTLY DURING A PORTION OF THE TEST. AT 2 MONTHS OF AGE, THE INFANTS WERE TESTED WITH THE NOW-FAMILIAR PATTERN PRESENTED SIMULTANEOUSLY WITH AN UNFAMILIAR ONE. SIMILAR TESTS WERE MADE WHEN THE INFANTS WERE 2 1/2 AND 3 MONTHS OLD. AT 3 1/4 MONTHS A NEW STIMULUS PATTERN WAS INTRODUCED FOR FAMILIARIZATION. FINALLY, AT 3 1/2 MONTHS THE NEWLY-FAMILIAR PATTERN WAS TESTED AGAINST AN UNFAMILIAR ONE. THE RESULTS DID DUPLICATE THOSE OF THE PREVIOUS STUDY: INFANTS GAVE MOST OF THEIR ATTENTION TO A FAMILIAR STIMULUS PATTERN, THEN SWITCHED THEIR PREFERENCE TO THE UNFAMILIAR PATTERN. (MH)

ED039940 PS003074
STATEMENT BY MARSDEN G. WAGNER, M. D. REPRESENTING THE AMERICAN PUBLIC HEALTH ASSOCIATION BEFORE THE SELECT SUBCOMMITTEE ON EDUCATION, MARCH 3, 1970. WAGNER, MARSDEN G., MAR 70 4P.
EDRS PRICE MF-$0.65 HC-$3.29

CRITICAL ISSUES IN DAY CARE AND EARLY CHILD EDUCATION ARE OUTLINED, AND HR BILL 13520 IS EVALUATED. THE ISSUES ARE: (1) THE SERIOUS SHORTAGE OF DAY CARE FOR CHILDREN OF WORKING MOTHERS, (2) RAPIDLY INCREASING EVIDENCE THAT INTERVENTION MUST BEGIN BEFORE THE AGE OF 3, IF THE POVERTY CYCLE IS TO BE BROKEN, (3) A NEED FOR COMPREHENSIVE, CONTINUOUS HEALTH AND EDUCATION SERVICES FOR CHILDREN, PREFERABLY IN THE SAME PHYSICAL LOCATION (PERHAPS AT A CHILDREN'S CENTER) FOR CONSISTENCY OF CARE AND LOWERED COSTS, (4) PARENT INVOLVEMENT IN AREAS OF PROGRAM DEVELOPMENT AND PARENT EDUCATION, (5) THE NEED FOR TRAINED MANPOWER TO ESTABLISH AND SUPERVISE DAY CARE AND EARLY EDUCATION PROGRAMS, AND (6) THE URGENT NEED OF CHILDREN FOR POWERFUL POLITICAL AND PROFESSIONAL ADVOCATES. HR 13520 IS VALUABLE BECAUSE IT WOULD MAKE FUNDS AVAILABLE FOR DAY CARE SERVICES, BUT IT SHOULD BE CHANGED TO INCLUDE CHILDREN UNDER 3. THE BILL CONTAINS THE POTENTIAL FOR DEVELOPMENT OF COMPREHENSIVE CHILD CARE PROGRAMS INCLUDING HEALTH, NUTRITIONS AND SOCIAL SERVICES AND DAILY PROGRAMS. HOWEVER, THE BILL SHOULD EITHER (1) DETAIL WHAT THESE SERVICES SHOULD INCLUDE AND HOW THEY WOULD BE COORDINATED, OR (2) PROVIDE AN ADMINISTRATIVE MECHANISM WITH AUTHORITY TO DEVELOP SERVICE MODELS, STANDARDS, COORDINATING MECHANISMS, AND QUALITY CONTROL METHODS. IF PASSED, A STRONG PROFESSIONAL ADVOCATE TO ADMINISTER THE PROGRAM IS ESSENTIAL. THE OFFICE OF CHILD DEVELOPMENT IS SUGGESTED AS THE BEST AGENCY AT PRESENT TO ACT IN THIS CAPACITY, BUT ITS AUTHORITY AND RESPONSIBILITIES NEED TO BE STRENGTHENED AND EXPANDED. (AUTHOR/NH)

ED039941 PS003075
STATEMENT ON COMPREHENSIVE PRESCHOOL EDUCATION AND CHILD DAY CARE ACT OF 1969 BEFORE THE SELECT SUBCOMMITTEE ON EDUCATION, FEBRUARY 27, 1970. FISCHER, GEORGE D., 27 FEB 70 4P.
EDRS PRICE MF-$0.65 HC-$3.29

THIS DOCUMENT IS AN OFFICIAL STATEMENT MADE BY GEORGE D. FISCHER, A SPOKESMAN FOR THE NATIONAL EDUCATION ASSOCIATION AND OTHER CONCERNED GROUPS. THE STATEMENT WAS MADE BEFORE THE SELECT COMMITTEE ON EDUCATION IN RESPONSE TO A HOUSE BILL ON PRESCHOOL EDUCATION. MR. FISCHER BEGINS BY PRAISING THE BILL, PARTICULARLY ITS EMPHASIS ON THE CHILD-DEVELOPING CONTENT OF THE PROGRAMS. HE ASKS, HOWEVER, THAT THE BILL BE ALTERED TO SAY THAT CHILDREN OTHER THAN THE ECONOMICALLY DEPRIVED SHOULD BE ENCOURAGED TO PARTICIPATE IN THE PROGRAMS. HE GOES ON TO EXPRESS PLEASURE AT THE PROVISIONS MENTIONED IN THE BILL FOR INVOLVING PARENTS IN THE PROGRAMS, BUT ASKS THAT ADDITIONAL PROVISIONS BE MADE FOR USING HIGH SCHOOL STUDENTS IN A WORK-STUDY SITUATION. HE SUGGESTS FURTHER (1) A SPECIFIC SECTION IN THE LAW WITH AN ADEQUATE APPROPRIATION FOR THE TRAINING OF PROFESSIONAL PERSONNEL, (2) AN INCREASE IN FEDERAL AID FOR THE CONSTRUCTION OF FACILITIES, (3) THE ESTABLISHMENT OF A FEDERAL BUILDING AUTHORITY, (4) A PROVISION PROHIBITING SECTARIAN INSTRUCTION, (5) A SPECIAL SECTION IN THE BILL TO AUTHORIZE PAYMENTS TO SCHOOL DISTRICTS TO ESTABLISH AFTER SCHOOL PROGRAMS FOR YOUNG SCHOOL AGED CHILDREN WHOSE MOTHERS WORK, AND (6) A PROVISION IN THE BILL TO ENCOURAGE EMPLOYERS TO PROVIDE MINIMUM-COST DAY CARE FOR THE CHILDREN OF WORKING MOTHERS. (MH)

ED039942 PS003076
BIBLIOGRAPHY ON THE BATTERED CHILD. (REVISED EDITION). , JUL 69 22P.
EDRS PRICE MF-$0.65 HC-$3.29
AVAILABLE FROM: CHILDREN'S BUREAU (DHEW), SOCIAL AND REHABILITATION SERVICE, 330 INDEPENDENCE AVENUE, S.W., WASHINGTON, D.C. 20003 (NO CHARGE)

TWO HUNDRED EIGHTY-TWO ARTICLES, BOOKS, REPORTS, EDITORIALS, THESES, DISSERTATIONS AND CONFERENCE PAPERS PUBLISHED BETWEEN 1946 AND 1969 ARE LISTED IN THIS BIBLIOGRAPHY. LEGAL, MEDICAL, PSYCHIATRIC, AND SOCIAL ASPECTS OF THE BATTERED CHILD SYNDROME ARE COVERED BY THESE PUBLICATIONS. AN ADDITIONAL SECTION INCLUDES 19 ABSTRACTS OF RESEARCH STUDIES OF CHILD NEGLECT AND ABUSE WHICH APPEARED IN VARIOUS ISSUES OF "RESEARCH RELATING TO CHILDREN." THESE STUDIES REPRESENT AN EXPLORATION OF MANY ASPECTS OF THE PROBLEM OF THE BATTERED CHILD: THE INCIDENCE OF CHILD ABUSE; THE ROLES OF FAMILY, COMMUNITY AND SOCIAL WORKER; CHILD CARE PRACTICES; UNDERLYING BEHAVIORAL FACTORS; LEGISLATION AND ITS EFFECTIVENESS; CHILD PROTECTIVE SERVICES AND THEIR EFFECTIVENESS; AN EPIDEMIOLOGIC STUDY; METHODS OF CASEWORK INTERVENTION. THIS BIBLIOGRAPHY IS OF POTENTIAL USE TO THE PROFESSIONAL WORKER OR STUDENT IN THE FIELD, AS WELL AS TO THE LAY READER. (NH)

ED039943 PS003082
DISCRIMINATING CHARACTERISTICS OF FAMILIES WATCHING SESAME STREET. EARLY DEVELOPMENTAL ADVERSITY PROGRAM: PHASE III, EDAP TECHNICAL NOTE 15.1. JORDAN, THOMAS E., MAR 70 5P.
EDRS PRICE MF-$0.65 HC-$3.29

"SESAME STREET" IS A TELEVISION PROGRAM AIMED AT STIMULATING YOUNG VIEWERS. THIS STUDY, A PART OF THE EARLY DEVELOPMENTAL ADVERSITY PROGRAM, ATTEMPTS TO DISCOVER WHAT DEMOGRAPHIC CHARACTERISTICS ARE ASSOCIATED WITH CHILDREN WHO VIEW OR DO NOT VIEW "SESAME STREET." THE SUBJECTS OF THE STUDY WERE 69 3-YEAR-OLD CHILDREN. BLACK AND WHITE, AS WELL AS MIDDLE CLASS AND LOWER CLASS CHILDREN, WERE REPRESENTED IN THE SAMPLE. THE DATA GENERATED BY THIS STUDY INDICATE THAT "SESAME STREET" IS WATCHED BY A DISPROPORTIONATELY SMALL NUMBER OF BLACK CHILDREN. FOR EVERY BLACK CHILD WATCHING THERE ARE FOUR OR FIVE WHO DO NOT, WHILE AMONG WHITES THERE IS AN EVEN SPLIT BETWEEN WATCHERS AND NONWATCHERS. A PREDICTABLY SIMILAR PATTERN OF RESULTS IS FOUND WHEN WATCHERS AND NONWATCHERS ARE COMPARED ON THE BASIS OF SOCIOECONOMIC STATUS. A SIGNIFICANTLY SMALLER PERCENTAGE OF LOWER CLASS CHILDREN THAN MIDDLE CLASS CHILDREN WATCH THE PROGRAM. THUS, VIEWERS ALREADY BELONG TO THE GROUP MOST PREPARED FOR SCHOOL, WHILE NONVIEWERS ARE THOSE WHO MOST NEED THE POSSIBLY BENEFICIAL EFFECTS OF "SESAME STREET." (MH)

ED039944 PS003104
EDUCATIONAL INTERVENTION AT HOME BY MOTHERS OF DISADVANTAGED INFANTS. KARNES, MERLE B.; AND OTHERS, 4 MAR 70 9P.
EDRS PRICE MF-$0.65 HC-$3.29

THE USE OF MOTHERS OF DISADVANTAGED CHILDREN AS AGENTS OF EDUCATIONAL INTERVENTION IS INVESTIGATED IN THIS STUDY. (THE COMPLETE REPORT WILL APPEAR IN THE DECEMBER, 1970, ISSUE OF "CHILD DEVELOPMENT.") THE PROGRAM WAS DESIGNED TO AID CHILDREN'S DEVELOPMENT AND TO FOSTER A SENSE OF DIGNITY AND VALUE IN THE MOTHERS. ONE CAUCASIAN AND 15 NEGRO MOTHERS, ALL FROM POVERTY ENVIRONMENTS, COMPLETED THE 15-MONTH TRAINING PROGRAM. THE INITIAL AGES OF THEIR CHILDREN WHO PARTICIPATED IN THE PROGRAM WERE BETWEEN 13 AND 27 MONTHS. THE TRAINING PROGRAM FOR THE MOTHERS CONSISTED OF A 2-HOUR MEETING EVERY WEEK AT WHICH THEY LEARNED TEACHING TECHNIQUES BASED ON THE PRINCIPLES OF POSITIVE REINFORCEMENT. THE MOTHERS WERE ASKED TO USE THESE TECHNIQUES WITH THEIR CHILDREN EVERY DAY. THOUGH AN ACTUAL CONTROL GROUP COULD NOT BE MAINTAINED, COMPARISONS WERE MADE WITH A MATCHED GROUP AND WITH A GROUP OF SIBLINGS WHO WERE NOT TAUGHT WITH THE REINFORCEMENT TECHNIQUES. COMPARISONS BASED ON THE STANFORD-BINET, AND THE ILLINOIS TEST OF PSYCHOLINGUISTIC ABILITIES REVEALED THE POST-PROGRAM SUPERIORITY OF THE EXPERIMENTAL GROUP OVER BOTH THE MATCHED GROUP AND THE SIBLING GROUP. (MH)

ED039945 PS003127

CULTURE OF THE SCHOOL: A CONSTRUCT FOR RESEARCH AND EXPLANATION IN EDUCATION. BURNETT, JACQUETTA H., MAR 70 14P.

EDRS PRICE MF-$0.65 HC-$3.29

THE CONFLICT OF CULTURES IN THE CLASSROOM IS THE URGENT EDUCATIONAL ISSUE TO WHICH THIS PAPER IS ADDRESSED. SCHOOL CULTURES ARE SUB-SETS OF THE CULTURE OF ORGANIZED INSTITUTIONS IN WHICH THEY ARE FORMED. IN OUR ETHNICALLY PLURALISTIC SOCIETY THE SCHOOL RUN AND STAFFED BY WHITE MIDDLE CLASS EDUCATORS (AS MOST ARE) FAILS TO MAKE A CULTURAL MATCH WITH THE COMMUNITIES IN WHICH THEY OPERATE. MISUNDERSTANDING OF THE RESULTING CONFLICT LED TO SUCH ETHNOCENTRIC AND CULTURALLY CHAUVINISTIC EXPLANATIONS AS THE "CULTURAL DEPRIVATION" OF BLACKS AND PUERTO RICANS. THOUGH WE CLAIM TO HAVE MOVED BEYOND THIS POINT OF MISUNDERSTANDING NOW, WE HAVE YET TO SOLVE THE PROBLEM OF THE CHILD WHO MUST NOT ONLY LEARN TO READ AND WRITE A DIFFERENT LANGUAGE OR DIALECT THAN HE HEARS AND SPEAKS OUTSIDE THE SCHOOL, BUT MUST ALSO DO SO THROUGH SITUATIONS AND PROCEDURES THAT ARE CULTURALLY FOREIGN TO HIS EXPERIENCE. THERE IS A NEED FOR COMMITMENT TO RESEARCH AND PRACTICE WITH A CULTURAL PERSPECTIVE, A PERSPECTIVE WHICH SUGGESTS THAT THE SCHOOL CULTURE IS A SECOND CULTURE TO BE ADDED TO A CHILD'S REPERTOIRE, RATHER THAN A REPLACEMENT FOR THE ETHNIC GROUP CULTURE ALREADY EXISTING. (MH)

ED039946 PS003268

ATTACHMENT AND RECIPROCITY IN THE TWO-YEAR-OLD CHILD. MARVIN, ROBERT S., II, APR 70 85P.

EDRS PRICE MF-$0.65 HC-$3.29

THIS PAPER REPORTED A PILOT STUDY ON ISSUES RELEVANT TO THE SOCIAL DEVELOPMENT OF THE 2-YEAR-OLD CHILD AND DISCUSSED THE RESULTS WITHIN THE FRAMEWORK OF THE EVOLUTIONARY-CONTROL-SYSTEMS THEORY PROPOSED BY BOWLBY (1958, 1969) AND AINSWORTH (1967, 1969). THE ISSUES EXAMINED WERE (1) ATTACHMENT AND (2) RECIPROCITY, OR THE ABILITY OF THE CHILD-MOTHER UNIT TO WORK TOGETHER UNDER A SINGLE GOAL-HIERARCHY. HYPOTHESES WERE PROPOSED THAT DEALT WITH (A) THE STABILITY OF ATTACHMENT, (B) MATERNAL VARIABLES WHICH WOULD SERVE AS THE OPTIMAL SETTING FOR THE FURTHER EXPRESSION OF ATTACHMENT BEHAVIORS, (C) THE NATURE OF THE CHILD'S ABILITY TO CARRY ON TRANSACTIONS WITH HIS MOTHER WHICH COULD BE LABELLED RECIPROCAL, (D) MATERNAL VARIABLES WHICH WOULD SERVE AS THE OPTIMAL SETTING FOR THIS DEVELOPMENT, AND (E) THE RELATIVE NATURE OF ATTACHMENT AND RECIPROCITY. SUBJECTS WERE THREE BOYS AND THREE GIRLS FROM WHITE, MIDDLE CLASS HOMES. DATA WERE COLLECTED BY MEANS OF NATURALISTIC OBSERVATIONS IN THE HOME, SUPPLEMENTED BY TWO STANDARDIZED SITUATIONS. INFANT AND MATERNAL RATING SCALES WERE USED FOR ANALYSIS. STUDY FINDINGS WERE DISCUSSED IN TERMS OF BOWLBY'S THEORIES AND SUGGEST THAT PARENTS SHOULD PROVIDE THE CHILD WITH STABLE AND WORKABLE BEHAVIOR MODELS ON HIS LEVEL OF ABILITY. (NH)

ED039947 PS003272

A COMPARISON OF THE NORMS OF THE PERSONAL SOCIAL DEVELOPMENT OF THE PRE-SCHOOL CHILDREN OF DELHI CENTRE AS OBTAINED BY THE CROSS-SECTIONAL STUDY AND THE LONGITUDINAL STUDY. MURALIDHARAN, RAJALAKSHMI, 69 17P.

EDRS PRICE MF-$0.65 HC-$3.29

THERE IS A MAJOR PROJECT IN INDIA TO COLLECT DATA FOR THE GENERATION OF DEVELOPMENTAL NORMS OF CHILDREN FROM 2 1/2 TO 5 YEARS OF AGE. THE PILOT STUDY OF THIS PROJECT, WHOSE MAIN OBJECTIVE WAS THE ADAPTATION OF MEASURES OF DEVELOPMENTAL PARAMETERS TO THE UNIQUE NEEDS OF INDIA, WAS REPORTED TO PS 003 284. THE PRESENT DOCUMENT REPRODUCES A STUDY THAT ATTEMPTS TO VALIDATE THE FINDINGS OF A CROSS-SECTIONAL STUDY OF INDIAN DEVELOPMENTAL NORMS BY COMPARING RESULTS (ONLY IN THE AREA OF PERSONAL-SOCIAL DEVELOPMENT) WITH THE DATA FROM A LONGITUDINAL STUDY. THE SAMPLE FOR THE CROSS-SECTIONAL STUDY WAS A GROUP OF 356 URBAN CHILDREN FROM A BROAD SOCIOECONOMIC RANGE, WHILE THE 42 SUBJECTS OF THE LONGITUDINAL STUDY WERE MOSTLY FROM A LOW INCOME RANGE. THE DATA WERE COLLECTED BY USE OF GESELL'S INTERVIEW SCHEDULES MODIFIED TO SUIT INDIAN CONDITIONS, AND, TO DETERMINE PERSONAL-SOCIAL DEVELOPMENT, ASPECTS OF BEHAVIOR SUCH AS EATING, DRESSING, AND PERSONAL HYGIENE WERE CONSIDERED. OF A TOTAL OF 156 ITEMS, THE RESULTS OF THE TWO STUDIES WERE IDENTICAL FOR 35 ITEMS AND VERY SIMILAR FOR 26 ITEMS. SIXTY-ONE ITEMS WERE NOT CHARACTERISTIC OF ANY AGE GROUP. (MH)

ED039948 PS003282

THE EFFECT OF SUPPLEMENTARY SMALL GROUP EXPERIENCE ON TASK ORIENTATION AND COGNITIVE PERFORMANCE IN KINDERGARTEN CHILDREN. A FINAL REPORT OF THE KINDERGARTEN 'LEARNING TO LEARN' PROGRAM EVALUATION PROJECT. LAY, MARGARET, 69 71P.

EDRS PRICE MF-$0.65 HC NOT AVAILABLE FROM EDRS.

A STUDY WAS DONE TO SEE IF A TEACHER-GUIDED, SEQUENTIALLY-ARRANGED PROGRAM OF INSTRUCTION FOR KINDERGARTEN CHILDREN USED IN ADDITION TO A REGULAR CLASSROOM PROGRAM IS MORE EFFECTIVE IN PRODUCING GENERAL INTELLECTUAL GAINS AND SPECIFIED BEHAVIORAL CHARACTERISTICS THAN TWO INSTRUCTIONAL ALTERNATIVES. THESE ALTERNATIVES WERE (1) PARTICIPATION IN A REGULAR KINDERGARTEN PROGRAM OR (2) PARTICIPATION IN A SPECIAL PROGRAM OF EXPRESSIVE ACTIVITIES (SUCH AS FINGER PAINTING, BLOCK PLAY) IN ADDITION TO A REGULAR KINDERGARTEN PROGRAM. SUBJECTS WERE 104 DISADVANTAGED KINDERGARTEN CHILDREN. EACH INSTRUCTIONAL GROUP HAD APPROXIMATELY 30 HOURS OF ACTUAL CONTACT TIME. THE STANFORD-BINET AND THE PEABODY PICTURE VOCABULARY TEST (PPVT), WERE USED TO MEASURE INTELLECTUAL FUNCTIONING, AND EXPERIMENTAL TASK SITUATIONS WERE USED TO OBTAIN MEASURES OF ATTENTION, VISUAL RETENTION, VISUAL DISCRIMINATION, TASK PERSISTENCE, DIVERGENT USES, AND CLASSIFICATION. RESULTS DID NOT SUPPORT THEORIES ON THE ADVANTAGES OF SEQUENTIAL INSTRUCTION OR A SPECIAL PROGRAM OF EXPRESSIVE ACTIVITIES IN ADDITION TO THE REGULAR CLASSROOM PROGRAM. APPENDIXES DESCRIBE THE PROGRAMS AND GIVE TEST DATA FOR SUBJECTS. [NOT AVAILABLE IN HARD COPY DUE TO MARGINAL LEGIBILITY OF ORIGINAL DOCUMENT] (DR)

ED039949 PS003284

DEVELOPMENTAL NORMS OF CHILDREN AGED 2 1/2-5 YEARS: A PILOT STUDY. MURALIDHARAN, RAJALAKSHMI, JAN 69 25P.

DOCUMENT NOT AVAILABLE FROM EDRS.

THE PURPOSE OF THIS PILOT STUDY, ASIDE FROM COLLECTION OF DEVELOPMENTAL DATA ON 38 NURSERY SCHOOL CHILDREN AGED 2 1/2 TO 5 YEARS, WAS (1) TO DEVELOP, MODIFY AND ADAPT THE TESTING EQUIPMENT USED IN GESELL'S DEVELOPMENTAL SCHEDULE, IN THE FIELD OF MOTOR, ADAPTIVE, LANGUAGE, AND PERSONAL-SOCIAL DEVELOPMENT; (2) TO DEVELOP ELABORATE, EXHAUSTIVE, OBSERVATIONAL RECORD BLANKS FOR ALL THE TESTS INCLUDED IN THE STUDY TO ENSURE OBJECTIVITY IN OBSERVATIONS; AND (3) TO DEVELOP STANDARD PROCEDURES FOR ADMINISTERING DIFFERENT TESTS IN ORDER TO MAINTAIN UNIFORMITY IN THE TESTING DONE BY DIFFERENT FIELD WORKERS. ADAPTIVE DEVELOPMENT, OR ABILITIES DEVELOPED WITHOUT SPECIFIC TRAINING, WAS MEASURED BY TESTS OF CUBE PLAY, FORM DISCRIMINATION, DRAWING, NUMBER CONCEPT, IMMEDIATE MEMORY, AND COMPARATIVE JUDGMENT. THE ACTION AGENT TEST, COMPREHENSION TEST, AND TESTS OF THE CONCEPTS OF NAME, AGE, ADDRESS, AND TIME WERE USED TO MEASURE LANGUAGE DEVELOPMENT. SUBJECTS WERE REQUIRED TO THROW A BALL, STAND ON ONE FOOT, THREAD BEADS, AND DO SIMILAR TASKS TO TEST MOTOR DEVELOPMENT. FINALLY, PERSONAL-SOCIAL DEVELOPMENT WAS MEASURED IN A STRUCTURED INTERVIEW SCHEDULE. THE OBJECTIVES OF THE STUDY WERE ACCOMPLISHED. (MH)

ED039950 PS003289

CONDITIONS FOSTERING THE USE OF INFORMATION FEEDBACK BY YOUNG CHILDREN. (REVISED REPORT). TEAGER, JOYCE, JUN 69 64P.

EDRS PRICE MF-$0.65 HC-$3.29

ISOLATION OF OPTIMAL INSTRUCTIONAL PROCESSES TO PROVIDE INFORMATION FEEDBACK AND TO MOTIVATE DISADVANTAGED CHILDREN WAS THE GOAL OF THIS COMPARATIVE STUDY OF REINFORCEMENT CONTIGENCIES. THE SUBJECTS WERE 21 BLACK CHILDREN FROM 45 TO 65 MONTHS OF AGE. CHILDREN WERE RANKED ON THE PPVT AND A LEARNING PROGRAM PRETEST, THEN RANDOMLY ASSIGNED TO THREE TREATMENT GROUPS. THE CONTINGENCY TREATMENTS COMPARED DURING A 3-DAY SOCIAL STUDIES LEARNING PROGRAM WERE: TREATMENT 1: TOKEN REINFORCEMENT (RAISINS), CHEMICAL FEEDBACK (GREEN OR RED DOT SHOWS ON BOOKLET WHEN CORRECT OR INCORRECT RESPONSE IS MARKED), AND VERBAL INFORMATION; TREATMENT 2: VERBAL REINFORCEMENT (PRAISE), CHEMICAL FEEDBACK, AND VERBAL INFORMATION; AND TREATMENT 3: CHEMICAL FEEDBACK AND VERBAL INFORMATION ONLY. ALSO, PAIRED ASSOCIATE TASKS WERE RUN WITH HALF OF THE SUBJECTS IN TREATMENT 1 RECEIVING TOKEN REINFORCEMENT AND HALF OF THE SUBJECTS IN TREATMENT 2 RECEIVING VERBAL REINFORCEMENT. ALL GROUPS PERFORMED SIGNIFICANTLY BETTER ON THE POST-TEST THAN ON THE PRETEST. THE SUBGROUP CONTINUING TO RECEIVE TOKEN REINFORCEMENT WAS SIGNIFICANTLY SUPERIOR TO ITS MATCHED SUBGROUP: THIS WAS NOT TRUE OF VERBAL REINFORCEMENT. NEITHER REINFORCER APPEARS TO BE NECESSARY AS CHILDREN CAN LEARN TO RECEIVE FEEDBACK STIMULI AS INFORMATION SIGNALS. (MH)

ED039951 PS003303

ADDRESS AT COMBINED MEETING OF N.Y.C. EARLY CHILDHOOD COUNCIL AND THE METROPOLITAN ASSOCIATION FOR CHILDHOOD EDUCATION ON "LANGUAGE ARTS MATERIALS IN EARLY CHILDHOOD" (TEACHERS COLLEGE, COLUMBIA UNIVERSITY, APRIL 6, 1968): COHEN, DOROTHY H., APR 68 16P.

EDRS PRICE MF-$0.65 HC-$3.29

WHILE THE INCREASED AVAILABILITY OF SPECIFIC MATERIALS DESIGNED FOR LANGUAGE ARTS CURRICULUMS OFFERS TEACHERS CONVENIENCE, IT IS IMPORTANT TO CONTINUE TO EVALUATE MATERIALS ACCORDING TO THEIR USEFULNESS AS TOOLS TO AID THE TEACHING-LEARNING PROCESS. LANGUAGE ARTS MATERIALS CAN BE CLASSIFIED ACCORDING TO FUNCTION: (1) THOSE THAT ENCOURAGE IMITATING THE ENGLISH LANGUAGE, (2) THOSE THAT ASSOCIATE SYMBOLS WITH MEANING, (3) THOSE THAT AID IN THE RECOGNITION OF SYMBOLS AND SYMBOL SYSTEMS, (4) THOSE THAT SUPPORT THE USE OF SYMBOLS FOR COMMUNICATION, (5) THOSE THAT AID THE DEVELOPMENT OF PHYSIOLOGICAL FUNCTION, (6) THOSE DESIGNED STRICTLY FOR READING, AND (7) THOSE THAT CAN BE CALLED LITERATURE. NEW RATIONALE SHOULD BE USED IN THE SELECTION OF CHILDREN'S LITERATURE, RATIONALE THAT WOULD WEIGH HEAVILY THE POSSIBILITY FOR CHILDREN TO ENJOY AND IDENTIFY WITH THE STORY. APPROACHES TO LANGUAGE ARTS CURRICULUM AND MATERIALS MUST CONSIDER (1) THE WAY ALL CHILDREN LEARN LANGUAGE, AND (2) THE PATTERN OF ANTICIPATORY BEHAVIOR AND THE RELATION OF ANTECEDENT PRACTICE TO LATER GOALS. THE YOUNGER THE CHILD, THE MORE LANGUAGE MUST PLAY A SUPPORTIVE ROLE TO SENSORY LEARNING. (MH)

ED039952 PS003340

DEPENDENCE AND COMPETENCE IN FOUR-YEAR-OLD BOYS AS RELATED TO PARENTAL TREATMENT OF THE CHILD. CLAPP, WILLIAM F., [69] 103P.

EDRS PRICE MF-$0.65 HC-$6.58

IN THIS STUDY 34 (17 DEPENDENT, 17 COMPETENT) 4-YEAR-OLD BOYS WERE CHOSEN FROM A GROUP OF 165 CHILDREN OBSERVED IN 11 NURSERIES. AN EPISODE SAMPLING TECHNIQUE WAS USED TO STUDY PATTERNED INTERACTIONS WITH CHILDREN, TEACHERS, AND OBSERVERS. EACH OF THE BOYS WAS OBSERVED IN INTERACTION WITH HIS MOTHER AND FATHER BY THREE OBSERVERS IN A SEMI-STRUCTURED LABORATORY SETTING. THE PARENTS WERE THEN INTERVIEWED WHILE THE CHILD WAS AGAIN STUDIED IN LABORATORY INTERACTION. SIX JUDGMENTS FOR DEPENDENCE AND COMPETENCE WERE MADE FOR THE CHILD WHILE THE PARENTS WERE ASSESSED BY MULTIPLE METHODS ON FOUR VARIABLES. VARIABLES INCLUDED THREE "TYPES" OF PARENTAL TREATMENT (TREATS CHILD AS AN ADULT, AS AN INFANT, OR AS A CHILD), AND THREE METHODS FOR ASSESSING PARENTAL CONSISTENCY. IT WAS FOUND THAT THE PARENTS OF COMPETENT CHILDREN TREATED THE CHILD AS A CHILD, RATHER THAN AS AN ADULT, TO A GREATER EXTENT THAN DID THE PARENTS OF DEPENDENT CHILDREN. THE PREDICTION OF A GREATER TENDENCY BY PARENTS OF DEPENDENT CHILDREN TO INFANTILIZE THE CHILD WAS NOT CLEARLY SUPPORTED. THE PARENTAL CONSISTENCY, AS ASSESSED BY THE DISCREPANCY BETWEEN GLOBAL JUDGMENTS FOR THE PARENTS' PHILOSOPHY AND NATURAL TENDENCIES, WAS SUPPORTED INDICATING THAT THE PARENTS OF DEPENDENT CHILDREN WERE NOT DOING (NATURE) WHAT THEY THOUGHT THEY SHOULD (PHILOSOPHY) TO THE EXTENT THE PARENTS OF COMPETENT CHILDREN WERE. (AUTHOR/DR)

ED039953 PS003403

THE NATIONAL LABORATORY ON EARLY CHILDHOOD EDUCATION: TOWARD CONSTRUCTIVE CHANGE. , 15 MAR 69 31P.

EDRS PRICE MF-$0.65 HC-$3.29

THIS PAPER DESCRIBES THE GOALS, MODEL, PROGRAMS AND ORGANIZATION OF THE NATIONAL LABORATORY ON EARLY CHILDHOOD EDUCATION, WHICH WAS ESTABLISHED IN 1967 AS THE FIRST NATIONAL RESEARCH AND DEVELOPMENT PROGRAM FOCUSED ON EARLY CHILDHOOD EDUCATION. THE CENTRAL GOAL IS THE DEVELOPMENT OF SPECIFICATIONS FOR THE BEST LEARNING ENVIRONMENTS OF CHILDREN FROM BIRTH TO NINE YEARS OF AGE. THE OPERATIONAL MODEL OF THE LABORATORY CONCERNS ITSELF WITH ALL FUNCTIONS, FROM RESEARCH THROUGH TRAINING; IT IS BUILT UPON THE PROGRAMS OR WORK TO BE ACCOMPLISHED AND ALLOWS FOR CONTINUOUS FEEDBACK. THE BASIC PROGRAM AREAS ARE: (1) RESEARCH AND SYNTHESIS ON THE EFFECTS OF INDIVIDUAL PERSONAL CHARACTERISTICS ON LEARNING PERFORMANCE, (2) RESEARCH AND SYNTHESIS OF ENVIRONMENTAL INFLUENCES ON THE EDUCABILITY OF YOUNG CHILDREN, (3) CURRICULUM RESEARCH AND DEVELOPMENT FOR THE DESIGN OF EDUCATIONAL INTERVENTION, (4) DEVELOPMENT AND EVALUATION OF EDUCATIONAL CHANGE AGENT ROLES, AND (5) DEVELOPMENT OF EVALUATION TECHNIQUES AND SUPPORTING TECHNOLOGY. A BRIEF DESCRIPTION IS GIVEN OF THE 8 GEOGRAPHICALLY DISPERSED COMPONENT CENTERS OF THE NATIONAL LABORATORY. THE WORK OF THE CENTERS IS ORGANIZED AROUND PROGRAMS OF RESEARCH AND DEVELOPMENT COORDINATION; INTRA- AND EXTRAMURAL COLLABORATION; COMMUNICATIONS; DEVELOPMENT OF HUMAN AND MATERIAL RESOURCES; FUNDING AND FISCAL MANAGEMENT; AND PLANNING AND MANAGEMENT. (AUTHOR/NH)

ED039954 PS003405

PARENT INVOLVEMENT IN COMPENSATORY EDUCATION. GORDON, IRA J., 70 89P.

EDRS PRICE MF-$0.65 HC-$3.29

AVAILABLE FROM: UNIVERSITY OF ILLINOIS PRESS, 54 EAST GREGORY, CHAMPAIGN, ILLINOIS 61820 ($2.50)

THIS MONOGRAPH CONSIDERS THE EFFECTS OF THE FAMILY ON THE INTELLECTUAL AND PERSONAL DEVELOPMENT OF THE CHILD, AND THE EFFECTS OF CULTURE UPON THE FAMILY'S WAY OF LIFE, AND THUS, ON THE CHILD. IN A SURVEY OF EARLY COMPENSATORY EDUCATION PROJECTS, UNIVERSITY BASED PROGRAMS, AND SCHOOL AND COMMUNITY PROGRAMS ARE DESCRIBED. PROGRAM ORGANIZATIONAL QUESTIONS DISCUSSED ARE: LOCUS OF CONTROL, LOCATION OF SERVICE, PURPOSES AND GOALS, AND USE OF PERSONNEL. A STATUS REPORT OF PARENTAL PARTICIPATION IN COMPENSATORY EDUCATION IS GIVEN AND PROGRAM CONTENT FOR PARENTAL INVOLVEMENT IS DISCUSSED, WITH EMPHASIS ON THE IMPORTANCE OF HOME VISITATION PROGRAMS. THE NEED FOR IMPROVED RESEARCH AND EVALUATION DESIGN AND METHODS IS STRESSED. (NH)

ED039955 PS003407

PROGRAMMED INSTRUCTION AS A MEANS OF ESTABLISHING "ERRORLESS" LEARNING WITH KINDERGARTEN LEVEL CHILDREN. FINAL REPORT. CRIST, ROBERT L., AUG 69 69P.

EDRS PRICE MF-$0.65 HC-$3.29

THE PURPOSE OF THIS STUDY WAS TO DETERMINE THE EFFECTIVENESS OF ERRORLESS DISCRIMINATION TRAINING IN TEACHING YOUNG RETARDED CHILDREN TO PAIR A GIVEN LETTER SYMBOL WITH A SPECIFIC SOUND. A SECONDARY OBJECTIVE WAS TO DETERMINE THE EXTENT TO WHICH THE LETTER-SOUND DISCRIMINATION WOULD GENERALIZE TO THE SKILL AREAS OF OMITTING THE DESIRED SOUND WHEN SHOWN THE LETTER, AND OF CONSTRUCTING THE LETTER WHEN THE APPROPRIATE SOUND WAS PRESENTED. SUBJECTS WERE 4 MENTALLY RETARDED MALES IN PRIMARY AND INTERMEDIATE SPECIAL AID CLASSES WHO WERE CHOSEN BECAUSE OF THEIR LACK OF KNOWLEDGE OF THE SOUNDS OF LETTERS. SUBJECTS PERFORMED ON TEACHING MACHINES FOR 15 MINUTES ON EACH OF 14 CONSECUTIVE SCHOOL DAYS. EACH SUBJECT WAS ALTERNATELY EXPOSED TO EACH OF TWO STIMULUS METHODS. EACH METHOD PROVIDED DISCRIMINATION TRAINING OF LETTER SOUNDS AND SYMBOLS FOR 13 OF THE 26 LETTERS IN THE ALPHABET. PRE- AND POST-TEST DATA SHOWED THAT ERRORLESS FORM DISCRIMINATION TRAINING WAS AS EFFECTIVE AS CUSTOMARY TRIAL-AND-ERROR DISCRIMINATION TRAINING IN PRODUCING GAINS. HOWEVER, THE ERRORLESS METHOD DIFFERED IN RESPECT TO DAILY PERFORMANCE, FOR IT GENERALLY RESULTED IN A HIGHER PERCENTAGE OF CORRECT RESPONSES MADE IN LESS TIME THAN DID THE TRIAL-AND-ERROR METHOD. THE LETTER-SOUND ASSOCIATIONS WHICH WERE MASTERED DID NOT OFTEN GENERALIZE TO RELATED VERBAL SKILLS. (AUTHOR/DR)

ED040738 PS001759

CHILD CARE ARRANGEMENTS OF WORKING MOTHERS IN THE UNITED STATES. LOW, SETH; SPINDLER, PEARL G., 68 123P.

EDRS PRICE MF-$0.65 HC NOT AVAILABLE FROM EDRS.

AVAILABLE FROM: SUPERINTENDENT OF DOCUMENTS, U.S. GOVERNMENT PRINTING OFFICE, WASHINGTON, D.C. 20402 ($1.25)

THIS REPORT PRESENTS BASIC DATA ON THE TYPES OF CHILD CARE ARRANGEMENTS AND THEIR FREQUENCY OF UTILIZATION BY WORKING MOTHERS BELONGING TO DIFFERENT SEGMENTS OF AMERICAN SOCIETY. THE SURVEY WAS CONDUCTED WITH THE HELP OF THE BUREA U OF CENSUS, WHICH INCLUDED SUPPLEMENTARY QUESTIONS ABOUT CHILD CARE IN ITS FEBRUARY, 1965 SURVEY, USING A SCIENTIFICALLY SELECTED SAMPLE REPRESENTING THE NON-INSTITUTIONAL CIVILIAN POPULATION. IT WAS FOUND THAT SINCE 1950 THE NUMBER OF WORKING MOTHERS HAS MORE THAN DOUBLED, TOTALING AS OF MARCH, 1967 4.1 MILLION WORKING MOTHERS WITH CHILDREN UNDER SIX YEARS OLD AND 6.4 MILLION WITH CHILDREN SIX TO SEVENTEEN. LICENSED DAY CARE FACILITIES WERE AVAILABLE FOR ONLY ABOUT 475,000 CHILDREN, AND THIS REPORT SHOWS THAT MANY OF THE REMAINING CHILDREN RECEIVE INADEQUATE CARE WHILE THEIR MOTHERS WORK. INCLUDED ARE A DETAILED PROFILE OF THE WORKING MOTHER, AND A REPORT OF THE CHILDREN AND ARRANGEMENTS FOR THEIR CARE. TABLES COMPRISE MORE THAN TWO-THIRDS OF THE REPORT. APPENDIXES A, B AND C PRESENT THE SCHEDULE FOR THE SURVEY OF CHILD CARE, DEFINITIONS AND EXPLANATIONS OF TERMS USED, AND SOURCE AND RELIABILITY OF THE ESTIMATES. APPENDIX D CONSISTS OF 184 TABLES WHICH SHOW DISTRIBUTIONS OF VARIOUS FACTORS OF WORKING MOTHERS, CHILDREN, AND CHILD CARE ARRANGEMENTS. (NH)

ED040739 PS002278
TELEVISION GUIDELINES FOR EARLY CHILDHOOD EDUCATION. MUKERJI, ROSE, 69 58P.
DOCUMENT NOT AVAILABLE FROM EDRS.
AVAILABLE FROM: NATIONAL INSTRUCTIONAL TELEVISION, BOX A, BLOOMINGTON, INDIANA 47401 ($2.00)

THIS DOCUMENT, A PROJECT OF THE NATIONAL INSTRUCTIONAL TELEVISION CENTER, ATTEMPTS TO IDENTIFY, TO EXPLAIN AND TO DEMONSTRATE DESIRABLE CONTENT AND TO PRESENT A PRODUCTION PLAN FOR TELEVISION PROGRAMS DESIGNED FOR YOUNG CHILDREN. GUIDELINES ARE GIVEN FOR UNDERSTANDING THE CHILD 3 TO 8 YEARS OLD, FOR IDENTIFYING LEARNING GOALS WHICH ARE SIGNIFICANT AND RELEVANT TO HIM, AND FOR USING PROCESSES WHICH FACILITATE HIS LEARNING. A MODEL FOR DEVELOPMENT AND EVALUATION OF THE TELEVISION SCRIPT IS PRESENTED, WITH SPECIFIC EXAMPLES OF PROGRAM DEVELOPMENT LEADING TO THE WRITING OF WORKING SCRIPTS. A MEMO FOR PRODUCTION AND EVALUATION LISTS SPECIFIC SUGGESTIONS FOR USE OF ADULT TALENT AND FOR PRODUCTION TECHNIQUES. RECOMMENDATIONS FOR UTILIZATION OF TELEVISION CONSISTENT WITH THE GUIDELINES, AND SUGGESTIONS FOR SUPPORTING MATERIAL FOR TEACHERS AND PARENTS, ARE GIVEN. THESE GUIDELINES ARE RELEVANT TO BOTH PUBLIC AND INSTRUCTIONAL TELEVISION. THEY ARE INTENDED TO BE USED FLEXIBLY, WITH LOCAL PLANNING AND PRODUCTION TEAMS USING THEIR OWN CREATIVITY. (AUTHOR/NH)

ED040740 PS002681
SOME CHARACTERISTICS OF NEURAL PROCESSING IN THE CHILD. ROBINSON, DANIEL N., 1 SEP 68 15P.
EDRS PRICE MF-$0.65 HC-$3.29

THIS REPORT TELLS OF THE PROCEDURES AND RESULTS OF A PSYCHOPHYSICAL STUDY OF 28 3.8-YEAR-OLD-BOYS FROM THE HARLEM TRAINING CENTER. IN SPITE OF AN EXPERIMENTAL SITUATION THAT WAS SOMETHING OF AN ORDEAL, SOME MEANINGFUL DATA WAS GENERATED. THE MAIN AREA INVESTIGATED IN THIS STUDY WAS THE EVOKED-RESPONSE INDICES OF TEMPORAL PROCESSING, THAT IS, THE RECORDABLE RESPONSE OF VISUAL CORTEX TO SINGLE FLASHES AND PAIRS OF FLASHES. THE FLASH PAIRS WERE PRESENTED WITH VARYING INTER-FLASH INTERVALS. STIMULI CONSISTED OF PULSES OF LIGHT PROVIDED BY A GRASS PS-2 PHOTOSTIMULATOR. DEPENDENT MEASURES OF SUBJECT RESPONDING WERE DERIVED FROM MONOPOLAR RECORDINGS THAT WERE TAKEN FROM THE RIGHT OCCIPITAL REGION CENTERED BETWEEN MIDLINE AND EAR. COMPUTER MEMORY WAS FED TO A MOSLEY X-Y PLOTTER, WHICH PROVIDED PERMANENT INK RECORDS OF THE DATA. SEVERAL FINDINGS ARE REPORTED BUT THE MAIN CONCLUSIONS CONCERN RELATIONS BETWEEN CHILDREN AND ADULTS REGARDING THE VISUAL EVOKED RESPONSE: (1) THE TIME REQUIRED BETWEEN SUCCESSIVE STIMULI FOR THE EMERGENCE OF COHERENT CORTICAL RESPONSES IS LONGER IN CHILDREN THAN IN ADULTS AND (2) BACKWARD MASKING OR INTER-STIMULUS INTERFERENCE IS MUCH MORE PRONOUNCED IN CHILDREN. (AUTHOR/MH)

ED040741 PS002824
PREACHING AND PRACTICING SELF-SACRIFICE: THEIR LOCUS OF EFFECT UPON CHILDREN'S BEHAVIOR AND COGNITION. BRYAN, JAMES H., 69 10P.
EDRS PRICE MF-$0.65 HC-$3.29

THIS RESEARCH IS PRIMARILY CONCERNED WITH DISCOVERING HOW CHILDREN'S BEHAVIOR (IN RELATION TO ALTRUISTIC GIVING) IS AFFECTED BY THE VERBAL ADVICE AND BEHAVIORAL EXAMPLE OF A SAME-SEX MODEL ON A TELEVISION SCREEN. THE SUBJECTS WERE A GROUP OF 600 CHILDREN DRAWN FROM FIRST THROUGH FIFTH GRADE. THEY WERE PLACED IN A SITUATION IN WHICH THEY COULD GIVE RECENTLY-WON MONEY TO THE MARCH OF DIMES. WHILE IN THIS SITUATION, THE CHILDREN OBSERVED THE MODEL GIVING THEM ADVICE (TO GIVE, NOT TO GIVE, OR NEUTRAL) AND RESPONDING TO THE SITUATION HIMSELF (GIVING OR NOT GIVING). EVERY POSSIBLE COMBINATION OF PREACHING AND PRACTICING WAS USED, SO THAT THERE WERE ALTRUISTIC MODELS, GREEDY MODELS, AND INCONSISTENT MODELS. DATA WAS COLLECTED CONCERNING (1) THE SUBJECTS' GIVING BEHAVIOR, (2) THE SUBJECTS' RATINGS OF THE MODEL, AND (3) THE SUBJECTS' ADVICE TO OTHER CHILDREN. THE RESULTS REVEALED THAT BEHAVIORAL EXAMPLE AFFECTED THE CHILDREN'S BEHAVIOR BUT NOT THEIR ADVICE TO OTHER CHILDREN, WHILE THE MODEL'S EXHORTATIONS AFFECTED THE CHILDREN'S ADVICE BUT NOT THEIR BEHAVIOR. BOTH THE MODEL'S BEHAVIOR AND HIS EXHORTATIONS AFFECTED THE CHILDREN'S JUDGMENT OF HIM, BUT THE RELATIONSHIP BETWEEN THE VARIABLES APPEARS TO BE ADDITIVE. (MH)

ED040742 PS002922
A FEASIBILITY STUDY OF PARENT AWARENESS PROGRAMS. FINAL REPORT. KEMBLE, VIRGINIA; AND OTHERS, NOV 69 23P.
EDRS PRICE MF-$0.65 HC-$3.29

THE PURPOSE OF THIS STUDY WAS TO EXPLORE THE FEASIBILITY OF GROUP MEETINGS OF HEAD START MOTHERS THAT ARE FOCUSED ON UNDERSTANDING OF ONE'S SELF AND OF OTHERS. A PARENT AWARENESS PROGRAM WAS DEVELOPED FOR USE WITH TWO GROUPS OF HEAD START MOTHERS OVER A 27-WEEK AND A 17-WEEK PERIOD, RESPECTIVELY. SPECIFIC OBJECTIVES WERE THAT MOTHERS WOULD (1) BECOME MORE AWARE OF THE NEEDS AND FEELINGS OF OTHERS, (2) DEVELOP A GREATER AWARENESS OF THEMSELVES, INCLUDING AN UNDERSTANDING OF THEIR STRENGTHS, ASSETS, AND THE EFFECT OF THEIR BEHAVIOR ON OTHERS, AND (3) LEARN EXPLICIT TECHNIQUES TO IMPROVE COMMUNICATION SKILLS THAT WOULD IN TURN RESULT IN BETTER INTERPERSONAL RELATIONSHIPS. TWO PARENT EDUCATORS TOOK THE ROLE OF FACILITATORS FOR THE INFORMAL GROUP DISCUSSIONS IN HELPING THE MOTHERS TRY OUT NEW WAYS OF HANDLING PROBLEMS AND OF EXPRESSING THEMSELVES IN THE GROUP SESSION. FOCUSES OF THE DISCUSSIONS INCLUDED PARENT-CHILD RELATIONSHIPS; METHODS OF DISCIPLINE; COMMUNICATION SKILLS; SELF-KNOWLEDGE; MARITAL STATUS; HETEROSEXUAL RELATIONSHIPS; DRUG, ALCOHOL, AND GLUE-SNIFFING ADDICTION; AND RACIAL FEELINGS. WHEN APPROPRIATE, THE PARENT EDUCATORS INTRODUCED AUDIO-VISUAL MEDIA, HANDOUTS, AND ROLE-PLAYING EXERCISES TO EXPAND DISCUSSION. THE SUSTAINED LEVEL OF PARTICIPATION AND THE FAVORABLE REACTIONS TO THE PROGRAM REPORTED BY THE PARENTS AND STAFF INDICATED THAT A PARENT AWARENESS PROGRAM IS FEASIBLE FOR THIS POPULATION. (AUTHOR/DR)

ED040743 PS002930
THE RELATION OF CONCEPTUAL STYLES AND MODE OF PERCEPTION TO GRAPHIC EXPRESSION. LOVANO, JESSIE J., [69] 29P.
EDRS PRICE MF-$0.65 HC-$3.29

THE PERCEPTUAL-DEVELOPMENTAL RESEARCH OF KAGAN AND WITKIN ELICITED THIS STUDY OF COGNITIVE STYLE. THE WORK OF THESE TWO RESEARCHERS LEADS TO THE CONCLUSION THAT DIFFERENCES BETWEEN GRAPHIC EXPRESSIONS OF CHILDREN OF THE SAME AGE REFLECT DIFFERENCES IN THE CHILDREN'S MODE OF INFORMATION PROCESSING. SPECIFICALLY, THIS STUDY SOUGHT TO TEST THE FOLLOWING HYPOTHESES: (1) THE SUBJECTS' COGNITIVE STYLE, AS MEASURED BY THE CONCEPTUAL STYLE TEST (CST), AND HIS MODE OF PERCEIVING AS MEASURED BY THE CHILDREN'S EMBEDDED FIGURES TEST (CEFT), WILL CORRELATE SIGNIFICANTLY WITH SPECIFIC CRITERIA OF HIS GRAPHIC EXPRESSIONS, AND (2) ANALYTICAL SCORES ON THE CST, CEFT, AND GRAPHIC EXPRESSIONS (DRAWINGS I, II, AND III AND SOPHISTICATION OF BODY CONCEPT) WILL INCREASE AS SUBJECTS ADVANCE IN GRADE. AFFIRMATION OF THE SECOND HYPOTHESIS WOULD INDICATE A DEVELOPMENTAL TREND FROM A GLOBAL (FIELD-DEPENDENT) MODE OF INFORMATION PROCESSING TO AN ANALYTICAL (FIELD-INDEPENDENT) MODE. THE TESTS WERE ADMINISTERED TO 114 BOYS, TWO OF EACH GRADE LEVEL, FROM GRADES 2 THROUGH 6. THE RESULTS, OBTAINED FROM TESTING OF SUB-HYPOTHESES, INDICATE GENERAL SUPPORT FOR THE SECOND HYPOTHESIS AND PARTIAL SUPPORT FOR THE FIRST. THE SPECIFIC DATA ARE DISCUSSED IN RELATION TO CONCEPTUAL STYLE, PERCEPTUAL MODE, AND GRAPHIC EXPRESSION. SPECIFIC RECOMMENDATIONS FOR FURTHER STUDY OF COGNITIVE STYLES ARE MADE. (AUTHOR/MH)

ED040744 PS002931
LANGUAGE TRAINING FOR TEACHERS OF DEPRIVED CHILDREN. HANSEN, HALVOR P., 13 NOV 69 21P.
EDRS PRICE MF-$0.65 HC-$3.29

THIS PAPER SUGGESTS THAT THE MAIN REASON FOR THE FAILURE OF MANY CHILDREN TO LEARN TO READ MAY BE THAT READING PROGRAMS OFTEN REQUIRE THE CHILD TO BEGIN READING BEFORE HE HAS DEVELOPED ORAL LANGUAGE SKILLS. BY 3 YEARS OF AGE THE CHILD HAS ACQUIRED ALMOST ALL THE LINGUISTIC RULES NEEDED TO PRODUCE BASIC, OR KERNEL, SENTENCES, WHICH CONSIST OF SUBJECT, AUXILIARY, AND PREDICATE. LANGUAGE PROGRAMS FOR YOUNG CHILDREN SHOULD WORK WITH THE TWO MAJOR ASPECTS OF LINGUISTIC ACTIVITY: COMPETENCE (INTERNALIZED KNOWLEDGE, OR RULES OF GRAMMAR), AND PERFORMANCE (THE USE THE CHILD MAKES OF THAT KNOWLEDGE WHEN SPEAKING.) TRANSFORMATIONAL GRAMMAR MAY BE USED AS A TOOL TO EXPAND THE CHILD'S LANGUAGE; THIS IS DISCUSSED IN TERMS OF JACOBS' (1968) WRITING ON DEEP STRUCTURE AND SURFACE STRUCTURE. A FIRST PRINCIPLE OF LANGUAGE TEACHERS IS TO LISTEN TO AND RESPECT THE LANGUAGE THE DEPRIVED CHILD BRINGS WITH HIM TO THE CLASSROOM, THEN EXTEND HIS ABILITY TO COMMUNICATE BY ADDITION OF A NEW SOCIAL DIALECT. TEACHERS MUST KNOW HOW TO ASSESS THE CHILD'S LINGUISTIC SKILLS, IDENTIFYING AREAS OF COMPETENCE AND PERFORMANCE, SO THAT INDIVIDUALIZED INSTRUCTION MAY BE PLANNED. CLASSES SHOULD STRESS STUDENT INVOLVEMENT AND UTILIZATION OF THE CHILD'S OWN SENTENCE PATTERNS, AS A MEANS FOR THE TEACHER TO DIRECT THE CHILD'S OWN DISCOVERY OF TRANSFORMATIONS OF MORE COMPLEX SPEECH PATTERNS. (AUTHOR/NH)

ED040745 PS002963
DESIGN AND MEASURES OF 1967-68 AND 1968-69 HEAD START E&R EVALUATION STUDIES. , [69] 20P.
EDRS PRICE MF-$0.65 HC-$3.29

EVALUATION OF HEAD START PROGRAMS IS APPROACHED THROUGH IDENTIFICATION OF INTERACTIONS WITH FAMILIES AND COMMUNITIES TO LEARN WHAT EFFECTS THE HEAD START EXPERIENCES HAVE HAD ON THE CHILDREN INVOLVED. AS A RESULT OF EARLIER STUDIES, MEASURES WERE DEVELOPED FOR SOCIAL-EMOTIONAL AND FAMILY FACTORS, AS WELL AS PROGRAM CHARACTERISTICS. IN 1966-67, THE NEWLY-ESTABLISHED EVALUATION AND RESEARCH (E&R) CENTERS CARRIED OUT THE FIRST FULL-YEAR HEAD START EVALUATION, USING CLASS SAMPLES REPRESENTING EXTREMES ON IMPORTANT DIMENSIONS. IN ADDITION,

FOR GREATER DEPTH OF MEASUREMENT OF COGNITION, SOCIAL-EMOTIONAL BEHAVIOR, PROGRAM, AND FAMILY, THE E&R CENTERS "CLUSTERED" TO COLLECT DATA FOR THE 1967-68 STUDY. TO MORE CLEARLY IDENTIFY THE FACTORS RELEVANT TO CHILD DEVELOPMENT, THE 1968-69 EVALUATION USED A DIFFERENT APPROACH, THAT OF "MAKING THINGS HAPPEN," IN CONTRAST TO PREVIOUS RELIANCE ON NATURAL VARIATION. COMMON CORE DATA WERE COLLECTED ON AT LEAST 120 CHILDREN 3 TO 5 YEARS OF AGE, ATTENDING HEAD START CLASSES FOR THE FIRST TIME. THE TESTS USED TO COLLECT COMMON CORE DATA, CLUSTER DATA, AND FOLLOW-UP DATA FOR THE 1967-68 AND 1068-69 STUDIES ARE IDENTIFIED AND DESCRIBED IN THIS PAPER. ALSO INDIVIDUALLY EXAMINED ARE EVALUATION STUDIES BY NINE E&R CENTERS, DESIGNED TO IDENTIFY RELEVANT DIMENSIONS OF HEAD START PROGRAMS AND TO DEVELOP ADEQUATE MEASURES OF THESE. DATA WILL BE PROVIDED ON WHAT OPTIMAL CHILD DEVELOPMENT PROGRAMS CAN BE, IN CONTRAST TO OTHER 1968-69 HEAD START EVALUATION STUDIES. (AUTHOR/NH)

ED040746 PS002965
AN ANALYSIS AND EVALUATION OF THE MONTESSORI THEORY OF INNER DISCIPLINE. BURNS, SISTER ALICIA, FEB 70 149P.
EDRS PRICE MF-$0.65 HC-$6.58

THE PRINCIPLES OF THE MONTESSORI THEORY OF INNER DISCIPLINE ARE DISCUSSED AND EVALUATED THROUGH EXAMINATION OF THE WRITINGS OF AND ABOUT MARIA MONTESSORI. THE PRINCIPLES ARE ALSO DISCUSSED IN RELATION TO AVAILABLE EMPIRICAL AND DESCRIPTIVE RESEARCH CONCERNING DISCIPLINE. THE PRINCIPLES OF INNER DISCIPLINE MAY BE SUMMARIZED AS FOLLOWS: THE CHILD IS A MAN DESERVING OF RESPECT. HE HAS AN INNER POWER WHICH FORCES HIS EXPANSION, AND HIS WILL LEADS HIM TO DEVELOP HIS ABILITIES. THE TEACHER ACTS AS A LOVING OBSERVER OF THE CHILD, WHO DOES NOT IMPART WHAT IS HERS BUT RATHER DEVELOPS THAT WHICH IS WITHIN THE CHILD. THE TEACHER PREPARES THE ENVIRONMENT IN WHICH CONCENTRATION CAN BE BEGUN AND CARRIED OUT, AND IN WHICH OBEDIENCE CAN BE CULTIVATED THROUGH THE GENTLE TRAINING OF THE WILL. ONCE THE CHILD HAS BEGUN TO CONCENTRATE, THE TEACHER DOES NOT INTERRUPT HIM. DISCIPLINE IS AN ON-GOING PROCESS DEPENDENT ON PERSONAL FREEDOM. IT IS BROUGHT ABOUT THROUGH AN INNER FORCE DEVELOPED IN THE CHILD BY SPONTANEOUS INTEREST IN AND CONCENTRATION ON AN EXTERNAL OBJECT (WORK). THE CHILD THUS LEARNS TO MOVE ABOUT ACTIVELY AND PURPOSEFULLY RATHER THAN WILDLY OR APATHETICALLY. HE FINDS HIS SATISFACTION IN THE NEED TO PRODUCE AND PERFECT HIS OWN WORK; THIS IS HIS INHERENT AND ONLY REWARD, A REWARD WHICH ELIMINATES THE NEED FOR PUNISHMENT. (AUTHOR/NH)

ED040747 PS003005
RULE AND ATTRIBUTE LEARNING IN THE USE AND IDENTIFICATION OF CONCEPTS WITH YOUNG DISADVANTAGED CHILDREN. SCHUTZ, SAMUEL, [69] 63P.
EDRS PRICE MF-$0.65 HC-$3.29

THIS STUDY ASSESSED THE VALUE OF TEACHING YOUNG CHILDREN THE RELEVANT ATTRIBUTES OF A CONCEPT AND THE CONCEPTUAL RULE BY WHICH THE ATTRIBUTES ARE ORGANIZED. IT WAS HYPOTHESIZED THAT ONLY IF CHILDREN HAD PRIOR KNOWLEDGE OF BOTH COMPONENTS COULD THEY FOLLOW INSTRUCTIONS DESIGNED TO TEACH A NEW CONCEPT. IT WAS FURTHER HYPOTHESIZED THAT CHILDREN WHO LEARNED TO FOLLOW INSTRUCTIONS INVOLVING A NEW RULE WOULD BE SUPERIOR AT DISCOVERING THIS RULE IN A CONCEPT IDENTIFICATION OR INDUCTIVE LEARNING PROBLEM. SIXTY HEAD START 4-YEAR-OLDS WHO COULD FOLLOW DIRECTIONS BUT DID NOT KNOW THE COMPONENTS TO BE TAUGHT WERE RANDOMLY ASSIGNED TO 1 OF 4 TREATMENT GROUPS: (1) LEARNED THE NEW RULE, (2) LEARNED NEW ATTRIBUTES, (3) LEARNED BOTH RULE AND ATTRIBUTES, AND (4) CONTROL. RESULTS OF PRE- AND POST-TESTS ON CONCEPT UTILIZATION AND CONCEPT IDENTIFICATION INDICATED THAT THE EXPERIMENTAL GROUPS PERFORMED BETTER THAN THE CONTROL GROUP IF AND ONLY IF THE CHILDREN HAD LEARNED BOTH COMPONENTS BEFORE OR DURING THE EXPERIMENT. TRANSFER OF THE NEW RULE TO THE CONCEPT IDENTIFICATION PROBLEM WAS DEMONSTRATED FOR THE RULE LEARNING GROUP, BUT NOT FOR THE RULE AND ATTRIBUTE LEARNING GROUP. (MH)

ED040748 PS003028
LONG DISTANCE INTERDISCIPLINARY EVALUATION OF DEVELOPMENTAL DISABILITIES. MEIER, JOHN, NOV 69 3P.
EDRS PRICE MF-$0.65 HC-$3.29

THE INCREASED EMPHASIS ON HAVING INDIVIDUAL DEVELOPMENTAL DISABILITIES DIAGNOSED BY INTERDISCIPLINARY TEAMS OF PROFESSIONALS HAS RAISED COMPLEX PROBLEMS INVOLVING TIME AND EXPENSE IN EVALUATING A CHILD IN HIS HOME SITUATION. THE JOHN F. KENNEDY CHILD DEVELOPMENT CENTER HAS A PLAN TO AVOID MOVING PROFESSIONALS TO OBSERVE A CHILD OR TO HAVING A CHILD'S FAMILY MOVE TO AN INTERDISCIPLINARY EVALUATION CENTER. THE PLAN IS BASED ON THE USE OF VIDEOTAPE RECORDING (VTR) IN THE CHILD'S OWN HOME SITUATION. IT CAUSES LITTLE INCONVENIENCE TO THE FAMILY, IS MORE UNOBTRUSIVE THAN A GROUP OF OBSERVERS, AND MAKES IT POSSIBLE FOR A TEAM OF SPECIALISTS MILES AWAY TO OBSERVE DIRECTLY THE DYNAMICS OF THE FAMILY AND THE BEHAVIOR OF THE CHILD. THESE STANDARD SAMPLES OF A CHILD'S BEHAVIORAL REPERTOIRE CAN ACCOMPANY REGULAR WRITTEN PROTOCOLS AND CAN RECORD THE ADMINISTRATION OF DEVELOPMENTAL TESTS. EVALUATION AND DIAGNOSTIC SESSIONS CAN INVOLVE THE PROFESSIONALS AT THE CENTER, THE VTR, AND PROFESSIONALS IN THE CHILD'S LOCALE, WHO CAN PARTICIPATE BY MEANS OF A LONG-DISTANCE AMPLIFIED TELEPHONE. THE TRAINING IMPACT OF A UNIVERSITY-AFFILIATED CENTER'S OPERATION WOULD THEREFORE BE EXTENDED. (MH)

ED040749 PS003030
AN EDUCATIONAL SYSTEM FOR DEVELOPMENTALLY DISABLED INFANTS. MEIER, JOHN; SEGNER, LESLIE, DEC 69 35P.
EDRS PRICE MF-$0.65 HC NOT AVAILABLE FROM EDRS.

THIS PAPER EXAMINES THE DEVELOPMENTAL PROBLEMS OF THE ENVIRONMENTALLY DISADVANTAGED IN LIGHT OF RECENT RESEARCH; MAKES A CASE FOR INTERVENTION DURING INFANCY, AND ATTEMPTS TO SPECIFY SOME CONCRETE DETAILS OF A CURRICULUM FOR AN INFANT EDUCATIONAL SYSTEM (IES). A RATIONALE FOR INFANT EDUCATION IS PRESENTED AND A VAST AMOUNT OF LITERATURE RELATED TO THE PROBLEM OF COMPENSATORY PROGRAMS IS REVIEWED. MUCH OF THIS LITERATURE INDICATES THE NECESSITY OF EXTREMELY EARLY INTERVENTION (E.G. THE IRREVERSIBILITY OF THE EFFECTS OF EARLY DEPRIVATION AND THE SOCIOECONOMIC CLASS DIFFERENCES IN INTELLECTUAL FUNCTIONING FOUND BY 18 MONTHS OF AGE). IT IS SUGGESTED THAT ON THE BASIS OF RESEARCH FINDINGS, THE RATIONALE AND TECHNIQUES FOR CONSTRUCTING A CURRICULUM BASED ON THE DEVELOPMENT OF AN INDIVIDUALIZED INSTRUCTION PROGRAM ARE QUITE APPROPRIATE FOR THE DESIGN OF AN IES CURRICULUM ARRANGED ACCORDING TO A SERIES OF DEVELOPMENTAL LEVELS. IT IS SPECIFICALLY RECOMMENDED THAT THE INFANT'S ENVIRONMENT BE CAREFULLY AND SCIENTIFICALLY STRUCTURED THROUGH THE USE OF AUTOTELIC STIMULATION. ALSO STRESSED ARE THE IMPORTANCE OF THE LEARNING FACILITATOR (PARENT) AND THE IMPORTANCE OF TRAINING PARENTS TO ENCOURAGE INFANTS' DEVELOPMENT. [NOT AVAILABLE IN HARD COPY DUE TO MARGINAL LEGIBILITY OF ORIGINAL DOCUMENT.] (MH)

ED040750 PS003062
NEED FOR EARLY AND CONTINUING EDUCATION. SCHAEFER, EARL S., 28 DEC 69 29P.
EDRS PRICE MF-$0.65 HC-$3.29

THE NECESSITY OF EARLY EDUCATION IS CONFIRMED BY A LARGE BODY OF RESEARCH, PARTICULARLY THAT WHICH REVEALS THE EMERGENCE OF MENTAL TEST SCORE DIFFERENCES BETWEEN CHILDREN OF DIFFERENT SOCIAL CLASSES DURING THE CRUCIAL PERIOD OF EARLY LANGUAGE DEVELOPMENT, THE SECOND YEAR OF LIFE. THE EVIDENCE INDICATES THAT VERBAL COMPREHENSION RELATES HIGHLY TO INTELLIGENCE TEST SCORES, TO READING ACHIEVEMENT, AND TO ACADEMIC AND OCCUPATIONAL SUCCESS, SUGGESTING THAT EDUCATION SHOULD BEGIN DURING OR BEFORE THE PERIOD OF EARLY, RAPID LANGUAGE DEVELOPMENT. HOWEVER, BECAUSE ENVIRONMENTAL STIMULATION DURING LATER YEARS PROFOUNDLY INFLUENCES INTELLECTUAL FUNCTIONING, EDUCATION MUST BE A CONTINUING PROCESS. IN FACT, DATA INDICATES THAT IQ SCORES INCREASE DURING INTENSIVE INTELLECTUAL STIMULATION AND DECREASE WHEN SUCH STIMULATION IS TERMINATED. THERE IS, THEREFORE, A NEED FOR FAMILY-CENTERED PROGRAMS DESIGNED TO INCREASE THE EDUCATIONAL QUALITY OF FAMILY INTERACTION THROUGHOUT THE PERIOD OF CHILD DEVELOPMENT. PARENT TRAINING PROGRAMS HAVE BEEN SUCCESSFUL IN IMPROVING PARENTAL BEHAVIOR. PARENTS SHOULD BE RECOGNIZED AS THE MOST INFLUENTIAL EDUCATORS OF THEIR OWN CHILDREN AND PROVIDED WITH TEACHING SKILLS. (MH)

ED040751 PS003070
ATTENTIONAL PREFERENCE AND EXPERIENCE: I. INTRODUCTION. HUNT, J. MCV., JAN 70 9P.
EDRS PRICE MF-$0.65 HC-$3.29

THIS PAPER INTRODUCES AND GIVES A REPORT OF THE FIRST OF A SERIES OF STUDIES CONCERNED WITH THE DEVELOPMENTAL ASPECTS OF INFORMATION PROCESSING. THE EXPERIMENTS ARE CONCERNED CHIEFLY WITH HOW REPEATED VISUAL ENCOUNTERS INFLUENCE INFANTS' ATTENTIONAL PREFERENCE FOR WHAT IS FAMILIAR OR UNFAMILIAR AND HOW INFANTS' PREFERENCE CAN BE AFFECTED BY RESPONSIVENESS TO THE INFANTS' SPONTANEOUS EFFORTS. IN THE FIRST EXPLORATORY STUDY OF THE SERIES, TWO STIMULUS PATTERNS WERE PLACED OVER THE CRIBS OF 15 INFANTS FOR THE INFANTS TO LOOK AT AND BE FAMILIAR WITH. ONE PATTERN WAS STATIONARY AND ONE MOVED. FOLLOWING 4 TO 5 WEEKS OF EXPOSURE, EACH BABY'S PREFERENCE FOR ONE OF THE PATTERNS WAS ASSESSED. NEXT, EACH OF THE FAMILIAR PATTERNS WAS PRESENTED SIMULTANEOUSLY WITH AN UNFAMILIAR ONE AND THEN REVERSED, AND A RECORD OF THE DIRECTION OF THE INFANT'S GAZE WAS KEPT. RESULTS FAVORED THE HYPOTHESIS OF ATTENTIONAL PREFERENCE FOR THE FAMILIAR PATTERN. THE GENERAL STRATEGY USED IN THIS STUDY IS TO BE FURTHER REFINED IN THE AUTHOR'S SUBSEQUENT STUDIES. (DR)

ED040752 PS003073
A STATEMENT ON THE COMPREHENSIVE PRESCHOOL EDUCATION AND CHILD DAY-CARE ACT OF 1969 BEFORE THE SELECT SUBCOMMITTEE ON EDUCATION OF THE HOUSE COMMITTEE ON EDUCATION AND LABOR, MARCH 3, 1970. MESSICK, SAMUEL, 3 MAR 70 10P.
EDRS PRICE MF-$0.65 HC-$3.29

THIS DOCUMENT PRAISES THE COMPREHENSIVE PRESCHOOL EDUCATION AND CHILD DAY-CARE ACT AND ADVOCATES AN EQUALLY COMPREHENSIVE COLLATERAL PROGRAM OF RESEARCH AND EVALUATION. IN ORDER TO AVOID DELAY IN STARTING PRESCHOOL AND CHILD CARE PROGRAMS, THE RESEARCH UNDERTAKEN SHOULD BE OF THE KIND CALLED EVALUATIVE RESEARCH IN WHICH PROGRAM AND RESEARCH ARE IN PROGRESS SIMULTANEOUSLY. THE RESEARCH MODEL IS THEREFORE INTEGRATED INTO THE PROGRAM AND FOCUSES ON PROCESS AS WELL AS PRODUCT MEASURES. ALTHOUGH TRADITIONAL RESEARCH HAS FOLLOWED AN ENGINEERING MODEL, THE RESEARCH ASSOCIATED WITH THESE PRESCHOOL PROGRAMS SHOULD FOLLOW A MEDICAL MODEL. THE IMPLICATIONS OF A MEDICAL MODEL INCLUDE ASSESSMENT OF BOTH INTENDED AND POSSIBLE OUTCOMES, AND FREQUENT MONITORING OF PARTICIPANTS' FEELINGS AND PROGRAM PROCESSES. AN EXAMPLE OF SUCH RESEARCH IS THE HEAD START LONGITUDINAL STUDY OF DISADVANTAGED CHILDREN BEING CARRIED ON BY EDUCATIONAL TESTING SERVICE. INCLUDED IS A DESCRIPTION OF SOME OF THE PROBLEMS ENCOUNTERED IN THIS PROJECT. (MH)

ED040753 PS003077
VIEWS ON PRE-SCHOOL EDUCATION AND DAY CARE. RAMBUSCH, NANCY MCCORMICK, [69] 10P.
EDRS PRICE MF-$0.65 HC-$3.29

THERE IS A CLEAR NEED IN OUR COUNTRY TODAY FOR EARLY EDUCATION PROGRAMS AIMED AT ACCELERATING THE COGNITIVE DEVELOPMENT OF DISADVANTAGED CHILDREN. ANOTHER NEED IS FOR CENTERS TO CARE FOR THE CHILDREN OF WORKING MOTHERS. OUR TRADITIONAL NURSERY SCHOOLS HAVE DEEMPHASIZED EARLY COGNITIVE DEVELOPMENT WHILE DAY CARE PROGRAMS HAVE BEEN FOCUSED ON DEPRIVED CHILDREN AND INADEQUATE PARENTS. THERE ARE SOME MARGINALLY SUCCESSFUL COMPENSATORY PRESCHOOL PROGRAMS UNDER HEAD START IMPETUS, BUT THESE PROGRAMS HAVE LITTLE IN COMMON WITH CONVENTIONAL PRESCHOOL EDUCATION. THE POPULAR CONCEPTIONS OF PRESCHOOL EDUCATION AND DAY CARE HAVE LITTLE TO DO WITH MEETING THE CHILD'S COGNITIVE NEEDS OR HIS MOTHER'S NEED FOR SELF-ESTEEM. WHAT WE NEED TODAY IS A NEW PROGRAM DESIGN THAT COMBINES TEMPORAL FLEXIBILITY WITH KNOWN EFFECTIVE CHILD CARE AND EDUCATIONAL PRACTICES. IT IS RECOMMENDED THAT THESE NEW BLENDS OF EARLY EDUCATION AND CHILD CARE BE DEVELOPED TO AVOID IDENTIFICATION WITH INDIGENCE AND MATERNAL INEPTNESS. THOSE PROGRAMS SHOULD PROVIDE INCENTIVES FOR MOTHERS TO BECOME INVOLVED SO THAT THROUGH TRAINING, THEY ACHIEVE SELF DETERMINATION. IT IS FURTHER RECOMMENDED THAT RESEARCHERS BE FUNDED TO CONTINUE TO SEARCH FOR THE MOST EFFECTIVE TECHNIQUES OF EARLY EDUCATION. (MH)

ED040754 PS003120
THE MISPLACED ADAPTATION TO INDIVIDUAL DIFFERENCES. HOLLAND, JAMES G., 69 6P.
EDRS PRICE MF-$0.65 HC-$3.29

THE CURRENT INTEREST IN AN EDUCATIONAL TECHNOLOGY THAT STRESSES ADAPTATION TO INDIVIDUAL STUDENT DIFFERENCES HAS RESULTED IN SUCH INDIVIDUALIZED SYSTEMS AS INDIVIDUALLY PRESCRIBED INSTRUCTION (IPI) AND COMPUTER ASSISTED INSTRUCTION (CAI). HOWEVER, SUCH SYSTEMS ARE NOT THE ANSWER TO AN AVOIDANCE OF STANDARDIZATION OF STUDENTS. NO ONE HAS YET RESOLVED THE BASIC DILEMMA BETWEEN THE COST IN TIME-AND-EFFORT EFFICIENCY AND THE DEMANDS OF TEST THEORY FOR VALIDITY AND RELIABILITY OF TESTS. THIS DILEMMA MEANS THAT WHILE GOOD TEACHING ITEMS SHOULD HAVE A LOW ERROR FACTOR IN ORDER TO ELICIT THE CORRECT RESPONSE AND THEN REINFORCE IT, GOOD DIAGNOSTIC ITEMS (NEEDED FOR INDIVIDUALIZATION) SHOULD NOT HAVE A LOW ERROR FACTOR. THUS, GOOD TEACHING ITEMS MEET CRITERIA INCOMPATIBLE WITH THOSE MET BY GOOD DIAGNOSTIC ITEMS. THIS PROBLEM IS NOT INSURMOUNTABLE, BUT NONE OF THE EXISTING PROGRAMS OF INDIVIDUALIZED INSTRUCTION HAVE SOLVED IT. THE MOST PERSUASIVE POINT AGAINST THE EXISTING PROGRAMS IS THAT THEY ARE INDIVIDUALIZED ONLY IN TERMS OF WHAT THE STUDENT BRINGS TO THE LESSON; THEY STILL RESULT IN THE PRODUCTION OF UNIFORMITY. (MH)

ED040755 PS003123
A SKILL DEVELOPMENT CURRICULUM FOR 3, 4, AND 5 YEAR OLD DISADVANTAGED CHILDREN. CAMP, JANET C., JUN 69 7P.
EDRS PRICE MF-$0.65 HC-$3.29

THIS PAPER DESCRIBES THE DARCEE CURRICULUM DESIGNED TO PREPARE YOUNG DISADVANTAGED CHILDREN FOR SCHOOL. THE EMPHASIS OF THE CURRICULUM IS ON THE DEVELOPMENT OF INFORMATION PROCESSING SKILLS, RATHER THAN ON THE LEARNING OF SPECIFIC INFORMATION. THE CURRICULUM IS IMPLEMENTED IN THE FORM OF A SEQUENTIALLY PROGRAMMED, STRUCTURED INSTRUCTIONAL PROGRAM. THE SKILL DEVELOPMENT OBJECTIVES FOLLOW THE BASIC STAGES IN THE PROCESSING OF INFORMATION AND ARE CATEGORIZED UNDER EITHER SENSORY SKILLS, ABSTRACTING AND MEDIATING SKILLS, OR RESPONSE SKILLS. SENSORY SKILLS INCLUDE ALL THE PROCESSES OF SUCCESSFUL INPUT AND DECODING OF ENVIRONMENTAL STIMULI, INVOLVING THE ORIENTING SKILL, THE DISCRIMINATORY SKILL, THE RELATIONAL SKILL, AND THE SEQUENTIAL SKILL. THE DARCEE CURRICULUM ALSO DEVELOPS THE ABSTRACTING AND MEDIATING SKILLS. THESE SKILLS COMPRISE THE ORGANIZATION PROCESS, THE AREAS OF WHICH HAVE BEEN DESIGNATED AS BASIC CONCEPT DEVELOPMENT ASSOCIATION, CLASSIFICATION SEQUENCING, AND CRITICAL THINKING. THE RESPONSE OR OUTPUT SKILLS CONCENTRATED ON BY THE DARCEE CURRICULUM ARE THOSE OF FINE EYE-HAND COORDINATION AND VERBALIZATION. THE CONTENT OF THE CURRICULUM IS ORDERED INTO INTERRELATED UNITS WHOSE THEMES WERE CHOSEN BECAUSE THEY WOULD BE OF INTEREST TO CHILDREN. THE NEED FOR A CHANGE IN ATTITUDES AND CURRICULA IN OUR PUBLIC SCHOOL SYSTEMS IS STRESSED. (MH)

ED040756 PS003125
TRANSPLANTING ENGLISH INFANT SCHOOL IDEAS TO AMERICAN CLASSROOMS AND SOME EFFECTS ON LANGUAGE USE. CAZDEN, COURTNEY B., 6 MAR 70 10P.
EDRS PRICE MF-$0.65 HC-$3.29

THE RESEARCH METHODOLOGY OF THIS STUDY IS AT LEAST AS IMPORTANT AS THE ACTUAL FINDINGS. FOR CERTAIN TYPES OF INFORMATION SEEKING, DIRECTED CONVERSATIONS, OR INTERVIEWS, SEEM MOST DESIRABLE. YET, ALTHOUGH SUCH CONVERSATIONS ARE EASY TO CARRY ON WITH TEACHERS, THEY ARE DIFFICULT TO MANAGE WITH 6-YEAR-OLD CHILDREN, ESPECIALLY WHEN THE INTERVIEWER IS UNFAMILIAR TO THE CHILD. IN THIS STUDY, ONE OF THE INTERVIEWER'S ASSISTANTS WROTE A DETAILED DESCRIPTION OF FIVE MINUTES OF THE CHILD'S BEHAVIOR WHILE ANOTHER ASSISTANT TOOK POLAROID PICTURES OF THE CHILD AT THE SAME TIME. IN THE AFTERNOON, THE INTERVIEWER TOOK EACH CHILD ASIDE AND ASKED HIM TO DESCRIBE WHAT HE WAS DOING IN THE PICTURES. THE CHILDREN SPOKE FREELY AND EASILY WITH THE INTERVIEWER ABOUT THE PICTURES AND THEIR OWN ACTIVITY. DATA COLLECTED IN THIS MANNER AND FROM OTHER TECHNIQUES WERE USED TO COMPARE THE FOLLOW-THROUGH CLASSROOMS OF TEACHER A (CHILD-DIRECTED INDIVIDUALIZED LEARNING) AND TEACHER B (TEACHER-DIRECTED GROUP INSTRUCTION). THE CHILDREN IN TEACHER A'S CLASS VALUED "OTHER ACTIVITIES" (BLOCK PLAY, WATER PLAY, LISTENING TO RECORDS) MORE THAN "DOING WHAT THE TEACHER LIKES" AND "DOING" TRADITIONAL ACADEMIC TASKS, WHILE TEACHER B'S STUDENTS DID NOT. ALSO, THE LANGUAGE USED BY TEACHER A'S STUDENTS WAS MORE DIFFERENTIATED AND VARIED THAN THAT USED BY THE OTHER CLASS. (MH)

ED040757 PS003130
PROCESS ACCOUNTABILITY IN CURRICULUM DEVELOPMENT. GOOLER, DENNIS D.; GROTELUESCHEN, ARDEN, [70] 11P.
EDRS PRICE MF-$0.65 HC-$3.29

THIS PAPER URGES THE CURRICULUM DEVELOPER TO ASSUME THE ACCOUNTABILITY FOR HIS DECISIONS NECESSITATED BY THE ACTUAL WAYS OUR SOCIETY FUNCTIONS. THE CURRICULUM DEVELOPER IS ENCOURAGED TO RECOGNIZE THAT HE IS A SALESMAN WITH A COMMODITY (THE CURRICULUM). HE IS URGED TO REALIZE THAT IF HE CANNOT MARKET THE PACKAGE TO THE CUSTOMERS (THE VARIOUS INTEREST GROUPS) THE CURRICULUM-COMMODITY WILL GO UNCONSUMED, NO MATTER WHAT ITS VIRTUES. THE ACCEPTANCE OR REJECTION OF A CURRICULUM BY THE CONSUMERS REPRESENTS THE ACCOUNTABILITY OF THE CURRICULUM DEVELOPER. HE HAS TO BE AWARE OF THE RELATIVE "CLOUT" WIELDED BY VARIOUS INTEREST GROUPS AND BE PREPARED, IN ADVANCE, TO DEMONSTRATE THAT HIS PRODUCT (CURRICULUM) IS WHAT THEY WANT AND NEED. HE MUST DO THIS PARTICULARLY AT THE "MAJOR MOMENTS" (NEED ASSESSMENT, CURRICULUM GOALS, CONTENT, METHODOLOGY AND FORMAT) IN THE DEVELOPMENTAL PROCESS, WHEN THE INTEREST GROUPS DIRECT THEIR CLAIMS OF ACCOUNTABILITY. THE CURRICULUM DEVELOPER NEEDS HELP TO PREPARE FOR THESE MAJOR MOMENTS, AND, THEREFORE, HAS NEED OF AN EVALUATOR. THE EVALUATOR CAN FUNCTION IN THE ROLE OF A SORT OF MARKET RESEARCH ANALYST, IDENTIFYING "POCKETS OF POTENTIAL PERSUASION" AND AIDING IN PACKAGING THE CURRICULUM-COMMODITY SO THAT IT WILL BE MOST INTERESTING AND USEFUL TO THE CONSUMERS. (MH)

ED040758 PS003133
A STUDY OF ONE LEARNER COGNITIVE STYLE AND THE ABILITY TO GENERALIZE BEHAVIORAL COMPETENCIES. CARTER, HEATHER L., [68] 6P.
EDRS PRICE MF-$0.65 HC-$3.29

THE GENERALIZATION OF ACQUIRED COMPETENCIES, SPECIFICALLY FLEXIBILITY OF CLOSURE, WAS THE SUBJECT OF THIS RESEARCH. FLEXIBILITY OF CLOSURE WAS DEFINED AS THE ABILITY TO DEMONSTRATE SELECTIVE ATTENTION TO A SPECIFIED SET OF ELEMENTS WHEN PRESENTED WITHIN VARIOUS SETTINGS (THE LARGER THE NUMBER OF SETTINGS FROM WHICH THE DESIRED SET OF ELEMENTS CAN BE SELECTED, THE HIGHER THE LEVEL OF FLEXIBILITY OF CLOSURE). THIS STUDY SOUGHT, SPECIFICALLY, TO DETERMINE WHETHER OR NOT THERE IS A SIGNIFICANT RELATIONSHIP BETWEEN FLEXIBILITY OF CLOSURE AND THE ABILITY TO GENERALIZE. THE SUBJECTS WERE A RANDOMLY SELECTED GROUP OF 64 FIRST, SECOND, THIRD, AND FOURTH GRADERS. FLEXIBILITY OF CLOSURE WAS MEASURED BY "THE CHILDREN'S EMBED-

DED FIGURES TEST." ABILITY TO GENERALIZE WAS MEASURED BY THE "SCIENCE PROCESS INSTRUMENT." THE SCIENCE TOPICS COVERED WERE CONTAINED IN THE ELEMENTARY SCIENCE PROGRAM "SCIENCE--A PROCESS APPROACH." ANALYSIS OF DATA REVEALED A SIGNIFICANT CORRELATION BETWEEN THE GENERALIZATION SCORES AND THE SCORES ON THE FLEXIBILITY OF CLOSURE MEASURE FOR THE TOTAL GROUP. WHEN THE DATA WAS BROKEN DOWN BY GRADE LEVEL AND SEX, HOWEVER, THE FINDINGS WERE NOT SIGNIFICANT FOR GIRLS OR THE FIRST AND SECOND GRADE. (MH)

ED040759 PS003157
A FACTOR ANALYTIC STUDY OF CHILDREN'S CAUSAL REASONING. BERZONSKY, MICHAEL D., 6 MAR 70 11P.
EDRS PRICE MF-$0.65 HC-$3.29

BECAUSE KNOWLEDGE OF THE COMPONENT SUBSKILLS OF CAUSAL REASONING WOULD AID IN PLANNING ELEMENTARY SCIENCE CURRICULA, THIS STUDY SOUGHT TO IDENTIFY COMPONENT ABILITIES THROUGH THE INDIVIDUAL ADMINISTRATION OF A BATTERY OF 29 TESTS TO A RANDOMLY-SELECTED SAMPLE OF 84 FIRST-GRADERS, EVENLY DIVIDED BY SEX. THESE TESTS WERE: (1) VERBAL TESTS OF CAUSALITY (3 VARIABLES), (2) HYPOTHESIZED CAUSAL COMPONENTS (10 VARIABLES), (3) CAUSAL DEMONSTRATIONS (8 VARIABLES), (4) PIAGETIAN CONCRETE OPERATIONAL TASKS (5 VARIABLES), (5) PIAGETIAN FORMAL OPERATIONAL TASKS (2 VARIABLES), (6) INTELLIGENCE (1 VARIABLE), AND (7) DESCRIPTIVE MEASURE (1 VARIABLE). THE RESULTS WERE ANALYZED BY SUBMITTING THE 30 VARIABLES TO A MAXIMUM-LIKELIHOOD FACTOR ANALYSIS WITH A VARIMAX ROTATION. THROUGH THIS PROCESS, A VERBAL CAUSAL REASONING FACTOR, INCLUDING THE 5 COMPONENT SUBSKILLS OF CHANCE, SKEPTICISM, PERSPECTIVES, COMPLETING "BECAUSE" STATEMENTS, AND DETECTING INCONGRUOUS CAUSAL RELATIONS, WAS IDENTIFIED. OTHER RESULTS FAIL TO SUPPORT BOTH PIAGET'S THEORY THAT PREOPERATIONAL THOUGHT LEADS TO PRECAUSAL EXPLANATIONS AND PIAGET AND INHELDER'S THEORY OF THE UNITARY NATURE OF LOGICAL THINKING. RATHER, RESULTS SUGGEST THAT AT LEAST 3 RELATIVELY INDEPENDENT ABILITIES ARE INVOLVED IN LOGICAL THINKING. (MH)

ED040760 PS003207
PERSPECTIVE ON THE JENSEN AFFAIR. BRAZZIEL, WILLIAM F., [70] 6P.
EDRS PRICE MF-$0.65 HC-$3.29

IN THE WINTER OF 1969, THE "HARVARD EDUCATION REVIEW" PUBLISHED AN ARTICLE BY ARTHUR JENSEN THAT SUGGESTED THAT RACIAL AND SOCIAL CLASS IQ DIFFERENCES WERE PRIMARILY DUE TO HEREDITARY FACTORS. FROM THE POINT OF VIEW OF THE OPPOSITION, THIS REPORT REVIEWS THE CONTROVERSY THAT ENSUED, INCLUDING JENSEN'S ORIGINAL STATEMENTS, THE CRITICS' REBUTTALS, AND JENSEN'S DEFENSES. IT IS POINTED OUT THAT JENSEN'S EXPLANATIONS HAVE FAILED TO SATISFY CRITICS WHO HAVE CITED ERRONEOUS STATISTICAL TRANSPOSITIONS AND SELECTIVE ATTENTION TO CO-TWIN STUDIES. IT IS SUGGESTED THAT THE WHOLE AFFAIR BE FORGOTTEN AND ATTENTION TURNED TOWARDS IMPROVING THE CONDITIONS OF THE POOR AND PROVIDING QUALITY EDUCATION FOR ALL. (MH)

ED040761 PS003208
[A STATEMENT REGARDING THE COMPREHENSIVE PRESCHOOL EDUCATION AND CHILD DAY CARE ACT OF 1969, AND OTHER RELATED BILLS.] GREER, WILLIAM C., 26 FEB 70 9P.
EDRS PRICE MF-$0.65 HC-$3.29

THIS SPEECH BEGINS WITH PRAISE FOR THE SUBCOMMITTEE'S PAST ACTION IN FURTHERING THE EDUCATION OF THE HANDICAPPED AND ENCOURAGING FEDERAL ASSISTANCE FOR THESE CHILDREN. THE GROWING NEED FOR ADDITIONAL AID FOR PRESCHOOL EDUCATION TO MEET THE DEVELOPMENTAL NEEDS OF HANDICAPPED CHILDREN IS EMPHASIZED. ALSO DISCUSSED ARE THE SPARSENESS OF GOVERNMENT PROGRAMS IN THE ABOVE AREA, THE EXPERTISE AND LEADERSHIP OF THE BUREAU OF EDUCATION FOR THE HANDICAPPED (BEH), AND THE PRESSING NEEDS OF CHILDREN LIVING IN HANDICAPPING ENVIRONMENTAL CONDITIONS. IT IS RECOMMENDED THAT (1) PROGRAMS BE ESTABLISHED FOR THE IDENTIFICATION AND AID OF HANDICAPPED CHILDREN, (2) SUCH PROGRAMS BE ADMINISTERED BY THE BEH, (3) PROJECTS BE AWARDED TO ANY AGENCY THAT DEMONSTRATES ITS CAPABILITY TO SERVE HANDICAPPED CHILDREN, (4) SUCH PROJECTS DEMONSTRATE COORDINATION WITH EXISTING CHILD DEVELOPMENT AND HANDICAPPED CHILDREN SERVICES, (5) TYPICAL PROJECTS SHOULD OFFER SEVERAL SERVICES (INCLUDING DIAGNOSIS, PREPARATION OF EDUCATIONAL PRESCRIPTIONS, AND A COMMUNICATION NETWORK), (6) THESE OBJECTIVES BE MET BY EXPANSION OF THE HANDICAPPED CHILDREN'S EARLY EDUCATION ASSISTANCE ACT OR BY SPECIFIC INCLUSION IN OTHER BILLS, AND (7) COST BE DEFRAYED BY FEDERAL AND STATE FUNDS. (MH)

ED040762 PS003209
[A STATEMENT REGARDING THE COMPREHENSIVE PRESCHOOL EDUCATION AND CHILD DAY CARE ACT OF 1969, AND OTHER RELATED BILLS.] MCCONNELL, FREEMAN, 26 FEB 70 8P.
EDRS PRICE MF-$0.65 HC-$3.29

THIS SPEECH WAS MADE IN FAVOR OF LEGISLATION DESIGNED TO PROVIDE COMPREHENSIVE PRESCHOOL EDUCATION FOR THE NATION'S CHILDREN. IT IS URGED THAT THE NEEDS OF THE HANDICAPPED CHILDREN OF OUR COUNTRY BE PARTICULARLY CONSIDERED. SIXTY TO EIGHTY PER CENT OF THE CHILDREN IN CLASSROOMS FOR THE RETARDED ARE CUMULATIVE PRODUCTS OF ENVIRONMENTAL FACTORS. THOSE CHILDREN SUFFERING FROM ORGANIC DISORDERS ALSO NEED AND DESERVE HELP. A CHILD IS BORN WITH AN "IMPAIRMENT"; WHETHER HE BECOMES "HANDICAPPED" OR NOT DEPENDS IN LARGE MEASURE ON THE FAVORABILITY OF HIS EARLY DEVELOPMENTAL ENVIRONMENT. SUPPORTIVE DATA IS PRESENTED FROM A 5-YEAR-STUDY IN EARLY INTERVENTION AT VANDERBILT UNIVERSITY. ALSO MENTIONED IS A PRESCHOOL PROGRAM FOR DEAF CHILDREN WHO WERE SUBSEQUENTLY ABLE TO ENTER NORMAL CLASSROOMS, BUT WHO, WITHOUT THE PROGRAM, WERE DESTINED TO BECOME DEAF MUTES. SUCH SPECIALIZED PROGRAMS ARE IMPOSSIBLE WITHOUT PUBLIC FINANCIAL ASSISTANCE. BOTH THE LEGISLATION ITSELF AND THE CONCEPT OF COMPREHENSIVE PRESCHOOL EDUCATION FOR ALL CHILDREN ARE SUPPORTED WITH THE RECOMMENDATION THAT ALLOWANCES BE MADE FOR ADDITIONAL MODELS FOR SENSORILY AND PHYSICALLY IMPAIRED CHILDREN AND CHILDREN FROM POVERTY AREAS. (MH)

ED040763 PS003646
LANGUAGE PROGRAMS FOR YOUNG CHILDREN: NOTES FROM ENGLAND AND WALES. CAZDEN, COURTNEY B., 70 46P.
EDRS PRICE MF-$0.65 HC-$3.29

BRITISH INFANT SCHOOL PROGRAMS TO AID LANGUAGE DEVELOPMENT FOR DISADVANTAGED CHILDREN 3 TO 8 YEARS OLD ARE DISCUSSED, WITH REFERENCE TO IDEAS AND PRACTICES IN THE UNITED STATES. IN GENERAL, ENGLISH INFANT SCHOOL TEACHERS BELIEVE THAT LANGUAGE DEVELOPMENT MUST BE NOURISHED BY THE TEACHER IN THE CONTEXT OF THE CHILD'S INTERACTION WITH HIS ENVIRONMENT. CENTRALLY IMPORTANT IS A HEIGHTENED TEACHER AWARENESS OF MEANS OF EXTENSION OF THE CHILD'S IDEAS AND LANGUAGE. OTHER TOPICS DISCUSSED ARE: (1) THE VALUE OF PEER GROUP TALK, (2) DAILY SCHEDULES RELATIVE TO THE CHILD'S SEX, (3) EXTRINSIC REINFORCEMENT, CONTRASTED WITH INTRINSIC REINFORCEMENT, (4) WHETHER OR NOT STANDARD ENGLISH SHOULD BE TAUGHT, (5) THE USE OF LOCAL CULTURAL CONTENT, (6) BILINGUALISM IN SCHOOL AND OUT, (7) COMMUNICATION SKILLS, (8) CHILDREN'S WRITTEN SENTENCES, (9) VERBAL FUNCTIONING EFFECTIVENESS, AND (10) COMPENSATORY EDUCATION: THE RECOMMENDATIONS OF THE PLOWDEN REPORT, AND THE GOALS OF THE 3 1/2-YEAR SCHOOLS COUNCIL PROJECT IN ENGLAND AND WALES. (NH)

ED040764 PS003647
ON THE HETEROGENEITY OF PSYCHOLOGICAL PROCESSES IN SYNTACTIC DEVELOPMENT. HASS, WILBUR A., 70 12P.
EDRS PRICE MF-$0.65 HC-$3.29

CHILDREN'S LANGUAGE ACQUISITION IS VIEWED BY DEVELOPMENTAL PSYCHOLINGUISTS AS A PROCESS OF CHANGE IN THE ORGANIZATION OF LANGUAGE PROCESSING OPERATIONS. NORMAL CHILDREN SEEM TO ACQUIRE THEIR NATIVE LANGUAGE BY THIS PROCESS, RATHER THAN BY ELIMINATING SPECIFIC MISTAKES. PRESCHOOL LANGUAGE DEVELOPS IN STAGES, AND KNOWLEDGE OF WHERE SYNTACTIC CHANGE IS LIKELY TO OCCUR SHOULD BE USED IN PLANNING AND EVALUATION OF EARLY EDUCATION PROGRAMS. IT IS USEFUL TO KNOW WHY CERTAIN SYNTACTIC CONSTRUCTIONS ARE TO OPEN TO CHANGE IN THE PRESCHOOL YEARS. FOR EXAMPLE, THREE PROCESSES ARE INVOLVED IN THE PRODUCTION OF ELABORATED NOUN PHRASES. THEY ARE (1) SURFACE SYNTACTIC STRUCTURE, (2) DEEP STRUCTURE, AND (3) SYNTACTIC TRANSFORMATIONS. THESE ASPECTS OF PROCESSING LANGUAGE CAN BE FACILITATED BY INSTRUCTION IN PERCEPTUAL-MOTOR SKILLS, BY USE OF REFERENTIAL CUES IN THE LANGUAGE SITUATION, AND BY ROLE PLAYING WITH SERIOUS COMMUNICATIONAL INTENT. CURRENT LANGUAGE CURRICULA COMBINE THESE ASPECTS IN UNSYSTEMATIC WAYS, SO THAT IT IS NOT CLEAR WHAT PROCESSES HAVE BEEN AFFECTED WHEN A CHANGE TAKES PLACE IN A CHILD'S GRAMMATICAL CONSTRUCTION. ULTIMATELY, LANGUAGE PROGRAMS SHOULD BE DIRECTED TO THE INDIVIDUAL'S SPECIFIC LANGUAGE NEEDS. COGNITIVE FACILITATION IS NOT NECESSARILY TO BE EXPECTED BUT IS DEPENDENT UPON THE PARTICULAR FEATURES INCLUDED IN EACH PROGRAM. (NH)

ED040765 PS003648
SOME LANGUAGE COMPREHENSION TESTS. BELLUGI-KLIMA, URSULA, 70 15P.
EDRS PRICE MF-$0.65 HC-$3.29

TO ASSESS A CHILD'S COMMUNICATIVE ABILITY, IT IS IMPORTANT TO DEVELOP NOT ONLY MEASURES OF HIS UNDERSTANDING OF VOCABULARY, BUT OF HIS UNDERSTANDING OF THE SYNTAX OF LANGUAGE: PATTERNS OF WORDS, REGULARITIES, AND RELATIONSHIPS OF WORDS IN A SENTENCE. CONTROLLED TEST SITUATIONS SHOULD BE ESTABLISHED IN WHICH THE CHILD RECEIVES MINIMAL CUES FROM THE SITUATION ITSELF. CHILDREN SHOULD CLEARLY UNDERSTAND THE MEANINGS OF

THE WORDS USED, AND TEST ITEMS SHOULD BE CONSTRUCTED SO CORRECT ANSWERS CANNOT BE GIVEN UNLESS THE CHILD COMPREHENDS THE SYNTAX BEING TESTED. THE CHILD IS VERBALLY INSTRUCTED ON WHAT TO DO WITH TOY TEST MATERIALS SUCH AS BOY AND GIRL DOLLS, BLOCKS, TOY ANIMALS, MARBLES, STICKS, AND CLAY. PROBLEMS ARE SET UP IN TERMS OF LEVELS OF DIFFICULTY. FIRST LEVEL ITEMS INCLUDE TESTING CHILDREN'S UNDERSTANDING OF ACTIVE SENTENCES SINGULAR/PLURAL NOUNS, AND POSSESSIVE NOUN INFLECTION. SECOND LEVEL ITEMS INCLUDE NEGATIVE/AFFIRMATIVE STATEMENTS, AND QUESTIONS, SINGULAR/PLURAL WITH NOUN AND VERB INFLECTIONS, AND ADJECTIVAL MODIFICATION. THIRD LEVEL PROBLEMS TEST FOR UNDERSTANDING OF NEGATIVE AFFIX, REFLEXIVIZATION, COMPARATIVES, PASSIVES, AND SELF-EMBEDDED SENTENCES. ALTHOUGH THE TESTS OF COMPREHENSION OF SYNTACTIC CONSTRUCTION HAVE NOT ALL BEEN TRIED OR STANDARDIZED, THEY ARE BASED ON LINGUISTIC THEORY, PSYCHOLINGUISTIC RESEARCH, AND DEVELOPMENTAL STUDIES OF CHILDREN'S SPEECH. (NH)

ED040766 PS003649
A TUTORIAL LANGUAGE PROGRAM FOR DISADVANTAGED INFANTS. PAINTER, GENEVIEVE, [69] 28P.
EDRS PRICE MF-$0.65 HC-$3.29

THIS STUDY ATTEMPTED TO AMELIORATE THE EDUCATIONAL DEFICITS OF INFANTS USING STRUCTURED TUTORIAL PROGRAMS OF LANGUAGE AND CONCEPT TRAINING IN THE HOME. IT WAS PART OF A LARGER PROJECT WHOSE PURPOSE WAS TO DETERMINE THE AGE AT WHICH INTERVENTION WILL PRODUCE MAXIMUM ACCELERATION OF COGNITIVE DEVELOPMENT. SUBJECTS WERE 20 DISADVANTAGED 8- AND 24-MONTH-OLD CHILDREN RANDOMLY ASSIGNED TO EXPERIMENTAL AND CONTROL GROUPS. FEMALE TUTORS WORKED WITH EACH EXPERIMENTAL SUBJECT IN HIS HOME 1 HOUR A DAY, 5 DAYS A WEEK, OVER 1 YEAR. IN THE FIRST 3 OR 4 WEEKS OF TRAINING RAPPORT WAS ESTABLISHED, AND THE CHILD'S DEVELOPMENT WAS STUDIED. LANGUAGE TRAINING STIMULATED INFANTS TO IMITATE ACTIONS AND SOUNDS, IDENTIFY AND NAME OBJECTS, VERBALIZE NEEDS, USE PICTURE BOOKS, DEVELOP ELABORATIVE LANGUAGE, AND USE INTERNAL DIALOGUE. CONCEPT TRAINING STIMULATED INFANTS TO UNDERSTAND CONCEPTS OF BODY IMAGE, SPACE, NUMBER, TIME, AND CLASSIFICATION. ON INITIAL TESTING BOTH GROUPS OF INFANTS WERE AVERAGE IN INTELLIGENCE AND MOTORIC DEVELOPMENT, BUT BELOW THEIR CHRONOLOGICAL AGE IN LANGUAGE AND CONCEPT DEVELOPMENT, AND IN INTERPRETATION OF SYMBOLIC REPRESENTATION. POSTTESTS SHOWED THAT THE EXPERIMENTAL GROUP HAD CONSISTENTLY HIGHER SCORES ON IQ, LANGUAGE, AND CONCEPTUAL DEVELOPMENT TESTS. THERE WERE NO SIGNIFICANT DIFFERENCES IN SENSORY-MOTOR DEVELOPMENT. (NH)

ED040767 PS003650
LANGUAGE RESEARCH AND PRESCHOOL LANGUAGE TRAINING. MOORE, DONALD R., [70] 57P.
EDRS PRICE MF-$0.65 HC-$3.29

THIS PAPER REVIEWS LITERATURE ON SUBCULTURAL DIFFERENCES IN LANGUAGE DEVELOPMENT TO FIND OUT WHAT THE LITERATURE SUGGESTS ABOUT THE NATURE OF A LANGUAGE PROGRAM FOR LOWER CLASS 4-YEAR-OLDS. THE FOLLOWING CONCLUSIONS ARE REACHED: (1) DIFFERENCES IN SYNTACTIC AND PHONOLOGICAL COMPETENCE ARE NOT IMPORTANT BARRIERS TO COMMUNICATION FOR THE LOWER CLASS PRESCHOOL CHILD AND SHOULD NOT BE THE FOCUS OF PRESCHOOL LANGUAGE TRAINING; (2) OF THE MANY SUBCULTURAL DIFFERENCES IN LANGUAGE, THE MAJOR ONE WHICH PUTS THE AVERAGE LOWER CLASS CHILD AT A "DISADVANTAGE" IS HIS RELATIVE LACK OF ABILITY TO USE A PRECISE LANGUAGE OF DESCRIPTION; (3) THE LITERATURE ON SUBCULTURAL DIFFERENCES IN LANGUAGE USE IDENTIFIES MANY OF THE SPECIFIC LANGUAGE SKILLS USED IN THIS ABSTRACT TYPE OF LANGUAGE; (4) THE TRADITIONAL PRESCHOOL IS NOT LIKELY TO FOSTER THE USE OF THE SPECIFIC LANGUAGE SKILLS WHICH THE LOWER CLASS CHILD MOST NEEDS TO MASTER; (5) OF TWO BROAD TYPES OF MORE FOCUSED LANGUAGE INTERVENTION PROGRAMS (ONE IN WHICH THE TEACHER'S RESPONSE IS CONTINGENT ON THE CHILD'S AND ONE IN WHICH THE CHILD'S RESPONSE IS CONTINGENT ON THE TEACHER'S), THE LATTER, MORE HIGHLY STRUCTURED, PROGRAM WILL PROBABLY BE MORE SUCCESSFUL IN TEACHING THE CRUCIAL LANGUAGE SKILLS. (AUTHOR/DR)

ED041614 PS002851
DEVELOPING COGNITIVE LEARNINGS WITH YOUNG CHILDREN. HAUPT, DOROTHY, 14 NOV 69 19P.
EDRS PRICE MF-$0.65 HC-$3.29

THIS PRELIMINARY STUDY EXPLORES (1) THE RELATIONSHIP BETWEEN CHILDREN'S BEHAVIORAL RESPONSES TO COGNITIVE TASKS IN A TESTING SITUATION AND IN A NURSERY SCHOOL ENVIRONMENT, AND (2) THE RELATIONSHIP OF THE ABOVE RESPONSES TO SEX, RACE, AND CLASS DIFFERENCES. STUDIES BY SIGEL INVESTIGATING THE CLASSIFICATION BEHAVIOR OF PRESCHOOL CHILDREN, AND BY HERTZIG, INVESTIGATING THE RESPONSES OF MIDDLE AND LOWER CLASS CHILDREN TO VERBAL AND PERFORMANCE TESTS, INFLUENCED THE FOCUS OF THE PRESENT STUDY. SUBJECTS WERE 30 4-YEAR-OLD MALE AND FEMALE CHILDREN OF DIFFERENT RACIAL AND SOCIO-ECONOMIC BACKGROUNDS. OBSERVATIONS WERE MADE OF THE INDIVIDUAL CHILD PRE- AND POSTTESTING SITUATIONS, WHICH USED THE SIGEL OBJECT AND PICTURE CATEGORIZATION TESTS AND A MOTOR ENCODING TASK. TEACHER REPORTS ASSESSED CHILDREN'S RESPONSES IN NURSERY SCHOOL. A TENTATIVE CONCLUSION IS THAT BOYS ATTEND LESS TO THE SPECIFICS OF A TASK DEMAND THAN DO GIRLS. LOW INCOME BLACK CHILDREN AND LOW INCOME WHITE MALES SHOWED A GREATER NUMBER OF BREAKAWAY AND NON-WORK RESPONSES DURING THE PICTURE CATEGORIZATION TASK THAN DID THE OTHER CHILDREN. LOW INCOME CHILDREN CHANGED THEIR RESPONSES TO TASK DEMANDS DURING THE PERIOD FROM PRE- TO POSTTESTING BY SHOWING INCREASED ATTENTION AND VERBALIZATION. (NH)

ED041615 PS002919
EXPERIMENTS IN HEAD START AND EARLY EDUCATION: THE EFFECTS OF TEACHER ATTITUDE AND CURRICULUM STRUCTURE ON PRESCHOOL DISADVANTAGED CHILDREN. FINAL REPORT. ERICKSON, EDSEL L.; AND OTHERS, NOV 69 186P.
EDRS PRICE MF-$0.65 HC-$6.58
AVAILABLE FROM: WESTERN'S CAMPUS BOOKSTORE, WESTERN MICHIGAN UNIVERSITY, KALAMAZOO, MICH 49001 ($6.25 PLUS .50 POST. & HANDLING, CK. PAYABLE TO W. CAMPUS BOOKSTORE)

THIS STUDY ASSESSES: (1) IMMEDIATE AND LONG TERM ACADEMIC AND PERSONAL ADJUSTMENT EFFECTS OF THE BEREITER-ENGELMANN PRESCHOOL PROGRAM AND OF THE TRADITIONAL ENRICHMENT PRESCHOOL PROGRAM, AS WELL AS THE EFFECTS OF NO PRESCHOOL EXPERIENCE; (2) EFFECTS OF THE ABOVE PROGRAMS ON CHILDREN AT THE KINDERGARTEN LEVEL; (3) INTERACTIVE EFFECTS OF EACH TYPE OF PRESCHOOL WHEN COMBINED WITH EACH TYPE OF KINDERGARTEN; AND (4) PROGRAM IMPACT ON TEACHERS AND PARENTS. SUBJECTS WERE INNER CITY PRESCHOOL CHILDREN: 180 RANDOMLY ASSIGNED TO EACH OF THE TWO EXPERIMENTAL PROGRAMS AND 640 TO THE CONTROL GROUP, GIVEN NO HEAD START TREATMENT. DATA WERE OBTAINED ON THE SUBJECT'S MEDICAL/DENTAL STATUS, USE OF LANGUAGE OTHER THAN ENGLISH, FAMILY CHARACTERISTICS, AND HOME AND CLASSROOM BEHAVIOR. FOR THE 2-YEAR PERIOD STUDIED, CONCLUSIONS WERE THAT THE BEREITER-ENGELMANN PROGRAM WAS SUPERIOR TO THE ENRICHMENT PRESCHOOL PROGRAM IN POSITIVELY MODIFYING EDUCATIONAL LEVELS. IT WAS FOUND THAT LONG TERM EFFECTS NEED NOT BE QUALIFIED BY SUBJECT DATA VARIABLES. INITIAL TEACHER ATTITUDES STACKED THE SUCCESS ODDS AGAINST, RATHER THAN FOR, THE SUPERIOR PROGRAM. IT IS RECOMMENDED THAT THE SUBJECTS IN THIS STUDY BE FOLLOWED FOR AT LEAST 2 MORE YEARS, THAT FURTHER RESEARCH BE DONE ON THE IMPACT OF TEACHER ATTITUDES; AND THAT CONTINUING PROGRAM EVALUATIONS BE MADE. APPENDIXES COMPRISE HALF OF THE DOCUMENT. (AUTHOR/NH)

ED041616 PS002961
A COMPARISON OF THREE INTERVENTION PROGRAMS WITH DISADVANTAGED PRESCHOOL CHILDREN. UNIVERSITY OF CALIFORNIA HEAD START RESEARCH AND EVALUATION CENTER. FINAL REPORT 1968-1969. EDWARDS, JOSEPH; STERN, CAROLYN, AUG 69 153P.
EDRS PRICE MF-$0.65 HC-$6.58

TO AID IN PROVIDING REMEDIATION FOR THE LANGUAGE AND COGNITIVE SKILLS OF DISADVANTAGED CHILDREN, THE UCLA HEAD START RESEARCH AND EVALUATION CENTER COMPARED THREE LANGUAGE PROGRAMS: THE UCLA PRESCHOOL LANGUAGE PROGRAM, THE BEHAVIORAL RESEARCH LABORATORIES' READINESS FOR LANGUAGE ARTS PROGRAM, AND AN UNSTRUCTURED PLACEBO PROGRAM. EACH OF THE SUBJECTS, 163 4-YEAR-OLD HEAD START CHILDREN, WAS RANDOMLY ASSIGNED BY SEX TO ONE OF THE PROGRAMS. A NO-TREATMENT HEAD START GROUP WAS USED FOR CONTROL. SUBJECTS WERE PRE- AND POSTTESTED ON THE PEABODY PICTURE VOCABULARY TEST, THE CALDWELL PRESCHOOL INVENTORY, THE GUMPGOOKIES, THE BEHAVIORAL RESEARCH LABORATORIES #1, THE VISUAL DISCRIMINATION INVENTORY, AND THE UCLA EARLY CHILDHOOD LANGUAGE TESTS FOR FOUR-YEAR-OLDS. EXPERIMENTAL TREATMENT EXTENDED OVER 24 WEEKS, 12 IN EACH OF 2 SEMESTERS. TESTING RESULTS (104 SUBJECTS) REVEALED THAT THE SUBJECTS IN THE TWO TASK-ORIENTED STRUCTURED LANGUAGE PROGRAMS WERE SUPERIOR IN PERFORMANCE TO BOTH PLACEBO AND CONTROL GROUPS. ALTHOUGH THE UCLA AND BRL PROGRAMS DIFFERED IN CONTENT, ACTIVITIES, AND MATERIALS, RESULTS WERE SIMILAR. AFRO-AMERICANS DID LESS WELL THAN ANGLO- OR MEXICAN-AMERICANS, GIRLS SLIGHTLY BETTER THAN BOYS, AND SUBJECTS WITH EXPERIENCED TEACHERS DID BETTER THAN THOSE WITH INEXPERIENCED TEACHERS. APPENDIXES COMPRISE FOUR-FIFTHS OF THIS REPORT. (MH/AUTHOR)

ED041617 PS003033
EXPERIMENTAL VARIATION OF HEAD START CURRICULA: A COMPARISON OF CURRENT APPROACHES. (NOVEMBER 1, 1969-JANUARY 31, 1970). MILLER, LOUISE B.; AND OTHERS, 31 JAN 70 42P.
EDRS PRICE MF-$0.65 HC-$3.29

THIS PAPER REPORTS RESULTS OF THE FIRST YEAR OF A 2-YEAR COMPARATIVE STUDY OF FOUR CURRICULA USED FOR DISADVANTAGED PRESCHOOL CHILDREN: BEREITER-ENGELMANN, DARCEE, MONTESSORI, AND TRADITIONAL (THE OFFICIAL HEAD START PROGRAM). DETAILS OF THE STUDY DESIGN AND PROCEDURES ARE CONTAINED IN THE ABBREVIATED ANNUAL PROGRESS REPORT FOR 1968-1969 (PS 003 034). TREATMENT (PROGRAM) DIMENSIONS WERE ASSESSED BY IN-CLASS MONITORING OF TEACHERS AND CHILDREN USING A TIME-SAMPLING

PROCEDURE, AND BY VIDEO-TAPE MONITORING OF TEACHERS IN THEIR CLASSROOMS. SIGNIFICANT DIFFERENCES WERE FOUND AMONG THE FOUR CURRICULA ON A NUMBER OF DIMENSIONS OF BEHAVIOR FOR BOTH TEACHERS AND CHILDREN, MOST OF THESE DIFFERENCES BEING IN PREDICTED DIRECTIONS. TREATMENT EFFECTS WERE ASSESSED BY USE OF A VARIETY OF COGNITIVE, SOCIAL, MOTIVATIONAL, PERCEPTUAL, AND ACHIEVEMENT MEASURES. PROGRAMS HAD SIGNIFICANTLY DIFFERENT EFFECTS ON THE CHILDREN WITH RESPECT TO A NUMBER OF VARIABLES MEASURED, SUCH AS CURIOSITY, INITIATIVE, ARITHMETIC, AND VERBAL PARTICIPATION. PRELIMINARY REGRESSION ANALYSES ON THE RELATIONSHIP BETWEEN TEACHING TECHNIQUES MONITORED IN CLASS AND DEPENDENT VARIABLES HAVE PRODUCED MULTIPLE R'S BETWEEN .229 AND .419 AND PARTIAL R'S BETWEEN - .293 AND .307. NO INTERPRETATION HAS BEEN MADE, PENDING THE INCLUSION OF VARIABLES FROM THE VIDEO-TAPE MONITORING. (AUTHOR/NH)

ED041618 PS003034
EXPERIMENTAL VARIATION OF HEAD START CURRICULA: A COMPARISON OF CURRENT APPROACHES. ANNUAL REPORT, JUNE 12, 1968-JUNE 11, 1969. MILLER, LOUISE B., 11 JUN 69 118P.
EDRS PRICE MF-$0.65 HC-$6.58

IN THIS STUDY, INVESTIGATORS MADE AN EXPERIMENTAL COMPARISON OF FOUR CURRICULA FOR HEAD START CLASSES: (1) THE OFFICIAL (OR "TRADITIONAL") HEAD START PROGRAM, EMPHASIZING ENRICHMENT OF EXPERIENCE, INDIVIDUAL DIFFERENCES, A CLIMATE OF FREEDOM, AND LEARNING BY DOING, (2) THE DARCEE PROGRAM, EMPHASIZING REINFORCEMENT OF ATTITUDES COMBINED WITH TRAINING IN BASIC SKILLS AND INTENSIVE WORK WITH MOTHERS, (3) THE ACADEMIC DRILLS APPROACH OF BEREITER AND ENGELMANN, EMPHASIZING THE ABILITY TO HANDLE LINGUISTIC AND NUMERICAL SYMBOLS, AND (4) THE MONTESSORI PROGRAM, CHARACTERIZED BY A HIGH DEGREE OF STRUCTURE IN RESPECT TO THE ANALYSIS AND SEQUENCING OF TASKS, COMBINED WITH GREAT FLEXIBILITY IN THAT EACH CHILD IS EXPECTED TO PURSUE HIS OWN INTERESTS. DURING THE 1968-69 SCHOOL YEAR 14 CLASSES WERE CONDUCTED--TWO MONTESSORI CLASSES, AND FOUR CLASSES IN EACH OF THE OTHER PROGRAM STYLES. THE 4-YEAR-OLDS IN THESE CLASSES WERE PRE- AND POSTTESTED WITH NINE INSTRUMENTS, SELECTED TO ASSESS GAINS IN COGNITIVE, MOTIVATIONAL, SOCIAL, AND PERCEPTUAL DEVELOPMENT. A NON-PRESCHOOL CONTROL GROUP WAS ALSO TESTED. CLASSES WERE MONITORED PERIODICALLY THROUGHOUT THE YEAR TO ASSESS TREATMENT DIMENSIONS. ALL PHASES OF THE FIRST YEAR OF THIS STUDY ARE NOW COMPLETE. DATA ANALYSIS IS IN PROCESS. TABLES AND APPENDICES ARE INCLUDED. (AUTHOR/NH)

ED041619 PS003149
DIRECT VERBAL INSTRUCTION CONTRASTED WITH MONTESSORI METHODS IN THE TEACHING OF NORMAL FOUR-YEAR-OLD CHILDREN. , [69] 21P.
EDRS PRICE MF-$0.65 HC-$3.29

THIS STUDY COMPARES THE EFFECTS OF MONTESSORI METHODS OF INSTRUCTION AND METHODS OF DIRECT VERBAL INSTRUCTION. MONTESSORI METHODS RELY ON THE ABILITY OF THE CHILD TO LEARN THROUGH PHYSICAL INTERACTION WITH INANIMATE OBJECTS AND MINIMIZE VERBAL BEHAVIOR BY TEACHER AND STUDENT, WHILE THE DIRECT VERBAL METHOD WORKS MAINLY THROUGH LANGUAGE USE, BOTH IN THE TEACHER'S PRESENTATION AND THE CHILD'S RESPONSES. IN THIS RESEARCH PROJECT, THE MONTESSORI GROUP WAS MADE UP OF 17 UPPER-MIDDLE CLASS 4-YEAR-OLDS WHO HAD ALREADY PARTICIPATED IN THE PROGRAM FOR A YEAR. THE DIRECT VERBAL GROUP, CALLED THE ACADEMIC PRESCHOOL, WAS COMPRISED OF 18 4-YEAR-OLDS FROM BACKGROUNDS SIMILAR TO THOSE OF THE MONTESSORI GROUP. ALL THE CHILDREN WERE PRE- AND POSTTESTED ON THE ILLINOIS TEST OF PSYCHOLINGUISTIC ABILITIES AND POSTTESTED ON THE WIDE-RANGE ACHIEVEMENT TEST (READING, ARITHMETIC AND SPELLING). THERE WERE NO SIGNIFICANT BETWEEN-GROUP DIFFERENCES AT PRETEST, AND POSTTEST TOTAL ITPA SCORES WERE ABOUT THE SAME AS THE PRETEST SCORES. THE SUBTEST DIFFERENCES IN THE SECOND TESTING FAVORED THE ACADEMIC PRESCHOOL ON TESTS INVOLVING ABSTRACTION AND THE MONTESSORI GROUP ON TESTS OF SIMPLE RECOGNITION OR MEMORY. THE ACADEMIC PRESCHOOL CHILDREN OUTSCORED THE MONTESSORI CHILDREN IN ALL AREAS OF THE ACHIEVEMENT TEST. (MH)

ED041620 PS003153
THE DEVELOPMENT OF THE CONTROL OF ADULT INSTRUCTIONS OVER NON-VERBAL BEHAVIOR. VAN DUYNE, H. JOHN, [67] 13P.
EDRS PRICE MF-$0.65 HC-$3.29

THE PURPOSE OF THE STUDY WAS (1) TO EXAMINE THE RESULTS FROM A TWO-ASSOCIATION PERCEPTUAL-MOTOR TASK AS TO THEIR IMPLICATIONS FOR LURIA'S THEORY ABOUT THE DEVELOPMENT OF VERBAL CONTROL OF NON-VERBAL BEHAVIOR; (2) TO EXPLORE THE EFFECTS OF VARIOUS LEARNING EXPERIENCES UPON THIS DEVELOPMENT. THE SAMPLE CONSISTED OF 20 RANDOMLY SELECTED CHILDREN IN EACH OF 3 AGE GROUPS (3-4-AND 5-YEAR-OLDS). THE CHILDREN IN EACH GROUP WERE RANDOMLY ASSIGNED TO 4 TREATMENTS. THE TREATMENTS WERE ADULT VERBAL INSTRUCTIONS, VISUAL OBSERVATION, SIMULATION DIRECT PRACTICE AND REPLICATION. LURIA'S BASIC TASK INVOLVED PRESSING A SQUARE BLOCK TO EITHER A YELLOW OR BLUE LIGHT AND A ROUND BLOCK TO EITHER A BLUE OR YELLOW LIGHT. FOUR CONDITIONS OF THE TASK WERE: (1) OVERT SELF-INSTRUCTIONS; (2) REMAINING SILENT; (3) A REVERSAL OF THE ASSOCIATIONS WITH CONDITIONS ONE AND TWO REPEATED. A THREE-WAY ANALYSIS OF VARIANCE AND SUBANALYSIS WERE PERFORMED ON NUMBER OF CORRECT RESPONSES. RESULTS INDICATED SIGNIFICANT DIFFERENCES IN PROFICIENCY BETWEEN AGE LEVELS--PROFICIENCY INCREASES WITH AGE. SIGNIFICANT DIFFERENCES WERE FOUND BETWEEN THE 4 CONDITIONS OF THE TASK--PERFORMANCE DECREASED FOLLOWING REVERSAL. THE TWO-ASSOCIATION TASK DID DIFFERENTIATE STAGES IN THE DEVELOPMENT OF VERBAL CONTROL OF NONVERBAL BEHAVIOR WITH HIGH SENSITIVITY FOR THE FULLY DEVELOPED SPECIFIC FUNCTION OF SPEECH. (AUTHOR/MH)

ED041621 PS003159
ISSUES AND REALITIES IN EARLY CHILDHOOD EDUCATION. SPODEK, BERNARD, 15 MAR 70 20P.
EDRS PRICE MF-$0.65 HC-$3.29

THIS PAPER INVESTIGATES THREE ISSUES VITAL TO EARLY CHILDHOOD EDUCATION: (1) SOURCES OF CURRICULUM, (2) SOURCES OF FINANCIAL SUPPORT, AND (3) THE RELATIONSHIP BETWEEN RACISM AND COMPENSATORY EDUCATION. "NATURAL" CHILDHOOD AND CHILD DEVELOPMENT THEORIES ARE DISCUSSED, AND THEIR USE AS A SOURCE OF CURRICULUM FOR YOUNG CHILDREN IS QUESTIONED, AS IS THE USE OF INTELLIGENCE TESTS. SOURCES OF FINANCIAL SUPPORT HAVE BEEN FEDERAL PROGRAMS, THE PUBLIC SCHOOLS, AND PRIVATE OWNERS. NEW TO THE FIELD ARE CORPORATE FRANCHISE AND CHAIN OPERATIONS WHICH HAVE INHERENT DANGERS: USE OF STANDARDIZED CURRICULUM AND PROCEDURE; THE POSSIBILITY THAT PROFIT MOTIVE MAY CUT COSTS AT THE EXPENSE OF THE CHILDREN; AND THE FREEDOM TO BE RACIALLY RESTRICTIVE. BENEFITS MAY BE INNOVATIVENESS AND INDEPENDENCE FROM POLITICAL PRESSURE. THE KERNER COMMISSION RECOMMENDATION THAT MORE PRESCHOOL COMPENSATORY EDUCATION PROGRAMS BE PROVIDED IN BLACK GHETTO AREAS SEEMS DESIGNED TO MAKE BLACK CHILDREN BEHAVE MORE LIKE WHITE, MIDDLE CLASS CHILDREN. THE IDENTIFICATION OF THE PROBLEM AS BEING IN THE CHILD IS A CONFORTABLE CONCEPT OF DISADVANTAGEMENT FOR WHITE GROUP MEMBERS. HOWEVER, THE PROBLEM MAY BE IN PUBLIC SCHOOL ATTITUDES, WHICH TEND TO PERPETUATE DISADVANTAGEMENT BY PROVIDING INADEQUATE EDUCATIONAL EXPERIENCES AND BY VIEWING THE CHILD THROUGH A NEGATIVE SET OF EXPECTATIONS. (AUTHOR/NH)

ED041622 PS003163
A DIAGNOSTIC-PRESCRIPTIVE APPROACH TO PRESCHOOL EDUCATION. HAYES, MABEL E.; DEMBO, MYRON H., MAR 70 15P.
EDRS PRICE MF-$0.65 HC-$3.29

THIS STUDY ATTEMPTED TO DEVELOP A DIAGNOSTIC-PRESCRIPTIVE CURRICULUM PROGRAM TO IMPROVE THE SCHOOL READINESS OF DISADVANTAGED PRESCHOOLERS. THE LANGUAGE DEVELOPMENT PATTERNS OF 32 3-, 4-, AND 5-YEAR-OLDS WERE DIAGNOSED BY USE OF THE ILLINOIS TEST OF PSYCHOLINGUISTIC ABILITIES (ITPA). TEACHERS WERE TRAINED TO USE THIS INFORMATION TO PROVIDE AN INSTRUCTIONAL PROGRAM BASED ON A CURRICULUM DEVELOPED AROUND THE SUBTESTS OF THE ITPA. STRATIFIED SAMPLING BASED ON INTELLIGENCE TEST SCORES WAS USED TO ASSIGN 16 SUBJECTS TO THE EXPERIMENTAL AND 16 TO THE CONTROL GROUP. BOTH GROUPS WERE PRE- AND POSTTESTED ON THE CALDWELL PRESCHOOL INVENTORY (CPI). THE ITPA WAS USED TO TEST THE LANGUAGE ABILITIES OF THE EXPERIMENTAL SUBJECTS WHO FOR FOUR MONTHS RECEIVED A SPECIAL HOUR-A-DAY LESSON BASED ON INDIVIDUAL LANGUAGE NEEDS. TEACHERS WERE FREE TO ADJUST OR ALTER LESSON PLANS. POSTTEST CPI SCORES INDICATED THAT THE DIAGNOSTIC-PRESCRIPTIVE PROGRAM SIGNIFICANTLY IMPROVED THE SCHOOL READINESS OF THE EXPERIMENTAL SUBJECTS. APPENDIXES A AND B LIST CLASSROOM DEFICIENCIES AND LANGUAGE ACTIVITIES RELATED TO ITPA SUBTESTS. (MH)

ED041623 PS003167
PROBLEM SOLVING PERFORMANCES OF FIRST GRADE CHILDREN. STEFFE, LESLIE P.; JOHNSON, DAVID C., MAR 70 25P.
EDRS PRICE MF-$0.65 HC-$3.29

THIS STUDY EXAMINED DIFFERENTIAL PERFORMANCES AMONG GROUPS (CATEGORIES) OF FIRST GRADE CHILDREN WHEN SOLVING EIGHT DIFFERENT TYPES OF ARITHMETICAL WORD PROBLEMS UNDER TWO DISTINCT EXPERIMENTAL CONDITIONS. THE CATEGORIES OF CHILDREN WERE ACTUALLY 4 ABILITY GROUPS: (1) LOW QUANTITATIVE COMPARISON SCORES AND LOW IQ (LORGE-THORNDIKE IQ TEST), (2) LOW QUANTITATIVE COMPARISON SCORES AND HIGH IQ, (3) HIGH QUANTITATIVE COMPARISON SCORES AND LOW IQ, AND (4) HIGH QUANTITATIVE COMPARISON SCORES AND HIGH IQ. THE 111 CHILDREN WHO FILLED THESE CATEGORIES WERE GIVEN A 48-ITEM PROBLEM SOLVING TEST, WITH SIX PROBLEMS FROM EACH OF THE EIGHT TYPES PRESENTED IN A RANDOMIZED SEQUENCE. HALF OF THE CHILDREN IN EACH ABILITY GROUP WERE RANDOMLY ASSIGNED TO THE CONDITION OF NO MANIPULATABLE OBJECTS, WHILE THE OTHER HALF WERE PROVIDED WITH MANIPULATABLE OBJECTS REFERRED TO IN THE PROBLEMS AND WERE ALLOWED TO USE THEM ANY WAY THEY WANTED TO HELP SOLVE THE PROBLEMS. ANALYSIS OF THE DATA REVEALED THAT IQ WAS NOT A SIGNIFICANT FACTOR, THAT PROBLEM CONDITION WAS SIGNIFICANT, THAT THERE WAS A SIGNIFICANT INTERACTION DUE TO QUANTITATIVE COMPARISONS AND PROBLEM CONDITIONS FOR ONE PROBLEM TYPE, AND THAT THERE WERE SIGNIFICANT MAIN EFFECTS DUE TO PROBLEM CONDITIONS FOR THE REMAINING SEVEN PROBLEM TYPES. THERE WAS

ALSO A SIGNIFICANT MAIN EFFECT DUE TO QUANTITATIVE COMPARISONS FOR ONE OF THE REMAINING SEVEN PROBLEM TYPES. (MH)

ED041624 PS003210
[A STATEMENT REGARDING THE COMPREHENSIVE PRESCHOOL EDUCATION AND CHILD DAY CARE ACT OF 1969, AND OTHER RELATED BILLS.] RIESSMAN, FRANK, 26 FEB 70 4P.
EDRS PRICE MF-$0.65 HC-$3.29

THIS PAPER SUPPORTS THE PROPOSED LEGISLATION, BUT RECOMMENDS THAT THE BILL (1) ASSURE LOCAL AUTONOMY FOR THE PROGRAMS AND EXCLUDE STATE DEPARTMENTS OF EDUCATION OR WELFARE FROM OPERATING RESPONSIBILITY, (2) INCLUDE ADDITIONAL LANGUAGE MANDATING CAREER DEVELOPMENT AS AN INTEGRAL PART OF THE STAFFING OF ALL PROGRAMS, AND (3) ENCOURAGE THE INVOLVEMENT OF LOCAL YOUTH TO SERVE THE CHILDREN IN THE PROGRAMS. THE FIRST RECOMMENDATION IS AN OUTGROWTH OF THE RECOGNITION THAT SOME STATE GOVERNMENTS HAVE, ON PREVIOUS OCCASIONS, BLOCKED NEW PROGRAMS, PARTICULARLY THOSE FOR THE POOR. CONCERN IS EXPRESSED THAT STATE AGENCIES MIGHT COME UNDER THE SWAY OF THE STATE DEPARTMENTS OF EDUCATION OR PUBLIC WELFARE, WHO ARE NOT NOTED FOR INNOVATIVENESS OR RESPONSIVENESS TO THE POOR. THE SECOND RECOMMENDATION REFLECTS THE BELIEF THAT CAREER DEVELOPMENT PROGRAMS ARE ESSENTIAL TO THE ECONOMIC UPGRADING OF THE POOR. FINALLY, THE INNOVATIVE USE OF NEIGHBORHOOD YOUTH CORPS YOUNGSTERS IN THE PROGRESS OF THE NATIONAL COMMISSION OF RESOURCES FOR YOUTH, ALONG WITH THE INCORPORATION OF THE "YOUTH TUTORING YOUTH" CONCEPT IN THE NEW CAREER OPPORTUNITIES PROGRAM, SUGGESTS THE POTENTIAL FOR PRODUCTIVE EMPLOYMENT OF THESE YOUNGSTERS. (MH)

ED041625 PS003214
EARLY CHILDHOOD EDUCATION LEARNING SYSTEM , OCT 69 67P.
EDRS PRICE MF-$0.65 HC-$3.29

A COMPARISON OF EFFECTS OF THREE PRESCHOOL INTERVENTION PROGRAMS DESIGNED TO PREPARE DISADVANTAGED MEXICAN-AMERICAN CHILDREN FOR SCHOOL IS THE SUBJECT OF THIS STUDY. THE SAN ANTONIO URBAN EDUCATIONAL DEVELOPMENT CENTER (SAUEDC) PRESCHOOL PROGRAM (N16) USES AN INSTRUCTIONAL PROGRAM BUILT ON FOUR STRUCTURAL COMPONENTS: (1) CONCEPT-AFFECT FORMATION, (2) DEVELOPMENT OF SENSORY MOTOR SKILLS, (3) DEVELOPMENT OF LANGUAGE SKILLS, AND (4) DEVELOPMENT OF THINKING PROCESSES. THE SECOND PROGRAM (N15) IS A SPECIAL PARENT-SCHOOL-COMMUNITY INVOLVEMENT PROJECT INTENDED TO ENCOURAGE PARENTAL ACTION TO FOSTER CHILD DEVELOPMENT. FINALLY, THREE SAN ANTONIO DAY CARE CENTERS (N14) FUNDED AS HEAD START PROGRAMS WERE EXAMINED. THE SUBJECTS WERE ALL 3-YEAR-OLD MEXICAN-AMERICAN CHILDREN. EACH GROUP WAS PRE- AND POSTTESTED ON THE LEITER INTERNATIONAL PERFORMANCE SCALE, THE PEABODY PICTURE VOCABULARY TEST (FORM A) IN ENGLISH, AND PEABODY (FORM B) IN SPANISH. ANALYSIS OF THE TEST-GENERATED DATA REVEALED THAT (AS PREDICTED) AT PRETEST ALL THE SUBJECTS SCORED SUBSTANTIALLY BELOW NATIONAL NORMS ON INSTRUMENTS THAT REQUIRED LANGUAGE IN TEST ADMINISTRATION AND APPROXIMATELY AT NATIONAL NORMS ON INSTRUMENTS THAT DIDN'T REQUIRE LANGUAGE IN TEST ADMINISTRATION. FURTHERMORE, CHILDREN IN THE SAUEDC PROGRAM ACHIEVED SIGNIFICANTLY GREATER GAINS IN I.Q. SCORES THAN CHILDREN IN EITHER OF THE OTHER GROUPS. (MH)

ED041626 PS003274
EVALUATION REPORT: EARLY CHILDHOOD EDUCATION PROGRAM, 1969 FIELD TEST. , MAR 70 204P.
EDRS PRICE MF-$0.65 HC-$9.87

REPORTED ARE FINDINGS FROM THE FIRST YEAR'S FIELD TEST OF THE HOME-ORIENTED APPALACHIA EDUCATIONAL LABORATORY (AEL) EARLY CHILDHOOD EDUCATION PROGRAM FOR 3-, 4-, AND 5-YEAR-OLDS. THE PROGRAM CONSISTS OF A 30-MINUTE DAILY TELEVISION LESSON, A WEEKLY HOME VISIT BY A PARAPROFESSIONAL, AND GROUP INSTRUCTION ONCE A WEEK IN A MOBILE CLASSROOM. THE SAMPLE WAS MADE UP OF A TOTAL OF 450 CHILDREN DIVIDED INTO THREE GROUPS. GROUP 1 RECEIVED TV INSTRUCTION AND HOME VISITS AND ATTENDED THE MOBILE CLASSROOM. GROUP 2 HAD TV AND HOME VISITS; GROUP 3, ONLY TV INSTRUCTION. 30 SUBJECTS FROM EACH GROUP WERE TESTED FOR EVALUATION PURPOSES. THE DATA ARE PRESENTED IN 5 CATEGORIES: PROGRAM EFFORT, PROGRAM PERFORMANCE, PROGRAM PERVASIVENESS, PROGRAM COST ANALYSIS, AND EVALUATION SYNTHESIS. APPENDIXES (ONE-SIXTH OF THIS REPORT) PRESENT DETAILED DATA ANALYSIS FOR (1) THE PROGRAM'S EVALUATION PLAN, (2) INTEREST LEVEL OF PROJECT CHILDREN, (3) IQ GAIN, (4) LANGUAGE DEVELOPMENT AND BEHAVIOR, (5) COGNITIVE GROWTH, (6) THE PARENT ATTITUDE QUESTIONNAIRE AND CHECKLIST, (7) PARAPROFESSIONAL ATTITUDE DATA INSTRUMENT AND RESULTS, AND (8) SOCIOECONOMIC FACTORS OF TREATMENT AND CONTROL GROUPS. IT WAS FOUND THAT TV LESSONS AND HOME VISITATIONS (BUT NOT THE MOBILE CLASSROOM) HAD A POSITIVE EFFECT ON CHILDREN'S COGNITIVE DEVELOPMENT. CHILDREN IN GROUP 1 SCORED HIGHEST ON VERBAL EXPRESSION. (DR)

ED041627 PS003276
STATEMENT OF THE INSTRUCTIONAL GOALS FOR CHILDREN'S TELEVISION WORKSHOP. , 31 DEC 68 11P.
EDRS PRICE MF-$0.65 HC-$3.29

CHILDREN'S TELEVISION WORKSHOP (CTW) IS AN EXPERIMENT IN THE INSTRUCTION OF PRESCHOOL CHILDREN THROUGH THE MEDIUM OF BROADCAST TELEVISION. THIS DOCUMENT, WHICH INCORPORATES, EXTENDS, AND SUPERSEDES AN EARLIER REPORT OF A MEETING TO ESTABLISH PRIORITIES AMONG GOALS FOR CTW, SERVES SIX RELATED PURPOSES: (1) IT ATTEMPTS TO REFLECT THE SUGGESTIONS OF THE MANY CONSULTANTS TO THE PROJECT; (2) IT PROVIDES A FRAMEWORK FOR ORGANIZING THE PROJECT'S GOALS; (3) IT PROPOSES PRIORITY OBJECTIVES TOWARD WHICH THE CTW EXPERIMENT SHOULD BE ESPECIALLY DIRECTED; (4) IT PROVIDES SPECIFIC OPERATIONAL EXAMPLES OF GOALS; (5) IT SERVES AS A COMMON REFERENCE FOR THE PRODUCTION AND SUMMATIVE EVALUATION PHASES OF THE PROJECT; AND (6) IT COMMUNICATES WITH THE PROJECT'S SPONSORS, ADVISORS, AND CONSULTANTS, AS WELL AS THE GENERAL PUBLIC. THE GOALS OF THE PROJECT FALL INTO THE OVERLAPPING CATEGORIES OF SYMBOLIC REPRESENTATION (LETTERS, NUMBERS, GEOMETRIC FORMS), REASONING AND PROBLEM SOLVING, AND FAMILIARITY WITH THE PHYSICAL AND SOCIAL ENVIRONMENT. SPECIFIC GOALS ARE EXTENSIVELY OUTLINED WITHIN THESE CATEGORIES AND THOSE WHICH ARE CONSIDERED THE PRIMARY INSTRUCTIONAL OBJECTIVES OF CTW ARE MARKED WITH AN ASTERISK. EVALUATION OF THE PROJECT WILL BE HANDLED BY EDUCATIONAL TESTING SERVICE. (MH)

ED041628 PS003278
PARENT PREFERENCE OF PRESCHOOL CHILDREN. LYNN, DAVID B.; CROSS, AMY R., [70] 5P.
EDRS PRICE MF-$0.65 HC-$3.29

AN EXPERIMENT WAS CONDUCTED TO TEST THE THEORY THAT YOUNG BOYS PREFER THE COMPANIONSHIP OF THEIR FATHERS IN PLAY ACTIVITIES TO THAT OF THEIR MOTHERS, WHILE YOUNG GIRLS HAVE NO PARTICULAR PREFERENCE. IT WAS HYPOTHESIZED THAT A BOY HAS THIS PREFERENCE BECAUSE HE HAS BEEN CARED FOR PRIMARILY BY HIS MOTHER, AND HIS DISCOVERY OF SEX-IDENTITY LEAVES HIM PARTICULARLY INSECURE IN HIS SHIFTING SEX-ROLE, THUS PRODUCING A STRONG AFFINITY FOR THE MOST AVAILABLE MASCULINITY MODEL, HIS FATHER. GIRLS DEVELOP NO SUCH PREFERENCE BECAUSE THEY HAVE BEEN PRIMARILY CARED FOR BY THE SAME-SEX PARENT, A LESS CONFUSING AND LESS TRAUMATIC SITUATION. THIS THEORY WAS TESTED BY PLACING CHILDREN IN SEVEN PLAY SITUATIONS AND ASKING THEM WHICH PARENT THEY WOULD LIKE TO HAVE JOIN THEM IN EACH OF THE ACTIVITIES. THE SUBJECTS WERE 150 2-, 3-, AND 4-YEAR-OLDS (76 BOYS AND 74 GIRLS). THE CRITERION FOR PARENT PREFERENCE WAS 4 OR MORE CHOICES OF ONE PARENT. ANALYSIS OF THE DATA REVEALED THAT THE BOYS SIGNIFICANTLY PREFERRED THE FATHER TO THE MOTHER. GIRLS SHOWED NO CONSISTENT PARENT PREFERENCE FOR THE TOTAL SAMPLE, BUT THIS WAS THE RESULT OF SIGNIFICANT PREFERENCES: FOR THE FATHER AT AGE 2 AND FOR THE MOTHER AT AGE 4. (MH)

ED041629 PS003286
THE PREVALENCE OF ANEMIA IN HEAD START CHILDREN. NUTRITION EVALUATION, 1968-69. MICKELSEN, OLAF; AND OTHERS, 69 22P.
EDRS PRICE MF-$0.65 HC-$3.29

CONCERN OVER THE NUTRITIONAL STATUS OF THE DISADVANTAGED IN AMERICA LED TO THIS STUDY DESCRIBING THE PREVALENCE OF ANEMIA AMONG HEAD START CHILDREN IN PONTIAC, MICHIGAN. HEMOGLOBIN AND HEMATOCRIT DETERMINATIONS, ALONG WITH MEASUREMENTS OF HEIGHT AND WEIGHT, WERE PERFORMED ON 77 CHILDREN, 4 TO 6 YEARS OLD, ENROLLED IN HEAD START CLASSES. THESE MEASUREMENTS WERE TAKEN TWICE, AT THE BEGINNING AND END OF A 6-MONTH INTERVAL. DUE TO ATTRITION DURING THE INTERVAL, ONLY 52 OF THE CHILDREN WERE AVAILABLE FOR THE SECOND SESSION. WHEN COMPARED TO THE STANDARDS COMMONLY USED IN NUTRITIONAL SURVEYS, ONLY ONE CHILD ON BOTH OCCASIONS HAD A HEMOGLOBIN LEVEL THAT WOULD BE CONSIDERED ANEMIC (I.E. BELOW 11 GM/100 ML.). THE MEHATOCRIT STANDARD OF ANEMIA, HOWEVER (LESS THAN 33%), INDICATED THAT 5.3% OF THE CHILDREN WERE ANEMIC AT THE FIRST READING AND 7.8% AT THE SECOND. EIGHTY PERCENT OF THE SUBJECTS AT BOTH READINGS WERE BLACK, AND, ALTHOUGH THE DIFFERENCES WERE NOT STATISTICALLY SIGNIFICANT, THESE CHILDREN HAD LOWER HEMOGLOBIN AND HEMATOCRIT VALUES THAN THEIR WHITE CLASSMATES. APPLYING TWO STANDARDS OF HEIGHT FOR AGE, THE STUART-MEREDITH PERCENTILE STANDARDS AND THE IOWA GROWTH CHARTS, IT APPEARS THAT THE HEAD START CHILDREN MEASURED WERE WELL WITHIN THE ACCEPTABLE RANGES OF "NORMAL." (MH)

ED041630 PS003292
TEACHER-PUPIL INTERACTION AS IT RELATES TO ATTEMPTED CHANGES IN TEACHER EXPECTANCY OF ACADEMIC ABILITY AND ACHIEVEMENT. JOSE, JEAN, MAR 70 8P.
EDRS PRICE MF-$0.65 HC-$3.29

THIS STUDY IS A PARTIAL REPLICATION OF ROSENTHAL'S (1968) STUDY OF TEACHER EXPECTATION IN WHICH STUDENTS FALSELY IDENTIFIED TO TEACHERS AS BEING CAPABLE OF DOING BETTER WORK SHOWED GREATER INTELLECTUAL GROWTH THAN CONTROL STUDENTS. THE PRESENT STUDY SOUGHT TO DETERMINE WHETHER OR NOT THIS RESULT COULD BE DUPLICATED AND WHETHER OR NOT TEACHER-

STUDENT CLASSROOM INTERACTION WOULD BE AFFECTED BY THE INFORMATION. FALSE INFORMATION WAS LEAKED TO FIRST AND SECOND GRADE TEACHERS ABOUT CERTAIN OF THEIR STUDENTS WHO WERE SUPPOSED TO HAVE SPECIAL LATE-BLOOMING ACADEMIC ABILITIES. FOUR EXPERIMENTAL STUDENTS AND FOUR CONTROL STUDENTS WERE RANDOMLY SELECTED FROM EACH OF 18 CLASSES. A TOTAL OF 144 STUDENTS WERE PRE- AND POSTTESTED ON THE TEST OF GENERAL ABILITY AND THE READING AND ARITHMETIC SUBTESTS OF THE METROPOLITAN ACHIEVEMENT TESTS. CLASSROOM INTERACTION WAS PRE- AND POST-MEASURED BY USE OF THE INTERACTION ANALYSIS SCALE. AFTER POSTTESTING, TEACHERS ALSO COMPLETED QUESTIONNAIRES CONCERNING STUDENT EXPECTANCY. RESULTS REVEALED THAT THE EXPERIMENTAL GROUP DID NOT MAKE SIGNIFICANTLY HIGHER GAINS THAN THE CONTROL GROUP ON ANY OF THE TESTS. IN ADDITION, CLASSROOM INTERACTION MEASURES SHOWED NO SPECIAL TREATMENT ACCORDED THE "SPECIAL" STUDENTS. (MH)

ED041631 PS003298
MAXIMIZING THE VALUE OF EVALUATION FOR THE HEAD START TEACHER. FINAL REPORT. STERN, CAROLYN, 31 AUG 69 188P.
EDRS PRICE MF-$0.65 HC-$6.58

THE PURPOSE OF THIS STUDY WAS TO FIND OUT WHETHER SYSTEMATIC EVALUATION FEEDBACK TO TEACHERS WOULD RESULT IN: (1) DEVELOPMENT OF MORE FAVORABLE ATTITUDES TOWARD EVALUATION, AS MEASURED BY TEACHER ATTITUDES TOWARD EVALUATION (TATE), AND INCREASED TEACHER USE OF A VARIETY OF CURRICULA AND MATERIALS, (2) GREATER CORRESPONDENCE BETWEEN TEACHERS' EXPECTATIONS AND CHILDREN'S PERFORMANCE, AS MEASURED BY TEACHERS EXPECTATIONS FOR ACHIEVEMENT OF CHILDREN IN HEAD START (TEACH), AND (3) GREATER GAINS ON COGNITIVE AND AFFECTIVE MEASURES FOR CHILDREN IN FEEDBACK CLASSES. 183 CHILDREN WERE TESTED ON A VARIETY OF MEASURES. DATA WERE ALSO COLLECTED FROM CLASSROOM OBSERVATIONS AND PARENT INTERVIEWS. OF THE 24 CLASSES IN THE STUDY, 10 CLASSES (20 TEACHERS) WERE IN THE FEEDBACK GROUP, WHICH ATTENDED MONTHLY MEETINGS WHERE THEY WERE INFORMED ABOUT CHILDREN'S TEST RESULTS, TEST INSTRUMENTS, AND CLASSROOM OBSERVATIONS. TEACHERS ALSO VIEWED VIDEO TAPES OF THEIR OWN CLASSES. ALTHOUGH CHILDREN SHOWED CONSISTENT GAINS, TEACHERS GIVEN FEEDBACK WERE NOT MEASURABLY MORE SUCCESSFUL IN REMEDIATING DEFICIENCIES THAN THOSE NOT RECEIVING FEEDBACK. WITH REFERENCE TO TEACHER ATTITUDES, THE INTERVENTION WAS MORE EFFECTIVE, AS SHOWN BY TEACH AND TATE SCORES AND BY INCREASED UNDERSTANDING AND RAPPORT BETWEEN TEACHERS AND EVALUATORS. (NH)

ED041632 PS003396
DEMONSTRATION INFANT DAY CARE AND EDUCATION PROGRAM. INTERIM REPORT, 1969-1970. , 70 8P.
EDRS PRICE MF-$0.65 HC-$3.29

THE ONTARIO INSTITUTE FOR STUDIES IN EDUCATION AND THE CANADIAN MOTHERCRAFT SOCIETY ARE RUNNING A DAY CARE PROGRAM FOR INFANTS (FROM 3 TO 30 MONTHS OF AGE) DESIGNED TO FACILITATE THEIR COGNITIVE, PERSONALITY, AND SOCIAL DEVELOPMENT THROUGH PERSONALIZED ADULT-CHILD INTERACTION, GUIDED LEARNING SITUATIONS, FREE PLAY, AND SPECIALIZED CARE. COLLABORATION WITH THE HOME IS EXTENSIVE. THIS DOCUMENT REPORTS UNCOMPLETED BUT ENCOURAGING MIDYEAR PROGRAM RESULTS. A SAMPLE OF INNER CITY DISADVANTAGED CHILDREN AND TWO SAMPLES OF MIDDLE CLASS CHILDREN WERE TESTED TWICE EACH ON THE BAYLEY MENTAL SCALE AND THE STANFORD-BINET IQ TEST. THE FIVE DISADVANTAGED CHILDREN WERE, ON THE AVERAGE, 4.9 MONTHS OLD WHEN THEY ENTERED THE PROGRAM AND HAD THEIR FIRST TESTING. THEIR SECOND TESTING, 8 MONTHS LATER, SHOWED A HIGHLY SIGNIFICANT GAIN. THE FIRST GROUP OF ADVANTAGED CHILDREN (N6) WAS TESTED AT AN AVERAGE AGE OF 21.6 MONTHS, AFTER 2 MONTHS IN THE PROGRAM, AND AGAIN 8 MONTHS LATER. THE GAIN SCORE FOR THIS GROUP WAS INCONSEQUENTIAL. THE OTHER GROUP OF MIDDLE CLASS CHILDREN (N7) WAS TESTED AT AN AVERAGE AGE OF 11.4 MONTHS, AFTER 2 MONTHS IN THE PROGRAM, AND AGAIN 6 MONTHS LATER. THIS GROUP WAS TESTED AGAIN AT AN AVERAGE OF 26.7 MONTHS AND THEIR GAIN SCORE WAS HIGHLY SIGNIFICANT. THE DIFFERENCE BETWEEN THE ADVANTAGED GROUPS WAS ATTRIBUTED TO TIME SPENT IN THE PROGRAM. (MH)

ED041633 PS003410
THE EFFECT OF A PERCEPTUAL-MOTOR TRAINING PROGRAM UPON THE READINESS AND PERCEPTUAL DEVELOPMENT OF CULTURALLY DISADVANTAGED KINDERGARTEN CHILDREN. TURNER, ROBERT V.; FISHER, MAURICE D., 6 MAR 70 7P.
EDRS PRICE MF-$0.65 HC-$3.29

AS A PART OF A TITLE III PROJECT, A PROGRAM WAS INITIATED TO PROVIDE DISADVANTAGED KINDERGARTEN CHILDREN WITH PLANNED PERCEPTUAL-MOTOR TRAINING EXERCISES. THIS STUDY INVESTIGATES THE EFFECTS OF THAT PROGRAM ON THE PERCEPTUAL DEVELOPMENT AND ACADEMIC READINESS OF A GROUP OF 76 SUCH CHILDREN. THE EXERCISES, DERIVED FROM THE KEPHART DEVELOPMENTAL PROGRAM, WERE USED FOR HALF OF EACH SCHOOL DAY, OVER A PERIOD OF SEVEN MONTHS. A CONTROL GROUP (N26) PARTICIPATED IN A CONVENTIONAL KINDERGARTEN PROGRAM. ALL THE CHILDREN WERE PRE- AND POSTTESTED ON THE SLOSSON INTELLIGENCE TEST, AND POSTTESTED ON THE METROPOLITAN READINESS TESTS FORM A, FROSTIG'S DEVELOPMENTAL TEST OF VISUAL PERCEPTION, AND KEPHART'S PURDUE PERCEPTUAL-MOTOR SURVEY. RESULTS UNCOVERED NO SIGNIFICANT GAIN SCORE DIFFERENCES BETWEEN GROUPS ON THE SIT. MEAN POSTTEST DIFFERENCES ON THE METROPOLITAN READINESS TESTS WERE SIGNIFICANT, FAVORING THE EXPERIMENTAL GROUP. THE KEPHART SURVEY REVEALED NO SIGNIFICANT BETWEEN-GROUP DIFFERENCES. THESE RESULTS WERE INTERPRETED AS SUGGESTING THAT THE PROGRAM WAS MORE EFFECTIVE AT IMPROVING FINE MOTOR BEHAVIORS THAN GROSS MOTOR BEHAVIORS. FINE MOTOR BEHAVIORS CORRELATE HIGHLY WITH SUCCESSFUL READING AND WRITING ACTIVITIES. INTENSIVE EXPOSURE TO VERBAL CONCEPTS, PAIRED WITH CONCRETE EXAMPLES AND MOVEMENT, MAY HAVE BEEN A MAJOR PROGRAM EFFECT. (MH)

ED041634 PS003420
RACE AND SEX IDENTIFICATION IN PRESCHOOL CHILDREN. RAYMER, ELIZABETH, AUG 69 102P.
EDRS PRICE MF-$0.65 HC-$6.58

IDENTIFICATION IS A LEARNING PROCESS IMPORTANT TO THE DEVELOPMENT OF SELF-CONCEPT AND TO THE ROLE BEHAVIOR OF AN INDIVIDUAL. THIS STUDY INVESTIGATED THE DEGREE OF RACE AND SEX IDENTIFICATION AND PREFERENCE IN BOTH BLACK AND WHITE DISADVANTAGED PRESCHOOL CHILDREN. THE MEASUREMENT INSTRUMENT DEVELOPED WAS A 96-ITEM PAIRED PICTURE SELECTION TASK CONSISTING OF 13 SUB-SERIES OF ITEMS THAT EXAMINED RACE AND SEX IDENTIFICATION, RACE AND SEX PREFERENCE, RACE LABELING, COLOR LABELING AND PREFERENCE, AND THE DOMINANCE OF RACE OR SEX CRITERIA IN SUBJECTS' RESPONSE PATTERNS. THE SAMPLE WAS COMPRISED OF 168 4-YEAR-OLD BLACK AND WHITE CHILDREN FROM HEAD START AND DAY CARE CENTERS. THE DATA REVEALED THAT: (1) WHITE CHILDREN IDENTIFIED WITH THEIR OWN SEX MORE THAN DID BLACK CHILDREN, (2) WHITE CHILDREN AND BLACK CHILDREN BOTH IDENTIFIED WITH AND PREFERRED THE WHITE RACE, (3) BLACK EXAMINERS DIDN'T INCREASE THE BLACK CHILDREN'S PREFERENCE FOR THE BLACK RACE, (4) BOYS PREFERRED THEIR OWN SEX LESS THAN DID GIRLS, WITH NO DIFFERENCE BETWEEN THE RACES, (5) SEX WAS THE DOMINANT SELECTION CRITERION FOR ALL GROUPS, (6) NO RELATIONSHIP APPEARED BETWEEN PREFERENCE FOR THE WHITE RACE AND EXPRESSED PREFERENCE FOR COLOR, AND (7) HALF THE SUBJECTS POINTED TO THE SAME PICTURE WHETHER IT WAS LABELED "GOOD" OR "BAD." (AUTHOR/MH)

ED041635 PS003451
BEHAVIOR MODIFICATION PROCEDURES APPLIED TO THE ISOLATE BEHAVIOR OF A NURSERY SCHOOL CHILD. BLASDEL, JOAN, AUG 68 21P.
EDRS PRICE MF-$0.65 HC-$3.29

THIS STUDY USED REINFORCEMENT PRINCIPLES TO INVESTIGATE SOME PROCEDURES FOR HELPING A 4-YEAR-OLD MEXICAN-AMERICAN GIRL ESTABLISH PEER CONTACT IN A HEAD START CLASS. ALTHOUGH DIANE WAS HEALTHY AND INTELLIGENT, SHE HAD A LOW RATE OF ATTENDANCE AT SCHOOL AND SPENT MOST OF HER TIME THERE IN ISOLATION. THE FIRST PROCEDURE EMPLOYED IN THE STUDY WAS THE CONTROLLED USE OF ADULT SOCIAL REINFORCEMENT. A TEACHER WAS SUPPOSED TO GO TO, TALK TO, SMILE AT, TOUCH, AND PRAISE DIANE FOR PARTICIPATING IN PEER INTERACTION. DUE TO DIANE'S IMPOVERISHED PEER-PLAY REPERTOIRE, HOWEVER, THERE WERE VERY FEW RESPONSES TO REINFORCE AND OTHER PROCEDURES HAD TO BE TRIED. THE ADULTS NEXT STRUCTURED PLAY SITUATIONS TO INCLUDE DIANE AND GAVE HER OTHER PROMPTS INTENDED TO LEAD TO PEER INTERACTION THAT COULD BE REINFORCED. AS A RESULT OF THIS PROCEDURE, PEER CONTACT WAS MARKEDLY INCREASED AND PROMPTING WAS SUBSEQUENTLY PHASED OUT. IT WAS ALSO SEEN THAT THE PROMPTING-REINFORCING PROCESS COULD BE USED TO INCREASE CERTAIN CLASSES OF BEHAVIOR (SUCH AS VERBAL OR NONVERBAL). IN THE FINAL PHASES OF THE STUDY, A RISE IN SPONTANEOUS, NONVERBAL BEHAVIOR WAS SEEN AND DIANE'S ATTENDANCE AT CLASS BECAME MORE REGULAR. BEHAVIOR MODIFICATION PRINCIPLES WERE THEREFORE JUDGED TO BE EFFECTIVE IN REMEDYING THE SUBJECT'S ISOLATE BEHAVIOR. (MH)

ED041636 PS003654
CHILDREN'S ACQUISITION OF VISUO-SPATIAL DIMENSIONALITY: A CONSERVATION STUDY. KERSHNER, JOHN R., JUN 70 30P.
EDRS PRICE MF-$0.65 HC-$3.29

THE EFFECTS OF LATERALITY, MOVEMENT, AND LANGUAGE ON CHILDREN'S ABILITY TO CONSERVE MULTIPLE SPACE RELATIONS WERE INVESTIGATED IN THIS STUDY OF VISUO-SPATIAL DIMENSIONALITY ACQUISITION. THE SAMPLE FOR THE EXPERIMENT CONSISTED OF 160 FIRST-GRADERS (80 BOYS, 80 GIRLS) WHO WERE MATCHED ON INTELLIGENCE AND SOCIOECONOMIC STATUS. THESE SUBJECTS WERE TESTED FOR THEIR FUNCTIONAL KNOWLEDGE OF LANGUAGE (PIAGET'S SCHEDULE) AND LATERAL DOMINANCE (D-K SCALE OF LATERAL DOMINANCE) AND THEN RANDOMLY ASSIGNED TO A SPECTATOR OR PARTICIPATION CONDITION. AN APPARATUS WAS DEVISED AND CONSTRUCTED TO TEST SPATIAL CONSERVATION. THOSE CHILDREN WHO WERE CLEARLY LATERALIZED HAD LESS SUCCESS IN REPRODUCING SPACE RELATIONS THAN DID CHILDREN WHO WERE MIXED IN THEIR LATERALITY. RESULTS WERE INTERPRETED TO BE IN SUPPORT OF AN ICONIC MODE OF REPRESENTATION AND DID NOT OFFER SUPPORT FOR

AN EXTREME EMPHASIS ON THE IMPORTANCE OF LANGUAGE OR ACTIVITY. FURTHER ANALYSIS OF THE DATA ON LATERALITY PATTERNS REVEALED THAT RIGHT-HANDED, LEFT-EYED CHILDREN PRODUCED THE MAIN LATERALITY EFFECT OBTAINED. RECENT NEUROPHYSIOLOGICAL EVIDENCE INDICATES THAT THE CEREBRAL HEMISPHERES FUNCTION ASYMMETRICALLY. THE RESULTS OF THIS STUDY ARE CONSISTENT WITH THAT EVIDENCE. (MH/AUTHOR)

ED041637 PS003659
A STUDY OF HOME ENVIRONMENT AND READINESS FOR ACHIEVEMENT AT SCHOOL. FINAL REPORT. REIMANIS, GUNARS, APR 70 43P.
EDRS PRICE MF-$0.65 HC-$3.29

INTERNAL REINFORCEMENT CONTROL IS DEFINED AS ONE'S BELIEF THAT HIS REWARDS OR PUNISHMENTS ARE CONTINGENT UPON HIS OWN BEHAVIOR. THIS STUDY TESTED TWO MAIN HYPOTHESES: (1) THAT INCONSISTENCY IN THE HOME ENVIRONMENT INTERFERES WITH THE DEVELOPMENT OF INTERNAL REINFORCEMENT CONTROL, AND (2) THAT INTERNAL REINFORCEMENT CONTROL CAN BE INCREASED BY SPECIAL TEACHER EFFORTS IN THE CLASSROOM, AND BY GROUP DISCUSSIONS OR COUNSELING OUTSIDE THE CLASS. A SECONDARY HYPOTHESIS WAS THAT INTERNAL REINFORCEMENT CONTROL RELATES POSITIVELY TO SCHOOL ACHIEVEMENT. THE HYPOTHESES WERE TESTED IN FOUR SEPARATE STUDIES USING SUBJECT POPULATION SAMPLES OF ELEMENTARY SCHOOL PUPILS AND COLLEGE FRESHMEN AND SOPHOMORES. THE STUDIES ASSESSED RELATIONSHIPS BETWEEN FAMILY ENVIRONMENT, INTELLIGENCE, SCHOOL ACHIEVEMENT AND TEACHER COUNSELING. THE FINDINGS PARTLY SUPPORTED THE FIRST HYPOTHESIS. INTERNAL REINFORCEMENT CONTROL WAS RELATED TO HOME ENVIRONMENT, WITH SEX DIFFERENCES. FOR MALES, A SUPPORTIVE, CONSISTENT HOME RELATED POSITIVELY TO INTERNALITY. FOR FEMALES, A SOMEWHAT REJECTANT HOME SEEMED TO FORCE INDEPENDENCE AND DEVELOPMENT OF INTERNAL CONTROL. THE SECOND HYPOTHESIS WAS SUPPORTED BY THE FINDING THAT FEELINGS OF INTERNAL REINFORCEMENT CONTROL INCREASED IN BOTH EARLY GRADERS AND COLLEGE STUDENTS AFTER SPECIAL COUNSELING. THE SECONDARY HYPOTHESIS WAS SUPPORTED FOR EARLY GRADERS, BUT NOT FOR COLLEGE STUDENTS. (AUTHOR/NH)

ED041638 PS003660
THE EFFECTIVENESS OF SPECIAL PROGRAMS FOR RURAL ISOLATED FOUR-YEAR-OLD CHILDREN. FINAL REPORT. PARKER, RONALD K., SEP 69 96P.
EDRS PRICE MF-$0.65 HC-$3.29

THE OBJECTIVE OF THIS STUDY WAS TO DEVELOP AND EVALUATE TWO PROCEDURES FOR PROVIDING PRESCHOOL EDUCATION FOR RURAL 4-YEAR-OLDS BY USING A MOBILE LABORATORY. THE PROJECT USED "READIMOBILES" TO DETERMINE THE EFFECTIVENESS OF A STRUCTURED, PSYCHOLINGUISTICALLY-BASED PRESCHOOL CURRICULUM ON BLACK, DISADVANTAGED CHILDREN. THERE WERE THREE TREATMENT GROUPS: (1) ADVANTAGED WHITE CHILDREN RECEIVING A GENERAL ENRICHMENT PROGRAM, (2) DISADVANTAGED BLACK CHILDREN RECEIVING THREE MONTHS OF LESSONS FROM THE PEABODY LANGUAGE DEVELOPMENT KIT, AND (3) DISADVANTAGED BLACK CHILDREN RECEIVING NINE MONTHS OF THE PEABODY PROGRAM. EACH CHILD IN THESE TREATMENT GROUPS WAS MATCHED TO A CONTROL CHILD BY AGE, RACE, SEX, AND SOCIOECONOMIC STATUS. BOTH GROUPS WERE POSTTESTED TWICE (TO DETERMINE RELIABILITY) ON THE STANFORD-BINET, THE CALDWELL PRESCHOOL INVENTORY AND THE ILLINOIS TEST OF PSYCHOLINGUISTIC ABILITIES. THE RESULTS SHOWED THAT THE EXPERIMENTAL SUBJECTS WERE SUPERIOR TO THE CONTROL SUBJECTS ON ALL MEASURES. THE TREATMENT GROUPS ALSO DIFFERED SIGNIFICANTLY FROM ONE ANOTHER. FINALLY, SUBJECTS IN ALL GROUPS SCORED SIGNIFICANTLY HIGHER ON THE SECOND POSTTEST. THE FINAL REPORT OF THIS DOCUMENT SUBMITTED TO THE OFFICE OF ECONOMIC OPPORTUNITY APPEARED AS ED 039 022. (MH)

ED041639 PS003661
DEVELOPMENT OF GRAMMATICAL STRUCTURES AND ATTRIBUTES IN PRE-SCHOOL AGE CHILDREN. FINAL REPORT. NURSS, JOANNE R.; DAY, DAVID E., JAN 70 83P.
EDRS PRICE MF-$0.65 HC-$3.29

THIS STUDY EXAMINED SEVERAL ASPECTS OF LANGUAGE DEVELOPMENT IN YOUNG CHILDREN. BASE LINE DATA WAS GATHERED FROM SOUTHERN URBAN HIGHER STATUS WHITE AND LOWER STATUS WHITE AND BLACK 4-YEAR-OLDS ON MEASURES OF: (1) PROFICIENCY IN CERTAIN ASPECTS OF STANDARD AMERICAN ENGLISH, (2) USE OF ATTRIBUTES IN DESCRIPTION, AND (3) ABILITY TO IMITATE, COMPREHEND, AND PRODUCE SELECTED GRAMMATICAL STRUCTURES. A TOTAL OF 147 CHILDREN ATTENDING PRESCHOOL CLASSES WERE PRE- AND POSTTESTED ON THE DAY LANGUAGE SCREEN AND THE BROWN, FRASER, BELLUGI TEST OF GRAMMATICAL CONTRASTS. DATA WERE ALSO COLLECTED CONCERNING THE LANGUAGE PROGRAM IN EACH OF THE CLASSROOMS AND THE DEMOGRAPHY OF THE SUBJECTS. THE RESULTS INDICATE THAT THERE ARE STATUS-RACE DIFFERENCES IN THE DEVELOPMENT OF LANGUAGE SKILLS IN 4-YEAR-OLDS, WITH THE HIGHER STATUS WHITE GROUP SCORING SIGNIFICANTLY HIGHER IN ALL THREE CATEGORIES ON THE PRE- AND POSTTESTS. HOWEVER, THE TWO LOWER STATUS GROUPS HAD SIGNIFICANTLY GREATER GAIN SCORES, INDICATING THAT THE REMEDIAL LANGUAGE PROGRAM USED IN THEIR CLASSES IMPROVED THEIR PROFICIENCY IN STANDARD AMERICAN ENGLISH AND RAISED THEIR LEVEL OF LANGUAGE MATURITY. IT IS SUGGESTED THAT DIRECT INSTRUCTION IN LANGUAGE SKILLS BE GIVEN TO THE LOWER STATUS PRESCHOOL CHILD, IN AN EFFORT TO AVOID LATER READING DIFFICULTY. (AUTHOR/NH)

ED041640 PS003662
THE EFFECTS OF SCHOOL ENVIRONMENT ON DISADVANTAGED KINDERGARTEN CHILDREN, WITH AND WITHOUT A HEAD START BACKGROUND. FINAL REPORT. LYNCH, DANIEL O.; HAMMES, RICHARD, 14 NOV 69 21P.
EDRS PRICE MF-$0.65 HC-$3.29

THIS STUDY INVESTIGATED THE COMPARATIVE EFFECTS OF 2 DISTINCT SCHOOL ENVIRONMENTS (STATE UNIVERSITY CAMPUS SCHOOLS AND LOCAL PUBLIC SCHOOLS) ON THE VERBALIZATION AND SOCIALIZATION SKILLS OF DISADVANTAGED KINDERGARTEN CHILDREN WITH AND WITHOUT A HEAD START BACKGROUND. IF SIGNIFICANT EFFECTS OCCURRED, IT WAS HOPED THAT ENVIRONMENTAL FACTORS THAT ENCOURAGE MAINTENANCE OF SIGNIFICANT RESIDUAL EFFECTS FROM THE HEAD START EXPERIENCE COULD BE IDENTIFIED. THE 75 SUBJECTS WERE DISTRIBUTED IN FIVE TREATMENT GROUPS: (1) CAMPUS SCHOOL, HIGH SES; (2) CAMPUS SCHOOL, LOW SES, HEAD START BACKGROUND; (3) PUBLIC SCHOOL, HIGH SES; (4) PUBLIC SCHOOL, LOW SES, HEAD START BACKGROUND; AND (5) PUBLIC SCHOOL, LOW SES, WITHOUT HEAD START BACKGROUND. VERBAL AND SOCIAL SKILLS WERE ASSESSED BY PRE- AND POSTTESTS ON THE ILLINOIS TEST OF PSYCHOLINGUISTIC ABILITIES, THE METROPOLITAN READING READINESS TEST, AND THE VINELAND SOCIAL MATURITY SCALE. ANALYSIS OF VARIANCE TREATMENT OF THE DATA REVEALED NO RESIDUAL HEAD START EFFECTS. THE ONLY SIGNIFICANT EFFECT POSSIBLY ATTRIBUTABLE TO SCHOOL ENVIRONMENT WAS THAT THE CHILDREN IN THE CAMPUS SCHOOL EXHIBITED GREATER SOCIAL GROWTH THAN THOSE IN THE PUBLIC SCHOOL. (MH)

ED041641 PS003667
LANGUAGE DEVELOPMENT OF SOCIALLY DISADVANTAGED PRESCHOOL CHILDREN. FINAL REPORT. LELER, HAZEL, JUN 70 127P.
EDRS PRICE MF-$0.65 HC-$6.58

THE RELATIONSHIP BETWEEN VARIOUS ASPECTS OF MOTHER-CHILD INTERACTION AND THE LANGUAGE PERFORMANCE OF YOUNG DISADVANTAGED NEGRO CHILDREN IS ASSESSED IN THIS STUDY. AN EXPLORATORY SURVEY WAS CONDUCTED TO DETERMINE IF MOTHERS IN SOCIALLY DISADVANTAGED FAMILIES WERE WILLING TO ENTER A PARENT PARTICIPATION PRESCHOOL PROGRAM. SUBJECTS FOR THIS STUDY, SELECTED FROM FAMILIES WHO WERE WILLING TO PARTICIPATE, WERE 53 CHILDREN AGES 2 1/2 TO 3 1/2 YEARS, SECOND OR LATER IN BIRTH ORDER, AND THEIR MOTHERS. DATA WERE COLLECTED BY LANGUAGE TESTING AND BY STRUCTURED ORDER, AND THEIR MOTHERS. DATA WERE COLLECTED BY LANGUAGE TESTING AND BY STRUCTURED OBSERVATION OF MOTHER-CHILD INTERACTION SCORED BY TWO RATERS ON VARIOUS SCALES. SIGNIFICANT POSITIVE CORRELATIONS WERE FOUND BETWEEN THE LANGUAGE TEST SCORES AND THE MOTHERS' ACCEPTANCE, USE OF PRAISE, AND REWARDING OF INDEPENDENCE, AND THE CHILD'S INDEPENDENCE AND VERBAL INITIATIVE. MOTHERS' NEGATIVE ACTIONS SUCH AS USE OF CRITICISM AND DISCOURAGEMENT OF VERBALIZATIONS WERE REFLECTED IN CHILDREN'S LOWER SCORES IN LANGUAGE PERFORMANCE. SOME SEX DIFFERENCES WERE SHOWN IN TEST SCORES AND IN MOTHER-CHILD INTERACTION. MUCH VARIATION WAS SHOWN AMONG THE SAMPLE CHILDREN. RECOMMENDATIONS ARE GIVEN FOR THE USE OF THE MEASURE OF MEAN LENGTH OF UTTERANCE. (NH)

ED041642 PS003668
A REVIEW OF THE EVALUATION OF THE FOLLOW THROUGH PROGRAM. ALKIN, MARVIN C., 15 MAY 70 9P.
EDRS PRICE MF-$0.65 HC-$3.29

THIS REVIEW OF A RESEARCH INSTITUTE'S EVALUATION OF THE NATIONAL FOLLOW THROUGH PROGRAM ASSERTS THAT BOTH THE CONTRACTING OFFICE AND THE RESEARCH INSTITUTE FAILED TO ADEQUATELY SPECIFY THE KIND OF STUDY INTENDED AND THE FUNCTIONS WHICH IT PROPOSED TO SERVE. ONE OF SEVERAL KINDS OF EVALUATION STUDIES MIGHT HAVE BEEN UNDERTAKEN: (1) A RESEARCH STUDY, DEMONSTRATING RELATIONSHIPS BETWEEN VARIABLES TO PROVIDE HYPOTHESES FOR PROGRAM APPROACHES, (2) A SUMMATIVE EVALUATION OF THE NATIONAL PROGRAM, (3) A SUMMATIVE EVALUATION OF THE RELATIVE EFFECTIVENESS OF VARIOUS SPONSOR PROGRAMS IN ACHIEVING THE FOLLOW THROUGH OBJECTIVES, OR (4) A FORMATIVE EVALUATION, PROVIDING INFORMATION TO THE DECISION-MAKER USEFUL IN MODIFYING THE PROGRAM OR IN UNDERSTANDING OUTCOME DIFFERENCES. IT IS DIFFICULT TO MAKE SPECIFIC RECOMMENDATIONS BECAUSE OF THE LACK OF STUDY DEFINITION. GENERAL RECOMMENDATIONS ARE: (A) THAT THE INSTITUTE'S EVALUATION STUDY BE CONTINUED FOR ONE MORE YEAR SINCE PRELIMINARY DATA COLLECTION HAS ALREADY BEEN DONE, (B) THE STUDY FOCUS BE CLARIFIED, WITH THE ASSISTANCE OF AN OUTSIDE PANEL, AND (C) THE BEST APPROACH FOR THE COMING YEAR WOULD PROBABLY BE ALTERNATIVE (3), LISTED ABOVE. (AUTHOR/NH)

ED041643 PS003671

A COMPARATIVE STUDY OF THE IMPACT OF TWO CONTRASTING EDUCATIONAL APPROACHES IN HEAD START, 1968-69. , 69 68P.

EDRS PRICE MF-$0.65 HC-$3.29

AS PART OF A NATIONAL EVALUATION OF HEAD START, A COMPARISON OF SCHOOL READINESS AND CHILDHOOD DEVELOPMENT APPROACHES TO PRESCHOOL EDUCATION WAS ATTEMPTED, BUT MAJOR METHODOLOGICAL PROBLEMS WERE ENCOUNTERED. IT WAS NOT POSSIBLE TO FIND THE STUDY SAMPLES CALLED FOR IN THE ORIGINAL PLAN, I.E. A CHILD-READINESS PROGRAM OF THE BEREITER-ENGELMANN TYPE, AND A CHILD DEVELOPMENT PROGRAM THAT WAS A SUITABLE EXAMPLE. A COMPROMISE SELECTION OF TWO HEAD START CENTERS INCLUDED ONE THAT WAS CHILD DEVELOPMENT-ORIENTED, AND ONE THAT HAD A MODIFIED MONTESSORI PROGRAM. A COMPARISON SAMPLE WAS SELECTED FROM A MIDDLE CLASS CHILD DEVELOPMENT-ORIENTED PRIVATE NURSERY SCHOOL. THE CHILDREN WERE PRE- AND POSTTESTED ON MEASURES OF COGNITIVE SKILLS, CURIOSITY, SELF-CONCEPT, AND SPONTANEOUS LANGUAGE. INDIVIDUAL CHILD OBSERVATIONS WERE ALSO MADE. HOWEVER, THE ORIGINAL DATA COLLECTION PLAN WAS SEVERELY CURTAILED BECAUSE OF LACK OF TIME AND TESTING SPACE. THE RESULTS OF THE STUDY ARE NOT DEFINITIVE BUT INDICATE THAT THE MIDDLE CLASS CHILDREN WERE MORE ABLE TO BENEFIT IN DEMONSTRABLE WAYS FROM A YEAR OF PRESCHOOL EDUCATION. HOWEVER, THE PRIVATE PROGRAM WAS JUDGED TO BE OF MUCH BETTER QUALITY THAN THE HEAD START PROGRAMS IN THE STUDY. (NH)

ED041644 PS003800

PRESCHOOLS AND THEIR GRADUATES. HANDLER, ELLEN OPPENHEIMER, 70 213P.

EDRS PRICE MF-$0.65 HC-$9.87

THIS EXPLORATORY STUDY CLARIFIES THE GOALS AND FUNCTIONS OF LONG DAY AND SHORT DAY PRESCHOOLS, AS RELATED TO THE REQUIREMENTS OF THE CLIENT GROUPS BEING SERVED, AND ANALYZES THEIR EFFECTS ON CHILDREN'S SOCIALIZATION AND ELEMENTARY SCHOOL ACHIEVEMENT. IT WAS HYPOTHESIZED THAT LOW SOCIOECONOMIC STATUS CHILDREN WHO HAD ATTENDED LONG DAY PRESCHOOLS WOULD BE MORE LIKELY TO MEET THE NORMATIVE EXPECTATIONS OF THE PRIMARY SCHOOL THAN LOW SOCIOECONOMIC STATUS CHILDREN WHO HAD ATTENDED SHORT DAY PRESCHOOLS. HIGH SOCIOECONOMIC STATUS CHILDREN WHO HAD ATTENDED LONG DAY PRESCHOOLS WERE EXPECTED TO DO ABOUT EQUALLY WELL AS THOSE WHO HAD ATTENDED SHORT DAY PRESCHOOLS OR NO PRESCHOOLS AT ALL. DATA WERE OBTAINED FROM CLASSROOM OBSERVATIONS AND INTERVIEWS WITH 21 TEACHERS IN SIX NURSERY SCHOOLS AND DAY CARE CENTERS. SCHOOL RECORDS OF 584 SECOND GRADE STUDENTS WERE ANALYZED. THE MEASURES OF SCHOOL ACHIEVEMENT USED WERE: (1) ABILITY TO ACHIEVE NORMAL PROMOTION, (2) THE ABSENCE OF TEACHER COMMENTS INDICATING UNACCEPTABLE CLASSROOM BEHAVIOR, AND (3) SCORES ON TWO OBJECTIVE ACHIEVEMENT TESTS, SCORED BY AN OUTSIDE AGENCY. THE CENTRAL HYPOTHESES WERE LARGELY SUPPORTED BY THE FINDINGS. (AUTHOR/NH)

ED042484 PS002981

COMPARATIVE STUDY OF THREE PRESCHOOL CURRICULA. WEIKART, DAVID P., MAR 69 18P.

EDRS PRICE MF-$0.65 HC-$3.29

THIS PROJECT WAS DESIGNED TO COMPARE THREE PRESCHOOL CURRICULA, WITH STAFF MODEL AND PROGRAM OPERATION HELD CONSTANT. THE CURRICULA WERE (1) A UNIT-BASED CURRICULUM EMPHASIZING THE SOCIAL-EMOTIONAL DEVELOPMENT GOALS OF THE TRADITIONAL NURSERY SCHOOL, (2) A COGNITIVELY-ORIENTED CURRICULUM DEVELOPED BY THE YPSILANTI PERRY PRESCHOOL PROJECT, AND (3) THE BEREITER-ENGLEMANN LANGUAGE TRAINING CURRICULUM. ALL THREE OF THESE PROGRAMS HAVE CAREFULLY PLANNED DAILY ACTIVITIES AND CLEARLY DEFINED WEEK-BY-WEEK GOALS. THE SUBJECTS FOR THE STUDY WERE 3- AND 4-YEAR-OLD FUNCTIONALLY RETARDED DISADVANTAGED CHILDREN. THERE WAS A NO-TREATMENT CONTROL GROUP. TEACHERS CONDUCTED CLASSROOMS AND HOME TEACHING SESSIONS WITHIN THE CURRICULUM STYLE THEY CHOSE. THE RESULTS OF PRE- AND POSTTEST TESTS (INCLUDING THE STANFORD-BINET AND PEABODY PICTURE VOCABULARY TEST) ARE HIGHLY UNUSUAL. THE GAIN SCORES OF THE TREATMENT GROUPS ARE REMARKABLY HIGH (SIGNIFICANTLY HIGHER THAN THE CONTROL GROUP'S SCORES), BUT THERE IS NO SIGNIFICANT DIFFERENCE IN SCORES AMONG THE THREE DIFFERENT CURRICULA SUGGESTING THAT THE VARIABLES HELD CONSTANT IN THIS EXPERIMENT (STAFF MODEL, METHOD OF PROJECT OPERATION, AND SPECIFIC TASK ORIENTATION OF THE CURRICULA) ARE AT LEAST AS IMPORTANT AS CURRICULUM CONTENT IN PRODUCING FAVORABLE DEVELOPMENTAL GAINS. (MH)

ED042485 PS003134

DEVELOPMENT OF GRAMMATICAL STRUCTURES IN PRESCHOOL AGE CHILDREN. NURSS, JOANNE R.; DAY, DAVID E., MAR 70 6P.

EDRS PRICE MF-$0.65 HC-$3.29

THE PURPOSE OF THIS STUDY WAS TO DESCRIBE THE LEVEL OF LANGUAGE MATURITY AND THE EFFECT OF A PRESCHOOL LANGUAGE PROGRAM ON THE LANGUAGE DEVELOPMENT OF URBAN, SOUTHERN 4-YEAR-OLDS. THE 147 SUBJECTS (57 LOWER STATUS BLACKS, 40 LOWER STATUS WHITES, AND 50 UPPER STATUS WHITES) ALL PARTICIPATED IN FIVE-DAY PER WEEK PREKINDERGARTEN PROGRAMS. DEPENDENT VARIABLES WERE MEASURED BY USE OF THE DAY LANGUAGE SCREEN AND THE BROWN, FRASER, BELLUGI TEST OF GRAMMATICAL CONTRASTS. THE DAY LANGUAGE SCREEN MEASURES PROFICIENCY IN CERTAIN RECEPTIVE AND EXPRESSIVE ASPECTS OF STANDARD AMERICAN ENGLISH, WHILE THE TEST OF GRAMMATICAL CONTRASTS ASSESSES ABILITY TO IMITATE, COMPREHEND, AND PRODUCE SELECTED GRAMMATICAL STRUCTURES. ANALYSIS OF THE LANGUAGE SCREEN DATA REVEALED THAT, WHILE NO SIGNIFICANT SEX OR SEX-STATUS-RACE INTERACTION EFFECTS OCCURRED, THERE WERE SIGNIFICANT STATUS-RACE EFFECTS ON PRETEST, POSTTEST, AND GAIN SCORES. UPPER CLASS SUBJECTS HAD HIGHER PRE- AND POSTTEST SCORES, BUT LOWER CLASS SUBJECTS OF BOTH RACES HAD LARGER GAIN SCORES. THE UPPER CLASS GROUP SCORED SIGNIFICANTLY HIGHER ON ALL THREE TASKS OF THE TEST OF GRAMMATICAL CONTRASTS, WHILE, BETWEEN THE TWO LOWER CLASS GROUPS, THE WHITES SCORED HIGHER ON THE COMPREHENSION TASK, BLACKS ON THE IMITATION, AND THERE WAS NO SIGNIFICANT DIFFERENCE ON THE PRODUCTION. (MH)

ED042486 PS003297

RISK-TAKING BEHAVIOR IN PRESCHOOL CHILDREN FROM THREE ETHNIC BACKGROUNDS. SILBERSTEIN, RUTH, JUN 69 45P.

EDRS PRICE MF-$0.65 HC-$3.29

COMPARED TO OTHER CHILDREN, MEXICAN-AMERICAN CHILDREN SEEM LESS RESPONSIVE IN TEST-TAKING AND CLASSROOM SITUATIONS. THIS BEHAVIOR MAY BE DUE TO A GENERALIZED TENDENCY TO BE CONSERVATIVE RISK-TAKERS. THIS STUDY INVESTIGATES ASPECTS OF THIS PROBLEM BY TESTING FOUR HYPOTHESES: (1) THAT MEXICAN-AMERICAN PRESCHOOLERS WOULD TAKE FEWER CHANCES ON A RISK-TAKING TEST THAN THEIR ANGLO-AMERICAN OR NEGRO PEERS, (2) THAT THIS INTER-GROUP DIFFERENCE WOULD INCREASE AS THE MATERIAL VALUE OF THE REWARD (CANDY, RATHER THAN PRAISE) INCREASED, (3) THAT FEWER CHANCES WOULD BE TAKEN FOLLOWING FAILURE THAN FOLLOWING SUCCESS, AND (4) THAT BOYS WOULD TAKE MORE CHANCES THAN GIRLS, REGARDLESS OF ETHNICITY OR REWARD. THE SUBJECTS, 60 NEGRO, 79 MEXICAN-AMERICAN, AND 25 ANGLO-AMERICAN HEAD START CHILDREN, WERE ALL GIVEN A RISK-TAKING TASK DEVELOPED FOR THIS STUDY. THE SUBJECTS WERE ASSIGNED ON A STRATIFIED RANDOM BASIS TO ONE OF THREE TREATMENT GROUPS BASED ON REWARD: BEADS, CANDY, OR VERBAL PRAISE. ANALYSIS OF THE DATA SHOWED NO SIGNIFICANT DIFFERENCES BETWEEN ETHNIC GROUPS, SEXES, TREATMENTS, OR FOR EFFECTS OF FAILURE AND SUCCESS. HOWEVER, AS PREDICTED, MEXICAN-AMERICANS TOOK SIGNIFICANTLY FEWER CHANCES WITH CANDY REWARD, WHILE NEGRO AND ANGLO-AMERICANS TOOK FEWER CHANCES WITH BEAD AND PRAISE REWARD. (MH)

ED042487 PS003315

A NUTRITIONAL SURVEY OF CHILDREN IN HEAD START CENTERS IN CENTRAL UNITED STATES. CROSS, MARIE Z., 30 NOV 67 6P.

EDRS PRICE MF-$0.65 HC-$3.29

THE PURPOSE OF THIS STUDY WAS TO INVESTIGATE THE EFFECTIVENESS OF A QUESTIONNAIRE IN EVALUATING THE NUTRITIONAL STATUS OF HEAD START CHILDREN IN RURAL, SMALL CITY, AND URBAN AREAS IN CENTRAL UNITED STATES. THE QUESTIONNAIRE, WHICH WAS PRIMARILY CONCERNED WITH THE FOOD PREFERENCES OF THE CHILDREN, WAS FILLED OUT BY THE MOTHER OF EACH OF THE 154 CHILDREN IN THE STUDY. NUTRITIONAL DATA WAS ALSO OBTAINED FROM ANALYSIS OF ONE WEEK'S MENUS FROM EACH OF THE HEAD START CENTERS INVOLVED IN THE STUDY. THE ONLY QUANTITATIVE DATA OBTAINED FROM THE QUESTIONNAIRES WAS THE AMOUNT OF MILK CONSUMED BY EACH CHILD. ANSWERS WERE SO NUTRITIONALLY FAVORABLE THAT IT IS SUSPECTED THAT THE MOTHERS MAY HAVE GIVEN ANSWERS THEY FELT THEY SHOULD GIVE, RATHER THAN ACTUAL MILK AMOUNTS. THE FOODS REPORTED AS BEING PREFERRED BY THE CHILDREN ARE VALUABLE SOURCES OF NUTRIENTS. THE HEAD START FOOD PROGRAMS, AS REPORTED IN THE MENUS, WERE NUTRITIONALLY ADEQUATE FOR THE ONE MEAL SERVED. THERE WERE NO SIGNIFICANT DIFFERENCES IN FOOD PREFERENCES OF THE CHILDREN IN THE THREE DIFFERENT AREAS STUDIED NOR IN THE TYPES OF FOOD SERVED IN THE CENTERS IN THESE AREAS. THE QUESTIONNAIRES PROVED TO BE OF QUESTIONABLE VALUE BECAUSE OF THE PAUCITY OF DATA THEY GENERATED CONCERNING QUANTITIES OF FOOD, BUT THE DATA WAS HELPFUL IN DETERMINING FOOD PREFERENCES. (MH)

ED042488 PS003316

ANTHROPOMETRIC MEASUREMENTS OF CHILDREN IN THE HEAD START PROGRAM. BASS, WILLIAM M.; FERRIS, M. SCOTT, 30 NOV 67 3P.

EDRS PRICE MF-$0.65 HC-$3.29

THIS IS A BRIEF PRELIMINARY REPORT OF AN ANTHROPOMETRIC MEASUREMENT STUDY OF A GROUP OF HEAD START CHILDREN. THE AREAS OF PRIMARY CONCERN WERE PATTERNS OF TOOTH ERUPTION AND BASIC HEAD AND BODY DIMENSIONS. PERMANENT HEAD START PERSONNEL WERE TRAINED TO MAKE THE OBSERVATIONS AND MEASUREMENTS. THE SAMPLE CONSISTED OF 148 CHILDREN (76 BOYS, 72 GIRLS) BETWEEN 4 YEARS 4 MONTHS AND 6 YEARS 7 MONTHS OLD. THE MEASUREMENTS TAKEN INCLUDED HEAD LENGTH, HEAD BREADTH, TOTAL FACIAL WIDTH, TOTAL FACIAL HEIGHT, WEIGHT, HEIGHT, ACROMIAL HEIGHT, STYLION HEIGHT, DACTYLION HEIGHT, SUPRASTERNAL HEIGHT, SYMPHYSEAL HEIGHT, AND VARIOUS DENTAL OBSERVATIONS. THE FOLLOWING OBSERVATIONS OF TOOTH ERUPTION PATTERNS WERE MADE: (1) BETWEEN 4 AND 5 YEARS, BOTH BOYS AND GIRLS WERE CONSISTENTLY MISSING THEIR FIRST PERMANENT MOLAR, (2) BETWEEN 5 AND 6 YEARS, GIRLS SHOWED THE LARGEST NUMBER OF ERUPTED 6-YEAR MOLARS AND BOTH CENTRAL AND LATERAL INCISORS, (3) GIRLS WERE ALSO MISSING THEIR DECIDUOUS TEETH AT THIS AGE, AND (4) BETWEEN 6 AND 7 YEARS, BOYS CATCH UP TO GIRLS IN INCIDENCE OF ERUPTED 6-YEAR MOLARS AND INCISORS. ACTUAL DATA IS NOT INCLUDED IN THIS REPORT. (MH)

ED042489 PS003318

INFLUENCE TECHNIQUES IN DYADS COMPOSED OF INTERDEPENDENT MIDDLE AND LOWER CLASS PRESCHOOL CHILDREN. FINAL REPORT ROSENFELD, HOWARD M.; RUSSELL, RICHARD L., 31 AUG 67 33P.

EDRS PRICE MF-$0.65 HC-$3.29

THE PROCEDURES BY WHICH CHILDREN FROM LOWER AND MIDDLE CLASS BACKGROUNDS ATTEMPT TO OBTAIN REWARDING OUTCOMES FROM EACH OTHER WERE OBSERVED UNDER SEMICONTROLLED CONDITIONS. TEN MALE AND 9 FEMALE DYADS, EACH COMPOSED OF 1 MIDDLE CLASS AND 1 LOWER CLASS PRESCHOOL CHILD, WERE REQUIRED TO COMPLETE 12 SIMPLE BLOCK PUZZLES IN WHICH EACH WAS GIVEN SOME OF THE PIECES HIS PARTNER NEEDED. REWARDS WERE GIVEN FOR COOPERATIVE OR COMPETITIVE PERFORMANCE. "S"S IN THE TWO SOCIOECONOMIC GROUPS DEMONSTRATED SIMILAR BEHAVIORAL REPERTOIRES. THEIR BEHAVIOR USUALLY INVOLVED THE PHYSICAL MANIPULATION OF PUZZLE PIECES, RATHER THAN ATTEMPTS TO INFLUENCE THEIR PARTNERS. ABOUT 3/4 OF ALL OBSERVED INTERPERSONAL ACTS COULD BE CATEGORIZED INTO TAKING, DELIVERING, AND DEMANDING PUZZLE PARTS. MIDDLE CLASS "S"S WERE MORE SUCCESSFUL IN GENERAL, BUT THEIR DEMANDS WERE COMPLIED WITH LESS THAN WERE THOSE OF LOWER CLASS "S"S. WHEN COMPETITIVE CONDITIONS WERE FIRST, "S"S EMITTED MORE ACTS IN BOTH PAYOFF CONDITIONS THAN WHEN COOPERATION WAS FIRST. THIS EFFECT WAS STRONGEST AMONG LOWER CLASS GIRLS, POSSIBLY BECAUSE OF DOMINANCE OF FEMALE MODELS IN THE LOWER CLASS HOME ENVIRONMENT. A FOLLOWUP STUDY ON 2 VERY LOW PERFORMING LOWER CLASS SUBJECTS REVEALED THAT THEIR RESPONSIVENESS INCREASED GREATLY WHEN PAIRED WITH FAMILIAR LOWER CLASS PARTNERS IN THEIR OWN PRESCHOOL ENVIRONMENT. (AUTHOR)

ED042490 PS003321

ERRORLESS ESTABLISHMENT OF A MATCH-TO-SAMPLE FORM DISCRIMINATION IN PRESCHOOL CHILDREN. I. A MODIFICATION OF ANIMAL LABORATORY PROCEDURES FOR CHILDREN, II. A COMPARISON OF ERRORLESS AND TRIAL-AND-ERROR DISCRIMINATION. PROGRESS REPORT. LEBLANC, JUDITH M., AUG 68 10P.

EDRS PRICE MF-$0.65 HC-$3.29

A SEQUENCE OF STUDIES COMPARED TWO TYPES OF DISCRIMINATION FORMATION: ERRORLESS LEARNING AND TRIAL-AND-ERROR PROCEDURES. THE SUBJECTS WERE THREE BOYS AND FIVE GIRLS FROM A UNIVERSITY PRESCHOOL. THE CHILDREN PERFORMED THE EXPERIMENTAL TASKS AT A TYPICAL MATCH-TO-SAMPLE APPARATUS WITH ONE SAMPLE WINDOW ABOVE AND FOUR MATCH (RESPONSE) WINDOWS BELOW. EACH OF THE CHILDREN PERFORMED EIGHT TASKS, EACH INVOLVING A FIFTY-TWO SLIDE PRESENTATION IN EIGHT DIFFERENT SESSIONS. THE ERRORLESS AND TRIAL-AND-ERROR TASKS WERE ALTERNATED. THE TASK SLIDES WERE PICTURES OF GEOMETRIC FIGURES THAT WERE ROTATED AT DIFFERENT ANGLES FROM THE SAMPLE ORIENTATION OF 0 DEGREES. RESULTS REVEALED THAT THE DESIGN OF THE TASKS WAS INSUFFICIENT FOR THE PURPOSES OF THE EXPERIMENT. NO ERRORLESS LEARNING OCCURRED, BECAUSE CRITERION DISCRIMINATION WAS TOO DIFFICULT. SUBSEQUENT EXPERIMENTATION WITH ADULTS INDICATED THAT THE TASKS WERE TOO SIMILAR TO PERMIT THE DESIRED COMPARISONS. (MH)

ED042491 PS003322

AN EXPERIMENTAL ANALYSIS OF ERROR INTERACTION ON "ERRORLESS" AND TRIAL-AND-ERROR PROGRAMS. PROGRESS REPORT. FAVELL, JUDITH ELBERT; AND OTHERS, AUG 68 7P.

EDRS PRICE MF-$0.65 HC-$3.29

IN THIS STUDY OF ERRORLESS LEARNING A PROCEDURE IS TESTED WHICH ALLOWS THE SUBJECT HIMSELF TO ADJUST THE SPEED AT WHICH A SUPPLEMENTARY STIMULUS AID IS WITHDRAWN. A STANDARD MATCH-TO-SAMPLE APPARATUS WITH 1 SAMPLE WINDOW ABOVE AND 4 MATCHING (RESPONSE) WINDOWS BELOW WAS USED. TOKENS WERE DELIVERED FOR CORRECT RESPONSES AND THE CORRECT MATCHING WINDO COULD RECEIVE EXTRA ILLUMINATION TO PROVIDE THE SUPPLEMENTARY STIMULUS AID. FOUR CHILDREN BETWEEN THE AGES OF FIVE AND EIGHT FROM A LOWER INCOME NEIGHBORHOOD SERVED AS SUBJECTS. THE RESEARCH INVOLVED 3 PHASES: (1) A PRELIMINARY MEASUREMENT OF TASK PERFORMANCE WITHOUT THE EXTRA-DIMENSIONAL CUE, (2) A SET OF TRIALS IN WHICH THE SUBJECT COULD PRODUCE THE SUPPLEMENTARY AID, AND (3) A SET OF TRIALS IN WHICH THE SUBJECT COULD PRODUCE THE EXTRA CUE, BUT ONLY AT THE COST OF A SUBSEQUENT LOSS OF TOKENS. IT WAS HOPED THAT IN THIS FINAL PHASE A SELF-PROGRAMMED FADING OUT WOULD OCCUR. HOWEVER, THE SUBJECTS NEVER PHASED OUT THE SUPPLEMENTARY STIMULUS AID, POSSIBLY BECAUSE OF THE TIME LAG BETWEEN TASK AID AND TOKEN LOSS. (MH)

ED042492 PS003323

A PROGRAM OF STIMULUS CONTROL FOR ESTABLISHING A ONE-MINUTE WAIT FOR REINFORCEMENT IN PRESCHOOL CHILDREN. PROGRESS REPORT. KOLB, DORIS H.; ETZEL, BARBARA C., AUG 68 30P.

EDRS PRICE MF-$0.65 HC-$3.29

AS A RESULT OF FINDINGS OF A PREVIOUS STUDY, THIS STUDY, WHICH SOUGHT TO PROGRAM PRESCHOOL SUBJECTS TO WAIT ONE MINUTE FOR REINFORCEMENT, USED PAUSE-BUILDING PROCEDURES BEFORE DELAY CONDITIONS WERE STARTED. THE CHILDREN, 3- TO 5-YEAR-OLDS, WERE DESIGNATED EITHER BASELINE (CONTROL) SUBJECTS (N3) OR PROGRAMMED (EXPERIMENTAL) SUBJECTS (N5). THOUGH PROCEDURES VARIED IN DETAIL FOR EACH SUBJECT, THE GENERAL PLAN FOLLOWED WAS FOR THE BASELINE SUBJECTS TO BE PUT RIGHT INTO 60 SECOND DELAY PERIODS (AFTER INITIAL PAUSE-BUILDING TRAINING) AND FOR THE PROGRAMMED SUBJECTS TO RECEIVE A PROGRAM OF TRAINING STEPS IN ADDITION TO THE PAUSE-BUILDING TRAINING BEFORE FACING THE 60 SECOND DELAY OF REINFORCEMENT. THESE TRAINING STEPS INVOLVED MULTIPLE SCHEDULES OF CONTINUOUS REINFORCEMENT AND PROGRESSIVE DIFFERENTIAL REINFORCEMENT, DISCRIMINATIVE STIMULI THAT WERE GRADUALLY FADED OUT, AND INCREASING DELAY OF REINFORCEMENT. THE PAUSE-BUILDING TRAINING, APPARENTLY A PREREQUISITE FOR SUCCESSFUL ENTRY INTO THE TRAINING PROGRAM, WAS EFFECTIVE, AND SO WAS THE PROGRAMMED TRAINING FOR THE EXPERIMENTAL GROUP, BUT ONLY UP TO THE POINT WHERE DISCRIMINATIVE STIMULI FOR NOT RESPONDING WERE FADED OUT. (MH)

ED042493 PS003324

SOCIAL FACILITATION OF HEAD START PERFORMANCE. PROGRESS REPORT. ROSENFELD, HOWARD M., AUG 69 18P.

EDRS PRICE MF-$0.65 HC-$3.29

A STUDY WAS DESIGNED TO TEST THE EFFECTS OF THE PRESENCE OF AGE-MATES ON THE PREACADEMIC PERFORMANCE OF SOCIALLY UNRESPONSIVE, DISADVANTAGED PRESCHOOL CHILDREN. EACH OF FOUR LOW PERFORMING MALE SUBJECTS WAS CONFRONTED WITH THREE HIGH PERFORMING MALE AND THREE LOW PERFORMING MALE PEERS. OF THE PEERS IN EACH OF THE TWO PERFORMANCE GROUPS, ONE WAS FROM A MIDDLE CLASS PRESCHOOL, ONE FROM A DIFFERENT LOWER CLASS PRESCHOOL, AND ONE FROM THE SUBJECT'S LOWER CLASS PRESCHOOL. THE SUBJECT WENT THROUGH A MATCH-TO-SAMPLE DISCRIMINATION TASK SESSION WITH EACH OF HIS 6 PEERS. ALL OF THESE SESSIONS INCLUDED 4 CONDITIONS: (1) BASELINE ALONE WITH EXPERIMENTER, (2) OBSERVED BY PEER, (3) COMPETING WITH PEER, AND (4) FINAL BASELINE. RESULTS, SHOWED THAT THE SUBJECTS DETERIORATED IN PERFORMANCE COMPARED TO BASELINE WHEN FAMILAR PEERS OBSERVED, BUT THAT THEIR PERFORMANCE IMPROVED WHEN THEY COMPETED WITH LOW PERFORMING FAMILIAR PEERS. SUBJECTS' PERFORMANCE IN THE OBSERVATION PHASE WAS ONLY SUPERIOR TO BASELINE WHEN THE OBSERVER WAS A MIDDLE CLASS HIGH PERFORMER. THE SMALL SAMPLE SIZE, HOWEVER, RENDERS ANY GENERALIZATIONS FROM THESE RESULTS HIGHLY SPECULATIVE (MH)

ED042494 PS003325

AN INVESTIGATION OF THE EFFECTS OF TEACHER VERBAL REINFORCEMENT AS IT RELATES TO SCHOLASTIC APTITUDE AND ACHIEVEMENT WITH ELEMENTARY SCHOOL CHILDREN. PROGRESS REPORT. HENNING, C. WALLIS, AUG 68 19P.

EDRS PRICE MF-$0.65 HC-$3.29

THE PURPOSE OF THIS STUDY WAS TO DETERMINE WHETHER OR NOT SYSTEMATIC VERBAL POSITIVE REINFORCEMENT ADMINISTERED BY TWO RELATIVELY UNSOPHISTICATED TEACHERS WOULD FAVORABLY AFFECT STUDENTS' ACHIEVEMENT SCORES. TWO KINDERGARTEN AND TWO FIRST GRADE CLASSES SERVED AS THE EXPERIMENTAL POPULATION WITH TEN STUDENTS FROM EACH CLASS AND ONE TEACHER FROM EACH GRADE COMPRISING THE EXPERIMENTAL GROUP. ALL CHILDREN WERE PRE- AND

POSTTESTED ON THE CALDWELL-SOULE PRESCHOOL INVENTORY AND THE PEABODY PICTURE VOCABULARY TEST (PPVT). SCORES OF THE PPVT PRETEST AND THE PINTNER-CUNNINGHAM (GIVEN TO ALL KINDERGARTEN CHILDREN) WERE HELD CONSTANT TO CONTROL FOR INTELLIGENCE DIFFERENCES. THE EXPERIMENTAL TEACHERS WERE TRAINED TO ADMINISTER APPROPRIATE POSITIVE REINFORCEMENT TO THEIR STUDENTS. STUDY RESULTS SHOWED THAT THEY CONSIDERABLY INCREASED THEIR POSITIVE REINFORCEMENT OUTPUT FROM EARLIER BASELINE MEASURES. THE CONTROL TEACHERS USED POSITIVE REINFORCEMENT ABOUT AS OFTEN AS THEY HAD AT BASELINE. ANALYSIS OF THE CALDWELL-SOULE PRE- AND POSTTEST SCORES REVEALED ENOUGH SIGNIFICANT DIFFERENCES TO SUPPORT THE CONTENTION THAT A PROGRAM OF SYSTEMATIC VERBAL POSITIVE REINFORCEMENT DOES FAVORABLY AFFECT THE ACHIEVEMENT OF KINDERGARTEN AND FIRST GRADE STUDENTS. (MH)

ED042495 PS003326
AN EXPERIMENTAL ANALYSIS OF PROCEDURES FOR INCREASING SPECIFIC VOCALIZATIONS OF CHILDREN WHO DO NOT DEVELOP FUNCTIONAL SPEECH. PROGRESS REPORT. LEBLANC, JUDITH M., AUG 68 13P.
EDRS PRICE MF-$0.65 HC-$3.29

TO GAIN SOME INSIGHT INTO THE PROBLEM OF DEVIANT SPEECH DEVELOPMENT IN LOW INCOME POPULATIONS, THIS STUDY INVESTIGATED THE ENVIRONMENTAL FACTORS THAT ENCOURAGE THE DEVELOPMENT OF NORMAL SPEECH. TWO SPECIFIC QUESTIONS WERE EXAMINED IN THIS STUDY: (1) IF SPECIFIC VOCALIZED ENVIRONMENTAL SOUNDS ARE PRESENTED CONTIGUOUSLY WITH REINFORCEMENT, WILL SUBJECT VOCALIZATIONS OF THAT SOUND INCREASE? AND (2) WOULD ESTABLISHING SPECIFIC ENVIRONMENTAL SOUNDS AS DISCRIMINATIVE FOR REINFORCEMENT PRODUCE INCREASES IN SUBJECT VOCALIZATIONS OF THOSE SOUNDS? SUBJECTS WERE A 13-MONTH-OLD FEMALE AND A 10-MONTH-OLD MALE. EXPERIMENTAL MANIPULATIONS INVOLVING RECORDING OF ENVIRONMENTAL SOUNDS AND A STIMULUS PRESENTATION TAPE ESTABLISHED THE CONDITIONS IN QUESTION: SPECIFIC VOCALIZED ENVIRONMENTAL SOUNDS PRESENTED CONTIGUOUSLY WITH REINFORCEMENT AND SPECIFIC ENVIRONMENTAL SOUNDS ESTABLISHED AS DISCRIMINATIVE FOR REINFORCEMENT. FINDINGS INDICATED THAT, FOR THESE SUBJECTS, PAIRING SOUNDS WITH REINFORCEMENT PRODUCED NO EFFECTS ON RATE OF VOCALIZATION OF THESE SOUNDS, BUT THAT MAKING THESE SOUNDS DISCRIMINATIVE FOR REINFORCEMENT DID INCREASE SUBJECTS' RATE OF VOCALIZATION. (MH)

ED042496 PS003327
CROSS-CULTURAL VERBAL COOPERATION. PROGRESS REPORT. REESE, NANCY MANN, AUG 68 16P.
EDRS PRICE MF-$0.65 HC-$3.29

THIS PILOT STUDY SOUGHT TO INVESTIGATE THE VERBAL COOPERATIVE BEHAVIOR OF MIDDLE CLASS AND LOWER CLASS CHILDREN WHEN PAIRED WITH SAME AND OPPOSITE SES PARTNERS. THE SUBJECTS WERE 12 BOYS AND 12 GIRLS RANGING IN AGE FROM 4-1 TO 5-4. IN THE EXPERIMENTAL SITUATION, 2 CHILDREN WERE SEATED FACING EACH OTHER ACROSS A TABLE. EACH OF THEM HAD FIVE PICTURES IN FRONT OF THEM THAT THEY HAD PREVIOUSLY BEEN TRAINED TO IDENTIFY AND MATCH BY NAME. A BOARD IN THE MIDDLE OF THE TABLE PREVENTED ONE SUBJECT FROM SEEING THE OTHER'S PICTURES. THE SUBJECTS WERE TOLD TO POINT TO THE PICTURES, ONE AT A TIME. IF THEY BOTH POINTED TO THE SAME PICTURE, THEY BOTH RECEIVED TOKEN REINFORCEMENT THAT COULD LATER BE REDEEMED FOR TOYS. TO ASSURE A MATCH, ONE SUBJECT WOULD HAVE TO TELL THE OTHER WHICH PICTURE HE WAS POINTING TO (INITIATION) AND THE OTHER SUBJECT WOULD HAVE TO POINT TO THE SAME ONE (MATCHING). CONTRARY TO EXPECTATION, ON BOTH OLDER AND YOUNGER AGE LEVELS, LOWER CLASS CHILDREN INITIATED RESPONSES MORE OFTEN THAN MIDDLE CLASS CHILDREN. (MH)

ED042497 PS003328
STIMULUS GENERALIZATION ACROSS INDIVIDUALS ALONG DIMENSIONS OF SEX AND RACE: SOME FINDINGS WITH CHILDREN FROM AN ALL-NEGRO NEIGHBORHOOD. PROGRESS REPORT. DOKE, LARRY A., AUG 69 39P.
EDRS PRICE MF-$0.65 HC-$3.29

FOUR MALE AND FIVE FEMALE NEGRO CHILDREN (RANGING IN AGE FROM 5 TO 9 YEARS) SERVED IN AN EXPERIMENTAL COMPARISON OF THE DISCRIMINATIVE CONTROL EXERTED BY SEX AND RACE ASPECTS OF OTHER CHILDREN. A BASELINE WAS ESTABLISHED IN WHICH COLOR PHOTOSLIDES OF A NEGRO GIRL AND A CAUCASIAN BOY DIFFERENTIALLY CONTROLLED RESPONDING ON TWO PUSH BUTTONS. RESPONSES DURING TEST PROBES PICTURING CHILDREN FROM EACH RACE-SEX GROUPING INDICATED PREDOMINANT CONTROL BY THE STIMULUS DIMENSION OF SEX. SIX OF THE SUBJECTS WERE THEN REINFORCED FOR DIFFERENTIALLY RESPONDING TO PHOTOSLIDES OF NEGRO AND CAUCASIAN CHILDREN. DURING SUBSEQUENT TRAINING, PHOTOSLIDES OF NEW INDIVIDUALS WERE INTRODUCED. RESPONSES DURING TEST PROBES WHICH FOLLOWED EACH OF THESE PHASES SHOWED NO GENERALIZATION ALONG A STIMULUS DIMENSION OF RACE. EFFECTS OF RACIAL STIMULUS CLASS LABELING UPON GENERALIZATION WERE STUDIED IN A FINAL PHASE FOLLOWING A MULTIPLE BASELINE DESIGN ACROSS SUBJECTS. IT WAS FOUND THAT FOR FOUR SUBJECTS A VERBAL STIMULUS CLASS LABELING REQUIREMENT, WHEN PAIRED WITH DIFFERENTIAL REINFORCEMENT FOR BUTTON-PUSHING, WAS SUFFICIENT TO SHIFT CONTROL TO A DIMENSION OF RACE. (AUTHOR)

ED042498 PS003329
EXPERIMENTAL ANALYSIS OF EFFECTS OF TEACHER ATTENTION OF PRESCHOOL CHILDREN'S BLOCK BUILDING BEHAVIOR. PROGRESS REPORT. COOPER, MARGARET L., AUG 69 13P.
EDRS PRICE MF-$0.65 HC-$3.29

THIS STUDY WAS DESIGNED TO DEMONSTRATE THE EFFECTS OF TEACHER ATTENTION GIVEN FOR SPECIFIC RESPONSES CHILDREN SHOW WHEN USING BUILDING BLOCKS. THESE INCLUDED THE RESPONSES OF COMBINING TRIANGLES TO MAKE RECTANGLES, STACKING DIVERSE PIECES TO MAKE A TOWER, MAKING STAIRS, MAKING A VARIATION ON A MODEL, AND MAKING A HOUSE-LIKE, ENCLOSED, ROOFED STRUCTURE. SOCIAL REINFORCEMENT INVOLVED THE TEACHER'S APPROVING ATTENTION, OCCASIONALLY SUPPLEMENTED BY A POLAROID SNAPSHOT OF A SUCCESSFUL OR NEAR-SUCCESSFUL CONSTRUCTION. EXPERIMENTALLY-PRODUCED CHANGES IN THESE BEHAVIORS DURING TEST SESSIONS WERE DISPLAYED FOR THREE PRESCHOOL CHILDREN. FOR TWO CHILDREN, TRAINING (PROMPTING AND REINFORCING DURING BLOCK PLAY) PRODUCED THE DESIRED BEHAVIOR ON THE TRAINED TASKS, BUT NO DEVELOPMENT WAS OBSERVED ON UNTRAINED TASKS. FOR THE THIRD CHILD, THE DESIRED BEHAVIORS FOLLOWED TRAINING ON THREE OF FOUR TRAINED TASKS; BUT THERE WAS NO CHANGE IN RESPONSE ON THE FOURTH TASK (AFTER FOUR DAYS OF TRAINING). A FIFTH TASK WAS NOT TRAINED; NEVERTHELESS, APPROPRIATE BEHAVIOR OCCURRED DURING THE LAST TWO DAYS OF THE STUDY. (MH)

ED042499 PS003330
THE MODIFICATION OF TEACHER BEHAVIORS WHICH MODIFY CHILD BEHAVIORS. PROGRESS REPORT. THOMSON, CAROLYN L.; COOPER, MARGARET L., AUG 69 22P.
EDRS PRICE MF-$0.65 HC-$3.29

THIS STUDY ON BEHAVIOR MODIFICATION TRAINING EXAMINED THE EFFECT OF FREQUENT FEEDBACK TO REINFORCE A TEACHER'S ATTENDING TO APPROPRIATE CHILD BEHAVIORS. TWO HEAD START TEACHERS WERE SELECTED AS SUBJECTS. BASELINE OBSERVATIONS, TRAINING, AND POSTTEST OBSERVATIONS WERE MADE OF BOTH TEACHERS. TRAINING INVOLVED FEEDBACK TO THE TEACHERS EVERY 10 MINUTES ON THE APPROPRIATENESS OF THEIR REINFORCING TECHNIQUES. DATA FROM OBSERVATIONS INDICATED THAT FEEDBACK WAS AN IMPORTANT FACTOR IN MODIFYING THE BEHAVIOR OF THE TEACHERS. IN ADDITION, TEACHERS WERE EQUIPPED WITH HEARING-AID TYPE RECEIVERS, SO THAT THEY COULD RECEIVE IMMEDIATE AND CONTINUAL FEEDBACK. THE DEPENDENT MEASURE OF THIS PHASE OF THE STUDY WAS THE BEHAVIOR OF THE CHILDREN THE TEACHER WAS ATTEMPTING TO HELP. THE DESIRED TEACHER BEHAVIORS AND STUDENT BEHAVIORS INCREASED GREATLY. ONE OF THE TEACHERS GENERALIZED TO THE ENTIRE CLASS THE LESSONS SHE HAD BEEN TAUGHT FOR A SPECIFIC TARGET CHILD. MEASUREMENT OF TEACHER EFFECTIVENESS THROUGH MEASUREMENT OF CHILD BEHAVIORS APPEARS WORTHY OF FURTHER EXPLORATION. (MH)

ED042500 PS003331
A SHOE IS TO TIE: A FILM DEMONSTRATION OF PROGRAMMING SELF-HELP SKILLS FOR PRESCHOOL CHILDREN. PROGRESS REPORT. COOPER, MARGARET L., AUG 69 6P.
EDRS PRICE MF-$0.65 HC-$3.29

AT THE EDNA A. HILL PRESCHOOL LABORATORIES AT THE UNIVERSITY OF KANSAS, CHILDREN BETWEEN THE AGES OF TWO AND FIVE ARE BEING TAUGHT TWO KINDS OF PRECISE SKILLS, SOME TO PREPARE THEM FOR THE ACADEMIC WORLD AND OTHERS TO ENABLE THEM TO CARE FOR THEMSELVES MORE INDEPENDENTLY. BEHAVIOR ANALYSIS AND APPLICATION OF REINFORCEMENT PRINCIPLES MAKE EARLIER SKILL DEVELOPMENT POSSIBLE. IN THIS PROGRAM, SKILLS ARE PROGRAMMED BY SIMPLIFYING THE STEPS, ISOLATING THE SPECIFIC RESPONSES, AND CONSISTENTLY REINFORCING CORRECT RESPONSES. THE AMOUNT OF TIME AND EFFORT EXERTED BY BOTH CHILD AND ADULT IS GREATLY DECREASED. AN EXAMPLE OF A SELF-HELP SKILL TAUGHT IN THIS PROGRAM IS SHOE-TYING. AS THE CHILD LEARNS THE SKILL, HE IS REINFORCED, THE EXTRA-LONG LACES ARE SHORTENED, AND THE INSTRUCTIONS ARE PHASED OUT UNTIL HE CAN TIE HIS OWN SHOES WITH NO INSTRUCTIONS. THROUGH SUCH PROGRAMMING, SKILLS HAVE BEEN SUCCESSFULLY AND EASILY TAUGHT TO CHILDREN IN THE PROGRAM AT EARLIER AGES THAN WOULD TRADITIONALLY BE EXPECTED. (MH)

ED042501 PS003393
STANDARDS AND COSTS FOR DAY CARE. , [69] 8P.
EDRS PRICE MF-$0.65 HC-$3.29

THIS ANALYSIS PROJECTS STANDARDS AND COSTS FOR THREE TYPES OF DAY CARE SITUATIONS: (1) CARE IN A CENTER FOR THE FULL DAY; (2) CARE IN A FOSTER HOME FOR THE FULL DAY; AND (3) CARE IN A CENTER BEFORE AND AFTER SCHOOL AND DURING THE SUMMER. STANDARDS ARE GIVEN FOR THREE LEVELS OF QUALITY OF DAY CARE: MINIMUM (MAINTAINS THE HEALTH AND SAFETY OF THE CHILD, BUT PROVIDES RELATIVELY LITTLE FOR HIS DEVELOPMENTAL NEEDS), ACCEPTABLE (PROVIDES A BASIC PROGRAM OF DEVELOPMENTAL ACTIVITIES AS WELL AS MINIMUM CARE), AND DESIRABLE (INCLUDES THE FULL RANGE OF GENERAL AND SPECIALIZED DEVELOPMENTAL ACTIVITIES SUITABLE FOR INDIVIDUALIZED DEVELOPMENT.) COSTS FOR DAY CARE PROGRAMS VARY GREATLY THROUGHOUT THE COUNTRY, REFLECTING SALARY AND OTHER VARIABLES AND DIFFERENCES IN KINDS OF SERVICES AVAILABLE TO THE CHILD (SUCH AS MEDICAID.) THE COSTS SHOWN MAY BE REDUCIBLE IF

SPACE OR TRANSPORTATION IS DONATED, IF SERVICES SUCH AS MEDICAL CARE ARE AVAILABLE THROUGH OTHER FUNDING SOURCES, OR IF FEES ARE PAID BY PARENTS. THE FOUR ATTACHED TABLES PRESENT STANDARDS AND COSTS FOR THE THREE DAY CARE SITUATIONS, PLUS A COMPARATIVE SUMMARY AND ESTIMATE OF NATIONAL COSTS. (AUTHOR/NH)

ED042502 PS003402
PREPRIMARY ENROLLMENT TRENDS OF CHILDREN UNDER SIX: 1964-1968. HURD, GORDON E., FEB 70 35P.
EDRS PRICE MF-$0.65 HC NOT AVAILABLE FROM EDRS.
AVAILABLE FROM: SUPERINTENDENT OF DOCUMENTS, U.S. GOVERNMENT PRINTING OFFICE, WASHINGTON, D.C. 20402 ($0.45, NO. HE 5.216:16001)

OFFICE OF EDUCATION ANNUAL REPORTS HAVE YIELDED THIS STATISTICAL DESCRIPTION OF PREPRIMARY ENROLLMENT TRENDS AND CHANGES DURING THE PERIOD FROM 1964 TO 1968. THIS REPORT CONTAINS FOUR PAGES OF TEXT, SUMMARIZING IN PROSE FORM THE SIGNIFICANT TRENDS AND ENROLLMENT PATTERNS AND CITING THE SOURCE AND RELIABILITY OF THE DATA. INFORMATION DESCRIBED AND GRAPHED INCLUDES TOTAL PREPRIMARY ENROLLMENT OF 3-5 YEAR OLDS; CUMULATIVE PERCENTAGE INCREASE OF PREPRIMARY ENROLLMENT OF 3-5 YEAR OLDS; AND ANALYSIS BY AGE, COLOR, REGION, FAMILY INCOME, OCCUPATION OF HEAD OF HOUSEHOLD, AND PLACE OF RESIDENCE. THE MOST STRIKING TREND IS THE YEARLY RISE IN THE NUMBER OF 3-5 YEAR OLDS ENROLLED EVEN THOUGH THERE WAS A YEARLY DECLINE IN THE POPULATION OF THIS AGE GROUP. IN 1968, 33% OF THIS POPULATION WAS ENROLLED. THE REPORT CONCLUDES WITH FOUR EXTENSIVE TABLES OF DATA. (MH)

ED042503 PS003404
PROGRAM-PROJECT RESUMES, 1969-1970. , [70] 360P.
EDRS PRICE MF-$0.65 HC-$13.16

THIS COLLECTION OF 120 PROJECT RESUMES IS A SURVEY OF PROGRAMS, PROJECTS, AND ACTIVITIES IN PROGRESS AT THE NATIONAL COORDINATION CENTER AND AT EACH OF THE SEVEN CENTERS ASSOCIATED WITH THE NATIONAL LABORATORY ON EARLY CHILDHOOD EDUCATION. EACH RESUME IS CODED ACCORDING TO LABORATORY CATEGORY AND NAME OF CENTER INVOLVED. THE TITLE OF EACH SPECIFIC PROJECT AND THE NAME OF THE PROJECTS' PRINCIPAL INVESTIGATOR IS GIVEN. EACH RESUME INCLUDES A CAPSULE STATEMENT OF GOALS, RATIONALE, METHOD, CHARACTERISTICS OF USERS, EXPECTED RESULTS, AND EVALUATION PROCEDURES. (WY)

ED042504 PS003412
AN ANALYSIS OF MOTHERS' SPEECH AS A FACTOR IN THE DEVELOPMENT OF CHILDREN'S INTELLIGENCE. ORTAR, GINA; CARMON, HANNA, AUG 69 116P.
EDRS PRICE MF-$0.65 HC-$6.58

THE PRESENT STUDY AIMED: (1) TO SYSTEMATICALLY DESCRIBE AND CLASSIFY THE SPEECH INPUT RECEIVED BY CHILDREN OF SPECIFIED AGES FROM THEIR MOTHERS IN THE HOME, (2) TO INVESTIGATE THE INTERDEPENDENCE BETWEEN THE QUALITY OF THE MOTHER'S SPEECH, HER SOCIO-CULTURAL BACKGROUND, AND HER CHILDREN'S LEVEL OF INTELLIGENCE, AND (3) TO DETERMINE WHETHER SOME ATTRIBUTES OF THE MOTHER'S SPEECH CAN BE MODIFIED IF SHE WISHES. THE SPEECH OF 57 MOTHERS FROM TWO ETHNO-CULTURAL GROUPS WAS RECORDED DURING TWO 60-MINUTE SESSIONS IN EACH HOME. SIBLINGS OF TWO AGES WERE OBSERVED: A CHILD NOT YET TALKING (ABOUT 1 YEAR OLD), AND A CHILD ALREADY TALKING (ABOUT 3 YEARS OLD). A THIRD VISIT YIELDED BACKGROUND INFORMATION FROM THE MOTHER, AND DURING A FOURTH VISIT (1 YEAR LATER), THE OLDER CHILD AND THE MOTHER WERE GIVEN INTELLIGENCE TESTS. THE UNITS OF SPEECH ANALYSES WERE WORDS AND SENTENCES, DEALING WITH SPEECH ASPECTS OF AMOUNT, CONTENT, AND FORM. ALTHOUGH ALL VARIABLE FACTORS AFFECTING VERBAL BEHAVIOR WERE NOT CONTROLLED, STUDY RESULTS YIELDED (1) MEANINGFUL MEASUREMENT OF FOUR ASPECTS OF SPEECH, AND ESTABLISHMENT OF PRELIMINARY NORMS TO EVALUATE A MOTHER'S MANNER OF SPEECH, (2) SIGNIFICANT CORRELATIONS OF THE CHILDREN'S INTELLIGENCE LEVEL WITH THE MEASURES OF MOTHERS' SPEECH, AND (3) PRELIMINARY INDICATIONS THAT READINESS AND ABILITY OF THE MOTHER TO MODIFY HER SPEECH IS CORRELATED WITH HER INTELLECTUAL LEVEL (PART OF AN ONGOING EXPERIMENT). APPENDIXES ARE INCLUDED. (AUTHOR/NH)

ED042505 PS003417
THE SOUTHSIDE EXPERIMENT IN PERSONALIZED EDUCATION. SPAULDING, ROBERT L., 10 APR 69 16P.
EDRS PRICE MF-$0.65 HC-$3.29

IN ORDER TO PROVIDE MORE PARTICIPATION BY STUDENTS IN MAKING THE DAY-TO-DAY DECISIONS OF ACADEMIC LIFE, THE SOUTHSIDE SCHOOL IN DURHAM, NORTH CAROLINA IS PRESENTLY INVOLVED IN A 5-YEAR EXPERIMENTAL PROGRAM FOR DISADVANTAGED CHILDREN. A PART OF THAT PROGRAM IS A PILOT PROJECT OF INDIVIDUALIZED INSTRUCTION WHICH PERMITS CONTINUOUS PROGRESS WITH INCREASING DEGREES OF FREEDOM, RESPONSIBILITY, AND DECISION-MAKING ON THE PART OF THE STUDENTS. THE PROJECT, CALLED PERSONALIZED EDUCATIONAL PROGRAMMING, INVOLVES 60 FIRST-, SECOND-, AND THIRD-GRADERS WHO ARE GROUPED INTO FOUR FAMILY GROUPS OR "PRIDES" THAT MEET PERIODICALLY FOR PLANNING OR GROUP ACTIVITY. EACH CHILD PLANS HIS OWN DAILY SCHEDULE WITH THE ASSISTANCE OF A TEACHER AND WITHIN THE SPECIFIC TIME CONSTRAINTS AND SUBJECT REQUIREMENTS FOR THAT DAY. GUIDELINES, SUGGESTED PROJECTS, AND SAMPLE SCHEDULES ARE POSTED FOR STUDENTS' PERUSAL. THE AMOUNT OF FREEDOM AND AUTONOMY AN INDIVIDUAL STUDENT IS PERMITTED DEPENDS ON HIS PAST DEMONSTRATIONS OF PERSONAL RESPONSIBILITY. THE PROJECT HAS BEEN OPERATING SINCE SEPTEMBER, 1968, AND EVALUATIONS ARE SCHEDULED FOR SUMMER, 1969, AND THE 1969-70 SCHOOL YEAR. (MH)

ED042506 PS003418
A PARENT-CHILD CENTER, NOVEMBER-DECEMBER 1968. HARRISON, FREDERICA; THOGERSON, ANN, DEC 68 25P.
EDRS PRICE MF-$0.65 HC-$3.29

A PARENT-CHILD CENTER PROGRAM WAS DESIGNED TO TEST THE THEORY THAT A MAJOR CAUSE OF A DISADVANTAGED CHILD'S ACADEMIC PROBLEMS IS THE LACK OF PROPER MATERNAL SUPPORT. THE 10 SUBJECTS FOR THIS STUDY OF PROGRAM EFFECTIVENESS WERE BLACK, WITHOUT HUSBANDS, AND EACH HAD A 1 1/2 TO 3-YEAR-OLD CHILD. MOTHERS MET TWICE A WEEK FOR 6 WEEKS IN A 2-PART PROGRAM THAT FOCUSED (1) ON THEIR CHILDREN'S LANGUAGE DEVELOPMENT AND (2) ON THEIR OWN DEVELOPMENT IN CHILD REARING, COOKING AND SEWING SKILLS. A PRESCHOOL TEACHER GAVE INSTRUCTIONS ON HOW TO STIMULATE CHILDREN'S LANGUAGE DEVELOPMENT AND MOTIVATION TO LEARN THROUGH APPROPRIATE USE OF DAY-TO-DAY EXPERIENCES. GROUP DISCUSSIONS WERE ENCOURAGED AT THESE MEETINGS. THE CHILDREN HAD A SPECIAL PROGRAM, TOO, THAT WAS INTENDED TO PROVIDE EXPERIENCES IN AN ENVIRONMENT THAT FOSTERED COGNITIVE, PERCEPTUAL, AND LANGUAGE DEVELOPMENT. THE PROGRAM TOOK PLACE IN A WELL-EQUIPPED KINDERGARTEN ROOM AND WAS BASED ON CHILDREN'S NEED FOR ORDER AND PREDICTABILITY, AN ALTERNATING PACE, MEDIATED EXPERIENCES, A SENSE OF SUCCESS AND A GENERAL LANGUAGE FACILITY. MEASURES TAKEN OF BOTH MOTHERS AND CHILDREN PROVIDED DESCRIPTION OF SUBJECTS, PROGRAM EVALUATION, AND EVALUATION OF THE MEASURING INSTRUMENTS USED. THE PROGRAM ACTIVITIES WERE JUDGED TO BE APPROPRIATE FOR THE SUBJECTS. (MH)

ED042507 PS003424
THE SOCIAL MATURITY OF DISADVANTAGED CHILDREN. SPECIAL STUDIES PROJECT #2: GALLAGHER, JAMES J.; AND OTHERS, FEB 67 9P.
EDRS PRICE MF-$0.65 HC-$3.29

TO DETERMINE DEVELOPMENT PATTERNS OF THE DISADVANTAGED CHILD AT THE AGE WHEN HE COMES INTO CONTACT WITH A SCHOOL PROGRAM, A COMPARISON WAS MADE OF THE TEST PERFORMANCES OF 25 PRIMARY SCHOOL CHILDREN ON THE STANFORD-BINET AND THE VINELAND SOCIAL MATURITY SCALE. TEST BATTERIES WERE GIVEN IN FALL AND IN SPRING. THE BINET TEST WAS ADMINISTERED AT SCHOOL, THE VINELAND AT HOME THROUGH SOCIAL WORK INTERVIEWS. EACH CHILD'S PERFORMANCE WAS EXAMINED IN TERMS OF ITEMS SUCCEEDED AND ITEMS FAILED ON THE VINELAND. EARLY FAILURES AND LATE SUCCESSES WERE CATEGORIZED, IDENTIFYING SUBAREAS OF GOOD AND POOR DEVELOPMENT. THERE WAS A SUBSTANTIAL DIFFERENCE BETWEEN THE MEAN SCORES ON THE BINET AND THE VINELAND SCALE. ONLY FOUR CHILDREN HAD A BINET QUOTIENT EQUAL TO OR SUPERIOR TO THEIR VINELAND QUOTIENT. CHILDREN EXCELLED PRIMARILY IN THE SELF-CARE AREAS, BEING ABLE TO FEED AND DRESS THEMSELVES AT AN AGE LEVEL MUCH BEYOND THEIR SKILLS IN OTHER AREAS. THEY WERE ALSO ABLE TO USE SMALL TOOLS TO DO ROUTINE HOUSEHOLD TASKS. FAILURES TENDED TO OCCUR IN THE AREAS OF COMMUNICATION, GENERAL SELF HELP, AND LOCOMOTION. IN REGARD TO NEIGHBORHOOD EXPLORATION, CHILDREN APPEAR TO BE OVERPROTECTED BY THEIR PARENTS. EVALUATION OF THE DISADVANTAGED CHILD'S SOCIAL SKILLS SHOULD INCLUDE MANY DEVELOPMENTAL DIMENSIONS. (NH)

ED042508 PS003428
CLASSIFICATION AND ATTENTION TRAINING CURRICULA FOR HEAD START CHILDREN. EARHART, EILEEN M., 6 MAR 70 6P.
EDRS PRICE MF-$0.65 HC-$3.29

THE NEEDS AND CAPABILITIES OF 4-YEAR-OLD HEAD START CHILDREN WERE CONSIDERED IN DEVELOPMENT OF CLASSIFICATION AND ATTENTION TRAINING CURRICULA, INCLUDING: (1) SENSORY EXPLORATION THROUGH OBJECT MANIPULATION, (2) VARIETY OF HIGH-INTEREST MATERIALS, (3) CHANGE OF PACE DURING THE LESSON, (4) PRESENTATION OF LEARNING ACTIVITIES AS GAMES, (5) RELATING OF NEW TERMS TO THE CHILD'S EXPERIENCE AND VOCABULARY, AND (6) INSTRUCTING THE CHILD IN CONCEPT MEANINGS BEFORE ASKING HIM TO FOLLOW DIRECTIONS USING THOSE CONCEPTS. TWENTY LESSONS WERE DEVELOPED IN CLASSIFICATION TRAINING, WHICH EMPHASIZED LABELING, DESCRIPTION, LIKENESSES AND DIFFERENCES, AND CATEGORICAL GROUPING OF SUCH OBJECTS AS PLASTIC FRUITS, TOY AIRPLANES, AND WEARING APPAREL. A GUIDED DISCOVERY METHOD ENCOURAGES THE CHILD TO DETECT AND RECOGNIZE RELATIONSHIPS FOR HIMSELF. ATTENTION TRAINING LESSONS USED MATERIALS SUCH AS STIMULUS SHAPES, PARQUETRY BLOCKS, AND THREE-DIMENSIONAL ANIMALS. THE CHILD LEARNS TO OBSERVE THE CHARACTERISTICS OF OBJECTS AND THEN SELECT LIKE OBJECTS. FOR ATTENTION TRAINING, A MINIMUM OF VERBALIZATION AND LABELING IS USED AS THE CHILD IS ENCOURAGED TO FOCUS ON VISUAL STIMULI. HEAD START TEACHERS HAVE REACTED POSITIVELY TO THESE CURRICULA. (NH)

ED042509 PS003437
THE DISTRIBUTION OF TEACHER APPROVAL AND DISAPPROVAL OF HEAD START CHILDREN. FINAL REPORT. MEYER, WILLIAM J.; LINDSTROM, DAVID, 69 57P.
EDRS PRICE MF-$0.65 HC-$3.29

THE MAIN PURPOSE OF THIS STUDY WAS TO DETERMINE WHETHER OR NOT A SAMPLE OF WHITE AND NEGRO HEAD START TEACHERS EXHIBITED ANY BIAS TOWARD A PARTICULAR SEX OR RACE AMONG THEIR STUDENTS. BIAS WAS DEFINED AS A DISPROPORTIONATE DISTRIBUTION OF VERBAL APPROVAL AND DISAPPROVAL. THE CHILDREN WERE ALSO OBSERVED TO DETERMINE THEIR FREQUENCY OF "BLAMEWORTHY" AND "PRAISEWORTHY" BEHAVIORS. A SECONDARY PURPOSE OF THE STUDY WAS THE OBSERVATION OF GENERAL CLASSROOM INTERACTION IN ORDER TO EXAMINE ITS RELATION TO THE PRINCIPLES OF REINFORCEMENT LEARNING THEORY. THIRTEEN CLASSES (126 CHILDREN IN ALL) SERVED AS SAMPLE, EACH WITH A TEACHER AND A TEACHER AIDE. MEASUREMENT INVOLVED PRE- AND POSTTESTING, 4 HOURS OF CLASSROOM OBSERVATION, AND EXTENSIVE INTERVIEWS. RESULTS INDICATE THAT, WITH ONE OR TWO EXCEPTIONS, THE TEACHERS EXHIBITED NO RACIAL OR SEXUAL BIAS. IT WAS ALSO FOUND THAT THE HEAD START TEACHERS USED MORE DISAPPROVAL THAN APPROVAL, A PATTERN OF BEHAVIOR INCONSISTENT WITH THE PRINCIPLES OF GENERAL REINFORCEMENT THEORY FOR CLASSROOM INTERACTION. FURTHERMORE, THE TEACHER'S USE OF DISAPPROVAL AND APPROVAL WAS NOT CONTINGENT ON SPECIFIC BEHAVIORS. THERE WAS A SIGNIFICANT NEGATIVE RELATIONSHIP BETWEEN TEACHER DISAPPROVAL AND AN INDEX OF MOTIVATION. (MH)

ED042510 PS003438
PSYCHOLINGUISTIC BEHAVIORS OF ISOLATED, RURAL CHILDREN WITH AND WITHOUT KINDERGARTEN. COWLES, MILLY; AND OTHERS, 24 APR 70 18P.
EDRS PRICE MF-$0.65 HC-$3.29

THIS PAPER REPORTS PART OF A LONGITUDINAL STUDY TO ASSESS THE PSYCHOLINGUISTIC ABILITIES OF RURAL CHILDREN GIVEN VARIOUS EDUCATIONAL OPPORTUNITIES. TWENTY-TWO KINDERGARTENS WERE ESTABLISHED, EACH WITH A TEACHER AND A TEACHER AIDE. PRIOR TO THE OPENING OF SCHOOL, THE STAFF WAS EXPOSED TO A SIX-WEEK INTENSIVE TRAINING SESSION. AN INSERVICE TRAINING PROGRAM STRESSED PERSONAL AND PROFESSIONAL PREPARATION THROUGHOUT THE YEAR. THE KINDERGARTEN PROGRAM WAS INFORMAL BUT EMPHASIZED LANGUAGE DEVELOPMENT ACTIVITIES. EVALUATION WAS BASED ON THE ILLINOIS TEST OF PSYCHOLINGUISTIC ABILITIES (ITPA) ADMINISTERED TO RANDOMLY SELECTED SAMPLES OF 32 NO-KINDERGARTEN AND 31 KINDERGARTEN CHILDREN AT THE END OF FIVE MONTHS IN THEIR "ENRICHED" FIRST GRADES IN HIGH PRIORITY (LOW ECONOMIC STATUS) SCHOOLS. DATA PROCESSED THROUGH BOTH MULTIVARIATE ANALYSIS OF VARIANCE AND ANALYSIS OF VARIANCE REVEALED THAT SUBJECTS WITH KINDERGARTEN EXPERIENCE SCORED SIGNIFICANTLY HIGHER THAN THOSE WITHOUT KINDERGARTEN ON SIX OF THE TEN SUBTESTS. WHILE THE NEED FOR MORE CAREFULLY CONTROLLED RESEARCH WAS INDICATED, EARLY EDUCATION DID APPEAR TO BE IMPORTANT FOR THIS POPULATION. (WY)

ED042511 PS003448
HAWAII HEAD START EVALUATION--1968-69. FINAL REPORT. ADKINS, DOROTHY C.; HERMAN, HANNAH, JAN 70 192P.
EDRS PRICE MF-$0.65 HC-$6.58

THE PRESENT STUDY COMPARED THE DEVELOPMENTAL EFFECTS OF TWO CURRICULA (UNIVERSITY OF HAWAII PRESCHOOL LANGUAGE CURRICULUM (UHPLC) AND A GENERAL ENRICHMENT CURRICULUM); TWO PARENT PROGRAMS (ONE EMPHASIZING THE MOTHER'S ROLE IN FOSTERING HER CHILD'S COGNITIVE DEVELOPMENT, P1, AND ONE FOCUSING ON MORE GENERAL CONCEPTS OF CHILD DEVELOPMENT, P2); AND TWO LEVELS OF PARENT PARTICIPATION (1/3 OR BETTER ATTENDANCE AT PARENT MEETINGS AND LESS THAN 1/3ATTENDANCE). DEPENDENT MEASURES INCLUDED CLASSROOM OBSERVATIONS, PRE- AND POSTTESTING ON A WIDE VARIETY OF TESTS, AND INTERVIEWS WITH MOTHERS HELD AT THE BEGINNING AND END OF THE PROGRAM. THE SAMPLE CONSISTED OF EIGHT HEAD START CLASSES. AMONG THE MAJOR RESULTS OF THE STUDY WAS THE SIGNIFICANTLY SUPERIOR PERFORMANCE OF UHPLC CHILDREN COMPARED TO CHILDREN IN THE ENRICHMENT CLASSES ON MANY OF THE TESTS, INCLUDING THE STANFORD-BINET, THE PRESCHOOL INVENTORY, AND SUBTESTS OF THE ILLINOIS TEST OF PSYCHOLINGUISTIC ABILITIES. THE CLASSROOM ATMOSPHERE, AS MEASURED BY THE POST OBSERVATION TEACHER RATING SCALES, WAS SIGNIFICANTLY BETTER IN UHPLC CLASSES. MOTHERS ACTIVE IN PARENT PROGRAMS SHOWED IMPROVED ATTITUDES TOWARDS CHILDREN'S EDUCATION AND INCREASED TOLERANCE TOWARDS CHILDREN'S CHOSEN COMPANIONS. (MH)

ED042512 PS003453
APPLICATION OF GROUP DYNAMICS PROCEDURES TO PROMOTE COMMUNICATION AMONG PARENTS AND TEACHERS. STERN, CAROLYN; AND OTHERS, JAN 70 34P.
EDRS PRICE MF-$0.65 HC-$3.29

THIS HEAD START STUDY SOUGHT TO DETERMINE WHETHER OR NOT INCREASED COMMUNICATION AMONG THE FOUR GROUPS OF ADULTS MOST INFLUENTIAL IN THE CHILD'S TRANSITION FROM PRESCHOOL TO KINDERGARTEN WOULD LEAD TO A GREATER SIMILARITY OF GOALS AND ATTITUDES AMONG THESE GROUPS, AND THUS HELP THE CHILD TO BRIDGE THE GAP BETWEEN PRESCHOOL AND SCHOOL. THE FOUR GROUPS OF ADULTS ARE THE PARENTS, KINDERGARTEN TEACHERS, HEAD START TEACHERS, AND DAY CARE TEACHERS. EIGHT MONTHLY MEETINGS WERE SCHEDULED FOR THESE GROUPS WITH PARENTS AND TEACHERS MEETING SEPARATELY. IT WAS HOPED THAT THROUGH THESE MEETINGS PARENTS AND TEACHERS WOULD DEMONSTRATE A GREATER SIMILARITY IN GOALS AND ATTITUDES. A CONTROL GROUP HAD NO SUCH MEETINGS. THE GROUPS WERE PRE- AND POSTTESTED ON THE ADRES (AN ALIENATION QUESTIONNAIRE, ATTITUDE DIFFERENCES RELATED TO ECONOMIC STATUS) AND THE TEACH SCALE (AN ASSESSMENT OF ACHIEVEMENT GOALS FOR 5-YEAR-OLD PUPILS, TEACHER EXPECTATIONS OF ACHIEVEMENT FOR CHILDREN IN HEAD START). PRETEST DIFFERENCES BETWEEN GROUPS WERE HIGHLY SIGNIFICANT, SHOWING A GAP BETWEEN THE EDUCATIONAL VALUES OF THE GROUPS. PRE-POST ANALYSIS OF TEACH REVEALED A TREND TOWARD SIMILARITY IN GOALS AMONG MEMBERS OF THE EXPERIMENTAL GROUP, ALTHOUGH THE SMALL SAMPLE AND POOR PARENT ATTENDANCE RENDER THE RESULTS STATISTICALLY UNDEPENDABLE. (MH)

ED042513 PS003454
THE "TELL-AND-FIND PICTURE GAME" FOR YOUNG CHILDREN. BLUMENFELD, PHYLLIS; KEISLAR, EVAN R., MAR 70 22P.
EDRS PRICE MF-$0.65 HC-$3.29

THE "TELL-AND-FIND PICTURE GAME" IS DESIGNED TO TEACH BOTH SPEAKING AND LISTENING COMPREHENSION SKILLS TO PRESCHOOL CHILDREN. THE GAME IS ARRANGED TO PROVIDE A COOPERATIVE EXPERIENCE FOR TWO PLAYERS WHO TAKE TURNS IN THE ROLE OF A SPEAKER AND OF A LISTENER. IN ORDER TO TEST THE EFFECTIVENESS OF THE GAME IN ENCOURAGING COGNITIVE GAINS, A PILOT STUDY WAS RUN IN WHICH THE GAME WAS ADAPTED TO PROVIDE SPECIFIC INSTRUCTION ON A NUMBER OF SPATIAL CONCEPTS. THIRTY 4-YEAR-OLD BLACK HEAD START CHILDREN WERE PRETESTED ON THESE SPATIAL CONCEPTS, AND THE 10 CHILDREN WHO MADE THE MOST ERRORS WERE SELECTED FOR THE PILOT STUDY. THESE CHILDREN PLAYED THE GAME FOR 20 MINUTES ON EACH OF SIX DAYS. ON THE SEVENTH DAY, POSTTESTS, WHICH WERE IDENTICAL WITH THE PRETESTS, WERE ADMINISTERED. THE CHILDREN WERE ALSO TESTED FOR AFFECTIVE RESPONSE TO THE GAME. THE OUTCOME OF THESE TESTS INDICATED THAT THE CHILDREN BOTH ENJOYED THE GAME AND IMPROVED THEIR LANGUAGE SKILLS OF LISTENING COMPREHENSION AND VERBAL EXPRESSION AS A RESULT OF IT. THE EMPHASIS ON COOPERATION SEEMED TO BE A GOOD FEATURE. THE STUDY ALSO SUGGESTED CERTAIN IMPROVEMENTS IN THE GAME, SOME OF WHICH WOULD DECREASE THE DEPENDENCE ON THE EXPERIMENTER AND MAKE THE PLAYERS MORE AUTONOMOUS. (MH)

ED042514 PS003455
THE EFFECT OF FOUR COMMUNICATION PATTERNS AND SEX ON LENGTH OF VERBALIZATION IN SPEECH OF FOUR YEAR OLD CHILDREN. FINAL REPORT. SMITH, DENNIS R., MAR 70 25P.
EDRS PRICE MF-$0.65 HC-$3.29

THE ASSUMPTION THAT THE DYADIC COMMUNICATION PATTERN (ONE TEACHER-ONE STUDENT) IS THE MOST EFFECTIVE PATTERN FOR ENCOURAGING LANGUAGE AND SPEECH DEVELOPMENT AMONG ELEMENTARY AND PRESCHOOL CHILDREN IS TESTED IN THIS STUDY. FIFTY-SIX 4-YEAR-OLD CHILDREN FROM THE TASK FORCE HEAD START PROGRAM OF BUFFALO, NEW YORK, WERE OBSERVED IN FOUR DIFFERENT COMMUNICATION PATTERNS AND THE MEAN LENGTH OF THEIR VERBALIZATIONS WAS RECORDED. ALSO NOTED WAS THE INTERACTION OF SEX WITH EACH OF THE CONDITIONS. THE PATTERNS USED WERE THE DYAD, THE TRIAD (1 EXPERIMENTER AND 2 CHILDREN), THE SMALL GROUP (1 EXPERIMENTER AND 3 CHILDREN), AND THE ROLE-PLAYING TRIAD (SAME AS TRIAD, BUT WITH CHILDREN ENCOURAGED TO ACT OUT ROLES). ANALYSIS OF THE DATA REVEALED NO SIGNIFICANT INTER-PATTERN DIFFERENCES IN MEAN VERBALIZATION LENGTH, EXCEPT THAT THE SMALL GROUP ELICITED A STATISTICALLY GREATER AMOUNT OF SPEECH THAN DID THE DYAD (BOTH WITH REPETITIONS LEFT IN AND WITH REPETITIONS DELETED). WITH AND WITHOUT REPETITIONS, GIRLS PRODUCED SIGNIFICANTLY MORE SPEECH THAN BOYS. WHILE THE ACTUAL DIFFERENCE BETWEEN THE SPEECH FROM THE SMALL GROUP AND FROM THE DYAD IS SMALL (LESS THAN ONE WORD PER RESPONSE), FINDINGS ARE IMPORTANT BECAUSE THEY DEMONSTRATE THAT THE DYADIC SITUATION MAY NOT BE JUSTIFIED IN TERMS OF SPEECH DEVELOPMENT, PARTICULARLY SINCE IT IS LESS ECONOMICAL OF THE TEACHER'S TIME. (MH)

ED042515 PS003456
HAWAII HEAD START EVALUATION FOLLOW-UP--1968-69. FINA L REPORT. HERMAN, HANNAH; ADKINS, DOROTHY C., JAN 70 47P.
EDRS PRICE MF-$0.65 HC-$3.29

THIS STUDY COMPARED THE PERFORMANCE OF KINDERGARTEN CHILDREN WHO HAD PARTICIPATED IN A FULL-YEAR HEAD START PROGRAM (FYHS) WITH THAT OF CHILDREN WHO HAD ATTENDED SUMMER HEAD START (SHS). FYHS SUBJECTS AT EACH OF TWO ELEMENTARY SCHOOLS WERE SELECTED AT RANDOM FROM ELIGIBLE APPLICANTS. SHS COMPARISON GROUPS WERE MADE UP PRIMARILY OF CHILDREN FROM THE SAME INITIAL LISTS OF SUBJECTS. ON A GROUP OF MEASURES ADMINISTERED ABOUT 8 MONTHS AFTER COMPLETION OF THE HEAD START PROGRAMS, NO SIGNIFICANT DIFFERENCES WERE SHOWN BETWEEN FHYS AND SHS CHILDREN, OR BETWEEN THE TWO ELEMENTARY SCHOOL GROUPS. SHS CHILDREN, HOWEVER, EARNED SIGNIFICANTLY HIGHER IQ SCORES AT THE END OF KINDERGARTEN THAN THEY HAD EARLY IN HEAD START, AND FYHS CHILDREN SHOWED A SIGNIFICANT PROGRESSIVE INCREASE IN IQ OVER A 2-YEAR PERIOD COVERING HEAD START AND KINDERGARTEN. THIS CONTINUOUS INCREASE IN IQ IS NOTEWORTHY, SINCE PREVIOUS STUDIES HAVE FOUND A LEVELING-OFF EFFECT FOLLOWING AN INITIAL GAIN IN HEAD START. IT IS RECOMMENDED THAT FOLLOW-UP STUDIES CONCENTRATE ON THE LONG-RANGE EFFECTS OF FYHS PROGRAMS WITH DEFINED CURRICULA FOCUSED ON COGNITIVE DEVELOPMENT. (AUTHOR/NH)

ED042516 PS003461
A FOLLOW-UP EVALUATION OF THE EFFECTS OF A UNIQUE SEQUENTIAL LEARNING PROGRAM, A TRADITIONAL PRESCHOOL PROGRAM AND A NO TREATMENT PROGRAM ON CULTURALLY DEPRIVED CHILDREN. FINAL REPORT. VAN DE RIET, VERNON; VAN DE RIET, HANI, DEC 69 35P.
EDRS PRICE MF-$0.65 HC-$3.29

THIS IS A FOLLOWUP STUDY OF SECOND AND THIRD GRADE CHILDREN WHO EXPERIENCED DIFFERENTIAL TREATMENT DURING THEIR KINDERGARTEN YEAR. A TOTAL OF 72 DISADVANTAGED BLACK CHILDREN COMPRISED THE SAMPLE WHICH WAS DIVIDED INTO THREE GROUPS. GROUP A RECEIVED A SPECIAL SEQUENTIAL LEARNING TO LEARN PROGRAM. GROUP B PARTICIPATED IN A TRADITIONAL KINDERGARTEN AND GROUP C REMAINED AT HOME. AT THE END OF THE YEAR, ALL SUBJECTS ENROLLED IN A REGULAR PUBLIC SCHOOL FIRST GRADE. DEVELOPMENTAL MEASURES OF THE CHILDREN TAKEN PERIODICALLY DURING THE FOUR-YEAR STUDY INCLUDED THE STANFORD ACHIEVEMENT TEST, SUBTESTS OF THE WECHSLER INTELLIGENCE SCALE FOR CHILDREN AND THE ILLINOIS TEST OF PSYCHOLINGUISTIC ABILITIES. EARLY RESULTS REVEALED THAT THE LEARNING TO LEARN PROGRAM ACCELERATED THE CHILDREN'S DEVELOPMENT, THAT THE REGULAR KINDERGARTEN GROUP MAINTAINED THEIR PREVIOUS DEVELOPMENTAL LEVEL, AND THAT THE NO-PROGRAM TREATMENT GROUP FELL BEHIND IN OVERALL DEVELOPMENT DURING THE KINDERGARTEN YEAR. HOWEVER, LATER RESULTS INDICATED THAT WHILE THE THREE GROUPS MAINTAINED THEIR ORDER OF MEAN DEVELOPMENTAL LEVEL, THE DIFFERENCES AMONG THEM DECREASED THROUGH THE YEARS, UNTIL, BY THE END OF THE THIRD GRADE, DIFFERENCES WERE NO LONGER STATISTICALLY SIGNIFICANT. (MH)

ED042517 PS003466
A SEQUENTIAL APPROACH TO EARLY CHILDHOOD AND ELEMENTARY EDUCATION, PHASE I. GRANT REPORT. VAN DE RIET, VERNON; VAN DE RIET, HANI, DEC 69 57P.
EDRS PRICE MF-$0.65 HC-$3.29

THE PROJECT ON WHICH THIS DOCUMENT REPORTS INTENDS TO (1) IMPLEMENT A THREE-YEAR AND A FOUR-YEAR SEQUENTIAL CURRICULUM BASED UPON DEVELOPMENTAL CONCEPTS, (2) CHANGE THE TRADITIONAL ROLES OF THE TEACHER AND THE STUDENT, (3) ACCOMMODATE INDIVIDUAL DIFFERENCES IN CHILDREN'S LEVELS AND LEARNING RATES, (4) INVOLVE PARENTS IN THE EDUCATION AND COGNITIVE DEVELOPMENT OF THEIR CHILDREN, (5) USE TEACHER ASSISTANTS TO FREE TEACHERS FOR SMALL GROUP ACTIVITY, AND (6) CARRY OUT AN EXTENSIVE EVALUATION OF THE CHILDREN IN THIS PROGRAM AND COMPARE THEM WITH CONTROL GROUPS. THE SEQUENTIAL CURRICULUM IS THE LEARNING TO LEARN PROGRAM AND THE SUBJECTS ARE 44 4-YEAR-OLDS AND 42 5-YEAR-OLDS . THE EXPERIMENTAL GROUPS WERE EXPOSED TO THE LEARNING TO LEARN PROGRAM, WHILE THE CONTROL GROUPS ENTERED A TRADITIONAL PRESCHOOL OR KINDERGARTEN. AT THE END OF THE FIRST YEAR OF THE PROJECT, EXTENSIVE DEVELOPMENTAL EVALUATION INDICATES LARGER GAINS FOR THE EXPERIMENTAL GROUPS, ESPECIALLY AMONG THE 4-YEAR-OLDS. LONG RANGE PLANS CALL FOR A CONTINUATION OF THE EXPERIMENTAL AND CONTROL CONDITIONS, ACCOMPANIED BY FURTHER TESTING, THROUGH THE SECOND GRADE. (MH)

ED042518 PS003677
THE NEW NURSERY SCHOOL RESEARCH PROJECT , 30 SEP 69 152P.
EDRS PRICE MF-$0.65 HC-$6.58

THIS FINAL REPORT DESCRIBES THE FOURTH YEAR OF THE NEW NURSERY SCHOOL PROGRAM (NNS) SET UP FOR ENVIRONMENTALLY DEPRIVED, SPANISH-SURNAMED 3- AND 4-YEAR-OLD CHILDREN. THE SCHOOL WAS ORGANIZED AS AN AUTOTELIC ENVIRONMENT WHICH THE CHILDREN (15 IN EACH OF TWO SESSIONS) ATTENDED FOR 3 HOURS A DAY. UPON ENTERING, CHILDREN WERE PRETESTED ON THE WECHSLER PRESCHOOL AND PRIMARY SCALE OF INTELLIGENCE (WPPSI) AND THE NNS DEVELOPED CATEGORIES ("C") TEST. RESULTS OF THESE TESTS AND OTHERS WERE LATER COMPARED AND CORRELATED WITH THOSE OF GROUP I, A SIMILAR SAMPLE OF SUBJECTS, AND GROUP II, ADVANTAGED PRESCHOOLERS. COMPARATIVE ANALYSIS REVEALED FEW SIGNIFICANT DIFFERENCES BUT INDICATED PROGRESSIVELY LESS MEAN DIFFERENCE BETWEEN THE PERFORMANCE OF NNS CHILDREN AND THE ADVANTAGED GROUP. THE CORRELATIONAL ANALYSIS REVEALED NO SIGNIFICANT RELATIONSHIPS, BUT IT HIGHLIGHTED THE NEED FOR OTHER APPROACHES TO MEASURE SELF-IMAGE. LONGITUDINALLY, PUBLIC SCHOOL TEACHERS REPORTED NO DIFFERENCE BETWEEN PRIOR NNS GRADUATES AND OTHER DEPRIVED CHILDREN IN TERMS OF CLASS STANDING. IMPROVED DAILY ATTENDANCE, INCREASED CONFIDENCE IN INDIVIDUAL ABILITY, AND POSITIVE ATTITUDE TOWARD SCHOOLWORK ARE LISTED AS QUALITATIVE GAINS FOR GRADUATES OF THE PROGRAM. ANOTHER REPORT ON THE NNS PROGRAM IS AVAILABLE AS ED 036 320. (WY)

ED043368 PS001935
A PILOT EXPERIMENT IN EARLY CHILDHOOD POLITICAL LEARNING. REPORT FROM THE PROJECT ON CONCEPTS IN POLITICAL SCIENCE. DENNIS, JACK; AND OTHERS, SEP 68 33P.
EDRS PRICE MF-$0.65 HC-$3.29

TO DETERMINE THE EFFECT OF EARLY POLITICAL INSTRUCTION, A SERIES OF BASIC POLITICAL CONCEPTS WERE INTRODUCED TO PRIMARY GRADE CHILDREN. USING ONE CLASS OF SECOND AND ONE CLASS OF FOURTH GRADERS AS CONTROL GROUPS AND ONE CLASS OF SECOND AND ANOTHER CLASS OF FOURTH GRADERS AS EXPERIMENTAL GROUPS, A UNIT OF CIVIC INSTRUCTION WAS TAUGHT DURING THE 2-WEEK PERIOD BEFORE A NATIONAL ELECTION. THE EXPERIMENTAL GROUPS RECEIVED FORMAL INSTRUCTION IN POLITICAL CONCEPTS OVER A 3-WEEK PERIOD AND ENGAGED IN CONCEPT-RELATED ROLE PLAYING ACTIVITIES. ALL CHILDREN WERE GIVEN STRUCTURED INTERVIEWS BEFORE AND AFTER THE PERIOD OF INSTRUCTION; THESE RESULTS WERE CODED. PRE- AND POST-TESTS WERE THE SCIENCE RESEARCH ASSOCIATES ACHIEVEMENT AND PRIMARY ABILITIES TESTS. INTERVIEW RESULTS SHOWED THAT ALL GROUPS INCREASED IN THE AVERAGE LEVEL OF POLITICAL CONCEPT-ATTAINMENT DURING THE ELECTION PERIOD, BUT THE EXPERIMENTAL GROUPS INCREASED MORE RAPIDLY EVEN WHEN INITIAL LEVELS OF POLITICAL CONCEPT ATTAINMENT AND GENERAL SCHOOL ACHIEVEMENT WERE HELD CONSTANT. IT IS SUGGESTED THAT THE YOUNG CHILD IS CAPABLE OF UNDERSTANDING MORE ABOUT THE POLITICAL REALM THAN IS GENERALLY ASSUMED AND THAT SCHOOL POLITICAL INSTRUCTION COULD PROFITABLY BEGIN EARLIER THAN IT NORMALLY DOES. APPENDIXES DESCRIBE CONCEPTS, INTERVIEWS, AND CHANGES IN POLITICAL CONCEPTUALIZATION. (AUTHOR/DR)

ED043369 PS003132
ENRICHMENT APPROACH VERSUS DIRECT INSTRUCTIONAL APPROACH AND THEIR EFFECTS ON DIFFERENTIAL PRESCHOOL EXPERIENCES. HALASA, OFELIA, MAR 70 11P.
EDRS PRICE MF-$0.65 HC-$3.29

THIS STUDY REPRESENTS A SEGMENT OF AN EVALUATION OF THE EFFECTS OF TWO DIAMETRICALLY-OPPOSED INSTRUCTIONAL STRATEGIES ON INNER-CITY KINDERGARTEN CHILDREN WHO HAD VARYING PRESCHOOL EXPERIENCES. THE CHILD- AND PARENT-ORIENTED "ENRICHMENT" APPROACH WAS USED IN ONE SCHOOL WHILE THE TEACHER- AND GOAL-ORIENTED "DIRECT INSTRUCTIONAL" APPROACH WAS PRACTICED IN A SEPARATE BUT COMPARABLE SCHOOL. CHILDREN RANDOMLY SELECTED FROM BOTH PROGRAMS WERE TESTED ON A VARIETY OF MEASURES IN OCTOBER AND MAY. DATA WERE COLLECTED ON SUCH INDEPENDENT VARIABLES AS SCHOOL POVERTY INDEX (PERCENT OF FAMILIES ON WELFARE), CHRONOLOGICAL AGE, NUMBER OF SIBLINGS, ORDINAL RANK OF CHILD IN FAMILY, AND SCHOOL YEAR ATTENDANCE. TWO STATISTICAL MEASURES WERE USED: STEPDOWN REGRESSION ANALYSIS AND ANALYSIS OF COVARIANCE. RESULTS INDICATED (1) DIRECT INSTRUCTIONAL STRATEGY WAS MORE EFFECTIVE THAN ENRICHMENT IN FOSTERING BASIC ACADEMIC SKILLS, (2) EFFECT OF PRESCHOOL EXPERIENCE ONE YEAR LATER WAS LIMITED TO READING SCORES ONLY, AND (3) PRETEST SCORES WERE THE BEST PREDICTORS OF CHILDREN'S PERFORMANCE ON POSTTESTS OF GENERAL MENTAL FUNCTIONING AND BASIC SKILLS. (AUTHOR/WY)

ED043370 PS003215
EARLY CHILDHOOD EDUCATION LEARNING SYSTEM FOR THREE-AND FOUR-YEAR-OLD MIGRANT CHILDREN, MCALLEN, TEXAS. EVALUATION REPORT, 1968-1969. , 31 JUL 69 101P.
EDRS PRICE MF-$0.65 HC-$6.58

THIS DOCUMENT REPORTS ON A PROGRAM SEEN AS AN INTEGRAL PART OF A TOTAL EDUCATIONAL DEVELOPMENT PLAN FOR MIGRANT CHILDREN. THE EARLY CHILDHOOD EDUCATION LEARNING SYSTEM IS AN INSTRUCTIONAL PROGRAM WHICH INCLUDES STAFF DEVELOPMENT AND PARENT-SCHOOL-COMMUNITY INVOLVEMENT. FOCUS IS ON THE SPECIAL LEARNING PROBLEMS OF MEXICAN-AMERICAN CHILDREN AND THE DEVELOPMENT OF BILINGUAL COMPETENCE. A TOTAL OF 98 3- AND 4-YEAR-OLD MIGRANT CHILDREN PARTICIPATED DURING 1968-1969. PROGRAM EVALUATION IS VIEWED AS A CONTINUING PROCESS. PART OF THIS EVALUATION WAS A PRE- AND POST-TESTING ON THE PRESCHOOL ATTAINMENT RECORD (PAR) OF 2 GROUPS OF CHILDREN, A MIGRANT GROUP FROM THE EARLY CHILDHOOD EDUCATION SYSTEM AND A NON-MIGRANT GROUP FROM REGULAR DAY CARE CENTERS. ON THE PRETEST, THE NON-MIGRANT CHILDREN SCORED HIGHER. HOWEVER, THE POSTTEST SHOWED THAT THE CHILDREN IN THE EXPERIMENTAL PROGRAM MADE GREATER DEVELOPMENTAL GAINS THAN THE OTHER CHILDREN. CHILDREN WHOSE TEACHERS HAD HIGH SCORES ON THE MINNESOTA TEACHER ATTITUDE INVENTORY PERFORMED BETTER ON THE PAR THAN STUDENTS WHOSE TEACHERS HAD LOW SCORES. PARENTS WHO PARTICIPATED IN THE PARENT ACTIVITIES SCORED HIGHER ON AN EDUCATIONAL ATTITUDE SCALE THAN NON-PARTICIPATING PARENTS. (MH)

ED043371 PS003288
SOCIAL CLASS AND PARENTS' ASPIRATIONS FOR THEIR CHILDREN. RESEARCH REPORT NO. 3 (REVISED). RODMAN, HYMAN; VOYDANOFF, PATRICIA, NOV 69 31P.
EDRS PRICE MF-$0.65 HC-$3.29

IN CONTRAST TO PREVIOUS RESEARCH, THIS STUDY ASSUMES A RANGE OF ASPIRATIONS FOR INDIVIDUALS, RATHER THAN A SINGLE LEVEL. THE BASIC HYPOTHESIS IS THAT SOCIAL CLASS IS RELATED TO THE WIDTH OF THE RANGE; THAT IS, THE LOWER THE SOCIAL CLASS LEVEL THE WIDER THE RANGE OF ASPIRATION. INTERVIEWS WERE CONDUCTED WITH PARENTS OF 255 NEGRO KINDERGARTEN AND PRE-SCHOOL CHILDREN, REPRESENTING BOTH LOWER CLASS AND MIDDLE CLASS BACKGROUNDS. THE CRITERION FOR SELECTION AS LOWER CLASS WAS THAT NEITHER PARENT HAD GONE BEYOND HIGH SCHOOL IN HIS EDUCATION; FOR MIDDLE CLASS, THAT BOTH PARENTS HAD FINISHED HIGH SCHOOL AND AT LEAST ONE PARENT HAD GONE BEYOND HIGH SCHOOL. THE HYPOTHESIS WAS SUPPORTED FOR BOTH EDUCATIONAL AND OCCUPATIONAL ASPIRATIONS, USING A VARIETY OF OPERATIONAL MEASURES. TO THE EXTENT THAT LOWER CLASS PARENTS HAVE A WIDER RANGE OF ASPIRATIONS, WITH A PEAK AS HIGH AS THE MIDDLE CLASS PEAK, THERE IS A BUILT-IN POTENTIAL FOR MOBILITY. TO ENCOURAGE MOBILITY IT IS IMPORTANT TO PROVIDE OPPORTUNITIES AND TO ESTABLISH A CONVICTION OF THEIR ATTAINABILITY. THIS DOCUMENT IS AN EXPANDED VERSION OF ED 030 482. (AUTHOR/NH)

ED043372 PS003307
A LONGITUDINAL STUDY OF PIAGET'S DEVELOPMENTAL STAGES AND OF THE CONCEPT OF REGRESSION. DUDEK, S. Z.; DYER, G. B., [69] 12P.
EDRS PRICE MF-$0.65 HC-$3.29

ANALYSIS OF 65 CHILDREN OVER A 4-YEAR PERIOD ON TESTS OF OPERATIONAL AND CAUSAL THINKING OFFERS SUPPORT FOR PIAGET'S NOTION OF STAGE PROGRESSION. IN KINDERGARTEN AND GRADE ONE, THE MAJORITY OF CHILDREN IN THIS LONGITUDINAL STUDY WERE BETWEEN PREOPERATIONAL AND THE ACHIEVEMENT STAGE OF OPERATIONAL THOUGHT. BY GRADE TWO, THE MAJORITY HAD ATTAINED THE TERMINAL STAGE ON SEVEN OF NINE TESTS GIVEN. BY GRADE THREE, THE CHILDREN ACHIEVED TERMINAL STAGES ON ALL TESTS. OVER A 3-YEAR PERIOD ONLY EIGHT TRUE REGRESSIONS OCCURRED. THIS NUMBER CONSTITUTED LESS THAN ONE PERCENT OF THE TOTAL POSSIBLE REGRESSIONS. BOTH THE PIAGET TEST SCORES AND THE WECHSLER INTELLIGENCE SCALE FOR CHILDREN MEASURES WERE SLIGHTLY HIGHER FOR THE REGRESSING CHILDREN. IN THIS STUDY, "REGRESSING CHILDREN" WERE NOT LESS INTELLIGENT THAN NONREGRESSING CHILDREN. HOWEVER, THE NUMBERS WERE TOO SMALL TO WARRANT ANY CONCLUSIONS. (WY)

ED043373 PS003310
INTELLECTUAL DEVELOPMENT AND THE ABILITY TO PROCESS VISUAL AND VERBAL INFORMATION. RANDHAWA, B. (RANDY), 2 MAR 70 22P.
EDRS PRICE MF-$0.65 HC-$3.29

FORTY RANDOMLY SELECTED SCHOOL CHILDREN, IN FOUR TREATMENT GROUPS OF TEN EACH (EACH COMPRISED OF CHILDREN FROM THE 5, 8, AND 12 YEAR AGE LEVELS) PARTICIPATED IN A STUDY TO DETERMINE THE EXTENT TO WHICH THE CAPACITY FOR INFORMATION PROCESSED BY A CHILD INCREASES IN AMOUNT WITH DEVELOPMENT. APPREHENSION SPAN (PERCEPTION AND TRANSFORMATION OF AURAL OR VISUAL INPUTS LEADING UP TO RECONSTRUCTION OR VERBAL DESCRIPTION OUTPUT) WAS MEASURED. A SPECIALLY DESIGNED FORM BOARD VARYING ON THREE BINARY DIMENSIONS AND THIRTY-TWO PLASTIC GEOMETRIC SHAPES VARYING ON FIVE BINARY DIMENSIONS WAS THE BASIC TEST MATERIAL TO WHICH A SUBJECT RESPONDED BY EITHER DESCRIBING OR RECONSTRUCTING A GIVEN STIMULUS DESIGN. SCORES WERE CALCULATED ON THE BASIS OF MATCH BETWEEN THE REFERENCE SUBSET OF SHAPES AND THE FORM BOARD PERFORMANCE. A 3 X 2 X 2 COMPLETE FACTORIAL DESIGN WAS USED. RESULTS INDICATE THAT THERE IS A DIFFERENTIAL DECREASE IN DIFFERENCES IN THE APPREHENSION SPAN OF CHILDREN WITH DEVELOPMENT. CORRELATIONS BETWEEN THE TOTAL OF EIGHT APPREHENSION SPAN TASKS AND THE PRIMARY MENTAL ABILITIES TEST SUPPORT THE CONCLUSION THAT INFORMATION IS PROCESSED THROUGH THE NON-VERBAL MODE AND BOTTLENECKS IN A CHILD'S PROCESSING OF INFORMATION ARE MAINLY THOSE INVOLVING TRANSLATION INTO AND OUT OF ANOTHER MEDIUM SUCH AS LANGUAGE. (WY)

ED043374 PS003336
REALISTIC PLANNING FOR THE DAY CARE CONSUMER. EMLEN, ARTHUR C., 18 MAR 70 29P.
EDRS PRICE MF-$0.65 HC-$3.29

THIS PAPER QUESTIONS PUBLIC ATTITUDES OF DISPARAGEMENT TOWARD CHILD CARE THAT IS PRIVATELY ARRANGED IN NEIGHBORHOOD HOMES, AND CITES RESEARCH TO SHOW THAT THE WIDESPREAD NON-USE OF ORGANIZED FACILITIES IS BASED ON REALISTIC ALTERNATIVE PATTERNS OF DAY CARE BEHAVIOR. SOME DETERMINANTS OF DAY CARE USE ARE DISCUSSED, AND AN UNDERSTANDING OF UTILIZATION BEHAVIOR IS SEEN AS THE KEY TO DEVELOPING QUALITY DAY CARE OF DIFFERENT KINDS. (AUTHOR)

ED043375 PS003345
BEHAVIORAL DATA FROM THE TULANE NUTRITION STUDY. SULZER, JEFFERSON L., 29 DEC 70 23P.
EDRS PRICE MF-$0.65 HC-$3.29

DOES NUTRITIONAL DEFICIENCY RETARD PSYCHOLOGICAL DEVELOPMENT? THE TULANE NUTRITION STUDY REPORTS THE FIRST SEGMENT OF ITS RESEARCH BASED ON EXTENSIVE ANALYSIS OF PSYCHOLOGICAL AND NUTRITIONAL DATA GATHERED PREDOMINATELY ON CHILDREN WHO ATTENDED FIVE, 6-WEEK HEAD START PROGRAMS. SCORES ON A BATTERY OF EIGHT PSYCHOLOGICAL TESTS AND TWO HEMATOLOGICAL MEASURES (HEMATOCRITS AND HEMOGLOBIN) PROVIDED BASELINE INDICES OF PSYCHOLOGICAL AND NUTRITIONAL STATUS. INITIAL STATISTICAL TESTS FAILED TO SHOW DIFFERENCES THAT COULD BE RELIABLY INTERPRETED AS DEVELOPMENTAL RETARDATION. FURTHER ANALYSIS INVOLVED A PILOT STUDY IN WHICH DIETARY INTERVENTION PRODUCED AN IMPROVEMENT IN BLOOD LEVELS FOR THE MOST DEFICIENT SUBGROUP. NO GENERALIZATIONS CAN BE MADE UNTIL SUBSEQUENT ANALYSIS (1) RESOLVES ISSUES RAISED BY AGE, (2) CONTROLS FOR INITIAL LACK OF EQUIVALENCE IN INTERVENTION GROUPS, AND (3) EXAMINES INDIVIDUAL DIFFERENCES IN NUTRITION AND BEHAVIOR PROFILES. FUTURE RESEARCH WILL FOCUS ON INDIVIDUAL CROSS-SECTIONAL APPROACHES AND ON FOLLOW-UP STUDIES INVOLVING SELECTED CHILDREN. (WY)

ED043376 PS003394
APPROACHES TO THE VALIDATION OF LEARNING HIERARCHIES. RESNICK, LAUREN B.; WANG, MARGARET C., JUN 69 42P.
EDRS PRICE MF-$0.65 HC-$3.29

THIS PAPER DESCRIBES A PROGRAM OF RESEARCH IN THE APPLICATION OF SCALOGRAM ANALYSIS TO THE VALIDATION OF LEARNING HIERARCHIES, TOGETHER WITH THE DEVELOPMENT OF AN ALTERNATIVE METHOD FOR ASSESSING HIERARCHICAL RELATIONSHIPS AMONG TESTS OF INSTRUCTIONAL OBJECTIVES. THE RELATIONSHIP BETWEEN SCALABILITY OF TESTS AND POSITIVE TRANSFER BETWEEN OBJECTIVES IN THE COURSE OF LEARNING IS DISCUSSED AND EXPERIMENTAL TRANSFER STUDIES TESTING HIERARCHICAL HYPOTHESES ARE DESCRIBED. RELATED RESEARCH BY DEVELOPMENTAL AND LEARNING PSYCHOLOGISTS AND BY TEST DESIGNERS IS DISCUSSED ALONG WITH THE AUTHORS' OWN RESEARCH. (AUTHOR)

ED043377 PS003401
ETHNIC AND SOCIOECONOMIC INFLUENCES ON THE HOME LANGUAGE EXPERIENCES OF CHILDREN. GORDON, SUSAN B., MAR 70 35P.
EDRS PRICE MF-$0.65 HC-$3.29

THE MAJOR HYPOTHESIS OF THIS STUDY IS THAT A SIGNIFICANT RELATIONSHIP EXISTS BETWEEN ENGLISH LANGUAGE ABILITY (AS MEASURED BY THE ILLINOIS TEST OF PSYCHOLINGUISTIC ABILITIES (ITPA) FULL-SCALE SCORE) AND LANGUAGE-MODELING BY THE MOTHER (AS MEASURED BY THE MOTHER-CHILD INTERACTION SCORE ON THE LANGUAGE MODEL MATRIX), AND BETWEEN ENGLISH LANGUAGE ABILITY AND TOTAL HOME LANGUAGE-MODELING (AS MEASURED BY THE TOTAL INTERACTION SCORE ON THE LANGUAGE MODEL MATRIX). SUB-HYPOTHESES STATE THAT ENGLISH LANGUAGE ABILITY, LANGUAGE-MODELING BY THE MOTHER, AND TOTAL HOME LANGUAGE-MODELING SIGNIFICANTLY DIFFER ACCORDING TO (1) ETHNICITY, (2) SOCIOECONOMIC STATUS (SES), AND (3) LANGUAGE MODEL TYPE. THE SAMPLE CONSISTED OF FIRST-GRADE CHILDREN: 50 NAVAJO INDIAN, 55 PUEBLO INDIAN, AND 50 RURAL SPANISH-AMERICAN. A LANGUAGE MODEL MATRIX WAS DESIGNED TO PROVIDE AN OPERATIONAL FRAMEWORK. TEST RESULTS SUPPORT THE MAJOR AND SUB-HYPOTHESES. AS ACCULTURATION AND SES INCREASE, SO DOES THE QUANTITY OF VERBAL INTERACTION IN THE HOME. PROGRAMS TO ALLEVIATE POVERTY, AND TO TEACH MOTHERS HOW TO TEACH THEIR CHILDREN, ARE OF VITAL IMPORTANCE IN THE ELIMINATION OF LINGUISTIC DISADVANTAGEMENT. (AUTHOR/NH)

ED043378 PS003406
MOTHERS' TRAINING PROGRAM: EDUCATIONAL INTERVENTION BY THE MOTHERS OF DISADVANTAGED INFANTS. BADGER, EARLADEEN, AUG 68 93P.
EDRS PRICE MF-$0.65 HC-$3.29

TWENTY MOTHERS OF CULTURALLY DISADVANTAGED CHILDREN TOOK PART IN A PROGRAM OF SELF-HELP WHICH WAS BOTH CHILD- AND MOTHER-CENTERED. TWO GROUPS OF TEN MOTHERS EACH MET WEEKLY WITH TWO STAFF MEMBERS OVER AN 8-MONTH PERIOD AND WERE TRAINED TO TUTOR THEIR INFANTS (1 TO 2-YEARS-OLD) IN THEIR HOMES. FIFTEEN OF THE INITIAL 20 MOTHERS REMAINED IN THE PROGRAM A SECOND YEAR. THE PROGRAM INCLUDED: (1) TRAINING MOTHERS TO USE EDUCATIONAL TOYS AND MATERIALS TO STIMULATE THEIR CHILDREN'S LEARNING IN SENSORY-MOTOR, CONCEPT, AND LANGUAGE DEVELOPMENT; (2) DISCUSSION OF CHILD-REARING PROBLEMS; (3) FOSTERING ATTITUDE CHANGE THROUGH SHARING IDEAS; AND (4) HELPING THE MOTHERS TO DEVELOP SELF-CONFIDENCE AND RESPONSIBILITY. REGULAR HOME VISITS WERE MADE BY STAFF MEMBERS TO OBSERVE MOTHERS WORKING WITH THEIR BABIES AND TO MAKE HELPFUL SUGGESTIONS. THE IMPLEMENTATION SECTION OF THIS REPORT DESCRIBES RECRUITMENT OF MOTHERS AND SELECTION OF EDUCATIONAL MATERIALS. ALSO GIVEN IS AN ACCOUNT OF THE WEEKLY MEETINGS WHICH EMPHASIZED VERBAL INTERACTION AND INVOLVEMENT OF THE GROUP AND THEIR LEADER. AT THE END OF THE TRAINING PERIOD EACH MOTHER COMPLETED A QUESTIONNAIRE EVALUATING THE PROGRAM. BOTH THESE EVALUATIONS AND STAFF JUDGMENTS INDICATED THAT THE PROGRAM WAS SUCCESSFUL IN MEETING ITS OBJECTIVES. (NH)

ED043379 PS003416
AN EDUCATION SYSTEM FOR HIGH-RISK INFANTS: A PREVENTIVE APPROACH TO DEVELOPMENTAL AND LEARNING DISABILITIES. MEIER, JOHN H.; AND OTHERS, MAR 70 59P.
DOCUMENT NOT AVAILABLE FROM EDRS.
AVAILABLE FROM: "DISADVANTAGED CHILD, VOLUME III," J. HELLMUTH (ED.) NOV. 1970. BRUNNER-MAZEL PUBLISHERS, 80 EAST 11TH STREET, NEW YORK, NY 10003 ($12.50)

THIS PAPER REVIEWS RECENT LITERATURE IN THE FIELD OF INFANT EDUCATION, PRESENTS A RATIONALE FOR DEVELOPING A SYSTEMATIC PROGRAM OF INFANT EDUCATION, AND SUGGESTS HOW THIS MIGHT BE ACCOMPLISHED. DEVELOPMENTAL RESEARCH HAS SHOWN THAT EXPERIENTIAL DEPRIVATION, WHETHER ENVIRONMENTALLY OR NEUROLOGICALLY CAUSED, IS THE MAJOR FACTOR IN MENTAL RETARDATION AND LEARNING DISABILITY. IF THIS FACTOR CAN BE MINIMIZED BY GIVING POTENTIALLY HANDICAPPED (HIGH-RISK) INFANTS APPROPRIATE AND THERAPEUTIC EXPERIENCES, THESE DISABILITIES CAN BE MINIMIZED OR PREVENTED. A MULTIPHASIC PROGRAM OF EDUCATION OF THE HIGH-RISK INFANT SHOULD BE INITIATED AT AS EARLY AN AGE AS POSSIBLE. TWO APPROACHES USED ARE THE ENRICHED DAY CARE SETTING, AND THE TRAINING OF MOTHERS IN PROGRAMS OF INFANT STIMULATION IN THE HOME. IT IS SUGGESTED THAT AN INFANT CURRICULUM INCLUDE: (1) A SOLID CONCEPTUAL RATIONALE, (2) AN INVENTORY OF INFANT DEVELOPMENT WHICH USES VALID ASSESSMENT INSTRUMENTS AND SKILLED OBSERVATIONS, (3) A SYSTEMATIC METHOD OF TEACHING THOSE WHO WILL TEACH PARENTS AND BABIES, (4) A DETAILED CURRICULUM OF SEQUENTIAL AND HIERARCHICAL EXPERIENCES, AND (5) AN ADDITIONAL REMEDIATION SYSTEM WHICH CAN BE USED WHEN SPECIAL INTERVENTION TECHNIQUES ARE NEEDED. (AUTHOR/NH)

ED043380 PS003421
EFFECTS OF AGE OF ENTRY AND DURATION OF PARTICIPATION IN A COMPENSATORY EDUCATION PROGRAM. SPAULDING, ROBERT L.; KATZENMEYER, WILLIAM G., 21 APR 69 11P.
EDRS PRICE MF-$0.65 HC-$3.29

ONE OF A SERIES OF REPORTS EVALUATING THE DURHAM EDUCATION IMPROVEMENT PROGRAM, THIS STUDY CONCENTRATES ON ASSESSING THE INFLUENCE OF AGE-OF-ENTRY ON SUBSEQUENT CHANGES IN PERFORMANCE ON INTELLIGENCE TESTS. CHANGES IN INTELLIGENCE QUOTIENT SCORES FOR TWO AGE-AT-ENTRY GROUPS (3-, 4-, 5-YEAR-OLDS COMBINED AND 6-YEAR-OLDS) WERE CORRELATED AFTER ONE AND TWO YEARS OF PARTICIPATION IN THE PROGRAM. ALTHOUGH SIGNIFICANT INCREASES IN MEASURED INTELLIGENCE WERE FOUND AFTER BOTH ONE AND TWO YEARS IN THE PROGRAM, NO ONE ENTRY AGE AFFORDED GREATER INCREASES IN SCORES THAN ANOTHER. (TABLES ARE INCLUDED). (WY)

ED043381 PS003422
MODIFICATION BY SOCIAL REINFORCEMENT OF DEFICIENT SOCIAL BEHAVIOR OF DISADVANTAGED KINDERGARTEN CHILDREN. SIBLEY, SALLY A.; AND OTHERS, [67] 16P.
EDRS PRICE MF-$0.65 HC-$3.29

POSITIVE SOCIAL REINFORCEMENT (TEACHER ATTENTION) WAS USED TO MODIFY THE DEFICIENT SOCIAL BEHAVIOR OF TWO DISADVANTAGED NEGRO KINDERGARTEN CHILDREN. SUBJECTS WERE A GIRL WHO SHOWED A VERY HIGH AMOUNT OF ISOLATE BEHAVIOR, AND A BOY WHO USUALLY PLAYED ALONE, OR WITH GIRLS TO THE EXCLUSION OF BOYS. DATA WERE COLLECTED FOR ONE MONTH DURING HALF HOUR PERIODS ON SUBJECTS' ISOLATE, PARALLEL, AND INTERACTIVE BEHAVIOR. INTERACTIONS OF TEACHERS WITH THE SUBJECTS WERE RECORDED AND CLASSIFIED AS POSITIVE, NEUTRAL, OR DIRECTIVE. FOR FOUR DAYS DISTRIBUTED THROUGHOUT THE STUDY, DATA IDENTICAL TO THAT ON THE SUBJECTS WERE COLLECTED ON THE REST OF THE CLASS TO PROVIDE NORMS. TREATMENT PROGRAMS PLANNED FOR THE TWO CHILDREN INVOLVED TEACHER ATTENTION (POSITIVE OR NEUTRAL), CONTINGENT ON PARALLEL OR INTERACTIVE PLAY. FOR THE BOY, ISOLATE PLAY AND PLAY WITH GIRLS WAS TO BE IGNORED; FOR THE GIRL, ISOLATE PLAY WAS TO BE IGNORED. DURING TREATMENT, THESE BEHAVIORS SHOWED SIGNIFICANT DECREASES. EXTINCTION AND REINTRODUCTION OF THE REINFORCEMENT PROGRAMS WERE INSTITUTED TO DEMONSTRATE THEIR CONTROL OVER THE SUBJECTS' SOCIAL BEHAVIOR. TEACHER REINFORCEMENT WAS EVIDENTLY THE CRUCIAL VARIABLE FACTOR AS SUBJECTS' PARALLEL AND INTERACTIVE PLAY DECREASED DURING THE EXTINCTION PERIOD. (NH)

ED043382 PS003427
78 BATTERED CHILDREN: A RETROSPECTIVE STUDY. SKINNER, ANGELA E.; CASTLE, RAYMOND L., SEP 69 24P.
DOCUMENT NOT AVAILABLE FROM EDRS.
AVAILABLE FROM: NSPCC INFORMATION DEPARTMENT, 1 RIDING HOUSE STREET, LONDON W1P 8AA. (FIVE SHILLINGS, $0.65)

THE NATIONAL SOCIETY FOR THE PREVENTION OF CRUELTY TO CHILDREN FINANCED THIS STUDY OF THE BATTERED-CHILD SYNDROME AND PROVIDED CASE STUDY DATA ON A SAMPLE OF 78 BATTERED CHILDREN UNDER THE AGE OF 4 YEARS, FROM LOW SOCIOECONOMIC STATUS FAMILIES. CASE STUDY INFORMATION WAS TRANSFERRED TO A PRECODED QUESTIONNAIRE. TABLES OF DEMOGRAPHIC AND MEDICAL DATA ON PARENTS AND CHILDREN ARE INCLUDED IN THIS REPORT. FIFTY-SIX PERCENT OF THE CHILDREN IN THE SAMPLE WERE LESS THAN A YEAR OLD, EMPHASIZING THAT RISK OCCURS AT A VERY YOUNG AGE. STUDY FINDINGS INDICATE THAT RELATIVELY MINOR BRUISES AND FACIAL TRAUMA OFTEN SIGNAL THE BEGINNING OF INCREASINGLY VIOLENT INJURY, AVERTIBLE BY EARLY DIAGNOSIS AND INTERVENTION. IN FAMILIES WHERE THE FIRST CHILD WAS BATTERED, CHANCES WERE 13 TO 1 THAT A SUBSEQUENT CHILD WOULD BE INJURED. THE RELIABILITY OF PREVIOUS SUGGESTIONS THAT ONE CHILD IS OFTEN SINGLED OUT FOR BATTERING IS THEREFORE QUESTIONABLE. THE PARENTS APPEARED TO HAVE LONG-STANDING PERSONALITY PROBLEMS (HABITUALLY AGRESSIVE AND/OR EMOTIONALLY IMPOVERISHED) HEIGHTENED BY THE DEMANDS OF PARENTHOOD. TOO FREQUENT OBSERVATION OF BATTERING FAMILIES BY MANY WORKERS WITHOUT SPECIFIC TREATMENT GOALS CAN INCREASE FAMILY STRESS AND IS NOT IN THE CHILD'S INTEREST. THERE IS A GREAT NEED FOR EARLIER RECOGNITION AND PROTECTION OF THE BATTERED CHILD AND FOR THERAPEUTIC SERVICES FOR THE PARENTS. (NH)

ED043383 PS003432
EMOTIONAL CHARACTERISTICS OF DISADVANTAGED CHILDREN OF APPALACHIA. ALEXANDER, THERON, [67] 11P.
EDRS PRICE MF-$0.65 HC-$3.29

CHILDREN LIVING IN THE DEPRIVED ENVIRONMENT OF APPALACHIA WERE STUDIED TO DETERMINE IF THEY SHOWED A LIMITED VERBAL RESPONSE TO STIMULI IN THEIR ENVIRONMENT, AND IF THEIR EMOTIONAL CHARACTERISTICS DIFFERED FROM THOSE OF ADVANTAGED CHILDREN. AN EARLIER STUDY (1957) OF AMERICAN INDIAN CHILDREN LIVING ON A RESERVATION PROVIDED THE STIMULUS FOR THIS RESEARCH. THE SUBJECTS WERE 93 WHITE, 6-YEAR-OLD BOYS AND GIRLS. OF THIS NUMBER, 34 WERE FROM A DISADVANTAGED, RURAL BACKGROUND AND 59 FROM A MIDDLE CLASS, URBAN BACKGROUND. THE SUBJECTS IN BOTH GROUPS WERE SHOWN FIVE CARDS WITH PHOTOGRAPHS OF HUMAN FIGURES WHOSE ACTIVITY AND EMOTION WERE AMBIGUOUS, AND THE VERBAL RESPONSES OF EACH CHILD WERE WRITTEN DOWN AS HE TALKED ABOUT THEM. THE PERCENTAGE OF THE CHILDREN IN THE TWO GROUPS USING POSITIVE WORDS WAS RELATIVELY SIMILAR. HOWEVER, THE PERCENTAGE OF DISADVANTAGED CHILDREN USING NEGATIVE WORDS SUCH AS "FIGHT," "MAD," "SAD," AND "SCOLD," WAS MORE THAN TWICE AS GREAT AS THE PERCENTAGE OF ADVANTAGED CHILDREN USING NEGATIVE WORDS. THE TENDENCY TO PERCEIVE NON-THREATENING OR NEUTRAL STIMULI AS HOSTILE, IF PERSISTING TO ADULTHOOD, MAY ADVERSELY AFFECT BOTH THE INDIVIDUAL AND SOCIETY, AND SHOULD BE TAKEN INTO ACCOUNT WHEN PLANNING AMELIORATIVE EDUCATIONAL PROGRAMS. (NH)

ED043384 PS003442
THE EFFECT ON AGGRESSION OF VARIATION IN AMOUNT OF OPPORTUNITY FOR PLAY. (INTERNAL REPORT). WUELLNER, LANCE, [69] 12P.
EDRS PRICE MF-$0.65 HC NOT AVAILABLE FROM EDRS.
AVAILABLE FROM: UNIVERSITY OF ILLINOIS, CHILDREN'S RESEARCH CENTER, URBANA, ILLINOIS

THE EFFECT OF A HIGH-OPPORTUNITY (HO) VERSUS A LOW-OPPORTUNITY (LO) PLAY ENVIRONMENT ON THE AGGRESSION OF PRESCHOOL CHILDREN WAS INVESTIGATED, HYPOTHESIZING THAT THE LO PLAY ENVIRONMENT WILL ELICIT SIGNIFICANTLY MORE AGGRESSION THAN THE HO PLAY ENVIRONMENT. THE TWO ENVIRONMENTS WERE PRESENTED RANDOMLY TO ONE GROUP OF 10 4-YEAR-OLDS, FIVE OF EACH SEX, ON 12 CONSECUTIVE 15-MINUTE PLAY SESSIONS, WITH THE STIPULATION THAT EACH ENVIRONMENT BE PRESENTED SIX TIMES. THERE WAS NO PRE-EXPERIMENTAL FAMILIARIZATION PERIOD DUE TO INFORMATION, LATER PROVEN INCORRECT, THAT THE SUBJECTS WERE ADEQUATELY FAMILIAR WITH ALL THE PLAY APPARATUS. RESULTS INDICATE THAT THE HIGH-LEVEL AGGRESSION IN THE FIRST TWO LO

SESSIONS IS SOLELY RESPONSIBLE FOR THE SIGNIFICANT DIFFERENCE BETWEEN THE AGGRESSION IN THE LO VERSUS THE HO ENVIRONMENTS. ANECDOTAL RECORDS INDICATE THAT THIS HIGH-LEVEL AGGRESSION CAN BE ATTRIBUTED TO A NOVEL PIECE OF EQUIPMENT, A ROCKER, RESULTING IN A RECOMMENDATION FOR FURTHER STUDY OF THE RELATION BETWEEN NOVELTY AND AGGRESSION. THE DISCUSSION IDENTIFIES SOME FACTORS RELEVANT IN THE AGGRESSION EDUCATION OF YOUNG CHILDREN. THE DESIGN OF SIMILAR STUDIES USING SUBJECTS WHO WOULD PRESUMABLY EXHIBIT HIGH-LEVEL AGGRESSION IN HIGH-OPPORTUNITY ENVIRONMENTS IS RECOMMENDED. (AUTHOR/NH)

ED043385 PS003443
GROSS ACTIVITY OF CHILDREN AT PLAY. (INTERNAL REPORT). WUELLNER, LANCE, [70] 10P.
EDRS PRICE MF-$0.65 HC NOT AVAILABLE FROM EDRS.
AVAILABLE FROM: UNIVERSITY OF ILLINOIS, CHILDREN'S RESEARCH CENTER, URBANA, ILLINOIS

TIME-LAPSE PHOTOGRAPHY WAS USED TO RECORD THE GROSS PLAY ACTIVITY OF PRESCHOOL CHILDREN, RATED ACCORDING TO THREE MEASURES OF EQUIPMENT USE AND THREE MEASURES OF MOVEMENT. THE DEFINITION AND DERIVATION OF THESE MEASURES WAS OUTLINED, AND FIVE HYPOTHESES WERE PRESENTED AND TESTED CONCERNING THE VARIABILITY AND INTERRELATION OF THE MEASURES. ANALYSIS OF THE DATA SUGGESTS THAT FACTORS INFLUENCING PLAY ARE SO COMPLEX THAT PRESENT ATTEMPTS AT PREDICTING GROUP ACTIVITY TRENDS MAY BE PREMATURE. FURTHER WORK IS NEEDED IN THE DEFINITION AND ISOLATION OF STIMULUS PARAMETERS OF THE PHYSICAL ENVIRONMENT SO THAT THE INTERPRETATION OF PLAY BEHAVIOR IS SIMPLIFIED AND MADE MORE RELEVANT FOR THE INDIVIDUAL CHILD. IT IS SUGGESTED THAT INDIVIDUAL TRENDS MUST BE INVESTIGATED BEFORE A COMPLETE UNDERSTANDING OF GROUP PLAY PATTERNS CAN BE ACHIEVED. (AUTHOR/NH)

ED043386 PS003444
PARENTAL CONCEPTUAL SYSTEMS, HOME PLAY ENVIRONMENT, AND POTENTIAL CREATIVITY IN CHILDREN. BISHOP, DOYLE W.; CHACE, CHARLES A., [69] 26P.
EDRS PRICE MF-$0.65 HC-$3.29

PARENTS DIFFERING ALONG A CONCRETENESS-ABSTRACTNESS DIMENSION OF CONCEPTUAL DEVELOPMENT, AS DEFINED BY THE MODEL OF HARVEY, HUNT, AND SCHRODER, DESCRIBED THEIR ATTITUDES AND PRACTICES REGARDING THEIR CHILDREN'S HOME PLAY ENVIRONMENT. THIS WAS DONE USING STRUCTURED QUESTIONNAIRES. POTENTIAL CREATIVITY OF THE 3- AND 4-YEAR-OLD CHILDREN THEMSELVES WAS MEASURED BY INDICATORS OF COMPLEXITY AND VARIETY OF PERFORMANCE ON A LABORATORY PLAY TASK. PARENTS' QUESTIONNAIRE RESPONSES WERE ANALYZED IN TERMS OF THE COMPLEXITY, NOVELTY, AUTONOMY, AND EXPLORATIVENESS OF THE HOME PLAY ENVIRONMENT. PARENTS' LEVELS OF CONCEPTUAL DEVELOPMENT WERE THAN COMPARED ON THE QUESTIONNAIRE RESPONSES AND THE CHILDREN'S PERFORMANCE SCORES. THE RESULTS FOR FATHERS SHOWED NO SIGNIFICANT DIFFERENCES. THE RESULTS FOR MOTHERS INDICATED THAT MORE ABSTRACT MOTHERS HAD MORE POSITIVE ATTITUDES TOWARD AND WERE MORE LIKELY THAN MORE CONCRETE MOTHERS TO PROVIDE COMPLEX, NOVEL, AUTONOMOUS, AND EXPLORATIVE PLAY SITUATIONS FOR THEIR CHILDREN. THE CHILDREN OF MORE ABSTRACT MOTHERS ALSO SHOWED MORE COMPLEX AND VARIED BEHAVIOR ON THE PREFORMANCE TASK. THESE RESULTS WERE UNRELATED TO DIFFERENCES AMONG PARENTS ON CERTAIN DEMOGRAPHIC VARIABLES--AGE, INCOME, EDUCATION, AND OCCUPATIONAL PRESTIGE. THE RESULTS WERE DISCUSSED IN TERMS OF THE ROLES OF PARENTAL CONCEPTUAL DEVELOPMENT AND THE HOME PLAY ENVIRONMENT IN AFFECTING POTENTIAL CREATIVITY. (AUTHOR)

ED043387 PS003457
ISSUES AND IMPLICATIONS OF THE DISTRIBUTION OF ATTENTION IN THE HUMAN INFANT. MCCALL, ROBERT B., APR 70 10P.
EDRS PRICE MF-$0.65 HC-$3.29

STUDIES OF THE INFANT'S DISTRIBUTION OF ATTENTION TO STIMULI OF VARYING COMPLEXITY, AND OF HIS DIFFERENTIAL ATTENTION TO FAMILIAR VERSUS NOVEL STIMULI (DISCREPANCY), HAVE ATTEMPTED TO SHED LIGHT ON THE DEVELOPMENT OF COGNITIVE STRUCTURES IN THE NON-VERBAL INFANT. THE SUBJECTS HAVE TYPICALLY BEEN NORMAL INFANTS AGES 4 TO 6 MONTHS. FOR TESTING, THE INFANT IS PLACED IN AN INFANT SEAT ON A TABLE IN A SMALL ROOM, WITH THE MOTHER SEATED TO THE SIDE AND REAR OF HIM. VISUAL OR AUDITORY STIMULI ARE PRESENTED TO THE INFANT AND HIS RESPONSE BEHAVIOR IS RECORDED. TWO DEPENDENT VARIABLES MEASURED HAVE BEEN FIRST FIXATION (THE LENGTH OF THE INFANT'S FIRST VISUAL FIXATION TO THE STIMULUS DURING ANY SINGLE PRESENTATION), AND CARDIAC DECELERATION (THE DEGREE TO WHICH THE INFANT'S HEART RATE SLOWS DURING A FIXATION). PAST STUDIES ARE CITED REGARDING THEIR DIFFERING EMPHASES ON PARTICULAR ASPECTS OF ATTENTION AND THEIR FINDINGS ON INDIVIDUAL DIFFERENCES. TYPICALLY, THE INFANT HABITUATES (RESPONDS LESS) TO REPEATED PRESENTATIONS OF STIMULI. WORK IN THIS AREA IS JUST BEGINNING, BUT STUDY RESULTS THUS FAR INDICATE THAT HABITUATION AND RESPONSE TO DISCREPANCY MAY BE IMPORTANT INDICES OF COGNITIVE FUNCTIONING. (NH)

ED043388 PS003460
CHILD DEVELOPMENT RESEARCH AND EVALUATION CENTER FOR HEAD START, TEMPLE UNIVERSITY, 1968 - 1969. ANNUAL REPORT. ALEXANDER, THERON; AND OTHERS, 31 AUG 69 278P.
EDRS PRICE MF-$0.65 HC-$9.87

THIS REPORT OF THE THIRD YEAR OF A HEAD START STUDY INDICATES THE DIVERSE RANGE OF INFORMATION GATHERED ON TWO TYPES OF PROGRAMS (PHILADELPHIA'S INNER CITY AND APPALACHIAN FOLLOW-UP) IN WHICH THE CHILD DEVELOPMENT RESEARCH AND EVALUATION CENTER AT TEMPLE UNIVERSITY PARTICIPATED. SUBJECTS IN THE PHILADELPHIA SAMPLE WERE 158 NEGRO CHILDREN EQUALLY BALANCED BETWEEN THE SEXES WHO HAD ATTENDED ANY ONE OF TWELVE HEAD START CENTERS. IN THE APPALACHIAN SAMPLE, THE MAJORITY OF THE 41 SUBJECTS WERE CAUCASIAN. THEY (1) HAD PREVIOUSLY EXPERIENCED AT LEAST A YEAR OF HEAD START (2) HAD BEEN TESTED IN THE 1967-1968 EVALUATION PROGRAM, AND (3) WERE CURRENTLY IN THE FIRST GRADE. INVESTIGATIONS OF COGNITIVE, SOCIAL-EMOTIONAL, AND PHYSICAL DEVELOPMENT WHICH UTILIZED BOTH STANDARDIZED AND SPECIALLY DEVELOPED INSTRUMENTS WERE UNDERTAKEN. TABULAR PRESENTATIONS OF TEST DATA ARE INCLUDED. FACULTY STUDIES AND RESEARCH PROJECTS WHICH RELATE TO ASSESSMENT OF THE CONTINUING INFLUENCE OF HEAD START ARE ALSO INCLUDED IN THIS DOCUMENT. (WY)

ED043389 PS003651
LONG TERM STUDY OF PREMATURES: SUMMARY OF PUBLISHED FINDINGS. WIENER, GERALD, [68] 56P.
EDRS PRICE MF-$0.65 HC-$3.29

ARE CHILDREN INTELLECTUALLY IMPAIRED AS A RESULT OF LOW BIRTH WEIGHT AND DOES RELATIVE IMPAIRMENT CHANGE AS CHILDREN GROW OLDER? PREMATURE INFANTS FROM A RANGE OF SOCIOECONOMIC GROUPS WERE STUDIED IN FIVE ROUNDS OVER 13 YEARS TO PROVIDE NEUROLOGICAL, PSYCHOLOGICAL, ACHIEVEMENT, AND SOCIOLOGICAL DATA ON 582 CHILDREN IN THREE BIRTH WEIGHT GROUPS. A SUMMARY BASED ON THE FINAL ROUND MAKES THESE POINTS: (1) BIRTH WEIGHT IS RELATED TO READING AND ARITHMETIC ACHIEVEMENT WHEN SOCIAL CLASS AND RACE ARE CONTROLLED, (2) BIRTH WEIGHT REMAINS A SIGNIFICANT CORRELATE WHEN AN ATTEMPT IS MADE TO CONTROL FOR NEUROLOGICAL STATUS (ESTIMATED AT AGE 40 WEEKS), (3) THE CORRELATION BETWEEN INDICES OF MENTAL DEVELOPMENT AND LATE ADOLESCENT INTELLECTUAL BEHAVIOR APPROACHES ZERO, (4) ARITHMETIC IS APPARENTLY MORE SENSITIVE AS AN INDICATOR OF IMPAIRMENT DUE TO BIRTH WEIGHT THAN IS READING, (5) NONE OF THE STATISTICAL INTERACTIONS BETWEEN RACE, SOCIAL CLASS, BIRTH WEIGHT, AND ACHIEVEMENT WERE SIGNIFICANT. (TABLES MAKE UP ONE-HALF OF THE DOCUMENT.) (WY)

ED043390 PS003653
WORDS AND DEEDS ABOUT ALTRUISM AND THE SUBSEQUENT REINFORCEMENT POWER OF THE MODEL. BRYAN, JAMES H.; AND OTHERS, [70] 13P.
EDRS PRICE MF-$0.65 HC-$3.29

NINETY-SIX SECOND AND THIRD GRADE CHILDREN WERE EXPOSED TO ONE OF SIX TYPES OF VIDEOTAPED MODELS. CHILDREN WITNESSED AN ADULT FEMALE PRACTICE EITHER CHARITABLE OR SELFISH BEHAVIOR. ONE-THIRD OF THE SUBJECTS IN EACH GROUP HEARD THE MODEL EXHORT EITHER CHARITY OR GREED OR VERBALIZE NORMATIVELY NEUTRAL MATERIAL. FOLLOWING THIS EXPOSURE, HALF THE CHILDREN WITHIN EACH GROUP RECEIVED SOCIAL REINFORCEMENTS FROM THE MODEL FOR RESPONSES MINIMIZING MATERIAL REWARDS, WHILE THE OTHER HALF OBTAINED NO SOCIAL REWARDS. AN INTERACTION OF MODEL'S PRACTICES, PREACHINGS AND SOCIAL REINFORCEMENTS WAS FOUND: THE MODEL WHO PRACTICED AND PREACHED CHARITY AND REWARDED SELF-DENIAL RESPONSES ELICITED THE GREATEST NUMBER OF SUCH RESPONSES FROM THE CHILDREN. THE MODEL WHO PREACHED AND PRACTICED CHARITY BUT DID NOT REWARD IT, ELICITED THE LEAST NUMBER OF THE RESPONSES. CHILDREN'S JUDGMENTS OF THE MODEL'S NICENESS WERE DETERMINED BY THE MODEL'S PREACHINGS AND PRACTICES, NOT BY THE REWARDS. (AUTHOR)

ED043391 PS003657
THE SAMPLE: OPERATIONS IN THE HEAD START YEAR. , FEB 70 41P.
EDRS PRICE MF-$0.65 HC-$3.29

THIS REPORT, THE THIRD IN A SERIES, DESCRIBES A HEAD START LONGITUDINAL STUDY OF THE COMPLEX INTERACTIONS THAT MAY TAKE PLACE AMONG CHILD, FAMILY, COMMUNITY AND PROGRAM VARIABLES. CHAPTER 1 DESCRIBES THE INITIAL LONGITUDINAL SAMPLE, BASED UPON INFORMATION ON SEX, RACE, HEAD START ENROLLMENT, AND SOCIOECONOMIC STATUS. ANALYSES ARE GIVEN OF MOTHERS' AND FATHERS' EDUCATION AND OCCUPATION. CHAPTER 2 GIVES AN ACCOUNT OF DATA COLLECTION DURING THE CURRENT YEAR OF THE STUDY, WHEN THE CHILDREN WERE FIRST ENROLLED IN HEAD START CLASSES. THE STUDY DESIGN CALLS FOR TWO LINES OF INVESTIGATION: FOLLOW-UP OF THE LONGITUDINAL SAMPLE, AND STUDY OF APPROPRIATE CROSS-SECTIONAL GROUPS (KINDERGARTEN THROUGH GRADE 3). THE PERSONAL RECORD OF SCHOOL EXPERIENCE (PROSE) AND THE CLASSROOM OBSERVATIONAL RATING SCALE (PERSONALITY) WERE USED THROUGHOUT THE PROGRAM YEAR TO RECORD THE CHILDREN'S RELATIONSHIPS WITH PEERS, TEACHERS, AND CLASSROOM MATERIALS. THE CHILDREN WERE TESTED

ALSO ON A VARIETY OF MEASURES OF MENTAL, MOTOR, AND PERSONALITY DEVELOPMENT. ADDITIONAL DATA WERE COLLECTED FROM PARENT INTERVIEWS AND CLASSROOM OBSERVATIONS. TEACHER AND SCHOOL ADMINISTRATOR QUESTIONNAIRES ARE IN PREPARATION. THE CROSS-SECTIONAL STUDY HAD NOT BEEN DONE AT THE TIME OF THIS REPORT. (NH)

ED043392 PS003663
CHILDREN'S JUDGMENTS OF AGE. LOOFT, WILLIAM R., MAR 70 12P.
EDRS PRICE MF-$0.65 HC-$3.29

SIXTY-THREE CHILDREN RANGING IN AGE FROM THREE TO NINE YEARS MADE AGE JUDGMENTS ON DRAWINGS OF HUMAN FIGURES. THE STIMULI CONSISTED OF FOUR DIFFERENT MALE FIGURES DRAWN ACCORDING TO TYPICAL PHYSICAL CHARACTERISTICS OF THE MIDDLE-AGED ADULT, ADOLESCENT, CHILD, AND INFANT. THE FIGURES WERE REPRODUCED IN TWO SIZES AND WERE PRESENTED TO THE SUBJECTS IN A PAIRED COMPARISON PROCEDURE. CHILDREN'S ACCURACY IN DETERMINING THE OLDER OF THE TWO FIGURES ON EACH STIMULUS CARD INCREASED STEADILY OVER THE SEVEN AGE LEVELS. THE ERRORS OF YOUNG SUBJECTS WERE PRIMARILY DUE TO A FIGURAL-SIZE RESPONSE SET. OLDER CHILDREN MADE INCREASING USE OF OTHER PHYSICAL FEATURES IN MAKING THEIR JUDGMENTS. (AUTHOR/WY)

ED043393 PS003856
PREDICTION OF READINESS IN KINDERGARTEN AND ACHIEVEMENT IN THE FIRST PRIMARY YEAR. STUDY NUMBER TWO. , JAN 70 15P.
EDRS PRICE MF-$0.65 HC-$3.29

A 4-YEAR UNITED STATES OFFICE OF EDUCATION PREKINDERGARTEN-KINDERGARTEN SERIES OF RESEARCH STUDIES HAS PROVIDED DATA USEFUL IN PREDICTING SCHOOL SUCCESS. THE PRESENT STUDY COMPARES TEST SCORES OF THE COMPLETE ASSESSMENT BATTERY ADMINISTERED BEFORE THE CHILDREN ENTERED KINDERGARTEN WITH SCORES OF THE SAME CHILDREN ON THE METROPOLITAN READINESS TESTS AT THE END OF KINDERGARTEN AND ON THE STANFORD ACHIEVEMENT TEST AT THE END OF THE FIRST PRIMARY YEAR. TEST SCORES OF 48 BOYS AND 55 GIRLS WERE COMBINED AS AGE AND SEX DIFFERENCES IN READINESS AND ACHIEVEMENT WERE NOT STATISTICALLY SIGNIFICANT. WHOLE AND PART TEST SCORES WERE TREATED SEPARATELY. THE ILLINOIS TEST OF PSYCHOLINGUISTIC ABILITIES, LANGUAGE QUOTIENT (ITPA-IQ) PROVED TO BE A REASONABLY GOOD PREDICTOR OF PERFORMANCE ON THE METROPOLITAN READINESS TESTS, AND PREDICTABILITY WAS INCREASED BY USING ONLY THREE ITPA SUBTESTS AND THE TEST OF VISUAL-MOTOR INTEGRATION (MVI) INSTEAD OF THE WHOLE ITPA BATTERY. PERFORMANCE ON THE STANFORD ACHIEVEMENT TEST COULD BE PREDICTED BEST BY USING ONE ITPA SUBTEST (AUDITORY-VOCAL ASSOCIATION) AND THE TEST OF VMI. THROUGHOUT THE STUDY, ITPA-3 PROVED TO BE THE BEST SINGLE PREDICTOR. (AUTHOR/NH)

ED043394 PS003920
AN INSTITUTIONAL ANALYSIS OF DAY CARE PROGRAM. PART II, GROUP DAY CARE: THE GROWTH OF AN INSTITUTION. FINAL REPORT. PRESCOTT, ELIZABETH; AND OTHERS, JUL 70 187P.
EDRS PRICE MF-$0.65 HC-$6.58

THIS MONOGRAPH CONTINUES AN ANALYSIS OF GROUP DAY CARE AS A SOCIAL INSTITUTION, PARTICULARLY AS IT HAS DEVELOPED IN SOUTHERN CALIFORNIA. PART I DISCUSSED WAYS IN WHICH COMMUNITIES OBTAIN DAY CARE FACILITIES, CONCENTRATING ON CHANGES IN COMMUNITY OPINION AND ENVIRONMENT WHICH INFLUENCE THE EXISTENCE OF DAY CARE CENTERS. PART II FOCUSES ON THE DECISION-MAKING PROCESS WITH REGARD TO THE BACKGROUND OF PROBLEMS MET IN SETTING UP COMMUNITY DAY CARE. THE ROLE OF MONEY AS A GREAT FACILITATOR IS EMPHASIZED THROUGHOUT THE REPORT. LICENSING, STANDARDS, AND STAFFING OF DAY CARE FACILITIES ARE EXAMINED. HOWEVER, COMMUNITIES SHOULD RECOGNIZE THAT IDEALIZED STANDARDS DO NOT, IN THEMSELVES, PROMOTE QUALITY. RATHER, COMMITTED LEADERS WHO CAN FIND A RESPONSIVE ENVIRONMENT FOR QUALITY DAY CARE PROGRAMS ARE VITALLY IMPORTANT. HOW THE LEADERSHIP NETWORK CAME INTO BEING AND HOW IT OPERATES TO PROMOTE ITS CONCERNS IS DISCUSSED. A CONSIDERATION OF ISSUES BEARING ON THE FUTURE OF DAY CARE CONCLUDES THE REPORT. APPENDIXES INCLUDE QUESTIONNAIRES USED IN THE PREPARATION OF THIS REPORT, QUALIFICATIONS FOR A CHILDREN'S CENTER PERMIT, AND THE PERMIT AUTHORIZING SERVICE IN INSTRUCTION IN CHILDREN'S CENTERS. (NH)

ED043395 PS003984
THE PRESCHOOL CHILD'S ABILITY TO FOLLOW DIRECTIONS. SMOTHERGILL, NANCY L., NOV 69 17P.
EDRS PRICE MF-$0.65 HC-$3.29

THE FIRST OF THIS SERIES OF STUDIES ON THE ABILITY OF YOUNG CHILDREN TO FOLLOW DIRECTIONS WAS DESIGNED TO FIND OUT WHICH IS EASIER FOR A PRESCHOOL CHILD: TO FOLLOW DIRECTIONS GIVEN ONLY BY DEMONSTRATION OR GIVEN ONLY VERBALLY. SUBJECTS WERE 108 WHITE, MIDDLE CLASS, 4-YEAR-OLDS ENROLLED IN A NURSERY SCHOOL. EACH TEACHER TESTED THE CHILDREN IN HER CLASS TO DETERMINE THEIR UNDERSTANDING OF RELATIONAL WORDS AND THEIR ABILITY TO FOLLOW INDIVIDUAL DIRECTIONS. STUDY RESULTS SHOWED NO SIGNIFICANT DIFFERENCE BETWEEN SCORES OF CHILDREN ASKED TO FOLLOW A VERBAL COMMAND AND THOSE ASKED TO FOLLOW DIRECTIONS GIVEN BY DEMONSTRATION. A SECOND STUDY INVESTIGATED CHILDREN'S ABILITY TO FOLLOW EITHER NOVEL OR ADDITIVE SEQUENTIAL DIRECTIONS. THERE WERE 30 CHILDREN IN EACH GROUP. IT WAS FOUND THAT CHILDREN COULD HANDLE SIGNIFICANTLY MORE DIRECTIONS IN THE ADDITIVE CONDITION THAN IN THE NOVEL. A REPLICATION-EXTENSION OF THIS STUDY (40 SUBJECTS) SHOWED THAT USE OF INCENTIVE DID NOT INCREASE THE NUMBER OF DIRECTIONS REMEMBERED. IN ANOTHER STUDY, CONDITIONAL DIRECTIONS SCALED FROM EASY TO DIFFICULT WERE USED AND MORE THAN ONE-HALF THE SUBJECTS SUCCESSFULLY COMPLETED ALL OF THE CONDITIONAL DIRECTIONS. A MAP STUDY INVOLVING THE NEED TO FOLLOW SYMBOLIC CODE DIRECTIONS SHOWED THAT CHILDREN WERE ABLE TO USE THE CODE WHEN THE TRANSFER OF THE CODE TO THE REAL LIFE ENVIRONMENT WAS FAIRLY OBVIOUS. (NH)

ED043396 PS004000
EARLY CHILDHOOD EDUCATION AS A DISCIPLINE. KATZ, LILIAN G., SEP 70 15P.
EDRS PRICE MF-$0.65 HC-$3.29

EARLY CHILDHOOD EDUCATION IS DEFINED AS GROUP SETTINGS WHICH ARE DELIBERATELY INTENDED TO EFFECT DEVELOPMENTAL CHANGES IN CHILDREN IN THE AGE RANGE FROM BIRTH UP TO THE AGE OF ENTERING FIRST GRADE. THE FOLLOWING PARAMETERS OF EARLY CHILDHOOD EDUCATION ARE PROPOSED AND EXPLORED: (A) CHARACTERISTICS OF CLIENTS, (B) CHARACTERISTICS OF TEACHERS AND ASSISTING ADULTS, (C) CURRICULUM, (D) PHILOSOPHICAL ORIENTATION AND HISTORICAL FACTORS, (E) PARENT POWER, (F) ADMINISTRATIVE FACTORS AND SPONSORSHIP, (G) LENGTH OF PROGRAM, AND (H) PHYSICAL PLANT AND CLIMATE. A MATRIX IS GENERATED FROM THESE PARAMETERS, IN ORDER TO DEMONSTRATE THAT EARLY CHILDHOOD EDUCATION IS A COMPLEX FIELD DESERVING OF EXTENSIVE ANALYSIS. THE FOCUS TODAY SEEMS TO BE EITHER ON CHARACTERISTICS OF CLIENTS OR ON PROGRAM ORGANIZATION, WITH THE ASSUMPTION THAT PACKAGED EARLY CHILDHOOD EDUCATION PROGRAMS MAY BE USED IN SITUATIONS WHICH ARE NOT ANALAGOUS, WITH POSITIVE RESULTS. ALTHOUGH THESE TWO PARAMETERS ARE OF MAJOR IMPORTANCE, IT IS EMPHASIZED THAT AN INCREASED UNDERSTANDING OF ALL THE PARAMETERS OF EARLY CHILDHOOD EDUCATION, AND THE WAYS IN WHICH THEY INTERACT AND INFLUENCE EACH OTHER, MAY MAKE IT MORE POSSIBLE TO SUCCESSFULLY TRANSLATE THEORY INTO PRACTICE. (AUTHOR/NH)

ED043397 PS004025
FROM THEORY TO OPERATIONS. DISADVANTAGED CHILDREN AND THEIR FIRST SCHOOL EXPERIENCES, ETS-HEAD START LONGITUDINAL STUDY. , AUG 69 259P.
EDRS PRICE MF-$0.65 HC-$9.87

IN THE SUMMER OF 1969, EDUCATIONAL TESTING SERVICE (ETS) BEGAN IDENTIFYING THE 1,650 3 1/2-YEAR-OLD CHILDREN IN FOUR SITES ACROSS THE COUNTRY WHO WOULD BECOME PART OF A SIX-YEAR LONGITUDINAL STUDY DESIGNED TO ASSESS THE IMPACT OF HEAD START. THE SITES WERE LEE COUNTY, ALABAMA, ST. LOUIS, MISSOURI, TRENTON, NEW JERSEY, AND PORTLAND, OREGON. THE CHILDREN WERE MEASURED ON A LARGE NUMBER OF RELEVANT VARIABLES BEFORE ANY OF THEM HAD EXPERIENCE WITH SOME OR NO HEAD START PROGRAM. THIS REPORT (THE SECOND OF THREE) DESCRIBES ATTEMPTS TO DESIGN AN EVALUATIVE PROGRAM BASED UPON CONCEPTIONS OF THE COMPLEXITY OF THE HUMAN ORGANISM AND AN INTERACTION MODEL OF HUMAN DEVELOPMENT. SIX CHAPTERS PRESENT: (1) A SHORT HISTORY OF THE ETS STUDY, (2) IMPRESSIONS OF THE STUDY COMMUNITIES, (3) MEASURES USED IN INITIAL ASSESSMENTS, (4) DATA COLLECTION PROCEDURES, (5) DATA STORAGE AND RETRIEVAL SYSTEM, (6) PLANS FOR DATA ANALYSIS. THE SEVENTH AND FINAL CHAPTER ANTICIPATES THE ACTIVITIES OF 1969-1970. FOUR APPENDIXES ARE INCLUDED: (A) TRYOUTS OF MEASURE, (B) WORKING PAPERS, (C) THE ETS-HEAD START LONGITUDINAL STUDY AND THE WESTINGHOUSE STUDY, (D) PROJECT PERSONNEL. ANOTHER PART OF THIS STUDY IS AVAILABLE AS PS 003 657. (WY)

ED044166 PS003058
ANCONA MONTESSORI RESEARCH PROJECT FOR CULTURALLY DISADVANTAGED CHILDREN. SEPTEMBER 1, 1968 TO AUGUST 31, 1969. FINAL REPORT. STODOLSKY, SUSAN S.; JENSEN, JUDITH, 31 AUG 69 83P.
EDRS PRICE MF-$0.65 HC-$3.29

THIS PAPER, PART OF A LONG TERM STUDY, REPORTS THE EFFECT OF A MODIFIED MONTESSORI PRESCHOOL EXPERIENCE ON COGNITIVE DEVELOPMENT, SCHOOL-RELATED BEHAVIORS, AND SOCIAL INTERACTIONS AND PERCEPTIONS OF DISADVANTAGED CHILDREN. EACH OF THIRTY-FIVE DISADVANTAGED NEGRO CHILDREN (31 IN NURSERY CLASSES AND 4 IN ELEMENTARY CLASSES) WAS PAIR-MATCHED WITH A MIDDLE CLASS CHILD. IN THE DISADVANTAGED GROUP, 17 CHILDREN WERE ATTENDING NURSERY CLASSES FOR THE FIRST TIME. PRE- AND POSTTESTS WERE MADE OF COGNITIVE ABILITY, ON THE STANFORD-BINET, PIAGET TESTS OF LENGTH CONSERVATION, AND SOCIOMETRIC FEATURES. ALSO, CHILDREN WERE RATED BY TESTERS ON PERFORMANCE AND BY TEACHERS RATED CLASSROOM BEHAVIORS. DATA FROM PREVIOUS YEARS ON SOME OF THE CHILDREN WERE USED IN REFERENCE TO LONG TERM CHANGE. PART I (NURSERY SCHOOL) TEST RESULTS SHOW THAT NEITHER FIRST NOR SECOND-YEAR CHILDREN SIGNIFICANTLY INCREASED THEIR I.Q. SCORES. BOTH DISADVANTAGED AND MIDDLE CLASS CHILDREN SCORED SIMILARLY ON TASK ORIENTATION. MIDDLE CLASS CHILDREN SHOWED MORE FRIENDSHIP CHOICES FORMING ACROSS

SOCIAL-CLASS LINES. PART II (ELEMENTARY SCHOOL) RESULTS PRESENT LIMITED SUPPORT FOR THE THEORY THAT CHILDREN WHO CONTINUE IN MONTESSORI, RATHER THAN PUBLIC, SCHOOL WILL SHOW BETTER SCHOOL ACHIEVEMENT. DATA INCLUDED SCHOOL RECORDS OF MORE THAN 30 CHILDREN. A FUTURE STUDY WILL INVESTIGATE DIFFUSION EFFECTS ON MOTHERS AND YOUNGER SIBLINGS, AND TESTING WITH MEASURES MORE DIRECTLY RELEVANT TO MONTESSORI CURRICULUM. (NH)

ED044167 PS003280
ON CLASS DIFFERENCES AND EARLY DEVELOPMENT. KAGAN, JEROME, 28 DEC 69 26P.
EDRS PRICE MF-$0.65 HC-$3.29

THERE ARE SEVEN MAJOR SETS OF DIFFERENCES BETWEEN YOUNG CHILDREN OF DIFFERENT ECONOMIC BACKGROUNDS. THE MIDDLE CLASS CHILD, COMPARED TO THE LOWER CLASS CHILD, GENERALLY EXHIBITS: (1) BETTER LANGUAGE COMPREHENSION AND EXPRESSION, (2) RICHER SCHEMA DEVELOPMENT, INVOLVING MENTAL PREPARATION FOR THE UNUSUAL, (3) STRONGER ATTACHMENT TO THE MOTHER, MAKING HIM MORE RECEPTIVE TO ADOPTION OF HER VALUES AND PROHIBITIONS, (4) LESS IMPULSIVE ACTION, (5) A BETTER SENSE OF HIS POTENTIAL EFFECTIVENESS, (6) MORE MOTIVATION FOR SCHOOL DEFINED TASKS, AND (7) GREATER EXCEPTATION OF SUCCESS AT INTELLECTUAL PROBLEMS. DATA FROM TWO STUDIES ARE OFFERED IN SUPPORT OF SOME OF THESE HYPOTHESES. ONE, A LONGITUDINAL STUDY OF 140 WHITE, MIDDLE AND LOWER CLASS INVOLVED OBSERVATIONS OF THEIR REACTIONS AT 4, 8, 13, AND 27 MONTHS OF AGE TO MASKS WITH SCRAMBLED FACIAL FEATURES. THE OTHER, A CROSS SECTIONAL STUDY OF 60 WHITE, 10-MONTH-OLD MIDDLE AND LOWER CLASS INFANTS INVOLVED HOME OBSERVATIONS OF MOTHER AND CHILD BEHAVIORS AND LABORATORY OBSERVATIONS OF CHILDREN'S REACTIONS TO MEANINGFUL AND NON-MEANINGFUL SPEECH, AND TO MOTHERS' AND STRANGERS' VOICES. TO BRING ABOUT IMPROVED DEVELOPMENTAL PATTERNS, IT IS IMPORTANT THAT LOWER CLASS MOTHERS BE SHOWN HOW THEY CAN BECOME EFFECTIVE CHANGE AGENTS IN THEIR CHILDREN'S LIVES. (NH)

ED044168 PS003285
PARENTS AS PRIMARY CHANGE AGENTS IN AN EXPERIMENTAL HEAD START PROGRAM OF LANGUAGE INTERVENTION. EXPERIMENTAL PROGRAM REPORT. BOGER, ROBERT P.; AND OTHERS, NOV 69 191P.
EDRS PRICE MF-$0.65 HC-$6.58

THE PURPOSE OF THIS STUDY WAS TO DETERMINE THE EFFECTIVENESS OF PARENTS AS CHANGE AGENTS IN AN ONGOING HEAD START PROGRAM. SUBJECTS WERE 72 RURAL WHITE DISADVANTAGED AND ADVANTAGED CHILDREN AND THEIR PARENTS WHO WERE ASSIGNED TO THREE TREATMENT GROUPS: DEVELOPMENTAL LANGUAGE, STRUCTURED LANGUAGE, AND PLACEBO (WORKSHOP). MOTHERS MET IN 12 WEEKLY 2-HOUR INSTRUCTIONAL SESSIONS WITH TEACHERS, USING SPECIFIC MATERIALS DEVELOPED IN TEACHER-DIRECTED WORKSHOPS. (THESE METERIALS WERE NOT USED IN THE HEAD START PROGRAM DURING THE EXPERIMENTAL PERIOD.) PRE- AND POSTTESTS ON A VARIETY OF MEASURING INSTRUMENTS EVALUATED CHILDREN'S INTELLECTUAL, LINGUISTIC AND SELF CONCEPT PERFORMANCE. ALSO EVALUATED WAS THE QUALITY OF MOTHER-CHILD INTERACTION AND THE MOTHER'S STORYTELLING ABILITY. RESULTS OF THE STUDY SUPPORT THE MAJOR HYPOTHESES WHICH PREDICTED IMPROVEMENT IN LANGUAGE PERFORMANCE, INTELLECTUAL PERFORMANCE, SELF CONCEPT DEVELOPMENT, AND MOTHER CHILD INTERACTION, AS A RESULT OF A DIFFERENTIATED PARENT EDUCATION LANGUAGE PROGRAM. NO PROGRAM APPROACH WAS CLEARLY SUPERIOR BUT MOTHERS IN THE SPECIFIC CONTENT ORIENTED INTERVENTION PROGRAM INCREASED THEIR OWN VERBAL AND LINGUISTIC SKILLS AS WELL AS THE QUALITY OF INTERACTION WITH THEIR CHILDREN. CHILDREN WHOSE PARENTS WORK WITH THEM APPEAR TO HAVE A LEARNING ADVANTAGE. APPENDIXES COMPRISE MORE THAN 1/3 OF THE DOCUMENT. (NH)

ED044169 PS003312
REPORT OF CHILD PLACEMENT STUDY COMMITTEE, JANUARY, 1969. , 20 FEB 69 78P.
EDRS PRICE MF-$0.65 HC-$3.29
AVAILABLE FROM: CHILD PLACEMENT STUDY, RHODE ISLAND COUNCIL OF COMMUNITY SERVICES, INC., 333 GROTTO AVENUE, PROVIDENCE, RI 02906 ($2.00)

AS A FIRST STEP IN DETERMINING THE EFFECTIVENESS OF PROGRAMS FOR CHILDREN AND FAMILIES, THE RHODE ISLAND COUNCIL OF COMMUNITY SERVICES MADE AN OVERALL STUDY OF THE NUMBER AND TYPE OF CHILDREN IN CHILD PLACEMENT SERVICES. THE COUNCIL BASED ITS REPORT ON THE CHARACTERISTICS OF 420 RANDOMLY-SELECTED CHILDREN OF WHICH 211 WERE IN FOSTER HOME; 214 IN INSTITUTIONS AND SIX IN GROUP HOME CARE. INCLUDED ARE A DEFINITION OF CHILD PLACEMENT AND TRENDS, AND A DESCRIPTION OF AGENCIES WHICH PROVIDE CHILD PLACEMENT SERVICES. THE THIRTEEN RECOMMENDATIONS MADE BY THE COUNCIL COMPRISE FOUR-FIFTHS OF THE REPORT. THE RECOMMENDATIONS INCLUDE DEVELOPING SERVICES THAT ARE ANCILLARY AND LONG-TERM, UPGRADING DIAGNOSTIC PROCEDURES, ESTABLISHING GROUP HOMES UNDER A VARIETY OF AUSPICES FOR A VARIETY OF CLIENTELE, INCREASING AND DIVERSIFYING RESIDENTIAL CARE FOR THE EMOTIONALLY DISTURBED, UPDATING AND REVISING STATE LAWS, MORE AGGRESSIVELY SEEKING THE RELEASE OF CHILDREN WHOSE PARENTS ARE NOT FULFILLING THEIR CHILDREN'S NEEDS ADEQUATELY, SUBSIDIZING THE ADOPTION PROCESS WITH STATE FUNDS, CENTRALIZING ADOPTION FILES, CENTRALIZING AND SYSTEMATIZING PROCEDURES FOR DATA COLLECTION AND EVALUATION, AND APPOINTING A COMMITTEE TO ENSURE IMPLEMENTATION OF THE FOREGOING RECOMMENDATIONS. THE REPORT CONCLUDES WITH AN APPENDIX ON CHILD PLACEMENT SURVEY PROPOSALS. (WY)

ED044170 PS003423
A COMPARATIVE STUDY OF FAILURE AVOIDANCE IN CULTURALLY DISADVANTAGED AND NON-CULTURALLY DISADVANTAGED FIRST GRADE CHILDREN. WEBBINK, PATRICIA G.; STEDMAN, DONALD J., 66 8P.
EDRS PRICE MF-$0.65 HC-$3.29

THIS STUDY TESTS THE HYPOTHESIS THAT CULTURALLY DISADVANTAGED (CD) CHILDREN WOULD RETURN MORE OFTEN TO A COMPLETED TASK (ONE ON WHICH THEY HAD HAD PREVIOUS SUCCESS), WHILE NON-CULTURALLY DISADVANTAGED (NCD) CHILDREN WOULD RETURN MORE OFTEN TO AN INCOMPLETED TASK (TO ACHIEVE CLOSURE OR TO RE-TRY A TASK WHICH THEY HAD PREVIOUSLY FAILED.) FAILURE AVOIDANCE WOULD BE SHOWN IN CD CHILDREN BECAUSE OF EXPECTANCY FOR AND TOLERANCE OF FAILURE IN RESPONSE TO EARLY ENVIRONMENTAL CONDITIONS WHICH LACK ACHIEVEMENT MOTIVATION, WITH THE OPPOSITE TRUE OF NCD CHILDREN. SUBJECTS WERE 24 NCD AND 20 CD FIRST GRADERS. THE NCD CHILDREN WERE ENROLLED IN A PRIVATE SCHOOL ATTENDED BY UPPER MIDDLE CLASS CHILDREN, AND THE CD CHILDREN WERE ENROLLED IN A PUBLIC SCHOOL ATTENDED BY LOWER CLASS CHILDREN. EACH GROUP INCLUDED TWO NEGRO CHILDREN. EACH SUBJECT WAS INDIVIDUALLY GIVEN TWO PUZZLES TO ASSEMBLE WITHIN CERTAIN TIME LIMITS. FAILURE WAS EXPERIMENTALLY INDUCED ON ONE PUZZLE EXPERIENCE BECAUSE THE EXPERIMENTER ANNOUNCED THE TIME WAS UP BEFORE PUZZLE COMPLETION, BUT SUCCESS WAS ALLOWED ON THE OTHER PUZZLE EXPERIENCE BECAUSE AS MUCH TIME WAS GIVEN AS WAS NEEDED FOR COMPLETION. AFTER AN INTERIM PERIOD, THE SUBJECT WAS ASKED WHICH PUZZLE HE WOULD LIKE TO MAKE AGAIN. AN ANALYSIS OF THE REPETITION CHOICE DATA UPHELD THE ORIGINAL HYPOTHESIS AND CONCOMITANT STATEMENT. (NH)

ED044171 PS003429
AN EXPERIMENTAL PROGRAM IN CLASSIFICATION AND ATTENTIONAL TRAINING WITH HEAD START CHILDREN. BOGER, ROBERT P., 6 MAR 70 8P.
EDRS PRICE MF-$0.65 HC-$3.29

THIS REPORT PRESENTS THE RESEARCH DESIGN OF AN EXPERIMENTAL INTERVENTION TRAINING PROGRAM DESIGNED TO DETERMINE THE SIMILARITIES AND DIFFERENCES IN COGNITIVE OUTCOMES AS A FUNCTION OF CURRICULA BASED ON CLASSIFICATION AND ATTENTIONAL TRAINING. ANSWERS TO TWO QUESTIONS OF PRACTICAL IMPORTANCE WERE SOUGHT. GIVEN THAT THE TRAINING PROGRAM DEVELOPED BY SIGEL AND ASSOCIATES POSITIVELY MODIFIED THE COGNITIVE SKILLS OF LOWER CLASS CHILDREN, COULD THE MATERIALS BE ADAPTED FOR YOUNGER CHILDREN WITHOUT LOSING THE CHARACTER OF THE TRAINING? ALSO, COULD THE PROGRAM BE CARRIED OUT BY HEAD START TEACHERS RATHER THAN RESEARCH PROJECT PERSONNEL? TWO CLASSROOMS IN EACH OF TWO INDEPENDENT PROGRAMS (DETROIT AND PONTIAC, MICHIGAN) ADMINISTERED CLASSIFICATION TRAINING AND MATCHING PLACEBO (LANGUAGE TRAINING) ALONG WITH ATTENTION TRAINING AND ITS PLACEBO (PERCEPTUAL MOTOR TRAINING). IN EACH LOCATION, ONE CLASSROOM WAS USED AS A PURE CONTROL. TEACHERS WERE SELECTED FROM A WELL QUALIFIED VOLUNTEER GROUP. A TOTAL OF TEN TEACHERS AND 160 CHILDREN PARTICIPATED IN THIS FIELD TEST. A CORE BATTERY OF MEASURES EMPLOYED BY THE 1968 NATIONAL HEAD START EVALUATION MODEL WAS GIVEN AND SUPPLEMENTED BY MEASURES CRITICAL TO THIS PROGRAM DESIGN. A TYPICAL PRE- AND POSTTEST RESEARCH DESIGN WAS USED. SEE COMPANION PAPER PS 003 428 WHICH DISCUSSES THE ACTUAL TRAINING INPUTS AND PS 003 430 WHICH PRESENTS THE STATISTICAL ANALYSIS AND RESULTS. (WY)

ED044172 PS003431
EVALUATION OF FOLLOW THROUGH, 1968 - 1969. , [69] 57P.
EDRS PRICE MF-$0.65 HC-$3.29

TO ASSESS THE IMPACT OF THE FOLLOW THROUGH PROGRAM IN PRINCE GEORGE'S COUNTY, MARYLAND, DATA FROM FIVE SOURCES WERE COLLECTED AND COMPILED. PARTICIPATING KINDERGARTEN AND FIRST GRADE TEACHERS SUBMITTED TEST SCORES FROM TWO READINESS MEASURES ADMINISTERED ON A PRE- AND POSTTEST BASIS FOR THE CHILDREN INVOLVED. REPORTS FROM SPECIALIZED PERSONNEL INDICATE THE KIND AND QUANTITY OF SERVICES PROVIDED: THE PSYCHOLOGIST, WHO WAS EMPLOYED ON A PART-TIME BASIS, EVALUATED SIXTEEN CHILDREN AND INITIATED EVALUATION PROCEDURES FOR SIX CHILDREN; THE SOCIAL WORKERS RENDERED SERVICES TO BENEFIT 1,848 PERSONS; SCHOOL HEALTH WORKERS ATTEMPTED TO MEET THE NEEDS OF 226 CHILDREN THROUGH SCREENING TESTS, REFERRALS AND AN IMMUNIZATION PROGRAM; PARENT HELPERS DESCRIBED WEEKLY CLASSES AND ACTIVITIES WHICH WERE GEARED TO ADVANCING PARENTS' PERSONAL, SCHOOL, AND COMMUNITY INTERESTS. PARENT PROGRAM CONTENT AND PARENT ATTENDANCE RECORDS ARE SEPARATELY LISTED. A LIST OF FIELD TRIPS AND VISITATIONS IN WHICH PARENTS PARTICIPATED IS ALSO PROVIDED. CHILDREN'S GAINS IN READINESS WERE INDICATED BY TEST SCORES ON BOTH TEST INSTRUMENTS. TOTAL PROGRAM EFFECTS WERE

DEEMED BENEFICIAL AND FOUR RECOMMENDATIONS FOR IMPROVING FUTURE PROGRAMS ARE MADE. (WY)

ED044173 PS003434
DEVELOPMENTAL-BEHAVIORAL PATTERNS IN TWENTY-SIX CULTURALLY DISADVANTAGED INFANTS. STEDMAN, DONALD J., [67] 8P.
EDRS PRICE MF-$0.65 HC-$3.29

THIS INTERIM REPORT IS PART OF A LONGITUDINAL STUDY OF DEVELOPMENTAL BEHAVIOR DESIGNED TO DETERMINE WHETHER INFANTS FROM CULTURALLY DISADVANTAGED HOMES HAVE DIFFERENT DEVELOPMENTAL PATTERNS THAN INFANTS FROM ADVANTAGED HOMES. TWENTY SIX CULTURALLY DISADVANTAGED INFANTS WERE INDIVIDUALLY EVALUATED ON THE BAYLEY SCALE OF INFANT MENTAL AND MOTOR DEVELOPMENT AND THE BAYLEY INFANT BEHAVIOR PROFILE AT 1, 2, 3 AND 6 MONTHS OF AGE. THE MOTHER OF THE INFANT AND A SPECIAL EVALUATOR/OBSERVER WERE PRESENT AS EACH BABY WAS EVALUATED. THE RESULTING MENTAL, MOTOR AND BEHAVIOR DATA INDICATED AVERAGE TO ABOVE AVERAGE MENTAL AND MOTOR QUOTIENTS AND "NORMAL" EARLY BEHAVIOR PATTERNS. SINCE OLDER DISADVANTAGED CHILDREN PERFORM AT SUBNORMAL LEVELS ON STANDARDIZED TESTS, IT WAS NOTED THAT THESE DATA HIGHLIGHT THE SECOND AND THIRD YEARS OF LIFE AS CRUCIAL TO THE DEVELOPMENT OF PATTERNS RELATED TO INTELLECTUAL DEVELOPMENT. (NH)

ED044174 PS003435
AN EXPERIMENTAL SUMMER KINDERGARTEN FOR CULTURALLY DEPRIVED CHILDREN. WASIK, BARBARA H.; SIBLEY, SALLY A., MAR 69 93P.
EDRS PRICE MF-$0.65 HC-$3.29

TWENTY CULTURALLY DEPRIVED CHILDREN PLANNING TO ENTER FIRST GRADE IN THE FALL ATTENDED AN 8-WEEK HALF-DAY SUMMER PROGRAM IN WHICH A SYSTEMATIC CLASSROOM MANAGEMENT PROGRAM UTILIZING TOKEN REINFORCEMENT AND ISOLATION TECHNIQUES WAS COMBINED WITH A STRONG ACADEMIC PROGRAM. ONE HOUR AND 40 MINUTES WAS ALLOTTED DAILY TO PRE-READING AND LANGUAGE PROGRAMS (SULLIVAN READING READINESS, 20 MINUTES; PHONICS, 20 MINUTES; SUPPLEMENTARY LANGUAGE ACTIVITIES, 20 MINUTES; LANGUAGE-ORIENTED ART, MUSIC OR OTHER SUPPLEMENTARY ACTIVITIES, 40 MINUTES). TWO ADDITIONAL PROGRAMS, STRESSING COGNITIVE SKILLS WERE DESIGNED TO INCREASE PROFICIENCY IN SUCH AREAS AS VERBAL FLUENCY, FOLLOWING INSTRUCTIONS, MANIPULATIVE ACTIVITIES, AND CLASSIFICATION. CUISENAIRE RODS WERE USED IN THE ARITHMETIC PROGRAM, SCHEDULED DAILY FOR ONE-HALF HOUR. THREE MAJOR AREAS OF SKILLS (INTELLIGENCE, LANGUAGE AND PRE-READING, AND SOCIAL MATURITY) WERE ASSESSED BY A BATTERY OF PRE- AND POSTTESTS. SIGNIFICANT GAINS WERE SHOWN IN THE AREAS OF LANGUAGE, SPEECH, PRE-READING AND ARITHMETIC, AND IN THE ABILITY TO HANDLE ABSTRACT CONCEPTS. CHILDREN WILL BE ASSESSED AGAIN AT THE END OF FIRST GRADE TO FIND OUT IF GAINS ARE BEING MAINTAINED. RESULTS OF TESTS ASSESSING SOCIAL MATURITY WERE INCONCLUSIVE. (NH)

ED044175 PS003439
THE EFFECT OF THREE HOME VISITING STRATEGIES UPON MEASURES OF CHILDREN'S ACADEMIC APTITUDE AND MATERNAL TEACHING BEHAVIORS. FINAL REPORT. BARBRACK, CHRISTOPHER R., FEB 70 72P.
EDRS PRICE MF-$0.65 HC-$3.29

HOME VISITORS WERE USED TO TEACH MOTHERS TO BE MORE EFFECTIVE EDUCATIONAL CHANGE AGENTS IN THEIR OWN HOMES. THE ONE-HOUR VISITS CONTINUED OVER 30 WEEKS. THE INITIAL SAMPLE CONSISTED OF 72 NEGRO MOTHERS AND THEIR FIRST GRADE CHILDREN. ALL CHILDREN HAS HAD 8-WEEK SUMMER HEAD START. FIVE TREATMENT GROUPS WERE (1) MOTHER-INVOLVED COGNITIVE HOME VISITOR ACTIVELY SOLICITED THE MOTHERS' PARTICIPATION, AND CONTENT SUPPLEMENTED THE FIRST GRADE CURRICULUM, (2) CHILD-CENTERED COGNITIVE HOME VISITOR WORKED ONLY WITH THE CHILDREN AND DID NOT SOLICIT MOTHER INVOLVEMENT, CONTENT SAME AS FOR FIRST GROUP, (3) MOTHER-INVOLVED PHYSICAL TRAINING HOME VISITOR ACTIVELY SOLICITED MOTHERS' PARTICIPATION, CONTENT DESIGNED TO TEACH GROSS MOTOR ACTIVITIES, (4) LOCAL CONTROL, AND (5) DISTAL CONTROL. THE CHILDREN WERE PRE- AND POSTTESTED ON MEASURES OF INTELLIGENCE, READINESS AND ACHIEVEMENT, AND THE MATERNAL TEACHING STYLE INSTRUMENT WAS USED TO ASSESS THE MOTHERS' TEACHING BEHAVIOR. RESULTS SUGGEST THAT A GOOD TREATMENT PROGRAM MIGHT BE A COGNITIVE PROGRAM WHICH WORKS TO INVOLVE THE MOTHER BY FIRST DEMONSTRATING IMPROVEMENTS IN THE CHILD'S BEHAVIOR. (NH)

ED044176 PS003440
SENSORHESIS AS A MOTIVE FOR PLAY AND STEREOTYPED BEHAVIOR. ELLIS, M. J., 17 DEC 69 27P.
EDRS PRICE MF-$0.65 HC-$3.29

THIS PAPER ATTEMPTS A UNIFIED EXPLANATION OF SUCH APPARENTLY NON-UTILITARIAN BEHAVIORS AS CURIOSITY, MANIPULATION, AND EXPLORATION AS MANIFESTATIONS OF "PLAYFUL BEHAVIORS" ON THE ONE HAND AND STEREOTYPED RESPONSES ON THE OTHER. SENSORHESIS NAMES THE NEW THEORY OFFERED TO EXPLAIN THE EXISTENCE AND NATURE OF PLAYFUL BEHAVIOR. PLAY AND STEREOTYPED BEHAVIORS ARE JUXTAPOSED ON THE SAME CONTINUUM BY VIRTUE OF THEIR POSSIBLE OPPOSITE ACTION IN MAINTAINING OPTIMAL STIMULUS INPUT IN AN ORGANISM (O). PLAY GENERATES LARGE INFORMATION LOADS BY VIRTUE OF ITS ELEMENTS OF NOVELY; STEREOTYPED BEHAVIOR GENERATES MINIMAL INFORMATION EITHER AS A SUBSTITUTION FOR STRESSFUL STIMULUS INPUT OR A BACUUM ACTIVITY UNDER CONDITIONS OF PERCEPTUAL DEPRIVATION. THE ADAPTATION OF THE O TO A GIVEN LEVEL OF STIMULUS COMPLEXITY REQUIRES AN INCREASINGLY COMPLEX INTERACTION WITH THE ENVIRONMENT TO MAINTAIN THE INFORMATION FLOW AND OPTIMAL AROUSAL. (WY)

ED044177 PS003449
MOTHER-CHILD INTERACTION: SOCIAL CLASS DIFFERENCES IN THE FIRST YEAR OF LIFE. TULKIN, STEVEN R.; KAGAN, JEROME, 70 2P.
DOCUMENT NOT AVAILABLE FROM EDRS.
AVAILABLE FROM: AMERICAN PSYCHOLOGICAL ASSOCIATION, 1201 17TH ST., N.W., WASHINGTON, D.C. 20036 (PROCEEDINGS, 78TH ANNUAL CONVENTION, APA, 1970

TO STUDY MATERNAL BEHAVIORS AS RELATED TO SOCIAL CLASS DIFFERENCES, 30 MIDDLE CLASS AND 30 WORKING CLASS WHITE MOTHERS WERE OBSERVED AT HOME ON TWO SEPARATE DAYS WITH THEIR 10-MONTH-OLD FIRSTBORN BABY GIRLS. PREDESIGNATED BEHAVIORS WHICH OCCURRED DURING 5-SECOND INTERVALS WERE RECORDED BY AN OBSERVER. TOTAL OBSERVATION TIME WAS 4 HOURS FOR EACH MOTHER AND CHILD. FINDINGS SHOWED THAT THE WORKING CLASS CHILDREN'S ENVIRONMENTS WERE MORE CROWDED AND PROVIDED LESS OPPORTUNITY FOR EXPLORATION AND MANIPULATION. LITTLE SOCIAL CLASS DIFFERENCE WAS FOUND FOR MOTHERS' NONVERBAL BEHAVIOR (SUCH AS TIME SPENT IN CLOSE PROXIMITY TO THE INFANT, KISSING, OR HOLDING). HOWEVER, DRAMATIC DIFFERENCES WERE FOUND FOR THE MOTHERS' VERBAL BEHAVIORS. MIDDLE CLASS MOTHERS MORE OFTEN: (1) INITIATED VOCALIZATION, (2) RESPONDED VOCALLY TO THEIR INFANT'S VOCALIZATIONS, (3) IMITATED INFANTS' VOCALIZATIONS, AND (4) PRAISED THEIR INFANTS VOCALLY. MIDDLE CLASS MOTHERS MORE OFTEN ENTERTAINED THEIR INFANTS AND RESPONDED MORE QUICKLY AND MORE FREQUENTLY TO THEIR INFANTS' FRETTING. MATERNAL DIFFERENCES SEEMED RELATED TO VARIOUS FACTORS, INCLUDING DIFFERENT CONCEPTIONS OF INFANCY AND DIFFERENT VALUES. WORKING CLASS MOTHERS LACKED CONFIDENCE IN THEIR ABILITY TO INFLUENCE THEIR CHILDRENS' DEVELOPMENT. (NH)

ED044178 PS003458
A PILOT INVESTIGATION OF THE EFFECTS OF TRAINING TECHNIQUES DESIGNED TO ACCELERATE CHILDRENS' ACQUISITION OF CONSERVATION OF DISCONTINUOUS QUANTITY. FINAL REPORT. FEIGENBAUM, KENNETH D., AUG 68 41P.
EDRS PRICE MF-$0.65 HC NOT AVAILABLE FROM EDRS.

THE PURPOSE OF THIS STUDY WAS TO TEST TRAINING TECHNIQUES DESIGNED (1) TO INDUCE CONSERVATION OF DISCONTINUOUS QUANTITY IN CHILDREN, AND (2) TO INDUCE ABILITY TO TAKE DIFFERENT SOCIAL ROLES. ALSO TESTED WAS THIS HYPOTHESIS: SUCCESSFULLY TRAINING CHILDREN IN CONSERVATION WILL IMPROVE THEIR ABILITY TO TAKE DIFFERENT SOCIAL ROLES, AND CONVERSELY, SUCCESSFULLY TRAINING CHILDREN TO TAKE DIFFERENT SOCIAL ROLES WILL INDUCE CONSERVATION IN THEM. A HETEROGENEOUS SAMPLE POPULATION OF 103 CHILDREN (AGED 45 TO 64 MONTHS) WAS GIVEN A BATTERY OF TESTS TO MEASURE GRASP OF CORRESPONDENCE, CONSERVATION, PHYSICAL PERSPECTIVE, AND SOCIAL ROLE PLAY. CHILDREN WERE PLACED IN 8 HETEROGENEOUS GROUPS. EACH OF SEVEN OF THESE GROUPS WAS GIVEN A 6-WEEK TRAINING PROGRAM INVOLVING A DIFFERENT COMBINATION OF THREE BASIC CONDITIONS: REVERSIBILITY-RECIPROCITY, PHYSICAL PERSPECTIVE-TAKING, AND SOCIAL ROLE-PLAY. THE EIGHTH GROUP (CONTROL) WAS GIVEN NO TRAINING. SUBJECTS WERE POSTTESTED ON THE PRETEST BATTERY. RESULTS INDICATE THAT REVERSIBILITY-RECIPROCITY TRAINING DOES INDUCE CONSERVATION OF DISCONTINUOUS QUANTITIES IN CHILDREN, AND THAT IMPROVEMENT IN CHILDREN'S SOCIAL ROLE-TAKING ABILITY IS MORE CLOSELY ASSOCIATED WITH REVERSIBILITY-RECIPROCITY TRAINING THAN WITH OTHER KINDS OF TRAINING. [NOT AVAILABLE IN HARD COPY DUE TO MARGINAL LEGIBILITY OF ORIGINAL DOCUMENT.] (AUTHOR/WY)

ED044179 PS003655
CHILDREN'S CONSERVATION OF MULTIPLE SPACE RELATIONS: EFFECTS OF PERCEPTION AND REPRESENTATION. KERSHNER, JOHN R., 1 APR 70 17P.
EDRS PRICE MF-$0.65 HC-$3.29

ONE HUNDRED AND SIXTY FIRST GRADE BOYS AND GIRLS OF NORMAL INTELLIGENCE WERE TESTED FOR ABILITY TO CONSERVE MULTIPLE SPACE RELATIONS. THE CRITERION TASK APPARATUS WAS A WOODEN T WITH A MODEL OF SCHOOLHOUSE ATTACHED AND CENTERED ABOVE THE POINT OF CONTACT OF THE HORIZONTAL AND VERTICAL AXIS. THE T HAD A TRACK RUNNING THE LENGTH OF BOTH ITS AXES ALONG WHICH A SMALL CAR COULD BE MANUALLY DIRECTED. THE CHILD WAS ASKED TO REPRODUCE THE SPACE RELATIONS REPRESENTED BY THE EXAMINER'S CONFIGURATION BY DIRECTING THE CAR AND/OR ROTATING THE T. AN ANALYSIS OF TASK-RELATED ERRORS SUPPORTED PIAGET'S NOTION OF REPRESENTATIONAL SPACE AND THE IMPORTANCE OF PARTICULAR FIELD CONFIGURATIONS. A FIGURE'S RELATIVE POSITION WAS HIGHLY IMPORTANT TO SUCCESSFUL PERFORMANCE WHEREAS ABSOLUTE ORIENTATION WAS A SECONDARY FACTOR. MORE DIFFICULTY IN REPRODUCING SPACE RELATIONS WAS EXPERIENCED BY THE CHILDREN ON A 180 DEGREE TRANSFORMED FIELD THAN IN 90 DEGREE RIGHT AND

90 DEGREE LEFT ROTATIONS. AN EXPLANATION FOR THE MANNER IN WHICH REVERSALS OF SYMMETRICAL FIGURES MAY OCCUR WAS ALSO PRESENTED. RESULTS SUGGEST THAT THE ABILITY TO FORM AND RETAIN A FLEXIBLE AND REVERSIBLE MEMORY IMAGE MAY BE OF PARAMOUNT IMPORTANCE IN THE ACQUISITION OF A HORIZONTAL-VERTICAL SYSTEM. (AUTHOR/WY)

ED044180 PS003855

PREDICTION OF ACHIEVEMENT IN THE FIRST PRIMARY YEAR. STUDY NUMBER ONE. , DEC 69 12P.

EDRS PRICE MF-$0.65 HC-$3.29

THIS REPORT IS PART OF A 4-YEAR STUDY OF PREKINDERGARTEN AND KINDERGARTEN CHILDREN DESIGNED TO PROVIDE DATA PREDICTIVE OF CHILDREN'S SCHOOL ACHIEVEMENT. A TOTAL OF 109 BOYS AND GIRLS WERE GIVEN THE COMPLETE ASSESSMENT BATTERY, METROPOLITAN READINESS TESTS (MRT), AND THE CALIFORNIA SHORT-FORM TEST OF MENTAL MATURITY AT THE END OF KINDERGARTEN OR IN THE MIDDLE OF THE FIRST PRIMARY YEAR. TEST SCORES WERE COMPARED WITH THE SAME CHILDREN'S SCORES ON THE STANFORD ACHIEVEMENT TEST GIVEN AT THE END OF THE FIRST PRIMARY YEAR. OF THE 24 FACTORS USED IN PREDICTION, EXCLUSIVE OF AGE AND SEX, THE TOTAL RAW SCORE OF THE MRT (WHICH CAN BE GIVEN TO GROUPS OF EIGHT OR TEN CHILDREN) ADMINISTERED AT THE END OF KINDERGARTEN APPEARED TO BE THE MOST PRACTICAL PREDICTOR OF PERFORMANCE AS MEASURED BY THE STANFORD ACHIEVEMENT TEST AT THE END OF THE FIRST PRIMARY YEAR. ONLY SLIGHT IMPROVEMENT IN PREDICTION WAS GAINED BY USING COMBINATIONS OF TESTS IN THE COMPLETE ASSESSMENT BATTERY, WITH MRT SUBTESTS. (AUTHOR/NH)

ED044181 PS003857

DEVELOPMENTAL SKILL AND ACHIEVEMENT DIFFERENCES OF CHILDREN IDENTIFIED AS EXCELLENT, GOOD, AND AVERAGE IN READING AND ARITHMETIC ACHIEVEMENT. STUDY NUMBER THREE. , APR 70 23P.

EDRS PRICE MF-$0.65 HC-$3.29

THIS STUDY SOUGHT TO IDENTIFY: (1) SPECIFIC DEVELOPMENTAL SKILLS OR PATTERNS OF SKILLS WHICH CONTRIBUTED SIGNIFICANTLY TO SUCCESS AND NONSUCCESS IN READING AND ARITHMETIC, AND (2) RELATIONSHIPS OF EXCELLENT, GOOD, AND AVERAGE ACHIEVERS IN READING AND ARITHMETIC TO SUCCESS IN OTHER ASPECTS OF ACHIEVEMENT. A COMPLETE ASSESSMENT BATTERY (ITPA, PPVT AND TESTS OF AUDITORY DISCRIMINATION, VISUAL-MOTOR INTEGRATION AND MOTOR COORDINATION) WAS GIVEN INDIVIDUALLY TO 103 BOYS AND GIRLS BEFORE THEY ENTERED KINDERGARTEN. THE CHILDREN WERE IDENTIFIED AS EXCELLENT, GOOD, OR AVERAGE ACHIEVERS BY A TABULATION OF GRADE EQUIVALENT SCORES ON THE STANFORD ACHIEVEMENT TEST GIVEN AT THE END OF THE FIRST PRIMARY YEAR. ANALYSIS INDICATES THAT ITPA-3 WHICH MEASURES ABILITY TO COMPLETE VERBAL ANALOGIES, DIFFERENTIATES BETWEEN ACHIEVERS IN 11 OF 12 COMPARISONS. THERE APPEARS TO BE A THRESHOLD IN CERTAIN READING AND ARITHMETIC SKILLS WHICH SEPARATES THE EXCELLENT AND GOOD ACHIEVERS FROM THE AVERAGE, AND FOR WHICH SEX DIFFERENCES ARE SHOWN. MORE DEVELOPMENTAL SKILLS TESTS DIFFERENTIATED THE THREE GROUPS OF ACHIEVERS IN ARITHMETIC THAN IN READING, AND DIFFERENTIATED AMONG BOYS MORE THAN GIRLS. GIRLS WHO RATED AVERAGE IN ONE ASPECT OF ACHIEVEMENT TENDED TO MAINTAIN AN AVERAGE LEVEL IN OTHER ASPECTS OF ACHIEVEMENT. (AUTHOR/NH)

ED044182 PS003858

REVIEW OF SELECTED EARLY EDUCATION RESEARCH IN THE SCHOOL DISTRICT OF UNIVERSITY CITY, MISSOURI, JUNE, 1970. , JUN 70 16P.

EDRS PRICE MF-$0.65 HC-$3.29

MAJOR FINDINGS FROM BOTH THE RESEARCH EFFORT IN EARLY EDUCATION AND THE PREKINDERGARTEN EXPERIMENTS UNDERTAKEN BY THE SCHOOL DISTRICT OF UNIVERSITY CITY ARE SUMMARIZED BRIEFLY IN THIS REPORT. THE RESEARCH EFFORT BEGAN IN 1963 UPON RECEIPT OF A THREE-YEAR FORD FOUNDATION GRANT. AS A FIRST STEP, A SURVEY WAS CONDUCTED AMONG TEACHERS TO IDENTIFY PROBLEMS OF MAJOR CONCERN. LEARNING PROBLEMS OF CHILDREN PROVED TO BE A HIGH PRIORITY ITEM. RESEARCH LITERATURE RELATED TO THE LEARNING PROBLEMS OF CHILDREN AFFECTING DEVELOPMENT OF SKILLS IN MOTOR, MULTI-SENSORY, VISUAL, COGNITIVE, AND LANGUAGE AREAS WAS INTENSELY EXAMINED BETWEEN 1963 AND 1965. IN 1966, A GRANT FROM THE FEDERAL GOVERNMENT MADE POSSIBLE THE ESTABLISHMENT OF EXPERIMENTAL PREKINDERGARTENS FOR 100 FOUR-YEAR-OLDS IN TWO CONSECUTIVE YEARS. DISCUSSED IN THIS REPORT ARE: EARLY LOCAL RESEARCH FINDINGS: INTERIM END OF YEAR FINDINGS; RESULTING PROGRAM IMPACT; PREDICTION OF ACHIEVEMENT AND LOGICAL REASONING TO STRENGTHEN LEARNING; TEACHERS' INTEREST IN RESEARCH; AND DISCUSSION. REFERENCES, TWO BIBLIOGRAPHIES, AND AN APPENDIX HIGHLIGHT BACKGROUND SOURCE MATERIAL. (WY)

ED044183 PS003865

THE PROFESSIONAL SELF IMAGE AND THE ATTRIBUTES OF A PROFESSION: AN EXPLORATORY STUDY OF THE PRESCHOOL TEACHER. HANDLER, ELLEN O., [70] 21P.

EDRS PRICE MF-$0.65 HC-$3.29

IN THIS STUDY OF THE PROFESSIONAL IMAGE OF 21 PRESCHOOL TEACHERS IN A SINGLE URBAN COMMUNITY, PARTICIPANTS WERE FIRST OBSERVED IN PROGRAM SETTINGS AND LATER INTERVIEWED. STUDY FINDINGS ARE BASED ON INTERVIEW RESULTS. TEACHERS WORKED IN SIX DIFFERENT TYPES OF PROGRAMS (REPRESENTING HALF DAY AND FULL DAY CARE) AND PUBLIC AND PRIVATE NURSERY SCHOOLS. ALL TEACHERS WERE FEMALE, 19 TO 66 YEARS OF AGE; EDUCATIONAL LEVEL RANGED FROM COMPLETION OF NINTH GRADE TO MASTER'S DEGREE LEVEL. SUBJECTS WERE ASKED TO NAME TRAITS ASSOCIATED WITH BEING A "PROFESSIONAL" AND ALL BUT SIX REFERRED TO THESE FOUR: ADEQUATE TRAINING, ACCREDITATION, WORK AS A VOCATION, AUTONOMY IN DECISION MAKING. MOST TEACHERS DEFINED THEIR OCCUPATIONAL GROUP AS PROFESSIONAL, AND ALMOST HALF THE GROUP DESCRIBED THEMSELVES AS FULL PROFESSIONALS. PROFESSIONAL SELF IMAGE SEEMED DIRECTLY ATTRIBUTABLE TO THE AMOUNT OF EDUCATION ATTAINED. A LACK OF TEACHER AGREEMENT ON THE RANKING OF BASIC GOALS IN PRESCHOOL TEACHING REFLECTED THE FUNDAMENTAL DISAGREEMENT AMONG LEADERS IN THE FIELD. LACK OF CONFIRMATION OF THE IMPORTANCE OF SHARED VALUES AND NORMS APPEARS TO HANDICAP DEVELOPMENT OF A PROFESSIONAL IMAGE. FINDINGS SUGGEST THAT DEVELOPMENT OF A PROFESSIONAL SELF IMAGE OCCURS RELATIVELY EARLY IN THE PROCESS OF PROFESSIONALIZATION. (NH)

ED044184 PS003917

THE EFFECTS OF DIFFERENT TYPES OF REINFORCEMENT ON YOUNG CHILDREN'S INCIDENTAL LEARNING. SIEGEL, ALEXANDER W.; VAN CARA, FLO, 70 18P.

EDRS PRICE MF-$0.65 HC-$3.29

ONE HUNDRED AND EIGHT KINDERGARTEN AND ELEMENTARY SCHOOL CHILDREN, 36 AT EACH OF THREE AGE LEVELS (5, 7, AND 9 YEARS) PARTICIPATED IN THE EXPERIMENT. ALL CHILDREN WERE PRESENTED A THREE-PART SUCCESSIVE DISCRIMINATION TASK; ORIGINAL LEARNING, PRESENTATION OF INCIDENTAL STIMULI, AND A TEST OF RECONGITION AND RECALL OF THE INCIDENTAL MATERIAL. ONE-THIRD OF THE SUBJECTS AT EACH AGE LEVEL LEARNED THE ORIGINAL TASK (INTENTIONAL LEARNING) UNDER ONE OF THREE REINFORCEMENT CONDITIONS; RIGHT-BLANK, RIGHT-WRONG, OR WRONG-BLANK. CONTRARY TO PREDICTION, THERE WERE NO AGE DIFFERENCES IN INCIDENTAL RECOGNITION OR RECALL (PREVIOUS STUDIES HAD FOUND A CURVILINEAR RELATION BETWEEN AGE AND INCIDENTAL LEARNING.) ALTHOUGH THE MAIN EFFECT OF REINFORCEMENT CONDITION WAS NOT SIGNIFICANT FOR TRAILS TO CRITERION ON INTENTIONAL LEARNING, CHILDREN OF ALL AGES WHO LEARNED THE ORIGINAL DISCRIMINATION UNDER THE WRONG-BLANK CONDITION SHOWED SIGNIFICANTLY HIGHER INCIDENTAL RECOGNITION AND RECALL THAN SUBJECTS TESTED UNDER THE RIGHT-WRONG AND WRONG-BLANK CONDITIONS. RESULTS WERE DISCUSSED IN TERMS OF THE EFFECTS OF A WRONG-BLANK REINFORCEMENT PROCEDURE ON THE CHILD'S ATTENTION TO THE TASK. (AUTHOR)

ED044185 PS004026

DISSEMINATION AND UTILIZATION OF KNOWLEDGE IN THE AREA OF EARLY CHILDHOOD EDUCATION: A DESCRIPTION OF SOME OF THE PROBLEMS. O'NEIL, BARBARA B., SEP 70 7P.

EDRS PRICE MF-$0.65 HC-$3.29

TO BE EFFECTIVE, INFORMATION ON EARLY CHILDHOOD EDUCATION SHOULD (1) BE DIRECTED TOWARDS THE APPROPRIATE AUDIENCE, (2) BE WRITTEN SO THAT IT IS UNDERSTANDABLE TO THAT AUDIENCE, AND (3) PROVIDE DATA TO HELP THE USER MAKE MEANINGFUL JUDGEMENTS. THE WIDE RANGE OF EDUCATIONAL AND OCCUPATIONAL LEVELS OF PEOPLE WORKING IN THE FIELD OF EARLY CHILDHOOD EDUCATION NECESSITATES DIFFERENT TREATMENTS OF THE SAME MESSAGE. MOREOVER, THERE IS A NEED FOR MORE FEEDBACK BETWEEN THE RESEARCHER AND THE PRACTITIONER TO DIRECT RESEARCH TO THE SALIENT PROBLEMS AND TO MAKE THE RESULTS OF RESEARCH MORE USEABLE. THE ERIC CLEARINGHOUSE ON EARLY CHILDHOOD EDUCATION (ERIC/ECE) IS AN INFORMATION ANALYSIS CENTER WHICH SERVES AS A SYNERGISTIC INFORMATION LINK BETWEEN RESOURCES AND THE USERS OF RESOURCES. THE ROLE OF ERIC/ECE AS A DISSEMINATOR OF NEW IDEA, NEW RESEARCH, AND NEW PRODUCTS IS DISCUSSED IN RELATION TO THE OVERALL GOAL OF PROVIDING BETTER EDUCATION FOR CHILDREN. THIS PAPER IS TO APPEAR AS PART OF A CHAPTER ENTITLED "STATE-OF-THE-ART IN EDUCATIONAL DIFFUSION" TO BE PUBLISHED BY THE TUSKEGEE INSTITUTE AND THE NATIONAL FEDERATION FOR THE IMPROVEMENT OF RURAL EDUCATION. (AUTHOR/NH)

ED044186 PS004128
INCREASING VERBAL COMMUNICATION SKILLS IN CULTURALLY DISADVANTAGED PRE-SCHOOL CHILDREN. FINAL REPORT. ROSS, ALAN O.; AND OTHERS, AUG 69 51P.
EDRS PRICE MF-$0.65 HC-$3.29

AFTER TAKING BASE RATE MEASURES OF VERBAL BEHAVIOR, USING A SPECIALLY DEVISED STORY TELLING TEST AND SELECTED SUB-TESTS FROM THE ILLINOIS TEST OF PSYCHOLINGUISTIC ABILITIES, 34 CHILDREN WITH A MEAN AGE OF 4-4, ATTENDING A YEAR-ROUND HEAD START PROGRAM, WERE ASSIGNED TO MATCHED EXPERIMENTAL AND CONTROL GROUPS. THE CHILDREN IN THE EXPERIMENTAL GROUP PARTICIPATED IN DAILY HALF-HOUR GROUP SESSIONS FOR A PERIOD OF SEVEN WEEKS DURING WHICH THEY WERE GIVEN SYSTEMATIC LANGUAGE TRAINING, BASED ON REINFORCEMENT PRINCIPLES. THE CHILDREN IN THE CONTROL GROUP CONTINUED TO PARTICIPATE IN THE REGULAR HEAD START PROGRAM. UPON CONCLUSION OF THE TRAINING PERIOD, ALL CHILDREN WERE RE-TESTED, WITH THE MEASURES USED IN THE PRE-TEST. SIGNIFICANT IMPROVEMENTS IN SCORES ON THE PART OF THE EXPERIMENTAL GROUP WERE FOUND FOR DECREASE-IN-VERB-OMISSION ON THE STORY TELLING TEST AND FOR THE VOCAL-ENCODING SUB-TEST OF THE ITPA. PRONOUNCED SEX DIFFERENCES WERE APPARENT. GIRLS IN BOTH GROUPS SHOWED IMPROVEMENT FOR DECREASE-IN-VERB OMISSION AND FOR VOCAL-ENCODING. AMONG THE BOYS, ONLY THOSE IN THE EXPERIMENTAL GROUP IMPROVED; THOSE IN THE CONTROL GROUP SHOWED SOME DECREASE IN SCORES. DISCUSSION OF RESULTS SUGGESTS THE POSSIBILITY OF A CROSS-SEX EFFECT. (AUTHOR/NH)

ED045174 PS001987
INFANT STIMULATION AND THE ETIOLOGY OF COGNITIVE PROCESSES. FOWLER, WILLIAM, JUN 66 110P.
EDRS PRICE MF-$0.65 HC-$6.58

WHAT DATA, PROBLEMS, AND CONCEPTS ARE MOST RELEVANT IN DETERMINING THE ROLE OF STIMULATION IN HUMAN DEVELOPMENT? A CRITICAL ANALYSIS OF THE RELATIONSHIPS BETWEEN LONG TERM STIMULATION, BEHAVIOR, AND COGNITIVE FUNCTIONING AND DEVELOPMENT POINTS UP BIASES AND GAPS IN PAST AS WELL AS CONTEMPORARY APPROACHES. EACH OF THE FOUR SECTIONS OF THIS PAPER FOCUSES UPON A CENTRAL TOPIC AND RELATED ISSUES. THEORETICAL AND METHODOLOGICAL BACKGROUND AND A REVIEW OF SALIENT FEATURES OF CERTAIN THEORIES OF INFANT AND CHILD DEVELOPMENT ARE THE FIRST TOPICS CONSIDERED. IN THE THIRD SECTION, A ROUGH CONCEPTUAL FRAMEWORK IS CONSTRUCTED TO AID IN INTERPRETING RESEARCH STUDIES AND TO FURNISH GUIDEPOSTS FOR FURTHER EMPIRICAL EXPLORATION. THE LAST SECTION PRESENTS SELECTIVELY REVIEWED STUDIES ON INFANT LEARNING AND COGNITION BY FIRST ANALYZING RESEARCH ON THE EARLY MONTHS OF INFANCY AND BY SURVEYING SUBSEQUENT DEVELOPMENT IN SENSORIMOTOR, PERCEPTUAL, AND SYMBOLIC MODES. AN EXTENSIVE BIBLIOGRAPHY IS INCLUDED. (WY)

ED045175 PS002888
CHILD CARE AND WORKING MOTHERS: A STUDY OF ARRANGEMENTS MADE FOR DAYTIME CARE OF CHILDREN. RUDERMAN, FLORENCE A., 68 392P.
DOCUMENT NOT AVAILABLE FROM EDRS.
AVAILABLE FROM: CHILD WELFARE LEAGUE OF AMERICA, INC., 44 E. 23RD ST., NEW YORK, N.Y. 10010 ($7.50)

IN 1960, THE CHILD WELFARE LEAGUE OF AMERICA BEGAN THE DAY CARE PROJECT TO SURVEY RESEARCH TO CLARIFY AND REVISE DAY CARE SERVICES. A THREE STAGE PROGRAM ASSESSED ATTITUDES AND PRACTICES IN SEVEN COMMUNITIES. STAGE I TAPPED COMMUNITY OPINIONS (NAMELY, WORKING MOTHERS) ON CHILD WELFARE ISSUES. STAGE II UTILIZED FIELD TECHNIQUES TO SURVEY SUPPLEMENTARY CHILD CARE PRACTICES IN 300 FAMILIES. STAGE III SURVEYED 1400 DAY CARE FACILITIES AND STUDIED LICENSING LAWS. WHEN COMPLETED IN 1964, THE STUDY REVEALED THAT (1) CLIENTELE CAME FROM NORMAL HOMES, (2) CHILDREN OF WORKING MOTHERS NEED SUPPLEMENTARY CHILD CARE SERVICES, (3) MUCH IN-HOME CARE FOR INFANTS IS IN A CARETAKER'S HOME, (4) MOTHERS WANT RESPONSIBLE CARE GIVEN AND DAY CARE IS FREQUENTLY OF POOR QUALITY, (5) STAFF REFLECTS LOW STANDARDS OF SELECTION AND STAFF IS DIFFICULT TO RECRUIT, (6) VIRTUES OF FAMILY DAY CARE ARE SELDOM REALIZED, AND (7) GOOD CARE MUST BE DIFFERENTIATED BY AGE OF CHILD. THE FINDINGS SUGGEST THAT CURRENT PRACTICES NEED TO MOVE TOWARD DEVELOPMENTS OF SUPPLEMENTARY CHILD CARE FACILITIES WHICH ARE INDEPENDENT OF CONNOTATIONS OF SOCIAL WORK AND PUBLIC UTILITY. (WY)

ED045176 PS003269
HETEROGENEOUS VS. HOMOGENEOUS SOCIAL CLASS GROUPING OF PRESCHOOL CHILDREN IN HEAD START CLASSROOMS. BOGER, ROBERT P.; AND OTHERS, 14 FEB 69 92P.
EDRS PRICE MF-$0.65 HC-$3.29

THIS STUDY TESTS THE HYPOTHESIS THAT DISADVANTAGED CHILDREN LEARN MORE FROM INTERACTION WITH ADVANTAGED CHILDREN IN HEAD START CLASSROOMS THAN WHEN GROUPED SOLELY WITH OTHER DISADVANTAGED CHILDREN. SUBJECTS WERE 32 DISADVANTAGED CHILDREN WHO WERE ASSIGNED TO TWO EXPERIMENTAL GROUPS OF EIGHT EACH AND A CONTROL GROUP OF 16. EIGHT ADVANTAGED CHILDREN WERE ADDED TO EACH OF THE EXPERIMENTAL GROUPS. TEACHERS ASSIGNED TO ALL THREE CLASSES WERE SIMILAR IN EXPERIENCE, TEACHING STYLE AND DEMOGRAPHIC CHARACTERISTICS. VARIABLES OF CHIEF INTEREST IN THIS STUDY WERE COGNITION, LANGUAGE, AND SOCIALIZATION. PRE- AND POSTTESTS ON A VARIETY OF STANDARDIZED AND SPECIALLY DEVELOPED INSTRUMENTS EVALUATED THE PERFORMANCE OF ALL CHILDREN. VIDEOTAPES WERE USED TO ASSESS SOCIO-EMOTIONAL BEHAVIORS SUCH AS AGGRESSION AND DEPENDENCY. WHEN COMPARISONS WERE MADE BETWEEN CONTROL AND EXPERIMENTAL GROUPS RESULTS INDICATED SUPPORT FOR INCREASED EDUCABILITY IN CLASSES HOLDING A HIGHER PERCENTAGE OF ADVANTAGED PEERS. CONSISTENT GAINS WERE EVIDENT ALTHOUGH SIGNIFICANCE AT THE .05 LEVEL WAS NOT REACHED. THE EXPERIMENTAL CHILDREN GAINED IN TASK PERSISTENCE AND VERBAL SKILLS; AGGRESSIVE AND DEPENDENT BEHAVIORS DECREASED; AND SELF CONCEPTS IMPROVED. (WY)

ED045177 PS003270
SUBPOPULATIONAL PROFILING OF THE PSYCHOEDUCATIONAL DIMENSIONS OF DISADVANTAGED PRESCHOOL CHILDREN: A CONCEPTUAL PROSPECTUS FOR AN INTERDISCIPLINARY RESEARCH. BOGER, ROBERT P.; AMBRON, SUEANN R., 68 65P.
EDRS PRICE MF-$0.65 HC NOT AVAILABLE FROM EDRS.

PROGRAM PLANNING FOR ECONOMICALLY DEPRIVED CHILDREN MIGHT BE IMPROVED IF BEHAVIORAL INFORMATION PERTINENT TO SPECIFIC SUBCULTURAL GROUPS WERE SYSTEMATICALLY OBTAINED. THIS PROSPECTUS FOCUSES ON DEVELOPING A THREE-PART BEHAVIORAL MODEL WHICH, WHEN INTEGRATED, WOULD IDENTIFY AND PROFILE THE NATURE OF DISADVANTAGEMENT IN TERMS IDIOSYNCRATIC AND MEANINGFUL TO A GIVEN SUBPOPULATION. THE FIRST PART OF THE MODEL SETS UP A SUBPOPULATION MATRIX FOR FIVE MAJOR SUBCULTURAL GROUPS (BLACK AMERICAN, MEXICAN AMERICAN, PUERTO RICAN, AMERICAN INDIAN, ANGLO AMERICAN) IN TERMS OF RURAL OR URBAN LOCALE, GEOGRAPHIC AREA, SOCIAL CLASS, AND SEX. THE SECOND MAJOR SECTION OF THE MODEL CONSIDERS PSYCHOEDUCATIONAL DIMENSIONS SUCH AS INTELLIGENCE, LANGUAGE SKILL, CONCEPTUAL ABILITY, PERCEPTUAL ABILITY, MOTIVATION, AND SELF CONCEPT. THE FINAL SECTION CONSIDERS PROCESS VARIABLES SUCH AS CHILD REARING PRACTICES, REINFORCEMENT PATTERNS, PARENTAL EXPECTATIONS, LANGUAGE PATTERNS, FAMILY COMPOSITION, STABILITY, MOBILITY, AND THE PHYSICAL SURROUNDINGS OF THE HOME. USED PRESCRIPTIVELY, THIS MODEL CAN HELP MOLD AN INTERVENTION PROGRAM APPROPRIATE TO FILL IN DEFICITS PROFILED FOR ETHNIC GROUPS ACROSS SOCIAL CLASS LEVELS. EXTENSIVE BIBLIOGRAPHY IS INCLUDED. [NOT AVAILABLE IN HARD COPY DUE TO MARGINAL LEGIBILITY OF ORIGINAL DOCUMENT.] (WY)

ED045178 PS003333
AN INVESTIGATION IN THE LEARNING OF EQUIVALENCE AND ORDER RELATIONS BY FOUR- AND FIVE-YEAR-OLD CHILDREN. CAREY, RUSSELL L.; STEFFE, LESLIE P., DEC 68 212P.
EDRS PRICE MF-$0.65 HC-$9.87

THIS STUDY IS ONE OF A SERIES WHICH ATTEMPTS TO ARRIVE AT GENERALIZATIONS ABOUT THE LEARNING OF MATHEMATICS AND THE USE OF ITS TERMINOLOGY IN THE CONTEXT OF MATHEMATICAL STRUCTURE BY YOUNG CHILDREN. THE FIRST HALF OF THE DOCUMENT DESCRIBES AN EXPERIMENTAL TRAINING PROGRAM DESIGNED TO INTEGRATE MATHEMATICAL CONCEPTS OF METRIC SPACE, ARC LENGTH, AND TRANSFORMATIONS WITH PIAGETAN NOTIONS OF CONSERVATION, TRANSITIVITY, AND SYMMETRY. SUBJECTS WERE 20 FOUR-YEAR-OLD AND 34 FIVE-YEAR-OLD CHILDREN WHO PARTICIPATED IN THREE UNITS OF SMALL GROUP INSTRUCTION. THEY WERE PRETESTED AND POSTTESTED INDIVIDUALLY. SEVENTY-FOUR TABLES AND NINE DIAGRAMS ARE INTERSPERSED WITHIN THE TEXT TO STATISTICALLY SUPPORT POINTS AS THEY ARE MADE. RESULTS, CONCLUSIONS, DISCUSSION, AND IMPLICATIONS ARE GIVEN AND INDICATE THAT GENERALLY THERE ARE SLIGHT SIGNIFICANT RELATIONSHIPS BETWEEN THE PSYCHOLOGICAL AND MATHEMATICAL CONSTRUCTS AFTER TRAINING. THE SECOND HALF OF THE DOCUMENT CONTAINS THE BIBLIOGRAPHY AND THREE APPENDIXES. APPENDIX I LISTS STUDENT CHARACTERISTICS IN TABULAR FORM; APPENDIX II GIVES THE DETAILS OF THE THREE INSTRUCTIONAL UNITS; AND APPENDIX III LISTS DIRECTIONS AND MATERIALS FOR MAKING THE FOUR MEASURING INSTRUMENTS USED IN THE PRE- AND POSTTESTS. (WY)

ED045179 PS003334
THE COGNITIVE ENVIRONMENTS OF URBAN PRESCHOOL CHILDREN. FINAL REPORT. HESS, ROBERT D.; AND OTHERS, NOV 68 364P.
EDRS PRICE MF-$0.65 HC-$13.16

THIS FINAL REPORT DESCRIBES A PROJECT BEGUN IN 1962 WHICH WAS DESIGNED TO ANALYZE THE EFFECT OF HOME AND MATERNAL INFLUENCE ON THE COGNITIVE DEVELOPMENT OF URBAN PRESCHOOL CHILDREN EVALUATED WHEN THEY WERE FOUR YEARS OLD. THE RESEARCH GROUP CONSISTED OF 163 MOTHER-CHILD PAIRS FROM THREE SOCIOECONOMIC STATUS LEVELS: MIDDLE CLASS, SKILLED WORKING CLASS, AND UNSKILLED WORKING CLASS. SUBJECTS WERE SELECTED FROM BOTH FATHER-PRESENT AND FATHER-ABSENT FAMILIES. THE TEXT OF THE REPORT ESTABLISHES EMPIRICAL BASELINES AND OFFERS CONCEPTS AND CONSTRUCTS RELATED TO FAMILY RESOURCES AND MATERNAL LIFE STYLES, MATERNAL CONTROL STRATEGIES AND COGNITIVE PROCESSES, MOTHER-CHILD INTERACTION, COGNITIVE BEHAV-

IOR OF MOTHER AND CHILD, MOTHER'S LANGUAGE AND THE CHILD'S COGNITIVE BEHAVIOR. A SUMMARY CHAPTER HIGHLIGHTS PROJECT RESULTS. EXTENSIVE APPENDIXES SUPPLEMENT THE TEXT BY PROVIDING DETAILED ANALYSIS OF TESTING TECHNIQUES, INTERVIEW PROCEDURES AND STATISTICAL DATA. REFERENCES ARE INCLUDED. A FOLLOW-UP REPORT OF ACADEMIC PERFORMANCE AND COGNITIVE ATTAINMENT DURING THE CHILDREN'S FIRST TWO YEARS OF SCHOOL IS AVAILABLE AS PS 003 335. (WY)

ED045180 PS003335
THE COGNITIVE ENVIRONMENTS OF URBAN PRESCHOOL CHILDREN: FOLLOW-UP PHASE. FINAL REPORT. HESS, ROBERT D.; AND OTHERS, JUN 69 347P.
EDRS PRICE MF-$0.65 HC-$13.16

THIS REPORT DESCRIBES THE SECOND OR FOLLOWUP PHASE OF A PROJECT BEGUN IN 1962, WHICH WAS DESIGNED TO ANALYZE THE EFFECT OF HOME AND MATERNAL INFLUENCE ON THE COGNITIVE DEVELOPMENT OF URBAN PRESCHOOL CHILDREN FROM THREE SOCIOECONOMIC LEVELS. REPORTED IS THE ACADEMIC PERFORMANCE AND COGNITIVE ATTAINMENT OF 158 ORIGINAL STUDY CHILDREN DURING THEIR FIRST TWO YEARS OF SCHOOL. THE TEXT OF THE REPORT OFFERS CONCEPTS AND CONSTRUCTS RELATED TO THE CHILD'S SCHOOL ACHIEVEMENT IN THE FIRST AND SECOND GRADES, STYLISTIC ASPECTS OF CHILDREN'S BEHAVIOR, THE CHILD'S COGNITIVE DEVELOPMENT, COGNITIVE BEHAVIOR OF MOTHER AND CHILD, THE CHILD'S LANGUAGE AND THE CHILD'S EXPLORATORY BEHAVIOR AND INTERESTS. A SUMMARY CHAPTER HIGHLIGHTS RESULTS OF THE FOLLOWUP PHASE. EXTENSIVE APPENDIXES SUPPLEMENT THE TEXT BY PROVIDING DETAILED ANALYSES OF TESTING TECHNIQUES, INTERVIEW PROCEDURES, AND STATISTICAL DATA. REFERENCES ARE INCLUDED. THE FINAL REPORT OF THE PRESCHOOL PHASE OF THIS STUDY IS AVAILABLE AS PS 003 334. (WY)

ED045181 PS003414
MODIFICATION OF THE CLASSROOM BEHAVIOR OF A "DISADVANTAGED" KINDERGARTEN BOY BY SOCIAL REINFORCEMENT AND ISOLATION. SIBLEY, SALLY A.; AND OTHERS, [67] 50P.
EDRS PRICE MF-$0.65 HC-$3.29

THE GOAL OF THE INVESTIGATION WAS TO ELIMINATE THE DISRUPTIVE, RESISTANT AND ASSAULTIVE BEHAVIORS AND INCREASE THE APPROPRIATE PEER INTERACTION OF AN ECONOMICALLY DISADVANTAGED KINDERGARTEN WHITE BOY. THE TREATMENT PROGRAM INVOLVED PRESENTATION OF ADULT (TEACHER) ATTENTION CONTINGENT UPON DESIRABLE CLASSROOM BEHAVIOR, WITHHOLDING OF ATTENTION CONTINGENT UPON INAPPROPRIATE BEHAVIOR, AND SOCIAL ISOLATION CONTINGENT UPON UNACCEPTABLE BEHAVIOR. THE SUBJECT'S BEHAVIOR WAS CLASSIFIED ACCORDING TO THE COPING ANALYSIS SCHEDULE FOR EDUCATIONAL SETTINGS, AND THE TEACHER'S INTERACTIONS WITH THE SUBJECT WERE CATEGORIZED ACCORDING TO THEIR CONTENT. BEHAVIOR AND INTERACTIONS WERE RECORDED BY AN OBSERVER. THE PROGRAM WAS CARRIED OUT DAILY IN THE ACTIVITIES OF FREE PLAY, DISCUSSION, AND REST. THE SUBJECT'S INAPPROPRIATE AND UNACCEPTABLE BEHAVIORS SIGNIFICANTLY DECREASED WHEN THEY WERE PUNISHED (ISOLATION) RATHER THAN IGNORED. A REVERSAL OF THE TREATMENT PROGRAM WAS INTRODUCED TO DEMONSTRATE THAT THE TEACHER'S INTERACTIONS WERE IN FACT THE CONTROLLING VARIABLES. REINSTATEMENT OF DATA TREATMENT HAD FAVORABLE RESULTS. THE STUDY INDICATES THAT THE SYSTEMATIC USE OF SOCIAL REINFORCEMENT TECHNIQUES IN THE CLASSROOM CAN SIGNIFICANTLY CHANGE A CHILD'S BEHAVIOR, EVEN WHEN THE TARGET IS MORE COMPREHENSIVE THAN THE SINGLE OPERANT. (AUTHOR/NH)

ED045182 PS003430
RESULTS AND IMPLICATIONS OF A HEAD START CLASSIFICATION AND ATTENTION TRAINING PROGRAM. MELCER, DONALD, MAR 70 19P.
EDRS PRICE MF-$0.65 HC-$3.29

THIS REPORT PRESENTS THE RESULTS, STATISTICAL ANALYSIS AND IMPLICATIONS OF CLASSIFICATION AND ATTENTION TRAINING CURRICULA FIELD TESTED WITH HEAD START CHILDREN BY THEIR TEACHERS. TEACHER, LOCATION OF PROGRAM, AND TREATMENT WERE THE VARIABLES CONSIDERED BUT ONLY TREATMENT EFFECTS WERE SIGNIFICANT. RESULTS, SUMMARIZED IN THREE LEVELS, INDICATE (1) ON SOME INTELLECTUAL DIMENSIONS, HEAD START PUPILS MADE GAINS REGARDLESS OF THE TYPE PROGRAM IN WHICH THEY PARTICIPATED, (2) SPECIFIC TREATMENTS ACROSS EXPERIMENTAL GROUPS PRODUCED TASK SPECIFIC GAINS, AND (3) PUPILS LEARN OPERATIONS BUT THEY DO NOT GENERALIZE THESE ACQUIRED ABILITIES TO OTHER THEORETICALLY RELATED AREAS OF COGNITIVE ACTIVITY. IMPLICATIONS ARE THAT A COMPREHENSIVE HEAD START PROGRAM MUST BEGIN WITH AN ASSESSMENT OF SPECIFIC LEARNING NEEDS FOLLOWED BY THE USE OF CURRICULA DESIGNED TO MEET THESE NEEDS. AN APPROACH WHICH BEGINS WITH PERCEPTUAL MOTOR MANIPULATION, PROCEEDS TO ATTENTION TRAINING, AND CONCLUDES WITH CLASSIFICATION TRAINING MIGHT BE MORE SUCCESSFUL THAN ANY OF ITS PREDECESSORS. SEE COMPANION PAPER PS 003 428 WHICH DISCUSSES THE ACTUAL TRAINING INPUTS AND DOCUMENT PS 003 429 WHICH PRESENTS THE RESEARCH AND SAMPLING DESIGN. (WY)

ED045183 PS003433
EARLY CHILDHOOD EDUCATION PROGRAM AND ITS COMPONENTS: PSYCHOLOGICAL EVALUATION, SENSORIMOTOR SKILLS PROGRAM, NEW VISIONS - A CHILDREN'S MUSEUM. PROJECT REPORTS, VOLUME 4, BOOK 1, 1969. LANE, ELIZABETH M., ED., FEB 70 82P.
EDRS PRICE MF-$0.65 HC-$3.29

ALTHOUGH THIS PROJECT REPORT EMPHASIZES 1968-1969, THE FOURTH YEAR OF DAYTON'S EARLY CHILDHOOD EDUCATION PROGRAM (ECE), IT ALSO REFERS TO EXPERIENCES ONGOING FROM 1965 WHEN ECE WAS INITIATED. THE 1968-1969 PROGRAM WAS A CONTINUATION OF EFFORTS TO PROVIDE CONCENTRATED AND CONTINUOUS LEARNING EXPERIENCES FOR 3-, 4-, AND 5-YEAR-OLD CHILDREN IN PERCEPTUAL, MOTIVATIONAL, AND SOCIAL SKILLS ACCORDING TO A PREVIOUSLY DEVELOPED PLAN. A SECOND GOAL WAS TO HELP PARENTS PROVIDE A SUPPORTIVE HOME ENVIRONMENT CONDUCIVE TO POSITIVE FAMILY DEVELOPMENT. THE PROGRAM SERVED 2,934 ECONOMICALLY DISADVANTAGED CHILDREN. THE FIRST PART OF THE REPORT EXPLAINS THE GOALS AND NATURE OF THE CHILDREN'S PRE-KINDERGARTEN CLASSROOM PROGRAM AND THE PARENT PROGRAM, DISCUSSES THE ORGANIZATION AND STAFF ROLES, CURRICULUM, AND THE PART PLAYED BY KINDERGARTEN IN THE ECE PROGRAM. ALSO OUTLINED ARE THE ACTIVITIES OF THE SOCIAL SERVICE STAFF AND THE ECE NURSE, THE NUTRITION PROGRAM, AND THE PARENT PROGRAM. THE REMAINDER OF THE DOCUMENT IS A COMPILATION OF THREE SEPARATE RESUMES WHICH PROVIDE DETAILED INFORMATION ON (1) PSYCHOLOGICAL EVALUATION OF ECE INCLUDING TESTS USED AND DATA ANALYSIS, (2) A LONGITUDINAL RESEARCH REPORT OF A SENSORIMOTOR SKILLS PROGRAM, AND (3) NEW VISIONS--A CHILDREN'S ART MUSEUM WHERE YOUNG CHILDREN ARE ENCOURAGED TO EXPLORE THE ARTIFACTS. (WY)

ED045184 PS003436
CHANGING THE LEARNING PATTERNS OF THE CULTURALLY DIFFERENT. SPAULDING, ROBERT L., 29 APR 69 12P.
EDRS PRICE MF-$0.65 HC-$3.29

THE DURHAM EDUCATION IMPROVEMENT PROGRAM (EIP) SEEKS TO DEVELOP NEW ORGANIZATIONAL PATTERNS AND INSTRUCTIONAL SYSTEMS IN ONGOING CLASSROOMS WHICH WOULD FOSTER THE EDUCATIONAL AND SOCIAL DEVELOPMENT OF DISADVANTAGED NORTH CAROLINA CHILDREN. A SMALL-SCALE MODEL SCHOOL SYSTEM (CONSISTING OF THREE SCHOOLS IN TARGET AREAS AND A LABORATORY SCHOOL) WAS CREATED TO SERVE 200 TO 300 CHILDREN FROM AGES 2 THROUGH 10. THE OVERALL STRATEGY FOR THE PROGRAM'S FIVE-YEAR PLAN IS (1) DEVELOPMENT OF NEW ORGANIZATIONAL PATTERNS AND PROCEDURES (2) INTRODUCTION OF NEW TECHNIQUES OF INSTRUCTION TO AND THROUGH THE LABORATORY FACILITY TO THE TARGET AREA SCHOOLS (3) CREATION OF A SERIES OF PRESCHOOL CLASSES (4) DEVELOPMENT OF SPECIAL TEACHER TRAINING PROCEDURES FOR USE IN TARGET AREA UNGRADED PRIMARY AND PRESCHOOL CLASSES. EFFECTS OF THE PROGRAM ARE TO BE EVALUATED BY A SERIES OF TESTS GIVEN BEFORE AND AFTER EACH SPECIAL INTERVENTION AS WELL AS BY A SERIES OF INTELLIGENCE AND ACHIEVEMENT TESTS ADMINISTERED OVER THE FULL LENGTH OF EACH CHILD'S INVOLVEMENT IN EIP CLASSES. REPORTS ON SEVERAL MAJOR RESEARCH QUESTIONS AND ON THE RESULTS OF EIP WILL BE PUBLISHED DURING THE NEXT TWO YEARS. (WY)

ED045185 PS003441
POSITION EFFECTS IN PLAY EQUIPMENT PREFERENCES OF NURSERY SCHOOL CHILDREN. WITT, PETER A.; GRAMZA, ANTHONY F., [69] 7P.
EDRS PRICE MF-$0.65 HC-$3.29
AVAILABLE FROM: PETER A. WITT, MOTOR PERFORMANCE AND PLAY RESEARCH LABORATORY, CHILDREN'S RESEARCH CENTER, UNIVERSITY OF ILLINOIS, CHAMPAIGN, ILLINOIS 61820

WITH REFERENCE TO THE NEED FOR DELINEATION OF PARAMETERS OPERATIVE IN CHILDREN'S PLAY, THE POSITION PREFERENCES OF FOUR GROUPS OF NURSERY SCHOOL SUBJECTS WERE STUDIED IN A LABORATORY PLAYROOM. A LARGE AND SMALL TRESTLE WERE INTERCHANGED BETWEEN CENTER AND CORNER POSITIONS IN A SERIES OF PLAY SESSIONS. THE FREQUENCY WITH WHICH THE SUBJECTS USED TRESTLES IN EACH POSITION WAS RECORDED. RESULTS REVEALED A SIGNIFICANT DIFFERENCE BETWEEN SESSIONS FOR THREE OF THE FOUR GROUPS OF CHILDREN TESTED, INDICATING THAT THE TRESTLE IN THE CENTER POSITION RECEIVED MORE USAGE THAN THE TRESTLE PLACED IN THE CORNER POSITION. IN ADDITION, THE LARGE TRESTLE PLACED IN THE CENTER OF THE ROOM RECEIVED EVEN GREATER USAGE THAN THE SMALL TRESTLE IN THIS FAVORED POSITION. THE INTERACTION OF POSITION AND TRESTLE SIZE WAS NOTED, ALONG WITH THE IMPORTANCE OF STUDYING OTHER SPECIFIABLE PARAMETERS AFFECTING A CHILD'S USE OF PLAY EQUIPMENT. RESULTS OF ADDITIONAL RESEARCH IN THIS AREA COULD HAVE IMPLICATIONS FOR UNOBTRUSIVELY MODIFYING CHILDREN'S PLAY BEHAVIOR PATTERNS BY THE PURPOSEFUL POSITIONING OF EQUIPMENT. (AUTHOR/NH)

ED045186 PS003447
INTELLECTUAL DEVELOPMENT OF CULTURALLY DEPRIVED CHILDREN IN A DAY CARE PROGRAM: A FOLLOW-UP STUDY. PRENTICE, NORMAN M.; BIERI, JAMES, 25 MAR 70 12P.
EDRS PRICE MF-$0.65 HC-$3.29

FOR THIS FOLLOWUP STUDY AN ATTEMPT WAS MADE TO RETEST ALL 136 CHILDREN EVALUATED IN THE AUSTIN, TEXAS DAY CARE PROGRAM NINE MONTHS EARLIER BUT ONLY 95 CHILDREN WERE AVAILABLE. SUBJECTS WERE NEGRO AND MEXICAN-AMERICAN. THE ORIGINAL STUDY INDICATED THAT SIGNIFICANTLY HIGHER SCORES WERE EARNED ON TESTS OF INTELLECTUAL PERFORMANCE AS A FUNCTION OF LENGTH OF TIME IN PROGRAM AND THAT "OLD" CHILDREN (IN PROGRAM APPROXIMATELY 14 MONTHS) GAINED AS MANY AS TEN IQ POINTS OVER "NEW" CHILDREN (IN PROGRAM AN AVERAGE OF 3 MONTHS). WERE THE OLD CHILDREN BRIGHTER TO BEGIN WITH OR DID THEY HAVE PARENTS MORE INTELLECTUALLY ALERT TO THE BENEFITS OF CONTINUED PARTICIPATION? TO ANSWER THIS QUESTION 57 OLD CHILDREN AND 38 NEW CHILDREN WERE RETESTED WITH TWO WELL-KNOWN, INDIVIDUALLY ADMINISTERED INTELLIGENCE TESTS. RESULTS INDICATE THAT THOSE WHO HAD BEEN IN THE PROGRAM AN AVERAGE OF 23 MONTHS WERE TO SOME EXTENT BRIGHTER AND THAT UPON RETESTING A SLIGHT BUT SIGNIFICANT DROP IN INTELLECTUAL LEVEL OCCURRED ON THE BINET. THE NEW CHILDREN, HOWEVER, MADE SLIGHT GAINS BETWEEN THE ORIGINAL AND THE FOLLOWUP TESTING WHICH UPON CLOSER ANALYSIS MIGHT BE DISMISSED AS ARTIFACTUAL. DIFFERENTIAL EFFECTS FOR SEX AND ETHNICITY OCCURRED. FIVE OTHER QUESTIONS ABOUT THE RELATIONSHIP OF INTELLECTUAL DEVELOPMENT TO DAY CARE ARE RAISED BY THIS STUDY AND REMAIN UNANSWERED. (BIBLIOGRAPHY PROVIDED). (WY)

ED045187 PS003452
THE DEVELOPMENT OF TEMPORAL DISCRIMINATION IN YOUNG CHILDREN. WALKER, JOHN, JUN 69 63P.
EDRS PRICE MF-$0.65 HC NOT AVAILABLE FROM EDRS.

THE PURPOSE OF THIS STUDY WAS TO PERFORM PILOT RESEARCH UPON TWO NORMAL CHILDREN AGED SIX YEARS (AN AGE MIDWAY BETWEEN COMPLETE ABSENCE OF TIME CONCEPTUALIZATION AND MATURATION OF TIME CONCEPTS) IN ORDER TO CHART THE CHARACTERISTIC RESPONSES WITHIN A CONDITIONING PARADIGM. PREVIOUS LITERATURE IN THE FIELD IS REVIEWED FOR THE PURPOSE OF PROVIDING A RATIONALE FOR THE USE OF AUTONOMIC VARIABLES (GALVANIC SKIN RESPONSE AND CEPHALIC VASOMOTOR RESPONSE) AND A DELAY CONDITIONING PROCEDURE. SPECIAL ATTENTION WAS DEVOTED TO DEVELOPMENT OF A TESTING TECHNIQUE WHICH WOULD OVERCOME FEAR OF THE TEST SITUATION AND EQUIPMENT. TESTING PROCEDURES WAS DIVIDED INTO THE FOLLOWING PHASES: (1) HABITUATION, (2) TEMPORAL CONDITIONING, AND (3) POST-CONDITIONING TEST SERIES. BOTH SUBJECTS DISPLAYED A FAR BETTER ABILITY TO INHIBIT RESPONDING, EVEN DURING EXTINCTION, THAN WAS ANTICIPATED. THE POSSIBILITY OF COUNTING BEHAVIOR WAS CONTROLLED. A DISCUSSION OF THE VARIOUS TEST FACTORS CONCLUDES THAT THE USE OF THE CURRENT EQUIPMENT AND PROCEDURE CAN BE EXPANDED INTO A LARGER, CROSS-SECTIONAL PROJECT TO ESTABLISH NORMATIVE PROFILES OF TEMPORAL DISCRIMINATION. TEST CHARTS OF THE SUBJECTS' RESPONSES ARE INCLUDED. [NOT AVAILABLE IN HARD COPY DUE TO MARGINAL LEGIBILITY OF ORIGINAL DOCUMENT.] (AUTHOR/NH)

ED045188 PS003459
THE DEFINITION, MEASUREMENT AND DEVELOPMENT OF SOCIAL MOTIVES UNDERLYING COOPERATIVE AND COMPETITIVE BEHAVIOR. MCCLINTOCK, CHARLES G.; MESSICK, DAVID M., [69] 52P.
EDRS PRICE MF-$0.65 HC-$3.29

THIS RESEARCH PROPOSAL SUPPORTS A PROGRAM IN SOCIAL PSYCHOLOGY WHICH USES A VARIETY OF GAME PARADIGMS AND RELATED TASKS TO OBTAIN ESTIMATES OF THE RELATIVE DOMINANCE OF VARIOUS SOCIAL MOTIVES INCLUDING THOSE OF MAXIMIZING OWN GAIN (INDIVIDUALISM), JOINT GAIN (COOPERATION), AND RELATIVE GAIN (COMPETITION). NUMEROUS MAJOR STUDIES COMPLETED OR IN PROGRESS PROVIDE BACKGROUND INFORMATION ON (1) THE IMPACT OF VARIOUS VARIABLES AFFECTING CHOICE BEHAVIOR; (2) PARADIGMS REVEALING MOTIVATIONAL DYNAMICS UNDERLYING CHOICES; (3) VALIDITY OF TWO TYPES OF MODELS IN DESCRIBING THE DOMINANCE OF MOTIVES FOR CHOICE; (4) DEVELOPMENT OF MOTIVES BETWEEN CHILDREN IN CROSS-CULTURAL STUDIES; (5) STRATEGIES OF PLAYERS IN TWO-PERSON BARGAINING SITUATIONS AND (6) THE UTILITY OF STATISTICAL AND OTHER METHODS FOR ANALYZING SOCIAL INTERACTION. THE PROPOSED PROGRAM WOULD CONTINUE THE FINAL ANALYSIS OF CROSS-CULTURAL DEVELOPMENTAL STUDIES; FURTHER DEVELOP AN INITIAL MODEL OF MOTIVATIONAL BASES OF COOPERATIVE AND COMPETITIVE CHOICE BEHAVIOR; CONTINUE INVESTIGATION OF CHANGES IN STRATEGY AT VARIOUS AGE LEVELS AND ACROSS VARIOUS BARGAINING SITUATIONS; AND INITIATE A NEW PROGRAM OF STUDIES ON THE EFFECTS OF VARIOUS SOCIAL MOTIVES UPON SEVERAL LEARNING AND PERFORMANCE TASKS AMONG CHILDREN AT THE SECOND, FOURTH, AND SIXTH GRADE LEVELS. (WY)

ED045189 PS003462
EVALUATION OF A PARENT AND CHILD CENTER PROGRAM. HAMILTON, MARSHALL L., JUN 70 16P.
EDRS PRICE MF-$0.65 HC-$3.29

IN THE PARTICULAR INTERVENTION PROGRAM DESCRIBED, CHILDREN UNDER 3 YEARS OF AGE ARE GIVEN A NURSERY SCHOOL TYPE OF EXPERIENCE FIVE DAYS A WEEK FOR EIGHT OR MORE HOURS A DAY, WITH PROGRAM EMPHASIS ON STIMULATING RETARDED DEVELOPMENT. MOTHERS ARE GIVEN INSERVICE TRAINING AVERAGING 3 HOURS PER WEEK, STRESSING DEVELOPMENT OF MOTHERS' SELF-CONCEPT, GENERAL HANDLING OF THE CHILD, LANGUAGE DEVELOPMENT OF THE CHILD, PHYSICAL CARE, AND DEVELOPMENT OF CHILD'S GROSS AND FINE MOTOR CONTROL. A MINIMUM OF 10 WEEKS OF PAID PARTICIPATION AS A TEACHER AIDE IS AVAILABLE FOR EACH OF THE MOTHERS. DATA ARE REPORTED FOR AN 11-MONTH PERIOD ON 18 FAMILIES FROM TWO CENTERS THAT PRIMARILY SERVE CHICANO MIGRANT FAMILIES. CHILDREN WERE PRE- AND POSTTESTED ON MEASURES TO DETERMINE MOTOR, LANGUAGE, AND SOCIAL DEVELOPMENT AND, IN ADDITION, A TEST WAS GIVEN TO ASSESS THE STIMULATION POTENTIAL OF EACH CHILD'S HOME. CONCLUSIONS MUST BE TENTAIVE IN THE ABSENCE OF A CONTROL GROUP, BUT POSTTEST SCORES INDICATED A SIGNIFICANT IMPROVEMENT IN THE AMOUNT AND QUALITY OF DEVELOPMENTAL HOME STIMULATION. SUBTEST SCORES SHOWED THE GREATEST IMPROVEMENT IN THE AREAS OF LANGUAGE DEVELOPMENT AND DEVELOPMENTAL AND VOCAL STIMULATION. (NH)

ED045190 PS003652
EDUCATIONAL INTERVENTION IN THE HOME AND PARAPROFESSIONAL CAREER DEVELOPMENT: A FIRST GENERATION MOTHER STUDY. BARBRACK, CHRISTOPHER R.; HORTON, DELLA M., 70 34P.
EDRS PRICE MF-$0.65 HC-$3.29

IN 1968 THE DEMONSTRATION AND RESEARCH CENTER FOR EARLY EDUCATION (DARCEE) INITIATED A SMALL STUDY TO BUILD AND UTILIZE MOTHERS' SKILLS (ESTABLISHED IN AN EARLIER AND MAJOR STUDY) AND TO BEGIN TO CONSTRUCT AND EXPLORE THE FEASIBILITY OF A "CAREER LADDER" FOR PERSONS INTERESTED IN EARLY EDUCATION. SUBJECTS WERE 12 NEGRO PRESCHOOLERS AND THEIR FAMILIES. THEY WERE EXPOSED TO A 40 WEEK PROGRAM OF HOME VISITS BY SELECTED MOTHERS. THE HOME VISITORS RECEIVED A BRIEF TWO-PHASE TRAINING PROGRAM EMPHASIZING THE (1) GOALS OF DARCEE AND (2) DEMONSTRATIONS AND ACTIVITIES TO BE USED IN SUBJECTS' HOMES. SUBJECTS WERE TESTED IN A PRETEST-POSTTEST DESIGN ON THREE MEASURES OF ACADEMIC APTITUDE, ONE OF WHICH WAS A SPECIALLY DEVELOPED DARCEE INSTRUMENT. RESULTS INDICATE THAT NO SIGNIFICANT INCREASES OR DECREASES OCCURRED. HOWEVER, MOTHERS INVOLVED AS HOME VISITORS APPEARED TO HAVE INCREASED SELF ESTEEM, ASPIRATIONS AND EXPECTATIONS AS A RESULT OF PROGRAM PARTICIPATION. APPENDIXES MAKE UP ALMOST 1/2 OF THIS DOCUMENT. (WY)

ED045191 PS003656
THE ITINERANT TEACHER. COLLINS, CAMILLA, [70] 10P.
EDRS PRICE MF-$0.65 HC-$3.29

THE USE OF A TRAVELING TEACHER IS ONE SOLUTION TO THE PROBLEM OF PROVIDING ON-THE-SPOT TRAINING FOR HEAD START TEACHERS IN SMALL RURAL COMMUNITIES IN REMOTE REGIONS OF NORTHERN CALIFORNIA. THE STATE DEPARTMENT OF EDUCATION, FUNDED THROUGH A GRANT TO CHICO STATE COLLEGE, IMPLEMENTED A STAFF DEVELOPMENT PROGRAM WHOSE CHIEF FEATURE WAS USE OF AN ITINERANT TEACHER WHO SPENT ONE WEEK IN EACH OF EIGHT CLASSROOMS IN SIX COUNTIES. IN ADDITION TO GIVING PRACTICAL HELPS IN CLASS, SHE TAUGHT A WORKSHOP COURSE FOR WHICH CHICO GRANTED ONE UNIT OF LOWER DIVISION CREDIT. THE CLASSES VISITED DIFFERED GREATLY IN SIZE, STRUCTURE, ETHNIC COMPOSITION AND STAFF BACKGROUND. THE TEACHER RESPONDED TO EACH CENTER'S PARTICULAR NEEDS AND WISHES, WORKING WITH BOTH TEACHING AND NONTEACHING PERSONNEL TO HELP THEM PLAN AND EVALUATE DAILY ACTIVITIES, ARRANGE SCHEDULES AND ROOM ORGANIZATION, USE CLASSROOM AND COMMUNITY RESOURCES MORE CREATIVELY, AND DEVELOP TECHNIQUES HELPFUL IN WORKING MORE EFFECTIVELY WITH CHILDREN AND PARENTS. THE ITINERANT TEACHER, ON AN EXTENDED CONTRACT, LATER PREPARED A MANUAL TO BE USED IN THOSE CLASSROOMS WHERE SHE HAD WORKED. RECOMMENDATIONS FOR THE CONTINUATION OF THE PROGRAM AND SPECIFIC SUGGESTIONS FOR ITS IMPROVEMENT ARE MADE. (WY)

ED045192 PS003666
ENVIRONMENTALLY ENRICHED CLASSROOMS AND THE DEVELOPMENT OF DISADVANTAGED PRESCHOOL CHILDREN. BUSSE, THOMAS V.; AND OTHERS, [70] 67P.
EDRS PRICE MF-$0.65 HC-$3.29

THIS STUDY EVALUATES THE EFFECTS OF PLACEMENT OF ADDITIONAL EQUIPMENT IN PRESCHOOL CLASSROOMS ON THE COGNITIVE, PERCEPTUAL, AND SOCIAL DEVELOPMENT OF URBAN NEGRO FOUR-YEAR-OLD CHILDREN. TWO GET SET CLASSROOMS IN EACH OF SIX AREAS OF PHILADELPHIA WERE PAIRED FOR TEACHERS, SUBJECTS, PHYSICAL FACILITIES AND EQUIPMENT. ONE CLASSROOM IN EACH PAIR WAS ENRICHED THROUGH THE ADDITION OF MATERIALS DESIGNED TO AUGMENT ONE OR MORE OF THE FOLLOWING: VERBAL ABILITY, PERFORMANCE ABILITY, VISUAL PERCEPTION, AUDITORY PERCEPTION, AND SOCIAL INTERACTION. ENRICHMENT ITEMS INCLUDED A TAPE

RECORDER AND TAPES, A POLAROID CAMERA WITH FILM AND FLASHBULBS, PUZZLE SETS, PRISMS, AND NEGRO DOLLS AND PUPPETS. PRETEST AND POSTTEST MEASURES ASSESSED COGNITIVE, PRECEPTUAL, AND SOCIAL DEVELOPMENT OF THE CHILDREN. THE FINDINGS SHOW THAT THE ENRICHMENT SIGNIFICANTLY ALTERED THE CLASSROOM ENVIRONMENT IN THE EXPERIMENTAL CLASSES. SIGNS OF THE ALTERATION WERE PRESENT IN THE COGNITIVE, PERCEPTUAL, AND SOCIAL DEVELOPMENT OF THE EXPERIMENTAL CHILDREN. HOWEVER, THE CONTROL CHILDREN SHOWED GREATER GAIN SCORES IN PERFORMANCE ABILITY. SINCE BOTH DESIRABLE AND UNDESIRABLE EFFECTS CAN RESULT FROM ENVIRONMENTAL ENRICHMENT, THE MORE EXTRAVAGANT CLAIMS FOR THE EFFICACY OF CERTAIN PLAY MATERIALS SHOULD BE MUTED AND A PROPERLY EQUIPPED CLASSROOM SHOULD NOT BE REGARDED AS A PANACEA FOR THE PROBLEMS OF DISADVANTAGED CHILDREN. (WY)

ED045193 PS003669
IMPACT OF THE HEAD START PROGRAM. PHASE I OF A PROJECTED LONGITUDINAL STUDY TO THE U. S. OFFICE OF ECONOMIC OPPORTUNITY. FINAL REPORT. , MAY 70 98P.
EDRS PRICE MF-$0.65 HC-$3.29

THIS FIRST PHASE OF A PROJECTED LONGITUDINAL STUDY DESIGNED TO ASSESS THE IMPACT OF HEAD START IN MONTGOMERY COUNTY, MARYLAND, CONCENTRATES ON REPORTING RESULTS OF DATA COLLECTION ACTIVITIES FROM 1966 TO THE END OF 1969. INSTRUMENTS WERE DEVELOPED TO MEASURE WHETHER HEAD START EVOLVED A CURRICULUM RELEVANT TO ITS GOALS AND WHETHER THE DEVELOPMENTAL CHARACTERISTICS OF FORMER HEAD STARTERS ARE DIFFERENT FROM THOSE OF COMPARABLE FIRST GRADERS WITHOUT HEAD START EXPERIENCE. METHODOLOGY INVOLVED OBSERVATION IN CLASSROOMS, TRIAL OF SPECIALLY DEVELOPED MATERIALS, AND ADMINISTRATION OF TESTS. CLASSROOM ADJUSTMENT WAS EVALUATED FOR PUPILS WORKING WITH TEACHERS, WITH OTHER ADULTS, AND WITHOUT DIRECT ADULT SUPERVISION. PUPILS IN HEAD START CLASSES, FORMER HEAD STARTERS CURRENTLY IN KINDERGARTEN, AND NON-HEAD STARTERS USED AS MATCHED CONTROLS WERE TESTED ON TESTS OF BASIC EXPERIENCE AND RATED FOR ADJUSTMENT. FIRST GRADERS WHO WERE FORMER HEAD STARTERS WERE TESTED ON STANDARDIZED INTELLIGENCE AND READINESS TESTS. EVEN THOUGH FEW SIGNIFICANT DIFFERENCES WERE FOUND BETWEEN HEAD STARTERS AND NON-HEAD STARTERS, THIS PHASE OF THE STUDY WAS JUDGED SUCCESSFUL BECAUSE INSTRUMENTS WERE DEVELOPED FOR THE DESCRIPTION OF HEAD START CLASSROOM ACTIVITIES AND FOR THE EVALUATION OF CLASSROOM ADJUSTMENT. SIXTEEN TABLES AND THIRTEEN FIGURES ARE PROVIDED ALONG WITH THREE APPENDIXES. (WY)

ED045194 PS003670
PROCEEDINGS: EARLY CHILDHOOD INTERVENTION RESEARCH CONFERENCE (UNIVERSITY OF SOUTH FLORIDA, TAMPA, MARCH 5 AND 6, 1970). , 6 MAR 70 111P.
EDRS PRICE MF-$0.65 HC-$6.58

WHAT EXPERIENCES AND KNOWLEDGE ACQUIRED DURING THE FIRST FIVE YEARS OF LIFE WILL ENABLE CHILDREN TO TAKE FULL ADVANTAGE OF A FORMAL EDUCATION SYSTEM DURING THEIR GROWING YEARS? THE CONFERENCE ON EARLY CHILDHOOD INTERVENTION AND RESEARCH EXAMINED AVAILABLE DATA WITHIN THE THEME "PROGRAMMING PARENTS TO PROGRAM CHILDREN." TOPICS AND SPEAKERS FOR THE FIVE PRESENTATIONS INCLUDE: (1) THE FAMILY AS AN EDUCATIONAL CHANGE AGENT-EARL SCHAEFER; (2) ENVIRONMENTAL CHANGES NEED FOR OPTIMAL CHILD DEVELOPMENT-BURTON WHITE; (3) CONTINGENCY CONTRACTING WITH PARENTS-CARL HAYWOOD; (4) PROCEDURES FOR THE DEVELOPMENT OF CONCEPTUAL AND THINKING SKILLS IN CHILDREN-CARL BEREITER; (5) THE CONFERENCE IN PERSPECTIVE: NEW DIRECTIONS-CARL HAYWOOD. BRIEF BIOGRAPHICAL SUMMARIES CITING RELEVANT RESEARCH AND FIELD WORK INVOLVING EACH OF THE FIVE PANELIST-PSYCHOLOGISTS ARE GIVEN. THE CONFERENCE PROCEEDINGS HAVE BEEN EDITED TO PRESERVE AN INFORMAL NARRATIVE STYLE. DISCUSSION BETWEEN PANELISTS IS REPORTED ALONG WITH QUESTIONS FROM THE AUDIENCE. FINAL COMMENTS BY CARL HAYWOOD SUMMARIZE AND ATTEMPT TO LINK INDIVIDUAL PRESENTATIONS. REFERENCES ARE GIVEN. (WY)

ED045195 PS003672
A NATIONAL SURVEY OF THE IMPACTS OF HEAD START CENTERS ON COMMUNITY INSTITUTIONS. , MAY 70 270P.
EDRS PRICE MF-$0.65 HC-$9.87

THE OBJECTIVES OF THE RESEARCH PROJECT DESCRIBED IN THIS REPORT ARE: (1) TO DETERMINE IF THERE HAVE BEEN CHANGES IN LOCAL EDUCATIONAL AND HEALTH INSTITUTIONS RELEVANT TO THE OBJECTIVES OF PROJECT HEAD START; (2) TO DETERMINE IF LOCAL HEAD START CENTERS WERE INFLUENTIAL IN BRINGING ABOUT RELEVANT CHANGES IN COMMUNITY INSTITUTIONS; (3) TO ANALYZE HOW HEAD START WAS INVOLVED IN THE INSTITUTIONAL CHANGE PROCESS; AND (4) TO DESCRIBE THE DIFFERENT IMPACTS ON COMMUNITY INSTITUTIONS OF VARIOUS HEAD START CHARACTERISTICS AND APPROACHES. FIELD RESEARCH WAS UNDERTAKEN IN A NATIONAL SAMPLE COMPOSED OF 58 COMMUNITIES WITH FULL-YEAR HEAD START PROGRAMS AND SEVEN COMMUNITIES WITH LITTLE EXPOSURE TO HEAD START. INTENSIVE STUDIES IN 42 OF THE HEAD START COMMUNITIES REVEALED THAT INDIVIDUALS AND GROUPS ASSOCIATED WITH HEAD START PROGRAMS HAD BEEN INVOLVED IN BRINGING ABOUT CHANGES IN HEALTH AND EDUCATIONAL INSTITUTIONS. A TOTAL OF 1,496 CHANGES CONSISTENT WITH HEAD START GOALS AND PHILOSOPHIES WERE IDENTIFIED. EXAMPLES OF CHANGES ARE: INCREASED INVOLVEMENT OF THE POOR WITH INSTITUTIONS, GREATER EMPLOYMENT OF LOCAL PEOPLE IN PARAPROFESSIONAL OCCUPATIONS, MORE EDUCATIONAL EMPHASIS ON THE PARTICULAR NEEDS OF THE POOR AND MINORITIES, AND MODIFICATION OF HEALTH SERVICES AND PRACTICES TO SERVE THE POOR MORE EFFECTIVELY. (AUTHOR/NH)

ED045196 PS003678
EXPERIMENTAL VARIATION OF HEAD START CURRICULA: A COMPARISON OF CURRENT APPROACHES. ANNUAL PROGRESS REPORT, JUNE 1, 1969 - MAY 31, 1970. MILLER, LOUISE B.; DYER, JEAN L., 31 MAY 70 119P.
EDRS PRICE MF-$0.65 HC-$6.58

TWO MAJOR QUESTIONS WERE RAISED IN REGARD TO FOUR TYPES OF PRESCHOOL PROGRAMS. (1) DO PROGRAMS DIFFER IN ACTUAL OPERATION AS WELL AS DESCRIPTIVELY? (2) DO PROGRAMS HAVE SIGNIFICANTLY DIFFERENT EFFECTS ON CHILDREN? ANALYSIS OF DATA OBTAINED ON SAMPLES OF FOUR CLASSROOMS IN EACH OF THREE PROGRAMS (BEREITER-ENGELMANN, DARCEE, TRADITIONAL) AND TWO CLASSROOMS IN THE FOURTH PROGRAM (MONTESSORI), SHOWED CLEAR DIFFERENCES. DESPITE WITHIN-PROGRAM TEACHER DIFFERENCES ON VARIABLES ASSESSED BY MONITORING PROCEDURES (OBSERVATION, TELEVISION), RESULTS PROVIDE NO EVIDENCE THAT THE TEACHERS' (N14) CHARACTERISTICS WERE A SOURCE OF DIFFERENCE AMONG PROGRAMS. RESULTS ALSO INDICATE THAT A BRIEF FOUR TO EIGHT WEEK TEACHER TRAINING PROGRAM SUPPLEMENTED BY VISITS FROM CONSULTANTS IS ADEQUATE FOR IDENTIFIABLE PROGRAM IMPLEMENTATION. THE FOUR PROGRAMS DID HAVE SIGNIFICANTLY DIFFERENT EFFECTS ON CHILDREN'S COGNITIVE, SOCIAL, AND/OR MOTIVATIONAL DEVELOPMENT. THE IMMEDIATE EFFECTS OF BEREITER-ENGELMANN AND DARCEE WERE STATISTICALLY SIGNIFICANT IN ACADEMIC AND MOTIVATIONAL DEVELOPMENT. THE EFFECTS OF BEREITER-ENGELMANN WERE LARGELY CONFINED TO COGNITIVE AND ACADEMIC AREAS. THE EFFECTS OF DARCEE WERE MORE DIFFUSE AND MOST EVIDENT IN THE AREAS OF MOTIVATION AND ATTITUDES. SEX DIFFERENCES OCCURRED. IN GENERAL, RESULTS INDICATE THAT THE IMMEDIATE IMPACT WAS SUPERIOR FOR THE TWO MOST DIDACTIC PROGRAMS. (WY)

ED045197 PS003680
EVALUATION AND RESEARCH CENTER FOR PROJECT HEAD START, UNIVERSITY OF SOUTH CAROLINA. INTERIM EVALUATION REPORT. FRIEDMAN, MYLES I., JAN 69 119P.
EDRS PRICE MF-$0.65 HC NOT AVAILABLE FROM EDRS.
AVAILABLE FROM: SOUTH CAROLINA UNIV., COLUMBIA, SOUTH CAROLINA. HEAD START EVALUATION AND RESEARCH CENTER

THIS DOCUMENT IS AN INTERIM EVALUATION REPORT OF LANGUAGE DEVELOPMENT CURRICULUMS IN FULL YEAR HEAD START PROGRAMS OPERATING IN THE FIVE STATE AREA THE RESEARCH AND EVALUATION CENTER SERVES. ONE EXPERIMENTAL STUDY IN LANGUAGE DEVELOPMENT CARRIED ON IN COOPERATION WITH THE TEXAS AND TULANE CENTERS IS REPORTED IN DEPTH. THE STUDY WAS IMPLEMENTED IN TEN CLASSROOMS IN TWO SITES (HENDERSON, NORTH CAROLINA AND VERO BEACH, FLORIDA) AND USED THE BUCHANAN READINESS IN LANGUAGE ARTS PROGRAM WITH VARIOUS COMBINATIONS OF SUPPLEMENTS, CAREFULLY MONITORED TEACHER TRAINING, AND PACKAGED REINFORCEMENT SCHEDULES. APPENDIXES COMPRISE FOUR-FIFTHS OF THE DOCUMENT AND INCLUDE TWO MANUALS FOR TEACHERS (BUCHANAN-SWANSON SUPPLEMENT AND THE REINSTEIN REINFORCEMENT PROGRAM), A COVER LETTER AND SAMPLE QUESTIONNAIRE USED IN THE LANGUAGE PROGRAM EVALUATION, A LISTING OF INSTRUMENTS COMMON TO NATIONAL EVALUATION PROJECTS, CENTER FORMS AND REPORTS USED FOR A VARIETY OF TESTS AND TESTING CONDITIONS, AND A DESCRIPTION OF CENTER QUALITY CONTROL PROCEDURES AND DATA PROCESSING. (WY)

ED045198 PS003854
THE EFFECTS OF ASSESSMENT AND PERSONALIZED PROGRAMMING ON SUBSEQUENT INTELLECTUAL DEVELOPMENT OF PREKINDERGARTEN AND KINDERGARTEN CHILDREN. FINAL REPORT. DUNLAP, JAMES M.; COFFMAN, ALICE O., JUL 70 52P.
EDRS PRICE MF-$0.65 HC-$3.29

THIS STUDY TESTS TWO HYPOTHESES: (1) PREKINDERGARTEN CHILDREN WHO ARE PROVIDED WITH A PERSONALIZED PROGRAM BASED ON INDIVIDUAL ASSESSMENT OF THEIR DEVELOPMENTAL SKILLS WILL INCREASE THEIR INTELLECTUAL ABILITIES AND WILL LEARN AT A HIGHER LEVEL THAN CHILDREN WITHOUT THIS PROGRAM, AND (2) THESE SAME CHILDREN WILL RETAIN THEIR ACQUIRED SUPERIORITY THROUGH THE FIRST AND SECOND PRIMARY YEARS. SUBJECTS WERE 126 FIRST AND 103 SECOND YEAR CHILDREN IN MATCHED EXPERIMENTAL AND CONTROL GROUPS. EXPERIMENTAL AND CONTROL GROUPS WERE COMPARED ON PRETESTS AND POSTTESTS GIVEN EACH YEAR OF THE EXPERIMENT OVER A SPAN OF FOUR YEARS. FINDINGS FROM THE 1969-1970 PHASE OF THE EXPERIMENT ARE REPORTED ALONG WITH THE FINAL FOUR YEAR FINDINGS (1967-1970). BOTH HYPOTHESES WERE SUPPORTED IN PART. AT PREKINDERGARTEN LEVEL, GAINS FROM PERSONALIZED PROGRAMMING WERE CONSISTENT ENOUGH TO POINT OUT THAT 4-YEAR-OLD CHILDREN HAD RESPONDED WELL TO BRIEF DAILY INDIVIDUALIZED SESSIONS OF WORK IN GAME-LIKE SITUATIONS WHICH

WERE GEARED TO DEVELOPMENT OF SENSORY, LANGUAGE, MOTOR, OR COGNITIVE SKILLS. THE POSITIVE EFFECTS DID NOT CARRY OVER TO THE END OF THE FOLLOWING YEAR. ALTHOUGH THE EXPERIMENTAL PROGRAM MADE NO LONG-RANGE IMPACT ON GIRLS, THE CUMULATIVE IMPACT ON BOYS INDICATED THEY OUTPERFORMED THEIR CONTROL COUNTERPARTS AS WELL AS THE GIRLS. SOME SUPPLEMENTARY STUDIES OF ACHIEVEMENT ARE REPORTED ALONG WITH UNANSWERED QUESTIONS PERTAINING TO CHILDREN WHO EVIDENCED DEVELOPMENTAL LAGS. (WY)

ED045199 PS003985
IMPLICATIONS OF MNEMONICS RESEARCH FOR COGNITIVE THEORY. REESE, HAYNE W., APR 70 19P.
EDRS PRICE MF-$0.65 HC-$3.29

A SKILLED COGNITIVE THEORIST MIGHT HELP BEHAVIORISTS RESOLVE INCONSISTENCIES FOUND FROM THEIR EXPERIMENTATION WITH IMAGINAL MNEMONICS IN PAIRED-ASSOCIATE AND SERIAL LEARNING TASKS. ICONIC COGNITION WHICH RELEGATES VERBAL PROCESSES TO SHORT-TERM STORAGE AND OUTPUT SYSTEMS IS INADEQUATE TO EXPLAIN THE VERBAL CODING AND ELABORATION PROCESSES SUGGESTED BY SOME RECENT RESEARCH FINDINGS. MOREOVER, VERBAL ELABORATION PLUS IMAGERY HAS BEEN FOUND TO BE EFFECTIVE IN PROMOTING LEARNING NOT ONLY FOR COLLEGE STUDENTS AND OLDER CHILDREN BUT ALSO FOR KINDERGARTEN CHILDREN AND OLDER PRESCHOOL CHILDREN. FOR YOUNG PRESCHOOL CHILDREN IMAGINAL ELABORATION SEEMS TO BE LESS EFFECTIVE THAN VERBAL ELABORATION. EXPERIMENTAL RESULTS THEMSELVES SEEM CONTRADICTORY AND ARE CONTRADICTORY TO BRUNER WHO THEORIZES THAT COGNITION IN YOUNG CHILDREN HAS AN ICONIC BASIS RATHER THAN A VERBAL BASIS. IN BEHAVIORISTIC MODELS, IMAGES ARE CONDITIONED SENSATIONS WHILE IN COGNITIVE MODELS THEY ARE DYNAMIC AND CHANGE ACCORDING TO FORMISTIC PRINCIPLES. A TOTAL OF 31 POSTULATES AND 17 DEDUCTIONS ILLUSTRATE SOME CONSIDERATIONS NECESSARY IN DEMONSTATING THAT MNEMONICS DATA MAY SEEM INCONSISTENT WITH BEHAVIORISTIC THEORIES, BUT ARE CONSISTENT WITH A COGNITIVE THEORY. COGNITIVISTS ARE INVITED TO ENGAGE IN RESEARCH ON THE PROBLEM. (WY)

ED045200 PS004012
FINAL REPORT ON PRESCHOOL EDUCATION TO OHIO DEPARTMENT OF EDUCATION. MCFADDEN, DENNIS N., SEP 69 120P.
EDRS PRICE MF-$0.65 HC-$6.58
AVAILABLE FROM: DR. RUSSELL A. WORKING, DIVISION OF RESEARCH, PLANNING, AND DEVELOPMENT, OHIO DEPARTMENT OF EDUCATION, COLUMBUS, OHIO 43215

THE OBJECTIVES OF THIS REPORT ARE TO DETERMINE WHETHER THERE IS A NEED TO ESTABLISH A STATEWIDE POLICY OF EARLY EDUCATION IN OHIO, TO DEFINE WHAT PRIORITIES ARE IMPLIED BY SUCH A NEED, AND TO SUGGEST RELEVANT RECOMMENDATIONS FOR THE ESTABLISHMENT OF A POLICY, IF NEEDED. SIXTEEN CHAPTERS (NINE-TENTHS) OF THIS REPORT PRESENT INFORMATION FROM RESEARCH LITERATURE ON THE DEVELOPMENT OF ABILITIES OR SKILLS OF YOUNG CHILDREN NECESSARY FOR SCHOOL ACHIEVEMENT. THE EFFECTS OF ENVIRONMENTAL DEPRIVATION ON LEARNING ARE ALSO DISCUSSED. THE REPORT URGES THAT OHIO ESTABLISH A POLICY IN EARLY EDUCATION TO ASSURE QUALITY PRESCHOOL AND KINDERGARTEN PROGRAMS FOR CHILDREN IN POVERTY-DEPRESSED AREAS. SPECIFIC RECOMMENDATIONS ARE MADE FOR CURRICULAR CONTENT, TEACHER TRAINING, WELFARE SERVICES, ADMINISTRATION, AND WORK IN CONJUNCTION WITH EXISTING AND NEEDED LEGISLATION. BIBLIOGRAPHIC REFERENCES ARE GIVEN. THREE APPENDIXES CONTAIN DATA ON (A) ESTIMATES OF CHILDREN BY AGE FOR OHIO COUNTIES, (B) TECHNICAL PROCEDURES FOR PROJECTING CHILDREN BY AGE FOR OHIO COUNTIES, AND (C) STATE REGULATIONS FOR KINDERGARTEN AS REPORTED IN A NATIONAL SURVEY. (WY)

ED045201 PS004018
PRELIMINARY ANALYSIS OF 1968-69 BOOTH ACHIEVEMENT. NIMNICHT, GLEN P.; AND OTHERS, NOV 69 10P.
EDRS PRICE MF-$0.65 HC-$3.29

THE RESPONSIVE MODEL PROGRAM USES THE TYPING OR LEARNING BOOTH AS AN IMPORTANT PART OF ITS AUTOTELIC (SELF-REWARDING) ENVIRONMENT, TO HELP CHILDREN DEVELOP THE MENTAL PROCESSES INVOLVED IN DISCOVERY OF RELATIONSHIPS, SUCH AS THE ASSOCIATION OF SOUND WITH SYMBOLS, OR DISCOVERING THE RULES OF A GAME. THE TYPING BOOTH ALSO HELPS CHILDREN TO DEVELOP INDEPENDENCE IN PROBLEM-SOLVING BEHAVIOR AND CAUSES RAPID LANGUAGE DEVELOPMENT. CHILD-CONTROL OVER INITIATION AND TERMINATION OF BOOTH ACTIVITIES IS EMPHASIZED. LANGUAGE DEVELOPMENT PHASES REFLECTING TYPING BOOTH ACHIEVEMENT ARE DESCRIBED: (1) FREE EXPLORATION, (2) SEARCH AND MATCH, (3) DISCRIMINATION, (4) TYPING WORDS AND STORIES, AND (5) CLASSROOM RELATED ACTIVITES. THIS PAPER REPORTS THE PROGRESS OF 801 KINDERGARTEN AND 300 FIRST GRADE CHILDREN, MOSTLY FROM LOW-INCOME HOMES, FROM 9 COMMUNITIES, DURING THE FIRST YEAR (1968-69) OF THE PROGRAM. TABLES GIVE DATA ON BOOTH ACHIEVEMENT FOR BOTH GROUPS OF CHILDREN, AND THE NUMBER OF MONTHS THE BOOTHS WERE IN OPERATION (A GROSS INDEX OF HOW LONG CHILDREN SPEND IN THE BOOTHS). IN GENERAL, DIFFERENCES IN BOOTH ACHIEVEMENT FROM DISTRICT TO DISTRICT, AND THE APPARENT RELATIONSHIP BETWEEN THE LENGTH OF TIME THE BOOTH WAS IN OPERATION AND BOOTH ACHIEVEMENT, REINFORCE THE IMPORTANCE OF BOOTH TRAINING FOR CHILDREN IN THE RESPONSIVE FOLLOW THROUGH MODEL (NH)

ED045202 PS004019
PRELIMINARY ANALYSIS ON KINDERGARTEN AND FIRST GRADE FOLLOW THROUGH TEST RESULTS FOR 1968-69. RAYDER, NICHOLAS F.; AND OTHERS, FEB 70 26P.
EDRS PRICE MF-$0.65 HC-$3.29

THIS PAPER IS A PRELIMINARY REPORT OF OBJECTIVE TEST RESULTS MADE BY APPROXIMATELY 300 POOR AND 100 NON-POOR KINDERGARTEN CHILDREN AND BY 417 FIRST GRADE CHILDREN DURING 1968-1969. TESTS ADMINISTERED TO THE KINDERGARTEN CLASSES IN THE FALL OF 1968 AND AGAIN IN THE SPRING OF 1969 WERE: SHORT-FORM WECHSLER PRESCHOOL AND PRIMARY SCALE OF INTELLIGENCE (WPPSI), CALDWELL PRESCHOOL INVENTORY (PSI), INNOVATIVE BEHAVIOR TEST (IB), AND CATEGORIES TEST (C). THE METROPOLITAN READINESS TEST WAS ADMINISTERED IN PRE-POST FASHION TO THE FIRST GRADE CLASSES. THE TEST RESULTS WERE USED TO MEASURE CHANGES IN A CHILD'S INTELLECTUAL ABILITY AS A RESULT OF ONE YEAR'S SCHOOLING IN A RESPONSIVE FOLLOW THROUGH CLASSROOM. EXCEPT FOR FOUR INSTANCES, AVERAGE TESTS SCORES MADE BY GROUPS OF BOTH POOR AND NON-POOR KINDERGARTEN FOLLOW THROUGH CHILDREN INCREASED FOR ALL TESTS IN EVERY COMMUNITY. THAT IS, OVER THE SEVEN TO NINE MONTH TIME PERIOD, KINDERGARTEN CHILDREN IN ALL COMMUNITIES INCREASED IN INTELLIGENCE, THE ABILITY TO FORM CONCEPTS, THE ABILITY TO SOLVE PROBLEMS AND THE ABILITY TO CATEGORIZE. RESULTS FOR FIRST GRADE CHILDREN WERE ALSO ENCOURAGING. THERE WERE CONSIDERABLE INCREASES IN METROPOLITAN TEST SCORES FOR BOTH FIRST GRADE COMMUNITIES FROM THE BEGINNING TO THE END OF THE SCHOOL YEAR. (AUTHOR/NH)

ED045203 PS004020
PRELIMINARY ANALYSIS OF 1968-69 HEAD START DATA. NIMNICHT, GLEN P.; AND OTHERS, 23 JUL 70 26P.
EDRS PRICE MF-$0.65 HC-$3.29

EIGHT HEAD START CENTERS WHICH USED THE RESPONSIVE MODEL PROGRAM DURING THE 1968-69 SCHOOL YEAR WERE ASSESSED TO DETERMINE COGNITIVE DEVELOPMENT OF CHILDREN, TEACHER PERFORMANCE IN THE CLASSROOM, ADEQUACY OF PHYSICAL FACILITIES, ADMINISTRATIVE SUPPORT AND THE INTERRELATIONSHIP BETWEEN THESE VARIABLES. TEACHERS WERE OBSERVED AT THE BEGINNING AND END OF THE SCHOOL YEAR AND RATED ON A SCALE DESIGNED TO INDICATE THE DEGREE TO WHICH THEY IMPLEMENTED THE PROCEDURES OF THE RESPONSIVE MODEL. FINDINGS INDICATED THAT THE MAJORITY OF TEACHERS INCREASED THEIR TEACHING SKILLS AND BECAME MORE CONSISTENT WITH THE MODEL CRITERIA. THE PRESCHOOL INVENTORY (PSI) MEASURING ACHIEVEMENT IN SKILLS AND CONCEPTS, WAS ADMINISTERED ON A PRE-POST BASIS TO 761 CHILDREN, AND AVERAGE SCORES IN ALL EIGHT COMMUNITIES DEMONSTRATED GROWTH THROUGHOUT THE YEAR. YEAR-END SCORES FOR THE RESPONSIVE MODEL CHILDREN WERE AT NATIONAL NORM LEVELS REPORTED FOR MIDDLE CLASS CHILDREN. (A LIMITATION OF THE PSI IS ITS LESS THAN ADEQUATE NORMS.) CHANGES IN CHILD TEST PERFORMANCE WERE GREATEST IN CLASSROOMS WITH ADEQUATE PHYSICAL FACILITIES, IN SITUATIONS WITH FEW ADMINISTRATIVE PROBLEMS AND WHERE TEACHER PERFORMANCE WAS CONSISTENT WITH RESPONSIVE MODEL OBJECTIVES. WHEN MEASURED BY PSI CHANGES, CHILD GROWTH WAS GREATEST FOR THOSE IN CLASSES WHOSE TEACHERS DEMONSTRATED A HIGH LEVEL OF TEACHING ABILITY. (AUTHOR/NH)

ED045204 PS004021
AN ASSESSMENT OF COGNITIVE GROWTH IN CHILDREN WHO HAVE PARTICIPATED IN THE TOY-LENDING COMPONENT OF THE PARENT-CHILD PROGRAM. RAYDER, NICHOLAS F.; AND OTHERS, 18 JUN 70 12P.
EDRS PRICE MF-$0.65 HC-$3.29

THIS REPORT IS ONE OF A SERIES EVALUATING THE PARENT/CHILD PROGRAM. THIS PROGRAM IS DESIGNED TO PROVIDE PRESCHOOL EDUCATION FOR 3- TO 4-YEAR-OLDS WHOSE PARENTS CANNOT AFFORD NURSERY SCHOOLS BUT YET ARE ABOVE THE INCOME LEVEL FOR HEAD START PARTICIPATION. TWO GROUPS OF PARENTS PARTICIPATED IN SEPARATE BUT EQUIVALENT PARENT/CHILD COURSES IN A CLASSROOM SETTING, 2 HOURS A WEEK FOR 10 WEEKS, AND WERE TAUGHT HOW TO TEACH THEIR CHILDREN THROUGH THE USE OF EDUCATIONAL TOYS. ALL 31 CHILDREN PARTICIPATING WERE PRE- AND POSTTESTED ON THE RESPONSIVE TEST, DEVELOPED TO MEASURE CHANGE IN THE INTELLECTUAL DEVELOPMENT OF CHILDREN WHO HAVE PARTICIPATED IN A RESPONSIVE ENVIRONMENT. A VARIETY OF SKILLS AND CONCEPTS WERE TESTED ON 13 SUBTESTS OF THE RESPONSIVE TEST. CONTROLS ALLOWED FOR THE EFFECTS OF MATURATION AND PRACTICE. FOR CHILDREN IN BOTH GROUPS OF PARENTS, THERE WERE SIGNIFICANT DIFFERENCES ON 9 OF THE 13 SUBTESTS. OF THE OTHER FOUR SUBTESTS, TWO WERE AT THE MAXIMUM LEVEL ON THE PRETEST, AND TWO MEASURED FACTORS FOR WHICH THE BOYS DID NOT PROVIDE PRACTICE. IT WAS CONCLUDED THAT THE CHILDREN LEARNED A CONSIDERABLE AMOUNT OVER THE 10 WEEKS OF INVOLVEMENT IN THE PARENT-CHILD COURSE AND THAT A LARGE PORTION OF THIS LEARNING CAN BE ATTRIBUTED TO THE COURSE ITSELF. PS 004 022 IS ANOTHER REPORT IN THIS SERIES. (NH)

ED045205 PS004022
AN EVALUATION OF NINE TOYS AND ACCOMPANYING LEARNING EPISODES IN THE RESPONSIVE MODEL PARENT/CHILD COMPONENT. NIMNICHT, GLEN P.; AND OTHERS, JUN 70 41P.
EDRS PRICE MF-$0.65 HC-$3.29

THIS SECOND OF A SERIES OF PAPERS EVALUATING THE PARENT/CHILD PROGRAM DESCRIBES THE PROCEDURE USED TO DECIDE WHETHER THE NINE TOYS AND THEIR ACCOMPANYING LEARNING EPISODES ARE APPROPRIATE FOR USE BY YOUNG CHILDREN IN THE PARENT/CHILD CONTEXT. PARENTS IN FOUR COURSES (PRELIMINARY AND PERFORMANCE TEST SITUATIONS) WERE GIVEN INSTRUCTIONS ON HOW TO PRESENT THE TOYS AND THE ASSOCIATED LEARNING EXPERIENCES TO THEIR CHILDREN. ONE TOY WAS PRESENTED EACH WEEK AND, AT THE END OF THAT TIME, EACH PARENT FILLED OUT A QUESTIONNAIRE ON THE CHILD'S INTEREST IN THE TOY. TO BE KEPT AS A PART OF THE PARENT/CHILD COURSE, A TOY (OR TASK) HAD TO HOLD THE INTEREST OF 80% OF THE CHILDREN. LOSS OF INTEREST BECAUSE OF MASTERY OF THE TASK DID NOT COUNT. IN ADDITION, DURING THE WEEK IN WHICH ANY GIVEN TOY WAS PRESENTED, THE CHILD HAD TO PLAY WITH THE TOY MORE THAN FIVE TIMES, AT LEAST ONCE WITHOUT THE PARENT SUGGESTING IT. DESCRIPTIONS OF TOYS, CRITERIA FOR EVALUATION AND A TABLE OF TEST RESULTS AND DECISIONS ON THE NINE EDUCATIONAL TOYS IS INCLUDED. PS 004 021 IS ANOTHER REPORT IN THIS SERIES. (NH)

ED045206 PS004023
A PROGRESS REPORT ON THE PARENT/CHILD COURSE AND TOY LIBRARY. NIMNICHT, GLEN P., 24 AUG 70 34P.
EDRS PRICE MF-$0.65 HC-$3.29

THIS REPORT GIVES AN OVERALL EVALUATION OF THE PARENT/CHILD PROGRAM OF PRESCHOOL EDUCATION FOR 3- TO 4-YEAR-OLDS. THE PROGRAM OBJECTIVES ARE: (1) TO AID PARENTS TO HELP THEIR CHILDREN DEVELOP A HEALTHY SELF-CONCEPT, (2) TO HELP PARENTS TO PROMOTE THEIR CHILDREN'S INTELLECTUAL DEVELOPMENT THROUGH EDUCATIONAL TOYS, (3) TO HELP PARENTS STIMULATE THEIR CHILDREN'S INTELLECTUAL ABILITIES BY IMPROVING INTERACTION BETWEEN PARENT AND CHILD, AND (4) TO AID PARENTS IN PARTICIPATING IN THE EDUCATION DECISION-MAKING PROCESS. THE RESULTS OF PARENTS' RESPONSES TO QUESTIONNAIRES AND CHILDREN'S PRE- AND POSTTEST SCORES ON THE RESPONSIVE ENVIRONMENT TEST ARE EVALUATED. WITH CERTAIN LIMITATIONS IN MIND (SUCH AS THE USE OF OPEN-ENDED QUESTIONS AND LACK OF A CONTROL GROUP), IT WAS CONCLUDED THAT: (A) PARENTS' ATTITUDES HAD CHANGED; THEY APPEARED TO BE MAKING MORE POSITIVE RESPONSES TO THEIR CHILDREN, HAVING A POSITIVE EFFECT ON SELF-CONCEPT, (B) RESULTS OF THE RESPONSVIE ENVIRONMENT TEST INDICATE THAT THE CHILDREN PROBABLY LEARNED SOME SPECIFIC SKILLS AND CONCEPTS AS A RESULT OF THE COURSE, (C) PARENTS BELIEVED THEIR CHILDREN WERE LEARNING, AND (D) THERE IS NO EVIDENCE TO SHOW THAT PARENTS WERE HELPED TO PARTICIPATE IN THE DECISION-MAKING PROCESS AFFECTING THEIR CHILDREN'S EDUCATION. (AUTHOR/NH)

ED045207 PS004024
OVERVIEW OF RESPONSIVE MODEL PROGRAM. NIMNICHT, GLEN P., JUL 70 12P.
EDRS PRICE MF-$0.65 HC-$3.29

THE RESPONSIVE MODEL PROGRAM ASSUMES THAT THE SCHOOL ENVIRONMENT SHOULD BE DESIGNED TO RESPOND TO THE LEARNER, AND THAT SCHOOL ACTIVITIES SHOULD BE AUTOTELIC, OR SELF-REWARDING, NOT DEPENDENT UPON REWARDS OR PUNISHMENT UNRELATED TO THE ACTIVITY. DEVELOPMENTAL THEORY, CERTAIN IDEAS OF OPERANT CONDITIONING, AND FLEXIBLE LEARNING SEQUENCES ARE USED IN THE PROGRAM. MAJOR OBJECTIVES ARE: (1) TO HELP CHILDREN DEVELOP A HEALTHY SELF-CONCEPT, AND (2) TO DEVELOP CHILDREN'S INTELLECTUAL ABILITY, SPECIFICALLY, THE ABILITY TO SOLVE PROBLEMS. ANOTHER OBJECTIVE IS TO GIVE THE CHILD AN UNDERSTANDING OF HIS CULTURAL BACKGROUND. THE PROGRAM HAS BEEN USED WITH LOW-INCOME MINORITY GROUP CHILDREN, AND WITH SOME MIDDLE CLASS WHITE CHILDREN, PRESCHOOL THROUGH GRADE 3. CURRICULUMS AND PROGRAMS FOR HEAD START AND FOLLOW THROUGH CLASSES ARE DESCRIBED. PARENT PARTICIPATION IN ADMINISTRATIVE DECISION-MAKING AND IN THE CLASSROOM IS ENCOURAGED. A PARENT/CHILD PROGRAM TEACHES PARENTS HOW TO TEACH THEIR CHILDREN THROUGH THE USE OF TOYS AND GAMES. AN INSERVICE PROGRAM TRAINS LOCAL PROGRAM ADVISORS, WHO TRAIN TEACHERS AND ASSISTANTS. ONGOING EVALUATION STUDIES EFFECTIVENESS OF TRAINING PROGRAM, CHILDREN'S GROWTH, AND DEVELOPMENT OF NEW WAYS TO ASSESS SELF-IMAGE AND ACHIEVEMENT. (AUTHOR/NH)

ED045208 PS004062
KEY ISSUES IN INFANT MORTALITY. FALKNER, FRANK, ED., 16 APR 69 92P.
EDRS PRICE MF-$0.65 HC NOT AVAILABLE FROM EDRS.
AVAILABLE FROM: SUPERINTENDENT OF DOCUMENTS, U.S. GOVERNMENT PRINTING OFFICE, WASHINGTON, D.C. 20402 ($1.00)

THIS PAMPHLET SUMMARIZES THE PROCEEDINGS OF A CONFERENCE ON INFANT MORTALITY SPONSORED BY THE NATIONAL INSTITUTE OF CHILD HEALTH AND HUMAN DEVELOPMENT. PARTICIPANTS WERE 25 PEOPLE ENGAGED IN VARIOUS DISCIPLINES (PHYSICIANS, NURSES, SOCIAL WORKERS, SOCIOLOGISTS, STATISTICIANS AND OTHERS) WHO DISCUSSED KEY ISSUES ON THE BASIS OF THEIR OWN KNOWLEDGE AND EXPERIENCE. THE TWO MAJOR POINTS MADE WERE: (1) THAT SOCIETY NEEDS TO CONCENTRATE LESS ON THE REDUCTION OF INFANT MORTALITY AS A GOAL IN ITSELF THAN ON ASSURING THAT CHILDREN WHO SURVIVE ARE WHOLE, HEALTHY INDIVIDUALS, AND (2) THAT NO MATTER HOW GOOD THE MEDICAL CARE SYSTEM IS, MORTALITY RATES CANNOT BE LOWERED BELOW A CERTAIN POINT UNLESS CERTAIN CHANGES ARE MADE IN THE SOCIAL ENVIRONMENT. WITHIN THIS CONTEXT, MANY ISSUES AND AREAS IN NEED OF RESEARCH WERE IDENTIFIED, PARTICULARLY IN CONNECTION WITH THE PERIOD WHEN THE MAJORITY OF DEATHS OCCUR: THE LAST EIGHT WEEKS BEFORE BIRTH AND THE FIRST FOUR WEEKS AFTER BIRTH. IT WAS ALSO EMPHASIZED THAT THERE IS ALREADY SUFFICIENT KNOWLEDGE TO SIGNIFICANTLY LOWER THE INFANT MORTALITY RATE IN THE UNITED STATES IF INSTITUTIONAL CHANGE, INCLUDING COMPREHENSIVE CARE PROGRAMS FOR THE POOR, COULD BE EFFECTED. (AUTHOR/NH)

ED045209 PS004063
AN OVERVIEW OF COGNITIVE AND LANGUAGE PROGRAMS FOR 3, 4, & 5 YEAR OLD CHILDREN. PARKER, RONALD K., COMP.; AND OTHERS, APR 70 209P.
DOCUMENT NOT AVAILABLE FROM EDRS.
AVAILABLE FROM: SOUTHEASTERN EDUCATION LABORATORY, 3450 INTERNATIONAL BOULEVARD, ATLANTA, GEORGIA 30354 ($2.00)

THIS REPORT WAS COMPILED TO SERVE AS A PARTIAL KNOWLEDGE BASE FOR THE SOUTHEASTERN EDUCATIONAL LABORATORY AND THE HARLEM RESEARCH CENTER IN THEIR EFFORT TO PLAN A RESEARCH PROGRAM IN EARLY EDUCATION. EDUCATIONAL PROGRAMS DESIGNED FOR 3-, 4-, AND 5-YEAR-OLD CHILDREN WHICH EMPHASIZE EITHER COGNITIVE-INTELLECTUAL DEVELOPMENT OR LANGUAGE DEVELOPMENT ARE BRIEFLY REVIEWED AND COMPARED. THE TEXT IS ORGANIZED INTO SIX MAJOR SECTIONS: (1) A SELECTION OF MAJOR REFERENCES IN THE GENERAL AREA OF EARLY EDUCATION, AND OF KEY REFERENCES TO ESTABLISH A RATIONALE FOR FOCUSING ON THE COGNITIVE-INTELLECTUAL AND LANGUAGE SKILLS IN EARLY EDUCATION FOR ECONOMICALLY DISADVANTAGED CHILDREN, (2) OUTLINES OF 18 PROGRAMS FOR WHICH A WRITTEN CURRICULUM EXISTS AND WHICH HAVE BEEN EVALUATED EMPIRICALLY, (3) ABSTRACTS OF SIX COMPARATIVE RESEARCH PROJECTS ON CURRICULUM, (4) OUTLINES OF SIX DEVELOPING PROGRAMS, (5) OUTLINES OF 17 EFFECTIVE CURRICULUM COMPONENTS AND IDEAS AND (6) IMPLICATIONS OF THE REVIEWS. BIBLIOGRAPHIC REFERENCES ARE INCLUDED ALONG WITH TWO APPENDIXES. APPENDIX A CONTAINS ABSTRACTS OF RESEARCH RELATING TO SPECIFIC PRESCHOOL PROGRAMS. APPENDIX B LISTS ADDRESSES OF PRESCHOOL PROGRAMS OR AUTHORS. (WY)

ED045210 PS004127
THE EFFECTS OF CARTOON CHARACTERS AS MOTIVATORS OF PRESCHOOL DISADVANTAGED CHILDREN. FINAL REPORT. GILL, ROBERT; AND OTHERS, JUL 70 100P.
EDRS PRICE MF-$0.65 HC-$3.29

A STUDY DESIGNED TO TEST EFFECTS OF CARTOON CHARACTERS ON THE BEHAVIOR OF PRESCHOOL DISADVANTAGED CHILDREN IN AN EDUCATIONAL SETTING EXPLORED THE USE OF CARTOONS AS COMPLEMENTARY ADDITIONS TO WORK MATERIALS. BECAUSE THE 83 HEAD START SUBJECTS HAD NOT BEEN INTRODUCED TO THE ALPHABET AN EXPERIMENTAL SET OF WORKSHEETS WAS MADE WHICH USED THE 26 LETTERS. ON MANY OF THESE WORKSHEETS A CAT CARTOON CHARACTER ACTED OUT SOME ASPECT OF THE MEANING OF A WORD ASSOCIATED WITH A PARTICULAR ALPHABET LETTER. OTHER WORKSHEETS USED WERE TRADITIONAL. ONE CONTROL AND THREE EXPERIMENTAL GROUPS WERE FORMED AND THE FOLLOWING AREAS OF CARTOON-EFFECT WERE MEASURED: EMOTIONAL ACTIONS, LEARNING ACTIVITY, SOCIAL ACTIVITY AND RESIDUAL ATTITUDES. FINDINGS INDICATE THAT THE CARTOON IS AN INTRINSIC STIMULATOR AND INFORMATION TRANSMITTER WHICH WOULD PROBABLY BE MORE EFFECTIVE IN ELEMENTARY SCHOOL CLASSES WITH OLDER CHILDREN AND THAT THE CARTOON SHOULD NOT BE USED FOR ROTE LEARNING. IT IS SUGGESTED THAT THE CARTOON CAN FILL A NEW ROLE IN THE CLASSROOM, HELPING THE TEACHER TO REACH CURRICULUM OBJECTIVES AND THE CHILD TO REACH HIGHER LEVELS OF LEARNING. APPENDIXES INCLUDE SAMPLE WORKSHEETS, PRE- AND POSTTESTS, A TEACHER QUESTIONNAIRE, DATA SUMMARY SHEETS, AND A HISTORY OF CARTOON DEVELOPMENT. (AUTHOR/NH)

ED045211 PS004195
HARTFORD EARLY CHILDHOOD PROGRAM, HARTFORD, CONNECTICUT: AN URBAN PUBLIC SCHOOL SYSTEM'S LARGE-SCALE APPROACH TOWARD RESTRUCTURING EARLY CHILDHOOD EDUCATION. MODEL PROGRAMS--CHILDHOOD EDUCATION. , 70 17P.
EDRS PRICE MF-$0.65 HC NOT AVAILABLE FROM EDRS.
AVAILABLE FROM: SUPERINTENDENT OF DOCUMENTS, U.S. GOVERNMENT PRINTING OFFICE, WASHINGTON, D.C. 20402 (HE 5.220:20162, $0.20)

THE HARTFORD EARLY CHILDHOOD PROGRAM INVOLVES MORE THAN 4,500 CHILDREN FROM 4 YEARS OLD TO FIRST GRADE LEVEL IN OVER 200 CLASSROOMS. CLASSROOMS ARE DESIGNED TO OFFER CHILDREN AN ENVIRONMENT THAT ENCOURAGES THEM TO LEARN INDEPENDENTLY. IDEAS HAVE BEEN BORROWED FROM THE MONTESSORI APPROACH AND

THE BRITISH INFANT SCHOOLS AND FITTED TO THE NEEDS OF THE HARTFORD SCHOOL DISTRICT'S URBAN STUDENTS. THE PROGRAM PHILOSOPHY EMBODIES NEW APPROACHES THAT CAN BE USED IN OLD SCHOOL BUILDINGS SUCH AS FORMAL EDUCATION BEGINNING AT 3 YEARS, MIXED-AGE "FAMILY" GROUPING, INTEREST CENTERS, AND EMPHASIS ON INTRINSIC MOTIVATION TOWARD PERSONEL SUCCESS. FUTURE PLANS CALL FOR EXTENSION OF THE PROGRAM TO ALL PUBLIC SCHOOL CLASSES IN GRADES K THROUGH 2. SOURCES OF MORE DETAILED INFORMATION ARE PROVIDED FOR THIS PROGRAM, SPECIFICALLY, AND FOR MODEL PROGRAMS CHILDHOOD EDUCATION, IN GENERAL. (AUTHOR/WY)

ED045212 PS004196
SANTA MONICA CHILDREN'S CENTERS, SANTA MONICA, CALIFORNIA: LOW-COST DAY CARE FACILITIES FOR CHILDREN OF WORKING MOTHERS MADE AVAILABLE THROUGH THE COOPERATION OF THE CALIFORNIA STATE GOVERNMENT AND LOCAL SCHOOL DISTRICT. MODEL PROGRAMS--CHILDHOOD EDUCATION. , 70 21P.
EDRS PRICE MF-$0.65 HC NOT AVAILABLE FROM EDRS.
AVAILABLE FROM: SUPERINTENDENT OF DOCUMENTS, U.S. GOVERNMENT PRINTING OFFICE, WASHINGTON, D.C. 20402 (HE 5.220:20135, $0.20)

TWO OF THE FOUR SANTA MONICA CHILDREN'S CENTERS ARE NURSERY SCHOOLS FOR CHILDREN AGED 3 TO 5; THE OTHER TWO CENTERS SERVE AS EXTENDED CARE FACILITIES FOR CHILDREN OF SCHOOL AGE. ALL CENTERS ARE CONCERNED WITH MEETING THE PHYSICAL, INTELLECTUAL, AND EMOTIONAL NEEDS OF CHILDREN ON A LONG-TERM BASIS AND STRESS A PROGRAM OFFERING A VARIETY OF PLAY EXPERIENCES. STAFF MEMBERS WORK WITH STUDENT ASSISTANTS FROM JUNIOR HIGH, CITY COLLEGE, AND THE NEIGHBORHOOD YOUTH CORPS. THIS AFFILIATION LIGHTENS THE TEACHERS' WORK LOAD AND BENEFITS THE STUDENTS BY GIVING THEM VALUEBLE EXPERIENCE IN CHILD CARE. PARENTS PARTICIPATE IN COMMUNICATION AND FUND RAISING ACTIVITIES AT BOTH STATE AND LOCAL LEVELS. LOCAL SCHOOL DISTRICTS AND THE STATE GOVERNMENT ALSO COOPERATE TO HELP ASSURE QUALITY DAY CARE AT A PRICE WORKING PARENTS CAN AFFORD. SOURCES OF MORE DETAILED INFORMATION ARE PROVIDED FOR THIS PROGRAM, SPECIFICALLY, AND FOR MODEL PROGRAMS CHILDHOOD EDUCATION, IN GENERAL. (AUTHOR/WY)

ED045213 PS004197
NEIGHBORHOOD HOUSE CHILD CARE SERVICES, SEATTLE, WASHINGTON: SEATTLE'S ANSWER TO CHILD CARE PROBLEMS OF LOW-INCOME FAMILIES. MODEL PROGRAMS--CHILDHOOD EDUCATION. , 70 22P.
EDRS PRICE MF-$0.65 HC NOT AVAILABLE FROM EDRS.
AVAILABLE FROM: SUPERINTENDENT OF DOCUMENTS, U.S. GOVERNMENT PRINTING OFFICE, WASHINGTON, D.C. 20402 (HE 5.220:20130, $0.20)

IN 1967 NEIGHBORHOOD HOUSE JOINED WITH THE SEATTLE DAY NURSERY, AN AGENCY WHICH HAS PROVIDED QUALITY CHILD CARE FOR MANY YEARS, TO INSTITUTE A HEAD START DAY CARE PROGRAM FOR CHILDREN FROM LOW-INCOME FAMILIES. THE PROGRAM ESTABLISHED HAS TWO COMPONENTS: THE ST. JAMES HEAD START CENTER WHICH HAS THREE CLASSROOMS AND THE DAY CARE HOME PROGRAM WHICH OPERATES IN INDIVIDUAL HOMES IN HOUSING PROJECTS. BOTH COMPONENTS PROVIDE HEALTH SERVICES, NUTRITION, EDUCATION, SOCIAL AND PSYCHOLOGICAL SERVICES PLUS OPPORTUNITIES FOR PARENT INVOLVEMENT ACCORDING TO HEAD START GOALS. THE ST. JAMES CENTER USES THREE MODELS AS THE BASIS OF CLASSROOM OPERATION AND INSTRUCTION: THE HUMAN DEVELOPMENT MODEL, THE RESPONSIVE ENVIRONMENT MODEL, AND THE SOCIAL REINFORCEMENT MODEL. EACH HEAD TEACHER CHOOSES THE MODEL SHE THINKS WILL BE MOST APPROPRIATE FOR HER CLASSROOM. THE DAY CARE HOME PROGRAM INCLUDES 10 HOMES IN FOUR SITES RUN BY MOTHERS CAREFULLY SCREENED FOR THE TASK. PERSONNEL ARE ENCOURAGED TO TAKE ADVANTAGE OF THE CAREER LADDER TO ADVANCE TO POSITIONS OF GREATER RESPONSIBILITY WITHIN THE PROGRAM. FUTURE PLANS INCLUDE ESTABLISHMENT OF ACTIVITY HOMES TO PROVIDE BEFORE- AND AFTER-SCHOOL CARE FOR SCHOOL-AGE CHILDREN AND PROVISIONS FOR CARE OF SICK CHILDREN. SOURCES OF MORE DETAILED INFORMATION ARE PROVIDED FOR THIS PROGRAM, SPECIFICALLY, AND FOR MODEL PROGRAMS CHILDHOOD EDUCATION, IN GENERAL. (AUTHOR/WY)

ED045214 PS004198
CROSS-CULTURAL FAMILY CENTER, SAN FRANCISCO, CALIFORNIA: A NURSERY SCHOOL PROVIDING A MULTICULTURAL CURRICULUM TO PROMOTE RACIAL UNDERSTANDING AND ACCEPTANCE. MODEL PROGRAMS--CHILDHOOD EDUCATION. , 70 16P.
EDRS PRICE MF-$0.65 HC NOT AVAILABLE FROM EDRS.
AVAILABLE FROM: SUPERINTENDENT OF DOCUMENTS, U.S. GOVERNMENT PRINTING OFFICE, WASHINGTON, D.C. 20402 (HE 5.220:20132, $0.15)

THE FAMILY CENTER IS THE DIRECT OUTGROWTH OF NURSERIES IN CROSS-CULTURAL EDUCATION (NICE) AND IS COMMITTED TO THE VALUES OF CROSS-CULTURAL ASSOCIATIONS. FAMILIES APPROACH THE EDUCATION OF CHILDREN 2 TO 5 YEARS AS AN INTERCULTURAL PRESCHOOL EXPERIENCE WHOSE INFLUENCE EXTENDS OUTWARD TO THE MULTI-ETHNIC NEIGHBORHOOD. PARENTS ARE ENCOURAGED TO PARTICIPATE, INTERACTING WITH THE STAFF AND EACH OTHER DURING FORMAL AND INFORMAL SESSIONS. THE PROJECT STAFF OFFER A COURSE ON WORKING WITH YOUNG CHILDREN TO INTERESTED MOTHERS. POSITIVE CONTRIBUTIONS STEMMING FROM THIS PROJECT ARE THAT THE CHILDREN INVOLVED SEEM TO BE DEVELOPING WITHOUT RACIAL OR CLASS PREJUDICE AND THE PARENTS ARE MORE OPEN-MINDED IN ACCEPTING MEMBERS OF OTHER SOCIOECONOMIC AND RACIAL GROUPS AS FRIENDS. THE MATERIALS AND FILMS DEVELOPED MAY BE USEFUL TO OTHER PROJECTS WHOSE AIM IS TO DEVELOP CROSS-CULTURAL UNDERSTANDINGS. SOURCES OF MORE DETAILED INFORMATION ARE PROVIDED FOR THIS PROGRAM, SPECIFICALLY, AND FOR MODEL PROGRAMS CHILDHOOD EDUCATION, IN GENERAL. (AUTHOR/WY)

ED045215 PS004199
DEMONSTRATION NURSERY CENTER FOR INFANTS AND TODDLERS, GREENSBORO, NORTH CAROLINA: A MODEL DAY CARE CENTER FOR CHILDREN UNDER 3 YEARS OLD. MODEL PROGRAMS--CHILDHOOD EDUCATION. , 70 19P.
EDRS PRICE MF-$0.65 HC NOT AVAILABLE FROM EDRS.
AVAILABLE FROM: SUPERINTENDENT OF DOCUMENTS, U.S. GOVERNMENT PRINTING OFFICE, WASHINGTON, D.C. 20402 (HE 5.220:20138, $0.20)

THE DEMONSTRATION NURSERY CENTER FOR INFANTS AND TODDLERS WAS ESTABLISHED IN 1967 TO CREATE A QUALITY DAY CARE PROGRAM THAT COULD BE REPLICATED ELSEWHERE, TO DEFINE THE COMPONENTS OF QUALITY CARE FOR INFANTS AND TO HELP THE STATE OF NORTH CAROLINA DEVELOP STANDARDS FOR INFANT CARE. THE CENTER MODELS ITSELF ON A WELL-FUNCTIONING HOME ENVIRONMENT AND NO ATTEMPT IS MADE TO ACCELERATE COGNITIVE OR MOTOR DEVELOPMENT; BUT THE STAFF MEMBERS STRIVE TO PROVIDE A WARM, HEALTHY, AND STIMULATING ENVIRONMENT FOR EACH OF THE 30 CHILDREN IN THE PROGRAM, RANGING IN AGE FROM 2 1/2 MONTHS TO 3 YEARS. SOURCES OF MORE DETAILED INFORMATION ARE PROVIDED FOR THIS PROGRAM, SPECIFICALLY, AND FOR MODEL PROGRAMS CHILDHOOD EDUCATION, IN GENERAL. (AUTHOR/WY)

ED045216 PS004200
APPALACHIA PRESCHOOL EDUCATION PROGRAM, CHARLESTON, WEST VIRGINIA: A THREE-PART PRESCHOOL PROGRAM COMBINING A TELEVISION PROGRAM, PARAPROFESSIONAL HOME VISITORS, AND A MOBILE CLASSROOM. MODEL PROGRAMS--CHILDHOOD EDUCATION. , 70 17P.
EDRS PRICE MF-$0.65 HC NOT AVAILABLE FROM EDRS.
AVAILABLE FROM: SUPERINTENDENT OF DOCUMENTS, U.S. GOVERNMENT PRINTING OFFICE, WASHINGTON, D.C. 20402 (HE 5.220:20143, $0.20)

A BREAKTHROUGH PROGRAM TO REACH RURALLY ISOLATED CHILDREN TO PREPARE THEM FOR FIRST GRADE, THE APPALACHIA PRESCHOOL EDUCATION PROGRAM WAS BEGUN IN SEPTEMBER, 1968. FOUR-HUNDRED FIFTY 3- TO 5-YEAR-OLDS ARE PARTICIPATING IN THREE TREATMENT GROUPS: (1) CHILDREN WHO, IN OR NEAR THEIR OWN HOMES, ARE SHOWN A DAILY EDUCATIONAL TELEVISION PROGRAM, HAVE A WEEKLY SESSION WITH A HOME VISITOR, AND A WEEKLY VISIT TO A MOBILE CLASSROOM, (2) CHILDREN WHO RECEIVE THE TELEVISION PROGRAM AND THE HOME VISITOR, BUT DO NOT ATTEND THE MOBILE CLASSROOM, AND (3) CHILDREN WHO RECEIVE THE TELEVISION PROGRAM ONLY. A CONTROL GROUP RECEIVES NO PRESCHOOL EDUCATION. SIGNIFICANT GAINS ON COGNITIVE AND LANGUAGE SKILLS WERE SHOWN BY CHILDREN IN GROUPS 1 AND 2. WITH CERTAIN MODIFICATIONS, SUCH AS INCREASED USE OF THE MOBILE CLASSROOM, THE PROGRAM WILL CONTINUE UNTIL THE SPRING OF 1971. EVALUATION WILL CONTINUE UNTIL 1972. SOURCES OF MORE DETAILED INFORMATION ARE PROVIDED FOR THIS PROGRAM, SPECIFICALLY, AND FOR MODEL PROGRAMS CHILDHOOD EDUCATION, IN GENERAL. (AUTHOR/NH)

ED045217 PS004201
COGNITIVELY ORIENTED CURRICULUM, YPSILANTI, MICHIGAN: A PROGRAM THAT EXPOSES PRESCHOOL CHILDREN TO A VARIETY OF MATERIALS AND EQUIPMENT TO TEACH CONCEPTS THROUGH PHYSICAL AND VERBAL EXPERIENCES. MODEL PROGRAMS--CHILDHOOD EDUCATION. , 70 28P.
EDRS PRICE MF-$0.65 HC NOT AVAILABLE FROM EDRS.
AVAILABLE FROM: SUPERINTENDENT OF DOCUMENTS, U.S. GOVERNMENT PRINTING OFFICE, WASHINGTON, D.C. 20402 (HE 5.220:20145, $0.25)

THE PERRY PRESCHOOL PROJECT, FOR EDUCABLE MENTALLY RETARDED 3- AND 4-YEAR-OLDS FROM DISADVANTAGED HOMES IS DESCRIBED. THIS PROGRAM USES A COGNITIVELY ORIENTED CURRICULUM (BASED ON PIAGETIAN THEORY) DESIGNED TO HELP THE CHILD CONSTRUCT THE MENTAL REPRESENTATIONS OF HIMSELF AND HIS ENVIRONMENT THAT WILL LEAD TO THE DEVELOPMENT OF LOGICAL MODES OF THOUGHT. SOURCES OF MORE DETAILED INFORMATION ARE PROVIDED FOR THIS PROGRAM, SPECIFICALLY, AND FOR MODEL PROGRAMS CHILDHOOD EDUCATION, IN GENERAL. (AUTHOR/NH)

ED045218 PS004202
THE DAY NURSERY ASSOCIATION OF CLEVELAND, CLEVELAND, OHIO: A LONG HISTORY OF CARE FOR CHILDREN, INVOLVEMENT OF PARENTS, AND SERVICE TO THE COMMUNITY. MODEL PROGRAMS--CHILDHOOD EDUCATION. , 70 22P.
EDRS PRICE MF-$0.65 HC NOT AVAILABLE FROM EDRS.
AVAILABLE FROM: SUPERINTENDENT OF DOCUMENTS, U.S. GOVERNMENT PRINTING OFFICE, WASHINGTON, D.C. 20402 (HE 5.220:20146, $0.20)
THE MULTI-FACETED PROGRAM OF THE DAY NURSERY ASSOCIATION OF CLEVELAND IS DESCRIBED IN THIS BOOKLET. SPECIFIC TOPICS INCLUDED ARE: A THERAPEUTIC NURSERY SCHOOL, DAY NURSERIES FOR LOW-INCOME NEIGHBORHOODS, NEIGHBORHOOD DAY CARE HOMES AND GROUP CENTERS, SUMMER CAMP, AND CONSULTATION SERVICES. SOURCES OF MORE DETAILED INFORMATION ARE PROVIDED FOR THIS PROGRAM, SPECIFICALLY, AND FOR MODEL PROGRAMS CHILDHOOD EDUCATION, IN GENERAL. (AUTHOR/NH)

ED045219 PS004203
MODEL OBSERVATION KINDERGARTEN AND FIRST GRADE, AMHERST, MASSACHUSETTS: MODEL CLASSROOMS WHICH OFFER COMPLETELY INDIVIDUALIZED SCHEDULING FOR MIXED AGE GROUPS OF KINDERGARTEN AND FIRST-GRADE STUDENTS. MODEL PROGRAMS--CHILDHOOD EDUCATION. , 70 19P.
EDRS PRICE MF-$0.65 HC NOT AVAILABLE FROM EDRS.
AVAILABLE FROM: SUPERINTENDENT OF DOCUMENTS, U.S. GOVERNMENT PRINTING OFFICE, WASHINGTON, D.C. 20402 (HE 5.220:20152, $0.20)
THIS BOOKLET DESCRIBES THE MODEL OBSERVATION KINDERGARTEN AND FIRST GRADE WHOSE APPROACH IS BASED ON THE PHILOSOPHY THAT EDUCATION SHOULD BE CENTERED IN THE LEARNER, THAT CHILDREN LEARN AT DIFFERENT RATES AND THAT CHILDREN LEARN SOMETHING ONLY WHEN THEY ARE READY. MANY ASPECTS OF THE BRITISH INFANT SCHOOLS ARE INCORPORATED IN THE PROGRAM. SOURCES OF MORE DETAILED INFORMATION ARE PROVIDED FOR THIS PROGRAM, SPECIFICALLY, AND FOR MODEL PROGRAMS CHILDHOOD EDUCATION, IN GENERAL. (AUTHOR/NH)

ED045220 PS004204
UNIVERSITY OF HAWAII PRESCHOOL LANGUAGE CURRICULUM, HONOLULU, HAWAII: A PROGRAM OF ENGLISH CONVERSATION FOR PRESCHOOL CHILDREN OF MULTIETHNIC BACKGROUNDS. MODEL PROGRAMS--CHILDHOOD EDUCATION. , 70 24P.
EDRS PRICE MF-$0.65 HC NOT AVAILABLE FROM EDRS.
AVAILABLE FROM: SUPERINTENDENT OF DOCUMENTS, U.S. GOVERNMENT PRINTING OFFICE, WASHINGTON, D.C. 20402 (HE 5.220:20156, $0.20)
THIS BOOKLET DESCRIBES THE UNIVERSITY OF HAWAII PRESCHOOL LANGUAGE CURRICULUM WHICH TEACHES PRESCHOOL CHILDREN OF MULTI-ETHNIC BACKGROUNDS TO SPEAK ENGLISH AND TO USE LANGUAGE AS A TOOL FOR COMMUNICATION, THOUGHT, AND PROBLEM SOLVING. THE PROGRAM WAS DESIGNED TO IMPROVE BOTH LINGUISTIC AND COGNITIVE ABILITIES. SOURCES OF MORE DETAILED INFORMATION ARE PROVIDED FOR THIS PROGRAM, SPECIFICALLY, AND FOR MODEL PROGRAMS CHILDHOOD EDUCATION, IN GENERAL. (AUTHOR/NH)

ED045221 PS004205
TACOMA PUBLIC SCHOOLS EARLY CHILDHOOD PROGRAM, TACOMA, WASHINGTON: COMBINED LOCAL, STATE, AND FEDERAL FUNDS SUPPORT A LARGE-SCALE EARLY CHILDHOOD PROGRAM IN THE PUBLIC SCHOOLS. MODEL PROGRAMS--CHILDHOOD EDUCATION. , 70 18P.
EDRS PRICE MF-$0.65 HC NOT AVAILABLE FROM EDRS.
AVAILABLE FROM: SUPERINTENDENT OF DOCUMENTS, U.S. GOVERNMENT PRINTING OFFICE, WASHINGTON, D.C. 20402 (HE 5.220:020160, $0.20)
THE TACOMA PUBLIC SCHOOLS EARLY CHILDHOOD PROGRAM IS A COMPREHENSIVE EFFORT TO GIVE ECONOMICALLY DISADVANTAGED CHILDREN AN EARLY EDUCATION PROGRAM WHICH WILL HAVE CONTINUITY AND LONG-RANGE EFFECTIVENESS. INVOLVING 5 YEARS OF EDUCATION (3-YEAR-OLDS THROUGH GRADE 3), THE PROGRAM USES THE RESPONSIVE ENVIRONMENT MODEL, WHICH HAS AS ITS OBJECTIVES THE DEVELOPMENT OF THE CHILD'S POSITIVE SELF-IMAGE AND HIS INTELLECTUAL ABILITY. SOURCES OF MORE DETAILED INFORMATION ARE PROVIDED FOR THIS PROGRAM, SPECIFICALLY, AND FOR MODEL PROGRAMS CHILDHOOD EDUCATION, IN GENERAL. (AUTHOR/NH)

ED045222 PS004206
COMMUNITY COOPERATIVE NURSERY SCHOOL, MENLO PARK, CALIFORNIA: A PRESCHOOL PROGRAM INVOLVING MOTHERS AS ORGANIZERS, HELPERS, AND DECISION-MAKERS. MODEL PROGRAMS--CHILDHOOD EDUCATION. , 70 15P.
EDRS PRICE MF-$0.65 HC NOT AVAILABLE FROM EDRS.
AVAILABLE FROM: SUPERINTENDENT OF DOCUMENTS, U.S. GOVERNMENT PRINTING OFFICE, WASHINGTON, D.C. 20402 (HE 5.220:20161, $0.15)
THIS BOOKLET DISCUSSES THE COMMUNITY COOPERATIVE NURSERY SCHOOL, A PROGRAM OF PRESCHOOL EDUCATION FOR CHILDREN FROM A WIDE RANGE OF SOCIOECONOMIC LEVELS. THE INVOLVEMENT OF MOTHERS IN THE CLASSROOM, IN SPECIAL CLASSES, AND IN DECISION-MAKING, IS AN INTEGRAL PART OF THE PROGRAM. SOURCES OF MORE DETAILED INFORMATION ARE PROVIDED FOR THIS PROGRAM, SPECIFICALLY, AND FOR MODEL PROGRAMS CHILDHOOD EDUCATION, IN GENERAL. (AUTHOR/NH)

ED045223 PS004208
THE DEVELOPMENT OF AN INFORMATION UNIT REVIEWING SELECTED WELL-DEVELOPED MODELS OF EARLY CHILDHOOD EDUCATION PROGRAMS. FINAL REPORT. CHOW, STANLEY H. L.; SIKORSKI, LINDA A., 30 OCT 70 119P.
EDRS PRICE MF-$0.65 HC-$6.58
THE INFORMATION UNIT ON EARLY CHILDHOOD EDUCATION WAS FORMED TO PROVIDE PRACTITIONERS IN THE FIELD WITH A READILY ACCESSIBLE SOURCE OF INFORMATION ON NEW PROGRAM DEVELOPMENTS, SO THAT DECISIONS ABOUT ADOPTING PROGRAMS MIGHT BE BASED ON A RATIONAL CONSIDERATION OF ALTERNATIVES. THE UNIT CONTAINS THE FOLLOWING FEATURES: A REVIEW OF TRENDS IN EARLY CHILDHOOD EDUCATION; A FILM-STRIP DESCRIBING SIGNIFICANT TRENDS; ABSTRACTS OF FIVE PROGRAMS WHICH DID NOT REQUIRE REPORT TREATMENT; AND DETAILED PROGRAM REPORTS FOR EACH OF SEVEN PROGRAMS (SUCH AS THE BANK STREET COLLEGE OF EDUCATION MODEL, THE RESPONSIVE ENVIRONMENT MODEL, THE ENGELMANN-BECKER MODEL, AND THE COGNITIVELY ORIENTED CURRICULUM). A PRELIMINARY FIELD TEST DETERMINED THE NEED FOR SUCH AN INFORMATION UNIT AND A MAIN FIELD TEST LATER JUDGED THE EFFECTIVENESS OF THE UNIT IN ACHIEVING ITS OBJECTIVES. RECOMMDNATIONS FOR IMPROVEMENT WERE ALSO COLLECTED IN THE SURVEY. QUESTIONNAIRES WERE USED IN THE EVALUATION. ACCORDING TO USERS, THE UNIT APPEARED TO BE SUCCESSFUL IN FULFILLING ITS INTENDED FUNCTIONS AND REACHING ITS OBJECTIVES. APPENDIXES COMPRISE ONE-HALF THE DOCUMENT AND INCLUDE SAMPLE QUESTIONNAIRE FORMS AND TABLES OF RELATED DATA ANALYSIS. (NH)

ED045224 PS004209
THE EFFECTS OF A PRESCHOOL LANGUAGE PROGRAM ON TWO-YEAR-OLD CHILDREN AND THEIR MOTHERS. FINAL REPORT. MANN, MARLIS, SEP 70 67P.
EDRS PRICE MF-$0.65 HC-$3.29
A STUDY WAS MADE TO DETERMINE WHETHER A STRUCTURED LANGUAGE PROGRAM FOR 2-YEAR-OLD EDUCATIONALLY DISADVANTAGED CHILDREN AND A COMPLEMENTARY STRUCTURED LANGUAGE PROGRAM FOR THEIR MOTHERS WOULD SIGNIFICANTLY AFFECT THE LANGUAGE BEHAVIOR OF MOTHERS AND CHILDREN. TWENTY-FOUR LOWER SOCIOECONOMIC STATUS MOTHERS AND THEIR 2-YEAR-OLDS WERE PLACED IN THE FOLLOWING THREE GROUPS: (1) LANGUAGE TREATMENT, (2) COUNSELING AND DAY CARE TREATMENT, AND (3) CONTROL WITH NO TREATMENT. HYPOTHESES WERE TESTED WHICH CONCERNED LANGUAGE STYLES AND MOTHER-CHILD INTERACTION PATTERNS. EXPERIMENTAL LANGUAGE GROUP CHILDREN AND MOTHERS RECEIVED TREATMENT (VERBAL REINFORCEMENT, ELABORATION AND EXTENSION) FOR 1 1/2 HOURS, 2 DAYS A WEEK FOR 10 WEEKS. MOTHERS IN THE COUNSELING GROUP RECEIVED COUNSELING ON MATTERS OF CONCERN TO LOW INCOME BLACK MOTHERS FOR 3 HOURS DAILY, ONCE A WEEK FOR 10 WEEKS. THEIR CHILDREN WERE IN DAY CARE FOR THAT PERIOD OF TIME. PRE- AND POSTTESTS OF MOTHERS AND CHILDREN IN THE TWO EXPERIMENTAL GROUPS WERE MADE USING A SYNTAX MEASURE AND THE CHILDREN WERE TESTED ON CONCEPT DEVELOPMENT. CONTROLS WERE POSTTESTED ONLY. IT WAS CONCLUDED THAT THE STRUCTURED LANGUAGE PROGRAM (A) PRODUCED A SIGNIFICANT CHANGE IN THE SYNTAX STYLE OF MOTHERS AND THE PATTERN OF VERBAL INTERACTION BETWEEN MOTHERS AND CHILDREN, AND (B) EFFECTIVELY CHANGED THE SYNTAX STYLE OF THE CHILDREN. (NH)

ED046486 PS003391
A GUIDE FOR MANAGERS OF CHILD DAY CARE AGENCIES. , MAY 69 70P.
EDRS PRICE MF-$0.65 HC-$3.29
THIS GUIDE WAS COMPILED BY A GROUP OF RURAL ARIZONA DAY CARE CENTER MANAGERS WORKING UNDER THE MIGRANT OPPORTUNITY PROGRAM (MOP) ESTABLISHED IN 1965. THE MANAGERS WERE PREVIOUSLY INEXPERIENCED AND, AT THE END OF TWO YEARS, WERE INTERESTED IN SELF-IMPROVEMENT AND MORE EFFICIENT WAYS TO PERFORM THEIR JOBS. THEIR COLLABORATION AND IDEA EXCHANGE, BASED ON THEIR ACTUAL EXPERIENCES, RESULTED IN THIS GUIDE. SUGGESTIONS FOR MORE EFFICIENT DAY CARE CENTER OPERATIONS ARE MADE. TOPICS INCLUDE STAFF SUPERVISION, PURCHASING GUIDELINES, AND IDEAS FOR EVALUATION OF CENTER EFFICIENCY. ANOTHER SECTION EXPLORES MEANS OF OBTAINING PUBLIC SUPPORT FROM VOLUNTEERS, PARENTS, AND AUXILLARY RESOURCES. THERE ARE GUIDELINES FOR COMPLIANCE WITH REGULATIONS AND ADEQUATE MAINTENANCE OF RECORDS (INCOME, EMPLOYMENT, HEALTH, PROGRESS, STATISTICS). THE GUIDE DEALS WITH THE PRACTICAL ASPECTS OF STAFF TRAINING INCLUDING LESSON PLANNING AND AN EXPLANATION OF METHODS EFFECTIVE IN ADULT EDUCATION. THIS PRACTICAL TEXT IS PARTICULARLY USEFUL FOR FEDERALLY FUNDED CENTERS FOR DISADVANTAGED CHILDREN. [FILMED FROM BEST AVAILABLE COPY.] (AJ)

ED046487 PS003674
PRESCHOOL EDUCATION AND SCHOOL ADMISSION PRACTICES IN NEW ZEALAND. BIRCH, JACK W.; BIRCH, JANE R., JUN 70 52P.
EDRS PRICE MF-$0.65 HC-$3.29

THE NEW ZEALAND EARLY CHILDHOOD EDUCATION EXPERIENCE IS STUDIED IN ORDER TO DISCOVER PRACTICES WHICH MIGHT BE ADAPTED FOR USE IN THE UNITED STATES. DATA ARE PRESENTED ON SOCIAL AND GOVERNMENTAL FACTORS INFLUENCING THE DEVELOPMENT OF EARLY CHILDHOOD EDUCATION IN NEW ZEALAND. PRESCHOOL EDUCATION IS CONDUCTED BY PRIVATE VOLUNTEER GROUPS SUBSIDIZED BY THE GOVERNMENT. THE PURPOSES AND ORGANIZATION OF THE TWO TYPES OF PRESCHOOL PROGRAM ARE PRESENTED. THE PLAY CENTER IS PARENT-OPERATED, EMPHASIZES PLAY AS A MEDIUM FOR SELF-REALIZATION, AND RECEIVES A SMALL AMOUNT OF FINANCIAL SUPPORT FROM THE GOVERNMENT. THE KINDERGARTEN, WHICH IS STAFFED BY GOVERNMENT TEACHERS, FOCUSES ON PREPARATION OF THE CHILD TO ENTER PRIMARY I, AND RECEIVES A LARGE AMOUNT OF FINANCIAL SUPPORT FROM THE GOVERNMENT. OF PARTICULAR INTEREST IS THE "DROP-IN" ADMISSION TO FIRST GRADE IMMEDIATELY AFTER EACH CHILD'S FIFTH BIRTHDAY. INTERVIEWS WITH 236 TEACHERS, ADMINISTRATORS, AND PARENTS FORM THE BASIS FOR POSITION STATEMENTS WHICH GIVE PROS AND CONS OF THE FIRST GRADE ADMISSION PROCEDURE. THE EDUCATIONAL DISADVANTAGE OF MAORI CHILDREN IS DISCUSSED. RESEARCH POSSIBILITIES ARE INDICATED. (NH)

ED046488 PS003676
ATTITUDINAL STUDY OF ROMAN CATHOLIC PARENTS OF PRE-SCHOOL CHILDREN REGARDING THE OPTION OF "CATHOLIC" OR PUBLIC SCHOOL EDUCATION FOR THEIR CHILDREN. MCGRATH, FRANCIS JOSEPH, JAN 70 55P.
EDRS PRICE MF-$0.65 HC-$3.29

THIS MASTER'S THESIS SURVEYED THE ATTITUDES OF CATHOLIC PARENTS TOWARDS THE OPTION OF PAROCHIAL OR PUBLIC SCHOOL EDUCATION FOR THEIR CHILDREN. THE SUBJECTS, MEMBERS OF ST. KIERAN'S PARISH IN CHICAGO HEIGHTS, ILLINOIS, WERE 85 FAMILIES WHO HAD ONLY PRESCHOOL AGE CHILDREN. PARENTS RESPONDED INDIVIDUALLY TO QUESTIONNAIRES. A SUMMARY OF QUESTIONNAIRE RESPONSES REVEALED: (1) YOUNG CATHOLIC PARENTS DO NOT FEEL A MORAL OBLIGATION BINDING UNDER SIN TO SEND THEIR CHILDREN TO PAROCHIAL SCHOOL; (2) THE MAJORITY OF CATHOLIC CHILDREN COMING OF SCHOOL AGE IN THE NEXT SIX YEARS ARE NOT LIKELY TO BE ENROLLED IN PAROCHIAL SCHOOLS; (3) YOUNG CATHOLIC PARENTS ARE IN FAVOR OF THE CATHOLIC CHURCH'S MAINTENANCE OF PAROCHIAL SCHOOLS; AND (4) THEY BELIEVE FEDERAL AND STATE GOVERNMENTS OUGHT TO GIVE FINANCIAL AID TO PRIVATE SCHOOLS. THE APPENDIXES INCLUDE COPIES OF THE COVER LETTER SENT TO PARENTS AND THE QUESTIONNAIRE. (AJ)

ED046489 PS003859
LICENSING OF CHILD CARE FACILITIES BY STATE WELFARE DEPARTMENTS: A CONCEPTUAL STATEMENT. CLASS, NORRIS E., 68 67P.
EDRS PRICE MF-$0.65 HC NOT AVAILABLE FROM EDRS.
AVAILABLE FROM: SUPERINTENDENT OF DOCUMENTS, U.S. GOVERNMENT PRINTING OFFICE, WASHINGTON, D.C. 20402 ($0.35)

IN THIS STATEMENT, STRUCTURAL AND OPERATIONAL ASPECTS OF LICENSING BY WELFARE DEPARTMENTS ARE ANALYZED. THE PHILOSOPHY OF LICENSING, AND THE UNDERLYING PRINCIPLES ARE DEFINED AND THE LICENSING OF CHILD CARE FACILITIES IS PRESENTED AS A PREVENTIVE SOCIAL SERVICE IN THE FORM OF LEGAL REGULATION. A COMPREHENSIVE DISCUSSION OF CHILD CARE LICENSING IS CONTAINED IN THE FOLLOWING CHAPTERS: CHILD CARE LICENSING; THE STATUTORY BASIS; THE FORMULATION OF LICENSING STANDARDS; ADMINISTRATIVE ORGANIZATION; APPLICATION, STUDY, AND LICENSE ISSUANCE; SUPERVISION-CONSULTATION; AND THE ACHIEVEMENT OF LICENSING GOALS. A HISTORICAL NOTE PROVIDES BACKGROUND ON THE DEVELOPMENT OF CHILD CARE LICENSING. THIS PUBLICATION SHOULD BE OF USE TO STATE WELFARE ADMINISTRATORS AND STAFFS IN IMPROVING THEIR LICENSING PROGRAMS, TO LEGISLATORS IN DRAFTING LICENSING STATUTES, TO CITIZENS SERVING ON BOARDS AND ADVISORY COMMITTEES OF WELFARE AGENCIES, AND TO SOCIAL WORK EDUCATORS. (AUTHOR/NH)

ED046490 PS003919
A TEST OF HABITUATION IN HUMAN INFANTS AS AN ACQUISITION PROCESS IN A RETROACTIVE INHIBITION PARADIGM. MILLER, DOLORES J.; AND OTHERS, SEP 70 18P.
EDRS PRICE MF-$0.65 HC-$3.29

HABITUATION AND DISHABITUATION TO A SIMPLE GEOMETRIC STIMULUS WERE EXAMINED FOR A SAMPLE OF 36 5-MONTH OLD SUBJECTS. ALL SUBJECTS VIEWED SUCCESSIVE PRESENTATIONS OF A STANDARD STIMULUS, AND, FOLLOWING A RETENTION INTERVAL, A SINGLE PRESENTATION OF THE STANDARD AND A NOVEL STIMULUS IN THE TEST PHASE. DURING THE INTERPOLATED INTERVAL, REPEATED PRESENTATIONS OF ANOTHER, DIFFERENT STIMULUS WERE SHOWN TO SUBJECTS IN THE RETROACTIVE INHIBITION CONDITION, WHILE THOSE IN THE CONTROL CONDITION WERE GIVEN AUDITORY STIMULATION. ANALYSES OF VISUAL FIXATION SCORES INDICATED THAT HABITUATION OCCURRED TO THE STANDARD STIMULUS AND THAT RESPONSE WITHIN CONDITIONS TO THIS STIMULUS IN THE TEST PHASE WAS IN DIRECTIONS PREDICTED BY THE INTERFERENCE THEORY OF FORGETTING. VISUAL RESPONSES OF SUBJECTS IN THE RETROACTIVE INHIBITION CONDITION APPEARED TO HAVE BEEN DISHABITUATED BY PRESENTATIONS OF A STIMULUS DURING THE RETENTION INTERVAL, WHEREAS THOSE OF SUBJECTS IN THE CONTROL CONDITION EVIDENCED CONTINUED HABITUATION TO THE STANDARD. THE BETWEEN-CONDITIONS COMPARISON ON THE TEST OF THE STANDARD STIMULUS, HOWEVER, ONLY APPROACHED SIGNIFICANCE. (AUTHOR)

ED046491 PS003921
UNDERSTANDING OF QUANTITATIVE CONCEPTS IN 3 1/2-4 1/2 YEAR-OLD CHILDREN. TANAKA, MASAKO N.; CHITTENDEN, EDWARD A., 3 MAR 70 9P.
EDRS PRICE MF-$0.65 HC-$3.29

THIS REPORT ANALYZES THE NONVERBAL PERFORMANCE OF 100 CHILDREN (3 1/2-4 1/2 YEAR OLD) ON TASKS OF DISCONTINUOUS QUANTITY. THE CHILDREN ARE PART OF A LARGER GROUP OF SUBJECTS PARTICIPATING IN A LONGITUDINAL STUDY OF EDUCATIONAL AND SOCIAL PROGRAMS FOR DISADVANTAGED CHILDREN CURRENTLY BEING CONDUCTED BY THE EDUCATIONAL TESTING SERVICE. THE PURPOSES OF THE ANALYSIS ARE: TO EXAMINE AND DESCRIBE SOME PSYCHOMETRIC PROPERTIES OF MEASURES APPROPRIATE FOR USE WITH VERY YOUNG CHILDREN; TO RELATE THE MEASURES T(THEORY IN DEVELOPMENTAL PSYCHOLOGY; AND TO CONSIDER SOME IMPLICATIONS FOR EDUCATIONAL RESEARCH AND PRACTICE. THE TWO PRINCIPAL MEASURES ARE A SPONTANEOUS CORRESPONDENCE TASK AND A TEST OF SPATIAL ENUMERATION, WITH A THIRD SUPPLEMENTARY TEST OF COUNTING. THE RESULTS SUGGEST THE FEASIBILITY OF MEASURES OF QUANTITATIVE THINKING WHICH ARE LESS DEPENDENT ON VERBAL RESPONSES AND WHICH ATTEMPT TO FOCUS ON THE PROCESSES OF RESPONDING. (AUTHOR/AJ)

ED046492 PS003941
INFORMATION ON INTERVENTION PROGRAMS OF THE DEMONSTRATION AND RESEARCH CENTER FOR EARLY EDUCATION. BARBRACK, CHRISTOPHER R.; AND OTHERS, [70] 36P.
EDRS PRICE MF-$0.65 HC-$3.29

THIS REPORT DESCRIBES THE DEMONSTRATION AND RESEARCH CENTER FOR EARLY CHILDHOOD EDUCATION (DARCEE), A CENTER INITIATED TO DEVELOP KNOWLEDGE TO IMPROVE THE EDUCABILITY OF YOUNG CHILDREN. THE REPORT INCLUDES A FOLD-OUT DIAGRAM OF DARCEE INTERVENTION PROGRAMS--COMPLETED, CURRENT, AND PLANNED. EACH PROGRAM IS LISTED WITH (1) AN EXPLANATION OF THE PURPOSE AND OBJECTIVES OF THE PROGRAM; (2) A LISTING OF PROGRAM PUBLICATIONS AND REPORTS; AND (3) A DESCRIPTION OF THE INDIVIDUAL PROJECT'S SETTING, SUBJECT POPULATION, AND THE TIME PERIOD INVOLVED. INCLUDED IN THE REPORT IS A GENERAL DESCRIPTION OF THE DARCEE PROGRAM ORGANIZED IN TERMS OF TWO CLASSES OF VARIABLES, APTITUDE FOR ACHIEVEMENT AND ATTITUDES TOWARD ACHIEVEMENT. PROGRAMS FOR LANGUAGE, SOCIAL, AND PHYSICAL DEVELOPMENT ARE DISCUSSED. ALSO EXPLAINED ARE PROGRAMS FOR PARENTS WHICH ARE BUILT ON THE IDEA THAT TRAINING THE MOTHER TO PROVIDE EXPERIENCES FOR HER CHILDREN WILL PROMOTE THEIR GROWTH AND DEVELOPMENT. DARCEE PROGRAM IMPLEMENTATION METHODS AND EVALUATION APPROACHES USED ARE INCLUDED IN THIS REPORT. (AJ)

ED046493 PS003942
A PLAN FOR CONTINUING GROWTH. ARMINGTON, DAVID E., NOV 69 22P.
EDRS PRICE MF-$0.65 HC-$3.29

TO RESHAPE OUR SCHOOLS, TOP PRIORITY MUST BE GIVEN TO PROGRAMS SUCH AS FOLLOW THROUGH WHICH EMPHASIZE CURRICULUM CHANGE AND TEACHER EDUCATION. THE EDUCATION DEVELOPMENT CENTER FOLLOW THROUGH PROGRAM, INSPIRED BY AN 8-YEAR ASSOCIATION WITH THE REVOLUTION IN ENGLISH PRIMARY SCHOOLS, FORMULATED THESE OBJECTIVES: (1) TO HELP SCHOOLS CREATE CLASSROOM ENVIRONMENTS RESPONSIVE TO THE INDIVIDUAL NEEDS OF CHILDREN AS WELL AS TO THE TALENTS AND STYLES OF THE TEACHERS; AND (2) TO DEVELOP THE ADVISORY CONCEPT TO FACILITATE GROWTH AND CHANGE IN SCHOOLS. THE KEY ELEMENTS OF THIS APPROACH ARE THE OPEN CLASSROOM; THE TEACHER AS RESEARCHER-EXPERIMENTER RATHER THAN AUTHORITY FIGURE; AND THE ADVISORY SERVICE. ADVISORS ARE EXPERIENCED EDUCATORS WHO WORK IN UNTHREATENING WAYS WITH SCHOOLS AND TEACHERS TO HELP THEM REALIZE THEIR POTENTIALS AND TO MAKE CHANGE SELF-SUSTAINING. THE THREE MAJOR FUNCTIONS OF THE ADVISORY ARE TO SUPPORT RESEARCH AND DEVELOPMENT; TO MAINTAIN A WORKSHOP AND RESOURCE CENTER; AND TO FACILITATE COMMUNICATIONS BETWEEN CLASSROOMS AND TEACHERS. IN 1969-70, TWELVE EDC ADVISORS SERVED NINE SCHOOL DISTRICTS IN EIGHT WIDELY-SCATTERED STATES. PLANS ARE BEING FORMULATED TO ESTABLISH LOCAL ADVISORY GROUPS IN SCHOOL DISTRICTS. (AJ)

ED046494 PS003976
TEACHER-CHILD RELATIONSHIPS IN DAY CARE CENTERS. WORKING PAPER. KATZ, LILIAN G., SEP 70 40P.
EDRS PRICE MF-$0.65 HC-$3.29

TEACHER-CHILD RELATIONSHIPS ARE COMPLEX PHENOMENA WHICH CAN BE DESCRIBED AND OBSERVED FROM A VARIETY OF ANGLES, ON MANY DIFFERENT LEVELS. RECENT RESEARCH CONTRIBUTES SOME INFORMATION APPLICABLE TO THE ANALYSIS OF TEACHER-CHILD RELATIONS AND IDENTIFIES ISSUES FOR FURTHER STUDY. TEACHER FUNCTIONS OR DUTIES MAY DEPEND, IN PART, UPON THE TEACHER'S BACKGROUND AND THE DEMANDS OF HER PROGRAM. ALTHOUGH FOUR TYPES OF FUNCTIONS ARE DEFINED (MATERNAL, THERAPEUTIC, FACILITATOR, INSTRUCTIONAL), NO RESEARCH HAS YET BEEN DONE TO INVESTIGATE TEACHERS' TIME DISTRIBUTION AMONG THESE ROLE FUNCTIONS. WHILE THE CHARACTERISTICS OF TEACHERS CAN BE EXAMINED IN TWO BROAD CLASSES, ATTRIBUTES AND BEHAVIORS, THE RESEARCH IS DIFFICULT TO SYNTHESIZE AND SUMMARIZE. HOWEVER, IT PROVIDES INDICATIONS THAT TEACHERS MAY NEED HELP IN DEVELOPING SKILLS TO EXTEND THE INFORMATION PROCESSING ABILITIES OF PUPILS AND TO BUILD MORE CONSTRUCTIVE CLASSROOM CLIMATES. THESE SKILLS NEED TO BE CLEARLY IDENTIFIED. RESEARCH INVOLVING LARGER SAMPLE SIZES IS NEEDED TO SUPPORT STUDIES ASSESSING THE PREDICTABILITY OF TEACHER BEHAVIOR FROM THE SPECIFICATIONS OF CURRICULUM MODELS. FEW STUDIES DEAL WITH THE EFFECTS OF TEACHERS ON CHILDREN. WELCOME ADDITIONS TO THE EXISTING BODY OF CONCEPTS ARE EXPECTED FROM THE PLANNED VARIATION EXPERIMENT WITH HEAD START CURRICULUM. REFERENCES ARE GIVEN. (WY)

ED046495 PS003986
NEGRO CULTURE AND EARLY CHILDHOOD EDUCATION. BARATZ, STEPHEN S., JUN 70 17P.
EDRS PRICE MF-$0.65 HC-$3.29

MOST COMPENSATORY EARLY CHILDHOOD PROGRAMS ARE BASED ON AN ASSUMPTION OF LINGUISTIC AND COGNITIVE DEFICITS WHICH MUST BE REMEDIED IF THE NEGRO CHILD IS TO SUCCEED IN SCHOOL, BUT MUCH COLLECTED DATA QUESTIONS THIS ASSUMPTION. THE LANGUAGE OF MANY LOWER CLASS NEGRO CHILDREN HAS BEEN SHOWN TO BE WELL-ORDERED AND HIGHLY STRUCTURED, ALTHOUGH THE DIALECT DIFFERS FROM STANDARD ENGLISH. A BODY OF LITERATURE HAS APPEARED WHICH TERMS THE NEGRO MOTHER INADEQUATE, BUT NEWER INSIGHT, ILLUSTRATED BY THE WORK OF VIRGINIA HEYER YOUNG, RECOGNIZES THAT THE NEGRO HAS A CULTURE AND LIFE STYLE WHICH IS MEANINGFUL AND WELL-DEFINED. CULTURE AND RACE ARE TOO OFTEN USED INTERCHANGEABLY, AND EARLY INTERVENTION PROGRAMS HAVE BEEN CREATED WHICH ARE ETHNOCENTRIC AND LACK CROSS-CULTURAL PERSPECTIVE. SUGGESTIONS ARE GIVEN FOR WAYS IN WHICH THE SCHOOL NEEDS TO BE RESTRUCTURED TO TAKE ADVANTAGE OF THESE OBSERVED CULTURAL DIFFERENCES, PARTICULARLY IN REGARD TO LANGUAGE AND READING. INTERVENTION IS SEEN AS NECESSARY, BUT IT SHOULD ASSUME A CULTURE CONFLICT, RATHER THAN A CULTURE DEFICIT, VIEWPOINT. (NH)

ED046496 PS004001
THE PHYSICAL ENVIRONMENT AS A MEDIATING FACTOR IN SCHOOL ACHIEVEMENT. MICHELSON, WILLIAM, JUN 68 24P.
EDRS PRICE MF-$0.65 HC-$3.29

AS PART OF A LONGITUDINAL STUDY OF 710 CHILDREN, THE ROLE OF THE HOME PHYSICAL ENVIRONMENT IN THE SCHOOL ACHIEVEMENT OF THIRD GRADE CHILDREN IS INVESTIGATED. HOME INTERVIEWS GATHERED INFORMATION ON FAMILY CHARACTERISTICS AND PHYSICAL ACCOMMODATIONS. CHILDREN'S ACHIEVEMENT DATA WAS OBTAINED BY ACHIEVEMENT TESTS AND TEACHER RATINGS. IT WAS HYPOTHESIZED THAT ACHIEVEMENT WOULD VARY DIRECTLY WITH BETTER QUALITY OF HOUSING AND PROVISION OF SUITABLE STUDY SPACE, AND THAT IT WOULD VARY INVERSELY WITH MEASURES OF CROWDING AND NOISE. TWO-WAY ANALYSIS OF VARIANCE TABLES WERE COMPUTED, WITH PHYSICAL AND SOCIAL FACTORS (SHARING OF HOMEWORK ROOM, HOUSING TYPE, AMOUNT OF NOISE, ETC.) AS INDEPENDENT VARIABLES, AND ACHIEVEMENT DATA AS DEPENDENT VARIABLES. THE HYPOTHESIS PROVED TRUE, WITH THE EXCEPTION OF ONE PHYSICAL VARIABLE, OVERCROWDING OF PERSONS PER ROOM OF THE DWELLING UNIT. CONCLUSIONS ARE TENTATIVE DUE TO CERTAIN LIMITATIONS OF THE STUDY. IT MAY BE THAT, WITHIN REASONABLE LIMITS, IT IS NOT THE NUMBER OF PEOPLE WHO OCCUPY A DWELLING THAT INFLUENCES STUDY AND RETENTION, BUT RATHER THE WAY THE AVAILABLE SPACE IS DIVIDED AND USED. (NH)

ED046497 PS004002
AN INVESTIGATION OF THE RELATIVE EFFECTIVENESS OF SELECTED CURRICULUM VARIABLES IN THE LANGUAGE DEVELOPMENT OF HEAD START CHILDREN. FRIEDMAN, MYLES I.; AND OTHERS, APR 70 133P.
EDRS PRICE MF-$0.65 HC-$6.58

THIS REPORT EVALUATES THE INFLUENCE OF FIVE LANGUAGE PROGRAMS ON THE LEARNING OF CHILDREN IN YEAR-ROUND HEAD START PROGRAMS. IT PRESENTS THE STATISTICAL ANALYSIS AND DESIGN OF AN INVESTIGATION CONDUCTED IN TEN CLASSROOMS IN TWO SITES (HENDERSON, NORTH CAROLINA AND VERO BEACH, FLORIDA). THE CORE OF THE PROGRAMS WAS THE BUCHANAN READINESS IN LANGUAGE ARTS PROGRAM WITH FOUR COMBINATIONS OF SUPPLEMENTS. A MONITORED AND AN UNMONITORED CONTROL GROUP WERE USED IN EACH SITE. IT WAS HYPOTHESIZED THAT THE EXPERIMENTAL CLASSES WOULD OUTRANK THE CONTROLS IN A PREDETERMINED ORDER. ALTHOUGH SIGNIFICANT DIFFERENCES WERE FOUND ON SEVERAL SUBTEST MEASURES, THE DATA DID NOT SUPPORT THE HYPOTHESIS. THE EXPERIMENTAL GROUPS, IN GENERAL, OUTPERFORMED THE CONTROL GROUPS ON ONLY TWO OF THE PRE- POSTTEST MEASURES (ALPHABET AND LETTER RECOGNITION). APPENDIXES COMPRISE ONE-HALF OF THE DOCUMENT AND INCLUDE TWO MANUALS FOR TEACHERS (BUCHANAN-SWANSON SUPPLEMENT AND THE REINSTEIN REINFORCEMENT PROGRAM), COVER LETTERS AND SAMPLE QUESTIONNAIRES USED IN THE LANGUAGE PROGRAM EVALUATION, A LISTING OF INSTRUMENTS COMMON TO NATIONAL EVALUATION PROJECTS, FORMS AND REPORTS USED FOR A VARIETY OF TESTS AND TESTING CONDITIONS, A LISTING OF PERSONNEL, AND THE TABLES FROM STATISTICAL ANALYSES. THE INTERIM REPORT EMPHASIZING THE GENERAL RATIONALE FOR THIS INVESTIGATION IS AVAILABLE AS PS 003 680. [FILMED FROM BEST AVAILABLE COPY.] (WY)

ED046498 PS004003
DEVELOPMENTAL TRENDS IN THE SELECTIVE PERCEPTION OF RACE AND AFFECT BY YOUNG NEGRO AND CAUCASIAN CHILDREN. STRAIN, BARBARA, AUG 70 49P.
EDRS PRICE MF-$0.65 HC-$3.29

THIS STUDY USED A "DISGUISED-STRUCTURED" TECHNIQUE FOR DETERMINING THE DIFFERENTIAL SALIENCY OF RACE AND AFFECT ON PREFERENCE BEHAVIOR OF 60 5-, 6-, AND 7-YEAR-OLD NEGRO AND CAUCASIAN CHILDREN. POSITIVELY AND NEGATIVELY VALUED OBJECTS WERE DISTRIBUTED BY SUBJECTS AMONG PHOTOGRAPHS OF HAPPY AND SAD NEGRO AND CAUCASIAN CHILDREN. NO RACIAL PREFERENCE WAS FOUND AMONG 5-YEAR-OLDS OF EITHER RACE OR AMONG OLDER NEGRO CHILDREN; 6- AND 7-YEAR-OLD CAUCASIAN CHILDREN SHOWED GROWING PREFERENCE FOR THE CAUCASIAN STIMULI. PREFERENCE FOR THE HAPPY STIMULI WAS SHOWN BY ALL GROUPS OF CHILDREN, THE AFFECT DIFFERENCES OVERRIDING ALL RACE PREFERENCES. INCLUDED ARE BOTH REFERENCES AND A BIBLIOGRAPHY OF SOURCES NOT CITED IN THE TEXT. APPENDIXES PROVIDED INCLUDE A DUPLICATION OF TASK PHOTOGRAPHS, SAMPLE DATA FORM, AND ADDITIONAL TASK TABLES. (AUTHOR/AJ)

ED046499 PS004011
PIAGET'S CONCEPT OF CLASSIFICATION: A COMPARATIVE STUDY OF SOCIALLY DISADVANTAGED AND MIDDLE-CLASS YOUNG CHILDREN. WEI, TAM THI DANG, [69] 20P.
EDRS PRICE MF-$0.65 HC-$3.29

THIS STUDY EXAMINES THE DIFFERENCES IN CLASSIFICATORY PERFORMANCE OF CHILDREN FROM MIDDLE CLASS (MC) AND FROM CULTURALLY DEPRIVED (CD) BACKGROUNDS AT KINDERGARTEN AND SECOND GRADE LEVELS. IT WAS HYPOTHESIZED THAT: (A) THE ABILITY TO CLASSIFY INCREASES WITH AGE (B) CD CHILDREN WOULD SCORE LOWER ON TALKS OF CLASSIFICATION THAN CHILDREN IN MC GROUPS (C) THE RANGE OF DIFFERENCES BETWEEN THE TWO SPECIAL GROUPS WOULD BE GREATER FOR THE SECOND GRADE THAN FOR THE KINDERGARTEN CHILDREN (D) THERE IS A DIFFERENCE IN THE JUSTIFICATION SCORES FAVORING THE ADVANTAGED OVER THE DEPRIVED GROUPS. EIGHTY SUBJECTS, IN FOUR GROUPS OF TWENTY EACH, PARTICIPATED. FOUR CLASSIFICATION TASKS OF PIAGET WERE USED (CHANGING CRITERIA, CLASSIFICATION, CLASS INCLUSION, AND MATRICES). SUBJECTS WERE INDIVIDUALLY INTERVIEWED, ASKED THE SAME QUESTIONS AND PRESENTED THE FOUR TASKS IN SEQUENCE. FINDINGS SUPPORTED THE HYPOTHESIS THAT THE ABILITY TO CLASSIFY INCREASES WITH AGE. THEY ALSO POINTED TO A SIGNIFICANT DIFFERENCE BETWEEN THE PERFORMANCE AND THE JUSTIFICATION SCORES OF THE TWO SOCIAL GROUPS. FINDINGS FROM THIS STUDY INDICATED AN ALMOST PARALLEL DEVELOPMENT BETWEEN THE TWO GRADE LEVELS OF THE TWO SOCIAL CLASSES. IT MIGHT BE PROFITABLE TO REPEAT THIS STUDY WITH A WIDER RANGE OF AGE LEVELS AND WITH A LARGER SAMPLE TO ASCERTAIN THE PRESENCE OR ABSENCE OF SOCIAL CLASS DIFFERENCES IN CLASSIFICATORY PERFORMANCE. (WY)

ED046500 PS004013
RULE STRUCTURE AND PROPORTION OF POSITIVE INSTANCES AS DETERMINANTS OF CONCEPT ATTAINMENT IN CHILDREN. SIEGEL, LINDA S.; FORBES, WILLIAM H., [69] 11P.
EDRS PRICE MF-$0.65 HC-$3.29
AVAILABLE FROM: LINDA S. SIEGEL, DEPARTMENT OF PSYCHIATRY, MCMASTER UNIVERSITY, HAMILTON, ONTARIO, CANADA

THIS STUDY TESTS THE FOLLOWING HYPOTHESES: (A) THE ABILITY TO SOLVE DISJUNCTIVE CONCEPTS INCREASES WITH AGE; (B) POSITIVE INSTANCES ARE OF GREATER USE IN SOLVING CONJUNCTIVE CONCEPTS WHILE NEGATIVE INSTANCES ARE OF GREATER USE IN SOLVING DISJUNCTIVE CONCEPTS; (C) OLDER CHILDREN WILL SHOW GREATER IMPROVEMENT THAN YOUNGER CHILDREN IN CONCEPT ATTAINMENT PERFORMANCE AS THE PROPORTION OF NEGATIVE INSTANCES INCREASES IN A DISJUNCTIVE PROBLEM. THE SUBJECTS WERE 36 SECOND GRADE CHILDREN AND 36 FIFTH GRADE CHILDREN. THE STIMULI CONSISTED OF 32 CARDS ON WHICH THERE WERE GEOMETRIC FORMS VARYING ON FIVE BINARY DIMENSIONS. SUBJECTS POINTED OUT THOSE CARDS IN THE ARRAY WHICH THEY FELT BEST MET THE EXAMINER'S VERBAL DESCRIPTION. RESULTS INDICATE THAT SECOND AND FIFTH GRADE CHILDREN SOLVED DISJUNCTIVE AND CONJUNCTIVE CONCEPT ATTAINMENT PROBLEMS WITH EITHER 20%, 50%, OR 80% POSITIVE INSTANCES. THE

OLDER CHILDREN SOLVED CONJUNCTIVE CONCEPTS MORE EASILY THAN DISJUNCTIVE CONCEPTS; BOTH WERE EQUALLY DIFFICULT FOR THE YOUNGER CHILDREN. AS THE PROPORTION OF NEGATIVE INSTANCES INCREASED, DISJUNCTIVE CONCEPTS WERE SOLVED MORE EASILY. (AUTHOR/WY)

ED046501 PS004017
PRESCHOOL EDUCATION AND POVERTY: THE DISTANCE IN BETWEEN. FINAL REPORT OF 1968-69 INTERVENTIONAL PROGRAM. GARFUNKEL, FRANK, JUL 70 49P.
EDRS PRICE MF-$0.65 HC-$3.29

AN EDUCATIONAL INTERVENTION PROGRAM FOR LOWER INCOME CHILDREN WAS CHARACTERIZED BY PARENT INVOLVEMENT IN ALL STAGES. ACTIVE DIALOGUE BETWEEN PARENTS, TEACHERS AND THE BOSTON UNIVERSITY HEAD START EVALUATION AND RESEARCH CENTER (BUER) WAS CONSIDERED A PRIMARY PURPOSE AND ENCOURAGED BY BUER TRAINING, RESEARCH AND SERVICE ACTIVITIES. AN ETHICAL CODE EVOLVED WHICH COMMITTED UNIVERSITY RESEARCHERS TO A NON-TRADITIONAL RESEARCH PROGRAM, OPEN TO COMMUNITY INVOLVEMENT AND CRITICISM. THE NEED FOR INSTITUTIONAL CHANGE WAS PERCEIVED AS MORE CRITICAL THAN ANY PARTICULAR CURRICULAR CONTENT, AND THE PROGRAM WAS CLOSELY INVOLVED WITH COMMUNITY PROBLEMS. PROGRAM COMPONENTS DISCUSSED ARE: PARENT INVOLVEMENT IN DECISION MAKING; INSERVICE TRAINING; OBSERVATION AND FEEDBACK; DIAGNOSTIC AND FOLLOW-UP WORK; AND DEVELOPMENT OF A NEW RESEARCH TOOL, THE CLASSROOM BEHAVIOR FORM. THE COMPLEX NATURE OF EVALUATION IS DISCUSSED, AND THE USE OF I.Q. GAINS TO MEASURE THE SUCCESS OF INTERVENTION PROGRAMS IS QUESTIONED. POLITICAL, SOCIAL, AND ECONOMIC GOALS OF HEAD START PROGRAMS ARE CITED AS MORE IMPORTANT TO THE NEEDS OF THE PEOPLE SERVED THAN THE EDUCATION PER SE OF YOUNG CHILDREN. HEAD START EVALUATION STUDIES SHOULD, THEREFORE, INCLUDE EVALUATION OF THESE GOALS. (NH)

ED046502 PS004055
AN APPLICATION OF PIAGET'S THEORY TO THE CONCEPTUALIZATION OF A PRESCHOOL CURRICULUM. KAMII, CONSTANCE, MAY 70 57P.
EDRS PRICE MF-$0.65 HC-$3.29

A PIAGETIAN PRESCHOOL EMPHASIZES THE CHILD'S ACTIVE CONSTRUCTION OF MENTAL IMAGES RATHER THAN PASSIVE ASSOCIATION OF WORDS AND PICTURES WITH REAL OBJECTS. THE ROLE OF THE TEACHER IS NEITHER TO DICTATE GOOD BEHAVIOR NOR TO TRANSMIT READY-MADE PREDIGESTED KNOWLEDGE. HER ROLE IS TO HELP THE CHILD TO CONTROL HIS OWN BEHAVIOR AND TO FIND THINGS OUT AS A RESULT OF HIS OWN CURIOSITY AND EXPLORATION. THE CHILD BUILDS KNOWLEDGE THROUGH HIS OWN ACTIONS ON OBJECTS, USING OBJECT FEEDBACK AND HIS OWN REASONING PROCESSES. TO ACCOMPLISH THIS TASK, THE TEACHER SELECTS A VARIETY OF OBJECTS TO GIVE A RANGE OF POSSIBLE ACTIVITIES FROM WHICH THE CHILD CAN CHOOSE. THE TEACHER DIAGNOSTICALLY PICKS UP ON THE CHILD'S INTERESTS BY MAKING SUGGESTIONS AND ASKING QUESTIONS. PIAGET'S DISTINCTION AMONG PHYSICAL, SOCIAL, AND LOGICO-MATHEMATICAL KNOWLEDGE AND REPRESENTATION GUIDES THE TEACHER IN DECIDING WHEN TO ANSWER A CHILD'S SPECIFIC QUESTIONS AND WHEN TO LEAVE THE QUESTION OPEN FOR THE CHILD TO FIND THE ANSWER. THE BASIC PRINCIPLE TO KEEP IN MIND IS THAT PLAY IS THE MOST POWERFUL ALLY ON THE TEACHER'S SIDE. A CURRICULUM WHICH REFLECTS AN UNDERSTANDING OF THE NATURE OF INTELLIGENCE FROM PIAGET'S BIOLOGICAL PERSPECTIVE WILL DEFINE ITS LONG-TERM GOALS FIRST AND THEN PROCEED TO CONCEPTUALIZE ITS SHORT-TERM GOALS. (AUTHOR/WY)

ED046503 PS004056
YPSILANTI PRESCHOOL CURRICULUM DEMONSTRATION PROJECT, 1968-1971. WEIKART, DAVID P., OCT 69 39P.
EDRS PRICE MF-$0.65 HC-$3.29

THIS REPORT DESCRIBES THE YPSILANTI PRESCHOOL CURRICULUM DEMONSTRATION PROJECT, A 5-YEAR PROGRAM CONDUCTED TO ASSESS THE EFFICACY OF PRESCHOOL INTERVENTION FOR CULTURALLY DISADVANTAGED CHILDREN DIAGNOSED AS FUNCTIONALLY RETARDED. FIVE GROUPS OF 3- AND 4-YEAR-OLDS PARTICIPATED IN THE PROGRAM OR SERVED AS CONTROLS. THE PROJECT SERVED AS A SOURCE OF DATA FOR RESEARCH ON DIFFERENT TYPES OF PRESCHOOL INTERVENTION AND AS A CENTER FOR DISSEMINATION OF INFORMATION TO TEACHERS, ADMINISTRATORS, AND RESEARCHERS IN EDUCATION. THE CURRICULA INCLUDED: (1) A COGNITIVELY OREIENTED CURRICULUM BASED PRIMARILY ON PIAGET'S PRINCIPLES OF COGNITIVE DEVELOPMENT, THE PRINCIPLES OF SOCIODRAMATIC PLAY AND IMPULSE CONTROL SUGGESTED BY SMILANSKY, AND SOME SPECIALLY DEVELOPED LANGUAGE TECHNIQUES; (2) A LANGUAGE TRAINING CURRICULUM EMPHASIZING LEARNING OF ACADEMIC SKILLS INCLUDING ARITHMETIC AND READING; AND (3) A UNIT-BASED CURRICULUM EMPHASIZING THE SOCIAL-EMOTIONAL DEVELOPMENT GOALS OF THE TRADITIONAL NURSERY SCHOOL PROGRAMS. THE PRESCHOOL SESSIONS WERE SUPPLEMENTED WITH HOME VISITS. THE RESULTS FOR THE FIRST TWO YEARS OF OPERATION (1967-69) DEMONSTRATED THAT CHILDREN MAY PROFIT FROM ANY STRUCTURED CURRICULUM WHICH OFFERS A WIDE RANGE OF EXPERIENCE AND INDIVIDUAL STUDENT ATTENTION. (AJ)

ED046504 PS004057
RELATIVE SOOTHING EFFECTS OF VERTICAL AND HORIZONTAL ROCKING. PEDERSON, DAVID R.; AND OTHERS, APR 69 16P.
EDRS PRICE MF-$0.65 HC-$3.29

IN THIS STUDY DESIGNED TO COMPARE THE RELATIVE PACIFYING PROPERTIES OF HORIZONTAL AND VERTICAL ROCKING, 13 INFANTS (MEAN AGE--58 DAYS) WERE EACH TESTED ON TWO SUBSEQUENT DAYS. THE ROCKING DEVICE WAS A CRADLE THAT COULD BE MANIPULATED TO PRODUCE SIDE-TO-SIDE ROCKING SIMILAR TO A COMMERCIAL CRADLE OR UP-AND-DOWN ROCKING. IN ITS UP-AND-DOWN MODE, THE CRADLE WAS MOVED THROUGH A 4-INCH VERTICAL EXCURSION. EACH SUBJECT RECEIVED ONE MODE OF ROCKING IN ONE DAILY SESSION AND THE OTHER MODE ON THE FOLLOWING DAY. THE SUBJECT'S ACTIVITY WAS INDEPENDENTLY RATED ON A 6-POINT SCALE EVERY 30 SECONDS BY TWO OBSERVERS, AND BY AN ELECTRO-CRAFT MOVEMENT TRANSDUCER PLACED UNDER THE MATTRESS OF THE CRADLE. EACH DAY THE INFANT RECEIVED TWO 5-MINUTE PERIODS OF ROCKING PRECEDED AND FOLLOWED BY A 5-MINUTE OBSERVATION PERIOD. SCORES SHOWED THAT ACTIVITY DURING ROCKING DECREASED; BUT WITH TERMINATION OF ROCKING, ACTIVITY RETURNED TO THE BASELINE LEVEL FOLLOWING THE FIRST ROCKING PERIOD. ACTIVITY AFTER THE SECOND ROCKING PERIOD DID NOT RISE TO THE INITIAL LEVEL. THE UP-AND-DOWN MODE WAS MORE EFFECTIVE AS A SOOTHER THAN THE SIDE-TO-SIDE MODE. TRANSDUCER SCORES WERE IN AGREEMENT WITH OBSERVER SCORES. (AUTHOR/AJ)

ED046505 PS004058
LEARNING TO LEARN ON A CONCEPT ATTAINMENT TASK AS A FUNCTION OF AGE AND SOCIOECONOMIC LEVEL. REPORT FROM THE PROJECT ON SITUATIONAL VARIABLES AND EFFICIENCY OF CONCEPT LEARNING. ADAMS, JANICE FREEMAN, SEP 70 47P.
EDRS PRICE MF-$0.65 HC-$3.29

AN EXPERIMENT TESTED THE ASSUMPTION THAT DIFFERENCES IN LEARNING TO LEARN (LTL) ARE TO A LARGE EXTENT EXPLAINED BY DIFFERENCES IN WHAT GROUPS OF DIFFERENT SOCIOECONOMIC STATUS (SES) HAVE LEARNED ABOUT WAYS TO LEARN A TASK. A 6-PROBLEM CONCEPT ATTAINMENT TASK NOT DEPENDENT ON VERBALIZATION WAS USED. SUBJECTS WERE 108 ELEMENTARY SCHOOL CAUCASIAN CHILDREN EQUALLY DIVIDED AMONG 7-, 9-, AND 11-YEAR-OLD AGE GROUPS, FROM LOW AND MIDDLE SES CATEGORIES. CERTAIN DIFFERENCES IN THE SHAPES OF THE SUBJECTS' LEARNING CURVES WERE PREDICTED. HOWEVER, RESULTS FAILED TO CONFIRM THAT THE 9- AND 11-YEAR-OLDS IN LOW SES GROUPS WOULD HAVE INCREASING GAINS ON THE EARLY PROBLEMS, WITH DECREASING GAINS ON THE FINAL PROBLEMS. THE LEARNING CURVES FOR THE LOW SES, 7-YEAR-OLD GROUP AND THE MIDDLE SES, 7-, 9-, AND 11-YEAR-OLD GROUPS WERE CURVES OF DECREASING GAINS ON ALL PROBLEMS, AS PREDICTED. IN SUMMARY, THE LEARNING CURVES ON PROBLEMS 1 THROUGH 6 WERE CURVES OF DECREASING GAINS FOR BOTH LOW AND MIDDLE SES CHILDREN AT THE THREE AGES STUDIED. SUGGESTIONS ARE MADE FOR FUTURE STUDIES. (AUTHOR/NH)

ED046506 PS004059
ATTITUDES OF PRESCHOOL AND ELEMENTARY SCHOOL CHILDREN TO AUTHORITY FIGURES. FORMANEK, RUTH; WOOG, PIERRE, MAR 70 15P.
EDRS PRICE MF-$0.65 HC-$3.29

THE PURPOSE OF THIS STUDY WAS TO EXAMINE CHILDREN'S PERCEPTIONS OF AUTHORITY FIGURES AS A FUNCTION OF THE VARIABLES OF SEX, AGE, ETHNIC GROUP AND SOCIO-ECONOMIC STATUS (SES). THE AUTHORITY FIGURES INCLUDED POLICEMAN, PRINCIPAL, TEACHER, FATHER, MOTHER, AND OVERALL (CUMULATIVE EFFECTS OF ALL AUTHORITY). QUESTIONS FROM THE CALDWELL PRESCHOOL INVENTORY WERE ADMINISTERED TO 90 PRESCHOOL CHILDREN. A MODIFICATION OF THIS INSTRUMENT WAS ADMINISTERED TO 526 ELEMENTARY SCHOOL CHILDREN (616--TOTAL POPULATION). RESPONSES WERE CATEGORIZED: THREATENING, PROTECTIVE, AMBIVALENT, OR NEUTRAL. INTERRATER AGREEMENT WAS GREATER THAN .90 IN ALL CASES. ANALYSIS OF THE DATA DEMONSTRATED THAT FOR PRESCHOOLERS, TEACHERS AND OVERALL WERE MORE THREATENING TO BOYS THAN TO GIRLS, AND THAT TEACHER, POLICEMAN, FATHER AND OVERALL WERE MORE THREATENING TO LOWER "SES" CHILDREN THAN TO MIDDLE "SES" CHILDREN. THE ELEMENTARY SCHOOL SAMPLE DEMONSTRATED THAT THREAT SCORES FOR THE PRINCIPAL AND OVERALL WERE GREATER FOR INTERMEDIATE AGE CHILDREN THAN FOR PRIMARY CHILDREN. THE FINDINGS SUGGEST THAT PERCEPTIONS OF AUTHORITY FIGURES ARE PROBABLY INITIALLY MODELED BY THE PARTICULAR SUBCULTURE OF THE CHILD AND THAT THESE PERCEPTIONS ARE SUBJECT TO CHANGE. (AUTHOR/AJ)

ED046507 PS004060

RELATIONSHIPS BETWEEN CHILDREN'S QUESTIONS AND NURSERY SCHOOL TEACHERS' RESPONSES. HAUPT, DOROTHY, 66 29P.

EDRS PRICE MF-$0.65 HC-$3.29

THIS STUDY (CONDENSED FROM AN UNPUBLISHED DOCTORAL DISSERTATION, "TEACHER-CHILD INTERACTION: A STUDY OF THE RELATIONSHIPS BETWEEN CHILD-INITIATED QUESTIONS AND NURSERY SCHOOL TEACHER BEHAVIOR," WAYNE STATE UNIVERSITY, 1966) EXAMINES THE TEACHING AND LEARNING PROCESSES SET IN MOTION WHEN FOUR-YEAR-OLD CHILDREN QUESTION THEIR TEACHERS IN NURSERY SCHOOL CLASSROOMS. THIRTEEN GIRLS, 13 BOYS, AND EIGHT TEACHERS, IN TWO MIDDLE CLASS NURSERY SCHOOLS WERE OBSERVED ON A ROTATED TIME AND PROGRAM AREA SCHEDULE. VERBATIM RECORDINGS WERE MADE OF CHILD-TEACHER-CHILD INTERACTIONS AND CODED TO PERMIT SYSTEMATIC COMPARISONS OF THE FORM, FUNCTION, AND CONTENT OF THE CHILDREN'S QUESTIONS AND THE TEACHERS' RESPONSES. RESULTS ARE PRESENTED IN TWO PARTS: (1) METHODOLOGICAL PROBLEMS AND (2) PATTERNS OF RELATIONSHIPS BETWEEN ACTS OF INSTIGATION, ACTS OF TEACHING, AND CHILD RESPONSE. MAJOR FINDINGS INCLUDE A DELINEATION OF DIFFERENCES BY SEX IN THE KINDS OF QUESTIONS ASKED, DIFFERENCES EVOKED IN STRUCTURED AND UNSTRUCTURED SITUATIONS, DIFFERENT RESPONSE PATTERNS USED BY TEACHERS FOR INITIAL QUESTIONS RATHER THAN RECIPROCAL QUESTIONS AND DIFFERENT RESPONSE PATTERNS USED FOR ANSWERS TO TYPICALLY BOY OR GIRL QUESTIONS. THE STUDY SUGGESTS THAT TEACHERS REINFORCE THEIR POSITION AS A PRIME VERBAL SOURCE OF INFORMATION AND THAT THEY NEED TO INCREASE THEIR SKILL IN HELPING CHILDREN LEARN HOW TO LEARN BY HELPING THEM POSE RELEVANT QUESTIONS IN A MORE ORDERLY SEQUENCE. (WY)

ED046508 PS004061

NUTRITION SURVEY OF WHITE MOUNTAIN APACHE PRESCHOOL CHILDREN. OWEN, GEORGE M.; AND OTHERS, [70] 22P.

EDRS PRICE MF-$0.65 HC-$3.29

AS PART OF A NATIONAL STUDY OF THE NUTRITION OF PRESCHOOL CHILDREN, DATA WERE COLLECTED ON 201 APACHE CHILDREN, 1 TO 6 YEARS OF AGE, LIVING ON AN INDIAN RESERVATION IN ARIZONA. THIS REPORT REVIEWS PROCEDURES AND CLINICAL FINDINGS, AND GIVES AN ANALYSIS OF GROWTH DATA INCLUDING SKELETAL MATURATION, NUTRIENT INTAKES AND CLINICAL BIOCHEMICAL DATA. IN THE STUDY, HOME INTERVIEWS WERE CONDUCTED AND CHILDREN WERE ALSO EXAMINED CLINICALLY. THE HIGH LEVEL OF VOLUNTARY PARTICIPATION OF FAMILIES REFLECTED GREAT INTEREST IN THE HEALTH STATUS OF THEIR CHILDREN. LIMITED SOCIOECONOMIC INFORMATION WAS OBTAINED ON THE PARTICIPANT FAMILIES BUT, GENERALLY, LIVING CONDITIONS WERE AT THE POVERTY OR NEAR-POVERTY LEVEL. IT IS NOTED THAT 36 OF THE CHILDREN WERE ENROLLED IN HEAD START AND RECEIVED A PORTION OF THEIR FOOD INTAKE THERE. THE PATTERN OF INSUFFICIENT OR INADEQUATE DIETARY INTAKES, GROWTH UNDERACHIEVEMENT AND BIOCHEMICAL EVIDENCE OF NUTRITIONAL RISK SEEN FOR APACHE CHILDREN WAS SIMILAR TO THAT OF CHILDREN LIVING IN POVERTY IN MISSISSIPPI. (NH)

ED046509 PS004064

A COMPARISON OF CONTRASTING PROGRAMS IN EARLY CHILDHOOD EDUCATION. WILLIAMS, CHARLES RAY, 70 128P.

EDRS PRICE MF-$0.65 HC-$6.58

THIS STUDY COMPARES THE PERFORMANCE OF PUPILS IN THE INDIVIDUALIZED EARLY CHILDHOOD PROGRAM AT THE UNIVERSITY OF CALIFORNIA AT LOS ANGELES ELEMENTARY SCHOOL WITH THAT OF KINDERGARTEN PUPILS IN THE MORE CONVENTIONAL PROGRAM OF THE LOS ANGELES CITY SCHOOLS. PROGRAMS OF BOTH INSTITUTIONS ARE ANALYZED AND RELATIONSHIPS BETWEEN SCHOOL PROGRAM AND STUDENT PERFORMANCE ARE NOTED. TO ASSESS PUPIL PERFORMANCE, THREE TESTS BASED ON PRECISE EDUCATIONAL OBJECTIVES FROM THREE CURRICULAR AREAS (SELF-RELATED SKILLS, READING READINESS, AND SOCIAL SKILLS) WERE ADMINISTERED TO A TOTAL OF 69 5-YEAR-OLDS. TO COMPARE THE PROGRAMS OF BOTH INSTITUTIONS, A SET OF OBSERVATIONAL CATEGORIES GUIDED DESCRIPTION OF ACTIVITIES FOR 21 CLASSROOMS. STATISTICAL EVIDENCE INDICATES THAT PERFORMANCE OF PUPILS IN THE UNIVERSITY SCHOOL PROGRAM WAS SIGNIFICANTLY (.01) HIGHER FOR ALL THREE CURRICULAR AREAS. AN ANALYSIS OF THE CLASSROOM OBSERVATIONS REVEALS A NUMBER OF AREAS OF GROSS DIFFERENCE BETWEEN THE TWO PROGRAMS WHICH APPEAR TO BE RELATED TO DIFFERENCES FOUND IN PUPIL PERFORMANCE. THE TEXT OF THIS DOCUMENT PROVIDES THE STUDY FORMAT AND FOUR EXTENSIVE APPENDIXES PROVIDE INSTRUMENTS DESIGNED TO EXPEDITE FURTHER RESEARCH INTO THE CAUSE AND EFFECT RELATIONSHIPS WHICH EXIST IN EDUCATIONAL PROGRAMS. (AUTHOR/WY)

ED046510 PS004065

ACTIVITIES FOR INFANT STIMULATION OR MOTHER-INFANT GAMES. BADGER, EARLADEEN, OCT 70 11P.

EDRS PRICE MF-$0.65 HC-$3.29

SPECIFIC SUGGESTIONS ARE OFFERED FOR MOTHER-INFANT ACTIVITIES, SEQUENCED ACCORDING TO DEVELOPMENTAL LEVELS, WHICH FOSTER THE PHYSICAL AND MENTAL DEVELOPMENT OF THE INFANT AND THE SOCIO-EMOTIONAL RELATIONSHIP BETWEEN MOTHER AND INFANT. THE ACTIVITIES ARE INTENDED FOR USE BY PROFESSIONALS, PARAPROFESSIONALS, AND MOTHER-TEACHER AIDES WHO WORK WITH INFANTS IN DAY CARE AND HOME BOUND PROGRAMS. THE PROGRAM IS BASED ON THE UZGIRIS-HUNT ORDINAL SCALES OF INFANT DEVELOPMENT AND INCLUDES THESE ACTIVITY CATEGORIES: (1) OBJECT PERMANENCE, (2) DEVELOPMENT OF MEANS, (3) IMITATION (VOCAL AND GESTURAL), (4) OPERATIONAL CAUSALITY, (5) OBJECT RELATIONS IN SPACE, AND (6) DEVELOPMENT OF SCHEMAS. A LIST IS GIVEN OF TOYS AND OTHER MATERIALS SUITABLE FOR INCLUSION IN A MOTHER-INFANT GAME KIT. (NH)

ED046511 PS004116

PRE-KINDERGARTEN PROGRAM, 1968-69. EVALUATION REPORT FOR THE PROJECT. NORTH, ROBERT D.; AND OTHERS, OCT 69 117P.

EDRS PRICE MF-$0.65 HC-$6.58

THE OBJECTIVES OF THE PRE-KINDERGARTEN PROGRAM WERE TO GIVE CHILDREN IN POVERTY AREAS OF NEW YORK CITY OPPORTUNITIES FOR INTELLECTUAL GROWTH THAT WOULD IMPROVE THEIR LATER CLASSROOM PERFORMANCE, HELP THEM ATTAIN A POSITIVE SELF-IMAGE AND A SOUND ATTITUDE TOWARD LEARNING, INCREASE PARENTAL INTEREST IN THEIR CHILDREN'S SCHOOL PROGRESS AND IMPROVE HOME-SCHOOL COOPERATION. OF THE 9,240 CHILDREN ENROLLED 49% WERE NEGRO AND 40% WERE SPANISH-SPEAKING. FOR PROGRAM EVALUATION, QUESTIONNAIRES WERE COMPLETED BY PRE-KINDERGARTEN TEACHERS AND PARAPROFESSIONALS, BY KINDERGARTEN TEACHERS, AND BY PARENTS. SAMPLE PRE-KINDERGARTEN AND KINDERGARTEN CLASSES WERE OBSERVED AND TESTED, TO DETERMINE WHETHER CHILDREN WHO HAD ATTENDED PRE-KINDERGARTEN DIFFERED FROM OTHERS, AND HOW WELL THE KINDERGARTENS BUILD UPON CHILDREN'S EARLIER LEARNING EXPERIENCES. SPECIAL EVALUATIVE INSTRUMENTS, THE PRE-KINDERGARTEN INVENTORY AND THE KINDERGARTEN INVENTORY, WERE DEVELOPED. THE MOST SIGNIFICANT RESULT OF THE PROGRAM WAS THE PUPILS' SUCCESS IN LEARNING BASIC CONCEPTS AND FUNDAMENTAL DISCRIMINATIONS HELPFUL IN LATER SCHOOL WORK. IT IS RECOMMENDED THAT THE PROGRAM BE CONTINUED AND EXTENDED TO MORE CHILDREN IN POVERTY AREAS. (NH)

ED046512 PS004117

MODELS, NORMS AND SHARING. HARRIS, MARY B., [70] 15P.

EDRS PRICE MF-$0.65 HC-$3.29

TO INVESTIGATE THE EFFECT OF MODELING ON ALTRUISM, 156 THIRD AND FIFTH GRADE CHILDREN WERE EXPOSED TO A MODEL WHO EITHER SHARED WITH THEM, GAVE TO A CHARITY, OR REFUSED TO SHARE. THE TEST APPARATUS, IDENTIFIED AS A GAME, CONSISTED OF A BOX WITH SIGNAL LIGHTS AND A CHUTE THROUGH WHICH MARBLES WERE DISPENSED. SUBJECTS AND THE MODEL PLAYED THE GAME TWICE. THE FIRST TIME THE MODEL WON AND DISPOSED OF PRIZE MARBLES IN ONE OF THREE WAYS. THE SECOND TIME THE SUBJECT WON AND WAS FREE TO DISPOSE OF OR SAVE PRIZE MARBLES. THE SUBJECTS' SUBSEQUENT SHARING WITH THE MODEL, SHARING WITH MENTAL HEALTH OR A TOYS FOR TOTS CHARITY, OR THEIR REFUSAL TO SHARE WAS OBSERVED THROUGH A ONE-WAY MIRROR IN THE TEST VAN. SUBJECTS ALSO RESPONDED TO A QUESTIONNAIRE DESIGNED TO ASSESS THE SALIENCE OF A NORM OF ALTRUISM. BOTH SPECIFIC AND GENERALIZED IMITATION OF ALTRUISM WERE FOUND AND SALIENCE OF SHARING APPEARED TO BE STRONGLY RELATED TO ACTUAL SHARING AND WEAKLY RELATED TO EXPERIMENTAL CONDITIONS. (AUTHOR/WY)

ED046513 PS004118

DEVELOPMENTAL GROUPINGS OF PRE-SCHOOL CHILDREN. FLAPAN, DOROTHY; NEUBAUER, PETER B., [70] 25P.

EDRS PRICE MF-$0.65 HC-$3.29

THIS PAPER REPORTS A LONGITUDINAL STUDY OF THE MENTAL HEALTH OR PATHOLOGY OF A NON-CLINICAL POPULATION OF 45 CHILDREN FROM 4 TO 6-YEARS-OLD FROM AN ENVIRONMENT OF ECONOMIC, EDUCATIONAL AND CULTURAL ADVANTAGE. DATA WAS COLLECTED ANNUALLY ON THESE CHILDREN FOR A PERIOD OF THREE YEARS. FINDINGS SHOWED THAT THE MAJORITY OF CHILDREN BETWEEN FOUR AND SIX YEARS OF AGE WERE JUDGED BY CLINICIANS TO HAVE PATHOLOGY, WITH OR WITHOUT INTERFERENCE WITH DEVELOPMENT, AND THAT RESEARCHERS WERE ABLE TO DETECT PSYCHIC CONSTELLATIONS AT AGE FOUR THAT MAINTAINED THEMSELVES DURING THE NEXT TWO YEARS. THESE FINDINGS POINT UP THE NEED TO DEVELOP MEANS FOR ASSESSING MENTAL HEALTH IN THE FIRST YEARS OF LIFE, AS WELL AS THE NEED TO EXPLORE THE VARIETY OF MENTAL HEALTH SERVICES THAT MAY BE USEFUL FOR CHILDREN BETWEEN FOUR AND SIX YEARS. (AJ)

ED046514 PS004120
DAME SCHOOL PROJECT (BI-LINGUAL PRE SCHOOL PROJECT), SANTA CLARA COUNTY OFFICE OF EDUCATION. FINAL REPORT, AUGUST 1, 1970. MICOTTI, ANTONIA R., AUG 70 32P.
EDRS PRICE MF-$0.65 HC-$3.29

THE OBJECTIVES OF THIS 1-YEAR PROJECT WERE (1) TO DEMONSTRATE AN AT-HOME PROCEDURE OF TEACHING IN ORDER TO IMPROVE THE CONCEPT FORMATION AND LANGUAGE DEVELOPMENT ENVIRONMENT OF 40 CHILDREN (3-5 YEARS) RESIDING IN LOW INCOME HOMES WHERE THE PRIMARY LANGUAGE WAS SPANISH; (2) TO TRAIN 11 WOMEN FROM THE COMMUNITY AS HOME TEACHERS; AND (3) TO GIVE TRAINING TO THE MOTHERS OF THE PROJECT CHILDREN SO THAT THEY COULD IMPROVE THEIR TEACHING TECHNIQUES WITH THEIR OWN CHILDREN. THE PRETESTS AND POSTTESTS ADMINISTERED WERE THE TEST OF BASIC LANGUAGE COMPETENCE, GIVEN IN SPANISH AND ENGLISH, THE INVENTORY OF DEVELOPMENTAL TASKS, GIVEN IN SPANISH, AND THE MATERNAL TEACHING STYLE INSTRUMENT (MOTHER/CHILD TEST) GIVEN IN SPANISH. AFTER THE YEAR, THE CHILDREN DEMONSTRATED MARKED IMPROVEMENT IN CONCEPT AND LANGUAGE DEVELOPMENT; ALL HOME TEACHERS HAD RECEIVED 370 HOURS OF INSERVICE AND PRESERVICE TRAINING; AND MOTHERS SHOWED CONSIDERABLE CHANGES IN TERMS OF ATTITUDES, EDUCATIONAL MATERIALS APPARENT IN THE HOMES, AND UPKEEP OF THEMSELVES AND THEIR HOMES. THE REPORT RECOMMENDS EXTENSION OF THE CURRICULUM TO KINDERGARTEN, REVISION OF TRAINING MODELS AND DEVELOPMENT OF "HOME PACKETS" FOR THE PROJECT CHILDREN. (AJ)

ED046515 PS004124
CONCEPT AND LANGUAGE DEVELOPMENT OF A GROUP OF FIVE YEAR OLDS WHO HAVE ATTENDED THE SYRACUSE UNIVERSITY CHILDREN'S CENTER INTERVENTION PROGRAM. LINDSTROM, DAVID; TANNENBAUM, JORDAN, SEP 70 20P.
EDRS PRICE MF-$0.65 HC-$3.29

TWO GROUPS OF 5-YEAR-OLD CHILDREN WERE EVALUATED USING SEVERAL MEASURES OF LANGUAGE AND CONCEPT ABILITY: STANFORD-BINET, FORM L-M; PRESCHOOL INVENTORY (PSI); BOEHM TEST OF BASIC CONCEPTS; PEABODY PICTURE VOCABULARY TEST, FORM B (PPVT); AND THE AUDITORY-VOCAL AUTOMATIC, MOTOR ENCODING, AUDITORY-VOCAL ASSOCIATION, AND VOCAL ENCODING SUBTESTS OF THE ILLINOIS TEST OF PSYCHLINGUISTIC ABILITIES (ITPA). THE EXPERIMENTAL (E) GROUP (N23) HAD ATTENDED THE SYRACUSE UNIVERSITY CHILDREN'S CENTER FOR A MINIMUM OF 32 MONTHS; A CONTROL (C) GROUP (N23) WITH LIMITED OR NO PRESCHOOL EXPERIENCE WAS USED FOR MATCHED CONTROL COMPARISONS. THE E GROUP SCORED CONSISTENTLY HIGHER THAN THE C GROUP ON THE MEASURES USED, AND AN EXAMINATION OF QUALITATIVE DIFFERENCES SHOWED THE E GROUP TO BE FUNCTIONING AT LEVELS WHICH WERE AT, OR ABOVE, THEIR CHRONOLOGICAL AGES. THE EMPHASIS WHICH THE CHILDREN'S CENTER PLACES ON LANGUAGE AND COGNITIVE DEVELOPMENTS CAN ACCOUNT FOR THESE RESULTS, AND SUGGESTS THAT LONG TERM ATTENDANCE IN SUCH A PROGRAM IS DESIRABLE. (AUTHOR/AJ)

ED046516 PS004178
A NATIONAL SURVEY OF THE IMPACTS OF HEAD START CENTERS ON COMMUNITY INSTITUTIONS. SUMMARY REPORT. , MAY 70 23P.
EDRS PRICE MF-$0.65 HC-$3.29

THIS PAMPHLET IS A CAPSULE COMMENTARY ON THE KIRSCHNER FIELD RESEARCH PROJECT WHICH ATTEMPTED TO OBTAIN A GREATER UNDERSTANDING OF HEAD START'S ROLE IN INFLUENCING COMMUNITY HEALTH AND EDUCATIONAL PROGRAMS. THE GENERAL GOALS FOR HEAD START ARE SUMMARIZED AND EXPANDED TO INCLUDE OBJECTIVES UNIQUE TO THIS SURVEY. SPECIFICALLY, THE KIRSCHNER PROJECT HOPED TO ILLUMINATE THE GENERAL QUESTION OF HOW TO ACHIEVE CHANGES IN LOCAL INSTITUTIONS UTILIZING A NATIONWIDE EDUCATIONAL INNOVATION AS THE INTERVENTION STRATEGY. FIELD WORK IN 42 COMMUNITIES REPRESENTING HIGH, MEDIUM, LOW, AND NO LEVELS OF HEAD START ACTIVITY IDENTIFIED FOUR KINDS OF CHANGES CONSISTENT WITH HEAD START PROGRAMS AND POLICIES. THE 1,496 CHANGES, WHEN PINPOINTED, COULD BE DISTRIBUTED INTO FOUR CATEGORIES: (1) INCREASED DECISION-MAKING, (2) GREATER EMPLOYMENT, (3) GREATER EDUCATIONAL EMPHASIS, AND (4) MODIFICATION OF HEALTH SERVICES. ALTHOUGH INSTITUTIONAL CHANGES TOOK PLACE IN A COMPLEX SOCIAL ENVIRONMENT, HEAD START DID SEEM TO HAVE A GENERALLY POSITIVE INFLUENCE IN MODIFYING LOCAL INSTITUTIONS SO THEY BECAME MORE RESPONSIVE TO THE NEEDS AND DESIRES OF THE POOR. A COMPLETE REPORT OF THIS RESEARCH PROJECT IS AVAILABLE AS PS 003 672. (WY)

ED046517 PS004192
HEAD START CURRICULUM MODELS: A REFERENCE LIST. , NOV 70 26P.
EDRS PRICE MF-$0.65 HC-$3.29

THIS BIBLIOGRAPHY LISTS REFERENCES TO BOOKS, ARTICLES, CURRICULUM AIDS, PROGRESS REPORTS AND OTHER WRITINGS RELATED TO THE 11 DIFFERENT HEAD START CURRICULUM MODELS NOW BEING TESTED EXPERIMENTALLY IN MANY COMMUNITIES. THE MODELS, DEVELOPED BY EXPERIENCED EDUCATORS, ARE: ACADEMICALLY ORIENTED PRESCHOOL; BEHAVIOR ANALYSIS MODEL; RESPONSIVE ENVIRONMENT CORPORATION; TUCSON EARLY EDUCATION MODEL; BANK STREET EARLY CHILDHOOD CENTER; PARENT EDUCATION PROJECT, FLORIDA MODEL; RESPONSIVE MODEL, BERKELEY; INSTITUTE FOR DEVELOPMENTAL STUDIES; PRIMARY EDUCATION PROJECT, PITTSBURGH; EDUCATIONAL DEVELOPMENT CENTER; AND COGNITIVELY ORIENTED CURRICULUM. READINGS GIVING AN OVERVIEW ARE ALSO LISTED. INFORMATION IS INCLUDED ON ORDERING THESE DOCUMENTS WHICH ARE AVAILABLE THROUGH THE ERIC SYSTEM. OTHER WORKS ARE AVAILABLE AT LIBRARIES OR FROM AUTHORS OR PUBLISHERS CITED. A LIST OF ADDRESSES OF THE EDUCATORS RESPONSIBLE FOR THE MODELS IS GIVEN. (NH)

ED046518 PS004194
PRESCHOOLER STUDY: THE MEDICAL, SOCIAL AND ECONOMIC CORRELATES OF POVERTY IN PRESCHOOL CHILDREN OF BRITISH COLUMBIA. A PILOT STUDY. TONKIN, ROGER S.; AND OTHERS, [70] 36P.
EDRS PRICE MF-$0.65 HC-$3.29

OVER 200 FAMILIES FROM LOWER AND MIDDLE INCOME AREAS OF BRITISH COLUMBIA, INCLUDING A GROUP REPRESENTING THE INDIAN COMMUNITIES, WERE STUDIED IN THIS EFFORT TO EXAMINE POVERTY AS IT RELATES TO FAMILIES, ESPECIALLY TO YOUNG CHILDREN. A WIDE VARIETY OF HEALTH, SOCIAL, AND ECONOMIC VARIABLES WERE EXAMINED IN THE HOPE OF DEVELOPING OUTPUT CRITERIA FOR THE EVALUATION OF POVERTY PROGRAMS. THE SUBJECTS WERE CHILDREN ENTERING KINDERGARTEN FOR THE FIRST TIME. INTERVIEWS WITH PARENTS GAVE MEDICAL HISTORIES OF THE CHILDREN AND PARENTAL ATTITUDES TOWARD COST OF LIVING AND INCOME. EXAMINATIONS GIVEN THE CHILDREN INCLUDED A ROUTINE PHYSICAL, DENTAL EXAMINATION, VISION AND HEARING SCREENING, AND A KINDERGARTEN READINESS TEST. CHILDREN OF POOR FAMILIES MORE FREQUENTLY DEMONSTRATED DENTAL DISEASE; SKIN, TONSIL, AND EAR INFECTIONS; AND POOR SCHOOL PERFORMANCE. THEIR FAMILIES WERE CHARACTERIZED BY FAMILY DISRUPTION, UNEMPLOYMENT, FREQUENT CHANGES IN RESIDENCE, AND LOWER LEVEL OF EDUCATION AND OCCUPATION. THE FAMILIES FROM MORE AFFLUENT SOCIOECONOMIC GROUPS MANIFESTED DIFFERENT ATTITUDES TOWARD EDUCATION. MORE THAN ONE-HALF THE DOCUMENT CONSISTS OF TABLES AND GRAPHS. (AJ)

ED046519 PS004210
MULTI-ETHNIC BOOKS FOR YOUNG CHILDREN: ANNOTATED BIBLIOGRAPHY FOR PARENTS AND TEACHERS. GRIFFIN, LOUISE, COMP., 70 77P.
EDRS PRICE MF-$0.65 HC NOT AVAILABLE FROM EDRS.
AVAILABLE FROM: PUBLICATIONS DEPARTMENT, NATIONAL ASSOCIATION FOR THE EDUCATION OF YOUNG CHILDREN, 1834 CONNECTICUT AVENUE, N.W., WASHINGTON, D.C. 20009 ($2.00)

THIS ANNOTATED BIBLIOGRAPHY LISTS BOOKS NOW AVAILABLE FOR CHILDREN WHO ARE NEITHER WHITE NOR MIDDLE CLASS. TEACHERS AND PARENTS WILL FIND THE BIBLIOGRAPHY EASY TO USE, BECAUSE BOOKS ARE GROUPED ACCORDING TO ACCENT ON RACE, NATIONAL BACKGROUND, ETHNIC GROUP, OR LIFE STYLE. SECTION HEADINGS ARE: AMERICAN INDIANS AND ESKIMOS, APPALACHIA AND THE SOUTHERN MOUNTAINS, AFRO-AMERICANS, HAWAII AND THE PHILIPPINES, LATIN-AMERICAN DERIVATION, ASIAN DERIVATION, JEWISH DERIVATION, EUROPEAN DERIVATION, AND MULTI-ETHNIC BOOKS WHICH ACCENT DIVERSITY. LISTS INCLUDE BOOKS IN OTHER LANGUAGES. A SUGGESTED AGE LEVEL OR LEVELS IS GIVEN FOR EACH BOOK. BOOKS FOR PARENTS AND TEACHERS AND A DIRECTORY OF PUBLISHERS ARE INCLUDED. (NH)

ED046520 PS004216
PROFILES OF CHILDREN: 1970 WHITE HOUSE CONFERENCE ON CHILDREN. , 70 174P.
EDRS PRICE MF-$0.65 HC NOT AVAILABLE FROM EDRS.
AVAILABLE FROM: SUPERINTENDENT OF DOCUMENTS, U.S. GOVERNMENT PRINTING OFFICE, WASHINGTON, D.C. 20402 ($3.00)

THIS BOOK OF CHARTS OF COMPARATIVE STATISTICS WAS COMPILED TO HELP THE 1970 WHITE HOUSE CONFERENCE ON CHILDREN EVALUATE PAST EFFORTS TO IMPROVE THE WELL-BEING OF AMERICA'S CHILDREN. FIRST, IT PRESENTS DATA ABOUT ASPECTS OF THE WORLD INTO WHICH AMERICAN CHILDREN ARE BORN, SUCH AS POPULATION, URBANIZATION, INCOME LEVELS, INCIDENCE OF DISEASE, DIVORCE AND DEATH RATES, AND POLLUTION LEVELS. IT THEN DEALS IN SUCCESSIVE SECTIONS WITH FOUR MAJOR STAGES OF CHILD DEVELOPMENT THROUGH AGE 3: THE PRENATAL PERIOD, THE FIRST YEAR OF LIFE, THE PRESCHOOL YEARS BETWEEN AGES ONE AND SIX, AND THE SCHOOL YEARS. BECAUSE THE CHILD IS TREATED AS AN ENTITY, THE MOST IMPORTANT ASPECTS OF EACH AGE GROUPING, SUCH AS HEALTH, EDUCATION, AND FAMILY LIFE ARE PRESENTED TOGETHER IN EACH SECTION. MANY THREE-COLOR CHARTS AND GRAPHS ILLUSTRATE THE TEXT. ILLUSTRATIONS ARE CROSS-REFERENCED TO AN APPENDIX (COMPRISING MORE THAN HALF THE BOOK) OF DETAILED TABLES OF THE DATA ON WHICH THE TEXT AND CHARTS ARE BASED. IT IS NOTED THAT THERE ARE SOME UNAVOIDABLE GAPS IN THE STATISTICS WITH REGARD TO MINORITY GROUPS SUCH AS SPANISH-AMERICANS, ORIENTALS, AND AMERICAN INDIANS. IMPROVEMENTS IN DATA COLLECTION WILL, HOPEFULLY, MAKE SUCH INFORMATION AVAILABLE TO FUTURE CONFERENCES. (AUTHOR/NH)

ED046521 PS004218
EMERGENCE OF IDENTITY: THE FIRST YEARS. 1970 WHITE HOUSE CONFERENCE ON CHILDREN, REPORT OF FORUM 2. (WORKING COPY). , 70 47P.
EDRS PRICE MF-$0.65 HC-$3.29

THIS FORUM IDENTIFIED SOME OF THE FACTORS INFLUENCING THE EMERGENCE OF IDENTITY DURING THE CRITICAL CHILDHOOD YEARS. TO HELP A CHILD DEVELOP A HEALTHY IDENTITY WHICH IS BOTH FAVORABLE AND REALISTIC, HE MUST BE TAUGHT ALMOST FROM BIRTH ABOUT HIS OWN INDIVIDUALITY. THE MANY ASPECTS OF TOTAL IDENTITY INCLUDE FAMILY, PHYSICAL SELF, SEX, ETHNIC AND CULTURAL, RELIGIOUS, AND INTELLECTUAL IDENTITY. SOME MAJOR OBSTACLES TO THE EMERGENCE OF HEALTHY IDENTITIES INCLUDE A VARIETY OF WIDELY HELD CULTURAL ASSUMPTIONS CONTRARY TO PRESENT-DAY EVIDENCE CONCERNING THE NATURE OF CHILD DEVELOPMENT. THESE ASSUMPTIONS, TYPICAL BEHAVIORS FOSTERED BY THEM, AND THEIR IDENTITY OUTCOMES ARE LISTED IN APPENDIX A. FORUM 2 PARTICIPANTS RECOMMEND (1) THE INITIATION OF A "SESAME STREET" TYPE OF TV PROGRAM FOR PARENTS, WHICH WOULD TEACH CHILD DEVELOPMENT PRINCIPLES AND GIVE PRACTICAL SUGGESTIONS FOR DAILY CHILD CARE; AND (2) THE ESTABLISHMENT OF CHILD-ORIENTED ENVIRONMENTAL COMMISSIONS ON NATIONAL AND LOCAL LEVELS, WHICH WOULD HELP PLAN, INSPECT, AND IMPROVE PROJECTS WHICH TRY TO MEET THE NEEDS OF CHILDREN. ADDITIONAL RECOMMENDATIONS ARE GIVEN IN APPENDIX B. (NH)

ED046522 PS004219
EXPRESSIONS OF IDENTITY: THE SCHOOL-AGE CHILD. 1970 WHITE HOUSE CONFERENCE ON CHILDREN, REPORT OF FORUM 3. (WORKING COPY). , 70 27P.
EDRS PRICE MF-$0.65 HC-$3.29

THE FOCUS OF FORUM 3 WAS TO RECOMMEND ACTION-ORIENTED PROGRAMS TO HELP THE SCHOOL-AGE CHILD FIND AND USE ALREADY-EXISTING COMMUNITY RESOURCES TO HELP HIM DEVELOP A POSITIVE IDENTITY. SPECIFICALLY, THE FOLLOWING COMPONENTS ARE RECOMMENDED: (1) THE CULTURAL VOUCHER SYSTEM, IN WHICH CHILDREN AGES 3 TO 16 WOULD BE ABLE TO PURCHASE ENRICHING GOODS AND SERVICES, WITH THE HELP OF A CULTURAL BROKER, OR ADVISER. (2) AN ENVIRONMENTAL PLANNING COMMISSION, COMPOSED OF PERSONS TRAINED IN DESIGN AND CHILD DEVELOPMENT, WHO COULD HELP DIRECT CITY PLANNING TO MAKE THE CITY A BETTER PLACE FOR CHILDREN TO LIVE, TO PLAY, AND TO LEARN. (3) THE GATEKEEPER OR SECOND FAMILY, A HELPING FAMILY OR PERSON TO WHOM CHILDREN CAN TURN FOR HELP IN PROBLEM SOLVING WHEN THE PARENT IS INAPPROPRIATE OR UNAVAILABLE. (4) THE ARTIST-TEACHER IN THE SCHOOL, A PROGRAM WHICH WOULD INVOLVE COMMUNITY ARTISTS IN THE EDUCATIONAL SYSTEM, MAKING THE CREATIVE PROCESS AN INTEGRAL PART OF LEARNING. (5) SUPPORT FOR CROSS-AGE TUTORING PROGRAMS, WHICH HELP BOTH THE OLDER AND THE YOUNGER YOUTHS INVOLVED, IN LEARNING AND IDENTITY FORMATION. THE UNDERLYING PHILOSOPHY OF THE RECOMMENDATIONS OF THIS FORUM IS THAT WHAT IS NEEDED IS NOT MORE AVAILABLE ACTIVITIES, BUT MORE GENUINE WAYS OF BEING AND OF RELATING TO OTHER PEOPLE. (AUTHOR/NH)

ED046523 PS004220
CRISIS IN VALUES. 1970 WHITE HOUSE CONFERENCE ON CHILDREN, REPORT OF FORUM 4. (WORKING COPY). , 70 46P.
EDRS PRICE MF-$0.65 HC-$3.29

TRADITIONALLY-EXPRESSED AMERICAN VALUES INCLUDE HEALTH, PERSONAL DIGNITY, FREEDOM OF CHOICE, RESPECT FOR THE RIGHTS AND HUMANITY OF OTHERS, THE RIGHT TO LOVE AND BE LOVED. A BIG GAP EXISTS, IN MANY INSTANCES, BETWEEN VALUES PROFESSED AND VALUES ACTUALLY LIVED IN PURSUIT OF "SUCCESS." OUR CHILDREN KNOW THIS, AND THE RESULT HAS BEEN A SENSE OF CONFUSION, OF FRUSTRATION, AND OF ALIENATION, OFTEN RESULTING IN EMBITTERMENT AND DROPPING OUT. THIS FORUM AFFIRMS THESE PRINCIPLES: (1) THAT SOCIETY ACCEPT THE RIGHT OF PERSONS TO PURSUE LIFE STYLES THAT DIFFER FROM THE AMERICAN MAINSTREAM, SO LONG AS OTHERS ARE NOT HURT; AND (2) THAT EVERY CHILD HAS THE RIGHT TO OPTIMUM DEVELOPMENT. TO ACHIEVE THESE GOALS, GENERAL RECOMMENDATIONS ARE MADE CONCERNING FAMILY, MEDIA, SCHOOL, RELIGION, RESEARCH, AND THE ROLE OF GOVERNMENT. INSTITUTIONS SHOULD JUDGE THE EFFECTS OF THEIR POLICIES ON THE LIVES OF CHILDREN AND CORRECT ANY PRACTICES WHICH BELIE THE VALUES THEY PROFESS. AN APPENDIX COMPRISING ONE HALF OF THE PAPER GIVES RESPONSES OF 10- TO 12-YEAR-OLDS, FROM THREE SECTIONS OF THE COUNTRY, TO A SOCIAL VALUES INVENTORY. (NH)

ED046524 PS004221
LEARNING INTO THE TWENTY-FIRST CENTURY. 1970 WHITE HOUSE CONFERENCE ON CHILDREN, REPORT OF FORUM 5. (WORKING COPY). , 70 26P.
EDRS PRICE MF-$0.65 HC-$3.29

IN THIS NATION, THE RIGHT TO LEARN WHAT THERE IS TO BE LEARNED HAS BEEN DENIED BECAUSE OF PREJUDICES AND ADHERENCE TO UNPRODUCTIVE TEACHING TECHNIQUES. THERE HAS BEEN TOO LITTLE ACCEPTANCE OF ADVANCED PRACTICES. FEDERALLY FUNDED EXPERIMENTAL SCHOOLS MUST BE INITIATED AS ALTERNATIVES TO PRESENT LEARNING MODES AND FOR THE DEVELOPMENT OF EXEMPLAR MODELS OF PHILOSOPHY AND PRACTICE. LEARNING MUST BECOME AN END IN ITSELF, AN INDIVIDUAL CHOICE, IMPLYING AN INDIVIDUAL DEFINITION OF SUCCESS. MODERN TECHNOLOGY WILL BE IMPLEMENTED FOR FLEXIBLE SCHEDULING AND PROGRESS RATES. ACKNOWLEDGING THE GROWING EMPHASIS ON TELEVISION IN THE HOME, THE FORUM SUGGESTS EACH HOME COULD HOUSE COMPUTERS AND MICROFILM LIBRARIES. "SCHOOL" WILL FOCUS ON HUMAN INTERACTION AND THE ABILITY TO KNOW ONESELF. TEACHERS WILL BE ENGAGED IN PREPARING COMPUTERIZED LESSONS, EVALUATING PROGRAMS, AND COUNSELING; THEREFORE, FUNDS MUST BE ALLOCATED FOR REDESIGN OF TEACHER EDUCATION. THE ACHIEVEMENT OF THIS PROGRAM MEANS COMMITMENT BACKED BY RESOURCES AND ACTION. THE REPORT RECOMMENDS MASSIVE EXPENDITURES OF FEDERAL FUNDS FOR THE DEVELOPMENT OF FORWARD-LOOKING PRACTICES AND LEARNING OPTIONS AND SUGGESTS THAT THE NATION'S 200TH BIRTHDAY, 1976, BE MADE AN OCCASION FOR NATIONWIDE DIALOGUE ABOUT OUR WHOLE LEARNING SITUATION. (AJ)

ED046525 PS004222
CREATIVITY AND THE LEARNING PROCESS. 1970 WHITE HOUSE CONFERENCE ON CHILDREN, REPORT OF FORUM 6. (WORKING PAPER). , 70 35P.
EDRS PRICE MF-$0.65 HC-$3.29

IN EXPLORING THE USE OF THE LEARNING PROCESS TO FOSTER CREATIVITY AMONG CHILDREN FROM 0-3 YEARS, WE MUST FREE OURSELVES FROM ANTIQUATED AND ERRONEOUS BELIEFS THAT SCHOOL IS THE ONLY ENVIRONMENT IN WHICH CREATIVITY AND LEARNING TAKES PLACE, AND THAT THE TEACHER IS THE SOLE AGENT OF SUCH ACHIEVEMENTS. OUR CULTURE, OUR ENVIRONMENT, AND OUR COMMUNICATION (INTERPERSONAL AND MASS MEDIA) ARE MORE PERVASIVE FACTORS. AN OVERWHELMING URGENCY EXISTS FOR REVOLUTIONARY CHANGES IN BOTH THE SCHOOLS AND SOCIETY. THE PRESIDENT AND THE U.S. OFFICE OF EDUCATION MUST ADVOCATE POLICY DECISIONS TO STIMULATE COMMUNICATION WITH CREATIVE COMMUNITY RESOURCE PERSONS, TO DEVELOP THE CREATIVE POTENTIAL IN TEACHERS AND TEACHERS-IN-TRAINING, TO ESTABLISH A NATIONAL INSTITUTE FOR CREATIVITY, AND TO NURTURE DEVELOPMENT OF NEW SOURCES FOR CREATIVE EDUCATION BEGINNING WITH THE BURGEONING FIELD OF EARLY CHILDHOOD, BECOMING AN INTEGRAL AND PERTINENT PART OF THE EDUCATIONAL PROGRAM IN THE SCHOOLS AND CULMINATING IN AESTHETIC EDUCATION AVAILABLE FOR THE GENERAL POPULATION. (WY)

ED046526 PS004223
MYTHOLOGY IN AMERICAN EDUCATION: A GUIDE TO CONSTRUCTIVE CONFRONTATION. 1970 WHITE HOUSE CONFERENCE ON CHILDREN, REPORT OF FORUM 8. (WORKING COPY). , 70 33P.
EDRS PRICE MF-$0.65 HC-$3.29

FORUM 8 IS CONCERNED WITH OBSTACLES TO EDUCATIONAL REFORM WHICH ARE BASED ON OBSOLETE MYTHS. FORUM MEMBERS URGENTLY ADVOCATE ALTERNATIVES TO THE TRADITIONAL PUBLIC SCHOOL APPROACH. SINCE THE IDEA THAT THERE IS "ONE BEST WAY" TO EDUCATE IS ONE OF THE MYTHS, REFORM MUST BE FLUID ENOUGH TO ACCOMMODATE INDIVIDUAL STUDENT STYLE, ATTITUDE, AND READINESS. THIS REPORT PROPOSES SUCH REFORM AND INCLUDES: (1) A BRIEF ANALYSIS OF THE CONTENT OF SEVERAL MYTHS CONSIDERED; (2) AN EXPLANATION OF THE EDUCATIONAL CONSEQUENCES OF MAINTAINING THE STATUS QUO BASED ON THOSE FALSE ASSUMPTIONS; (3) A LOOK AT THE EVIDENCE WHICH UNDERMINES THE MYTH'S VALIDITY; AND IN SOME CASES (4) CONSIDERATION OF POSSIBLE ALTERNATIVES. ENCOURAGING A VARIETY OF ALTERNATIVE EDUCATIONAL MODELS, THE FORUM RECOMMENDS NEW PUBLIC SCHOOL SYSTEMS INDEPENDENT OF STATE AND LOCAL REGULATIONS, OPEN EDUCATION APPROACHES, OPEN ENROLLMENT POLICIES, AND CROSS-AGE CLASSROOM PATTERNS. WITH PARENTS AND TEACHERS JOINING TOGETHER, EXISTING REGULATIONS AND REQUIREMENTS MUST BE SUSPENDED TO PROVIDE SUFFICIENT AUTONOMY FOR EXPERIMENTATION. THE REPORT INCLUDES AN APPENDIX OF THE MYTHS DISCUSSED AND AN EXTENSIVE BIBLIOGRAPHY OF REFERENCES USED. (AUTHOR/AJ)

ED046527 PS004224
KEEPING CHILDREN HEALTHY: HEALTH PROTECTION AND DISEASE PREVENTION. 1970 WHITE HOUSE CONFERENCE ON CHILDREN, REPORT OF FORUM 10. (WORKING PAPER).
GREEN, MORRIS, 70 54P.
EDRS PRICE MF-$0.65 HC-$3.29

THIS FORUM CONSIDERS PREVENTIVE HEALTH CARE TO INCLUDE NOT ONLY GOOD PHYSICAL AND DENTAL CARE, GOOD NUTRITION, AND GOOD SANITATION, BUT ALSO ADEQUATE HOUSING, QUALITY EDUCATION, SUFFICIENT CLOTHING AS WELL AS OPPORTUNITIES TO EXPERIENCE LOVE, ACHIEVE SELF RESPECT, PARTICIPATE IN PLAY AND BECOME MEANINGFULLY INVOLVED WITH OTHERS. SEVERAL POPULATION GROUPS IN OUR COUNTRY ARE SUBJECT TO UNUSUAL HEALTH HAZARDS AND HAVE PARTICULAR NEED FOR HEALTH CARE. POOR CHILDREN, EXPECTANT MOTHERS, YOUNG INFANTS, HANDICAPPED AND EMOTIONALLY DISTURBED CHILDREN, AND CHILDREN OF MIGRANT WORKERS ARE THE ESPECIALLY VULNERABLE GROUPS. THE SOCIAL PATHOLOGY OF NARCOTIC ADDICTION, PREJUDICE, UNDERSTIMULATION, VIOLENCE, AND INDIFFERENCE TO HUMAN NEEDS CONSTITUTES OTHER PRESSING PROBLEMS THAT THREATEN THE QUALITY OF PHYSICAL AND EMOTIONAL HEALTH IN OUR SOCIETY. A HIGH PRIORITY SHOULD BE SET ON THE DEVELOPMENT AND DELIVERY OF NEEDED SERVICES TO INSURE IMMEDIATE ACCESS TO DECENT CARE FOR THE MOST VULNERABLE GROUPS. OTHER RECOMMEN-

DATIONS CALL FOR ACCEPTANCE OF NATIONAL STANDARDS FOR PREVENTIVE HEALTH SERVICES, MANPOWER AUGMENTATION, RESEARCH IN THE HEALTH SCIENCES, ADEQUATE INCOME, GOOD NUTRITION, IMPROVED HOUSING, AND A REINSTITUTIONALIZATION RECONSTRUCTION OF THE SYSTEMS FOR DELIVERING HUMAN SERVICES AS A NATIONAL COMMITMENT. (WY)

ED046528 PS004225
DELIVERY OF CHILD HEALTH SERVICES. 1970 WHITE HOUSE CONFERENCE ON CHILDREN, REPORT OF FORUM 11. (WORKING PAPER). , DEC 70 62P.
EDRS PRICE MF-$0.65 HC-$3.29

THIS REPORT EXAMINES THE CURRENT STATUS OF CHILD HEALTH SERVICES IN THE UNITED STATES AND IDENTIFIES PRIORITIES FOR AN IMPROVED HEALTH CARE PROGRAM FOR MOTHERS AND CHILDREN. ITS RECOMMENDATIONS ARE DESIGNED AS GUIDELINES FOR CONSTRUCTIVE DISCUSSION BY PARTICIPANTS IN THE 1970 WHITE HOUSE CONFERENCE ON CHILDREN. A MAJOR THESIS OF THE REPORT IS THAT THE EXISTING CHILD HEALTH SYSTEM IN THE UNITED STATES IS COSTLY BUT CUMBERSOME, WELL-INTENTIONED BUT DEPLORABLY PIECEMEAL, A SYSTEM WHICH MUDDLES ALONG RATHER THAN MOVING FORTHRIGHTLY AHEAD. IN THE 1970'S, WE SHALL BE RESPONSIBLE FOR MEETING THE HEALTH NEEDS OF AN ANTICIPATED 100 MILLION YOUNG PEOPLE AT VARIOUS STAGES OF DEVELOPMENT. THE FORUM MEMBERS HAVE CONCLUDED THAT NOTHING LESS THAN A RATIONALLY PLANNED AND SOUNDLY SUPPORTED MATERNAL AND CHILD HEALTH PROGRAM CAN BE EXPECTED TO CORRECT CURRENT INEQUITIES AND INADEQUACIES. SPECIFICALLY RECOMMENDED ARE: (1) A FEDERALLY-FINANCED NATIONAL CHILD HEALTH CARE PROGRAM, (2) AUGMENTATION OF ILLNESS PREVENTION AND HEALTH PROMOTION SERVICES, (3) REVITALIZATION OF CERTAIN EXISTING CHILD HEALTH PROGRAM, (4) THE ESTABLISHMENT OF A UNIFIED CHILD HEALTH UNIT WITHIN THE DEPARTMENT OF HEALTH, EDUCATION AND WELFARE, UNDER A NEWLY CREATED DEPUTY ASSISTANT SECRETARY, AND (5) ONGOING ADVOCACY OF CHILD HEALTH PROGRAMS, THROUGH A PRESIDENTIAL COUNCIL. TWO PAPERS ARE ATTACHED WHICH COMPARE VARIOUS PROPOSALS FOR NATIONAL HEALTH INSURANCE. (AUTHOR/NH)

ED046529 PS004226
CHILDREN WHO ARE INJURED. 1970 WHITE HOUSE CONFERENCE ON CHILDREN, REPORT OF FORUM 13. (WORKING COPY). , 70 28P.
EDRS PRICE MF-$0.65 HC-$3.29

THREE MAJOR PREMISES FORM THE BASIS OF THE RECOMMENDATIONS OF FORUM 13. FIRST, THE TRADITIONAL DEFINITION OF INJURY SHOULD BE EXPANDED TO INCLUDE PSYCHOLOGICAL, SOCIOLOGICAL, AND ENVIRONMENTAL FACTORS LEADING TO CHILDREN'S INJURIES. SECOND, APPROACHES TO PREVENTING AND TREATING INJURIES CANNOT BE SEPARATED FROM THE ENVIRONMENTS WITH WHICH CHILDREN CONSTANTLY INTERACT. THIRD, CHILDREN MUST BE GIVEN HIGHER PRIORITY, BOTH BY GOVERNMENT AND PRIVATE ENTERPRISE, AT ALL LEVELS THROUGHOUT THE NATION. THE FOLLOWING RECOMMENDATIONS ARE MADE: (1) THAT GOVERNMENTAL UNITS CLOSEST TO THE NEIGHBORHOOD SELECT PERSONS TO BE TRAINED IN PROBLEM-SOLVING TECHNIQUES AND INFORMED ABOUT AVAILABLE RESOURCES RELATED TO CHILDREN'S INJURIES; (2) THAT GOVERNMENTS, AIDED BY PRIVATE AND VOLUNTEER ORGANIZATIONS, DEVELOP PROGRAMS OF TRAINING AND ONGOING CONSULTATION FOR THOSE COMMUNITY WORKERS; (3) THAT A CABINET LEVEL POSITION WITH MAJOR RESPONSIBILITY FOR CHILDREN AND YOUTH BE CONSIDERED; AND (4) THAT CONGRESS ESTABLISH A PERMANENT STAFF TO STUDY PROBLEMS RELATED TO CHILDREN AND THEIR ENVIRONMENTS. (AUTHOR/NH)

ED046530 PS004227
CHANGING FAMILIES IN A CHANGING SOCIETY. 1970 WHITE HOUSE CONFERENCE ON CHILDREN, REPORT OF FORUM 14. (WORKING COPY). , 70 18P.
EDRS PRICE MF-$0.65 HC-$3.29

FORUM 14 ADVOCATES THE DEVELOPMENT OF FLEXIBLE POLICIES FOR VARIANT FAMILY FORMS AND LEGISLATIVE PROGRAMS WHICH ARE RESPONSIVE TO FAMILY NEEDS WHETHER THE FAMILY IS A SINGLE PARENT, NUCLEAR FAMILY, OR SOME OTHER FORM. HUMAN SERVICE SYSTEMS MUST BE BUILT AROUND PEOPLE; FAMILIES SHOULD NOT BE EXPECTED TO FIT INTO MASS PRODUCED FORMAL SYSTEMS BASED ON THE PRINCIPLE OF LEAST COST AND ON THE PRESUMED EXPERTISE OF THE PROFESSIONAL. A FAMILY'S MAIN TASKS ARE TO DEVELOP CAPACITIES TO SOCIALIZE CHILDREN, TO ENHANCE THE COMPETENCE OF FAMILY MEMBERS TO COPE WITH THE DEMANDS OF BUREAUCRATIC ORGANIZATIONS, TO USE THESE ORGANIZATIONS AND TO PROVIDE SATISFACTIONS AND A MENTALLY HEALTHY ENVIRONMENT. THE FORUM RECOMMENDS THE INITIATION OF AN "INSTITUTE FOR THE STUDY OF THE FAMILY" TO CONDUCT RESEARCH INTO FAMILY NEEDS AND TO CREATE MARRIAGE AND FAMILY LIVING INSTITUTES AT UNIVERSITIES TO INCREASE THE EFFECTIVENESS OF SPECIALISTS AND PROFESSIONALS. THE FORUM FURTHER ADVOCATES THE EXAMINATION AND REORDERING OF CURRENT SYSTEMS AND LEGISLATION, INCLUDING A REVIEW EVERY FIVE YEARS EVALUATING HEW ON THE INTER-AGENCY LEVEL TO INSURE QUALITY CHILD CARE. (AJ)

ED046531 PS004228
CHILDREN AND PARENTS: TOGETHER IN THE WORLD. 1970 WHITE HOUSE CONFERENCE ON CHILDREN, REPORT OF FORUM 15. (WORKING COPY). , 70 32P.
EDRS PRICE MF-$0.65 HC-$3.29

THE LOW PRIORITY ACCORDING TO CHILDREN AND FAMILIES IN OUR WAY OF LIFE IS REFLECTED IN POLICIES AND ACTIONS AT NATIONAL, STATE, AND LOCAL LEVELS. WE LIKE TO THINK OF AMERICA AS A CHILD-ORIENTED SOCIETY BUT, IN FACT, OUR PRIORITIES LIE MORE IN THE PURSUIT OF AFFLUENCE, AND THE WORSHIP OF MATERIAL THINGS AND TECHNOLOGY. A BROKEN TELEVISION SET OR A BROKEN COMPUTER MAY PROVOKE MORE INDIGNATION AND MORE ACTION THAN A BROKEN FAMILY OR A BROKEN CHILD. NEW NATIONAL GOALS SHOULD BE PURSUED BY MANY DIFFERENT PARTS OF OUR SOCIETY TO ENHANCE THE QUALITY OF LIFE FOR AMERICA'S CHILDREN. ADULT-CHILD INTERACTION MUST BE INCREASED ON ALL LEVELS. TO BENEFIT CHILDREN AND FAMILIES, SPECIFIC RECOMMENDATIONS ARE PRESENTED WHICH CAN BE UNDERTAKEN BY PRIVATE INDUSTRY AND SMALL BUSINESSES, THE MASS MEDIA, THE COMMUNITY, SCHOOLS, FEDERAL, STATE AND LOCAL GOVERNMENTS, AND INDIVIDUAL FAMILIES. (WY)

ED046532 PS004229
FAMILY PLANNING AND FAMILY ECONOMICS. 1970 WHITE HOUSE CONFERENCE ON CHILDREN, REPORT OF FORUM 16. (WORKING COPY). , 70 27P.
EDRS PRICE MF-$0.65 HC-$3.29

FEW ACTIONS OF THE NEXT DECADE WILL BE MORE PERTINENT TO THE WELFARE OF AMERICA'S CHILDREN THAN WHAT WE DO ABOUT TWO OF THE MOST BASIC DETERMINANTS OF THE QUALITY OF LIFE OF OUR CHILDREN AND THEIR FAMILIES--DISTRIBUTION OF INCOME AMONG FAMILIES IN AND BY OUR SOCIETY AND SIZE OF THE FAMILY AND OF OUR SOCIETY. IN REGARD TO THESE FUNDAMENTAL ISSUES, FOUR CHALLENGES TO THE SEVENTIES EMERGE: (1) ACHIEVEMENT OF MORE EQUITABLE DISTRIBUTION OF FAMILY INCOME, (2) HELPING CHILDREN AND THEIR FAMILIES UNDERSTAND THE FULL MEANING OF HUMAN SEXUALITY AND FAMILY PLANNING IN THEIR LIVES, (3) MAKING FAMILY PLANNING SERVICES AVAILABLE TO ALL AMERICANS BY 1974 AND (4) STABILIZATION OF A POPULATION FIGURE FOR OUR NATION. BEFORE ANY OF THE FORUM RECOMMENDATIONS CAN BECOME A REALITY, TWO FUNDAMENTAL SHIFTS IN ECONOMIC DIRECTION MUST OCCUR (REALLOCATION OF NATIONAL EXPENDITURES FROM MILITARY USES AND RESTRUCTURING THE DISTRIBUTION OF GOVERNMENT INCOME FROM FEDERAL TO STATE LEVELS). ONLY THEN CAN FEDERALLY FINANCED AND ADMINISTERED SYSTEMS OF INCOME SUPPORT, SUPPORTIVE HUMAN SERVICES, FAMILY PLANNING SERVICES, AND A POPULATION STABILIZATION FIGURE BE REALIZED. (AUTHOR/WY)

ED046533 PS004230
DEVELOPMENTAL DAY CARE SERVICES FOR CHILDREN. 1970 WHITE HOUSE CONFERENCE ON CHILDREN, REPORT OF FORUM 17. (WORKING COPY). , 70 33P.
EDRS PRICE MF-$0.65 HC-$3.29

WHEN PROPERLY FUNDED AND PROVIDED WITH ADEQUATE EDUCATIONAL, HEALTH, AND OTHER NEEDED RESOURCES, DAY CARE PROGRAMS CAN MAKE AN IMPORTANT CONTRIBUTION TO THE LIFE OF MANY AMERICAN FAMILIES. FOR A VARIETY OF REASONS, PRESENT SERVICES FOR PROVIDING SUPPLEMENTARY CHILD CARE ARE INSUFFICIENT. TO RESPOND TO THE CHANGES IN OUR NATIONAL LIFE STYLE, WE MUST DEVELOP A NETWORK OF SUPPLEMENTARY CHILD CARE FACILITIES READILY AVAILABLE TO ALL FAMILIES WITH CHILDREN FLEXIBLE ENOUGH TO BE PART OF A FAMILY'S LIFE, AND GOOD ENOUGH TO PROMOTE FULL DEVELOPMENT OF OUR NATION'S CHILDREN. AS A START TOWARD SUCH A SYSTEM, THIS FORUM RECOMMENDS ESTABLISHING AND ALLOCATING THE TOTAL OF FINANCIAL COMMITMENT NEEDED FOR DAY CARE, DEVELOPING A PREVENTIVE APPROACH TO CHILDREN'S NEEDS AND PROBLEMS, MOBILIZING CONTINUING PUBLIC SUPPORT FOR DAY CARE, AND COORDINATING OPERATIONAL PROCEDURES AT FEDERAL, STATE, AND LOCAL LEVELS. (WY)

ED046534 PS004231
CHILDREN WITHOUT PREJUDICE. 1970 WHITE HOUSE CONFERENCE ON CHILDREN, REPORT OF FORUM 18. (WORKING PAPER). , 70 15P.
EDRS PRICE MF-$0.65 HC-$3.29

PREJUDICIAL ATTITUDES ARE COMMONPLACE IN OUR SOCIETY, AND THEY ADVERSELY AFFECT ALL OF OUR CHILDREN. CHILDREN OF A MINORITY OR POOR GROUP ARE DIRECTLY AFFECTED BECAUSE THEY ARE LIKELY TO SUFFER HUNGER, POOR HEALTH AND HOUSING, AND INADEQUATE SCHOOLS. WHITE, MIDDLE CLASS CHILDREN ARE AFFECTED IN WAYS WHICH ARE LESS OBVIOUS, BUT JUST AS DAMAGING. IN TRYING TO RESOLVE THE CONFLICT BETWEEN WHAT INSTITUTIONS PREACH ABOUT THE BROTHERHOOD OF MAN, AND WHAT THESE SAME INSTITUTIONS TEACH BY EXAMPLE THROUGH VIOLATING CONCEPTS OF LOVE AND JUSTICE, THESE CHILDREN MAY DEVELOP UNHEALTHY AND UNDESIRABLE ATTITUDES AND BEHAVIOR PATTERNS. MINORITY RACES AND POOR PEOPLE ARE NOT THE ONLY TARGETS OF PREJUDICE. THE PHYSICALLY AND MENTALLY HANDICAPPED, MEMBERS OF MINORITY RELIGIONS, FEMALES, AND THE AGED SUFFER AS WELL. FORUM 18 VIEWS THESE PREJUDICIAL ATTITUDES AS A SERIOUS THREAT TO OUR SOCIETY, WHOSE STRENGTH DEPENDS UPON FULL OPPORTUNITY FOR ALL. THE FORUM MAKES SEVERAL SPECIFIC RECOMMENDATIONS FOR GOVERNMEN-

TAL CHANGE, SPEARHEADED BY THE PRESIDENT OF THE UNITED STATES, IN THE AREAS OF EDUCATION, HOUSING, HEALTH, AND CIVIL RIGHTS. (NH)

ED046535 PS004232
CHILDREN AND THEIR PHYSICAL AND SOCIAL ENVIRONMENT. 1970 WHITE HOUSE CONFERENCE ON CHILDREN, REPORT OF FORUM 19. (WORKING COPY). , 70 17P.
EDRS PRICE MF-$0.65 HC-$3.29

WE WANT AN ENVIRONMENT THAT IS GOOD FOR ALL OUR CHILDREN TO GROW UP IN AND REACH THEIR FULL POTENTIAL. THEY NEED AN ENVIRONMENT THAT GIVES THEM MANY KINDS OF EXPERIENCES, THAT PROVIDES BOTH PRIVACY AND OPPORTUNITIES TO FORM SOCIAL BONDS, AND THAT IS ENRICHED BY BEAUTY. TO PROVIDE SUCH AN ENVIRONMENT FOR OUR CHILDREN, WE MUST ALSO PROVIDE IT FOR ADULTS. UNFORTUNATELY, OUR PUBLIC POLICIES AND PROGRAMS HAVE SHAPED A WORLD WHICH IS INHOSPITABLE TO BOTH. POLICIES FOR LAND USE, TRANSPORTATION, TAXATION, ZONING, AND HOUSING HAVE LIMITED OPPORTUNITIES FOR COOPERATION AMONG GROUPS SEGREGATED BY THESE POLICIES. ONE OF OUR MAJOR NATIONAL GOALS SHOULD FOCUS ON PLANNING AND PROVIDING FOR AN ENVIRONMENT THAT IS GOOD IN EVERY SENSE FOR THE CREATIVE GROWTH OF BOTH CHILDREN AND ADULTS. WE RECOMMEND THE ESTABLISHMENT OF A STANDING COMMISSION FOR THE COMING GENERATION. THE COMMISSION WOULD TAKE A BROAD VIEW OF NATIONAL POLICIES AND PROGRAMS--NOT ONLY THOSE SPECIFICALLY DIRECTED TOWARD CHILDREN--AND ACT AS AN ADVOCATE FOR THE YOUNG IN ALL FIELDS. (AUTHOR/WY)

ED046536 PS004233
THE CHILD AND LEISURE TIME. 1970 WHITE HOUSE CONFERENCE ON CHILDREN, REPORT OF FORUM 21. (WORKING COPY). , 70 17P.
EDRS PRICE MF-$0.65 HC-$3.29

CREATIVE LEISURE ACTIVITIES MAKE A PROFOUND CONTRIBUTION TO THE CHILD'S EMOTIONAL, PSYCHOLOGICAL, PHYSICAL, AESTHETIC, AND SPIRITUAL GROWTH. WE, AS A NATION, HAVE FAILED TO EMPHASIZE THE IMPORTANCE OF LEISURE EXPERIENCES UPON THE INDIVIDUAL. THE PRIME OBSTACLES HAVE BEEN TWO PREJUDICIAL ATTITUDES: (1) THAT LEISURE IS INTRINSICALLY LESS WORTHY THAN WORK, AND (2) THAT SURVIVAL SKILLS ARE MORE WORTHY THAN THOSE ACTIVITIES ENJOYED FOR THEIR OWN SAKE. A VARIETY OF LEISURE OPTIONS SHOULD EXIST IN THE HOME, AT SCHOOL, AND IN THE COMMUNITY. OUR COUNTRY HAS PROVIDED, AT BEST, AN UNCOORDINATED PATCHWORK OF PUBLIC, PRIVATE, COMMERCIAL, AND VOLUNTARY PROGRAMS THAT MAY NEGLECT THE LESS AFFLUENT CHILD. ONE BASIC NATIONAL GOAL SHOULD BE TO DESIGN A TOTAL LEISURE CLIMATE TO FACILITATE GROWTH IN EVERY CHILD. SPECIFIC RECOMMENDATIONS TO ACCOMPLISH THIS GOAL INCLUDE HAVING THE GOVERNMENT INITIATE POLICIES TO PLAN AND DELIVER LEISURE OPPORTUNITIES FOR CHILDREN, MAKING MORE EFFECTIVE USE OF MOBILE AND PORTABLE UNITS TO EXTEND CULTURAL AND RECREATIONAL OPPORTUNITIES INTO RURAL AND URBAN ENVIRONMENTS, HAVING UNIVERSITIES DEVELOP PROPER ATTITUDES CONCERNING LEISURE AND LEISURE PROFICIENCIES IN THEIR STUDENTS, AND EXPANDING RESEARCH AND DEVELOPMENT ENDEAVORS IN THE AREA. (WY)

ED046537 PS004234
THE RIGHTS OF CHILDREN. 1970 WHITE HOUSE CONFERENCE ON CHILDREN, REPORT OF FORUM 22. (WORKING COPY). , 70 36P.
EDRS PRICE MF-$0.65 HC-$3.29

CHILDREN'S RIGHTS CAN BE SERVED BY MAXIMIZING FROM BIRTH THE OPPORTUNITIES FOR EACH INDIVIDUAL CHILD'S HEALTHY GROWTH, WELL-BEING, AND FULLFILLMENT. KNOWLEDGE OF THE DEVELOPMENTAL NEEDS AND CHARACTERISTICS OF CHILDREN MUST BE THE FOUNDATION FOR ACTION AND POLICY BY GOVERNMENT AND OTHER AGENCIES AND INSTITUTIONS--NATIONAL, STATE AND LOCAL. CHILDREN HAVE THE RIGHT TO GROW UP IN A SOCIETY WHICH RESPECTS THE DIGNITY OF LIFE, THE RIGHT TO BE BORN HEALTHY AND WANTED, THE RIGHT TO GROW UP IN NURTURING FAMILY AND COMMUNITY ENVIRONMENTS, THE RIGHT TO BE EDUCATED TO CAPACITY, AND THE RIGHT TO HAVE SOCIETAL MECHANISMS EFFECT THE FOREGOING RIGHTS. THREE MAJOR CONCERNS MUST GUIDE THE DEVELOPMENT OF ANY RECOMMENDATIONS DESIGNED TO SECURE THE RIGHTS OF CHILDREN: (1) COMMITMENT TO CHILDREN AS A PRIMARY FACTOR, (2) COMMITMENT TO INDIVIDUALIZE CARE OF CHILDREN BY ALL PERSONS SERVING THEM, AND (3) SPECIAL CONCERN FOR THE MENTAL AND PHYSICAL HEALTH OF MINORITY CHILDREN. (AUTHOR/WY)

ED046538 PS004235
THE CHILD ADVOCATE. 1970 WHITE HOUSE CONFERENCE ON CHILDREN, REPORT OF FORUM 24. (WORKING COPY). , 70 27P.
EDRS PRICE MF-$0.65 HC-$3.29

THIS FORUM SUGGESTS THE INITIATION OF A FEDERALLY FUNDED NATIONAL SYSTEM OF CHILD ADVOCACY INCLUDING A PRESIDENTIALLY-APPOINTED COUNCIL TO RECOMMEND LEGISLATION, PROVIDE FOR AND REPORT ON THE WELFARE AND PROGRESS OF CHILDREN. THE NATIONAL COUNCIL, COMPOSED OF PARENTS AS WELL AS PROFESSIONALS, WOULD SUPPORT NEIGHBORHOOD CHILD ADVOCATE COUNCILS BY PROVIDING FUNDING AND ACTING AS NATIONAL SPOKESMEN. THE ADVOCATE HIMSELF WOULD BE AN EMPATHETIC ADMINISTRATOR WITH ACCESS TO SOCIAL, ECONOMIC, AND LEGAL RESOURCES. HE WOULD WORK TO SECURE THE INDIVIDUAL CHILD'S BASIC NEEDS THROUGH HIS STAFF OF PROFESSIONALS AND LAY VOLUNTEERS. AN ADVOCATE MIGHT SPECIFICALLY CONCENTRATE ON STRENGTHENING PARENTAL CONCERN, SECURING BASIC CHILD RIGHTS IN THE SCHOOL, IMPROVING RELATIONSHIPS WITH LAW ENFORCERS, COURTS, AND WORKING WITH OTHER CHILD CARE AGENCIES. THE NATIONAL COUNCIL WOULD ESTABLISH AN INFORMATION CENTER FOR CLASSIFYING MATERIALS ON CHILD CARE PROBLEMS. A PILOT PROGRAM TO ESTABLISH GUIDELINES WOULD BE A FIRST STEP TOWARDS AN ADVOCACY PROGRAM. (AJ)

ED046539 PS004407
CONDITION WITH CAUTION: THINK THRICE BEFORE CONDITIONING. (ROUGH DRAFT). KATZ, LILIAN G., FEB 71 7P.
EDRS PRICE MF-$0.65 HC-$3.29

INNOVATIVE MODELS FOR EDUCATION ARE OFTEN QUICKLY ADOPTED. BEHAVIOR MODIFICATION, OR OPERANT CONDITIONING, IS AN EXAMPLE OF A TECHNIQUE WHICH HAS BEEN WIDELY USED BECAUSE, WHEN PROPERLY APPLIED IN THE CLASSROOM, IT "WORKS." HOWEVER, THE APPLICATION OF A TECHNIQUE SHOULD BE CAREFULLY THOUGHT THROUGH IN TERMS OF THE MEANING OF THE BEHAVIOR IN QUESTION. FOR EXAMPLE, THREE CHILDREN MAY EXHIBIT THE SAME DISRUPTIVE BEHAVIOR, OR PHENOTYPE. YET THE GENESES, OR GENOTYPES, OF THE BEHAVIOR MAY BE VERY DIFFERENT. THE CHILD MAY HAVE LEARNED THIS BEHAVIOR THROUGH REINFORCEMENT AT HOME OR AT SCHOOL; THE BEHAVIOR MAY BE AN EXPRESSION OF AN EMOTIONAL INJURY; IT MAY INDICATE A LACK OF SOCIAL SKILL OR KNOWLEDGE OF ALTERNATIVE WAYS OF RESPONSE; OR THERE MAY BE OTHER CAUSES. FOR ALL GENOTYPES, BEHAVIOR MODIFICATION MAY BE SUCCESSFUL IN CHANGING UNDESIRABLE BEHAVIOR, BUT IT DOES NOT ALWAYS ADDRESS ITSELF TO THE UNDERLYING CAUSE OF BEHAVIOR. A PARADIGM IS GIVEN SHOWING POSSIBLE PHENOTYPE/GENOTYPE/TREATMENT RELATIONSHIPS. (AUTHOR/NH)

ED046540 PS004408
THE VICARIOUS CONDITIONING OF EMOTIONAL RESPONSES IN NURSERY SCHOOL CHILDREN. FINAL REPORT. VENN, JERRY R., 30 SEP 70 47P.
EDRS PRICE MF-$0.65 HC-$3.29

TO VICARIOUSLY CONDITION EITHER FEAR OR A POSITIVE EMOTIONAL RESPONSE, FILMS IN WHICH A 5-YEAR-OLD MALE MODEL MANIFESTED ONE OR THE OTHER RESPONSE WERE SHOWN TO NURSERY SCHOOL CHILDREN. THE MEASURE OF VICARIOUS CONDITIONING WAS THE CHILDREN'S RATE OF RESPONSE TO THE CONDITIONED STIMULUS AND A CONTROLLED STIMULUS IN SEVERAL OPERANT SITUATIONS AFTER WATCHING THE FILM. IN EXPERIMENTS 1 AND 2, FEAR RESPONSES WERE VICARIOUSLY CONDITIONED; AFTER VIEWING THE FILM, THE CHILDREN RATED LOWER IN OPERANT RESPONSES TO THE FEAR STIMULUS THAN TO THE CONTROL STIMULUS. IN EXPERIMENTS 3 AND 4, AFTER VIEWING A POSITIVE FILM, THE CHILDREN SHOWED A HIGHER RATE OF OPERANT RESPONSE TO THE POSITIVE EMOTIONAL STIMULUS THAN TO THE CONTROL STIMULUS. THE EXPERIMENTS SHOW THAT HUMAN OPERANT RESPONSES CAN BE AFFECTED BY BOTH VICARIOUS FEAR CONDITIONING AND VICARIOUS POSITIVE EMOTIONAL CONDITIONING. IN ALL EXPERIMENTS THE CONDITIONING EFFECT WAS SHORT TERM AND EASILY NEUTRALIZED. FURTHER RESEARCH SUGGESTED INCLUDES: CONSIDERATION OF THE AGE FACTOR; USE OF LIVE MODELS RATHER THAN FILMS; AND REDUCTION OF EXPERIMENTER BIAS, EXPECTATIONS, AND GENERALIZATION BY EMPLOYMENT OF AUTOMATED APPARATUS AND MAXIMALLY DIFFERENT TEST STIMULI. REFERENCES AND APPENDIX ARE INCLUDED. (AJ)

ED046541 PS004409
A PILOT STUDY OF A PRESCHOOL METHOD OF PREVENTIVE EDUCATION. FINAL REPORT. MCGILLIGAN, ROBERT P., 30 SEP 70 32P.
EDRS PRICE MF-$0.65 HC-$3.29

THE SCHOOL DISTRICT OF JENNINGS, MISSOURI, UNDERTOOK A STUDY OF THE EFFECTIVENESS OF GROUPING ON ACADEMIC ACHIEVEMENT IN KINDERGARTEN. IT WAS HYPOTHESIZED THAT GROUPING CHILDREN ACCORDING TO DEVELOPMENTAL LAGS WOULD BE BENEFICIAL TO THE SUBJECTS IN TERMS OF THEIR ACADEMIC AND PERSONAL DEVELOPMENT; THAT THE CURRICULA WOULD BE PARTIALLY RESPONSIBLE FOR THESE BENEFITS; AND THAT THE STUDENTS' ACADEMIC PERFORMANCES WOULD BE RELATED TO FAMILY DEMOGRAPHIC, MATERNAL ATTITUDINAL VARIABLES AND PERCEPTION OF THE CHILD'S BEHAVIOR. POST-TREATMENT SCORES OBTAINED FROM 73 SUBJECTS REVEALED THAT OF THE DEMOGRAPHIC VARIABLES INVESTIGATED, FATHER'S OCCUPATION AND THE NUMBER OF BROTHERS WERE THE ONLY ONES SIGNIFICANTLY RELATED TO MEASURED ACHIEVEMENT. MATERNAL ATTITUDES WERE NOT RELATED. IT WAS RECOMMENDED THAT THE STUDY BE REPLICATED WITH BETTER CONTROL OF VARIABLES AND CROSS-VALIDATED WITH DIFFERENT POPULATIONS; THAT THE SUBJECTS BE FOLLOWED THROUGH SECOND GRADE; THAT THE EFFECT OF KINDERGARTEN ON SELF-CONCEPT GROWTH AND THE RELATIONSHIP BETWEEN MATERNAL ATTITUDES AND FAMILY VARIABLES TO ACHIEVEMENT BE FURTHER EXPLORED. REFERENCES AND APPENDIXES CONTAINING A DESCRIPTION OF THE TEST BATTERY, PARENT QUESTIONNAIRE, AND STATISTICAL ANALYSIS OF STUDY DATA ARE INCLUDED. (AUTHOR/AJ)

ED046542 PS004414
DIFFERENTIAL RESPONSE PATTERNS AS THEY AFFECT THE SELF ESTEEM OF THE CHILD. MILLER, THOMAS W., 8 JAN 71 20P.
EDRS PRICE MF-$0.65 HC-$3.29
THE EFFECTS OF DIFFERENTIAL VERBAL RESPONSE PATTERNS OF MOTHERS ON THE SELF ESTEEM OF THEIR CHILDREN WERE EXPLORED BY MEANS OF A STRATIFIED RANDOM SAMPLING OF 203 EIGHTH GRADE CHILDREN AND THEIR MOTHERS. TEST RESULTS SHOWED THAT THERE IS A RELATIONSHIP BETWEEN THE WAY IN WHICH A MOTHER RESPONDS TO HER CHILD IN NEGATIVE SITUATIONS AND THE CHILD'S SELF ESTEEM FOR THE INNER CITY SAMPLE ONLY. SIGNIFICANT DIFFERENCES ARE OBSERVED BETWEEN THE RESPONSES OF THE INNER CITY BLACK SAMPLE AND THE SUBURBAN WHITE SAMPLE. INNER CITY MOTHERS WERE FOUND TO BE LESS DESCRIPTIVE AND THEIR CHILDREN HAD LOWER ESTIMATES OF SELF ESTEEM THAN DID PERIPHERAL CITY AND SUBURBAN MOTHERS AND THEIR CHILDREN. DISCUSSION FOCUSES ON THEORETICAL SUPPORT, CULTURAL DIFFERENCES, AND IMPORT FOR FUTURE INQUIRY. IT IS SUGGESTED THAT PRACTICAL APPLICATION OF THE FINDINGS EXTEND BEYOND THE PARENT-CHILD HOME RELATIONSHIP TO THE TEACHER AND OTHER MEMBERS OF THE COMMUNITY. (AUTHOR/NH)

ED046543 PS004420
THE EFFECT OF AGGRESSIVE CARTOONS: CHILDREN'S INTERPERSONAL PLAY. HAPKIEWICZ, WALTER G.; RODEN, AUBREY H., [70] 19P.
EDRS PRICE MF-$0.65 HC-$3.29
SIXTY SECOND GRADE CHILDREN WERE RANDOMLY ASSIGNED TO SAME SEX PAIRS AND EACH PAIR WAS RANDOMLY ASSIGNED TO ONE OF THREE TREATMENT GROUPS: AGGRESSIVE CARTOON, NONAGGRESSIVE CARTOON, AND NO CARTOON. RESULTS INDICATED THAT THERE WAS NO DIFFERENCE AMONG THE GROUPS ON MEASURES OF INTERPERSONAL AGGRESSION ALTHOUGH BOYS EXHIBITED SIGNIFICANTLY MORE AGGRESSION THAN GIRLS. BOYS ALSO DEMONSTRATED MORE PROSOCIAL BEHAVIOR (SHARING) THAN GIRLS, ALTHOUGH THOSE WHO VIEWED THE AGGRESSIVE CARTOON PERFORMED THIS RESPONSE AT A REDUCED RATE. ON THE BASIS OF EXISTING EVIDENCE IT WAS CONCLUDED THAT AGGRESSIVE CARTOONS HAVE LITTLE EFFECT ON CHILDREN'S AGGRESSION IN INTERPERSONAL PLAY. (AUTHOR)

ED046544 PS004433
THE RELATIONSHIP OF INDIVIDUAL DIFFERENCES IN THE ORIENTING RESPONSE TO COMPLEX LEARNING IN KINDERGARTNERS. REPORT FROM THE MOTIVATION AND INDIVIDUAL DIFFERENCES IN LEARNING AND RETENTION PROJECT. FARLEY, FRANK H.; MANSKE, MARY E., JUL 70 13P.
EDRS PRICE MF-$0.65 HC-$3.29
HEART RATE CHANGE WAS USED AS THE INDEX OF THE ORIENTING RESPONSE (OR) OF 102 KINDERGARTEN CHILDREN. HEART RATE CHANGE WAS MEASURED BY RECORDING HEART RATE UPON THE PRESENTATION OF TONES. 15 SIMILAR TONES FOLLOWED BY A DIFFERENT, 16TH TONE, WERE USED. FROM THIS DATA THE CHILDREN WERE DIVIDED INTO HIGH, MEDIUM, OR LOW ORIENTORS. FOLLOWING THE "OR" TESTING SESSION, 96 SUBJECTS RECEIVED TWO PICTORIAL ANALOGUES OF VERBAL DISCRIMINATION TASKS. SUBSEQUENTLY, 65 SUBJECTS RECEIVED A PAIRED-ASSOCIATE (P-A) TASK. LEARNING ON THESE TASKS, WHEN RELATED TO "OR" CLASSIFICATION, SHOWED THAT LOW "OR" MALES AND MEDIUM "OR" FEMALES PERFORMED BEST, WHILE MEDIUM "OR" MALES AND LOW "OR" FEMALES PERFORMED WORST. THIS FINDING WAS SIGNIFICANT FOR THE P-A TASK, INDICATING A RELATIONSHIP BETWEEN "OR" CLASSIFICATION AND LEARNING PERFORMANCE ON THIS PARTICULAR P-A TASK. IT IS DIFFICULT TO EXPLAIN THE FACT THAT PERFORMANCE WAS REVERSED BETWEEN THE SEXES. (WD)

ED046545 PS004477
EFFECTS OF PRESCHOOL STIMULATION UPON SUBSEQUENT SCHOOL PERFORMANCE AMONG THE CULTURALLY DISADVANTAGED. PLANT, WALTER T.; SOUTHERN, MARA L., 30 SEP 70 77P.
EDRS PRICE MF-$0.65 HC-$3.29
THIS DOCUMENT REPORTS THE RATIONALE, DESIGN, AND EXECUTION OF A LONGITUDINAL INVESTIGATION OF THE INTELLECTUAL ACHIEVEMENT EFFECTS OF A COGNITIVELY ORIENTED PRESCHOOL FOR DISADVANTAGED MEXICAN-AMERICAN CHILDREN IN SAN JOSE, CALIFORNIA. SEVEN GROUPS OF CHILDREN AGES 3-5 WERE STUDIED. TWO GROUPS WERE EXPOSED TO TWO TEN-WEEK SUCCESSIVE SUMMER SESSIONS OF TRAINING PRIOR TO ENTRY INTO KINDERGARTEN. THEIR PROGRAM EMPHASIZED COGNITIVELY STRUCTURED SMALL GROUP EXPERIENCES WITH 4-5 CHILDREN IN EACH GROUP. GROUP LEADERS WERE LOCAL MEXICAN-AMERICAN HIGH SCHOOL STUDENTS WORKING UNDER THE SUPERVISION OF EXPERIENCED PRIMARY TEACHERS. THE OTHER FIVE GROUPS WERE COMPARISON GROUPS; TWO WERE FROM OUTSIDE THE GEOGRAPHICAL AREA AND THREE WERE FROM THE SCHOOL ATTENDANCE AREA OF THE TRAINING GROUPS. SEVEN HYPOTHESES WERE TESTED THROUGH GATHERING AND PROCESSING PSYCHOMETRIC DATA FROM SCHOOL-RELATED ACHIEVEMENT ABILITY TESTS. RESULTS WERE COMPARED LONGITUDINALLY ACROSS GROUPS TO DETERMINE THE EARLY ADVANTAGE OF SPECIFIC COGNITIVE TRAINING. ALL GROUPS WERE TESTED AT REGULAR INTERVALS AND EVALUATIONS OF IN-SCHOOL PERFORMANCE WERE MADE THROUGH KINDERGARTEN, FIRST AND SECOND GRADES. IN GENERAL, THERE WERE SHORT-TERM GAINS BUT LATER, FEW DIFFERENCES EXISTED BETWEEN THE TRAINING AND COMPARISON GROUPS. AN APPENDIX PROVIDES SAMPLES OF THE TRAINING LESSONS PLUS INFORMATION ABOUT PROJECT MATTERS. (WY)

ED047771 PS003271
MICHIGAN STATE UNIVERSITY, HEAD START EVALUATION AND RESEARCH, 1967-68 RESEARCH ABSTRACTS AND PROGRESS REPORTS. , 68 47P.
EDRS PRICE MF-$0.65 HC-$3.29
THIS DOCUMENT CONTAINS NINE RESEARCH ABSTRACTS AND FIVE PROGRESS REPORTS OF PROJECTS, COMPLETE AND INCOMPLETE, INITIATED IN 1967-1968 BY THE MICHIGAN STATE UNIVERSITY HEAD START AND EVALUATION CENTER. THE TABLE OF CONTENTS LISTS 14 PROJECTS UNDER TWO SUBHEADINGS (1) RESEARCH ABSTRACTS, 1967-1968 REPORT, AND (2) PROGRESS REPORTS, 1967-1968 RESEARCH PROJECTS. (WY)

ED047772 PS003419
FIELD STUDIES OF SOCIAL REINFORCEMENT IN A PRESCHOOL. HARRIS, FLORENCE R., 16 OCT 67 18P.
EDRS PRICE MF-$0.65 HC-$3.29
THIS SEMINAR PAPER REPORTS CASE STUDIES IN THE SUCCESSFUL USE OF ADULT SOCIAL REINFORCEMENT TO MODIFY PROBLEM BEHAVIORS OF INDIVIDUAL CHILDREN IN THE LABORATORY PRESCHOOL AT THE UNIVERSITY OF WASHINGTON, SEATTLE. AFTER INITIALLY DETERMINING THAT TEACHER BEHAVIOR FUNCTIONED AS A REINFORCER IN ACCORDANCE WITH REINFORCEMENT PRINCIPLES, IT BECAME POSSIBLE TO STUDY THE EFFECTS OF ADULT ATTENTION ON BEHAVIOR DEFICITS SUCH AS EXCESSIVE CRYING, EXTREME PASSIVITY, EXCESSIVE ISOLATE BEHAVIOR, LACK OF SPEECH, AND HYPERACTIVITY. THROUGH TEXT AND TABLES, A BRIEF DESCRIPTION OF THE REINFORCEMENT PROGRAM FOR EACH OF NINE "PROBLEM" CHILDREN IS PRESENTED. COLLECTIVELY, THE CASE STUDIES DEMONSTRATE THE EFFECTIVENESS OF ADULT SOCIAL REINFORCEMENT AS A TOOL FOR HELPING CHILDREN MODIFY BEHAVIORS THAT HANDICAP THEM. WY)

ED047773 PS003679
PROCEEDINGS OF FOLLOW THROUGH CONFERENCE (GAINESVILLE, FLORIDA, DECEMBER 9-10, 1969). BREIVOGEL, WILLIAM F., ED., APR 70 91P.
EDRS PRICE MF-$0.65 HC-$3.29
THIS BULLETIN CONTAINS THE PROCEEDINGS OF A CONFERENCE ON FOLLOW THROUGH HELD ON DECEMBER 9-10, 1969, AT THE UNIVERSITY OF FLORIDA. THE CONFERENCE WAS SPONSORED BY THE FLORIDA DEPARTMENT OF EDUCATION, THE INSTITUTE FOR DEVELOPMENT OF HUMAN RESOURCES, AND THE FLORIDA EDUCATIONAL RESEARCH AND DEVELOPMENT COUNCIL. THE PURPOSE OF THIS CONFERENCE WAS TO INFORM FLORIDA SCHOOL SYSTEMS WITH YEAR-ROUND HEAD START, SUMMER HEAD START, AND EARLY CHILDHOOD PEOPLE, IN GENERAL, ABOUT FOLLOW THROUGH--WHAT IT IS, WHAT EDUCATIONAL INNOVATIONS ARE BEING DEVELOPED AND TRIED, WHAT PRACTICES MIGHT BE ADAPTED TO LOCAL PROGRAMS. INCLUDED IS A DISCUSSION OF FOLLOW THROUGH FROM PEOPLE AT VARIOUS LEVELS OF THE PROGRAM: THE NATIONAL DIRECTOR OF FOLLOW THROUGH, THE FLORIDA DEPARTMENT OF EDUCATION'S EARLY CHILDHOOD CONSULTANT, TWO FOLLOW THROUGH MODEL SPONSORS, THREE FLORIDA PEOPLE AT THE SCHOOL DISTRICT LEVEL WHO ARE INVOLVED DAILY IN THE PROGRAM, A VIEW OF SUPPLEMENTAL SERVICES AVAILABLE THROUGH FOLLOW THROUGH, A RESEARCHER'S VIEW OF THE EVALUATION PROCESS USED ON FOLLOW THROUGH MODELS, AND A PROJECTION OF WHAT PROBLEMS EDUCATION WILL FACE IN THE 70'S. THE APPENDIX INCLUDES A LIST OF FOLLOW THROUGH PROGRAM SPONSORS. (AUTHOR/AJ)

ED047774 PS003943
A REVISION OF THE BASIC PROGRAM PLAN OF EDUCATION AT AGE THREE. NIMNICHT, GLEN P., AUG 70 37P.
EDRS PRICE MF-$0.65 HC-$3.29
A MODEL RESPONSIVE EDUCATIONAL SYSTEM BEING EVOLVED BY THE FAR WEST LABORATORY IS DESIGNED TO SERVE CHILDREN FROM AGES 3 TO 9. THE MAJOR OBJECTIVES OF THE EDUCATIONAL SYSTEM ARE TO HELP CHILDREN DEVELOP SELF-CONCEPT AS IT RELATES TO LEARNING IN THE SCHOOL AND THE HOME, AND TO DEVELOP INTELLECTUAL ABILITY. AN AUTOTELIC ENVIRONMENT IS STRESSED. THE SYSTEM INTEGRATES FOUR COMPONENT PARTS: (A) HEAD START, (B) FOLLOW THROUGH, (C) PARENT-CHILD LIBRARY, AND (D) DAY CARE PROGRAM. COMPONENT E, THE SYSTEMS COMPONENT, CAN STAND ALONE OR BECOME A PART OF THE TOTAL SYSTEM. THE TIMETABLE CHARTS SPAN 1966-76 AND INDICATE THE NUMBER OF YEARS INVOLVED IN PROGRAM DEVELOPMENT, TRAINING TASKS, PARENT INVOLVEMENT ACTIVITIES, IMPLEMENTATION IN CLASSROOMS, EVALUATION FOR EACH COMPONENT AND FOR THE TOTAL SYSTEM. FEEDBACK FROM THE HEAD START COMPONENT HAS ALREADY PROVIDED ENOUGH INFORMATION TO PERMIT THIS FIRST REVISION OF THE BASIC PLAN AND TO RESHAPE THE TASKS AND OBJECTIVES OF SUBSEQUENT PHASES. (WY)

ED047775 PS004015
THE BEHAVIOR ANALYSIS CLASSROOM. BUSHELL, DON, JR., 70 22P.
EDRS PRICE MF-$0.65 HC-$3.29
AVAILABLE FROM: FOLLOW THROUGH PROJECT, DEPARTMENT OF HUMAN DEVELOPMENT, UNIVERSITY OF KANSAS, LAWRENCE, KANSAS 66044 ($0.30)

IN A BEHAVIOR ANALYSIS CLASSROOM THE FIRST STEP IS TO DEFINE INSTRUCTIONAL OBJECTIVES FOR ACADEMIC OR SOCIAL SKILLS. THE SECOND STEP IS TO DETERMINE HOW MUCH THE CHILD ALREADY KNOWS ABOUT WHAT IS TO BE TAUGHT. AN ENTRY BEHAVIOR INVENTORY AND DIAGNOSTIC TESTS HELP TEACHERS DECIDE WHERE EACH CHILD NEEDS TO BEGIN WORKING IN THE SEQUENCE LEADING TO ACADEMIC OBJECTIVES. MOTIVATION IS TAUGHT WITH THE HELP OF INCENTIVES SUCH AS TEACHER-PRAISE AND CHILD SELECTION OF FAVORITE ACTIVITIES. A TOKEN SYSTEM REWARDS THE CHILD WITH TOKENS FOR BEHAVIOR AND IMPROVEMENT AT LEARNING TASKS. TOKENS MAY BE ACCUMULATED AND EXCHANGED LATER FOR ACTIVITIES SUCH AS RECESS AND A CHANCE TO PLAY GAMES WITH CLASSMATES. TO BE EFFECTIVE, TOKENS MUST BE USED FOR IMMEDIATE REINFORCEMENT AND DELIVERED AT FREQUENT INTERVALS WHEN THE CHILD IS LEARNING STEPS OF A NEW AND DIFFICULT TASK. A CLASSROOM TEAM OF TEACHER AND AIDES MAKES IT POSSIBLE FOR EACH CHILD TO RECEIVE PERSONAL ATTENTION AND REINFORCEMENT. PARENT PARTICIPATION, IN THE CLASSROOM AND AT HOME, IS A KEY FACTOR IN THE SUCCESS OF THE BEHAVIOR ANALYSIS APPROACH. THE CURRICULUM, THE DAILY SCHEDULE, AND THE USE OF REINFORCEMENT TECHNIQUES FOR DISCIPLINE ARE DISCUSSED. PROGRAM AND STAFF DEVELOPMENT AND EVALUATION ARE DESCRIBED. (NH)

ED047776 PS004016
A TOKEN MANUAL FOR BEHAVIOR ANALYSIS CLASSROOMS. BUSHELL, DON, JR., 70 15P.
EDRS PRICE MF-$0.65 HC-$3.29
AVAILABLE FROM: FOLLOW THROUGH PROJECT, DEPARTMENT OF HUMAN DEVELOPMENT, UNIVERSITY OF KANSAS, LAWRENCE, KANSAS 66044 ($0.30)

THIS DUAL LANGUAGE MANUAL, WRITTEN IN BOTH SPANISH AND ENGLISH, WILL HELP THE TEACHER IN A BEHAVIOR ANALYSIS CLASSROOM UTILIZE THE TOKEN SYSTEM TO MOTIVATE, REINFORCE, AND FOSTER INDEPENDENCE IN PUPILS' LEARNING ACTIVITIES. THE RATIONALE AND PROCEDURES FOR EARNING, GIVING, AND EXCHANGING TOKENS IS CLEARLY EXPLAINED. THE USE OF HELPFUL ACCESSORIES SUCH AS A KITCHEN TIMER TO ANNOUNCE WHEN IT IS TIME TO EXCHANGE TOKENS EARNED FOR ITEMS OR EVENTS, TOKEN APRONS WITH POCKETS, AND TICKETS (ALTERNATIVES TO TOKENS) ARE DESCRIBED. SOME SOLUTIONS ARE PRESENTED TO COMMON PROBLEMS (TOKENS PUT IN MOUTH, STEALING TOKENS, AND THE HAVE-NOT-CHILD WHO HAS NOT EARNED ENOUGH TOKENS FOR EXCHANGE). THE MANUAL SERVES AS A PRACTICAL GUIDE FOR ELEMENTARY OR PRESCHOOL TEACHERS WHO WORK IN CLASSROOMS WHERE POSITIVE REINFORCEMENT FOR GOOD LEARNING BEHAVIOR IS PRACTICED. (WY)

ED047777 PS004123
SCHOOL ACHIEVEMENT: A PRELIMINARY LOOK AT THE EFFECTS OF THE HOME. CRAWFORD, PATRICIA; EASON, GARY, JAN 70 50P.
EDRS PRICE MF-$0.65 HC-$3.29

A LONGITUDINAL STUDY (1960-1966) INVESTIGATED THE EFFECTS OF HOME ENVIRONMENT ON SCHOOL ACHIEVEMENT. THIS PRELIMINARY REPORT FOCUSES ON CHILDREN WHO WERE ENROLLED IN JUNIOR KINDERGARTEN IN 1960. THE FOLLOWING YEAR ALL CHILDREN ENROLLED IN SENIOR KINDERGARTEN BECAME PART OF THE STUDY. THE FIRST SECTION OF THE DOCUMENT OUTLINES DATA COLLECTION PROCEDURES USING A PARENT INTERVIEW QUESTIONNAIRE, AND DESCRIBES ITEMS SELECTED FOR ANALYSIS. PUPIL SCORES ON ONE SPECIALLY DEVELOPED TEST AND TWO STANDARDIZED MENTAL TESTS WERE USED ALONG WITH TEACHER RATINGS IN A MULTIPLE REGRESSION ANALYSIS. THE DOCUMENT SECTION CONCERNED WITH RESULTS AND DISCUSSION ANSWERS FOUR QUESTIONS THAT GUIDED THE STUDY: (1) WHAT NONSCHOOL VARIABLES ARE THE BEST PREDICTORS OF SCHOOL ACHIEVEMENT? (2) DOES HOME ENVIRONMENT MAKE MORE OF A DIFFERENCE TO SCORES ON AN OBJECTIVE STANDARDIZED TEST OR IS IT MORE LIKELY TO AFFECT THE TEACHER'S JUDGMENTS OF A CHILD? IS SOCIOECONOMIC STATUS RELEVANT IN TRYING TO EXPLAIN SCHOOL ACHIEVEMENT? AND (4) DOES IQ MAKE A DIFFERENCE OR DO ACTIONS IN THE HOME PROVIDE A BETTER EXPLANATION OF A CHILD'S PERFORMANCE? APPENDIXES COMPRISE ONE-HALF OF THE DOCUMENT. (WY)

ED047778 PS004125
A COMPARATIVE ANALYSIS OF THE PIAGETIAN DEVELOPMENT OF TWELVE MONTH OLD DISADVANTAGED INFANTS IN AN ENRICHMENT CENTER WITH OTHERS NOT IN SUCH A CENTER. HONIG, ALICE S.; BRILL, SHEILA, SEP 70 27P.
EDRS PRICE MF-$0.65 HC-$3.29

THIS STUDY TESTED THE HYPOTHESIS THAT A 6-MONTH, HALF-DAY PROGRAM OF ENRICHMENT IN LANGUAGE AND PIAGETIAN SENSORIMOTOR SKILLS TAILORED TO THE COGNITIVE-DEVELOPMENTAL LEVEL OF INFANTS WOULD ACCELERATE THE DEVELOPMENT OF PARTICIPATING INFANTS. THE EXPERIMENTAL POPULATION CONSISTED OF 16 12-MONTH-OLD INFANTS ATTENDING ENRICHMENT SESSIONS AT SYRACUSE UNIVERSITY'S CHILDREN'S CENTER. THE CONTROL GROUP CONSISTED OF 16 12-MONTH-OLD INFANTS WHO RECEIVED NO INTERVENTION. ALL THE INFANTS WERE BLACK AND FROM LOW INCOME HOMES. THE TESTS USED IN ASSESSMENT WERE: A STANDARDIZED INFANT GLOBAL IQ TEST, THE CATTELL INFANT INTELLIGENCE SCALE, THE EARLY LANGUAGE ASSESSMENT SCALE, AND THE PIAGETIAN INFANCY SCALES. THE RESULTS DEMONSTRATED THAT FEMALES BENEFITED MORE THAN MALES FROM THE ENRICHMENT PROGRAM, POSSIBLY DUE TO DIFFERENTIAL HOME TREATMENT. THE ADVANCES MADE BY THE EXPERIMENTAL INFANTS BOTH ON THE OBJECT PERMANENCE SCALE AND THE MEANS-ENDS SCALE COMPARED TO THEIR CONTROLS OFFERS ENCOURAGEMENT TO EXPLICITLY PLANNED ENRICHMENT EFFORTS, BASED ON A PIAGETIAN COGNITIVE-DEVELOPMENTAL MODEL AND DESIGNED TO OFFSET COGNITIVE DEFICITS THAT SOMETIMES RESULT WHEN AN INFANT IS NOT PROVIDED THE VARIETY, SEQUENCING AND CHALLENGE APPROPRIATE TO HIS LEVEL OF EXPERIENCES. (AJ)

ED047779 PS004126
PRE-SCHOOL EDUCATION IN EUROPE. BLACKSTONE, TESSA, APR 70 43P.
EDRS PRICE MF-$0.65 HC-$3.29

THE EXTENT AND NATURE OF PRESCHOOL EDUCATION IN EUROPE IS DISCUSSED, WITH REFERENCE TO ENGLAND AND WALES, FRANCE, THE NETHERLANDS, NORWAY AND SWEDEN. REPORTS ON PRESCHOOL EDUCATION IN THESE COUNTRIES GIVE EXAMPLES OF BOTH AN EARLY AND A LATE START TO COMPULSORY EDUCATION, VERY EXTENSIVE AND VERY LIMITED PRESCHOOL PROVISION, AND THE EFFECTS OF PRIVATE AND STATE SUPPORT. EDUCATIONAL PROVISION IS MADE FOR VERY SMALL NUMBERS OF CHILDREN UNDER THREE YEARS OF AGE, IF AT ALL. IN MOST OF THE COUNTRIES PRIMARY EDUCATION IS SEPARATE FROM PRESCHOOL EDUCATION AND CONTACTS BETWEEN THE TWO SYSTEMS ARE USUALLY LIMITED. COUNTRIES ARE COMPARED ON SUCH MATTERS AS PRESCHOOL STAFFING, CURRICULUM, CLASS SIZE, AND PARENT INVOLVEMENT. LACK OF RESOURCES AND CONFLICTING VALUES ARE CONSIDERED THE MAIN REASONS FOR THE SLOW GROWTH OF NURSERY, (OR PRESCHOOL) EDUCATION IN EUROPE. SUGGESTIONS ARE MADE ABOUT THE POLICIES THAT GOVERNMENTS SHOULD ADOPT IN THIS SPHERE, AND ABOUT THE IMPORTANT ROLES THAT PARENTS AND TEACHERS SHOULD TAKE AS PARTNERS IN THE EDUCATIONAL PROCESS. NH)

ED047780 PS004211
PROCEEDINGS OF THE CONFERENCE ON INDUSTRY AND DAY CARE (URBAN RESEARCH CORPORATION, CHICAGO, 1970). , 70 94P.
DOCUMENT NOT AVAILABLE FROM EDRS.
AVAILABLE FROM: URBAN RESEARCH CORPORATION, 5464 SOUTH SHORE DRIVE, CHICAGO, ILL. 60615 ($15.00)

THIS BOOKLET OF CONFERENCE PROCEEDINGS REFLECTS THE EFFORTS OF THE URBAN RESEARCH CORPORATION TO CONTINUE CONVERSATION BETWEEN INDUSTRY AND DAY CARE SPECIALISTS. A GROUP OF 175 INDUSTRY REPRESENTATIVES, EARLY CHILDHOOD SPECIALISTS, COMMUNITY AGENCY REPRESENTATIVES, AND DAY CARE OPERATORS AND FRANCHISERS CONVENED TO DISCUSS THEIR MUTUAL CONCERNS. TOPICS INCLUDED IN THE BOOKLET ARE: MAJOR ISSUES IN DAY CARE, MODELS OF INDUSTRY-RELATED DAY CARE, THE CONSUMERS, COSTS AND FUNDING, FEDERAL LEGISLATION FOR DAY CARE, MODELS OF THE MIND, INDUSTRIAL DAY CARE'S ROOTS IN AMERICA. THE FOUR APPENDIXES SUMMARIZE WORKSHOPS HELD ON PROGRAM GOALS, FRANCHISE ARRANGEMENTS, 4-C PROGRAMS, AND LICENSING. TWO OTHER TOPICS, A COMPARATIVE ANALYSIS OF LEGISLATION, AND STANDARDS AND COSTS ARE INCLUDED ALONG WITH A LISTING OF PARTICIPANTS AND THEIR ADDRESSES. (WY)

ED047781 PS004212
MARGINAL CHILDREN OF WAR: AN EXPLORATORY STUDY OF AMERICAN-KOREAN CHILDREN. HURH, WON MOO, JUL 67 61P.
EDRS PRICE MF-$0.65 HC-$3.29

THE NATURE AND EXTENT OF THE PROBLEMS INVOLVED IN THE SOCIALIZATION OF MIXED-RACE CHILDREN OF AMERICAN SERVICEMEN AND KOREAN WOMEN IS DISCUSSED. OBSERVATIONS AND INTERVIEWS FIND THESE FACTORS SIGNIFICANT IN CONSTITUTING THE SOCIAL MARGINALITY OF SUCH CHILDREN: (A) THE STIGMA OF ILLEGITIMACY, (B) THE MOTHERS' UNDESIRABLE OCCUPATIONAL STATUS (PROSTITUTION), (C) CHILDREN'S ECONOMIC AND EDUCATIONAL DEPRIVATION, AND (D) PHYSICAL DIFFERENCES, EXPECIALLY COLOR OF HAIR AND SKIN. AMERO-KOREAN CHILDREN ARE RACIAL HYBRIDS, BUT NOT CULTURAL HYBRIDS, FOR THEY ARE SOCIALIZED IN THE RELATIVELY HOMOGENEOUS KOREAN CULTURE AND HAVE NO ALTERNATE COURSE BUT TO BECOME PART OF THE IN-GROUP. THE OFTEN DISASTROUS EFFECT (OF BEING RACIALLY HYBRID) ON CHILDREN'S SELF-IMAGE AND EMOTIONAL DEVELOPMENT IS DISCUSSED. THESE CHILDREN HAVE RARELY BEEN ADOPTED IN KOREA, LARGELY BECAUSE OF CULTURAL ATTITUDES FAVORING KINSHIP LINEAGE AND BECAUSE OF SOCIAL APATHY. A MULTI-DIMENSIONAL SOLUTION TO THE PROBLEM IS PROPOSED, WHICH INVOLVES AN UNDERLYING ATTITUDINAL CHANGE ON THE PART OF THE KOREAN PEOPLE, INTEGRATION OF THESE CHILDREN INTO SOCIETY, POOLING OF WELFARE INSTITUTION RESOURCES, AND A STRONGER GOVERNMENT ROLE IN CHILD WELFARE. TABLES ARE INCLUDED OF THE STATUS OF HYBRID CHILDREN IN KOREA, AND OF INTERCOUNTRY ADOPTION. (NH)

ED047782 PS004215
HEAD START PLANNED VARIATION STUDY. , SEP 70 17P.
EDRS PRICE MF-$0.65 HC-$3.29

PROJECT HEAD START AND PROJECT FOLLOW THROUGH ARE JOINTLY EXPLORING THE EFFECTIVENESS OF 12 DIFFERENT EDUCATIONAL APPROACHES, OR MODELS, FOR THE EDUCATION OF YOUNG CHILDREN FROM POVERTY FAMILIES. INVESTIGATIONS INCLUDE STUDY OF (1) THE EFFECT OF A CONTINUOUS INTERVENTION PROGRAM WHICH BEGINS WITH HEAD START AND EXTENDS THROUGH THIRD GRADE, (2) THE INITIAL IMPACT AND LASTING EFFECT OF VARIOUS APPROACHES DURING THIS PERIOD OF TIME, AND (3) THE MOST EFFECTIVE AGE FOR PUPIL ENTRANCE. PLANNED VARIATION PROGRAM SPONSORS AND SHORT PROGRAM DESCRIPTIONS ARE LISTED. PROGRAM APPROACHES REPRESENTED INCLUDE STRUCTURED ACADEMIC, COGNITIVELY-ORIENTED, DEVELOPMENTAL SELF-DIRECTED, PRAGMATIC ACTION-ORIENTED, RESPONSIVE ENVIRONMENT, AND PARENT EDUCATOR. THE ENABLING MODEL IS ALSO DISCUSSED. CRITERIA ARE GIVEN FOR THE SELECTION OF THE 30 COMMUNITIES IN THE 1970-71 STUDY, WHICH INCLUDE 15 OF THE 1969-70 SITES. THE OVERALL DESIGN AND PLANS FOR MEASUREMENT, ASSESSMENT, AND ANALYSIS ARE PRESENTED. (NH)

ED047783 PS004217
CLASSIFYING DAY CARE CENTERS FOR COST ANALYSIS. MCCLELLAN, KEITH, NOV 70 25P.
EDRS PRICE MF-$0.65 HC-$3.29

THE PURPOSE OF THIS INVESTIGATION WAS TO DESIGN A CLASSIFICATION SYSTEM FOR DETERMINING THE OPERATING COSTS OF DAY CARE CENTERS FOR PRESCHOOLERS. THE BASIC HYPOTHESIS OF THE STUDY WAS THAT OWNERSHIP ARRANGEMENTS AND PROGRAMS OF DAY CARE CENTERS COULD BOTH BE USED TO PREDICT SUCH CHARACTERISTICS AS VARIATIONS IN CLIENTELE, FACILITIES, STAFFING PATTERNS, AND ORGANIZATIONAL ARRANGEMENTS. A CENSUS WAS TAKEN OF 543 STATE-LICENSED PRESCHOOL DAY CARE CENTERS IN CHICAGO. PROGRAMS WERE CLASSIFIED ACCORDING TO FOUR FACTORS: (1) SUCCESS-ORIENTATION: MASTERY OF SKILLS/MASTERY OF INTERPERSONAL RELATIONSHIPS; (2) SUPERVISION: DIRECTED LEARNING/NON-DIRECTED LEARNING; (3) SKILL DEVELOPMENT: FIXED TASKS/FLEXIBLE TASKS; AND (4) REWARD-MOTIVATION: OPERANT CONDITIONING/POSITIVE REINFORCEMENT. THE REPORT SUGGESTS THAT THE TEST OF ACCURACY OF THE COST ANALYSIS PROCEDURES WILL BE THEIR ABILITY TO PROVIDE INSIGHT INTO SUCH MATTERS AS GOOD MANAGEMENT STRATEGIES, OPTIMUM SIZES OF DAY CARE CENTERS, SUITABLE FEE SCHEDULES, PROPER RATIOS BETWEEN INDEBTEDNESS AND NET INCOME, AND APPROPRIATE STAFFING PATTERNS. EVIDENCE GATHERED TO DATE INDICATES THAT THE CLASSIFICATION SYSTEM MAY BE USED AS A PREDICTIVE DEVICE. [FILMED FROM BEST AVAILABLE COPY]. (AJ)

ED047784 PS004236
RELATIONSHIPS BETWEEN SELECTED FAMILY VARIABLES AND MATERNAL AND INFANT BEHAVIOR IN A DISADVANTAGED POPULATION. A SUPPLEMENTARY REPORT. GORDON, IRA J.; AND OTHERS, 15 APR 69 84P.
EDRS PRICE MF-$0.65 HC-$3.29

THIS PAMPHLET CONTAINS A SERIES OF STUDIES THAT GREW OUT OF THE PARENT EDUCATION PROJECT OF THE INSTITUTE FOR DEVELOPMENT OF HUMAN RESOURCES. THE OBJECTIVES AND GENERAL DESIGN OF THE PROJECT CONSISTED OF INSTRUCTION OF 200 ENVIRONMENTALLY DISADVANTAGED MOTHERS BY PARENT EDUCATORS USING A SEQUENCE OF INFANT STIMULATION EXERCISES CONDUCTED IN THE HOME. THE INDIVIDUAL STUDIES PRESENTED REPRESENT A MIX OF GRADUATE STUDENT PILOT EFFORTS, DISSERTATION RESEARCH, FACULTY INVESTIGATIONS, AND REPLICATIONS OF PILOT WORK. ALL HAVE BEEN EDITED AND ADAPTED TO HIGHLIGHT THE RELATIONSHIP BETWEEN HOME FACTORS, MOTHER'S ATTITUDE AND BEHAVIOR IN THE PROJECT, AND HER BEHAVIOR TOWARD CHILDREN. TITLES INCLUDE: RELATIONSHIP BETWEEN MATERNAL BEHAVIOR AND INFANT PERFORMANCE IN ENVIRONMENTALLY DISADVANTAGED HOMES; A SURVEY OF LOW INCOME NEGROES IN ALACHUO AND SURROUNDING COUNTIES; MEASUREMENT OF SELF ESTEEM; A STUDY OF THE RELATIONSHIPS BETWEEN TRAINED AND UNTRAINED TWELVE MONTH OLD ENVIRONMENTALLY DEPRIVED INFANTS ON THE "GRIFFITHS MENTAL DEVELOPMENT SCALE"; RELATIONSHIP BETWEEN MATERNAL BEHAVIOR AND INFANT PERFORMANCE IN ENVIRONMENTALLY DISADVANTAGED HOMES; AND RELATIONSHIPS BETWEEN OBSERVED HOME BEHAVIOR VARIABLES AND INFANT PERFORMANCE. (WY)

ED047785 PS004237
NUTRITIONAL STATUS OF NEW ORLEANS, MISSISSIPPI AND ALABAMA HEAD START CHILDREN. FINAL REPORT. SMITH, JACK L., 31 AUG 69 93P.
EDRS PRICE MF-$0.65 HC-$3.29

THREE PURPOSES GUIDED COMPILATION OF THIS FINAL REPORT ON THE NUTRITIONAL STATUS OF NEW ORLEANS, MISSISSIPPI, AND ALABAMA HEAD START CHILDREN: (1) TO EVALUATE THE CAUSES OF ANEMIA THROUGH DETAILED STUDIES OF URBAN NEW ORLEANS PRESCHOOL CHILDREN AND THEIR MOTHERS, (2) TO STUDY THE EFFECT OF DIETARY SUPPLEMENTATION OF SCHOOL FEEDING PROGRAMS UPON THE NUTRITIONAL STATUS OF GROUPS OF ANEMIC AND NON-ANEMIC CHILDREN IN PRESCHOOL AND KINDERGARTEN PROGRAMS, (3) TO USE NATIONALLY STANDARDIZED PROCEDURES TO COLLECT AND INTEGRATE NEW ORLEANS DATA WITH DATA OBTAINED FROM MISSISSIPPI AND ALABAMA STUDIES ON RURAL AND SEMI-URBAN CHILDREN. THE NEW ORLEANS STUDY WAS CONDUCTED IN THREE PHASES AND UTILIZED CONTROL AND NUTRITIONALLY SUPPLEMENTED GROUPS WHEN THEY WERE AVAILABLE. COMPARISON PROCEDURES WERE USED, BASED ON THIRTEEN ANALYSES OF BLOOD AND URINE DATA. THE REPORT'S GENERAL CONCLUSION WAS THAT IT IS NOT POSSIBLE TO ASCERTAIN OR TO INFLUENCE THE HEMATOLOGICAL STATUS OF THE POPULATIONS INVESTIGATED. ONE THIRD OF THIS DOCUMENT IS MADE UP OF TABLES WHICH PERMIT AN EXAMINATION OF THE NUMBER OF INDIVIDUALS TESTED FOR EACH PARAMETER, FOR EACH SCHOOL, AND FOR VARIATION BETWEEN SCHOOLS. (WY)

ED047786 PS004240
AN ANALYSIS OF PUBLISHED PRESCHOOL LANGUAGE PROGRAMS. BARTLETT, ELSA JAFFE, NOV 70 15P.
EDRS PRICE MF-$0.65 HC-$3.29

FOR PURPOSES OF ANALYSIS, PRESCHOOL LANGUAGE PROGRAMS CAN BE SORTED INTO FOUR GENERAL CATEGORIES ACCORDING TO THE DOMINANT TYPE OF LEARNING ACTIVITY (1) PATTERN PRACTICE, (2) COGNITIVE VERBALIZATION, (3) DISCUSSION, (4) ROLE PLAY. ALONG WITH DEFINITIONS OF LANGUAGE, THE PROGRAM TYPES DIFFER IN THE KINDS OF INTERACTIONS WHICH OCCUR BETWEEN TEACHER AND CHILD AND AMONG CHILDREN THEMSELVES. THE KIND OF INTERACTION A PROGRAM PROMOTES SHOULD BE A KEY FEATURE IN CHOOSING A PUBLISHED PACKAGE FOR PRESCHOOL USE. IT IS IMPORTANT TO KNOW EXACTLY THE KIND OF LEARNING RELATIONSHIPS THAT ARE BEING REWARDED AND WHETHER THEY ARE THE KIND OF LEARNING BEHAVIORS THE SCHOOL WISHES TO FOSTER. OTHER MAJOR POINTS OF COMPARISON AMONG PROGRAMS COME FROM INSPECTION OF THE TEACHER'S GUIDE. PROGRAMS DIFFER IN THE AMOUNT OF ORGANIZATION AND SEQUENCING PROVIDED FOR THE TEACHER AND THEY ALSO VARY IN THE AMOUNT OF DETAILED INFORMATION GIVEN TO GUIDE THE TEACHER. THE SINGLE MOST IMPORTANT FACTOR IN CHOOSING A PROGRAM SEEMS TO BE WHETHER THE TEACHER IS ABLE TO SPEND THE 15 TO 30 MINUTES PER DAY CARRYING OUT THE RECOMMENDED CLASSROOM PROCEDURES. FOUR CHARTS IDENTIFY SPECIFIC PROGRAMS, MATERIALS, LEARNING ACTIVITIES AND TYPES OF TEACHERS' GUIDES ANALYZED FOR THIS STUDY. [FILMED FROM BEST AVAILABLE COPY.] (WY)

ED047787 PS004241
FOLLOW THROUGH: PROGRAM APPROACHES, SCHOOL YEAR 1970-71. RESNICK, LAUREN B.; AND OTHERS, 70 51P.
EDRS PRICE MF-$0.65 HC-$3.29

THE 1970-71 FOLLOW THROUGH PLANNED VARIATION STUDY WILL EVALUATE NEW APPROACHES TO EARLY EDUCATION FOR CHILDREN FROM LOW INCOME FAMILIES. BRIEF DESCRIPTIONS ARE GIVEN OF THE 20 PROGRAM APPROACHES BEING USED IN 160 PUBLIC SCHOOLS SELECTED FOR THE STUDY. PROGRAMS REFLECT A WIDE SPECTRUM OF THEORETICAL POSITIONS, WHICH RANGE FROM LESS STRUCTURED CHILD-CENTERED APPROACH WHICH EMPHASIZES NOT CURRICULUM CONTENT SO MUCH AS THE DEVELOPMENT OF THE CHILD'S CONFIDENCE AND OTHER BEHAVIORAL CHARACTERISTICS. TWO OF THE APPROACHES EMPHASIZE PARENT TRAINING AND PARTICIPATION. INCLUDED IS A LIST OF ADDRESSES OF THE 20 PROGRAM SPONSORS, FROM WHOM MORE DETAILED PRESENTATIONS ARE AVAILABLE. (AUTHOR/NH)

ED047788 PS004412
SESAME STREET. A SURVEY OF TWO CITIES: VIEWING PATTERNS IN INNER CITY LOS ANGELES AND CHICAGO. FILEP, ROBERT; AND OTHERS, 21 AUG 70 127P.
EDRS PRICE MF-$0.65 HC-$6.58

THIS SURVEY WAS CONDUCTED: (1) TO DEVELOP A SURVEY INSTRUMENT FOR THE COLLECTION OF VIEWER INTERVIEWS WITH THE GUIDANCE AND INVOLVEMENT OF PERSONNEL RECRUITED FROM INNER CITY COMMUNITIES; (2) TO ASCERTAIN IF SESAME STREET WAS BEING RECEIVED BY A SIGNIFICANT NUMBER OF INNER CITY HOUSEHOLDS IN THE LOW-INCOME, MINORITY, COMMUNITIES OF LOS ANGELES AND CHICAGO; (3) TO IDENTIFY TELEVISION VIEWING PATTERNS OF THE PRESCHOOLERS AND THEIR PARENTS; (4) TO OBTAIN DATA ABOUT THE PERCEIVED VALUE OF THE EDUCATIONAL ASPECTS OF SESAME STREET; AND (5) TO IDENTIFY POTENTIAL VOLUNTEER PARTICIPANTS TO MAXIMIZE THE EFFECTIVENESS OF EACH PRESCHOOLER'S VIEWING. THE DIRECTION OF THE SURVEY (COVERING 8,000 HOUSEHOLDS) IS TOWARD DETERMINING IF SESAME STREET REACHES THE POPULATION FOR WHICH IT IS INTENDED--POOR INNER CITY PRESCHOOLERS. OBSERVATIONS ARE PROVIDED THAT COMPARE THE AUDIENCES IN THE TWO CITIES AND SUGGEST FUTURE PROGRAM MODIFICATIONS. APPROXIMATELY ONE-THIRD OF THE DOCUMENT CONSISTS OF TABLES AND SURVEY FORMS. (AJ)

ED047789 PS004415
INSTRUCTIONAL SPECIFICITY AND OUTCOME-EXPECTATION IN OBSERVATIONALLY-INDUCED QUESTION FORMULATION. ROSENTHAL, TED L.; ZIMMERMAN, BARRY J., NOV 70 17P.
EDRS PRICE MF-$0.65 HC-$3.29

SPONTANEOUS AND MODEL-INDUCED PRODUCTION OF A VALUATIONAL STYLE OF INQUIRY WAS STUDIED IN 128 THIRD GRADE CHILDREN. PROVISION OF A FAVORABLE VERSUS A NEUTRAL OUTCOME-EXPECTATION, AND SEX OF CHILD FAILED TO INFLUENCE THE RESULTS. ALL MODELING GROUPS DISPLAYED STRONG VALUE-QUESTION INCREASES OVER BASELINE WHICH, WITHOUT FURTHER TUTELAGE, THEY GENERALIZED TO A NEW SET OF STIMULUS PICTURES. FOUR INSTRUCTIONAL VARIATIONS, IMPLICIT, EXPLICIT, PATTERN (CALLING NOTICE TO AN UNDERLYING SIMILARITY AMONG THE MODEL'S QUESTIONS), AND

MAPPING (EXEMPLIFYING ESSENTIAL FEATURES OF THE MODEL'S PARADIGM) PROVED TO DIFFER SIGNIFICANTLY IN THE POSTMODELING IMITATION PHASE BUT NOT IN GENERALIZATION. THE CONCEPTUAL AND PEDAGOGICAL RELEVANCE OF THE RESULTS WERE DISCUSSED. (AUTHOR)

ED047790 PS004416
MODELING BY EXEMPLIFICATION AND INSTRUCTION IN TRAINING CONSERVATION. ROSENTHAL, TED L.; ZIMMERMAN, BARRY J., [70] 32P.
EDRS PRICE MF-$0.65 HC-$3.29

FOUR EXPERIMENTS (INVOLVING A TOTAL OF 158 CHILDREN) DEMONSTRATED OBSERVATIONALLY-INDUCED LEARNING EFFECTS ON MULTIDIMENSIONAL CONSERVATION TASKS USING BRIEF, SINGLE SESSION TRAINING. FIRST GRADE SAMPLES OF MIDDLE CLASS ANGLO-AMERICAN, AND ECONOMICALLY DISADVANTAGED MEXICAN-AMERICAN CHILDREN DISPLAYED GAINS IN VICARIOUSLY-INDUCED CONSERVATION AS DID A SEPARATE GROUP OF 4-YEAR-OLDS. ON INITIAL (IMITATIVE) TASK STIMULI, MODELING INCREASED CONSERVATION RESPONSES WHICH THEN GENERALIZED TO A NEW SET OF STIMULUS ITEMS WITHOUT FURTHER INTERVENTION. VERBAL FEEDBACK PRAISING THE MODEL'S RESPONSES DID NOT AFFECT PERFORMANCE. A NONCONSERVING MODEL REDUCED CONSERVATION IN INITIALLY-CONSERVING CHILDREN. A NONMODELING INSTRUCTION PROCEDURE FAILED TO MODIFY CONSERVATION SCORES. THE MODEL'S PROVISION OF A RULE TO EXPLAIN STIMULUS EQUIVALENCE IMPROVED PERFORMANCE WHEN CRITERION RESPONSE REQUIRED JUDGED EQUIVALENCE PLUS EXPLANATION, BUT NOT WHEN THE RESPONSE CRITERION WAS JUDGED EQUIVALENCE ALONE. CHILDREN WHO OBSERVED THE MODEL CONSERVE WITHOUT GIVING AN EXPLANATION NEVERTHELESS INCREASED THEIR CORRECT JUDGMENTS-PLUS-RULE RESPONSES IN THE IMITATION PHASE, THUS DEMONSTRATING THAT OBSERVATIONAL LEARNING CAN PRODUCE INFERENTIAL THINKING. THEORETICAL IMPLICATIONS OF THE RESULTS WERE DISCUSSED. (AUTHOR)

ED047791 PS004421
A SEQUENTIAL APPROACH TO EARLY CHILDHOOD AND ELEMENTARY EDUCATION, PHASE II. GRANT REPORT. VAN DE RIET, VERNON; AND OTHERS, DEC 70 99P.
EDRS PRICE MF-$0.65 HC-$3.29

THIS REPORT IS THE 2-YEAR FOLLOWUP EVALUATION OF A PROPOSED 4-YEAR GRANT, STUDYING THE EFFECTS OF A SEQUENTIAL LEARNING PROGRAM ON DISADVANTAGED CHILDREN. FOUR- AND 5-YEAR-OLDS (N86) WERE MATCHED ON SEVERAL DEVELOPMENTAL VARIABLES, WITH ONE GROUP AT EACH AGE ENTERING THE LEARNING TO LEARN PROGRAM AT EITHER THE NURSERY OR KINDERGARTEN LEVEL. THE OTHER TWO GROUPS SERVED AS CONTROLS AND ENTERED DAY CARE CENTERS OR TRADITIONAL TYPE KINDERGARTENS. DURING THE SECOND YEAR OF THE PROJECT THE EXPERIMENTAL GROUPS EITHER ATTENDED KINDERGARTEN OR FIRST GRADE AT THE LEARNING TO LEARN SCHOOL, AND THE CONTROL GROUPS ATTENDED EITHER TITLE I KINDERGARTEN OR TRADITIONAL FIRST GRADE CLASSES IN PUBLIC SCHOOLS. EXPERIMENTAL AND CONTROL GROUPS WERE TESTED ON MEASURES OF INTELLIGENCE, PSYCHOLINGUISTIC ABILITY, VISUAL MOTOR ABILITY, PRIMARY MENTAL ABILITIES, READINESS AND ACHIEVEMENT. RESULTS INDICATE THAT THE CHILDREN WHO BEGAN THE PROGRAM AT AGE 4 HAVE MADE MUCH LARGER DEVELOPMENTAL GAINS THAN CHILDREN IN THE MATCHED CONTROL GROUP. TO A LESSER EXTENT, THE CHILDREN WHO BEGAN THE PROGRAM AT AGE 5 HAVE ADVANCED MORE RAPIDLY THAN THEIR CONTROL GROUP. AN APPENDIX GIVES INDIVIDUAL RAW DATA COLLECTED, DESCRIPTIONS OF TESTS USED, AND RATING SCALES. (AUTHOR/NH)

ED047792 PS004422
THE IMPLICATIONS OF DESIGN AND MODEL SELECTION FOR THE EVALUATION OF PROGRAMS FOR THE DISADVANTAGED CHILD. HODGES, WALTER L., 28 DEC 70 24P.
EDRS PRICE MF-$0.65 HC-$3.29

THE DIFFICULT WORK OF IDENTIFYING EFFECTIVE RESEARCH STRATEGIES IN EARLY EDUCATION HAS RECENTLY BEGUN. SECOND GENERATION MODEL-DERIVED PROGRAMS ARE JUST BEGINNING TO EMERGE. TO LEARN FROM THESE PROGRAMS, EVALUATORS MUST IDENTIFY FOUR CRITERIA OF CRITICAL DIFFERENCES EXISTING AMONG PROGRAMS AND ATTACK THE PROGRAMMATIC ANALYSIS OF THESE DIFFERENCES WITH VIGOR. THE FOUR CRITERIA ARE SPECIFICATION OF: (1) THE PROCESS THROUGH WHICH PROGRAM GOALS AND INSTRUCTIONAL OBJECTIVES ARE GENERATED OR SELECTED (THE VIEW OF CHILD DEVELOPMENT INVOLVED AND THE MANNER OF ACCOUNTING FOR SOCIETAL PRESS), (2) THE CONDITIONS OR PROCESSES TO BE USED TO INSURE THE WILLFUL INTERACTION OF THE TARGET POPULATION WITH THESE GOALS AND INSTRUCTIONAL OBJECTIVES (THE APPROPRIATE INCENTIVE CONDITIONS), (3) THE APPROPRIATE SEQUENCE FOR THE INTRODUCTION OF LEARNING OPPORTUNITIES OR THE STRATEGIES REQUIRED TO ENABLE THE PROGRAMMER TO ORDER INSTRUCTIONAL OBJECTIVES IN SOME SEQUENCE, AND (4) THE STRATEGIES REQUIRED OF THE TEACHER OR PROGRAMMER FOR ORGANIZING THE LEARNING SITUATION FOR OPTIMAL BENEFIT TO CHILDREN. ADMITTEDLY, GENERIC APPROACHES AND THE FUNCTIONAL EQUIVALENCE OF MODELS POSE ADDITIONAL DIFFICULTIES FOR EVALUATORS BUT THESE CAN BE OVERCOME BY DIRECTING PRELIMINARY EFFORTS TOWARD UNDERSTANDING THE RELATIONSHIP OF A MODEL TO A COMPLETE EDUCATIONAL SYSTEM. (WY)

ED047793 PS004424
THE EFFECTS OF ADULT VERBAL MODELING AND FEEDBACK ON THE ORAL LANGUAGE OF HEAD START CHILDREN. HUTINGER, PATRICIA; BRUCE, TERRI, [AUG 70] 19P.
EDRS PRICE MF-$0.65 HC-$3.29

THIS STUDY EXAMINES SOME VARIABLES THAT MAY AFFECT TWO ASPECTS OF SYNTAX IN HEAD START CHILDREN; THE USE OF DESCRIPTORS AND THE USE OF COMPLETE SENTENCES. THIRTY-SIX CHILDREN WERE ASSIGNED TO SIX EXPERIMENTAL CONDITIONS IN A DESIGN WHICH VARIED ADULT VERBAL MODELING, FEEDBACK, AND SEX. CHILDREN GIVEN ADULT VERBAL MODELING PRODUCED SIGNIFICANTLY MORE ADJECTIVES, PLACED THEM CORRECTLY MORE OFTEN AND PRODUCED MORE GRAMMATICALLY COMPLETE SENTENCES THAN SS GIVEN NO MODEL. THE SS GIVEN DISCRIMINATION LEARNING SHOWED CONSISTENTLY SUPERIOR PERFORMANCE OVER SS GIVEN INDISCRIMINATE PRAISE. SEX DIFFERENCES, EXCEPT FOR ONE, WERE NONSIGNIFICANT. A RETENTION TEST, 12-14 DAYS LATER, SHOWED THAT RESULTS ATTRIBUTABLE TO MAIN EFFECTS STOOD UP OVER A PERIOD OF TIME, BUT WERE NOT SIGNIFICANTLY DIFFERENT FROM SCORES OBTAINED IMMEDIATELY AFTER LEARNING. (AUTHOR)

ED047794 PS004425
THE MEANING OF AN ORIENTING RESPONSE: A STUDY IN THE HIERARCHICAL ORDER OF ATTENDING. LEWIS, MICHAEL; HARWITZ, MARCIA, APR 69 41P.
EDRS PRICE MF-$0.65 HC-$3.29

THE PURPOSES OF THIS STUDY ARE: (1) TO ATTEMPT TO SHOW THE WEAKNESS OF THE THEORY OF A TWO-STAGE PROCESS OF ATTENDING, I.E. HAVING BOTH SEPARATE AND ORDERED FOCUSING AND ELABORATING ASPECTS; AND (2) TO OFFER AN ALTERNATIVE APPROACH WHEREBY BOTH FOCUSING AND ELABORATING ARE UNDER THE SERVICE OF COGNITIVE VARIABLES. THE DISCUSSION COVERS THE ISSUE OF THE DEFINITION OF A "NEW" STIMULUS EVENT, THE INHERENT DIFFICULTIES IN A SIMPLE MATCHING PROCESS, AND PRESENTS AN ALTERNATIVE MODEL FOR ATTENDING TO STIMULUS EVENTS. AN EXPERIMENT IS PRESENTED WHICH DEMONSTRATES AN ORIENTING REFLEX (OR) HIERARCHY COMPARABLE TO HIERARCHIES OF CONCEPT FORMATION ATTAINMENT IN THE SAME AGE CHILD. SPECIFICALLY, A REDUNDANT VISUAL SIGNAL IS FOLLOWED BY FOUR VARIATIONS OF THAT SIGNAL; CHANGES IN COLOR, SIZE, NUMBER, AND ROTATION. THE RESULTS, ACCOUNTING FOR BOTH DISCRIMINABILITY AND INTRINSIC VALUE DEMONSTRATE A HIERARCHY OF STIMULUS SALIENCE. THIS HIERARCHY OF COLOR, SIZE, NUMBER, AND ROTATION IS CONSISTENT WITH CONCEPT FORMATION ACQUISITION AND THESE RESULTS ARE USED TO ARGUE FOR THE PROPOSED MODEL OF ATTENDING WHICH EMPHASIZES THE NEED TO CONSIDER COGNITIVE PRINCIPLES IN UNDERSTANDING AN OR. (AUTHOR/AJ)

ED047795 PS004434
CURRICULAR INTERVENTION IN LANGUAGE ARTS READINESS FOR HEAD START CHILDREN. TULANE UNIVERSITY, HEAD START EVALUATION AND RESEARCH CENTER, 1968-1969 INTERVENTION REPORT. SUPPLEMENT TO THE ANNUAL REPORT TO THE OFFICE OF ECONOMIC OPPORTUNITY. JONES, SHUELL H., 31 AUG 69 19P.
EDRS PRICE MF-$0.65 HC-$3.29

IN A PREVIOUS STUDY, (ED 038 175) MISSISSIPPI CHILDREN, WHO WERE A YEAR YOUNGER (3 1/2 TO 4 1/2) THAN ALABAMA CHILDREN, HAD SCORED HIGHER THAN THE ALABAMA CHILDREN ON POSTTESTING. THIS SUPPLEMENTARY REPORT GIVES THE RESULTS OF FURTHER INVESTIGATION OF THIS FINDING. EXPLANATIONS MAY BE: (1) THE YOUNGER CHILDREN BEGAN WITH HIGHER IQ SCORES; (2) MORE THAN EIGHT TIMES AS MANY CHILDREN IN ALABAMA LIVE WITH FAMILIES RECEIVING WELFARE; AND (3) MORE ALABAMA CHILDREN HAVE NO ADULT MALE RESIDING IN THE HOME. SUPPLEMENTAL DATA IN TABULAR FORM INCLUDE: STANDARD DEVIATIONS OF PRETEST AND POSTTEST MEANS, AGE MEANS AND STANDARD DEVIATIONS, TIME INTERVAL IN WEEKS, PREVIOUS HEAD START EXPERIENCE, TESTER RELIABILITY, AGE RANGE AND ANALYSES OF CORRELATION OF IQ TO FAMILY STATUS. WHETHER THESE FACTORS HAVE PLAYED A PART IN THE PHENOMENON STUDIED IS ACTUALLY UNKNOWN. FURTHER INVESTIGATION IS NEEDED. (AUTHOR/AJ)

ED047796 PS004435
FACTORS? IN CHILD DEVELOPMENT: PEER RELATIONS. PHILLIS, JUDITH A., 6 FEB 71 10P.
EDRS PRICE MF-$0.65 HC-$3.29

RELATIONSHIPS BETWEEN SOCIAL DEVELOPMENT, PEER POPULARITY, AND PUPIL JUSTIFICATIONS OF FRIENDSHIP CHOICES WERE INVESTIGATED. SUBJECTS WERE 30 BOYS AND 30 GIRLS, 13 OF WHOM WERE NEGRO. THE CHILDREN WERE ENROLLED IN A LABORATORY SUMMER SCHOOL PROGRAM AND RANGED IN AGE FROM 5 TO 8 YEARS. DURING TAPED INTERVIEWS, EACH CHILD WAS ASKED: (1) TO SELECT THE CHILD HE WOULD MOST LIKE TO PLAY WITH, AND WHY, AND THE CHILD HE WOULD NEXT MOST LIKE TO PLAY WITH, AND (2) TO SELECT THE CHILD HE WOULD WANT TO BE THE LEADER OF HIS PHYSICAL EDUCATION TEAM, AND WHY, AND WHICH CHILD HE WOULD NEXT SELECT. CORRELATIONS WERE MADE FOR A PERSONAL RELATIONS CONTENT SCORING CATEGORY, AND FOR A PERSONALITY INDEX. RESULTS SHOWED THAT THE JUSTIFICATIONS WHICH CHILDREN GAVE FOR CHOOSING OTHERS VARIED

WITH AGE, SEX, AND THE ACTIVITY TO BE SHARED. NEITHER RACE DIFFERENCES NOR DIFFERENCES IN LENGTH OF TIME OF ENROLLMENT AT THE SCHOOL AFFECTED POPULARITY. TWO SOCIALIZATION FACTORS, REFLECTIVITY AND SOCIALIZATION, WERE DEFINED, BOTH OF WHICH APPEAR TO REFLECT SOCIAL SENSITIVITY ON THE PART OF POPULAR CHILDREN. (NH)

ED047797 PS004436
DISADVANTAGED CHILDREN AND THEIR FIRST SCHOOL EXPERIENCES. ETS-HEAD START LONGITUDINAL STUDY: PRELIMINARY DESCRIPTION OF THE INITIAL SAMPLE PRIOR TO SCHOOL ENROLLMENT. A REPORT IN TWO VOLUMES: VOLUME 1. , AUG 70 300P.
EDRS PRICE MF-$0.65 HC-$9.87

THIS PRELIMINARY REPORT IS THE FOURTH IN A SERIES DESCRIBING THE PROGRESS OF A 6-YEAR LONGITUDINAL STUDY BY THE EDUCATIONAL TESTING SERVICE (ETS). THE PRESENT REPORT SPECIFICALLY DESCRIBES INITIAL DIFFERENCES BETWEEN CHILDREN WHO GO ON TO HEAD START, AND THOSE WHO DO NOT, BASED ON RESULTS OF 16 OF THE 33 MEASURES ADMINISTERED IN YEAR 1 (1969) IN THREE OF THE STUDY SITES: PORTLAND, OREGON; ST. LOUIS, MISSOURI; AND TRENTON, NEW JERSEY. IN ADDITION TO TEST SCORES, INFORMATION WAS COLLECTED ON FAMILY AND HEALTH. COMPARISONS ARE MADE IN RELATION TO THE CHILDREN THEMSELVES (SEX, AGE, RACE, MONTH OF TESTING, TEST SCORES, AND HEALTH INFORMATION) AND TO THEIR FAMILY SITUATIONS. THE RESULTS OF THE COMPARISONS ARE DISCUSSED IN RELATION TO (A) RELEVANT ADDITIONAL INFORMATION ON CHARACTERISTICS OF HEAD START POPULATION PROVIDED BY THE OFFICE OF CHILD DEVELOPMENT/HEAD START; AND (B) RELATED FINDINGS IN THE LITERATURE ON DISADVANTAGED CHILDREN, ESPECIALLY IN RESPECT TO HEAD START ATTENDANCE OR NON-ATTENDANCE. VARIABLES RELATING TO THE PARENTAL DECISION TO SEND A CHILD TO HEAD START ARE: HEAD START ATTENDANCE BY AN OLDER SIBLING, THE MOTHER'S EMPLOYMENT STATUS, THE EDUCATIONAL LEVEL OF THE PARENTS, PARENTAL ATTITUDES TOWARDS JOBS AND EDUCATION, SIZE OF THE FAMILY, RACE, AND THE CHILD'S SEX. OTHER PARTS OF THE LONGITUDINAL STUDY CAN BE LOCATED AS ED 037 486, ED 043 391, AND ED 043 397. (AUTHOR/AJ)

ED047798 PS004437
DISADVANTAGED CHILDREN AND THEIR FIRST SCHOOL EXPERIENCES. ETS-HEAD START LONGITUDINAL STUDY: PRELIMINARY DESCRIPTION OF THE INITIAL SAMPLE PRIOR TO SCHOOL ENROLLMENT. A REPORT IN TWO VOLUMES: VOLUME 2--TABLES. , AUG 70 1,262P.
EDRS PRICE MF-$0.65 HC-$42.77

AS PART OF ITS 6-YEAR LONGITUDINAL STUDY DESIGNED TO ASSESS THE IMPACT OF HEAD START, EDUCATIONAL TESTING SERVICE (ETS) HAS SUMMARIZED AND COMPILED TABLES OF DATA COLLECTED ON 16 OF THE 33 INSTRUMENTS ADMINISTERED TO CHILDREN IN 1969 IN THREE SITES (ST. LOUIS, MISSOURI; TRENTON, NEW JERSEY; AND PORTLAND, OREGON). DATA FROM THE PARENT INTERVIEW AND THE CHILD'S MEDICAL EXAMINATION IS ALSO INCLUDED. THE 806 TABLES ARE REPRODUCED AS COMPUTER PRINTOUTS. TOPICS ARE: (1) HEALTH INFORMATION, (2) PARENT INTERVIEW, (3) BOY-GIRL IDENTITY TASK, (4) BROWN IDS SELF-CONCEPT REFERENTS TEST, (5) COOPERATIVE PRESCHOOL INVENTORY (CALDWELL), (6) ETS ENUMERATION TASK I, (7) ETS MATCHED PICTURES LANGUAGE COMPREHENSION TASK I, (8) ETS STORY SEQUENCE TASK, (9) FIXATION TIME, (10) HESS AND SHIPMAN TOY SORTING TASK, (11) JOHNS HOPKINS PERCEPTUAL TEST, (12) MATCHING FAMILIAR FIGURES TEST, (13) MOTOR INHIBITION TEST, (14) OPEN FIELD TEST, (15) RISK TAKING TASK 2, (16) SEGUIN FORM BOARD, (17) VIGOR. THE NARRATIVE PORTION OF THIS REPORT (VOLUME 1) IS PS 004 436. OTHER REPORTS OF THE ETS STUDY ARE ED 037 486, ED 043 391, AND ED 043 397. (WY)

ED047799 PS004439
HEARING LEVELS OF CHILDREN BY AGE AND SEX: UNITED STATES. ROBERTS, JEAN; HUBER, PAUL, FEB 70 56P.
EDRS PRICE MF-$0.65 HC NOT AVAILABLE FROM EDRS.
AVAILABLE FROM: SUPERINTENDENT OF DOCUMENTS, U.S. GOVERNMENT PRINTING OFFICE, WASHINGTON, D.C. 20402 (PUBLIC HEALTH SERVICE PUBLICATION NO. 1000-SERIES 11-NO. 102 $.55)

THIS REPORT CONTAINS ESTIMATES OF HEARING LEVELS FOR CHILDREN 6 TO 11 YEARS OF AGE IN THE UNITED STATES AS DETERMINED IN THE SECOND CYCLE OF THE HEALTH EXAMINATION SURVEY, CONDUCTED DURING 1963-1965. A PROBABILITY SAMPLE (N7,119) WAS SELECTED TO REPRESENT THE 24 MILLION CHILDREN 6 TO 11 YEARS OF AGE IN THE NONINSTITUTIONAL POPULATION. HEARING THRESHOLD LEVELS FOR THE RIGHT EAR AND LEFT EAR OF EACH CHILD EXAMINED WERE DETERMINED INDIVIDUALLY BY AIR CONDUCTION WITH STANDARD PURE-TONE AUDIOMETERS AT EIGHT FREQUENCIES. TESTING WAS DONE UNDER CAREFULLY CONTROLLED CONDITIONS IN A SPECIALLY CONSTRUCTED TRAILER. THE REPORT GIVES FINDINGS BY AGE AND SEX FOR THE RIGHT EAR, LEFT EAR AND BETTER EAR AT EACH OF THE TEST FREQUENCIES, AND ALSO PRESENTS ESTIMATES OF HEARING LEVELS FOR SPEECH. COMPARISON OF THE PRESENT STUDY FINDINGS WITH FINDINGS FROM SOME OF THE PREVIOUS LARGE-SCALE HEARING SURVEYS, SUCH AS THE 1935-1936 NATIONAL HEALTH SURVEY AND THE PITTSBURGH SURVEYS, IS INCLUDED. TABLES AND APPENDIXES COMPRISE TWO THIRDS OF THE DOCUMENT. (AUTHOR/NH)

ED047800 PS004440
NON-VERBAL INFORMATION STORAGE IN HUMANS AND DEVELOPMENTAL INFORMATION PROCESSING CHANNEL CAPACITY. RANDHAWA, BIKKAR S., 7 FEB 71 14P.
EDRS PRICE MF-$0.65 HC-$3.29

THIS STUDY WAS DESIGNED TO ASCERTAIN THE NATURE OF INFORMATION STORAGE IN HUMANS AND TO DETERMINE THE CHANNEL CAPACITY OF SS AT VARIOUS STAGES OF DEVELOPMENT. A 3 X 2 X 2 MULTIVARIATE COMPLETE FACTORIAL DESIGN WAS EMPLOYED: THE THREE LEVELS OF THE FIRST FACTOR (AGE) WERE 5, 8, AND 12 YEARS; THE TWO LEVELS OF THE SECOND FACTOR WERE VISUAL AND VERBAL INPUTS; AND THE TWO LEVELS OF THE THIRD FACTOR WERE RECONSTRUCTION AND VERBAL DESCRIPTION. ONE HUNDRED AND TWENTY CHILDREN, 40 AT EACH AGE LEVEL, WERE RANDOMLY SELECTED AND ASSIGNED 10 EACH TO EACH TREATMENT. SS WERE TESTED INDIVIDUALLY. THE RESULTS INDICATED THAT INFORMATION IS STORED IN NONVERBAL FORM IN SUCH TASKS. THE NONVERBAL IMAGE STORAGE IS AFFECTED DIFFERENTLY BY THE DEVELOPMENTAL LEVEL OF THE SS. (AUTHOR)

ED047801 PS004441
THE ACQUISITION OF CONSERVATION THROUGH SOCIAL INTERACTION. MURRAY, FRANK B., 4 FEB 71 13P.
EDRS PRICE MF-$0.65 HC-$3.29

THE PURPOSE OF THIS STUDY WAS TO DETERMINE IF AN EFFECTIVE CONSERVATION TRAINING PROCEDURE WOULD BE ONE IN WHICH A CHILD WAS CONFRONTED WITH OPPOSING POINTS OF VIEW. SUBJECTS WERE 108 CHILDREN WITH A MEAN AGE OF 6.7 YEARS. IN TWO EXPERIMENTS, A GROUP OF THREE CHILDREN (GENERALLY ONE NONCONSERVER AND TWO CONSERVERS) WAS REQUIRED TO RESPOND WITH ONE GROUP ANSWER TO A SERIES OF STANDARDIZED CONSERVATION PROBLEMS. WHEN TESTED AGAIN INDIVIDUALLY, ALL SUBJECTS MADE SIGNIFICANT GAINS IN CONSERVATION JUDGMENTS AND EXPLANATIONS ON THE SAME PROBLEMS, ON A PARALLEL FORM OF THOSE PROBLEMS, AND ON NEW PROBLEMS. NONCONSERVERS MADE THE GREATEST GAINS. CONSERVATION WAS FOUND TO BE RELATED TO AN ANALYTICAL COGNITIVE STYLE IN ONE STUDY. (AUTHOR/AJ)

ED047802 PS004442
IMPLICATIONS OF POST-NATAL CORTICAL DEVELOPMENT FOR CREATIVITY RESEARCH. GORDON, MARJORY; DACEY, JOHN, 6 FEB 71 10P.
EDRS PRICE MF-$0.65 HC-$3.29

MAN'S LONG PERIOD OF CEREBRAL GROWTH HAS IMPORTANT IMPLICATIONS FOR EDUCATION. THE BRAIN GOES THROUGH MAJOR DEVELOPMENTAL CHANGES AFTER BIRTH, AND RESEARCHERS HAVE SUGGESTED THAT THIS GROWTH PROCESS PRESENTS AN OPPORTUNITY FOR FOSTERING THE PLASTICITY OF GENETICALLY DETERMINED CONNECTIONS. ANIMAL STUDIES SHOW THAT POSTNATAL GROWTH OF THE BRAIN IS INFLUENCED BY INCREASING THE SENSORY INPUT FROM THE ENVIRONMENT. THIS INFLUENCE IS MANIFESTED IN TERMS OF INCREASED INTERCONNECTIVITY OF NERVE CELLS AND MICRONEURON DEVELOPMENT. IT IS PROPOSED THAT, IN THE HUMAN LEARNER, TWO DIMENSIONS OF ENVIRONMENTAL ENRICHMENT ARE NECESSARY: INTERACTION WITH OBJECTS AND INTERPERSONAL INTERACTION. IMPLICATIONS ARE DISCUSSED FOR TEACHING THE DISADVANTAGED CHILD AND FOR HELPING TO ESTABLISH CREATIVE MODES OF THOUGHT. DEVELOPMENT OF BETTER MEASUREMENT TECHNIQUES FOR ASCERTAINING THE MICRONEURONAL GROWTH PATTERN AND ITS BEHAVIORAL CORRELATES SHOULD PRECEDE FURTHER RESEARCH. (AUTHOR/NH)

ED047803 PS004443
A STUDY IN TRAINING NURSERY CHILDREN ON LOGICAL OPERATIONAL SKILLS. KINCAID, CAROLYN; AND OTHERS, 7 FEB 71 10P.
EDRS PRICE MF-$0.65 HC-$3.29

PIAGET'S ORGANISMIC-DEVELOPMENTAL THEORY OF INTELLIGENCE WAS INVESTIGATED IN THIS STUDY TO DETERMINE THE EFFECTIVENESS OF TRAINING MIDDLE CLASS 3 AND 4 YEAR OLDS ON TWO LOGICO-MATHEMATICAL STRUCTURES: CLASSIFICATION AND SERIATION. TWENTY-FOUR CHILDREN WERE DIVIDED INTO TWO MAIN AGE GROUPS (MEAN AGES: 3 YEARS 8 MONTHS; 4 YEARS 5 MONTHS). WITHIN EACH AGE CATEGORY, CHILDREN WERE RANDOMLY ASSIGNED TO GROUPS OF FOUR FOR SERIATION TRAINING, CLASSIFICATION TRAINING, AND A CONTROL GROUP. TO ASSESS IQ AND VERBAL ABILITY, THE PEABODY PICTURE VOCABULARY TEST WAS UTILIZED AS A PRETEST-POSTTEST MEASURE; PIAGETIAN TASKS AS A POSTTEST ONLY. TASKS INCLUDED A SERIATION SERIES OF SIX PROBLEMS AND A CLASSIFICATION SERIES OF SEVEN PROBLEMS. THREE CONSERVATION TASKS (QUANTITY, NUMBER AND AREA) WERE ADMINISTERED AS FAR-TRANSFER TESTS. COVARIANCE ANALYSIS OF THE SERIATION TASK BATTERY INDICATED THERE WERE SIGNIFICANT TREATMENT MAIN EFFECTS AND AN AGE-TREATMENT INTERACTION WITH THE HIGH AGE SERIATION GROUP INDICATING SUPERIOR PERFORMANCE. CLASSIFICATION IN BOTH AGE GROUPS WAS NOT FOUND TO BE EFFECTIVE. LEARNING WAS NOT FOUND TO GENERALIZE TO THE FAR-TRANSFER TASKS. THE AGE-RELATED FINDINGS FROM THIS STUDY WERE INTERPRETED AS SUPPORTING THE STAGE-DEPENDENT ASPECTS OF PIAGET'S THEORY. (AUTHOR/AJ)

ED047804 PS004444

THE EFFECT OF VARYING OBJECT NUMBER AND TYPE OF ARRANGEMENT ON CHILDREN'S ABILITY TO COORDINATE PERSPECTIVES. BARRAGY, SISTER MICHELEEN, [69] 15P.

EDRS PRICE MF-$0.65 HC-$3.29

THIS STUDY WAS CONCERNED WITH CHILDREN'S ABILITY TO CONSERVE SPATIAL RELATIONSHIPS AMONG OBJECTS IN DIFFERENT ARRANGEMENTS, IN THE PRESENCE OF PROJECTED CHANGES IN THE OBSERVER'S VISUAL FIELD. THE OBJECTIVES WERE: (1) TO DETERMINE THE EFFECTS OF VARYING TYPES OF ARRANGEMENT AND NUMBER OF OBJECTS IN THE ARRANGEMENT ON PERSPECTIVE ABILITY PERFORMANCE, (2) TO INVESTIGATE THE RELATIONSHIP OF AGE AND SEX TO THE ACQUISITION AND PERFORMANCE OF PERSPECTIVE COORDINATION, AND (3) TO COMPARE THE DIFFICULTY LEVEL OF LEFT-RIGHT, FOREGROUND-BACKGROUND RELATIONS. TEN BOYS AND TEN GIRLS EACH FROM KINDERGARTEN, THIRD, AND SIXTH GRADES (N60) WERE RANDOMLY SELECTED FROM PUPILS HAVING AN IQ WITHIN THE 83 TO 117 RANGE. THE MEASURE WAS AN ADAPTATION OF PIAGET'S THREE-MOUNTAIN COORDINATION OF PERSPECTIVE TASK. WHILE VIEWING SIX DIFFERENT OBJECT ARRANGEMENTS FROM A STATIC POSITION, SUBJECTS WERE ASKED TO MATCH PHOTOGRAPHS OF THE OBJECT GROUPS WITH THE POSITION OF THE CAMERA WHEN THE PICTURE WAS TAKEN. THE DOCUMENT PROVIDES RESULTS REGARDING (1) OBJECT NUMBER AND ARRANGEMENT EFFECTS OF TASK DIFFICULTY, (2) THE EFFECT OF MASKING FACTORS ON PERFORMANCE LEVELS, AND (3) CONCLUSIONS ABOUT SEX AND AGE IN RELATION TO PERFORMANCE. (AUTHOR/AJ)

ED047805 PS004446

EFFECTS OF VIEWING VIDEOTAPED SAME AND OPPOSITE COLOR CHILD-TEACHERS ON INTEGRATED AND ALL-WHITE KINDERGARTNERS. COLTON, FRANK V.; GORDON, JACK, 7 FEB 71 10P.

EDRS PRICE MF-$0.65 HC-$3.29

THIS PILOT STUDY SOUGHT TO DETERMINE WHAT WERE THE EFFECTS, IF ANY, OF HAVING INTEGRATED AND ALL-WHITE KINDERGARTEN CHILDREN VIEW SPECIALLY PREPARED VIDEO-TAPED TELEVISION SEQUENCES. THESE SEQUENCES FEATURED BLACK AND WHITE CHILDREN WHO WERE UNKNOWN TO THE VIEWERS AND WHO PORTRAYED ROLES IN WHICH THEY DEMONSTRATED SIMPLE CONCEPTS. DATA FROM THIS PRELIMINARY STUDY (N59) INDICATED THAT: (1) BOTH TYPES OF KINDERGARTNERS CAN ACQUIRE CONCEPTS (OVER, AROUND, THROUGH, ETC.) BY PASSIVELY VIEWING EITHER AN UNKNOWN, SAME OR OPPOSITE COLOR CHILD TEACHING, (2) VIEWING AN UNKNOWN CHILD-TEACHER OF THE OPPOSITE COLOR DID NOT ALTER THE INITIAL SAME COLOR PREFERENCES OF "PREFERRED COMPANIONS" OF EITHER TYPE OF KINDERGARTNER, AND (3) HIGH CONCEPT ATTAINERS DID NOT DEMONSTRATE MORE PRE-POST CHANGE TO OPPOSITE COLOR CHILD-TEACHERS AS "PREFERRED COMPANIONS" THAN LOW CONCEPT ATTAINERS. RECOMMENDATIONS FOR FURTHER RESEARCH ARE GIVEN. (AUTHOR/NH)

ED047806 PS004448

COMMUNICATIVE COMPETENCE AND THE DISADVANTAGED CHILD: A STUDY OF THE RELATIONSHIP BETWEEN LANGUAGE MODELS AND THE DEVELOPMENT OF COMMUNICATION SKILLS IN DISADVANTAGED PRESCHOOLERS. FINAL REPORT. MCCAFFREY, ARTHUR; AND OTHERS, SEP 70 126P.

EDRS PRICE MF-$0.65 HC NOT AVAILABLE FROM EDRS.

TWO PARALLEL AND COMPLEMENTARY STUDIES OF LANGUAGE MODELLING AND ITS RELATION TO THE DEVELOPMENT OF COMMUNICATIVE COMPETENCE IN THE YOUNG CHILD ARE REPORTED. OVER A 6-MONTH PERIOD, STUDY 1 INVOLVED WEEKLY NATURALISTIC OBSERVATIONS (IN THE HOME) OF THE NATURE AND QUALITY OF THE LINGUISTIC STIMULATION OFFERED BY MOTHERS TO THEIR CHILDREN BETWEEN 2 AND 4 YEARS OF AGE. THE EIGHT HOMES VISITED REPRESENTED BLACK AND WHITE FAMILIES, WITH HIGH AND LOW INCOMES, IN SUBURBAN AND INNER CITY SETTINGS. THE DIFFERING MATERNAL LANGUAGE BEHAVIORS OBSERVED SEEMED TO REFLECT DIFFERING BASIC PREMISES HELD BY MIDDLE AND WORKING CLASS MOTHERS ABOUT INFANCY AND EARLY CHILDHOOD. LANGUAGE USAGE IS ONE OF THE AREAS AFFECTED. IT IS SUGGESTED THAT INTERVENTION PROGRAMS HELP MOTHERS TO LEARN MORE ABOUT CHILD DEVELOPMENT AND INCLUDE LANGUAGE PROGRAMS. STUDY 2 TESTED THE LANGUAGE USAGE OF 40 PRESCHOOL CHILDREN OF DIFFERING SOCIOECONOMIC BACKGROUNDS IN THREE BASIC AREAS OF COMPETENCE: PERCEPTUAL, COGNITIVE, AND LINGUISTIC. THE RESULTS WERE USED TO PLAN TRAINING SESSIONS IN COMMUNICATION SKILLS APPROPRIATE TO EACH CHILD'S NEEDS. PRETESTS AND POSTTESTS INDICATE THAT CHILDREN BENEFITTED BY SUCH TRAINING OVER THE SHORT TERM. APPENDIXES ARE INCLUDED. [NOT AVAILABLE IN HARD COPY DUE TO MARGINAL LEGIBILITY OF ORIGINAL DOCUMENT.] (NH)

ED047807 PS004449

PROGRAMS FOR INFANTS AND YOUNG CHILDREN. PART I: EDUCATION AND DAY CARE. SILVERSTONE, NAOMI, ED., OCT 70 221P.

EDRS PRICE MF-$0.65 HC-$9.87

THIS BOOK IS INTENDED FOR USE BY LOCAL COMMITTEES WHO ARE PLANNING AND ORGANIZING DAY CARE AND EDUCATION PROGRAMS FOR INFANTS AND YOUNG CHILDREN. DESCRIPTIONS ARE GIVEN OF VARIOUS TYPES OF PROGRAMS THAT ARE ALREADY IN OPERATION: 32 IN THE UNITED STATES AND THREE IN OTHER COUNTRIES. SOME OF THESE PROGRAMS ARE COMPREHENSIVE BUT HIGHLIGHT EDUCATIONAL SKILLS; SOME ARE PRIMARILY CONCERNED WITH EDUCATION, EITHER AT HOME OR IN LEARNING CENTERS AND SOME PROVIDE DAY CARE. OTHER PROGRAMS PROVIDE SERVICES FOR THE MENTALLY RETARDED OR OTHERS WITH SPECIAL NEEDS. EACH PROGRAM SUMMARY IS FOLLOWED BY FOUR SECTIONS: (1) OBJECTIVES; (2) PROGRAM DESCRIPTIONS; (3) EFFECTIVENESS; AND (4) REPLICATION. FURTHER INFORMATION MAY BE OBTAINED BY WRITING TO INDIVIDUAL PROGRAM DIRECTORS; ADDRESSES ARE INCLUDED. A BIBLIOGRAPHY GIVES OTHER SOURCES OF INFORMATION ON EARLY CHILDHOOOD PROGRAMS AND INCLUDES FILM SUGGESTIONS. (NH)

ED047808 PS004450

PROGRAMS FOR INFANTS AND YOUNG CHILDREN. PART II: NUTRITION. , OCT 70 86P.

EDRS PRICE MF-$0.65 HC-$3.29

THIS REPORT DESCRIBES VARIOUS GOVERNMENT NUTRITION PROGRAMS DESIGNED TO AID PREGNANT WOMEN AND CHILDREN UNDER SIX. PROGRAMS DESCRIBED INCLUDE: THE AGRICULTURE EXTENSION PROGRAM, A HOME PROGRAM IN ALLEGHANY COUNTY, MARYLAND; SUPPLEMENTAL FOOD PROGRAMS IN WASHINGTON, D.C. AND DENVER; AND THE CHICAGO SUPPLEMENTAL FOOD VOUCHER EXPERIMENTAL PROGRAM. ALSO DISCUSSED ARE SPECIAL FOOD SERVICE PROGRAMS FOR GROUPS OF CHILDREN AWAY FROM HOME WHICH ARE PROVIDED IN GREENVILLE, SOUTH CAROLINA; SAN FRANCISCO; RALEIGH COUNTY, WEST VIRGINIA; VINCENNES, INDIANA; SAN DIEGO, TEXAS; AND IN DAY CARE CENTERS AT THE UNIVERSITY OF NORTH CAROLINA CAMPUSES AT GREENSBORO AND CHAPEL HILL. THE APPENDIX INCLUDES REPRINTS OF ARTICLES WRITTEN BY MARGARET MEAD AND JAMES ROPER, A BIBLIOGRAPHY ON FOOD AND NUTRITION, FILM SUGGESTIONS, A LISTING OF FEDERAL AND STATE PERSONNEL INVOLVED IN FOOD PROGRAMS, AND EXAMPLES OF PROGRAM MATERIALS USED IN THE DISTRICT OF COLUMBIA. (AJ)

ED047809 PS004451

PROGRAMS FOR INFANTS AND YOUNG CHILDREN. PART III: HEALTH. , OCT 70 166P.

EDRS PRICE MF-$0.65 HC-$6.58

DIRECTED TOWARD THE IMPROVEMENT OF HEALTH CARE FOR MOTHERS AND YOUNG CHILDREN, THIS REPORT DESCRIBES A NUMBER OF COMPREHENSIVE PROGRAMS FOCUSED ON HEALTH AND REPORTS ON PROJECTS WHICH HAVE SINGLED OUT ONE OR MORE SPECIFIC MATERNAL OR CHILD HEALTH SERVICES. INCLUDED ARE DESCRIPTIONS OF EXISTING COMMUNITY PROGRAMS FOR PREGNANT SCHOOLGIRLS, HEALTH POLICIES AND PROCEDURES FOR DAY CARE CENTERS, FAMILY PLANNING SERVICES, AND SERVICES FOR CRIPPLED CHILDREN. CONSIDERABLE ATTENTION IS GIVEN TO A DISCUSSION OF THE ACUTE MANPOWER SHORTAGE, ESPECIALLY THAT OF TRAINED MEDICAL PERSONNEL. (AJ)

ED047810 PS004452

PROGRAMS FOR INFANTS AND YOUNG CHILDREN. PART IV: FACILITIES AND EQUIPMENT. SALE, JUNE, OCT 70 72P.

EDRS PRICE MF-$0.65 HC-$3.29

THIS MANUAL IS DESIGNED TO FACILITATE PLANNING FOR DAY CARE CENTER FACILITIES. GOALS AND PRINCIPLES OF DAY CARE ARE DISCUSSED IN RELATION TO PROGRAMS FOR INFANTS, TODDLERS, AND PRESCHOOLERS WITH SPECIAL ATTENTION TO STAFF, PARENTS, AND COMMUNITY. SUGGESTIONS ARE PRESENTED FOR INDOOR AND OUTDOOR PLANNING FOR SUCH TOPICS AS EQUIPMENT, SUPPLIES, VENTILATION, ACOUSTICS, LIGHTING, TEMPERATURE CONTROL, STORAGE, AND NUMBEROUS OTHER AREAS OF CONCERN. PROVIDED IN THE MANUAL IS A PARTIAL LIST OF RESOURCES FOR THE PURCHASE OF EQUIPMENT AND SUPPLIES. THE MANUAL OFFERS VARIOUS FLOOR AND PLOT PLANS AND PRACTICAL PATTERNS FOR THE CONSTRUCTION OF EQUIPMENT, SUCH AS SHELVES, CUPBOARDS, BOOK AND COAT RACKS. A BIBLIOGRAPHY IS INCLUDED TO PROVIDE FURTHER SOURCES OF INFORMATION. (AJ)

ED047811 PS004453

FEDERAL PROGRAMS FOR YOUNG CHILDREN. , OCT 70 475P.

EDRS PRICE MF-$0.65 HC-$16.45

THIS MANUAL IS A GUIDE TO HELP INDIVIDUALS, COMMUNITY AND STATE GROUPS CONCERNED WITH THE PROBLEMS OF YOUNG CHILDREN LOCATE SPECIFIC KINDS OF FEDERAL PROGRAMS. SPECIFIC SECTION HEADINGS OF THE MANUAL ARE: CHILD CARE AND EARLY CHILDHOOD EDUCATION, HEALTH, MEDICAL, AND WELFARE SERVICES, INDIVIDUAL GRANTS PROGRAMS, TRAINING PROGRAMS, FOOD AND NUTRITION PROGRAMS, FACILITIES AND EQUIPMENT PROGRAMS, RESEARCH PROGRAMS, RESEARCH AND DEMONSTRATION PROGRAMS SPECIAL CENTER PROGRAMS, AND INFORMATION AND TECHNICAL ASSISTANCE. INDIVIDUAL PROGRAM ENTRIES GIVE INFORMATION IN SUCH CATEGORIES AS:

AUTHORIZING STATUTE, ADMINISTRATOR, NATURE OF PROGRAM ACTIVITY, ELIGIBILITY, AVAILABLE ASSISTANCE, USE RESTRICTIONS, APPROPRIATIONS, OBLIGATIONS, AVERAGE ASSISTANCE, ASSISTANCE PREREQUISITES, POSTGRANT REQUIREMENTS, WASHINGTON CONTACT, LOCAL CONTACT, APPLICATION DEADLINES, APPROVAL/DISAPPROVAL TIME, REWORKING TIME, RELATED PROGRAMS, PROGRAM ACCOMPLISHMENTS. (AUTHOR/AJ)

ED047812 PS004454
EFFECTS OF DURATION OF A NURSERY SCHOOL SETTING ON ENVIRONMENTAL CONSTRAINTS AND CHILDREN'S MODES OF ADAPTATION. BERK, LAURA E., 7 FEB 71 23P.
EDRS PRICE MF-$0.65 HC-$3.29

THIS STUDY IS CONCERNED WITH THE WAY IN WHICH CHILDREN'S NATURALLY OCCURRING BEHAVIORS CHANGE OVER A PERIOD OF TIME AS THEY ADAPT TO A NURSERY SCHOOL SETTING. A SET OF SEVEN VARIETIES OF ENVIRONMENTAL CONSTRAINTS AND FOURTEEN ADAPTATIONS TO THESE CONSTRAINTS WAS OBSERVED AMONG 18 3-, 4-, AND 5-YEAR-OLDS IN A NURSERY SCHOOL CLASSROOM FIRST IN THE FALL, WHEN THE SETTING WAS NEWLY INITIATED, AND SECONDLY IN THE SPRING, WHEN THE SETTING HAD BEEN IN EXISTENCE FOR AN EXTENSIVE PERIOD OF TIME. THE FINDINGS SHOWED THAT DURATION OF THE SETTING WAS SIGNIFICANTLY RELATED TO CHANGES IN SEVERAL VARIETIES OF CONSTRAINTS AND ADAPTATIONS. THE RESULTS ILLUSTRATE A BASIC CONCEPTION OF ECOLOGICAL PSYCHOLOGY, THAT THE PROGRAM OF AN ENVIRONMENT'S INPUTS TO INDIVIDUALS CHANGES IF ITS ECOLOGICAL PROPERTIES CHANGE--IN THIS CASE, IF THE DURATION OF THE SETTING INCREASES. ED 040 421 IS AN EARLIER VERSION OF THIS STUDY. (AUTHOR)

ED047813 PS004478
CHILD WELFARE SERVICES: A SOURCEBOOK. KADUSHIN, ALFRED, 70 557P.
DOCUMENT NOT AVAILABLE FROM EDRS.
AVAILABLE FROM: THE MACMILLIAN COMPANY, 866 THIRD AVENUE, NEW YORK, NEW YORK 10022 ($8.95)

THIS SOURCEBOOK MAKES CONVENIENTLY AVAILABLE THE RELEVANT MATERIALS ON CHILD WELFARE THAT WERE FORMERLY SCATTERED IN CONFERENCE PROCEEDINGS, PROFESSIONAL JOURNALS, GOVERNMENT PUBLICATIONS, AND SPECIAL MEETING REPORTS. THE BOOK IS A SUPPLEMENTARY TOOL FOR THOSE INTERESTED IN TEACHING AND LEARNING ABOUT CHILD WELFARE AND EMPHASIZES RESEARCH IN THIS AREA. SELECTION OF MATERIAL FOR THE SOURCEBOOK WAS BASED ON A DEFINITION OF CHILD WELFARE SERVICES WITHIN THE CONTEXT OF THE PROFESSION OF SOCIAL WORK AND IS PRIMARILY CONCERNED WITH SERVICES PERFORMED BY THOSE WHO ARE CHILD WELFARE SOCIAL WORKERS EMPLOYED BY INSTITUTIONS, ORGANIZATIONS, AND AGENCIES. TOPICS INCLUDED ARE: PROTECTIVE SERVICES, HOMEMAKER AND DAY-CARE SERVICES, FOSTER-CARE SERVICES, ADOPTION SERVICES, AND THE CHILD-CARING INSTITUTION. (AUTHOR/AJ)

ED047814 PS004480
STARTING NURSERY SCHOOL, II: PREDICTION OF CHILDREN'S INITIAL EMOTIONAL REACTIONS FROM BACKGROUND INFORMATION. FINAL REPORT. SCHWARZ, J. CONRAD; WYNN, RUTH, NOV 70 22P.
EDRS PRICE MF-$0.65 HC-$3.29

THE RELATIONSHIP OF BACKGROUND FACTORS TO SEPARATION REACTION AND SOCIAL EMOTIONAL ADJUSTMENT AT THE START OF NURSERY SCHOOL WAS EXAMINED IN 106 MIDDLE-CLASS 4-YEAR-OLDS. MOTHERS COMPLETED THE CAIN-LEVINE SOCIAL COMPETENCY SCALE AND QUESTIONNAIRES ON THE SOCIAL EXPERIENCE OF THEIR CHILDREN. RATINGS OF REACTIONS TO SEPARATION AND OF ADJUSTMENT WERE OBTAINED ON THE FIRST DAY OF NURSERY SCHOOL AND ONE AND FIVE WEEKS LATER. EXPERIENCE WITH PLAYMATES AT HOME, EXPERIENCE IN GROUP SETTINGS AWAY FROM HOME, AND CONTACT WITH DIFFERENT BABY SITTERS IN THE HOME WERE EACH INDEPENDENTLY RELATED TO EASE OF INITIAL SEPARATION. A TOTAL SOCIAL EXPERIENCE SCORE CORRELATED -.46 (P.001) WITH SEPARATION DISTRESS. THE SOCIAL EXPERIENCE SCORE WAS NOT RELATED TO FIFTH-WEEK SEPARATION PROBLEMS BUT WAS CORRELATED WITH ADJUSTMENT THROUGH THE FIFTH WEEK. SOCIAL COMPETENCY WAS NOT RELATED TO SEPARATION REACTION RATINGS OR SOCIAL EXPERIENCE BUT WAS CORRELATED WITH ADJUSTMENT THROUGH THE FIFTH WEEK. THE RESULTS SUPPORTED THE VIEW THAT THE DISTRESS WHICH SOME CHILDREN EXHIBIT AT THE START OF NURSERY SCHOOL IS A FUNCTION OF THE NOVELTY OF THE SITUATION FOR THE CHILD IN QUESTION. [FILMED FROM BEST AVAILABLE COPY.] (AUTHOR)

ED047815 PS004481
LEARNING TO OBSERVE--OBSERVING TO LEARN. COHEN, DOROTHY H., FEB 71 13P.
EDRS PRICE MF-$0.65 HC-$3.29

IN THIS ADDRESS, DOROTHY H. COHEN ADMONISHES TEACHERS TO REMAIN AWARE THAT IN THE CLASSROOM THEY ARE BOTH TEACHERS AND OBSERVERS TRYING TO FIND CLUES TO UNDERSTANDING AND INTERACTION. BECAUSE TEACHERS ARE HUMAN BEINGS WITH ATTITUDES AND BELIEFS OF THEIR OWN, IT IS DIFFICULT TO BE OBJECTIVE IN MAKING OBSERVATIONS OF CHILDREN. AN OPEN MIND READY TO ACCEPT ANYTHING THAT THERE IS TO SEE, WITHOUT JUDGMENT, IS A PREREQUISITE. OBSERVATIONS OF CHILDREN MUST BEGIN WITHOUT ANY PRECONCEIVED NOTIONS OF WHAT ONE OUGHT TO FIND OR WILL FIND. PERCEPTIONS OF CHILDREN CAN BE INFLUENCED BY THE OBSERVER'S PERSONAL ASSOCIATIONS, MORAL JUDGMENTS, AGE, AND PHYSICAL WELL-BEING. ADULTS MUST LEARN TO PERCEIVE CHILDREN'S BEHAVIOR FIRST AS IT IS MEANT, AND ONLY SECONDARILY AS IT IS INTERPRETED BY ADULT STANDARDS. BODY MOVEMENT IS THE MAJOR LANGUAGE OF EXPRESSION IN EARLY CHILDHOOD AND TELLS MORE ABOUT THE MEANING OF CHILDREN'S BEHAVIOR THAN THEIR WORDS. TEACHERS MUST LEARN TO READ BODY LANGUAGE TO INTERPRET CHILDREN'S DEVELOPMENTAL STAGES OF COMPETENCE, EXPERIMENTATION, TESTING, AND GENERAL ATTITUDES TOWARD SELF. (AUTHOR/AJ)

ED047816 PS004483
PROJECT HEAD START 1968: A DESCRIPTIVE REPORT OF PROGRAMS AND PARTICIPANTS. , SEP 70 282P.
EDRS PRICE MF-$0.65 HC-$9.87

THIS REPORT IS THE SECOND IN A SERIES DESIGNED TO DESCRIBE CHILDREN, THEIR FAMILIES, AND STAFF MEMBERS WHO HAVE PARTICIPATED IN PROJECT HEAD START CENTER ACTIVITIES. THE DATA DEPICTS CENTER AND PARTICIPANT CHARACTERISTICS FOR THE FULL YEAR 1967-1968 AND SUMMER 1968 HEAD START PROGRAMS, AND, IN COMBINATION WITH DATA IN THE REPORT ON PREVIOUS PROGRAMS (SEE PROJECT HEAD START 1965-1967: A DESCRIPTIVE REPORT OF PROGRAMS AND PARTICIPANTS, ED 034 569), PROVIDE COMPARATIVE INFORMATION OVER TIME. THE BUREAU OF THE CENSUS SELECTED SEPARATE SAMPLES FOR THE FULL YEAR 1968 AND SUMMER 1968 PROGRAMS. THE SAMPLING DESIGN AND PROCEDURES FOR CENTERS, CLASSES, AND CHILDREN REMAINED THE SAME AS THOSE EMPLOYED IN THE 1965-1967 PROGRAM. DATA IS PROVIDED ON (A) CHILDREN AND THEIR FAMILIES, (B) MEDICAL AND DENTAL INFORMATION, (C) CENTER INFORMATION, (D) STAFF MEMBER CHARACTERISTICS, AND (E) PARENT PARTICIPATION. THE APPENDIX CONTAINS DIRECTIONS AND QUESTIONNAIRES SENT TO CENTER DIRECTORS REQUESTING PROGRAM INFORMATION. (WY)

ED047817 PS004484
BASIC FACTS ABOUT LICENSING OF DAY CARE. , OCT 70 12P.
EDRS PRICE MF-$0.65 HC-$3.29

THIS OVERVIEW OF STATE DAY CARE LICENSING PROCEDURES ANSWERS EIGHT QUESTIONS BASIC TO AN UNDERSTANDING OF LICENSING POLICIES IN THE NATION. THE QUESTIONS ARE: (1) WHY IS DAY CARE LICENSED? (2) HOW IS DAY CARE DEFINED FOR LICENSING PURPOSES? (3) WHICH STATES LICENSE DAY CARE SERVICES? (4) WHICH DEPARTMENTS OF STATE GOVERNMENT LICENSE DAY CARE? (5) WHAT PROCEDURES ARE INVOLVED IN LICENSING? (6) WHAT FACILITIES ARE COVERED BY STATE LICENSING LAWS? (7) IS THERE A LICENSING FEE? (8) HOW CAN DAY CARE LICENSING BECOME MORE RESPONSIVE TO COMMUNITY NEEDS? THE APPENDIX CONTAINS TWO TABLES. THE FIRST LISTS DAY CARE LICENSING BY STATE AND THE SECOND LISTS THE CHIEF STATUTORY PROVISIONS INTERFERING WITH PROTECTION OF CHILDREN THROUGH DAY CARE LICENSURE. (WY)

ED047818 PS004485
FILMS SUITABLE FOR HEAD START CHILD DEVELOPMENT PROGRAMS. , NOV 70 12P.
EDRS PRICE MF-$0.65 HC-$3.29

THIS BROCHURE LISTS 31 FILMS AVAILABLE ON A FREE-LOAN BASIS THROUGH THE 28 LIBRARIES OF THE MOTION PICTURE TALKING SERVICE, INC. THE TITLE, LENGTH, AVAILABILITY IN BLACK/WHITE OR COLOR, AND AN ANNOTATION IS GIVEN FOR EACH FILM. ALL THE FILMS ARE ORIENTED TOWARD STAFF DEVELOPMENT FOR HEAD START PERSONNEL. SOME OF THE FILMS ARE AVAILABLE IN SPANISH. ADDRESSES AND MANAGERS OF THE MODERN TALKING PICTURE SERVICE FILM LIBRARIES ARE LISTED ON THE BACK COVER. (WY)

ED047819 PS004486
THE EFFECTS OF EXTRANEOUS MATERIAL AND NEGATIVE EXEMPLARS ON A SOCIAL SCIENCE CONCEPT-LEARNING TASK FOR PRE-SCHOOL CHILDREN. MARTORELLA, PETER H.; WOOD, ROGER, 6 FEB 71 7P.
EDRS PRICE MF-$0.65 HC-$3.29

THIS STUDY ANALYZES THE RELATIVE EFFECTS OF TWO CATEGORIES OF VARIABLES UPON THE LEARNING OF A BASIC SOCIAL SCIENCE CONCEPT BY A KINDERGARTEN POPULATION. MAJOR HYPOTHESES WERE: (1) SUBJECTS RECEIVING TREATMENTS WITH LOW DEGREES OF IRRELEVANT MATERIAL WOULD SCORE SIGNIFICANTLY HIGHER ON CONCEPT-LEARNING MEASURES RELATED TO THE TASK THAN THOSE RECEIVING TREATMENTS WITH MEDIUM AND HIGH DEGREES OF IRRELEVANT DATA, (2) SUBJECTS RECEIVING TREATMENTS WITH THE GREATER NUMBER OF NEGATIVE EXEMPLARS WOULD SCORE SIGNIFICANTLY HIGHER ON CONCEPT-LEARNING MEASURES THAN THOSE RECEIVING LESSER NUMBERS, (3) SUBJECTS RECEIVING TREATMENTS WITH THE GREATER NUMBER OF NEGATIVE EXEMPLARS WOULD HAVE AN INTERACTION EFFECT UPON LEARNING MEASURES. SUBJECTS WERE 789,225 KINDERGARTEN CHILDREN REPRESENTING A CROSS SECTION OF SEATTLE'S POPULATION, ACCORDING TO SES DATA. TEACHING MATERIALS WERE CASSETTE RECORDINGS MANUALLY SYNCHRONIZED WITH 2X2 COLORED SLIDES OF CONCEPT EXEMPLARS AND NONEXEMPLARS SHOWN ON A SLIDE PROJECTOR. THE CONCEPT "ISLAND" WAS TAUGHT TO CHILDREN IN GROUPS OF TWO AND THREE, AND THREE CRITICAL ATTRIBUTES WERE DELINEATED. ANALYSIS OF VARIANCE INDICATED NO SIGNIFICANT DIFFERENCES. THE STUDY SEEMS TO SUGGEST THAT FOR PRESCHOOL CHILDREN INCREASING IRRELEVANT DIMENSIONS AND REDUCING CON-

TRAST IN A SOCIAL SCIENCE CONCEPT-LEARNING TASK ARE NOT SIGNIFICANT FACTORS. (WY)

ED047820 PS004487
IMPULSIVITY & REFLECTIVITY AS REFLECTED BY THE VARIABLES OF TIME AND ERROR. SHEPPARD, JEAN B., [66] 8P.
EDRS PRICE MF-$0.65 HC-$3.29

THIS EXPERIMENT WAS DESIGNED TO DETERMINE THE RELATIONSHIP BETWEEN REACTION TIME, ERROR RATE AND PERFORMANCE ON A VARIETY OF COGNITIVE AND SOCIAL MEASURES, AS WELL AS IN RELATION TO DEMOGRAPHIC VARIABLES (RACE, MONTHS AT YONGE SCHOOL, GRADE, AND SEX). SIXTY STUDENTS (FIRST THROUGH THIRD GRADE) WERE TESTED ON THE FIRST FIFTEEN ITEMS OF THE VISUAL-MOTOR ASSOCIATION PORTION OF THE ILLINOIS TEST OF PSYCHOLINGUISTIC ABILITIES, 1961 VERSION. AN ITEM ANALYSIS OF THE SUBTEST WAS PERFORMED AND A FREQUENCY DISTRIBUTION OF THE ERRORS WAS PLOTTED. THE DATA INDICATE THAT THE MEASURE DID NOT DISCRIMINATE BETWEEN IMPULSIVITY AND REFLECTIVITY. CORRELATIONAL ANALYSIS FAILED TO SUPPORT PREVIOUS RESEARCH BY KAGAN ON REFLECTIVE BEHAVIOR. A POST HOC ANALYSIS SHOWED A REVERSAL OF WHAT WOULD NORMALLY BE EXPECTED; SUBJECTS WHO TOOK THE LEAST TIME MADE THE LEAST ERRORS AND SUBJECTS WHO TOOK THE MOST TIME MADE THE MOST ERRORS. (WY)

ED047821 PS004492
THE FIRST YEAR OF SESAME STREET: A HISTORY AND OVERVIEW. FINAL REPORT, VOLUME I OF V VOLUMES. COONEY, JOAN GANZ, DEC 70 25P.
EDRS PRICE MF-$0.65 HC-$3.29

THIS PAPER DESCRIBES THE EVOLUTION OF THE CHILDREN'S TELEVISION WORKSHOP, WHICH WAS ORIGINALLY SUGGESTED IN A STUDY MADE BY JOAN GANZ COONEY FOR THE CARNEGIE CORPORATION, AND WHICH WAS RESPONSIBLE FOR THE DEVELOPMENT AND PRODUCTION OF THE DAILY, 1-HOUR EDUCATIONAL PROGRAM, "SESAME STREET:" AS ENVISIONED IN THE CARNEGIE PROPOSAL, THE PROGRAM WAS TO COMBINE ENTERTAINMENT VALUE WITH SOLID EDUCATIONAL MATTER. THE TARGET AUDIENCE WAS TO BE INNER-CITY DISADVANTAGED CHILDREN FROM 3 TO 5 YEARS OF AGE. BRIEFLY OUTLINED IN THIS OVERVIEW ARE INSTRUCTIONAL GOALS, PRE-PRODUCTION RESEARCH AND PLANNING, FUNDING, METHODS OF EVALUATION, FUTURE PLANS, AND GENERAL CONCLUSIONS OF THE FIRST-YEAR EVALUATION REPORT SUBMITTED BY THE EDUCATIONAL TESTING SERVICE. (NH)

ED047822 PS004493
THE FIRST YEAR OF SESAME STREET: THE FORMATIVE RESEARCH. FINAL REPORT, VOLUME II OF V VOLUMES. REEVES, BARBARA FRENGEL, DEC 70 200P.
EDRS PRICE MF-$0.65 HC-$6.58

THIS PAPER REPORTS THE RESULTS OF FORMATIVE RESEARCH CONDUCTED BY THE CHILDREN'S TELEVISION WORKSHOP FROM THE TIME OF THE INITIAL STAFFING OF THE "SESAME STREET" PROJECT IN 1968 UNTIL THE END OF THE PROGRAM'S FIRST BROADCAST SEASON, TWO YEARS LATER. CHAPTER I DESCRIBES PREBROADCAST RESEARCH, WHICH WAS CENTERED AROUND THREE MAJOR PROBLEM AREAS: (1) ESTABLISHING INSTRUCTIONAL GOALS; (2) TESTING FOR THE DETERMINANTS OF APPEAL, AND (3) TESTING FOR ACHIEVEMENT. A DESCRIPTION OF EVALUATION RESEARCH ON FIVE 1-HOUR PILOT SHOWS IS INCLUDED. CHAPTER II REPORTS ON PROGRESS TESTING CONDUCTED DURING THE BROADCAST PERIOD WITH 200 3- TO 5-YEAR-OLD VIEWERS (EXPERIMENTAL GROUP) AND NONVIEWERS (CONTROL GROUP) OF "SESAME STREET" IN DAY CARE CENTERS. DETAILED APPENDIXES, TABLES AND FIGURES ARE INCLUDED. (NH)

ED047823 PS004494
THE FIRST YEAR OF SESAME STREET: AN EVALUATION. FINAL REPORT, VOLUME III OF V VOLUMES. BALL, SAMUEL; AND OTHERS, OCT 70 442P.
EDRS PRICE MF-$0.65 HC-$16.45

THIS STUDY EVALUATES THE IMPACT OF THE FIRST YEAR OF "SESAME STREET" ON PRESCHOOL TELEVIEWING AUDIENCES IN FIVE SITES (BOSTON, MASS., DURHAM, N.C., PHOENIX, ARIZ., SUBURBAN PHILADELPHIA, AND NORTHEASTERN CALIFORNIA). CHAPTER I INTRODUCES EVALUATIONAL QUESTIONS AND THE RESEARCH STRATEGY. CHAPTER II PRESENTS SAMPLING PROCEDURES FOR PRETEST AND POSTTEST DATA ON 943 CHILDREN, EXPLAINS CRITERIA FOR DEVELOPMENT AND SELECTION OF MEASUREMENT INSTRUMENTS ASSESSING CHILDREN'S LEARNING, PROGRAM CONTENT, PARENT AND TEACHER ATTITUDES, AND DESCRIBES FIELD OPERATIONS. CHAPTER III ANALYZES RESULTS IN THREE PARTS: (1) A DESCRIPTIVE ANALYSIS OF THE VIEWING POPULATION (AGE, SEX, ADVANTAGED CHILDREN, SPANISH-SPEAKING CHILDREN, RURAL CHILDREN, AND DISADVANTAGED AT-HOME AND IN-SCHOOL VIEWERS), (2) A PROBING ANALYSIS INVESTIGATING IN DEPTH THE CHARACTERISTICS OF AT-HOME, DISADVANTAGED, HIGH-VIEWING CHILDREN IN RELATION TO HOME BACKGROUND AND HIGH OR LOW LEARNING, (3) AN INFERENTIAL ANALYSIS EXAMINING THE OVERALL EFFECTIVENESS OF THE TELEVISION SERIES IN ACHIEVING ITS GOALS. CHAPTER IV PRESENTS THE SUMMARY, CONCLUSIONS AND RECOMMENDATIONS. EXTENSIVE APPENDIXES INCLUDE DETAILED INFORMATION ON "SESAME STREET" GOALS AND EVALUATION INSTRUMENTS. (WY)

ED047824 PS004495
THE FIRST YEAR OF SESAME STREET: A SUMMARY OF AUDIENCE SURVEYS. FINAL REPORT, VOLUME IV OF V VOLUMES. SAMUELS, BRUCE, COMP., DEC 70 31P.
EDRS PRICE MF-$0.65 HC-$3.29

WHO WATCHED "SESAME STREET" AND WITH WHAT FREQUENCY AT DIFFERENT SOCIOECONOMIC LEVELS? THIS UTILIZATION STUDY PROVIDES ANSWERS TO THE QUESTION BY COMPILING DATA FROM NATIONAL RATINGS, SPECIAL SURVEYS COMMISSIONED BY THE CHILDREN'S TELEVISION WORKSHOP, AND UNSOLICITED, INDEPENDENTLY CONDUCTED SURVEYS WHICH WERE BROUGHT TO THE WORKSHOP'S ATTENTION. NINE PROJECTS WERE REVIEWED AND SUMMARIZED INTO A VIEWING PROFILE CHART. THE CHART PRESENTS INFORMATION ON TITLE AND DATE OF SURVEY, SURVEYOR, PURPOSES OF SURVEY, CHARACTER OF SAMPLE, SIZE OF SAMPLE, AVAILABILITY ON UHF, VHF, AND CABLE TV AND PERCENT OF PENETRATION. THE RESULTS OF THE PROJECTS SHOWED A HIGHLY ENCOURAGING RATE OF VIEWING AND SUPPORTED THE NEED FOR SPECIAL EFFORTS TO PROMOTE WIDER VIEWING, ESPECIALLY IN LOW INCOME NEIGHBORHOODS AND IN COMMUNITIES SERVED ONLY BY UHF STATIONS. (WY)

ED047825 PS004496
PRE-READING ON SESAME STREET. FINAL REPORT, VOLUME V OF V VOLUMES. GIBBON, SAMUEL Y., JR.; PALMER, EDWARD L., DEC 70 89P.
EDRS PRICE MF-$0.65 HC-$3.29

THIS PAPER REVIEWS THE EVOLUTION AND IMPLEMENTATION OF THE "SESAME STREET" CURRICULUM RELATING TO THE DEVELOPMENT OF LANGUAGE AND PREREADING SKILLS. THE FIRST SECTION GIVES A BRIEF HISTORY OF THE CHILDREN'S TELEVISION WORKSHOP, DESCRIBES THE OPERATIONAL MODEL FOLLOWED BY THE WORKSHOP IN CARRYING OUT ITS INITIAL EXPERIMENT, AND SUGGESTS APPLICATION OF THE MODEL TO FUTURE WORKSHOP PRODUCTIONS. THE SECOND SECTION SPECIFIES THE LANGUAGE AND PREREADING GOALS REPRESENTED IN THE "SESAME STREET" CURRICULUM AND DISCUSSES THE REASONS FOR THEIR INCLUSION. THESE GOALS INCLUDE IMPROVING SELF-CONCEPT, GENERAL CONCEPT DEVELOPMENT, AND THE DEVELOPMENT OF SPECIFIC PERCEPTUAL SKILLS. BEHAVIORAL GOALS RELATED TO THE LEARNING OF LETTERS ARE LISTED AND DISCUSSED IN DETAIL. THE THIRD SECTION DESCRIBES MANY OF THE PRODUCTION TECHNIQUES AND TEACHING STRATEGIES USED TO IMPLEMENT THESE LETTER-LEARNING GOALS. THE PROBLEMS OF SEQUENCING AND SCHEDULING INSTRUCTION FOR BROADCAST TELEVISION ARE CONSIDERED. THE FOURTH SECTION PROVIDES SOME PRELIMINARY DATA ON THE ABILITY OF VIEWERS TO NAME CERTAIN LETTERS. THE EVIDENCE SUGGESTS THAT SOME SUCCESS HAS BEEN ACHIEVED IN TEACHING LETTER IDENTIFICATION. THE FINAL SECTION IS A SUMMARY. A STATEMENT OF INSTRUCTIONAL GOALS FOR THE 1970-1971 EXPERIMENTAL SEASON OF "SESAME STREET" IS APPENDED. (AUTHOR/WY)

ED047826 PS004538
PARENTS ARE TEACHERS: A CHILD MANAGEMENT PROGRAM. BECKER, WESLEY C., 71 199P.
DOCUMENT NOT AVAILABLE FROM EDRS.
AVAILABLE FROM: RESEARCH PRESS COMPANY, P.O. BOX 3327, COUNTRY FAIR STATION, CHAMPAIGN, ILL. 61820 ($3.75)

THIS MANUAL IS DESIGNED TO HELP PARENTS APPLY REINFORCEMENT THEORY IN MANAGING THEIR CHILDREN. THE PROGRAM EXPLAINS HOW PARENTS CAN SYSTEMATICALLY USE CONSEQUENCES TO TEACH CHILDREN IN POSITIVE WAYS. UNITS INCLUDE: WHEN TO REINFORCE; HOW TO REINFORCE; REINFORCEMENT AND PUNISHMENT IN EVERYDAY LIFE; AND WHY PARENTS (AND TEACHERS) GOOF; THE CRITICISM TRAP. TEN UNITS IN THE TEXT ILLUSTRATE PRACTICAL SITUATIONS IN WHICH REINFORCEMENT THEORY MIGHT OPERATE TO MODIFY ADULT AND CHILD BEHAVIOR. WRITE-IN EXERCISES FOLLOW EACH UNIT AND ANSWER KEYS APPEAR AT THE END OF THE BOOKLET. THE AUTHOR SUGGESTS THAT THIS PROGRAM SHOULD BE OF CONSIDERABLE VALUE TO TEACHER AIDES, TO CLINICAL PSYCHOLOGISTS SERVING AS GROUP LEADERS FOR PARENT PROGRAMS, TO SCHOOL SOCIAL WORKERS, TO ELEMENTARY GUIDANCE COUNSELORS, TO SPECIAL EDUCATION TEACHERS AND TO THE AVERAGE PARENT. (WY)

ED048916 PS003131
A SUCCESSFUL ATTEMPT TO TRAIN CHILDREN IN COORDINATION OF PROJECTIVE SPACE. MILLER, JACK W.; MILLER, HAROLDINE G., MAR 70 29P.
EDRS PRICE MF-$0.65 HC-$3.29

THE OBJECTIVE OF THE INVESTIGATION WAS TO DEVELOP AND TEST PROCEDURES FOR TRAINING CHILDREN IN COORDINATION OF PROJECTIVE SPACE. (PROJECTIVE CONCEPTS INVOLVE APPARENT DISTANCE, RELATIVE POSITION, SHAPE OF FIGURES, AND OTHER TOPOLOGICAL FACTORS. A PERSON WITH A COMMAND OF PROJECTIVE SPACE SEES OBJECTS AS A COORDINATED SYSTEM OF FIGURES IN SPACE.) A TOTAL OF 36 8-YEAR-OLD MIDDLE CLASS CHILDREN WHO COULD NOT COORDINATE PROJECTIVE SPACE WERE TRAINED IN A CAREFULLY SEQUENCED INSTRUCTIONAL PROGRAM EMBODYING HEIRARCHIES BASED ON PIAGETIAN THEORY AS ONE DIMENSION, BRUNERIAN MODES OF REPRESENTATION AS A SECOND, AND COMPLEXITY OF TASK AS THE THIRD. GAINS IN ABILITY TO COORDINATE PROJECTIVE SPACE, AS MEASURED BY THE PERSPECTIVE ABILITY TEST DEVELOPED BY THE SENIOR AUTHOR, EXCEEDED THOSE OF

A CONTROL GROUP. THERE WERE NO SIGNIFICANT DIFFERENCES BETWEEN PERFORMANCE GAINS OF MALES AND FEMALES. IT IS RECOMMENDED THAT PREVIOUS STUDIES THAT SUGGESTED PIAGET'S NORMATIVE PROCESS IS IMMUTABLE--AND THAT BASIC COGNITIVE DEVELOPMENT CANNOT BE ENHANCED SIGNIFICANTLY THROUGH INSTRUCTION--BE REEVALUATED IN TERMS OF THEORETICAL DEFICIENCIES, INAPPROPRIATE METHODOLOGY, MEASUREMENT PROBLEMS, AND OTHER FACTORS. THE POSSIBILITY OF SUCCESSFUL TRAINING ON OTHER SPATIAL TASKS AND WITH YOUNGER CHILDREN SHOULD BE CONSIDERED. APPENDIXES PROVIDE STATISTICAL DATA, TRAINING LESSONS, AND EXPLANATIONS OF PIAGETIAN THEORY. (AUTHORS/DR)

ED048917 PS003311
THE ROLE OF EXPERIENCE IN THE BEHAVIORAL DEVELOPMENT OF HUMAN INFANTS: CURRENT STATUS AND RECOMMENDATIONS. WHITE, BURTON L., 70 78P.
EDRS PRICE MF-$0.65 HC-$3.29
AVAILABLE FROM: "REVIEW OF CHILD DEVELOPMENT." ED. BY BETTYE CALDWELL AND H. RICCIUTI. NEW YORK: RUSSELL SAGE FOUNDATION (IN PRESS)

THIS PAPER IS DESIGNED AS AN INFORMATION GUIDE FOR THOSE PERSONS RESPONSIBLE FOR REARING HUMAN INFANTS FROM BIRTH TO 18 MONTHS. THE AUTHOR PROVIDES AN EXTENSIVE REVIEW OF THE LITERATURE AND TRENDS OF RESEARCH IN THIS AREA NOTING THAT THE CURRENT VOLUMES OF KNOWLEDGE IN THIS AREA ARE NOT YET DEPENDABLE ENOUGH TO PROVIDE RELIABLE BASES FOR PRACTICE. HE NOTES THAT AMONG THE PROBLEMS PRESENTED IN THE STUDY OF INFANTS ARE (1) AVAILABILITY OF SUBJECTS IN NATURAL ENVIRONMENT, AND (2) THE LACK OF RELIABLE MEASURES FOR RESEARCH. PROVIDED IS AN ENUMERATION, EXPLANATION AND EVALUATION OF KINDS OF STUDIES AND KNOWN INFORMATION ABOUT INFANT DEVELOPMENT. INCLUDED ARE LONGITUDINAL STUDIES, CROSS-SECTIONAL STUDIES, AND ASSESSMENTS OF DIRECT AND INDIRECT EVIDENCE. THE AUTHOR FEELS THAT PRACTITIONERS SHOULD DEMAND AND SUPPORT THE PRODUCTION OF MORE DEPENDABLE KNOWLEDGE BY SPONSORING FIELD AND BASIC RESEARCH THROUGHOUT INFANCY ON THE WHOLE INFANT (RATHER THAN ON HIS SEPARATE BEHAVIORS) AS HE FUNCTIONS IN REAL LIFE. WHITE ADMONISHES PRACTITIONERS TO ACCEPT THE FACT THAT, FOR THE TIME BEING, CHILD-REARING PRACTICES MUST BE DESIGNED ON AN ADMITTED BEST GUESS BASIS. AN EXTENSIVE BIBLIOGRAPHY IS PROVIDED. (AUTHOR/AJ)

ED048918 PS003795
MINIMUM STANDARDS FOR LICENSED DAY CARE CENTERS AND NIGHT-TIME CENTERS. REVISED EDITION. , 1 JAN 70 86P.
EDRS PRICE MF-$0.65 HC-$3.29

THIS DOCUMENT GIVES THE MINIMUM STANDARDS REQUIRED FOR LICENSING DAY CARE CENTERS AND NIGHTTIME CENTERS IN THE STATE OF ILLINOIS. THE STANDARDS WERE ESTABLISHED BY THE DEPARTMENT OF CHILDREN AND FAMILY SERVICES UNDER THE CHILD CARE ACT OF 1969. INCLUDED IN THE PUBLICATION ARE: (1) AN EXPLANATION OF THE LEGAL BASIS AND APPLICATION OF STANDARDS; (2) STANDARDS FOR ORGANIZATION AND ADMINISTRATION OF CENTERS; (3) DISCUSSION OF PERSONNEL AND WORKING CONDITIONS; (4) ENUMERATION OF SERVICES TO CHILDREN (THOSE ELIGIBLE FOR SERVICE, DISCIPLINE MEASURES ALLOWED, HEALTH AND MEDICAL STANDARDS, ETC.); AND (5) SPECIAL SECTIONS DEALING WITH PHYSICAL PLANT, RECORDS AND REPORTS REQUIRED. (AJ)

ED048919 PS003833
LEAD POISONING IN CHILDREN. LIN-FU, JANE S., 70 27P.
EDRS PRICE MF-$0.65 HC NOT AVAILABLE FROM EDRS.
AVAILABLE FROM: SUPERINTENDENT OF DOCUMENTS, U.S. GOVERNMENT PRINTING OFFICE, WASHINGTON, D.C. 20402 ($0.25, PUBLICATION NUMBER 2108-1970)

THIS PUBLICATION IS A GUIDE TO HELP SOCIAL AND HEALTH WORKERS PLAN A PREVENTIVE CAMPAIGN AGAINST LEAD POISONING, A CAUSE OF MENTAL RETARDATION OTHER NEUROLOGICAL HANDICAPS, AND DEATH AMONG CHILDREN. THE MAIN VICTIMS ARE 1- TO 6-YEAR-OLDS LIVING IN AREAS WHERE DETERIORATING HOUSING PREVAILS. AMONG THE CAUSES OF LEAD POISONING ARE: INGESTION OF LEAD-BASE PAINT, INHALATION OF FUMES WHEN LEADED BATTERY CASINGS ARE BURNED FOR FUEL, AND INGESTION OF HOME-GROWN VEGETABLES GROWN IN SOIL CONTAINING LEADED BATTERY CASINGS. LEAD POISONING ASSOCIATED WITH PICA, THE CRAVING FOR UNNATURAL FOODS, IS A CHRONIC PROCESS REQUIRING FROM 3 TO 6 MONTHS OF STEADY LEAD INGESTION. EVEN THOUGH THE EARLY SYMPTOMS ARE NONSPECIFIC--ANOREXIA, ABDOMINAL PAIN, CONSTIPATION, VOMITING, ANEMIA--AN INCREASED AWARENESS OF THE PROBLEM BY PHYSICIANS AND OTHER HEALTH WORKERS CAN LEAD TO EARLY DETECTION. THE PUBLIC IS POORLY INFORMED AND EVEN PARENTS OF CHILDREN ONCE STRIKEN ARE UNAWARE OF THE HIGH RATES OF RECURRENCE AND OF OCCURRENCE IN SIBLINGS. CONTROL AND PREVENTION INVOLVE PROFESSIONAL AND PUBLIC EDUCATION, LEGISLATION, RESEARCH, AND IMPROVED HOUSING. (AJ)

ED048920 PS004115
PLAY BEHAVIOR AND EFFICACY IN GHETTO FOUR-YEAR-OLDS: ORGANIZATION AND PSYCHOSEXUAL CONTENT OF PLAY. BOROWITZ, GENE H.; AND OTHERS, 70 31P.
EDRS PRICE MF-$0.65 HC-$3.29

EFFECTANCE, DEFINED AS THE CHILD'S INDEPENDENT, EFFECTIVE INTERACTION WITH PEOPLE AND THINGS, IS STUDIED THROUGH OBSERVATION OF THE PLAY OF 36 PRESCHOOL LOW INCOME BLACK CHILDREN. THE CHILDREN WERE OBSERVED AND FILMED IN SEMI-STRUCTURED PLAY SESSIONS, PRIMARILY WITH FAMILY DOLLS, DOLL FURNITURE, AND SMALL BABY BOTTLE. INSTRUMENTS USED WERE: (1) THE PLAY SESSION BEHAVIOR SCALE, WHICH INCLUDES 22 VARIABLES DEFINING ORGANIZATION, INVOLVEMENT, AND INTERPERSONAL RESPONSIVENESS IN PLAY, AND (2) THE PSYCHOSEXUAL CONTENT OF PLAY SCALE, WHICH INCLUDES 13 VARIABLES DEFINING THE AMOUNT OF CONTENT REFLECTING EACH OF THE FIVE EARLY PSYCHOSEXUAL STAGES OF DEVELOPMENT. IT IS CONCLUDED THAT: (A) EFFECTIVE FUNCTIONING AS A LEARNER AT AGE 4 REQUIRES SKILLS WHICH BECAME CRYSTALLIZED DURING THE ANAL RETENTIVE STAGE, SUCH AS THE ABILITY TO PERSIST IN TASKS, TAKE PLEASURE IN ACCOMPLISHMENTS, AND LOOK FOR RULES AND ORDER; AND (B) OPTIMAL FUNCTIONING AS A LEARNER AT AGE 4 IS FACILITATED BY SKILLS ARISING OUT OF THE PHALLIC STAGE, SUCH AS CURIOSITY, SELF-ASSERTION, AND AN EMERGING SENSE OF WHERE ONE FITS IN THE SOCIAL ORDER. STATISTICAL TABLES AND AN APPENDIX CONSISTING OF THE INSTRUMENTS AND RATER'S MANUAL USED COMPRISE ALMOST HALF OF THE DOCUMENT. (AUTHOR/NH)

ED048921 PS004238
THE PSYCHOLOGICAL EFFECTS OF PREGNANCY AND NEONATAL HEALTH THREATS ON CHILD DEVELOPMENT. CECIL, HENRY S.; AND OTHERS, 69 31P.
EDRS PRICE MF-$0.65 HC NOT AVAILABLE FROM EDRS.

THIS STUDY FOLLOWED A SMALL GROUP OF CHILDREN EXPOSED TO PRE- AND PERINATAL HEALTH THREATS TO DETERMINE WHETHER ANY PSYCHOLOGICAL EFFECTS OF THE HEALTH THREAT COULD BE IDENTIFIED AND IF SO, WHETHER THERE IS POTENTIAL IN PEDIATRIC CARE TO PREVENT SUCH CONSEQUENCES. THE 67 INFANTS WERE ALL MEMBERS OF LOW INCOME FAMILIES. THE TESTS USED INCLUDED THE PARENTAL ATTITUDES RESEARCH INSTRUMENT (PARI) AND MATERNAL INTERVAL HISTORIES (ABOUT FINANCIAL STRESS, HOUSING DIFFICULTIES AND ILLNESSES) TAKEN EVERY FOUR MONTHS. INTERVAL HISTORIES ON THE CHILDREN'S BEHAVIOR WERE TAKEN WHEN THE CHILDREN WERE 18 MONTHS OLD. THE FINDINGS INDICATE THAT MATERNAL CONCERN ABOUT HEALTH OR OUTCOME INCREASES THE LIKELIHOOD OF DEVIANT BEHAVIOR IN CHILDREN WITH HISTORIES OF THREAT. THESE CONCERNED MOTHERS CAN BE IDENTIFIED AT THE POINT OF STRESS FOR INTERVENTION DUE TO THEIR FEARS OF LOSS OR DEFECT IN THEIR CHILDREN. THOUGH ENVIRONMENTAL STRESSES DO NOT INCREASE THE INCIDENCE OF DEVIATIONS, THEY MAY OBSCURE FOR THE PHYSICIAN THE EFFECT OF MATERNAL CONCERN ABOUT A HEALTH THREAT. INTENSIVE SOCIAL WORK SERVICES IN COLLABORATION WITH THE MEDICAL CARE IS REQUIRED IF AN INTERVENTION PROGRAM IS TO REACH VULNERABLE MOTHER-INFANT PAIRS. [NOT AVAILABLE IN HARD COPY DUE TO MARGINAL LEGIBILITY OF ORIGINAL DOCUMENT.] (AUTHOR/AJ)

ED048922 PS004410
THE PROFESSIONAL RESPONSE. RUBOW, CAROL L.; FILLERUP, JOSEPH M., NOV 70 36P.
EDRS PRICE MF-$0.65 HC-$3.29

TEACHERS IN THE TUCSON EARLY CHILDHOOD EDUCATION MODEL (TEEM) ARE BEING ENCOURAGED TO EMPLOY "THE PROFESSIONAL RESPONSE" IN CLASSROOM INTERACTIONS TO STIMULATE PUPIL THINKING. THE TEACHER USES THE PROFESSIONAL RESPONSE WHEN SHE RESPONDS TO A CHILD IN SUCH A WAY AS TO INVITE HIM TO RECALL PREVIOUS EXPERIENCES AND TO PREDICT IN TERMS OF THESE, TO CATEGORIZE, TO THINK ABOUT HIS RESPONSE, TO BECOME DESCRIPTIVE AND SPECIFIC, AND TO STRENGTHEN THE MEANING THAT WORDS AND PHRASES HAVE FOR HIM. TEACHERS AND AIDES ARE TRAINED TO UTILIZE (1) REINFORCEMENT, (2) INDIVIDUALIZATION, (3) MODELING, AND (4) ORCHESTRATION (IDENTIFYING SKILLS TO EVOLVE OUT OF ACTIVITY) IN HARMONY WITH THE PHILOSOPHY AND ORGANIZATION OF TEEM. BASIC TO DEVELOPMENT OF THE PROFESSIONAL RESPONSE IS A TEACHER'S ABILITY TO PICK UP CUES FROM THE TOTAL CLASSROOM ENVIRONMENT. THE TEACHER MUST LISTEN TO PUPILS SO THAT SHE WILL KEEP THE ENVIRONMENT IN TUNE WITH THEIR INTERESTS AND DEVELOPMENT. TWO TEEM CHECKLISTS FOR TEACHER SELF-EVALUATION ARE APPENDED TO THIS THEORETICAL MODEL OF THE TEACHER'S ROLE IN TEACHER-PUPIL INTERACTIONS. BOTH CHECKLISTS MAY HELP TEACHERS TO DEVELOP THEIR OWN STYLE OF PROFESSIONAL RESPONSE. (WY)

ED048923 PS004423
THE EFFICACY OF A MATHEMATICS READINESS PROGRAM FOR INDUCING CONSERVATION OF NUMBER, WEIGHT, AREA, MASS, AND VOLUME IN DISADVANTAGED PRESCHOOL CHILDREN IN THE SOUTHERN UNITED STATES. YOUNG, BEVERLY S., 4 FEB 71 9P.
EDRS PRICE MF-$0.65 HC-$3.29

THE PRESENT STUDY WAS DESIGNED TO DETERMINE WHETHER CONSERVATION OF NUMBER, WEIGHT, VOLUME, AREA, AND MASS COULD BE LEARNED AND RETAINED BY DISADVANTAGED PRESCHOOL CHILDREN WHEN TAUGHT BY AN INEXPERIENCED CLASSROOM TEACHER. AN

INSTRUCTIONAL SEQUENCE OF 10-MINUTE LESSONS WAS PRESENTED ON ALTERNATE DAYS OVER A 3 1/2 WEEK PERIOD BY PRESERVICE ELEMENTARY EDUCATION MAJORS TO 93 CHILDREN 3-5 YEARS OF AGE. INSTRUCTIONS TO THE TEACHER CONSISTED OF TEN TYPED LESSON PLANS WHICH PERMITTED FLEXIBILITY IN WORDING AND PHRASING BUT WERE STRUCTURED IN TERMS OF SPECIFIC TASKS AND EXPERIENCES. CHILDREN IN THE EXPERIMENTAL GROUP WERE SUBDIVIDED INTO SMALLER, HOMOGENEOUS GROUPS OF 4-6 CHILDREN FOR TRAINING. A CONTROL GROUP WAS EXPOSED TO AN ENRICHED ENVIRONMENT BUT RECEIVED NO TRAINING. RESULTS SHOWED SIGNIFICANT GAINS FOR THE EXPERIMENTAL GROUP IN 15 OF THE 18 CRITERION SUBTESTS AND SIGNIFICANT INTERACTION BETWEEN CHRONOLOGICAL AGE (CA), MENTAL AGE (MA), AND INTELLIGENCE QUOTIENT (IQ) LEVELS. AN ANALYSIS FOR RETENTION SHOWED NO EXTINCTION. INSTRUCTION APPEARED TO BE EFFECTIVE FOR STUDENTS ABOVE THE 3-YEAR-OLD LEVEL IN MA AND CA, AND FOR IQ LEVELS ABOVE 65. WHEN DISADVANTAGED CHILDREN WERE COMPARED WITH ADVANTAGED CHILDREN OF THE SAME MA LEVEL, OR OF THE SAME IQ LEVEL, SIGNIFICANT DIFFERENCES APPEARED. (WY)

ED048924 PS004447
FIELD TEST OF THE UNIVERSITY OF HAWAII PRESCHOOL LANGUAGE CURRICULUM. FINAL REPORT. ADKINS, DOROTHY C.; CROWELL, DORIS C., DEC 70 53P.
EDRS PRICE MF-$0.65 HC-$3.29

REPORTS ON A PROJECT DESIGNED (1) TO EXPLORE THE UTILITY OF THE UNIVERSITY OF HAWAII PRESCHOOL LANGUAGE CURRICULUM IN A BROAD FIELD-TESTING SITUATION WITH TEACHERS OF VARYING SKILL AND BACKGROUND; (2) TO DETERMINE WHETHER OR NOT THERE IS LOSS OF EFFECTIVENESS WHEN THE AMOUNT OF SUPERVISION AND CONSULTATION HAS BEEN REDUCED FROM THAT PROVIDED IN LOCALLY ADMINISTERED PROJECTS; AND (3) TO MEASURE THE EFFECTIVENESS OF THE CURRICULUM WITH GROUPS USING SEVERAL NONSTANDARD DIALECTS OTHER THAN HAWAIIAN PIDGIN. THE CURRICULUM WAS TAUGHT IN 16 CLASSES OF APPALACHIAN, HAWAIIAN, INDIAN, MEXICAN-AMERICAN, NORTHERN URBAN, SOUTHERN NEGRO, AND PUERTO RICAN CHILDREN. CHILDREN WERE GIVEN THE PPVT AND THE ITPA INITIALLY AND AGAIN AFTER A 6-MONTH INTERVAL. THE CHANGE FROM PRETEST TO POSTTEST ON EACH MEASURE WAS COMPUTED FOR EACH CLASS. THE EXPERIMENTAL TEACHER WAS RANKED IN TERMS OF THE TOTAL NET GAIN AND WAS ALSO RANKED INDEPENDENTLY BY THE PROJECT STAFF IN TERMS OF EFFECTIVENESS IN USING THE LANGUAGE CURRICULUM. BOTH THE RANK ORDER AND TETRACHORIC CORRELATION COEFFICIENTS BETWEEN THESE TWO VARIABLES WERE SIGNIFICANTLY DIFFERENT FROM ZERO BEYOND THE .01 LEVEL OF CONFIDENCE. APPENDIXES COMPRISE MORE THAN HALF THE DOCUMENT. (AUTHOR/AJ)

ED048925 PS004455
COMMUNITY COORDINATED CHILD CARE: A FEDERAL PARTNERSHIP IN BEHALF OF CHILDREN. FINAL REPORT. , 31 DEC 70 516P.
EDRS PRICE MF-$0.65 HC-$19.74

DURING 1969 AND 1970, THE DAY CARE AND CHILD DEVELOPMENT COUNCIL OF AMERICA, INC. (DCCDCA) PROVIDED TECHNICAL ASSISTANCE TO CITIZENS' COMMITTEES FORMED IN A NUMBER OF COMMUNITIES AND STATES TO PARTICIPATE IN THE FEDERALLY SPONSORED COMMUNITY COORDINATED CHILD CARE (4-C) PROGRAM. THIS FINAL OMNIBUS REPORT ON THE CONTRACT DESCRIBES (DCCDCA'S TECHNICAL ASSISTANCE EFFORT AND PRESENTS THE COUNCIL'S FINDINGS AND RECOMMENDATIONS CONCERNING THE 4-C PROGRAM. A HISTORY OF THE 4-C EFFORT NATIONALLY AND A REPORT ON EACH OF THE 24 PILOT PROGRAMS ARE INCLUDED. THE SUMMARY PRESENTED AT THE BEGINNING OF THIS DOCUMENT ALSO HAS BEEN PUBLISHED SEPARATELY AS PS 004 541. MATERIAL IN THIS REPORT IS DRAWN FROM MANY SOURCES: EXPERIENCES OF DCCDCA STAFF MEMBERS, CONTRIBUTIONS FROM INDIVIDUALS IN EARLY CHILDHOOD PROGRAMS, DOCUMENTS, MEMOS, AND OTHER WRITTEN MATERIAL OBTAINED FROM NATIONAL, REGIONAL, STATE, AND LOCAL SOURCES. APPENDIXES INCLUDED. (AUTHOR/AJ)

ED048926 PS004482
DECENTRATION IN CHILDREN: ITS GENERALITY AND CORRELATES. SCOTT, GAIL S., [69] 10P.
EDRS PRICE MF-$0.65 HC-$3.29

THIS STUDY TESTED 60 CHILDREN, 5 TO 8 YEARS OLD, ON A VARIETY OF MENTAL, MORAL, SOCIAL, CREATIVE AND COGNITIVE TASKS TO DETERMINE THE INTERRELATEDNESS OF THOSE VARIABLES AND THEIR RELATIONSHIPS TO THE INTELLECTUAL PROCESS OF DECENTRATION. THE SUBJECTS WERE OBSERVED WHILE ATTENDING A SUMMER PROGRAM PRIOR TO ENTERING GRADES ONE THROUGH THREE. OBSERVERS RATED EACH PUPIL ON SPECIFIC BEHAVIORS ASSOCIATED WITH EGOCENTRICITY AND DECENTRATION, AS WELL AS FOR POSITIVE-NEGATIVE AFFECT AND VERBAL-NONVERBAL BEHAVIOR. IDENTIFYING THE UNDERLYING STRUCTURE OF THE INTERRELATIONSHIPS OF THE DECENTERING, VERBAL, AND POSITIVE IN ADDITION TO THE REMAINING 27 VARIABLES WAS ACCOMPLISHED THROUGH A FACTOR ANALYSIS. THE DECENTERING MEASURES RESULTED IN LARGE LOADINGS; VERBAL AND POSITIVE VARIABLES LOADED HEAVILY ON CONFORMITY. RESULTS DEFINE AND STRESS THE DECENTERING FACTOR AS AN INDEPENDENT VARIABLE HAVING VERY LITTLE INTERACTION ON THE REMAINING COGNITIVE VARIABLES. IT APPEARS THAT NEITHER COGNITIVE NOR SOCIAL VARIABLES ARE PROMINENTLY INVOLVED WITH DECENTERING; HOWEVER, STAGE BY STAGE COMPARISONS SHOW THAT THIS IS A FINDING PECULIAR TO THE LEVEL OF DEVELOPMENT ASSESSED. WHILE THIS STUDY AFFORDS NO ASSESSMENT OF THE DIVIDING LINE BETWEEN EGOCENTRIC AND DECENTERING BEHAVIOR, IT PROVIDES BASELINE DATA FROM WHICH OTHER STUDIES MAY BE CARRIED OUT. OBSERVATION FORM INCLUDED. (WY)

ED048927 PS004498
TINY DRAMAS: VOCAL COMMUNICATION BETWEEN MOTHER AND INFANT IN JAPANESE AND AMERICAN FAMILIES. CAUDILL, WILLIAM, MAR 69 43P.
EDRS PRICE MF-$0.65 HC NOT AVAILABLE FROM EDRS.

WHY DO AMERICAN INFANTS HAVE A GREATER AMOUNT OF VOCALIZATION, AND PARTICULARLY OF HAPPY VOCALIZATION, THAN DO JAPANESE INFANTS? TO ANSWER THIS QUESTION, 30 JAPANESE AND 30 AMERICAN FIRST-BORN, 3- TO 4-MONTH OLD INFANTS EQUALLY DIVIDED BY SEX, AND LIVING IN INTACT MIDDLE CLASS URBAN FAMILIES WERE OBSERVED IN THEIR HOMES ON TWO CONSECUTIVE DAYS DURING 1961-1964. TWO SPECIFIC STYLES OF CHILD CARE WERE SHOWN TO BE AT WORK INFLUENCING THE PROCESS BY WHICH LEARNING OF CULTURAL EXPECTATIONS FOR BEHAVIOR COMES ABOUT. AMERICAN MOTHERS WERE BUSIER, LIVELIER, AND DIFFERENTIATED IN THEIR RESPONSE TO THEIR BABY'S HAPPY OR UNHAPPY VOCALIZATIONS. THE JAPANESE MOTHER'S PACE WAS MORE LEISURELY. SHE WAS MORE ATTENTIVE TO THE BABY WHEN HE WAS GOING TO SLEEP OR WAKING UP AND LESS RESPONSIVE TO VOCALIZATION IN GENERAL. APPARENTLY, THESE DIFFERENCES IN MATERNAL STYLE OF CHILD CARE ELICIT BEHAVIORS FROM INFANTS THAT ARE IN LINE WITH LATER EXPECTANCIES FOR BEHAVIOR IN THE TWO CULTURES. A FOLLOWUP STUDY OF THE FIRST 20 OF THESE SAME CHILDREN IN EACH CULTURE AS THEY BECAME 2 1/2 AND 6 YEARS OF AGE IS BEING COMPLETED. IT IS EXPECTED THAT THE EARLY DIFFERENCES IN BEHAVIOR SEEN IN INFANCY WILL CONTINUE ALONG THE LINES LAID DOWN BY THE TWO CULTURES. [NOT AVAILABLE IN HARD COPY DUE TO MARGINAL LEGIBILITY OF ORIGINAL DOCUMENT.] (WY)

ED048928 PS004499
SOME EUROPEAN NURSERY SCHOOLS AND PLAYGROUNDS. UTZINGER, ROBERT C., 70 79P.
DOCUMENT NOT AVAILABLE FROM EDRS.
AVAILABLE FROM: PUBLICATIONS DISTRIBUTION SERVICES, UNIVERSITY OF MICHIGAN, ANN ARBOR, MICHIGAN 48104 ($3.50

THIS MONOGRAPH, INTERDISCIPLINARY IN SCOPE, IS A NARRATIVE AND PHOTOGRAPHIC ACCOUNT OF SOME SEVENTEEN FACILITIES EXISTING FOR CHILD CARE IN EUROPE. IT PRESENTS PROTOTYPE PLANS, DIAGRAMS AND PICTURES OF PLAYROOMS AND PLAYGROUNDS IN DAY NURSERIES, NURSERY SCHOOLS, PLAYGROUNDS, AND RECREATION CENTERS IN LONDON, ENGLAND; COPENHAGEN, DENMARK; STOCKHOLM AND UPPSALA, SWEDEN; AND ZURICH, SWITZERLAND. THE SECTION TITLED "CONCLUSIONS AND RECOMMENDATIONS" SUMMARIZES WHAT THE AUTHOR LEARNED ABOUT FACILITIES FOR THE YOUNG CHILD WHILE HE WAS ON THE STUDY TOUR. THIRTEEN OF THE RECOMMENDATIONS ARE GENERAL IN NATURE, 25 PERTAIN TO INDOOR PLAY AREAS, AND 15 PERTAIN TO OUTDOOR PLAY AREAS. (WY)

ED048929 PS004500
HEAD START GRADUATES: ONE YEAR LATER. NUMMEDAL, SUSAN G.; STERN, CAROLYN, 6 FEB 71 33P.
EDRS PRICE MF-$0.65 HC-$3.29

TO DETERMINE THE CONTINUING IMPACT OF HEAD START EXPERIENCE, THIS FOLLOW-UP STUDY COMPARED (1) THE BEHAVIOR OF CHILDREN WHO HAD FULL YEAR HEAD START (FYHS) EXPERIENCE UNDER THREE DIFFERENT TYPES OF AGENCIES, AND (2) WITHIN EACH AGENCY, WHERE POSSIBLE, THE BEHAVIOR OF CHILDREN WHO DID NOT HAVE FYHS EXPERIENCE. SUBJECTS WERE 102 FYHS CHILDREN AND 39 NON HEAD START CHILDREN. DATA WERE GATHERED TO ASSESS THE CHILD'S HOME BACKGROUND AS WELL AS HIS CURRENT SCHOOL ENVIRONMENT. A PRETEST AND POSTTEST BATTERY OF FOUR INSTRUMENTS WAS ADMINISTERED TO EACH CHILD AND FIVE SETS OF OBSERVATIONS WERE MADE IN CLASSROOMS WHERE SUBJECTS WERE ENROLLED. RESULTS INDICATE THAT CHILDREN ATTENDED MARKEDLY CONTRASTING FIRST YEAR OF PRIMARY SCHOOL PROGRAMS. CHANGES IN INTELLECTUAL FUNCTIONING WERE COMPLEX AND FOR THE MOST PART INCONCLUSIVE. DIFFICULTIES IN RESEARCH DESIGN REFLECTED PROBLEMS CONSISTENT WITH COMPARATIVE STUDIES OF THIS TYPE. RATHER THAN CONCLUDE THAT FYHS FAILED TO AFFECT A LASTING CHANGE IN CHILDREN, THIS STUDY POINTS UP THE IMPORTANCE OF CAREFULLY DESCRIBING THE DIFFERENT CLASSROOM ENVIRONMENTS AND SELECTING APPROPRIATE COMPARISON GROUPS WHEN ATTEMPTING TO EVALUATE THE LONG-RANGE EFFECTS OF HEAD START. NUMEROUS TABLES ARE INCLUDED. (WY)

ED048930 PS004501
EDUCATION OF THE INFANT AND YOUNG CHILD. DENENBERG, VICTOR H., ED., 70 150P.
DOCUMENT NOT AVAILABLE FROM EDRS.
AVAILABLE FROM: ACADEMIC PRESS INC., PUBLISHERS, 111 FIFTH AVENUE, NEW YORK, NEW YORK 10003 ($6.75, BOOK CODE: 2091-50)

THE PURPOSE OF THIS BOOK IS TO BRING TOGETHER INFORMATION ON THE CONDITIONS WHICH WOULD AID IN MAXIMIZING THE LEARNING POTENTIAL AND BEHAVIORAL DEVELOPMENT OF THE VERY YOUNG CHILD WITH PARTICULAR EMPHASIS ON THE TYPES OF EXPERIENCES THAT SHOULD BE RECEIVED BY YOUNG BABIES WHO SPEND PART OF THEIR TIME IN A DAY CARE CENTER. THE PAPERS PRESENTED BY JEROME KAGAN, WILLIAM MASON, HANUS PAPOUSEK, EARL SCHAEFER, DAVID WEIKART, AND DOLORES LAMBIE DISCUSS: (1) WHY POOR CHILDREN DO BADLY IN SCHOOL SITUATIONS AND POSSIBLE REMEDIES, (2) THE EFFECTS OF EARLY DEPRIVATION ON ANIMALS, (3) RECENT EUROPEAN EXPERIENCE WITH DAY CARE CENTERS, (4) THE NEED FOR EDUCATION TO START VERY EARLY IN THE INFANT'S LIFE, AND (5) SOME EXPERIMENTAL REGIMENS FOR ENRICHING THE EDUCATIONAL EXPERIENCE OF VERY YOUNG CHILDREN. DISCUSSIONS OF THE THEMES OF THESE PAPERS BY PSYCHOLOGIST JEROME BRUNER AND BY RICHARD ORTON, THE ASSOCIATE DIRECTOR OF PROJECT HEAD START, FOLLOW. FINALLY, EDITOR VICTOR DENENBERG ABSTRACTS FROM THE PREVIOUS MATERIAL A NUMBER OF FACTORS WHICH ARE OF CRITICAL CONCERN WHEN SETTING UP A DAY CARE CENTER. (AUTHOR/WY)

ED048931 PS004502
FEDERAL INVOLVEMENT IN DAY CARE. MALONE, MARGARET, 3 MAR 69 45P.
EDRS PRICE MF-$0.65 HC-$3.29

BECAUSE OF THE EXPANDING NEED FOR CHILD CARE FOR PRESCHOOL CHILDREN, AND FOR OLDER CHILDREN IN AFTER-SCHOOL HOURS, THERE IS GREATER INTEREST IN PROGRAMS FOR DAY CARE, AND INCREASING ACCEPTANCE OF THE CONCEPT OF PUBLICLY-FINANCED DAY CARE. THIS PAPER DESCRIBES THE MARKET FOR DAY CARE, THE FEDERAL PROGRAMS WHICH EXIST AND THE STANDARDS WHICH HAVE BEEN ESTABLISHED FOR FEDERALLY-AIDED DAY CARE. THE ISSUES INVOLVED IN THE EXPANSION OF DAY CARE PROGRAMS IN THE UNITED STATES ARE DISCUSSED, AND VARIOUS PROPOSALS MADE TO EXPAND THESE SERVICES THROUGH FEDERAL LEGISLATION ARE POINTED OUT. AN ATTACHMENT SUMMARIZES LEGISLATIVE PROPOSALS ON DAY CARE AND PRESCHOOL EDUCATION WHICH HAVE BEEN MADE SINCE 1961. (AUTHOR/NH)

ED048932 PS004504
A BRIEF GUIDE TO NEWSLETTERS IN EARLY CHILDHOOD EDUCATION. ALLGAIER, JANET FAGAN, COMP., MAR 71 13P.
EDRS PRICE MF-$0.65 HC-$3.29

THIS DOCUMENT IS A BRIEF LISTING OF 31 INFORMATIVE NEWSLETTERS AND BULLETINS CONCERNED DIRECTLY WITH, OR RELATED TO, THE FIELD OF EARLY CHILDHOOD EDUCATION. EACH LISTING CONTAINS THE PUBLICATION'S TITLE, SCOPE, FREQUENCY OF PUBLICATION AND SUBSCRIPTION INFORMATION. THE GUIDE OFFERS A WIDE VARIETY OF MATERIALS OF INTEREST TO TEACHERS, PARENTS, AIDES, ADMINISTRATORS AND RESEARCHERS INVOLVED IN EARLY CHILDHOOD EDUCATION. (AUTHOR/WY)

ED048933 PS004505
A NATIONAL SURVEY OF THE PARENT-CHILD CENTER PROGRAM. LAZAR, IRVING; AND OTHERS, MAR 70 539P.
EDRS PRICE MF-$0.65 HC-$19.74

THIS RESEARCH REPORT IS A DESCRIPTION AND ANALYSIS OF THE DEVELOPMENT AND STATUS OF THE FIRST YEAR OF OPERATION OF THE PARENT-CHILD CENTER (PCC) PROGRAM WITHIN PROJECT HEAD START. THE PERSPECTIVE OF THE REPORT IS NATIONAL, INDIVIDUAL CENTERS BEING REGARDED AS ILLUSTRATIVE EXAMPLES OF THE NATIONAL PROGRAM. BECAUSE OF THE EARLY STAGE OF DEVELOPMENT AND COMPLEXITY OF PCC ACTIVITIES, LITTLE ATTENTION IS FOCUSED ON OUTCOMES AND IMPACTS. THE CONCLUSIONS AND RECOMMENDATIONS OFFERED IN THIS REPORT MUST BE CONSIDERED IN THE CONTEXT OF THE EVOLUTIONARY NATURE OF PCC. CHAPTER TITLES INCLUDE: ORGANIZATIONAL DEVELOPMENT OF THE PARENT-CHILD CENTERS; THE PHYSICAL FACILITIES; THE PARENT-CHILD CENTER STAFF; THE FAMILIES SERVED; PROGRAMS FOR CHILDREN; PROGRAMS FOR PARENTS AND OTHER FAMILY MEMBERS; HEALTH SERVICES; SOCIAL SERVICES; AND COST ANALYSIS. SIX EXTENSIVE APPENDIXES, 45 TABLES, 12 GRAPHS, FOUR FIGURES, AND A BIBLIOGRAPHY ARE PROVIDED. A REVIEW AND SUMMARY OF THE REPORT IS AVAILABLE AS PS 004 526. (WY)

ED048934 PS004507
RADICAL SCHOOL REFORM. GROSS, BEATRICE, ED.; GROSS, RONALD, ED., 69 350P.
DOCUMENT NOT AVAILABLE FROM EDRS.
AVAILABLE FROM: SIMON & SCHUSTER, INC., 630 FIFTH AVENUE, ROCKEFELLER CENTER, NEW YORK, NEW YORK 10020 ($2.95, PAPERBACK)

THIS BOOK PROVIDES A COMPREHENSIVE EXAMINATION OF THE NATURE OF THE SCHOOL CRISIS AND THE WAYS IN WHICH RADICAL THINKERS AND EDUCATORS ARE DEALING WITH IT. EXCERPTS FROM THE WRITINGS OF JONATHAN KOZOL, JOHN HOLT, KENNETH CLARK, AND OTHERS ARE CONCERNED WITH THE REALITIES OF EDUCATION IN GHETTOS AND SUBURBS. PAUL GOODMAN, MARSHALL MCLUHAN, SYLVIA ASHTON-WARNER, AND OTHERS RAISE BASIC QUESTIONS ABOUT THE ROLE OF THE SCHOOL IN MODERN SOCIETY, AND DISCUSS NEW DIRECTIONS FOR GHETTO EDUCATION, COMMUNITY-RUN SCHOOLS, STUDENT FREEDOM AND PARTICIPATION, AND RELEVANT CURRICULA. ALMOST HALF THE BOOK CONSISTS OF FIRSTHAND REPORTS OF RADICAL SCHOOL REFORM IN PRACTICE FROM SUMMERHILL TO HARLEM. AMONG THE CONTRIBUTORS TO THIS SECTION ARE JOSEPH FEATHERSTONE, GEORGE DENNISON, HERBERT KOHL, AND OMAR KHAYYAM MOORE. (AJ)

ED048935 PS004514
PROGRAMS OF HEAD START PARENT INVOLVEMENT IN HAWAII. A SECTION OF THE FINAL REPORT FOR 1969-70. ADKINS, DOROTHY C., JAN 71 13P.
EDRS PRICE MF-$0.65 HC-$3.29

PRESENTS THE EVOLUTION OF PARTICIPATION PROGRAMS FOR HEAD START PARENTS WHICH WERE CONDUCTED BY THE UNIVERSITY OF HAWAII CENTER FOR RESEARCH IN EARLY CHILDHOOD EDUCATION FROM 1967-1968 THROUGH 1970. EACH YEAR'S SHIFTING EMPHASIS WAS BASED ON EXPERIENCE WITH PROGRAMS TRIED EARLIER, ON SHIFTING INTERESTS OF STAFF AND PARTICULAR COMMUNITIES INVOLVED IN OTHER ASPECTS OF THE YEAR'S RESEARCH PROGRAM, AND ON ASPECTS OF THE OVERALL RESEARCH DESIGN OF THAT YEAR. PROGRAMS OF GROUP MEETINGS AND INDIVIDUAL HOME VISITS WERE EXPLORED. VARIOUS TYPES OF PARENT PARTICIPATION PROGRAMS IN CONJUNCTION WITH CURRICULAR MODULES IN THE COGNITIVE AND MOTIVATIONAL REALMS WERE ASSESSED. THE MAJOR CONCLUSION IS THAT BROAD GENERALIZATION IS NOT POSSIBLE FROM SMALL AND SHORT TERM ATTEMPTS TO ALTER PARENTAL ATTITUDES AND PRACTICES. PARENT PROGRAMS MAY NOT BE THE MOST EFFECTIVE WAY TO IMPROVE COGNITIVE ABILITIES AND BEHAVIOR OF PRESCHOOL CHILDREN. (AUTHOR/WY)

ED048936 PS004515
THE ABILITY OF KINDERGARTEN AND FIRST GRADE CHILDREN TO USE THE TRANSITIVE PROPERTY OF THREE LENGTH RELATIONS IN THREE PERCEPTUAL SITUATIONS. DIVERS, BENJAMIN P., JR.; STEFFE, LESLIE P., 4 FEB 71 33P.
EDRS PRICE MF-$0.65 HC NOT AVAILABLE FROM EDRS.

ONE MAJOR PURPOSE OF THIS INVESTIGATION WAS TO DETERMINE AND COMPARE THE EFFECTS OF THREE DIFFERENT PERCEPTUAL SITUATIONS (SCREENING, NEUTRAL, AND CONFLICT) ON KINDERGARTEN AND FIRST GRADE CHILDREN'S ABILITY TO USE THE TRANSITIVE PROPERTY OF THE EQUIVALENCE RELATION "SAME LENGTH AS" AND THE TWO ORDER RELATIONS "LONGER THAN" AND "SHORTER THAN". A TOTAL OF 96 SUBJECTS (49 KINDERGARTEN AND 47 FIRST GRADE CHILDREN) WERE CHOSEN FROM THE LOCAL PUBLIC SCHOOL POPULATION. TRAINED EXAMINERS ADMINISTERED THE SPECIALLY DEVELOPED KNOWLEDGE OF TERMS TEST AND THE CONSERVATION OF LENGTH RELATIONS TEST (CLRT) INDIVIDUALLY TO THE CHILDREN. ON THE BASIS OF CLRT SCORES, SUBJECTS WERE CLASSIFIED AS BEING HIGH, MEDIUM, OR LOW IN CONSERVATION ABILITY. CLRT MATERIALS WERE RED, GREEN, AND BLUE STICKS, SODA STRAWS, AND PIPE CLEANERS WHICH THE CHILDREN JUDGED AND COMPARED FOR EQUIVALENCE IN LENGTH. RESULTS INDICATE (1) CHILDREN IN BOTH GRADE LEVELS AND IN ALL THREE CONSERVATION LEVELS WERE ABLE TO USE THE TRANSITIVE PROPERTY IN THE NEUTRAL SITUATION IN MANY MORE INSTANCES THAN IN EITHER THE SCREENING OR CONFLICT SITUATION AND (2) FIRST GRADE CHILDREN SIGNIFICANTLY OUTPERFORMED THE KINDERGARTEN CHILDREN. (WY)

ED048937 PS004517
AN INTEGRATED PROGRAM OF GROUP CARE AND EDUCATION FOR SOCIOECONOMICALLY ADVANTAGED AND DISADVANTAGED INFANTS. FOWLER, WILLIAM; AND OTHERS, 7 FEB 71 14P.
EDRS PRICE MF-$0.65 HC-$3.29

THE ONTARIO INSTITUTE FOR STUDIES IN EDUCATION AND THE CANADIAN MOTHERCRAFT SOCIETY COMPLETED THE FIRST YEAR OF THEIR 3-YEAR DAY CARE DEMONSTRATION PROJECT FOR ADVANTAGED AND DISADVANTAGED INFANTS FROM 3 TO 30 MONTHS OF AGE. THE PROGRAM WAS DESIGNED TO FACILITATE INFANTS' COGNITIVE, PERSONALITY, AND SOCIAL DEVELOPMENT THROUGH PERSONALIZED ADULT-CHILD INTERACTION, GUIDED LEARNING SITUATIONS, FREE PLAY AND SPECIALIZED CARE. PARENT GUIDANCE, TRAINING OF HIGH SCHOOL STUDENTS AS INFANT CARETAKER-TEACHERS, AND TEACHER INSERVICE EDUCATION WERE ALSO PROJECT COMPONENTS. INFANTS IN THE PROGRAM MADE SIGNIFICANT GAINS OVER THE FIRST YEAR IN MENTAL, SOCIAL, AND LANGUAGE DEVELOPMENT, ESPECIALLY FOR YOUNGER VERSUS OLDER INFANTS COMPARED WITH EXCLUSIVELY HOME-REARED CONTROLS. SUBSAMPLES OF ADVANTAGED INFANTS SHOWED MEAN TEST GAINS OF 30 TO 40 POINTS OVER 17 MONTHS AND DISADVANTAGED INFANTS 30 POINTS OVER 13 MONTHS. OTHER MEASURES OF SOCIOEMOTIONAL AND COGNITIVE DEVELOPMENT AND MEASURES OF STUDENT AND PARENT FUNCTIONING SHOWED GENERALLY POSITIVE RESULTS. THIS PAPER IS A MORE COMPLETE REPORT OF ED 041 632. (AUTHOR/WY)

ED048938 PS004520
EVALUATION GUIDE FOR EARLY CHILDHOOD EDUCATION PROGRAMS. , 69 23P.
EDRS PRICE MF-$0.65 HC-$3.29
AVAILABLE FROM: TEACHER EDUCATION, STATE DEPARTMENT OF EDUCATION, STATE OFFICE BUILDING, MONTGOMERY, ALABAMA 36104

THIS PUBLICATION IS A BULLETIN OF THE STANDARDS USED BY THE ALABAMA STATE DEPARTMENT OF EDUCATION IN 1969, FOR THE EVALUATION AND APPROVAL OF PROGRAMS OF TEACHER EDUCATION IN THE AREA OF EARLY CHILDHOOD. THE 14 STANDARDS ENUMERATED INCLUDE: INSTITUTION'S STATEMENT OF PURPOSE, ORGANIZATION AND ADMINISTRATION, PROGRAM OF INSTRUCTION, FACULTY, LIBRARY AND RELATED SOURCES, AND PHYSICAL FACILITIES. UNDER EACH STANDARD IS A NARRATIVE EXPLANATION OF STANDARD CONTENT. THESE INSTITUTION STANDARDS, DESIGNED FOR BACCALAUREATE AND MASTER'S DEGREE PROGRAMS IN EARLY CHILDHOOD EDUCATION, ARE USEFUL TO INSTITUTIONS WHICH PLAN TO DESIGN AND DEVELOP EARLY CHILDHOOD EDUCATION PROGRAMS. (AUTHOR/AJ)

ED048939 PS004524
INCREASING THE EFFECTIVENESS OF PARENTS-AS-TEACHERS. STERN, CAROLYN; AND OTHERS, DEC 70 43P.
EDRS PRICE MF-$0.65 HC-$3.29

THIS STUDY INVOLVED THE USE OF GROUP PROCESS TECHNIQUES IN MEETINGS AT WHICH PARENTS AND TEACHERS WERE ENCOURAGED TO EXPRESS THEIR FEELINGS, FRUSTRATIONS, NEEDS AND EXPECTATIONS. THE TWO HYPOTHESES TESTED WERE: (1) PARENTS PARTICIPATING IN THE ENCOUNTERS WILL EVIDENCE MORE DIRECT CONCERN FOR THEIR CHILDREN'S PRESCHOOL EDUCATION AND MORE FAVORABLE ATTITUDES TOWARD HEAD START THAN THOSE NOT ATTENDING SUCH MEETINGS; AND (2) THAT THE CHILDREN OF PARENTS PARTICIPATING WILL SCORE HIGHER ON TESTS OF LANGUAGE PERFORMANCE AND INFORMATION ACQUISITION THAN CHILDREN OF PARENTS NOT ATTENDING. THE STUDY INCLUDED TWO HEAD START CLASSES INVOLVING 30 BLACK, MEXICAN-AMERICAN, AND ANGLO CHILDREN. THE CHILDREN WERE PRETESTED AND POSTTESTED WITH THE PEABODY PICTURE VOCABULARY TEST, CALDWELL PRESCHOOL INVENTORY AND SITUATIONAL TEST OF COMPETENCE (MID-MEASURE). PARENTS WERE TESTED WITH PARENTS EXPECTATIONS FOR ACHIEVEMENT OF CHILDREN IN HEAD START (PEACH), PARENTS ATTITUDES TOWARD HEAD START (PATHS), AND THE "HOW I FEEL" MEASURE OF ALIENATION. DEMOGRAPHIC DATA WAS ALSO COLLECTED AND PARENTS AND TEACHERS COMPLETED THE SITUATION TEST OF COMPETENCE AS THEY EXPECTED THE CHILD TO RESPOND. RESULTS OF THE STUDY SHOWED THAT ONLY THE SECOND HYPOTHESIS TESTED WAS SUPPORTED. (AUTHOR/AJ)

ED048940 PS004525
THE NEW NURSERY SCHOOL RESEARCH PROJECT , 31 OCT 70 147P.
EDRS PRICE MF-$0.65 HC-$6.58

THE PRIMARY OBJECTIVES OF THE NEW NURSERY SCHOOL WERE TO INCREASE CHILDREN'S SENSORY AND PERCEPTUAL ACUITY, DEVELOP POSITIVE SELF CONCEPT, AND INCREASE LANGUAGE, CONCEPTUAL AND PROBLEM SOLVING ABILITIES. DURING 1969-1970 THE LONGITUDINAL STUDY, BEGUN IN 1964, INCLUDED 28 CHILDREN WHO WERE 3- AND 4-YEAR-OLDS FROM LOWER SOCIOECONOMIC HOMES CHARACTERIZED BY USE OF DIALECT OR PRIMARY SPEECH OF ANOTHER LANGUAGE AND LACK OF ENGLISH FLUENCY. TO DETERMINE THE EFFECTIVENESS OF AN OPEN, RESPONSIVE ENVIRONMENT IN LESSENING THE EDUCATIONAL GAP BETWEEN ADVANTAGED AND DISADVANTAGED CHILDREN, SEVERAL PROJECTS WERE UNDERTAKEN TO EXTEND AND EVALUATE THE WORK DONE IN PREVIOUS YEARS. THROUGH THE USE OF A MOBILE INSTRUCTIONAL LIBRARY, A HOME VISITATION PROGRAM WAS CONTINUED WHICH BROUGHT THE NEW NURSERY SCHOOL TEACHING STRATEGIES AND RELATED EDUCATIONAL MATERIALS DIRECTLY INTO THE HOMES OF THE PUPILS. A SMALL SCALE PROJECT TO STUDY THE FEASIBILITY OF A SPANISH TUTORIAL PROGRAM FOR PREKINDERGARTEN CHILDREN WAS BEGUN. A METHOD OF EVALUATING YOUNG CHILDREN'S COMPREHENSION OF KEY GRAMMATICAL ELEMENTS WAS USED, EVALUATED AND REVISED. RESULTS ARE DISCUSSED IN TERMS OF A COMPARATIVE ANALYSIS OF SEVERAL TESTING MEASURES. MORE THAN HALF OF THIS DOCUMENT CONSISTS OF TABLES AND SUPPLEMENTAL INFORMATION. (AUTHOR/AJ)

ED048941 PS004526
REVIEW AND SUMMARY OF A NATIONAL SURVEY OF THE PARENT-CHILD CENTER PROGRAM. COSTELLO, JOAN; BINSTOCK, ELEANOR, AUG 70 52P.
EDRS PRICE MF-$0.65 HC-$3.29

THIS DOCUMENT IS A SUMMARY OF THE COMPREHENSIVE FINAL REPORT, "A NATIONAL SURVEY OF THE PARENT-CHILD CENTER PROGRAM" (PS 004 505). THE SURVEY IS A DESCRIPTION AND ANALYSIS OF THE DEVELOPMENT AND STATUS OF THE FIRST YEAR'S OPERATION OF HEAD START'S PARENT-CHILD CENTER (PCC) PROGRAM. THE SECTIONAL HEADINGS DENOTE THE SCOPE OF THE REPORT: (1) HISTORY AND ORGANIZATIONAL PLAN OF THE PARENT AND CHILD CENTERS; (2) PCC FAMILIES; (3) CENTER FACILITIES; (4) HEALTH SERVICES; (5) PROGRAMS FOR CHILDREN; (6) PROGRAMS FOR PARENTS AND FAMILY MEMBERS; (7) PERSONNEL PRACTICES; (8) IMPACT OF PCC PROGRAM ON CHILDREN, FAMILIES AND COMMUNITIES; (9) COST ANALYSIS; AND (10) LESSONS FROM THE FIRST YEAR. THE EXTENSIVE TABLES, GRAPHS, AND REFERENCES AVAILABLE IN THE COMPREHENSIVE REPORT ARE NOT INCLUDED IN THIS SUMMARY. (AJ)

ED048942 PS004530
DIFFERENTIAL PERFORMANCE OF KINDERGARTEN CHILDREN ON TRANSITIVITY OF THREE MATCHING RELATIONS. OWENS, DOUGLAS T.; STEFFE, LESLIE P., 4 FEB 71 26P.
EDRS PRICE MF-$0.65 HC NOT AVAILABLE FROM EDRS.

THE MAJOR OBJECTIVE OF THIS STUDY WAS TO INVESTIGATE DIFFERENTIAL PERFORMANCES AMONG 5-YEAR-OLD CHILDREN WHEN USING TRANSITIVITY OF MATCHING RELATIONS. INSTRUMENTS WERE CONSTRUCTED TO MEASURE THE SUBJECTS' (1) KNOWLEDGE OF MATCHING RELATIONS, (2) ABILITY TO CONSERVE THE RELATIONS, AND (3) PROFICIENCY IN MAKING INFERENCES USING THE TRANSITIVE PROPERTY OF THE RELATIONS. THREE SPECIALLY DESIGNED TESTS, ADMINISTERED INDIVIDUALLY TO 21 BOYS AND 21 GIRLS, ASSESSED KNOWLEDGE OF RELATIONAL TERMINOLOGY, LEVEL OF CONSERVATION AND PERFORMANCE ON MANIPULATIVE TASKS (MATCHING, COMPARING, JUDGING QUANTITATIVE RELATIONS AMONG OBJECTS). A SURPRISING RESULT OF THIS INVESTIGATION WAS THAT SUBJECTS IN THE HIGH CATEGORY OF CONSERVATION DID NOT PERFORM SIGNIFICANTLY BETTER ON TRANSITIVITY THAN SUBJECTS IN THE LOW CATEGORY OF CONSERVATION FOR EACH RELATION. IN GENERAL, DIFFERENTIAL PERFORMANCE ON TRANSITIVITY BETWEEN EQUIVALENCE AND ORDER RELATIONAL GROUPS OCCURRED ONLY WITHIN THE HIGH CONSERVATION LEVEL. AN EXTENSIVE COMPARISON IS MADE BETWEEN PRESENT RESULTS AND SMEDSLUND'S (1963A) DATA FOR CONSERVATION AND TRANSITIVITY OF DISCONTINUOUS QUANTITY. (WY)

ED048943 PS004537
"NEED ACHIEVEMENT" TRAINING FOR HEAD START CHILDREN AND THEIR MOTHERS. KOWATRAKUL, SURANG; AND OTHERS, [70] 36P.
EDRS PRICE MF-$0.65 HC NOT AVAILABLE FROM EDRS.

THIS PAPER REPORTS A SHORT TERM INTERVENTION IN THE AREA OF "NEED TO ACHIEVE" AMONG DISADVANTAGED PRESCHOOLERS. CHANGES IN MEASURED INTELLIGENCE WERE ALSO EXAMINED. THE STUDY HYPOTHESIZED THAT CHILDREN RECEIVING NEED FOR ACHIEVEMENT ("N"-ACH) TRAINING WOULD SCORE HIGHER ON INTELLIGENCE TESTS AND EVIDENCE MORE OF AN INCREASE IN NEED FOR ACHIEVEMENT, AS MEASURED BY THE ARONSON GRAPHIC EXPRESSIONS, THAN CHILDREN NOT RECEIVING SUCH TRAINING. THE 84 BLACK SUBJECTS, 46 BOYS AND 38 GIRLS, WERE DIVIDED INTO TWO "N"-ACH TRAINING GROUPS AND TWO CONTROL GROUPS. ALL SUBJECTS WERE PRETESTED WITH THE ARONSON GRAPHIC EXPRESSIONS DESIGN. "N"-ACH TREATMENT FOR THE EXPERIMENTAL GROUPS CONSISTED OF ONE HOUR OF TRAINING EACH MORNING ON HEAD START SCHOOL DAYS FOR THREE MONTHS. THE TASKS OF THE TRAINER WERE: (1) TRAINING IN GOAL SETTING; (2) DEVELOPMENT OF ACHIEVEMENT LANGUAGE ("I WILL TRY HARDER," "I DID IT"); (3) DEVELOPMENT OF COGNITIVE SUPPORTS; AND (4) DEVELOPMENT OF GROUP SUPPORTS. POSTTESTS GIVEN WERE THE STANDFORD BINET AND ARONSON GRAPHIC EXPRESSIONS. THE TESTED IQ CHANGE OCCURRED IN THE PREDICTED DIRECTION BUT WAS NOT SIGNIFICANT AND THERE WERE NO SIGNIFICANT DIFFERENCES BETWEEN THE TWO GROUPS IN "N"-ACH. THE MOTHERS OF THE CHILDREN TESTED WERE ALSO SUBJECTS IN A SEPARATE "N"-ACH TRAINING PROGRAM. [NOT AVAILABLE IN HARD COPY DUE TO MARGINAL LEGIBILITY OF ORIGINAL DOCUMENT.] (AJ)

ED048944 PS004541
COMMUNITY COORDINATED CHILD CARE: A FEDERAL PARTNERSHIP IN BEHALF OF CHILDREN. SUMMARY. , 31 DEC 70 29P.
EDRS PRICE MF-$0.65 HC-$3.29

DURING 1969 AND 1970, THE DAY CARE AND CHILD DEVELOPMENT COUNCIL OF AMERICA, INC. (DCCDCA) PROVIDED TECHNICAL ASSISTANCE TO CITIZENS' COMMITTEES FORMED IN A NUMBER OF COMMUNITIES AND STATES TO PARTICIPATE IN THE FEDERALLY SPONSORED COMMUNITY COORDINATED CHILD CARE (4-C) PROGRAM. THIS SUMMARY OF THE PILOT 4-C PROGRAM INCLUDES BACKGROUND, RESULTS, SUCCESS FACTORS, HIGHLIGHTS OF FINDINGS AND RECOMMENDATIONS, AND IS CONDENSED FROM A 506 PAGE FINAL REPORT (PS 004 455) ON THE PROGRAM SUBMITTED BY THE DCCDCA TO HEW'S OFFICE OF CHILD DEVELOPMENT. AN EXTENSIVE GROUP OF CHARTS AND TABLES IS INCLUDED IN THE DOCUMENT. (AUTHOR/AJ)

ED048945 PS004542
SIMULATION ACTIVITIES FOR TRAINING PARENTS AND TEACHERS AS EDUCATIONAL PARTNERS: A REPORT AND EVALUATION. CHAMPAGNE, DAVID W.; GOLDMAN, RICHARD M., 6 FEB 71 31P.
EDRS PRICE MF-$0.65 HC-$3.29

THIS REPORT SUMMARIZES A PROGRAM TO HELP PARENTS LEARN SOME SPECIFIC TEACHING SKILLS TO HELP THEIR CHILDREN LEARN. TO DEVELOP A POSITIVE REINFORCEMENT TEACHING STYLE WAS THE BASIC OBJECTIVE BECAUSE IT IS BOTH THE MOST SIMPLE STYLE TO LEARN AND THE MOST POWERFUL STYLE FOR BUILDING SUCCESS IN LEARNING. ROLE-PLAY STIMULATION IN SMALL GROUPS WAS THE BASIC STRATEGY FOR BOTH THE TEACHERS' LEARNING TO TEACH PARENTS AND FOR PARENTS LEARNING TO TEACH THEIR CHILDREN. TEACHERS WERE TRAINED FOR THREE DAYS ON MATERIALS EXPLAINING PROGRAM PURPOSE, STRATE-

GIES, ROLE-PLAY EXPERIENCES, AND THE KINDS OF SENSITIVITY NECESSARY TO BE EFFECTIVE TEACHERS OF PARENTS. EACH OF THESE TEACHERS TRAINED THREE TO FIVE PARENTS FOR 2 1/2 DAYS. NEXT, THE PARENTS UNDER DIRECT SUPERVISION OF THE PROFESSIONAL TEACHERS TAUGHT KINDERGARTEN AGE CHILDREN IN A HEAD START SUMMER PROGRAM. EVALUATIONS OF THE PROGRAM WERE CONDUCTED UTILIZING: (1) ANALYSIS OF AUDIO-TAPED SAMPLES OF PARENTS' TEACHING, (2) WRITTEN OBSERVATIONS OF PARENTS' AND TEACHERS' TRAINING, (3) DAILY LOGS AND INTERVIEWS WITH TEACHERS AND SUPERVISOR. ELEVEN OF THE 12 PARENTS INCREASED THEIR USE OF POSITIVE REINFORCEMENT. EIGHT OF THE 12 PARENTS INCREASED THE VARIETY OF REINFORCERS USED. APPENDIXES AND TABLES INCLUDED. (AUTHOR/AJ)

ED048946 PS004653
A LONGITUDINAL ASSESSMENT OF THINKING ABILITY OF PRELITERATE CHILDREN DURING A TWO-YEAR PERIOD. FINAL REPORT. BALL, RACHEL S., MAR 71 48P.
EDRS PRICE MF-$0.65 HC-$3.29

THE PRESENT REPORT IS THE FOURTH OF A SERIES CONCERNED WITH MENTAL FUNCTIONING AND ITS DEVELOPMENT IN EARLY CHILDHOOD. THE STUDY ATTEMPTED TO DISCOVER WHETHER THE SAME CHILDREN TESTED AT INTERVALS OF ONE OR MORE YEARS SHOWED SIMILAR DEVELOPMENT IN THINKING ABILITY FROM AGE TO AGE. LONGITUDINAL TEST PROTOCOLS WERE OBTAINED FOR 92 CHILDREN AT 3 YEARS WHO WERE RETESTED AT 5 YEARS AND 55 CHILDREN AT 4 YEARS WHO WERE RETESTED AT 5 YEARS, MAKING 147 CHILDREN INCLUDED FOR TESTS AT THE 5-YEAR LEVEL. A QUESTIONNAIRE COVERING THE ENVIRONMENTAL INFLUENCE IN THE LIFE OF THE 5-YEAR-OLD WAS ASKED OF EACH MOTHER. QUESTIONNAIRE RESULTS WERE ANALYZED TO SEE WHAT RELATIONSHIPS TO CHILDREN'S THINKING ABILITY COULD BE FOUND. FACTOR PATTERNS WERE COMPARED ACROSS THE THREE AGE LEVELS. RESULTS INDICATE THAT FIVE SPECIFIC SORTS OF THINKING ABILITY CAN BE IDENTIFIED. IN GENERAL, THE PATTERNS OF THINKING SHOWN BY PRESCHOOL CHILDREN ARE RETAINED THROUGHOUT THE THREE YEAR AGE RANGE. HOWEVER, THE PATTERN OF DEVELOPMENT OF EACH CHILD VARIES NOT ONLY IN GENERAL RATE OF CHANGE BUT ALSO FOR EACH APTITUDE. ONE CLEAR IMPLICATION OF THIS STUDY IS THAT ASSIGNMENT TO A "TRACK" RESULTS IN A GREAT WASTE OF POTENTIAL BECAUSE INDIVIDUAL RATES OF DEVELOPMENT AND DIFFERENT APTITUDES VARY SO GREATLY FROM YEAR TO YEAR. (WY)

ED048947 PS004665
HEAD START CURRICULUM MODELS: A REFERENCE LIST. (REVISED EDITION). , FEB 71 27P.
EDRS PRICE MF-$0.65 HC-$3.29

THIS BIBLIOGRAPHY LISTS REFERENCES TO BOOKS, ARTICLES, CURRICULUM AIDS, PROGRESS REPORTS AND OTHER WORK RELATED TO THE 11 DIFFERENT HEAD START CURRICULUM MODELS NOW BEING TESTED EXPERIMENTALLY IN MANY COMMUNITIES. THE MODELS, DEVELOPED BY EXPERIENCED EDUCATORS, ARE: ACADEMICALLY ORIENTED PRESCHOOL; BEHAVIOR ANALYSIS MODEL; RESPONSIVE ENVIRONMENT CORPORATION; TUCSON EARLY EDUCATION MODEL; BANK STREET EARLY CHILDHOOD CENTER; PARENT EDUCATION PROJECT; RESPONSIVE MODEL; INSTITUTE FOR DEVELOPMENTAL STUDIES; PRIMARY EDUCATION PROJECT; EDUCATIONAL DEVELOPMENT CENTER; AND COGNITIVELY ORIENTED CURRICULUM. READINGS WHICH GIVE AN OVERVIEW OF THE CURRICULUM MODELS PROJECT ARE ALSO LISTED. INFORMATION IS INCLUDED ON ORDERING THOSE DOCUMENTS WHICH ARE AVAILABLE THROUGH THE ERIC SYSTEM. OTHER WORKS ARE AVAILABLE AT LIBRARIES OR FROM AUTHORS OR PUBLISHERS CITED. A LIST OF ADDRESSES OF THE EDUCATORS RESPONSIBLE FOR THE MODELS IS GIVEN. (NH)

ED049809 PS002532
CAN I LOVE THIS PLACE? A STAFF GUIDE TO OPERATING CHILD CARE CENTERS FOR THE DISADVANTAGED. MCKEE, CHARLES J. L., ED.; WEIL, LINN B., ED., 69 60P.
EDRS PRICE MF-$0.65 HC-$3.29

THIS STAFF GUIDE IS DIRECTED TO INDIVIDUALS OR GROUPS WHO ARE INTERESTED IN THE ESTABLISHMENT AND OPERATION OF CHILD CARE CENTERS FOR DISADVANTAGED CHILDREN AND INCLUDES DISCUSSIONS OF STAFF SCHEDULES, DUTIES, SUPPLIES, HEALTH AND SAFETY. THE FIRST SECTION DEALS WITH DAILY ROUTINES AND DISCUSSES CARE FOR INFANTS, TODDLERS, PRE-SCHOOL AND SCHOOL-AGE CHILDREN. HELPFUL FOOD SERVICE IDEAS ARE PROVIDED, INCLUDING CHECK LISTS AND ENUMERATION OF SUPPLIES NEEDED. THE SECOND SECTION DESCRIBES SPECIFIC ACTIVITIES SUCH AS A RHYTHM BAND, PAINTING, COOKING, GROUP GAMES, SCIENCE, AND STORIES. A LIST OF MATERIALS NEEDED, STEP-BY-STEP INSTRUCTIONS, AND AGE GROUP RECOMMENDATIONS ARE GIVEN FOR EACH ACTIVITY. (AJ)

ED049810 PS003152
THE DAY CARE NEIGHBOR SERVICE: A HANDBOOK FOR THE ORGANIZATION AND OPERATION OF A NEW APPROACH TO FAMILY DAY CARE. COLLINS, ALICE H.; WATSON, EUNICE L., 69 63P.
EDRS PRICE MF-$0.65 HC-$3.29
AVAILABLE FROM: FIELD STUDY OF THE NEIGHBORHOOD FAMILY DAY CARE SYSTEM, 2856 NORTHWEST SAVIER, PORTLAND, OREGON 97210

THE DAY CARE NEIGHBOR SERVICE MAKES IT POSSIBLE TO PROVIDE SOCIAL SERVICE AT THE NEIGHBORHOOD LEVEL WHERE WORKING MOTHERS, WITHOUT BENEFIT OF ANY SOCIAL AGENCY, MAKE PRIVATE AND INFORMAL DAY CARE ARRANGEMENTS WITH NEIGHBORHOOD SITTERS. IT MAKES USE OF A SOCIAL WORK CONSULTANT TO FIND THE KEY INDIVIDUAL IN EACH NEIGHBORHOOD WHO IS ALREADY INFORMALLY HELPING HER NEIGHBORS TO MAKE DAY CARE ARRANGEMENTS. THE AIM OF THE SERVICE IS TO CONTRIBUTE TO THE QUALITY AND STABILITY OF THESE PRIVATE FAMILY DAY CARE ARRANGEMENTS. THIS BOOKLET DESCRIBES THE SERVICE METHODS AND TECHNIQUES OF INTERVENTION WHICH ARE BASED ON A SUBTLE FORM OF SOCIAL WORK CONSULTATION. ALSO EXAMINED ARE CRITICAL ISSUES AND PROBLEMS AN INNOVATOR MIGHT ENCOUNTER IN ESTABLISHING A SIMILAR PROGRAM. THE SHARP FOCUS OF THE SERVICE, AS WELL AS ITS ECONOMY, RECOMMEND IT AS AN ADJUNCT OF DAY CARE PROGRAMS WHEREVER PRIVATE FAMILY DAY CARE ARRANGEMENTS ARE SOUGHT. (WY)

ED049811 PS003673
LANGUAGE ACQUISITION AND COGNITIVE DEVELOPMENT. OLSON, DAVID R., 12 JUN 68 137P.
DOCUMENT NOT AVAILABLE FROM EDRS.
AVAILABLE FROM: HAYWOOD, C.H. "SOCIAL-CULTURAL ASPECTS OF MENTAL RETARDATION." SEPTEMBER 1970 APPLETON-CENTURY-CROFTS, 440 PARK AVE., S., NEW YORK, NEW YORK 10016 (PAPER, $6.25)

THIS PAPER ANALYTICALLY REVIEWS THE LITERATURE ON COGNITIVE DEVELOPMENT, PARTICULARLY AS IT RELATES TO THE ACQUISITION OF LANGUAGE. OF PRIMARY CONCERN ARE THE BASIC COGNITIVE PROCESSES OF PERCEPTUAL GROUPINGS, CONCEPTS AND RELATIONS, AND MEMORY. DISCUSSED ARE THE ACQUISITION OF LANGUAGE, SOME ASPECTS OF THE NATURE OF LANGUAGE AND LANGUAGE DEVELOPMENT. ANOTHER SECTION DEALS WITH COGNITIVE DEVELOPMENT, WHICH IS DIVIDED INTO DISCUSSIONS OF PERCEPTION AND PERCEPTUAL SCHEMATA AND CONCEPTS AND CONCEPTUAL SYSTEMS. A FINAL SECTION ON LANGUAGE AND THOUGHT SUMMARIZES AND CONCLUDES THE DOCUMENT. EXTENSIVE REFERENCES ARE INCLUDED. (WY)

ED049812 PS004490
A TEACHING LEARNING SCHEMA FOR TEACHER TRAINING AND CURRICULUM DEVELOPMENT IN EARLY EDUCATION. HODGES, WALTER L., 23 OCT 70 41P.
EDRS PRICE MF-$0.65 HC-$3.29

THE PROCESS ORIENTED INTERACTIVE LEARNING SYSTEM POSTULATED IN THIS PAPER STARTS WITH THE GENERATION OF A SET OF PROCESS OBJECTIVES FOR CHILDREN WHICH ARE BASED ON THE PRINCIPLES OF DEVELOPMENT - INTELLECTUAL AND SOCIAL - AND RELATED TO THE SUBSTANCE OF THE BASIC GOALS WHICH SOCIETY HOLDS FOR EDUCATION: READING, LANGUAGE, NUMBER, INDEPENDENCE, AND COOPERATION. A SEQUENTIAL FLOW OF ACTIVITIES FOR BOTH TEACHERS AND PUPILS IS OUTLINED AND FIVE IMPLICATIONS ARISE. (1) TEACHERS MUST PROVIDE OPPORTUNITIES FOR THE KINDS OF PUPIL BEHAVIOR THAT CAN BE REINFORCED. (2) PRIORITY MUST BE GIVEN TO PROCESSES WHICH PERMIT THE CHILD TO TRANSFER THESE PROCESSES FROM ONE LEARNING SITUATION TO ANOTHER. (3) THE TEACHER SHOULD APPROACH TEACHING WITH AN EXPERIMENTAL ATTITUDE. (4) TEACHING INCLUDES BOTH ACTIVE AND PASSIVE PROCESSES. (5) EARLY CHILDHOOD EDUCATION MUST CONTINUE TO BE ACUTELY SENSITIVE TO THE SOCIAL AND PERSONAL CONSEQUENCES OF THE PROGRESSIVE ACHIEVEMENT DECREMENT IN DISADVANTAGED CHILDREN. IF THIS LEARNING SYSTEM BECOMES SUCCESSFUL IN GUIDING PROGRAM DEVELOPMENT, THERE SHOULD BE LESS NEED FOR SPECIALIZED PROGRAMS SUCH AS THOSE DESIGNED FOR CHILDREN WITH LEARNING DISABILITIES. (WY)

ED049813 PS004497
CORRELATION OF PAIRED-ASSOCIATE PERFORMANCE WITH SCHOOL ACHIEVEMENT AS A FUNCTION OF TASK AND SAMPLE VARIATION. FELDMAN, DAVID H.; JOHNSON, LEE ELLEN, FEB 71 24P.
EDRS PRICE MF-$0.65 HC-$3.29

TO STUDY THE EFFECTS OF TASK AND SAMPLE VARIATION UPON PAIRED-ASSOCIATES (PA) PERFORMANCE, SIX THIRD-GRADE AND SIX SIXTH-GRADE CLASSES IN TWO URBAN SCHOOLS WERE TESTED ON TWO PA TASKS, ONE PAIRING PICTURES OF FAMILIAR OBJECTS (PA-CF), THE OTHER PAIRING NONSENSE SYLLABLES WITH JAPANESE "KANJI" (PA-K). HYPOTHESES TESTED WERE: (1) MEAN LEVEL OF PERFORMANCE IS HIGHER FOR PA-CF THAN FOR PA-K; (2) THERE IS AN SES-RELATED DIFFERENCE IN PERFORMANCE ON PA-K BUT NOT ON PA-CF; (3) PA-K IS MORE HIGHLY CORRELATED WITH SCHOOL ACHIEVEMENT THAN IS PA-CF; (4) THE VARIANCE SHARED BY PA-K AND SCHOOL ACHIEVEMENT IS INDEPENDENT OF VARIANCE SHARED BY THE TWO PA TASKS. RESULTS PROVIDED GENERAL SUPPORT FOR THE HYPOTHESES, BUT SOME INCONSISTENT RESULTS ARE DISCUSSED. (AUTHOR)

ED049814 PS004506
THE NEW YORK STATE EXPERIMENTAL PREKINDERGARTEN PROGRAM. SUMMARY REPORT, 1969-70. , NOV 70 55P.
EDRS PRICE MF-$0.65 HC-$3.29

THIS FOURTH YEAR REPORT SUMMARIZES THE SERVICES RENDERED DURING 1969-1970 BY THE NEW YORK STATE EXPERIMENTAL PREKINDERGARTEN PROGRAM AND INCLUDES A PARTIAL EVALUATION OF THE ACCOMPLISHMENTS OF THE PROGRAM AS COMPARED TO ITS STATED GOALS. THE REPORT IS BASED ON QUESTIONNAIRE RESPONSES BY 49 OF THE 50 PROGRAMS, INCLUDING NEW YORK CITY. BECAUSE OF ITS COMPLEXITY, THE NEW YORK CITY DATA IS PRESENTED IN A SEPARATE

SECTION. SEVEN DEMONSTRATION CENTERS FOR INSERVICE EDUCATION ARE INCLUDED IN THE 50 PROGRAMS. ANSWERS TO THE SURVEY QUESTIONNAIRE PROVIDE ANECDOTAL RECORDS, STATISTICAL DATA, AND SUBJECTIVE DESCRIPTIONS OF TECHNIQUES USED TO ACHIEVE GOALS. TOPICS COVERED ARE: RECRUITMENT AND SELECTION OF CHILDREN; PLANNING AND PROGRAMING IN THE CLASSROOM; PARENT INVOLVEMENT; EVIDENCE OF GROWTH AND DEVELOPMENT; AND PLANNING FOR CONTINUING GOALS IN KINDERGARTEN AND PRIMARY PROGRAMS. (NH)

ED049815 PS004509
RESEARCH AND DEVELOPMENT REGISTER IN EARLY CHILDHOOD EDUCATION, 1970. , MAR 71 229P.
EDRS PRICE MF-$0.65 HC-$9.87
AVAILABLE FROM: NATIONAL PROGRAM ON EARLY CHILDHOOD EDUCATION, CEMREL, INC., 10646 ST. CHARLES ROCK ROAD, ST. ANN, MISSOURI 63074 ($2.30)

THE PURPOSE OF THIS REGISTER IS TO IDENTIFY PERSONS WORKING IN THE FIELD OF EARLY CHILDHOOD EDUCATION, 1479 LISTINGS ARE INCLUDED. EACH ENTRY GIVES NAME, ADDRESS, PRESENT POSITION; EDUCATION, WORK IN PROGRESS AND CURRENT INTEREST. TWENTY FIVE PAGES OF CHARTS CATEGORIZE SPECIFIC INTEREST INFORMATION FOR EACH RESPONDENT. LISTINGS FOR THE REGISTER WERE OBTAINED AS A RESULT OF RESPONSES TO REQUESTS FOR VITA INFORMATION. (AJ)

ED049816 PS004511
PREPRIMARY ENROLLMENT, OCTOBER 1969. HURD, GORDON E., 70 29P.
EDRS PRICE MF-$0.65 HC NOT AVAILABLE FROM EDRS.
AVAILABLE FROM: SUPERINTENDENT OF DOCUMENTS, U.S. GOVERNMENT PRINTING OFFICE, WASHINGTON, D.C. 20402 ($0.35, DOCUMENT CATALOG NO. HE5.220:20079-69)

THIS STUDY, BASED ON INFORMATION COLLECTED BY THE U.S. BUREAU OF THE CENSUS IN ITS CURRENT POPULATION SURVEY, SHOWS THE NUMBER OF CHILDREN 3 TO 5 YEARS OLD IN THE UNITED STATES AND THE EXTENT OF THEIR ENROLLMENT IN PUBLIC AND NONPUBLIC PREPRIMARY PROGRAMS. THIS SURVEY RELATED THE PREPRIMARY ENROLLMENT TO SEVERAL SOCIOECONOMIC FACTORS: FAMILY INCOME, OCCUPATION OF HEAD OF HOUSEHOLD, RESIDENCE (METROPOLITAN, RURAL, ETC.), FULL-DAY OR PART-DAY ATTENDANCE, AND GEOGRAPHICAL REGION. THE DATA REVEALED THAT OVER 40% OF 3- AND 4-YEAR-OLDS ENROLLED WERE FROM FAMILIES WITH INCOME ABOVE $10,000; YET, REGARDLESS OF INCOME, SIGNIFICANTLY MORE NEGRO 3- AND 4-YEAR-OLDS WERE ENROLLED. CHILDREN FROM FARM FAMILIES HAD THE LOWEST ENROLLMENT RATES, WHILE THOSE FROM WHITE-COLLAR FAMILIES RATED HIGHEST. RELATIVELY HIGH ENROLLMENT RATES ARE SHOWN FOR CHILDREN FROM FAMILIES WHO REPORTED NO HOUSEHOLD HEAD. HIGHEST RATES WERE COMPUTED FOR CHILDREN LIVING IN METROPOLITAN AREAS OUTSIDE THE CENTRAL CITIES. THE WEST HAD THE HIGHEST ENROLLMENT PERCENTAGE; THE SOUTH, THE LOWEST. MOST CHILDREN ATTENDED PART-DAY CLASSES. APPROXIMATELY THREE-FOURTHS OF THE DOCUMENT CONSISTS OF TABLES AND AN APPENDIX. (AJ)

ED049817 PS004512
A RESOURCE AND REFERENCE BIBLIOGRAPHY IN EARLY CHILDHOOD EDUCATION AND DEVELOPMENTAL PSYCHOLOGY: THE AFFECTIVE DOMAIN. FELDMAN, RONALD, COMP.; COOPERSMITH, STANLEY, COMP., 71 155P.
EDRS PRICE MF-$0.65 HC-$6.58

THIS BIBLIOGRAPHY PROVIDES A COMPREHENSIVE LISTING OF THE REFERENCE LITERATURE IN EARLY CHILDHOOD (AGES 2-9) PSYCHOLOGY AND EDUCATION DEALING WITH THE AFFECTIVE DOMAIN. CATEGORIES SUCH AS ACHIEVEMENT MOTIVATION; AGGRESSION; ANGER AND FRUSTRATION; CHARACTER AND MORAL DEVELOPMENT; CREATIVITY; GAMES; AND SOCIAL BEHAVIOR ARE INCLUDED. ONE OF THE 27 SECTIONS LISTS GENERAL REFERENCES IN THE FIELD OF EDUCATION AND CHILD DEVELOPMENT AND INCLUDES BOOKS, ANTHOLOGIES, AND PAPERS. (REFERENCES AND MATERIAL RELEVANT TO THE COGNITIVE DOMAIN WILL APPEAR IN A SEPARATE REPORT.) THE BIBLIOGRAPHY WAS PREPARED FOR USE BY BOTH THE PRACTITIONER AND THE RESEARCHER AND INCLUDES NONTECHNICAL TREATMENTS OF SUBJECTS AS WELL AS MAJOR RESEARCH ARTICLES. ARTICLES PUBLISHED WITHIN THE PAST TEN YEARS (1960-1969), AND ESPECIALLY WITHIN THE PAST FIVE YEARS (1965-1969), ARE EMPHASIZED. FOUR DIFFERENT TYPES OF ARTICLES ARE ENTERED FOR EACH TOPIC: THEORETICAL TREATMENTS; SPECIFIC RESEARCH FINDINGS; TEACHER PRACTICES; AND CURRICULAR MATERIAL. A CODE IDENTIFIES LISTINGS OF PARTICULAR USE TO PERSONS INVOLVED IN TEACHING OR CURRICULUM DESIGN, AND LISTINGS WHICH CONTAIN A REVIEW OF THE LITERATURE. AVAILABILITY INFORMATION IS ALSO GIVEN. (AUTHOR/NH)

ED049818 PS004516
A DEVELOPMENTAL LEARNING APPROACH TO INFANT CARE IN A GROUP SETTING. FOWLER, WILLIAM, FEB 71 51P.
EDRS PRICE MF-$0.65 HC-$3.29

THIS CONFERENCE PAPER HIGHLIGHTS ONE INFANT EDUCATION PROJECT AS A SUCCESSFUL EXAMPLE OF A GENERAL, PERVASIVE APPROACH TO STIMULATION IN A GROUP SETTING. THE ONTARIO INSTITUTE AND THE CANADIAN MOTHERCRAFT SOCIETY HAVE COMPLETED THE FIRST YEAR OF THEIR 3-YEAR DAY CARE DEMONSTRATION PROJECT FOR ADVANTAGED AND DISADVANTAGED INFANTS FROM 3 TO 30 MONTHS OF AGE. THE PROGRAM HAD BEEN DESIGNED TO FACILITATE INFANTS' COGNITIVE, PERSONALITY, AND SOCIAL DEVELOPMENT THROUGH PERSONALIZED ADULT-CHILD INTERACTION, GUIDED LEARNING SITUATIONS, FREE PLAY AND SPECIALIZED CARE. INFANTS IN THE PROGRAM MADE SIGNIFICANT GAINS OVER THE FIRST YEAR IN MENTAL, SOCIAL, AND LANGUAGE DEVELOPMENT, ESPECIALLY FOR YOUNGER VERSUS OLDER INFANTS COMPARED WITH EXCLUSIVELY HOME-REARED CONTROLS. MEASURES OF CARETAKER AND PARENT FUNCTIONING ALSO SHOWED GENERALLY POSITIVE RESULTS. IT IS SUGGESTED THAT INVOLVEMENT, ENTHUSIASM, AND COORDINATION OF PARENT CARE AND TEACHING ACTIVITIES WERE ESPECIALLY INFLUENTIAL IN THE PROJECT'S SUCCESS. THE IMPORTANCE OF WARM, SENSITIVE RELATIONS WITH BABIES IN BOTH TEACHING AND NONTEACHING SITUATIONS IS EMPHASIZED. THE MAGNITUDE OF GAINS FOR BOTH ADVANTAGED AND DISADVANTAGED CHILDREN SUGGESTS A RANGE OF POTENTIAL GREATER THAN USUALLY REALIZED. SEE ALSO PS 004 517 AND ED 041 632. (WY)

ED049819 PS004521
CHILD DEVELOPMENT RESEARCH UNIT PROGRESS REPORT, FEBRUARY, 1970. , FEB 70 35P.
EDRS PRICE MF-$0.65 HC-$3.29

TO INSURE THE MOST ACCURATE RESEARCH, IT IS NECESSARY TO HAVE TEAMS OF SCIENTISTS FROM THE CULTURE BEING STUDIED AND FROM A CONTRASTING CULTURE. THE INDIGENOUS MEMBERS OF THE TEAM PROVIDE A SENSITIVITY TO NUANCES OF MEANING AND INTERPRETATIONS OF INTENT OF BEHAVIOR THAT CANNOT EASILY BE RECOGNIZED BY AN OUTSIDER. THE OUTSIDER TEAM MEMBERS WILL CONTRIBUTE OBJECTIVITY TO THE RESEARCH. WORKING UNDER THIS PRINCIPLE, THE CHILD DEVELOPMENT RESEARCH UNIT PROVIDES AN APPRENTICE PROGRAM TO TRAIN INDIGENOUS BEHAVIORAL SCIENTISTS FOR RESEARCH IN KENYA. STUDENTS AT THE UNIVERSITY OF EAST AFRICA ARE HIRED AS APPRENTICES DURING THEIR SUMMER VACATIONS. EACH FIELD TEAM ESTABLISHES A PANEL COMMUNITY, A SET OF HOUSEHOLDS AMONG WHICH THE MOTHERS PARTICIPATE TOGETHER IN ACTIVITIES AND FORM A SOCIAL NETWORK INCLUDING AT LEAST 100 PREADOLESCENT CHILDREN. SINCE EACH FIELD TEAM DESIGNS ITS OWN RESEARCH, MANY VARIED FACTORS INFLUENCING THE WAY IN WHICH CHILDREN LEARN HAVE BEEN EXPLORED, INCLUDING: SALIENCE OF THE FATHER, COMPOSITION OF THE HOUSEHOLD, SIBLING ORDER, KINSHIP NETWORK, NATURE OF TASK ASSIGNMENT, SCHOOLING, MOTHER'S TEACHING STYLE, AND THE EXPERIENCE OF INITIATION. OTHER STUDIES HAVE DEALT WITH PHYSICAL GROWTH, HEALTH, MOTIVATION, SOCIAL BEHAVIOR, AND SOCIAL INSTITUTIONS. BRIEF SUMMARY STATEMENTS OF THESE STUDIES ARE INCLUDED IN THIS DOCUMENT. (AUTHOR/AJ)

ED049820 PS004522
PROJECT GENESIS. FINAL REPORT. JENS, DOROTHY, 70 123P.
EDRS PRICE MF-$0.65 HC-$6.58

PROJECT GENESIS IS A PREVENTATIVE PROGRAM WHICH TRIES TO IDENTIFY POTENTIAL LEARNING DEVIANCIES BEFORE CHILDREN ENTER KINDERGARTEN, AND WHICH PROVIDES INDIVIDUALIZED PROGRAMMING TO OFFSET FUTURE LEARNING PROBLEMS. CLINICS HELD IN THE SPRING TEST EACH CHILD ENTERING KINDERGARTEN THE FOLLOWING FALL ON PERCEPTUAL-MOTOR ABILITIES, HEARING, SPEECH, LANGUAGE DEVELOPMENT, VISION, DEVELOPMENTAL MATURITY, AND LEARNING READINESS. ANY CHILD WHO DISPLAYS A POTENTIAL LEARNING PROBLEM DURING THE SCREENING HAS AN INDIVIDUALIZED PROGRAM OF LEARNING ACTIVITIES DEVELOPED FOR HIM BY A MASTER TEACHER TRAINED IN DEVELOPMENTAL LEARNING. A PERCEPTUAL-MOTOR AIDE AND A VISION CONSULTANT ASSIST IN PROGRAM PLANNING. THE PRESCRIBED PROGRAM IS CARRIED OUT THROUGH INDIVIDUAL WEEKLY OR DAILY SESSIONS. THE TEACHER IN EACH CHILD'S REGULAR CLASSROOM AND THE CHILD'S PARENTS ALSO PARTICIPATE. (NH)

ED049821 PS004523
THE EFFECTS OF INSTRUCTION ON THE DEVELOPMENT OF THE CONCEPT OF CONSERVATION OF NUMEROUSNESS BY KINDERGARTEN CHILDREN. REPORT FROM THE PROJECT ON INDIVIDUALLY GUIDED ELEMENTARY MATHEMATICS BENZINGER, THOMAS L., OCT 70 46P.
EDRS PRICE MF-$0.65 HC-$3.29

FORTY KINDERGARTEN CHILDREN AT THE STEPHEN BULL SCHOOL IN RACINE, WISCONSIN WERE TESTED TO DETERMINE THE EFFECTS OF A SEQUENCE OF 12 EXPERIMENTAL LESSONS ON THE ABILITY OF KINDERGARTEN CHILDREN TO RECOGNIZE AND CONSERVE NUMEROUSNESS. SUBJECTS WERE 40-LOW-TO-MIDDLE SOCIOECONOMIC LEVEL CHILDREN DIVIDED INTO TREATMENT AND CONTROL GROUPS. A SPECIALLY DEVELOPED TEST OF NUMEROUSNESS (ARITHMETIC READINESS) SERVED AS A PRE- AND POSTTEST. THE LESSONS WERE DESIGNED TO GIVE EXPERIENCE WITH ONE-TO-ONE CORRESPONDENCE AND

COMPARISONS BY COUNTING, RELATIVE SIZE AND/OR RELATIVE DENSITY. NO SIGNIFICANT DIFFERENCES WERE OBSERVED BETWEEN THE MEAN GAIN SCORES OF THE EXPERIMENTAL AND CONTROL GROUPS. HOWEVER, SIGNIFICANT DIFFERENCES WERE OBSERVED BETWEEN THE MEAN GAIN SCORES OF CHILDREN IN THE TREATMENT GROUPS WHO ATTENDED THE HALF-DAY SESSION AND THOSE ATTENDING A SPECIAL FULL-DAY PROGRAM. A SIMILAR RESULT WAS OBSERVED WITHIN THE CONTROL GROUPS. RESULTS INDICATE THAT THE LESSONS USED IN THIS EXPERIMENT DID NOT ALONE SUFFICIENTLY ENHANCE THE SUBJECTS' ABILITY TO CONSERVE NUMEROUSNESS, BUT THAT THEY SHOULD PROVIDE AN EFFECTIVE SUPPLEMENT TO FORMAL ACTIVITY WITH NUMBER CONCEPTS. (AUTHOR/WY)

ED049822 PS004527
AN ANNOTATED BIBLIOGRAPHY ON EARLY CHILDHOOD. 70 107P.
DOCUMENT NOT AVAILABLE FROM EDRS.
AVAILABLE FROM: PUBLICATIONS DISTRIBUTION SERVICES, UNIVERSITY OF MICHIGAN, ANN ARBOR, MICHIGAN 47104 ($4.00, MONOGRAPH ECF/1)

THIS ANNOTATED BIBLIOGRAPHY OF MORE THAN 150 BOOKS AND ARTICLES COVERS A WIDE RANGE OF TOPICAL AREAS CONCERNED WITH THE RELATIONSHIP OF THE YOUNG CHILD TO HIS ENVIRONMENT. AMONG THE 18 TOPICS INCLUDED ARE: CHILD DEVELOPMENT; HEALTH, EDUCATIONAL, STAFF, AND COMMUNITY PROGRAMS; INFANTS AND TODDLERS, HANDICAPPED CHILDREN; PROJECT HEAD START; DAY CARE; AND DISADVANTAGED CHILDREN. SOURCES FOR PERIODICALS, BIBLIOGRAPHIES, AND FILMS ARE ALSO LISTED. THE BIBLIOGRAPHY IS INTENDED TO BE A SOURCE OF INFORMATION WITHIN ITSELF AS WELL AS A DIRECTORY TO INFORMATION SOURCES. ANNOTATIONS ARE EXTENSIVE. THE SELECTION OF PUBLICATIONS TO BE INCLUDED WAS GUIDED BY THE PROFESSIONAL INTERESTS OF THE PROJECT STAFF RATHER THAN BY ANY EXPLICIT THEORY OF EARLY CHILD CARE AND DEVELOPMENT. (AUTHOR/AJ)

ED049823 PS004528
INFLUENCES OF A PIAGET-ORIENTED CURRICULUM ON INTELLECTUAL FUNCTIONING OF LOWER-CLASS KINDERGARTEN CHILDREN. RAPH, JANE; AND OTHERS, 5 FEB 71 22P.
EDRS PRICE MF-$0.65 HC-$3.29

INTELLECTUAL FUNCTIONING OF A LOWER CLASS KINDERGARTEN CLASS EXPOSED TO THE INTRODUCTION OF A PIAGET-ORIENTED CURRICULUM WAS COMPARED WITH INTELLECTUAL FUNCTIONING OF ONE COMPARISON LOWER CLASS AND ONE COMPARISON MIDDLE CLASS GROUP OF CHILDREN TAUGHT IN A TRADITIONAL, ACTIVITY-CENTERED KINDERGARTEN PROGRAM. CHANGE SCORES BETWEEN THE BEGINNING AND END OF A SCHOOL YEAR WERE SIGNIFICANTLY HIGHER FOR THE EXPERIMENTAL LOWER CLASS GROUP ON ONE STANDARDIZED MEASURE AND ON SEVERAL PIAGETIAN TASKS. MAIN FEATURES OF THE PIAGET-ORIENTED CURRICULUM AND IMPLICATIONS OF THE RESULTS ARE DISCUSSED. ONE-HALF OF THE DOCUMENT CONSISTS OF THE BIBLIOGRAPHY, TABLES, AND SUMMARY MATERIAL. (AUTHOR)

ED049824 PS004529
PARENT-CHILD VERBAL INTERACTION: A STUDY OF DIALOGUE STRATEGIES AND VERBAL ABILITY. PLUMER, DAVENPORT, 4 FEB 71 44P.
EDRS PRICE MF-$0.65 HC-$3.29

TO DEVELOP AND TEST A SCHEME FOR ANALYZING ADULT-CHILD VERBAL INTERACTION, TAPE RECORDINGS OF SUCH INTERACTIONS WERE MADE IN 12 HOMES REPRESENTING HIGH VERBAL ABILITY AND AVERAGE VERBAL ABILITY. DIALOGUES OBTAINED WERE CODED IN NINE CATEGORIES OF UTTERANCES, AND THEIR FREQUENCY AND PATTERNING WERE RELATED TO THE VERBAL ABILITY OF THE 12 7 1/2- TO 8 1/2-YEAR-OLD MALE SUBJECTS. THESE CHILDREN WERE PART OF A LONGITUDINAL STUDY OF THE PRE AND POST NATAL PERIOD AS IT RELATES TO LEARNING ABILITIES AND DISABILITIES, AND HAD BEEN TESTED ON VERBAL ABILITY AT AGE 4 AND AT AGE 7. A COMPLETE MEDICAL, SOCIAL, AND PSYCHOLOGICAL HISTORY WAS ALSO AVAILABLE FOR EACH CHILD. DATA FROM THE PRESENT RESEARCH INCLUDED SEVEN HOURS OF TAPE FROM EACH FAMILY, REPRESENTING 21 20-MINUTE SESSIONS; THE FAMILY'S COMMENTARY ON EACH OF THE SESSIONS; THE RESEARCHER'S NOTES FROM HOME VISITS; AND THE MOTHERS' ATTITUDE RESPONSES TO A QUESTIONNAIRE. APPARENT WITHIN-GROUP DIFFERENCES PRODUCED VERY LARGE STANDARD DEVIATIONS AND HENCE FINDINGS OF NON-SIGNIFICANCE. IT WAS CONCLUDED THAT FURTHER NATURALISTIC STUDY WOULD BE PRODUCTIVE, BUT THAT TIGHTER EXPERIMENTAL CONTROLS SHOULD BE ESTABLISHED. (NH)

ED049825 PS004531
STATE AS VARIABLE, AS OBSTACLE AND AS MEDIATOR OF STIMULATION IN INFANT RESEARCH. KORNER, ANNELIESE F., 12 FEB 71 29P.
EDRS PRICE MF-$0.65 HC-$3.29

THIS PAPER IS A DISCUSSION OF THE DIFFERENT CONTEXTS IN WHICH THE CONCEPT OF THE INFANT'S STATE IS USED IN INFANT RESEARCH. THE INFANT STATES DISCUSSED ARE: REGULAR SLEEP, IRREGULAR SLEEP, DROWSINESS, ALERT INACTIVITY, WAKING ACTIVITY, AND CRYING. ALSO INCLUDED ARE HUNGER PERIODS AND INDETERMINATE STATES, THOSE INSTANCES IN WHICH AN INFANT'S STATE DOES NOT CLEARLY MEET THE CRITERIA OF ANY OF THE OTHER STATES. A BRIEF SUMMARY OF NEONATAL STUDIES WHICH EXPLORE BOTH INNATE AND EXPERIENTIAL FACTORS AFFECTING BEHAVIOR AND DEVELOPMENT OF NEWBORNS IS GIVEN. WITHOUT CONTROLLING FOR STATE, INFANT STUDIES MAY YIELD BOTH FALSE POSITIVE AND FALSE NEGATIVE RESULTS. STATE CAN BE CONSIDERED A VARIABLE, THE PRIMARY FOCUS OF RESEARCH RATHER THAN AN INTERVENING FACTOR. RESEARCH IN THE AREA OF STATE PROPOSED INCLUDED THOSE DEALING WITH DISTINCTNESS, PREDICTABILITY, RANGE, AND FLEXIBILITY OF STATE. STATE MAY ALSO BE A MEDIATOR OF STIMULATION. IN STUDIES ASSESSING THE EFFECTS OF EARLY STIMULATION, IT IS IMPORTANT TO DETERMINE WHICH TYPES OF STIMULATION ARE MOST EFFECTIVE AT VARIOUS DEVELOPMENTAL STAGES AND THE OPTIMAL STATE OF THE INFANT DURING WHICH SUCH STIMULATION CAN TAKE EFFECT. BIBLIOGRAPHY AND TABLES INCLUDED. (AUTHOR/AJ)

ED049826 PS004532
CHILD ABUSE LEGISLATION IN THE 1970'S. DE FRANCIS, VINCENT, 70 134P.
DOCUMENT NOT AVAILABLE FROM EDRS.
AVAILABLE FROM: THE AMERICAN HUMANE ASSOCIATION, CHILDREN'S DIVISION, P.O. BOX 1266, DENVER, COLORADO 80201 ($1.50)

THIS DOCUMENT IS A STUDY OF EXISTING CHILD ABUSE REPORTING LEGISLATION. IT REFLECTS LAW CHANGES OVER THE LAST FIVE YEARS, RECORDS THE STATUS OF THE LAW IN EACH OF THE STATES AND TERRITORIES, NOTES NOVEL APPROACHES, DISCUSSES PROBLEM AREAS, AND CHALLENGES SOME EXISTING CONCEPTS. THE MONOGRAPH PROVIDES GUIDELINES FOR COMMUNITIES SEEKING TO MODIFY THEIR LAWS BY PRESENTING UNDER THIS COVER SELECTED PORTIONS OF EXISTING STATE LAWS CHOSEN AS MOST REPRESENTATIVE OF CURRENT TRENDS. DATA FOR THIS PUBLICATION WAS COLLECTED THROUGH RESPONSE TO QUESTIONNAIRES SENT TO THE STATE DEPARTMENT OF WELFARE IN EACH STATE. THE REPORT RECOGNIZES THAT AMONG THE TRENDS IN THIS AREA ARE: (1) A GROWING NUMBER OF PROFESSIONALS REQUIRED BY LAW TO REPORT ABUSE CASES, AND (2) A MOVE AWAY FROM A CRIME-AND-PUNISHMENT APPROACH TO A PHILOSOPHY OF LEGISLATION DESIGNED TO PROTECT THE CHILD AND IMPROVE PARENTAL RESPONSIBILITY. (AUTHOR/AJ)

ED049827 PS004533
MODELS FOR NONGRADING SCHOOLS: A REPORT OF A NATIONAL SEMINAR. , 70 28P.
DOCUMENT NOT AVAILABLE FROM EDRS.
AVAILABLE FROM: INSTITUTE FOR DEVELOPMENT OF EDUCATIONAL ACTIVITIES, INC., P.O. BOX 628, FAR HILLS BRANCH, DAYTON, OHIO 45419 ($1.50)

THE PURPOSE OF THE NATIONAL SEMINAR REPORTED IN THIS BOOKLET WAS TO BRING TOGETHER A GROUP OF THEORETICIANS AND PRACTITIONERS TO (1) EXAMINE THE PRESENT STATUS OF THE NONGRADED SCHOOL IN THE UNITED STATES, AND (2) ESTABLISH GUIDELINES FOR TEACHERS AND ADMINISTRATORS WHO WANT INFORMATION DEMONSTRATING HOW NONGRADING AND CONTINUOUS PROGRESS WORKS IN ACTUAL PRACTICE. SPEAKERS STRESSED THE IMPORTANCE OF CAREFULLY DEFINING WHAT A NONGRADED SCHOOL SHOULD BE, AND OF USING THAT DEFINITION TO ASSESS ATTEMPTS TO ESTABLISH NONGRADED SCHOOLS, AND PRESENTED A CONCEPTUAL MODEL OF THE NONGRADED SCHOOL. (NH)

ED049828 PS004535
THE VALUE OF CLASSROOM REWARDS IN EARLY EDUCATION. HODGES, WALTER L., JAN 71 13P.
EDRS PRICE MF-$0.65 HC-$3.29

EXTERNAL REINFORCEMENT PARADIGMS ARE USEFUL AND NECESSARY IN A COMPLETE INSTRUCTIONAL SYSTEM AND EXTERNAL REINFORCEMENT IS NOT ANTITHETICAL TO A BELIEF IN AN INTRINSIC MOTIVATION HYPOTHESIS. TEACHER TRAINING, PARENT EDUCATION, AND CLASSROOM MANAGEMENT, AS WELL AS COMPLEX LEARNING SEQUENCES, CAN BE IMPROVED BY THE USE OF PRINCIPLES EMERGING FROM THE EXPERIMENTAL ANALYSIS OF BEHAVIOR. TEACHERS ESPECIALLY NEED TO PAY ATTENTION TO ALL THE VARIABLES WHICH MEDIATE THEIR EFFECTIVENESS WITH CHILDREN. IT IS TIME TO INTERRELATE LEARNING AND DEVELOPMENTAL PRINCIPLES FROM DIFFERING POINTS OF VIEW WHICH HAVE MET THE EMPIRICAL TEST OF EFFECTIVENESS. ON THE WHOLE, THE APPROACH TO INSTRUCTION REQUIRED BY THE SYSTEMATIC USE OF EXTERNAL REINFORCEMENT CAN STRENGTHEN SYSTEMS DERIVED FROM OTHER THEORIES. (WY)

ED049829 PS004539
KINDERGARTEN: WHO? WHAT? WHERE? OSBORN, D. KEITH, ED., 69 68P.
DOCUMENT NOT AVAILABLE FROM EDRS.
AVAILABLE FROM: SACUS, SCHOOL OF HOME ECONOMICS, DAWSON HALL, THE UNIVERSITY OF GEORGIA, ATHENS, GEORGIA 30601 ($1.50)

THIS PAMPHLET PRESENTS ARTICLES AND PAPERS WHICH EXPLORE THE ROLE OF A GOOD KINDERGARTEN IN THE MENTAL, PHYSICAL AND SOCIAL DEVELOPMENT OF THE CHILD. THE IMPORTANCE OF THE PRESCHOOL YEARS, WHEN THE FOUNDATION OF LEARNING IS LAID, IS EMPHASIZED THROUGHOUT THE PUBLICATION. INDIVIDUAL ARTICLES BY EDUCATORS DISCUSS A VARIETY OF TOPICS, INCLUDING EARLY CHILDHOOD NEEDS AND THE SIGNIFICANCE OF THE KINDERGARTEN PROGRAM; CURRICULUM AND MATERIALS; CHARACTERISTICS OF THE 5-YEAR-OLD;

THE PERSONALITY AND ROLE OF A GOOD KINDERGARTEN TEACHER; PARENT INVOLVEMENT; WHEN READING SHOULD (AND SHOULD NOT) BE TAUGHT; AND RESEARCH RELATED TO THE ADVANTAGES OF KINDERGARTEN. (NH)

ED049830 PS004627
LENIN'S GRANDCHILDREN: PRESCHOOL EDUCATION IN THE SOVIET UNION. WEAVER, KITTY D., APR 71 254P.
DOCUMENT NOT AVAILABLE FROM EDRS.
AVAILABLE FROM: SIMON AND SCHUSTER, ROCKEFELLER CENTER, 630 FIFTH AVENUE, NEW YORK, NEW YORK 10020 ($7.50)

THE SOVIETS HAVE LONG BEEN DEVOTING EDUCATIONAL AND INSTITUTIONAL ENERGIES TO THE FIELD OF EARLY CHILDHOOD EDUCATION. THIS BOOK STRESSES WHAT RUSSIAN PRESCHOOL EDUCATION DOES RATHER THAN WHAT ITS THEORISTS CLAIM IT DOES FOR CHILDREN AGED 2 MONTHS TO 6 YEARS WHO ARE IN GROUP CARE. CHILDREN, TEACHERS AND PARENTS TELL THEIR OWN STORIES. OBVIOUSLY SOVIET SCHOOL PREPARES FOR LIFE IN THE COMMUNIST STATE, JUST AS THE AMERICAN SCHOOL TRIES TO CONDITION CHILDREN FOR LIFE IN THE AMERICAN TYPE OF REPRESENTATIVE DEMOCRACY. HOWEVER, THERE IS ROOM FOR SOME CROSSBREEDING OF AMERICAN AND RUSSIAN PEDAGOGY BECAUSE, QUITE APART FROM POLITICS, CHILDREN AND THEIR BASIC NEEDS ARE REMARKABLY ALIKE EVERYWHERE. (AUTHOR/WY)

ED049831 PS004629
THE UNIT-BASED CURRICULUM. YPSILANTI PRESCHOOL CURRICULUM DEMONSTRATION PROJECT. MCCLELLAND, DONNA; AND OTHERS, MAY 70 57P.
EDRS PRICE MF-$0.65 HC-$3.29

THIS DOCUMENT IS A COMPILATION OF WEEKLY REPORTS WRITTEN BY THE UNIT-BASED TEACHERS IN THE YPSILANTI PRESCHOOL DEMONSTRATION PROJECT. THE PURPOSE OF THE UNIT-BASED PROGRAM IS TO SUPPLY PRESCHOOLERS WITH THE NECESSARY EDUCATIONAL AND SOCIAL SKILLS TO ADAPT READILY TO A KINDERGARTEN CURRICULUM. THE SUCCESS OF THE PROGRAM DEPENDS ALMOST ENTIRELY UPON THE TEACHERS' ABILITY TO USE INTUITION IN FOLLOWING THE CHILDREN'S LEAD AND TO SHAPE TENTATIVE EXPLORATIONS INTO SOLID LEARNING EXPERIENCES. THE WEEKLY REPORTS VIEW THE PROGRAM FROM FIVE ANGLES TO PROVIDE DIFFERENT PERSPECTIVES ON THE CURRICULUM AS IT IS BROUGHT TO LIFE IN THE CLASSROOM. THE PROGRAM IS REVIEWED IN TERMS OF THE GOALS THE TEACHERS HAVE SET, THE UNITS AROUND WHICH THE ACTIVITIES REVOLVE, THE PROBLEMS AND SMALL TRIUMPHS OF PARTICULAR CHILDREN, THE COGNITIVE THEMES EMPHASIZED DURING THE RELATIVELY STRUCTURED CIRCLE TIME, AND THE TEACHER'S OBSERVATIONS OF THE CHILDREN DURING DISCOVERY TIME (FREE PLAY). (AUTHOR/AJ)

ED049832 PS004630
THE COGNITIVE CURRICULUM. YPSILANTI PRESCHOOL CURRICULUM DEMONSTRATION PROJECT. MCCLELLAND, DONNA; AND OTHERS, MAY 70 50P.
EDRS PRICE MF-$0.65 HC-$3.29

THE COGNITIVE CURRICULUM FOCUSES PRIMARILY ON INTELLECTUAL, OR COGNITIVE DEVELOPMENT OF THE CHILD. MUCH OF ITS THEORY IS BASED ON THE WORK OF PIAGET AND IS CONCERNED WITH THE DEVELOPMENT OF LOGICAL THINKING AND REPRESENTATION. A CENTRAL TENET IS THAT THE CHILD LEARNS THROUGH ACTIVE INVOLVEMENT WITH HIS ENVIRONMENT AND THAT THE CHILD UNDERGOES STAGES OF DEVELOPMENT. FOUR COGNITIVE SKILL AREAS: CLASSIFICATION AND SERIATION, SPATIAL AND TEMPORAL RELATIONS, PREDICTABILITY, AND TRANSFORMATION ARE OBJECTIVES SUITABLE FOR THE PRESCHOOL CHILD. THE STRUCTURED CLASSROOM ENVIRONMENT IS NOT INTENDED TO BE A SUBSTITUTE FOR GOOD TEACHING NOR DOES IT REPLACE THE NEED FOR ACTION AND INTERACTION AMONG CHILDREN. IT SIMPLY PROVIDES THE CHILD WITH SUPPORT AND THE OPPORTUNITY TO ACHIEVE ACADEMIC SUCCESSES IN THE PROGRAM. DESCRIPTIONS OF THE ROLE OF THE COGNITIVE TEACHER, SPECIFIC CURRICULUM ACTIVITIES, AND LESSON PLANS MAKE THIS DOCUMENT A PRACTICAL GUIDE TO UNDERSTANDING THE OPERATION OF A COGNITIVE CURRICULUM IN PRESCHOOL. (WY)

ED049833 PS004632
A DESCRIPTIVE ACCOUNT OF FOUR MODES OF CHILDREN'S PLAY BETWEEN ONE AND FIVE YEARS. SUTTON-SMITH, BRIAN, DEC 70 26P.
EDRS PRICE MF-$0.65 HC-$3.29

THE PRESENT DESCRIPTIONS OF PLAY OF CHILDREN TWO TO FIVE ARE BASED ON THE THEORY THAT THE FOUR PROCESSES OF UNDERSTANDING INCLUDE FOUR DIFFERENT EMPHASES: (1) IMITATION, (2) EXPLORATION, (3) PREDICTION, AND (4) CONSTRUCTION (BUILDING, ETC.). THEREFORE, THE CATEGORIES OF CHILDREN'S PLAY DISCUSSED ARE TRANSFORMATIONS OF EACH OF THESE TYPES. PLAY IS A REVERSAL OF THE USUAL ADAPTIVE BEHAVIOR SEQUENCES AND PERMITS THE SUBJECT MORE VARIATION AND CONTROL OVER THE INSTRUMENTAL BEHAVIOR WITHIN THESE SEQUENCES. PLAY, WHILE NOT ALWAYS SELF-EVIDENT, USUALLY OCCURS IN A SPACE SET ASIDE FOR TOYS AND PLAY ACTIVITY AT ESTABLISHED TIMES AFTER ADULT-REQUIRED ACTIVITIES, AND IS ACCOMPANIED BY SIGNS OF PLEASURE, RELAXATION, AND EXCITEMENT. PLAY IS VOLUNTARY AND OFTEN INCLUDES ROLE PLAYING. THE OBSERVER OF PLAY MUST NOTE WHO IS BEING PORTRAYED, WHAT ACTS ARE BEING EXPRESSED, AND WHAT THE SETTING AND TIME ARE WITHIN THE PLAY ACTIVITY. THE CATEGORIES INCLUDED IN THIS PAPER DEAL ONLY WITH SELF-PLAY AS DISTINGUISHED FROM SOCIAL PLAY. EXTENSIVE DESCRIPTIONS OF PLAY AT SPECIFIC AGES MAKE UP MOST OF THE DOCUMENT. (AJ)

ED049834 PS004634
HAS PRESCHOOL COMPENSATORY EDUCATION FAILED? WEIKART, DAVID P., 69 9P.
EDRS PRICE MF-$0.65 HC-$3.29

DISCUSSES EVALUATION OF PRESCHOOL COMPENSATORY EDUCATION PROGRAMS AND REVIEWS RESEARCH LITERATURE. SUGGESTS THAT THE FOLLOWING IDEAS ARE CRUCIAL FOR EFFECTIVE PRESCHOOL EDUCATION (1) CHILDREN CAN PROFIT INTELLECTUALLY FROM ANY PRESCHOOL CURRICULUM THAT IS BASED ON A WIDE RANGE OF EXPERIENCE; (2) THE PRIMARY ROLE OF CURRICULUM IS TO HELP THE TEACHER TO TEACH; (3) THE SELECTION OF CURRICULUM IS CRITICAL, FOR ONE THAT IS TOO EASY AND LIMITED IN SCOPE WILL NOT CHALLENGE THE TEACHER; AND (4) STAFF INVOLVEMENT IS MORE IMPORTANT THAN THE PARTICULAR CURRICULUM USED, AND NECESSARY INGREDIENTS INCLUDE PLANNING TIME FOR TEACHERS, SYSTEMATIC LANGUAGE INTERACTION BETWEEN TEACHER AND CHILD, AND HOME VISITS BY TEACHERS. AN OVERVIEW OF RESEARCH IN THE FIELD OF PRESCHOOL EDUCATION IS ALSO GIVEN IN THIS PAPER. [FILMED FROM BEST AVAILABLE COPY.] (NH)

ED049835 PS004635
THE INFLUENCE OF SELECTED VARIABLES ON THE EFFECTIVENESS OF PRESCHOOL PROGRAMS FOR DISADVANTAGED CHILDREN. SPICKER, HOWARD H., 69 14P.
EDRS PRICE MF-$0.65 HC-$3.29

THE PURPOSE OF THIS PAPER IS TO IDENTIFY SOME VARIATIONS AMONG EXPERIMENTAL PROGRAMS AND DISCUSS THE MANNER IN WHICH SUCH VARIATIONS SEEM TO AFFECT A PROGRAM'S SUCCESS. TO ACCOMPLISH THIS PURPOSE AN IN-DEPTH ANALYSIS OF A FEW MAJOR PRESCHOOL INTERVENTION STUDIES IS MADE IN TERMS OF FOUR PERTINENT VARIABLES: (1) CURRICULUM MODEL (2) HOME INTERVENTION (3) AGE AT INTERVENTION AND (4) DURATION OF INTERVENTION. THE WESTINGHOUSE REPORT EVALUATING THE IMPACT OF HEAD START, THE GRAY AND KLAUS PROGRAM, THE INDIANA PROJECT, THE KARNES PROGRAM, THE WEIKART PROGRAM, MONTESSORI, AND THE BEREITER-ENGELMANN PROGRAM ARE COMPARED. A FEW GENERAL OBSERVATIONS AND TENTATIVE SPECULATIONS ARE MADE ABOUT SEVERAL OTHER VARIABLES WHICH APPEAR TO AFFECT THE OUTCOME OF PRESCHOOL INTERVENTIONS. THE EVALUATION OF PRESCHOOL OUTCOMES MIGHT INVOLVE THE FOUR MAJOR VARIABLES IN DETERMINING WHAT MODIFICATIONS WOULD IMPROVE PRESCHOOL INTERVENTION RESULTS WITH DISADVANTAGED CHILDREN. (WY)

ED049836 PS004638
INFANT DEVELOPMENT IN LOWER CLASS AMERICAN FAMILIES. LEWIS, MICHAEL; WILSON, CORNELIA D., APR 71 24P.
EDRS PRICE MF-$0.65 HC-$3.29

THIS STUDY WAS CONDUCTED TO OBSERVE THE EFFECTS OF SOCIAL CLASS ON THE INTERACTION OF MOTHERS AND THEIR 12-WEEK-OLD INFANTS. DATA ON THE INFANTS' COGNITIVE AND ATTENTIVE BEHAVIOR WAS ALSO OBTAINED. EACH OF 32 WHITE AND BLACK INFANTS FROM FIVE DIFFERENT LEVELS OF SOCIAL CLASS WAS OBSERVED AT HOME FOR TWO FULL HOURS OF WAKING TIME. OBSERVED INFANT BEHAVIOR INCLUDED MOVE, VOCALIZE, FRET/CRY, PLAY, NOISE, AND SMILE. FINDINGS INDICATE THAT LOWER SES INFANTS VOCALIZE AND SMILE MORE AND FRET/CRY LESS THAN UPPER MIDDLE SES INFANTS. MATERNAL BEHAVIORS OF TOUCH, HOLD, SMILE, LOOK, AND PLAY WERE MORE FREQUENT AMONG LOWER SES THAN MIDDLE SES MOTHERS, AND LOWER SES MOTHERS SPEND MORE TIME WATCHING TV THAN THE MIDDLE SES MOTHERS. THERE IS A RELATIVELY STRONG RELATIONSHIP BETWEEN INFANT AND MATERNAL BEHAVIOR. MIDDLE SES MOTHERS VOCALIZE WHEN THEIR INFANTS VOCALIZE, TOUCH AND HOLD THEM WHEN THEY FRET AND WATCH THEM PLAY. LOWER SES MOTHERS TEND TO TOUCH THEIR INFANTS WHEN THEY VOCALIZE, WHEN THEY CRY AND WHEN THEY ARE AT PLAY. THERE WERE NO CLASS DIFFERENCES ON THE TWO INFANT MENTAL TESTS. PERFORMANCE ON A MEASURE OF ATTENTION INDICATED THAT TWO-THIRDS OF THE MIDDLE CLASS INFANTS FAILED TO SHOW RESPONSE DECREMENT WHILE ALL THE LOWER CLASS INFANTS DEMONSTRATED RESPONSE DECREMENT. IN GENERAL, THIS STUDY SUPPORTS THE PRESENCE OF SOCIAL CLASS DIFFERENCES IN TERMS OF BOTH COGNITIVE AND ATTENTIVE BEHAVIORS.

ED049837 PS004656
RELATIONSHIP OF CURRICULUM, TEACHING, AND LEARNING IN PRESCHOOL EDUCATION. WEIKART, DAVID P., FEB 71 35P.
EDRS PRICE MF-$0.65 HC-$3.29

THREE BASIC QUESTIONS CONCERNING PRESCHOOL EDUCATION ARE DISCUSSED USING INFORMATION DERIVED FROM RESEARCH IN EARLY CHILDHOOD EDUCATION THROUGH 1963-1971. THE QUESTIONS ARE: (1) DOES PRESCHOOL EDUCATION MAKE A DIFFERENCE IN LATER SCHOOL PERFORMANCE OF DISADVANTAGED CHILDREN? (2) IF PRESCHOOL EDUCATION DOES MAKE A DIFFERENCE, DOES IT MATTER WHICH CURRICULUM THEORY IS EMPLOYED? AND (3) HOW CAN EDUCATORS GUARANTEE EFFECTIVE PRESCHOOL EDUCATION? FINDINGS INDICATE THAT (1) PRESCHOOL EXPERIENCE CAN MAKE A DIFFERENCE FOR DISADVANTAGED CHILDREN. A FEW SPECIAL SITUATIONS HAVE OFFERED

IMMEDIATE POSITIVE IMPACT IN TERMS OF THEIR STATED GOALS. LONG-TERM DATA ARE NOT YET AVAILABLE. (2) FROM FOUR TYPES OF CURRICULA (PROGRAMMED, OPEN FRAMEWORK, CHILD-CENTERED, AND CUSTODIAL) TWO POINTS CAN BE MADE. FIRST, CHILDREN PROFIT FROM ANY CURRICULUM THAT IS BASED ON A WIDE RANGE OF EXPERIENCES AND SECOND, THE SUCCESSFUL CURRICULUM GUIDES THE TEACHER IN ADAPTING THEORY TO THE ACTUAL BEHAVIORS OF CHILDREN AND (3) A SUCCESSFUL PROGRAM REQUIRES AN EFFECTIVE STAFF MODEL WHICH IN TURN RELIES ON PLANNING AND SUPERVISION. EDUCATORS SHOULD FEEL FREE TO DEVELOP ANY CURRICULUM THAT CAN BE ADAPTED TO THE NEEDS OF THE CHILDREN AND THE REQUIREMENTS OF THEIR STAFF MODEL. (WY)

ED049838 PS004668
A GUIDE TO THE PLANNING AND OPERATION OF A CHILD DEVELOPMENT CENTER FOR MIGRANT CHILDREN AND A REPORT OF THE HOOPESTON CHILD DEVELOPMENT CENTER YORK, MARY ELIZABETH, AUG 70 314P.
EDRS PRICE MF-$0.65 HC-$13.16

THIS REPORT DESCRIBES IN DETAIL THE PLANNING AND OPERATION OF AN 8-WEEK PILOT DAY CARE PROGRAM FOR MIGRANT CHILDREN IN HOOPESTON, ILLINOIS. PLANNING BEGAN A YEAR IN ADVANCE AND INVOLVED ARRANGEMENTS FOR FUNDING, STAFF, AND PHYSICAL FACILITIES, AS WELL AS THE IMPORTANT HUMAN RELATIONS TASK OF ESTABLISHING HONEST COMMUNICATION BETWEEN REPRESENTATIVES OF TWO SEGMENTS OF THE COMMUNITY: BUSINESS AND PROFESSIONAL PEOPLE, AND ADULT MIGRANT WORKERS. THE STRUCTURE AND MEETINGS OF THE PLANNING-ADVISORY COMMITTEE ARE DESCRIBED. OTHER AREAS DISCUSSED ARE THE ROLE OF MIGRANT REPRESENTATIVES, LICENSING AND REGULATIONS, FINANCING AND BUDGET, FEES, BUILDING, THE CHILDREN, PROFESSIONAL AND VOLUNTEER STAFF, STAFF RECRUITMENT AND TRAINING, COMPREHENSIVE SERVICES, PARENT INVOLVEMENT, AND THE EDUCATIONAL PROGRAM--ITS GOALS, METHODS, AND CURRICULUM. EVALUATION IS IN PROGRESS. APPENDIXES COMPRISE APPROXIMATELY 3/4 OF THE DOCUMENT AND INCLUDE SUPPLEMENTAL MATERIALS AND REPORTS. (NH)

ED049839 PS004679
SOCIAL INTERACTION IN HETEROGENEOUS PRE-SCHOOLS IN ISRAEL. FEITELSON, DINA; AND OTHERS, 5 FEB 71 13P.
EDRS PRICE MF-$0.65 HC-$3.29

A 2-YEAR-PROJECT WITH 48 DISADVANTAGED (D) AND 48 MIDDLE CLASS (P) ISRAELI 2-YEAR-OLDS WAS SET UP TO STUDY HOW HETEROGENEOUS OR HOMOGENEOUS GROUPING INFLUENCES SOCIAL INTERACTION. TWENTY-FOUR D'S WERE THE HOMOGENEOUS GROUP, 48 P'S AND 24 D'S WERE EQUALLY DIVIDED INTO THREE HETEROGENEOUS GROUPS WITH A RATIO OF 2:1. THIS REPORT IS BASED ON AN ANALYSIS OF NARRATIVE RECORDS OF SUBJECTS DURING 1-HOUR FREE PLAY OBSERVATIONS. THE RECORDS WERE FIRST DIVIDED INTO SOCIAL INTERACTION UNITS (SIU'S). SIU'S WERE THEN CLASSIFIED INTO SEVEN CATEGORIES, AND THE PERCENTAGE OF SIU'S OF EACH CHILD IN ANY ONE OF THE CATEGORIES AND WITH ANY TYPE OF POSSIBLE INTERACTEE (ADULT, D CHILD, P CHILD) COMPUTED. THE OVERALL AMOUNT OF SOCIAL INTERACTIONS INCREASED MORE FOR THE HETEROGENEOUS D'S THAN FOR THE HOMOGENEOUS D'S. HOWEVER, BOTH HETEROGENEOUS D'S AS WELL AS P'S INTERACTED MORE WITHIN THEIR OWN GROUP THAN WITH EACH OTHER, DESPITE THE 2:1 RATIO OF P'S TO D'S IN EACH GROUP WHICH SHOULD HAVE FAVORED INTERACTION WITH P'S BY THE HETEROGENEOUS D'S. MOREOVER, THE HOMOGENEOUS D'S (LIKE THE P'S) DEVELOPED A BETTER ABILITY TO COOPERATE WITH PEERS WHILE THE HETEROGENEOUS D'S REMAINED VERY DEPENDENT ON ADULTS. (AUTHOR)

ED049840 PS004686
NEIGHBORHOOD FAMILY DAY CARE AS A CHILD-REARING ENVIRONMENT. EMLEN, ARTHUR C., 19 NOV 70 29P.
EDRS PRICE MF-$0.65 HC-$3.29

THE FIELD STUDY REPORTED EXAMINED THE ATTITUDES AND BEHAVIOR OF WORKING MOTHERS AND THEIR NEIGHBORHOOD CAREGIVERS (NONRELATIVES). DATA WERE OBTAINED FROM INTERVIEWS WITH 104 MOTHER-SITTER PAIRS, 39 OF WHOM WERE FRIENDS WHEN THE ARRANGEMENT BEGAN, AND 65 OF WHOM WERE STRANGERS. THE DYNAMICS OF MOTHER-SITTER RELATIONS PROVE TO BE DRAMATICALLY DIFFERENT FOR THE TWO GROUPS. BETWEEN WOMEN WHO ALREADY KNOW EACH OTHER, FRIENDSHIP IS APPARENTLY THE BOND THAT HOLDS THE DAY CARE ARRANGEMENT TOGETHER. DISSATISFACTIONS MAY INVOLVE STRAINS CENTERING AROUND STATUS, DOMINANCE, AND INTERPERSONAL ISSUES, BUT MAY BE TOLERATED BECAUSE OF FRIENDSHIP. BY CONTRAST, THOSE WHO START OUT AS STRANGERS TEND TO DEVELOP A SYSTEM OF MUTUAL SATISFACTIONS NOT ASSOCIATED WITH DEGREE OF FRIENDSHIP ALTHOUGH FRIENDSHIP MAY LATER DEVELOP. MOTIVATION FOR CAREGIVERS WHO SIT FOR STRANGERS WAS FOUND TO BE PERSONAL ROLE SATISFACTION, AS WELL AS ECONOMIC. THE GOALS AND METHODS OF THE DAY CARE NEIGHBOR SERVICE, A 2-YEAR DEMONSTRATION PROJECT, ARE DESCRIBED. THROUGH A CREATIVE USE OF CONSULTATION, SOCIAL WORKERS REACH "DAY CARE NEIGHBORS" WHO, IN TURN, HELP POTENTIAL USERS AND GIVERS OF DAY CARE TO FIND EACH OTHER AND TO MAKE SATISFACTORY ARRANGEMENTS. THE SOCIAL IMPACT OF THE SERVICE IS DISCUSSED. TABLES ARE INCLUDED. (NH)

ED050802 PS004510
ENVIRONMENTAL FORCES IN THE HOME LIVES OF THREE-YEAR-OLD CHILDREN IN THREE POPULATION SUBGROUPS. SCHOGGEN, MAXINE; SCHOGGEN, PHIL, JAN 71 117P.
EDRS PRICE MF-$0.65 HC-$6.58

THIS RESEARCH WAS DESIGNED TO SERVE TWO MAJOR PURPOSES: (1) TO CREATE A SUBSTANTIAL LIBRARY OF THEORETICALLY NEUTRAL OBSERVATIONAL DATA AS PERMANENT DOCUMENTATION OF ACTUAL LIFE EXPERIENCES IN THE LIVES OF 3-YEAR-OLD CHILDREN FROM DIFFERENT SOCIOECONOMIC BACKGROUNDS AND (2) TO ANALYZE SPECIMEN RECORDS IN ORDER (A) TO DESCRIBE AND QUANTIFY THE KINDS OF ACTIVE ENVIRONMENTAL INPUTS RECEIVED BY THE CHILDREN, (B) TO ASSESS RELATIONSHIPS BETWEEN HOME EXPERIENCES AND SOCIOECONOMIC STATUS, (3) TO EXPLORE THE CHARACTERISTICS OF THE SOCIAL ENVIRONMENT OF CHILDREN IN DISADVANTAGED HOMES, AND (D) TO RELATE FINDINGS TO CERTAIN DATA IN THE RESEARCH LITERATURE ON CHILD-REARING. NARRATIVE DESCRIPTIONS OF BEHAVIOR OF 8 LOW-INCOME URBAN, 8 LOW-INCOME RURAL AND 8 MIDDLE-INCOME URBAN CHILDREN PROVIDE THE BASIC OBSERVATIONAL DATA RECORDED AS ENVIRONMENTAL FORCE UNITS (UNITS OF BEHAVIOR OF AGENTS ACTING WITH RESPECT TO THE CHILD). CHILD BEHAVIOR IS THEN CODED AND DESCRIBED ACCORDING TO A SET OF 26 VARIABLES. SIMILARITIES AND DIFFERENCES ACROSS GROUPS ON SOME DIMENSIONS OF THE VARIABLES ARE PRESENTED. RESULTS OF THIS ANALYSIS FEATURE WIDE INDIVIDUAL DIFFERENCES, SOME IMPORTANT SIMILARITIES ACROSS THE THREE SOCIOECONOMIC GROUPS, AND SOME INTERESTING INTERGROUP DIFFERENCES IN ORIENTATION TO CHILD-REARING. (NH)

ED050803 PS004536
PRESCHOOL INSTRUCTION MOBILE FACILITIES: DESCRIPTION AND ANALYSIS. SCHOOL PRACTICES REPORT NO. 3. HOWSE, JENNIFER, 71 134P.
EDRS PRICE MF-$0.65 HC-$6.58
AVAILABLE FROM: SOUTHEASTERN EDUCATION LABORATORY, 3450 INTERNATIONAL BOULEVARD, ATLANTA, GEORGIA 30354

THIS REPORT ON THE USE OF MOBILE FACILITIES IN PRESCHOOL INSTRUCTION PROGRAMS IS DIVIDED INTO FOUR PARTS. PART I DESCRIBES THE THREE MAJOR MOBILE PRESCHOOL INSTRUCTION PROGRAMS. THE APPALACHIA PRESCHOOL PROGRAM AND SOUTHEASTERN EDUCATION LABORATORY'S READIMOBILE PROGRAM ARE BEING FIELD TESTED AS POSSIBLE STRATEGIES FOR THE DELIVERY OF INSTRUCTIONAL SERVICES TO RURAL CHILDREN WHILE THE FLORIDA MOBILE EARLY LEARNING PROGRAM REPRESENTS AN APPROACH TO THE PRESCHOOL EDUCATION OF MIGRANT CHILDREN. INFORMATION PRESENTED INCLUDES BACKGROUND, PHYSICAL DESCRIPTION OF THE UNIT, DESCRIPTION OF THE POPULATION, PROGRAM OPERATION, STAFFING AND CURRICULUM, EVALUATION, COST ANALYSIS, AND A LINE DRAWING OF THE UNIT. PART II OF THE MONOGRAPH DEALS WITH MOBILE PRESCHOOL TRAINING PROGRAMS. PART III DESCRIBES SELECTED ELEMENTARY SCHOOL MOBILE PROGRAMS AND ONE QUASI-MOBILE PRESCHOOL PROGRAM. PART IV CONTAINS GENERAL CONCLUSIONS AND RECOMMENDATIONS AND ATTEMPTS TO DEAL WITH SOME OF THE MAJOR ISSUES GERMANE TO MOBILE EDUCATION, TO SYNTHESIZE THE PROGRAMS REVIEWED AND GIVE SOME IDEA OF THE STATE OF THE ART IN MOBILE PRESCHOOL INSTRUCTION, AND TO FORMULATE SOME OF THE UNANSWERED QUESTIONS PERTINENT TO THE FUTURE DEVELOPMENT OF SIMILAR PROGRAMS. (AUTHOR/AJ)

ED050804 PS004540
HEALTH CARE OF CHILDREN: A CHALLENGE. COCHRANE, HORTENCE S.; DIBUONO, THEODORE, 70 94P.
DOCUMENT NOT AVAILABLE FROM EDRS.
AVAILABLE FROM: THE SCHOOL OF SOCIAL WORK, SYRACUSE UNIVERSITY, 926 SOUTH CROUSE AVENUE, SYRACUSE, N.Y. 13210 ($2.50)

THIS PUBLICATION, WRITTEN FOR PERSONS PREPARING FOR OR ENGAGED IN CHILD CARE SERVICES, PROVIDES INFORMATION THAT WILL PROMOTE IMPROVED HEALTH AWARENESS, INITIATE ACTION AND ENABLE PARENTS TO COPE MORE ADEQUATELY WITH PROBLEMS OF THEIR CHILDREN'S HEALTH. THE PUBLICATION WILL ENABLE SOCIAL WORK, CHILD WELFARE, DAY CARE, PRESCHOOL, AND NURSING SCHOOL STUDENTS AND CHILD CARE WORKERS TO (1) COMPREHEND THE NORMAL FUNCTIONING OF SMALL CHILDREN; (2) PLACE THE EMOTIONAL AND PHYSICAL GROWTH NEEDS OF CHILDREN IN PROPER PERSPECTIVE; (3) IDENTIFY DEFECTS, ILLNESSES, AND HANDICAPS IN CHILDREN; (4) DEVELOP SKILL IN APPROPRIATE USE OF HEALTH AND MEDICAL CARE RESOURCES; (5) GROW IN THEIR CREATIVITY, INGENUITY, AND CAPACITY TO PROVIDE THE NECESSARY SUPPLEMENTATION TO THE HEALTH CARE WHICH THE FAMILY OFFERS THE PRESCHOOL CHILD; (6) IMPROVE COMPETENCE IN OFFERING HEALTH GUIDANCE PLANNING EFFECTIVELY WITH PARENTS; (7) INCREASE A SENSITIVITY TO HEALTH NEEDS OF PRESCHOOL CHILDREN IN LOWER SOCIOECONOMIC FAMILIES; AND (8) STRENGTHEN FAMILY LIFE THROUGH APPROPRIATE MEDICAL CARE SERVICE FOR CHILDREN. CHAPTER HEADINGS INCLUDE: CHILD HEALTH CARE, GROWTH AND DEVELOPMENT, HEALTH SUPERVISION OF CHILDREN, A CONTINUUM OF HEALTH AND DISEASE, DISEASE STATES, AND HANDICAPPING CONDITIONS. AN APPENDIX AND BIBLIOGRAPHY OF FURTHER SOURCES ARE INCLUDED. (AUTHOR/AJ)

ED050805 PS004626
AN ANALYSIS OF EXCELLENT EARLY EDUCATIONAL PRACTICES: PRELIMINARY REPORT. WHITE, BURTON L., 71 78P.
EDRS PRICE MF-$0.65 HC-$3.29

THIS DOCUMENT REPORTS THE FIRST PHASE OF A LONGITUDINAL RESEARCH PROJECT DESIGNED TO PRODUCE INFORMATION ON HOW TO RAISE CHILDREN SO THEIR BASIC ABILITIES MAY DEVELOP OPTIMALLY DURING THE FIRST SIX YEARS OF LIFE. ALTHOUGH THIS PRESCHOOL PROJECT HAS BEEN IN OPERATION FIVE YEARS, THE STUDY IS NOT YET COMPLETED BECAUSE STATEMENTS ABOUT THE EFFECTS OF VARIOUS CHILD REARING PRACTICES AND EXPERIENCES HAVE NOT BEEN PUT TO EXPERIMENTAL TEST. NONTHELESS, PRELIMINARY RESULTS CONCERNING OPTIMAL AND RESTRICTED DEVELOPMENT OF 48 CHILDREN IN A NATURAL ENVIRONMENT CAN BE REPORTED. IN GENERAL, CHILD REARING INTERACTIONS DURING YEARS 1-3 APPEAR TO OFFER THE MOST RELEVANCE FOR INTENSE INVESTIGATION. THE MOTHER'S DIRECT AND INDIRECT ACTIVITIES APPEAR TO BE THE MOST POWERFUL FORMATIVE FACTORS IN THE DEVELOPMENT OF THE PRESCHOOL CHILD. SOME "BEST GUESSES" ABOUT THE MOST EFFECTIVE CHILD REARING PRACTICES CAN BE MADE. FINDINGS SUGGEST THAT EFFECTIVE MOTHERS (1) ARE GENERALLY PERMISSIVE, (2) USUALLY BUT NOT ALWAYS RESPOND TO THEIR CHILD'S APPEALS FOR IMMEDIATE HELP (3) ACT IN RESPONSE TO OVERTURES BY THE CHILD AND (4) HAVE A HIGH ENERGY LEVEL. REFERENCES AND TABLES OF DATA ARE INCLUDED. (WY)

ED050806 PS004633
THE PLAYFUL MODES OF KNOWING. SUTTON-SMITH, BRIAN, [70] 15P.
EDRS PRICE MF-$0.65 HC-$3.29

ALL FORMS OF PLAY ARE TRANSFORMATIONS OF FOUR BASIC MODES BY WHICH PEOPLE KNOW THE WORLD: COPYING, ANALYSIS, PREDICTION, AND SYNTHESIS. TRANSFORMATION INVOLVES FOREGOING THE USUAL OUTCOMES OF ADAPTED INTELLIGENCE FOR THE SAKE OF VOLUNTARY CONTROL OF ONE'S OWN BEHAVIOR IN GAMES, AND FOR THE EXCITEMENT OF NOVEL AFFECTIVE, COGNITIVE AND BEHAVIORAL VARIATIONS WHICH THEN BECOME POSSIBLE. IMITATIVE PLAY, EXPLORATORY PLAY, TESTING PLAY, AND CONTESTING ARE DISCUSSED IN TERMS OF THEIR SOCIAL AND PERSONAL MEANINGS. SEVERAL CONTESTING GAMES ENJOYED BY CHILDREN OF VARYING AGE LEVELS, SUCH AS HIDE AND SEEK, RED ROVER AND PRISONER'S BASE, ARE DESCRIBED AND CLASSIFIED ACCORDING TO ACTORS, ACTS, SPACE, AND TIME. GAMES REFLECT SOCIETY IN GENERAL IN THAT THEY EMBODY BOTH RULE AND REASON, CHANCE AND MADNESS, AND SOCIETIES IN PARTICULAR IN THAT SPECIFIC TYPES OF GAMES ENJOYED REFLECT DIFFERING MODES OF LIFE. IT IS SUGGESTED THAT THE PRIMARY FUNCTION OF PLAY MAY BE THE ENJOYMENT OF A COMMITMENT TO ONE'S OWN EXPERIENCE. (NH)

ED050807 PS004636
SURVIVAL SKILLS AND FIRST GRADE ACADEMIC ACHIEVEMENT. REPORT #1. COBB, JOSEPH A., DEC 70 71P.
EDRS PRICE MF-$0.65 HC-$3.29

AS PART OF A CONTINUING EFFORT TO FIND EDUCATIONALLY RELEVANT VARIABLES FOR HANDICAPPED CHILDREN THE PRESENT INVESTIGATION FOCUSED ON THE RELATIONSHIP OF OBSERVABLE BEHAVIORS TO FIRST GRADE ACHIEVEMENT. SUBJECTS WERE 134 FIRST GRADERS WHO WERE OBSERVED IN READING AND ARITHMETIC PERIODS (SURVIVAL SKILLS) FOR 10 TO 14 DAYS. THE DATA COLLECTED WERE CORRELATED WITH ACHIEVEMENT AS MEASURED ON STANDARDIZED ACHIEVEMENT TESTS. THERE WAS A MODERATE COMPOSITE SURVIVAL SKILL RELATIONSHIP. A STEPWISE REGRESSION ANALYSIS USING SPECIFIC ASPECTS OF SURVIVAL SKILLS BEHAVIOR AS INDEPENDENT VARIABLES AND ACHIEVEMENT SCORES AS DEPENDENT VARIABLES WAS PERFORMED. IN GENERAL, A RELATIONSHIP WAS FOUND BETWEEN SOCIAL CLASS, SURVIVAL SKILLS AND FIRST GRADE ACHIEVEMENT. LOWER CLASS CHILDREN WERE MORE VARIABLE AND MORE PREDICTABLE IN THEIR SURVIVAL SKILLS BEHAVIOR THAN UPPER CLASS CHILDREN. THE COMBINED VARIABLES OF SEX OF CHILD AND SES PROVED TO BE THE MOST POWERFUL PREDICTORS FOR ACHIEVEMENT FROM SURVIVAL SKILLS. A MIXTURE OF STABILITY AND FLUX CHARACTERIZED THE FINDINGS REGARDING SURVIVAL SKILLS ACROSS ACADEMIC SETTINGS. THE EVIDENCE GAINED IN THIS STUDY PROVIDES SUPPORT FOR THE THEORETICAL SIGNIFICANCE OF SITUATIONAL VARIABLES IN ACCOUNTING FOR BEHAVIOR AND POINTS TO THE IMPLICATIONS OF THE PRACTICAL SIGNIFICANCE OF SEARCHING OUT EDUCATIONALLY RELEVANT VARIABLES IN THE CLASSROOM ENVIRONMENT. (WY)

ED050808 PS004639
HEIGHT AND WEIGHT OF CHILDREN: UNITED STATES. HAMILL, PETER V. V.; AND OTHERS, SEP 70 55P.
EDRS PRICE MF-$0.65 HC NOT AVAILABLE FROM EDRS.
AVAILABLE FROM: SUPERINTENDENT OF DOCUMENTS, U.S. GOVERNMENT PRINTING OFFICE, WASHINGTON, D.C. 20402 ($0.55, PUBLIC HEALTH SERVICE PUBLICATION NO. 1000-SERIES 11-NO. 104)

THIS REPORT CONTAINS NATIONAL ESTIMATES BASED ON FINDINGS FROM THE HEALTH EXAMINATION SURVEY IN 1963-65 ON HEIGHT AND WEIGHT MEASUREMENTS OF CHILDREN 6- TO 11-YEARS-OLD. A NATIONWIDE PROBABILITY SAMPLE OF 7,119 CHILDREN WAS SELECTED TO REPRESENT THE NONINSTITUTIONALIZED CHILDREN (ABOUT 24 MILLION) IN THIS AGE GROUP. HEIGHT WAS OBTAINED IN STOCKING FEET WITH THE HEAD IN THE FRANKFORT PLANE, SUBJECT STANDING ERECT BUT NOT MANUALLY ELONGATED, AND RECORDED BY MEANS OF A POLAROID CAMERA MOUNTED ON THE MEASURING ROD. WEIGHT WAS MEASURED IN STANDARDIZED CLOTHING ON A SELF-RECORDING SCALE. THE PRESENT FINDINGS ARE COMPARED WITH OTHER FINDINGS, BOTH IN THE PAST AND IN OTHER COUNTRIES. THERE HAS BEEN A STEADY AND VERY REGULAR INCREASE IN BOTH HEIGHT AND WEIGHT OF CHILDREN IN THE UNITED STATES OVER THE PAST 90 YEARS. AMERICAN CHILDREN ARE AMONG THE LARGEST IN THE WORLD. AMERICAN BOYS AT AGE 6 ARE SLIGHTLY TALLER AND HEAVIER THAN THE GIRLS, BUT, BY AGE 11, THE GIRLS ARE LARGER. WHILE HEIGHTS FOR WHITE AND BLACK BOYS IN THIS AGE RANGE ARE COMPARABLE, WHITE BOYS ARE SLIGHTLY HEAVIER THAN BLACK BOYS AT EVERY AGE. BLACK GIRLS ARE TALLER AND WEIGH SLIGHTLY LESS THAN WHITE GIRLS UNTIL AGE 11. HEIGHT AND WEIGHT AS MEASURES OF GROWTH OF THE DEVELOPING HUMAN AND THE USE OF THESE FINDINGS AS STANDARDS, BOTH CLINICAL AND EPIDEMIOLOGIC, IS DISCUSSED. THREE-FIFTHS OF THIS DOCUMENT CONSISTS OF DETAILED TABLES. (AUTHOR/AJ)

ED050809 PS004661
INTERVENTION WITH MOTHERS AND YOUNG CHILDREN: A STUDY OF INTRAFAMILY EFFECTS. GILMER, BARBARA R.; AND OTHERS, DEC 70 63P.
EDRS PRICE MF-$0.65 HC-$3.29

THIS STUDY COMPARES THREE METHODS OF INTERVENTION CONDUCTED OVER 2 1/2 YEARS TO PROMOTE COGNITIVE DEVELOPMENT AND COMPETENCY OF DISADVANTAGED YOUNG CHILDREN. SUBJECTS WERE ABOUT 80 BLACK MOTHER-CHILD-YOUNGER SIBLING TRIADS, DIVIDED INTO THREE GROUPS (AND MATCHED WITH COMPARISON GROUPS): (1) MAXIMUM IMPACT, A TRAINING PROGRAM FOR THE TARGET CHILD (3 TO 4 YEARS OF AGE) AT A CENTER 5 DAYS A WEEK, AND FOR THE MOTHER AT A CENTER ONCE A WEEK; (2) CURRICULUM, WHICH GAVE THE OLDER CHILDREN A CLASSROOM PROGRAM LIKE THAT OF THE FIRST GROUP BUT OFFERED NO PROGRAM FOR MOTHER OR SIBLINGS; AND (3) HOME VISITOR, IN WHICH THE FAMILY HAD NO DIRECT CONTACT WITH THE CENTER BUT RECEIVED 1-HOUR HOME VISITS ONCE A WEEK FROM A TEACHER WHO SHOWED THE MOTHER HOW TO INSTRUCT HER CHILDREN. THE CENTER PROGRAM FOR MOTHERS TAUGHT THEM HOW TO STIMULATE THEIR CHILDREN INTELLECTUALLY AND IMPROVED MOTHERS' SELF-CONCEPT AND HOME MANAGEMENT. THE CHILDREN'S CLASS PROGRAM EMPHASIZED SKILL DEVELOPMENT AND AN ORDERED ENVIRONMENT. INTELLIGENCE PRETESTS AND POSTTESTS WERE GIVEN TO MOTHERS AND CHILDREN. PROGRAM EFFECTS ON TARGET CHILDREN, DIFFERENTIAL EFFECT OF THE MOTHERS' INVOLVEMENT, VERTICAL DIFFUSION TO SIBLINGS, AND THE EFFECT OF THE HOME VISITOR ARE DISCUSSED. (NH)

ED050810 PS004666
A REVIEW OF EXPERIENCE: ESTABLISHING, OPERATING, EVALUATING A DEMONSTRATION NURSERY CENTER FOR THE DAYTIME CARE OF INFANTS AND TODDLERS, 1967-1970. FINAL REPORT. KEISTER, MARY ELIZABETH, JUN 70 72P.
EDRS PRICE MF-$0.65 HC-$3.29

THIS DOCUMENT IS THE FINAL REPORT OF PHASE ONE (1967-1970) OF THE GROUP CARE OF INFANTS DEMONSTRATION (CENTER) PROJECT. THIS REPORT DEVOTES MAJOR ATTENTION TO THE PROBLEMS OF ESTABLISHING, OPERATING, AND EVALUATING A GROUP DAY CARE CENTER FOR INFANT AND TODDLER CARE. THE CENTER PROJECT DESCRIBES WHAT IS REQUIRED TO PROVIDE HOUSING, EQUIPMENT, FOOD, SUPPLIES, SERVICES, PROPER RATIO OF ADULTS TO CHILDREN, DAILY PROGRAMS AND COSTS FOR THIS ONE PROGRAM. EVALUATIONS OF CHILD GROWTH WERE BASED ON DATA FROM 15 PAIRS OF MATCHED HOME AND CENTER CHILDREN (FROM MIDDLE CLASS FAMILIES) BETWEEN THE AGES OF THREE MONTHS AND THREE YEARS. DATA ANALYSIS REVEALED FEW SIGNIFICANT DIFFERENCES BETWEEN GROUPS ON MENTAL, MOTOR, OR SOCIAL DEVELOPMENT. THOSE DIFFERENCES WHICH WERE SIGNIFICANT FAVORED THE CENTER CHILDREN. ILLNESS DATA WERE DIFFICULT TO COLLECT AND INDICATED THAT CENTER CHILDREN APPEARED TO HAVE HAD MORE DIAPER RASH AND MORE COLDS. OUTGROWTHS OF THE CENTER PROJECT WERE PUBLICATION OF GUIDELINES FOR THE STATE LEGISLATURE, A LEAFLET FOR PARENTS, AND A DESCRIPTIVE BOOKLET DETAILING GROUP CARE OF YOUNG CHILDREN. ALTHOUGH THIS ONE PROGRAM DEMONSTRATED THAT BABIES IN GROUP CARE ARE NOT HARMED BY THE EXPERIENCE, THE REPORT STRESSES THE PIONEERING NATURE AND UNIQUENESS OF THE CENTER ENDEAVOR. (WY)

ED050811 PS004671
THE SWEDISH CHILD: A SURVEY OF THE LEGAL, ECONOMIC, EDUCATIONAL, MEDICAL AND SOCIAL SITUATION OF CHILDREN AND YOUNG PEOPLE IN SWEDEN. WESTER, ASTRID, 70 47P.
EDRS PRICE MF-$0.65 HC NOT AVAILABLE FROM EDRS.
AVAILABLE FROM: SWEDISH INSTITUTE, HAMNGATAN 27, P.O. BOX 7072, S-103 82 STOCKHOLM, SWEDEN

THIS REPORT SURVEYS THE VARIOUS PROVISIONS MADE BY THE SWEDISH GOVERNMENT TO PROTECT AND INSURE THE RIGHTS OF ITS CHILDREN. TOPICS DISCUSSED INCLUDE: THE LEGAL STATUS OF CHILDREN BORN IN OR OUT OF WEDLOCK; CUSTODY AND GUARDIANSHIP, ECONOMIC STATUS OF THE CHILD (CHILDREN'S ALLOWANCES, SOCIAL INSURANCE, MATERNITY BENEFITS, INHERITANCE); THE CHILD AT

SCHOOL; MEDICAL PROVISIONS; DAY CARE SERVICES; FOSTER CARE; AND SOCIAL CARE FOR THE HANDICAPPED. THE SWEDISH GOVERNMENT PROVIDES NINE YEARS OF FREE COMPULSORY EDUCATION FOR CHILDREN UNTIL THE AGE OF SIXTEEN. EIGHTY-FIVE PERCENT OF CHILD CARE ACTIVITIES ARE NOW RUN BY THE MUNICIPAL AUTHORITIES. THE ATTITUDE OF THE SWEDISH GOVERNMENT ON THE SUBJECT OF CHILD CARE IS THAT SUCCESS IN THE CARE AND TREATMENT OF CHILDREN DEPENDS NOT ONLY ON HOW CHILD CARE IS DESIGNED BUT ALSO ON HOW THE TOTAL ENVIRONMENT IN WHICH PEOPLE LIVE IS SHAPED. (AJ)

ED050812 PS004673
3 ON 2 PROGRAM: ADMINISTRATIVE GUIDE AND IMPLEMENTATION HANDBOOK. (REVISED EDITION). , AUG 70 53P.
EDRS PRICE MF-$0.65 HC-$3.29

IN THIS PROGRAM, BASED ON THE CONCEPTS OF INDIVIDUALIZED INSTRUCTION THROUGH THE TEAM APPROACH TO TEACHING, A TEAM OF THREE PROFESSIONALLY EQUAL TEACHERS TEACH A GROUP THE SIZE OF TWO CLASSES WHICH IS A COMBINATION OF GRADE LEVELS SUCH AS K-1, 1-2, OR 2-3. THE PROGRAM GOALS ARE THAT THE STUDENT SHOULD (1) ACQUIRE BASIC ACADEMICS, (2) DEVELOP SELF-DIRECTION, (3) DEVELOP A REALISTIC AND POSITIVE SELF-CONCEPT, AND (4) ESTABLISH SATISFYING INTERPERSONAL RELATIONSHIPS. THE PROGRAM INCLUDES UNGRADED ACTIVITIES, IMPROVED COUNSELING AND GUIDANCE, FLEXIBLE SCHEDULING, VARIABLE INSTRUCTIONAL GROUPING BASED ON THE LEARNER'S NEEDS, FLEXIBLE PHYSICAL FACILITIES, MULTI-MEDIA INSTRUCTIONAL MATERIALS, PARENT CONFERENCES, AND AMPLE PREPARATION TIME FOR TEACHERS. CONTENT AREAS INCLUDE LANGUAGE ARTS, MATHEMATICS, SOCIAL STUDIES, SCIENCE, ART, MUSIC, PHYSICAL EDUCATION, AND HEALTH. THIS DOCUMENT PROVIDES ADMINISTRATIVE GUIDELINES AND IMPLEMENTATION SUGGESTIONS IN AREAS SUCH AS CURRICULUM, FACILITIES, INSTRUCTION STRATEGIES, IN-SERVICE TEACHER WORKSHOPS, STUDENT PROGRESS EVALUATION, PROMOTION, COUNSELING, HOME-SCHOOL RELATIONS. EXTENSIVE SUPPLEMENTARY INFORMATION AND BIBLIOGRAPHIES ARE PROVIDED ON (1) INDIVIDUALIZED DIFFERENCES; (2) INDIVIDUALIZED INSTRUCTION; (3) THE CONCEPT OF CONTINUOUS, INDIVIDUAL PUPIL PROGRESS; AND (4) GUIDANCE AND COUNSELING. TABLES PROVIDE SAMPLE SCHEDULES, STAFF UTILIZATION, CLASSROOM ARRANGEMENTS, ETC. (AUTHOR/AJ)

ED050813 PS004674
NON-PUBLIC PRESCHOOL PROGRAMS IN INDIANA. GIBBS, VANITA; MCCARTHY, JAN, MAR 71 46P.
EDRS PRICE MF-$0.65 HC-$3.29
AVAILABLE FROM: CURRICULUM RESEARCH AND DEVELOPMENT CENTER, SCHOOL OF EDUCATION, INDIANA STATE UNIVERSITY, TERRE HAUTE, INDIANA 47809 ($0.50)

DURING THE SCHOOL YEAR, 1969-70, THE INDIANA CHAPTER OF DELTA KAPPA GAMMA, INTERNATIONAL HONORARY FOR WOMEN IN EDUCATION, AND THE INDIANA ASSOCIATION FOR THE EDUCATION OF YOUNG CHILDREN (IAEYC) CONDUCTED A SURVEY BY QUESTIONNAIRE OF THE NON-PUBLIC PRESCHOOL PROGRAMS IN THE STATE OF INDIANA. IN AN EFFORT TO GIVE DIRECTION TO PRESCHOOL PROGRAM DEVELOPMENT, THE RESEARCH COMMITTEES FROM LOCAL CHAPTERS OF THE SORORITY LOCATED NON-PUBLIC PRESCHOOL PROGRAMS IN THEIR RESPECTIVE COMMUNITIES AND CONDUCTED INTERVIEWS WITH THE DIRECTORS OF THESE PROGRAMS. THE DATA FOUND IN THIS DOCUMENT BASED ON 526 QUESTIONNAIRE RESPONSES, INCLUDE INFORMATION REGARDING THE EDUCATIONAL CONTENTS OF EXISTING PROGRAMS, PREPARATION OF STAFF, NUMBER OF CHILDREN SERVED, PHYSICAL FACILITIES, SOCIOECONOMIC LEVEL OF FAMILIES SERVED, PARENT PARTICIPATION, TYPES OF PROGRAMS AND SOURCES OF FUNDING. THE DOCUMENT INCLUDES A DIRECTORY OF THE PROGRAMS INCLUDED AND A COPY OF THE INDIANA LAW FOR LICENSING. (AUTHOR/AJ)

ED050814 PS004675
EDUCATIONAL INTERVENTION IN EARLY CHILDHOOD: A REPORT OF A FIVE-YEAR LONGITUDINAL STUDY OF THE EFFECTS OF EARLY EDUCATIONAL INTERVENTION IN THE LIVES OF DISADVANTAGED CHILDREN IN DURHAM, NORTH CAROLINA. FINAL REPORT, VOLUME I. SPAULDING, ROBERT L., 70 312P.
EDRS PRICE MF-$0.65 HC-$13.16

THIS VOLUME IS THE FIRST OF THREE WHICH REPORT THE RESULTS OF THE FIVE-YEAR EDUCATION IMPROVEMENT PROGRAM IN DURHAM, NORTH CAROLINA. VOLUME I DESCRIBES THE ORIGINAL PROPOSAL, THE RESEARCH STRATEGIES EMPLOYED, THE INTERVENTION RATIONALE, THE CURRICULAR PROGRAMS DEVELOPED, THE CHARACTERISTICS OF THE SUBJECTS AND THEIR FAMILIES, AND THE RESULTS OF THE OVERALL PROGRAM OF EDUCATIONAL INTERVENTION. APPROXIMATELY ONE-HALF THE DOCUMENT CONSISTS OF TABLES, CHARTS, AND GRAPHS. THE THREE VOLUMES TOGETHER CONSTITUTE THE FINAL REPORT TO THE FORD FOUNDATION. FOLLOWUP STUDIES USING THE DATA GATHERED DURING THE FIVE-YEAR SPAN OF THE PROGRAM WILL BE CONDUCTED DURING THE NEXT FEW YEARS AND REPORTED IN THE APPROPRIATE PROFESSIONAL JOURNALS. VOLUME II IS CATALOGUED UNDER PS 004 676 AND VOLUME III IS PS 004 677. (NH)

ED050815 PS004676
EDUCATIONAL INTERVENTION IN EARLY CHILDHOOD: APPENDIXES. FINAL REPORT, VOLUME II. SPAULDING, ROBERT L., 70 122P.
EDRS PRICE MF-$0.65 HC-$6.58

THIS VOLUME IS THE SECOND OF THREE WHICH REPORT THE RESULTS OF THE FIVE-YEAR EDUCATION IMPROVEMENT PROGRAM (EIP) IN DURHAM, NORTH CAROLINA. VOLUME II CONTAINS APPENDIXES TO THE FIRST VOLUME. APPENDIXES INCLUDE INFORMATION ON EIP PUBLICATIONS, DISSEMINATION ACTIVITIES, INSTRUCTIONAL RESOURCES MADE AVAILABLE TO EIP TEACHERS, EVALUATIONS BY OUTSIDE AGENTS INCLUDING THE EDUCATIONAL TESTING SERVICE, HEALTH CONDITIONS OF PROJECT CHILDREN AND FAMILIES, AND INSTRUMENTS USED IN DATA COLLECTION. THE THREE VOLUMES TOGETHER REPRESENT THE FINAL REPORT PRESENTED TO THE FORD FOUNDATION. FOLLOWUP STUDIES USING THE DATA GATHERED DURING THE FIVE-YEAR SPAN OF THE PROGRAM WILL BE CONDUCTED DURING THE NEXT FEW YEARS AND REPORTED IN THE APPROPRIATE PROFESSIONAL JOURNALS. VOLUME I APPEARS AS PS 004 675, AND VOLUME III IS PS 004 677. (AJ)

ED050816 PS004677
EDUCATIONAL INTERVENTION IN EARLY CHILDHOOD: ABSTRACTS OF THE 1965-1970 SPECIAL STUDIES RESEARCH AND EVALUATION REPORT. FINAL REPORT, VOLUME III. SPAULDING, ROBERT L., APR 70 179P.
EDRS PRICE MF-$0.65 HC-$6.58

THIS VOLUME IS THE LAST OF THREE WHICH REPORT THE RESULTS OF THE FIVE-YEAR EDUCATION IMPROVEMENT PROGRAM IN DURHAM, NORTH CAROLINA. VOLUME III CONSISTS OF ABSTRACTS OF SPECIAL STUDIES CONDUCTED BY THE INVESTIGATORS IN THE PROGRAM. SOME OF THE STUDIES HAVE BEEN PUBLISHED IN PROFESSIONAL JOURNALS. THE THREE VOLUMES, TOGETHER, CONSTITUTE THE FINAL REPORT TO THE FORD FOUNDATION. FOLLOWUP STUDIES USING THE DATA GATHERED DURING THE FIVE-YEAR SPAN OF THE PROGRAM WILL BE CONDUCTED DURING THE NEXT FEW YEARS AND REPORTED IN THE APPROPRIATE PROFESSIONAL JOURNALS. A 25-PAGE ANNOTATED BIBLIOGRAPHY IS INCLUDED IN THIS DOCUMENT. VOLUME I OF THIS REPORT APPEARS AS PS 004 675, AND VOLUME II IS PS 004 676. (AJ)

ED050817 PS004678
CURRICULUM FOR THE INFANT AND TODDLER. A COLOR SLIDE SERIES WITH SCRIPT. (SCRIPT ONLY). SAUNDERS, MINTA M.; KEISTER, MARY ELIZABETH, 71 38P.
EDRS PRICE MF-$0.65 HC NOT AVAILABLE FROM EDRS.
AVAILABLE FROM: INFANT CARE PROJECT, INSTITUTE FOR CHILD AND FAMILY DEVELOPMENT, UNIVERSITY OF NORTH CAROLINA, GREENSBORO, NC 27412 (SCRIPT, $2.00

THIS SCRIPT WAS WRITTEN TO ACCOMPANY A SERIES OF 118 COLOR SLIDES AND PRESENTS THE VIEW THAT THE IMPORTANT ELEMENTS IN CARING FOR AND TEACHING VERY YOUNG CHILDREN CANNOT BE PACKAGED AS A CURRICULUM. EVERYTHING THAT GOES INTO AFFECTIONATE AND SATISFYING CHILD CARE, DAY AFTER DAY, OFFERS MANY OPPORTUNITIES FOR LEARNING BY BABIES, TODDLERS, AND THEIR CAREGIVERS. EXPENSIVE TOYS AND EQUIPMENT ARE FOR THIS TYPE OF "CURRICULUM." SOME CHILD DEVELOPMENT THEORIES ARE BRIEFLY PRESENTED, AND INFANTS AND TODDLERS ARE SHOWN LEARNING THROUGH VARIOUS ASPECTS OF ROUTINE DAILY CARE, EXPLORATION AND PLAY, AND VISITS TO DOCTOR'S OFFICE AND NURSERY SCHOOL. RESULTS ARE REPORTED OF A STUDY OF 20 BABIES UNDER THE AGE OF 2 RECEIVING ALL-DAY CARE IN A NURSERY USING THE OLD-FASHIONED "CURRICULUM" PRESENTED IN THIS SLIDE SERIES. PAIRED WITH BABIES BROUGHT UP IN THEIR OWN HOMES BY INTERESTED, INVOLVED MOTHERS, THEY KEPT PACE IN MENTAL, MOTOR, AND SOCIAL DEVELOPMENT. INSTRUCTIONS ARE INCLUDED FOR ORDERING THE SLIDE SERIES. (AJ)

ED050818 PS004680
MEASURING DIFFERENTIAL DEVELOPMENT IN YOUNG CHILDREN. GARBER, HOWARD L., 7 FEB 71 10P.
EDRS PRICE MF-$0.65 HC-$3.29

THE PURPOSE OF THIS STUDY WAS TO INVESTIGATE THE IVANOV-SMOLENSKY PROCEDURE AS AN EFFECTIVE CLINICAL DEVICE FOR THE ASSESSMENT OF COGNITIVE DEVELOPMENT IN CHILDREN UNDER FOUR YEARS OLD. THIS PROCEDURE, EXPRESSLY DEVELOPED FOR ASSESSING DEVELOPMENT IN CHILDREN WITH LIMITED VERBAL SKILLS, MINIMIZES SOME OF THE RESEARCH PROBLEMS ASSOCIATED WITH YOUNG CHILDREN SINCE IT REQUIRES ONLY THAT A CHILD RESPOND TO SIMPLE VERBAL COMMANDS AND COLORED LIGHTS BY SQUEEZING A RUBBER BULB. FOUR GROUPS OF CHILDREN (N27), VARYING IN AGE AND IQ, WERE FORMED TO TEST THE SENSITIVITY OF THE PROCEDURE TO DETECT DIFFERENTIAL DEVELOPMENT. IT WAS EXPECTED THAT IF THE PROCEDURE WAS SENSITIVE, SUPERIOR PERFORMANCE WOULD BE SHOWN IN THE FORM OF AN INCREASE IN REGULATORY CONTROL WITH INCREASED LEVELS OF DEVELOPMENT. PERFORMANCE SCORES WERE SUBMITTED TO ANALYSIS OF VARIANCE AND THEN MULTIVARIATE ANALYSIS. RESULTS SHOWED THAT THE IVANOV-SMOLENSKY PROCEDURE HAS PROMISE AS A RESEARCH DEVICE. (AJ)

ED050819 PS004681
MODIFYING RESPONSE LATENCY AND ERROR RATE OF IMPULSIVE CHILDREN. EGELAND, BYRON; RUTNER, MURRAY, 7 FEB 71 12P.
EDRS PRICE MF-$0.65 HC-$3.29

THE PURPOSE OF THIS STUDY WAS TO MODIFY THE CONCEPTUAL TEMPO (RESPONSE STYLE ON A REFLECTIVE-IMPULSIVE DIMENSION) BY TRAINING IMPULSIVE CHILDREN TO INCREASE THEIR RESPONSE LATENCY OR BY TEACHING MORE EFFECTIVE SEARCH STRATEGIES AND SCANNING TECHNIQUES. SUBJECTS WERE 169 SECOND GRADERS FROM TWO LOWER CLASS AREA SCHOOLS. EACH SUBJECT WAS ASSIGNED TO ONE OF FOUR GROUPS: SC-SEARCH AND SCAN, TI-DELAY RESPONSES, CI-IMPULSIVE BUT GIVEN NO TRAINING, CR-RANDOMLY SELECTED CONTROLS. SC AND TI CHILDREN WERE TAUGHT A SERIES OF MATCH-TO-SAMPLE DISCRIMINATION TASKS. THE TI GROUP WAS TRAINED TO "THINK ABOUT ANSWERS AND TAKE TIME" BEFORE RESPONDING. THE SC GROUP WAS TRAINED TO APPLY RULES AND BASIC STRATEGIES. ALL SUBJECTS HAD BEEN PRETESTED ON A PORTION OF THE MATCHING FAMILIAR FIGURES (MFF). AS A POSTTEST, EIGHT UNFAMILIAR MFF ITEMS WERE GIVEN INDIVIDUALLY AND THE REMAINING EIGHT ITEMS WERE USED 7-9 DAYS LATER AS A DELAYED POSTTEST. CHANGES IN RESPONSE LATENCY AND NUMBER OF ERRORS FROM PRETEST TO POSTTESTS WERE ANALYZED. RESULTS INDICATE THAT THE TRAINING RECEIVED BY SC AND TI GROUPS DID AFFECT RESPONSE LATENCY BUT DID NOT HAVE MUCH EFFECT ON ERROR SCORES. (WY)

ED050820 PS004750
CHILDREN COME FIRST: THE INSPIRED WORK OF ENGLISH PRIMARY SCHOOLS. MURROW, CASEY; MURROW, LIZA, 71 271P.
DOCUMENT NOT AVAILABLE FROM EDRS.
AVAILABLE FROM: AMERICAN HERITAGE PRESS, 330 WEST 42ND STREET, NEW YORK, N.Y. 10036 ($6.95)

THIS BOOK, A STUDY OF THE INFORMAL CLASSROOM METHODS USED SUCCESSFULLY IN MANY ENGLISH INFANT AND JUNIOR SCHOOLS, IS THE REPORT OF TWO YOUNG AMERICAN TEACHERS WHO, FOR ONE YEAR, OBSERVED SCHOOLS IN ENGLAND AND TALKED WITH TEACHERS, PARENTS, AND CHILDREN. STRONG ACCEPTANCE OF INFORMAL APPROACHES IS CONVEYED BECAUSE, DESPITE SOME WEAKNESSES, SUCH APPROACHES MAKE LEARNING A PRODUCTIVE AND BALANCED EXPERIENCE FOR CHILDREN. WHILE SOME COMPARISONS OF ENGLISH AND AMERICAN CHILDREN ARE VALID, IT SHOULD NOT BE ASSUMED THAT THE SUM TOTAL OF WORK NOW TAKING PLACE IN THE BETTER ENGLISH SCHOOLS SHOULD OR COULD BE EXPORTED WHOLE TO THE UNITED STATES. A STUDY OF ENGLISH FAILURES AS WELL AS ACHIEVEMENTS IS NEEDED TO PROMOTE A MORE COMPLETE UNDERSTANDING OF THE INNER WORKINGS AND PHILOSOPHY OF THE BEST ENGLISH PROGRAMS. (WY)

ED050821 PS004753
THE DAY CARE CHALLENGE: THE UNMET NEEDS OF MOTHERS AND CHILDREN. KEYSERLING, MARY DUBLIN, 4 MAR 71 12P.
EDRS PRICE MF-$0.65 HC-$3.29

AN OVERVIEW OF THE PRESENT SHORTAGE OF DAY CARE FACILITIES IN THE UNITED STATES IS PRESENTED IN THIS SPEECH. STATISTICS CITED ON THE NUMBER OF WORKING MOTHERS WITH CHILDREN UNDER THE AGE OF 6 AND THE NUMBER OF DAY CARE LICENSED HOMES AND CENTERS SHOW THAT THE SHORTAGE OF LICENSED DAY CARE FACILITIES IS MUCH MORE ACUTE THAN IT WAS FIVE YEARS AGO. ALSO, THERE ARE A GREAT NUMBER OF MOTHERS WHO ARE INELIGIBLE FOR SUBSIDIZED DAY CARE, BUT WHOSE INCOMES ARE TOO LOW TO BUY GOOD PRIVATE CARE. GOVERNMENT PROGRAMS PROVIDE DAY CARE FOR ONLY 2% OF THE MIGRANT CHILDREN WHO NEED IT, AND FOR ONLY ABOUT 10% OF THE CHILDREN AT POVERTY OR NEAR POVERTY LEVELS. MOTHERS IN FEDERALLY SPONSORED WORK TRAINING PROGRAMS ARE OFTEN UNABLE TO CONTINUE PARTICIPATION BECAUSE OF LACK OF CHILD CARE. IT IS RECOMMENDED THAT OVER THE NEXT FIVE YEARS A GOAL BE SET FOR PROVISION OF DEVELOPMENTAL DAY CARE SERVICES FOR AT LEAST 2 MILLION ADDITIONAL CHILDREN, MERELY TO CATCH UP WITH THE CURRENT NEED. PARTICIPATION OF THE CLOTHING INDUSTRY, SOME HOSPITALS, AND SOME GOVERNMENTAL DEPARTMENTS IN PROVIDING DAY CARE FOR CHILDREN OF THEIR EMPLOYEES AND THE GROWING EMERGENCE OF FRANCHISED DAY CARE SYSTEMS ARE DISCUSSED. [FILMED FROM BEST AVAILABLE COPY.] (NH)

ED050822 PS004755
THE ASSESSMENT OF "SELF-CONCEPT" IN EARLY CHILDHOOD EDUCATION. COLLER, ALAN R., APR 71 79P.
EDRS PRICE MF-$0.65 HC-$3.29

THIS PAPER (1) REVIEWS THE LITERATURE AND EXAMINES HISTORICALLY SOME OF THE MORE IMPORTANT THEORETICAL HIGHLIGHTS THAT PERTAIN TO BOTH SELF-AS-SUBJECT AND SELF-AS-OBJECT DEFINITIONS OF SELF, (2) BRIEFLY DESCRIBES AND DISCUSSES THE VARIOUS ASSESSMENT APPROACHES DESIGNED TO ASSESS "SELF CONCEPT" IN YOUNG CHILDREN ACCORDING TO A SPECIALLY DEVELOPED CLASSIFICATORY SCHEMA, (3) ENUMERATES SUGGESTIONS TO AID THE FUTURE EVALUATION OF CHILDREN IN EARLY CHILDHOOD EDUCATION PROGRAMS. EXTENSIVE REFERENCES ARE PROVIDED. (WY)

ED050823 PS004757
PARENTS: ACTIVE PARTNERS IN EDUCATION. A STUDY/ACTION PUBLICATION. SAYLER, MARY LOU, 71 33P.
EDRS PRICE MF-$0.65 HC NOT AVAILABLE FROM EDRS.
AVAILABLE FROM: PUBLICATIONS-SALES SECTION, NATIONAL EDUCATION ASSOCIATION, 1201 SIXTEENTH STREET, N.W., WASHINGTON, D.C. 20036 ($1.00, NEA STOCK NUMBER 281-08890)

THIS PAMPHLET DESCRIBES A PROGRAM TO PROMOTE EFFECTIVE HOME-SCHOOL RELATIONS AND REFLECTS THE BELIEF THAT PARENT-TEACHER COOPERATION IS ESSENTIAL FOR THE BEST EDUCATION FOR CHILDREN. DISCUSSED ARE SPECIFIC STEPS THAT TEACHERS CAN TAKE TO INVOLVE PARENTS IN THE CLASSROOM AND SOME OF THE FEARS AND ATTITUDES THAT MAY INFLUENCE THE BEHAVIOR AND EFFECTIVENESS OF PARENTS. SUGGESTIONS ARE GIVEN TO HELP TEACHERS PLAN ACTIVITIES WHICH ARE APPROPRIATE FOR PARENTAL HELP IN CLASS (NURSERY THROUGH GRADE 6). A FINAL CHAPTER SUMS UP PROBLEMS WHICH MAY BE ENCOUNTERED, ENUMERATING TEACHER FEARS AND REWARDS IN A PARENT PARTICIPATION PROGRAM. (NH)

ED050824 PS004760
TWO KINDS OF KINDERGARTEN AFTER FOUR TYPES OF HEAD START. MILLER, LOUISE B.; DYER, JEAN L., [71] 52P.
EDRS PRICE MF-$0.65 HC-$3.29

RESULTS ARE REPORTED AT THE END OF THE SECOND YEAR OF A 3-YEAR COMPARISON OF FOUR PREKINDERGARTEN PROGRAMS: BEREITER-ENGELMANN, DARCEE, MONTESSORI AND TRADITIONAL. A NUMBER OF CLASSES IN EACH PROGRAM STYLE WERE USED WITH 246 FOUR-YEAR-OLDS IN HEAD START. CHILDREN WERE TESTED EARLY IN THE YEAR, AT THE END OF THE YEAR, AND AT THE END OF KINDERGARTEN ON A BATTERY OF TESTS AND RATING SCALES, INCLUDING STANFORD-BINET, PRESCHOOL INVENTORY, CURIOSITY BOX, REPLACEMENT PUZZLE, DOG & BONE, BEHAVIOR INVENTORY AND EMBEDDED FIGURES. THE KINDERGARTEN EXPERIENCE WAS SYSTEMATICALLY VARIED. ONE REPLICATION OF THE ORIGINAL EXPERIMENT ENTERED A FOLLOW THROUGH KINDERGARTEN, THE REMAINDER OF THE EXPERIMENTAL CHILDREN ENTERED REGULAR KINDERGARTEN, A NON-ACADEMIC PROGRAM. A VIDEO-TAPE MONITORING PROCEDURE DEVELOPED PREVIOUSLY WAS USED TO ANALYZE DIFFERENCES AMONG KINDERGARTEN PROGRAMS. DATA WERE EXAMINED FROM SEVERAL ASPECTS. (1) DID FOLLOW THROUGH AND REGULAR KINDERGARTEN CLASSES DIFFER IN EXPECTED DIMENSIONS? (2) DID FOLLOW THROUGH PRODUCE GREATER GAINS THAN REGULAR KINDERGARTEN? (3) WERE THERE INTERACTIONS BETWEEN TYPE OF HEAD START AND TYPE OF KINDERGARTEN? (4) TO WHAT EXTENT WERE HEAD START GAINS MAINTAINED IRRESPECTIVE OF TYPE OF KINDERGARTEN? (5) WERE THERE SEX EFFECTS OR SEX INTERACTIONS? RESULTS ARE DISCUSSED IN TERMS OF NEED FOR FINER ANALYSIS OF PROGRAM DIMENSIONS AS RELATED TO SPECIFIC EFFECTS. (AUTHOR/AJ)

ED050825 PS004761
CONTROL OF LEAD POISONING IN CHILDREN. (PRE-PUBLICATION DRAFT). , DEC 70 142P.
EDRS PRICE MF-$0.65 HC-$6.58

THIS DOCUMENT PRESENTS INFORMATION ABOUT ASPECTS OF THE LEAD POLLUTION PROBLEM THAT RELATE TO CHILDREN, SUGGESTS A COMMUNITY ACTION PROGRAM FOR CONTROLLING LEAD HAZARDS, ESTIMATES THE STAFF AND OTHER COSTS INVOLVED IN DEVELOPING SUCH A PROGRAM, AND TELLS HOW TO SYNTHESIZE THE PROGRAM COMPONENTS FOR MAXIMUM EFFECTIVENESS. THE SEVEN PARTS OF THE DOCUMENT CONCERN THEMSELVES WITH VARIOUS ASPECTS OF THE PROBLEM: (1) EPIDEMIOLOGY, ETIOLOGY, CLINICAL SIGNS AND SYMPTOMS OF LEAD POISONING; (2) PLANNING A CITY PROGRAM FOR LEAD CONTROL; (3) COMMUNITY AWARENESS AND EDUCATION; (4) CASEFINDING TO IDENTIFY CHILDREN WITH INCREASED LEAD INTAKE; (5) GUIDELINES FOR DEVELOPMENT AND ENACTMENT OF LEAD CONTROL LEGISLATION; (6) FINANCING A LEAD-CONTROL PROGRAM; AND (7) IDENTIFICATION AND MANAGEMENT OF ENVIRONMENTAL LEAD SOURCES IN THE RESIDENTIAL NEIGHBORHOOD. APPENDIX I GIVES AN ALTERNATE APPROACH TO ASPECT (7). APPENDIX II CONTAINS WORK SHEETS FOR ENVIRONMENTAL EVALUATION FROM UNITED STATES CENSUS DATA, AND CENSUS TRACTS. (AUTHOR/NH)

ED050826 PS004765
THE WORLD OF THE CHILD. PALMER, LEE, ED., 71 62P.
DOCUMENT NOT AVAILABLE FROM EDRS.
AVAILABLE FROM: THE ONTARIO INSTITUTE FOR STUDIES IN EDUCATION, 252 BLOOR STREET WEST, TORONTO 5, ONTARIO, CANADA ($1.50)

THE EARLY SCHOOL ENVIRONMENT STUDY (ESES), DEVELOPED BY PAUL PARK AND A TEAM OF TEN TEACHERS, BEGINS WITH THE PHILOSOPHY THAT CHILDREN LEARN THROUGH THE SOLUTION OF PRACTICAL PROBLEMS THAT ARE MEANINGFUL TO THEM, AND EXPANDS THIS APPROACH BEYOND THE SCIENCE FRAMEWORK INTO THE LEARNING OF LANGUAGE, MATHEMATICS, AND SOCIAL STUDIES. THIS BOOKLET WAS PREPARED PARTLY AS A SURVEY OF THE WORK OF THE ESES STUDY TO DATE, AND PARTLY AS AN INTERIM GUIDE FOR TEACHERS AND PRINCIPALS. IT OFFERS A STRUCTURED AND PRACTICAL METHODOLOGY FOR IMPLEMENTING THE CHILD-CENTERED APPROACH TO TEACHING AND LEARNING. SUGGESTIONS ARE GIVEN FOR PROGRAM PLANNING, COVERING SUCH TOPICS AS METHODS OF MOTIVATION, SUPPLIES, BOOKS, RESOURCE PEOPLE, GROUPING OF CHILDREN, TIME ARRANGEMENTS, AND

SO ON. EACH PROJECT HAS A STARTING POINT (ROCKS, WOODS, FAMILIES, STAMPS, PIRATES, THE HUMAN BODY) THAT SERVES AS A SPRINGBOARD INTO THE SELF-MOTIVATED PROCESS OF INQUIRY AND DISCOVERY CHARACTERIZING ESES. ACTIVITY FLOW CHARTS USED IN PROJECTS SHOW SAMPLE EXPLORATIONS OF THE CHILDREN'S ENVIRONMENT. OTHER TOPICS DISCUSSED ARE: THE ROLES OF TEACHER AND PRINCIPAL; THE DISINTERESTED CHILD; EVALUATION; TEACHER WORKSHOPS. LISTS OF RESOURCE MATERIALS ARE INCLUDED. (NH)

ED050827 PS004792
INDIVIDUAL DIFFERENCES IN THE DEVELOPMENT OF SOME ATTACHMENT BEHAVIORS. AINSWORTH, MARY D. SALTER; AND OTHERS, 11 FEB 71 41P.
EDRS PRICE MF-$0.65 HC-$3.29

THIS REPORT IS A PORTION OF A STUDY OF ATTACHMENT BEHAVIOR: BEHAVIOR PROMOTING CONTACT AND/OR PROXIMITY OF AN INFANT TO HIS MOTHER FIGURE. THIS REPORT DEALS SPECIFICALLY WITH CRYING, RESPONSE TO BRIEF EVERYDAY SEPARATIONS FROM THE MOTHER AND TO HER RETURN, AND BEHAVIOR RELEVANT TO PHYSICAL CONTACT WITH HER. THE SUBJECTS, 26 INFANT-MOTHER PAIRS FROM WHITE, MIDDLE CLASS FAMILIES, WERE VISITED AT HOME ONCE EVERY THREE WEEKS FROM 3 TO 54 WEEKS, EACH VISIT LASTING APPROXIMATELY FOUR HOURS. FROM THE OBSERVER'S DETAILED NOTES, A NARRATIVE RECORD WAS MADE OF INFANT BEHAVIOR AND MOTHER-INFANT INTERACTION. THE FINDINGS REPORTED IN QUARTER-YEAR SETS ILLUSTRATE DEVELOPMENTAL TRENDS, INDIVIDUAL DIFFERENCES IN THE BEHAVIOR OF BOTH MOTHER AND INFANT, AND THE RELATIONSHIP BETWEEN MATERNAL AND INFANT BEHAVIOR. THE RESEARCHERS CONCLUDE THAT (1) THERE ARE IMPORTANT QUALITATIVE DIFFERENCES IN INFANT-MOTHER ATTACHMENT RELATIONSHIPS; (2) NO SINGLE CRITERION OF ATTACHMENT CAN SERVE AS AN ADEQUATE BASIS IN ALL CASES FOR DETERMINING THE PRESENCE OF INFANT ATTACHMENT; (3) THERE IS NO PRESENT BASIS FOR ASSESSING STRENGTH OF ATTACHMENT; AND (4) MOTHER-INFANT INTERACTION SEEMS TO BE LINKED TO ATTACHMENT BEHAVIORS AND THE QUALITY OF THE ATTACHMENT RELATIONSHIP. MORE THAN ONE-FOURTH OF THIS DOCUMENT CONSISTS OF REFERENCES, FOOTNOTES, AND TABLES. (AUTHOR/AJ)

ED050828 PS004802
VISUAL IMAGERY INSTRUCTION AND NON-ACTION VERSUS ACTION SITUATIONS RELATIVE TO RECALL BY CHILDREN. FINAL REPORT. TAYLOR, ARTHUR M., 15 APR 70 108P.
EDRS PRICE MF-$0.65 HC-$6.58

THE REPORTS OF EIGHT STUDIES TESTING THE EFFECTS OF ELABORATION ON THE LEARNING OF CHILDREN ARE COMPILED IN THIS DOCUMENT. MENTAL ELABORATION IS "THINKING WHILE LEARNING" WHICH OCCURS AS THE LEARNER ACTIVELY ADDS CONTEXT TO THE MATERIAL HE IS ASKED TO PROCESS. SUPPLIED ELABORATION, INCLUDED IN THESE STUDIES, OCCURS WHEN THE LEARNER IS PROVIDED WITH ELABORATIVE LEARNING AIDS SUCH AS PICTURES AND SENTENCES. ATTEMPTS ARE MADE TO STATE THE DIFFERENTIAL EFFECTS ON LEARNING OF THE TWO TYPES OF ELABORATION. A MODEL FOR RESEARCH ON ELABORATION WAS PRESENTED, AND IT WAS HYPOTHESIZED THAT CHILDREN COULD LEARN MUCH MORE RAPIDLY WHEN SUPPLIED WITH CONTEXTS OR INSTRUCTED IN HOW TO MAKE UP THEIR OWN CONTEXTS. THE GENERAL APPROACH WAS TO TEST A RANGE OF TASKS FOR WHICH IMAGERY OR VERBAL ELABORATION WOULD BE EFFECTIVE. SEVEN OF THE STUDIES INVOLVED THE PAIRED-ASSOCIATE RECALL OF NOUNS, WHILE THE OTHER INVOLVED THE LEARNING OF A FINGER MAZE. THE MOST STRIKING FINDING WAS THAT INSTRUCTING CHILDREN IN MENTAL ELABORATION (IMAGERY AND SENTENCE GENERATION) SIGNIFICANTLY INCREASED THE RECALL OF NOUNS WHEN COMPARED WITH ROTE REPETITION, AND IT SEEMS THAT INSTRUCTING CHILDREN IN "HOW TO LEARN" STRATEGIES MAY BE APPROPRIATE FOR SEVERAL SCHOOL LEARNING TASKS. (AJ)

ED050829 PS004803
A STUDY OF THE DEVELOPMENT OF EGOCENTRISM AND THE COORDINATION OF SPATIAL PERCEPTIONS IN ELEMENTARY SCHOOL CHILDREN. FINAL REPORT. TOWLER, JOHN O., DEC 69 39P.
EDRS PRICE MF-$0.65 HC-$3.29

THIS STUDY DEVELOPED FROM THE HYPOTHESES: (1) THERE IS A SEQUENTIAL PATTERN IN THE DEVELOPMENT OF CHILDREN'S ABILITIES TO COORDINATE PERSPECTIVES, AND (2) USE OF AN URBAN ENVIRONMENT IN THE TEST OF COORDINATION OF PERSPECTIVES WILL RESULT IN AN EARLIER DEVELOPMENT OF THE AGE-STAGE RELATIONSHIPS TESTED BY PIAGET AND INHELDER (SWITZERLAND, 1963). STATISTICALLY TESTED HYPOTHESES WERE: (1) THERE ARE SIGNIFICANT CORRELATIONS BETWEEN THE ABILITY TO COORDINATE PERSPECTIVES AND CHRONOLOGICAL AGE, INTELLIGENCE, SOCIO-ECONOMIC STATUS, AND KNOWLEDGE OF LEFT-RIGHT RELATIONSHIPS; AND (2) THERE IS A SIGNIFICANT DIFFERENCE IN THE MEAN SCORES OF HIGH AND LOW SOCIO-ECONOMIC GROUPS ON THE TEST OF COORDINATION OF PERSPECTIVES WHEN THE EFFECT OF INTELLIGENCE IS REMOVED, AND ALSO A DIFFERENCE BETWEEN SUBJECTS LIVING IN URBAN AS OPPOSED TO RURAL ENVIRONMENTS ON THE SAME TEST. THE STUDY INVOLVED THE ADMINISTRATION OF AN INTELLIGENCE TEST, A TEST OF RIGHT-LEFT RELATIONSHIPS AND THE TEST OF COORDINATION OF PERSPECTIVES TO 140 CHILDREN FROM KINDERGARTEN TO GRADE SIX, 5.0 TO 12.7 YEARS OF AGE, ENROLLED IN TWO SCHOOLS REFLECTING HIGH AND LOW SOCIO-ECONOMIC CLASSES, RURAL AND URBAN ENVIRONMENTS. RESULTS PROVED HYPOTHESIS 1 ACCEPTABLE; 2 WAS NOT. THE FINDING THAT THERE ARE DIFFERENCES IN THE DEVELOPMENTAL STAGES OF CHILDREN OF THE SAME AGE BUT WITH DIFFERENT IQS INDICATES THAT PIAGET'S AGE-STAGE RELATIONSHIPS MAY BE MORE CLOSELY ALLIED TO INTELLIGENCE THAN TO MATURATION AND EXPERIENCE. (AJ)

ED050830 PS004804
A STUDY OF CAUSAL THINKING IN ELEMENTARY SCHOOL CHILDREN. FINAL REPORT. WARD, EDNA M., JUN 70 123P.
EDRS PRICE MF-$0.65 HC-$6.58

THIS STUDY, WHICH IS A PARTIAL REPLICATION AND VALIDATION OF THE 1962 LAURENDEAU AND PINARD STUDY OF CAUSAL THINKING, INVESTIGATES CROSS-CULTURAL DIFFERENCES AMONG THREE AGE LEVELS OF CANADIAN AND AMERICAN SCHOOL CHILDREN IN THE DEVELOPMENT OF CAUSAL THINKING. ALSO STUDIED IS THE RELATIONSHIP BETWEEN LEVEL OF DEVELOPMENT OF CAUSAL THINKING AND VARIABLES OF AGE, SEX, IQ, AND GRADE PLACEMENT. SEVENTY-FIVE BOYS AND 75 GIRLS, AGES 6, 8, AND 11 YEARS, WERE ADMINISTERED THE LAURENDEAU AND PINARD QUESTIONNAIRES (INCLUDED IN APPENDIXES) TO ELICIT RESPONSES ABOUT CONCEPTS OF DREAM, LIFE, THE ORIGIN OF NIGHT, THE MOVEMENT OF CLOUDS, AND THE FLOATING AND SINKING OF OBJECTS. RESPONSES WERE EVALUATED FOR INSTANCES OF PRECAUSAL THINKING, I.E. REALISM, ANIMISM, ARTIFICIALISM, FINALISM, AND DYNAMISM. ANALYSES OF THE DATA SUPPORT THE PIAGET (1927) AND THE LAURENDEAU AND PINARD (1962) FINDINGS WITH REGARD TO THE THREE AGE-RELATED STAGES OF DEVELOPMENT OF CAUSAL THINKING, AND THE MANIFESTATION OF PRECAUSAL FORMS OF THINKING. SIGNIFICANT DIFFERENCES APPEAR FOR THE DIMENSIONS OF AGE AND SCHOOL GRADE FOR THE AMERICAN SUBJECTS. SIGNIFICANT DIFFERENCES BETWEEN CANADIAN AND AMERICAN CHILDREN ARE FOUND IN LEVEL OF DEVELOPMENT ATTAINED IN ALL THE CONCEPTS; EXCEPTION WAS THE CONCEPT OF LIFE. (NH)

ED050831 PS004807
EFFECTS OF SOCIAL CLASS INTEGRATION OF PRESCHOOL NEGRO CHILDREN ON TEST PERFORMANCE AND SELF-CONCEPT. FINAL REPORT. GEIGER, EDWIN L.; EPPS, EDGAR G., JUN 70 18P.
EDRS PRICE MF-$0.65 HC-$3.29

THIS STUDY, DESIGNED TO ASSESS THE EFFECTS OF SOCIAL CLASS INTEGRATION, TESTED THE FOLLOWING HYPOTHESIS: PRESCHOOL AGE BLACK CHILDREN FROM MIDDLE CLASS SOCIOECONOMIC (SES) BACKGROUNDS WILL NOT BE ADVERSELY AFFECTED BY ATTENDING A DAILY PROGRAM WITH A SMALLER GROUP OF BLACK PEERS FROM LOWER SES BACKGROUNDS. A PRE- AND POSTTEST BATTERY ADMINISTERED TO ALL THE SUBJECTS INCLUDED THE STANDFORD-BINET INTELLIGENCE TEST, THE ILLINOIS TEST OF PSYCHOLINGUISTIC ABILITIES (ITPA), THE CALDWELL PRESCHOOL INVENTORY, AND THE BROWN IDS SELF-CONCEPT REFERENTS TEST. THE SUBJECTS WERE BLACK CHILDREN, 46- TO 57-MONTHS OLD AT THE BEGINNING OF THE STUDY, DIVIDED INTO THREE CLASSROOM GROUPS: AN EXPERIMENTAL GROUP OF 10 MIDDLE CLASS AND FIVE LOWER CLASS CHILDREN, A MIDDLE CLASS CONTROL GROUP (N15), AND A LOWER CLASS CONTROL GROUP (N15). RESULTS FOR THE BINET, ITPA, AND SELF-CONCEPT TEST SUPPORT THE HYPOTHESIS; RESULTS FOR THE CALDWELL PRESCHOOL INVENTORY DO NOT. BECAUSE OF THE SMALL SIZE OF THE GROUPS STUDIED AND THE PRESENCE OF CONFOUNDING FACTORS IN THE DESIGN, THE RESULTS ARE VIEWED AS TENTATIVE. (AUTHOR/AJ)

ED051871 PS004488
DIRECTED RESEARCH PROGRAM IN READING, EARLY CHILDHOOD, VOCATIONAL EDUCATION, SCHOOL ORGANIZATION AND ADMINISTRATION, FY 72 - FY 76. , MAY 70 73P.
EDRS PRICE MF-$0.65 HC-$3.29

IN 1970 THE NATIONAL CENTER FOR EDUCATIONAL RESEARCH AND DEVELOPMENT (CER) REVIEWED UNITED STATES OFFICE OF EDUCATION (USOE) BUREAU OF RESEARCH POLICIES OVER THE PREVIOUS 15 YEARS, AND AS A RESULT OF THIS REVIEW, INITIATED THE DIRECTED RESEARCH PROGRAM. THIS PROGRAM WILL CONCENTRATE FUNDS IN FOUR AREAS OF HIGH EDUCATIONAL SIGNIFICANCE AND WILL BE CONDUCTED SO THAT CUMULATIVE RESULTS CAN BE EMPLOYED RELATIVELY SOON TO IMPROVE THE SCHOOLS: (1) READING, (2) EARLY CHILDHOOD, (3) VOCATIONAL EDUCATION, AND (4) SCHOOL ORGANIZATION AND ADMINISTRATION. IN THIS DOCUMENT, DEVELOPMENT PLANS FOR EACH OF THESE FOUR AREAS ARE PROFILED AGAINST A TIMETABLE SPANNING FISCAL YEARS 1971-1976 WITH POSSIBLE COST ALLOCATIONS PER ACTIVITY PER YEAR. PROBLEMS, OBJECTIVES, AND STRATEGIES FOR DEVELOPMENT OF ACTIVITIES ARE DESCRIBED AND MAJOR PROBLEM AREAS WITHIN ACTIVITIES ARE DELINEATED. RESEARCH WHICH CONCENTRATES ON DISADVANTAGED POPULATIONS, WHICH IS LINKED TO OTHER USOE PROGRAMS, WHICH CAN BE DISSEMINATED TO THE SCHOOLS, AND WHICH CAN BE IMPLEMENTED IN EXPERIMENTAL SCHOOLS OR REGIONAL EDUCATIONAL LABORATORIES WILL OFFER MAXIMAL RETURN FOR THE INVESTMENT OF RESOURCES. (WY)

ED051872 PS004672
GUIDE FOR RIPPLES. POLLAK, RUTH S., 70 34P.
EDRS PRICE MF-$0.65 HC-$3.29
AVAILABLE FROM: NATIONAL INSTRUCTIONAL TELEVISION CENTER, BOX A, BLOOMINGTON, INDIANA 47401 ($1.00)

THE "RIPPLES" SERIES OF EDUCATIONAL TELEVISION PROGRAMS FOR CHILDREN FROM 5 TO 7 YEARS OLD IS DESCRIBED IN THIS GUIDE. THE PROGRAMS PRESENT BASIC IDEAS ABOUT MAN IN RELATION TO HIMSELF AND HIS ENVIRONMENT, LEADING THE CHILD INTO MANY SUBJECT AREAS AND STIMULATING CURIOSITY ABOUT HIMSELF AND THE WIDER WORLD. THE INFORMATION PRESENTED IN THIS GUIDE IS PLANNED TO HELP TEACHERS USE 36 DIFFERENT "RIPPLES" PROGRAMS EFFECTIVELY AND INCLUDES PROGRAM DESCRIPTION, BASIC EMPHASIS, AND SUGGESTIONS FOR FURTHER ACTIVITIES FOR EACH PROGRAM. WHEN SPECIFIC PREPARATIONS ARE DESIRABLE, THESE ARE ALSO MENTIONED. THE "RIPPLES" TELEVISION APPROACH IS DIFFERENT IN THAT IT DEPARTS FROM TRADITIONAL SUBJECT MATTER AND EMPHASIZES THE IMPORTANCE OF THE TEACHER ROLE IN LATER DISCUSSION AND ACTIVITIES. THE PROGRAMS ARE PLANNED TO REINFORCE EACH OTHER BY APPROACHING THE SAME IDEAS FROM DIFFERENT POINTS OF VIEW. FOR EXAMPLE, THE IDEA THAT CHILDREN CAN COPE WITH NEW SITUATIONS IS DEALT WITH IN SEVERAL WAYS IN THESE PROGRAMS: "EVERYBODY'S DIFFERENT, ALL BY MYSELF, HOW DO YOU KNOW?, OVERNIGHT AT THE HOSPITAL, AND LOST". (NH)

ED051873 PS004682
BEFORE SCHOOL STARTS. FOR CHILDREN'S MINDS--NOT JUST TO MIND THE CHILDREN. THE CHILD CENTRE--AS SEEN BY A PARENT. THORSELL, SIV; KARRE, MARIANNE, 69 27P.
EDRS PRICE MF-$0.65 HC NOT AVAILABLE FROM EDRS.
AVAILABLE FROM: SWEDISH INSTITUTE, HAMNGATAN 27, P.O. BOX 7072, S-103 82 STOCKHOLM, SWEDEN

THE TWO ARTICLES IN THIS DOCUMENT DESCRIBE SWEDISH CHILD CENTERS (DAY NURSERIES, NURSERY SCHOOLS, AND AFTER SCHOOL CENTERS). IN ONE ARTICLE, A GOVERNMENT OFFICIAL DISCUSSES THE OVERALL AIMS OF THE CHILD CENTERS, THEIR FACILITIES AND USE, AND THE STANDARDS AND STAFF. THE ROLE OF NATIONAL AND LOCAL GOVERNMENTS IN ADMINISTRATION AND FINANCES IS OUTLINED AND THE NEED FOR EXPANSION OF PRESCHOOL FACILITIES IN SWEDEN IS STRESSED. THE SECOND ARTICLE, WRITTEN BY A JOURNALIST, IS A CRITIQUE OF SWEDISH CHILD CENTERS FROM THE PARENT'S POINT OF VIEW. THE NEED FOR ADDITIONAL AND BETTER CENTERS TO REACH WIDER AND MORE DIVERSE GROUPS OF CHILDREN IS EMPHASIZED. PHYSICAL PLANNING, AGE GROUPING, TEACHERS, AND LENGTH OF THE CENTER DAY ARE DISCUSSED. (NH)

ED051874 PS004758
A COMPARISON STUDY OF THE COGNITIVE DEVELOPMENT OF DISADVANTAGED FIRST GRADE PUPILS (AS MEASURED BY SELECTED PIAGETIAN TASKS). HILLIARD, EVERETT, 29 APR 71 11P.
EDRS PRICE MF-$0.65 HC-$3.29

THE PURPOSE OF THIS STUDY WAS TO TEST THE EFFECTS OF AN EXPERIMENTAL METHOD OF INSTRUCTION UPON THE COGNITIVE DEVELOPMENT OF DISADVANTAGED FIRST GRADE CHILDREN. THE HYPOTHESES FORMULATED WERE: (1) THERE IS NO DIFFERENCE BETWEEN THE MEDIANS OF THE CONTROL AND EXPERIMENTAL GROUPS OR BETWEEN THE NUMBERS OF SUBJECTS IN EACH GROUP PLACING AT THE VARIOUS STAGES OF CONSERVATION ON CONSERVATION OF SUBSTANCE TASKS, CONSERVATION OF QUANTITY (DISCONTINUOUS) TASKS, AND SERIATION TASKS; AND (2) THERE IS NO DIFFERENCE BETWEEN THE MEDIANS OF THE CONTROL AND EXPERIMENTAL GROUPS ON THE NUMBERS SUBTEST OF THE METROPOLITAN READINESS TESTS. THE SAMPLE CONSISTED OF 38 FIRST GRADE PUPILS (MEAN AGE 6 YEARS AND 3 MONTHS AT THE BEGINNING OF THE YEAR) PRIMARILY FROM MEXICAN-AMERICAN, LOW INCOME HOMES. THE STUDENTS WERE PRETESTED IN SEPTEMBER. NEAR THE END OF THE YEAR, A 6-WEEK TRAINING PROGRAM CONSISTING OF 30-MINUTE DAILY LESSONS USING PIAGET'S TASKS WAS ADMINISTERED TO THE EXPERIMENTAL GROUP BY TEACHER AIDES. THE CONTROLS WERE SIMULTANEOUSLY GIVEN A TRADITIONAL ARITHMETIC PROGRAM. THE EXPERIMENTAL PROGRAM EMPHASIZED CHILDREN'S MANIPULATION AND CLASSIFICATION OF MATERIALS AND THE DEVELOPMENT OF LANGUAGE AND CONCEPTS OF NUMBER, SIZE, WEIGHT AND LENGTH AS WELL AS AN AWARENESS OF REVERSIBILITY IN RELATION TO MANY DIFFERENT KINDS OF TRANSFORMATIONS. BOTH HYPOTHESES WERE SUPPORTED. (AUTHOR/AJ)

ED051875 PS004763
CONFERENCE ON READING AND EARLY CHILDHOOD. , 70 60P.
EDRS PRICE MF-$0.65 HC-$3.29

COLLECTED IN THIS DOCUMENT ARE SEVEN PAPERS PRESENTED AT THE OHIO CONFERENCE ON READING AND EARLY CHILDHOOD: (1) "KIDS," JEROME KAGEN; (2) "PARENTS AS PARTNERS," CHRISTINE F. BRANCHE; (3) "WHEN THE YOUNG CHILD FINDS IMPORTANCE IN READING," LELAND B. JACOBS; (4) "FOUR QUESTIONS ON EARLY CHILDHOOD EDUCATION," LILIAN G. KATZ; (5) "HOW TO TEACH POOR BLACKS AND RICH WHITES TO READ," S. ALAN COHEN; (6) "COORDINATION OF REGULAR AND SPECIAL PROGRAMS," MARTIN L. STAHL; AND (7) "DISSEMINATION," JOSEPH L. DAVIS. (AJ)

ED051876 PS004766
ON EARLY LEARNING: THE MODIFIABILITY OF HUMAN POTENTIAL. GORDON, IRA J., 71 52P.
EDRS PRICE MF-$0.65 HC NOT AVAILABLE FROM EDRS.
AVAILABLE FROM: ASSOCIATION FOR SUPERVISION AND CURRICULUM DEVELOPMENT, NEA, 1201 SIXTEENTH ST., N.W., WASHINGTON, D.C. 20036 ($2.00, NEA STOCK NO. 611-17842)

THREE MAJOR EDUCATIONAL GOALS SUGGESTED FOR THE CHILD ARE: (1) THAT HE LEARN TO BALANCE A CONCEPT OF HIMSELF AS BOTH AN INDIVIDUAL AND A GROUP MEMBER; (2) THAT HE BECAME COMPETENT SO THAT HE WILL FEEL HE CAN INFLUENCE THE EVENTS THAT AFFECT HIS LIFE; AND (3) THAT HE DEVELOP A POSITIVE SENSE OF SELF-ESTEEM. A TRANSACTIONAL VIEW OF DEVELOPMENT AND THE ROLE OF CULTURE ARE DISCUSSED, AND AN OVERVIEW OF LONGITUDINAL STUDIES WHICH EXPLORE RELATIONSHIPS BETWEEN EARLY CHILD EXPERIENCE AND LATER PERSONALITY AND INTELLECTUAL DEVELOPMENT IS PRESENTED. STUDIES WHICH INVESTIGATE THE EFFECTS OF DIFFERENT TYPES OF STIMULATION UPON THE DEVELOPMENT OF THE YOUNG CHILD ARE DISCUSSED. THE NEED FOR NEW MEASURES OF INTELLECTUAL DEVELOPMENT IN THE EARLY YEARS IS EMPHASIZED, FOR MEASURES CURRENTLY IN USE HAVE NO PREDICTIVE VALIDITY. EDUCATORS SHOULD NOT CONFINE THEIR EFFORTS TO THE COGNITIVE DOMAIN, BUT SHOULD INVOLVE PARENTS AND THE GENERAL COMMUNITY IN ALL ASPECTS OF EDUCATION, INCLUDING DECISION MAKING. (NH)

ED051877 PS004768
ANALYSIS OF EARLY CHILDHOOD PROGRAMS: A SEARCH FOR COMPARATIVE DIMENSIONS. LAY, MARGARET; DOPYERA, JOHN, [70] 15P.
EDRS PRICE MF-$0.65 HC-$3.29

TO HELP EDUCATORS OBTAIN MORE SPECIFIC COMPARATIVE DATA ON PRESCHOOL PROGRAMS, THIS PAPER DEVELOPS SOME COMMON CONSTRUCTS FOR THE OBJECTIVE ASSESSMENT OF ANY PROGRAM. THE CONSTRUCTS PROPOSED ARE: (1) DENSITY, THE TOTAL AMOUNT OF SENSORY STIMULATION ENCOUNTERED WITHIN A GIVEN TIME SPAN; (2) VARIETY, THE EXTENT TO WHICH THE PROGRAM PROVIDES ENCOUNTERS TO DIVERSE STIMULI/SITUATIONS; (3) COMPLEXITY, THE EXTENT TO WHICH CHILDREN ENCOUNTER STIMULI/SITUATIONS IN THEIR NATURAL COMPLEX STATE AS COMPARED WITH ENCOUNTERING PREPARED SIMPLIFIED VERSIONS; (4) SEQUENCE, PROVISION FOR FUTURE ENCOUNTERS AND/OR EMPHASIS GIVEN TO PREVIOUS EXPERIENCE; (5) REGULARITY, THE EXTENT TO WHICH A PATTERN OF ENCOUNTERS RECURS ON A DAILY OR WEEKLY BASIS; (6) EMERGENCE, EXTENT TO WHICH NEW MATERIALS ARE INTRODUCED AS THE PROGRAM PROGRESSES AND/OR WHICH EXPECTATIONS FOR USE OF MATERIALS AND INTERACTIONS ARE ALTERED DURING THE PROGRAM; (7) UNIFORMITY, EXTENT TO WHICH CHILDREN WITHIN A PROGRAM HAVE SIMILAR ENCOUNTERS; (8) CONTRAST; (9) PACING; (10) SCOPE, AND (11) CONTROLLABILITY. THE CONSIDERATION OF DIMENSIONS WOULD FACILITATE THE COMBINATION OF VARIOUS ASPECTS OF SEVERAL PROGRAMS TO PRODUCE PROGRAMS MORE CLOSELY TAILORED TO A CHILD'S ASSESSED PERSONOLOGICAL CHARACTERISTICS OR STAGE OF DEVELOPMENT. (AUTHOR/AJ)

ED051878 PS004794
AN ACADEMIC PRESCHOOL FOR DISADVANTAGED CHILDREN: REVIEW OF FINDINGS. PRELIMINARY DRAFT. BEREITER, CARL, [70] 16P.
EDRS PRICE MF-$0.65 HC-$3.29

THIS PAPER PRESENTS SOME INFERENCES ABOUT PRESCHOOL EDUCATION, BASED ON EVALUATIVE RESEARCH DONE ON THE BEREITER-ENGLEMANN PROGRAM. THESE INFERENCES MAY BE SUMMARIZED AS FOLLOWS: (1) THE BEREITER-ENGLEMANN PROGRAM HAS CLEARLY HAD MORE IMPACT ON IQ AND ACHIEVEMENT THAN THE TRADITIONAL CHILD-CENTERED APPROACH, BUT NOT NECESSARILY MORE IMPACT THAN OTHER PROGRAMS HAVING A STRONG INSTRUCTIONAL EMPHASIS; (2) THE TRADITIONAL NURSERY SCHOOL AND KINDERGARTEN PROGRAM HAS FAILED TO ACHIEVE AS GOOD RESULTS IN COGNITIVE LEARNING AS THE MORE INSTRUCTIONAL APPROACHES, AND AT THE SAME TIME HAS NOT DEMONSTRATED ANY REDEEMING ADVANTAGES; AND (3) HOWEVER ENCOURAGING THE IMMEDIATE RESULTS AND FOLLOW-UP ACHIEVEMENT DATA OF A PRESCHOOL COMPENSATORY EDUCATION PROGRAM, NO PRESCHOOL PROGRAM SHOWS PROMISE OF MAKING, BY ITSELF, A PERMANENT DIFFERENCE IN POOR CHILDREN'S SCHOLASTIC SUCCESS. IT IS SUGGESTED THAT NO MORE RESOURCES BE DEVOTED TO THE SEARCH FOR BETTER PRESCHOOL PROGRAMS BECAUSE THE EXISTING TECHNOLOGY ENABLES YOUNG CHILDREN TO BE TAUGHT FAR MORE THAN THEY CAN BENEFIT FROM. IT IS PROPOSED THAT EDUCATORS DIRECT MORE EFFORT TOWARD CONSTRUCTING ARTICULATED PROGRAMS THAT PERMIT TEACHING IN PRESCHOOL WHAT WILL BE USEFUL LATER, AND TEACHING IN THE ELEMENTARY SCHOOL WHAT BUILDS UPON THE CHILD'S LEARNING IN PRESCHOOL. (NH)

ED051879 PS004801
TO LAUGH IS TO KNOW: A DISCUSSION OF THE COGNITIVE ELEMENT IN CHILDREN'S HUMOR. BYERS, LIBBY, [70] 11P.
EDRS PRICE MF-$0.65 HC-$3.29

THE DEVELOPMENT OF CHILDREN'S HUMOR IS DESCRIBED, FOCUSING ON THE COGNITIVE ASPECT OF WHAT IS FUNNY AND HOW THIS RELATES TO CHILDREN'S INTELLECTUAL GROWTH. COGNITIVE ELEMENTS THAT FACILITATE CHILDREN'S HUMOR ARE IDENTIFIED AS: (1) THE ABILITY TO GRASP INCONGRUITIES, (2) THE PRESENCE OF AN INTELLECTUAL CHALLENGE, (3) TIMING, (4) NOVELTY, AND (5) A SENSE OF DETACHMENT FROM THE SITUATION IN THE JOKE. HUMOR, AS USED ON SESAME STREET, IS DISCUSSED AS AN INSTRUCTIONAL TECHNIQUE TO REINFORCE AND EXPAND RECENTLY LEARNED CONCEPTS. (NH)

ED051880 PS004808
DAY CARE SURVEY-1970. SUMMARY REPORT AND BASIC ANALYSIS. , APR 71 246P.
EDRS PRICE MF-$0.65 HC-$9.87

THIS COMPREHENSIVE STUDY WAS DESIGNED TO PROVIDE ESSENTIAL INFORMATION FOR FEDERAL, STATE, AND LOCAL POLICY PLANNERS TO DESIGN AND TEST NEW PROGRAM CONCEPTS IN DAY CARE SERVICES FOR CHILDREN. FINDINGS FROM THE SURVEY PROVIDE DATA ON EXISTING DAY CARE PROGRAMS, AVAILABILITY OF DAY CARE SERVICES, AND THE NATURE AND EXTENT OF THE NEED FOR DAY CARE SERVICE. THE RESULTS OF THE SURVEY INDICATE THAT THERE IS A SIZEABLE POTENTIAL DEMAND AMONG LOW TO MODERATE INCOME WORKING MOTHERS FOR BETTER DAY CARE CENTER CAPACITY, THAT FOR SCHOOL-AGE CHILDREN THERE IS LITTLE ORGANIZED CARE OR OTHER SUPERVISED RECREATION TO MEET NEEDS BEFORE AND AFTER SCHOOL; AND LOW TO MODERATE INCOME WORKING MOTHERS PAY A NOMINAL AMOUNT OF LESS THAN $100 A YEAR FOR IN-HOME CARE, AND $400 TO $700 A YEAR FOR OUT-OF-HOME CARE. INFORMATION WAS OBTAINED FROM DAY CARE CENTER OPERATORS ON EXPENSES AND INCOME, AND PARENTS WERE ASKED WHAT THEY WERE WILLING TO PAY FOR ADEQUATE DAY CARE AND WHAT THEY COULD AFFORD. THIS VOLUME CONTAINS THE TEXT OF THE REPORT, WHILE A SEPARATE VOLUME PRESENTS THE PROJECT METHODOLOGY AND SURVEY INSTRUMENTS. APPROXIMATELY THREE-FOURTHS OF THIS DOCUMENT CONSISTS OF TABLES. (AUTHOR/AJ)

ED051881 PS004809
LANGUAGE TRAINING IN EARLY CHILDHOOD EDUCATION. LAVATELLI, CELIA STENDLER, ED., 71 196P.
DOCUMENT NOT AVAILABLE FROM EDRS.
AVAILABLE FROM: UNIVERSITY OF ILLINOIS PRESS, 54 EAST GREGORY, CHAMPAIGN, ILL. 61820 ($4.00)

THE PURPOSE OF THIS BOOK IS TO MAKE READERS, ESPECIALLY TEACHERS, MORE CONSCIOUS OF LANGUAGE PROCESSES AND OF THE COMPONENTS OF TEACHER-CHILD INTERACTIONS THAT AFFECT LANGUAGE ACQUISITION. THE PAPERS IN THIS VOLUME, DEVOTED TO BOTH THE THEORY AND PRACTICE OF LANGUAGE TRAINING, WERE SELECTED ON THE BASIS OF WHAT APPEAR TO BE PROMISING PRACTICES IN LANGUAGE TRAINING DERIVED FROM CURRENT PSYCHOLINGUISTIC THOUGHT. PART I CONTAINS THE FOLLOWING PAPERS: "LANGUAGE RESEARCH AND PRESCHOOL LANGUAGE TRAINING," DONALD R. MOORE; "ON THE HETEROGENEITY OF PSYCHOLOGICAL PROCESSES IN SYNTACTIC DEVELOPMENT," WILBUR A. HASS; AND "LANGUAGE OF THE DISADVANTAGED: THE DISTANCING HYPOTHESIS," IRVING SIGEL. PART II CONTAINS: "A TUTORIAL LANGUAGE PROGRAM FOR DISADVANTAGED INFANTS," GENEVIEVE PAINTER; "A SYSTEMATIZED APPROACH TO THE TUCSON METHOD OF LANGUAGE TEACHING," CELIA LAVATELLI, ED.; AND "LANGUAGE PROGRAMS FOR YOUNG CHILDREN: NOTES FROM ENGLAND AND WALES," COURTNEY B. CAZDEN. PART III PAPERS ARE: "SOME LANGUAGE COMPREHENSION TESTS," URSULA BELLUGI-KLIMA; AND "ELICITED IMITATION AS A RESEARCH TOOL IN DEVELOPMENTAL PSYCHOLINGUISTICS," DANIEL I. SLOBIN AND CHARLES A. WELSH. (AUTHOR/AJ)

ED051882 PS004810
RACIAL ATTITUDES AMONG WHITE KINDERGARTEN CHILDREN FROM THREE DIFFERENT ENVIRONMENTS. OROST, JEAN H., JAN 71 27P.
EDRS PRICE MF-$0.65 HC-$3.29

THIS RESEARCH WAS INITIATED TO DETERMINE WHETHER THE EXTENT OF A WHITE CHILD'S FIRST-HAND CONTACTS WITH BLACK PEERS WOULD INFLUENCE HIS ATTITUDES TOWARD BLACKS. THE SUBJECTS, 49 WHITE, MIDDLE TO UPPER CLASS KINDERGARTEN CHILDREN, ALL FROM TWO-PARENT HOMES WITH MOTHERS WHO DID NOT WORK OUTSIDE THE HOME, WERE DIVIDED INTO THREE GROUPS: (A) CHILDREN WITH NO ASSOCIATION WITH BLACK CHILDREN, (B) CHILDREN WITH INTERRACIAL CONTACTS IN SCHOOL ONLY, AND (C) CHILDREN WITH INTERRACIAL CONTACTS BOTH IN SCHOOL AND RESIDENTIAL ENVIRONMENT. THE TEST USED WAS THE SOCIAL EPISODES TEST DESIGNED BY TRAGER AND RADKE-YARROW, BUT WITH PICTURES DESIGNED ESPECIALLY FOR THIS PROJECT. THE THREE PICTURES SHOWN AND DISCUSSED WERE: (1) THREE WHITE CHILDREN PLAYING AND A BLACK CHILD APPROACHING THE GROUP, (2) THREE WHITE CHILDREN PLAYING, AND (3) THREE WHITE CHILDREN AND ONE BLACK CHILD PLAYING TOGETHER. AN INTERVIEW WAS CONDUCTED TO DETERMINE THE EXTENT OF THE CHILD'S ASSOCIATIONS WITH AND FEELINGS TOWARD BLACK CHILDREN. 79.7% OF THE SAMPLE DISPLAYED SOME FORM OF TENSION AFTER BEING SHOWN THE FIRST PICTURE. ABOUT HALF THAT NUMBER OF CHILDREN DISPLAYED TENSION AFTER PICTURE NUMBER THREE OF RACIAL HARMONY. REFUSAL TO DISCUSS PICTURE NUMBER ONE WAS MOST PREVALENT AMONG GROUP B SUBJECTS. TENSION DISPLAYED BY DISTRACTION WAS MOST EVIDENT AMONG GROUP A SUBJECTS. (AUTHOR/AJ)

ED051883 PS004811
EFFECT OF LABELS ON MEMORY IN THE ABSENCE OF REHEARSAL. WARD, WILLIAM C.; LEGANT, PATRICIA, OCT 70 11P.
EDRS PRICE MF-$0.65 HC-$3.29

THIS STUDY TESTS THE HYPOTHESIS THAT LABELING FACILITATES RECALL IN NURSERY SCHOOL CHILDREN IF AND ONLY IF IT LEADS TO REHEARSAL. SUBJECTS WERE 34 CHILDREN RANGING IN AGE FROM 47 TO 53 MONTHS. DURING PRETRAINING, THOSE CHILDREN IN THE LABEL GROUP NAMED PICTURES OF ANIMALS AND FRUITS AS THEY WERE PRESENTED, WHILE THOSE IN THE NO LABEL GROUP MATCHED EACH PICTURE TO THE SAME CARD IN A SECOND SET OF PICTURES. EIGHT TEST TRIALS FOLLOWED. DURING EACH ONE THE CHILD WAS SHOWN TWO PICTURES, ONE AT A TIME, WITH EXPOSURE ENDED AS SOON AS HE NAMED THEM (OR IN THE NO LABEL GROUP, AFTER A COMPARABLY BRIEF EXPOSURE.) FOR ALL SUBJECTS THERE WAS A 20-SECOND DELAY BETWEEN PRESENTATION AND RECALL, DURING WHICH THE TESTER CONVERSED WITH THE CHILD TO PREVENT REHEARSAL. SUBJECTS WHO LABELED SHOWED RECALL SUPERIOR TO THAT OF SUBJECTS WHO DID NOT, INDICATING THAT THE FACILITATING EFFECT OF LABELS IN SHORT-TERM MEMORY IS NOT SOLELY ATTRIBUTABLE EITHER TO AN INCREASED TENDENCY TO REHEARSE OR TO THE STRENGTHENING OF A PRIMARY MEMORY SOURCE. (AUTHOR/NH)

ED051884 PS004815
CONSULTATION IN DAY CARE. KIESTER, DOROTHY J., 69 82P.
DOCUMENT NOT AVAILABLE FROM EDRS.
AVAILABLE FROM: INSTITUTE OF GOVERNMENT, UNIVERSITY OF NORTH CAROLINA, CHAPEL HILL, NC 27514 ($1.00)

THIS HANDBOOK CLARIFIES THE RESPONSIBILITY, ROLE AND FUNCTIONS OF THE DAY CARE CONSULTANT. A CHAPTER ON THE PHILOSOPHY OF DAY CARE IS INTENDED TO STIMULATE THOUGHTFUL CONSIDERATION OF HOW EXISTING PATTERNS OF DAY CARE AFFECT CHILDREN, PARENTS, AND THE FAMILY. A VARIETY OF METHODS AND STRATEGIES FOR TRANSLATING DAY CARE PHILOSOPHY INTO PRACTICE ARE DESCRIBED. THE TOOLS NEEDED BY THE DAY CARE CONSULTANT ARE KNOWLEDGE, COMMUNICATION SKILLS, RELATIONSHIP SKILLS, CONSTRUCTIVE USE OF AUTHORITY, AND SKILLS OF DIAGNOSIS AND PROBLEM SOLVING. A FINAL CHAPTER ON TRAINING DISCUSSES CONFERENCES AND INSTITUTES, WORKSHOPS, AND INSERVICE TRAINING. THIS BOOKLET WAS WRITTEN PRIMARILY FOR DAY CARE CONSULTANTS, BUT IT SHOULD ALSO BE HELPFUL TO BOARDS OF DIRECTORS AND PLANNING COMMITTEES IN COMMUNITIES WHERE SKILLED CONSULTANTS ARE NOT READILY AVAILABLE. (NH)

ED051885 PS004817
MOTHER-INFANT INTERACTION AND INFANT DEVELOPMENT AMONG THE WOLOF OF SENEGAL. LUSK, DIANE; LEWIS, MICHAEL, MAR 71 21P.
EDRS PRICE MF-$0.65 HC-$3.29

TEN MOTHER-INFANT DYADS WERE OBSERVED IN THEIR HOMES FOR FOUR HOURS EACH DURING ONE MONTH IN ORDER TO MEASURE INTERACTIVE ASPECTS OF THEIR BEHAVIOR. DEMOGRAPHIC DATA ARE INCLUDED FOR THE PARTICIPATING FAMILIES, WHO ARE MEMBERS OF THE WOLOF IN SENEGAL, AFRICA. FOR THIS STUDY, INTERACTION WAS DEFINED AS A SEQUENCE OF BEHAVIORS INVOLVING BOTH CARETAKER AND INFANT WHICH FELL (A) WITHIN ONE 10-SECOND TIME COLUMN OR (B) EXTENDED OVER TWO OR MORE TIME COLUMNS BUT WHICH THE OBSERVED JUDGED TO BE A CONTINUOUS SEQUENCE. SIX DIFFERENT INFANT BEHAVIORS (FRET/CRY, EXTREME MOVEMENT, LOOK, VOCALIZE, SMILE, TOUCH) AND FIVE ADULT BEHAVIORS (TOUCH-GROSS, TOUCH-FINE, VOCALIZE, SMILE, APPROACH) WERE RECORDED. AFTER COLLECTING THE OBSERVATIONAL DATA, THE NEW BAYLEY SCALES OF INFANT DEVELOPMENT WERE GIVEN TO THE INFANTS IN THEIR HOMES. THE MOST IMPORTANT RESULT TO EMERGE WAS THAT THE PATTERN OF CARETAKER-INFANT INTERACTION WAS RELATED MORE STRONGLY TO THE AGE OF THE INFANT THAN TO ANY OTHER VARIABLE INVESTIGATED. THE RESULTS OF THE DEVELOPMENTAL TESTING ARE IN AGREEMENT WITH OTHER FINDINGS THAT AFRICAN INFANTS SHOW PRECOCIOUS DEVELOPMENT WITHIN THE FIRST YEAR. NO RELATIONSHIP BETWEEN THE INTERACTION MEASURES AND TESTS OF COGNITIVE AND MOTOR SKILLS WAS FOUND. (AUTHOR/NH)

ED051886 PS004818
INTERRELATIONS IN CHILDREN'S LEARNING OF VERBAL AND PICTORIAL PAIRED ASSOCIATES. HALE, GORDON A., JAN 71 25P.
EDRS PRICE MF-$0.65 HC-$3.29

THIS STUDY WAS DESIGNED TO INVESTIGATE THE FUNCTIONAL SIMILARITY OF THE MENTAL PROCESSES CHILDREN USE TO LEARN VERBAL TASKS AND PICTORIAL TASKS. CHILDREN IN GRADES 3 AND 6 (N144) AND IN GRADE 9 (N112) WERE GIVEN FOUR SHORT PAIRED-ASSOCIATE TASKS ENTITLED PICTURES, CONCRETE WORDS, ABSTRACT WORDS, AND JAPANESE CHARACTERS. THE TASKS CONSISTED OF SIX STIMULUS-RESPONSE PAIRS PRESENTED OVER TWO TRIALS. PLANNED COMPARISONS IN MEAN LEVEL OF PERFORMANCE INVOLVED THE FIRST

THREE TASKS. PERFORMANCE ON PICTURES WAS FOUND TO BE SUPERIOR TO CONCRETE WORDS, AND CONCRETE WORDS WAS SUPERIOR TO ABSTRACT WORDS, WITH THE FORMER EFFECT REACHING SIGNIFICANCE FOR GRADES 3 AND 9 AND THE LATTER FOR GRADES 3 AND 6. AN ANALYSIS OF ALL FOUR TASKS FOUND THAT CORRELATION BETWEEN PICTURES AND CONCRETE WORDS INCREASED ACROSS GRADE LEVELS TO A GREATER DEGREE THAN CORRELATION BETWEEN ANY OTHER PAIR OF TASKS. THIS LAST RESULT PARALLELED DATA FROM AN AUXILLARY EXPERIMENT AND SUGGESTS A DEVELOPMENTAL INCREASE IN CHILDREN'S USE OF VERBAL PROCESSES ALONG WITH IMAGERY TO LEARN PICTORIAL MATERIALS. (AUTHOR/NH)

ED051887 PS004823
LIVING WITH CHILDREN: NEW METHODS FOR PARENTS AND TEACHERS. PATTERSON, GERALD R.; GULLION, M. ELIZABETH, 68 128P.
DOCUMENT NOT AVAILABLE FROM EDRS.
AVAILABLE FROM: RESEARCH PRESS, COUNTRY FAIR STATION, BOX 3177, CHAMPAIGN, ILL. 61820 ($3.00)

WRITTEN IN THE FORM OF PROGRAMMED INSTRUCTION, THIS BOOK IS DESIGNED TO HELP PARENTS AND TEACHERS UNDERSTAND AND CORRECT SITUATIONS IN WHICH A CHILD'S BEHAVIOR IS DISTRESSING. THE BOOK UTILIZES THE SOCIAL LEARNING APPROACH (THAT PEOPLE LEARN MOST BEHAVIOR PATTERNS FROM OTHER PEOPLE). THE FIRST SECTION DISCUSSES HOW PARENTS AND CHILDREN LEARN AND TEACHES ABOUT REINFORCERS, HOW CHILDREN TRAIN PARENTS, ACCIDENTAL TRAINING, AND HOW TO OBSERVE AND RETRAIN ONE'S CHILD. THE SECOND SECTION ON CHANGING UNDESIRABLE BEHAVIOR PRESENTS CLUES FOR HELPING BELLIGERENT, RELUCTANT, OVERLY ACTIVE, DEPENDENT, FRIGHTENED OR WITHDRAWN CHILDREN. SAMPLE BEHAVIOR GRAPHS ARE PROVIDED. (AJ)

ED051888 PS004824
ISSUES IN HUMAN DEVELOPMENT: AN INVENTORY OF PROBLEMS, UNFINISHED BUSINESS AND DIRECTIONS FOR RESEARCH. VAUGHAN, VICTOR C., III, ED., NOV 67 222P.
EDRS PRICE MF-$0.65 HC NOT AVAILABLE FROM EDRS.
AVAILABLE FROM: SUPERINTENDENT OF DOCUMENTS, U.S. GOVERNMENT PRINTING OFFICE, WASHINGTON, D.C. 20402 ($1.75)

THE PAPERS PRESENTED AT THE SYMPOSIUM ON ISSUES IN HUMAN DEVELOPMENT IN PHILADELPHIA, NOVEMBER 1967, ARE COLLECTED IN THIS DOCUMENT. INCLUDED ARE LENGTHY EXTRACTS FROM THE DISCUSSION. PARTICIPANTS AT THE CONFERENCE WERE FROM THE BIOLOGIC AND SOCIAL SCIENCES. THE GOAL OF THE CONFERENCE WAS NOT SO MUCH TO REVEAL ANSWERS TO PROBLEMS AS TO MAKE SURE THE RIGHT QUESTIONS WERE BEING ASKED, IN THE HOPE THAT THE ULTIMATE ANSWERS MIGHT SERVE AS GUIDES TO SOCIAL AND POLITICAL ACTION. THE SEVEN PARTS INTO WHICH THE CONFERENCE WAS DIVIDED EMPHASIZED THESE ASPECTS OF HUMAN DEVELOPMENT: EARLIEST INFLUENCES; PHYSICAL AND CHEMICAL GROWTH AND DEVELOPMENT; SOCIALIZATION IN EARLY CHILDHOOD; COGNITION AND LEARNING; ADOLESCENCE; THE CITY; INSTITUTIONS, ECONOMICS AND THE LAW. ALL OF THE PAPERS ARE TIMELY; SOME WERE FRESHLY UPDATED BEFORE THIS PUBLICATION. THE ISSUES DISCUSSED PRESENT THE NEED FOR STUDY AND RESEARCH, AND FOR COMMUNITY ACTION THAT WILL HELP CHILDREN TO LIVE CREATIVE AND PRODUCTIVE LIVES. (AUTHOR/NH)

ED051889 PS004833
A PRESCHOOL ARTICULATION AND LANGUAGE SCREENING FOR THE IDENTIFICATION OF SPEECH DISORDERS. FINAL REPORT. WRIGHT, REVILLA; LEVIN, BARBARA, JUN 71 25P.
EDRS PRICE MF-$0.65 HC-$3.29

THIS REPORT DESCRIBES THE VALIDITY AND RELIABILITY STUDIES DONE TO STANDARDIZE A PRESCHOOL SCREENING TEST DEVELOPED FOR IDENTIFICATION OF ARTICULATION AND LANGUAGE DISORDERS. THE TEST MEETS THE NEED FOR A BRIEF PROCEDURE WHICH (1) IDENTIFIES ARTICULATION AND LANGUAGE DISORDERS, (2) IS NOT DIALECT BOUND AND GOES ACROSS CULTURAL AND REGIONAL DIFFERENCES IN ENGLISH, AND (3) IS STANDARDIZED ON A PREDOMINATELY BLACK POPULATION. THE TEST TAKES 5 TO 8 MINUTES TO ADMINISTER AND INCLUDES BASIC AREAS OF VOCABULARY, ARTICULATION, AND LANGUAGE. A FAILURE IN ARTICULATION AND/OR LANGUAGE INDICATES THE NEED FOR A LONGER EVALUATION. THE RESULTS OF THE SHORT SCREENING TEST ARE COMPARED WITH THE RESULTS OF MORE EXTENSIVE TESTING FOR 152 CHILDREN ENROLLED IN DAY CARE AND HEAD START TYPE PROGRAMS. AGES RANGED FROM 2 1/2 TO 5 1/2 YEARS, WITH 25 CHILDREN IN EACH 6 MONTH AGE GROUP. NINETY-FOUR PERCENT OF THE TIME THE SCREENING EITHER AGREED WITH THE EVALUATION (135 CHILDREN) OR GAVE A FALSE POSITIVE (10 CHILDREN), INDICATING THAT THIS TEST IS AN EFFICIENT AND VALID INDICATOR OF ARTICULATION AND LANGUAGE DISORDERS. COMMUNICATION OF RESULTS TO SCHOOL PERSONNEL AND PARENTS FOR EFFECTIVE FOLLOW UP IS DISCUSSED. TABLES ARE INCLUDED. A TESTING KIT AND MANUAL ARE AVAILABLE. (AUTHOR/NH)

ED051890 PS004834
CONDITIONING TASKS PERFORMANCE IN INFANCY AND EARLY CHILDHOOD AS A STABLE AND MEASURABLE ASPECT OF BEHAVIOR. FINAL REPORT. STRONG, EMILY; VALLERY, ARLEE, SEP 70 34P.
EDRS PRICE MF-$0.65 HC-$3.29

PRIMARILY A FEASIBILITY STUDY, THE RESEARCH REPORTED IS BASED ON EYSENCK'S HYPOTHESIS THAT CONDITIONABILITY IS A UNITARY FACTOR RELATED TO INTROVERSION-EXTROVERSION AND ATTENTION SPAN. THIRTY INFANTS, REPRESENTING A RANDOM SAMPLING OF RACE, SEX, AND SOCIOECONOMIC BACKGROUND, WERE TESTED ON THREE CONSECUTIVE DAYS AT AGES 3 MONTHS, 5 MONTHS, 9 MONTHS, AND 12 MONTHS. TESTS BASED ON EXISTING METHODS OF SUCCESSFUL INFANT CONDITIONING WERE ADAPTED TO INFANTS' ABILITIES AT EACH AGE, BUT AT EACH TEST TIME INCLUDED EYE BLINK, VOCALIZATION, HEAD TURN, DISCRIMINATION AND SINGLE-STIMULUS CONDITIONING. TESTS OF ATTENTION-SPAN AND THE BAYLEY TEST OF MENTAL AND MOTOR DEVELOPMENT WERE ALSO GIVEN EACH TIME. THE SUBJECTS WILL BE TESTED AGAIN AT AGE 3 AND AT AGE 7, USING STANDARD IQ AND PERSONALITY TESTS. THE FEASIBILITY OF THIS LONGITUDINAL STUDY WAS ESTABLISHED, AND CONCLUSIONS WERE DRAWN ABOUT THE USEFULNESS OF THE VARIOUS CONDITIONING PROCEDURES EMPLOYED. FURTHER RESEARCH LEADING TO STANDARDIZED PROCEDURES AND A TEST OF CONDITIONABILITY IS NEEDED, TO GIVE CLUES TO THE CHILD'S INDIVIDUAL LEARNING STYLE. FIGURES SHOWING THE APPARATUS FOR THE TESTS USED IN THIS STUDY ARE INCLUDED. (AUTHOR/NH)

ED051891 PS004845
A STUDY IN CHILD CARE (CASE STUDY FROM VOLUME II-A): "A HOUSE FULL OF CHILDREN." DAY CARE PROGRAMS REPRINT SERIES. ZECKHAUSER, SALLY; RUOPP, RICHARD R., NOV 70 49P.
EDRS PRICE MF-$0.65 HC-$3.29

THE UTE INDIAN TRIBE DAY CARE CENTER AT FORT DUCHESNE, UTAH, IS AN EXPANDED HEAD START PROGRAM SERVING UTE AND ANGLO CHILDREN. THE COMMUNITY CONTROL OF THE CENTER IS SIGNIFICANT: TWO-THIRDS OF THE STAFF ARE UTE; PARENTS WORK AS PAID STAFF AND VOLUNTEERS IN TEACHING SITUATIONS; MONTHLY PARENT MEETINGS ARE HELD; 40% OF THE PARENTS ARE INVOLVED IN A CAREER DEVELOPMENT PROGRAM; AND THE CENTER DISTRIBUTES ITS OWN MONTHLY NEWSLETTER. ETHNIC IDENTITY AND BILINGUAL COMMUNICATION ARE STRESSED IN THE DAY CARE PROGRAM. CHILDREN ARE TAUGHT ABOUT THEIR NATIVE LEGENDS, FOODS, CRAFTS AND DANCES. CENTER PERSONNEL FEEL THAT THE EMPHASIS ON UTE CULTURE GIVES UTE CHILDREN INCREASED TRIBAL PRIDE AND ANGLO CHILDREN A BETTER UNDERSTANDING OF THEIR INDIAN NEIGHBORS. CHILDREN IN THE CENTER ARE FREE TO CHOOSE THEIR OWN ACTIVITIES AND SELF-RELIANCE IS ENCOURAGED. THE CENTER PROVIDES A FULL-TIME NUTRITIONAL AND HEALTH PROGRAM. A FLOOR PLAN OF THE CENTER, A COMMUNITY HISTORY, AN EXPLANATION OF CENTER AND STAFF ORGANIZATION, A CHART OF THE USE OF THE COORDINATOR'S TIME, AND PARENT COMMENTS ARE INCLUDED IN THIS DOCUMENT. AN APPENDIX PROVIDES A SAMPLE DAILY SCHEDULE, WEEKLY MENU, PHYSICAL EXAM FORM AND CHILD INFORMATION FORM. (AJ)

ED051892 PS004846
A STUDY IN CHILD CARE (CASE STUDY FROM VOLUME II-A): "THEY UNDERSTAND." DAY CARE PROGRAMS REPRINT SERIES. O'FARRELL, BRIGID, NOV 70 44P.
EDRS PRICE MF-$0.65 HC-$3.29

THIS DAY CARE CENTER, OPERATED BY SYRACUSE UNIVERSITY AND SERVING 100 CHILDREN (BIRTH TO 3-YEAR-OLD), ADMITS ONLY ONE CHILD PER FAMILY. THE CHILD MUST BE THE FIRST OR SECOND CHILD IN A FAMILY WHERE BOTH PARENTS HAVE HIGH SCHOOL EDUCATION OR LESS AND EARN LESS THAN $5,000 PER YEAR. THE PROGRAM PHILOSOPHY MAINTAINS THAT QUALITY DAY CARE MUST CARRY OVER INTO THE CHILD'S HOME LIFE AND COMMUNITY. THE CENTER SUPPORTS A HOME VISIT PROGRAM DESIGNED TO HELP FULFILL THE EDUCATIONAL, NUTRITIONAL AND HEALTH NEEDS OF EXPECTANT MOTHERS THROUGH THE CHILD'S THIRD YEAR. MANY OF THE WOMEN SELECTED FOR THE PROGRAM ARE UNMARRIED HIGH SCHOOL STUDENTS. THE PRIMARY GOAL OF THE EDUCATIONAL PROGRAM IS TO GIVE YOUNG CHILDREN AND THEIR FAMILIES OPPORTUNITY FOR MAXIMUM INTELLECTUAL, EMOTIONAL AND SOCIAL GROWTH. THE INFANT PROGRAM EMPHASIZES THE YOUNG CHILD'S EMOTIONAL NEED FOR ATTACHMENT TO A SPECIAL PERSON, FOLLOWS PIAGETIAN TASK SEQUENCING, PROVIDES INFANT STIMULATION AND ENCOURAGES LANGUAGE DEVELOPMENT. THE "FAMILY STYLE" TODDLER PROGRAM ALLOWS THE CHILD TO CHOOSE BETWEEN VARIOUS LEARNING EXPERIENCES, WITH OLDER CHILDREN HELPING YOUNGER ONES. CREATIVITY, SENSE PERCEPTION, AND SMALL AND LARGE MUSCLE ACTIVITY ARE IMPORTANT PARTS OF THE CURRICULUM. THE DOCUMENT PROVIDES INFORMATION CONCERNING TRANSPORTATION, HEALTH, FOOD, POLICYMAKING, STAFF ORGANIZATION, VOLUNTEERS, AND RESOURCE USE. "INTELLECTUAL STIMULATION FOR INFANTS AND TODDLERS," LEARNING GAMES AND ACTIVITIES DESIGNED BY IRA J. GORDON AND J. RONALD LALLY, HAS BEEN REMOVED FROM THIS REPORT. (AJ)

ED051893 PS004847
A STUDY IN CHILD CARE (CASE STUDY FROM VOLUME II-A): "TACOS AND TULIPS." DAY CARE PROGRAMS REPRINT SERIES. O'FARRELL, BRIGID, NOV 70 57P.
EDRS PRICE MF-$0.65 HC-$3.29

THE HOLLAND DAY CARE CENTER IN MICHIGAN SERVES A DIVERSE COMMUNITY OF ANGLO CHILDREN OF DUTCH ANCESTRY AND CHILDREN OF FORMER MIGRANT WORKERS OF CHICANO, BLACK, PUERTO RICAN AND CUBAN ORIGINS WHO HAVE SETTLED IN THE AREA. LOCATED IN TWO CHURCHES WHICH ARE ABOUT THREE BLOCKS APART, THE PROGRAM DIVIDES CHILDREN BY ABILITY AND AGE INTO FIVE CLASSROOMS WITH ABOUT 15 CHILDREN PER CLASS. THE PROGRAM PHILOSOPHY EMPHASIZES SOCIAL-EMOTIONAL GROWTH IN A RELAXED AND UNSTRUCTURED ATMOSPHERE. CHILDREN ARE TAUGHT BOTH ANGLO AND SPANISH CULTURES IN A BILINGUAL APPROACH. VOLUNTEERS FROM THE COMMUNITY SERVE ON THE BOARD OF DIRECTORS, POLICY ADVISORY COMMITTEE, PERSONNEL AND FINANCE COMMITTEES. THEY ALSO AID COOKS AND TEACHING STAFF, AND MALE VOLUNTEERS PROVIDE ROLE MODELS. REGULAR NUTRITION AND HEALTH PROGRAMS ARE PROVIDED BY VOLUNTEER PROFESSIONALS AND SOCIAL SERVICES ARE AVAILABLE. INCLUDED IN THIS REPORT IS INFORMATION ON CENTER AND STAFF ORGANIZATION, STAFF TRAINING, EXECUTIVE DIRECTOR'S TIME-USE CHART, A TABLE CONCERNING USE OF RESOURCES AND COMMENTS MADE BY PARENTS. AN APPENDIX PROVIDES SAMPLE PARENT INVOLVEMENT LITERATURE, WORD BOOK SAMPLES FOR SPANISH-SPEAKING STUDENTS, CHILD GUIDANCE MATERIALS, AND A CAREER DEVELOPMENT PLAN FOR STAFF MEMBERS. (AJ)

ED051894 PS004848
A STUDY IN CHILD CARE (CASE STUDY FROM VOLUME II-A): "GOOD VIBES." DAY CARE PROGRAMS REPRINT SERIES. ELBOW, LINDA, NOV 70 61P.
EDRS PRICE MF-$0.65 HC-$3.29

THE HAIGHT-ASHBURY CHILDREN'S CENTER DESCRIBED IN THIS BOOKLET HAS THESE IMPORTANT ASPECTS: (1) IT IS A COMMUNITY CENTER, OFFERING DAY CARE FOR CHILDREN 2 1/2 TO 6 YEARS OF AGE AND COMMUNITY SERVICES FOR PARENTS; (2) ITS CURRICULUM USES A MODIFICATION OF THE BRITISH INFANT SCHOOL SYSTEM; AND (3) PARENTS ARE AN INTEGRAL PART OF THE PLANNING AND FINANCING OF THE CENTER. FAMILIES SERVED BY THE CENTER ARE PRIMARILY LOW INCOME, FROM A VARIETY OF ETHNIC GROUPS. THE PROGRAM INCLUDES A SOCIAL WORKER AND PARENT-COMMUNITY WORKER, WHEN FUNDS PERMIT. CENTER MEETINGS PROVIDE A FORUM FOR DISCUSSION OF PLANS FOR THE DAY CARE CENTER AND SPECIFIC COMMUNITY ISSUES. INFORMATION ON THE CENTER'S HISTORY, FUNDING, PROGRAM, STAFF ORGANIZATION AND TRAINING, AND USE OF RESOURCES IS INCLUDED. AN APPENDIX PRESENTS THE PARENTS' PARTICIPATION SHARE PLAN AND OTHER MATERIAL. (NH)

ED051895 PS004849
A STUDY IN CHILD CARE (CASE STUDY FROM VOLUME II-A): "A ROLLS-ROYCE OF DAY CARE." DAY CARE PROGRAMS REPRINT SERIES. O'FARRELL, BRIGID, NOV 70 43P.
EDRS PRICE MF-$0.65 HC-$3.29

THE AMALGAMATED DAY CARE CENTER IS AN INDEPENDENT TRUST ESTABLISHED THROUGH A COLLECTIVE BARGAINING AGREEMENT BETWEEN THE AMALGAMATED CLOTHING WORKERS OF AMERICA, AFL-CIO, AND THE EMPLOYERS OF THE GARMENT INDUSTRY. THE FREE CENTER, OPEN FROM 6:00 A.M. TO 6:00 P.M., IS LOCATED NEAR THE CHICAGO GARMENT INDUSTRIES TO MINIMIZE TRANSPORTATION PROBLEMS FOR PARENTS. NO ATTEMPT IS MADE TO DETERMINE FAMILY INCOME AND THE SOLE CRITERION FOR ADMITTANCE IS UNION MEMBERSHIP. THE CENTER PLACES PRIMARY EMPHASIS ON INTELLECTUAL AND LANGUAGE DEVELOPMENT TO PREPARE ITS STUDENTS TO ENTER PUBLIC SCHOOLS. IT ALSO SEEKS TO DEVELOP SELF-RELIANCE, A STRONG SELF-IMAGE, AND INNER CONTROLS, AND EMPHASIZES THE PRESENTATION OF POSITIVE ETHNIC MODELS AND ATTITUDES FOR THE BLACK, CHICANO, PUERTO RICAN, AND ANGLO CHILDREN. THE FREE HEALTH PROGRAM IS SUPPLEMENTED BY A NUTRITION PROGRAM OF BREAKFAST, HOT LUNCH AND SNACKS. THE 60 CHILDREN ARE DIVIDED INTO FOUR CLASSROOMS WITH ONE TEACHER AND ONE ASSISTANT TEACHER SERVING EACH GROUP. INFORMATION IS PROVIDED ON POLICY MAKING, CENTER AND STAFF ORGANIZATION, USE OF RESOURCES, PARENT, TEACHER, AND OBSERVER COMMENTS. AN APPENDIX INCLUDES A DAILY CLASSROOM SCHEDULE, SAMPLE MENU, CHILD PROGRESS REPORT AND A UNION PAMPHLET. (AJ)

ED051896 PS004850
A STUDY IN CHILD CARE (CASE STUDY FROM VOLUME II-A): "IT'S A WELL-RUN BUSINESS, TOO." DAY CARE PROGRAMS REPRINT SERIES. ROSENTHAL, KRISTINE, NOV 70 53P.
EDRS PRICE MF-$0.65 HC-$3.29

A DAY CARE CENTER OPERATED BY AMERICAN CHILD CENTERS, INC. OF NASHVILLE, TENNESSEE, A PRIVATE NONFRANCHISE CORPORATION, IS DESCRIBED. PROGRAM EMPHASIS IS PLACED ON THE EMOTIONAL, SOCIAL AND PHYSICAL DEVELOPMENT OF THE CHILD, AS OPPOSED TO CUSTODIAL CARE, OR SERVICES TO PARENTS OR THE COMMUNITY. CAREFUL COST-ACCOUNTING METHODS ARE USED TO MAKE THE CENTER PROFITABLE WITHOUT SACRIFICE OF QUALITY. ADMISSIONS ARE ON AN OPEN BASIS, BUT BECAUSE OF THE LOCATION AND HIGH COST OF THE CENTER'S SERVICES, 92% OF THE FAMILIES SERVED ARE WHITE, AND 80% OF THE FATHERS HAVE COLLEGE DEGREES. THE PROGRAM USES AN EXPERIMENTAL APPROACH INVOLVING MUCH CREATIVE PLAY, MULTI-AGE GROUPING, AND TEAM TEACHING. ACADEMIC ADVISORS MONITOR THE PROGRAM. PARENTAL INTEREST IS ENCOURAGED, BUT PARENTS DO NOT MAKE POLICY. STAFF ORGANIZATION AND DUTIES ARE DESCRIBED; A FUNCTIONAL BREAKDOWN IS GIVEN OF HOW INCOME IS USED; AND FINANCIAL AND STAFFING PROBLEMS FACED BY THE CENTERS ARE DISCUSSED. AN APPENDIX CONTAINS ILLUSTRATIVE MATERIALS. (NH)

ED051897 PS004851
A STUDY IN CHILD CARE (CASE STUDY FROM VOLUME II-B): "I'M A NEW WOMAN NOW." DAY CARE PROGRAMS REPRINT SERIES. WILLIS, ERLINE, NOV 70 74P.
EDRS PRICE MF-$0.65 HC-$3.29

THE FAMILY DAY CARE CAREER PROGRAM PLAN OF NEW YORK CITY PROVIDES DAY CARE FOR APPROXIMATELY 3500 CHILDREN OF PUBLIC ASSISTANCE OR LOW INCOME CAREER MOTHERS (WORKING, IN SCHOOL, OR IN TRAINING) IN THE HOMES OF TEACHER MOTHERS (DAY CARE MOTHERS). THE DAY CARE HOMES ARE ADMINISTERED BY 21 SUB-CENTERS, WHICH PROVIDE SUPPORT FOR TEACHER MOTHERS THROUGH HOME VISITS BY EDUCATIONAL AIDES AND DAY CARE AIDES. TWO CAREER DEVELOPMENT PATHS ARE AVAILABLE TO WOMEN IN THE PROGRAM: INTERNAL (TEACHER MOTHERS MAY MOVE UPWARD TO OTHER STAFF POSITIONS) AND OUTSIDE THE SYSTEM (CAREER MOTHERS ARE GIVEN COUNSELING AND HELPED TO RECEIVE TRAINING AND JOB PLACEMENT). THE SYSTEM PROVIDES A MEANS FOR TEACHER MOTHERS TO EARN NEEDED MONEY AT HOME AND TO INCREASE THEIR FEELINGS OF SELF-WORTH. WITH GOOD DAY CARE FOR THEIR CHILDREN AVAILABLE FREE OF CHARGE, CAREER MOTHERS ARE ABLE TO IMPROVE THEIR LIVES THROUGH EMPLOYMENT OR TRAINING. INFORMATION ON THE PROGRAM'S HISTORY, ORGANIZATION, STAFF, POLICYMAKING, AND USE OF RESOURCES IS INCLUDED. AN APPENDIX CONTAINS ILLUSTRATIVE MATERIALS. (NH)

ED051898 PS004852
A STUDY IN CHILD CARE (CASE STUDY FROM VOLUME II-B): "A SENSE OF BELONGING." DAY CARE PROGRAMS REPRINT SERIES. ELBOW, LINDA, NOV 70 68P.
EDRS PRICE MF-$0.65 HC-$3.29

THE BERKELEY CHILDREN'S CENTERS SYSTEM OF SEVEN DAY CARE CENTERS, 3 PRESCHOOL AND 4 SCHOOL-AGE, FOR CHILDREN OF WORKING PARENTS OF LOW INCOME HOMES (BELOW $6,000/YEAR) IS SPONSORED BY THE BERKELEY UNIFIED SCHOOL DISTRICT. THE 285 BLACK, ANGLO AND CHICANO CHILDREN ENROLLED ARE UNDER THE SUPERVISION OF 83 STAFF MEMBERS. THE CENTERS' ASSOCIATION WITH THE PUBLIC SCHOOL DISTRICT ALLOWS THEM TO SHARE IN THE HIGHER SALARIES AND EMPLOYEE BENEFITS, SPECIALIZED STAFF, INFORMATION RESOURCES, PERSONNEL SERVICES, STABILITY AND COMMUNITY SUPPORT OF THE LARGER SYSTEM. THE SYSTEM COMBINES CENTRALIZED ORGANIZATION FOR RESOURCES WHILE MAINTAINING LOCAL AUTONOMY FOR EACH CENTER. THE BASIC PROGRAM TRIES TO RESPOND TO THE INDIVIDUAL NEEDS OF CHILD, STAFF MEMBER AND PARENT. CHILDREN ARE GROUPED BY DEVELOPMENTAL STAGE RATHER THAN AGE, AND HAVE FREE CHOICE BETWEEN SELF-HELP MATERIALS AND PLANNED ACTIVITIES. SOME CENTERS UTILIZE A NIMNICHT RESPONSIVE ENVIRONMENT MODEL. A PART-TIME NURSE FOR THE CHILDREN AND SOCIAL SERVICES FOR PARENTS ARE AVAILABLE. ALTHOUGH HOME VISITS ARE MADE WHEN PROBLEMS ARISE, PARENTAL INVOLVEMENT IS MINIMAL. IN THIS REPORT, INFORMATION IS PROVIDED ON POLICYMAKING, STAFF ORGANIZATION AND TRAINING, USE OF SCHEDULE, TEACHER EVALUATION FORMS AND CHILD DEVELOPMENT ASSESSMENT FORMS. (AJ)

ED051899 PS004853
A STUDY IN CHILD CARE (CASE STUDY FROM VOLUME II-A): "LIKE BEING AT HOME." DAY CARE PROGRAMS REPRINT SERIES. RUOPP, RICHARD R., NOV 70 42P.
EDRS PRICE MF-$0.65 HC-$3.29

THE GREELEY PARENT CHILD CENTER IN GREELEY, COLORADO IS A YEAR-ROUND CENTER SERVING PRIMARILY A CHICANO MIGRANT OR SETTLED-OUT MIGRANT POPULATION. A COMPREHENSIVE CHILD CARE PROGRAM IS OFFERED DURING THE DAY, AND EDUCATIONAL PROGRAMS FOR THE PARENTS ARE AVAILABLE DURING THE EVENING. THE CENTER WAS ORIGINALLY FUNDED BY HEAD START AND WAS DEVELOPED AS A MODEL TO BE DUPLICATED IN OTHER MIGRANT AREAS. LATER, FUNDING CAME FROM PRIVATE SOURCES. RECENTLY THE PARENTS OF CHILDREN ATTENDING THE CENTER FORMED A NONPROFIT CORPORATION AND ARE INVOLVED IN POLICYMAKING DECISIONS. THE CENTER IS CURRENTLY UNDERSTAFFED, AND AT TIMES THE CARE OFFERED THE CHILDREN IS MAINLY CUSTODIAL, BUT IS AIMED AT SELF-IMAGE ENRICHMENT AND BETTER HEALTH. HOWEVER, THERE ARE SOME STRUCTURED ACTIVITIES: ART, STORYTELLING, SINGING, NUMBERS, NAMES, AND LETTERS. VOLUNTEERS AND AIDES ASSIST THE HEAD TEACHER. WITH NO MONEY AVAILABLE FOR STAFF TRAINING, AN INFORMAL SELF-TEACHING AND EACH-ONE-TEACH-ONE ATMOSPHERE PREVAILS. ESTIMATED AND IN-KIND EXPENDITURES ARE ITEMIZED. AN APPENDIX INCLUDES STIMULATION KITS (DIRECTIONS FOR SIMPLE, HOMEMADE TOYS), WEEKLY FEE SCHEDULE, AND RECORD CARDS. (NH)

ED051900 PS004854
A STUDY IN CHILD CARE (CASE STUDY FROM VOLUME II-A): "CHILDREN AS 'KIDS'." DAY CARE PROGRAMS REPRINT SERIES. O'FARRELL, BRIGID, NOV 70 50P.
EDRS PRICE MF-$0.65 HC-$3.29

THE GEORGETOWN DAY CARE CENTER, IN WASHINGTON, D.C., IS DUALLY SPONSORED BY A LARGE HOSPITAL AND A PRIVATE NON-PROFIT ORGANIZATION AND OFFERS DAY CARE SERVICES TO A SMALL NUMBER OF THE CHILDREN OF PARENTS WHO WORK AT THE HOSPITAL. THE CENTER ALSO FUNCTIONS AS A HALFWAY HOUSE FOR CHILDREN IN A DIAGNOSTIC CENTER WHICH IDENTIFIES PRESCHOOL CHILDREN WITH OBSERVABLE OR POTENTIAL HANDICAPS. THE DAY CARE PROGRAM ALLOWS THESE CHILDREN TO BE GRADUALLY INTRODUCED INTO A NORMAL PRESCHOOL SETTING, WHILE THEY ARE BEING WORKED WITH AND OBSERVED. THE PRIMARY EMPHASIS OF THE PROGRAM IS THE CHILD'S SOCIAL AND EMOTIONAL DEVELOPMENT, BUT SOME PRE-READING AND PRE-KINDERGARTEN MATH MATERIALS ARE USED. A UNIQUE COMBINATION OF USE OF PRIVATE AND PUBLIC RESOURCES IS DEMONSTRATED IN THIS CENTER, FOR THE HOSPITAL PROVIDES PHYSICAL FACILITIES, HEALTH CARE, AND FOOD SERVICES; THE PRIVATE ORGANIZATION RAISES FUNDS FOR TEACHERS' SALARIES AND SUPPLIES, AND PROVIDES VOLUNTEER HELP IN THE CLASSROOM; AND THE PARENTS PAY ON A SLIDING SCALE BASED ON INCOME. PARENTS MEET REGULARLY AND ARE REPRESENTED ON THE ADVISORY COMMITTEES. APPENDIXES INCLUDE SAMPLES OF PARENT AND VOLUNTEER INVOLVEMENT MATERIALS. (NH)

ED051901 PS004855
A STUDY IN CHILD CARE (CASE STUDY FROM VOLUME II-A): "LIFE IS GOOD, RIGHT? RIGHT!" DAY CARE PROGRAMS REPRINT SERIES. O'FARRELL, BRIGID, NOV 70 57P.
EDRS PRICE MF-$0.65 HC-$3.29

HOUSED IN STRUCTURES FORMERLY USED BY A CHURCH, THE 5TH CITY PRESCHOOL IS LOCATED IN ONE OF CHICAGO'S POOREST BLACK GHETTOS. THE 228 INFANT-TO-KINDERGARTEN-AGE CHILDREN (78% BLACK, 22% WHITE) ARE ALL FROM FAMILIES LIVING IN THE 5TH CITY AREA. THE PROGRAM EMPHASIZES THE DEVELOPMENT OF THE TOTAL CHILD AND CONCENTRATES ON HELPING CHILDREN TO BUILD A STRONG SELF-IMAGE. THE CURRICULUM ENCOMPASSES READING, LANGUAGE, MATH, WRITING, DRAMA, MUSICAL INSTRUMENTS, ARCHITECTURE, POETRY, DRAMA, SCULPTURE, PROSE, SONGS, AND PICTORIALS. A STABLE DAILY SEQUENCE OF EVENTS IS FOLLOWED. TO CREATE STRUCTURED RELATIONSHIPS WITHIN A CLASS, CHILDREN ARE GIVEN PRACTICAL ROLES AND JOBS, WEAR UNIFORMS, MARCH IN GROUPS, SIT, WAIT AND STAND TOGETHER. DAILY TEACHER MEETINGS ARE HELD ON CURRICULUM PLANNING AND TRAINING. THE PROGRAM IS AN IMPORTANT SEGMENT OF A COMPREHENSIVE COMMUNITY REFORMATION EXPERIMENT AND PERSONNEL WILL GRADUALLY BE REPLACED BY COMMUNITY MEMBERS. SPONSORED BY THE CHURCH FEDERATION OF GREATER CHICAGO, OTHER CENTERS OPERATED ON THE SAME BASIS ARE LOCATED IN 18 OTHER CITIES INCLUDING BOMBAY, INDIA, SIDNEY, AUSTRALIA, AND HONG KONG. THE DIRECTORS OF THESE SCHOOLS ARE TRAINED AT THE 5TH CITY PRESCHOOL. INFORMATION IS INCLUDED ON ORGANIZATION, STAFF TRAINING AND RESOURCE USE. (AJ)

ED051902 PS004856
A STUDY IN CHILD CARE (CASE STUDY FROM VOLUME II-A): "HEY, GEORGIE GET YOURSELF TOGETHER." DAY CARE PROGRAMS REPRINT SERIES. BERGSTEIN, PATRICIA, NOV 70 39P.
EDRS PRICE MF-$0.65 HC-$3.29

AVCO, A PRIVATE INDUSTRY IN THE BOSTON AREA, HAS PROVIDED THE FINANCIAL AND CORPORATE SUPPORT FOR THE AVCO DAY CARE CENTER DESCRIBED IN THIS BOOKLET. THE POPULATION SERVED BY THE CENTER IS 88 PERCENT BLACK AND 12 PERCENT WHITE. ADMISSION DOES NOT DEPEND UPON INCOME, EMPLOYMENT AT AVCO, OR PERSONAL BACKGROUND BUT IS ON A FIRST-COME, FIRST-SERVED BASIS, PROVIDED PARENTS CAN PAY THE MODERATE RATES. THE PRIMARY CONCERN OF THE STAFF IS THE PROMOTION OF THE SOCIAL AND EMOTIONAL DEVELOPMENT OF THE CHILDREN, WHO RANGE IN AGE FROM 1 TO 5 YEARS. EMPHASIS IS PLACED ON POSITIVE SELF-IMAGE, SELF-RELIANCE, FRIENDLY INTERACTION, AND A FLEXIBLE ATMOSPHERE. THE CODIRECTORS SPEND ABOUT HALF TIME WORKING DIRECTLY WITH THE CHILDREN RATHER THAN CONFINING THEMSELVES STRICTLY TO ADMINISTRATION. STAFF ORGANIZATION IS DEMOCRATIC, FRIENDLY AND INFORMAL. THE CENTER IS NOT INVOLVED IN SOCIAL SERVICE WORK, PARENT EDUCATION, OR COMMUNITY ORGANIZATION. HOWEVER, A STATE SOCIAL WORKER VISITS THE CENTER BIMONTHLY TO CONSULT WITH STAFF AND PARENTS ON SPECIAL CHILD PROBLEMS. THE HISTORY, ORGANIZATION, PEOPLE SERVED, STAFF, AND BUDGET ARE DESCRIBED AND AN APPENDIX GIVES ADDITIONAL ILLUSTRATIVE MATERIALS. (NH)

ED051903 PS004857
A STUDY IN CHILD CARE (CASE STUDY FROM VOLUME II-A): "ALL KINDS OF LOVE--IN A CHINESE RESTAURANT." DAY CARE PROGRAMS REPRINT SERIES. ROWE, MARY, NOV 70 35P.
EDRS PRICE MF-$0.65 HC-$3.29

THE WEST 80TH STREET DAY CARE CENTER REPRESENTS A COMMUNITY EFFORT TO MEET THE NEEDS OF THE CHILDREN AND PARENTS IN THE NEW YORK GHETTO AREA IT SERVES. THE HEART OF THE PROGRAM AND A MAJOR REASON FOR ITS SUCCESS IS THE FACT THAT THE CENTER IS COMMUNITY-CONTROLLED, WITH AN UNUSUALLY HIGH DEGREE OF PARENT INVOLVEMENT. TO HELP IMPROVE THE LIVES OF WHOLE FAMILIES, NOT JUST THE CHILDREN IN THE DAY CARE PROGRAM, THE CENTER IS VERY INVOLVED IN SOCIAL ACTION PROGRAMS, COUNSELING AND REFERRALS, OFFERS HELP TO OLDER CHILDREN, AND ACTS IN SPECIAL EMERGENCY SITUATIONS. THE EDUCATIONAL PROGRAM IS BASED ON THE PREMISE THAT A CHILD'S EDUCATION CANNOT BE ISOLATED FROM THE SOCIAL SYSTEM IN WHICH IT TAKES PLACE. THE CHILDREN ARE TAUGHT ABOUT THE DANGERS OF DRUGS ON THE STREETS, AND IN ALL EDUCATIONAL ACTIVITIES (WHICH INCLUDE MANY FIELD TRIPS) THE CENTER TRIES TO LINK WHAT THE CHILDREN SEE IN THE CLASSROOM WITH WHAT THEY EXPERIENCE DAILY IN THE COMMUNITY. A SPECIAL EMPHASIS IS PLACED ON DEVELOPMENT OF LANGUAGE SKILLS AND A GOOD SELF IMAGE. IN THIS REPORT, BACKGROUND INFORMATION IS GIVEN ON THE CENTER, AND ALSO DETAILS OF PROGRAM ORGANIZATION, STAFFING, AND BUDGET. PHYSICAL FACILITIES ARE VERY POOR (THE CENTER IS LOCATED IN AN OLD RESTAURANT), BUT THROUGH COMMUNITY EFFORTS MONEY HAS BEEN RAISED FOR A NEW BUILDING. (NH)

ED051904 PS004858
A STUDY IN CHILD CARE (CASE STUDY FROM VOLUME II-A): "A SMALL U. N." DAY CARE PROGRAMS REPRINT SERIES. RUOPP, RICHARD R., NOV 70 62P.
EDRS PRICE MF-$0.65 HC-$3.29

THE CENTRAL CITY HEAD START DAY CARE CENTER IN SALT LAKE CITY SERVES 62 PRESCHOOLERS FROM FAMILIES MEETING THE OEO POVERTY GUIDELINES. THE ETHNIC DISTRIBUTION IS WIDE INCLUDING CHICANO, BLACK, ANGLO, NAVAJO AND CHINESE CHILDREN. SIGNIFICANT TO THE PROGRAM'S SUCCESS ARE: THE COMPLEMENTARY MIX OF STAFF PERSONALITIES, THE EMPHASIS ON CAREER DEVELOPMENT OF PARAPROFESSIONALS, THE EXTENSIVE PARENTAL INVOLVEMENT, CROSS-CULTURAL EDUCATION, HEALTH CARE AND SOCIAL SERVICE RESOURCES. THE EDUCATIONAL PROGRAM EMPHASIZES THAT AS A CHILD GAINS CONFIDENCE AND MASTERS SKILLS, HE DEVELOPS SOCIALLY AND EMOTIONALLY. TEACHERS PLAN UNITS AROUND VARIOUS SUBJECTS AND ORGANIZE FIELD TRIPS AND ACTIVITIES TO ACCOMPANY THEM. CHILDREN ARE ENCOURAGED TO BE AWARE OF AND EXPRESS THEIR FEELINGS THROUGH DRAMATIC PLAY, NURSERY RHYMES AND GAMES. PRAISE IS FREQUENTLY GIVEN TO BUILD CONFIDENCE AND BOLSTER SELF-IMAGES. ACTIVITIES ARE STRUCTURED AROUND LANGUAGE GROWTH, TEACHING OF PRE-READING SKILLS, "SESAME STREET," MUSIC AND ART. OTHER INFORMATION PROVIDED IN THIS DOCUMENT INCLUDES DISCUSSION OF CENTER AND STAFF ORGANIZATION AND RESOURCE USES, SAMPLES OF CLASSROOM SCHEDULES AND LEARNING GAMES, AND COPIES OF A VOLUNTEER ORIENTATION SCHEDULE, AND CENTER REGULATIONS. (AJ)

ED051905 PS004859
A STUDY IN CHILD CARE (CASE STUDY FROM VOLUME II-A) RUOPP, RICHARD R.; O'FARRELL, BRIGID, NOV 70 57P.
EDRS PRICE MF-$0.65 HC-$3.29

THE CASPER DAY CARE CENTER IN CASPER, WYOMING, CONSISTS OF TWO DAY CARE CENTERS, LOCATED IN CHURCHES, SERVES 91 CHILDREN INCLUDING PHYSICALLY OR MENTALLY HANDICAPPED CHILDREN (TODDLERS AND SCHOOL AGE) OF WORKING MOTHERS IN LOW-INCOME FAMILIES. THE PROGRAM IS DESIGNED TO FACILITATE THE ASSOCIATION OF HANDICAPPED CHILDREN WITH NORMAL CHILDREN (ONE DISTURBED CHILD/FIVE NORMAL CHILDREN). THE PROFESSIONAL STAFF IS HEAVILY DEPENDENT ON 26 VOLUNTEERS. ACTIVITIES ARE GENERALLY THE SAME FOR ALL CHILDREN EXCEPT FOR SPEECH THERAPY AND SPECIAL ATTENTION AT MEALTIME. THE PROGRAM INTEGRATES EDUCATIONAL AND SOCIAL-EMOTIONAL DEVELOPMENT, LANGUAGE DEVELOPMENT, "SESAME STREET" VIEWING, SENSORIMOTOR AND PERCEPTUAL DEVELOPMENT, MATH AND READING TUTORING FOR SCHOOL AGE CHILDREN. NUTRITION AND HEALTH PROGRAMS AND SOCIAL SERVICES ARE PROVIDED. FUNDING HAS DEVELOPED INTO A MAJOR PROBLEM AND THE CENTER IS DEPENDENT ON DONATED LABOR, FACILITIES AND SERVICES. PARENT INVOLVEMENT IS MINIMAL. INFORMATION IS PROVIDED ON CENTER ORGANIZATION, RESOURCE USES, ADMISSION POLICIES, MENUS AND PROGRAM PURPOSE. (AJ)

ED051906 PS004860
A STUDY IN CHILD CARE (CASE STUDY FROM VOLUME II-B): "WILL YOU MARRY ME?" DAY CARE PROGRAM REPRINT SERIES. COOK, PATRICIA, NOV 70 50P.
EDRS PRICE MF-$0.65 HC-$3.29

THE SPRINGFIELD DAY NURSERY SYSTEM IN SPRINGFIELD, MASSACHUSETTS IS ONE OF A SYSTEM OF FOUR DAY CARE CENTERS. IT IS IN AN URBAN AREA, AND OVER ONE-HALF OF THE FAMILIES SERVED ARE PUERTO RICAN, MANY OF WHOM HAVE UNEMPLOYMENT AND LANGUAGE BARRIER PROBLEMS. A BILINGUAL PROGRAM (ENGLISH-SPANISH) IS ONE OF THE OUTSTANDING FEATURES OF THE DAY CARE CENTER. THE PROGRAM STRONGLY EMPHASIZES THE DEVELOPMENT OF ENGLISH LANGUAGE SKILLS, IN AN ATMOSPHERE WHICH ACCEPTS THE CHILD'S DIFFICULTY WITH ENGLISH AND REINFORCES HIS ATTEMPTS TO LEARN. EACH AGE-GROUPED CLASSROOM HAS BOTH ENGLISH- AND SPANISH-SPEAKING TEACHERS WHO WORK FOR THE DEVELOPMENT OF POSITIVE SELF-IMAGES IN THE CHILDREN AND FOR THE ACQUIRING OF LANGUAGE SKILLS THROUGH A FLEXIBLE CURRICULUM. DEVELOPMENT LEARNING MATERIALS ARE USED EXTENSIVELY FOR SERIATION AND SENSORIMOTOR DEVELOPMENT. COUNSELING IS AVAILABLE TO PARENTS AT THE CENTER, WITH REFERRALS TO COMMUNITY SOCIAL SERVICES IF FURTHER HELP IS NEEDED. THE HISTORY AND ORGANIZATION OF THE SYSTEM, STAFF, AND EXPENDITURES ARE DESCRIBED. AN APPENDIX OF ADDITIONAL ILLUSTRATIVE MATERIALS IS INCLUDED. (NH)

ED051907 PS004861
A STUDY IN CHILD CARE (CASE STUDY FROM VOLUME II-B): "WE COME WITH THE DUST AND WE GO WITH THE WIND." DAY CARE PROGRAMS REPRINT SERIES. ELBOW, LINDA, NOV 70 67P.
EDRS PRICE MF-$0.65 HC-$3.29

APPROXIMATELY 468 CHILDREN OF MIGRANT AGRICULTURAL WORKERS IN THE STATE OF WASHINGTON ARE SERVED IN THE NINE NORTHWEST RURAL OPPORTUNITIES (NRO) DAY CARE CENTERS DESCRIBED HERE. A COMMUNITY ORGANIZATION PROGRAM WAS ALSO FORMED BY THE NRO SYSTEM. NINETY PERCENT OF THE FAMILIES SERVED ARE CHICANO, AND ALL ARE BELOW THE POVERTY LEVEL. THESE ASPECTS OF THE DAY CARE PROGRAM ARE PARTICULARLY NOTEWORTHY: THE TRAILER FACILITIES (FORMERLY USED AS MOBILE UNITS, NOW PERMANENTLY LOCATED); THE EDUCATIONAL PROGRAM FOR CHILDREN FROM 1 MONTH THROUGH 5 YEARS OF AGE, WHICH IS BASED ON THE SPECIAL NEEDS OF MIGRANT CHILDREN AND USES A COMBINATION OF APPROACHES TO ADEQUATELY PREPARE THE CHILDREN FOR PUBLIC SCHOOL; AND TEACHER TRAINING WHICH INSURES THAT NEW CURRICULUM IS INTRODUCED EFFICIENTLY AND UNIFORMLY THROUGHOUT THE NRO SYSTEM. INFORMATION IS PRESENTED ON THE BACKGROUND OF THE SYSTEM, BASIC PROGRAM (INCLUDING HEALTH, PARENT EDUCATION, AND COMMUNITY INVOLVEMENT), ORGANIZATION, STAFF, VOLUNTEER HELP, AND BUDGET. AN APPENDIX CONTAINS SAMPLES OF THE DAILY SCHEDULE, CURRICULUM MATERIALS, INFANT BEHAVIOR GOALS, AND TEACHER TRAINING MATERIALS. (NH)

ED051908 PS004862
A STUDY IN CHILD CARE (CASE STUDY FROM VOLUME II-B): "SOMEPLACE SECURE." DAY CARE PROGRAMS REPRINT SERIES. ROSENTHAL, KRISTINE, NOV 70 50P.
EDRS PRICE MF-$0.65 HC-$3.29

THE NEIGHBORHOOD CENTERS DAY CARE ASSOCIATION (NCDCA) IS A PRIVATE, NONPROFIT CORPORATION WHICH FOR 18 YEARS HAS PROVIDED DAY CARE SERVICES TO LOW INCOME AND WELFARE FAMILIES IN THE HOUSTON AREA. MORE THAN 1,100 CHILDREN ARE PRESENTLY BEING SERVED. THERE ARE EIGHT CENTERS AND ABOUT 180 DAY HOMES WHICH ARE USED TO SUPPLEMENT THE CARE AVAILABLE AT THE CENTERS, EITHER BECAUSE NO CENTER EXISTS IN THE NEIGHBORHOOD OR BECAUSE IT IS FELT THE HOME ENVIRONMENT WOULD BE MORE SUITED TO A PARTICULAR CHILD. OTHER OUTSTANDING ASPECTS OF THE NCDCA PROGRAM ARE ITS STABILITY OVER MANY YEARS OF OPERATION, THE JOB SECURITY IT PROVIDES FOR STAFF, AND ITS CAPACITY FOR DELIVERING SOCIAL SERVICES THROUGH COUNSELING AND REFERRALS. CREATIVITY AND INDEPENDENCE ARE IMPORTANT TO THE NCDCA EDUCATION PROGRAM, AND A HIGH VALUE IS PLACED BY TEACHERS AND PARENTS ON MANNERS AND AN ORDERED ROUTINE. DEVELOPMENT PROGRAMS IN THE DAY HOMES ARE SOMEWHAT LIMITED BECAUSE OF LACK OF TRAINING OF THE DAY HOME OPERATORS, BUT WARM AND CONTINUING CARE IS PROVIDED. THE ORGANIZATION, STAFF AND BUDGET OF THE NCDCA IS DESCRIBED. AN APPENDIX GIVES ADDITIONAL ILLUSTRATIVE MATERIALS. (NH)

ED051909 PS004863
A STUDY IN CHILD CARE (CASE STUDY FROM VOLUME II-B): "...WHILE [THEY TOOK] CARE OF OUR CHILDREN, THEIRS WEREN'T BEING CARED FOR." DAY CARE PROGRAMS REPRINT SERIES. ROSENTHAL, KRISTINE, NOV 70 70P.
EDRS PRICE MF-$0.65 HC-$3.29

THE MECKLENBURG COUNTY DEPARTMENT OF SOCIAL SERVICES IN CHARLOTTE, NORTH CAROLINA, OPERATES NINE CHILD DEVELOPMENT DAY CARE CENTERS AND 5 DAY HOMES WHICH PROVIDE CARE FOR 257 BLACK AND ANGLO CHILDREN, 2- TO 5-YEARS-OLD, PRIMARILY FROM LOW-INCOME HOMES. THE CENTERS ARE LOCATED IN CHURCHES, SCHOOLS, AND FACILITIES IN LOW INCOME HOUSING PROJECTS. THE SYSTEM'S BASIC EMPHASIS IS TO TEACH "CULTURALLY ISOLATED" CHILDREN TO FUNCTION IN AN INTEGRATED WORLD USING A VARIETY OF ETHNIC MATERIALS. EMPHASIS IS PLACED ON LANGUAGE DEVELOPMENT, MOTOR AND COORDINATION SKILLS, CREATIVE EXPRESSION, AND SOCIAL-EMOTIONAL DEVELOPMENT. UNIQUE TO THE CENTERS' PROGRAM IS THE STYLE AND SCOPE OF THE NUTRITION PROGRAM. MANY CHILDREN SUFFER FROM MALNUTRITION, ANEMIA, AND PSYCHOLOGICAL ANXIETIES RESULTING FROM CHRONIC HUNGER AT HOME. DOUBLE AMOUNTS OF FOOD ARE SERVED ON MONDAYS WHEN CHILDREN ARE HUNGRY FROM THE WEEKEND AND ON FRIDAYS IN ANTICIPATION OF THE WEEKEND. MEALTIME BECOMES A PERIOD FOR LEARNING SOCIALIZATION. ANOTHER SIGNIFICANT ASPECT OF THE PROGRAM IS THE PRIVATE HOME AFTER-SCHOOL CARE FACILITIES THAT PROVIDE RELAXED, YET STIMULATING, ATMOSPHERES FOR CHILDREN AFTER THE REGIMENTED PUBLIC SCHOOL DAY. ALTHOUGH PROGRAM DATA VARIES FROM CENTER TO CENTER, GENERAL TOPICS DISCUSSED IN THIS REPORT INCLUDE PARENTAL INVOLVEMENT, TRANSPORTATION, HEALTH PROGRAMS, STAFF TRAINING, CENTER ORGANIZATION, AND RESOURCE USES. (AUTHOR/AJ)

ED051910 PS004864
A STUDY IN CHILD CARE (CASE STUDY FROM VOLUME II-B): "THEY BRAG ON A CHILD TO MAKE HIM FEEL GOOD." DAY CARE PROGRAMS REPRINT SERIES. ROSENTHAL, KRISTINE, NOV 70 69P.
EDRS PRICE MF-$0.65 HC-$3.29

THIS DOCUMENT DESCRIBES 19 APPALACHIAN DAY CARE CENTERS, OPERATED BY THE KENTUCKY CHILD WELFARE RESEARCH FOUNDATION, SERVING 639 PRESCHOOLERS FOR NINE SCHOOL MONTHS AND 247 DURING THE 9-WEEK SUMMER SESSION. THE CENTERS,LOCATED IN CHURCHES, ABANDONED SCHOOL HOUSES AND STORE FRONTS ARE STAFFED LARGELY BY PARAPROFESSIONALS FROM THE COMMUNITY. SOCIAL SERVICES ARE EXTENDED BEYOND THE CHILD TO THE FAMILY. FOR INSTANCE, A HOMEMAKER SERVICE IS OFFERED THE MOTHERS DURING WHICH THE HOMEMAKER VISITS PARENTS AND OFFERS TO HELP IN COOKING, CLEANING, OR CARING FOR A DISABLED PARENT. THE HOMEMAKER OFTEN STIMULATES PARENTS' INTEREST IN THEIR CHILDREN AND HELPS FAMILIES TO HELP THEMSELVES. PARENTS ARE INVOLVED IN ALL LEVELS OF THE PROJECT'S POLICYMAKING APPARATUS AND ACTIVE IN ALL ASPECTS OF THE PROGRAM. THE TRAINING OF PARAPROFESSIONALS HELPS THEM TO DEVELOP A WIDE VARIETY OF JOB SKILLS. VOLUNTEERS ARE USED EXTENSIVELY IN MANY CAPACITIES. THE CHILDREN'S EDUCATION PROGRAM IS NOT FORMAL AND WRITTEN CURRICULUM IS AVOIDED. EMPHASIS IS PLACED ON INDIVIDUAL EXPRESSION THROUGH THE USE OF CREATIVE MATERIALS. NUTRITION AND HEALTH ARE EMPHASIZED AND PROVIDING TRANSPORTATION FOR CHILDREN OVER THE MOUNTAIN ROADS IS A CONTINUING CONCERN. INFORMATION IS GIVEN ON THE CENTERS' ORGANIZATION AND USE OF RESOURCES. (AJ)

ED051911 PS004865
A STUDY IN CHILD CARE. VOLUME I: FINDINGS. DAY CARE PROGRAMS REPRINT SERIES. FITZSIMMONS, STEPHEN J.; ROWE, MARY P., APR 71 82P.
EDRS PRICE MF-$0.65 HC-$3.29

THIS IS THE FIRST OF FOUR VOLUMES OF A STUDY DESIGNED TO SEEK AND DESCRIBE FORMAL CHILD CARE ARRANGEMENTS OF GOOD QUALITY AND TO INVESTIGATE THE COST OF REPRODUCING THESE CENTERS AND HOME CARE ARRANGEMENTS. THE TWENTY CENTERS AND SYSTEMS DESCRIBED INCLUDE CENTERS ALL AROUND THE COUNTRY: ON INDIAN RESERVATIONS, IN THE INNER CITY, IN HOSPITALS, RURAL SETTINGS AND MIGRANT COMMUNITIES. SPONSORS RANGE FROM WELFARE DEPARTMENTS TO LABOR UNIONS. THIS VOLUME PRESENTS AN OVERVIEW OF EACH OF THE TWENTY CENTERS. APPENDIXES COMPRISE 7/8 OF THE DOCUMENT. APPENDIX A IS CONCERNED WITH GENERAL PROGRAM INFORMATION, NOTABLE PROGRAM ELEMENTS, CHILD AND FAMILY CHARACTERISTICS, FUNDING AND EXPENDITURES. APPENDIX B CONTAINS SUMMARY CENTER DESCRIPTIONS AND COST DATA. (AJ)

ED051912 PS004866
A STUDY IN CHILD CARE. VOLUME III: COST AND QUALITY ISSUES FOR OPERATORS. DAY CARE PROGRAMS REPRINT SERIES. THOMPSON, LYNN C., APR 71 165P.
EDRS PRICE MF-$0.65 HC-$6.58

ONE OF A SERIES OF FOUR VOLUMES ON CHILD CARE, THIS OVERVIEW FURNISHES INFORMATION FOR OPERATORS OR POTENTIAL OPERATORS OF CHILD CARE CENTERS, WITH SPECIAL ATTENTION PAID TO ORGANIZATIONAL FEATURES THAT FOSTER EFFICIENT OPERATION. CHAPTER ONE DISCUSSES GOALS FOR THE CARE OF PRESCHOOL CHILDREN AND DESCRIBES AND ASSESSES THE EXTENT TO WHICH GOALS WERE MET IN 19 DAY CARE CENTERS WHICH WERE STUDIED IN DEPTH. TABLES PROVIDE BASIC DATA ON THESE CENTERS AND INCLUDE INFORMATION ON BACKGROUND; NOTABLE ELEMENTS; CHILD, STAFF AND FAMILY CHARACTERISTICS; AND ESTIMATIONS OF FUNDING AND EXPENDITURES FOR 1970-1971. CHAPTER TWO DISCUSSES FACTORS INVOLVED IN THE EFFECTIVE OPERATION OF A CENTER AND PRESENTS DETAILED RECOMMENDATIONS. DESIGNS ARE PRESENTED FOR THREE PROTOTYPE CENTERS SERVING RESPECTIVELY 25, 50 AND 75 CHILDREN IN AVERAGE DAILY ATTENDANCE. THESE DESIGNS DETAIL CENTER ORGANIZATION, STAFFING, OPERATION, AND FINANCE. CHAPTER THREE GIVES SPECIFIC INFORMATION ABOUT THE PROVISION OF SERVICES BEYOND A CORE PROGRAM FOR PRESCHOOLERS. BOTH OPERATIONS AND FINANCES ARE DISCUSSED. REFERENCE IS MADE TO APPROPRIATE CASE STUDIES.

APPENDIXES GIVE FURTHER INFORMATION ON WORKING WITH STAFF, CORE PROGRAMS, STAFF DUTIES AND DAILY SCHEDULES FOR THE PROTOTYPE CENTERS. REGIONAL ADJUSTMENTS ARE SUGGESTED FOR THE MODEL BUDGET. (NH)

ED052814 PS003914
EDUCATIONAL INTERVENTION IN THE HOME AND PARAPROFESSIONAL CAREER DEVELOPMENT: A SECOND GENERATION MOTHER STUDY WITH AN EMPHASIS ON COSTS AND BENEFITS. FINAL REPORT. BARBRACK, CHRISTOPHER R.; HORTON, DELLA M., JUL 70 45P.
EDRS PRICE MF-$0.65 HC-$3.29

THE PRESENT STUDY COMPARED THE RELATIVE EFFECTIVENESS OF THREE HOME VISITING PROJECTS WHOSE PURPOSE WAS TO TRAIN LOW INCOME MOTHERS TO USE COMMONLY AVAILABLE MATERIALS AND EVERYDAY EVENTS FOR THE EDUCATIONAL STIMULATION OF THEIR PRESCHOOL CHILDREN. THE HOME VISITING PROJECTS VARIED IN TERMS OF EXPENSE AND PROFESSIONAL QUALIFICATIONS OF THE HOME VISITORS. DATA ON GENERAL INTELLIGENCE, CONCEPT DEVELOPMENT AND MATERNAL TEACHING STYLE WERE ANALYZED TO DETERMINE THE EFFECT OF HOME VISITS ON THE CHILD AND MOTHER AND TO COMPARE TREATMENT EFFECTS ASSOCIATED WITH EACH OF THE PROJECTS. IN ADDITION TO THE STANFORD BINET AND PEABODY PICTURE VOCABULARY TEST USED TO TEST CHILDREN'S APTITUDE, TWO RELATIVELY NEW INSTRUMENTS WERE USED: THE DARCEE CONCEPT TEST FOR CHILDREN, AND AN ABRIDGED VERSION OF THE MATERNAL TEACHING STYLE INSTRUMENT. RESULTS OF TESTING SHOWED LITTLE DIFFERENCE BETWEEN TREATMENT GROUPS AND SUGGEST A USEFUL PLAN FOR INVOLVING PARAPROFESSIONALS IN A MEANINGFUL "CAREER LADDER" WHICH RESULTS IN AN EDUCATIONAL INTERVENTION PROJECT STAFFED ENTIRELY BY PARAPROFESSIONALS. (NH)

ED052815 PS004534
PRESCHOOL PROGRAMS. IJR PRESCHOOL PROJECT REPORT, VOLUME I. COSTELLO, JOAN; AND OTHERS, 70 200P.
EDRS PRICE MF-$0.65 HC-$6.58

THIS PAPER IS THE FIRST OF THREE REPORTS BASED ON FOUR YEARS (1965-1969) WITH A RESEARCH PRESCHOOL FOR DISADVANTAGED BLACKS ON CHICAGO'S WESTSIDE. THE NINE CHAPTERS INCLUDED ARE TITLED: (1) FOUNDATIONS FOR PLANNING PRESCHOOL PROGRAMS--A POSITION STATEMENT, (2) CURRICULUM: THE TRANSLATION OF LEARNING GOALS INTO TEACHING PRACTICE, (3) THE TEACHER-CHILD RELATIONSHIP IN THE PRESCHOOL, (4) SPACE AND TIME IN THE PRESCHOOL, (5) CURRICULUM GUIDE (WHAT HAPPENED IN 1968-1969), (6) FIRST WEEK OF SCHOOL: A TEACHING PLAN, (7) A WEEK IN MID-YEAR: A TEACHING PLAN, (8) CLASSROOM OBSERVATIONS, AND (9) CATALOG OF TEACHING-LEARNING ACTIVITIES. AN APPENDIX INCLUDES A BIBLIOGRAPHY OF RESEARCH REPORTS AND PUBLICATIONS DERIVED FROM THIS PROJECT. (WY)

ED052816 PS004657
HEALTH AND NUTRITION IN DISADVANTAGED CHILDREN AND THEIR RELATIONSHIP WITH INTELLECTUAL DEVELOPMENT. COLLABORATIVE RESEARCH REPORT. CARTER, JAMES; AND OTHERS, [70] 73P.
EDRS PRICE MF-$0.65 HC-$3.29

THREE GROUPS OF CHILDREN (URBAN BLACK, URBAN WHITE, RURAL WHITE) FROM MIDDLE TENNESSEE WHO LIVE IN AN APPALACHIAN-TYPE ENVIRONMENT WERE STUDIED TO ASSESS THEIR HEALTH AND NUTRITIONAL STATUS. IN ADDITION, SOME ATTEMPT WAS MADE TO RELATE ASPECTS OF PHYSICAL STATUS TO INTELLECTUAL ADEQUACY AS MEASURED BY THE STANFORD-BINET OR THE WECHSLER PRESCHOOL AND PRIMARY SCALE OF INTELLIGENCE. THE THREE TARGET GROUPS ATTENDED DAY CARE PROGRAMS WITH A SCHOOL LUNCH AND SNACK PROGRAM. A COMPARISON GROUP DID NOT. FINDINGS OF INTEREST WERE: (1) THE GENERAL HEALTH STATUS OF CHILDREN EXAMINED WAS NOT INFERIOR ON NATIONAL NORMS. (2) THERE WAS A SUFFICIENTLY HIGH INCIDENCE OF VISUAL, AUDITORY, AND SPEECH PROBLEMS TO WARRANT SPECIFIC ATTENTION. (3) THE COMPOSITE SPECIMEN ANALYSIS TECHNIQUE WAS SUCCESSFULLY USED BECAUSE IT PRESENTED A PRECISE PICTURE OF WHAT A CHILD ATE RATHER THAN WHAT HE WAS SERVED. (4) NO PARTICULAR MEANING WAS FOUND IN CORRELATIONS BETWEEN VARIOUS INDICES OF SKELETAL AGE, HEIGHT, WEIGHT, BONE DENSITY AND INDICES OF LEARNING ABILITY. THE STUDY WAS DESIGNED AND EXECUTED SOLELY TO PROVIDE DESCRIPTIVE INFORMATION. FIGURES AND TABLES OF PHYSIOLOGICAL DATA ARE PROVIDED. (WY)

ED052817 PS004659
A COMPARISON OF THE EFFECT OF VERBAL AND MATERIAL REWARD ON THE LEARNING OF LOWER CLASS PRESCHOOL CHILDREN. FARBER, ANNE E., MAY 71 30P.
EDRS PRICE MF-$0.65 HC-$3.29

THIS STUDY COMPARED THE EFFECTIVENESS OF VERBAL AND CANDY REWARD ON THE LEARNING OF 72 LOWER CLASS, BLACK PRESCHOOL CHILDREN. A COMBINATION OF THE TWO REWARD CONDITIONS WAS INCLUDED TO INVESTIGATE IF MATERIAL REWARD HAD A DISTRACTING EFFECT. THE INFORMATIONAL VALUE OF THE TWO TYPES OF REWARDS WAS MANIPULATED TO DETERMINE IF THEY DIFFERED IN INFORMATIONAL PROPERTIES AS WELL AS IN INCENTIVE VALUE. THE CHILDREN LEARNED MOST EFFECTIVELY WHEN GIVEN VERBAL REWARD IN COMPARISON TO CANDY REWARD; IT DID NOT APPEAR THAT CANDY FUNCTIONED AS A DISTRACTOR. NO DIFFERENCES IN INFORMATIONAL PROPERTIES IN THE TWO REWARDS WERE FOUND. AN APPENDIX GIVES A REVIEW OF THE EXPERIMENTAL LITERATURE. (AUTHOR)

ED052818 PS004660
REEXAMINING VARIABLES AFFECTING COGNITIVE FUNCTIONING IN PRESCHOOL CHILDREN: A FOLLOW-UP. MUMBAUER, CORINNE C., DEC 70 11P.
EDRS PRICE MF-$0.65 HC-$3.29

A TOTAL OF 28 ADVANTAGED AND 28 DISADVANTAGED 5-YEAR-OLD CHILDREN WHO HAD BEEN TESTED IN A PREVIOUS STUDY DESIGNED TO MEASURE SOME OF THE SKILLS AND CHARACTERISTICS THOUGHT TO BE RELATED TO ACADEMIC SUCCESS (ED 032 929) WERE RETESTED AFTER A 6-MONTH INTERVAL DURING WHICH THEY HAD HAD A PRESCHOOL EXPERIENCE. TWO MEASURES OF OBJECT EXPLORATORY BEHAVIOR, ONE OF ABILITY TO INHIBIT MOTOR BEHAVIOR UNDER VERBAL AND MODELED REQUEST AND ONE OF IMPULSIVITY-REFLECTIVITY WERE USED. STIMULUS RATHER THAN SUBJECT CHARACTERISTICS SEEMED TO ACCOUNT FOR OBJECT EXPLORATORY BEHAVIOR. REFLECTIVITY WAS FOUND TO INCREASE WITH AGE. (AUTHOR/AJ)

ED052819 PS004662
INFLUENCE OF SUBJECT AND SITUATIONAL VARIABLES ON THE PERSISTENCE OF FIRST GRADE CHILDREN IN A TEST-LIKE SITUATION. MUMBAUER, CORINNE C., 70 7P.
EDRS PRICE MF-$0.65 HC-$3.29

THIS STUDY WAS DESIGNED TO INVESTIGATE THE EFFECT OF SITUATIONAL VARIABLES ON THE PERSISTENCE OF 6-YEAR-OLD CHILDREN FROM VARYING SOCIOECONOMIC AND EDUCATIONAL BACKGROUNDS. SUBJECTS WERE 24 MALE AND 24 FEMALE CHILDREN SELECTED RANDOMLY FROM EACH OF FOUR GROUPS OF FIRST GRADE NEGRO CHILDREN: ONE GROUP OF ADVANTAGED CHILDREN WHO HAD ATTENDED PRESCHOOL AND THREE GROUPS OF DISADVANTAGED CHILDREN WHOSE PRESCHOOL BACKGROUND VARIED. IN THE TEST-LIKE SITUATION, NINE BLOCK DESIGNS WERE ADMINISTERED FROM THE KOHS BLOCK DESIGN SERIES TO PROVIDE RELATIVELY INSOLUBLE TASKS TO MEASURE PERSISTENCE. THE DIFFICULTY LEVEL OF THE TASK WAS DESCRIBED TO EACH CHILD WHO WAS TESTED INDIVIDUALLY UNDER CONDITIONS OF REWARD AND NON-REWARD. EXPECTATIONS BASED ON THE EFFECTS OF SOCIOECONOMIC AND PRESCHOOL EXPERIENCE DIFFERENCES IN BACKGROUND OF THE FOUR SUBJECT GROUPS WERE NOT MET. ALSO UNSUBSTANTIATED WERE THE EXPECTATIONS ABOUT THE SITUATIONAL VARIABLES OF REWARD PRESENCE AND ABSENCE OR SET FOR TASK DIFFICULTY. IMPLICATIONS OF THE FINDINGS AND POSSIBLE DESIGN CHANGES ARE DISCUSSED. (WY)

ED052820 PS004791
EARLY CHILDHOOD EDUCATION PROGRAM, ESEA TITLE I, FY 1970. PROJECT REPORTS, VOLUME 5, BOOK 2, 1970. LANE, ELIZABETH M., ED., 70 159P.
EDRS PRICE MF-$0.65 HC-$6.58

THIS REPORT ON THE 1969-70 DAYTON EARLY CHILDHOOD EDUCATION PROGRAM IS DIVIDED INTO THREE PARTS: (1) AN OVERVIEW OF THE ECE PROGRAM, (2) A DESCRIPTION OF THE PROGRAM COMPONENTS OF ECE, AND (3) AN EVALUATION. SECTION 1 INCLUDES AN INTRODUCTION AND REPORTS ON THE GROWTH OF THE PROGRAM, HOW THE PROGRAM CONTRIBUTES TO THE KINDERGARTEN PROGRAM, THE OBJECTIVES, PROGRAM ORGANIZATION AND STAFF ROLES, AND THE CURRICULUM. SECTION 2 EXPLAINS THE VALUE OF CURRICULUM CONSULTANTS TO INSURE UNIFIED CURRICULUM DESIGN, ENUMERATES THE SPECIAL STAFF SERVICES, DESCRIBES THE HEALTH AND NUTRITION PROGRAM, AND DISCUSSES THE TASKS OF SOCIAL WORKERS AND INVOLVEMENT OF PARENTS. SECTION 3 REPORTS THAT ALTHOUGH TESTS DEMONSTRATE THAT CHILDREN DO IMPROVE COGNITIVE SKILLS FROM THEIR EXPERIENCE IN THE ECE PROGRAM, GAINS ARE QUICKLY LOST WITHOUT REINFORCEMENT AND ARE NOT EVIDENT IN KINDERGARTEN OR FIRST GRADE. TABLES ARE INCLUDED. (AUTHOR/AJ)

ED052821 PS004793
THE IMPLICATIONS OF PARENT EFFECTIVENESS TRAINING FOR FOSTER PARENTS. THOMPSON, JACK M.; PATRICK, RAYMOND, [70] 7P.
EDRS PRICE MF-$0.65 HC-$3.29

THIS PAPER DESCRIBES THE PARENT EFFECTIVENESS TRAINING (PET) PROGRAM AND POINTS OUT ITS SPECIFIC IMPLICATIONS FOR FOSTER PARENTS. THE ROLE OF A FOSTER PARENT IS EXTREMELY DIFFICULT, AND THERE IS A NEED FOR TRAINING FOSTER PARENTS TO BECOME MORE EFFECTIVE WHICH, IN TURN, WILL HAVE POSITIVE EFFECTS UPON FOSTER CHILDREN. THE PET PROGRAM, DEVELOPED IN 1962 BY DR. THOMAS GORDON, CONSISTS OF EIGHT 3-HOUR TRAINING SESSIONS AND IS LIMITED TO 25 PARTICIPANTS. THROUGH LECTURES, ROLE-PLAYING AND PRACTICE, PARENTS LEARN THESE COMMUNICATION SKILLS: (1) ACTIVE LISTENING--THE PARENT LEARNS TO REFLECT BACK WHAT THE CHILD IS TRYING TO COMMUNICATE ABOUT HIS PROBLEMS IN A WAY THAT FACILITATES THE CHILD'S GROWTH; (2) "I" MESSAGES--THE PARENT LEARNS TO COMMUNICATE PERSONAL FEELINGS WHEN THE PROBLEM IS HIS, RATHER THAN PLACING THE BLAME ON THE CHILD AND (3) CONFLICT RESOLUTION--WORKING OUT CONFLICTS SO THAT BOTH PARENT AND CHILD ARE ACTIVELY ENGAGED IN REACHING A SATISFACTORY SOLUTION. THE PROGRAM ALSO FOCUSES ON THE PROBLEMS OF USING POWER IN THE PARENT-CHILD RELATIONSHIP, AND ON ASSESSMENT AND MODIFICATION OF PARENT VALUES. (AUTHOR/AJ)

ED052822 PS004805
PRESCHOOL PROGRAMS: AN ANNOTATED BIBLIOGRAPHY. JOHNSON, ADELE M., COMP., JUN 71 48P.
EDRS PRICE MF-$0.65 HC-$3.29

THIS BIBLIOGRAPHY PROVIDES ANNOTATIONS FOR RECENT RESEARCH STUDIES AND LISTS JOURNAL ARTICLES ON PRESCHOOL PROGRAMS. THE 180 ENTRIES OFFER INFORMATION FOR PROGRAM ORGANIZERS AND ADMINISTRATORS, TEACHERS AND PARENTS. INCLUDED ARE ENTRIES FROM THE ERIC MONTHLY ABSTRACT JOURNAL, "RESEARCH IN EDUCATION," COVERING A PERIOD FROM JANUARY 1970 THROUGH MARCH 1971, AND JOURNAL ARTICLES REPORTED IN "CURRENT INDEX TO JOURNALS IN EDUCATION" FROM JANUARY 1970 THROUGH FEBRUARY 1971. TITLES WERE SELECTED FROM THESE CATEGORIES: PRESCHOOL EDUCATION, PRESCHOOL PROGRAMS, EARLY CHILDHOOD EDUCATION, NURSERY SCHOOLS, EXPERIMENTAL PROGRAMS, AND DEMONSTRATION PROGRAMS. INFORMATION RELATED SPECIFICALLY TO DAY CARE IS NOT INCLUDED IN THIS BIBLIOGRAPHY BUT HAS BEEN COMPILED IN A SEPARATE BIBLIOGRAPHY. (AJ)

ED052823 PS004806
DAY CARE: AN ANNOTATED BIBLIOGRAPHY. HOWARD, NORMA KEMEN, COMP., JUN 71 19P.
EDRS PRICE MF-$0.65 HC-$3.29

THIS BIBLIOGRAPHY CONTAINS ANNOTATIONS OF RECENT RESEARCH REPORTS, PAPERS, AND BOOKLETS AND A LIST OF JOURNAL ARTICLES DEALING WITH DIFFERENT ASPECTS OF DAY CARE. SPECIFIC TOPICS COVERED INCLUDE PROGRAM, STAFF, BUILDING, EQUIPMENT, LICENSING AND STANDARDS, FINANCING, GOVERNMENTAL INVOLVEMENT, AND COMMUNITY SUPPORT. THE BIBLIOGRAPHY SHOULD BE OF PARTICULAR USE TO TEACHERS, ADMINISTRATORS, AND PARENTS INTERESTED IN DAY CARE. ORDERING INFORMATION FOR ALL TITLES IS INCLUDED. (NH)

ED052824 PS004814
THE EVALUATION OF "SESAME STREET'S" SOCIAL GOALS: THE INTERPERSONAL STRATEGIES OF COOPERATION, CONFLICT RESOLUTION, AND DIFFERING PERSPECTIVES. MCDONALD, D. LYNN; PAULSON, F. LEON, APR 71 16P.
EDRS PRICE MF-$0.65 HC-$3.29

THIS REPORT REVIEWS "SESAME STREET'S" DEVELOPMENT OF PROCEDURE AND MATERIALS FOR THE 1970-1971 SEASON WITH EMPHASIS ON THE SOCIAL GOALS OF COOPERATION, CONFLICT RESOLUTION, AND REALIZATION OF DIFFERING PERSPECTIVES. THESE GOALS MARK A DEPARTURE FROM THE FIRST YEAR OF PROGRAMING WHICH EMPHASIZED COGNITIVE LEARNING OBJECTIVES. RESEARCH DESIGN, SITUATIONAL TESTING OF SOCIAL GOALS, AND DEVELOPMENT OF SCORING PROCEDURES ARE DISCUSSED. THE RESULTS OF PILOT TESTING WILL LEAD TO FURTHER PROGRAM AND TEST REFINEMENT IN ANTICIPATION OF A LARGER SCALE EFFORT TO TEACH SOCIAL GOALS DURING THE THIRD SEASON. (AUTHOR/AJ)

ED052825 PS004819
INFANT REACTIVITY TO REDUNDANT PROPRIOCEPTIVE AND AUDITORY STIMULATION: A TWIN STUDY. VAN DEN DAELE, LELAND D., FEB 71 19P.
EDRS PRICE MF-$0.65 HC-$3.29

THE ROLE OF GENETIC FACTORS IN INFANT RESPONSE TO REDUNDANCY WAS EVALUATED THROUGH OBSERVATION OF THE BEHAVIOR OF THREE SETS OF SAME-SEX FRATERNAL TWINS AND SIX SETS OF SAME-SEX IDENTICAL TWINS TO COMBINATIONS OF REDUNDANT PROPRIOCEPTIVE AND AUDITORY STIMULATION. THE TWINS RANGED IN AGE FROM 6 WEEKS TO 24 WEEKS. ONE MEMBER OF EACH TWIN SET WAS PLACED ON EACH SIDE OF A PARTITION IN A MOTOR-DRIVEN ROCKERBOX, AND FOUR 1-MINUTE TREATMENTS WERE ADMINISTERED IN MIXED ORDER, WITH 1-MINUTE PRE-TREATMENT AND POST-TREATMENT PERIODS. THE TREATMENTS CONSISTED OF COMBINATIONS OF FAST AND SLOW ROCKING UNDER CONDITIONS OF SOUND AND NO SOUND. AN OBSERVER RATED THE ACTIVITY LEVEL OF EACH TWIN ON A 5-POINT SCALE AT 30-SECOND INTERVALS. TREATMENT WAS ASSOCIATED WITH A SIGNIFICANT DECLINE OF INFANT ACTIVITY INDEPENDENT OF ZYGOSITY. IDENTICAL TWINS EXHIBITED MARKED BEHAVIORAL CONSISTENCY COMPARED TO FRATERNAL TWINS DURING AND AFTER TREATMENT. THE RESULTS APPEAR TO PROVIDE POSITIVE EVIDENCE FOR THE ROLE OF ENDOGENOUS, GENETICALLY LINKED REGULATION OF INFANT RESPONSE TO REDUNDANT STIMULATION. (AUTHOR/NH)

ED052826 PS004821
CURRENT EXPENDITURES BY LOCAL EDUCATION AGENCIES FOR FREE PUBLIC ELEMENTARY AND SECONDARY EDUCATION, 1968-69. BARR, RICHARD H.; FOSTER, BETTY J., SEP 70 4P.
DOCUMENT NOT AVAILABLE FROM EDRS.
AVAILABLE FROM: SUPERINTENDENT OF DOCUMENTS, U.S. GOVERNMENT PRINTING OFFICE, WASHINGTON, D.C. 20402 ($0.10, CATALOG NO. HE 5.222:22026-69)

LOCAL EDUCATION AGENCIES SPENT $28.5 BILLION ON FREE PUBLIC ELEMENTARY AND SECONDARY EDUCATION DURING 1968-69, WHICH REPRESENTS 92 PERCENT OF PUBLIC SCHOOL EXPENDITURES DURING THAT YEAR. THESE DATA DO NOT INCLUDE MONEY SPENT FOR ADMINISTRATION AT STATE AND INTERMEDIATE LEVELS, COMMUNITY SERVICES, ADULT EDUCATION, AND SUMMER SCHOOLS FOR WHICH TUITION IS CHARGED. ALSO EXCLUDED ARE EXPENDITURES OF FEDERAL FUNDS RECEIVED UNDER THE ELEMENTARY AND SECONDARY EDUCATION ACT OF 1965 (ESEA) TITLES I, II AND III; THE VALUE OF COMMODITIES DONATED FOR THE SCHOOL LUNCH PROGRAM; AND EXPENDITURES OF INCOME RECEIVED FROM NONTAX REVENUES (TUITION AND FEES). THE EXPENDITURES OF $28.5 BILLION WERE THOSE ALLOWABLE EXPENDITURES USED TO ESTABLISH THE "AVERAGE PER PUPIL EXPENDITURE IN A STATE," AND THE NATIONAL AVERAGE EXPENDITURE PER PUPIL IN AVERAGE DAILY ATTENDANCE (ADA) REQUIRED BY FEDERAL LAW. THE NATIONAL AVERAGE EXPENDITURE PER PUPIL IN ADA WAS $685, AN INCREASE OF 11.8 PERCENT OVER THE $612 REPORTED FOR THE 1967-68 SCHOOL YEAR. A TABLE GIVES THE FOLLOWING INFORMATION BY REGION AND STATE: CURRENT TOTAL EXPENDITURES FOR FREE PUBLIC ELEMENTARY AND SECONDARY EDUCATION; AVERAGE DAILY ATTENDANCE; CURRENT EXPENDITURES PER PUPIL; PERCENT INCREASE. INCLUDED IS A GRAPH WHICH PRESENTS A 5-YEAR COMPARISON OF STATE AVERAGE EXPENDITURES PER PUPIL IN ADA. (NH)

ED052827 PS004826
THE HEALTH OF CHILDREN--1970: SELECTED DATA FROM THE NATIONAL CENTER FOR HEALTH STATISTICS. , 70 73P.
EDRS PRICE MF-$0.65 HC NOT AVAILABLE FROM EDRS.
AVAILABLE FROM: SUPERINTENDENT OF DOCUMENTS, U.S. GOVERNMENT PRINTING OFFICE, WASHINGTON, D.C. 20402 ($0.50)

IN THIS BOOKLET, CHARTS AND GRAPHS PRESENT DATA FROM FOUR DIVISIONS OF THE NATIONAL CENTER FOR HEALTH STATISTICS. THE DIVISIONS REPRESENTED ARE THOSE CONCERNED WITH VITAL STATISTICS (BIRTHS, DEATHS, FETAL DEATHS, MARRIAGES AND DIVORCES); HEALTH INTERVIEW STATISTICS (INFORMATION ON HEALTH AND DEMOGRAPHIC FACTORS RELATED TO ILLNESS); HEALTH EXAMINATION STATISTICS (DATA ON PREVALENCE OF ILLNESS AND ON VARIOUS HEALTH-RELATED MEASURES); AND HEALTH RESOURCES STATISTICS (CHARACTERISTICS AND UTILIZATION OF HEALTH RESOURCES SUCH AS HOSPITALS, CLINICS, NURSING HOMES AND FAMILY PLANNING CENTERS.) INFANT MORTALITY IS RECOGNIZED AS A MAJOR PROBLEM AND IS THE FOCUS OF PART I OF THE BOOKLET. PART II DEALS WITH CHILDREN'S ACUTE CONDITIONS AND ACCIDENTS. PART III PRESENTS STATISTICS ON THE IMPACT OF ILLNESS ON CHILDREN AGES 6 TO 11 YEARS AND INCLUDES FIGURES ON SPEECH AND HEARING DEFECTS, DAYS OF RESTRICTED ACTIVITY AND DAYS IN BED, SCHOOL DAYS LOST, AND REASONS FOR HOSPITALIZATION. HEALTH CARE IS DISCUSSED IN PART IV, WITH STATISTICS GIVEN ON NUMBERS OF VISITS OF CHILDREN TO DOCTORS AND DENTISTS. PART V PRESENTS DATA ON THE GROWTH AND DEVELOPMENT OF CHILDREN AGES 6 TO 11 YEARS. (NH)

ED052828 PS004829
REPORT TO THE PRESIDENT: WHITE HOUSE CONFERENCE ON CHILDREN 1970. , 71 439P.
EDRS PRICE MF-$0.65 HC NOT AVAILABLE FROM EDRS.
AVAILABLE FROM: SUPERINTENDENT OF DOCUMENTS, U.S. GOVERNMENT PRINTING OFFICE, WASHINGTON, D.C. 20402 ($4.75)

MOST OF THIS DOCUMENT CONSISTS OF THE INDIVIDUAL REPORTS APPROVED BY THE 25 FORUMS AT THE 1970 WHITE HOUSE CONFERENCE ON CHILDREN. ALSO INCLUDED ARE THE CONFERENCE PREAMBLE THAT SET THE TONE OF THE CONFERENCE PROCEEDINGS; THE LETTER OF TRANSMITTAL SUBMITTED TO THE PRESIDENT BY THE NATIONAL CONFERENCE CHAIRMAN, STEPHEN HESS; AND AN APPENDIX CONTAINING LISTS OF CONFERENCE STAFF, CONSULTANTS, ADVISORY COMMITTEES, AND CONTRIBUTORS. (AJ)

ED052829 PS004830
STATE AS AN INFANT-ENVIRONMENT INTERACTION: AN ANALYSIS OF MOTHER-INFANT BEHAVIOR AS A FUNCTION OF SEX. LEWIS, MICHAEL, MAY 71 57P.
EDRS PRICE MF-$0.65 HC-$3.29

THE LITERATURE ON THE PSYCHOLOGICAL CONSTRUCT OF STATE IS REVIEWED, AND IT IS PROPOSED THAT STATE BE DEFINED IN TERMS OF AN INFANT-ENVIRONMENT INTERACTION. INTERACTIVE BEHAVIOR OF 32 MOTHER-INFANT DYADS WAS OBSERVED IN THE HOME FOR A TOTAL OF 2 HOURS FOR EACH PAIR, IN ORDER TO EXPLORE VARIOUS TYPES OF INTERACTIVE PROCESSES AND ANALYSES. A CHECKLIST DIVIDED INTO 10-SECOND INTERVALS INCLUDED VARIOUS OBSERVED BEHAVIORS, FOR EXAMPLE; INFANT FRET/CRY, VOCALIZE, PLAY, SMILE, AND EAT; AND MOTHER TOUCH, HOLD, VOCALIZE, PLAY, CHANGE, AND FEED. THE DATA SEEMED TO SUPPORT THE PROPOSED MODEL OF STATE, NAMELY THAT INFANT CONDITION (BEHAVIOR) ALONE WAS INSUFFICIENT TO DESCRIBE STATE SINCE OFTEN THE SAME CONDITION HAD WIDELY DIFFERENT CONSEQUENCES WHICH IN TURN SHOULD AFFECT FUTURE CONDITIONS. THE DATA ALSO REVEALED INDIVIDUAL DIFFERENCES AS A FUNCTION OF THE SEX OF THE INFANT. BRIEFLY, GIRLS RECEIVED MORE DISTAL RESPONSES TO THE SAME BEHAVIOR FOR WHICH BOYS RECEIVED PROXIMAL RESPONSES. THIS FINDING WAS DISCUSSED AS AN IMPORTANT SOURCE OF INDIVIDUAL VARIANCE AND ITS EFFECT ON SUBSEQUENT COGNITIVE FUNCTIONING. (AUTHOR/NH)

ED052830 PS004831
PREVENTION OF IRON-DEFICIENCY ANEMIA IN INFANTS AND CHILDREN OF PRESCHOOL AGE. FOMON, SAMUEL J., 70 19P.
EDRS PRICE MF-$0.65 HC NOT AVAILABLE FROM EDRS.
AVAILABLE FROM: SUPERINTENDENT OF DOCUMENTS, U.S. GOVERNMENT PRINTING OFFICE, WASHINGTON, D.C. 20402 ($0.20, PUBLIC HEALTH SERVICE PUBLICATION NO. 2085)

IRON-DEFICIENCY ANEMIA IS ALMOST CERTAINLY THE MOST PREVALENT NUTRITIONAL DISORDER AMONG INFANTS AND YOUNG CHILDREN IN THE UNITED STATES. ANEMIA IS FREQUENTLY SEEN AMONG CHILDREN OF LOW SOCIOECONOMIC STATUS BUT IS PROBABLY ALSO THE MOST FREQUENT NUTRITIONAL DEFICIENCY DISEASE SEEN AMONG CHILDREN CARED FOR BY PRIVATE DOCTORS. POSSIBLE REASONS FOR THE WIDESPREAD OCCURRENCE OF THIS DISEASE ARE: (1) AN ERRONEOUS BELIEF AMONG MANY PHYSICIANS THAT IRON IS NOT ABSORBED BEFORE 2 OR 3 MONTHS OF AGE AND THAT THEREFORE IT IS USELESS TO GIVE IRON TO YOUNG INFANTS, (2) LACK OF AWARENESS AMONG PROFESSIONAL WORKERS AND PARENTS THAT MOST UNFORTIFIED FOODS PROVIDE LIMITED AMOUNTS OF IRON, (3) INABILITY OF MANY PARENTS TO CARRY OUT A PROGRAM OF DAILY ADMINISTRATION OF MEDICINAL IRON, AND (4) FEEDING OF MILK, A POOR IRON SOURCE, TO INFANTS IN LARGE QUANTITIES TO THE EXCLUSION OF IRON-RICH FOODS. RECOMMENDATIONS ARE GIVEN FOR AVERAGE DAILY INTAKE OF IRON. A MASSIVE EDUCATIONAL EFFORT DIRECTED TO PROFESSIONAL WORKERS AND TO PARENTS IS URGED, AND SUGGESTIONS ARE MADE FOR EVALUATION OF MATERNAL AND CHILD PROGRAMS. TABLES GIVE DATA ON THE PREVALENCE OF IRON-DEFICIENCY ANEMIA AND THE IRON CONTENT OF COMMERCIAL INFANT FOODS. (NH)

ED052831 PS004832
THREE DEGREES OF PARENT INVOLVEMENT IN A PRESCHOOL PROGRAM: IMPACT ON MOTHERS AND CHILDREN. RADIN, NORMA, 8 MAY 71 16P.
EDRS PRICE MF-$0.65 HC-$3.29

TO DETERMINE THE EFFECT OF DIFFERENT AMOUNTS OF PARENTAL INVOLVEMENT, 80 4-YEAR-OLD CHILDREN FROM LOWER CLASS HOMES, ENROLLED IN A COMPENSATORY PRESCHOOL PROGRAM (CLASS FOR ONE-HALF DAY, FOUR DAYS PER WEEK FOR A FULL YEAR) WERE DIVIDED INTO THREE GROUPS. GROUP I RECEIVED SUPPLEMENTARY BI-WEEKLY TUTORING FROM TEACHERS WITH NO PARENTAL INVOLVEMENT. GROUP II WAS TUTORED BUT IN THE PRESENCE OF THEIR MOTHERS WHO BECAME INVOLVED. GROUP III WAS OFFERED THE SAME TUTORING AS GROUP II, AND MOTHERS PARTICIPATED IN SMALL GROUP DISCUSSIONS ABOUT CHILDREARING. THE STANFORD-BINET AND THE PEABODY PICTURE VOCABULARY TEST (PPVT) WERE GIVEN AS PRETESTS AND POSTTESTS TO ALL CHILDREN. A REVISED VERSION OF THE PUPIL BEHAVIOR INVENTORY WAS COMPLETED BY TEACHERS AND TWO STANDARDIZED QUESTIONNAIRES WERE COMPLETED BY MOTHERS TO TAP ATTITUDES TOWARD CHILDREARING AND COGNITIVE STIMULATION IN THE HOME. NO SIGNIFICANT DIFFERENCES WERE FOUND BETWEEN GROUPS IN IQ GAIN ON EITHER THE STANFORD-BINET OR THE PPVT, ALTHOUGH ALL GROUPS GAINED SIGNIFICANTLY. SIGNIFICANT DIFFERENCES DID EMERGE ON FACTORS OF PARENTAL MEASURES, BUT NOT ON THE TEACHER RATING FORM. DESIRABLE CHANGES IN MATERNAL ATTITUDES WERE FOUND IN THE MOTHERS WHO HAD BEEN OFFERED OPPORTUNITY FOR MAXIMUM PARTICIPATION. (AUTHOR/AJ)

ED052832 PS004884
DEMOGRAPHIC AND SOCIO-ECONOMIC DATA OF THE BECKLEY, WEST VIRGINIA AREA AND 1968-1970 DEVELOPMENTAL COSTS OF THE EARLY CHILDHOOD EDUCATION FIELD STUDY. TECHNICAL REPORT NO. 1. BERTRAM, CHARLES L., FEB 71 17P.
EDRS PRICE MF-$0.65 HC-$3.29

THIS REPORT INCLUDES DEMOGRAPHIC INFORMATION ABOUT THE EIGHT COUNTY FIELD TEST AREA, SOCIOECONOMIC INFORMATION ABOUT THE PARENTS OF EARLY CHILDHOOD EDUCATION (ECE) PROGRAM CHILDREN; AND INFORMATION ON THE NUMBER OF STAFF AND DEVELOPMENTAL COST OF THE ECE FIELD STUDY (1968-69 AND 1969-70). A SUMMARY OF DATA RESULTS IS GIVEN. (AUTHOR/AJ)

ED052833 PS004885
ATTAINMENT OF COGNITIVE OBJECTIVES. TECHNICAL REPORT NO. 3. HINES, BRAINARD, FEB 71 10P.
EDRS PRICE MF-$0.65 HC-$3.29

TO DETERMINE THE EFFECTS OF THE TELEVISION PROGRAM, "AROUND THE BEND" AND THE RELATED ACTIVITIES OF THE HOME VISITOR AND MOBILE VAN TEACHERS, THE APPALACHIA PRESCHOOL TEST (APT) WAS DEVELOPED BY THE APPALACHIAN EDUCATIONAL LABORATORY. APT IS USED TO SUPPLEMENT THE STANDARDIZED INSTRUMENTS BEING USED TO MEASURE PROGRAM PERFORMANCE. THE TEST CONSISTS OF FOUR SUBTESTS AND AN EXPERIMENTAL SECTION: PART 1 DEALS WITH COLOR NAMING, IDENTIFYING BODY PARTS, AND RIGHT-LEFT DISCRIMINATION; PART 2 (DESCRIBED IN THIS REPORT) IS THE BASIS FOR DETERMINING SPECIFIC COGNITIVE LEARNING FROM THE EARLY CHILDHOOD EDUCATION CURRICULUM; PARTS 3 AND 4 ARE PIAGET-TYPE, CONSERVATION OF NUMBER AND SIZE TASKS; PART 5 IS AN EXPERIMENTAL SUBTEST DESIGNED TO MEASURE UNDERSTANDING OF CAUSE AND EFFECT, LOGICAL CLASSIFICATION AND LETTER RECOGNITION. TO MEASURE THE ACHIEVEMENT OF COGNITIVE OBJECTIVES PART 2 WAS GIVEN TO 273 CHILDREN IN THREE TREATMENT GROUPS, AND SUBSEQUENTLY TO A 60-CHILD SAMPLE IN A COMPARISON GROUP. CHILDREN WHO VIEWED ONLY THE TELEVISION PROGRAM AND WERE NOT EXPOSED TO THE HOME VISITOR AND MOBILE VAN TEACHERS SCORED SIGNIFICANTLY LOWER ON THE TEST. RESULTS INDICATE THAT THE HOME VISITOR, MORE THAN ANY OTHER PART OF THE PROGRAM, HAS A GREAT POTENTIAL FOR INFLUENCING THE CHILD'S BEHAVIOR, ESPECIALLY IF SHE CAN PRODUCE CHANGES IN THE CHILD'S ENVIRONMENT. A SUMMARY OF AEL EARLY CHILDHOOD EDUCATION PROGRAM IS AVAILABLE AS PS 004 889. (AUTHOR/AJ)

ED052834 PS004886
DETAILED ANALYSIS OF LANGUAGE DEVELOPMENT OF PRESCHOOL CHILDREN IN ECE PROGRAM. TECHNICAL REPORT NO. 4. HINES, BRAINARD W., 71 49P.
EDRS PRICE MF-$0.65 HC-$3.29

THIS REPORT IS CONCERNED WITH THE LANGUAGE SKILLS CATEGORY OF OBJECTIVES OF THE EARLY CHILDHOOD EDUCATION (ECE) PROGRAM. THE ILLINOIS TEST OF PSYCHOLINGUISTIC ABILITY (ITPA) WAS THE PRIMARY INSTRUMENT USED FOR EVALUATION OF 3-, 4-, AND 5-YEAR-OLD CHILDREN IN THREE TREATMENT GROUPS: (1) MOBILE EDUCATIONAL FACILITY, TV, AND PARAPROFESSIONAL, (2) TV AND PARAPROFESSIONAL, AND (3) TV ONLY. A CONTROL GROUP RECEIVED NO TREATMENT. AN OVERVIEW OF THE ITPA IS GIVEN, AS WELL AS SEPARATE DESCRIPTIONS OF EACH OF THE TEN SUBTESTS. THE SUBTESTS OVERLAP SOMEWHAT IN THE FUNCTIONS THEY MEASURE, BUT COVER THE BROAD AREAS OF AUDITORY MEMORY AND ACUITY, VERBAL EXPRESSION AND GRAMMAR, SYNTAX AND TRANSFORMATIONS, AND THE ABILITY TO ASSOCIATE VARIOUS AUDITORY AND VISUAL STIMULI. STATISTICAL DESCRIPTIONS AND INFERENCES ARE PRESENTED FOR EACH SUBTEST. AN OVERALL SUMMARY OF THE FINDINGS OF THE EFFECTS FOR THE SECOND YEAR'S PROGRAMMING IN LANGUAGE DEVELOPMENT IS PRESENTED. TRENDS REPORTED INDICATE THAT THE ECE PROGRAM IS HAVING AN EFFECT ON A BROAD RANGE OF PSYCHOLINGUISTIC ABILITIES. TABLES AND FIGURES COMPRISE ABOUT ONE-HALF OF THE DOCUMENT. A SUMMARY OF AEL EARLY CHILD EDUCATION PROGRAM IS AVAILABLE AS PS 004 889. (AUTHOR/NH)

ED052835 PS004887
SOCIAL SKILLS DEVELOPMENT IN THE EARLY CHILDHOOD EDUCATION PROJECT. TECHNICAL REPORT NO. 7. PENA, DEAGELIA; MILLER, GEORGE, FEB 71 86P.
EDRS PRICE MF-$0.65 HC-$3.29

A TOTAL OF 105 CHILDREN (3, 4, AND 5 YEARS OLD) PARTICIPATED IN A STUDY TO DETERMINE THE EXTENT TO WHICH THE EXPERIENCE OF ATTENDING A MOBILE CLASSROOM FOR AN HOUR AND A HALF, ONCE A WEEK (32 WEEKS) CONTRIBUTED TO THE DEVELOPMENT OF SOCIAL SKILLS. SINCE THIS WAS ONE OF THE FIRST ATTEMPTS TO MEASURE THESE SKILLS IN YOUNG CHILDREN, ANOTHER OBJECTIVE WAS TO LEARN AS MUCH AS POSSIBLE ABOUT THE DEVELOPMENT OF THESE SKILLS. THE CHILDREN WERE DIVIDED INTO TWO GROUPS. ONE WATCHED THE DAILY TELEVISION PROGRAM, "AROUND THE BEND," AND WAS VISITED WEEKLY BY A HOME VISITOR. THE OTHER GROUP WATCHED THE PROGRAM, HAD HOME VISITS AND VISITED A MOBILE CLASSROOM ONCE A WEEK. A TASK WHICH INVOLVED PLACING MODEL FURNITURE IN A MODEL HOUSE WAS SELECTED AS THE TASK WHICH WOULD MOST STIMULATE THE OCCURRENCE OF BEHAVIORS THAT FACILITATE THE PROCESS OF LEARNING IN GROUP SITUATIONS. OBSERVERS CODED CHILDREN'S BEHAVIOR UNDER SIX MAJOR CATEGORIES: INITIATION, REQUEST FOR HELP OR QUESTIONS, GIVING HELP, REFUSING HELP, GROUP CONSCIOUSNESS, AND RESPONSE TO PEERS. RESULTS GAVE STRONG INDICATION THAT THE MOBILE CLASSROOM CONTRIBUTED TO THE DEVELOPMENT OF SOCIAL SKILLS ASSUMED IMPORTANT IN THE LEARNING PROCESS WITHIN A SOCIALLY STRUCTURED ENVIRONMENT. TABLES AND GRAPHS COMPRISE MORE THAN HALF THE DOCUMENT. A SUMMARY OF AEL EARLY CHILDHOOD EDUCATION PROGRAM IS AVAILABLE AS PS 004 889. (AUTHOR/AJ)

ED052836 PS004888
RESULTS OF PARENT AND STUDENT REACTION QUESTIONNAIRE. TECHNICAL REPORT NO. 8. HINES, BRAINARD, JAN 71 6P.
EDRS PRICE MF-$0.65 HC-$3.29

IN ORDER TO EVALUATE THE CHANGES IN PARENT AND STUDENT ATTITUDES TOWARD THE VARIOUS COMPONENTS OF THE EARLY CHILDHOOD EDUCATION (ECE) PROGRAM, THE PARAPROFESSIONAL HOME VISITORS WERE ASKED TO COMPLETE A TEN ITEM QUESTIONNAIRE BASED ON THEIR OBSERVATIONS OF THE FAMILY'S REACTIONS TO EACH OF THREE COMPONENTS (TV PROGRAM, HOME VISIT, AND MOBILE CLASSROOM). THE QUESTIONNAIRE WAS COMPLETED ON A WEEKLY BASIS FOR A SAMPLE OF APPROXIMATELY 80 FAMILIES NORMALLY VISITED BY THE PARAPROFESSIONALS. GRAPHICAL ANALYSIS OF THE WEEKLY CHANGES IN ATTITUDE OF PARENTS AND CHILDREN SHOWED A SIMILAR PATTERN FOR INDIVIDUALS EXPOSED TO THE MOBILE FACILITY AND THOSE WHO WERE ONLY VISITED BY THE PARAPROFESSIONAL. ALTHOUGH ATTITUDE TOWARD THE PROGRAM REMAINED AT A HIGHLY POSITIVE LEVEL THROUGHOUT THE YEAR, IT DECREASED SLIGHTLY IN LATE OCTOBER, EARLY JANUARY, AND LATE FEBRUARY. BOTH PARENTS' AND CHILDREN'S ATTITUDES FOLLOWED THIS SAME PATTERN, ALTHOUGH THE PARENTS WERE CONSISTENTLY MORE ENTHUSIASTIC ABOUT THE PROGRAM. A

SUMMARY OF AEL EARLY CHILD EDUCATION PROGRAM IS AVAILABLE AS PS 004 889. (AJ)

ED052837 PS004889
EVALUATION REPORT: EARLY CHILDHOOD EDUCATION PROGRAM, 1969-1970 FIELD TEST. SUMMARY REPORT. BERTRAM, CHARLES L.; AND OTHERS, MAY 71 30P.
EDRS PRICE MF-$0.65 HC-$3.29

THIS REPORT IS BASED ON DATA OBTAINED DURING THE SECOND YEAR OF A 3-YEAR FIELD TEST CYCLE OF THE APPALACHIA EDUCATIONAL LABORATORY (AEL) EARLY CHILDHOOD EDUCATION (ECE) PROGRAM. THE ECE PROGRAM IS A HOME-ORIENTED INSTRUCTIONAL SYSTEM DESIGNED FOR 3-, 4-, AND 5-YEAR-OLDS, WHICH IS BEING USED ON A REGIONAL BASIS FOR APPROXIMATELY 25,000 CHILDREN. IT CONSISTS OF 30-MINUTE TELEVISION LESSONS BROADCAST INTO THE HOME EACH DAY; A WEEKLY HOME VISIT BY PARAPROFESSIONALS TO DISCUSS THE PROGRAM WITH PARENTS AND CHILDREN, AND TO DELIVER MATERIALS FOR THE PARENTS TO USE WITH THE CHILDREN; AND GROUP INSTRUCTION ONCE A WEEK IN A MOBILE CLASSROOM. TESTS USED, METHODS, AND RESULTS ARE REPORTED FOR CHILDREN'S GAINS IN COGNITIVE, LANGUAGE, PSYCHOMOTOR, AND SOCIAL SKILLS CATEGORIES. FIELD TEST RESULTS ARE PRESENTED IN FOUR AREAS: PROGRAM EFFORT (DESCRIBES MATERIAL AND PERSONNEL REQUIREMENTS); PROGRAM PERFORMANCE (CHILDREN'S ACHIEVEMENT GAINS AND PARENTS' AND CHILDREN'S ATTITUDES TOWARD THE PROGRAM), PROGRAM PERVASIVENESS (DESCRIBES THE POPULATION WHICH MIGHT BE SERVED), AND EVALUATION SYNTHESIS (SUMMARY). THE PROGRAM PERVASIVENESS STUDY AND COST ANALYSIS INDICATE THAT THE APPALACHIAN EDUCATIONAL LABORATORY ECE PROGRAM IS AN ECONOMICAL ALTERNATIVE TO OTHER PROGRAMS OF EARLY CHILDHOOD EDUCATION. (AUTHOR/NH)

ED052838 PS004893
ANALYSIS OF INTELLIGENCE SCORES. HINES, BRAINARD W., FEB 71 16P.
EDRS PRICE MF-$0.65 HC-$3.29

THE THEORY UNDERLYING THE MEASUREMENT OF INTELLECTUAL GROWTH BY THE PEABODY PICTURE VOCABULARY TEST (PPVT) AND ITS CONGRUENCE WITH THE OBJECTIVES OF THE APPALACHIA EDUCATIONAL LABORATORY (AEL) EARLY CHILDHOOD EDUCATION PROGRAM IS EXPLORED. THE PPVT WAS ADMINISTERED TO A SAMPLE OF 160 3- AND 4-YEAR-OLD CHILDREN IN THREE TREATMENT GROUPS: (1) PACKAGE (MOBILE CLASSROOM, TV, AND HOME VISITOR), (2) TV-HOME VISITOR (HV), (3) TV ONLY, AND A CONTROL GROUP. DATA ARE ANALYZED BY A THREE-WAY ANALYSIS OF VARIANCE AND AN ANALYSIS OF COVARIANCE PROCEDURE. BECAUSE OF THE HIGHLY SPECIFIC NATURE OF THE TEST ITEMS ON THE PPVT, IT IS NOT LIKELY THAT IT REFLECTS GENERAL PROGRAM EFFECTS AS WELL AS THE MORE BROADLY BASED INSTRUMENT IN A TEST BATTERY. TWO GROUPS OF CHILDREN (PACKAGE AND TV-HV) SCORED NEAR THE NATIONAL MEAN (50TH PERCENTILE) IN IQ AND TWO GROUPS (TV ONLY AND CONTROL) SCORED NEAR THE 40TH PERCENTILE WHEN COMPARED TO THE NATIONAL SAMPLE. THE LACK OF OVERALL DEFICIT INDICATES THAT MANY OF THE CHILDREN HAVE AN ADEQUATE VOCABULARY LEVEL. RAW SCORE ANALYSIS SUGGESTS THE PROBABILITY OF A TREATMENT EFFECT IN THE VERBAL AREA WHICH IS REFLECTED BY THE PPVT AND WHICH FAVORS THE PACKAGE AND TV-HV GROUPS. A SUMMARY OF THE AEL EARLY CHILDHOOD PROGRAM IS AVAILABLE AS PS 004 889. (AUTHOR/NH)

ED052839 PS004894
ANALYSIS OF VISUAL PERCEPTION OF CHILDREN IN THE EARLY CHILDHOOD EDUCATION PROGRAM (RESULTS OF THE MARIANNE FROSTIG DEVELOPMENTAL TEST OF VISUAL PERCEPTION). HINES, BRAINARD W., FEB 71 31P.
EDRS PRICE MF-$0.65 HC-$3.29

THIS REPORT INCLUDES A DESCRIPTION OF THE FROSTIG AS A TOTAL INSTRUMENT AND AN OVERALL ANALYSIS, AS WELL AS SEPARATE ANALYSES AND DESCRIPTIONS OF EACH SUBTEST. A BRIEF SUMMARY OF THE EXPERIMENTAL DESIGN AND SAMPLING PLAN ALSO IS INCLUDED. A SUMMARY OF THE AEL EARLY CHILDHOOD PROGRAM IS AVAILABLE AS PS 004 889. (AUTHOR/NH)

ED052840 PS004895
FACTOR ANALYSIS OF THE EARLY CHILDHOOD EDUCATION TEST DATA. PENA, DEAGELIA, FEB 71 29P.
EDRS PRICE MF-$0.65 HC-$3.29

TWENTY VARIABLES COMPRISING THE SUBTESTS OF THE FROSTIG, ILLINOIS TEST OF PSYCHOLINGUISTIC ABILITY, APPALACHIA PRESCHOOL TEST AND THE PEABODY PICTURE VOCABULARY TEST RAW SCORE WERE FACTOR ANALYZED BY A PRINCIPAL COMPONENT SOLUTION AND AN ORTHOGONAL ROTATION OF THE FACTOR MATRIX. ALTHOUGH THE DIFFERENT SUBTESTS WERE DESIGNED TO MEASURE SPECIFIC ABILITIES, THESE ABILITIES COULD BE MASKED BY THE PRESENCE OF UNKNOWN UNDERLYING FACTORS COMMON TO THESE TESTS. EIGHT FACTORS WERE IDENTIFIED: VOCABULARY; REASONING; GENERAL RECEPTION; IDENTIFYING BODY PARTS; GENERAL COGNITIVE SKILLS; VISUAL PERCEPTION; AUDITORY MEMORY; AND VERBAL EXPRESSION. THE RESULTS OF THE FACTOR ANALYSIS SHOWED THAT, TO SOME EXTENT, THE FACTORS REVEALED CERTAIN ABILITIES WHICH DISCRIMINATED BETWEEN GROUPS OF CHILDREN TESTED. THE EFFECTIVENESS OF THE EARLY CHILDHOOD EDUCATION (ECE) PROGRAM ON AT LEAST A FEW FACTORS WAS INDICATED. WITH THE EXCEPTION OF THE CATEGORY OF "VERBAL EXPRESSION," IN WHICH THE COMPARISON GROUP SCORED THE HIGHEST, THE ECE SUBJECTS HAD HIGHER FACTOR SCORES. A SUMMARY OF THE AEL EARLY CHILDHOOD PROGRAM IS AVAILABLE AS PS 004 889. (AUTHOR/NH)

ED052841 PS004896
ANALYSIS OF CHILDREN'S REACTIONS TO AEL'S PRESCHOOL TELEVISION PROGRAM. MILLER, GEORGE L., DEC 70 9P.
EDRS PRICE MF-$0.65 HC-$3.29

THIS REPORT DESCRIBES A TECHNIQUE WHICH CAN BE USED TO PROVIDE BOTH FORMATIVE AND SUMMATIVE EVALUATION OF TELEVISION PROGRAMS DESIGNED TO PROMOTE EDUCATIONAL DEVELOPMENT IN 3-, 4-, AND 5-YEAR-OLD CHILDREN. THE DAILY HALF-HOUR PROGRAM EVALUATED IS PART OF AN APPALACHIA EDUCATIONAL LABORATORY PROJECT, NOW IN ITS SECOND YEAR. (OTHER PROJECT COMPONENTS ARE WEEKLY VISITS IN HOMES BY PARAPROFESSIONALS, AND WEEKLY VISITS BY A MOBILE CLASSROOM.) OF THE 170 TV PROGRAMS TRANSMITTED IN THE FIRST TWO YEARS, OBSERVATIONAL DATA WAS COLLECTED ON 133. THE TELECASTS, DESIGNED TO ELICIT OVERT RESPONSES FROM CHILDREN, MADE POSSIBLE A SYSTEMATIC OBSERVATIONAL EVALUATION OF VIEWER RESPONSES. EACH OF EIGHT PARAPROFESSIONALS WATCHED THE PROGRAM WITH A DIFFERENT CHILD EVERY MORNING SO THAT, IN A RANDOM FASHION, ALL 270 CHILDREN WERE OBSERVED AN EQUAL NUMBER OF TIMES. THE OBSERVER CODED CHILDREN'S RESPONSES WHILE VIEWING THE TV PROGRAM AND RATED THEM ON A STANDARD TALLY SHEET. FIRST YEAR AND SECOND YEAR PROGRAMS WERE COMPARED ON (1) THE RATIO OF RESPONSES TO QUESTIONS ASKED BY THE TV TEACHER, (2) THE RATIO OF NEGATIVE REACTIONS TO ENTHUSIASTIC REACTIONS, AND (3) THE AVERAGE NUMBER OF ENTHUSIASTIC REACTIONS. RESULTS INDICATE THAT SYSTEMATIC OBSERVATIONAL SYSTEMS CAN PROVIDE FORMATIVE EVALUATION OF PRESCHOOL TV PROGRAMS TO GUIDE CHANGES IN PRESENTATION TECHNIQUES, CONTENT, AND EMPHASIS. A SUMMARY OF THE AEL EARLY CHILDHOOD PROGRAM IS AVAILABLE AS PS 004 889. (AJ)

ED052842 PS004897
A COMPARISON OF PARENTS' ATTITUDES TOWARD AEL'S "AROUND THE BEND" AND OTHER CHILDREN'S TELEVISION PROGRAMS. BERTRAM, CHARLES L., DEC 70 16P.
EDRS PRICE MF-$0.65 HC-$3.29

THIS STUDY COMPARED THE PARENTAL APPEAL OF THE APPALACHIA EDUCATIONAL LABORATORY'S TELEVISION PROGRAM, "AROUND THE BEND," WITH "CAPTAIN KANGAROO" AND "ROMPER ROOM." DATA WAS SOLITITED FROM 150 PARENTS OF CHILDREN IN EACH OF THE THREE TREATMENT GROUPS OF THE EARLY CHILDHOOD EDUCATION PROGRAM: (1) CHILDREN WHO OBSERVED THE TELEVISION PROGRAM ONLY; (2) THOSE WHO WATCHED THE PROGRAM AND WERE VISITED AT HOME ONCE WEEKLY BY A PARAPROFESSIONAL; AND (3) THOSE RECEIVING THE TV PROGRAM AND THE HOME VISITS, WHO WERE ALSO EXPOSED ONCE A WEEK TO A MOBILE CLASSROOM. THE SURVEY FORMS WERE DESIGNED TO DETERMINE WHICH PROGRAMS WERE VIEWED BY THE CHILDREN, IF PARENTS WATCHED THE PROGRAMS WITH THE CHILDREN, IF PARENTS THOUGHT THE CHILDREN ENJOYED AND/OR LEARNED FROM THE PROGRAMS, AND IF PARENTS THOUGHT THE DIFFERENT PROGRAMS WERE GOOD FOR THE CHILDREN. PARENTS WERE ASKED TO RATE THE PROGRAMS FROM THE BEST TO THE VERY WORST AND GIVE THE PROGRAM SPONSORS' NAMES. EIGHTY-ONE PERCENT OF THE 150 PARENTS TO WHOM FORMS WERE MAILED RESPONDED. "AROUND THE BEND" WAS RATED BEST BY 51% OF THE PARENTS; "CAPTAIN KANGAROO," BY 38% AND "ROMPER ROOM," BY 11%: THE RATINGS VARIED AMONG THE PARENTS OF CHILDREN IN DIFFERENT TREATMENT GROUPS. MANY OF THE CHILDREN WATCHED TWO OR MORE CHILDREN'S PROGRAMS EACH DAY. MANY PARENTS WATCHED THE PROGRAMS WITH THEIR CHILDREN AND FELT THAT INSTRUCTIONAL TELEVISION COMBINED WITH HOME VISITS WAS AN ACCEPTABLE PROCEDURE FOR EARLY CHILDHOOD EDUCATION. A SUMMARY OF THE AEL EARLY CHILDHOOD PROGRAM IS AVAILABLE AS PS 004 889. (AUTHOR/AJ)

ED052843 PS004904
BRITISH PRIMARY EDUCATION: AN ANNOTATED BIBLIOGRAPHY. HASKELL, LUCY A., COMP., JUL 71 18P.
EDRS PRICE MF-$0.65 HC-$3.29

THIS ANNOTATED BIBLIOGRAPHY LISTS BRITISH PUBLICATIONS USEFUL TO AMERICAN EDUCATORS' UNDERSTANDING OF EDUCATIONAL REFORM IN ENGLAND AND THE BRITISH PRIMARY SCHOOLS. SINCE AMERICAN ENTHUSIASM FOR OPEN AND INFORMAL EDUCATIONAL METHODS HAS GROWN SO QUICKLY, THIS BIBLIOGRAPHIC TOOL IS A NECESSARY FIRST STEP IN THE SYSTEMATIC, THOROUGH STUDY OF BRITISH SCHOOLS AS POTENTIAL MODELS FOR UNITED STATES SCHOOL REFORM. THE BIBLIOGRAPHY IS DIVIDED INTO FOUR SECTIONS: "A BRIEF SURVEY OF ENGLISH EDUCATION," DESCRIBING THE MAJOR TRENDS OF EDUCATION IN THE CONTEXT OF BRITISH HISTORY; "PIONEERS IN EDUCATIONAL THOUGHT," ACCOUNTS OF SOME OF THE MAJOR EDUCATIONAL INNOVATORS OF THE PAST 150 YEARS; "CONTEMPORARY TRENDS IN PRIMARY EDUCATION," DESCRIPTIONS OF "INFORMAL" PROGRAMS AND SAMPLES OF THE CONTINUING BRITISH DEBATE OVER THE SCHOOLS AND WHERE THEY SHOULD BE HEADING; AND "CURRICULUM INNOVATIONS," DESCRIPTIONS OF INNOVATIONS IN VARIOUS SUBJECT AREAS. TWO BRIEF SECTIONS ARE ADDED FOR THOSE WHO ARE INTERESTED IN AN AMERICAN VIEW OF BRITISH PRIMARY SCHOOLS AND IN GENERAL BACKGROUND MATERIAL. (AUTHOR/AJ)

ED052844 PS004916
IMPLEMENTATION OF PLANNED VARIATION IN HEAD START: PRELIMINARY EVALUATIONS OF PLANNED VARIATION IN HEAD START ACCORDING TO FOLLOW THROUGH APPROACHES (1969-1970). INTERIM REPORT: FIRST YEAR OF EVALUATION, PART II. , MAY 71 446P.
EDRS PRICE MF-$0.65 HC-$16.45

TO EVALUATE THE FOLLOW THROUGH PORTION OF THE PLANNED VARIATION PROGRAM (1967-1970) EIGHT DISTINCT APPROACHES WERE STUDIED. THE APPROACHES REST ON DIFFERING PHILOSOPHICAL AND PSYCHOLOGICAL PREMISES AND EMPLOY A VARIETY OF PEDAGOGICAL STRATEGIES. A BATTERY OF 14 EXISTING AND SPECIALLY DEVELOPED MEASURES WERE USED TO COVER THE COGNITIVE AREA. FACTORS SUCH AS ORGANIZATION OF CLASSROOMS, PARENT-CHILD INTERACTION, SUPERVISION, CHILD PERFORMANCE DATA AND DIFFUSION EFFECTS WERE ANALYZED. AMONG THE MOST IMPORTANT OUTCOMES OF THE FIRST YEAR OF THIS 3-YEAR ASSESSMENT STUDY ARE (1) CATALOGUING THE PROCESS OF PROGRAM IMPLEMENTATION (2) DESCRIBING CLASSROOM PROCESSES (3) ESTABLISHING THE SCHEME AND INSTRUMENTS TO BE USED FOR THE SECOND AND THIRD YEARS OF THE STUDY. THE GENERAL CONCLUSION OF THIS DOCUMENT IS THAT FIRST YEAR OUTCOMES ARE ENCOURAGING BUT IT IS TOO EARLY TO ASSESS WITH CONFIDENCE THE SPECIFIC OUTCOMES OF SPECIFIC PROGRAM MODELS. ONE FOURTH OF THE DOCUMENT CONSISTS OF BIBLIOGRAPHIC REFERENCES AND APPENDIXES DETAILING TEST INSTRUMENTS. A REVIEW AND SUMMARY OF THIS DOCUMENT IS AVAILABLE AS PS 004 917. (WY)

ED052845 PS004917
IMPLEMENTATION OF PLANNED VARIATION IN HEAD START. I. REVIEW AND SUMMARY OF THE STANFORD RESEARCH INSTITUTE INTERIM REPORT: FIRST YEAR OF EVALUATION. BISSELL, JOAN S., APR 71 51P.
EDRS PRICE MF-$0.65 HC-$3.29

THIS PAMPHLET SUMMARIZES THE INTERIM REPORT OF THE HEAD START PLANNED VARIATION STUDY ALTHOUGH INFORMATION FROM OTHER SOURCES IS INCLUDED. DURING THE PILOT PHASE (1969-1970) EIGHT DISTINCT APPROACHES TO PRESCHOOL EDUCATION WERE ANALYZED WITH REGARD TO THE NATURE AND EXTENT OF IMPLEMENTATION OF EARLY EDUCATION MODELS AND PROGRAM EFFECTS. THE FIRST GROUP OF FINDINGS DEALS WITH DIFFERENCES IN EASE OF IMPLEMENTATION IN NEW LOCATIONS AND WITH EXTERNAL FACTORS WHICH FACILITATE IMPLEMENTATION. THE SECOND GROUP CONCERNS THE NATURE OF EXPERIENCES PROVIDED TO CHILDREN BY PRESCHOOLS BASED ON DIFFERENT EDUCATIONAL PHILOSOPHIES AND METHODS. THE THIRD SET OF FINDINGS CONCERNS THE EFFECTS OF PRESCHOOL PROGRAMS ON CHILDREN AND THEIR FAMILIES. THE PRELIMINARY AND TENTATIVE NATURE OF ALL OF THESE FINDINGS IS STRESSED BECAUSE THEY ARE BASED ON ONLY THE FIRST YEAR OF A 3-YEAR PROGRAM OF EVALUATION. THE COMPLETE INTERIM REPORT IS AVAILABLE AS PS 004 916. (WY)

ED052846 PS004935
EARLY CHILDHOOD EDUCATION PROGRAM FOR NURSERY, KINDERGARTEN CHILDREN. , 7 AUG 70 41P.
EDRS PRICE MF-$0.65 HC-$3.29

A SUMMER PROGRAM CONDUCTED IN TWO SCHOOLS INVOLVED 154 NURSERY SCHOOL AND KINDERGARTEN CHILDREN. ELIGIBILITY WAS DETERMINED BY ECONOMIC CRITERIA, ABILITY TO ATTEND THE FULL 5-WEEK PROGRAM, AND PROBABILITY OF BENEFIT FROM THE PROGRAM. PUPIL-TEACHER RATIOS WERE GENERALLY 9 TO 1; PART-TIME PSYCHOLOGICAL AND SPEECH SERVICES AND A NURSE WERE ALSO AVAILABLE. THE GENERAL PROGRAM DESIGN WAS TO PROVIDE ENRICHMENT ACTIVITIES TO CHILDREN IN AN OPEN CLASSROOM ATMOSPHERE. BECAUSE A CONTROL GROUP WAS NOT AVAILABLE, EVALUATION OF PROGRAM EFFECTS WAS UNDERTAKEN BY PRETESTING AND POSTTESTING WITH THE CHILD BEHAVIOR RATING SCALE (CBRS) AND THE PEABODY PICTURE VOCABULARY TEST (PPVT). THE CBRS WAS ALSO ADMINISTERED OVER THE TELEPHONE TO A SAMPLE OF 20 PARENTS. TEACHERS KEPT A RECORD OF CONTACTS WITH PARENTS TO ASSESS GENERAL PARENTAL INVOLVEMENT IN THE PROGRAM. EVALUATION FINDINGS INDICATE THAT: (1) STUDENTS MADE SIGNIFICANT IMPROVEMENT IN TWO OF THE CBRS SCALES (SELF-ADJUSTMENT AND SCHOOL ADJUSTMENT); (2) PARENTS TENDED TO RATE THEIR CHILDREN LOWER ON THE SELF-ADJUSTMENT SCALE THAN DID THE TEACHERS; (3) THE MEAN IQ SCORES AS MEASURED BY THE PPVT WERE COMPARABLE TO THE NATIONAL AVERAGE; AND (4) ALMOST ALL PARENTS WERE INVOLVED IN THE PROGRAM, AND THEIR ASSESSMENTS OF THE PROGRAM WERE POSITIVE. THE DOCUMENT ALSO INCLUDES PROGRAM REPORTS AND PHOTOGRAPHS FROM THE TWO SCHOOLS, A REPLICA OF A NEWSLETTER SENT HOME WEEKLY, AND SELECTED LETTERS FROM PARENTS. (AJ)

ED052847 PS004957
STUDY OF SELECTED CHILDREN IN HEAD START PLANNED VARIATION, 1969-1970. FIRST YEAR REPORT: 3 - CASE STUDIES OF CHILDREN. DITTMANN, LAURA L.; AND OTHERS, 71 39P.
EDRS PRICE MF-$0.65 HC-$3.29

TO TEST THE FEASIBILITY OF USING CASE STUDY TECHNIQUES IN NATIONAL EVALUATIONS, THE CASE STUDY APPROACH WAS USED TO STUDY THE EXPERIENCES OF A BOY AND A GIRL IN EACH OF EIGHT HEAD START CURRICULAR MODELS AND TWO CHILDREN IN A CLASSROOM NOT UNDER THE SPONSORSHIP OF A PROGRAM DEVELOPER. TEACHERS AND MOTHERS WERE ALSO INTERVIEWED. THE PURPOSE OF THE STUDY WAS TO CAPTURE THE CHILDREN'S EXPERIENCES IN THE DIFFERENT SETTINGS, NOT TO EVALUATE THE MODEL ITSELF. SUMMARIES OF CASE STUDIES OF 16 CHILDREN ARE PRESENTED. CLASSROOM OBSERVERS AGREED ON THESE FINDINGS: (1) THE HEAD START EXPERIENCE IS VALUABLE TO THE CHILDREN; (2) THERE IS NOT ENOUGH CONTACT BETWEEN THE HOME AND THE SCHOOL; (3) CONCENTRATION ON COGNITIVE ASPECTS OF THE MODEL TENDS TO MAKE TEACHERS LESS AWARE OF OTHER IMPORTANT ASPECTS OF THE CHILD'S LIFE; (4) THE MODELS RESTRICTED THE TEACHERS IN TAILORING THE PROGRAM TO THE INDIVIDUAL CHILD; AND (5) IN MANY INSTANCES THE CURRICULUM SEEMS BETTER GEARED TO BOYS. INVESTIGATORS CONCLUDED THAT THE CASE STUDY APPROACH IS FEASIBLE. A FINAL SECTION COMMENTS ON THE FUNCTIONING OF THE MODELS AND THE EXTENT TO WHICH HEAD START GOALS ARE BEING MET. (NH)

ED053787 PS004658
THE TRAINING OF FAMILY DAY-CARE WORKERS: A FEASIBILITY STUDY AND INITIAL PILOT EFFORTS. FINAL REPORT. DOKECKI, PAUL R.; AND OTHERS, JAN 71 37P.
EDRS PRICE MF-$0.65 HC-$3.29

INITIAL STUDIES ASSESSED EXISTING DAY CARE FACILITIES IN AREA HOMES AND CENTERS, AND SOLICITED DAY CARE INFORMATION FROM OTHER STATES. AN OBVIOUS NEED FOR QUALITY PROGRAMS WAS INDICATED. A PILOT PROGRAM TO IMPROVE THE QUALITY OF CARE RECEIVED BY CHILDREN IN DAY CARE HOMES IS DESCRIBED. THE HOME VISITOR METHOD FOR TRAINING FAMILY DAY CARE WORKERS, MODELED AFTER AN EXISTING DARCEE PROGRAM FOR MOTHERS, WAS SELECTED AS PARTICULARLY SUITABLE FOR THE APPALACHIAN REGION. TO DEVELOP THE TRAINING PROGRAM, THE PREPARATION OF FAMILY DAY CARE WORKERS WAS ANALYZED WITH REGARD TO: (1) MEETING THE BASIC NEEDS OF CHILDREN; (2) SUBSTITUTING FOR THE MOTHER IN MEETING THE CHILD'S EMOTIONAL NEEDS; (3) GENERAL MANAGEMENT OF THE FAMILY DAY CARE SITUATION; (4) ADAPTING TO CHILDREN'S DEVELOPMENT AND HETEROGENEITY OF AGES; AND (5) SERVING AS EFFECTIVE EDUCATIONAL CHANGE AGENTS. CRITERIA FOR THE SELECTION OF FAMILY DAY CARE WORKERS AND PLANS TO UTILIZE THEIR EDUCATIONAL POTENTIAL ARE DISCUSSED. EVALUATION INVOLVES ONGOING ASSESSMENT OF THE DAY CARE HOME VISITING PROGRAM, DEVELOPMENT OF INSTRUMENTATION FOR FUTURE RESEARCH, AND CONTINUED DEVELOPMENT OF FAMILY DAY CARE PROGRAMS. APPENDIXES PRESENT SAMPLE MENUS, AND SUGGESTIONS FOR BEHAVIOR MANAGEMENT AND PLAY. (NH)

ED053788 PS004667
CHILD CARE WORKER TRAINING PROJECT. OPERATIONAL PHASE AND EMPLOYMENT. FINAL REPORT. , JAN 70 111P.
EDRS PRICE MF-$0.65 HC-$6.58

THE RESPONSIBILITY OF THE CHILD CARE WORKER TRAINING PROJECT WAS TO TRAIN 500 UNEMPLOYED PEOPLE FROM FIVE CITIES IN AN EXPERIMENTAL AND DEMONSTRATION PROJECT DESIGNED TO OVERCOME THE SHORTAGE OF CHILD CARE PERSONNEL. EACH OF THE CENTERS (BALTIMORE, CHICAGO, CLEVELAND, NEWARK AND NEW YORK) DEVELOPED ITS OWN METHOD OF RECRUITMENT, SHORT-TERM PRE-EMPLOYMENT TRAINING AND JOB PLACEMENT. THE MAJOR OBJECTIVE OF THE OVERALL PROJECT WAS TO PROVIDE MORE AND BETTER CARE FOR CHILDREN IN NEED OF CHILD WELFARE SERVICES WHILE AT THE SAME TIME OPENING NEW CAREER OPPORTUNITIES FOR PREVIOUSLY UNEMPLOYED OR UNDEREMPLOYED PERSONS. THE PLAN ITSELF, HOW IT EVOLVED, WHO PARTICIPATED, THE SEQUENCE OF EVENTS, WHAT PROBLEMS AND SUCCESSES WERE ENCOUNTERED, PROJECT RESULTS AND IMPLICATIONS FOR THE FUTURE ARE DESCRIBED. (AUTHOR/WY)

ED053789 PS004684
ALL ABOUT ME. UNIT 1 CURRICULUM GUIDE. CAMP, JANET; WILKERSON, PEGGY, 70 110P.
EDRS PRICE MF-$0.65 HC-$6.58
AVAILABLE FROM: INFORMATION OFFICE, DARCEE, BOX 151, GEORGE PEABODY COLLEGE, NASHVILLE, TENNESSEE 37203 ($1.50)

THIS CURRICULUM GUIDE PRESENTS A 2- OR 3-WEEK UNIT CONCERNED WITH THE INDIVIDUAL CHILD AND HIS RELATIONSHIPS WITH MEMBERS OF THE CLASSROOM SOCIAL GROUP. ONE IN A SERIES OF RESOURCE UNITS, THIS UNIT IS PLACED FIRST FOR SEVERAL REASONS: (1) ITS CONTENT IS HIGHLY MOTIVATIONAL; (2) IT PROVIDES A MEANINGFUL CONTEXT FOR ACQUAINTING CHILDREN WITH EACH OTHER; (3) IT ENCOURAGES THE DEVELOPMENT OF BASIC SENSORY SKILLS; (4) IT CONTRIBUTES TO DEVELOPMENT OF A POSITIVE SELF-CONCEPT; AND (5) IT IS DESIGNED TO REVIEW AND EXTEND PREVIOUSLY DEVELOPED CONCEPTS AND SKILLS. THE CONTENT IS ORDERED FROM THE MOST

SIMPLE TO THE MOST COMPLEX, ENABLING THE TEACHER TO TERMINATE THE UNIT AT ANY POINT WHERE THE CONTENT BECOMES TOO COMPLEX OR ABSTRACT FOR THE CHILDREN TO GRASP. INSTRUCTIONAL MATERIALS AND UNIT CONTENT SHOULD BE ADAPTED TO REFLECT THE PHYSICAL CHARACTERISTICS OF THE DIFFERENT CHILDREN IN THE CLASSROOM. PROVIDED IS A LISTING AND EXPLANATION OF EACH OF THE SKILLS TO BE DEVELOPED ACCOMPANIED BY SUGGESTED INSTRUCTIONAL ACTIVITIES. INSTRUCTIONAL MATERIALS ARE LISTED WITH SOURCES; AND THE APPENDIX PROVIDES ADDITIONAL INSTRUCTIONAL AIDS. (AUTHOR/AJ)

ED053790 PS004685
AUTUMN. UNIT 3 CURRICULUM GUIDE. CAMP, JANET; AND OTHERS, 70 113P.
EDRS PRICE MF-$0.65 HC-$6.58
AVAILABLE FROM: INFORMATION OFFICE, DARCEE, BOX 151, GEORGE PEABODY COLLEGE, NASHVILLE, TENNESSEE 37203 ($1.50)

THIS CURRICULUM GUIDE PRESENTS A 3-WEEK SCIENCE UNIT FOCUSING ON CHANGES WHICH OCCUR IN LIVING THINGS AS A RESULT OF WEATHER CHANGES. THIS UNIT, THE THIRD IN A SERIES, IS INTENDED TO REVIEW AND EXTEND THE UNDERSTANDINGS, CONCEPTS, AND SKILLS WHICH A CHILD HAS DEVELOPED PREVIOUSLY. THE MAJOR CONTENT OBJECTIVES ARE TO DEVELOP THE CHILD'S AWARENESS AND UNDERSTANDING OF CHANGES IN HIS ENVIRONMENT, TO EXPAND HIS CONCEPTS REGARDING PEOPLE AND CLOTHING INTRODUCED IN THE UNIT "ALL ABOUT ME" AND TO DEVELOP UNDERSTANDINGS CONCERNING PLANTS INTRODUCED IN THE UNIT "PLANTS". MAJOR SKILL OBJECTIVES INCLUDE THE DEVELOPMENT AND REFINEMENT OF SENSORY, ABSTRACTING, ASSOCIATION, AND MOTOR RESPONSE SKILLS AS WELL AS CONCEPT DEVELOPMENT. THE UNIT CONTENT IS DESIGNED TO BE ALTERED TO BE APPROPRIATE FOR THE AREA AND THE GROUP OF CHILDREN INVOLVED. PROVIDED IS A LISTING AND EXPLANATION OF EACH OF THE SKILLS TO BE DEVELOPED AND APPROPRIATE INSTRUCTIONAL ACTIVITIES. INSTRUCTIONAL MATERIALS ARE LISTED WITH SOURCES; AND AN APPENDIX PROVIDES ADDITIONAL INSTRUCTIONAL AIDS. (AUTHOR/AJ)

ED053791 PS004754
AN EVALUATION OF LOGICAL OPERATIONS INSTRUCTION IN THE PRESCHOOL. HOOPER, FRANK H., 22 MAY 70 63P.
EDRS PRICE MF-$0.65 HC-$3.29

AS A PREPARATORY STEP TO THE DESIGN OF A PRESCHOOL CURRICULUM, THIS STUDY EXAMINES THREE OF THE COMPLEX COGNITIVE BEHAVIORS EXEMPLIFIED BY THE CONCRETE OPERATIONS PERIOD AND ITS DEVELOPMENTAL PREREQUISITES. MIDDLE-CLASS CHILDREN IN A UNIVERSITY LABORATORY NURSERY SETTING WERE PRETESTED, MATCHED FOR AGE AND RANDOMLY ASSIGNED TO AN INSTRUCTION OR A COMPARISON CONTROL GROUP. THE INSTRUCTION GROUP WAS TRAINED IN TWO CLUSTERS OF FOUR CHILDREN PER TEACHER ON LABELING-CLASSIFICATION, DISCRIMINATION-MEMORY, AND SERIATION TASKS. EACH CLUSTER CONSISTED OF A YOUNGER BOY, A YOUNGER GIRL, AN OLDER BOY AND AN OLDER GIRL. EACH SESSION CONSISTED OF 20-30 MINUTES OF ORGANIZED ACTIVITY AND THERE WERE 12 SESSIONS OVER A 3-WEEK PERIOD FOR EACH TRAINING CONDITION. THE CONTROL GROUP CHILDREN HAD AN EQUIVALENT AMOUNT OF SEPARATE SMALL GROUP ACTIVITY WITH A PRESCHOOL TEACHER. THE RESULTS OF POSTTESTING AND TRANSFER TASKS SUPPORT THE CONTENTION THAT THE DEVELOPMENTAL STATUS OF THE CURRICULUM TARGET POPULATION WILL DETERMINE TO A GREAT EXTENT THE SUCCESS OR FAILURE OF AN EDUCATIONAL INTERVENTION EFFORT. AGE-RELATED MATURATIONAL COMPONENTS ARE IMPORTANT CONSIDERATIONS IN ANY CURRICULUM ATTEMPT TO MODIFY THE COURSE OF COGNITIVE DEVELOPMENT. ONE HALF THE DOCUMENT PRESENTS BIBLIOGRAPHY AND APPENDIXES DETAILING THE TRAINING PROGRAMS. (WY)

ED053792 PS004800
COGNITIVE STUDIES VOLUME 2: DEFICITS IN COGNITION. HELLMUTH, JEROME, ED., 71 374P.
DOCUMENT NOT AVAILABLE FROM EDRS.
AVAILABLE FROM: BRUNNER/MAZEL, INC., 80 EAST 11TH STREET, NEW YORK, NEW YORK 10003 ($15.00)

THIS BOOK IS A COLLECTION OF 15 ORIGINAL ARTICLES ON THE RAPIDLY GROWING AREA OF COGNITION. IT PRESENTS SEMINAL STUDIES IN SUCH AREAS AS SCHIZOPHRENIA, DYSLEXIA, BLINDNESS, CURRICULUM AND TEACHING, CHILD DEVELOPMENT, LEARNING DISABILITIES, LANGUAGE, PROBLEM-SOLVING AND BODY AWARENESS. SOME ARTICLES REPRESENT WORK OF A PIONEERING NATURE WHILE OTHERS PRESENT ESTABLISHED POINTS OF VIEW. (AUTHOR/WY)

ED053793 PS004812
LEARNING BY DISCOVERY: A REVIEW OF THE RESEARCH METHODOLOGY. REPORT FROM THE PROJECT ON VARIABLES AND PROCESSES IN COGNITIVE LEARNING. SCOTT, JOSEPH A.; FRAYER, DOROTHY A., DEC 70 35P.
EDRS PRICE MF-$0.65 HC-$3.29

RESEARCH COMPARING DISCOVERY AND EXPOSITORY METHODS OF PRESENTATION HAS YIELDED CONFLICTING RESULTS. A REVIEW OF THE RESEARCH ON DISCOVERY LEARNING IS PROVIDED IN THIS PAPER, FOCUSING ON THE METHODOLOGY OF EACH STUDY. CONCLUSIONS ARE DRAWN CONCERNING THE EFFECTS OF DISCOVERY METHODS OF PRESENTATION ON INITIAL LEARNING, TRANSFER, AND RETENTION. USE OF A STANDARDIZED CONCEPT LEARNING TASK IS RECOMMENDED FOR FUTURE RESEARCH ON DISCOVERY METHODS OF PRESENTATION. (AUTHOR)

ED053794 PS004825
STANDARDS FOR DAY CARE CENTERS FOR INFANTS AND CHILDREN UNDER 3 YEARS OF AGE. , 71 29P.
DOCUMENT NOT AVAILABLE FROM EDRS.
AVAILABLE FROM: AMERICAN ACADEMY OF PEDIATRICS, P.O. BOX 1034, EVANSTON, ILLINOIS 60204 ($2.00)

THE COMMITTEE ON INFANT AND PRESCHOOL CHILD OF THE AMERICAN ACADEMY OF PEDIATRICS HAS DEVELOPED BASIC STANDARDS FOR QUALITY DAY CARE FOR CHILDREN UNDER 3 YEARS OF AGE. THE AVAILABILITY OF DAY CARE PROVIDES A MOTHER WITH THE CHOICE OF GROUP DAY CARE AS ONE OF THE MEANS OF PROVIDING FOR HER CHILDREN. OPTIONS SHOULD INCLUDE FULL-TIME OR PART-TIME DAY CARE UNDER A VARIETY OF SPONSORSHIPS AND IN A VARIETY OF LOCATIONS SUCH AS NEIGHBORHOOD SCHOOLS OR PARENTS' PLACE OF EMPLOYMENT. THE PRIMARY PURPOSE OF DAY CARE SHOULD BE TO OFFER A SOUND BASIS FOR PROMOTING LEARNING AND FURTHER DEVELOPMENT OF THE YOUNG INFANT AND SUPPORT AND ENCOURAGEMENT FOR THE MOTHER IN HER EFFORTS TO CARE FOR HER CHILD. PARENT INVOLVEMENT IN THE DAY CARE CENTER IS SEEN AS ESSENTIAL. THE EIGHT CHAPTERS IN THIS MANUAL COVER THE FOLLOWING AREAS: BASIC PRINCIPLES; ADMINISTRATION; PERSONNEL; RECORDS; PROGRAM; HEALTH SERVICES; NUTRITION; AND FACILITIES. (AUTHOR/NH)

ED053795 PS004827
PLANNING A DAY CARE CENTER. , 71 21P.
EDRS PRICE MF-$0.65 HC-$3.29

THE PURPOSE OF THIS GUIDE IS TO GIVE INDIVIDUALS, COMMUNITY GROUPS, AND OTHER ORGANIZATIONS A CHECKLIST OF IMPORTANT POINTS THAT MUST BE CONSIDERED IN DAY CARE PROGRAM PLANNING IF QUALITY SERVICES ARE TO BE ESTABLISHED FOR CHILDREN AND FAMILIES. THE GUIDE PROVIDES INFORMATION CONCERNING THE PRELIMINARY STEPS NEEDED TO ESTABLISH A DAY CARE PROGRAM; DIFFERENT TYPES OF DAY CARE PROGRAMS; AND PROGRAMS WITH SPECIAL EMPHASIS (SUCH AS EDUCATION, RECREATION, OR THERAPEUTIC). ALSO DISCUSSED ARE SOURCES FOR FUNDING DAY CARE; SERVICES OFFERED IN GROUP CENTERS, DAY CARE HOME PROGRAMS; LEGAL REQUIREMENTS; ADMINISTRATIVE FRAMEWORK; AND VARIOUS COST CONSIDERATIONS. (AUTHOR/AJ)

ED053796 PS004836
MOVEMENT AND MOVEMENT PATTERNS OF EARLY CHILDHOOD. SINCLAIR, CAROLINE B., JUN 71 25P.
EDRS PRICE MF-$0.65 HC-$3.29
AVAILABLE FROM: DIVISION OF EDUCATIONAL RESEARCH AND STATISTICS, STATE DEPARTMENT OF EDUCATION, RICHMOND, VIRGINIA 23216

THIS STUDY WAS UNDERTAKEN TO DETERMINE THE PROGRESSIVE DEVELOPMENT IN MOVEMENT AND MOVEMENT PATTERNS (COORDINATED MOVEMENTS OF BODY PARTS USED INVOLUNTARILY TO ACHIEVE AN OBJECTIVE) OF CHILDREN 2- TO 6-YEARS-OLD, TO IDENTIFY GENERAL CHARACTERISTICS WHICH MAY BE STUDIED FOR APPRAISAL OF GROWTH AND DEVELOPMENT, AND TO STUDY VARIATIONS IN MOVEMENT AMONG NORMAL SUBJECTS IN THIS AGE RANGE. THE STUDY WAS CONDUCTED BY OBSERVATION, MOTION PHOTOGRAPHY, AND ANALYSIS OF THE PERFORMANCE OF SUBJECTS IN 18 TO 25 MOVEMENT TASKS IN EACH OF SIX SCHOOL SEMESTERS. MOVEMENT PERFORMANCE RECORDED ON FILM WAS ANALYZED ACCORDING TO THE MOVEMENT TASK ANALYSIS FORM DEVELOPED FOR EACH TASK. TO ESTABLISH A SUITABLE CONTEXT FOR DETERMINING MOVEMENT DEVELOPMENT, THE FACTORS OF AGE, SEX, INTELLIGENCE, MATURITY, TEACHER'S ESTIMATE OF ACHIEVEMENT, AND READING READINESS WERE STUDIED IN RELATION TO THE SUBJECT'S MOTOR SCORES. MOVEMENT TASK SCORES WERE SUMMARIZED FOR EACH AGE GROUP. THE STUDY CONCLUDED THAT NORMAL PRESCHOOL CHILDREN WILL PERFORM A VARIETY OF MOVEMENT TASKS WHICH ARE SIMILAR AND WHICH DEVELOP ACCORDING TO A PREDICTABLE TIMETABLE; ALTHOUGH MOTOR PERFORMANCE AND MOVEMENT DEVELOPMENT VARY WITH AGE, SEX, AND AMONG INDIVIDUALS. SEVEN CHARACTERISTICS SIGNIFICANT IN THE MOVEMENT DEVELOPMENT OF YOUNG CHILDREN WERE IDENTIFIED. (AUTHOR/AJ)

ED053797 PS004837
CONTEMPORARY INFLUENCES IN EARLY CHILDHOOD EDUCATION. EVANS, ELLIS D., 71 377P.
DOCUMENT NOT AVAILABLE FROM EDRS.
AVAILABLE FROM: HOLT, RINEHART AND WINSTON, INC., 383 MADISON AVENUE, NEW YORK, NEW YORK 10017 ($7.50)

THE SUBJECT OF THIS BOOK IS PREPRIMARY EDUCATIONAL PROGRAMS; THE FOCUS IS UPON BROAD EDUCATIONAL STRATEGIES VARIOUSLY APPLICABLE TO CHILDREN AGES 3-6. THIS BOOK COMMUNICATES TO READERS THE GREAT VARIETY IN EDUCATIONAL AND PSYCHOLOGICAL THINKING ABOUT CHILDREN IN THE EARLY 1970'S. THE BOOK MAINTAINS A CONSISTENT RESEARCH PERSPECTIVE AND WHENEVER POSSIBLE EMPIRICAL INVESTIGATIONS IN EARLY CHILDHOOD EDUCATION ARE PRESENTED. THE APPENDIXES INCLUDE: APPENDIX A, SOME FREQUENTLY USED TESTS; APPENDIX B, SCHOOL READINESS; APPENDIX C, A LISTING OF PRINCIPAL PREPRIMARY PROGRAMS. (AUTHOR/WY)

ED053798 PS004839
BIBLIOGRAPHY OF BOOKS FOR CHILDREN. 1971 EDITION. SUNDERLIN, SYLVIA, ED., 71 134P.
DOCUMENT NOT AVAILABLE FROM EDRS.
AVAILABLE FROM: ASSOCIATION FOR CHILDHOOD EDUCATION INTERNATIONAL, 3615 WISCONSIN AVENUE, N.W., WASHINGTON, D.C. 20016 ($2.25)

THIS IS AN ANNOTATED BIBLIOGRAPHY OF BOOKS SUITABLE FOR CHILDREN AGED 2 TO 12. ABOUT 1500 TITLES ARE INCLUDED. BOOKS ARE LISTED UNDER GENERAL HEADINGS SUCH AS ANIMALS IN FICTION, ART, BIOGRAPHIES, BOOKS FOR BEGINNING READERS, BOOKS FOR FUN, BOOKS FOR THE VERY YOUNG, FANTASY AND FAIRY TALES, FICTION, FOLKLORE, FOREIGN LANGUAGE, HOLIDAYS, MOTHER GOOSE, MUSIC, POETRY, RELIGION, SCIENCE, REFERENCE, SOCIAL STUDIES, AND STORY COLLECTIONS. (WY)

ED053799 PS004840
CHILD HEALTH AND HUMAN DEVELOPMENT: PROGRESS 1963-1970. A REPORT OF THE NATIONAL INSTITUTE OF CHILD HEALTH AND HUMAN DEVELOPMENT. FALKNER, FRANK, ED.; REASER, GEORGIA PERKINS, ED., 70 125P.
EDRS PRICE MF-$0.65 HC-$6.58
AVAILABLE FROM: SUPERINTENDENT OF DOCUMENTS, U.S. GOVERNMENT PRINTING OFFICE, WASHINGTON, D.C. 20402 ($L.00)

THIS PROGRESS REPORT IS BASED ON SEVEN YEARS OF BASIC RESEARCH IN MATERNAL HEALTH, CHILD HEALTH AND HUMAN DEVELOPMENT. TOPICS INCLUDE: THE BEGINNING OF LIFE: PRENATAL DEVELOPMENT; EARLY PREVENTION, DETECTION, AND THERAPY OF CONGENITAL, STRUCTURAL AND METABOLIC DEFECTS; PROBLEMS OF BIRTH AND POSTNATAL ADAPTATION; CHILD DEVELOPMENT: NORMAL AND ABNORMAL; THE REPRODUCTIVE PROCESS: BASIC BIOLOGY AND ITS RELATION TO FAMILY PLANNING; FAMILY PLANNING, MATURATION AND AGING. TRENDS IN FUNDING AND PROGRAM DEVELOPMENT ARE ALSO LISTED. (WY)

ED053800 PS004843
CHILD CARE PARAPROFESSIONALS: CHARACTERISTICS FOR SELECTION. MAZYCK, HAROLD EUGENE, JR., 71 149P.
EDRS PRICE MF-$0.65 HC-$6.58

THE PURPOSE OF THIS STUDY WAS TO ANALYZE THE CHARACTERISTICS OF PARAPROFESSIONAL CHILD CARE WORKERS AS DETERMINED BY RATINGS GIVEN ON THE MAZYCK RATING SCALE FOR PARAPROFESSIONALS (MRSP). THE SCALE WAS DEVELOPED FOR THIS STUDY AND COMPRISED TWO CATEGORIES OF CHARACTERISTICS, PERSONAL-SOCIAL, AND EDUCATIONAL-BIOGRAPHICAL-WORKING RELATIONSHIPS. RATERS SELECTED WERE CHILD DEVELOPMENT SPECIALISTS, HEAD START PROGRAM DIRECTORS, AND TWO GROUPS OF PARAPROFESSIONALS, ONE TRAINED AND THE OTHER UNTRAINED. A MAJOR HYPOTHESIS WAS THAT SUBJECTS WOULD DIFFER SIGNIFICANTLY IN THEIR RATINGS OF CHARACTERISTICS OF PARAPROFESSIONALS, AND THIS HYPOTHESIS WAS VERIFIED. STATISTICAL ANALYSIS IDENTIFIED NINE FACTORS TO BE CONSIDERED IN CHARACTERIZING PARAPROFESSIONALS: GENERAL PERSONAL QUALITIES; DEMOGRAPHIC FACTS; EDUCATION; TEMPERAMENT; MATURITY; WORK EFFECTIVENESS; FRUSTRATING SITUATIONS; POSITIVE WORK ATTITUDES; AND FEELINGS OF SECURITY. ANY FUTURE USE OF THE MRSP SCALE SHOULD ADD A STATISTICALLY DERIVED THIRD CHARACTERISTICS CATEGORY: REACTION TO STRESS, AND SCALE ITEMS SHOULD BE REWRITTEN TO BE MORE EASILY UNDERSTOOD BY PARAPROFESSIONALS. APPENDIXES INCLUDE A SAMPLE OF THE MRSP; LIST OF CHARACTERISTICS; DATA FORMS; CORRESPONDENCE; AND A LIST OF CHILD DEVELOPMENT SPECIALISTS PARTICIPATING IN THE STUDY. (AUTHOR/NH)

ED053801 PS004872
WHAT'S THROWN OUT WITH THE BATH WATER: A BABY? LEWIS, MICHAEL; JOHNSON, NORMA, JUN 70 7P.
EDRS PRICE MF-$0.65 HC-$3.29

THIS STUDY INVESTIGATED THE COMMON PRACTICE IN INFANT RESEARCH OF ELIMINATING FROM REPORTED DATA LARGE NUMBERS OF SUBJECTS WHO PROVE UNCOOPERATIVE (SLEEPY, FATIGUED, FUSSY) DURING THE EXPERIMENT. IT WAS SUGGESTED THAT THESE EXCLUDED INFANTS CONSTITUTE A SPECIAL CLASS OF SUBJECTS AND THAT THE INCLUSION OF THEIR DATA WOULD GREATLY ALTER THE RESEARCH RESULTS. SUBJECTS COMPARED WERE 37 3- TO 6-MONTH-OLD INFANTS, 15 OF WHOM WERE UNABLE TO FINISH THE EXPERIMENT SESSIONS. TWO VISUAL AND TWO AUDITORY TESTS WERE ADMINISTERED AND MEASURED ACCORDING TO FIXATION TIME AND CARDIAC DECELERATION. ACTIVITY DATA WERE COLLECTED BY USE OF AN INFANT STABILIMETER. RESULTS DEMONSTRATE THAT INFANTS UNABLE TO COMPLETE THE EXPERIMENT SHOW DIFFERENT ATTENTIVE PATTERNS FROM THOSE ABLE TO COMPLETE THE SESSIONS. THE FINDINGS SUGGEST THAT ELIMINATION OF LARGE NUMBERS OF INFANTS MAY RESULT IN SERIOUS BIASING OF OBTAINED DATA. (AUTHOR/AJ)

ED053802 PS004891
THE EFFECTS OF EXPERIENCE ON INFANTS' REACTIONS TO SEPARATION FROM THEIR MOTHERS. TULKIN, STEVEN R., APR 71 12P.
DOCUMENT NOT AVAILABLE FROM EDRS.
AVAILABLE FROM: STEVEN R. TULKIN, STATE UNIVERSITY OF NEW YORK, DEPARTMENT OF PSYCHOLOGY, BUFFALO, NEW YORK 14214

THE PRESENT STUDY EXAMINED INFANTS' REACTIONS TO SEPARATION FROM AND REUNION WITH THEIR MOTHERS, AND ATTEMPTED TO DETERMINE IF THESE BEHAVIORS WERE RELATED TO THE INFANTS' EXPERIENCES WITH THEIR MOTHERS AT HOME. THE SUBJECTS, 60 CAUCASIAN MOTHER-INFANT PAIRS, WERE OBSERVED AT HOME TWO HOURS ON EACH OF TWO DAYS AND IN A LABORATORY SETTING. THE INFANTS, FIRST-BORN 10-MONTH-OLD GIRLS, WERE HALF FROM MIDDLE CLASS FAMILIES AND HALF FROM WORKING CLASS FAMILIES. THERE WERE NO SOCIAL CLASS DIFFERENCES IN THE FREQUENCY OF CRYING UPON SEPARATION. INFANTS OF WORKING CLASS MOTHERS WHO WORKED COULD BETTER TOLERATE BRIEF SEPARATIONS FROM THEIR MOTHERS THAN CHILDREN OF NON-WORKING MOTHERS OF THE SAME CLASS. ALSO EXAMINED WAS THE INFLUENCE OF EXPERIENCES AT HOME ON THE VARIOUS LABORATORY MEASUREMENTS. TWO-WAY ANALYSES OF VARIANCE REVEALED THAT MIDDLE CLASS INFANTS WHO CRIED AND/OR CRAWLED UPON SEPARATION FROM MOTHER SPENT MORE TIME FACE-TO-FACE WITH THEIR MOTHERS AT HOME, WHILE WORKING CLASS INFANTS WHO CRIED AND/OR CRAWLED SPENT LESS TIME IN THIS POSITION. (AUTHOR/AJ)

ED053803 PS004899
SCHOOLS WHERE CHILDREN LEARN. FEATHERSTONE, JOSEPH, 25 MAY 71 190P.
DOCUMENT NOT AVAILABLE FROM EDRS.
AVAILABLE FROM: LIVERIGHT, 386 PARK AVENUE SOUTH, NEW YORK, NEW YORK 10016 ($5.95)

THIS COLLECTION OF ESSAYS FROM "THE NEW REPUBLIC" OFFERS A FRESH LOOK AT AMERICA'S CURRENT EDUCATIONAL CRISIS. THE APPROACH USED IN THE ENGLISH PRIMARY SCHOOLS IS ANALYZED AND FOUND VALUABLE. ALSO DETAILED ARE VARIETIES OF SOUND EDUCATIONAL PRACTICE FOUND IN A NEW ZEALAND PRIMARY SCHOOL, IN A COLORADO CLASSROOM, AND IN A HARLEM STREET ACADEMY FOR HIGH SCHOOL DROP OUTS. IN ALL THESE NEW LEARNING ENVIRONMENTS, THE AUTHOR FINDS COMMON THREADS OF FREEDOM, A NEW CONCEPTION OF THE TEACHER'S ROLE, AN EMPHASIS ON STANDARDS OF WORKMANSHIP, AND AN IMPLICIT UNDERSTANDING THAT A FULL CHILDHOOD IS THE BEST PREPARATION FOR LIFE. BY CONTRAST, SEVERAL REPORTS EMPHASIZE THE "SHODDINESS AND CONFUSION" PREVALENT ON THE AMERICAN SCENE--IN THE MIDDLE CLASS HIGH SCHOOL, IN EDUCATIONAL TECHNOLOGY, IN FRANCHISED DAY CARE, IN THE "PATHOLOGICAL PROFESSIONALISM" OF THE EDUCATIONAL SYSTEM. (AUTHOR/WY)

ED053804 PS004901
CHILDREN DANCE IN THE CLASSROOM. DIMONDSTEIN, GERALDINE, 12 JUL 71 282P.
DOCUMENT NOT AVAILABLE FROM EDRS.
AVAILABLE FROM: THE MACMILLAN COMPANY, 866 THIRD AVENUE, NEW YORK, NEW YORK 10022 ($7.95)

THE AUTHOR PRESENTS A PRACTICAL, WORKABLE FRAMEWORK FOR TEACHING DANCE IN THE CLASSROOM. THIS BOOK, ESSENTIALLY DESIGNED FOR THE NONSPECIALIST TEACHER, IS A COMPILATION OF IDEAS AND MATERIALS THAT HAVE EVOLVED OVER TWENTY YEARS OF TEACHING MUSIC AND MOVEMENT TO CHILDREN IN NURSERY AND ELEMENTARY SCHOOLS AND OF INTRODUCING CONCEPTS OF DANCE TO STUDENTS AND TEACHERS. LESSONS ARE PRESENTED AS CREATIVE DANCE PROBLEMS. SOME OF THE CLASSROOM PROBLEMS ARE ELABORATIONS OF AN EXPERIMENTAL DEVELOPMENT PROJECT IN THE ARTS AND HUMANITIES FOR YOUNG CHILDREN. THE CONTENT AND FORMAT OF LESSONS REPRESENTS A SYNTHESIS OF CHILDREN'S EXPLORATIONS IN DIVERSE EDUCATIONAL ENVIRONMENTS AND ARE SUGGESTED AS A WORKING MODEL FOR TEACHERS. NUMEROUS PHOTOGRAPHS ARE INCLUDED TO SUPPLEMENT THE TEXT. THE AUTHOR MAKES TWO ADDITIONAL POINTS. FIRST, SHE FOCUSES ON THE ROLE OF OBSERVATION AND EXPERIENCE IN EXTENDING A CHILD'S CREATIVE IMAGINATION. SECOND, SHE CRITICIZES CURRENT PRACTICES IN RHYTHMIC AND DANCE EDUCATION AND MAKES PRACTICAL SUGGESTIONS FOR IMPROVEMENT. THE FINAL CHAPTER LISTS RESOURCES FOR USE IN DANCE AND MOVEMENT EDUCATION PROGRAMS. (AUTHOR/WY)

ED053805 PS004903
TEACHING THE YOUNG CHILD: GOALS FOR ILLINOIS. KATZ, LILIAN G., 15 MAY 71 8P.
EDRS PRICE MF-$0.65 HC-$3.29

THIS PAPER, OUTLINING THE PRESENT GOALS, PURPOSES AND FUTURE ROLE OF THE ILLINOIS ASSOCIATION FOR THE EDUCATION OF YOUNG CHILDREN (ILLAEYC), DISCUSSES WHAT IS INVOLVED IN PROVIDING HIGH QUALITY PROGRAMS FOR YOUNG CHILDREN EVERYWHERE, NOT ONLY IN ILLINOIS. AMONG ILLAEYC'S OBJECTIVES: (1) TO PROVIDE A CHANNEL OF INFORMATION FOR PEOPLE WORKING WITH YOUNG CHILDREN; (2) TO MAINTAIN A CLOSE WATCH ON THE STANDARDS, QUALITY AND AVAILABILITY OF SERVICES OFFERED TO YOUNG CHILDREN; (3) TO DEVELOP POSITIONS AS A STATE GROUP ON THE PROPER PRIORITIES IN TERMS OF YOUNG CHILDREN'S NEEDS; AND (4) TO FOSTER

STRONG WORKING RELATIONSHIPS WITH OTHER GROUPS CONCERNED WITH YOUNG CHILDREN. TO ACHIEVE HIGH QUALITY PROGRAMS, THERE MUST BE EYE-TO-EYE CONTACT AND INTENSIVE INTERACTION WITH EACH CHILD, AND THERE MUST BE TIME FOR REFLECTION ON EACH DAY'S ACTIVITIES. THE EDUCATOR'S PRIMARY RESPONSIBILITY IS THE QUALITY OF DAY-TO-DAY ENCOUNTERS OF INDIVIDUAL ADULTS WITH INDIVIDUAL CHILDREN. BY CONCENTRATING ON THIS APPROACH, EDUCATORS CAN ACHIEVE TWO GOALS SIMULTANEOUSLY: PROVIDE HIGH QUALITY SERVICE TO CHILDREN AND IMPRESS (RATHER THAN PRESSURE) THOSE WHO SEEK COUNSEL ON EDUCATION PROGRAMS FOR YOUNG CHILDREN. (AJ)

ED053806 PS004905
DESIGNS AND PROPOSAL FOR EARLY CHILDHOOD RESEARCH: A NEW LOOK: A MULTIPLE SYSTEMS-SERVICE APPROACH TO PROGRAMS AND RESEARCH FOR HELPING POOR CHILDREN. (ONE IN A SERIES OF SIX PAPERS). CHILMAN, CATHERINE; GROTBERG, EDITH H., ED., 71 63P.
EDRS PRICE MF-$0.65 HC-$3.29

AN OVERVIEW IS GIVEN OF CONDITIONS LINKED TO THE CAUSES AND PERPETUATION OF POVERTY. THESE FACTORS INCLUDE LARGE FAMILY SIZE, UNEMPLOYMENT, LACK OF EDUCATION, AND SOCIAL AND PERSONAL DISORGANIZATION. FAMILY PLANNING SERVICES ARE IMPORTANT BUT BY THEMSELVES TEND TO BE INEFFECTIVE AND PROGRAMS SHOULD BE LAUNCHED WHICH WOULD IMPROVE THE TOTAL LIFE SITUATION OF THE POOR. RESEARCH-BASED EVIDENCE IS PRESENTED REGARDING VARIOUS ANTI-POVERTY PROGRAMS, INCLUDING PARENT EDUCATION, INDIVIDUAL COUNSELING, JOB TRAINING, AND USE OF PARAPROFESSIONALS. AN EXAMINATION OF "PARTICIPATION OF THE POOR" IN DECISION MAKING CAPACITIES IN PROGRAMS WHICH AFFECT THEM IS INCLUDED. MULTI-PRONGED INTERVENTION IN RESPECT TO CHANGING THE SECONDARY AND TERTIARY SYSTEMS OF THE POVERTY ENVIRONMENT (HOUSING, EMPLOYMENT OPPORTUNITIES, HEALTH, WELFARE, LEGAL, EDUCATIONAL AND VOCATIONAL SERVICES) IS RECOMMENDED. SUCH AN APPROACH CALLS FOR MULTI-VARIATE PROGRAM RESEARCH, FOR WHICH A PROPOSAL IS PRESENTED. (AUTHOR/NH)

ED053807 PS004906
DESIGNS AND PROPOSAL FOR EARLY CHILDHOOD RESEARCH: A NEW LOOK: ON ATTAINING THE GOALS OF EARLY CHILDHOOD EDUCATION. (ONE IN A SERIES OF SIX PAPERS). ROHWER, WILLIAM D., JR.; GROTBERG, EDITH H., ED., 71 29P.
EDRS PRICE MF-$0.65 HC-$3.29

A DETAILED ANALYSIS OF THE OBJECTIVES OF EDUCATION AND THE PRACTICES OF SCHOOLING LEADS TO THE SUGGESTION THAT NEITHER ARE BEING ACHIEVED. PROPOSED IS A REVISED STATEMENT OF THE GOAL OF EDUCATION: EDUCATION IS TO ASSIST THE STUDENT TO BE ADAPTIVE WITH RESPECT TO EXTRA-SCHOOL TASKS. THE FOLLOWING EDUCATIONAL OBJECTIVES SEEM RELEVANT TO REALIZING THIS GOAL: TO PROMOTE THE STUDENT'S ACQUISITION OF: (1) A REPERTORY OF SKILLS FOR ACCURATELY LOCATING AND EFFICIENTLY LEARNING NEW INFORMATION AND NEW SKILLS; (2) A REPERTORY OF SKILLS FOR SOLVING PROBLEMS; AND (3) MOTIVATIONAL SYSTEMS THAT WILL INCLINE HIM TO ENGAGE IN LEARNING AND PROBLEM SOLVING ON A CONTINUING BASIS. ONE OBLIGATION IS TO DETERMINE THE CHARACTER OF THE SKILLS NEEDED, THE OPTIMAL TIMING FOR INSTRUCTION IN THESE SKILLS, AND THE OPTIMAL METHODS OF INSTRUCTION. THE MAJOR PORTION OF THIS PAPER IS CONCERNED WITH EXAMINATION OF THIS OBLIGATION. INCLUDED ARE A DESCRIPTION OF SELECTED PREREQUISITE SKILLS, ACCOUNTS OF WHAT IS KNOWN ABOUT THE EMERGENCE OF SUCH SKILLS DEPENDING ON CHARACTERISTICS OF THE STUDENT, INFORMATION ON WHAT IS KNOWN ABOUT INSTRUCTION DESIGNED TO PROMOTE THE EMERGENCE OF THE SKILLS, AND NOTES ON WHAT IS NOT KNOWN ABOUT THESE SKILLS. (NH)

ED053808 PS004907
DESIGNS AND PROPOSAL FOR EARLY CHILDHOOD RESEARCH: A NEW LOOK: PRESCHOOL RESEARCH AND PRESCHOOL EDUCATIONAL OBJECTIVES GROTBERG, EDITH H., ED.; AND OTHERS, 71 43P.
EDRS PRICE MF-$0.65 HC-$3.29

LONGITUDINAL STUDIES TO CLARIFY AND VALIDATE OBJECTIVES AND STANDARDS OF PRESCHOOL EDUCATION ARE ADVOCATED. UNTIL THE RESULT OF SUCH RESEARCH IS AVAILABLE, STUDIES OF METHODS AND PROCESSES HAVE LITTLE PRACTICAL OR THEORETICAL USE. PRESCHOOL GOALS GENERALLY AGREED UPON BY AMERICAN EDUCATORS ARE THE PROMOTION OF THE CHILD'S EMOTIONAL AND SOCIAL DEVELOPMENT, AND THE IMPROVEMENT OF MENTAL PROCESSES AND SKILLS. CURRENT STRATEGIES FOR FURTHER DEFINING THESE GOALS INCLUDE: (1) "BAG OF VIRTUES" APPROACH, WHICH ADVOCATES THAT THE CHILD ACQUIRE SELF CONFIDENCE, SPONTANEITY, CURIOSITY, SELF-DISCIPLINE, AND SPECIFIC APTITUDES AND SKILLS; (2) THE CLASS COMPARISON STRATEGY, WHICH ASSUMES A MIDDLE CLASS SUPERIORITY IN ATTITUDES, GOALS, AND GENERAL LIFE STYLE; (3) THE INDUSTRIAL PSYCHOLOGY STRATEGY, WHICH SAYS THAT IN ORDER TO MAKE IT IN THE SYSTEM, CHILDREN MUST MEET CERTAIN STANDARDS OF LANGUAGE AND SKILLS, EVEN THOUGH THEY ARE NOT TERMED "DEPRIVED" IN TERMS OF THEIR OWN CULTURE. IN CONTRAST, THE COGNITIVE-DEVELOPMENTAL APPROACH, WHICH IS EXEMPLIFIED BY PIAGETIAN STAGE THEORY, IS FAVORED AND IS USED IN THIS PAPER TO ARRIVE AT A STRATEGY FOR THE DEFINITION OF EDUCATION OBJECTIVES. THE CHILD AND HIS DEVELOPMENT, THE USE OF LONGITUDINAL DATA, AND SOME RECENT RESEARCH DEMONSTRATING RELATIONSHIPS BETWEEN PIAGETIAN STAGES OF COGNITION AND EGO STAGES ARE ALSO DISCUSSED. (NH)

ED053809 PS004908
DESIGNS AND PROPOSAL FOR EARLY CHILDHOOD RESEARCH: A NEW LOOK: A SYSTEMS APPROACH TO PRESCHOOL EDUCATION. (ONE IN A SERIES OF SIX PAPERS). WOOLMAN, MYRON; GROTBERG, EDITH H., ED., 71 152P.
EDRS PRICE MF-$0.65 HC-$6.58

SUGGESTED IS A LEARNING SYSTEMS APPROACH DESIGNED TO BE CONSISTENT WITH THE OBJECTIVES AND SCOPE OF DEVELOPMENTAL PSYCHOLOGY AND YET SOPHISTICATED AND APPROPRIATE ENOUGH TO FIT THE UNIQUE DEMANDS OF EARLY CHILDHOOD EDUCATION. IDENTIFIED ARE EIGHT CONTINGENCIES FOR LEARNING THAT ANY EDUCATIONAL SYSTEM MUST POSSESS. ADDED TO THESE ARE FEATURES CONSIDERED DISTINCTIVE TO LEARNING ENVIRONMENTS FOR PRESCHOOL CHILDREN. AMONG THESE FEATURES ARE THE FAMILY AS A LEARNING SYSTEM, A SYSTEMS PERSPECTIVE, A PSYCHO-SOCIAL THEORY OF CLASSROOM LEARNING, THE PHILOSOPHIC POSITION, CRITERIA AND SPECIFICATIONS, THE OPERATIONAL STAGE, EVALUATING AND MEASURING LEARNING SYSTEMS, AN EDUCATIONAL RESEARCH SUPERSTRUCTURE, AND THE EDUCATIONAL RESEARCH TESTING SYSTEM. EIGHT FIGURES SPECIFY DESIGNS AND RELATIONSHIPS IMPORTANT IN CONCEPTUALIZING AND OPERATIONALIZING THIS APPROACH. (WY)

ED053810 PS004909
DESIGNS AND PROPOSAL FOR EARLY CHILDHOOD RESEARCH: A NEW LOOK: THE UNACKNOWLEDGED ROLE OF CULTURE CONFLICT IN NEGRO EDUCATION. (ONE IN A SERIES OF SIX PAPERS). STEWART, WILLIAM A.; GROTBERG, EDITH H., ED., 71 52P.
EDRS PRICE MF-$0.65 HC-$3.29

AS A PLAUSIBLE EXPLANATION OF NEGRO ACADEMIC UNDERACHIEVEMENT, CULTURE CONFLICT HAS BEEN IGNORED BY EDUCATORS AND SOCIAL SCIENTISTS TO A DEGREE NOT INDICATED BY THE WIDE RANGE OF EVIDENCE WHICH POINTS TO ITS IMPORTANCE AS A CONTRIBUTING FACTOR. REASONS SUGGESTED FOR THIS THEORETICAL IMBALANCE CAN BE SUMMARIZED BY SAYING THAT IT HAS BEEN CONTROVERSIAL TO USE A CULTURAL-DIFFERENCE MODEL IN DEALING WITH AMERICAN NEGROES, AND IT IS LIKELY TO REMAIN SO IN THE FUTURE. THIS POSES A DILEMMA FOR THOSE WHO WANT TO HELP NEGRO CHILDREN ACHIEVE SATISFACTORILY IN SCHOOL. IF CULTURAL DIFFERENCES BETWEEN NEGROES AND WHITES ACCOUNT AT LEAST IN PART FOR THEIR DIFFERENT SCHOOL PERFORMANCE, IT IS UNLIKELY THAT EFFORTS TO RAISE THE LEVEL OF NEGRO ACADEMIC ACHIEVEMENT WILL BE SUCCESSFUL AS LONG AS CULTURAL FACTORS ARE IGNORED. FOR AWHILE, HOWEVER, MOST SOCIAL SCIENTISTS WILL PROBABLY PREFER TO STAY WITHIN THE BOUNDS OF ENVIRONMENTALISM IN THEIR SEARCH FOR THE CAUSES OF NEGRO ACADEMIC UNDERACHIEVEMENT. THE SOCIAL PENALTIES FOR FAILING WITH AN ENVIRONMENTAL-DIFFERENCE MODEL ARE STILL LESS SEVERE THAN THOSE WHICH ACCOMPANY SUCCESS WITH A GENETIC-DIFFERENCE OR CULTURAL-DIFFERENCE MODEL. (AUTHOR/NH)

ED053811 PS004910
DESIGNS AND PROPOSAL FOR EARLY CHILDHOOD RESEARCH: A NEW LOOK: MALNUTRITION, LEARNING AND INTELLIGENCE. (ONE IN A SERIES OF SIX PAPERS). BIRCH, HERBERT G.; GROTBERG, EDITH H., ED., 71 38P.
EDRS PRICE MF-$0.65 HC-$3.29

A SURVEY OF THE EVIDENCE SHOWS THAT SOME DEGREES OF MALNUTRITION IS RELATIVELY WIDESPREAD AMONG POOR CHILDREN. HOWEVER, THE EFFECTS OF INADEQUATE NUTRITION ON GROWTH AND MENTAL DEVELOPMENT DEPEND TO A LARGE EXTENT ON THE SEVERITY, THE TIMING (PRE AND POSTNATAL), AND THE DURATION OF THE NUTRITIONAL DEPRIVATION. THE DATA ARE INADEQUATE ON THE TRUE PREVALENCE OF MALNUTRITION AMONG CHILDREN IN THIS COUNTRY, BUT THERE IS EVEN LESS INFORMATION ABOUT ITS ONSET OR ABOUT ITS SEVERITY AND QUALITY. THE ABSENCE OF SUCH KNOWLEDGE REFLECTS NOT THE ABSENCE OF THE PROBLEM, BUT THE LACK OF ATTENTION DEVOTED TO IT. THERE IS STRONG INDICATION THAT NUTRITIONAL FACTORS AT A NUMBER OF DIFFERENT LEVELS CONTRIBUTE SIGNIFICANTLY TO DEPRESSED INTELLECTUAL LEVEL AND LEARNING FAILURE. MOREOVER, AN ADEQUATE STATE OF NUTRITION IS NECESSARY FOR GOOD ATTENTION AND FOR APPROPRIATE AND SENSITIVE RESPONSIVENESS TO THE ENVIRONMENT. FURTHER, WOMEN WHO WERE MALNOURISHED AS CHILDREN ARE MORE LIKELY TO HAVE DISTURBED PREGNANCIES AND CHILDREN OF LOW BIRTH WEIGHT AND INCREASED RISK OF NEUROINTEGRATIVE ABNORMALITY. IT MUST BE RECOGNIZED, HOWEVER, THAT IMPROVEMENT OF NUTRITION ALONE CANNOT FULLY SOLVE THE PROBLEM OF INTELLECTUAL DEFICIT AND SCHOOL FAILURE. RATHER, AN OVERALL EFFORT TO IMPROVE THE CONDITION OF DISADVANTAGED CHILDREN IS REQUIRED. (AUTHOR/NH)

ED053812 PS004912
DEMONSTRATION AND TRAINING PROJECT FOR MIGRANT CHILDREN, MCALLEN, TEXAS. EARLY CHILDHOOD LEARNING SYSTEM. FINAL EVALUATION REPORT, 1970-71. , JUL 71 43P.
EDRS PRICE MF-$0.65 HC-$3.29

THIS IS A REPORT OF THE FINAL YEAR OF A 3-YEAR PROJECT TO DEVELOP A SEQUENTIAL EARLY CHILDHOOD EDUCATION PROGRAM TO MEET THE UNIQUE NEEDS OF 3-, 4-, AND 5-YEAR-OLD MIGRANT MEXICAN AMERICAN CHILDREN. THE BILINGUAL PROGRAM'S MAJOR COMPONENTS ARE INSTRUCTIONAL MATERIALS, STAFF DEVELOPMENT, AND PARENT-SCHOOL-COMMUNITY INVOLVEMENT. NINETY CHILDREN PARTICIPATED IN THE PROGRAM IN 1970-71, WITH TWO CLASSES OF 15 PUPILS EACH IN EACH OF THE THREE AGE GROUPS. EVALUATION WAS BASED ON CRITERION-REFERENCED TESTS GIVEN TO EXPERIMENTAL PUPILS AT THE BEGINNING AND END OF THE SCHOOL YEAR; AND NORM-REFERENCED TESTS, GIVEN TO EXPERIMENTAL CLASSES AND COMPARISON GROUPS OF THE SAME AGE, ETHNICITY, AND SOCIOECONOMIC BACKGROUND WHO ATTENDED DAY CARE CENTERS WITHOUT PLANNED INSTRUCTIONAL PROGRAMS. TEST FINDINGS REVEALED THAT CHILDREN IN THE LABORATORY PROGRAM MET THE CRITERION ON THE CURRICULUM-REFERENCED TESTS ON ALL BUT A FEW OF THE 25 UNITS. EXPERIMENTAL PUPILS SCORED HIGHER THAN COMPARISON PUPILS ON TESTS OF SPANISH AND ENGLISH COMPREHENSION, GENERAL CONCEPTS, AND NONVERBAL INTELLIGENCE. (AUTHOR/AJ)

ED053813 PS004918
APPLICATION OF MARKOV PROCESSES TO THE CONCEPT OF STATE. FREEDLE, ROY; LEWIS, MICHAEL, 71 15P.
EDRS PRICE MF-$0.65 HC-$3.29

THE PURPOSE OF THIS PAPER IS TO OUTLINE SOME APPLICATION OF THE MARKOV PROCESS TO THE STUDY OF STATE AND STATE CHANGES. THE ESSENCE OF THIS MATHEMATICAL CONCEPT CONSISTS OF THE ANALYSIS OF SEQUENCES OF INFANT RESPONSES IN INTERACTION WITH ITS ENVIRONMENT. CATEGORIES CAN BE DEFINED WHICH REFLECT THE JOINT OCCURRENCE OF AN INFANT'S BEHAVIOR (OR CONDITION) ALONG WITH SOME ASSOCIATIVE EVENT(S) IN THE INFANT'S IMMEDIATE ENVIRONMENT. EACH OF THESE CATEGORIES OF INFANT-ENVIRONMENT INTERACTION CAN BE USED AS A DEFINITION OF STATE FOR THE PURPOSES OF STUDYING THE SEQUENTIAL UNFOLDING AMONG CATEGORIES. AN EXAMPLE UTILIZING CHILD VOCALIZATION DATA COLLECTED BY LEWIS IS GIVEN. WHEN APPLIED TO MOTHER-INFANT INTERACTION, A PARTICULAR MOTHER-INFANT PAIR MAY YIELD DATA WHICH GIVE A POOR FIT IN TERMS OF MATCHING STATISTICS WITH THE MARKOV MODEL. THEREFORE, THREE ALTERNATIVE PROCEDURES ARE SUGGESTED. (AUTHOR/WY)

ED053814 PS004919
EXPERIMENTAL VARIATION OF HEAD START CURRICULA: A COMPARISON OF CURRENT APPROACHES. PROGRESS REPORT NO. 9, MARCH 1, 1971 - MAY 31, 1971. MILLER, LOUISE B.; AND OTHERS, 31 MAY 71 26P.
EDRS PRICE MF-$0.65 HC-$3.29

THIS STUDY SEEKS TO DETERMINE WHAT DIFFERENCES IN READINESS EXISTED IN LOUISVILLE, KENTUCKY CHILDREN WHO HAD BEEN EXPOSED TO VARIOUS COMBINATIONS OF HEAD START, FOLLOW-THROUGH AND REGULAR KINDERGARTEN. ALL FIRST GRADE CHILDREN IN LOUISVILLE WERE TESTED WITH THE METROPOLITAN READINESS TEST DURING THE FIRST MONTH OF FIRST GRADE. DATA WAS ANALYZED WITH ANALYSIS OF COVARIANCE, ANALYSIS OF VARIANCE AND CORRELATION. ALTHOUGH ADDITIONAL DATA ANALYSIS IS IN PROCESS, FIVE TENTATIVE CONCLUSIONS ARE OFFERED: (1) THE TOKEN-ECONOMY FOLLOW-THROUGH KINDERGARTEN WAS BETTER FOR THESE CHILDREN THAN THE REGULAR KINDERGARTEN; (2) THE BEST COMBINATION OF HEAD START AND KINDERGARTEN WAS TRADITIONAL HEAD START FOLLOWED BY FOLLOW-THROUGH KINDERGARTEN; (3) THE WORST COMBINATION WAS BEREITER-ENGELMANN HEAD START FOLLOWED BY REGULAR KINDERGARTEN; (4) FOR CHILDREN ENTERING THE FOLLOW-THROUGH PROGRAM IN KINDERGARTEN THERE IS NO EVIDENCE THAT THERE WAS AN ADVANTAGE IN HAVING HAD HEAD START AT ALL; AND (5) FOR MALES ENTERING THE REGULAR KINDERGARTEN PROGRAM, ANY TYPE OF HEAD START APPEARED TO BE BETTER THAN NONE. (WY)

ED053815 PS004928
NURSERIES IN CROSS-CULTURAL EDUCATION. FINAL REPORT. LANE, MARY B.; AND OTHERS, 71 465P.
EDRS PRICE MF-$0.65 HC-$16.45
AVAILABLE FROM: MARY B. LANE, SAN FRANCISCO STATE COLLEGE, SCHOOL OF EDUCATION, 1600 HOLLOWAY, SAN FRANCISCO, CALIFORNIA 94132

NURSERIES IN CROSS-CULTURAL EDUCATION (NICE) INITIATED AND IMPLEMENTED A 5-YEAR PROGRAM INVOLVING THREE NURSERY SCHOOLS IN PREVENTIVE MENTAL HEALTH IN A SAN FRANCISCO POVERTY AREA. IT WAS A DEMONSTRATION PROJECT CARRIED OUT TO STUDY PROCESSES OF INVOLVING INNER-CITY FAMILIES IN COPING WITH PROBLEMS THAT OFTEN OVERWHELM CITY DWELLERS. NICE FOCUSED ON THE EDUCATION OF CHILDREN 2 TO 5 YEARS OLD AS AN INTERCULTURAL PRESCHOOL EXPERIENCE WHOSE INFLUENCE EXTENDED OUTWARD TO THE MULTI-ETHNIC NEIGHBORHOOD. THE PROCESSES DEVELOPED IN NICE COMPRISE AN INTERACTION MODEL THAT MIGHT BE UTILIZED WITH GROUPS OF PEOPLE EVERYWHERE. CHAPTER TITLES INCLUDE: THE SETTING OF THE STUDY, INDIVIDUALIZED CROSS-CULTURAL FAMILY MODEL, REVIEW OF RESEARCH IN PRESCHOOL PROGRAMS, DESCRIPTION OF THE SAMPLE, DESCRIPTION OF PROJECT SETTING AND OF STAFF, PROGRAM FOR CHILDREN, PROGRAM FOR ADULT MEMBERS, MOTHER AS TEACHER AT HOME, THE ACQUISITION AND ANALYSIS OF EVALUATIONAL DATA, ANALYSIS OF PROCESSES USED TO OBTAIN GROWTH, AND VIGNETTE OF A NICE PROJECT. EXTENSIVE APPENDIXES PRESENT SCHEDULES, TIMETABLES, BEHAVIOR RATING SCALES AND STAFF INFORMATION. (WY)

ED053816 PS004929
THE USE OF INDIVIDUAL GOAL-SETTING CONFERENCES AS A MOTIVATIONAL TECHNIQUE. GAA, JOHN P., [70] 13P.
EDRS PRICE MF-$0.65 HC-$3.29

THIS STUDY EXAMINED THE EFFECT OF GOAL-SETTING ON THE ACHIEVEMENT AND ATTITUDES OF 108 BOYS AND GIRLS FROM GRADES 1-4. PUPILS IN GROUP I PARTICIPATED IN FOUR GOAL-SETTING CONFERENCES WITH THE EXPERIMENTER. PUPILS IN GROUP II ALSO HAD CONFERENCES BUT CLASS STUDY TOPICS WERE DISCUSSED AND STUDENTS DID NOT SET GOALS. GROUP III WAS A CONTROL GROUP RECEIVING ONLY CLASSROOM INSTRUCTION IN READING SKILLS. TWO ATTITUDE MEASURES WERE ADMINISTERED TO ALL PUPILS ALONG WITH AN EXPERIMENTER-DEVELOPED AND A CRITERION-REFERENCED ACHIEVEMENT TEST. THE EXPERIMENTAL DESIGN WAS A 3X3X2 RANDOMIZED BLOCK DESIGN WITH THREE TREATMENTS, THREE LEVELS OF PREVIOUS ACHIEVEMENT, AND TWO SEXES. FINDINGS INDICATE THAT THE USE OF AN INDIVIDUAL GOAL-SETTING CONFERENCE CAN IMPROVE THE CLASSROOM MOTIVATION OF PUPILS. THE CONFOUNDING OF OTHER FACTORS MAKES PRESENT FINDINGS TENTATIVE. SUGGESTIONS FOR FUTURE RESEARCH INCLUDE BEGINNING WITH A MORE PRECISE DELINEATION OF THE ATTRIBUTES OF GOAL-SETTING. (WY)

ED053817 PS005000
OPENING UP THE CLASSROOM: A WALK AROUND THE SCHOOL. HUCKLESBY, SYLVIA, AUG 71 12P.
EDRS PRICE MF-$0.65 HC-$3.29

OPEN EDUCATION PRACTICES ARE ILLUSTRATED IN THIS PAPER IN WHICH CHILDREN'S NATURAL INTEREST IN THE OUTDOOR WORLD IS USED TO OUTLINE LEARNING ACTIVITIES WHICH MIGHT RESULT FROM A SHORT NATURE WALK. THE TEACHERS' OBJECTIVE IS TO HELP THE CHILD LEARN STRATEGIES AND SKILLS WHICH WILL ENABLE HIM TO ACQUIRE, SORT, STORE AND USE INFORMATION, IN CONTRAST TO LEARNING A BODY OF FACTS. THE PAPER ARGUES THAT TEACHERS SHOULD ENCOURAGE THE CHILD THROUGH DIALOGUE AND DISCUSSION, LEADING HIM TO A LEVEL OF INTEREST WHICH WILL THEN SUSTAIN SELF-DIRECTED ACTIVITY. SPECIFICALLY DISCUSSED ARE WAYS TO TEACH MATH CONCEPTS, SCIENCE, LANGUAGE ARTS, AND ART USING VARIOUS NATURAL MATERIALS SUCH AS STONES, STICKS, LEAVES AND FLOWERS. (NH)

ED053818 PS005011
A STUDY IN THE UTILIZATION OF TECHNOLOGICALLY ADVANCED TECHNIQUES FOR TEACHER-PARENT-CHILD ASSESSMENT. FINAL REPORT. RAVEY, PHYLLIS; AND OTHERS, DEC 69 16P.
EDRS PRICE MF-$0.65 HC-$3.29

THIS REPORT DESCRIBES A PILOT STUDY IN THE USE OF VIDEO TAPE AS A RECORDING AND REPORTING DEVICE FOR A CHILD'S RESPONSES IN A LEARNING SITUATION. IT WAS BELIEVED THAT VIDEO TAPE COULD BE USED AS AN IMPROVED MEANS OF HOME-SCHOOL COMMUNICATION. NINETEEN 5-YEAR-OLD SUBJECTS IN GROUPS OF SIX WERE VIDEOTAPED FOR 12-MINUTE SEGMENTS IN ACTUAL CLASSROOM SITUATIONS. AT A SCHEDULED PARENT-TEACHER CONFERENCE, BOTH PARENTS OF EACH CHILD (SEPARATED BY A SCREEN TO ELIMINATE PARTNER INFLUENCE) VIEWED THE TAPE AND RECORDED 5 SPECIFIC ITEMS OF THEIR CHILD'S BEHAVIOR ON THE FORM PROVIDED. STUDENT BEHAVIOR CATEGORIES WERE: (1) INTENT ON ONGOING WORK, (2) REMARK WHICH IS TASK ORIENTED, (3) NON-TASK ORIENTED REMARK, (4) DAYDREAMING, AND (5) FIDGETING. USING THE TAPE METHOD, PARENTS WERE ABLE TO SEE THEIR CHILD'S PROBLEMS AND POTENTIALS DIRECTLY AND WITHOUT INITIAL ELABORATION BY THE TEACHER AT THE PARENT CONFERENCE. PARENTS INITIATED THE COMMENTS AND THE TEACHER BECAME A PARTICIPANT IN THE EVALUATION RATHER THAN THE JUDGE. PARENTS COMPARED THEIR TABULATIONS AFTER VIEWING THE TAPE, OFTEN REVEALING INCONSISTENT EXPECTATIONS BETWEEN PARENTS. FATHERS WERE USUALLY RESPONSIVE TO MORE ITEMS IN A GIVEN SEGMENT OF TIME THAN THE MOTHERS. STUDY FINDINGS SUGGEST THAT USE OF VIDEO TAPE MIGHT HELP IDENTIFY A CHILD'S LEARNING PATTERN OR CONSISTENT SCHOOL LIFE PATTERN. (AUTHOR/AJ)

ED053819 PS005035
A GUIDE TO READING PIAGET. BREARLEY, MOLLY; HITCHFIELD, ELIZABETH, 69 180P.
DOCUMENT NOT AVAILABLE FROM EDRS.
AVAILABLE FROM: SCHOCKEN BOOKS, INC., 67 PARK AVENUE, NEW YORK, NEW YORK 10016 ($2.25, PAPER)

A METHOD FOR READING PIAGET IS PRESENTED IN THIS GUIDE, WRITTEN FOR PRACTICING TEACHERS WHO WANT BETTER UNDERSTANDING OF PIAGET'S WRITINGS. AN ACCOUNT OF A PIAGETIAN EXPERIMENT IS GIVEN, FOLLOWED BY A DISCUSSION OF ITS THEORETICAL AND PRACTICAL IMPLICATIONS. EIGHT TOPICS ARE EXPLORED: NUMBER, MEASUREMENT, KNOTS, PERSPECTIVES, COORDINATES, FLOATING AND SINKING, MORAL JUDGMENT, AND THE BEHAVIOR OF BABIES. THE

CONCLUSION PROVIDES A SYNOPSIS OF PIAGET'S THEORY OF STAGES OF COGNITIVE DEVELOPMENT. THE EXPERIMENTAL EXAMPLES CHOSEN COVER A WIDE AGE RANGE TO EMPHASIZE THE GENETIC APPROACH AND TO EXTEND THE APPEAL OF THE GUIDE TO AS LARGE A GROUP OF TEACHERS AS POSSIBLE. EXAMPLES WERE ALSO CHOSEN BECAUSE THEY ARE ESPECIALLY APPLICABLE IN SCHOOLS. (AUTHOR/AJ)

ED053820 PS005067
CLASSROOM LANGUAGE OF TEACHERS OF YOUNG CHILDREN. STERN, CAROLYN; FRITH, SANDRA, OCT 70 45P.
EDRS PRICE MF-$0.65 HC-$3.29

THE PURPOSE OF THIS STUDY WAS TO DETERMINE IF (1) KINDERGARTEN READING READINESS CAN BE ENHANCED BY DIFFERENTIATED INSTRUCTION IN VISUO-MOTOR (V-M) SKILLS, (2) THE GESELL DEVELOPMENTAL PLACEMENT EXAMINATION IS EFFECTIVE FOR INTER-CLASS GROUPING, AND (3) DEVELOPMENTAL GROWTH CAN BE ACCELERATED WITH DIFFERENTIATED INSTRUCTION IN V-M SKILLS. MATERIALS AND MEDIA APPROPRIATE FOR KINDERGARTEN INSTRUCTION WERE ALSO TO BE IDENTIFIED. SUBJECTS WERE RANDOMLY ASSIGNED BY GESELL DEVELOPMENTAL PLACEMENT EXAMINATION (GDPE) SCORES TO EXPERIMENTAL AND CONTROL HIGH, LOW, AND HETEROGENEOUS DEVELOPMENT CLASSES. DIFFERENTIATED INSTRUCTION IN V-M SKILLS WAS ADMINISTERED. AFTER 8 MONTHS, GDPE POSTTEST AND GATES-MACGINITIE READINESS SKILLS TEST WERE ADMINISTERED. RESULTS REVEALED THAT (1) DIFFERENTIATED V-M INSTRUCTION DOES NOT SIGNIFICANTLY ENHANCE KINDERGARTEN READING READINESS; (2) THERE ARE NO EDUCATIONAL ADVANTAGES IN INNER-CITY GROUPING ON BASIS OF DEVELOPMENTAL AGE; AND (3) DEVELOPMENTAL GROWTH IS NOT ACCELERATED BY A PROGRAM IN V-M SKILLS; (4) SLIDE-TAPE SELF-INSTRUCTIONAL PACKAGES AND LANGUAGE MASTERS ARE USEFUL MEDIA FOR KINDERGARTEN INSTRUCTION. APPENDIXES COMPRISE MORE THAN ONE-HALF OF THE DOCUMENT. (AUTHOR/AJ)

ED053821 PS005068
THE EFFECTS OF DIFFERENTIATED INSTRUCTION IN VISUO-MOTOR SKILLS ON DEVELOPMENTAL GROWTH AND READING READINESS AT KINDERGARTEN LEVEL. FINAL REPORT. KELLY, INGA K., AUG 71 133P.
EDRS PRICE MF-$0.65 HC-$6.58

THE FOCUS OF THIS STUDY WAS TO ANALYZE THE CLASSROOM LANGUAGE OF KINDERGARTEN TEACHERS AND TO RELATE THIS INFORMATION TO VARIOUS NORMATIVE ESTIMATES OF THE LANGUAGE REPERTOIRE OF YOUNG CHILDREN. A TOTAL OF 104 5-MINUTE SAMPLES WERE TAPE RECORDED FOR 15 KINDERGARTEN TEACHERS. TRANSCRIPTS WERE LATER CHECKED BY AN INDEPENDENT LISTNER. THESE SCRITS FORMED THE DATA BASE FOR ALL TEACHER LANGUAGE ANALYSES. IN HE FIRST ANALYSIS, THE WORDS WERE LISTED ACCORDING TO PARTS OF SPEECH, AND CORRELATIONS BETWEEN THIS LANGUAGE CORPUS AND 2 MAJOR LISTINGS OF CHILDREN'S VOCABULARY (THORNDIKE-LORGE AND RINSLAND) WERE FOUND TO BE SIGNIFICANT. OVER 60 PERCENT OF THE LANGUAGE USED BY TEACHERS IS WITHIN THE EXPECTED LEVEL OF FAMILIARITY. THE 40 PERCENT BALANCE OF UNFAMILIAR WORDS MAY BE CONSIDERED THE WORD LOAD TO WHICH THESE CHILDREN WERE EXPOSED IN THE PROCESS OF VOCABULARY ACQUISITION. A FLANDERS-TYPE ANALYSIS OF THE NATURE OF THE COMMUNICATIONS CONVEYED BY THE TEACHERS' LANGUAGE WITH REFERENCE TO TEACHER STYLE ACROSS ETHNIC AND SOCIOECONOMIC (SES) GROUPS REVEALED THAT CAUCASIAN TEACHERS OF BOTH HIGH SES BLACK CHILDREN AND LOW SES WHITE CHILDREN USE MORE VERBAL REINFORCEMENT THAN WAS NOTED WITH CAUCASIAN TEACHERS WITH HIGH SES WHITE CHILDREN OR BLACK TEACHERS WITH LOW SES BLACK CHILDREN. IN GENERAL, CAUCASIAN TEACHERS OF HIGH SES CAUCASIAN CHILDREN GIVE FEWER VERBAL SUPPORTS, WHEREAS BLACK TEACHERS OF LOW SES BLACK CHILDREN ARE THE WARMEST AND MOST SUPPORTIVE. (AUTHOR/AJ)

ERIC JOURNAL ARTICLES

EJ 000 191 PS 500 002
THE NATURE AND NURTURE OF PREJUDICE REDL, FRITZ, *CHILDHOOD EDUC*, V45 N5, PP254-57, 69 JAN
CONDENSED FROM AN ADDRESS GIVEN AT A CONVOCATION OF STUDENTS AT WAYNE STATE UNIVERSITY IN THE SUMMER OF 1968.

EJ 000 192 PS 500 006
CONCERNED CITIZENS IN THE MAKING VOLKERS, JANICE J., *CHILDHOOD EDUC*, V45 N5, PP269-72, 69 JAN

EJ 000 391 PS 500 000
THE TEMPER OF THE TIMES VAN TIL, WILLIAM, *CHILDHOOD EDUC*, V45 N5, PP243-46, 69 JAN

EJ 000 392 PS 500 001
THE DEVELOPMENT OF CHILDREN'S VIEWS OF FOREIGN PEOPLES LAMBERT, WALLACE E.; KLINEBERG, OTTO, *CHILDHOOD EDUC*, V45 N5, PP247-53, 69 JAN
A SELECTION, SLIGHTLY REVISED, FROM CHILDREN'S VIEWS OF FOREIGN PEOPLES: A CROSS NATIONAL STUDY, BY WALLACE E. LAMBERT AND OTTO KLINEBERG. N.Y., MEREDITH PUBLISHING CO, 1967.

EJ 000 393 PS 500 005
CHOOSING CHILDREN'S BOOKS ABOUT OTHER COUNTRIES EDMAN, MARION; BATCHELDER, MILDRED L., *CHILDHOOD EDUC*, V45 N5, PP265-68, 69 JAN

EJ 001 116 PS 500 004
STRONG WORDS MADDOX, G. A.; ROSS, R. S., *CHILDHOOD EDUC*, V45 N5, PP260-64, 69 JAN

EJ 001 498 PS 500 003
PREJUDICE IN THE SCHOOLS BURNETT, ALICE, *CHILDHOOD EDUC*, V45 N5, PP258-59, 69 JAN

EJ 001 672 PS 500 007
NURSERIES IN THE CZECHOSLOVAK SOCIALIST REPUBLIC BARTUSKOVA, MARIA, *CHILDHOOD EDUC*, V45 N5, PP273-76, 69 JAN

EJ 001 912 PS 500 015
CLASSROOM OPPORTUNITIES TO EXPRESS FEELINGS ELLISOR, MILDRED, *CHILDHOOD EDUC*, V45 N7, PP373-78, 69 MAR

EJ 002 018 PS 500 014
HELPING CHILDREN COPE WITH FEELINGS. LONG, NICHOLAS; AND OTHERS, *CHILDHOOD EDUC*, V45 N7, PP367-72, 69 MAR

EJ 002 313 PS 500 019
TO KEEP AN INNER BALANCE HAUPT, CHARLOTTE, *CHILDHOOD EDUC*, V45 N7, PP391-95, 69 MAR

EJ 002 421 PS 500 022
EVALUATION OF CLASSROOM CLIMATE WITHALL, JOHN, *CHILDHOOD EDUC*, V45 N7, PP403-08, 69 MAR

EJ 002 654 PS 500 018
LITERATURE FOR YOUNG CHILDREN LEWIS, CLAUDIA, *CHILDHOOD EDUC*, V45 N7, PP385-90, 69 MAR

EJ 002 655 PS 500 021
BILLY MEARNS: FRIEND AND TEACHER. HUGHES MEARNS, 1875-1965 GILLIES, EMILY, *CHILDHOOD EDUC*, V45 N7, PP398-402, 69 MAR

EJ 003 029 PS 500 017
"THIS IS ME!" LAMBERT, CARROLL, *CHILDHOOD EDUC*, V45 N7, PP381-84, 69 MAR

EJ 003 082 PS 500 013
THE FEELINGS OF LEARNING BEATTY, WALCOTT H., *CHILDHOOD EDUC*, V45 N7, PP363-66, 69 MAR

EJ 003 083 PS 500 016
CLARIFYING FEELINGS THROUGH PEER INTERACTION PERKINS, HUGH V., *CHILDHOOD EDUC*, V45 N7, PP379-80, 69 MAR

EJ 003 416 PS 500 031
SYMPOSIUM: FOR AND AGAINST STRIKES CAUSEY, J. P.; PFAU, DONALD W., *CHILDHOOD EDUC*, V45 N8, PP438-44, 69 APR

EJ 003 417 PS 500 032
STRIKES, SANCTIONS, OR SURRENDER? SELDEN, DAVID, *CHILDHOOD EDUC*, V45 N8, PP445-47, 69 APR

EJ 003 418 PS 500 033
LABOR'S VIEWS ON TEACHER STRIKES ROTH, HERRICK S., *CHILDHOOD EDUC*, V45 N8, PP448-9, 69 APR

EJ 003 419 PS 500 034
CHILDREN AND THE SCHOOL STRIKE LESTER, SEELIG; RISIKOFF, ROSE, *CHILDHOOD EDUC*, V45 N8, PP450-53, 69 APR

EJ 003 459 PS 500 037
BODY SIZE OF CONTEMPORARY GROUPS OF EIGHT-YEAR-OLD CHILDREN STUDIED IN DIFFERENT PARTS OF THE WORLD MEREDITH, HOWARD V., *MONGR SOC RES CHILD DEVELOP*, V34 N1, PP1-93, 69 JAN/FEB

EJ 003 552 PS 500 039
INTRODUCTION TO THE 1968 INFANT CONFERENCE PAPERS SIGEL, IRVING E., *MERRILL-PALMER QUART*, V15 N1, PP3-5, 69 JAN
PAPER PRESENTED AT THE MERRILL-PALMER INSTITUTE ON RESEARCH AND TRAINING OF INFANT DEVELOPMENT (DETROIT, MICH., FEB. 15-17, 1968).

EJ 003 553 PS 500 042
PERCEPTUAL-COGNITIVE DEVELOPMENT IN INFANCY: A GENERALIZED EXPECTANCY MODEL AS A FUNCTION OF THE MOTHER-INFANT INTERACTION LEWIS, MICHAEL; GOLDBERG, SUSAN, *MERRILL-PALMER QUART*, V15 N1, PP81-100, 69 JAN
PAPER PRESENTED AT THE MERRILL-PALMER INSTITUTE ON RESEARCH AND TRAINING OF INFANT DEVELOPMENT (DETROIT, MICH., FEB. 15-17, 1968).

EJ 003 554 PS 500 043
CONTINUNITY IN COGNITIVE DEVELOPMENT DURING THE FIRST YEAR KAGAN, JEROME, *MERRILL-PALMER QUART*, V15 N1, PP101-119, 69 JAN
PAPER PRESENTED AT THE MERRILL-PALMER INSTITUTE ON RESEARCH AND TRAINING OF INFANT DEVELOPMENT (DETROIT, MICH., FEB. 15-17, 1968).

EJ 003 595 PS 500 024
EARLY CHILDHOOD EDUCATION - FOR WHAT GOALS? SENN, MILTON J. E., *CHILDREN*, V16 N1, PP8-13, 69 JAN-FEB
CONDENSED FROM THE FIRST EVANGELINE BURGESS MEMORIAL LECTURE PRESENTED AT PACIFIC OAKS COLLEGE AND CHILDREN'S SCHOOL, PASADENA, CALIF., APRIL 3, 1968.

EJ 003 629 PS 500 030
NEA VIEWS ON TEACHER STRIKES KOONTZ, ELIZABETH D., *CHILDHOOD EDUC*, V45 N8, PP435-37, 69 APR

EJ 003 630 PS 500 035
LOOKING BEYOND THE STRIKES ANDREWS, J. EDWARD, JR., *CHILDHOOD EDUC*, V45 N8, PP454-56, 69 APR

EJ 003 658 PS 500 038
A FOLLOW-UP NORMATIVE STUDY OF NEGRO INTELLIGENCE AND ACHIEVEMENT KENNEDY, WALLACE A., *MONGR SOC RES CHILD DEVELOP*, V34 N2, PP1-40, 69 MAR/APR

EJ 003 743 PS 500 027
NEW HOPE FOR BABIES OF RH NEGATIVE MOTHERS LIN-FU, JANE S., *CHILDREN*, V16 N1, PP23-27, 69 JAN-FEB

EJ 003 946 PS 500 036
DANISH RECREATION HOMES FOR YOUNG CHILDREN HENRIKSEN, GRETHE, *CHILDHOOD EDUC*, V45 N8, PP457-59, 69 APR

EJ 003 955 PS 500 025
CASE CONFERENCE: A PSYCHOTHERAPEUTIC AIDE IN A HEADSTART PROGRAM. I. THEORY AND PRACTICE ANDRONICO, MICHAEL P.; GUERNEY, BERNARD G., JR., *CHILDREN*, V16 N1, PP14-17, 69 JAN-FEB

EJ 003 956 PS 500 026
CASE CONFERENCE: A PSYCHOTHERAPEUTIC AIDE IN A HEADSTART PROGRAM. II. COMMENTARY MURPHY, LOIS BARCLAY; AND OTHERS, *CHILDREN*, V16 N1, PP18-22, 69 JAN-FEB

EJ 003 972 PS 500 023
SEPARATION REACTIONS IN YOUNG, MILDLY RETARDED CHILDREN. KESSLER, JANES W.; AND OTHERS, *CHILDREN*, V16 N1, PP2-7, 69 JAN-FEB
BASED ON A PAPER PRESENTED AT THE 1968 ANNUAL MEETING OF THE AMERICAN ORTHOPSYCHIATRIC ASSOC.

EJ 004 044 PS 500 040
LEVELS OF CONCEPTUAL ANALYSIS IN ENVIRONMENT-INFANT INTERACTION RESEARCH GEWIRTZ, JACOB L., *MERRILL-PALMER QUART*, V15 N1, PP7-47, 69 JAN
PAPER PRESENTED AT THE MERRILL-PALMER INSTITUTE ON RESEARCH AND TRAINING OF INFANT DEVELOPMENT (DETROIT, MICH., FEB. 15-17, 1968).

EJ 004 045 PS 500 041
CHILD DEVELOPMENT RESEARCH: AN EDIFICE WITHOUT A FOUNDATION WHITE, BURTON L., *MERRILL-PALMER QUART*, V15 N1, PP49-79, 69 JAN
PAPER PRESENTED AT THE MERRILL-PALMER INSTITUTE ON RESEARCH AND TRAINING OF INFANT DEVELOPMENT (DETROIT, MICH., FEB. 15-17, 1968).

EJ 004 046 PS 500 044
HUMAN BEHAVIOR GENETICS: PRESENT STATUS AND SUGGESTIONS FOR FUTURE RESEARCH VANDENBERG, STEVEN G., *MERRILL-PALMER QUART*, V15 N1, PP121-154, 69 JAN
PAPER PRESENTED AT THE MERRILL-PALMER INSTITUTE ON RESEARCH AND TRAINING OF INFANT DEVELOPMENT (DETROIT, MICH., FEB. 15-17, 1968).

EJ 004 092 PS 500 028
A SOCIAL WORK MISSION TO HIPPIELAND CRYSTAL, DAVID; GOLD, IRWIN H., *CHILDREN*, V16 N1, PP28-32, 69 JAN-FEB
BASED ON A PAPER PRESENTED AT THE 1968 FORUM OF THE NATIONAL CONFERENCE ON SOCIAL WELFARE.

EJ 004 093 PS 500 029
DEVELOPING MANPOWER FOR THE WORLD'S SOCIAL WELFARE NEEDS. SOME OBSERVATIONS FROM THE CONFERENCE OF MINISTERS RESPONSIBLE FOR SOCIAL WELFARE.. DELLIQUADRI, P. FREDERICK, *CHILDREN*, V16 N1, PP33-35, 69 JAN-FEB

EJ 006 811 PS 500 065
MUSIC IN THE BEGINNING READING PROGRAM KUHMERKER, LISA, *YOUNG CHILDREN*, V24 N3, PP157-63, 69 JAN

EJ 006 854 PS 500 068
AUDIO-VISUAL MATERIALS IN EARLY CHILDHOOD EDUCATION HENDRICKSON, NOREJANE; WILLIAMS, BRUCE M., *YOUNG CHILDREN*, V24 N4, PP209-16, 69 MAR

EJ 006 855 PS 500 081
TELEVISION VIOLENCE OSBORN, D. KEITH; HALE, WILLIAM, *CHILDHOOD EDUC*, V45 N9, PP505-07, 69 MAY
THE PROJECT DESCRIBED IS FINANCED IN PART BY FUNDS FROM FIELD ENTERPRISES EDUCATIONAL CORP., CHICAGO, ILL.

EJ 006 876 PS 500 070
SOME EFFECTS OF PUNISHMENT ON CHILDREN'S BEHAVIOR PARKE, ROSS D., *YOUNG CHILDREN*, V24 N4, PP225-40, 69 MAR
THE PREPARATION OF THIS PAPER AND SOME OF THE STUDIES THAT ARE REPORTED HERE WERE SUPPORTED IN PART BY RESEARCH GRANT GS 1847, NATIONAL SCIENCE FOUNDATION

EJ 006 877 PS 500 089
INTERACTION OF SEX OF SUBJECT AND DEPENDENCY-TRAINING PROCEDURES IN A SOCIAL-REINFORCEMENT STUDY HILL, DOROTHY L.; WALTERS, RICHARD H., *MERRILL-PALMER QUART*, V15 N2, PP185-98, 69 APR
BASED ON A DOCTORAL DISSERTATION PRESENTED BY THE FIRST-NAMED AUTHOR IN PARTIAL FULFILLMENT OF THE REQUIREMENTS FOR THE PH.D. DEGREE UNDER THE SUPERVISION OF THE SECOND-NAMED AUTHOR

EJ 006 921 PS 500 087
THE EFFECT OF EARLY STIMULATION: THE PROBLEM OF FOCUS IN DEVELOPMENTAL STIMULATION FOWLER, WILLIAM, *MERRILL-PALMER QUART*, V15 N2, PP157-70, 69 APR
PAPER, REVISED FOR PUBLICATION, PRESENTED AT A SYMPOSIUM ON HEREDITY AND ENVIRONMENT (AERA, NEW YORK CITY, FEB. 16, 1967)

EJ 006 922 PS 500 097
OF DREAMS AND REALITY: KIBBUTZ CHILDREN RABIN, ALBERT I., *CHILDREN*, V16 N4, PP160-62, 69 JUL-AUG

EJ 006 980 PS 500 045
CHILDREN UNDER THREE - FINDING WAYS TO STIMULATE DEVELOPMENT. I. ISSUES IN RESEARCH MURPHY, LOIS BARCLAY, *CHILDREN*, V16 N2, PP46-52, 69 MAR-APR

EJ 006 981 PS 500 061
AN ESSAY FOR TEACHERS KAGAN, JEROME, *YOUNG CHILDREN*, V24 N3, PP132-42, 69 JAN
ADDRESS PRESENTED AT THE NATIONAL ASSOC. FOR THE EDUCATION OF YOUNG CHILDREN (NEW YORK, N.Y., NOVEMBER 6, 1968)

EJ 006 982 PS 500 064
A MOBILE PRESCHOOL LIPSON, ROSELLA, *YOUNG CHILDREN*, V24 N3, PP154-56, 69 JAN

EJ 006 983 PS 500 067
CHALLENGES AHEAD FOR EARLY CHILDHOOD EDUCATION BIBER, BARBARA, *YOUNG CHILDREN*, V24 N4, PP196-205, 69 MAR
BASED ON A SPEECH PRESENTED AT THE NATIONAL ASSOCIATION FOR THE EDUCATION OF YOUNG CHILDREN (NEW YORK, N.Y., NOVEMBER 9, 1968)

EJ 006 984 PS 500 080
CRUCIAL ISSUES IN CONTEMPORARY EARLY CHILDHOOD EDUCATION MARGOLIN, EDYTHE, *CHILDHOOD EDUC*, V45 N9, PP500-04, 69 MAY

EJ 007 047 PS 500 066
EVALUATION OF EDUCATIONAL PROGRAMS FRANK, LAWRENCE K., *YOUNG CHILDREN*, V24 N3, PP167-74, 69 JAN

EJ 007 062 PS 500 084
CUES FOR OBSERVING CHILDREN'S BEHAVIOR DOWLEY, EDITH, *CHILDHOOD EDUC*, V45 N9, PP517-21, 69 MAY

EJ 007 071 PS 500 079
CREATIVE LEARNING IN CHILDREN'S PLAYGROUNDS GREY, ALEXANDER, *CHILDHOOD EDUC*, V45 N9, PP491-99, 69 MAY

EJ 007 089 PS 500 051
PARENT AND CHILD CENTERS--WHAT THEY ARE, WHERE THEY ARE GOING KELIHER, ALICE V., *CHILDREN*, V16 N2, PP63-66, 69 MAR-APR

EJ 007 090 PS 500 054
THE 4-C PROGRAM SUGARMAN, JULE M., *CHILDREN*, V16 N2, PP76-77, 69 MAR-APR

EJ 007 091 PS 500 071
STATEMENT BY THE PRESIDENT ON THE ESTABLISHMENT OF AN OFFICE OF CHILD DEVELOPMENT NIXON, RICHARD M., *YOUNG CHILDREN*, V24 N5, PP262-64, 69 MAY

EJ 007 092 PS 500 093
A NEW LOOK AT THE COURTS AND CHILDREN'S RIGHTS WADLINGTON, WALTER, *CHILDREN*, V16 N4, PP138-42, 69 JUL-AUG

EJ 007 161 PS 500 052
COMBATING MALNUTRITION THROUGH MATERNAL AND CHILD HEALTH PROGRAMS EGAN, MARY C., *CHILDREN*, V16 N2, PP67-71, 69 MAR-APR
BASED ON A PAPER PRESENTED AT THE ANNUAL MEETING OF THE AMERICAN PUBLIC HEALTH ASSOCIATION, DETROIT, MICHIGAN, NOVEMBER, 1968

EJ 007 162 PS 500 053
NEW ZEALAND'S DENTAL SERVICE FOR CHILDREN ESPIE, J. G., *CHILDREN*, V16 N2, PP72-75, 69 MAR-APR

EJ 007 163 PS 500 055
RUBELLA AND ITS AFTERMATH HARDY, JANET B., *CHILDREN*, V16 N3, PP90-96, 69 MAY-JUN

EJ 007 164 PS 500 056
PLANNING FOR A MASS ATTACK ON RUBELLA CHENOWETH, ALICE D., *CHILDREN*, V16 N3, PP94-95, 69 MAY-JUN

EJ 007 165 PS 500 092
PROMOTING CHILD HEALTH THROUGH COMPREHENSIVE CARE CLOSE, KATHRYN, *CHILDREN*, V16 N4, PP130-37, 69 JUL-AUG

EJ 007 178 PS 500 082
IS THERE A LITERATURE FOR THE DISADVANTAGED CHILD? SEABERG, DOROTHY I., *CHILDHOOD EDUC*, V45 N9, PP508-12, 69 MAY

EJ 007 205 PS 500 073
FIRST STEPS IN SCHOOL HICKS, RUTH; SINCLAIR, WARD, *YOUNG CHILDREN*, V24 N5, PP273-74, 69 MAY

EJ 007 214 PS 500 075
DISTORTIONS IN THE KINDERGARTEN HARRIS, BEECHER H.; FISCHER, ROBERT J., *YOUNG CHILDREN*, V24 N5, PP279-84, 69 MAY

EJ 007 220 PS 500 085
THE CHILD WHO STUTTERS POTTER, ROBERT E., *CHILDHOOD EDUC*, V45 N9, PP522-24, 69 MAY

EJ 007 221 PS 500 086
THE BILINGUAL CHILD MEYERSON, MARION D., *CHILDHOOD EDUC*, V45 N9, PP525-27, 69 MAY

EJ 007 273 PS 500 062
NUMBER GAMES WITH YOUNG CHILDREN HEARD, IDA MAE, *YOUNG CHILDREN*, V24 N3, PP147-50, 69 JAN

EJ 007 274 PS 500 076
BOOKS WHICH GIVE MATHEMATICAL CONCEPTS TO YOUNG CHILDREN: AN ANNOTATED BIBLIOGRAPHY MCINTYRE, MARGARET, *YOUNG CHILDREN*, V24 N5, PP287-91, 69 MAY

EJ 007 301 PS 500 078
NURSES GAIN FROM FIELD WORK WITH YOUNG CHILDREN MAYNARD, MARJORIE; DONDERO, ANNE E., *YOUNG CHILDREN*, V24 N5, PP298-308, 69 MAY

EJ 007 311 PS 500 063
ACTIVITIES TO TEACH THE CONCEPT OF CONSERVATION FEIGENBAUM, KENNETH, *YOUNG CHILDREN*, V24 N3, PP151-53, 69 JAN

EJ 007 316 PS 500 069
PLAY FOR HOSPITALIZED CHILDREN BROOKS, MARY M., *YOUNG CHILDREN*, V24 N4, PP219-24, 69 MAR

EJ 007 362 PS 500 057
ON BEING A WHITEY IN THE MIDST OF A RACIAL CRISIS MIDDLEMAN, RUTH R., *CHILDREN*, V16 N3, PP97-102, 69 MAY-JUN

EJ 007 363 PS 500 077
A NONSEGREGATED APPROACH TO HEAD START FREIS, RUTH; AND OTHERS, *YOUNG CHILDREN*, V24 N5, PP292-96, 69 MAY

EJ 007 408 PS 500 046
CHILDREN UNDER THREE - FINDING WAYS TO STIMULATE DEVELOPMENT. II. SOME CURRENT EXPERIMENTS: A THREE PRONGED PROJECT PROVENCE, SALLY, *CHILDREN*, V16 N2, PP53-55, 69 MAR-APR

EJ 007 409 PS 500 047
CHILDREN UNDER THREE - FINDING WAYS TO STIMULATE DEVELOPMENT. II. SOME CURRENT EXPERIMENTS: LEARNING AT TWO PALMER, FRANCIS H., *CHILDREN*, V16 N2, PP55-57, 69 MAR-APR

EJ 007 410 PS 500 048
CHILDREN UNDER THREE - FINDING WAYS TO STIMULATE DEVELOPMENT. II. SOME CURRENT EXPERIMENTS: STIMULATION VIA PARENT EDUCATION GORDON, IRA J., *CHILDREN*, V16 N2, PP57-59, 69 MAR-APR

EJ 007 411 PS 500 049
CHILDREN UNDER THREE - FINDING WAYS TO STIMULATE DEVELOPMENT. II. SOME CURRENT EXPERIMENTS: A HOME TUTORING PROGRAM SCHAEFER, EARL S., *CHILDREN*, V16 N2, PP59-61, 69 MAR-APR

EJ 007 412 PS 500 050
CHILDREN UNDER THREE - FINDING WAYS TO STIMULATE DEVELOPMENT. II. SOME CURRENT EXPERIMENTS: FROM INFANCY THROUGH SCHOOL ROBINSON, HALBERT B., *CHILDREN*, V16 N2, PP61-62, 69 MAR-APR

EJ 007 413 PS 500 094
INFORMED CONSENT IN PEDIATRIC RESEARCH LEWIS, MELVIN; AND OTHERS, *CHILDREN*, V16 N4, PP143-48, 69 JUL-AUG

EJ 007 425 PS 500 083
BING NURSERY SCHOOL , *CHILDHOOD EDUC*, V45 N9, PP513-16, 69 MAY

EJ 007 431 PS 500 091
SELF-DISCLOSURE AND RELATIONSHIP TO THE TARGET PERSON PEDERSEN, DARHL M.; HIGBEE, KENNETH L., *MERRILL-PALMER QUART*, V15 N2, PP213-20, 69 APR

EJ 007 444 PS 500 058
AGGRESSIVE GROUP WORK WITH TEENAGE DELINQUENT BOYS GROB, HARRY E., JR.; VAN DOREN, ERIC E., *CHILDREN*, V16 N3, PP103-08, 69 MAY-JUN

EJ 007 445 PS 500 059
SERVICES TO CHILDREN LIVING WITH RELATIVES OR GUARDIANS HUGHES, SHIRLEY L., *CHILDREN*, V16 N3, PP109-13, 69 MAY-JUN

EJ 007 446 PS 500 060
PARENTAL AND COMMUNITY NEGLECT--TWIN RESPONSIBILITIES OF PROTECTIVE SERVICES LEWIS, HAROLD, *CHILDREN*, V16 N3, PP114-18, 69 MAY-JUN

EJ 007 447 PS 500 072
UPBRINGING OF CHILDREN IN KIBBUTZIM OF ISRAEL BRANDWINE, ALIZA, *YOUNG CHILDREN*, V24 N5, PP265-72, 69 MAY

EJ 007 448 PS 500 074
NEW OPPORTUNITIES IN DAY CARE: AN INTERVIEW WITH GERTRUDE HOFFMANN , *YOUNG CHILDREN*, V24 N5, PP275-78, 69 MAY

EJ 007 449 PS 500 088
KINSHIP INTERACTION AND MARITAL SOLIDARITY BLOOD, ROBERT O., *MERRILL-PALMER QUART*, V15 N2, PP171-84, 69 APR

EJ 007 450 PS 500 090
ADOLESCENT NORMS AND BEHAVIOR: ORGANIZATION AND CONFORMITY GOODMAN, NORMAN, *MERRILL-PALMER QUART*, V15 N2, PP199-211, 69 APR
AN EARLIER VERSION OF THIS PAPER WAS PRESENTED AT THE ANNUAL MEETING OF THE AMERICAN SOCIOLOGICAL ASSOC. (SAN FRANCISCO, CALIF., AUG. 29, 1967)

EJ 007 451 PS 500 095
INVOLVING PARENTS IN THEIR CHILDREN'S DAY-CARE EXPERIENCES LARRABEE, MARGERY M., *CHILDREN*, V16 N4, PP149-54, 69 JUL-AUG

EJ 007 452 PS 500 096
FAMILIES OF CHILDREN IN FOSTER CARE JENKINS, SHIRLEY; NORMAN, ELAINE, *CHILDREN*, V16 N4, PP155-59, 69 JUL-AUG

EJ 007 690 PS 500 099
SEX DIFFERENCES IN CHILDREN'S MODES OF AGGRESSIVE RESPONSES TOWARD OUTSIDERS FESHBACH, NORMA D., *MERRILL-PALMER QUART*, V15 N3, PP249-58, 69 JUL

EJ 007 691 PS 500 100
SOCIAL REINFORCEMENT FOR EXPRESSION VS. SUPPRESSION OF AGGRESSION NELSEN, EDWARD A., *MERRILL-PALMER QUART*, V15 N3, PP259-78, 69 JUL
THIS PAPER IS BASED UPON A THESIS SUBMITTED IN PARTIAL FULFILLMENT OF THE REQUIREMENTS FOR THE PH.D. AT STANFORD UNIVERSITY

EJ 007 713 PS 500 105
A HOTLINE TELEPHONE SERVICE FOR YOUNG PEOPLE IN CRISIS GARELL, DALE C., *CHILDREN*, V16 N5, PP177-80, 69 SEP-OCT

EJ 007 727 PS 500 109
WORKING WITH FAMILIES OF DELINQUENT BOYS O'NEIL, CARLE F., *CHILDREN*, V16 N5, PP198-202, 69 SEP-OCT

EJ 007 790 PS 500 103
OR PSYCHOANALYTIC THEORY OF ADOLESCENCE? TOOLEY, KAY, *MERRILL-PALMER QUART*, V15 N3, PP305-6, 69 JUL

EJ 007 791 PS 500 118
THE ECOLOGY OF GROWTH AND DEVELOPMENT IN A MEXICAN PREINDUSTRIAL COMMUNITY. REPORT 1: METHOD AND FINDINGS FROM BIRTH TO ONE MONTH OF AGE CRAVIOTO, J.; AND OTHERS, *MONOGR SOC RES CHILD DEVELOP*, V34 N5, PP1-76, 69 AUG

EJ 007 875 PS 500 107
A SCHOOL GUIDANCE CLASS FOR EMOTIONALLY DISTURBED CHILDREN LEHRMAN, WENDY, *CHILDREN*, V16 N5, PP187-91, 69 SEP-OCT

EJ 007 876 PS 500 112
A ROOM PLANNED BY CHILDREN PFLUGER, LUTHER W.; ZOLA, JESSIE M., *YOUNG CHILDREN*, V24 N6, PP337-41, 69 SEP

EJ 008 042 PS 500 106
COMPREHENSIVE CHILD PSYCHIATRY THROUGH A TEAM APPROACH LIVINGSTONE, JOHN B.; AND OTHERS, *CHILDREN*, V16 N5, PP181-86, 69 SEP-OCT

EJ 008 043 PS 500 111
AN INTERVIEW WITH ANN DEHUFF PETERS , *YOUNG CHILDREN*, V24 N6, PP334-36, 69 SEP

EJ 008 119 PS 500 117
AN APPROACH TO LANGUAGE LEARNING LAVATELLI, CELIA STENDLER, *YOUNG CHILDREN*, V24 N6, PP368-76, 69 SEP

EJ 008 171 PS 500 102
ESSAYS ON EQUILIBRIUM SHANTZ, CAROLYN UHLINGER, *MERRILL-PALMER QUART*, V15 N3, PP295-304, 69 JUL

EJ 008 172 PS 500 113
CHILDREN AND TEACHERS IN TWO TYPES OF HEAD START CLASSES KATZ, LILIAN G., *YOUNG CHILDREN*, V24 N6, PP342-49, 69 SEP

EJ 008 263 PS 500 116
"TUBE" PLAY TAYLOR, T. WILLIAM, *YOUNG CHILDREN*, V24 N6, PP364-67, 69 SEP

EJ 008 272 PS 500 101
THE EFFECT OF A STRUCTURED TUTORIAL PROGRAM ON THE COGNITIVE AND LANGUAGE DEVELOPMENT OF CULTURALLY DISADVANTAGED INFANTS PAINTER, GENEVIEVE, *MERRILL-PALMER QUART*, V15 N3, PP279-94, 69 JUL
THE RESEARCH PROJECT IS BEING SUPPORTED BY A GRANT FROM THE BUREAU OF RESEARCH, U.S. OFFICE OF EDUCATION (OEC 6-10-235)

EJ 008 273 PS 500 110
HEAD START IN ALASKA SHELDON, BERNICE S., *YOUNG CHILDREN*, V24 N6, PP329-33, 69 SEP

EJ 008 274 PS 500 114
COMPARISON OF VERBAL INTERACTION IN TWO PRESCHOOL PROGRAMS SEIFERT, KELVIN, *YOUNG CHILDREN*, V24 N6, PP350-55, 69 SEP
THIS STUDY WAS MADE ON BEHALF OF THE FOREIGN LANGUAGE INNOVATIVE CURRICULA STUDY, ANN ARBOR, MICHIGAN

EJ 008 318 PS 500 098
EARLY ANTECEDENTS OF ROLE-TAKING AND ROLE-PLAYING ABILITY KERCKHOFF, ALAN C., *MERRILL-PALMER QUART*, V15 N3, PP229-47, 69 JUL

EJ 008 319 PS 500 108
COMBINING SOCIAL CASEWORK AND GROUP WORK METHODS IN A CHILDREN'S HOSPITAL HAGBERG, KATHERINE L., *CHILDREN*, V16 N5, PP192-97, 69 SEP-OCT

EJ 008 461 PS 500 104
BLACK IDENTITY AND THE HELPING PERSON BRIELAND, DONALD, *CHILDREN*, V16 N5, PP170-76, 69 SEP-OCT

EJ 008 462 PS 500 115
INFANT EDUCATION: A COMMUNITY PROJECT STABENAU, JOAN C.; AND OTHERS, *YOUNG CHILDREN*, V24 N6, PP358-63, 69 SEP

EJ 008 780 PS 500 119
A DEVELOPMENTAL INVESTIGATION OF VISUAL AND HAPTIC PREFERENCES FOR SHAPE AND TEXTURE GLINER, CYNTHIA R.; AND OTHERS, *MONGR SOC RES CHILD DEVELOP*, V34 N6, PP1-40, 69 SEP

EJ 009 029 PS 500 120
LOOKING FORWARD TO THE SEVENTIES ALLEN, JAMES E., JR., *CHILDHOOD EDUC*, V46 N1, PP3, 69 SEP-OCT

EJ 009 030 PS 500 121
THE SEVENTIES: A TIME FOR GIANT STEPS FROST, JOE L.; ROWLAND, G. THOMAS, *CHILDHOOD EDUC*, V46 N1, PP4-13, 69 SEP-OCT
REPRINT FROM CURRICULA FOR THE SEVENTIES: EARLY CHILDHOOD THROUGH EARLY ADOLESCENCE, PP. 431-442, BOSTON, MASS., HOUGHTON MIFFLIN CO., 1969

EJ 009 031 PS 500 122
WHAT'S AHEAD IN TEACHER EDUCATION? DAVIES, DON, *CHILDHOOD EDUC*, V46 N1, PP14-16, 69 SEP-OCT

EJ 009 032 PS 500 123
TWO CONGRESSMEN LOOK AT AMERICAN EDUCATION PELL, CLAIBORNE; QUIE, ALBERT H., *CHILDHOOD EDUC*, V46 N1, PP17-21, 69 SEP-OCT

EJ 009 033 PS 500 124
LABOR AND EDUCATION PETERSON, ESTHER, *CHILDHOOD EDUC*, V46 N1, PP22-23, 69 SEP-OCT

EJ 009 034 PS 500 125
WHAT'S AHEAD FOR PREADOLESCENCE? FRASER, DAVID W., *CHILDHOOD EDUC*, V46 N1, PP24-28, 69 SEP-OCT

EJ 009 815 PS 500 126
A DAY CARE PROGRAM IN THE MIDDLE EAST PETERS, EVELYN, *CHILDHOOD EDUC*, V46 N1, PP29-33, 69 SEP-OCT

EJ 010 125 PS 500 130
THE CARE AND EDUCATION OF PRESCHOOL NONWHITES IN THE REPUBLIC OF SOUTH AFRICA IRELAND, RALPH R., *YOUNG CHILDREN*, V25 N1, PP23-29, 69 OCT
DESCRIBES HOW THE BANTU, FIVE-SIXTHS OF THE SOUTH AFRICAN POPULATION, OPERATE 120 NURSERY SCHOOLS FOR WORKING MOTHERS' CHILDREN. SEPARATE FROM WHITE FACILITIES, THE SCHOOLS EMPHASIZE PERSONAL HYGIENE, PLAY AND TASK ACTIVITIES, AND KNOWLEDGE OF BANTU AND WHITE CULTURES. (DR)

EJ 010 312 PS 500 139
BODY SIZE OF CONTEMPORARY YOUTH IN DIFFERENT PARTS OF THE WORLD MEREDITH, HOWARD V., *MONOGR SOC RES CHILD DEVELOP*, V34 N7, PP1-120, 69 OCT
BASED ON BODY SIZE MEASUREMENTS ACCUMULATED BETWEEN 1950-1960, COMPARISONS WERE MADE OF 13-YEAR-OLD GIRLS AND 15-YEAR-OLD BOYS FROM NORTH AND SOUTH AMERICA, NORTHERN, CENTRAL, AND SOUTHWEST ASIA, OCEANIA, AUSTRALIA, AFRICA, THE NEAR EAST, AND EUROPE. (DO)

EJ 010 443 PS 500 128
WHAT IS LEARNED AND WHAT IS TAUGHT CHITTENDEN, EDWARD A., *YOUNG CHILDREN*, V25 N1, PP12-19, 69 OCT
DESCRIBES RESEARCH ON PIAGET'S THEORIES ON THE IMPORTANCE OF EXPLORATION, USE OF CONCRETE OBJECTS, AND SELF-DIRECTED LEARNING FOR CHILDREN. RELATES THE CONCEPTS OF CONSTRUCTION AND INSTRUCTION TO EDUCATIONAL MODELS AND TEACHING ROLES. (DR)

EJ 010 444 PS 500 131
THE KINDNESSES OF CHILDREN ROSENHAN, DAVID, *YOUNG CHILDREN*, V25 N1, PP30-44, 69 OCT
REVIEWS RESEARCH ON PROSOCIAL BEHAVIORS (KINDNESSES) IN CHILDREN. EMPHASIZES EMOTIONAL FACTORS, MODELING, AND MORAL PRINCIPLES IN THE DEVELOPMENT OF PROSOCIAL BEHAVIOR. DISCUSSES THE RELATIONSHIP OF KINDNESS TO COGNITIVE AND SOCIAL BEHAVIOR. EDITOR/DR

EJ 010 588 PS 500 127
FOUNDATIONS FOR GOOD BEGINNINGS MURPHY, LOIS BARCLAY, *YOUNG CHILDREN*, V25 N1, PP5-11, 69 OCT
ENCOURAGES USE OF HEAD START AND COMMUNITY RESOURCES, PROFESSIONALS, AND MOTHERS IN SHAPING CHILDREN'S EARLY EXPERIENCES TO MAXIMIZE EDUCATIONAL POTENTIAL. STRESSES NEED TO GIVE MOTHERS INFORMATION ON CHILD DEVELOPMENT FROM THE PRENATAL PERIOD THROUGH THE PRESCHOOL YEARS. (DR)

EJ 010 653 PS 500 132
L'EDUCATION PRESCOLAIRE ET L'APPRENTISSAGE DE LA LECTURE (PRE SCHOOL EDUCATION AND INTRODUCTION TO READING) FILHO, M. B. LOURENCO, *INT J EARLY CHILDHOOD*, V1 N1, PP5-8, 69
A SERIES OF TESTS MEASURES THE CORRECT STAGE OF MENTAL MATURITY NECESSARY FOR A CHILD TO LEARN TO READ AND WRITE. PURPOSE IS TO PREVENT CHILDREN FROM BEING TAUGHT TO READ IN NURSERY SCHOOLS BEFORE THEY ARE READY. (JF)

EJ 010 859 PS 500 136
FAMILY PROBLEMS CONCERNING THE MENTALLY RETARDED CHILD KLACKENBERG, GUNNAR, *INT J EARLY CHILDHOOD*, V1 N1, PP29-34, 69
A MENTALLY HANDICAPPED CHILD CAUSES FAMILIAL PRESSURES: CONCERNS OVER FUTURE PREGNANCIES, EMOTIONAL STRAIN, AND THE NECESSITY FOR AN ULTIMATE DECISION ON WHETHER OR NOT THE CHILD SHOULD BE INSTITUTIONALIZED. (JF)

EJ 011 253 PS 500 134
SELF-MADE TOYS IN CHILDREN'S GAMES VINCE-BAKONYI, AGNES, *INT J EARLY CHILDHOOD*, V1 N1, PP15-19, 69
A 2-YEAR EXPERIMENT WITH HUNGARIAN KINDERGARTENERS CONCLUDED THAT HANDICRAFT ACTIVITY WHICH EVOLVED OUT OF PLAY EXPERIENCES HAD THE MOST POSITIVE EFFECTS ON DIFFERENT KINDS OF CHILDREN. (JF)

EJ 011 302 PS 500 135
INTRODUCTION OF NEW CHILDREN INTO A DAY CARE CENTER PETERS, EVELYN, *INT J EARLY CHILDHOOD*, V1 N1, PP20-24, 69
SUGGESTIONS FOR TEACHERS TO HELP THEM EASE A CHILD'S TRANSITION FROM HOME AND FAMILY TO A STRANGE DAY CARE CENTER.

EJ 011 344 PS 500 133
CHILD PSYCHOLOGY IN FUTURE SOCIETY SKARD, AASE GRUDA, *INT J EARLY CHILDHOOD*, V1 N1, PP9-14, 69

EJ 011 345 PS 500 137
SLEEP PROBLEMS APLEY, JOHN; MACKEITH, RONALD, *INT J EARLY CHILDHOOD*, V1 N1, PP35-40, 69
EXCERPT FROM CHAPTER IN THE SECOND EDITION OF THEIR BOOK, THE CHILD AND HIS SYMPTOMS, A COMPREHENSIVE APPROACH. GREAT BRITAIN: BLACKWELL SCIENTIFIC PUBLICATIONS

EJ 011 346 PS 500 138
THE ROLE OF WOMEN IN THE DEVELOPMENT OF THEIR COUNTRIES: COMMENTS FROM OMEP ON A QUESTIONNAIRE FROM U.N SKARD, AASE GRUDA, *INT J EARLY CHILDHOOD*, V1 N1, PP42-45, 69
DISCUSSES DOUBLE ROLE OF WOMEN AS MOTHERS AND CONTRIBUTING CITIZENS OF SOCIETY. EMPHASIZES NEED FOR DAY CARE CENTERS TO FREE OLDER GIRLS AND WOMEN FOR EDUCATION AND EMPLOYMENT. (MS)

EJ 011 595 PS 500 129
NUTRITION IN DAY CARE CENTERS ROCKWELL, ROBERT E.; ENDRES, JEANNETTE, *YOUNG CHILDREN*, V25 N1, PP20-22, 69 OCT
LUNCH TIME CAN PROVIDE NUTRITIONALLY ADEQUATE MEALS AND ALSO CREATE SETTINGS IN WHICH CHILDREN LEARN MECHANICAL AND SOCIAL SKILLS. EDITOR/DR

EJ 011 784 PS 500 142
WHAT DO YOUNG PEOPLE WANT? RICHARDS, CATHERINE V., *CHILDREN*, V16 N6, PP223-225, 69 NOV-DEC

EJ 011 785 PS 500 155
PINK IS A GOOD COLOR. ? HANDLER, JUNE MOSS, *CHILDHOOD EDUC*, V46 N2, PP76-8, 69 NOV
ATTITUDES OF RACIAL PREJUDICE MIGHT BE CHANGED IN CHILDREN THROUGH ART EXPERIENCES AS CHILDREN EXPRESS IDEAS AND EMOTIONS IN BLACK AND BROWN COLORS. (JF)

EJ 011 823 PS 500 156
THE POVERTY CULTURE BRADSHAW, CAROL E., *CHILDHOOD EDUC*, V46 N2, PP79-84, 69 NOV
ENVIRONMENT AND BEHAVIOR OF DISADVANTAGED RURAL FAMILIES AFFECT THE GROWTH AND DEVELOPMENT OF CHILDREN. SPECIFICALLY, INFANT PUNISHMENT, REWARDING BEHAVIOR, SIBLING INDEPENDENCE, HEALTH, HOUSING, AND WORKING MOTHERS ARE DISCUSSED. (THIS STUDY WAS SUPPORTED IN PART BY A GRANT (RE: IF 4-NU-27,028-01) FROM THE DIV. OF NURSING, HEW) (JF)

EJ 011 838 PS 500 141
COMMUNICATING WITH TODAY'S TEENAGERS; AN EXERCISE BETWEEN GENERATIONS SCHINDLER-RAINMAN, EVA, *CHILDREN*, V16 N6, PP218-223, 69 NOV-DEC
A ONE WEEK "COURSE-HAPPENING" INVOLVING ADULTS AND TEENAGERS USED SELF-INQUIRY, ROLE PLAYING, AND GROUP DISCUSSIONS TO DEVELOP INTERGENERATIONAL COMMUNICATION AND UNDERSTANDING. TECHNIQUES AND RESULTS ARE DISCUSSED. (DR)

EJ 011 839 PS 500 159
THE RELATIONSHIP BETWEEN THE TEACHER AND THE TAUGHT. FIRST IMPRESSIONS OF A STUDENT TEACHER ASCHER, MICHELLE, *CHILDHOOD EDUC*, V46 N2, PP93-5, 69 NOV

EJ 011 840 PS 500 160
ON VALUING DIVERSITY IN LANGUAGE GOODMAN, KENNETH S., *CHILDHOOD EDUC*, V46 N3, PP123-26, 69 DEC
WHEN EDUCATORS IMPOSE THEIR OWN LANGUAGE FORMS ON CHILDREN THEY CREATE LEARNING DISABILITIES. ACCEPTANCE AND USE OF DIFFERENCES IN CHILDREN'S LANGUAGE AND EXPERIENCE CAN INSTEAD AID GROWTH. (DR)

EJ 011 841 PS 500 162
TOO MUCH SHUSHING - LET CHILDREN TALK BROMAN, BETTY L., *CHILDHOOD EDUC*, V46 N3, PP132-34, 69 DEC
SUGGESTIONS AND SPECIFIC TEACHING TECHNIQUES FOR LANGUAGE GROWTH ADAPTABLE TO THE CLASSROOM. LISTS ACTIVITIES STRESSING LANGUAGE SKILLS TO ENCOURAGE COMMUNICATION. (DR)

EJ 011 842 PS 500 163
EXPERIENCES AND LANGUAGE DEVELOPMENT NIELSEN, WILHELMINE R., *CHILDHOOD EDUC*, V46 N3, PP135-38, 69 DEC
USE OF DIRECT EXPERIENCES FOR CHILDREN TO FOSTER LEARNING AND LANGUAGE DEVELOPMENT IS ENCOURAGED. CLASSROOM MATERIALS AND STUDY TRIPS ARE SUGGESTED. (DR)

EJ 011 843 PS 500 165
COMO CONTESTAN LOS PADRES LAS PREGUNTAS DE SUS NINOS? (HOW DO PARENTS RESPOND TO CHILDREN'S QUESTIONS?) LESHAN, EDA J., *CHILDHOOD EDUC*, V46 N3, PP146-48, 69 DEC
THIS ARTICLE, TRANSLATED BY LUZ S. GONZALEZ GOMEZ, FIRST APPEARED IN AN ENGLISH VERSION IN THE OCTOBER 1968 ISSUE OF CHILDHOOD EDUC (P. 79-82). (DR)

EJ 011 844 PS 500 167
BRINGING THEIR OWN: LANGUAGE DEVELOPMENT IN THE MIDDLE GRADES HORNBURGER, JANE M., *CHILDHOOD EDUC*, V46 N3, PP155-57, 69 DEC
ENCOURAGES THE TEACHER TO ACCEPT THE DISADVANTAGED CHILD'S LANGUAGE. LISTS SELECTED REFERENCES TO HELP DEVELOP LANGUAGE SKILLS. (DR)

EJ 011 845 PS 500 168
THE ELEMENTS OF EFFECTIVE COMMUNICATION HUNTER, MADELINE, *CHILDHOOD EDUC*, V46 N3, PP158-61, 69 DEC
EXPLAINS ELEMENTS OF HELPING CHILDREN COMMUNICATE: (1) RECOGNIZE THE NEED FOR CHILD SENDING A MESSAGE, (2) HELP HIM TO PUT THE MESSAGE INTO LANGUAGE, (3) ALLOW TRANSMISSION OF THE MESSAGE, AND (4) DECODE THE MESSAGE. (DR)

EJ 011 874 PS 500 164
LANGUAGE LEARNING AT ROUGH ROCK HOFFMAN, VIRGINIA, *CHILDHOOD EDUC*, V46 N3, PP139-45, 69 DEC
DESCRIBES A BILINGUAL, BICULTURAL CURRICULUM IN A RESERVATION SCHOOL, COURSES ON NAVAJO CULTURE, ENGLISH AND NAVAJO READING PROGRAMS; AND OPPORTUNITIES FOR PARENT PARTICIPATION. (DR)

EJ 011 914 PS 500 140
EARLY MALNUTRITION AND HUMAN DEVELOPMENT DAYTON, DELBERT H., *CHILDREN*, V16 N6, PP210-217, 69 NOV-DEC
RELATES STUDIES OF THE EFFECTS OF PRE- AND POST-NATAL AND CHILDHOOD MALNUTRITION ON PHYSICAL AND MENTAL DEVELOPMENT. DISCUSSES NATIONAL AND INTERNATIONAL NUTRITION PROBLEMS AND SOLUTIONS. (DR)

EJ 011 915 PS 500 148
PIAGET MISUNDERSTOOD: A CRITIQUE OF THE CRITICISMS OF HIS THEORY OF MORAL DEVELOPMENT LICKONA, THOMAS, *MERRILL-PALMER QUART*, V15 N4, PP337-50, 69 OCT
A DEFENCE OF PIAGET'S THEORY OF MORAL DEVELOPMENT AGAINST MISUNDERSTANDINGS OF HIS OVEREMPHASIS ON GENETIC MATURATION, UNDEREMPHASIS ON ROLE OF INTELLIGENCE, AND IMPOSITION OF A "UNIVERSAL" ORDER. (MH)

EJ 011 916 PS 500 149
STAGES OF SENSORIMOTOR DEVELOPMENT: A REPLICATION STUDY CORMAN, HARVEY H.; ESCALONA, SIBYLLE K., *MERRILL-PALMER QUART*, V15 N4, PP351-61, 69 OCT
PIAGET'S THEORY OF STAGES OF SENSORIMOTOR DEVELOPMENT IS SUPPORTED IN CROSS-SECTIONAL AND LONGITUDINAL VALIDATION EMPLOYING GUTTMAN'S SCALOGRAM ANALYSIS. (MH)

EJ 011 917 PS 500 150
A DEVELOPMENTAL STUDY OF NONCONSERVATION CHOICES IN YOUNG CHILDREN ROTHENBERG, BARBARA B.; COURTNEY, ROSALEA G., *MERRILL-PALMER QUART*, V15 N4, PP363-73, 69 OCT
THIS STUDY WAS SUPPORTED BY A GRANT FROM THE CARNEGIE CORPORATION TO EDUCATIONAL TESTING SERVICE. (MH)

EJ 011 982 PS 500 153
THE IMPACT OF CHANGE GOODMAN, MARY ELLEN, *CHILDHOOD EDUC*, V46 N2, PP67-72, 69 NOV
KEYNOTE ADDRESS DELIVERED AT THE ACEI STUDY CONFERENCE, HOUSTON, TEXAS, APRIL 7, 1969. (JF)

EJ 011 983 PS 500 154
THE IMPACT OF CHANGE. A REBUTTAL ADAMS, PAUL L., *CHILDHOOD EDUC*, V46 N2, PP73-74, 69 NOV
A REJOINDER STATEMENT TO M.L. GOODMAN'S KEYNOTE ADDRESS GIVEN AT THE ACEI STUDY CONFERENCE, HOUSTON, TEXAS, APRIL 8, 1969. (JF)

EJ 011 984 PS 500 158
FREEDOM OF CHOICE- WHO'S KIDDING WHOM?; FREEDOM-CHOICE AND RESPONSIBILITY. A SYMPOSIUM COURSON, CLIFFORD C.; RUTHERFORD, RICHARD, *CHILDHOOD EDUC*, V46 N2, PP88-92, 69 NOV

EJ 012 199 PS 500 144
RETARDED CHILDREN AT CAMP WITH NORMAL CHILDREN FLAX, NORMAN; PETERS, EDWARD N., *CHILDREN*, V16 N6, PP232-237, 69 NOV-DEC
STATISTICAL ANALYSIS OF DATA FROM WRITTEN FORMS AND SCALES (DESIGNED TO MEASURE CHILDREN'S BEHAVIOR IN GROUPS), OBSERVATIONS, AND INTERVIEWS INDICATED THAT MANY EDUCALBLE MENTALLY RETARDED CHILDREN CAN PARTICIPATE SUCCESSFULLY IN CAMP ACTIVITIES WITH NORMAL CHILDREN. (DR)

EJ 012 207 PS 500 151
EARLY MALNUTRITION AND CENTRAL NERVOUS SYSTEM FUNCTION SCRIMSHAW, NEVIN S., *MERRILL-PALMER QUART*, V15 N4, PP375-88, 69 OCT
DISCUSSES THE CONSEQUENCES OF SEVERE MALNUTRITION IN YOUNG EXPERIMENTAL ANIMALS. DEVELOPMENT OF THE BRAIN IS PERMANENTLY IMPAIRED. STUDIES OF THE EFFECTS OF MALNUTRITION ON CHILDREN ARE INCLUDED. (THIS PAPER WAS PRESENTED AT THE EIGHTH ANNUAL LECTURE OF THE MERRILL-PALMER HISTORICAL LIBRARY IN CHILD DEVELOPMENT AND FAMILY LIFE, OCTOBER 25, 1968.) (MH)

EJ 012 396 PS 500 161
SUGGESTIONS FROM STUDIES OF EARLY LANGUAGE ACQUISITION CAZDEN, COURTNEY B., *CHILDHOOD EDUC*, V46 N3, PP127-31, 69 DEC
OVERVIEW OF CURRENT RESEARCH ON HOW CHILDREN LEARN THEIR NATIVE LANGUAGE BEFORE SCHOOL. IMPLICATIONS TO AID LEARNING IN SCHOOL ARE DISCUSSED. (DR)

EJ 012 397 PS 500 166
MEXICAN-AMERICANS AND LANGUAGE LEARNING ARNOLD, RICHARD D.; TAYLOR, THOMASINE H, *CHILDHOOD EDUC*, V46 N3, PP149-54, 69 DEC

EJ 012 579 PS 500 143
FAMILY TIES AND THE INSTITUTIONAL CHILD MEYER, MARGRIT, *CHILDREN*, V16 N6, PP226-231, 69 NOV-DEC
GIVES SUGGESTIONS FOR PLACEMENT AGENCIES' PROCEDURES TO BENEFIT INSTITUTIONALIZED CHILDREN AND THEIR PARENTS. DESCRIBES METHODS FOR DEVELOPING VISITING RELATIONSHIPS AND CHOOSING FOSTER FAMILIES TO ENSURE STABLE AND LASTING ADULT-CHILD RELATIONSHIPS. (DR)

EJ 012 580 PS 500 157
ASK ME SOMETHING I KNOW SELLARS, SOPHIA N., *CHILDHOOD EDUC*, V46 N2, PP85-7, 69 NOV

EJ 012 676 PS 500 145
PSYCHOLOGICAL DEPRIVATION: WHAT WE DO, DON'T, AND SHOULD KNOW ABOUT IT HERZOG, ELIZABETH, *CHILDREN*, V16 N6, PP238-240, 69 NOV-DEC
A REVIEW OF RESEARCH FINDINGS ON BIOLOGICAL, PSYCHOLOGICAL, AND SOCIAL DEPRIVATION PUBLISHED BY THE NATIONAL INSTITUTE OF CHILD HEALTH AND HUMAN DEVELOPMENT. DISCUSSES IMPLICATIONS FOR INTERVENTION PROGRAMS AND FUTURE RESEARCH. (DR)

EJ 012 677 PS 500 169
EDUCATIONAL RESEARCH POLICIES OF SCHOOL DISTRICTS NATIONWIDE GOWAN, JOHN C.; WYETH, EZRA, *CALIF J EDUC RES*, V20 N5, PP204-12, 69 NOV
REPORTS NATIONAL SURVEY RESULTS OF LARGE SCHOOL DISTRICTS' POLICIES ON PARTICIPATING IN RESEARCH PROJECTS ORIGINATING OUTSIDE THE DISTRICT. INCLUDED ARE EXCERPTS FROM SPECIFIC SCHOOL DISTRICT POLICIES AND A REPORT ON DATA ACCESSIBILITY BY WILLIAM G. MONAHAN OF THE UNIVERSITY OF IOWA. (DR)

EJ 012 678 PS 500 170
AN EXPERIMENTAL APPROACH TO THE EFFECT OF GROUP ANIMADVERSION WENZEL, LAWRENCE A., *CALIF J EDUC RES*, V20 N5, PP213-20, 69 NOV
RESULTS OF A STUDY OF THE EFFECTS OF NEGATIVE CRITICISM INDICATED THAT GROUP CRITICISM REDUCES THE COGNITIVE PERFORMANCE OF COLLEGE STUDENTS. (DR)

EJ 012 679 PS 500 171
IMAGES OF THE IDEAL PUPIL HELD BY TEACHERS IN PREPARATION YAMAMOTO, KAORU, *CALIF J EDUC RES*, V20 N5, PP221-33, 69 NOV

EJ 012 717 PS 500 146
LOCATION AS A FEATURE OF INSTRUCTIONAL INTERACTION ADAMS, RAYMOND S., *MERRILL-PALMER QUART*, V15 N4, PP309-21, 69 OCT
AN ANALYSIS OF TEACHER-PUPIL INTERACTION IN GRADES 1,6, AND 11 SHOWED THAT COMMUNICATORY BEHAVIOR WAS CONCENTRATED IN THE FRONT OF THE ROOM AND ALONG THE CENTER AISLE. (PORTIONS OF THE RESEARCH REPORTED WERE SUPPORTED AT THE UNIVERSITY OF MISSOURI BY THE EDUCATIONAL MEDIA BRANCH OF USOE.) (MS)

EJ 012 718 PS 500 147
SIMILARITIES IN VALUES AND OTHER PERSONALITY CHARACTERISTICS IN COLLEGE STUDENTS AND THEIR PARENTS TROLL, LILLIAN E., *MERRILL-PALMER QUART*, V15 N4, PP323-36, 69 OCT
THE GENERATION GAP WAS ANALYZED IN INTERVIEWS OF 100 WHITE COLLEGE STUDENTS AND THEIR PARENTS. INTRA-FAMILIAL SIMILARITIES IN VALUES WERE GREATER THAN IN OTHER DOMAINS, WITH SOMEWHAT GREATER LIKENESS BETWEEN PARENT-PARENT THAN BETWEEN PARENT-CHILD. (THIS STUDY WAS SUPPORTED BY GRANT MH-08062 FROM NIMH, AND WAS PART OF A LARGER STUDY OF TWO-GENERATION FAMILIES UNDERTAKEN BY PROFS. NEUGARTEN OF THE COMM. ON HUMAN DEVELOPMENT AND RICHARD FLACKS OF DEPT. OF SOCIOLOGY, UNIVERSITY OF CHICAGO.) (MH)

EJ 012 719 PS 500 152
SETTING AND THE EMERGENCE OF COMPETENCE DURING ADULT SOCIALIZATION: WORKING AT HOME VS. WORKING "OUT THERE" EZEKIEL, RAPHAEL S., *MERRILL-PALMER QUART*, V15 N4, PP389-96, 69 OCT
EXAMINES THE EMERGENCE OF COMPETENCE AMONG PEACE CORPS VOLUNTEERS AND TRIES TO DETERMINE WHAT CONDITIONS CAUSE SUCH EMERGENCE. CONCLUDES THAT IT IS DUE IN PART TO THE NOVEL SITUATION. (TAKEN IN PART FROM A PAPER DELIVERED AT AM. PSYCHOLOGICAL ASSOC., CHICAGO, SEP 1965. DISCUSSION IS BASED ON A STUDY AT INSTITUTE OF HUMAN DEVELOPMENT, UNIVERSITY OF CALIFORNIA, BERKELEY UNDER CONTRACT NO. PC-(W)-55 WITH THE PEACE CORPS.) (MH)

EJ 012 815 PS 500 177
DIACRITICAL MARKS IN TEXTBOOK ADOPTION JOHNSON, DONNA JEAN, *ELEM SCH J*, V70 N4, PP206-209, 70 JAN
DECRIES LACK OF CONSISTENCY OF DIACRITICAL MARKINGS ACROSS DIFFERENT DICTIONARIES, TEXTBOOKS, ETC; URGES TEXTBOOK COMMITTEES TO KEEP THIS FACTOR IN MIND. (MH)

EJ 012 871 PS 500 174
WHICH PUPILS DO TEACHERS CALL ON? GOOD, THOMAS L., *ELEM SCH J*, V70 N4, PP190-98, 70 JAN
REPORTS ON A STUDY OF TEACHER EXPECTANCY SHOWING THAT TEACHERS GIVE "TALENTED" STUDENTS MORE OPPORTUNITY TO PARTICIPATE IN CLASS, THUS INCREASING THEIR SKILLS, WHILE LOW ACHIEVERS ARE RELATIVELY IGNORED. (MH)

EJ 013 022 PS 500 183
BUILDING ON EXPERIENCES IN LITERATURE PAIGE, MARJORIE L., *YOUNG CHILDREN*, V25 N2, PP85-88, 69 DEC

EJ 013 062 PS 500 195
THE COMPLEXITY OF INFANT DEVELOPMENT. AN ESSAY REVIEW PROVENCE, SALLY, *CHILDREN*, V17 N1, PP31-2, 70 JAN-FEB

EJ 013 227 PS 500 176
TESTING IN THE SCHOOLS: A RESPONSE TO JOHN HOLT SHAPIRO, BERNARD J.; SHAPIRO, PHYLLIS P., *ELEM SCH J*, V70 N4, PP202-205, 70 JAN
OPPOSES HOLT'S SUGGESTION TO ELIMINATE TESTING; STATES THAT THE EVILS HE SUGGESTED ARE NOT INHERENT IN TESTING BUT IN TEST ADMINISTRATION AND INTERPRETATION. SUPPORTS MATERIAL-IMBEDDED TESTS USING UNOBTRUSIVE MEASURES. (MH)

EJ 013 228 PS 500 178
DO STUDENTS' IDEAS AND ATTITUDES SURVIVE PRACTICE TEACHING? WEINSTOCK, HENRY R.; PECCOLO, CHARLES M., *ELEM SCH J*, V70 N4, PP210-18, 70 JAN
ANSWERS TITLE QUESTION AFFIRMATIVELY BUT CONTENDS THAT ELEMENTARY STUDENT TEACHERS ARE MORE LOGICAL AND CONSISTENT IN THEIR IDEAS AND ATTITUDES THAN SECONDARY STUDENT TEACHERS. CURRICULUM CHANGES ARE SUGGESTED FOR TRAINING OF SECONDARY TEACHERS. (MH)

EJ 013 229 PS 500 182
THE EDUCATION OF YOUNG CHILDREN: AT THE CROSSROADS? HEATH, DOUGLAS H., *YOUNG CHILDREN*, V25 N2, PP73-84, 69 DEC
DISCUSSES GAP WHICH HAS DEVELOPED BECAUSE EDUCATORS EMPHASIZE ACADEMIC EXCELLENCE WHILE ADOLESCENTS ARE CHARACTERIZED BY AN INTEREST IN HUMAN VALUES AND GROWING EMOTIONAL ISOLATION. SUGGESTIONS FOR MEETING THE NEEDS OF THIS GENERATION ARE OFFERED. (ADDRESS PRESENTED AT THE 1969 CONFERENCE OF THE NATIONAL ASSOCIATION FOR THE EDUCATION OF YOUNG CHILDREN, SALT LAKE CITY, UTAH, NOVEMBER 12.) (DR)

EJ 013 230 PS 500 184
HIS OWN HELLO HARRIS, CORNELIA C., *YOUNG CHILDREN*, V25 N2, PP89-95, 69 DEC
GIVES REASONS FOR OPPOSING KINDERGARTEN TEACHERS, TEACHING DOUBLE SESSIONS BECAUSE OF RESULTING PROBLEMS RELATING TO CLOSE SCHEDULING, LACK OF SPACE, LACK OF TIME FOR PARENT CONFERENCES AND, INABILITY OF TEACHERS TO ADEQUATELY RESPOND TO INDIVIDUAL CHILDREN'S NEEDS. (DR)

EJ 013 231 PS 500 185
CREATIVE SUPERVISION OF HEAD START CENTERS HATCH, VIRGINIA B., *YOUNG CHILDREN*, V25 N2, PP96-101, 69 DEC
THE JOB OF EDUCATIONAL SUPERVISOR IS OFTEN STEREOTYPED AND DOES NOT PROVIDE FOR COMMUNICATION WITH TEACHERS AND CHILDREN. HEAD START OFFERS AN OPPORTUNITY FOR THE SUPERVISOR TO EFFECTIVELY OBSERVE AND AT THE SAME TIME PARTICIPATE IN THE LEARNING PROCESS AT THE CENTER. (EDITOR/DR)

EJ 013 232 PS 500 187
THE ROLE OF THE PRIMARY TEACHER IN CHARACTER EDUCATION RAINS, SYLVESTER; MORRIS, RUBY, *YOUNG CHILDREN*, V25 N2, PP105-108, 69 DEC

EJ 013 233 PS 500 188
WHAT MOTHERS NEED HENDRICK, JOANNE, *YOUNG CHILDREN*, V25 N2, PP109-114, 69 DEC
DISCUSSES WAYS TO IMPROVE HOME-SCHOOL RELATIONS, STRESSING THAT BOTH TEACHER AND PARENT ARE INTERESTED IN THE CHILD'S WELFARE. ENCOURAGES FREQUENT COMMUNICATION AND CONFERENCES TO DISCUSS GOALS AND PROBLEMS. (DR)

EJ 013 234 PS 500 191
A PRESCHOOL WORKSHOP FOR EMOTIONALLY DISTURBED CHILDREN BLOCH, JUDITH, *CHILDREN*, V17 N1, PP10-14, 70 JAN-FEB

EJ 013 296 PS 500 186
A DOLL CORNER UPSTAIRS NOECKER, ALBERTINE, *YOUNG CHILDREN*, V25 N2, PP102-104, 69 DEC

EJ 013 329 PS 500 193
WHY CHILDREN ARE IN JAIL AND HOW TO KEEP THEM OUT DOWNEY, JOHN J., *CHILDREN*, V17 N1, PP21-26, 70 JAN-FEB
EVALUATES AND ANALYZES DETENTION PROCEDURES AND DESCRIBES FACILITIES REQUIRED TO END CURRENT DEFICIENCIES. (JF)

EJ 013 330 PS 500 194
FACTS AGAINST IMPRESSIONS: MOTHERS SEEKING TO RELINQUISH CHILDREN FOR ADOPTION PLATTS, HAL K., *CHILDREN*, V17 N1, PP27-30, 70 JAN-FEB
DESCRIBES A QUESTIONNAIRE SURVEY ON AGENCY POLICIES BY LOS ANGELES COUNTY DEPARTMENT OF ADOPTIONS WHICH COVERED 1,513 CASES. (JF)

EJ 013 482 PS 500 190
CHILDHOOD LEAD POISONING...AN ERADICABLE DISEASE LIN-FU, JANE S., *CHILDREN*, V17 N1, PP2-9, 70 JAN-FEB
LACK OF AWARENESS AND INADEQUATE HOUSING CODES ARE THE CHIEF CAUSES CONTRIBUTING TO THE PERSISTENCE OF LEAD POISONING AMONG CHILDREN. (JF)

EJ 013 560 PS 500 172
WHAT DO YOU MEAN, "AUDITORY PERCEPTION"? SEYMOUR, DOROTHY, *ELEM SCH J*, V70 N4, PP175-79, 70 JAN
TO CLARIFY THE CONFUSION OF BEGINNING READING TEACHERS AND LINGUISTS ABOUT GOALS AND PROCEDURES OF AUDITORY TRAINING, THIS ARTICLE INTRODUCES PRECISE INSTRUCTION TERMINOLOGY. (MH)

EJ 013 561 PS 500 173
PERSONALIZED EDUCATION IN SOUTHSIDE SCHOOL SPAULDING, ROBERT L., *ELEM SCH J*, V70 N4, PP180-89, 70 JAN
THIS ARTICLE IS BASED ON REMARKS PRESENTED AT THE ANNUAL CONVENTION OF THE NATIONAL SOCIETY FOR PROGRAMMED INSTRUCTION, SHERATON PARK HOTEL, WASH., D.C., APR 10, 1969. URGES PERSONALIZED (NOT JUST INDIVIDUALIZED) INSTRUCTION, IN WHICH RELEVANCY IS ACHIEVED BY HAVING THE STUDENTS THEMSELVES PARTICIPATE IN DECISION MAKING AND DAILY PROGRAMMING. (MH)

EJ 013 562 PS 500 175
FOR BETTER READING - A MORE POSITIVE SELF-IMAGE COHN, MAXINE; KORNELLY, DONALD, *ELEM SCH J*, V70 N4, PP199-201, 70 JAN
UNDERACHIEVERS IN A SEVENTH GRADE CLASS IMPROVE THEIR READING LEVELS THROUGH A PROGRAM OF INDIVIDUAL PACING AND IMMEDIATE POSITIVE FEEDBACK. (MH)

EJ 013 624 PS 500 179
DEVELOPMENTAL SPEECH INACCURACY AND SPEECH THERAPY IN THE EARLY SCHOOL YEARS MORENCY, ANNE S.; AND OTHERS, *ELEM SCH J*, V70 N4, PP219-24, 70 JAN
REPORTS A STUDY THAT INDICATES MANY FUNCTIONAL SPEECH DEFECTS AT THE FIRST GRADE LEVEL ARE MANIFESTATIONS OF SLOW DEVELOPMENT AND SHOULD NOT BE SUBJECT TO THERAPY. (MH)

EJ 013 625 PS 500 180
THE EFFECTS OF INSTRUCTION ON LANGUAGE DEVELOPMENT DAY, DAVID E.; NURSS, JOANNE R., *ELEM SCH J*, V70 N4, PP225-31, 70 JAN
THE STUDY INDICATED SOME SUPERIORITY OF THE BEREITER-ENGELMANN PROGRAM, A STRUCTURED, BEHAVIORISTIC METHOD, OVER TRADITIONAL LANGUAGE INSTRUCTION METHODS. (MH)

EJ 013 800 PS 500 192
GOALS AND METHODS IN A PRESCHOOL PROGRAM FOR DISADVANTAGED CHILDREN BIBER, BARBARA, *CHILDREN*, V17 N1, PP15-20, 70 JAN-FEB
PRIMARY GOALS ARE TO ADVANCE CHILDREN'S ABILITY TO USE LANGUAGE FUNCTIONALLY AND MASTER CONCEPTUAL-COGNITIVE PROCESSES, AND TO DEVELOP POSITIVE SELF-CONCEPTS. (DEVELOPED FROM A PAPER FOR A MEETING OF HEAD START REGIONAL TRAINING OFFICERS.) (JF)

EJ 013 946 PS 500 181
THE PARENTAL ROLE, A FUNCTIONAL-COGNITIVE APPROACH EMMERICH, WALTER, *MONOGR SOC RES CHILD DEVELOP*, V34 N8, PP1-71, 69 NOV
A NOVEL APPROACH THAT CONCEPTUALIZES AND MEASURES A THEORETICALLY DERIVED SET OF PARENTAL ROLE COMPONENTS, CONSIDERS THEIR INTERRELATIONS, AND EXAMINES SOME OF THEIR ATTITUDE AND PERSONALITY CORRELATES. (THIS STUDY WAS SUPPORTED BY PURDUE UNIVERSITY AND BY NICHHD UNDER A RESEARCH GRANT TO EDUCATIONAL TESTING SERVICE.) (AUTHOR/DR)

EJ 013 947 PS 500 189
A DEVELOPMENTAL STUDY OF INFORMATION PROCESSING WITHIN THE FIRST THREE YEARS OF LIFE: RESPONSE DECREMENT TO A REDUNDANT SIGNAL LEWIS, MICHAEL; AND OTHERS, *MONOGR SOC RES CHILD DEVELOP*, V34 N9, PP1-41, 69 DEC
SEVEN EXPERIMENTS STUDY THE DECREASE IN RESPONSE TO REPEATED VISUAL STIMULATION IN CHILDREN'S FIRST FOUR YEARS. (DR)

EJ 014 139 PS 500 225
TELL IT LIKE IT IS FERGUSON, BESS, *YOUNG CHILDREN*, V25 N3, PP159-161, 70 JAN
SUGGESTIONS FOR WELL-WRITTEN NEWSPAPER ARTICLES THAT INFORM THE COMMUNITY AND PUBLICIZE THE NURSERY SCHOOL OR DAY CARE CENTER. (DR)

EJ 014 228 PS 500 202
SHOULD EDUCATIONAL OBJECTIVES BE STATED IN BEHAVIORAL TERMS? - PART III OJEMANN, RALPH H., *ELEM SCH J*, V70 N5, PP271-78, 70 FEB
EXPLAINS HOW THE OBSERVATION OF OVERT BEHAVIOR CAN BE USED AS AN INDICATOR OF KNOWLEDGE OF CONCEPTS OR OTHER INTERNAL CHANGES IN LEARNING. (AUTHOR/DR)

EJ 014 292 PS 500 200
VISIT TO A MISSION SCHOOL FOR ABORIGINAL CHILDREN WOLMAN, MARIANNE, *ELEM SCH J*, V70 N5, PP261-64, 70 FEB
EMPHASIZES THE EFFECT OF SOCIAL VALUES AND TEACHER EXPECTATIONS ON CHILDREN'S SCHOLASTIC SUCCESS. (DR)

EJ 014 306 PS 500 199
BEHAVIORAL SCIENCE FOR ELEMENTARY-SCHOOL PUPILS LONG, BARBARA ELLIS, *ELEM SCH J*, V70 N5, PP253-60, 70 FEB
DESCRIBES A BEHAVIORAL SCIENCE-MENTAL HEALTH CURRICULUM WHICH USES AN EXPERIMENTAL, NON-DIRECTIVE APPROACH AND MOVES FROM SPECIFIC EXPERIENCE TO ABSTRACT PRINCIPLES. (DR)

EJ 014 433 PS 500 196
WANTED: RX FOR THE EQUITABLE MANAGEMENT OF PARENT-SCHOOL CONFLICT FIRESTER, LEE; FIRESTER, JOAN, *ELEM SCH J*, V70 N5, PP239-43, 70 FEB

EJ 014 521 PS 500 198
LEARNING DISABILITIES: A TEAM APPROACH JACQUOT, WILLARD S.; AND OTHERS, *ELEM SCH J*, V70 N5, PP248-52, 70 FEB
EXPLAINS HOW TO COORDINATE PUBLIC SCHOOL PERSONNEL TO PROVIDE DIAGNOSIS AND THERAPY TO CHILDREN WITH LEARNING DISABILITIES. (DR)

EJ 014 522 PS 500 201
DIAGNOSTIC TEACHING: A MODEST PROPOSAL PROUTY, ROBERT W.; PRILLAMAN, DOUGLAS, *ELEM SCH J*, V70 N5, PP265-70, 70 FEB
PRESENTS A MODEL FOR DIAGNOSTIC TEACHING, A DESIGN FOR PREPARATION OF DIAGNOSTIC TEACHERS, AND A LIST OF ADMINISTRATIVE CONSIDERATIONS FOR IMPLEMENTING THE MODEL. (DR)

EJ 014 918 PS 500 222
CHILDREN WHO SPEAK NAVAJO BECENTI, MAEBAH, *YOUNG CHILDREN*, V25 N3, PP141-142, 70 JAN

EJ 014 945 PS 500 223
CONCEPT LEARNING THROUGH MOVEMENT IMPROVISATION: THE TEACHER'S ROLE AS CATALYST STECHER, MIRIAM B., *YOUNG CHILDREN*, V25 N3, PP143-153, 70 JAN
AN APPROACH TO TEACHING FUNDAMENTAL CONCEPTS OF MUSIC AND MOVEMENT IS PRESENTED THROUGH ILLUSTRATION AND DESCRIPTION. CREATIVE PHYSICAL AND VERBAL RESPONSES ARE EMPHASIZED. (AN EXPANDED WORK BY STECHER AND MCELHENY IS ENTITLED MUSICAL ARTS IN THE EARLY CHILDHOOD CURRICULUM). (DR)

EJ 015 059 PS 500 221
THE CASE FOR THE ACADEMIC PRESCHOOL: FACT OR FICTION? ELKIND, DAVID, *YOUNG CHILDREN*, V25 N3, PP132-140, 70 JAN
QUESTIONS THE EFFICIENCY, ECONOMY, AND LEARNING BENEFITS OF FORMAL INSTRUCTIONAL PROGRAMS AT THE PRESCHOOL LEVEL, PARTICULARLY FOR MIDDLE CLASS CHILDREN. CONCLUDES THAT ACADEMIC PRESCHOOL FOR THIS GROUP IS UNDESIRABLE. (DR)

EJ 015 060 PS 500 224
HOW ELSE? FLURRY, RUTH, *YOUNG CHILDREN*, V25 N3, PP155-158, 70 JAN
A REPORT ON THE PRINCIPLES AND PRACTICES OF THE BRITISH PRIMARY SCHOOLS. (DR)

EJ 015 096 PS 500 205
RACIAL DIFFERENCES IN INDICES OF EGO FUNCTIONING RELEVANT TO ACADEMIC ACHIEVEMENT LESSING, ELISE E., *J GENET PSYCHOL*, V115 N2, PP153-167, 69 DEC
THIS STUDY OF EIGHTH GRADERS AND ELEVENTH GRADERS FOUND THAT BLACKS SCORE LOWER THAN WHITES ON ACADEMIC ACHIEVEMENT AND ON THE EGO VARIABLES OF SENSE OF PERSONAL CONTROL AND WILLINGNESS TO DELAY GRATIFICATION. (MH)

EJ 015 097 PS 500 206
THE INTERSITUATIONAL GENERALITY OF FORMAL THOUGHT STONE, MARY ANN; AUSUBEL, DAVID P., *J GENET PSYCHOL*, V115 N2, PP169-180, 69 DEC
SHOWS THAT, CONTRARY TO PIAGETIAN THEORY, FORMAL THOUGHT IN A VARIETY OF SUBJECT MATTERS IS NOT POSSIBLE UNTIL SUFFICIENT REQUISITE CONCRETE BACKGROUND EXPERIENCE IN EACH CONTENT AREA INVOLVED HAS BEEN ATTAINED. (MH)

EJ 015 098 PS 500 208
COMPARISON OF GROSS, INTENSIVE, AND EXTENSIVE QUANTITIES BY RETARDATES MCMANIS, DONALD L., *J GENET PSYCHOL*, V115 N2, PP229-236, 69 DEC
GROSS COMPARISONS (EASIEST) WERE SOLVABLE BY ALL; INTENSIVE COMPARISONS (MEDIUM DIFFICULTY) WERE INVERSELY RELATED TO IQ, AND EXTENSIVE COMPARISONS (HARDEST) WERE EASIEST FOR LOW IQ, LOW M.A. AND HIGH IQ, HIGH M.A. RETARDATES. (MH)

EJ 015 099 PS 500 209
CHILDREN'S FEAR IN A DENTAL SITUATION AS A FUNCTION OF BIRTH ORDER DEFEE, JR., JOHN F.; HIMELSTEIN, PHILIP, *J GENET PSYCHOL*, V115 N2, PP253-255, 69 DEC
FIRSTBORN CHILDREN WERE FOUND TO BE BOTH MORE FEARFUL AND MORE SENSITIVE TO PAIN IN A DENTAL SITUATION THAN LATER BORN CHILDREN. (MH)

EJ 015 100 PS 500 210
PRESCHOOL CHILDREN'S UNDERSTANDING OF THE COORDINATED CONCEPTS OF DISTANCE, MOVEMENT, NUMBER, AND TIME ROTHENBERG, BARBARA B., *J GENET PSYCHOL*, V115 N2, PP263-276, 69 DEC
PROBLEMS WERE SOLVED MOST EASILY WHEN THERE WAS A DIFFERENCE IN ONLY ONE DIMENSION. DISTANCE UNDERSTANDING CORRELATED HIGHLY WITH AGE, INTELLIGENCE, AND CONSERVATION. LARGE SOCIAL CLASS DIFFERENCES FOR THE TASK ALSO APPEARED. (MH)

EJ 015 101 PS 500 211
INSTRUMENTAL AND AFFECTIONAL DEPENDENCY AND NURTURANCE IN PRESCHOOL CHILDREN EININGER, MARY ANN; HILL, JOHN P., *J GENET PSYCHOL*, V115 N2, PP277-284, 69 DEC
IN A STUDY TO EXPLORE RESPONSES FROM A ROLE THEORY POINT OF VIEW, AFFECTION-SEEKING CHILDREN SHOWED MORE OVERT NURTURANCE OF AN AFFECTION-GIVING (PERSON-ORIENTED) TYPE THAN DID INSTRUMENTAL (TASK-ORIENTED) HELP-SEEKING CHILDREN. (MH)

EJ 015 125 PS 500 197
READING - DIRECTED OR NOT? GOUDEY, CHARLES E., *ELEM SCH J*, V70 N5, PP245-47, 70 FEB
REPORTS A STUDY DESIGNED TO MEASURE THE USEFULNESS OF DIRECTED READING IN WHICH QUESTIONS TO BE ANSWERED ARE PRESENTED TO THE CHILDREN BEFORE THE READING SELECTIONS. VALUE OF DIRECTED READING IS QUESTIONED. (DR)

EJ 015 126 PS 500 226
SOME BASIC PERCEPTUAL PROCESSES IN READING PICK, ANNE D., *YOUNG CHILDREN*, V25 N3, PP162-181, 70 JAN
ASSESSES THE CURRENT STATE OF KNOWLEDGE CONCERNING CHILDREN'S PERCEPTION AND THE PROCESSES OF LEARNING TO READ. CONSIDERS RESEARCH STUDIES AND THE REASONS FOR THEIR SUCCESS OR FAILURE. (DR)

EJ 015 160 PS 500 204
ESTEEM AND ACHIEVEMENT IN ARITHMETIC PEPER, JOHN B.; CHANSKY, NORMAN M., *ELEM SCH J*, V70 N5, PP284-88, 70 FEB
RESULTS OF A STUDY THAT MEASURED RANKINGS OF ACHIEVEMENT IN ARITHMETIC BY SELF, PEERS, AND TEACHERS, AND THEIR RELATION TO ARITHMETIC ACHIEVEMENT MEASURED BY STANDARDIZED TESTS. (DR)

EJ 015 184 PS 500 203
BLACK HISTORY ELLIOTT, JR., RAYMOND N.; FERRER, LEONA, *ELEM SCH J*, V70 N5, PP279-83, 70 FEB
EXPLAINS WHY BLACK HISTORY SHOULD BE INCLUDED IN ELEMENTARY SCHOOL CURRICULUMS, HOW THIS CAN BE ACCOMPLISHED, AND THE PROBABLE EFFECTS. (DR)

EJ 015 199 PS 500 207
INDUSTRIALIZATION, CHILD-REARING PRACTICES, AND CHILDREN'S PERSONALITY MUSSEN, PAUL; BEYTAGH, LUZ A. MALDONADO, *J GENET PSYCHOL*, V115 N2, PP195-216, 69 DEC

EJ 015 258 PS 500 232
AUDITORY DISCRIMINATION ABILITIES OF DISADVANTAGED ANGLO- AND MEXICAN-AMERICAN CHILDREN ARNOLD, RICHARD D.; WIST, ANNE H., *ELEM SCH J*, V70 N6, PP295-299, 70 MAR
LENDS SUPPORT TO THE HYPOTHESIS THAT CHILDREN FROM MINORITY ETHNIC GROUPS WITH A LOW SOCIOECONOMIC STATUS ARE LIKELY TO HAVE MORE PROBLEMS IN AUDITORY DISCRIMINATION THAN CHILDREN WITH ONLY ONE OF THESE BACKGROUND FACTORS. (AUTHOR/DR)

EJ 015 382 PS 500 231
EFFECT OF VISUAL STIMULI IN COMPLEMENTING TELEVISED INSTRUCTION DWYER, JR., FRANCIS M., *CALIF J EDUC RES*, V21 N1, PP43-47, 70 JAN
CONCLUDES THAT MANY VARIABLES AFFECT THE EFFECTIVENESS OF VISUAL ILLUSTRATIONS IN FACILITATING LEARNING. (MS)

EJ 015 393 PS 500 215
THE DEVELOPMENT OF COOPERATION IN ALTERNATIVE TASK SITUATIONS MITHAUG, DENNIS E., *J EXP CHILD PSYCHOL*, V8 N3, PP443-460, 69 DEC
IN THIS FOLLOW-UP STUDY, IT WAS FOUND THAT COOPERATION COULD BE DEVELOPED WHEN REWARDS FOR COOPERATING WERE GREATER THAN FOR PERFORMING INDIVIDUAL TASKS AND WHEN SUBJECTS COULD DISCRIMINATE BETWEEN TASK ALTERNATIVES AND RELATIVE REWARDS. FOR REPRINTS, WRITE TO THE EXPERIMENTAL EDUCATION UNIT, CHILD DEVELOPMENT AND MENTAL RETARDATION CENTER, UNIV. OF WASHINGTON, SEATTLE, WASHINGTON 98105. (MH)

EJ 015 394 PS 500 217
THE OCULAR RESPONSE OF HUMAN NEWBORNS TO INTERMITTANT VISUAL MOVEMENT WICKELGREN, LYN W., *J EXP CHILD PSYCHOL*, V8 N3, PP469-482, 69 DEC
THE RESEARCH REPORTED HERE IS BASED ON A THESIS SUBMITTED BY THE AUTHOR TO YALE UNIVERSITY IN PARTIAL FULFILLMENT OF REQUIREMENTS FOR THE PH.D. DEGREE. (MH)

EJ 015 395 PS 500 218
FACTORS AFFECTING LATERAL DIFFERENTIATION IN THE HUMAN NEWBORN TURKEWITZ, GERALD; AND OTHERS, *J EXP CHILD PSYCHOL*, V8 N3, PP483-493, 69 DEC
CONCLUDES THAT BOTH ASYMMETRY OF MUSCLE TONUS AND SOMESTHETIC STIMULATION CONTRIBUTE TO THE NORMALLY OCCURRING LATERAL DIFFERENCES IN RESPONSIVENESS, THOUGH OTHER FACTORS ARE INVOLVED. (MH)

EJ 015 487 PS 500 238
HOW DO INNER-CITY TEACHERS USE A SYSTEM-WIDE CURRICULUM? LARSON, RICHARD G.; BEAUCHAMP, GEORGE A., *ELEM SCH J*, V70 N6, PP331-341, 70 MAR
COMPARES INNER-CITY AND OUTER-CITY TEACHERS IN THE SAME SYSTEM ACCORDING TO CURRICULUM OMISSIONS AND ADDITIONS, DEVIATION FROM PRESCRIBED CURRICULUM TIME ALLOTMENTS, AND EXTENT OF CURRICULUM COVERAGE. (DR)

EJ 015 850 PS 500 214
DIGIT SPAN, PRACTICE AND DICHOTIC LISTENING PERFORMANCE IN THE MENTALLY RETARDED URBANO, RICHARD C.; SCOTT, KEITH G., *J EXP CHILD PSYCHOL*, V8 N3, PP432-442, 69 DEC
IN TWO EXPERIMENTS WITH MENTALLY RETARDED CHILDREN, DIGIT SPAN HAD A SIGNIFICANT EFFECT ON DICHOTIC LISTENING PERFORMANCE, WHILE PRACTICE AND MENTAL AGE DID NOT. THE FIRST STUDY WAS SUBMITTED BY THE FIRST AUTHOR IN PARTIAL FULFILLMENT OF THE M.A. REQUIREMENTS AT THE UNIVERSITY OF ILLINOIS. (MH)

EJ 015 851 PS 500 220
CUE NOVELTY AND TRAINING LEVEL IN THE DISCRIMINATION SHIFT PERFORMANCE OF RETARDATES BILSKY, LINDA; HEAL, LAIRD W., *J EXP CHILD PSYCHOL*, V8 N3, PP503-511, 69 DEC
SUBJECTS USED MORE EXTRA-DIMENSIONAL SHIFT SOLUTIONS IN THE PRESENCE OF NOVEL CUES THAN IN THE PRESENCE OF FAMILIAR CUES, EXCEPT AT THE HIGHEST TRAINING LEVEL. (MH)

EJ 015 979 PS 500 229
HUMAN RELATIONS TRAINING FOR TEACHERS: THE EFFECTIVENESS OF SENSITIVITY TRAINING LEE, WALTER S., *CALIF J EDUC RES*, V21 N1, PP28-34, 70 JAN
REPORTS THAT 51 ELEMENTARY TEACHERS IN THIS IN-SERVICE TRAINING PROGRAM IMPROVED IN THEIR ATTITUDES TOWARD CHILDREN, TEACHING, AND INTERPERSONAL RELATIONSHIPS. (THIS STUDY IS BASED UPON A DOCTORAL DISSERTATION COMPLETED AT THE UNIVERSITY OF CALIFORNIA AT LOS ANGELES.) (DR)

EJ 015 980 PS 500 235
THE NON-STRUCTURED APPROACH TO CHILDREN'S LITERATURE GROFF, PATRICK, *ELEM SCH J*, V70 N6, PP308-316, 70 MAR
EXPLAINS THE REASOS FOR USING THIS APPROACH IN ELEMENTARY SCHOOL. DISCUSSES CHILDREN'S INTERESTS, SUITABLE BOOKS AND STORIES, AND QUESTIONS TO BE USED IN TEACHER PLANNING. (DR)

EJ 015 981 PS 500 236
THE SCHOOL AND THE UNIVERSITY: CO-OPERATIVE ROLES IN STUDENT TEACHING KNIGHT, DON A.; WAYNE, JACK I., *ELEM SCH J*, V70 N6, PP317-320, 70 MAR
DESCRIBES AN EXPLORATORY PROGRAM FOR STUDENT TEACHERS CONSISTING OF A COURSE IN SOCIAL STUDIES CURRICULUM AND METHODS, STUDENT TEACHING SEMINARS, AND SUPERVISION AND DIRECTION OF CLASSROOM ACTIVITIES BY THEIR CO-OPERATING TEACHERS. (DR)

EJ 016 163 PS 500 212
SEMANTIC RELATIONSHIP AND THE LEARNING OF SYNTACTIC WORD PAIRS IN CHILDREN GALLAGHER, JOSEPH W., *J EXP CHILD PSYCHOL*, V8 N3, PP411-417, 69 DEC
THIS STUDY EXAMINED THE INFLUENCE OF SEMANTIC CONSISTENCY (MEANINGFULNESS) AND ANOMALY ON THE LEARNING OF THREE TYPES OF SYNTACTIC PAIRS. THE RESULTS SHOWED THAT MEANINGFUL PAIRS ARE LEARNED WITH FEWER ERRORS THAN ANOMALOUS PAIRS. (AUTHOR)

EJ 016 164 PS 500 213
THE DISCRIMINABILITY OF FORM AMONG YOUNG CHILDREN GAINES, ROSSLYN, *J EXP CHILD PSYCHOL*, V8 N3, PP418-431, 69 DEC
THOUGH INCREASING COMPLEXITY INCREASED THE DIFFICULTY OF DISCRIMINATION OF FORM, NURSERY SCHOOL, KINDERGARTEN, AND FIRST GRADE CHILDREN WERE ALL ABOVE CHANCE IN PERFORMANCE, OLDER CHILDREN BEING SUPERIOR. THE RESULTS ARE DISCUSSED IN RELATION TO DEVELOPMENTAL PERCEPTUAL THEORY. PORTIONS OF THIS PAPER WERE PRESENTED AT THE AMERICAN PSYCHOLOGICAL ASSOCIATION MEETING, WASHINGTON, D.C., 1967. (MH)

EJ 016 165 PS 500 219
TRANSFER FROM PERCEPTUAL PRETRAINING AS A FUNCTION OF NUMBER OF TASK DIMENSIONS TIGHE, LOUISE S.; TIGHE, THOMAS J, *J EXP CHILD PSYCHOL*, V8 N3, PP494-502, 69 DEC

EJ 016 166 PS 500 230
A THIRD STUDY OF SOME RELATIONSHIPS BETWEEN CREATIVITY AND PERCEPTION IN 6TH GRADE CHILDREN MCWHINNIE, HAROLD J., *CALIF J EDUC RES*, V21 N1, PP35-42, 70 JAN
CONCLUDES THAT THERE IS LITTLE OR NO RELATIONSHIP BETWEEN CREATIVITY AND PERCEPTION VARIABLES AND RELATES CONCLUSIONS TO ART EDUCATION. (THIS REPORT IS PART OF A LARGER STUDY IN CREATIVITY AND PERCEPTUAL LEARNING IN ART, DONE UNDER A U.S.O.E. GRANT.) (DR)

EJ 016 350 PS 500 216
EFFECTS OF STIMULUS-RESPONSE SIMILARITY AND DISSIMILARITY ON CHILDREN'S MATCHING PERFORMANCE PARTONG, DAVID A.; FOUTS, GREGORY T., *J EXP CHILD PSYCHOL*, V8 N3, PP461-468, 69 DEC

EJ 016 351 PS 500 239
EDUCATIONAL AND GROWTH NEEDS OF CHILDREN IN DAY CARE GILBERT, DOROTHEA, *CHILD WELFARE*, V49 N1, PP15-20, 70 JAN
A GENERAL LOOK AT DAY CARE FROM A DEVELOPMENTAL VIEWPOINT. STRESSES NEED TO MOLD THE PRESCHOOL EXPERIENCE TO THE CHILD'S NATURAL GROWTH STAGES AND TO INTEGRATE THE WORLDS OF HOME AND NURSERY SCHOOL. THIS PAPER WAS PRESENTED AT THE CWLA EASTERN REGIONAL CONFERENCE AT PHILADELPHIA IN 1968. (MH)

EJ 016 352 PS 500 240
PRESCHOOL PROGRAMS OF THE U.S.S.R RADIN, NORMA, *CHILD WELFARE*, V49 N1, PP29-36, 70 JAN
TAKES A LOOK AT THE 30-YEAR-OLD SYSTEM OF NURSERIES AND CRECHES, EXAMINING EXTENT, ADMINISTRATION, ORGANIZATION, ADDITIONAL SERVICES, CURRICULA, AND UNDERLYING PHILOSOPHY. (MH)

EJ 016 380 PS 500 241
THE USE OF PLAY TECHNIQUES IN THE TREATMENT OF CHILDREN BURNS, BRENDA S., *CHILD WELFARE*, V49 N1, PP37-41, 70 JAN
DESCRIPTION AND EXAMPLES OF 7 WAYS TO USE PLAY TECHNIQUES IN PSYCHOANALYTICALLY-ORIENTED THERAPY FOR EMOTIONALLY DISTURBED CHILDREN. GOALS INCLUDE EMOTIONAL VENTILATION, COMMUNICATION, AND DEVELOPMENT OF SKILLS. (MH)

EJ 016 381 PS 500 243
THE PRESCHOOL COOPERATIVE AS A THERAPY FOR MOTHERS FENBY, BARBARA LOU, *CHILD WELFARE*, V49 N2, PP108-110, 70 FEB
A USEFUL RESOURCE FOR CHILD CARE AGENCIES IS THE COOPERATIVE, MOTHER-RUN PRESCHOOL, WHICH OFFERS MOTHERS PERSPECTIVE, IDENTITY, EMOTIONAL SUPPORT, AND SOCIALLY APPROVED RESPITE FROM THEIR CHILDREN. THE ASSOCIATION WITH OTHER MOTHERS HAS THE GREATEST POSITIVE EFFECT. (MH)

EJ 016 463 PS 500 233
HAVE YOU DISABLED A POTENTIAL READ'N' DROPOUT LATELY? GOLDSMITH, VIRGINIA G., *ELEM SCH J*, V70 N6, PP300-303, 70 MAR
EXPLAINS WHY THE PRACTICE OF ROUND-ROBIN ORAL READING LEADS TO FRUSTRATION, REJECTION AND FAILURE FOR SLOWER STUDENTS, BOREDOM FOR BETTER STUDENTS. (DR)

EJ 016 464 PS 500 237
INITIAL TEACHING ALPHABET AND TRADITIONAL ORTHOGRAPHY--THEIR IMPACT ON SPELLING AND WRITINGS NIKAS, GEORGE B., *ELEM SCH J*, V70 N6, PP321-330, 70 MAR
IN ONE OSWEGO, NEW YORK SCHOOL, A STUDY SHOWED NO SIGNIFICANT DIFFERENCES IN SPELLING OR SPONTANEOUS WRITING FOR CHILDREN TAUGHT DIFFERENT ALPHABETS IN BEGINNING READING. (DR)

EJ 016 606 PS 500 227
STEPS PURSUANT TO SECURING ACCREDITATION BY PRIVATE SECONDARY SCHOOLS MONROE, CHARLES E., *CALIF J EDUC RES*, V21 N1, PP5-13, 70 JAN
BASED ON A STUDY INVOLVING 230 SCHOOLS IN CALIFORNIA, RECOMMENDATIONS ARE OFFERED FOR PRIVATE SECONDARY SCHOOL ACCREDITATION. (DR)

EJ 016 607 PS 500 234
HERO MODELS PUNKE, HAROLD H., *ELEM SCH J*, V70 N6, PP304-307, 70 MAR
DESCRIBES HOW HERO IMAGES OR HUMAN MODELS CAN BE USEFUL IN DEVELOPING SOCIALLY APPROVED IDEALS IN YOUNG PEOPLE. (MG)

EJ 016 608 PS 500 242
NEW DIRECTIONS IN THE LICENSING OF CHILD CARE FACILITIES COSTIN, LELA B., *CHILD WELFARE*, V49 N2, PP64-71, 70 FEB
SOCIAL WORKERS' CONFERENCE CONCLUDES THAT BETTER OUT-OF-HOME CARE FOR CHILDREN COULD RESULT FROM CENTRAL INVOLVEMENT OF SOCIAL WORKERS IN REGULATION OF CHILD-CARE FACILITIES. (MH)

EJ 016 653 PS 500 228
IMPROVING HIGH SCHOOL LEARNING PREDICTIONS WITH MULTIPLE JUNIOR HIGH TEST SCORES CASSEL, RUSSELL N.; KNOX, PATRICIA, *CALIF J EDUC RES*, V21 N1, PP14-20, 70 JAN

EJ 016 716 PS 500 265
THE PRINCIPAL AND THE KINDERGARTEN THURMAN, ROBERT S., *CHILDHOOD EDUC*, V46 N4, PP205-208, 70 JAN

EJ 016 773 PS 500 245
A PARENT'S GIFT CRABB, PAULINE, *YOUNG CHILDREN*, V25 N4, PP221-222, 70 MAR

EJ 016 774 PS 500 254
ROLE PERCEPTIONS AND JOB SATISFACTION AMONG LOWER AND MIDDLE LEVEL JUNIOR COLLEGE ADMINISTRATORS DAHL, ERNEST W., *CALIF J EDUC RES*, V21 N2, PP57-63, 70 MAR
INTERVIEWS WITH 24 ADMINISTRATORS INDICATED VERY HIGH JOB SATISFACTION WITH 80 PERCENT SEEING THEIR ROLES AS INCLUDING AND PROVIDING INNOVATIVE-TYPE LEADERSHIP. (DR)

EJ 016 775 PS 500 267
SOCIOECONOMIC STATUS AND CHILDREN'S INTERESTS SELIG, HANNAH, *CHILDHOOD EDUC*, V46 N4, PP225-227, 70 JAN
DESCRIBES RESEARCH STUDY COMPARING EXPRESSED INTERESTS OF UPPER MIDDLE AND UPPER LOWER CLASS FOURTH GRADE CHILDREN AND THE IMPLICATIONS OF RESULTS FOR SCHOOL PROGRAM PLANNING. (DR)

EJ 016 776 PS 500 268
TEACHING AND THE NEW MORALITY WEISER, MARGARET G., *CHILDHOOD EDUC*, V46 N5, PP234-238, 70 FEB

EJ 016 777 PS 500 344
CHANGES IN SUCCESS-FAILURE ATTITUDES DURING ADOLESCENCE DISTEFANO, M. K., JR.; AND OTHERS, *J GENET PSYCHOL*, V116 N1, PP11-13, 70 MAR
FOUND THROUGH ADMINISTERING OF SUCCESS-FAILURE INVENTORY TO 100 ADOLESCENTS FROM 7TH THROUGH 11TH GRADE THAT SUCCESS MOTIVATION INCREASES AND FEAR OF FAILURE DECREASES DURING THIS PERIOD. (DR)

EJ 016 819 PS 500 266
MORE ON LEARNING-RESOURCE CENTERS LIKE, DORIS W., *CHILDHOOD EDUC*, V46 N4, PP209-212, 70 JAN
PRACTICAL SUGGESTIONS FOR BRINGING TOGETHER HUMAN RESOURCES AND MULTIMEDIA RESOURCES. (EDITOR/DR)

EJ 016 839 PS 500 264
PREADOLESCENTS - WHAT MAKES THEM TICK? A CHILDHOOD EDUCATION SPECIAL (FIRST IN A SERIES): CLASSIC STATEMENTS FROM THE EDUCATOR'S ARCHIVES REDL, FRITZ, *CHILDHOOD EDUC*, V46 N4, PP201-204, 70 JAN
DISCUSSES THE INDIVIDUAL AND GROUP PSYCHOLOGY OF PREADOLESCENCE AND OFFERS SUGGESTIONS FOR IMPROVING ADULT-CHILD RELATIONSHIPS. (EXCERPT FROM "PREADOLESCENTS - WHAT MAKES THEM TICK?" BY DR. FRITZ REDL, PUBLISHED IN CHILD STUDY IN 1943.) (DR)

EJ 016 840 PS 500 346
SHARING IN CHILDREN AS A FUNCTION OF THE NUMBER OF SHAREES AND RECIPROCITY PRESBIE, ROBERT J.; KANAREFF, VERA T., *J GENET PSYCHOL*, V116 N1, PP31-44, 70 MAR

EJ 016 930 PS 500 255
A STUDY IN THE USE OF A PROGRAMMED GEOGRAPHY UNIT AVEN, SAMUEL D.; AND OTHERS, *CALIF J EDUC RES*, V21 N2, PP64-67, 70 MAR
A STUDY SHOWED THAT STUDENTS USING PROGRAMED MATERIAL COMPLETED THEIR UNITS OF WORK FASTER AND HAD A HIGHER ACHIEVEMENT RATE THAN STUDENTS TAUGHT CONVENTIONALLY. (DR)

EJ 016 966 PS 500 260
ENJOYING PREADOLESCENCE: THE FORGOTTEN YEARS MURPHY, LOIS BARCLAY, *CHILDHOOD EDUC*, V46 N4, PP178-180, 70 JAN
DISCUSSES THE DISTINCTIVE PROBLEMS OF THE YEARS FROM 10 TO 14 AND THEIR RELATION TO EDUCATION. (DR)

EJ 017 097 PS 500 277
COLLEGE TRAINING FOR HEAD START WORKERS: A BOOST TOWARD CAREER ADVANCEMENT FLYNN, JOHN, *CHILDREN*, V17 N2, PP49-52, 70 MAR-APR
DISCUSSES OPPORTUNITIES FOR HIGHER EDUCATION FOR EMPLOYEES IN HEAD START CENTERS, PROVIDED THROUGH THE HEAD START SUPPLEMENTARY TRAINING PROGRAM. (NH)

EJ 017 244 PS 500 257
PERFORMANCES OF AVERAGE ABILITY STUDENTS IN A JUNIOR COLLEGE AND IN FOUR-YEAR INSTITUTIONS, 1953 TO 1968 HALL, LINCOLN H., *CALIF J EDUC RES*, V21 N2, PP74-83, 70 MAR

EJ 017 245 PS 500 259
THE EFFECT OF STUDENT EVALUATIONS OF COLLEGE INSTRUCTION UPON SUBSEQUENT EVALUATIONS MCCLELLAND, JAMES N., *CALIF J EDUC RES*, V21 N2, PP88-95, 70 MAR
A STUDY SHOWED THAT STUDENT OPINION COULD BE AFFECTED BY PUBLISHING RESULTS OF EARLIER STUDENT RATINGS, BUT THAT THESE INFLUENCES WERE NOT PERMANENT; COURSE CHANGES WOULD BE REFLECTED IN LATER RATINGS. (DR)

EJ 017 421 PS 500 256
EDUCATIONAL APPLICATION OF BEHAVIOR MODIFICATION TECHNIQUES WITH SEVERELY RETARDED CHILDREN IN A CHILD DEVELOPMENT CENTER JACKSON, MARTHA E.; JACKSON, NEWTON L. P., JR., *CALIF J EDUC RES*, V21 N2, PP68-73, 70 MAR
REPORTS BEHAVIOR CHANGES ACHIEVED AFTER A 3-WEEK TRAINING PROGRAM WITH 2 PROFOUNDLY RETARDED CHILDREN WHO WERE ACUTE MANAGEMENT PROBLEMS. (DR)

EJ 017 422 PS 500 273
I WAS A SLOW-LEARNER MURFIN, MARK, *CHILDHOOD EDUC*, V46 N5, PP259-260, 70 FEB
TEACHERS SHOULD RECOGNIZE THAT A WIDE RANGE OF ABILITY AND ACADEMIC ACHIEVEMENT IN A CLASSROOM IS NORMAL, ALWAYS PRESENT, AND DESIRABLE. SUCH A RANGE WILL NOT DISCOURAGE OR HUMILIATE THE SLOW-LEARNER, BUT ENCOURAGE HIM TO PROCEED AT HIS OWN PACE. (NH)

EJ 017 423 PS 500 280
THE GOAL OF LIFE ENHANCEMENT FOR A FATALLY ILL CHILD MORSE, JOAN, *CHILDREN*, V17 N2, PP63-68, 70 MAR-APR

EJ 017 424 PS 500 348
RELATIONSHIP OF SOCIOECONOMIC STATUS, SEX, AND AGE TO AGGRESSION OF EMOTIONALLY DISTURBED CHILDREN IN MOTHERS' PRESENCE RAU, MARGOT; AND OTHERS, *J GENET PSYCHOL*, V116 N1, PP95-100, 70 MAR

EJ 017 445 PS 500 252
A CHILD PROTECTION SERVICE ON A 24-HOUR, 365-DAY BASIS , *CHILD WELFARE*, V49 N3, PP168, 70 MAR
DESCRIBES METROPOLITAN EMERGENCY NIGHT SERVICE PROVIDED BY LAW STUDENTS TO ENSURE CHILD PROTECTION. (THIS ARTICLE IS A REPRINT OF "DANGER OF ABUSE OR NEGLECT REQUIRES 24-HOUR, 365-DAY PROTECTION SERVICE BY CAS." OUR CHILDREN V5, N1, 1968-69.) (MS)

EJ 017 446 PS 500 262
I AM--I WANT--I NEED: PREADOLESCENTS LOOK AT THEMSELVES AND THEIR VALUES LEWIS, GERTRUDE M., *CHILDHOOD EDUC*, V46 N4, PP186-194, 70 JAN
QUESTIONS AND OPINIONS OF STUDENTS IN GRADES 5 THROUGH 8 REFLECT CONCERN ABOUT PHYSICAL DEVELOPMENT AND EMOTIONAL FACTORS, SEX EDUCATION, RELATIONSHIPS WITH OTHERS, AND SOCIAL CONCERNS. (TAKEN FROM TEACH US WHAT WE WANT TO KNOW BY RUTH V. BYLER (ED.) AND OTHERS. MENTAL HEALTH MATERIALS CENTER, INC., 419 PARK AVENUE SOUTH, NEW YORK 10016, 1969.) (DR)

EJ 017 447 PS 500 281
SOME HIGHLIGHTS FROM THE NUTRITION CONFERENCE SIMMS, MIMI, *CHILDREN*, V17 N2, PP69-71, 70 MAR-APR
GUIDELINES FOR ENDING HUNGER AND MALNUTRITION DUE TO POVERTY IN THE UNITED STATES. (NH)

EJ 017 608 PS 500 244
CHILDREN'S QUESTIONS: THEIR FORMS, FUNCTIONS AND ROLES IN EDUCATION CAZDEN, COURTNEY B., *YOUNG CHILDREN*, V25 N4, PP202-220, 70 MAR
DISCUSSES CURRENT RESEARCH IN CHILD LANGUAGE TO HELP TEACHERS UNDERSTAND HOW YOUNG CHILDREN ACQUIRE LANGUAGE SKILLS. (DR)

EJ 017 709 PS 500 246
PSYCHOLOGIST AND TEACHER: COOPERATION OR CONFLICT? LACROSSE, E. ROBERT, JR., *YOUNG CHILDREN*, V25 N4, PP223-229, 70 MAR
URGES COOPERATION BETWEEN NURSERY SCHOOL TEACHERS WHO PREFER THE INTUITIVE APPROACH TO EDUCATION AND RESEARCH PSYCHOLOGISTS WHO EMPHASIZE THE NEED FOR USING SCIENTIFIC METHODOLOGY IN STUDYING CHILDREN AND THEIR DEVELOPMENT. (DR)

EJ 017 710 PS 500 247
PLAY IN DEWEY'S THEORY OF EDUCATION DENNIS, LAWRENCE, *YOUNG CHILDREN*, V25 N4, PP230-235, 70 MAR
EXPLAINS DEWEY'S THEORY OF PLAY AS A PURPOSEFUL ACTIVITY WHICH HAS SOCIAL VALUE AND WHICH PROVIDES THE BASIS FOR WORK AND EDUCATIONAL PRACTICE. (DR)

EJ 017 711 PS 500 345
THE INFUENCE OF SOME TASK VARIABLES AND OF SOCIOECONOMIC CLASS ON THE MANIFESTATION OF CONSERVATION OF NUMBER BAKER, NANCY E.; SULLIVAN, EDMUND V., *J GENET PSYCHOL*, V116 N1, PP21-30, 70 MAR
A TOTAL OF 156 KINDERGARTEN CHILDREN WERE GIVEN PIAGETIAN CONSERVATION OF INEQUALITY TASKS. THE RESULTS INDICATED THAT NUMBER CONSERVATION IS MORE LIKELY WITH HIGHER INTEREST MATERIALS, WITH SMALLER AGGREGATE SIZES, WITH HIGHER SOCIOECONOMIC CLASS FEMALES, AND WITH CHILDREN WHO PERFORM BETTER ON ADDITION AND SUBTRACTION TASKS. (DR)

EJ 017 712 PS 500 349
ACQUISITION OF COGNITIVE RESPONSES UNDER DIFFERENT PATTERNS OF VERBAL REWARDS FELKER, DONALD W.; MILHOLLAN, FRANK, *J GENET PSYCHOL*, V116 N1, PP113-123, 70 MAR
ANALYSES OF DATA FROM TASK MEASURING IMITATIVE ACQUISITION OF COGNITIVE RESPONSES INDICATED THAT DIFFERENCES IN PERFORMANCE WERE RELATED TO DIFFERENCES IN (A) TREATMENT, (B) SEX AND ROLE OF REWARDER, AND (C) SEX OF REWARDER AND SEX OF SUBJECT. (DR)

EJ 017 848 PS 500 248
THE EXECUTIVE DIRECTOR'S TESTIMONY BEFORE THE HOUSE EDUCATION AND LABOR COMMITTEE AKERS, MILTON E., *YOUNG CHILDREN*, V25 N4, PP236-246, 70 MAR
DEFINES PRIORITIES IN THE FIELD OF EARLY CHILDHOOD EDUCATION IN RELATION TO CHILDREN'S EXPERIENCES, LEADERSHIP, NONPROFESSIONALS, PARENTS, FACILITIES, AND COORDINATION AND INTEGRATION OF SERVICES. (DR)

EJ 017 849 PS 500 249
A REPORT ON A CWLA PILOT PROJECT TO TRAIN NEW CHILD CARE WORKERS BERMAN, SAMUEL P., *CHILD WELFARE*, V49 N3, PP156-160, 70 MAR
REPORT OF A PILOT PROJECT THAT TRAINED 542 UNEMPLOYED OR UNDEREMPLOYED PERSONS IN 5 CITIES TO BECOME CHILD CARE WORKERS. DISCUSSES REWARDS AND PROBLEMS OF THE PROJECT. (DR)

EJ 017 850 PS 500 251
USING A STEP TOWARD PROFESSIONALISM IN TRAINING OF CHILD CARE STAFF MALUCCIO, ANTHONY N., *CHILD WELFARE*, V49 N3, PP165-167, 70 MAR
DESCRIBES A STAFF TRAINING PROGRAM THAT USED A SERIES OF TAPED LESSONS TO HELP INEXPERIENCED CHILD CARE WORKERS DEVELOP UNDERSTANDING OF CONCEPTS OF HUMAN BEHAVIOR AND CHILD CARE. (DR)

EJ 017 851 PS 500 269
CONTRASTING VIEWS OF EARLY CHILDHOOD EDUCATION LAVATELLI, CELIA STENDLER, *CHILDHOOD EDUC*, V46 N5, PP239-246, 70 FEB
COMPARES ACADEMICALLY-ORIENTED, MONTESSORI, BRITISH INFANT SCHOOLS AND CHILD DEVELOPMENT OR TRADITIONAL NURSERY SCHOOLS. SUGGESTS THAT A COMBINATION OF STRUCTURED LEARNING ACTIVITIES AND FREE PLAY PERIODS IS DESIRABLE. (NH)

EJ 017 852 PS 500 270
REACHING THE YOUNG CHILD THROUGH PARENT EDUCATION GORDON, IRA J., *CHILDHOOD EDUC*, V46 N5, PP247-249, 70 FEB

EJ 017 900 PS 500 250
SMALL GROUPS - AN EFFECTIVE TREATMENT APPROACH IN RESIDENTIAL PROGRAMS FOR ADOLESCENTS SCOTT, MAX L., *CHILD WELFARE*, V49 N3, PP161-164, 70 MAR
EXPLAINS HOW GROUP SESSIONS HAVE HELPED RESIDENT DELINQUENTS TO GOVERN THEMSELVES AND READJUST TO COMMUNITY SETTINGS. (DR)

EJ 017 901 PS 500 261
THE CHANGING CHILDREN OF PREADOLESCENCE (OR THE QUESTIONABLE JOY OF BEING PRE-ANYTHING) MCNEIL, ELTON B., *CHILDHOOD EDUC*, V46 N4, PP181-185, 70 JAN

EJ 017 902 PS 500 271
ON SEPARATION AND SCHOOL ENTRANCE GROSS, DOROTHY W., *CHILDHOOD EDUC*, V46 N5, PP250-253, 70 FEB
SUGGESTS HOW PARENTS AND TEACHERS CAN WORK TOGETHER TO HELP CHILDREN DEAL WITH THE TRAUMAS OF SEPARATION UPON SCHOOL ENTRANCE. (NH)

EJ 017 903 PS 500 343
STAGES OF THE DREAM CONCEPT AMONG HASIDIC CHILDREN KAHANA, BOAZ, *J GENET PSYCHOL*, V116 N1, PP3-9, 70 MAR
ADMINISTERING OF KOHLBERG'S ADAPTATION OF PINARD AND LAURENDEAU'S DREAM INTERVIEW TO 24 HASIDIC BOYS AGED 4 TO 16 YIELDED DATA THAT FAILED TO SUPPORT THE INVARIANCE OF THE PROCESS OF EMERGING COGNITIVE STRUCTURES IN THE DEVELOPMENT OF THE DREAM CONCEPT AND UNDERSCORED THE IMPORTANCE OF CULTURAL INFLUENCES IN AFFECTING THE SEQUENCE OF COGNITIVE DEVELOPMENT. (DR)

EJ 017 904 PS 500 347
THE FATHER-DAUGHTER RELATIONSHIP AND THE PERSONALITY DEVELOPMENT OF THE FEMALE BILLER, HENRY B.; WEISS, STEPHAN D., *J GENET PSYCHOL*, V116 N1, PP79-93, 70 MAR
CONCLUDES FROM CITED LITERATURE AND SPECULATIVE DISCUSSION THAT THE FATHER'S INFLUENCE ON FEMALE IDENTIFICATION AND PERSONALITY ADJUSTMENT IS EXTREMELY SIGNIFICANT. (DR)

EJ 018 016 PS 500 253
CALIFORNIA ADVISORY COUNCIL ON EDUCATIONAL RESEARCH SUGGESTED POLICY ON EDUCATIONAL RESEARCH FOR CALIFORNIA SCHOOL DISTRICTS , *CALIF J EDUC RES*, V21 N2, PP52-56, 70 MAR

EJ 018 047 PS 500 263
WHEN CHILDREN ENJOY SCHOOL: SOME LESSONS FROM BRITAIN BARTH, ROLAND S., *CHILDHOOD EDUC*, V46 N4, PP195-200, 70 JAN

EJ 018 066 PS 500 272
SOCIAL ACTION FOR THE PRIMARY SCHOOLS JOYCE, BRUCE R., *CHILDHOOD EDUC*, V46 N5, PP254-258, 70 FEB
ARGUES THAT SCHOOL PRIORITIES SHOULD BE CHANGED FROM EMPHASIS ON LANGUAGE SKILLS AND TECHNICAL PROFICIENCY TO DEVELOPMENT OF POSITIVE ATTITUDES OF LOVE AND COMMITMENT TO OTHERS, BOTH IN THE SCHOOL AND IN THE WIDER COMMUNITY. (NH)

EJ 018 067 PS 500 278
THE GENERATION GAP IN THE EYES OF YOUTH HERZOG, ELIZABETH; SUDIA, CECELIA E., *CHILDREN*, V17 N2, PP53-58, 70 MAR-APR
SUMMARIZES TEENAGERS' RESPONSES TO A QUESTIONNAIRE ON THE GENERATION GAP. TEENS DISCUSS VALUE CONFLICTS, PROBLEMS OF SOCIETY, PARENTS' AND TEENAGERS' FAULTS AND VIRTUES, AND THEIR OWN HOPES FOR THE FUTURE. (NH)

EJ 018 068 PS 500 279
YOUTH AS ADVISERS TO ADULTS AND VICE VERSA STREAN, HERBERT S., *CHILDREN*, V17 N2, PP59-62, 70 MAR-APR
CHILDREN AND YOUNG PEOPLE CAN HELP GUIDE AN ADULT AS HE TRIES TO COUNSEL, TEACH AND LIVE WITH THEM. PERSONAL INTEGRITY IS MAINTAINED WITH A MINIMUM OF BELLIGERENCY WHEN EACH SIDE FEELS IT HAS A VOICE IN DECISION-MAKING. (NH)

EJ 018 130 PS 500 258
A NOTE ON TEACHING FOR CREATIVITY LINDSEY, JAMES F.; HICKS, DAVID, *CALIF J EDUC RES*, V21 N2, PP84-87, 70 MAR

EJ 018 131 PS 500 274
RECIPES FOR MOM BRANTLEY, MABEL, *CHILDHOOD EDUC*, V46 N5, PP261-262, 70 FEB
TEACHERS WHO ARE AWARE CAN HELP PARENTS TO ACCEPT THEIR CHILDREN'S IDEAS WITH RESPECT AND APPRECIATION. IN THIS ARTICLE, A COLLECTION OF RECIPES DICTATED BY CLASSROOM CHILDREN IS USED TO REACH MOTHERS. (NH)

EJ 018 132 PS 500 275
FANTASIZING AND POETRY CONSTRUCTION IN PRESCHOOLERS SPITZE, GLENNYS S., *CHILDHOOD EDUC*, V46 N5, PP283-286, 70 FEB
THE CHILD'S CREATIVE POTENTIAL MAY BE FOSTERED IN THE CLASSROOM BY (1) STORY-TELLING, (2) EXPRESSING INTEREST IN THE CHILD'S ATTEMPTS TO WRITE STORIES AND POETRY, (3) ALLOWING FREEDOM AND TIME FOR THE CHILD'S CREATIVE EFFORTS AND (4) HELPING THE CHILD TO ASSOCIATE CREATIVE EFFORT WITH PLEASURE. (NH)

EJ 018 133 PS 500 276
TEACHING IN PRESCHOOLS: ROLES AND GOALS KATZ, LILIAN G., *CHILDREN*, V17 N2, PP42-48, 70 MAR-APR
DISCUSSES MATERNAL, THERAPEUTIC AND INSTRUCTIONAL TEACHER ROLE MODELS AND EFFECTS OF TEACHING STYLES ON PRESCHOOL CHILDREN. SUGGESTS NEED FOR PRESCHOOL EDUCATORS TO BE MORE SENSITIVE TO PARENTS' GOALS, WHICH MAY BE MORE INSTRUCTIONAL AND CONTROL ORIENTED THAN THE TEACHER'S. (NH)

EJ 018 198 PS 500 339
PSYCHOLINGUISTIC ABILITIES OF GOOD AND POOR READING DISADVANTAGED FIRST-GRADERS BRUININKS, ROBERT H.; AND OTHERS, *ELEM SCH J*, V70 N7, PP378-386, 70 APR
RESULTS OF THE STUDY SEEM TO SUGGEST THE PRESENCE OF GENERAL DEFICITS IN THE AUDITORY RECEPTIVE AND VOCAL EXPRESSIVE ABILITIES OF POOR READING DISADVANTAGED CHILDREN, WHO LEARNED TO READ USING THE INITIAL TEACHING ALPHABET SERIES RATHER THAN THE TRADITIONAL ORTHOGRAPHY APPROACH. (AUTHOR)

EJ 018 259 PS 500 283
CHILDREN'S JUDGMENTS OF KINDNESS BALDWIN, CLARA P.; BALDWIN, ALFRED L., *CHILD DEVELOP*, V41 N1, PP29-47, 70 MAR
THE KINDNESS PICTURE-STORY MEASURE WAS CONSTRUCTED AND GIVEN TO SUBJECTS BETWEEN THE AGES OF 4 AND YOUNG ADULTHOOD. RESULTS SHOWED THAT CHILDREN ACQUIRE AN UNDERSTANDING OF DIFFERENT ASPECTS OF KINDNESS AT DIFFERENT AGES. (DR)

EJ 018 260 PS 500 287
THE EFFECTS OF TEMPERATURE AND POSITION ON THE SUCKING PRESSURE OF NEWBORN INFANTS ELDER, MARY SCOVILL, *CHILD DEVELOP*, V41 N1, PP95-102, 70 MAR

EJ 018 306 PS 500 335
THE COMPUTER CAN HELP INDIVIDUALIZE INSTRUCTION DEEP, DONALD, *ELEM SCH J*, V70 N7, PP351-358, 70 APR
EXPLAINS THE DIFFERENCE BETWEEN COMPUTER-ASSISTED INSTRUCTION AND COMPUTER-MANAGED INSTRUCTION, DEFINES AND DISCUSSES INDIVIDUALIZED INSTRUCTION, DESCRIBES AND POINTS OUT THE COMPUTER FUNCTION IN PLAN (PROGRAM FOR LEARNING IN ACCORDANCE WITH NEEDS). (AUTHOR)

EJ 018 307 PS 500 354
A MULTIPLE-CHOICE AUDIO-VISUAL DISCRIMINATION APPARATUS WITH QUICK INTER-CHANGE DISPLAY AND RESPONSE PANELS SCOTT, KEITH G., *J EXP CHILD PSYCHOL*, V9 N1, PP43-50, 70 FEB
DESCRIPTION OF AN APPARATUS THAT PRESENTS AUTOMATED AUDIOVISUAL DISPLAYS REQUIRING MULTIPLE RESPONSE CHOICES. (MH)

EJ 018 320 PS 500 284
ATTACHMENT, EXPLORATION, AND SEPARATION: ILLUSTRATED BY THE BEHAVIOR OF ONE-YEAR-OLDS IN A STRANGE SITUATION AINSWORTH, MARY D. SALTER; BELL, SILVIA M., *CHILD DEVELOP*, V41 N1, PP49-67, 70 MAR
AN EARLIER VERSION OF THIS PAPER WAS PRESENTED AT THE ANNUAL MEETING OF THE AMERICAN PSYCHOLOGICAL ASSOCIATION AT SAN FRANCISCO, SEPTEMBER 1968, IN A SYMPOSIUM, "ATTACHMENT BEHAVIOR IN HUMANS AND ANIMALS." (DR)

EJ 018 321 PS 500 299
NEED FOR APPROVAL, CHILDREN'S SHARING BEHAVIOR, AND RECIPROCITY IN SHARING STAUB, ERVIN; SHERK, LINDA, *CHILD DEVELOP*, V41 N1, PP243-252, 70 MAR

EJ 018 322 PS 500 321
PERCEPTUAL CORRELATES OF IMPULSIVE AND REFLECTIVE BEHAVIOR DRAKE, DIANA MACK, *DEVELOP PSYCHOL*, V2 N2, PP202-214, 70 MAR

EJ 018 323 PS 500 324
IMITATION AS A FUNCTION OF VICARIOUS AND DIRECT REWARD LIEBERT, ROBERT M.; FERNANDEZ, LUIS E., *DEVELOP PSYCHOL*, V2 N2, PP230-232, 70 MAR
BOTH VICARIOUS AND DIRECT REWARDS IMPROVE IMITATIVE MATCHING BEHAVIOR. THIS RESULT IS DISCUSSED IN TERMS OF THE HYPOTHESIS THAT VICARIOUS REWARD SERVES PRIMARILY TO INCREASE ATTENTION TO RELEVANT MODELING CUES. (AUTHOR/MH)

EJ 018 324 PS 500 326
INDIVIDUAL DIFFERENCES IN THE CONSIDERATION OF INFORMATION AMONG TWO-YEAR-OLD CHILDREN REPPUCCI, N. DICKON, *DEVELOP PSYCHOL*, V2 N2, PP240-246, 70 MAR
TWENTY-FIVE 2-YEAR-OLDS WERE OBSERVED IN FREE-PLAY AND PROBLEM-SOLVING SESSIONS. IT WAS CONCLUDED THAT SUSTAINED INVOLVEMENT WITH TOYS WAS POSITIVELY RELATED TO RESPONSE TIMES IN CONFLICT SITUATIONS AND NEGATIVELY RELATED TO MOTOR ACTIVITY. (MH)

EJ 018 325 PS 500 357
VICARIOUS REINFORCEMENT EFFECTS ON EXTINCTION HAMILTON, MARSHALL L., *J EXP CHILD PSYCHOL*, V9 N1, PP108-114, 70 FEB

EJ 018 326 PS 500 361
CHILD NEGLECT AMONG THE POOR: A STUDY OF PARENTAL ADEQUACY IN FAMILIES OF THREE ETHNIC GROUPS GIOVANNONI, JEANNE M.; BILLINGSLEY, ANDREW, *CHILD WELFARE*, V49 N4, PP196-204, 70 APR
EXAMINES FACTORS FOUND AMONG LOW INCOME GROUPS THAT DIFFERENTIATE THE ADEQUATE PARENT FROM THE NEGLECTFUL PARENT. A MORE EXTENSIVE VERSION OF THIS PAPER WAS PRESENTED AT THE CWLA SOUTH PACIFIC REGIONAL CONFERENCE AT SAN FRANCISCO IN 1969. (NH)

EJ 018 422 PS 500 337
WHAT INFLUENCES THE MATHEMATICAL UNDERSTANDING OF ELEMENTARY-SCHOOL TEACHERS? GIBNEY, THOMAS C.; AND OTHERS, *ELEM SCH J*, V70 N7, PP367-372, 70 APR
THERE WERE SIGNIFICANT MEAN DIFFERENCES IN THE MATHEMATICAL UNDERSTANDINGS OF TEACHERS WHEN CLASSIFIED BY POPULATION OF THE COMMUNITY WHERE THEY GRADUATED FROM HIGH SCHOOL, OR BY SUBJECTS THEY MOST OR LEAST PREFERRED TO TEACH. (NH)

EJ 018 423 PS 500 342
MATERIAL REINFORCEMENT AND SUCCESS IN SPELLING THOMSON, ERIC W.; GALLOWAY, CHARLES G., *ELEM SCH J*, V70 N7, PP395-398, 70 APR
STUDY OF 91 ELEMENTARY SCHOOL PUPILS INDICATES THAT IN REGULAR CLASSROOM SITUATIONS SPELLING PROFICIENCY CAN BE INCREASED THROUGH THE USE OF MATERIAL AND SOCIAL REINFORCEMENT. (AUTHOR)

EJ 018 465 PS 500 285
INFANT DEVELOPMENT, PRESCHOOL IQ, AND SOCIAL CLASS WILLERMAN, LEE; AND OTHERS, *CHILD DEVELOP*, V41 N1, PP69-77, 70 MAR
THIS PAPER WAS PRESENTED AT THE BIENNIAL MEETING OF THE SOCIETY FOR RESEARCH IN CHILD DEVELOPMENT, SANTA MONICA, CALIFORNIA, MARCH 25-29, 1969. (DR)

EJ 018 707 PS 500 362
MINIMAL BRAIN DAMAGE: A MEANINGFUL DIAGNOSIS OR AN IRRELEVANT LABEL? LACEY, HARVEY M., *CHILD WELFARE*, V49 N4, PP205-211, 70 APR
GROUPS SYMPTOMS, AND SUGGESTS RESOURCES AND ENERGY BE CONCENTRATED ON EDUCATIONAL AND PSYCHOLOGICAL INTERVENTION, RATHER THAN ON CAUSES. (NH)

EJ 018 815 PS 500 350
THE LEARNING OF SPEECHLIKE STIMULI BY CHILDREN GILBERT, JOHN H., *J EXP CHILD PSYCHOL*, V9 N1, PP1-11, 70 FEB
USING AUDITORY ENSEMBLES OF SOUND THAT DIFFERED IN FREQUENCY, INTENSITY, AND DURATION, IT WAS FOUND THAT FIFTH GRADERS MORE EASILY LEARN STIMULI THAT ARE UNLIKE SPEECH THAN THOSE WHICH CLOSELY APPROXIMATE SPEECH. (MH)

EJ 018 816 PS 500 351
VOWEL PRODUCTIONS AND IDENTIFICATION BY NORMAL AND LANGUAGE DELAYED CHILDREN GILBERT, JOHN H., *J EXP CHILD PSYCHOL*, V9 N1, PP12-19, 70 FEB
LISTENERS HAD MORE DIFFICULTY IDENTIFYING VOWELS UTTERED BY 4-YEAR-OLDS CLASSIFIED AS LATE LANGUAGE USERS THAN THOSE UTTERED BY 4-YEAR-OLDS CLASSIFIED AS NORMAL. (MH)

EJ 018 817 PS 500 352
THE LEARNING OF VERBAL STRINGS AS A FUNCTION OF CONNECTIVE FORM CLASS ROHWER, WILLIAM D., JR.; SUZUKI, NANCY, *J EXP CHILD PSYCHOL*, V9 N1, PP20-28, 70 FEB
CONCLUDES THAT CONNECTIVE FORM CLASS AFFECTS THE LEARNING OF ENTIRE GRAMMATICAL STRINGS. (MH)

EJ 018 818 PS 500 359
SYNTACTIC MATURITY IN SCHOOL CHILDREN AND ADULTS HUNT, KELLOGG W., *MONOGR SOC RES CHILD DEVELOP*, V35 N1, PP1-67, 70 FEB
INVESTIGATES THE DIFFERENCES IN SYNTACTICAL STRUCTURE OF SENTENCES WRITTEN BY SCHOOL CHILDREN OF DIFFERENT AGES AND OF DIFFERENT ABILITIES WITHIN THE SAME GRADE. WRITING OF CERTAIN ADULTS IS ALSO STUDIED. (MH)

EJ 018 871 PS 500 288
THE DISTRACTING EFFECTS OF MATERIAL REINFORCERS IN THE DISCRIMINATION LEARNING OF LOWER- AND MIDDLE-CLASS CHILDREN SPENCE, JANET TAYLOR, *CHILD DEVELOP*, V41 N1, PP103-111, 70 MAR

EJ 018 872 PS 500 291
REASONS FOR FAILURE ON THE CLASS INCLUSION PROBLEM AHR, PAUL R.; YOUNISS, JAMES, *CHILD DEVELOP*, V41 N1, PP131-143, 70 MAR

EJ 018 873 PS 500 292
SHORT-TERM RECOGNITION MEMORY IN CHILDREN CALFEE, ROBERT C., *CHILD DEVELOP*, V41 N1, PP145-161, 70 MAR
A SERIES OF STUDIES INDICATED THAT PERFORMANCE ON SERIAL RECOGNITION MEMORY TASKS WAS RELATIVELY CONSTANT OVER A WIDE RANGE OF AGE AND IQ, AND EXCEPT FOR RESPONSE BIASES AND FORGETTING RATE, RECOGNITION MEMORY PROCESSES OF NORMAL AND RETARDED CHILDREN APPEARED TO BE IDENTICAL WITH THOSE OF ADULTS. (AUTHOR/DR)

EJ 018 874 PS 500 293
OPERATIONAL THOUGHT INDUCEMENT STRAUSS, SIDNEY; LANGER, JONAS, *CHILD DEVELOP*, V41 N1, PP163-175, 70 MAR
REPORTS RESULTS OF SHORT-TERM TRAINING PROCEDURES UPON THE ACQUISITION OF THE CONCEPT OF CONSERVATION IN CHILDREN. (DR)

EJ 018 875 PS 500 295
PREDICTIVE VERSUS PERCEPTUAL RESPONSES TO PIAGET'S WATER-LINE TASK AND THEIR RELATION TO DISTANCE CONSERVATION FORD, LEROY H., JR., *CHILD DEVELOP*, V41 N1, PP193-204, 70 MAR
PORTIONS OF THIS PAPER WERE READ AT THE EASTERN PSYCHOLOGICAL ASSOCIATION MEETING, APRIL 1968, WASHINGTON, D.C. (DR)

EJ 018 876 PS 500 296
A DISCRIMINATION TASK WHICH INDUCES CONSERVATION OF NUMBER HALFORD, G. S.; FULLERTON, T. J., *CHILD DEVELOP*, V41 N1, PP205-213, 70 MAR
RESULTS INDICATED THAT THE TRAINING METHOD (DISCRIMINATION) INDUCED 8 OF THE 12 SUBJECTS TO ACQUIRE CONSERVATION OF A STABLE KIND. (AUTHOR/DR)

EJ 018 877 PS 500 297
PROJECTIVE VISUAL IMAGERY AS A FUNCTION OF AGE AND DEAFNESS YOUNISS, JAMES; ROBERTSON, ANNE DE SHAZO, *CHILD DEVELOP*, V41 N1, PP215-224, 70 MAR
RESULTS SUPPORTED PIAGET'S VIEWPOINT THAT MENTAL IMAGERY AND GENERAL SYMBOLIC FUNCTIONING ARE DEPENDENT ON THE GROWTH OF INTELLIGENCE WITH RESPECT TO THE PREADOLESCENT PERIOD. (AUTHOR)

EJ 018 878 PS 500 304
CONCEPT LEARNING IN DISCRIMINATION TASKS CALDWELL, EDWARD C.; HALL, VERNON C., *DEVELOP PSYCHOL*, V2 N1, PP41-48, 70 JAN

EJ 018 879 PS 500 306
WHAT IS LEARNED IN PROBABILITY LEARNING SULLIVAN, FRANK J.; ROSS, BRUCE M., *DEVELOP PSYCHOL*, V2 N1, PP58-65, 70 JAN
EXAMINES WEIR'S HYPOTHESIS OF A U-SHAPED RELATIONSHIP BETWEEN AGE AND TERMINAL LEVEL OF CORRECT RESPONDING; STUDIES USE OF ALTERNATION PATTERNING AS A RESPONSE STRATEGY; INVESTIGATES EXTENT TO WHICH IMMEDIATE REINFORCEMENT CONTROLLED THE SUBJECTS' CHOICES. THE RESULTS REPORTED HERE ARE BASED ON PART OF A DOCTORAL DISSERTATION SUBMITTED BY THE FIRST AUTHOR TO THE CATHOLIC UNIVERSITY OF AMERICA IN 1967. (MG)

EJ 018 880 PS 500 308
REPRESENTATIONAL LEVEL AND CONCEPT PRODUCTION IN CHILDREN AND ADOLESCENTS ELKIND, DAVID; AND OTHERS, *DEVELOP PSYCHOL*, V2 N1, PP85-89, 70 JAN
STUDY INDICATES THAT FOR CHILDREN, BUT NOT FOR ADOLESCENTS, THE NUMBER OF CONCEPTS PRODUCED WAS INVERSELY RELATED TO THE LEVEL OF ABSTRACTNESS OF THE STIMULI. (AUTHOR/MG)

EJ 018 881 PS 500 312
CHILDREN'S REACTIONS TO DISTRACTORS IN A LEARNING SITUATION TURNURE, JAMES E., *DEVELOP PSYCHOL*, V2 N1, PP115-122, 70 JAN
FINDINGS OF THIS STUDY INDICATE THAT CHILDREN CAN LEARN TO CONTROL THEIR ATTENDING OR ORIENTING RESPONSES IN THE FACE OF SOME DISTRACTING STIMULI BY THE AGE OF 6 1/2 TO 7 1/2 YEARS. THIS STUDY WAS ADAPTED FROM A DISSERTATION SUBMITTED TO THE GRADUATE SCHOOL OF YALE UNIVERSITY, IN PARTIAL FULFILLMENT OF THE REQUIREMENTS FOR THE PH.D. DEGREE. (AUTHOR/MG)

EJ 018 882 PS 500 318
TRANSITIVE INFERENCE WITH NONTRANSITIVE SOLUTIONS CONTROLLED YOUNISS, JAMES; MURRAY, JOHN P., *DEVELOP PSYCHOL*, V2 N2, PP169-175, 70 MAR
EIGHT-YEAR-OLDS WERE ABLE TO MAKE INFERENTIAL JUDGMENTS BASED ON TRANSITIVE SIZE RELATIONS, WHILE 6-YEAR-OLDS WERE NOT. IN ADDITION, MORE OLDER THAN YOUNGER SUBJECTS EVIDENCED SERIAL ORDERING, PRESUMABLY A PREREQUISITE FOR TRANSITIVE INFERENCE. (MH)

EJ 018 883 PS 500 319
EFFECT OF VERBAL PRETRAINING AND SINGLE-PROBLEM MASTERY ON WEIGL LEARNING-SET FORMATION IN CHILDREN ROUTH, DONALD K.; WISCHNER, GEORGE J., *DEVELOP PSYCHOL*, V2 N2, PP176-180, 70 MAR
VERBAL PRETRAINING AIDED BOTH SINGLE-PROBLEM DISCRIMINATION AND LEARNING-SET PERFORMANCE, WHILE SINGLE-PROBLEM MASTERY MANIPULATIONS HAD NO SIGNIFICANT EFFECT. THESE RESULTS SUPPORT THE THEORY OF ACQUIRED DISTINCTIVENESS OF CUES. (MH)

EJ 018 884 PS 500 323
INFORMATION PROCESSING IN PROBLEM SOLVING AS A FUNCTION OF DEVELOPMENTAL LEVEL AND STIMULUS SALIENCY EIMAS, PETER D., *DEVELOP PSYCHOL*, V2 N2, PP224-229, 70 MAR
PORTIONS OF THIS PAPER WERE PRESENTED AT THE MEETINGS OF THE SOCIETY FOR RESEARCH IN CHILD DEVELOPMENT, SANTA MONICA, CALIFORNIA, MARCH 1969. (MH)

EJ 018 885 PS 500 325
AGE CHANGES IN CHILDREN'S LEARNING SET WITH WIN-STAY, LOSE-SHIFT PROBLEMS BERMAN, PHYLLIS W.; AND OTHERS, *DEVELOP PSYCHOL*, V2 N2, PP233-239, 70 MAR

EJ 018 886 PS 500 327
PERCEPTUAL AND SENSORIMOTOR SUPPORTS FOR CONSERVATION TASKS WHITEMAN, MARTIN; PEISACH, ESTELLE, *DEVELOP PSYCHOL*, V2 N2, PP247-256, 70 MAR

EJ 018 887 PS 500 329
TRANSFER EFFECTS IN CHILDREN'S ODDITY LEARNING SARAVO, ANNE; AND OTHERS, *DEVELOP PSYCHOL*, V2 N2, PP273-282, 70 MAR
INVESTIGATES THE RELATIVE ROLES OF POSITIVE AND NEGATIVE CUE RETENTION ON ODDITY TRANSFER, AND SEEKS TO LEARN HOW THESE ROLES CHANGE WITH AGE AND PRACTICE. AGE RANGE STUDIED IS FROM 3 TO 7 YEARS OLD. (MH)

EJ 018 888 PS 500 332
CONTINUITY IN THE DEVELOPMENT OF CONCEPTUAL BEHAVIOR IN PRESCHOOL CHILDREN: A REJOINDER VAN DEN DAELE, LELAND D., *DEVELOP PSYCHOL*, V2 N2, PP303-305, 70 MAR
RECONSIDERATION OF MCGAUGHRAN AND WYLIE'S INTERPRETATION OF QUALITATIVE VERSUS QUANTITATIVE FORMS OF ANALYSIS OF CONCEPTUAL BEHAVIOR OF PRESCHOOL CHILDREN. (AUTHOR)

EJ 018 889 PS 500 333
CONTINUITY IN THE DEVELOPMENT OF CONCEPTUAL BEHAVIOR IN PRESCHOOL CHILDREN: RESPONSE TO A REJOINDER MCGAUGHRAN, LAURENCE S.; WYLIE, ALEXANDER A., *DEVELOP PSYCHOL*, V2 N2, PP306-309, 70 MAR
A REPLY TO VAN DEN DAELE'S RECONSIDERATION OF THEIR INTERPRETATION OF QUALITATIVE VERSUS QUANTITATIVE FORMS OF BEHAVIOR ANALYSIS. (MH)

EJ 018 890 PS 500 353
A PARTIAL TEST OF A SOCIAL LEARNING THEORY OF CHILDREN'S CONFORMITY HAMM, NORMAN H., *J EXP CHILD PSYCHOL*, V9 N1, PP29-42, 70 FEB
THIS STUDY IS BASED ON A DISSERTATION SUBMITTED TO THE GRADUATE SCHOOL OF KENT STATE UNIVERSITY IN PARTIAL FULFILLMENT OF THE REQUIREMENTS FOR A PH.D. DEGREE. (MH)

EJ 018 891 PS 500 356
A METHODOLOGICAL INVESTIGATION OF PIAGET'S THEORY OF OBJECT CONCEPT DEVELOPMENT IN THE SENSORY-MOTOR PERIOD MILLER, DELORES J.; AND OTHERS, *J EXP CHILD PSYCHOL*, V9 N1, PP59-85, 70 FEB
CONSISTENT AGE CHANGES SUGGEST 2 OVERLAPPING DEVELOPMENTAL DIMENSIONS: (1) THE ABILITY TO DEAL WITH VISIBLE VERSUS INVISIBLE DISPLACEMENTS, AND (2) WITH NONSEQUENTIAL VERSUS SEQUENTIAL DISPLACEMENTS. OTHER FINDINGS ARE INCLUDED. (MH)

EJ 018 892 PS 500 358
FACTORS INFLUENCING IMITATIVE LEARNING IN PRESCHOOL CHILDREN WAXLER, CAROLYN ZAHN; YARROW, MARIAN RADKE, *J EXP CHILD PSYCHOL*, V9 N1, PP115-130, 70 FEB

EJ 018 956 PS 500 334
A DAY IN THE LIFE OF A SCHOOL PSYCHOLOGIST LASSEGARD, DICK, *ELEM SCH J*, V70 N7, PP345-350, 70 APR
CHRONICLES THE EFFORTS OF A SCHOOL PSYCHOLOGIST TO HELP STUDENTS THROUGH INDIVIDUAL COUNSELING AND REMEDIAL PROGRAMS AND TO COMMUNICATE EFFECTIVELY WITH PARENTS, TEACHERS, AND COMMUNITY GROUPS. (NH)

EJ 018 957 PS 500 336
THE TEACHER'S VIEW OF THE PRINCIPAL'S ROLE IN INNOVATION MAHAN, JAMES M., *ELEM SCH J*, V70 N7, PP359-365, 70 APR
QUESTIONNAIRE RESPONSES BY 113 TEACHERS FROM 28 ELEMENTARY SCHOOLS INDICATED THAT TEACHERS REGARD THE PRINCIPAL AND SUBJECT SPECIALISTS AS BEING MOST INFLUENTIAL IN INITIATING INNOVATION. (NH)

EJ 018 958 PS 500 340
ARE MOVERS LOSERS? CRAMER, WARD; DORSEY, SUZANNE, *ELEM SCH J*, V70 N7, PP387-390, 70 APR
STUDY OF 366 SIXTH-GRADE CHILDREN OF ENLISTED AIR FORCE PERSONNEL SHOWED THAT MOBILITY HAD NO ADVERSE EFFECT ON THEIR READING ACHIEVEMENT AND, ON THE CONTRARY, MAY HAVE CONTRIBUTED TO THEIR READING PROFICIENCY. (NH)

EJ 018 969 PS 500 341
ACHIEVEMENT OF FIRST- AND SECOND-YEAR PUPILS IN GRADED AND NONGRADED CLASSROOMS BRODY, ERNESS BRIGHT, *ELEM SCH J*, V70 N7, PP391-394, 70 APR

EJ 018 970 PS 500 363
DEVELOPING PUBLIC DAY CARE FACILITIES IN MARYLAND HUNT, GRACE B., *CHILD WELFARE*, V49 N4, PP220-223, 70 APR

EJ 019 003 PS 500 282
AN ONTOGENY OF OPTIONAL SHIFT BEHAVIOR KENDLER, TRACY S.; KENDLER, HOWARD H., *CHILD DEVELOP*, V41 N1, PP1-27, 70 MAR
STUDIED DEVELOPMENTAL CHANGES IN OPTIONAL SHIFT DISCRIMINATIONS USING KINDERGARTNERS, SECOND GRADERS, SIXTH GRADERS, AND COLLEGE STUDENTS. (DR)

EJ 019 004 PS 500 289
CHANGES IN FRIENDSHIP STATUS AS A FUNCTION OF REINFORCEMENT BLAU, BURTON; RAFFERTY, JANET, *CHILD DEVELOP*, V41 N1, PP113-121, 70 MAR
RESULTS REVEALED THAT ALL SUBJECTS RECEIVING REINFORCEMENT INCREASED IN FRIENDSHIP STATUS AS RATED BY THEIR PARTNERS IN A COOPERATIVE TASK. (DR)

EJ 019 005 PS 500 290
SELF-CONCEPTS OF HIGH- AND LOW-CURIOSITY BOYS MAW, WALLACE H.; MAW, ETHEL W., *CHILD DEVELOP*, V41 N1, PP123-129, 70 MAR
HIGH-CURIOSITY BOYS HAD HIGHER SELF-CONCEPTS THAN LOW-CURIOSITY BOYS AND TENDED TO EXHIBIT BETTER INTERPERSONAL ATTITUDES AND TO PARTICIPATE IN ACTIVITIES WHICH SEEM TO BE AN INDICATION OF CURIOSITY. (AUTHOR/DR)

EJ 019 006 PS 500 294
THE EFFECTS OF STIMULUS TYPE ON PERFORMANCE IN A COLOR-FORM SORTING TASK WITH PRESCHOOL, KINDERGARTEN, FIRST-GRADE, AND THIRD-GRADE CHILDREN HARRIS, LAUREN; AND OTHERS, *CHILD DEVELOP*, V41 N1, PP177-191, 70 MAR
REPORTS THAT FORM MATCHING INCREASED WITH AGE BOTH IN NUMBER OF SUBJECTS WITH RELIABLE PREFERENCES AND IN STRENGTH OF PREFERENCES, BUT THAT AT ALL AGES FORM MATCHES PREDOMINATED. (AUTHOR/DR)

EJ 019 007 PS 500 298
CHILDREN'S MANIPULATION OF ILLUSORY AND AMBIGUOUS STIMULI, DISCRIMINATIVE PERFORMANCE, AN IMPLICATIONS FOR CONCEPTUAL DEVELOPMENT DAEHLER, MARVIN W., *CHILD DEVELOP*, V41 N1, PP225-241, 70 MAR
STUDIED DISCRIMINATIVE AND INVESTIGATORY RESPONSE BEHAVIOR AND EFFECTS OF RESPONSE TRAINING ON CHILDREN 4-5 TO 6-5 YEARS OF AGE. (DR)

EJ 019 008 PS 500 300
PERCEIVED MATERNAL CHILD-REARING EXPERIENCE AND THE EFFECTS OF VICARIOUS AND DIRECT REINFORCEMENT ON MALES HEILBRUN, ALFRED B., JR., *CHILD DEVELOP*, V41 N1, PP253-262, 70 MAR

EJ 019 009 PS 500 301
EFFECTS OF REINFORCEMENT BASE-LINE-INPUT DISCREPANCY UPON IMITATION IN CHILDREN EPSTEIN, RALPH; PRICE, FRANK, *DEVELOP PSYCHOL*, V2 N1, PP12-21, 70 JAN
STUDY DEMONSTRATES THAT PERFORMANCE OF IMITATIVE ACTS MAY BE HIGHLY RELATED TO A COMPLEX INTERACTION BETWEEN THE CHILD'S REINFORCEMENT HISTORY AND CURRENT REINFORCEMENT INPUTS. (AUTHOR)

EJ 019 010 PS 500 302
EFFECTS OF BRIEF OBSERVATION OF MODEL BEHAVIOR ON CONCEPTUAL TEMPO OF IMPULSIVE CHILDREN DEBUS, RAY L., *DEVELOP PSYCHOL*, V2 N1, PP22-32, 70 JAN

EJ 019 011 PS 500 303
FEAR OF VISUAL NOVELTY: DEVELOPMENTAL PATTERNS IN MALES AND FEMALES BRONSON, GORDON W., *DEVELOP PSYCHOL*, V2 N1, PP33-40, 70 JAN
LONGITUDINAL DATA CONCERNING FEAR RESPONSES IN 30 BOYS AND 30 GIRLS OBSERVED FROM AGES ONE MONTH TO 8 1/2 YEARS SUGGEST THAT IN MALES--BUT NOT IN FEMALES--A PREDISPOSITION TO A PARTICULAR LEVEL OF FEARFULNESS IS SET BY EVENTS THAT OCCURRED BEFORE 6 MONTHS OF AGE. (AUTHOR/MG)

EJ 019 012 PS 500 305
EFFECT OF VERBAL RESPONSE CLASS ON SHIFT IN THE PRESCHOOL CHILD'S JUDGMENT OF LENGTH IN RESPONSE TO AN ANCHOR STIMULUS SALZINGER, SUZANNE; AND OTHERS, *DEVELOP PSYCHOL*, V2 N1, PP49-57, 70 JAN

EJ 019 013 PS 500 307
SENSORY ORGANIZATION IN RETARDATES AND NORMALS STAYTON, SAMUEL E., *DEVELOP PSYCHOL*, V2 N1, PP66-70, 70 JAN

EJ 019 014 PS 500 309
INDIVIDUAL DIFFERENCES IN THE INFANT'S DISTRIBUTION OF ATTENTION TO STIMULUS DISCREPANCY MCCALL, ROBERT B.; KAGAN, JEROME, *DEVELOP PSYCHOL*, V2 N1, PP90-98, 70 JAN
RESULTS OF THIS STUDY OF 72 4-MONTH-OLD INFANTS SUGGEST CAUTION IN USING AN OVERT DEMONSTRATION OF HABITUATION AS A NECESSARY INDEX OF PERCEPTUAL LEARNING. (AUTHOR/MG)

EJ 019 015 PS 500 311
COMPARATIVE PERCEPTUAL MOTOR PERFORMANCE OF NEGRO AND WHITE YOUNG MENTAL RETARDATES ALLEY, GORDON R.; SNIDER, BILL, *DEVELOP PSYCHOL*, V2 N1, PP110-114, 70 JAN
RESULTS OF THIS STUDY SUGGEST THAT NEGRO MENTALLY RETARDED CHILDREN ARE MORE PROFICIENT ON SENSORY MOTOR TASKS THAN ARE THEIR WHITE COUNTERPARTS. (AUTHOR/MG)

EJ 019 016 PS 500 314
ON RELATING AN INFANT'S OBSERVATION TIME OF VISUAL STIMULI WITH CHOICE-THEORY ANALYSIS FREEDLE, ROY; LEWIS, MICHAEL, *DEVELOP PSYCHOL*, V2 N1, PP129-133, 70 JAN
OUTLINES A METHOD BY WHICH OBSERVATION TIME AS MEASURED BY VISUAL FIXATION ON AN OBJECT IN THE VISUAL FIELD CAN BE PREDICTED FOR N ITEMS VIEWED SIMULTANEOUSLY IN THE FIELD WHEN THE TIME FOR OBSERVING EACH ITEM PRESENTED SINGLY IS KNOWN. (AUTHOR/MG)

EJ 019 017 PS 500 315
MAGNITUDE-PROBABILITY PREFERENCES OF PRESCHOOL CHILDREN FROM TWO SOCIOECONOMIC LEVELS SILVERMAN, STEPHAN M.; SHAPIRO, MARTIN M., *DEVELOP PSYCHOL*, V2 N1, PP134-139, 70 JAN
THIS ARTICLE IS BASED ON A THESIS SUBMITTED BY THE FIRST AUTHOR TO EMORY UNIVERSITY IN PARTIAL FULFILLMENT OF THE REQUIREMENTS FOR THE MA DEGREE. (AUTHOR)

EJ 019 018 PS 500 320
FATHER ABSENCE AND THE PERSONALITY DEVELOPMENT OF THE MALE CHILD BILLER, HENRY B., *DEVELOP PSYCHOL*, V2 N2, PP181-201, 70 MAR

EJ 019 019 PS 500 322
ATTACHMENT BEHAVIORS IN HUMAN INFANTS: DISCRIMINATIVE VOCALIZATION ON MATERNAL SEPARATION FLEENER, DON E.; CAIRNS, ROBERT B., *DEVELOP PSYCHOL*, V2 N2, PP215-223, 70 MAR
STUDY OF 64 INFANTS SHOWED THAT (1) ONCE INFANTS BEGAN TO CRY, THEY TENDED TO PERSIST, (2) ONLY OLDER INFANTS SPECIFICALLY MISSED THEIR MOTHERS, AND (3) TENDENCY TO CRY WAS NOT RELATED TO MATERNAL RESPONSIVENESS OR SEX OF CHILD. (MH)

EJ 019 020 PS 500 328
PATERNAL ABSENCE, SEX TYPING, AND IDENTIFICATION SANTROCK, JOHN W., *DEVELOP PSYCHOL*, V2 N2, PP264-272, 70 MAR
THROUGH MATERNAL INTERVIEWS AND OBSERVATIONS OF STRUCTURED DOLL-PLAY, THIS STUDY ASSESSES THE EFFECTS OF FATHER ABSENCE ON THE DEPENDENCY, AGGRESSION, AND MASCULINITY-FEMININITY OF PRESCHOOL NEGRO CHILDREN. (MH)

EJ 019 021 PS 500 330
STANDARDIZATION OF A RESEARCH INSTRUMENT FOR IDENTIFYING ASSOCIATIVE RESPONDING IN CHILDREN ACHENBACH, THOMAS M., *DEVELOP PSYCHOL*, V2 N2, PP283-291, 70 MAR
CROSS-VALIDATION AND STANDARDIZATION OF A MULTIPLE CHOICE ANALOGY TEST DESIGNED TO IDENTIFY CHILDREN WHO RELY ON FREE ASSOCIATION RATHER THAN ANALOGICAL REASONING. (AUTHOR)

EJ 019 022 PS 500 360
STRUCTURED FAMILY-ORIENTED THERAPY FOR SCHOOL BEHAVIOR AND LEARNING DISORDERS FRIEDMAN, ROBERT, *CHILD WELFARE*, V49 N4, PP187-195, 70 APR

EJ 019 323 PS 500 316
A METHODOLOGICAL AND PHILOSOPHICAL CRITIQUE OF INTERVENTION-ORIENTED RESEARCH SROUFE, L. ALAN, *DEVELOP PSYCHOL*, V2 N1, PP140-145, 70 JAN
RAISES QUESTIONS CONCERNING THE METHODS AND PROCEDURES FOR OBTAINING CLASS DIFFERENCES, INTERPRETATIONS OF THESE DIFFERENCES, AND THE DECISION TO INTERVENE. (AUTHOR/MG)

EJ 019 324 PS 500 317
DEFICITS AND VALUE JUDGMENTS: A COMMENT ON SROUFE'S CRITIQUE BEE, HELEN L.; AND OTHERS, *DEVELOP PSYCHOL*, V2 N1, PP146-149, 70 JAN

EJ 019 359 PS 500 310
YOUNG CHILDREN IN INSTITUTIONS: SOME ADDITIONAL EVIDENCE WOLINS, MARTIN, *DEVELOP PSYCHOL*, V2 N1, PP99-109, 70 JAN
STUDY EVIDENCE DOES NOT SUPPORT FAMILIAR ASSUMPTIONS OF DEFICIENCIES IN INTELLIGENCE, PERSONALITY AND VALUE DEVELOPMENT, RESULTING BECAUSE YOUNG CHILDREN WERE SEPARATED FROM THEIR NATURAL MOTHERS AND GIVEN MANY YEARS OF INSTITUTIONAL CARE. THIS PAPER WAS PRESENTED AT THE 45TH ANNUAL MEETING OF THE AMERICAN ORTHOPSYCHIATRIC ASSOCIATION, CHICAGO, MARCH 20-23, 1968. (AUTHOR/MG)

EJ 019 386 PS 500 313
ROLE MODELSHIP AND INTERACTION IN ADOLESCENCE AND YOUNG ADULTHOOD BELL, ALAN P., *DEVELOP PSYCHOL*, V2 N1, PP123-128, 70 JAN
FINDINGS OF THIS STUDY SUPPORT THE POSITION THAT THE GLOBAL CONCEPT OF IDENTIFICATION IS TOO VAGUE TO BE USEFUL IN ASSESSING ITS EFFECTS ON, OR RELATION TO ADOLESCENT BEHAVIORS. THE STUDY WAS BASED ON PART OF A DOCTORAL DISSERTATION ("ROLE MODELS: THEIR RELATIONSHIP TO EDUCATIONAL AND OCCUPATIONAL BEHAVIORS") SUBMITTED TO TEACHERS COLLEGE, COLUMBIA UNIVERSITY. (AUTHOR/MG)

EJ 019 387 PS 500 331
PARENTAL DETERMINANTS OF PEER-ORIENTATION AND SELF-ORIENTATION AMONG PREADOLESCENTS HOLLANDER, EDWIN P.; MARCIA, JAMES E., *DEVELOP PSYCHOL*, V2 N2, PP292-302, 70 MAR

EJ 019 388 PS 500 338
PRAISE, CRITICISM, AND RACE BROWN, WILLIAM E.; AND OTHERS, *ELEM SCH J*, V70 N7, PP373-377, 70 APR
ATTITUDES OF TEACHERS TOWARD BI-RACIAL SITUATIONS SEEM TO BE AN ADDED VARIABLE IN THE PRAISE-CRITICISM DIMENSION OF TEACHER BEHAVIOR. CLASSES IN WHICH THE TEACHER'S RACE DIFFERS FROM THAT OF THE PUPILS HAVE A MORE POSITIVE SITUATION, WHICH AIDS IN PUPIL MOTIVATION. (AUTHOR)

EJ 019 414 PS 500 286
MOTHERS AS TEACHERS OF THEIR OWN PRESCHOOL CHILDREN: THE INFLUENCE OF SOCIOECONOMIC STATUS AND TASK STRUCTURE ON TEACHING SPECIFICITY BROPHY, JERE EDWARD, *CHILD DEVELOP*, V41 N1, PP79-94, 70 MAR
THIS PAPER IS BASED ON A DISSERTATION SUBMITTED TO THE FACULTY OF THE COMMITTEE ON HUMAN DEVELOPMENT AT THE UNIVERSITY OF CHICAGO IN PARTIAL FULFILLMENT OF THE REQUIREMENTS FOR THE PH.D. DEGREE. (DR)

EJ 019 415 PS 500 355
CHILDREN'S REACTIONS TO FAILURE AS A FUNCTION OF INSTRUCTIONS AND GOAL DISTANCE PEDERSON, DAVID R.; MCEWAN, ROBERT C., *J EXP CHILD PSYCHOL*, V9 N1, PP51-58, 70 FEB
THIS PAPER IS BASED ON AN M.A. THESIS PRESENTED TO THE GRADUATE SCHOOL OF THE UNIVERSITY OF WESTERN ONTARIO BY THE SECOND AUTHOR AND SUPERVISED BY THE FIRST AUTHOR. (MH)

EJ 019 443 PS 500 404
ILLEGIBILITIES IN THE CURSIVE HANDWRITING OF SIXTH-GRADERS HORTON, LOWELL W., *ELEM SCH J*, V70 N8, PP446-450, 70 MAY

EJ 019 506 PS 500 367
VALUING THE DIGNITY OF BLACK CHILDREN: A BLACK TEACHER SPEAKS WOLFE, DEBORAH PARTRIDGE, *CHILDHOOD EDUC*, V46 N7, PP348-350, 70 APR
EXPLAINS THE EXPERIENCE OF BEING BLACK IN AMERICA AND URGES TEACHERS TO VALUE THE DIGNITY OF EVERY CHILD IN THEIR CLASSROOMS. (DR)

EJ 019 507 PS 500 372
WHEN WORDS FAIL...DANCE MUKERJI, ROSE, *CHILDHOOD EDUC*, V46 N7, PP374-375, 70 APR
A DESCRIPTION OF HOW ONE GROUP OF SIX-YEAR-OLDS USED THE MEDIUM OF DANCE TO EXPRESS THEIR EMOTIONS AND REACTIONS TO THE DEATH OF MARTIN LUTHER KING, JR. (DR)

EJ 019 594 PS 500 365
EARLY MOTHER-INFANT INTERACTION AND 24-HOUR PATTERNS OF ACTIVITY AND SLEEP SANDER, LOUIS W.; AND OTHERS, *J AMER ACAD CHILD PSYCHIAT*, V9 N1, PP103-123, 70 JAN
THIS PAPER REPRESENTS PORTIONS OF A PRESENTATION GIVEN DECEMBER 9, 1968, TO THE DENVER PSYCHOANALYTIC SOCIETY AND TO THE DIVISION OF PSYCHIATRY OF THE UNIVERSITY OF COLORADO MEDICAL CENTER. (NH)

EJ 019 595 PS 500 407
DIFFERENTIAL VISUAL BEHAVIOR TO HUMAN AND HUMANOID FACES IN EARLY INFANCY CARPENTER, GENEVIEVE C.; AND OTHERS, *MERRILL-PALMER QUART*, V16 N1, PP91-108, 70 JAN
THIS PAPER WAS PRESENTED BY THE SENIOR AUTHOR AT THE MERRILL-PALMER INSTITUTE CONFERENCE ON RESEARCH AND TEACHING OF INFANT DEVELOPMENT, FEBRUARY 13-15, 1969. (MH)

EJ 019 669 PS 500 400
BEHAVIORAL COUNSELING FOR ELEMENTARY-SCHOOL CHILDREN BLAKER, KENNETH E.; BENNETT, ROGER W., *ELEM SCH J*, V70 N8, PP411-417, 70 MAY
GIVES EXAMPLES OF CLASSROOM SITUATIONS IN WHICH REINFORCEMENT THEORY IS USED TO COPE WITH SOME PRACTICAL PROBLEMS OF EDUCATING CHILDREN. (AUTHOR/DR)

EJ 019 862 PS 500 373
SEX EDUCATION OF THE YOUNG CHILD BERGER, ALLAN S., *YOUNG CHILDREN*, V25 N5, PP261-267, 70 MAY
THIS PAPER WAS PRESENTED TO A RECENT STAFF CONFERENCE OF THE TAKOMA PARK DAY CARE CENTER, TAKOMA PARK, MARYLAND. (DR)

EJ 019 966 PS 500 378
EVALUATING SETTINGS FOR LEARNING HARMS, THELMA, *YOUNG CHILDREN*, V25 N5, PP304-308, 70 MAY
A CHECKLIST IS PROVIDED TO EVALUATE THE SCHOOL ENVIRONMENT AS EXPERIENCED BY THE CHILD. A SELECTED LIST OF FILMS, BOOKS, AND PAMPHLETS FOR THE TEACHER IS INCLUDED. (DR)

EJ 020 103 PS 500 364
FROM THE TEACHER'S NOTEBOOK JEROME, ALICE, *J AMER ACAD CHILD PSYCHIAT*, V9 N1, PP12-32, 70 JAN
DESCRIPTION OF PSYCHOTHERAPEUTIC TECHNIQUES USED WITH TWO HIGHLY-DISTURBED GIRLS, BOTH 5 1/2 YEARS OLD. (NH)

EJ 020 104 PS 500 366
SECOND STAGE TEACHING PROBLEMS IN A PUBLIC SCHOOL CLASS FOR EMOTIONALLY DISTURBED CHILDREN TURNER, RUTH M.; CLAMAN, LAWRENCE, *J AMER ACAD CHILD PSYCHIAT*, V9 N1, PP144-156, 70 JAN
SUGGESTS THAT ONCE MAJOR BEHAVIORAL PROBLEMS HAVE BEEN SOLVED, THE TEACHER SHOULD CONCENTRATE ON THE SPECIFIC LEARNING PROBLEMS OF EACH CHILD. THIS PAPER IS A REVISED VERSION OF A PAPER PRESENTED AT THE ANNUAL MEETING OF THE AMERICAN ASSOCIATION OF PSYCHIATRIC CLINICS FOR CHILDREN, NOVEMBER 9, 1968, NEW YORK. (NH)

EJ 020 294 PS 500 376
WHAT ABOUT THE SCHOOL BUS? OVITT, JEAN M., *YOUNG CHILDREN*, V25 N5, PP293-296, 70 MAY

EJ 020 295 PS 500 377
A BACKWARD GLANCE--A FORWARD STEP? CHRISTOPHERSON, JOAN, *YOUNG CHILDREN*, V25 N5, PP297-303, 70 MAY
DESCRIBES THE KINDERGARTEN OF THE DECROLY SCHOOL OF BARCELONA, A PRIVATE SCHOOL THAT EMPHASIZES FLEXIBILITY AND THE USE OF THE NATURAL ENVIRONMENT AS A LESSON RESOURCE. (DR)

EJ 020 395 PS 500 401
TOY TALK: THE NEW CONVERSATION BETWEEN GENERATIONS STROM, ROBERT D., *ELEM SCH J*, V70 N8, PP418-428, 70 MAY
EXPLAINS HOW A TEACHING STRATEGY USING TOYS CAN DEVELOP VERBAL SKILLS IN YOUNG CHILDREN. (DR)

EJ 020 396 PS 500 405
RECEPTIVE LANGUAGE DEVELOPMENT IN INFANCY: ISSUES AND PROBLEMS FRIEDLANDER, BERNARD Z., *MERRILL-PALMER QUART*, V16 N1, PP7-51, 70 JAN
SUGGESTS THAT THE GROWTH OF RECEPTIVE LANGUAGE FUNCTIONING IN VERY YOUNG CHILDREN IS A CRUCIAL DEVELOPMENTAL AREA AND SUMMARIZES SOME MAJOR ISSUES INVOLVED IN ATTEMPTING TO LEARN MORE ABOUT IT. PORTIONS OF THIS TEXT WERE INCLUDED IN AN INVITED PRESENTATION AT THE 1969 CONFERENCE ON RESEARCH AND TEACHING OF INFANT DEVELOPMENT, MERRILL-PALMER INSTITUTE, DETROIT, FEBRUARY, 1969. (MH)

EJ 020 519 PS 500 371
PERSPECTIVE ON THE JENSEN AFFAIR BRAZZIEL, WILLIAM F., *CHILDHOOD EDUC*, V46 N7, PP371-373, 70 APR

EJ 020 520 PS 500 375
EFFECT OF VERBALIZATION ON YOUNG CHILDREN'S LEARNING OF A MANIPULATIVE SKILL LOMBARD, AVIMA; STERN, CAROLYN, *YOUNG CHILDREN*, V25 N5, PP282-288, 70 MAY
RESULTS OF A STUDY INVOLVING HEAD START CHILDREN SHOWED THAT PRACTICE IN VERBALIZATION WAS MOST EFFECTIVE IN HELPING CHILDREN TO ACQUIRE VERBAL SKILLS. THE AMOUNT OF EXPERIENCE WITH THE ACTUAL TASK WAS THE CRITICAL VARIABLE IN LEARNING A MOTOR OR ASSEMBLY SKILL. A VERSION OF THIS PAPER WAS PRESENTED AT THE ANNUAL MEETING OF THE AMERICAN PSYCHOLOGICAL ASSOCIATION, SAN FRANCISCO, AUGUST 1968. IT WAS ALSO SUBMITTED AS PART OF A DOCTORAL DISSERTATION BY THE SENIOR AUTHOR. (DR)

EJ 020 521 PS 500 409
PRECURSORS OF INTELLIGENCE AND CREATIVITY: A LONGITUDINAL STUDY OF ONE CHILD'S DEVELOPMENT BROWN, JANET L., *MERRILL-PALMER QUART*, V16 N1, PP117-137, 70 JAN
THIS PAPER WAS PRESENTED AT THE MERRILL-PALMER CONFERENCE ON RESEARCH AND TEACHING OF INFANT DEVELOPMENT, FEBRUARY 13, 1969. (MH)

EJ 020 522 PS 500 410
COGNITIVE SYNTHESIS IN NEGRO AND WHITE CHILDREN FARNHAM-DIGGORY, SYLVIA, *MONOGR SOC RES CHILD DEVELOP*, V35 N2, 70 MAR
THREE EXPERIMENTS EXPLORE FACTORS ASSOCIATED WITH THE DEVELOPMENT OF CERTAIN SYMBOLIC ABILITIES (VERBAL, MAPLIKE, AND MATHEMATICAL) IN 4-10 YEAR OLD NEGRO AND WHITE CHILDREN. THE EXPERIMENTAL TASKS REQUIRED A SYNTHESIS OF CONCEPTS WITH SYMBOLIC STIMULI. (MH)

EJ 020 541 PS 500 370
THE BEAUTIFUL PEOPLE IN CHILDREN'S BOOKS GLANCY, BARBARA, *CHILDHOOD EDUC*, V46 N7, PP365-370, 70 APR

EJ 020 717 PS 500 368
UNDERSTANDING THE BLACK CHILD WILKERSON, DOXEY A., *CHILDHOOD EDUC*, V46 N7, PP351-354, 70 APR
SUGGESTS THAT PSEUDOSCIENTIFIC THEORIES ABOUT WHY CHILDREN CANNOT LEARN BE ABANDONED AND REPLACED WITH MEANINGFUL TEACHING AND CURRICULUM THAT PROMOTE LEARNING. ENCOURAGES POSITIVE EXPECTATIONS BY TEACHERS AND COOPERATIVE RELATIONSHIPS WITH PARENTS. (DR)

EJ 020 718 PS 500 406
PATTERNS OF FEAR DEVELOPMENT DURING INFANCY SCARR, SANDRA; SALAPATEK, PHILIP, *MERRILL-PALMER QUART*, V16 N1, PP53-90, 70 JAN
TAKES AN EXPLORATORY LOOK AT THE RELATIONSHIPS BETWEEN (1) THE VARIOUS FEARS THAT DEVELOP DURING INFANCY, (2) PERCEPTUAL-COGNITIVE DEVELOPMENT AND THE EXHIBITION OF SPECIFIC FEARS, AND (3) INDIVIDUAL DIFFERENCES IN TEMPERAMENT AND THE MANIFESTATION OF SPECIFIC FEARS. THIS PAPER WAS PRESENTED AT THE MERRILL-PALMER INSTITUTE CONFERENCE ON RESEARCH AND TEACHING OF INFANT DEVELOPMENT, FEBRUARY 13-15, 1969. (MH)

EJ 020 719 PS 500 408
PROGRAMMING LIFE HISTORIES: EFFECTS OF STRESS IN ONTOGENY UPON EMOTIONAL REACTIVITY DENENBERG, VICTOR H.; AND OTHERS, *MERRILL-PALMER QUART*, V16 N1, PP109-116, 70 JAN

EJ 020 773 PS 500 397
TAKE A GIANT STEP --A REMEDIAL PROGRAM IN A CAMP SETTING REMER, VICTOR, *CHILD WELFARE*, V49 N5, PP270-274, 70 MAY
PRE- AND POSTTESTS OF 268 CHILDREN FROM THE FIFTH, SIXTH AND SEVENTH GRADES SHOWED THAT 179 GAINED 1 TO 5 YEARS IN READING GRADE LEVELS AFTER A 4 1/2- WEEK REMEDIAL READING PROGRAM IN A CAMP SETTING. FOLLOWUP REVEALED THAT NONE OF THE PARTICIPANTS BECAME SCHOOL DROPOUTS, AND ATTITUDES AND ACHIEVEMENT WERE IMPROVED. (NH)

EJ 020 774 PS 500 403
PARENTS TEACH KINDERGARTEN READING AT HOME NIEDERMEYER, FRED C., *ELEM SCH J*, V70 N8, PP438-445, 70 MAY

EJ 020 839 PS 500 399
A.S. NEILL: LATTER-DAY DEWEY? KEOHANE, MARY, *ELEM SCH J*, V70 N8, PP401-410, 70 MAY
COMPARES AND CONTRASTS THE BELIEFS AND PRACTICES OF A.S. NEILL, HEADMASTER OF SUMMERHILL SCHOOL, WITH JOHN DEWEY'S EDUCATIONAL PHILOSOPHY. (DR)

EJ 020 840 PS 500 402
SOVIET PRESCHOOL EDUCATION KREUSLER, ABRAHAM, *ELEM SCH J*, V70 N8, PP429-437, 70 MAY
EXPLAINS THE HISTORY, PHILOSOPHY, AND PRACTICES OF PUBLIC PRESCHOOLS IN RUSSIA. (DR)

EJ 020 857 PS 500 369
CHOICES, CHOICES, CHOICES! PEAK EXPERIENCES FROM THE AFRO-AMERICAN HERITAGE ADAIR, THELMA, *CHILDHOOD EDUC*, V46 N7, PP355-364, 70 APR
DESCRIBES METHODS, TECHNIQUES, AND RESOURCES FOR STUDYING THE BLACK CULTURAL HERITAGE THROUGH SOCIAL STUDIES, COMMUNICATIONS, MUSIC, AND ART. (DR)

EJ 020 858 PS 500 395
THE GHETTO AS A SOURCE OF FOSTER HOMES GARBER, MICHAEL; AND OTHERS, *CHILD WELFARE*, V49 N5, PP246-251, 70 MAY
PLACEMENT OF 20 MINORITY GROUP CHILDREN IN LOW INCOME MINORITY GROUP FOSTER HOMES PROVED HIGHLY SUCCESSFUL IN TERMS OF FAMILY ADJUSTMENT AND CHILD BEHAVIOR MODIFICATION. (NH)

EJ 020 859 PS 500 396
FOSTER CARE FOR MENTALLY RETARDED CHILDREN: HOW DOES CHILD WELFARE MEET THIS CHALLENGE? ADAMS, MARGARET E., *CHILD WELFARE*, V49 N5, PP260-269, 70 MAY
FOSTER CARE, IN FAMILY OR GROUP HOME, HAS PROVED A WORKABLE ALTERNATIVE TO TRADITIONAL INSTITUTIONAL CARE FOR RETARDED CHILDREN. ROLE OF CHILD WELFARE AGENCIES IS DISCUSSED. THIS PAPER WAS PRESENTED AT THE NATIONAL CONFERENCE ON SOCIAL WELFARE AT NEW YORK IN 1969. (AUTHOR/NH).

EJ 020 860 PS 500 398
WILLINGNESS TO ADOPT ATYPICAL CHILDREN CHAMBERS, DONALD E., *CHILD WELFARE*, V49 N5, PP275-279, 70 MAY
WILLINGNESS TO ADOPT ATYPICAL CHILDREN APPEARS TO BE HIGH FOR CHILDREN WHO ARE UNDER 5 YEARS OF AGE, WHO ARE PHYSICALLY HANDICAPPED, ARE SLOW LEARNERS, OR ARE OF AMERICAN INDIAN OR SPANISH-AMERICAN PARENTAGE. (AUTHOR)

EJ 020 892 PS 500 374
THE CALIFORNIA CREDENTIAL STORY: A NEW SPECIALIZATION FOR TEACHERS OF YOUNG CHILDREN MORRIS, MARJORIE SIMPSON, *YOUNG CHILDREN*, V25 N5, PP268-281, 70 MAY

EJ 021 026 PS 500 417
CONSISTENCY OF MATERNAL ATTITUDES AND PERSONALITY FROM PREGNANCY TO EIGHT MONTHS FOLLOWING CHILDBIRTH DAVIDS, ANTHONY; HOLDEN, RAYMOND H., *DEVELOP PSYCHOL*, V2 N3, PP364-366, MAY '70

EJ 021 027 PS 500 419
DEVELOPMENT OF MORAL ATTITUDES IN WHITE AND NEGRO BOYS HARRIS, HELENA, *DEVELOP PSYCHOL*, V2 N3, PP376-383, MAY '70
A PIAGETIAN-TYPE INTERVIEW AND W.I.S.C. VOCABULARY TEST ADMINISTERED TO 200 BIRACIAL BOYS OF FOUR SOCIAL CLASS LEVELS REVEALED THAT MATURITY OF MORAL ATTITUDES IS POSITIVELY RELATED TO SOCIAL CLASS, VOCABULARY SKILLS, AND WHITE RACE. THIS STUDY IS BASED ON A DISSERTATION PRESENTED TO COLUMBIA UNIVERSITY IN CANDIDACY FOR THE DEGREE OF DOCTOR OF PHILOSOPHY. (MH)

EJ 021 077 PS 500 386
EASE OF HABITUATION TO REPEATED AUDITORY AND SOMESTHETIC STIMULATION IN THE HUMAN NEWBORN MOREAU, TINA; AND OTHERS, *J EXP CHILD PSYCHOL*, V9 N2, PP193-207, APR '70
DIFFERENCES WERE FOUND IN THE EASE WITH WHICH NEWBORN INFANTS HABITUATE TO STIMULI IN DIFFERENT MODALITIES AND IN THE EASE WITH WHICH DIFFERENT RESPONSES HABITUATE TO THE SAME STIMULUS. (MH)

EJ 021 078 PS 500 387
RECOVERY OF HABITUATION IN INFANTS PANCRATZ, CHARITY N.; COHEN, LESLIE B., *J EXP CHILD PSYCHOL*, V9 N2, PP208-216, APR '70
MALE INFANTS HABITUATED THEIR FIXATION TIME OVER TRIALS AND DIFFERENTIATED BETWEEN THE NOVEL AND FAMILIAR STIMULI WHEN THE POSTHABITUATION INTERVAL WAS 15 SECONDS, BUT NEITHER MALE NOR FEMALE INFANTS DID SO WHEN THE INTERVAL WAS 5 MINUTES. THIS PAPER IS BASED UPON A THESIS SUBMITTED BY THE FIRST AUTHOR IN PARTIAL FULFILLMENT OF THE REQUIREMENTS FOR THE DEGREE OF MASTER OF ARTS IN PSYCHOLOGY AT THE UNIVERSITY OF ILLINOIS. (MH)

EJ 021 079 PS 500 437
AN EXAMINATION OF CHILDREN'S DAILY SCHEDULES IN THREE SOCIAL CLASSES AND THEIR RELATION TO FIRST-GRADE READING ACHIEVEMENT MILLER, WILMA H., *CALIF J EDUC RES*, V21 N3, PP100-110, MAY '70
AMOUNT OF PARENT-CHILD INTERACTION WAS RELATED TO SOCIAL CLASS, ALTHOUGH VARIATION WITHIN CLASSES WAS FOUND. HOME ACTIVITIES WERE NOT SIGNIFICANTLY CORRELATED WITH READING READINESS OR ACHIEVEMENT. RESEARCH WAS TAKEN FROM A DOCTORAL DISSERTATION DONE BY WILMA H. MILLER UNDER THE DIRECTION OF DR. RUTH STRANG AT THE UNIVERSITY OF ARIZONA, 1967. (DR)

EJ 021 080 PS 500 456
PROGRAMMING CREATIVE BEHAVIOR REESE, HAYNE W.; PARNES, SIDNEY J., *CHILD DEVELOP*, V41 N2, PP413-423, JUN '70
CREATIVITY, AS MEASURED BY STANDARD TESTS, WAS IMPROVED IN HIGH SCHOOL STUDENTS AS A CONSEQUENCE OF A 1-SEMESTER COURSE WITH SPECIAL PROGRAMED MATERIALS. (MH) CREATIVE DEVELOPMENT

EJ 021 081 PS 500 458
INTRAFAMILY COMPARISON OF LOVING-REJECTING CHILD-REARING PRACTICES COX, SAMUEL H., *CHILD DEVELOP*, V41 N2, PP437-448, JUN '70
EXTRA-FAMILIAL MEASURES OF CHILD'S BEHAVIOR MORE RELATED TO: (1) CHILD'S PERCEPTION OF EACH PARENT THAN TO THE PARENT'S OWN REPORT, (2) MOTHER'S REPORT THAN TO FATHER'S REPORT, AND (3) CHILD'S PERCEPTION OF FATHER THAN TO CHILD'S PERCEPTION OF MOTHER. (MH)

EJ 021 082 PS 500 465
THE RELATION BETWEEN THE AMOUNT OF TIME INFANTS SPEND AT VARIOUS STATES AND THE DEVELOPMENT OF VISUAL BEHAVIOR MOSS, HOWARD A.; ROBSON, KENNETH S., *CHILD DEVELOP*, V41 N2, PP509-517, JUN '70

EJ 021 083 PS 500 467
PLAY AS A FUNCTION OF TOY STRUCTURE AND FANTASY PREDISPOSITION PULASKI, MARY ANN SPENCER, *CHILD DEVELOP*, V41 N2, PP531-537, JUN '70
THIS STUDY IS BASED ON A DOCTORAL DISSERTATION SUBMITTED TO THE CITY UNIVERSITY OF NEW YORK IN PARTIAL FULFILLMENT OF THE REQUIREMENTS FOR THE DEGREE OF DOCTOR OF PHILOSOPHY IN PSYCHOLOGY. (MH)

EJ 021 188 PS 500 466
TWINNING: A MARKER FOR BIOLOGICAL INSULTS HOWARD, ROBERT G.; BROWN, ANNE M., *CHILD DEVELOP*, V41 N2, PP519-530, JUN '70
ANALYSIS OF VARIOUS STATISTICS FROM BIRTH RECORDS OF 317 CONSECUTIVE BIRTHS REVEALED THAT TWINS ARE NONREPRESENTATIVE OF NEWBORNS WITH RESPECT TO BIRTH WEIGHT AND GESTATION, WITH MALE PAIRS TO SAME-SEX PAIRS THE LEAST REPRESENTATIVE. DIFFERENCES BETWEEN NEGRO AND CAUCASIAN TWINS WERE ALSO FOUND. (MH)

EJ 021 380 PS 500 442
EDUCATIONAL EVALUATION AS RESEARCH FOR PROGRAM IMPROVEMENT MESSICK, SAMUEL, *CHILDHOOD EDUC*, V46 N8, PP413-414, MAY '70

EJ 021 381 PS 500 447
RESEARCH, EVALUATION, AND PUBLIC POLICY: AN INVITED EDITORIAL SUGARMAN, JULE M., *CHILD DEVELOP*, V41 N2, PP263-266, JUN '70

EJ 021 411 PS 500 444
NATURAL ASSESSMENT OF EDUCATIONAL PROGRESS MEHRENS, WILLIAM A., *CHILDHOOD EDUC*, V46 N8, PP422-425, MAY '70
OFFERS AN OVERVIEW OF NAEP, A PROJECT DESIGNED TO COMPILE DATA FOR ASSESSING AND IMPROVING AMERICAN EDUCATION. (DR)

EJ 021 514 PS 500 438
TEACHING THE UNTEACHABLES GLAVACH, MATHEW; STONER, DONOVAN, *CALIF J EDUC RES*, V21 N3, PP111-119, MAY '70

EJ 021 523 PS 500 430
INFANT MORTALITY: AN URGENT NATIONAL PROBLEM FALKNER, FRANK, *CHILDREN*, V17 N3, PP83-87, MAY-JUN '70

EJ 021 524 PS 500 431
INFANT MORTALITY TRENDS AND MATERNAL AND INFANT CARE HUNT, ELEANOR, *CHILDREN*, V17 N3, PP88-90, MAY-JUN '70

EJ 021 629 PS 500 443
INDIVIDUALIZING INSTRUCTION THROUGH DIAGNOSIS AND EVALUATION MILLER, JACK W.; MILLER, HAROLDINE G., *CHILDHOOD EDUC*, V46 N8, PP417-421, MAY '70

EJ 021 683 PS 500 425
MEASURES OF VOCABULARY AND GRAMMATICAL SKILLS FOR CHILDREN UP TO AGE SIX MEHRABIAN, ALBERT, *DEVELOP PSYCHOL*, V2 N3, PP439-446, MAY '70
SIX MEASURES OF CHILDREN'S VERBAL SKILLS WERE FOUND TO HAVE INTERNAL CONSISTENCY, AND INTERJUDGE AND TEST-RETEST RELIABILITY. (MH)

EJ 021 755 PS 500 381
PROBLEM SOLVING AND THE PERCEPTUAL SALIENCE OF VARIABILITY AND CONSTANCY: A DEVELOPMENTAL STUDY ODOM, RICHARD D.; GUZMAN, RICHARD D., *J EXP CHILD PSYCHOL*, V9 N2, PP156-165, APR '70
AGE AND CONDITION (EITHER CONSTANCY-RELEVANT OR VARIABILITY-RELEVANT) INTERACT, WITH THE YOUNGEST GROUP IN THE CONSTANCY-RELEVANT CONDITION PERFORMING MOST POORLY ON CONCEPT IDENTIFICATION TASKS. (MH)

EJ 021 756 PS 500 382
DIMENSIONAL LEARNING ACROSS SENSORY MODALITIES IN NURSERY SCHOOL CHILDREN BLANK, MARION; KLIG, SALLY, *J EXP CHILD PSYCHOL*, V9 N2, PP166-173, APR '70
RESULTS INDICATE THAT DIMENSIONAL SHIFTING REPRESENTS SOME FORM OF NONVERBALLY MEDIATED LEARNING RATHER THAN A MORE LIMITED FORM OF DISCRIMINATION LEARNING BOUND TO THE SPECIFIC SENSORY MODALITY OF TRAINING. (MH)

EJ 021 757 PS 500 383
IMAGERY IN CHILDREN'S PAIRED-ASSOCIATE LEARNING REESE, HAYNE W., *J EXP CHILD PSYCHOL*, V9 N2, PP174-178, APR '70

EJ 021 758 PS 500 384
SPATIO-TEMPORAL SERIAL PERFORMANCE IN CHILDREN AND ADULTS FOLEY, WAYNE EDWARD; LIPPMAN, LOUIS G., *J EXP CHILD PSYCHOL*, V9 N2, PP179-186, APR '70
NEITHER ADULTS' NOR CHILDREN'S PERFORMANCES ON A RECONSTRUCTION TASK WAS AFFECTED BY SPATIAL VARIATION, BUT CHILDREN'S PERFORMANCE WAS INFLUENCED BY VARIATION IN THE TEMPORAL SEQUENCE OF STIMULUS PRESENTATION. THIS ARTICLE IS BASED UPON AN M.A. THESIS BY THE FIRST AUTHOR UNDER SUPERVISION OF THE SECOND AUTHOR. A VERSION OF THIS PAPER WAS PRESENTED AT THE 1969 MEETINGS OF THE WESTERN PSYCHOLOGICAL ASSOCIATION, VANCOUVER. (MH)

EJ 021 759 PS 500 385
RESPONSE STRATEGIES IN THE ODDITY DISCRIMINATION OF PRESCHOOL CHILDREN CROLL, WILLIAM L., *J EXP CHILD PSYCHOL*, V9 N2, PP187-192, APR '70

EJ 021 760 PS 500 388
MEMORY IN THE INFANT FAGAN, JOSEPH F., III, *J EXP CHILD PSYCHOL*, V9 N2, PP217-226, APR '70
FOR INFANTS FROM 3 TO 6 MONTHS OLD, NOVEL STIMULI COMMANDED SIGNIFICANTLY MORE ATTENTION THAN FAMILIAR STIMULI ON BOTH IMMEDIATE AND DELAYED TESTS OF STIMULUS RECOGNITION. (MH)

EJ 021 761 PS 500 391
TRAINING IN CONSERVATION OF WEIGHT OVERBECK, CARLA; SCHWARTZ, MARIAN, *J EXP CHILD PSYCHOL*, V9 N2, PP253-264, APR '70
REINFORCEMENT TRAINING WAS SHOWN TO FACILITATE ACQUISITION OF CONSERVATION OF WEIGHT, WHILE ACTIVE PARTICIPATION WAS NO MORE EFFECTIVE THAN PASSIVE OBSERVATION. THIS REPORT IS BASED ON A THESIS SUBMITTED IN PARTIAL FULFILLMENT OF REQUIREMENTS FOR THE M.S. DEGREE BY THE FIRST AUTHOR UNDER THE SUPERVISION OF THE SECOND AUTHOR. (MH)

EJ 021 762 PS 500 392
THE INTERACTION OF PRONUNCIABILITY AND RESPONSE PRETRAINING ON THE PAIRED-ASSOCIATE PERFORMANCE OF THIRD-GRADE CHILDREN KELLAS, GEORGE; BUTTERFIELD, EARL C., *J EXP CHILD PSYCHOL*, V9 N2, PP265-271, APR '70
FREE PAIRED-ASSOCIATE TASK PERFORMANCE IS AIDED BY PRONUNCIABILITY, AND FACILITATION OF PERFORMANCE DUE TO RELEVANT PRETRAINING INCREASES AS PRONUNCIABILITY DECREASES. (MH)

EJ 021 763 PS 500 411
THE INTELLIGENCE OF CHILDREN OF SCHIZOPHRENICS LANE, ELLEN A.; AND OTHERS, *DEVELOP PSYCHOL*, V2 N3, PP315-317, MAY '70
ANALYSIS OF IQ'S OF 262 CHILDREN AND THEIR 129 SCHIZOPHRENIC PARENTS REVEALED NO DELETERIOUS EFFECTS ON THE INTELLECTUAL DEVELOPMENT OF THE CHILDREN. (MH)

EJ 021 764 PS 500 416
THE ROLE OF COMPREHENSION IN CHILDREN'S PROBLEM SOLVING BEM, SANDRA L., *DEVELOP PSYCHOL*, V2 N3, PP351-358, MAY '70
THIS ARTICLE IS BASED ON A DOCTORAL DISSERTATION SUBMITTED TO THE DEPARTMENT OF PSYCHOLOGY, UNIVERSITY OF MICHIGAN. (MH)

EJ 021 765 PS 500 418
CHILD VERSUS ADULT PERCEPTION OF EVALUATIVE MESSAGES IN VERBAL, VOCAL, AND VISUAL CHANNELS BUGENTAL, DAPHNE E.; AND OTHERS, *DEVELOP PSYCHOL*, V2 N3, PP367-375, MAY '70
ONLY AGE DIFFERENCE IN PERCEPTION INDICATED YOUNG CHILDREN SAW PICTURES OF WOMEN SMILING AS ONLY NEUTRAL OR WEAKLY POSITIVE. (MH)

EJ 021 766 PS 500 420
PROBABILITY LEARNING AS A FUNCTION OF AGE, SEX, AND TYPE OF CONSTRAINT PECAN, ERENE V.; SCHVANEVELDT, ROGER W., *DEVELOP PSYCHOL*, V2 N3, PP384-388, MAY '70
HIGHER LEVELS OF PREDICTING THE MORE FREQUENT EVENT WERE ACHIEVED WITH MALES THAN FEMALES; WITH THE CONTINGENT THAN THE NONCONTINGENT SITUATION; AND WITH ADULT MALES THAN BOYS IN THE NONCONTINGENT SITUATION. FEMALES WERE MORE LIKELY TO REPEAT AN INCORRECT PREDICTION. (MH)

EJ 021 767 PS 500 422
DEVELOPMENT CHANGES IN PROBLEM-SOLVING STRATEGIES: PERMUTATION LESKOW, SONIA; SMOCK, CHARLES D., *DEVELOP PSYCHOL*, V2 N3, PP412-422, MAY '70
INDICATES THAT TWO MAJOR NONEXCLUSIVE PERMUTATION PROBLEM-SOLVING STRATEGIES INCREASE WITH AGE: (1) MATHEMATICAL GROUP STRUCTURE, AND (2) HOLDING INITIAL MARKS CONSTANT WHILE PERMUTING THE REMAINDER. SIGNIFICANT SEX DIFFERENCES ARE SUGGESTED. THIS REPORT IS BASED ON A DISSERTATION SUBMITTED TO THE GRADUATE SCHOOL OF PURDUE UNIVERSITY BY THE FIRST AUTHOR IN PARTIAL FULFILLMENT OF THE REQUIREMENTS OF THE PH.D. DEGREE AND CONDUCTED UNDER THE SUPERVISION OF THE SECOND AUTHOR. (MH)

EJ 021 768 PS 500 423
COGNITIVE SYNTHESIS, CONSERVATION, AND TASK ANALYSIS HALL, VERNON C.; AND OTHERS, *DEVELOP PSYCHOL*, V2 N3, PP423-428, MAY '70
TRAINING FOR OR ALTERING THE "SET" RESULTED IN BETTER PERFORMANCE. SUBJECTS TRAINED TO PERFORM CORRECTLY ON THE SYNTHESIS TASK DID NOT DO SIGNIFICANTLY BETTER ON CONSERVATION. (MH)

EJ 021 769 PS 500 427
MOTOR ACTIVITY: EFFECTS ON MEMORY WEINER, BARBARA; GOODNOW, JACQUELINE J., *DEVELOP PSYCHOL*, V2 N3, PP448, MAY '70
RESULTS INDICATED THAT HANDLING, IN ADDITION TO SEEING AN OBJECT, FACILITATES MEMORY ONLY BECAUSE IT MAINTAINS VISUAL ATTENTION. (MH)

EJ 021 770 PS 500 451
BACKWARD ASSOCIATIONS IN PAIRED-ASSOCIATE LEARNING OF RETARDATES AND NORMAL CHILDREN BAUMEISTER, ALFRED A.; AND OTHERS, *CHILD DEVELOP*, V41 N2, PP355-364, JUN '70

EJ 021 771 PS 500 453
COMPARISON OF RATIOS AND THE CHANCE CONCEPT IN CHILDREN FISCHBEIN, EFRAIM; AND OTHERS, *CHILD DEVELOP*, V41 N2, PP377-389, JUN '70
SHORT INSTRUCTION ENABLED THIRD- AND SIXTH-GRADERS TO MAKE CORRECT RATIO DECISIONS. (MH)

EJ 021 772 PS 500 454
DETERMINANTS OF PART-WHOLE PERCEPTION IN CHILDREN ELKIND, DAVID; AND TOTHERS, *CHILD DEVELOP*, V41 N2, PP391-398, JUN '70
RESULTS SUPPORT VIEW THAT DEVELOPMENT OF PART-WHOLE PERCEPTION IS MEDIATED BY LOGICLIKE PERCEPTUAL REGULATIONS. (MH)

EJ 021 773 PS 500 459
INFERENCE AND PREFERENCE IN CHILDREN'S CONCEPTUAL PERFORMANCE SCHOLNICK, ELLIN KOFSKY, *CHILD DEVELOP*, V41 N2, PP449-460, JUN '70

EJ 021 774 PS 500 461
SOCIOECONOMIC BACKGROUND AND COGNITIVE FUNCTIONING IN PRESCHOOL CHILDREN MUMBAUER, CORINNE C.; MILLER, J. O., *CHILD DEVELOP*, V41 N2, PP471-480, JUN '70
DISADVANTAGED PRESCHOOL CHILDREN, ALTHOUGH LESS EFFICIENT IN INTELLECTUAL PERFORMANCE THAN ADVANTAGED CHILDREN, WERE NOT LESS LIKELY TO INHIBIT MOTOR RESPONSES UPON VERBAL REQUEST OR LESS CURIOUS. (MH)

EJ 021 775 PS 500 463
PATTERNS OF WISC SCORES FOR CHILDREN OF TWO SOCIOECONOMIC CLASSES AND RACES BURNES, KAY, *CHILD DEVELOP*, V41 N2, PP493-499, JUN '70
DISADVANTAGED SUBJECTS OBTAINED LOWER SCORES THAN ADVANTAGED. DIFFERENCES WERE BETWEEN SOCIOECONOMIC GROUPS, NOT BETWEEN RACES. (MH)

EJ 021 776 PS 500 464
REVERSIBILITY TRAINING AND STIMULUS DESIRABILITY AS FACTORS IN CONSERVATION OF NUMBER ROLL, SAMUEL, *CHILD DEVELOP*, V41 N2, PP501-507, JUN '70
TRAINING INCREASED CONSERVATION RESPONDING BUT NOT VERBALIZATION OF CONSERVATION PRINCIPLES. STIMULUS DESIRABILITY DID NOT AFFECT PRESENCE OF CONSERVATION EVEN IN LABORING-CLASS SUBJECTS. (MH)

EJ 021 777 PS 500 468
NONVERBAL MNEMONIC MEDIATION IN PRESCHOOL CHILDREN RYAN, SARAH M.; AND OTHERS, *CHILD DEVELOP*, V41 N2, PP539-550, JUN '70
CONTRARY TO PREVIOUS FINDINGS, CHILDREN AS YOUNG AS 3 1/2-4 YEARS OF AGE EXHIBITED THE ABILITY TO USE NONVERBAL, IKONIC MEDIATION. PRODUCTION DEFICIENCIES AND INEFFICIENCIES WERE MORE COMMON THAN MEDIATION DEFICIENCIES AND INEFFICIENCIES. (MH)

EJ 021 849 PS 500 393
OPTIONAL SHIFT BEHAVIOR OF CHILDREN AS A FUNCTION OF AGE, TYPE OF PRETRAINING AND STIMULUS SALIENCE TIGHE, THOMAS J.; TIGHE, LOUISE S., *J EXP CHILD PSYCHOL*, V9 N2, PP272-285, APR '70

EJ 021 965 PS 500 445
THE IMPACT OF HEAD START: AN EVALUATION OF THE EFFECTS OF HEAD START ON CHILDREN'S COGNITIVE AND AFFECTIVE DEVELOPMENT BY VICTOR G. CICIRELLI KEAN, JOHN M., *CHILDHOOD EDUC*, V46 N8, PP449-452, MAY '70
DISCUSSES THE FINDINGS OF THE WESTINGHOUSE REPORT AND SUGGESTS THEY BE CONSIDERED A LIMITED AND PARTIAL DESCRIPTION OF THE EFFECTS OF USING HEAD START TO EDUCATE CHILDREN. (DR)

EJ 021 986 PS 500 380
EFFECTS OF ARITHMETIC PROBLEM DIFFICULTY ON PUPILLARY DILATION IN NORMALS AND EDUCABLE RETARDATES BOERSMA, FREDERIC; AND OTHERS, *J EXP CHILD PSYCHOL*, V9 N2, PP142-155, APR '70

EJ 021 987 PS 500 389
GENERALIZATION IN A STIMULUS CLASSIFICATION TASK: STIMULUS SELECTION WITHIN AND AMONG DIMENSIONS CROLL, WILLIAM L., *J EXP CHILD PSYCHOL*, V9 N2, PP227-238, APR '70

EJ 021 988 PS 500 390
THE STABILITY OF DIMENSIONAL PREFERENCE FOLLOWING ODDITY TRAINING BROWN, ANN L., *J EXP CHILD PSYCHOL*, V9 N2, PP239-252, APR '70

EJ 021 989 PS 500 412
COGNITIVE FACTORS IN THE CONDITIONING OF CHILDREN'S PREFERENCES WALLS, RICHARD T.; DIVESTA, FRANCIS J., *DEVELOP PSYCHOL*, V2 N3, PP318-324, MAY '70
DEVELOPMENT OF PREFERENCE FOUND TO BE RELATED TO FREQUENCY OF ASSOCIATION OF REWARDS WITH A CRITICAL STIMULUS. THIS ARTICLE IS BASED ON A DISSERTATION SUBMITTED IN PARTIAL FULFILLMENT OF THE REQUIREMENTS FOR THE DEGREE OF DOCTOR OF PHILOSOPHY FROM THE PENNSYLVANIA STATE UNIVERSITY BY THE FIRST AUTHOR. (MH)

EJ 021 990 PS 500 413
NATURE OF CREATIVITY IN HIGH- AND LOW-CURIOSITY BOYS MAW, WALLACE H.; MAW, ETHEL W., *DEVELOP PSYCHOL*, V2 N3, PP325-329, MAY '70
IN A STUDY BASED ON OPERATIONAL DEFINITIONS, HIGH-CURIOSITY FIFTH GRADED BOYS WERE FOUND TO RATE HIGH ON CERTAIN CREATIVITY FACTORS, WHILE LOW-CURIOSITY BOYS RATED LOW ON THE SAME FACTORS. (MH)

EJ 021 991 PS 500 414
USE OF THE IT SCALE FOR CHILDREN IN ASSESSING SEX-ROLE PREFERENCE IN PRESCHOOL NEGRO CHILDREN SUMMERS, DARRYL L.; FELKER, DONALD W., *DEVELOP PSYCHOL*, V2 N3, PP330-334, MAY '70
RESULTS SUPPORTED THE VALIDITY OF THE IT SCALE FOR CHILDREN (ITSC) FOR PRESCHOOL NEGRO CHILDREN. THIS ARTICLE IS BASED UPON A THESIS SUBMITTED IN PARTIAL FULFILLMENT OF THE REQUIREMENTS FOR THE MASTER'S DEGREE AT THE UNIVERSITY OF MARYLAND. (MH)

EJ 021 992 PS 500 421
EFFECTS OF INCONSISTENT PUNISHMENT ON AGGRESSION IN CHILDREN DEUR, JAN L.; PARKE, ROSS D., *DEVELOP PSYCHOL*, V2 N3, PP403-411, MAY '70
DEMONSTRATES THE SUPPRESSIVE EFFECT OF PUNISHMENT ON THE STRENGTH AND PERSISTENCE OF AN AGGRESSIVE RESPONSE IN CHILDREN. AN EARLIER VERSION OF THIS PAPER WAS PRESENTED AT THE MEETING OF THE SOCIETY FOR RESEARCH IN CHILD DEVELOPMENT, SANTA MONICA, 1969. (MH)

EJ 021 993 PS 500 424
LONGITUDINAL STUDY OF DEVELOPMENT OF THE BODY CONCEPT FATERSON, HANNA F.; WITKIN, HERMAN A., *DEVELOP PSYCHOL*, V2 N3, PP429-438, MAY '70
ARTICULATION-OF-BODY-CONCEPT SCORES INCREASED BETWEEN AGES 8 AND 14, WITH LITTLE CHANGE THEREAFTER. (MH)

EJ 021 994 PS 500 426
SOME CORRELATES OF AVERAGE LEVEL OF HAPPINESS AMONG COLLEGE STUDENTS CONSTANTINOPLE, ANNE, *DEVELOP PSYCHOL*, V2 N3, PP447, MAY '70
LEVEL OF HAPPINESS IS MOST CLOSELY ASSOCIATED WITH BASIC TRUST, IDENTITY, BASIC MISTRUST, AND ISOLATION ON THE INVENTORY OF PSYCHOSOCIAL DEVELOPMENT. (MH)

EJ 021 995 PS 500 429
NURTURANCE, NURTURANCE WITHDRAWAL, AND RESISTANCE TO TEMPTATION AMONG THREE AGE GROUPS SAADATMAND, BIJAN; AND OTHERS, *DEVELOP PSYCHOL*, V2 N3, PP450, MAY '70

EJ 021 996 PS 500 440
CREATIVITY AND ALIENATION: AN EXPLORATION OF THEIR RELATIONSHIP IN ADOLESCENCE HEUSSENSTAMM, FRANCES K., *CALIF J EDUC RES*, V21 N3, PP140-146, MAY '70
COMPARES CREATIVITY MEASURES FOR THREE GROUPS OF STUDENTS: TEACHER-NOMINATED, PEER-NOMINATED, AND CONTROL. TEACHERS WERE MORE EFFECTIVE IN RECOGNIZING CREATIVITY THAN PEERS. PEER NOMINEES WERE LESS ALIENATED THAN THE OTHER GROUPS. (DR)

EJ 021 997 PS 500 447
RELATION OF EARLY SOCIALIZATION EXPERIENCES TO SELF-CONCEPTS AND GENDER ROLE IN MIDDLE CHILDHOOD SEARS, ROBERT R., *CHILD DEVELOP*, V41 N2, PP267-289, JUN '70
HIGH SELF-CONCEPTS SIGNIFICANTLY ASSOCIATED WITH (1) HIGH READING AND ARITHMETIC ACHIEVEMENT, (2)OR SELF-CONCEPTS ASSOCIATED WITH FEMINITY. (MH)

EJ 021 998 PS 500 448
THE DEVELOPMENT OF THE CONCEPT OF OBJECT AS RELATED TO INFANT-MOTHER ATTACHMENT BELL, SILVIA M., *CHILD DEVELOP*, V41 N2, PP291-311, JUN '70
RESULTS INDICATE THAT (1) BABIES HAVE BETTER CONCEPT OF PERSON THAN OBJECT AS PERMANENT, BUT THERE ARE IMPORTANT INDIVIDUAL DIFFERENCES, (2) RATE OF PERSON PERMANENCE DEVELOPMENT IS RELATED TO INFANT-MOTHER ATTACHMENT, AND (3) RATE OF PERSON PERMANENCE DEVELOPMENT AFFECTS OBJECT PERMANENCE DEVELOPMENT. (MH)

EJ 021 999 PS 500 455
A DEVELOPMENTAL STUDY OF THE RELATIONSHIP BETWEEN CONCEPTUAL, EGO, AND MORAL DEVELOPMENT SULLIVAN, EDMUND V.; AND OTHERS, *CHILD DEVELOP*, V41 N2, PP399-411, JUN '70

EJ 022 000 PS 500 460
BIRTH ORDER AND PHYSIOLOGICAL STRESS RESPONSE WEISS, JONATHAN H., *CHILD DEVELOP*, V41 N2, PP461-470, JUN '70
OBJECTIVE MEASURES REVEAL ELEVATED HEART RATES FOR FIRST-BORNS. (MH)

EJ 022 057 PS 500 462
CERTAIN ANTENATAL, PERINATAL, AND DEVELOPMENTAL VARIABLES AND READING RETAR RETARDATION IN MIDDLE-CLASS BOYS LYLE, J. G., *CHILD DEVELOP*, V41 N2, PP481-491, JUN '70

EJ 022 136 PS 500 415
CHILDREN'S SOCIAL SENSITIVITY AND THE RELATIONSHIP TO INTERPERSONAL COMPETENCE, INTRAPERSONAL COMFORT, AND INTELLECTUAL LEVEL ROTHENBERG, BARBARA B., *DEVELOP PSYCHOL*, V2 N3, PP335-350, MAY '70
AGE, INTELLECTUAL ABILITY, AND INTERPERSONAL ADJUSTMENT WERE THE FACTORS WHICH CONTRIBUTED MOST TO ACCURATE SOCIAL PERCEPTIONS BY STUDENTS IN GRADES 3 AND 5. THIS ARTICLE IS BASED ON A DISSERTATION SUBMITTED TO THE FACULTY OF THE GRADUATE SCHOOL OF CORNELL UNIVERSITY IN PARTIAL FULFILLMENT OF THE REQUIREMENTS FOR THE PH.D. DEGREE. (MH)

EJ 022 137 PS 500 432
A PRESCHOOL EXCHANGE: BLACK MOTHERS SPEAK AND A WHITE TEACHER LISTENS KUNREUTHER, SYLVIA CLIFFORD, *CHILDREN*, V17 N3, PP91-96, MAY-JUN '70
TEACHER IN THE ROLE OF LISTENER AT WEEKLY GROUP MEETINGS WITH EIGHT MOTHERS HELPS THEM GAIN CONFIDENCE AS SHE HERSELF GAINS UNDERSTANDING OF MOTHERS' GOALS FOR THEIR CHILDREN. (NH)

EJ 022 138 PS 500 441
THE ENVIRONMENTAL MYSTIQUE: TRAINING THE INTELLECT VERSUS DEVELOPMENT OF THE CHILD ZIGLER, EDWARD, *CHILDHOOD EDUC*, V46 N8, PP402-412, MAY '70
ANALYZES SELECTED RESEARCH ON EMOTIONAL AND MOTIVATIONAL DEVELOPMENT. CITES SOME EXCESSES ASSOCIATED WITH POPULAR STRESS ON COGNITIVE GROWTH; DISCUSSES SOME NOT-SO-EASILY MEASURABLE AREAS OF AFFECTIVE BEHAVIOR. THIS PAPER IS A MODIFIED VERSION OF A PAPER PRESENTED TO THE AMERICAN EDUCATION RESEARCH ASSOCIATION, 1969. (DR)

EJ 022 139 PS 500 449
RECIPROCITY AND GENEROSITY: SOME DETERMINANTS OF SHARING IN CHILDREN HARRIS, MARY B., *CHILD DEVELOP*, V41 N2, PP313-328, JUN '70
THIS PAPER IS BASED UPON A DOCTORAL DISSERTATION SUBMITTED TO STANFORD UNIVERSITY.

EJ 022 140 PS 500 450
PREACHING AND PRACTICING GENEROSITY: CHILDREN'S ACTIONS AND REACTIONS BRYAN, JAMES H.; WALBEK, NANCY HODGES, *CHILD DEVELOP*, V41 N2, PP329-353, JUN '70
CHILDREN'S BEHAVIOR AFFECTED BY MODEL'S ACTS BUT NOT HIS WORDS. CHILDREN'S JUDGMENT OF MODEL AFFECTED BY BOTH ACTS AND WORDS. CHILDREN FAIL TO RECALL ACCURATELY CONDITIONS IN WHICH THE MODEL ACTED INCONSISTENTLY. (MH)

EJ 022 141 PS 500 452
INTERACTIVE EFFECTS OF INFORMATIONAL AND AFFECTIVE COMPONENTS OF SOCIAL AND NONSOCIAL REINFORCERS ON INDEPENDENT AND DEPENDENT CHILDREN TODD, JUDY; NAKAMURA, CHARLES Y., *CHILD DEVELOP*, V41 N2, PP365-376, JUN '70
A SHORT VERSION OF THIS PAPER WAS DELIVERED AT THE SEVENTY-SIXTH ANNUAL CONVENTION OF THE APA, 1968.

EJ 022 142 PS 500 457
IT SCORE VARIATIONS BY INSTRUCTIONAL STYLE THOMPSON, NORMAN L., JR.; MCCANDLESS, BOYD R., *CHILD DEVELOP*, V41 N2, PP425-436, JUN '70
THIS PAPER WAS PRESENTED MARCH 1, 1969 AT THE MEETING OF THE SOUTHEASTERN PSYCHOLOGICAL ASSOCIATION, NEW ORLEANS.

EJ 022 180 PS 500 434
ONE-PARENT ADOPTIONS BRANHAM, ETHEL, *CHILDREN*, V17 N3, PP103-107, MAY-JUN '70
THE LOS ANGELES COUNTY DEPARTMENT OF ADOPTIONS DISCUSSES ITS POLICY OF PERMITTING ONE-PARENT ADOPTIONS FOR HARD-TO-PLACE CHILDREN, SUCCESSFUL SO FAR IN A REVIEW OF 36 OUT OF 40 CASES. A LONGITUDINAL STUDY IS PLANNED. (NH)

EJ 022 181 PS 500 435
A SERVICE PATTERN FOR HELPING UNMARRIED PREGNANT TEENAGERS MIDDLEMAN, RUTH R., *CHILDREN*, V17 N3, PP108-112, MAY-JUN '70
VERBAL AND NON-VERBAL COMMUNICATION BETWEEN SOCIAL WORKERS AND UNWED PREGNANT TEENS IS FACILITATED BY USE OF CONCRETE TASKS WHICH HELP THE TEEN TO EXPRESS HER IDENTITY AND FACE HER SITUATION. (NH)

EJ 022 182 PS 500 436
THE RIGHTS OF FOSTER PARENTS GARRETT, BEATRICE L., *CHILDREN*, V17 N3, PP113, MAY-JUN '70
LIST OF LEGAL AND MORAL RIGHTS AND RESPONSIBILITIES OF FOSTER PARENTS, TO WHICH READERS ARE INVITED TO SUBMIT ADDITIONS OR REVISIONS IN PREPARATION FOR A NATIONAL CONFERENCE OF FOSTER PARENTS, OCTOBER, 1970. (NH)

EJ 022 213 PS 500 379
THE INFLUENCE OF DIFFERENT RESPONSE CONSEQUENCES ON CHILDREN'S PREFERENCE FOR TIME-OUT WILLOUGHBY, R. H., *J EXP CHILD PSYCHOL*, V9 N2, PP133-141, APR '70
TIME-OUT FROM POSITIVE REINFORCEMENT WAS FOUND TO HAVE A SUPPRESSIVE EFFECT WHEN THE RESPONSE ALTERNATIVE WAS REINFORCED WITH THE SAME FREQUENCY AS THE PUNISHED RESPONSE. WHEN THE RESPONSE ALTERNATIVE WAS A RESPONSE FOR WHICH POSITIVE REINFORCEMENT HAD BEEN WITHDRAWN, TIME-OUT WAS SIGNIFICANTLY PREFERRED. (MH)

EJ 022 214 PS 500 394
GENERALIZATION OF ADULT'S STIMULUS CONTROL OF CHILDREN'S BEHAVIOR REDD, WILLIAM H., *J EXP CHILD PSYCHOL*, V9 N2, PP286-296, APR '70
GENERALIZATION OF STIMULUS CONTROL IN DIFFERENT SITUATIONS AND WITH NOVEL ADULTS OCCURRED WITH THOSE CHILDREN WHO WERE TRAINED BY CONTINGENT REINFORCEMENT, BUT NOT WITH THOSE TRAINED BY BOTH CONTINGENT AND NONCONTINGENT REINFORCEMENT. THIS RESEARCH WAS SUBMITTED AS PART OF THE AUTHOR'S DISSERTATION. (MH)

EJ 022 215 PS 500 433
HELPING HOUSEPARENTS FIND AND USE THEIR CREATIVITY GROB, HARRY E., JR.; VAN DOREN, ERIC E., *CHILDREN*, V17 N3, PP97-102, MAY-JUN '70
PROFESSIONAL STAFF AT AN INSTITUTE FOR JUVENILE DELINQUENTS REPORT AN APPROACH WHICH ENCOURAGED HOUSEPARENTS TO PARTICIPATE IN PROGRAM PLANNING AND TO USE THEIR CREATIVE POTENTIALITY. THIS RESULTED IN HOUSEPARENTS ENCOURAGING BOYS IN THEIR CHARGE TO DO THE SAME. (NH)

EJ 022 247 PS 500 428
REPORT ON THE UTILITY OF A PIAGET-BASED INFANT SCALE WITH OLDER RETARDED CHILDREN WACHS, THEODORE D., *DEVELOP PSYCHOL*, V2 N3, PP449, MAY '70
THE POTENTIAL OF THE INFANT PSYCHOLOGICAL DEVELOPMENT SCALE FOR MEASURING THE INTELLECTUAL ABILITIES OF RETARDED CHILDREN IS FOUND TO BE FAVORABLE. (MH)

EJ 022 248 PS 500 439
COMPARING VALIDITY OF CHANCE LEVEL AND HIGHER TEST SCORES HANNA, GERALD S.; ROSCOE, JOHN T., *CALIF J EDUC RES*, V21 N3, PP127-131, MAY '70
TO INVESTIGATE THE RELATIONSHIP BETWEEN MULTIPLE-CHOICE AND COMPLETION GEOMETRY TEST SCORES, THIS STUDY USED A TECHNIQUE FOR QUANTIFYING AND COMPARING THE VALIDITY OF SCORES OF DIFFERENT LEVELS. (AUTHOR/DR)

EJ 022 334 PS 500 472
THE ARTS ARE ALIVE AND THRIVING IN ST. LOUIS , *CHILDHOOD EDUC*, V46 N6, PP304-305, MAR '70

EJ 022 371 PS 500 480
EPILOGUE AND A NEW BEGINNING BERMAN, STIDNEY, *J AMER ACAD CHILD PSYCHIAT*, V9 N2, PP193-201, APR '70
THIS IS THE PRESIDENTIAL ADDRESS GIVEN AT THE ANNUAL MEETING OF THE AMERICAN ACADEMY OF CHILD PSYCHIATRY, OCTOBER 18, 1969. (MH)

EJ 022 475 PS 500 487
BEHAVIOR DEVIATIONS IN MENTALLY RETARDED CHILDREN CHESS, STELLA; HASSIBI, MAHIN, *J AMER ACAD CHILD PSYCHIAT*, V9 N2, PP282-297, APR '70
PSYCHIATRIST STUDIES 52 RETARDED CHILDREN AND ANALYZES THEIR DEVIANT BEHAVIOR FROM A PSYCHIATRIC PERSPECTIVE. (MH)

EJ 022 476 PS 500 491
TRANSITIONAL OBJECTS AND THE PROCESS OF INDIVIDUATION: A STUDY IN THREE DIFFERENT SOCIAL GROUPS GADDINI, RENATA; GADDINI, EUGENIO, *J AMER ACAD CHILD PSYCHIAT*, V9 N2, PP347-365, APR '70
STUDIES THE SPECIAL TECHNIQUES THAT CHILDREN USE TO GO TO SLEEP APART FROM THEIR MOTHERS. (MH)

EJ 022 477 PS 500 496
EARLY RECOLLECTIONS AND THE PERCEPTION OF OTHERS: A STUDY OF DELINQUENT ADOLESCENTS WOLMAN, RICHARD N., *J GENET PSYCHOL*, V116 N2D, PP157-163, '70
EARLY MEMORIES OF A SUCCORANT NEED-FULFILLING NATURE ALONG WITH MEMORIES OF SELF-ABASEMENT AND ABNEGATION IMPAIR THE OBJECTIVE PERCEPTION OF SIGNIFICANT OTHERS, WHILE EARLY MEMORIES OF INDEPENDENT ACTIVITY AND CONFRONTATION ENHANCE PERCEPTION. (MH)

EJ 022 478 PS 500 511
THE FAMILY ROMANCE FANTASY IN CHILDREN ADOPTED IN INFANCY SCHWARTZ, EDWARD M., *CHILD WELFARE*, V49 N7, PP386-391, JUL '70
PROBLEMS OF IDENTIFICATION BEHAVIOR ASSOCIATED WITH THE FAMILY ROMANCE FANTASY WERE NOT CHARACTERISTIC OF 25 ADOPTEES STUDIED. (NH)

EJ 022 532 PS 500 510
PEER- OBSERVER CONSULTATION FOSTERLING, CHARLES; MCNAMARA, FRANK P., *CHILD WELFARE*, V49 N7, PP379-385, JUL '70
A VIEW ROOM WAS USED IN TREATMENT OF 2 DYSFUNCTIONAL CHILDREN. SOCIAL WORKERS FOUND IT USEFUL FOR PEER CONSULTATION, WHICH BENEFITED CHILDREN IN THERAPY. (NH)

EJ 022 533 PS 500 512
EARLY LEGAL ADOPTION OLDS, CHARLES B., *CHILD WELFARE*, V49 N7, PP392-394, JUL '70
SUGGESTS THAT ADOPTIVE FAMILY, RATHER THAN THE AGENCY, DECIDE HOW SOON AFTER PLACEMENT OF THE CHILD, THE FAMILY IS READY TO LEGALLY ADOPT HIM. (NH)

EJ 022 536 PS 500 482
CERTAIN CULTURAL AND FAMILIAL FACTORS CONTRIBUTING TO ADOLESCENT ALIENATION NOSHPITZ, JOSEPH D., *J AMER ACAD CHILD PSYCHIAT*, V9 N2, PP216-223, APR '70

EJ 022 582 PS 500 516
GROWTH OF HEAD, FACE, TRUNK, AND LIMBS IN PHILADEPHIA WHITE AND NEGRO CHILDREN OF ELEMENTARY AND HIGH SCHOOL AGE KROGMAN, WILTON MARION, *MONOGR SOC RES CHILD DEVELOP*, V35 N3, PP1-80, MAY '70

EJ 022 975 PS 500 469
HELPING CHILDREN WITH EMOTIONAL PROBLEMS AT SCHOOL PERRY, MARY H., *CHILDHOOD EDUC*, V46 N6, PP290-292, MAR '70

EJ 022 976 PS 500 470
WHO ARE THEY? IDENTIFYING DISTURBED CHILDREN IN THE CLASSROOM FAULK, CHARLES J.; AND OTHERS, *CHILDHOOD EDUC*, V46 N6, PP293-298, MAR '70

EJ 022 977 PS 500 471
IF SCHOOLS ARE TO MEET THEIR RESPONSIBILITIES TO ALL CHILDREN MORSE, WILLIAM C., *CHILDHOOD EDUC*, V46 N6, PP299-303, MAR '70
DESCRIBES THE ELEMENTS OF AN ADEQUATE EDUCATIONAL SETTING FOR EMOTIONALLY DISTURBED CHILDREN. (AUTHOR/DR)

EJ 022 978 PS 500 473
ECOLOGICAL PLANNING FOR DISTURBED CHILDREN LEWIS, WILBERT W., *CHILDHOOD EDUC*, V46 N6, PP306-310, MAR '70

EJ 022 979 PS 500 488
A MULTIHANDICAPPED RUBELLA BABY: THE FIRST EIGHTEEN MONTHS FREEDMAN, DAVID A.; AND OTHERS, *J AMER ACAD CHILD PSYCHIAT*, V9 N2, PP298-317, APR '70

EJ 022 980 PS 500 490
RESIDENTIAL TREATMENT OF CHILDREN; A SURVEY OF INSTITUTIONAL CHARACTERISTICS MARSDEN, GERALD; AND OTHERS, *J AMER ACAD CHILD PSYCHIAT*, V9 N2, PP332-346, APR '70

EJ 023 013 PS 500 551
1. OBSTETRICAL MEDICATION AND INFANT OUTCOME: A REVIEW OF THE LITERATURE BOWES, WATSON A., JR., *MONOGR SOC RES CHILD DEV*, V35 N4, PP3-23, JUN '70

MONOGR SOC RES CHILD DEV, V35 N4, PP24-34, JUN '70

EJ 023 015 PS 500 553
III. OBSTETRICAL MEDICATION AND INFANT OUTCOME: SOME SUMMARY CONSIDERATIONS STEINSCHNEIDER, ALFRED, *MONOGR SOC RES CHILD DEV*, V35 N4, PP35-37, JUN '70

EJ 023 189 PS 500 497
A TEST OF PIAGET'S THEORY OF "NOMINAL REALISM" BROOK, JUDITH S., *J GENET PSYCHOL*, V116 N2D, PP165-75, '70

PIAGET'S SUPPORT PIAGET'S THOUGH NOMINAL REALISM DOESN'T SEEM TO DEVELOP IN AS UNIFIED A PATTERN AS HE DESCRIBED. A VERSION OF THIS PAPER WAS READ AT THE ANNUAL MEETING OF THE NEW JERSEY STATE PSYCHOLOGICAL ASSOCIATION, MAY 1968. THIS RESEARCH IS BASED ON A DISSERTATION SUBMITTED IN PARTIAL FULFILLMENT OF THE REQUIREMENTS FOR THE DOCTORAL DEGREE AT TEACHERS COLLEGE, COLUMBIA UNIVERSITY. (MH)

EJ 023 190 PS 500 498
CHILDREN'S SPATIAL REPRESENTATIONS AND HORIZONTAL DIRECTIONALITY KERSHNER, JOHN R., *J GENET PSYCHOL*, V116 N2D, PP177-189, '70

EJ 023 191 PS 500 499
THE RELATION OF PARENTAL TRAINING TO CONCEPTUAL STRUCTURE IN PREADOLESCENTS CROSS, HERBERT J., *J GENET PSYCHOL*, V116 N2D, PP197-202, '70

EJ 023 192 PS 500 502
A PRELIMINARY SEARCH FOR FORMAL OPERATIONS STRUCTURES NEIMARK, EDITH D., *J GENET PSYCHOL*, V116 N2D, PP223-232, '70

RESULTS INDICATE THAT THE FORMAL OPERATIONS TASKS EMPLOYED IN THE STUDY ARE CORRELATED, EXCEPT FOR THE INHELDER AND PIAGET CHEMICAL BODIES TASKS. (MH)

EJ 023 193 PS 500 506
THE DEVELOPMENT OF PROBABILISTIC THINKING IN CHILDREN: A COMPARISON OF TWO METHODS OF ASSESSMENT CARLSON, JERRY S., *J GENET PSYCHOL*, V116 N2D, PP263-269, '70

FINDINGS INDICATE THAT (1) DEVELOPMENT OF PROBABILITY REASONING CAN BE SHOWN BY AN INCREASING MONOTONIC TREND WITH AGE, (2) VERBAL TESTS ASSESS DIFFERENT ASPECTS OF THIS DEVELOPMENT THAN DO NONVERBAL TESTS, (3) PIAGET'S ONTOGENETIC AGE BRACKETS ARE ACCURATE, AND (4) SEX AND INTELLIGENCE ARE NOT SIGNIFICANT VARIABLES. (MH)

EJ 023 283 PS 500 509
THE RIGHTS OF CHILDREN EMERGE: HISTORICAL NOTES ON THE FIRST WHITE HOUSE CONFERENCE ON CHILDREN STRETCH, JOHN J., *CHILD WELFARE*, V49 N7, PP365-372, JUL '70

EJ 023 391 PS 500 478
THE FAMILY DAY CARE PROGRAM IN MILWAUKEE: A 3-FACETED APPROACH TO COMMUNITY ENRICHMENT WADE, CAMILLE, *CHILD WELFARE*, V49 N6, PP336-341, JUN '70

THIS ARTICLE IS REPRINTED FROM BAEYC REPORTS, V10 N5 MAY, 1969 (MG)

EJ 023 392 PS 500 479
COMMUNITY ACTION ON BEHALF OF PREGNANT SCHOOL-AGE GIRLS: EDUCATIONAL POLICIES AND BEYOND MCMURRAY, GEORGIA L., *CHILD WELFARE*, V49 N6, PP342-346, JUN '70

THIS PAPER IS BASED ON A PRESENTATION AT THE CWLA EASTERN REGIONAL CONFERENCE AT BALTIMORE IN 1969 (MG)

EJ 023 424 PS 500 476
TWO MODES OF MATERNAL IMMATURITY AND THEIR CONSEQUENCES *CHILD WELFARE*, V49 N6, PP312-323, JUN '70

STUDIES MOTHERS FROM POVERTY-STRICKEN APPALACHIA WHO EXHIBIT THE APATHY-FUTILITY SYNDROME OR CHILDISH IMPULSIVITY. SUGGESTIONS FOR TREATMENT ARE MADE. (MG)

EJ 023 425 PS 500 483
"YOUTH UNREST": REFLECTIONS OF A PSYCHOANALYST FRIEND, MAURICE R., *J AMER ACAD CHILD PSYCHIAT*, V9 N2, PP224-232, APR '70

THIS ARTICLE IS A REVISION OF AN ADDRESS GIVEN BEFORE THE COMBINED WASHINGTON PSYCHIATRIC AND WASHINGTON PSYCHOANALYTIC SOCIETIES IN WASHINGTON, D.C., NOVEMBER 22, 1968. (MH)

EJ 023 426 PS 500 484
ALIENATION: AN ESSENTIAL PROCESS OF THE PSYCHOLOGY OF ADOLESCENCE BERMAN, SIDNEY, *J AMER ACAD CHILD PSYCHIAT*, V9 N2, PP233-250, APR '70

MENT PRINCIPLES AND SOCIAL CHANGES TO MAKE ADOLESCENCE LESS DISRUPTIVE. (MH)

EJ 023 427 PS 500 485
ALIENATION OF YOUTH AS REFLECTED IN THE HIPPIE MOVEMENT WILLIAMS, FRANK S., *J AMER ACAD CHILD PSYCHIAT*, V9 N2, PP251-263, APR '70

EJ 023 428 PS 500 486
ALIENATION OF PRESENT-DAY ADOLESCENTS WISE, LOUIS J., *J AMER ACAD CHILD PSYCHIAT*, V9 N2, PP264-277, APR '70

EJ 023 429 PS 500 489
PSYCHOPHYSIOLOGIC AND CONVERSION REACTIONS IN CHILDREN: SELECTIVE INCIDENCE IN VERBAL AND NONVERBAL FAMILIES LOOFF, DAVID H., *J AMER ACAD CHILD PSYCHIAT*, V9 N2, PP318-331, APR '70

ENUMERATES CHARACTERISTICS OF CHILDREN EXHIBITING THE BEHAVIORAL DEVIANCIES IN QUESTION, AND MAKES SUGGESTIONS FOR THEORY AND CLINICAL APPLICATION. THIS REPORT IS BASED ON A PAPER READ BEFORE THE SOUTHERN PSYCHIATRIC ASSOCIATION, ATLANTA, GEORGIA, OCTOBER 7, 1968. (MH)

EJ 023 430 PS 500 492
THE ROLE OF GEOGRAPHIC MOBILITY IN SOME ADJUSTMENT PROBLEMS OF CHILDREN AND FAMILIES TOOLEY, KAY, *J AMER ACAD CHILD PSYCHIAT*, V9 N2, PP366-378, APR '70

EJ 023 431 PS 500 500
SUGGESTIBILITY IN RELATION TO SCHOOL GRADE, SEX, AND SOURCE OF INFLUENCE ZOHNER, DORIN, *J GENET PSYCHOL*, V116 N2D, PP203-209, '70

EJ 023 432 PS 500 501
ENVIRONMENTAL DISCONTINUITY, STRESS, AND SEX EFFECTS UPON SUSCEPTIBILITY TO SOCIAL INFLUENCE ZOHNER, DORIN, *J GENET PSYCHOL*, V116 N2D, PP211-217, '70

SOCIAL INFLUENCE WAS INFLUENCED MOST BY PRESTIGE SUGGESTION, CONFORMITY, AND BASELINE SUGGESTION, IN THAT ORDER. DIFFERENTIAL EFFECTS OF SUGGESTION DEPENDED ON THE EFFECTS OF TYPE OF DISCONTINUITY AND SEX. (MH)

EJ 023 433 PS 500 504
ONTOGENY OF THE LOCUS AND ORIENTATION OF THE PERCEIVER: A CONFIRMATION AND AN ADDITION PEDROW, DONALD P.; BUSSE, THOMAS V., *J GENET PSYCHOL*, V116 N2D, PP247-250, '70

EJ 023 434 PS 500 505
THE EFFECTS OF PERSONALITY VARIABLES ON DISTORTION THRESHOLDS IN THE AMES ROOM SILBERFARB, ROBERT M.; CALDWELL, WILLARD E., *J GENET PSYCHOL*, V116 N2D, PP251-261, '70

THIS STUDY WAS BASED ON A THESIS SUBMITTED BY THE FIRST AUTHOR AS PARTIAL FULFILLMENT OF THE DEGREE OF MASTER OF ARTS AT THE GEORGE WASHINGTON UNIVERSITY, WASHINGTON, D. C.

EJ 023 435 PS 500 507
SEX IDENTITY IN LONDON CHILDREN: MEMORY, KNOWLEDGE AND PREFERENCE TESTS NADELMAN, LORRAINE, *HUMAN DEVELOP*, V13 N1, PP28-42, '70

EJ 023 436 PS 500 508
THE EFFECTS OF A PAY-OFF MATRIX ON SELECTIVE ATTENTION HAGEN, J. W.; WEST, R. F., *HUMAN DEVELOP*, V13 N1, PP43-52, '70

SUBJECTS RECALLED THE MORE REWARDING STIMULI SIGNIFICANTLY BETTER. (MH)

EJ 023 611 PS 500 481
ADOLESCENCE AND SOCIAL CHANGE SETTLAGE, CALVIN F., *J AMER ACAD CHILD PSYCHIAT*, V9 N2, PP203-215, APR '70
THIS PAPER WAS PRESENTED TO THE JOINT MEETING OF THE AMERICAN PSYCHIATRIC ASSOCIATION AND THE AMERICAN PSYCHOANALYTIC ASSOCIATION IN BOSTON, MAY, 1968; IT WAS PUBLISHED IN SUMMARY FORM IN THE AMERICAN JOURNAL OF PSYCHIATRY (SOLNIT ET AL., 1969). (MH)

EJ 023 612 PS 500 494
AN EXPLORATORY STUDY OF THE 3-, 5-, AND 7-YEAR OLD FEMALE'S COMPREHENSION OF COOPERATIVE AND UNCOOPERATIVE SOCIAL INTERACTION FEIGENBAUM, KENNETH D.; AND OTHERS, *J GENET PSYCHOL*, V116 N2D, PP141-148, '70
THE GIRLS UNDERSTOOD COMPETITION BETTER THAN COOPERATION AND INTERACTIONS WHICH ONLY INVOLVED CHILDREN BETTER THAN THOSE INVOLVING ADULTS OR ADULTS AND CHILDREN. COMPREHENSION IMPROVED WITH AGE AND RELATED TO PIAGET'S CONCEPT OF DECENTERING. (MH)

EJ 023 613 PS 500 495
CHILDREARING PRACTICES AMONG SELECTED CULTURALLY DEPRIVED MINORITIES KEARNS, BESSIE JEAN RULEY, *J GENET PSYCHOL*, V116 N2D, PP149-155, '70
SIGNIFICANT DIFFERENCES IN CHILD REARING PRACTICES DO EXIST AMONG PAPAGO INDIAN, MEXICAN-AMERICAN, AND ANGLO MOTHERS. (MH)

EJ 023 614 PS 500 503
SOCIOECONOMIC STATUS AND SEX DIFFERENCES IN ADOLESCENT REFERENCE-GROUP ORIENTATION PURNELL, RICHARD F., *J GENET PSYCHOL*, V116 N2D, PP233-239, '70
NO SIGNIFICANT DIFFERENCES IN ORIENTATION WERE FOUND FOR ADOLESCENTS (1) OF DIFFERENT SOCIAL CLASSES, (2) OF DIFFERENT SEX, AND (3) OF DIFFERENT SOCIAL CLASS WITHIN SEX. THE STUDY REPORTED HERE IS FROM THE AUTHOR'S DOCTORAL DISSERTATION SUBMITTED TO THE DEPARTMENT OF EDUCATIONAL PSYCHOLOGY, UNIVERSITY OF TEXAS. (MH)

EJ 023 678 PS 500 477
A SUMMARY OF THE REPORT OF THE JOINT COMMISSION ON MENTAL HEALTH OF CHILDREN , *CHILD WELFARE*, V49 N6, PP324-326, JUN '70
THIS ARTICLE IS AN ABSTRACT FROM DIGEST OF CRISIS IN CHILD MENTAL HEALTH: CHALLENGE FOR THE 1970'S, THE FINAL REPORT OF THE JOINT COMMISSION ON MENTAL HEALTH OF CHILDREN (MG)

EJ 023 702 PS 500 474
SENSITIVITY TRAINING: WHAT IS IT? HOW CAN IT HELP STUDENTS, TEACHERS, ADMINISTRATORS? LIPPITT, RONALD, *CHILDHOOD EDUC*, V46 N6, PP311-313, MAR '70

EJ 023 703 PS 500 475
THE TEACHER AS COUNSELOR: THERAPEUTIC APPROACHES TO UNDERSTANDING SELF AND OTHERS DINKMEYER, DON, *CHILDHOOD EDUC*, V46 N6, PP314-317, MAR '70

EJ 023 704 PS 500 493
SPECIAL CONSIDERATIONS IN THE OPERATION OF A HEAD START PROGRAM BY A COMMUNITY CHILD GUIDANCE CLINIC NIR, YEHUDA; EAGLE, CAROL J., *J AMER ACAD CHILD PSYCHIAT*, V9 N2, PP379-393, APR '70

EJ 023 858 PS 500 562
CONSCIENCE, PERSONALITY, AND SOCIALIZATION TECHNIQUES HOFFMAN, MARTIN L., *HUM DEVELOP*, V13 N2, PP90-126, '70
PARENTS OF 7TH GRADERS WHOSE MORAL JUDGMENTS WERE "HUMANISTIC" WERE FOUND TO USE DISCIPLINE TECHNIQUES THAT VARIED ACCORDING TO THE OCCASION, TO USE INDUCTION METHODS AND TO FOCUS ON ISSUES AND POSSIBLE REPARATION. THE DISCIPLINE OF PARENTS OF CHILDREN WHOSE MORAL JUDGMENTS WERE "CONVENTIONAL," FREQUENTLY INVOLVED LOVE WITHDRAWAL AND EMPHASIZED PARENT POWER ASPECT. (NH)

EJ 023 964 PS 500 514
DEPENDENCE OF LAUGHTER ON COGNITIVE STRATEGIES KREITLER, HANS; KREITLER, SHULAMITH, *MERRILL PALMER QUART*, V16 N2, PP163-177, APR '70
COGNITIVE STRATEGIES OF IDENTIFICATION OF THE ABSURD WITH CRITICISM, WONDER, OR MOCKERY WERE FOUND TO ELICIT LAUGHTER IN AN ABOVE CHANCE FREQUENCY. (MH)

EJ 023 965 PS 500 528
THE MODIFICATION OF CHILDHOOD STUTTERING: SOME RESPONSE-RESPONSE RELATIONSHIPS WAHLER, R. G.; AND OTHERS, *J EXP CHILD PSYCHOL*, V9 N3, PP411-428, JUN '70
WHEN CONTINGENCY MANAGEMENT PROCEDURES WERE APPLIED TO THE SECONDARY BEHAVIORAL DEVIANCIES OF 2 STUTTERERS, BOTH THE SECONDARY PROBLEMS AND THE STUTTERING WERE REDUCED. (MH)

EJ 024 027 PS 500 554
A LEARNING EXPERIENCE IN HELPING PARENTS GET WHAT THEY WANT BOYLE, JOHN, *CHILDREN*, V17 N4, PP127-131, JUL-AUG '70
STUDENT SOCIAL WORKER HELPS PARENTS OF RETARDED CHILDREN GET A SCHOOL FOR THEIR CHILDREN. (NH)

EJ 024 028 PS 500 557
A DIFFERENTIAL USE OF GROUP HOMES FOR DELINQUENT BOYS PEARSON, JOHN W., *CHILDREN*, V17 N4, PP143-148, JUL-AUG '70

EJ 024 033 PS 500 536
COOPERATIVE AND COMPETITIVE BEHAVIOR OF URBAN AFRO-AMERICAN, ANGLO-AMERICAN, MEXICAN-AMERICAN, AND MEXICAN VILLAGE CHILDREN MADSEN, MILLARD, C.; SHAPIRA, ARIELLA, *DEVELOP PSYCHOL*, V3 N1, PP16-20, JUL '70

EJ 024 034 PS 500 563
CULTURAL DIFFERENCES IN COLOR/FORM PREFERENCE AND IN CLASSIFICATORY BEHAVIOR SCHMIDT, W. H. O.; NZIMANDE, A., *HUM DEVELOP*, V13 N2, PP140-48, '70
CROSS-CULTURAL DATA WAS COLLECTED ON COLOR/FORM PREFERENCE AND THE ABILITY TO CLASSIFY AMONG ZULU CHILDREN AND ADULTS. SIGNIFICANT DIFFERENCES WERE FOUND ATTRIBUTABLE TO FACTORS OF WESTERN-TYPE SCHOOLING, LITERACY, AND URBAN OR RURAL LIFE. (NH)

EJ 024 470 PS 500 530
AN EXPERIMENTAL STUDY OF THE SOCIAL RESPONSIVENESS OF CHILDREN WITH AUTISTIC BEHAVIORS FREITAG, GILBERT, *J EXP CHILD PSYCHOL*, V9 N3, PP436-453, JUN '70
THIS ARTICLE IS BASED UPON A DISSERTATION SUBMITTED IN PARTIAL FULFILLMENT OF THE REQUIREMENTS FOR THE DEGREE OF DOCTOR OF PHILOSOPHY FROM YALE UNIVERSITY. (MH)

EJ 024 471 PS 500 556
A CLINIC FOR CHILDREN WITH LEARNING DISABILITIES KAPPELMAN, MURRAY M.; GANTER, ROBERT L., *CHILDREN*, V17 N4, PP137-142, JUL-AUG '70

EJ 024 496 PS 500 558
HEALTH CARE THROUGH HEAD START HUNTER, GERTRUDE T., *CHILDREN*, V17 N4, PP149-153, JUL-AUG '70
DESCRIBES LOCAL HEAD START PROGRAMS DESIGNED TO PROVIDE A SYSTEM OF COMPREHENSIVE HEALTH CARE FOR CHILDREN TO RECEIVE AFTER THEY LEAVE HEAD START. (NH)

EJ 024 497 PS 500 559
A REPORT FROM ABROAD...FAMILY PARTICIPATION IN HOSPITAL CARE FOR CHILDREN BELL, JOHN E.; BELL, ELISABETH A., *CHILDREN*, V17 N4, PP154-157, JUL-AUG '70

EJ 024 691 PS 500 513
PROBLEMS OF DEPRIVATION AND DEVELOPMENTAL LEARNING FOWLER, WILLIAM, *MERRILL PALMER QUART*, V16 N2, PP141-161, APR '70
REVISION OF PAPER FOR TASK FORCE ON SOCIAL AND BIOLOGICAL DEPRIVATION INFLUENCES ON LEARNING AND PERFORMANCE FOR THE NATIONAL INSTITUTE OF CHILD HEALTH AND HUMAN DEVELOPMENT, U.S. DEPARTMENT OF HEALTH, EDUCATION, AND WELFARE, JUNE 15, 1968. (MH)

EJ 024 692 PS 500 518
TRANSFER PERFORMANCE IN CHILDREN'S ODDITY LEARNING AS A FUNCTION OF DIMENSIONAL PREFERENCE, SHIFT PARADIGM AND OVERTRAINING BROWN, ANN L., *J EXP CHILD PSYCHOL*, V9 N3, PP307-19, JUN '70

EJ 024 693 PS 500 519
IMITATION OF AN ANIMATED PUPPET AS A FUNCTION OF MODELING, PRAISE, AND DIRECTIONS PARTON, DAVID A., *J EXP CHILD PSYCHOL*, V9 N3, PP320-9, JUN '70
A BRIEF REPORT OF THIS RESEARCH WAS PRESENTED AT THE 1967 BIENNIAL MEETING OF THE SOCIETY FOR RESEARCH IN CHILD DEVELOPMENT. (MH)

EJ 024 694 PS 500 521
CHILDREN'S PERFORMANCE ON AN ODDITY PROBLEM AS A FUNCTION OF THE NUMBER OF VALUES ON THE RELEVANT DIMENSION SMALL, MELINDA Y., *J EXP CHILD PSYCHOL*, V9 N3, PP336-41, JUN '70
A SERIES OF TRIALS WITH 4 VALUES ON THE RELEVANT DIMENSION WAS EASIER FOR KINDERGARTEN AND FIRST-GRADE CHILDREN THAN A SERIES WITH 2 VALUES. (MH)

EJ 024 695 PS 500 524
THE ROLE OF OBJECT ORIENTATION IN INFANT PERCEPTION MCGURK, HARRY, *J EXP CHILD PSYCHOL*, V9 N3, PP363-373, JUN '70
SERIES OF EXPERIMENTS INDICATES THAT YOUNG INFANTS ARE MORE SENSITIVE TO THE SPATIAL ORIENTATION OF FORMS THAN WAS PREVIOUSLY THOUGHT. THIS REPORT IS BASED ON A DISSERTATION SUBMITTED TO THE UNIVERSITY OF STRATHCLYDE, AUGUST, 1969, IN PARTIAL FULFILLMENT OF THE REQUIREMENTS FOR THE DEGREE OF MSC. (MH)

EJ 024 696 PS 500 525
VISUAL ORIENTATION IN CHILDREN'S DISCRIMINATION LEARNING UNDER CONSTANT, VARIABLE, AND COVARIABLE DELAY OF REINFORCEMENT BERCH, DANIEL B., *J EXP CHILD PSYCHOL*, V9 N3, PP374-87, JUN '70
THIS ARTICLE IS BASED UPON A DISSERTATION SUBMITTED TO THE UNIVERSITY OF NEW MEXICO IN PARTIAL FULFILLMENT OF THE REQUIREMENTS FOR THE DEGREE OF DOCTOR OF PHILOSOPHY. (MH)

EJ 024 697 PS 500 526
EFFECTS OF ENFORCED ATTENTION AND STIMULUS PHASING UPON RULE LEARNING IN CHILDREN JOHNSON, PEDER J.; AND OTHERS, *J EXP CHILD PSYCHOL*, V9 N3, PP388-399, JUN '70
BOTH ENFORCED ATTENTION AND STIMULUS PHASING FOUND TO IMPROVE TASK PERFORMANCE. (MH)

EJ 024 698 PS 500 527
SINGLE-LETTER CUE SELECTION IN THE PAIRED-ASSOCIATE LEARNING OF NORMAL CHILDREN AND RETARDATES BAUMEISTER, ALFRED A.; BERRY, FRANKLIN M., *J EXP CHILD PSYCHOL*, V9 N3, PP400-410, JUN '70

EJ 024 699 PS 500 529
VERBAL AND IMAGERY PROCESSES IN CHILDREN'S PAIRED-ASSOCIATE LEARNING DAVIDSON, ROBERT E.; ADAMS, JANICE FREEMAN, *J EXP CHILD PSYCHOL*, V9 N3, PP429-435, JUN '70
RESULTS INDICATE THAT VERBALIZATION IS THE PREFERRED SYMBOLIC PROCESS IN YOUNG CHILDREN. PORTIONS OF THIS PAPER WERE PRESENTED AT THE ANNUAL MEETING OF THE AMERICAN EDUCATIONAL RESEARCH ASSOCIATION, LOS ANGELES, CALIFORNIA, 1969. (MH)

EJ 024 700 PS 500 531
SHORT-TERM MEMORY FOR VISUAL INFORMATION IN CHILDREN AND ADULTS HAITH, MARSHALL M.; AND OTHERS, *J EXP CHILD PSYCHOL*, V9 N3, PP454-469, JUN '70
ADULTS AND CHILDREN USED SIMILAR REPORT STRATEGIES IN A TACHISTOSCOPIC MEMORY TASK, BUT THE CAPACITY OF THE CHILDREN'S SHORT TERM MEMORY WAS STRIKINGLY LIMITED. PORTIONS OF THIS PAPER WERE READ AT THE EASTERN PSYCHOLOGICAL MEETINGS, WASHINGTON, D.C., APRIL, 1968. (MH)

EJ 024 701 PS 500 533
TRANSFER OF MATCHING AND MISMATCHING BEHAVIOR IN PRESCHOOL CHILDREN SHERMAN, JAMES A.; AND OTHERS, *J EXP CHILD PSYCHOL*, V9 N3, PP489-498, JUN '70
CHILDREN CONSISTENTLY TRANSFERRED THEIR MATCHING OR NON-MATCHING BEHAVIOR TO A PROBE SAMPLE STIMULUS. A PORTION OF THIS RESEARCH WAS PRESENTED AT THE SOUTHEASTERN PSYCHOLOGICAL ASSOCIATION MEETING, NEW ORLEANS, LOUISIANA, 1969. (MH)

EJ 024 702 PS 500 544
MOTIVATIONAL EFFECTS OF PRAISE AND CRITICISM ON CHILDREN'S LEARNING SPEAR, PAUL S., *DEVELOP PSYCHOL*, V3 N1, PP124-132, JUL '70
INDICATES THAT APPROVAL AND DISAPPROVAL AFFECT THE SUBJECT'S MOTIVATIONAL LEVEL (ASSESSED BY RATE OF RESPONDING) RATHER THAN HIS LEARNING (ASSESSED BY ACQUISITION MEASURES). THIS STUDY IS BASED ON A DISSERTATION SUBMITTED IN PARTIAL FULFILLMENT FOR THE PH.D. DEGREE AT THE UNIVERSITY OF DENVER. (MH)

EJ 024 703 PS 500 545
LEVEL OF ASPIRATION AND THE PROBABILITY LEARNING OF MIDDLE- AND LOWER-CLASS CHILDREN GRUEN, GERALD; AND OTHERS, *DEVELOP PSYCHOL*, V3 N1, PP133-142, JUL '70

EJ 024 704 PS 500 547
TRANSFER IN NURSERY SCHOOL CHILDREN BETWEEN TWO RELATIONAL TASKS SCOTT, MARCIA S., *DEVELOP PSYCHOL*, V3 N1, PP145, JUL '70
SUGGESTS THAT 5-YEAR-OLD CHILDREN ARE CAPABLE OF QUITE SUBTLE PROBLEM SOLVING. (MH)

EJ 024 705 PS 500 561
DEVELOPMENTAL PROCESSES IN DISCRIMINATION LEARNING KENDLER, H. H.; KENDLER, T. S., *HUM DEVELOP*, V13 N2, PP65-89, '70
DISCRIMINATION - LEARNING BEHAVIOR OF CHILDREN IS ANALYZED IN TERMS OF TWO THEORETICAL ORIENTAITONS: THE MEDIATIONAL - ATTENTION CONCEPTION, AND A COORDINATED SINGLE-UNIT AND MEDIATIONAL S-R FORMULATION. THE INFLUENCE OF VERBAL LABELS AND OTHER SYMBOLIC REPRESENTATIONAL RESPONSES IS DISCUSSED. (NH)

EJ 024 934 PS 500 520
INSTRUMENTAL PERFORMANCE AS A FUNCTION OF REINFORCEMENT SCHEDULE, LUCK VERSUS SKILL INSTRUCTIONS, AND SEX OF CHILD STABLER, JOHN R.; JOHNSON, EDWARD E., *J EXP CHILD PSYCHOL*, V9 N3, PP330-5, JUN '70
SPEED DURING EXTINCTION WAS HIGHER FOLLOWING PARTIAL REINFORCEMENT, FOLLOWING SKILL INSTRUCTIONS, AND FOR FEMALES. (MH)

EJ 024 935 PS 500 522
EFFECT OF FAMILIAR AND UNFAMILIAR ENVIRONMENTS ON PROXIMITY BEHAVIOR OF YOUNG CHILDREN CASTELL, ROLF, *J EXP CHILD PSYCHOL*, V9 N3, PP342-7, JUN '70
THE RESULTS OF THIS EXPERIMENT WERE PRESENTED AT THE 11TH INTERNATIONAL ETHOLOGICAL CONFERENCE, RENNES, FRANCE, SEPTEMBER 2-5, 1969. (MH)

EJ 024 936 PS 500 523
EFFECTS OF REINFORCEMENT HISTORY ON TIMING (DRL) PERFORMANCE IN YOUNG CHILDREN WEISBERG, PAUL, *J EXP CHILD PSYCHOL*, V9 N3, PP348-362, JUN '70
SHOWS THAT SPECIAL REPERTOIRES SHAPED BY DIFFERENTIAL REINFORCEMENT SCHEDULE HISTORY AFFECT THE VERY YOUNG CHILD'S ABILITY TO LEARN TO WITHHOLD AND TO SPACE RESPONSES IN A FREE OPERANT, TEMPORAL DISCRIMINATION TASK. (MH)

EJ 024 937 PS 500 532
ROLE OF DISCRIMINATIVE STIMULI IN THE FORMATION OF FUNCTIONAL RESPONSE CLASSES ARNOLD, CAROLE REVELLE, *J EXP CHILD PSYCHOL*, V9 N3, PP470-488, JUN '70
THIS PAPER IS BASED ON A DISSERTATION SUBMITTED IN PARTIAL FULFILLMENT OF THE PH.D. DEGREE TO THE GRADUATE COLLEGE OF THE UNIVERSITY OF ILLINOIS. (MH)

EJ 024 938 PS 500 534
SOCIOECONOMIC STATUS AND INTELLECTIVE PERFORMANCE AMONG NEGRO PRESCHOOL BOYS PALMER, FRANCIS H., *DEVELOP PSYCHOL*, V3 N1, PP1-9, JUL '70
NO INTELLECTUAL DIFFERENCES WERE FOUND BY SOCIOECONOMIC STATUS AMONG NEGRO CHILDREN UP TO AGE 3 YEARS 8 MONTHS, WHEN SAMPLING PROCEDURES AND ADAPTATION TO THE TESTING SITUATION WERE CONTROLLED. (MH)

EJ 024 939 PS 500 535
SEX DIFFERENCES IN PRESCHOOL CHILDREN WITHOUT HISTORIES OF COMPLICATIONS OF PREGNANCY AND DELIVERY PEDERSEN, FRANK A.; BELL, RICHARD Q., *DEVELOP PSYCHOL*, V3 N1, PP10-15, JUL '70
DESPITE THE PRECAUTIONS IN SUBJECT SELECTION MANY OF THE USUAL SEX DIFFERENCES APPEARED, INCLUDING BOYS' HIGHER LEVEL OF AGGRESSION TOWARD PEERS. (MH)

EJ 024 940 PS 500 537
LONGITUDINAL STUDY OF COGNITIVE DICTIONARIES FROM AGES NINE TO SEVENTEEN MORAN, LOUIS J.; SWARTZ, JON D., *DEVELOP PSYCHOL*, V3 N1, PP21-28, JUL '70
IN FREE WORD ASSOCIATION LISTS ADMINISTERED TO CHILDREN AND ADOLESCENTS 3 TIMES AT 1-YEAR INTERVALS, IDIODYNAMIC ASSOCIATIVE SETS REMAINED STABLE, THOUGH SPECIFIC WORDS DID NOT. (MH)

EJ 024 941 PS 500 538
LONG-TERM RETENTION OF VERBAL IMITATION THELEN, MARK H., *DEVELOP PSYCHOL*, V3 N1, PP29-31, JUL '70
GROUPS OF ELEMENTARY SCHOOL CHILDREN WHO OBSERVED AN ADULT MODEL MAKING SELF-BLAME STATEMENTS MADE SIGNIFICANTLY MORE IMITATIVE SELF-BLAME RESPONSES ON A TEST 7 MONTHS LATER THAN DID A NO-MODEL CONTROL GROUP. (MH)

EJ 024 942 PS 500 539
CHILDREN'S UTILIZATION OF LOGICAL SYMBOLS: AN INTERPRETATION OF CONCEPTUAL BEHAVIOR BASED ON PIAGETIAN THEORY FURTH, HANS G.; AND OTHERS, *DEVELOP PSYCHOL*, V3 N1, PP36-57, JUL '70

EJ 024 943 PS 500 540
A COMPARISON OF RETARDATES AND NORMALS ON THE POGGENDORFF AND OPPEL-KUNDT ILLUSIONS SPITZ, HERMAN H.; AND OTHERS, *DEVELOP PSYCHOL*, V3 N1, PP58-65, JUL '70
CONTRARY TO PIAGET'S PREDICTIONS, ADOLESCENT RETARDATES AND 9-YEAR-OLD NORMALS WERE MORE SUSCEPTIBLE TO THE OPPEL-KUNDT ILLUSION THAN HIGH SCHOOL SOPHOMORES AND ADULTS. NO GROUP DIFFERENCES WERE FOUND ON THE POGGENDORF ILLUSION. (MH)

EJ 024 944 PS 500 541
MATERNAL CHILD-REARING EXPERIENCE AND SELF- REINFORCEMENT EFFECTIVENESS HEILBRUN, ALFRED B., JR.; NORBERT, NANCYANN, *DEVELOP PSYCHOL*, V3 N1, PP81-87, JUL '70
CONFIRMS THAT SUBJECTS WITH HIGH-NURTURANT MOTHERS ARE MORE EFFECTIVE SELF-REINFORCERS THAN SUBJECTS WITH LOW-NURTURANT MOTHERS. (MH)

EJ 024 945 PS 500 546
AGGRESSION IN CHILDREN AS A FUNCTION OF SEX OF SUBJECT AND SEX OF OPPONENT SHORTELL, JAMES R.; BILLER, HENRY B., *DEVELOP PSYCHOL*, V3 N1, PP143-144, JUL '70
THIS ARTICLE IS BASED ON A DOCTORAL DISSERTATION SUBMITTED BY THE FIRST AUTHOR, UNDER THE DIRECTION OF THE SECOND AUTHOR, TO THE UNIVERSITY OF MASSACHUSETTS.

EJ 024 946 PS 500 548
SENSORY ORGANIZATION AND INTELLIGENCE: A MODIFICATION AND REPLICATION STAYTON, SAMUEL E., *DEVELOP PSYCHOL*, V3 N1, PP146, JUL '70

EJ 024 947 PS 500 549
SELF-REINFORCEMENT VERSUS EXTERNAL REINFORCEMENT IN BEHAVIOR MODIFICATION WITH CHILDREN JOHNSON, STEPHEN M., *DEVELOP PSYCHOL*, V3 N1, PP147-148, JUL '70

EJ 024 948 PS 500 550
INTERACTION OF REWARD, PUNISHMENT, AND SEX IN A TWO-CHOICE DISCRIMINATION TASK WITH CHILDREN RATLIFF, RICHARD G.; TINDALL, ROBERT C., *DEVELOP PSYCHOL*, V3 N1, PP150, JUL '70

EJ 024 982 PS 500 517
AN INCREASING EFFECT OF DISORIENTATION ON THE DISCRIMINATION OF PRINT: A DEVELOPMENTAL STUDY CLAY, MARIE M., *J EXP CHILD PSYCHOL*, V9 N3, PP297-306, JUN '70
EXPLORES THE VARIOUS EFFECTS OF CHANGING THE FAMILIAR ORIENTATION OF WORDS WITH BEGINNING READERS. (MH)

EJ 025 047 PS 500 560
RECOLLECTIONS OF CHILDHOOD: A STUDY OF THE RETROSPECTIVE METHOD YARROW, MARIAN RADKE; AND OTHERS, *MONOGR SOC RES CHILD DEV*, V35 N5, PP1-83, AUG '70
INVESTIGATES AND SUGGESTS CAUTION IN USE OF RETROSPECTIVE REPORTS AS A SOURCE OF INFORMATION IN THE AREA OF PERSONALITY DEVELOPMENT. (NH)

EJ 025 078 PS 500 555
REACHING FOR THE DREAM: AN EXPERIMENT IN TWO-WAY BUSING GROSS, NORMAN M., *CHILDREN*, V17 N4, PP133-136, JUL-AUG '70
PARENT INVOLVEMENT PLAYS A CRUCIAL ROLE IN THE SUCCESS OF A TWO-WAY BUSING PROGRAM. (NH)

EJ 025 149 PS 500 542
EFFECTS OF SOCIAL CLASS ON CHILDREN'S MOTORIC EXPRESSION WALLACH, MICHAEL A.; MARTIN, MARILYN L., *DEVELOP PSYCHOL*, V3 N1, PP106-113, JUL '70

EJ 025 231 PS 500 515
PSYCHOLOGICAL ASSESSMENT INSTRUMENTS FOR USE WITH HUMAN INFANTS THOMAS, HOBEN, *MERRILL PALMER QUART*, V16 N2, PP179-223, APR '70

EJ 025 232 PS 500 543
CHILDREN'S DEPENDENCY SCALE GOLIGHTLY, CAROLE; AND OTHERS, *DEVELOP PSYCHOL*, V3 N1, PP114-118, JUL '70

EJ 025 268 PS 500 624
SEASON OF BIRTH AND INTELLIGENCE MARTINDALE, COLIN; BLACK, F. WILLIAM, *J GENET PSYCHOL*, V117 N1, PP137-138, SEP '70
120 CHILDREN, MOST WITH A DIAGNOSISOF CHRONIC ENCEPHALOPATHY, WERE SELECTED FROM THE PSYCHOLOGY DEPARTMENT OF A BOSTON HOSPITAL IN THIS ATTEMPT TO REPLICATE ORME'S FINDINGS. RESULTS INDICATE A CLEAR CURVILINEAR RELATIONSHIP WITH MODEST TEMPERATURES IN THE BIRTH MONTH BEING ASSOCIATED WITH HIGH IQ, WHILE BOTH HIGHER AND LOWER TEMPERATURES ARE ASSOCIATED WITH LOWER IQ. (AUTHOR/WY)

EJ 025 304 PS 500 581
CHILDREN'S SENSITIVITY TO PAINTING STYLES GARDNER, HOWARD, *CHILD DEVELOP*, V41 N3, PP813-21, SEP '70

EJ 025 305 PS 500 619
BODY PROPORTIONS IN CHILDREN'S DRAWINGS OF A MAN NASH, HARVEY; HARRIS, DALE B., *J GENET PSYCHOL*, V117 N1, PP85-90, SEP '70
FOUR CLASSES OF FIRST GRADE CHILDREN PRODUCED A DRAWING A DAY FOR TEN DAYS. THE LENGTH OF THE HEAD, TRUNK, AND LEGS WAS MEASURED TO THE NEAREST MILIMETER. THE CHILDREN CLEARLY MAGNIFIED HEAD LENGTH AND SOMEWHAT LESS CLEARLY DIMINISHED LEG LENGTH. (WY)

EJ 025 318 PS 500 616
SOME RELATIONSHIPS AMONG CHILDREN'S PERCEPTIONS OF PARENTAL CHARACTERISTICS HEAPS, RICHARD A., *J GENET PSYCHOL*, V117 N1, PP7-11, SEP '70
A TOTAL OF 63 FIFTH GRADE CHILDREN WERE GIVEN SEMANTIC DIFFERENTIAL MEASURES. IT WAS FOUND THAT THERE IS A POSITIVE RELATIONSHIP BETWEEN GIRLS' PERCEPTIONS OFTHEIR MOTHERS' AND FATHERS' CHARACTERISTICS. FOR GIRLS, ONE CAN USE PERCEPTIONS OF THE CONCEPT "PARENTS" TO MAKE INFERENCES ABOUT THE PERCEIVED CHARACTERISTICS OF BOTH PARENTS. THERE ARE NO SUCH RELATIONSHIPS FOR BOYS. (AUTHOR/WY)

EJ 025 360 PS 500 570
SYMPTOM PATTERNS IN HYPERKINETIC, NEUROTIC, AND NORMAL CHILDREN CONNERS, C. KEITH, *CHILD DEVELOP*, V41 N3, PP667-682, SEP '70
CONCLUDES THAT THERE ARE FEW QUALITATIVE DIFFERENCES BETWEEN NORMAL AND PSYCHIATRICALLY ILL CHILDRE, THOUGH THEY DIFFER IN THE SEVERITY OF SYMPTOMATOLOGY. (AUTHOR/WY)

EJ 025 361 PS 500 577
THE DEVELOPMENT OF ROLE-TAKING AS REFLECTED BY BEHAVIOR OF BRIGHT, AVERAGE, AND RETARDED CHILDREN IN A SOCIAL GUESSING GAME DEVRIES, RHETA, *CHILD DEVELOP*, V41 N3, PP759-770, SEP '70
SUGGESTS A 5-STAGE SEQUENCE OF DEVELOPMENT FROM A TOTAL LACK OF RECOGNITION OF THE NEED FOR SECRECY AND DECEPTIVENESS IN THE FIRST STAGE TO THE FIFTH STAGE IN WHICH THE CHILD WAS COMPETITIVE AND ATTEMPTED TO OUTWIT THE OPPONENT BY UTILIZING AN IRREGULAR SHIFTING STRATEGY. (AUTHOR/WY)

EJ 025 362 PS 500 587
AMOUNT OF SHORT-TERM FAMILIARIZATION AND THE RESPONSE TO AUDITORY DISCREPANCIES MCCALL, ROBERT B.; MELSON, WILLIAM H., *CHILD DEVELOP*, V41 N3, PP861-869, SEP '70

EJ 025 363 PS 500 622
ATTENTIONAL PREFERENCE AND EXPERIENCE: II. AN EXPLORATORY LONGITUDINAL STUDY OF THE EFFECT OF VISUAL FAMILIARITY AND RESPONSIVENESS UZGIRIS, INA C.; HUNT, J. MCV., *J GENET PSYCHOL*, V117 N1, PP109-121, SEP '70
AN EARLIER VERSION OF THIS PAPER WAS PRESENTED BY UZGIRIS AT THE MEETING OF THE SOCIETY FOR RESEARCH IN CHILD DEVELOPMENT, MINNEAPOLIS, MINNESOTA, MARCH, 1965. (WY)

EJ 025 364 PS 500 623
ATTENTIONAL PREFERENCE AND EXPERIENCE: III. VISUAL FAMILIARITY AND LOOKING TIME GREENBERG, DAVID; AND OTHERS, *J GENET PSYCHOL*, V117 N1, PP123-135, SEP '70
ATTEMPTS TO IMPROVE METHODS EMPLOYED BY UZGIRIS AND HUNT. THE LONGITUDINAL SCHEDULE OF EVENTS IN THIS EXPERIMENT INVOLVED 24 INFANTS ONE MONTH OLD IN AN EXPERIMENTAL GROUP WHOSE MOTHERS WERE INSTRUCTED TO PRESENT AND CHANGE A VISUAL STIMULUS PATTERN. (WY)

EJ 025 374 PS 500 571
AGE PATTERNS IN CHILDREN'S PSYCHIATRIC SYMPTOMS SHECHTMAN, AUDREY, *CHILD DEVELOP*, V41 N3, PP683-693, SEP '70

EJ 025 375 PS 500 578
CARDIAC CLASSICAL CONDITIONING AND REVERSAL IN THE MONGOLOID, ENCEPHALOPATHIC, AND NORMAL CHILD BLOCK, JAMES D.; AND OTHERS, *CHILD DEVELOP*, V41 N3, PP771-785, SEP '70

EJ 025 376 PS 500 580
AN EXPLORATORY STUDY OF RESTING CARDIAC RATE AND VARIABILITY FROM THE LAST TRIMESTER OF PRENATAL LIFE THROUGH THE FIRST YEAR OF POSTNATAL LIFE LEWIS, MICHAEL; AND OTHERS, *CHILD DEVELOP*, V41 N3, PP799-811, SEP '70
THE DATA INDICATE NO RELATIONSHIP BETWEEN MATERNAL AND FETAL DATA. MOREOVER, THERE ARE CLEAR DEVELOPMENTAL PATTERNS OF RESTING CARDIAC RESPONSE OVER THE FIRST YEAR OF LIFE, WITH RATE AND VARIABILITY SHOWING LINEAR DECREASES. (AUTHOR/WY)

EJ 025 377 PS 500 620
AWARENESS, AFFECTION, AND PERCEIVED SIMILARITY IN THE PARENT-CHILD RELATIONSHIP WAKEFIELD, WILLIAM M., *J GENET PSYCHOL*, V117 N1, PP91-97, SEP '70
SIXTY ADOLESCENTS AND THEIR PARENTS PROVIDED DATA WHICH REVEALED THAT ALTHOUGH PARENTS WERE ABLE TO PREDICT THEIR ADOLESCENTS' RESPONSES TO A PROBLEM CHECKLIST WITH ACCURACY GREATER THAN CHANGE, THIS FORM OF "PARENTAL AWARENESS" APPEARS UNRELATED TO THE DEGREE TO WHICH THE ADOLESCENT LIKES THE PARENT OR SEES HIMSELF AS SIMILAR TO THE PARENT. (AUTHOR/WY)

EJ 025 386 PS 500 590
SOME NONVERBAL ASPECTS OF COMMUNICATION BETWEEN MOTHER AND PRESCHOOL CHILD SCHMIDT, WILFRED H. O.; HORE, TERENCE, *CHILD DEVELOP*, V41 N3, PP889-896, SEP '70

EJ 025 469 PS 500 564
BODY SIZE OF CONTEMPORARY GROUPS OF ONE-YEAR-OLD INFANTS STUDIED IN DIFFERENT PARTS OF THE WORLD MEREDITH, HOWARD V., *CHILD DEVELOP*, V41 N3, PP551-600, SEP '70
INFANTS LIVING IN VARIOUS GEOGRAPHIC LOCATIONS ARE FOUND TO DIFFER AS MUCH AS 9 POUNDS IN AVERAGE BODY WEIGHT, 5.5 INCHES IN AVERAGE BODY LENGTH, AND 2.5 INCHES IN AVERAGE CHEST CIRCUMFERENCE. (AUTHOR/WY)

EJ 025 470 PS 500 579
MATRICES, THREE BY THREE: CLASSIFICATION AND SERIATION MACKAY, C. K.; AND OTHERS, *CHILD DEVELOP*, V41 N3, PP787-797, SEP '70
INVESTIGATES THE DEVELOPMENT OF THE ABILITY FOR DOUBLE SERIATION IN CHILDREN AGE 5-8 YEARS AND FINDS THAT THERE IS A DEVELOPMENTAL LAG BETWEEN THE EMERGENCE OF THE ABILITY FOR CROSS-CLASSIFICATION AND THAT FOR DOUBLE SERIATION. (WY)

EJ 025 471 PS 500 617
THE CONNOTATIVE MEANING OF PARENT-CHILD RELATIONSHIPS AS RELATED TO PERCEIVED MATERNAL WARMTH AND CONTROL MAGARO, PETER A., *J GENET PSYCHOL*, V117 N1, PP25-35, SEP '70

EJ 025 626 PS 500 608
PSYCHOLOGICAL DEVELOPMENT--PREDICTIONS FROM INFANCY RUTTER, MICHAEL, *J CHILD PSYCHOL PSYCHIAT*, V11 N1, PP49-62, MAY '70
A CONSIDERATION OF THE FACTORS WHICH INFLUENCE DEVELOPMENT AND DEVELOPMENT PREDICTIONS LEADS TO THE VIEW THAT, WITH BETTER INSTRUMENTS, IMPROVED BUT STILL VERY MODEST PREDICTIONS MIGHT BECOME POSSIBLE DURING LATER INFANCY. PAPER READ TO THE STANDING CONFERENCE OF SOCIETIES REGISTERED FOR ADOPTION: MEDICAL GROUP: DAY CONFERENCE ON "GENETIC AND PSYCHOLOGICAL ASPECTS OF ADOPTION," ROYAL SOCIETY OF MEDICINE, LONDON, 23 OCTOBER, 1968. (WY)

EJ 025 635 PS 500 585
EFFECTS OF VICARIOUS CONSEQUENCES ON IMITATIVE PERFORMANCE LIEBERT, ROBERT M.; FERNANDEZ, LUIS E., *CHILD DEVELOP*, V41 N3, PP847-852, SEP '70

EJ 025 803 PS 500 591
COMMENTS ON SOCIAL DESIRABILITY AND PERSUASION GOZALI, JOAV, *CHILD DEVELOP*, V41 N3, PP897-898, SEP '70

EJ 025 953 PS 500 566
THINKING ABOUT PEOPLE THINKING ABOUT PEOPLE THINKING ABOUT...: A STUDY OF SOCIAL COGNITIVE DEVELOPMENT MILLER, PATRICIA H.; AND OTHERS, *CHILD DEVELOP*, V41 N3, PP613-623, SEP '70
TRACES THE CHILD'S GROWING UNDERSTANDING OF THE RECURSIVE NATURE OF THOUGHT THROUGH MASTERY OF A SEQUENCE OF FOUR STEPS. RECURSIVE THINKING MAY WELL BE A PREREQUISITE FOR COMPLEX, ROLE TAKING-TYPE INFERENCES FOUND IN ADOLESCENT THOUGHT. (WY)

EJ 025 954 PS 500 567
INTERRELATIONS AND CORRELATES OVER TIME IN CHILDREN'S LEARNING STEVENSON, HAROLD W.; AND OTHERS, *CHILD DEVELOP*, V41 N3, PP625-637, SEP '70
SEVENTY-THREE SUBJECTS TESTED AT GRADE 4 WERE RETESTED AT GRADE 7 ON FIVE TASKS. IN ADDITION, 138 SEVENTH GRADERS WERE TESTED ON THESE TASKS FOR THE FIRST TIME. USING PERFORMANCE AT GRADE 4 TO PREDICT PERFORMANCE ON DIFFERENT TASKS AT GRADE 7 OFTEN WAS MORE SATISFACTORY THAN USING SEVENTH-GRADE PREDICTORS. (AUTHOR/WY)

EJ 025 955 PS 500 568
EFFECTS OF NAMING RELEVANT AND IRRELEVANT STIMULI ON THE DISCRIMINATION LEARNING OF CHILDREN DICKERSON, DONALD J., *CHILD DEVELOP*, V41 N3, PP639-650, SEP '70

EJ 025 956 PS 500 569
A TEST OF LURIA'S HYPOTHESES CONCERNING THE DEVELOPMENT OF VERBAL SELF-REGULATION MILLER, SCOTT A.; AND OTHERS, *CHILD DEVELOP*, V41 N3, PP651-665, SEP '70
CONTRARY TO LURIA'S HYPOTHESIS, VERBAL CONTROL DID NOT AFFECT SENSORI-MOTOR PERFORMANCE IN THIS EXPERIMENT INVOLVING 160 PRESCHOOL CHILDREN IN FOUR AGE GROUPS TESTED ON LURIA'S 2-CHOICE TASKS. (WY)

EJ 025 957 PS 500 572
SCALOGRAM ANALYSIS OF LOGICAL AND PERCEPTUAL COMPONENTS OF CONSERVATION OF DISCONTINUOUS QUANTITY SCHWARTZ, MARILYN MILLER; SCHOLINICK, ELLIN KOFSKY, *CHILD DEVELOP*, V41 N3, PP695-705, SEP '70

EJ 025 958 PS 500 573
VERBAL MEDIATORS AND CUE DISCRIMINATION IN THE TRANSITION FROM NONCONSERVATION TO CONSERVATION OF NUMBER PETERS, DONALD L., *CHILD DEVELOP*, V41 N3, PP707-721, SEP '70
FOUR GROUPS OF KINDERGARTEN CHILDREN WERE INVOLVED IN A PRETEST-POSTTEST EXPERIMENT COMPARING VERBAL CUED, VISUAL CUED, VERBAL RULE SULPPLEMENTED INSTRUCTION ON CONSERVATION TASKS. BOTH LANGUAGE LEVEL AND ANALYTIC SORTING BEHAVIOR WERE RELIABLE PREDICTIONS OF NUMBER CONSERVATION PERFORMANCE IN INDIVIDUAL CHILDREN. (AUTHOR/WY)

EJ 025 959 PS 500 575
DIMENSIONAL PREFERENCE AND DISCRIMINATION SHIFT LEARNING IN CHILDREN TIGHE, LOUISE S.; AND OTHERS, *CHILD DEVELOP*, V41 N3, PP737-746, SEP '70

EJ 025 960 PS 500 582
LOGICAL THINKING IN CHILDREN AGES SIX THROUGH THIRTEEN SHAPIRO, BERNARD J.; O'BRIEN, THOMAS C., *CHILD DEVELOP*, V41 N3, PP823-29, SEP '70

EJ 025 961 PS 500 583
THE EFFECT OF INFORMATIVE FEEDBACK ON PROBLEM SOLVING SCHROTH, MARVIN L., *CHILD DEVELOP*, V41 N3, PP831-37, SEP '70

EJ 025 962 PS 500 586
SEMANTICS, PHRASE STRUCTURE, AND AGE AS VARIABLES IN SENTENCE RECALL VANEVERY, HARDYN; ROSENBERG, SHELDON, *CHILD DEVELOP*, V41 N3, PP853-859, SEP '70
INDICATES THAT THE VARIABLES ASSOCIATED WITH AGE NOT ONLY INCREASE RECALL PERFORMANCE AND CHUNKING BUT THEY INFLUENCE THE MANNER IN WHICH SEMANTIC AND SYNTACTIC INFORMATION IN SENTENCES IS PROCESSED AS WELL. (AUTHOR/WY)

EJ 025 963 PS 500 606
AGE DIFFERENCES IN THE DISCRIMINATION SHIFT LEARNING OF YOUNG CHILDREN GARNER, JOHN, *J CHILD PSYCHOL PSYCHIAT*, V11 N1, PP29-36, MAY '70

EJ 025 964 PS 500 615
SELF-REINFORCEMENT ESTABLISHED FOR A DISCRIMINATION TASK MILLER, ADAM W., JR.; CLARK, NORMA, *J GENET PSYCHOL*, V117 N1, PP1-6, SEP '70
RESULTS INDICATED THAT A COMBINATION OF PRIMARY AND CONDITIONAL REINFORCERS WAS MOST EFFECTIVE IN DEVELOPING A VERBAL CONDITIONED REINFORCER WHICH EFFECTIVELY FUNCTIONED AS A SELF-REINFORCER TO FACILITATE NEW LEARNING FOR 80 SECOND GRADE SS. (AUTHOR/WY)

EJ 025 988 PS 500 621
ATTENTIONAL PREFERENCE AND EXPERIENCE: I. INTRODUCTION HUNT, J. MCV., *J GENET PSYCHOL*, V117 N1, PP99-107, SEP '70
REVIEWS A SERIES OF PAPERS WHICH REPORT A SEQUENCE OF EXPERIMENTS CONCERNED WITH HOW REPEATED VISUAL ENCOUNTERS WITH OBJECTS OR PATTERNS INFLUENCE ATTENTIONAL PREFERENCE FOR WHAT IS FAMILIAR OF WHAT IS UNFAMILIAR OR NOVEL. (WY)

EJ 026 152 PS 500 565
EXPERIMENTAL ANALYSIS OF THE FACTORS DETERMINING OBEDIENCE OF FOUR-YEAR-OLD CHILDREN TO ADULT FEMALES LANDAUER, T. K.; AND OTHERS, *CHILD DEVELOP*, V41 N3, PP601-611, SEP '70
NURSERY SCHOOL CHILDREN WERE ASKED TO PERFORM TASKS BY THEIR OWN AND OTHER MOTHERS. THERE WAS ONLY SLIGHT CONSISTENCY ACROSS MOTHERS IN THE TENDENCY OF CHILDREN TO OBEY. HOWEVER, OBEDIENCE WAS STRONGLY DETERMINED BY THE PREEXISTING RELATIONSHIP BETWEEN ADULT AND CHILD, 44 TO 52 CHILDREN WERE LESS OBEDIENT TO THEIR OWN MOTHERS. (AUTHOR/WY)

EJ 026 153 PS 500 574
THE EFFECT OF ANXIETY OVER INTELLECTUAL PERFORMANCE ON REFLECTION-IMPULSIVITY IN CHILDREN MESSER, STANLEY, *CHILD DEVELOP*, V41 N3, PP723-35, SEP '70
SUPPORTS THE PROPOSITION THAT ANXIETY OVER INTELLECTUAL PERFORMANCE IS ONE ANTECEDENT OF A REFLECTIVE COGNITIVE DISPOSITION. (AUTHOR/WY)

EJ 026 154 PS 500 576
THE IMPACT OF WORDS AND DEEDS CONCERNING ALTRUISM UPON CHILDREN BRYAN, JAMES H.; WALBEK, NANCY H., *CHILD DEVELOP*, V41 N3, PP747-757, SEP '70
SEVENTY-TWO SECOND-, THIRD-, AND FOURTH- GRADE GIRLS WERE EXPOSED TO A VIDEO-TAPED ADULT MODEL WHO PRACTICED AND/OR PREACHED GENEROSITY OR SELFISHNESS. THE EFFECT OF THE MODEL'S PRACTICES UPON SS DONATION BEHAVIOR WAS MARGINALLY SIGNIFICANT, BUT DONATION BEHAVIOR WAS UNAFFECTED BY EITHER THE POWER OR THE EXHORTATIONS OF THE MODEL. (WY)

EJ 026 155 PS 500 604
SOME PSYCHIATRIC OBSERVATIONS ON A GROUP OF MALADJUSTED DEAF CHILDREN WILLIAMS, CYRIL E., *J CHILD PSYCHOL PSYCHIAT*, V11 N1, PP1-18, MAY '70
IN A GROUP OF 51 MALADJUSTED DEAF CHILDREN THE PSYCHIATRIC DISORDERS ENCOUNTERED WERE SIMILAR TO THOSE FOUND IN NORMAL CHILDREN AND THOSE HANDICAPPED IN OTHER WAYS. (WY)

EJ 026 156 PS 500 605
PSYCHIATRIC DISORDER AND ADULT AND PEER GROUP REJECTION OF THE CHILD'S NAME BAGLEY, CHRISTOPHER; EVAN-WONG, LOUISE, *J CHILD PSYCHOL PSYCHIAT*, V11 N1, PP19-27, MAY '70

EJ 026 157 PS 500 607
A FOLLOW-UP STUDY OF SCHOOL PHOBIC ADOLESCENTS ADMITTED TO AN IN-PATIENT UNIT BERG, JAN, *J CHILD PSYCHOL PSYCHIAT*, V11 N1, PP37-47, MAY '70
OF THE 1/3 TO 2/3 OF SCHOOL PHOBIC ADOLESCENTS WHO HAD RETURNED TO SCHOOL AFTER TREATMENT AT THE IN-PATIENT UNIT, 1/3 OF THE GROUP WERE WELL-ADJUSTED, 1/3 HAD LIMITED FUNCTIONING, AND 1/3 WERE SEVERELY INCAPACITATED BY NEUROTIC PROBLEMS AND INTERPERSONAL DIFFICULTIES. THIS PAPER IS THE BASIS OF A TALK DELIVERED, BY INVITATION, AT THE CHARLES BURNS CLINIC, BIRMINGHAM, (ENGLAND) ON 19 SEPTEMBER 1969. (AUTHOR/WY)

EJ 026 208 PS 500 589
REPRESENTATIONAL AND SYNTACTIC COMPETENCE OF PROBLEM READERS DENNER, BRUCE, *CHILD DEVELOP*, V41 N3, PP881-887, SEP '70
PROBLEM READERS WERE AS COMPETENT AS AVERAGE READERS IN ASSOCIATING NON-REPRESENTATIONAL LINEAR FORMS WITH WORDS, BUT WERE LESS COMPETENT IN SYNTHESIZING WHOLE SENTENCES FROM INDIVIDUAL LINEAR FORMS. (AUTHOR/WY)

EJ 026 313 PS 500 588
CHILDREN'S BEHAVIOR PROBLEMS AS VIEWED BY TEACHERS, PSYCHOLOGISTS, AND CHILDREN ZIV, AVNER, *CHILD DEVELOP*, V41 N3, PP871-879, SEP '70
THIRTY BEHAVIOR PROBLEMS WERE RANKED ACCORDING TO SEVERITY BY 165 EIGHTH-GRADE BOYS AND GIRLS, 82 TEACHERS, AND 45 PSYCHOLOGISTS. A SIGNIFICANT POSITIVE CORRELATION WAS FOUND BETWEEN TEACHERS' AND PSYCHOLOGISTS' RANKINGS. (AUTHOR/WY)

EJ 026 324 PS 500 584
MATERNAL BEHAVIOR TOWARD OWN AND OTHER PRESCHOOL CHILDREN: THE PROBLEM OF "OWNNESS" HALVERSON, CHARLES F., JR.; WALDROP, MARY F., *CHILD DEVELOP*, V41 N3, PP839-45, SEP '70
INTERACTIONS BETWEEN MOTHERS AND THEIR OWN AND OTHER 2 1/2 YEAR OLDS WERE EXPLORED TO IDENTIFY MATERNAL BEHAVIORS WHICH WERE CONSISTENT ACROSS CHILDREN AND THOSE WHICH WERE TIED TO INDIVIDUAL CHILDREN. ARTICLE BASED ON PAPER PRESENTED AT THE BIENNIAL MEETING OF THE SOCIETY FOR RESEARCH IN CHILD DEVELOPMENT, SANTA MONICA, CALIFORNIA, MARCH, 1969. (WY)

EJ 026 325 PS 500 618
A COMPARISON OF THE CHARACTERISTICS OF JUNIOR HIGH SCHOOL STUDENTS GREENFELD, NORMAN; FINKELSTEIN, ELSIE L., *J GENET PSYCHOL*, V117 N1, PP37-50, SEP '70
THIS STUDY COMPARED SOME PERSONAL- SOCIAL CHARACTERISTICS OF A SAMPLE (250 SS) OF JUNIOR HIGH SCHOOL STUDENTS WHICH WAS STUDIED IN 1930-1935 WITH A SOMEWHAT SIMILAR SAMPLE (211 SS) OF STUDENTS AT THE SAME SCHOOL TODAY. RESULTS INDICATE SIGNIFICANT CHANGE IN OVERALL PERSONAL-SOCIAL CHARACTERISTICS OF THE CHILDREN IN THESE TWO SAMPLES. (AUTHOR/WY)

EJ 026 373 PS 500 603
NEW LIGHT ON THE HUMAN POTENTIAL OTTO, HERBERT A., *CHILDHOOD EDUC*, V47 N1, PP23-28, OCT '70
REVISION BY THE AUTHOR OF AN ARTICLE PUBLISHED IN SATURDAY REVIEW. DECEMBER 20, 1969.

EJ 026 374 PS 500 649
SEMANTIC AND PHONETIC RELATIONS IN THE FALSE RECOGNITION OF WORDS BY THIRD- AND SIXTH-GRADE CHILDREN FELZEN, ENID; ANISFELD, MOSHE, *DEVELOP PSYCHOL*, V3 N2, PP163-168, SEP '70

EJ 026 375 PS 500 652
AGE DIFFERENCES IN JUDGMENTS OF RECENCY FOR SHORT SEQUENCES OF PICTURES MATHEWS, MARY ELIZABETH; FOZARD, JAMES L., *DEVELOP PSYCHOL*, V3 N2, PP208-217, SEP '70
PARTS OF THE DATA DESCRIBED WERE PRESENTED AT THE MEETING OF THE EASTERN PSYCHOLOGICAL ASSOCIATION, PHILADELPHIA, PENNSYLVANIA, APRIL 10-12, 1969. (MS)

EJ 026 376 PS 500 653
A SEX DIFFERENCE IN THE WECHSLER IQ VOCABULARY SCORE AS A PREDICTOR OF STRATEGY IN A PROBABILITY-LEARNING TASK PERFORMED BY ADOLESCENTS WEINBERG, SHEILA; RABINOWITZ, JOSHUA, *DEVELOP PSYCHOL*, V3 N2, PP218-224, SEP '70

EJ 026 450 PS 500 650
HONESTY AND ALTRUISM AMONG PREADOLESCENTS MUSSEN, PAUL; AND OTHERS, *DEVELOP PSYCHOL*, V3 N2, PP169-194, SEP '70

EJ 026 493 PS 500 595
MODIFYING BEHAVIOR OF KINDERGARTEN CHILDREN SIBLEY, SALLY A.; AND OTHERS, *YOUNG CHILDREN*, V25 N6, PP345-352, SEP '70
SYSTEMATIC APPLICATION OF POSITIVE REINFORCEMENT PRINCIPLES CAN BE A POWERFUL TOOL FOR TEACHERS IN THE CLASSROOM SETTING. (NH)

EJ 026 494 PS 500 668
IMITATION AND ECHOING IN YOUNG SCHIZOPHRENIC CHILDREN SHAPIRO, THEODORE; AND OTHERS, *J AMER ACAD CHILD PSYCHIAT*, V9 N3, PP548-567, JUL '70
PRESENTED AT THE ANNUAL MEETING OF THE AMERICAN ACADEMY OF CHILD PSYCHIATRY, CHICAGO, ILLINOIS, OCTOBER 18, 1969. (WY)

EJ 026 506 PS 500 659
VISUAL AND HAPTIC DIMENSIONAL PREFERENCE: A DEVELOPMENTAL STUDY SIEGEL, ALENXANDER W.,; VANCE, BILLIE J., *DEVELOP PSYCHOL*, V3 N2, PP264-266, SEP '70

EJ 026 507 PS 500 661
A DEVELOPMENTAL INVESTIGATION OF THE EFFECT OF SENSORY MODALITY ON FORM RECOGNITION IN CHILDREN BUTTER, ELIOT J.; ZUNG, BURTON J., *DEVELOP PSYCHOL*, V3 N2, PP276, SEP '70

EJ 026 508 PS 500 663
MOTHER-INFANT RELATIONSHIP AND WEIGHT GAIN IN THE FIRST MONTH OF LIFE SHAW, JON A.; AND OTHERS, *J AMER ACAD CHILD PSYCHIAT*, V9 N3, PP428-444, JUL '70
PAPER PRESENTED AT THE ANNUAL MEETING OF THE AMERICAN ASSOCIATION OF PSYCHIATRIC CLINICS FOR CHILDREN, BOSTON, MASS., NOVEMBER, 1969. (WY)

EJ 026 640 PS 500 613
COMBATTING RETARDATION IN INFANTS WITH DOWN'S SYNDROME KUGEL, ROBERT B., *CHILDREN*, V17 N5, PP188-92, SEP-OCT '70

EJ 026 734 PS 500 600
CHILDREN AND THEIR EXPANDING WORLD OF KNOWLEDGE FRAZIER, ALEXANDER, *CHILDHOOD EDUC*, V47 N1, PP6-13, OCT '70
PAPER PRESENTED AT THE ANNUAL STUDY CONFERENCE OF THE ASSOCIATION FOR CHILDHOOD EDUCATION INTERNATIONAL, ATLANTA, GEORGIA, APRIL 1, 1970.

EJ 026 735 PS 500 611
THE EFFECT OF BLACK HISTORY ON AN INTERRACIAL GROUP OF CHILDREN LIKOVER, BELLE, *CHILDREN*, V17 N5, PP177-82, SEP-OCT '70

EJ 026 771 PS 500 599
MAKING TOMORROW NOW: BUILDING A QUALITATIVE ENVIRONMENT FOR ALL CHILDREN BRENNAN, MATTHEW J., *CHILDHOOD EDUC*, V47 N1, PP2-5, OCT '70
EDUCATORS SHOULD DEVELOP PROGRAMS TO PROMOTE UNDERSTANDINGS OF ENVIRONMENTAL CHANGE, THE INTERDEPENDENCY OF LIVING THINGS, AND THE INFLUENCES OF HEREDITY AND ENVIRONMENT. (NH)

EJ 026 772 PS 500 601
ENVIRONMENTAL EDUCATION: THE STATE OF THE ART HILL, WILHELMINA, *CHILDHOOD EDUC*, V47 N1, PP14-18, OCT '70

EJ 026 773 PS 500 614
HEAD START'S INFLUENCE ON COMMUNITY CHANGE DATTA, LOIS-ELLIN, *CHILDREN*, V17 N5, PP193-96, SEP-OCT '70

EJ 026 774 PS 500 666
THE USE OF A PLAY PROGRAM BY HOSPITALIZED CHILDREN TISZA, VERONICA B.; AND OTHERS, *J AMER ACAD CHILD PSYCHIAT*, V9 N3, PP515-531, JUL '70

EJ 026 810 PS 500 646
THE USE OF METROPOLITCAN READINESS TESTS WITH MEXICAN-AMERICAN CHILDREN MISHRA, SHITALA P.; HURT, MAURE, JR., *CALIF J EDUC RES,* V21 N4, PP182-7, SEP '70

EJ 026 814 PS 500 597
EXPERIMENTAL LEARNING REEVALUATED RAND, HELENE, *YOUNG CHILDREN,* V25 N6, PP363-366, SEP '70
ADULT-CHILD INTERACTION AS CHILD VERBALIZES HIS EXPERIENCES HELPS CHILD TO INTEGRATE THIS NEW INFORMATION INTO HIS STORE OF KNOWLEDGE. (NH)

EJ 026 815 PS 500 629
THE EFFECTS OF PSYCHOSOCIAL DEPRIVATION ON HUMAN DEVELOPMENT IN INFANCY CALDWELL, BETTYE M., *MERRILL PALMER QUART,* V16 N3, PP260-77, JUL '70

EJ 026 835 PS 500 593
AN OVERVIEW OF BRITISH INFANT SCHOOLS HETZEL, DONNA C., *YOUNG CHILDREN,* V25 N6, PP336-339, SEP '70

EJ 026 915 PS 500 598
CANDIDATE FOR INTEGRATION: A HEARING-IMPAIRED CHILD IN A REGULAR NURSERY SCHOOL NORTHCOTT, WINIFRED H., *YOUNG CHILDREN,* V25 N6, PP367-380, SEP '70
THE HEARING-IMPAIRED CHILD IN A NURSERY SCHOOL FOR CHILDREN WITH NORMAL HEARING IS SURROUNDED BY EXPERIENCES WHICH HELP HIM TO REGARD SPEECH AS A NATURAL OUTLET FOR EXPRESSION. (NH)

EJ 026 935 PS 500 662
TANGIBLE REINFORCERS AND CHILD GROUP THERAPY CLEMENT, PAUL W.; AND OTHERS, *J AMER ACAD CHILD PSYCHIAT,* V9 N3, PP409-427, JUL '70

EJ 027 028 PS 500 602
DEVELOPING A LEARNING ENVIRONMENT OF QUALITY TILLMAN, RODNEY, *CHILDHOOD EDUC,* V47 N1, PP19-22, OCT '70

EJ 027 029 PS 500 644
A STUDY OF THE EFFECTIVENESS OF SPECIFIC TEACHING OF CONSERVATION TO CHILDREN IN SELECTED ELEMENTARY SCHOOLS OF BUTTE COUNTY, CALIFORNIA GLADEN, FRANK H.; CARKIN, HELEN S., *CALIF J EDUC RES,* V21 N4, PP152-69, SEP '70

EJ 027 030 PS 500 645
A PILOT STUDY OF COMPUTER-ASSISTED DRILL AND PRACTICE IN SEVENTH GRADE REMEDIAL MATHEMATICS CRAWFORD, ALAN N., *CALIF J EDUC RES,* V21 N4, PP170-81, SEP '70

EJ 027 031 PS 500 647
THE INFLUENCE OF SET INDUCTION UPON STUDENT ACHIEVEMENT AND ASSESSMENT OF EFFECTIVE TEACHING SCHUCK, ROBERT F., *CALIF J EDUC RES,* V21 N4, PP188098, SEP '70
REPORTS AN EXPERIMENT IN WHICH THE EFFECTIVENESS OF "SET INDUCTION" (ESTABLISHING A FRAME OF REFERENCE DELIBERATELY DESIGNED TO FACILITATE THE COMMUNICATIVE LINK BETWEEN THE PUPILS AND THEIR LESSON) IS EXAMINED AS AN INSTRUCTIONAL STRATEGY. (WY)

EJ 027 181 PS 500 651
PROBABILITY LEARNING AS A FUNCTION OF SEX OF THE SUBJECT, TEST ANXIETY, AND PERCENTAGE OF REINFORCEMENT DUSEK, JEROME B.; HILL, KENNEDY T., *DEVELOP PSYCHOL,* V3 N2, PP195-207, SEP '70

EJ 027 182 PS 500 654
CONTINUITY AND DISCONTINUITY HYPOTHESES IN STUDIES OF CONSERVATION BRAINERD, CHARLES J., *DEVELOP PSYCHOL,* V3 N2, PP225-228, SEP '70

EJ 027 183 PS 500 655
DISCRIMINATION SHIFT PERFORMANCE OF KINDERGARTEN CHILDREN AS A FUNCTION OF VARIATION OF THE IRRELEVANT SHIFT DIMENSION DICKERSON, DONALD J.; AND OTHERS, *DEVELOP PSYCHOL,* V3 N2, PP229-235, SEP '70

EJ 027 184 PS 500 656
DISCRIMINATION SHIFTS IN THREE-YEAR-OLDS AS A FUNCTION OF SHIFT PROCEDURE CARON, ALBERT J., *DEVELOP PSYCHOL,* V3 N2, PP236-241, SEP '70

EJ 027 185 PS 500 658
INSTITUTIONALIZATION AND THE EFFECTIVENESS OF SOCIAL REINFORCEMENT: A FIVE- AND EIGHT-YEAR FOLLOW-UP STUDY ZIGLER, EDWARD; AND OTHERS, *DEVELOP PSYCHOL,* V3 N2, PP255-263, SEP '70

EJ 027 341 PS 500 610
THE HOSPITAL AND THE PRESCHOOL CHILD MILLAR, T. P., *CHILDREN,* V17 N5, PP171-76, SEP-OCT '70

EJ 027 342 PS 500 612
REUNITING CHILDREN AND PARENTS THROUGH CASEWORK AND GROUP WORK EDINGER, HANNI B., *CHILDREN,* V17 N5, PP183-87, SEP-OCT '70

EJ 027 343 PS 500 657
ANXIETY, AFFILIATION, AND SOCIAL ISOLATION MACDONALD, A. P., JR., *DEVELOP PSYCHOL,* V3 N2, PP242-254, SEP '70
THE DATA FROM THIS ANXIETY-AFFILIATION EXPERIMENT INDICATE THAT THE LINK BETWEEN ANXIETY AND AFFILIATION IS EXPECIALLY PRONOUNCED IN FIRSTBORN MALES AND LATER BORN FEMALES. DATA REPORTED IS TAKEN FROM A DISSERTATION SUBMITTED IN PARTIAL FULFILLMENT OF THE REQUIREMENTS FOR THE PHD DEGREE AT CORNELL UNIVERSITY. (AUTHOR/WY)

EJ 027 344 PS 500 664
THE FUNCTION OF AMBIGUITY IN CHILD CRISES STEIN, MYRON, *J AMER ACAD CHILD PSYCHIAT,* V9 N3, PP462-476, JUL '70
DISCUSSES THE FUNCTION OF "AMBIGUITY" (AN ATTITUDE OF HATIBUAL UNCERTAINTY, VAGUENESS, AND IMPRECISION OF COMMUNICATION) IN CRISIS SITUATIONS INVOLVING ADULT-CHILD INTERCHANGES. MAKES SUGGESTIONS FOR MEDICAL AND PSYCHIATRIC COUNSELORS. PAPER WAS PRESENTED AT THE MEETING OF THE AMERICAN ASSOCIATION OF PSYCHIATRIC CLINICS FOR CHILDREN, BOSTON, MASS., NOVEMBER, 1969. (WY)

EJ 027 345 PS 500 667
THE EFFECTS OF OBJECT LOSS ON THE BODY IMAGE OF SCHIZOPHRENIC GIRLS GREEN, ARTHUR H., *J AMER ACAD CHILD PSYCHIAT,* V9 N3, PP532-547, JUL '70

EJ 027 435 PS 500 596
ABOUT RESEARCH: PART I, THE NATURE OF RESEARCH... CHANGING EMPHASES SCOTT, PHYLLIS M., *YOUNG CHILDREN,* V25 N6, PP353-362, SEP '70

EJ 027 436 PS 500 625
RESEARCH STRATEGIES AND CONCEPTS OF DEVELOPMENT AND LEARNING. INTRODUCTION HOROWITZ, FRANCES DEGEN, *MERRILL PALMER QUART,* V16 N3, PP235-37, JUL '70

EJ 027 437 PS 500 626
AN AGE-IRRELEVANT CONCEPT OF DEVELOPMENT BAER, DONALD M., *MERRILL PALMER QUART,* V16 N3, PP238-45, JUL '70
REWRITTEN AND SHORTENED VERSION OF PRESENTATION GIVEN AT A SYMPOSIUM OF THE AMERICAN PSYCHOLOGICAL ASSOCIATION MEETING, NEW YORK, NEW YORK, 1966. (MS)

EJ 027 438 PS 500 627
AN ORGANISM ORIENTED CONCEPT OF DEVELOPMENT GOLLIN, EUGENE S., *MERRILL PALMER QUART,* V16 N3, PP246-52, JUL '70
REWRITTEN AND SHORTENED VERSION OF PRESENTATION GIVEN AT A SYMPOSIUM OF THE AMERICAN PSYCHOLOGICAL ASSOCIATION MEETING, NEW YORK 1966. (MS)

EJ 027 439 PS 500 628
DEVELOPMENTAL LAWS AND THE EXPERIMENTALIST'S ONTOLOGY SUTTON-SMITH, BRIAN, *MERRILL PALMER QUART,* V16 N3, PP253-59, JUL '70
REWRITTEN AND SHORTENED VERSION OF PRESENTATION GIVEN AT A SYMPOSIUM OF THE AMERICAN PSYCHOLOGICAL ASSOCIAITON MEETING, NEW YORK 1966 (MS)

EJ 027 448 PS 500 665
TEACHER-PARENT WORK IN THE HOME: AN ASPECT OF CHILD GUIDANCE CLINIC SERVICES BRAUN, SAMUEL J.; REISER, NANCY R., *J AMER ACAD CHILD PSYCHIAT,* V9 N3, PP495-514, JUL '70

EJ 027 501 PS 500 609
A NATIONAL PRIORITY: RAISING THE QUALITY OF CHILDREN'S LIVES ZIGLER, EDWARD F., *CHILDREN,* V17 N5, PP166-70, SEP-OCT '70

EJ 027 502 PS 500 631
PSYCHOLOGICAL SOURCES OF "RESISTANCE" TO FAMILY PLANNING KELLER, ALAN B.; AND OTHERS, *MERRILL PALMER QUART,* V16 N3, PP286-302, JUL '70

EJ 027 531 PS 500 592
THE FUNDAMENTAL LEARNING NEEDS OF TODAY'S YOUNG CHILDREN , *YOUNG CHILDREN,* V25 N6, PP326-335, SEP '70

EJ 027 551 PS 500 594
AWARENESS--ONE KEY TO READING READINESS WEISER, MARGARET, *YOUNG CHILDREN,* V25 N6, PP340-344, SEP '70
SUGGESTS METHODS AND MATERIALS FOR IMPROVING THE PERCEPTION ABILITIES OF YOUNG CHILDREN. (NH)

EJ 027 552 PS 500 648
SEPARATING ENDOGENOUS, EXOGENOUS, ECOGENIC, AND EPOGENIC COMPONENT CURVES IN DEVELOPMENTAL DATA CATTELL, RAYMOND B., *DEVELOP PSYCHOL*, V3 N2, PP151-162, SEP '70
STUDY WAS FIRST PRESENTED AT THE ANNUAL INVITATIONAL ADDRESS TO DIVISION 20, MATURITY AND OLD AGE, AT THE MEETING OF THE AMERICAN PSYCHOLOGICAL ASSOCIATION, AUGUST 30, 1968. (MS)

EJ 027 585 PS 500 630
DIAGNOSING MINIMAL BRAIN DAMAGE IN CHILDREN: A COMPARISON OF TWO BENDER SCORING SYSTEMS HAYDEN, BENJAMIN S.; AND OTHERS, *MERRILL PALMER QUART*, V16 N3, PP278-85, JUL '70

EJ 027 586 PS 500 660
AN INSTRUMENT FOR MEASURING CREATIVITY IN YOUNG CHILDREN: THE GROSS GEOMETRIC FORMS GROSS, RUTH B.; MARSH, MARION, *DEVELOP PSYCHOL*, V3 N2, PP267, SEP '70

EJ 027 613 PS 500 643
STUDIES IN PATTERN DETECTION IN NORMAL AND AUTISTIC CHILDREN. II. REPRODUCTION AND PRODUCTION OF COLOR SEQUENCES FRITH, UTA, *JOURNAL OF EXPERIMENTAL CHILD PSYCHOLOGY*, V10 N1, PP120-135, AUG '70
FINDINGS ARE CONSISTENT WITH THE HYPOTHESIS OF AN INPUT PROCESSING DEFICIT IN AUTISTIC CHILDREN. AUTISTIC CHILDREN WERE INSENSITIVE TO DIFFERENCES IN THE STRUCTURES PRESENT AND TENDED TO IMPOSE THEIR OWN SIMPLE STEREOTYPED PATTERNS. NORMAL CHILDREN IMPOSED SUCH PATTERNS IN THE ABSENCE OF STRUCTURED INPUT ONLY. PAPER REPORTS WORK WHICH HAS BEEN SUBMITTED TO THE UNIVERSITY OF LONDON AS PART OF A PH.D THESIS. (AUTHOR/WY)

EJ 027 614 PS 500 677
SCHOOL ACHIEVERS AND UNDERACHIEVERS IN AN URBAN GHETTO HIRSCH, JAY G.; COSTELLO, JOAN, *ELEMENTARY SCHOOL JOURNAL*, V71 N2, PP78-85, NOV '70
IN A STUDY OF 23 BLACK GHETTO BOYS AND GIRLS, THE VARIABLES RATED MOST IMPORTANT FOR DISTINGUISHING BETWEEN ACHIEVERS ANDUNDERACHIEVERS WERE THE NATURE AND QUALITY OF THE CHILDREN'S INTERPERSONAL RELATIONSHIPS AND SELF-CONCEPTS. (NH)

EJ 027 644 PS 500 684
ADOPTIVE PLACEMENT OF THE OLDER CHILD CHEMA, REGINA; AND OTHERS, *CHILD WELFARE*, V49 N8, PP450-458, OCT '70
THE IMPORTANCE OF DEALING IMMEDIATELY WITH THE TRAUMA OF THE CHILD'S SEPARATION FROM NATURAL PARENTS, SIBLINGS, AND FOSTER PARENTS IS STRESSED. PLACEMENT TECHNIQUES AND PROCEDURES INVOLVING ADOPTIVE PARENTS, FOSTER PARENTS AND THE CHILD ARE DESCRIBED. (MG)

EJ 027 673 PS 500 707
WRITE YOUR OWN SONGS DUBNER, EDITH SCHELL, *ELEMENTARY SCHOOL JOURNAL*, V71 N3, PP152-161, DEC '70

EJ 027 704 PS 500 675
THE ORGANIZATIONAL CLIMATE OF SCHOOLS IN FIVE URBAN AREAS KENNEY, JAMES B.; RENTZ, R. ROBERT, *ELEMENTARY SCHOOL JOURNAL*, V71 N2, PP61-69, NOV '70
ANALYSIS OF TEACHER RESPONSES TO THE ORGANIZATIONAL CLIMATE DESCRIPTION QUESTIONNAIRE SHOWED THAT THE URBAN SCHOOL SITUATION OUTSIDE THE IMMEDIATE CLASSROOM ENVIRONMENT WAS AN IMPORTANT INFLUENCE ON URBAN TEACHERS' PERCEPTIONS OF THEIR SCHOOLS. (NH)

EJ 027 825 PS 500 635
ODDITY PREFERENCE BY MENTAL RETARDATES DICKERSON, DONALD J., *JOURNAL OF EXPERIMENTAL CHILD PSYCHOLOGY*, V10 N1, PP28-32, AUG '70
THREE GROUPS OF SEVERELY RETARDED AND THREE GROUPS OF MILDLY RETARDED INDIVIDUALS RESPONDED TO A SERIES OF FIVE 10-TRIAL ODDITY PROBLEMS UNDER NONREWARD CONDITIONS. RESULTS SUGGEST THAT ODDITY IS A STIMULUS CHARACTERISTIC TO WHICH AN APPROACH RESPONSE IS MADE, INDEPENDENT OF ITS CONCURRENT ASSOCIATION WITH REWARD, AND THAT STIMULUS VALUE OF ODDITY DIFFERS FOR MILDLY AND SEVERELY RETARDED SS. (AUTHOR/WY)

EJ 027 826 PS 500 703
A CASE AGAINST BEHAVIORAL OBJECTIVES MACDONALD, JAMES B.; WOLFSON, BERNICE J., *ELEMENTARY SCHOOL JOURNAL*, V71 N3, PP119-128, DEC '70

EJ 027 827 PS 500 708
CLASSROOM MANAGEMENT--MORE THAN CONDITIONING PALARDY, J. MICHAEL, *ELEMENTARY SCHOOL JOURNAL*, V71 N3, PP162-165, DEC '70
DISCUSSES LIMITATIONS TO THE BEHAVIORIST APPROACH TO CLASSROOM MANAGEMENT AND SUGGESTS THAT SCHOOLS MUST DESIGN STRATEGIES OF PREVENTION AS WELL AS REMEDIATION. (NH)

EJ 027 846 PS 500 637
NEWBORN ATTENTION: DIFFERENTIAL RESPONSE DECREMENT TO VISUAL STIMULI FRIEDMAN, STEVEN; AND OTHERS, *JOURNAL OF EXPERIMENTAL CHILD PSYCHOLOGY*, V10 N1, PP44-51, AUG '70

EJ 027 847 PS 500 639
VISUAL ALERTNESS IN NEONATES AS EVOKED BY MATERNAL CARE KORNER, ANNELIESE F.; THOMAN, EVELYN B., *JOURNAL OF EXPERIMENTAL CHILD PSYCHOLOGY*, V10 N1, PP67-78, AUG '70
FORTY CRYING AND 24 SLEEPING 2- TO 3-DAY-OLD HEALTHY, FULL-TERM NEWBORNS WERE GIVEN SIX INTERVENTIONS WHICHENTAILED CONTACT AND/OR VESTIBULAR STIMULATION. SCORES OBTAINED ON A SIX-POINT SCALE ASSESSING LEVELS OF ALERTNESS IMPLY THAT THE VESTIBULAR STIMULATION WHICH ATTENDS MATERNAL CARETAKING ACTIVITIES IS CRUCIAL, AT LEAST DURING THE NEONATAL PERIOD. (AUTHOR/WY)

EJ 027 848 PS 500 642
CHANGES IN THE NONNUTRITIVE SUCKING RESPONSE TO STIMULATION DURING INFANCY SAMEROFF, ARNOLD J., *JOURNAL OF EXPERIMENTAL CHILD PSYCHOLOGY*, V10 N1, PP112-119, AUG '70

EJ 027 880 PS 500 681
PUPILS' PERCEPTION OF TEACHERS' VERBAL FEEDBACK ZAHORIK, JOHN A., *ELEMENTARY SCHOOL JOURNAL*, V71 N2, PP105-114, NOV '70

EJ 027 881 PS 500 698
THE OTHER MOUTH: WRITING IN THE SCHOOLS HOFFMAN, MARVIN, *CHILDHOOD EDUCATION*, V47 N2, PP79-83, NOV '70
DESCRIBES THE TEACHERS AND WRITERS COLLABORATIVE, A PROGRAM IN WHICH A PROFESSIONAL WRITER WORKS CLOSELY ON A LONG-TERM BASIS WITH A PARTICULAR GROUP OF PUBLIC SCHOOL STUDENTS AND THEIR TEACHER. OBJECT: TO ENCOURAGE, CHILDREN TO WRITE CREATIVELY, OUT OF THEIR OWN EXPERIENCES, ABOUT WHAT IS REAL TO THEM. (MG)

EJ 027 916 PS 500 727
MEETING SOCIO-EDUCATIONAL NEEDS WADSWORTH, H. G., *CHILDHOOD EDUCATION*, V47 N3, PP148-151, DEC '70
SCHOOL SYSTEMS CAN ADOPT A PREVENTIVE APPROACH TOWARD IMPROVING MENTAL HEALTH OFITS STUDENTS AND STAFF, THROUGH SUPPORTIVE SERVICES ANDINDIVIDUALIZED PROGRAMMING. (NH)

EJ 027 917 PS 500 730
A PLAN FOR PROTECTION: THE CHILD-ABUSE CENTER HELFER, RAY E., *CHILD WELFARE*, V49 N9, PP486-494, NOV '70

EJ 027 918 PS 500 731
COLLABORATION IN SCHOOL GUIDANCE: TASK-ORIENTED GUIDANCE AND ITS STRUCTURE SARVIS, MARY A.; PENNEKAMP, MARIANNE, *CHILD WELFARE*, V49 N9, PP502-508, NOV '70
SUCCESSFUL GUIDANCE WORK IN A PUBLIC SCHOOL SETTING CALLS FOR AN APPROACH ORIENTED TOWARD IMPLEMENTING EDUCATIONAL GOALS. A MAJOR FACTOR IN THIS PROCESS IS THE STRUCTURE OF THE GUIDANCE DEPARTMENT. (AUTHOR/WY)

EJ 027 919 PS 500 732
THE CHILD CARE COUNSELOR: NEW THERAPIST IN CHILDREN'S INSTITUTIONS DIGGLES, MARY W., *CHILD WELFARE*, V49 N9, PP509-513, NOV '70
IN THE TREATMENT OF CHILDREN IN INSTITUTIONS, THE EMPHASIS IS SHIFTING FROM ONE-TO-ONE THERAPY TO THE GROUP LIVING UNIT AS A MEANS OF SOCIALIZATION. SUCH AN APPROACH HIGHLIGHTS THE ROLE OF THE CHILD CARE COUNSELOR AS A PRIMARY THERAPEUTIC AGENT. (AUTHOR)

EJ 027 920 PS 500 733
A GROUP METHOD FOR FINDING AND DEVELOPING FOSTER HOMES GROSS, PAULA KUHN; BUSSARD, FRAN, *CHILD WELFARE*, V49 N9, PP521-524, NOV '70

EJ 027 943 PS 500 693
WHAT ARE THE SOURCES OF EARLY CHILDHOOD CURRICULUM? SPODEK, BERNARD, *YOUNG CHILDREN*, V26 N1, PP48-50, OCT '70
ADAPTED FROM A PAPER PRESENTED AT THE ASCD CONFERENCE, SAN FRANCISCO, CALIF., MARCH 5, 1970.

EJ 028 100 PS 500 679
CONTINUOUS PUPIL PROGRESS IN THE NON-GRADED SCHOOL: HOPE OR HOAX? MCLOUGHLIN, WILLIAM P., *ELEMENTARY SCHOOL JOURNAL*, V71 N2, PP90-96, NOV '70

EJ 028 101 PS 500 701
THE RIGHTS OF THE CHILD - THE REALIZATION OF HIS POTENTIAL ESSEX, MARY LANGMUIR, *INTERNATIONAL JOURNAL OF EARLY CHILDHOOD*, V1 N2, PP71-92, '69
PRESENTED AT THE TWELFTH ASSEMBLY OF THE WORLD ORGANIZATION FOR EARLY CHILDHOOD EDUCATION, WASHINGTON, D. C. (MS)

EJ 028 102 PS 500 702
L'EDUCATEUR ET L'EPANOUISSEMENT DE LA PERSONNALITE DE L'ENFANT LAPOINTE, ROGER E., *INTERNATIONAL JOURNAL OF EARLY CHILDHOOD*, V1 N2, PP93-114, '69
PRESENTED AT THE TWELFTH ASSEMBLY OF THE WORLD ORGANIZATION FOR EARLY CHILDHOOD EDUCATION, WASHINGTON, D.C. (MS)

EJ 028 200 PS 500 722
MAKING TOMORROW NOW: THE PEOPLE ENVIRONMENT HYMES, JAMES L., JR., *CHILDHOOD EDUCATION*, V47 N3, PP122-125, DEC '70

EJ 028 239 PS 500 709
SELF-PERCEPTIONS OF PUPILS IN AN EXPERIMENTAL ELEMENTARY SCHOOL PURKEY, WILLIAM W.; AND OTHERS, *ELEMENTARY SCHOOL JOURNAL*, V71 N3, PP166-171, DEC '70

EJ 028 310 PS 500 690
AND A FRIENDLY GOODBYE CUNNINGHAM, JANE, *YOUNG CHILDREN*, V26 N1, PP25-26, OCT '70
INADEQUACIES IN PRESCHOOL ACCOMMODATIONS NEED NOT HAMPER TRUE EDUCATIONAL GOALS. A RESOURCEFUL TEACHER CAN OFFSET SOME OF THE DISADVANTAGES FOUND IN DOUBLE SESSION PRESCHOOLS BY EXERCISING HER INGENUITY AND IMAGINATION. (AUTHOR/WY)

EJ 028 383 PS 500 697
THE OFF-KILTERED KIDS SCHECHTER, MARSHALL D.; TEMKIN, POLLY B., *CHILDHOOD EDUCATION*, V47 N2, PP75-78, NOV '70
MANY CHILDREN WRONGLY DIAGNOSED AS EMOTIONALLY DISTURBED, ACTUALLY HAVE A FAULTY SENSE OF PERCEPTION, KNOWN AS MINIMAL CEREBRAL DISFUNCTION. THIS ARTICLE DESCRIBES SOME TYPICAL SYMPTOMS, AND DISCUSSES WAYS SUCH CHILDREN MIGHT BE HELPED. (MG)

EJ 028 501 PS 500 674
THE STUDENT IN PROJECT PLAN: A FUNCTIONING PROGRAM OF INDIVIDUALIZED EDUCATION QUIRK, THOMAS J., *ELEMENTARY SCHOOL JOURNAL*, V71 N1, PP42-54, OCT '70

EJ 028 502 PS 500 691
A TRAINING PROGRAM FOR VOLUNTEERS PARTEN, CARROLL B., *YOUNG CHILDREN*, V26 N1, PP27-33, OCT '70

EJ 028 503 PS 500 706
THE EFFECT OF PLANNING ON TEACHING ZAHORIK, JOHN A., *ELEMENTARY SCHOOL JOURNAL*, V71 N3, PP143-151, DEC '70
SUGGESTS THAT TYPICAL LESSON PLANNING MAY MAKE TEACHER'S THINKING RIGID AND TEACHER LESS SENSITIVE TO PUPILS. SCOPE OF PLANNING SHOULD, THEREFORE INCLUDE SPECIFIC TEACHER BEHAVIORS. (NH)

EJ 028 577 PS 500 678
KEYS TO STANDARD ENGLISH CASELLI, RON, *ELEMENTARY SCHOOL JOURNAL*, V71 N2, PP86-89, NOV '70
TEACHERS SHOULD BUILD ON STUDENTS' EXISTING SPEECH PATTERNS, HELPING STUDENTS TO GAIN AURAL UNDERSTANDING OF STANDARD ENGLISH, AND PROVIDING ORAL AND WRITTEN PRACTICE. (NH)

EJ 028 578 PS 500 700
THE ROLE OF SYNTAX IN CHILDREN'S COMPREHENSION FROM AGES SIX TO TWELVE KESSEL, FRANK S., *MONOGRAPHS OF THE SOCIETY FOR RESEARCH IN CHILD DEVELOPMENT*, V35 N6, PP1-95, SEP '70
THIS MONOGRAPH IS BASED ON A DOCTORAL THESIS SUBMITTED TO THE FACULTY OF THE GRADUATE SCHOOL OF THE UNIVERSITY OF MINNESOTA IN AUGUST 1969. (MG)

EJ 028 633 PS 500 632
THE EFFECTS OF OVERLEARNING ON CHILDREN'S NONREVERSAL AND REVERSAL LEARNING USING UNRELATED STIMULI SCHAEFFER, BENSON; ELLIS, STEPHEN, *JOURNAL OF EXPERIMENTAL CHILD PSYCHOLOGY*, V10 N1, PP1-7, AUG '70
TWO EXPERIMENTS SHOW THAT RESPONSE TO EXPLICIT DIMENSIONS IS NOT CRUCIAL TO THE CHANGE FROM EASIER NONREVERSAL TO EASIER REVERSAL SHIFTS DURING OVERLEARNING IN GRAMMAR SCHOOL CHILDREN AGES 7, 8, AND 9. (WY)

EJ 028 634 PS 500 636
THE APPLICATION OF PREMACK'S GENERALIZATION ON REINFORCEMENT TO THE MANAGEMENT OF CLASSROOM BEHAVIOR WASIK, BARBARA H., *JOURNAL OF EXPERIMENTAL CHILD PSYCHOLOGY*, V10 N1, PP33-43, AUG '70
A BEHAVIOR MANAGEMENT PROCEDURE WAS SUCCESSFULLY EMPLOYED IN A DEMONSTRATION SCHOOL FOR CULTURALLY DEPRIVED CHILDREN TO INCREASE APPROPRIATE BEHAVIOR IN A SECOND-GRADE CLASSROOM OF TWENTY CHILDREN. (AUTHOR/WY)

EJ 028 635 PS 500 638
TRANSPOSITION AND TRANSFER OF ABSOLUTE RESPONDING AS FUNCTIONS OF LEARNING-SET TRAINING AND STIMULUS SIMILARITY YEH, JOYCE CHING-YI WU, *JOURNAL OF EXPERIMENTAL CHILD PSYCHOLOGY*, V10 N1, PP57-66, AUG '70
PAPER IS BASED ON A DISSERTATION SUBMITTED TO BROWN UNIVERSITY IN PARTIAL FULFILLMENT OF THE REQUIREMENTS FOR THE PH.D. DEGREE IN PSYCHOLOGY, JUNE, 1966.

EJ 028 636 PS 500 640
GENERALIZED IMITATION AND THE DISCRIMINATION HYPOTHESIS STEINMAN, WARREN M., *JOURNAL OF EXPERIMENTAL CHILD PSYCHOLOGY*, V10 N1, PP79-99, AUG '70
THE RESULTS OF THREE EXPERIMENTS INVOLVING 6 YOUNG CHILDREN SUGGEST THAT THE GENERALIZED IMITATION EFFECT MAY NOT BE ENTIRELY DUE TO THE CHILD'S INABILITY TO DISCRIMINATE REINFORCED FRON NONREINFORCED OCCASIONS. INSTRUCTIONAL AND SOCIAL VARIABLES MAY STRONGLY INFLUENCE THE GENERALIZED IMITATION EFFECT. (WY)

EJ 028 637 PS 500 641
CONJUNCTIVE AND DISJUNCTIVE RULE LEARNING AS A FUNCTION OF AGE AND FORCED VERBALIZATION KING, WILLIAM L.; HOLT, JULIA RAE, *JOURNAL OF EXPERIMENTAL CHILD PSYCHOLOGY*, V10 N1, PP100-111, AUG '70
INFORMATION OBTAINED IN THIS STUDY INVOLVING 72 GIRLS (6-, 9-, AND 12-YEAR-OLDS) DOCUMENTS THE FACILITATING EFFECT OF FORCED VERBALIZATION AT THREE AGE LEVELS. (AUTHOR/WY)

EJ 028 638 PS 500 704
LEARNING: THE ROLE OF FACTS AND GENERALIZATIONS BUSER, ROBERT L.; ROOZE, GENE E., *ELEMENTARY SCHOOL JOURNAL*, V71 N3, PP129-133, DEC '70

EJ 028 676 PS 500 687
CHILDREN'S REACTIONS TO TV VIOLENCE: A REVIEW OF RESEARCH ENDSLEY, RICHARD C.; OSBORN, D. KEITH, *YOUNG CHILDREN*, V26 N1, PP4-11, OCT '70

EJ 028 677 PS 500 688
BIBLIOGRAPHY ON HOSPITALIZED AND HANDICAPPED CHILDREN , *YOUNG CHILDREN*, V26 N1, PP12-15, OCT '70
PRESENTS LIST OF RESOURCES USEFUL TO TEACHERS AND PARENTS IN HELPING CHILDREN COPE WITH HANDICAPS AND HOSPITAL EXPERIENCES. (MS)

EJ 028 717 PS 500 670
TEACHING NUMBER SENSE THROUGH RHYTHMICAL COUNTING OGLETREE, EARL J.; AND OTHERS, *ELEMENTARY SCHOOL JOURNAL*, V71 N1, PP11-17, OCT '70

EJ 028 718 PS 500 671
BEYOND NUFFIELD RAPPAPORT, DAVID, *ELEMENTARY SCHOOL JOURNAL*, V71 N1, PP18-25, OCT '70

EJ 028 792 PS 500 682
POSTADOPTION COUNSELING: A PROFESSIONAL OBLIGATION LAWDER, ELIZABETH A., *CHILD WELFARE*, V49 N8, PP435-442, OCT '70

EJ 028 793 PS 500 695
WORKING MOTHERS AND THEIR CHILDREN MEAD, MARGARET, *CHILDHOOD EDUCATION*, V47 N2, PP66-71, NOV '70
DISCUSSES POSSIBLE WAYS OF PROVIDING CONTINUITY OF CARE FOR YOUNG CHILDREN OF WORKING MOTHERS, INCLUDING INDUSTRY - SPONSORED DAY NURSERIES, COOPERATIVE NURSERY SCHOOLS, COMMUNAL CLUSTERS WHERE WORKING AND NONWORKING WOMEN SHARE HOUSEHOLD TASKS AND CHILD CARE, AND EXPANDED NEIGHBORHOOD DAY CARE. (MG)

EJ 028 795 PS 500 726
"OF HAIRY ARMS AND A DEEP BARITONE VOICE": A SYMPOSIUM MEN IN YOUNG CHILDREN'S LIVES WILLIAMS, BRUCE W.; JOHNSTON, JOHN M., *CHILDHOOD EDUCATION*, V47 N3, PP139-147, DEC '70

EJ 028 845 PS 500 723
INVOLVING PARENTS IN CHILDREN'S LEARNING JONES, ELIZABETH, *CHILDHOOD EDUCATION*, V47 N3, PP126-130, DEC '70

EJ 028 846 PS 500 728
LET DO IT MY WAY RICH, IRENE S., *CHILDHOOD EDUCATION,* V47 N3, PP152-155, DEC '70
DESCRIBES INNOVATIVE CLASSROOM PRACTICES DEVELOPED BY TEACHERS WITH SUPPORT FROM THE TEACHER INNOVATION FUND AWARD PROGRAM (TIF), ESTABLISHED LAST YEAR IN THE DISTRICT OF COLUMBIA. (NH)

EJ 028 894 PS 500 633
THE MODELING OF SHARING: EFFECTS ASSOCIATED WITH VICARIOUS REINFORCEMENT, SYMBOLIZATION, AGE, AND GENERALIZATION ELLIOTT, ROGERS; VASTA, ROSS, *JOURNAL OF EXPERIMENTAL CHILD PSYCHOLOGY,* V10 N1, PP8-15, AUG '70

EJ 028 895 PS 500 634
RECENCY AND SUMMATION EFFECTS OF NONREWARD IN CHILDREN DAVIDSON, NANCY HENDERSHOTT; FITZGERALD, HIRAM E., *JOURNAL OF EXPERIMENTAL CHILD PSYCHOLOGY,* V10 N1, PP16-27, AUG '70
THIRTY KINDERGARTEN CHILDREN IN THREE SESSIONS PERFORMED A LEVER-PULLING TASK UNDER THREE PARTIAL REINFORCEMENT CONDITIONS. THE RESULTS OF THE EXPERIMENT DEMONSTRATED THAT BOTH RECENCY AND SUMMATION OF NONREWARD INFLUENCED PERFORMANCE AS MEASURED BY LATENCY. BASED IN PART ON A MASTER'S THESIS SUBMITTED BU THE FIRST AUTHOR IN PARTIAL FULLFILLMENT OF THE REQUIREMENTS FOR THE MA DEGREE. (AUTHOR/WY)

EJ 028 896 PS 500 676
ANXIETY - A CLASSROOM CLOSE-UP KAPLAN, BERT L., *ELEMENTARY SCHOOL JOURNAL,* V71 N2, PP70-77, NOV '70
TEACHERS CAN BE MORE EFFECTIVE IF THEY DEVELOP AN UNDERSTANDING OF THE CAUSES OF ANXIETY AND THE INNER CONFLICTS IT MAY REPRESENT. (NH)

EJ 028 897 PS 500 699
LOOK--I SEE ME BROWN, STANLEY B.; BROWN, L. BARBARA, *CHILDHOOD EDUCATION,* V47 N2, PP84-85, NOV '70
SUGGESTS HOW SIMPLE ROLE-PLAYING CAN BE USED TO IMPROVE SOCIAL INTERACTION OF PRIMARY STUDENTS. (MG)

EJ 028 898 PS 500 729
THE SHORT ATTENTION SPAN: FACT AND MYTH BROMAN, BETTY L., *CHILDHOOD EDUCATION,* V47 N3, PP156-158, DEC '70

EJ 028 926 PS 500 689
RACIAL AWARENESS IN YOUNG MEXICAN-AMERICAN, NEGRO AND ANGLO CHILDREN DURRETT, MARY ELLEN; DAVY, ACHSAH J., *YOUNG CHILDREN,* V26 N1, PP16-24, OCT '70

EJ 028 959 PS 500 669
READING: AN ETERNAL DYNAMIC JENKINSON, MARION D., *ELEMENTARY SCHOOL JOURNAL,* V71 N1, PP1-10, OCT '70
A CRITICAL REVIEW OF THE NATIONAL SOCIETY FOR THE STUDY OF EDUCATION YEARBOOK ENTITLED INNOVATION AND CHANGE IN READING INSTRUCTION. (WY)

EJ 028 960 PS 500 680
ORGANIZING FOR READING INSTRUCTION OLIVER, MARVIN E., *ELEMENTARY SCHOOL JOURNAL,* V71 N2, PP97-104, NOV '70
HOMOGENEOUS GROUPING DOES NOT NECESSARILY PROVIDE A SETTING FOR GREATER GAINS IN READING ACHIEVEMENT. TEACHER-USE OF INFORMAL READING INVENTORIES, SUCH AS CLOZE IS OS SUGGESTED FOR ACCURATE PLACEMENT OF CHILDREN IN READING GROUPS. (NH)

EJ 029 015 PS 500 692
ABOUT RESEARCH: PART II. IS A BEHAVIORAL APPROACH SUPERFICIAL? IS OPERANT CONDITIONING FAIR? WHY DO RESEARCH? SCOTT, PHYLLIS M., *YOUNG CHILDREN,* V26 N1, PP36-47, OCT '70

EJ 029 042 PS 500 672
THE ECONOMIC LITERACY OF ELEMENTARY-SCHOOL PUPILS MCKENZIE, RICHARD B., *ELEMENTARY SCHOOL JOURNAL,* V71 N1, PP26-35, OCT '70

EJ 029 043 PS 500 673
TURNBOW CABIN ROACH, JAMES L., *ELEMENTARY SCHOOL JOURNAL,* V71 N1, PP36-41, OCT '70
DESCRIBES A PROJECT IN WHICH FOURTH AND SIXTH GRADERS INVESTIGATED MAN'S RELATIONSHIP TO THE ENVIRONMENT AS THEY EXPLORED THE PHYSICAL AREA AND LEARNED THE HISTORY OF TURNBOW CABIN, ARCHES NATIONAL MONUMENT, UTAH. (WY)

EJ 029 102 PS 500 683
TERMINATION OF RESIDENTIAL TREATMENT OF CHILDREN HIRSCHBERG, J. COTTER, *CHILD WELFARE,* V49 N8, PP443-447, OCT '70
EXAMINES THE PROCESS OF TERMINATION FROM THE STAND POINT OF THE PARENTS OF THE CHILD WHO IS ENDING TREATMENT, POINTING OUT SOME INEVITABLE CONSEQUENCES OF TERMINATION WHICH THE PARENTS NEED TO BE AWARE OF. THIS PAPER WAS PRESENTED AT THE ANNUAL MEETING OF THE AMERICAN ORTHOPSYCHIATRIC ASSOCIATION AT NEW YORK, N.Y., APRIL 1, 1969. (MG)

EJ 029 103 PS 500 694
THE CHILD'S RIGHT TO QUALITY DAY CARE: AN ACEI POSITION PAPER BUTLER, ANNIE L., *CHILDHOOD EDUCATION,* V47 N2, PP58-65, NOV '70

EJ 029 104 PS 500 705
HEALTH, EDUCATION, AND WELFARE: THE PROGRESSIVE IMPULSE IN THE NEW YORK CITY PUBLIC SCHOOLS BERROL, SELMA C., *ELEMENTARY SCHOOL JOURNAL,* V71 N3, PP134-142, DEC '70

EJ 029 166 PS 500 685
SOME HELPFUL TECHNIQUES WHEN PLACING OLDER CHILDREN FOR ADOPTION SHARRAR, MARY LOU, *CHILD WELFARE,* V49 N8, PP459-463, OCT '70
DESCRIBES TECHNIQUES WHICH FAMILIES ADOPTING CHILDREN 6 MONTHS OLD OR OLDER MIGHT USE TO HELP COMMUNICATE FEELINGS OF LOVE, CONTINUITY OF AFFECTION, AND PERMANENCE OF THE NEW HOME TO BOTH VERBAL AND NON-VERBAL CHILDREN. INCLUDES SONGS AND STORIES. (MG)

EJ 029 167 PS 500 686
AN INTERDISCIPLINARY APPROACH IN DAY TREATMENT OF EMOTIONALLY DISTURBED CHILDREN GRITZKA, KAREN; AND OTHERS, *CHILD WELFARE,* V49 N8, PP468-472, OCT '70
EXPLAINS HOW NURSES, PSYCHIATRY AIDES, OCCUPATIONAL THERAPISTS, AND TEACHERS COMBINE SKILLS TO DEFINE EACH CHILD'S MAJOR PROBLEM AREAS AND DEVELOP TREATMENT PLANS. THE APPROACH PROVIDES CONSISTENCY IN THE CLINIC AND IN RELATIONS BETWEEN THE CLINIC AND THE HOME. (MG)

EJ 029 168 PS 500 696
INDEPENDENT STUDY AT SEVEN WINN, MILDRED, *CHILDHOOD EDUCATION,* V47 N2, PP72-74, NOV '70

EJ 029 169 PS 500 724
DEVELOPING NEW TEACHING TEAMS ENZMANN, ARTHUR M., *CHILDHOOD EDUCATION,* V47 N3, PP131-134, DEC '70

EJ 029 217 PS 500 748
FREEDOM TO MANIPULATE OBJECTS AND QUESTION-ASKING PERFORMANCE OF SIX-YEAR-OLDS TORRANCE, E. PAUL, *YOUNG CHILDREN,* V26 N2, PP93-97, DEC '70
AN EXPERIMENT WITH 66 SIX-YEAR-OLD CHILDREN SHOWED THAT CHILDREN ASKED MORE AND BETTER QUESTIONS ABOUT UNFAMILIAR OBJECTS (TOYS) WHEN THEY HAD BEEN GIVEN AN OPPORTUNITY TO MANIPULATE THEM THAN WHEN THEY SAW ONLY DEMONSTRATIONS OF THE TOYS. (NH)

EJ 029 218 PS 500 757
MATERNAL FOOD RESTRICTION: EFFECTS ON OFFSPRING DEVELOPMENT, LEARNING, AND A PROGRAM OF THERAPY VORE, DAVID A.; OTTINGER, DONALD R., *DEVELOPMENTAL PSYCHOLOGY,* V3 N3, PP337-342, NOV '70

EJ 029 219 PS 500 779
WISC SUBTEST AND IQ SCORE CORRELATES OF FATHER ABSENCE LESSING, ELISE E.; AND OTHERS, *JOURNAL OF GENETIC PSYCHOLOGY,* V117 N2, PP181-95, DEC '70

EJ 029 280 PS 500 747
LISTEN TO WHAT I MADE. FROM MUSICAL THEORY TO USABLE INSTRUMENT MYERSON, EDITH S., *YOUNG CHILDREN,* V26 N2, PP90-92, DEC '70
SUGGESTS INEXPENSIVE RHYTHM INSTRUMENTS CHILDREN CAN MAKE FROM FAMILIAR MATERIALS FOUND AT HOME. (NH)

EJ 029 281 PS 500 786
A THIRD STUDY OF THE EFFECTS OF A LEARNING EXPERIENCE UPON PREFERENCE FOR COMPLEXITY-ASYMMETRY IN FOURTH, FIFTH, AND SIXTH GRADE CHILDREN MCWHINNIE, HAROLD J., *CALIFORNIA JOURNAL OF EDUCATIONAL RESEARCH,* V21 N5, PP216-225, NOV '70
INVESTIGATES EFFECTS OF A SPECIFIC METHOD OF ART INSTRUCTION DESIGNED TO INCREASE THE INDIVIDUAL'S ABILITY TO HANDLE VISUAL COMPLEXITY AND DETAIL. IMPLICATIONS OF FINDINGS FOR ART EDUCATION ARE ALSO DISCUSSED. (MG)

EJ 029 341 PS 500 740
CHILDREN AND THE MASS MED!A WINSTON, SHIRLEY, *CHILDREN,* V17 N6, PP242, NOV-DEC '70
RESUME OF TESTIMONY GIVEN AT HEARINGS AT THE WHITE HOUSE CONFERENCE ON CHILDREN, SEPTEMBER, 1970. TOPICS CONSIDERED WERE THE INFLUENCE OF THE MASS MEDIA ON CHILDREN AND WAYS TO IMPROVE MEDIA PRODUCTS. (NH)

EJ 029 342 PS 500 745
THE CHILD'S EYE VIEW: EXPERIMENTAL PHOTOGRAPHY WITH PRESCHOOL CHILDREN LANDMAN, GEORGE; ATHEY, IRENE, *YOUNG CHILDREN,* V26 N2, PP77-81, DEC '70

EJ 029 343 PS 500 801
EDUCATIONAL TECHNOLOGY: A CRITIQUE OHANIAN, VERA, *ELEMENTARY SCHOOL JOURNAL,* V71 N4, PP182-197, JAN '71

EJ 029 358 PS 500 751
IT MAKES ME FEEL BAD WHEN YOU CALL ME "STINKY" OLSEN, MARY, *YOUNG CHILDREN,* V26 N2, PP120-122, DEC '70
DISCUSSION OF FEELINGS AND EMOTIONS CAN BECOME A REGULAR PART OF THE CLASSROOM CURRICULUM TO HELP CHILDREN ACCEPT AND UNDERSTAND THEIR FEELINGS AND TO BECOME MORE AWARE OF THEIR ENVIRONMENT. (NH)

EJ 029 359 PS 500 752
DEVELOPMENTAL ASPECTS OF REACTION TO POSITIVE INDUCEMENTS LINDSKOLD, SVENN; AND OTHERS, *DEVELOPMENTAL PSYCHOLOGY,* V3 N3, PP277-284, NOV '70
PROBES CHILDREN'S BEHAVIORAL SENSITIVITY TO VARIATION IN REWARD PROBABILITY AND MAGNITUDE (BRIBES) AND SUGGESTS THAT PREADOLESCENT CHILDREN DO RESPOND TO PROMISES OF POSITIVE INDUCEMENTS FOR COOPERATION IN A MIXED-MOTIVE SITUATION. (WY)

EJ 029 360 PS 500 753
REACTION TIME AND REMOTE ASSOCIATION IN TALENTED MALE ADOLESCENTS LIBLEY, WILLIAM L., JR., *DEVELOPMENTAL PSYCHOLOGY,* V3 N3, PP285-297, NOV '70

EJ 029 361 PS 500 758
COMPLEXITY, CONTOUR, AND AREA AS DETERMINANTS OF ATTENTION IN INFANTS MCCALL, ROBERT B.; MELSON, WILLIAM H., *DEVELOPMENTAL PSYCHOLOGY,* V3 N3, PP343-349, NOV '70

EJ 029 362 PS 500 759
DEVELOPMENTAL CHANGES IN THE USE OF EMOTION CUES IN A CONCEPT-FORMATION TASK SAVITSKY, JEFFREY C.; IZARD, CARROLL E., *DEVELOPMENTAL PSYCHOLOGY,* V3 N3, PP350-357, NOV '70

EJ 029 363 PS 500 764
FIXATION TIME AND TEMPO OF PLAY IN INFANTS MESSER, STANLEY B.; AND OTHERS, *DEVELOPMENTAL PSYCHOLOGY,* V3 N3, PP406, NOV '70

EJ 029 382 PS 500 710
EXAMINATION AND REEVALUATION OF PROSTHETIC LENSES EMPLOYING AN OPERANT PROCEDURE FOR MEASURING SUBJECTIVE VISUAL ACUITY IN A RETARDED CHILD MACHT, JOEL, *JOURNAL OF EXPERIMENTAL CHILD PSYCHOLOGY,* V10 N2, PP139-145, OCT '70

EJ 029 383 PS 500 760
SENSORY-MODALITY EFFECTS ON SHAPE PERCEPTION IN PRESCHOOL CHILDREN DELEON, J. L.; AND OTHERS, *DEVELOPMENTAL PSYCHOLOGY,* V3 N3, PP358-362, NOV '70

EJ 029 384 PS 500 770
HOW ADULTS AND CHILDREN SEARCH AND RECOGNIZE PICTURES MACKWORTH, N. H.; BRUNNER, J. S., *HUMAN DEVELOPMENT,* V13 N3, PP149-177, '70

EJ 029 385 PS 500 771
BIOLOGICAL AND ECOLOGICAL INFLUENCES ON DEVELOPMENT AT 12 MONTHS OF AGE JORDAN, T. E.; SPANER, S. D., *HUMAN DEVELOPMENT,* V13 N3, PP178-187, '70

EJ 029 386 PS 500 772
DEVELOPMENTAL DIFFERENCES IN THE INTEGRATION OF PICTURE SERIES: EFFECTS OF VARIATIONS IN OBJECT-ATTRIBUTE RELATIONSHIPS KASDORF, C. A., III; SCHNALL, M., *HUMAN DEVELOPMENT,* V13 N3, PP188-200, '70

EJ 029 387 PS 500 774
PHYSICAL GROWTH AND BODY COMPOSITION: PAPERS FROM THE KYOTO SYMPOSIUM ON ANTHROPOLOGICAL ASPECTS OF HUMAN GROWTH BROZEK, JOSEF, E., *MONOGRAPHS OF THE SOCIETY FOR RESEARCH IN CHILD DEVELOPMENT,* V35 N7, '70

EJ 029 388 PS 500 792
THE LIVING WORLD: THE PHYSICAL ENVIRONEMNT STAPP, WILLIAM B., *CHILDHOOD EDUCATION,* V47 N4, PP178-181, JAN '71
AN APPEAL FOR SCHOOLS TO EMBARK ON A COMPREHENSIVE ENVIRONMENTAL EDUCATION PROGRAM. (WY)

EJ 029 389 PS 500 793
AN ENVIRONMENT THAT SUPPORTS MAN GRATZ, PAULINE, *CHILDHOOD EDUCATION,* V47 N4, PP182-185, JAN '71
CONSIDERS TWO INTERLINKING THREATS TO HUMAN EXISTENCE - THE DEPLETION OF OXYGEN AND THE LEACHING OF NITROGEN-AND EXPLORES WHAT CAN BE DONE TO OVERCOME THEM. (WY)

EJ 029 390 PS 500 794
ROCKS, RIVERS AND CITY CHILDREN KERLIN, SARAH M., *CHILDHOOD EDUCATION,* V47 N4, PP186-190, JAN '71
REPORTS A SERIES OF URBAN-CENTERED ENCOUNTERS WHICH HELPED SOME NEW YORK CITY CHILDREN BECOME AWARE OF THE PROCESSES THAT SHAPE THEIR ENVIRONMENT AND THE EARTH. (WY)

EJ 029 391 PS 500 795
OCEANS AND CHILDREN: MARINE SCIENCE AND ECOLOGICAL UNDERSTANDING LINSKY, RONALD B., *CHILDHOOD EDUCATION,* V47 N4, PP191-194, JAN '71
TEACHERS AND CHILDREN ALIKE LEARN A REVERENCE FOR LIFE IN THIS HANDS-ON APPROACH TO THE STUDY OF OCEANOGRAPHY AND MARINE ECOLOGY. (WY)

EJ 029 392 PS 500 797
RESOURCES FOR ENVIRONMENTAL EDUCATORS: ECOLOGY AND TEACHERS ABBOTT, MARGARET, COMP., *CHILDHOOD EDUCATION,* V47 N4, PP200-201, JAN '71

EJ 029 393 PS 500 798
ENVIRONMENTAL ECOLOGICAL EDUCATION IN CHILDREN'S BOOKS WATT, LOIS B., COMP., *CHILDHOOD EDUCATION,* V47 N4, PP202-204, JAN '71

EJ 029 413 PS 500 716
REACTION TO SUCESS AND FAILURE IN COMPLEX LEARNING: A POSTFEEDBACK EFFECT HENDERSON, KENT, *JOURNAL OF EXPERIMENTAL CHILD PSYCHOLOGY,* V10 N2, PP206-215, OCT '70

EJ 029 414 PS 500 802
ENCOURAGEMENT FOR THE YOUNG WRITER NIEDERER, MARGARET; RAIM, JOAN, *ELEMENTARY SCHOOL JOURNAL,* V71 N4, PP198-205, JAN '71

EJ 029 444 PS 50 175
SHORT-TERM MEMORY IN CHILDREN: KEEPING TRACK OF VARIABLES WITH FEW OR MANY STATES MORIN, ROBERT E.; AND OTHERS, *JOURNAL OF EXPERIMENTAL CHILD PSYCHOLOGY,* V10 N2, PP181-188, OCT '70

EJ 029 531 PS 500 715
VISUAL ABILITIES AND PATTERN PREFERENCES OF PREMATURE INFANTS AND FULL-TERM NEONATES MIRANDA, SIMON B., *JOURNAL OF EXPERIMENTAL CHILD PSYCHOLOGY,* V10 N2, PP189-205, OCT '70
PAPER IS BASED ON A DISSERTATION SUBMITTED IN PARTIAL FULFILLMENT OF THE REQUIREMENTS FOR THE DEGREE OF DOCTOR OF PHILOSOPHY FROM CASE WESTERN RESERVE UNIVERSITY. (WY)

EJ 029 532 PS 500 773
SEQUENCE EFFECTS IN THE ABSTRACTION OF THE CONCEPT OF PROGRESSIVE CHANGE SCHWEITZER, THOMAS M.; SCHNALL, M., *HUMAN DEVELOPMENT,* V13 N3, PP201-212, '70
PAPER IS BASED ON A MASTER'S THESIS SUBMITTED BY THE SENIOR AUTHOR TO THE DEPARTMENT OF PSYCHOLOGY, BRANDEIS UNIVERSITY, 1967. (IR)

EJ 029 533 PS 500 781
TIMING AND SOURCES OF INFORMATION ABOUT, AND ATTITUDES TOWARD, MENSTRUATION AMONG COLLEGE FEMALES DUNHAM, FRANCES Y., *JOURNAL OF GENETIC PSYCHOLOGY,* V117 N2, PP205-217, DEC '70
A VERSION OF THIS PAPER WAS PRESENTED AT THE SOUTHEASTERN PSYCHOLOGICAL ASSOCIATION MEETINGS, NEW ORLEANS, LOUISIANA, APRIL, 1966. (WY)

EJ 029 617 PS 500 746
EARLY CHILDHOOD EDUCATION AS A DISCIPLINE KATZ, LILIAN G., *YOUNG CHILDREN,* V26 N2, PP82-89, DEC '70
INCREASED UNDERSTANDING OF THE PARAMETERS OF EARLY CHILDHOOD EDUCATION, AND THE WAYS THEY INTERACT AND INFLUENCE EACH OTHER, MAY HELP EDUCATORS TO MORE SUCCESSFULLY TRANSLATE THEORY INTO PRACTICE. (NH)

EJ 029 618 PS 500 785
A COMPARISON OF CHARACTERISTICS OF PROSPECTIVE SECONDARY SCHOOL TEACHERS ENROLLED IN TWO DIFFERENT DEGREE PROGRAMS RICHEK, HERBERT G., *CALIFORNIA JOURNAL OF EDUCATIONAL RESEARCH*, V21 N5, PP204-207, NOV '70

EJ 029 619 PS 500 787
PRE-SCHOOL EDUCATION IN THE WORK OF J.A. COMENIUS (KOMENSKY) CAPKOVA, DAGMAR, *INTERNATIONAL JOURNAL OF EARLY CHILDHOOD*, V2 N1, PP1-7, '70

EJ 029 620 PS 500 788
EARLY AGE EDUCATION HOFFMANN, ERIKA, *INTERNATIONAL JOURNAL OF EARLY CHILDHOOD*, V2 N1, PP8-14, '70

EJ 029 621 PS 500 789
RESISTING PRESSURES IN THE PRE-SCHOOL CENTRE P 15-27 STUBBS, BETH, *INTERNATIONAL JOURNAL OF EARLY CHILDHOOD*, V2 N1, '70

SUGGESTS A NON-STATIC APPROACH TO PRESCHOOL CURRICULUM PLANNING WHICH WOULD INCORPORATE COGNITIVE LEARNING, WHILE AT THE SAME TIME RETAINING IMPORTANT PROGRAM ASPECTS WHICH PERTAIN TO THE CHILD'S PHYSICAL, SOCIAL AND EMOTIONAL DEVELOPMENT. (NH)

EJ 029 622 PS 500 791
LA EDUCACION PRE-ESCOLAR EN LAS ESCUELAS PUBLICAS DE PUERTO RICO UNDERWOOD, ANA R., *INTERNATIONAL JOURNAL OF EARLY CHILDHOOD*, V2 N1, PP38-43, '70

EJ 029 623 PS 500 796
"ENVIRONMENT," AN OLD CONCEPT IN EDUCATION: A CHILDHOOD EDUCATION SPECIAL (SECOND IN A SERIES), CLASSICAL STATEMENTS FROM THE EDUCATOR'S ARCHIVES SNYDER, AGNES, COMP., *CHILDHOOD EDUCATION*, V47 N4, PP195-199, JAN '71

EJ 029 768 PS 500 762
EFFECT OF SUCCESS AND FAILURE ON THE REFLECTIVE AND IMPULSIVE CHILD REALI, NORMA; HALL, VERNON, *DEVELOPMENTAL PSYCHOLOGY*, V3 N3, PP392-402, NOV '70

EJ 029 769 PS 500 776
COMPARISON OF PICTORIAL AND VERBAL SEMANTIC SCALES AS USED BY CHILDREN HELPER, MALCOLM M., *JOURNAL OF GENETIC PSYCHOLOGY*, V117 N2, PP149-156, DEC '70

EJ 029 916 PS 500 712
AN APPLIANCE FOR AUTOINDUCED ADVERSE CONTROL OF SELF-INJURIOUS BEHAVIOR YEAKEL, MARY H.; AND OTHERS, *JOURNAL OF EXPERIMENTAL CHILD PSYCHOLOGY*, V10 N2, PP159-169, OCT '70

EJ 029 917 PS 500 799
LETTER TO THE TEACHER OF A HARD-OF-HEARING CHILD POLLOCK, MARGARET B.; POLLOCK, KENNETH C., *CHILDHOOD EDUCATION*, V47 N4, PP206-209, JAN '71

PRACTICAL SUGGESTIONS ARE OFFERED TO HELP THE TEACHER UNDERSTAND AND WORK WITH THE HARD-OF-HEARING CHILD IN A REGULAR ELEMENTARY SCHOOL CLASSROOM. (WY)

EJ 029 950 PS 500 734
DRUG USE AMONG THE YOUNG: AS TEENAGERS SEE IT HERZOG, ELIZABETH; AND OTHERS, *CHILDREN*, V17 N6, PP207-212, NOV-DEC '70

REPORTS RESPONSES OF 205 STUDENTS TO A CHILDREN'S BUREAU INQUIRY ON TEENAGE DRUG USAGE. YOUTH WERE ASKED HOW TEENAGERS FEEL ABOUT USE OF VARIOUS KINDS OF DRUGS, WHAT MAKES SOME TEENAGERS USE DRUGS AND KEEPS OTHERS FROM USING THEM, AND WHAT ADULTS SHOULD DO ABOUT TEENAGE DRUG USAGE. (NH)

EJ 029 951 PS 500 736
A PLAY PROGRAM IN A PEDIATRIC CLINIC AZARNOFF, PAT, *CHILDREN*, V17 N6, PP218-221, NOV-DEC '70

EJ 029 952 PS 500 737
CHANGING PROSPECTS FOR CHILDREN WITH HEMOPHILIA BRINKHOUS, KENNETH M., *CHILDREN*, V17 N6, PP222-227, NOV-DEC '70

EJ 029 953 PS 500 790
NUTRITION REHABILITATION CENTRES BENGOA, JOSE M., *INTERNATIONAL JOURNAL OF EARLY CHILDHOOD*, V2 N1, PP28-37, '70

DISCUSSES THE SPECIFIC FUNCTION OF NUTRITION REHABILITATION CENTERS IN DEVELOPING COUNTRIES: TO EDUCATE THE MOTHERS THROUGH THE NUTRITIONAL REHABILITATION OF THEIR CHILDREN. (NH)

EJ 030 178 PS 500 763
SUBJECT-MODEL SEXUAL STATUS AND VERBAL IMITATIVE PERFORMANCE IN KINDERGARTEN CHILDREN RICKARD, HENRY C.; AND OTHERS, *DEVELOPMENTAL PSYCHOLOGY*, V3 N3, PP405, NOV '70

EJ 030 285 PS 500 718
THE UTILIZATION BY CHILDREN AND ADULTS OF BINARY PROPOSITIONAL THINKING IN CONCEPT LEARNING SEGGIE, J. L., *JOURNAL OF EXPERIMENTAL CHILD PSYCHOLOGY*, V10 N2, PP235-247, OCT '70

EJ 030 286 PS 500 719
SYNTACTICAL MEDIATION OF PAIRED-ASSOCIATE LEARNING AS A FUNCTION OF AGE FULD, PAULA ALTMAN, *JOURNAL OF EXPERIMENTAL CHILD PSYCHOLOGY*, V10 N2, PP248-256, OCT '70

EJ 030 287 PS 500 720
VERBAL-DISCRIMINATION LEARNING AND TRANSFER WITH VERBAL AND PICTORIAL MATERIALS GOULET, L. R.; STERNS, HARVEY L., *JOURNAL OF EXPERIMENTAL CHILD PSYCHOLOGY*, V10 N2, PP257-263, OCT '70

EJ 030 288 PS 500 721
THE ROLE OF MEMORY IN MAKING TRANSITIVE JUDGMENTS ROODIN, MARLENE L.; GRUEN, GERALD E., *JOURNAL OF EXPERIMENTAL CHILD PSYCHOLOGY*, V10 N2, PP264-275, OCT '70

EJ 030 289 PS 500 743
MODEL FOR A THINKING MCHINE: AN INFORMATION-PROCESSING FRAMEWORK FOR THE STUDY OF COGNITIVE DEVELOPMENT NEIMARK, EDITH D., *MERRILL-PALMER QUARTERLY*, V16 N4, PP345-368, OCT '70

EJ 030 290 PS 500 754
LEARNING AND PROBLEM SOLVING BY THE MENTALLY RETARDED UNDER THREE TESTING CONDITIONS STEVENSON, HAROLD W.; AND OTHERS, *DEVELOPMENTAL PSYCHOLOGY*, V3 N3, PP307-312, NOV '70

EJ 030 291 PS 500 756
CREATIVITY CHANGE IN STUDENT NURSES: A CROSS-SECTIONAL AND LONGITUDINAL STUDY EISENMAN, RUSSELL, *DEVELOPMENTAL PSYCHOLOGY*, V3 N3, PP320-325, NOV '70

EJ 030 292 PS 500 765
EFFECTS OF PROBING CHILDREN'S PHENOMENISTIC EXPLANATIONS OF CAUSE AND EFFECT BERZONSKY, MICHAEL D., *DEVELOPMENTAL PSYCHOLOGY*, V3 N3, PP407, NOV '70

EJ 030 293 PS 500 766
THE DEVELOPMENT OF FREE CLASSIFICATION AND FREE RECALL IN CHILDREN LANGE, GARRETT W.; HULTSCH, DAVID F., *DEVELOPMENTAL PSYCHOLOGY*, V3 N3, PP408, NOV '70

EJ 030 294 PS 500 768
WORD ASSOCIATION AND DEFINITION IN MIDDLE CHILDHOOD SHEPARD, WINIFRED O., *DEVELOPMENTAL PSYCHOLOGY*, V3 N3, PP412, NOV '70

EJ 030 295 PS 500 778
RELATIONSHIP OF CONSERVATION EXPLANATIONS TO ITEM DIFFICULTY PEISACH, ESTELLE; WEIN, NORMAN, *JOURNAL OF GENETIC PSYCHOLOGY*, V117 N2, PP167-180, DEC '70

EJ 030 296 PS 500 780
AGE-DEVELOPMENT IN THE LINEAR REPRESENTATION OF WORDS AND OBJECTS NATHAN, SUSAN W.; HASS, WILBUR A., *JOURNAL OF GENETIC PSYCHOLOGY*, V117 N2, PP197-204, DEC '70

DESCRIBES A DEVELOPMENTAL STUDY OF SEMANTIC STRUCTURES IN CHILDREN WHO ARE ASKED TO DETERMINE THE FITNESS OF DESCRIPTIVE LABELS FOR LINE DRAWINGS REPRESENTING A VARIETY OF PERCEPTUAL STIMULI. (AUTHOR/WY)

EJ 030 297 PS 500 783
PRIOR REINFORCEMENT HISTORY AS AN EXPLANATION FOR THE EFFECTS OF SEX OF SUBJECT AND EXPERIMENTER IN SOCIAL REINFORCEMENT PARADIGMS PALETZ, MERRILL, D., *JOURNAL OF GENETIC PSYCHOLOGY*, V117 N2, PP227-138, DEC '70

PAPER IS BASED ON A DISSERTATION SUBMITTED TO THE UNIVERSITY OF ILLINOIS IN PARTIAL FULFILLMENT OF THE REQUIREMENTS FOR THE PH.D. (WY)

EJ 030 298 PS 500 784
DIFFERENTIAL FACTOR STRUCTURE OF SEVENTH GRADE STUDENTS VERY, PHILIP S.; IACONO, CARMINE H., *JOURNAL OF GENETIC PSYCHOLOGY*, V117 N2, PP239-252, DEC '70
ANALYSIS OF THE MENTAL FACTORS OF SEVENTH GRADE STUDENTS INDICATES THAT NUMERICAL FACILITY AND PERCEPTUAL SPEED ARE A SINGLE FACTOR AT THIS AGE LEVEL AND THAT NO PURELY VERBAL FACTOR EXISTS. SEVEN CLEARLY DIFFERENTIATED FACTORS ARE FOUND FOR MALES AND FIVE FOR FEMALES. (AUTHOR/WY)

EJ 030 430 PS 500 761
CONSEQUENCES OF LOW BIRTH WEIGHT CAPUTO, DANIEL V.; MANDELL, WALLACE, *DEVELOPMENTAL PSYCHOLOGY*, V3 N3, PP363-383, NOV '70

EJ 030 431 PS 500 782
A PRELIMINARY VIEW OF TRENDS IN AGE, EDUCATION, AND INTELLIGENCE OF PROBLEM YOUTH CREEK, LEON VANDE; BATH, JOHN, *JOURNAL OF GENETIC PSYCHOLOGY*, V117 N2, PP219-225, DEC '70

EJ 030 432 PS 500 809
CLINICAL IMPLICATIONS OF MATERNAL EMPLOYMENT: A REVIEW OF RESEARCH POZNANSKI, ELVA; AND OTHERS, *JOURNAL OF THE AMERICAN ACADEMY OF CHILD PSYCHIATRY*, V9 N4, PP741-761, OCT '70

EJ 030 469 PS 500 744
PARENT AND CHILD CENTERS--IMPETUS, IMPLEMENTATION, IN-DEPTH VIEW PIEPER, ALICE M., *YOUNG CHILDREN*, V26 N2, PP70-76, DEC '70

EJ 030 510 PS 500 750
SOCIALIZATION AND INSTRUMENTAL COMPETENCE IN YOUNG CHILDREN BAUMRIND, DIANA, *YOUNG CHILDREN*, V26 N2, PP104-119, DEC '70
DISCUSSES RELATIONSHIPS BETWEEN PARENTAL AUTHORITY PATTERNS BY WHICH CHILDREN ARE INFLUENCED AND THE DEVELOPMENT OF SOCIALLY RESPONSIBLE AND INDEPENDENT BEHAVIOR IN YOUNG CHILDREN (ESPECIALLY GIRLS). (NH)

EJ 030 511 PS 500 755
SOME DETERMINANTS OF CHILDREN'S SELF-REWARD BEHAVIOR AFTER EXPOSURE TO DISCREPANT REWARD CRITERIA STOUWIE, ROGER J.; AND OTHERS, *DEVELOPMENTAL PSYCHOLOGY*, V3 N3, PP313-319, NOV '70

EJ 030 512 PS 500 767
CHILDREN'S JUDGMENTS OF PERSONALITY ON THE BASIS OF VOICE QUALITY PHILLIS, JUDITH A., *DEVELOPMENTAL PSYCHOLOGY*, V3 N3, PP411, NOV '70

EJ 030 513 PS 500 777
PATTERNS OF MOTHER-INFANT CONTACT: THE SIGNIFICANCE OF LATERAL PREFERENCE WEILAND, I. HYMAN; SPERBER, ZANWIL, *JOURNAL OF GENETIC PSYCHOLOGY*, V117 N2, PP157-165, DEC '70

EJ 030 514 PS 500 806
THE IMPACT OF OBJECT LOSS ON A SIX-YEAR-OLD CHETHIK, MORTON, *JOURNAL OF THE AMERICAN ACADEMY OF CHILD PSYCHIATRY*, V9 N4, PP624-643, OCT '70
TRACES THE EVENTS IN THE LIFE OF A 6-YEAR-OLD EMOTIONALLY DISTURBED BOY DURING THE TEN MONTHS OF HIS MOTHER'S DETERIORATION AND DEATH FROM CANCER. (WY)

EJ 030 515 PS 500 807
PREVENTIVE THERAPY WITH SIBLINGS OF A DYING CHILD FEINBERG, DANIEL, *JOURNAL OF THE AMERICAN ACADEMY OF CHILD PSYCHIATRY*, V9 N4, PP644-668, OCT '70

EJ 030 516 PS 500 808
ISSUES IN ASSESSING DEVELOPMENT FLAPAN, DOROTHY; NEUBAUER, PETER B., *JOURNAL OF THE AMERICAN ACADEMY OF CHILD PSYCHIATRY*, V9 N4, PP669-687, OCT '70
AMONG THE ISSUES CONSIDERED ARE: THE CONCEPTUALIZATION OF HEALTH; THE PROBLEMS OF VALIDITY AND RELIABILITY; THE PREDICTION OF DEVELOPMENTAL PROGRESSION AND POSTDICTION: THE ROLE OF SYMPTOMS: THE DETERMINATION OF DEVELOPMENTAL INFLUENCE AND THE DEFINITION OF VARIATIONS IN DEVELOPMENT. A SHORTER VERSION OF THIS PAPER WAS PRESENTED TO THE AMERICAN ACADEMY OF CHILD PSYCHIATRY, UNDER THE TITLE "DEVELOPMENTAL ASSESSMENT OF CHILDREN IN EARLY CHILDHOOD," IN OCTOBER 1968. (AUTHOR/WY)

EJ 030 547 PS 500 800
ON THE PSYCHOLINGUISTIC METHOD OF TEACHING READING SMITH, FRANK; GOODMAN, KENNETH S., *ELEMENTARY SCHOOL JOURNAL*, V71 N4, PP177-181, JAN '71
THE VALUE OF PSYCHOLINGUISTICS LIES IN THE INSIGHTS IT CAN GIVE RESEARCHERS AND PRACTITIONERS INTO THE LEARNING-TO-READ AND READING PROCESSES. THE TERM "PSYCHOLINGUISTIC" IS MEANINGLESS WHEN USED IN CONNECTION WITH FAD READING KITS AND INSTRUCTIONAL MATERIALS. (NH)

EJ 030 548 PS 500 804
ORAL READING ACHIEVEMENT OF SCOTTISH AND AMERICAN CHILDREN ELDER, RICHARD D., *ELEMENTARY SCHOOL JOURNAL*, V71 N4, PP216-230, JAN '71

EJ 030 589 PS 500 711
A METHODOLOGY FOR CONDUCTING AN EXPERIMENTAL ANALYSIS OF CHEATING BEHAVIOR BURCHARD, JOHN D., *JOURNAL OF EXPERIMENTAL CHILD PSYCHOLOGY*, V10 N2, PP146-158, OCT '70

EJ 030 590 PS 500 713
ESTIMATION OF LINE LENGTH AND NUMBER: A DEVELOPMENTAL STUDY SIEGEL, ALEXANDER W.; MCBURNEY, DONALD H., *JOURNAL OF EXPERIMENTAL CHILD PSYCHOLOGY*, V10 N2, PP170-180, OCT '70
RESULTS OF PAPER WERE REPORTED AT THE 1969 MEETING OF THE SOCIETY FOR RESEARCH IN CHILD DEVELOPMENT. (WY)

EJ 030 591 PS 500 717
INDIVIDUAL DIFFERENCES IN CHILDREN'S REACTIONS TO FRUSTRATIVE NONREWARD WATSON, PETER, *JOURNAL OF EXPERIMENTAL CHILD PSYCHOLOGY*, V10 N2, PP216-234, OCT '70
REPORTS A SERIES OF THREE EXPLORATORY STUDIES. (WY)

EJ 030 652 PS 500 735
ADOLESCENCE, IDENTITY, AND FOSTER FAMILY CARE MACINTYRE, J. MCEWAN, *CHILDREN*, V17 N6, PP213-217, NOV-DEC '70

EJ 030 653 PS 500 738
FOSTER FAMILY SERVICES FOR MENTALLY RETARDED CHILDREN GARRETT, BEATRICE L., *CHILDREN*, V17 N6, PP228-233, NOV-DEC '70

EJ 030 713 PS 500 741
SOCIAL SCHEMATA OF SCHOOL BEGINNERS: SOME DEMOGRAPHIC CORRELATES LONG, BARBARA H.; HENDERSON, EDMUND H., *MERRILL-PALMER QUARTERLY*, V16 N4, PP305-324, OCT '70

EJ 030 714 PS 500 749
PATTERNS OF FAMILY ORGANIZATION: AN APPROACH TO CHILD STUDY PATON, CORA L., *YOUNG CHILDREN*, V26 N2, PP98-102, DEC '70

EJ 030 715 PS 500 805
A STUDY OF WED AND UNWED MOTHERHOOD IN ADOLESCENTS AND YOUNG ADULTS AUG, ROBERT G.; BRIGHT, THOMAS P., *JOURNAL OF THE AMERICAN ACADEMY OF CHILD PSYCHIATRY*, V9 N4, PP577-594, OCT '70

EJ 030 792 PS 500 775
FAKABILITY OF SCORES ON THE GROUP PERSONALITY PROJECTIVE TEST BROZOVICH, RICHARD, *JOURNAL OF GENETIC PSYCHOLOGY*, V117 N2, PP143-148, DEC '70

EJ 031 049 PS 500 810
"THERE WAS A CHILD WENT FORTH"--A PHILOSOPHY OF EARLY EDUCATION HEFFERNAN, HELEN, *CHILD WELFARE*, V49 N10, PP545-552, DEC '70
PAPER WAS PRESENTED AT THE CWLA SOUTHWEST REGIONAL CONFERENCE, FORTH WORTH, TEXAS, 1970. (NH)

EJ 031 445 PS 500 815
SCHOOL PHOBIA AND SELF-EVALUATION NICHOLS, KEITH A.; BEERG, IAN, *JOURNAL OF CHILD PSYCHOLOGY AND PSYCHIATRY*, V11 N2, PP133-141, NOV '70
CONTRARY TO THE RESEARCH HYPOTHESIS, HIGHER LEVELS OF SELF-EVALUATION WERE NOT OBSERVED IN A SAMPLE OF SCHOOL PHOBIC CHILDREN WHEN THESE CHILDREN WERE COMPARED WITH A CONTROL GROUP OF DISTURBED, BUT NONPHOBIC CHILDREN WHO WERE ALSO ATTENDING A PSYCHIATRIC CLINIC. (WY)

EJ 031 540 PS 500 811
OPTIMAL OPERATION OF PUBLIC/PRIVATE CHILD WELFARE DELIVERY SYSTEMS LOUGHERY, DONALD L., JR., *CHILD WELFARE*, V49 N10, PP553-560, DEC '70
COOPERATION OF PUBLIC AND PRIVATE AGENCIES IN NEW SYSTEM OF MULTISERVICE CENTERS IS DISCUSSED AS A PARTIAL SOLUTION TO URGENT CHILD WELFARE NEEDS. (NH)

EJ 031 541 PS 500 816
THE RELATIONSHIP BETWEEN CONTROLLED PROJECTION RESPONSES AND SOCIOMETRIC STATUS DUROJAIYE, M. O. A., *JOURNAL OF CHILD PSYCHOLOGY AND PSYCHIATRY*, V11 N2, PP143-148, NOV '70
THIS STUDY DEMONSTRATES THAT RAVEN'S CONTROLLED PROJECTION TEST IS A SENSITIVE TOOL FOR DIFFERENTIATING BETWEEN POPULAR AND UNPOPULAR BOYS. (WY)

EJ 031 629 PS 500 813
THE WORLD TEST: DEVELOPMENTAL ASPECTS OF A PLAY TECHNIQUE KAMP, L. N. J.; KESSLER, E. S., *JOURNAL OF CHILD PSYCHOLOGY AND PSYCHIATRY*, V11 N2, PP81-108, NOV '70

EJ 031 630 PS 500 814
ON THE RELIABILITY OF THE GRAHAM/ROSENBLITH BEHAVIOUR TEST FOR NEONATES BENCH, JOHN; PARKER, ANNE, *JOURNAL OF CHILD PSYCHOLOGY AND PSYCHIATRY*, V11 N2, PP121-131, NOV '70

EJ 031 644 PS 500 819
BRIDGING THE CONCEPT GAP IN WORK WITH YOUTH ALISSI, ALBERT S., *CHILDREN*, V18 N1, PP13-18, JAN-FEB '71
EMPHASIZES THE NEED TO VIEW ADOLESCENTS AND ADULTS AS AN INTERACTING UNIT AND TO AVOID OVERSPECIALIZATION OF SOCIAL SERVICES AIMED AT PARTICULAR AGE GROUPS. PROGRAMS SHOULD BE RESTRUCTURED TO INCREASE YOUTH-ADULT INTERACTION, GIVING THEM MORE DECISION-MAKING POWER, AND ALSO MORE RESPONSIBILITY. (NH)

EJ 031 780 PS 500 826
CLASSROOM BEHAVIOR: MESSAGES FROM CHILDREN LIPTON, AARON, *ELEMENTARY SCHOOL JOURNAL*, V71 N5, PP254-261, FEB '71

EJ 031 781 PS 500 833
HAVE YOU EVER THOUGHT OF A PROP BOX? BENDER, JUDITH, *YOUNG CHILDREN*, V26 N3, PP164-169, JAN '71
A PROP BOX IS COMPOSED OF SPECIALIZED ITEMS (ORDINARY HOUSEWARES) COMBINED TO FOSTER A SPECIFIC TYPE OF PLAY. (AUTHOR/AJ)

EJ 031 848 PS 500 818
PLANNED VARIATION IN HEAD START PROGRAMS KLEIN, JENNY W., *CHILDREN*, V18 N1, PP8-12, JAN-FEB '71

EJ 031 849 PS 500 827
WHO SELECTS THE OBJECTIVES FOR LEARNING--AND WHY? OJEMANN, RALPH H., *ELEMENTARY SCHOOL JOURNAL*, V71 N5, PP262-273, FEB '71

EJ 031 850 PS 500 828
DO YOU REALLY WANT TO IMPROVE THE CURRICULUM? VAUGHN, JOHN W.; RANDS, RALPH C., *ELEMENTARY SCHOOL JOURNAL*, V71 N5, PP274-278, FEB '71

EJ 031 872 PS 500 834
THE DEVELOPMENT OF CLASSIFICATORY SKILLS IN YOUNG CHILDREN: A TRAINING PROGRAM SIGEL, IRVING E., *YOUNG CHILDREN*, V26 N3, PP170-184, JAN '71
REFERS TO CLASSIFICATION SKILLS AS "PRELUDES" TO CONCEPT ATTAINMENT. (AUTHOR)

EJ 032 059 PS 500 831
CONTEMPORARY CONCERNS IN EARLY CHILDHOOD EDUCATION ZIGLER, EDWARD, *YOUNG CHILDREN*, V26 N3, PP141-156, JAN '71
ADDRESS PRESENTED AT THE 1970 CONFERENCE OF THE NATIONAL ASSOCIATION FOR THE EDUCATION OF YOUNG CHILDREN, BOSTON, MASS., NOVEMBER 21, 1970. (AJ)

EJ 032 108 PS 500 823
ADVOCACY FOR CHILDREN: CHALLENGE FOR THE 1970'S WORK, HENRY, *CHILDREN*, V18 N1, PP31-32, JAN-FEB '71

EJ 032 192 PS 500 825
THE CAMERA FOCUSES ON READING LIEBERMAN, JANET E.; AND OTHERS, *ELEMENTARY SCHOOL JOURNAL*, V71 N5, PP244-251, FEB '71
REPORTS ON PROJECT MUSE, HUNTER COLLEGE, NEW YORK, WHICH HAS EXPLORED WAYS OF USING THE CAMERA IN THE TEACHING OF READING. (NH)

EJ 032 359 PS 500 830
BEFORE CHILDREN CAN MEASURE CAREY, RUSSELL L.; STEFFE, LESLIE P., *ELEMENTARY SCHOOL JOURNAL*, V71 N5, PP268-292, FEB '71

EJ 032 412 PS 500 821
VOLUNTEERING TO HELP INDIANS HELP THEMSELVES DIMOCK, EDMUND; RIEGEL, BARBARA, *CHILDREN*, V18 N1, PP23-27, JAN-FEB '71

EJ 032 509 PS 500 812
LEARNING AND COGNITIVE DEVELOPMENT: REPRESENTATIVE SAMPLES, CUMULATIVE-HIERARCHICAL LEARNING, AND EXPERIMENTAL-LONGITUDINAL METHODS STAATS, ARTHUR W.; AND OTHERS, *MONOGRAPHS OF THE SOCIETY FOR RESEARCH IN CHILD DEVELOPMENT*, V35 N8, NOV '70
THE COGNITIVE LEARNING OF CHILDREN IS EXPLORED IN FOUR STUDIES: (1) ALPHABET READING, (2) LEARNING READING UNITS AND CLASSICAL CONCEPT FORMATION, (3) COUNTING LEARNING AND COUNTING LEARNING MEDIATED BY VERBAL-RESPONSE CHAINS, AND (4) WRITING LEARNING, IMITATION, AND THE COGNITIVE-LEARNING ACCELERATION. (NH)

EJ 032 510 PS 500 829
PARENTS: SUMMER READING TEACHERS SULLIVAN, HOWARD J.; LABEAUNE, CAROL, *ELEMENTARY SCHOOL JOURNAL*, V71 N5, PP279-285, FEB '71

EJ 032 553 PS 500 820
AN ATTACK ON IMPEDIMENTS TO EFFECTIVE CROSS-CULTURAL TEACHING CARTER, LAMORE J.; HENSLEY, OLIVER D., *CHILDREN*, V18 N1, PP19-22, JAN-FEB '71
REPORTS A MULTI-STATE BI-RACIAL APPROACH TO IMPROVING EDUCATION FOR DISADVANTAGED CHILDREN. (NH)

EJ 032 563 PS 500 822
RECENT DEVELOPMENTS IN KOREAN SERVICES FOR CHILDREN MILLER, HELEN, *CHILDREN*, V18 N1, PP28-30, JAN-FEB '71

EJ 032 564 PS 500 824
IS IT TIME TO BREAK THE SILENCE ON VIOLENCE? MUNNELLY, ROBERT J., *ELEMENTARY SCHOOL JOURNAL*, V71 N5, PP237-243, FEB '71
THE SOCIAL STUDIES ELEMENTARY SCHOOL CURRICULUM SHOULD HELP CHILDREN EXPLORE THE NATURE AND CAUSES OF CONFLICT, AND HELP THEM DISCOVER NON-VIOLENT, CONSTRUCTIVE WAYS OF RESOLVING CONFLICT SITUATIONS. (NH)

EJ 032 565 PS 500 832
WHO CARES FOR AMERICA'S CHILDREN? BRONFENBRENNER, URIE, *YOUNG CHILDREN*, V26 N3, PP157-163, JAN '71
EXPRESSES THE VIEW THAT RADICAL REFORMS, INCLUDING REORDERING OF NATIONAL PRIORITIES, ARE NEEDED TO PROVIDE A HUMAN ENVIRONMENT FOR CHILDREN. GIVES A CONCRETE SUGGESTION TO MAKE MAJOR INSTITUTIONS BECOME FAMILY- AND CHILD- ORIENTED. (AUTHOR/AJ)

EJ 032 611 PS 500 817
PRIORITIES FOR CHANGE--SOME PRELIMINARY PROPOSALS FROM THE WHITE HOUSE CONFERENCE ON CHILDREN EPSTEIN, NOEL, *CHILDREN*, V18 N1, PP2-7, JAN-FEB '71

EJ 032 675 PS 500 837
INFANT MENTAL DEVELOPMENT AND NEUROLOGICAL STATUS, FAMILY SOCIOECONOMIC STATUS, AND INTELLIGENCE AT AGE FOUR IRETON, HAROLD; AND OTHERS, *CHILD DEVELOPMENT*, V41 N4, PP937-45, DEC '70

EJ 032 676 PS 500 849
RECOGNITION OF FLASHED WORDS BY CHILDREN SAMUELS, S. JAY, *CHILD DEVELOPMENT*, V41 N4, PP1089-94, DEC '70

EJ 032 677 PS 500 876
THEORETICAL NOTES ON POWER MOTIVATION VEROFF, JOSEPH; VEROFF, JOANNE B., *MERRILL-PALMER QUARTERLY OF BEHAVIOR AND DEVELOPMENT*, V17 N1, PP59-69, JAN '71
OUTLINES A THEORY OF THE DEVELOPMENT OF SOCIAL MOTIVES FOR POWER; SPECULATES THAT POWER CONCERNS ARE ELICITED BY NORMAL DEVELOPMENTAL PRESSURES. (NH)

EJ 032 678 PS 500 881
HOME LANGUAGE AND PERFORMANCE ON STANDARDIZED TESTS SPENCE, ALLYN G.; AND OTHERS, *ELEMENTARY SCHOOL JOURNAL*, V71 N6, PP309-313, MAR '71
THIS STUDY IS DESIGNED TO INVESTIGATE THE RELATIONSHIP BETWEEN THE LANGUAGE THAT MEXICAN-AMERICAN PARENTS OF LOWER SOCIOECONOMIC STATUS SPEAK TO THEIR CHILDREN AND THE CHILDREN'S PERFORMANCE ON STANDARDIZED TESTS DESIGNED TO MEASURE INTELLECTUAL ABILITIES. (AJ)

EJ 032 679 PS 500 885
PIAGETIAN TASKS AS CLASSROOM EVALUATIVE TOOLS WEISMAN, LORRAINE I.; SAFFORD, PHILIP L., *ELEMENTARY SCHOOL JOURNAL*, V71 N6, PP329-338, MAR '71

EJ 032 763 PS 500 869
WHAT GENERATION GAP? LARSEN, MARIE, *CHILDHOOD EDUCATION*, V47 N5, PP259-260, FEB '71
AN ART INSTRUCTOR OF A SENIOR CITIZENS' CLASS BRINGS TOGETHER A KINDERGARTEN CLASS AND HER OWN PUPILS TO SEE AGE DIFFERENCES VANISH THROUGH COMRADESHIP. (AJ)

EJ 032 796 PS 500 871
THE CHILDCARE ATTITUDES OF TWO GENERATIONS OF MOTHERS COHLER, BERTRAM J.; AND OTHERS, *MERRILL-PALMER QUARTERLY OF BEHAVIOR AND DEVELOPMENT*, V17 N1, PP3-17, JAN '71
REVISION OF PAPER PRESENTED AT THE ANNUAL MEETINGS OF THE AMERICAN ORTHOPSYCHIATRIC ASSOCIATION, NEW YORK, N.Y., 1969. (NH)

EJ 032 865 PS 500 903
ON SELECTING MATERIALS FOR THE CLASSROOM BARTH, ROLAND S., *CHILDHOOD EDUCATION*, V47 N6, PP311-314, MAR '71

EJ 032 890 PS 500 846
PATTERNS OF INFORMATION PROCESSING USED BY AND WITH YOUNG CHILDREN IN A NURSERY SCHOOL SETTING HONIG, ALICE S.; AND OTHERS, *CHILD DEVELOPMENT*, V41 N4, PP1045-65, DEC '70
PRESENTS DATA USING AN OBSERVATIONAL TECHNIQUE, APPROACH, WHICH DESCRIBES THE BEHAVIORS OF YOUNG CHILDREN IN NATURALISTIC SOCIAL SITUATIONS. (WY)

EJ 032 891 PS 500 848
MODIFYING RISK-TAKING BEHAVIOR WEST, JOEL D.; AND OTHERS, *CHILD DEVELOPMENT*, V41 N4, PP1083-88, DEC '70
A SIX-WEEK PROGRAM IN A PHYSICAL DEVELOPMENT CLINIC WAS SUCCESSFUL IN INCREASING RISK-TAKING BEHAVIOR IN 49 BOYS. THE CHANGE SEEMED TO REPRESENT A GENERALIZED BEHAVIOR SHIFT. (WY)

EJ 032 892 PS 500 851
NEONATE-MOTHER INTERACTION: EFFECTS OF PARITY ON FEEDING BEHAVIOR THOMAN, EVELYN B.; AND OTHERS, *CHILD DEVELOPMENT*, V41 N4, PP1103-11, DEC '70

EJ 032 893 PS 500 857
ATTENTIONAL RESPONSES OF FIVE-MONTH GIRLS TO DISCREPANT AUDITORY STIMULI MELSON, WILLIAM H.; MCCALL, ROBERT B., *CHILD DEVELOPMENT*, V41 N4, PP1159-71, DEC '70

EJ 032 894 PS 500 862
RESISTANCE TO TEMPTATION IN YOUNG NEGRO CHILDREN MUMBAUER, CORINNE C.; GRAY, SUSAN W., *CHILD DEVELOPMENT*, V41 N4, PP1203-7, DEC '70
INVESTIGATES THE RESISTANCE TO TEMPTATION OF DISADVANTAGED 5-YEAR-OLD NEGRO CHILDREN IN A GAME-LIKE SITUATION. (WY)

EJ 032 895 PS 500 872
INTELLECTUAL OPERATIONS IN TEACHER QUESTION-ASKING BEHAVIOR ZIMMERMAN, BARRY J.; BERGAN, JOHN R., *MERRILL-PALMER QUARTERLY OF BEHAVIOR AND DEVELOPMENT*, V17 N1, PP19-26, JAN '71
REPORTS A STUDY OF TEACHER QUESTION-ASKING BEHAVIOR AS A MEANS FOR INITIATING INTELLECTUAL OPERATIONS IN STUDENTS. (NH)

EJ 032 896 PS 500 884
CLASSROOM DISCIPLINE: A NEW APPROACH PURKEY, WILLIAM W.; AVILA, DON, *ELEMENTARY SCHOOL JOURNAL*, V71 N6, PP325-328, MAR '71
THE APPROACH TO DISCIPLINE PRESENTED HERE SUGGESTS THAT OPTIMAL CLASSROOM DISCIPLINE IS DIRECTLY RELATED TO TEACHER BELIEFS REGARDING PUPILS, HIMSELF, AND TEACHING. (AJ)

EJ 032 909 PS 500 841
YOUNG CHILDREN'S ORIENTATION OF LETTERS AS A FUNCTION OF AXIS OF SYMMETRY AND STIMULUS ALIGNMENT CAIRNS, NANCY U.; STEWARD, MARGARET S., *CHILD DEVELOPMENT*, V41 N4, PP993-1002, DEC '70

EJ 032 932 PS 500 859
PERSISTENCE AS A FUNCTION OF CONCEPTUAL STRUCTURE AND QUALITY OF FEEDBACK STUEMPFIG, DANIEL W.; MAEHR, MARTIN L., *CHILD DEVELOPMENT*, V41 N4, PP1183-90, DEC '70

EJ 032 933 PS 500 900
SHOWING AND SHARING IN THE KINDERGARTEN COWE, EILEEN, *CHILDHOOD EDUCATION*, V47 N6, PP300-302, MAR '71

EJ 032 934 PS 500 901
INVISIBLE FACTORS IN A CHILD'S REACTION TO TELEVISION PAUL, NORMAN L., *CHILDHOOD EDUCATION*, V47 N6, PP303-306, MAR '71
PAPER PRESENTED AT THE ACTION FOR CHILDREN'S TELEVISION FIRST NATIONAL SYMPOSIUM ON CHILDREN AND TELEVISION, KENNEDY MEMORIAL HOSPITAL FOR CHILDREN, BOSTON, MASSACHUSETTS, OCTOBER 16, 1970. (NH)

EJ 033 052 PS 500 844
THE GENERALITY OF COLOR-FORM PREFERENCE AS A FUNCTION OF MATERIALS AND TASK REQUIREMENTS AMONG LOWER-CLASS NEGRO CHILDREN OLMSTED, PATRICIA P.; SIGEL, IRVING E., *CHILD DEVELOPMENT*, V41 N4, PP1025-32, DEC '70

EJ 033 053 PS 500 850
CHILDREN'S USE OF CONTEXT IN JUDGMENT OF WEIGHT O'REILLY, EDMOND; STEGER, JOSEPH A., *CHILD DEVELOPMENT*, V41 N4, PP1095-1101, DEC '70

EJ 033 054 PS 500 853
PERCEPTUAL EXPLORATION IN ISRAELI CHILDREN KUGELMASS, SOL; LIEBLICH, AMIA, *CHILD DEVELOPMENT*, V41 N4, PP1125-31, DEC '70
REPORTS REPLICATION AND EXTENSION OF ELKIND AND WEISS'S STUDY OF PERCEPTUAL EXPLORATION USING 122 ISRAELI CHILDREN. IN GENERAL, RESULTS WERE UPHELD AND REFLECTED THE INFLUENCE OF SCHOOL EXPERIENCES SEEN MOST SPECIFICALLY IN THE RIGHT-LEFT DIRECTIONALITY EXPECTED TO RESULT FROM LEARNING TO READ HEBREW. (WY)

EJ 033 055 PS 500 864
ASSESSING THE ALTERNATIVES RATHBONE, CHARLES H., *CHILDHOOD EDUCATION*, V47 N5, PP234-238, FEB '71
DISCUSSES THE RECENT GROWTH OF "FREE SCHOOLS" AND THE NEED FOR CHANGE; MAKES A PLEA FOR ALTERNATIVES TO TRADITIONAL SCHOOLING. (AJ)

EJ 033 056 PS 500 873
THE USEFULNESS OF CUMULATIVE DEPRIVATION AS AN EXPLANATION OF EDUCATIONAL DEFICIENCIES SCHULTZ, CHARLES B.; AURBACH, HERBERT A., *MERRILL-PALMER QUARTERLY OF BEHAVIOR AND DEVELOPMENT*, V17 N1, PP27-39, JAN '71
EXAMINES THE QUESTION OF WHETHER ENVIRONMENTAL FACTORS RESTRICT ONLY THE CAPACITY TO PERFORM THE TYPE OF TASKS SCHOOLS REQUIRE, OR IF THEY INHIBIT THE GENERAL CAPACITY TO LEARN. (NH)

EJ 033 057 PS 500 898
A CHILD'S FIRST STEPS: SOME SPECULATIONS STEWART, MARY LOU, *CHILDHOOD EDUCATION*, V47 N6, PP290-295, MAR '71
PATTERNS OF MOTOR PERCEPTUAL DEVELOPMENT IN BOTH BLACK AND WHITE AMERICAN INFANTS ARE DISCUSSED, WITH IMPLICATIONS FOR EARLY CHILDHOOD EDUCATORS. (NH)

EJ 033 156 PS 500 865
ALTERNATIVE LEARNING ENVIRONMENTS: A PHILADELPHIA STORY KIES, KATHLEEN M., *CHILDHOOD EDUCATION*, V47 N5, PP239-244, FEB '71

EJ 033 157 PS 500 866
NEW DAY IN NORTH DAKOTA: CHANGING TEACHERS AND CHANGING SCHOOLS PEDERSON, CLARA A., *CHILDHOOD EDUCATION*, V47 N5, PP245-249, FEB '71
IN AN ATTEMPT TO CREATE MORE INDIVIDUALIZED MODES OF INSTRUCTION FOR ELEMENTARY PUPILS, THE UNIVERSITY OF NORTH DAKOTA ESTABLISHED AN ALTERNATIVE TEACHER EDUCATION PROGRAM TO PREPARE BOTH PROSPECTIVE AND EXPERIENCED TEACHERS FOR THEIR NEW ROLES IN CHANGING SCHOOLS. (AJ)

EJ 033 158 PS 500 870
TOUCH-FEEL LEARNING AT THE TALLAHASSEE JUNIOR MUSEUM GRISSETT, HELEN T., *CHILDHOOD EDUCATION*, V47 N5, PP261-264, FEB '71
THIS IS A TEACHER'S ACCOUNT OF THE EXCITING AND UNEXPECTED ENCOUNTERS THAT NATURE CAN PROVIDE. (AUTHOR/AJ)

EJ 033 159 PS 500 882
AN INTEGRATED DAY WORKSHOP MUSKOPF, ALLAN; MOSS, JOY, *ELEMENTARY SCHOOL JOURNAL*, V71 N6, PP315-319, MAR '71

EJ 033 279 PS 500 877
A METHOD OF INCREASING THE ABILITY OF FIRST GRADE PUPILS TO USE PHONETIC GENERALIZATIONS HARTLEY, RUTH N., *CALIFORNIA JOURNAL OF EDUCATIONAL RESEARCH*, V22 N1, PP9-16, JAN '71

EJ 033 313 PS 500 855
RELIABILITY ASSESSMENT OF OBSERVATION DATA: A POSSIBLE METHODOLOGICAL PROBLEM REID, JOHN B., *CHILD DEVELOPMENT*, V41 N4, PP1143-50, DEC '70

EJ 033 510 PS 500 902
LITERATURE, CREATIVITY AND IMAGINATION ALEXANDER, LLOYD, *CHILDHOOD EDUCATION*, V47 N6, PP307-310, MAR '71
LITERATURE CAN STIMULATE CREATIVITY AND IMAGINATION NECESSARY FOR THE DEVELOPMENT OF PERSONAL AWARENESS AND SOCIAL CONSCIOUSNESS. (NH)

EJ 033 573 PS 500 840
CHILDREN'S SELECTIVE ATTENTION TO STIMULI: STAGE OR SET? GAINES, ROSSLYN, *CHILD DEVELOPMENT*, V41 N4, PP979-91, DEC '70
THE RESULTS SHOW THAT SELECTIVE ATTENTION TO COLOR OR FORM CAN BE EXPERIMENTALLY CHANGED AND IS NOT DEVELOPMENTALLY DETERMINED FOR ALL SS. (WY)

EJ 033 574 PS 500 879
THE USE OF HIERARCHIES IN CURRICULUM ANALYSIS AND INSTRUCTIONAL PLANNING AIRASIAN, PETER W., *CALIFORNIA JOURNAL OF EDUCATIONAL RESEARCH*, V22 N1, PP34-41, JAN '71

EJ 033 700 PS 500 838
A REEXAMINATION OF SOME ASSUMPTIONS ABOUT THE LANGUAGE OF THE DISADVANTAGED CHILD HOUSTON, SUSAN H., *CHILD DEVELOPMENT*, V41 N4, PP948-63, DEC '70

ALTHOUGH RESEARCH ON THE LANGUAGE OF THE DISADVANTAGED CHILD IS RECEIVING MUCH IMPETUS, FEW EXTANT STUDIES HAVE BEEN HELPFUL TO THE TEACHER. THIS ARTICLE REEXAMINES WIDELY HELD MISCONCEPTIONS ABOUT DISADVANTAGED CHILD LANGUAGE IN LIGHT OF MODERN LINGUISTIC AND PSYCHOLINGUISTIC ADVANCES. (WY)

EJ 033 701 PS 500 861
COMPETENCE VERSUS PERFORMANCE IN YOUNG CHILDREN'S USE OF ADJECTIVAL COMPARATIVES STERN, CAROLYN; BRYSON, JUANITA, *CHILD DEVELOPMENT*, V41 N4, PP1197-1201, DEC '70

EJ 033 702 PS 500 874
NON-SOCIAL SPEECH IN FOUR-YEAR-OLD CHILDREN AS A FUNCTION OF BIRTH ORDER AND INTERPERSONAL SITUATION RUBIN, KENNETH H.; AND OTHERS, *MERRILL-PALMER QUARTERLY OF BEHAVIOR AND DEVELOPMENT*, V17 N1, PP41-50, JAN '71

EJ 033 777 PS 500 835
THE EARLY TRAINING PROJECT: A SEVENTH-YEAR REPORT GRAY, SUSAN W.; KLAUS, RUPERT A., *CHILD DEVELOPMENT*, V41 N4, PP909-24, DEC '70

EJ 033 778 PS 500 839
VERBAL FACTORS IN COMPENSATION PERFORMANCE AND THE RELATION BETWEEN CONSERVATION AND COMPENSATION LARSEN, GARY Y.; FLAVELL, JOHN H., *CHILD DEVELOPMENT*, V41 N4, PP965-77, DEC '70

EJ 033 779 PS 500 842
FUNCTIONS OF VISUAL IMAGERY IN THE LEARNING AND CONCEPT FORMATION OF CHILDREN HOLLENBERG, CLEMENTINA KUHLMAN, *CHILD DEVELOPMENT*, V41 N4, PP1003-15, DEC '70

EJ 033 780 PS 500 845
THE RELATIONSHIP BETWEEN AUDITORY AND VISUAL SHORT-TERM MEMORY AND READING ACHIEVEMENT DORNBUSH, RHEA L.; BASOW, SUSAN, *CHILD DEVELOPMENT*, V41 N4, PP1033-44, DEC '70

EJ 033 781 PS 500 847
MEANING AND ATTENTION AS DETERMINANTS OF SOCIAL REINFORCER EFFECTIVENESS CAIRNS, ROBERT B., *CHILD DEVELOPMENT*, V41 N4, PP1067-82, DEC '70

EJ 033 782 PS 500 854
LEARNING OF MEDIA CONTENT: A DEVELOPMENTAL STUDY COLLINS, W. ANDREW, *CHILD DEVELOPMENT*, V41 N4, PP1133-42, DEC '70

SUGGESTS AN INCREASE WITH AGE IN CHILDREN'S ABILITY TO FOCUS ON ESSENTIAL CONTENT FROM A MEDIA PRESENTATION. CHILDREN IN EARLY ADOLESCENCE SEEMED BETTER ABLE THAN YOUNGER ONES TO IGNORE NONESSENTIAL INFORMATION. (WY)

EJ 033 783 PS 500 856
THE RELATIONSHIP BETWEEN INTENTIONAL LEARNING, INCIDENTAL LEARNING, AND TYPE OF REWARD IN PRESCHOOL, EDUCABLE, MENTAL RETARDATES ROSS, DOROTHEA, *CHILD DEVELOPMENT*, V41 N4, PP1151-1158, DEC '70

EJ 033 784 PS 500 868
DESIGNING TOMORROW'S SCHOOL TODAY: THE MULTISENSORY EXPERIENCE CENTER RAY, HENRY W., *CHILDHOOD EDUCATION*, V47 N5, PP254-258, FEB '71

EJ 033 785 PS 500 887
TRANSFER OF VERBAL PAIRED ASSOCIATES IN MENTALLY RETARDED INDIVIDUALS AND NORMAL CHILDREN AS A FUNCTION OF INTERLIST SIMILARITY WILCOX, STEPHEN J.; BAUMEISTER, ALFRED A., *JOURNAL OF EXPERIMENTAL CHILD PSYCHOLOGY*, V10 N3, PP277-286, DEC '70

EJ 033 786 PS 500 888
CHILDREN'S SHIFT PERFORMANCE IN THE ABSENCE OF DIMENSIONALITY AND A LEARNED REPRESENTATIONAL RESPONSE GOULET, L. R.; WILLIAMS, KERRY G., *JOURNAL OF EXPERIMENTAL CHILD PSYCHOLOGY*, V10 N3, PP287-294, DEC '70

EJ 033 787 PS 500 889
TIME ESTIMATION BY YOUNG CHILDREN WITH AND WITHOUT INFORMATIONAL FEEDBACK CROWDER, ALETHA M. H.; HOHLE, RAYMOND H., *JOURNAL OF EXPERIMENTAL CHILD PSYCHOLOGY*, V10 N3, PP295-307, DEC '70

EJ 033 788 PS 500 890
ARE THESE TWO STIMULI FROM THE SAME SET? RESPONSE TIMES OF CHILDREN AND ADULTS WITH FAMILIAR AND ARBITRARY SETS MORIN, ROBERT E.; AND OTHERS, *JOURNAL OF EXPERIMENTAL CHILD PSYCHOLOGY*, V10 N3, PP308-318, DEC '70

EJ 033 789 PS 500 891
EFFECTS OF MEMORY AIDS ON HYPOTHESIS BEHAVIOR AND FOCUSING IN YOUNG CHILDREN AND ADULTS EIMAS, PETER D., *JOURNAL OF EXPERIMENTAL CHILD PSYCHOLOGY*, V10 N3, PP319-336, DEC '70

EJ 033 790 PS 500 892
SEQUENTIAL CONTIGUITY AND SHORT-TERM MEMORY IN CHILDREN'S DISCRIMINATION LEARNING CROLL, WILLIAM L.; AND OTHERS, *JOURNAL OF EXPERIMENTAL CHILD PSYCHOLOGY*, V10 N3, PP337-343, DEC '70

EJ 033 791 PS 500 893
CHILDREN'S TWO-CHOICE LEARNING OF PREDOMINANTLY ALTERNATING AND REPEATING SEQUENCES JONES, SANDRA J., *JOURNAL OF EXPERIMENTAL CHILD PSYCHOLOGY*, V10 N3, PP344-362, DEC '70

EJ 033 792 PS 500 894
YOUNG CHILDREN'S USE OF THE SPEECH CODE IN A RECALL TASK LOCKE, JOHN L.; FEHR, FRED S., *JOURNAL OF EXPERIMENTAL CHILD PSYCHOLOGY*, V10 N3, PP367-373, DEC '70

EJ 033 793 PS 500 895
FACILITATING AND INTERFERING EFFECTS OF STIMULUS NAMING ON CHILDREN'S MOTOR PAIRED-ASSOCIATE LEARNING CANTOR, JOAN H., *JOURNAL OF EXPERIMENTAL CHILD PSYCHOLOGY*, V10 N3, PP374-389, DEC '70

EJ 033 794 PS 500 896
EMOTIONAL CONCOMITANTS OF VISUAL MASTERY IN INFANTS: THE EFFECTS OF STIMULUS MOVEMENT ON SMILING AND VOCALIZING SHULTZ, THOMAS R.; ZIGLER, EDWARD, *JOURNAL OF EXPERIMENTAL CHILD PSYCHOLOGY*, V10 N3, PP390-402, DEC '70

EJ 033 795 PS 500 897
A DECREMENTAL EFFECT OF REDUNDANCY IN DISCRIMINATION LEARNING HOUSE, BETTY J., *JOURNAL OF EXPERIMENTAL CHILD PSYCHOLOGY*, V10 N3, PP403-412, DEC '70

EJ 033 863 PS 500 878
AN EXPERIMENTAL STUDY OF TWO METHODS OF PRESENTING THE INVERSION ALGORITHM IN DIVISION OF FRACTIONS INGERSOLL, GARY M., *CALIFORNIA JOURNAL OF EDUCATIONAL RESEARCH*, V22 N1, PP17-25, JAN '71

EJ 033 864 PS 500 880
THE NUFFIELD MATHEMATICS PROJECT RAPPAPORT, DAVID, *ELEMENTARY SCHOOL JOURNAL*, V71 N6, PP295-308, MAR '71

EJ 034 002 PS 500 836
EDUCATIONAL INTERVENTION AT HOME BY MOTHERS OF DISADVANTAGED INFANTS KARNES, MERLE B.; AND OTHERS, *CHILD DEVELOPMENT*, V41 N4, PP925-35, DEC '70

EJ 034 042 PS 500 843
SELF-DESCRIPTION AS A FUNCTION OF EVALUATIVE AND ACTIVITY RATINGS AMONG AMERICAN AND INDIAN ADOLESCENTS LONG, BARBARA H.; AND OTHERS, *CHILD DEVELOPMENT*, V41 N4, PP1017-24, DEC '70

RESULTS OF CROSS-CULTURAL COMPARISONS OF VERBAL RESPONSES INDICATE THAT SOCIAL DESIRABILITY HAS A HIGHER VALUE FOR INDIAN ADOLESCENTS AND ACTIVITY HAS A GREATER VALUE FOR AMERICAN ADOLESCENTS. GREATER SEX DIFFERENCES IN SELF-PERCEPTION OCCURRED FOR AMERICANS, AND GREATER CULTURAL DIFFERENCES FOR BOYS. (WY)

EJ 034 043 PS 500 852
CONCEPTUAL EMPHASIS IN THE HISTORY OF DEVELOPMENTAL PSYCHOLOGY: EVOLUTIONARY THEORY, TELEOLOGY, AND THE NATURE-NURTURE ISSUE ANANDALAKSHMY, S.; GRINDER, ROBERT E., *CHILD DEVELOPMENT*, V41 N4, PP1113-23, DEC '70

EJ 034 044 PS 500 858
THE ABILITY OF PERSONALITY VARIABLES IN DISCRIMINATING AMONG THREE INTELLECTUAL GROUPS OF PREADOLESCENT BOYS AND GIRLS KIRKENDALL, DON R.; ISMAIL, A. H., *CHILD DEVELOPMENT*, V41 N4, PP1173-81, DEC '70

EJ 034 045 PS 500 863
A NOTE ON SELECTIVE IMITATION BY A SIX-WEEK-OLD INFANT GARDNER, JUDITH; GARDNER, HOWARD, *CHILD DEVELOPMENT*, V41 N4, PP1209-13, DEC '70

EJ 034 069 PS 500 899
WRITE FIRST, READ LATER CHOMSKY, CAROL, *CHILDHOOD EDUCATION*, V47 N6, PP296-299, MAR '71
SUGGESTS THAT CHILDREN SHOULD LEARN TO READ BY CREATING THEIR OWN SPELLINGS FOR FAMILIAR WORDS. (NH)

EJ 034 133 PS 500 867
WIDER WINDOWS FOR ELEMENTARY SCHOOLS DIXON, NATHANIEL R., *CHILDHOOD EDUCATION*, V47 N5, PP250-253, FEB '71
SEVERAL WASHINGTON, D. C. EXPERIMENTAL SCHOOLS BROADENED THE CLASSROOMS TO ENCOMPASS THE OUTSIDE WORLD. (AJ)

EJ 034 158 PS 500 860
THE EFFECT OF INDIVIDUAL-CONTINGENT GROUP REINFORCEMENT ON POPULARITY ALDEN, STEVEN E.; AND OTHERS, *CHILD DEVELOPMENT*, V41 N4, PP1191-96, DEC '70

EJ 034 159 PS 500 886
INDIVIDUALLY GUIDED MOTIVATION: DEVELOPING SELF-DIRECTION AND PROSOCIAL BEHAVIORS KLAUSMEIER, HERBERT J.; AND OTHERS, *ELEMENTARY SCHOOL JOURNAL*, V71 N6, PP339-350, MAR '71

EJ 034 231 PS 500 883
TURNING THE TIDE IN TEACHER QUALITY METZNER, SEYMOUR; SHARP, RICHARD M., *ELEMENTARY SCHOOL JOURNAL*, V71 N6, PP320-324, MAR '71
THIS ARTICLE ADVOCATES NEW PROGRAMS FOR TEACHER-PREPARATION INSTITUTIONS TO INSURE THE FINISHED QUALITY OF TEACHERS. (AJ)

EJ 034 298 PS 500 875
THE MANIPULATION AND MEASUREMENT OF SELF-DISCLOSURE IN PREADOLESCENTS VONDRACEK, SARAH I.; VONDRACEK, FRED W., *MERRILL-PALMER QUARTERLY OF BEHAVIOR AND DEVELOPMENT*, V17 N1, PP51-58, JAN '71
AN ATTEMPT WAS MADE TO DEVELOP A RELIABLE MEASURE OF PREADOLESCENTS' WILLINGNESS TO SHARE INFORMATION ABOUT THEMSELVES (SELF-DISCLOSURE). THE COMPLETED INSTRUMENT WAS USED TO STUDY THE EFFECTS OF INTERVIEWER SEX, SUBJECT'S SEX, AND INTERVIEWER DISCLOSURE INPUT ON DISCLOSURE OUTPUT IN THIS AGE GROUP. (AUTHOR/NH)

EJ 034 312 PS 500 982
CHILDREN: THEIR POTENTIALS MURPHY, GARDNER; MURPHY, LOIS BARCLAY, *CHILDHOOD EDUCATION*, V47 N7, PP356-359, APR 71

EJ 034 313 PS 500 988
WORD FLUENCY--INTELLECT OR PERSONALITY? MARTIN, WILLIAM A., *JOURNAL OF GENETIC PSYCHOLOGY*, V118 N1, PP17-24, MAR 71
AN ATTEMPT TO SECURE FURTHER EVIDENCE FOR, OR AGAINST, THE INTELLECTUAL EXPLANATION OF MAORI SUPERIORITY IN WORD FLUENCY. (WY)

EJ 034 420 PS 500 950
LA FORMATION THEATRALE DANS L'EDUCATION PRESCOLAIRE MILLER, ROMANA, *INTERNATIONAL JOURNAL OF EARLY CHILDHOOD*, V2 N2, PP85-91, 70
THEATRE, PARTICULARLY THE USE OF PUPPET SHOWS AND GAMES, CAN PLAY AN IMPORTANT ROLE IN THE DEVELOPMENT OF THE PERSONALITY OF THE PRESCHOOL CHILD. (NH)

EJ 034 421 PS 500 983
EXPANDING THE CHILD'S WORLD THROUGH DRAMA AND MOVEMENT HAYES, ELOISE, *CHILDHOOD EDUCATION*, V47 N7, PP360-367, APR 71

EJ 034 422 PS 500 984
VALUES AND TECHNIQUES OF CREATIVE DRAMATICS DUBOIS, ELIOSE BARCLAY, *CHILDHOOD EDUCATION*, V47 N7, PP368-370, APR 71
CREATIVE DRAMATICS HELPS INCREASE AND RELEASE CHILDREN'S CREATIVE POTENTIAL. THIS ARTICLE STRESSES SELECTION OF QUALITATIVE MATERIALS. (WY)

EJ 034 452 PS 500 909
ATTITUDES OF PRESCHOOL AND ELEMENTARY SCHOOL CHILDREN TO AUTHORITY FIGURES FORMANEK, RUTH; WOOG, PIERRE, *CHILD STUDY JOURNAL*, V1 N2, PP100-110, WIN 70-71
AT THE PRESCHOOL LEVEL, THIS STUDY FOUND THAT VARIABLES OF SEX AND SOCIOECONOMIC STATUS BECOME PREDICTORS OF PERCEPTIONS OF AUTHORITY FIGURES, BUT THESE EFFECTS LESSEN AS THE CHILDREN BECOME OLDER. OLDER CHILDREN BECOME MORE THREATENED BY THOSE OUTSIDE THE HOME AND ARE MORE PROTECTIVE IN THEIR PERCEPTION OF THOSE IN THE HOME. (AUTHOR/NH)

EJ 034 453 PS 500 927
OCCUPATIONAL PRESTIGE AS SEEN BY DISADVANTAGED BLACK CHILDREN LEFEBVRE, ANDRE; BOHN, MARTIN J., JR., *DEVELOPMENTAL PSYCHOLOGY*, V4 N2, PP173-177, MAR 71

EJ 034 454 PS 500 931
THE EFFECTS OF SEX-ROLE STANDARDS FOR ACHIEVEMENT AND SEX-ROLE PREFERENCE ON THREE DETERMINANTS OF ACHIEVEMENT MOTIVATION STEIN, ALETHA HUSTON, *DEVELOPMENTAL PSYCHOLOGY*, V4 N2, PP219-231, MAR 71

EJ 034 509 PS 500 910
CAN POVERTY CHILDREN LIVE ON "SESAME STREET?" SPRIGLE, HERBERT A., *YOUNG CHILDREN*, V26 N4, PP202-217, MAR 71
AN ASSESSMENT BY AN EDUCATOR WHO HAS INCORPORATED SESAME STREET INTO HIS PROGRAM FOR DISADVANTAGED CHILDREN. HIS CONCLUSION: THERE ARE NO SIMPLE SOLUTIONS TO COMPLEX PROBLEMS. (WY)

EJ 034 527 PS 500 905
SUB-PROFESSIONAL BEHAVIOR MODIFICATION AND THE DEVELOPMENT OF TOKEN-REINFORCEMENT SYSTEMS IN INCREASING ACADEMIC MOTIVATION AND ACHIEVEMENT RYBACK, DAVID; AND OTHERS, *CHILD STUDY JOURNAL*, V1 N2, PP52-68, WIN 70-71
THE USE OF TOKEN-REINFORCER SYSTEMS IS DISCUSSED, WITH PARTICULAR REFERENCE TO THE STAATS MOTIVATION ACHIEVEMENT READING TECHNIQUE. (NH)

EJ 034 528 PS 500 907
THE SYSTEMATIC USE OF THE PEMACK PRINCIPLE IN MODIFYING CLASSROOM BEHAVIORS ANDREWS, HENRY B., JR., *CHILD STUDY JOURNAL*, V1 N2, PP74-79, WIN 70-71

EJ 034 529 PS 500 924
NOVELTY, FAMILIARITY, AND THE DEVELOPMENT OF INFANT ATTENTION WEIZMANN, FREDRIC; AND OTHERS, *DEVELOPMENTAL PSYCHOLOGY*, V4 N2, PP149-154, MAR 71
IN THIS STUDY, CHANGES IN INFANT'S ATTENTION TO NOVEL ON FAMILIAR STIMULI IN NOVEL AND FAMILIAR ENVIRONMENTS AS A FUNCTION OF AGE WERE EXAMINED. BY 8 WEEKS, MALES FIXATED A NOVEL STABILE MORE IF IN A FAMILIAR ENVIRONMENT WHILE FEMALES FIXATED THE NOVEL STABILE MORE IF IN A NOVEL ENVIRONMENT. (AUTHOR/WY)

EJ 034 530 PS 500 933
A STIMULUS SIMILARITY SCALE FOR TEMPORAL MEASURES OF ATTENTION IN INFANTS AND CHILDREN FREEDLE, ROY, *DEVELOPMENTAL PSYCHOLOGY*, V4 N2, PP240-247, MAR 71

EJ 034 531 PS 500 936
A TEST OF THE GENERALITY OF THE EFFECTS OF DEVIANT PRESCHOOL MODELS ROSS, SHEILA A., *DEVELOPMENTAL PSYCHOLOGY*, V4 N2, PP262-267, MAR 71

EJ 034 532 PS 500 942
PLAY PERSISTENCE: SOME EFFECTS OF INTERRUPTION, SOCIAL REINFORCEMENT, AND DEFECTIVE TOYS FARNHAM-DIGGORY, S.; RAMSEY, BARBARA, *DEVELOPMENTAL PSYCHOLOGY*, V4 N2, PP297-298, MAR 71
CONSTANT INSTRUSIANS UPON THE PLAY ACTIVITIES OF YOUNG CHILDREN MAY SET UP EMOTIONAL TENSIONS AND/OR SCRAMBLED EXPECTANCIES THAT INTERFERE SIGNIFICANTLY WITH SUBSEQUENT PLAY PERSISTENCE. (AUTHOR)

EJ 034 533 PS 500 948
CHILDREN AND WAR GAMES HAMMAR, STINA, *INTERNATIONAL JOURNAL OF EARLY CHILDHOOD*, V2 N2, PP74-77, 70
THE CHILD'S WAR GAME IS AN EXPRESSION OF HOW HE EXPERIENCES THE WORLD. ADULTS SHOULD NOT PROHIBIT THE WAR GAME, BUT RATHER SHOULD LISTEN TO IT FOR CLUES TO SOME OF THE PROBLEMS AND TENSIONS THE CHILD CANNOT EXPRESS VERBALLY, AND FOR OPPORTUNITIES TO SUGGEST ALTERNATIVES TO VIOLENCE. (NH)

EJ 034 534 PS 500 949
UN EXEMPLE D'OBSERVATION INTENSIVE DU COMPORTEMENT DE JEUNES ENFANTS DANS LE CADRE D'UNE GARDERIE VERSELE, BERNARD-ALEXANDER; CAMBIER, ANNE, *INTERNATIONAL JOURNAL OF EARLY CHILDHOOD*, V2 N2, PP78-84, 70
NATURAL OBSERVATIONS OF 15- TO 20-MONTH-OLD NURSERY SCHOOL CHILDREN SHOWED THAT CHILDREN EXHIBITED MORE SOCIAL BEHAVIORS INVOLVING SEVEN CATEGORIES OF CONTACT (SMILING, GOING TOWARDS, SPEAKING TO, ETC.) AFTER EATING TOGETHER AROUND A COMMUNAL TABLE THAN BEFORE, AND SHOWED LESS AGGRESSIVE BEHVIOR. FURTHER RESEARCH IS RECOMMENDED. (NH)

EJ 034 535 PS 500 952
CONTROL OF ORIENTING BEHAVIOR IN CHILDREN UNDER FIVE YEARS OF AGE TURNURE, JAMES E., *DEVELOPMENTAL PSYCHOLOGY*, V4 N1, PP16-24, JAN 71

THE CAPABILITY OF YOUNG HIGH ABILITY CHILDREN TO COPE WITH EXTRANEOUS DISTRACTIVE STIMULI DURING PERFORMANCE ON A TWO-CHOICE DISCRIMINATION TASK WAS INVESTIGATED. RESULTS INDICATE THAT EXISTING INTERPRETATIONS OF THE DEVELOPMENT OF ATTENTIVE ABILITIES IN CHILDREN BASED ON THE NOTION OF AN INCREASING ATTENTION SPAN ARE IN NEED OF ELABORATION OR REFORMULATION. (AUTHOR/WY)

EJ 034 536 PS 500 954
SMILING TO SOCIAL STIMULI: ELICITING AND CONDITIONING EFFECTS ZELAZO, PHILIP R., *DEVELOPMENTAL PSYCHOLOGY*, V4 N1, PP32-42, JAN 71

EJ 034 537 PS 500 955
STIMULUS AND RESPONSE ALTERNATION IN YOUNG CHILDREN RABINWITZ, F. MICHAEL; DEMYER, SANDRA, *DEVELOPMENTAL PSYCHOLOGY*, V4 N1, PP43-54, JAN 71

EJ 034 538 PS 500 957
STIMULUS CONTROL OF PARENT OR CARETAKER BEHAVIOR BY OFFSPRING BELL, RICHARD Q., *DEVELOPMENTAL PSYCHOLOGY*, V4 N1, PP63-72, JAN 71

A WAY OF THINKING ABOUT THE CHILD'S STIMULUS EFFECTS IS ADVANCED AND APPLIED TO PARENT-CHILD INTERACTIONS OBSERVED IN HOME SETTINGS. (AUTHOR/WY)

EJ 034 539 PS 500 959
DELAY OF GRATIFICATION AND INTERNAL VERSUS EXTERNAL CONTROL AMONG ADOLESCENTS OF LOW SOCIOECONOMIC STATUS ZYTKOSKEE, ADRIAN; AND OTHERS, *DEVELOPMENTAL PSYCHOLOGY*, V4 N1, PP93-98, JAN 71

EJ 034 540 PS 500 969
LINGUISTIC AND PSYCHOLOGICAL FACTORS IN THE SPEECH REGULATION OF BEHAVIOR IN YOUNG CHILDREN BEISWENGER, HUGO, *JOURNAL OF EXPERIMENTAL CHILD PSYCHOLOGY*, V11 N1, PP63-75, FEB 71

EJ 034 541 PS 500 972
ESTIMATES AND ESTIMATE-BASED INFERENCES IN YOUNG CHILDREN HEXCOX, KURT E.; HAGEN, JOHN W., *JOURNAL OF EXPERIMENTAL CHILD PSYCHOLOGY*, V11 N1, PP106-123, FEB 71

EJ 034 542 PS 500 994
THE OBJECTIVE MEASUREMENT OF CHILDREN'S INTRAFAMILIAL ATTITUDE AND SENTIMENT STRUCTURE AND THE INVESTMENT-SUBSIDIATION MODEL DELHEES, KARL H.; AND OTHERS, *JOURNAL OF GENETIC PSYCHOLOGY*, V118 N1, PP87-113, MAR 71

EJ 034 565 PS 500 965
DISCRIMINATION OF SPATIALLY CONFUSABLE LETTERS BY YOUNG CHILDREN ASSO, DOREEN; WYKE, MARIA, *JOURNAL OF EXPERIMENTAL CHILD PSYCHOLOGY*, V11 N1, PP11-20, FEB 71

A STUDY OF THE ABILITY OF YOUNG CHILDREN TO DISCRIMINATE AMONG SUCH LETTERS AS P AND Q, D AND B, USING FOUR DIFFERENT METHODS OF DISCRIMINATION (MATCHING, COPYING, NAMING, AND WRITING TO DICTATION). RESULTS SHOW THAT THE ACCURACY OF DISCRIMINATION IS DEPENDENT UPON THE METHOD OF ASSESSMENT EMPLOYED. (AUTHOR/WY)

EJ 034 566 PS 500 970
TERMINOLOGY AND METHODOLOGY RELATED TO THE USE OF HEART RATE RESPONSIVITY IN INFANCY RESEARCH WOODCOCK, JAMES M., *JOURNAL OF EXPERIMENTAL CHILD PSYCHOLOGY*, V11 N1, PP76-92, FEB 71

METHODOLOGICAL PROBLEMS IN MEASURING AND INTERPRETING INFANTILE HEART RATE REACTIVITY IN RESEARCH ARE DISCUSSED. VARIOUS WAYS OF DESCRIBING CARDIAC ACTIVITY ARE LISTED. ATTENTION IS GIVEN TO THE RELATIONSHIP BETWEEN RESTING STATE AND HEART RATE RESPONSIVITY. (AUTHOR/WY)

EJ 034 567 PS 500 976
TACTILE IDENTIFICATION OF LETTERS: A COMPARISON OF DEAF AND HEARING CHILDRENS' PERFORMANCES SCHIFF, WILLIAM; DYTELL, RITA SCHER, *JOURNAL OF EXPERIMENTAL CHILD PSYCHOLOGY*, V11 N1, PP150-164, FEB 71

EJ 034 611 PS 500 941
MEASURES OF FORM CONSTANCY: DEVELOPMENTAL TRENDS KAESS, DALE W., *DEVELOPMENTAL PSYCHOLOGY*, V4 N2, PP296, MAR 71

EJ 034 707 PS 500 925
STIMULUS CORRELATES OF AREA JUDGMENTS: A PSYCHOPHYSICAL DEVELOPMENTAL STUDY KEMPLER, BERNHARD, *DEVELOPMENTAL PSYCHOLOGY*, V4 N2, PP158-163, MAR 71

EJ 034 708 PS 500 960
HARMONIOUS PARENTS AND THEIR PRESCHOOL CHILDREN BAUMRIND, DIANA, *DEVELOPMENTAL PSYCHOLOGY*, V4 N1, PP99-102, JAN 71

THIS BRIEF REPORT DESCRIBES HARMONIOUS PARENTS AND THEIR CHILDREN. THE SIX PRESCHOOL DAUGHTERS WHOSE PARENTS WERE HARMONIOUS WERE OUTSTANDINGLY COMPETENT BUT THE OPPOSITE WAS TRUE OF THE TWO SONS. (AUTHOR/WY)

EJ 034 709 PS 500 977
THE CAPACITY TO LOVE: A POSSIBLE REFORMULATION JOSSELYN, IRENE M., *JOURNAL OF THE AMERICAN ACADEMY OF CHILD PSYCHIATRY*, V10 N1, PP6-22, JAN 71

THIS PAPER SUGGESTS GUIDELINES FOR WORKING WITH THE CURRENT SOCIAL PATHOLOGY OF BOTH ADOLESCENTS AND ADULTS. THE AUTHOR SUGGESTS THAT TODAY'S ADOLESCENTS OFTEN HAVE NOT EXPERIENCED THE MUTUALITY OF INTERPERSONAL RELATIONSHIPS THAT REQUIRE NOT ONLY A CAPACITY TO SEEK LOVE, BUT EQUALLY TO LOVE. (AUTHOR/AJ)

EJ 034 710 PS 500 980
INCREASING AND RELEASING HUMAN POTENTIALS ELKIND, DAVID, *CHILDHOOD EDUCATION*, V47 N7, PP346-348, APR 71

THE AUTHOR SUGGESTS THAT A BALANCED VIEW OF FREEDOM TEMPERED WITH CONSTRAINT CAN OVERCOME BARRIERS TO THE HUMAN POTENTIALS MOVEMENT. (AUTHOR/WY)

EJ 034 711 PS 500 981
NEW CONCEPTS OF HUMAN POTENTIALS: NEW CHALLENGE FOR TEACHERS COMBS, ARTHUR W., *CHILDHOOD EDUCATION*, V47 N7, PP349-355, APR 71

EJ 034 712 PS 501 004
TRAINING, TRANSFER, AND THE DEVELOPMENT OF COMPLEX BEHAVIOR GOULET, L. R., *HUMAN DEVELOPMENT*, V13 N4, PP213-240, 70

CONTRASTS DEVELOPMENTAL MODELS IN TERMS OF THEIR ASSUMPTIONS ABOUT THE JOINT ROLES OF EXPERIENCE AND MATURATION IN BEHAVIOR, AND THE SIMILARITIES OF THESE ASSUMPTIONS TO THOSE MADE IN LEARNING THEORIES. PRESENTS EXPERIMENTAL METHODS FOR SEPARATING MATURATION AND EXPERIENCE EFFECTS. (AUTHOR/NH)

EJ 034 713 PS 501 005
ON LANGUAGE AND KNOWING IN PIAGET'S DEVELOPMENTAL THEORY FURTH, H. G., *HUMAN DEVELOPMENT*, V13 N4, PP241-257, 70

CLARIFIES DISTINCTION BETWEEN FIGURATIVE AND OPERATIVE KNOWING AND ITS RELATIONSHIP TO SYMBOLIC FUNCTIONING. OUTLINES HOW THE CONCEPTS OF SYMBOL, LANGUAGE AND SIGNIFICATION FIT WITHIN THE PIAGETIAN THEORY OF KNOWING. (AUTHOR/NH)

EJ 034 714 PS 501 006
THE RELATIONSHIP BETWEEN TIME OF MEASUREMENT AND AGE IN COGNITIVE DEVELOPMENT OF CHILDREN: AN APPLICATION OF CROSS-SECTIONAL SEQUENCES BALTES, P. B.; AND OTHERS, *HUMAN DEVELOPMENT*, V13 N4, PP258-268, 70

EJ 034 784 PS 500 904
FOUR QUESTIONS ON EARLY CHILDHOOD EDUCATION KATZ, LILIAN G., *CHILD STUDY JOURNAL*, V1 N2, PP43-51, WIN 70-71

DISCUSSES GOALS OF EARLY EDUCATION, AND THE QUALITIES OF PROGRAMS, TEACHERS AND ADMINISTRATION WHICH WOULD HELP TO IMPLEMENT THESE GOALS. (NH)

EJ 034 901 PS 500 921
OLDER BROTHERS' INFLUENCE ON SEX-TYPED, AGGRESSIVE, AND DEPENDENT BEHAVIOR IN FATHER-ABSENT CHILDREN WOHLFORD, PAUL; AND OTHERS, *DEVELOPMENTAL PSYCHOLOGY*, V4 N2, PP124-134, MAR 71

EJ 034 902 PS 500 935
MASCULINITY AND FEMININITY IN THE ELEMENTARY AND JUNIOR HIGH SCHOOL YEARS VROEGH, KAREN, *DEVELOPMENTAL PSYCHOLOGY*, V4 N2, PP254-261, MAR 71

EJ 034 903 PS 500 943
DISADVANTAGED AND NONDISADVANTAGED CHILDREN'S EXPECTANCY IN SKILL AND CHANCE OUTCOMES WALLS, RICHARD T.; COX, JANET, *DEVELOPMENTAL PSYCHOLOGY*, V4 N2, PP299, MAR 71

EJ 034 921 PS 500 963
EFFECT OF INSTRUCTIONAL SET ON TWELVE-YEAR-OLD CHILDREN'S PERCEPTION OF INTERRUPTION MACMILLAN, DONALD L.; KEOGH, BARBARA K., *DEVELOPMENTAL PSYCHOLOGY*, V4 N1, PP106, JAN 71

EJ 035 078 PS 500 987
CHILDHOOD PSYCHOSIS COMBINED WITH XYZ ABNORMALITIES ABRAMS, NAOMI; PERGAMENT, EUGENE, *JOURNAL OF GENETIC PSYCHOLOGY*, V118 N1, PP13-16, MAR 71
SUMMARIZES THE DIAGNOSTIC EVALUATION OF ONE PREPUBESCENT MALE WITH THE DOUBLE Y SYNDROME AND SUGGESTS A NEED TO INVESTIGATE FURTHER THE BIOCHEMICAL, PHYSIOLOGICAL, AND GENETIC ROLES UNDERLYING SUCH GROSS BEHAVIORAL ABNORMALITIES. (WY)

EJ 035 168 PS 500 911
THE CREATIVE ENVIRONMENT WORKSHOP BAKER, WILLIAM E.; AND OTHERS, *YOUNG CHILDREN*, V26 N4, PP219-223, MAR 71
THE CREATIVE WORKSHOP IS FACILITATING CHANGE IN OUR PRESENT EDUCATIONAL APPROACH THROUGH THE REEDUCATION OF ADULTS WHO WORK WITH CHILDREN. THE PROGRAM ACTIVELY ENGAGES ADULTS IN ADAPTING TO AND EXPLORING OUR DYNAMIC ENVIRONMENT IN THE HOPE THAT CHILDREN TAUGHT BY THESE ADULTS WILL LEARN TO CHALLENGE FACTS AND THEIR RELEVANCE RATHER THAN PASSIVELY ACCEPTING WHAT HAS PREVIOUSLY BEEN DISCOVERED. (WY)

EJ 035 169 PS 500 919
USING SENSITIVITY TRAINING WITH JUNIOR HIGH SCHOOL STUDENTS RUEVENI, URI, *CHILDREN*, V18 N2, PP69-72, MAR-APR 71
THIS IS A DISCUSSION OF A PHILADELPHIA JUNIOR HIGH SCHOOL'S USE OF SENSITIVITY TRAINING SESSIONS TO MODIFY THE CLASSROOM BEHAVIOR OF DISRUPTIVE STUDENTS. (AUTHOR/AJ)

EJ 035 170 PS 500 945
LA FORMATION DU PERSONNEL NON MEDICAL S'OCCUPANT DU PETIT ENFANT DE 1 A 6 ANS MIALARET, GASTON, *INTERNATIONAL JOURNAL OF EARLY CHILDHOOD*, V2 N2, PP49-54, 70
OBJECTIVES OF PROFESSIONAL TRAINING PROGRAMS FOR PRESCHOOL STAFF ARE DISCUSSED, WITH EMPHASIS ON THE IMPORTANCE OF THE CHILD'S EARLY YEARS FOR HIS EMOTIONAL, AS WELL AS PHYSICAL DEVELOPMENT. (NH)

EJ 035 171 PS 500 998
A TEACHER DISCOVERS INDIVIDUALIZED INSTRUCTION DUGGER, CHESTER W., *ELEMENTARY SCHOOL JOURNAL*, V71 N7, PP357-360, APR 71
AN ACCOUNT OF A BEGINNING TEACHER'S SUCCESSFUL EXPERIENCE WITH AN INDIVIDUALIZED CLASSROOM PROGRAM IN THIRD GRADE. (WY)

EJ 035 172 PS 501 003
REMEDIAL READING INSTRUCTION BY TRAINED PUPIL TUTORS NIEDERMEYER, FRED C.; ELLIS, PATRICIA, *ELEMENTARY SCHOOL JOURNAL*, V71 N7, PP400-405, APR 71
DESCRIBES A TUTORIAL PROGRAM IN WHICH SCHOOL PERSONNEL TRAINED FIFTH- AND SIXTH-GRADE PUPILS TO TUTOR KINDERGARTENERS IN READING. (WY)

EJ 035 243 PS 500 946
WHAT IS A GOOD KINDERGARTEN? VEDEL-PETERSEN, JACOB, *INTERNATIONAL JOURNAL OF EARLY CHILDHOOD*, V2 N2, PP55-64, 70
THIS PAPER IS CONCERNED WITH THE KINDERGARTEN AS AN EDUCATIONAL INSTITUTE AND IS PART OF A LARGER SURVEY OF THE LITERATURE... ON ALL ASPECTS OF THE CHILD'S DEVELOPMENT AS AFFECTED BY THE KINDERGARTEN EXPERIENCE. (AUTHOR)

EJ 035 269 PS 500 929
RESPONSE TO VOICE OF MOTHER AND STRANGER BY BABIES IN THE FIRST YEAR TURNURE, CYNTHIA, *DEVELOPMENTAL PSYCHOLOGY*, V4 N2, PP182-190, MAR 71

EJ 035 359 PS 500 920
DEVELOPMENT OF FREE RECALL LEARNING IN CHILDREN COLE, MICHAEL; AND OTHERS, *DEVELOPMENTAL PSYCHOLOGY*, V4 N2, PP109-123, MAR 71
IN THREE EXPERIMENTS, PERFORMANCE OF CHILDREN IN GRADES RANGING FROM 1 TO 9 WAS INVESTIGATED IN A REPEATED TRIALS, FREE RECALL EXPERIMENT. ALTHOUGH PERFORMANCE ON THE ACCURACY AND CLUSTERING MEASURES INCREASED WITH GRADE, INTERACTIONS BETWEEN GRADE AND OTHER INDEPENDENT VARIABLES WERE GENERALLY LACKING. (AUTHOR/WY)

EJ 035 360 PS 500 922
DIMENSIONAL SALIENCE AND IDENTIFICATION OF THE RELEVANT DIMENSION IN PROBLEM SOLVING: A DEVELOPMENTAL STUDY ODOM, RICHARD D.; MUMBAUER, CORINNE C., *DEVELOPMENTAL PSYCHOLOGY*, V4 N2, PP135-140, MAR 71

EJ 035 361 PS 500 926
INTERRELATIONS AMONG LEARNING AND PERFORMANCE TASKS AT THE PRESCHOOL LEVEL FRIEDRICHS, ANN G.; AND OTHERS, *DEVELOPMENTAL PSYCHOLOGY*, V4 N2, PP164-172, MAR 71

EJ 035 362 PS 500 930
DEVELOPMENTAL PATTERNS FOR CHILDREN'S CLASS AND CONDITIONAL REASONING ABILITIES ROBERGE, JAMES J.; PAULUS, DIETER H., *DEVELOPMENTAL PSYCHOLOGY*, V4 N2, PP191-200, MAR 71

EJ 035 363 PS 500 932
CHILDREN'S ABILITY TO OPERATE WITHIN A MATRIX: A DEVELOPMENTAL STUDY SIEGEL, ALEXANDER W.; KRESH, ESTHER, *DEVELOPMENTAL PSYCHOLOGY*, V4 N2, PP232-239, MAR 71

EJ 035 364 PS 500 934
PARENTAL EDUCATION, SEX DIFFERENCES, AND PERFORMANCE ON COGNITIVE TASKS AMONG TWO-YEAR-OLD CHILDREN REPPUCCI, N. DICKON, *DEVELOPMENTAL PSYCHOLOGY*, V4 N2, PP248-253, MAR 71
THE RELATION BETWEEN SEX OF CHILD, PARENTAL EDUCATIONAL LEVEL, AND PERFORMANCE ON THREE DIFFERENT TYPES OF COGNITIVE TASKS WAS INVESTIGATED AMONG 48 2-YEAR-OLD CHILDREN. RESULTS CONFIRMED THE EXPECTATION THAT PARENTAL EDUCATION WOULD BE POSITIVELY RELATED TO SUPERIOR PERFORMANCE ON ALL OF THE TASKS FOR GIRLS BUT UNRELATED FOR BOYS. (AUTHOR/WY)

EJ 035 365 PS 500 937
MEDIATION AND PERCEPTUAL TRANSFER IN CHILDREN KATZ, PHYLLIS A.; AND OTHERS, *DEVELOPMENTAL PSYCHOLOGY*, V4 N2, PP268-276, MAR 71

EJ 035 366 PS 500 938
OUTERDIRECTEDNESS IN THE PROBLEM-SOLVING OF INSTITUTIONALIZED AND NONINSTITUTIONALIZED NORMAL AND RETARDED CHILDREN YANDO, REGINA; ZIGLER, EDWARD, *DEVELOPMENTAL PSYCHOLOGY*, V4 N2, PP277-288, MAR 71

EJ 035 367 PS 500 939
ASSOCIATION AND ABSTRACTION AS MECHANISMS OF IMITATIVE LEARNING LIEBERT, ROBERT M.; SWENSON, SHARON A., *DEVELOPMENTAL PSYCHOLOGY*, V4 N2, PP289-294, MAR 71

EJ 035 368 PS 500 940
FREE RECALL OF OBJECT NAMES IN PRESCHOOL CHILDREN AS A FUNCTION OF INTRACATEGORY VARIATION MCCARSON, CAROLE; DAVES, WALTER F., *DEVELOPMENTAL PSYCHOLOGY*, V4 N2, PP295, MAR 71

EJ 035 369 PS 500 944
PAIRED-ASSOCIATE LEARNING OF CHILDREN WITH MIXED LIST DESIGNS GALLAGHER, JOSEPH W.; REID, DONALD R., *DEVELOPMENTAL PSYCHOLOGY*, V4 N2, PP300, MAR 71

EJ 035 370 PS 500 947
I SEE WHAT YOU MEAN BRANNIGAN, CHRISTOPHER; HUMPHRIES, DAVID, *INTERNATIONAL JOURNAL OF EARLY CHILDHOOD*, V2 N2, PP65-73, 70
STUDIES OF COMMUNICATION BY FACIAL EXPRESSIONS AND BY GESTURE, WITH DAY NURSERY CHILDREN BETWEEN 3- AND 5-YEARS-OLD, ARE REPORTED. PRACTICAL APPLICATION IS DISCUSSED, SUCH AS IN CASES OF MENTAL ILLNESS WHERE VERBAL COMMUNICATION IS INADEQUATE. (NH)

EJ 035 371 PS 500 958
CHAOTIC REINFORCEMENT: A SOCIOECONOMIC LEVELER BRESNAHAN, JEAN L.; BLUM, WILLIAM L., *DEVELOPMENTAL PSYCHOLOGY*, V4 N1, PP89-92, JAN 71
DATA PROVIDES EVIDENCE THAT THE INCONSISTENT REINFORCEMENT HISTORIES OF LOWER SOCIOECONOMIC CHILDREN CONTRIBUTE TO THEIR TYPICAL INEFFECTUAL PERFORMANCE. (AUTHOR/WY)

EJ 035 372 PS 500 961
THE "MENTAL STEP" HYPOTHESIS IN SOLVING VERBAL PROBLEMS: EFFECTS OF VARIATIONS IN QUESTION-PHRASING ON A GRADE SCHOOL POPULATION ZERN, DAVID, *DEVELOPMENTAL PSYCHOLOGY*, V4 N1, PP103-104, JAN 71

EJ 035 373 PS 500 962
TRAINING CREATIVITY IN YOUNG CHILDREN CROPLEY, A. J.; FEURING, ELSIE, *DEVELOPMENTAL PSYCHOLOGY*, V4 N1, PP105, JAN 71

EJ 035 374 PS 500 964
CUE AND INCENTIVE MOTIVATIONAL PROPERTIES OF REINFORCERS IN CHILDREN'S DISCRIMINATION LEARNING HAAF, ROBERT A., *JOURNAL OF EXPERIMENTAL CHILD PSYCHOLOGY*, V11 N1, PP1-10, FEB 71

EJ 035 375 PS 500 966
DEVELOPMENTAL TRENDS IN THE INTENTIONAL AND INCIDENTAL LEARNING COMPONENTS OF A VERBAL DISCRIMINATION TASK DEICHMANN, JOHN W.; AND OTHERS, *JOURNAL OF EXPERIMENTAL CHILD PSYCHOLOGY*, V11 N1, PP21-34, FEB 71

EJ 035 376 PS 500 967
THE EFFECTS OF CONNOTATIVE SIMILARITY IN CHILDREN'S LEARNING OF A PAIRED-ASSOCIATE TASK DI VESTA, FRANCIS J., *JOURNAL OF EXPERIMENTAL CHILD PSYCHOLOGY*, V11 N1, PP35-44, FEB 71

EJ 035 377 PS 500 971
THE EFFECTS OF REHEARSAL AND CHUNKING INSTRUCTIONS ON CHILDREN'S MULTITRIAL FREE RECALL ROSNER, SUE R., *JOURNAL OF EXPERIMENTAL CHILD PSYCHOLOGY*, V11 N1, PP93-105, FEB 71

EJ 035 378 PS 500 973
LEARNING, CURIOSITY, AND SOCIAL GROUP MEMBERSHIP NICKI, R. M.; SHEA, J. F., *JOURNAL OF EXPERIMENTAL CHILD PSYCHOLOGY*, V11 N1, PP124-132, FEB 71

EJ 035 379 PS 500 975
TRANSFER AND SEQUENCE IN LEARNING DOUBLE CLASSIFICATION SKILLS RESNICK, LAUREN B.; AND OTHERS, *JOURNAL OF EXPERIMENTAL CHILD PSYCHOLOGY*, V11 N1, PP139-149, FEB 71

EJ 035 380 PS 500 986
CREATIVITY AS RELATED TO FIELD INDEPENDENCE AND MOBILITY BLOOMBERG, MORTON, *JOURNAL OF GENETIC PSYCHOLOGY*, V118 N1, PP3-12, MAR 71

THE DIFFERENTIAL ROLE OF MOBILITY IN CREATIVITY AND IN INTELLIGENCE SUGGESTS THAT HORIZONTAL MOBILITY MAY BE ESSENTIAL IN CREATIVITY AND VERTICAL MOBILITY IN INTELLIGENCE. (AUTHOR/WY)

EJ 035 381 PS 500 991
SEQUENTIAL LEARNING BY CHILDREN LIVESEY, P. J.; LITTLE, AUDREY, *JOURNAL OF GENETIC PSYCHOLOGY*, V118 N1, PP33-38, MAR 71

EJ 035 382 PS 500 992
THE ROLE OF VERBAL MEDIATION IN MENTAL DEVELOPMENT JENSEN, ARTHUR R., *JOURNAL OF GENETIC PSYCHOLOGY*, V118 N1, PP39-70, MAR 71

EJ 035 383 PS 500 995
SOME RELATIONSHIPS BETWEEN VERBAL AND PERCEPTUAL CAPABILITIES AND THE DEVELOPMENT OF RELATIVE THINKING CARLSON, JERRY S., *JOURNAL OF GENETIC PSYCHOLOGY*, V118 N1, PP115-119, MAR 71

EJ 035 466 PS 500 999
WHAT PUPILS KNOW ABOUT VOCABULARY IN MATHEMATICS--1930 AND 1968 OLANDER, HERBERT T.; EHMER, CHARLES L., *ELEMENTARY SCHOOL JOURNAL*, V71 N7, PP361-367, APR 71

EJ 035 537 PS 500 000
THE CULTURE OF THE CULTURALLY DEPRIVED GOODMAN, YETTA M., *ELEMENTARY SCHOOL JOURNAL*, V71 N7, PP376-383, APR 71

AN INFORMAL INVESTIGATION OF RHYTHMS AND RHYMES IN "DEPRIVED" CHILDREN'S GAMES AND SONGS ATTESTS TO CULTURAL DIFFERENCE RATHER THAN CULTURAL DEPRIVATION. (WY)

EJ 035 538 PS 500 917
GROUP SERVICES FOR UNMARRIED MOTHERS: AN INTERDISCIPLINARY APPROACH DANFORTH, JOYCE; AND OTHERS, *CHILDREN*, V18 N2, PP59-64, MAR-APR 71

REPORTS ON A GROUP PROGRAM IN WHICH A PUBLIC HEALTH NURSE AND TWO SOCIAL WORKERS HAVE BEEN WORKING TOGETHER TO HELP UNMARRIED MOTHERS PREPARE FOR DELIVERY AND PLAN FOR THE CARE OF THEIR BABIES. (AUTHOR/AJ)

EJ 035 539 PS 500 979
AN ATTEMPT TO COMBINE CLINICAL AND EDUCATIONAL RESOURCES: A REPORT ON THE FIRST YEAR'S EXPERIENCE OF A THERAPEUTIC SCHOOL LEVE, ROBERT M.; AND OTHERS, *JOURNAL OF THE AMERICAN ACADEMY OF CHILD PSYCHIATRY*, V10 N1, PP108-123, JAN 71

THIS REPORT IS THE STORY OF ONE CLINIC'S DEPARTURE FROM TRADITIONAL METHODS OF DEALING WITH DISTURBED INNER-CITY SCHOOL CHILDREN. THE PAPER INCLUDES A DISCUSSION OF A COOPERATIVE VENTURE BETWEEN A CHILD GUIDANCE CLINIC AND THE PUBLIC SCHOOL SYSTEM AND AN EXAMINATION OF THE PRACTICAL ASPECTS OF THE PROBLEMS ARISING FROM SUCH A JOINT PROJECT. (AUTHOR/AJ)

EJ 035 579 PS 501 002
A CAREER DEVELOPMENT PROGRAM IN THE CHICAGO PUBLIC SCHOOLS NORWICH, ANTHONY L., *ELEMENTARY SCHOOL JOURNAL*, V71 N7, PP391-399, APR 71

CHILDREN IN GRADES FOUR TO SIX BENEFITED FROM AN INNOVATIVE UNIT OF INSTRUCTION ORGANIZED AROUND WORKERS AND THEIR JOBS. (WY)

EJ 035 618 PS 500 906
SELF CONCEPTS OF DISADVANTAGED AND ADVANTAGED STUDENTS SOARES, LOUISE M.; SOARES, ANTHONY T., *CHILD STUDY JOURNAL*, V1 N2, PP69-73, WIN 70-71

RESULTS OF A STUDY OF 707 STUDENTS SHOW THAT ALL DISADVANTAGED CHILDREN DO NOT NECESSARILY HAVE NEGATIVE SELF CONCEPTS. IN FACT, THEY SHOW JUST THE OPPOSITE AT THE ELEMENTARY SCHOOL LEVEL; HOWEVER, SELF CONCEPT DIMINISHES FOR BOTH DISADVANTAGED AND ADVANTAGED STUDENTS AT THE SECONDARY SCHOOL LEVEL. (NH)

EJ 035 619 PS 500 914
SELECTING PRIORITIES AT THE WHITE HOUSE CONFERENCE ON CHILDREN CLOSE, KATHRYN, *CHILDREN*, V18 N2, PP42-48, MAR-APR 71

EJ 035 620 PS 500 923
MEXICAN-AMERICAN CULTURAL MEMBERSHIP AND ADJUSTMENT TO SCHOOL RAMIREZ, MANUEL, III.; AND OTHERS, *DEVELOPMENTAL PSYCHOLOGY*, V4 N2, PP141-148, MAR 71

MEXICAN-AMERICAN AND ANGLO-AMERICAN JUNIOR HIGH AND HIGH SCHOOL STUDENTS OF THE LOWER SOCIOECONOMIC CLASS WERE ADMINISTERED AN ATTITUDE TOWARDS EDUCATION SCALE AND A PROJECTIVE TECHNIQUE CONSISTING OF PICTURES FOR WHICH THEY WERE ASKED TO CONSTRUCT STORIES. THE RESULTS SHOWED THAT MEXICAN-AMERICANS HAD EXPRESSED VIEWS TOWARD EDUCATION WHICH WERE LESS POSITIVE THAN THOSE OF ANGLO-AMERICANS. (AUTHOR/WY)

EJ 035 621 PS 500 951
SELF-ESTEEM, SUCCESS-FAILURE, AND LOCUS OF CONTROL IN NEGRO CHILDREN EPSTEIN, RALPH; KOMORITA, S. S., *DEVELOPMENTAL PSYCHOLOGY*, V4 N1, PP2-8, JAN 71

EJ 035 622 PS 500 953
PATTERN COPYING UNDER THREE CONDITIONS OF AN EXPANDED SPATIAL FIELD KEOGH, BARBARA K., *DEVELOPMENTAL PSYCHOLOGY*, V4 N1, PP25-31, JAN 71

EJ 035 623 PS 500 968
OPERANT LEARNING OF VISUAL PATTERN DISCRIMINATION IN YOUNG INFANTS MCKENZIE, BERYL; DAY, R. H., *JOURNAL OF EXPERIMENTAL CHILD PSYCHOLOGY*, V11 N1, PP45-53, FEB 71

AN OPERANT CONDITIONING TECHNIQUE WAS USED TO STUDY VISUAL DISCRIMINATION OF SIMPLE PATTERNS BY INFANTS AGED 6-12 WEEKS. THE APPROPRIATE DIRECTION OF HEAD TURNING TO THE PATTERNS WAS DEVELOPED AND MAINTAINED BY SOCIAL REINFORCEMENT. RESULTS SHOWED THAT VISUAL DISCRIMINATIVE CONTROL OF THE DIRECTION OF HEAD TURNING CAN BE ACHIEVED. (WY)

EJ 035 624 PS 500 974
EFFECT OF PRETRAINING AND INSTRUCTIONS ON AVOIDANCE CONDITIONING IN PRESCHOOL CHILDREN MOFFAT, GENE H.; MILLER, FRANK D., *JOURNAL OF EXPERIMENTAL CHILD PSYCHOLOGY*, V11 N1, PP133-138, FEB 71

EJ 035 625 PS 500 978
A THERAPEUTIC APPROACH TO SPEECH PHOBIA: ELECTIVE MUTISM REEXAMINED HALPERN, WERNER I.; AND OTHERS, *JOURNAL OF THE AMERICAN ACADEMY OF CHILD PSYCHIATRY*, V10 N1, PP94-107, JAN 71

THIS ARTICLE IS PRIMARILY A REVIEW OF THE LITERATURE ON ELECTIVE MUTISM (THE DISORDER MANIFEST IN A CHILD WHO SPEAKS ONLY TO A FEW SELECT INTIMATES, USUALLY PARENTS AND SIBLINGS). THE DISCUSSION THAT FOLLOWS STRUCTURES THE ROLE OF THE THERAPIST AND VARIOUS EFFECTIVE THERAPEUTIC TECHNIQUES. (AUTHOR/AJ)

EJ 035 626 PS 500 990
SEX-ROLE IDENTITY AND SIBLING COMPOSITION ROSENBERG, B. G.; SUTTON-SMITH, B., *JOURNAL OF GENETIC PSYCHOLOGY*, V118 N1, PP29-32, MAR 71

EXAMINES RESPONSES OF PARENTS AND CHILDREN IN TWO-CHILD FAMILIES (BOY-BOY, BOY-GIRL) TO THE GOUGH SCALE OF PSYCHOLOGICAL FEMINITY (89 FAMILIES). RESULTS INDICATE THAT SIBLING SEX STATUS IS A SIGNIFICANT SOURCE OF VARIANCE IN FATHER SEX-ROLE SCORES. (WY)

EJ 035 627 PS 500 993
BODY BUILD, SEX-ROLE PREFERENCE, AND SEX-ROLE ADOPTION IN JUNIOR HIGH SCHOOL BOYS BILLER, HENRY B.; LIEBMAN, DONALD A., *JOURNAL OF GENETIC PSYCHOLOGY*, V118 N1, PP81-86, MAR 71

EJ 035 628 PS 500 996
AN EXAMINATION OF FRUSTRATION AGGRESSION RELATIONS IN BOYS DURING MIDDLE CHILDHOOD COHEN, STEWART, *JOURNAL OF GENETIC PSYCHOLOGY*, V118 N1, PP129-140, MAR 71

EJ 035 662 PS 500 908
TEACHERS' RATINGS OF URBAN CHILDREN'S READING PERFORMANCE FLEMING, JAMES T., *CHILD STUDY JOURNAL*, V1 N2, PP80-99, WIN 70-71
MANY READING TEACHERS, PARTICULARLY THOSE WHOSE SPEECH DIFFERS CONSIDERABLY FROM THE CHILDREN THEY TEACH, CONFUSE NORMS OF SPEAKING AND READING PERFORMANCE VARIABLES. TEACHER'S ATTITUDES TOWARDS CHILDREN'S SPEECH INFLUENCE THEIR JUDGMENT OF CHILDREN'S READING. (NH)

EJ 035 663 PS 500 985
SIX SUCCESSFUL READING PROGRAMS FOR INNER-CITY SCHOOLS CRISCUOLO, NICHOLAS P., *CHILDHOOD EDUCATION*, V47 N7, PP371-372, APR 71
EMPHASIZES THE NEED FOR A STRONG PARTNERSHIP BETWEEN COMMUNITY AND SCHOOL IN DEVELOPING SUCCESSFUL READING PROGRAMS FOR INNER-CITY CHILDREN. (WY)

EJ 035 664 PS 501 001
SOME NOTES ON STRATEGY AND CONTENT FOR ELEMENTARY READING PROGRAMS IN THE '70'S HILTON, ERNEST, *ELEMENTARY SCHOOL JOURNAL*, V71 N7, PP384-390, APR 71
OUTLINES FIVE INCERNIBLE TRENDS IN THE TEACHING OF READING THAT WILL BECOME MAIN CURRENTS IN THE SEVENTIES. (WY)

EJ 035 710 PS 500 956
EXPERIMENTER BIAS IN PERFORMANCE OF CHILDREN AT A SIMPLE MOTOR TASK DUSEK, JEROME B., *DEVELOPMENTAL PSYCHOLOGY*, V4 N1, PP55-62, JAN 71

EJ 035 711 PS 500 989
SEX DIFFERENCES IN YIELDING TO TEMPTATION: A FUNCTION OF THE SITUATION KEASEY, CHARLES BLAKE, *JOURNAL OF GENETIC PSYCHOLOGY*, V118 N1, PP25-28, MAR 71

EJ 035 800 PS 500 913
THE EFFECTS OF FATHER ABSENCE ON CHILD DEVELOPMENT HETHERINGTON, E. MAVIS; DEUR, JAN L., *YOUNG CHILDREN*, V26 N4, PP233-248, MAR 71
THE AUTHORS BRING TOGETHER FINDINGS FROM RESEARCH DEALING WITH THE EFFECTS OF FATHER ABSENCE IN CHILDREN'S DEVELOPMENT. (WY)

EJ 035 801 PS 500 915
ADOPTION RESOURCES FOR BLACK CHILDREN GALLAGHER, URSULA M., *CHILDREN*, V18 N2, PP49-53, MAR-APR 71
THE GROWING NUMBER OF ADOPTIONS IN THIS COUNTRY, INCLUDING RACIALLY MIXED ADOPTIONS, ATTEST TO THE GENERAL ACCEPTANCE OF ADOPTION AS A WAY OF BRINGING LOVE TO CHILDREN IN NEED OF FAMILIES OF THEIR OWN AND THE SATISFACTIONS OF PARENTHOOD TO CHILDLESS COUPLES, SINGLE MEN AND WOMEN, AND FAMILIES WHO HAVE ROOM FOR ONE MORE. (AUTHOR/AJ)

EJ 035 802 PS 500 916
DAY CARE FOR CHILDREN: ASSETS AND LIABILITIES PRESCOTT, ELIZABETH; JONES, ELIZABETH, *CHILDREN*, V18 N2, PP54-58, MAR-APR 71
THESE TWO SPECIALISTS IN EARLY CHILDHOOD EDUCATION, ON THE BASIS OF EXTENSIVE RESEARCH, QUESTION THE ASSUMPTION THAT GROUP DAY CARE NECESSARILY WILL PROVIDE ALL OF THE EXPERIENCES A CHILD NEEDS. (AJ)

EJ 035 803 PS 500 918
THE USE OF DEVELOPMENTAL PLANS FOR MENTALLY RETARDED CHILDREN IN FOSTER FAMILY CARE MAMULA, RICHARD A., *CHILDREN*, V18 N2, PP65-68, MAR-APR 71
FOSTER MOTHERS OF CHILDREN PLACED IN FAMILY CARE FROM A STATE HOSPITAL FOR THE MENTALLY RETARDED WERE PROVIDED WITH INDIVIDUALIZED DEVELOPMENTAL PLANS WITH SPECIFIC TIME-RELATED OBJECTIVES. THE PROGRESS OF THE CHILDREN WAS MORE RAPID THAN THAT OF CONTROLS AND THE FOSTER MOTHERS INTEREST AND PRIDE IN BEING FAMILY CARETAKERS INCREASED. (AUTHOR/AJ)

EJ 035 804 PS 500 928
FATHER ABSENCE, PERCEIVED MATERNAL BEHAVIOR, AND MASCULINITY OF SELF-CONCEPT AMONG JUNIOR HIGH SCHOOL BOYS BILLER, HENRY B.; BAHM, ROBERT M., *DEVELOPMENTAL PSYCHOLOGY*, V4 N2, PP178-181, MAR 71

EJ 035 842 PS 500 912
GOING ON A TRIP BUSCHHOFF, LOTTE K., *YOUNG CHILDREN*, V26 N4, PP224-232, MAR 71
ACTUAL EXPERIENCE IS AN IMPORTANT PART OF A CHILD'S EARLY EDUCATION. OUTINGS (THOUGH NOT WITHOUT PROBLEMS) OFFER SENSORY EXCITEMENT AND ASSIST IN COMPLETION OF THE LEARNING CYCLE. (WY)

EJ 035 887 PS 500 997
THE RELATIONSHIP BETWEEN INTELLIGENCE AND PERFORMANCE ON THE STROOP COLOR-WORD TEST IN SECOND- AND FIFTH-GRADE CHILDREN FRIEDMAN, RONALD, *JOURNAL OF GENETIC PSYCHOLOGY*, V118 N1, PP147-148, MAR 71

EJ 035 912 PS 501 007
LANGUAGE DIALECT, REINFORCEMENT, AND THE INTELLIGENCE-TEST PERFORMANCE OF NEGRO CHILDREN QUAY, LORENE C., *CHILD DEVELOPMENT*, V42 N1, PP5-15, MAR 71
NO RELIABLE IQ DIFFERENCES WERE FOUND WHEN THE STANFORD-BINET WAS ADMINISTERED TO 100 4-YEAR-OLD NEGRO CHILDREN UNDER TWO CONDITIONS OF LANGUAGE (STANDARD ENGLISH AND NEGRO DIALECT) AND TWO CONDITIONS OF REINFORCEMENT (PRAISE AND CANDY). (AUTHOR/WY)

EJ 035 949 PS 501 042
WHEN IS SUBSIDIZED ADOPTION PREFERABLE TO LONG-TERM FOSTER CARE? ANDREWS, ROBERTA G., *CHILD WELFARE*, V50 N4, PP194-200, APR 71
PAPER WAS PRESENTED AT THE CWLA SOUTHWEST REGIONAL CONFERENCE AT FORT WORTH, TEXAS, 1970 (JE)

EJ 035 989 PS 501 011
AGE DIFFERENCES IN PLEASANTNESS OF VISUAL PATTERNS OF DIFFERENT VARIABILITY IN LATE CHILDHOOD AND ADOLESCENCE BALTES, PAUL B.; WENDER, KARL, *CHILD DEVELOPMENT*, V42 N1, PP47-55, MAR 71

EJ 035 990 PS 501 012
A DEVELOPMENTAL STUDY OF PRESCHOOL CHILDREN'S PREFERENCE FOR RANDOM FORMS BLACK, KATHRYN NORCROSS; AND OTHERS, *CHILD DEVELOPMENT*, V42 N1, PP57-61, MAR 71

EJ 035 991 PS 501 015
THE RELATION OF ROLE TAKING TO THE DEVELOPMENT OF MORAL JUDGMENT IN CHILDREN SELMAN, ROBERT L., *CHILD DEVELOPMENT*, V42 N1, PP79-91, MAR 71
REPORTS TWO STUDIES WHOSE PURPOSE WAS TO EXPLORE THE RELATIONSHIP IN MIDDLE CHILDHOOD OF THE CHILD'S ABILITY TO TAKE THE ROLE OF ANOTHER AND HIS ABILITY TO MAKE QUALITATIVELY HIGHER-LEVEL MORAL JUDGMENTS. (WY)

EJ 036 075 PS 501 008
CUMULATIVE EFFECTS OF CONTINUOUS STIMULATION ON AROUSAL LEVEL IN INFANTS BRACKBILL, YVONNE, *CHILD DEVELOPMENT*, V42 N1, PP17-26, MAR 71
THE RESULTS OF THIS EXPERIMENT INDICATE THAT CONTINUOUS STIMULATION HAS A MARKED PACIFYING EFFECT ON YOUNG INFANTS. (WY)

EJ 036 076 PS 501 014
IRRELEVANCE OF NEWBORN WAKING STATES TO SOME MOTOR AND APPETITIVE RESPONSES BELL, RICHARD Q.; HAAF, ROBERT A., *CHILD DEVELOPMENT*, V42 N1, PP69-77, MAR 71

EJ 036 077 PS 501 016
POWER AND THE INTERNALIZATION OF SELF-DENIAL GRUSEC, JOAN E., *CHILD DEVELOPMENT*, V42 N1, PP90-105, MAR 71

EJ 036 078 PS 501 017
CAN NEWBORNS SHOW CARDIAC ORIENTING? JACKSON, JAN C.; AND OTHERS, *CHILD DEVELOPMENT*, V42 N1, PP107-121, MAR 71

EJ 036 079 PS 501 019
GIRLS' ATTITUDES TOWARD MODELED BEHAVIORS AND THE CONTENT OF IMITATIVE PRIVATE PLAY HICKS, DAVID J., *CHILD DEVELOPMENT*, V42 N1, PP139-147, MAR 71

EJ 036 080 PS 501 021
CHILDREN'S "IMITATION" AS A FUNCTION OF THE PRESENCE OR ABSENCE OF A MODEL AND THE DESCRIPTION OF HIS INSTRUMENTAL BEHAVIORS MASTERS, JOHN C.; DRISCOLL, SALLY A., *CHILD DEVELOPMENT*, V42 N1, PP161-170, MAR 71

EJ 036 081 PS 501 028
THE BEHAVIOR OF TWINS: EFFECTS OF BIRTH WEIGHT AND BIRTH SEQUENCE MATHENY, ADAM P., JR.; BROWN, ANNE M., *CHILD DEVELOPMENT*, V42 N1, PP251-257, MAR 71

EJ 036 082 PS 501 035
EMOTIONAL REACTIONS OF YOUNG CHILDREN TO TV VIOLENCE OSBORN, D. K.; ENDSLEY, R. C., *CHILD DEVELOPMENT*, V42 N1, PP321-331, MAR 71

EJ 036 083 PS 501 039
A CASE AGAINST A CASE AGAINST BEHAVIORAL OBJECTIVES HERSH, RICHARD H.; COHEN, STUART J., *ELEMENTARY SCHOOL JOURNAL*, V71 N8, PP430-437, MAY 71
ARGUES THAT THE EFFORT TO CLEARLY DEFINE AND ASSESS OUR INSTRUCTIONAL GOALS IS NOT ONLY WORTH DOING, BUT WORTH DOING WELL. (WY)

EJ 036 091 PS 501 030
THE BEHAVIORAL AROUSAL THRESHOLD IN INFANT SLEEP AS A FUNCTION OF TIME AND SLEEP STATE SCHMIDT, KATALIN; BIRNS, BEVERLY, *CHILD DEVELOPMENT*, V42 N1, PP269-277, MAR 71

EJ 036 092 PS 501 034
INDIVIDUAL DIFFERENCES IN THE VISUAL PURSUIT BEHAVIOR OF NEONATES BARTEN, SYBIL; AND OTHERS, *CHILD DEVELOPMENT*, V42 N1, PP313-319, MAR 71

EJ 036 126 PS 501 013
FATHERS' VERBAL INTERACTION WITH INFANTS IN THE FIRST THREE MONTHS OF LIFE REBELSKY, FREDA; HANKS, CHERYL, *CHILD DEVELOPMENT*, V42 N1, PP63-68, MAR 71
THE DATA FROM THIS STUDY SHOWS THAT FATHERS SPEND LITTLE TIME VOCALIZING TO THEIR INFANTS AND THAT THE NUMBER OF INTERACTIONS VARIES BY TIME OF DAY, AGE AND SEX OF INFANT AND THE KIND OF ACTIVITY OCCURRING DURING THE INTERACTION. (AUTHOR/WY)

EJ 036 127 PS 501 032
DELAYED REINFORCEMENT AND VOCALIZATION RATES OF INFANTS RAMEY, CRAIG T.; OURTH, L. LYNN, *CHILD DEVELOPMENT*, V42 N1, PP291-297, MAR 71
RESULTS OF THIS STUDY INDICATE THAT LEARNING OCCURRED ONLY UNDER IMMEDIATE REINFORCEMENT AND THAT THERE WAS NO DEVELOPMENTAL TREND IN THE ABILITY TO WITHSTAND THE DETRIMENTAL EFFECTS OF DELAYED REINFORCEMENT. (WY)

EJ 036 210 PS 501 063
CHILD-REARING PRACTICES IN MOUNTAIN COUNTY, KENTUCKY HENRY, JIM G., *BUREAU OF SCHOOL SERVICE BULLETIN*, V43 N3, PP55-72, MAR 71

EJ 036 211 PS 501 064
LANGUAGE DEVELOPMENT OF DISADVANTAGED CHILDREN KODMAN, FRANK, JR., *BUREAU OF SCHOOL SERVICE BULLETIN*, V43 N3, PP73-80, MAR 71

EJ 036 327 PS 501 037
THE NEW SCHOOL PERRONE, VITO; STRANDBERG, WARREN, *ELEMENTARY SCHOOL JOURNAL*, V71 N8, PP409-422, MAY 71
DESCRIBLES THE ESTABLISHMENT OF A NEW KIND OF PREPARATION PROGRAM FOR BOTH PROSPECTIVE AND EXPERIENCED ELEMENTARY-SCHOOL TEACHERS, IN WHICH THE UNIVERSITY OF NORTH DAKOTA AND LOCAL COMMUNITIES SUPPORT A MORE INDIVIDUALIZED, PERSONALIZED LEARNING ENVIRONMENT FOR THE ELEMENTARY CLASSROOM. (WY)

EJ 036 328 PS 501 047
SEX EDUCATION FOR THE CHILD IN FOSTER CARE SANCTUARY, GERALD P., *CHILD WELFARE*, V50 N3, PP154-159, MAR 71
SEX EDUCATION FOR CHILDREN IN FOSTER CARE RAISES SPECIAL PROBLEMS IN PART BECAUSE THE BACKGROUND OF MOST YOUNGSTERS IN PLACEMENT USUALLY INCLUDES INSECURE RELATIONSHIPS WITH THE FAMILY ADULTS. ANOTHER SPECIAL RISK MAY LIE IN THE SEX ATTITUDES OF FOSTER PARENTS AND CHILD CARE WORKERS. ORIENTATION PROGRAMS FOR THEM ARE A FIRST STEP TOWARD SEX EDUCATION OF THE CHILDREN. (AUTHOR/WY)

EJ 036 329 PS 501 050
THE PLACE OF PRESCHOOL EDUCATION IN THE EDUCATIONAL SYSTEM PANANDIKAR, S., *NIE JOURNAL*, V5 N2, PP6-9, NOV 70
DISCUSSES THE PLACE OF PRESCHOOL EDUCATION IN INDIA'S EDUCATIONAL SYSTEM. (WY)

EJ 036 330 PS 501 051
DEVELOPMENT OF THE MONTESSORI METHOD JOOSTEN, A. M., *NIE JOURNAL*, V5 N2, PP10-17, NOV 70
INTENDED TO BRIEFLY SURVEY THE MONTESSORI METHOD AND DISPEL MISUNDERSTANDINGS ABOUT ITS PURPOSE AND USE. (WY)

EJ 036 331 PS 501 052
COMMUNITY PARTICIPATION IN PRESCHOOL EDUCATION--WHY AND HOW SWAMINATHAN, MINA, *NIE JOURNAL*, V5 N2, PP18-23, NOV 70
DESCRIBES SOME EXPERIMENTS IN COMMUNITY PARTICIPATION IN PRESCHOOL EDUCATION. VOLUNTEERS ATTEMPT TO ENCOURAGE PARENTS AND OTHERS IN THIS FORM OF SOCIAL ACTION. (WY)

EJ 036 332 PS 501 053
THE ROLE OF A LABORATORY NURSERY SCHOOL VERMA, AMITA, *NIE JOURNAL*, V5 N2, PP24-29, NOV 70
CITES ADVANTAGES TO BE GAINED BY ESTABLISHING MORE LABORATORY NURSERY SCHOOLS THROUGH OUT INDIA. (WY)

EJ 036 333 PS 501 054
PRESCHOOL EDUCATION, PARENTS AND THE COMMUNITY IN A DEVELOPING SOCIETY SWAMINATHAN, INDIRA, *NIE JOURNAL*, V5 N2, PP33-39, NOV 70
ENVISIONS THE TEACHER-EDUCATOR'S ROLE AS VITAL IN INVOLVING PARENTS AND COMMUNITY IN PRESCHOOL EDUCATION. (WY)

EJ 036 334 PS 501 055
THE PRESCHOOL IN RURAL INDIA KHALAKDINA, MARGARET, *NIE JOURNAL*, V5 N2, PP44-51, NOV 70
TEACHERS' ACUMEN AND IMAGINATION CAN SHAPE A SYLLABUS TO HELP INDIA'S RURAL PRESCHOOLER PREPARE FOR THE TECHNOLOGICAL ERA IN WHICH HE WILL BE AN ADULT. (WY)

EJ 036 335 PS 501 056
CLASSROOM PRACTICES IN PRE-BASIC SCHOOLS PANKAJAM, G., *NIE JOURNAL*, V5 N2, PP52-56, NOV 70
LINKS GANDHI'S IDEAS OF EDUCATION TO THE SYSTEM OF EDUCATION DEEMED MOST SUITABLE FOR RURAL INDIA. (WY)

EJ 036 336 PS 501 058
EDUCATION OF TEACHERS FOR NURSERY SCHOOLS: A CREATIVE APPROACH SAHGAL, S. P., *NIE JOURNAL*, V5 N2, PP61-64, NOV 70
REPORTS THE PAINFUL PARADOX THAT THE PRESCHOOL YEARS IN A CHILD'S LIFE ARE HIS MOST FORMATIVE AND VITAL AND HIS TEACHERS ARE AMONG THE LEAST SUITABLE IN INDIA. THE ARTICLE SUGGESTS A TWO-YEAR TRAINING PROGRAM TO HELP RESOLVE THE DILEMMA. (WY)

EJ 036 337 PS 501 059
TOWARDS AN INDIAN PHILOSOPHY OF PRIMARY EDUCATION SINGH, R. P., *NIE JOURNAL*, V5 N2, PP65-70, NOV 70

EJ 036 395 PS 501 065
EXPERIMENTAL PRESCHOOL INTERVENTION IN THE APPALACHIAN HOME WILLIAMSON, JACK, *BUREAU OF SCHOOL SERVICE BULLETIN*, V43 N3, PP81-92, MAR 71

EJ 036 580 PS 501 043
THE ADMINISTRATION OF "SELECTIVITY" IN THE BREAKFAST PROGRAM OF A PUBLIC ELEMENTARY SCHOOL HOSHINO, GEORGE; RUTH, MARY K., *CHILD WELFARE*, V50 N4, PP201-207, APR 71
IN THE DISTRIBUTION OF BENEFITS UNDER A SOCIAL WELFARE PROGRAM, THE FRAME OF REFERENCE IS EXTREMELY IMPORTANT AS A GUIDE TO SOCIAL POLICY. THE SCHOOL BREAKFAST PROGRAM DISCUSSED HERE IS ANALYZED ON THE BASIS OF TWO CONCEPTS--AND THE EXAMINATION POINTS UP SOME BASIC PROBLEMS. (WY)

EJ 036 581 PS 501 062
HEAD START: A HEAD START TO HEALTH? LEIGH, TERRENCE M., *BUREAU OF SCHOOL SERVICE BULLETIN*, V43 N3, PP32-54, MAR 71
PROVIDES A MODEL FOR COMPARING THE HEALTH SERVICES COMPONENT OF HEAD START PROGRAMS. (WY)

EJ 036 745 PS 501 027
THE ACQUISITION OF DIRECT AND INDIRECT OBJECTS IN JAPANESE MCNEILL, DAVID; AND OTHERS, *CHILD DEVELOPMENT*, V42 N1, PP237-249, MAR 71

EJ 036 746 PS 501 029
INTERVENTION STRATEGIES FOR SPANISH-SPEAKING PRESCHOOL CHILDREN NEDLER, SHARI; SEBERA, PEGGY, *CHILD DEVELOPMENT*, V42 N1, PP259-267, MAR 71
COMPARES THREE STRATEGIES OF EARLY INTERVENTION DESIGNED TO INCREASE THE LANGUAGE AND COMMUNICATION SKILLS OF DISADVANTAGED 3-YEAR-OLD MEXICAN-AMERICAN CHILDREN. (WY)

EJ 036 747 PS 501 031
PROCESSING OF PHONOLOGICAL SEQUENCES BY YOUNG CHILDREN AND ADULTS MOREHEAD, DONALD M., *CHILD DEVELOPMENT*, V42 N1, PP279-289, MAR 71

EJ 036 748 PS 501 033
STORY RECALL IN KINDERGARTEN CHILDREN: EFFECT OF METHOD OF PRESENTATION ON PSYCHOLINGUISTIC PERFORMANCE BLANK, MARION; FRANK, SHELDON M., *CHILD DEVELOPMENT*, V42 N1, PP299-312, MAR 71

EJ 036 818 PS 501 009
AN EXPERIMENTAL STUDY OF BASIC LEARNING ABILITY AND INTELLIGENCE IN LOW-SOCIOECONOMIC-STATUS CHILDREN GUINAGH, BARRY J., *CHILD DEVELOPMENT*, V42 N1, PP27-36, MAR 71

EJ 036 819 PS 501 010
SOCIAL-CLASS DIFFERENTIATION IN COGNITIVE DEVELOPMENT AMONG BLACK PRESCHOOL CHILDREN GOLDEN, MARK; AND OTHERS, *CHILD DEVELOPMENT*, V42 N1, PP37-45, MAR 71

EJ 036 820 PS 501 018
COGNITIVE DEVELOPMENT AND CHILDREN'S COMPREHENSION OF HUMOR MCGHEE, PAUL E., *CHILD DEVELOPMENT*, V42 N1, PP123-138, MAR 71
LEVEL OF COGNITIVE DEVELOPMENT WAS NOT SIGNIFICANTLY RELATED TO HUMOR APPRECIATION FOR EITHER NOVELTY OR INCONGRUITY HUMOR IN 30 BOYS AT EACH OF THREE AGE LEVELS: 5, 7, AND 9. (WY)

EJ 036 821 PS 501 020
THE LEARNING AND TRANSFER OF DOUBLE-CLASSIFICATION SKILLS BY FIRST GRADERS JACOBS, PAUL I.; VANDEVENTER, MARY, *CHILD DEVELOPMENT*, V42 N1, PP149-159, MAR 71
BRIEF TRAINING SESSIONS CAN IMPROVE FIRST-GRADERS' PERFORMANCE ON DOUBLE-CLASSIFICATION PROBLEMS. QUESTIONS ARE RAISED ABOUT WHETHER OR NOT THE BASIC INTELLECTUAL ABILITY UNDERLYING PERFORMANCE HAS ALSO BEEN INCREASED. (WY)

EJ 036 822 PS 501 023
EFFECTS OF STIMULUS AVAILABILITY ON CHILDREN'S INFERENCES SCHOLNICK, ELLIN KOFSKY, *CHILD DEVELOPMENT*, V42 N1, PP183-194, MAR 71

EJ 036 823 PS 501 025
CONDITIONAL DISCRIMINATION LEARNING IN CHILDREN: TWO RELEVANT FACTORS DOAN, HELEN MCK.; COOPER, DEBORAH L., *CHILD DEVELOPMENT*, V42 N1, PP209-220, MAR 71

EJ 036 824 PS 501 026
CHILDREN'S UNDERSTANDING OF PROBABILITY CONCEPTS HOEMANN, HARRY W.; ROSS, BRUCE M., *CHILD DEVELOPMENT*, V42 N1, PP221-236, MAR 71

EJ 036 825 PS 501 036
DEVELOPMENTAL SHIFTS IN VERBAL RECALL BETWEEN MENTAL AGES TWO AND FIVE ROSSI, SHEILA; WITTROCK, M. C., *CHILD DEVELOPMENT*, V42 N1, PP333-338, MAR 71

EJ 036 826 PS 501 041
EVALUATION UNDER INDIVIDUALIZED INSTRUCTION WANG, MARGARET C.; YEAGER, JOHN L., *ELEMENTARY SCHOOL JOURNAL*, V71 N8, PP448-452, MAY 71

EJ 036 827 PS 501 057
A PERSPECTIVE ON COGNITIVE DEVELOPMENT: THE PRESCHOOL CHILD'S PERFORMANCE IN CLASSIFICATION TASKS ANANDALAKSHMY, S., *NIE JOURNAL*, V5 N2, PP57-60, NOV 70
SUGGESTS THAT CATEGORIZATION TASKS BE INCLUDED IN INDIA'S PRESCHOOL PROGRAMS. (WY)

EJ 037 021 PS 501 061
THE KINDERGARTEN AGAINST APPALACHIAN POVERTY STREET, PAUL, *BUREAU OF SCHOOL SERVICE BULLETIN*, V43 N3, PP19-31, MAR 71
GRADUATES OF COMPENSATORY EARLY CHILDHOOD PROGRAMS IN KNOX COUNTY, KENTUCKY DEMONSTRATED FEW DIFFERENCES WHEN COMPARED WITH MATCHED SUBJECTS IN FIRST GRADE. (WY)

EJ 037 066 PS 501 022
SPATIAL ABILITIES AND SPATIAL EGOCENTRISM IN THE YOUNG CHILD SHANTZ, CAROLYN U.; WATSON, JOHN S., *CHILD DEVELOPMENT*, V42 N1, PP171-181, MAR 71

EJ 037 099 PS 501 040
THE DEVELOPMENT OF PRE-READING SKILLS IN AN EXPERIMENTAL KINDERGARTEN PROGRAM STANCHFIELD, JO M., *ELEMENTARY SCHOOL JOURNAL*, V71 N8, PP438-447, MAY 71
KINDERGARTEN CHILDREN WHO WERE TAUGHT IN A STRUCTURED, SEQUENTIAL PROGRAM ACHIEVED SIGNIFICANTLY MORE THAN KINDERGARTEN CHILDREN TAUGHT THE REGULAR CURRICULUM. (WY)

EJ 037 183 PS 501 044
INTERPERSONAL RELATIONSHIPS IN RESIDENTIAL TREATMENT CENTERS FOR DISTURBED CHILDREN ADLER, JACK, *CHILD WELFARE*, V50 N4, PP208-217, APR 71
THE THERAPEUTIC EFFECTIVENESS OF A RESIDENTIAL TREATMENT CENTER FOR DISTURBED CHILDREN IS LARGELY DEPENDENT ON THE RELATIONSHIPS WITHIN AND AMONG THE GROUPS INVOLVED--CHILDREN, STAFF, AND ADMINISTRATION. SOLUTION OF THE PROBLEMS THAT ARISE DEMANDS KNOWLEDGE, AWARENESS, SKILL, AND COOPERATION. (AUTHOR/WY)

EJ 037 184 PS 501 046
CHILDREN'S ENVIRONMENTS AND CHILD WELFARE MAAS, HENRY S., *CHILD WELFARE*, V50 N3, PP132-142, MAR 71
RELATIONSHIPS BETWEEN ENVIRONMENTS AND CHILDREN IN CARE HAVE DEEP AND IMPORTANT IMPLICATIONS FOR CHILD WELFARE PRACTICE AND POLICY. WITHIN ECOLOGICAL AND SOCIAL INTERACTIONAL FRAMEWORKS, PREVENTIVE PROGRAMS ARE PROPOSED. (AUTHOR/WY)

EJ 037 235 PS 501 038
TEACHERS IN CHILDREN'S ROLES? RUST, VAL, *ELEMENTARY SCHOOL JOURNAL*, V71 N8, PP423-429, MAY 71
IF OUR SCHOOLS ARE TO BECOME SOCIALLY FUNCTIONAL, IT IS IMPERATIVE THAT WE ADDRESS OURSELVES TO THE BASIC THEME THAT TEACHING MUST BE IN HARMONY WITH CHILDLIKE PERCEPTIONS AND BIASES. (AUTHOR/WY)

EJ 037 236 PS 501 045
FAMILY TREATMENT WITHIN THE MILIEU OF A RESIDENTIAL TREATMENT CENTER KEMP, CLAIRE JACKSON, *CHILD WELFARE*, V50 N4, PP229-235, APR 71
THIS PAPER DESCRIBES A PROCESS OF INVOLVING THE FAMILY IN A RESIDENTIAL TREATMENT CENTER PROGRAM, A TREATMENT MODALITY TO WHICH THE WISCONSIN CHILDREN'S TREATMENT CENTER HAS BECOME COMMITTED. (AUTHOR/WY)

EJ 037 237 PS 501 048
DAY CARE IN THE 1970S: PLANNING FOR EXPANSION PIERCE, WILLIAM L., *CHILD WELFARE*, V50 N3, PP160-163, MAR 71
A COMBINATION OF MANY FACTORS INDICATES THAT DURING THIS DECADE THE NUMBER OF CHILDREN REQUIRING DAY CARE WILL INCREASE ENORMOUSLY. PLANNING THE EXPANSION OF DAY CARE SERVICES TO MEET THIS NEED INVOLVES PUBLIC POLICY DECISIONS ON SEVERAL FRONTS--WELFARE, MANPOWER, EDUCATION--WITH POSSIBILITIES OF GREAT BENEFIT OR LOSS TO SOCIETY. (AUTHOR/WY)

EJ 037 238 PS 501 049
HELPING FOSTER PARENTS UNDERSTAND DISTURBED CHILDREN THOMAS, CAROLYN B., *CHILD WELFARE*, V50 N3, PP168-175, MAR 71

EJ 037 283 PS 501 060
SUFFER THE LITTLE KENTUCKY FIRST-GRADERS STREET, PAUL; LEIGH, TERRENCE M., *BUREAU OF SCHOOL SERVICE BULLETIN*, V43 N3, PP5-18, MAR 71
THIS FOLLOW-UP STUDY REPORTS THE FAILURE-PROMOTION EXPERIENCE OF KENTUCKY FIRST-GRADERS OF 1968-69 AND RELATES THEIR ACADEMIC SUCCESS OR FAILURE TO THEIR AGES OF ENTERING FIRST GRADE. THE RATE OF FIRST GRADE REPEATERS IN KENTUCKY IS DISAPPOINTINGLY HIGH AND A YOUNGSTER WHO ATTEMPTS FIRST GRADE TWICE IS NOT SUBSTANTIALLY BETTER OFF THAN HE WAS THE FIRST TIME. (WY)

EJ 037 318 PS 501 024
THE INFLUENCE OF MASCULINE, FEMININE, AND NEUTRAL TASKS ON CHILDREN'S ACHIEVEMENT BEHAVIOR, EXPECTANCIES OF SUCCESS, AND ATTAINMENT VALUES STEIN, ALETHA HUSTON; AND OTHERS, *CHILD DEVELOPMENT*, V42 N1, PP195-207, MAR 71

EJ 037 342 PS 501 077
INFANTS' RECOGNITION MEMORY FOR A SERIES OF VISUAL STIMULI FAGAN, JOSEPH F., III, *JOURNAL OF EXPERIMENTAL CHILD PSYCHOLOGY*, V11 N2, PP244-250, APR 71

EJ 037 426 PS 501 090
UNDERSTANDING ONE ANOTHER: UNESCO'S ASSOCIATED SCHOOLS PROJECT BIZOT, JUDITHE, *CHILDHOOD EDUCATION*, V47 N8, PP429-433, MAY 71
DESCRIBES CURRICULUM, METHODS AND MATERIALS USED IN THIS UNIQUE INTERNATIONAL ATTEMPT TO PROMOTE IDENTIFICATION OF CHILDREN WITH MANKIND AS A WHOLE, WHILE RESPECTING DIVERSITY OF CULTURES. (NH)

EJ 037 493 PS 501 069
COGNITIVE DEVELOPMENT IN INFANCY: ASSESSMENT, ACCELERATION, AND ACTUALIZATION STARR, RAYMOND H., JR., *MERRILL-PALMER QUARTERLY OF BEHAVIOR AND DEVELOPMENT*, V17 N2, PP153-186, APR 71
PAPER PRESENTED AT THE MERRILL-PALMER CONFERENCE ON RESEARCH AND TEACHING OF INFANT DEVELOPMENT, FEBRUARY 13-15, 1970. (JE)

EJ 037 494 PS 501 076
THE MEASUREMENT OF VISUAL ATTENTION IN INFANTS: A COMPARISON OF TWO METHODOLOGIES GREENBERG, DAVID J.; WEIZMANN, FREDRIC, *JOURNAL OF EXPERIMENTAL CHILD PSYCHOLOGY*, V11 N2, PP234-243, APR 71

EJ 037 495 PS 501 081
CHILDREN'S ACQUISITION AND REVERSAL BEHAVIOR IN A PROBABILITY LEARNING SITUATION AS A FUNCTION OF PROGRAMMED INSTRUCTION, INTERNAL-EXTERNAL CONTROL, AND SCHEDULES OF REINFORCEMENT KELLER, HAROLD R., *JOURNAL OF EXPERIMENTAL CHILD PSYCHOLOGY*, V11 N2, PP281-295, APR 71

EJ 037 516 PS 501 070
DEVELOPMENTAL GENETICS OF BEHAVIORAL CAPACITIES: THE NATURE-NURTURE PROBLEM RE-EVALUATED GINSBURG, BENSON E., *MERRILL-PALMER QUARTERLY OF BEHAVIOR AND DEVELOPMENT*, V17 N2, PP187-202, APR 71
PAPER PRESENTED AT THE MERRILL-PALMER CONFERENCE ON RESEARCH AND TEACHING OF INFANT DEVELOPMENT, FEBRUARY 13-15, 1970. (JE)

EJ 037 517 PS 501 075
EFFECT OF CORRELATED VISUAL AND TACTUAL FEEDBACK ON AUDITORY PATTERN LEARNING AT DIFFERENT AGE LEVELS WOHLWILL, JOACHIM F., *JOURNAL OF EXPERIMENTAL CHILD PSYCHOLOGY*, V11 N2, PP213-228, APR 71

EJ 037 534 PS 501 073
DEVELOPMENTAL GENERALITY OF A FORM RECOGNITION STRATEGY OWEN, DEAN H., *JOURNAL OF EXPERIMENTAL CHILD PSYCHOLOGY*, V11 N2, PP194-205, APR 71
COMPARISONS OF THE REGRESSION PROFILE AND CORRELATIONS OF PHYSICAL MEASURES WITH LATENCY FOR A 5-YEAR-OLD SUBJECT (WHO PERFORMED 1250 TRIALS IN A FORM RECOGNITION TASK) WITH THOSE FOR A GROUP OF 25 ADULTS INDICATED THAT USE OF FORM INFORMATION WAS HIGHLY CONSISTENT ACROSS AGE LEVELS. (AUTHOR/WY)

EJ 037 535 PS 501 079
EFFECT OF INCENTIVES AND AGE ON THE VISUAL RECOGNITION OF RETARDED READERS GOYEN, JUDITH D.; LYLE, J. G., *JOURNAL OF EXPERIMENTAL CHILD PSYCHOLOGY*, V11 N2, PP266-273, APR 71
INCENTIVES PRODUCED NO DISCERNIBLE EFFECT UPON THE PERFORMANCE OF EITHER OF TWO TREATMENT GROUPS. THE DATA WERE ALSO ANALYZED FOR LATENCY OF RESPONSE, PRACTICE EFFECTS AND REVERSAL ERRORS, NONE OF WHICH WAS RELATED TO READING RETARDATION. (WY)

EJ 037 577 PS 501 091
MEDICAL GENETICS AND ADOPTION SCHULTZ, AMELIA L.; MOTULSKY, ARNO G., *CHILD WELFARE*, V50 N1, PP4-17, JAN 71
DISCUSSES BASIC CONCEPTS IN HUMAN AND MEDICAL GENETICS AND THEIR RELEVANCE TO THE FIELD OF ADOPTION. DESCRIBES GENETIC COUNSELING AND SUGGESTS THAT ADOPTION AGENCIES USE SUCH SERVICES. (AUTHOR)

EJ 037 578 PS 501 097
ETHICAL ISSUES IN RESEARCH IN EARLY CHILDHOOD INTERVENTION GRAY, SUSAN W., *CHILDREN*, V18 N3, PP83-89, MAY-JUN 71

EJ 037 635 PS 501 098
THINKING SKILLS AS A GOAL IN AN AFTER-SCHOOL PROGRAM SUNLEY, ROBERT, *CHILDREN*, V18 N3, PP90-94, MAY-JUN 71
FIVE-TO NINE-YEAR-OLDS ENGAGE IN AN AFTER SCHOOL PROGRAM DESIGNED TO DEVELOP THEIR COGNITIVE SKILLS. (AJ)

EJ 037 736 PS 501 085
THE WORLD HOUSE: BUILDING A QUALITATIVE ENVIRONMENT FOR ALL THE WORLD'S CHILDREN MIEL, ALICE, *CHILDHOOD EDUCATION*, V47 N8, PP402-405, MAY 71
DISCUSSES FIVE BASIC CHARACTERISTICS OF SCHOOLING PLANNED TO PRODUCE A QUALITATIVE ENVIRONMENT. (NH)

EJ 037 737 PS 501 086
SWEDISH PRESCHOOLS: ENVIRONMENTS OF SENSITIVITY PASSANTINO, RICHARD J., *CHILDHOOD EDUCATION*, V47 N8, PP406-411, MAY 71
SWEDISH PRESCHOOL PROGRAMS EVIDENCE RESPECT FOR THE ABILITY OF THE CHILD AND A SENSE THAT EVERY ASPECT OF DAILY LIFE HAS ITS LEARNING AS WELL AS ESTHETIC VALUE. (NH)

EJ 037 738 PS 501 087
LETTERS FROM ENGLAND HAPGOOD, MARILYN, *CHILDHOOD EDUCATION*, V47 N8, PP412-417, MAY 71
A VIEW OF OPEN EDUCATION IS GIVEN IN THIS ANECDOTAL REPORT OF VISITS TO PRIMARY SCHOOLS IN ENGLAND. (NH)

EJ 038 021 PS 501 099
SOME THOUGHTS ON PLANNING HEALTH CARE FOR CHILDREN AND YOUTH WALLACE, HELEN M., *CHILDREN*, V18 N3, PP95-100, MAY-JUN 71
DISCUSSES EXISTING CHILD AND MATERNAL HEALTH CARE SERVICES, THE GROWING NEED FOR NEW PROJECTS AND MANPOWER, AND THE COSTS OF SUCH PROGRAMS. (AJ)

EJ 038 022 PS 501 103
THE USE OF STIMULANT DRUGS IN TREATING HYPERACTIVE CHILDREN , *CHILDREN*, V18 N3, PP111, MAY-JUN 71

EJ 038 170 PS 501 082
THE GROWTH OF CHILDREN'S SEMANTIC MEMORY: SEMANTIC ELEMENTS SCHAEFFER, BENSON; AND OTHERS, *JOURNAL OF EXPERIMENTAL CHILD PSYCHOLOGY*, V11 N2, PP296-309, APR 71
SUPPORTS THE POSITION THAT CHILDREN LEARN SUPERORDINATE ELEMENTS LATER THAN SUBORDINATE ONES. (WY)

EJ 038 171 PS 501 084
THE EFFECTS OF SOCIAL ISOLATION AND CHARACTERISTICS OF THE MODEL ON ACCENT IMITATION IN FOURTH-GRADE CHILDREN HANLON, CAMILLE C., *CONTEMPORARY EDUCATION*, V42 N5, PP322-336, APR 71

EJ 038 262 PS 501 068
COGNITIVE-PERCEPTUAL DEVELOPMENT IN INFANCY: SETTING FOR THE SEVENTIES WATSON, JOHN S., *MERRILL-PALMER QUARTERLY OF BEHAVIOR AND DEVELOPMENT*, V17 N2, PP139-152, APR 71
PAPER PRESENTED AT THE MERRILL-PALMER CONFERENCE ON RESEARCH AND TEACHING OF INFANT DEVELOPMENT, FEBRUARY 13-15, 1970. (JE)

EJ 038 263 PS 501 071
A NONARBITRARY BEHAVIORAL CRITERION FOR CONSERVATION OF ILLUSION-DISTORTED LENGTH IN FIVE-YEAR-OLDS KING, WILLIAM L., *JOURNAL OF EXPERIMENTAL CHILD PSYCHOLOGY*, V11 N2, PP171-181, APR 71

EJ 038 264 PS 501 072
DEVELOPMENT OF THE OBJECT CONCEPT AS MANIFESTED IN CHANGES IN THE TRACKING BEHAVIOR OF INFANTS BETWEEN 7 AND 20 WEEKS OF AGE BOWER, T. G. R.; AND OTHERS, *JOURNAL OF EXPERIMENTAL CHILD PSYCHOLOGY*, V11 N2, PP182-193, APR 71
THE TRACKING BEHAVIOR OF INFANTS UP TO 5 MONTHS OF AGE WAS STUDIED USING LINEAR AND CIRCULAR TRAJECTORIES, WITH PARTIAL OCCLUSION OF THE TRAJECTORIES. RESULTS INDICATE THAT IT IS NOT UNTIL THE AGE OF ABOUT 16 WEEKS THAT INFANTS CAN BE SAID TO BE TRACKING A MOVING OBJECT AS AN OBJECT. (AUTHOR/WY)

EJ 038 265 PS 501 074
DECISION PROCESSES IN MULTIDIMENSIONAL GENERALIZATION CROLL, WILLIAM L., *JOURNAL OF EXPERIMENTAL CHILD PSYCHOLOGY*, V11 N2, PP206-212, APR 71

EJ 038 266 PS 501 080
EFFECT OF INCENTIVES UPON RETARDED AND NORMAL READERS ON A VISUAL-ASSOCIATE LEARNING TASK GOYEN, JUDITH D.; LYLE, J. G., *JOURNAL OF EXPERIMENTAL CHILD PSYCHOLOGY*, V11 N2, PP274-280, APR 71
REPORTS THAT INCENTIVES HAD AN INCREMENTAL EFFECT UPON LEARNING, THAT INCENTIVES WERE EQUALLY EFFECTIVE FOR BOTH RETARDED AND NORMAL READERS, AND THAT THE PERFORMANCE OF THE RETARDED AND NORMAL READERS DID NOT DIFFER SIGNIFICANTLY. (AUTHOR/WY)

EJ 038 267 PS 501 083
REINFORCER EFFECTI MASSARI, DAVID J., *JOURNAL OF EXPERIMENTAL CHILD PSYCHOLOGY*, V11 N2, APR 71

EJ 038 393 PS 501 089
HUMAN RESOURCES FOR INTERNATIONAL STUDIES PLOGHOFT, MILTON E.; GERHARDT, FRANK, *CHILDHOOD EDUCATION*, V47 N8, PP424-426, MAY 71
URGES GREATER INVOLVEMENT OF INTERNATIONAL STUDENTS AND PROFESSORS IN SOCIAL SCIENCE EDUCATION. (MS)

EJ 038 394 PS 501 101
PSYCHOLOGICAL CONSULTATION IN A PRESCHOOL BALTER, LAWRENCE, *CHILDREN*, V18 N3, PP105-108, MAY-JUN 71
DISCUSSES THE ROLE OF THE PSYCHOLOGICAL CONSULTANT IN NURSERY SCHOOLS FOR DISADVANTAGED CHILDREN AS IT DIFFERS FROM THE SERVICE PROVIDED FOR MORE ECONOMICALLY ADVANTAGED CHILDREN. SPECIAL ATTENTION IS FOCUSED ON STAFF TENSIONS AND STAFF-PARENT RELATIONSHIPS. (AJ)

EJ 038 407 PS 501 088
THE DAYS THAT MAKE US HAPPY: GAMES AROUND THE WORLD MCWHIRTER, MARY ESTHER, *CHILDHOOD EDUCATION*, V47 N8, PP418-423, MAY 71
SPECIFIC GAMES ARE DESCRIBED WHICH MAY CONTRIBUTE TO A PROGRAM OF EDUCATION FOR PEACE, BY DEEPENING CHILDREN'S INSIGHTS AND FEELINGS OF AFFINITY TO PEOPLE OF OTHER COUNTRIES. (NH)

EJ 038 454 PS 501 066
A DECADE OF INFANT CONDITIONING AND LEARNING RESEARCH FITZGERALD, HIRAM E.; PORGES, STEPHEN W., *MERRILL-PALMER QUARTERLY OF BEHAVIOR AND DEVELOPMENT*, V17 N2, PP79-117, APR 71
SUMMARIZES RESEARCH PROJECTS ON INFANT BEHAVIOR CONDUCTED DURING THE 1960'S AND INCLUDES AN EXTENSIVE LIST OF REFERENCES. (AJ)

EJ 038 455 PS 501 078
GENERALIZED IMITATION AS A FUNCTION OF DISCRIMINATION DIFFICULTY AND CHOICE STEINMAN, WARREN M.; BOYCE, KATHLEEN D., *JOURNAL OF EXPERIMENTAL CHILD PSYCHOLOGY*, V11 N2, PP251-265, APR 71
RESULTS OF THIS STUDY INVOLVING FOUR KINDERGARTEN GIRLS SUGGEST THAT GENERALIZED IMITATION MAY BE A FUNCTION OF THE METHODS USED AND IS NOT NECESSARILY RELATED TO A FAILURE TO DISCRIMINATE RESPONSE CONTINGENCIES. (MS)

EJ 038 471 PS 501 102
DEMOCRATIZATION OF EDUCATIONAL OPPORTUNITY. AN ESSAY REVIEW GORDON, EDMUND W., *CHILDREN*, V18 N3, PP109-110, MAY-JUN 71

EJ 038 531 PS 501 100
RESEARCH FOR SERVICE TO SEVERELY RETARDED CHILDREN ARNOLD, IRENE L.; BUDNER, STANLEY, *CHILDREN*, V18 N3, PP101-104, MAY-JUN 71
BASED ON A PAPER PRESENTED AT THE ANNUAL CONVENTION OF THE AMERICAN ASSOCIATION ON MENTAL DEFICIENCY, WASHINGTON, D.C., MAY 1970. (JE)

EJ 038 570 PS 501 067
ORIGINS OF SOCIAL DEVELOPMENT IN INFANCY FERGUSON, LUCY RAU, *MERRILL-PALMER QUARTERLY OF BEHAVIOR AND DEVELOPMENT*, V17 N2, PP119-137, APR 71
PAPER PRESENTED AT THE MERRILL-PALMER CONFERENCE ON RESEARCH AND TEACHING OF INFANT DEVELOPMENT, FEBRUARY 13-15, 1970. (JE)

EJ 038 571 PS 501 092
TRENDS AND DILEMMAS IN CHILD WELFARE RESEARCH NEEL, ANN F., *CHILD WELFARE*, V50 N1, PP25-32, JAN 71

EJ 038 643 PS 501 093
UNIONS AND DAY CARE CENTERS FOR THE CHILDREN OF WORKING MOTHERS MILLER, JOYCE D., *CHILD WELFARE*, V50 N1, PP38-39, JAN 71
REPORTS INVOLVEMENT OF THE AMALGAMATED CLOTHING WORKERS OF AMERICA IN ESTABLISHING A PILOT DAY CARE CENTER FOR WORKERS' CHILDREN. PARENT EDUCATION AND CENTER PROGRAM ARE DESCRIBED. (NH)

EJ 038 730 PS 501 104
FATHER AVAILABILITY AND ACADEMIC PERFORMANCE AMONG THIRD-GRADE BOYS BLANCHARD, ROBERT W.; BILLER, HENRY B., *DEVELOPMENTAL PSYCHOLOGY*, V4 N3, PP301-305, MAY 71
ACADEMIC PERFORMANCE OF BOYS IN A HIGH FATHER-PRESENT (MORE THAN 2 HOURS PER DAY) GROUP WAS FOUND TO BE VERY SUPERIOR TO THAT OF BOYS IN EARLY FATHER-ABSENT (BEFORE AGE 5), LATE FATHER-ABSENT (AFTER AGE 5), AND LOW FATHER-PRESENT (LESS THAN 6 HOURS PER WEEK) GROUPS. (NH)

EJ 038 792 PS 501 142
ATTITUDE OF BLACK NATURAL PARENTS REGARDING ADOPTION SHARRAR, MARY LOU, *CHILD WELFARE*, V50 N5, PP286-289, MAY 71
MEETINGS BETWEEN BLACK UNWED EXPECTANT SCHOOLGIRLS AND BLACK AND WHITE ADOPTIVE PARENTS AND SOCIAL WORKERS ARE DISCUSSED. (NH)

EJ 038 853 PS 501 108
SHIFTS IN CHILD-REARING ATTITUDES LINKED WITH PARENTHOOD AND OCCUPATION HURLEY, JOHN R.; HOHN, ROBERT L., *DEVELOPMENTAL PSYCHOLOGY*, V4 N3, PP324-328, MAY 71
CHILD-REARING ATTITUDE MEASURES WERE ADMINISTERED TO UNDERGRADUATE STUDENTS AND 6 YEARS LATER TO 63 PERCENT (N75) OF THE ORIGINAL SAMPLE. GENERAL SHIFTS TOWARD INCREASED MANIFEST REJECTION (ESPECIALLY FOR PARENTS WHO WERE MORE PROLIFIC) AND DECREASED OVERPROTECTION OCCURRED, BUT PRESSURE FOR ACHIEVEMENT REMAINED THE SAME. (NH)

EJ 038 854 PS 501 119
FATHER ABSENCE AND CONSCIENCE DEVELOPMENT HOFFMAN, MARTIN L., *DEVELOPMENTAL PSYCHOLOGY*, V4 N3, PP400-406, MAY 71
FATHER-ABSENT AND FATHER-PRESENT SEVETH GRADERS WERE COMPARED ON MORAL ATTRIBUTES AND OVERT AGGRESSION. SOME EVIDENCE SUGGESTS THAT SOME BUT NOT ALL OF THE EFFECTS OF FATHER ABSENCE ARE ATTRIBUTABLE TO THE LACK OF A PATERNAL MODEL. EFFECTS MAY BE MEDIATED IN PART BY CHANGES IN THE MOTHER'S CHILD-REARING PATTERN. (NH)

EJ 038 855 PS 501 133
A FACTOR ANALYSIS OF FIFTH AND SIXTH GRADERS' REPORTS OF PARENTAL CHILD-REARING BEHAVIOR BURGER, GARY K.; ARMENTROUT, JAMES A., *DEVELOPMENTAL PSYCHOLOGY*, V4 N3, PP483, MAY 71

EJ 038 906 PS 501 145
WHY NOT FEELINGS AND VALUES IN INSTRUCTIONAL TELEVISION? MUKERJI, ROSE, *YOUNG CHILDREN*, V26 N5, PP273-281, MAY 71
TELEVISION FOR CHILDREN CAN HELP THEM BROADEN THEIR EXPERIENCES, DEVELOP VALUES AND UNDERSTAND MORE ABOUT HUMAN FEELINGS. AN EXAMPLE OF THIS TYPE OF EDUCATIONAL TELEVISION IS "RIPPLES," A SERIES OF 15-MINUTE COLOR PROGRAMS FOR IN-SCHOOL VIEWING BY CHILDREN IN KINDERGARTEN AND EARLY PRIMARY GRADES. (AJ)

EJ 038 907 PS 501 147
AUDIO-VISUAL MATERIALS IN EARLY CHILDHOOD EDUCATION HENDRICKSON, NOREJANE; WILLIAMS, BRUCE M., *YOUNG CHILDREN*, V26 N5, PP287-289, MAY 71
LISTS 21 FILMS AND TWO FILMSTRIPS AVAILABLE ON INFANT DEVELOPMENT, EXCEPTIONAL CHILDREN, AND PLAY AREAS. (AJ)

EJ 038 935 PS 501 107
BEHAVIORAL COMPLIANCE AND DEVALUATION OF THE FORBIDDEN OBJECT AS A FUNCTION OF PROBABILITY OF DETECTION AND SEVERITY OF THREAT BIAGGIO, ANGELA; RODRIGUES, AROLDO, *DEVELOPMENTAL PSYCHOLOGY*, V4 N3, PP320-323, MAY 71
THIRTY-NINE SECOND GRADE CHILDREN WERE SUBJECTS OF AN EXPERIMENT DEVISED TO TEST THE PREDICTION DERIVED FROM COGNITIVE DISSONANCE THEORY THAT MILD THREATS ARE MORE EFFECTIVE THAN SEVERE THREATS IN OBTAINING INTERNALIZATION OF PROHIBITIONS. (AUTHOR/NH)

EJ 038 936 PS 501 110
CONFORMITY IN EARLY AND LATE ADOLESCENCE LANDSBAUM, JANE B.; WILLIS, RICHARD H., *DEVELOPMENTAL PSYCHOLOGY*, V4 N3, PP334-337, MAY 71

EJ 038 937 PS 501 112
RACE AND CONFORMITY AMONG CHILDREN MOCK, RONALD L.; TUDDENHAM, READ D., *DEVELOPMENTAL PSYCHOLOGY*, V4 N3, PP349-365, MAY 71
THE RELATIONSHIP BETWEEN SUSCEPTIBILITY TO GROUP PRESSURE AND THE RACIAL COMPOSITION OF SMALL GROUPS WAS EXPLORED IN THIS STUDY OF 280 FOURTH, FIFTH AND SIXTH GRADERS. ON TESTS OF PERCEPTUAL JUDGMENT, NEGRO CHILDREN SHOWED MORE CONFORMITY THAN WHITES, AND GIRLS MORE THAN BOYS. (AUTHOR/NH)

EJ 038 943 PS 501 130
EYE CONTACT IN CHILDREN AS A FUNCTION OF AGE, SEX, SOCIAL AND INTELLECTIVE VARIABLES ASHEAR, VICTOR; SNORTUM, JOHN R., *DEVELOPMENTAL PSYCHOLOGY*, V4 N3, PP479, MAY 71

EJ 038 944 PS 501 154
NORMAL PSYCHOSEXUAL DEVELOPMENT RUTTER, MICHAEL, *JOURNAL OF CHILD PSYCHOLOGY AND PSYCHIATRY AND ALLIED DISCIPLINES*, V11 N4, PP259-283, APR 71
NORMAL SEXUAL DEVELOPMENT IS REVIEWED WITH RESPECT TO PHYSICAL MATURATION, SEXUAL INTERESTS, SEX "DRIVE", PSYCHOSEXUAL COMPETENCE AND MATURITY, GENDER ROLE, OBJECT CHOICE, CHILDREN'S CONCEPTS OF SEXUAL DIFFERENCES, SEX ROLE PREFERENCE AND STANDARDS, AND PSYCHOSEXUAL STAGES. BIOLOGIC, PSYCHOANALYTIC AND PSYCHOSOCIAL THEORIES ARE BRIEFLY CONSIDERED. (AUTHOR/AJ)

EJ 038 985 PS 501 141
SCHOOL COUNSELING BY CONTRACT MYERS, ROBERT M., *CHILD WELFARE*, V50 N5, PP283-285, MAY 71
REPORTS A PLAN USED IN MASSACHUSETTS WHEREBY SCHOOL SYSTEMS PURCHASE THE SCHOOL ADJUSTMENT COUNSELING SERVICES OF SOCIAL WORKERS, WITH A WELFARE AGENCY ACTING IN A SUPERVISORY CAPACITY. (NH)

EJ 039 057 PS 501 125
"FOCAL" COLOR AREAS AND THE DEVELOPMENT OF COLOR NAMES HEIDER, ELEANOR ROSCH, *DEVELOPMENTAL PSYCHOLOGY*, V4 N3, PP447-455, MAY 71
THREE EXPERIMENTS USING 3- AND 4-YEAR-OLDS AS SUBJECTS TESTED THE HYPOTHESIS THAT FOCAL COLORS ARE MORE SALIENT THAN NONFOCAL COLORS FOR YOUNG CHILDREN AND ARE THE AREAS TO WHICH COLOR NAMES INITIALLY BECOME ATTACHED. (NH)

EJ 039 058 PS 501 146
CONTINUITY FROM PREKINDERGARTEN TO KINDERGARTEN COHEN, DOROTHY H., *YOUNG CHILDREN*, V26 N5, PP282-286, MAY 71
EARLY CHILDHOOD TEACHERS NEED NOT WORRY ABOUT PROGRAM CONTENT DUPLICATION BUT SHOULD REALIZE THAT THE STANDARD MATERIALS FOR EARLY CHILDHOOD PROGRAMS ARE MERELY TOOLS TO BE USED FOR THE SATISFACTION OF THE THREE MAJOR EARLY CHILDHOOD DRIVES; CURIOSITY, INTEREST IN OTHER CHILDREN, AND THE HANDLING OF EMOTIONAL IMPULSES. (AJ)

EJ 039 266 PS 501 111
NORMAL AND RETARDED CHILDREN'S EXPECTANCY FOR FAILURE MACMILLAN, DONALD L.; KEOGH, BARBARA K., *DEVELOPMENTAL PSYCHOLOGY*, V4 N3, PP343-348, MAY 71

EJ 039 286 PS 501 139
A PARENTING SCALE AND SEPARATION DECISIONS GOLDSTEIN, HARRIET, *CHILD WELFARE*, V50 N5, PP271-276, MAY 71
A PARENTAL CONTINUUM SCALE DESIGNED TO MEASURE PARENTING CAPACITIES IS PRESENTED AS A TOOL TO HELP CHILD WELFARE AGENCIES DECIDE WHETHER AND WHEN TO SEPARATE CHILDREN FROM THEIR NATURAL PARENTS. (NH)

EJ 039 501 PS 501 095
A SENSITIVITY-TRAINING APPROACH TO GROUP THERAPY WITH CHILDREN POLLACK, DONALD, *CHILD WELFARE*, V50 N2, PP86-89, FEB 71

EJ 039 572 PS 501 132
EARLY GRADE SCHOOL PERFORMANCE OF INNER CITY NEGRO HIGH SCHOOL HIGH ACHIEVERS, LOW ACHIEVERS, AND DROPOUTS SOLOMON, DANIEL; AND OTHERS, *DEVELOPMENTAL PSYCHOLOGY*, V4 N3, PP482, MAY 71

EJ 039 587 PS 501 124
LANGUAGE, SOCIALIZATION, AND DELINQUENCY KULIK, JAMES A.; AND OTHERS, *DEVELOPMENTAL PSYCHOLOGY*, V4 N3, PP434-439, MAY 71

EJ 039 627 PS 501 106
SEVERE PROTEIN-CALORIE MALNUTRITION AND COGNITIVE DEVELOPMENT IN INFANCY AND EARLY CHILDHOOD BROCKMAN, LOIS M.; RICCIUTI, HENRY N., *DEVELOPMENTAL PSYCHOLOGY*, V4 N3, PP312-319, MAY 71
FOLLOWING NUTRITIONAL RECOVERY FROM SEVERE PROTEIN-CALORIE DEFICIENCY, 20 YOUNG CHILDREN EVIDENCED A RETARDED LEVEL OF CATEGORIZATION BEHAVIOR COMPARED TO A CONTROL GROUP OF 19 ADEQUATELY NOURISHED CHILDREN FROM SIMILAR SOCIOECONOMIC BACKGROUND. (NH)

EJ 039 628 PS 501 109
CHRONOLOGICAL AGE AND PERFORMANCE ON PROBLEMS WITH REPEATED PRESOLUTION SHIFTS DOUGLASS, H. JEFF; BOURNE, L. E., JR., *DEVELOPMENTAL PSYCHOLOGY*, V4 N3, PP329-333, MAY 71

EJ 039 629 PS 501 113
IDEATIONAL CREATIVITY AND EXPRESSIVE ASPECTS OF HUMAN FIGURE DRAWING IN KINDERGARTEN-AGE CHILDREN SINGER, DAVID L.; WHITON, MARY BETH, *DEVELOPMENTAL PSYCHOLOGY*, V4 N3, PP366-369, MAY 71

EJ 039 630 PS 501 117
THE INFLUENCE OF AGE AND STIMULUS DIMENSIONALITY ON FORM PERCEPTION BY PRESCHOOL CHILDREN KRAYNAK, AUDREY R.; RASKIN, LARRY M., *DEVELOPMENTAL PSYCHOLOGY*, V4 N3, PP389-393, MAY 71

EJ 039 631 PS 501 118
RETENTION FOLLOWING A CHANGE IN AMBIENT CONTEXTUAL STIMULI FOR SIX AGE GROUPS JENSEN, LARRY C.; AND OTHERS, *DEVELOPMENTAL PSYCHOLOGY*, V4 N3, PP394-399, MAY 71

EJ 039 632 PS 501 122
PERSONALITY, COGNITIVE, AND ACADEMIC CORRELATES OF PROBLEM-SOLVING FLEXIBILITY GREENBERGER, ELLEN; AND OTHERS, *DEVELOPMENTAL PSYCHOLOGY*, V4 N3, PP416-424, MAY 71

EJ 039 633 PS 501 128
INTERDEPENDENCE OF INHELDER AND PIAGET'S MODEL OF LOGICAL THINKING BERZONSKY, MICHAEL D., *DEVELOPMENTAL PSYCHOLOGY*, V4 N3, PP469-476, MAY 71

EJ 039 634 PS 501 131
FREE RECALL OF WORDS AND OBJECTS KOSSUTH, GINA L.; AND OTHERS, *DEVELOPMENTAL PSYCHOLOGY*, V4 N3, PP480, MAY 71

EJ 039 635 PS 501 135
YOUNG CHILDREN'S PERFORMANCE ON A TWO-CHOICE TASK AS A FUNCTION OF SOCIAL REINFORCEMENT, BASELINE PREFERENCE, AND RESPONSE STRATEGY HILL, KENNEDY T.; WATTS, GRAEME H., *DEVELOPMENTAL PSYCHOLOGY*, V4 N3, PP487-488, MAY 71

EJ 039 636 PS 501 137
FREE RECALL AND CLUSTERING AT FOUR AGE LEVELS: EFFECTS OF LEARNING TO LEARN AND PRESENTATION METHOD MOELY, BARBARA E.; SHAPIRO, S. I., *DEVELOPMENTAL PSYCHOLOGY*, V4 N3, PP490, MAY 71

EJ 039 637 PS 501 143
WHAT THE WORLD NEEDS NOW: ENVIRONMENTAL EDUCATION FOR YOUNG CHILDREN KLUGE, JEAN, *YOUNG CHILDREN*, V26 N5, PP260-263, MAY 71
THROUGH OBSERVATION AND FIRST-HAND EXPERIENCES, CHILDREN WILL BECOME SENSITIVE TO THEIR ENVIRONMENT; AND AS THEY MATURE, THEIR AWARENESS WILL FORM THE BASIS FOR INTELLIGENT ACTION NECESSARY TO PROTECT OUR NATURAL RESOURCES. (AUTHOR)

EJ 039 638 PS 501 148
THE EFFECTS OF ATTENTION AND MEDIATION ON CHILDREN'S MEMORY HAGEN, JOHN WILLIAM, *YOUNG CHILDREN*, V26 N5, PP290-304, MAY 71

EJ 039 639 PS 501 150
SOME RELATIONSHIPS BETWEEN CLASS INCLUSION, PERCEPTUAL CAPABILITIES, VERBAL CAPABILITIES AND RACE CARLSON, J. S., *HUMAN DEVELOPMENT*, V14 N1, PP30-38, 71

EJ 039 640 PS 501 151
ON THE CONSERVATION OF LIQUIDS HAMEL, B. REMMO, *HUMAN DEVELOPMENT*, V14 N1, PP39-46, 71
SIXTY MIDDLE CLASS CHILDREN (MEAN AGE 78.6 MONTHS) WERE TESTED TO DETERMINE IF RECOGNITION OF IDENTITY PRECEDES RECOGNITION OF QUANTITATIVE EQUIVALENCE WHEN DEALING WITH QUANTITIES OF LIQUIDS. WHEN MEASURING CONSERVATION, THE IMPORTANCE OF TWO ASPECTS OF LANGUAGE (SEMANTICS AND SYNTAX) IS STRESSED. (AUTHOR/AJ)

EJ 039 798 PS 501 094
THE EXIT OF CHILDREN FROM FOSTER CARE: AN INTERIM RESEARCH REPORT FANSHEL, DAVID, *CHILD WELFARE*, V50 N2, PP65-81, FEB 71
THIS IS AN INTERIM REPORT ON A 5-YEAR STUDY OF A GROUP OF 624 CHILDREN TO DETERMINE FACTORS INFLUENCING LENGTH OF FOSTER CARE. (AUTHOR)

EJ 039 799 PS 501 096
WHITE STAFF, BLACK CHILDREN: IS THERE A PROBLEM? BURNS, CRAWFORD E., *CHILD WELFARE*, V50 N2, PP90-96, FEB 71
THIS ARTICLE ILLUSTRATES THE PROBLEMS EXISTING IN THE RELATIONSHIPS BETWEEN WHITE SOCIAL WORKERS AND BLACK CHILDREN CLIENTS. (AJ)

EJ 039 800 PS 501 144
WHO ARE THE DISADVANTAGED? ORNSTEIN, ALLAN C., *YOUNG CHILDREN*, V26 N5, PP264-272, MAY 71
THE AUTHOR OBJECTS TO THE NEBULOUS LABEL "DISADVANTAGED" WHEN USED TO REFER TO VARIOUS ECONOMIC, RACIAL, SOCIAL, PSYCHOLOGICAL, INTELLECTUAL AND/OR GEOGRAPHICAL GROUPS. THE IMPORTANCE OF "EQUAL EDUCATIONAL OPPORTUNITY" IS EMPHASIZED. (AUTHOR/AJ)

EJ 039 898 PS 501 105
A TEST OF ERIKSON'S THEORY OF EGO EPIGENESIS CIACCIO, N. V., *DEVELOPMENTAL PSYCHOLOGY*, V4 N3, PP306-311, MAY 71
TWO BASIC POSTULATES, (1) EGO STAGE PROGRESSION WITH INCREASING AGE, AND (2) DEVELOPMENT OF THE EGO AS IT MEETS THE DIFFERENT CRISIS ELEMENTS OF THE EGO STAGES, WERE TESTED ON A SAMPLE OF 120 5-, 8-, AND 11-YEAR-OLD BOYS, USING A PROJECTIVE INSTRUMENT AND A CODING SYSTEM. THE FIRST POSTULATE FOUND PRELIMINARY CONFIRMATION; THE VALIDITY OF THE SECOND WAS CALLED INTO QUESTION. (NH)

EJ 039 899 PS 501 115
SEX DIFFERENCES IN ADOLESCENT REACTIONS TOWARD NEWCOMERS FESHBACH, NORMA; SONES, GITTELLE, *DEVELOPMENTAL PSYCHOLOGY*, V4 N3, PP381-386, MAY 71
FINDINGS SUGGEST A STABLE SEX DIFFERENCE IN RESPONSE TO OUTSIDERS WHICH HAS ROOTS IN CHILD'S EARLY DEVELOPMENTAL HISTORY. BOYS WERE MORE FRIENDLY TO NEWCOMERS THAN GIRLS WERE. (NH)

EJ 039 900 PS 501 116
COGNITIVE COMPONENTS OF SEPARATION ANXIETY LITTENBERG, RONNIE; AND OTHERS, *DEVELOPMENTAL PSYCHOLOGY*, V4 N3, PP387-388, MAY 71

EJ 039 901 PS 501 120
THE RELATIONSHIP OF BIRTH ORDER AND SEX OF SIBLINGS TO GENDER ROLE IDENTITY VROEGH, KAREN, *DEVELOPMENTAL PSYCHOLOGY*, V4 N3, PP407-411, MAY 71

EJ 039 902 PS 501 121
CHANGE IN EFFICIENCY OF EGO FUNCTIONING AND COMPLEXITY FROM ADOLESCENCE TO YOUNG ADULTHOOD NAWAS, M. MIKE, *DEVELOPMENTAL PSYCHOLOGY*, V4 N3, PP412-415, MAY 71
STUDY FINDINGS SUGGEST THAT BEHAVIOR IS MORE A FUNCTION OF THE PSYCHOSOCIAL AND SITUATIONAL DEMANDS OF CURRENT CIRCUMSTANCES THAN IT IS OF THE PAST. (NH)

EJ 039 903 PS 501 126
DIFFERENTIAL ADJUSTMENT TO PUBESCENCE AND COGNITIVE STYLE PATTERNS DREYER, ALBERT S.; AND OTHERS, *DEVELOPMENTAL PSYCHOLOGY*, V4 N3, PP456-462, MAY 71
DISCUSSES HOW DIFFERING COGNITIVE STYLE IN ADOLESCENTS RELATES TO THEIR ADAPTATION TO PUBESCENT BODY CHANGE. (NH)

EJ 039 904 PS 501 127
EFFECT OF THE PRESENCE OF A HUMAN MODEL ON IMITATIVE BEHAVIOR IN CHILDREN DUBANOSKI, RICHARD A.; PARTON, DAVID A., *DEVELOPMENTAL PSYCHOLOGY*, V4 N3, PP463-468, MAY 71

EJ 039 905 PS 501 129
CORRELATES OF LOCUS OF CONTROL IN A SECONDARY SCHOOL POPULATION NOWICKI, STEPHEN, JR.; ROUNDTREE, JULIA, *DEVELOPMENTAL PSYCHOLOGY*, V4 N3, PP477-478, MAY 71

EJ 039 906 PS 501 134
LEVEL OF "N" ACHIEVEMENT AND PROBABILITY IN CHILDREN OLLENDICK, RHOMAS H.; GRUEN, GERALD E., *DEVELOPMENTAL PSYCHOLOGY*, V4 N3, PP486, MAY 71

EJ 039 907 PS 501 136
IMITATIVE AGGRESSION IN CHILDREN AS A FUNCTION OF OBSERVING A HUMAN MODEL DUBANOSKI, RICHARD A.; PARTON, DAVID A., *DEVELOPMENTAL PSYCHOLOGY*, V4 N3, PP489, MAY 71

EJ 039 908 PS 501 149
THE IMPACT OF MOTHER'S PRESENCE UPON BEHAVIOR: THE FIRST YEAR ESCALONA, S. K.; CORMAN, H. H., *HUMAN DEVELOPMENT*, V14 N1, PP2-15, 71

STUDIES THE EFFECTS OF MOTHERS' PRESENCE AND ABSENCE ON TWO INFANTS FROM BIRTH TO TWO YEARS. (AJ)

EJ 039 909 PS 501 152
THE PART PLAYED BY MEDIATION PROCESSES IN THE RETENTION OF TEMPORAL SEQUENCES BY TWO READING GROUPS GROENENDAAL, H. A.; BAKKER, D. J., *HUMAN DEVELOPMENT*, V14 N1, PP62-70, 71

THIRTY 7-YEAR-OLD AND 26 10-YEAR-OLD BOYS WERE PRESENTED WITH TEMPORAL SEQUENCES OF MEANINGFUL AND MEANINGLESS FIGURES TO DETERMINE THE DIFFERENCES IN PERCEPTION AND RETENTION OF ABOVE- AND BELOW-AVERAGE READERS. (AUTHOR/AJ)

EJ 039 947 PS 501 153
AN EXPERIMENT ON EYEBROW-RAISING AND VISUAL SEARCHING IN CHILDREN JONES, N. G. BLURTON; KONNER, M. J., *JOURNAL OF CHILD PSYCHOLOGY AND PSYCHIATRY AND ALLIED DISCIPLINES*, V11 N4, PP233-240, APR 71

EJ 039 987 PS 501 123
MODIFICATION OF PEER PREFERENCE OF FIRST-GRADE CHILDREN HASKETT, GARY JOSH, *DEVELOPMENTAL PSYCHOLOGY*, V4 N3, PP429-433, MAY 71

EVALUATES THE EFFECTS OF SIX KINDS OF SOCIAL INTERACTION ON PEER PREFERENCE AMONG FIRST GRADE CHILDREN. (NH)

EJ 040 041 PS 501 114
GROUP CARE AND INTELLECTUAL DEVELOPMENT MOYLES, E. WILLIAM; WOLINS, MARTIN, *DEVELOPMENTAL PSYCHOLOGY*, V4 N3, PP370-380, MAY 71

SEVERAL HUNDRED CHILDREN IN VARIOUS GROUP CARE PROGRAMS WERE COMPARED FOR COGNITIVE DEVELOPMENT WITH SAME-AGE CHILDREN REARED AT HOME. THE GROUP-REARED CHILDREN DID NOT SHOW ANY OF THE DEVELOPMENTAL DEFICIENCIES USUALLY ATTRIBUTED TO INSTITUTIONAL CARE. (NH)

EJ 040 042 PS 501 138
UNWED MOTHERS AND THEIR DECISIONS TO KEEP OR SURRENDER CHILDREN FESTINGER, TRUDY BRADLEY, *CHILD WELFARE*, V50 N5, PP253-263, MAY 71

FACTORS THAT MIGHT ALLOW PREDICTION OF THE UNWED MOTHER'S DECISION TO KEEP HER CHILD OR TO SURRENDER IT FOR ADOPTION ARE EXAMINED IN THIS STUDY OF 137 WHITE AND BLACK CLIENTS OF A SOCIAL AGENCY. (NH)

EJ 040 043 PS 501 140
THE PARENTS' CENTER PROJECT: A MULTISERVICE APPROACH TO THE PREVENTION OF CHILD ABUSE BEAN, SHIRLEY L., *CHILD WELFARE*, V50 N5, PP277-282, MAY 71

DESCRIBES A CENTER WHICH HAS A PROGRAM OF GROUP THERAPY FOR PARENTS IN FAMILIES WHERE PATTERNS OF CHILD ABUSE WERE DEVELOPING AND ALSO OFFERS FULL DAYTIME CARE FOR THEIR CHILDREN. (NH)

EJ 040 210 PS 501 187
INCORPORATION OF VALUES BY LOWER AND MIDDLE SOCIOECONOMIC CLASS PRESCHOOL BOYS ERMALINSKI, RICHARD; RUSCELLI, VINCENT, *CHILD DEVELOPMENT*, V42 N2, PP629-632, JUN 71

EJ 040 294 PS 501 161
CONFORMITY IN CHILDREN AS A FUNCTION OF GRADE LEVEL, AND REAL VERSUS HYPOTHETICAL ADULT AND PEER MODELS HAMM, NORMAN H.; HOVING, KENNETH L., *JOURNAL OF GENETIC PSYCHOLOGY*, V118 N2, PP253-63, JUN 71

EJ 040 295 PS 501 167
RHYTHMIC HABIT PATTERNS IN INFANCY: THEIR SEQUENCE, AGE OF ONSET, AND FREQUENCY KRAVITZ, HARVEY; BOEHM, JOHN J., *CHILD DEVELOPMENT*, V42 N2, PP399-413, JUN 71

EJ 040 296 PS 501 169
ATTENTION DISTRIBUTION IN THE 24-MONTH-OLD CHILD: VARIATIONS IN COMPLEXITY AND INCONGRUITY OF THE HUMAN FORM LEWIS, MICHAEL; AND OTHERS, *CHILD DEVELOPMENT*, V42 N2, PP429-438, JUN 71

EJ 040 297 PS 501 172
PRESTIMULUS ACTIVITY LEVEL AND RESPONSIVITY IN THE NEONATE LAMPER, CELIA; EISDORFER, CARL, *CHILD DEVELOPMENT*, V42 N2, PP465-473, JUN 71

EJ 040 298 PS 501 184
HUNGER AND MOTOR RESTRAINT ON AROUSAL AND VISUAL ATTENTION IN THE INFANT GIACOMAN, SHARON L., *CHILD DEVELOPMENT*, V42 N2, PP605-614, JUN 71

EJ 040 319 PS 501 181
A COMPARATIVE STUDY OF PIAGET'S DEVELOPMENTAL SCHEMA OF SIGHTED CHILDREN WITH THAT OF A GROUP OF BLIND CHILDREN GOTTESMAN, MILTON, *CHILD DEVELOPMENT*, V42 N2, PP573-580, JUN 71

EJ 040 359 PS 501 163
CHILDREN'S COMMUNICATION ACCURACY RELATED TO RACE AND SOCIOECONOMIC STATUS BALDWIN, THELMA L.; AND OTHERS, *CHILD DEVELOPMENT*, V42 N2, PP345-357, JUN 71

EJ 040 360 PS 501 195
THE EFFECTS OF FEEDBACK VARIATIONS ON REFERENTIAL COMMUNICATION OF CHILDREN FISHBEIN, HAROLD D.; OSBORNE, MARTA, *MERRILL-PALMER QUARTERLY OF BEHAVIOR AND DEVELOPMENT*, V17 N3, PP243-250, JUL 71

EJ 040 453 PS 501 171
KNOWLEDGE OF ACTION AND OBJECT WORDS: A COMPARISON OF LOWER- AND MIDDLE-CLASS NEGRO PRESCHOOLERS JERUCHIMOWICZ, RITA; AND OTHERS, *CHILD DEVELOPMENT*, V42 N2, PP455-464, JUN 71

EJ 040 454 PS 501 188
A DEVELOPMENTAL STUDY OF SIZE CONSTANCY FOR TWO- VERSUS THREE-DIMENSIONAL STIMULI KUBZANSKY, PHILIP E.; AND OTHERS, *CHILD DEVELOPMENT*, V42 N2, PP633-635, JUN 71

EJ 040 455 PS 501 193
RELATIONSHIPS BETWEEN INFANTS' VOCALIZATIONS AND THEIR MOTHERS' BEHAVIORS BECKWITH, LEILA, *MERRILL-PALMER QUARTERLY OF BEHAVIOR AND DEVELOPMENT*, V17 N3, PP211-226, JUL 71

EJ 040 456 PS 501 194
THE MOTHER-CHILD RELATIONSHIP AND THE FATHER-ABSENT BOY'S PERSONALITY DEVELOPMENT 27-241 BILLER, HENRY B., *MERRILL-PALMER QUARTERLY OF BEHAVIOR AND DEVELOPMENT*, V17 N3, JUL 71

EJ 040 685 PS 501 229
THE PSYCHOLOGICAL CORRELATES OF SPEECH CHARACTERISTICS OF SOUNDING "DISADVANTAGED": A SOUTHERN REPLICATION SHAMO, G. WAYNE, *CHILD STUDY JOURNAL*, V1 N3, PP111-122, SPR 71

IN THIS REPLICATION STUDY BOTH NORTHERN AND SOUTHERN TEACHERS TENDED TO CLASSIFY A CHILD "CULTURALLY DISADVANTAGED" EVEN AFTER VERY SHORT EXPOSURE TO HIS SPEECH, IF HIS SPEECH EXHIBITED IRREGULARITIES IN GRAMMAR, SILENT PAUSING, AND PRONUNCIATION. (NH)

EJ 040 722 PS 501 157
CONSIDERATIONS IN DAY CARE COST ANALYSIS MCCLELLAN, KEITH, *CHILD WELFARE*, V50 N6, PP341-48, JUN 71

EJ 040 723 PS 501 183
NEGRO-WHITE, MALE-FEMALE EIGHT-MONTH DEVELOPMENTAL SCORES COMPARED WITH SEVEN-YEAR WISC AND BENDER TEST SCORES GOFFENEY, BARBARA; AND OTHERS, *CHILD DEVELOPMENT*, V42 N2, PP595-604, JUN 71

EJ 040 724 PS 501 225
EFFECTS OF INSTRUCTIONS ON THEME GRADING: GRAMMATICAL VS. HOLISTIC FOLLMAN, JOHN; AND OTHERS, *CHILD STUDY JOURNAL*, V1 N3, PP135-141, SPR 71

TWELVE COLLEGE SENIORS IN AN ENGLISH METHODS COURSE WERE ASSIGNED TO THREE TREATMENT GROUPS, GRAMMATICAL, HOLISTIC, AND BOTH. EACH GROUP RECEIVED DIFFERENT INSTRUCTIONS BUT GRADED THE SAME 10 THEMES. THEMES GRADED FOR GRAMMATICAL ERRORS RECEIVED LOWER GRADES THAN THE SAME THEMES GRADED HOLISTICALLY. (NH)

EJ 040 799 PS 501 196
A DISCONTINUITY IN THE SOCIALIZATION OF MALES IN THE UNITED STATES KNOX, WILLIAM E.; KUPFERER, HARRIET J., *MERRILL-PALMER QUARTERLY OF BEHAVIOR AND DEVELOPMENT*, V17 N3, PP251-261, JUL 71
EXPLORES THE INCONSISTENCY IN SOCIETAL EXPECTATIONS FOR AMERICAN MALES FROM YOUTH TO ADULTHOOD. (AJ)

EJ 041 056 PS 501 178
ACOUSTIC ANALYSIS OF THE ACQUISITION OF ACCEPTABLE "R" IN AMERICAN ENGLISH KLEIN, ROBERT P., *CHILD DEVELOPMENT*, V42 N2, PP543-550, JUN 71

EJ 041 133 PS 501 159
DEVELOPMENT OF RETENTION AND ORGANIZATION OCCURRING IN FREE RECALL IN TURKISH CHILDREN YAVUZ, HALIDE S., *JOURNAL OF GENETIC PSYCHOLOGY*, V118 N2, PP203-209, JUN 71
THIS STUDY COMPARES THE FREE RECALL OF SMALL COMMON OBJECTS AS PERCEPTUAL STIMULI IN NORMAL MALE AND FEMALE CHILDREN OF TWO AGE LEVELS (8 YEARS AND 12 YEARS). THE DATA SHOW THAT GIRLS ARE SUPERIOR TO BOYS IN FREE RECALL, AND WITH INCREASING AGE, CAPACITY TO RECALL INCREASES. EIGHT-YEAR-OLDS EVIDENCE CLUSTERING IN THEIR ORGANIZED RECALL OF CONCRETE OBJECTS. (NH)

EJ 041 134 PS 501 164
STATE IV OF PIAGET'S THEORY OF INFANT'S OBJECT CONCEPTS: A LONGITUDINAL STUDY GRATH, GERALD; LANDERS, WILLIAM F., *CHILD DEVELOPMENT*, V42 N2, PP359 372, JUN 71

EJ 041 135 PS 501 168
STUDIES OF CONSERVATION WITH YORUBA CHILDREN OF DIFFERING AGES AND EXPERIENCE LLOYD, BARBARA B., *CHILD DEVELOPMENT*, V42 N2, PP415-428, JUN 71
QUESTIONS CONCERNING THE EFFECTS OF FAMILIAR AND ALIEN MATERIALS, AGE AND CULTURE, AND THE ETIOLOGY OF CONSERVATION ARE EXAMINED IN NUMBER AND CONTINOUS QUANTITY TASKS ASSESSING CONSERVATION IN YORUBA CHILDREN FROM TRADITIONAL AND EDUCATIONALLY ADVANTAGED HOMES. (AUTHOR/AJ)

EJ 041 136 PS 501 176
THE DISCRIMINATION LEARNING OF NORMAL AND RETARDED CHILDREN AS A FUNCTION OF PENALTY CONDITIONS AND ETIOLOGY OF THE RETARDED HARTER, SUSAN; AND OTHERS, *CHILD DEVELOPMENT*, V42 N2, PP517-536, JUN 71

EJ 041 137 PS 501 177
THE EFFECTS OF REWARD AND PUNISHMENT UPON CHILDREN'S ATTENTION, MOTIVATION, AND DISCRIMINATION LEARNING WITTE, KENNETH L.; GROSSMAN, EUGENE E., *CHILD DEVELOPMENT*, V42 N2, PP537-542, JUN 71

EJ 041 138 PS 501 179
THE EFFECTS OF STIMULUS REDUNDANCY ON TRANSFER OF STIMULUS PRETRAINING CAMPIONE, JOSEPH C., *CHILD DEVELOPMENT*, V42 N2, PP551-559, JUN 71

EJ 041 139 PS 501 180
NUMBER CONSERVATION IN VERY YOUNG CHILDREN: THE EFFECT OF AGE AND MODE OF RESPONDING CALHOUN, L. G., *CHILD DEVELOPMENT*, V42 N2, PP561-572, JUN 71

EJ 041 140 PS 501 182
CLASSIFICATION PATTERNS OF UNDERPRIVILEGED CHILDREN IN ISRAEL SHARAN, SHLOMO; WELLER, LEONARD, *CHILD DEVELOPMENT*, V42 N2, PP581-594, JUN 71

EJ 041 141 PS 501 185
ANTICIPATORY IMAGERY AND MODIFIED ANAGRAM SOLUTIONS: A DEVELOPMENTAL STUDY LIPTON, CHERYL; OVERTON, WILLIS F., *CHILD DEVELOPMENT*, V42 N2, PP615-623, JUN 71
A MODIFIED ANAGRAM TASK IS EMPLOYED TO EXPLORE THE DEVELOPMENT OF ANTICIPATORY IMAGERY AND ITS RELATIONSHIP TO READING ACHIEVEMENT, COMPLEXITY OF STIMULUS MATERIAL, AND PRACTICE EFFECTS. (AUTHOR/AJ)

EJ 041 142 PS 501 189
LINGUISTIC AND THEMATIC VARIABLES IN RECALL OF A STORY BY DISADVANTAGED CHILDREN MILGRAM, NORMAN A.; AND OTHERS, *CHILD DEVELOPMENT*, V42 N2, PP637-640, JUN 71

EJ 041 143 PS 501 190
LABELING AND IMAGING AS AIDS TO MEMORY ROBINSON, JAMES P.; LONDON, PERRY, *CHILD DEVELOPMENT*, V42 N2, PP641-644, JUN 71
CLARIFIES SOME OF THE CONDITIONS UNDER WHICH VERBAL PROCESSES FACILITATE OR INHIBIT LEARNING OF VISUAL STIMULI. (AUTHOR/AJ)

EJ 041 144 PS 501 192
CONSERVATION OF NUMBER IN VERY YOUNG CHILDREN: A FAILURE TO REPLICATE MEHLER AND BEVER WILLOUGHBY, ROBERT H.; TRACHY, SHARON, *MERRILL-PALMER QUARTERLY OF BEHAVIOR AND DEVELOPMENT*, V17 N3, PP205-209, JUL 71

EJ 041 145 PS 501 224
THE DEVELOPMENT OF COGNITIVE BALANCE AND THE TRANSITION FROM CONCRETE TO FORMAL OPERATIONAL THOUGHT BLANCHARD, EDWARD B.; BINDSEIL, BEVERLY D., *CHILD STUDY JOURNAL*, V1 N3, PP126-134, SPR 71
THIS STUDY COMPARED AFFECTIVE RESPONSES TO WRITTEN AND ORAL PRESENTATIONS OF TRIADIC SITUATIONS OF THREE GROUPS: FOURTH GRADERS (CONCRETE OPERATIONAL), EIGHTH GRADERS, AND FRESHMEN IN COLLEGE (FORMAL OPERATIONAL) TO SEE WHETHER THE VARIATION IN STIMULUS MODE PRODUCES A DIFFERENT KIND OF RESPONSE IN THE EIGHTH GRADERS. (AUTHOR/NH)

EJ 041 146 PS 501 226
THE ASSESSMENT OF DIFFERENCES IN CONCEPTUAL STYLE DENNEY, DOUGLAS, *CHILD STUDY JOURNAL*, V1 N3, PP142-155, SPR 71

EJ 041 342 PS 501 158
PARENTHOOD: SOME ANTECEDENTS AND CONSEQUENCES: A PRELIMINARY SURVEY OF THE MENTAL HEALTH LITERATURE ARASTEH, JOSEPHINE D., *JOURNAL OF GENETIC PSYCHOLOGY*, V118 N2, PP179-202, JUN 71
RESEARCH FINDINGS ARE PRESENTED ON BIRTH CONTROL METHODS AND USAGE; UNWANTED CHILDREN; AND THE EFFECTS OF FAMILY SIZE, BIRTH ORDER AND SOCIAL CLASS ON THE CHILD. (NH)

EJ 041 343 PS 501 160
SOME LANGUAGE-RELATED COGNITIVE ADVANTAGES OF BILINGUAL FIVE-YEAR-OLDS FELDMAN, CAROL; SHEN, MICHAEL, *JOURNAL OF GENETIC PSYCHOLOGY*, V118 N2, PP235 44, JUN 71
MONOLINGUAL AND BILINGUAL HEAD START CHILDREN WERE COMPARED IN THEIR ABILITY ON TASKS INVOLVING OBJECT CONSTANCY, NAMING, AND THE USE OF NAMES IN SENTENCES. ALL TASKS (PARTICULARLY NONVERBAL MEASURES) WERE FOUND TO BE EASIER FOR BILINGUALS THAN MONOLINGUALS. (AUTHOR/NH)

EJ 041 446 PS 501 162
EXPRESSIONS OF PERSONALITY IN CREATIONS OF LATENCY AGE CHILDREN CARMICHAEL, LARAINE MORES; MCFARLAND, MARGARET B., *JOURNAL OF GENETIC PSYCHOLOGY*, V118 N2, PP271-79, JUN 71
THIS STUDY SHOWS A DEMONSTRABLE RELATIONSHIP BETWEEN CHILDREN'S PERSONALITY TRAITS AND THE CHARACTERISTICS OF THEIR CREATIONS AND USE OF MATERIALS. (NH)

EJ 041 447 PS 501 165
CURIOSITY AND THE PARENT-CHILD RELATIONSHIP SAXE, ROBERT M.; STOLLAK, GARY E., *CHILD DEVELOPMENT*, V42 N2, PP373-384, JUN 71
OBSERVATIONS OF PARENT-CHILD INTERACTION INDICATE THAT MOTHER'S POSITIVE FEELING IS CORRELATED WITH HER CHILD'S SOCIABILITY, CURIOSITY, ATTENTIVENESS, MANIPULATION, AND OFFERING INFORMATION. (AJ)

EJ 041 448 PS 501 166
EFFECTS OF CONTINGENT AND NONCONTINGENT REINFORCEMENT UPON GENERALIZED IMITATION MASTERS, JOHN C.; MORRIS, RICHARD J., *CHILD DEVELOPMENT*, V42 N2, PP385-397, JUN 71

EJ 041 449 PS 501 174
THE DEVELOPMENT OF HYPNOTIC SUSCEPTIBILITY: A LONGITUDINAL (CONVERGENCE) STUDY COOPER, LESLIE M.; LONDON, PERRY, *CHILD DEVELOPMENT*, V42 N2, PP487-503, JUN 71

EJ 041 450 PS 501 175
CONCEPTUAL TEMPO IN YOUNG GRADE-SCHOOL CHILDREN ESKA, BRUNHILDE; BLACK, KATHRYN NORCROSS, *CHILD DEVELOPMENT*, V42 N2, PP505-516, JUN 71
DESIGNED TO REASSESS THE RELATIONSHIP BETWEEN RESPONSE SPEED, ERRORS, AND IQ FOR BOTH SEXES, AND TO EVALUATE THE FINDINGS IN RELATION TO THE OVERALL PATTERN OF DATA ACCUMULATED FROM PREVIOUS INVESTIGATIONS. (AUTHOR/AJ)

EJ 041 451 PS 501 223
VERBAL OPERANT CONDITIONING OF AN ACTIVE-NON-ACTIVE VERBAL DIFFERENTIAL IN EARLY SCHOOL CHILDREN RYBACK, DAVID, *CHILD STUDY JOURNAL*, V1 N3, PP123-125, SPR 71
RESULTS OF THIS STUDY SUGGEST THAT EARLY SCHOOL-AGE CHILDREN RESPOND TO THE ACTIVE-PASSIVE DIMENSION IN VERBAL CONDITIONING AS WELL AS TO THE HARD-SOFT AND GOOD-BAD DIMENSIONS. (AUTHOR/NH)

EJ 041 591 PS 501 170
CHILDREN'S DESCRIPTIONS OF PEERS: A WERNERIAN DEVELOPMENTAL ANALYSIS SCARLETT, HELAINE H.; AND OTHERS, *CHILD DEVELOPMENT,* V42 N2, PP439-453, JUN 71

EJ 041 630 PS 501 156
AN ISRAELI EXPERIMENTAL GROUP WITH PRIMARY SCHOOL DROPOUTS OUTSIDE THE SCHOOL SETTING BERMAN, YITZCHAK, *CHILD WELFARE,* V50 N6, PP336-40, JUN 71

EJ 041 631 PS 501 186
INCENTIVE PREFERENCE AND RESISTANCE TO TEMPTATION DMITRUK, VICTOR M., *CHILD DEVELOPMENT,* V42 N2, PP625-628, JUN 71

EJ 041 632 PS 501 197
ROLE MODEL INFLUENCES ON COLLEGE WOMEN'S CAREER ASPIRATIONS ALMQUIST, ELIZABETH M.; ANGRIST, SHIRLEY S., *MERRILL-PALMER QUARTERLY OF BEHAVIOR AND DEVELOPMENT,* V17 N3, PP263-279, JUL 71

EJ 041 722 PS 501 173
VALIDITY OF THE DENVER DEVELOPMENTAL SCREENING TEST FRANKENBURG, WILLIAM K.; AND OTHERS, *CHILD DEVELOPMENT,* V42 N2, PP475-485, JUN 71

EVALUATES VALIDITY OF THE DENVER DEVELOPMENTAL SCREENING TEST USED FOR ASSESSING THE DEVELOPMENT OF PRESCHOOLERS. (AJ)

EJ 041 723 PS 501 191
FIVE-YEAR STABILITY OF INTELLIGENCE QUOTIENTS FROM LANGUAGE AND NONLANGUAGE GROUP TESTS HOPKINS, KENNETH D.; BIBELHEIMER, MILO, *CHILD DEVELOPMENT,* V42 N2, PP645-649, JUN 71

EJ 041 724 PS 501 227
A SHORT, RELIABLE, EASY TO ADMINISTER INDIVIDUAL INTELLIGENCE TEST FOR SPECIAL CLASS PLACEMENT ARMSTRONG, ROBERT J.; AND OTHERS, *CHILD STUDY JOURNAL,* V1 N3, PP156-163, SPR 71

EJ 041 725 PS 501 228
THE RELATIONSHIP BETWEEN THE WECHSLER INTELLIGENCE SCALE FOR CHILDREN AND THE SLOSSON INTELLIGENCE TEST MAXWELL, MICHAEL T., *CHILD STUDY JOURNAL,* V1 N3, PP164-171, SPR 71

THE RELATIONSHIP BETWEEN THE SLOSSON (1953) INTELLIGENCE TEST (SIT) AND THE WECHSLER (1949) INTELLIGENCE SCALE FOR CHILDREN (WISC) WAS STUDIED TO PROVIDE INFORMATION ABOUT THE SIT'S USEFULNESS AS A MEASURE OF INTELLIGENCE, FOR PLACEMENT PURPOSES AND FOR SCREENING PURPOSES. (NH)

EJ 041 758 PS 501 255
AN EXPLORATORY STUDY OF THE RELATIONSHIP BETWEEN COGNITIVE PRETESTING AND COURSE ACHIEVEMENT SODERBERG, LANNY O., *CALIFORNIA JOURNAL OF EDUCATIONAL RESEARCH,* V22 N2, PP64-67, MAR 71

COMPARISON OF TWO GROUPS OF GRADUATE STUDENTS ON EACH OF THREE ACHIEVEMENT CRITERIA GAVE NO EVIDENCE THAT EITHER OF TWO PRETESTS (ONE COURSE-RELEVANT COGNITIVE, THE OTHER NON-RELEVANT AFFECTIVE) WAS INFLUENTIAL. (NH)

EJ 041 829 PS 501 250
ART - FOR THE CHILD'S SAKE TIMBERLAKE, PATRICIA, *YOUNG CHILDREN,* V26 N6, PP355-357, AUG 71

EMPHASIZES THE VALUE OF KINDERGARTEN ART STUDY TO PROVIDE INTELLECTUAL STIMULATION AND PROMOTE EMOTIONAL GROWTH. (AJ)

EJ 041 830 PS 501 256
A THIRD STUDY OF PERCEPTUAL BEHAVIOR IN SIXTH GRADE CHILDREN IN RELATION TO THEIR BEHAVIOR IN ART MCWHINNIE, HAROLD J., *CALIFORNIA JOURNAL OF EDUCATIONAL RESEARCH,* V22 N2, PP68-73, MAR 71

THE RELATIONSHIP AMONG FOUR PERCEPTUAL VARIABLES IS STUDIED AND THE RESULTS DISCUSSED WITH REFERENCE TO IMPLICATIONS FOR THE TEACHING OF ART AND FURTHER RESEARCH INTO VARIABLES OF THE PSYCHOLOGY OF ART. (NH)

EJ 041 856 PS 501 204
EFFECTS OF SOCIAL COMPARISON UPON CHILDREN'S SELF-REINFORCEMENT AND ALTRUISM TOWARD COMPETITORS AND FRIENDS MASTERS, JOHN C., *DEVELOPMENTAL PSYCHOLOGY,* V5 N1, PP64-72, JUL 71

EJ 041 857 PS 501 219
KINDERGARTEN CHILDREN'S ACTIVE VOCABULARY ABOUT BODY BUILD LERNER, RICHARD M.; SCHROEDER, CHRISTINE, *DEVELOPMENTAL PSYCHOLOGY,* V5 N1, PP179, JUL 71

EJ 041 858 PS 501 263
RACIAL ATTITUDES OF NEGRO PRESCHOOLERS O'REILLY, ALORA, *CALIFORNIA JOURNAL OF EDUCATIONAL RESEARCH,* V22 N3, PP126-130, MAY 71

EJ 041 956 PS 501 198
CAN CONDITIONED RESPONSES BE ESTABLISHED IN THE NEWBORN INFANT: 1971? SAMEROFF, ARNOLD J., *DEVELOPMENTAL PSYCHOLOGY,* V5 N1, PP1-12, JUL 71

EVIDENCE INDICATES THAT THE NEWBORN INFANT MUST FIRST DEVELOP COGNITIVE SYSTEMS, THROUGH HIS EXPERIENCE WITH VARIOUS STIMULI, TO DIFFERENTIATE EACH MODALITY SEPARATELY BEFORE HE CAN INTEGRATE ANY TWO MODALITIES IN CLASSICAL CONDITIONING. (AUTHOR/NH)

EJ 041 957 PS 501 200
COOPERATION AND COMPETITION OF MEXICAN, MEXICAN-AMERICAN, AND ANGLO-AMERICAN CHILDREN OF TWO AGES UNDER FOUR INSTRUCTIONAL SETS KAGAN, SPENCER; MADSEN, MILLARD C., *DEVELOPMENTAL PSYCHOLOGY,* V5 N1, PP32-39, JUL 71

EJ 041 958 PS 501 207
PRESCHOOL PLAY NORMS: A REPLICATION BARNES, KEITH E., *DEVELOPMENTAL PSYCHOLOGY,* V5 N1, PP99-103, JUL 71

PRESCHOOL PLAY BEHAVIOR OF TODAY WAS COMPARED WITH PLAY NORMS COLLECTED MORE THAN 40 YEARS AGO. PRESENT PLAY BEHAVIOR WAS JUDGED TO BE SIGNIFICANTLY LESS SOCIAL. (NH)

EJ 041 959 PS 501 212
NEWBORN'S RESPONSE TO THE CRY OF ANOTHER INFANT SIMNER, MARVIN L., *DEVELOPMENTAL PSYCHOLOGY,* V5 N1, PP136-150, JUL 71

A SERIES OF INVESTIGATIONS WERE CONDUCTED TO DETERMINE WHETHER REFLEXIVE CRYING OCCURS IN NEWBORNS AND TO DEFINE THE PARAMETERS THAT CONTROL HIS BEHAVIOR. (NH)

EJ 041 960 PS 501 230
THE INFLUENCE OF STIMULUS EXPOSURE ON RATED PREFERENCE: EFFECTS OF AGE, PATTERN OF EXPOSURE, AND STIMULUS MEANINGFULNESS FAW, TERRY T.; PIEN, DIANA, *JOURNAL OF EXPERIMENTAL CHILD PSYCHOLOGY,* V11 N3, PP339-346, JUN 71

EJ 041 961 PS 501 247
THE DECLINE OF PLAY IN URBAN KINDERGARTENS ROBISON, HELEN F., *YOUNG CHILDREN,* V26 N6, PP333-341, AUG 71

PRESENTS THE PURPOSE AND VALUE OF TEACHER INVOLVEMENT IN PLAY, ITS POSSIBLE CONTRIBUTIONS TO CREATIVITY AND SOCIALIZATION. (AJ)

EJ 041 962 PS 501 264
ADJUSTMENT DIFFERENCES OF SELECTED FOREIGN-BORN PUPILS OSBORN, WILLIAM P., *CALIFORNIA JOURNAL OF EDUCATIONAL RESEARCH,* V22 N3, PP131-139, MAY 71

EJ 041 963 PS 501 266
COGNITIVE STYLES IN HYPERACTIVE CHILDREN AND THE EFFECT OF METHYLPHENIDATE CAMPBELL, SUSAN B.; AND OTHERS, *JOURNAL OF CHILD PSYCHOLOGY AND PSYCHIATRY AND ALLIED DISCIPLINES,* V12 N1, PP55-67, JUN 71

EJ 041 981 PS 501 233
ORIENTATION DISCRIMINATION IN INFANTS: A COMPARISON OF VISUAL FIXATION AND OPERANT TRAINING METHODS MCKENZIE, BERYL; DAY, R. H., *JOURNAL OF EXPERIMENTAL CHILD PSYCHOLOGY,* V11 N3, PP366-375, JUN 71

EJ 042 208 PS 501 242
THE EFFECTS OF DIFFERENT COMPETITIVE CONTINGENCIES ON COOPERATIVE BEHAVIOR STEWART, JEFFREY E.; AND OTHERS, *JOURNAL OF EXPERIMENTAL CHILD PSYCHOLOGY,* V11 N3, PP461-479, JUN 71

EJ 042 347 PS 501 253
EVALUATIVE USES OF UNCONVENTIONAL MEASUREMENT TECHNIQUES IN AN EDUCATIONAL SYSTEM JUNG, STEVEN M., *CALIFORNIA JOURNAL OF EDUCATIONAL RESEARCH,* V22 N2, PP48-57, MAR 71

TO DETERMINE THE DEGREE TO WHICH PLAN (PROGRAM FOR LEARNING IN ACCORDANCE WITH NEEDS) GOALS WERE ATTAINED, AND TO COMPARE PLAN WITH A MORE CONVENTIONAL EDUCATIONAL PROGRAM USED IN CONTROL CLASSES, THE CRITICAL INCIDENTS METHOD WAS USED. PLAN GOALS ARE DEVELOPMENT OF STUDENT SELF-RESPONSIBILITY, SELF-MANAGEMENT, AND RESOURCEFULNESS. (NH)

EJ 042 348 PS 501 254
VERBAL PARTICIPATION AS A FUNCTION OF THE PRESENCE OF PRIOR INFORMATION CONCERNING APTITUDE MEANS, GLADYS H.; AND OTHERS, *CALIFORNIA JOURNAL OF EDUCATIONAL RESEARCH,* V22 N2, PP58-63, MAR 71

THE PURPOSE OF THE STUDY WAS TO INVESTIGATE THE POSSIBLE MOTIVATIONAL EFFECT THAT KNOWLEDGE OF RESULTS OF PERFORMANCE ON SOME COMPLEX ACADEMIC TASK MIGHT HAVE ON VERBAL PARTICIPATION IN A RELATED ACADEMIC AREA. (AUTHOR/NH)

EJ 042 349 PS 501 265
A BEHAVIOURAL SCREENING QUESTIONNAIRE FOR USE WITH THREE-YEAR-OLD CHILDREN. PRELIMINARY FINDINGS RICHMAN, N.; GRAHAM, P. J., *JOURNAL OF CHILD PSYCHOLOGY AND PSYCHIATRY AND ALLIED DISCIPLINES*, V12 N1, PP5-33, JUN 71

THE QUESTIONNAIRE DEVELOPED COULD BE USED TO IDENTIFY CHILDREN WITH BEHAVIOR DIFFICULTIES AND DEVELOPMENTAL DELAY. (MS)

EJ 042 406 PS 501 248
A CREATIVE PLAYGROUND MCCORD, IVALEE H., *YOUNG CHILDREN*, V26 N6, PP342-347, AUG 71

AT KANSAS STATE UNIVERSITY CHILD DEVELOPMENT LABORATORY, AN OUTDOOR PLAY SPACE HAS BEEN IMAGINATIVELY DESIGNED TO PROVIDE VARIED PHYSICAL EXPERIENCES FOR YOUNG CHILDREN. (AUTHOR/AJ)

EJ 042 506 PS 501 238
THE CONTROL OF RELATIVE SIZE BY PICTORIAL DEPTH CUES IN CHILDREN AND ADULTS WILCOX, BARBARA LEE; TEGHTSOONIAN, MARTHA, *JOURNAL OF EXPERIMENTAL CHILD PSYCHOLOGY*, V11 N3, PP413-429, JUN 71

A DEVELOPMENTAL STUDY OF THE RELATION BETWEEN APPARENT SIZE AND PICTORIAL DEPTH DEMONSTRATED THE USEFULNESS OF OPERANT TECHNIQUES IN ESTABLISHING EQUIVALENT DIFFERENTIAL RESPONDING AND INTERESTING STIMULUS EQUIVALENCE IN ADULTS, 9- AND 3-YEAR-OLDS. (AUTHOR/AJ)

EJ 042 791 PS 501 260
RELATIONSHIP OF CLASSROOM GROUPING PRACTICES TO DIFFUSION OF STUDENTS' SOCIOMETRIC CHOICES AND DIFFUSION OF STUDENTS' PERCEPTION OF SOCIOMETRIC CHOICE O'REILLY, ROBERT P.; ILLENBERG, GREGORY J., *CALIFORNIA JOURNAL OF EDUCATIONAL RESEARCH*, V22 N3, PP104-114, MAY 71

EJ 042 880 PS 501 203
DEVELOPMENTAL CHANGES IN IDIODYNAMIC SET RESPONSES OF CHILDREN'S WORD ASSOCIATIONS PENK, WALTER, *DEVELOPMENTAL PSYCHOLOGY*, V5 N1, PP55-63, JUL 71

THE EFFECT OF SUBJECT AGE, SEX, EXAMINER, AND STIMULUS WORD DIFFERENCES ON DEVELOPMENTAL SEQUENCES OF IDIODYNAMIC SET RESPONSES IN CHILDREN'S WORD ASSOCIATIONS WAS INVESTIGATED. SUBJECTS WERE 100 CHILDREN, AGES 7-11. THE FINDINGS COULD NOT BE INTERPRETED AS EVIDENCE OF STAGE PROGRESSIONS, OR HIERARCHICAL RANKINGS IN MEDIATIONAL PROCESSES. (NH)

EJ 042 881 PS 501 261
OF TIME AND THE PRONOUN: A NEW METHODOLOGY FOR RESEARCH IN HIGHER EDUCATION PETERS, DIANNE S., *CALIFORNIA JOURNAL OF EDUCATIONAL RESEARCH*, V22 N3, PP115-121, MAY 71

REPORTS THAT THE PATTERN OF A FACULTY'S SOCIAL ENVIRONMENT AND THE PRONOUN PATTERN OF THEIR SPEECH ARE PARALLEL. (AUTHOR/AJ)

EJ 042 955 PS 501 199
VARIETY OF EXEMPLARS VERSUS LINGUISTIC CONTEXTS IN CONCEPT ATTAINMENT IN YOUNG CHILDREN MARTIN, CLAUDE; OLSON, DAVID, *DEVELOPMENTAL PSYCHOLOGY*, V5 N1, PP13-17, JUL 71

TO TEST THE HYPOTHESIS THAT CHILDREN LEARN CONCEPTS BETTER THROUGH LINGUISTIC CUES THAN THROUGH EXEMPLARS, 58 KINDERGARTEN CHILDREN IN FOUR MATCHED GROUPS WERE TAUGHT FOUR NEW CONCEPTS USING DIFFERENT COMBINATIONS OF SENTENCES AND EXEMPLARS. NEITHER MAIN EFFECT, VARIETY OF EXEMPLARS, NOR LEVEL OF LINGUISTIC CONTEXT WAS SIGNIFICANT. HOWEVER, A STRONG INTERACTION BETWEEN FACTORS WAS OBTAINED. (NH)

EJ 042 956 PS 501 202
EFFECTS OF DIFFERENTIAL EXPERIENCE ON INFANTS' PERFORMANCE IN A PIAGETIAN STAGE IV OBJECT-CONCEPT TASK LANDERS, WILLIAM F., *DEVELOPMENTAL PSYCHOLOGY*, V5 N1, PP48-54, JUL 71

REPORTS ON AN EXPERIMENT WHICH INVOLVED 42 7 1/2-10 1/2-MONTH-OLD INFANTS PLAYING A TWO-POSITION HIDDEN-OBJECT GAME. RESULTS WERE INTERPRETED TO SUPPORT AND EXTEND PREVIOUS EXPLANATIONS OF STAGE IV OF OBJECT-CONCEPT DEVELOPMENT. THIS REPORT IS A REVISED VERSION OF A PAPER PRESENTED AT THE BIENNIAL MEETING OF THE SOCIETY FOR RESEARCH IN CHILD DEVELOPMENT, SANTA MONICA, CALIFORNIA, 1969. (NH)

EJ 042 957 PS 501 205
EFFECTS OF SOCIAL REINFORCEMENT ON LEARNING AND RETENTION IN CHILDREN ALLEN, SARA A.; AND OTHERS, *DEVELOPMENTAL PSYCHOLOGY*, V5 N1, PP73-80, JUL 71

REINFORCEMENT CONDITIONS OF APPROVAL, DISAPPROVAL, OR SILENCE WERE USED DURING A DISCRIMINATION TASK ASSIGNED TO 96 BOYS AND 96 GIRLS. CHILDREN RECEIVING CRITICISM RESPONDED AT SLOWER RATES AND MADE MORE ERRORS THAN CHILDREN RECEIVING PRAISE OR SILENCE. RETENTION WAS MEASURED AFTER 8 DAYS. RESULTS SUGGEST THAT DISAPPROVAL NEGATIVELY AFFECTS BOTH MOTIVATION AND LEARNING. (NH)

EJ 042 958 PS 501 206
IDENTIFICATION OF VERBAL CONCEPTS BY PRESCHOOL CHILDREN DI VESTA, FRANCIS J.; STAUBER, KATHLEEN A., *DEVELOPMENTAL PSYCHOLOGY*, V5 N1, PP81-85, JUL 71

EJ 042 959 PS 501 209
VERBAL PAIRED-ASSOCIATE LEARNING IN CHILDREN AND ADULTS WITH ANTICIPATION, RECOGNITION, AND RECALL METHODS MC CULLERS, JOHN C., *DEVELOPMENTAL PSYCHOLOGY*, V5 N1, PP112-117, JUL 71

EJ 042 960 PS 501 210
CHARACTERISTICS OF WORD ASSOCIATION RESPONSES OBTAINED FROM CHILDREN IN GRADES ONE THROUGH FOUR PALERMO, DAVID S., *DEVELOPMENTAL PSYCHOLOGY*, V5 N1, PP118-123, JUL 71

EJ 042 961 PS 501 216
NAMING AND MEMORY IN NURSERY SCHOOL CHILDREN IN THE ABSENCE OF REHEARSAL WARD, WILLIAM C.; LEGANT, PATRICIA, *DEVELOPMENTAL PSYCHOLOGY*, V5 N1, PP174-175, JUL 71

EJ 042 962 PS 501 218
INFORMATION SEEKING ABOUT UNCERTAIN BUT UNAVOIDABLE OUTCOMES: EFFECTS OF PROBABILITY, VALENCE, AND INTERVENING ACTIVITY GRUSEC, THEODORE; GRUSEC, JOAN E., *DEVELOPMENTAL PSYCHOLOGY*, V5 N1, PP177, JUL 71

EJ 042 963 PS 501 231
THE "FEATURE POSITIVE EFFECT" AND SIMULTANEOUS DISCRIMINATION LEARNING SAINSBURY, ROBERT, *JOURNAL OF EXPERIMENTAL CHILD PSYCHOLOGY*, V11 N3, PP347-356, JUN 71

FOUR- AND FIVE-YEAR-OLD CHILDREN (N24) WERE PUT INTO TWO GROUPS AND TRAINED TO DISCRIMINATE BETWEEN TWO DISPLAYS WHICH COULD ONLY BE DIFFERENTIATED BY A SINGLE DISTINCTIVE FEATURE LOCATED ON ONE OF THE DISPLAYS. SUBJECTS TRAINED WITH THE DISTINCTIVE FEATURE LOCATED ON THE POSITIVE DISPLAY LEARNED THE SIMULTANEOUS DISCRIMINATION WHILE FEATURE NEGATIVE SUBJECTS DID NOT. (AJ)

EJ 042 964 PS 501 237
RECOGNITION MEMORY FOR PICTURES IN PRESCHOOL CHILDREN BROWN, ANN L.; SCOTT, MARCIA S., *JOURNAL OF EXPERIMENTAL CHILD PSYCHOLOGY*, V11 N3, PP401-412, JUN 71

EJ 042 965 PS 501 239
FACTORS INFLUENCING CHILDREN'S CONCEPT IDENTIFICATION PERFORMANCE WITH NONPREFERRED RELEVANT ATTRIBUTES JOHNSON, PEDER J.; AND OTHERS, *JOURNAL OF EXPERIMENTAL CHILD PSYCHOLOGY*, V11 N3, PP430-441, JUN 71

EXPERIMENTS WERE CONDUCTED TO DETERMINE THE INFLUENCE UPON TASK DIFFICULTY OF THESE FACTORS: AGE; PERCENTAGE OF REDUNDANCY BETWEEN RELEVANT AND IRRELEVANT CUES; SALIENCY OF REINFORCEMENT, DISCRIMINABILITY OF RELEVANT NONPREFERRED DIMENSION, AND LEARNING SET PRETRAINING TO REJECT PREFERRED IRRELEVANT DIMENSIONS. (AUTHOR/AJ)

EJ 042 966 PS 501 241
MEMORY AND ATTENTION IN CHILDREN'S DOUBLE-ALTERNATION LEARNING BALLING, JOHN D.; MYERS, NANCY A., *JOURNAL OF EXPERIMENTAL CHILD PSYCHOLOGY*, V11 N3, PP448-460, JUN 71

ASSESSED THE INFLUENCE OF MNEMONIC AND ATTENTIONAL AIDS ON CHILDREN'S DOUBLE-ALTERNATION LEARNING, IN A PREDICTION SITUATION IN WHICH SUBJECT HAD TO LEARN TO PRODUCE TWO CONSECUTIVE RESPONSES OF THE ALTERNATE TYPES. (AUTHOR/AJ)

EJ 042 967 PS 501 243
THE PERFORMANCE OF PRESCHOOL CHILDREN ON REVERSAL AND TWO TYPES OF EXTRADIMENSIONAL SHIFTS CAMPIONE, JOSEPH C., *JOURNAL OF EXPERIMENTAL CHILD PSYCHOLOGY*, V11 N3, PP480-490, JUN 71

EJ 042 968 PS 501 245
EFFECTS OF CONTEXT ON PRESCHOOL CHILDREN'S JUDGMENTS CANTOR, GORDON N., *JOURNAL OF EXPERIMENTAL CHILD PSYCHOLOGY*, V11 N3, PP505-512, JUN 71

EJ 043 020 PS 501 246
BOOKS FOR YOUNG CHILDREN MCPHEE, MIRIAM; LEWIS, CLAUDIA, *YOUNG CHILDREN*, V26 N6, PP329-332, AUG 71
REVIEWS SELECTED NEW PUBLICATIONS FOR CHILDREN AND DESIGNATES AGE LEVELS WITHIN OVERLAPPING RANGES. (AJ)

EJ 043 058 PS 501 213
SELECTIVE ATTENTION IN MENTAL RETARDATES HAGEN, JOHN W.; HUNTSMAN, NANCY J., *DEVELOPMENTAL PSYCHOLOGY*, V5 N1, PP151-160, JUL 71

EJ 043 089 PS 501 251
FLORIDA'S EARLY CHILDHOOD LEARNING PROGRAM FOR MIGRANT CHILDREN COMBS, ELOYCE F., *YOUNG CHILDREN*, V26 N6, PP359-363, AUG 71

EJ 043 192 PS 501 214
AGGRESSION AS A FUNCTION OF EXPECTED RETALIATION AND AGGRESSION LEVEL OF TARGET AND AGGRESSOR PETERSON, ROLF A., *DEVELOPMENTAL PSYCHOLOGY*, V5 N1, PP161-166, JUL 71

EJ 043 193 PS 501 215
A LONGITUDINAL STUDY OF CHANGES IN EGO IDENTITY STATUS DURING THE FRESHMAN YEAR AT COLLEGE WATERMAN, ALAN S.; WATERMAN, CAROLINE K., *DEVELOPMENTAL PSYCHOLOGY*, V5 N1, PP167-173, JUL 71

EJ 043 194 PS 501 222
AN ACTIVITY GROUP APPROACH TO SERIOUSLY DISTURBED LATENCY BOYS SCOY, HOLLY VAN, *CHILD WELFARE*, V50 N7, PP413-419, JUL 71

EJ 043 195 PS 501 235
INFANT HABITUATION AND GENERALIZATION TO DIFFERING DEGREES OF STIMULUS NOVELTY COHEN, LESLIE B.; AND OTHERS, *JOURNAL OF EXPERIMENTAL CHILD PSYCHOLOGY*, V11 N3, PP379-389, JUN 71

EJ 043 196 PS 501 236
THE CONTROL OF IMITATIVE AND NONIMITATIVE BEHAVIORS IN SEVERELY RETARDED CHILDREN THROUGH "GENERALIZED-INSTRUCTION FOLLOWING" MARTIN, JERRY A., *JOURNAL OF EXPERIMENTAL CHILD PSYCHOLOGY*, V11 N3, PP390-400, JUN 71

EJ 043 197 PS 501 240
TELEVISED AGGRESSION AND THE INTERPERSONAL AGGRESSION OF PRESCHOOL CHILDREN STEUER, FAYE B.; AND OTHERS, *JOURNAL OF EXPERIMENTAL CHILD PSYCHOLOGY*, V11 N3, PP442-447, JUN 71

EJ 043 198 PS 501 244
LEARNING OF AGGRESSION AS A FUNCTION OF PRESENCE OF A HUMAN MODEL, RESPONSE INTENSITY, AND TARGET OF THE RESPONSE PARTON, DAVID A.; GESHURI, YOSSEF, *JOURNAL OF EXPERIMENTAL CHILD PSYCHOLOGY*, V11 N3, PP491-504, JUN 71

EJ 043 199 PS 501 252
CHILDREN'S AGGRESSION FESHBACH, NORMA; FESHBACH, SEYMOUR, *YOUNG CHILDREN*, V26 N6, PP364-377, AUG 71
REVIEWS AND ASSESSES CURRENT KNOWLEDGE ON CHILDREN'S AGGRESSION: THE DETERMINANTS AND REGULATION MECHANISMS. (AJ)

EJ 043 200 PS 501 259
IMPROVING THE SELF-CONCEPTS OF ACADEMIC UNDERACHIEVERS THROUGH MATERNAL GROUP COUNSELING WECHSLER, JILL D., *CALIFORNIA JOURNAL OF EDUCATIONAL RESEARCH*, V22 N3, PP96-103, MAY 71

EJ 043 239 PS 501 257
COGNITIVE STYLE AND READING ABILITY WINEMAN, JOHN, *CALIFORNIA JOURNAL OF EDUCATIONAL RESEARCH*, V22 N2, PP74-79, MAR 71

EJ 043 283 PS 501 201
EFFECT ON RESISTANCE TO DEVIATION OF OBSERVING A MODEL'S AFFECTIVE REACTION TO RESPONSE CONSEQUENCES SLABY, RONALD G.; PARKE, ROSS D., *DEVELOPMENTAL PSYCHOLOGY*, V5 N1, PP40-47, JUL 71
ELEMENTARY SCHOOL CHILDREN OF BOTH SEXES (N132) SAW A MALE PEER FILM MODEL EITHER REWARDED OR PUNISHED FOR TOUCHING PROHIBITED TOYS. THE MODEL EITHER SMILED, CRIED, OR SHOWED NO REACTION, AND SUBSEQUENTLY HAD A DIFFERENTIAL INFLUENCE ON THE BEHAVIOR OF CHILDREN WHO OBSERVED. (NH)

EJ 043 284 PS 501 208
EFFECTS OF COMPETITION-INDUCED FRUSTRATION ON TWO CLASSES OF MODELED BEHAVIOR CHRISTY, PAULINE R.; AND OTHERS, *DEVELOPMENTAL PSYCHOLOGY*, V5 N1, PP104-111, JUL 71

EJ 043 285 PS 501 232
A NONVERBAL TECHNIQUE FOR STUDYING MUSIC PREFERENCE COTTER, VANCE W.; SPRADLIN, JOSEPH E., *JOURNAL OF EXPERIMENTAL CHILD PSYCHOLOGY*, V11 N3, PP357-365, JUN 71
EVALUATES THE PREFERENCE AMONG RETARDED CHILDREN AND ADOLESCENTS FOR MUSIC AS COMPARED TO SILENCE, FOR MUSIC AS COMPARED TO WHITE NOISE (NONMUSICAL AUDITORY STIMULUS) AND FOR TWO PARTICULAR TYPES OF MUSIC. (AUTHOR/AJ)

EJ 043 314 PS 501 211
A CHILD IN DISTRESS: THE INFLUENCE OF NURTURANCE AND MODELING ON CHILDREN'S ATTEMPTS TO HELP STAUB, ERVIN, *DEVELOPMENTAL PSYCHOLOGY*, V5 N1, PP124-132, JUL 71

EJ 043 315 PS 501 221
COLONIAL CHILD CARE INSTITUTIONS: OUR HERITAGE OF CARE WHITTAKER, JAMES K., *CHILD WELFARE*, V50 N7, PP396-400, JUL 71

EJ 043 316 PS 501 234
AN AUDITORY PROMPTING DEVICE FOR BEHAVIOR OBSERVATION LEIFER, A. D.; LEIFER, L. J., *JOURNAL OF EXPERIMENTAL CHILD PSYCHOLOGY*, V11 N3, PP376-378, JUN 71
HARDWARE IS DESCRIBED FOR A LIGHTWEIGHT, MOBILE DEVICE THAT FACILITATES SYSTEMATIC SAMPLING OF BEHAVIOR IN TIME AND THE ACCURATE INDICATION OF SHORT TIME INTERVALS. (AUTHOR/AJ)

EJ 043 352 PS 501 217
STEREOTYPIC AFFECTIVE PROPERTIES OF PERSONAL NAMES AND SOMATOTYPES IN CHILDREN JOHNSON, PETER A.; STAFFIERI, J. ROBERT, *DEVELOPMENTAL PSYCHOLOGY*, V5 N1, PP176, JUL 71

EJ 043 353 PS 501 220
A SOCIOCULTURAL PERSPECTIVE ON PHYSICAL CHILD ABUSE GIL, DAVID G., *CHILD WELFARE*, V50 N7, PP389-395, JUL 71
SUGGESTS A SERIES OF MEASURES FOR PREVENTION OF CHILD ABUSE THROUGH EDUCATION, LEGISLATION, ELIMINATION OF POVERTY, AND SOCIAL SERVICES. (AUTHOR/AJ)

EJ 043 354 PS 501 249
UNIVERSAL CHILD CARE WILLIAMS, A. KENTON, *YOUNG CHILDREN*, V26 N6, PP348-354, AUG 71
AN OVERVIEW OF THE FACTORS INFLUENCING GROWING EMPHASIS ON DAY CARE AND AN EXAMINATION OF THE HISTORICAL DEVELOPMENT, CURRENT TRENDS AND FUTURE GOALS OF DAY CARE. (AUTHOR/AJ)

EJ 043 415 PS 501 258
EFFECTS OF TUTORIAL EXPERIENCES ON THE PROBLEM-SOLVING BEHAVIOR OF SIXTH-GRADERS RAMIREZ, JUDITH VALLA, *CALIFORNIA JOURNAL OF EDUCATIONAL RESEARCH*, V22 N2, PP80-90, MAR 71
THE EFFECTS OF A PROBLEM SOLVING-ORIENTED TUTORIAL PROGRAM ON THE PROBLEM SOLVING BEHAVIOR OF STUDENT TUTORS IS STUDIED. HALF OF A SIXTH GRADE CLASS WERE TUTORS; THE OTHER HALF A CONTROL GROUP. RESULTS ON TWO TASKS MEASURING PROBLEM SOLVING SKILLS SHOWED SIGNIFICANT DIFFERENCE BETWEEN THE TWO GROUPS ONLY ON THE SKILL OF PROBLEM DEFINING. (NH)

EJ 043 456 PS 501 262
A GEOMETRIC REPRESENTATION OF THE NOTIONS OF RELIABILITY, RELEVANCE, AND VALIDITY KAISER, HENRY F.; CARTER, HAROLD D., *CALIFORNIA JOURNAL OF EDUCATIONAL RESEARCH*, V22 N3, PP122-125, MAY 71

EJ 043 480 PS 501 268
DEVELOPMENT OF SYNTACTIC COMPREHENSION IN PRESCHOOL CHILDREN AS A FUNCTION OF SOCIOECONOMIC LEVEL PARISI, DOMENICO, *DEVELOPMENTAL PSYCHOLOGY*, V5 N2, PP186-189, SEP 71

EJ 043 481 PS 501 289
SEX DIFFERENCES IN THE EXPRESSION OF VOCATIONAL ASPIRATIONS BY ELEMENTARY SCHOOL CHILDREN LOOFT, WILLIAM R., *DEVELOPMENTAL PSYCHOLOGY*, V5 N2, PP366, SEP 71

EJ 043 482 PS 501 339
LEVELS OF ASPIRATION, ACHIEVEMENT, AND SOCIOCULTURAL DIFFERENCES IN PRESCHOOL CHILDREN VERSTEEG, ARLEN; HALL, ROBERT, *JOURNAL OF GENETIC PSYCHOLOGY*, V119, PP137-142, SEP 71

EJ 043 605 PS 501 270
SOCIAL PARTICIPATION AS A FACTOR IN THE MORAL DEVELOPMENT OF PREADOLESCENTS KEASEY, CHARLES BLAKE, *DEVELOPMENTAL PSYCHOLOGY*, V5 N2, PP216-220, SEP 71
STAGE OF MORAL DEVELOPMENT WAS FOUND TO BE POSITIVELY RELATED TO EXTENT OF SOCIAL PARTICIPATION WHETHER JUDGED BY SELF, PEERS, OR TEACHERS. (AUTHOR/WY)

EJ 043 606 PS 501 276
INTERPERSONAL PERCEPTION OF YOUNG CHILDREN: EGOCENTRISM OR EMPATHY? BORKE, HELENE, *DEVELOPMENTAL PSYCHOLOGY*, V5 N2, PP263-269, SEP 71
THIS STUDY SUGGESTS THAT CHILDREN 3-8 YEARS OLD ARE NOT TOTALLY EGOCENTRIC BUT HAVE SOME CAPACITY FOR RESPONDING EMPATHICALLY TO ANOTHER PERSON'S PERSPECTIVE AND POINT OF VIEW. (AUTHOR/WY)

EJ 043 666 PS 501 277
SATIATION OF VISUAL REINFORCEMENT IN YOUNG INFANTS CARON, ROSE F.; AND OTHERS, *DEVELOPMENTAL PSYCHOLOGY*, V5 N2, PP279-289, SEP 71
EXPERIMENT DEMONSTRATES THAT THE REINFORCING EFFICACY OF VISUAL FEEDBACK IS RELATED TO ITS DEGREE OF REDUNDANCY. (WY)

EJ 043 667 PS 501 282
AGE CHANGES IN CARDIAC DECELERATION WITHIN A FIXED FOREPERIOD REACTION-TIME TASK: AN INDEX OF ATTENTION SROUFE, L. ALAN, *DEVELOPMENTAL PSYCHOLOGY*, V5 N2, PP338-343, SEP 71
THIRTY 6-, 8-, AND 10-YEAR-OLD BOYS WERE SUBJECTS IN THIS STUDY WHOSE FINDINGS SUGGEST THAT THE OBTAINED DIFFERENCES IN ANTICIPATORY HEART-RATE DECELERATION REFLECT DEVELOPMENTAL CHANGES IN THE ABILITY TO MAINTAIN ATTENTION. (WY)

EJ 043 668 PS 501 293
EVIDENCE FOR COMPETITION AND COORDINATION BETWEEN VOCAL AND MANUAL RESPONSES IN PRESCHOOL CHILDREN BIRCH, DAVID, *JOURNAL OF EXPERIMENTAL CHILD PSYCHOLOGY*, V12 N1, PP10-26, AUG 71
COMPARISONS AMONG MEASURES OF VOCAL AND MANUAL RESPONSES INDICATE THE TWO RESPONSE SYSTEMS ARE NOT INDEPENDENT AND SUGGEST THE HYPOTHESIS THAT PROCESSES OF COORDINATION OCCUR WITH CHILDREN 4 YEARS OR OLDER THAT DO NOT CCCUR WITH YOUNGER CHILDREN. (AUTHOR/WY)

EJ 043 669 PS 501 326
ATTENTION IN HYPERACTIVE CHILDREN AND THE EFFECT OF METHYLPHENIDATE (RITALIN) SYKES, DONALD H.; AND OTHERS, *JOURNAL OF CHILD PSYCHOLOGY AND PSYCHIATRY*, V12 N2, PP129-139, AUG 71
HYPERACTIVE CHILDREN TREATED WITH METHYLPHENIDATE (RITALIN) SHOWED A SIGNIFICANT IMPROVEMENT IN ALL ASPECTS OF PERFORMANCE IN AN EXPERIMENTER-PACED TASK WHEN COMPARED TO A CONTROL GROUP OF HYPERACTIVE CHILDREN GIVEN A PLACEBO. (AUTHOR/WY)

EJ 043 670 PS 501 345
INFANT-CARETAKER INTERACTIONS BENNETT, STEPHEN, *JOURNAL OF CHILD PSYCHIATRY*, V10 N2, PP321-335, APR 71
AN INFANT'S UNIQUE STYLE AND TEMPERAMENT IS THOUGHT TO DEVELOP DURING A GIVEN SMALL TIME SEGMENT AS A CONSEQUENCE OF THE INITIATIVES TAKEN BY CARETAKER OR INFANT; USUALLY AN INTERACTION OF THE TWO. (WY)

EJ 043 671 PS 501 346
VIOLENCE BEGINS AT HOME. THE PARENTS' CENTER PROJECT FOR THE STUDY AND PREVENTION OF CHILD ABUSE GALDSTON, RICHARD, *JOURNAL OF CHILD PSYCHIATRY*, V10 N2, PP336-350, APR 71
DESCRIBES A PROJECT IN OPERATION FOR OVER TWO YEARS WHICH OFFERS PROTECTIVE INTERVENTION FOR CHILDREN AND GROUP MEETINGS FROM PARENTS. SUGGESTS THE CREATION OF A NUMBER OF CENTERS TO HELP VULNERABLE PARENTS OF PRESCHOOL CHILDREN IN AN EFFORT TO INTERRUPT THE CIRCULAR SPREAD OF VIOLENCE AS A FAMILY PHENOMENON. (WY)

EJ 043 672 PS 501 350
SOCIAL COMPARISON BY YOUNG CHILDREN MASTERS, JOHN C., *YOUNG CHILDREN*, V27 N1, PP37-60, OCT 71
BEGINNING WITH PRESCHOOL YEARS, CHILDREN COMPARE THE REWARDS THEY RECEIVE WITH THOSE RECEIVED BY OTHER CHILDREN. THESE COMPARISONS HAVE POWERFUL EFFECTS UPON SUBSEQUENT SELF-REWARDING BEHAVIOR, EVALUATION OF REWARDS AND THE SHARING OF REWARDS WITH OTHERS. A KEY PROCESS IN THESE DEVELOPMENTS, "SOCIAL COMPARISON," IS REVIEWED IN THIS ARTICLE. (AUTHOR/WY)

EJ 043 703 PS 501 271
DEVELOPMENT OF VISUAL SCANNING STRATEGIES FOR DIFFERENTIATING WORDS NODINE, CALVIN F.; LANG, NORMA J., *DEVELOPMENTAL PSYCHOLOGY*, V5 N2, PP221-32, SEP 71
EYE MOVEMENT OF NONREADERS (KINDERGARTEN SUBJECTS) AND READERS (THIRD-GRADE SUBJECTS) WERE MEASURED DURING A VISUAL DISCRIMINATION TASK INVOLVING MATCHED AND UNMATCHED PAIRS OF FOUR-LETTER PSEUDOWORDS. BOTH QUANTITATIVE AND QUALITATIVE ANALYSES SUPPORT THE CONCLUSION THAT THE DEVELOPMENT OF PERCEPTUAL STRATEGIES IS A DIRECT RESULT OF INCREASING COGNITIVE CONTROL OVER EYE MOVEMENTS. (AUTHOR/WY)

EJ 043 704 PS 501 284
APPARENT VISUAL SIZE AS A FUNCTION OF AGE, INTELLIGENCE, AND A SURROUNDING FRAME OF REFERENCE FOR NORMAL AND MENTALLY RETARDED SUBJECTS HILL, A. LEWIS; BURKE, DEBORAH, *DEVELOPMENTAL PSYCHOLOGY*, V5 N2, PP349-356, SEP 71

EJ 043 705 PS 501 287
STIMULUS SELECTION AS A FUNCTION OF LETTER COLOR AND AGE IN PAIRED-ASSOCIATE LEARNING RABINOWITZ, F. MICHAEL; MCCLINTON, SANDRA, *DEVELOPMENTAL PSYCHOLOGY*, V5 N2, PP364, SEP 71

EJ 043 706 PS 501 294
METHODOLOGICAL STUDY OF FORM CONSTANCY DEVELOPMENT KAESS, DALE W., *JOURNAL OF EXPERIMENTAL CHILD PSYCHOLOGY*, V12 N1, PP27-34, AUG 71

EJ 043 707 PS 501 334
A STUDY OF RECOGNITION AND REPRODUCTION OF BENDER GESTALT FIGURES BY CHILDREN OF AVERAGE AND BELOW INTELLIGENCE ALLEN, ROBERT M.; AND OTHERS, *JOURNAL OF GENETIC PSYCHOLOGY*, V119, PP75-78, SEP 71
THIS STUDY OF EDUCABLE MENTAL RETARDATES AND INTELLECTUALLY AVERAGE CHILDREN SUPPORTED THE COMMONSENSE NOTION THAT RECOGNITION SKILL IS MORE HIGHLY DEVELOPED THAN REPRODUCTION SKILL IN SAME AGE CHILDREN OF BOTH GROUPS. (WY)

EJ 043 856 PS 501 283
A DEVELOPMENTAL STUDY OF COGNITIVE BALANCE BLANCHARD, EDWARD B.; PRICE, KATINA C., *DEVELOPMENTAL PSYCHOLOGY*, V5 N2, PP344-348, SEP 71

EJ 043 857 PS 501 305
EARLY COGNITIVE DEVELOPMENT AND PRESCHOOL EDUCATION GOLDSCHMID, MARCEL L., *INTERNATIONAL JOURNAL OF EARLY CHILDHOOD*, V3 N1, PP1-9, 71

EJ 043 858 PS 501 315
NEW DIMENSIONS IN STAFF DEVELOPMENT IN A JUVENILE CORRECTIONAL SYSTEM GRENIER, WALTER J., *CHILDREN*, V18 N5, PP187-191, SEP-OCT 71
RECOGNIZING THAT THERE MUST BE MUTUAL COMMUNICATION AND RESPECT BETWEEN ADMINISTRATORS AND EMPLOYEES, THE JUVENILE DIVISION OF THE ILLINOIS DEPARTMENT OF CORRECTIONS HAS IMPLEMENTED EXTENSIVE IN-SERVICE TRAINING FOR ALL EMPLOYEES. (MK)

EJ 043 859 PS 501 323
EMOTIONAL SENSITIVITY AND INTELLIGENCE IN CHILDREN FROM ORPHANAGES AND NORMAL HOMES CHEYNE, WILLIAM M.; JAHODA, GUSTAV, *JOURNAL OF CHILD PSYCHOLOGY AND PSYCHIATRY*, V12 N2, PP77-90, AUG 71
EIGHTY ORPHANAGE CHILDREN, 6-10 YEARS OLD, WERE MATCHED WITH CHILDREN IN NORMAL HOMES AND TESTED FOR RECOGNITION OF EMOTION IN SPEECH. RECOGNITION SCORES WERE HIGHER FOR (A) NEGATIVE THAN POSITIVE EMOTIONS, (B) FEMALE THAN MALE VOICES, AND (C) EDUCATED AND UNEDUCATED SPEECH, THOUGH THESE EFFECTS INTERACTED WITH AGE. (AUTHOR/WY)

EJ 043 860 PS 501 337
DEVELOPMENTAL CHARACTERISTICS OF EMOTIONAL EXPERIENCE ALEXANDER, THERON, *JOURNAL OF GENETIC PSYCHOLOGY*, V119, PP109-117, SEP 71

EJ 044 006 PS 501 308
EARLY CHILD STIMULATION THROUGH PARENT EDUCATION GORDON, IRA J., *INTERNATIONAL JOURNAL OF EARLY CHILDHOOD*, V3 N1, PP26-36, 71

EJ 044 007 PS 501 311
A MOTHERS' TRAINING PROGRAM--THE ROAD TO A PURPOSEFUL EXISTENCE BADGER, EARLADEEN D., *CHILDREN*, V18 N5, PP168-173, SEP-OCT 71
IN A TRAINING PROGRAM, 20 SOCIALLY AND ECONOMICALLY DISADVANTAGED MOTHERS LEARN THEY CAN HAVE A MOST IMPORTANT PART IN HELPING PREPARE THEIR PRESCHOOL CHILDREN FOR PUBLIC SCHOOL. (MK)

EJ 044 008 PS 501 317
LEARNING FROM EACH OTHER SCHAEFER, EARL S., *CHILDHOOD EDUCATION*, V48 N1, PP2-7, OCT 71
ARGUES THAT EDUCATION MUST BE A CONTINUING PROCESS THROUGHOUT AN INDIVIDUAL'S LIFE SPAN, TAKING PLACE IN THE FAMILY, SCHOOL, AND COMMUNITY. (AJ)

EJ 044 009 PS 501 333
EFFECTS OF HEMOPHILIA UPON INTELLECTUAL GROWTH AND ACADEMIC ACHIEVEMENT OLCH, DORIS, *JOURNAL OF GENETIC PSYCHOLOGY*, V119, PP63-74, SEP 71

EJ 044 010 PS 501 349
ON THE VALUE OF BOTH PLAY AND STRUCTURE IN EARLY EDUCATION FOWLER, WILLIAM, *YOUNG CHILDREN*, V27 N1, PP24-36, OCT 71
THIS DISCUSSION OF THE ROLE OF STRUCTURED GUIDANCE IN FACILITATING COGNITIVE DEVELOPMENT PRESENTS THE AUTHOR'S POINT OF VIEW REGARDING A CURRENT ISSUE IN EARLY CHILDHOOD EDUCATION. (WY)

EJ 044 118 PS 501 291
EARLY AUDITORY DEPRIVATION AND SENSORY COMPENSATION MACDOUGALL, JAMES C.; RABINOVITCH, M. SAM, *DEVELOPMENTAL PSYCHOLOGY*, V5 N2, PP368, SEP 71

EJ 044 119 PS 501 292
THE EFFECTS OF THE ENVIRONMENT UPON STATE CYCLES IN THE HUMAN NEWBORN ASHTON, R., *JOURNAL OF EXPERIMENTAL CHILD PSYCHOLOGY*, V12 N1, PP1-9, AUG 71
A DIMMER LIGHT CONDITION WAS FOUND TO AFFECT THE RESPIRATION RATE OF 10 NEWBORNS IN AN EXPERIMENT INVESTIGATING THE EFFECTS OF SOUND AND LIGHT INTENSITY. (WY)

EJ 044 157 PS 501 295
DISCRIMINATION AND INSTRUCTIONS AS FACTORS IN THE CONTROL OF NONREINFORCED IMITATION BUFFORD, RODGER K., *JOURNAL OF EXPERIMENTAL CHILD PSYCHOLOGY*, V12 N1, PP35-50, AUG 71
REPORTS THREE EXPERIMENTS CONDUCTED TO INVESTIGATE FACTORS CONTROLLING PERFORMANCE OF NONREINFORCED VERBAL IMITATION. (WY)

EJ 044 186 PS 501 272
SOME DEVELOPMENTAL CHANGES IN THE ORGANIZATION OF SELF-EVALUATIONS MULLENER, NATHANAEL; LAIRD, JAMES D., *DEVELOPMENTAL PSYCHOLOGY*, V5 N2, PP233-236, SEP 71
STUDIES AGE-RELATED DIFFERENCES IN THE KIND AND COMPLEXITY OF INFORMATION INDIVIDUALS RECEIVE ABOUT THEMSELVES. (WY)

EJ 044 230 PS 501 313
THIRTY YEARS OF INNOVATION IN FOSTER CARE TIEDER, MYRA, *CHILDREN*, V18 N5, PP179-182, SEP-OCT 71

EJ 044 285 PS 501 318
LEARNING FROM CHILDREN: THE ROLE OF OCD ZIGLER, EDWARD, *CHILDHOOD EDUCATION*, V48 N1, PP8-11, OCT 71
DISCUSSES GOALS OF THE OFFICE OF CHILD DEVELOPMENT AND DESCRIBES SOME OCD EXPERIMENTAL PROJECTS NOW IN PROGRESS. (AJ)

EJ 044 507 PS 501 290
THE EFFECT OF TRAINING CHILDREN TO MAKE MORAL JUDGMENTS THAT ARE INDEPENDENT OF SANCTIONS JENSEN, LARRY; HUGHSTON, KAREN, *DEVELOPMENTAL PSYCHOLOGY*, V5 N2, PP367, SEP 71

EJ 044 508 PS 501 319
EVERY CHILD A TEACHER GARTNER, ALAN; AND OTHERS, *CHILDHOOD EDUCATION*, V48 N1, PP12-16, OCT 71
REPORTS ON THE GROWTH OF TUTORIAL PROGRAMS IN WHICH CHILDREN LEARN THROUGH TEACHING. (AJ)

EJ 044 509 PS 501 320
"THIS YEAR I GOT MY BUDDY TO LAUGH" SWETT, MANETTE, *CHILDHOOD EDUCATION*, V48 N1, PP17-20, OCT 71
AN EXAMPLE OF CROSS-AGE TEACHING IS DESCRIBED IN THIS ACCOUNT OF A FOURTH GRADE CLASS' ADOPTION OF A KINDERGARTEN CLASS. (AJ)

EJ 044 510 PS 501 322
WORKING TOGETHER WORKS MAJORS, HUGHIE LEE, *CHILDHOOD EDUCATION*, V48 N1, PP25-28, OCT 71
DESCRIBES CROSS-AGE TUTORING EXPERIMENT IN WHICH SIXTH GRADERS PROVIDED INDIVIDUAL HELP AND COMPANIONSHIP TO FIRST-GRADERS. TUTOR GAINS WERE SUBJECT REINFORCEMENT, EXTENDED CREATIVITY, AND MEANINGFUL PERSONAL RELATIONSHIPS. (AJ)

EJ 044 511 PS 501 347
CREATING A CLIMATE FOR INDIVIDUALIZING INSTRUCTION WHEELER, ALAN H., *YOUNG CHILDREN*, V27 N1, PP12-16, OCT 71
THE ROLE OF THE TEACHER IS BASIC IN CREATING A LEARNING ENVIRONMENT WHICH WILL RECOGNIZE AND RESPOND TO INDIVIDUAL NEEDS AND DIFFERENCES. INNOVATIVE TEACHER EDUCATION IS NECESSARY IN ORDER TO DEVELOP TEACHERS WHO WILL FACILITATE EFFECTIVE LEARNING FOR CHILDREN. (AUTHOR)

EJ 044 512 PS 501 348
CARPENTRY FOR YOUNG CHILDREN BRANDHOFER, MARIJANE, *YOUNG CHILDREN*, V27 N1, PP17-23, OCT 71
THE AUTHOR PRESENTS PRACTICAL, SPECIFIC SUGGESTIONS FOR HEPLING YOUNG CHILDREN HAVE SUCCESSFUL CARPENTRY EXPERIENCES. SELECTION OF TOOLS AND MATERIALS AS WELL AS GUIDES FOR THEIR USE AND CARE ARE INCLUDED. (AUTHOR/WY)

EJ 044 613 PS 501 321
LANGUAGE LEARNING--FRESH VIVID AND THEIR OWN BEYER, EVELYN, *CHILDHOOD EDUCATION*, V48 N1, PP21-24, OCT 71
EXPLORES THE IMPORTANCE OF ENCOURAGING CHILDREN TO PLAY WITH LANGUAGE, TO USE IT AS AN ART MEDIUM, TO EXPERIMENT WITH SOUNDS AND WORDS, AND TO EXTEND MEANINGS. (AUTHOR/AJ)

EJ 044 691 PS 501 267
THE PRIORITY OF CUES IN SEX DISCRIMINATION BY CHILDREN AND ADULTS THOMPSON, SPENCER K.; BENTLER, P. M., *DEVELOPMENTAL PSYCHOLOGY*, V5 N2, PP181-185, SEP 71
REALISTIC MALE AND FEMALE PLASTIC DOLLS WERE USED IN THIS STUDY WHICH EXAMINED THE RELATIVE IMPORTANCE OF CUES ASSOCIATED WITH PHYSICAL SEX CHARACTERISTICS (GENITALS, BODY TYPE, AND HAIR LENGTH). (WY)

EJ 044 692 PS 501 269
PHONETIC COMPATIBILITY IN PAIRED-ASSOCIATE LEARNING OF FIRST- AND THIRD-GRADE CHILDREN FRAUNFELKER, BARBARA S., *DEVELOPMENTAL PSYCHOLOGY*, V5 N2, PP211-215, SEP 71
STUDIES THE EFFECT OF PHONETIC COMPATIBILITY UPON VERBAL LEARNING AND CONCLUDES THAT IT IS A TASK VARIABLE OF CONSIDERABLE MAGNITUDE. (WY)

EJ 044 693 PS 501 273
LANGUAGE STRUCTURE AND THE FREE RECALL OF VERBAL MESSAGES BY CHILDREN WEENER, PAUL, *DEVELOPMENTAL PSYCHOLOGY*, V5 N2, PP237-243, SEP 71

EJ 044 694 PS 501 285
THE SEQUENCE OF DEVELOPMENT OF CERTAIN NUMBER CONCEPTS IN PRESCHOOL CHILDREN SIEGEL, LINDA S., *DEVELOPMENTAL PSYCHOLOGY*, V5 N2, PP357-361, SEP 71

EJ 044 695 PS 501 286
THE DEVELOPMENT OF THE UNDERSTANDING OF CERTAIN NUMBER CONCEPTS SIEGEL, LINDA S., *DEVELOPMENTAL PSYCHOLOGY*, V5 N2, PP362-363, SEP 71

EJ 044 696 PS 501 297
GENERALIZED LABELING ON THE BASIS OF STRUCTURAL RESPONSE CLASSES BY TWO YOUNG CHILDREN WHITEHURST, GROVER J., *JOURNAL OF EXPERIMENTAL CHILD PSYCHOLOGY*, V12 N1, PP59-71, AUG 71

EJ 044 697 PS 501 298
CONCEPTUAL BEHAVIOR IN YOUNG CHILDREN: LEARNING TO SHIFT DIMENSIONAL ATTENTION SCHELL, DONNA J., *JOURNAL OF EXPERIMENTAL CHILD PSYCHOLOGY*, V12 N1, PP72-87, AUG 71

EJ 044 698 PS 501 299
VISUAL AND HAPTIC CUE UTILIZATION BY PRESCHOOL CHILDREN: THE RECOGNITION OF VISUAL AND HAPTIC STIMULI PRESENTED SEPARATELY AND TOGETHER MILLAR, SUSANNA, *JOURNAL OF EXPERIMENTAL CHILD PSYCHOLOGY*, V12 N1, PP88-94, AUG 71

EJ 044 699 PS 501 300
THE USE OF VERBAL MEDIATION IN THE RETARDED AS A FUNCTION OF DEVELOPMENTAL LEVEL AND RESPONSE AVAILABILITY GORDON, DONALD A.; BAUMEISTER, ALFRED A., *JOURNAL OF EXPERIMENTAL CHILD PSYCHOLOGY*, V12 N1, PP95-105, AUG 71
THE FOCUS OF THE STUDY WAS ON THE PAIRED-ASSOCIATE PERFORMANCE OF RETARDED SUBJECTS OF DIFFERENT LEVELS OF MENTAL AGE UNDER VARIOUS INSTRUCTIONAL CONDITIONS. (WY)

EJ 044 700 PS 501 301
CHILDREN'S RECALL STRATEGIES IN DICHOTIC LISTENING WITELSON, SANDRA F.; RABINOVITCH, M. SAM, *JOURNAL OF EXPERIMENTAL CHILD PSYCHOLOGY*, V12 N1, PP106-113, AUG 71
THE RESULTS OF THIS STUDY OF 24 9- AND 10-YEAR-OLD NORMAL CHILDREN INDICATED THAT BY 9 YEARS OF AGE, CHILDREN SPONTANEOUSLY ADOPT BOTH EAR AND TEMPORAL RECALL STRATEGIES UNDER THE SAME CONDITIONS AS DO ADULTS. THE CHILDREN READILY SWITCH FROM ONE RECALL STRATEGY TO THE OTHER AS A FUNCTION OF THE RATE INPUT OF THE MATERIAL. (WY)

EJ 044 701 PS 501 303
THE EFFECTS OF VISUALLY REPRESENTED CUES ON LEARNING OF LINEAR FUNCTION RULES LEE, SEONG-SOO, *JOURNAL OF EXPERIMENTAL CHILD PSYCHOLOGY*, V12 N1, PP129-145, AUG 71

EJ 044 702 PS 501 304
OBSERVATIONAL LEARNING: THE EFFECTS OF AGE, TASK DIFFICULTY, AND OBSERVERS' MOTORIC REHEARSAL WILLIAMS, MELANIE L.; WILLOUGHBY, R. H., *JOURNAL OF EXPERIMENTAL CHILD PSYCHOLOGY*, V12 N1, PP146-156, AUG 71

EJ 044 703 PS 501 306
ANALYSE DE L'ADOPTION DE LA NOTION DE "FLEUR" CHEZ LES ENFANTS DE 6 ANS MONATOVA, LILY, *INTERNATIONAL JOURNAL OF EARLY CHILDHOOD*, V3 N1, PP10-21, 71

A GROUP OF 20 6-YEAR-OLD CHILDREN WERE EXAMINED TO FIND OUT THEIR CONCEPT OF "FLOWER" AND THE AMOUNT OF DETAILED KNOWLEDGE THEY POSSESSED ABOUT FLOWERS. DATA WAS COLLECTED ON THE TECHNIQUES TEACHERS USE TO INTRODUCE SUCH INFORMATION. (AJ)

EJ 044 704 PS 501 328
THE FRANCK DRAWING COMPLETION TEST AS A MEASURE OF CREATIVITY ANASTASI, ANNE; SCHAEFER, CHARLES E., *JOURNAL OF GENETIC PSYCHOLOGY*, V119, PP3-12, SEP 71

A STUDY INVOLVING 800 NEW YORK METROPOLITAN HIGH SCHOOL STUDENTS CONCLUDED THAT THE FRANCK DRAWING COMPLETION TEST CAN DISCRIMINATE AMONG HIGH LEVELS OF CREATIVITY. (WY)

EJ 044 705 PS 501 329
A PILOT INVESTIGATION OF THE EFFECTS OF TRAINING TECHNIQUES DESIGNED TO ACCELERATE CHILDREN'S ACQUISITION OF CONSERVATION OF DISCONTINOUS QUANTITY FEIGENBAUM, KENNETH D., *JOURNAL OF GENETIC PSYCHOLOGY*, V119, PP13-23, SEP 71

EJ 044 706 PS 501 335
COGNITIVE STYLE AND CLASSIFICATION GARRETTSON, JUDY, *JOURNAL OF GENETIC PSYCHOLOGY*, V119, PP79-87, SEP 71

BEHAVIOR OF 60 SECOND-GRADE BOYS TESTED ON THREE TASKS DESIGNED BY PIAGET AND ON TWO COGNITIVE STYLE TASKS SHOWED GREAT VARIABILITY IN EACH CHILD'S RESPONSES. (WY)

EJ 044 707 PS 501 336
DIVERGENT THINKING AND PERSONALITY MEASURES OF ENGLISH AND AMERICAN EDUCATION MAJORS DI SCIPIO, WILLIAM J., *JOURNAL OF GENETIC PSYCHOLOGY*, V119, PP99-107, SEP 71

ENGLISH TEACHER-TRAINING COEDS WERE FOUND TO BE SIGNIFICANTLY MORE VERBALLY FLUENT THAN A MATCHED AMERICAN SAMPLE ON THREE MEASURES OF DIVERGENT THINKING. (WY)

EJ 044 757 PS 501 316
THE LIFE AND WORKS OF ERIK ERIKSON SOLNIT, ALBERT J., *CHILDREN*, V18 N5, PP192-193, SEP-OCT 71

REVIEW OF A BOOK BY ROBERT COLES, WHO WAS A STUDENT OF ERIKSON'S, ENTITLED "ERIK H. ERIKSON: THE GROWTH OF HIS WORK." (MK)

EJ 044 825 PS 501 280
THE USE OF PERCEPTUAL, FUNCTIONAL, AND ABSTRACT ATTRIBUTES IN MULTIPLE CLASSIFICATION PARKER, RONALD K.; DAY, MARY C., *DEVELOPMENTAL PSYCHOLOGY*, V5 N2, PP312-319, SEP 71

EJ 044 946 PS 501 331
INK-BLOT RESPONSES OF IDENTICAL AND FRATERNAL TWINS HAMILTON, J., *JOURNAL OF GENETIC PSYCHOLOGY*, V119, PP37-41, SEP 71

EJ 045 011 PS 501 309
LE NOUVEAU PROGRAMME D'ACTIVITES EDUCATRICES DANS LES ESTABLISSEMENTS PRESCOLAIRES EN YOUGOSLAVIE LOVRIC, MILENA, *INTERNATIONAL JOURNAL OF EARLY CHILDHOOD*, V3 N1, PP37-38, 71

DESCRIBES A NEW PRESCHOOL PROGRAM IN YUGOSLAVIA THAT STRESSES THE IMPORTANCE OF CHILDREN'S PLAY AND OF SPECIAL FORMS OF WORK. (AJ)

EJ 045 012 PS 501 312
A PLAY CENTER FOR DEVELOPMENTALLY HANDICAPPED INFANTS DIAMOND, FLORENCE, *CHILDREN*, V18 N5, PP174-178, SEP-OCT 71

EJ 045 042 PS 501 274
CONDITIONS GOVERNING NONREINFORCED IMITATION BANDURA, ALBERT; BARAB, PETER G., *DEVELOPMENTAL PSYCHOLOGY*, V5 N2, PP244-255, SEP 71

FINDINGS OF THE PRESENT EXPERIMENT REVEAL THAT DISCRIMINATION PROCESSES PLAY AN INFLUENTIAL ROLE IN NONREINFORCED IMITATION IN SEVERLY RETARDED CHILDREN. (WY)

EJ 045 043 PS 501 296
CHILDREN'S REACTIONS TO FAILURE AS A FUNCTION OF INTERRESPONSE INTERVAL PEDERSON, DAVID R., *JOURNAL OF EXPERIMENTAL CHILD PSYCHOLOGY*, V12 N1, PP51-58, AUG 71

THIS STUDY EXAMINED THE EFFECTS OF .5-, 1.0- AND 5.0-SECOND INTERRESPONSE INTERVALS ON CHILDREN'S LEVER-PULLING RESPONSES FOLLOWING SUCCESS AND FAILURE ON A BALL TOWER TASK. (WY)

EJ 045 044 PS 501 302
GENERALIZED IMITATION: THE EFFECTS OF EXPERIMENTER ABSENCE, DIFFERENTIAL REINFORCEMENT, AND STIMULUS COMPLEXITY PETERSON, ROBERT F.; AND OTHERS, *JOURNAL OF EXPERIMENTAL CHILD PSYCHOLOGY*, V12 N1, PP114-128, AUG 71

EJ 045 045 PS 501 332
GENETIC FACTORS IN TESTS OF PERCEPTION AND THE RORSCHACH MURAWSKI, BENJAMIN J., *JOURNAL OF GENETIC PSYCHOLOGY*, V119, PP43-52, SEP 71

EJ 045 046 PS 501 340
SEX DIFFERENCES IN ADAPTIVE STYLES BRANNIGAN, GARY G.; TOLOR, ALEXANDER, *JOURNAL OF GENETIC PSYCHOLOGY*, V119, PP143-149, SEP 71

BOTH MEXICAN- AND ANGLO-AMERICAN HEAD START PUPILS WERE SIGNIFICANTLY HIGHER IN THEIR LEVEL OF ASPIRATION AS COMPARED TO THEIR LEVEL OF ACHIEVEMENT. HOWEVER, THE MEXICAN-AMERICAN GROUP'S ACHIEVEMENT LEVEL WAS CONSIDERABLY NEARER TO THEIR LEVEL OF ASPIRATION AND THEY CONSISTENTLY SET MORE REALISTIC GOALS IN A RISK-TAKING SITUATION. (AUTHOR/WY)

EJ 045 047 PS 501 341
SELF-PARENTAL DISTANCE, CONTROL OF REINFORCEMENT, AND PERSONAL FUTURE TIME PERSPECTIVE BRANNIGAN, GARY G.; TOLOR, ALEXANDER, *JOURNAL OF GENETIC PSYCHOLOGY*, V119, PP151-157, SEP 71

THE RESULTS OF THIS STUDY CONFIRM THE PREDICTED RELATIONSHIP BETWEEN CLOSE SELF-PARENTAL DISTANCE AND INTERNAL CONTROL OF REINFORCEMENT FOR BOTH MALES AND FEMALES. (AUTHOR/WY)

EJ 045 048 PS 501 344
RECIPROCAL CONTRIBUTIONS BETWEEN PSYCHOANALYSIS AND PSYCHOEDUCATION NEFF, LEONARD; HAYWARD, RUTH, *JOURNAL OF CHILD PSYCHIATRY*, V10 N2, PP204-241, APR 71

DESCRIBES A WAY IN WHICH EGO FUNCTIONS MAY BE DEVELOPED TO HELP CHILDREN WITH A CERTAIN TYPE OF LEARNING DISORDER GAIN A SECOND CHANCE THROUGH PSYCHOEDUCATION. (WY)

EJ 045 049 PS 501 346
ANXIETY IN YOUNG CHILDREN BERGER, ALLAN S., *YOUNG CHILDREN*, V27 N1, PP5-11, OCT 71

A PSYCHIATRIST CONTRIBUTES TO AN UNDERSTANDING OF ANXIETY BY DETAILING THE SOURCES OF YOUNG CHILDREN'S FEARS. HE SUGGESTS WAYS ADULTS MAY HELP CHILDREN DEAL WITH THESE FEARS. (AUTHOR/WY)

EJ 045 068 PS 501 278
THE INFLUENCE OF NEGRO AND WHITE TEACHERS RATED AS EFFECTIVE OR NONEFFECTIVE ON THE PERFORMANCE OF NEGRO AND WHITE LOWER-CLASS CHILDREN YANDO, REGINA; AND OTHERS, *DEVELOPMENTAL PSYCHOLOGY*, V5 N2, PP290-299, SEP 71

STUDY FINDINGS SHOW THAT THE PERFORMANCE OF 72 NEGRO AND 72 WHITE CHILDREN WAS INFLUENCED BY INDIVIDUAL VARIATIONS IN THE PERSONAL CHARACTERISTICS OF THE ADULTS WITH WHOM THEY WERE INTERACTING IN TASK SITUATIONS RATHER THAN BY THE ADULTS' RACE. FURTHER, THIS INFLUENCE WAS RELATIVELY CONSTANT FOR BOTH NEGRO AND WHITE CHILDREN. (AUTHOR/WY)

EJ 045 083 PS 501 275
READING DISABILITY AND DIFFICULTIES IN FINGER LOCALIZATION AND RIGHT-LEFT DISCRIMINATION CROXEN, MARY E.; LYTTON, HUGH, *DEVELOPMENTAL PSYCHOLOGY*, V5 N2, PP256-262, SEP 71

EJ 045 084 PS 501 343
MOTIVATIONAL AND ATTITUDINAL CONTENT OF FIRST GRADE READING TEXTBOOKS BLOM, GASTON E., *JOURNAL OF CHILD PSYCHIATRY*, V10 N2, PP191-203, APR 71

EJ 045 107 PS 501 279
CHILD EFFECTS ON ADULT BEHAVIOR YARROW, MARIAN R.; AND OTHERS, *DEVELOPMENTAL PSYCHOLOGY*, V5 N2, PP300-311, SEP 71

EJ 045 108 PS 501 324
RESEARCH IN READING RETARDATION: TWO CRITICAL PROBLEMS APPLEBEE, ARTHUR N., *JOURNAL OF CHILD PSYCHOLOGY AND PSYCHIATRY*, V12 N2, PP91-113, AUG 71

THE FIRST PROBLEM CONFUSING RESULTS OF READING RESEARCH IS ONE OF DEFINITION, WITH ALL ITS ATTENDANT QUESTIONS OF GENERALIZATION AND REPLICATION. THE SECOND PROBLEM IS ONE OF INFERENCE AND HAS AT ITS HEART A FUNDAMENTAL DISJUNCTION BETWEEN THE STATISTICAL MODEL WHICH MOST STUDIES HAVE ASSUMED AND THE MODEL WHICH MAY IN FACT DESCRIBE THE UNDERLYING RELATIONSHIPS. (AUTHOR/WY)

EJ 045 109 PS 501 325
AUTONOMIC RESPONSES OF MALE ADOLESCENTS EXHIBITING REFRACTORY BEHAVIOUR IN SCHOOL DAVIES, JOHN G. V.; MALIPHANT, RODNEY, *JOURNAL OF CHILD PSYCHOLOGY AND PSYCHIATRY*, V12 N2, PP115-127, AUG 71
ADOLESCENT BOYS, JUDGED BY THE MAJORITY OF THEIR TEACHERS TO BE REFRACTORY (UNMANAGABLE IN BEHAVIOR), WERE FOUND TO HAVE SIGNIFICANTLY LOWER BASE HEART-RATES THAN THEIR MATCHED CONTROLS IN THREE EXPERIMENTAL SITUATIONS. (AUTHOR/WY)

EJ 045 110 PS 501 327
NEWBORN AND PRESCHOOLER: ORGANIZATION OF BEHAVIOR AND RELATIONS BETWEEN PERIODS BELL, RICHARD Q.; AND OTHERS, *MONOGRAPHS OF THE SOCIETY FOR RESEARCH IN CHILD DEVELOPMENT*, V36 N1-2, PP1-145, APR-JUL 71

EJ 045 111 PS 501 330
THE RELATIONSHIP OF ORDINAL POSITION AND SEX TO INTEREST PATTERNS OBERLANDER, MARK I.; AND OTHERS, *JOURNAL OF GENETIC PSYCHOLOGY*, V119, PP29-36, SEP 71
STUDY RESULTS SUGGEST THAT THE DISPOSITION OF FIRSTBORNS SEEMS TO BE TOWARD INTELLECTUAL ACTIVITIES AND THAT OF THE LATER BORNS TOWARD SOCIAL ACTIVITIES HAVING A HIGH DEGREE OF SOCIAL PARTICIPATION AND CONCERN. (WY)

EJ 045 159 PS 501 288
CHILD-PARENT SPATIAL PATTERNS UNDER PRAISE AND REPROOF GUARDO, CAROL J.; MEISELS, MURRAY, *DEVELOPMENTAL PSYCHOLOGY*, V5 N2, PP365, SEP 71

EJ 045 190 PS 501 281
CORRESPONDENCE BETWEEN BEHAVIORAL AND DOLL-PLAY MEASURES OF CONSCIENCE BURTON, ROGER V., *DEVELOPMENTAL PSYCHOLOGY*, V5 N2, PP320-332, SEP 71

EJ 045 191 PS 501 338
EFFECTS OF SEX-TYPED INFORMATION ON CHILDREN'S TOY PREFERENCES LIEBERT, ROBERT M., *JOURNAL OF GENETIC PSYCHOLOGY*, V119, PP133-136, SEP 71
IN ORDER TO TEST THE HYPOTHESIS THAT CHILDREN'S TOY PREFERENCES MAY BE INFLUENCED BY KNOWLEDGE OF THE USUAL PREFERENCES OF THEIR OWN SEX, THE EFFECT OF EXPERIMENTALLY MANIPULATING SEX-TYPED INFORMATION WERE EXAMINED, AS EXPECTED, THE DATA REVEALED THAT CHILDREN MATCHED THE ALLEGED PREFERENCES OF THEIR OWN SEX AT A LEVEL SIGNIFICANTLY ABOVE CHANCE. (WY)

EJ 045 232 PS 501 307
METODO DE ARCHIVAR LAS OBSERVACIONES DEL COMPORTAMIENTO DEL NINO, COMO GUIA PARA ENTENDERLO MEJOR STAMP, ISLA M., *INTERNATIONAL JOURNAL OF EARLY CHILDHOOD*, V3 N1, PP22-25, 71
PRESENTS A QUESTIONNAIRE FOR THE RECORDING OF TEACHERS' OBSERVATIONS OF INDIVIDUAL CHILDREN. (AJ)

EJ 045 233 PS 501 310
INVOLVING PARENTS IN RESIDENTIAL TREATMENT OF CHILDREN HEITING, KENNETH H., *CHILDREN*, V18 N5, PP163-167, SEP-OCT 71
INSTEAD OF COMPLETELY SEPARATING CHILDREN FROM THE PARENTS WHO CAUSED THEIR ORIGINAL PROBLEMS, PARENTAL-CHILD INTERACTION AND PARENTAL HELP ARE ENCOURAGED AT THIS RESIDENTIAL TREATMENT CENTER. (MK)

EJ 045 234 PS 501 314
OCCUPATIONAL THERAPY AND SPECIAL EDUCATION MITCHELL, MARLYS MARIE, *CHILDREN*, V18 N5, PP183-186, SEP-OCT 71
IN TREATING THE HANDICAPPED, OCCUPATIONAL THERAPISTS ARE MAINLY INTERESTED IN DEVELOPING PHYSICAL SKILLS, WHILE SPECIAL EDUCATION TEACHERS WORK WITH ACADEMIC ACHIEVEMENT. HELP IS NEEDED FROM BOTH THESE KINDS OF PROFESSIONALS, AS WELL AS FROM ADMINISTRATORS, SUPERVISORS AND DIRECTORS OF EACH OF THE PROGRAMS FOR HANDICAPPED CHILDREN. (MK)

EJ 045 388 PS 501 368
A CHECK ON THE STRUCTURE OF PARENTAL REPORTS OF CHILD-REARING PRACTICES DIELMAN, T. E.; AND OTHERS, *CHILD DEVELOPMENT*, V42 N3, PP893-903, SEP 71

EJ 045 389 PS 501 386
AN EXPERIENCE WITH FEAR IN THE LIVES OF CHILDREN MEATHENIA, PEGGY SUE, *CHILDHOOD EDUCATION*, V48 N2, PP75-79, NOV 71
A KINDERGARTEN TEACHER NARRATES HER CLASSROOM EXPERIENCES WITH TERROR-STRICKEN SPANISH-AMERICAN CHILDREN AFTER A DEVASTATING TORNADO. (AJ)

EJ 045 390 PS 501 402
STUDENT EVALUATION OF A HIGH SCHOOL SEX EDUCATION PROGRAM JUHASZ, ANNE MCCREARY, *CALIFORNIA JOURNAL OF EDUCATIONAL RESEARCH*, V22 N4, PP144-155, SEP 71
RESEARCH EXAMINING HIGH SCHOOL STUDENTS' (GRADES 7 TO 12) EVALUATIONS OF A SEX EDUCATION PROGRAM IN TERMS OF METHOD, CONTENT, ATTITUDE, UNDERSTANDING, TEACHER EFFECTIVENESS, VALUE AND NEED. (AUTHOR/AJ)

EJ 045 391 PS 501 403
EFFECT OF CLASSROOM NOISE ON NUMBER IDENTIFICATION BY RETARDED CHILDREN PIERSON, JEANNE, *CALIFORNIA JOURNAL OF EDUCATIONAL RESEARCH*, V22 N4, PP156-163, SEP 71
RESULTS OF A QUESTIONNAIRE SURVEY OF 1137 FOURTH, FIFTH AND SIXTH GRADE STUDENTS COMPARING THE ATTITUDES OF STUDENTS IN TEAM TEACHING AND THOSE IN SELF-CONTAINED CLASSES. QUESTIONS MEASURE ATTITUDES OF STUDENTS' SOCIAL-SELF, INTEREST IN SCHOOL, SCHOOL ACHIEVEMENT, TEACHERS, AND RESPONSIBILITY. (AUTHOR/AJ)

EJ 045 392 PS 501 408
PERCEPTIONS OF NEGRO BOYS REGARDING COLOR AND OCCUPATIONAL STATUS SCIARA, FRANK J., *CHILD STUDY JOURNAL*, V1 N4, PP203-211, SUM 71
IN A CONTROLLED STUDY, 70 FOURTH GRADE NEGRO BOYS ASCRIBED HIGH STATUS OCCUPATIONS TO NEGRO MEN WITH LIGHT COLORING AND LOW STATUS OCCUPATIONS TO NEGRO MEN WITH DARK COLORING. FINDINGS SEEM TO INDICATE THAT THE NEW SENSE OF UNITY AND EMPHASIS UPON BLACK PRIDE HAS HAD LITTLE EFFECT UPON THESE YOUNG SUBJECTS. (AUTHOR/MK)

EJ 045 393 PS 501 410
PEER TUTORING AS A TECHNIQUE FOR TEACHING THE UNMOTIVATED MOHAN, MADAN, *CHILD STUDY JOURNAL*, V1 N4, PP217-225, SUM 71
IN AN 8-MONTH PEER TUTORING PROGRAM, UNMOTIVATED CHILDREN IN GRADES 7 AND 8 TUTORED UNMOTIVATED CHILDREN IN GRADES 2 AND 3. IMPROVEMENTS IN ATTITUDE AND BEHAVIOR RESULTED FOR BOTH TUTORS AND TUTEES, WITH THE EXCEPTION OF ONE EMOTIONALLY DISTURBED CHILD. (MK)

EJ 045 394 PS 501 411
CHILDREN AND THE POLITICS OF TRUST RICCARDS, MICHAEL P., *CHILD STUDY JOURNAL*, V1 N4, PP227-232, SUM 71
EXAMINES THE HAZARDS OF TEACHING SCHOOL CHILDREN TO HAVE UNQUESTIONING TRUST IN THE GOVERNMENT AND ITS LEADERS. SUGGESTS THAT STUDENTS SHOULD BE TAUGHT THE ACTUAL RATHER THAN AN IDEALIZED MECHANISM VERSION OF THE AMERICAN POLITICS, AND ALSO THE IMPORTANCE OF THE DEMOCRATIC CITIZEN AS BOTH SUPPORTER AND CRITIC OF THE SYSTEM. (MK)

EJ 045 423 PS 501 389
THEY BECAME WHAT THEY BEHELD PRYKE, DAVID, *CHILDHOOD EDUCATION*, V48 N2, PP90-93, NOV 71
URGES EDUCATORS AND PARENTS TO ARM CHILDREN WITH THE TOOLS TO MASTER THE CODES OF THE NEW MEDIA (FILM, TELEVISION, RADIO, PHOTOGRAPHY) TO ENABLE THEM TO ACTIVATE, UNDERSTAND AND CONTROL THEIR MEDIA ENVIRONMENT. (AJ)

EJ 045 424 PS 501 405
VISUAL LEARNING: AN ANALYSIS BY SEX AND GRADE LEVEL DWYER, FRANCIS M., JR., *CALIFORNIA JOURNAL OF EDUCATIONAL RESEARCH*, V22 N4, PP170-176, SEP 71
EVALUATION TO DETERMINE IF IDENTICAL ILLUSTRATIONS USED IN LEARNING AND TESTING SITUATIONS ARE EQUALLY EFFECTIVE FOR BOYS AND GIRLS OF THE SAME GRADE LEVEL. SUBJECTS WERE MEMBERS OF GRADES 9, 10, 11, AND 12. (AJ)

EJ 045 453 PS 501 342
COOPERATION AND COMPETITION IN FOUR-YEAR-OLDS AS A FUNCTION OF REWARD CONTINGENCY AND SUBCULTURE NELSON, LINDEN; MADSEN, MILLARD C., *DEVELOPMENTAL PSYCHOLOGY*, V1 N4, PP340-344, JUL 69
THIRTY-SIX PAIRS OF 4-YEAR-OLDS PLAYED A GAME WHICH REQUIRED COOPERATIVE INTERACTION IN ORDER TO GET PRIZES. SUBJECTS WERE HIGHLY RESPONSIVE TO THE CUE OF LIMITED REWARD AND RELATIVELY INSENSITIVE TO THE NECESSITY OF MUTUAL ASSISTANCE AND THE POSSIBILITY OF SHARING BY TAKING TURNS. (AUTHOR/WY)

EJ 045 454 PS 501 361
THE INCENTIVE VALUE OF UNCERTAINTY REDUCTION FOR CHILDREN FELDSTEIN, JEROME H.; WITRYOL, SAM L., *CHILD DEVELOPMENT*, V42 N3, PP793-804, SEP 71
THE MAJOR HYPOTHESIS, THAT UNCERTAINTY REDUCTION ACTS AS AN INCENTIVE WAS GENERALLY CONFIRMED FOR 60 FOURTH GRADES. (WY)

EJ 045 455 PS 501 365
EFFECTS OF VARIATIONS IN THE NURSERY SCHOOL SETTING ON ENVIRONMENTAL CONSTRAINTS AND CHILDREN'S MODES OF ADAPTATION BERK, LAURA E., *CHILD DEVELOPMENT*, V42 N3, PP839-869, SEP 71

EJ 045 456 PS 501 372
CORRELATES OF CURIOSITY AND EXPLORATORY BEHAVIOR IN PRESCHOOL DISADVANTAGED CHILDREN MINUCHIN, PATRICIA, *CHILD DEVELOPMENT*, V42 N3, PP939-950, SEP 71
DESCRIBES A PILOT PROJECT WITH TWO OBJECTIVES: 1) TO DEVELOP MEASURES OF CURIOSITY AND EXPLORATION APPLICABLE TO PRESCHOOL CHILDREN, AND 2) TO INVESTIGATE THE RELATIONSHIP BETWEEN VARIATIONS IN EXPLORATORY BEHAVIOR AND OTHER ASPECTS OF EMOTIONAL AND COGNITIVE GROWTH. (WY)

EJ 045 457 PS 501 376
NIGHT TRAINING THROUGH PARENTS' IMPLICIT USE OF OPERANT CONDITIONING BENJAMIN, LORNA S.; AND OTHERS, *CHILD DEVELOPMENT*, V42 N3, PP963-966, SEP 71

EJ 045 458 PS 501 378
THE EFFECT OF SUBJECT RACE, MODEL RACE, AND VICARIOUS PRAISE ON VICARIOUS LEARNING THELEN, MARK H., *CHILD DEVELOPMENT*, V42 N3, PP972-977, SEP 71

EJ 045 459 PS 501 393
INDIVIDUAL DIFFERENCES IN CHILDREN'S REACTIONS TO REWARD AND NONREWARD WATSON, PETER, *JOURNAL OF EXPERIMENTAL CHILD PSYCHOLOGY*, V12 N2, PP170-181, OCT 71

EJ 045 460 PS 501 395
EFFECTS OF AN ADULT'S PRESENCE AND PRAISE ON YOUNG CHILDREN'S PERFORMANCE MEDDOCK, TERRY D.; AND OTHERS, *JOURNAL OF EXPERIMENTAL CHILD PSYCHOLOGY*, V12 N2, PP197-211, OCT 71
ON A SIMPLE MOTOR TASK THE PERFORMANCE OF 32 4-YEAR-OLD CHILDREN OF EACH SEX INCREASED UNDER BOTH ADULT PRAISE AND ADULT PRESENCE WITH THE EFFECTS BEING ADDITIVE. (WY)

EJ 045 505 PS 501 352
A CROSS-CULTURAL COMPARISON OF MATERNAL COMMUNICATION GREENGLASS, ESTHER R., *CHILD DEVELOPMENT*, V42 N3, PP685-692, SEP 71
AN EXPERIMENT USING 132 ITALIAN-BORN AND CANADIAN-BORN MOTHERS PAIRED WITH THEIR CHILDREN EXAMINED THE RELATIONSHIP BETWEEN MATERNAL COMMUNICATION AND ETHNICITY, SEX AND AGE OF CHILD. DIRECT OBSERVATION OF MATERNAL COMMUNICATION WAS EMPLOYED DURING THREE DISCUSSION TASKS IN WHICH THE MOTHER AND CHILD WERE REQUIRED TO REACH A CONSENSUS. (WY)

EJ 045 532 PS 501 385
LEARNING FROM PLAY IN OTHER CULTURES EBBECK, FREDERICK N., *CHILDHOOD EDUCATION*, V48 N2, PP69-74, NOV 71
UNDERSTANDING THE DIFFERENCES IN VALUES THAT DIFFERING CULTURES ATTACH TO PLAY MAY HELP EDUCATORS (1) TO CLARIFY THE ROLE OF SPONTANEOUS PLAY, (2) TO RECOGNIZE THE LIMITATIONS OF COMPETITIVE PLAY, (3) TO BETTER BALANCE DIRECTED AND SPONTANEOUS PLAY, AND (4) TO VIEW PLAY AS ABSORBED, JOYFUL, EDUCATIVE ACTIVITY. (AUTHOR/AJ)

EJ 045 597 PS 501 355
CONSONANT CUE PERCEPTION BY TWENTY- TO TWENTY-FOUR-WEEK-OLD INFANTS MOFFITT, ALAN R., *CHILD DEVELOPMENT*, V42 N3, PP717-731, SEP 71
INFANTS WERE ABLE TO DISCRIMINATE BETWEEN "BAH" AND "GAH" SYLLABLES, INDICATING THAT LINGUISTIC-PERCEPTUAL CAPACITIES ARE PRESENT DURING EARLY LIFE. (WY)

EJ 045 598 PS 501 369
ACCELERATING VISUAL COMPLEXITY LEVELS IN THE HUMAN INFANT GREENBERG, DAVID J., *CHILD DEVELOPMENT*, V42 N3, PP905-918, SEP 71

EJ 045 599 PS 501 371
JUDGING OUTLINE FACES: A DEVELOPMENTAL STUDY BRADSHAW, J. L.; MCKENZIE, B. E., *CHILD DEVELOPMENT*, V42 N3, PP929-937, SEP 71
OUTLINE FACES WERE PRESENTED FOR RATING ALONG SIX DICHOTOMOUS ATTRIBUTES WITH FEATURES VARYING SYSTEMATICALLY. DIFFERENCES WERE FOUND TO BE LARGELY ATTENTIONAL, WITH CERTAIN FEATURES INVARIABLY BEING DIFFERENTIALLY EMPLOYED AND ASSOCIATED WITH CERTAIN ATTRIBUTES ACROSS ALL SAMPLES. (WY)

EJ 045 793 PS 501 404
EFFECT OF CLASSROOM NOISE ON NUMBER IDENTIFICATION BY RETARDED CHILDREN JOINER, LEE M.; KOTTMEYER, WAYNE A., *CALIFORNIA JOURNAL OF EDUCATIONAL RESEARCH*, V22 N4, PP164-169, SEP 71

EJ 045 797 PS 501 375
AN INEXPENSIVE AND PORTABLE MEANS FOR ONE-WAY OBSERVATION BURTON, ROGER V., *CHILD DEVELOPMENT*, V42 N3, PP959-962, SEP 71
PLANS FOR AN INEXPENSIVE EASILY CONSTRUCTED PORTABLE APPARATUS FOR ONE-WAY OBSERVATION ARE PRESENTED. (WY)

EJ 045 798 PS 501 407
AUTOMATED READING INSTRUCTION IN THE GHETTO STRANG, HAROLD R.; WOLF, MONTROSE M., *CHILD STUDY JOURNAL*, V1 N4, PP187-201, SUM 71
TO IMPROVE READING SKILLS, AN AUTOMATED TUTORIAL PROGRAM WITH IMMEDIATE FEEDBACK AND A TOKEN REWARDS INCENTIVE SYSTEM, WAS GIVEN TO A SIXTH GRADE CLASS OF CULTURALLY DISADVANTAGED RETARDED READERS. SIGNIFICANT IMPROVEMENT IN READING SKILLS WAS SHOWN AFTER A 4-MONTH PROGRAM PERIOD. (MK)

EJ 046 057 PS 501 388
ON TEAM TEACHING PRYKE, DAVID, *CHILDHOOD EDUCATION*, V48 N2, PP85-89, NOV 71

EJ 046 058 PS 501 406
THE USE OF CREATIVITY TRAINING MATERIALS WITH SPECIAL CHILDREN: A REPORT OF A FEASIBILITY EXPERIENCE NICKSE, RUTH S.; RIPPLE, RICHARD E., *CHILD STUDY JOURNAL*, V1 N4, PP175-185, SUM 71
CREATIVITY TRAINING MATERIALS WERE USED WITH A GROUP OF ELEMENTARY SCHOOL CHILDREN WHO EXHIBITED ACADEMIC, SOCIAL OR EMOTIONAL PROBLEMS. STUDY RECOMMENDS INCREASED USE OF SUCH MATERIALS, WITH MORE TIME AND ATTENTION ALLOWED FOR GROUP DISCUSSIONS AND ROLE-PLAYING DURING THESE PERIODS. (MK)

EJ 046 231 PS 501 353
TRAINING AND GENERALIZATION OF DENSITY CONSERVATION: EFFECTS OF FEEDBACK AND CONSECUTIVE SIMILAR STIMULI BRAINERD, CHARLES J.; ALLEN, TERRY WALTER, *CHILD DEVELOPMENT*, V42 N3, PP693-704, SEP 71

EJ 046 232 PS 501 354
THE ROLE OF FAMILIARITY IN CHILDREN'S EXPLANATIONS OF PHYSICAL CAUSALITY BERZONSKY, MICHAEL D., *CHILD DEVELOPMENT*, V42 N3, PP705-715, SEP 71
THIS STUDY INVESTIGATES THE RESPONSES OF 84 CHILDREN, AGED 6 YEARS 3 MONTHS TO 7 YEARS 5 MONTHS, TO QUESTIONS DEALING WITH THE CATEGORIES OF PHYSICAL CAUSALITY AND 2 CAUSAL DEMONSTRATIONS. (WY)

EJ 046 233 PS 501 356
THE ROLE OF OPERATIONAL THINKING IN CHILDREN'S COMPREHENSION AND APPRECIATION OF HUMOR MCGHEE, PAUL E., *CHILD DEVELOPMENT*, V42 N3, PP734-743, SEP 71

EJ 046 234 PS 501 357
REFLECTION-IMPULSIVITY AND COLOR-FORM SORTING KATZ, JUDITH MILSTEIN, *CHILD DEVELOPMENT*, V42 N3, PP745-754, SEP 71
A STUDY TO DETERMINE WHETHER THE DIFFERENTIAL DEVELOPMENT OF CONCEPTUAL TEMPO CAN PREDICT PREFERENCES. CONCEPTUAL TEMPO PREDICTED PREFERENCES IN COLOR-FORM SORTING AMONG 67 CHILDREN RANGING IN AGE FROM 44 TO 65 MONTHS. (WY)

EJ 046 235 PS 501 359
SEMANTIC DIFFERENTIAL ANALYSIS OF RELATIONAL TERMS USED IN CONSERVATION HARASYM, CAROLYN R.; AND OTHERS, *CHILD DEVELOPMENT*, V42 N3, PP767-779, SEP 71
SIXTY-ONE CHILDREN IN GRADES 1, 2, AND 3 IN RURAL COUNTY SCHOOLS WERE COMPARED IN THEIR SEMANTIC DIFFERENTIAL JUDGMENTS OF RELATIONAL TERMS USED IN ASSESSING CONSERVATION. (WY)

EJ 046 236 PS 501 360
COMPLEX MOTOR LEARNING IN FOUR-YEAR-OLDS LEITHWOOD, K. A.; FOWLER, W., *CHILD DEVELOPMENT*, V42 N3, PP781-792, SEP 71
THE EFFECTS OF 4 MONTHS OF GYMNOSTIC TRAINING UPON COMPLEX AND SIMPLE GROSS MOTOR ABILITIES AND GENERAL COGNITIVE AND PSYCHOSOCIAL FUNCTIONING IN 4-YEAR-OLDS WERE COMPARED WITH THE EFFECTS OF MUSIC TRAINING AND NO TREATMENT. (WY)

EJ 046 237 PS 501 364
A REEXAMINATION OF THE ROLE OF INCENTIVE IN CHILDREN'S DISCRIMINATION LEARNING MCCULLERS, JOHN C.; MARTIN, JUDITH A. GARDNER, *CHILD DEVELOPMENT*, V42 N3, PP827-838, SEP 71

EJ 046 238 PS 501 367
THE INFLUENCE OF COGNITIVE STYLE ON PERCEPTUAL LEARNING ODOM, RICHARD D.; AND OTHERS, *CHILD DEVELOPMENT*, V42 N3, PP883-891, SEP 71

EJ 046 239 PS 501 370
PIAGET'S CONCEPT OF CLASSIFICATION: A COMPARATIVE STUDY OF SOCIALLY DISADVANTAGED AND MIDDLE-CLASS YOUNG CHILDREN WEI, TAM T. D.; AND OTHERS, *CHILD DEVELOPMENT*, V42 N3, PP919-927, SEP 71

EJ 046 240 PS 501 373
EFFECTS OF EXPOSURE TO MODELS ON CONCEPT IDENTIFICATION IN KINDERGARTEN AND SECOND-GRADE CHILDREN RYAN, DAVID; KOBASIGAWA, AKIRA, *CHILD DEVELOPMENT*, V42 N3, PP951-955, SEP 71

EJ 046 241 PS 501 374
EFFECTS OF STIMULUS ABSTRACTNESS AND FAMILIARITY ON LISTENER'S PERFORMANCE IN A COMMUNICATION TASK GRUSHCOW, ROCHELLE; GAUTHIER, JOAN PRESTON, *CHILD DEVELOPMENT*, V42 N3, PP956-958, SEP 71

TWO IMPLICATIONS FOR COMMUNICATION RESEARCH ARE EVIDENCED BY THE RESULTS OF THIS STUDY. 1) JUNIOR KINDERGARTEN CHILDREN ARE CAPABLE OF DECODING INFORMATION COMMUNICATED IN TERMS OF DESCRIPTIONS RATHER THAN OBJECT NAMES; 2) THE YOUNG LISTENER'S PERFORMANCE IS A FUNCTION OF THE DEGREE OF ABSTRACTNESS OF THE REFERENT. (WY)

EJ 046 242 PS 501 377
ACTIVITY LEVEL AND MOTOR INHIBITION: THEIR RELATIONSHIP TO INTELLIGENCE-TEST PERFORMANCE IN NORMAL CHILDREN LOO, CHALSA; WENAR, CHARLES, *CHILD DEVELOPMENT*, V42 N3, PP967-971, SEP 71

FORTY MIDDLE CLASS KINDERGARTEN CHILDREN'S ACTIVITY LEVEL WAS NOT FOUND TO BE CORRELATED WITH MOTOR INHIBITION, IMPULSIVITY, OR IA, WHILE MOTOR INHIBITION WAS SIGNIFICANTLY CORRELATED WITH IQ BUT NOT WITH IMPULSIVITY. (WY)

EJ 046 243 PS 501 379
EFFECTS OF SPATIAL SEPARATION OF STIMULUS, RESPONSE, AND REWARD IN DISCRIMINATION LEARNING BY CHILDREN RAMEY, CRAIG T.; GOULET, L. R., *CHILD DEVELOPMENT*, V42 N3, PP978-982, SEP 71

MALE SCHOOL CHILDREN OF THREE AGE LEVELS WERE TESTED ON A 2-CHOICE VISUAL DISCRIMINATION TASK THAT VARIED IN SPATIAL CONTINGUITY OF STIMULUS, RESPONSE, AND REWARD. SEPARATION OF STIMULUS FROM RESPONSE AND REWARD WAS FOUND TO RETARD LEARNING. (WY)

EJ 046 244 PS 501 380
COGNITIVE DEVELOPMENT IN INFANTS OF DIFFERENT AGE LEVELS AND FROM DIFFERENT ENVIRONMENTAL BACKGROUNDS: AN EXPLANATORY INVESTIGATION WACHS, THEODORE D.; AND OTHERS, *MERRILL-PALMER QUARTERLY*, V17 N4, PP283-317, OCT 71

REPORTS A CROSS-SECTIONAL STUDY EXAMINING INTENSITY OF STIMULATION AND VERBAL STIMULATION IN HOME CIRCUMSTANCES AS THESE FACTORS RELATE TO PSYCHOLOGICAL DEVELOPMENT ACROSS SEVERAL AGE GROUPS (7TH, 11TH, 15TH, OR 22ND MONTH OF LIFE). (WY)

EJ 046 245 PS 501 381
EXTINCTION OF CONSERVATION: A METHODOLOGICAL AND THEORETICAL ANALYSIS MILLER, SCOTT A., *MERRILL-PALMER QUARTERLY*, V17 N4, PP319-334, OCT 71

EJ 046 246 PS 501 382
SCHOOL AND HOME: NOT EITHER-OR SCOTT, RALPH; SATTEL, LUDWIG, *MERRILL-PALMER QUARTERLY*, V17 N4, PP335-345, OCT 71

PRESENTS A CASE VIGNETTE WHICH SUGGESTS THAT PAST FAILURE IN COMPENSATORY EDUCATION PROGRAMS SPRINGS FROM THE FAILURE OF EDUCATORS TO 1) RECOGNIZE THE RELATIONSHIPS BETWEEN FLUID INTELLIGENCE AND CULTURAL DEPRIVATION, 2) UTILIZE TEACHER SKILLS IN THE PSYCHODYNAMICS OF FAMILY RELATIONSHIPS, AND 3) CHANGES METHODS OF TESTING AND CATEGORIZING CHILDREN. (WY)

EJ 046 247 PS 501 383
ARTISTIC STYLE AS CONCEPT FORMATION FOR CHILDREN AND ADULTS WALK, RICHARD D.; AND OTHERS, *MERRILL-PALMER QUARTERLY*, V17 N4, PP347-356, OCT 71

REPORTS TWO STUDIES. THE FIRST STUDY COMPARED ADULTS AND CHILDREN (AGED FOUR, SIX, AND EIGHT) ON ABILITY TO SORT PAINTINGS ACCORDING TO ARTIST, A CONCEPTUAL TASK THAT CAN REVEAL COGNITIVE ORGANIZATION. THE SECOND STUDY COMPARED THREE GROUPS OF EIGHT- TO NINE-YEAR-OLDS USING SLIGHTLY DIFFERENT PROCEDURES. THE RESULTS SHOWED STRONG DEVELOPMENTAL TRENDS THAT SUGGEST HYPOTHESES ABOUT COGNITIVE DEVELOPMENT. (WY)

EJ 046 248 PS 501 387
PLAY, THE ESSENTIAL INGREDIENT HARTLEY, RUTH E., *CHILDHOOD EDUCATION*, V48 N2, PP80-84, NOV 71

EMPHASIZES THE IMPORTANCE OF SPONTANEOUS PLAY FOR GROWTH IN COGNITION AND SOCIAL VALUES. THE AUTHOR SPECIFICALLY DISCUSSES FINGER PAINTING, WATER, BLOCKS AND DRAMATIC PLAY. (AJ)

EJ 046 249 PS 501 392
EYE MOVEMENTS, PERCEPTUAL ACTIVITY, AND CONSERVATION DEVELOPMENT O'BRYAN, KENNETH G.; BOERSMA, FREDERIC J., *JOURNAL OF EXPERIMENTAL CHILD PSYCHOLOGY*, V12 N2, PP157-169, OCT 71

DATA GATHERED ON 92 GIRLS (6-10 YEARS OF AGE) TESTED ON PIAGETIAN CONSERVATION TASKS SUPPORTS A THEORY OF PERCEPTUAL ACTIVITY LEADING TO DECENTRATION AND INDICATES A CHANGE IN VIEWING STRATEGY ASSOCIATED WITH CHANGE IN CONSERVATION STATUS. (WY)

EJ 046 250 PS 501 394
ACCOMMODATION OF VISUAL TRACKING PATTERNS IN HUMAN INFANTS TO OBJECT MOVEMENT PATTERNS NELSON, KEITH E., *JOURNAL OF EXPERIMENTAL CHILD PSYCHOLOGY*, V12 N2, PP182-196, OCT 71

SHORT-TERM CHANGES IN VISUAL BEHAVIOR OBSERVED IN 80 INFANTS (3-9 MONTHS) PARALLEL CHANGES OBSERVED ACROSS AGE BY PIAGET AND FIT WELL HIS ASSUMPTION THAT THE INFANT'S INCREASINGLY SOPHISTICATED ACTION PATTERNS EVOLVE BY SUCCESSIVE ACCOMODATIONS TO ENCOUNTERED PHENOMENON. (WY)

EJ 046 251 PS 501 396
THE STABILITY AND TRANSFERABILITY OF CONCEPTUAL CODING IN CHILDREN JOHNSON, PEDER J.; AND OTHERS, *JOURNAL OF EXPERIMENTAL CHILD PSYCHOLOGY*, V12 N2, PP212-222, OCT 71

EJ 046 252 PS 501 397
IMITATION LEARNING OF INFORMATION-PROCESSING LAMAL, PETER A., *JOURNAL OF EXPERIMENTAL CHILD PSYCHOLOGY*, V12 N2, PP223-227, OCT 71

MODIFIED TWENTY-QUESTIONS AND PROBLEMS WERE SOLVED BY 72 SUBJECTS IN A STUDY OF THE INFLUENCE OF AN ADULT MODEL ON THE INFORMATION-PROCESSING STRATEGY USED BY CHILDREN OF VARIOUS GRADE LEVELS. (WY)

EJ 046 253 PS 501 398
THE ROLE OF REINFORCEMENT PROCEDURE IN CHILDREN'S PROBABILITY LEARNING AS A FUNCTION OF AGE AND NUMBER OF RESPONSE ALTERNATIVES WITTIG, MICHELE ANDRISIN; WEIR, MORTON W., *JOURNAL OF EXPERIMENTAL CHILD PSYCHOLOGY*, V12 N2, PP228-239, OCT 71

EJ 046 254 PS 501 399
THE LEARNING AND TRANSFER OF DOUBLE-CLASSIFICATION SKILLS: A REPLICATION AND EXTENSION JACOBS, PAUL I.; VANDEVENTER, MARY, *JOURNAL OF EXPERIMENTAL CHILD PSYCHOLOGY*, V12 N2, PP240-257, OCT 71

EJ 046 255 PS 501 400
EFFECTS OF IMITATION OF DIFFERENT REINFORCEMENT COMBINATIONS TO A MODEL CHEYNE, J. A., *JOURNAL OF EXPERIMENTAL CHILD PSYCHOLOGY*, V12 N2, PP258-269, OCT 71

EJ 046 256 PS 501 401
RECOGNITION MEMORY: THE RELATIONSHIP OF ACCURACY AND LATENCY OF RESPONSE UNDER DIFFERENT MEMORY LOADS IN RETARDATES URBANO, RICHARD C.; AND OTHERS, *JOURNAL OF EXPERIMENTAL CHILD PSYCHOLOGY*, V12 N2, PP270-277, OCT 71

EJ 046 257 PS 501 409
MOTOR COORDINATION AND YOUNG CHILDREN'S DRAWING ABILITIES GROSSMAN, MARVIN, *CHILD STUDY JOURNAL*, V1 N4, PP213-215, SUM 71

A STUDY OF 90 FIRST GRADE CHILDREN INDICATES THAT, FOR YOUNG CHILDREN, VISUAL-MOTOR COORDINATION IS A BEHAVIOR THAT FACILITATES EFFECTIVE EXPRESSION IN ART. (AUTHOR/MK)

EJ 046 401 PS 501 391
THE SCHOOL SOCIAL WORKER'S ROLE IN OVERCOMING LEARNING HANDICAPS PRUNTY, ODESSA, *CHILD WELFARE*, V50 N8, PP442-446, OCT 71

EJ 046 455 PS 501 384
DAY CARE: CRISIS AND CHALLENGE KEYSERLING, MARY DUBLIN, *CHILDHOOD EDUCATION*, V48 N2, PP59-68, NOV 71

INFORMS PARENTS AND EDUCATORS OF THE SHOCKING CONDITIONS OF DAY CARE FACILITIES IN THE U. S. AND URGES NEW APPROACHES AND LEGISLATION. (AJ)

EJ 046 456 PS 501 390
DAY CARE CHALLENGE: THE UNMET NEEDS OF MOTHERS AND CHILDREN KEYSERLING, MARY DUBLIN, *CHILD WELFARE*, V50 N8, PP434-441, OCT 71

EJ 046 466 PS 501 351
OBSERVATION STUDIES OF PARENT-CHILD INTERACTION: A METHODOLOGICAL REVIEW. LYTTON, HUGH, *CHILD DEVELOPMENT*, V42 N3, PP651-684, SEP 71

REVIEWS PARENT-CHILD INTERACTION STUDIES, THE MAJOR SOURCE OF INFORMATION ABOUT THE SOCIALIZATION PROCESS OF THE CHILD. DEALS FULLY WITH OBSERVATION STUDIES--NATURALISTIC OBSERVATION AND EXPERIMENTALLY ARRANGED INTERACTION IN THE LABORATORY--BUT ALSO DRAWS ON INTERVIEW AND QUESTIONNAIRE METHODS FOR COMPARISON. (WY)

EJ 046 467 PS 501 362
THE USE OF ROLE PLAYING AND INDUCTION IN CHILDREN'S LEARNING OF HELPING AND SHARING BEHAVIOR STAUB, ERVIN, *CHILD DEVELOPMENT*, V42 N3, PP805-816, SEP 71

EJ 046 468 PS 501 363
BLOCK MANIPULATION BY CHILDREN AS A FUNCTION OF SOCIAL REINFORCEMENT, ANXIETY, AROUSAL, AND ABILITY PATTERN BARTON, KEITH, *CHILD DEVELOPMENT*, V42 N3, PP817-826, SEP 71

EJ 046 469 PS 501 366
THE EFFECTS OF MOTHERS' PRESENCE AND PREVISITS ON CHILDREN'S EMOTIONAL REACTION TO STARTING NURSERY SCHOOL SCHWARZ, J. CONRAD; WYNN, RUTH, *CHILD DEVELOPMENT*, V42 N3, PP871-881, SEP 71
COMPARED THE PERCEPTUAL LEARNING OF REFLECTIVE AND IMPULSIVE KINDERGARTEN CHILDREN. (WY)

EJ 046 672 PS 501 358
THE RELATIONSHIP BETWEEN PRIMARY STUDENTS' RATIONALIZATION OF CONSERVATION AND THEIR MATHEMATICAL ACHIEVEMENT CATHCART, W. GEORGE, *CHILD DEVELOPMENT*, V42 N3, PP755-765, SEP 71

EJ 046 727 PS 501 415
IQ CHANGES IN HOSPITALIZED MENTAL RETARDATES ROSS, ROBERT T., *DEVELOPMENTAL PSYCHOLOGY*, V5 N3, PP395-397, NOV 71
AN ANALYSIS OF CHANGES IN CA, MA, AND IQ IN 324 PATIENTS, REPRESENTATIVE OF THE POPULATION OF A HOSPITAL FOR MENTALLY RETARDED, INDICATED THAT THE DECREMENT IN IQ IN MENTALLY RETARDED CHILDREN IS DUE PRIMARILY TO INCREASES IN CA AND NOT TO DECREASES IN MA. IT APPEARS THAT MA IS THE MORE MEANINGFUL INDEX OF INTELLIGENCE LEVEL. (AUTHOR/WY)

EJ 046 782 PS 501 414
JUDGMENTS OF PATTERN GOODNESS AND PATTERN PREFERENCE AS FUNCTIONS OF AGE AND PATTERN UNCERTAINTY CLEMENT, DAVID E.; SISTRUNK, FRANK, *DEVELOPMENTAL PSYCHOLOGY*, V5 N3, PP389-394, NOV 71
RATINGS OF PATTERN GOODNESS AND OF PATTERN PREFERENCE WERE MADE BY 96 SUBJECTS FOR EACH OF 50 STIMULUS PATTERNS OF KNOWN PATTERN UNCERTAINTY. EQUAL NUMBERS OF MALE AND FEMALE SUBJECTS WERE USED IN EACH OF FOUR AGE GROUPS (9-10), (13-14), (5817-18), (20-21). PATTERN PREFERENCE WAS SIMILAR FOR ALL AGE GROUPS, WITH THE LEAST UNCERTAIN PATTERNS PREFERRED. (AUTHOR/WY)

EJ 046 783 PS 501 421
AGE, SEX, RACE, AND THE PERCEPTION OF FACIAL BEAUTY CROSS, JOHN F.; CROSS, JANE, *DEVELOPMENTAL PSYCHOLOGY*, V5 N3, PP433-439, NOV 71

EJ 046 784 PS 501 427
A METHOD FOR STUDYING THE DEVELOPMENT OF GENDER IDENTITY MAY, ROBERT R., *DEVELOPMENTAL PSYCHOLOGY*, V5 N3, PP484-487, NOV 71
A GROUP OF 75 GRADE-SCHOOL CHILDREN SHOWED A SIGNIFICANT SEX DIFFERENCE IN DEPRIVATION/ENHANCEMENT FANTASY PATTERNS INDICATING THAT THESE PATTERNS MEANINGFULLY REFLECT ISSUES OF GENDER IDENTITY. (AUTHOR/WY)

EJ 046 785 PS 501 438
PHYSIQUE IDENTIFICATION, PREFERENCE, AND AVERSION IN KINDERGARTEN CHILDREN LERNER, RICHARD M.; SCHROEDER, CHRISTINE, *DEVELOPMENTAL PSYCHOLOGY*, V5 N3, PP538, NOV 71
KINDERGARTEN CHILDREN DO APPEAR TO SHOW A PHYSIQUE PREFERENCE CONSISTENT WITH THEIR SOCIETY'S FAVORABLE ORIENTATION TOWARD AVERAGE BODY BUILDS. (AUTHOR/WY)

EJ 046 786 PS 501 447
TEENAGERS DISCUSS AGE RESTRICTIONS SUDIA, CECELIA; REA, JANE HARWOOD, *CHILDREN*, V18 N6, PP232-236, NOV-DEC 71
REPORTS THE RESULTS OF A MAY, 1970 SURVEY OF 430 HIGH SCHOOL STUDENTS' ATTITUDES TOWARD AGE RESTRICTIONS AFFECTING SUCH AREAS AS VOTING, ARMED FORCES, MOVIE ATTENDANCE, DRIVING, CONFIDENTIAL MEDICAL CARE, MARRIAGE, ETC. (AJ)

EJ 046 787 PS 501 449
144 FOSTER CHILDREN BRYCE, MARVIN E.; EHLERT, ROGER C., *CHILD WELFARE*, V50 N9, PP499-503, NOV 71
CHILDREN KEPT IN "TEMPORARY" FOSTER CARE FOR LONG PERIODS EVEN THOUGH THERE IS NO POSSIBILITY OF RETURN TO THE NATURAL PARENTS ARE DEPRIVED OF THEIR CHANCE FOR NORMAL DEVELOPMENTAL GROWTH. THIS STUDY EXAMINES FACTORS INVOLVED IN THE PROBLEM. (AJ)

EJ 046 788 PS 501 454
WHAT'S A SCHOOL FOR? SAXE, RICHARD W., *ELEMENTARY SCHOOL JOURNAL*, V72 N1, PP7-11, OCT 1971
REPORTS RESULTS OF ANSWERS GIVEN BY PUPILS IN ONE SCHOOL (GRADES 1-6) TO THE QUESTION "WHAT'S A SCHOOL FOR?" (WY)

EJ 046 887 PS 501 417
THE YOUNG CHILD'S UNDERSTANDING OF SOCIAL JUSTICE IRWIN, D. MICHELLE; MOORE, SHIRLEY G., *DEVELOPMENTAL PSYCHOLOGY*, V5 N3, PP406-410, NOV 71
RESULTS OF TWO STUDIES FOUND THAT BOTH YOUNGER AND OLDER PRESCHOOLERS WERE MORE JUST THAN UNJUST, THAT THE OLDER SUBJECTS UNDERSTOOD NOTIONS OF JUSTICE BETTER THAN DID YOUNGER SUBJECTS AND THAT THE PRESCHOOLER'S UNDERSTANDING OF GUILT-INNOCENCE, AND APOLOGY-RESTITUTION IS CLEARER THAN HIS UNDERSTANDING OF INTENTIONALITY. (AUTHOR/WY)

EJ 046 888 PS 501 418
PSYCHOSOCIAL DEVELOPMENT IN CROSS-CULTURAL PERSPECTIVE: A NEW LOOK AT AN OLD ISSUE GOLDMAN, RUTH K., *DEVELOPMENTAL PSYCHOLOGY*, V5 N3, PP411-419, NOV 71
THIS STUDY SUPPORTS THE HYPOTHESIS THAT CHILDREN REARED IN GROUP-CARE SETTINGS ARE NOT NECESSARILY RETARDED IN THEIR PSYCHOSOCIAL DEVELOPMENT IN COMPARISON TO FAMILY-REARED CHILDREN. THEY MAY, IN FACT, DEPENDING UPON GROUP-CARE PHILOSOPHY AND PRACTICE, AS WELL AS REASONS FOR ADMISSION, SURPASS THEIR HOME-REARED COUNTERPARTS IN PSYCHOLOGICAL MATURITY. (AUTHOR/WY)

EJ 046 889 PS 501 422
THE ACQUISITION AND PERFORMANCE OF A SOCIALLY NEUTRAL RESPONSE AS A FUNCTION OF VICARIOUS REWARD AKAMATSU, T. JOHN; THELEN, MARK H., *DEVELOPMENTAL PSYCHOLOGY*, V5 N3, PP440-445, NOV 71
RESULTS OF AN EXPERIMENTAL TASK ADMINISTERED TO 7-8 YEAR OLD CHILDREN (24 BOYS AND 24 GIRLS) SHOWED THAT ACQUISITION OF MODELED BEHAVIOR OCCURRED IN THE ABSENCE OF VICARIOUS REWARD, AND THAT, CONTRARY TO PREDICTION, VICARIOUS REWARD HAD NO SIGNIFICANT EFFECT ON THE PERFORMANCE OF IMITATIVE BEHAVIOR. (AUTHOR/WY)

EJ 046 890 PS 501 429
A CROSS-CULTURAL STUDY OF THE CHILD'S COMMUNICATION WITH HIS MOTHER GREENGLASS, ESTHER R., *DEVELOPMENTAL PSYCHOLOGY*, V5 N3, PP494-499, NOV 71

EJ 046 891 PS 501 435
CARDIAC DECELERATION AND ITS STABILITY IN HUMAN NEWBORNS LIPSITT, LEWIS P.; JACKLIN, CAROL N., *DEVELOPMENTAL PSYCHOLOGY*, V5 N3, PP535, NOV 71

EJ 046 892 PS 501 436
DEVELOPMENTAL CONFORMITY BISHOP, BARBARA R.; BECKMAN, LINDA, *DEVELOPMENTAL PSYCHOLOGY*, V5 N3, PP536, NOV 71
THE DATA COLLECTED ON 144 LOWER-MIDDLE INCOME MALE AND FEMALE SUBJECTS SUGGESTS THAT AS THE AGE OF THE CHILD INCREASES, EITHER THE NEED FOR SOCIAL APPROVAL MUST DECREASE OR THE EXPECTANCY OF SUCCESS THROUGH NONCONFORMING RESPONSES MUST INCREASE. (AUTHOR/WY)

EJ 046 893 PS 501 453
WORKING WITH SEPARATION KRUGMAN, DOROTHY C., *CHILD WELFARE*, V50 N9, PP528-537, NOV 71
DISCUSSES THE ROLE OF THE CASEWORKER IN PROVIDING SUPPORT TO CHILDREN EXPERIENCING SEPARATION FROM THEIR FAMILIES AND EMPHASIZES THE NEED TO RECOGNIZE THAT THERE ARE DIFFERENCES BETWEEN THOSE SEPARATION EXPERIENCES DICTATED BY THE NEEDS OF CHILDREN AND THOSE DICTATED BY ARBITRARY OR NONCASEWORK FACTORS. (AJ)

EJ 046 963 PS 501 450
HELPING PARENTS IN A PEDIATRIC CLINIC COKIN, MOLLY; AND OTHERS, *CHILD WELFARE*, V50 N9, PP504-509, NOV 71
TWO SOCIAL WORKERS AND A PEDIATRICIAN WORKING AS A TEAM HELPED PARENTS WHO BROUGHT THEIR CHILDREN TO A MEDICAL CENTER TO PERCEIVE THE PARENT-CHILD RELATIONSHIP AS A CAUSATIVE FACTOR IN DEVELOPMENTAL DIFFICULTIES. (AUTHOR/AJ)

EJ 046 968 PS 501 455
WHAT'S DEPRIVED ABOUT BEING DIFFERENT? LA BELLE, THOMAS J., *ELEMENTARY SCHOOL JOURNAL*, V72 N1, PP13-19, OCT 1971
SUGGESTS EIGHT PRINCIPLES THAT MIGHT BE USED IN FORMULATING A SCHOOL PROGRAM THAT IS MORE RELEVANT TO CULTURALLY DIFFERENT GROUPS. (WY)

EJ 047 001 PS 501 451
ADOPTION TRENDS: JANUARY-JUNE 1971 SMITH, MICHAEL J., *CHILD WELFARE*, V50 N9, PP510-511, NOV 71

EJ 047 103 PS 501 456
SAY YOU COME FROM MISSOURI WHITELEY, JACK, *ELEMENTARY SCHOOL JOURNAL*, V72 N1, PP20-28, OCT 1971
THE HEADMASTER OF A BRITISH SCHOOL ADVISES U.S. TEACHERS TO EXERCISE A CERTAIN AMOUNT OF SKEPTICISM AND ASK QUESTIONS BEFORE ACCEPTING SOME OF THE EXCITING PRACTICES OF THE NEW BRITISH PRIMARY SCHOOLS. (WY)

EJ 047 339 PS 501 432
LOGICAL SYMBOL USE IN DEAF AND HEARING CHILDREN AND ADOLESCENTS YOUNISS, JAMES; AND OTHERS, *DEVELOPMENTAL PSYCHOLOGY*, V5 N3, PP511-517, NOV 71
RESULTS OF TWO EXPERIMENTS SUPPORT THE VIEW THAT LOGICAL DEVELOPMENT CAN OCCUR WHEN THERE IS NO DIRECT INTERNALIZATION OF A SOCIETAL LANGUAGE AND THAT DEAF ADOLESCENTS ARE CAPABLE OF PROPOSITIONAL THOUGHT DESPITE THEIR LANGUAGE DEFICIENCY. (AUTHOR/WY)

EJ 047 340 PS 501 440
LONGITUDINAL ASSESSMENT OF THE RELATION BETWEEN MEASURED INTELLIGENCE OF INSTITUTIONALIZED RETARDATES AND HOSPITAL AGE SACHS, LEWIS B.; FRISK, GUY C., *DEVELOPMENTAL PSYCHOLOGY*, V5 N3, PP541, NOV 71

EJ 047 341 PS 501 448
AN ESSAY REVIEW: MENTAL RETARDATION AS A SOCIAL PROBLEM MEDNICK, MIRIAM F., *CHILDREN*, V18 N6, PP237-238, NOV-DEC 71
REVIEW OF MARGARET ADAM'S BOOK, MENTAL RETARDATION AND ITS SOCIAL DIMENSIONS. NEW YORK: COLUMBIA UNIVERSITY PRESS, 1971. (AJ)

EJ 047 342 PS 501 452
ESTABLISHMENT OF DAY CARE PROGRAMS FOR THE MENTALLY RETARDED DONOHUE, DANIEL T., *CHILD WELFARE*, V50 N9, PP519-523, NOV 71
DESCRIBES MARYLAND'S EXTENSIVE NETWORK OF DAY CARE CENTERS FOR SEVERELY MENTALLY RETARDED CHILDREN. SPECIFIC CHARACTERISTICS, STIPULATED FOR ALL THE PROGRAMS, ARE REVIEWED. (AUTHOR/AJ)

EJ 047 353 PS 501 442
INVOLVING PARENTS IN A CHILDREN'S CLINIC LANGELLOTTO, EUGENE, *CHILDREN*, V18 N6, PP202-207, NOV-DEC 71
ACTIVITIES OF LOW INCOME PARENTS OF CHILDREN SERVED BY A COMPREHENSIVE PEDIATRIC CLINIC ILLUSTRATE HOW INCLUSION OF CLIENTS IN THE STRUCTURE OF HEALTH PROJECTS ENCOURAGES THEM TO SPEAK AND ACT FOR THEMSELVES. (AUTHOR/AJ)

EJ 047 354 PS 501 443
ADOLESCENT MATERNITY SERVICES: A TEAM APPROACH SMITH, ELEANOR W.; AND OTHERS, *CHILDREN*, V18 N6, PP208-213, NOV-DEC 71

EJ 047 355 PS 501 446
CARING FOR CHILDREN WITH SICKLE CELL ANEMIA DUCKETT, CAMILLE L., *CHILDREN*, V18 N6, PP227-231, NOV-DEC 71
A CLINICAL SPECIALIST IN PUBLIC HEALTH NURSING DISCUSSES THE ROLE OF THE NURSE IN WORKING WITH THE FAMILY AND CHILD AFFECTED BY SICKLE CELL ANEMIA. (AJ)

EJ 047 594 PS 501 416
THE CHRONOLOGY OF THE DEVELOPMENT OF COVERT SPEECH IN CHILDREN CONRAD, R., *DEVELOPMENTAL PSYCHOLOGY*, V5 N3, PP398-405, NOV 71
RESULTS OF AN EXPERIMENT WITH CHILDREN AGES 3-11 YEARS PERFORMING SERIAL RECALL TASKS SUGGEST THAT IT IS NOT UNTIL ABOUT AGE 5 YEARS THAT CHILDREN'S OVERT SPEECH REACHES A FUNCTIONAL STAGE THAT WOULD JUSTIFY INTERNALIZATION. (AUTHOR/WY)

EJ 047 676 PS 501 412
MODIFICATION OF IMPULSIVE AND REFLECTIVE COGNITIVE STYLES THROUGH OBSERVATION OF FILM-MEDIATED MODELS RIDBERG, EUGENE H.; AND OTHERS, *DEVELOPMENTAL PSYCHOLOGY*, V5 N3, PP369-377, NOV 71
COGNITIVE STYLE WAS MODIFIED IN A SAMPLE OF 50 IMPULSIVE AND 50 REFLECTIVE FOURTH-GRADE BOYS. SUBJECTS VIEWED A FILM-MEDIATED MODEL DISPLAYING A RESPONSE STYLE OPPOSITE TO THEIR OWN COGNITIVE STYLE. THE SPECIFIC CUES IN THE MODEL'S BEHAVIOR WHICH FACILITATED SHIFTS IN COGNITIVE STYLE VARIED WITH THE INTELLECTUAL LEVELS OF THE SUBJECT. (AUTHOR/WY)

EJ 047 677 PS 501 413
DELAY OF FEEDBACK INTERVAL, POSTFEEDBACK INTERVAL, DISTRACTION, AND TASK DIFFICULTY AS FACTORS IN A MODIFIED CONCEPT-IDENTIFICATION TASK WITH JUNIOR HIGH SCHOOL SUBJECTS RABINOWITZ, F. MICHAEL; BEATON, VIRGINIA L., *DEVELOPMENTAL PSYCHOLOGY*, V5 N3, PP378-388, NOV 71
THE EFFECTS OF DELAY OF INFORMATION FEEDBACK INTERVAL (0 OR 7 SECONDS), POSTINFORMATION FEEDBACK INTERVAL (1, 8, OR 15 SECONDS), DIFFICULTY (ONE OR THREE VARIABLE IRRELEVANT DIMENSIONS), AND PRESENCE OR ABSENCE OF A TRACTOR IN THE POSTINFORMATION FEEDBACK INTERVAL WERE INVESTIGATED WITH 240 JUNIOR HIGH SCHOOL CHILDREN IN A MODIFIED CONCEPT-IDENTIFICATION TASK. (AUTHOR/WY)

EJ 047 678 PS 501 419
SINGLE VERSUS CUMULATIVE PRESENTATION OF STIMULI TO KINDERGARTNERS IN REVERSAL SHIFT BEHAVIOR KENDLER, HOWARD H.; WARD, JAMES W., *DEVELOPMENTAL PSYCHOLOGY*, V5 N3, PP420-426, NOV 71

EJ 047 679 PS 501 420
DEVELOPMENT OF MEMORIZATION STRATEGIES NEIMARK, EDITH; AND OTHERS, *DEVELOPMENTAL PSYCHOLOGY*, V5 N3, PP427-432, NOV 71
DATA FROM A DEVELOPMENTAL TASK ADMINISTERED TO CHILDREN IN GRADES 1, 3, 4, 5, AND 6 WERE INTERPRETED AS EVIDENCE THAT MEMORIZATION IS NOT AN ISOLATED SKILL BUT, RATHER, ONE OF MANY MANIFESTATIONS OF AN INDIVIDUAL'S CHARACTERISTIC AGE-RELATED APPROACH TO PROBLEMS. (AUTHOR/WY)

EJ 047 680 PS 501 423
SEX AND AGE DIFFERENCES IN PATTERN ORGANIZATION IN A FIGURAL-CONCEPTUAL TASK GUTTMAN, RUTH; KAHNEMAN, IRAH, *DEVELOPMENTAL PSYCHOLOGY*, V5 N3, PP446-453, NOV 71

EJ 047 681 PS 501 424
CHILDREN'S ACQUISITION OF VISUO-SPATIAL DIMENSIONALITY: A CONSERVATION STUDY KERSHNER, JOHN R., *DEVELOPMENTAL PSYCHOLOGY*, V5 N3, PP454-462, NOV 71
RESULTS OF AN EXPERIMENT INVESTIGATING THE EFFECTS OF LATERALITY, MOVEMENT, AND LANGUAGE ON 160 FIRST GRADE CHILDREN'S ABILITY TO CONSERVE MULTIPLE-SPACE RELATIONS SEEM TO BE CONSISTENT WITH NEUROPHYSIOLOGICAL EVIDENCE ATTESTING TO THE ASYMMETRICAL FUNCTIONING OF THE CEREBRAL HEMISPHERES. (AUTHOR/WY)

EJ 047 682 PS 501 425
THE DEVELOPMENT OF THE PROPORTIONALITY SCHEME IN CHILDREN AND ADOLESCENTS BRAINERD, CHARLES J., *DEVELOPMENTAL PSYCHOLOGY*, V5 N3, PP469-476, NOV 71
IN GENERAL, THIS CROSS-SECTIONAL VALIDATION STUDY SUPPORTS INHELDER AND PIAGET'S CLAIMS ABOUT THE DEVELOPMENT OF CONCEPTS OF VOLUME AND DENSITY MORE EASILY THAN YOUNGER SUBJECTS. (AUTHOR/WY)

EJ 047 683 PS 501 426
THE CHILDREN'S ASSOCIATIVE RESPONDING TEST: A TWO-YEAR FOLLOW-UP ACHENBACH, THOMAS M., *DEVELOPMENTAL PSYCHOLOGY*, V5 N3, PP477-483, NOV 71
PREVIOUSLY TESTED 5TH AND 6TH GRADERS IN THE TWO-YEAR FOLLOW-UP SAMPLE CONTINUED TO RESPOND ASSOCIATIVELY ON THE CHILDREN'S ASSOCIATIVE RESPONDING TEST, INDICATING STABILITY IN RESPONSE PATTERNS. TEST-RETEST RELIABILITY OF THE NUMBER OF ERRORS WAS HIGH. (AUTHOR/WY)

EJ 047 684 PS 501 428
TITRATING DELAYED MATCHING TO SAMPLE IN CHILDREN FERRARO, DOUGLAS P.; AND OTHERS, *DEVELOPMENTAL PSYCHOLOGY*, V5 N3, PP488-493, NOV 71

EJ 047 685 PS 501 430
ABSTRACTION, INFERENCE, AND THE PROCESS OF IMITATIVE LEARNING LIEBERT, ROBERT M.; SWENSON, SHARON A., *DEVELOPMENTAL PSYCHOLOGY*, V5 N3, PP500-504, NOV 71
IN THIS STUDY INVOLVING 32 FIRST GRADERS, RESULTS INDICATED THAT IMITATIVE LEARNING WAS ACCOMPLISHED AND TRANSLATED INTO ACTION BY A TWO-STEP PROCESS OF INFORMATIONAL ANALYSIS INVOLVING ABSTRACTION AND SUBSEQUENT INFERENCE. (AUTHOR/WY)

EJ 047 686 PS 501 431
STIMULUS PREFERENCE AND MULTIPLICATIVE CLASSIFICATION IN CHILDREN OVERTON, WILLIS F.; JORDAN, ROSALIE, *DEVELOPMENTAL PSYCHOLOGY*, V5 N3, PP505-510, NOV 71
THE ROLE OF STIMULUS PREFERENCE AND VARIOUS SUBJECT AND TASK VARIABLES IN THE SOLUTION OF MATRIX-COMPLETION PROBLEMS WERE EXAMINED USING CHILDREN AT 4 AND 6 YEARS OF AGE. AGE, THE NUMBER OF STIMULUS CATEGORIES, THE TYPE OF DRAWING, AND THE SPECIFIC MATRIX STIMULUS CATEGORIES TAKEN INDIVIDUALLY AND IN COMBINATION WERE FOUND TO HAVE SIGNIFICANT EFFECTS UPON PERFORMANCE. (AUTHOR/WY)

EJ 047 687 PS 501 434
CONCEPTUAL RULE LEARNING AND CHRONOLOGICAL AGE BOURNE, L. E., JR.; O'BANION, KATY, *DEVELOPMENTAL PSYCHOLOGY*, V5 N3, PP525-534, NOV 71

EJ 047 688 PS 501 439
COGNITIVE MEDIATION OF DEVELOPMENTAL TRENDS IN EXTREME RESPONSE CHOICE EMMERICH, WALTER, *DEVELOPMENTAL PSYCHOLOGY*, V5 N3, PP540, NOV 71
THE PRESENT FINDINGS SUGGEST THAT "NEVER" AS A RESPONSE AND "VERY OFTEN" AS A RESPONSE ARE MEDIATED BY DIFFERENT UNDERLYING PROCESSES, AT LEAST BETWEEN THE AGES OF 8 AND 17. (AUTHOR/WY)

EJ 047 689 PS 501 441
THE EFFECTS OF ENRICHED NEONATAL EXPERIENCES UPON LATER COGNITIVE FUNCTIONING WACHS, THEODORE D.; CUCINOTTA, PATTIANN, *DEVELOPMENTAL PSYCHOLOGY*, V5 N3, PP542, NOV 71
THE DATA REPORTED IN THIS SMALL STUDY CONFIRM PREVIOUS RESEARCH INDICATING THAT EARLY STIMULATION, THOUGH INITIALLY AFFECTING HUMAN BEHAVIOR, HAS LITTLE PERMANENT EFFECT UPON LATER FUNCTIONING. (AUTHOR/WY)

EJ 047 893 PS 501 433
RECOGNITION OF ENGLISH AND HEBREW LETTERS AS A FUNCTION OF AGE AND DISPLAY PREDICTABILITY DAVES, WALTER F.; WERZBERGER, JONAS B., *DEVELOPMENTAL PSYCHOLOGY*, V5 N3, PP518-524, NOV 71

EJ 047 894 PS 501 457
A BASIC VOCABULARY FOR BEGINNING READING JOHNSON, DALE D., *ELEMENTARY SCHOOL JOURNAL*, V72 N1, PP29-34, OCT 1971
COMPILES VOCABULARY FROM THE SPONTANEOUS SPEAKING VOCABULARY OF CHILDREN IN KINDERGARTEN-FIRST GRADE AND FROM A LIST OF 500 WORDS FREQUENTLY USED IN PRINTED AMERICAN ENGLISH. (WY)

EJ 047 968 PS 501 444
A FRESH LOOK AT INTERCOUNTRY ADOPTIONS ADAMS, JOHN E.; KIM, HYUNG BOK, *CHILDREN*, V18 N6, PP214-221, NOV-DEC 71
DISCUSSION OF INTERCOUNTRY ADOPTIONS COVERS CURRENT ADOPTION TRENDS AND LEGISLATION, RESEARCH, PROBLEMS OF ADJUSTMENT, BENEFITS AND RISKS TO FAMILY AND CHILD, THE ROLE OF THE AGENCY AND THE IMPACT OF SUCH PRACTICES TOWARD PROVIDING FOR THE WELFARE OF ALL CHILDREN. (AJ)

EJ 048 045 PS 501 458
EARLY ADMISSION: OPINION VERSUS EVIDENCE BRAGA, JOSEPH L., *ELEMENTARY SCHOOL JOURNAL*, V72 N1, PP35-46, OCT 1971
DESPITE EVIDENCE OF MANY RESEARCH STUDIES SUPPORTING EARLY SCHOOL ADMISSION FOR MENTALLY ADVANCED CHILDREN, ATTITUDES AND PRACTICE IN THE MAJORITY OF SCHOOLS HAVE PREVENTED ITS INSTITUTION. THIS ARTICLE DISCUSSES THE MAJOR QUESTIONS RAISED ABOUT EARLY ADMISSION, EXAMINES TEACHER ATTITUDES, AND CONCLUDES THAT TEACHERS NEED TO BE REEDUCATED ON THIS ISSUE. (WY)

EJ 048 099 PS 501 437
THE RATIONAL ZERO POINT ON INCENTIVE-OBJECT PREFERENCE SCALES: A DEVELOPMENTAL STUDY HAAF, ROBERT A., *DEVELOPMENTAL PSYCHOLOGY*, V5 N3, PP537, NOV 71
PREFERENCE JUDGMENTS MADE BY 20 MALES AND 20 FEMALES (GRADES K-4) ABOUT THE INCENTIVE VALUE OF 10 OBJECTS (I.E. BUBBLE GUM, CHICLET, CANDY CORN, DRIED LIMA BEAN) HELPED DETERMINE RELATIVE AND ABSOLUTE SCALES FOR USE OF THESE OBJECTS AS REWARDS. THE ASSUMPTION THAT THE SAME OBJECT IS EQUALLY REWARDING AT DIFFERENT AGE LEVELS MAY BE UNWARRANTED. (AUTHOR/WY)

EJ 048 234 PS 501 471
PARENTAL CONCEPTUAL SYSTEMS, HOME PLAY ENVIRONMENT, AND POTENTIAL CREATIVITY IN CHILDREN BISHOP, DOYLE W.; CHACE, CHARLES A., *JOURNAL OF EXPERIMENTAL CHILD PSYCHOLOGY*, V12 N3, PP318-338, DEC 71

EJ 048 235 PS 501 480
THE INFLUENCE OF TEACHER-CHILD INTERACTION ON THE LEARNING PROCESS MARCUS, IRWIN M., *JOURNAL OF THE AMERICAN ACADEMY OF CHILD PSYCHIATRY*, V10 N3, PP481-500, JUL 71
THREE GROUPS OF CHILDREN WHO HAD COMPLETED THE FIRST GRADE AND WERE IN A SUMMER LANGUAGE IMPROVEMENT PROGRAM WERE STUDIED WITH REGARD TO GAIN IN READING ACHIEVEMENT DIFFERENCES IN TEACHING STYLE AND THE EFFECTS OF RACE OF THE TEACHER. (NH)

EJ 048 296 PS 501 469
INTERACTION EFFECTS OF SOCIAL AND TANGIBLE REINFORCEMENT BROWN, RICHARD A., *JOURNAL OF EXPERIMENTAL CHILD PSYCHOLOGY*, V12 N3, PP289-303, DEC 71

EJ 048 297 PS 501 475
EFFECTS OF COOPERATIVE RESPONSE ACQUISITION ON SOCIAL BEHAVIOR DURING FREE-PLAY ALTMAN, KARL, *JOURNAL OF EXPERIMENTAL CHILD PSYCHOLOGY*, V12 N3, PP387-395, DEC 71

EJ 048 298 PS 501 476
SMILING IN CHILDREN AS A FUNCTION OF THEIR SENSE OF MASTERY HARTER, SUSAN; AND OTHERS, *JOURNAL OF EXPERIMENTAL CHILD PSYCHOLOGY*, V12 N3, PP396-404, DEC 71
EXAMINES THE RELATIONSHIP BETWEEN SMILING BEHAVIOR AND THE CORRECTNESS OF RESPONSES ON A PICTORIAL WORD-RECOGNITION TASK FOR 4-AND 8-YEAR-OLD CHILDREN. (AUTHOR/AJ)

EJ 048 299 PS 501 479
A STUDY OF SLEEP BEHAVIOR IN TWO-YEAR-OLD CHILDREN RAGINS, NAOMI; SCHACHTER, JOSEPH, *JOURNAL OF THE AMERICAN ACADEMY OF CHILD PSYCHIATRY*, V10 N3, PP464-480, JUL 71
INTERVIEWS AND QUESTIONNAIRES YIELDED INFORMATION FROM MOTHERS OF 2-YEAR-OLDS ABOUT THEIR CHILDREN'S SLEEP PRACTICES AND PATTERNS, AND ABOUT THE MOTHER'S CONCERNS ABOUT THEIR CHILDREN'S SLEEP BEHAVIOR. (NH)

EJ 048 300 PS 501 481
A MICRO-ANALYSIS OF MOTHER-INFANT INTERACTION. BEHAVIOR REGULATING SOCIAL CONTACT BETWEEN A MOTHER AND HER 3 1/2 MONTH-OLD TWINS STERN, DANIEL N., *JOURNAL OF THE AMERICAN ACADEMY OF CHILD PSYCHIATRY*, V10 N3, PP501-517, JUL 71
AN EXAMPLE OF "CONTROLLING" MATERNAL BEHAVIOR WITH 3 1/2-MONTH-OLD TWINS IS STUDIED BY A METHOD OF FRAME-BY-FRAME FILM ANALYSIS. CHARACTERISTIC INFANT BEHAVIORS REGULATING SOCIAL CONTACT WITH THE MOTHER ARE IDENTIFIED AND FOLLOWED THROUGH 15 MONTHS. (AUTHOR)

EJ 048 301 PS 501 482
PLAYROOM OBSERVATIONS OF HYPERACTIVE CHILDREN ON MEDICATION RAPOPORT, JUDITH; AND OTHERS, *JOURNAL OF THE AMERICAN ACADEMY OF CHILD PSYCHIATRY*, V10 N3, PP524-534, JUL 71
A CONTROLLED OUTPATIENT STUDY OF 19 HYPERACTIVE BOYS (AGED 4-10 YEARS) OF NORMAL INTELLIGENCE EXAMINED THE EFFECTS OF PLACEBO AND TWO DIFFERENT DRUGS ON THE BOYS' PLAYROOM BEHAVIOR. (AUTHOR/NH)

EJ 048 302 PS 501 497
MATERNAL CHILD REARING AND CREATIVITY IN SONS HEILBRUN, ALFRED B., JR., *JOURNAL OF GENETIC PSYCHOLOGY*, V119 PT.2, PP175-9, DEC 71

EJ 048 303 PS 501 499
PLAY BEHAVIOR IN YOUNG CHILDREN: A CROSS-CULTURAL STUDY FINLEY, GORDON E.; LAYNE, OTTIS, JR., *JOURNAL OF GENETIC PSYCHOLOGY*, V119 PT.2, PP203-210, DEC 71

EJ 048 304 PS 501 501
SENSORY-SET FACTORS IN AGE DIFFERENCES IN REACTION TIME BOTWINICK, JACK, *JOURNAL OF GENETIC PSYCHOLOGY*, V119 PT.2, PP241-9, DEC 71
AGE DIFFERENCES IN REACTION TIME (ELDERLY VS. YOUNG ADULTS) WERE FOUND TO PERSIST EVEN WHEN STIMULUS INTENSITIES WERE ADJUSTED ON AN INDIVIDUAL BASIS OF REPORTED LOUDNESS. (WY)

EJ 048 305 PS 501 505
OBJECT CONSTRUCTION AND IMITATION UNDER DIFFERING CONDITIONS OF REARING PARASKEVOPOULOS, JOHN; HUNT, J. MCV., *JOURNAL OF GENETIC PSYCHOLOGY*, V119 PT.2, PP301-321, DEC 71
COMPARES THE AGES AT WHICH INFANTS LIVING UNDER DIFFERENT CONDITIONS IN TWO ORPHANGES IN ATHENS, GREECE ACHIEVE LEVELS OF OBJECT CONSTRUCTION AND IMITATION, BOTH VERBAL AND GESTURAL. HOME-REARED INFANTS OF THE SAME AGE RANGE WERE ALSO EXAMINED USING TWO OF THE UZGIRIS-HUNT ORDINAL SCALES OF INFANT PSYCHOLOGICAL DEVELOPMENT. (WY)

EJ 048 306 PS 501 513
BEHAVIOUR PROBLEMS IN THE INFANT SCHOOL CHAZAN, MAURICE; JACKSON, SUSAN, *JOURNAL OF CHILD PSYCHOLOGY AND PSYCHIATRY*, V12 N3, PP191-210, OCT 71
ANALYZES INFORMATION OBTAINED FROM TEACHERS RELATING TO THE INCIDENCE OF BEHAVIOR PROBLEMS IN A SAMPLE OF CHILDREN IN THEIR FIRST YEAR IN THE INFANT SCHOOL. (WY)

EJ 048 395 PS 501 485
STUDYING HUMAN ECOLOGY: TEACHER EDUCATION AND THE CULTURALLY DIVERSE ANTES, JOHN M., *CHILDHOOD EDUCATION*, V48 N4, PP182-186, JAN 72
DESCRIBES AN INTERNSHIP PROGRAM TO HELP STUDENT TEACHERS DEVELOP SENSITIVITY TO ENVIRONMENTAL INFLUENCES ON CHILDREN FROM MINORITY AND POVERTY CULTURES. (NH)

EJ 048 396 PS 501 494
CONCEPTS OF SOCIAL SEX ROLES AMONG CHILEAN ADOLESCENTS WILLIAMSON, R. C.; SEWARD, GEORGENE H., *HUMAN DEVELOPMENT*, V14 N3, PP184-194, 71
REPORTS THE FINDINGS OF A STUDY OF 210 CHILEAN MALE AND FEMALE ADOLESCENTS ON A 12-PONT SEMANTIC DIFFERENTIAL SCALE. COMPARISONS WERE MADE FOR 7 CONCEPTS RELATED TO SEX ROLES. SIGNIFICANT DIFFERENCES OCCURRED BETWEEN THE BOYS' AND GIRLS' RATING OF THE TRAITS OF MEN AND WOMEN, BUT THE DIFFERENCES WERE NO LARGER THAN FOR OTHER NATIONAL SAMPLES. (AUTHOR/WY)

EJ 048 397 PS 501 496
CHANGES IN PARENTAL BEHAVIOR REPORTED BY CHILDREN IN WEST GERMANY AND THE UNITED STATES RODGERS, R. R., *HUMAN DEVELOPMENT*, V14 N3, PP208-224, 71

CHANGES IN PARENTAL BEHAVIOR WERE INVESTIGATED IN COLOGNE, WEST GERMANY, IN 1960 AND 1968, AND UPSTATE NEW YORK IN 1960-1962 AND 1965 USING RATINGS MADE BY 6TH GRADE SCHOOL CHILDREN. THE HYPOTHESIZED CHANGES WERE CONFIRMED FOR 7 PARENTAL BEHAVIORS. (AUTHOR/WY)

EJ 048 472 PS 501 492
EXPLORATION OF DEVELOPMENTAL VARIABLES BY MANIPULATION AND SIMULATION OF AGE DIFFERENCES IN BEHAVIOR BALTES, PAUL B.; GOULET, L. R., *HUMAN DEVELOPMENT*, V14 N3, PP149-170, 71

EXPLORES STRATEGIES FREQUENTLY UTILIZED IN DEVELOPMENTAL RESEARCH LABORATORIES AND DISCUSSES THE POWER OF THESE STRATEGIES IN ISOLATING THE MAJOR VARIABLES WHOSE EFFECTS ARE AGE (OR TIME)-RELATED. THE PAPER ALSO PROVIDES INFORMATION ABOUT THE KEY DEVELOPMENTAL ANTECEDENTS OF AGE DIFFERENCES. (AUTHOR/WY)

EJ 048 473 PS 501 495
DESIRABILITY JUDGMENTS AS A FUNCTION OF ITEM CONTENT, INSTRUCTIONAL SET, AND SET: A LIFE-SPAN DEVELOPMENTAL STUDY AHAMMER, INGE M., *HUMAN DEVELOPMENT*, V14 N3, PP195-207, 71

DESIRABILITY JUDGMENTS (VALUES) OF 4 PERSONALITY DIMENSIONS (AFFILIATION, AUTONOMY, ACHIEVEMENT, NURTURANCE) AND 2 CONTROL SCALES WERE INVESTIGATED IN A TOTAL OF 120 MALE AND FEMALE SUBJECTS FROM 4 DIFFERENT AGE GROUPS REPRESENTING CHILDHOOD, ADOLESCENCE, ADULTHOOD, AND OLD AGE. CLEAR AGE AND SEX DIFFERENCES REFLECTED MULTIPLE VALUE SYSTEMS. (AUTHOR/WY)

EJ 048 697 PS 501 487
WHAT TO DO TILL THE MALE MAN COMES SCIARRA, DOROTHY JUNE, *CHILDHOOD EDUCATION*, V48 N4, PP190-191, JAN 72

SUGGESTS CLASSROOM MATERIALS AND ACTIVITIES WHICH, IN THE ABSENCE OF MALE TEACHERS, MAY BE USED IN PRESCHOOL AND PRIMARY CLASSROOMS TO PROVIDE MALE SEX-ROLE MODELS. (NH)

EJ 048 904 PS 501 478
INTERVENTION IN INFANCY: A PROGRAM FOR BLIND INFANTS FRAIBERG, SELMA, *JOURNAL OF THE AMERICAN ACADEMY OF CHILD PSYCHIATRY*, V10 N3, PP381-405, JUL 71

REPORTS LONGITUDINAL STUDIES OF THE UNIQUE DEVELOPMENTAL PATTERNS OF THE BLIND BABY, AND DISCUSSES THE USE OF HOME VISITS TO SHOW PARENTS HOW TO ASSIST THEIR INFANT'S DEVELOPMENT. (NH)

EJ 048 905 PS 501 512
THE EFFECTS OF OWN-HOME AND INSTITUTION-REARING ON THE BEHAVIOURAL DEVELOPMENT OF NORMAL AND MONGOL CHILDREN FRANCIS, SARAH H., *JOURNAL OF CHILD PSYCHOLOGY AND PSYCHIATRY*, V12 N3, PP173-190, OCT 71

BEHAVIORAL DIFFERENCES WERE FOUND FOR BOTH MONGOLS AND NORMAL CHILDREN (MENTAL AGE BELOW 2 YEARS) BETWEEN THOSE WHO LIVED AT HOME WITH THEIR PARENTS AND THOSE IN INSTITUTIONS. (AUTHOR/WY)

EJ 048 998 PS 501 488
PLANNING TRIPS FOR VULNERABLE CHILDREN COHEN, SHIRLEY, *CHILDHOOD EDUCATION*, V48 N4, PP192-196, JAN 72

PRACTICAL SUGGESTIONS TO HELP TEACHERS PLAN FIELD TRIPS THAT WILL BE HELPFUL EXPERIENCES FOR SCHOOL CHILDREN WHO ARE MORE VULNERABLE, FEARFUL, CONFUSED AND DESTRUCTIVE THAN MOST OF THEIR PEERS. (NH)

EJ 048 999 PS 501 491
HANDWRITING: THE STATE OF THE CRAFT HUITT, RAY, *CHILDHOOD EDUCATION*, V48 N4, PP219-223, JAN 72

EJ 049 117 PS 501 470
YOUNG CHILDREN'S COMPREHENSION OF LOGICAL CONNECTIVES SNUPPES, PATRICK; FELDMAN, SHIRLEY, *JOURNAL OF EXPERIMENTAL CHILD PSYCHOLOGY*, V12 N3, PP304-317, DEC 71

REPORTS TWO EXPERIMENTS: 1) AN INVESTIGATION OF THE EXTENT TO WHICH 4-TO 6-YEAR-OLD CHILDREN COMPREHEND THE LOGICAL CONNECTIVES OF CONJUNCTION, DISJUNCTION, AND NEGATION; AND 2) AN INVESTIGATION OF THE ROLE OF IDIOMS IN CHILDREN'S UNDERSTANDING OF SENTENTIAL CONNECTIVES. (AUTHOR/AJ)

EJ 049 167 PS 501 472
A DEVELOPMENTAL COMPARISON OF IDENTITY AND EQUIVALENCE CONSERVATIONS PAPALIA, DIANE E.; HOOPER, FRANK H., *JOURNAL OF EXPERIMENTAL CHILD PSYCHOLOGY*, V12 N3, PP347-361, DEC 71

INVESTIGATES THE DEVELOPMENTAL PRIORITY OF IDENTITY CONSERVATION AS CONTRASTED WITH EQUIVALENCE CONSERVATION USING QUANTITY AND NUMBER CONSERVATION TASKS. (AUTHOR/AJ)

EJ 049 168 PS 501 473
EFFECT OF REINFORCEMENT CONTINGENCIES IN INCREASING PROGRAMMED READING AND MATHEMATICS BEHAVIORS IN FIRST-GRADE CHILDREN HOLT, GARY L., *JOURNAL OF EXPERIMENTAL CHILD PSYCHOLOGY*, V12 N3, PP362-369, DEC 71

EJ 049 169 PS 501 474
STRENGTH OF DIMENSIONAL PREFERENCES AS A PREDICTOR OF NURSERY-SCHOOL CHILDREN'S PERFORMANCE ON A CONCEPT-SHIFT TASK SEITZ, VICTORIA; WEIR, MORTON W., *JOURNAL OF EXPERIMENTAL CHILD PSYCHOLOGY*, V12 N3, PP370-386, DEC 71

EJ 049 170 PS 501 477
CHILDREN'S PERFORMANCE IN SIMPLE AND SUCCESSIVE-REVERSAL CONCEPT IDENTIFICATION PROBLEMS SMALL, MELINDA Y.; LUCAS, MARK, *JOURNAL OF EXPERIMENTAL CHILD PSYCHOLOGY*, V12 N3, PP405-415, DEC 71

REPORTS TWO EXPERIMENTS: 1) TO DETERMINE WHETHER CHILDREN PERFORM AS ADULTS IN THE SIMPLE AND SUCCESSIVE-REVERSAL CONCEPT IDENTIFICATION PROBLEMS AND TO ASSESS THEIR RETENTION OF STIMULUS-RESPONSE INFORMATION; AND 2) TO DETERMINE THE ASSOCIATIVE STRENGTH OF THE PAIN OF RESPONSE WORDS. (AUTHOR/AJ)

EJ 049 171 PS 501 493
CLASSIFICATORY SCHEMES IN RELATION TO CLASS INCLUSION BEFORE AND AFTER TRAINING YOUNISS, J., *HUMAN DEVELOPMENT*, V14 N3, PP171-183, 71

RESULTS OF THIS INVESTIGATION SUPPORT THE VIEW THAT OPERATING CLASS INCLUSION REQUIRES COORDINATION BETWEEN LOGICAL INTENSION AND EXTENSION, A PROCESS WHICH CAN BE FACILITATED THROUGH TRAINING. (AUTHOR/WY)

EJ 049 172 PS 501 502
DIFFERENTIAL COGNITIVE DEVELOPMENT WITHIN AND BETWEEN RACIAL AND ETHNIC GROUPS OF DISADVANTAGED PRESCHOOL AND KINDERGARTEN CHILDREN SOUTHERN, MARA L.; PLANT, WALTER T., *JOURNAL OF GENETIC PSYCHOLOGY*, V119 PT.2, PP259-266, DEC 71

YOUNG CHILDREN FROM ECONOMICALLY IMPOVERISHED FAMILIES DISPLAYED DEFICIENT GENERAL INTELLECTUAL AND LANGUAGE ABILITIES PARTLY AS A FUNCTION OF THEIR SPECIFIC RACIAL OR ETHNIC BACKGROUNDS. (WY)

EJ 049 173 PS 501 503
EFFECTS OF PERCEPTUAL TRAINING ON CHILDREN'S HUMAN FIGURE DRAWINGS ARMENTROUT, JAMES A., *JOURNAL OF GENETIC PSYCHOLOGY*, V119 PT.2, PP281-7, DEC 71

EJ 049 426 PS 501 498
MEANING CONDITIONING AND AWARENESS AMONG CHILDREN MILLER, ADAM; KNOLL, CHERYL, *JOURNAL OF GENETIC PSYCHOLOGY*, V119 PT.2, PP187-194, DEC 71

PRE-EXPERIMENTAL PREDICTIONS THAT AN INCREASE IN GRADE WOULD BE PARALLELED BY AN INCREASE IN DEGREE OF MEANING CONDITIONING, IN AMOUNT OF AWARENESS, AND IN AMOUNT OF CONDITIONING WITH AWARENESS WERE NOT SUPPORTED IN THIS INVESTIGATION. CONSIDERATION OF POSSIBLE REASONS FOR SUCH A RESULT HELP CLARIFY THE NATURE OF MEANING CONDITIONING. (WY)

EJ 049 427 PS 501 500
TRANSFERENCE TOWARD THE CHILD THERAPIST AND OTHER PARENT SURROGATES SUBOTNIK, LEO, *JOURNAL OF GENETIC PSYCHOLOGY*, V119 PT.2, PP215-231, DEC 71

THE ATTITUDES OF AN INSTITUTIONALIZED 7-YEAR-OLD MENTALLY RETARDED, WHITE BOY TOWARD HIS THERAPIST, TEACHERS, AND COTTAGE WORKERS BEFORE, DURING, AND FOLLOWING TWO MONTHS OF PSYCHOTHERAPY WERE INFERRED TO SUPPORT THE TRANSFERENCE HYPOTHESIS. (WY)

EJ 049 428 PS 501 504
THE INFLUENCE OF INCENTIVES ON MEMORY STAGES IN CHILDREN CUVO, ANTHONY J.; WITRYOL, SAM L., *JOURNAL OF GENETIC PSYCHOLOGY*, V119 PT.2, PP289-300, DEC 71

EJ 049 429 PS 501 506
MEMORY: INTERACTION OF STIMULUS AND ORGANISMIC FACTORS CORSINI, D. A., *HUMAN DEVELOPMENT*, V14 N4, PP227-235, 71
SEVERAL ASPECTS OF MEMORY DEVELOPMENT ARE DISCUSSED WITHIN THE FRAMEWORK OF MEMORY RESEARCH: THE DEVELOPMENT OF REPRESENTATIONAL ABILITIES; THE DEVELOPMENT OF THE PROPENSITY TO REPRESENT; THE DEVELOPMENT OF MNEMONIC STRATEGIES; THE DEVELOPMENT OF A GENERAL INFORMATION BASE; THE DEVELOPMENT OF FAMILIARITY WITH DIFFERENT TYPES OF STIMULUS REPRESENTATION; AND THE DEVELOPMENT OF THE COGNITIVE OPERATIVE SYSTEM. (AUTHOR/WY)

EJ 049 430 PS 501 507
WHAT THE DEVELOPMENT OF SHORT-TERM MEMORY IS BELMONT, J. M.; BUTTERFIELD, E. C., *HUMAN DEVELOPMENT*, V14 N4, PP236-248, 71
DEVELOPMENT OF MEMORY DEPENDS UPON CHANGES IN SEVERAL MNEMONIC PROCESSES, WHICH ARE ILLUSTRATED IN EXPERIMENTS WITH NORMAL AND MENTALLY RETARDED ADULTS AND CHILDREN. (AUTHOR/WY)

EJ 049 431 PS 501 508
DEVELOPMENTAL CHANGES IN VISUAL INFORMATION PROCESSING AND SHORT-TERM VISUAL MEMORY HAITH, M. M., *HUMAN DEVELOPMENT*, V14 N4, PP249-261, 71

EJ 049 432 PS 501 509
SOME THOUGHTS ON HOW CHILDREN LEARN TO REMEMBER HAGEN, J. W., *HUMAN DEVELOPMENT*, V14 N4, PP262-271, 71
REVIEWS RESEARCH ON VERBAL LABELING AND SHORTTERM MEMORY. (AUTHOR/WY)

EJ 049 433 PS 501 510
FIRST DISCUSSANT'S COMMENTS: WHAT IS MEMORY DEVELOPMENT THE DEVELOPMENT OF? FLAVELL, H. H., *HUMAN DEVELOPMENT*, V14 N4, PP272-278, 71

EJ 049 434 PS 501 511
SECOND DISCUSSANT'S COMMENTS: WHAT'S LEFT TO SAY? JENKINS, J. J., *HUMAN DEVELOPMENT*, V14 N4, PP279-86, 71

EJ 049 526 PS 501 486
SOURCES OF MANPOWER FOR THE PRESCHOOL CLASSROOM MILGRAM, JOEL I., *CHILDHOOD EDUCATION*, V48 N4, PP187-189, JAN 72

EJ 049 562 PS 501 483
A CITY FOR CHILDREN: THE YEAR 2005 BLOOMBERG, WARNER, JR., *CHILDHOOD EDUCATION*, V48 N4, PP170-174, JAN 72
COMMUNITY PRIORITIES TO CREATE A BETTER QUALITY OF LIFE FOR CHILDREN ARE OUTLINED. (NH)

EJ 049 656 PS 501 484
FAMILIES WITHOUT FATHERS HERZOG, ELIZABETH; SUDIA, CECELIA E., *CHILDHOOD EDUCATION*, V48 N4, PP175-181, JAN 72
COMMON GENERALIZATIONS ABOUT CHILDREN GROWING UP IN FATHERLESS FAMILIES ARE REEXAMINED. TOPICS INCLUDE SCHOOL ACHIEVEMENT, DELINQUENCY, MASCULINE IDENTITY, ROLE OF THE MOTHER, AND SOCIETAL ATTITUDES. (NH)

EJ 049 657 PS 501 489
SYMPOSIUM ON ALTERNATIVE COMMUNITIES: CHILDREN OF THE GROUP FAMILY BERSON, DEBBIE, *CHILDHOOD EDUCATION*, V48 N4, PP197-200, JAN 72
PERSONAL ACCOUNTS OF INNOVATIVE SOCIAL ARRANGEMENTS IN TWO COMMUNES FOCUS ON COMMUNITY RESPONSIBILITY FOR CHILD REARING. (NH)

EJ 049 658 PS 501 490
SOME THOUGHTS ON COMMUNAL CHILDREARING GROSS, LOUISE, *CHILDHOOD EDUCATION*, V48 N4, PP201-203, JAN 72
ONE MOTHER DESCRIBES HER COMMUNAL CHILD REARING EXPERIENCES. (NH)

EJ 049 895 PS 501 540
LE MONDE DES TOUT PETITS EST-IL INFLUENCE PAR NOTRE MONDE MODERNE? (IS THE WORLD OF CHILDREN INFLUENCED BY OUR MODERN WORLD?) DUPARC, GERMAINE, *INTERNATIONAL JOURNAL OF EARLY CHILDHOOD*, V3 N2, PP49-57, 71
ALTHOUGH THE MODERN CHILD IS "UP TO THE MINUTE" IN HIS LANGUAGE, INTERESTS, AND MEMORY FOR TECHNOLOGICAL DETAILS, IN MANY ESSENTIAL RESPECTS HIS VISION HAS REMAINED UNCHANGED FROM THAT OF CHILDREN OF PREVIOUS GENERATIONS. (EDITOR)

EJ 049 896 PS 501 540
A REPORT ON EVALUATION STUDIES OF PROJECT HEAD START DATTA, LOIS-ELLIN, *INTERNATIONAL JOURNAL OF EARLY CHILDHOOD*, V3 N2, PP58-69, 71
COPIES OF THE EXTENSIVE REFERENCE LIST FOR THIS ARTICLE MAY BE OBTAINED FROM THE EDITOR ON REQUEST. (EDITOR)

EJ 049 937 PS 501 532
"STRUCTURE" CAN IMPROVE THE GROUP BEHAVIOR OF FIVE-YEAR-OLD CHILDREN TORRANCE, E. PAUL, *ELEMENTARY SCHOOL JOURNAL*, V72 N2, PP102-6, NOV 71
"IN SUMMARY, THE RESULTS SUGGEST THAT, WITH FIVE-YEAR-OLD CHILDREN, MORE MIGHT BE GAINED BY STRUCTURING THE TASK THAN BY STRUCTURING THE GROUP." (AUTHOR)

EJ 049 938 PS 501 543
METODO DE ARCHIVAR LAS OBSERVACIONES DEL COMPORTAMIENTO DEL NINO, COMO GUIA PARA ENTENDERLO MEJOR (METHODS OF RECORDING OBSERVATIONS OF CHILDREN'S BEHAVIOR, A GUIDE FOR BETTER UNDERSTANDING) STAMP, ISLA M., *INTERNATIONAL JOURNAL OF EARLY CHILDHOOD*, V3 N2, PP78-81, 71
COPIES OF THE BEHAVIOUR STUDY TECHNIQUE DESCRIBED IN THIS ARTICLE MAY BE OBTAINED IN ENGLISH FROM THE AUSTRALIAN COUNCIL FOR EDUCATIONAL RESEARCH, FREDERICK ST., HAWTHORN, VICTORIA, AUSTRALIA 3122. (RY)

EJ 050 038 PS 501 530
STRUCTURE OF-OR FOR-KNOWLEDGE? THOMAS, JOHN I., *ELEMENTARY SCHOOL JOURNAL*, V72 N2, PP81-7, NOV 71
CURRICULUM DESIGN MUST ENCOMPASS NOT ONLY SUBJECT STRUCTURE BUT ALSO STUDENT EXPERIENCE AND INQUISITIVENESS. (AN)

EJ 050 072 PS 501 527
TOP PRIORITY: UNDERSTANDING SELF AND OTHERS DINKMEYER, DON, *ELEMENTARY SCHOOL JOURNAL*, V72 N2, PP62-71, NOV 71
ANALYZES THE EDUCATIONAL PROBLEM OF TEACHERS BEING UNABLE TO DEAL WITH THE SOCIAL AND EMOTIONAL DEVELOPMENT OF THEIR PUPILS, AND DESCRIBES A PROGRAM OF STUDENT SELF ACTUALIZATION AND UNDERSTANDING OF OTHERS. (AN)

EJ 050 073 PS 501 536
INTELLECTUAL EVOLUTION FROM ADOLESCENCE TO ADULTHOOD PIAGET, J., *HUMAN DEVELOPMENT*, V15 N1, PP1-12, 72
GROWING OUT OF A CHILD'S COGNITIVE DEVELOPMENTAL HISTORY, FORMAL OPERATION BECOMES ESTABLISHED AT ABOUT THE AGE OF 12-15 YEARS. THE ESSENCE OF THE LOGIC OF CULTURED ADULTS AND THE BASIS FOR ELEMENTARY SCIENTIFIC THOUGHT ARE THEREBY PROVIDED. THE RATE AT WHICH A CHILD PROGRESSES THROUGH THE DEVELOPMENTAL SUCCESSION MAY VARY, ESPECIALLY FROM ONE CULTURE TO ANOTHER. (AUTHOR)

EJ 050 074 PS 501 537
VERBAL REGULATION OF MOTOR BEHAVIOR-SOVIET RESEARCH AND NON-SOVIET REPLICATIONS WOZNIAK, R. H., *HUMAN DEVELOPMENT*, V15 N1, PP13-57, 72
SOVIET INVESTIGATION OF THE DEVELOPMENT OF VERBAL INHIBITION OF PRESEVERATIVE MANUAL BEHAVIOR ARE REVIEWED. NON-SOVIET INVESTIGATIONS OF VERBAL-MANUAL INTERACTION ARE CONSIDERED IN RELATION TO THE SOVIET VIEW OF THE DEVELOPMENT OF VOLUNTARY BEHAVIOR; AND IT IS ARGUED, ON THE BASIS OF THIS EVIDENCE, THAT THE SOVIET POSITION NEED NOT STAND OR FALL ON THE REPLICABILITY OF THE SPECIFIC VERBAL-INHIBITION-OF-PERSEVERATION PHENOMENA DESCRIBED BY LURIA. (AUTHOR)

EJ 050 075 PS 501 561
THINKING BEFORE LANGUAGE? A SYMPOSIUM: 1. RELATIONSHIPS BETWEEN LANGUAGE AND THOUGHT VOYAT, GILBERT, *CHILDHOOD EDUCATION*, V48 N5, PP248-51, FEB 72
WHAT IS QUESTIONED HERE IS NOT THE TEACHING OF WORDS BUT THEIR PREMATURE IMPOSITION UPON THE CHILD BEFORE HE HAS ACQUIRED THE CONCEPTS THAT UNDERLIE THEM. (AUTHOR)

EJ 050 199 PS 501 544
PRESCHOOL EDUCATION IN ISRAEL LOMBARD, AVIMA D., *INTERNATIONAL JOURNAL OF EARLY CHILDHOOD*, V3 N2, PP82-9, 71
WHILE PRESCHOOL EDUCATION IN ISRAEL IS EXTENSIVE AND HAS A RELATIVELY LONG HISTORY, ITS SCOPE AND TRADITIONS ACT TO DETER INNOVATION AND CHANGE. THE PRESSING NEEDS OF THE DISADVANTAGED MAY, IN THE NEXT FEW YEARS, CREATE ENOUGH FORCE TO BRING ABOUT LONG-AWAITED CHANGES. (AUTHOR)

EJ 050 200 PS 501 562
THINKING BEFORE LANGUAGE? A SYMPOSIUM: 2. A SCHOOL FOR THINKING WACHS, HARRY; FURTH, HANS G., *CHILDHOOD EDUCATION*, V48 N5, PP252-5, FEB 72
THE AUTHORS CHALLENGE PROPONENTS OF INFORMAL "OPEN CLASSROOMS" AS WELL AS OF TRADITIONAL SCHOOL ORGANIZATION. (EDITOR)

EJ 050 274 PS 501 553
AN INTERVIEW WITH GEORGIA MCMURRAY, NEW YORK CITY'S COMMISSIONER FOR CHILD DEVELOPMENT WARREN, VIRGINIA LEE, *CHILDREN TODAY*, V1 N1, PP28-9, JAN-FEB 72
NEW YORK'S COMMISSIONER FOR CHILD DEVELOPMENT HEADS AN AGENCY WITH A YEARLY BUDGET OF $101.2 MILLION AND A STAFF OF 450. (RY)

EJ 050 320 PS 501 559
LEARNING FROM EACH OTHER: PREDIATRICIANS AND TEACHERS HOLMAN, GERALD H., *CHILDHOOD EDUCATION*, V48 N5, PP240-3, FEB 72
TEACHERS AND PHYSICIANS MUST WORK COOPERATIVELY IN THE ASSESSMENT, MANAGEMENT AND RE-EVALUATION OF CHILDREN WITH ANY MEDICAL, DENTAL, SOCIAL, EMOTIONAL PROBLEM THAT MIGHT INTERFERE WITH LEARNING. (AUTHOR)

EJ 050 321 PS 501 560
THE DIAGNOSTIC EVALUATION OF CHILDREN WITH LEARNING PROBLEMS: A COMMUNICATION PROCESS OZER, MARK N.; RICHARDSON, H. BURTT, JR., *CHILDHOOD EDUCATION*, V48 N5, PP244-7, FEB 72
THIS ACCOUNT OF "INTERACTIVE EXAMINATIONS" AFFORDS MORE INSIGHT ABOUT WAYS OF IMPROVING COLLABORATION AMONG DOCTORS, PARENTS AND TEACHERS TO HELP CHILDREN SUCCEED IN LEARNING. (EDITOR)

EJ 050 379 PS 501 554
NIGHT CARE CENTER WARREN, VIRGINIA LEE, *CHILDREN TODAY*, V1 N1, PP29, 40, JAN-FEB 72
A DESCRIPTION OF SAMUEL'S TEMPLE DAY CARE CENTER, ONE OF NEW YORK CITY'S TWO LICENSED 24-HOUR FACILITIES. (RY)

EJ 050 380 PS 501 555
INDUSTRY AND DAY CARE SIMMS, MIMI, *CHILDREN TODAY*, V1 N1, PP30-1, JAN-FEB 72
WHEN COMPANIES OPERATE CHILD CARE CENTERS FOR THEIR EMPLOYEES, THEY ATTRACT STEADY AND DEPENDABLE WORKERS, REDUCE ABSENTEEISM AND LABOR TURNOVER, AND EVEN INCREASE PRODUCTION. (AUTHOR)

EJ 050 423 PS 501 564
CHILDREN: OUR CHALLENGE MONDALE, WALTER F., *YOUNG CHILDREN*, V27 N2, PP75-81, DEC 71
ADDRESS PRESENTED BY THE SENATOR FROM MINNESOTA AT THE ANNUAL CONFERENCE OF THE NATIONAL ASSOCIATION FOR THE EDUCATION OF YOUNG CHILDREN, MINNEAPOLIS, MINN., NOV. 6, 1971. (RY)

EJ 050 487 PS 501 542
AN ADVENTURE PLAYGROUND FOR HANDICAPPED CHILDREN IN LONDON LADY ALLEN OF HURTWOOD, *INTERNATIONAL JOURNAL OF EARLY CHILDHOOD*, V3 N2, PP70-7, 71
A 20-MINUTE FILM SHOWING THE REACTION OF THE CHILDREN TO THIS SPECIALLY DESIGNED PLAYGROUND IS AVAILABLE ON LOAN FROM ANY BRITISH EMBASSY, CONSULATE, OR BRITISH INFORMATION SERVICES, 845 THIRD AVENUE, N.Y. 10022. (EDITOR/RY)

EJ 050 496 PS 501 545
CHILDREN AND ROAD ACCIDENTS VAN DER DOES, V. I., *INTERNATIONAL JOURNAL OF EARLY CHILDHOOD*, V3 N2, PP90-3, 71
ALL RESEARCH WORK ON THE SUBJECT OF ACCIDENT PREVENTION POINTS TO THE FACT THAT FEW ACCIDENTS ARE OUTSIDE THE POWER OF MAN TO PREVENT. (AUTHOR)

EJ 050 497 PS 501 572
EARLY INTERVENTION AND SOCIAL CLASS: DIAGNOSIS AND TREATMENT OF PRESCHOOL CHILDREN IN A DAY CARE CENTER SILVERMAN, MARTIN A.; WOLFSON, EVA, *JOURNAL OF THE AMERICAN ACADEMY OF CHILD PSYCHIATRY*, V10 N4, PP603-18, OCT 71
A DESCRIPTION OF A TEAM CONSISTING OF PSYCHIATRIST, PSYCHIATRIC SOCIAL WORKER AND EDUCATIONAL CONSULTANT, AND THEIR FIVE YEARS OF WORK IN A DAY CARE CENTER SITUATED IN THE HEART OF A CRIME-RIDDEN, DRUG-RIDDEN SECTION OF MANHATTAN'S WEST SIDE. (AUTHORS/RY)

EJ 050 591 PS 501 531
INSTRUCTIONAL PROGRAMMING FOR THE INDIVIDUAL PUPIL IN THE MULTIUNIT ELEMENTARY SCHOOL KLAUSMEIER, HERBERT J.; AND OTHERS, *ELEMENTARY SCHOOL JOURNAL*, V72 N2, PP88-101, NOV 71
DESCRIBES THE DEVELOPMENT AND ORGANIZATION OF ELEMENTARY, INDIVIDUALIZED, PROGRAMMED INSTRUCTION IN THE PAST DECADE. (AN)

EJ 050 794 PS 501 515
MOTHER'S MODE OF DISCIPLINE AND CHILD'S VERBAL ABILITY KOENIG, FREDRICK; AND OTHERS, *CHILD STUDY JOURNAL*, V2 N1, PP19-22, 71
CHILDREN WHO LEARN TO SPEAK AT AN EARLY AGE HAVE MOTHERS WHOSE BASIC MODE OF DISCIPLINING IS VERBAL. CHARTS; BIBLIOGRAPHY. (AF)

EJ 050 795 PS 501 516
CONDITIONING INDEPENDENT WORK BEHAVIOR IN READING WITH SEVEN YEAR OLD CHILDREN IN A REGULAR EARLY CHILDHOOD CLASSROOM YAWKEY, THOMAS D., *CHILD STUDY JOURNAL*, V2 N1, PP23-34, 71
THE MAJOR CONCERN OF THE STUDY WAS TO DETERMINE WHAT DIFFERENCES, IF ANY, IN INDEPENDENT READING-WORK BEHAVIORS WERE OBSERVED BETWEEN BASELINE AND EXPERIMENTAL CONDITIONS USING THE RULES, IGNORE, PRAISE TECHNIQUE WITH TWO SEVEN YEAR OLD CHILDREN. DURING THE REINFORCEMENT PERIOD CHILDREN WORKED HARDER. BIBLIOGRAPHY. (AUTHOR/AF)

EJ 050 935 PS 501 549
TRAINING WORKERS FOR CHILD CARE CENTERS WILLIAMS, F. NEIL; SCHERMOLY, GERALDINE, *CHILDREN TODAY*, V1 N1, PP18-9, JAN-FEB 72
PENN VALLEY COMMUNITY COLLEGE, KANSAS CITY, MO. RECEIVED AN EDUCATION PROFESSIONS DEVELOPMENT ACT GRANT THAT ENABLED IT TO ESTABLISH A DEVELOPMENTAL TRAINING PROJECT FOR DAY CARE AND NURSERY SCHOOL WORKERS. (AUTHORS)

EJ 050 936 PS 501 557
RELATING AND RESPONDING: THE ADULT DEUTSCH, KARL W., *CHILDHOOD EDUCATION*, V48 N5, PP227-35, FEB 72
THIS ANALYSIS WAS ADAPTED BY THE AUTHOR FROM HIS KEYNOTE ADDRESS AT THE ANNUAL STUDY CONFERENCE OF THE ASSOCIATION FOR CHILDHOOD EDUCATION INTERNATIONAL AT MILWAUKEE, WISCONSIN, APRIL 12, 1971. (EDITOR/RY)

EJ 050 937 PS 501 563
A NEW CHILD CARE PROFESSION: THE CHILD DEVELOPMENT ASSOCIATE ZIGLER, EDWARD, *YOUNG CHILDREN*, V27 N2, PP71-4, DEC 71
THIS ANNOUNCEMENT OF A NEW PROFESSION -- CHILD DEVELOPMENT ASSOCIATE -- WAS MADE AT THE ANNUAL CONFERENCE OF THE NATIONAL ASSOCIATION FOR THE EDUCATION OF YOUNG CHILDREN, MINNEAPOLIS, MINN., NOVEMBER 6, 1971, BY THE CHIEF OF THE OFFICE OF CHILD DEVELOPMENT AND THE CHILDREN'S BUREAU. (RY)

EJ 050 938 PS 501 574
A PROGRAM FOR HOSPITALIZED PSYCHOTIC CHILDREN: REGULAR ATTENDANCE, AWAY FROM THE HOSPITAL, AT A COMMUNITY NURSERY SCHOOL TANGUAY, PETER E.; AND OTHERS, *JOURNAL OF THE AMERICAN ACADEMY OF CHILD PSYCHIATRY*, V10 N4, PP661-72, OCT 71
EMPHASIS IS GIVEN TO PROBLEMS WHICH AROSE BETWEEN THE NURSERY SCHOOL TEACHERS AND THE HOSPITAL PERSONNEL TAKING PART IN THE PROGRAM. (AUTHORS/RY)

EJ 050 982 PS 501 526
DIRECTION SPORTS: A TUTORIAL PROGRAM FOR ELEMENTARY-SCHOOL PUPILS KLEIN, STEPHEN P.; NIEDERMEYER, FRED C., *ELEMENTARY SCHOOL JOURNAL*, V72 N2, PP53-61, NOV 71
DESCRIBES AN AFTER-SCHOOL PROGRAM OF SPORTS DIRECTED EDUCATION IN MATHEMATICS AND SPELLING FOR MINORITY GROUP STUDENTS, USING MINORITY GROUP COLLEGE STUDENTS AS COACHES. (AN)

EJ 051 013 PS 501 514
STUDYING AGGRESSIVE CHILDREN THROUGH RESPONSE TO FRUSTRATING SITUATIONS FELDHUSEN, JOHN F.; AND OTHERS, *CHILD STUDY JOURNAL*, V2 N1, PP1-17, 71
VERBAL SITUATION EXERCISES COMPOSED BY ROSENZWEIG SHOWED DEGREES OF ADJUSTMENT OR MALADJUSTMENT TO FRUSTRATING SITUATIONS. MIXTURE OF SOCIALLY-ACCEPTED AND NON-ACCEPTED CLASS DISRUPTORS FROM GRADES 3,6,9 PARTICIPATED. MORE MALADJUSTED BEHAVIOR CHOICES WERE ELICITED FROM RURAL CHILDREN IN COMPARISON TO THEIR URBAN COUNTERPARTS. VERY LITTLE VARIATION OCCURED AMONG JUST RURAL CHILDREN. CHARTS; BIBLIOGRAPHY. (AF)

EJ 051 014 PS 501 517
SEX-ROLE AND NEED FOR APPROVAL IN ADOLESCENTS MIKESELL, RICHARD H.; CALHOUN, LAWRENCE G., *CHILD STUDY JOURNAL*, V2 N1, PP35-37, 71
THE NEED FOR APPROVAL AND SEX ROLE IS AT BEST DIFFICULT TO DEMONSTRATE IN AN ADOLESCENT POPULATION; THE RELATIONSHIP MAY BE LIMITED TO ELEMENTARY AGED CHILDREN, IF IT OCCURS AT ALL. BIBLIOGRAPHY. (AUTHOR)

EJ 051 015 PS 501 518
SELF-ESTEEM, PARENT IDENTIFICATION AND SEX ROLE DEVELOPMENT IN PRESCHOOL AGE BOYS AND GIRLS FLAMMER, DONALD P., *CHILD STUDY JOURNAL*, V2 N1, PP39-47, 71
SELF ESTEEM WAS SHOWN TO BE ASSOCIATED MORE CLOSELY TO HIGH SEX ROLE ORIENTATION FOR BOYS AND LOW SEX ROLE ADOPTION FOR GIRLS; WHILE FATHER IDENTIFICATION, FOR BOYS ONLY, WAS RELATED TO MODERATE LEVELS OF SEX ROLE ORIENTATION AND SEX ROLE PREFERENCE. BIBLIOGRAPHY. (AUTHOR)

EJ 051 016 PS 501 519
PHYSIOLOGICAL INDICATIONS OF ORGANIC INVOLVEMENT BURROWS, ROY E., *CHILD STUDY JOURNAL*, V2 N1, PP47-52, 71
THE PRESENCE OF THREE OR MORE MINOR AND/OR MAJOR ANOMALIES IN AN INDIVIDUAL WITH MENTAL RETARDATION MAY INDICATE NOT JUST A DEVELOPMENTAL RELATIONSHIP BETWEEN THE RETARDATION AND MALFORMATION SYNDROMES, BUT A COMMON CAUSE FOR THE ENTIRE RETARDATION MALFORMATION SYNDROME. TABLES, BIBLIOGRAPHY. (AUTHOR)

EJ 051 017 PS 501 538
MOTHER-INFANT INTERACTION AND INFANT DEVELOPMENT AMONG THE WOLOF OF SENEGAL LUSK, DIANE; LEWIS, M., *HUMAN DEVELOPMENT*, V15 N1, PP58-69, 72
CARETAKER-INFANT INTERACTION WITHIN THE FIRST YEAR OF LIFE WAS STUDIED IN A GROUP OF 10 WOLOF INFANTS. THE PATTERN OF CARETAKER-INFANT INTERACTION WAS MORE STRONGLY RELATED TO AGE OF INFANT THAN ANY OTHER VARIABLE INVESTIGATED. THE OFTEN-FOUND RESULT THAT AFRICAN INFANTS SHOW PRECOCIOUS DEVELOPMENT WITHIN THE FIRST YEAR WAS CONFIRMED FOR THE WOLOF. (AUTHOR)

EJ 051 018 PS 501 567
ANXIETY IN THE EVALUATIVE CONTEXT HILL, KENNEDY T., *YOUNG CHILDREN*, V27 N2, PP97-116, DEC 71
THIS ARTICLE DETAILS SOME OF THE DEVELOPMENTAL PATTERNS THAT CHARACTERIZE THE CHILD'S EXPERIENCES WITH ANXIETY ABOUT BEING EVALUATED. (AUTHOR)

EJ 051 019 PS 501 568
PARENT-CHILD SEPARATION: PSYCHOLOGICAL EFFECTS ON THE CHILDREN RUTTER, MICHAEL, *JOURNAL OF CHILD PSYCHOLOGY AND PSYCHIATRY*, V12 N4, PP233-60, DEC 71
IT IS CONCLUDED THAT A CHILD'S SEPARATION FROM HIS FAMILY CONSTITUTES A POTENTIAL CAUSE OF SHORT-TERM DISTRESS BUT SEPARATION IS OF LITTLE DIRECT IMPORTANCE AS A CAUSE OF LONG-TERM DISORDER. (AUTHOR)

EJ 051 020 PS 501 573
DEVELOPMENTAL FACTORS IN ADOLESCENT DRUG USE: A STUDY OF PSYCHEDELIC DRUG USERS PITTEL, STEPHEN M.; AND OTHERS, *JOURNAL OF THE AMERICAN ACADEMY OF CHILD PSYCHIATRY*, V10 N4, PP640-60, OCT 71
THIS PAPER IS CONCRNED WITH THE BACKGROUNDS AND DEVELOPMENTAL HISTORIES OF A GROUP OF APPROXIMATELY 250 VOLUNTEER SUBJECTS WHO IDENTIFY THEMSELVES WITH THE HIPPIE COMMUNITY OF SAN FRANCISCO. (AUTHORS)

EJ 051 062 PS 501 534
BLACK CLIENTS AND WHITE WORKERS; A REPORT FROM THE FIELD BARRETT, FRANKLIN T.; PERLMUTTER, FELICE, *CHILD WELFARE*, V51 N1, PP19-24, JAN 72
"A NEW STUDY ON BLACK CLIENTS' PREFERENCE FOR BLACK SERVICE-GIVERS SUPPORTS THE FINDINGS IN EARLIER RESEARCH THAT THE COMPETENCE, NOT THE RACE, OF THE SERVERS IS VIEWED AS THE CRUCIAL VARIABLE." (EDITOR)

EJ 051 082 PS 501 528
MY MON CAN TEACH READING TOO! CRAMER, WARD, *ELEMENTARY SCHOOL JOURNAL*, V72 N2, PP72-5, NOV 71
DESCRIBES A TUTORIAL METHOD OF INDIVIDUALIZED, PROGRAMMED READING INSTRUCTION THAT DOESN'T REQUIRE AND SOPHISTICATED MATERIALS FOR ITS IMPLEMENTATION. (AN)

EJ 051 150 PS 501 566
RESEARCH FOR UNDERSTANDING VAN WYCK, BETTY, *YOUNG CHILDREN*, V27 N2, PP93-6, DEC 71
"WILL CHILDREN EAT THEIR MEAL JUST AS WELL IF THEY EAT DESSERT FIRST?" A DAY CARE CENTER STAFF PLANNED AND CARRIED OUT A RESEARCH PROJECT TO ANSWER THIS QUESTION. THE PROJECT YIELDED THE UNPLANNED RESULT OF INCREASED STAFF COOPERATION AND UNDERSTANDING OF CHILDREN'S BEHAVIOR. (EDITOR)

EJ 051 151 PS 501 569
SEX DIFFERENCES IN BEHAVIOURAL IMPULSIVITY, INTELLECTUAL IMPULSIVITY, AND ATTAINMENT IN YOUNG CHILDREN GARNER, JOHN; AND OTHERS, *JOURNAL OF CHILD PSYCHOLOGY AND PSYCHIATRY*, V12 N4, PP261-71, DEC 71
INTER-RELATIONSHIPS BETWEEN SUBTESTS OF THE WISC, INTELLECTUAL AND BEHAVIORAL IMPULSIVITY, WERE EXAMINED SEPARATELY FOR BOYS AND GIRLS IN AN ATTEMPT TO CONFIRM THAT IMPULSIVITY IS DIFFERENTLY RELATED TO ATTAINMENT FOR THE TWO SEXES. (AUTHORS)

EJ 051 152 PS 501 570
PSYCHIATRIC DISORDER IN THE CHILDREN OF CARIBBEAN IMMIGRANTS NICOL, A. R., *JOURNAL OF CHILD PSYCHOLOGY AND PSYCHIATRY*, V12 N4, PP273-87, DEC 71
THE NOTES OF 204 CHILDREN OF CARIBBEAN IMMIGRANTS ATTENDING A CHILD GUIDANCE UNIT WERE EXAMINED. CHILDREN BORN IN THE WEST INDIES WERE COMPARED WITH THOSE BORN IN BRITAIN. (AUTHOR)

EJ 051 153 PS 501 571
THE RELIABILITY OF RATING SCALES FOR ASSESSING THE BEHAVIOUR OF DISTURBED CHILDREN IN A RESIDENTIAL UNIT CUNNINGHAM, MORRIS A., *JOURNAL OF CHILD PSYCHOLOGY AND PSYCHIATRY*, V12 N4, PP289-304, DEC 71
NINETEEN CHILDREN WERE RATED ON 24 BEHAVIOR TRAITS BY TEN NURSES IN A CHILDREN'S IN-PATIENT UNIT. (AUTHOR)

EJ 051 205 PS 501 533
CHILDREN AS VICTIMS OF INSTITUTIONALIZATION RUBIN, SOL, *CHILD WELFARE*, V51 N1, PP6-18, JAN 72
"AMERICAN SOCIAL AND LEGAL PROCEDURES IN DEALING WITH CHILDREN OFTEN RESULT NOT IN NURTURE AND PROTECTION, BUT IN CURTAILING OF CHILDREN'S RIGHTS AND ARBITRARY COMMITMENT TO INSTITUTIONS." (EDITOR)

EJ 051 206 PS 501 558
LEARNING FROM GEOGRAPHERS SCARFE, NEVILLE V., *CHILDHOOD EDUCATION*, V48 N5, PP236-9, FEB 72
"...NOTHING COULD BE MORE EXCITING THAN LEARNING ABOUT THE SPLENDOR OF OUR EARTH WITH ITS GREAT DIVERSITY OF ATTRACTIVE AND INGENIOUS HUMAN BEINGS." (AUTHOR)

EJ 051 234 PS 501 535
A PERSPECTIVE ON RESIDENTIAL CHILD CARE PROGRAMS , *CHILD WELFARE*, V51 N1, PP30-7, JAN 72
THE CONCLUSIONS OF A SURVEY OF LUTHERAN RESIDENTIAL CHILD CARE PROGRAMS PUBLISHED IN DECEMBER 1970 BY THE LUTHERAN COUNCIL IN THE U.S.A. (EDITOR)

EJ 051 235 PS 501 546
EDUCATIONAL COMPONENT OF DAY CARE KLEIN, JENNY W., *CHILDREN TODAY*, V1 N1, PP2-5, JAN-FEB 72
THE QUESTION OF WHETHER OR NOT WE SHOULD HAVE A NATIONAL DAY CARE PROGRAM HAS LARGELY BEEN SUPPLANTED BY A MORE SEARCHING QUESTION: WHAT KIND OF DAY CARE PROGRAM SHOULD WE HAVE? (AUTHOR)

EJ 051 236 PS 501 547
WHAT DOES RESEARCH TEACH US ABOUT DAY CARE: FOR CHILDREN UNDER THREE CALDWELL, BETTYE M., *CHILDREN TODAY*, V1 N1, PP6-11, JAN-FEB 72
ACCUMULATING EVIDENCE SUGGESTED THAT DURING THE FIRST 3 YEARS A CHILD NEEDS A CERTAIN AMOUNT AND QUALITY OF EXPERIENCE FOR AN OPTIMAL RATE OF INTELLECTUAL DEVELOPMENT. (AUTHOR)

EJ 051 237 PS 501 548
WHAT DOES RESEARCH TEACH US ABOUT DAY CARE: FOR CHILDREN OVER THREE GROTBERG, EDITH H., *CHILDREN TODAY*, V1 N1, PP12-7, JAN-FEB 72
BY ACCEPTING BOTH THE IMPORTANCE OF THE GROUP ON ACHIEVEMENT BEHAVIOR IN GENERAL AND THE IMPORTANCE OF BETTER FACILITIES, TEACHERS, AND CURRICULA ON THE BEHAVIOR OF CHILDREN FROM MINORITIES AND LOWER SOCIAL AND ECONOMIC LEVELS, WE WILL HAVE A GOOD BASIS FOR HELPING ALL CHILDREN DEVELOP AND LEARN. (AUTHOR)

EJ 051 238 PS 501 550
ONE MORNING A WEEK ELWELL, RICHARD R., *CHILDREN TODAY*, V1 N1, PP20-2, JAN-FEB 72
A DESCRIPTION OF A COMMUNITY DAY CARE CENTER IN CHEVY CHASE, MD. (RY)

EJ 051 239 PS 501 552
CREATING CHILD CARE COMMUNITIES THROUGH 4-C PROGRAMS MEYER, DOLORES A., *CHILDREN TODAY*, V1 N1, PP25-7, JAN-FEB 72
MANY COMMUNITIES HAVE EXPRESSED THEIR CONCERN ABOUT INADEQUACIES IN CHILD CARE BY SETTING UP A COMMUNITY COORDINATED CHILD CARE (4-C) COUNCIL THAT BRINGS TOGETHER ALL THOSE INVOLVED WITH SERVICES TO CHILDREN AND FAMILIES. (AUTHOR/RY)

EJ 051 240 PS 501 556
A PARENT SPEAKS , *CHILDREN TODAY*, V1 N1, PP32-3, JAN-FEB 72
THE REACTION OF A PARENT WHOSE TWO DAUGHTERS ATTENDED ONE OF THE NURSERY SCHOOLS KNOWN AS NURSERIES IN CROSS-CULTURAL EDUCATION (NICE). THESE SCHOOLS ARE PART OF A PROJECT DESIGNED TO PROMOTE INTERFAMILY, INTERRACE RELATIONS. (RY)

EJ 051 241 PS 501 565
CHILD ADVOCACY -- REFLECTIONS GREEN, FREDERICK C., *YOUNG CHILDREN*, V27 N2, PP82-8, DEC 71
ADDRESS PRESENTED AT THE ANNUAL CONFERENCE OF THE NATIONAL ASSOCIATION FOR THE EDUCATION OF YOUNG CHILDREN, MINNEAPOLIS, MINN., NOV. 6, 1971, BY THE ASSOCIATE CHIEF OF THE CHILDREN'S BUREAU WHICH WAS RECENTLY ESTABLISHED WITHIN THE OFFICE OF CHILD DEVELOPMENT. (RY)

EJ 051 270 PS 501 529
MORALS, MORALS EVERYWHERE: VALUES IN CHILDREN'S FICTION EISENBERG, WILLIAM D., *ELEMENTARY SCHOOL JOURNAL*, V72 N2, PP76-80, NOV 71
THERE IS A NEED FOR LESS DIDACTICISM, MORE STORY, AND LESS PROGRAMMING IN CHILDREN'S LITERATURE. (AN)

EJ 051 271 PS 501 551
DAY CARE LICENSING GRANATO, SAM J.; LYNCH, E. DOLLIE, *CHILDREN TODAY*, V1 N1, PP23-4, JAN-FEB 72
THE HELP STATE AND LOCAL AGENCIES SET UP REALISTIC LICENSING CODES THAT ASSURE ADEQUATE PROTECTION OF CHILDREN IN DAY CARE, THE OFFICE OF CHILD DEVELOPMENT AND THE OFFICE OF ECONOMIC OPPORTUNITY INITIATED A THREE-PHASE DAY CARE LICENSING PROJECT IN SEPTEMBER, 1970. (AUTHORS)

EJ 051 352 PS 501 577
THE TEACHER STRUCTURE CHECKLIST: A POSSIBLE TOOL FOR COMMUNICATION WEBSTER, PATRICIA ROWE, *YOUNG CHILDREN*, V27 N3, PP149-53, FEB 72
THE CHECKLIST IS USEFUL IN PROVIDING A COMMUNICATION TOOL FOR INSERVICE TEACHER TRAINING AT ALL LEVELS AND FOR TEACHERS' EVALUATION AND ASSESSMENT OF THEIR PRACTICES. (AUTHOR/JB)

EJ 051 410 PS 501 579
WHAT CAN TEACHERS LEARN FROM DIRECTORS IN THE PERFORMING ARTS? SEABERG, DOROTHY I.; ZINSMASTER, WANNA M., *ELEMENTARY SCHOOL JOURNAL*, V72 N4, PP67-75, JAN 72
AUTHOR CONCLUDES THAT PERHAPS IT IS TIME IN TEACHER EDUCATION TO STRESS INTUITION AND THE AESTHETICS OF TEACHING. (AUTHOR/JB)

EJ 051 470 PS 501 601
DEVELOPMENTAL COMPARISONS OF CONFORMITY ACROSS TWO CULTURES SISTRUNK, FRANK; AND OTHERS, *CHILD DEVELOPMENT*, V42 N4, PP1175-85, OCT 71
THIS STUDY INVESTIGATED THE RELATIVE CONFORMITY OF AMERICAN AND BRAZILIAN STUDENTS ACROSS AGES FROM 9 TO 21 YEARS OLD. (AUTHORS)

EJ 051 471 PS 501 619
ON PLAY D'HEURLE, ADMA; FEIMER, JOEL N., *ELEMENTARY SCHOOL JOURNAL*, V72 N3, PP118-24, DEC 71
SERIOUS EFFORTS IN THE DIRECTION OF A THEORY OF EDUCATION MUST RE-EVALUATE THE BROADER SIGNIFICANCE OF PLAY AND REAPPRAISE ITS ROLE IN HUMAN EXPERIENCE. (AUTHORS)

EJ 051 472 PS 501 623
MODIFICATION OF BEHAVIOR PATTERNS OF INDIAN CHILDREN GALLOWAY, CHARLES G.; MICKELSON, NORMA I., *ELEMENTARY SCHOOL JOURNAL*, V72 N3, PP150-5, DEC 71
DESCRIBED IS AN EDUCATIONAL PROGRAM CONDUCTED DURING THE SUMMER OF 1968 FOR THREE GROUPS OF INDIAN CHILDREN. (RY)

EJ 051 473 PS 501 626
THE USE OF BEHAVIOR-MODIFICATION TECHNIQUES WITH FEMALE DELINQUENTS FODOR, IRIS E., *CHILD WELFARE*, V51 N2, PP93-103, FEB 72
ARTICLE DESCRIBES TECHNIQUES USED IN DEALING WITH DELINQUENT GIRLS IN A TRAINING SCHOOL. (EDITOR/RY)

EJ 051 563 PS 501 522
AN EXAMINATION OF THE DEVELOPMENTAL RELATIONS BETWEEN CERTAIN SPATIAL TASKS LARSEN, GARY Y.; ABRAVANEL, EUGENE, *MERRILL-PALMER QUARTERLY*, V18 N1, PP39-52, JAN 72
THE CONSERVATION OF DISTANCE AND OF LENGTH AND THE AWARENESS OF THE HORIZONTAL AND OF THE VERTICAL DO SEEM TO SIGNIFICANTLY PRECEDE THE MEASUREMENT OF LENGTH, BUT THE RESULTS DID NOT INDICATE THAT THESE FOUR TASKS HAVE ANY DEVELOPMENTAL ORDER AMONG THEMSELVES. BIBLIOGRAPHY, CHARTS. (AUTHOR)

EJ 051 564 PS 501 524
THE ROLE OF RETROSPECTIVE ACCOUNTS IN THE STUDY OF INTERGENERATIONAL ATTITUDES COHLER, BERTRAM J., *MERRILL-PALMER QUARTERLY*, V18 N1, PP59-60, JAN 72
AUTHOR DISCUSSES WHAT HE FEELS IS BURTON'S MISINTERPRETATION OF HIS STUDY, "RETROSPECTIVE ACCOUNTS IN THE STUDY OF INTERGENERATIONAL ACCOUNTS" (PS 501 525). (AF)

EJ 051 565 PS 501 525
THE INTERPRETATION OF INTERGENERATIONAL ATTITUDES BURTON, ROGER V., *MERRILL-PALMER QUARTERLY*, V18 N1, PP61-2, JAN 72
AUTHOR FEELS THAT A RECENT STUDY BY COHLER ET AL. DISCUSSING "INTERGENERATIONAL ATTITUDES" OF CHILD REARING IS MISLEADING BECAUSE THE ATTITUDES PRESENTED ARE NOT TRULY REPRENTATIVE OF GRANDMOTHERS AND MOTHERS BELIEFS BUT OF PRESENT DAY CHILD REARING PRACTICES. (AF)

EJ 051 566 PS 501 575
THE TEACHER'S ROLE IN HELPING YOUNG CHILDREN DEVELOP LANGUAGE COMPETENCE MATTICK, ELSE, *YOUNG CHILDREN*, V27 N3, PP133-42, FEB 72

EJ 051 567 PS 501 578
MOTHER-CHILD INTERACTIONS AND COGNITIVE DEVELOPMENT IN CHILDREN STREISSGUTH, ANN PYTKOWICS; BEE, HELEN L., *YOUNG CHILDREN*, V27 N3, PP154-73, FEB 72
THE RATE AND NATURE OF MOTHER-CHILD INTERACTION - VERBAL AND NONVERBAL- AND ITS EFFECTS ARE HERE DISCUSSED AND RECENT RESEARCH IS PRESENTED AND ANALYZED. (EDITOR/JB)

EJ 051 568 PS 501 593
RELATIONSHIPS BETWEEN ATTRIBUTES OF MOTHERS AND THEIR INFANTS' IQ SCORES BECKWITH, LEILA, *CHILD DEVELOPMENT*, V42 N4, PP1083-97, OCT 71
THE PRESENT STUDY EXPLORES THE SPECIFIC ENVIRONMENTAL INFLUENCES IN THE INTELLECTUAL DEVELOPMENT OF 24 ADOPTIVE INFANTS LIVING IN MIDDLE CLASS FAMILIES. (AUTHOR)

EJ 051 569 PS 501 602
MATCHING AUDITORY AND VISUAL SERIES: MODALITY PROBLEM OR TRANSLATION PROBLEM? GOODNOW, JACQUELINE J., *CHILD DEVELOPMENT*, V42 N4, PP1187-201, OCT 71
AN INVESTIGATION TO ACCOUNT FOR AGE CHANGES IN THE ACCURACY WITH WHICH CHILDREN MATCH AUDITORY TO VISUAL SERIES. (AUTHOR)

EJ 051 772 PS 501 624
CHILDREN'S PERCEPTIONS OF A TEACHING TEAM WHITTINGTON, KATHRYN D.; LAWLER, PATRICIA R., *ELEMENTARY SCHOOL JOURNAL*, V72 N3, PP156-60, DEC 71
PURPOSE OF THE STUDY WAS TO LEARN TO WHAT EXTENT CHILDREN MADE DISCRIMINATIONS ABOUT TEACHERS ON A TEAM. (AUTHORS)

EJ 051 779 PS 501 585
THE HISTORY OF LONGITUDINAL RESEARCH: IMPLICATIONS FOR THE FUTURE SONTAG, LESTER, *CHILD DEVELOPMENT*, V42 N4, PP987-1002, OCT 71
PAPER PRESENTED AT THE MEETING OF THE AMERICAN PSYCHOLOGICAL ASSOCIATION, MIAMI, FLORIDA, SEPTEMBER, 1970. (RY)

EJ 052 065 PS 501 576
PRACTICAL APPROACHES FOR RESOLVING THE PROBLEM OF NUTRITION AMONG LOW-INCOME FAMILIES SADOW, SUE, *YOUNG CHILDREN*, V27 N3, PP143-8, FEB 72
THE AUTHOR SKETCHES EARLY EFFORTS AT NUTRITION AND FOODS INSTRUCTION FOR IMMIGRANTS AND GOES ON TO DESCRIBE CURRENT PROGRAMS AND APPROACHES TO SOLVING THE POOR'S NUTRITION PROBLEMS. (JB)

EJ 052 066 PS 501 583
READING INSTRUCTION AND COGNITIVE DEVELOPMENT ARTLEY, A. STERL, *ELEMENTARY SCHOOL JOURNAL*, V72 N4, PP203-11, JAN 72
THE AUTHOR RECOMMENDS NONRESTRICTIVE QUESTIONING AS ONE TECHNIQUE OF PROVOKING THOUGHT. (AUTHOR/JB)

EJ 052 067 PS 501 620
INDIVIDUALIZATION - TEACHERS' VIEWS BOSCO, JAMES, *ELEMENTARY SCHOOL JOURNAL*, V72 N3, PP125-31, DEC 71

EJ 052 068 PS 501 622
MICRO-TEACHING FOR PREPARING TEACHERS OF CULTURALLY DIVERSE CHILDREN ANDERSEN, DAN W.; ANTES, JOHN M., *ELEMENTARY SCHOOL JOURNAL*, V72 N3, PP142-9, DEC 71
OBJECTIVES OF THIS STUDY WERE TO SURVEY AND APPRAISE THE REACTIONS OF THE GRADUATE INTERNS CONCERNING THE VALUE AND EFFECTIVENESS OF THEIR MICRO TEACHING EXPERIENCE, AND TO DETERMINE THE RELATIONSHIP BETWEEN EFFECTIVENESS IN PRESENTING A "MICRO" LESSON AND EFFECTIVENESS IN TEACHING IN A REGULAR CLASSROOM LATER. (AUTHORS/RY)

EJ 052 126 PS 501 584
THE MYTH BEHIND GRADED CONTENT ELLISON, ALFRED, *ELEMENTARY SCHOOL JOURNAL*, V72 N4, PP212-21, JAN 72
AUTHOR SAYS GRADED CLASSROOMS AND GRADED TEXTBOOKS BASED ON THEM ARE THE KEY STUMBLING BLOCKS TO PROGRESS IN OUR WHOLE EDUCATIONAL SYSTEM. (AUTHOR/JB)

EJ 052 175 PS 501 539
SENTENCE REPETITION: ELICITED IMITATION OF A CONTROLLED SET OF SYNTACTIC STRUCTURES BY FOUR LANGUAGE GROUPS CLAY, MARIE M., *MONOGRAPH OF THE SOCIETY FOR RESEARCH IN CHILD DEVELOPMENT*, V36 N3, PP1+, SEP 71

EJ 052 176 PS 501 580
CREATIVE DRAMA AND LANGUAGE GROWTH STEWIG, JOHN WARREN, *ELEMENTARY SCHOOL JOURNAL*, V72 N4, PP176-88, JAN 72
A REGULAR CONTINUING PROGRAM OF CREATIVE DRAMA CAN PROVIDE CHILDREN WITH MANY OPPORTUNITIES FOR GROWTH IN KNOWLEDGE OF LANGUAGE. (AUTHOR/JB)

EJ 052 177 PS 501 581
REGISTER: SOCIAL VARIATION IN LANGUAGE USE DESTEFANO, JOHANNA S., *ELEMENTARY SCHOOL JOURNAL*, V72 N4, PP189-94, JAN 72
TEACHERS CAN HELP STUDENTS INCREASE THEIR RANGE OF REGISTERS BY BEING AWARE OF AND ENCOURAGING THEIR STUDENTS' LINGUISTIC EFFORTS AND ENCOURAGING STUDENTS' CONTROL OVER "LITERATE" FORMS. (AUTHOR/JB)

EJ 052 178 PS 501 582
READING, WRITING, AND BLACK ENGLISH GOLUB, LESTER S., *ELEMENTARY SCHOOL JOURNAL*, V72 N4, PP195-202, JAN 72
THE AUTHOR DESCRIBES AN APPROACH TO TEACHING READING AND WRITING IN WHICH EMPHASIS IS ON THE CHILD'S PRODUCTION OF LANGUAGE. (AUTHOR/JB)

EJ 052 179 PS 501 600
NOUN PLURAL DEVELOPMENT IN PRIMARY GRADE CHILDREN GRAVES, MICHAEL F.; KOZIOL, STEPHEN, *CHILD DEVELOPMENT*, V42 N4, PP1165-73, OCT 71
THIS PAPER REPORTS AN INVESTIGATION INTO THE ABILITY OF A GROUP OF PRIMARY GRADE CHILDREN TO PRODUCE PLURAL FORMS OF SELECTED TYPES OF REAL AND NONSENSE WORDS. (AUTHORS)

EJ 052 180 PS 501 618
DICTIONARY SYLLABICATION - HOW USEFUL GROFF, PATRICK, *ELEMENTARY SCHOOL JOURNAL*, V72 N3, PP107-17, DEC 71
AUTHOR CONCLUDES THAT THE EVIDENCE FROM THE SCIENCE OF PHONETICS AND FROM THE EXPERIMENTATION WITH DICTIONARY SYLLABICATION SHOWS THAT DICTIONARY FORMS OF WORD DIVISION ARE INAPPROPRIATE FOR USE IN TEACHING READING AND SPELLING. (AUTHOR/RY)

EJ 052 237 PS 501 523
PREDICTION OF INTELLECTUAL PERFORMANCE AT 3 YEARS FROM INFANT TESTS AND PERSONALITY MEASURES BIRNS, BEVERLY; GOLDEN, MARK, *MERRILL-PALMER QUARTERLY*, V18 N1, PP53-8, JAN 72

EJ 052 310 PS 501 627
THE BOY WHO DID NOT CRY AMENT, AARON, *CHILD WELFARE*, V51 N2, PP104-9, FEB 72
REBUILDING THE CAPACITY TO FORM MEANINGFUL HUMAN RELATIONSHIPS IS OFTEN THE ESSENTIAL TASK IN THE TREATMENT OF DISTURBED FOSTER CHILDREN. (EDITOR)

EJ 052 391 PS 501 613
THE DEVELOPMENT OF THE LANGUAGE OF EMOTIONS: CONDITIONS OF EMOTIONAL AROUSAL WOLMAN, RICHARD N.; AND OTHERS, *CHILD DEVELOPMENT*, V42 N4, PP1288-93, OCT 71
THIS STUDY DEMONSTRATES THE GENERAL DEVELOPMENTAL PROGRESSION OF THE INCREASED INTERNALIZATION OF THE CONDITIONS OF EMOTIONAL AROUSAL. FEMALES SHOW A TENDENCY TO BE MORE DEPENDENT THAN MALES ON EXTERNAL AROUSAL CUES. (AUTHORS)

EJ 052 420 PS 501 621
FOSTERING A NEED TO READ BRAUN, CARL, *ELEMENTARY SCHOOL JOURNAL*, V72 N3, PP132-41, DEC 71
A NUMBER OF SUGGESTIONS ARE OFFERED THAT CAN BE INCORPORATED INTO THE CLASSROOM READING PROGRAM TO HELP THE YOUNG LEARNER DISCOVER WHAT READING IS -- ITS PURPOSE AS WELL AS THE PROCESS. (AUTHOR/RY)

EJ 052 440 PS 501 521
CONSIDERATIONS FOR THE STUDY OF LANGUAGE IN YOUNG LOW-INCOME MINORITY GROUP CHILDREN DICKIE, JOYCE; BAGUR, J. SUSANA, *MERRILL-PALMER QUARTERLY*, V18 N1, PP25-38, JAN 72

EJ 052 441 PS 501 586
EXPLORATORY AND PLAY BEHAVIORS OF INFANTS REARED IN AN INSTITUTION AND IN LOWER- AND MIDDLE-CLASS HOMES COLLARD, ROBERTA R., *CHILD DEVELOPMENT*, V42 N4, PP1003-15, OCT 71

EJ 052 442 PS 501 587
HELPING BEHAVIOR AMONG NORMAL AND RETARDED CHILDREN SEVERY, LAWRENCE J.; DAVIS, KEITH E., *CHILD DEVELOPMENT*, V42 N4, PP1017-31, OCT 71
DISTINCTIONS BETWEEN PSYCHOLOGICAL VERSUS TASK HELPING AND ATTEMPTED VERSUS ACHIEVED HELP WERE APPLIED TO THE HELPING BEHAVIORS OF NORMAL AND RETARDED CHILDREN OF 2 AGE GROUPS OBSERVED IN NATURAL SETTINGS. (AUTHORS)

EJ 052 443 PS 501 588
LEARNING TO BE GENEROUS OR STINGY: IMITATION OF SHARING BEHAVIOR AS A FUNCTION OF MODEL GENEROSITY AND VICARIOUS REINFORCEMENT PRESBIE, ROBERT J.; COITEUX, PAUL F., *CHILD DEVELOPMENT*, V42 N4, PP1033-8, OCT 71
CHILDREN WHO OBSERVED A VERY GENEROUS ADULT MODEL SHARING, LATER SHARED MORE THAN THOSE WHO OBSERVED A VERY STINGY MODEL. THE EFFECTS OF VICARIOUS REINFORCEMENT ON THE AMOUNT SHARED, DELIVERED BY EITHER THE EXPERIMENTER OR THE MODEL ALONE, WERE ALSO DEMONSTRATED. (AUTHORS)

EJ 052 444 PS 501 589
AGE, STATE, AND MATERNAL BEHAVIOR ASSOCIATED WITH INFANT VOCALIZATIONS JONES, SANDRA J.; MOSS, HOWARD A., *CHILD DEVELOPMENT*, V42 N4, PP1039-51, OCT 71
THE RELATION BETWEEN MATERNAL PRESENCE AND INFANT'S VOCALIZATION DEPENDED UPON THE INFANT'S STATE: WHEN THE INFANT WAS IN THE ACTIVE AWAKE STATE, HE VOCALIZED LESS IN THE PRESENCE OF THE MOTHER THAN WHEN ALONE, THUS INDICATING THAT THE MAJORITY OF EARLY VOCALIZATIONS ARE ASSOCIATED WITH A NON-SOCIAL SITUATION. (AUTHORS/RY)

EJ 052 445 PS 501 590
WHAT'S THROWN OUT WITH THE BATH WATER: A BABY? LEWIS, MICHAEL; JOHNSON, NORMA, *CHILD DEVELOPMENT*, V42 N4, PP1053-5, OCT 71
DATA FROM INFANTS UNABLE TO COMPLETE EXPERIMENTAL SESSIONS WERE COMPARED TO THOSE FOR WHOM THERE WERE COMPLETE DATA. RESULTS SUGGEST THAT THE ELIMINATION OF LARGE NUMBERS OF INFANTS MAY HAVE A POTENTIALLY BIASING EFFECT ON REPORTED DATA. (AUTHORS)

EJ 052 446 PS 501 591
INFANT OBEDIENCE AND MATERNAL BEHAVIOR: THE ORIGINS OF SOCALIZATION RECONSIDERED STAYTON, DONELDA J.; AND OTHERS, *CHILD DEVELOPMENT*, V42 N4, PP1057-69, OCT 71
BASED ON 25 WHITE MIDDLE-CLASS INFANTS FROM 9 TO 12 MONTHS OF AGE, THE EARLIEST MANIFESTATION OF OBEDIENCE TO APPEAR WAS A SIMPLE DISPOSITION TO COMPLY WITH MATERNAL COMMANDS AND PROHIBITIONS, INDEPENDENT OF EFFORTS TO TRAIN OR DISCIPLINE THE BABY. (AUTHORS/RY)

EJ 052 447 PS 501 592
IDENTIFICATION AND CONSCIENCE DEVELOPMENT HOFFMAN, MARTIN L., *CHILD DEVELOPMENT*, V42 N4, PP1071-82, OCT 71
IT WAS TENTATIVELY CONCLUDED THAT IDENTIFICATION MAY CONTRIBUTE TO THE RECOGNITION THAT MORAL PRINCIPLES AND NOT EXTERNAL SANCTIONS FORM THE BASIS OF RIGHT AND WRONG, BUT NOT TO THE APPLICATION OF THESE PRINCIPLES TO ONE'S OWN BEHAVIOR IN THE ABSENCE OF AUTHORITY. (AUTHOR)

EJ 052 448 PS 501 594
LOCUS OF CONTROL AND ACHIEVEMENT IN MIDDLE- AND LOWER-CLASS CHILDREN BARTEL, NETTIE R., *CHILD DEVELOPMENT*, V42 N4, PP1099-107, OCT 71
RESULTS OF THIS STUDY WERE INTERPRETED IN TERMS OF THE SOCIAL CONTROL FUNCTION SERVED BY THE PUBLIC SCHOOLS. (AUTHOR/RY)

EJ 052 449 PS 501 595
MOTHERS' TEST OF ANXIETY AND TASK SELECTION AND CHILDREN'S PERFORMANCE WITH MOTHER OR A STRANGER BLECHMAN, ELAINE A.; NAKAMURA, CHARLES Y., *CHILD DEVELOPMENT*, V42 N4, PP1109-18, OCT 71
WHEN HIGH ANXIOUS MOTHERS ADMINISTERED TASKS TO THEIR CHILDREN, THEY FACILITATED THE TASK PERFORMANCE OF THEIR DAUGHTERS BUT WERE STRONGLY DETRIMENTAL TO THAT OF THEIR SONS. LOW ANXIOUS MOTHERS CHOSE MORE DIFFICULT TASKS FOR SONS THAN FOR DAUGHTERS, AND THEY FACILITATED THE TASK PERFORMANCE OF SONS MORE THAN THAT OF DAUGHTERS. (AUTHORS/RY)

EJ 052 450 PS 501 596
SPEECH REGISTERS IN YOUNG CHILDREN WEEKS, THELMA E., *CHILD DEVELOPMENT*, V42 N4, PP1119-31, OCT 71
RESULTS SUGGEST THAT CHILDREN ACQUIRE SPEECH REGISTERS CONCURRENTLY WITH LANGUAGE AND THAT THE PROGRESSION OF ACQUISITION VARIES MORE FOR REGISTERS THAN FOR GRAMMATICAL FORMS. (AUTHOR)

EJ 052 451 PS 501 597
A FACTOR-ANALYTIC STUDY OF THE RELATIONSHIP OF MOTOR FACTORS TO ACADEMIC CRITERIA FOR FIRST- AND THIRD-GRADE BOYS CHISSOM, BRAD S., *CHILD DEVELOPMENT*, V42 N4, PP1133-43, OCT 71
A SIGNIFICANT RELATIONSHIP WAS FOUND BETWEEN MOTOR ABILITIES AND MEASURES OF ACADEMIC APTITUDE AND ACADEMIC ACHIEVEMENT FOR FIRST-GRADE BOYS. NO SIGNIFICANT RELATIONSHIP WAS OBTAINED BETWEEN MOTOR ABILITIES AND THE 2 CRITERION MEASURES OF ACADEMIC APTITUDE AND ACADEMIC ACHIEVEMENT FOR THE GROUP OF THIRD-GRADE BOYS. (AUTHOR)

EJ 052 452 PS 501 598
THE DEVELOPMENT OF SOME INTENTION CONCEPTS IN YOUNG CHILDREN KING, MICHAEL, *CHILD DEVELOPMENT*, V42 N4, PP1145-52, OCT 71
ABILITY TO DISTINGUISH INTENTION FROM ACCIDENT AND UNDERSTANDING OF UNCONSCIOUS INTENTION WERE EXAMINED IN PRESCHOOL, KINDERGARTEN, AND THIRD-GRADE-AGE CHILDREN. (AUTHOR)

EJ 052 453 PS 501 599
BIRTH ORDER, NUMBER OF SIBLINGS AND SOCIAL REINFORCER EFFECTIVENESS IN CHILDREN UNRUH, SUSAN GULICK; AND OTHERS, *CHILD DEVELOPMENT*, V42 N4, PP1153-63, OCT 71

EJ 052 454 PS 501 604
THE EFFECTS OF CHRONOLOGICAL AGE, TRIALS, AND LIST CHARACTERISTICS UPON CHILDREN'S CATEGORY CLUSTERING WACHS, THEODORE D.; GRUEN, GERALD E., *CHILD DEVELOPMENT*, V42 N4, PP1217-27, OCT 71
RESULTS INDICATED THAT AVAILABILITY OF CATEGORIES RATHER THAN FREQUENCY OF WORDS SEEMED MOST CRUCIAL IN DETERMINING DEVELOPMENTAL CHANGES IN CLUSTERING EFFICIENCY. (AUTHORS)

EJ 052 455 PS 501 605
THE EFFECTS OF MANIPULATION OF TEACHER COMMUNICATION STYLE IN THE PRESCHOOL SMOTHERGILL, NANCY L.; AND OTHERS, *CHILD DEVELOPMENT*, V42 N4, PP1229-39, OCT 71
THIS STUDY WAS DESIGNED TO ASSESS THE INFLUENCE OF AN ELABORATIVE VERSUS NONELABORATIVE TEACHING STYLE ON CHILDREN'S NURSERY SCHOOL BEHAVIOR. (AUTHORS)

EJ 052 456 PS 501 606
A REEXAMINATION OF THE DEVELOPMENT OF MORAL JUDGMENTS IN CHILDREN ARMSBY, RICHARD E., *CHILD DEVELOPMENT*, V42 N4, PP1241-8, OCT 71

EJ 052 457 PS 501 607
SOME PARAMETERS OF PUNISHMENT AFFECTING RESISTANCE TO DEVIATION AND GENERALIZATION OF A PROHIBITION CHEYNE, J. A., *CHILD DEVELOPMENT*, V42 N4, PP1249-61, OCT 71
AN EXPERIMENT WAS CONDUCTED COMPARING THE EFFECTIVENESS FOR PRODUCING RESPONSE INHIBITION OF HIGH- AND LOW-INTENSITY PHYSICAL PUNISHMENT AND ELABORATED VERBAL PUNISHMENT WHEN PUNISHMENT WAS DELIVERED EITHER EARLY OR LATE IN A RESPONSE SEQUENCE. (AUTHOR)

EJ 052 458 PS 501 608
POSITION STRATEGIES IN AN OBJECT DISCRIMINATION TASK CARMEAN, STEPHEN L.; CARMEAN, C. JEAN, *CHILD DEVELOPMENT*, V42 N4, PP1263-70, OCT 71
RESULTS OF 5 EXPERIMENTS SUPPORTED THE HYPOTHESIS THAT MANY NONLEARNERS IN A MULTIPAIR VISUAL DISCRIMINATION LEARNING TASK WERE FOLLOWING POSITION RATHER THAN OBJECT STRATEGIES AND THAT IT WAS POSSIBLE TO PREDICT INDIVIDUAL SUBJECTS' STRATEGIES FROM PREVIOUS PERFORMANCES. (AUTHORS)

EJ 052 459 PS 501 609
EFFECTS OF ADULT AND PEER OBSERVERS ON BOYS' AND GIRLS' RESPONSES TO AN AGGRESSIVE MODEL MARTIN, MARIAN F.; AND OTHERS, *CHILD DEVELOPMENT*, V42 N4, PP1271-5, OCT 71
RESULTS INDICATE THAT THERE IS NO SIMPLE RELATIONSHIP BETWEEN TYPE OF OBSERVER PRESENT AND CHILDREN'S AGGRESSIVE RESPONDING FOLLOWING EXPOSURE TO AN AGGRESSIVE MODEL. (AUTHORS)

EJ 052 460 PS 501 610
INFORMATION PROCESSING AND THE MODIFICATION OF AN "IMPULSIVE CONCEPTUAL TEMPO" HEIDER, ELEANOR ROSCH, *CHILD DEVELOPMENT*, V42 N4, PP1276-81, OCT 71
EIGHTY MIDDLE-CLASS AND 80 LOWER-CLASS BOYS WERE TESTED ON A VISUAL AND A VERBAL TASK UNDER 3 CONDITIONS DESIGNED TO MODIFY AN "IMPULSIVE TEMPO." (AUTHOR)

EJ 052 461 PS 501 611
CHILDREN'S JUDGMENTS OF AGE LOOFT, WILLIAM R., *CHILD DEVELOPMENT*, V42 N4, PP1282-4, OCT 71
CHILDREN MADE AGE JUDGMENTS ON DRAWING OF HUMAN FIGURES, WHICH CONSISTED OF ADULT, ADOLESCENT, CHILD, AND INFANT CHARACTERIZATIONS. (AUTHOR)

EJ 052 462 PS 501 612
SELF-INITIATED VERBAL REINFORCEMENT AND POSITIVE SELF-CONCEPT FELKER, DONALD W.; THOMAS, SUSAN BAHLKE, *CHILD DEVELOPMENT*, V42 N4, PP1285-7, OCT 71
FOUR HYPOTHESES WERE DERIVED FROM THE PROPOSITION THAT POSITIVE SELF-CONCEPT IS DUE PARTLY TO AN ABILITY TO UTILIZE SELF-INITIATED VERBAL REINFORCEMENT. (AUTHORS)

EJ 052 463 PS 501 614
THE EFFECT OF SOCIAL INTERACTION ON ACTIVITY LEVELS IN SIX-TO EIGHT-YEAR-OLD BOYS KASPAR, J. C.; LOWENSTEIN, R., *CHILD DEVELOPMENT*, V42 N4, PP1294-8, OCT 71
THIS STUDY INVESTIGATED THE EFFECT OF AN INTERACTION BETWEEN RELATIVELY ACTIVE AND RELATIVELY QUIET BOYS ON THEIR JOINT ACTIVITY LEVEL. (AUTHOR/RY)

EJ 052 464 PS 501 615
THE CONCEPT OF DEATH IN EARLY CHILDHOOD CHILDERS, PERRY; WIMMER, MARY, *CHILD DEVELOPMENT*, V42 N4, PP1293-301, OCT 71
EVIDENCE INDICATED THAT THE AWARENESS OF DEATH AS UNIVERSAL IS A FUNCTION OF AGE; THE UNDERSTANDING OF DEATH AS IRREVOCABLE WAS NOT DEMONSTRATED SYSTEMATICALLY THROUGH AGE 10. (AUTHORS)

EJ 052 465 PS 501 616
A COMPARATIVE STUDY OF ENGLISH PLURALIZATION BY NATIVE AND NON-NATIVE ENGLISH SPEAKERS NATALICIO, DIANA S.; NATALICIO, LUIZ F. S., *CHILD DEVELOPMENT*, V42 N4, PP1302-6, OCT 71
RESULTS INDICATE THAT THE PATTERN OF ACQUISITION OF NOUN PLURALS IN ENGLISH IS COMPARABLE FOR BOTH CHILDREN HAVING ENGLISH AS THEIR FIRST LANGUAGE AND THOSE ACQUIRING ENGLISH AS A SECOND LANGUAGE. (AUTHORS)

EJ 052 466 PS 501 617
FACTOR STRUCTURE OF CHILDREN'S PERSONAL SPACE SCHEMATA GUARDO, CAROL J.; MEISELS, MURRAY, *CHILD DEVELOPMENT*, V42 N4, PP1307-12, OCT 71
DATA FROM 431 CHILDREN IN GRADES 3-10 ON A PERSONAL SPACE TASK WERE POOLED INTO 4 SEX-AGE GROUPS AND SEPARATELY FACTOR ANALYZED. (AUTHORS)

EJ 052 493 PS 501 625
THE CHILD WELFARE AGENCY AS THE EXTENDED FAMILY TAYLOR, JOSEPH L., *CHILD WELFARE*, V51 N2, PP74-83, FEB 72
IN HELPING DISTURBED, DEPRIVED CHILDREN AND THEIR FAMILIES, AN AGENCY'S CONCEPT OF ITS TREATMENT TASK IS OF VITAL IMPORTANCE. AN EFFECTIVE APPROACH FOCUSES ON AN AGENCY'S FUNCTIONING AS AN EXTENDED FAMILY, AND ASSUMING A PARENTING ROLE. (EDITOR)

EJ 052 529 PS 501 520
ROLE ORIENTATIONS, MARITAL AGE, AND LIFE PATTERNS IN ADULTHOOD ELDER, GLEN H., JR., *MERRILL-PALMER QUARTERLY*, V18 N1, PP3-24, JAN 72
A STUDY OF THE DETERMINANTS OF WOMEN MARRYING EARLY AVERAGE AND LATE. CHARTS. BIBLIOGRAPHY. (AF)

EJ 052 581 PS 501 603
THE DEVELOPMENT OF ELEMENTARY SCHOOL CHILDREN'S JUDGMENT OF INTENT HEBBLE, PETER W., *CHILD DEVELOPMENT*, V42 N4, PP1203-15, OCT 71
A RATING-SCALE INSTRUMENT WAS DEVISED TO CLARIFY THE RELATIONSHIP BETWEEN CHILDREN'S JUDGMENTS OF NAUGHTINESS OF A STORY CHARACTER AND THE STORY'S DESCRIPTION OF THE CHARACTER'S INTENT AND THE CONSEQUENCES OF HIS BEHAVIOR. (AUTHOR)

EJ 052 594 PS 501 683
THE MODIFICATION OF INTELLIGENCE BY TRAINING IN THE VERBALIZATION OF WORD DEFINITIONS AND SIMPLE CONCEPTS LEVINSON, ELIZABETH J., *CHILD DEVELOPMENT*, V42 N5, PP1361-80, NOV 71

EJ 052 652 PS 501 686
THE FORMATION AND REVERSAL OF AN ATTITUDE AS FUNCTIONS OF ASSUMED SELF-CONCEPT, RACE, AND SOCIOECONOMIC CLASS BERNSTEIN, MARTIN E.; DI VESTA, FRANCIS J., *CHILD DEVELOPMENT*, V42 N5, PP1417-31, NOV 71

EJ 052 653 PS 501 712
VALUES OF MEXICAN-AMERICAN, NEGRO, AND ANGLO BLUE-COLLAR AND WHITE-COLLAR CHILDREN WASSERMAN, SUSAN A., *CHILD DEVELOPMENT*, V42 N5, PP1624-8, NOV 71
STUDY INVESTIGATED RELATIONSHIPS BETWEEN 4-YEAR OLDS' EXPRESSED HUMANITARIAN AND SUCCESS VALUE PREFERENCES AND THEIR ETHNICITY, SOCIOECONOMIC STATUS, AND SEX. (AUTHOR)

EJ 052 654 PS 501 722
"OPENNESS" OF SCHOOL CLIMATE AND ALIENATION OF HIGH SCHOOL STUDENTS HARTLEY, MARVIN C.; HOY, WAYNE K., *CALIFORNIA JOURNAL OF EDUCATIONAL RESEARCH*, V23 N1, PP17-24, JAN 72
STUDY SUGGESTS THAT ONE POSSIBLE WAY TO BEGIN TO INCREASE THE ATTRACTIVENESS OF SECONDARY SCHOOLS IS TO "OPEN" THE CLIMATE. (AUTHORS)

EJ 052 723 PS 501 656
SEX DIFFERENCES IN EFFECTS OF KINDERGARTEN ATTENDANCE ON DEVELOPMENT OF SCHOOL READINESS AND LANGUAGE SKILLS RUBIN, ROSALYN, *ELEMENTARY SCHOOL JOURNAL*, V72 N5, PP265-74, FEB 72
THE WIDELY RECOGNIZED DEVELOPMENTAL AGE DIFFERENCES BETWEEN BOYS AND GIRLS OF THE SAME CHRONOLOGICAL AGE IS ALMOST UNIVERSALLY IGNORED IN EDUCATIONAL PLANNING FOR CHILDREN IN THEIR EARLY SCHOOL YEARS. (AUTHOR)

EJ 052 766 PS 501 651
CURRICULUM BOON OR BANE? KLEIN, M. FRANCES; TYLER, LOUIS L., *ELEMENTARY SCHOOL JOURNAL*, V72 N5, PP225-9, FEB 72
THIS PAPER SUGGESTS SEVEN GENERAL CATEGORIES OF QUESTIONS THAT SHOULD BE CONSIDERED IN MAKING CURRICULUM CHOICES. (RY)

EJ 052 767 PS 501 652
SOCIAL ISSUES, SOCIAL ACTION, AND THE SOCIAL STUDIES OCHOA, ANNA; MANSON, GARY, *ELEMENTARY SCHOOL JOURNAL*, V72 N5, PP230-7, FEB 72
AUTHORS ADVOCATE INCORPORATING SOCIAL ACTION INTO THE SOCIAL STUDIES CURRICULUM. (RY)

EJ 052 878 PS 501 654
SELF-GUIDANCE AS AN EDUCATIONAL GOAL AND THE SELECTION OF OBJECTIVES OJEMANN, RALPH H., *ELEMENTARY SCHOOL JOURNAL*, V72 N5, PP247-57, FEB 72
THE ACCEPTANCE OF SELF-GUIDANCE AS AN EDUCATIONAL GOAL REQUIRES A CONSIDERABLE REORIENTATION OF THINKING WITH RESPECT TO THE PURPOSE OF EDUCATION, THE CONTENT OF THE SCHOOL CURRICULUM, AND THE ROLE OF THE TEACHER. (AUTHOR)

EJ 052 992 PS 501 717
SOME EFFECTS OF TESTING PROCEDURE ON DIVERGENT THINKING NICHOLLS, JOHN G., *CHILD DEVELOPMENT*, V42 N5, PP1647-51, NOV 71
GAME-LIKE AND TEST-LIKE METHODS OF DIVERGENT THINKING ASSESSMENT WERE COMPARED WITH 10-YEAR OLDS. EFFECTS OF METHOD ON SCORE CORRELATES WERE SUFFICIENT TO ALLOW THE POSSIBILITY THAT METHOD MAY BE IMPLICATED IN OUTCOMES OF MANY STUDIES OF DIVERGENT THINKING. (AUTHOR)

EJ 053 399 PS 501 655
CUE SYSTEMS AVAILABLE DURING THE READING PROCESS: A PSYCHOLINGUISTIC VIEWPOINT ALLEN, P. DAVID, *ELEMENTARY SCHOOL JOURNAL*, V72 N5, PP258-64, FEB 72
WE CAN IMPROVE READING INSTRUCTION BY USING THE STRENGTHS ANY CHILD BRINGS TO THE READING TASK. (AUTHOR)

EJ 053 479 PS 501 635
AUDITORY-LINGUISTIC SENSITIVITY IN EARLY INFANCY TREHUB, SANDRA E.; RABINOVITCH, M. SAM, *DEVELOPMENTAL PSYCHOLOGY*, V6 N1, PP74-7, JAN 72
THREE INVESTIGATIONS ARE REPORTED WHICH INDICATE THAT INFANTS BETWEEN 4 AND 17 WEEKS OF AGE ARE ABLE TO DETECT SOME DIFFERENCES IN SOUNDS UPON WHICH PHONEMIC CONTRASTS ARE BASED. (AUTHORS)

EJ 053 480 PS 501 661
STIMULUS INTERACTION AND PROBLEM DIFFICULTY IN CHILDREN'S DISCRIMINATION LEARNING BERCH, DANIEL B., *JOURNAL OF EXPERIMENTAL CHILD PSYCHOLOGY*, V13 N1, PP115-27, FEB 72

EJ 053 481 PS 501 662
PAIRED-ASSOCIATE LEARNING AND BIDIRECTIONAL ASSOCIATIVE RECALL IN FIRST, THIRD, FIFTH AND SEVENTH GRADERS COLE, LAWRENCE E.; KANAK, N. JACK, *JOURNAL OF EXPERIMENTAL CHILD PSYCHOLOGY*, V13 N1, PP128-37, FEB 72
RESULTS SHOW THAT PAIRED-ASSOCIATE LEARNING PROCEEDS AT A FASTER RATE BEYOND THE THIRD GRADE. (AUTHORS)

EJ 053 482 PS 501 688
COGNITIVE STYLE: METHODOLOGICAL AND DEVELOPMENTAL CONSIDERATIONS DAVIS, ALBERT J., *CHILD DEVELOPMENT*, V42 N5, PP1447-59, NOV 71
FINDINGS SUGGESTED A RELIABILITY PROBLEM AND RAISED A QUESTION OF VALIDITY WITH THE USE OF TOTAL RESPONSE FREQUENCIES BASED ON RELATIVELY UNLIMITED FREE RESPONSES TO THE SCST-FORM A. (AUTHOR)

EJ 053 483 PS 501 713
THE NAMING OF PRIMARY COLORS BY CHILDREN ANYAN, WALTER R., JR.; QUILLIAN, WARREN W., II, *CHILD DEVELOPMENT*, V42 N5, PP1629-32, NOV 71
IN THE FIFTH AND SIXTH YEARS OF LIFE, THE ABILITY OF GIRLS TO IDENTIFY PRIMARY COLORS BY NAME IS GREATER THAN THAT OF BOYS. CHILDREN IN THE SIXTH YEAR WHO ATTEND SCHOOL OUTPERFORM THOSE WHO HAVE NOT BEEN TO SCHOOL, AND GIRLS OF THIS AGE WHO HAVE NOT BEEN TO SCHOOL NAME COLORS AS WELL AS BOYS WHO ATTEND SCHOOL. (AUTHORS)

EJ 053 484 PS 501 718
CONCEPTUAL STYLE AND CONCEPTUAL ABILITY IN KINDERGARTEN THROUGH THE EIGHTH GRADE WHITE, KATHLEEN M., *CHILD DEVELOPMENT*, V42 N5, PP1652-6, NOV 71

EJ 053 485 PS 501 721
LEARNING TO LISTEN: A STUDY IN AUDITORY PERCEPTION MARASCUILO, LEONARD A.; PENFIELD, DOUGLAS A., *CALIFORNIA JOURNAL OF EDUCATIONAL RESEARCH*, V23 N1, PP4-16, JAN 72
A LISTENING PROGRAM USING PRE-RECORDED TAPES AND WORKBOOKS TO TEACH SECOND, FIFTH, EIGHTH, AND ELEVENTH GRADE STUDENTS HOW TO IMPROVE THEIR LISTENING TO ORAL COMMUNICATION. (AUTHORS/MB)

EJ 053 506 PS 501 653
A CHILD-CENTERED DICTIONARY DOWNING, JOHN, *ELEMENTARY SCHOOL JOURNAL*, V72 N5, PP239-46, FEB 72
MISCONCEPTION OF THE ROLE OF THE DICTIONARY RESULTS IN POOR ATTITUDES TOWARD REFERENCE BOOKS AND, CONSEQUENTLY, INADEQUATE SKILLS IN READING THEM. (AUTHOR/RY)

EJ 053 600 PS 501 648
SHARING PARENTS WITH STRANGERS: THE ROLE OF THE GROUP HOME FOSTER FAMILY'S OWN CHILDREN ELLIS, LILLIAN, *CHILD WELFARE*, V51 N3, PP165-70, MAR 72
SPECIAL PROBLEMS ARISE IN A GROUP FOSTER HOME FOR EMOTIONALLY DISTURBED CHILDREN WHEN THE FOSTER PARENTS HAVE CHILDREN OF THEIR OWN. MANY DIFFICULTIES MAY DEVELOP AS THEIR OWN CHILDREN TRY TO ADJUST TO SHARING THE HOME. (EDITOR)

EJ 053 601 PS 501 650
THE TEAM APPROACH IN HOME CARE OF MENTALLY RETARDED CHILDREN GREEN, MELVENA, *CHILD WELFARE*, V51 N3, PP178-81, MAR 72
AN EXPERIMENTAL HOME CARE PROGRAM UTILIZING A TEAM APPROACH HAS PROVED EFFECTIVE IN DEVELOPING MAXIMUM POTENTIAL FOR MENTALLY RETARDED CHILDREN IN FOSTER HOMES. (EDITOR)

EJ 053 647 PS 501 633
EXPERIMENTAL ANALYSES OF COOPERATION AND COMPETITION OF ANGLO-AMERICAN AND MEXICAN CHILDREN KAGAN, SPENCER; MADSEN, MILLARD C., *DEVELOPMENTAL PSYCHOLOGY*, V6 N1, PP49-59, JAN 72
THE RESULTS OF FOUR EXPERIMENTS COMPARING THE BEHAVIOR OF CHILDREN FROM TWO SETTINGS ARE REPORTED IN THIS ARTICLE. (AUTHORS)

EJ 053 648 PS 501 634
DEVELOPMENTAL COURSE OF RESPONSIVENESS TO SOCIAL REINFORCEMENT IN NORMAL CHILDREN AND INSTITUTIONALIZED RETARDED CHILDREN ZIGLER, EDWARD; BALLA, DAVID, *DEVELOPMENTAL PSYCHOLOGY*, V6 N1, PP66-73, JAN 72
IMPLICATIONS OF THE FINDINGS FOR THE PROGRAMMING OF INSTITUTIONS FOR THE RETARDED ARE DISCUSSED. (AUTHORS)

EJ 053 649 PS 501 637
PERCEPTUAL AND LOGICAL FACTORS IN THE DEVELOPMENT OF MULTIPLICATIVE CLASSIFICATION OVERTON, WILLIS F.; BRODZINSKY, DAVID, *DEVELOPMENTAL PSYCHOLOGY*, V6 N1, PP104-9, JAN 72
THE DEVELOPMENT OF MULTIPLICATIVE CLASSIFICATORY SKILLS IN CHILDREN BETWEEN 4 AND 9 YEARS OF AGE WAS INVESTIGATED BY MEANS OF TWO FORMS OF THE MATRIX-COMPLETION TASK. (AUTHORS)

EJ 053 650 PS 501 638
DEVELOPMENT OF THE CONCEPT OF SERIATION SIEGEL, LINDA S., *DEVELOPMENTAL PSYCHOLOGY*, V6 N1, PP135-7, JAN 72
THE ABILITY TO ORDER OBJECTS IN A SERIES ACCORDING TO SOME DIMENSION, SUCH AS SIZE, IS RECOGNIZED AS AN IMPORTANT ASPECT OF A CHILD'S ABILITY TO UNDERSTAND LOGICAL CONCEPTS. (AUTHOR)

EJ 053 651 PS 501 640
DEVELOPMENT OF CONSERVATION IN NORMAL AND RETARDED CHILDREN GRUEN, GERALD E.; VORE, DAVID A., *DEVELOPMENTAL PSYCHOLOGY*, V6 N1, PP146-57, JAN 72
IN THE PRESENT STUDY, THE AUTHORS COLLECTED DATA THAT WOULD HELP RESOLVE THE CONTROVERSEY BETWEEN DEVELOPMENTAL AND DEFECT THEORISTS OF MENTAL RETARDATION. (AUTHORS/RY)

EJ 053 652 PS 501 646
THE THREE WISHES OF LATENCY AGE CHILDREN ABLES, BILLIE, *DEVELOPMENTAL PSYCHOLOGY*, V6 N1, PP186, JAN 72
ASKING A CHILD WHAT HE WOULD WISH FOR IF HE HAD THREE WISHES FORMED THE BASIS OF THIS STUDY. (AUTHOR/RY)

EJ 053 653 PS 501 649
THE EFFECT OF EMOTION ON GROWTH STEWART, ANN H., *CHILD WELFARE*, V51 N3, PP171-7, MAR 72
PHYSIOLOGICAL CHANGES REFLECTING PSYCHOLOGICAL OR EMOTIONAL STRESS MAY BE EVIDENCED PARTICULARLY STRONGLY DURING THE FIRST 2 OR 3 YEARS OF A CHILD'S LIFE IF THE NORMAL "DIALOGUE" WITH THE MOTHER DOES NOT TAKE PLACE. (EDITOR)

EJ 053 654 PS 501 666
ACQUIRED DISTINCTIVENESS AND EQUIVALENCE OF CUES IN YOUNG CHILDREN REESE, HAYNE W., *JOURNAL OF EXPERIMENTAL CHILD PSYCHOLOGY*, V13 N1, PP171-82, FEB 72
STUDY WAS DESIGNED TO PROVIDE FURTHER EVIDENCE ON THE SPEED OF DEVELOPMENT OF THE ACQUIRED DISTINCTIVENESS AND EQUIVALENCE EFFECTS DURING THE TRANSFER TASK. (AUTHOR)

EJ 053 668 PS 501 724
FRIENDSHIPS AMONG STUDENTS IN DESEGREGATED SCHOOLS SACHDEVA, DARSHAN, *CALIFORNIA JOURNAL OF EDUCATIONAL RESEARCH*, V23 N1, PP45-51, JAN 72
FINDINGS SUGGEST THAT PERSONAL CONTACT HAS BEEN EFFECTIVE IN THE DEVELOPMENT OF INTERRACIAL FRIENDSHIPS IN DESEGREGATED SCHOOLS. (AUTHOR)

EJ 053 676 PS 501 723
TITLE I AND REMEDIAL READING COMPONENTS FOR DISADVANTAGED STUDENTS RIDER, GERALD S., *CALIFORNIA JOURNAL OF EDUCATIONAL RESEARCH*, V23 N1, PP24-44, JAN 72
FOCUS OF THE STUDY WAS TO IDENTIFY AND ANALYZE THE COMMON ELEMENTS OF THE INSTRUCTIONAL ORGANIZATIONAL SYSTEMS USED IN NINE OF THE MOST EFFECTIVE TITLE I READING COMPONENTS IN 1968-69 FOR DISADVANTAGED PUPILS IN GRADES 1-6. (AUTHOR)

EJ 053 708 PS 501 628
ACQUISITION OF CONSERVATION THROUGH SOCIAL INTERACTION MURRAY, FRANK B., *DEVELOPMENTAL PSYCHOLOGY*, V6 N1, PP1-6, JAN 72
THE EXPECTATION THAT AN EFFECTIVE CONSERVATION TRAINING PROCEDURE WOULD BE ONE IN WHICH THE CHILD WAS CONFRONTED WITH OPPOSING POINTS OF VIEW WAS INVESTIGATED IN AN EXPERIMENT AND A REPLICATION EXPERIMENT IN WHICH THE CHILD'S POINT OF VIEW WAS BROUGHT INTO CONFLICT WITH THOSE OF OTHER CHILDREN. (AUTHOR/RY)

EJ 053 709 PS 501 630
THE UNSUPERVISED CHILD OF THE WORKING MOTHER WOODS, MERILYN B., *DEVELOPMENTAL PSYCHOLOGY*, V6 N1, PP14-25, JAN 72
THE PRIMARY FOCUS OF THIS RESEARCH IS UPON A SECONDARY OR DERIVED ASPECT OF MATERNAL EMPLOYMENT, NAMELY, THE SUPERVISION OF CHILDREN WHOSE MOTHERS WORK. (AUTHOR)

EJ 053 710 PS 501 631
EFFECT OF OVERT VERBAL LABELING ON SHORT-TERM MEMORY IN CULTURALLY DEPRIVED AND NONDEPRIVED CHILDREN MCCARVER, RONALD B.; ELLIS, NORMAN R., *DEVELOPMENTAL PSYCHOLOGY*, V6 N1, PP38-41, JAN 72
THE INVESTIGATORS ASSESSED THE EFFECTS OF TWO VARIABLES, OVERT LABELING AND CULTURAL DIFFERENCES, ON THE SHORT-TERM MEMORY PERFORMANCE OF YOUNG CHILDREN. (AUTHORS)

EJ 053 711 PS 501 632
EFFECT OF A CHILD'S SEX ON ADULT INTERPRETATIONS OF ITS BEHAVIOR MEYER, JOHN W.; SOBIESZEK, BARBARA I., *DEVELOPMENTAL PSYCHOLOGY*, V6 N1, PP42-8, JAN 72
VIDEOTAPES OF TWO 17-MONTH OLD CHILDREN -- EACH CHILD SOMETIMES DESCRIBED AS A BOY AND SOMETIMES AS A GIRL -- WERE SHOWN TO 85 ADULT MIDDLE-CLASS SUBJECTS, WHO RATED ATTRIBUTES OF THE CHILDREN ON QUESTIONNAIRES CONTAINING SEX ROLE ITEMS. (AUTHORS/RY)

EJ 053 712 PS 501 636
EFFECTS OF RATE OF STIMULUS PRESENTATION AND PENALTY CONDITIONS ON THE DISCRIMINATION LEARNING OF NORMAL AND RETARDED CHILDREN HARTER, SUSAN; ZIGLER, EDWARD, *DEVELOPMENTAL PSYCHOLOGY*, V6 N1, PP88-91, JAN 72
THE EFFECTS OF RATE OF STIMULUS PRESENTATION AND REINFORCEMENT CONDITIONS ON THE TWO-CHOICE DISCRIMINATION LEARNING PERFORMANCE OF MA MATCHED NORMAL AND FAMILIAL RETARDED CHILDREN WERE EXAMINED. (AUTHORS)

EJ 053 713 PS 501 639
TOYS DELAY THE INFANT'S FOLLOWING OF HIS MOTHER CORTER, CARL M.; AND OTHERS, *DEVELOPMENTAL PSYCHOLOGY*, V6 N1, PP138-45, JAN 72
THE PRESENT STUDY INVESTIGATED SOME PROPERTIES OF THE ENVIRONMENT THAT CONTROL AN INFANT'S RESPONSE TO HIS MOTHER'S DEPARTURE AND, IN PARTICULAR, THE READINESS WITH WHICH HE FOLLOWS HER. (AUTHORS)

EJ 053 714 PS 501 641
RACE, SOCIAL CLASS, AND AGE OF ACHIEVEMENT OF CONSERVATION ON PIAGET'S TASKS GAUDIA, GIL, *DEVELOPMENTAL PSYCHOLOGY*, V6 N1, PP158-65, JAN 72
THE PRIMARY PURPOSE OF THIS STUDY WAS TO INVESTIGATE CONSERVATION ACQUISITION ACROSS SUBCULTURAL GROUPS. (AUTHOR)

EJ 053 715 PS 501 642
RESPONSE TO SOCIAL REINFORCEMENT RATES AS A FUNCTION OF REINFORCEMENT HISTORY HAMILTON, MARSHALL L., *DEVELOPMENTAL PSYCHOLOGY*, V6 N1, PP180, JAN 72
A CHILD'S HISTORY OF REINFORCEMENT IS REGARDED AS SETTING A STANDARD THAT DETERMINES WHAT CURRENT RATES OF REINFORCEMENT WILL BE DEPRIVATIONAL OR SATIATIONAL FOR HIM. (AUTHOR)

EJ 053 716 PS 501 643
THE DEVELOPMENT OF MEMORY-ENCODING PROCESSES IN YOUNG CHILDREN HALL, JAMES W.; HALPERIN, MARCIA S., *DEVELOPMENTAL PSYCHOLOGY*, V6 N1, PP181, JAN 72
THE PRESENT STUDY TESTED THE FEASIBILITY OF USING A PURELY VERBAL RECOGNITION-MEMORY PROCEDURE WITH YOUNG CHILDREN AND EXAMINED THE ROLE OF VERBAL ASSOCIATIONS IN THE MEMORY ENCODING OF SUCH CHILDREN. (AUTHOR)

EJ 053 717 PS 501 644
DISCRIMINATION LEARNING BY REFLECTIVE AND IMPULSIVE CHILDREN AS A FUNCTION OF REINFORCEMENT SCHEDULE MASSARI, DAVID J.; SCHACK, MARY LOU, *DEVELOPMENTAL PSYCHOLOGY*, V6 N1, PP183, JAN 72
THESE FINDINGS SUGGEST THAT A HIGH DENSITY OF NEGATIVE FEEDBACK INDUCES BOTH REFLECTIVE AND IMPULSIVE CHILDREN TO MAKE FEWER ERRORS THAN DOES POSITIVE FEEDBACK. (AUTHORS)

EJ 053 718 PS 501 645
DEVELOPMENTAL DETERMINANTS OF ATTENTION: A CROSS-CULTURAL REPLICATION SELLERS, MARTHA JULIA; AND OTHERS, *DEVELOPMENTAL PSYCHOLOGY*, V6 N1, PP185, JAN 72
A REPLICATION OF A PREVIOUS LONGITUDINAL STUDY OF AMERICAN CHILDREN -- THIS TIME WITH GUATAMALAN CHILDREN. (RY)

EJ 053 719 PS 501 657
AVOIDANCE CONDITIONING IN YOUNG CHILDREN WITH INTERRUPTION OF A POSITIVE STIMULUS AS THE AVERSIVE EVENT MOFFAT, GENE H., *JOURNAL OF EXPERIMENTAL CHILD PSYCHOLOGY*, V13 N1, PP21-8, FEB 72

EJ 053 720 PS 501 658
NONVERBAL INFORMATION STORAGE IN CHILDREN AND DEVELOPMENTAL INFORMATION PROCESSING CHANNEL CAPACITY RANDHAWA, BIKKAR S., *JOURNAL OF EXPERIMENTAL CHILD PSYCHOLOGY*, V13 N1, PP58-70, FEB 72
GLANZER AND CLARK'S "VERBAL LOOP HYPOTHESIS" APPEARED TO BE CONTRADICTED BY THESE DATA. (AUTHOR)

EJ 053 721 PS 501 659
EFFECTS OF HEBREW AND ENGLISH LETTERS ON CHILDREN'S PERCEPTUAL SET KEENAN, VERNE, *JOURNAL OF EXPERIMENTAL CHILD PSYCHOLOGY*, V13 N1, PP71-84, FEB 72
DATA SUGGESTS THAT PERCEPTUAL PROCESSING IN THE LANGUAGE-APPROPRIATE DIRECTION IS AN ESTABLISHED SKILL BY THE TIME A CHILD FINISHES SECOND GRADE. (AUTHOR)

EJ 053 722 PS 501 660
TRANSFER OF TRAINING: SOME BOUNDARY CONDITIONS AND INITIAL THEORY CAMPIONE, JOSEPH C.; BEATON, VIRGINIA L., *JOURNAL OF EXPERIMENTAL CHILD PSYCHOLOGY*, V13 N1, PP94-114, FEB 72
DATA WERE DISCUSSED IN TERMS OF AN OUTLINE OF AN EMPIRICALLY BASED THEORY OF TRANSFER. (AUTHORS)

EJ 053 723 PS 501 663
MODIFICATION OF FORM AND COLOR RESPONDING IN YOUNG CHILDREN AS A FUNCTION OF DIFFERENTIAL REINFORCEMENT GUSINOW, JOAN F.; PRICE, LOUIS E., *JOURNAL OF EXPERIMENTAL CHILD PSYCHOLOGY*, V13 N1, PP145-53, FEB 72

EJ 053 724 PS 501 664
MEANINGFULNESS, SERIAL POSITION AND RETENTION INTERVAL IN RECOGNITION SHORT-TERM MEMORY GLIDDEN, LARAINE MASTERS, *JOURNAL OF EXPERIMENTAL CHILD PSYCHOLOGY*, V13 N1, PP154-64, FEB 72

EJ 053 725 PS 501 665
AGE, ICONIC STORAGE, AND VISUAL INFORMATION PROCESSING GUMMERMAN, KENT; GRAY, CYNTHIA ROBERTS, *JOURNAL OF EXPERIMENTAL CHILD PSYCHOLOGY*, V13 N1, PP165-70, FEB 72
YOUNG CHILDREN'S ICONIC STORAGE IS LONGER THAN THAT OF OLDER CHILDREN AND ADULTS BUT YOUNG CHILDREN PROCESS THE INFORMATION IN ICONIC STORAGE RELATIVELY SLOWLY. (AUTHORS)

EJ 053 726 PS 501 667
CONCEPT ATTAINMENT, GENERALIZATION, AND RETENTION THROUGH OBSERVATION AND VERBAL CODING ROSENTHAL, TED L.; AND OTHERS, *JOURNAL OF EXPERIMENTAL CHILD PSYCHOLOGY,* V13 N1, PP183-94, FEB 72

EJ 053 727 PS 501 668
VERBAL-LABELING AND CUE-TRAINING IN REVERSAL-SHIFT BEHAVIOR KENDLER, HOWARD H.; AND OTHERS, *JOURNAL OF EXPERIMENTAL CHILD PSYCHOLOGY,* V13 N1, PP195-209, FEB 72
THREE EXPERIMENTS ARE REPORTED THAT WERE DESIGNED TO TEST THE EFFECTIVENESS OF TWO TRAINING PROCEDURES, ONE PERCEPTUAL, THE OTHER VERBAL, ON UPGRADING THE CONCEPTUAL BEHAVIOR OF PRESCHOOL CHILDREN. (AUTHORS/MB)

EJ 053 728 PS 501 669
DEVELOPMENT OF THE ABILITY TO ENCODE WITHIN EVALUATIVE DIMENSIONS CERMAK, LAIRD S.; AND OTHERS, *JOURNAL OF EXPERIMENTAL CHILD PSYCHOLOGY,* V13 N1, PP210-19, FEB 72

EJ 053 729 PS 501 670
PRIMACY IN PRESCHOOLERS' SHORT-TERM MEMORY: THE EFFECTS OF REPEATED TESTS AND SHIFT TRIALS ROSNER, SUE R., *JOURNAL OF EXPERIMENTAL CHILD PSYCHOLOGY,* V13 N1, PP220-30, FEB 72

EJ 053 730 PS 501 671
STEADY-STATE BEHAVIOR IN CHILDREN: A METHOD AND SOME DATA DECASPER, ANTHONY J.; ZEILER, MICHAEL D., *JOURNAL OF EXPERIMENTAL CHILD PSYCHOLOGY,* V13 N1, PP231-9, FEB 72
RESEARCH EMANATED FROM THE NEED TO FIND A SITUATION FOR EXPERIMENTING WITH CHILDREN FOR AN EXTENDED NUMBER OF SESSIONS. (AUTHOR)

EJ 053 731 PS 501 681
INFANT SMILING TO NONSOCIAL STIMULI AND THE RECOGNITION HYPOTHESIS ZELAZO, PHILIP R.; KOMER, M. JOAN, *CHILD DEVELOPMENT,* V42 N5, PP1327-39, NOV 71
RESULTS DEMONSTRATE THAT 12 - 15 - WEEK-OLD MALE INFANTS SMILE TO NONSOCIAL STIMULI, AND OFFERS SUPPORT FOR THE RECOGNITION HYPOTHESIS OF INFANT SMILING. (AUTHORS/MB)

EJ 053 732 PS 501 684
EMERGENCE AND PERSISTENCE OF BEHAVIORAL DIFFERENCES IN TWINS WILSON, RONALD S.; AND OTHERS, *CHILD DEVELOPMENT,* V42 N5, PP1381-98, NOV 71
MOTHERS OF 232 PAIRS OF TWINS WERE INTERVIEWED PERIODICALLY ABOUT THE SIMILARITIES AND DIFFERENCES IN BEHAVIOR DISPLAYED BY THEIR TWINS DURING INFANCY AND EARLY CHILDHOOD. (AUTHORS)

EJ 053 733 PS 501 685
EFFECTS OF AGE, SEX, SYSTEMATIC CONCEPTUAL LEARNING, ACQUISITION OF LEARNING SETS, AND PROGRAMMED SOCIAL INTERACTION ON THE INTELLECTUAL AND CONCEPTUAL DEVELOPMENT OF PRESCHOOL CHILDREN FROM POVERTY BACKGROUNDS JACOBSON, LEONARD I.; AND OTHERS, *CHILD DEVELOPMENT,* V42 N5, PP1399-415, NOV 71

EJ 053 734 PS 501 687
INTERACTIONS BETWEEN THE FACILITATIVE AND INHIBITORY EFFECTS OF A PUNISHING STIMULUS IN THE CONTROL OF CHILDREN'S HITTING BEHAVIOR KATZ, ROGER C., *CHILD DEVELOPMENT,* V42 N5, PP1433-46, NOV 71
STUDY INVESTIGATED THE EFFECTS OF A RESPONSE-PRODUCED INTENSE-NOISE STIMULUS (PUNISHMENT) ON THE EXTINCTION OF CHILDREN'S HITTING BEHAVIOR. (AUTHOR)

EJ 053 735 PS 501 689
DO MATERIAL REWARDS ENHANCE THE PERFORMANCE OF LOWER-CLASS CHILDREN? SPENCE, JANET T., *CHILD DEVELOPMENT,* V42 N5, PP1461-70, NOV 71

EJ 053 736 PS 501 690
FEEDING BEHAVIORS OF NEWBORN INFANTS AS A FUNCTION OF PARITY OF THE MOTHER THOMAS, EVELYN B.; AND OTHERS, *CHILD DEVELOPMENT,* V42 N5, PP1471-83, NOV 71

EJ 053 737 PS 501 691
FAMILY INTERACTION VARIABLES AND ADJUSTMENT OF NONCLINIC BOYS MURRELL, STANLEY A., *CHILD DEVELOPMENT,* V42 N5, PP1485-94, NOV 71
MEMBERS OF AVERAGE (ADJUSTMENT) FAMILIES MADE DECISIONS FASTER AND TALKED MORE EQUALLY TO ONE ANOTHER THAN MEMBERS OF LOW (ADJUSTMENT) FAMILIES AND HAD HIGHER NORMALITY SCORES THAN EITHER HIGH OR LOWS. (AUTHOR)

EJ 053 738 PS 501 692
COLOR DOMINANCE IN PRESCHOOL CHILDREN AS A FUNCTION OF SPECIFIC CUE PREFERENCES BROWN, ANN L.; CAMPIONE, JOSEPH C., *CHILD DEVELOPMENT,* V42 N5, PP1495-1500, NOV 71

EJ 053 739 PS 501 693
WORDS AND DEEDS ABOUT ALTRUISM AND THE SUBSEQUENT REINFORCEMENT POWER OF THE MODEL BRYAN, JAMES H.; AND OTHERS, *CHILD DEVELOPMENT,* V42 N5, PP1501-8, NOV 71
EXPERIMENT STUDIED THE EFFECTIVENESS OF SOCIAL REINFORCEMENT BY A MODEL WHO DEMONSTRATED VARYING DEGREES OF COMMITMENT TO THE NORM OF GIVING OR SOCIAL RESPONSIBILITY. (AUTHORS)

EJ 053 740 PS 501 694
DEVELOPMENTAL ASPECTS OF VARIABLES RELEVANT TO OBSERVATIONAL LEARNING LEIFER, AIMEE DORR; AND OTHERS, *CHILD DEVELOPMENT,* V42 N5, PP1509-16, NOV 71
RELEVANCE OF COGNITIVE AND DEVELOPMENTAL VARIABLES TO OBSERVATIONAL LEARNING AND IMITATION IS ALSO DISCUSSED. (AUTHORS/MB)

EJ 053 741 PS 501 695
INCONSISTENT VERBAL INSTRUCTIONS AND CHILDREN'S RESISTANCE-TO-TEMPTATION BEHAVIOR STOUWIE, ROGER J., *CHILD DEVELOPMENT,* V42 N5, PP1517-31, NOV 71
STUDY INVESTIGATED THE EFFECTS OF INCONSISTENCY OF INSTRUCTIONS, ORDER OF PRESENTATION OF INSTRUCTIONS, AND SEX OF CHILD UPON CHILDREN'S BEHAVIOR IN A RESISTANCE-TO-TEMPTATION SITUATION. (AUTHOR)

EJ 053 742 PS 501 696
CONCEPT CONSERVATION IN CHILDREN: THE DEPENDENCE OF BELIEF SYSTEMS ON SEMANTIC REPRESENTATION SALTZ, ELI; MEDOW, MIRIAM LUCAS, *CHILD DEVELOPMENT,* V42 N5, PP1533-42, NOV 71
RESULTS APPEAR TO INDICATE THAT THE BELIEF SYSTEMS OF THE YOUNG CHILD ABOUT THE ATTRIBUTES OF A STIMULUS PERSON CAN BE ALTERED EXTENSIVELY BY INTRODUCING CHARACTERISTICS COMPLETELY UNRELATED TO THESE ATTRIBUTES INTO THE SEMANTIC REPRESENTATION OF THAT PERSON. (AUTHORS)

EJ 053 743 PS 501 697
DEVELOPMENTAL DIFFERENCES IN THE FIELD OF VIEW DURING TACHISTOSCOPIC PRESENTATION MILLER, LEON K., *CHILD DEVELOPMENT,* V42 N5, PP1543-51, NOV 71
RESEARCH WAS DESIGNED TO DETERMINE WHETHER DEVELOPMENTAL DIFFERENCES IN SENSITIVITY TO MORE PERIPHERALLY PRESENTED MATERIAL COULD BE FOUND UNDER CONDITIONS IN WHICH OVERT EYE MOVEMENTS DURING THE PRESENTATION OF TASK MATERIAL WERE NOT POSSIBLE. (AUTHOR)

EJ 053 744 PS 501 698
ARTICULATION OF THE BODY CONCEPT AMONG FIRST-GRADE ISRAELI CHILDREN WELLER, LEONARD; SHLOMO, SHARAN (SINGER), *CHILD DEVELOPMENT,* V42 N5, PP1553-9, NOV 71
EFFECTS OF COUNTRY OF ORIGIN AND SOCIAL CLASS ON SEX DIFFERENCES IN BODY ARTICULATION WERE ALSO ANALYZED. (AUTHORS)

EJ 053 745 PS 501 699
MATERNAL WARMTH, ACHIEVEMENT MOTIVATION, AND COGNITIVE FUNCTIONING IN LOWER-CLASS PRESCHOOL CHILDREN RADIN, NORMA, *CHILD DEVELOPMENT,* V42 N5, PP1560-5, NOV 71
FINDINGS SUGGEST THAT MATERNAL CHILD-REARING PRACTICES SIGNIFICANTLY AFFECT THE CHILD'S RESPONSE TO A GIVEN COMPENSATORY PRESCHOOL PROGRAM. (AUTHOR)

EJ 053 746 PS 501 700
CONTINUITY IN THE DEVELOPMENT OF VISUAL BEHAVIOR IN YOUNG INFANTS BARTEN, SYBIL; RONCH, JUDAH, *CHILD DEVELOPMENT,* V42 N5, PP1566-71, NOV 71
STUDY INVESTIGATED WHETHER THE OBSERVED INDIVIDUAL DIFFERENCES IN VISUAL PURSUIT ENDURE BEYOND THE NEONATAL PERIOD. (AUTHORS/MB)

EJ 053 747 PS 501 701
DIALECT, RACE, AND LANGUAGE PROFICIENCY: ANOTHER DEAD HEAT ON THE MERRY-GO-ROUND FOREIT, KAREN G.; DONALDSON, PATRICIA L., *CHILD DEVELOPMENT,* V42 N5, PP1572-4, NOV 71
AUTHORS SUGGEST A REANALYSIS OF THE DATA AND A REPLICATION OF THE EXPERIMENT DESCRIBED BY J. S. BARATZ IN A PREVIOUS ISSUE OF CHILD DEVELOPMENT (EJ 008 114). (MB)

EJ 053 748 PS 501 702
PROXIMITY AND INTERACTIONAL BEHAVIOR OF YOUNG CHILDREN TO THEIR "SECURITY" BLANKETS WEISSBERG, PAUL; RUSSELL, JAMES E., *CHILD DEVELOPMENT,* V42 N5, PP1575-9, NOV 71

EJ 053 749 PS 501 703
DISCRIMINATION OF STEREOMETRIC OJBECTS AND PHOTOGRAPHS OF OBJECTS BY CHILDREN ETAUGH, CLAIRE FALK; VAN SICKLE, DOUGLAS, *CHILD DEVELOPMENT*, V42 N5, PP1580-2, NOV 71

EJ 053 750 PS 501 704
THE EFFECT OF AGGRESSIVE CARTOONS ON CHILDREN'S INTERPERSONAL PLAY HAPKIEWICZ, WALTER G.; RODEN, AUBREY H., *CHILD DEVELOPMENT*, V42 N5, PP1583-5, NOV 71

EJ 053 751 PS 501 706
STIMULUS NOVELTY AS A VARIABLE IN CHILDREN'S WIN-STAY, LOSE-SHIFT DISCRIMINATION LEARNING SET BERMAN, PHYLLIS W., *CHILD DEVELOPMENT*, V42 N5, PP1591-5, NOV 71

EJ 053 752 PS 501 707
THE EFFECTS OF DIFFERENT TYPES OF REINFORCEMENT ON YOUNG CHILDREN'S INCIDENTAL LEARNING SIEGEL, ALEXANDER W.; VAN CARA, FLO, *CHILD DEVELOPMENT*, V42 N5, PP1596-601, NOV 71

EJ 053 753 PS 501 708
FAMILY FACTORS RELATED TO COMPETENCE IN YOUNG DISADVANTAGED MEXICAN-AMERICAN CHILDREN STEDMAN, JAMES M.; MCKENZIE, RICHARD E., *CHILD DEVELOPMENT*, V42 N5, PP1602-7, NOV 71

EJ 053 754 PS 501 709
OBSERVING BEHAVIOR AND CHILDREN'S DISCRIMINATION LEARNING GOLDSTEIN, SONDRA BLEVINS; SIEGEL, ALEXANDER W., *CHILD DEVELOPMENT*, V42 N5, PP1608-13, NOV 71
STUDY FOUND THAT STIMULUS PRESENCE DURING A DELAY OF REINFORCEMENT INTERVAL ENHANCED PERFORMANCE, AND TO A LARGE EXTENT PREVENTED THE USUAL DELAY-PRODUCED DECREMENT. (AUTHORS)

EJ 053 755 PS 501 710
CROSS-MODAL MATCHING AMONG NORMAL AND RETARDED CHILDREN ZUNG, BURTON J., *CHILD DEVELOPMENT*, V42 N5, PP1614-8, NOV 71
RESULTS REAFFIRM THE NOTION THAT RETARDED INDIVIDUALS ARE LESS ADEPT AT RECOGNIZING FAMILIAR FORMS HAPTICALLY THAN VISUALLY. (AUTHOR)

EJ 053 756 PS 501 711
EFFECTS OF TYPE AND SOURCE OF LABELS ON CHILDREN'S PERCEPTUAL JUDGMENTS AND DISCRIMINATION LEARNING ETAUGH, CLAIRE F.; AVERILL, BONNIE E., *CHILD DEVELOPMENT*, V42 N5, PP1619-23, NOV 71

EJ 053 757 PS 501 716
THE ROLE OF BODY PARTS AND READINESS IN ACQUISITION OF NUMBER CONSERVATION CURCIO, FRANK; AND OTHERS, *CHILD DEVELOPMENT*, V42 N5, PP1641-6, NOV 71
A COMBINATION OF READINESS AND BODY-PART TRAINING WAS THE MOST EFFECTIVE IN PRODUCING NUMBER CONSERVATION WITH EXTERNAL OBJECTS. (AUTHORS)

EJ 053 758 PS 501 719
NEONATAL SMILING IN REM STATES, IV: PREMATURE STUDY EMDE, ROBERT N.; AND OTHERS, *CHILD DEVELOPMENT*, V42 N5, PP1657-61, NOV 71
IN A NATURALISTIC BEHAVIORAL STDY, IT WAS FOUND THAT PREMATURES HAVE SIGNIFICANTLY MORE ENDOGENOUS SMILING THAN FULL-TERM NEWBORNS. (AUTHORS)

EJ 053 759 PS 501 720
THE EFFECTS OF A FAMILIAR TOY AND MOTHER'S PRESENCE ON EXPLORATORY AND ATTACHMENT BEHAVIORS IN YOUNG CHILDREN GERSHAW, N. JAME; SCHWARZ, J. CONRAD, *CHILD DEVELOPMENT*, V42 N5, PP1662-6, NOV 71

EJ 053 853 PS 501 647
ON TRANSRACIAL ADOPTION OF BLACK CHILDREN JONES, EDMOND D., *CHILD WELFARE*, V51 N3, PP156-64, MAR 72
TRANSRACIAL ADOPTIONS HAVE BEEN ENCOURAGED WIDELY AS A WAY TO MEET THE NEEDS OF MANY BLACK CHILDREN. THIS PRACTICE AND THE AGENCY PHILOSOPHY BEHIND IT ARE CHALLENGED IN THE LIGHT OF TODAY'S SOCIAL REALITIES. (EDITOR)

EJ 053 887 PS 501 629
RACIAL FACTORS IN TEST PERFORMANCE BUCKY, STEVEN F.; BANTA, THOMAS J., *DEVELOPMENTAL PSYCHOLOGY*, V6 N1, PP7-13, JAN 72
THE PURPOSE OF THE STUDY WAS TO DETERMINE (A) WHETHER THERE ARE DIFFERENCES IN THE WAY IN WHICH NEGRO AND WHITE EXPERIMENTERS INTERACT WITH NEGRO AND WHITE SUBJECTS; AND (B) WHETHER SUCH DIFFERENCES INFLUENCE PERFORMANCE ON TESTS OF MOTOR IMPULSE CONTROL, REFLECTIVITY, INNOVATIVE BEHAVIOR, AND CURIOSITY. (AUTHORS)

EJ 053 905 PS 501 680
RELIABILITY AND STABILITY OF THE DENVER DEVELOPMENTAL SCREENING TEST FRANKENBURG, WILLIAM K.; AND OTHERS, *CHILD DEVELOPMENT*, V42 N5, PP1315-25, NOV 71
RESULTS INDICATE THAT THE TEST-RETEST STABILITY OF THE DDST IS QUITE SATISFACTORY FOR A SCREENING TEST. (AUTHORS/MB)

EJ 053 906 PS 501 705
PERFORMANCE OF CULTURALLY DEPRIVED CHILDREN ON THE CONCEPT ASSESSMENT KIT--CONSERVATION WASIK, BARBARA H.; WASIK, JOHN L., *CHILD DEVELOPMENT*, V42 N5, PP1586-90, NOV 71

EJ 053 907 PS 501 714
A PIAGETIAN QUESTIONNAIRE APPLIED TO PUPILS IN A SECONDARY SCHOOL TISHER, R. P., *CHILD DEVELOPMENT*, V42 N5, PP1633-6, NOV 71
AUTHOR CONCLUDES THAT A PIAGETIAN BASED PAPER-AND-PENCIL TECHNIQUE CAN BE SUCCESSFULLY USED FOR OLDER SUBJECTS RATHER THAN THE CONVERSATION-INTERVIEW TECHNIQUE USED FOR ELEMENTARY SCHOOL CHILDREN. (MB)

EJ 053 908 PS 501 715
SOCIAL CLASS DIFFERENCES IN TEACHER ATTITUDES TOWARD CHILDREN GOLDENBERG, IRENE, *CHILD DEVELOPMENT*, V42 N5, PP1637-40, NOV 71
MIDDLE-CLASS TEACHERS WERE SIGNIFICANTLY MORE PERMISSIVE AND LESS PURITANICAL IN OUTLOOK, TOOK MORE PLEASURE IN THE EMOTIONAL ASPECTS OF TEACHER-PUPIL RELATIONSHIPS, AND SHOWED LESS AUTHORITARIAN ATTITUDES TOWARD CHILDREN THAN DID LOWER-CLASS TEACHERS. (AUTHOR/MB)

EJ 053 927 PS 501 682
PIAGET AND GESELL: A PSYCHOMETRIC ANALYSIS OF TESTS BUILT FROM THEIR TASKS KAUFMAN, ALAN S., *CHILD DEVELOPMENT*, V42 N5, PP1341-60, NOV 71
AIM OF THE STUDY IS TO ASSESS EMPIRICALLY THE INTERRELATIONSHIPS AMONG SOME OF PIAGET-S AND GESELL'S BEHAVIORAL TASKS. (AUTHOR)

EJ 053 929 PS 501 737
THE SORE-FOOTED DUCK THOMPSON, ALICE C., *CHILDHOOD EDUCATION*, V48 N6, PP303-6, MAR 72
AS MANY AS ONE-THIRD OF OUR CHILDREN, WHO ARE SOMETIMES LABELED "NONRETARDED EXCEPTIONALS," ARE BEING SHUNTED OFF TO SPECIAL CLASSROOMS OR IF IN A REGULAR CLASSROOM ARE NEGLECTED AND EVEN IGNORED BY THE TEACHER. (EDITOR)

EJ 054 049 PS 501 745
EVALUATION DIMENSION OF THE AFFECTIVE MEANING SYSTEM OF THE PRESCHOOL CHILD MCMURTRY, C. ALLEN; WILLIAMS, JOHN E., *DEVELOPMENTAL PSYCHOLOGY*, V6 N2, PP238-46, MAR 72
STUDY WAS AIMED AT DETERMINING WHETHER POSITIVE ADJECTIVES AND NEGATIVE ADJECTIVES POSSESS THE "OPPOSITENESS" (MUTUAL EXCLUSIVENESS) NECESSARY FOR THEIR CONCEPTUALIZATION AS DEFINING THE EXTREMES OF A SINGLE DIMENSION OF MEANING. (AUTHORS)

EJ 054 162 PS 501 726
SOME ANGLES ON PARENT-TEACHER LEARNING CHILMAN, CATHERINE S., *CHILDHOOD EDUCATION*, V48 N3, PP119-25, DEC 71
COUNSEL ON WAYS TO OVERCOME COMMUNICATIONS BLOCKS. (EDITOR)

EJ 054 289 PS 501 733
LEARNING FROM OUR CRITICS GROSS, BEATRICE; GROSS, RONALD, *CHILDHOOD EDUCATION*, V48 N6, PP282-6, MAR 72
DISCUSSES THE CRITICISM OF THE RADICAL REFORMERS IN EDUCATION AND WHAT CAN BE LEARNED FROM THEM. (MB)

EJ 054 290 PS 501 752
FATHER-CHILD INTERACTION AND THE INTELLECTUAL FUNCTIONING OF FOUR-YEAR-OLD BOYS RADIN, NORMA, *DEVELOPMENTAL PSYCHOLOGY*, V6 N2, PP353-61, MAR 72
BOYS IQ WAS POSITIVELY CORRELATED WITH PATERNAL NURTURANCE, AND NEGATIVELY CORRELATED WITH PATERNAL RESTRICTIVENESS. (AUTHOR)

EJ 054 377 PS 501 727
SYMPOSIUM ON PARENT-CENTERED EDUCATION: 1. THE CHILD'S FIRST TEACHER GRAY, SUSAN W., *CHILDHOOD EDUCATION*, V48 N3, PP127-9, DEC 71
NOT ALWAYS APPARENT IS THE FACT THAT THE MOTHER BECOMES LITERALLY THE CHILD'S FIRST TEACHER. (AUTHOR)

EJ 054 378 PS 501 728
SYMPOSIUM ON PARENT-CENTERED EDUCATION: 2. LEARNING THROUGH (AND FROM) MOTHERS LEVENSTEIN, PHYLLIS, *CHILDHOOD EDUCATION*, V48 N3, PP130-4, DEC 71
DESCRIBES THE MOTHER CHILD HOME PROGRAM WHEREIN "TOY DEMONSTRATORS" SHOW MOTHERS HOW TO INCREASE DAILY VERBAL INTERACTION WITH THEIR CHILDREN. (MB)

EJ 054 379 PS 501 729
SYMPOSIUM ON PARENT-CENTERED EDUCATION: 3. LEARNING THROUGH PARENTS: LESSONS FOR TEACHERS WEIKART, DAVID P., *CHILDHOOD EDUCATION*, V48 N3, PP135-7, DEC 71
THE PRIMARY LESSON TO BE LEARNED BY TEACHERS FROM PARENTS IS THAT THE TEACHER'S ROLE IS TO PROVIDE SERVICE TO THE PARENTS RATHER THAN "EXPERT" TRANSLATION OF MIDDLE-CLASS SOCIAL WISDOM INTO UNIVERSAL CHILD-REARING PRACTICE. (AUTHOR)

EJ 054 380 PS 501 731
AREAS OF RECENT RESEARCH IN EARLY CHILDHOOD EDUCATION BUTLER, ANNIE L., *CHILDHOOD EDUCATION*, V48 N3, PP143-7, DEC 71
AN ADAPTATION OF A PAPER PRESENTED AT THE XIIITH WORLD ASSEMBLY OF OMEP (WORLD ORGANIZATION FOR EARLY CHILDHOOD EDUCATION) IN BONN, GERMANY. (MB)

EJ 054 381 PS 501 734
CONTRIBUTIONS OF CRITICISM TO PARENT, FAMILY-LIFE AND SEX EDUCATION GRAMS, ARMIN, *CHILDHOOD EDUCATION*, V48 N6, PP287-91, MAR 72
ALTHOUGH CRITICISM HEARD MOST OFTEN ABOUT SEX EDUCATION IS FROM EXTREMIST SOURCES, THERE ARE CRITICS WHOSE ARGUMENTS DEAL WITH TIMING, METHODS, AND ESPECIALLY THE READINESS OF TEACHERS TO DO THE JOB. (AUTHOR/MB)

EJ 054 382 PS 501 735
CONFRONTING PERSISTENT CONCERNS ALLEN, AUDRIANNA, *CHILDHOOD EDUCATION*, V48 N6, PP292-7, MAR 72
A COMPREHENSIVE OVERVIEW OF OVERSTRESS AND UNDERSTRESSES IN TODAY'S SCHOOLS -- AND SPECIFIC WAYS FOR INDIVIDUALS TO BRING ABOUT CHANGE. (EDITOR)

EJ 054 472 PS 501 736
CHILDREN OF TECHNOLOGY: IMAGES OR THE REAL THING COHEN, DOROTHY H., *CHILDHOOD EDUCATION*, V48 N6, PP298-302, MAR 72
AUTHOR ASKS WHETHER CHILDREN IN BECOMING OVERDEPENDENT ON TECHNOLOGY ARE LOSING STRENGTH TO FUNCTION AS HUMAN BEINGS. (AUTHOR/MB)

EJ 054 508 PS 501 768
OVERLAP: HYPOTHESIS OR TAUTOLOGY? ETAUGH, ALFRED F.; ETAUGH, CLAIRE FALK, *DEVELOPMENTAL PSYCHOLOGY*, V6 N2, PP340-2, MAR 72
AUTHORS DEMONSTRATE THAT A SIMPLE ALGEBRAIC ANALYSIS RENDERS PREVIOUS INTERPRETATIONS SUPERFLUOUS, MAKING "OVERLAP" A TAUTOLOGY AND NOT A HYPOTHESIS. (AUTHORS/MB)

EJ 054 727 PS 501 757
A CHANGE AGENT STRATEGY: PRELIMINARY REPORT ORLICH, DONALD C.; AND OTHERS, *ELEMENTARY SCHOOL JOURNAL*, V72 N6, PP281-93, MAR 72
DESCRIBES A PROJECT THAT CHANGED THE SOCIAL STUDIES CURRICULUM BY CHANGING THE METHOD OF TEACHING. (MB)

EJ 054 804 PS 501 746
RELATION BETWEEN IDENTITY CONSERVATION AND EQUIVALENCE CONSERVATION WITHIN FOUR CONCEPTUAL DOMAINS MOYNAHAN, ELLEN; GLICK, JOSEPH, *DEVELOPMENTAL PSYCHOLOGY*, V6 N2, PP247-51, MAR 72
RESULTS INDICATE THAT IDENTITY CONSERVATION GENERALLY DOES NOT PRECEDE EQUIVALENCE CONSERVATION; INSTEAD THE TWO CONSERVATIONS TEND TO CO-OCCUR. (AUTHORS)

EJ 054 805 PS 501 754
MEMORY FOR RHYTHMIC SERIES: AGE CHANGES IN ACCURACY AND NUMBER CODING LEHMAN, ELYSE BRAUCH; GOODNOW, JACQUELINE, *DEVELOPMENTAL PSYCHOLOGY*, V6 N2, PP363, MAR 72

EJ 054 806 PS 501 763
VERBAL RECALL AS A FUNCTION OF PERSONALITY CHARACTERISTICS FISHER, DENNIS F.; KEEN, SUSAN P., *JOURNAL OF GENETIC PSYCHOLOGY*, V120 PT1, PP83-92, MAR 72
RESULTS FAILED TO CONFIRM THE FINDINGS OF PREVIOUS INVESTIGATORS, WHICH SHOWED ANAL RETENTIVES TO BE SUPERIOR IN VERBAL RECALL. (AUTHORS)

EJ 055 093 PS 501 672
AGE OF SUBJECT, TYPE OF SOCIAL CONTACT, AND RESPONSIVENESS TO SOCIAL REINFORCEMENT ATEMA, JAN M.; AND OTHERS, *JOURNAL OF GENETIC PSYCHOLOGY*, V120 PT1, PP3-12, MAR 72
STUDY IS AN EXPERIMENTAL INVESTIGATION OF DEVELOPMENTAL ASPECTS OF THE VALENCE THEORY. (AUTHORS)

EJ 055 094 PS 501 673
ANXIETY AND MORAL JUDGMENT IN EARLY ADOLESCENCE BIRNBAUM, MORTON P., *JOURNAL OF GENETIC PSYCHOLOGY*, V120 PT1, PP13-26, MAR 72
ONE MAJOR ASPECT OF MORAL JUDGMENT SELECTED FOR THIS STUDY IS THE CHILD'S FLEXIBILITY TOWARD RULES. (MB)

EJ 055 095 PS 501 674
SPONTANEOUS MEASUREMENT IN YOUNG CHILDREN: A RE-EXAMINATION DAEHLER, MARVIN W., *JOURNAL OF GENETIC PSYCHOLOGY*, V120 PT1, PP27-38, MAR 72

EJ 055 096 PS 501 675
WORD-ASSOCIATION RESPONSES OF CHILDREN AS A FUNCTION OF AGE, SEX AND INSTRUCTIONS KAHANA, BOAZ; STERNECK, ROSALIE, *JOURNAL OF GENETIC PSYCHOLOGY*, V120 PT1, PP39-48, MAR 72
STUDY EXAMINED WORD ASSOCIATIONS FROM THE PERSPECTIVE OF COGNITIVE LEVEL AND THOUGHT PROCESSES. (AUTHORS/MB)

EJ 055 097 PS 501 676
CHILDREN'S MORAL REASONING HARDEMAN, MILDRED, *JOURNAL OF GENETIC PSYCHOLOGY*, V120 PT1, PP49-60, MAR 72
PURPOSE OF THE STUDY IS TO TEST PIAGET'S HYPOTHESIS OF A PARALLEL RELATIONSHIP BETWEEN MORAL CONCEPTS AND LOGICAL STRUCTURES IN HUMAN DEVELOPMENT. (AUTHOR)

EJ 055 098 PS 501 678
SEX DIFFERENCES IN PERFORMANCE AS A FUNCTION OF PRAISE AND BLAME ZIV, ABNER, *JOURNAL OF GENETIC PSYCHOLOGY*, V120 PT1, PP111-20, MAR 72
RESEARCH EXAMINED THREE INDEPENDENT VARIABLES: TYPE OF REINFORCEMENT GIVEN TO EXAMINEE, SEX OF EXAMINEE, AND SEX OF REINFORCER. (AUTHOR/MB)

EJ 055 099 PS 501 679
HAPTIC RECOGNITION OF OBJECTS IN CHILDREN KRANTZ, MURRAY, *JOURNAL OF GENETIC PSYCHOLOGY*, V120 PT1, PP121-34, MAR 72
PURPOSE OF THE INVESTIGATION IS TO DESCRIBE THE MULTIDIMENSIONAL HAPTIC CLASSIFICATION SYSTEM IN ITS SIMPLEST FORM AND DEMONSTRATE ITS FUNCTIONING IN THE HAPTIC RECOGNITION OF EVERYDAY PHYSICAL OBJECTS. (AUTHOR/MB)

EJ 055 100 PS 501 739
COMING OF AGE WITH THE DELBOEUF ILLUSION: BRIGHTNESS CONTRAST, COGNITION AND PERCEPTUAL DEVELOPMENT WEINTRAUB, DANIEL J.; COOPER, LYNN A., *DEVELOPMENTAL PSYCHOLOGY*, V6 N2, PP187-97, MAR 72
TESTING POLLACK'S HYPOTHESIS THAT DECREASES IN EFFECTIVE CONTOUR CONTRAST (RESULTING FROM A DECREASE IN RECEPTOR SENSITIVITY WITH AGE OR FROM A CHANGE IN ACTUAL STIMULUS CONTRAST) LEAD TO DECREASES IN ILLUSION MAGNITUDE. CONCLUSIONS ARE QUESTIONED BY SJOSTROM AND POLLACK (PS 501 740). (AUTHOR/MB)

EJ 055 101 PS 501 740
THE ROLE OF LIGHTNESS CONTRAST IN DETERMINING THE MAGNITUDE OF THE DELBOEUF ILLUSION: A REJOINDER TO WEINTRAUB AND COOPER SJOSTROM, KRISTEN; POLLACK, ROBERT H., *DEVELOPMENTAL PSYCHOLOGY*, V6 N2, PP198-200, MAR 72
QUESTIONS THE CONCLUSIONS DESCRIBED IN PS 501 739. (MB)

EJ 055 102 PS 501 747
DEVELOPMENT OF HIERARCHIES OF DIMENSIONAL SALIENCE ODOM, RICHARD; BUZMAN, RICHARD D., *DEVELOPMENTAL PSYCHOLOGY*, V6 N2, PP271-87, MAR 72
IT WAS SHOWN THAT HIERARCHIES CHANGE WITH DEVELOPMENT AND THAT RELATIVE SALIENCE OF A DIMENSION IS NEGATIVELY ASSOCIATED WITH BOTH REACTION TIME OF CHOICE AND NUMBER OF ERRORS ON THE IDENTITY TASK. (AUTHORS)

EJ 055 103 PS 501 748
DEVELOPMENT OF YOUNG CHILDREN'S ATTENTION TO NORMAL AND DISTORTED STIMULI: A CROSS CULTURAL STUDY FINLEY, GORDON E., *DEVELOPMENTAL PSYCHOLOGY*, V6 N2, PP288-92, MAR 72
STUDY SHOWS THAT AGE-RELATED EXPERIENCE HAS A MARKED IMPACT ON THE COGNITIVE STRUCTURES OF YOUNG CHILDREN. (AUTHORS/MB)

EJ 055 104 PS 501 751
ACADEMIC CHEATING: THE CONTRIBUTION OF SEX, PERSONALITY AND SITUATIONAL VARIABLES JOHNSON, CHARLES D.; GORMLY, JOHN, *DEVELOPMENTAL PSYCHOLOGY*, V6 N2, PP320-5, MAR 72

FEMALES CHEATED IN RESPONSE TO CONSISTENTLY UNFAVORABLE SELF-PERCEPTIONS, WHILE MALES WERE INFLUENCED BY IMMEDIATE SITUATIONAL FACTORS. (AUTHORS)

EJ 055 105 PS 501 755
STYLE OF ADAPTATION TO AVERSIVE MATERNAL CONTROL AND PARANOID BEHAVIOR HEILBRUN, ALFRED B., JR.; NORBERT, NANCYANN, *JOURNAL OF GENETIC PSYCHOLOGY*, V120 PT1, PP145-54, MAR 72

TESTED WAS THE HYPOTHESIS THAT MALES WHO HAVE ADOPTED AN OPEN STYLE OF ADAPTING TO AVERSIVE CONTROL WILL SHOW EVIDENCE OF PARANOID BEHAVIOR, WHEREAS THOSE WHO HAVE ADOPTED A CLOSED STYLE OF ADAPTING TO AVERSIVE MATERNAL CONTROL WILL NOT. (AUTHORS/MB)

EJ 055 106 PS 501 756
SIBLING RESEMBLANCES IN DIVERGENT THINKING OLIVE, HELEN, *JOURNAL OF GENETIC PSYCHOLOGY*, V120 PT1, PP155-62, MAR 72

INVESTIGATION COMBINED TWO HERETOFORE UNCONNECTED RESEARCH AREAS: THE NEWLY STRUCTURED OPERATION OF DIVERGENT THINKING AND THE OLDER DOMAIN OF FAMILY RESEMBLANCES. (AUTHOR)

EJ 055 107 PS 501 761
SOME SOCIAL EFFECTS OF CROSS-GRADE GROUPING AHLBRAND, WILLIAM P., JR.; REYNOLDS, JAMES A., *ELEMENTARY SCHOOL JOURNAL*, V72 N6, PP327-32, MAR 72

PURPOSE OF THE STUDY WAS TO EXAMINE THE EFFECT OF AGE-GROUP MEMBERSHIP ON SOCIOMETRIC NOMINATIONS MADE ON THE BASIS OF SCHOLARSHIP, LEADERSHIP, AND POPULARITY. (AUTHORS)

EJ 055 108 PS 501 764
INSTITUTIONALIZED RETARDATES' ANIMAL DRAWINGS; THEIR MEANINGS AND SIGNIFICANCE PUSTEL, GABRIEL; AND OTHERS, *JOURNAL OF GENETIC PSYCHOLOGY*, V120 PT1, PP103-10, MAR 72

AN IMAGE OF THE RETARDED EMERGED FROM THE DRAWINGS, WHICH, GENERALLY, WERE CONVERGENT ON THE ADULT LEVEL BUT DIVERGENT FOR THE ADOLESCENTS. (AUTHORS)

EJ 055 109 PS 501 765
EFFECTS OF AGE UPON RETRIEVAL FROM SHORT-TERM MEMORY ANDERS, TERRY R.; AND OTHERS, *DEVELOPMENTAL PSYCHOLOGY*, V6 N2, PP214-7, MAR 72

RESULTS INDICATE THAT RETRIEVAL TIME BECAME SLOWER WITH AGE. (MB)

EJ 055 110 PS 501 766
AGE CHANGES AND COHORT DIFFERENCES IN PERSONALITY WOODRUFF, DIANA S.; BIRREN, JAMES E., *DEVELOPMENTAL PSYCHOLOGY*, V6 N2, PP252-9, MAR 72

AUTHORS SUGGEST THAT SEPARATING THE EFFECTS OF AGE CHANGES AND COHORT DIFFERENCES IN PERSONALITY CAN ADD NEW DIMENSIONS TO THE EXISTING BODY OF DEVELOPMENTAL LITERATURE ON PERSONALITY. (AUTHORS/MB)

EJ 055 111 PS 501 767
AN ANALYSIS OF THE CONCEPT OF CULTURAL DEPRIVATION TULKIN, STEVEN R., *DEVELOPMENTAL PSYCHOLOGY*, V6 N2, PP326-39, MAR 72

SUGGESTIONS ARE PRESENTED FOR SPECIFIC CHANGES IN SOCIAL SCIENTISTS' APPROACHES TO MINORITY GROUP PROBLEMS. (AUTHOR)

EJ 055 112 PS 501 769
FACTORIAL STRUCTURE OF SELECTED PSYCHO-EDUCATIONAL MEASURES AND PIAGETIAN REASONING ASSESSMENTS STEPHENS, BETH; AND OTHERS, *DEVELOPMENTAL PSYCHOLOGY*, V6 N2, PP343-8, MAR 72

REVIEW OF THE FACTOR MATRIX INDICATED THAT PIAGETIAN REASONING TASKS INVOLVE ABILITIES SEPARATE FROM THOSE MEASURED BY STANDARD TESTS OF INTELLIGENCE AND ACHIEVEMENT. (AUTHORS)

EJ 055 113 PS 501 770
DEVELOPMENT OF CUTANEOUS AND KINESTHETIC LOCALIZATION BY BLIND AND SIGHTED CHILDREN JONES, BILL, *DEVELOPMENTAL PSYCHOLOGY*, V6 N2, PP349-52, MAR 72

RESULTS ARE DISCUSSED IN TERMS OF THE INTERACTIVE EFFECTS OF SENSORY SYSTEMS. (AUTHOR)

EJ 055 153 PS 501 738
TEACHING READING IN THE KINDERGARTEN: A REVIEW OF RECENT STUDIES VUKILICH, CAROL; BEATTIE, IAN, *CHILDHOOD EDUCATION*, V48 N6, PP327-30, MAR 72

RESULTS OF RESEARCH REPORTS CAN BE INTERPRETED TO SUIT PERSONAL PREJUDICES, SAY THE AUTHORS, SINCE MANY RESEARCH STUDIES ARE NOT CAREFULLY REPORTED. (AUTHORS/MB)

EJ 055 154 PS 501 759
GROWTH IN READING IN AN INTEGRATED DAY CLASSROOM MOSS, JOY F., *ELEMENTARY SCHOOL JOURNAL*, V72 N6, PP304-20, MAR 72

ARTICLE IS A RECORD OF AUTHOR'S EXPERIENCE IN DEVELOPING WAYS OF INTEGRATING CHILDREN'S BEGINNING READING INTO THE TOTAL PROCESS OF LEARNING AND LIVING. (AUTHOR/MB)

EJ 055 204 PS 501 677
DISCRIMINATION LEARNING AND TRANSFER OF TRAINING IN THE AGED COPPINGER, N. W.; NEHRKE, MILTON F., *JOURNAL OF GENETIC PSYCHOLOGY*, V120 PT1, PP93-102, MAR 72

STUDIES OF THE ABILITY OF ELDERLY DEBILITATED PATIENTS TO RESPOND TO CONCEPTUAL TRAINING AND THEIR DIFFERENTIAL RESPONSE TO DIFFERENT KINDS OF CONCEPTUAL SHIFTS. (AUTHORS/MB)

EJ 055 205 PS 501 732
RESEARCH ON ASPECTS OF LEADERSHIP ROLES IN EARLY AND ELEMENTARY EDUCATION YONEMURA, MARGARET, *CHILDHOOD EDUCATION*, V48 N3, PP163-6, DEC 71

DESCRIBES INVESTIGATIONS TO EXPLORE WAYS OF IDENTIFYING EFFECTIVE ADMINISTRATORS. (AUTHOR)

EJ 055 206 PS 501 741
COMPARISONS OF VOCAL IMITATION, TACTILE STIMULATION, AND FOOD AS REINFORCERS FOR INFANT VOCALIZATIONS HAUGAN, GERTRUDE M.; MCINTYRE, ROGER W., *DEVELOPMENTAL PSYCHOLOGY*, V6 N2, PP201-9, MAR 72

EJ 055 207 PS 501 742
PERSON SPECIFICITY OF THE "SOCIAL DEPRIVATION-SATIATION EFFECT" BABAD, ELISHA Y., *DEVELOPMENTAL PSYCHOLOGY*, V6 N2, PP210-3, MAR 72

THE "SOCIAL DEPRIVATION-SATIATION EFFECT" IS CHARACTERIZED BY AN INVERSE RELATION BETWEEN THE FREQUENCY OF SOCIAL REINFORCEMENT RECEIVED IN A STANDARD TREATMENT PERIOD AND THE EFFECTIVENESS OF THAT REINFORCER IN A SUBSEQUENT TEST. (AUTHOR)

EJ 055 208 PS 501 743
INTERRELATIONS IN THE ATTACHMENT BEHAVIOR OF HUMAN INFANTS COATES, BRIAN; AND OTHERS, *DEVELOPMENTAL PSYCHOLOGY*, V6 N2, PP218-30, MAR 72

EJ 055 209 PS 501 744
THE STABILITY OF ATTACHMENT BEHAVIORS IN THE HUMAN INFANT COATES, BRIAN; AND OTHERS, *DEVELOPMENTAL PSYCHOLOGY*, V6 N2, PP231-7, MAR 72

EJ 055 210 PS 501 749
EFFECTS OF CONCURRENT AND SERIAL TRAINING ON GENERALIZED VOCAL IMITATION IN RETARDED CHILDREN SCHROEDER, GERALD L.; BAER, DONALD M., *DEVELOPMENTAL PSYCHOLOGY*, V6 N2, PP293-301, MAR 72

INCREASE IN PROBE ACCURACY FOLLOWING CONCURRENT TRAINING WAS CONSISTENTLY GREATER THAN FOLLOWING SERIAL TRAINING. (AUTHORS)

EJ 055 211 PS 501 750
MOTIVATIONAL EFFECTS OF BOREDOM ON CHILDREN'S RESPONSE SPEEDS KUBOSE, SUNNAN K., *DEVELOPMENTAL PSYCHOLOGY*, V6 N2, PP302-5, MAR 72

RESULTS CONFIRMED PREVIOUS FINDINGS THAT RESPONSE SPEEDS WOULD BE FASTER FOLLOWING AN 18- THAN A 8-SECOND STIMULUS DURATION. (AUTHOR)

EJ 055 212 PS 501 753
CHILDREN'S OBSERVATION AND INTEGRATION OF AGGRESSIVE EXPERIENCES COHEN, STEWART, *DEVELOPMENTAL PSYCHOLOGY*, V6 N2, PP362, MAR 72

THE ACQUISITION OF AGGRESSIVE RESPONSES MAY LIKELY BE A FUNCTION OF THE ENVIRONMENT'S COPIOUS PROVISION OF IMITATIVE MODELS. (AUTHOR)

EJ 055 213 PS 501 760
CHANGES IN SELF-PERCEPTIONS OF HEAD-START TRAINEES DURRETT, MARY ELLEN; RADOV, ANEITA SHARPLES, *ELEMENTARY SCHOOL JOURNAL*, V72 N6, PP321-6, MAR 72

THE BROWN SELF-REPORT INVENTORY WAS ADMINISTERED TO THREE GROUPS OF TRAINEES AT THE BEGINNING AND AT THE END OF THE HEAD START LEADERSHIP DEVELOPMENT PROGRAM. (AUTHORS)

EJ 055 214 PS 501 762
CONDITIONING OF INFANT VOCALIZATIONS IN THE HOME ENVIRONMENT TOMLINSON-KEASEY, C., *JOURNAL OF GENETIC PSYCHOLOGY*, V120 PT1, PP75-82, MAR 72

EJ 055 215 PS 501 771
FORMAL OPERATIONS IN FEMALES FROM ELEVEN TO FIFTY-FOUR YEARS OF AGE TOMLINSON-KEASEY, C., *DEVELOPMENTAL PSYCHOLOGY*, V6 N2, PP364, MAR 72

STUDY WAS DESIGNED TO OBTAIN CROSS-SECTIONAL DATA ON THE LEVEL OF COGNITIVE DEVELOPMENT OF THREE AGE GROUPS. (AUTHOR)

EJ 055 362 PS 501 725
TEACHERS AND PARENTS: CHANGING ROLES AND GOALS CONANT, MARGARET M., *CHILDHOOD EDUCATION*, V48 N3, PP114-8, DEC 71
NEW KINDS OF "PRODUCTIVE LIAISON" ARE DEVELOPING BETWEEN PARENTS AND SCHOOL PROFESSIONALS, BASED ON MUTUAL RESPECT AND SHARED UNDERSTANDINGS. (EDITOR)

EJ 055 363 PS 501 730
LISTENING BEYOND WORDS: LEARNING FROM PARENTS IN CONFERENCES GRISSOM, CATHERINE E., *CHILDHOOD EDUCATION*, V48 N3, PP138-42, DEC 71
STRAIGHT TALK FOR TEACHERS WITH THE COURAGE TO ACKNOWLEDGE NEED FOR HELP IN TALKING WITH URBAN, WORKING-CLASS PARENTS WHO MAY HAVE DIFFERING VALUES BUT WHO SHARE A COMMON CONCERN ABOUT THE WELFARE OF THEIR CHILDREN. (EDITOR)

EJ 055 364 PS 501 758
A PROCESS FOR POETRY-WRITING RODGERS, DENIS, *ELEMENTARY SCHOOL JOURNAL*, V72 N6, PP294-303, MAR 72
DESCRIBES A PROCESS WHICH TOOK 5 LESSON PERIODS AND ENABLED THE CHILDREN TO WRITE THEIR OWN POETRY. (MB)

EJ 055 488 PS 501 779
SON OF ROBOT COMMANDO OSBORN, D. KEITH, *CHILDHOOD EDUCATION*, V48 N7, PP375-6, APR 72
DESCRIPTIONS OF TOYS THAT INVITE AGGRESSIVE AND VIOLENT BEHAVIOR, AND SUGGESTIONS ON WHAT PARENTS AND TEACHERS CAN DO TO PROTECT CHILDREN. (SP)

EJ 055 489 PS 501 863
THE STRUCTURING OF SOCIAL ATTITUDES IN CHILDREN NIAS, D. K. B., *CHILD DEVELOPMENT*, V43 N1, PP211-9, MAR 72
BY COMPARING THE RESULTS OF THIS INVESTIGATION WITH THE ATTITUDE ORGANIZATION OF ADULTS, AN UNDERSTANDING MAY BE GAINED OF THE PROCESSES INVOLVED IN ATTITUDE DEVELOPMENT. (MB)

EJ 055 533 PS 501 772
SUCCESS AND ACCOUNTABILITY GORDON, IRA J., *CHILDHOOD EDUCATION*, V48 N7, PP338-47, APR 72
THE AUTHOR DISCUSSES COGNITION AND AFFECT AS TWO ASPECTS OF THE "WHOLE CHILD" CONCEPT, DESCRIBES POSITIVE AND NEGATIVE ITEMS RELATING TO THE HOME ENVIRONMENT AND PARENT BEHAVIOR, SUGGESTS IMPLICATIONS FOR SCHOOL PROGRAMS TO ENCOURAGE SUCCESS, AND REDEFINES ACCOUNTABILITY IN TERMS OF THE CHILD'S TOTAL SELF-CONCEPT. (SP)

EJ 055 534 PS 501 774
INSTANT LAW AND ORDER METALITZ, BEATRICE R., *CHILDHOOD EDUCATION*, V48 N7, PP354-5, APR 72
A KINDERGARTEN TEACHER, AWARE OF THE NEED FOR "A GENERATION OF PEACEMAKERS", DESCRIBES ONE METHOD OF TRAINING CHILDREN TO DISCUSS DIFFERENCES INSTEAD OF RESORTING TO VIOLENCE. (AUTHOR/SP)

EJ 055 535 PS 501 781
HOW FREE IS FREE PLAY? VAN CAMP, SARAH S., *YOUNG CHILDREN*, V27 N4, PP205-7, APR 72
IF DISTINCT AND WELL-EQUIPPED "ACTIVITY CENTERS" ARE AVAILABLE, THE KINDERGARTEN BECOMES "AN ABSORBING CHILD-CENTERED OPEN CLASSROOM" WITH THE ENTIRE TIME "FREE PLAY/FREE WORK TIME." (AUTHOR/SP)

EJ 055 536 PS 501 786
VIOLENCE AS A SYMPTOM OF CHILDHOOD EMOTIONAL ILLNESS LITTNER, NER, *CHILD WELFARE*, V51 N4, PP208-19, APR 72
THE LEVEL OF KNOWLEDGE ABOUT CHILDHOOD EMOTIONAL DISTURBANCE IS ADEQUATE TO THE TASK OF EARLY PREVENTION AND REHABILITATION, BUT THE CHALLENGE IS TO STIMULATE THE ESSENTIAL COMMUNITY COOPERATION. (ML)

EJ 055 537 PS 501 862
SELECTIVE STRATEGIES IN CHILDREN'S ATTENTION TO TASK-RELEVANT INFORMATION LEHMAN, ELYSE BRAUCH, *CHILD DEVELOPMENT*, V43 N1, PP197-209, MAR 72
RESULTS SUGGEST THAT SELECTIVE ATTENTION IS A MULTIFACETED SKILL, WITH DEVELOPMENT OF ITS PARTS PROGRESSING AT DIFFERENT RATES. (AUTHOR)

EJ 055 547 PS 501 858
MOTIVATIONAL AND ACHIEVEMENT DIFFERENCES AMONG CHILDREN OF VARIOUS ORDINAL BIRTH POSITIONS ADAMS, RUSSEL L.; PHILLIPS, BEEMAN N., *CHILD DEVELOPMENT*, V43 N1, PP155-64, MAR 72
WHEN DIFFERENCES IN LEVEL OF MOTIVATION WERE CONTROLLED, ALL OF THE PREVIOUSLY FOUND DIFFERENCES BETWEEN FIRSTBORN AND LATER BORN DISAPPEARED. (AUTHORS)

EJ 055 655 PS 501 805
SOME COGNITIVE AND AFFECTIVE ASPECTS OF EARLY LANGUAGE DEVELOPMENT EVELOFF, HERBERT H., *CHILD DEVELOPMENT*, V42 N6, PP1895-907, DEC 71
NORMAL AND ABNORMAL LANGUAGE DEVELOPMENT DEPENDS TO A GREAT DEGREE ON THE NATURE OF THE INFANT-MOTHER RELATIONSHIP. (AUTHOR)

EJ 055 656 PS 501 870
AN EXPLORATORY STUDY OF SOCIALIZATION EFFECTS ON BLACK CHILDREN: SOME BLACK-WHITE COMPARISONS BAUMRIND, DIANA, *CHILD DEVELOPMENT*, V43 N1, PP261-7, MAR 72
MAJOR CONCLUSION FROM THIS EXPLORATORY ANALYSIS WAS THAT IF THE BLACK FAMILIES WERE VIEWED BY WHITE NORMS THEY APPEARED AUTHORITARIAN, BUT THAT, UNLIKE THEIR WHITE COUNTERPARTS, THE MOST AUTHORITARIAN OF THESE FAMILIES PRODUCED THE MOST SELF-ASSERTIVE AND INDEPENDENT GIRLS. (AUTHOR)

EJ 055 736 PS 501 782
NURSERY SCHOOLS FIFTY YEARS AGO ELIOT, ABIGAIL ADAMS, *YOUNG CHILDREN*, V27 N4, PP209-13, APR 72
THE AUTHOR, ONE OF THE PIONEERS IN EARLY CHILDHOOD EDUCATION, DESCRIBES HER EARLY EXPERIENCES. (SP)

EJ 055 875 PS 501 815
AN EVALUATION OF A THEORY OF SPECIFIC DEVELOPMENTAL DYSLEXIA SATZ, PAUL; AND OTHERS, *CHILD DEVELOPMENT*, V42 N6, PP2009-21, DEC 71
BEHAVIORAL PATTERN OF DEFICITS OBSERVED IN DYSLEXIC CHILDREN IS QUITE SIMILAR TO ADULTS WHO HAVE SUSTAINED DAMAGE TO THE LEFT CEREBRAL HEMISPHERE. (AUTHORS)

EJ 055 876 PS 501 829
HYPERACTIVITY AND THE MACHINE: THE ACTOMETER JOHNSON, CHARLES F., *CHILD DEVELOPMENT*, V42 N6, PP2105-10, DEC 71
AN ACTOMETER IS A MODIFIED SELF-WINDING CALENDAR WATCH WHICH RECORDS ACCELERATION AND DECELERATION OF MOVEMENTS WITH A "SIGNIFICANT COMPONENT" IN THE SAME PLANE AS THE FACE OF THE WATCH. ACTOMETERS TESTED IN THIS STUDY WERE NOT RELIABLE. (AUTHOR/MB)

EJ 055 897 PS 501 860
FREEDOM FROM EXTERNAL EVALUATION MAEHR, MARTIN L.; STALLINGS, WILLIAM M., *CHILD DEVELOPMENT*, V43 N1, PP177-85, MAR 72
TWO EXPERIMENTS WERE CONDUCTED TO ASSESS THE EFFECTS OF VARYING DEGREES OF EXTERNAL EVALUATION NOT ONLY ON PERFORMANCE BUT ALSO ON CONTINUING MOTIVATION. (AUTHORS)

EJ 056 090 PS 501 775
LITERATURE, CREATIVITY AND IMAGINATION LIVINGSTON, MYRA COHN, *CHILDHOOD EDUCATION*, V48 N7, PP356-61, APR 72
THE AUTHOR IS CONCERNED ABOUT THE OVEREMPHASIS ON FORM AND TECHNIQUES IN TEACHING LITERATURE, AND SUGGESTS THAT TEACHERS ENCOURAGE THE RELEASE OF EMOTION AND FEELINGS IN THEIR STUDENTS BY MEANS OF LITERATURE AND WRITTEN EXPRESSION. (SP)

EJ 056 391 PS 501 776
THE SPANISH-SPEAKING FIVE-YEAR-OLD BROMAN, BETTY L., *CHILDHOOD EDUCATION*, V48 N7, PP362-4, APR 72
AUTHOR OBSERVED FOUR KINDERGARTEN CLASSES WHERE TEACHERS WERE ABLE TO SPEAK SPANISH; SPANISH-SPEAKING CHILDREN, BY VARIOUS METHODS, LEARNED SKILLS AND CONTENT AT THE SAME RATE AS ENGLISH-SPEAKING CHILDREN DID. (SP)

EJ 056 392 PS 501 847
RELATIONS OF AGE AND INTELLIGENCE TO SHORT-TERM COLOR MEMORY BELMONT, JOHN M., *CHILD DEVELOPMENT*, V43 N1, PP19-29, MAR 72
IT WAS CONCLUDED THAT AGE AND IQ HAVE STRONG INFLUENCES ON ACQUISITION-RETRIEVAL, BUT THAT FORGETTING RATE IS INDEPENDENT OF THESE VARIABLES. (AUTHOR)

EJ 056 393 PS 501 851
THE RELATION OF FORM RECOGNITION TO CONCEPT DEVELOPMENT NELSON, KATHERINE, *CHILD DEVELOPMENT*, V43 N1, PP67-74, MAR 72
HYPOTHESIS WAS CONFIRMED THAT MORE FAMILIAR AND MORE AMBIGUOUS CONCEPTS WOULD BE LESS READILY NAMED IN THEIR LESS DETAILED REPRESENTATIONS. (AUTHOR/MB)

EJ 056 394 PS 501 852
LOGICAL CAPACITY OF VERY YOUNG CHILDREN: NUMBER INVARIANCE RULES GELMAN, ROCHEL, *CHILD DEVELOPMENT*, V43 N1, PP75-90, MAR 72
RESULTS ARE DISCUSSED IN TERMS OF WHY CHILDREN OF THE SAME AGE FAIL TO CONSERVE NUMBER IN THE STANDARD CONSERVATION TASK AND HOW COMPLEX NUMBER CONCEPTS MIGHT DEVELOP. (AUTHOR)

EJ 056 395 PS 501 853
INFORMATION AND STRATEGY IN THE YOUNG CHILD'S SEARCH FOR HIDDEN OBJECTS WEBB, ROGER A.; AND OTHERS, *CHILD DEVELOPMENT*, V43 N1, PP91-104, MAR 72
FINDINGS ARE INTERPRETED IN TERMS OF SEARCH STRATEGY AND MEMORY. (AUTHORS)

EJ 056 396 PS 501 854
MODELING EFFECTS UPON CONCEPTUAL STYLE AND COGNITIVE TEMPO DENNEY, DOUGLAS R., *CHILD DEVELOPMENT*, V43 N1, PP105-19, MAR 72
PERFORMANCE DEMONSTRATED THAT THE CONCEPTUAL STYLE AND COGNITIVE TEMPO OF THE MODEL CHANGED THE STYLES AND TEMPOS OF THE SS AND THAT THESE EFFECTS GENERALIZED TO INDEPENDENT TASKS. (AUTHOR)

EJ 056 397 PS 501 866
DEVELOPMENT OF RELATIONAL CONCEPTS AND WORD DEFINITION IN CHILDREN FIVE THROUGH ELEVEN SWARTZ, KARYL; HALL, ALFRED E., *CHILD DEVELOPMENT*, V43 N1, PP239-44, MAR 72
COMPARISON BETWEEN RELATIONAL CONCEPTS AND WORD DEFINITIONS COINCIDED WITH LOWER LEVELS OF THINKING, AND ABSTRACT DEFINITIONS WITH THE HIGHEST LEVEL. (AUTHOR)

EJ 056 398 PS 501 868
THE EFFECTS OF DIFFERENTIAL REINFORCEMENT ON THE DISCRIMINATION LEARNING OF NORMAL AND LOW-ACHIEVING MIDDLE-CLASS BOYS BLAIR, JOHN RAYMOND, *CHILD DEVELOPMENT*, V43 N1, PP251-5, MAR 72
RESULTS INDICATED THAT THE NORMAL ACHIEVERS LEARNED MORE EFFECTIVELY UNDER PERSON AND PERFORMANCE REINFORCEMENT THAN UNDER TANGIBLE REINFORCEMENT, WHEREAS THE REVERSE WAS TRUE FOR LOW ACHIEVERS. (AUTHOR)

EJ 056 399 PS 501 873
THE EFFECT OF SIBLING RELATIONSHIP ON CONCEPT LEARNING OF YOUNG CHILDREN TAUGHT BY CHILD-TEACHERS CICIRELLI, VICTOR G., *CHILD DEVELOPMENT*, V43 N1, PP282-7, MAR 72
RESULTS ARE INTERPRETED IN TERMS OF ROLE THEORY AND SIBLING RIVALRY, AND HAVE APPLICATION FOR SCHOOL PRACTICE. (AUTHOR)

EJ 056 400 PS 501 874
VARIABLES AFFECTING ASSOCIATIVE RECALL IN CHILDREN BERNSTEIN, ALAN; LURIA, ZELLA, *CHILD DEVELOPMENT*, V43 N1, PP388-92, MAR 72
RESULTS ARE DISCUSSED IN TERMS OF POSSIBLE PERCEPTUAL AND MNEMONIC DEVICES USED FOR RECALL. (AUTHORS)

EJ 056 401 PS 501 875
THE EFFECTS OF TRAINING AND SOCIOECONOMIC CLASS UPON THE ACQUISITION OF CONSERVATION CONCEPTS FIGURELLI, JENNIFER C.; KELLER, HAROLD R., *CHILD DEVELOPMENT*, V43 N1, PP293-8, MAR 72
LOWER-CLASS CHILDREN REQUIRED SIGNIFICANTLY MORE TRAINING TASK REPETITIONS TO LEARN A CONSERVATION TASK THAN DID MIDDLE-CLASS CHILDREN. (AUTHORS)

EJ 056 402 PS 501 876
NOUN-PAIR LEARNING IN CHILDREN AND ADULTS: UNDERLYING STRINGS AND RETRIEVAL TIME SUZUKI, NANCY S., *CHILD DEVELOPMENT*, V43 N1, PP299-307, MAR 72
STUDY WAS AN ATTEMPT TO EXPLAIN THE OBSERVED DIFFERENCE ASSOCIATED WITH SENTENCE TYPE IN THE PERFORMANCE OF CHILDREN AND THE ABSENCE OF A SIMILAR DIFFERENCE IN THE PERFORMANCE OF COLLEGE STUDENTS. (AUTHOR)

EJ 056 569 PS 501 788
EVALUATION OF A PARENT AND CHILD CENTER PROGRAM HAMILTON, MARSHALL L., *CHILD WELFARE*, V51 N4, PP248-58, APR 72
ARTICLE DESCRIBES CHANGES THAT OCCURRED IN CHILDREN AND PARENTS WHO PARTICIPATED IN A PRESCHOOL INTERVENTION PROGRAM. (AUTHOR)

EJ 056 607 PS 501 780
SESAME STREET: MAGIC OR MALEVOLENCE? RATLIFF, ANNE R.; RATLIFF, RICHARD G., *YOUNG CHILDREN*, V27 N4, PP199-204, APR 72
"DESPITE ITS UNUSUAL POTENTIAL, BOTH EDUCATIONAL AND SOCIAL, IT SEEMS THAT SESAME STREET MAY BE EXPOSING CHILDREN TO UNNECESSARY AGGRESSION...(WHICH) OFTEN GOES UNPUNISHED AND, OCCASIONALLY, IS ACTIVELY REWARDED." (AUTHOR)

EJ 056 608 PS 501 784
PARENTS AS EDUCATORS: EVIDENCE FROM CROSS-SECTIONAL, LONGITUDINAL AND INTERVENTION RESEARCH SCHAEFER, EARL S., *YOUNG CHILDREN*, V27 N4, PP227-39, APR 72
"THE EVIDENCE SUGGESTS THAT PARENTS HAVE GREAT INFLUENCE UPON THE BEHAVIOR OF THEIR CHILDREN, PARTICULARLY THEIR INTELLECTUAL AND ACADEMIC ACHIEVEMENT, AND THAT PROGRAMS WHICH TEACH PARENTS SKILLS IN EDUCATING THEIR CHILDREN ARE EFFECTIVE SUPPLEMENTS OR ALTERNATIVES FOR PRESCHOOL EDUCATION." (AUTHOR)

EJ 056 609 PS 501 791
MULTIDIMENSIONAL SCALING OF DIMENSIONAL PREFERENCES: A METHODOLOGICAL STUDY SEITZ, VICTORIA R., *CHILD DEVELOPMENT*, V42 N6, PP1701-20, DEC 71
IT WAS CONCLUDED THAT THE SCALED PREFERENCE VALUES HAVE HIGH FACE VALIDITY AND THAT THEY SUGGEST THE NEED FOR REEXAMINATION OF SOME PREVIOUS EXPERIMENTAL RESULTS. (AUTHOR)

EJ 056 610 PS 501 792
TAKING ANOTHER'S PERSPECTIVE: ROLE-TAKING DEVELOPMENT IN EARLY CHILDHOOD SELMAN, ROBERT L., *CHILD DEVELOPMENT*, V42 N6, PP1721-34, DEC 71
ROLE-TAKING, A PROTOTYPICAL SOCIAL-COGNITIVE SKILL, IS THE ABILITY TO VIEW THE WORLD (INCLUDING THE SELF) FROM ANOTHER'S PERSPECTIVE. (AUTHOR/MB)

EJ 056 611 PS 501 794
PARENTAL ATTITUDES AND INTERACTIONS IN DELINQUENCY DUNCAN, PAM, *CHILD DEVELOPMENT*, V42 N6, PP1751-65, DEC 71
RESULTS INDICATE THAT THE PARENTS OF NON-DELINQUENTS CAN BE CLEARLY DIFFERENTIATED FROM PARENTS OF DELINQUENTS IN TERMS OF DISPLAYING A HIGHER ACTIVITY LEVEL, LESS REJECTION, HIGHER PARENTAL ADJUSTMENT, LOWER CONSISTENCY OF CONTROLS, BUT HIGHER CONSISTENCY OF FEELINGS. (AUTHOR)

EJ 056 612 PS 501 797
PROBLEM-SOLVING THINKING AND ADJUSTMENT AMONG DISADVANTAGED PRESCHOOL CHILDREN SHURE, MYRNA B.; AND OTHERS, *CHILD DEVELOPMENT*, V42 N6, PP1791-803, DEC 71
IMPLICATIONS ARE THAT INCREASING A CHILD'S ABILITY TO THINK IN TERMS OF ALTERNATIVE SOLUTIONS TO REAL-LIFE PROBLEMS COULD SUPPLEMENT A PRIMARY PREVENTIVE MENTAL HEALTH PROGRAM. (AUTHORS)

EJ 056 613 PS 501 798
VERBAL MEDIATION AND SATIATION IN YOUNG CHILDREN COOK, HAROLD; SMOTHERGILL, DANIEL, *CHILD DEVELOPMENT*, V42 N6, PP1805-12, DEC 71
THE LOGICAL EXTENSION OF RESULTS MAY BE VALUABLE IN ADDING TO OUR UNDERSTANDING OF THE VARIETY OF PHENOMENA INVOLVING MEDIATIONAL PROCESSES, SUCH AS TRANSPOSITION, REVERSAL AND NONREVERSAL SHIFTS, IMAGERY, CONCEPT FORMATION, WORD MEANING, AND THE EFFECTIVENESS OF VERBAL STIMULI IN DISCRIMINATION AND GENERALIZATION. (AUTHORS)

EJ 056 614 PS 501 799
FACTORS RELATED TO SCHOOL ACHIEVEMENT IN AN ECONOMICALLY DISADVANTAGED GROUP BUCK, MILDREN R.; AUSTRIN, HARVEY R., *CHILD DEVELOPMENT*, V42 N6, PP1813-26, DEC 71
FINDINGS ARE DISCUSSED IN THE LIGHT OF SOCIAL-LEARNING THEORY. (AUTHORS)

EJ 056 615 PS 501 800
EFFECTS OF SYNTACTICAL MEDIATION, AGE, AND MODES OF REPRESENTATION ON PAIRED-ASSOCIATE LEARNING HUGHES, S. EILEEN DOLORES; WALSH, JOHN F., *CHILD DEVELOPMENT*, V42 N6, PP1827-36, DEC 71
SYNTACTICAL MEDIATION REFERS TO THE PHENOMENSON IN WHICH THE GRAMMATICAL STRUCTURE OF LANGUAGE CAN BE EMPLOYED IN THE STRUCTURE OF VERBAL MEDIATORS. (AUTHORS/MB)

EJ 056 616 PS 501 801
FIGURATIVE AND OPERATIVE ASPECTS OF CHILDREN'S INFERENCE YOUNISS, JAMES; DENNISON, ANN, *CHILD DEVELOPMENT*, V42 N6, PP1837-47, DEC 71
STUDY ATTEMPTED TO SPECIFY TWO COMPLEMENTARY ASPECTS OF CHILDREN'S INFERENTIAL SIZE JUDGMENTS WITHIN THE CONTEXT OF PIAGET'S THEORY. (AUTHORS)

EJ 056 617 PS 501 806
DEVELOPMENT OF A SENSE OF SELF-IDENTITY IN CHILDREN GUARDO, CAROL J.; BOHAN, JANIS BEEBE, *CHILD DEVELOPMENT*, V42 N6, PP1909-21, DEC 71
DISTINCTION IS MADE BETWEEN SELF (SELF AS A SUBJECT) AND SELF-CONCEPT. (MB)

EJ 056 618 PS 501 808
GENERALITY OF PERCEPTUAL BIASES IN INFERENCE AND CONCEPT USAGE SCHOLNICK, ELLIN KOBSKY, *CHILD DEVELOPMENT*, V42 N6, PP1937-49, DEC 71

EXPERIMENT EXAMINED THE GENERALITY OF DIMENSIONAL AND CUE-LOCATION BIASES IN INFERENCE AND ROLE OF DIRECTNESS OF INFORMATION. (AUTHOR)

EJ 056 619 PS 501 809
SOCIAL-CLASS DIFFERENCES AND TASK VARIABLES IN THE DEVELOPMENT OF MULTIPLICATIVE CLASSIFICATION OVERTON, WILLIS F.; AND OTHERS, *CHILD DEVELOPMENT*, V42 N6, PP1951-58, DEC 71

RESULTS ARE DISCUSSED IN TERMS OF THE DEVELOPMENT AND ACTIVATION OF COGNITIVE STRUCTURES. (AUTHORS)

EJ 056 620 PS 501 810
SEMANTIC INTEGRATION, AGE, AND THE RECALL OF SENTENCES ROSENBERG, SHELDON; AND OTHERS, *CHILD DEVELOPMENT*, V42 N6, PP1959-66, DEC 71

RESULTS INDICATE THAT THE SEMANTIC CONSTRAINTS REVEALED BY ADULT ASSOCIATIVE SENTENCES USED HERE ARE A FUNCTIONAL PART OF THE LINGUISTIC KNOWLEDGE A 5-YEAR-OLD CHILD BRINGS TO THE TASK OF MEMORIZING SENTENCES. (AUTHORS)

EJ 056 621 PS 501 813
THE INFLUENCE OF NONINTELLECTIVE FACTORS ON THE IQ SCORES OF MIDDLE- AND LOWER-CLASS CHILDREN KINNIE, ERNEST J.; STERNLOF, RICHARD E., *CHILD DEVELOPMENT*, V42 N6, PP1989-95, DEC 71

BY "NONINTELLECTIVE" ARE MEANT FACTORS WHICH ARE PRESENT IN A TEST SITUATION AND WHICH INFLUENCE THE TEST SCORES OBTAINED BUT ARE NOT OBVIOUSLY RELATED TO THE SKILLS OR KNOWLEDGE OSTENSIBLY BEING MEASURED BY THE TEST. (AUTHORS)

EJ 056 622 PS 501 814
THE RELATIONSHIP BETWEEN VALUES AND BEHAVIOR: A DEVELOPMENTAL HYPOTHESIS HENSHEL, ANNE-MARIE, *CHILD DEVELOPMENT*, V42 N6, PP1997-2007, DEC 71

IT WAS FOUND THAT THERE WAS A STRONGER NEGATIVE CORRELATION BETWEEN HONESTY SCORES AND CHEATING INCIDENTS AMONG OLDER CHILDREN THAN YOUNGER. (AUTHOR)

EJ 056 623 PS 501 816
THE CURIOSITY DIMENSION OF FIFTH-GRADE CHILDREN: A FACTORIAL DISCRIMINANT ANALYSIS MAW, WALLACE H.; MAGOON, A. JON, *CHILD DEVELOPMENT*, V42 N6, PP2023-31, DEC 71

FINDINGS SUGGEST THAT, IF CURIOSITY IS TO BE DEVELOPED MEANINGFULLY IN THE SCHOOLS, AFFECTIVE DEVELOPMENT MUST BE FOSTERED AT THE SAME TIME THAT COGNITIVE SKILLS ARE TAUGHT. (AUTHORS)

EJ 056 624 PS 501 817
UNILATERAL DOMINANCE IS NOT RELATED TO NEUROPSYCHOLOGICAL INTEGRITY CRINELLA, FRANCIS M.; AND OTHERS, *CHILD DEVELOPMENT*, V42 N6, PP2033-54, DEC 71

AUTHORS SUGGEST THAT CONSIDERATION BE GIVEN TO MAXIMIZING THE OPPORTUNIES FOR SYSTEMS IN EITHER CEREBRAL HEMISPHERE TO DEVELOP FULLY IN EARLY LIFE, WHEN THE CHILD IS ESSENTIALLY "SPLIT-BRAINED," SO THAT DEVELOPMENTAL IMBALANCE DOES NOT EXIST WHEN THE TWO HEMISPHERES LATER BEGIN TO COMMUNICATE. (AUTHORS/MB)

EJ 056 625 PS 501 821
RACE AND SEX DIFFERENCES IN THE CHILD'S PERCEPTION OF EMOTION GITTER, A. GEORGE; AND OTHERS, *CHILD DEVELOPMENT*, V42 N6, PP2071-5, DEC 71

EJ 056 626 PS 501 822
RACIAL PREFERENCES IN YOUNG CHILDREN KIRCHER, MARY; FURBY, LITA, *CHILD DEVELOPMENT*, V42 N6, PP2076-8, DEC 71

THIRTY NEGRO AND WHITE PRESCHOOL CHILDREN WERE TESTED FOR DIFFERENTIAL PREFERENCE FOR NEGRO AND WHITE CHARACTERISTICS ON FOUR FACIAL FEATURES. (AUTHORS/MB)

EJ 056 627 PS 501 824
PERCEPTUAL INADEQUACY AND COMMUNICATIVE INEFFECTIVENESS IN INTERPERSONAL COMMUNICATION LONGHURST, THOMAS M.; TURNURE, JAMES E., *CHILD DEVELOPMENT*, V42 N6, PP2064-88, DEC 71

INVESTIGATION INDICATES THAT PERCEPTUAL INADEQUACY MUST BE CONTROLLED IN STUDIES THAT UTILIZE AMBIGUOUS, NOVEL OR NONSENSE DESIGNS IN STIMULUS MATERIALS. (AUTHORS)

EJ 056 628 PS 501 825
CONCEPTUAL ENCODING AND CONCEPT RECALL-RECOVERY IN CHILDREN LIBBY, WILLIAM L., JR.; KROES, WILLIAM H., *CHILD DEVELOPMENT*, V42 N6, PP2089-93, DEC 71

MAJOR FINDING IS THAT RECALL IN THE SHIFT CONDITION DRAMATICALLY EXCEEDED RECALL IN THE NO SHIFT CONDITION. (AUTHORS/MB)

EJ 056 629 PS 501 826
THE MEASUREMENT OF CHILDREN'S SELF-CONCEPT AS RELATED TO RACIAL MEMBERSHIP STABLER, JOHN R.; AND OTHERS, *CHILD DEVELOPMENT*, V42 N6, PP2094-97, DEC 71

ATTITUDES TOWARD THE COLORS BLACK AND WHITE MAY INFLUENCE THE WAY BLACK AND WHITE CHILDREN VIEW EACH OTHER AND THEMSELVES. (AUTHORS)

EJ 056 630 PS 501 832
A DEVELOPMENTAL STUDY OF THE EFFECTS OF PRETRAINING ON A PERCEPTUAL RECOGNITION TASK HENNINGS, JAMES S., S. J.; KORNREICH, L. BERELL, *CHILD DEVELOPMENT*, V42 N6, PP2117-9, DEC 71

FINDING SUPPORTS THE EDUCATIONAL THEORY AND PRACTICES OF MONTESSORI EDUCATORS. (AUTHORS)

EJ 056 631 PS 501 846
AN ONTOGENY OF MEDIATIONAL DEFICIENCY KENDLER, TRACY S., *CHILD DEVELOPMENT*, V43 N1, PP1-17, MAR 72

MEDIATIONAL DEFICIENCY IS USED HERE AS A GENERIC TERM TO APPLY TO A FAILURE TO MEDIATE DUE TO EITHER A PRODUCTION DEFICIENCY (EXTERNAL EVENT) OR A CONTROL DEFICIENCY (POTENTIAL MEDIATOR). (MB)

EJ 056 632 PS 501 848
MOTHER-CHILD INTERACTION IN THE FIRST YEAR OF LIFE TULKIN, STEVEN R.; KAGAN, JEROME, *CHILD DEVELOPMENT*, V43 N1, PP31-41, MAR 72

IT WAS SUGGESTED THAT WORKING-CLASS MOTHERS LESS FREQUENTLY BELIEVED THAT THEIR INFANTS WERE CAPABLE OF COMMUNICATING WITH OTHER PEOPLE, AND HENCE FELT IT WAS FUTILE TO ATTEMPT TO INTERACT WITH THEM VERBALLY. (AUTHORS)

EJ 056 633 PS 501 849
HABITUATION AND MEMORY: INFANT CARDIAC RESPONSES TO FAMILIAR AND DISCREPANT AUDITORY STIMULI HOROWITZ, ALAN B., *CHILD DEVELOPMENT*, V43 N1, PP43-53, MAR 72

EJ 056 634 PS 501 850
PATTERNS OF RESPONDING IN THE WORD ASSOCIATIONS OF WEST AFRICAN CHILDREN SHARP, DONALD; COLE, MICHAEL, *CHILD DEVELOPMENT*, V43 N1, PP55-65, MAR 72

STUDIES CONDUCTED AMONG THE KPELLE OF NORTH CENTRAL LIBERIA WHOSE PRESENT CULTURAL MILIEU OFFERS UNIQUE POSSIBILITIES FOR STUDYING THE ROLE OF PARTICULAR EXPERIENTIAL FACTORS, PARTICULARLY EDUCATION, ON THE DEVELOPMENT OF PARADIGMATIC RESPONSE. (AUTHORS)

EJ 056 635 PS 501 859
THE ONSET OF WARINESS SCHAFFER, H. RUDOLPH; AND OTHERS, *CHILD DEVELOPMENT*, V43 N1, PP165-75, MAR 72

WARINESS DID NOT SET IN GRADUALLY OVER A PERIOD OF TIME BUT, ON THE CONTRARY, WAS FOUND IN ITS FULLY DEVELOPED FORM AT 9 MONTHS, HAVING BEEN COMPLETELY ABSENT AT 8 MONTHS. (AUTHORS/MB)

EJ 056 636 PS 501 861
THE EFFECT OF SYSTEMATIC STORY CHANGES ON INTENTIONALITY IN CHILDREN'S MORAL JUDGMENTS GUTKIN, DANIEL C., *CHILD DEVELOPMENT*, V43 N1, PP187-95, MAR 72

EJ 056 707 PS 501 789
LONGITUDINAL DEVELOPMENT OF VERY YOUNG CHILDREN IN A COMPREHENSIVE DAY CARE PROGRAM: THE FIRST TWO YEARS ROBINSON, HALBERT B.; ROBINSON, NANCY M., *CHILD DEVELOPMENT*, V42 N6, PP1673-83, DEC 71

A MUCH GREATER POSITIVE EFFECT OF THE PROGRAM WAS FOUND WITH CULTURALLY DEPRIVED, PRESCHOOL NEGRO CHILDREN THAN WITH MORE ADVANTAGED CAUCASIAN CHILDREN. (AUTHORS)

EJ 056 708 PS 501 790
PEER INTERACTION AND COGNITIVE DEVELOPMENT RARDIN, DONALD R.; MOAN, CHARLES E., *CHILD DEVELOPMENT*, V42 N6, PP1685-99, DEC 71

IMPLICATIONS OF THIS STUDY ON CHILD-DEVELOPMENT THEORY, EDUCATION, AND PSYCHOTHERAPY ARE DISCUSSED. (MB)

EJ 056 709 PS 501 793
COMPARISON OF IMITATION AND COMPREHENSION SCORES BETWEEN TWO LOWER-CLASS GROUPS AND THE EFFECTS OF TWO WARM-UP CONDITIONS ON IMITATION OF THE SAME GROUPS HALL, VERNON C.; TURNER, RALPH R., *CHILD DEVELOPMENT*, V42 N6, PP1735-50, DEC 71

EJ 056 710 PS 501 795
THE SEQUENCE OF DEVELOPMENT OF SOME EARLY MATHEMATICS BEHAVIORS WANG, MARGARET C.; AND OTHERS, *CHILD DEVELOPMENT*, V42 N6, PP1767-78, DEC 71

IMPLICATION OF FINDINGS FOR DESIGNING AN INTRODUCTORY MATHEMATICS CURRICULUM ARE DISCUSSED. (AUTHORS)

EJ 056 711 PS 501 796
TEACHING MULTIPLE CLASSIFICATION TO YOUNG CHILDREN PARKER, RONALD K.; AND OTHERS, *CHILD DEVELOPMENT,* V42 N6, PP1779-89, DEC 71
PURPOSE OF THE STUDY WAS TO EVALUATE THE EFFECTIVENESS OF A HIERARCHICALLY ARRANGED INSTRUCTIONAL PROGRAM IN MULTIPLE CLASSIFICATION, WHICH REFERS TO THE ABILITY TO DEFINE A CLASS BY TWO OR MORE ATTRIBUTES SIMULTANEOUSLY. (AUTHORS/MB)

EJ 056 712 PS 501 802
USE OF LABELS AND CUES IN CHILDREN'S CONCEPT IDENTIFICATION SCHOLNICK, ELLIN KOFSKY, *CHILD DEVELOPMENT,* V42 N6, PP1849-58, DEC 71
DATA SUGGEST THAT THE EFFECTIVENESS OF VERBALIZATION IN CONCEPT IDENTIFICATION DEPENDS ON THE ASPECT OF THE TASK WHICH IS VERBALIZED. (AUTHOR)

EJ 056 713 PS 501 803
A TRANSFORMATIONAL ANALYSIS OF ORAL SYNTACTIC STRUCTURES OF CHILDREN REPRESENTING VARYING ETHNOLINGUISTIC COMMUNITIES BRAUN, CARL; KLASSEN, BERNARD, *CHILD DEVELOPMENT,* V42 N6, PP1859-71, DEC 71
TO WHAT EXTENT AND IN WHAT SPECIFIC WAYS ETHNIC BACKGROUND, PARTICULARLY BLINGUALISM, RELATE TO LINGUISTIC DEVELOPMENT IS A MATTER OF CONCERN WITH RESPECT TO CURRICULUM DEVELOPMENT AND INSTRUCTION. (AUTHORS/MB)

EJ 056 714 PS 501 804
MATERNAL CONTROL AND OBEDIENCE IN THE TWO-YEAR-OLD MINTON, CHERYL; AND OTHERS, *CHILD DEVELOPMENT,* V42 N6, PP1873-94, DEC 71
MAJOR RESULTS INDICATED THAT (A) MOTHERS WHO HAD NOT ATTENDED COLLEGE WERE MARKEDLY MORE PROHIBITIVE AND INTRUSIVE THAN COLLEGE-EDUCATED MOTHERS; (B) MOTHERS WERE MORE INTRUSIVE WITH SONS THAN WITH DAUGHTERS; AND (C) THE CHILDREN WERE GENERALLY OBEDIENT. (AUTHORS)

EJ 056 715 PS 501 807
CHILDREN'S COMPREHENSION OF RELATIVIZED ENGLISH SENTENCES BROWN, H, DOUGLAS, *CHILD DEVELOPMENT,* V42 N6, PP1923-36, DEC 71
RESULTS IMPLY THAT IN EARLY CHILDHOOD EDUCATION THE LANGUAGE OF TEST INSTRUCTIONS AND READING PROGRAMS COULD BE BETTER GEARED TO THE CHILD'S LINGUISTIC COMPETENCE. (AUTHOR)

EJ 056 716 PS 501 811
VISUAL RESPONSE DECREMENT AS A FUNCTION OF AGE OF HUMAN NEWBORNS FRIEDMAN, STEVEN; CARPENTER, GENEVIEVE C., *CHILD DEVELOPMENT,* V42 N6, PP1967-73, DEC 71
RESULTS SUGGEST THAT THE HUMAN INFANT'S RESPONSE TO VISUAL STIMULATION UNDERGOES CHANGE DURING THE NEONATAL PERIOD. (AUTHORS)

EJ 056 717 PS 501 812
SURFACE STRUCTURE AND THE TOPIC-COMMENT DISTINCTION: A DEVELOPMENTAL STUDY HORNBY, PETER A., *CHILD DEVELOPMENT,* V42 N6, PP1975-88, DEC 71
IN THIS STUDY THE PART OF THE SENTENCE WHICH CONSTITUTES WHAT THE SPEAKER IS TALKING ABOUT IS CALLED THE "TOPIC" OF THE SENTENCE, AND THE REST OF THE SENTENCE IS THE "COMMENT", WHICH PROVIDES NEW INFORMATION ABOUT THE TOPIC. (AUTHOR/MB)

EJ 056 718 PS 501 818
RELATIONSHIP BETWEEN LATERAL PREFERENCE AND SELECTED BEHAVIORAL VARIABLES FOR CHILDREN FAILING ACADEMICALLY SABATINO, DAVID A.; BECKER, JOHN TO., *CHILD DEVELOPMENT,* V42 N6, PP2055-60, DEC 71
FINDINGS SUPPORT THE HYPOTHESIS THAT LATERAL PREFERENCE, PER SE, HAS LITTLE EFFECT ON INFORMATION-PROCESSING BEHAVIORS. (AUTHORS)

EJ 056 719 PS 501 819
MODEL AFFECT AND CHILDREN'S IMITATIVE ALTRUISM BRYAN, JAMES H., *CHILD DEVELOPMENT,* V42 N6, PP2061-5, DEC 71
AN INVESTIGATION OF IMMEDIATE AND DELAYED VICARIOUS REINFORCEMENTS UPON CHILDREN'S IMITATIVE SELF-SACRIFICING BEHAVIOR. (AUTHOR/MB)

EJ 056 720 PS 501 820
STABILITY OF THE ORIENTING REFLEX IN INFANTS TO AUDITORY AND VISUAL STIMULI AS INDEXED BY CARDIAC DECELERATION BROTSKY, S. JOYCE; KAGAN, JEROME, *CHILD DEVELOPMENT,* V42 N6, PP2066-70, DEC 71

EJ 056 721 PS 501 823
BEHAVIOR MODIFICATION IN THE HOME WITH THE MOTHER AS THE EXPERIMENTER: THE EFFECT OF DIFFERENTIAL REINFORCEMENT ON SIBLING NEGATIVE RESPONSE RATES VEENSTRA, MARJORIE SHAFER, *CHILD DEVELOPMENT,* V42 N6, PP2079-83, DEC 71

EJ 056 722 PS 501 827
BEHAVIORAL SLEEP CYCLES IN THE HUMAN NEWBORN ASHTON, R., *CHILD DEVELOPMENT,* V42 N6, PP2098-2100, DEC 71

EJ 056 723 PS 501 828
THE EXPERIMENTAL FACILITATION OF CHILDREN'S COMPREHENSION AND PRODUCTION OF FOUR SYNTACTIC STRUCTURES ELARDO, RICHARD, *CHILD DEVELOPMENT,* V42 N6, PP2101-4, DEC 71
STUDY OFFERS SOME EVIDENCE WHICH BEARS ON THE AMOUNT OF INFLUENCE OF THE ENVIRONMENT UPON LINGUISTIC CAPACITY. (AUTHOR)

EJ 056 724 PS 501 830
THE YOUNG CHILD'S COMPREHENSION OF TIME CONNECTIVES HATCH, EVELYN, *CHILD DEVELOPMENT,* V42 N6, PP2111-3, DEC 71
SUBJECTS RESPONDED MOST ACCURATELY TO SENTENCES REPRESENTING TEMPORAL ORDER AND TO "AND THEN BUT FIRST" COMMANDS THAN TO "BEFORE/AFTER" COMMANDS. (AUTHOR)

EJ 056 725 PS 501 831
SOCIAL CLASS INTELLIGENCE, AND COGNITIVE STYLE IN INFANCY GOLDEN, MARK; BIRNS, BEVERLY, *CHILD DEVELOPMENT,* V42 N6, PP2114-6, DEC 71
AUTHORS CONCLUDE THAT SOCIAL CLASS DIFFERENCES IN INTELLECTUAL DEVELOPMENT OR COGNITIVE STYLE ARE PROBABLY NOT PRESENT DURING THE SENSORIMOTOR PERIOD. (AUTHORS/MB)

EJ 056 726 PS 501 833
EFFECTS OF SOCIOECONOMIC STATUS AND THE VALUE OF A REINFORCER UPON SELF-REINFORCEMENT BY CHILDREN PESKAY, JOEL; MASTERS, JOHN C., *CHILD DEVELOPMENT,* V42 N6, PP2120-3, DEC 71

EJ 056 727 PS 501 855
THE DEVELOPMENT OF COMPETENCE IN AN EXCEPTIONAL LANGUAGE STRUCTURE IN OLDER CHILDREN AND YOUNG ADULTS KRAMER, PAMELA E.; AND OTHERS, *CHILD DEVELOPMENT,* V43 N1, PP121-30, MAR 72
SUBJECTS BETWEEN 8 AND 20 YEARS OF AGE WERE TESTED FOR COMPETENCE ON AN EXCEPTION TO A GRAMMATICAL RULE, THE MINIMAL DISTANCE RULE. (AUTHORS)

EJ 056 728 PS 501 856
EFFECTS OF SOCIAL COMPARISON UPON THE IMITATION OF NEUTRAL AND ALTRUISTIC BEHAVIORS BY YOUNG CHILDREN MASTERS, JOHN C., *CHILD DEVELOPMENT,* V43 N1, PP131-42, MAR 72
THE THEORY OF SOCIAL COMPARISON POSTULATES THAT THE TENDENCY TO COMPARE ONE'S PERFORMANCE TO OTHERS' WILL DECREASE AS A FUNCTION OF THE DISCREPANCY BETWEEN THE QUALITY OF ONE'S OWN PERFORMANCE AND THAT OF THE COMPARISON PERSON. (AUTHOR/MB)

EJ 056 729 PS 501 857
WHITE ADULT BEHAVIOR TOWARD BLACK AND WHITE CHILDREN COATES, BRIAN, *CHILD DEVELOPMENT,* V43 N1, PP143-54, MAR 72
WHITE MALE ADULTS WERE MORE NEGATIVE WITH BLACK CHILDREN THAN WITH WHITE CHILDREN WHEREAS THERE WAS A NONSIGNIFICANT DIFFERENCE BETWEEN THE 2 RACES FOR WHITE FEMALE ADULTS. ON TRAIT RATINGS OF THE CHILDREN FOLLOWING THE TRAINING SESSION, BOTH MALES AND FEMALES RATED BLACK CHILDREN MORE NEGATIVELY THAN WHITE CHILDREN. (AUTHOR/MB)

EJ 056 730 PS 501 864
A DEVELOPMENTAL STUDY OF FREE CLASSIFICATION IN CHILDREN DENNEY, NANCY WADSWORTH, *CHILD DEVELOPMENT,* V43 N1, PP221-32, MAR 72
STUDY CONCERNED WITH THE EFFECTS OF PROCEDURAL DIFFERENCES ON THE CLASSIFICATION OF GEOMETRICAL STIMULI. (AUTHOR)

EJ 056 731 PS 501 865
INFANTS' RESPONSES TO NOVELTY IN FAMILIAR AND UNFAMILIAR SETTINGS PARRY, MEYER H., *CHILD DEVELOPMENT,* V43 N1, PP233-7, MAR 72

EJ 056 732 PS 501 869
EXECUTIVE COMPETENCE AND SPONTANEOUS SOCIAL BEHAVIOR IN ONE-YEAR-OLDS WENAR, CHARLES, *CHILD DEVELOPMENT,* V43 N1, PP256-60, MAR 72
EXECUTIVE COMPETENCE IS DEFINED AS THE CHILD'S ABILITY TO INITIATE AND SUSTAIN LOCOMOTOR, MANIPULATIVE, AND VISUALLY REGARDING ACTIVITIES AT A GIVEN LEVEL OF COMPLEXITY AND INTENSITY, AND WITH A GIVEN DEGREE OF SELF-SUFFICIENCY. (AUTHOR)

EJ 056 733 PS 501 871
THE EFFECT OF A TELEVISION MODEL UPON RULE ADOPTION BEHAVIOR OF CHILDREN STEIN, GERALD M.; BRYAN, JAMES H., *CHILD DEVELOPMENT*, V43 N1, PP268-73, MAR 72
RESULTS INDICATED THAT GIRLS' RULE VIOLATIONS WERE AFFECTED BY THE MODEL'S SKILL LEVEL, AND BY INTERACTION OF THE MODEL'S VERBAL AND BEHAVIORAL EXPRESSIONS RELEVANT TO THOSE RULES. (AUTHORS)

EJ 056 734 PS 501 872
SITUATIONAL EFFECTS ON JUSTIFIABLENESS OF AGGRESSION AT THREE AGE LEVELS SHANTZ, DAVID W.; PENTZ, THOMAS, *CHILD DEVELOPMENT*, V43 N1, PP274-81, MAR 72
STUDY IS AN INITIAL EFFORT AT DETERMINING THE SEQUENCE AND DEVELOPMENTAL LEVEL AT WHICH CHILDREN FIRST USE A VARIETY OF SITUATIONAL VARIABLES IN MAKING DECISIONS CONCERNING THE APPROPRIATENESS OF VARIOUS TYPES OF AGGRESSIVE RESPONSES. (AUTHORS)

EJ 056 762 PS 501 787
CHILD WELFARE: SEARCHING FOR RELEVANT LEARNING ON THE UNDERGRADUATE LEVEL FORTHMAN, ROBERT C., *CHILD WELFARE*, V51 N4, PP231-9, APR 72
ARTICLE DESCRIBES A SPECIAL COURSE DEVELOPED FOR CHILD WELFARE AND CONCLUDES THAT A HEAVY EMPHASIS ON FIELD OBSERVATION PROVED A SUCCESSFUL EDUCATIONAL METHOD. (ML)

EJ 056 860 PS 501 773
ASPEN MORNINGS WITH SYLVIA ASHTON-WARNER WASSERMANN, SELMA, *CHILDHOOD EDUCATION*, V48 N7, PP348-53, APR 72
AUTHOR DESCRIBES A WORKSHOP WHERE SHE EXPERIENCED THE "ORGANIC CURRICULUM" INCLUDING THE "KEY VOCABULARY". (SP)

EJ 056 861 PS 501 777
SYMPOSIUM ON CHILD-OBSERVATION: 1. FILM-MAKING AS AN OBSERVATION TECHNIQUE WINICK, MARIANN PEZZELLA, *CHILDHOOD EDUCATION*, V48 N7, PP365-9, APR 72
A COLLEGE SUPERVISOR DESCRIBES HER OBSERVATIONS IN AN ITALIAN MONTESSORI SCHOOL, WHERE SHE FILMED THE CHILDREN, AND SUGGESTS THAT STUDENT TEACHERS FILM THEIR CLASSES AS AN AID TO OBSERVATION. (SP)

EJ 056 862 PS 501 778
SYMPOSIUM ON CHILD-OBSERVATION: 2. THE TWO-A-DAY OBSERVATION PLAN WILLS, CLARICE, *CHILDHOOD EDUCATION*, V48 N7, PP370-4, APR 72
DESCRIBES AND GIVES EXAMPLES OF PLAN WHEREBY THE TEACHER OBSERVES TWO PUPILS PER DAY, RECORDING THEIR BEHAVIOR AT VARIOUS INTERVALS. (SP)

EJ 056 863 PS 501 783
SCIENCING FOR YOUNG CHILDREN NEUMAN, DONALD, *YOUNG CHILDREN*, V27 N4, PP215-26, APR 72
"SPECIFIC SUGGESTIONS ARE GIVEN FOR ACTIVITIES WHICH WILL INTEREST YOUNG CHILDREN AND HELP THEM DEVELOP IMPORTANT SKILLS BASIC TO INTELLECTUAL DEVELOPMENT. THE EMPHASIS IS ON INVOLVEMENT WITH MATERIALS AS A METHOD OF LEARNING." (EDITOR)

EJ 056 864 PS 501 785
TEACHING RACE RELATIONS IN THE NURSERY SCHOOL KERCKHOFF, RICHARD K.; TRELLA, SHERRY CRANE, *YOUNG CHILDREN*, V27 N4, PP240-8, APR 72
"A REPORT OF SOME SPECIFIC EXPERIMENTAL CURRICULUM APPROACHES DESIGNED TO PROMOTE CONSTRUCTIVE RACIAL ATTITUDES THROUGH A FOCUS ON GENERAL, BROAD PRINCIPLES. THIS PROJECT WAS EVALUATED IN TERMS OF THE CHILDREN'S REACTIONS AND THE ABILITY OF THESE LEARNING EXPERIENCES TO FIT INTO THE NURSERY SCHOOL PROGRAM." (EDITOR)

EJ 056 914 PS 501 867
NEGRO DIALECT AND BINET PERFORMANCE IN SEVERELY DISADVANTAGED BLACK FOUR-YEAR-OLDS QUAY, LORENE C., *CHILD DEVELOPMENT*, V43 N1, PP245-50, MAR 72
FINDINGS, CONFIRMING THE RESULTS OF AN EARLIER STUDY USING A LESS DEPRIVED POPULATION, INDICATED THAT YOUNG BLACK CHILDREN DO NOT BENEFIT FROM HAVING THE BINET ADMINISTERED IN NEGRO DIALECT. (AUTHOR)

EJ 057 016 PS 501 835
COGNITIVE AND AFFECTIVE REACTIONS OF KINDERGARTNERS TO VIDEO DISPLAYS COLTON, FRANK V., *CHILD STUDY JOURNAL*, V2 N2, PP63-6, 72
CHILDREN WERE SHOWN TELEVISION SEQUENCES DEPICTING BLACK AND WHITE CHILDREN "TEACHING" CONCEPTS, TO TEST WHETHER CONCEPTS WOULD BE LEARNED AND WHETHER SOCIAL PREFERENCES WOULD CHANGE; THE CHILDREN LEARNED THE CONCEPTS BUT PREFERRED COMPANIONS OF THEIR OWN COLOR BOTH BEFORE AND AFTER VIEWING. (SP)

EJ 057 017 PS 501 836
CIVIC BOOKS AND CIVIC CULTURE RICCARDS, MICHAEL P., *CHILD STUDY JOURNAL*, V2 N2, PP67-74, 72
A NUMBER OF THIRD-GRADE SOCIAL STUDIES TEXTS WERE ANALYZED WITH REGARD TO SIX CATEGORIES: CIVIC ORIENTATIONS, BENEFITS RECEIVED, VALUE WORDS, SYMBOLIC REFERENCES, AUTHORITY FIGURES AND HERO IMAGES. THE POLITICAL WORLD...PRESENTED IN THESE TEXTBOOKS IS ONE IN WHICH AUTHORITY IS BENEVOLENT AND SOCIAL CONFLICT IS MINIMAL. (AUTHOR)

EJ 057 018 PS 501 929
TEACHER EXPECTANCY AS RELATED TO THE ACADEMIC AND PERSONAL GROWTH OF PRIMARY-AGE CHILDREN FLEMING, ELYSE S.; ANTTONEN, RALPH G., *MONOGRAPHS OF THE SOCIETY FOR RESEARCH IN CHILD DEVELOPMENT*, V36 N5, PP1-31, DEC 71
THE GENERALIZED SELF-FULFILLING PROPHECY PHENOMENON FAILED TO BE SUPPORTED IN THIS STUDY, BUT THE SIGNIFICANT DIFFERENCES RELATED TO THE TEACHER-OPINION DIMENSION UNDERSCORE THE COMPLEXITY OF TEACHER-PUPIL INTERACTION. (AUTHORS/MB)

EJ 057 116 PS 501 922
HABITUATION AND RECOVERY OF VISUAL RESPONSE IN THE ALERT HUMAN NEWBORN FRIEDMAN, STEVEN, *JOURNAL OF EXPERIMENTAL CHILD PSYCHOLOGY*, V13 N2, PP339-49, APR 72
SOME INFANTS, SOON AFTER BIRTH, ARE CAPABLE OF STORING VISUAL INFORMATION AS REFLECTED IN THEIR ABILITY TO DETECT AND RESPOND TO CHANGE IN THE IMMEDIATE ENVIRONMENT. (AUTHOR)

EJ 057 133 PS 501 888
EFFECTS OF SEX AND BIRTH ORDER ON SEX-ROLE DEVELOPMENT AND INTELLIGENCE AMONG KINDERGARTEN CHILDREN LAOSA, LUIS M.; BROPHY, JERE E., *DEVELOPMENTAL PSYCHOLOGY*, V6 N3, PP409-15, MAY 72

EJ 057 326 PS 501 841
LEARNING FROM LOOKING WITHIN: A DIFFERENT FOCUS, RELATING AND RESPONDING THROUGH THE ARTS FLEMING, ROBERT S., *CHILDHOOD EDUCATION*, V48 N8, PP394-9, MAY 72
THIS REFORM-PROPOSAL COMES NOT SO MUCH FROM CHANGES IN STAFFING OR IN ORGANIZATION OR IN NEW CURRICULUM GUIDES, AS IT DOES FROM DEEP COMMITMENTS AND STRONG BELIEFS. (AUTHOR)

EJ 057 327 PS 501 910
LEARNING FROM THE BRITISH PRIMARY SCHOOLS HEYMAN, MARK, *ELEMENTARY SCHOOL JOURNAL*, V72 N7, PP335-42, APR 72
CONCLUSION DRAWN FROM THIS ANALYSIS IS THAT IT IS NECESSARY TO PAY MORE ATTENTION TO CULTURAL BACKGROUND AND SOCIAL ENVIRONMENT OF SCHOOLS, NOT SIMPLY THE OPEN CLASSROOM. (MB)

EJ 057 441 PS 501 843
REPORT CARDS FOR TEACHERS HUNTER, ELIZABETH, *CHILDHOOD EDUCATION*, V48 N8, PP410-1, MAY 72
AN EVALUATION FORM IS GIVEN FOR TEACHERS TO TUNE IN TO WHAT THEIR STUDENTS THINK AND FEEL ABOUT THEIR CLASSROOM LIVES. (AUTHOR/MB)

EJ 057 442 PS 501 908
A DEVELOPMENTAL LEARNING APPROACH TO INFANT CARE IN A GROUP SETTING FOWLER, WILLIAM, *MERRILL-PALMER QUARTERLY*, V18 N2, PP145-75, APR 72
OBJECTIVES OF THE INVESTIGATION WERE: (A) TO PROBE THE SIGNIFICANCE OF EARLY EXPERIENCE AS A FOUNDATION PERIOD FOR DEVELOPMENTAL LEARNING, THROUGH (B) ESTABLISHING A QUALITY PROGRAM OF GROUP DAY CARE AND EDUCATION FOR INFANTS. (AUTHOR)

EJ 057 475 PS 501 840
DELINQUENCY PREDICTION SCALES AND PERSONALITY INVENTORIES FOLLMAN, JOHN; AND OTHERS, *CHILD STUDY JOURNAL*, V2 N2, PP99-103, 72
STUDY OF 18-21 YEAR OLD MEN IN A REFORMATORY INDICATED BOTH DELINQUENCY PREDICTION SCALES GENERALLY CORRELATED LOW WITH MOST OF THE PERSONALITY INVENTORY SCALES; SCALE SCORES OF BOTH INVENTORIES WERE GENERALLY ELEVATED. (AUTHOR)

EJ 057 476 PS 501 891
A SOCIAL COMPETENCE SCALE AND SYMPTOM CHECKIST FOR THE PRESCHOOL CHILD: FACTOR DIMENSIONS, THEIR CROSS-INSTRUMENT GENERALITY, AND LONGITUDINAL PERSISTENCE KOHN, MARTIN; ROSMAN, BERNICE L., *DEVELOPMENTAL PSYCHOLOGY*, V6 N3, PP430-44, MAY 72
PURPOSE OF THE PRESENT STUDY WAS THE DEVELOPMENT OF TWO RESEARCH INSTRUMENTS DESIGNED TO ASSESS YOUNG CHILDREN'S FUNCTIONING IN PRESCHOOL SETTINGS. (AUTHORS)

EJ 057 584 PS 501 928
LEARNING DISORDERS IN CHILDREN: SIBLING STUDIES OWEN, FREYA WEAVER; AND OTHERS, *MONOGRAPHS OF THE SOCIETY FOR RESEARCH IN CHILD DEVELOPMENT*, V36 N4, PP1-74, NOV 71
PURPOSE OF THE STUDY WAS TO DISCOVER WHETHER THE CHARACTERISTICS OF ACADEMICALLY HANDICAPPED CHILDREN COULD BE MORE PRECISELY IDENTIFIED AND DESCRIBED, AND TO CLARIFY FURTHER THE CAUSES AND THE FAMILIAL PATTERNS OF LEARNING DISABILITIES. (AUTHORS/MB)

EJ 057 733 PS 501 911
DESIGNING INSTRUCTIONAL SETTINGS FOR CHILDREN LABELED "RETARDED": SOME REFLECTIONS BAUER, DAVID H.; YAMAMOTO, KAORU, *ELEMENTARY SCHOOL JOURNAL*, V72 N7, PP343-50, APR 72
BEFORE TRYING TO DESIGN ENVIRONMENTS FOR LEARNING, TEACHERS OUGHT TO EXAMINE THE FORCES IN THE SOCIAL AND THE INDIVIDUAL LIVES OF CHILDREN THAT INFLUENCE THE INSTRUCTIONAL PROCESS. (AUTHORS)

EJ 057 895 PS 501 839
RETROACTIVE AND PROACTIVE MULTIPLE LIST INTERFERENCE WITH DISADVANTAGED CHILDREN WALLS, RICHARD T.; KALBAUGH, JANET COX, *CHILD STUDY JOURNAL*, V2 N2, PP91-7, 72
RESULTS OF A STUDY INVOLVING 60 HEADSTART CHILDREN AND PAIRED ASSOCIATE LISTS; THE RELATIONSHIP BETWEEN RI AND PI IS AS WOULD BE PREDICTED UNDER THESE CONDITIONS WITH CHILDREN. (AUTHOR/SP)

EJ 057 896 PS 501 884
VERBAL AND NONVERBAL REWARDS AND PUNISHMENT IN THE DISCRIMINATION LEARNING OF CHILDREN OF VARYING SOCIOECONOMIC STATUS SPENCE, JANET TAYLOR, *DEVELOPMENTAL PSYCHOLOGY*, V6 N3, PP381-4, MAY 72

EJ 057 897 PS 501 885
EVOLUTION OF THE HUMAN FIGURE IN A THREE-DIMENSIONAL MEDIUM GOLOMB, CLAIRE, *DEVELOPMENTAL PSYCHOLOGY*, V6 N3, PP385-91, MAY 72
STUDY ANALYZES FIGURES CHILDREN MAKE WITH PLAYDOUGH, A DIFFERENT MEDIUM THAT PROVIDES EVIDENCE RELATED TO TWO OPPOSING THEORIES OF THE DEVELOPMENT OF REPRESENTATION. (AUTHOR)

EJ 057 898 PS 501 886
MODELING BY EXEMPLIFICATION AND INSTRUCTION IN TRAINING CONSERVATION ROSENTHAL, TED L.; ZIMMERMAN, BARRY J., *DEVELOPMENTAL PSYCHOLOGY*, V6 N3, PP392-401, MAY 72
FOUR EXPERIMENTS ARE DESCRIBED IN WHICH OBSERVATIONAL LEARNING WAS FOUND ON MULTIDIMENSIONAL CONSERVATION TASKS. (MB)

EJ 057 899 PS 501 890
REINSTATEMENT EFFECTS IN CHILDREN HOVING, KENNETH L.; AND OTHERS, *DEVELOPMENTAL PSYCHOLOGY*, V6 N3, PP426-9, MAY 72
AIM OF THIS EXPERIMENT WAS TO DETERMINE WHETHER THE INCREASED RETENTION OF EARLY LEARNED BEHAVIOR IN ANIMALS MIGHT ALSO BE OPERABLE IN CHILDREN. (AUTHORS/MB)

EJ 057 900 PS 501 897
INTERMODAL AND INTRAMODAL RETENTION OF VISUAL AND TACTUAL INFORMATION IN YOUNG CHILDREN ROSE, SUSAN A.; AND OTHERS, *DEVELOPMENTAL PSYCHOLOGY*, V6 N3, PP482-6, MAY 72
IT WAS CONCLUDED THAT THE YOUNG CHILD'S DIFFICULTY IN RETAINING TACTUAL INFORMATION IS PROBABLY ONE OF THE MAJOR DETERMINANTS OF HIS ESTABLISHED DIFFICULTY IN INTERSENSORY INTEGRATION. (AUTHORS)

EJ 057 901 PS 501 901
IDENTITY AND EQUIVALENCE CONSERVATION AT TWO AGE LEVELS ELKIND, DAVID; SCHOENFELD, EVA, *DEVELOPMENTAL PSYCHOLOGY*, V6 N3, PP529-33, MAY 72
RESULTS CONFIRM THE HYPOTHESIS THAT IDENTITY AND EQUIVALENCE CONSERVATION REQUIRE DIFFERENT MENTAL PROCESSES. (AUTHORS/MB)

EJ 057 902 PS 501 902
PERSEVERATION AND ALTERNATION PRETRAINING AND BINARY PREDICTION MYERS, NANCY ANGRIST, *DEVELOPMENTAL PSYCHOLOGY*, V6 N3, PP534-5, MAY 72
A STUDY OF PROBABILITY LEARNING USING A NONCONTINGENT BINARY PREDICTION SITUATION TO EVALUATE THE EFFECT OF PRETRAINING REINFORCEMENT SCHEDULE. (AUTHOR/MB)

EJ 057 903 PS 501 916
INITIAL PROBABILITY REHEARSAL, AND CONSTRAINT IN ASSOCIATIVE CLASS SELECTION ROSENTHAL, TED L.; WHITE, GLENN M., *JOURNAL OF EXPERIMENTAL CHILD PSYCHOLOGY*, V13 N2, PP261-74, APR 72
EXTENSIVE, YET SELECTIVE, CHANGES IN WORD ASSOCIATE CHOICES WERE OBTAINED WITH THE PROCEDURES PRESENTLY STUDIED; SUGGESTING THAT SIMPLE "NONVERBAL," RESPONSE FORMATS MAY FACILITATE INVESTIGATION OF COGNITIVE AND SOCIAL BEHAVIOR IN YOUNG CHILDREN. (AUTHORS)

EJ 057 904 PS 501 920
IMAGERY AND MULTIPLE-LIST PAIRED ASSOCIATE LEARNING IN YOUNG CHILDREN REESE, HAYNE W., *JOURNAL OF EXPERIMENTAL CHILD PSYCHOLOGY*, V13 N2, PP310-23, APR 72
RESULTS SHOW THAT THE MOST EFFICIENT WAY TO LEARN A SERIES OF LISTS IS TO FORM A NEW INTERACTIVE IMAGE FOR EACH NEW RESPONSE TO A GIVEN STIMULUS, BUT THE MOST EFFICIENT WAY TO RETAIN THE LISTS IS TO REPEAT THE PREVIOUS RESPONSE ITEMS WHILE EACH NEW LIST IS BEING LEARNED. (AUTHOR)

EJ 057 905 PS 501 921
DEVELOPMENTAL AND EXPERIMENTAL FACTORS ASSOCIATED WITH INFERENTIAL BEHAVIOR DAEHLER, MARVIN W., *JOURNAL OF EXPERIMENTAL CHILD PSYCHOLOGY*, V13 N2, PP324-38, APR 72
RESULTS OF THESE EXPERIMENTS INDICATE THAT THE ABILITY TO DEAL WITH POSITIVE AND NEGATIVE INSTANCES IS NOT ONLY CONTINGENT UPON DEVELOPMENTAL LEVEL, BUT ALSO UPON THE DIMENSIONAL CHARACTERISTICS OF THE STIMULI. (AUTHOR)

EJ 057 906 PS 501 923
TRANSFER BETWEEN THE ODDITY AND RELATIVE SIZE CONCEPTS: REVERSAL AND EXTRADIMENSIONAL SHIFTS BROWN, ANN L.; SCOTT, MARCIA S., *JOURNAL OF EXPERIMENTAL CHILD PSYCHOLOGY*, V13 N2, PP350-67, APR 72
THE ABILITY OF CHILDREN OF 3-5 YEARS TO ACQUIRE MEDIATED SOLUTIONS TO CONCEPTUAL PROBLEMS AND TO EXECUTE RAPID REVERSAL SHIFTS WITHIN THESE CONCEPTS SUGGESTS THAT THEIR PROBLEM SOLVING CAPACITY IS NOT NECESSARILY LIMITED TO SIMPLE ASSOCIATIVE RESPONSES. (AUTHORS)

EJ 057 907 PS 501 924
QUANTITATIVE AND QUALITATIVE ASPECTS OF MEMORY FOR PICTURE STIMULI DAVIES, GRAHAM M., *JOURNAL OF EXPERIMENTAL CHILD PSYCHOLOGY*, V13 N2, PP382-93, APR 72
IMPLICATIONS OF THE FINDINGS FOR SUPPORT OF TRACE MODALITY HYPOTHESES ARE DISCUSSED. (MB)

EJ 057 908 PS 501 925
INSTABILITY OF DIMENSIONAL PREFERENCE FOLLOWING CHANGES IN RELATIVE CUE SIMILARITY SMILEY, SANDRA S., *JOURNAL OF EXPERIMENTAL CHILD PSYCHOLOGY*, V13 N2, PP394-403, APR 72
COLOR AND FORM PREFERENCES OF KINDERGARTEN, FIRST AND THIRD GRADE SS WERE TESTED USING STANDARD TWO-DIMENSIONAL GEOMETRIC FORMS. (AUTHOR)

EJ 057 909 PS 501 926
GENERALIZATION AS A FUNCTION OF THE RANGE OF TEST STIMULI: THE ROLES OF DISCRIMINABILITY AND RESPONSE BIAS CROLL, WILLIAM L., *JOURNAL OF EXPERIMENTAL CHILD PSYCHOLOGY*, V13 N2, PP404-12, APR 72
ANALYSES INDICATED THAT VARYING THE RANGE OF TEST STIMULI CHANGES THE DISCRIMINABILITY OF THE STIMULI WITHIN THAT RANGE, EVEN THOUGH THE PHYSICAL DIFFERENCES AMONG THESE STIMULI REMAIN CONSTANT. (AUTHOR)

EJ 057 910 PS 501 927
GRADE INTERACTION WITH WORDS AND PICTURES IN A PAIRED-ASSOCIATE TASK: A PROPOSED EXPLANATION LYNCH, STEVE; ROHWER, WILLIAM D., JR., *JOURNAL OF EXPERIMENTAL CHILD PSYCHOLOGY*, V13 N2, PP413-21, APR 72
EXPERIMENT WAS DESIGNED TO TEST THE EXPLANATION OF THE DEVELOPMENTAL INTERACTION SEPARATELY FOR THE ITEM LEARNING AND ASSOCIATIVE LEARNING COMPONENTS. (AUTHOR)

EJ 058 054 PS 501 845
LOOKING BACK WITH APPRECIATION ELSTER, RUTH, *CHILDHOOD EDUCATION*, V48 N8, PP416-20, MAY 72
AUTHOR, A RETIRED TEACHER, LOOKS BACK ON HER TEACHING CAREER. (MB)

EJ 058 055 PS 501 878
HELPING PARENTS TO HELP THEIR CHILDREN IN PLACEMENT WILLIAMS, CAROL J., *CHILD WELFARE*, V51 N5, PP297-303, MAY 72
DESCRIBES THE MERRIFIELD PROGRAM OF THE WORCESTER CHILDREN'S FRIEND SOCIETY WHICH WAS DESIGNED TO MEET THE NEEDS OF A SMALL NUMBER OF EMOTIONALLY DISTURBED, SCHOOL-AGE CHILDREN UNTREATABLE WHILE LIVING IN THEIR OWN HOMES. (AUTHOR/MB)

EJ 058 132 PS 501 834
THE EFFECTS OF THE DUSO GUIDANCE PROGRAM ON THE SELF-CONCEPTS OF PRIMARY SCHOOL CHILDREN HALES, LOYDE W.; KOVAL, CALISTA B., *CHILD STUDY JOURNAL,* V2 N2, PP57-61, 72
CHILDREN WHO PARTICIPATED IN THE DUSO PROGRAM FELT MORE CAPABLE OF DOING THINGS INDEPENDENTLY OF OTHERS, MORE CAPABLE OF DIRECTING THEIR OWN ACTIVITIES, AND GREATER ACCEPTANCE BY OTHERS. (AUTHOR)

EJ 058 133 PS 501 842
STOP, LOOK, LISTEN -- AND KEEP ON!! CORNELIUS, RUTH, *CHILDHOOD EDUCATION,* V48 N8, PP400-9, MAY 72
BY LISTENING TO THE VERY YOUNG, TO YOUTH, TO OTHERS IN OUR LIVES, WE CAN ENCOURAGE THEM AND OURSELVES TO MOVE LIKE BEAUTIFUL PEOPLE. (AUTHOR)

EJ 058 134 PS 501 844
LOOKING IN -- TO SELF DISCOVERY TWINING, GERALDINE, *CHILDHOOD EDUCATION,* V48 N8, PP412-5, MAY 72
"LOOKING IN" SHOWS US HOW WE CAN GROW ALONG WITH THE CHILDREN WHEN EVERYBODY SHARES IN THE LEARNING PROCESS. (AUTHOR)

EJ 058 135 PS 501 877
RESIDENTIAL TREATMENT OF EMOTIONALLY DISTURBED CHILDREN IN NORWAY ZIEGLER, STAN, *CHILD WELFARE,* V51 N5, PP290-6, MAY 72
MILIEU THERAPY IS CENTRAL TO RESIDENTIAL TREATMENT OF EMOTIONALLY DISTURBED CHILDREN IN NORWAY. THE TREND IS AWAY FROM THE AMERICAN EMPHASIS ON INDIVIDUAL PSYCHOTHERAPY AS A MAJOR TREATMENT COMPONENT. (EDITOR)

EJ 058 136 PS 501 882
CROSS-SEX IDENTITY IN BARBADOS BURTON, ROGER V., *DEVELOPMENTAL PSYCHOLOGY,* V6 N3, PP365-74, MAY 72
EVIDENCE SUGGESTS THAT BOTH CONFLICT OF CROSS-SEX IDENTITY AND CONSISTENCY OF FEMININE IDENTIFICATION OCCUR IN FATHER ABSENT MALES IN CARIBBEAN CULTURE. (AUTHOR)

EJ 058 137 PS 501 883
DEVELOPMENT OF DIRECTIONALITY IN CHILDREN: AGES SIX THROUGH TWELVE LONG, ATAN B.; LOOFT, WILLIAM R., *DEVELOPMENTAL PSYCHOLOGY,* V6 N3, PP375-80, MAY 72
TEST PERFORMANCE ACROSS AGE GROUPS FOLLOWED A HIGHLY SIGNIFICANT LINEAR TREND. (AUTHORS)

EJ 058 138 PS 501 892
RELATIONSHIP OF PRESCHOOL SOCIAL-EMOTIONAL FUNCTIONING TO LATER INTELLECTUAL ACHIEVEMENT KOHN, MARTIN; ROSMAN, BERNICE, *DEVELOPMENTAL PSYCHOLOGY,* V6 N3, PP445-52, MAY 72
FINDINGS SUGGEST THAT THE CHILD WHO IS CURIOUS, ALERT, AND ASSERTIVE WILL LEARN MORE FROM HIS ENVIRONMENT AND THAT THE CHILD WHO IS PASSIVE, APATHETIC, AND WITHDRAWN WILL LEARN LESS ABOUT HIS ENVIRONMENT BECAUSE OF HIS DIMINISHED CONTACT. (AUTHORS)

EJ 058 139 PS 501 893
EFFECTS OF VICARIOUS CONSEQUENCES AND RACE OF MODEL UPON IMITATIVE PERFORMANCE BY BLACK CHILDREN LIEBERT, ROBERT M.; AND OTHERS, *DEVELOPMENTAL PSYCHOLOGY,* V6 N3, PP453-6, MAY 72
IN THIS STUDY BLACK CHILDREN WERE MORE LIKELY TO MATCH THE RESPONSES OF WHITE MODELS THAN OF BLACK ONES. (AUTHORS/MB)

EJ 058 140 PS 501 894
EXTENSION OF PERSONAL FUTURE TIME PERSPECTIVE, AGE, AND LIFE-SATISFACTION OF CHILDREN AND ADOLESCENTS LESSING, ELISE E., *DEVELOPMENTAL PSYCHOLOGY,* V6 N3, PP457-68, MAY 72
FUTURE TIME PERSPECTIVE IS DEFINED AS THE FORWARD EXPANSE OF TIME OVER WHICH FUTURE IMAGES OF THE SELF ARE PROJECTED. (AUTHOR/MB)

EJ 058 141 PS 501 898
EGO IDENTITY STATUS AND MORALITY: THE RELATIONSHIP BETWEEN TWO DEVELOPMENTAL CONSTRUCTS PODD, MARVIN H., *DEVELOPMENTAL PSYCHOLOGY,* V6 N3, PP497-507, MAY 72
RESULTS OF THE STUDY GENERALLY SUPPORT THE POSITION THAT MORAL IDEOLOGY IS RELATED TO IDENTITY STATUS. (AUTHORS)

EJ 058 142 PS 501 899
AN APPLICATION OF BRUNSWIK'S LENS MODEL TO DEVELOPMENTAL CHANGES IN PROBABILITY LEARNING DEFFENBACHER, KENNETH; HAMM, NORMAN H., *DEVELOPMENTAL PSYCHOLOGY,* V6 N3, PP508-19, MAY 72

EJ 058 143 PS 501 900
ACHIEVEMENT MOTIVATION AND FEAR OF FAILURE IN FAMILY AND SCHOOL HERMANS, HUBERT J. M.; AND OTHERS, *DEVELOPMENTAL PSYCHOLOGY,* V6 N3, PP520-8, MAY 72
RESULTS INDICATE THAT THE ACHIEVEMENT MOTIVATION AND THE DEBILITATING ANXIETY OF THE CHILD MANIFEST THEMSELVES IN THE SOCIAL INTERACTION PATTERNS BOTH WITHIN THE FAMILY AND WITHIN THE CLASSROOM. (AUTHORS)

EJ 058 144 PS 501 915
SOCIAL REINFORCEMENT SATIATION: AN OUTCOME OF FREQUENCY OR AMBIGUITY? WARREN, VERA L.; CAIRNS, ROBERT B., *JOURNAL OF EXPERIMENTAL CHILD PSYCHOLOGY,* V13 N2, PP249-60, APR 72
THE TASK FOR THE RESEARCH REPORTED IN THIS PAPER WAS TO CLARIFY THE CONDITIONS THAT ARE RESPONSIBLE FOR THE DIMINISHED EFFECTIVENESS OF SOCIAL APPROVAL FOLLOWING PRE-EXPOSURE. (AUTHORS)

EJ 058 145 PS 501 917
DEVELOPMENTAL CHANGES IN CLUSTERING CRITERIA DENNEY, NANCY WADSWORTH; ZIOBROWSKI, MARTIN, *JOURNAL OF EXPERIMENTAL CHILD PSYCHOLOGY,* V13 N2, PP275-82, APR 72
STUDY SUGGESTS THAT, RATHER THAN BEING LESS ABLE TO ORGANIZE INFORMATION, YOUNG CHILDREN SIMPLY ORGANIZE ACCORDING TO DIFFERENT CRITERIA THAN ADULTS. (AUTHORS)

EJ 058 146 PS 501 918
PSYCHOPHYSICALLY SCALED CUE DIFFERENCES, LEARNING RATE, AND ATTENTIONAL STRATEGIES IN A TACTILE DISCRIMINATION TASK BROWN, ANN L.; AND OTHERS, *JOURNAL OF EXPERIMENTAL CHILD PSYCHOLOGY,* V13 N2, PP283-302, APR 72
A SERIES OF THREE EXPERIMENTS WITH NURSERY SCHOOL CHILDREN IS REPORTED USING TEXTURE CUES TO INVESTIGATE THE RELATIONSHIP BETWEEN CUE DIFFERENCES AND LEARNING RATE. (AUTHORS/MB)

EJ 058 171 PS 501 913
THE SUGAR-COATED WORLD OF THE THIRD-GRADE READER D'HEURLE, ADMA; AND OTHERS, *ELEMENTARY SCHOOL JOURNAL,* V72 N7, PP362-71, APR 72
A CRITICAL ANALYSIS OF CURRENT READING TEXTBOOKS. (MB)

EJ 058 212 PS 501 838
CREATIVITY: IDEA QUANTITY AND IDEA QUALITY ROWETON, WILLIAM E., *CHILD STUDY JOURNAL,* V2 N2, PP83-9, 72
STUDY SHOWED THAT CREATIVITY WAS NOT HIGHLY INFLUENCED BY PERCEPTUAL SENSITIVITY OR ACADEMIC ACHIEVEMENT; VERBAL PRETRAINING FACILITATED IDEA FLUENCY BUT NOT ORIGINALITY. (AUTHOR/SP)

EJ 058 213 PS 501 881
PROJECT PLAYPEN -- PRIMARY PREVENTION FINCK, GEORGE H.; AND OTHERS, *CHILD WELFARE,* V51 N5, PP318-26, MAY 72
A PILOT PROJECT OF SUBSIDIZED FAMILY DAY CARE, DESIGNED FOR LOW-INCOME WORKING MOTHERS AND AIMED AT FOSTERING A CHILD'S DEVELOPMENTAL NEEDS, TURNED OUT TO BE A COMPREHENSIVE SERVICE THAT ALSO ALTERED ATTITUDES OF MIDDLE-CLASS VOLUNTEERS. (EDITOR)

EJ 058 214 PS 501 887
INFLUENCE OF MODELING, EXHORTATIVE VERBALIZATION, AND SURVEILLANCE ON CHILDREN'S SHARING POULOS, RITA W.; LIEBERT, ROBERT M., *DEVELOPMENTAL PSYCHOLOGY,* V6 N3, PP402-8, MAY 72

EJ 058 215 PS 501 889
PROBLEMS OF CONTROL IN SIMULTANEOUS DISCRIMINATION TASKS MOODY, MARK; GOLLIN, EUGENE S., *DEVELOPMENTAL PSYCHOLOGY,* V6 N3, PP416-25, MAY 72
ARTICLE ATTEMPTS TO PROVIDE GUIDELINES FOR A SYSTEMATIC APPROACH IN DEALING WITH POSITION BIASES IN ORDER TO IMPROVE THE ADEQUACY OF DECISIONS ABOUT HYPOTHETICAL STATEMENTS. (MB)

EJ 058 216 PS 501 895
SOME IMMEDIATE EFFECTS OF TELEVISED VIOLENCE ON CHILDREN'S BEHAVIOR LIEBERT, ROBERT M.; BARON, ROBERT A., *DEVELOPMENTAL PSYCHOLOGY,* V6 N3, PP469-75, MAY 72
RESULTS INDICATED THAT CHILDREN EXPOSED TO THE AGGRESSIVE PROGRAM ENGAGED IN LONGER ATTACKS AGAINST AN OSTENSIBLE CHILD VICTIM THAN SUBJECTS EXPOSED TO THE NONAGGRESSIVE PROGRAM. (AUTHORS)

EJ 058 217 PS 501 896
MALE AND FEMALE AUDITORY REINFORCEMENT OF INFANT VOCALIZATIONS BANIKIOTES, FLORENCE G.; AND OTHERS, *DEVELOPMENTAL PSYCHOLOGY,* V6 N3, PP476-81, MAY 72

EJ 058 218 PS 501 903
A DEVELOPMENTAL INVESTIGATION OF TELEVISED MODELED VERBALIZATIONS ON RESISTANCE TO DEVIATION WOLF, THOMAS M., *DEVELOPMENTAL PSYCHOLOGY*, V6 N3, PP537, MAY 72
IN THIS STUDY BOYS WERE EXPOSED TO A TELEVISED VERBAL PEER MODEL WHO CONFORMED TO OR DEVIATED FROM A PROHIBITION RULE. (AUTHOR)

EJ 058 219 PS 501 904
NONSOCIAL REINFORCEMENT OF INFANTS' VOCALIZATIONS RAMEY, CRAIN T.; WATSON, JOHN S., *DEVELOPMENTAL PSYCHOLOGY*, V6 N3, PP538, MAY 72
FINDINGS INDICATE THAT INFANT BOYS MAY BE MORE EASILY CONDITIONED BY VISUAL REINFORCEMENT THAN ARE GIRLS. (AUTHOR/MB)

EJ 058 220 PS 501 905
STATE AS VARIABLE, AS OBSTACLE, AND AS MEDIATOR OF STIMULATION IN INFANT RESEARCH KORNER, ANNELIESE F., *MERRILL-PALMER QUARTERLY*, V18 N2, PP77-94, APR 72
AUTHOR DISCUSSES THE DIFFERENT CONTEXTS IN WHICH THE CONCEPT OF STATE IS USED, DRAWING ON EXAMPLES FROM HER OWN RESEARCH WITH NEWBORNS. (MB)

EJ 058 221 PS 501 906
STATE AS AN INFANT-ENVIRONMENT INTERACTION: AN ANALYSIS OF MOTHER-INFANT INTERACTIONS AS A FUNCTION OF SEX LEWIS, MICHAEL, *MERRILL-PALMER QUARTERLY*, V18 N2, PP95-122, APR 72

EJ 058 222 PS 501 907
INDIVIDUAL DIFFERENCES IN THE DEVELOPMENT OF SOME ATTACHMENT BEHAVIORS AINSWORTH, MARY D. SALTER; AND OTHERS, *MERRILL-PALMER QUARTERLY*, V18 N2, PP123-5, APR 72

EJ 058 223 PS 501 909
NUTRITION AND BRAIN DEVELOPMENT IN INFANTS COURSIN, DAVID BAIRD, *MERRILL-PALMER QUARTERLY*, V18 N2, PP177-202, APR 72

EJ 058 224 PS 501 919
CHARITY IN CHILDREN: THE INFLUENCE OF "CHARITY" STIMULI AND AN AUDIENCE FOUTS, GREGORY, *JOURNAL OF EXPERIMENTAL CHILD PSYCHOLOGY*, V13 N2, PP303-9, APR 72
MAIN PURPOSE OF THIS STUDY IS TO DEMONSTRATE A CONTROL PROCEDURE WHICH ALLOWS THE RESEARCHER TO INVESTIGATE BEHAVIORS WHICH ARE LAWFULLY RELATED TO CHARITY STIMULI AND ASSESS THE INFLUENCE OF UNCONTROLLED VARIABLES IN CHARITY SITUATIONS. (AUTHOR)

EJ 058 307 PS 501 880
ADOPTION: IDENTIFICATION AND SERVICE O'NEILL, MARY M., *CHILD WELFARE*, V51 N5, PP314-7, MAY 72
COLLABORATION OF A PUBLIC SOCIAL SERVICE DEPARTMENT AND A PUBLIC ADOPTION DEPARTMENT DEMONSTRATED THAT IT WAS POSSIBLE TO FIND PERMANENT ADOPTIVE HOMES FOR MANY CHILDREN WHO WERE IN FOSTER CARE. (EDITOR)

EJ 058 308 PS 501 914
TOWARD A DEMOCRATIC ELEMENTARY-SCHOOL CLASSROOM GUERNEY, BERNARD G.; MERRIAM, MARY-LINDA, *ELEMENTARY SCHOOL JOURNAL*, V72 N7, PP372-83, APR 72
AUTHORS PROPOSE SEVERAL HYPOTHESES THAT CAN BE SCIENTIFICALLY TESTED TO ANSWER THE QUESTION AS TO WHAT BENEFITS MIGHT REASONABLY BE EXPECTED IF CHILDREN ARE TAUGHT IN A SETTING WITH ATTITUDES AND BEHAVIORS CONGRUENT WITH A DEMOCRATIC IDEOLOGY. (AUTHORS/MB)

EJ 058 353 PS 501 837
EFFECTS OF PROVISION FOR INDIVIDUAL DIFFERENCES AND TEACHER ATTENTION UPON STUDY BEHAVIOR AND ASSIGNMENTS COMPLETED STILLWELL, CONNIE; AND OTHERS, *CHILD STUDY JOURNAL*, V2 N2, PP75-81, 72
PRESCRIPTIVE ASSIGNMENTS OF AN APPROPRIATE ACHIEVEMENT LEVEL DURING MATH PERIOD RESULTED IN INCREASED ATTENDING DURING MATH PERIOD AND SLIGHT INCREASES IN COMPLETION OF ALL ACADEMIC ASSIGNMENTS. (RESULTS WERE) MAINTAINED EVEN AFTER EXPERIMENTAL PROCEDURES WERE WITHDRAWN. (AUTHOR)

EJ 058 354 PS 501 879
MODELING AND THE FEARFUL CHILD PATIENT ADELSON, RICHARD; GOLDFRIED, MARVIN R., *CHILD WELFARE*, V51 N5, PP304-9, MAY 72
THIS ARTICLE MAY BE USEFUL TO WORKERS WHO NEED TO HELP YOUNG CHILDREN TO ACCEPT DENTAL CARE. (EDITOR)

EJ 058 395 PS 501 912
A PERCEPTUAL TEST BATTERY: DEVELOPMENT AND STANDARDIZATION TURAIDS, DAINIS; AND OTHERS, *ELEMENTARY SCHOOL JOURNAL*, V72 N7, PP351-61, APR 72
TEST BATTERY WAS DESIGNED TO EXPLORE THE AUDITORY AND THE VISUAL PERCEPTUAL PROCESSING ABILITIES OF CHILDREN FROM FIVE THROUGH EIGHT. (AUTHORS)

EJ 058 411 PS 501 942
LEARNING DISABILITY: A NEW LOOK AT UNDERACHIEVING HARTLAGE, LAWRENCE C., *CHILD STUDY JOURNAL*, V2 N3, PP105-8, 72
"THE ULTIMATE RESPONSIBILITY FOR EDUCATING ALL CHILDREN SHOULD BE RETURNED TO EDUCATORS, BUT TRESSED BY THE SUPPORTIVE DIAGNOSTIC AND REMEDIAL EXPERTISE OF SPECIALISTS IN CHILD PSYCHOLOGY." (AUTHOR)

EJ 058 412 PS 501 955
CREATIVE ABILITY OVER A FIVE-YEAR SPAN KOGAN, NATHAN; PANKOVE, ETHEL, *CHILD DEVELOPMENT*, V43 N2, PP427-42, JUN 72
A POSSIBLE INTERPRETATION OF THE DIFFERENTIAL PREDICTABILITY ACROSS SCHOOL SYSTEMS AS REVEALED IN THIS STUDY, IS OFFERED. (AUTHORS/MB)

EJ 058 413 PS 501 958
TASK ORIENTATION VERSUS SOCIAL ORIENTATION IN YOUNG CHILDREN AND THEIR ATTENTION TO RELEVANT SOCIAL CUES RUBLE, DIANE N.; NAKAMURA, CHARLES Y., *CHILD DEVELOPMENT*, V43 N2, PP471-80, JUN 72
RESULTS SUPPORTED THE EXPECTATIONS REGARDING FIELD DEPENDENCE-INDEPENDENCE BUT FAILED TO SUPPORT THOSE REGARDING SEX DIFFERENCES. (AUTHORS)

EJ 058 414 PS 501 972
THE RELATIONSHIP BETWEEN CHILDREN'S ACADEMIC PERFORMANCE AND ACHIEVEMENT ACCOUNTABILITY CLIFFORD, MARGARET M.; CLEARY, T. ANNE, *CHILD DEVELOPMENT*, V43 N2, PP647-55, JUN 72
PURPOSE OF THE STUDY IS TO EXAMINE RELATIONSHIPS BETWEEN INTERNALITY AND ACHIEVEMENT-RELATED VARIABLES IN A PERFORMANCE SITUATION WHERE STUDENTS DETERMINE THE DIFFICULTY LEVEL AT WHICH THEY DESIRE TO WORK. (AUTHORS)

EJ 058 463 PS 501 930
A GUIDE FOR COLLECTING AND ORGANIZING INFORMATION ON EARLY CHILDHOOD PROGRAMS SMITH, MARILYN; GIESY, ROSEMARY, *YOUNG CHILDREN*, V27 N5, PP264-71, JUN 72
TWO CHARTS ARE GIVEN: ONE TO ASSESS PROGRAM OBJECTIVES; THE OTHER, RESOURCES. (MB)

EJ 058 507 PS 501 936
WINDOW BEGINS WITH AN "L" MCGLATHERY, GLENN, *YOUNG CHILDREN*, V27 N5, PP299-301, JUN 72
BY PUSHING A CHILD TO AN EARLY ACCEPTANCE OF OUR PERCEPTIONS, WE OFTEN FAIL TO LISTEN TO HIM AND UNDERSTAND WHAT HE IS SAYING. (EDITOR)

EJ 058 508 PS 501 967
FAMILY HARMONY: AN ETIOLOGIC FACTOR IN ALIENATION PAULSON, MORRIS J.; AND OTHERS, *CHILD DEVELOPMENT*, V43 N2, PP591-603, JUN 72
RESULTS SUGGEST THAT RECOLLECTIONS OF EARLIER EXPERIENCED PARENTAL ATTITUDES CAN BE RETROSPECTIVE CLUES OF EARLIER PARENT-CHILD INTERACTION ALONG THE ALIENATION DIMENSION OF AN ANTI-ESTABLISHMENT VS. ESTABLISHMENT PHILOSOPHY OF EARLY CHILD REARING. (AUTHORS/MB)

EJ 058 509 PS 501 970
THE DEVELOPMENT OF DEMOCRATIC VALUES AND BEHAVIOR AMONG MEXICAN-AMERICAN CHILDREN SOLOMON, DANIEL; AND OTHERS, *CHILD DEVELOPMENT*, V43 N2, PP625-38, JUN 72
IT IS THE THESIS OF THIS STUDY THAT VALUES WHICH GOVERN POLITICAL BEHAVIOR DEVELOP OUT OF MORE GENERAL VALUES WHICH CAN APPLY TO VIRTUALLY AND KIND OF GROUP INTERACTION. (AUTHORS)

EJ 058 510 PS 501 975
SOME DISCRIMINATIVE PROPERTIES OF RACE AND SEX FOR CHILDREN FROM AN ALL-NEGRO NEIGHBORHOOD DOKE, LARRY A.; RISLEY, TODD R., *CHILD DEVELOPMENT*, V43 N2, PP677-81, JUN 72
STUDY DIRECTED AT DETERMINING WHICH ASPECT OF PHOTOGRAPHIC REPRESENTATIONS OF CHILDREN DIFFERING ALONG DIMENSIONS OF RACE AND SEX WOULD ACQUIRE CONTROL OVER RESPONSES OF NEGRO CHILDREN. (AUTHORS)

EJ 058 585 PS 501 932
CONDITION WITH CAUTION KATZ, LILIAN G., *YOUNG CHILDREN*, V27 N5, PP277-80, JUN 72
AUTHOR DISCUSSES THE APPLICATION OF BEHAVIOR MODIFICATION TECHNIQUES TO CERTAIN DISRUPTIVE BEHAVIORS. (MB)

EJ 058 586 PS 501 937
ATTACHMENT: ITS ORIGINS AND COURSE YARROW, LEON J.; PEDERSON, FRANK A., *YOUNG CHILDREN*, V27 N5, PP302-12, JUN 72

IN THIS PAPER SOME BEHAVIORAL INDICES OF ATTACHMENT ARE DEFINED AND SOME OF THE FACTORS THAT AFFECT ITS DEVELOPMENT ARE CONSIDERED. (EDITOR)

EJ 058 587 PS 501 953
RELATIONSHIPS BETWEEN INFANTS' SOCIAL BEHAVIOR AND THEIR MOTHERS' BEHAVIOR BECKWITH, LEILA, *CHILD DEVELOPMENT*, V43 N2, PP397-411, JUN 72

QUALITATIVELY, THE MORE SUPPRESSIVE AND CRITICAL THE MOTHER, THE LESS RESPONSIVE THE BABY WAS IN SOCIAL PLAY WITH HER. THE MORE THE BABY RESPONDED TO HIS MOTHER, THE LESS HE RESPONDED TO A STRANGER. (AUTHOR)

EJ 058 588 PS 501 956
THE RELATIVE EFFICACY OF CONTACT AND VESTIBULAR-PROPRIOCEPTIVE STIMULATION IN SOOTHING NEONATES KORNER, ANNELIESE F.; THOMAN, EVELYN B., *CHILD DEVELOPMENT*, V43 N2, PP443-53, JUN 72

DATA INDICATE THAT THE INTERVENTIONS PROVIDED DIFFERED IN THEIR EFFECTIVENESS IN CALMING NEWBORNS TO A HIGHLY SIGNIFICANT DEGREE. (AUTHORS)

EJ 058 589 PS 501 961
EVIDENCE FOR THE UNCONDITIONABILITY OF THE BABKIN REFLEX IN NEWBORNS SOSTEK, ANITA M.; AND OTHERS, *CHILD DEVELOPMENT*, V43 N2, PP509-519, JUN 72

THE BABKIN REFLEX IS A REACTION TO THE SIMULTANEOUS PRESSING OF THE PALMS OF THE HANDS OF THE INFANT. (AUTHORS)

EJ 058 590 PS 501 965
EGOCENTRISM AND SOCIAL INFLUENCE IN CHILDREN WEINHEIMER, SIDNEY, *CHILD DEVELOPMENT*, V43 N2, PP567-78, JUN 72

EGOCENTRIC CHILDREN WERE SHOWN TO HAVE INADEQUATE SOCIAL SCHEMA TO UNDERSTAND THE ADULT MEANING OF CONFORMITY AND INDEPENDENCE. (AUTHOR)

EJ 058 594 PS 501 969
A STUDY OF THE RELATIVE DOMINANCE OF VISION AND TOUCH IN SIX-MONTH-OLD INFANTS GRATCH, GERALD, *CHILD DEVELOPMENT*, V43 N2, PP615-23, JUN 72

A SIX-MONTH-OLD INFANT WHO CAN REMOVE A TRANSPARENT CLOTH FROM HIS HAND WHEN IT IS COVERED AFTER HE GRASPS A TOY MAY NOT BE ABLE TO REMOVE AN OPAQUE COVER. ALTERNATIVE INTERPRETATIONS OF THE PHENOMENON, THAT IS, DEGREE OF BIMANUAL COORDINATION AND FOCUS OF ATTENTION, ARE DISCUSSED. (AUTHOR/MB)

EJ 058 606 PS 501 978
TRAINING COMMUNICATION SKILLS IN YOUNG CHILDREN SHANTZ, CAROLYN UHLINGER; WILSON, KARL E., *CHILD DEVELOPMENT*, V43 N2, PP693-8, JUN 72

STUDY IS AN ATTEMPT TO INCREASE COMMUNICATION PROFICIENCY IN YOUNG CHILDREN BY USING TRAINING PROCEDURES WHICH FOCUS PRIMARILY ON MAKING THE LISTENER'S NEEDS MORE SALIENT TO THE CHILD AS HE FORMS AND GIVES MESSAGES. (AUTHORS/MB)

EJ 058 628 PS 501 944
A COMPARATIVE STUDY OF COUNSELEE PREFERENCES FOR BEHAVIORIST AND CLIENT-CENTERED COUNSELING APPROACHES BARABASZ, ARREED F.; AND OTHERS, *CHILD STUDY JOURNAL*, V2 N3, PP117-22, 72

RESULTS OF STUDY SHOWED HIGH SCHOOL STUDENTS PREFERRED BEHAVIORIST RATHER THAN CLIENT-CENTERED COUNSELING; THE FINDINGS ARE OF IMPORTANCE TO HIGH SCHOOL COUNSELORS. (SP)

EJ 058 693 PS 501 950
DEVELOPMENTAL DIFFERENCES IN THE PERCEPTION AND PRODUCTION OF FACIAL EXPRESSIONS ODOM, RICHARD D.; LEMOND, CAROLYN M., *CHILD DEVELOPMENT*, V43 N2, PP359-69, JUN 72

FOR THE AGE RANGE TESTED THERE IS A LAG BETWEEN THE PERCEPTION AND PRODUCTION OF CERTAIN FACIAL EXPRESSIONS. (AUTHORS)

EJ 058 694 PS 501 954
OUTERDIRECTEDNESS AND IMITATIVE BEHAVIOR OF INSTITUTIONALIZED AND NONINSTITUTIONALIZED YOUNGER AND OLDER CHILDREN ZIGLER, EDWARD; YANDO, REGINA, *CHILD DEVELOPMENT*, V43 N2, PP413-25, JUN 72

OUTERDIRECTEDNESS HAS BEEN DEFINED BY FIRST AUTHOR AND HIS COLLEAGUES AS A STYLE OF PROBLEM SOLVING CHARACTERIZED BY RELIANCE ON CONCRETE SITUATIONAL CUES RATHER THAN BY ACTIVE ATTEMPTS TO DEDUCE ABSTRACT RELATIONSHIPS. (AUTHORS/MB)

EJ 058 695 PS 501 957
RELATION OF TYPE AND ONSET OF FATHER ABSENCE TO COGNITIVE DEVELOPMENT SANTROCK, JOHN W., *CHILD DEVELOPMENT*, V43 N2, PP455-69, JUN 72

WHILE FATHER ABSENCE DUE TO DIVORCE, DESERTION, OR SEPARATION HAD THE MOST NEGATIVE INFLUENCE IN THE INITIAL 2 YEARS OF THE CHILD'S LIFE FOR BOYS AND GIRLS, FATHER ABSENCE DUE TO DEATH WAS THE MOST DETRIMENTAL WHEN IT OCCURRED IN THE 6 - 9 PERIOD OF THE BOY'S LIFE. (AUTHOR)

EJ 058 696 PS 501 964
MOTHERS' SPEECH TO CHILDREN LEARNING LANGUAGE SNOW, CATHERINE E., *CHILD DEVELOPMENT*, V43 N2, PP549-65, JUN 72

FINDINGS INDICATE THAT CHILDREN WHO ARE LEARNING LANGUAGE HAVE AVAILABLE A SAMPLE OF SPEECH WHICH IS SIMPLER, MORE REDUNDANT, AND LESS CONFUSING THAN NORMAL ADULT SPEECH. (AUTHOR)

EJ 058 697 PS 501 971
INFANCY AND THE OPTIMAL LEVEL OF STIMULATION GREENBERG, DAVID J.; O'DONNELL, WILLIAM J., *CHILD DEVELOPMENT*, V43 N2, PP639-45, JUN 72

STUDY ATTEMPTED TO DETERMINE THE VIABILITY OF OPTIMAL LEVEL THEORY AS IT PERTAINS TO INFANT PERCEPTUAL AND COGNITIVE DEVELOPMENT. (AUTHORS)

EJ 058 768 PS 501 931
A GLANCE AT A HEAD START PROGRAM IN AN ALASKAN CITY CONNET, MARGARET, *YOUNG CHILDREN*, V27 N5, PP273-6, JUN 72

AN HOUR BY HOUR DESCRIPTION OF CHILDREN'S ACTIVITIES FOR ONE DAY. (MB)

EJ 058 769 PS 501 935
BIG STEPS ON BEHALF OF LITTLE PEOPLE NASH, HARRIETT; TOBIN, MICHAEL F., *YOUNG CHILDREN*, V27 N5, PP289-92, JUN 72

TEACHERS, ADMINISTRATORS, COLLEGE FACULTIES AND A STATE DEPARTMENT OF EDUCATION JOIN TOGETHER IN A UNIQUE AND FORWARD THINKING MOVEMENT TO IMPROVE EARLY CHILDHOOD EDUCATION PROGRAMS WITH SPECIAL FOCUS ON TEACHER EDUCATION. (EDITOR)

EJ 058 859 PS 501 949
ENVIRONMENTAL EFFECTS ON LANGUAGE DEVELOPMENT: A STUDY OF YOUNG CHILDREN IN LONG-STAY RESIDENTIAL NURSERIES TIZARD, BARBARA; AND OTHERS, *CHILD DEVELOPMENT*, V43 N2, PP337-58, JUN 72

SIGNIFICANT CORRELATIONS WERE OBTAINED BETWEEN THE LANGUAGE COMPREHENSION SCORES OF THE CHILDREN AND BOTH THE QUALITY OF THE TASK DIRECTED TO THEM AND THE WAY IN WHICH THE NURSERY WAS ORGANIZED. (AUTHORS)

EJ 058 927 PS 501 960
PREDICTION OF DEVELOPMENTAL OUTCOME AT SEVEN YEARS FROM PRENATAL, PERINATAL, AND POSTNATAL EVENTS SMITH, A. C.; AND OTHERS, *CHILD DEVELOPMENT*, V43 N2, PP495-507, JUN 72

SPECIFIC AIM OF THE STUDY WAS TO DETERMINE THE PREDICTIVE ACCURACY OF SELECTED OBSERVATIONS OBTAINED DURING DEVELOPMENTAL PERIODS ON LATER DEVELOPMENTAL OUTCOME. (AUTHORS)

EJ 058 928 PS 501 962
TESTS BUILT FROM PIAGET'S AND GESELL'S TASKS AS PREDICTORS OF FIRST-GRADE ACHIEVEMENT KAUFMAN, ALAN S.; KAUFMAN, NADEEN L., *CHILD DEVELOPMENT*, V43 N2, PP521-35, JUN 72

RESULTS OFFER EMPIRICAL SUPPORT TO ILG AND AMES'S CLAIM THAT THE GESELL BATTERY IS AN EXCELLENT PREDICTOR OF SCHOOL READINESS. THE CLOSE SIMILARITY OF THE PIAGET AND GESELL TESTS ACCORDS WELL WITH PREVIOUS FINDINGS THAT THE TWO TESTS HAVE MUCH IN COMMON. (AUTHORS/MB)

EJ 058 929 PS 501 966
LOCUS OF CONTROL: AN EXAMPLE OF DANGERS IN USING CHILDREN'S SCALES WITH CHILDREN GORSUCH, RICHARD L.; AND OTHERS, *CHILD DEVELOPMENT*, V43 N2, PP579-90, JUN 72

IN RESEARCH WITH CHILDREN, THERE IS A COMMON PROBLEM WHICH COULD REDUCE THE RELIABILITY OF A QUESTIONNAIRE FOR SOME CHILDREN BUT NOT OTHERS: VERBAL COMPREHENSION. (AUTHORS)

EJ 058 964 PS 501 938
SOS CHILDREN'S VILLAGES THROUGHOUT THE WORLD: SUBSTITUTE OR SUPERIOR SERVICE? DODGE, JAMES, *CHILD WELFARE*, V51 N6, PP344-54, JUN 72

AUTHOR EXAMINES THE QUESTION OF WHETHER CHILDREN'S VILLAGES COULD BE OF GREAT BENEFIT TO THE UNITED STATES. (MB)

EJ 059 313 PS 501 951
THE RELATIONSHIP BETWEEN LIQUID CONSERVATION AND COMPENSATION GELMAN, ROCHEL; WEINBERG, DENISE HOOTSTEIN, *CHILD DEVELOPMENT,* V43 N2, PP371-83, JUN 72
COMPENSATION AS ASSESSED BY ANY ONE TEST OR CRITERION USED IS MORE DIFFICULT THAN CONSERVATION. AND, THE UNDERSTANDING OF THE COMPENSATION PRINCIPLE, AS MANIFESTED IN VERBAL STATEMENTS, CONTINUES TO DEVELOP WELL AFTER THE AGE AT WHICH LIQUID CONSERVATION MAY BE TAKEN FOR GRANTED. (AUTHORS)

EJ 059 314 PS 501 952
VIOLATION OF A RULE AS A METHOD OF DIAGNOSING INFANTS' LEVELS OF OBJECT CONCEPT LECOMPTE, GUNEY K.; GRATCH, GERALD, *CHILD DEVELOPMENT,* V43 N2, PP385-96, JUN 72
DEVELOPMENT OF OBJECT IDENTITY WAS STUDIED WITHIN THE FRAMEWORK OF A HIDING GAME THAT VARIED THE OBJECTS THEMSELVES INSTEAD OF THEIR SPATIAL POSITIONS. (AUTHORS)

EJ 059 315 PS 501 963
THE ROLE OF OVERT ACTIVITY IN CHILDREN'S IMAGERY PRODUCTION WOLFF, PETER; LEVIN, JOEL R., *CHILD DEVELOPMENT,* V43 N2, PP537-47, JUN 72
THE ROLE OF MOTOR ACTIVITY IN CHILDREN'S FORMATION OF DYNAMIC MENTAL IMAGERY WAS INVESTIGATED IN 2 EXPERIMENTS USING A PAIRED-ASSOCIATE RECOGNITION TASK. (AUTHORS)

EJ 059 316 PS 501 968
OBSERVATION, REPETITION, AND ETHNIC BACKGROUND IN CONCEPT ATTAINMENT AND GENERALIZATION ZIMMERMAN, BARRY J.; ROSENTHAL, TED L., *CHILD DEVELOPMENT,* V43 N2, PP605-13, JUN 72
ATTAINING AND GENERALIZING A NEW CONCEPT WERE STUDIED IN MEXICAN- AND ANGLO-AMERICAN FIFTH GRADERS. BOTH MODELING AND REPETITION IMPROVED PERFORMANCE. (AUTHORS/MB)

EJ 059 317 PS 501 974
INCENTIVE EFFECTS IN CHILDREN'S CREATIVITY WARD, WILLIAM C.; AND OTHERS, *CHILD DEVELOPMENT,* V43 N2, PP669-676, JUN 72
DATA PROVIDE EVIDENCE FOR THE SITUATIONAL INVARIANCE OF INDIVIDUAL DIFFERENCES, AND FOR THE GREATER IMPORTANCE OF CAPACITY THAN OF MOTIVATIONAL VARIABLES IN ACCOUNTING FOR SUCH DIFFERENCES. (AUTHORS)

EJ 059 318 PS 501 976
THE STAGE IV ERROR IN PIAGET'S THEORY OF OBJECT CONCEPT DEVELOPMENT: DIFFICULTIES IN OBJECT CONCEPTUALIZATION OR SPATIAL LOCALIZATION? EVANS, WILSON; GRATCH, GERALD, *CHILD DEVELOPMENT,* V43 N2, PP682-8, JUN 72
RESULTS DO NOT SUPPORT PIAGET'S EXPLANATION OF OBJECT CONCEPTUALIZATION. (MB)

EJ 059 319 PS 501 977
STABILITY OF FIRST-GRADE CHILDREN'S DIMENSIONAL PREFERENCES OFFENBACH, STUART I.; AND OTHERS, *CHILD DEVELOPMENT,* V43 N2, PP689-92, JUN 72
RESULTS INDICATE THAT CHILDREN'S PREFERENCES WERE RELATIVELY STABLE OVER TIME. (AUTHORS/MB)

EJ 059 320 PS 501 981
THE EFFECTS OF GROUPING ON SHORT-TERM SERIAL RECALL OF DIGITS BY CHILDREN: DEVELOPMENTAL TRENDS HARRIS, GILBERT J.; BURKE, DEBORAH, *CHILD DEVELOPMENT,* V43 N2, PP710-6, JUN 72
STUDY INVESTIGATES THE EFFECTS OF SPATIAL AND TEMPORAL GROUPING ON SHORT-TERM SERIAL RECALL BY ELEMENTARY SCHOOL CHILDREN OF THREE DIFFERENT GRADE LEVELS. (AUTHORS)

EJ 059 445 PS 501 933
A YOUNG MAN AROUND THE CLASS MENDELSON, ANNA, *YOUNG CHILDREN,* V27 N5, PP281-3, JUN 72
DISCUSSES THE BENEFITS OF STUDENTS FROM THE LOCAL HIGH SCHOOL SERVING AS AIDES IN KINDERGARTEN CLASSES. (MB)

EJ 059 509 PS 501 945
SELF CONCEPT AND SOCIO-ECONOMIC STATUS TROWBRIDGE, NORMA; AND OTHERS, *CHILD STUDY JOURNAL,* V2 N3, PP123-43, 72
STUDY SHOWED THAT LOWER-CLASS CHILDREN HAVE HIGHER SELF-CONCEPT SCORES THAN MIDDLE-CLASS CHILDREN; DATA ON SPECIFIC CSEI ITEMS ARE PRESENTED IN TABLES. (AUTHOR/SP)

EJ 059 510 PS 501 948
ANALYSIS AND MODIFICATION OF SEARCH STRATEGIES OF IMPULSIVE AND REFLECTIVE CHILDREN ON THE MATCHING FAMILIAR FIGURES TEST ZELNIKER, TAMAR; AND OTHERS, *CHILD DEVELOPMENT,* V43 N2, PP321-5, JUN 72

EJ 059 511 PS 501 959
VISUAL HABITUATION IN THE HUMAN INFANT MILLER, DOLORES J., *CHILD DEVELOPMENT,* V43 N2, PP481-93, JUN 72
PURPOSE OF THIS STUDY WAS TO TEST THE ADEQUACY OF THE SERIAL HABITUATION HYPOTHESIS AS AN ACCOUNT OF THE INFANT'S PERCEPTUAL COMMERCE WITH VISUAL STIMULI. (AUTHOR)

EJ 059 512 PS 501 973
CONCEPTUAL TEMPO AND INHIBITION OF MOVEMENT IN BLACK PRESCHOOL CHILDREN HARRISON, ALGEA; NADELMAN, LORRAINE, *CHILD DEVELOPMENT,* V43 N2, PP657-68, JUN 72
OBJECTIVES OF THIS STUDY WERE TO ATTEMPT TO CLASSIFY PRESCHOOL CHILDREN ON CONCEPTUAL TEMPO, TO INVESTIGATE A RELATIONSHIP BETWEEN CONCEPTUAL TEMPO AND ABILITY TO INHIBIT MOVEMENT, AND TO INVESTIGATE THE RELATIONSHIP OF INTELLIGENCE TO BOTH DIMENSIONS. (AUTHORS)

EJ 059 513 PS 501 979
EXPECTANCY TO PERFORM AND VICARIOUS REWARD: THEIR EFFECTS UPON IMITATION THELEN, MARK H.; AND OTHERS, *CHILD DEVELOPMENT,* V43 N2, PP699-703, JUN 72
WITH NO EXPECTANCY TO PERFORM, VICARIOUS REWARD HAD NO EFFECT ON SPONTANEOUS IMITATION. (AUTHORS)

EJ 059 514 PS 501 980
VISUAL MASKING AND DEVELOPMENTAL DIFFERENCES IN INFORMATION PROCESSING MILLER, LEON K., *CHILD DEVELOPMENT,* V43 N2, PP704-9, JUN 72
RESULTS WERE INTERPRETED IN TERMS OF CURRENT CONCEPTIONS OF AGE DIFFERENCES IN INFORMATION-PROCESSING SPEED. (AUTHOR)

EJ 059 537 PS 501 946
LINGUISTIC FACTORS IN READING RYSTROM, RICHARD, *CHILD STUDY JOURNAL,* V2 N3, PP145-51, 72
EXAMINES THE PRESENT STATE OF THE RELATIONSHIP BETWEEN LINGUISTICS AND READING, PROPOSES HOW READING INSTRUCTION COULD BE IMPROVED USING CURRENTLY KNOW LINGUISTIC INFORMATION, AND DISCUSSES ONE TYPE OF LINGUISTIC FINDING USEFUL TO READING SPECIALISTS. (AUTHOR)

EJ 059 555 PS 501 947
CHILDREN'S IMITATION OF GRAMMATICAL AND UNGRAMMATICAL SENTENCES LOVE, JOHN M.; PARKER-ROBINSON, CLEO, *CHILD DEVELOPMENT,* V43 N2, PP309-19, JUN 72
GRAMMATICAL SENTENCES WERE EASIER TO IMITATE THAN UNGRAMMATICAL ONES ONLY WHEN FUNCTION WORDS WERE INCLUDED IN THE SENTENCE; WITH FUNCTION WORDS ABSENT, THERE WAS NO SIGNIFICANT DIFFERENCE. (AUTHORS)

EJ 059 593 PS 501 939
HOMER FOLKS'S "THE CARE OF DESTITUTE, NEGLECTED AND DELINQUENT CHILDREN" TRATTNER, WALTER I., *CHILD WELFARE,* V51 N6, PP361-8, JUN 72
REPUBLICATION OF HOMER FOLKS'S BOOK ON CHILD CARE IN THE 19TH CENTURY -- A MILESTONE IN A CHILD WELFARE LITERATURE -- HAS VALUE FOR TODAY, BOTH AS HISTORY AND AS A REMINDER OF THE TASKS AHEAD. (EDITOR)

EJ 059 643 PS 501 934
NUTRITION AND EDUCATIONAL EXPERIENCE: INTERRELATED VARIABLES IN CHILDREN'S LEARNING FOSTER, FLORENCE P., *YOUNG CHILDREN,* V27 N5, PP284-8, JUN 72
ARTICLE DEALS WITH THE INTERRELATEDNESS OF THE FOOD PROGRAM, INTELLECTUAL DEVELOPMENT, AND CURRICULUM ACTIVITIES OF YOUNG CHILDREN THROUGH THE LONG DAY AT THE CHILD CARE CENTER. (EDITOR)

EJ 059 644 PS 501 940
SEX ROLE IDENTITY OF ADOLESCENT GIRLS IN FOSTER HOMES AND INSTITUTIONS STEELE, CAROLYN I., *CHILD WELFARE,* V51 N6, PP375-84, JUN 72
CAUTION IS NECESSARY IN CONTEMPLATING PLACEMENT OF ADOLESCENT GIRLS WITH SEX ROLE IDENTITY PROBLEMS: POSTPLACEMENT VISITING BETWEEN DAUGHTER AND MOTHER IS IMPORTANT. (EDITOR)

EJ 059 671 PS 501 941
PREVENTING ILLEGITIMATE TEENAGE PREGNANCY THROUGH SYSTEMS INTERACTION JARVIS, D. L., *CHILD WELFARE,* V51 N6, PP396-400, JUN 72
AUTHOR DESCRIBES APPROACH TAKEN BY THE CHILDREN'S AID SOCIETY OF VANCOUVER IN SPONSORING A DEMONSTRATION PROJECT AIMED AT ILLEGITIMACY PREVENTION THROUGH HOSPITAL OBSERVATION AND FAMILY LIFE DIALOGUE WITH HIGHSCHOOLERS. (AUTHOR/MB)

EJ 059 672 PS 501 943
THE EFFECTS OF IMMEDIATE FEEDBACK ON THE BEHAVIOR OF TEACHERS-IN-TRAINING SILVERMAN, STUART; KIMMEL, ELLEN, *CHILD STUDY JOURNAL*, V2 N3, PP109-16, 72
RESULTS OF EXPERIMENT SHOWED THAT THE USE OF AN FM WIRELESS MICROPHONE AND AN FM RADIO WERE EFFECTIVE IN MODIFYING THE BEHAVIOR OF STUDENT INTERNS WITHIN THE CONTEXT OF THE CLASSROOM ITSELF. (AUTHOR)

EJ 059 699 PS 501 994
CHILDREN'S ABILITY TO ORDER FACIAL AND NONFACIAL CONTINUA AS A FUNCTION OF MA, CA, AND IQ KIER, RAE JEANNE; HARTER, SUSAN, *JOURNAL OF GENETIC PSYCHOLOGY*, V120 PT 2, PP241-51, JUN 72
FINDINGS HIGHLIGHT A GENERAL CONSIDERATION FOR DEVELOPMENTAL RESEARCH: NAMELY, WHETHER CA OR MA IS THE MORE APPROPRIATE DEVELOPMENTAL PARAMETER. (AUTHORS)

EJ 059 746 PS 502 044
A MATTER OF LIFE AND DEATH GALEN, HARLENE, *YOUNG CHILDREN*, V27 N6, PP351-6, AUG 72
AUTHOR DESCRIBES PRACTICAL GUIDELINES FOR TEACHERS IN HANDLING THE SUBJECT OF DEATH WITH YOUNG CHILDREN. (EDITOR)

EJ 059 813 PS 501 991
EYE CONTACT, ATTITUDES, AND ATTITUDE CHANGE AMONG MALES BREED, GEORGE; PORTER, MAYNARD, *JOURNAL OF GENETIC PSYCHOLOGY*, V120 PT 2, PP211-7, JUN 72
EXPERIMENT DESIGNED TO MANIPULATE THE PERCEIVED PERSON'S LOOKING BEHAVIOR AND THE PERCEIVER'S ATTITUDES TOWARD HIM IN AN EFFORT TO DETERMINE IF ONE IS MORE POTENT OR IF THEY INTERACT IN AFFECTING THE PERCEIVER'S DEGREE OF SEARCH FOR EYE CONTACT. (AUTHORS/MB)

EJ 059 870 PS 501 996
RELATIONSHIPS OF PARENTAL BEHAVIOR TO "DISADVANTAGED" CHILDREN'S INTRINSIC-EXTRINSIC MOTIVATION FOR TASK STRIVING SOLOMON, DANIEL; HOULIHAN, KEVIN A., *JOURNAL OF GENETIC PSYCHOLOGY*, V120 PT 2, PP257-74, JUN 72
IN THIS STUDY, THE RELEVANCE OF STRIVING SITUATIONS TO INTRINSIC AND EXTRINSIC MOTIVATION WAS MANIPULATED BY VARYING THE DEGREE OF INVOLVEMENT IN THE CHILD'S PERFORMANCE DISPLAYED BY THE EXPERIMENTER. (AUTHORS)

EJ 059 871 PS 501 998
NEGRO PARENTAL BEHAVIOR AND SOCIAL CLASS VARIABLES BUSSE, THOMAS V.; BUSSE, PAULINE, *JOURNAL OF GENETIC PSYCHOLOGY*, V120 PT 2, PP297-94, JUN 72
RESEARCH MEASURED ACCEPTED DIMENSIONS OF CHILD-REARING BEHAVIOR BY MEANS OF OBSERVATIONS OF BOTH NEGRO MOTHERS AND FATHERS TEACHING THEIR FIFTH GRADE SONS. (AUTHORS)

EJ 059 872 PS 502 022
FEMINIZATION IN PRESCHOOL BIBER, HENRY; AND OTHERS, *DEVELOPMENTAL PSYCHOLOGY*, V7 N1, PP86, JUL 72
RESULTS REFLECT PRIMARILY A HIGHER NUMBER OF INSTRUCTIONAL CONTACTS TO GIRLS RATHER THAN A TENDENCY OF TEACHERS TO BE MORE REINFORCING TO THEM. (AUTHORS)

EJ 059 873 PS 502 027
DIMENSIONS OF EARLY STIMULATION AND THEIR DIFFERENTIAL EFFECTS ON INFANT DEVELOPMENT YARROW, LEON J.; AND OTHERS, *MERRILL-PALMER QUARTERLY*, V18 N3, PP205-18, JUL 72
AUTHORS LOOK AT A RANGE OF VARIATION IN EXPERIENCE OF FIVE-TO SIX-MONTH-OLD INFANTS ON A CONCRETE BEHAVIORAL LEVEL, AND CONCEPTUALIZE THESE DISCRETE BEHAVIORS. (AUTHORS/MB)

EJ 059 874 PS 502 028
REACTIONS TO RESPONSE-CONTINGENT STIMULATION IN EARLY INFANCY WATSON, JOHN S.; RAMEY, CRAIG T., *MERRILL-PALMER QUARTERLY*, V18 N3, PP218-27, JUL 72
DATA IS FROM A SHORT-TERM LONGITUDINAL STUDY CONDUCTED AT THE INSTITUTE OF HUMAN DEVELOPMENT WHICH INVOLVED PRESENTING TWO WEEKS OF A SPECIAL CONTINGENCY EXPERIENCE TO INFANTS BETWEEN THEIR EIGHTH AND TENTH WEEKS. (AUTHORS/MB)

EJ 059 875 PS 502 029
PRINCIPLES OF INTERACTION IN LANGUAGE LEARNING MOERK, ERNST, *MERRILL-PALMER QUARTERLY*, V18 N3, PP229-57, JUL 72
INVESTIGATION CONCENTRATED ON VERBAL AND NONVERBAL VARIABLES OF CHILD-MOTHER INTERACTIONS AS IT PERTAINS TO THE CHILD'S LANGUAGE DEVELOPMENT. (MB)

EJ 059 876 PS 502 050
PIAGET'S CONSTRUCTIONIST THEORY SMILLIE, D., *HUMAN DEVELOPMENT*, V15 N3, PP171-86, 72
AUTHOR CLAIMS THAT PIAGET'S ACCOUNT OF THE CONSTRUCTION OF REALITY NEEDS MODIFICATION AND A SHIFT IN EMPHASIS. (AUTHOR/MB)

EJ 059 877 PS 502 055
RESPONSE DEPRESSION AND FACILITATION COMPONENTS OF THE FRUSTRATION EFFECT IN CHILDREN'S BEHAVIOR OWEN, NEVILLE, *JOURNAL OF EXPERIMENTAL CHILD PSYCHOLOGY*, V13 N3, PP478-87, JUN 72
GREATER RESPONSE VIGOR FOLLOWING NONREWARD COMPARED TO REWARD IS TERMED THE FRUSTRATION EFFECT. (AUTHOR)

EJ 059 878 PS 502 059
ATTENTION SPAN AND GENERALIZATION OF TASK-RELATED STIMULUS CONTROL: EFFECTS OF REINFORCEMENT CONTINGENCIES REDD, WILLIAM H., *JOURNAL OF EXPERIMENTAL CHILD PSYCHOLOGY*, V13 N3, PP527-39, JUN 72
STUDY CONDUCTED TO INVESTIGATE ATTENTION SPAN IN RELATION TO VARIOUS SCHEDULES OR REGIMES OF REINFORCEMENT. (AUTHOR/MB)

EJ 060 012 PS 502 005
INFANT DEVELOPMENT IN LOWER-CLASS AMERICAN FAMILIES LEWIS, M.; WILSON, CORNIELIA, *HUMAN DEVELOPMENT*, V15 N2, PP112-27, 72
FROM A SYMPOSIUM ON CROSS-CULTURAL STUDIES OF MOTHER-INFANT INTERACTION AT THE BIENNIAL MEETING FOR RESEARCH IN CHILD DEVELOPMENT, MINNEAPOLIS, MINN., APRIL 2, 1971. (MB)

EJ 060 013 PS 502 046
DEVELOPMENTAL THEORY: ITS PLACE AND RELEVANCE IN EARLY INTERVENTION PROGRAMS SIGEL, IRVING E., *YOUNG CHILDREN*, V27 N6, PP364-72, AUG 72
AUTHOR FOCUSES ON THE NEED TO BEGIN TO SPECIFY IN GREATER DETAIL WHAT THE INPUTS ARE FOR THE CHILD, TO DEFINE HIS REASONABLE LIVING SPACE, AND TO DEFINE WHICH OF THOSE FACTORS MAY ALTER THE COURSE OF GROWTH IN SPITE OF WHAT HAPPENS IN THE NURSERY SCHOOL. (AUTHOR/MB)

EJ 060 014 PS 502 048
LIMITATIONS ON THE GENERALIZABILITY OF GROWTH CURVES OF INTELLIGENCE: A REANALYSIS OF SOME DATA FROM THE HARVARD GROWTH STUDY SCHAIE, K. W., *HUMAN DEVELOPMENT*, V15 N3, PP141-52, 72

EJ 060 015 PS 502 049
SEX DIFFERENCES IN HUMAN DEVELOPMENT HUTT, CORINNE, *HUMAN DEVELOPMENT*, V15 N3, PP153-70, 72
SEX DIFFERENCES IN MANY ASPECTS OF EARLY HUMAN DEVELOPMENT ARE REVIEWED: IN PHYSICAL GROWTH AND MATURATION, IN MOTOR ACTIVITY AND SENSORY CAPACITIES IN INFANCY, IN MOTHER-INFANT INTERACTION, IN THE ONSET OF FEAR, IN THE SOCIAL BEHAVIOUR OF PRE-SCHOOL CHILDREN, IN EXPLORATION, PLAY AND CREATIVITY, AND IN INTELLECTUAL FUNCTIONS. (AUTHOR)

EJ 060 105 PS 501 983
AESTHETIC EDUCATION IN SOVIET SCHOOLS PUTKO, ALEXANDER, *ELEMENTARY SCHOOL JOURNAL*, V72 N8, PP397-401, MAY 72
AUTHOR IS WITH THE NOVOSTI PRESS AGENCY, MOSCOW. (MB)

EJ 060 106 PS 501 984
SUPERINTENDENT JULIA RICHMAN: A SOCIAL PROGRESSIVE IN THE PUBLIC SCHOOLS BERROL, SELMA C., *ELEMENTARY SCHOOL JOURNAL*, V72 N8, PP402-11, MAY 72
DESCRIBES THE PROBLEMS IN NEW YORK CITY'S SCHOOLS DURING THE PERIOD FROM 1898 TO 1914 AND SUPERINTENDENT JULIA RICHMAN'S INNOVATIVE APPROACHES TO SOLUTIONS. (MB)

EJ 060 107 PS 502 042
REFLECTIONS ON REVISITING VIENNA'S YOUNG CITIZENS GITTER, LENA L., *YOUNG CHILDREN*, V27 N6, PP340-4, AUG 72
AUTHOR BEGAN HER CAREER AS A MONTESSORI TEACHER IN A VIENNESE KINDERGARTEN 40 YEARS AGO. (MB)

EJ 060 108 PS 502 043
HEAD START IN MICRONESIA WITHYCOMBE, JERALDINE S., *YOUNG CHILDREN*, V27 N6, PP346-9, AUG 72
AUTHOR IS DIRECTOR OF THE HEAD START LEADERSHIP DEVELOPMENT PROGRAM IN MICRONESIA. (MB)

EJ 060 109 PS 502 058
AGE DIFFERENCES IN VISUAL REACTION TIME OF "BRAIN DAMAGED" AND NORMAL CHILDREN UNDER IRREGULAR PREPARATORY INTERVAL CONDITIONS CZUDNER, G.; ROURKE, B. P., *JOURNAL OF EXPERIMENTAL CHILD PSYCHOLOGY*, V13 N3, PP516-26, JUN 72
RESULTS SUPPORT THE CONTENTION THAT WITH ADVANCING YEARS BRAIN-DAMAGED CHILDREN MAY ADAPT TO AND/OR RECOVER FROM THE DEFICIT(S) INVOLVED IN THE INABILITY TO DEVELOP AND MAINTAIN A READINESS TO RESPOND. (AUTHOR/MB)

EJ 060 203 PS 502 040
VIEWPOINT: GAP AND THE JOINT COMMISSION ON MENTAL HEALTH OF CHILDREN COHEN, DONALD J., *CHILDREN TODAY*, V1 N4, PP34-8, JUL-AUG 72
A CRITICAL APPRAISAL OF THE GAP'S REVIEW OF THE MAJOR REPORT OF THE JOINT COMMISSION ON MENTAL HEALTH OF CHILDREN. (MB)

EJ 060 330 PS 501 986
DIFFERENTIAL OUTCOMES OF A MONTESSORI CURRICULUM STODOLSKY, SUSAN S.; KARLSON, ALFRED L., *ELEMENTARY SCHOOL JOURNAL*, V72 N8, PP419-33, MAY 72
AUTHORS BELIEVE THAT THEY HAVE TENTATIVELY DEMONSTRATED THAT THE MONTESSORI CURRICULUM IS EFFECTIVE OVER A PERIOD OF TWO YEARS IN NURTURING CONTINUING DEVELOPMENT IN CHILDREN IN THE AREAS OF VISUAL-MOTOR INTEGRATION, MATCHING AND SORTING SKILLS, PSYCHO-MOTOR SKILLS, AND TO SOME EXTENT NUMBER CONCEPTS. (AUTHORS/MB)

EJ 060 385 PS 502 014
CHILDREN'S REPORTS OF PARENTAL CHILD-REARING BEHAVIOR AT FIVE GRADE LEVELS ARMENTROUT, JAMES A.; BURGER, GARY K., *DEVELOPMENTAL PSYCHOLOGY*, V7 N1, PP44-8, JUL 72
FACTOR ANALYSES OF MALES' AND FEMALES' REPORTS OF MATERNAL AND PATERNAL BEHAVIORS YIELDED THE SAME THREE FACTORS AS EARLIER STUDIES--ACCEPTANCE VERSUS REJECTION, PSYCHOLOGICAL AUTONOMY VERSUS PSYCHOLOGICAL CONTROL, AND FIRM CONTROL VERSUS LAX CONTROL. (AUTHORS)

EJ 060 452 PS 502 037
FUNDING CHILD CARE PROGRAMS UNDER TITLE IV-A LOURIE, NORMAN V., *CHILDREN TODAY*, V1 N4, PP23-5, JUL-AUG 72
DESCRIBES THE OPPORTUNITIES FOR USING TITLE IV-A OF THE SOCIAL SECURITY ACT IN CHILD CARE PROGRAMING. (MB)

EJ 060 473 PS 502 041
THE RIGHTS OF CHILDREN FORER, LOIS G., *YOUNG CHILDREN*, V27 N6, PP332-9, AUG 72
A PROMINENT ATTORNEY SPEAKS OUT ON THOUGHT-PROVOKING PROBLEMS INVOLVING THE LAW AND CHILDREN. (EDITOR)

EJ 060 501 PS 502 007
TREATMENT OF PROBLEMS ASSOCIATED WITH COGNITIVE AND PERCEPTUAL-MOTOR DEFICITS MILLMAN, HOWARD L., *CHILD WELFARE*, V51 N7, PP447-451, JUL 72

EJ 060 502 PS 502 016
PERCEPTION OF RHYTHM BY SUBJECTS WITH NORMAL AND DEFICIENT HEARING RILEIGH, KATHRYN K.; ODOM, PENELOPE B., *DEVELOPMENTAL PSYCHOLOGY*, V7 N1, PP54-61, JUL 72
STUDY FOUND THAT AUDITORY EXPERIENCE HAS AN INDIRECT INFLUENCE ON RHYTHM PERCEPTION, BUT AUDITORY INVOLVEMENT DURING THE TASK DOES NOT. (AUTHORS/MB)

EJ 060 522 PS 502 036
PARENTS OF CHILDREN WITH PKU SCHILD, SYLVIA, *CHILDREN TODAY*, V1 N4, PP20-2, JUL-AUG 72
EXCERPTED FROM "WHAT DO YOU KNOW ABOUT PKU," A PAMPHLET PUBLISHED BY THE U.S. DEPARTMENT OF HEALTH, EDUCATION, AND WELFARE, PUBLIC HEALTH SERVICE, HEALTH SERVICES AND MENTAL HEALTH ADMINISTRATION, (HSM)71-5703. (AUTHOR)

EJ 060 523 PS 502 038
CHILD HEALTH ISSUES IN NEW YORK MAYER, SHIRLEY, *CHILDREN TODAY*, V1 N4, PP30-5, JUL-AUG 72
EXCERPTS FROM A FULL REPORT WHICH APPEARED IN THE CITY ALMANAC, A PUBLICATION OF THE CENTER OF NEW YORK CITY AFFAIRS OF THE NEW SCHOOL FOR SOCIAL RESEARCH. (MB)

EJ 060 720 PS 502 031
LANGUAGE PATTERNS WITHIN THE YOUTH SUBCULTURE: DEVELOPMENT OF SLANG VOCABULARIES NELSON, EDWARD A.; ROSENBAUM, EDWARD, *MERRILL-PALMER QUARTERLY*, V18 N3, PP273-85, JUL 72
REPORT CONCERNS RESEARCH TO DEVELOP A BROAD AND FLEXIBLE METHOD FOR ASSESSING FAMILIARITY WITH SLANG FOR VARIOUS TOPICS. (AUTHORS)

EJ 060 773 PS 501 990
PERCEPTION AND LANGUAGE: A GERMAN REPLICATION OF THE PIAGET-INHELDER POSITION SCOTT, RALPH; SATTEL, LUDWIG, *JOURNAL OF GENETIC PSYCHOLOGY*, V120 PT 2, PP203-10, JUN 72
RESULTS SUGGEST THAT CULTURAL DISADVANTAGE MAY ACT TO DETER GROWTH IN BOTH PERCEPTUAL AND LANGUAGE SPHERES AND THAT PERCEPTUAL MEASURES MAY BE SOMEWHAT LESS RESISTANT TO CULTURAL INFLUENCE THAN ARE LANGUAGE MEASURES. (AUTHORS/MB)

EJ 060 774 PS 501 997
"RIGHT," "WRONG," AND DISCRIMINATION LEARNING IN CHILDREN ROTHBERG, CAROLE; HARRIS, MARY B., *JOURNAL OF GENETIC PSYCHOLOGY*, V120 PT 2, PP275-86, JUN 72
IN GENERAL, THE STUDY CONFIRMED THE PREDICTION THAT LEARNING OF A DISCRIMINATION UNDER PUNISHMENT OR A REWARD-PUNISHMENT CONDITION IS SUPERIOR TO THAT UNDER REWARD ALONE. (AUTHORS)

EJ 060 775 PS 502 001
AN EXPERIMENTAL STUDY OF THE SELECTIVE ATTENTION OF CHILDREN OF 1896 AND 1966 NELSON, THOMAS M.; AND OTHERS, *JOURNAL OF GENETIC PSYCHOLOGY*, V120 PT 2, PP317-24, JUN 72
LITTLE EVIDENCE IS PROVIDED FOR COGNITIVE CHANGES IN CHILDREN OVER THE LAST 70 YEARS. (AUTHORS)

EJ 060 776 PS 502 017
PRECOCIOUS THOUGHTS ON NUMBER: THE LONG AND THE SHORT OF IT PUFALL, PETER B.; SHAW, ROBERT E., *DEVELOPMENTAL PSYCHOLOGY*, V7 N1, PP62-9, JUL 72
IN THIS STUDY CHILDREN BETWEEN THE AGES OF 3 AND 6 YEARS WERE EACH PRESENTED WITH SIX NUMBER PROBLEMS IN WHICH LENGTH AND DENSITY WERE VARIED ACCORDING TO THE PROPOSED COMPOSITION RULES. (AUTHORS)

EJ 060 777 PS 502 030
THE ROLE OF FRONT-BACK FEATURES IN CHILDREN'S "FRONT," "BACK," AND "BESIDE" PLACEMENTS OF OBJECTS HARRIS, LAUREN JAY; STROMMEN, ELLEN A., *MERRILL-PALMER QUARTERLY*, V18 N3, PP259-71, JUL 72
AUTHORS' FINDINGS SUBSTANTIATE THE VIEW THAT RELIANCE ON ANY SINGLE TEST OF FRONT-BACK (WHICH IS BASED UPON THE CHILD'S OWN BODY) IS LIKELY TO YIELD A MISLEADING PICTURE OF THE QUALITY OF THE CHILD'S KNOWLEDGE OF FRONT-BACK, (AUTHORS/MB)

EJ 060 778 PS 502 032
CONCRETE OPERATIONAL THINKING IN MENTALLY ILL ADOLESCENTS LERNER, SANDRA; AND OTHERS, *MERRILL-PALMER QUARTERLY*, V18 N3, PP287-91, JUL 72
DATA SUGGEST AN ABILITY TO USE CONCRETE-OPERATIONAL REASONING IS NOT REQUIRED FOR DOING COMPLEX ARITHMETIC, EVEN THOUGH IT MAY BE NECESSARY FOR LEARNING THESE ARITHMETIC SKILLS. (AUTHORS)

EJ 060 779 PS 502 052
HYPOTHESES, STRATEGIES, AND STEREOTYPES IN DISCRIMINATION LEARNING GHOLSON, BARRY; AND OTHERS, *JOURNAL OF EXPERIMENTAL CHILD PSYCHOLOGY*, V13 N3, PP423-46, JUN 72
IN THE COURSE OF TWO EXPERIMENTS, GROUPS OF KINDERGARTEN, SECOND, FOURTH, SIXTH GRADE AND COLLEGE STUDENTS RECEIVED SEVERAL DISCRIMINATION PROBLEMS TO INVESTIGATE HYPOTHESIS TESTING BEHAVIOR. (AUTHORS/MB)

EJ 060 780 PS 502 053
SOME FACTORS AFFECTING THE COMPLEXITY OF CHILDREN'S SENTENCES: THE EFFECTS OF MODELING, AGE, SEX, AND BILINGUALISM HARRIS, MARY B.; HASSEMER, WENDY G., *JOURNAL OF EXPERIMENTAL CHILD PSYCHOLOGY*, V13 N3, PP447-55, JUN 72
RESULTS SUGGEST THAT MODELING CAN INDEED AFFECT THE COMPLEXITY OF CHILDREN'S SENTENCES EVEN IN THE ABSENCE OF REINFORCEMENT OR INSTRUCTIONS OF IMITATE. (AUTHORS)

EJ 060 781 PS 502 054
THE ROLE OF INCONGRUITY AND RESOLUTION IN CHILDREN'S APPRECIATION OF CARTOON HUMOR SCHULTZ, THOMAS R., *JOURNAL OF EXPERIMENTAL CHILD PSYCHOLOGY*, V13 N3, PP456-77, JUN 72
TWO EXPERIMENTS WERE CONDUCTED TO TEST A NUMBER OF PREDICTIONS DERIVED FROM A COGNITIVE THEORY OF HUMOR. (AUTHOR)

EJ 060 782 PS 502 056
REVERSALS PRIOR TO SOLUTION OF CONCEPT IDENTIFICATION IN CHILDREN TIGHE, THOMAS J.; TIGHE, LOUISE S., *JOURNAL OF EXPERIMENTAL CHILD PSYCHOLOGY*, V13 N3, PP488-500, JUN 72
PRESOLUTION REVERSAL PREVENTED OR SIGNIFICANTLY RETARDED LEARNING IN KINDERGARTEN AND FIRST-GRADE CHILDREN BUT DID NOT HINDER LEARNING IN FIFTH-GRADE CHILDREN. (AUTHORS)

EJ 060 783 PS 502 057
PRODUCTION OF NOVEL AND GRAMMATICAL UTTERANCES BY YOUNG CHILDREN WHITEHURST, GROVER J., *JOURNAL OF EXPERIMENTAL CHILD PSYCHOLOGY*, V13 N3, PP502-15, JUN 72
STUDY WAS CONDUCTED IN ORDER TO OBTAIN PRELIMINARY CONFIRMATION OF THE HYPOTHESIS THAT NOVEL AND APPROPRIATE LINGUISTIC BEHAVIOR CAN BE UNDERSTOOD THROUGH AN ANALYSIS OF STIMULUS CONTROL. (AUTHOR)

EJ 060 784 PS 502 061
THE EFFECTS OF VERBAL PRETRAINING ON THE MULTIDIMENSIONAL GENERALIZATION BEHAVIOR OF CHILDREN SPIKER, CHARLES C.; AND OTHERS, *JOURNAL OF EXPERIMENTAL CHILD PSYCHOLOGY*, V13 N3, PP558-72, JUN 72
PREDICTIONS FOR MULTIDIMENSIONAL GENERALIZATION WERE DERIVED FROM HULL-SPENCE LEARNING THEORY, AND AN EXPERIMENT IS REPORTED THAT WAS DESIGNED TO TEST THIS ASPECT OF THE THEORY. ALTERNATIVE TO THIS ANALYSIS IS PRESENTED IN PS 502 062; AUTHORS RESPOND IN PS 502 063. (AUTHORS/MB)

EJ 060 785 PS 502 062
THREE-CUE SELECTION MODELS APPLIED TO MULTIDIMENSIONAL STIMULUS CLASSIFICATION: ALTERNATIVES TO THE SPIKER, CROLL, AND MILLER ANALYSIS BOGARTZ, RICHARD S., *JOURNAL OF EXPERIMENTAL CHILD PSYCHOLOGY,* V13 N3, PP573-84, JUN 72
ALTERNATIVE ANALYSIS TO STUDY REPORTED IN PS 502 061. REJOINDER PRESENTED IN PS 502 063. (MB)

EJ 060 786 PS 502 063
ON THE COMPARISON OF PSYCHOLOGICAL THEORIES: A REPLY TO PROFESSOR BOGARTZ SPIKER, CHARLES C.; AND OTHERS, *JOURNAL OF EXPERIMENTAL CHILD PSYCHOLOGY,* V13 N3, PP585-92, JUN 72
REJOINDER TO PS 502 062 WHICH IN TURN IS AN ALTERNATIVE ANALYSIS OF AUTHORS' STUDY PRESENTED IN PS 502 061. (MB)

EJ 060 900 PS 502 033
JOINING TOGETHER TO HELP FOSTER CHILDREN ROSENDORF, SIDNEY, *CHILDREN TODAY,* V1 N4, PP2-6, JUL-AUG 72
DESCRIBES THE SECOND NATIONAL FOSTER PARENT CONFERENCE, UNDER THE SPONSORSHIP OF HEW'S OFFICE OF CHILD DEVELOPMENT, WHICH DEVELOPED THE NATIONAL FOSTER PARENT ASSOCIATION. (MB)

EJ 060 929 PS 502 045
WE HAVE MEN ON THE STAFF KENDALL, EARLINE, *YOUNG CHILDREN,* V27 N6, PP358-62, AUG 72
DESCRIBES THE NASHVILLE CHILD CENTER, WHICH HAS A LARGE PERCENTAGE OF MEN ON ITS TEACHING STAFF. (MB)

EJ 060 930 PS 502 047
THE ITINERANT TEACHER COLLINS, CAMILLA, *YOUNG CHILDREN,* V27 N6, PP374-9, AUG 72
TEACHER TRAINING IS EFFECTIVELY PROVIDED BY AN INSTRUCTOR WHO BRINGS HER SKILLS IN PRESCHOOL EDUCATION TO TEACHERS IN OUTLYING COMMUNITIES. (EDITOR)

EJ 060 999 PS 502 008
A DEMONSTRATION SUMMER PRESCHOOL PROGRAM PURNELL, JOHN C., *CHILD WELFARE,* V51 N7, PP452-59, JUL 72
A HIGH FREQUENCY OF UNMET MEDICAL NEEDS AND A BREAKDOWN IN FAMILY STRUCTURE AMONG LOW-INCOME PRESCHOOL CHILDREN WERE DISCOVERED AMONG TEN YOUNGSTERS ENROLLED IN A DEMONSTRATION DAY CARE PROJECT. THIS PAPER REPORTS ON HOW A CHILD CARE CENTER ATTEMPTED TO MEET THE DEVELOPMENTAL NEEDS OF SUCH CHILDREN. (EDITOR)

EJ 061 000 PS 502 009
PROJECT TREAT: A NEW APPROACH TO THE SEVERELY DISTURBED CHILD WILLNER, MILTON; AND OTHERS, *CHILD WELFARE,* V51 N7, PP460-64, JUL 72
DESCRIBES AN INNOVATIVE PROGRAM FOR THE TREATMENT OF SEVERELY DISTURBED CHILDREN IN AN AREA LACKING A 7-DAY-WEEK RESIDENTIAL TREATMENT CENTER. THE PROJECT, DEVELOPED BY A CHILD WELFARE AGENCY, A BOARD OF EDUCATION AND A MENTAL HEALTH DEPARTMENT, REPORTS CONSIDERABLE SUCCESS. (EDITOR/RB)

EJ 061 001 PS 502 035
A TEAM APPROACH USING CASSETTE TAPES SCOGGINS, ROY T., JR.; AND OTHERS, *CHILDREN TODAY,* V1 N4, PP16-9, JUL-AUG 72
DESCRIBES A NEW PROGRAM AT THE COASTAL CENTER, AN INSTITUTION FOR MENTALLY RETARDED CHILDREN NEAR CHARLESTON, SOUTH CAROLINA. (MB)

EJ 061 058 PS 501 982
HOW TO TEACH FEAR ROGERS, DONALD J., *ELEMENTARY SCHOOL JOURNAL,* V72 N8, PP391-5, MAY 72
FORMULA FOR TEACHING FEAR IS CREATE AN ATMOSPHERE IN WHICH ACHIEVEMENT IS VALUED OVER PERSONAL WORTH, IN WHICH BLAME IS MORE COMMON THAN UNDERSTANDING, AND IN WHICH THE OPINION OF OTHERS IS MORE IMPORTANT THAN THE OPINION OF SELF. (AUTHOR)

EJ 061 059 PS 501 987
THE DEVELOPMENT OF THE LANGUAGE OF EMOTIONS: I. THEORETICAL AND METHODOLOGICAL INTRODUCTION WOLMAN, RICHARD N.; AND OTHERS, *JOURNAL OF GENETIC PSYCHOLOGY,* V120 PT 2, PP167-76, JUN 72
INQUIRY FOCUSES ON THE LANGUAGE BY WHICH CHILDREN DESCRIBE VARIOUS ALTERED BODILY STATES IN ORDER TO COMMUNICATE THEM TO OTHERS. PARTS II AND III OF THIS STUDY ARE PS 502 000 AND PS 502 002. (AUTHORS/MB)

EJ 061 060 PS 501 988
PARAMETERS OF THE SPIRAL AFTER-EFFECT IN ORGANICS, SCHIZOPHRENICS, AND NORMALS HERSEN, MICHEL; AND OTHERS, *JOURNAL OF GENETIC PSYCHOLOGY,* V120 PT 2, PP177-87, JUN 72
PREDICTION THAT ORGANICS WILL REPORT FEWER AFTER-EFFECTS THAN BOTH NORMALS AND SCHIZOPHRENICS WAS CONFIRMED. (AUTHORS)

EJ 061 061 PS 501 989
HYPOTHESIS OF ORIGIN AND NATURE FOR THE "SOMINDENCE-DISSOFRUSTANCE" PERSONALITY FACTOR, U.I. 30 DELHEES, KARL H., *JOURNAL OF GENETIC PSYCHOLOGY,* V120 PT 2, PP189-201, JUN 72
SOMINDENCE (SOBER MATURE INDEPENDENCE) IS FOUND IN THE STOLID, MATURE, INDEPENDENT; AND BY CONTRAST, DISSOFRUSTANCE (DISSOCIATIVE REJECTION OF FRUSTRATING IDEAS) CHARACTERIZES THE MORE CAREFUL, LESS ENTHUSIASTIC PERSON WITH INCREASED DEPENDENCE ON EXTERNAL CONTROL. (AUTHOR/MB)

EJ 061 062 PS 501 992
DEVELOPMENTAL TRENDS IN GENERAL AND TEST ANXIETY AMONG JUNIOR AND SENIOR HIGH SCHOOL STUDENTS MANLEY, MERLIN J.; ROSEMEIR, ROBERT A., *JOURNAL OF GENETIC PSYCHOLOGY,* V120 PT 2, PP219-26, JUN 72
RESULTS SUGGEST DISTINCT PATTERNS BY SEX AND GRADE LEVEL FOR BOTH GENERAL AND TEST ANXIETY. (MB)

EJ 061 063 PS 501 995
PHENOMENAL ENVIRONMENTAL OPPRESSIVENESS IN SUICIDAL ADOLESCENTS LEVENSON, MARVIN; NEURINGER, CHARLES, *JOURNAL OF GENETIC PSYCHOLOGY,* V120 PT 2, PP253-6, JUN 72
IF THE MEASURES USED IN THIS STUDY WERE VALID INDICATORS OF PHENOMENAL ENVIRONMENTAL OPPRESSIVENESS, THEN IT WOULD SEEM THAT SUICIDAL ADOLESCENTS DO NOT SEE THEIR WORLD AS ANY MORE OVERWHELMING OR OVERPOWERING THAN DO OTHERS OF THE SAME AGE. (AUTHORS)

EJ 061 064 PS 502 000
THE DEVELOPMENT OF THE LANGUAGE OF EMOTIONS: II. INTENTIONALITY IN THE EXPERIENCE OF AFFECT LEWIS, WILLIAM C.; AND OTHERS, *JOURNAL OF GENETIC PSYCHOLOGY,* V120 PT 2, PP303-16, JUN 72
ONE OF A SERIES OF STUDIES OF HOW CHILDREN COME TO NAME THEIR FEELINGS. FOR PARTS I AND III SEE PS 501 987 AND PS 502 002. (MB)

EJ 061 065 PS 502 002
THE DEVELOPMENT OF THE LANGUAGE OF EMOTIONS: III. TYPE OF ANXIETY IN THE EXPERIENCE OF AFFECT LEWIS, WILLIAM C.; AND OTHERS, *JOURNAL OF GENETIC PSYCHOLOGY,* V120 PT 2, PP325-42, JUN 72
ONE OF A SERIES OF STUDIES OF HOW CHILDREN COME TO NAME THEIR FEELINGS. PARTS I AND II ARE PS 501 987 AND PS 502 000. (MB)

EJ 061 066 PS 502 010
AGE- AND SEX-RELATED VARIATION IN PERFORMANCE ON A FIGURAL-CONCEPTUAL TASK GUTTMAN, RUTH; KAHNEMAN, IRAH, *DEVELOPMENTAL PSYCHOLOGY,* V7 N1, PP4-9, JUL 72
STUDY DEALS WITH A COMPARATIVE DEVELOPMENTAL ANALYSIS OF PERFORMANCES ON THE SAME TASK BY FOUR AGE GROUPS. (MB)

EJ 061 067 PS 502 011
ORIENTATION IN CHILDREN'S HUMAN FIGURE DRAWINGS: AN ASPECT OF GRAPHIC LANGUAGE GOODNOW, JACQUELINE J.; FRIEDMAN, SARAH, *DEVELOPMENTAL PSYCHOLOGY,* V7 N1, PP10-6, JUL 72
RESULTS OF THIS STUDY SUGGEST THE FEASIBILITY OF USING CONCEPTS FROM STUDIES OF SPOKEN LANGUAGE FOR EXPERIMENTAL STUDIES OF GRAPHIC PERFORMANCE. (AUTHORS)

EJ 061 068 PS 502 012
CHILDREN'S UNDERSTANDING OF SPATIAL RELATIONS: COORDINATION OF PERSPECTIVES FISHBEIN, HAROLD D.; AND OTHERS, *DEVELOPMENTAL PSYCHOLOGY,* V7 N1, PP21-33, JUL 72
A THEORETICAL FRAMEWORK STEMMING FROM THE EVOLUTIONARY PSYCHOLOGY OF HERBERT SPENCER, ALONG WITH TWO EXPERIMENTS WITH YOUNG CHILDREN AS SUBJECTS, ARE PRESENTED. (AUTHORS)

EJ 061 069 PS 502 015
FAMILY CORRELATES OF VERBAL REASONING ABILITY KELLAGHAN, THOMAS; MACNAMARA, JOHN, *DEVELOPMENTAL PSYCHOLOGY,* V7 N1, PP49-53, JUL 72
THE RELATIONSHIP BETWEEN VERBAL REASONING ABILITY ON THE ONE HAND AND SEX, SOCIAL CLASS, FAMILY SIZE, AND ORDINAL POSITION IN THE FAMILY ON THE OTHER WERE EXAMINED FOR A REPRESENTATIVE SAMPLE OF 11-YEAR-OLD IRISH CHILDREN. (AUTHORS)

EJ 061 070 PS 502 020
IMITATION OF TEACHER PREFERENCES IN A FIELD SETTING FESHBACH, NORMA D.; FESHBACH, SEYMOUR, *DEVELOPMENTAL PSYCHOLOGY,* V7 N1, PP84, JUL 72
DATA PROVIDE AN EXPERIMENTAL DEMONSTRATION THAT TEACHERS' BRIEF AND MILD EXPRESSIONS OF OPINION, INCIDENTAL TO THE CURRICULUM OBJECTIVES, CAN SIGNIFICANTLY INFLUENCE THE ATTITUDES OF THEIR PUPILS. (AUTHORS)

EJ 061 071 PS 502 021
AGGRESSION ANXIETY, PERCEPTION OF AGGRESSIVE CUES, AND EXPECTED RETALIATION HEBDA, MARY ELLEN; AND OTHERS, *DEVELOPMENTAL PSYCHOLOGY*, V7 N1, PP85, JUL 72
AUTHORS INVESTIGATED THE HYPOTHESIS THAT DIFFERENCES IN AGGRESSIVE BEHAVIOR MAY PARTLY BE A FUNCTION OF DIFFERENCES (A) IN THE PERCEPTION OF AGGRESSIVE CUES, OR (B) IN THE DEGREE IN WHICH RETALIATION IS EXPECTED. (AUTHORS)

EJ 061 072 PS 502 026
PERSONAL ORIENTATION TO SUCCESS AND FAILURE IN URBAN BLACK CHILDREN GARRETT, ALICE M.; WILLOUGHBY, R. H., *DEVELOPMENTAL PSYCHOLOGY*, V7 N1, PP92, JUL 72
EXAMINES THE HYPOTHESIS THAT LOWER-CLASS BLACK CHILDREN ARE MORE "EXTERNAL" IN THEIR PERSONAL ORIENTATION THAN MIDDLE-CLASS WHITE CHILDREN. (AUTHORS/MB)

EJ 061 073 PS 502 034
FOUR CHILDREN GREY, CATHERINE, *CHILDREN TODAY*, V1 N4, PP7-12, JUL-AUG 72
ARTICLE ATTEMPTS TO DESCRIBE THE EMOTIONAL REBIRTH OF FOUR OF THE EIGHT CHILDREN BROUGHT TOGETHER AS ONE FAMILY BY THE REMARRIAGE OF PARENTS WHO EACH HAD FOUR CHILDREN. (MB)

EJ 061 074 PS 502 051
THE EVOLUTION OF DEVELOPMENTAL PSYCHOLOGY: A COMPARISON OF HANDBOOKS LOOFT, W. R., *HUMAN DEVELOPMENT*, V15 N3, PP187-201, 72
THREE DIFFERENT HANDBOOKS FROM CHILD PSYCHOLOGY, WHOSE PUBLICATION DATES SPAN 40 YEARS, AND A HANDBOOK ON THE PSYCHOLOGY OF AGING WERE SUBJECTED TO QUANTITATE AND QUALITATE COMPARATIVE ANALYSES. (AUTHOR/MB)

EJ 061 075 PS 502 060
SIMPLE REACTION TIME IN CHILDREN: EFFECTS OF INCENTIVE, INCENTIVE-SHIFT AND OTHER TRAINING VARIABLES ELLIOTT, ROGERS, *JOURNAL OF EXPERIMENTAL CHILD PSYCHOLOGY*, V13 N3, PP540-57, JUN 72
IMPLICATION OF FINDINGS FOR CLASSICAL MATURATION THEORIES OF THE DEVELOPMENT OF REACTION SPEED ARE DISCUSSED. (AUTHOR/MB)

EJ 061 085 PS 502 018
RACE OF EXPERIMENTER AS A VARIABLE IN RESEARCH WITH CHILDREN SOLKOFF, NORMAN, *DEVELOPMENTAL PSYCHOLOGY*, V7 N1, PP70-5, JUL 72
FINDINGS INDICATE THAT WHITE EXAMINERS DO NOT DEPRESS IQ SCORES OF BLACK CHILDREN. (MB)

EJ 061 138 PS 501 999
THE DEVELOPMENT OF THE CONTROL OF ADULT INSTRUCTIONS OVER NONVERBAL BEHAVIOR VAN DUYNE, H. JOHN, *JOURNAL OF GENETIC PSYCHOLOGY*, V120 PT 2, PP295-302, JUN 72
STUDY BASICALLY SUPPORTS THE RUSSIAN THEORY OF THE SECOND SIGNAL SYSTEM AND ITS REGULATORY CONTROL OF CONSCIOUS BEHAVIOR. (AUTHOR)

EJ 061 139 PS 502 013
CHANGES IN INFANTS' VOCALIZATIONS AS A FUNCTION OF DIFFERENTIAL ACOUSTIC STIMULATION WEBSTER, R. L.; AND OTHERS, *DEVELOPMENTAL PSYCHOLOGY*, V7 N1, PP39-43, JUL 72
RESULTS OF THIS STUDY INDICATED THAT THE FREQUENCY OF AN AUDITORY STIMULUS IS A DIMENSION TO WHICH INFANTS DIFFERENTIALLY RESPOND IN TERMS OF RESPONSE RATE AND ACOUSTIC CHARACTERISTICS OF THEIR VOCALIZATIONS. (AUTHORS)

EJ 061 140 PS 502 019
EFFECTS OF SOCIAL AND VOCAL STIMULATION ON INFANT BABBLING DODD, BARBARA J., *DEVELOPMENTAL PSYCHOLOGY*, V7 N1, PP80-3, JUL 72
IT WAS CONCLUDED THAT BOTH SOCIAL AND VOCAL ELEMENTS ARE NECESSARY TO STIMULATE A GENERAL INCREASE IN THE NUMBER AND LENGTH OF CONSONANT UTTERANCES, BUT THERE WAS NO EVIDENCE THAT STIMULATION ENCOURAGED INFANTS TO IMITATE THE CONSONANT PHONEMES PRESENTED. (AUTHOR)

EJ 061 141 PS 502 023
DEVELOPMENTAL CHANGE IN INFANT VISUAL FIXATION TO DIFFERING COMPLEXITY LEVELS AMONG CROSS-SECTIONALLY AND LONGITUDINALLY STUDIED INFANTS HOROWITZ, FRANCES DEGEN; AND OTHERS, *DEVELOPMENTAL PSYCHOLOGY*, V7 N1, PP88-9, JUL 72

EJ 061 142 PS 502 024
AN INFANT CONTROL PROCEDURE FOR STUDYING INFANT VISUAL FIXATIONS HOROWITZ, FRANCES DEGEN; AND OTHERS, *DEVELOPMENTAL PSYCHOLOGY*, V7 N1, PP90, JUL 72
IN THIS STUDY INSTEAD OF THE EXPERIMENTER CONTROLLING THE DURATION OF STIMULUS EXPOSURE, THE INFANTS' BEHAVIOR WAS ALLOWED TO CONTROL STIMULUS DURATION. (AUTHORS/MB)

EJ 061 184 PS 501 985
SCHOOL IN CHEROKEE AND ENGLISH HOLLAND, R. FOUNT, *ELEMENTARY SCHOOL JOURNAL*, V72 N8, PP412-8, MAY 72
DESCRIBES THE ACTIVITIES OF THE CHEROKEE BILINGUAL EDUCATION CENTER, CREATED IN 1969 BY NORTHEASTERN STATE COLLEGE AT TAHLEQUAH, OKLAHOMA. (MB)

EJ 061 194 PS 501 993
PERSONALITY, COGNITIVE, AND DEMOGRAPHIC CHARACTERISTICS OF STUDENT ACTIVISTS AND ACTIVE STUDENTS DEVINE, HOWARD F.; CLARK, PHILIP M., *JOURNAL OF GENETIC PSYCHOLOGY*, V120 PT 2, PP227-39, JUN 72
DATA CLEARLY FAILED TO SUPPORT THE GENERAL HYPOTHESIS THAT ACTIVE STUDENTS WOULD BE QUITE SIMILAR TO STUDENT ACTIVISTS ALONG THE DIMENSIONS STUDIED; INSTEAD, WHEN DIFFERENCES WERE FOUND, THE RESULTS TENDED TO GROUP ACTIVE STUDENTS WITH PASSIVE STUDENTS AND DIFFERENTIATE BOTH FROM STUDENT ACTIVISTS. (AUTHORS/MB)

EJ 061 231 PS 502 003
INFANT CARE AND GROWTH IN URBAN ZAMBIA GOLDBERG, SUSAN, *HUMAN DEVELOPMENT*, V15 N2, PP77-89, 72
FROM A SYMPOSIUM ON CROSS-CULTURAL STUDIES OF MOTHER-INFANT INTERACTION AT THE BIENNIAL MEETING FOR RESEARCH IN CHILD DEVELOPMENT, MINNEAPOLIS, MINN., APRIL 2, 1971. (MB)

EJ 061 232 PS 502 004
IMPLICATIONS OF INFANT DEVELOPMENT AMONG THE MAYAN INDIANS OF MEXICO BRAZELTON, T. B., *HUMAN DEVELOPMENT*, V15 N2, PP90-111, 72
FROM A SYMPOSIUM ON CROSS-CULTURAL STUDIES OF MOTHER-INFANT INTERACTION AT THE BIENNIAL MEETING FOR RESEARCH IN CHILD DEVELOPMENT, MINNEAPOLIS, MINN., APRIL 2, 1971. (MB)

EJ 061 233 PS 502 006
GROUP HOME CARE AS AN ADJUNCT TO RESIDENTIAL TREATMENT GREENBERG, ARTHUR; MAYER, MORRIS F., *CHILD WELFARE*, V51 N7, PP423-35, JUL 72
FOR SOME CHILDREN WHO HAVE BEEN IN RESIDENTIAL TREATMENT, LIFE IN A GROUP HOME CAN PROVIDE A TRANSITIONAL EXPERIENCE TO PREPARE THEM FOR RETURN TO THEIR OWN HOME OR FOR INDEPENDENT LIVING. (EDITOR)

EJ 061 234 PS 502 025
GIVEN NAMES AND STEREOTYPING BRUNING, JAMES L.; HUSA, FREDERICK T., *DEVELOPMENTAL PSYCHOLOGY*, V7 N1, PP91, JUL 72
STUDY DESIGNED TO DETERMINE WHETHER BEHAVIORAL STEREOTYPES ARE ASSOCIATED WITH ACTIVE VERSUS PASSIVE NAMES, AND ALSO, THE AGE WHEN THESE STEREOTYPES APPEAR. (AUTHORS/MB)

EJ 061 235 PS 502 039
CLARIFYING THE ROLE OF FOSTER PARENTS GALAWAY, BURT, *CHILDREN TODAY*, V1 N4, PP32-3, JUL-AUG 72
DESCRIBES A 12-WEEK COURSE FOR FOSTER PARENTS SPONSORED BY THE UNIVERSITY OF MINNESOTA IN COOPERATION WITH MINNESOTA STATE AND COUNTY DEPARTMENTS OF WELFARE AND THE MINNESOTA FOSTER PARENTS ASSOCIATION. (MB)

EJ 061 442 PS 502 066
IS SESAME STREET EXPORTABLE? LAMBERT, WILLIAM W., *INTERNATIONAL JOURNAL OF EARLY CHILDHOOD*, V4 N1, PP18-20, 72
AUTHOR'S ATTITUDE TOWARD THE ADAPTATION OF SESAME STREET IN FOREIGN COUNTRIES IS THAT IT IS WORTH DOING, IF DONE WELL, BUT THE PROJECT SHOULD BE APPROACHED CRITICALLY AND WARILY. (AUTHOR/MB)

EJ 061 465 PS 502 064
LE PROBLEME DE LA LIBERTE ET DE LA DISCIPLINE DANS LE JEU (PROBLEMS OF FREEDOM AND DISCIPLINE IN PLAY) TOPINSKA, ZOFIA, *INTERNATIONAL JOURNAL OF EARLY CHILDHOOD*, V4 N1, PP5-10, 72
DISCUSSES THE PROTECTION OF THE INDIVIDUAL'S FREEDOM TO PLAY AND THE GROWTH OF SOCIAL RELATIONS THROUGH PLAY. (AUTHOR/MB)

EJ 061 692 PS 502 070
EARLY CHILDHOOD EDUCATION IN JAPAN YAMASHITA, T., *INTERNATIONAL JOURNAL OF EARLY CHILDHOOD*, V4 N1, PP35-8, 72
THE TWO KINDS OF EDUCATIONAL FACILITIES FOR EARLY CHILDHOOD IN JAPAN ARE THE KINDERGARTEN, ESTABLISHED IN ACCORDANCE WITH THE SCHOOL EDUCATION LAW, AND THE DAY NURSERY, BASED UPON THE CHILDREN'S WELFARE LAW. (AUTHOR/MB)

EJ 062 417 PS 502 069
ENRICHING CHILDREN'S LIVES: INTERNATIONAL CO-OPERATION THROUGH UNICEF AND OMEP CRAIG, MARJORIE L.; MOORE, WINIFRED A., *INTERNATIONAL JOURNAL OF EARLY CHILDHOOD*, V4 N1, PP31-4, 72
A DESCRIPT OF UNICEF'S ACTIVITIES WITH SUGGESTIONS FOR COOPERATION IN MANY OF THESE PROGRAMS BY THE WORLD ORGANIZATION FOR EARLY CHILDHOOD EDUCATION (OMEP). (MB)

EJ 062 549 PS 502 068
THE IMPORTANCE OF SECURITY IN THE EDUCATION OF YOUNG CHILDREN SCARFE, N. V., *INTERNATIONAL JOURNAL OF EARLY CHILDHOOD,* V4 N1, PP27-30, 72

AUTHOR SPEAKS OF THE NECESSITY FOR SKILLED GUIDANCE ON THE PART OF TEACHER AND PARENTS BUT THAT CREATIVE ACTIVITIES DO NOT TAKE PLACE IN AN ATMOSPHERE OF INSECURITY OR FEAR OR ANXIETY. (AUTHOR/MB)

EJ 062 592 PS 502 065
TELEVISION INSTRUCTION AND THE PRESCHOOL CHILD PALMER, EDWARD L., *INTERNATIONAL JOURNAL OF EARLY CHILDHOOD,* V4 N1, PP11-7, 72

AUTHOR, VICE-PRESIDENT AND DIRECTOR OF RESEARCH AT THE CHILDREN'S TELEVISION WORKSHOP, DESCRIBES THE RESEARCH CONDUCTED FOR SESAME STREET. (MB)

EJ 062 593 PS 502 067
INVESTIGACIONES EN EL CAMPO EDUCATIVE (INVESTIGATIONS IN EDUCATION FIELD) MAZZELLA DE BEVILACQUA, ANUNCIACION, *INTERNATIONAL JOURNAL OF EARLY CHILDHOOD,* V4 N1, PP21-6, 72

ARTICLE REFERS TO SOME OF THE ACTIVITIES CARRIED OUT UNDER THE AUSPICES OF THE DEPARTMENT OF PEDAGOGIC INVESTIGATIONS OF THE INSTITUTE OF HIGHER EDUCATION OF URUGUAY. (EDITOR/MB)

EJ 062 594 PS 502 071
MOTHER-ATTACHMENT AND STRANGER-REACTIONS IN THE THIRD YEAR OF LIFE MACCOBY, ELEANOR E.; FELDMAN, S. SHIRLEY, *MONOGRAPHS OF THE SOCIETY FOR RESEARCH IN CHILD DEVELOPMENT,* V37 N1, PP1-86, 72

TWO STUDIES ARE REPORTED: (1) THE GROWTH AND CHANGE, FROM AGE 2 TO 3, IN CERTAIN ASPECTS OF ATTACHMENT TO MOTHER AND STRANGER-FEAR AMONG A GROUP OF AMERICAN CHILDREN, AND (2) A CROSS-SECTIONAL STUDY OF A GROUP OF 2 1/2 YEAR-OLD KIBBUTZ-REARED ISRAELI CHILDREN. (AUTHORS/MB)

SUBJECT INDEX

ABILITY
[COMPETENCE IN YOUNG CHILDREN.] ED032124
CHILDREN: THEIR POTENTIALS EJ 034 312
THE SORE-FOOTED DUCK EJ 053 929

ABILITY IDENTIFICATION
THE PRESCHOOL CHILD'S ABILITY TO FOLLOW DIRECTIONS. ED043395
PIAGETIAN TASKS AS CLASSROOM EVALUATIVE TOOLS EJ 032 679
INCREASING AND RELEASING HUMAN POTENTIALS EJ 034 710

ABSTRACT REASONING
A METHODOLOGY FOR FOSTERING ABSTRACT THINKING IN DEPRIVED CHILDREN. ED026131
THE EFFECT OF VARYING OBJECT NUMBER AND TYPE OF ARRANGEMENT ON CHILDREN'S ABILITY TO COORDINATE PERSPECTIVES. ED047804
THE ABILITY OF KINDERGARTEN AND FIRST GRADE CHILDREN TO USE THE TRANSITIVE PROPERTY OF THREE LENGTH RELATIONS IN THREE PERCEPTUAL SITUATIONS. ED048936
SPATIAL ABILITIES AND SPATIAL EGOCENTRISM IN THE YOUNG CHILD EJ 037 066
INTERDEPENDENCE OF INHELDER AND PIAGET'S MODEL OF LOGICAL THINKING EJ 039 633
SPONTANEOUS MEASUREMENT IN YOUNG CHILDREN: A RE-EXAMINATION EJ 055 095
DEVELOPMENT OF RELATIONAL CONCEPTS AND WORD DEFINITION IN CHILDREN FIVE THROUGH ELEVEN EJ 056 397
FAMILY CORRELATES OF VERBAL REASONING ABILITY EJ 061 069

ABSTRACTION LEVELS
THE DISTANCING HYPOTHESIS: A HYPOTHESIS CRUCIAL TO THE DEVELOPMENT OF REPRESENTATIONAL COMPETENCE. ED024466
STIMULUS ABSTRACTNESS AND THE CONSERVATION OF WEIGHT. ED035441
THE DEVELOPMENT OF THE LANGUAGE OF EMOTIONS: CONDITIONS OF EMOTIONAL AROUSAL EJ 052 391

ABSTRACTION TESTS
DEVELOPMENTAL LEVEL AND CONCEPT-LEARNING--A REPLICATION AND EXTENSION. ED016528
A DEVELOPMENTAL STUDY OF THE RELATIONSHIP BETWEEN REACTION-TIME AND PROBLEM-SOLVING EFFICIENCY. FINAL REPORT. ED020018
HEAD START EVALUATION AND RESEARCH CENTER, UNIVERSITY OF KANSAS. REPORT NO. IX, DEVELOPMENT OF "MATCHING" ABSTRACTIONS IN YOUNG CHILDREN. ED021645

ABSTRACTS
ABSTRACTS OF RESEARCH PERTAINING TO--UNGRADED VS SELF-CONTAINED CLASSROOM ORGANIZATION IN THE ELEMENTARY SCHOOL (GRADES 1-7). ED019129
EARLY CHILDHOOD SELECTED BIBLIOGRAPHIES SERIES. NUMBER 2, LANGUAGE. ED022538
EARLY CHILDHOOD SELECTED BIBLIOGRAPHIES SERIES. NUMBER 3, EDUCATION. ED022546
EARLY CHILDHOOD SELECTED BIBLIOGRAPHIES SERIES. NUMBER 4, COGNITION. ED023488
EARLY CHILDHOOD SELECTED BIBLIOGRAPHIES SERIES. NUMBER 5, SOCIAL. ED024472
EARLY CHILDHOOD SELECTED BIBLIOGRAPHIES SERIES. NUMBER 6, PERSONALITY. ED024475
HEAD START CRIB. CHILDHOOD RESEARCH INFORMATION BULLETIN: SELECTED RESUMES OF EARLY CHILDHOOD RESEARCH REPORTS. BULLETIN NO. 1. ED025318
BIBLIOGRAPHY: TEACHER CHARACTERISTICS. ED029716

ACADEMIC ABILITY
AN EVALUATION AND FOLLOW-UP STUDY OF SUMMER 1966 HEAD START CHILDREN IN WASHINGTON, D.C. ED020794
INTELLIGENCE QUOTIENT VERSUS LEARNING QUOTIENT: IMPLICATIONS FOR ELEMENTARY CURRICULA. ED031304

ACADEMIC ACHIEVEMENT
STUDY OF ACHIEVEMENT--REPORT POPULATION STUDY OF JUNIOR AND SENIOR KINDERGARTEN PUPILS, 1960-61 AND 1961-62. ED017321
STUDY OF ACHIEVEMENT, TORONTO INFORMATION BULLETIN NO. 1. ED017323
PRESCHOOL INTERVENTION--A PRELIMINARY REPORT OF THE PERRY PRESCHOOL PROJECT. ED018251
FINAL REPORT ON HEAD START EVALUATION AND RESEARCH--1966-67 TO THE INSTITUTE FOR EDUCATIONAL DEVELOPMENT. SECTION III, INFLUENCING ATTITUDES OF PARENTS AND TEACHERS THROUGH REWARDING CHILDREN. ED019119
REPORT OF THE EFFECTIVENESS OF PROJECT HEAD START, LUBBOCK, TEXAS. PARTS I, II, AND APPENDICES. ED019131
AN EVALUATION OF A PRESCHOOL TRAINING PROGRAM FOR CULTURALLY DEPRIVED CHILDREN. FINAL REPORT. ED019135
EFFECT OF TRIMESTER SCHOOL OPERATION ON THE ACHIEVEMENT AND ADJUSTMENT OF KINDERGARTEN AND FIRST THROUGH THIRD GRADE CHILDREN. FINAL REPORT. ED020003
HEAD START RESEARCH AND EVALUATION OFFICE, UNIVERSITY OF CALIFORNIA AT LOS ANGELES. ANNUAL REPORT, NOVEMBER 1967. SECTION II. ED021613
HEAD START EVALUATION AND RESEARCH CENTER, THE UNIVERSITY OF CHICAGO. REPORT B, MATERNAL ANTECEDENTS OF INTELLECTUAL ACHIEVEMENT BEHAVIORS IN LOWER CLASS PRESCHOOL CHILDREN. ED022551
HEAD START EVALUATION AND RESEARCH CENTER, THE UNIVERSITY OF CHICAGO. REPORT D, THE INTERACTION OF INTELLIGENCE AND BEHAVIOR AS ONE PREDICTOR OF EARLY SCHOOL ACHIEVEMENT IN WORKING CLASS AND CULTURALLY DISADVANTAGED HEAD START CHILDREN. ED022553
HEAD START EVALUATION AND RESEARCH CENTER, THE UNIVERSITY OF CHICAGO. REPORT F, SOCIALIZATION INTO THE ROLE OF PUPIL. ED023456
A STANDARDIZED NEUROLOGICAL EXAMINATION: ITS VALIDITY IN PREDICTING SCHOOL ACHIEVEMENT IN HEAD START AND OTHER POPULATIONS. FINAL REPORT. ED023475
ACADEMIC PRESCHOOL, CHAMPAIGN, ILLINOIS ED027979
A STUDY OF PUBLIC AND PRIVATE KINDERGARTEN AND NON-KINDERGARTEN CHILDREN IN THE PRIMARY GRADES. ED028837
AN EXPLORATORY INVESTIGATION OF THE CARROLL LEARNING MODEL AND THE BLOOM STRATEGY FOR MASTERY LEARNING. ED028841
AGE OF ENTRANCE INTO THE FIRST GRADE AS RELATED TO RATE OF SCHOLASTIC ACHIEVEMENT. ED028843
INTERRELATIONS BETWEEN SOCIAL-EMOTIONAL BEHAVIOR AND INFORMATION ACHIEVEMENT OF HEAD START CHILDREN. REPORT NUMBER 5. ED030479
EFFECTIVENESS OF DIRECT VERBAL INSTRUCTION ON IQ PERFORMANCE AND ACHIEVEMENT IN READING AND ARITHMETIC. ED030496
DOES THE USE OF CUISENAIRE RODS IN KINDERGARTEN, FIRST AND SECOND GRADES UPGRADE ARITHMETIC ACHIEVEMENT? ED032128
RELATIONSHIPS BETWEEN TEACHER BEHAVIOR, PUPIL BEHAVIOR, AND PUPIL ACHIEVEMENT. ED038189
PREDICTION OF READINESS IN KINDERGARTEN AND ACHIEVEMENT IN THE FIRST PRIMARY YEAR. STUDY NUMBER TWO. ED043393
THE EFFECT OF THREE HOME VISITING STRATEGIES UPON MEASURES OF CHILDREN'S ACADEMIC APTITUDE AND MATERNAL TEACHING BEHAVIORS. FINAL REPORT. ED044175
PREDICTION OF ACHIEVEMENT IN THE FIRST PRIMARY YEAR. STUDY NUMBER ONE. ED044180
DEVELOPMENTAL SKILL AND ACHIEVEMENT DIFFERENCES OF CHILDREN IDENTIFIED AS EXCELLENT, GOOD, AND AVERAGE IN READING AND ARITHMETIC ACHIEVEMENT. STUDY NUMBER THREE. ED044181
THE COGNITIVE ENVIRONMENTS OF URBAN PRESCHOOL CHILDREN: FOLLOW-UP PHASE. FINAL REPORT. ED045180
CHANGING THE LEARNING PATTERNS OF THE CULTURALLY DIFFERENT. ED045184
FINAL REPORT ON PRESCHOOL EDUCATION TO OHIO DEPARTMENT OF EDUCATION. ED045200
THE PHYSICAL ENVIRONMENT AS A MEDIATING FACTOR IN SCHOOL ACHIEVEMENT. ED046496
A PILOT STUDY OF A PRESCHOOL METHOD OF PREVENTIVE EDUCATION. FINAL REPORT. ED046541
SCHOOL ACHIEVEMENT: A PRELIMINARY LOOK AT THE EFFECTS OF THE HOME. ED047777
CORRELATION OF PAIRED-ASSOCIATE PERFORMANCE WITH SCHOOL ACHIEVEMENT AS A FUNCTION OF TASK AND SAMPLE VARIATION. ED049813
SURVIVAL SKILLS AND FIRST GRADE ACADEMIC ACHIEVEMENT. REPORT #1. ED050807
DESIGNS AND PROPOSAL FOR EARLY CHILDHOOD RESEARCH: A NEW LOOK: THE UNACKNOWLEDGED ROLE OF CULTURE CONFLICT IN NEGRO EDUCATION. (ONE IN A SERIES OF SIX PAPERS). ED053810

RACIAL DIFFERENCES IN INDICES OF EGO FUNCTIONING RELEVANT TO ACADEMIC ACHIEVEMENT EJ 015 096
IMPROVING HIGH SCHOOL LEARNING PREDICTIONS WITH MULTIPLE JUNIOR HIGH TEST SCORES EJ 016 653
PERFORMANCES OF AVERAGE ABILITY STUDENTS IN A JUNIOR COLLEGE AND IN FOUR-YEAR INSTITUTIONS, 1953 TO 1968 EJ 017 244
ACHIEVEMENT OF FIRST- AND SECOND-YEAR PUPILS IN GRADED AND NONGRADED CLASSROOMS EJ 018 969
SCHOOL ACHIEVERS AND UNDERACHIEVERS IN AN URBAN GHETTO EJ 027 614
PIAGETIAN TASKS AS CLASSROOM EVALUATIVE TOOLS EJ 032 679
THE KINDERGARTEN AGAINST APPALACHIAN POVERTY EJ 037 021
EARLY GRADE SCHOOL PERFORMANCE OF INNER CITY NEGRO HIGH SCHOOL HIGH ACHIEVERS, LOW ACHIEVERS, AND DROPOUTS EJ 039 572
CORRELATES OF LOCUS OF CONTROL IN A SECONDARY SCHOOL POPULATION EJ 039 905
EFFECTS OF HEMOPHILIA UPON INTELLECTUAL GROWTH AND ACADEMIC ACHIEVEMENT EJ 044 009
A FACTOR-ANALYTIC STUDY OF THE RELATIONSHIP OF MOTOR FACTORS TO ACADEMIC CRITERIA FOR FIRST- AND THIRD-GRADE BOYS EJ 052 451
AREAS OF RECENT RESEARCH IN EARLY CHILDHOOD EDUCATION EJ 054 380
MOTIVATIONAL AND ACHIEVEMENT DIFFERENCES AMONG CHILDREN OF VARIOUS ORDINAL BIRTH POSITIONS EJ 055 547
RELATIONSHIP OF PRESCHOOL SOCIAL-EMOTIONAL FUNCTIONING TO LATER INTELLECTUAL ACHIEVEMENT EJ 058 138
EFFECTS OF PROVISION FOR INDIVIDUAL DIFFERENCES AND TEACHER ATTENTION UPON STUDY BEHAVIOR AND ASSIGNMENTS COMPLETED EJ 058 353
LEARNING DISABILITY: A NEW LOOK AT UNDERACHIEVING EJ 058 411

ACADEMIC APTITUDE

AN EXPLORATORY INVESTIGATION OF THE CARROLL LEARNING MODEL AND THE BLOOM STRATEGY FOR MASTERY LEARNING. ED028841
PERFORMANCES OF AVERAGE ABILITY STUDENTS IN A JUNIOR COLLEGE AND IN FOUR-YEAR INSTITUTIONS, 1953 TO 1968 EJ 017 244
A FACTOR-ANALYTIC STUDY OF THE RELATIONSHIP OF MOTOR FACTORS TO ACADEMIC CRITERIA FOR FIRST- AND THIRD-GRADE BOYS EJ 052 451

ACADEMIC ASPIRATION

SOCIAL CLASS AND PARENT'S ASPIRATIONS FOR THEIR CHILDREN. REPORT NUMBER 8. ED030482
LEVEL OF ASPIRATION AND THE PROBABILITY LEARNING OF MIDDLE- AND LOWER-CLASS CHILDREN EJ 024 703
HOW TO TEACH FEAR EJ 061 058

ACADEMIC FAILURE

PREVENTION OF FAILURE. ED020777
SUFFER THE LITTLE KENTUCKY FIRST-GRADERS EJ 037 283

ACADEMIC PERFORMANCE

A SOCIAL PSYCHOLOGICAL ANALYSIS OF THE TRANSITION FROM HOME TO SCHOOL. FINAL REPORT. ED015017
MONTESSORI PRE-SCHOOL EDUCATION. FINAL REPORT. ED017320
TEACHERS' BELIEFS, CLASSROOM ATMOSPHERE AND STUDENT BEHAVIOR. FINAL REPORT. ED018249
MOTIVATIONAL EFFECTS OF INDIVIDUAL CONFERENCES AND GOAL SETTING ON PERFORMANCE AND ATTITUDES IN ARITHMETIC. REPORT FROM THE PROJECT ON SITUATIONAL VARIABLES AND EFFICIENCY OF CONCEPT LEARNING. ED032113
A COMPARISON OF CONTRASTING PROGRAMS IN EARLY CHILDHOOD EDUCATION. ED046509
EFFECTS OF PRESCHOOL STIMULATION UPON SUBSEQUENT SCHOOL PERFORMANCE AMONG THE CULTURALLY DISADVANTAGED. ED046545
RELATIONSHIP OF CURRICULUM, TEACHING, AND LEARNING IN PRESCHOOL EDUCATION. ED049837
HOME LANGUAGE AND PERFORMANCE ON STANDARDIZED TESTS EJ 032 678
SUFFER THE LITTLE KENTUCKY FIRST-GRADERS EJ 037 283
FATHER AVAILABILITY AND ACADEMIC PERFORMANCE AMONG THIRD-GRADE BOYS EJ 038 730
EARLY GRADE SCHOOL PERFORMANCE OF INNER CITY NEGRO HIGH SCHOOL HIGH ACHIEVERS, LOW ACHIEVERS, AND DROPOUTS EJ 039 572
PERSONALITY, COGNITIVE, AND ACADEMIC CORRELATES OF PROBLEM-SOLVING FLEXIBILITY EJ 039 632
TEACHER EXPECTANCY AS RELATED TO THE ACADEMIC AND PERSONAL GROWTH OF PRIMARY-AGE CHILDREN EJ 057 018
THE RELATIONSHIP BETWEEN CHILDREN'S ACADEMIC PERFORMANCE AND ACHIEVEMENT ACCOUNTABILITY EJ 058 414

ACADEMICALLY HANDICAPPED

EFFECT OF SENSORIMOTOR ACTIVITY ON PERCEPTION AND LEARNING IN THE NEUROLOGICALLY HANDICAPPED CHILD. FINAL PROGRESS REPORT. ED033757
RACIAL DIFFERENCES IN INDICES OF EGO FUNCTIONING RELEVANT TO ACADEMIC ACHIEVEMENT EJ 015 096

ACCELERATION

THE EFFECT OF A STRUCTURED TUTORIAL PROGRAM ON THE COGNITIVE AND LANGUAGE DEVELOPMENT OF CULTURALLY DISADVANTAGED INFANTS EJ 008 272

ACCIDENT PREVENTION

CHILDREN AND ROAD ACCIDENTS EJ 050 496

ACCIDENTS

CHILDREN WHO ARE INJURED. 1970 WHITE HOUSE CONFERENCE ON CHILDREN, REPORT OF FORUM 13. (WORKING COPY). ED046529

ACCOUNTING

CONSIDERATIONS IN DAY CARE COST ANALYSIS EJ 040 722

ACCREDITATION (INSTITUTIONS)

STEPS PURSUANT TO SECURING ACCREDITATION BY PRIVATE SECONDARY SCHOOLS EJ 016 606

ACHIEVEMENT

THE FORMATION OF ADDITION AND SUBTRACTION CONCEPTS BY PUPILS IN GRADES ONE AND TWO. FINAL REPORT. ED015015
THE RELATIONSHIPS BETWEEN CERTAIN TEACHER CHARACTERISTICS AND ACHIEVEMENT AND CREATIVITY OF GIFTED ELEMENTARY SCHOOL STUDENTS. FINAL REPORT SUMMARY. ED015787
FINAL REPORT ON HEAD START EVALUATION AND RESEARCH--1966-67 TO THE INSTITUTE FOR EDUCATIONAL DEVELOPMENT. SECTION VIII, RELATIONSHIPS BETWEEN SELF-CONCEPT AND SPECIFIC VARIABLES IN A LOW-INCOME CULTURALLY DIFFERENT POPULATION. ED019124
THE ASSESSMENT OF ACHIEVEMENT ANXIETIES IN CHILDREN: HOW IMPORTANT IS RESPONSE SET AND MULTIDIMENSIONALITY IN THE TEST ANXIETY SCALE FOR CHILDREN? ED025313
A THEORETICAL APPROACH FOR SELECTING ELEMENTARY SCHOOL ENVIRONMENTAL VARIABLES. ED028834
A COMPARATIVE STUDY OF FAILURE AVOIDANCE IN CULTURALLY DISADVANTAGED AND NON-CULTURALLY DISADVANTAGED FIRST GRADE CHILDREN. ED044170
PRELIMINARY ANALYSIS OF 1968-69 BOOTH ACHIEVEMENT. ED045201
THE USE OF INDIVIDUAL GOAL-SETTING CONFERENCES AS A MOTIVATIONAL TECHNIQUE. ED053816
SOME DETERMINANTS OF CHILDREN'S SELF-REWARD BEHAVIOR AFTER EXPOSURE TO DISCREPANT REWARD CRITERIA EJ 030 511
THE EFFECTS OF SEX-ROLE STANDARDS FOR ACHIEVEMENT AND SEX-ROLE PREFERENCE ON THREE DETERMINANTS OF ACHIEVEMENT MOTIVATION EJ 034 454
THE INFLUENCE OF MASCULINE, FEMININE, AND NEUTRAL TASKS ON CHILDREN'S ACHIEVEMENT BEHAVIOR, EXPECTANCIES OF SUCCESS, AND ATTAINMENT VALUES EJ 037 318
LEVEL OF "N" ACHIEVEMENT AND PROBABILITY IN CHILDREN EJ 034 906
AN EXPLORATORY STUDY OF THE RELATIONSHIP BETWEEN COGNITIVE PRETESTING AND COURSE ACHIEVEMENT EJ 041 758
THE EFFECTS OF DIFFERENT COMPETITIVE CONTINGENCIES ON COOPERATIVE BEHAVIOR EJ 042 208
LEVELS OF ASPIRATION, ACHIEVEMENT, AND SOCIOCULTURAL DIFFERENCES IN PRESCHOOL CHILDREN EJ 043 482
THE RELATIONSHIP BETWEEN PRIMARY STUDENTS' RATIONALIZATION OF CONSERVATION AND THEIR MATHEMATICAL ACHIEVEMENT EJ 046 672
LOCUS OF CONTROL AND ACHIEVEMENT IN MIDDLE- AND LOWER-CLASS CHILDREN EJ 052 448

ACHIEVEMENT GAINS

AN ASSESSMENT OF INTELLIGENCE, PSYCHOLINGUISTIC ABILITIES AND LEARNING APTITUDES AMONG PRESCHOOL CHILDREN. ED014323
AN EVALUATION OF THE EFFECTS OF A SUMMER HEAD START PROGRAM. ED014327
IMPACT OF SUMMER 1965 HEAD START ON CHILDREN'S CONCEPT ATTAINMENT DURING KINDERGARTEN. FINAL REPORT. ED015773
HEADSTART OPERATIONAL FIELD ANALYSIS. PROGRESS REPORT IV. ED015777
THE EARLY TRAINING PROJECT FOR DISADVANTAGED CHILDREN--A REPORT AFTER FIVE YEARS. ED016514
SECOND-YEAR REPORT ON AN EVALUATIVE STUDY OF PREKINDERGARTEN PROGRAMS FOR EDUCATIONALLY DISADVANTAGED CHILDREN. ED016523
THE EFFECTS OF JUNIOR KINDERGARTEN ON ACHIEVEMENT--THE FIRST FIVE YEARS. APPENDIX. ED016527
EVALUATION OF CHANGES OCCURRING IN CHILDREN WHO PARTICIPATED IN PROJECT HEAD START. ED017316
AN APPROACH FOR WORKING WITH MOTHERS OF DISADVANTAGED PRESCHOOL CHILDREN. ED017335
THE EFFECTS OF A HIGHLY STRUCTURED PRESCHOOL PROGRAM ON THE MEASURED INTELLIGENCE OF CULTURALLY DISADVANTAGED FOUR-YEAR-OLD CHILDREN. INTERIM REPORT. ED019116
A FOLLOW-UP STUDY OF INTELLIGENCE CHANGES IN CHILDREN WHO PARTICIPATED IN PROJECT HEADSTART. ED020786
THE EFFECTS OF ASSESSMENT AND PERSONALIZED PROGRAMMING ON SUBSEQUENT INTELLECTUAL DEVELOPMENT OF PREKINDERGARTEN AND KINDERGARTEN CHILDREN. FINAL REPORT OF PHASE II. ED023487

THE ELEMENTARY MATHEMATICS STUDY: AN INTERIM REPORT ON KINDERGARTEN YEAR RESULTS. ED027937
EFFECT OF MATERNAL ATTITUDES, TEACHER ATTITUDES, AND TYPE OF NURSERY SCHOOL TRAINING ON THE ABILITIES OF PRESCHOOL CHILDREN. FINAL REPORT. ED028844
A COMPARISON OF READING READINESS ACHIEVEMENT OF KINDERGARTEN CHILDREN OF DISPARATE ENTRANCE AGES. ED033745
THE EFFECTS OF SCHOOL ENVIRONMENT ON DISADVANTAGED KINDERGARTEN CHILDREN, WITH AND WITHOUT A HEAD START BACKGROUND. FINAL REPORT. ED041640
A COMPARATIVE STUDY OF THE IMPACT OF TWO CONTRASTING EDUCATIONAL APPROACHES IN HEAD START, 1968-69. ED041643
AN INVESTIGATION OF THE EFFECTS OF TEACHER VERBAL REINFORCEMENT AS IT RELATES TO SCHOLASTIC APTITUDE AND ACHIEVEMENT WITH ELEMENTARY SCHOOL CHILDREN. PROGRESS REPORT. ED042494
HAWAII HEAD START EVALUATION FOLLOW-UP--1968-69. FINA L REPORT. ED042515
THE FIRST YEAR OF SESAME STREET: THE FORMATIVE RESEARCH. FINAL REPORT, VOLUME II OF V VOLUMES. ED047822
A PILOT STUDY OF COMPUTER-ASSISTED DRILL AND PRACTICE IN SEVENTH GRADE REMEDIAL MATHEMATICS EJ 027 030

ACHIEVEMENT NEED
"NEED ACHIEVEMENT" TRAINING FOR HEAD START CHILDREN AND THEIR MOTHERS. ED048943
INFLUENCE OF SUBJECT AND SITUATIONAL VARIABLES ON THE PERSISTENCE OF FIRST GRADE CHILDREN IN A TEST-LIKE SITUATION. ED052819
SHIFTS IN CHILD-REARING ATTITUDES LINKED WITH PARENTHOOD AND OCCUPATION EJ 038 853

ACHIEVEMENT RATING
FROM THEORY TO THE CLASSROOM, BACKGROUND INFORMATION ON THE FIRST GRADE PROJECT IN NEW YORK CITY SCHOOLS. ED015770
PROBABILITY LEARNING AS A FUNCTION OF SEX OF THE SUBJECT, TEST ANXIETY, AND PERCENTAGE OF REINFORCEMENT EJ 027 181
THE EFFECTS OF DIFFERENTIAL REINFORCEMENT ON THE DISCRIMINATION LEARNING OF NORMAL AND LOW-ACHIEVING MIDDLE-CLASS BOYS EJ 056 398

ACHIEVEMENT TESTS
A STUDY OF THE FULL-YEAR 1966 HEAD START PROGRAMS. ED015010
PROJECT TOBI, THE DEVELOPMENT OF A PRE-SCHOOL ACHIEVEMENT TEST. FINAL REPORT. ED016520
MATCHED-PAIR SCORING TECHNIQUE USED ON A FIRST-GRADE YES-NO TYPE ECONOMICS ACHIEVEMENT TEST. ED029699
SRA ECONOMICS MATERIALS IN GRADES ONE AND TWO. EVALUATION REPORTS. ED029700
COMPARISON OF YES-NO, MATCHED-PAIRS, AND ALL-NO SCORING OF A FIRST-GRADE ECONOMICS ACHIEVEMENT TEST. ED029701
TESTS BUILT FROM PIAGET'S AND GESELL'S TASKS AS PREDICTORS OF FIRST-GRADE ACHIEVEMENT EJ 058 928

ACOUSTICAL ENVIRONMENT
CHANGES IN INFANTS' VOCALIZATIONS AS A FUNCTION OF DIFFERENTIAL ACOUSTIC STIMULATION EJ 061 139

ACTION PROGRAMS (COMMUNITY)
EXPRESSIONS OF IDENTITY: THE SCHOOL-AGE CHILD. 1970 WHITE HOUSE CONFERENCE ON CHILDREN, REPORT OF FORUM 3. (WORKING COPY). ED046522

ACTION RESEARCH
THE EVALUATION OF PROJECT HEAD START--A CONCEPTUAL STATEMENT. ED015792
PROBLEMS OF EDUCATIONAL EVALUATION IN PROJECT HEAD START--SAMPLING, DESIGN, AND CONTROL GROUPS. ED015793
THE EFFECT OF SOCIAL INTERACTION ON ACTIVITY LEVELS IN SIX-TO EIGHT-YEAR-OLD BOYS EJ 052 463

ACTIVISM
PERSONALITY, COGNITIVE, AND DEMOGRAPHIC CHARACTERISTICS OF STUDENT ACTIVISTS AND ACTIVE STUDENTS EJ 061 194

ACTIVITIES
CURRICULUM GUIDE FOR CHILDREN'S ACTIVITIES, PARENT PRESCHOOL PROGRAM. ED027078
INDIVIDUALIZED MOTOR-PERCEPTUAL STUDY. ED029692
EXEL ED029698
CHILDHOOD RESOURCES INFORMATION BULLETIN. VOLUME 1, NUMBER 2, FALL 1969. ED032948
WHAT ABOUT THE SCHOOL BUS? EJ 020 294

ACTIVITY LEARNING
SPONTANEOUS PLAY: AN AVENUE FOR INTELLECTUAL DEVELOPMENT. ED023444
AN OVERVIEW OF BRITISH INFANT SCHOOLS EJ 026 835

ADAPTATION LEVEL THEORY
STYLE OF ADAPTATION TO AVERSIVE MATERNAL CONTROL AND PARANOID BEHAVIOR EJ 055 105

ADJECTIVES
COMPETENCE VS. PERFORMANCE IN YOUNG CHILDREN'S USE OF COMPLEX LINGUISTIC STRUCTURES. ED029687

ADJUSTMENT (TO ENVIRONMENT)
A FOLLOWUP STUDY OF ADOPTIONS: POST-PLACEMENT FUNCTIONING OF ADOPTION FAMILIES. ED039018
INTRODUCTION OF NEW CHILDREN INTO A DAY CARE CENTER EJ 011 302
THE USE OF A PLAY PROGRAM BY HOSPITALIZED CHILDREN EJ 026 774
POSTADOPTION COUNSELING: A PROFESSIONAL OBLIGATION EJ 028 792
ADJUSTMENT DIFFERENCES OF SELECTED FOREIGN-BORN PUPILS EJ 041 962
THE EFFECTS OF MOTHERS' PRESENCE AND PREVISITS ON CHILDREN'S EMOTIONAL REACTION TO STARTING NURSERY SCHOOL EJ 046 469
FAMILY INTERACTION VARIABLES AND ADJUSTMENT OF NONCLINIC BOYS EJ 053 737
FAMILY FACTORS RELATED TO COMPETENCE IN YOUNG DISADVANTAGED MEXICAN-AMERICAN CHILDREN EJ 053 753
PROBLEM-SOLVING THINKING AND ADJUSTMENT AMONG DISADVANTAGED PRESCHOOL CHILDREN EJ 056 612

ADJUSTMENT PROBLEMS
THE WARRIOR DROPOUTS. ED016529
SHARING PARENTS WITH STRANGERS: THE ROLE OF THE GROUP HOME FOSTER FAMILY'S OWN CHILDREN EJ 053 600

ADMINISTRATION
THE KINDERGARTEN, A PLACE FOR LEARNING. BULLETIN TWO: OPERATIONAL GUIDELINES FOR ADMINISTRATORS. ED039024
PRESCHOOL PROGRAMS OF THE U.S.S.R EJ 016 352

ADMINISTRATIVE ORGANIZATION
CO-OPERATIVE NURSERY SCHOOLS--A HANDBOOK FOR PARENTS. A GUIDE FOR ORGANIZATION AND ADMINISTRATION. REVISED EDITION. ED020022

ADMINISTRATIVE PERSONNEL
EXPANDED PREKINDERGARTEN PROGRAM, EVALUATION OF NEW YORK CITY TITLE I EDUCATIONAL PROJECTS 1966-67. ED019115

ADMINISTRATIVE PROBLEMS
HEAD START EVALUATION AND RESEARCH CENTER. PROGRESS REPORT OF RESEARCH STUDIES, 1966-1967. ED021612
HEAD START EVALUATION AND RESEARCH CENTER. PROGRESS REPORT OF RESEARCH STUDIES 1966 TO 1967. DOCUMENT 2, STUDIES OF THE SOCIAL ORGANIZATION OF HEAD START CENTERS. ED021624
PROJECT HEAD START, THE URBAN AND RURAL CHALLENGE. FINAL REPORT. ED022527

ADMINISTRATOR GUIDES
TEACHER AIDES: HANDBOOK FOR INSTRUCTORS AND ADMINISTRATORS. ED024461
THE KINDERGARTEN, A PLACE FOR LEARNING. BULLETIN TWO: OPERATIONAL GUIDELINES FOR ADMINISTRATORS. ED039024
A GUIDE FOR MANAGERS OF CHILD DAY CARE AGENCIES. ED046486

ADMINISTRATOR RESPONSIBILITY
THE CHILD ADVOCATE. 1970 WHITE HOUSE CONFERENCE ON CHILDREN, REPORT OF FORUM 24. (WORKING COPY). ED046538

ADMINISTRATOR ROLE
THE PRINCIPAL AND THE KINDERGARTEN EJ 016 716
RESEARCH ON ASPECTS OF LEADERSHIP ROLES IN EARLY AND ELEMENTARY EDUCATION EJ 055 205

ADMISSION (SCHOOL)
PRESCHOOL EDUCATION AND SCHOOL ADMISSION PRACTICES IN NEW ZEALAND. ED046487
EARLY ADMISSION: OPINION VERSUS EVIDENCE EJ 048 045

ADMISSION CRITERIA
PRESCHOOL EDUCATION AND SCHOOL ADMISSION PRACTICES IN NEW ZEALAND. ED046487
EARLY ADMISSION: OPINION VERSUS EVIDENCE EJ 048 045

ADOLESCENCE
OR PSYCHOANALYTIC THEORY OF ADOLESCENCE? EJ 007 790
CERTAIN CULTURAL AND FAMILIAL FACTORS CONTRIBUTING TO ADOLESCENT ALIENATION EJ 022 536
ALIENATION: AN ESSENTIAL PROCESS OF THE PSYCHOLOGY OF ADOLESCENCE EJ 023 426
ALIENATION OF PRESENT-DAY ADOLESCENTS EJ 023 428
ADOLESCENCE AND SOCIAL CHANGE EJ 023 611
AWARENESS, AFFECTION, AND PERCEIVED SIMILARITY IN THE PARENT-CHILD RELATIONSHIP EJ 025 377
ADOLESCENCE, IDENTITY, AND FOSTER FAMILY CARE EJ 030 652
BRIDGING THE CONCEPT GAP IN WORK WITH YOUTH EJ 031 644
LEARNING OF MEDIA CONTENT: A DEVELOPMENTAL STUDY EJ 033 782
INTELLECTUAL EVOLUTION FROM ADOLESCENCE TO ADULTHOOD EJ 050 073
ANXIETY AND MORAL JUDGMENT IN EARLY ADOLESCENCE EJ 055 094

ADOLESCENTS
ADOLESCENT NORMS AND BEHAVIOR: ORGANIZATION AND CONFORMITY EJ 007 450
A HOTLINE TELEPHONE SERVICE FOR YOUNG PEOPLE IN CRISIS EJ 007 713
COMMUNICATING WITH TODAY'S TEENAGERS; AN EXERCISE BETWEEN GENERATIONS EJ 011 838
SMALL GROUPS - AN EFFECTIVE TREATMENT APPROACH IN RESIDENTIAL PROGRAMS FOR ADOLESCENTS EJ 017 900
PERCEIVED MATERNAL CHILD-REARING EXPERIENCE AND THE EFFECTS OF VICARIOUS AND DIRECT REINFORCEMENT ON MALES EJ 019 008
SOCIOECONOMIC STATUS AND SEX DIFFERENCES IN ADOLESCENT REFERENCE-GROUP ORIENTATION EJ 023 614
A FOLLOW-UP STUDY OF SCHOOL PHOBIC ADOLESCENTS ADMITTED TO AN IN-PATIENT UNIT EJ 026 157
A SEX DIFFERENCE IN THE WECHSLER IQ VOCABULARY SCORE AS A PREDICTOR OF STRATEGY IN A PROBABILITY-LEARNING TASK PERFORMED BY ADOLESCENTS EJ 026 376
REACTION TIME AND REMOTE ASSOCIATION IN TALENTED MALE ADOLESCENTS EJ 029 360
LEARNING AND PROBLEM SOLVING BY THE MENTALLY RETARDED UNDER THREE TESTING CONDITIONS EJ 030 290
SELF-DESCRIPTION AS A FUNCTION OF EVALUATIVE AND ACTIVITY RATINGS AMONG AMERICAN AND INDIAN ADOLESCENTS EJ 034 042
DELAY OF GRATIFICATION AND INTERNAL VERSUS EXTERNAL CONTROL AMONG ADOLESCENTS OF LOW SOCIOECONOMIC STATUS EJ 034 539
FATHER ABSENCE, PERCEIVED MATERNAL BEHAVIOR, AND MASCULINITY OF SELF-CONCEPT AMONG JUNIOR HIGH SCHOOL BOYS EJ 035 804
CONFORMITY IN EARLY AND LATE ADOLESCENCE EJ 038 936
SEX DIFFERENCES IN ADOLESCENT REACTIONS TOWARD NEWCOMERS EJ 039 899
CHANGE IN EFFICIENCY OF EGO FUNCTIONING AND COMPLEXITY FROM ADOLESCENCE TO YOUNG ADULTHOOD EJ 039 902
DIFFERENTIAL ADJUSTMENT TO PUBESCENCE AND COGNITIVE STYLE PATTERNS EJ 039 903
AUTONOMIC RESPONSES OF MALE ADOLESCENTS EXHIBITING REFRACTORY BEHAVIOUR IN SCHOOL EJ 045 109
ADOLESCENT MATERNITY SERVICES: A TEAM APPROACH EJ 047 354
CONCEPTS OF SOCIAL SEX ROLES AMONG CHILEAN ADOLESCENTS EJ 048 396
VIOLENCE AS A SYMPTOM OF CHILDHOOD EMOTIONAL ILLNESS EJ 055 536
SEX ROLE IDENTITY OF ADOLESCENT GIRLS IN FOSTER HOMES AND INSTITUTIONS EJ 059 644
LANGUAGE PATTERNS WITHIN THE YOUTH SUBCULTURE: DEVELOPMENT OF SLANG VOCABULARIES EJ 060 720
CONCRETE OPERATIONAL THINKING IN MENTALLY ILL ADOLESCENTS EJ 060 778
PHENOMENAL ENVIRONMENTAL OPPRESSIVENESS IN SUICIDAL ADOLESCENTS EJ 061 063

ADOPTED CHILDREN
THE FAMILY ROMANCE FANTASY IN CHILDREN ADOPTED IN INFANCY EJ 022 478
POSTADOPTION COUNSELING: A PROFESSIONAL OBLIGATION EJ 028 792
WHEN IS SUBSIDIZED ADOPTION PREFERABLE TO LONG-TERM FOSTER CARE? EJ 035 949
ADOPTION TRENDS: JANUARY-JUNE 1971 EJ 047 001

ADOPTION
AN INFANT RATING SCALE, ITS VALIDATION AND USEFULNESS. ED016513
A FOLLOWUP STUDY OF ADOPTIONS: POST-PLACEMENT FUNCTIONING OF ADOPTION FAMILIES. ED039018
CHILD WELFARE SERVICES: A SOURCEBOOK. ED047813
FACTS AGAINST IMPRESSIONS: MOTHERS SEEKING TO RELINQUISH CHILDREN FOR ADOPTION EJ 013 330
WILLINGNESS TO ADOPT ATYPICAL CHILDREN EJ 020 860
ONE-PARENT ADOPTIONS EJ 022 180
EARLY LEGAL ADOPTION EJ 022 533
ADOPTIVE PLACEMENT OF THE OLDER CHILD EJ 027 644
SOME HELPFUL TECHNIQUES WHEN PLACING OLDER CHILDREN FOR ADOPTION EJ 029 166
ADOPTION RESOURCES FOR BLACK CHILDREN EJ 035 801
WHEN IS SUBSIDIZED ADOPTION PREFERABLE TO LONG-TERM FOSTER CARE? EJ 035 949
MEDICAL GENETICS AND ADOPTION EJ 037 577
UNWED MOTHERS AND THEIR DECISIONS TO KEEP OR SURRENDER CHILDREN EJ 040 042
ADOPTION TRENDS: JANUARY-JUNE 1971 EJ 047 001
A FRESH LOOK AT INTERCOUNTRY ADOPTIONS EJ 047 968
ON TRANSRACIAL ADOPTION OF BLACK CHILDREN EJ 053 853
ADOPTION: IDENTIFICATION AND SERVICE EJ 058 307

ADOPTION (IDEAS)
RECENT DEVELOPMENTS IN KOREAN SERVICES FOR CHILDREN EJ 032 563
ADOPTION RESOURCES FOR BLACK CHILDREN EJ 035 801
WHEN IS SUBSIDIZED ADOPTION PREFERABLE TO LONG-TERM FOSTER CARE? EJ 035 949
ATTITUDE OF BLACK NATURAL PARENTS REGARDING ADOPTION EJ 038 792
THE EFFECT OF A TELEVISION MODEL UPON RULE ADOPTION BEHAVIOR OF CHILDREN EJ 056 733

ADULT CHARACTERISTICS
RELATING AND RESPONDING: THE ADULT EJ 050 936

ADULT DEVELOPMENT
SETTING AND THE EMERGENCE OF COMPETENCE DURING ADULT SOCIALIZATION: WORKING AT HOME VS. WORKING "OUT THERE" EJ 012 719
SEPARATING ENDOGENOUS, EXOGENOUS, ECOGENIC, AND EPOGENIC COMPONENT CURVES IN DEVELOPMENTAL DATA EJ 027 552

ADULTS
COMMUNICATING WITH TODAY'S TEENAGERS; AN EXERCISE BETWEEN GENERATIONS EJ 011 838
YOUTH AS ADVISERS TO ADULTS AND VICE VERSA EJ 018 068
HOW ADULTS AND CHILDREN SEARCH AND RECOGNIZE PICTURES EJ 029 384
RECOGNITION OF FLASHED WORDS BY CHILDREN EJ 032 676
DEVELOPMENTAL GENERALITY OF A FORM RECOGNITION STRATEGY EJ 037 534
CHANGE IN EFFICIENCY OF EGO FUNCTIONING AND COMPLEXITY FROM ADOLESCENCE TO YOUNG ADULTHOOD EJ 039 902
CONFORMITY IN CHILDREN AS A FUNCTION OF GRADE LEVEL, AND REAL VERSUS HYPOTHETICAL ADULT AND PEER MODELS EJ 040 294
A DEVELOPMENTAL STUDY OF SIZE CONSTANCY FOR TWO-VERSUS THREE-DIMENSIONAL STIMULI EJ 040 454
RELATING AND RESPONDING: THE ADULT EJ 050 936
EFFECT OF A CHILD'S SEX ON ADULT INTERPRETATIONS OF ITS BEHAVIOR EJ 053 711
WHITE ADULT BEHAVIOR TOWARD BLACK AND WHITE CHILDREN EJ 056 729

ADVISORY COMMITTEES
A PLAN FOR CONTINUING GROWTH. ED046493

AESTHETIC EDUCATION
AESTHETIC EDUCATION IN SOVIET SCHOOLS EJ 060 105

AFFECTION
EXTRA-CURRICULAR PARENT-CHILD CONTACT AND CHILDREN'S SOCIALLY REINFORCED TASK BEHAVIOR. ED023447
ATTACHMENT, EXPLORATION, AND SEPARATION: ILLUSTRATED BY THE BEHAVIOR OF ONE-YEAR-OLDS IN A STRANGE SITUATION EJ 018 320
THE CAPACITY TO LOVE: A POSSIBLE REFORMULATION EJ 034 709

AFFECTIVE BEHAVIOR
SOUTHWESTERN COOPERATIVE EDUCATIONAL LABORATORY INTERACTION OBSERVATION SCHEDULE (SCIOS): A SYSTEM FOR ANALYZING TEACHER-PUPIL INTERACTION IN THE AFFECTIVE DOMAIN. ED038188
EMOTIONAL DEVELOPMENT IN THE FIRST TWO YEARS. ED039936
DEVELOPMENTAL TRENDS IN THE SELECTIVE PERCEPTION OF RACE AND AFFECT BY YOUNG NEGRO AND CAUCASIAN CHILDREN. ED046498
A RESOURCE AND REFERENCE BIBLIOGRAPHY IN EARLY CHILDHOOD EDUCATION AND DEVELOPMENTAL PSYCHOLOGY: THE AFFECTIVE DOMAIN. ED049817
INDIVIDUAL DIFFERENCES IN THE DEVELOPMENT OF SOME ATTACHMENT BEHAVIORS. ED050827
THE KINDNESSES OF CHILDREN EJ 010 444
ATTACHMENT, EXPLORATION, AND SEPARATION: ILLUSTRATED BY THE BEHAVIOR OF ONE-YEAR-OLDS IN A STRANGE SITUATION EJ 018 320
IT MAKES ME FEEL BAD WHEN YOU CALL ME "STINKY" EJ 029 358
DEVELOPMENTAL CHANGES IN THE USE OF EMOTION CUES IN A CONCEPT-FORMATION TASK EJ 029 362
I SEE WHAT YOU MEAN EJ 035 370
EFFECT ON RESISTANCE TO DEVIATION OF OBSERVING A MODEL'S AFFECTIVE REACTION TO RESPONSE CONSEQUENCES EJ 043 283
SMILING IN CHILDREN AS A FUNCTION OF THEIR SENSE OF MASTERY EJ 048 298
THE RELATIONSHIP BETWEEN VALUES AND BEHAVIOR: A DEVELOPMENTAL HYPOTHESIS EJ 056 622
MODEL AFFECT AND CHILDREN'S IMITATIVE ALTRUISM EJ 056 719
IMITATION OF TEACHER PREFERENCES IN A FIELD SETTING EJ 061 070

AFFECTIVE OBJECTIVES
SUCCESS AND ACCOUNTABILITY EJ 055 533
COGNITIVE AND AFFECTIVE REACTIONS OF KINDERGARTNERS TO VIDEO DISPLAYS EJ 057 016

AFFILIATION NEED
ANXIETY, AFFILIATION, AND SOCIAL ISOLATION EJ 027 343

AFRICAN AMERICAN STUDIES
BLACK HISTORY EJ 015 184
CHOICES, CHOICES, CHOICES! PEAK EXPERIENCES FROM THE AFRO-AMERICAN HERITAGE EJ 020 857

AFTER SCHOOL CENTERS
BEFORE SCHOOL STARTS. FOR CHILDREN'S MINDS--NOT JUST TO MIND THE CHILDREN. THE CHILD CENTRE--AS SEEN BY A PARENT. ED051873

AFTER SCHOOL PROGRAMS
[THE JUNIPER GARDENS CHILDREN'S PROJECT.] FINAL PROGRESS REPORT FOR OEO GRANT CG-8180. ED027947
THE STORY OF AN AFTER - SCHOOL PROGRAM. ED035464
A STUDY IN CHILD CARE (CASE STUDY FROM VOLUME II-B): "...WHILE [THEY TOOK] CARE OF OUR CHILDREN, THEIRS WEREN'T BEING CARED FOR." DAY CARE PROGRAMS REPRINT SERIES. ED051909
THINKING SKILLS AS A GOAL IN AN AFTER-SCHOOL PROGRAM EJ 037 635
DIRECTION SPORTS: A TUTORIAL PROGRAM FOR ELEMENTARY-SCHOOL PUPILS EJ 050 982

AGE
AGE OF ENTRANCE INTO THE FIRST GRADE AS RELATED TO RATE OF SCHOLASTIC ACHIEVEMENT. ED028843
CHILD HEALTH AND HUMAN DEVELOPMENT: PROGRESS 1963-1970. A REPORT OF THE NATIONAL INSTITUTE OF CHILD HEALTH AND HUMAN DEVELOPMENT. ED053799
A PRELIMINARY VIEW OF TRENDS IN AGE, EDUCATION, AND INTELLIGENCE OF PROBLEM YOUTH EJ 030 431
CHILDREN'S JUDGMENTS OF AGE EJ 052 461
EFFECTS OF AGE UPON RETRIEVAL FROM SHORT-TERM MEMORY EJ 055 109
CHILDREN'S ABILITY TO ORDER FACIAL AND NONFACIAL CONTINUA AS A FUNCTION OF MA, CA, AND IQ EJ 059 699

AGE DIFFERENCES
AGE OF ENTRANCE INTO THE FIRST GRADE AS RELATED TO ARITHMETIC ACHIEVEMENT. ED020801
CENTRAL AND INCIDENTAL LEARNING IN CHILDREN. ED023450
STIMULUS DIMENSIONALITY AND MANIPULABILITY IN VISUAL PERCEPTUAL LEARNING. ED023452
METHODOLOGICAL ISSUES IN THE STUDY OF AGE DIFFERENCES IN INFANTS' ATTENTION TO STIMULI VARYING IN MOVEMENT AND COMPLEXITY. ED023477
AGE AND MEMORY AS FACTORS IN PROBLEM SOLVING. ED025327
WORD ASSOCIATIONS AS RELATED TO CHILDREN'S VERBAL HABITS. ED025329
ACQUISTION AND TRANSFER DIFFERENCES BETWEEN KINDERGARTENERS AND SECOND-GRADERS ON AURALLY AND VISUALLY PRESENTED PAIRED-ASSOCIATES USING AN A-B, A-C DESIGN RESEARCH PROJECT NUMBER 2 OF PROJECT HEAD START RESEARCH AND EVALUATION CENTER, SYRACUSE UNIVERSITY RESEARCH INSTITUTE. FINAL REPORT, NOVEMBER 1, 1967. ED026139
CONCEPT IDENTIFICATION STRATEGIES. RESEARCH PROJECT NUMBER 3 OF PROJECT HEAD START RESEARCH AND EVALUATION CENTER, SYRACUSE UNIVERSITY RESEARCH INSTITUTE, NOVEMBER 1, 1967. ED026140
THE DEVELOPMENT OF ROLE-TAKING AND COMMUNICATION SKILLS IN CHILDREN. ED027082
THE AUDITORY MEMORY OF CHILDREN FROM DIFFERENT SOCIO-ECONOMIC BACKGROUNDS. ED027092
CHILDREN'S ABILITY TO OPERATE WITHIN A MATRIX: A DEVELOPMENTAL STUDY. ED029715
DISCRIMINATION OF RECENCY IN CHILDREN. FINAL REPORT. ED030493
THE UTILIZATIONS OF CONCRETE, FUNCTIONAL, AND DESIGNATIVE CONCEPTS IN MULTIPLE CLASSIFICATION. ED032112
DEVELOPMENT OF THE UNDERSTANDING OF LOGICAL CONNECTIVES. ED032125
LANGUAGE STRUCTURE AND THE FREE RECALL OF VERBAL MESSAGES BY CHILDREN. ED032933
DETERMINANTS OF CHILDREN'S ATTEMPTS TO HELP ANOTHER CHILD IN DISTRESS. ED039023
CHILDREN'S JUDGMENTS OF AGE. ED043392
DEVELOPMENTAL TRENDS IN THE SELECTIVE PERCEPTION OF RACE AND AFFECT BY YOUNG NEGRO AND CAUCASIAN CHILDREN. ED046498
RULE STRUCTURE AND PROPORTION OF POSITIVE INSTANCES AS DETERMINANTS OF CONCEPT ATTAINMENT IN CHILDREN. ED046500
LEARNING TO LEARN ON A CONCEPT ATTAINMENT TASK AS A FUNCTION OF AGE AND SOCIOECONOMIC LEVEL. REPORT FROM THE PROJECT ON SITUATIONAL VARIABLES AND EFFICIENCY OF CONCEPT LEARNING. ED046505
MOTHER-INFANT INTERACTION AND INFANT DEVELOPMENT AMONG THE WOLOF OF SENEGAL. ED051885
INTERRELATIONS IN CHILDREN'S LEARNING OF VERBAL AND PICTORIAL PAIRED ASSOCIATES. ED051886
A DEVELOPMENTAL INVESTIGATION OF VISUAL AND HAPTIC PREFERENCES FOR SHAPE AND TEXTURE EJ 008 780
REASONS FOR FAILURE ON THE CLASS INCLUSION PROBLEM EJ 018 872
TRANSITIVE INFERENCE WITH NONTRANSITIVE SOLUTIONS CONTROLLED EJ 018 882
CHILD VERSUS ADULT PERCEPTION OF EVALUATIVE MESSAGES IN VERBAL, VOCAL, AND VISUAL CHANNELS EJ 021 765
PROBABILITY LEARNING AS A FUNCTION OF AGE, SEX, AND TYPE OF CONSTRAINT EJ 021 766
THE EFFECTS OF PERSONALITY VARIABLES ON DISTORTION THRESHOLDS IN THE AMES ROOM EJ 023 434
CHILDREN'S SENSITIVITY TO PAINTING STYLES EJ 025 304
AGE PATTERNS IN CHILDREN'S PSYCHIATRIC SYMPTOMS EJ 025 374
DEVELOPMENTAL CHANGES IN THE USE OF EMOTION CUES IN A CONCEPT-FORMATION TASK EJ 029 362
HOW ADULTS AND CHILDREN SEARCH AND RECOGNIZE PICTURES EJ 029 384
DEVELOPMENTAL DIFFERENCES IN THE INTEGRATION OF PICTURE SERIES: EFFECTS OF VARIATIONS IN OBJECT-ATTRIBUTE RELATIONSHIPS EJ 029 386
SYNTACTICAL MEDIATION OF PAIRED-ASSOCIATE LEARNING AS A FUNCTION OF AGE EJ 030 286
THE DEVELOPMENT OF FREE CLASSIFICATION AND FREE RECALL IN CHILDREN EJ 030 293
VERBAL FACTORS IN COMPENSATION PERFORMANCE AND THE RELATION BETWEEN CONSERVATION AND COMPENSATION EJ 033 778
LEARNING OF MEDIA CONTENT: A DEVELOPMENTAL STUDY EJ 033 782
CHILDREN'S TWO-CHOICE LEARNING OF PREDOMINANTLY ALTERNATING AND REPEATING SEQUENCES EJ 033 791
THE EFFECTS OF SEX-ROLE STANDARDS FOR ACHIEVEMENT AND SEX-ROLE PREFERENCE ON THREE DETERMINANTS OF ACHIEVEMENT MOTIVATION EJ 034 454
STIMULUS AND RESPONSE ALTERNATION IN YOUNG CHILDREN EJ 034 537
STIMULUS CORRELATES OF AREA JUDGMENTS: A PSYCHOPHYSICAL DEVELOPMENTAL STUDY EJ 034 707
RESPONSE TO VOICE OF MOTHER AND STRANGER BY BABIES IN THE FIRST YEAR EJ 035 269
DEVELOPMENT OF FREE RECALL LEARNING IN CHILDREN EJ 035 359
DEVELOPMENTAL PATTERNS FOR CHILDREN'S CLASS AND CONDITIONAL REASONING ABILITIES EJ 035 362
CHILDREN'S ABILITY TO OPERATE WITHIN A MATRIX: A DEVELOPMENTAL STUDY EJ 035 363
MEDIATION AND PERCEPTUAL TRANSFER IN CHILDREN EJ 035 365
THE EFFECTS OF REHEARSAL AND CHUNKING INSTRUCTIONS ON CHILDREN'S MULTITRIAL FREE RECALL EJ 035 377
AGE DIFFERENCES IN PLEASANTNESS OF VISUAL PATTERNS OF DIFFERENT VARIABILITY IN LATE CHILDHOOD AND ADOLESCENCE EJ 035 989
A DEVELOPMENTAL STUDY OF PRESCHOOL CHILDREN'S PREFERENCE FOR RANDOM FORMS EJ 035 990
FATHERS' VERBAL INTERACTION WITH INFANTS IN THE FIRST THREE MONTHS OF LIFE EJ 036 126
COGNITIVE DEVELOPMENT AND CHILDREN'S COMPREHENSION OF HUMOR EJ 036 820
DEVELOPMENTAL SHIFTS IN VERBAL RECALL BETWEEN MENTAL AGES TWO AND FIVE EJ 036 825
SUFFER THE LITTLE KENTUCKY FIRST-GRADERS EJ 037 283
EFFECT OF CORRELATED VISUAL AND TACTUAL FEEDBACK ON AUDITORY PATTERN LEARNING AT DIFFERENT AGE LEVELS EJ 037 517
THE GROWTH OF CHILDREN'S SEMANTIC MEMORY: SEMANTIC ELEMENTS EJ 038 170
CHRONOLOGICAL AGE AND PERFORMANCE ON PROBLEMS WITH REPEATED PRESOLUTION SHIFTS EJ 039 628
THE INFLUENCE OF AGE AND STIMULUS DIMENSIONALITY ON FORM PERCEPTION BY PRESCHOOL CHILDREN EJ 039 630
RETENTION FOLLOWING A CHANGE IN AMBIENT CONTEXTUAL STIMULI FOR SIX AGE GROUPS EJ 039 631
THE EFFECTS OF FEEDBACK VARIATIONS ON REFERENTIAL COMMUNICATION OF CHILDREN EJ 040 360
A DEVELOPMENTAL STUDY OF SIZE CONSTANCY FOR TWO-VERSUS THREE-DIMENSIONAL STIMULI EJ 040 454
DEVELOPMENT OF RETENTION AND ORGANIZATION OCCURRING IN FREE RECALL IN TURKISH CHILDREN EJ 041 133
NUMBER CONSERVATION IN VERY YOUNG CHILDREN: THE EFFECT OF AGE AND MODE OF RESPONDING EJ 041 139
ANTICIPATORY IMAGERY AND MODIFIED ANAGRAM SOLUTIONS: A DEVELOPMENTAL STUDY EJ 041 141
THE DEVELOPMENT OF COGNITIVE BALANCE AND THE TRANSITION FROM CONCRETE TO FORMAL OPERATIONAL THOUGHT EJ 041 145
THE DEVELOPMENT OF HYPNOTIC SUSCEPTIBILITY: A LONGITUDINAL (CONVERGENCE) STUDY EJ 041 449
CHILDREN'S DESCRIPTIONS OF PEERS: A WERNERIAN DEVELOPMENTAL ANALYSIS EJ 041 591
INCENTIVE PREFERENCE AND RESISTANCE TO TEMPTATION EJ 041 631
THE INFLUENCE OF STIMULUS EXPOSURE ON RATED PREFERENCE: EFFECTS OF AGE, PATTERN OF EXPOSURE, AND STIMULUS MEANINGFULNESS EJ 041 960
THE CONTROL OF RELATIVE SIZE BY PICTORIAL DEPTH CUES IN CHILDREN AND ADULTS EJ 042 506
FACTORS INFLUENCING CHILDREN'S CONCEPT IDENTIFICATION PERFORMANCE WITH NONPREFERRED RELEVANT ATTRIBUTES EJ 042 965
MEMORY AND ATTENTION IN CHILDREN'S DOUBLE-ALTERNATION LEARNING EJ 042 966
APPARENT VISUAL SIZE AS A FUNCTION OF AGE, INTELLIGENCE, AND A SURROUNDING FRAME OF REFERENCE FOR NORMAL AND MENTALLY RETARDED SUBJECTS EJ 043 704
STIMULUS SELECTION AS A FUNCTION OF LETTER COLOR AND AGE IN PAIRED-ASSOCIATE LEARNING EJ 043 705
A DEVELOPMENTAL STUDY OF COGNITIVE BALANCE EJ 043 856

DEVELOPMENTAL CHARACTERISTICS OF EMOTIONAL EXPERIENCE EJ 043 860
SOME DEVELOPMENTAL CHANGES IN THE ORGANIZATION OF SELF-EVALUATIONS EJ 044 186
OBSERVATIONAL LEARNING: THE EFFECTS OF AGE, TASK DIFFICULTY, AND OBSERVERS' MOTORIC REHEARSAL EJ 044 702
THE USE OF PERCEPTUAL, FUNCTIONAL, AND ABSTRACT ATTRIBUTES IN MULTIPLE CLASSIFICATION EJ 044 825
LE NOUVEAU PROGRAMME D'ACTIVITES EDUCATRICES DANS LES ESTABLISSEMENTS PRESCOLAIRES EN YOUGOSLAVIE EJ 045 011
JUDGMENTS OF PATTERN GOODNESS AND PATTERN PREFERENCE AS FUNCTIONS OF AGE AND PATTERN UNCERTAINTY EJ 046 782
DEVELOPMENTAL CONFORMITY EJ 046 892
DEVELOPMENT OF MEMORIZATION STRATEGIES EJ 047 679
SEX AND AGE DIFFERENCES IN PATTERN ORGANIZATION IN A FIGURAL-CONCEPTUAL TASK EJ 047 680
TITRATING DELAYED MATCHING TO SAMPLE IN CHILDREN EJ 047 684
CONCEPTUAL RULE LEARNING AND CHRONOLOGICAL AGE EJ 047 687
SENSORY-SET FACTORS IN AGE DIFFERENCES IN REACTION TIME EJ 048 304
EXPLORATION OF DEVELOPMENTAL VARIABLES BY MANIPULATION AND SIMULATION OF AGE DIFFERENCES IN BEHAVIOR EJ 048 472
DESIRABILITY JUDGMENTS AS A FUNCTION OF ITEM CONTENT, INSTRUCTIONAL SET, AND SET: A LIFE-SPAN DEVELOPMENTAL STUDY EJ 048 473
DEVELOPMENTAL CHANGES IN VISUAL INFORMATION PROCESSING AND SHORT-TERM VISUAL MEMORY EJ 049 431
MATCHING AUDITORY AND VISUAL SERIES: MODALITY PROBLEM OR TRANSLATION PROBLEM? EJ 051 569
THE EFFECTS OF CHRONOLOGICAL AGE, TRIALS, AND LIST CHARACTERISTICS UPON CHILDREN'S CATEGORY CLUSTERING EJ 052 454
THE DEVELOPMENT OF ELEMENTARY SCHOOL CHILDREN'S JUDGMENT OF INTENT EJ 052 581
AGE OF SUBJECT, TYPE OF SOCIAL CONTACT, AND RESPONSIVENESS TO SOCIAL REINFORCEMENT EJ 055 093
AGE CHANGES AND COHORT DIFFERENCES IN PERSONALITY EJ 055 110
RELATIONS OF AGE AND INTELLIGENCE TO SHORT-TERM COLOR MEMORY EJ 056 392
THE RELATIONSHIP BETWEEN VALUES AND BEHAVIOR: A DEVELOPMENTAL HYPOTHESIS EJ 056 622
RACIAL PREFERENCES IN YOUNG CHILDREN EJ 056 626
IDENTITY AND EQUIVALENCE CONSERVATION AT TWO AGE LEVELS EJ 057 901
GRADE INTERACTION WITH WORDS AND PICTURES IN A PAIRED-ASSOCIATE TASK: A PROPOSED EXPLANATION EJ 057 910
EXTENSION OF PERSONAL FUTURE TIME PERSPECTIVE, AGE, AND LIFE-SATISFACTION OF CHILDREN AND ADOLESCENTS EJ 058 140
CREATIVE ABILITY OVER A FIVE-YEAR SPAN EJ 058 412
RELATION OF TYPE AND ONSET OF FATHER ABSENCE TO COGNITIVE DEVELOPMENT EJ 058 695
VIOLATION OF A RULE AS A METHOD OF DIAGNOSING INFANTS' LEVELS OF OBJECT CONCEPT EJ 059 314
VISUAL MASKING AND DEVELOPMENTAL DIFFERENCES IN INFORMATION PROCESSING EJ 059 514
AGE DIFFERENCES IN VISUAL REACTION TIME OF "BRAIN DAMAGED" AND NORMAL CHILDREN UNDER IRREGULAR PREPARATORY INTERVAL CONDITIONS EJ 060 109
HYPOTHESES, STRATEGIES, AND STEREOTYPES IN DISCRIMINATION LEARNING EJ 060 779
REVERSALS PRIOR TO SOLUTION OF CONCEPT IDENTIFICATION IN CHILDREN EJ 060 782
AGE- AND SEX-RELATED VARIATION IN PERFORMANCE ON A FIGURAL-CONCEPTUAL TASK EJ 061 066
GIVEN NAMES AND STEREOTYPING EJ 061 234

AGE GRADE PLACEMENT

MULTI-AGE GROUPING--ENRICHING THE LEARNING ENVIRONMENT. ED017343

AGENCY ROLE

REPORT OF CHILD PLACEMENT STUDY COMMITTEE, JANUARY, 1969. ED044169
144 FOSTER CHILDREN EJ 046 787
THE CHILD WELFARE AGENCY AS THE EXTENDED FAMILY EJ 052 493

AGGRESSION

HEAD START EVALUATION AND RESEARCH CENTER, BOSTON UNIVERSITY. REPORT C-II, THE EXPRESSION OF AGGRESSION IN PRE-SCHOOL CHILDREN. ED022562
THE RELATIONSHIP BETWEEN INSTRUMENTAL ASSERTION AND THE STANFORD-BINET. ED030474
THE EFFECT ON AGGRESSION OF VARIATION IN AMOUNT OF OPPORTUNITY FOR PLAY. (INTERNAL REPORT). ED043384
THE EFFECT OF AGGRESSIVE CARTOONS: CHILDREN'S INTERPERSONAL PLAY. ED046543
SEX DIFFERENCES IN CHILDREN'S MODES OF AGGRESSIVE RESPONSES TOWARD OUTSIDERS EJ 007 690
SOCIAL REINFORCEMENT FOR EXPRESSION VS. SUPPRESSION OF AGGRESSION EJ 007 691
RELATIONSHIP OF SOCIOECONOMIC STATUS, SEX, AND AGE TO AGGRESSION OF EMOTIONALLY DISTURBED CHILDREN IN MOTHERS' PRESENCE EJ 017 424
EFFECTS OF INCONSISTENT PUNISHMENT ON AGGRESSION IN CHILDREN EJ 021 992
SEX DIFFERENCES IN PRESCHOOL CHILDREN WITHOUT HISTORIES OF COMPLICATIONS OF PREGNANCY AND DELIVERY EJ 024 939
AGGRESSION IN CHILDREN AS A FUNCTION OF SEX OF SUBJECT AND SEX OF OPPONENT EJ 024 945
CHILDREN AND WAR GAMES EJ 034 533
AN EXAMINATION OF FRUSTRATION AGGRESSION RELATIONS IN BOYS DURING MIDDLE CHILDHOOD EJ 035 628
SEX DIFFERENCES IN ADOLESCENT REACTIONS TOWARD NEWCOMERS EJ 039 899
IMITATIVE AGGRESSION IN CHILDREN AS A FUNCTION OF OBSERVING A HUMAN MODEL EJ 039 907
AGGRESSION AS A FUNCTION OF EXPECTED RETALIATION AND AGGRESSION LEVEL OF TARGET AND AGGRESSOR EJ 043 192
TELEVISED AGGRESSION AND THE INTERPERSONAL AGGRESSION OF PRESCHOOL CHILDREN EJ 043 197
LEARNING OF AGGRESSION AS A FUNCTION OF PRESENCE OF A HUMAN MODEL, RESPONSE INTENSITY, AND TARGET OF THE RESPONSE EJ 043 198
CHILDREN'S AGGRESSION EJ 043 199
THE EFFECT OF SUBJECT RACE, MODEL RACE, AND VICARIOUS PRAISE ON VICARIOUS LEARNING EJ 045 458
STUDYING AGGRESSIVE CHILDREN THROUGH RESPONSE TO FRUSTRATING SITUATIONS EJ 051 013
EFFECTS OF ADULT AND PEER OBSERVERS ON BOYS' AND GIRLS' RESPONSES TO AN AGGRESSIVE MODEL EJ 052 459
CHILDREN'S OBSERVATION AND INTEGRATION OF AGGRESSIVE EXPERIENCES EJ 055 212
SON OF ROBOT COMMANDO EJ 055 488
INSTANT LAW AND ORDER EJ 055 534
SESAME STREET: MAGIC OR MALEVOLENCE? EJ 056 607
SITUATIONAL EFFECTS ON JUSTIFIABLENESS OF AGGRESSION AT THREE AGE LEVELS EJ 056 734
SOME IMMEDIATE EFFECTS OF TELEVISED VIOLENCE ON CHILDREN'S BEHAVIOR EJ 058 216
AGGRESSION ANXIETY, PERCEPTION OF AGGRESSIVE CUES, AND EXPECTED RETALIATION EJ 061 071

ALPHABETS

INITIAL TEACHING ALPHABET AND TRADITIONAL ORTHOGRAPHY--THEIR IMPACT ON SPELLING AND WRITINGS EJ 016 464
TACTILE IDENTIFICATION OF LETTERS: A COMPARISON OF DEAF AND HEARING CHILDRENS' PERFORMANCES EJ 034 567

AMERICAN CULTURE

ADAPTATIONAL TASKS IN CHILDHOOD IN OUR CULTURE. ED021632
COMPARISON OF AMERICAN AND NORWEGIAN NURSERY SCHOOL CHILDREN ON INDEPENDENCE BEHAVIOR AND TRAINING. ED024457
COMPARISON OF AMERICAN AND NORWEGIAN NURSERY SCHOOL CHILDREN OF INDEPENDENCE BEHAVIOR AND TRAINING. SUMMARY REPORT. ED024476

AMERICAN ENGLISH

AN INVESTIGATION OF THE STANDARD-NONSTANDARD DIMENSION OF CENTRAL TEXAN ENGLISH. PART OF THE FINAL REPORT. ED026130

AMERICAN HISTORY

COLONIAL CHILD CARE INSTITUTIONS: OUR HERITAGE OF CARE EJ 043 315

AMERICAN INDIANS

SUMMARY AND OBSERVATIONS IN THE DAKOTAS AND MINNESOTA. INDIAN COMMUNITIES AND PROJECT HEAD START. ED013670
AN APPRAISAL OF POSSIBILITIES FOR A HEAD START PROGRAM AMONG THE POTAWATOMI INDIANS OF KANSAS. INDIAN COMMUNITIES AND PROJECT HEAD START. ED013671
PROJECT HEAD START IN AN INDIAN COMMUNITY. ED014329
INDIAN COMMUNITIES AND PROJECT HEAD START. SUMMARY AND OBSERVATIONS IN THE DAKOTAS AND MINNESOTA, TOGETHER WITH AN APPRAISAL OF POSSIBILITIES FOR A HEAD START PROGRAM AMONG THE POTAWATOMI INDIANS OF KANSAS. ED016510
THE WARRIOR DROPOUTS. ED016529
INDIAN HERITAGE: A SELECTED BOOK LIST FOR ALL AGES. ED036345
THE INFLUENCE OF TWO COUNSELING METHODS ON THE PHYSICAL AND VERBAL AGGRESSION OF PRESCHOOL INDIAN CHILDREN. PART OF THE FINAL REPORT ON HEAD START EVALUATION AND RESEARCH: 1968-69 TO THE OFFICE OF ECONOMIC OPPORTUNITY. ED037243
NUTRITION SURVEY OF WHITE MOUNTAIN APACHE PRESCHOOL CHILDREN. ED046508
A STUDY IN CHILD CARE (CASE STUDY FROM VOLUME II-A): "A HOUSE FULL OF CHILDREN." DAY CARE PROGRAMS REPRINT SERIES. ED051891
VOLUNTEERING TO HELP INDIANS HELP THEMSELVES EJ 032 412
MODIFICATION OF BEHAVIOR PATTERNS OF INDIAN CHILDREN EJ 051 472
SCHOOL IN CHEROKEE AND ENGLISH EJ 061 184

ANALYSIS OF VARIANCE

HEADSTART OPERATIONAL FIELD ANALYSIS. PROGRESS REPORT III. ED015776
DEVELOPMENT OF GRAMMATICAL STRUCTURES AND ATTRIBUTES IN PRE-SCHOOL AGE CHILDREN. FINAL REPORT. ED041639
FREE RECALL OF OBJECT NAMES IN PRESCHOOL CHILDREN AS A FUNCTION OF INTRACATEGORY VARIATION EJ 035 368
PAIRED-ASSOCIATE LEARNING OF CHILDREN WITH MIXED LIST DESIGNS EJ 035 369

ANCILLARY SERVICES

A PLAY PROGRAM IN A PEDIATRIC CLINIC EJ 029 951

ANGLO AMERICANS

CHILDREARING PRACTICES AMONG SELECTED CULTURALLY DEPRIVED MINORITIES EJ 023 613
MEXICAN-AMERICAN CULTURAL MEMBERSHIP AND ADJUSTMENT TO SCHOOL EJ 035 620
COOPERATION AND COMPETITION OF MEXICAN, MEXICAN-AMERICAN, AND ANGLO-AMERICAN CHILDREN OF TWO AGES UNDER FOUR INSTRUCTIONAL SETS EJ 041 957
VALUES OF MEXICAN-AMERICAN, NEGRO, AND ANGLO BLUE-COLLAR AND WHITE-COLLAR CHILDREN EJ 052 653
EXPERIMENTAL ANALYSES OF COOPERATION AND COMPETITION OF ANGLO-AMERICAN AND MEXICAN CHILDREN EJ 053 647

ANIMAL BEHAVIOR

DETERMINANTS OF INFANT BEHAVIOUR IV. ED032947
PROGRAMMING LIFE HISTORIES: EFFECTS OF STRESS IN ONTOGENY UPON EMOTIONAL REACTIVITY EJ 020 719
MATERNAL FOOD RESTRICTION: EFFECTS ON OFFSPRING DEVELOPMENT, LEARNING, AND A PROGRAM OF THERAPY EJ 029 218
SEQUENTIAL LEARNING BY CHILDREN EJ 035 381

ANNOTATED BIBLIOGRAPHIES

A BIBLIOGRAPHY (WITH SELECTED ANNOTATIONS) ON NONGRADED ELEMENTARY SCHOOLS. ED015024
AN ANNOTATED BIBLIOGRAPHY OF BEHAVIOR MODIFICATION WITH CHILDREN AND RETARDATES. ED020025
EARLY CHILDHOOD SELECTED BIBLIOGRAPHIES SERIES. NUMBER 1, PHYSICAL. ED022532
EARLY CHILDHOOD SELECTED BIBLIOGRAPHIES SERIES. NUMBER 2, LANGUAGE. ED022538
EARLY CHILDHOOD SELECTED BIBLIOGRAPHIES SERIES. NUMBER 3, EDUCATION. ED022546
CHILD DEVELOPMENT AND SOCIAL SCIENCE EDUCATION. PART III: ABSTRACTS OF RELEVANT LITERATURE. ED023466
EARLY CHILDHOOD SELECTED BIBLIOGRAPHIES SERIES. NUMBER 4, COGNITION. ED023488
EARLY CHILDHOOD SELECTED BIBLIOGRAPHIES SERIES. NUMBER 5, SOCIAL. ED024472
URBAN EDUCATION BIBLIOGRAPHY: AN ANNOTATED LISTING. ED024474
EARLY CHILDHOOD SELECTED BIBLIOGRAPHIES SERIES. NUMBER 6, PERSONALITY. ED024475
GOOD REFERENCES ON DAY CARE. ED027969
PROBLEM SOLVING AND CONCEPT FORMATION: ANNOTATED LISTING OF NATIONAL AND INTERNATIONAL CURRICULAR PROJECTS AT THE EARLY CHILDHOOD LEVEL. ED029685
BIBLIOGRAPHY: TEACHER CHARACTERISTICS. ED029716
MULTI-ETHNIC BOOKS FOR HEAD START CHILDREN. PART I: BLACK AND INTEGRATED LITERATURE. ED031312
LIVING AND LEARNING: AN ANNOTATED BIBLIOGRAPHY FOR THOSE WHO LIVE AND LEARN WITH YOUNG CHILDREN. ED032935
SOURCE BOOK OF SELECTED MATERIALS FOR EARLY CHILDHOOD EDUCATION IN THE ARTS. ED033746
SELECTED BOOKS ABOUT THE AFRO-AMERICAN FOR VERY YOUNG CHILDREN K-2. ED039029
MULTI-ETHNIC BOOKS FOR YOUNG CHILDREN: ANNOTATED BIBLIOGRAPHY FOR PARENTS AND TEACHERS. ED046519
AN ANNOTATED BIBLIOGRAPHY ON EARLY CHILDHOOD. ED049822
DAY CARE: AN ANNOTATED BIBLIOGRAPHY. ED052823
BIBLIOGRAPHY OF BOOKS FOR CHILDREN. 1971 EDITION. ED053798
BOOKS WHICH GIVE MATHEMATICAL CONCEPTS TO YOUNG CHILDREN: AN ANNOTATED BIBLIOGRAPHY EJ 007 274
BIBLIOGRAPHY ON HOSPITALIZED AND HANDICAPPED CHILDREN EJ 028 677
ENVIRONMENTAL ECOLOGICAL EDUCATION IN CHILDREN'S BOOKS EJ 029 393
BOOKS FOR YOUNG CHILDREN EJ 043 020

ANNUAL REPORTS

HEAD START EVALUATION AND RESEARCH CENTER, THE UNIVERSITY OF CHICAGO. REPORT A, MATERNAL INFLUENCES UPON DEVELOPMENT OF COGNITION. ED022550
HEAD START EVALUATION AND RESEARCH CENTER, THE UNIVERSITY OF CHICAGO. REPORT B, MATERNAL ANTECEDENTS OF INTELLECTUAL ACHIEVEMENT BEHAVIORS IN LOWER CLASS PRESCHOOL CHILDREN. ED022551
HEAD START EVALUATION AND RESEARCH CENTER, THE UNIVERSITY OF CHICAGO. REPORT C, COGNITIVE INTERACTION BETWEEN TEACHER AND PUPIL IN A PRESCHOOL SETTING. ED022552
HEAD START EVALUATION AND RESEARCH CENTER, THE UNIVERSITY OF CHICAGO. REPORT D, THE INTERACTION OF INTELLIGENCE AND BEHAVIOR AS ONE PREDICTOR OF EARLY SCHOOL ACHIEVEMENT IN WORKING CLASS AND CULTURALLY DISADVANTAGED HEAD START CHILDREN. ED022553
HEAD START EVALUATION AND RESEARCH CENTER, THE UNIVERSITY OF CHICAGO. ANNUAL REPORT, 1966-1967. ED023445
HEAD START EVALUATION AND RESEARCH CENTER, THE UNIVERSITY OF CHICAGO. REPORT F, SOCIALIZATION INTO THE ROLE OF PUPIL. ED023456
ANNUAL RESEARCH REPORT OF COMPLETED AND INCOMPLETE INVESTIGATIONS FOR NATIONAL HEAD START EVALUATION. ED025320
HEAD START EVALUATION AND RESEARCH CENTER, TULANE UNIVERSITY. ANNUAL REPORT. ED029705
PROJECT HEAD START RESEARCH AND EVALUATION CENTER, SYRACUSE UNIVERSITY, RESEARCH INSTITUTE. FINAL REPORT. ED030486
CHILD DEVELOPMENT RESEARCH AND EVALUATION CENTER FOR HEAD START, TEMPLE UNIVERSITY. ANNUAL REPORT. ED030487
ARIZONA CENTER FOR EARLY CHILDHOOD EDUCATION ANNUAL REPORT, JUNE 1968 - JUNE 1969. ED034586

ANOMALIES

CHILD HEALTH AND HUMAN DEVELOPMENT: PROGRESS 1963-1970. A REPORT OF THE NATIONAL INSTITUTE OF CHILD HEALTH AND HUMAN DEVELOPMENT. ED053799
PHYSIOLOGICAL INDICATIONS OF ORGANIC INVOLVEMENT EJ 051 016

ANTHOLOGIES

SOCIAL STUDIES EDUCATION: THE ELEMENTARY SCHOOL. ED027061

ANXIETY

THE RELATION BETWEEN TEST ANXIETY AND NEED FOR MEMORY SUPPORT IN PROBLEM SOLVING. REVISED RESEARCH MEMORANDUM NO. 11. ED021616
FURTHER EVIDENCE ON THE STABILITY OF THE FACTOR STRUCTURE OF THE TEST ANXIETY SCALE FOR SCHILDREN. ED023485
THE ASSESSMENT OF ACHIEVEMENT ANXIETIES IN CHILDREN: HOW IMPORTANT IS RESPONSE SET AND MULTIDIMENSIONALITY IN THE TEST ANXIETY SCALE FOR CHILDREN? ED025313
ANXIETY AS A FACTOR IN THE CHILD'S RESPONSIVENESS TO SOCIAL REINFORCEMENT. ED027074
NURTURANCE, NURTURANCE WITHDRAWAL, AND RESISTANCE TO TEMPTATION AMONG THREE AGE GROUPS EJ 021 995
BIRTH ORDER AND PHYSIOLOGICAL STRESS RESPONSE EJ 022 000
THE EFFECT OF ANXIETY OVER INTELLECTUAL PERFORMANCE ON REFLECTION-IMPULSIVITY IN CHILDREN EJ 026 153
PROBABILITY LEARNING AS A FUNCTION OF SEX OF THE SUBJECT, TEST ANXIETY, AND PERCENTAGE OF REINFORCEMENT EJ 027 181
THE FUNCTION OF AMBIGUITY IN CHILD CRISES EJ 027 344
ANXIETY - A CLASSROOM CLOSE-UP EJ 028 896
SCHOOL PHOBIA AND SELF-EVALUATION EJ 031 445
COGNITIVE COMPONENTS OF SEPARATION ANXIETY EJ 039 900
ANXIETY IN YOUNG CHILDREN EJ 045 049
BLOCK MANIPULATION BY CHILDREN AS A FUNCTION OF SOCIAL REINFORCEMENT, ANXIETY, AROUSAL, AND ABILITY PATTERN EJ 046 468
ANXIETY IN THE EVALUATIVE CONTEXT EJ 051 018
MOTHERS' TEST OF ANXIETY AND TASK SELECTION AND CHILDREN'S PERFORMANCE WITH MOTHER OR A STRANGER EJ 052 449
ANXIETY AND MORAL JUDGMENT IN EARLY ADOLESCENCE EJ 055 094
ACHIEVEMENT MOTIVATION AND FEAR OF FAILURE IN FAMILY AND SCHOOL EJ 058 143
MODELING AND THE FEARFUL CHILD PATIENT EJ 058 354
DEVELOPMENTAL TRENDS IN GENERAL AND TEST ANXIETY AMONG JUNIOR AND SENIOR HIGH SCHOOL STUDENTS EJ 061 062
THE DEVELOPMENT OF THE LANGUAGE OF EMOTIONS: III. TYPE OF ANXIETY IN THE EXPERIENCE OF AFFECT EJ 061 065
AGGRESSION ANXIETY, PERCEPTION OF AGGRESSIVE CUES, AND EXPECTED RETALIATION EJ 061 071

APTITUDE

VERBAL PARTICIPATION AS A FUNCTION OF THE PRESENCE OF PRIOR INFORMATION CONCERNING APTITUDE EJ 042 348

ARITHMETIC

THE EFFECTS OF TWO VARIABLES ON THE PROBLEM-SOLVING ABILITIES OF FIRST-GRADE CHILDREN. ED019113
MAKING PRIMARY ARITHMETIC MEANINGFUL TO CHILDREN. ED020015
AGE OF ENTRANCE INTO THE FIRST GRADE AS RELATED TO ARITHMETIC ACHIEVEMENT. ED020801
ARITHMETIC AND MATHEMATICS. DIMENSIONS IN EARLY LEARNING SERIES. ED026136
IDENTIFICATION IN THE KINDERGARTEN OF FACTORS THAT MAKE FOR FUTURE SUCCESS IN READING AND IDENTIFICATION AND DIAGNOSIS IN THE KINDERGARTEN OF POTENTIAL READING DISABILITY CASES. FINAL REPORT. ED029710
DOES THE USE OF CUISENAIRE RODS IN KINDERGARTEN, FIRST AND SECOND GRADES UPGRADE ARITHMETIC ACHIEVEMENT? ED032128
PROBLEM SOLVING PERFORMANCES OF FIRST GRADE CHILDREN. ED041623

DEVELOPMENTAL SKILL AND ACHIEVEMENT DIFFERENCES OF CHILDREN IDENTIFIED AS EXCELLENT, GOOD, AND AVERAGE IN READING AND ARITHMETIC ACHIEVEMENT. STUDY NUMBER THREE. ED044181
SURVIVAL SKILLS AND FIRST GRADE ACADEMIC ACHIEVEMENT. REPORT #1. ED050807
ESTEEM AND ACHIEVEMENT IN ARITHMETIC EJ 015 160

AROUSAL PATTERNS
CUMULATIVE EFFECTS OF CONTINUOUS STIMULATION ON AROUSAL LEVEL IN INFANTS EJ 036 075
HUNGER AND MOTOR RESTRAINT ON AROUSAL AND VISUAL ATTENTION IN THE INFANT EJ 040 298

ART
ART - FOR THE CHILD'S SAKE EJ 041 829
A THIRD STUDY OF PERCEPTUAL BEHAVIOR IN SIXTH GRADE CHILDREN IN RELATION TO THEIR BEHAVIOR IN ART EJ 041 830
AESTHETIC EDUCATION IN SOVIET SCHOOLS EJ 060 105

ART ACTIVITIES
AN EXPLORATION OF THE USES OF RHYTHMIC MOVEMENT TO DEVELOP AESTHETIC CONCEPTS IN THE PRIMARY GRADES. ED020770
THE EFFECTS OF TEACHER IN-SERVICE EDUCATION ON THE DEVELOPMENT OF ART IDEAS WITH SIX-YEAR OLD CULTURALLY DEPRIVED CHILDREN. FINAL REPORT. ED027066
CLASSROOM OPPORTUNITIES TO EXPRESS FEELINGS EJ 001 912
ART - FOR THE CHILD'S SAKE EJ 041 829

ART EDUCATION
INCREASING THE AWARENESS OF ART IDEAS OF CULTURALLY DEPRIVED KINDERGARTEN CHILDREN THROUGH EXPERIENCES WITH CERAMICS. FINAL REPORT. ED016519
ART EDUCATION IN THE ELEMENTARY SCHOOL. ED018274
CHILDREN LEARN AND GROW THROUGH ART EXPERIENCES. ILLINOIS CURRICULUM PROGRAM, THE SUBJECT FIELD SERIES. ED019132
AN EXPLORATION OF THE USES OF RHYTHMIC MOVEMENT TO DEVELOP AESTHETIC CONCEPTS IN THE PRIMARY GRADES. ED020770
CHILDREN AND THE ARTS. PRESENTATIONS FROM A WRITING CONFERENCE. ED025317
THE EFFECTS OF A LEARNING PROGRAM IN PERCEPTUAL-MOTOR ACTIVITY UPON THE VISUAL PERCEPTION OF SHAPE. FINAL REPORT. ED030494
SOURCE BOOK OF SELECTED MATERIALS FOR EARLY CHILDHOOD EDUCATION IN THE ARTS. ED033746
THE ARTS ARE ALIVE AND THRIVING IN ST. LOUIS EJ 022 334
A THIRD STUDY OF THE EFFECTS OF A LEARNING EXPERIENCE UPON PREFERENCE FOR COMPLEXITY-ASYMMETRY IN FOURTH, FIFTH, AND SIXTH GRADE CHILDREN EJ 029 281
A THIRD STUDY OF PERCEPTUAL BEHAVIOR IN SIXTH GRADE CHILDREN IN RELATION TO THEIR BEHAVIOR IN ART EJ 041 830

ART EXPRESSION
A COMPARISON OF THE DEVELOPMENTAL DRAWING CHARACTERISTICS OF CULTURALLY ADVANTAGED AND CULTURALLY DISADVANTAGED CHILDREN. FINAL REPORT. ED015783
STUDY OF ACHIEVEMENT, TORONTO INFORMATION BULLETIN NO. 1. ED017323
CHILDREN LEARN AND GROW THROUGH ART EXPERIENCES. ILLINOIS CURRICULUM PROGRAM, THE SUBJECT FIELD SERIES. ED019132
PINK IS A GOOD COLOR. ? EJ 011 785
WHAT GENERATION GAP? EJ 032 763
ARTISTIC STYLE AS CONCEPT FORMATION FOR CHILDREN AND ADULTS EJ 046 247
LE MONDE DES TOUT PETITS EST-IL INFLUENCE PAR NOTRE MONDE MODERNE? (IS THE WORLD OF CHILDREN INFLUENCED BY OUR MODERN WORLD?) EJ 049 895

ARTICULATION (SPEECH)
REPORT ON THE ARTICULATORY AND INTELLIGIBILITY STATUS OF SOCIALLY DISADVANTAGED PRE-SCHOOL CHILDREN. ED014321
AN ARTICULATION STUDY OF 15,255 SEATTLE FIRST GRADE CHILDREN WITH AND WITHOUT KINDERGARTEN. ED024438
A PRESCHOOL ARTICULATION AND LANGUAGE SCREENING FOR THE IDENTIFICATION OF SPEECH DISORDERS. FINAL REPORT. ED051889
DEVELOPMENTAL SPEECH INACCURACY AND SPEECH THERAPY IN THE EARLY SCHOOL YEARS EJ 013 624
VOWEL PRODUCTIONS AND IDENTIFICATION BY NORMAL AND LANGUAGE DELAYED CHILDREN EJ 018 816
ACOUSTIC ANALYSIS OF THE ACQUISITION OF ACCEPTABLE "R" IN AMERICAN ENGLISH EJ 041 056
PHONETIC COMPATIBILITY IN PAIRED-ASSOCIATE LEARNING OF FIRST- AND THIRD-GRADE CHILDREN EJ 044 692

ASPIRATION
FINAL REPORT ON HEAD START EVALUATION AND RESEARCH: 1967-68 TO THE OFFICE OF ECONOMIC OPPORTUNITY. SECTION II: ACHIEVEMENT MOTIVATION AND PATTERNS OF REINFORCEMENT IN HEAD START CHILDREN. ED023458
DISADVANTAGED AND NONDISADVANTAGED CHILDREN'S EXPECTANCY IN SKILL AND CHANCE OUTCOMES EJ 034 903
ROLE MODEL INFLUENCES ON COLLEGE WOMEN'S CAREER ASPIRATIONS EJ 041 632
LEVELS OF ASPIRATION, ACHIEVEMENT, AND SOCIOCULTURAL DIFFERENCES IN PRESCHOOL CHILDREN EJ 043 482

ASSOCIATE DEGREES
TRAINING WORKERS FOR CHILD CARE CENTERS EJ 050 935

ASSOCIATION (PSYCHOLOGICAL)
FREE-ASSOCIATION NORMS AND ASSOCIATIVE STRUCTURE. ED025328
WORD ASSOCIATIONS AS RELATED TO CHILDREN'S VERBAL HABITS. ED025329
LANGUAGE STRUCTURE AND THE FREE RECALL OF VERBAL MESSAGES BY CHILDREN. ED032933
STRONG WORDS EJ 001 116
BACKWARD ASSOCIATIONS IN PAIRED-ASSOCIATE LEARNING OF RETARDATES AND NORMAL CHILDREN EJ 021 770
ROLE OF DISCRIMINATIVE STIMULI IN THE FORMATION OF FUNCTIONAL RESPONSE CLASSES EJ 024 937
THE CHILDREN'S ASSOCIATIVE RESPONDING TEST: A TWO-YEAR FOLLOW-UP EJ 047 683
PATTERNS OF RESPONDING IN THE WORD ASSOCIATIONS OF WEST AFRICAN CHILDREN EJ 056 634

ASSOCIATION TESTS
HEAD START EVALUATION AND RESEARCH CENTER, TULANE UNIVERSITY. FINAL REPORT. (TITLE SUPPLIED). ED020782
STANDARDIZATION OF A RESEARCH INSTRUMENT FOR IDENTIFYING ASSOCIATIVE RESPONDING IN CHILDREN EJ 019 021
CHARACTERISTICS OF WORD ASSOCIATION RESPONSES OBTAINED FROM CHILDREN IN GRADES ONE THROUGH FOUR EJ 042 960
INITIAL PROBABILITY REHEARSAL, AND CONSTRAINT IN ASSOCIATIVE CLASS SELECTION EJ 057 903

ASSOCIATIVE LEARNING
CONCEPT FORMATION BY KINDERGARTEN CHILDREN IN A CARD-SORTING TASK. PSYCHOLOGY SERIES. ED013665
LEARNING OF INCENTIVE-VALUE BY CHILDREN. ED023473
INDUCED VERSUS SPONTANEOUS REHEARSAL IN SHORT-TERM MEMORY IN NURSERY SCHOOL CHILDREN. STUDY M: DEVELOPMENT OF SELECTIVE ATTENTION ABILITIES. ED024444
FREE-ASSOCIATION NORMS AND ASSOCIATIVE STRUCTURE. ED025328
IMPLICIT VERBAL BEHAVIOR IN ELEMENTARY SCHOOL CHILDREN, (INTERNAL VERBAL RESPONSES OF ELEMENTARY SCHOOL CHILDREN ELICITED BY THE ASSOCIATION OF WORDS). FINAL REPORT. ED028848
THE EFFECT OF MEDIATIONAL INSTRUCTIONS ON ASSOCIATIVE SKILLS OF FIRST GRADE INNERCITY CHILDREN. ED038177
INTERRELATIONS IN CHILDREN'S LEARNING OF VERBAL AND PICTORIAL PAIRED ASSOCIATES. ED051886
SEMANTIC RELATIONSHIP AND THE LEARNING OF SYNTACTIC WORD PAIRS IN CHILDREN EJ 016 163
REPRESENTATIONAL AND SYNTACTIC COMPETENCE OF PROBLEM READERS EJ 026 208
SEMANTIC AND PHONETIC RELATIONS IN THE FALSE RECOGNITION OF WORDS BY THIRD- AND SIXTH-GRADE CHILDREN EJ 026 374
WORD ASSOCIATION AND DEFINITION IN MIDDLE CHILDHOOD EJ 030 294
ASSOCIATION AND ABSTRACTION AS MECHANISMS OF IMITATIVE LEARNING EJ 035 367
THE EFFECTS OF CONNOTATIVE SIMILARITY IN CHILDREN'S LEARNING OF A PAIRED-ASSOCIATE TASK EJ 035 376
DEVELOPMENTAL CHANGES IN IDIODYNAMIC SET RESPONSES OF CHILDREN'S WORD ASSOCIATIONS EJ 042 880
CHARACTERISTICS OF WORD ASSOCIATION RESPONSES OBTAINED FROM CHILDREN IN GRADES ONE THROUGH FOUR EJ 042 960
THE INFLUENCE OF INCENTIVES ON MEMORY STAGES IN CHILDREN EJ 049 428
THE DEVELOPMENT OF MEMORY-ENCODING PROCESSES IN YOUNG CHILDREN EJ 053 716
WORD-ASSOCIATION RESPONSES OF CHILDREN AS A FUNCTION OF AGE, SEX AND INSTRUCTIONS EJ 055 096
VARIABLES AFFECTING ASSOCIATIVE RECALL IN CHILDREN EJ 056 400
PATTERNS OF RESPONDING IN THE WORD ASSOCIATIONS OF WEST AFRICAN CHILDREN EJ 056 634
INITIAL PROBABILITY REHEARSAL, AND CONSTRAINT IN ASSOCIATIVE CLASS SELECTION EJ 057 903
GRADE INTERACTION WITH WORDS AND PICTURES IN A PAIRED-ASSOCIATE TASK: A PROPOSED EXPLANATION EJ 057 910

ATHLETIC PROGRAMS
DESIRABLE ATHLETIC COMPETITION FOR CHILDREN OF ELEMENTARY SCHOOL AGE. ED027086

ATTENDANCE
EFFECTS OF KINDERGARTEN ATTENDANCE ON DEVELOPMENT OF SCHOOL READINESS AND LANGUAGE SKILLS. INTERIM REPORT. ED029706

ATTENDANCE PATTERNS
A STUDY OF SOME ECOLOGICAL, ECONOMIC AND SOCIAL FACTORS INFLUENCING PARENTAL PARTICIPATION IN PROJECT HEAD START. ED014331
STUDY OF ACHIEVEMENT--JUNIOR KINDERGARTEN, WHO IS SERVED AND WHO GOES. ED017322

ATTENDANT TRAINING
THE TRAINING OF FAMILY DAY-CARE WORKERS: A FEASIBILITY STUDY AND INITIAL PILOT EFFORTS. FINAL REPORT. ED053787
A TEAM APPROACH USING CASSETTE TAPES EJ 061 001

ATTENTION
HEAD START EVALUATION AND RESEARCH CENTER, UNIVERSITY OF KANSAS. REPORT NO. I, THE OBSERVATION OF REINFORCEMENT BEHAVIOR OF TEACHERS IN HEAD START CLASSROOMS AND THE MODIFICATION OF A TEACHER'S ATTENDING BEHAVIOR. ED021633
SOCIO-CULTURAL INFLUENCES ON ATTENTION IN ELEMENTARY SCHOOL CHILDREN. FINAL REPORT. ED024456
ATTENTIONAL PREFERENCE AND EXPERIENCE: II. AN EXPLORATORY LONGITUDINAL STUDY OF THE EFFECTS OF VISUAL FAMILIARITY AND RESPONSIVENESS. ED039938
ATTENTIONAL PREFERENCE AND EXPERIENCE: III. VISUAL FAMILIARITY AND LOOKING TIME. ED039939
ATTENTIONAL PREFERENCE AND EXPERIENCE: I. INTRODUCTION. ED040751
CLASSIFICATION AND ATTENTION TRAINING CURRICULA FOR HEAD START CHILDREN. ED042508
ISSUES AND IMPLICATIONS OF THE DISTRIBUTION OF ATTENTION IN THE HUMAN INFANT. ED043387
AN EXPERIMENTAL PROGRAM IN CLASSIFICATION AND ATTENTIONAL TRAINING WITH HEAD START CHILDREN. ED044171
RESULTS AND IMPLICATIONS OF A HEAD START CLASSIFICATION AND ATTENTION TRAINING PROGRAM. ED045182
THE MEANING OF AN ORIENTING RESPONSE: A STUDY IN THE HIERARCHICAL ORDER OF ATTENDING. ED047794
THE RELATION BETWEEN THE AMOUNT OF TIME INFANTS SPEND AT VARIOUS STATES AND THE DEVELOPMENT OF VISUAL BEHAVIOR EJ 021 082
THE SHORT ATTENTION SPAN: FACT AND MYTH EJ 028 898
REACTION TIME AND REMOTE ASSOCIATION IN TALENTED MALE ADOLESCENTS EJ 029 360
COMPLEXITY, CONTOUR, AND AREA AS DETERMINANTS OF ATTENTION IN INFANTS EJ 029 361
FIXATION TIME AND TEMPO OF PLAY IN INFANTS EJ 029 363
ATTENTIONAL RESPONSES OF FIVE-MONTH GIRLS TO DISCREPANT AUDITORY STIMULI EJ 032 893
NOVELTY, FAMILIARITY, AND THE DEVELOPMENT OF INFANT ATTENTION EJ 034 529
A STIMULUS SIMILARITY SCALE FOR TEMPORAL MEASURES OF ATTENTION IN INFANTS AND CHILDREN EJ 034 530
CONTROL OF ORIENTING BEHAVIOR IN CHILDREN UNDER FIVE YEARS OF AGE EJ 034 535
THE EFFECTS OF ATTENTION AND MEDIATION ON CHILDREN'S MEMORY EJ 039 638
ATTENTION DISTRIBUTION IN THE 24-MONTH-OLD CHILD: VARIATIONS IN COMPLEXITY AND INCONGRUITY OF THE HUMAN FORM EJ 040 296
HUNGER AND MOTOR RESTRAINT ON AROUSAL AND VISUAL ATTENTION IN THE INFANT EJ 040 298
THE EFFECTS OF REWARD AND PUNISHMENT UPON CHILDREN'S ATTENTION, MOTIVATION, AND DISCRIMINATION LEARNING EJ 041 137
MEMORY AND ATTENTION IN CHILDREN'S DOUBLE-ALTERNATION LEARNING EJ 042 966
SELECTIVE ATTENTION IN MENTAL RETARDATES EJ 043 058
AGE CHANGES IN CARDIAC DECELERATION WITHIN A FIXED FOREPERIOD REACTION-TIME TASK: AN INDEX OF ATTENTION EJ 043 667
ATTENTION IN HYPERACTIVE CHILDREN AND THE EFFECT OF METHYLPHENIDATE (RITALIN) EJ 043 669
DEVELOPMENTAL DETERMINANTS OF ATTENTION: A CROSS-CULTURAL REPLICATION EJ 053 718
DEVELOPMENT OF YOUNG CHILDREN'S ATTENTION TO NORMAL AND DISTORTED STIMULI: A CROSS CULTURAL STUDY EJ 055 103
SELECTIVE STRATEGIES IN CHILDREN'S ATTENTION TO TASK-RELEVANT INFORMATION EJ 055 537
TASK ORIENTATION VERSUS SOCIAL ORIENTATION IN YOUNG CHILDREN AND THEIR ATTENTION TO RELEVANT SOCIAL CUES EJ 058 413
AN EXPERIMENTAL STUDY OF THE SELECTIVE ATTENTION OF CHILDREN OF 1896 AND 1966 EJ 060 775

ATTENTION CONTROL
HEAD START EVALUATION AND RESEARCH CENTER, UNIVERSITY OF KANSAS. REPORT NO. X, ENHANCEMENT OF THE SOCIAL REINFORCING VALUE OF A PRESCHOOL TEACHER. ED021646
CENTRAL AND INCIDENTAL LEARNING IN CHILDREN. ED023450
LEARNING OF INCENTIVE-VALUE BY CHILDREN. ED023473
CHILDREN'S REACTIONS TO DISTRACTORS IN A LEARNING SITUATION EJ 018 881
CONTROL OF ORIENTING BEHAVIOR IN CHILDREN UNDER FIVE YEARS OF AGE EJ 034 535

ATTENTION SPAN
NOVELTY AND FAMILIARITY AS DETERMINANTS OF INFANT ATTENTION WITHIN THE FIRST YEAR. ED023483
A COMPARATIVE STUDY OF CURRENT EDUCATIONAL TELEVISION PROGRAMS FOR PRESCHOOL CHILDREN. FINAL REPORT. ED032123
A TEST OF HABITUATION IN HUMAN INFANTS AS AN ACQUISITION PROCESS IN A RETROACTIVE INHIBITION PARADIGM. ED046490
CONDITIONING TASKS PERFORMANCE IN INFANCY AND EARLY CHILDHOOD AS A STABLE AND MEASURABLE ASPECT OF BEHAVIOR. FINAL REPORT. ED051890
CONTINUNITY IN COGNITIVE DEVELOPMENT DURING THE FIRST YEAR EJ 003 554
INDIVIDUAL DIFFERENCES IN THE INFANT'S DISTRIBUTION OF ATTENTION TO STIMULUS DISCREPANCY EJ 019 014
ATTENTIONAL PREFERENCE AND EXPERIENCE: II. AN EXPLORATORY LONGITUDINAL STUDY OF THE EFFECT OF VISUAL FAMILIARITY AND RESPONSIVENESS EJ 025 363
ATTENTIONAL PREFERENCE AND EXPERIENCE: III. VISUAL FAMILIARITY AND LOOKING TIME EJ 025 364
FIXATION TIME AND TEMPO OF PLAY IN INFANTS EJ 029 363
CONTROL OF ORIENTING BEHAVIOR IN CHILDREN UNDER FIVE YEARS OF AGE EJ 034 535
INFANTS' RECOGNITION MEMORY FOR A SERIES OF VISUAL STIMULI EJ 037 342
THE MEASUREMENT OF VISUAL ATTENTION IN INFANTS: A COMPARISON OF TWO METHODOLOGIES EJ 037 494
SELECTIVE ATTENTION IN MENTAL RETARDATES EJ 043 058
PSYCHOPHYSICALLY SCALED CUE DIFFERENCES, LEARNING RATE, AND ATTENTIONAL STRATEGIES IN A TACTILE DISCRIMINATION TASK EJ 058 146
ANALYSIS AND MODIFICATION OF SEARCH STRATEGIES OF IMPULSIVE AND REFLECTIVE CHILDREN ON THE MATCHING FAMILIAR FIGURES TEST EJ 059 510
ATTENTION SPAN AND GENERALIZATION OF TASK-RELATED STIMULUS CONTROL: EFFECTS OF REINFORCEMENT CONTINGENCIES EJ 059 878

ATTITUDE TESTS
THE COGNITIVE ENVIRONMENTS OF URBAN PRE-SCHOOL CHILDREN. MANUAL OF INSTRUCTIONS FOR ADMINISTERING AND SCORING "SCHOOLS" QUESTION. ED018254
ATTITUDES OF PRESCHOOL AND ELEMENTARY SCHOOL CHILDREN TO AUTHORITY FIGURES. ED046506
TIMING AND SOURCES OF INFORMATION ABOUT, AND ATTITUDES TOWARD, MENSTRUATION AMONG COLLEGE FEMALES EJ 029 533
THE DEVELOPMENT OF ELEMENTARY SCHOOL CHILDREN'S JUDGMENT OF INTENT EJ 052 581
SOCIAL CLASS DIFFERENCES IN TEACHER ATTITUDES TOWARD CHILDREN EJ 053 908
EVALUATION DIMENSION OF THE AFFECTIVE MEANING SYSTEM OF THE PRESCHOOL CHILD EJ 054 049
THE STRUCTURING OF SOCIAL ATTITUDES IN CHILDREN EJ 055 489

ATTITUDES
THE MAKING OF A PUPIL: CHANGING CHILDREN INTO SCHOOL CHILDREN. ED037235
ATTITUDES OF PRESCHOOL AND ELEMENTARY SCHOOL CHILDREN TO AUTHORITY FIGURES. ED046506
THE NATURE AND NURTURE OF PREJUDICE EJ 000 191
LABOR'S VIEWS ON TEACHER STRIKES EJ 003 418
CHANGES IN SUCCESS-FAILURE ATTITUDES DURING ADOLESCENCE EJ 016 777
AGE DIFFERENCES IN PLEASANTNESS OF VISUAL PATTERNS OF DIFFERENT VARIABILITY IN LATE CHILDHOOD AND ADOLESCENCE EJ 035 989
A DEVELOPMENTAL STUDY OF PRESCHOOL CHILDREN'S PREFERENCE FOR RANDOM FORMS EJ 035 990
GIRLS' ATTITUDES TOWARD MODELED BEHAVIORS AND THE CONTENT OF IMITATIVE PRIVATE PLAY EJ 036 079
TEENAGERS DISCUSS AGE RESTRICTIONS EJ 046 786
THE FORMATION AND REVERSAL OF AN ATTITUDE AS FUNCTIONS OF ASSUMED SELF-CONCEPT, RACE, AND SOCIOECONOMIC CLASS EJ 052 652
TEACHERS AND PARENTS: CHANGING ROLES AND GOALS EJ 055 362
EYE CONTACT, ATTITUDES, AND ATTITUDE CHANGE AMONG MALES EJ 059 813

AUDIENCES
THE FIRST YEAR OF SESAME STREET: A SUMMARY OF AUDIENCE SURVEYS. FINAL REPORT, VOLUME IV OF V VOLUMES. ED047824

AUDIOLINGUAL SKILLS
CANDIDATE FOR INTEGRATION: A HEARING-IMPAIRED CHILD IN A REGULAR NURSERY SCHOOL EJ 026 915

AUDIOMETRIC TESTS
THRESHOLD BY IDENTIFICATION OF PICTURES (TIP) TEST AND DISCRIMINATION BY IDENTIFICATION OF PICTURES (DIP) TEST. ED015784

AUDIOVISUAL AIDS
THE SOUTHSIDE EXPERIMENT IN PERSONALIZED EDUCATION. ED042505
THE EFFECTS OF EXTRANEOUS MATERIAL AND NEGATIVE EXEMPLARS ON A SOCIAL SCIENCE CONCEPT-LEARNING TASK FOR PRE-SCHOOL CHILDREN. ED047819
AUDIO-VISUAL MATERIALS IN EARLY CHILDHOOD EDUCATION EJ 006 854
AUDIO-VISUAL MATERIALS IN EARLY CHILDHOOD EDUCATION EJ 038 907

AUDIOVISUAL INSTRUCTION
AUTOMATED READING INSTRUCTION IN THE GHETTO EJ 045 798

AUDITION (PHYSIOLOGY)
HEARING LEVELS OF CHILDREN BY AGE AND SEX: UNITED STATES. ED047799

AUDITORY DISCRIMINATION
HEAD START EVALUATION AND RESEARCH CENTER, UNIVERSITY OF KANSAS. REPORT NO. IIA, A STUDY OF AUDITORY DISCRIMINATION AND VERBAL RESPONDING. ED021634
AN EXPERIMENTAL PROGRAM DESIGNED TO INCREASE AUDITORY DISCRIMINATION WITH HEAD START CHILDREN. ED029680
INITIAL AND FINAL CONSONANT RELATIONSHIPS IN SPEECH-SOUND TESTS: A DISCRIMINATION OR RESPONSE SET PROBLEM? ED032131
HEARING LEVELS OF CHILDREN BY AGE AND SEX: UNITED STATES. ED047799
THE LEARNING OF SPEECHLIKE STIMULI BY CHILDREN EJ 018 815
VOWEL PRODUCTIONS AND IDENTIFICATION BY NORMAL AND LANGUAGE DELAYED CHILDREN EJ 018 816
EFFECT OF CORRELATED VISUAL AND TACTUAL FEEDBACK ON AUDITORY PATTERN LEARNING AT DIFFERENT AGE LEVELS EJ 037 517
SENSORY-SET FACTORS IN AGE DIFFERENCES IN REACTION TIME EJ 048 304
AUDITORY-LINGUISTIC SENSITIVITY IN EARLY INFANCY EJ 053 479

AUDITORY EVALUATION
HEARING LEVELS OF CHILDREN BY AGE AND SEX: UNITED STATES. ED047799

AUDITORY PERCEPTION
LISTENING. WHAT RESEARCH SAYS TO THE TEACHER, NO. 29. ED026120
PERCEPTUAL MODE DOMINANCE: AN APPROACH TO ASSESSMENT OF FIRST GRADE READING AND SPELLING. ED026132
EXPERIMENTS IN GRAMMATICAL PROCESSING IN CHILDREN. RESEARCH PROJECT NUMBER 1 OF PROJECT HEAD START RESEARCH AND EVALUATION CENTER, SYRACUSE UNIVERSITY RESEARCH INSTITUTE. FINAL REPORT, NOVEMBER 1, 1967. ED026138
WHAT DO YOU MEAN, "AUDITORY PERCEPTION"? EJ 013 560
AMOUNT OF SHORT-TERM FAMILIARIZATION AND THE RESPONSE TO AUDITORY DISCREPANCIES EJ 025 362
EARLY AUDITORY DEPRIVATION AND SENSORY COMPENSATION EJ 044 118
LEARNING TO LISTEN: A STUDY IN AUDITORY PERCEPTION EJ 053 485

AUDITORY TESTS
INITIAL AND FINAL CONSONANT RELATIONSHIPS IN SPEECH-SOUND TESTS: A DISCRIMINATION OR RESPONSE SET PROBLEM? ED032131
ECHOIC RESPONSE INVENTORY FOR CHILDREN (ERIC). ED039931

AUDITORY TRAINING
LISTENING. WHAT RESEARCH SAYS TO THE TEACHER, NO. 29. ED026120
WHAT DO YOU MEAN, "AUDITORY PERCEPTION"? EJ 013 560

AUDITORY VISUAL TESTS
THRESHOLD BY IDENTIFICATION OF PICTURES (TIP) TEST AND DISCRIMINATION BY IDENTIFICATION OF PICTURES (DIP) TEST. ED015784

AURAL LEARNING
THE LEARNING OF SPEECHLIKE STIMULI BY CHILDREN EJ 018 815
AUDITORY-LINGUISTIC SENSITIVITY IN EARLY INFANCY EJ 053 479

AURAL STIMULI
AUDITORY COMPONENTS OF NEONATAL EXPERIENCE: A PRELIMINARY REPORT. ED025336
ACQUISTION AND TRANSFER DIFFERENCES BETWEEN KINDERGARTENERS AND SECOND-GRADERS ON AURALLY AND VISUALLY PRESENTED PAIRED-ASSOCIATES USING AN A-B, A-C DESIGN RESEARCH PROJECT NUMBER 2 OF PROJECT HEAD START RESEARCH AND EVALUATION CENTER, SYRACUSE UNIVERSITY RESEARCH INSTITUTE. FINAL REPORT, NOVEMBER 1, 1967. ED026139
INFANT REACTIVITY TO REDUNDANT PROPRIOCEPTIVE AND AUDITORY STIMULATION: A TWIN STUDY. ED052825
CHANGES IN THE NONNUTRITIVE SUCKING RESPONSE TO STIMULATION DURING INFANCY EJ 027 848
ATTENTIONAL RESPONSES OF FIVE-MONTH GIRLS TO DISCREPANT AUDITORY STIMULI EJ 032 893
THE RELATIONSHIP BETWEEN AUDITORY AND VISUAL SHORT-TERM MEMORY AND READING ACHIEVEMENT EJ 033 780
RESPONSE TO VOICE OF MOTHER AND STRANGER BY BABIES IN THE FIRST YEAR EJ 035 269
EFFECT OF PRETRAINING AND INSTRUCTIONS ON AVOIDANCE CONDITIONING IN PRESCHOOL CHILDREN EJ 035 624
THE DEVELOPMENT OF COGNITIVE BALANCE AND THE TRANSITION FROM CONCRETE TO FORMAL OPERATIONAL THOUGHT EJ 041 145
NEWBORN'S RESPONSE TO THE CRY OF ANOTHER INFANT EJ 041 959
EFFECT OF CLASSROOM NOISE ON NUMBER IDENTIFICATION BY RETARDED CHILDREN EJ 045 793
HABITUATION AND MEMORY: INFANT CARDIAC RESPONSES TO FAMILIAR AND DISCREPANT AUDITORY STIMULI EJ 056 633

AURALLY HANDICAPPED
CANDIDATE FOR INTEGRATION: A HEARING-IMPAIRED CHILD IN A REGULAR NURSERY SCHOOL EJ 026 915
LETTER TO THE TEACHER OF A HARD-OF-HEARING CHILD EJ 029 917

AUTHORITARIANISM
ATTITUDES OF PRESCHOOL AND ELEMENTARY SCHOOL CHILDREN TO AUTHORITY FIGURES EJ 034 452
AN EXPLORATORY STUDY OF SOCIALIZATION EFFECTS ON BLACK CHILDREN: SOME BLACK-WHITE COMPARISONS EJ 055 656

AUTISM
PSYCHOLOBIOLOGICAL REFERENTS FOR THE TREATMENT OF AUTISM. ED028814
AN EXPERIMENTAL STUDY OF THE SOCIAL RESPONSIVENESS OF CHILDREN WITH AUTISTIC BEHAVIORS EJ 024 470
STUDIES IN PATTERN DETECTION IN NORMAL AND AUTISTIC CHILDREN. II. REPRODUCTION AND PRODUCTION OF COLOR SEQUENCES EJ 027 613
AN APPLIANCE FOR AUTOINDUCED ADVERSE CONTROL OF SELF-INJURIOUS BEHAVIOR EJ 029 916
CHILDHOOD PSYCHOSIS COMBINED WITH XYZ ABNORMALITIES EJ 035 078

AUTOINSTRUCTIONAL PROGRAMS
RESEARCH ON THE NEW NURSERY SCHOOL. PART I, A SUMMARY OF THE EVALUATION OF THE EXPERIMENTAL PROGRAM FOR DEPRIVED CHILDREN AT THE NEW NURSERY SCHOOL USING SOME EXPERIMENTAL MEASURES. INTERIM REPORT. ED027076
THE NEW NURSERY SCHOOL RESEARCH PROJECT ED042518

AUTOMATION
AUTOMATED READING INSTRUCTION IN THE GHETTO EJ 045 798

BASIC READING
THERE IS A BETTER WAY. A PREMISE POINTS THE WAY, A PROFILE WITH PROMISE, A COMPOSITE OF THE SURVEY. ED023471

BASIC SKILLS
THE EFFECTS OF ASSESSMENT AND PERSONALIZED PROGRAMMING ON SUBSEQUENT INTELLECTUAL DEVELOPMENT OF PREKINDERGARTEN AND KINDERGARTEN CHILDREN. ED013663
THE PRESCHOOL INVENTORY. ED014334
ADAPTATIONAL TASKS IN CHILDHOOD IN OUR CULTURE. ED021632
MOTHER'S MODE OF DISCIPLINE AND CHILD'S VERBAL ABILITY EJ 050 794

BASIC VOCABULARY
A REPLICATIVE INVESTIGATION OF THE BUCKINGHAM-DOLCH FREE-ASSOCIATION WORD STUDY. FINAL REPORT. ED017333

BEGINNING READING
THE DIRECT INSTRUCTION PROGRAM FOR TEACHING READING. ED015022
CHILDREN WHO READ EARLY, TWO LONGITUDINAL STUDIES. ED019107
GRADE EQUIVALENT COMPARISONS BETWEEN DISADVANTAGED NEGRO URBAN CHILDREN WITH AND WITHOUT KINDERGARTEN EXPERIENCE WHEN TAUGHT TO READ BY SEVERAL METHODS. ED020798
AN EARLY INTERVENTION PROGRAM THAT FAILED. ED021609
LEARNING TO READ THROUGH EXPERIENCE. SECOND EDITION. ED027067
READING. DIMENSIONS IN EARLY LEARNING SERIES. ED027070
MUSIC IN THE BEGINNING READING PROGRAM EJ 006 811
PARENTS TEACH KINDERGARTEN READING AT HOME EJ 020 774
MOTIVATIONAL AND ATTITUDINAL CONTENT OF FIRST GRADE READING TEXTBOOKS EJ 045 084
A BASIC VOCABULARY FOR BEGINNING READING EJ 047 894
MY MON CAN TEACH READING TOO! EJ 051 082
TEACHING READING IN THE KINDERGARTEN: A REVIEW OF RECENT STUDIES EJ 055 153
GROWTH IN READING IN AN INTEGRATED DAY CLASSROOM EJ 055 154
LINGUISTIC FACTORS IN READING EJ 059 537

BEHAVIOR
CODING MANUAL FOR APPROACH (A PROCEDURE FOR PATTERNING RESPONSES OF ADULTS AND CHILDREN). ED015005
THE STATUS OF BEHAVIORAL MEASUREMENT AND ASSESSMENT IN CHILDREN. ED018252
A STUDY OF FOOD AND POVERTY AMONG 113 HEAD START CHILDREN IN MISSOULA, MONTANA. ED028829
THE RELATIONSHIP BETWEEN HEMOGLOBIN LEVEL AND INTELLECTUAL FUNCTION. ED028830
THE PLAYFUL MODES OF KNOWING. ED050806
REEXAMINING VARIABLES AFFECTING COGNITIVE FUNCTIONING IN PRESCHOOL CHILDREN: A FOLLOW-UP. ED052818
STATE AS AN INFANT-ENVIRONMENT INTERACTION: AN ANALYSIS OF MOTHER-INFANT BEHAVIOR AS A FUNCTION OF SEX. ED052829
CLINICAL IMPLICATIONS OF MATERNAL EMPLOYMENT: A REVIEW OF RESEARCH EJ 030 432
THEORETICAL NOTES ON POWER MOTIVATION EJ 032 677
TRAINING, TRANSFER, AND THE DEVELOPMENT OF COMPLEX BEHAVIOR EJ 034 712
BEHAVIORAL COMPLIANCE AND DEVALUATION OF THE FORBIDDEN OBJECT AS A FUNCTION OF PROBABILITY OF DETECTION AND SEVERITY OF THREAT EJ 038 935
EFFECT OF THE PRESENCE OF A HUMAN MODEL ON IMITATIVE BEHAVIOR IN CHILDREN EJ 039 904

AN EXPERIMENT ON EYEBROW-RAISING AND VISUAL SEARCHING IN CHILDREN EJ 039 947
THE DEVELOPMENT OF HYPNOTIC SUSCEPTIBILITY: A LONGITUDINAL (CONVERGENCE) STUDY EJ 041 449
A THIRD STUDY OF PERCEPTUAL BEHAVIOR IN SIXTH GRADE CHILDREN IN RELATION TO THEIR BEHAVIOR IN ART EJ 041 830
THE ACQUISITION AND PERFORMANCE OF A SOCIALLY NEUTRAL RESPONSE AS A FUNCTION OF VICARIOUS REWARD EJ 046 889
A STUDY OF SLEEP BEHAVIOR IN TWO-YEAR-OLD CHILDREN EJ 048 299
METODO DE ARCHIVAR LAS OBSERVACIONES DEL COMPORTAMIENTO DEL NINO, COMO GUIA PARA ENTENDERLO MEJOR (METHODS OF RECORDING OBSERVATIONS OF CHILDREN'S BEHAVIOR, A GUIDE FOR BETTER UNDERSTANDING) EJ 049 938

BEHAVIOR CHAINING

EFFECTS OF NAMING RELEVANT AND IRRELEVANT STIMULI ON THE DISCRIMINATION LEARNING OF CHILDREN EJ 025 955
MODIFICATION OF BEHAVIOR PATTERNS OF INDIAN CHILDREN EJ 051 472
CONDITION WITH CAUTION EJ 058 585

BEHAVIOR CHANGE

EVALUATION OF TWO ASSOCIATED YM-YWHA HEADSTART PROGRAMS. FINAL REPORT. ED014318
AN ASSESSMENT OF INTELLIGENCE, PSYCHOLINGUISTIC ABILITIES AND LEARNING APTITUDES AMONG PRESCHOOL CHILDREN. ED014323
BEHAVIOR PATTERNS OF NORMAL CHILDREN. ED015016
SUMMARY OF BEHAVIOR PATTERNS OF NORMAL CHILDREN. ED016531
PROJECT HEAD START--SUMMER 1966. FINAL REPORT. SECTION THREE, PUPILS AND PROGRAMS. ED018248
EFFECTS OF ADULT SOCIAL REINFORCEMENT ON CHILD BEHAVIOR. ED019997
AN ANNOTATED BIBLIOGRAPHY OF BEHAVIOR MODIFICATION WITH CHILDREN AND RETARDATES. ED020025
HEAD START EVALUATION AND RESEARCH CENTER, UNIVERSITY OF KANSAS. REPORT NO. I, THE OBSERVATION OF REINFORCEMENT BEHAVIOR OF TEACHERS IN HEAD START CLASSROOMS AND THE MODIFICATION OF A TEACHER'S ATTENDING BEHAVIOR. ED021633
MODIFICATION OF A DEVIANT SIBLING INTERACTION PATTERN IN THE HOME. ED023461
BEHAVIOR MODIFICATION OF AN ADJUSTMENT CLASS: A TOKEN REINFORCEMENT PROGRAM. ED023462
LINGUISTIC AND PSYCHOLOGICAL FACTORS IN THE SPEECH REGULATION OF BEHAVIOR IN VERY YOUNG CHILDREN. ED024442
MOTIVATIONAL AND SOCIAL COMPONENTS IN COMPENSATORY EDUCATION PROGRAMS: SUGGESTED PRINCIPLES, PRACTICES, AND RESEARCH DESIGNS. ED024464
FUN WHILE LEARNING AND EARNING. A LOOK INTO CHATTANOOGA PUBLIC SCHOOLS' TOKEN REINFORCEMENT PROGRAM. ED027952
THE SIMULTANEOUS REHABILITATION OF MOTHERS AND THEIR CHILDREN. ED034591
A TOKEN REINFORCEMENT SYSTEM IN THE PUBLIC SCHOOLS. ED036323
BEHAVIORAL RESEARCH RELEVANT TO THE CLASSROOM. ED039036
PREACHING AND PRACTICING SELF-SACRIFICE: THEIR LOCUS OF EFFECT UPON CHILDREN'S BEHAVIOR AND COGNITION. ED040741
BEHAVIOR MODIFICATION PROCEDURES APPLIED TO THE ISOLATE BEHAVIOR OF A NURSERY SCHOOL CHILD. ED041635
A PROGRAM OF STIMULUS CONTROL FOR ESTABLISHING A ONE-MINUTE WAIT FOR REINFORCEMENT IN PRESCHOOL CHILDREN. PROGRESS REPORT. ED042492
THE MODIFICATION OF TEACHER BEHAVIORS WHICH MODIFY CHILD BEHAVIORS. PROGRESS REPORT. ED042499
THE SOCIAL MATURITY OF DISADVANTAGED CHILDREN. SPECIAL STUDIES PROJECT #2: ED042507
MODIFICATION BY SOCIAL REINFORCEMENT OF DEFICIENT SOCIAL BEHAVIOR OF DISADVANTAGED KINDERGARTEN CHILDREN. ED043381
MODIFICATION OF THE CLASSROOM BEHAVIOR OF A "DISADVANTAGED" KINDERGARTEN BOY BY SOCIAL REINFORCEMENT AND ISOLATION. ED045181
CONDITION WITH CAUTION: THINK THRICE BEFORE CONDITIONING. (ROUGH DRAFT). ED046539
FIELD STUDIES OF SOCIAL REINFORCEMENT IN A PRESCHOOL. ED047772
EFFECTS OF DURATION OF A NURSERY SCHOOL SETTING ON ENVIRONMENTAL CONSTRAINTS AND CHILDREN'S MODES OF ADAPTATION. ED047812
PARENTS ARE TEACHERS: A CHILD MANAGEMENT PROGRAM. ED047826
EDUCATIONAL INTERVENTION IN EARLY CHILDHOOD: ABSTRACTS OF THE 1965-1970 SPECIAL STUDIES RESEARCH AND EVALUATION REPORT. FINAL REPORT, VOLUME III. ED050816
LIVING WITH CHILDREN: NEW METHODS FOR PARENTS AND TEACHERS. ED051887
SOME EFFECTS OF PUNISHMENT ON CHILDREN'S BEHAVIOR EJ 006 876
EDUCATIONAL APPLICATION OF BEHAVIOR MODIFICATION TECHNIQUES WITH SEVERELY RETARDED CHILDREN IN A CHILD DEVELOPMENT CENTER EJ 017 421
ACQUISITION OF COGNITIVE RESPONSES UNDER DIFFERENT PATTERNS OF VERBAL REWARDS EJ 017 712
CHANGES IN FRIENDSHIP STATUS AS A FUNCTION OF REINFORCEMENT EJ 019 004
EFFECTS OF BRIEF OBSERVATION OF MODEL BEHAVIOR ON CONCEPTUAL TEMPO OF IMPULSIVE CHILDREN EJ 019 010
TEACHING THE UNTEACHABLES EJ 021 514
EFFECTS OF INCONSISTENT PUNISHMENT ON AGGRESSION IN CHILDREN EJ 021 992
PREACHING AND PRACTICING GENEROSITY: CHILDREN'S ACTIONS AND REACTIONS EJ 022 140
ECOLOGICAL PLANNING FOR DISTURBED CHILDREN EJ 022 978
THE MODIFICATION OF CHILDHOOD STUTTERING: SOME RESPONSE-RESPONSE RELATIONSHIPS EJ 023 965
THE DEVELOPMENT OF ROLE-TAKING AS REFLECTED BY BEHAVIOR OF BRIGHT, AVERAGE, AND RETARDED CHILDREN IN A SOCIAL GUESSING GAME EJ 025 361
MODIFYING BEHAVIOR OF KINDERGARTEN CHILDREN EJ 026 493
THE EFFECT OF BLACK HISTORY ON AN INTERRACIAL GROUP OF CHILDREN EJ 026 735
TANGIBLE REINFORCERS AND CHILD GROUP THERAPY EJ 026 935
CLASSROOM MANAGEMENT--MORE THAN CONDITIONING EJ 027 827
THE APPLICATION OF PREMACK'S GENERALIZATION ON REINFORCEMENT TO THE MANAGEMENT OF CLASSROOM BEHAVIOR EJ 028 634
CREATIVITY CHANGE IN STUDENT NURSES: A CROSS-SECTIONAL AND LONGITUDINAL STUDY EJ 030 291
MODIFYING RISK-TAKING BEHAVIOR EJ 032 891
SUB-PROFESSIONAL BEHAVIOR MODIFICATION AND THE DEVELOPMENT OF TOKEN-REINFORCEMENT SYSTEMS IN INCREASING ACADEMIC MOTIVATION AND ACHIEVEMENT EJ 034 527
THE SYSTEMATIC USE OF THE PEMACK PRINCIPLE IN MODIFYING CLASSROOM BEHAVIORS EJ 034 528
LINGUISTIC AND PSYCHOLOGICAL FACTORS IN THE SPEECH REGULATION OF BEHAVIOR IN YOUNG CHILDREN EJ 034 540
USING SENSITIVITY TRAINING WITH JUNIOR HIGH SCHOOL STUDENTS EJ 035 169
CHAOTIC REINFORCEMENT: A SOCIOECONOMIC LEVELER EJ 035 371
A SENSITIVITY-TRAINING APPROACH TO GROUP THERAPY WITH CHILDREN EJ 039 501
EFFECTS OF COMPETITION-INDUCED FRUSTRATION ON TWO CLASSES OF MODELED BEHAVIOR EJ 043 284
CHANGES IN PARENTAL BEHAVIOR REPORTED BY CHILDREN IN WEST GERMANY AND THE UNITED STATES EJ 048 397
CONDITIONING INDEPENDENT WORK BEHAVIOR IN READING WITH SEVEN YEAR OLD CHILDREN IN A REGULAR EARLY CHILDHOOD CLASSROOM EJ 050 795
THE USE OF BEHAVIOR-MODIFICATION TECHNIQUES WITH FEMALE DELINQUENTS EJ 051 473
THE BOY WHO DID NOT CRY EJ 052 310
INSTANT LAW AND ORDER EJ 055 534
BEHAVIOR MODIFICATION IN THE HOME WITH THE MOTHER AS THE EXPERIMENTER: THE EFFECT OF DIFFERENTIAL REINFORCEMENT ON SIBLING NEGATIVE RESPONSE RATES EJ 056 721
MODELING AND THE FEARFUL CHILD PATIENT EJ 058 354

BEHAVIOR DEVELOPMENT

SCHOOL READINESS, BEHAVIOR TESTS USED AT THE GESELL INSTITUTE. ED023449
REINFORCEMENT GROWS UP: THE EXPERIMENTAL ANALYSIS OF BEHAVIOR AS A SYSTEMATIC APPROACH TO THE TEACHING OF DEVELOPMENTAL PSYCHOLOGY. ED023479
LINGUISTIC AND PSYCHOLOGICAL FACTORS IN THE SPEECH REGULATION OF BEHAVIOR IN VERY YOUNG CHILDREN. ED024442
INFANTS' RESPONSES TO FACIAL STIMULI DURING THE FIRST YEAR OF LIFE: EXPLORATORY STUDIES IN THE DEVELOPMENT OF A FACE SCHEMA. ED024455
CHILD DEVELOPMENT AND MATERIAL SURVEY. PART I, TECHNICAL REPORT. FINAL REPORT. ED027084
ATTACHMENT AND RECIPROCITY IN THE TWO-YEAR-OLD CHILD. ED039946
DEVELOPMENTAL-BEHAVIORAL PATTERNS IN TWENTY-SIX CULTURALLY DISADVANTAGED INFANTS. ED044173
THE ROLE OF EXPERIENCE IN THE BEHAVIORAL DEVELOPMENT OF HUMAN INFANTS: CURRENT STATUS AND RECOMMENDATIONS. ED048917
EDUCATION OF THE INFANT AND YOUNG CHILD. ED048930
LIVING WITH CHILDREN: NEW METHODS FOR PARENTS AND TEACHERS. ED051887
FACTORS INFLUENCING IMITATIVE LEARNING IN PRESCHOOL CHILDREN EJ 018 892
FEAR OF VISUAL NOVELTY: DEVELOPMENTAL PATTERNS IN MALES AND FEMALES EJ 019 011
ATTACHMENT BEHAVIORS IN HUMAN INFANTS: DISCRIMINATIVE VOCALIZATION ON MATERNAL SEPARATION EJ 019 019
PATTERNS OF FEAR DEVELOPMENT DURING INFANCY EJ 020 718
OPTIONAL SHIFT BEHAVIOR OF CHILDREN AS A FUNCTION OF AGE, TYPE OF PRETRAINING AND STIMULUS SALIENCE EJ 021 849
SOCIALIZATION AND INSTRUMENTAL COMPETENCE IN YOUNG CHILDREN EJ 030 510
INDIVIDUALLY GUIDED MOTIVATION: DEVELOPING SELF-DIRECTION AND PROSOCIAL BEHAVIORS EJ 034 159

THE OBJECTIVE MEASUREMENT OF CHILDREN'S INTRAFAMILIAL ATTITUDE AND SENTIMENT STRUCTURE AND THE INVESTMENT-SUBSIDIATION MODEL EJ 034 542
THE BEHAVIOR OF TWINS: EFFECTS OF BIRTH WEIGHT AND BIRTH SEQUENCE EJ 036 081
DEVELOPMENTAL GENETICS OF BEHAVIORAL CAPACITIES: THE NATURE-NURTURE PROBLEM RE-EVALUATED EJ 037 516
THE IMPACT OF MOTHER'S PRESENCE UPON BEHAVIOR: THE FIRST YEAR EJ 039 908
THE SEQUENCE OF DEVELOPMENT OF SOME EARLY MATHEMATICS BEHAVIORS EJ 056 710
SITUATIONAL EFFECTS ON JUSTIFIABLENESS OF AGGRESSION AT THREE AGE LEVELS EJ 056 734

BEHAVIOR PATTERNS

BEHAVIOR PATTERNS OF NORMAL CHILDREN. ED015016
POSITIVE SOCIAL REINFORCEMENT IN THE NURSERY SCHOOL PEER GROUP. ED016515
SUMMARY OF BEHAVIOR PATTERNS OF NORMAL CHILDREN. ED016531
THE CHILD WHO DISLIKES GOING TO SCHOOL. ED019999
HEAD START EVALUATION AND RESEARCH CENTER, UNIVERSITY OF KANSAS. REPORT NO. V, A COMPARATIVE BEHAVIORAL ANALYSIS OF PEER-GROUP INFLUENCE TECHNIQUES IN HEAD START AND MIDDLE CLASS POPULATIONS. ED021638
HEAD START EVALUATION AND RESEARCH CENTER, THE UNIVERSITY OF CHICAGO. REPORT D, THE INTERACTION OF INTELLIGENCE AND BEHAVIOR AS ONE PREDICTOR OF EARLY SCHOOL ACHIEVEMENT IN WORKING CLASS AND CULTURALLY DISADVANTAGED HEAD START CHILDREN. ED022553
HEAD START EVALUATION AND RESEARCH CENTER, BOSTON UNIVERSITY. REPORT C-II, THE EXPRESSION OF AGGRESSION IN PRE-SCHOOL CHILDREN. ED022562
INTERACTION PATTERNS AS A SOURCE OF ERROR IN TEACHERS' EVALUATIONS OF HEAD START CHILDREN. FINAL REPORT. ED023453
PROCESSES OF CURIOSITY AND EXPLORATION IN PRESCHOOL DISADVANTAGED CHILDREN. ED023470
INFANTS' RESPONSES TO FACIAL STIMULI DURING THE FIRST YEAR OF LIFE: EXPLORATORY STUDIES IN THE DEVELOPMENT OF A FACE SCHEMA. ED024455
PARENT-CHILD INTERACTION AND THE CHILD'S APPROACH TO TASK SITUATIONS. ED025307
COOPERATIVE, TRUSTING BEHAVIOR AS A FUNCTION OF ETHNIC GROUP SIMILARITY-DISSIMILARITY AND OF IMMEDIATE AND DELAYED REWARD IN A TWO-PERSON GAME. PART OF THE FINAL REPORT. ED025322
THE RELATIONSHIP BETWEEN INSTRUMENTAL ASSERTION AND THE STANFORD-BINET. ED030474
ENVIRONMENT INFLUENCES ON THE DEVELOPMENT OF ABILITIES. ED032126
AN ECOLOGICAL STUDY OF THREE-YEAR-OLDS AT HOME. FINAL REPORT. ED037238
A REPLICATION AND EXTENSION STUDY ON N-LENGTH, INHIBITION AND COOPERATIVE BEHAVIOR WITH A MEXICAN-AMERICAN POPULATION. PART OF THE FINAL REPORT ON HEAD START EVALUATION AND RESEARCH: 1968-69 TO THE OFFICE OF ECONOMIC OPPORTUNITY. ED037249
CHARACTERIZATION OF THE EFFECT OF SPACE, MATERIALS, AND TEACHER BEHAVIOR ON PRESCHOOL CHILDREN'S FREE PLAY ACTIVITY PATTERNS. RESEARCH REPORT NO. 1. ED037251
THE EFFECT OF N-LENGTH ON THE DEVELOPMENT OF COOPERATIVE AND NON-COOPERATIVE BEHAVIOR IN A TWO-PERSON GAME. PART OF THE FINAL REPORT ON HEAD START EVALUATION AND RESEARCH: 1968-69 TO THE OFFICE OF ECONOMIC OPPORTUNITY. ED038172
ANALYSIS OF THE OBJECT CATEGORIZATION TEST AND THE PICTURE CATEGORIZATION TEST FOR PRESCHOOL CHILDREN. ED038174
THE PREVALENCE OF BEHAVIOR SYMPTOMS IN YOUNGER ELEMENTARY SCHOOL CHILDREN. ED039040
PREACHING AND PRACTICING SELF-SACRIFICE: THEIR LOCUS OF EFFECT UPON CHILDREN'S BEHAVIOR AND COGNITION. ED040741
INFLUENCE TECHNIQUES IN DYADS COMPOSED OF INTERDEPENDENT MIDDLE AND LOWER CLASS PRESCHOOL CHILDREN. FINAL REPORT ED042489
WORDS AND DEEDS ABOUT ALTRUISM AND THE SUBSEQUENT REINFORCEMENT POWER OF THE MODEL. ED043390
RELATIVE SOOTHING EFFECTS OF VERTICAL AND HORIZONTAL ROCKING. ED046504
A DESCRIPTIVE ACCOUNT OF FOUR MODES OF CHILDREN'S PLAY BETWEEN ONE AND FIVE YEARS. ED049833
INFANT DEVELOPMENT IN LOWER CLASS AMERICAN FAMILIES. ED049836
NEIGHBORHOOD FAMILY DAY CARE AS A CHILD-REARING ENVIRONMENT. ED049840
ENVIRONMENTAL FORCES IN THE HOME LIVES OF THREE-YEAR-OLD CHILDREN IN THREE POPULATION SUBGROUPS. ED050802
INTERACTION OF SEX OF SUBJECT AND DEPENDENCY-TRAINING PROCEDURES IN A SOCIAL-REINFORCEMENT STUDY EJ 006 877
PERCEPTUAL CORRELATES OF IMPULSIVE AND REFLECTIVE BEHAVIOR EJ 018 322
TWO MODES OF MATERNAL IMMATURITY AND THEIR CONSEQUENCES EJ 023 424
COOPERATIVE AND COMPETITIVE BEHAVIOR OF URBAN AFRO-AMERICAN, ANGLO-AMERICAN, MEXICAN-AMERICAN, AND MEXICAN VILLAGE CHILDREN EJ 024 033
SEX DIFFERENCES IN PRESCHOOL CHILDREN WITHOUT HISTORIES OF COMPLICATIONS OF PREGNANCY AND DELIVERY EJ 024 939
THE CONNOTATIVE MEANING OF PARENT-CHILD RELATIONSHIPS AS RELATED TO PERCEIVED MATERNAL WARMTH AND CONTROL EJ 025 471
EXPERIMENTAL ANALYSIS OF THE FACTORS DETERMINING OBEDIENCE OF FOUR-YEAR-OLD CHILDREN TO ADULT FEMALES EJ 026 152
THE USE OF A PLAY PROGRAM BY HOSPITALIZED CHILDREN EJ 026 774
STUDIES IN PATTERN DETECTION IN NORMAL AND AUTISTIC CHILDREN. II. REPRODUCTION AND PRODUCTION OF COLOR SEQUENCES EJ 027 613
DEVELOPMENTAL ASPECTS OF REACTION TO POSITIVE INDUCEMENTS EJ 029 359
AN APPLIANCE FOR AUTOINDUCED ADVERSE CONTROL OF SELF-INJURIOUS BEHAVIOR EJ 029 916
CLASSROOM BEHAVIOR: MESSAGES FROM CHILDREN EJ 031 780
NEONATE-MOTHER INTERACTION: EFFECTS OF PARITY ON FEEDING BEHAVIOR EJ 032 892
AN EXAMINATION OF FRUSTRATION AGGRESSION RELATIONS IN BOYS DURING MIDDLE CHILDHOOD EJ 035 628
IRRELEVANCE OF NEWBORN WAKING STATES TO SOME MOTOR AND APPETITIVE RESPONSES EJ 036 076
THE BEHAVIOR OF TWINS: EFFECTS OF BIRTH WEIGHT AND BIRTH SEQUENCE EJ 036 081
TEACHERS IN CHILDREN'S ROLES? EJ 037 235
CHILDREN'S ACQUISITION AND REVERSAL BEHAVIOR IN A PROBABILITY LEARNING SITUATION AS A FUNCTION OF PROGRAMMED INSTRUCTION, INTERNAL-EXTERNAL CONTROL, AND SCHEDULES OF REINFORCEMENT EJ 037 495
RHYTHMIC HABIT PATTERNS IN INFANCY: THEIR SEQUENCE, AGE OF ONSET, AND FREQUENCY EJ 040 295
PRESTIMULUS ACTIVITY LEVEL AND RESPONSIVITY IN THE NEONATE EJ 040 297
CURIOSITY AND THE PARENT-CHILD RELATIONSHIP EJ 041 447
EFFECTS OF CONTINGENT AND NONCONTINGENT REINFORCEMENT UPON GENERALIZED IMITATION EJ 041 448
COOPERATION AND COMPETITION OF MEXICAN, MEXICAN-AMERICAN, AND ANGLO-AMERICAN CHILDREN OF TWO AGES UNDER FOUR INSTRUCTIONAL SETS EJ 041 957
EFFECTS OF DIFFERENTIAL EXPERIENCE ON INFANTS' PERFORMANCE IN A PIAGETIAN STAGE IV OBJECT-CONCEPT TASK EJ 042 956
NEWBORN AND PRESCHOOLER: ORGANIZATION OF BEHAVIOR AND RELATIONS BETWEEN PERIODS EJ 045 110
LE MONDE DES TOUT PETITS EST-IL INFLUENCE PAR NOTRE MONDE MODERNE? (IS THE WORLD OF CHILDREN INFLUENCED BY OUR MODERN WORLD?) EJ 049 895
ANXIETY IN THE EVALUATIVE CONTEXT EJ 051 018
RESEARCH FOR UNDERSTANDING EJ 051 150
MODIFICATION OF BEHAVIOR PATTERNS OF INDIAN CHILDREN EJ 051 472
HELPING BEHAVIOR AMONG NORMAL AND RETARDED CHILDREN EJ 052 442
EMERGENCE AND PERSISTENCE OF BEHAVIORAL DIFFERENCES IN TWINS EJ 053 732
INTERRELATIONS IN THE ATTACHMENT BEHAVIOR OF HUMAN INFANTS EJ 055 208
THE STABILITY OF ATTACHMENT BEHAVIORS IN THE HUMAN INFANT EJ 055 209
AN EVALUATION OF A THEORY OF SPECIFIC DEVELOPMENTAL DYSLEXIA EJ 055 875
SESAME STREET: MAGIC OR MALEVOLENCE? EJ 056 607
FACTORS RELATED TO SCHOOL ACHIEVEMENT IN AN ECONOMICALLY DISADVANTAGED GROUP EJ 056 614
DESIGNING INSTRUCTIONAL SETTINGS FOR CHILDREN LABELED "RETARDED": SOME REFLECTIONS EJ 057 733
ATTACHMENT: ITS ORIGINS AND COURSE EJ 058 586
PIAGET'S CONSTRUCTIONIST THEORY EJ 059 876
MOTHER-ATTACHMENT AND STRANGER-REACTIONS IN THE THIRD YEAR OF LIFE EJ 062 594

BEHAVIOR PROBLEMS

COVERT PROJECT, YEAR 1. ED019137
EFFECTS OF ADULT SOCIAL REINFORCEMENT ON CHILD BEHAVIOR. ED019997
[THE JUNIPER GARDENS CHILDREN'S PROJECT.] FINAL PROGRESS REPORT FOR OEO GRANT CG-8180. ED027947
THE MAGIC YEARS: UNDERSTANDING AND HANDLING THE PROBLEMS OF EARLY CHILDHOOD. ED029712
REDUCING BEHAVIOR PROBLEMS: AN OPERANT CONDITIONING GUIDE FOR TEACHERS. ED034570
A TOKEN REINFORCEMENT SYSTEM IN THE PUBLIC SCHOOLS. ED036323
CONDITION WITH CAUTION: THINK THRICE BEFORE CONDITIONING. (ROUGH DRAFT). ED046539
FIELD STUDIES OF SOCIAL REINFORCEMENT IN A PRESCHOOL. ED047772

THE PSYCHOLOGICAL EFFECTS OF PREGNANCY AND NEONATAL HEALTH THREATS ON CHILD DEVELOPMENT. ED048921
LIVING WITH CHILDREN: NEW METHODS FOR PARENTS AND TEACHERS. ED051887
THE IMPLICATIONS OF PARENT EFFECTIVENESS TRAINING FOR FOSTER PARENTS. ED052821
DIAGNOSTIC TEACHING: A MODEST PROPOSAL EJ 014 522
MINIMAL BRAIN DAMAGE: A MEANINGFUL DIAGNOSIS OR AN IRRELEVANT LABEL? EJ 018 707
BEHAVIORAL COUNSELING FOR ELEMENTARY-SCHOOL CHILDREN EJ 019 669
AGE PATTERNS IN CHILDREN'S PSYCHIATRIC SYMPTOMS EJ 025 374
CLINICAL IMPLICATIONS OF MATERNAL EMPLOYMENT: A REVIEW OF RESEARCH EJ 030 432
USING SENSITIVITY TRAINING WITH JUNIOR HIGH SCHOOL STUDENTS EJ 035 169
THE USE OF STIMULANT DRUGS IN TREATING HYPERACTIVE CHILDREN EJ 038 022
COGNITIVE STYLES IN HYPERACTIVE CHILDREN AND THE EFFECT OF METHYLPHENIDATE EJ 041 963
A BEHAVIOURAL SCREENING QUESTIONNAIRE FOR USE WITH THREE-YEAR-OLD CHILDREN. PRELIMINARY FINDINGS EJ 042 349
CHILDREN'S AGGRESSION EJ 043 199
AUTONOMIC RESPONSES OF MALE ADOLESCENTS EXHIBITING REFRACTORY BEHAVIOUR IN SCHOOL EJ 045 109
HELPING PARENTS IN A PEDIATRIC CLINIC EJ 046 963
PLAYROOM OBSERVATIONS OF HYPERACTIVE CHILDREN ON MEDICATION EJ 048 301
STUDYING AGGRESSIVE CHILDREN THROUGH RESPONSE TO FRUSTRATING SITUATIONS EJ 051 013
PARENT-CHILD SEPARATION: PSYCHOLOGICAL EFFECTS ON THE CHILDREN EJ 051 019
CONDITION WITH CAUTION EJ 058 585
PHENOMENAL ENVIRONMENTAL OPPRESSIVENESS IN SUICIDAL ADOLESCENTS EJ 061 063

BEHAVIOR RATING SCALES

THE COGNITIVE ENVIRONMENTS OF URBAN PRE-SCHOOL CHILDREN. MANUAL FOR CODING MOTHER-CHILD INTERACTION ON THE EIGHT-BLOCK SORTING TASK. ED018266
DEVELOPMENT OF A SOCIAL COMPETENCY SCALE FOR PRESCHOOL CHILDREN. FINAL REPORT. ED020004
HEAD START EVALUATION AND RESEARCH CENTER, THE UNIVERSITY OF CHICAGO. REPORT B, MATERNAL ANTECEDENTS OF INTELLECTUAL ACHIEVEMENT BEHAVIORS IN LOWER CLASS PRESCHOOL CHILDREN. ED022551
HEAD START EVALUATION AND RESEARCH CENTER, BOSTON UNIVERSITY. REPORT A-III, OBSERVATIONAL STRATEGIES FOR OBTAINING DATA ON CHILDREN AND TEACHERS IN HEAD START CLASSES. (OSOD). ED022559
THE DEVELOPMENT OF A BEHAVIOR CHECKLIST FOR BOYS. ED023468
DEPENDENCY AND SOCIAL PERFORMANCE: THE DEVELOPMENT OF A SCALE TO MEASURE LEVEL OF INDEPENDENCE IN SMALL CHILDREN. PART OF THE FINAL REPORT. ED026129
PROJECT HEAD START RESEARCH AND EVALUATION CENTER, SYRACUSE UNIVERSITY, RESEARCH INSTITUTE. FINAL REPORT. ED030486
PRIMARY INFLUENCES ON THE DEVELOPMENT OF COMPETENCE: THE DEVELOPMENT OF A MATERNAL BEHAVIOR SCALE. PROGRESS REPORT. ED032127
INDIVIDUAL DIFFERENCES IN GHETTO FOUR-YEAR-OLDS. ED034572
CHILD BEHAVIOR SURVEY INSTRUMENT: MANUAL OF INSTRUCTIONS AND DEFINITIONS. ED037230
RELATIVE SOOTHING EFFECTS OF VERTICAL AND HORIZONTAL ROCKING. ED046504
PLAY BEHAVIOR AND EFFICACY IN GHETTO FOUR-YEAR-OLDS: ORGANIZATION AND PSYCHOSEXUAL CONTENT OF PLAY. ED048920
A STUDY IN THE UTILIZATION OF TECHNOLOGICALLY ADVANCED TECHNIQUES FOR TEACHER-PARENT-CHILD ASSESSMENT. FINAL REPORT. ED053818
CHILDREN'S DEPENDENCY SCALE EJ 025 232
CHILDREN'S BEHAVIOR PROBLEMS AS VIEWED BY TEACHERS, PSYCHOLOGISTS, AND CHILDREN EJ 026 313
PATTERNS OF INFORMATION PROCESSING USED BY AND WITH YOUNG CHILDREN IN A NURSERY SCHOOL SETTING EJ 032 890
IRRELEVANCE OF NEWBORN WAKING STATES TO SOME MOTOR AND APPETITIVE RESPONSES EJ 036 076
A BEHAVIOURAL SCREENING QUESTIONNAIRE FOR USE WITH THREE-YEAR-OLD CHILDREN. PRELIMINARY FINDINGS EJ 042 349
THE RELIABILITY OF RATING SCALES FOR ASSESSING THE BEHAVIOUR OF DISTURBED CHILDREN IN A RESIDENTIAL UNIT EJ 051 153

BEHAVIOR STANDARDS

INTERACTION PATTERNS AS A SOURCE OF ERROR IN TEACHERS' EVALUATIONS OF HEAD START CHILDREN. FINAL REPORT. ED023453

BEHAVIOR THEORIES

THE HIERARCHICAL ORGANIZATION OF INTELLECTUAL STRUCTURES. ED022534
LURIA'S MODEL OF THE VERBAL CONTROL OF BEHAVIOR. STUDY F: MOTIVATIONAL AND CONTROL IN THE DEVELOPMENT OF LANGUAGE FUNCTIONS, D. BIRCH. ED024443
A THEORY OF PARENT EFFECTIVENESS. ED028815
AN ATTRIBUTIONAL (COGNITIVE) MODEL OF MOTIVATION. ED038173
SENSORHESIS AS A MOTIVE FOR PLAY AND STEREOTYPED BEHAVIOR. ED044176
SUBPOPULATIONAL PROFILING OF THE PSYCHOEDUCATIONAL DIMENSIONS OF DISADVANTAGED PRESCHOOL CHILDREN: A CONCEPTUAL PROSPECTUS FOR AN INTERDISCIPLINARY RESEARCH. ED045177
THE FAMILY ROMANCE FANTASY IN CHILDREN ADOPTED IN INFANCY EJ 022 478
CLASSROOM MANAGEMENT--MORE THAN CONDITIONING EJ 027 827
SEX DIFFERENCES IN YIELDING TO TEMPTATION: A FUNCTION OF THE SITUATION EJ 035 711
CHILDREN'S "IMITATION" AS A FUNCTION OF THE PRESENCE OR ABSENCE OF A MODEL AND THE DESCRIPTION OF HIS INSTRUMENTAL BEHAVIORS EJ 036 080
THE CONTROL OF IMITATIVE AND NONIMITATIVE BEHAVIORS IN SEVERELY RETARDED CHILDREN THROUGH "GENERALIZED-INSTRUCTION FOLLOWING" EJ 043 196
CHILDREN'S AGGRESSION EJ 043 199
A STUDY OF THE RELATIVE DOMINANCE OF VISION AND TOUCH IN SIX-MONTH-OLD INFANTS EJ 058 594
PIAGET'S CONSTRUCTIONIST THEORY EJ 059 876

BEHAVIORAL COUNSELING

THE FUNCTION OF AMBIGUITY IN CHILD CRISES EJ 027 344
A COMPARATIVE STUDY OF COUNSELEE PREFERENCES FOR BEHAVIORIST AND CLIENT-CENTERED COUNSELING APPROACHES EJ 058 628

BEHAVIORAL OBJECTIVES

LONG TERM EFFECT OF STRUCTURED TRAINING ON 3 YOUNG CHILDREN. ED023480
CURRICULUM GUIDE FOR EARLY CHILDHOOD EDUCATION. BEHAVIORAL GOALS - PRE-K THROUGH ONE. ED027940
ASSESSING PROCESS AND PRODUCT WITH YOUNG CHILDREN IN SCHOOL SETTINGS. ED035453
SHOULD EDUCATIONAL OBJECTIVES BE STATED IN BEHAVIORAL TERMS? - PART III EJ 014 228
A CASE AGAINST BEHAVIORAL OBJECTIVES EJ 027 826
A CASE AGAINST A CASE AGAINST BEHAVIORAL OBJECTIVES EJ 036 083
CONDITION WITH CAUTION EJ 058 585
TREATMENT OF PROBLEMS ASSOCIATED WITH COGNITIVE AND PERCEPTUAL-MOTOR DEFICITS EJ 060 501

BEHAVIORAL SCIENCE RESEARCH

OUTCOMES OF INDIVIDUAL AND PROGRAMMATIC VARIATIONS AMONG PROJECT HEAD START CENTERS, SUMMER, 1965. FINAL REPORT. ED014325
CODING MANUAL FOR APPROACH (A PROCEDURE FOR PATTERNING RESPONSES OF ADULTS AND CHILDREN). ED015005
SOCIAL AND EMOTIONAL BEHAVIOR IN INFANCY--SOME DEVELOPMENTAL ISSUES AND PROBLEMS. ED015789
THE STATUS OF BEHAVIORAL MEASUREMENT AND ASSESSMENT IN CHILDREN. ED018252
THE COGNITIVE ENVIRONMENTS OF URBAN PRE-SCHOOL CHILDREN. MANUAL OF INSTRUCTIONS FOR ADMINISTERING AND SCORING THE HOME INTERVIEW. ED018253
EXTINCTION IN DISCRIMINATION LEARNING--PRESENTATION AND CONTINGENCY VARIABLES AND ASSOCIATED SIDE EFFECTS. ED019139
REPORT ON ACTIVITIES, 1964-1966. ED020016
AN ANNOTATED BIBLIOGRAPHY OF BEHAVIOR MODIFICATION WITH CHILDREN AND RETARDATES. ED020025
RESPONSE TO VARYING LEVELS OF CONDITIONING REWARDS. FINAL REPORT. ED020803
THE EFFECT OF SUBJECT-DETERMINED VERBALIZATION ON DISCRIMINATION LEARNING IN PRESCHOOLERS. ED021620
REINFORCEMENT GROWS UP: THE EXPERIMENTAL ANALYSIS OF BEHAVIOR AS A SYSTEMATIC APPROACH TO THE TEACHING OF DEVELOPMENTAL PSYCHOLOGY. ED023479
ENGINEERING VERBAL BEHAVIOR. ED025308
THE DEVELOPMENT OF LANGUAGE FUNCTIONS. REPORT NUMBER 8, DEVELOPMENT OF LANGUAGE FUNCTIONS: A RESEARCH PROGRAM PROJECT. ED025325
TANGENT TO EXPERIMENTAL TECHNIQUES OF VERBAL CONTROL. ED025334
SUBJECTS' HYPOTHESES, EXPERIMENTAL INSTRUCTIONS AND AUTONOMIC "CONDITIONING". ED025335
CONCEPT GROWTH AND THE EDUCATION OF THE CHILD: A SURVEY OF RESEARCH ON CONCEPTUALIZATION. NATIONAL FOUNDATION FOR EDUCATIONAL RESEARCH IN ENGLAND AND WALES OCCASIONAL PUBLICATION SERIES NO. 12. ED026121
PROJECT HEAD START RESEARCH AND EVALUATION CENTER, SYRACUSE UNIVERSITY RESEARCH INSTITUTE. FINAL REPORT, NOVEMBER 1, 1967. ED026137
COGNITIVE FACTORS IN SEMANTIC CONDITIONING. A THESIS IN EDUCATIONAL PSYCHOLOGY. ED027069
THE DEVELOPMENT OF ROLE-TAKING AND COMMUNICATION SKILLS IN CHILDREN. ED027082
REVIEW OF SELECTED INTERVENTION RESEARCH WITH YOUNG CHILDREN. ED027091
CHILDREN'S UNDERSTANDING OF SOCIAL INTERACTION. ED031298

[COMPETENCE IN YOUNG CHILDREN.] ED032124
THE EFFECTS OF PSYCHOSOCIAL DEPRIVATION ON HUMAN DEVELOPMENT IN INFANCY. ED034574
THE EFFECTS OF MOTHERS' PRESENCE AND PREVISITS ON CHILDREN'S EMOTIONAL REACTIONS TO STARTING NURSERY SCHOOL. ED034596
NURTURANCE, DEPENDENCE, AND EXPLORATORY BEHAVIOR IN PREKINDERGARTENERS. ED035443
BEHAVIORAL RESEARCH RELEVANT TO THE CLASSROOM. ED039036
SENSORHESIS AS A MOTIVE FOR PLAY AND STEREOTYPED BEHAVIOR. ED044176
MICHIGAN STATE UNIVERSITY, HEAD START EVALUATION AND RESEARCH, 1967-68 RESEARCH ABSTRACTS AND PROGRESS REPORTS. ED047771
PLAY BEHAVIOR AND EFFICACY IN GHETTO FOUR-YEAR-OLDS: ORGANIZATION AND PSYCHOSEXUAL CONTENT OF PLAY. ED048920
CHILD DEVELOPMENT RESEARCH UNIT PROGRESS REPORT, FEBRUARY, 1970. ED049819
THE VALUE OF CLASSROOM REWARDS IN EARLY EDUCATION. ED049828
THE PLAYFUL MODES OF KNOWING. ED050806
HUMAN BEHAVIOR GENETICS: PRESENT STATUS AND SUGGESTIONS FOR FUTURE RESEARCH EJ 004 046
CUES FOR OBSERVING CHILDREN'S BEHAVIOR EJ 007 062
ABOUT RESEARCH: PART II. IS A BEHAVIORAL APPROACH SUPERFICIAL? IS OPERANT CONDITIONING FAIR? WHY DO RESEARCH? EJ 029 015
LEARNING AND COGNITIVE DEVELOPMENT: REPRESENTATIVE SAMPLES, CUMULATIVE-HIERARCHICAL LEARNING, AND EXPERIMENTAL-LONGITUDINAL METHODS EJ 032 509
SEX DIFFERENCES IN YIELDING TO TEMPTATION: A FUNCTION OF THE SITUATION EJ 035 711
GIRLS' ATTITUDES TOWARD MODELED BEHAVIORS AND THE CONTENT OF IMITATIVE PRIVATE PLAY EJ 036 079
CHILDREN'S "IMITATION" AS A FUNCTION OF THE PRESENCE OR ABSENCE OF A MODEL AND THE DESCRIPTION OF HIS INSTRUMENTAL BEHAVIORS EJ 036 080
AN EXPERIMENT ON EYEBROW-RAISING AND VISUAL SEARCHING IN CHILDREN EJ 039 947
AGGRESSION AS A FUNCTION OF EXPECTED RETALIATION AND AGGRESSION LEVEL OF TARGET AND AGGRESSOR EJ 043 192
EFFECT ON RESISTANCE TO DEVIATION OF OBSERVING A MODEL'S AFFECTIVE REACTION TO RESPONSE CONSEQUENCES EJ 043 283
EFFECTS OF COMPETITION-INDUCED FRUSTRATION ON TWO CLASSES OF MODELED BEHAVIOR EJ 043 284
A CHILD IN DISTRESS: THE INFLUENCE OF NURTURANCE AND MODELING ON CHILDREN'S ATTEMPTS TO HELP EJ 043 314
CHILD EFFECTS ON ADULT BEHAVIOR EJ 045 107
NEWBORN AND PRESCHOOLER: ORGANIZATION OF BEHAVIOR AND RELATIONS BETWEEN PERIODS EJ 045 110
CORRESPONDENCE BETWEEN BEHAVIORAL AND DOLL-PLAY MEASURES OF CONSCIENCE EJ 045 190
OBSERVATION STUDIES OF PARENT-CHILD INTERACTION: A METHODOLOGICAL REVIEW EJ 046 466
CONDITIONING INDEPENDENT WORK BEHAVIOR IN READING WITH SEVEN YEAR OLD CHILDREN IN A REGULAR EARLY CHILDHOOD CLASSROOM EJ 050 795
SEX DIFFERENCES IN BEHAVIOURAL IMPULSIVITY, INTELLECTUAL IMPULSIVITY, AND ATTAINMENT IN YOUNG CHILDREN EJ 051 151
PSYCHIATRIC DISORDER IN THE CHILDREN OF CARIBBEAN IMMIGRANTS EJ 051 152
THE RELIABILITY OF RATING SCALES FOR ASSESSING THE BEHAVIOUR OF DISTURBED CHILDREN IN A RESIDENTIAL UNIT EJ 051 153
DEVELOPMENTAL COMPARISONS OF CONFORMITY ACROSS TWO CULTURES EJ 051 470
HELPING BEHAVIOR AMONG NORMAL AND RETARDED CHILDREN EJ 052 442
LEARNING TO BE GENEROUS OR STINGY: IMITATION OF SHARING BEHAVIOR AS A FUNCTION OF MODEL GENEROSITY AND VICARIOUS REINFORCEMENT EJ 052 443
AGE, STATE, AND MATERNAL BEHAVIOR ASSOCIATED WITH INFANT VOCALIZATIONS EJ 052 444
INFANT OBEDIENCE AND MATERNAL BEHAVIOR: THE ORIGINS OF SOCALIZATION RECONSIDERED EJ 052 446
IDENTIFICATION AND CONSCIENCE DEVELOPMENT EJ 052 447
LOCUS OF CONTROL AND ACHIEVEMENT IN MIDDLE- AND LOWER-CLASS CHILDREN EJ 052 448
MOTHERS' TEST OF ANXIETY AND TASK SELECTION AND CHILDREN'S PERFORMANCE WITH MOTHER OR A STRANGER EJ 052 449
BIRTH ORDER, NUMBER OF SIBLINGS AND SOCIAL REINFORCER EFFECTIVENESS IN CHILDREN EJ 052 453
THE EFFECTS OF MANIPULATION OF TEACHER COMMUNICATION STYLE IN THE PRESCHOOL EJ 052 455
A REEXAMINATION OF THE DEVELOPMENT OF MORAL JUDGMENTS IN CHILDREN EJ 052 456
SOME PARAMETERS OF PUNISHMENT AFFECTING RESISTANCE TO DEVIATION AND GENERALIZATION OF A PROHIBITION EJ 052 457
EFFECTS OF ADULT AND PEER OBSERVERS ON BOYS' AND GIRLS' RESPONSES TO AN AGGRESSIVE MODEL EJ 052 459
INFORMATION PROCESSING AND THE MODIFICATION OF AN "IMPULSIVE CONCEPTUAL TEMPO" EJ 052 460
SELF-INITIATED VERBAL REINFORCEMENT AND POSITIVE SELF-CONCEPT EJ 052 462
THE EFFECT OF SOCIAL INTERACTION ON ACTIVITY LEVELS IN SIX-TO EIGHT-YEAR-OLD BOYS EJ 052 463
EXPERIMENTAL ANALYSES OF COOPERATION AND COMPETITION OF ANGLO-AMERICAN AND MEXICAN CHILDREN EJ 053 647
TOYS DELAY THE INFANT'S FOLLOWING OF HIS MOTHER EJ 053 713
RESPONSE TO SOCIAL REINFORCEMENT RATES AS A FUNCTION OF REINFORCEMENT HISTORY EJ 053 715
DEVELOPMENTAL DETERMINANTS OF ATTENTION: A CROSS-CULTURAL REPLICATION EJ 053 718
VERBAL-LABELING AND CUE-TRAINING IN REVERSAL-SHIFT BEHAVIOR EJ 053 727
STEADY-STATE BEHAVIOR IN CHILDREN: A METHOD AND SOME DATA EJ 053 730
INFANT SMILING TO NONSOCIAL STIMULI AND THE RECOGNITION HYPOTHESIS EJ 053 731
EMERGENCE AND PERSISTENCE OF BEHAVIORAL DIFFERENCES IN TWINS EJ 053 732
INTERACTIONS BETWEEN THE FACILITATIVE AND INHIBITORY EFFECTS OF A PUNISHING STIMULUS IN THE CONTROL OF CHILDREN'S HITTING BEHAVIOR EJ 053 734
DO MATERIAL REWARDS ENHANCE THE PERFORMANCE OF LOWER-CLASS CHILDREN? EJ 053 735
FEEDING BEHAVIORS OF NEWBORN INFANTS AS A FUNCTION OF PARITY OF THE MOTHER EJ 053 736
COLOR DOMINANCE IN PRESCHOOL CHILDREN AS A FUNCTION OF SPECIFIC CUE PREFERENCES EJ 053 738
WORDS AND DEEDS ABOUT ALTRUISM AND THE SUBSEQUENT REINFORCEMENT POWER OF THE MODEL EJ 053 739
DEVELOPMENTAL ASPECTS OF VARIABLES RELEVANT TO OBSERVATIONAL LEARNING EJ 053 740
INCONSISTENT VERBAL INSTRUCTIONS AND CHILDREN'S RESISTANCE-TO-TEMPTATION BEHAVIOR EJ 053 741
CONCEPT CONSERVATION IN CHILDREN: THE DEPENDENCE OF BELIEF SYSTEMS ON SEMANTIC REPRESENTATION EJ 053 742
ARTICULATION OF THE BODY CONCEPT AMONG FIRST-GRADE ISRAELI CHILDREN EJ 053 744
MATERNAL WARMTH, ACHIEVEMENT MOTIVATION, AND COGNITIVE FUNCTIONING IN LOWER-CLASS PRESCHOOL CHILDREN EJ 053 745
CONTINUITY IN THE DEVELOPMENT OF VISUAL BEHAVIOR IN YOUNG INFANTS EJ 053 746
PROXIMITY AND INTERACTIONAL BEHAVIOR OF YOUNG CHILDREN TO THEIR "SECURITY" BLANKETS EJ 053 748
DISCRIMINATION OF STEREOMETRIC OJBECTS AND PHOTOGRAPHS OF OBJECTS BY CHILDREN EJ 053 749
THE EFFECT OF AGGRESSIVE CARTOONS ON CHILDREN'S INTERPERSONAL PLAY EJ 053 750
STIMULUS NOVELTY AS A VARIABLE IN CHILDREN'S WIN-STAY, LOSE-SHIFT DISCRIMINATION LEARNING SET EJ 053 751
NEONATAL SMILING IN REM STATES, IV: PREMATURE STUDY EJ 053 758
THE EFFECTS OF A FAMILIAR TOY AND MOTHER'S PRESENCE ON EXPLORATORY AND ATTACHMENT BEHAVIORS IN YOUNG CHILDREN EJ 053 759
COMPARISONS OF VOCAL IMITATION, TACTILE STIMULATION, AND FOOD AS REINFORCERS FOR INFANT VOCALIZATIONS EJ 055 206
PERSON SPECIFICITY OF THE "SOCIAL DEPRIVATION-SATIATION EFFECT" EJ 055 207
INTERRELATIONS IN THE ATTACHMENT BEHAVIOR OF HUMAN INFANTS EJ 055 208
THE STABILITY OF ATTACHMENT BEHAVIORS IN THE HUMAN INFANT EJ 055 209
MOTIVATIONAL EFFECTS OF BOREDOM ON CHILDREN'S RESPONSE SPEEDS EJ 055 211
CHILDREN'S OBSERVATION AND INTEGRATION OF AGGRESSIVE EXPERIENCES EJ 055 212
CONDITIONING OF INFANT VOCALIZATIONS IN THE HOME ENVIRONMENT EJ 055 214
HYPERACTIVITY AND THE MACHINE: THE ACTOMETER EJ 055 876
THE SEQUENCE OF DEVELOPMENT OF SOME EARLY MATHEMATICS BEHAVIORS EJ 056 710
MATERNAL CONTROL AND OBEDIENCE IN THE TWO-YEAR-OLD EJ 056 714
VISUAL RESPONSE DECREMENT AS A FUNCTION OF AGE OF HUMAN NEWBORNS EJ 056 716
RELATIONSHIP BETWEEN LATERAL PREFERENCE AND SELECTED BEHAVIORAL VARIABLES FOR CHILDREN FAILING ACADEMICALLY EJ 056 718
MODEL AFFECT AND CHILDREN'S IMITATIVE ALTRUISM EJ 056 719
STABILITY OF THE ORIENTING REFLEX IN INFANTS TO AUDITORY AND VISUAL STIMULI AS INDEXED BY CARDIAC DECELERATION EJ 056 720
BEHAVIOR MODIFICATION IN THE HOME WITH THE MOTHER AS THE EXPERIMENTER: THE EFFECT OF DIFFERENTIAL REINFORCEMENT ON SIBLING NEGATIVE RESPONSE RATES EJ 056 721
BEHAVIORAL SLEEP CYCLES IN THE HUMAN NEWBORN EJ 056 722
EFFECTS OF SOCIOECONOMIC STATUS AND THE VALUE OF A REINFORCER UPON SELF-REINFORCEMENT BY CHILDREN EJ 056 726
EFFECTS OF SOCIAL COMPARISON UPON THE IMITATION OF NEUTRAL AND ALTRUISTIC BEHAVIORS BY YOUNG CHILDREN EJ 056 728
WHITE ADULT BEHAVIOR TOWARD BLACK AND WHITE CHILDREN EJ 056 729

INFANTS' RESPONSES TO NOVELTY IN FAMILIAR AND UNFAMILIAR SETTINGS EJ 056 731
EXECUTIVE COMPETENCE AND SPONTANEOUS SOCIAL BEHAVIOR IN ONE-YEAR-OLDS EJ 056 732
THE EFFECT OF A TELEVISION MODEL UPON RULE ADOPTION BEHAVIOR OF CHILDREN EJ 056 733
SITUATIONAL EFFECTS ON JUSTIFIABLENESS OF AGGRESSION AT THREE AGE LEVELS EJ 056 734
INFLUENCE OF MODELING, EXHORTATIVE VERBALIZATION, AND SURVEILLANCE ON CHILDREN'S SHARING EJ 058 214
SOME IMMEDIATE EFFECTS OF TELEVISED VIOLENCE ON CHILDREN'S BEHAVIOR EJ 058 216
MALE AND FEMALE AUDITORY REINFORCEMENT OF INFANT VOCALIZATIONS EJ 058 217
A DEVELOPMENTAL INVESTIGATION OF TELEVISED MODELED VERBALIZATIONS ON RESISTANCE TO DEVIATION EJ 058 218
NONSOCIAL REINFORCEMENT OF INFANTS' VOCALIZATIONS EJ 058 219
STATE AS VARIABLE, AS OBSTACLE, AND AS MEDIATOR OF STIMULATION IN INFANT RESEARCH EJ 058 220
STATE AS AN INFANT-ENVIRONMENT INTERACTION: AN ANALYSIS OF MOTHER-INFANT INTERACTIONS AS A FUNCTION OF SEX EJ 058 221
INDIVIDUAL DIFFERENCES IN THE DEVELOPMENT OF SOME ATTACHMENT BEHAVIORS EJ 058 222
CHARITY IN CHILDREN: THE INFLUENCE OF "CHARITY" STIMULI AND AN AUDIENCE EJ 058 224
THE RELATIVE EFFICACY OF CONTACT AND VESTIBULAR-PROPRIOCEPTIVE STIMULATION IN SOOTHING NEONATES EJ 058 588
EGOCENTRISM AND SOCIAL INFLUENCE IN CHILDREN EJ 058 590
THE DEVELOPMENT OF THE CONTROL OF ADULT INSTRUCTIONS OVER NONVERBAL BEHAVIOR EJ 061 138
EFFECTS OF SOCIAL AND VOCAL STIMULATION ON INFANT BABBLING EJ 061 140

BEHAVIORAL SCIENCES
BEHAVIORAL SCIENCE FOR ELEMENTARY-SCHOOL PUPILS EJ 014 306
AN AUDITORY PROMPTING DEVICE FOR BEHAVIOR OBSERVATION EJ 043 316

BEHVIORAL SCIENCE RESEARCH
POWER AND THE INTERNALIZATION OF SELF-DENIAL EJ 036 077

BELIEFS
PARENTAL ANTECEDENTS OF CHILDREN'S BELIEFS IN INTERNAL-EXTERNAL CONTROL OF REINFORCEMENTS IN INTELLECTUAL ACHIEVEMENT SITUATIONS. ED024447
CONCEPT CONSERVATION IN CHILDREN: THE DEPENDENCE OF BELIEF SYSTEMS ON SEMANTIC REPRESENTATION EJ 053 742

BIAS
CHILDREN WITHOUT PREJUDICE. 1970 WHITE HOUSE CONFERENCE ON CHILDREN, REPORT OF FORUM 18. (WORKING PAPER). ED046534
WHAT'S THROWN OUT WITH THE BATH WATER: A BABY? ED053801
EXPERIMENTER BIAS IN PERFORMANCE OF CHILDREN AT A SIMPLE MOTOR TASK EJ 035 710
THE FORMATION AND REVERSAL OF AN ATTITUDE AS FUNCTIONS OF ASSUMED SELF-CONCEPT, RACE, AND SOCIOECONOMIC CLASS EJ 052 652

BIBLIOGRAPHIES
REPORT ON ACTIVITIES, 1964-1966. ED020016
BIBLIOGRAPHY OF PAPERS COVERING WORK UNDER OEO CONTRACT NUMBER 510. FINAL REPORT. (TITLE SUPPLIED). ED020773
A BIBLIOGRAPHY OF RESEARCH ON FOREIGN STUDENT AFFAIRS. ED021629
USING MUSIC WITH HEAD START CHILDREN. ED022543
BIBLIOGRAPHY, EARLY CHILDHOOD EDUCATION. ED022544
BIBLIOGRAPHY OF RESEARCH STUDIES IN ELEMENTARY SCHOOL AND PRE-SCHOOL MATHEMATICS. ED023464
THE MIDDLE SCHOOL: A SELECTED BIBLIOGRAPHY WITH INTRODUCTION. ED029714
BIBLIOGRAPHY ON THE BATTERED CHILD. (REVISED EDITION). ED039942
HEAD START CURRICULUM MODELS: A REFERENCE LIST. ED046517
HEAD START CURRICULUM MODELS: A REFERENCE LIST. (REVISED EDITION). ED048947
A RESOURCE AND REFERENCE BIBLIOGRAPHY IN EARLY CHILDHOOD EDUCATION AND DEVELOPMENTAL PSYCHOLOGY: THE AFFECTIVE DOMAIN. ED049817
THE BEAUTIFUL PEOPLE IN CHILDREN'S BOOKS EJ 020 541
RESOURCES FOR ENVIRONMENTAL EDUCATORS: ECOLOGY AND TEACHERS EJ 029 392

BICULTURALISM
WHAT'S DEPRIVED ABOUT BEING DIFFERENT? EJ 046 968

BILINGUAL EDUCATION
THE COMPARATIVE EFFICACIES OF SPANISH, ENGLISH AND BILINGUAL COGNITIVE VERBAL INSTRUCTION WITH MEXICAN-AMERICAN HEAD START CHILDREN. FINAL REPORT. ED030473
ESOL-SESD GUIDE: KINDERGARTEN. ED033748
A BILINGUAL ORAL LANGUAGE AND CONCEPTUAL DEVELOPMENT PROGRAM FOR SPANISH-SPEAKING PRE-SCHOOL CHILDREN. ED034568
AN EARLY CHILDHOOD EDUCATION MODEL: A BILINGUAL APPROACH. ED038167
EARLY CHILDHOOD EDUCATION LEARNING SYSTEM ED041625
A STUDY IN CHILD CARE (CASE STUDY FROM VOLUME II-B): "WILL YOU MARRY ME?" DAY CARE PROGRAM REPRINT SERIES. ED051906
DEMONSTRATION AND TRAINING PROJECT FOR MIGRANT CHILDREN, MCALLEN, TEXAS. EARLY CHILDHOOD LEARNING SYSTEM. FINAL EVALUATION REPORT, 1970-71. ED053812
LANGUAGE LEARNING AT ROUGH ROCK EJ 011 874

BILINGUAL SCHOOLS
SCHOOL IN CHEROKEE AND ENGLISH EJ 061 184

BILINGUAL STUDENTS
AN EVALUATION OF OPERATION HEAD START BILINGUAL CHILDREN, SUMMER, 1965. ED013667
FINAL REPORT ON HEAD START EVALUATION AND RESEARCH--1966-67 TO THE INSTITUTE FOR EDUCATIONAL DEVELOPMENT. SECTION VI, THE MEASUREMENT OF BILINGUALISM AND BICULTURAL SOCIALIZATION OF THE CHILD IN THE SCHOOL SETTING--THE DEVELOPMENT OF INSTRUMENTS. ED019122
SAN ANTONIO LANGUAGE RESEARCH PROJECT, 1965-66 (YEAR TWO) FINDINGS. ED022528
HEAD START EVALUATION AND RESEARCH CENTER, THE UNIVERSITY OF CHICAGO. REPORT E, COMPARATIVE USE OF ALTERNATIVE MODES FOR ASSESSING COGNITIVE DEVELOPMENT IN BILINGUAL OR NON-ENGLISH SPEAKING CHILDREN. ED022554
ADMINISTRATION MANUAL FOR THE INVENTORY OF SOCIALIZATION OF BILINGUAL CHILDREN AGES THREE TO TEN. PART OF THE FINAL REPORT. ED027062
ADMINISTRATION MANUAL FOR TESTS OF BASIC LANGUAGE COMPETENCE IN ENGLISH AND SPANISH. LEVEL I (PRESCHOOL) ED027063
ADMINISTRATION MANUAL FOR TESTS OF BASIC LANGUAGE COMPETENCE IN ENGLISH AND SPANISH. LEVEL II (PRIMARY GRADES): CHILDREN AGES SIX TO TEN, ENGLISH AND SPANISH VERSIONS, FORMS A AND B. PART OF THE FINAL REPORT. ED027064
THE BILINGUAL CHILD EJ 007 221
THE USE OF METROPOLITCAN READINESS TESTS WITH MEXICAN-AMERICAN CHILDREN EJ 026 810
SOME LANGUAGE-RELATED COGNITIVE ADVANTAGES OF BILINGUAL FIVE-YEAR-OLDS EJ 041 343
THE SPANISH-SPEAKING FIVE-YEAR-OLD EJ 056 391
SOME FACTORS AFFECTING THE COMPLEXITY OF CHILDREN'S SENTENCES: THE EFFECTS OF MODELING, AGE, SEX, AND BILINGUALISM EJ 060 780

BILINGUAL TEACHER AIDES
SCHOOL IN CHEROKEE AND ENGLISH EJ 061 184

BILINGUALISM
SOME LANGUAGE-RELATED COGNITIVE ADVANTAGES OF BILINGUAL FIVE YEAR OLDS. ED031307
A STUDY IN CHILD CARE (CASE STUDY FROM VOLUME II-A): "A HOUSE FULL OF CHILDREN." DAY CARE PROGRAMS REPRINT SERIES. ED051891
THE BILINGUAL CHILD EJ 007 221
CHILDREN WHO SPEAK NAVAJO EJ 014 918
A TRANSFORMATIONAL ANALYSIS OF ORAL SYNTACTIC STRUCTURES OF CHILDREN REPRESENTING VARYING ETHNOLINGUISTIC COMMUNITIES EJ 056 713

BIOGRAPHIES
BILLY MEARNS: FRIEND AND TEACHER. HUGHES MEARNS, 1875-1965 EJ 002 655
SUPERINTENDENT JULIA RICHMAN: A SOCIAL PROGRESSIVE IN THE PUBLIC SCHOOLS EJ 060 106

BIOLOGICAL INFLUENCES
SEX DIFFERENCES IN MENTAL AND BEHAVIORAL TRAITS. ED026117
CURRENT ISSUES IN RESEARCH ON EARLY DEVELOPMENT. ED028813
THE DEVELOPMENT OF EARLY SOCIAL INTERACTION--AN ETHOLOGICAL APPROACH. ED031291
BIOGENETICS OF RACE AND CLASS. ED036317
BEHAVIORAL DATA FROM THE TULANE NUTRITION STUDY. ED043375
TWINNING: A MARKER FOR BIOLOGICAL INSULTS EJ 021 188
BIOLOGICAL AND ECOLOGICAL INFLUENCES ON DEVELOPMENT AT 12 MONTHS OF AGE EJ 029 385
SEX DIFFERENCES IN HUMAN DEVELOPMENT EJ 060 015

BIRACIAL ELEMENTARY SCHOOLS
PRAISE, CRITICISM, AND RACE EJ 019 388

BIRACIAL SCHOOLS
AN ATTACK ON IMPEDIMENTS TO EFFECTIVE CROSS-CULTURAL TEACHING EJ 032 553

BIRTH ORDER
CHILDREN'S FEAR IN A DENTAL SITUATION AS A FUNCTION OF BIRTH ORDER EJ 015 099
BIRTH ORDER AND PHYSIOLOGICAL STRESS RESPONSE EJ 022 000
NON-SOCIAL SPEECH IN FOUR-YEAR-OLD CHILDREN AS A FUNCTION OF BIRTH ORDER AND INTERPERSONAL SITUATION EJ 033 702
THE BEHAVIOR OF TWINS: EFFECTS OF BIRTH WEIGHT AND BIRTH SEQUENCE EJ 036 081

THE RELATIONSHIP OF BIRTH ORDER AND SEX OF SIBLINGS TO GENDER ROLE IDENTITY EJ 039 901
THE RELATIONSHIP OF ORDINAL POSITION AND SEX TO INTEREST PATTERNS EJ 045 111
BIRTH ORDER, NUMBER OF SIBLINGS AND SOCIAL REINFORCER EFFECTIVENESS IN CHILDREN EJ 052 453
MOTIVATIONAL AND ACHIEVEMENT DIFFERENCES AMONG CHILDREN OF VARIOUS ORDINAL BIRTH POSITIONS EJ 055 547
EFFECTS OF SEX AND BIRTH ORDER ON SEX-ROLE DEVELOPMENT AND INTELLIGENCE AMONG KINDERGARTEN CHILDREN EJ 057 133
FAMILY CORRELATES OF VERBAL REASONING ABILITY EJ 061 069

BLACK COMMUNITY
ADOPTION RESOURCES FOR BLACK CHILDREN EJ 035 801

BLACK POWER
WHITE STAFF, BLACK CHILDREN: IS THERE A PROBLEM? EJ 039 799

BLIND CHILDREN
A COMPARATIVE STUDY OF PIAGET'S DEVELOPMENTAL SCHEMA OF SIGHTED CHILDREN WITH THAT OF A GROUP OF BLIND CHILDREN EJ 040 319
INTERVENTION IN INFANCY: A PROGRAM FOR BLIND INFANTS EJ 048 904
DEVELOPMENT OF CUTANEOUS AND KINESTHETIC LOCALIZATION BY BLIND AND SIGHTED CHILDREN EJ 055 113

BOARD OF EDUCATION POLICY
COMMUNITY ACTION ON BEHALF OF PREGNANT SCHOOL-AGE GIRLS: EDUCATIONAL POLICIES AND BEYOND EJ 023 392

BODY HEIGHT
HEIGHT AND WEIGHT OF CHILDREN: UNITED STATES. ED050808

BODY IMAGE
LONGITUDINAL STUDY OF DEVELOPMENT OF THE BODY CONCEPT EJ 021 993
THE EFFECTS OF OBJECT LOSS ON THE BODY IMAGE OF SCHIZOPHRENIC GIRLS EJ 027 345
DIFFERENTIAL ADJUSTMENT TO PUBESCENCE AND COGNITIVE STYLE PATTERNS EJ 039 903
KINDERGARTEN CHILDREN'S ACTIVE VOCABULARY ABOUT BODY BUILD EJ 041 857
STEREOTYPIC AFFECTIVE PROPERTIES OF PERSONAL NAMES AND SOMATOTYPES IN CHILDREN EJ 043 352
ARTICULATION OF THE BODY CONCEPT AMONG FIRST-GRADE ISRAELI CHILDREN EJ 053 744

BODY WEIGHT
LONG TERM STUDY OF PREMATURES: SUMMARY OF PUBLISHED FINDINGS. ED043389
HEIGHT AND WEIGHT OF CHILDREN: UNITED STATES. ED050808
MOTHER-INFANT RELATIONSHIP AND WEIGHT GAIN IN THE FIRST MONTH OF LIFE EJ 026 508
CONSEQUENCES OF LOW BIRTH WEIGHT EJ 030 430
THE BEHAVIOR OF TWINS: EFFECTS OF BIRTH WEIGHT AND BIRTH SEQUENCE EJ 036 081
PHYSIQUE IDENTIFICATION, PREFERENCE, AND AVERSION IN KINDERGARTEN CHILDREN EJ 046 785

BOOK REVIEWS
THE COMPLEXITY OF INFANT DEVELOPMENT. AN ESSAY REVIEW EJ 013 062
READING: AN ETERNAL DYNAMIC EJ 028 959
THE LIFE AND WORKS OF ERIK ERIKSON EJ 044 757
AN ESSAY REVIEW: MENTAL RETARDATION AS A SOCIAL PROBLEM EJ 047 341
HOMER FOLKS'S "THE CARE OF DESTITUTE, NEGLECTED AND DELINQUENT CHILDREN" EJ 059 593
THE EVOLUTION OF DEVELOPMENTAL PSYCHOLOGY: A COMPARISON OF HANDBOOKS EJ 061 074

BOOKLISTS
MULTI-ETHNIC BOOKS FOR HEAD START CHILDREN. PART I: BLACK AND INTEGRATED LITERATURE. ED031312
MONTESSORI INDEX. THIRD EDITION. ED035435
NEGRO HERITAGE: A SELECTED BOOK LIST FOR ALL AGES. ED036341
HISPANIC HERITAGE: A SELECTED BOOK LIST FOR ALL AGES. ED036342
INDIAN HERITAGE: A SELECTED BOOK LIST FOR ALL AGES. ED036345
MULTI-ETHNIC BOOKS FOR YOUNG CHILDREN: ANNOTATED BIBLIOGRAPHY FOR PARENTS AND TEACHERS. ED046519
RESOURCES FOR ENVIRONMENTAL EDUCATORS: ECOLOGY AND TEACHERS EJ 029 392
BOOKS FOR YOUNG CHILDREN EJ 043 020

BOOKS
BIBLIOGRAPHY, EARLY CHILDHOOD EDUCATION. ED022544
ELEMENTARY EDUCATION RESPONDS TO A CHANGING SOCIETY ED024448
ANNUAL PROGRESS IN CHILD PSYCHIATRY AND CHILD DEVELOPMENT 1969. ED032941

BREAKFAST PROGRAMS
THE ADMINISTRATION OF "SELECTIVITY" IN THE BREAKFAST PROGRAM OF A PUBLIC ELEMENTARY SCHOOL EJ 036 580
NUTRITION AND EDUCATIONAL EXPERIENCE: INTERRELATED VARIABLES IN CHILDREN'S LEARNING EJ 059 643

BROADCAST INDUSTRY
CHILDREN AND THE MASS MEDIA EJ 029 341

BUDGETS
FEDERAL PROGRAMS ASSISTING CHILDREN AND YOUTH. REVISED EDITION. ED038161

BUILDING PLANS
SOME EUROPEAN NURSERY SCHOOLS AND PLAYGROUNDS. ED048928

BUS TRANSPORTATION
REACHING FOR THE DREAM: AN EXPERIMENT IN TWO-WAY BUSING EJ 025 078

BUSINESS RESPONSIBILITY
CHILDREN AND PARENTS: TOGETHER IN THE WORLD. 1970 WHITE HOUSE CONFERENCE ON CHILDREN, REPORT OF FORUM 15. (WORKING COPY). ED046531
WHO CARES FOR AMERICA'S CHILDREN? EJ 032 565
SON OF ROBOT COMMANDO EJ 055 488

CARDIOVASCULAR SYSTEM
THE PREVALENCE OF ANEMIA IN HEAD START CHILDREN. NUTRITION EVALUATION, 1968-69. ED041629

CAREER OPPORTUNITIES
EDUCATIONAL INTERVENTION IN THE HOME AND PARAPROFESSIONAL CAREER DEVELOPMENT: A FIRST GENERATION MOTHER STUDY. ED045190
A STUDY IN CHILD CARE (CASE STUDY FROM VOLUME II-B): "I'M A NEW WOMAN NOW." DAY CARE PROGRAMS REPRINT SERIES. ED051897
EDUCATIONAL INTERVENTION IN THE HOME AND PARAPROFESSIONAL CAREER DEVELOPMENT: A SECOND GENERATION MOTHER STUDY WITH AN EMPHASIS ON COSTS AND BENEFITS. FINAL REPORT. ED052814
CHILD CARE WORKER TRAINING PROJECT. OPERATIONAL PHASE AND EMPLOYMENT. FINAL REPORT. ED053788

CAREER PLANNING
ROLE MODEL INFLUENCES ON COLLEGE WOMEN'S CAREER ASPIRATIONS EJ 041 632

CAREERS
A CAREER DEVELOPMENT PROGRAM IN THE CHICAGO PUBLIC SCHOOLS EJ 035 579

CARTOONS
THE EFFECTS OF CARTOON CHARACTERS AS MOTIVATORS OF PRESCHOOL DISADVANTAGED CHILDREN. FINAL REPORT. ED045210
THE EFFECT OF AGGRESSIVE CARTOONS: CHILDREN'S INTERPERSONAL PLAY. ED046543
THE EFFECT OF AGGRESSIVE CARTOONS ON CHILDREN'S INTERPERSONAL PLAY EJ 053 750
THE ROLE OF INCONGRUITY AND RESOLUTION IN CHILDREN'S APPRECIATION OF CARTOON HUMOR EJ 060 781

CASE RECORDS
78 BATTERED CHILDREN: A RETROSPECTIVE STUDY. ED043382

CASE STUDIES
STUDY OF SELECTED CHILDREN IN HEAD START PLANNED VARIATION, 1969-1970. FIRST YEAR REPORT: 3 - CASE STUDIES OF CHILDREN. ED052847
A STUDY OF WED AND UNWED MOTHERHOOD IN ADOLESCENTS AND YOUNG ADULTS EJ 030 715
RECIPROCAL CONTRIBUTIONS BETWEEN PSYCHOANALYSIS AND PSYCHOEDUCATION EJ 045 048
SCHOOL AND HOME: NOT EITHER-OR EJ 046 246
THE BOY WHO DID NOT CRY EJ 052 310
GROUP HOME CARE AS AN ADJUNCT TO RESIDENTIAL TREATMENT EJ 061 233

CASE STUDIES (EDUCATION)
OPERATION HEAD START--AN EVALUATION. FINAL REPORT. ED013117
AN INSTITUTIONAL ANALYSIS OF DAY CARE PROGRAM. PART I, GROUP DAY CARE: A STUDY IN DIVERSITY. FINAL REPORT. ED036319
FIELD STUDIES OF SOCIAL REINFORCEMENT IN A PRESCHOOL. ED047772

CASEWORKER APPROACH
TEACHER-PARENT WORK IN THE HOME: AN ASPECT OF CHILD GUIDANCE CLINIC SERVICES EJ 027 448

CASEWORKERS
COMBINING SOCIAL CASEWORK AND GROUP WORK METHODS IN A CHILDREN'S HOSPITAL EJ 008 319

CATALOGS
EQUIPMENT AND SUPPLIES TESTED AND APPROVED FOR PRESCHOOL/SCHOOL/ HOME. ED017325

CATHARSIS
SOCIAL REINFORCEMENT FOR EXPRESSION VS. SUPPRESSION OF AGGRESSION EJ 007 691

CATHOLIC PARENTS
ATTITUDINAL STUDY OF ROMAN CATHOLIC PARENTS OF PRE-SCHOOL CHILDREN REGARDING THE OPTION OF "CATHOLIC" OR PUBLIC SCHOOL EDUCATION FOR THEIR CHILDREN. ED046488

CATHOLIC SCHOOLS
ATTITUDINAL STUDY OF ROMAN CATHOLIC PARENTS OF PRE-SCHOOL CHILDREN REGARDING THE OPTION OF "CATHOLIC" OR PUBLIC SCHOOL EDUCATION FOR THEIR CHILDREN. ED046488

CAUCASIANS
A CHILD'S FIRST STEPS: SOME SPECULATIONS EJ 033 057
THE EFFECT OF SUBJECT RACE, MODEL RACE, AND VICARIOUS PRAISE ON VICARIOUS LEARNING EJ 045 458

CENSUS FIGURES
PREPRIMARY ENROLLMENT OF CHILDREN UNDER SIX: OCTOBER 1967. ED027094

CEREBRAL DOMINANCE
CHILDREN'S ACQUISITION OF VISUO-SPATIAL DIMENSIONALITY: A CONSERVATION STUDY. ED041636
YOUNG CHILDREN'S ORIENTATION OF LETTERS AS A FUNCTION OF AXIS OF SYMMETRY AND STIMULUS ALIGNMENT EJ 032 909
UNILATERAL DOMINANCE IS NOT RELATED TO NEUROPSYCHOLOGICAL INTEGRITY EJ 056 624

CERTIFICATION
PRELIMINARY REPORT OF THE AD HOC JOINT COMMITTEE ON THE PREPARATION OF NURSERY AND KINDERGARTEN TEACHERS. ED032924
LICENSING OF CHILD CARE FACILITIES BY STATE WELFARE DEPARTMENTS: A CONCEPTUAL STATEMENT. ED046489
BASIC FACTS ABOUT LICENSING OF DAY CARE. ED047817
MINIMUM STANDARDS FOR LICENSED DAY CARE CENTERS AND NIGHT-TIME CENTERS. REVISED EDITION. ED048918
NEW DIRECTIONS IN THE LICENSING OF CHILD CARE FACILITIES EJ 016 608

CERTIFICATION BUDGETING
DEVELOPING PUBLIC DAY CARE FACILITIES IN MARYLAND EJ 018 970

CHAINING
ROLE OF DISCRIMINATIVE STIMULI IN THE FORMATION OF FUNCTIONAL RESPONSE CLASSES EJ 024 937

CHANGE AGENTS
ON CLASS DIFFERENCES AND EARLY DEVELOPMENT. ED044167
PARENTS AS PRIMARY CHANGE AGENTS IN AN EXPERIMENTAL HEAD START PROGRAM OF LANGUAGE INTERVENTION. EXPERIMENTAL PROGRAM REPORT. ED044168
A NATIONAL SURVEY OF THE IMPACTS OF HEAD START CENTERS ON COMMUNITY INSTITUTIONS. ED045195
A NATIONAL SURVEY OF THE IMPACTS OF HEAD START CENTERS ON COMMUNITY INSTITUTIONS. SUMMARY REPORT. ED046516
HEAD START'S INFLUENCE ON COMMUNITY CHANGE EJ 026 773
DO YOU REALLY WANT TO IMPROVE THE CURRICULUM? EJ 031 850
THE CREATIVE ENVIRONMENT WORKSHOP EJ 035 168
A CHANGE AGENT STRATEGY: PRELIMINARY REPORT EJ 054 727

CHANGING ATTITUDES
AFFECTIVE DIMENSIONS OF TEACHERS OF DISADVANTAGED CHILDREN IN SIX MAJORITY NEGRO SCHOOL DISTRICTS. ED028833
PEDAGOGICAL ATTITUDES OF CONVENTIONAL AND SPECIALLY-TRAINED TEACHERS. ED034587
CHANGING FAMILIES IN A CHANGING SOCIETY. 1970 WHITE HOUSE CONFERENCE ON CHILDREN, REPORT OF FORUM 14. (WORKING COPY). ED046530
THE TEMPER OF THE TIMES EJ 000 391
FACTS AGAINST IMPRESSIONS: MOTHERS SEEKING TO RELINQUISH CHILDREN FOR ADOPTION EJ 013 330
CHANGES IN SUCCESS-FAILURE ATTITUDES DURING ADOLESCENCE EJ 016 777
ABOUT RESEARCH: PART I, THE NATURE OF RESEARCH... CHANGING EMPHASES EJ 027 435
RECENT DEVELOPMENTS IN KOREAN SERVICES FOR CHILDREN EJ 032 563
ASSESSING THE ALTERNATIVES EJ 033 055
ATTITUDE OF BLACK NATURAL PARENTS REGARDING ADOPTION EJ 038 792

CHARTS
CURRICULUM GUIDE FOR EARLY CHILDHOOD EDUCATION. BEHAVIORAL GOALS - PRE-K THROUGH ONE. ED027940
A GUIDE FOR COLLECTING AND ORGANIZING INFORMATION ON EARLY CHILDHOOD PROGRAMS EJ 058 463

CHEATING
A METHODOLOGY FOR CONDUCTING AN EXPERIMENTAL ANALYSIS OF CHEATING BEHAVIOR EJ 030 589
RESISTANCE TO TEMPTATION IN YOUNG NEGRO CHILDREN EJ 032 894
ACADEMIC CHEATING: THE CONTRIBUTION OF SEX, PERSONALITY AND SITUATIONAL VARIABLES EJ 055 104
THE RELATIONSHIP BETWEEN VALUES AND BEHAVIOR: A DEVELOPMENTAL HYPOTHESIS EJ 056 622

CHECK LISTS
CREATIVITY: IDEA QUANTITY AND IDEA QUALITY EJ 058 212

CHEROKEE
SCHOOL IN CHEROKEE AND ENGLISH EJ 061 184

CHILD ABUSE
BIBLIOGRAPHY ON THE BATTERED CHILD. (REVISED EDITION). ED039942
78 BATTERED CHILDREN: A RETROSPECTIVE STUDY. ED043382
CHILD ABUSE LEGISLATION IN THE 1970'S. ED049826
PARENTAL AND COMMUNITY NEGLECT--TWIN RESPONSIBILITIES OF PROTECTIVE SERVICES EJ 007 446
A PLAN FOR PROTECTION: THE CHILD-ABUSE CENTER EJ 027 917
THE PARENTS' CENTER PROJECT: A MULTISERVICE APPROACH TO THE PREVENTION OF CHILD ABUSE EJ 040 043
A SOCIOCULTURAL PERSPECTIVE ON PHYSICAL CHILD ABUSE EJ 043 353
VIOLENCE BEGINS AT HOME. THE PARENTS' CENTER PROJECT FOR THE STUDY AND PREVENTION OF CHILD ABUSE EJ 043 671

CHILD CARE
OPTOMETRIC CHILD VISION CARE AND GUIDANCE. A SERIES OF PAPERS RELEASED BY THE OPTOMETRIC EXTENSION PROGRAM TO ITS MEMBERSHIP 1966-1967. ED032111
DAY CARE AND CHILD DEVELOPMENT IN YOUR COMMUNITY. ED034576
CHILD CARE ARRANGEMENTS OF WORKING MOTHERS IN THE UNITED STATES. ED040738
VIEWS ON PRE-SCHOOL EDUCATION AND DAY CARE. ED040753
REPORT OF CHILD PLACEMENT STUDY COMMITTEE, JANUARY, 1969. ED044169
DEMONSTRATION NURSERY CENTER FOR INFANTS AND TODDLERS, GREENSBORO, NORTH CAROLINA: A MODEL DAY CARE CENTER FOR CHILDREN UNDER 3 YEARS OLD. MODEL PROGRAMS--CHILDHOOD EDUCATION. ED045215
DEVELOPMENTAL DAY CARE SERVICES FOR CHILDREN. 1970 WHITE HOUSE CONFERENCE ON CHILDREN, REPORT OF FORUM 17. (WORKING COPY). ED046533
COMMUNITY COORDINATED CHILD CARE: A FEDERAL PARTNERSHIP IN BEHALF OF CHILDREN. FINAL REPORT. ED048925
TINY DRAMAS: VOCAL COMMUNICATION BETWEEN MOTHER AND INFANT IN JAPANESE AND AMERICAN FAMILIES. ED048927
COMMUNITY COORDINATED CHILD CARE: A FEDERAL PARTNERSHIP IN BEHALF OF CHILDREN. SUMMARY. ED048944
CAN I LOVE THIS PLACE? A STAFF GUIDE TO OPERATING CHILD CARE CENTERS FOR THE DISADVANTAGED. ED049809
THE DAY CARE NEIGHBOR SERVICE: A HANDBOOK FOR THE ORGANIZATION AND OPERATION OF A NEW APPROACH TO FAMILY DAY CARE. ED049810
HEALTH CARE OF CHILDREN: A CHALLENGE. ED050804
THE SWEDISH CHILD: A SURVEY OF THE LEGAL, ECONOMIC, EDUCATIONAL, MEDICAL AND SOCIAL SITUATION OF CHILDREN AND YOUNG PEOPLE IN SWEDEN. ED050811
THE DAY CARE CHALLENGE: THE UNMET NEEDS OF MOTHERS AND CHILDREN. ED050821
REPORT TO THE PRESIDENT: WHITE HOUSE CONFERENCE ON CHILDREN 1970. ED052828
PROMOTING CHILD HEALTH THROUGH COMPREHENSIVE CARE EJ 007 165
UPBRINGING OF CHILDREN IN KIBBUTZIM OF ISRAEL EJ 007 447
FAMILY TIES AND THE INSTITUTIONAL CHILD EJ 012 579
INFANT MORTALITY TRENDS AND MATERNAL AND INFANT CARE EJ 021 524
THE CHILDCARE ATTITUDES OF TWO GENERATIONS OF MOTHERS EJ 032 796
STIMULUS CONTROL OF PARENT OR CARETAKER BEHAVIOR BY OFFSPRING EJ 034 538
GROUP CARE AND INTELLECTUAL DEVELOPMENT EJ 040 041
COLONIAL CHILD CARE INSTITUTIONS: OUR HERITAGE OF CARE EJ 043 315
UNIVERSAL CHILD CARE EJ 043 354
DAY CARE: CRISIS AND CHALLENGE EJ 046 455
DAY CARE CHALLENGE: THE UNMET NEEDS OF MOTHERS AND CHILDREN EJ 046 456
144 FOSTER CHILDREN EJ 046 787
WORKING WITH SEPARATION EJ 046 893
THE UNSUPERVISED CHILD OF THE WORKING MOTHER EJ 053 709
FUNDING CHILD CARE PROGRAMS UNDER TITLE IV-A EJ 060 452
INFANT CARE AND GROWTH IN URBAN ZAMBIA EJ 061 231

CHILD CARE CENTERS
WHERE IS DAY CARE HEADING. ED016530
LICENSING OF CHILD CARE FACILITIES BY STATE WELFARE DEPARTMENTS: A CONCEPTUAL STATEMENT. ED046489
CAN I LOVE THIS PLACE? A STAFF GUIDE TO OPERATING CHILD CARE CENTERS FOR THE DISADVANTAGED. ED049809
A REVIEW OF EXPERIENCE: ESTABLISHING, OPERATING, EVALUATING A DEMONSTRATION NURSERY CENTER FOR THE DAYTIME CARE OF INFANTS AND TODDLERS, 1967-1970. FINAL REPORT. ED050810
A STUDY IN CHILD CARE. VOLUME I: FINDINGS. DAY CARE PROGRAMS REPRINT SERIES. ED051911

A STUDY IN CHILD CARE. VOLUME III: COST AND QUALITY ISSUES FOR OPERATORS. DAY CARE PROGRAMS REPRINT SERIES. ED051912
A PLAN FOR PROTECTION: THE CHILD-ABUSE CENTER EJ 027 917
AN INTERDISCIPLINARY APPROACH IN DAY TREATMENT OF EMOTIONALLY DISTURBED CHILDREN EJ 029 167
VIOLENCE BEGINS AT HOME. THE PARENTS' CENTER PROJECT FOR THE STUDY AND PREVENTION OF CHILD ABUSE EJ 043 671
AN INTERVIEW WITH GEORGIA MCMURRAY, NEW YORK CITY'S COMMISSIONER FOR CHILD DEVELOPMENT EJ 050 274
NIGHT CARE CENTER EJ 050 379
INDUSTRY AND DAY CARE EJ 050 380
A PERSPECTIVE ON RESIDENTIAL CHILD CARE PROGRAMS EJ 051 234
SOS CHILDREN'S VILLAGES THROUGHOUT THE WORLD: SUBSTITUTE OR SUPERIOR SERVICE? EJ 058 964
FUNDING CHILD CARE PROGRAMS UNDER TITLE IV-A EJ 060 452
WE HAVE MEN ON THE STAFF EJ 060 929

CHILD CARE OCCUPATIONS

A REPORT ON A CWLA PILOT PROJECT TO TRAIN NEW CHILD CARE WORKERS EJ 017 849
A NEW CHILD CARE PROFESSION: THE CHILD DEVELOPMENT ASSOCIATE EJ 050 937

CHILD CARE WORKERS

THE TRAINING OF FAMILY DAY-CARE WORKERS: A FEASIBILITY STUDY AND INITIAL PILOT EFFORTS. FINAL REPORT. ED053787
CHILD CARE WORKER TRAINING PROJECT. OPERATIONAL PHASE AND EMPLOYMENT. FINAL REPORT. ED053788
CHILD CARE PARAPROFESSIONALS: CHARACTERISTICS FOR SELECTION. ED053800
USING A STEP TOWARD PROFESSIONALISM IN TRAINING OF CHILD CARE STAFF EJ 017 850
THE FAMILY DAY CARE PROGRAM IN MILWAUKEE: A 3-FACETED APPROACH TO COMMUNITY ENRICHMENT EJ 023 391
THE CHILD CARE COUNSELOR: NEW THERAPIST IN CHILDREN'S INSTITUTIONS EJ 027 919
SEX EDUCATION FOR THE CHILD IN FOSTER CARE EJ 036 328
HELPING PARENTS IN A PEDIATRIC CLINIC EJ 046 963
TRAINING WORKERS FOR CHILD CARE CENTERS EJ 050 935
WE HAVE MEN ON THE STAFF EJ 060 929

CHILD DEVELOPMENT

THE CHILDREN'S CENTER--A MICROCOSMIC HEALTH, EDUCATION, AND WELFARE UNIT. PROGRESS REPORT. ED013116
YOUNG CHILDREN'S THINKING, STUDIES OF SOME ASPECTS OF PIAGET'S THEORY. ED013662
THE HOUSING ENVIRONMENT AS A FACTOR IN CHILD DEVELOPMENT. FINAL REPORT. ED014322
AN EVALUATION OF DIFFERENCES AMONG DIFFERENT CLASSES OF HEAD START PARTICIPANTS. FINAL REPORT. ED015012
A COMPARISON OF THE DEVELOPMENTAL DRAWING CHARACTERISTICS OF CULTURALLY ADVANTAGED AND CULTURALLY DISADVANTAGED CHILDREN. FINAL REPORT. ED015783
AN INFANT RATING SCALE, ITS VALIDATION AND USEFULNESS. ED016513
SEQUENCE IN LEARNING--FACT OR FICTION. ED017330
EARLY CHILDHOOD EDUCATION AND THE WALDORF SCHOOL PLAN. ED019114
A FRESH APPROACH TO EARLY CHILDHOOD EDUCATION AND A STUDY OF ITS EFFECTIVENESS. LEARNING TO LEARN PROGRAM. ED019117
AGE OF ENTRANCE INTO THE FIRST GRADE AS RELATED TO ARITHMETIC ACHIEVEMENT. ED020801
SPONTANEOUS PLAY: AN AVENUE FOR INTELLECTUAL DEVELOPMENT. ED023444
PROMISING DIRECTIONS FOR RESEARCH AND DEVELOPMENT IN EARLY CHILDHOOD EDUCATION. ED023448
CHILD DEVELOPMENT AND SOCIAL SCIENCE EDUCATION. PART III: ABSTRACTS OF RELEVANT LITERATURE. ED023466
REINFORCEMENT GROWS UP: THE EXPERIMENTAL ANALYSIS OF BEHAVIOR AS A SYSTEMATIC APPROACH TO THE TEACHING OF DEVELOPMENTAL PSYCHOLOGY. ED023479
EARLY CHILDHOOD SELECTED BIBLIOGRAPHIES SERIES. NUMBER 4, COGNITION. ED023488
INDEX AND DESCRIPTION OF TESTS. ED025304
CONCEPT GROWTH AND THE EDUCATION OF THE CHILD: A SURVEY OF RESEARCH ON CONCEPTUALIZATION. NATIONAL FOUNDATION FOR EDUCATIONAL RESEARCH IN ENGLAND AND WALES OCCASIONAL PUBLICATION SERIES NO. 12. ED026121
ELEMENTARY SCHOOL MATHEMATICS: A GUIDE TO CURRENT RESEARCH. THIRD EDITION. ED026123
CHILD DEVELOPMENT AND MATERIAL SURVEY. PART I, TECHNICAL REPORT. FINAL REPORT. ED027084
THE PROGRAM OF RESEARCH OF THE MERRILL-PALMER INSTITUTE IN CONJUNCTION WITH THE HEAD START EVALUATION AND RESEARCH CENTER, MICHIGAN STATE UNIVERSITY. ANNUAL REPORT. VOLUME II: RESEARCH. ED027088
CURRICULUM GUIDE FOR EARLY CHILDHOOD EDUCATION. BEHAVIORAL GOALS - PRE-K THROUGH ONE. ED027940
CHILD PSYCHIATRY: THE PAST QUARTER CENTURY. ED027951
CURRENT ISSUES IN RESEARCH ON EARLY DEVELOPMENT. ED028813
PSYCHOMOTOR EDUCATION - THEORY AND PRACTICE. ED029684
THE NURSERY YEARS: THE MIND OF THE CHILD FROM BIRTH TO SIX YEARS. ED029711
THE MAGIC YEARS: UNDERSTANDING AND HANDLING THE PROBLEMS OF EARLY CHILDHOOD. ED029712
CHILDREN'S ABILITY TO OPERATE WITHIN A MATRIX: A DEVELOPMENTAL STUDY. ED029715
RELATION OF SPATIAL EGOCENTRISM AND SPATIAL ABILITIES OF THE YOUNG CHILD. REPORT NUMBER 7. ED030481
CHILDREN'S UNDERSTANDING OF SOCIAL INTERACTION. ED031298
A COMPARISON OF RELATIVE STRUCTURAL LEVELS ON A VARIETY OF COGNITIVE TASKS. ED032923
ANNUAL PROGRESS IN CHILD PSYCHIATRY AND CHILD DEVELOPMENT 1969. ED032941
INFANT DAY CARE AND ATTACHMENT. ED033755
THE INFLUENCE OF THEORETICAL CONCEPTIONS OF HUMAN DEVELOPMENT ON THE PRACTICE OF EARLY CHILDHOOD EDUCATION. ED033766
TRAINING THE INTELLECT VERSUS DEVELOPMENT OF THE CHILD. ED034573
CHARACTERISTICS OF PRIMARY LEVEL CHILDREN. ED036343
CHILD REARING. AN INQUIRY INTO RESEARCH AND METHODS. ED036344
NUTRITION AND MENTAL DEVELOPMENT. RESEARCH REPORT NO. 5. ED037252
THE ETS-OEO LONGITUDINAL STUDY OF DISADVANTAGED CHILDREN. ED039927
SOCIAL INFLUENCES ON CHILDREN'S HUMOR RESPONSES. ED039933
ATTENTIONAL PREFERENCE AND EXPERIENCE: II. AN EXPLORATORY LONGITUDINAL STUDY OF THE EFFECTS OF VISUAL FAMILIARITY AND RESPONSIVENESS. ED039938
ATTENTIONAL PREFERENCE AND EXPERIENCE: III. VISUAL FAMILIARITY AND LOOKING TIME. ED039939
A COMPARISON OF THE NORMS OF THE PERSONAL SOCIAL DEVELOPMENT OF THE PRE-SCHOOL CHILDREN OF DELHI CENTRE AS OBTAINED BY THE CROSS-SECTIONAL STUDY AND THE LONGITUDINAL STUDY. ED039947
DEVELOPMENTAL NORMS OF CHILDREN AGED 2 1/2-5 YEARS: A PILOT STUDY. ED039949
THE DEVELOPMENT OF THE CONTROL OF ADULT INSTRUCTIONS OVER NON-VERBAL BEHAVIOR. ED041620
A LONGITUDINAL STUDY OF PIAGET'S DEVELOPMENTAL STAGES AND OF THE CONCEPT OF REGRESSION. ED043372
ON CLASS DIFFERENCES AND EARLY DEVELOPMENT. ED044167
PROCEEDINGS: EARLY CHILDHOOD INTERVENTION RESEARCH CONFERENCE (UNIVERSITY OF SOUTH FLORIDA, TAMPA, MARCH 5 AND 6, 1970). ED045194
FINAL REPORT ON PRESCHOOL EDUCATION TO OHIO DEPARTMENT OF EDUCATION. ED045200
ACTIVITIES FOR INFANT STIMULATION OR MOTHER-INFANT GAMES. ED046510
CREATIVITY AND THE LEARNING PROCESS. 1970 WHITE HOUSE CONFERENCE ON CHILDREN, REPORT OF FORUM 6. (WORKING PAPER). ED046525
DEVELOPMENTAL DAY CARE SERVICES FOR CHILDREN. 1970 WHITE HOUSE CONFERENCE ON CHILDREN, REPORT OF FORUM 17. (WORKING COPY). ED046533
THE CHILD AND LEISURE TIME. 1970 WHITE HOUSE CONFERENCE ON CHILDREN, REPORT OF FORUM 21. (WORKING COPY). ED046536
THE RIGHTS OF CHILDREN. 1970 WHITE HOUSE CONFERENCE ON CHILDREN, REPORT OF FORUM 22. (WORKING COPY). ED046537
THE ROLE OF EXPERIENCE IN THE BEHAVIORAL DEVELOPMENT OF HUMAN INFANTS: CURRENT STATUS AND RECOMMENDATIONS. ED048917
A RESOURCE AND REFERENCE BIBLIOGRAPHY IN EARLY CHILDHOOD EDUCATION AND DEVELOPMENTAL PSYCHOLOGY: THE AFFECTIVE DOMAIN. ED049817
CHILD DEVELOPMENT RESEARCH UNIT PROGRESS REPORT, FEBRUARY, 1970. ED049819
AN ANNOTATED BIBLIOGRAPHY ON EARLY CHILDHOOD. ED049822
A DESCRIPTIVE ACCOUNT OF FOUR MODES OF CHILDREN'S PLAY BETWEEN ONE AND FIVE YEARS. ED049833
AN ANALYSIS OF EXCELLENT EARLY EDUCATIONAL PRACTICES: PRELIMINARY REPORT. ED050805
TO LAUGH IS TO KNOW: A DISCUSSION OF THE COGNITIVE ELEMENT IN CHILDREN'S HUMOR. ED051879
MOTHER-INFANT INTERACTION AND INFANT DEVELOPMENT AMONG THE WOLOF OF SENEGAL. ED051885
A STUDY IN CHILD CARE (CASE STUDY FROM VOLUME II-A): "THEY UNDERSTAND." DAY CARE PROGRAMS REPRINT SERIES. ED051892
A STUDY IN CHILD CARE (CASE STUDY FROM VOLUME II-A): "LIFE IS GOOD, RIGHT? RIGHT!" DAY CARE PROGRAMS REPRINT SERIES. ED051901
A STUDY IN CHILD CARE (CASE STUDY FROM VOLUME II-A) ED051905
THE HEALTH OF CHILDREN--1970: SELECTED DATA FROM THE NATIONAL CENTER FOR HEALTH STATISTICS. ED052827
REPORT TO THE PRESIDENT: WHITE HOUSE CONFERENCE ON CHILDREN 1970. ED052828
COGNITIVE STUDIES VOLUME 2: DEFICITS IN COGNITION. ED053792
MOVEMENT AND MOVEMENT PATTERNS OF EARLY CHILDHOOD. ED053796

DESIGNS AND PROPOSAL FOR EARLY CHILDHOOD RESEARCH: A NEW LOOK: PRESCHOOL RESEARCH AND PRESCHOOL EDUCATIONAL OBJECTIVES ED053808
INTRODUCTION TO THE 1968 INFANT CONFERENCE PAPERS EJ 003 552
LEVELS OF CONCEPTUAL ANALYSIS IN ENVIRONMENT-INFANT INTERACTION RESEARCH EJ 004 044
CHILD DEVELOPMENT RESEARCH: AN EDIFICE WITHOUT A FOUNDATION EJ 004 045
CHILDREN UNDER THREE - FINDING WAYS TO STIMULATE DEVELOPMENT. I. ISSUES IN RESEARCH EJ 006 980
THE ECOLOGY OF GROWTH AND DEVELOPMENT IN A MEXICAN PREINDUSTRIAL COMMUNITY. REPORT 1: METHOD AND FINDINGS FROM BIRTH TO ONE MONTH OF AGE EJ 007 791
WHAT'S AHEAD FOR PREADOLESCENCE? EJ 009 034
WHAT IS LEARNED AND WHAT IS TAUGHT EJ 010 443
THE KINDNESSES OF CHILDREN EJ 010 444
FOUNDATIONS FOR GOOD BEGINNINGS EJ 010 588
SLEEP PROBLEMS EJ 011 345
EARLY MALNUTRITION AND HUMAN DEVELOPMENT EJ 011 914
PIAGET MISUNDERSTOOD: A CRITIQUE OF THE CRITICISMS OF HIS THEORY OF MORAL DEVELOPMENT EJ 011 915
EARLY MALNUTRITION AND CENTRAL NERVOUS SYSTEM FUNCTION EJ 012 207
THE COMPLEXITY OF INFANT DEVELOPMENT. AN ESSAY REVIEW EJ 013 062
EDUCATIONAL AND GROWTH NEEDS OF CHILDREN IN DAY CARE EJ 016 351
ENJOYING PREADOLESCENCE: THE FORGOTTEN YEARS EJ 016 966
PLAY IN DEWEY'S THEORY OF EDUCATION EJ 017 710
CONTRASTING VIEWS OF EARLY CHILDHOOD EDUCATION EJ 017 851
INDIVIDUAL DIFFERENCES IN THE CONSIDERATION OF INFORMATION AMONG TWO-YEAR-OLD CHILDREN EJ 018 324
INFANT DEVELOPMENT, PRESCHOOL IQ, AND SOCIAL CLASS EJ 018 465
REASONS FOR FAILURE ON THE CLASS INCLUSION PROBLEM EJ 018 872
PROJECTIVE VISUAL IMAGERY AS A FUNCTION OF AGE AND DEAFNESS EJ 018 877
TRANSFER EFFECTS IN CHILDREN'S ODDITY LEARNING EJ 018 887
CONTINUITY IN THE DEVELOPMENT OF CONCEPTUAL BEHAVIOR IN PRESCHOOL CHILDREN: A REJOINDER EJ 018 888
CONTINUITY IN THE DEVELOPMENT OF CONCEPTUAL BEHAVIOR IN PRESCHOOL CHILDREN: RESPONSE TO A REJOINDER EJ 018 889
AN ONTOGENY OF OPTIONAL SHIFT BEHAVIOR EJ 019 003
CHILDREN'S MANIPULATION OF ILLUSORY AND AMBIGUOUS STIMULI, DISCRIMINATIVE PERFORMANCE, AN IMPLICATIONS FOR CONCEPTUAL DEVELOPMENT EJ 019 007
THE ENVIRONMENTAL MYSTIQUE: TRAINING THE INTELLECT VERSUS DEVELOPMENT OF THE CHILD EJ 022 138
TRANSITIONAL OBJECTS AND THE PROCESS OF INDIVIDUATION: A STUDY IN THREE DIFFERENT SOCIAL GROUPS EJ 022 476
THE RELATION OF PARENTAL TRAINING TO CONCEPTUAL STRUCTURE IN PREADOLESCENTS EJ 023 191
ONTOGENY OF THE LOCUS AND ORIENTATION OF THE PERCEIVER: A CONFIRMATION AND AN ADDITION EJ 023 433
AN EXPLORATORY STUDY OF THE 3-, 5-, AND 7-YEAR OLD FEMALE'S COMPREHENSION OF COOPERATIVE AND UNCOOPERATIVE SOCIAL INTERACTION EJ 023 612
AN AGE-IRRELEVANT CONCEPT OF DEVELOPMENT EJ 027 437
AN ORGANISM ORIENTED CONCEPT OF DEVELOPMENT EJ 027 438
DEVELOPMENTAL LAWS AND THE EXPERIMENTALIST'S ONTOLOGY EJ 027 439
CHILDREN'S REACTIONS TO TV VIOLENCE: A REVIEW OF RESEARCH EJ 028 676
CHILDREN AND THE MASS MEDIA EJ 029 341
ISSUES IN ASSESSING DEVELOPMENT EJ 030 516
"THERE WAS A CHILD WENT FORTH"--A PHILOSOPHY OF EARLY EDUCATION EJ 031 049
WHO CARES FOR AMERICA'S CHILDREN? EJ 032 565
CHILDREN: THEIR POTENTIALS EJ 034 312
THE CAPACITY TO LOVE: A POSSIBLE REFORMULATION EJ 034 709
TRAINING, TRANSFER, AND THE DEVELOPMENT OF COMPLEX BEHAVIOR EJ 034 712
ON LANGUAGE AND KNOWING IN PIAGET'S DEVELOPMENTAL THEORY EJ 034 713
THE EFFECTS OF FATHER ABSENCE ON CHILD DEVELOPMENT EJ 035 800
CLASSROOM PRACTICES IN PRE-BASIC SCHOOLS EJ 036 335
CHILDREN'S ENVIRONMENTS AND CHILD WELFARE EJ 037 184
HELPING FOSTER PARENTS UNDERSTAND DISTURBED CHILDREN EJ 037 238
SWEDISH PRESCHOOLS: ENVIRONMENTS OF SENSITIVITY EJ 037 737
CONTINUITY FROM PREKINDERGARTEN TO KINDERGARTEN EJ 039 058
UNIVERSAL CHILD CARE EJ 043 354
A MOTHERS' TRAINING PROGRAM--THE ROAD TO A PURPOSEFUL EXISTENCE EJ 044 007
THE CHRONOLOGY OF THE DEVELOPMENT OF COVERT SPEECH IN CHILDREN EJ 047 594
LEARNING FROM EACH OTHER: PREDIATRICIANS AND TEACHERS EJ 050 320
THE DIAGNOSTIC EVALUATION OF CHILDREN WITH LEARNING PROBLEMS: A COMMUNICATION PROCESS EJ 050 321
CHILDREN: OUR CHALLENGE EJ 050 423
MOTHER-INFANT INTERACTION AND INFANT DEVELOPMENT AMONG THE WOLOF OF SENEGAL EJ 051 017
EDUCATIONAL COMPONENT OF DAY CARE EJ 051 235
CHILD ADVOCACY -- REFLECTIONS EJ 051 241
ON PLAY EJ 051 471
RELATIONSHIPS BETWEEN ATTRIBUTES OF MOTHERS AND THEIR INFANTS' IQ SCORES EJ 051 568
MATCHING AUDITORY AND VISUAL SERIES: MODALITY PROBLEM OR TRANSLATION PROBLEM? EJ 051 569
THE HISTORY OF LONGITUDINAL RESEARCH: IMPLICATIONS FOR THE FUTURE EJ 051 779
EXPLORATORY AND PLAY BEHAVIORS OF INFANTS REARED IN AN INSTITUTION AND IN LOWER- AND MIDDLE-CLASS HOMES EJ 052 441
THE DEVELOPMENT OF SOME INTENTION CONCEPTS IN YOUNG CHILDREN EJ 052 452
THE DEVELOPMENT OF ELEMENTARY SCHOOL CHILDREN'S JUDGMENT OF INTENT EJ 052 581
SEX DIFFERENCES IN EFFECTS OF KINDERGARTEN ATTENDANCE ON DEVELOPMENT OF SCHOOL READINESS AND LANGUAGE SKILLS EJ 052 723
DEVELOPMENTAL COURSE OF RESPONSIVENESS TO SOCIAL REINFORCEMENT IN NORMAL CHILDREN AND INSTITUTIONALIZED RETARDED CHILDREN EJ 053 648
AN EVALUATION OF A THEORY OF SPECIFIC DEVELOPMENTAL DYSLEXIA EJ 055 875
PARENTS AS EDUCATORS: EVIDENCE FROM CROSS-SECTIONAL, LONGITUDINAL AND INTERVENTION RESEARCH EJ 056 608
DEVELOPMENT OF A SENSE OF SELF-IDENTITY IN CHILDREN EJ 056 617
PEER INTERACTION AND COGNITIVE DEVELOPMENT EJ 056 708
A DEVELOPMENTAL LEARNING APPROACH TO INFANT CARE IN A GROUP SETTING EJ 057 442
DEVELOPMENT OF DIRECTIONALITY IN CHILDREN: AGES SIX THROUGH TWELVE EJ 058 137
DEVELOPMENTAL DIFFERENCES IN THE PERCEPTION AND PRODUCTION OF FACIAL EXPRESSIONS EJ 058 693
PREDICTION OF DEVELOPMENTAL OUTCOME AT SEVEN YEARS FROM PRENATAL, PERINATAL, AND POSTNATAL EVENTS EJ 058 927
CHILDREN'S ABILITY TO ORDER FACIAL AND NONFACIAL CONTINUA AS A FUNCTION OF MA, CA, AND IQ EJ 059 699
DIMENSIONS OF EARLY STIMULATION AND THEIR DIFFERENTIAL EFFECTS ON INFANT DEVELOPMENT EJ 059 873
INFANT DEVELOPMENT IN LOWER-CLASS AMERICAN FAMILIES EJ 060 012
DEVELOPMENTAL THEORY: ITS PLACE AND RELEVANCE IN EARLY INTERVENTION PROGRAMS EJ 060 013
CHILDREN'S UNDERSTANDING OF SPATIAL RELATIONS: COORDINATION OF PERSPECTIVES EJ 061 068
INFANT CARE AND GROWTH IN URBAN ZAMBIA EJ 061 231

CHILD DEVELOPMENT CENTERS

THE DEUTSCH MODEL--INSTITUTE FOR DEVELOPMENTAL STUDIES. ED020009
INKSTER PUBLIC SCHOOLS IMPLEMENT CHILD DEVELOPMENT CENTER. ED025303
ENGINEERING VERBAL BEHAVIOR. ED025308
CHILD DEVELOPMENT RESEARCH AND EVALUATION CENTER FOR HEAD START, TEMPLE UNIVERSITY. ANNUAL REPORT. ED030487
PROCEEDINGS OF THE CONFERENCE ON INDUSTRY AND DAY CARE (URBAN RESEARCH CORPORATION, CHICAGO, 1970). ED047780
PROGRAMS FOR INFANTS AND YOUNG CHILDREN. PART IV: FACILITIES AND EQUIPMENT. ED047810
A GUIDE TO THE PLANNING AND OPERATION OF A CHILD DEVELOPMENT CENTER FOR MIGRANT CHILDREN AND A REPORT OF THE HOOPESTON CHILD DEVELOPMENT CENTER ED049838
A STUDY IN CHILD CARE (CASE STUDY FROM VOLUME II-A): "IT'S A WELL-RUN BUSINESS, TOO." DAY CARE PROGRAMS REPRINT SERIES. ED051896
CHILDREN UNDER THREE - FINDING WAYS TO STIMULATE DEVELOPMENT. II. SOME CURRENT EXPERIMENTS: FROM INFANCY THROUGH SCHOOL EJ 007 412
ASK ME SOMETHING I KNOW EJ 012 580
EVALUATION OF A PARENT AND CHILD CENTER PROGRAM EJ 056 569

CHILD DEVELOPMENT SPECIALISTS

A STUDY OF EARLY ELEMENTARY TEACHER EVALUATION OF SELECTED EYE-HAND COORDINATION SKILLS OF KINDERGARTEN CHILDREN. INGHAM INTERMEDIATE COOPERATIVE RESEARCH PROJECT, 1967-68: SUMMARY REPORT. ED030488
A NEW CHILD CARE PROFESSION: THE CHILD DEVELOPMENT ASSOCIATE EJ 050 937

CHILD LANGUAGE

A STUDY OF THE COMMUNICATIVE ABILITIES OF DISADVANTAGED CHILDREN. FINAL REPORT. ED032119
A TRANSFORMATIONAL ANALYSIS OF THE LANGUAGE OF KINDERGARTEN AND ELEMENTARY SCHOOL CHILDREN. ED034592

ON THE HETEROGENEITY OF PSYCHOLOGICAL PROCESSES IN SYNTACTIC DEVELOPMENT. ED040764
SOME LANGUAGE COMPREHENSION TESTS. ED040765
LANGUAGE RESEARCH AND PRESCHOOL LANGUAGE TRAINING. ED040767
SUGGESTIONS FROM STUDIES OF EARLY LANGUAGE ACQUISITION EJ 012 396
CHILDREN'S QUESTIONS: THEIR FORMS, FUNCTIONS AND ROLES IN EDUCATION EJ 017 608
A TEST OF PIAGET'S THEORY OF "NOMINAL REALISM" EJ 023 189
A REEXAMINATION OF SOME ASSUMPTIONS ABOUT THE LANGUAGE OF THE DISADVANTAGED CHILD EJ 033 700
NON-SOCIAL SPEECH IN FOUR-YEAR-OLD CHILDREN AS A FUNCTION OF BIRTH ORDER AND INTERPERSONAL SITUATION EJ 033 702
WRITE FIRST, READ LATER EJ 034 069
THE PSYCHOLOGICAL CORRELATES OF SPEECH CHARACTERISTICS OF SOUNDING "DISADVANTAGED": A SOUTHERN REPLICATION EJ 040 685
LANGUAGE LEARNING--FRESH VIVID AND THEIR OWN EJ 044 613
MOTHER'S MODE OF DISCIPLINE AND CHILD'S VERBAL ABILITY EJ 050 794
THE TEACHER'S ROLE IN HELPING YOUNG CHILDREN DEVELOP LANGUAGE COMPETENCE EJ 051 566
SENTENCE REPETITION: ELICITED IMITATION OF A CONTROLLED SET OF SYNTACTIC STRUCTURES BY FOUR LANGUAGE GROUPS EJ 052 175
A CHILD-CENTERED DICTIONARY EJ 053 506
SOME COGNITIVE AND AFFECTIVE ASPECTS OF EARLY LANGUAGE DEVELOPMENT EJ 055 655
INVESTIGACIONES EN EL CAMPO EDUCATIVE (INVESTIGATIONS IN EDUCATION FIELD) EJ 062 593

CHILD PSYCHOLOGY

CHILD PSYCHIATRY: THE PAST QUARTER CENTURY. ED027951
ANNUAL PROGRESS IN CHILD PSYCHIATRY AND CHILD DEVELOPMENT 1969. ED032941
THE PREVALENCE OF BEHAVIOR SYMPTOMS IN YOUNGER ELEMENTARY SCHOOL CHILDREN. ED039040
PARENT PREFERENCE OF PRESCHOOL CHILDREN. ED041628
THE FEELINGS OF LEARNING EJ 003 082
CHILD PSYCHOLOGY IN FUTURE SOCIETY EJ 011 344
PREADOLESCENTS - WHAT MAKES THEM TICK? A CHILDHOOD EDUCATION SPECIAL (FIRST IN A SERIES): CLASSIC STATEMENTS FROM THE EDUCATOR'S ARCHIVES EJ 016 839
THE CHANGING CHILDREN OF PREADOLESCENCE (OR THE QUESTIONABLE JOY OF BEING PRE-ANYTHING) EJ 017 901
COGNITIVE FACTORS IN THE CONDITIONING OF CHILDREN'S PREFERENCES EJ 021 989
TANGIBLE REINFORCERS AND CHILD GROUP THERAPY EJ 026 935
"STRUCTURE" CAN IMPROVE THE GROUP BEHAVIOR OF FIVE-YEAR-OLD CHILDREN EJ 049 937
THE EVOLUTION OF DEVELOPMENTAL PSYCHOLOGY: A COMPARISON OF HANDBOOKS EJ 061 074

CHILD REARING

CHILD REARING IN CALIFORNIA, A STUDY OF MOTHERS WITH YOUNG CHILDREN. ED020783
EARLY CHILDHOOD SELECTED BIBLIOGRAPHIES SERIES. NUMBER 3, EDUCATION. ED022546
PARENT-CHILD INTERACTION AND THE CHILD'S APPROACH TO TASK SITUATIONS. ED025307
PARENTAL BEHAVIOR TOWARD BOYS AND GIRLS OF PRESCHOOL AGE. ED026119
A THEORY OF PARENT EFFECTIVENESS. ED028815
THE NURSERY YEARS: THE MIND OF THE CHILD FROM BIRTH TO SIX YEARS. ED029711
ATTITUDES, EXPECTATIONS, AND BEHAVIOR OF PARENTS OF HEAD START AND NON-HEAD START CHILDREN. REPORT NUMBER 1. ED030475
A NOTE ON PUNISHMENT PATTERNS IN PARENTS OF PRESCHOOL CHILDREN. REPORT NUMBER 3. ED030477
COMPETENCE AND DEPENDENCE IN CHILDREN: PARENTAL TREATMENT OF FOUR-YEAR-OLD GIRLS. FINAL REPORT. ED030497
INFANCY IN HOLLAND: THE FIRST THREE MONTHS. ED031296
ENVIRONMENT INFLUENCES ON THE DEVELOPMENT OF ABILITIES. ED032126
DEPENDENCE AND COMPETENCE IN FOUR-YEAR-OLD BOYS AS RELATED TO PARENTAL TREATMENT OF THE CHILD. ED039952
THE ROLE OF EXPERIENCE IN THE BEHAVIORAL DEVELOPMENT OF HUMAN INFANTS: CURRENT STATUS AND RECOMMENDATIONS. ED048917
AN ANALYSIS OF EXCELLENT EARLY EDUCATIONAL PRACTICES: PRELIMINARY REPORT. ED050805
OF DREAMS AND REALITY: KIBBUTZ CHILDREN EJ 006 922
INDUSTRIALIZATION, CHILD-REARING PRACTICES, AND CHILDREN'S PERSONALITY EJ 015 199
CHILD NEGLECT AMONG THE POOR: A STUDY OF PARENTAL ADEQUACY IN FAMILIES OF THREE ETHNIC GROUPS EJ 018 326
PERCEIVED MATERNAL CHILD-REARING EXPERIENCE AND THE EFFECTS OF VICARIOUS AND DIRECT REINFORCEMENT ON MALES EJ 019 008
INTRAFAMILY COMPARISON OF LOVING-REJECTING CHILD-REARING PRACTICES EJ 021 081
CHILDREARING PRACTICES AMONG SELECTED CULTURALLY DEPRIVED MINORITIES EJ 023 613
MATERNAL CHILD-REARING EXPERIENCE AND SELF- REINFORCEMENT EFFECTIVENESS EJ 024 944
THE CONNOTATIVE MEANING OF PARENT-CHILD RELATIONSHIPS AS RELATED TO PERCEIVED MATERNAL WARMTH AND CONTROL EJ 025 471
THE CHILD'S RIGHT TO QUALITY DAY CARE: AN ACEI POSITION PAPER EJ 029 103
SOCIALIZATION AND INSTRUMENTAL COMPETENCE IN YOUNG CHILDREN EJ 030 510
HARMONIOUS PARENTS AND THEIR PRESCHOOL CHILDREN EJ 034 708
CHILD-REARING PRACTICES IN MOUNTAIN COUNTY, KENTUCKY EJ 036 210
SHIFTS IN CHILD-REARING ATTITUDES LINKED WITH PARENTHOOD AND OCCUPATION EJ 038 853
A FACTOR ANALYSIS OF FIFTH AND SIXTH GRADERS' REPORTS OF PARENTAL CHILD-REARING BEHAVIOR EJ 038 855
A PARENTING SCALE AND SEPARATION DECISIONS EJ 039 286
A CHECK ON THE STRUCTURE OF PARENTAL REPORTS OF CHILD-REARING PRACTICES EJ 045 388
A CITY FOR CHILDREN: THE YEAR 2005 EJ 049 562
SYMPOSIUM ON ALTERNATIVE COMMUNITIES: CHILDREN OF THE GROUP FAMILY EJ 049 657
SOME THOUGHTS ON COMMUNAL CHILDREARING EJ 049 658
THE ROLE OF RETROSPECTIVE ACCOUNTS IN THE STUDY OF INTERGENERATIONAL ATTITUDES EJ 051 564
THE INTERPRETATION OF INTERGENERATIONAL ATTITUDES EJ 051 565
AN EXPLORATORY STUDY OF SOCIALIZATION EFFECTS ON BLACK CHILDREN: SOME BLACK-WHITE COMPARISONS EJ 055 656
PARENTS AS EDUCATORS: EVIDENCE FROM CROSS-SECTIONAL, LONGITUDINAL AND INTERVENTION RESEARCH EJ 056 608
IMPLICATIONS OF INFANT DEVELOPMENT AMONG THE MAYAN INDIANS OF MEXICO EJ 061 232

CHILD RESPONSIBILITY

THE RELATIONSHIP BETWEEN THE TEACHER AND THE TAUGHT. FIRST IMPRESSIONS OF A STUDENT TEACHER EJ 011 839
FREEDOM OF CHOICE- WHO'S KIDDING WHOM?; FREEDOM- CHOICE AND RESPONSIBILITY. A SYMPOSIUM EJ 011 984

CHILD ROLE

CHILDREN AS VICTIMS OF INSTITUTIONALIZATION EJ 051 205

CHILD WELFARE

CHILD WELFARE LEAGUE OF AMERICA STANDARDS FOR DAY CARE SERVICE. REVISED EDITION. ED039019
REALISTIC PLANNING FOR THE DAY CARE CONSUMER. ED043374
78 BATTERED CHILDREN: A RETROSPECTIVE STUDY. ED043382
THE CHILD ADVOCATE. 1970 WHITE HOUSE CONFERENCE ON CHILDREN, REPORT OF FORUM 24. (WORKING COPY). ED046538
CHILD WELFARE SERVICES: A SOURCEBOOK. ED047813
BASIC FACTS ABOUT LICENSING OF DAY CARE. ED047817
CHILD ABUSE LEGISLATION IN THE 1970'S. ED049826
THE SWEDISH CHILD: A SURVEY OF THE LEGAL, ECONOMIC, EDUCATIONAL, MEDICAL AND SOCIAL SITUATION OF CHILDREN AND YOUNG PEOPLE IN SWEDEN. ED050811
SERVICES TO CHILDREN LIVING WITH RELATIVES OR GUARDIANS EJ 007 445
FAMILIES OF CHILDREN IN FOSTER CARE EJ 007 452
A CHILD PROTECTION SERVICE ON A 24-HOUR, 365-DAY BASIS EJ 017 445
FOSTER CARE FOR MENTALLY RETARDED CHILDREN: HOW DOES CHILD WELFARE MEET THIS CHALLENGE? EJ 020 859
THE RIGHTS OF CHILDREN EMERGE: HISTORICAL NOTES ON THE FIRST WHITE HOUSE CONFERENCE ON CHILDREN EJ 023 283
OPTIMAL OPERATION OF PUBLIC/PRIVATE CHILD WELFARE DELIVERY SYSTEMS EJ 031 540
ADVOCACY FOR CHILDREN: CHALLENGE FOR THE 1970'S EJ 032 108
RECENT DEVELOPMENTS IN KOREAN SERVICES FOR CHILDREN EJ 032 563
PRIORITIES FOR CHANGE--SOME PRELIMINARY PROPOSALS FROM THE WHITE HOUSE CONFERENCE ON CHILDREN EJ 032 611
WHEN IS SUBSIDIZED ADOPTION PREFERABLE TO LONG-TERM FOSTER CARE? EJ 035 949
CHILDREN'S ENVIRONMENTS AND CHILD WELFARE EJ 037 184
TRENDS AND DILEMMAS IN CHILD WELFARE RESEARCH EJ 038 571
A PARENTING SCALE AND SEPARATION DECISIONS EJ 039 286
THE EXIT OF CHILDREN FROM FOSTER CARE: AN INTERIM RESEARCH REPORT EJ 039 798
THE PARENTS' CENTER PROJECT: A MULTISERVICE APPROACH TO THE PREVENTION OF CHILD ABUSE EJ 040 043
COLONIAL CHILD CARE INSTITUTIONS: OUR HERITAGE OF CARE EJ 043 315
THIRTY YEARS OF INNOVATION IN FOSTER CARE EJ 044 230
CHILDREN AS VICTIMS OF INSTITUTIONALIZATION EJ 051 205
THE CHILD WELFARE AGENCY AS THE EXTENDED FAMILY EJ 052 493
CHILD WELFARE: SEARCHING FOR RELEVANT LEARNING ON THE UNDERGRADUATE LEVEL EJ 056 762
HOMER FOLKS'S "THE CARE OF DESTITUTE, NEGLECTED AND DELINQUENT CHILDREN" EJ 059 593

CHILD WELFARE CENTERS

A DEMONSTRATION SUMMER PRESCHOOL PROGRAM EJ 060 999

CHILDHOOD
ADAPTATIONAL TASKS IN CHILDHOOD IN OUR CULTURE. ED021632
THE DEVELOPMENT OF ROLE-TAKING AND COMMUNICATION SKILLS IN CHILDREN. ED027082
LOOKING BACK WITH APPRECIATION EJ 058 054

CHILDHOOD ATTITUDES
THE IMPACT OF COGNITIVE MATURITY ON THE DEVELOPMENT OF SEX-ROLE ATTITUDES IN THE YEARS 4 TO 8. ED019109
PARENTAL ANTECEDENTS OF CHILDREN'S BELIEFS IN INTERNAL-EXTERNAL CONTROL OF REINFORCEMENTS IN INTELLECTUAL ACHIEVEMENT SITUATIONS. ED024447
CHILDREN'S JUDGMENTS OF AGE. ED043392
RACIAL ATTITUDES AMONG WHITE KINDERGARTEN CHILDREN FROM THREE DIFFERENT ENVIRONMENTS. ED051882
CONCERNED CITIZENS IN THE MAKING EJ 000 192
THE DEVELOPMENT OF CHILDREN'S VIEWS OF FOREIGN PEOPLES EJ 000 392
SHARING IN CHILDREN AS A FUNCTION OF THE NUMBER OF SHAREES AND RECIPROCITY EJ 016 840
DEVELOPMENT OF MORAL ATTITUDES IN WHITE AND NEGRO BOYS EJ 021 027
ATTITUDES OF PRESCHOOL AND ELEMENTARY SCHOOL CHILDREN TO AUTHORITY FIGURES EJ 034 452
GIRLS' ATTITUDES TOWARD MODELED BEHAVIORS AND THE CONTENT OF IMITATIVE PRIVATE PLAY EJ 036 079
A FACTOR ANALYSIS OF FIFTH AND SIXTH GRADERS' REPORTS OF PARENTAL CHILD-REARING BEHAVIOR EJ 038 855
KINDERGARTEN CHILDREN'S ACTIVE VOCABULARY ABOUT BODY BUILD EJ 041 857
EFFECTS OF SEX-TYPED INFORMATION ON CHILDREN'S TOY PREFERENCES EJ 045 191
TRANSFERENCE TOWARD THE CHILD THERAPIST AND OTHER PARENT SURROGATES EJ 049 427
RACIAL PREFERENCES IN YOUNG CHILDREN EJ 056 626
THE MEASUREMENT OF CHILDREN'S SELF-CONCEPT AS RELATED TO RACIAL MEMBERSHIP EJ 056 629
MODELING AND THE FEARFUL CHILD PATIENT EJ 058 354
CHILDREN'S REPORTS OF PARENTAL CHILD-REARING BEHAVIOR AT FIVE GRADE LEVELS EJ 060 385
GIVEN NAMES AND STEREOTYPING EJ 061 234
TELEVISION INSTRUCTION AND THE PRESCHOOL CHILD EJ 062 592

CHILDHOOD INTERESTS
AN EVALUATION OF NINE TOYS AND ACCOMPANYING LEARNING EPISODES IN THE RESPONSIVE MODEL PARENT/CHILD COMPONENT. ED045205
SOCIOECONOMIC STATUS AND CHILDREN'S INTERESTS EJ 016 775
ON SELECTING MATERIALS FOR THE CLASSROOM EJ 032 865
LE MONDE DES TOUT PETITS EST-IL INFLUENCE PAR NOTRE MONDE MODERNE? (IS THE WORLD OF CHILDREN INFLUENCED BY OUR MODERN WORLD?) EJ 049 895

CHILDHOOD NEEDS
A CREATIVE GUIDE FOR PRESCHOOL TEACHERS. GOALS, ACTIVITIES, AND SUGGESTED MATERIALS FOR AN ORGANIZED PROGRAM. ED016512
WHERE IS DAY CARE HEADING. ED016530
FREEDOM TO MOVE. ED020778
CHILD'S PLAY, A CREATIVE APPROACH TO PLAYSPACES FOR TODAY'S CHILDREN. ED021630
GROUP DAY CARE AS A CHILD-REARING ENVIRONMENT. AN OBSERVATIONAL STUDY OF DAY CARE PROGRAM. ED024453
ATTACHMENT AND RECIPROCITY IN THE TWO-YEAR-OLD CHILD. ED039946
EXPRESSIONS OF IDENTITY: THE SCHOOL-AGE CHILD. 1970 WHITE HOUSE CONFERENCE ON CHILDREN, REPORT OF FORUM 3. (WORKING COPY). ED046522
CHILDREN AND THEIR PHYSICAL AND SOCIAL ENVIRONMENT. 1970 WHITE HOUSE CONFERENCE ON CHILDREN, REPORT OF FORUM 19. (WORKING COPY). ED046535
THE CHILD AND LEISURE TIME. 1970 WHITE HOUSE CONFERENCE ON CHILDREN, REPORT OF FORUM 21. (WORKING COPY). ED046536
THE RIGHTS OF CHILDREN. 1970 WHITE HOUSE CONFERENCE ON CHILDREN, REPORT OF FORUM 22. (WORKING COPY). ED046537
THE CHILD ADVOCATE. 1970 WHITE HOUSE CONFERENCE ON CHILDREN, REPORT OF FORUM 24. (WORKING COPY). ED046538
FEDERAL PROGRAMS FOR YOUNG CHILDREN. ED047811
KINDERGARTEN: WHO? WHAT? WHERE? ED049829
HEALTH CARE OF CHILDREN: A CHALLENGE. ED050804
A STUDY IN CHILD CARE (CASE STUDY FROM VOLUME II-B): "A SENSE OF BELONGING." DAY CARE PROGRAMS REPRINT SERIES. ED051898
TEACHING THE YOUNG CHILD: GOALS FOR ILLINOIS. ED053805
EDUCATIONAL AND GROWTH NEEDS OF CHILDREN IN DAY CARE EJ 016 351
THE FUNDAMENTAL LEARNING NEEDS OF TODAY'S YOUNG CHILDREN EJ 027 531
THE RIGHTS OF THE CHILD - THE REALIZATION OF HIS POTENTIAL EJ 028 101
MAKING TOMORROW NOW: THE PEOPLE ENVIRONMENT EJ 028 200
WORKING MOTHERS AND THEIR CHILDREN EJ 028 793
ADVOCACY FOR CHILDREN: CHALLENGE FOR THE 1970'S EJ 032 108
WHO CARES FOR AMERICA'S CHILDREN? EJ 032 565
PRIORITIES FOR CHANGE--SOME PRELIMINARY PROPOSALS FROM THE WHITE HOUSE CONFERENCE ON CHILDREN EJ 032 611
SELECTING PRIORITIES AT THE WHITE HOUSE CONFERENCE ON CHILDREN EJ 035 619
DAY CARE FOR CHILDREN: ASSETS AND LIABILITIES EJ 035 802
EDUCATIONAL COMPONENT OF DAY CARE EJ 051 235
CHILD ADVOCACY -- REFLECTIONS EJ 051 241
THE IMPORTANCE OF SECURITY IN THE EDUCATION OF YOUNG CHILDREN EJ 062 549

CHILDREN
WHEN THE CHILD IS ANGRY. ED017331
DIFFERENTIATION BETWEEN NORMAL AND DISORDERED CHILDREN BY A COMPUTER ANALYSIS OF EMOTIONAL AND VERBAL BEHAVIOR. ED019138
EVALUATING THE CHILD'S LANGUAGE COMPETENCE. ED019141
A DIGEST OF THE RESEARCH ACTIVITIES OF REGIONAL EVALUATION AND RESEARCH CENTERS FOR PROJECT HEAD START (SEPTEMBER 1, 1966 TO NOVEMBER 30, 1967). ED023446
SOME STUDIES OF THE MORAL DEVELOPMENT OF CHILDREN. ED024445
MOTIVATIONAL AND SOCIAL COMPONENTS IN COMPENSATORY EDUCATION PROGRAMS: SUGGESTED PRINCIPLES, PRACTICES, AND RESEARCH DESIGNS. ED024464
THE ASSESSMENT OF ACHIEVEMENT ANXIETIES IN CHILDREN: HOW IMPORTANT IS RESPONSE SET AND MULTIDIMENSIONALITY IN THE TEST ANXIETY SCALE FOR CHILDREN? ED025313
EXPERIMENTS IN GRAMMATICAL PROCESSING IN CHILDREN. RESEARCH PROJECT NUMBER 1 OF PROJECT HEAD START RESEARCH AND EVALUATION CENTER, SYRACUSE UNIVERSITY RESEARCH INSTITUTE. FINAL REPORT, NOVEMBER 1, 1967. ED026138
THE THOMAS SELF-CONCEPT VALUES TEST. ED027068
COGNITIVE FACTORS IN SEMANTIC CONDITIONING. A THESIS IN EDUCATIONAL PSYCHOLOGY. ED027069
THE AUDITORY MEMORY OF CHILDREN FROM DIFFERENT SOCIO-ECONOMIC BACKGROUNDS. ED027092
FEDERAL PROGRAMS ASSISTING CHILDREN AND YOUTH. ED028840
AN EXPERIMENTAL STUDY OF SYNTACTICAL FACTORS INFLUENCING CHILDREN'S COMPREHENSION OF CERTAIN COMPLEX RELATIONSHIPS. FINAL REPORT. ED030492
FEDERAL PROGRAMS ASSISTING CHILDREN AND YOUTH. REVISED EDITION. ED038161
PROFILES OF CHILDREN: 1970 WHITE HOUSE CONFERENCE ON CHILDREN. ED046520
DELIVERY OF CHILD HEALTH SERVICES. 1970 WHITE HOUSE CONFERENCE ON CHILDREN, REPORT OF FORUM 11. (WORKING PAPER). ED046528
CHILDREN WHO ARE INJURED. 1970 WHITE HOUSE CONFERENCE ON CHILDREN, REPORT OF FORUM 13. (WORKING COPY). ED046529
BODY SIZE OF CONTEMPORARY GROUPS OF EIGHT-YEAR-OLD CHILDREN STUDIED IN DIFFERENT PARTS OF THE WORLD EJ 003 459
CUES FOR OBSERVING CHILDREN'S BEHAVIOR EJ 007 062
COMPREHENSIVE CHILD PSYCHIATRY THROUGH A TEAM APPROACH EJ 008 042
BUILDING ON EXPERIENCES IN LITERATURE EJ 013 022
A SUMMARY OF THE REPORT OF THE JOINT COMMISSION ON MENTAL HEALTH OF CHILDREN EJ 023 678
DEPENDENCE OF LAUGHTER ON COGNITIVE STRATEGIES EJ 023 964
DEVELOPMENTAL CHANGES IN THE USE OF EMOTION CUES IN A CONCEPT-FORMATION TASK EJ 029 362
HOW ADULTS AND CHILDREN SEARCH AND RECOGNIZE PICTURES EJ 029 384
THE DEVELOPMENT OF FREE CLASSIFICATION AND FREE RECALL IN CHILDREN EJ 030 293
PERCEPTUAL EXPLORATION IN ISRAELI CHILDREN EJ 033 054
SON OF ROBOT COMMANDO EJ 055 488
DEVELOPMENTAL AND EXPERIMENTAL FACTORS ASSOCIATED WITH INFERENTIAL BEHAVIOR EJ 057 905
SOME IMMEDIATE EFFECTS OF TELEVISED VIOLENCE ON CHILDREN'S BEHAVIOR EJ 058 216
VIEWPOINT: GAP AND THE JOINT COMMISSION ON MENTAL HEALTH OF CHILDREN EJ 060 203
THE RIGHTS OF CHILDREN EJ 060 473
CHILD HEALTH ISSUES IN NEW YORK EJ 060 523
FOUR CHILDREN EJ 061 073

CHILDRENS BOOKS
MULTI-ETHNIC BOOKS FOR HEAD START CHILDREN. PART I: BLACK AND INTEGRATED LITERATURE. ED031312
BOOKS IN PRESCHOOL: A GUIDE TO SELECTING, PURCHASING, AND USING CHILDREN'S BOOKS. ED038178
SELECTED BOOKS ABOUT THE AFRO-AMERICAN FOR VERY YOUNG CHILDREN K-2. ED039029
MULTI-ETHNIC BOOKS FOR YOUNG CHILDREN: ANNOTATED BIBLIOGRAPHY FOR PARENTS AND TEACHERS. ED046519
BIBLIOGRAPHY OF BOOKS FOR CHILDREN. 1971 EDITION. ED053798
CHOOSING CHILDREN'S BOOKS ABOUT OTHER COUNTRIES EJ 000 393
IS THERE A LITERATURE FOR THE DISADVANTAGED CHILD? EJ 007 178

THE BEAUTIFUL PEOPLE IN CHILDREN'S BOOKS EJ 020 541
MORALS, MORALS EVERYWHERE: VALUES IN CHILDREN'S FICTION EJ 051 270
THE SUGAR-COATED WORLD OF THE THIRD-GRADE READER EJ 058 171

CHILDRENS GAMES
"TUBE" PLAY EJ 008 263
SELF-MADE TOYS IN CHILDREN'S GAMES EJ 011 253
THINKING SKILLS AS A GOAL IN AN AFTER-SCHOOL PROGRAM EJ 037 635
THE DAYS THAT MAKE US HAPPY: GAMES AROUND THE WORLD EJ 038 407

CITY PROBLEMS
DAY CARE AS A SOCIAL INSTRUMENT: A POLICY PAPER. ED027065

CIVIL LIBERTIES
THE RIGHTS OF THE CHILD - THE REALIZATION OF HIS POTENTIAL EJ 028 101

CIVIL RIGHTS
A NEW LOOK AT THE COURTS AND CHILDREN'S RIGHTS EJ 007 092
THE RIGHTS OF CHILDREN EJ 060 473

CLASS ACTIVITIES
MAKING A CHILD'S OWN BOOK. ED035452
THE COGNITIVE CURRICULUM. YPSILANTI PRESCHOOL CURRICULUM DEMONSTRATION PROJECT. ED049832
CHILDREN DANCE IN THE CLASSROOM. ED053804
RECIPES FOR MOM EJ 018 131
A GLANCE AT A HEAD START PROGRAM IN AN ALASKAN CITY EJ 058 768

CLASS ATTENDANCE
THE CHILD WHO DISLIKES GOING TO SCHOOL. ED019999

CLASS MANAGEMENT
THE SIMULTANEOUS REHABILITATION OF MOTHERS AND THEIR CHILDREN. ED034591
THE TEACHER, TEACHER STYLE, AND CLASSROOM MANAGEMENT. PROCEEDINGS OF THE HEAD START RESEARCH SEMINARS: SEMINAR NO. 2, THE TEACHER AND CLASSROOM MANAGEMENT (1ST, WASHINGTON, D.C., JULY 22, 1968). ED035463
EXTENDING OPEN EDUCATION IN THE UNITED STATES. ED038182
SECOND STAGE TEACHING PROBLEMS IN A PUBLIC SCHOOL CLASS FOR EMOTIONALLY DISTURBED CHILDREN EJ 020 104
CLASSROOM MANAGEMENT--MORE THAN CONDITIONING EJ 027 827
THE APPLICATION OF PREMACK'S GENERALIZATION ON REINFORCEMENT TO THE MANAGEMENT OF CLASSROOM BEHAVIOR EJ 028 634
CLASSROOM DISCIPLINE: A NEW APPROACH EJ 032 896

CLASS ORGANIZATION
MULTI-AGE GROUPING--ENRICHING THE LEARNING ENVIRONMENT. ED017343
EDUCATION FOR INITIATIVE AND RESPONSIBILITY, COMMENTS ON A VISIT TO THE SCHOOLS OF LEICESTERSHIRE COUNTY, APRIL 1967. SECOND EDITION. ED020795

CLASSICAL CONDITIONING
A DECADE OF INFANT CONDITIONING AND LEARNING RESEARCH EJ 038 454
EVIDENCE FOR THE UNCONDITIONABILITY OF THE BABKIN REFLEX IN NEWBORNS EJ 058 589

CLASSIFICATION
THE COGNITIVE ENVIRONMENTS OF URBAN PRE-SCHOOL CHILDREN. MANUAL OF INSTRUCTIONS FOR ADMINISTERING AND SCORING SIGEL CONCEPTUAL STYLE SORTING TASKS. ED018263
MODIFICATION OF CLASSIFICATORY COMPETENCE AND LEVEL OF REPRESENTATION AMONG LOWER-CLASS NEGRO KINDERGARTEN CHILDREN. ED021608
THE DISTANCING HYPOTHESIS: A HYPOTHESIS CRUCIAL TO THE DEVELOPMENT OF REPRESENTATIONAL COMPETENCE. ED024466
THE IDENTIFICATION AND ASSESSMENT OF THINKING ABILITY IN YOUNG CHILDREN. FINAL REPORT. ED025316
THE SHIFT FROM COLOR TO FORM PREFERENCE IN YOUNG CHILDRE N OF DIFFERENT ETHNIC BACKGROUNDS. PART OF THE FINAL REPORT. ED025321
CHILDREN'S ABILITY TO OPERATE WITHIN A MATRIX: A DEVELOPMENTAL STUDY. ED029715
MODIFICATION OF COGNITIVE SKILLS AMONG LOWER-CLASS NEGRO CHILDREN: A FOLLOW-UP TRAINING STUDY. REPORT NUMBER 6. ED030480
CONCEPT FORMATION IN CHILDREN: A STUDY USING NONSENSE STIMULI AND A FREE-SORT TASK. ED031306
THE UTILIZATIONS OF CONCRETE, FUNCTIONAL, AND DESIGNATIVE CONCEPTS IN MULTIPLE CLASSIFICATION. ED032112
ANALYSIS OF THE OBJECT CATEGORIZATION TEST AND THE PICTURE CATEGORIZATION TEST FOR PRESCHOOL CHILDREN. ED038174
A PIAGETIAN METHOD OF EVALUATING PRESCHOOL CHILDREN'S DEVELOPMENT IN CLASSIFICATION. ED039013
CLASSIFICATION AND ATTENTION TRAINING CURRICULA FOR HEAD START CHILDREN. ED042508
CLASSIFYING DAY CARE CENTERS FOR COST ANALYSIS. ED047783
REASONS FOR FAILURE ON THE CLASS INCLUSION PROBLEM EJ 018 872
THE EFFECTS OF STIMULUS TYPE ON PERFORMANCE IN A COLOR-FORM SORTING TASK WITH PRESCHOOL, KINDERGARTEN, FIRST-GRADE, AND THIRD-GRADE CHILDREN EJ 019 006
GENERALIZATION IN A STIMULUS CLASSIFICATION TASK: STIMULUS SELECTION WITHIN AND AMONG DIMENSIONS EJ 021 987
CULTURAL DIFFERENCES IN COLOR/FORM PREFERENCE AND IN CLASSIFICATORY BEHAVIOR EJ 024 034
DECISION PROCESSES IN MULTIDIMENSIONAL GENERALIZATION EJ 038 265
SEVERE PROTEIN-CALORIE MALNUTRITION AND COGNITIVE DEVELOPMENT IN INFANCY AND EARLY CHILDHOOD EJ 039 627
SOME RELATIONSHIPS BETWEEN CLASS INCLUSION, PERCEPTUAL CAPABILITIES, VERBAL CAPABILITIES AND RACE EJ 039 639
CLASSIFICATION PATTERNS OF UNDERPRIVILEGED CHILDREN IN ISRAEL EJ 041 140
COGNITIVE STYLE AND CLASSIFICATION EJ 044 706
THE USE OF PERCEPTUAL, FUNCTIONAL, AND ABSTRACT ATTRIBUTES IN MULTIPLE CLASSIFICATION EJ 044 825
THE LEARNING AND TRANSFER OF DOUBLE-CLASSIFICATION SKILLS: A REPLICATION AND EXTENSION EJ 046 254
THE EFFECTS OF CHRONOLOGICAL AGE, TRIALS, AND LIST CHARACTERISTICS UPON CHILDREN'S CATEGORY CLUSTERING EJ 052 454
PERCEPTUAL AND LOGICAL FACTORS IN THE DEVELOPMENT OF MULTIPLICATIVE CLASSIFICATION EJ 053 649
A DEVELOPMENTAL STUDY OF FREE CLASSIFICATION IN CHILDREN EJ 056 730

CLASSROOM ARRANGEMENT
A ROOM PLANNED BY CHILDREN EJ 007 876

CLASSROOM COMMUNICATION
PRELIMINARY RESULTS FROM RELATIONSHIP BETWEEN TEACHERS' VOCABULARY USAGE AND THE VOCABULARY OF KINDERGARTEN AND FIRST GRADE STUDENTS. ED032135
VERBAL BEHAVIOR OF PRESCHOOL TEACHERS. A VERY PRELIMINARY REPORT. ED034577
THE EFFECTS OF DIFFERENTIATED INSTRUCTION IN VISUO-MOTOR SKILLS ON DEVELOPMENTAL GROWTH AND READING READINESS AT KINDERGARTEN LEVEL. FINAL REPORT. ED053821
LOCATION AS A FEATURE OF INSTRUCTIONAL INTERACTION EJ 012 717
THE EFFECTS OF MANIPULATION OF TEACHER COMMUNICATION STYLE IN THE PRESCHOOL EJ 052 455

CLASSROOM ENVIRONMENT
TEACHERS BELIEF SYSTEMS AND PRESCHOOL ATMOSPHERES. ED014320
REPORT OF A RESEARCH AND DEMONSTRATION PROJECT FOR CULTURALLY DISADVANTAGED CHILDREN IN THE ANCONA MONTESSORI SCHOOL. ED015014
PROJECT HEAD START--SUMMER 1966. FINAL REPORT. SECTION THREE, PUPILS AND PROGRAMS. ED018248
TEACHERS' BELIEFS, CLASSROOM ATMOSPHERE AND STUDENT BEHAVIOR. FINAL REPORT. ED018249
THINKING, FEELING, EXPERIENCING--TOWARD REALIZATION OF FULL POTENTIAL. ED020012
LEICESTERSHIRE REPORT: THE CLASSROOM ENVIRONMENT. ED027964
THE ANALYSIS OF DATA GENERATED IN A RESEARCH DESIGNED TO SECURE BASELINE INFORMATION ON A HEAD START PROGRAM. A REPORT TO THE U.S. OFFICE OF ECONOMIC OPPORTUNITY FROM THE DEPARTMENT OF RESEARCH, MONTGOMERY COUNTY, MARYLAND PUBLIC SCHOOLS. ED037232
RESEARCH, CHANGE, AND SOCIAL RESPONSIBILITY: STUDIES OF THE IMPRINT OF THE LOW-INCOME HOME ON YOUNG CHILDREN. ED039935
THE EFFECTS OF SCHOOL ENVIRONMENT ON DISADVANTAGED KINDERGARTEN CHILDREN, WITH AND WITHOUT A HEAD START BACKGROUND. FINAL REPORT. ED041640
HARTFORD EARLY CHILDHOOD PROGRAM, HARTFORD, CONNECTICUT: AN URBAN PUBLIC SCHOOL SYSTEM'S LARGE-SCALE APPROACH TOWARD RESTRUCTURING EARLY CHILDHOOD EDUCATION. MODEL PROGRAMS--CHILDHOOD EDUCATION. ED045211
THE COGNITIVE CURRICULUM. YPSILANTI PRESCHOOL CURRICULUM DEMONSTRATION PROJECT. ED049832
CHILDREN COME FIRST: THE INSPIRED WORK OF ENGLISH PRIMARY SCHOOLS. ED050820
AWARENESS--ONE KEY TO READING READINESS EJ 027 551
MAKING TOMORROW NOW: THE PEOPLE ENVIRONMENT EJ 028 200
CLASSROOM BEHAVIOR: MESSAGES FROM CHILDREN EJ 031 780
ON SELECTING MATERIALS FOR THE CLASSROOM EJ 032 865
THE SYSTEMATIC USE OF THE PEMACK PRINCIPLE IN MODIFYING CLASSROOM BEHAVIORS EJ 034 528
LETTERS FROM ENGLAND EJ 037 738
CREATING A CLIMATE FOR INDIVIDUALIZING INSTRUCTION EJ 044 511
EFFECT OF CLASSROOM NOISE ON NUMBER IDENTIFICATION BY RETARDED CHILDREN EJ 045 793
GROWTH IN READING IN AN INTEGRATED DAY CLASSROOM EJ 055 154
DESIGNING INSTRUCTIONAL SETTINGS FOR CHILDREN LABELED "RETARDED": SOME REFLECTIONS EJ 057 733

TOWARD A DEMOCRATIC ELEMENTARY-SCHOOL CLASSROOM EJ 058 308

CLASSROOM FURNITURE

WORKTABLE ON WHEELS. ED035451

CLASSROOM MATERIALS

ENVIRONMENTALLY ENRICHED CLASSROOMS AND THE DEVELOPMENT OF DISADVANTAGED PRESCHOOL CHILDREN. ED045192
ON SELECTING MATERIALS FOR THE CLASSROOM EJ 032 865
WHAT TO DO TILL THE MALE MAN COMES EJ 048 697
HOW FREE IS FREE PLAY? EJ 055 535

CLASSROOM OBSERVATION TECHNIQUES

A METHOD TO INVESTIGATE THE MOVEMENT PATTERNS OF CHILDREN. ED027938
CHILD BEHAVIOR SURVEY INSTRUMENT: MANUAL OF INSTRUCTIONS AND DEFINITIONS. ED037230
RECORDING INDIVIDUAL PUPIL EXPERIENCES IN THE CLASSROOM: A MANUAL FOR PROSE RECORDERS. ED038163
SOUTHWESTERN COOPERATIVE EDUCATIONAL LABORATORY INTERACTION OBSERVATION SCHEDULE (SCIOS): A SYSTEM FOR ANALYZING TEACHER-PUPIL INTERACTION IN THE AFFECTIVE DOMAIN. ED038188
RELATIONSHIPS BETWEEN TEACHER BEHAVIOR, PUPIL BEHAVIOR, AND PUPIL ACHIEVEMENT. ED038189
OSCAR GOES TO NURSERY SCHOOL: A NEW TECHNIQUE FOR RECORDING PUPIL BEHAVIOR. ED039923
TRANSPLANTING ENGLISH INFANT SCHOOL IDEAS TO AMERICAN CLASSROOMS AND SOME EFFECTS ON LANGUAGE USE. ED040756
MAXIMIZING THE VALUE OF EVALUATION FOR THE HEAD START TEACHER. FINAL REPORT. ED041631
SURVIVAL SKILLS AND FIRST GRADE ACADEMIC ACHIEVEMENT. REPORT #1. ED050807
A STUDY IN THE UTILIZATION OF TECHNOLOGICALLY ADVANCED TECHNIQUES FOR TEACHER-PARENT-CHILD ASSESSMENT. FINAL REPORT. ED053818
THE SHORT ATTENTION SPAN: FACT AND MYTH EJ 028 898
PATTERNS OF INFORMATION PROCESSING USED BY AND WITH YOUNG CHILDREN IN A NURSERY SCHOOL SETTING EJ 032 890
METODO DE ARCHIVAR LAS OBSERVACIONES DEL COMPORTAMIENTO DEL NINO, COMO GUIA PARA ENTENDERLO MEJOR EJ 045 232
SYMPOSIUM ON CHILD-OBSERVATION: 1. FILM-MAKING AS AN OBSERVATION TECHNIQUE EJ 056 861
SYMPOSIUM ON CHILD-OBSERVATION: 2. THE TWO-A-DAY OBSERVATION PLAN EJ 056 862
THE EFFECTS OF IMMEDIATE FEEDBACK ON THE BEHAVIOR OF TEACHERS-IN-TRAINING EJ 059 672

CLASSROOM RESEARCH

HEADSTART OPERATIONAL FIELD ANALYSIS. PROGRESS REPORT I. ED015774
HEAD START EVALUATION AND RESEARCH CENTER, BOSTON UNIVERSITY. REPORT A-III, OBSERVATIONAL STRATEGIES FOR OBTAINING DATA ON CHILDREN AND TEACHERS IN HEAD START CLASSES. (OSOD). ED022559
THE ROLE OF THE TEACHER IN THE INFANT AND NURSERY SCHOOL. ED029703
THE MONTESSORI RESEARCH PROJECT. FOUR PROGRESS REPORTS. ED030489
SOME PARAMETERS OF TEACHER EFFECTIVENESS AS ASSESSED BY AN ECOLOGICAL APPROACH. ED032928
AN INTEGRATIVE APPROACH TO CLASSROOM LEARNING. ED033749
LOCATION AS A FEATURE OF INSTRUCTIONAL INTERACTION EJ 012 717

CLASSROOM TECHNIQUES

REDUCING BEHAVIOR PROBLEMS: AN OPERANT CONDITIONING GUIDE FOR TEACHERS. ED034570
THE SIMULTANEOUS REHABILITATION OF MOTHERS AND THEIR CHILDREN. ED034591
THE VALUE OF CLASSROOM REWARDS IN EARLY EDUCATION. ED049828
CHILDREN COME FIRST: THE INSPIRED WORK OF ENGLISH PRIMARY SCHOOLS. ED050820
A TEACHER DISCOVERS INDIVIDUALIZED INSTRUCTION EJ 035 171
RELATIONSHIP OF CLASSROOM GROUPING PRACTICES TO DIFFUSION OF STUDENTS' SOCIOMETRIC CHOICES AND DIFFUSION OF STUDENTS' PERCEPTION OF SOCIOMETRIC CHOICE EJ 042 791

CLINICAL DIAGNOSIS

HEAD START EVALUATION AND RESEARCH CENTER, BOSTON UNIVERSITY. REPORT B-I, PRIMARY AND SECONDARY PREVENTION STUDYING CLINICAL PROCESS AND DISTURBANCE WITH PRESCHOOL CHILDREN. ED022560
A CLINIC FOR CHILDREN WITH LEARNING DISABILITIES EJ 024 471
HEAD START: A HEAD START TO HEALTH? EJ 036 581

CLINICS

A PLAY PROGRAM IN A PEDIATRIC CLINIC EJ 029 951
AN ATTEMPT TO COMBINE CLINICAL AND EDUCATIONAL RESOURCES: A REPORT ON THE FIRST YEAR'S EXPERIENCE OF A THERAPEUTIC SCHOOL EJ 035 539
INTERPERSONAL RELATIONSHIPS IN RESIDENTIAL TREATMENT CENTERS FOR DISTURBED CHILDREN EJ 037 183
FAMILY TREATMENT WITHIN THE MILIEU OF A RESIDENTIAL TREATMENT CENTER EJ 037 236
INVOLVING PARENTS IN A CHILDREN'S CLINIC EJ 047 353

CLUSTER GROUPING

CONCEPT FORMATION IN CHILDREN: A STUDY USING NONSENSE STIMULI AND A FREE-SORT TASK. ED031306
FREE RECALL OF WORDS AND OBJECTS EJ 039 634
FREE RECALL AND CLUSTERING AT FOUR AGE LEVELS: EFFECTS OF LEARNING TO LEARN AND PRESENTATION METHOD EJ 039 636
THE EFFECTS OF CHRONOLOGICAL AGE, TRIALS, AND LIST CHARACTERISTICS UPON CHILDREN'S CATEGORY CLUSTERING EJ 052 454
A DEVELOPMENTAL STUDY OF FREE CLASSIFICATION IN CHILDREN EJ 056 730
DEVELOPMENTAL CHANGES IN CLUSTERING CRITERIA EJ 058 145
THE EFFECTS OF GROUPING ON SHORT-TERM SERIAL RECALL OF DIGITS BY CHILDREN: DEVELOPMENTAL TRENDS EJ 059 320

COCURRICULAR ACTIVITIES

CORRELATES OF LOCUS OF CONTROL IN A SECONDARY SCHOOL POPULATION EJ 039 905

CODIFICATION

CODING MANUAL FOR APPROACH (A PROCEDURE FOR PATTERNING RESPONSES OF ADULTS AND CHILDREN). ED015005
HEAD START EVALUATION AND RESEARCH CENTER, THE UNIVERSITY OF CHICAGO. REPORT C, COGNITIVE INTERACTION BETWEEN TEACHER AND PUPIL IN A PRESCHOOL SETTING. ED022552
A TEST OF ERIKSON'S THEORY OF EGO EPIGENESIS EJ 039 898
LABELING AND IMAGING AS AIDS TO MEMORY EJ 041 143
THE STABILITY AND TRANSFERABILITY OF CONCEPTUAL CODING IN CHILDREN EJ 046 251

COGNITIVE ABILITY

THE COGNITIVE ENVIRONMENTS OF URBAN PRE-SCHOOL CHILDREN. MANUAL OF INSTRUCTIONS FOR ADMINISTERING AND SCORING THE TWENTY QUESTIONS TASK. ED018261
AN ANALYSIS OF A CLASS OF PROBLEM SOLVING BEHAVIOR. FINAL REPORT. ED020776
HEAD START RESEARCH AND EVALUATION OFFICE, UNIVERSITY OF CALIFORNIA AT LOS ANGELES. APPENDIX I TO THE ANNUAL REPORT, NOVEMBER 1967. ED020793
SOME EFFECTS OF SOCIAL CLASS AND RACE ON CHILDREN'S LANGUAGE AND INTELLECTUAL ABILITIES. ED022540
COGNITIVE AND LINGUISTIC DEFICITS IN PSYCHOTIC CHILDREN. STUDY M: DEVELOPMENT OF SELECTIVE ATTENTION ABILITIES. ED024440
ROLE OF MOTHERS' LANGUAGE STYLES IN MEDIATING THEIR PRESCHOOL CHILDREN'S COGNITIVE DEVELOPMENT. ED025298
THE INITIAL PHASE OF A PRESCHOOL CURRICULUM DEVELOPMENT PROJECT. FINAL REPORT. ED027071
THE FACTORIAL STRUCTURE OF REASONING, MORAL JUDGMENT, AND MORAL CONDUCT. ED031302
THE EFFECTS OF MODE OF PRESENTATION AND NUMBER OF CATEGORIES ON 4-YEAR-OLDS' PROPORTION ESTIMATES. ED032132
MEASURING PERCEPTUAL MOTOR ABILITY IN PRESCHOOL CHILDREN. ED032932
INFLUENCES OF A PIAGET-ORIENTED CURRICULUM ON INTELLECTUAL FUNCTIONING OF LOWER-CLASS KINDERGARTEN CHILDREN. ED049823
WISC SUBTEST AND IQ SCORE CORRELATES OF FATHER ABSENCE EJ 029 219
DIFFERENTIAL FACTOR STRUCTURE OF SEVENTH GRADE STUDENTS EJ 030 298
COMPETENCE VERSUS PERFORMANCE IN YOUNG CHILDREN'S USE OF ADJECTIVAL COMPARATIVES EJ 033 701
TRANSFER AND SEQUENCE IN LEARNING DOUBLE CLASSIFICATION SKILLS EJ 035 379
CREATIVITY AS RELATED TO FIELD INDEPENDENCE AND MOBILITY EJ 035 380
AN EXPERIMENTAL STUDY OF BASIC LEARNING ABILITY AND INTELLIGENCE IN LOW-SOCIOECONOMIC-STATUS CHILDREN EJ 036 818
PERSONALITY, COGNITIVE, AND ACADEMIC CORRELATES OF PROBLEM-SOLVING FLEXIBILITY EJ 039 632
SOME LANGUAGE-RELATED COGNITIVE ADVANTAGES OF BILINGUAL FIVE-YEAR-OLDS EJ 041 343
SEX AND AGE DIFFERENCES IN PATTERN ORGANIZATION IN A FIGURAL-CONCEPTUAL TASK EJ 047 680
THE CHILDREN'S ASSOCIATIVE RESPONDING TEST: A TWO-YEAR FOLLOW-UP EJ 047 683
STIMULUS PREFERENCE AND MULTIPLICATIVE CLASSIFICATION IN CHILDREN EJ 047 686
SMILING IN CHILDREN AS A FUNCTION OF THEIR SENSE OF MASTERY EJ 048 298
PREDICTION OF INTELLECTUAL PERFORMANCE AT 3 YEARS FROM INFANT TESTS AND PERSONALITY MEASURES EJ 052 237
CONCEPTUAL STYLE AND CONCEPTUAL ABILITY IN KINDERGARTEN THROUGH THE EIGHTH GRADE EJ 053 484

COGNITIVE DEVELOPMENT

THE EFFECTS OF ASSESSMENT AND PERSONALIZED PROGRAMMING ON SUBSEQUENT INTELLECTUAL DEVELOPMENT OF PREKINDERGARTEN AND KINDERGARTEN CHILDREN. ED013663

EVALUATION OF TWO ASSOCIATED YM-YWHA HEADSTART PROGRAMS. FINAL REPORT. ED014318
COGNITIVE DEVELOPMENT IN INFANTS OF DIFFERENT AGE LEVELS AND FROM DIFFERENT ENVIRONMENTAL BACKGROUNDS. ED015786
DEVELOPMENTAL LEVEL AND CONCEPT-LEARNING--A REPLICATION AND EXTENSION. ED016528
THE COGNITIVE ENVIRONMENTS OF URBAN PRE-SCHOOL CHILDREN. MANUAL OF INSTRUCTIONS FOR ADMINISTERING AND SCORING TOY SORTING TASK. ED018264
THE IMPACT OF COGNITIVE MATURITY ON THE DEVELOPMENT OF SEX-ROLE ATTITUDES IN THE YEARS 4 TO 8. ED019109
SOCIAL CLASS AND COGNITIVE DEVELOPMENT IN INFANCY. ED019111
TEACHING FORMAL OPERATIONS TO PRESCHOOL ADVANTAGED AND DISADVANTAGED CHILDREN. ED019990
AN EVALUATION OF THE EFFECTS OF A UNIQUE SEQUENTIAL LEARNING PROGRAM ON CULTURALLY DEPRIVED PRESCHOOL CHILDREN. FINAL REPORT. ED019994
A DEVELOPMENTAL STUDY OF THE RELATIONSHIP BETWEEN REACTION-TIME AND PROBLEM-SOLVING EFFICIENCY. FINAL REPORT. ED020018
THE INTERACTION OF FATHER-ABSENCE AND SIBLING-PRESENCE ON COGNITIVE ABILITIES. ED020024
THE EFFECT OF HEADSTART ON DEVELOPMENTAL PROCESSES. ED020026
REGIONAL EVALUATION AND RESEARCH CENTER FOR PROJECT HEAD START, SUPPLEMENTARY RESEARCH REPORT, SEPTEMBER 1, 1967-DECEMBER 31, 1967. ED020791
INFLUENCES OF CULTURAL PATTERNS ON THE THINKING OF CHILDREN IN CERTAIN ETHNIC GROUPS, A STUDY OF THE EFFECT OF JEWISH SUB-CULTURE ON THE FIELD-DEPENDENCE-INDEPENDENCE DIMENSION OF COGNITION. ED020796
THE HIERARCHICAL ORGANIZATION OF INTELLECTUAL STRUCTURES. ED022534
THE EFFECT OF EARLY STIMULATION: THE PROBLEM OF FOCUS IN DEVELOPMENTAL STIMULATION. ED022535
THE TWO YEAR OLD. ED022536
HEAD START EVALUATION AND RESEARCH CENTER, THE UNIVERSITY OF CHICAGO. REPORT A, MATERNAL INFLUENCES UPON DEVELOPMENT OF COGNITION. ED022550
SPONTANEOUS PLAY: AN AVENUE FOR INTELLECTUAL DEVELOPMENT. ED023444
HEAD START EVALUATION AND RESEARCH CENTER, THE UNIVERSITY OF CHICAGO. ANNUAL REPORT, 1966-1967. ED023445
HEAD START EVALUATION AND RESEARCH CENTER, THE UNIVERSITY OF CHICAGO. REPORT F, SOCIALIZATION INTO THE ROLE OF PUPIL. ED023456
CHILD DEVELOPMENT AND SOCIAL SCIENCE EDUCATION. PART IV: A TEACHING STRATEGY DERIVED FROM SOME PIAGETIAN CONCEPTS. ED023467
PROCEEDINGS OF THE ANNUAL CONVENTION OF THE CHRISTIAN ASSOCIATION FOR PSYCHOLOGICAL STUDIES ON THE DYNAMICS OF LEARNING CHRISTIAN CONCEPTS (12TH, GRAND RAPIDS, MICHIGAN, MARCH 31-APRIL 1, 1965). ED023476
METHODOLOGICAL ISSUES IN THE STUDY OF AGE DIFFERENCES IN INFANTS' ATTENTION TO STIMULI VARYING IN MOVEMENT AND COMPLEXITY. ED023477
THE CONCEPT OF DEVELOPMENTAL LEARNING. ED023484
CONCEPT LEARNING IN EARLY CHILDHOOD. ED024454
THE DISTANCING HYPOTHESIS: A HYPOTHESIS CRUCIAL TO THE DEVELOPMENT OF REPRESENTATIONAL COMPETENCE. ED024466
PERCEPTUAL-COGNITIVE DEVELOPMENT IN INFANCY: A GENERALIZED EXPECTANCY MODEL AS A FUNCTION OF THE MOTHER-INFANT INTERACTION. ED024470
A PRELIMINARY SEARCH FOR FORMAL OPERATIONS STRUCTURES. ED024471
A STUDY OF COGNITIVE AND SOCIAL FUNCTIONING. PROJECT II ED025310
A RATIONALE FOR A STRUCTURED EDUCATIONAL PROGRAM AND SUGGESTED ACTIVITIES FOR CULTURALLY DISADVANTAGED INFANTS. ED026112
AN EVALUATION OF A SIX-WEEK HEADSTART PROGRAM USING AN ACADEMICALLY ORIENTED CURRICULUM: CANTON, 1967. ED026114
CONCEPT GROWTH AND THE EDUCATION OF THE CHILD: A SURVEY OF RESEARCH ON CONCEPTUALIZATION. NATIONAL FOUNDATION FOR EDUCATIONAL RESEARCH IN ENGLAND AND WALES OCCASIONAL PUBLICATION SERIES NO. 12. ED026121
COGNITIVE GROWTH IN PRESCHOOL CHILDREN. ED027057
CHILD DEVELOPMENT AND MATERIAL SURVEY. PART I, TECHNICAL REPORT. FINAL REPORT. ED027084
PIAGET, SKINNER, AND AN INTENSIVE PRESCHOOL PROGRAM FOR LOWER CLASS CHILDREN AND THEIR MOTHERS. ED027966
PERRY PRESCHOOL PROJECT, YPSILANTI, MICHIGAN ED027975
REPLICATION OF THE "MOTIVATED LEARNING" COGNITIVE TRAINING PROCEDURES WITH CULTURALLY DEPRIVED PRESCHOOLERS. REPORT FROM PROJECT MOTIVATED LEARNING. ED029708
CHILDREN'S ABILITY TO OPERATE WITHIN A MATRIX: A DEVELOPMENTAL STUDY. ED029715
MODIFICATION OF COGNITIVE SKILLS AMONG LOWER-CLASS NEGRO CHILDREN: A FOLLOW-UP TRAINING STUDY. REPORT NUMBER 6. ED030480
CONCEPT FORMATION IN CHILDREN: A STUDY USING NONSENSE STIMULI AND A FREE-SORT TASK. ED031306
SOME LANGUAGE-RELATED COGNITIVE ADVANTAGES OF BILINGUAL FIVE YEAR OLDS. ED031307
THE UTILIZATIONS OF CONCRETE, FUNCTIONAL, AND DESIGNATIVE CONCEPTS IN MULTIPLE CLASSIFICATION. ED032112
UNDERSTANDING READINESS: AN OCCASIONAL PAPER. ED032117
DEVELOPMENT OF THE UNDERSTANDING OF LOGICAL CONNECTIVES. ED032125
A COMPARISON OF RELATIVE STRUCTURAL LEVELS ON A VARIETY OF COGNITIVE TASKS. ED032923
SOCIOECONOMIC BACKGROUND AND COGNITIVE FUNCTIONING IN PRES-CHOOL CHILDREN. ED032929
A STRUCTURE-PROCESS APPROACH TO COGNITIVE DEVELOPMENT OF PRESCHOOL NEGRO CHILDREN: RATIONALE AND EFFECTS. ED033743
SOCIAL CLASS DIFFERENTIATION IN COGNITIVE DEVELOPMENT: A LONGITU-DINAL STUDY. ED033754
YOUNG CHILDREN'S COMPREHENSION OF LOGICAL CONNECTIVES. ED033756
"CONSERVATION" BELOW AGE THREE: FACT OR ARTIFACT? ED035438
PAPER-AND-PENCIL VERSUS CONCRETE PERFORMANCE OF NORMALS AND RETARDATES ON THE ETS WRITTEN EXERCISES. ED035442
CLASSIFICATION AND INFERENTIAL THINKING IN CHILDREN OF VARYING AGE AND SOCIAL CLASS. ED035446
THE ROLE OF UNDERDETERMINACY AND REFERENCE IN THE SENTENCE RECALL OF YOUNG CHILDREN. ED035449
AN INVESTIGATION OF THE MANNER IN WHICH YOUNG CHILDREN PROCESS INTELLECTUAL INFORMATION. FINAL REPORT. ED036313
THE EFFECT OF SELECTED TRAINING EXPERIENCES ON PERFORMANCE ON A TEST OF CONSERVATION OF NUMEROUSNESS. REPORT FROM PHASE 2 OF THE PROTOTYPIC INSTRUCTIONAL SYSTEMS IN ELEMENTARY MATHEMATICS PROJECT. ED036334
AN INTRODUCTION OF LENGTH CONCEPTS TO KINDERGARTEN CHILDREN. REPORT FROM THE PROJECT ON ANALYSIS OF MATHEMATICS INSTRUCTION. ED036335
A STUDY OF NON-VERBAL REPRESENTATION IN YOUNG CHILDREN. ED036336
PIAGET'S THEORY AND SPECIFIC INSTRUCTION: A RESPONSE TO BEREITER AND KOHLBERG. ED038164
CONDITIONAL LOGIC AND PRIMARY CHILDREN. ED038186
MALNUTRITION, LEARNING AND INTELLECTUAL DEVELOPMENT: RESEARCH AND REMEDIATION. ED039017
THE RELATION OF CERTAIN HOME ENVIRONMENT FACTORS TO THE THINKING ABILITIES OF THREE-YEAR-OLD CHILDREN. FINAL REPORT. ED039041
A FACTOR ANALYSIS OF A THREE-YEAR LONGITUDINAL STUDY OF CONSERVATION OF NUMBER AND RELATED MATHEMATICAL CON-CEPTS. ED039934
A FACTOR ANALYTIC STUDY OF CHILDREN'S CAUSAL REASONING. ED040759
EXPERIMENTS IN HEAD START AND EARLY EDUCATION: THE EFFECTS OF TEACHER ATTITUDE AND CURRICULUM STRUCTURE ON PRESCHOOL DISADVANTAGED CHILDREN. FINAL REPORT. ED041615
A COMPARISON OF THREE INTERVENTION PROGRAMS WITH DISADVAN-TAGED PRESCHOOL CHILDREN. UNIVERSITY OF CALIFORNIA HEAD START RESEARCH AND EVALUATION CENTER. FINAL REPORT 1968-1969. ED041616
DIRECT VERBAL INSTRUCTION CONTRASTED WITH MONTESSORI METHODS IN THE TEACHING OF NORMAL FOUR-YEAR-OLD CHILDREN. ED041619
DEMONSTRATION INFANT DAY CARE AND EDUCATION PROGRAM. INTERIM REPORT, 1969-1970. ED041632
A PARENT-CHILD CENTER, NOVEMBER-DECEMBER 1968. ED042506
HAWAII HEAD START EVALUATION--1968-69. FINAL REPORT. ED042511
HAWAII HEAD START EVALUATION FOLLOW-UP--1968-69. FINA L REPORT. ED042515
A FOLLOW-UP EVALUATION OF THE EFFECTS OF A UNIQUE SEQUENTIAL LEARNING PROGRAM, A TRADITIONAL PRESCHOOL PROGRAM AND A NO TREATMENT PROGRAM ON CULTURALLY DEPRIVED CHILDREN. FINAL REPORT. ED042516
EARLY CHILDHOOD EDUCATION LEARNING SYSTEM FOR THREE-AND FOUR-YEAR-OLD MIGRANT CHILDREN, MCALLEN, TEXAS. EVALUATION RE-PORT, 1968-1969. ED043370
A LONGITUDINAL STUDY OF PIAGET'S DEVELOPMENTAL STAGES AND OF THE CONCEPT OF REGRESSION. ED043372
APPROACHES TO THE VALIDATION OF LEARNING HIERARCHIES. ED043376
INFANT STIMULATION AND THE ETIOLOGY OF COGNITIVE PROCESSES. ED045174
THE COGNITIVE ENVIRONMENTS OF URBAN PRESCHOOL CHILDREN. FINAL REPORT. ED045179
THE COGNITIVE ENVIRONMENTS OF URBAN PRESCHOOL CHILDREN: FOLLOW-UP PHASE. FINAL REPORT. ED045180
CHANGING THE LEARNING PATTERNS OF THE CULTURALLY DIFFERENT. ED045184
PRELIMINARY ANALYSIS OF 1968-69 HEAD START DATA. ED045203
AN OVERVIEW OF COGNITIVE AND LANGUAGE PROGRAMS FOR 3, 4, & 5 YEAR OLD CHILDREN. ED045209

COGNITIVELY ORIENTED CURRICULUM, YPSILANTI, MICHIGAN: A PROGRAM THAT EXPOSES PRESCHOOL CHILDREN TO A VARIETY OF MATERIALS AND EQUIPMENT TO TEACH CONCEPTS THROUGH PHYSICAL AND VERBAL EXPERIENCES. MODEL PROGRAMS--CHILDHOOD EDUCATION. ED045217
HEAD START GRADUATES: ONE YEAR LATER. ED048929
LANGUAGE ACQUISITION AND COGNITIVE DEVELOPMENT. ED049811
THE NEW YORK STATE EXPERIMENTAL PREKINDERGARTEN PROGRAM. SUMMARY REPORT, 1969-70. ED049814
THE COGNITIVE CURRICULUM. YPSILANTI PRESCHOOL CURRICULUM DEMONSTRATION PROJECT. ED049832
INTERVENTION WITH MOTHERS AND YOUNG CHILDREN: A STUDY OF INTRAFAMILY EFFECTS. ED050809
EDUCATIONAL INTERVENTION IN EARLY CHILDHOOD: ABSTRACTS OF THE 1965-1970 SPECIAL STUDIES RESEARCH AND EVALUATION REPORT. FINAL REPORT, VOLUME III. ED050816
MEASURING DIFFERENTIAL DEVELOPMENT IN YOUNG CHILDREN. ED050818
A COMPARISON STUDY OF THE COGNITIVE DEVELOPMENT OF DISADVANTAGED FIRST GRADE PUPILS (AS MEASURED BY SELECTED PIAGETIAN TASKS). ED051874
TO LAUGH IS TO KNOW: A DISCUSSION OF THE COGNITIVE ELEMENT IN CHILDREN'S HUMOR. ED051879
ATTAINMENT OF COGNITIVE OBJECTIVES. TECHNICAL REPORT NO. 3. ED052833
SOCIAL SKILLS DEVELOPMENT IN THE EARLY CHILDHOOD EDUCATION PROJECT. TECHNICAL REPORT NO. 7. ED052835
AN EVALUATION OF LOGICAL OPERATIONS INSTRUCTION IN THE PRESCHOOL. ED053791
COGNITIVE STUDIES VOLUME 2: DEFICITS IN COGNITION. ED053792
A GUIDE TO READING PIAGET. ED053819
PERCEPTUAL-COGNITIVE DEVELOPMENT IN INFANCY: A GENERALIZED EXPECTANCY MODEL AS A FUNCTION OF THE MOTHER-INFANT INTERACTION EJ 003 553
CONTINUNITY IN COGNITIVE DEVELOPMENT DURING THE FIRST YEAR EJ 003 554
THE EFFECT OF EARLY STIMULATION: THE PROBLEM OF FOCUS IN DEVELOPMENTAL STIMULATION EJ 006 921
WHAT IS LEARNED AND WHAT IS TAUGHT EJ 010 443
STAGES OF SENSORIMOTOR DEVELOPMENT: A REPLICATION STUDY EJ 011 916
A DEVELOPMENTAL STUDY OF NONCONSERVATION CHOICES IN YOUNG CHILDREN EJ 011 917
THE INTERSITUATIONAL GENERALITY OF FORMAL THOUGHT EJ 015 097
COMPARISON OF GROSS, INTENSIVE, AND EXTENSIVE QUANTITIES BY RETARDATES EJ 015 098
STAGES OF THE DREAM CONCEPT AMONG HASIDIC CHILDREN EJ 017 903
OPERATIONAL THOUGHT INDUCEMENT EJ 018 874
PREDICTIVE VERSUS PERCEPTUAL RESPONSES TO PIAGET'S WATER-LINE TASK AND THEIR RELATION TO DISTANCE CONSERVATION EJ 018 875
REPRESENTATIONAL LEVEL AND CONCEPT PRODUCTION IN CHILDREN AND ADOLESCENTS EJ 018 880
TRANSITIVE INFERENCE WITH NONTRANSITIVE SOLUTIONS CONTROLLED EJ 018 882
INFORMATION PROCESSING IN PROBLEM SOLVING AS A FUNCTION OF DEVELOPMENTAL LEVEL AND STIMULUS SALIENCY EJ 018 884
AGE CHANGES IN CHILDREN'S LEARNING SET WITH WIN-STAY, LOSE-SHIFT PROBLEMS EJ 018 885
PERCEPTUAL AND SENSORIMOTOR SUPPORTS FOR CONSERVATION TASKS EJ 018 886
TRANSFER EFFECTS IN CHILDREN'S ODDITY LEARNING EJ 018 887
A METHODOLOGICAL INVESTIGATION OF PIAGET'S THEORY OF OBJECT CONCEPT DEVELOPMENT IN THE SENSORY-MOTOR PERIOD EJ 018 891
THE EFFECTS OF STIMULUS TYPE ON PERFORMANCE IN A COLOR-FORM SORTING TASK WITH PRESCHOOL, KINDERGARTEN, FIRST-GRADE, AND THIRD-GRADE CHILDREN EJ 019 006
CHILDREN'S MANIPULATION OF ILLUSORY AND AMBIGUOUS STIMULI, DISCRIMINATIVE PERFORMANCE, AN IMPLICATIONS FOR CONCEPTUAL DEVELOPMENT EJ 019 007
COGNITIVE SYNTHESIS IN NEGRO AND WHITE CHILDREN EJ 020 522
THE ROLE OF COMPREHENSION IN CHILDREN'S PROBLEM SOLVING EJ 021 764
DEVELOPMENT CHANGES IN PROBLEM-SOLVING STRATEGIES: PERMUTATION EJ 021 767
DETERMINANTS OF PART-WHOLE PERCEPTION IN CHILDREN EJ 021 772
INFERENCE AND PREFERENCE IN CHILDREN'S CONCEPTUAL PERFORMANCE EJ 021 773
SOCIOECONOMIC BACKGROUND AND COGNITIVE FUNCTIONING IN PRESCHOOL CHILDREN EJ 021 774
REVERSIBILITY TRAINING AND STIMULUS DESIRABILITY AS FACTORS IN CONSERVATION OF NUMBER EJ 021 776
NONVERBAL MNEMONIC MEDIATION IN PRESCHOOL CHILDREN EJ 021 777
THE DEVELOPMENT OF THE CONCEPT OF OBJECT AS RELATED TO INFANT-MOTHER ATTACHMENT EJ 021 998
A PRELIMINARY SEARCH FOR FORMAL OPERATIONS STRUCTURES EJ 023 192
THE DEVELOPMENT OF PROBABILISTIC THINKING IN CHILDREN: A COMPARISON OF TWO METHODS OF ASSESSMENT EJ 023 193
AN EXPLORATORY STUDY OF THE 3-, 5-, AND 7-YEAR OLD FEMALE'S COMPREHENSION OF COOPERATIVE AND UNCOOPERATIVE SOCIAL INTERACTION EJ 023 612
MATRICES, THREE BY THREE: CLASSIFICATION AND SERIATION EJ 025 470
CONTINUITY AND DISCONTINUITY HYPOTHESES IN STUDIES OF CONSERVATION EJ 027 182
RESISTING PRESSURES IN THE PRE-SCHOOL CENTRE P 15-27 EJ 029 621
MODEL FOR A THINKING MCHINE: AN INFORMATION-PROCESSING FRAMEWORK FOR THE STUDY OF COGNITIVE DEVELOPMENT EJ 030 289
THE DEVELOPMENT OF CLASSIFICATORY SKILLS IN YOUNG CHILDREN: A TRAINING PROGRAM EJ 031 872
LEARNING AND COGNITIVE DEVELOPMENT: REPRESENTATIVE SAMPLES, CUMULATIVE-HIERARCHICAL LEARNING, AND EXPERIMENTAL-LONGITUDINAL METHODS EJ 032 509
CHILDREN'S USE OF CONTEXT IN JUDGMENT OF WEIGHT EJ 033 053
THE USEFULNESS OF CUMULATIVE DEPRIVATION AS AN EXPLANATION OF EDUCATIONAL DEFICIENCIES EJ 033 056
THE RELATIONSHIP BETWEEN TIME OF MEASUREMENT AND AGE IN COGNITIVE DEVELOPMENT OF CHILDREN: AN APPLICATION OF CROSS-SECTIONAL SEQUENCES EJ 034 714
CHILDREN'S ABILITY TO OPERATE WITHIN A MATRIX: A DEVELOPMENTAL STUDY EJ 035 363
PARENTAL EDUCATION, SEX DIFFERENCES, AND PERFORMANCE ON COGNITIVE TASKS AMONG TWO-YEAR-OLD CHILDREN EJ 035 364
OUTERDIRECTEDNESS IN THE PROBLEM-SOLVING OF INSTITUTIONALIZED AND NONINSTITUTIONALIZED NORMAL AND RETARDED CHILDREN EJ 035 366
THE ROLE OF VERBAL MEDIATION IN MENTAL DEVELOPMENT EJ 035 382
SOCIAL-CLASS DIFFERENTIATION IN COGNITIVE DEVELOPMENT AMONG BLACK PRESCHOOL CHILDREN EJ 036 819
COGNITIVE DEVELOPMENT AND CHILDREN'S COMPREHENSION OF HUMOR EJ 036 820
CHILDREN'S UNDERSTANDING OF PROBABILITY CONCEPTS EJ 036 824
A PERSPECTIVE ON COGNITIVE DEVELOPMENT: THE PRESCHOOL CHILD'S PERFORMANCE IN CLASSIFICATION TASKS EJ 036 827
COGNITIVE DEVELOPMENT IN INFANCY: ASSESSMENT, ACCELERATION, AND ACTUALIZATION EJ 037 493
THINKING SKILLS AS A GOAL IN AN AFTER-SCHOOL PROGRAM EJ 037 635
COGNITIVE-PERCEPTUAL DEVELOPMENT IN INFANCY: SETTING FOR THE SEVENTIES EJ 038 262
WHY NOT FEELINGS AND VALUES IN INSTRUCTIONAL TELEVISION? EJ 038 906
SEVERE PROTEIN-CALORIE MALNUTRITION AND COGNITIVE DEVELOPMENT IN INFANCY AND EARLY CHILDHOOD EJ 039 627
DIFFERENTIAL ADJUSTMENT TO PUBESCENCE AND COGNITIVE STYLE PATTERNS EJ 039 903
ATTENTION DISTRIBUTION IN THE 24-MONTH-OLD CHILD: VARIATIONS IN COMPLEXITY AND INCONGRUITY OF THE HUMAN FORM EJ 040 296
STATE IV OF PIAGET'S THEORY OF INFANT'S OBJECT CONCEPTS: A LONGITUDINAL STUDY EJ 041 134
STUDIES OF CONSERVATION WITH YORUBA CHILDREN OF DIFFERING AGES AND EXPERIENCE EJ 041 135
NUMBER CONSERVATION IN VERY YOUNG CHILDREN: THE EFFECT OF AGE AND MODE OF RESPONDING EJ 041 139
ANTICIPATORY IMAGERY AND MODIFIED ANAGRAM SOLUTIONS: A DEVELOPMENTAL STUDY EJ 041 141
THE DEVELOPMENT OF COGNITIVE BALANCE AND THE TRANSITION FROM CONCRETE TO FORMAL OPERATIONAL THOUGHT EJ 041 145
CAN CONDITIONED RESPONSES BE ESTABLISHED IN THE NEWBORN INFANT: 1971? EJ 041 956
COGNITIVE STYLE AND READING ABILITY EJ 043 239
A DEVELOPMENTAL STUDY OF COGNITIVE BALANCE EJ 043 856
EARLY COGNITIVE DEVELOPMENT AND PRESCHOOL EDUCATION EJ 043 857
ON THE VALUE OF BOTH PLAY AND STRUCTURE IN EARLY EDUCATION EJ 044 010
CORRELATES OF CURIOSITY AND EXPLORATORY BEHAVIOR IN PRESCHOOL DISADVANTAGED CHILDREN EJ 045 456
THE ROLE OF OPERATIONAL THINKING IN CHILDREN'S COMPREHENSION AND APPRECIATION OF HUMOR EJ 046 233
COMPLEX MOTOR LEARNING IN FOUR-YEAR-OLDS EJ 046 236
COGNITIVE DEVELOPMENT IN INFANTS OF DIFFERENT AGE LEVELS AND FROM DIFFERENT ENVIRONMENTAL BACKGROUNDS: AN EXPLANATORY INVESTIGATION EJ 046 244
ARTISTIC STYLE AS CONCEPT FORMATION FOR CHILDREN AND ADULTS EJ 046 247
PLAY, THE ESSENTIAL INGREDIENT EJ 046 248
ACCOMMODATION OF VISUAL TRACKING PATTERNS IN HUMAN INFANTS TO OBJECT MOVEMENT PATTERNS EJ 046 250
DELAY OF FEEDBACK INTERVAL, POSTFEEDBACK INTERVAL, DISTRACTION, AND TASK DIFFICULTY AS FACTORS IN A MODIFIED CONCEPT-IDENTIFICATION TASK WITH JUNIOR HIGH SCHOOL SUBJECTS EJ 047 677

THE DEVELOPMENT OF THE PROPORTIONALITY SCHEME IN CHILDREN AND ADOLESCENTS EJ 047 682
COGNITIVE MEDIATION OF DEVELOPMENTAL TRENDS IN EXTREME RESPONSE CHOICE EJ 047 688
THE EFFECTS OF ENRICHED NEONATAL EXPERIENCES UPON LATER COGNITIVE FUNCTIONING EJ 047 689
OBJECT CONSTRUCTION AND IMITATION UNDER DIFFERING CONDITIONS OF REARING EJ 048 305
A DEVELOPMENTAL COMPARISON OF IDENTITY AND EQUIVALENCE CONSERVATIONS EJ 049 167
STRENGTH OF DIMENSIONAL PREFERENCES AS A PREDICTOR OF NURSERY-SCHOOL CHILDREN'S PERFORMANCE ON A CONCEPT-SHIFT TASK EJ 049 169
CLASSIFICATORY SCHEMES IN RELATION TO CLASS INCLUSION BEFORE AND AFTER TRAINING EJ 049 171
INTELLECTUAL EVOLUTION FROM ADOLESCENCE TO ADULTHOOD EJ 050 073
VERBAL REGULATION OF MOTOR BEHAVIOR-SOVIET RESEARCH AND NON-SOVIET REPLICATIONS EJ 050 074
THINKING BEFORE LANGUAGE? A SYMPOSIUM: 1. RELATIONSHIPS BETWEEN LANGUAGE AND THOUGHT EJ 050 075
AN EXAMINATION OF THE DEVELOPMENTAL RELATIONS BETWEEN CERTAIN SPATIAL TASKS EJ 051 563
MOTHER-CHILD INTERACTIONS AND COGNITIVE DEVELOPMENT IN CHILDREN EJ 051 567
READING INSTRUCTION AND COGNITIVE DEVELOPMENT EJ 052 066
PREDICTION OF INTELLECTUAL PERFORMANCE AT 3 YEARS FROM INFANT TESTS AND PERSONALITY MEASURES EJ 052 237
MATERNAL WARMTH, ACHIEVEMENT MOTIVATION, AND COGNITIVE FUNCTIONING IN LOWER-CLASS PRESCHOOL CHILDREN EJ 053 745
WORD-ASSOCIATION RESPONSES OF CHILDREN AS A FUNCTION OF AGE, SEX AND INSTRUCTIONS EJ 055 096
FORMAL OPERATIONS IN FEMALES FROM ELEVEN TO FIFTY-FOUR YEARS OF AGE EJ 055 215
SUCCESS AND ACCOUNTABILITY EJ 055 533
PEER INTERACTION AND COGNITIVE DEVELOPMENT EJ 056 708
A DEVELOPMENTAL STUDY OF FREE CLASSIFICATION IN CHILDREN EJ 056 730
DEVELOPMENTAL AND EXPERIMENTAL FACTORS ASSOCIATED WITH INFERENTIAL BEHAVIOR EJ 057 905
ATTACHMENT: ITS ORIGINS AND COURSE EJ 058 586
OUTERDIRECTEDNESS AND IMITATIVE BEHAVIOR OF INSTITUTIONALIZED AND NONINSTITUTIONALIZED YOUNGER AND OLDER CHILDREN EJ 058 694
RELATION OF TYPE AND ONSET OF FATHER ABSENCE TO COGNITIVE DEVELOPMENT EJ 058 695
INFANCY AND THE OPTIMAL LEVEL OF STIMULATION EJ 058 697
TREATMENT OF PROBLEMS ASSOCIATED WITH COGNITIVE AND PERCEPTUAL-MOTOR DEFICITS EJ 060 501
PERCEPTION AND LANGUAGE: A GERMAN REPLICATION OF THE PIAGET-INHELDER POSITION EJ 060 773
AN EXPERIMENTAL STUDY OF THE SELECTIVE ATTENTION OF CHILDREN OF 1896 AND 1966 EJ 060 775
CHILDREN'S UNDERSTANDING OF SPATIAL RELATIONS: COORDINATION OF PERSPECTIVES EJ 061 068

COGNITIVE MEASUREMENT

DEVELOPMENT OF APPROPRIATE EVALUATION TECHNIQUES FOR SCREENING CHILDREN IN A HEAD START PROGRAM. A PILOT PROJECT. ED015006
COGNITIVE DEVELOPMENT IN INFANTS OF DIFFERENT AGE LEVELS AND FROM DIFFERENT ENVIRONMENTAL BACKGROUNDS. ED015786
TRAINING EFFECTS AND CONCEPT DEVELOPMENT--A STUDY OF THE CONSERVATION OF CONTINUOUS QUANTITY IN CHILDREN. ED016533
EVALUATION OF THE CLEVELAND CHILD DEVELOPMENT PROGRAM. A LONGITUDINAL STUDY (FIRST YEAR REPORT). ED020000
DEVELOPING COGNITIVE LEARNINGS WITH YOUNG CHILDREN. ED041614
A LONGITUDINAL STUDY OF PIAGET'S DEVELOPMENTAL STAGES AND OF THE CONCEPT OF REGRESSION. ED043372
CHILD DEVELOPMENT RESEARCH AND EVALUATION CENTER FOR HEAD START, TEMPLE UNIVERSITY, 1968 - 1969. ANNUAL REPORT. ED043388
IMPULSIVITY & REFLECTIVITY AS REFLECTED BY THE VARIABLES OF TIME AND ERROR. ED047820

SOCIAL CLASS INTELLIGENCE, AND COGNITIVE STYLE IN INFANCY EJ 056 725

COGNITIVE OBJECTIVES

COGNITIVE STYLE: METHODOLOGICAL AND DEVELOPMENTAL CONSIDERATIONS EJ 053 482
COGNITIVE AND AFFECTIVE REACTIONS OF KINDERGARTNERS TO VIDEO DISPLAYS EJ 057 016

DELAY OF FEEDBACK INTERVAL, POSTFEEDBACK INTERVAL, DISTRACTION, AND TASK DIFFICULTY AS FACTORS IN A MODIFIED CONCEPT-IDENTIFICATION TASK WITH JUNIOR HIGH SCHOOL SUBJECTS EJ 047 677

COGNITIVE PROCESSES

COGNITIVE PROCESSES IN THE DEVELOPMENT OF CHILDREN'S APPRECIATION OF HUMOR. ED020784
THE RELATION BETWEEN TEST ANXIETY AND NEED FOR MEMORY SUPPORT IN PROBLEM SOLVING. REVISED RESEARCH MEMORANDUM NO. 11. ED021616
THE EFFECT OF SUBJECT-DETERMINED VERBALIZATION ON DISCRIMINATION LEARNING IN PRESCHOOLERS. ED021620
SIX STRUCTURE-OF-INTELLECT HYPOTHESES IN SIX-YEAR-OLD CHILDREN. ED023469
A PRELIMINARY SEARCH FOR FORMAL OPERATIONS STRUCTURES. ED024471
THE IDENTIFICATION AND ASSESSMENT OF THINKING ABILITY IN YOUNG CHILDREN. FINAL REPORT. ED025316
ERROR, RESPONSE TIME AND IQ: SEX DIFFERENCES IN COGNITIVE STYLE OF PRESCHOOL CHILDREN. ED026122
COGNITIVE FACTORS IN SEMANTIC CONDITIONING. A THESIS IN EDUCATIONAL PSYCHOLOGY. ED027069
THE ELEMENTARY MATHEMATICS STUDY: AN INTERIM REPORT ON KINDERGARTEN YEAR RESULTS. ED027937
A STUDY OF LANGUAGE DEVIATIONS AND COGNITIVE PROCESSES. PROGRESS REPORT NO. 3. ED027958
A COMPARISON OF RELATIVE STRUCTURAL LEVELS ON A VARIETY OF COGNITIVE TASKS. ED032923
ON COGNIZING COGNITIVE PROCESSES. ED035437
AN INVESTIGATION OF THE MANNER IN WHICH YOUNG CHILDREN PROCESS INTELLECTUAL INFORMATION. FINAL REPORT. ED036313
ATTENTIONAL PREFERENCE AND EXPERIENCE: I. INTRODUCTION. ED040751
A STUDY OF ONE LEARNER COGNITIVE STYLE AND THE ABILITY TO GENERALIZE BEHAVIORAL COMPETENCIES. ED040758
AN EXPERIMENTAL PROGRAM IN CLASSIFICATION AND ATTENTIONAL TRAINING WITH HEAD START CHILDREN. ED044171
CHILDREN'S CONSERVATION OF MULTIPLE SPACE RELATIONS: EFFECTS OF PERCEPTION AND REPRESENTATION. ED044179
INFANT STIMULATION AND THE ETIOLOGY OF COGNITIVE PROCESSES. ED045174
RESULTS AND IMPLICATIONS OF A HEAD START CLASSIFICATION AND ATTENTION TRAINING PROGRAM. ED045182
IMPLICATIONS OF MNEMONICS RESEARCH FOR COGNITIVE THEORY. ED045199
PRELIMINARY ANALYSIS OF 1968-69 BOOTH ACHIEVEMENT. ED045201
PIAGET'S CONCEPT OF CLASSIFICATION: A COMPARATIVE STUDY OF SOCIALLY DISADVANTAGED AND MIDDLE-CLASS YOUNG CHILDREN. ED046499
RULE STRUCTURE AND PROPORTION OF POSITIVE INSTANCES AS DETERMINANTS OF CONCEPT ATTAINMENT IN CHILDREN. ED046500
AN APPLICATION OF PIAGET'S THEORY TO THE CONCEPTUALIZATION OF A PRESCHOOL CURRICULUM. ED046502
NON-VERBAL INFORMATION STORAGE IN HUMANS AND DEVELOPMENTAL INFORMATION PROCESSING CHANNEL CAPACITY. ED047800
IMPLICATIONS OF POST-NATAL CORTICAL DEVELOPMENT FOR CREATIVITY RESEARCH. ED047802
A STUDY IN TRAINING NURSERY CHILDREN ON LOGICAL OPERATIONAL SKILLS. ED047803
THE EFFECT OF VARYING OBJECT NUMBER AND TYPE OF ARRANGEMENT ON CHILDREN'S ABILITY TO COORDINATE PERSPECTIVES. ED047804
DECENTRATION IN CHILDREN: ITS GENERALITY AND CORRELATES. ED048926
A STUDY OF CAUSAL THINKING IN ELEMENTARY SCHOOL CHILDREN. FINAL REPORT. ED050830
COGNITIVE STUDIES VOLUME 2: DEFICITS IN COGNITION. ED053792
AN EXPERIMENTAL APPROACH TO THE EFFECT OF GROUP ANIMADVERSION EJ 012 678
THE INFUENCE OF SOME TASK VARIABLES AND OF SOCIOECONOMIC CLASS ON THE MANIFESTATION OF CONSERVATION OF NUMBER EJ 017 711
CHILDREN'S JUDGMENTS OF KINDNESS EJ 018 259
DEPENDENCE OF LAUGHTER ON COGNITIVE STRATEGIES EJ 023 964
LONGITUDINAL STUDY OF COGNITIVE DICTIONARIES FROM AGES NINE TO SEVENTEEN EJ 024 940
FREEDOM TO MANIPULATE OBJECTS AND QUESTION-ASKING PERFORMANCE OF SIX-YEAR-OLDS EJ 029 217
MODEL FOR A THINKING MCHINE: AN INFORMATION-PROCESSING FRAMEWORK FOR THE STUDY OF COGNITIVE DEVELOPMENT EJ 030 289
THE DEVELOPMENT OF FREE CLASSIFICATION AND FREE RECALL IN CHILDREN EJ 030 293
THE DEVELOPMENT OF CLASSIFICATORY SKILLS IN YOUNG CHILDREN: A TRAINING PROGRAM EJ 031 872
PATTERNS OF INFORMATION PROCESSING USED BY AND WITH YOUNG CHILDREN IN A NURSERY SCHOOL SETTING EJ 032 890
INTELLECTUAL OPERATIONS IN TEACHER QUESTION-ASKING BEHAVIOR EJ 032 895
LEARNING OF MEDIA CONTENT: A DEVELOPMENTAL STUDY EJ 033 782
ARE THESE TWO STIMULI FROM THE SAME SET? RESPONSE TIMES OF CHILDREN AND ADULTS WITH FAMILIAR AND ARBITRARY SETS EJ 033 788

EFFECTS OF MEMORY AIDS ON HYPOTHESIS BEHAVIOR AND FOCUSING IN YOUNG CHILDREN AND ADULTS EJ 033 789
CHILDREN'S TWO-CHOICE LEARNING OF PREDOMINANTLY ALTERNATING AND REPEATING SEQUENCES EJ 033 791
EMOTIONAL CONCOMITANTS OF VISUAL MASTERY IN INFANTS: THE EFFECTS OF STIMULUS MOVEMENT ON SMILING AND VOCALIZING EJ 033 794
NOVELTY, FAMILIARITY, AND THE DEVELOPMENT OF INFANT ATTENTION EJ 034 529
ESTIMATES AND ESTIMATE-BASED INFERENCES IN YOUNG CHILDREN EJ 034 541
DIMENSIONAL SALIENCE AND IDENTIFICATION OF THE RELEVANT DIMENSION IN PROBLEM SOLVING: A DEVELOPMENTAL STUDY EJ 035 360
INTERRELATIONS AMONG LEARNING AND PERFORMANCE TASKS AT THE PRESCHOOL LEVEL EJ 035 361
DEVELOPMENTAL PATTERNS FOR CHILDREN'S CLASS AND CONDITIONAL REASONING ABILITIES EJ 035 362
THE RELATIONSHIP BETWEEN INTELLIGENCE AND PERFORMANCE ON THE STROOP COLOR-WORD TEST IN SECOND- AND FIFTH-GRADE CHILDREN EJ 035 887
THE RELATION OF ROLE TAKING TO THE DEVELOPMENT OF MORAL JUDGMENT IN CHILDREN EJ 035 991
STORY RECALL IN KINDERGARTEN CHILDREN: EFFECT OF METHOD OF PRESENTATION ON PSYCHOLINGUISTIC PERFORMANCE EJ 036 748
EFFECTS OF STIMULUS AVAILABILITY ON CHILDREN'S INFERENCES EJ 036 822
A PERSPECTIVE ON COGNITIVE DEVELOPMENT: THE PRESCHOOL CHILD'S PERFORMANCE IN CLASSIFICATION TASKS EJ 036 827
IDEATIONAL CREATIVITY AND EXPRESSIVE ASPECTS OF HUMAN FIGURE DRAWING IN KINDERGARTEN-AGE CHILDREN EJ 039 629
THE INFLUENCE OF AGE AND STIMULUS DIMENSIONALITY ON FORM PERCEPTION BY PRESCHOOL CHILDREN EJ 039 630
COGNITIVE COMPONENTS OF SEPARATION ANXIETY EJ 039 900
CLASSIFICATION PATTERNS OF UNDERPRIVILEGED CHILDREN IN ISRAEL EJ 041 140
THE ASSESSMENT OF DIFFERENCES IN CONCEPTUAL STYLE EJ 041 146
CHILDREN'S DESCRIPTIONS OF PEERS: A WERNERIAN DEVELOPMENTAL ANALYSIS EJ 041 591
COGNITIVE STYLE AND CLASSIFICATION EJ 044 706
REFLECTION-IMPULSIVITY AND COLOR-FORM SORTING EJ 046 234
THE INFLUENCE OF COGNITIVE STYLE ON PERCEPTUAL LEARNING EJ 046 238
PIAGET'S CONCEPT OF CLASSIFICATION: A COMPARATIVE STUDY OF SOCIALLY DISADVANTAGED AND MIDDLE-CLASS YOUNG CHILDREN EJ 046 239
EXTINCTION OF CONSERVATION: A METHODOLOGICAL AND THEORETICAL ANALYSIS EJ 046 245
RECOGNITION MEMORY: THE RELATIONSHIP OF ACCURACY AND LATENCY OF RESPONSE UNDER DIFFERENT MEMORY LOADS IN RETARDATES EJ 046 256
MODIFICATION OF IMPULSIVE AND REFLECTIVE COGNITIVE STYLES THROUGH OBSERVATION OF FILM-MEDIATED MODELS EJ 047 676
THE DEVELOPMENT OF THE PROPORTIONALITY SCHEME IN CHILDREN AND ADOLESCENTS EJ 047 682
TITRATING DELAYED MATCHING TO SAMPLE IN CHILDREN EJ 047 684
COGNITIVE MEDIATION OF DEVELOPMENTAL TRENDS IN EXTREME RESPONSE CHOICE EJ 047 688
COGNITIVE STYLE: METHODOLOGICAL AND DEVELOPMENTAL CONSIDERATIONS EJ 053 482
THE NAMING OF PRIMARY COLORS BY CHILDREN EJ 053 483
CHILDREN'S MORAL REASONING EJ 055 097
COMING OF AGE WITH THE DELBOEUF ILLUSION: BRIGHTNESS CONTRAST, COGNITION AND PERCEPTUAL DEVELOPMENT EJ 055 100
DEVELOPMENT OF HIERARCHIES OF DIMENSIONAL SALIENCE EJ 055 102
INFORMATION AND STRATEGY IN THE YOUNG CHILD'S SEARCH FOR HIDDEN OBJECTS EJ 056 395
MODELING EFFECTS UPON CONCEPTUAL STYLE AND COGNITIVE TEMPO EJ 056 396
IDENTITY AND EQUIVALENCE CONSERVATION AT TWO AGE LEVELS EJ 057 901
RELATIONSHIP OF PRESCHOOL SOCIAL-EMOTIONAL FUNCTIONING TO LATER INTELLECTUAL ACHIEVEMENT EJ 058 138
CONCRETE OPERATIONAL THINKING IN MENTALLY ILL ADOLESCENTS EJ 060 778
THE ROLE OF INCONGRUITY AND RESOLUTION IN CHILDREN'S APPRECIATION OF CARTOON HUMOR EJ 060 781

COGNITIVE TESTS
HEAD START EVALUATION AND RESEARCH CENTER. PROGRESS REPORT OF RESEARCH STUDIES 1966 TO 1967. DOCUMENT 1, DEVELOPMENT OF THE MATRIX TEST. ED021623
HEAD START EVALUATION AND RESEARCH CENTER, THE UNIVERSITY OF CHICAGO. REPORT E, COMPARATIVE USE OF ALTERNATIVE MODES FOR ASSESSING COGNITIVE DEVELOPMENT IN BILINGUAL OR NON-ENGLISH SPEAKING CHILDREN. ED022554
PAPER-AND-PENCIL VERSUS CONCRETE PERFORMANCE OF NORMALS AND RETARDATES ON THE ETS WRITTEN EXERCISES. ED035442
AN EXPLORATORY STUDY OF THE RELATIONSHIP BETWEEN COGNITIVE PRETESTING AND COURSE ACHIEVEMENT EJ 041 758

COLLECTIVE BARGANING
STRIKES, SANCTIONS, OR SURRENDER? EJ 003 417

COLLECTIVE SETTLEMENTS
SYMPOSIUM ON ALTERNATIVE COMMUNITIES: CHILDREN OF THE GROUP FAMILY EJ 049 657
SOME THOUGHTS ON COMMUNAL CHILDREARING EJ 049 658

COLLEGE BOUND STUDENTS
EFFECTS OF PARENTAL EXPECTATIONS OF EDUCATIONAL PLANS OF WHITE AND NONWHITE ADOLESCENTS. FINAL REPORT. ED027096

COLLEGE CURRICULUM
LEARNING AND TEACHING, GRADES N-9 (EMPHASIS ON MIDDLE GRADES). ED024467

COLLEGE FRESHMEN
A LONGITUDINAL STUDY OF CHANGES IN EGO IDENTITY STATUS DURING THE FRESHMAN YEAR AT COLLEGE EJ 043 193

COLLEGE PROGRAMS
ENCOURAGING STUDENTS' RESEARCH ON COGNITIVE DEVELOPMENT. ED031301

COLLEGE SCHOOL COOPERATION
THE SCHOOL AND THE UNIVERSITY: CO-OPERATIVE ROLES IN STUDENT TEACHING EJ 015 981

COLLEGE STUDENTS
ANXIETY, AFFILIATION, AND SOCIAL ISOLATION EJ 027 343
PERCEPTUAL EXPLORATION IN ISRAELI CHILDREN EJ 033 054
RELIABILITY ASSESSMENT OF OBSERVATION DATA: A POSSIBLE METHODOLOGICAL PROBLEM EJ 033 313
ARE THESE TWO STIMULI FROM THE SAME SET? RESPONSE TIMES OF CHILDREN AND ADULTS WITH FAMILIAR AND ARBITRARY SETS EJ 033 788
EFFECTS OF MEMORY AIDS ON HYPOTHESIS BEHAVIOR AND FOCUSING IN YOUNG CHILDREN AND ADULTS EJ 033 789
SENSORY-SET FACTORS IN AGE DIFFERENCES IN REACTION TIME EJ 048 304
DEVELOPMENTAL CHANGES IN CLUSTERING CRITERIA EJ 058 145
CREATIVITY: IDEA QUANTITY AND IDEA QUALITY EJ 058 212

COLOR
CULTURAL DIFFERENCES IN COLOR/FORM PREFERENCE AND IN CLASSIFICATORY BEHAVIOR EJ 024 034
THE GENERALITY OF COLOR-FORM PREFERENCE AS A FUNCTION OF MATERIALS AND TASK REQUIREMENTS AMONG LOWER-CLASS NEGRO CHILDREN EJ 033 052
DIMENSIONAL SALIENCE AND IDENTIFICATION OF THE RELEVANT DIMENSION IN PROBLEM SOLVING: A DEVELOPMENTAL STUDY EJ 035 360
"FOCAL" COLOR AREAS AND THE DEVELOPMENT OF COLOR NAMES EJ 039 057
STIMULUS SELECTION AS A FUNCTION OF LETTER COLOR AND AGE IN PAIRED-ASSOCIATE LEARNING EJ 043 705
REFLECTION-IMPULSIVITY AND COLOR-FORM SORTING EJ 046 234
RELATIONS OF AGE AND INTELLIGENCE TO SHORT-TERM COLOR MEMORY EJ 056 392
VARIABLES AFFECTING ASSOCIATIVE RECALL IN CHILDREN EJ 056 400

COLORS
THE NAMING OF PRIMARY COLORS BY CHILDREN EJ 053 483

COMMUNICATION (THOUGHT TRANSFER)
THE COGNITIVE ENVIRONMENTS OF URBAN PRE-SCHOOL CHILDREN. MANUAL OF INSTRUCTIONS FOR ADMINISTERING AND SCORING FIRST DAY. ED018258
HEAD START EVALUATION AND RESEARCH CENTER, BOSTON UNIVERSITY. REPORT C-I, PERCEPTION OF EMOTION AMONG CHILDREN: RACE AND SEX DIFFERENCES. ED022561
LANGUAGE EXPERIENCES WHICH PROMOTE READING. ED034571
OBSERVED COGNITIVE COMMUNICATION PATTERNS OF ADULTS AND CHILDREN IN FOUR PRE-SCHOOL AGE GROUPS. ED036325
A STUDY OF COMMUNICATION PATTERNS IN DISADVANTAGED CHILDREN. ED037250
HELPING CHILDREN COPE WITH FEELINGS. EJ 002 018
TOY TALK: THE NEW CONVERSATION BETWEEN GENERATIONS EJ 020 395
CHILD VERSUS ADULT PERCEPTION OF EVALUATIVE MESSAGES IN VERBAL, VOCAL, AND VISUAL CHANNELS EJ 021 765
CHILDREN'S COMMUNICATION ACCURACY RELATED TO RACE AND SOCIOECONOMIC STATUS EJ 040 359
EFFECTS OF STIMULUS ABSTRACTNESS AND FAMILIARITY ON LISTENER'S PERFORMANCE IN A COMMUNICATION TASK EJ 046 241
SOME ANGLES ON PARENT-TEACHER LEARNING EJ 054 162
SOME COGNITIVE AND AFFECTIVE ASPECTS OF EARLY LANGUAGE DEVELOPMENT EJ 055 655

COMMUNICATION PROBLEMS
DISSEMINATION AND UTILIZATION OF KNOWLEDGE IN THE AREA OF EARLY CHILDHOOD EDUCATION: A DESCRIPTION OF SOME OF THE PROBLEMS. ED044185
COMMUNICATING WITH TODAY'S TEENAGERS; AN EXERCISE BETWEEN GENERATIONS EJ 011 838
THE ELEMENTS OF EFFECTIVE COMMUNICATION EJ 011 845

WHAT MOTHERS NEED EJ 013 233
PSYCHOPHYSIOLOGIC AND CONVERSION REACTIONS IN CHILDREN: SELECTIVE INCIDENCE IN VERBAL AND NONVERBAL FAMILIES EJ 023 429
THE FUNCTION OF AMBIGUITY IN CHILD CRISES EJ 027 344
SOME ANGLES ON PARENT-TEACHER LEARNING EJ 054 162
PERCEPTUAL INADEQUACY AND COMMUNICATIVE INEFFECTIVENESS IN INTERPERSONAL COMMUNICATION EJ 056 627

COMMUNICATION SKILLS
THE HUMAN CONNECTION--LANGUAGE AND LITERATURE. ED018271
THE DEVELOPMENT OF ROLE-TAKING AND COMMUNICATION SKILLS IN CHILDREN. ED027082
CREATIVITY AND THE LEARNING PROCESS. 1970 WHITE HOUSE CONFERENCE ON CHILDREN, REPORT OF FORUM 6. (WORKING PAPER). ED046525
COMMUNICATING WITH TODAY'S TEENAGERS; AN EXERCISE BETWEEN GENERATIONS EJ 011 838
THE ELEMENTS OF EFFECTIVE COMMUNICATION EJ 011 845
SUGGESTIONS FROM STUDIES OF EARLY LANGUAGE ACQUISITION EJ 012 396
INTERVENTION STRATEGIES FOR SPANISH-SPEAKING PRESCHOOL CHILDREN EJ 036 746
THE TEACHER STRUCTURE CHECKLIST: A POSSIBLE TOOL FOR COMMUNICATION EJ 051 352
TRAINING COMMUNICATION SKILLS IN YOUNG CHILDREN EJ 058 606

COMMUNICATIONS
THEY BECAME WHAT THEY BEHELD EJ 045 423

COMMUNITY ACTION
COMMUNITY COORDINATED CHILD CARE: 1. INTERIM POLICY GUIDANCE FOR THE 4-C PROGRAM ED034579
CONTROL OF LEAD POISONING IN CHILDREN. (PRE-PUBLICATION DRAFT). ED050825
A STUDY IN CHILD CARE (CASE STUDY FROM VOLUME II-A): "GOOD VIBES." DAY CARE PROGRAMS REPRINT SERIES. ED051894

COMMUNITY AGENCIES (PUBLIC)
HEAD START'S INFLUENCE ON COMMUNITY CHANGE EJ 026 773
OPTIMAL OPERATION OF PUBLIC/PRIVATE CHILD WELFARE DELIVERY SYSTEMS EJ 031 540
ESTABLISHMENT OF DAY CARE PROGRAMS FOR THE MENTALLY RETARDED EJ 047 342

COMMUNITY ATTITUDES
AN EVALUATION OF OPERATION HEAD START BILINGUAL CHILDREN, SUMMER, 1965. ED013667
EVALUATION OF PROJECT HEAD START READING READINESS IN ISSAQUENA AND SHARKEY COUNTIES, MISSISSIPPI, SUMMER, 1965. FINAL REPORT. ED014319
RESEARCH IN A BLACK COMMUNITY: FOUR YEARS IN REVIEW. ED039035
VOLUNTEERING TO HELP INDIANS HELP THEMSELVES EJ 032 412
THE PRESCHOOL IN RURAL INDIA EJ 036 334

COMMUNITY CONTROL
A STUDY IN CHILD CARE (CASE STUDY FROM VOLUME II-A): "ALL KINDS OF LOVE--IN A CHINESE RESTAURANT." DAY CARE PROGRAMS REPRINT SERIES. ED051903

COMMUNITY COOPERATION
RESEARCH IN A BLACK COMMUNITY: FOUR YEARS IN REVIEW. ED039035
ESTABLISHMENT OF DAY CARE PROGRAMS FOR THE MENTALLY RETARDED EJ 047 342

COMMUNITY COORDINATION
THE 4-C PROGRAM EJ 007 090

COMMUNITY EDUCATION
A NATIONAL SURVEY OF THE IMPACTS OF HEAD START CENTERS ON COMMUNITY INSTITUTIONS. ED045195
A NATIONAL SURVEY OF THE IMPACTS OF HEAD START CENTERS ON COMMUNITY INSTITUTIONS. SUMMARY REPORT. ED046516

COMMUNITY HEALTH SERVICES
INVOLVING PARENTS IN A CHILDREN'S CLINIC EJ 047 353
PROJECT TREAT: A NEW APPROACH TO THE SEVERELY DISTURBED CHILD EJ 061 000

COMMUNITY INFLUENCE
HEAD START'S INFLUENCE ON COMMUNITY CHANGE EJ 026 773

COMMUNITY INVOLVEMENT
THE IMPACT OF OPERATION HEAD START ON GREENE COUNTY, OHIO, AN EVALUATION REPORT. ED020772
PRESCHOOL EDUCATION AND POVERTY: THE DISTANCE IN BETWEEN. FINAL REPORT OF 1968-69 INTERVENTIONAL PROGRAM. ED046501
PROCEEDINGS OF THE CONFERENCE ON INDUSTRY AND DAY CARE (URBAN RESEARCH CORPORATION, CHICAGO, 1970). ED047780
A STUDY IN CHILD CARE (CASE STUDY FROM VOLUME II-A): "LIKE BEING AT HOME." DAY CARE PROGRAMS REPRINT SERIES. ED051899
A STUDY IN CHILD CARE (CASE STUDY FROM VOLUME II-A): "LIFE IS GOOD, RIGHT? RIGHT!" DAY CARE PROGRAMS REPRINT SERIES. ED051901
HEAD START IN ALASKA EJ 008 273
FOUNDATIONS FOR GOOD BEGINNINGS EJ 010 588
COMMUNITY PARTICIPATION IN PRESCHOOL EDUCATION--WHY AND HOW EJ 036 331
PRESCHOOL EDUCATION, PARENTS AND THE COMMUNITY IN A DEVELOPING SOCIETY EJ 036 333
THE SCHOOL SOCIAL WORKER'S ROLE IN OVERCOMING LEARNING HANDICAPS EJ 046 401

COMMUNITY MIGRANT PROJECTS
A GUIDE TO THE PLANNING AND OPERATION OF A CHILD DEVELOPMENT CENTER FOR MIGRANT CHILDREN AND A REPORT OF THE HOOPESTON CHILD DEVELOPMENT CENTER ED049838

COMMUNITY ORGANIZATIONS
A STUDY IN CHILD CARE (CASE STUDY FROM VOLUME II-A): "ALL KINDS OF LOVE--IN A CHINESE RESTAURANT." DAY CARE PROGRAMS REPRINT SERIES. ED051903

COMMUNITY PLANNING
A SURVEY AND EVALUATION OF PROJECT HEAD START AS ESTABLISHED AND OPERATED IN COMMUNITIES OF THE COMMONWEALTH OF MASSACHUSETTS DURING THE SUMMER OF 1965. ED014324

COMMUNITY PROBLEMS
PARENTAL AND COMMUNITY NEGLECT--TWIN RESPONSIBILITIES OF PROTECTIVE SERVICES EJ 007 446

COMMUNITY PROGRAMS
A PRELIMINARY INVESTIGATION TO ESTABLISH A REGIONAL CENTER FOR EDUCATIONAL DEVELOPMENTAL STUDIES OF DISADVANTAGED PRESCHOOL CHILDREN. FINAL REPORT. ED017318
DISTURBANCE AND DISSONANCE - COMMUNITY UNIVERSITY COLLABORATION IN DIAGNOSIS AND TREATMENT OF DISTURBANCES. ED030485

COMMUNITY RESOURCES
EXPRESSIONS OF IDENTITY: THE SCHOOL-AGE CHILD. 1970 WHITE HOUSE CONFERENCE ON CHILDREN, REPORT OF FORUM 3. (WORKING COPY). ED046522

COMMUNITY RESPONSIBILITY
CHILDREN AND PARENTS: TOGETHER IN THE WORLD. 1970 WHITE HOUSE CONFERENCE ON CHILDREN, REPORT OF FORUM 15. (WORKING COPY). ED046531
PARENTAL AND COMMUNITY NEGLECT--TWIN RESPONSIBILITIES OF PROTECTIVE SERVICES EJ 007 446
A CITY FOR CHILDREN: THE YEAR 2005 EJ 049 562

COMMUNITY ROLE
AN INSTITUTIONAL ANALYSIS OF DAY CARE PROGRAM. PART II, GROUP DAY CARE: THE GROWTH OF AN INSTITUTION. FINAL REPORT. ED043394

COMMUNITY SERVICE PROGRAMS
CREATING CHILD CARE COMMUNITIES THROUGH 4-C PROGRAMS EJ 051 239

COMMUNITY SERVICES
COMMUNITY COORDINATED CHILD CARE: A FEDERAL PARTNERSHIP IN BEHALF OF CHILDREN. FINAL REPORT. ED048925
COMMUNITY COORDINATED CHILD CARE: A FEDERAL PARTNERSHIP IN BEHALF OF CHILDREN. SUMMARY. ED048944
A STUDY IN CHILD CARE (CASE STUDY FROM VOLUME II-A): "GOOD VIBES." DAY CARE PROGRAMS REPRINT SERIES. ED051894

COMMUNITY STUDY
PROJECT HEAD START AND THE CULTURALLY DEPRIVED IN ROCHESTER, NEW YORK, A STUDY OF PARTICIPATING AND NON-PARTICIPATING FAMILIES IN AREAS SERVED BY PROJECT HEAD START IN ROCHESTER, FINAL REPORT. ED013669
A SURVEY AND EVALUATION OF PROJECT HEAD START AS ESTABLISHED AND OPERATED IN COMMUNITIES OF THE COMMONWEALTH OF MASSACHUSETTS DURING THE SUMMER OF 1965. ED014324
PROJECT HEAD START IN AN INDIAN COMMUNITY. ED014329
NORTHFIELD, VERMONT--A COMMUNITY DEPTH STUDY. ED018245
A NATIONAL SURVEY OF THE IMPACTS OF HEAD START CENTERS ON COMMUNITY INSTITUTIONS. ED045195
A NATIONAL SURVEY OF THE IMPACTS OF HEAD START CENTERS ON COMMUNITY INSTITUTIONS. SUMMARY REPORT. ED046516

COMPARATIVE ANALYSIS
AN EVALUATION OF HEAD START PRESCHOOL ENRICHMENT PROGRAMS AS THEY AFFECT THE INTELLECTUAL ABILITY, THE SOCIAL ADJUSTMENT, AND THE ACHIEVEMENT LEVEL OF FIVE-YEAR-OLD CHILDREN ENROLLED IN LINCOLN, NEBRASKA. ED015011
COMPARATIVE STUDIES OF A GROUP OF HEAD START AND A GROUP OF NON-HEAD START PRESCHOOL CHILDREN. FINAL REPORT. ED015013
A COMPARISON OF THE DEVELOPMENTAL DRAWING CHARACTERISTICS OF CULTURALLY ADVANTAGED AND CULTURALLY DISADVANTAGED CHILDREN. FINAL REPORT. ED015783
A COMPARATIVE STUDY OF TWO PRESCHOOL PROGRAMS FOR CULTURALLY DISADVANTAGED CHILDREN--A HIGHLY STRUCTURED AND A TRADITIONAL PROGRAM. ED016524
THE EFFECTS OF JUNIOR KINDERGARTEN ON ACHIEVEMENT--THE FIRST FIVE YEARS. APPENDIX. ED016527
MONTESSORI PRE-SCHOOL EDUCATION. FINAL REPORT. ED017320

PROJECT HEAD START--SUMMER 1966. FINAL REPORT. SECTION TWO, FACILITIES AND RESOURCES OF HEAD START CENTERS. ED018247
DIFFERENTIATION BETWEEN NORMAL AND DISORDERED CHILDREN BY A COMPUTER ANALYSIS OF EMOTIONAL AND VERBAL BEHAVIOR. ED019138
THE SYNTACTIC STRUCTURES OF 5-YEAR-OLD CULTURALLY DEPRIVED CHILDREN. ED020788
PILOT STUDY OF FIVE METHODS OF PRESENTING THE SUMMER HEAD START CURRICULAR PROGRAM. ED021622
HEAD START EVALUATION AND RESEARCH CENTER. PROGRESS REPORT OF RESEARCH STUDIES 1966 TO 1967. DOCUMENT 5, COMPARATIVE ITEM-CONTENT ANALYSIS OF ACHIEVEMENT TEST PERFORMANCE IN YOUNG CHILDREN. ED021627
A COMPARISON OF WISC AND OSA IN ASSESSING THE INTELLIGENCE OF IMMIGRANT CHILDREN OF NON-ENGLISH SPEAKING BACKGROUND. A PILOT PROJECT. ED022526
A COMPARISON OF THE PSYCHOLINGUISTIC FUNCTIONING OF "EDUCATIONALLY-DEPRIVED" AND "EDUCATIONALLY-ADVANTAGED" CHILDREN. ED022537
AN EVALUATION OF THE PRESCHOOL READINESS CENTERS PROGRAM IN EAST ST. LOUIS, ILLINOIS, JULY 1, 1967-JUNE 30, 1968. FINAL REPORT. ED023472
COGNITIVE AND LINGUISTIC DEFICITS IN PSYCHOTIC CHILDREN. STUDY M: DEVELOPMENT OF SELECTIVE ATTENTION ABILITIES. ED024440
COMPARATIVE EFFECTIVENESS OF ECHOIC AND MODELING PROCEDURES IN LANGUAGE INSTRUCTION WITH CULTURALLY DISADVANTAGED CHILDREN. ED025314
LEARNING READINESS IN TWO JEWISH GROUPS: A STUDY IN "CULTURAL DEPRIVATION." AN OCCASIONAL PAPER. ED026126
ACQUISTION AND TRANSFER DIFFERENCES BETWEEN KINDERGARTENERS AND SECOND-GRADERS ON AURALLY AND VISUALLY PRESENTED PAIRED-ASSOCIATES USING AN A-B, A-C DESIGN RESEARCH PROJECT NUMBER 2 OF PROJECT HEAD START RESEARCH AND EVALUATION CENTER, SYRACUSE UNIVERSITY RESEARCH INSTITUTE. FINAL REPORT, NOVEMBER 1, 1967. ED026139
FURTHER EVIDENCE ON THE RELATION BETWEEN AGE OF SEPARATION AND SIMILARITY IN IQ AMONG PAIRS OF SEPARATED IDENTICAL TWINS. ED027058
AN APPRAISAL OF HEAD START PARTICIPANTS AND NON-PARTICIPANTS: EXPANDED CONSIDERATIONS ON LEARNING DISABILITIES AMONG DISADVANTAGED CHILDREN. ED027939
A COMPARATIVE STUDY OF THE SELF-IMAGES OF DISADVANTAGED CHILDREN. ED028821
A COMPARISON OF THE READING READINESS OF KINDERGARTEN PUPILS EXPOSED TO CONCEPTUAL-LANGUAGE AND BASAL READER PREREADING PROGRAMS. A PILOT STUDY. FINAL REPORT. ED029709
SIX SCHOOL READINESS SCREENING DEVICES USED IN PEDIATRIC OFFICES: CONCURRENT VALIDITY. FINAL REPORT. ED029719
A STUDY OF EARLY ELEMENTARY TEACHER EVALUATION OF SELECTED EYE-HAND COORDINATION SKILLS OF KINDERGARTEN CHILDREN. INGHAM INTERMEDIATE COOPERATIVE RESEARCH PROJECT, 1967-68: SUMMARY REPORT. ED030488
LANGUAGE AND ENVIRONMENT: AN INTERIM REPORT ON A LONGITUDINAL STUDY. ED032136
A LONGITUDINAL INVESTIGATION OF MONTESSORI AND TRADITIONAL PREKINDERGARTEN TRAINING WITH INNER CITY CHILDREN: A COMPARATIVE ASSESSMENT OF LEARNING OUTCOMES. THREE PART STUDY. ED034588
INFORMATION EXCHANGE IN MOTHER-CHILD INTERACTIONS. ED034599
FOUR YEARS ON. A FOLLOW-UP STUDY AT SCHOOL LEAVING AGE OF CHILDREN FORMERLY ATTENDING A TRADITIONAL AND A PROGRESSIVE JUNIOR SCHOOL. ED035434
CLASSIFICATION AND INFERENTIAL THINKING IN CHILDREN OF VARYING AGE AND SOCIAL CLASS. ED035446
A COMPARATIVE STUDY OF THREE FORMS OF THE METROPOLITAN READINESS TEST AT TWO SOCIO-ECONOMIC LEVELS. ED035448
CHILDREN AND TEACHERS IN TWO TYPES OF HEAD START CLASSES. ED036324
A LONGITUDINAL STUDY OF DISADVANTAGED CHILDREN WHO PARTICIPATED IN THREE DIFFERENT PRESCHOOL PROGRAMS. ED036338
A STUDY OF COMMUNICATION PATTERNS IN DISADVANTAGED CHILDREN. ED037250
HEAD START PLANNED VARIATION PROGRAM. ED038170
EXPERIMENTAL VARIATION OF HEAD START CURRICULA: A COMPARISON OF CURRENT APPROACHES. (NOVEMBER 1, 1969-JANUARY 31, 1970). ED041617
A COMPARATIVE STUDY OF THE IMPACT OF TWO CONTRASTING EDUCATIONAL APPROACHES IN HEAD START, 1968-69. ED041643
COMPARATIVE STUDY OF THREE PRESCHOOL CURRICULA. ED042484
A COMPARATIVE STUDY OF FAILURE AVOIDANCE IN CULTURALLY DISADVANTAGED AND NON-CULTURALLY DISADVANTAGED FIRST GRADE CHILDREN. ED044170
IMPACT OF THE HEAD START PROGRAM. PHASE I OF A PROJECTED LONGITUDINAL STUDY TO THE U. S. OFFICE OF ECONOMIC OPPORTUNITY. FINAL REPORT. ED045193
PIAGET'S CONCEPT OF CLASSIFICATION: A COMPARATIVE STUDY OF SOCIALLY DISADVANTAGED AND MIDDLE-CLASS YOUNG CHILDREN. ED046499
YPSILANTI PRESCHOOL CURRICULUM DEMONSTRATION PROJECT, 1968-1971. ED046503
A COMPARISON OF CONTRASTING PROGRAMS IN EARLY CHILDHOOD EDUCATION. ED046509
CONCEPT AND LANGUAGE DEVELOPMENT OF A GROUP OF FIVE YEAR OLDS WHO HAVE ATTENDED THE SYRACUSE UNIVERSITY CHILDREN'S CENTER INTERVENTION PROGRAM. ED046515
HEAD START GRADUATES: ONE YEAR LATER. ED048929
THE INFLUENCE OF SELECTED VARIABLES ON THE EFFECTIVENESS OF PRESCHOOL PROGRAMS FOR DISADVANTAGED CHILDREN. ED049835
TWO KINDS OF KINDERGARTEN AFTER FOUR TYPES OF HEAD START. ED050824
ANALYSIS OF EARLY CHILDHOOD PROGRAMS: A SEARCH FOR COMPARATIVE DIMENSIONS. ED051877
AN ACADEMIC PRESCHOOL FOR DISADVANTAGED CHILDREN: REVIEW OF FINDINGS. PRELIMINARY DRAFT. ED051878
EXPERIMENTAL VARIATION OF HEAD START CURRICULA: A COMPARISON OF CURRENT APPROACHES. PROGRESS REPORT NO. 9, MARCH 1, 1971 - MAY 31, 1971. ED053814
SOCIAL REINFORCEMENT FOR EXPRESSION VS. SUPPRESSION OF AGGRESSION EJ 007 691
CHILDREN AND TEACHERS IN TWO TYPES OF HEAD START CLASSES EJ 008 172
COMPARISON OF VERBAL INTERACTION IN TWO PRESCHOOL PROGRAMS EJ 008 274
SIMILARITIES IN VALUES AND OTHER PERSONALITY CHARACTERISTICS IN COLLEGE STUDENTS AND THEIR PARENTS EJ 012 718
COMPARISON OF GROSS, INTENSIVE, AND EXTENSIVE QUANTITIES BY RETARDATES EJ 015 098
ILLEGIBILITIES IN THE CURSIVE HANDWRITING OF SIXTH-GRADERS EJ 019 443
CREATIVITY AND ALIENATION: AN EXPLORATION OF THEIR RELATIONSHIP IN ADOLESCENCE EJ 021 996
SELF-PERCEPTIONS OF PUPILS IN AN EXPERIMENTAL ELEMENTARY SCHOOL EJ 028 239
THE ECONOMIC LITERACY OF ELEMENTARY-SCHOOL PUPILS EJ 029 042
THE DEVELOPMENT OF CLASSIFICATORY SKILLS IN YOUNG CHILDREN: A TRAINING PROGRAM EJ 031 872
RECOGNITION OF FLASHED WORDS BY CHILDREN EJ 032 676
OUTERDIRECTEDNESS IN THE PROBLEM-SOLVING OF INSTITUTIONALIZED AND NONINSTITUTIONALIZED NORMAL AND RETARDED CHILDREN EJ 035 366
SEQUENTIAL LEARNING BY CHILDREN EJ 035 381
WHAT PUPILS KNOW ABOUT VOCABULARY IN MATHEMATICS--1930 AND 1968 EJ 035 466
THE MEASUREMENT OF VISUAL ATTENTION IN INFANTS: A COMPARISON OF TWO METHODOLOGIES EJ 037 494
EFFECT OF INCENTIVES UPON RETARDED AND NORMAL READERS ON A VISUAL-ASSOCIATE LEARNING TASK EJ 038 266
A COMPARATIVE STUDY OF PIAGET'S DEVELOPMENTAL SCHEMA OF SIGHTED CHILDREN WITH THAT OF A GROUP OF BLIND CHILDREN EJ 040 319
THE DISCRIMINATION LEARNING OF NORMAL AND RETARDED CHILDREN AS A FUNCTION OF PENALTY CONDITIONS AND ETIOLOGY OF THE RETARDED EJ 041 136
AN EXPLORATORY STUDY OF THE RELATIONSHIP BETWEEN COGNITIVE PRETESTING AND COURSE ACHIEVEMENT EJ 041 758
PRESCHOOL PLAY NORMS: A REPLICATION EJ 041 958
SELECTIVE ATTENTION IN MENTAL RETARDATES EJ 043 058
PIAGET'S CONCEPT OF CLASSIFICATION: A COMPARATIVE STUDY OF SOCIALLY DISADVANTAGED AND MIDDLE-CLASS YOUNG CHILDREN EJ 046 239
OBJECT CONSTRUCTION AND IMITATION UNDER DIFFERING CONDITIONS OF REARING EJ 048 305
DEVELOPMENTAL COMPARISONS OF CONFORMITY ACROSS TWO CULTURES EJ 051 470
NOUN-PAIR LEARNING IN CHILDREN AND ADULTS: UNDERLYING STRINGS AND RETRIEVAL TIME EJ 056 402
THE RELATIONSHIP BETWEEN LIQUID CONSERVATION AND COMPENSATION EJ 059 313
AN EXPERIMENTAL STUDY OF THE SELECTIVE ATTENTION OF CHILDREN OF 1896 AND 1966 EJ 060 775
THREE-CUE SELECTION MODELS APPLIED TO MULTIDIMENSIONAL STIMULUS CLASSIFICATION: ALTERNATIVES TO THE SPIKER, CROLL, AND MILLER ANALYSIS EJ 060 785
ON THE COMPARISON OF PSYCHOLOGICAL THEORIES: A REPLY TO PROFESSOR BOGARTZ EJ 060 786
THE EVOLUTION OF DEVELOPMENTAL PSYCHOLOGY: A COMPARISON OF HANDBOOKS EJ 061 074

COMPARATIVE EDUCATION

THE INTERNATIONAL WALDORF SCHOOL MOVEMENT. ED015019
UNDERSTANDING THE FOURTH GRADE SLUMP IN CREATIVE THINKING. FINAL REPORT. ED018273
A LONDON INFANT SCHOOL. AN INTERVIEW. ED027963
PRE-SCHOOL EDUCATION IN EUROPE. ED047779
SCHOOLS WHERE CHILDREN LEARN. ED053803
ORAL READING ACHIEVEMENT OF SCOTTISH AND AMERICAN CHILDREN EJ 030 548
LEARNING FROM THE BRITISH PRIMARY SCHOOLS EJ 057 327
REFLECTIONS ON REVISITING VIENNA'S YOUNG CITIZENS EJ 060 107

COMPARATIVE STATISTICS

PROJECT HEAD START--SUMMER 1966. FINAL REPORT. SECTION ONE, SOME CHARACTERISTICS OF CHILDREN IN THE HEAD START PROGRAM. ED018246
INFANT MORTALITY: A CHALLENGE TO THE NATION. ED032122
CURRICULAR INTERVENTION IN LANGUAGE ARTS READINESS FOR HEAD START CHILDREN. TULANE UNIVERSITY, HEAD START EVALUATION AND RESEARCH CENTER, 1968-1969 INTERVENTION REPORT. SUPPLEMENT TO THE ANNUAL REPORT TO THE OFFICE OF ECONOMIC OPPORTUNITY. ED047795
DISADVANTAGED CHILDREN AND THEIR FIRST SCHOOL EXPERIENCES. ETS-HEAD START LONGITUDINAL STUDY: PRELIMINARY DESCRIPTION OF THE INITIAL SAMPLE PRIOR TO SCHOOL ENROLLMENT. A REPORT IN TWO VOLUMES: VOLUME 2--TABLES. ED047798
BODY SIZE OF CONTEMPORARY YOUTH IN DIFFERENT PARTS OF THE WORLD EJ 010 312

COMPARATIVE TESTING

AN EVALUATION OF DIFFERENCES AMONG DIFFERENT CLASSES OF HEAD START PARTICIPANTS. FINAL REPORT. ED015012
SECOND-YEAR REPORT ON AN EVALUATIVE STUDY OF PREKINDERGARTEN PROGRAMS FOR EDUCATIONALLY DISADVANTAGED CHILDREN. ED016523
SENSORIMOTOR EXPERIENCE AND CONCEPT FORMATION IN EARLY CHILDHOOD. FINAL REPORT. ED019143
IDENTIFICATION AND EVALUATION OF CHARACTERISTICS OF KINDERGARTEN CHILDREN THAT FORETELL EARLY LEARNING PROBLEMS. FINAL REPORT. ED020006
IDENTIFICATION AND EVALUATION OF CHARACTERISTICS OF KINDERGARTEN CHILDREN THAT FORETELL EARLY LEARNING PROBLEMS. SUMMARY REPORT. ED020007
SOCIOECONOMIC STATUS AND LEARNING PROFICIENCY IN YOUNG CHILDREN. ED020023
HEAD START EVALUATION AND RESEARCH CENTER. PROGRESS REPORT OF RESEARCH STUDIES 1966 TO 1967. DOCUMENT 1, DEVELOPMENT OF THE MATRIX TEST. ED021623
CHILDREN'S JUDGMENTS OF AGE. ED043392
INFLUENCES OF A PIAGET-ORIENTED CURRICULUM ON INTELLECTUAL FUNCTIONING OF LOWER-CLASS KINDERGARTEN CHILDREN. ED049823
TWO KINDS OF KINDERGARTEN AFTER FOUR TYPES OF HEAD START. ED050824
A METHOD OF INCREASING THE ABILITY OF FIRST GRADE PUPILS TO USE PHONETIC GENERALIZATIONS EJ 033 279

COMPENSATORY EDUCATION

HANDBOOK FOR PROJECT HEAD START. ED015018
A COMPARATIVE STUDY OF TWO PRESCHOOL PROGRAMS FOR CULTURALLY DISADVANTAGED CHILDREN--A HIGHLY STRUCTURED AND A TRADITIONAL PROGRAM. ED016524
A REPORT OF THE SOUTHERN REGIONAL CONFERENCE ON EARLY CHILDHOOD EDUCATION. ED019112
FINAL REPORT ON HEAD START EVALUATION AND RESEARCH--1966-67 TO THE INSTITUTE FOR EDUCATIONAL DEVELOPMENT. SECTION III, INFLUENCING ATTITUDES OF PARENTS AND TEACHERS THROUGH REWARDING CHILDREN. ED019119
FINAL REPORT ON HEAD START EVALUATION AND RESEARCH--1966-67 TO THE INSTITUTE FOR EDUCATIONAL DEVELOPMENT. SECTION IV, AN EXPLORATORY STUDY OF ORAL LANGUAGE DEVELOPMENT AMONG CULTURALLY DIFFERENT CHILDREN. ED019120
EARLY LEARNING IN THE HOME. ED019127
REPORT OF THE EFFECTIVENESS OF PROJECT HEAD START, LUBBOCK, TEXAS. PARTS I, II, AND APPENDICES. ED019131
AN EVALUATION OF A PRESCHOOL TRAINING PROGRAM FOR CULTURALLY DEPRIVED CHILDREN. FINAL REPORT. ED019135
PRELIMINARY FINDINGS FROM A LONGITUDINAL EDUCATIONAL IMPROVEMENT PROJECT BEING CONDUCTED FOR INSTRUCTIONALLY IMPOVERISHED PUPILS IN INTACT SCHOOLS IN THE URBAN SOUTH. ED020021
COMMUNICATIVE COMPETENCE OF LOW-INCOME CHILDREN--ASSUMPTIONS AND PROGRAMS. ED020775
PRE-SCHOOL EDUCATION. ED020785
HEAD START EVALUATION AND RESEARCH CENTER, UNIVERSITY OF KANSAS. REPORT NO. III, EFFECTS OF A LANGUAGE PROGRAM ON CHILDREN IN A HEAD START NURSERY. ED021636
PROBLEMS AND PROSPECTS OF EDUCATION IN THE BIG CITIES AS EXEMPLIFIED BY PITTSBURGH, PENNSYLVANIA. ED022542
SAN MATEO COUNTY HUMAN RESOURCES COMMISSION PROJECT HEAD START - SUMMER 1966. AN EVALUATIONAL REPORT. ED023478
MOTIVATIONAL AND SOCIAL COMPONENTS IN COMPENSATORY EDUCATION PROGRAMS: SUGGESTED PRINCIPLES, PRACTICES, AND RESEARCH DESIGNS. ED024464
PRESCHOOL PROGRAMS AND THE INTELLECTUAL DEVELOPMENT OF DISADVANTAGED CHILDREN. ED024473
A STUDY OF FAMILY INFLUENCES ON THE EDUCATION OF NEGRO LOWER-CLASS CHILDREN. PROJECT I. ED025309
ANNUAL RESEARCH REPORT OF COMPLETED AND INCOMPLETE INVESTIGATIONS FOR NATIONAL HEAD START EVALUATION. ED025320
HEAD START PROGRAMS OPERATED BY PUBLIC SCHOOL SYSTEMS, 1966-67. ED026115
PRESCHOOL PARENT EDUCATION PROGRAM: A CURRICULUM GUIDE FOR USE BY TEACHERS CONDUCTING PARENT EDUCATION PROGRAMS AS A PART OF OVER-ALL COMPENSATORY PRESCHOOL PROJECTS. EXPERIMENTAL EDITION. ED026118
A CURRICULUM OF TRAINING FOR PARENT PARTICIPATION IN PROJECT HEAD START. ED026144
AN APPRAISAL OF HEAD START PARTICIPANTS AND NON-PARTICIPANTS: EXPANDED CONSIDERATIONS ON LEARNING DISABILITIES AMONG DISADVANTAGED CHILDREN. ED027939
EARLY CHILDHOOD PROJECT, NEW YORK CITY ED027974
PERRY PRESCHOOL PROJECT, YPSILANTI, MICHIGAN ED027975
INFANT EDUCATION RESEARCH PROJECT, WASHINGTON, D.C. ED027976
PRESCHOOL PROGRAM, FRESNO, CALIFORNIA ED027977
ACADEMIC PRESCHOOL, CHAMPAIGN, ILLINOIS ED027979
TOWARD THE PREVENTION OF INCOMPETENCE. ED028812
EVALUATION OF THE EFFECTS OF HEAD START EXPERIENCE IN THE AREA OF SELF-CONCEPT, SOCIAL SKILLS, AND LANGUAGE SKILLS. PRE-PUBLICATION DRAFT. ED028832
HEAD START EVALUATION AND RESEARCH CENTER, TULANE UNIVERSITY. ANNUAL REPORT. ED029705
A REPORT ON THE 1967-68 PROGRAM FOR PRESCHOOL CHILDREN AND THEIR PARENTS. RESEARCH REPORT SERIES 1968-69, NO. 4. ED029713
SPOTLIGHT ON FOLLOW THROUGH. ED029720
HEAD START IN ACTION. ED030471
ATTITUDES, EXPECTATIONS, AND BEHAVIOR OF PARENTS OF HEAD START AND NON-HEAD START CHILDREN. REPORT NUMBER 1. ED030475
INTERRELATIONS BETWEEN SOCIAL-EMOTIONAL BEHAVIOR AND INFORMATION ACHIEVEMENT OF HEAD START CHILDREN. REPORT NUMBER 5. ED030479
MODIFICATION OF COGNITIVE SKILLS AMONG LOWER-CLASS NEGRO CHILDREN: A FOLLOW-UP TRAINING STUDY. REPORT NUMBER 6. ED030480
EFFECTIVENESS OF DIRECT VERBAL INSTRUCTION ON IQ PERFORMANCE AND ACHIEVEMENT IN READING AND ARITHMETIC. ED030496
TECHNOLOGY AND THE EDUCATION OF THE DISADVANTAGED. ED031293
EVALUATION OF AN INTERDISCIPLINARY APPROACH TO PREVENTION OF EARLY SCHOOL FAILURE. FOLLOW-UP STUDY, FINAL REPORT. ED031295
[THE JUNIPER GARDENS PARENT COOPERATIVE NURSERY.] FINAL PROGRESS REPORT FOR OEO CAP GRANT CG-8474 A/O. ED032920
MOTHERS' TRAINING PROGRAM: THE GROUP PROCESS. ED032926
INFANT EDUCATION. ED033760
THE EFFECTS OF SOCIODRAMATIC PLAY ON DISADVANTAGED PRESCHOOL CHILDREN. ED033761
SELECTED LONGITUDINAL STUDIES OF COMPENSATORY EDUCATION--A LOOK FROM THE INSIDE. ED033762
EFFECTS OF SOCIAL REINFORCEMENT ON SELF-ESTEEM OF MEXICAN-AMERICAN CHILDREN. LONG ABSTRACT. ED033767
HEAD START PROGRAMS AND PARTICIPANTS 1965-1967. ED034569
A SOCIALLY INTEGRATED KINDERGARTEN. ED034578
AN EVALUATION OF THE PRESCHOOL READINESS CENTERS PROGRAM IN EAST ST. LOUIS, ILLINOIS, JULY 1, 1968 - JUNE 30, 1969. FINAL REPORT. ED034585
AN EVALUATION OF A PILOT PROJECT TO ASSESS THE INTRODUCTION OF THE MODERN ENGLISH INFANT SCHOOL APPROACH TO LEARNING WITH SECOND AND THIRD YEAR DISADVANTAGED CHILDREN. ED034595
THE ADVANTAGED: A PRESCHOOL PROGRAM FOR THE DISADVANTAGED. ED035436
ANALYSIS OF HOME ENVIRONMENT AND DEVELOPMENT OF PARENT INTERVENTION. ED035458
PROJECT HEAD START AT WORK. REPORT OF A SURVEY STUDY OF 335 PROJECT HEAD START CENTERS, SUMMER, 1965. ED036311
INSTITUTE FOR DEVELOPMENTAL STUDIES INTERIM PROGRESS REPORT. PART II: RESEARCH AND EVALUATION. ED036312
PRESCHOOL INTERVENTION THROUGH SOCIAL LEARNING. ED036316
EARLY LEARNING AND COMPENSATORY EDUCATION: CONTRIBUTION OF BASIC RESEARCH. ED036318
THE IMPACT OF HEAD START: AN EVALUATION OF THE EFFECTS OF HEAD START ON CHILDREN'S COGNITIVE AND AFFECTIVE DEVELOPMENT. (EXECUTIVE SUMMARY). ED036321
PLANNING PARENT-IMPLEMENTED PROGRAMS: A GUIDE FOR PARENTS, SCHOOLS AND COMMUNITIES. ED036322
PARENTAL BEHAVIOR AND CHILDREN'S SCHOOL ACHIEVEMENT: IMPLICATIONS FOR HEAD START. PROCEEDINGS OF THE HEAD START RESEARCH SEMINARS: SEMINAR NO. 5, INTERVENTION IN FAMILY LIFE (1ST, WASHINGTON, D.C., JANUARY 13, 1969). ED036332
THE ROLE OF THE TEACHER IN INTERVENTION PROGRAMS. PROCEEDINGS OF THE HEAD START RESEARCH SEMINARS: SEMINAR NO. 6, THE TEACHER IN INTERVENTION PROGRAMS (1ST, WASHINGTON, D.C., APRIL 18, 1969). ED036333
A LONGITUDINAL STUDY OF DISADVANTAGED CHILDREN WHO PARTICIPATED IN THREE DIFFERENT PRESCHOOL PROGRAMS. ED036338
THE ANALYSIS OF DATA GENERATED IN A RESEARCH DESIGNED TO SECURE BASELINE INFORMATION ON A HEAD START PROGRAM. A REPORT TO THE U.S. OFFICE OF ECONOMIC OPPORTUNITY FROM THE DEPARTMENT OF RESEARCH, MONTGOMERY COUNTY, MARYLAND PUBLIC SCHOOLS. ED037232

INTRA-FAMILY DIFFUSION OF SELECTED COGNITIVE SKILLS AS A FUNCTION OF EDUCATIONAL STIMULATION. ED037233
A REPORT ON EVALUATION STUDIES OF PROJECT HEAD START. ED037239
RESEARCH AND CONSULTATION IN THE NATURAL ENVIRONMENT. ED037240
PARENT INVOLVEMENT IN PROJECT HEAD START. PART OF THE FINAL REPORT ON HEAD START EVALUATION AND RESEARCH: 1968-1969 TO THE OFFICE OF ECONOMIC OPPORTUNITY. ED037244
A PILOT PROJECT USING A LANGUAGE DEVELOPMENT PROGRAM WITH PRESCHOOL DISADVANTAGED CHILDREN. PART OF THE FINAL REPORT ON HEAD START EVALUATION AND RESEARCH: 1968-69 TO THE OFFICE OF ECONOMIC OPPORTUNITY. ED037245
A COMPARISON OF HEAD START CHILDREN WITH A GROUP OF HEAD START ELIGIBLES AFTER ONE YEAR IN ELEMENTARY SCHOOL. PART OF THE FINAL REPORT ON HEAD START EVALUATION AND RESEARCH: 1968-69 TO THE OFFICE OF ECONOMIC OPPORTUNITY. ED037247
EVALUATION OF EDUCATIONAL PROGRAMS AS RESEARCH ON EDUCATIONAL PROCESS. ED038165
EARLY CHILD STIMULATION THROUGH PARENT EDUCATION. ED038166
AN EARLY CHILDHOOD EDUCATION MODEL: A BILINGUAL APPROACH. ED038167
HEAD START PLANNED VARIATION PROGRAM. ED038170
CURRICULAR INTERVENTION IN LANGUAGE ARTS READINESS FOR HEAD START CHILDREN. TULANE UNIVERSITY, HEAD START EVALUATION AND RESEARCH CENTER ANNUAL REPORT TO THE OFFICE OF ECONOMIC OPPORTUNITY. ED038175
WAKULLA COUNTY PRESCHOOL. FINAL REPORT. ED039022
A SOCIAL LEARNING APPROACH TO EARLY CHILDHOOD EDUCATION. ED039025
FOLLOW THROUGH PROJECT, WICHITA UNIFIED SCHOOL DISTRICT 259: INITIAL YEAR, SEPTEMBER 1968 - MAY 1969 EVALUATION REPORT. ED039027
THE EFFECT OF A PRESCHOOL EXPERIENCE UPON INTELLECTUAL FUNCTIONING AMONG FOUR-YEAR-OLD, WHITE CHILDREN IN RURAL MINNESOTA. ED039030
CURRICULAR INTERVENTION TO ENHANCE THE ENGLISH LANGUAGE COMPETENCE OF HEAD START CHILDREN. PART OF THE FINAL REPORT ON HEAD START EVALUATION AND RESEARCH: 1968-69 TO THE OFFICE OF ECONOMIC OPPORTUNITY. ED039032
EDUCATIONAL DAY CARE: AN INSTALLATION MANUAL. ED039918
A SUPPLEMENTARY REPORT ON EVALUATION OF THE NEW NURSERY SCHOOL PROGRAM AT COLORADO STATE COLLEGE. ED039919
A REPORT ON THE EVALUATION OF THE STATE PRESCHOOL PROGRAM CONTRASTED WITH THE WESTINGHOUSE REPORT ON HEAD START. ED039920
ENVIRONMENTALLY DEPRIVED CHILDREN. ED039937
EDUCATIONAL INTERVENTION AT HOME BY MOTHERS OF DISADVANTAGED INFANTS. ED039944
PARENT INVOLVEMENT IN COMPENSATORY EDUCATION. ED039954
A FEASIBILITY STUDY OF PARENT AWARENESS PROGRAMS. FINAL REPORT. ED040742
DESIGN AND MEASURES OF 1967-68 AND 1968-69 HEAD START E&R EVALUATION STUDIES. ED040745
AN EDUCATIONAL SYSTEM FOR DEVELOPMENTALLY DISABLED INFANTS. ED040749
NEED FOR EARLY AND CONTINUING EDUCATION. ED040750
PERSPECTIVE ON THE JENSEN AFFAIR. ED040760
ISSUES AND REALITIES IN EARLY CHILDHOOD EDUCATION. ED041621
A REVIEW OF THE EVALUATION OF THE FOLLOW THROUGH PROGRAM. ED041642
PSYCHOLINGUISTIC BEHAVIORS OF ISOLATED, RURAL CHILDREN WITH AND WITHOUT KINDERGARTEN. ED042510
APPLICATION OF GROUP DYNAMICS PROCEDURES TO PROMOTE COMMUNICATION AMONG PARENTS AND TEACHERS. ED042512
EFFECTS OF AGE OF ENTRY AND DURATION OF PARTICIPATION IN A COMPENSATORY EDUCATION PROGRAM. ED043380
PRE-KINDERGARTEN PROGRAM, 1968-69. EVALUATION REPORT FOR THE PROJECT. ED046511
HAS PRESCHOOL COMPENSATORY EDUCATION FAILED? ED049834
CHILDREN UNDER THREE - FINDING WAYS TO STIMULATE DEVELOPMENT. I. ISSUES IN RESEARCH EJ 006 980
A NONSEGREGATED APPROACH TO HEAD START EJ 007 363
FLORIDA'S EARLY CHILDHOOD LEARNING PROGRAM FOR MIGRANT CHILDREN EJ 043 089
A REPORT ON EVALUATION STUDIES OF PROJECT HEAD START EJ 049 896
DEVELOPMENTAL THEORY: ITS PLACE AND RELEVANCE IN EARLY INTERVENTION PROGRAMS EJ 060 013

COMPLEXITY LEVEL

CONCEPT IDENTIFICATION STRATEGIES. RESEARCH PROJECT NUMBER 3 OF PROJECT HEAD START RESEARCH AND EVALUATION CENTER, SYRACUSE UNIVERSITY RESEARCH INSTITUTE, NOVEMBER 1, 1967. ED026140
SYNTACTIC COMPLEXITY IN MOTHER-CHILD INTERACTIONS. ED035454
AN EXAMINATION OF CHANGES IN ATTITUDES TO VISUAL COMPLEXITY WITH INCREASING AGE. ED039930
A THIRD STUDY OF THE EFFECTS OF A LEARNING EXPERIENCE UPON PREFERENCE FOR COMPLEXITY-ASYMMETRY IN FOURTH, FIFTH, AND SIXTH GRADE CHILDREN EJ 029 281
RELATIONSHIP OF CONSERVATION EXPLANATIONS TO ITEM DIFFICULTY EJ 030 295
LINGUISTIC AND PSYCHOLOGICAL FACTORS IN THE SPEECH REGULATION OF BEHAVIOR IN YOUNG CHILDREN EJ 034 540
AGE DIFFERENCES IN PLEASANTNESS OF VISUAL PATTERNS OF DIFFERENT VARIABILITY IN LATE CHILDHOOD AND ADOLESCENCE EJ 035 989
A DEVELOPMENTAL STUDY OF PRESCHOOL CHILDREN'S PREFERENCE FOR RANDOM FORMS EJ 035 990
ATTENTION DISTRIBUTION IN THE 24-MONTH-OLD CHILD: VARIATIONS IN COMPLEXITY AND INCONGRUITY OF THE HUMAN FORM EJ 040 296
GENERALIZED IMITATION: THE EFFECTS OF EXPERIMENTER ABSENCE, DIFFERENTIAL REINFORCEMENT, AND STIMULUS COMPLEXITY EJ 045 044
ACCELERATING VISUAL COMPLEXITY LEVELS IN THE HUMAN INFANT EJ 045 598
SOME FACTORS AFFECTING THE COMPLEXITY OF CHILDREN'S SENTENCES: THE EFFECTS OF MODELING, AGE, SEX, AND BILINGUALISM EJ 060 780
DEVELOPMENTAL CHANGE IN INFANT VISUAL FIXATION TO DIFFERING COMPLEXITY LEVELS AMONG CROSS-SECTIONALLY AND LONGITUDINALLY STUDIED INFANTS EJ 061 141

COMPONENTIAL ANALYSIS

APPROACHES TO THE VALIDATION OF LEARNING HIERARCHIES. ED043376
SEMANTIC DIFFERENTIAL ANALYSIS OF RELATIONAL TERMS USED IN CONSERVATION EJ 046 235

COMPOSITION (LITERARY)

EFFECTS OF INSTRUCTIONS ON THEME GRADING: GRAMMATICAL VS. HOLISTIC EJ 040 724

COMPOSITION SKILLS (LITERARY)

A COMPARISON BETWEEN THE ORAL AND WRITTEN RESPONSES OF FIRST-GRADE CHILDREN IN I.T.A. AND T.O. CLASSES. ED019144
ANALYSES OF STORIES DICTATED IN CLASSES OF THE COOPERATIVE PROJECT. ED019993
A STUDY OF COMPOSITION ABILITY AS ASSESSED WITH A STANDARDIZED INSTRUMENT FOR SECOND AND THIRD GRADE CHILDREN. ED029696
A STUDY COMPARING GLOBAL QUALITY AND SYNTACTIC MATURITY IN THE WRITING COMPOSITION OF SECOND AND THIRD GRADE STUDENTS. ED029697
SYNTACTIC MATURITY IN SCHOOL CHILDREN AND ADULTS EJ 018 818

COMPREHENSION

COGNITIVE PROCESSES IN THE DEVELOPMENT OF CHILDREN'S APPRECIATION OF HUMOR. ED020784
THE PRESCHOOL CHILD'S ABILITY TO FOLLOW DIRECTIONS. ED043395
THE ROLE OF COMPREHENSION IN CHILDREN'S PROBLEM SOLVING EJ 021 764
REACTION TIME AND REMOTE ASSOCIATION IN TALENTED MALE ADOLESCENTS EJ 029 360
THE ACQUISITION OF DIRECT AND INDIRECT OBJECTS IN JAPANESE EJ 036 745
COGNITIVE DEVELOPMENT AND CHILDREN'S COMPREHENSION OF HUMOR EJ 036 820
ON THE CONSERVATION OF LIQUIDS EJ 039 640
DEVELOPMENT OF SYNTACTIC COMPREHENSION IN PRESCHOOL CHILDREN AS A FUNCTION OF SOCIOECONOMIC LEVEL EJ 043 480
THE ROLE OF OPERATIONAL THINKING IN CHILDREN'S COMPREHENSION AND APPRECIATION OF HUMOR EJ 046 233
COMPARISON OF IMITATION AND COMPREHENSION SCORES BETWEEN TWO LOWER-CLASS GROUPS AND THE EFFECTS OF TWO WARM-UP CONDITIONS ON IMITATION OF THE SAME GROUPS EJ 056 709
THE EXPERIMENTAL FACILITATION OF CHILDREN'S COMPREHENSION AND PRODUCTION OF FOUR SYNTACTIC STRUCTURES EJ 056 723
THE YOUNG CHILD'S COMPREHENSION OF TIME CONNECTIVES EJ 056 724
A MATTER OF LIFE AND DEATH EJ 059 746
THE ROLE OF INCONGRUITY AND RESOLUTION IN CHILDREN'S APPRECIATION OF CARTOON HUMOR EJ 060 781

COMPREHENSION DEVELOPMENT

AN EXPERIMENTAL STUDY OF SYNTACTICAL FACTORS INFLUENCING CHILDREN'S COMPREHENSION OF CERTAIN COMPLEX RELATIONSHIPS. FINAL REPORT. ED030492
YOUNG CHILDREN'S COMPREHENSION OF LOGICAL CONNECTIVES. ED033756
THE ROLE OF SYNTAX IN CHILDREN'S COMPREHENSION FROM AGES SIX TO TWELVE EJ 028 578

COMPREHENSIVE PROGRAMS

EVALUATION OF A PARENT AND CHILD CENTER PROGRAM. ED045189
PRESCHOOL EDUCATION AND POVERTY: THE DISTANCE IN BETWEEN. FINAL REPORT OF 1968-69 INTERVENTIONAL PROGRAM. ED046501
PROGRAMS FOR INFANTS AND YOUNG CHILDREN. PART I: EDUCATION AND DAY CARE. ED047807
A STUDY IN CHILD CARE (CASE STUDY FROM VOLUME II-A): "LIKE BEING AT HOME." DAY CARE PROGRAMS REPRINT SERIES. ED051899

PARENT AND CHILD CENTERS--IMPETUS, IMPLEMENTATION, IN-DEPTH VIEW EJ 030 469
INVOLVING PARENTS IN A CHILDREN'S CLINIC EJ 047 353

COMPUTER ASSISTED INSTRUCTION

THE COMPUTER CAN HELP INDIVIDUALIZE INSTRUCTION EJ 018 306
A PILOT STUDY OF COMPUTER-ASSISTED DRILL AND PRACTICE IN SEVENTH GRADE REMEDIAL MATHEMATICS EJ 027 030

COMPUTER PROGRAMS

FOLLOW-UP OF OPERATION HEAD START PARTICIPANTS IN THE STATE OF IOWA. FINAL REPORT. ED015771
PROBLEMS OF CONTROL IN SIMULTANEOUS DISCRIMINATION TASKS EJ 058 215

CONCEPT FORMATION

YOUNG CHILDREN'S THINKING, STUDIES OF SOME ASPECTS OF PIAGET'S THEORY. ED013662
CONCEPT FORMATION BY KINDERGARTEN CHILDREN IN A CARD-SORTING TASK. PSYCHOLOGY SERIES. ED013665
IMPACT OF SUMMER 1965 HEAD START ON CHILDREN'S CONCEPT ATTAINMENT DURING KINDERGARTEN. FINAL REPORT. ED015773
HEADSTART OPERATIONAL FIELD ANALYSIS. PROGRESS REPORT II. ED015775
HEADSTART OPERATIONAL FIELD ANALYSIS. PROGRESS REPORT III. ED015776
HEADSTART OPERATIONAL FIELD ANALYSIS. PROGRESS REPORT IV. ED015777
CONCEPT FORMATION AS A FUNCTION OF METHOD OF PRESENTATION AND RATIO OF POSITIVE TO NEGATIVE INSTANCES. ED015779
DEVELOPMENT OF CHILDREN'S ABILITY TO COORDINATE PERSPECTIVES. ED016516
TRAINING EFFECTS AND CONCEPT DEVELOPMENT--A STUDY OF THE CONSERVATION OF CONTINUOUS QUANTITY IN CHILDREN. ED016533
ORAL OR WRITTEN LANGUAGE--THE CONSEQUENCES FOR COGNITIVE DEVELOPMENT IN AFRICA AND THE UNITED STATES. ED018279
DEVELOPMENT OF A GROUP MEASURE TO ASSESS THE EXTENT OF PRE-LOGICAL AND PRE-CAUSAL THINKING IN PRIMARY SCHOOL AGE CHILDREN. ED019136
SENSORIMOTOR EXPERIENCE AND CONCEPT FORMATION IN EARLY CHILDHOOD. FINAL REPORT. ED019143
NUMBER TRAINING TECHNIQUES AND THEIR EFFECTS ON DIFFERENT POPULATIONS. FINAL REPORT. ED019988
LOGICAL OPERATIONS AND CONCEPTS OF CONSERVATION IN CHILDREN, A TRAINING STUDY. FINAL REPORT. ED020010
AN ANALYSIS OF A CLASS OF PROBLEM SOLVING BEHAVIOR. FINAL REPORT. ED020776
CONCEPT GROWTH AND THE EDUCATION OF THE CHILD: A SURVEY OF RESEARCH ON CONCEPTUALIZATION. NATIONAL FOUNDATION FOR EDUCATIONAL RESEARCH IN ENGLAND AND WALES OCCASIONAL PUBLICATION SERIES NO. 12. ED026121
CONCEPT IDENTIFICATION STRATEGIES. RESEARCH PROJECT NUMBER 3 OF PROJECT HEAD START RESEARCH AND EVALUATION CENTER, SYRACUSE UNIVERSITY RESEARCH INSTITUTE, NOVEMBER 1, 1967. ED026140
CONCEPT AND LANGUAGE DEVELOPMENT IN A KINDERGARTEN OF DISADVANTAGED CHILDREN. ED027967
PERFORMANCE OF KINDERGARTEN CHILDREN FROM LOW INCOME FAMILIES ON SELECTED CONCEPT CATEGORIES. ED028847
YOUNG CHILDREN'S USE OF LANGUAGE IN INFERENTIAL BEHAVIOR. ED029691
THE EFFECT OF VERBALIZATION OF RELEVANT AND IRRELEVANT DIMENSIONS ON CONCEPT FORMATION. ED030484
INVESTIGATION OF CONCEPT LEARNING IN YOUNG CHILDREN. FINAL REPORT. ED030498
A STUDY OF THE INTERRELATIONSHIPS OF CONSERVATION OF LENGTH RELATIONS, CONSERVATIONS OF LENGTH, AND TRANSITIVITY OF LENGTH RELATIONS OF THE AGE OF FOUR AND FIVE YEARS. ED031303
TEACHING KINDERGARTEN CHILDREN TO APPLY CONCEPT-DEFINING RULES. ED037231
TEACHING MATHEMATICAL CONCEPTS TO TWO- AND THREE-YEAR-OLDS: SOME EXPERIMENTAL STUDIES. ED037234
RULE AND ATTRIBUTE LEARNING IN THE USE AND IDENTIFICATION OF CONCEPTS WITH YOUNG DISADVANTAGED CHILDREN. ED040747
A PILOT EXPERIMENT IN EARLY CHILDHOOD POLITICAL LEARNING. REPORT FROM THE PROJECT ON CONCEPTS IN POLITICAL SCIENCE. ED043368
COGNITIVELY ORIENTED CURRICULUM, YPSILANTI, MICHIGAN: A PROGRAM THAT EXPOSES PRESCHOOL CHILDREN TO A VARIETY OF MATERIALS AND EQUIPMENT TO TEACH CONCEPTS THROUGH PHYSICAL AND VERBAL EXPERIENCES. MODEL PROGRAMS--CHILDHOOD EDUCATION. ED045217
PIAGET'S CONCEPT OF CLASSIFICATION: A COMPARATIVE STUDY OF SOCIALLY DISADVANTAGED AND MIDDLE-CLASS YOUNG CHILDREN. ED046499
RULE STRUCTURE AND PROPORTION OF POSITIVE INSTANCES AS DETERMINANTS OF CONCEPT ATTAINMENT IN CHILDREN. ED046500
AN APPLICATION OF PIAGET'S THEORY TO THE CONCEPTUALIZATION OF A PRESCHOOL CURRICULUM. ED046502
LEARNING TO LEARN ON A CONCEPT ATTAINMENT TASK AS A FUNCTION OF AGE AND SOCIOECONOMIC LEVEL. REPORT FROM THE PROJECT ON SITUATIONAL VARIABLES AND EFFICIENCY OF CONCEPT LEARNING. ED046505
DAME SCHOOL PROJECT (BI-LINGUAL PRE SCHOOL PROJECT), SANTA CLARA COUNTY OFFICE OF EDUCATION. FINAL REPORT, AUGUST 1, 1970. ED046514
CONCEPT AND LANGUAGE DEVELOPMENT OF A GROUP OF FIVE YEAR OLDS WHO HAVE ATTENDED THE SYRACUSE UNIVERSITY CHILDREN'S CENTER INTERVENTION PROGRAM. ED046515
THE EFFECTS OF EXTRANEOUS MATERIAL AND NEGATIVE EXEMPLARS ON A SOCIAL SCIENCE CONCEPT-LEARNING TASK FOR PRE-SCHOOL CHILDREN. ED047819
THE NEW NURSERY SCHOOL RESEARCH PROJECT ED048940
LANGUAGE ACQUISITION AND COGNITIVE DEVELOPMENT. ED049811
A STUDY OF THE DEVELOPMENT OF EGOCENTRISM AND THE COORDINATION OF SPATIAL PERCEPTIONS IN ELEMENTARY SCHOOL CHILDREN. FINAL REPORT. ED050829
A STUDY OF CAUSAL THINKING IN ELEMENTARY SCHOOL CHILDREN. FINAL REPORT. ED050830
AUTUMN. UNIT 3 CURRICULUM GUIDE. ED053790
A GUIDE TO READING PIAGET. ED053819
PRESCHOOL CHILDREN'S UNDERSTANDING OF THE COORDINATED CONCEPTS OF DISTANCE, MOVEMENT, NUMBER, AND TIME EJ 015 100
CHILDREN'S JUDGMENTS OF KINDNESS EJ 018 259
CONCEPT LEARNING IN DISCRIMINATION TASKS EJ 018 878
REPRESENTATIONAL LEVEL AND CONCEPT PRODUCTION IN CHILDREN AND ADOLESCENTS EJ 018 880
A METHODOLOGICAL INVESTIGATION OF PIAGET'S THEORY OF OBJECT CONCEPT DEVELOPMENT IN THE SENSORY-MOTOR PERIOD EJ 018 891
COMPARISON OF RATIOS AND THE CHANCE CONCEPT IN CHILDREN EJ 021 771
DETERMINANTS OF PART-WHOLE PERCEPTION IN CHILDREN EJ 021 772
INFERENCE AND PREFERENCE IN CHILDREN'S CONCEPTUAL PERFORMANCE EJ 021 773
THE DEVELOPMENT OF THE CONCEPT OF OBJECT AS RELATED TO INFANT-MOTHER ATTACHMENT EJ 021 998
A DEVELOPMENTAL STUDY OF THE RELATIONSHIP BETWEEN CONCEPTUAL, EGO, AND MORAL DEVELOPMENT EJ 021 999
A TEST OF PIAGET'S THEORY OF "NOMINAL REALISM" EJ 023 189
THE RELATION OF PARENTAL TRAINING TO CONCEPTUAL STRUCTURE IN PREADOLESCENTS EJ 023 191
VERBAL AND IMAGERY PROCESSES IN CHILDREN'S PAIRED-ASSOCIATE LEARNING EJ 024 699
CHILDREN'S UTILIZATION OF LOGICAL SYMBOLS: AN INTERPRETATION OF CONCEPTUAL BEHAVIOR BASED ON PIAGETIAN THEORY EJ 024 942
LEARNING: THE ROLE OF FACTS AND GENERALIZATIONS EJ 028 638
THE UTILIZATION BY CHILDREN AND ADULTS OF BINARY PROPOSITIONAL THINKING IN CONCEPT LEARNING EJ 030 285
FUNCTIONS OF VISUAL IMAGERY IN THE LEARNING AND CONCEPT FORMATION OF CHILDREN EJ 033 779
INTERRELATIONS AMONG LEARNING AND PERFORMANCE TASKS AT THE PRESCHOOL LEVEL EJ 035 361
CHILDREN'S UNDERSTANDING OF PROBABILITY CONCEPTS EJ 036 824
DEVELOPMENT OF THE OBJECT CONCEPT AS MANIFESTED IN CHANGES IN THE TRACKING BEHAVIOR OF INFANTS BETWEEN 7 AND 20 WEEKS OF AGE EJ 038 264
SOME RELATIONSHIPS BETWEEN CLASS INCLUSION, PERCEPTUAL CAPABILITIES, VERBAL CAPABILITIES AND RACE EJ 039 639
STATE IV OF PIAGET'S THEORY OF INFANT'S OBJECT CONCEPTS: A LONGITUDINAL STUDY EJ 041 134
CONSERVATION OF NUMBER IN VERY YOUNG CHILDREN: A FAILURE TO REPLICATE MEHLER AND BEVER EJ 041 144
THE ASSESSMENT OF DIFFERENCES IN CONCEPTUAL STYLE EJ 041 146
VARIETY OF EXEMPLARS VERSUS LINGUISTIC CONTEXTS IN CONCEPT ATTAINMENT IN YOUNG CHILDREN EJ 042 955
EFFECTS OF DIFFERENTIAL EXPERIENCE ON INFANTS' PERFORMANCE IN A PIAGETIAN STAGE IV OBJECT-CONCEPT TASK EJ 042 956
IDENTIFICATION OF VERBAL CONCEPTS BY PRESCHOOL CHILDREN EJ 042 958
FACTORS INFLUENCING CHILDREN'S CONCEPT IDENTIFICATION PERFORMANCE WITH NONPREFERRED RELEVANT ATTRIBUTES EJ 042 965
THE SEQUENCE OF DEVELOPMENT OF CERTAIN NUMBER CONCEPTS IN PRESCHOOL CHILDREN EJ 044 694
THE DEVELOPMENT OF THE UNDERSTANDING OF CERTAIN NUMBER CONCEPTS EJ 044 695
CONCEPTUAL BEHAVIOR IN YOUNG CHILDREN: LEARNING TO SHIFT DIMENSIONAL ATTENTION EJ 044 697
ANALYSE DE L'ADOPTION DE LA NOTION DE "FLEUR" CHEZ LES ENFANTS DE 6 ANS EJ 044 703
SEMANTIC DIFFERENTIAL ANALYSIS OF RELATIONAL TERMS USED IN CONSERVATION EJ 046 235
PIAGET'S CONCEPT OF CLASSIFICATION: A COMPARATIVE STUDY OF SOCIALLY DISADVANTAGED AND MIDDLE-CLASS YOUNG CHILDREN EJ 046 239
EFFECTS OF EXPOSURE TO MODELS ON CONCEPT IDENTIFICATION IN KINDERGARTEN AND SECOND-GRADE CHILDREN EJ 046 240
ARTISTIC STYLE AS CONCEPT FORMATION FOR CHILDREN AND ADULTS EJ 046 247

PLAY, THE ESSENTIAL INGREDIENT EJ 046 248
THE STABILITY AND TRANSFERABILITY OF CONCEPTUAL CODING IN CHILDREN EJ 046 251
CONCEPTUAL RULE LEARNING AND CHRONOLOGICAL AGE EJ 047 687
A DEVELOPMENTAL COMPARISON OF IDENTITY AND EQUIVALENCE CONSERVATIONS EJ 049 167
STRENGTH OF DIMENSIONAL PREFERENCES AS A PREDICTOR OF NURSERY-SCHOOL CHILDREN'S PERFORMANCE ON A CONCEPT-SHIFT TASK EJ 049 169
CHILDREN'S PERFORMANCE IN SIMPLE AND SUCCESSIVE-REVERSAL CONCEPT IDENTIFICATION PROBLEMS EJ 049 170
THINKING BEFORE LANGUAGE? A SYMPOSIUM: 1. RELATIONSHIPS BETWEEN LANGUAGE AND THOUGHT EJ 050 075
THINKING BEFORE LANGUAGE? A SYMPOSIUM: 2. A SCHOOL FOR THINKING EJ 050 200
THE DEVELOPMENT OF SOME INTENTION CONCEPTS IN YOUNG CHILDREN EJ 052 452
CHILDREN'S JUDGMENTS OF AGE EJ 052 461
THE CONCEPT OF DEATH IN EARLY CHILDHOOD EJ 052 464
CONCEPTUAL STYLE AND CONCEPTUAL ABILITY IN KINDERGARTEN THROUGH THE EIGHTH GRADE EJ 053 484
DEVELOPMENT OF THE CONCEPT OF SERIATION EJ 053 650
DEVELOPMENT OF CONSERVATION IN NORMAL AND RETARDED CHILDREN EJ 053 651
ACQUISITION OF CONSERVATION THROUGH SOCIAL INTERACTION EJ 053 708
RACE, SOCIAL CLASS, AND AGE OF ACHIEVEMENT OF CONSERVATION ON PIAGET'S TASKS EJ 053 714
CONCEPT ATTAINMENT, GENERALIZATION, AND RETENTION THROUGH OBSERVATION AND VERBAL CODING EJ 053 726
VERBAL-LABELING AND CUE-TRAINING IN REVERSAL-SHIFT BEHAVIOR EJ 053 727
EFFECTS OF AGE, SEX, SYSTEMATIC CONCEPTUAL LEARNING, ACQUISITION OF LEARNING SETS, AND PROGRAMMED SOCIAL INTERACTION ON THE INTELLECTUAL AND CONCEPTUAL DEVELOPMENT OF PRESCHOOL CHILDREN FROM POVERTY BACKGROUNDS EJ 053 733
THE ROLE OF BODY PARTS AND READINESS IN ACQUISITION OF NUMBER CONSERVATION EJ 053 757
PERFORMANCE OF CULTURALLY DEPRIVED CHILDREN ON THE CONCEPT ASSESSMENT KIT--CONSERVATION EJ 053 906
RELATION BETWEEN IDENTITY CONSERVATION AND EQUIVALENCE CONSERVATION WITHIN FOUR CONCEPTUAL DOMAINS EJ 054 804
SPONTANEOUS MEASUREMENT IN YOUNG CHILDREN: A RE-EXAMINATION EJ 055 095
CHILDREN'S MORAL REASONING EJ 055 097
HAPTIC RECOGNITION OF OBJECTS IN CHILDREN EJ 055 099
FORMAL OPERATIONS IN FEMALES FROM ELEVEN TO FIFTY-FOUR YEARS OF AGE EJ 055 215
THE RELATION OF FORM RECOGNITION TO CONCEPT DEVELOPMENT EJ 056 393
LOGICAL CAPACITY OF VERY YOUNG CHILDREN: NUMBER INVARIANCE RULES EJ 056 394
MODELING EFFECTS UPON CONCEPTUAL STYLE AND COGNITIVE TEMPO EJ 056 396
DEVELOPMENT OF RELATIONAL CONCEPTS AND WORD DEFINITION IN CHILDREN FIVE THROUGH ELEVEN EJ 056 397
THE EFFECT OF SIBLING RELATIONSHIP ON CONCEPT LEARNING OF YOUNG CHILDREN TAUGHT BY CHILD-TEACHERS EJ 056 399
THE EFFECTS OF TRAINING AND SOCIOECONOMIC CLASS UPON THE ACQUISITION OF CONSERVATION CONCEPTS EJ 056 401
TAKING ANOTHER'S PERSPECTIVE: ROLE-TAKING DEVELOPMENT IN EARLY CHILDHOOD EJ 056 610
FIGURATIVE AND OPERATIVE ASPECTS OF CHILDREN'S INFERENCE EJ 056 616
DEVELOPMENT OF A SENSE OF SELF-IDENTITY IN CHILDREN EJ 056 617
GENERALITY OF PERCEPTUAL BIASES IN INFERENCE AND CONCEPT USAGE EJ 056 618
USE OF LABELS AND CUES IN CHILDREN'S CONCEPT IDENTIFICATION EJ 056 712
EVOLUTION OF THE HUMAN FIGURE IN A THREE-DIMENSIONAL MEDIUM EJ 057 897
MODELING BY EXEMPLIFICATION AND INSTRUCTION IN TRAINING CONSERVATION EJ 057 898
IDENTITY AND EQUIVALENCE CONSERVATION AT TWO AGE LEVELS EJ 057 901
DEVELOPMENTAL AND EXPERIMENTAL FACTORS ASSOCIATED WITH INFERENTIAL BEHAVIOR EJ 057 905
TRANSFER BETWEEN THE ODDITY AND RELATIVE SIZE CONCEPTS: REVERSAL AND EXTRADIMENSIONAL SHIFTS EJ 057 906
DEVELOPMENT OF DIRECTIONALITY IN CHILDREN: AGES SIX THROUGH TWELVE EJ 058 137
AN APPLICATION OF BRUNSWIK'S LENS MODEL TO DEVELOPMENTAL CHANGES IN PROBABILITY LEARNING EJ 058 142
THE RELATIONSHIP BETWEEN LIQUID CONSERVATION AND COMPENSATION EJ 059 313
VIOLATION OF A RULE AS A METHOD OF DIAGNOSING INFANTS' LEVELS OF OBJECT CONCEPT EJ 059 314
OBSERVATION, REPETITION, AND ETHNIC BACKGROUND IN CONCEPT ATTAINMENT AND GENERALIZATION EJ 059 316
THE STAGE IV ERROR IN PIAGET'S THEORY OF OBJECT CONCEPT DEVELOPMENT: DIFFICULTIES IN OBJECT CONCEPTUALIZATION OR SPATIAL LOCALIZATION? EJ 059 318
PRECOCIOUS THOUGHTS ON NUMBER: THE LONG AND THE SHORT OF IT EJ 060 776
THE ROLE OF FRONT-BACK FEATURES IN CHILDREN'S "FRONT," "BACK," AND "BESIDE" PLACEMENTS OF OBJECTS EJ 060 777
REVERSALS PRIOR TO SOLUTION OF CONCEPT IDENTIFICATION IN CHILDREN EJ 060 782

CONCEPT TEACHING

CONCEPT FORMATION AS A FUNCTION OF METHOD OF PRESENTATION AND RATIO OF POSITIVE TO NEGATIVE INSTANCES. ED015779
THE STUDY OF MUSIC IN THE ELEMENTARY SCHOOL--A CONCEPTUAL APPROACH. ED017328
NUMBER TRAINING TECHNIQUES AND THEIR EFFECTS ON DIFFERENT POPULATIONS. FINAL REPORT. ED019988
TEACHING FORMAL OPERATIONS TO PRESCHOOL ADVANTAGED AND DISADVANTAGED CHILDREN. ED019990
TEACHING MUSICAL CONCEPTS RELATED TO MELODY, RHYTHM, FORM, AND HARMONY, TEACHER RESOURCE MATERIAL KINDERGARTEN, GRADES 1 AND 2. ED019991
LOGICAL OPERATIONS AND CONCEPTS OF CONSERVATION IN CHILDREN, A TRAINING STUDY. FINAL REPORT. ED020010
MODIFICATION OF CLASSIFICATORY COMPETENCE AND LEVEL OF REPRESENTATION AMONG LOWER-CLASS NEGRO KINDERGARTEN CHILDREN. ED021608
SKILL GAMES FOR MATHEMATICS. ED022548
HEAD START EVALUATION AND RESEARCH CENTER, BOSTON UNIVERSITY. REPORT D-II, TRAINING FOR NUMBER CONCEPT. ED022564
CHILD DEVELOPMENT AND SOCIAL SCIENCE EDUCATION. PART I: THE PROBLEM, PART II: CONFERENCE REPORT. ED023465
TEACHING MOTHERS TO TEACH: A HOME COUNSELING PROGRAM FOR LOW-INCOME PARENTS. ED028819
INDUCING CONSERVATION OF NUMBER, WEIGHT, VOLUME, AREA, AND MASS IN PRE-SCHOOL CHILDREN. ED028822
KINDERGARTEN: THE CHILD IN HIS HOME AND SCHOOL ENVIRONMENTS. COURSE OF STUDY AND RELATED LEARNING ACTIVITIES. (CURRICULUM BULLETIN, 1967-68 SERIES, NO. 2A.) ED029681
GRADE 1: LIVING AND WORKING TOGETHER IN THE COMMUNITY. COURSE OF STUDY AND RELATED LEARNING ACTIVITIES. (CURRICULUM BULLETIN, 1967-68 SERIES, NO. 2B.) ED029682
COMPETENCE VS. PERFORMANCE IN YOUNG CHILDREN'S USE OF COMPLEX LINGUISTIC STRUCTURES. ED029687
EFFECT OF VARIETY ON THE LEARNING OF A SOCIAL STUDIES CONCEPT BY PRESCHOOL CHILDREN. ED029690
GRADE 2: HOW PEOPLE LIVE IN CITY COMMUNITIES AROUND THE WORLD. COURSE OF STUDY AND RELATED LEARNING ACTIVITIES. (CURRICULUM BULLETIN, 1968-69 SERIES, NO. 2.) ED029694
INVESTIGATION OF CONCEPT LEARNING IN YOUNG CHILDREN. FINAL REPORT. ED030498
A STUDY OF THE INTERRELATIONSHIPS OF CONSERVATION OF LENGTH RELATIONS, CONSERVATIONS OF LENGTH, AND TRANSITIVITY OF LENGTH RELATIONS OF THE AGE OF FOUR AND FIVE YEARS. ED031303
INFORMATION VALUE OF FEEDBACK WITH PRESCHOOL CHILDREN. ED031311
TEACHING MATHEMATICAL CONCEPTS TO TWO- AND THREE-YEAR-OLDS: SOME EXPERIMENTAL STUDIES. ED037234
RULE AND ATTRIBUTE LEARNING IN THE USE AND IDENTIFICATION OF CONCEPTS WITH YOUNG DISADVANTAGED CHILDREN. ED040747
EFFECTS OF VIEWING VIDEOTAPED SAME AND OPPOSITE COLOR CHILD-TEACHERS ON INTEGRATED AND ALL-WHITE KINDERGARTNERS. ED047805
A SUCCESSFUL ATTEMPT TO TRAIN CHILDREN IN COORDINATION OF PROJECTIVE SPACE. ED048916
BOOKS WHICH GIVE MATHEMATICAL CONCEPTS TO YOUNG CHILDREN: AN ANNOTATED BIBLIOGRAPHY EJ 007 274
ACTIVITIES TO TEACH THE CONCEPT OF CONSERVATION EJ 007 311
CHILDREN UNDER THREE - FINDING WAYS TO STIMULATE DEVELOPMENT. II. SOME CURRENT EXPERIMENTS: LEARNING AT TWO EJ 007 409
A DISCRIMINATION TASK WHICH INDUCES CONSERVATION OF NUMBER EJ 018 876

CONCEPTUAL SCHEMES

THE EVALUATION OF PROJECT HEAD START--A CONCEPTUAL STATEMENT. ED015792
A STUDY OF LANGUAGE DEVELOPMENT FROM INFANCY TO AGE 5. ED022539
INTELLECTUAL DEVELOPMENT AND THE ABILITY TO PROCESS VISUAL AND VERBAL INFORMATION. ED043373
SUBPOPULATIONAL PROFILING OF THE PSYCHOEDUCATIONAL DIMENSIONS OF DISADVANTAGED PRESCHOOL CHILDREN: A CONCEPTUAL PROSPECTUS FOR AN INTERDISCIPLINARY RESEARCH. ED045177
CONTINUITY IN THE DEVELOPMENT OF CONCEPTUAL BEHAVIOR IN PRESCHOOL CHILDREN: A REJOINDER EJ 018 888
CONTINUITY IN THE DEVELOPMENT OF CONCEPTUAL BEHAVIOR IN PRESCHOOL CHILDREN: RESPONSE TO A REJOINDER EJ 018 889

CONCEPTUAL TEMPO
ANALYSIS AND MODIFICATION OF SEARCH STRATEGIES OF IMPULSIVE AND REFLECTIVE CHILDREN ON THE MATCHING FAMILIAR FIGURES TEST EJ 059 510
CONCEPTUAL TEMPO AND INHIBITION OF MOVEMENT IN BLACK PRESCHOOL CHILDREN EJ 059 512

CONDITIONED RESPONSE
RESPONSE TO VARYING LEVELS OF CONDITIONING REWARDS. FINAL REPORT. ED020803
HEAD START EVALUATION AND RESEARCH CENTER, UNIVERSITY OF KANSAS. REPORT NO. VIIC, ERRORLESS DISCRIMINATION IN PRESCHOOL CHILDREN: A PROGRAM FOR ESTABLISHING A ONE-MINUTE DELAY OF REINFORCEMENT. ED021642
HEAD START EVALUATION AND RESEARCH CENTER, UNIVERSITY OF KANSAS. REPORT NO. IX, DEVELOPMENT OF "MATCHING" ABSTRACTIONS IN YOUNG CHILDREN. ED021645
COGNITIVE FACTORS IN SEMANTIC CONDITIONING. A THESIS IN EDUCATIONAL PSYCHOLOGY. ED027069
A PROGRAM OF STIMULUS CONTROL FOR ESTABLISHING A ONE-MINUTE WAIT FOR REINFORCEMENT IN PRESCHOOL CHILDREN. PROGRESS REPORT. ED042492
COGNITIVE FACTORS IN THE CONDITIONING OF CHILDREN'S PREFERENCES EJ 021 989
EFFECT OF PRETRAINING AND INSTRUCTIONS ON AVOIDANCE CONDITIONING IN PRESCHOOL CHILDREN EJ 035 624
A DECADE OF INFANT CONDITIONING AND LEARNING RESEARCH EJ 038 454
CAN CONDITIONED RESPONSES BE ESTABLISHED IN THE NEWBORN INFANT: 1971? EJ 041 956
INTERACTIONS BETWEEN THE FACILITATIVE AND INHIBITORY EFFECTS OF A PUNISHING STIMULUS IN THE CONTROL OF CHILDREN'S HITTING BEHAVIOR EJ 053 734
EVIDENCE FOR THE UNCONDITIONABILITY OF THE BABKIN REFLEX IN NEWBORNS EJ 058 589

CONDITIONED STIMULUS
STIMULUS GENERALIZATION ACROSS INDIVIDUALS ALONG DIMENSIONS OF SEX AND RACE: SOME FINDINGS WITH CHILDREN FROM AN ALL-NEGRO NEIGHBORHOOD. PROGRESS REPORT. ED042497

CONDITIONING
A TEST OF HABITUATION IN HUMAN INFANTS AS AN ACQUISITION PROCESS IN A RETROACTIVE INHIBITION PARADIGM. ED046490
THE VICARIOUS CONDITIONING OF EMOTIONAL RESPONSES IN NURSERY SCHOOL CHILDREN. FINAL REPORT. ED046540
CONDITIONING TASKS PERFORMANCE IN INFANCY AND EARLY CHILDHOOD AS A STABLE AND MEASURABLE ASPECT OF BEHAVIOR. FINAL REPORT. ED051890
ATTENTIONAL RESPONSES OF FIVE-MONTH GIRLS TO DISCREPANT AUDITORY STIMULI EJ 032 893
SMILING TO SOCIAL STIMULI: ELICITING AND CONDITIONING EFFECTS EJ 034 536
EFFECT OF PRETRAINING AND INSTRUCTIONS ON AVOIDANCE CONDITIONING IN PRESCHOOL CHILDREN EJ 035 624
CONDITIONAL DISCRIMINATION LEARNING IN CHILDREN: TWO RELEVANT FACTORS EJ 036 823
A DECADE OF INFANT CONDITIONING AND LEARNING RESEARCH EJ 038 454
CAN CONDITIONED RESPONSES BE ESTABLISHED IN THE NEWBORN INFANT: 1971? EJ 041 956
MEANING CONDITIONING AND AWARENESS AMONG CHILDREN EJ 049 426

CONDUCT
THE IMPACT OF WORDS AND DEEDS CONCERNING ALTRUISM UPON CHILDREN EJ 026 154

CONFERENCE REPORTS
CHILDREN AND THE ARTS. PRESENTATIONS FROM A WRITING CONFERENCE. ED025317
REPORT TO THE PRESIDENT: WHITE HOUSE CONFERENCE ON CHILDREN 1970. ED052828

CONFERENCES
THE USE OF INDIVIDUAL GOAL-SETTING CONFERENCES AS A MOTIVATIONAL TECHNIQUE. ED053816

CONFLICT
IS IT TIME TO BREAK THE SILENCE ON VIOLENCE? EJ 032 564
COOPERATION AND COMPETITION IN FOUR-YEAR-OLDS AS A FUNCTION OF REWARD CONTINGENCY AND SUBCULTURE EJ 045 453

CONFLICT RESOLUTION
THE COGNITIVE ENVIRONMENTS OF URBAN PRE-SCHOOL CHILDREN. MANUAL OF INSTRUCTIONS FOR ADMINISTERING AND SCORING MOTHER'S ROLE IN TEACHER/CHILD AND CHILD/PEER SCHOOL SITUATIONS. ED018257
HEAD START EVALUATION AND RESEARCH CENTER, UNIVERSITY OF KANSAS. REPORT NO. V, A COMPARATIVE BEHAVIORAL ANALYSIS OF PEER-GROUP INFLUENCE TECHNIQUES IN HEAD START AND MIDDLE CLASS POPULATIONS. ED021638
A THEORY OF PARENT EFFECTIVENESS. ED028815
IS IT TIME TO BREAK THE SILENCE ON VIOLENCE? EJ 032 564
FOUR CHILDREN EJ 061 073

CONFORMITY
A PARTIAL TEST OF A SOCIAL LEARNING THEORY OF CHILDREN'S CONFORMITY EJ 018 890
A TEST OF THE GENERALITY OF THE EFFECTS OF DEVIANT PRESCHOOL MODELS EJ 034 531
CONFORMITY IN EARLY AND LATE ADOLESCENCE EJ 038 936
RACE AND CONFORMITY AMONG CHILDREN EJ 038 937
CONFORMITY IN CHILDREN AS A FUNCTION OF GRADE LEVEL, AND REAL VERSUS HYPOTHETICAL ADULT AND PEER MODELS EJ 040 294
DEVELOPMENTAL CONFORMITY EJ 046 892
DEVELOPMENTAL COMPARISONS OF CONFORMITY ACROSS TWO CULTURES EJ 051 470
EGOCENTRISM AND SOCIAL INFLUENCE IN CHILDREN EJ 058 590

CONSERVATION (CONCEPT)
NUMBER TRAINING TECHNIQUES AND THEIR EFFECTS ON DIFFERENT POPULATIONS. FINAL REPORT. ED019988
HEAD START EVALUATION AND RESEARCH CENTER, BOSTON UNIVERSITY. REPORT D-II, TRAINING FOR NUMBER CONCEPT. ED022564
INDUCING CONSERVATION OF NUMBER, WEIGHT, VOLUME, AREA, AND MASS IN PRE-SCHOOL CHILDREN. ED028822
SUCCESSFUL NUMBER CONSERVATION TRAINING. ED031297
A STUDY OF THE INTERRELATIONSHIPS OF CONSERVATION OF LENGTH RELATIONS, CONSERVATIONS OF LENGTH, AND TRANSITIVITY OF LENGTH RELATIONS OF THE AGE OF FOUR AND FIVE YEARS. ED031303
"CONSERVATION" BELOW AGE THREE: FACT OR ARTIFACT? ED035438
STIMULUS ABSTRACTNESS AND THE CONSERVATION OF WEIGHT. ED035441
THE EFFECT OF SELECTED TRAINING EXPERIENCES ON PERFORMANCE ON A TEST OF CONSERVATION OF NUMEROUSNESS. REPORT FROM PHASE 2 OF THE PROTOTYPIC INSTRUCTIONAL SYSTEMS IN ELEMENTARY MATHEMATICS PROJECT. ED036334
AN INTRODUCTION OF LENGTH CONCEPTS TO KINDERGARTEN CHILDREN. REPORT FROM THE PROJECT ON ANALYSIS OF MATHEMATICS INSTRUCTION. ED036335
A FACTOR ANALYSIS OF A THREE-YEAR LONGITUDINAL STUDY OF CONSERVATION OF NUMBER AND RELATED MATHEMATICAL CONCEPTS. ED039934
PROBLEM SOLVING PERFORMANCES OF FIRST GRADE CHILDREN. ED041623
A PILOT INVESTIGATION OF THE EFFECTS OF TRAINING TECHNIQUES DESIGNED TO ACCELERATE CHILDRENS' ACQUISITION OF CONSERVATION OF DISCONTINUOUS QUANTITY. FINAL REPORT. ED044178
CHILDREN'S CONSERVATION OF MULTIPLE SPACE RELATIONS: EFFECTS OF PERCEPTION AND REPRESENTATION. ED044179
AN INVESTIGATION IN THE LEARNING OF EQUIVALENCE AND ORDER RELATIONS BY FOUR- AND FIVE-YEAR-OLD CHILDREN. ED045178
MODELING BY EXEMPLIFICATION AND INSTRUCTION IN TRAINING CONSERVATION. ED047790
THE ACQUISITION OF CONSERVATION THROUGH SOCIAL INTERACTION. ED047801
THE EFFECT OF VARYING OBJECT NUMBER AND TYPE OF ARRANGEMENT ON CHILDREN'S ABILITY TO COORDINATE PERSPECTIVES. ED047804
THE EFFICACY OF A MATHEMATICS READINESS PROGRAM FOR INDUCING CONSERVATION OF NUMBER, WEIGHT, AREA, MASS, AND VOLUME IN DISADVANTAGED PRESCHOOL CHILDREN IN THE SOUTHERN UNITED STATES. ED048923
THE ABILITY OF KINDERGARTEN AND FIRST GRADE CHILDREN TO USE THE TRANSITIVE PROPERTY OF THREE LENGTH RELATIONS IN THREE PERCEPTUAL SITUATIONS. ED048936
DIFFERENTIAL PERFORMANCE OF KINDERGARTEN CHILDREN ON TRANSITIVITY OF THREE MATCHING RELATIONS. ED048942
THE EFFECTS OF INSTRUCTION ON THE DEVELOPMENT OF THE CONCEPT OF CONSERVATION OF NUMEROUSNESS BY KINDERGARTEN CHILDREN. REPORT FROM THE PROJECT ON INDIVIDUALLY GUIDED ELEMENTARY MATHEMATICS ED049821
A COMPARISON STUDY OF THE COGNITIVE DEVELOPMENT OF DISADVANTAGED FIRST GRADE PUPILS (AS MEASURED BY SELECTED PIAGETIAN TASKS). ED051874
ACTIVITIES TO TEACH THE CONCEPT OF CONSERVATION EJ 007 311
A DEVELOPMENTAL STUDY OF NONCONSERVATION CHOICES IN YOUNG CHILDREN EJ 011 917
THE INFUENCE OF SOME TASK VARIABLES AND OF SOCIOECONOMIC CLASS ON THE MANIFESTATION OF CONSERVATION OF NUMBER EJ 017 711
OPERATIONAL THOUGHT INDUCEMENT EJ 018 874
A DISCRIMINATION TASK WHICH INDUCES CONSERVATION OF NUMBER EJ 018 876
PERCEPTUAL AND SENSORIMOTOR SUPPORTS FOR CONSERVATION TASKS EJ 018 886
TRAINING IN CONSERVATION OF WEIGHT EJ 021 761
REVERSIBILITY TRAINING AND STIMULUS DESIRABILITY AS FACTORS IN CONSERVATION OF NUMBER EJ 021 776
SCALOGRAM ANALYSIS OF LOGICAL AND PERCEPTUAL COMPONENTS OF CONSERVATION OF DISCONTINUOUS QUANTITY EJ 025 957
VERBAL MEDIATORS AND CUE DISCRIMINATION IN THE TRANSITION FROM NONCONSERVATION TO CONSERVATION OF NUMBER EJ 025 958

CONTINUITY AND DISCONTINUITY HYPOTHESES IN STUDIES OF CONSERVATION EJ 027 182
RELATIONSHIP OF CONSERVATION EXPLANATIONS TO ITEM DIFFICULTY EJ 030 295
BEFORE CHILDREN CAN MEASURE EJ 032 359
CHILDREN'S USE OF CONTEXT IN JUDGMENT OF WEIGHT EJ 033 053
VERBAL FACTORS IN COMPENSATION PERFORMANCE AND THE RELATION BETWEEN CONSERVATION AND COMPENSATION EJ 033 778
STIMULUS CORRELATES OF AREA JUDGMENTS: A PSYCHOPHYSICAL DEVELOPMENTAL STUDY EJ 034 707
A NONARBITRARY BEHAVIORAL CRITERION FOR CONSERVATION OF ILLUSION-DISTORTED LENGTH IN FIVE-YEAR-OLDS EJ 038 263
INTERDEPENDENCE OF INHELDER AND PIAGET'S MODEL OF LOGICAL THINKING EJ 039 633
ON THE CONSERVATION OF LIQUIDS EJ 039 640
STUDIES OF CONSERVATION WITH YORUBA CHILDREN OF DIFFERING AGES AND EXPERIENCE EJ 041 135
NUMBER CONSERVATION IN VERY YOUNG CHILDREN: THE EFFECT OF AGE AND MODE OF RESPONDING EJ 041 139
CONSERVATION OF NUMBER IN VERY YOUNG CHILDREN: A FAILURE TO REPLICATE MEHLER AND BEVER EJ 041 144
A PILOT INVESTIGATION OF THE EFFECTS OF TRAINING TECHNIQUES DESIGNED TO ACCELERATE CHILDREN'S ACQUISITION OF CONSERVATION OF DISCONTINOUS QUANTITY EJ 044 705
TRAINING AND GENERALIZATION OF DENSITY CONSERVATION: EFFECTS OF FEEDBACK AND CONSECUTIVE SIMILAR STIMULI EJ 046 231
SEMANTIC DIFFERENTIAL ANALYSIS OF RELATIONAL TERMS USED IN CONSERVATION EJ 046 235
EXTINCTION OF CONSERVATION: A METHODOLOGICAL AND THEORETICAL ANALYSIS EJ 046 245
EYE MOVEMENTS, PERCEPTUAL ACTIVITY, AND CONSERVATION DEVELOPMENT EJ 046 249
THE RELATIONSHIP BETWEEN PRIMARY STUDENTS' RATIONALIZATION OF CONSERVATION AND THEIR MATHEMATICAL ACHIEVEMENT EJ 046 672
CHILDREN'S ACQUISITION OF VISUO-SPATIAL DIMENSIONALITY: A CONSERVATION STUDY EJ 047 681
THE DEVELOPMENT OF THE PROPORTIONALITY SCHEME IN CHILDREN AND ADOLESCENTS EJ 047 682
A DEVELOPMENTAL COMPARISON OF IDENTITY AND EQUIVALENCE CONSERVATIONS EJ 049 167
AN EXAMINATION OF THE DEVELOPMENTAL RELATIONS BETWEEN CERTAIN SPATIAL TASKS EJ 051 563
DEVELOPMENT OF CONSERVATION IN NORMAL AND RETARDED CHILDREN EJ 053 651
ACQUISITION OF CONSERVATION THROUGH SOCIAL INTERACTION EJ 053 708
RACE, SOCIAL CLASS, AND AGE OF ACHIEVEMENT OF CONSERVATION ON PIAGET'S TASKS EJ 053 714
CONCEPT CONSERVATION IN CHILDREN: THE DEPENDENCE OF BELIEF SYSTEMS ON SEMANTIC REPRESENTATION EJ 053 742
THE ROLE OF BODY PARTS AND READINESS IN ACQUISITION OF NUMBER CONSERVATION EJ 053 757
PERFORMANCE OF CULTURALLY DEPRIVED CHILDREN ON THE CONCEPT ASSESSMENT KIT--CONSERVATION EJ 053 906
RELATION BETWEEN IDENTITY CONSERVATION AND EQUIVALENCE CONSERVATION WITHIN FOUR CONCEPTUAL DOMAINS EJ 054 804
LOGICAL CAPACITY OF VERY YOUNG CHILDREN: NUMBER INVARIANCE RULES EJ 056 394
THE EFFECTS OF TRAINING AND SOCIOECONOMIC CLASS UPON THE ACQUISITION OF CONSERVATION CONCEPTS EJ 056 401
MODELING BY EXEMPLIFICATION AND INSTRUCTION IN TRAINING CONSERVATION EJ 057 898
IDENTITY AND EQUIVALENCE CONSERVATION AT TWO AGE LEVELS EJ 057 901
THE RELATIONSHIP BETWEEN LIQUID CONSERVATION AND COMPENSATION EJ 059 313
PRECOCIOUS THOUGHTS ON NUMBER: THE LONG AND THE SHORT OF IT EJ 060 776
CONCRETE OPERATIONAL THINKING IN MENTALLY ILL ADOLESCENTS EJ 060 778

CONSERVATION EDUCATION
CHILDREN AND THEIR EXPANDING WORLD OF KNOWLEDGE EJ 026 734
A STUDY OF THE EFFECTIVENESS OF SPECIFIC TEACHING OF CONSERVATION TO CHILDREN IN SELECTED ELEMENTARY SCHOOLS OF BUTTE COUNTY, CALIFORNIA EJ 027 029
LEARNING FROM GEOGRAPHERS EJ 051 206

CONSONANTS
INITIAL AND FINAL CONSONANT RELATIONSHIPS IN SPEECH-SOUND TESTS: A DISCRIMINATION OR RESPONSE SET PROBLEM? ED032131

CONSTRUCTED RESPONSE
PSYCHOLOGICAL BASES FOR INSTRUCTIONAL DESIGN. ED013121
EXTINCTION IN DISCRIMINATION LEARNING--PRESENTATION AND CONTINGENCY VARIABLES AND ASSOCIATED SIDE EFFECTS. ED019139

CONSTRUCTION (PROCESS)
EVOLUTION OF THE HUMAN FIGURE IN A THREE-DIMENSIONAL MEDIUM EJ 057 897

CONSULTANTS
LONG DISTANCE INTERDISCIPLINARY EVALUATION OF DEVELOPMENTAL DISABILITIES. ED040748
CONSULTATION IN DAY CARE. ED051884
PSYCHOLOGICAL CONSULTATION IN A PRESCHOOL EJ 038 394

CONSULTATION PROGRAMS
SEMO PROJECT HEAD START, PSYCHOLOGICAL SERVICES REPORT, SUMMER 1967. PHASE THREE FINAL REPORT. ED020779

CONSUMER EDUCATION
THE ECONOMIC LITERACY OF ELEMENTARY-SCHOOL PUPILS EJ 029 042

CONTENT ANALYSIS
EFFECTS OF INSTRUCTIONS ON THEME GRADING: GRAMMATICAL VS. HOLISTIC EJ 040 724
LINGUISTIC AND THEMATIC VARIABLES IN RECALL OF A STORY BY DISADVANTAGED CHILDREN EJ 041 142
THE SUGAR-COATED WORLD OF THE THIRD-GRADE READER EJ 058 171

CONTEXT CLUES
EFFECTS OF CONTEXT ON PRESCHOOL CHILDREN'S JUDGMENTS EJ 042 968

CONTINUOUS PROGRESS PLAN
MODELS FOR NONGRADING SCHOOLS: A REPORT OF A NATIONAL SEMINAR. ED049827
CONTINUOUS PUPIL PROGRESS IN THE NON-GRADED SCHOOL: HOPE OR HOAX? EJ 028 100

CONTRACTS
SCHOOL COUNSELING BY CONTRACT EJ 038 985

CONTRAST
EFFECTS OF CONTEXT ON PRESCHOOL CHILDREN'S JUDGMENTS EJ 042 968
COMING OF AGE WITH THE DELBOEUF ILLUSION: BRIGHTNESS CONTRAST, COGNITION AND PERCEPTUAL DEVELOPMENT EJ 055 100

CONTROLLED ENVIRONMENT
THE PREPARED ENVIRONMENT AND ITS RELATIONSHIP TO LEARNING. ED025302

CONVENTIONAL INSTRUCTION
AN ACADEMIC PRESCHOOL FOR DISADVANTAGED CHILDREN: REVIEW OF FINDINGS. PRELIMINARY DRAFT. ED051878

COOPERATIVE PLANNING
OPTIMAL OPERATION OF PUBLIC/PRIVATE CHILD WELFARE DELIVERY SYSTEMS EJ 031 540
BIG STEPS ON BEHALF OF LITTLE PEOPLE EJ 058 769

COOPERATIVE PROGRAMS
CO-OPERATIVE NURSERY SCHOOLS--A HANDBOOK FOR PARENTS. A GUIDE FOR ORGANIZATION AND ADMINISTRATION. REVISED EDITION. ED020022
A STUDY IN CHILD CARE (CASE STUDY FROM VOLUME II-A): "CHILDREN AS 'KIDS'." DAY CARE PROGRAMS REPRINT SERIES. ED051900
ENRICHING CHILDREN'S LIVES: INTERNATIONAL CO-OPERATION THROUGH UNICEF AND OMEP EJ 062 417

CORRECTIVE INSTITUTIONS
WHY CHILDREN ARE IN JAIL AND HOW TO KEEP THEM OUT EJ 013 329
HELPING HOUSEPARENTS FIND AND USE THEIR CREATIVITY EJ 022 215
THE USE OF BEHAVIOR-MODIFICATION TECHNIQUES WITH FEMALE DELINQUENTS EJ 051 473

CORRELATION
PROJECT HEAD START--SUMMER 1966. FINAL REPORT. SECTION THREE, PUPILS AND PROGRAMS. ED018248
A COMPARISON BETWEEN THE ORAL AND WRITTEN RESPONSES OF FIRST-GRADE CHILDREN IN I.T.A. AND T.O. CLASSES. ED019144
SOME EFFECTS OF SOCIAL CLASS AND RACE ON CHILDREN'S LANGUAGE AND INTELLECTUAL ABILITIES. ED022540
AN INVESTIGATION OF SIMILARITIES IN PARENT-CHILD TEST SCORES FOR EVIDENCE OF HEREDITARY COMPONENTS. ED027060
THE FACTORIAL STRUCTURE OF REASONING, MORAL JUDGMENT, AND MORAL CONDUCT. ED031302
FIGURAL CREATIVITY, INTELLIGENCE, AND PERSONALITY IN CHILDREN: A FACTOR ANALYTIC STUDY. ED032931
LONG TERM STUDY OF PREMATURES: SUMMARY OF PUBLISHED FINDINGS. ED043389
INTERRELATIONS AND CORRELATES OVER TIME IN CHILDREN'S LEARNING EJ 025 954
CHILDREN'S BEHAVIOR PROBLEMS AS VIEWED BY TEACHERS, PSYCHOLOGISTS, AND CHILDREN EJ 026 313
HONESTY AND ALTRUISM AMONG PREADOLESCENTS EJ 026 450
INFANT MENTAL DEVELOPMENT AND NEUROLOGICAL STATUS, FAMILY SOCIOECONOMIC STATUS, AND INTELLIGENCE AT AGE FOUR EJ 032 675
CLASSROOM DISCIPLINE: A NEW APPROACH EJ 032 896

COST EFFECTIVENESS
CLASSIFYING DAY CARE CENTERS FOR COST ANALYSIS. ED047783
CONSIDERATIONS IN DAY CARE COST ANALYSIS EJ 040 722

COSTS
STANDARDS AND COSTS FOR DAY CARE. ED042501
SOME THOUGHTS ON PLANNING HEALTH CARE FOR CHILDREN AND YOUTH EJ 038 021

COUNSELING
A DAY IN THE LIFE OF A SCHOOL PSYCHOLOGIST EJ 018 956
MEETING SOCIO-EDUCATIONAL NEEDS EJ 027 916
ADOLESCENT MATERNITY SERVICES: A TEAM APPROACH EJ 047 354

COUNSELING EFFECTIVENESS
GROUP WORK WITH PARENTS OF CHILDREN WITH LEARNING DISORDERS. ED019130
THE TEACHER AS COUNSELOR: THERAPEUTIC APPROACHES TO UNDERSTANDING SELF AND OTHERS EJ 023 703

COUNSELING GOALS
GROUP WORK WITH PARENTS OF CHILDREN WITH LEARNING DISORDERS. ED019130

COUNSELING INSTRUCTIONAL PROGRAMS
A CAREER DEVELOPMENT PROGRAM IN THE CHICAGO PUBLIC SCHOOLS EJ 035 579

COUNSELING PROGRAMS
THE TEACHER AS COUNSELOR: THERAPEUTIC APPROACHES TO UNDERSTANDING SELF AND OTHERS EJ 023 703
THE CHILD CARE COUNSELOR: NEW THERAPIST IN CHILDREN'S INSTITUTIONS EJ 027 919

COUNSELING SERVICES
A HOTLINE TELEPHONE SERVICE FOR YOUNG PEOPLE IN CRISIS EJ 007 713
EARLY LEGAL ADOPTION EJ 022 533
MEDICAL GENETICS AND ADOPTION EJ 037 577
SCHOOL COUNSELING BY CONTRACT EJ 038 985

COUNSELOR EVALUATION
A COMPARATIVE STUDY OF COUNSELEE PREFERENCES FOR BEHAVIORIST AND CLIENT-CENTERED COUNSELING APPROACHES EJ 058 628

COUNSELOR QUALIFICATIONS
BLACK CLIENTS AND WHITE WORKERS; A REPORT FROM THE FIELD EJ 051 062

COUNSELOR ROLE
YOUTH AS ADVISERS TO ADULTS AND VICE VERSA EJ 018 068

COUNSELORS
THE CHILD CARE COUNSELOR: NEW THERAPIST IN CHILDREN'S INSTITUTIONS EJ 027 919

COURSE DESCRIPTIONS
LEARNING AND TEACHING, GRADES N-9 (EMPHASIS ON EARLY CHILDHOOD). ED023459
CHILD WELFARE: SEARCHING FOR RELEVANT LEARNING ON THE UNDERGRADUATE LEVEL EJ 056 762

COURSE EVALUATION
THE EFFECT OF STUDENT EVALUATIONS OF COLLEGE INSTRUCTION UPON SUBSEQUENT EVALUATIONS EJ 017 245

COURSE ORGANIZATION
TEACHING GENERAL MUSIC, A RESOURCE HANDBOOK FOR GRADES 7 AND 8. ED018277
CLARIFYING THE ROLE OF FOSTER PARENTS EJ 061 235

COURT ROLE
A NEW LOOK AT THE COURTS AND CHILDREN'S RIGHTS EJ 007 092

COURTS
A NEW LOOK AT THE COURTS AND CHILDREN'S RIGHTS EJ 007 092

CREATIVE ABILITY
PARENTAL CONCEPTUAL SYSTEMS, HOME PLAY ENVIRONMENT, AND POTENTIAL CREATIVITY IN CHILDREN. ED043386
CREATIVITY AND ALIENATION: AN EXPLORATION OF THEIR RELATIONSHIP IN ADOLESCENCE EJ 021 996
CREATIVE ABILITY OVER A FIVE-YEAR SPAN EJ 058 412
INCENTIVE EFFECTS IN CHILDREN'S CREATIVITY EJ 059 317

CREATIVE ACTIVITIES
THE CREATIVE-AESTHETIC APPROACH TO SCHOOL READINESS AND MEASURED CREATIVE GROWTH. ED017344
MAKING A CHILD'S OWN BOOK. ED035452
THE CHILD AND LEISURE TIME. 1970 WHITE HOUSE CONFERENCE ON CHILDREN, REPORT OF FORUM 21. (WORKING COPY). ED046536
WHAT GENERATION GAP? EJ 032 763
THE CREATIVE ENVIRONMENT WORKSHOP EJ 035 168
THE USE OF CREATIVITY TRAINING MATERIALS WITH SPECIAL CHILDREN: A REPORT OF A FEASIBILITY EXPERIENCE EJ 046 058

CREATIVE DEVELOPMENT
THE CREATIVE-AESTHETIC APPROACH TO SCHOOL READINESS AND MEASURED CREATIVE GROWTH. ED017344
UNDERSTANDING THE FOURTH GRADE SLUMP IN CREATIVE THINKING. FINAL REPORT. ED018273
THINKING, FEELING, EXPERIENCING--TOWARD REALIZATION OF FULL POTENTIAL. ED020012
CREATIVITY AND THE LEARNING PROCESS. 1970 WHITE HOUSE CONFERENCE ON CHILDREN, REPORT OF FORUM 6. (WORKING PAPER). ED046525
FANTASIZING AND POETRY CONSTRUCTION IN PRESCHOOLERS EJ 018 132
THE USE OF CREATIVITY TRAINING MATERIALS WITH SPECIAL CHILDREN: A REPORT OF A FEASIBILITY EXPERIENCE EJ 046 058

CREATIVE DRAMATICS
EXPANDING THE CHILD'S WORLD THROUGH DRAMA AND MOVEMENT EJ 034 421
VALUES AND TECHNIQUES OF CREATIVE DRAMATICS EJ 034 422
CREATIVE DRAMA AND LANGUAGE GROWTH EJ 052 176

CREATIVE EXPRESSION
CHILDREN DANCE IN THE CLASSROOM. ED053804
LETTERS FROM ENGLAND EJ 037 738
IDEATIONAL CREATIVITY AND EXPRESSIVE ASPECTS OF HUMAN FIGURE DRAWING IN KINDERGARTEN-AGE CHILDREN EJ 039 629
A CREATIVE PLAYGROUND EJ 042 406
A PROCESS FOR POETRY-WRITING EJ 055 364

CREATIVE TEACHING
WHAT CAN TEACHERS LEARN FROM DIRECTORS IN THE PERFORMING ARTS? EJ 051 410

CREATIVE THINKING
PRODUCTIVE THINKING IN EDUCATION. ED024459
IMPLICATIONS OF POST-NATAL CORTICAL DEVELOPMENT FOR CREATIVITY RESEARCH. ED047802
PRODUCTION OF NOVEL AND GRAMMATICAL UTTERANCES BY YOUNG CHILDREN EJ 060 783

CREATIVE WRITING
THE OTHER MOUTH: WRITING IN THE SCHOOLS EJ 027 881
ENCOURAGEMENT FOR THE YOUNG WRITER EJ 029 414

CREATIVITY
THE RELATIONSHIPS BETWEEN CERTAIN TEACHER CHARACTERISTICS AND ACHIEVEMENT AND CREATIVITY OF GIFTED ELEMENTARY SCHOOL STUDENTS. FINAL REPORT SUMMARY. ED015787
HELPING THE CHILD DEVELOP HIS CREATIVE POTENTIAL. ED026113
CREATIVITY AND THE LEARNING PROCESS. 1970 WHITE HOUSE CONFERENCE ON CHILDREN, REPORT OF FORUM 6. (WORKING PAPER). ED046525
PRECURSORS OF INTELLIGENCE AND CREATIVITY: A LONGITUDINAL STUDY OF ONE CHILD'S DEVELOPMENT EJ 020 521
NATURE OF CREATIVITY IN HIGH- AND LOW-CURIOSITY BOYS EJ 021 990
AN INSTRUMENT FOR MEASURING CREATIVITY IN YOUNG CHILDREN: THE GROSS GEOMETRIC FORMS EJ 027 586
THE CHILD'S EYE VIEW: EXPERIMENTAL PHOTOGRAPHY WITH PRESCHOOL CHILDREN EJ 029 342
CREATIVITY CHANGE IN STUDENT NURSES: A CROSS-SECTIONAL AND LONGITUDINAL STUDY EJ 030 291
ON SELECTING MATERIALS FOR THE CLASSROOM EJ 032 865
LITERATURE, CREATIVITY AND IMAGINATION EJ 033 510
EXPANDING THE CHILD'S WORLD THROUGH DRAMA AND MOVEMENT EJ 034 421
INCREASING AND RELEASING HUMAN POTENTIALS EJ 034 710
TRAINING CREATIVITY IN YOUNG CHILDREN EJ 035 373
CREATIVITY AS RELATED TO FIELD INDEPENDENCE AND MOBILITY EJ 035 380
IDEATIONAL CREATIVITY AND EXPRESSIVE ASPECTS OF HUMAN FIGURE DRAWING IN KINDERGARTEN-AGE CHILDREN EJ 039 629
EXPRESSIONS OF PERSONALITY IN CREATIONS OF LATENCY AGE CHILDREN EJ 041 446
THE FRANCK DRAWING COMPLETION TEST AS A MEASURE OF CREATIVITY EJ 044 704
SEX AND AGE DIFFERENCES IN PATTERN ORGANIZATION IN A FIGURAL-CONCEPTUAL TASK EJ 047 680
PARENTAL CONCEPTUAL SYSTEMS, HOME PLAY ENVIRONMENT, AND POTENTIAL CREATIVITY IN CHILDREN EJ 048 234
MATERNAL CHILD REARING AND CREATIVITY IN SONS EJ 048 302
LITERATURE, CREATIVITY AND IMAGINATION EJ 056 090
CREATIVITY: IDEA QUANTITY AND IDEA QUALITY EJ 058 212

CREATIVITY RESEARCH
THE CREATIVE-AESTHETIC APPROACH TO SCHOOL READINESS AND MEASURED CREATIVE GROWTH. ED017344
UNDERSTANDING THE FOURTH GRADE SLUMP IN CREATIVE THINKING. FINAL REPORT. ED018273
HELPING THE CHILD DEVELOP HIS CREATIVE POTENTIAL. ED026113
IDENTIFICATION AND DEVELOPMENT OF CREATIVE ABILITIES. ED027965
SOME DIMENSIONS OF CREATIVE THINKING ABILITY ACHIEVEMENT, AND INTELLIGENCE IN FIRST GRADE. ED028818
FIGURAL CREATIVITY, INTELLIGENCE, AND PERSONALITY IN CHILDREN: A FACTOR ANALYTIC STUDY. ED032931
RATE AND UNIQUENESS IN CHILDREN'S CREATIVE RESPONDING. ED034581

A THIRD STUDY OF SOME RELATIONSHIPS BETWEEN CREATIVITY AND PERCEPTION IN 6TH GRADE CHILDREN EJ 016 166
PROGRAMMING CREATIVE BEHAVIOR EJ 021 080
PLAY AS A FUNCTION OF TOY STRUCTURE AND FANTASY PREDISPOSITION EJ 021 083
TRAINING CREATIVITY IN YOUNG CHILDREN EJ 035 373
CREATIVITY AS RELATED TO FIELD INDEPENDENCE AND MOBILITY EJ 035 380
CREATIVITY: IDEA QUANTITY AND IDEA QUALITY EJ 058 212
INCENTIVE EFFECTS IN CHILDREN'S CREATIVITY EJ 059 317

CREATIVITY TESTS
EXPRESSIONS OF PERSONALITY IN CREATIONS OF LATENCY AGE CHILDREN EJ 041 446
THE FRANCK DRAWING COMPLETION TEST AS A MEASURE OF CREATIVITY EJ 044 704

CREDENTIALS
THE CALIFORNIA CREDENTIAL STORY: A NEW SPECIALIZATION FOR TEACHERS OF YOUNG CHILDREN EJ 020 892

CRISIS THERAPY
PREVENTIVE THERAPY WITH SIBLINGS OF A DYING CHILD EJ 030 515

CRITERIA
A NONARBITRARY BEHAVIORAL CRITERION FOR CONSERVATION OF ILLUSION-DISTORTED LENGTH IN FIVE-YEAR-OLDS EJ 038 263

CRITICAL INCIDENTS METHOD
EVALUATIVE USES OF UNCONVENTIONAL MEASUREMENT TECHNIQUES IN AN EDUCATIONAL SYSTEM EJ 042 347

CRITICAL PATH METHOD
FINAL REPORT ON HEAD START EVALUATION AND RESEARCH--1966-67 TO THE INSTITUTE FOR EDUCATIONAL DEVELOPMENT. SECTION II, ON THE INTERPRETATION OF MULTIVARIATE SYSTEMS. ED019118

CRITICAL THINKING
DEVELOPMENT OF A GROUP MEASURE TO ASSESS THE EXTENT OF PRE-LOGICAL AND PRE-CAUSAL THINKING IN PRIMARY SCHOOL AGE CHILDREN. ED019136

CROSS AGE TEACHING
REMEDIAL READING INSTRUCTION BY TRAINED PUPIL TUTORS EJ 035 172
EFFECTS OF TUTORIAL EXPERIENCES ON THE PROBLEM-SOLVING BEHAVIOR OF SIXTH-GRADERS EJ 043 415
"THIS YEAR I GOT MY BUDDY TO LAUGH" EJ 044 509
WORKING TOGETHER WORKS EJ 044 510
THE EFFECT OF SIBLING RELATIONSHIP ON CONCEPT LEARNING OF YOUNG CHILDREN TAUGHT BY CHILD-TEACHERS EJ 056 399
A YOUNG MAN AROUND THE CLASS EJ 059 445

CROSS CULTURAL STUDIES
INFANCY IN HOLLAND: THE FIRST THREE MONTHS. ED031296
A DISCUSSION OF RESEARCH AIMS AND STRATEGIES FOR STUDYING EDUCATION IN THE INNER-CITY (A CRITIQUE OF NON-PARTICIPANT OBSERVATIONS). PRELIMINARY DRAFT. ED038187
TINY DRAMAS: VOCAL COMMUNICATION BETWEEN MOTHER AND INFANT IN JAPANESE AND AMERICAN FAMILIES. ED048927
A STUDY OF CAUSAL THINKING IN ELEMENTARY SCHOOL CHILDREN. FINAL REPORT. ED050830
A STUDY IN CHILD CARE (CASE STUDY FROM VOLUME II-A): "A SMALL U. N." DAY CARE PROGRAMS REPRINT SERIES. ED051904
NURSERIES IN CROSS-CULTURAL EDUCATION. FINAL REPORT. ED053815
CULTURAL DIFFERENCES IN COLOR/FORM PREFERENCE AND IN CLASSIFICATORY BEHAVIOR EJ 024 034
BODY SIZE OF CONTEMPORARY GROUPS OF ONE-YEAR-OLD INFANTS STUDIED IN DIFFERENT PARTS OF THE WORLD EJ 025 469
PHYSICAL GROWTH AND BODY COMPOSITION: PAPERS FROM THE KYOTO SYMPOSIUM ON ANTHROPOLOGICAL ASPECTS OF HUMAN GROWTH EJ 029 387
SELF-DESCRIPTION AS A FUNCTION OF EVALUATIVE AND ACTIVITY RATINGS AMONG AMERICAN AND INDIAN ADOLESCENTS EJ 034 042
TEACHERS IN CHILDREN'S ROLES? EJ 037 235
HUMAN RESOURCES FOR INTERNATIONAL STUDIES EJ 038 393
BEHAVIORAL COMPLIANCE AND DEVALUATION OF THE FORBIDDEN OBJECT AS A FUNCTION OF PROBABILITY OF DETECTION AND SEVERITY OF THREAT EJ 038 935
GROUP CARE AND INTELLECTUAL DEVELOPMENT EJ 040 041
STUDIES OF CONSERVATION WITH YORUBA CHILDREN OF DIFFERING AGES AND EXPERIENCE EJ 041 135
DIVERGENT THINKING AND PERSONALITY MEASURES OF ENGLISH AND AMERICAN EDUCATION MAJORS EJ 044 707
A CROSS-CULTURAL COMPARISON OF MATERNAL COMMUNICATION EJ 045 505
LEARNING FROM PLAY IN OTHER CULTURES EJ 045 532
PSYCHOSOCIAL DEVELOPMENT IN CROSS-CULTURAL PERSPECTIVE: A NEW LOOK AT AN OLD ISSUE EJ 046 888
A CROSS-CULTURAL STUDY OF THE CHILD'S COMMUNICATION WITH HIS MOTHER EJ 046 890
PLAY BEHAVIOR IN YOUNG CHILDREN: A CROSS-CULTURAL STUDY EJ 048 303
CONCEPTS OF SOCIAL SEX ROLES AMONG CHILEAN ADOLESCENTS EJ 048 396
DEVELOPMENTAL COMPARISONS OF CONFORMITY ACROSS TWO CULTURES EJ 051 470
DEVELOPMENTAL DETERMINANTS OF ATTENTION: A CROSS-CULTURAL REPLICATION EJ 053 718
DEVELOPMENT OF YOUNG CHILDREN'S ATTENTION TO NORMAL AND DISTORTED STIMULI: A CROSS CULTURAL STUDY EJ 055 103
OBSERVATION, REPETITION, AND ETHNIC BACKGROUND IN CONCEPT ATTAINMENT AND GENERALIZATION EJ 059 316
PERCEPTION AND LANGUAGE: A GERMAN REPLICATION OF THE PIAGET-INHELDER POSITION EJ 060 773
INFANT CARE AND GROWTH IN URBAN ZAMBIA EJ 061 231
IMPLICATIONS OF INFANT DEVELOPMENT AMONG THE MAYAN INDIANS OF MEXICO EJ 061 232
MOTHER-ATTACHMENT AND STRANGER-REACTIONS IN THE THIRD YEAR OF LIFE EJ 062 594

CROSS CULTURAL TRAINING
EFFECTS OF SOCIAL REINFORCEMENT ON SELF-ESTEEM OF MEXICAN-AMERICAN CHILDREN. LONG ABSTRACT. ED033767

CROSS SECTIONAL STUDIES
FORMAL OPERATIONS IN FEMALES FROM ELEVEN TO FIFTY-FOUR YEARS OF AGE EJ 055 215
SOCIAL CLASS INTELLIGENCE, AND COGNITIVE STYLE IN INFANCY EJ 056 725
MOTHER-ATTACHMENT AND STRANGER-REACTIONS IN THE THIRD YEAR OF LIFE EJ 062 594

CUES
INVESTIGATIONS OF THE ROLE OF SELECTED CUES IN CHILDREN'S PAIRED-ASSOCIATE LEARNING. REPORT FROM THE READING PROJECT. ED036315
AN EXPERIMENTAL ANALYSIS OF ERROR INTERACTION ON "ERRORLESS" AND TRIAL-AND-ERROR PROGRAMS. PROGRESS REPORT. ED042491
CUE NOVELTY AND TRAINING LEVEL IN THE DISCRIMINATION SHIFT PERFORMANCE OF RETARDATES EJ 015 851
CHILDREN'S JUDGMENTS OF PERSONALITY ON THE BASIS OF VOICE QUALITY EJ 030 512
A DECREMENTAL EFFECT OF REDUNDANCY IN DISCRIMINATION LEARNING EJ 033 795
MEDIATION AND PERCEPTUAL TRANSFER IN CHILDREN EJ 035 365
CUE AND INCENTIVE MOTIVATIONAL PROPERTIES OF REINFORCERS IN CHILDREN'S DISCRIMINATION LEARNING EJ 035 374
PATTERN COPYING UNDER THREE CONDITIONS OF AN EXPANDED SPATIAL FIELD EJ 035 622
EFFECTS OF STIMULUS AVAILABILITY ON CHILDREN'S INFERENCES EJ 036 822
CONDITIONAL DISCRIMINATION LEARNING IN CHILDREN: TWO RELEVANT FACTORS EJ 036 823
THE CONTROL OF RELATIVE SIZE BY PICTORIAL DEPTH CUES IN CHILDREN AND ADULTS EJ 042 506
VARIETY OF EXEMPLARS VERSUS LINGUISTIC CONTEXTS IN CONCEPT ATTAINMENT IN YOUNG CHILDREN EJ 042 955
FACTORS INFLUENCING CHILDREN'S CONCEPT IDENTIFICATION PERFORMANCE WITH NONPREFERRED RELEVANT ATTRIBUTES EJ 042 965
THE PRIORITY OF CUES IN SEX DISCRIMINATION BY CHILDREN AND ADULTS EJ 044 691
VISUAL AND HAPTIC CUE UTILIZATION BY PRESCHOOL CHILDREN: THE RECOGNITION OF VISUAL AND HAPTIC STIMULI PRESENTED SEPARATELY AND TOGETHER EJ 044 698
THE EFFECTS OF VISUALLY REPRESENTED CUES ON LEARNING OF LINEAR FUNCTION RULES EJ 044 701
CONSONANT CUE PERCEPTION BY TWENTY- TO TWENTY-FOUR-WEEK-OLD INFANTS EJ 045 597
EFFECTS OF EXPOSURE TO MODELS ON CONCEPT IDENTIFICATION IN KINDERGARTEN AND SECOND-GRADE CHILDREN EJ 046 240
CUE SYSTEMS AVAILABLE DURING THE READING PROCESS: A PSYCHOLINGUISTIC VIEWPOINT EJ 053 399
VERBAL-LABELING AND CUE-TRAINING IN REVERSAL-SHIFT BEHAVIOR EJ 053 727
COLOR DOMINANCE IN PRESCHOOL CHILDREN AS A FUNCTION OF SPECIFIC CUE PREFERENCES EJ 053 738
USE OF LABELS AND CUES IN CHILDREN'S CONCEPT IDENTIFICATION EJ 056 712
INSTABILITY OF DIMENSIONAL PREFERENCE FOLLOWING CHANGES IN RELATIVE CUE SIMILARITY EJ 057 908
TASK ORIENTATION VERSUS SOCIAL ORIENTATION IN YOUNG CHILDREN AND THEIR ATTENTION TO RELEVANT SOCIAL CUES EJ 058 413
STABILITY OF FIRST-GRADE CHILDREN'S DIMENSIONAL PREFERENCES EJ 059 319
REVERSALS PRIOR TO SOLUTION OF CONCEPT IDENTIFICATION IN CHILDREN EJ 060 782
AGGRESSION ANXIETY, PERCEPTION OF AGGRESSIVE CUES, AND EXPECTED RETALIATION EJ 061 071

CULTURAL AWARENESS
CROSS-CULTURAL FAMILY CENTER, SAN FRANCISCO, CALIFORNIA: A NURSERY SCHOOL PROVIDING A MULTICULTURAL CURRICULUM TO PROMOTE RACIAL UNDERSTANDING AND ACCEPTANCE. MODEL PROGRAMS--CHILDHOOD EDUCATION. ED045214

UNDERSTANDING ONE ANOTHER: UNESCO'S ASSOCIATED SCHOOLS PROJECT EJ 037 426
HUMAN RESOURCES FOR INTERNATIONAL STUDIES EJ 038 393
WHO ARE THE DISADVANTAGED? EJ 039 800
WHAT'S DEPRIVED ABOUT BEING DIFFERENT? EJ 046 968
STUDYING HUMAN ECOLOGY: TEACHER EDUCATION AND THE CULTURALLY DIVERSE EJ 048 395

CULTURAL BACKGROUND
NEGRO HERITAGE: A SELECTED BOOK LIST FOR ALL AGES. ED036341
HISPANIC HERITAGE: A SELECTED BOOK LIST FOR ALL AGES. ED036342
INDIAN HERITAGE: A SELECTED BOOK LIST FOR ALL AGES. ED036345
MULTI-ETHNIC BOOKS FOR YOUNG CHILDREN: ANNOTATED BIBLIOGRAPHY FOR PARENTS AND TEACHERS. ED046519
EXPERIMENTAL ANALYSES OF COOPERATION AND COMPETITION OF ANGLO-AMERICAN AND MEXICAN CHILDREN EJ 053 647
LEARNING FROM THE BRITISH PRIMARY SCHOOLS EJ 057 327
AN EXPERIMENTAL STUDY OF THE SELECTIVE ATTENTION OF CHILDREN OF 1896 AND 1966 EJ 060 775

CULTURAL DIFFERENCES
PROJECT HEAD START IN AN INDIAN COMMUNITY. ED014329
UNDERSTANDING THE FOURTH GRADE SLUMP IN CREATIVE THINKING. FINAL REPORT. ED018273
COMPARISON OF AMERICAN AND NORWEGIAN NURSERY SCHOOL CHILDREN ON INDEPENDENCE BEHAVIOR AND TRAINING. ED024457
COMPARISON OF AMERICAN AND NORWEGIAN NURSERY SCHOOL CHILDREN OF INDEPENDENCE BEHAVIOR AND TRAINING. SUMMARY REPORT. ED024476
GRAMMATICAL DEVELOPMENT IN RUSSIAN-SPEAKING CHILDREN. ED025332
LEARNING READINESS IN TWO JEWISH GROUPS: A STUDY IN "CULTURAL DEPRIVATION." AN OCCASIONAL PAPER. ED026126
PUERTO RICAN CHILDREN IN MAINLAND SCHOOLS. A SOURCE BOOK FOR TEACHERS. ED027953
A DISCUSSION OF RESEARCH AIMS AND STRATEGIES FOR STUDYING EDUCATION IN THE INNER-CITY (A CRITIQUE OF NON-PARTICIPANT OBSERVATIONS). PRELIMINARY DRAFT. ED038187
LANGUAGE RESEARCH AND PRESCHOOL LANGUAGE TRAINING. ED040767
EMOTIONAL CHARACTERISTICS OF DISADVANTAGED CHILDREN OF APPALACHIA. ED043383
NEGRO CULTURE AND EARLY CHILDHOOD EDUCATION. ED046495
TINY DRAMAS: VOCAL COMMUNICATION BETWEEN MOTHER AND INFANT IN JAPANESE AND AMERICAN FAMILIES. ED048927
PERCEPTUAL EXPLORATION IN ISRAELI CHILDREN EJ 033 054
THE CULTURE OF THE CULTURALLY DEPRIVED EJ 035 537
COOPERATION AND COMPETITION OF MEXICAN, MEXICAN-AMERICAN, AND ANGLO-AMERICAN CHILDREN OF TWO AGES UNDER FOUR INSTRUCTIONAL SETS EJ 041 957
LEVELS OF ASPIRATION, ACHIEVEMENT, AND SOCIOCULTURAL DIFFERENCES IN PRESCHOOL CHILDREN EJ 043 482
LEARNING FROM PLAY IN OTHER CULTURES EJ 045 532
WHAT'S DEPRIVED ABOUT BEING DIFFERENT? EJ 046 968
ARTICULATION OF THE BODY CONCEPT AMONG FIRST-GRADE ISRAELI CHILDREN EJ 053 744
LISTENING BEYOND WORDS: LEARNING FROM PARENTS IN CONFERENCES EJ 055 363
MODELING BY EXEMPLIFICATION AND INSTRUCTION IN TRAINING CONSERVATION EJ 057 898

CULTURAL DISADVANTAGEMENT
PROJECT HEAD START AND THE CULTURALLY DEPRIVED IN ROCHESTER, NEW YORK, A STUDY OF PARTICIPATING AND NON-PARTICIPATING FAMILIES IN AREAS SERVED BY PROJECT HEAD START IN ROCHESTER, FINAL REPORT. ED013669
SOME EFFECTS OF SOCIAL CLASS AND RACE ON CHILDREN'S LANGUAGE AND INTELLECTUAL ABILITIES. ED022540
A STUDY OF VISUAL PERCEPTIONS IN EARLY CHILDHOOD. ED023451
THE EFFECTS OF PSYCHOSOCIAL DEPRIVATION ON HUMAN DEVELOPMENT IN INFANCY. ED034574
INSTITUTE FOR DEVELOPMENTAL STUDIES INTERIM PROGRESS REPORT. PART II: RESEARCH AND EVALUATION. ED036312
LANGUAGE DEVELOPMENT OF SOCIALLY DISADVANTAGED PRESCHOOL CHILDREN. FINAL REPORT. ED041641
PSYCHOLOGICAL DEPRIVATION: WHAT WE DO, DON'T, AND SHOULD KNOW ABOUT IT EJ 012 676
THE EFFECTS OF PSYCHOSOCIAL DEPRIVATION ON HUMAN DEVELOPMENT IN INFANCY EJ 026 815
WHAT'S DEPRIVED ABOUT BEING DIFFERENT? EJ 046 968
AN ANALYSIS OF THE CONCEPT OF CULTURAL DEPRIVATION EJ 055 111

CULTURAL ENRICHMENT
DEVELOPMENT OF AN ENLARGED MUSIC REPERTORY FOR KINDERGARTEN THROUGH GRADE SIX (JUILLIARD REPERTORY PROJECT). FINAL REPORT. ED016521
A THIRD STUDY OF THE EFFECTS OF A LEARNING EXPERIENCE UPON PREFERENCE FOR COMPLEXITY-ASYMMETRY IN FOURTH, FIFTH, AND SIXTH GRADE CHILDREN EJ 029 281
THE DAYS THAT MAKE US HAPPY: GAMES AROUND THE WORLD EJ 038 407
ART - FOR THE CHILD'S SAKE EJ 041 829

CULTURAL ENVIRONMENT
"YOUTH UNREST": REFLECTIONS OF A PSYCHOANALYST EJ 023 425

CULTURAL FACTORS
THE EFFECTS OF MONTESSORI EDUCATIONAL TECHNIQUES ON CULTURALLY DISADVANTAGED HEAD START CHILDREN. ED015009
UNDERSTANDING THE FOURTH GRADE SLUMP IN CREATIVE THINKING. FINAL REPORT. ED018273
INFLUENCES OF CULTURAL PATTERNS ON THE THINKING OF CHILDREN IN CERTAIN ETHNIC GROUPS, A STUDY OF THE EFFECT OF JEWISH SUBCULTURE ON THE FIELD-DEPENDENCE-INDEPENDENCE DIMENSION OF COGNITION. ED020796
MODIFICATION OF CLASSIFICATORY COMPETENCE AND LEVEL OF REPRESENTATION AMONG LOWER-CLASS NEGRO KINDERGARTEN CHILDREN. ED021608
EMERGENCE OF IDENTITY: THE FIRST YEARS. 1970 WHITE HOUSE CONFERENCE ON CHILDREN, REPORT OF FORUM 2. (WORKING COPY). ED046521
STAGES OF THE DREAM CONCEPT AMONG HASIDIC CHILDREN EJ 017 903
CHOICES, CHOICES, CHOICES! PEAK EXPERIENCES FROM THE AFRO-AMERICAN HERITAGE EJ 020 857
ADOLESCENCE AND SOCIAL CHANGE EJ 023 611
CHILD-REARING PRACTICES IN MOUNTAIN COUNTY, KENTUCKY EJ 036 210
TEACHERS IN CHILDREN'S ROLES? EJ 037 235
A SOCIOCULTURAL PERSPECTIVE ON PHYSICAL CHILD ABUSE EJ 043 353
RACE, SOCIAL CLASS, AND AGE OF ACHIEVEMENT OF CONSERVATION ON PIAGET'S TASKS EJ 053 714

CULTURAL PLURALISM
CULTURE OF THE SCHOOL. A CONSTRUCT FOR RESEARCH AND EXPLANATION IN EDUCATION. ED039945
ON VALUING DIVERSITY IN LANGUAGE EJ 011 840

CULTURALLY ADVANTAGED
AN ASSESSMENT AND COMPARISON OF SELECTED CHARACTERISTICS AMONG CULTURALLY DISADVANTAGED HEADSTART CHILDREN (SUMMER PROGRAM 1965), CULTURALLY DISADVANTAGED NON-HEADSTART CHILDREN, AND NON-CULTURALLY DISADVANTAGED CHILDREN. (TITLE SUPPLIED). ED014330
A COMPARISON OF THE DEVELOPMENTAL DRAWING CHARACTERISTICS OF CULTURALLY ADVANTAGED AND CULTURALLY DISADVANTAGED CHILDREN. FINAL REPORT. ED015783
A COMPARATIVE STUDY OF THE SELF-IMAGES OF DISADVANTAGED CHILDREN. ED028821
SOCIOECONOMIC BACKGROUND AND COGNITIVE FUNCTIONING IN PRESCHOOL CHILDREN. ED032929
DEVELOPMENTAL GROUPINGS OF PRE-SCHOOL CHILDREN. ED046513
REEXAMINING VARIABLES AFFECTING COGNITIVE FUNCTIONING IN PRESCHOOL CHILDREN: A FOLLOW-UP. ED052818
HERO MODELS EJ 016 607
SELF CONCEPTS OF DISADVANTAGED AND ADVANTAGED STUDENTS EJ 035 618

CULTURALLY DISADVANTAGED
EVALUATION OF PROJECT HEAD START READING READINESS IN ISSAQUENA AND SHARKEY COUNTIES, MISSISSIPPI, SUMMER, 1965. FINAL REPORT. ED014319
AN ASSESSMENT OF INTELLIGENCE, PSYCHOLINGUISTIC ABILITIES AND LEARNING APTITUDES AMONG PRESCHOOL CHILDREN. ED014323
AN EVALUATION OF THE EFFECTS OF A SUMMER HEAD START PROGRAM. ED014327
AN ASSESSMENT AND COMPARISON OF SELECTED CHARACTERISTICS AMONG CULTURALLY DISADVANTAGED HEADSTART CHILDREN (SUMMER PROGRAM 1965), CULTURALLY DISADVANTAGED NON-HEADSTART CHILDREN, AND NON-CULTURALLY DISADVANTAGED CHILDREN. (TITLE SUPPLIED). ED014330
REPORT OF A RESEARCH AND DEMONSTRATION PROJECT FOR CULTURALLY DISADVANTAGED CHILDREN IN THE ANCONA MONTESSORI SCHOOL. ED015014
A COMPARISON OF THE DEVELOPMENTAL DRAWING CHARACTERISTICS OF CULTURALLY ADVANTAGED AND CULTURALLY DISADVANTAGED CHILDREN. FINAL REPORT. ED015783
A NATIONAL DEMONSTRATION PROJECT UTILIZING TELEVISED MATERIALS FOR THE FORMAL EDUCATION OF CULTURALLY DISADVANTAGED PRESCHOOL CHILDREN. FINAL REPORT. ED015788
THE EARLY TRAINING PROJECT FOR DISADVANTAGED CHILDREN--A REPORT AFTER FIVE YEARS. ED016514
A COMPARATIVE STUDY OF TWO PRESCHOOL PROGRAMS FOR CULTURALLY DISADVANTAGED CHILDREN--A HIGHLY STRUCTURED AND A TRADITIONAL PROGRAM. ED016524
EVALUATION OF CHANGES OCCURRING IN CHILDREN WHO PARTICIPATED IN PROJECT HEAD START. ED017316
THE EFFECTS OF NEUROLOGICAL AND ENVIRONMENTAL FACTORS ON THE LANGUAGE DEVELOPMENT OF HEAD START CHILDREN--A EVALUATION OF THE HEAD START PROGRAM. ED017317

HEAD START, WEST VIRGINIA, SUMMER 1966--A SEVEN-COUNTY OVERVIEW, A SPECIAL ASSIGNMENT OF THE WEST VIRGINIA DEPARTMENT OF MENTAL HEALTH. ED017338
A PARENT EDUCATION APPROACH TO PROVISION OF EARLY STIMULATION FOR THE CULTURALLY DISADVANTAGED. FINAL REPORT. ED017339
RESULTS OF THE SUMMER 1965 PROJECT HEAD START. VOLUMES I AND II. ED018250
FINAL REPORT ON HEAD START EVALUATION AND RESEARCH--1966-67 TO THE INSTITUTE FOR EDUCATIONAL DEVELOPMENT. SECTION V, THE ROLE OF DIALECT IN THE SCHOOL-SOCIALIZATION OF LOWER CLASS CHILDREN. ED019121
EARLY LEARNING IN THE HOME. ED019127
A COMPARATIVE STUDY OF VARIOUS PROJECT HEAD START PROGRAMS. ED019987
AN EVALUATION OF THE EFFECTS OF A UNIQUE SEQUENTIAL LEARNING PROGRAM ON CULTURALLY DEPRIVED PRESCHOOL CHILDREN. FINAL REPORT. ED019994
EVALUATION OF THE CLEVELAND CHILD DEVELOPMENT PROGRAM. A LONGITUDINAL STUDY (FIRST YEAR REPORT). ED020000
LANGUAGE LEARNING ACTIVITIES FOR THE DISADVANTAGED CHILD. ED020002
THE DEUTSCH MODEL--INSTITUTE FOR DEVELOPMENTAL STUDIES. ED020009
MOTIVATIONAL FACTORS AND IQ-CHANGES IN CULTURALLY DEPRIVED CHILDREN ATTENDING NURSERY SCHOOL. ED020017
THE EFFECT OF HEADSTART ON DEVELOPMENTAL PROCESSES. ED020026
EFFECTIVENESS OF THE HEAD START PROGRAM IN ENHANCING SCHOOL READINESS OF CULTURALLY DEPRIVED CHILDREN. ED020771
THE IMPACT OF OPERATION HEAD START ON GREENE COUNTY, OHIO, AN EVALUATION REPORT. ED020772
PRE-SCHOOL EDUCATION. ED020785
A FOLLOW-UP STUDY OF INTELLIGENCE CHANGES IN CHILDREN WHO PARTICIPATED IN PROJECT HEADSTART. ED020786
AN EVALUATION AND FOLLOW-UP STUDY OF SUMMER 1966 HEAD START CHILDREN IN WASHINGTON, D.C. ED020794
MAKING WAVES, DENVER HEAD START. ED020802
AN EARLY INTERVENTION PROGRAM THAT FAILED. ED021609
CULTURAL ENVIRONMENTAL ACHIEVEMENT PROJECT, A SUMMARIZATION AND EVALUATION OF AN EXPERIMENTAL PRE-SCHOOL PROGRAM. ED021610
PROJECT HEAD START, REPORT ON THE PREKINDERGARTEN PROGRAM, 1965. ED021611
HEAD START EVALUATION AND RESEARCH CENTER. PROGRESS REPORT OF RESEARCH STUDIES, 1966-1967. ED021612
HEAD START RESEARCH AND EVALUATION OFFICE, UNIVERSITY OF CALIFORNIA AT LOS ANGELES. ANNUAL REPORT, NOVEMBER 1967. SECTION II. ED021613
PILOT STUDY OF FIVE METHODS OF PRESENTING THE SUMMER HEAD START CURRICULAR PROGRAM. ED021622
HEAD START EVALUATION AND RESEARCH CENTER. PROGRESS REPORT OF RESEARCH STUDIES 1966 TO 1967. DOCUMENT 1, DEVELOPMENT OF THE MATRIX TEST. ED021623
HEAD START EVALUATION AND RESEARCH CENTER. PROGRESS REPORT OF RESEARCH STUDIES 1966 TO 1967. DOCUMENT 3, AN EXPERIMENTAL APPROACH TO STUDYING NON-VERBAL REPRESENTATION IN YOUNG CHILDREN. ED021625
HEAD START EVALUATION AND RESEARCH CENTER. PROGRESS REPORT OF RESEARCH STUDIES 1966 TO 1967. DOCUMENT 5, COMPARATIVE ITEM-CONTENT ANALYSIS OF ACHIEVEMENT TEST PERFORMANCE IN YOUNG CHILDREN. ED021627
HEAD START EVALUATION AND RESEARCH CENTER. PROGRESS REPORT OF RESEARCH STUDIES 1966 TO 1967. DOCUMENT 6, INDIVIDUAL INSTRUCTION PROJECT I. ED021628
HEAD START EVALUATION AND RESEARCH CENTER, UNIVERSITY OF KANSAS. REPORT NO. III, EFFECTS OF A LANGUAGE PROGRAM ON CHILDREN IN A HEAD START NURSERY. ED021636
HEAD START EVALUATION AND RESEARCH CENTER, UNIVERSITY OF KANSAS. REPORT NO. XI, VERBAL RECALL RESEARCH. ED021647
PRE-SCHOOL RESEARCH AND EVALUATION PROJECT. ED022541
USING MUSIC WITH HEAD START CHILDREN. ED022543
FINAL REPORT ON HEAD START EVALUATION AND RESEARCH: 1967-68 TO THE OFFICE OF ECONOMIC OPPORTUNITY. SECTION I: PART A, MIDDLE CLASS MOTHER-TEACHERS IN AN EXPERIMENTAL PRESCHOOL PROGRAM FOR SOCIALLY DISADVANTAGED CHILDREN. ED023454
FINAL REPORT ON HEAD START EVALUATION AND RESEARCH: 1967-68 TO THE OFFICE OF ECONOMIC OPPORTUNITY. SECTION I: PARTS A AND B. ED023457
GUIDELINES FOR PLANNING PRESCHOOL PROGRAMS FOR EDUCATIONALLY DEPRIVED CHILDREN UNDER TITLE I OF THE ELEMENTARY AND SECONDARY EDUCATION ACT OF 1965. ED023463
PROCESSES OF CURIOSITY AND EXPLORATION IN PRESCHOOL DISADVANTAGED CHILDREN. ED023470
AN EVALUATION OF THE PRESCHOOL READINESS CENTERS PROGRAM IN EAST ST. LOUIS, ILLINOIS, JULY 1, 1967-JUNE 30, 1968. FINAL REPORT. ED023472
A STANDARDIZED NEUROLOGICAL EXAMINATION: ITS VALIDITY IN PREDICTING SCHOOL ACHIEVEMENT IN HEAD START AND OTHER POPULATIONS. FINAL REPORT. ED023475
THE PRESCHOOL LANGUAGE PROJECT. A REPORT OF THE FIRST YEAR'S WORK. ED023482
CONCEPT LEARNING IN EARLY CHILDHOOD. ED024454
MOTIVATIONAL AND SOCIAL COMPONENTS IN COMPENSATORY EDUCATION PROGRAMS: SUGGESTED PRINCIPLES, PRACTICES, AND RESEARCH DESIGNS. ED024464
PRESCHOOL PROGRAMS AND THE INTELLECTUAL DEVELOPMENT OF DISADVANTAGED CHILDREN. ED024473
LANGUAGE ABILITY AND READINESS FOR SCHOOL OF CHILDREN WHO PARTICIPATED IN HEAD START PROGRAMS. A DISSERTATION ABSTRACT. ED025299
COMPARATIVE EFFECTIVENESS OF ECHOIC AND MODELING PROCEDURES IN LANGUAGE INSTRUCTION WITH CULTURALLY DISADVANTAGED CHILDREN. ED025314
HEAD START CRIB. CHILDHOOD RESEARCH INFORMATION BULLETIN: SELECTED RESUMES OF EARLY CHILDHOOD RESEARCH REPORTS. BULLETIN NO. 1. ED025318
METHODOLIGICAL CONSIDERATIONS IN DEVISING HEAD START PROGRAM EVALUATIONS. ED025319
THE EFFECT OF A STRUCTURED TUTORIAL PROGRAM ON THE COGNITIVE AND LANGUAGE DEVELOPMENT OF CULTURALLY DISADVANTAGED INFANTS. ED026110
A RATIONALE FOR A STRUCTURED EDUCATIONAL PROGRAM AND SUGGESTED ACTIVITIES FOR CULTURALLY DISADVANTAGED INFANTS. ED026112
THE EFFECTIVENESS OF THE PEABODY LANGUAGE DEVELOPMENT KITS AND THE INITIAL TEACHING ALPHABET WITH DISADVANTAGED CHILDREN IN THE PRIMARY GRADES: AFTER TWO YEARS. ED026125
A METHODOLOGY FOR FOSTERING ABSTRACT THINKING IN DEPRIVED CHILDREN. ED026131
THE EFFECTS OF TEACHER IN-SERVICE EDUCATION ON THE DEVELOPMENT OF ART IDEAS WITH SIX-YEAR OLD CULTURALLY DEPRIVED CHILDREN. FINAL REPORT. ED027066
RESEARCH ON THE NEW NURSERY SCHOOL. PART II: A REPORT ON THE USE OF TYPEWRITERS AND RELATED EQUIPMENT WITH THREE- AND FOUR-YEAR-OLD CHILDREN AT THE NEW NURSERY SCHOOL. INTERIM REPORT. ED027077
A STUDY OF THE EFFECTS OF TEACHER ATTITUDE AND CURRICULUM STRUCTURE ON PRESCHOOL DISADVANTAGED CHILDREN. ANNUAL PROGRESS REPORT I. ED027079
THE PROGRAM OF RESEARCH OF THE MERRILL-PALMER INSTITUTE IN CONJUNCTION WITH THE HEAD START EVALUATION AND RESEARCH CENTER, MICHIGAN STATE UNIVERSITY. ANNUAL REPORT. VOLUME II: RESEARCH. ED027088
CONCEPT AND LANGUAGE DEVELOPMENT IN A KINDERGARTEN OF DISADVANTAGED CHILDREN. ED027967
DIAGNOSTICALLY BASED CURRICULUM, BLOOMINGTON, INDIANA ED027978
TOWARD THE PREVENTION OF INCOMPETENCE. ED028812
TEACHING MOTHERS TO TEACH: A HOME COUNSELING PROGRAM FOR LOW-INCOME PARENTS. ED028819
A COMPARATIVE STUDY OF THE SELF-IMAGES OF DISADVANTAGED CHILDREN. ED028821
PROJECT HEAD START: EVALUATION AND RESEARCH SUMMARY 1965-1967. ED028826
A STUDY OF FOOD AND POVERTY AMONG 113 HEAD START CHILDREN IN MISSOULA, MONTANA. ED028829
THE RELATIONSHIP BETWEEN HEMOGLOBIN LEVEL AND INTELLECTUAL FUNCTION. ED028830
[REGIONAL RESEARCH AND RESOURCE CENTER IN EARLY CHILDHOOD.] FINAL REPORT. ED028846
AN EXPERIMENTAL PROGRAM DESIGNED TO INCREASE AUDITORY DISCRIMINATION WITH HEAD START CHILDREN. ED029680
REPLICATION OF THE "MOTIVATED LEARNING" COGNITIVE TRAINING PROCEDURES WITH CULTURALLY DEPRIVED PRESCHOOLERS. REPORT FROM PROJECT MOTIVATED LEARNING. ED029708
SOCIAL ANTECEDENTS OF PRESCHOOL CHILDREN'S BEHAVIORS. REPORT NUMBER 2. ED030476
PRELIMINARY RESULTS FROM A LONGITUDINAL STUDY OF DISADVANTAGED PRESCHOOL CHILDREN. ED030490
THE ROLE OF INCENTIVES IN DISCRIMINATION LEARNING OF CHILDREN WITH VARYING PRE-SCHOOL EXPERIENCE. ED031290
PERSONALITY DEVELOPMENT IN DISADVANTAGED FOUR-YEAR-OLD BOYS: OBSERVATIONS WITH PLAY TECHNIQUES. ED031310
A DESCRIPTIVE STUDY OF COGNITIVE AND AFFECTIVE TRENDS DIFFERENTIATING SELECTED GROUPS OF PRE-SCHOOL CHILDREN. ED031314
EVAULATION OF THE DEMONSTRATION PHASE OF THE TEEN TUTORIAL PROGRAM: A MODEL OF INTERRELATIONSHIP OF SEVENTH GRADERS, KINDERGARTEN PUPILS AND PARENTS TO MEET THE DEVELOPMENTAL NEEDS OF DISADVANTAGED CHILDREN. ED032115
INVESTIGATION OF METHODS TO ASSESS THE EFFECTS OF CULTURAL DEPRIVATION. FINAL REPORT. ED032121
CHILDREN'S PERCEPTIONS OF ADULT ROLES AS AFFECTED BY CLASS, FATHER-ABSENCE AND RACE. ED032134
RESISTANCE TO TEMPTATION IN YOUNG NEGRO CHILDREN IN RELATION TO SEX OF THE SUBJECT, SEX OF THE EXPERIMENTER AND FATHER ABSENCE OR PRESENCE. ED032138
RESEARCH, CHANGE, AND SOCIAL RESPONSIBILITY: AN ILLUSTRATIVE MODEL FROM EARLY EDUCATION. ED032922

SOCIOECONOMIC BACKGROUND AND COGNITIVE FUNCTIONING IN PRESCHOOL CHILDREN. ED032929
THE EARLY TRAINING PROJECT: A SEVENTH YEAR REPORT. ED032934
MODIFICATION OF THE PEABODY PICTURE VOCABULARY TEST. ED033752
PENNSYLVANIA PRESCHOOL AND PRIMARY EDUCATION PROJECT: 1968-1969 FINAL REPORT TO THE FORD FOUNDATION. ED033759
THE SATURDAY SCHOOL: AN INSTALLATION MANUAL. ED033765
STANDARDIZED TESTS AND THE DISADVANTAGED. ED034594
THE ADVANTAGED: A PRESCHOOL PROGRAM FOR THE DISADVANTAGED. ED035436
POPULATION CHARACTERISTICS OF DISADVANTAGED PRESCHOOL CHILDREN. PROCEEDINGS OF THE HEAD START RESEARCH SEMINARS: SEMINAR NO. 3, HEAD START POPULATIONS (1ST, WASHINGTON, D.C., OCTOBER 9, 1968). ED036330
NUTRITION AND MENTAL DEVELOPMENT. RESEARCH REPORT NO. 5. ED037252
DEVELOPMENT OF A READINESS TEST FOR DISADVANTAGED PRE-SCHOOL CHILDREN IN THE UNITED STATES. FINAL REPORT. ED037253
PSYCHOLINGUISTIC BEHAVIORS OF BLACK, DISADVANTAGED RURAL CHILDREN. ED039037
THE ETS-OEO LONGITUDINAL STUDY OF DISADVANTAGED CHILDREN. ED039927
A PARENT-CHILD CENTER, NOVEMBER-DECEMBER 1968. ED042506
A FOLLOW-UP EVALUATION OF THE EFFECTS OF A UNIQUE SEQUENTIAL LEARNING PROGRAM, A TRADITIONAL PRESCHOOL PROGRAM AND A NO TREATMENT PROGRAM ON CULTURALLY DEPRIVED CHILDREN. FINAL REPORT. ED042516
MOTHERS' TRAINING PROGRAM: EDUCATIONAL INTERVENTION BY THE MOTHERS OF DISADVANTAGED INFANTS. ED043378
CHILD DEVELOPMENT RESEARCH AND EVALUATION CENTER FOR HEAD START, TEMPLE UNIVERSITY, 1968 - 1969. ANNUAL REPORT. ED043388
ANCONA MONTESSORI RESEARCH PROJECT FOR CULTURALLY DISADVANTAGED CHILDREN. SEPTEMBER 1, 1968 TO AUGUST 31, 1969. FINAL REPORT. ED044166
DEVELOPMENTAL-BEHAVIORAL PATTERNS IN TWENTY-SIX CULTURALLY DISADVANTAGED INFANTS. ED044173
SUBPOPULATIONAL PROFILING OF THE PSYCHOEDUCATIONAL DIMENSIONS OF DISADVANTAGED PRESCHOOL CHILDREN: A CONCEPTUAL PROSPECTUS FOR AN INTERDISCIPLINARY RESEARCH. ED045177
A GUIDE FOR MANAGERS OF CHILD DAY CARE AGENCIES. ED046486
YPSILANTI PRESCHOOL CURRICULUM DEMONSTRATION PROJECT, 1968-1971. ED046503
EFFECTS OF PRESCHOOL STIMULATION UPON SUBSEQUENT SCHOOL PERFORMANCE AMONG THE CULTURALLY DISADVANTAGED. ED046545
A SEQUENTIAL APPROACH TO EARLY CHILDHOOD AND ELEMENTARY EDUCATION, PHASE II. GRANT REPORT. ED047791
THE EFFECTS OF ADULT VERBAL MODELING AND FEEDBACK ON THE ORAL LANGUAGE OF HEAD START CHILDREN. ED047793
REEXAMINING VARIABLES AFFECTING COGNITIVE FUNCTIONING IN PRESCHOOL CHILDREN: A FOLLOW-UP. ED052818
IS THERE A LITERATURE FOR THE DISADVANTAGED CHILD? EJ 007 178
THE POVERTY CULTURE EJ 011 823
BRINGING THEIR OWN: LANGUAGE DEVELOPMENT IN THE MIDDLE GRADES EJ 011 844
HERO MODELS EJ 016 607
PSYCHOLINGUISTIC ABILITIES OF GOOD AND POOR READING DISADVANTAGED FIRST-GRADERS EJ 018 198
A LEARNING EXPERIENCE IN HELPING PARENTS GET WHAT THEY WANT EJ 024 027
HEALTH CARE THROUGH HEAD START EJ 024 496
THE USEFULNESS OF CUMULATIVE DEPRIVATION AS AN EXPLANATION OF EDUCATIONAL DEFICIENCIES EJ 033 056
OCCUPATIONAL PRESTIGE AS SEEN BY DISADVANTAGED BLACK CHILDREN EJ 034 453
THE CULTURE OF THE CULTURALLY DEPRIVED EJ 035 537
SELF CONCEPTS OF DISADVANTAGED AND ADVANTAGED STUDENTS EJ 035 618
CHILDREN'S ENVIRONMENTS AND CHILD WELFARE EJ 037 184
THE PSYCHOLOGICAL CORRELATES OF SPEECH CHARACTERISTICS OF SOUNDING "DISADVANTAGED": A SOUTHERN REPLICATION EJ 040 685
RACIAL ATTITUDES OF NEGRO PRESCHOOLERS EJ 041 858
DIFFERENTIAL COGNITIVE DEVELOPMENT WITHIN AND BETWEEN RACIAL AND ETHNIC GROUPS OF DISADVANTAGED PRESCHOOL AND KINDERGARTEN CHILDREN EJ 049 172
DO MATERIAL REWARDS ENHANCE THE PERFORMANCE OF LOWER-CLASS CHILDREN? EJ 053 735
PERFORMANCE OF CULTURALLY DEPRIVED CHILDREN ON THE CONCEPT ASSESSMENT KIT--CONSERVATION EJ 053 906
LONGITUDINAL DEVELOPMENT OF VERY YOUNG CHILDREN IN A COMPREHENSIVE DAY CARE PROGRAM: THE FIRST TWO YEARS EJ 056 707

CULTURE CONFLICT

THE WARRIOR DROPOUTS. ED016529
CULTURE OF THE SCHOOL: A CONSTRUCT FOR RESEARCH AND EXPLANATION IN EDUCATION. ED039945
DESIGNS AND PROPOSAL FOR EARLY CHILDHOOD RESEARCH: A NEW LOOK: THE UNACKNOWLEDGED ROLE OF CULTURE CONFLICT IN NEGRO EDUCATION. (ONE IN A SERIES OF SIX PAPERS). ED053810

CULTURE FREE TESTS

THE JOHNS HOPKINS PERCEPTUAL TEST, THE DEVELOPMENT OF A RAPID INTELLIGENCE TEST FOR THE PRE-SCHOOL CHILD. ED020787
THE USE OF THE GOODENOUGH DRAW-A-MAN TEST AS A PREDICTOR OF ACADEMIC ACHIEVEMENT. ED029695
DEVELOPMENT OF A READINESS TEST FOR DISADVANTAGED PRE-SCHOOL CHILDREN IN THE UNITED STATES. FINAL REPORT. ED037253

CURIOSITY

THE COGNITIVE ENVIRONMENTS OF URBAN PRE-SCHOOL CHILDREN. MANUAL OF INSTRUCTIONS FOR ADMINISTERING AND SCORING PLUTCHIK EXPLORATORY-INTEREST QUESTIONNAIRE. ED018262
THE COGNITIVE ENVIRONMENTS OF URBAN PRE-SCHOOL CHILDREN. MANUAL OF INSTRUCTIONS FOR ADMINISTERING AND SCORING THE CURIOSITY TASK. ED018268
PROCESSES OF CURIOSITY AND EXPLORATION IN PRESCHOOL DISADVANTAGED CHILDREN. ED023470
SELF-CONCEPTS OF HIGH- AND LOW-CURIOSITY BOYS EJ 019 005
NATURE OF CREATIVITY IN HIGH- AND LOW-CURIOSITY BOYS EJ 021 990
LEARNING, CURIOSITY, AND SOCIAL GROUP MEMBERSHIP EJ 035 378
CURIOSITY AND THE PARENT-CHILD RELATIONSHIP EJ 041 447
CORRELATES OF CURIOSITY AND EXPLORATORY BEHAVIOR IN PRESCHOOL DISADVANTAGED CHILDREN EJ 045 456
THE CURIOSITY DIMENSION OF FIFTH-GRADE CHILDREN: A FACTORIAL DISCRIMINANT ANALYSIS EJ 056 623

CURRENT EVENTS

THE TEMPER OF THE TIMES EJ 000 391

CURRICULUM

A STUDY OF THE EFFECTS OF TEACHER ATTITUDE AND CURRICULUM STRUCTURE ON PRESCHOOL DISADVANTAGED CHILDREN. ANNUAL PROGRESS REPORT I. ED027079
ADDRESS AT COMBINED MEETING OF N.Y.C. EARLY CHILDHOOD COUNCIL AND THE METROPOLITAN ASSOCIATION FOR CHILDHOOD EDUCATION ON "LANGUAGE ARTS MATERIALS IN EARLY CHILDHOOD" (TEACHERS COLLEGE, COLUMBIA UNIVERSITY, APRIL 6, 1968): ED039951
COMPARATIVE STUDY OF THREE PRESCHOOL CURRICULA. ED042484
KINDERGARTEN: WHO? WHAT? WHERE? ED049829
THE SEVENTIES: A TIME FOR GIANT STEPS EJ 009 030
PRESCHOOL PROGRAMS OF THE U.S.S.R EJ 016 352
NUTRITION AND EDUCATIONAL EXPERIENCE: INTERRELATED VARIABLES IN CHILDREN'S LEARNING EJ 059 643

CURRICULUM DESIGN

SEQUENCE IN LEARNING--FACT OR FICTION. ED017330
THE NEW ELEMENTARY SCHOOL. ED017341
EXPERIMENTAL VARIATION OF HEAD START CURRICULA: A COMPARISON OF CURRENT APPROACHES. (NOVEMBER 1, 1969-JANUARY 31, 1970). ED041617
RELATIONSHIP OF CURRICULUM, TEACHING, AND LEARNING IN PRESCHOOL EDUCATION. ED049837
THE NON-STRUCTURED APPROACH TO CHILDREN'S LITERATURE EJ 015 980
STRUCTURE OF-OR FOR-KNOWLEDGE? EJ 050 038
CURRICULUM BOON OR BANE? EJ 052 766

CURRICULUM DEVELOPMENT

PRELIMINARY EVALUATION OF A LANGUAGE CURRICULUM FOR PRESCHOOL CHILDREN. FINAL REPORT. ED021618
THE YPSILANTI EARLY EDUCATION PROGRAM. ED022531
CHILD DEVELOPMENT AND SOCIAL SCIENCE EDUCATION. PART I: THE PROBLEM, PART II: CONFERENCE REPORT. ED023465
CHILD DEVELOPMENT AND SOCIAL SCIENCE EDUCATION. PART III: ABSTRACTS OF RELEVANT LITERATURE. ED023466
CHILD DEVELOPMENT AND SOCIAL SCIENCE EDUCATION. PART IV: A TEACHING STRATEGY DERIVED FROM SOME PIAGETIAN CONCEPTS. ED023467
CHILDREN AND THE ARTS. PRESENTATIONS FROM A WRITING CONFERENCE. ED025317
THE INITIAL PHASE OF A PRESCHOOL CURRICULUM DEVELOPMENT PROJECT. FINAL REPORT. ED027071
PIAGET, SKINNER, AND AN INTENSIVE PRESCHOOL PROGRAM FOR LOWER CLASS CHILDREN AND THEIR MOTHERS. ED027966
DIAGNOSTICALLY BASED CURRICULUM, BLOOMINGTON, INDIANA ED027978
AN EVALUATION OF THE INTERIM CLASS: AN EXTENDED READINESS PROGRAM. ED028820
ECONOMICS IN THE ELEMENTARY SCHOOL ED028839
A TWO-YEAR LANGUAGE ARTS PROGRAM FOR PRE-FIRST GRADE CHILDREN: FIRST YEAR REPORT. ED029686
PROGRESS REPORT ON RESEARCH AT THE NEW NURSERY SCHOOL: GENERAL BACKGROUND AND PROGRAM RATIONALE. ED032930
DEVELOPMENT OF A DANCE CURRICULUM FOR YOUNG CHILDREN. CAREL ARTS AND HUMANITIES CURRICULUM DEVELOPMENT PROGRAM FOR YOUNG CHILDREN. ED032936

DEVELOPMENT OF A THEATRE ARTS CURRICULUM FOR YOUNG CHILDREN. CAREL ARTS AND HUMANITIES CURRICULUM DEVELOPMENT PROGRAM FOR YOUNG CHILDREN. ED032937
DEVELOPMENT OF A MUSIC CURRICULUM FOR YOUNG CHILDREN. CAREL ARTS AND HUMANITIES CURRICULUM DEVELOPMENT PROGRAM FOR YOUNG CHILDREN. ED032938
DEVELOPMENT OF A VISUAL ARTS CURRICULUM FOR YOUNG CHILDREN. CAREL ARTS AND HUMANITIES CURRICULUM DEVELOPMENT PROGRAM FOR YOUNG CHILDREN. ED032939
DEVELOPMENT OF A LITERATURE CURRICULUM FOR YOUNG CHILDREN. CAREL ARTS AND HUMANITIES CURRICULUM DEVELOPMENT PROGRAM FOR YOUNG CHILDREN. ED032940
ARTS AND HUMANITIES FOR YOUNG SCHOOL CHILDREN. ED032945
A STRUCTURE-PROCESS APPROACH TO COGNITIVE DEVELOPMENT OF PRESCHOOL NEGRO CHILDREN: RATIONALE AND EFFECTS. ED033743
THE TUCSON EARLY EDUCATION MODEL. ED033753
ORCHESTRATED INSTRUCTION: A COOKING EXPERIENCE. ED034593
NEW NURSERY SCHOOL RESEARCH PROJECT, OCTOBER 1, 1968 TO SEPTEMBER 30, 1969. ANNUAL PROGRESS REPORT. ED036320
INDEPENDENT LEARNING IN THE ELEMENTARY SCHOOL CLASSROOM. ED036326
PIAGET'S THEORY AND SPECIFIC INSTRUCTION: A RESPONSE TO BEREITER AND KOHLBERG. ED038164
AN EARLY CHILDHOOD EDUCATION MODEL: A BILINGUAL APPROACH. ED038167
PRESCHOOL MATHEMATICS CURRICULUM PROJECT. FINAL REPORT. ED038168
A PIAGETIAN METHOD OF EVALUATING PRESCHOOL CHILDREN'S DEVELOPMENT IN CLASSIFICATION. ED039013
A STUDY OF THE ABILITY OF PRIMARY SCHOOL CHILDREN TO GENERALIZE BEHAVIORAL COMPETENCIES SPECIFIED FOR "SCIENCE--A PROCESS APPROACH" TO OTHER CONTENT SETTINGS. ED039038
AN EDUCATIONAL SYSTEM FOR DEVELOPMENTALLY DISABLED INFANTS. ED040749
PROCESS ACCOUNTABILITY IN CURRICULUM DEVELOPMENT. ED040757
ISSUES AND REALITIES IN EARLY CHILDHOOD EDUCATION. ED041621
CLASSIFICATION AND ATTENTION TRAINING CURRICULA FOR HEAD START CHILDREN. ED042508
AN APPLICATION OF PIAGET'S THEORY TO THE CONCEPTUALIZATION OF A PRESCHOOL CURRICULUM. ED046502
A TEACHING LEARNING SCHEMA FOR TEACHER TRAINING AND CURRICULUM DEVELOPMENT IN EARLY EDUCATION. ED049812
THE UNIT-BASED CURRICULUM. YPSILANTI PRESCHOOL CURRICULUM DEMONSTRATION PROJECT. ED049831
A STUDY IN CHILD CARE (CASE STUDY FROM VOLUME II-A): "LIFE IS GOOD, RIGHT? RIGHT!" DAY CARE PROGRAMS REPRINT SERIES. ED051901
LANGUAGE LEARNING AT ROUGH ROCK EJ 011 874
CHOICES, CHOICES, CHOICES! PEAK EXPERIENCES FROM THE AFRO-AMERICAN HERITAGE EJ 020 857
WHAT ARE THE SOURCES OF EARLY CHILDHOOD CURRICULUM? EJ 027 943
DO YOU REALLY WANT TO IMPROVE THE CURRICULUM? EJ 031 850
ASSESSING THE ALTERNATIVES EJ 033 055
DESIGNING TOMORROW'S SCHOOL TODAY: THE MULTI-SENSORY EXPERIENCE CENTER EJ 033 784
STRUCTURE OF-OR FOR-KNOWLEDGE? EJ 050 038
THINKING BEFORE LANGUAGE? A SYMPOSIUM: 2. A SCHOOL FOR THINKING EJ 050 200
SOCIAL ISSUES, SOCIAL ACTION, AND THE SOCIAL STUDIES EJ 052 767
A CHANGE AGENT STRATEGY: PRELIMINARY REPORT EJ 054 727

CURRICULUM ENRICHMENT
CHILDREN LEARN AND GROW THROUGH ART EXPERIENCES. ILLINOIS CURRICULUM PROGRAM, THE SUBJECT FIELD SERIES. ED019132

CURRICULUM EVALUATION
GUIDELINES FOR ELEMENTARY SOCIAL STUDIES. ED019998
GUIDEBOOK FOR TEACHERS. ED020001
PILOT STUDY OF FIVE METHODS OF PRESENTING THE SUMMER HEAD START CURRICULAR PROGRAM. ED021622
SRA ECONOMICS MATERIALS IN GRADES ONE AND TWO. EVALUATION REPORTS. ED029700
LOGICAL THINKING IN SECOND GRADE. FINAL REPORT. ED033747
PENNSYLVANIA PRESCHOOL AND PRIMARY EDUCATION PROJECT: 1968-1969 FINAL REPORT TO THE FORD FOUNDATION. ED033759
CURRICULAR INTERVENTION TO ENHANCE THE ENGLISH LANGUAGE COMPETENCE OF HEAD START CHILDREN. PART OF THE FINAL REPORT ON HEAD START EVALUATION AND RESEARCH: 1968-69 TO THE OFFICE OF ECONOMIC OPPORTUNITY. ED039032
THE EFFECTIVENESS OF SPECIAL PROGRAMS FOR RURAL ISOLATED FOUR-YEAR-OLD CHILDREN. FINAL REPORT. ED041638
BEHAVIORAL SCIENCE FOR ELEMENTARY-SCHOOL PUPILS EJ 014 306
STUDENT EVALUATION OF A HIGH SCHOOL SEX EDUCATION PROGRAM EJ 045 390
CURRICULUM BOON OR BANE? EJ 052 766
DIFFERENTIAL OUTCOMES OF A MONTESSORI CURRICULUM EJ 060 330

CURRICULUM GUIDES
THE STUDY OF MUSIC IN THE ELEMENTARY SCHOOL--A CONCEPTUAL APPROACH. ED017328
BIG QUESTIONS AND LITTLE CHILDREN: SCIENCE AND HEAD START. ED024458
LEARNING AND TEACHING, GRADES N-9 (EMPHASIS ON MIDDLE GRADES). ED024467
PRESCHOOL PARENT EDUCATION PROGRAM: A CURRICULUM GUIDE FOR USE BY TEACHERS CONDUCTING PARENT EDUCATION PROGRAMS AS A PART OF OVER-ALL COMPENSATORY PRESCHOOL PROJECTS. EXPERIMENTAL EDITION. ED026118
A CURRICULUM OF TRAINING FOR PARENT PARTICIPATION IN PROJECT HEAD START. ED026144
SCIENCE ADVENTURES IN CHILDREN'S PLAY. ED026146
A GUIDE FOR PERCEPTUAL-MOTOR TRAINING ACTIVITIES. ED027075
CURRICULUM GUIDE FOR CHILDREN'S ACTIVITIES, PARENT PRESCHOOL PROGRAM. ED027078
CONCEPT AND LANGUAGE DEVELOPMENT IN A KINDERGARTEN OF DISADVANTAGED CHILDREN. ED027967
KINDERGARTEN: THE CHILD IN HIS HOME AND SCHOOL ENVIRONMENTS. COURSE OF STUDY AND RELATED LEARNING ACTIVITIES. (CURRICULUM BULLETIN, 1967-68 SERIES, NO. 2A.) ED029681
GRADE 1: LIVING AND WORKING TOGETHER IN THE COMMUNITY. COURSE OF STUDY AND RELATED LEARNING ACTIVITIES. (CURRICULUM BULLETIN, 1967-68 SERIES, NO. 2B.) ED029682
GRADE 2: HOW PEOPLE LIVE IN CITY COMMUNITIES AROUND THE WORLD. COURSE OF STUDY AND RELATED LEARNING ACTIVITIES. (CURRICULUM BULLETIN, 1968-69 SERIES, NO. 2.) ED029694
THE INTERGROUP RELATIONS CURRICULUM: A PROGRAM FOR ELEMENTARY SCHOOL EDUCATION. VOLUMES I AND II. ED029704
CONCEPT AND LANGUAGE DEVELOPMENT. A RESOURCE GUIDE FOR TEACHING YOUNG CHILDREN. ED030472
FAMILY LIFE AROUND THE WORLD, LEVEL I. ED032116
KINDERGARTEN CURRICULUM GUIDE: EARLY CHILDHOOD EDUCATION. ED034575
SOCIAL STUDIES IN THE PRIMARY GRADES. ED035460
PRESCHOOL CURRICULUM GUIDE FOR CHILDREN'S CENTERS IN CALIFORNIA. ED037241
CURRICULUM GUIDE FOR PHYSICAL EDUCATION: KINDERGARTEN AND UNGRADED PRIMARY. ED038169
EDUCATIONAL DAY CARE: AN INSTALLATION MANUAL. ED039918
LANGUAGE FOR LEARNING: ORAL LANGUAGE AND COGNITIVE DEVELOPMENT, PRE-K, K, GRADE 1. SECTION 1, TEACHER'S GUIDE. ED039921
KINDERGARTEN CURRICULUM GUIDE. ED039929
ALL ABOUT ME. UNIT 1 CURRICULUM GUIDE. ED053789
AUTUMN. UNIT 3 CURRICULUM GUIDE. ED053790

CURRICULUM PLANNING
A CREATIVE GUIDE FOR PRESCHOOL TEACHERS. GOALS, ACTIVITIES, AND SUGGESTED MATERIALS FOR AN ORGANIZED PROGRAM. ED016512
THE SOUTHSIDE EXPERIMENT IN PERSONALIZED EDUCATION. ED042505
AN EDUCATION SYSTEM FOR HIGH-RISK INFANTS: A PREVENTIVE APPROACH TO DEVELOPMENTAL AND LEARNING DISABILITIES. ED043379
HOW DO INNER-CITY TEACHERS USE A SYSTEM-WIDE CURRICULUM? EJ 015 487
CHILDREN AND THEIR EXPANDING WORLD OF KNOWLEDGE EJ 026 734
WHO SELECTS THE OBJECTIVES FOR LEARNING--AND WHY? EJ 031 849
IS IT TIME TO BREAK THE SILENCE ON VIOLENCE? EJ 032 564
SAY YOU COME FROM MISSOURI EJ 047 103

CURRICULUM PROBLEMS
SOCIAL STUDIES IN ELEMENTARY SCHOOLS (THIRTY-SECOND YEARBOOK). ED018275

CURRICULUM RESEARCH
PROGRAMED INSTRUCTION AS A STRATEGY FOR DEVELOPING CURRICULA FOR CHILDREN FROM DISADVANTAGED BACKGROUNDS. ED015782
PRELIMINARY EVALUATION OF A LANGUAGE CURRICULUM FOR PRESCHOOL CHILDREN. FINAL REPORT. ED021618
ELEMENTARY SCHOOL MATHEMATICS: A GUIDE TO CURRENT RESEARCH. THIRD EDITION. ED026123
DEVELOPMENT OF A MUSIC CURRICULUM FOR YOUNG CHILDREN. CAREL ARTS AND HUMANITIES CURRICULUM DEVELOPMENT PROGRAM FOR YOUNG CHILDREN. ED032938
YPSILANTI PRESCHOOL CURRICULUM DEMONSTRATION PROJECT, 1968-1971. ED046503
PLANNED VARIATION IN HEAD START PROGRAMS EJ 031 848

CUTANEOUS SENSE
TACTILE IDENTIFICATION OF LETTERS: A COMPARISON OF DEAF AND HEARING CHILDRENS' PERFORMANCES EJ 034 567
DEVELOPMENT OF CUTANEOUS AND KINESTHETIC LOCALIZATION BY BLIND AND SIGHTED CHILDREN EJ 055 113

DANCE
A PILOT STUDY INTEGRATING VISUAL FORM AND ANTHROPOLOGICAL CONTENT FOR TEACHING CHILDREN AGES 6 TO 11 ABOUT CULTURES AND PEOPLES OF THE WORLD ED027095

DEVELOPMENT OF A DANCE CURRICULUM FOR YOUNG CHILDREN. CAREL ARTS AND HUMANITIES CURRICULUM DEVELOPMENT PROGRAM FOR YOUNG CHILDREN. ED032936
CHILDREN DANCE IN THE CLASSROOM. ED053804
CONCEPT LEARNING THROUGH MOVEMENT IMPROVISATION: THE TEACHER'S ROLE AS CATALYST EJ 014 945
WHEN WORDS FAIL...DANCE EJ 019 507

DATA ANALYSIS

CODING MANUAL FOR APPROACH (A PROCEDURE FOR PATTERNING RESPONSES OF ADULTS AND CHILDREN). ED015005
PROJECT HEAD START--SUMMER 1966. FINAL REPORT. SECTION THREE, PUPILS AND PROGRAMS. ED018248
IQ CHANGES IN HOSPITALIZED MENTAL RETARDATES EJ 046 727
WHAT'S THROWN OUT WITH THE BATH WATER: A BABY? EJ 052 445

DATA BASES

ENVIRONMENTAL FORCES IN THE HOME LIVES OF THREE-YEAR-OLD CHILDREN IN THREE POPULATION SUBGROUPS. ED050802

DATA COLLECTION

A TECHNIQUE FOR GATHERING CHILDREN'S LANGUAGE SAMPLES FROM NATURALISTIC SETTINGS. ED016532
A DISTINCTIVE FEATURES ANALYSIS OF PRE-LINGUISTIC INFANT VOCALIZATIONS. ED025330
AN ECOLOGICAL STUDY OF THREE-YEAR-OLDS AT HOME. FINAL REPORT. ED037238
RECOLLECTIONS OF CHILDHOOD: A STUDY OF THE RETROSPECTIVE METHOD EJ 025 047
A GUIDE FOR COLLECTING AND ORGANIZING INFORMATION ON EARLY CHILDHOOD PROGRAMS EJ 058 463

DATA PROCESSING

CODING MANUAL FOR APPROACH (A PROCEDURE FOR PATTERNING RESPONSES OF ADULTS AND CHILDREN). ED015005

DAY CARE CENTERS

REFLECTIONS ON REVISITING VIENNA'S YOUNG CITIZENS EJ 060 107
EARLY CHILDHOOD EDUCATION IN JAPAN EJ 061 692

DAY CARE PROGRAMS

THE CHILDREN'S CENTER--A MICROCOSMIC HEALTH, EDUCATION, AND WELFARE UNIT. PROGRESS REPORT. ED013116
GROUP DAY CARE AS A CHILD-REARING ENVIRONMENT. AN OBSERVATIONAL STUDY OF DAY CARE PROGRAM. ED024453
REACHING THE HARD-TO-REACH: THE USE OF PARTICIPANT GROUP METHODS WITH MOTHERS OF CULTURALLY DISADVANTAGED PRESCHOOL CHILDREN. ED024469
FEDERAL INTERAGENCY DAY CARE REQUIREMENTS, PURSUANT TO SEC. 522 (D) OF THE ECONOMIC OPPORTUNITY ACT. ED026145
DAY CARE AS A SOCIAL INSTRUMENT: A POLICY PAPER. ED027065
JDC GUIDE FOR DAY CARE CENTERS, A HANDBOOK TO AID COMMUNITIES IN DEVELOPING DAY CARE CENTER PROGRAMS FOR PRE-SCHOOL CHILDREN. ED027961
JDC HANDBOOK FOR TEACHERS IN DAY CARE CENTERS. ED027962
FEDERAL FUNDS FOR DAY CARE PROJECTS. (REVISED EDITION). ED033741
INFANT DAY CARE AND ATTACHMENT. ED033755
AN INSTITUTIONAL ANALYSIS OF DAY CARE PROGRAM. PART I, GROUP DAY CARE: A STUDY IN DIVERSITY. FINAL REPORT. ED036319
PLANNING ENVIRONMENTS FOR YOUNG CHILDREN: PHYSICAL SPACE. ED038162
COMMUNITY COORDINATED CHILD CARE (4-C) MANUAL. ED039016
CHILD WELFARE LEAGUE OF AMERICA STANDARDS FOR DAY CARE SERVICE. REVISED EDITION. ED039019
EDUCATIONAL DAY CARE: AN INSTALLATION MANUAL. ED039918
STATEMENT BY MARSDEN G. WAGNER, M. D. REPRESENTING THE AMERICAN PUBLIC HEALTH ASSOCIATION BEFORE THE SELECT SUBCOMMITTEE ON EDUCATION, MARCH 3, 1970. ED039940
STATEMENT ON COMPREHENSIVE PRESCHOOL EDUCATION AND CHILD DAY CARE ACT OF 1969 BEFORE THE SELECT SUBCOMMITTEE ON EDUCATION, FEBRUARY 27, 1970. ED039941
A STATEMENT ON THE COMPREHENSIVE PRESCHOOL EDUCATION AND CHILD DAY-CARE ACT OF 1969 BEFORE THE SELECT SUBCOMMITTEE ON EDUCATION OF THE HOUSE COMMITTEE ON EDUCATION AND LABOR, MARCH 3, 1970. ED040752
DEMONSTRATION INFANT DAY CARE AND EDUCATION PROGRAM. INTERIM REPORT, 1969-1970. ED041632
CHILD CARE AND WORKING MOTHERS: A STUDY OF ARRANGEMENTS MADE FOR DAYTIME CARE OF CHILDREN. ED045175
INTELLECTUAL DEVELOPMENT OF CULTURALLY DEPRIVED CHILDREN IN A DAY CARE PROGRAM: A FOLLOW-UP STUDY. ED045186
SANTA MONICA CHILDREN'S CENTERS, SANTA MONICA, CALIFORNIA: LOW-COST DAY CARE FACILITIES FOR CHILDREN OF WORKING MOTHERS MADE AVAILABLE THROUGH THE COOPERATION OF THE CALIFORNIA STATE GOVERNMENT AND LOCAL SCHOOL DISTRICT. MODEL PROGRAMS--CHILDHOOD EDUCATION. ED045212
NEIGHBORHOOD HOUSE CHILD CARE SERVICES, SEATTLE, WASHINGTON: SEATTLE'S ANSWER TO CHILD CARE PROBLEMS OF LOW-INCOME FAMILIES. MODEL PROGRAMS--CHILDHOOD EDUCATION. ED045213
DEMONSTRATION NURSERY CENTER FOR INFANTS AND TODDLERS, GREENSBORO, NORTH CAROLINA: A MODEL DAY CARE CENTER FOR CHILDREN UNDER 3 YEARS OLD. MODEL PROGRAMS--CHILDHOOD EDUCATION. ED045215
THE DAY NURSERY ASSOCIATION OF CLEVELAND, CLEVELAND, OHIO: A LONG HISTORY OF CARE FOR CHILDREN, INVOLVEMENT OF PARENTS, AND SERVICE TO THE COMMUNITY. MODEL PROGRAMS--CHILDHOOD EDUCATION. ED045218
A GUIDE FOR MANAGERS OF CHILD DAY CARE AGENCIES. ED046486
DEVELOPMENTAL DAY CARE SERVICES FOR CHILDREN. 1970 WHITE HOUSE CONFERENCE ON CHILDREN, REPORT OF FORUM 17. (WORKING COPY). ED046533
PROCEEDINGS OF THE CONFERENCE ON INDUSTRY AND DAY CARE (URBAN RESEARCH CORPORATION, CHICAGO, 1970). ED047780
CLASSIFYING DAY CARE CENTERS FOR COST ANALYSIS. ED047783
BASIC FACTS ABOUT LICENSING OF DAY CARE. ED047817
MINIMUM STANDARDS FOR LICENSED DAY CARE CENTERS AND NIGHT-TIME CENTERS. REVISED EDITION. ED048918
FEDERAL INVOLVEMENT IN DAY CARE. ED048931
AN INTEGRATED PROGRAM OF GROUP CARE AND EDUCATION FOR SOCIOECONOMICALLY ADVANTAGED AND DISADVANTAGED INFANTS. ED048937
A DEVELOPMENTAL LEARNING APPROACH TO INFANT CARE IN A GROUP SETTING. ED049818
THE DAY CARE CHALLENGE: THE UNMET NEEDS OF MOTHERS AND CHILDREN. ED050821
DAY CARE SURVEY-1970. SUMMARY REPORT AND BASIC ANALYSIS. ED051880
CONSULTATION IN DAY CARE. ED051884
A STUDY IN CHILD CARE (CASE STUDY FROM VOLUME II-A): "A HOUSE FULL OF CHILDREN." DAY CARE PROGRAMS REPRINT SERIES. ED051891
A STUDY IN CHILD CARE (CASE STUDY FROM VOLUME II-A): "THEY UNDERSTAND." DAY CARE PROGRAMS REPRINT SERIES. ED051892
A STUDY IN CHILD CARE (CASE STUDY FROM VOLUME II-A): "TACOS AND TULIPS." DAY CARE PROGRAMS REPRINT SERIES. ED051893
A STUDY IN CHILD CARE (CASE STUDY FROM VOLUME II-A): "GOOD VIBES." DAY CARE PROGRAMS REPRINT SERIES. ED051894
A STUDY IN CHILD CARE (CASE STUDY FROM VOLUME II-A): "A ROLLS-ROYCE OF DAY CARE." DAY CARE PROGRAMS REPRINT SERIES. ED051895
A STUDY IN CHILD CARE (CASE STUDY FROM VOLUME II-A): "IT'S A WELL-RUN BUSINESS, TOO." DAY CARE PROGRAMS REPRINT SERIES. ED051896
A STUDY IN CHILD CARE (CASE STUDY FROM VOLUME II-B): "I'M A NEW WOMAN NOW." DAY CARE PROGRAMS REPRINT SERIES. ED051897
A STUDY IN CHILD CARE (CASE STUDY FROM VOLUME II-B): "A SENSE OF BELONGING." DAY CARE PROGRAMS REPRINT SERIES. ED051898
A STUDY IN CHILD CARE (CASE STUDY FROM VOLUME II-A): "LIKE BEING AT HOME." DAY CARE PROGRAMS REPRINT SERIES. ED051899
A STUDY IN CHILD CARE (CASE STUDY FROM VOLUME II-A): "CHILDREN AS 'KIDS'." DAY CARE PROGRAMS REPRINT SERIES. ED051900
A STUDY IN CHILD CARE (CASE STUDY FROM VOLUME II-A): "LIFE IS GOOD, RIGHT? RIGHT!" DAY CARE PROGRAMS REPRINT SERIES. ED051901
A STUDY IN CHILD CARE (CASE STUDY FROM VOLUME II-A): "HEY, GEORGIE GET YOURSELF TOGETHER." DAY CARE PROGRAMS REPRINT SERIES. ED051902
A STUDY IN CHILD CARE (CASE STUDY FROM VOLUME II-A): "ALL KINDS OF LOVE--IN A CHINESE RESTAURANT." DAY CARE PROGRAMS REPRINT SERIES. ED051903
A STUDY IN CHILD CARE (CASE STUDY FROM VOLUME II-A): "A SMALL U. N." DAY CARE PROGRAMS REPRINT SERIES. ED051904
A STUDY IN CHILD CARE (CASE STUDY FROM VOLUME II-A) ED051905
A STUDY IN CHILD CARE (CASE STUDY FROM VOLUME II-B): "WILL YOU MARRY ME?" DAY CARE PROGRAM REPRINT SERIES. ED051906
A STUDY IN CHILD CARE (CASE STUDY FROM VOLUME II-B): "WE COME WITH THE DUST AND WE GO WITH THE WIND." DAY CARE PROGRAMS REPRINT SERIES. ED051907
A STUDY IN CHILD CARE (CASE STUDY FROM VOLUME II-B): "SOMEPLACE SECURE." DAY CARE PROGRAMS REPRINT SERIES. ED051908
A STUDY IN CHILD CARE (CASE STUDY FROM VOLUME II-B): "...WHILE [THEY TOOK] CARE OF OUR CHILDREN, THEIRS WEREN'T BEING CARED FOR." DAY CARE PROGRAMS REPRINT SERIES. ED051909
A STUDY IN CHILD CARE (CASE STUDY FROM VOLUME II-B): "THEY BRAG ON A CHILD TO MAKE HIM FEEL GOOD." DAY CARE PROGRAMS REPRINT SERIES. ED051910
A STUDY IN CHILD CARE. VOLUME I: FINDINGS. DAY CARE PROGRAMS REPRINT SERIES. ED051911
A STUDY IN CHILD CARE. VOLUME III: COST AND QUALITY ISSUES FOR OPERATORS. DAY CARE PROGRAMS REPRINT SERIES. ED051912
DAY CARE: AN ANNOTATED BIBLIOGRAPHY. ED052823
THE TRAINING OF FAMILY DAY-CARE WORKERS: A FEASIBILITY STUDY AND INITIAL PILOT EFFORTS. FINAL REPORT. ED053787
STANDARDS FOR DAY CARE CENTERS FOR INFANTS AND CHILDREN UNDER 3 YEARS OF AGE. ED053794
PLANNING A DAY CARE CENTER. ED053795
CHILDREN UNDER THREE - FINDING WAYS TO STIMULATE DEVELOPMENT. II. SOME CURRENT EXPERIMENTS: A THREE PRONGED PROJECT EJ 007 408

NEW OPPORTUNITIES IN DAY CARE: AN INTERVIEW WITH GERTRUDE HOFFMANN EJ 007 448
INVOLVING PARENTS IN THEIR CHILDREN'S DAY-CARE EXPERIENCES EJ 007 451
A DAY CARE PROGRAM IN THE MIDDLE EAST EJ 009 815
AN INTERDISCIPLINARY APPROACH IN DAY TREATMENT OF EMOTIONALLY DISTURBED CHILDREN EJ 029 167
DAY CARE FOR CHILDREN: ASSETS AND LIABILITIES EJ 035 802
UNIONS AND DAY CARE CENTERS FOR THE CHILDREN OF WORKING MOTHERS EJ 038 643
CONSIDERATIONS IN DAY CARE COST ANALYSIS EJ 040 722
UNIVERSAL CHILD CARE EJ 043 354
DAY CARE: CRISIS AND CHALLENGE EJ 046 455
DAY CARE CHALLENGE: THE UNMET NEEDS OF MOTHERS AND CHILDREN EJ 046 456
CHILDREN: OUR CHALLENGE EJ 050 423
EDUCATIONAL COMPONENT OF DAY CARE EJ 051 235
WHAT DOES RESEARCH TEACH US ABOUT DAY CARE: FOR CHILDREN UNDER THREE EJ 051 236
WHAT DOES RESEARCH TEACH US ABOUT DAY CARE: FOR CHILDREN OVER THREE EJ 051 237
CREATING CHILD CARE COMMUNITIES THROUGH 4-C PROGRAMS EJ 051 239
LONGITUDINAL DEVELOPMENT OF VERY YOUNG CHILDREN IN A COMPREHENSIVE DAY CARE PROGRAM: THE FIRST TWO YEARS EJ 056 707
A DEVELOPMENTAL LEARNING APPROACH TO INFANT CARE IN A GROUP SETTING EJ 057 442
NUTRITION AND EDUCATIONAL EXPERIENCE: INTERRELATED VARIABLES IN CHILDREN'S LEARNING EJ 059 643
FUNDING CHILD CARE PROGRAMS UNDER TITLE IV-A EJ 060 452

DAY CARE SERVICES

WHERE IS DAY CARE HEADING. ED016530
FEDERAL INTERAGENCY DAY CARE REQUIREMENTS, PURSUANT TO SEC. 522 (D) OF THE ECONOMIC OPPORTUNITY ACT. ED026145
JDC GUIDE FOR DAY CARE CENTERS, A HANDBOOK TO AID COMMUNITIES IN DEVELOPING DAY CARE CENTER PROGRAMS FOR PRE-SCHOOL CHILDREN. ED027961
GOOD REFERENCES ON DAY CARE. ED027969
COMMUNITY COORDINATED CHILD CARE: 1. INTERIM POLICY GUIDANCE FOR THE 4-C PROGRAM ED034579
THE STORY OF AN AFTER - SCHOOL PROGRAM. ED035464
AN INSTITUTIONAL ANALYSIS OF DAY CARE PROGRAM. PART I, GROUP DAY CARE: A STUDY IN DIVERSITY. FINAL REPORT. ED036319
CHILD WELFARE LEAGUE OF AMERICA STANDARDS FOR DAY CARE SERVICE. REVISED EDITION. ED039019
EDUCATIONAL DAY CARE: AN INSTALLATION MANUAL. ED039918
CHILD CARE ARRANGEMENTS OF WORKING MOTHERS IN THE UNITED STATES. ED040738
STANDARDS AND COSTS FOR DAY CARE. ED042501
REALISTIC PLANNING FOR THE DAY CARE CONSUMER. ED043374
AN INSTITUTIONAL ANALYSIS OF DAY CARE PROGRAM. PART II, GROUP DAY CARE: THE GROWTH OF AN INSTITUTION. FINAL REPORT. ED043394
CHILD CARE AND WORKING MOTHERS: A STUDY OF ARRANGEMENTS MADE FOR DAYTIME CARE OF CHILDREN. ED045175
SANTA MONICA CHILDREN'S CENTERS, SANTA MONICA, CALIFORNIA: LOW-COST DAY CARE FACILITIES FOR CHILDREN OF WORKING MOTHERS MADE AVAILABLE THROUGH THE COOPERATION OF THE CALIFORNIA STATE GOVERNMENT AND LOCAL SCHOOL DISTRICT. MODEL PROGRAMS--CHILDHOOD EDUCATION. ED045212
DEMONSTRATION NURSERY CENTER FOR INFANTS AND TODDLERS, GREENSBORO, NORTH CAROLINA: A MODEL DAY CARE CENTER FOR CHILDREN UNDER 3 YEARS OLD. MODEL PROGRAMS--CHILDHOOD EDUCATION. ED045215
DEVELOPMENTAL DAY CARE SERVICES FOR CHILDREN. 1970 WHITE HOUSE CONFERENCE ON CHILDREN, REPORT OF FORUM 17. (WORKING COPY). ED046533
PROCEEDINGS OF THE CONFERENCE ON INDUSTRY AND DAY CARE (URBAN RESEARCH CORPORATION, CHICAGO, 1970). ED047780
CLASSIFYING DAY CARE CENTERS FOR COST ANALYSIS. ED047783
CHILD WELFARE SERVICES: A SOURCEBOOK. ED047813
MINIMUM STANDARDS FOR LICENSED DAY CARE CENTERS AND NIGHT-TIME CENTERS. REVISED EDITION. ED048918
EDUCATION OF THE INFANT AND YOUNG CHILD. ED048930
FEDERAL INVOLVEMENT IN DAY CARE. ED048931
THE DAY CARE NEIGHBOR SERVICE: A HANDBOOK FOR THE ORGANIZATION AND OPERATION OF A NEW APPROACH TO FAMILY DAY CARE. ED049810
A GUIDE TO THE PLANNING AND OPERATION OF A CHILD DEVELOPMENT CENTER FOR MIGRANT CHILDREN AND A REPORT OF THE HOOPESTON CHILD DEVELOPMENT CENTER ED049838
NEIGHBORHOOD FAMILY DAY CARE AS A CHILD-REARING ENVIRONMENT. ED049840
A REVIEW OF EXPERIENCE: ESTABLISHING, OPERATING, EVALUATING A DEMONSTRATION NURSERY CENTER FOR THE DAYTIME CARE OF INFANTS AND TODDLERS, 1967-1970. FINAL REPORT. ED050810
THE DAY CARE CHALLENGE: THE UNMET NEEDS OF MOTHERS AND CHILDREN. ED050821
BEFORE SCHOOL STARTS. FOR CHILDREN'S MINDS--NOT JUST TO MIND THE CHILDREN. THE CHILD CENTRE--AS SEEN BY A PARENT. ED051873
DAY CARE SURVEY-1970. SUMMARY REPORT AND BASIC ANALYSIS. ED051880
CONSULTATION IN DAY CARE. ED051884
A STUDY IN CHILD CARE (CASE STUDY FROM VOLUME II-A): "A HOUSE FULL OF CHILDREN." DAY CARE PROGRAMS REPRINT SERIES. ED051891
A STUDY IN CHILD CARE (CASE STUDY FROM VOLUME II-A): "THEY UNDERSTAND." DAY CARE PROGRAMS REPRINT SERIES. ED051892
A STUDY IN CHILD CARE (CASE STUDY FROM VOLUME II-A): "TACOS AND TULIPS." DAY CARE PROGRAMS REPRINT SERIES. ED051893
A STUDY IN CHILD CARE (CASE STUDY FROM VOLUME II-A): "GOOD VIBES." DAY CARE PROGRAMS REPRINT SERIES. ED051894
A STUDY IN CHILD CARE (CASE STUDY FROM VOLUME II-A): "A ROLLS-ROYCE OF DAY CARE." DAY CARE PROGRAMS REPRINT SERIES. ED051895
A STUDY IN CHILD CARE (CASE STUDY FROM VOLUME II-A): "IT'S A WELL-RUN BUSINESS, TOO." DAY CARE PROGRAMS REPRINT SERIES. ED051896
A STUDY IN CHILD CARE (CASE STUDY FROM VOLUME II-B): "I'M A NEW WOMAN NOW." DAY CARE PROGRAMS REPRINT SERIES. ED051897
A STUDY IN CHILD CARE (CASE STUDY FROM VOLUME II-B): "A SENSE OF BELONGING." DAY CARE PROGRAMS REPRINT SERIES. ED051898
A STUDY IN CHILD CARE (CASE STUDY FROM VOLUME II-A): "LIKE BEING AT HOME." DAY CARE PROGRAMS REPRINT SERIES. ED051899
A STUDY IN CHILD CARE (CASE STUDY FROM VOLUME II-A): "CHILDREN AS 'KIDS'." DAY CARE PROGRAMS REPRINT SERIES. ED051900
A STUDY IN CHILD CARE (CASE STUDY FROM VOLUME II-A): "LIFE IS GOOD, RIGHT? RIGHT!" DAY CARE PROGRAMS REPRINT SERIES. ED051901
A STUDY IN CHILD CARE (CASE STUDY FROM VOLUME II-A): "HEY, GEORGIE GET YOURSELF TOGETHER." DAY CARE PROGRAMS REPRINT SERIES. ED051902
A STUDY IN CHILD CARE (CASE STUDY FROM VOLUME II-A): "ALL KINDS OF LOVE--IN A CHINESE RESTAURANT." DAY CARE PROGRAMS REPRINT SERIES. ED051903
A STUDY IN CHILD CARE (CASE STUDY FROM VOLUME II-A): "A SMALL U. N." DAY CARE PROGRAMS REPRINT SERIES. ED051904
A STUDY IN CHILD CARE (CASE STUDY FROM VOLUME II-A) ED051905
A STUDY IN CHILD CARE (CASE STUDY FROM VOLUME II-B): "WILL YOU MARRY ME?" DAY CARE PROGRAM REPRINT SERIES. ED051906
A STUDY IN CHILD CARE (CASE STUDY FROM VOLUME II-B): "WE COME WITH THE DUST AND WE GO WITH THE WIND." DAY CARE PROGRAMS REPRINT SERIES. ED051907
A STUDY IN CHILD CARE (CASE STUDY FROM VOLUME II-B): "SOMEPLACE SECURE." DAY CARE PROGRAMS REPRINT SERIES. ED051908
A STUDY IN CHILD CARE (CASE STUDY FROM VOLUME II-B): "...WHILE [THEY TOOK] CARE OF OUR CHILDREN, THEIRS WEREN'T BEING CARED FOR." DAY CARE PROGRAMS REPRINT SERIES. ED051909
A STUDY IN CHILD CARE (CASE STUDY FROM VOLUME II-B): "THEY BRAG ON A CHILD TO MAKE HIM FEEL GOOD." DAY CARE PROGRAMS REPRINT SERIES. ED051910
A STUDY IN CHILD CARE. VOLUME I: FINDINGS. DAY CARE PROGRAMS REPRINT SERIES. ED051911
A STUDY IN CHILD CARE. VOLUME III: COST AND QUALITY ISSUES FOR OPERATORS. DAY CARE PROGRAMS REPRINT SERIES. ED051912
DAY CARE: AN ANNOTATED BIBLIOGRAPHY. ED052823
STANDARDS FOR DAY CARE CENTERS FOR INFANTS AND CHILDREN UNDER 3 YEARS OF AGE. ED053794
PLANNING A DAY CARE CENTER. ED053795
LABOR AND EDUCATION EJ 009 033
INTRODUCTION OF NEW CHILDREN INTO A DAY CARE CENTER EJ 011 302
NUTRITION IN DAY CARE CENTERS EJ 011 595
NEW DIRECTIONS IN THE LICENSING OF CHILD CARE FACILITIES EJ 016 608
DEVELOPING PUBLIC DAY CARE FACILITIES IN MARYLAND EJ 018 970
WHAT ABOUT THE SCHOOL BUS? EJ 020 294
THE FAMILY DAY CARE PROGRAM IN MILWAUKEE: A 3-FACETED APPROACH TO COMMUNITY ENRICHMENT EJ 023 391
WORKING MOTHERS AND THEIR CHILDREN EJ 028 793
THE CHILD'S RIGHT TO QUALITY DAY CARE: AN ACEI POSITION PAPER EJ 029 103
SELECTING PRIORITIES AT THE WHITE HOUSE CONFERENCE ON CHILDREN EJ 035 619
DAY CARE FOR CHILDREN: ASSETS AND LIABILITIES EJ 035 802
DAY CARE IN THE 1970S: PLANNING FOR EXPANSION EJ 037 237
UNIONS AND DAY CARE CENTERS FOR THE CHILDREN OF WORKING MOTHERS EJ 038 643
CONSIDERATIONS IN DAY CARE COST ANALYSIS EJ 040 722
FLORIDA'S EARLY CHILDHOOD LEARNING PROGRAM FOR MIGRANT CHILDREN EJ 043 089
UNIVERSAL CHILD CARE EJ 043 354
DAY CARE: CRISIS AND CHALLENGE EJ 046 455
DAY CARE CHALLENGE: THE UNMET NEEDS OF MOTHERS AND CHILDREN EJ 046 456
ESTABLISHMENT OF DAY CARE PROGRAMS FOR THE MENTALLY RETARDED EJ 047 342

EARLY INTERVENTION AND SOCIAL CLASS: DIAGNOSIS AND TREATMENT OF PRESCHOOL CHILDREN IN A DAY CARE CENTER EJ 050 497
RESEARCH FOR UNDERSTANDING EJ 051 150
ONE MORNING A WEEK EJ 051 238
CREATING CHILD CARE COMMUNITIES THROUGH 4-C PROGRAMS EJ 051 239
DAY CARE LICENSING EJ 051 271
PROJECT PLAYPEN -- PRIMARY PREVENTION EJ 058 213

DAY PROGRAMS
GOOD REFERENCES ON DAY CARE. ED027969
EDUCATIONAL APPLICATION OF BEHAVIOR MODIFICATION TECHNIQUES WITH SEVERELY RETARDED CHILDREN IN A CHILD DEVELOPMENT CENTER EJ 017 421

DEAF CHILDREN
SOME PSYCHIATRIC OBSERVATIONS ON A GROUP OF MALADJUSTED DEAF CHILDREN EJ 026 155
TACTILE IDENTIFICATION OF LETTERS: A COMPARISON OF DEAF AND HEARING CHILDRENS' PERFORMANCES EJ 034 567
LOGICAL SYMBOL USE IN DEAF AND HEARING CHILDREN AND ADOLESCENTS EJ 047 339
PERCEPTION OF RHYTHM BY SUBJECTS WITH NORMAL AND DEFICIENT HEARING EJ 060 502

DEAF RESEARCH
LOGICAL SYMBOL USE IN DEAF AND HEARING CHILDREN AND ADOLESCENTS EJ 047 339

DEATH
INFANT MORTALITY: A CHALLENGE TO THE NATION. ED032122
KEY ISSUES IN INFANT MORTALITY. ED045208
THE GOAL OF LIFE ENHANCEMENT FOR A FATALLY ILL CHILD EJ 017 423
THE IMPACT OF OBJECT LOSS ON A SIX-YEAR-OLD EJ 030 514
PREVENTIVE THERAPY WITH SIBLINGS OF A DYING CHILD EJ 030 515
THE CONCEPT OF DEATH IN EARLY CHILDHOOD EJ 052 464
A MATTER OF LIFE AND DEATH EJ 059 746

DECISION MAKING
FAMILY SOCIOLOGY OR WIVES' FAMILY SOCIOLOGY? A COMPARISON OF HUSBANDS' AND WIVES' ANSWERS ABOUT DECISION MAKING IN THE GREEK AND AMERICAN CULTURE. REPORT NUMBER 4. ED030478
PLANNING PARENT-IMPLEMENTED PROGRAMS: A GUIDE FOR PARENTS, SCHOOLS AND COMMUNITIES. ED036322
AN INSTITUTIONAL ANALYSIS OF DAY CARE PROGRAM. PART II, GROUP DAY CARE: THE GROWTH OF AN INSTITUTION. FINAL REPORT. ED043394
THE DEFINITION, MEASUREMENT AND DEVELOPMENT OF SOCIAL MOTIVES UNDERLYING COOPERATIVE AND COMPETITIVE BEHAVIOR. ED045188
LOOKING BEYOND THE STRIKES EJ 003 630
WHO SELECTS THE OBJECTIVES FOR LEARNING--AND WHY? EJ 031 849
DECISION PROCESSES IN MULTIDIMENSIONAL GENERALIZATION EJ 038 265
EFFECTS OF CONTEXT ON PRESCHOOL CHILDREN'S JUDGMENTS EJ 042 968
SELF-GUIDANCE AS AN EDUCATIONAL GOAL AND THE SELECTION OF OBJECTIVES EJ 052 878

DECISION MAKING SKILLS
STUDIES IN PATTERN DETECTION IN NORMAL AND AUTISTIC CHILDREN. II. REPRODUCTION AND PRODUCTION OF COLOR SEQUENCES EJ 027 613

DEDUCTIVE METHODS
LOGICAL INFERENCE IN DISCRIMINATION LEARNING OF YOUNG CHILDREN. REPORT FROM THE RULE LEARNING PROJECT. ED036314
DEVELOPMENTAL PATTERNS FOR CHILDREN'S CLASS AND CONDITIONAL REASONING ABILITIES EJ 035 362

DEFINITIONS
EARLY CHILDHOOD EDUCATION AS A DISCIPLINE. ED043396
WORD ASSOCIATION AND DEFINITION IN MIDDLE CHILDHOOD EJ 030 294
THE MODIFICATION OF INTELLIGENCE BY TRAINING IN THE VERBALIZATION OF WORD DEFINITIONS AND SIMPLE CONCEPTS EJ 052 594
A CHILD-CENTERED DICTIONARY EJ 053 506

DELINQUENCY
WHY CHILDREN ARE IN JAIL AND HOW TO KEEP THEM OUT EJ 013 329
LANGUAGE, SOCIALIZATION, AND DELINQUENCY EJ 039 587

DELINQUENCY CAUSES
EARLY RECOLLECTIONS AND THE PERCEPTION OF OTHERS: A STUDY OF DELINQUENT ADOLESCENTS EJ 022 477

DELINQUENT BEHAVIOR
THE USE OF BEHAVIOR-MODIFICATION TECHNIQUES WITH FEMALE DELINQUENTS EJ 051 473

DELINQUENT IDENTIFICATION
DELINQUENCY PREDICTION SCALES AND PERSONALITY INVENTORIES EJ 057 475

DELINQUENT REHABILITATION
AGGRESSIVE GROUP WORK WITH TEENAGE DELINQUENT BOYS EJ 007 444
WORKING WITH FAMILIES OF DELINQUENT BOYS EJ 007 727
HELPING HOUSEPARENTS FIND AND USE THEIR CREATIVITY EJ 022 215
A DIFFERENTIAL USE OF GROUP HOMES FOR DELINQUENT BOYS EJ 024 028

DELINQUENTS
AGGRESSIVE GROUP WORK WITH TEENAGE DELINQUENT BOYS EJ 007 444
A PRELIMINARY VIEW OF TRENDS IN AGE, EDUCATION, AND INTELLIGENCE OF PROBLEM YOUTH EJ 030 431
PARENTAL ATTITUDES AND INTERACTIONS IN DELINQUENCY EJ 056 611

DEMOCRATIC VALUES
THE INTERNATIONAL WALDORF SCHOOL MOVEMENT. ED015019
CIVIC BOOKS AND CIVIC CULTURE EJ 057 017
TOWARD A DEMOCRATIC ELEMENTARY-SCHOOL CLASSROOM EJ 058 308
THE DEVELOPMENT OF DEMOCRATIC VALUES AND BEHAVIOR AMONG MEXICAN-AMERICAN CHILDREN EJ 058 509

DEMOGRAPHY
DEMOGRAPHIC AND SOCIO-ECONOMIC DATA OF THE BECKLEY, WEST VIRGINIA AREA AND 1968-1970 DEVELOPMENTAL COSTS OF THE EARLY CHILDHOOD EDUCATION FIELD STUDY. TECHNICAL REPORT NO. 1. ED052832

DEMONSTRATION PROGRAMS
[REGIONAL RESEARCH AND RESOURCE CENTER IN EARLY CHILDHOOD.] FINAL REPORT. ED028846
THE STORY OF AN AFTER - SCHOOL PROGRAM. ED035464
MODEL OBSERVATION KINDERGARTEN AND FIRST GRADE, AMHERST, MASSACHUSETTS: MODEL CLASSROOMS WHICH OFFER COMPLETELY INDIVIDUALIZED SCHEDULING FOR MIXED AGE GROUPS OF KINDERGARTEN AND FIRST-GRADE STUDENTS. MODEL PROGRAMS--CHILDHOOD EDUCATION. ED045219
FOLLOW THROUGH: PROGRAM APPROACHES, SCHOOL YEAR 1970-71. ED047787
A REVIEW OF EXPERIENCE: ESTABLISHING, OPERATING, EVALUATING A DEMONSTRATION NURSERY CENTER FOR THE DAYTIME CARE OF INFANTS AND TODDLERS, 1967-1970. FINAL REPORT. ED050810

DEMONSTRATION PROJECTS
A NATIONAL DEMONSTRATION PROJECT UTILIZING TELEVISED MATERIALS FOR THE FORMAL EDUCATION OF CULTURALLY DISADVANTAGED PRESCHOOL CHILDREN. FINAL REPORT. ED015788
CHILD CARE WORKER TRAINING PROJECT. OPERATIONAL PHASE AND EMPLOYMENT. FINAL REPORT. ED053788
PREVENTING ILLEGITIMATE TEENAGE PREGNANCY THROUGH SYSTEMS INTERACTION EJ 059 671

DEMONSTRATIONS (EDUCATIONAL)
[THE JUNIPER GARDENS CHILDREN'S PROJECT.] FINAL PROGRESS REPORT FOR OEO GRANT CG-8180. ED027947

DENTAL EVALUATION
ANTHROPOMETRIC MEASUREMENTS OF CHILDREN IN THE HEAD START PROGRAM. ED042488

DENTAL HEALTH
NEW ZEALAND'S DENTAL SERVICE FOR CHILDREN EJ 007 162

DENTISTRY
MODELING AND THE FEARFUL CHILD PATIENT EJ 058 354

DEVELOPING NATIONS
HEAD START IN MICRONESIA EJ 060 108

DEVELOPMENT
SOME STUDIES OF THE MORAL DEVELOPMENT OF CHILDREN. ED024445
EARLY CHILDHOOD EDUCATION AS A DISCIPLINE. ED043396
THE DEVELOPMENT OF CHILDREN'S VIEWS OF FOREIGN PEOPLES EJ 000 392

DEVELOPMENTAL GUIDANCE
A RATIONALE FOR DEVELOPMENTAL TESTING AND TRAINING. ED028835

DEVELOPMENTAL PROGRAMS
THE EFFECTS OF MONTESSORI EDUCATIONAL TECHNIQUES ON CULTURALLY DISADVANTAGED HEAD START CHILDREN. ED015009
OPTIMIZING EDUCATIONAL INVESTMENT STRATEGIES. ED015780
ACTIVITIES FOR INFANT STIMULATION OR MOTHER-INFANT GAMES. ED046510
A DEVELOPMENTAL LEARNING APPROACH TO INFANT CARE IN A GROUP SETTING. ED049818
PROJECT GENESIS. FINAL REPORT. ED049820
A STUDY IN CHILD CARE (CASE STUDY FROM VOLUME II-B): "WILL YOU MARRY ME?" DAY CARE PROGRAM REPRINT SERIES. ED051906
THE USE OF DEVELOPMENTAL PLANS FOR MENTALLY RETARDED CHILDREN IN FOSTER FAMILY CARE EJ 035 803
ON THE VALUE OF BOTH PLAY AND STRUCTURE IN EARLY EDUCATION EJ 044 010

DEVELOPMENTAL THEORY: ITS PLACE AND RELEVANCE IN EARLY INTERVENTION PROGRAMS EJ 060 013
A TEAM APPROACH USING CASSETTE TAPES EJ 061 001

DEVELOPMENTAL PSYCHOLOGY
REINFORCEMENT GROWS UP: THE EXPERIMENTAL ANALYSIS OF BEHAVIOR AS A SYSTEMATIC APPROACH TO THE TEACHING OF DEVELOPMENTAL PSYCHOLOGY. ED023479
PERSONALITY DEVELOPMENT IN INFANCY ED024439
CURRENT ISSUES IN RESEARCH ON EARLY DEVELOPMENT. ED028813
EIDETIC IMAGERY IN CHILDREN. FINAL REPORT. ED029707
DECENTRATION IN CHILDREN: ITS GENERALITY AND CORRELATES. ED048926
PROBLEMS OF DEPRIVATION AND DEVELOPMENTAL LEARNING EJ 024 691
RESEARCH STRATEGIES AND CONCEPTS OF DEVELOPMENT AND LEARNING. INTRODUCTION EJ 027 436
CONCEPTUAL EMPHASIS IN THE HISTORY OF DEVELOPMENTAL PSYCHOLOGY: EVOLUTIONARY THEORY, TELEOLOGY, AND THE NATURE-NURTURE ISSUE EJ 034 043
CREATIVITY AS RELATED TO FIELD INDEPENDENCE AND MOBILITY EJ 035 380
DEVELOPMENTAL SHIFTS IN VERBAL RECALL BETWEEN MENTAL AGES TWO AND FIVE EJ 036 825
DEVELOPMENTAL COURSE OF RESPONSIVENESS TO SOCIAL REINFORCEMENT IN NORMAL CHILDREN AND INSTITUTIONALIZED RETARDED CHILDREN EJ 053 648
DEVELOPMENT OF CONSERVATION IN NORMAL AND RETARDED CHILDREN EJ 053 651
ACQUIRED DISTINCTIVENESS AND EQUIVALENCE OF CUES IN YOUNG CHILDREN EJ 053 654
CHILDREN'S MORAL REASONING EJ 055 097
AN ANALYSIS OF THE CONCEPT OF CULTURAL DEPRIVATION EJ 055 111
THE RELATIONSHIP BETWEEN VALUES AND BEHAVIOR: A DEVELOPMENTAL HYPOTHESIS EJ 056 622
A DEVELOPMENTAL STUDY OF THE EFFECTS OF PRETRAINING ON A PERCEPTUAL RECOGNITION TASK EJ 056 630
AN ONTOGENY OF MEDIATIONAL DEFICIENCY EJ 056 631
THE ONSET OF WARINESS EJ 056 635
DEVELOPMENT OF DIRECTIONALITY IN CHILDREN: AGES SIX THROUGH TWELVE EJ 058 137
EGO IDENTITY STATUS AND MORALITY: THE RELATIONSHIP BETWEEN TWO DEVELOPMENTAL CONSTRUCTS EJ 058 141
AN APPLICATION OF BRUNSWIK'S LENS MODEL TO DEVELOPMENTAL CHANGES IN PROBABILITY LEARNING EJ 058 142
RELATION OF TYPE AND ONSET OF FATHER ABSENCE TO COGNITIVE DEVELOPMENT EJ 058 695
THE EFFECTS OF GROUPING ON SHORT-TERM SERIAL RECALL OF DIGITS BY CHILDREN: DEVELOPMENTAL TRENDS EJ 059 320
VISUAL MASKING AND DEVELOPMENTAL DIFFERENCES IN INFORMATION PROCESSING EJ 059 514
PIAGET'S CONSTRUCTIONIST THEORY EJ 059 876
HYPOTHESES, STRATEGIES, AND STEREOTYPES IN DISCRIMINATION LEARNING EJ 060 779
DEVELOPMENTAL TRENDS IN GENERAL AND TEST ANXIETY AMONG JUNIOR AND SENIOR HIGH SCHOOL STUDENTS EJ 061 062
AGE- AND SEX-RELATED VARIATION IN PERFORMANCE ON A FIGURAL-CONCEPTUAL TASK EJ 061 066
CHILDREN'S UNDERSTANDING OF SPATIAL RELATIONS: COORDINATION OF PERSPECTIVES EJ 061 068
THE EVOLUTION OF DEVELOPMENTAL PSYCHOLOGY: A COMPARISON OF HANDBOOKS EJ 061 074
DEVELOPMENTAL CHANGE IN INFANT VISUAL FIXATION TO DIFFERING COMPLEXITY LEVELS AMONG CROSS-SECTIONALLY AND LONGITUDINALLY STUDIED INFANTS EJ 061 141

DEVELOPMENTAL TASKS
MODIFICATION OF CLASSIFICATORY COMPETENCE AND LEVEL OF REPRESENTATION AMONG LOWER-CLASS NEGRO KINDERGARTEN CHILDREN. ED021608
EARLY INFANT STIMULATION AND MOTOR DEVELOPMENT. ED038179
AN ONTOGENY OF OPTIONAL SHIFT BEHAVIOR EJ 019 003
MEASURES OF FORM CONSTANCY: DEVELOPMENTAL TRENDS EJ 034 611
THE ROLE OF OVERT ACTIVITY IN CHILDREN'S IMAGERY PRODUCTION EJ 059 315

DIACRITICAL MARKING
DIACRITICAL MARKS IN TEXTBOOK ADOPTION EJ 012 815

DIAGNOSTIC TEACHING
A DIAGNOSTIC-PRESCRIPTIVE APPROACH TO PRESCHOOL EDUCATION. ED041622
DIAGNOSTIC TEACHING: A MODEST PROPOSAL EJ 014 522

DIAGNOSTIC TESTS
AN ASSESSMENT AND COMPARISON OF SELECTED CHARACTERISTICS AMONG CULTURALLY DISADVANTAGED HEADSTART CHILDREN (SUMMER PROGRAM 1965), CULTURALLY DISADVANTAGED NON-HEADSTART CHILDREN, AND NON-CULTURALLY DISADVANTAGED CHILDREN. (TITLE SUPPLIED). ED014330
LONG DISTANCE INTERDISCIPLINARY EVALUATION OF DEVELOPMENTAL DISABILITIES. ED040748
DIAGNOSING MINIMAL BRAIN DAMAGE IN CHILDREN: A COMPARISON OF TWO BENDER SCORING SYSTEMS EJ 027 585
THE DIAGNOSTIC EVALUATION OF CHILDREN WITH LEARNING PROBLEMS: A COMMUNICATION PROCESS EJ 050 321

DIALECT STUDIES
THE EFFECTS OF STANDARD DIALECT TRAINING ON NEGRO. FIRST-GRADERS LEARNING TO READ. FINAL REPORT. ED029717

DIALECTS
PROBLEMS OF DIALECT. ED025300
A STUDY OF THE COMMUNICATIVE ABILITIES OF DISADVANTAGED CHILDREN. FINAL REPORT. ED032119
ON VALUING DIVERSITY IN LANGUAGE EJ 011 840

DICTIONARIES
A CHILD-CENTERED DICTIONARY EJ 053 506

DIETETICS
A STUDY OF FOOD AND POVERTY AMONG 113 HEAD START CHILDREN IN MISSOULA, MONTANA. ED028829
PROGRAMS FOR INFANTS AND YOUNG CHILDREN. PART II: NUTRITION. ED047808
MATERNAL FOOD RESTRICTION: EFFECTS ON OFFSPRING DEVELOPMENT, LEARNING, AND A PROGRAM OF THERAPY EJ 029 218

DIFFUSION
DIFFUSION OF INTERVENTION EFFECTS IN DISADVANTAGED FAMILIES. ED026127
INTRA-FAMILY DIFFUSION OF SELECTED COGNITIVE SKILLS AS A FUNCTION OF EDUCATIONAL STIMULATION. ED037233
DISSEMINATION AND UTILIZATION OF KNOWLEDGE IN THE AREA OF EARLY CHILDHOOD EDUCATION: A DESCRIPTION OF SOME OF THE PROBLEMS. ED044185

DIMENSIONAL PREFERENCE
INSTABILITY OF DIMENSIONAL PREFERENCE FOLLOWING CHANGES IN RELATIVE CUE SIMILARITY EJ 057 908
STABILITY OF FIRST-GRADE CHILDREN'S DIMENSIONAL PREFERENCES EJ 059 319

DIRECTORIES
NON-PUBLIC PRESCHOOL PROGRAMS IN INDIANA. ED050813

DISADVANTAGED ENVIRONMENT
ENVIRONMENTALLY DEPRIVED CHILDREN. ED039937
THE POVERTY CULTURE EJ 011 823
PROBLEMS OF DEPRIVATION AND DEVELOPMENTAL LEARNING EJ 024 691
LANGUAGE DEVELOPMENT OF DISADVANTAGED CHILDREN EJ 036 211
EXPERIMENTAL PRESCHOOL INTERVENTION IN THE APPALACHIAN HOME EJ 036 395

DISADVANTAGED GROUPS
NORTHFIELD, VERMONT--A COMMUNITY DEPTH STUDY. ED018245
SEX AND RACE DIFFERENCES IN THE DEVELOPMENT OF UNDERPRIVILEGED PRESCHOOL CHILDREN. ED019992
SUBPOPULATIONAL PROFILING OF THE PSYCHOEDUCATIONAL DIMENSIONS OF DISADVANTAGED PRESCHOOL CHILDREN: A CONCEPTUAL PROSPECTUS FOR AN INTERDISCIPLINARY RESEARCH. ED045177
RELATIONSHIPS BETWEEN SELECTED FAMILY VARIABLES AND MATERNAL AND INFANT BEHAVIOR IN A DISADVANTAGED POPULATION. A SUPPLEMENTARY REPORT. ED047784
DISADVANTAGED CHILDREN AND THEIR FIRST SCHOOL EXPERIENCES. ETS-HEAD START LONGITUDINAL STUDY: PRELIMINARY DESCRIPTION OF THE INITIAL SAMPLE PRIOR TO SCHOOL ENROLLMENT. A REPORT IN TWO VOLUMES: VOLUME 1. ED047797
INTERVENTION WITH MOTHERS AND YOUNG CHILDREN: A STUDY OF INTRAFAMILY EFFECTS. ED050809
HEALTH AND NUTRITION IN DISADVANTAGED CHILDREN AND THEIR RELATIONSHIP WITH INTELLECTUAL DEVELOPMENT. COLLABORATIVE RESEARCH REPORT. ED052816
WHO ARE THE DISADVANTAGED? EJ 039 800

DISADVANTAGED YOUTH
A SURVEY AND EVALUATION OF PROJECT HEAD START AS ESTABLISHED AND OPERATED IN COMMUNITIES OF THE COMMONWEALTH OF MASSACHUSETTS DURING THE SUMMER OF 1965. ED014324
SUMMARY REPORT OF A STUDY OF THE FULL-YEAR 1966 HEAD START PROGRAMS. ED014328
HANDBOOK FOR PROJECT HEAD START. ED015018
TEACHING A TEACHING LANGUAGE TO DISADVANTAGED CHILDREN. ED015021
MEMORANDUM ON--FACILITIES FOR EARLY CHILDHOOD EDUCATION. ED015023
HEADSTART OPERATIONAL FIELD ANALYSIS. PROGRESS REPORT II. ED015775
PROGRAMED INSTRUCTION AS A STRATEGY FOR DEVELOPING CURRICULA FOR CHILDREN FROM DISADVANTAGED BACKGROUNDS. ED015782
THE DEVELOPMENT OF A TEST TO ASSESS THE OCCURRENCE OF SELECTED FEATURES OF NON-STANDARD ENGLISH IN THE SPEECH OF DISADVANTAGED PRIMARY CHILDREN. ED015790

THE EFFECTS OF DIFFERENT LANGUAGE INSTRUCTION ON THE USE OF ATTRIBUTES OF PRE-KINDERGARTEN DISADVANTAGED CHILDREN. ED016522
SECOND-YEAR REPORT ON AN EVALUATIVE STUDY OF PREKINDERGARTEN PROGRAMS FOR EDUCATIONALLY DISADVANTAGED CHILDREN. ED016523
A PRELIMINARY INVESTIGATION TO ESTABLISH A REGIONAL CENTER FOR EDUCATIONAL DEVELOPMENTAL STUDIES OF DISADVANTAGED PRESCHOOL CHILDREN. FINAL REPORT. ED017318
A RESEARCH PROGRAM TO DETERMINE THE EFFECTS OF VARIOUS PRESCHOOL INTERVENTION PROGRAMS ON THE DEVELOPMENT OF DISADVANTAGED CHILDREN AND THE STRATEGIC AGE FOR SUCH INTERVENTION. ED017319
THE NATIONAL TEACHER CORPS PROGRAM, 1966-67 EVALUATION REPORT. ED019110
THE EFFECTS OF A HIGHLY STRUCTURED PRESCHOOL PROGRAM ON THE MEASURED INTELLIGENCE OF CULTURALLY DISADVANTAGED FOUR-YEAR-OLD CHILDREN. INTERIM REPORT. ED019116
FINAL REPORT ON HEAD START EVALUATION AND RESEARCH--1966-67 TO THE INSTITUTE FOR EDUCATIONAL DEVELOPMENT. SECTION IV, AN EXPLORATORY STUDY OF ORAL LANGUAGE DEVELOPMENT AMONG CULTURALLY DIFFERENT CHILDREN. ED019120
FINAL REPORT ON HEAD START EVALUATION AND RESEARCH--1966-67 TO THE INSTITUTE FOR EDUCATIONAL DEVELOPMENT. SECTION VIII, RELATIONSHIPS BETWEEN SELF-CONCEPT AND SPECIFIC VARIABLES IN A LOW-INCOME CULTURALLY DIFFERENT POPULATION. ED019124
THE EFFECT OF PRESCHOOL GROUP EXPERIENCE ON VARIOUS LANGUAGE AND SOCIAL SKILLS IN DISADVANTAGED CHILDREN. FINAL REPORT. ED019989
REPORT ON ACTIVITIES, 1964-1966. ED020016
PRELIMINARY FINDINGS FROM A LONGITUDINAL EDUCATIONAL IMPROVEMENT PROJECT BEING CONDUCTED FOR INSTRUCTIONALLY IMPOVERISHED PUPILS IN INTACT SCHOOLS IN THE URBAN SOUTH. ED020021
SEMO PROJECT HEAD START, PSYCHOLOGICAL SERVICES REPORT, SUMMER 1967. PHASE THREE FINAL REPORT. ED020779
SEMO PROJECT HEAD START, PSYCHOLOGICAL SERVICES REPORT, 1966-67 YEAR PROGRAM. ED020780
REGIONAL EVALUATION AND RESEARCH CENTER FOR PROJECT HEAD START, SUPPLEMENTARY RESEARCH REPORT, SEPTEMBER 1, 1967-DECEMBER 31, 1967. ED020791
AN EVALUATION AND FOLLOW-UP STUDY OF SUMMER 1966 HEAD START CHILDREN IN WASHINGTON, D.C. ED020794
GRADE EQUIVALENT COMPARISONS BETWEEN DISADVANTAGED NEGRO URBAN CHILDREN WITH AND WITHOUT KINDERGARTEN EXPERIENCE WHEN TAUGHT TO READ BY SEVERAL METHODS. ED020798
EXPERIMENTS IN HEAD START AND EARLY EDUCATION: THE EFFECTS OF TEACHER ATTITUDE AND CURRICULUM STRUCTURE ON PRESCHOOL DISADVANTAGED CHILDREN. FINAL REPORT. ED041615
A COMPARISON OF THREE INTERVENTION PROGRAMS WITH DISADVANTAGED PRESCHOOL CHILDREN. UNIVERSITY OF CALIFORNIA HEAD START RESEARCH AND EVALUATION CENTER. FINAL REPORT 1968-1969. ED041616
EARLY CHILDHOOD EDUCATION LEARNING SYSTEM ED041625
THE PREVALENCE OF ANEMIA IN HEAD START CHILDREN. NUTRITION EVALUATION, 1968-69. ED041629
THE EFFECT OF A PERCEPTUAL-MOTOR TRAINING PROGRAM UPON THE READINESS AND PERCEPTUAL DEVELOPMENT OF CULTURALLY DISADVANTAGED KINDERGARTEN CHILDREN. ED041633
RACE AND SEX IDENTIFICATION IN PRESCHOOL CHILDREN. ED041634
THE EFFECTS OF SCHOOL ENVIRONMENT ON DISADVANTAGED KINDERGARTEN CHILDREN, WITH AND WITHOUT A HEAD START BACKGROUND. FINAL REPORT. ED041640
PRESCHOOLS AND THEIR GRADUATES. ED041644
COMPARATIVE STUDY OF THREE PRESCHOOL CURRICULA. ED042484
THE SAMPLE: OPERATIONS IN THE HEAD START YEAR. ED043391
AN EXPERIMENTAL SUMMER KINDERGARTEN FOR CULTURALLY DEPRIVED CHILDREN. ED044174
EARLY CHILDHOOD EDUCATION PROGRAM AND ITS COMPONENTS: PSYCHOLOGICAL EVALUATION, SENSORIMOTOR SKILLS PROGRAM, NEW VISIONS - A CHILDREN'S MUSEUM. PROJECT REPORTS, VOLUME 4, BOOK 1, 1969. ED045183
INTELLECTUAL DEVELOPMENT OF CULTURALLY DEPRIVED CHILDREN IN A DAY CARE PROGRAM: A FOLLOW-UP STUDY. ED045186
IMPACT OF THE HEAD START PROGRAM. PHASE I OF A PROJECTED LONGITUDINAL STUDY TO THE U. S. OFFICE OF ECONOMIC OPPORTUNITY. FINAL REPORT. ED045193
EVALUATION AND RESEARCH CENTER FOR PROJECT HEAD START, UNIVERSITY OF SOUTH CAROLINA. INTERIM EVALUATION REPORT. ED045197
PRELIMINARY ANALYSIS OF 1968-69 BOOTH ACHIEVEMENT. ED045201
PRELIMINARY ANALYSIS OF 1968-69 HEAD START DATA. ED045203
OVERVIEW OF RESPONSIVE MODEL PROGRAM. ED045207
THE EFFECTS OF CARTOON CHARACTERS AS MOTIVATORS OF PRESCHOOL DISADVANTAGED CHILDREN. FINAL REPORT. ED045210
APPALACHIA PRESCHOOL EDUCATION PROGRAM, CHARLESTON, WEST VIRGINIA: A THREE-PART PRESCHOOL PROGRAM COMBINING A TELEVISION PROGRAM, PARAPROFESSIONAL HOME VISITORS, AND A MOBILE CLASSROOM. MODEL PROGRAMS--CHILDHOOD EDUCATION. ED045216
COGNITIVELY ORIENTED CURRICULUM, YPSILANTI, MICHIGAN: A PROGRAM THAT EXPOSES PRESCHOOL CHILDREN TO A VARIETY OF MATERIALS AND EQUIPMENT TO TEACH CONCEPTS THROUGH PHYSICAL AND VERBAL EXPERIENCES. MODEL PROGRAMS--CHILDHOOD EDUCATION. ED045217
AN INVESTIGATION OF THE RELATIVE EFFECTIVENESS OF SELECTED CURRICULUM VARIABLES IN THE LANGUAGE DEVELOPMENT OF HEAD START CHILDREN. ED046497
THE IMPLICATIONS OF DESIGN AND MODEL SELECTION FOR THE EVALUATION OF PROGRAMS FOR THE DISADVANTAGED CHILD. ED047792
THE FIRST YEAR OF SESAME STREET: A HISTORY AND OVERVIEW. FINAL REPORT, VOLUME I OF V VOLUMES. ED047821
CAN I LOVE THIS PLACE? A STAFF GUIDE TO OPERATING CHILD CARE CENTERS FOR THE DISADVANTAGED. ED049809
THE NEW YORK STATE EXPERIMENTAL PREKINDERGARTEN PROGRAM. SUMMARY REPORT, 1969-70. ED049814
RELATIONSHIP OF CURRICULUM, TEACHING, AND LEARNING IN PRESCHOOL EDUCATION. ED049837
A COMPARISON STUDY OF THE COGNITIVE DEVELOPMENT OF DISADVANTAGED FIRST GRADE PUPILS (AS MEASURED BY SELECTED PIAGETIAN TASKS). ED051874
PRESCHOOL PROGRAMS. IJR PRESCHOOL PROJECT REPORT, VOLUME I. ED052815
EARLY CHILDHOOD EDUCATION PROGRAM FOR NURSERY, KINDERGARTEN CHILDREN. ED052846
DESIGNS AND PROPOSAL FOR EARLY CHILDHOOD RESEARCH: A NEW LOOK: A MULTIPLE SYSTEMS-SERVICE APPROACH TO PROGRAMS AND RESEARCH FOR HELPING POOR CHILDREN. (ONE IN A SERIES OF SIX PAPERS). ED053806
AUDITORY DISCRIMINATION ABILITIES OF DISADVANTAGED ANGLO- AND MEXICAN-AMERICAN CHILDREN EJ 015 258
HOW DO INNER-CITY TEACHERS USE A SYSTEM-WIDE CURRICULUM? EJ 015 487
SPECIAL CONSIDERATIONS IN THE OPERATION OF A HEAD START PROGRAM BY A COMMUNITY CHILD GUIDANCE CLINIC EJ 023 704
HEALTH, EDUCATION, AND WELFARE: THE PROGRESSIVE IMPULSE IN THE NEW YORK CITY PUBLIC SCHOOLS EJ 029 104
THE CAMERA FOCUSES ON READING EJ 032 192
AN ATTACK ON IMPEDIMENTS TO EFFECTIVE CROSS-CULTURAL TEACHING EJ 032 553
RESISTANCE TO TEMPTATION IN YOUNG NEGRO CHILDREN EJ 032 894
A REEXAMINATION OF SOME ASSUMPTIONS ABOUT THE LANGUAGE OF THE DISADVANTAGED CHILD EJ 033 700
COMPETENCE VERSUS PERFORMANCE IN YOUNG CHILDREN'S USE OF ADJECTIVAL COMPARATIVES EJ 033 701
WIDER WINDOWS FOR ELEMENTARY SCHOOLS EJ 034 133
CAN POVERTY CHILDREN LIVE ON "SESAME STREET?" EJ 034 509
PLAY PERSISTENCE: SOME EFFECTS OF INTERRUPTION, SOCIAL REINFORCEMENT, AND DEFECTIVE TOYS EJ 034 532
THE ROLE OF VERBAL MEDIATION IN MENTAL DEVELOPMENT EJ 035 382
AN ATTEMPT TO COMBINE CLINICAL AND EDUCATIONAL RESOURCES: A REPORT ON THE FIRST YEAR'S EXPERIENCE OF A THERAPEUTIC SCHOOL EJ 035 539
SIX SUCCESSFUL READING PROGRAMS FOR INNER-CITY SCHOOLS EJ 035 663
ETHICAL ISSUES IN RESEARCH IN EARLY CHILDHOOD INTERVENTION EJ 037 578
THINKING SKILLS AS A GOAL IN AN AFTER-SCHOOL PROGRAM EJ 037 635
WHO ARE THE DISADVANTAGED? EJ 039 800
LINGUISTIC AND THEMATIC VARIABLES IN RECALL OF A STORY BY DISADVANTAGED CHILDREN EJ 041 142
FLORIDA'S EARLY CHILDHOOD LEARNING PROGRAM FOR MIGRANT CHILDREN EJ 043 089
AUTOMATED READING INSTRUCTION IN THE GHETTO EJ 045 798
COGNITIVE DEVELOPMENT IN INFANTS OF DIFFERENT AGE LEVELS AND FROM DIFFERENT ENVIRONMENTAL BACKGROUNDS: AN EXPLANATORY INVESTIGATION EJ 046 244
EARLY INTERVENTION AND SOCIAL CLASS: DIAGNOSIS AND TREATMENT OF PRESCHOOL CHILDREN IN A DAY CARE CENTER EJ 050 497
TITLE I AND REMEDIAL READING COMPONENTS FOR DISADVANTAGED STUDENTS EJ 053 676
RACE, SOCIAL CLASS, AND AGE OF ACHIEVEMENT OF CONSERVATION ON PIAGET'S TASKS EJ 053 714
DIALECT, RACE, AND LANGUAGE PROFICIENCY: ANOTHER DEAD HEAT ON THE MERRY-GO-ROUND EJ 053 747
FAMILY FACTORS RELATED TO COMPETENCE IN YOUNG DISADVANTAGED MEXICAN-AMERICAN CHILDREN EJ 053 753
PROBLEM-SOLVING THINKING AND ADJUSTMENT AMONG DISADVANTAGED PRESCHOOL CHILDREN EJ 056 612
NEGRO DIALECT AND BINET PERFORMANCE IN SEVERELY DISADVANTAGED BLACK FOUR-YEAR-OLDS EJ 056 914
A DEMONSTRATION SUMMER PRESCHOOL PROGRAM EJ 060 999

DISCIPLINE

AN ANALYSIS AND EVALUATION OF THE MONTESSORI THEORY OF INNER DISCIPLINE. ED040746
PARENTS ARE TEACHERS: A CHILD MANAGEMENT PROGRAM. ED047826

SOME EFFECTS OF PUNISHMENT ON CHILDREN'S BEHAVIOR EJ 006 876
BEHAVIORAL COMPLIANCE AND DEVALUATION OF THE FORBIDDEN OBJECT AS A FUNCTION OF PROBABILITY OF DETECTION AND SEVERITY OF THREAT EJ 038 935
LE PROBLEME DE LA LIBERTE ET DE LA DISCIPLINE DANS LE JEU (PROBLEMS OF FREEDOM AND DISCIPLINE IN PLAY) EJ 061 465

DISCIPLINE POLICY

CHILD REARING IN CALIFORNIA, A STUDY OF MOTHERS WITH YOUNG CHILDREN. ED020783
A NOTE ON PUNISHMENT PATTERNS IN PARENTS OF PRESCHOOL CHILDREN. REPORT NUMBER 3. ED030477

DISCOVERY LEARNING

INDEPENDENT AND GROUP LEARNING. ED017332
EARLY CHILDHOOD EDUCATION AND THE WALDORF SCHOOL PLAN. ED019114
SUPERMARKET DISCOVERY CENTER, PILOT STUDY, MAY - SEPTEMBER, 1968. INITIAL REPORT. ED027941
PRELIMINARY ANALYSIS OF 1968-69 BOOTH ACHIEVEMENT. ED045201
THE WORLD OF THE CHILD. ED050826
LEARNING BY DISCOVERY: A REVIEW OF THE RESEARCH METHODOLOGY. REPORT FROM THE PROJECT ON VARIABLES AND PROCESSES IN COGNITIVE LEARNING. ED053793
OPENING UP THE CLASSROOM: A WALK AROUND THE SCHOOL. ED053817
THE NUFFIELD MATHEMATICS PROJECT EJ 033 864

DISCOVERY PROCESSES

AN ANALYSIS OF A CLASS OF PROBLEM SOLVING BEHAVIOR. FINAL REPORT. ED020776
WHAT THE WORLD NEEDS NOW: ENVIRONMENTAL EDUCATION FOR YOUNG CHILDREN EJ 039 637
PLAY, THE ESSENTIAL INGREDIENT EJ 046 248

DISCRIMINANT ANALYSIS

THE CURIOSITY DIMENSION OF FIFTH-GRADE CHILDREN: A FACTORIAL DISCRIMINANT ANALYSIS EJ 056 623

DISCRIMINATION LEARNING

COMPARATIVE STUDIES OF A GROUP OF HEAD START AND A GROUP OF NON-HEAD START PRESCHOOL CHILDREN. FINAL REPORT. ED015013
CONCEPT FORMATION AS A FUNCTION OF METHOD OF PRESENTATION AND RATIO OF POSITIVE TO NEGATIVE INSTANCES. ED015779
DISCRIMINATION LEARNING, PROBLEM SOLVING, AND CHOICE PATTERNING BY CHILDREN AS A FUNCTION OF INCENTIVE VALUE, MOTIVATION, AND SEQUENTIAL DEPENDENCIES. FINAL REPORT. ED016518
EXTINCTION IN DISCRIMINATION LEARNING--PRESENTATION AND CONTINGENCY VARIABLES AND ASSOCIATED SIDE EFFECTS. ED019139
REGIONAL EVALUATION AND RESEARCH CENTER FOR HEAD START, SOUTHERN UNIVERSITY. ANNUAL REPORT. ED020792
VARIABLES AFFECTING THE PERFORMANCE OF YOUNG CHILDREN ON A LETTER DISCRIMINATION TASK. ED020797
HEAD START EVALUATION AND RESEARCH CENTER, UNIVERSITY OF KANSAS. FINAL REPORT ON RESEARCH ACTIVITIES. ED021614
HEAD START EVALUATION AND RESEARCH CENTER, UNIVERSITY OF KANSAS. REPORT NO. VIIB, ESTABLISHMENT OF NONVERBAL COLOR DISCRIMINATION RESPONSES TO AUDITORY COLOR-LABELING STIMULI AND SUBSEQUENT EFFECTS ON COLOR-LABELING RESPONSES. ED021641
HEAD START EVALUATION AND RESEARCH CENTER, UNIVERSITY OF KANSAS. REPORT NO. VIIC, ERRORLESS DISCRIMINATION IN PRESCHOOL CHILDREN: A PROGRAM FOR ESTABLISHING A ONE-MINUTE DELAY OF REINFORCEMENT. ED021642
HEAD START EVALUATION AND RESEARCH CENTER, UNIVERSITY OF KANSAS. REPORT NO. IX, DEVELOPMENT OF "MATCHING" ABSTRACTIONS IN YOUNG CHILDREN. ED021645
CENTRAL AND INCIDENTAL LEARNING IN CHILDREN. ED023450
STIMULUS DIMENSIONALITY AND MANIPULABILITY IN VISUAL PERCEPTUAL LEARNING. ED023452
LEARNING OF INCENTIVE-VALUE BY CHILDREN. ED023473
THE EFFECT OF VERBALIZATION OF RELEVANT AND IRRELEVANT DIMENSIONS ON CONCEPT FORMATION. ED030484
PROJECT HEAD START RESEARCH AND EVALUATION CENTER, SYRACUSE UNIVERSITY, RESEARCH INSTITUTE. FINAL REPORT. ED030486
DISCRIMINATION OF RECENCY IN CHILDREN. FINAL REPORT. ED030493
THE EFFECTS OF A LEARNING PROGRAM IN PERCEPTUAL-MOTOR ACTIVITY UPON THE VISUAL PERCEPTION OF SHAPE. FINAL REPORT. ED030494
LOGICAL INFERENCE IN DISCRIMINATION LEARNING OF YOUNG CHILDREN. REPORT FROM THE RULE LEARNING PROJECT. ED036314
PROGRAMMED INSTRUCTION AS A MEANS OF ESTABLISHING "ERRORLESS" LEARNING WITH KINDERGARTEN LEVEL CHILDREN. FINAL REPORT. ED039955
ERRORLESS ESTABLISHMENT OF A MATCH-TO-SAMPLE FORM DISCRIMINATION IN PRESCHOOL CHILDREN. I. A MODIFICATION OF ANIMAL LABORATORY PROCEDURES FOR CHILDREN, II. A COMPARISON OF ERRORLESS AND TRIAL-AND-ERROR DISCRIMINATION. PROGRESS REPORT. ED042490
AN EXPERIMENTAL ANALYSIS OF ERROR INTERACTION ON "ERRORLESS" AND TRIAL-AND-ERROR PROGRAMS. PROGRESS REPORT. ED042491
STIMULUS GENERALIZATION ACROSS INDIVIDUALS ALONG DIMENSIONS OF SEX AND RACE: SOME FINDINGS WITH CHILDREN FROM AN ALL-NEGRO NEIGHBORHOOD. PROGRESS REPORT. ED042497
A DEVELOPMENTAL INVESTIGATION OF VISUAL AND HAPTIC PREFERENCES FOR SHAPE AND TEXTURE EJ 008 780
CUE NOVELTY AND TRAINING LEVEL IN THE DISCRIMINATION SHIFT PERFORMANCE OF RETARDATES EJ 015 851
THE DISCRIMINABILITY OF FORM AMONG YOUNG CHILDREN EJ 016 164
CONCEPT LEARNING IN DISCRIMINATION TASKS EJ 018 878
EFFECT OF VERBAL PRETRAINING AND SINGLE-PROBLEM MASTERY ON WEIGL LEARNING-SET FORMATION IN CHILDREN EJ 018 883
AGE CHANGES IN CHILDREN'S LEARNING SET WITH WIN-STAY, LOSE-SHIFT PROBLEMS EJ 018 885
AN ONTOGENY OF OPTIONAL SHIFT BEHAVIOR EJ 019 003
EFFECT OF VERBAL RESPONSE CLASS ON SHIFT IN THE PRESCHOOL CHILD'S JUDGMENT OF LENGTH IN RESPONSE TO AN ANCHOR STIMULUS EJ 019 012
PROBLEM SOLVING AND THE PERCEPTUAL SALIENCE OF VARIABILITY AND CONSTANCY: A DEVELOPMENTAL STUDY EJ 021 755
DIMENSIONAL LEARNING ACROSS SENSORY MODALITIES IN NURSERY SCHOOL CHILDREN EJ 021 756
RESPONSE STRATEGIES IN THE ODDITY DISCRIMINATION OF PRESCHOOL CHILDREN EJ 021 759
OPTIONAL SHIFT BEHAVIOR OF CHILDREN AS A FUNCTION OF AGE, TYPE OF PRETRAINING AND STIMULUS SALIENCE EJ 021 849
THE STABILITY OF DIMENSIONAL PREFERENCE FOLLOWING ODDITY TRAINING EJ 021 988
TRANSFER PERFORMANCE IN CHILDREN'S ODDITY LEARNING AS A FUNCTION OF DIMENSIONAL PREFERENCE, SHIFT PARADIGM AND OVERTRAINING EJ 024 692
VISUAL ORIENTATION IN CHILDREN'S DISCRIMINATION LEARNING UNDER CONSTANT, VARIABLE, AND COVARIABLE DELAY OF REINFORCEMENT EJ 024 696
DEVELOPMENTAL PROCESSES IN DISCRIMINATION LEARNING EJ 024 705
AN INCREASING EFFECT OF DISORIENTATION ON THE DISCRIMINATION OF PRINT: A DEVELOPMENTAL STUDY EJ 024 982
EFFECTS OF NAMING RELEVANT AND IRRELEVANT STIMULI ON THE DISCRIMINATION LEARNING OF CHILDREN EJ 025 955
AGE DIFFERENCES IN THE DISCRIMINATION SHIFT LEARNING OF YOUNG CHILDREN EJ 025 963
DISCRIMINATION SHIFT PERFORMANCE OF KINDERGARTEN CHILDREN AS A FUNCTION OF VARIATION OF THE IRRELEVANT SHIFT DIMENSION EJ 027 183
DISCRIMINATION SHIFTS IN THREE-YEAR-OLDS AS A FUNCTION OF SHIFT PROCEDURE EJ 027 184
THE EFFECTS OF OVERLEARNING ON CHILDREN'S NONREVERSAL AND REVERSAL LEARNING USING UNRELATED STIMULI EJ 028 633
TRANSPOSITION AND TRANSFER OF ABSOLUTE RESPONDING AS FUNCTIONS OF LEARNING-SET TRAINING AND STIMULUS SIMILARITY EJ 028 635
GENERALIZED IMITATION AND THE DISCRIMINATION HYPOTHESIS EJ 028 636
VERBAL-DISCRIMINATION LEARNING AND TRANSFER WITH VERBAL AND PICTORIAL MATERIALS EJ 030 287
CHILDREN'S SELECTIVE ATTENTION TO STIMULI: STAGE OR SET? EJ 033 573
SEQUENTIAL CONTIGUITY AND SHORT-TERM MEMORY IN CHILDREN'S DISCRIMINATION LEARNING EJ 033 790
CHILDREN'S TWO-CHOICE LEARNING OF PREDOMINANTLY ALTERNATING AND REPEATING SEQUENCES EJ 033 791
FACILITATING AND INTERFERING EFFECTS OF STIMULUS NAMING ON CHILDREN'S MOTOR PAIRED-ASSOCIATE LEARNING EJ 033 793
A DECREMENTAL EFFECT OF REDUNDANCY IN DISCRIMINATION LEARNING EJ 033 795
DISCRIMINATION OF SPATIALLY CONFUSABLE LETTERS BY YOUNG CHILDREN EJ 034 565
CUE AND INCENTIVE MOTIVATIONAL PROPERTIES OF REINFORCERS IN CHILDREN'S DISCRIMINATION LEARNING EJ 035 374
DEVELOPMENTAL TRENDS IN THE INTENTIONAL AND INCIDENTAL LEARNING COMPONENTS OF A VERBAL DISCRIMINATION TASK EJ 035 375
CONDITIONAL DISCRIMINATION LEARNING IN CHILDREN: TWO RELEVANT FACTORS EJ 036 823
THE DISCRIMINATION LEARNING OF NORMAL AND RETARDED CHILDREN AS A FUNCTION OF PENALTY CONDITIONS AND ETIOLOGY OF THE RETARDED EJ 041 136
THE EFFECTS OF REWARD AND PUNISHMENT UPON CHILDREN'S ATTENTION, MOTIVATION, AND DISCRIMINATION LEARNING EJ 041 137
THE EFFECTS OF STIMULUS REDUNDANCY ON TRANSFER OF STIMULUS PRETRAINING EJ 041 138
THE "FEATURE POSITIVE EFFECT" AND SIMULTANEOUS DISCRIMINATION LEARNING EJ 042 963
THE PERFORMANCE OF PRESCHOOL CHILDREN ON REVERSAL AND TWO TYPES OF EXTRADIMENSIONAL SHIFTS EJ 042 967
CONDITIONS GOVERNING NONREINFORCED IMITATION EJ 045 042
A REEXAMINATION OF THE ROLE OF INCENTIVE IN CHILDREN'S DISCRIMINATION LEARNING EJ 046 237
EFFECTS OF SPATIAL SEPARATION OF STIMULUS, RESPONSE, AND REWARD IN DISCRIMINATION LEARNING BY CHILDREN EJ 046 243

SINGLE VERSUS CUMULATIVE PRESENTATION OF STIMULI TO KINDERGARTNERS IN REVERSAL SHIFT BEHAVIOR EJ 047 678
TITRATING DELAYED MATCHING TO SAMPLE IN CHILDREN EJ 047 684
STIMULUS INTERACTION AND PROBLEM DIFFICULTY IN CHILDREN'S DISCRIMINATION LEARNING EJ 053 480
EFFECTS OF RATE OF STIMULUS PRESENTATION AND PENALTY CONDITIONS ON THE DISCRIMINATION LEARNING OF NORMAL AND RETARDED CHILDREN EJ 053 712
DISCRIMINATION LEARNING BY REFLECTIVE AND IMPULSIVE CHILDREN AS A FUNCTION OF REINFORCEMENT SCHEDULE EJ 053 717
TRANSFER OF TRAINING: SOME BOUNDARY CONDITIONS AND INITIAL THEORY EJ 053 722
DISCRIMINATION OF STEREOMETRIC OJBECTS AND PHOTOGRAPHS OF OBJECTS BY CHILDREN EJ 053 749
STIMULUS NOVELTY AS A VARIABLE IN CHILDREN'S WIN-STAY, LOSE-SHIFT DISCRIMINATION LEARNING SET EJ 053 751
OBSERVING BEHAVIOR AND CHILDREN'S DISCRIMINATION LEARNING EJ 053 754
EFFECTS OF TYPE AND SOURCE OF LABELS ON CHILDREN'S PERCEPTUAL JUDGMENTS AND DISCRIMINATION LEARNING EJ 053 756
DISCRIMINATION LEARNING AND TRANSFER OF TRAINING IN THE AGED EJ 055 204
DEVELOPMENT OF RELATIONAL CONCEPTS AND WORD DEFINITION IN CHILDREN FIVE THROUGH ELEVEN EJ 056 397
THE EFFECTS OF DIFFERENTIAL REINFORCEMENT ON THE DISCRIMINATION LEARNING OF NORMAL AND LOW-ACHIEVING MIDDLE-CLASS BOYS EJ 056 398
VERBAL AND NONVERBAL REWARDS AND PUNISHMENT IN THE DISCRIMINATION LEARNING OF CHILDREN OF VARYING SOCIOECONOMIC STATUS EJ 057 896
INSTABILITY OF DIMENSIONAL PREFERENCE FOLLOWING CHANGES IN RELATIVE CUE SIMILARITY EJ 057 908
PROBLEMS OF CONTROL IN SIMULTANEOUS DISCRIMINATION TASKS EJ 058 215
"RIGHT," "WRONG," AND DISCRIMINATION LEARNING IN CHILDREN EJ 060 774
HYPOTHESES, STRATEGIES, AND STEREOTYPES IN DISCRIMINATION LEARNING EJ 060 779
REVERSALS PRIOR TO SOLUTION OF CONCEPT IDENTIFICATION IN CHILDREN EJ 060 782
THE EFFECTS OF VERBAL PRETRAINING ON THE MULTIDIMENSIONAL GENERALIZATION BEHAVIOR OF CHILDREN EJ 060 784
THREE-CUE SELECTION MODELS APPLIED TO MULTIDIMENSIONAL STIMULUS CLASSIFICATION: ALTERNATIVES TO THE SPIKER, CROLL, AND MILLER ANALYSIS EJ 060 785

DISCRIMINATORY ATTITUDES (SOCIAL)
CHILDREN WITHOUT PREJUDICE. 1970 WHITE HOUSE CONFERENCE ON CHILDREN, REPORT OF FORUM 18. (WORKING PAPER). ED046534
MARGINAL CHILDREN OF WAR: AN EXPLORATORY STUDY OF AMERICAN-KOREAN CHILDREN. ED047781
RACIAL ATTITUDES AMONG WHITE KINDERGARTEN CHILDREN FROM THREE DIFFERENT ENVIRONMENTS. ED051882
CHILDREN AS VICTIMS OF INSTITUTIONALIZATION EJ 051 205
SOME DISCRIMINATIVE PROPERTIES OF RACE AND SEX FOR CHILDREN FROM AN ALL-NEGRO NEIGHBORHOOD EJ 058 510

DISCRIMINATORY LEGISLATION
CHILDREN AS VICTIMS OF INSTITUTIONALIZATION EJ 051 205

DISCUSSION GROUPS
A FEASIBILITY STUDY OF PARENT AWARENESS PROGRAMS. FINAL REPORT. ED040742

DISCUSSION PROGRAMS
ON BEING A WHITEY IN THE MIDST OF A RACIAL CRISIS EJ 007 362

DISEASE CONTROL
CHILDHOOD LEAD POISONING...AN ERADICABLE DISEASE EJ 013 482

DISEASES
CHANGING PROSPECTS FOR CHILDREN WITH HEMOPHILIA EJ 029 952
EFFECTS OF HEMOPHILIA UPON INTELLECTUAL GROWTH AND ACADEMIC ACHIEVEMENT EJ 044 009
PARENTS OF CHILDREN WITH PKU EJ 060 522

DISTANCE
CHILD-PARENT SPATIAL PATTERNS UNDER PRAISE AND REPROOF EJ 045 159

DIVERGENT THINKING
DIVERGENT THINKING AND PERSONALITY MEASURES OF ENGLISH AND AMERICAN EDUCATION MAJORS EJ 044 707
SOME EFFECTS OF TESTING PROCEDURE ON DIVERGENT THINKING EJ 052 992
SIBLING RESEMBLANCES IN DIVERGENT THINKING EJ 055 106

DOCTORAL THESES
A STUDY OF THE INFLUENCE OF CERTAIN PRESCHOOL EDUCATIONAL MOVEMENTS ON CONTEMPORARY PRESCHOOL PRACTICES. ED035450

DRAMATIC PLAY
LA FORMATION THEATRALE DANS L'EDUCATION PRESCOLAIRE EJ 034 420

AN EXPERIENCE WITH FEAR IN THE LIVES OF CHILDREN EJ 045 389

DRAMATICS
LA FORMATION THEATRALE DANS L'EDUCATION PRESCOLAIRE EJ 034 420

DROPOUT PROGRAMS
AN ISRAELI EXPERIMENTAL GROUP WITH PRIMARY SCHOOL DROPOUTS OUTSIDE THE SCHOOL SETTING EJ 041 630

DROPOUT TEACHING
AN ISRAELI EXPERIMENTAL GROUP WITH PRIMARY SCHOOL DROPOUTS OUTSIDE THE SCHOOL SETTING EJ 041 630

DROPOUTS
THE WARRIOR DROPOUTS. ED016529
AN ISRAELI EXPERIMENTAL GROUP WITH PRIMARY SCHOOL DROPOUTS OUTSIDE THE SCHOOL SETTING EJ 041 630

DRUG ABUSE
DRUG USE AMONG THE YOUNG: AS TEENAGERS SEE IT EJ 029 950
DEVELOPMENTAL FACTORS IN ADOLESCENT DRUG USE: A STUDY OF PSYCHEDELIC DRUG USERS EJ 051 020

DRUG THERAPY
II. DELIVERY MEDICATION AND INFANT OUTCOME: AN EMPIRICAL STUDY EJ 023 014
THE USE OF STIMULANT DRUGS IN TREATING HYPERACTIVE CHILDREN EJ 038 022
COGNITIVE STYLES IN HYPERACTIVE CHILDREN AND THE EFFECT OF METHYLPHENIDATE EJ 041 963
ATTENTION IN HYPERACTIVE CHILDREN AND THE EFFECT OF METHYLPHENIDATE (RITALIN) EJ 043 669
PLAYROOM OBSERVATIONS OF HYPERACTIVE CHILDREN ON MEDICATION EJ 048 301

DYSLEXIA
AN EVALUATION OF A THEORY OF SPECIFIC DEVELOPMENTAL DYSLEXIA EJ 055 875

EARLY ADMISSION
EARLY ADMISSION: OPINION VERSUS EVIDENCE EJ 048 045

EARLY CHILDHOOD
TRAINING EFFECTS AND CONCEPT DEVELOPMENT--A STUDY OF THE CONSERVATION OF CONTINUOUS QUANTITY IN CHILDREN. ED016533
A STUDY OF A MEASUREMENT RESOURCE IN CHILD RESEARCH, PROJECT HEAD START. ED020790
THE EFFECT OF EARLY STIMULATION: THE PROBLEM OF FOCUS IN DEVELOPMENTAL STIMULATION. ED022535
THE TWO YEAR OLD. ED022536
A STUDY OF LANGUAGE DEVELOPMENT FROM INFANCY TO AGE 5. ED022539
PROCEEDINGS OF THE ANNUAL CONVENTION OF THE CHRISTIAN ASSOCIATION FOR PSYCHOLOGICAL STUDIES ON THE DYNAMICS OF LEARNING CHRISTIAN CONCEPTS (12TH, GRAND RAPIDS, MICHIGAN, MARCH 31-APRIL 1, 1965). ED023476
THE ACQUISITION OF LINGUISTIC STRUCTURE. TECHNICAL REPORT VIII, A STUDY IN THE ACQUISITION OF LANGUAGE: FREE RESPONSES TO COMMANDS. ED023486
EARLY CHILDHOOD SELECTED BIBLIOGRAPHIES SERIES. NUMBER 4, COGNITION. ED023488
PARENTAL BEHAVIOR TOWARD BOYS AND GIRLS OF PRESCHOOL AGE. ED026119
CHILD DEVELOPMENT AND MATERIAL SURVEY. PART II, MATERIAL SURVEY. FINAL REPORT. ED027085
RESEARCH ISSUES IN THE HEALTH AND NUTRITION IN EARLY CHILDHOOD. ED027970
THE NURSERY YEARS: THE MIND OF THE CHILD FROM BIRTH TO SIX YEARS. ED029711
THE MAGIC YEARS: UNDERSTANDING AND HANDLING THE PROBLEMS OF EARLY CHILDHOOD. ED029712
THE DEVELOPMENT OF EARLY SOCIAL INTERACTION--AN ETHOLOGICAL APPROACH. ED031291
SEX DIFFERENCES IN GENERALITY AND CONTINUITY OF VERBAL RESPONSIVITY. ED035444
RESEARCH ISSUES IN CHILD HEALTH, I-IV. PROCEEDINGS OF THE HEAD START RESEARCH SEMINARS: SEMINAR NO. 4, HEALTH AND NUTRITION IN EARLY CHILDHOOD (1ST, WASHINGTON, D.C., NOVEMBER 1, 1968). ED036331
EMERGENCE OF IDENTITY: THE FIRST YEARS. 1970 WHITE HOUSE CONFERENCE ON CHILDREN, REPORT OF FORUM 2. (WORKING COPY). ED046521
A LONGITUDINAL ASSESSMENT OF THINKING ABILITY OF PRELITERATE CHILDREN DURING A TWO-YEAR PERIOD. FINAL REPORT. ED048946
A RESOURCE AND REFERENCE BIBLIOGRAPHY IN EARLY CHILDHOOD EDUCATION AND DEVELOPMENTAL PSYCHOLOGY: THE AFFECTIVE DOMAIN. ED049817
SEX IDENTITY IN LONDON CHILDREN: MEMORY, KNOWLEDGE AND PREFERENCE TESTS EJ 023 435

CHILDREN AND THEIR EXPANDING WORLD OF KNOWLEDGE EJ 026 734
THE FUNDAMENTAL LEARNING NEEDS OF TODAY'S YOUNG CHILDREN EJ 027 531
AN INSTRUMENT FOR MEASURING CREATIVITY IN YOUNG CHILDREN: THE GROSS GEOMETRIC FORMS EJ 027 586
DAY CARE IN THE 1970S: PLANNING FOR EXPANSION EJ 037 237
SEVERE PROTEIN-CALORIE MALNUTRITION AND COGNITIVE DEVELOPMENT IN INFANCY AND EARLY CHILDHOOD EJ 039 627
BOOKS FOR YOUNG CHILDREN EJ 043 020
ANXIETY IN YOUNG CHILDREN EJ 045 049
A STUDY OF SLEEP BEHAVIOR IN TWO-YEAR-OLD CHILDREN EJ 048 299
THE CONCEPT OF DEATH IN EARLY CHILDHOOD EJ 052 464
TRANSFER OF TRAINING: SOME BOUNDARY CONDITIONS AND INITIAL THEORY EJ 053 722
SPONTANEOUS MEASUREMENT IN YOUNG CHILDREN: A RE-EXAMINATION EJ 055 095
INFORMATION AND STRATEGY IN THE YOUNG CHILD'S SEARCH FOR HIDDEN OBJECTS EJ 056 395
TEACHING MULTIPLE CLASSIFICATION TO YOUNG CHILDREN EJ 056 711
PRECOCIOUS THOUGHTS ON NUMBER: THE LONG AND THE SHORT OF IT EJ 060 776
ORIENTATION IN CHILDREN'S HUMAN FIGURE DRAWINGS: AN ASPECT OF GRAPHIC LANGUAGE EJ 061 067
THE IMPORTANCE OF SECURITY IN THE EDUCATION OF YOUNG CHILDREN EJ 062 549

EARLY CHILDHOOD EDUCATION

PROJECT HEAD START AND THE CULTURALLY DEPRIVED IN ROCHESTER, NEW YORK, A STUDY OF PARTICIPATING AND NON-PARTICIPATING FAMILIES IN AREAS SERVED BY PROJECT HEAD START IN ROCHESTER, FINAL REPORT. ED013669
PROJECT HEAD START IN AN INDIAN COMMUNITY. ED014329
MEMORANDUM ON--FACILITIES FOR EARLY CHILDHOOD EDUCATION. ED015023
MEMO--COMMENTS ON THE WOLFF AND STEIN STUDY. ED015029
MONTESSORI PRE-SCHOOL EDUCATION. FINAL REPORT. ED017320
A STUDY OF THE KINDERGARTEN PROGRAM, FULL-DAY OR HALF-DAY. ED017327
THE ROLE OF SOCIALIZATION AND SOCIAL INFLUENCE IN A COMPENSATORY PRESCHOOL PROGRAM. ED017337
NORTHFIELD, VERMONT--A COMMUNITY DEPTH STUDY. ED018245
A REPORT OF THE SOUTHERN REGIONAL CONFERENCE ON EARLY CHILDHOOD EDUCATION. ED019112
EARLY CHILDHOOD EDUCATION AND THE WALDORF SCHOOL PLAN. ED019114
A POSITION PAPER ON EARLY CHILDHOOD EDUCATION. ED019128
CRITICAL OVERVIEW OF EARLY CHILDHOOD EDUCATION PROGRAMS. ED019142
PREVENTION OF FAILURE. ED020777
PRE-SCHOOL EDUCATION. ED020785
EARLY CHILDHOOD EDUCATION TODAY. ED021631
EARLY CHILDHOOD SELECTED BIBLIOGRAPHIES SERIES. NUMBER 2, LANGUAGE. ED022538
BIBLIOGRAPHY, EARLY CHILDHOOD EDUCATION. ED022544
EARLY CHILDHOOD SELECTED BIBLIOGRAPHIES SERIES. NUMBER 3, EDUCATION. ED022546
PROMISING DIRECTIONS FOR RESEARCH AND DEVELOPMENT IN EARLY CHILDHOOD EDUCATION. ED023448
EARLY CHILDHOOD SELECTED BIBLIOGRAPHIES SERIES. NUMBER 4, COGNITION. ED023488
EARLY CHILDHOOD SELECTED BIBLIOGRAPHIES SERIES. NUMBER 5, SOCIAL. ED024472
EARLY CHILDHOOD SELECTED BIBLIOGRAPHIES SERIES. NUMBER 6, PERSONALITY. ED024475
ARITHMETIC AND MATHEMATICS. DIMENSIONS IN EARLY LEARNING SERIES. ED026136
READING. DIMENSIONS IN EARLY LEARNING SERIES. ED027070
THE SPIRIT OF THE TIMES IN CHILDHOOD EDUCATION. THE FIRST EVANGELINE BURGESS MEMORIAL LECTURE. ED027081
VISUAL LEARNING. DIMENSIONS IN EARLY LEARNING SERIES. ED027089
REVIEW OF SELECTED INTERVENTION RESEARCH WITH YOUNG CHILDREN. ED027091
CURRICULUM GUIDE FOR EARLY CHILDHOOD EDUCATION. BEHAVIORAL GOALS - PRE-K THROUGH ONE. ED027940
PROGRAM FOR EARLY CHILDHOOD EDUCATION. ED027957
A PLAN OF ACTION FOR PARENT-CHILD EDUCATIONAL CENTERS. ED027959
A LONDON INFANT SCHOOL. AN INTERVIEW. ED027963
EARLY EDUCATION: THE CREATION OF CAPACITY. ED028824
LITERATURE AND THE YOUNG CHILD. ED028828
PROBLEM SOLVING AND CONCEPT FORMATION: ANNOTATED LISTING OF NATIONAL AND INTERNATIONAL CURRICULAR PROJECTS AT THE EARLY CHILDHOOD LEVEL. ED029685
EARLY CHILDHOOD EDUCATION IN AMERICAN SAMOA, 1968. ED032114
PHILOSOPHY: A CRUCIAL DISTINCTION. ED032129
RESEARCH, CHANGE, AND SOCIAL RESPONSIBILITY: AN ILLUSTRATIVE MODEL FROM EARLY EDUCATION. ED032922
PRELIMINARY REPORT OF THE AD HOC JOINT COMMITTEE ON THE PREPARATION OF NURSERY AND KINDERGARTEN TEACHERS. ED032924
EVALUATION OF SELECTED COMPONENTS OF: A SUPPLEMENTARY CENTER FOR EARLY CHILDHOOD EDUCATION. TITLE III. ED032927
LIVING AND LEARNING: AN ANNOTATED BIBLIOGRAPHY FOR THOSE WHO LIVE AND LEARN WITH YOUNG CHILDREN. ED032935
THE SOCIOLOGY OF EARLY CHILDHOOD EDUCATION: A REVIEW OF LITERATURE. TECHNICAL REPORT NO. 1. ED032944
CHILDHOOD RESOURCES INFORMATION BULLETIN. VOLUME 1, NUMBER 2, FALL 1969. ED032948
SOURCE BOOK OF SELECTED MATERIALS FOR EARLY CHILDHOOD EDUCATION IN THE ARTS. ED033746
THE TUCSON EARLY EDUCATION MODEL. ED033753
THE INFLUENCE OF THEORETICAL CONCEPTIONS OF HUMAN DEVELOPMENT ON THE PRACTICE OF EARLY CHILDHOOD EDUCATION. ED033766
DESIGNING A PROGRAM FOR BROADCAST TELEVISION. ED033768
TRAINING THE INTELLECT VERSUS DEVELOPMENT OF THE CHILD. ED034573
ARIZONA CENTER FOR EARLY CHILDHOOD EDUCATION ANNUAL REPORT, JUNE 1968 - JUNE 1969. ED034586
STAFFING PRESCHOOLS: BACKGROUND INFORMATION. ED034589
AN EDUCATIONAL IMPERATIVE AND ITS FALLOUT IMPLICATIONS. ED034590
ORCHESTRATED INSTRUCTION: A COOKING EXPERIENCE. ED034593
MONTESSORI INDEX. THIRD EDITION. ED035435
A STUDY OF THE INFLUENCE OF CERTAIN PRESCHOOL EDUCATIONAL MOVEMENTS ON CONTEMPORARY PRESCHOOL PRACTICES. ED035450
POSTDOCTORAL RESEARCH TRAINING PROGRAM IN EDUCATIONAL STIMULATION. FINAL REPORT. ED035455
EARLY LEARNING AND COMPENSATORY EDUCATION: CONTRIBUTION OF BASIC RESEARCH. ED036318
EARLY CHILDHOOD EDUCATION: AN INTRODUCTION TO THE PROFESSION. ED036328
MATERIALS FOR KINDERGARTEN. ED037237
DEVELOPMENT OF THE EARLY CHILDHOOD EDUCATION PROGRAM. BASIC PLAN. ED038181
[NATIONAL LABORATORY ON EARLY CHILDHOOD EDUCATION PROGRAM ED039012
COMMUNITY COORDINATED CHILD CARE (4-C) MANUAL. ED039016
AN ANALYSIS OF EARLY CHILDHOOD EDUCATION RESEARCH AND DEVELOPMENT. ED039028
THE NATIONAL LABORATORY ON EARLY CHILDHOOD EDUCATION: TOWARD CONSTRUCTIVE CHANGE. ED039953
TELEVISION GUIDELINES FOR EARLY CHILDHOOD EDUCATION. ED040739
AN EDUCATIONAL SYSTEM FOR DEVELOPMENTALLY DISABLED INFANTS. ED040749
NEED FOR EARLY AND CONTINUING EDUCATION. ED040750
ISSUES AND REALITIES IN EARLY CHILDHOOD EDUCATION. ED041621
EVALUATION REPORT: EARLY CHILDHOOD EDUCATION PROGRAM, 1969 FIELD TEST. ED041626
PREPRIMARY ENROLLMENT TRENDS OF CHILDREN UNDER SIX: 1964-1968. ED042502
PROGRAM-PROJECT RESUMES, 1969-1970. ED042503
A SEQUENTIAL APPROACH TO EARLY CHILDHOOD AND ELEMENTARY EDUCATION, PHASE I. GRANT REPORT. ED042517
AN EDUCATION SYSTEM FOR HIGH-RISK INFANTS: A PREVENTIVE APPROACH TO DEVELOPMENTAL AND LEARNING DISABILITIES. ED043379
EARLY CHILDHOOD EDUCATION AS A DISCIPLINE. ED043396
REVIEW OF SELECTED EARLY EDUCATION RESEARCH IN THE SCHOOL DISTRICT OF UNIVERSITY CITY, MISSOURI, JUNE, 1970. ED044182
DISSEMINATION AND UTILIZATION OF KNOWLEDGE IN THE AREA OF EARLY CHILDHOOD EDUCATION: A DESCRIPTION OF SOME OF THE PROBLEMS. ED044185
EARLY CHILDHOOD EDUCATION PROGRAM AND ITS COMPONENTS: PSYCHOLOGICAL EVALUATION, SENSORIMOTOR SKILLS PROGRAM, NEW VISIONS - A CHILDREN'S MUSEUM. PROJECT REPORTS, VOLUME 4, BOOK 1, 1969. ED045183
THE EFFECTS OF ASSESSMENT AND PERSONALIZED PROGRAMMING ON SUBSEQUENT INTELLECTUAL DEVELOPMENT OF PREKINDERGARTEN AND KINDERGARTEN CHILDREN. FINAL REPORT. ED045198
AN OVERVIEW OF COGNITIVE AND LANGUAGE PROGRAMS FOR 3, 4, & 5 YEAR OLD CHILDREN. ED045209
TACOMA PUBLIC SCHOOLS EARLY CHILDHOOD PROGRAM, TACOMA, WASHINGTON: COMBINED LOCAL, STATE, AND FEDERAL FUNDS SUPPORT A LARGE-SCALE EARLY CHILDHOOD PROGRAM IN THE PUBLIC SCHOOLS. MODEL PROGRAMS--CHILDHOOD EDUCATION. ED045221
THE DEVELOPMENT OF AN INFORMATION UNIT REVIEWING SELECTED WELL-DEVELOPED MODELS OF EARLY CHILDHOOD EDUCATION PROGRAMS. FINAL REPORT. ED045223
NEGRO CULTURE AND EARLY CHILDHOOD EDUCATION. ED046495
A COMPARISON OF CONTRASTING PROGRAMS IN EARLY CHILDHOOD EDUCATION. ED046509
HEAD START CURRICULUM MODELS: A REFERENCE LIST. ED046517
THE BEHAVIOR ANALYSIS CLASSROOM. ED047775

A TOKEN MANUAL FOR BEHAVIOR ANALYSIS CLASSROOMS. ED047776
THE IMPLICATIONS OF DESIGN AND MODEL SELECTION FOR THE EVALUATION OF PROGRAMS FOR THE DISADVANTAGED CHILD. ED047792
PROGRAMS FOR INFANTS AND YOUNG CHILDREN. PART I: EDUCATION AND DAY CARE. ED047807
A BRIEF GUIDE TO NEWSLETTERS IN EARLY CHILDHOOD EDUCATION. ED048932
EVALUATION GUIDE FOR EARLY CHILDHOOD EDUCATION PROGRAMS. ED048938
HEAD START CURRICULUM MODELS: A REFERENCE LIST. (REVISED EDITION). ED048947
A TEACHING LEARNING SCHEMA FOR TEACHER TRAINING AND CURRICULUM DEVELOPMENT IN EARLY EDUCATION. ED049812
RESEARCH AND DEVELOPMENT REGISTER IN EARLY CHILDHOOD EDUCATION, 1970. ED049815
AN ANNOTATED BIBLIOGRAPHY ON EARLY CHILDHOOD. ED049822
KINDERGARTEN: WHO? WHAT? WHERE? ED049829
LENIN'S GRANDCHILDREN: PRESCHOOL EDUCATION IN THE SOVIET UNION. ED049830
THE ASSESSMENT OF "SELF-CONCEPT" IN EARLY CHILDHOOD EDUCATION. ED050822
DIRECTED RESEARCH PROGRAM IN READING, EARLY CHILDHOOD, VOCATIONAL EDUCATION, SCHOOL ORGANIZATION AND ADMINISTRATION, FY 72 - FY 76. ED051871
CONFERENCE ON READING AND EARLY CHILDHOOD. ED051875
ANALYSIS OF EARLY CHILDHOOD PROGRAMS: A SEARCH FOR COMPARATIVE DIMENSIONS. ED051877
LANGUAGE TRAINING IN EARLY CHILDHOOD EDUCATION. ED051881
PRESCHOOL PROGRAMS: AN ANNOTATED BIBLIOGRAPHY. ED052822
CONTEMPORARY INFLUENCES IN EARLY CHILDHOOD EDUCATION. ED053797
DESIGNS AND PROPOSAL FOR EARLY CHILDHOOD RESEARCH: A NEW LOOK: A MULTIPLE SYSTEMS-SERVICE APPROACH TO PROGRAMS AND RESEARCH FOR HELPING POOR CHILDREN. (ONE IN A SERIES OF SIX PAPERS). ED053806
DESIGNS AND PROPOSAL FOR EARLY CHILDHOOD RESEARCH: A NEW LOOK: ON ATTAINING THE GOALS OF EARLY CHILDHOOD EDUCATION. (ONE IN A SERIES OF SIX PAPERS). ED053807
DESIGNS AND PROPOSAL FOR EARLY CHILDHOOD RESEARCH: A NEW LOOK: A SYSTEMS APPROACH TO PRE-SCHOOL EDUCATION. (ONE IN A SERIES OF SIX PAPERS). ED053809
DESIGNS AND PROPOSAL FOR EARLY CHILDHOOD RESEARCH: A NEW LOOK: MALNUTRITION, LEARNING AND INTELLIGENCE. (ONE IN A SERIES OF SIX PAPERS). ED053811
DEMONSTRATION AND TRAINING PROJECT FOR MIGRANT CHILDREN, MCALLEN, TEXAS. EARLY CHILDHOOD LEARNING SYSTEM. FINAL EVALUATION REPORT, 1970-71. ED053812
EARLY CHILDHOOD EDUCATION - FOR WHAT GOALS? EJ 003 595
MUSIC IN THE BEGINNING READING PROGRAM EJ 006 811
AUDIO-VISUAL MATERIALS IN EARLY CHILDHOOD EDUCATION EJ 006 854
TELEVISION VIOLENCE EJ 006 855
SOME EFFECTS OF PUNISHMENT ON CHILDREN'S BEHAVIOR EJ 006 876
INTERACTION OF SEX OF SUBJECT AND DEPENDENCY-TRAINING PROCEDURES IN A SOCIAL-REINFORCEMENT STUDY EJ 006 877
THE EFFECT OF EARLY STIMULATION: THE PROBLEM OF FOCUS IN DEVELOPMENTAL STIMULATION EJ 006 921
OF DREAMS AND REALITY: KIBBUTZ CHILDREN EJ 006 922
CHILDREN UNDER THREE - FINDING WAYS TO STIMULATE DEVELOPMENT. I. ISSUES IN RESEARCH EJ 006 980
AN ESSAY FOR TEACHERS EJ 006 981
A MOBILE PRESCHOOL EJ 006 982
CHALLENGES AHEAD FOR EARLY CHILDHOOD EDUCATION EJ 006 983
CRUCIAL ISSUES IN CONTEMPORARY EARLY CHILDHOOD EDUCATION EJ 006 984
EVALUATION OF EDUCATIONAL PROGRAMS EJ 007 047
CREATIVE LEARNING IN CHILDREN'S PLAYGROUNDS EJ 007 071
PARENT AND CHILD CENTERS--WHAT THEY ARE, WHERE THEY ARE GOING EJ 007 089
THE 4-C PROGRAM EJ 007 090
STATEMENT BY THE PRESIDENT ON THE ESTABLISHMENT OF AN OFFICE OF CHILD DEVELOPMENT EJ 007 091
COMBATING MALNUTRITION THROUGH MATERNAL AND CHILD HEALTH PROGRAMS EJ 007 161
NEW ZEALAND'S DENTAL SERVICE FOR CHILDREN EJ 007 162
IS THERE A LITERATURE FOR THE DISADVANTAGED CHILD? EJ 007 178
DISTORTIONS IN THE KINDERGARTEN EJ 007 214
THE CHILD WHO STUTTERS EJ 007 220
THE BILINGUAL CHILD EJ 007 221
NUMBER GAMES WITH YOUNG CHILDREN EJ 007 273
BOOKS WHICH GIVE MATHEMATICAL CONCEPTS TO YOUNG CHILDREN: AN ANNOTATED BIBLIOGRAPHY EJ 007 274
NURSES GAIN FROM FIELD WORK WITH YOUNG CHILDREN EJ 007 301
ACTIVITIES TO TEACH THE CONCEPT OF CONSERVATION EJ 007 311
A NONSEGREGATED APPROACH TO HEAD START EJ 007 363
CHILDREN UNDER THREE - FINDING WAYS TO STIMULATE DEVELOPMENT. II. SOME CURRENT EXPERIMENTS: A THREE PRONGED PROJECT EJ 007 408
CHILDREN UNDER THREE - FINDING WAYS TO STIMULATE DEVELOPMENT. II. SOME CURRENT EXPERIMENTS: LEARNING AT TWO EJ 007 409
CHILDREN UNDER THREE - FINDING WAYS TO STIMULATE DEVELOPMENT. II. SOME CURRENT EXPERIMENTS: STIMULATION VIA PARENT EDUCATION EJ 007 410
CHILDREN UNDER THREE - FINDING WAYS TO STIMULATE DEVELOPMENT. II. SOME CURRENT EXPERIMENTS: A HOME TUTORING PROGRAM EJ 007 411
CHILDREN UNDER THREE - FINDING WAYS TO STIMULATE DEVELOPMENT. II. SOME CURRENT EXPERIMENTS: FROM INFANCY THROUGH SCHOOL EJ 007 412
BING NURSERY SCHOOL EJ 007 425
UPBRINGING OF CHILDREN IN KIBBUTZIM OF ISRAEL EJ 007 447
NEW OPPORTUNITIES IN DAY CARE: AN INTERVIEW WITH GERTRUDE HOFFMANN EJ 007 448
A DAY CARE PROGRAM IN THE MIDDLE EAST EJ 009 815
THE CARE AND EDUCATION OF PRESCHOOL NONWHITES IN THE REPUBLIC OF SOUTH AFRICA EJ 010 125
WHAT IS LEARNED AND WHAT IS TAUGHT EJ 010 443
FOUNDATIONS FOR GOOD BEGINNINGS EJ 010 588
L'EDUCATION PRESCOLAIRE ET L'APPRENTISSAGE DE LA LECTURE (PRE SCHOOL EDUCATION AND INTRODUCTION TO READING) EJ 010 653
FAMILY PROBLEMS CONCERNING THE MENTALLY RETARDED CHILD EJ 010 859
SELF-MADE TOYS IN CHILDREN'S GAMES EJ 011 253
INTRODUCTION OF NEW CHILDREN INTO A DAY CARE CENTER EJ 011 302
CHILD PSYCHOLOGY IN FUTURE SOCIETY EJ 011 344
SLEEP PROBLEMS EJ 011 345
THE ROLE OF WOMEN IN THE DEVELOPMENT OF THEIR COUNTRIES: COMMENTS FROM OMEP ON A QUESTIONNAIRE FROM U.N EJ 011 346
NUTRITION IN DAY CARE CENTERS EJ 011 595
EARLY MALNUTRITION AND HUMAN DEVELOPMENT EJ 011 914
CREATIVE SUPERVISION OF HEAD START CENTERS EJ 013 231
HOW ELSE? EJ 015 060
THE PRINCIPAL AND THE KINDERGARTEN EJ 016 716
THE EXECUTIVE DIRECTOR'S TESTIMONY BEFORE THE HOUSE EDUCATION AND LABOR COMMITTEE EJ 017 848
CONTRASTING VIEWS OF EARLY CHILDHOOD EDUCATION EJ 017 851
A BACKWARD GLANCE--A FORWARD STEP? EJ 020 295
SOVIET PRESCHOOL EDUCATION EJ 020 840
THE CALIFORNIA CREDENTIAL STORY: A NEW SPECIALIZATION FOR TEACHERS OF YOUNG CHILDREN EJ 020 892
THE ENVIRONMENTAL MYSTIQUE: TRAINING THE INTELLECT VERSUS DEVELOPMENT OF THE CHILD EJ 022 138
ABOUT RESEARCH: PART I, THE NATURE OF RESEARCH... CHANGING EMPHASES EJ 027 435
TEACHER-PARENT WORK IN THE HOME: AN ASPECT OF CHILD GUIDANCE CLINIC SERVICES EJ 027 448
A NATIONAL PRIORITY: RAISING THE QUALITY OF CHILDREN'S LIVES EJ 027 501
WHAT ARE THE SOURCES OF EARLY CHILDHOOD CURRICULUM? EJ 027 943
L'EDUCATEUR ET L'EPANOUISSEMENT DE LA PERSONNALITE DE L'ENFANT EJ 028 102
ABOUT RESEARCH: PART II. IS A BEHAVIORAL APPROACH SUPERFICIAL? IS OPERANT CONDITIONING FAIR? WHY DO RESEARCH? EJ 029 015
EARLY CHILDHOOD EDUCATION AS A DISCIPLINE EJ 029 617
EARLY AGE EDUCATION EJ 029 620
"THERE WAS A CHILD WENT FORTH"--A PHILOSOPHY OF EARLY EDUCATION EJ 031 049
BEFORE CHILDREN CAN MEASURE EJ 032 359
FOUR QUESTIONS ON EARLY CHILDHOOD EDUCATION EJ 034 784
THE PLACE OF PRESCHOOL EDUCATION IN THE EDUCATIONAL SYSTEM EJ 036 329
ETHICAL ISSUES IN RESEARCH IN EARLY CHILDHOOD INTERVENTION EJ 037 578
WHY NOT FEELINGS AND VALUES IN INSTRUCTIONAL TELEVISION? EJ 038 906
AUDIO-VISUAL MATERIALS IN EARLY CHILDHOOD EDUCATION EJ 038 907
FLORIDA'S EARLY CHILDHOOD LEARNING PROGRAM FOR MIGRANT CHILDREN EJ 043 089
LEARNING FROM EACH OTHER EJ 044 008
ON THE VALUE OF BOTH PLAY AND STRUCTURE IN EARLY EDUCATION EJ 044 010
SAY YOU COME FROM MISSOURI EJ 047 103
WHAT TO DO TILL THE MALE MAN COMES EJ 048 697
PLANNING TRIPS FOR VULNERABLE CHILDREN EJ 048 998
THE TEACHER STRUCTURE CHECKLIST: A POSSIBLE TOOL FOR COMMUNICATION EJ 051 352
THE TEACHER'S ROLE IN HELPING YOUNG CHILDREN DEVELOP LANGUAGE COMPETENCE EJ 051 566
SENTENCE REPETITION: ELICITED IMITATION OF A CONTROLLED SET OF SYNTACTIC STRUCTURES BY FOUR LANGUAGE GROUPS EJ 052 175
AREAS OF RECENT RESEARCH IN EARLY CHILDHOOD EDUCATION EJ 054 380
SUCCESS AND ACCOUNTABILITY EJ 055 533
HOW FREE IS FREE PLAY? EJ 055 535

NURSERY SCHOOLS FIFTY YEARS AGO EJ 055 736
SYMPOSIUM ON CHILD-OBSERVATION: 2. THE TWO-A-DAY OBSERVATION PLAN EJ 056 862
SCIENCING FOR YOUNG CHILDREN EJ 056 863
A GUIDE FOR COLLECTING AND ORGANIZING INFORMATION ON EARLY CHILDHOOD PROGRAMS EJ 058 463
A GLANCE AT A HEAD START PROGRAM IN AN ALASKAN CITY EJ 058 768
BIG STEPS ON BEHALF OF LITTLE PEOPLE EJ 058 769
REFLECTIONS ON REVISITING VIENNA'S YOUNG CITIZENS EJ 060 107
EARLY CHILDHOOD EDUCATION IN JAPAN EJ 061 692

EARLY CHILDHOOD METHODS
PSYCHOLOGIST AND TEACHER: COOPERATION OR CONFLICT? EJ 017 709

EARLY EXPERIENCE
EVALUATION OF TWO ASSOCIATED YM-YWHA HEADSTART PROGRAMS. FINAL REPORT. ED014318
DEVELOPMENT OF APPROPRIATE EVALUATION TECHNIQUES FOR SCREENING CHILDREN IN A HEAD START PROGRAM. A PILOT PROJECT. ED015006
THE EARLY TRAINING PROJECT FOR DISADVANTAGED CHILDREN--A REPORT AFTER FIVE YEARS. ED016514
A PARENT EDUCATION APPROACH TO PROVISION OF EARLY STIMULATION FOR THE CULTURALLY DISADVANTAGED. FINAL REPORT. ED017339
AN EVALUATION OF A PRESCHOOL TRAINING PROGRAM FOR CULTURALLY DEPRIVED CHILDREN. FINAL REPORT. ED019135
THE EFFECT OF EARLY STIMULATION: THE PROBLEM OF FOCUS IN DEVELOPMENTAL STIMULATION. ED022535
THE CONCEPT OF DEVELOPMENTAL LEARNING. ED023484
THE DISTANCING HYPOTHESIS: A HYPOTHESIS CRUCIAL TO THE DEVELOPMENT OF REPRESENTATIONAL COMPETENCE. ED024466
AUDITORY COMPONENTS OF NEONATAL EXPERIENCE: A PRELIMINARY REPORT. ED025336
[COMPETENCE IN YOUNG CHILDREN.] ED032124
LANGUAGE AND ENVIRONMENT: AN INTERIM REPORT ON A LONGITUDINAL STUDY. ED032136
PSYCHOLINGUISTIC BEHAVIORS OF ISOLATED, RURAL CHILDREN WITH AND WITHOUT KINDERGARTEN. ED042510
ANCONA MONTESSORI RESEARCH PROJECT FOR CULTURALLY DISADVANTAGED CHILDREN. SEPTEMBER 1, 1968 TO AUGUST 31, 1969. FINAL REPORT. ED044166
ON CLASS DIFFERENCES AND EARLY DEVELOPMENT. ED044167
PROCEEDINGS: EARLY CHILDHOOD INTERVENTION RESEARCH CONFERENCE (UNIVERSITY OF SOUTH FLORIDA, TAMPA, MARCH 5 AND 6, 1970). ED045194
THE ROLE OF EXPERIENCE IN THE BEHAVIORAL DEVELOPMENT OF HUMAN INFANTS: CURRENT STATUS AND RECOMMENDATIONS. ED048917
EDUCATION OF THE INFANT AND YOUNG CHILD. ED048930
A DEVELOPMENTAL LEARNING APPROACH TO INFANT CARE IN A GROUP SETTING. ED049818
AN ANALYSIS OF EXCELLENT EARLY EDUCATIONAL PRACTICES: PRELIMINARY REPORT. ED050805
CURRICULUM FOR THE INFANT AND TODDLER. A COLOR SLIDE SERIES WITH SCRIPT. (SCRIPT ONLY). ED050817
ON EARLY LEARNING: THE MODIFIABILITY OF HUMAN POTENTIAL. ED051876
ISSUES IN HUMAN DEVELOPMENT: AN INVENTORY OF PROBLEMS, UNFINISHED BUSINESS AND DIRECTIONS FOR RESEARCH. ED051888
REEXAMINING VARIABLES AFFECTING COGNITIVE FUNCTIONING IN PRESCHOOL CHILDREN: A FOLLOW-UP. ED052818
EARLY ANTECEDENTS OF ROLE-TAKING AND ROLE-PLAYING ABILITY EJ 008 318
FOUNDATIONS FOR GOOD BEGINNINGS EJ 010 588
PROGRAMMING LIFE HISTORIES: EFFECTS OF STRESS IN ONTOGENY UPON EMOTIONAL REACTIVITY EJ 020 719
EARLY RECOLLECTIONS AND THE PERCEPTION OF OTHERS: A STUDY OF DELINQUENT ADOLESCENTS EJ 022 477
RECOLLECTIONS OF CHILDHOOD: A STUDY OF THE RETROSPECTIVE METHOD EJ 025 047
EARLY COGNITIVE DEVELOPMENT AND PRESCHOOL EDUCATION EJ 043 857
LEARNING FROM EACH OTHER EJ 044 008
WORKING WITH SEPARATION EJ 046 893
THE EFFECTS OF ENRICHED NEONATAL EXPERIENCES UPON LATER COGNITIVE FUNCTIONING EJ 047 689
WHAT DOES RESEARCH TEACH US ABOUT DAY CARE: FOR CHILDREN UNDER THREE EJ 051 236
MOTHER-CHILD INTERACTIONS AND COGNITIVE DEVELOPMENT IN CHILDREN EJ 051 567
DIMENSIONS OF EARLY STIMULATION AND THEIR DIFFERENTIAL EFFECTS ON INFANT DEVELOPMENT EJ 059 873

EARLY READING
A TWO-YEAR LANGUAGE ARTS PROGRAM FOR PRE-FIRST GRADE CHILDREN: FIRST YEAR REPORT. ED029686
DEVELOPMENTAL LEARNING AS A CONCEPT IN EARLY READING. ED031289
CONFERENCE ON READING AND EARLY CHILDHOOD. ED051875
WRITE FIRST, READ LATER EJ 034 069

EATING HABITS
HEAD START EVALUATION AND RESEARCH CENTER, UNIVERSITY OF KANSAS. REPORT NO. VIII, PHYSICAL DEVELOPMENT OF CHILDREN IN THE HEAD START PROGRAM IN THE CENTRAL UNITED STATES. ED021644
BETTER FEEDING CAN MEAN BETTER SPEAKING. ED025306
AN ANALYSIS OF BEHAVIORAL MECHANISMS INVOLVED IN CONTROL OVER INFANT FEEDING BEHAVIOR ED037236
UN EXEMPLE D'OBSERVATION INTENSIVE DU COMPORTEMENT DE JEUNES ENFANTS DANS LE CADRE D'UNE GARDERIE EJ 034 534
RESEARCH FOR UNDERSTANDING EJ 051 150
PRACTICAL APPROACHES FOR RESOLVING THE PROBLEM OF NUTRITION AMONG LOW-INCOME FAMILIES EJ 052 065

ECHOLALIA
IMITATION AND ECHOING IN YOUNG SCHIZOPHRENIC CHILDREN EJ 026 494

ECOLOGICAL FACTORS
A STUDY OF SOME ECOLOGICAL, ECONOMIC AND SOCIAL FACTORS INFLUENCING PARENTAL PARTICIPATION IN PROJECT HEAD START. ED014331
THE ECOLOGY OF GROWTH AND DEVELOPMENT IN A MEXICAN PREINDUSTRIAL COMMUNITY. REPORT 1: METHOD AND FINDINGS FROM BIRTH TO ONE MONTH OF AGE EJ 007 791
AN ENVIRONMENT THAT SUPPORTS MAN EJ 029 389

ECOLOGY
EDUCATION FOR SURVIVAL. ED039021
AUTUMN. UNIT 3 CURRICULUM GUIDE. ED053790
MAKING TOMORROW NOW: BUILDING A QUALITATIVE ENVIRONMENT FOR ALL CHILDREN EJ 026 771
THE LIVING WORLD: THE PHYSICAL ENVIRONEMNT EJ 029 388
ENVIRONMENTAL ECOLOGICAL EDUCATION IN CHILDREN'S BOOKS EJ 029 393

ECONOMIC DISADVANTAGEMENT
EVALUATION OF HEADSTART EDUCATIONAL PROGRAM IN CAMBRIDGE, MASSACHUSETTS. FINAL REPORT. ED013668
PRESCHOOLER STUDY: THE MEDICAL, SOCIAL AND ECONOMIC CORRELATES OF POVERTY IN PRESCHOOL CHILDREN OF BRITISH COLUMBIA. A PILOT STUDY. ED046518
SOME HIGHLIGHTS FROM THE NUTRITION CONFERENCE EJ 017 447
CHILD-REARING PRACTICES IN MOUNTAIN COUNTY, KENTUCKY EJ 036 210
STUDYING HUMAN ECOLOGY: TEACHER EDUCATION AND THE CULTURALLY DIVERSE EJ 048 395

ECONOMIC FACTORS
HEAD START EVALUATION AND RESEARCH CENTER, THE UNIVERSITY OF CHICAGO. REPORT A, MATERNAL INFLUENCES UPON DEVELOPMENT OF COGNITION. ED022550

ECONOMICALLY DISADVANTAGED
FACTORS AFFECTING COGNITIVE GROWTH IN PROJECT HEAD START CHILDREN--WHAT KINDS OF CHANGES OCCUR IN WHAT KINDS OF CHILDREN UNDER WHAT KINDS OF PROGRAMS. ED015794
THE LIMITATIONS OF BRIEF INTELLIGENCE TESTING WITH YOUNG CHILDREN. ED020774
DAY CARE AS A SOCIAL INSTRUMENT: A POLICY PAPER. ED027065
MODIFICATION OF THE CLASSROOM BEHAVIOR OF A "DISADVANTAGED" KINDERGARTEN BOY BY SOCIAL REINFORCEMENT AND ISOLATION. ED045181
SOME THOUGHTS ON PLANNING HEALTH CARE FOR CHILDREN AND YOUTH EJ 038 021
EFFECTS OF AGE, SEX, SYSTEMATIC CONCEPTUAL LEARNING, ACQUISITION OF LEARNING SETS, AND PROGRAMMED SOCIAL INTERACTION ON THE INTELLECTUAL AND CONCEPTUAL DEVELOPMENT OF PRESCHOOL CHILDREN FROM POVERTY BACKGROUNDS EJ 053 733
FACTORS RELATED TO SCHOOL ACHIEVEMENT IN AN ECONOMICALLY DISADVANTAGED GROUP EJ 056 614

ECONOMICS
ECONOMICS IN THE ELEMENTARY SCHOOL ED028839
SRA ECONOMICS MATERIALS IN GRADES ONE AND TWO. EVALUATION REPORTS. ED029700
THE ECONOMIC LITERACY OF ELEMENTARY-SCHOOL PUPILS EJ 029 042

EDUCABLE MENTALLY HANDICAPPED
YPSILANTI PRESCHOOL CURRICULUM DEMONSTRATION PROJECT, 1968-1971. ED046503
EFFECTS OF ARITHMETIC PROBLEM DIFFICULTY ON PUPILLARY DILATION IN NORMALS AND EDUCABLE RETARDATES EJ 021 986
LEARNING AND PROBLEM SOLVING BY THE MENTALLY RETARDED UNDER THREE TESTING CONDITIONS EJ 030 290
THE RELATIONSHIP BETWEEN INTENTIONAL LEARNING, INCIDENTAL LEARNING, AND TYPE OF REWARD IN PRESCHOOL, EDUCABLE, MENTAL RETARDATES EJ 033 783
EFFECT OF INSTRUCTIONAL SET ON TWELVE-YEAR-OLD CHILDREN'S PERCEPTION OF INTERRUPTION EJ 034 921
NORMAL AND RETARDED CHILDREN'S EXPECTANCY FOR FAILURE EJ 039 266

A STUDY OF RECOGNITION AND REPRODUCTION OF BENDER GESTALT FIGURES BY CHILDREN OF AVERAGE AND BELOW INTELLIGENCE EJ 043 707

EDUCATION
PRODUCTIVE THINKING IN EDUCATION. ED024459
FROM LEARNING FOR LOVE TO LOVE OF LEARNING: ESSAYS ON PSYCHOANALYSIS AND EDUCATION. ED032925
PROFILES OF CHILDREN: 1970 WHITE HOUSE CONFERENCE ON CHILDREN. ED046520
A BRIEF GUIDE TO NEWSLETTERS IN EARLY CHILDHOOD EDUCATION. ED048932

EDUCATION SERVICE CENTERS
SCHOOL IN CHEROKEE AND ENGLISH EJ 061 184

EDUCATIONAL ADMINISTRATION
FOUR QUESTIONS ON EARLY CHILDHOOD EDUCATION EJ 034 784

EDUCATIONAL ATTITUDES
THE COGNITIVE ENVIRONMENTS OF URBAN PRE-SCHOOL CHILDREN. MANUAL OF INSTRUCTIONS FOR ADMINISTERING AND SCORING EDUCATIONAL ATTITUDE SURVEY. ED018255
THE SPIRIT OF THE TIMES IN CHILDHOOD EDUCATION. THE FIRST EVANGELINE BURGESS MEMORIAL LECTURE. ED027081
HOW TO TEACH FEAR EJ 061 058

EDUCATIONAL BACKGROUND
INFLUENCE OF SUBJECT AND SITUATIONAL VARIABLES ON THE PERSISTENCE OF FIRST GRADE CHILDREN IN A TEST-LIKE SITUATION. ED052819
A PRELIMINARY VIEW OF TRENDS IN AGE, EDUCATION, AND INTELLIGENCE OF PROBLEM YOUTH EJ 030 431
MATERNAL CONTROL AND OBEDIENCE IN THE TWO-YEAR-OLD EJ 056 714

EDUCATIONAL CHANGE
EARLY EDUCATION: THE CREATION OF CAPACITY. ED028824
AN EDUCATIONAL IMPERATIVE AND ITS FALLOUT IMPLICATIONS. ED034590
PLANNING PARENT-IMPLEMENTED PROGRAMS: A GUIDE FOR PARENTS, SCHOOLS AND COMMUNITIES. ED036322
EXTENDING OPEN EDUCATION IN THE UNITED STATES. ED038182
IMPLEMENTING DIFFERENT AND BETTER SCHOOLS. ED039926
LEARNING INTO THE TWENTY-FIRST CENTURY. 1970 WHITE HOUSE CONFERENCE ON CHILDREN, REPORT OF FORUM 5. (WORKING COPY). ED046524
MYTHOLOGY IN AMERICAN EDUCATION: A GUIDE TO CONSTRUCTIVE CONFRONTATION. 1970 WHITE HOUSE CONFERENCE ON CHILDREN, REPORT OF FORUM 8. (WORKING COPY). ED046526
THE SEVENTIES: A TIME FOR GIANT STEPS EJ 009 030
WHAT'S AHEAD IN TEACHER EDUCATION? EJ 009 031
TWO CONGRESSMEN LOOK AT AMERICAN EDUCATION EJ 009 032
WHAT'S AHEAD FOR PREADOLESCENCE? EJ 009 034
DEVELOPING A LEARNING ENVIRONMENT OF QUALITY EJ 027 028
DO YOU REALLY WANT TO IMPROVE THE CURRICULUM? EJ 031 850
AN ATTACK ON IMPEDIMENTS TO EFFECTIVE CROSS-CULTURAL TEACHING EJ 032 553
ASSESSING THE ALTERNATIVES EJ 033 055
NEW DAY IN NORTH DAKOTA: CHANGING TEACHERS AND CHANGING SCHOOLS EJ 033 157
THE NEW SCHOOL EJ 036 327
LEARNING FROM OUR CRITICS EJ 054 289
CONFRONTING PERSISTENT CONCERNS EJ 054 382
LEARNING FROM LOOKING WITHIN: A DIFFERENT FOCUS, RELATING AND RESPONDING THROUGH THE ARTS EJ 057 326

EDUCATIONAL DEVELOPMENT
A SEQUENTIAL APPROACH TO EARLY CHILDHOOD AND ELEMENTARY EDUCATION, PHASE I. GRANT REPORT. ED042517
EFFECTS OF AGE OF ENTRY AND DURATION OF PARTICIPATION IN A COMPENSATORY EDUCATION PROGRAM. ED043380

EDUCATIONAL DIAGNOSIS
PROJECT HEAD START, PSYCHOLOGICAL SERVICES REPORT, RESEARCH, SUMMER 1968. ED024460
DIAGNOSTICALLY BASED CURRICULUM, BLOOMINGTON, INDIANA ED027978
LONG DISTANCE INTERDISCIPLINARY EVALUATION OF DEVELOPMENTAL DISABILITIES. ED040748
A DIAGNOSTIC-PRESCRIPTIVE APPROACH TO PRESCHOOL EDUCATION. ED041622
PROJECT GENESIS. FINAL REPORT. ED049820
LEARNING DISABILITIES: A TEAM APPROACH EJ 014 521
LEARNING DISORDERS IN CHILDREN: SIBLING STUDIES EJ 057 584
LEARNING DISABILITY: A NEW LOOK AT UNDERACHIEVING EJ 058 411

EDUCATIONAL DISCRIMINATION
CHILDREN WITHOUT PREJUDICE. 1970 WHITE HOUSE CONFERENCE ON CHILDREN, REPORT OF FORUM 18. (WORKING PAPER). ED046534

EDUCATIONAL ENVIRONMENT
THE COGNITIVE ENVIRONMENTS OF URBAN PRE-SCHOOL CHILDREN. MANUAL OF INSTRUCTIONS FOR ADMINISTERING AND SCORING MOTHER'S ROLE IN TEACHER/CHILD AND CHILD/PEER SCHOOL SITUATIONS. ED018257
A THEORETICAL APPROACH FOR SELECTING ELEMENTARY SCHOOL ENVIRONMENTAL VARIABLES. ED028834
"THERE WAS A CHILD WENT FORTH"--A PHILOSOPHY OF EARLY EDUCATION EJ 031 049
FOUR QUESTIONS ON EARLY CHILDHOOD EDUCATION EJ 034 784

EDUCATIONAL EQUIPMENT
EQUIPMENT AND SUPPLIES TESTED AND APPROVED FOR PRESCHOOL/SCHOOL/ HOME. ED017325
ENVIRONMENTALLY ENRICHED CLASSROOMS AND THE DEVELOPMENT OF DISADVANTAGED PRESCHOOL CHILDREN. ED045192

EDUCATIONAL EXPERIENCE
A POSITION PAPER ON EARLY CHILDHOOD EDUCATION. ED019128
AN ARTICULATION STUDY OF 15,255 SEATTLE FIRST GRADE CHILDREN WITH AND WITHOUT KINDERGARTEN. ED024438
THE SAMPLE: OPERATIONS IN THE HEAD START YEAR. ED043391
DISADVANTAGED CHILDREN AND THEIR FIRST SCHOOL EXPERIENCES. ETS-HEAD START LONGITUDINAL STUDY: PRELIMINARY DESCRIPTION OF THE INITIAL SAMPLE PRIOR TO SCHOOL ENROLLMENT. A REPORT IN TWO VOLUMES: VOLUME 1. ED047797
HAVE YOU EVER THOUGHT OF A PROP BOX? EJ 031 781
PERCEPTUAL EXPLORATION IN ISRAELI CHILDREN EJ 033 054
A CAREER DEVELOPMENT PROGRAM IN THE CHICAGO PUBLIC SCHOOLS EJ 035 579
DAY CARE FOR CHILDREN: ASSETS AND LIABILITIES EJ 035 802
THEY BECAME WHAT THEY BEHELD EJ 045 423

EDUCATIONAL EXPERIMENTS
ON RESPONSIVE ENVIRONMENTS. ED018278
THE EFFECTS OF MANIPULATION OF TEACHER COMMUNICATION STYLE IN THE PRESCHOOL. ED034598
DEVELOPMENT OF GRAMMATICAL STRUCTURES IN PRE-SCHOOL AGE CHILDREN. ED042485
PRESCHOOL EDUCATION IN ISRAEL EJ 050 199

EDUCATIONAL FACILITIES
OPERATION HEAD START--AN EVALUATION. FINAL REPORT. ED013117
MEMORANDUM ON--FACILITIES FOR EARLY CHILDHOOD EDUCATION. ED015023

EDUCATIONAL FINANCE
CURRENT EXPENDITURES BY LOCAL EDUCATION AGENCIES FOR FREE PUBLIC ELEMENTARY AND SECONDARY EDUCATION, 1968-69. ED052826

EDUCATIONAL GAMES
PROGRAMED INSTRUCTION AS A STRATEGY FOR DEVELOPING CURRICULA FOR CHILDREN FROM DISADVANTAGED BACKGROUNDS. ED015782
LANGUAGE LEARNING ACTIVITIES FOR THE DISADVANTAGED CHILD. ED020002
SKILL GAMES FOR MATHEMATICS. ED022548
GAMES AND OTHER ACTIVITIES FOR DEVELOPING LANGUAGE SKILLS. ED022555
EXEL ED029698
AN EXPERIMENTAL GAME IN ORAL LANGUAGE COMPREHENSION. ED038171
THE "TELL-AND-FIND PICTURE GAME" FOR YOUNG CHILDREN. ED042513
THINKING BEFORE LANGUAGE? A SYMPOSIUM: 2. A SCHOOL FOR THINKING EJ 050 200

EDUCATIONAL HISTORY
HEALTH, EDUCATION, AND WELFARE: THE PROGRESSIVE IMPULSE IN THE NEW YORK CITY PUBLIC SCHOOLS EJ 029 104
DEVELOPMENT OF THE MONTESSORI METHOD EJ 036 330
NURSERY SCHOOLS FIFTY YEARS AGO EJ 055 736
SUPERINTENDENT JULIA RICHMAN: A SOCIAL PROGRESSIVE IN THE PUBLIC SCHOOLS EJ 060 106

EDUCATIONAL IMPROVEMENT
UNDERSTANDING THE BLACK CHILD EJ 020 717
THE WORLD HOUSE: BUILDING A QUALITATIVE ENVIRONMENT FOR ALL THE WORLD'S CHILDREN EJ 037 736
BIG STEPS ON BEHALF OF LITTLE PEOPLE EJ 058 769

EDUCATIONAL INNOVATION
LEICESTERSHIRE REPORT: THE CLASSROOM ENVIRONMENT. ED027964
LEICESTERSHIRE REVISITED. ED029683
IMPLEMENTING DIFFERENT AND BETTER SCHOOLS. ED039926
VIEWS ON PRE-SCHOOL EDUCATION AND DAY CARE. ED040753
LEARNING INTO THE TWENTY-FIRST CENTURY. 1970 WHITE HOUSE CONFERENCE ON CHILDREN, REPORT OF FORUM 5. (WORKING COPY). ED046524
MYTHOLOGY IN AMERICAN EDUCATION: A GUIDE TO CONSTRUCTIVE CONFRONTATION. 1970 WHITE HOUSE CONFERENCE ON CHILDREN, REPORT OF FORUM 8. (WORKING COPY). ED046526
PROCEEDINGS OF FOLLOW THROUGH CONFERENCE (GAINESVILLE, FLORIDA, DECEMBER 9-10, 1969). ED047773

RADICAL SCHOOL REFORM. ED048934
CHILDREN COME FIRST: THE INSPIRED WORK OF ENGLISH PRIMARY SCHOOLS. ED050820
BRITISH PRIMARY EDUCATION: AN ANNOTATED BIBLIOGRAPHY. ED052843
LOOKING FORWARD TO THE SEVENTIES EJ 009 029
LANGUAGE LEARNING AT ROUGH ROCK EJ 011 874
THE TEACHER'S VIEW OF THE PRINCIPAL'S ROLE IN INNOVATION EJ 018 957
ASSESSING THE ALTERNATIVES EJ 033 055
ALTERNATIVE LEARNING ENVIRONMENTS: A PHILADELPHIA STORY EJ 033 156
AN INTEGRATED DAY WORKSHOP EJ 033 159
THE CREATIVE ENVIRONMENT WORKSHOP EJ 035 168
SIX SUCCESSFUL READING PROGRAMS FOR INNER-CITY SCHOOLS EJ 035 663
SOME NOTES ON STRATEGY AND CONTENT FOR ELEMENTARY READING PROGRAMS IN THE '70'S EJ 035 664
THE NEW SCHOOL EJ 036 327
THINKING BEFORE LANGUAGE? A SYMPOSIUM: 2. A SCHOOL FOR THINKING EJ 050 200

EDUCATIONAL INTEREST

FACTORS INFLUENCING THE RECRUITMENT OF CHILDREN INTO THE HEAD START PROGRAM, SUMMER 1965--A CASE STUDY OF SIX CENTERS IN NEW YORK CITY. STUDY II. ED015026
EFFECTS OF PARENTAL EXPECTATIONS OF EDUCATIONAL PLANS OF WHITE AND NONWHITE ADOLESCENTS. FINAL REPORT. ED027096

EDUCATIONAL LEGISLATION

WHERE IS DAY CARE HEADING. ED016530
STATEMENT BY MARSDEN G. WAGNER, M. D. REPRESENTING THE AMERICAN PUBLIC HEALTH ASSOCIATION BEFORE THE SELECT SUBCOMMITTEE ON EDUCATION, MARCH 3, 1970. ED039940
STATEMENT ON COMPREHENSIVE PRESCHOOL EDUCATION AND CHILD DAY CARE ACT OF 1969 BEFORE THE SELECT SUBCOMMITTEE ON EDUCATION, FEBRUARY 27, 1970. ED039941
A STATEMENT ON THE COMPREHENSIVE PRESCHOOL EDUCATION AND CHILD DAY-CARE ACT OF 1969 BEFORE THE SELECT SUBCOMMITTEE ON EDUCATION OF THE HOUSE COMMITTEE ON EDUCATION AND LABOR, MARCH 3, 1970. ED040752
FINAL REPORT ON PRESCHOOL EDUCATION TO OHIO DEPARTMENT OF EDUCATION. ED045200

EDUCATIONAL METHODS

FACTORS ASSOCIATED WITH A PROGRAM FOR ENCOURAGING SELF-INITIATED ACTIVITIES BY FIFTH AND SIXTH GRADE STUDENTS IN A SELECTED ELEMENTARY SCHOOL EMPHASIZING INDIVIDUALIZED INSTRUCTION. ED015785
THE ROLE OF SOCIALIZATION AND SOCIAL INFLUENCE IN A COMPENSATORY PRESCHOOL PROGRAM. ED017337
THE INFLUENCE OF THEORETICAL CONCEPTIONS OF HUMAN DEVELOPMENT ON THE PRACTICE OF EARLY CHILDHOOD EDUCATION. ED033766
EARLY CHILDHOOD EDUCATION: AN INTRODUCTION TO THE PROFESSION. ED036328
GOALS AND METHODS IN A PRESCHOOL PROGRAM FOR DISADVANTAGED CHILDREN EJ 013 800

EDUCATIONAL NEEDS

PUERTO RICAN CHILDREN IN MAINLAND SCHOOLS. A SOURCE BOOK FOR TEACHERS. ED027953
ECONOMICS IN THE ELEMENTARY SCHOOL ED028839
LEARNING INTO THE TWENTY-FIRST CENTURY. 1970 WHITE HOUSE CONFERENCE ON CHILDREN, REPORT OF FORUM 5. (WORKING COPY). ED046524
VOLUNTEERING TO HELP INDIANS HELP THEMSELVES EJ 032 412
LA FORMATION DU PERSONNEL NON MEDICAL S'OCCUPANT DU PETIT ENFANT DE 1 A 6 ANS EJ 035 170
SELECTING PRIORITIES AT THE WHITE HOUSE CONFERENCE ON CHILDREN EJ 035 619
THE PLACE OF PRESCHOOL EDUCATION IN THE EDUCATIONAL SYSTEM EJ 036 329
EFFECTS OF HEMOPHILIA UPON INTELLECTUAL GROWTH AND ACADEMIC ACHIEVEMENT EJ 044 009

EDUCATIONAL OBJECTIVES

ART EDUCATION IN THE ELEMENTARY SCHOOL. ED018274
EARLY LEARNING IN THE HOME. ED019127
THINKING, FEELING, EXPERIENCING--TOWARD REALIZATION OF FULL POTENTIAL. ED020012
AN EXPLORATION OF THE USES OF RHYTHMIC MOVEMENT TO DEVELOP AESTHETIC CONCEPTS IN THE PRIMARY GRADES. ED020770
INKSTER PUBLIC SCHOOLS IMPLEMENT CHILD DEVELOPMENT CENTER. ED025303
THE SPIRIT OF THE TIMES IN CHILDHOOD EDUCATION. THE FIRST EVANGELINE BURGESS MEMORIAL LECTURE. ED027081
THE CHANGE PROCESS IN ACTION: KINDERGARTEN ED027949
EARLY EDUCATION: THE CREATION OF CAPACITY. ED028824
INSTRUCTIONAL AND EXPRESSIVE EDUCATIONAL OBJECTIVES: THEIR FORMULATION AND USE IN CURRICULUM. ED028838
PSYCHOMOTOR EDUCATION - THEORY AND PRACTICE. ED029684
FROM LEARNING FOR LOVE TO LOVE OF LEARNING: ESSAYS ON PSYCHOANALYSIS AND EDUCATION. ED032925
DEVELOPMENT OF A MUSIC CURRICULUM FOR YOUNG CHILDREN. CAREL ARTS AND HUMANITIES CURRICULUM DEVELOPMENT PROGRAM FOR YOUNG CHILDREN. ED032938
AN INTEGRATIVE APPROACH TO CLASSROOM LEARNING. ED033749
THE TUCSON EARLY EDUCATION MODEL. ED033753
PENNSYLVANIA PRESCHOOL AND PRIMARY EDUCATION PROJECT: 1968-1969 FINAL REPORT TO THE FORD FOUNDATION. ED033759
TRAINING THE INTELLECT VERSUS DEVELOPMENT OF THE CHILD. ED034573
AN EDUCATIONAL IMPERATIVE AND ITS FALLOUT IMPLICATIONS. ED034590
EARLY LEARNING AND COMPENSATORY EDUCATION: CONTRIBUTION OF BASIC RESEARCH. ED036318
NEW NURSERY SCHOOL RESEARCH PROJECT, OCTOBER 1, 1968 TO SEPTEMBER 30, 1969. ANNUAL PROGRESS REPORT. ED036320
EARLY CHILDHOOD EDUCATION: AN INTRODUCTION TO THE PROFESSION. ED036328
EDUCATION FOR SURVIVAL. ED039021
NEED FOR EARLY AND CONTINUING EDUCATION. ED040750
THE MISPLACED ADAPTATION TO INDIVIDUAL DIFFERENCES. ED040754
A SKILL DEVELOPMENT CURRICULUM FOR 3, 4, AND 5 YEAR OLD DISADVANTAGED CHILDREN. ED040755
STATEMENT OF THE INSTRUCTIONAL GOALS FOR CHILDREN'S TELEVISION WORKSHOP. ED041627
A PLAN FOR CONTINUING GROWTH. ED046493
A TEACHING LEARNING SCHEMA FOR TEACHER TRAINING AND CURRICULUM DEVELOPMENT IN EARLY EDUCATION. ED049812
DESIGNS AND PROPOSAL FOR EARLY CHILDHOOD RESEARCH: A NEW LOOK: ON ATTAINING THE GOALS OF EARLY CHILDHOOD EDUCATION. (ONE IN A SERIES OF SIX PAPERS). ED053807
DESIGNS AND PROPOSAL FOR EARLY CHILDHOOD RESEARCH: A NEW LOOK: PRESCHOOL RESEARCH AND PRESCHOOL EDUCATIONAL OBJECTIVES ED053808
"THIS IS ME!" EJ 003 029
EARLY CHILDHOOD EDUCATION - FOR WHAT GOALS? EJ 003 595
AN ESSAY FOR TEACHERS EJ 006 981
CHALLENGES AHEAD FOR EARLY CHILDHOOD EDUCATION EJ 006 983
LOOKING FORWARD TO THE SEVENTIES EJ 009 029
ON VALUING DIVERSITY IN LANGUAGE EJ 011 840
TOO MUCH SHUSHING - LET CHILDREN TALK EJ 011 841
THE EDUCATION OF YOUNG CHILDREN: AT THE CROSSROADS? EJ 013 229
GOALS AND METHODS IN A PRESCHOOL PROGRAM FOR DISADVANTAGED CHILDREN EJ 013 800
SHOULD EDUCATIONAL OBJECTIVES BE STATED IN BEHAVIORAL TERMS? - PART III EJ 014 228
THE CASE FOR THE ACADEMIC PRESCHOOL: FACT OR FICTION? EJ 015 059
HOW ELSE? EJ 015 060
EFFECT OF VISUAL STIMULI IN COMPLEMENTING TELEVISED INSTRUCTION EJ 015 382
THE NON-STRUCTURED APPROACH TO CHILDREN'S LITERATURE EJ 015 980
MORE ON LEARNING-RESOURCE CENTERS EJ 016 819
PLAY IN DEWEY'S THEORY OF EDUCATION EJ 017 710
THE CHANGING CHILDREN OF PREADOLESCENCE (OR THE QUESTIONABLE JOY OF BEING PRE-ANYTHING) EJ 017 901
WHEN CHILDREN ENJOY SCHOOL: SOME LESSONS FROM BRITAIN EJ 018 047
SOCIAL ACTION FOR THE PRIMARY SCHOOLS EJ 018 066
SOVIET PRESCHOOL EDUCATION EJ 020 840
CHOICES, CHOICES, CHOICES! PEAK EXPERIENCES FROM THE AFRO-AMERICAN HERITAGE EJ 020 857
THE RIGHTS OF THE CHILD - THE REALIZATION OF HIS POTENTIAL EJ 028 101
L'EDUCATEUR ET L'EPANOUISSEMENT DE LA PERSONNALITE DE L'ENFANT EJ 028 102
THE EFFECT OF PLANNING ON TEACHING EJ 028 503
EARLY AGE EDUCATION EJ 029 620
INDIVIDUALLY GUIDED MOTIVATION: DEVELOPING SELF-DIRECTION AND PROSOCIAL BEHAVIORS EJ 034 159
FOUR QUESTIONS ON EARLY CHILDHOOD EDUCATION EJ 034 784
A CASE AGAINST A CASE AGAINST BEHAVIORAL OBJECTIVES EJ 036 083
DEMOCRATIZATION OF EDUCATIONAL OPPORTUNITY. AN ESSAY REVIEW EJ 038 471
WHAT'S A SCHOOL FOR? EJ 046 788
TOP PRIORITY: UNDERSTANDING SELF AND OTHERS EJ 050 072
INDIVIDUALIZATION - TEACHERS' VIEWS EJ 052 067
SELF-GUIDANCE AS AN EDUCATIONAL GOAL AND THE SELECTION OF OBJECTIVES EJ 052 878
LEARNING FROM OUR CRITICS EJ 054 289
LISTENING BEYOND WORDS: LEARNING FROM PARENTS IN CONFERENCES EJ 055 363
BIG STEPS ON BEHALF OF LITTLE PEOPLE EJ 058 769

EDUCATIONAL OPPORTUNITIES

DEMOCRATIZATION OF EDUCATIONAL OPPORTUNITY. AN ESSAY REVIEW EJ 038 471
WHO ARE THE DISADVANTAGED? EJ 039 800

EDUCATIONAL PHILOSOPHY

A POSITION PAPER ON EARLY CHILDHOOD EDUCATION. ED019128
THE SPIRIT OF THE TIMES IN CHILDHOOD EDUCATION. THE FIRST EVANGELINE BURGESS MEMORIAL LECTURE. ED027081
LEICESTERSHIRE REVISITED. ED029683
EXTENDING OPEN EDUCATION IN THE UNITED STATES. ED038182
AN ANALYSIS AND EVALUATION OF THE MONTESSORI THEORY OF INNER DISCIPLINE. ED040746
LENIN'S GRANDCHILDREN: PRESCHOOL EDUCATION IN THE SOVIET UNION. ED049830
CHILDREN COME FIRST: THE INSPIRED WORK OF ENGLISH PRIMARY SCHOOLS. ED050820
BRITISH PRIMARY EDUCATION: AN ANNOTATED BIBLIOGRAPHY. ED052843
SCHOOLS WHERE CHILDREN LEARN. ED053803
SOCIAL ACTION FOR THE PRIMARY SCHOOLS EJ 018 066
A BACKWARD GLANCE--A FORWARD STEP? EJ 020 295
A.S. NEILL: LATTER-DAY DEWEY? EJ 020 839
MAKING TOMORROW NOW: THE PEOPLE ENVIRONMENT EJ 028 200
PRE-SCHOOL EDUCATION IN THE WORK OF J.A. COMENIUS (KOMENSKY) EJ 029 619
EARLY AGE EDUCATION EJ 029 620
"ENVIRONMENT," AN OLD CONCEPT IN EDUCATION: A CHILDHOOD EDUCATION SPECIAL (SECOND IN A SERIES), CLASSICAL STATEMENTS FROM THE EDUCATOR'S ARCHIVES EJ 029 623
"THERE WAS A CHILD WENT FORTH"--A PHILOSOPHY OF EARLY EDUCATION EJ 031 049
THE NUFFIELD MATHEMATICS PROJECT EJ 033 864
DEVELOPMENT OF THE MONTESSORI METHOD EJ 036 330
CLASSROOM PRACTICES IN PRE-BASIC SCHOOLS EJ 036 335
TOWARDS AN INDIAN PHILOSOPHY OF PRIMARY EDUCATION EJ 036 337
SAY YOU COME FROM MISSOURI EJ 047 103
STRUCTURE OF-OR FOR-KNOWLEDGE? EJ 050 038
ON PLAY EJ 051 471

EDUCATIONAL PLANNING

THE EVALUATION OF PROJECT HEAD START--A CONCEPTUAL STATEMENT. ED015792
INSTRUCTIONAL AND EXPRESSIVE EDUCATIONAL OBJECTIVES: THEIR FORMULATION AND USE IN CURRICULUM. ED028838
NATURAL ASSESSMENT OF EDUCATIONAL PROGRESS EJ 021 411
THE USE OF HIERARCHIES IN CURRICULUM ANALYSIS AND INSTRUCTIONAL PLANNING EJ 033 574

EDUCATIONAL POLICY

THE PLACE OF PRESCHOOL EDUCATION IN THE EDUCATIONAL SYSTEM EJ 036 329

EDUCATIONAL PRACTICE

A STUDY OF THE INFLUENCE OF CERTAIN PRESCHOOL EDUCATIONAL MOVEMENTS ON CONTEMPORARY PRESCHOOL PRACTICES. ED035450
THE MAKING OF A PUPIL: CHANGING CHILDREN INTO SCHOOL CHILDREN. ED037235
PRE-SCHOOL EDUCATION IN EUROPE. ED047779
RADICAL SCHOOL REFORM. ED048934
LENIN'S GRANDCHILDREN: PRESCHOOL EDUCATION IN THE SOVIET UNION. ED049830
SCHOOLS WHERE CHILDREN LEARN. ED053803
TESTING IN THE SCHOOLS: A RESPONSE TO JOHN HOLT EJ 013 227

EDUCATIONAL PRINCIPLES

FUNCTIONAL PRINCIPLES OF LEARNING. ED032946

EDUCATIONAL PROBLEMS

EVALUATION OF PROJECT HEAD START READING READINESS IN ISSAQUENA AND SHARKEY COUNTIES, MISSISSIPPI, SUMMER, 1965. FINAL REPORT. ED014319
PROJECT HEAD START IN AN INDIAN COMMUNITY. ED014329
PROBLEMS AND PROSPECTS OF EDUCATION IN THE BIG CITIES AS EXEMPLIFIED BY PITTSBURGH, PENNSYLVANIA. ED022542
EARLY CHILDHOOD SELECTED BIBLIOGRAPHIES SERIES. NUMBER 3, EDUCATION. ED022546
MBD - AN EDUCATIONAL PUZZLEMENT. ED032130
AN EDUCATIONAL IMPERATIVE AND ITS FALLOUT IMPLICATIONS. ED034590
CULTURE OF THE SCHOOL: A CONSTRUCT FOR RESEARCH AND EXPLANATION IN EDUCATION. ED039945
PERSPECTIVE ON THE JENSEN AFFAIR. ED040760
EARLY CHILDHOOD EDUCATION AS A DISCIPLINE. ED043396
CRUCIAL ISSUES IN CONTEMPORARY EARLY CHILDHOOD EDUCATION EJ 006 984
THE SEVENTIES: A TIME FOR GIANT STEPS EJ 009 030
EARLY CHILDHOOD EDUCATION AS A DISCIPLINE EJ 029 617

EDUCATIONAL PROGRAMS

A READING READINESS TRAINING PROGRAM FOR PERCEPTUALLY HANDICAPPED KINDERGARTEN PUPILS OF NORMAL VISION. FINAL REPORT. ED013119
PRESCHOOL AND PRIMARY EDUCATION PROJECT. 1967-68 ANNUAL PROGRESS REPORT TO THE FORD FOUNDATION. ED027936
POSTDOCTORAL RESEARCH TRAINING PROGRAM IN EDUCATIONAL STIMULATION. FINAL REPORT. ED035455
MOTHERS' TRAINING PROGRAM: EDUCATIONAL INTERVENTION BY THE MOTHERS OF DISADVANTAGED INFANTS. ED043378
RESULTS AND IMPLICATIONS OF A HEAD START CLASSIFICATION AND ATTENTION TRAINING PROGRAM. ED045182
THE ITINERANT TEACHER. ED045191
PRE-SCHOOL EDUCATION IN EUROPE. ED047779
PROGRAMS FOR INFANTS AND YOUNG CHILDREN. PART I: EDUCATION AND DAY CARE. ED047807
FEDERAL PROGRAMS FOR YOUNG CHILDREN. ED047811
A TEACHING LEARNING SCHEMA FOR TEACHER TRAINING AND CURRICULUM DEVELOPMENT IN EARLY EDUCATION. ED049812
AN ANNOTATED BIBLIOGRAPHY ON EARLY CHILDHOOD. ED049822
EDUCATIONAL INTERVENTION IN EARLY CHILDHOOD: A REPORT OF A FIVE-YEAR LONGITUDINAL STUDY OF THE EFFECTS OF EARLY EDUCATIONAL INTERVENTION IN THE LIVES OF DISADVANTAGED CHILDREN IN DURHAM, NORTH CAROLINA. FINAL REPORT, VOLUME I. ED050814
EDUCATIONAL INTERVENTION IN EARLY CHILDHOOD: APPENDIXES. FINAL REPORT, VOLUME II. ED050815
EDUCATIONAL INTERVENTION IN EARLY CHILDHOOD: ABSTRACTS OF THE 1965-1970 SPECIAL STUDIES RESEARCH AND EVALUATION REPORT. FINAL REPORT, VOLUME III. ED050816
A STUDY IN CHILD CARE (CASE STUDY FROM VOLUME II-A): "ALL KINDS OF LOVE--IN A CHINESE RESTAURANT." DAY CARE PROGRAMS REPRINT SERIES. ED051903
A STUDY IN CHILD CARE (CASE STUDY FROM VOLUME II-B): "WE COME WITH THE DUST AND WE GO WITH THE WIND." DAY CARE PROGRAMS REPRINT SERIES. ED051907
PRESCHOOL PROGRAMS. IJR PRESCHOOL PROJECT REPORT, VOLUME I. ED052815
CHILD CARE WORKER TRAINING PROJECT. OPERATIONAL PHASE AND EMPLOYMENT. FINAL REPORT. ED053788
CONTEMPORARY INFLUENCES IN EARLY CHILDHOOD EDUCATION. ED053797
SCHOOLS WHERE CHILDREN LEARN. ED053803
TOUCH-FEEL LEARNING AT THE TALLAHASSEE JUNIOR MUSEUM EJ 033 158
NIGHT CARE CENTER EJ 050 379
TRAINING WORKERS FOR CHILD CARE CENTERS EJ 050 935
MODIFICATION OF BEHAVIOR PATTERNS OF INDIAN CHILDREN EJ 051 472
CHANGES IN SELF-PERCEPTIONS OF HEAD-START TRAINEES EJ 055 213
EVALUATION OF A PARENT AND CHILD CENTER PROGRAM EJ 056 569
PREVENTING ILLEGITIMATE TEENAGE PREGNANCY THROUGH SYSTEMS INTERACTION EJ 059 671
HEAD START IN MICRONESIA EJ 060 108

EDUCATIONAL QUALITY

THE EXECUTIVE DIRECTOR'S TESTIMONY BEFORE THE HOUSE EDUCATION AND LABOR COMMITTEE EJ 017 848
A NATIONAL PRIORITY: RAISING THE QUALITY OF CHILDREN'S LIVES EJ 027 501
THE CHILD'S RIGHT TO QUALITY DAY CARE: AN ACEI POSITION PAPER EJ 029 103

EDUCATIONAL RESEARCH

HEAD START, WEST VIRGINIA, SUMMER 1966--A SEVEN-COUNTY OVERVIEW, A SPECIAL ASSIGNMENT OF THE WEST VIRGINIA DEPARTMENT OF MENTAL HEALTH. ED017338
DEVELOPMENT OF A GROUP MEASURE TO ASSESS THE EXTENT OF PRE-LOGICAL AND PRE-CAUSAL THINKING IN PRIMARY SCHOOL AGE CHILDREN. ED019136
THE EFFECTS OF ASSESSMENT AND PERSONALIZED PROGRAMMING ON SUBSEQUENT INTELLECTUAL DEVELOPMENT OF PREKINDERGARTEN AND KINDERGARTEN CHILDREN. FINAL REPORT OF PHASE II. ED023487
EFFECTS OF PARENTAL EXPECTATIONS OF EDUCATIONAL PLANS OF WHITE AND NONWHITE ADOLESCENTS. FINAL REPORT. ED027096
PRESCHOOL AND PRIMARY EDUCATION PROJECT. 1967-68 ANNUAL PROGRESS REPORT TO THE FORD FOUNDATION. ED027936
THE USE OF COLOURED RODS IN TEACHING PRIMARY NUMBERWORK. ED028823
A STUDY OF PUBLIC AND PRIVATE KINDERGARTEN AND NON-KINDERGARTEN CHILDREN IN THE PRIMARY GRADES. ED028837
HEAD START EVALUATION AND RESEARCH CENTER, TULANE UNIVERSITY. ANNUAL REPORT. ED029705
CHILD DEVELOPMENT RESEARCH AND EVALUATION CENTER FOR HEAD START, TEMPLE UNIVERSITY. ANNUAL REPORT. ED030487
CHILDHOOD RESOURCES INFORMATION BULLETIN. VOLUME 1, NUMBER 2, FALL 1969. ED032948
AN INTEGRATIVE APPROACH TO CLASSROOM LEARNING. ED033749
ARIZONA CENTER FOR EARLY CHILDHOOD EDUCATION ANNUAL REPORT, JUNE 1968 - JUNE 1969. ED034586

A LONGITUDINAL INVESTIGATION OF MONTESSORI AND TRADITIONAL PREKINDERGARTEN TRAINING WITH INNER CITY CHILDREN: A COMPARATIVE ASSESSMENT OF LEARNING OUTCOMES. THREE PART STUDY. ED034588
FOUR YEARS ON. A FOLLOW-UP STUDY AT SCHOOL LEAVING AGE OF CHILDREN FORMERLY ATTENDING A TRADITIONAL AND A PROGRESSIVE JUNIOR SCHOOL. ED035434
THE NATIONAL LABORATORY ON EARLY CHILDHOOD EDUCATION: TOWARD CONSTRUCTIVE CHANGE. ED039953
CHANGING THE LEARNING PATTERNS OF THE CULTURALLY DIFFERENT. ED045184
MICHIGAN STATE UNIVERSITY, HEAD START EVALUATION AND RESEARCH, 1967-68 RESEARCH ABSTRACTS AND PROGRESS REPORTS. ED047771
HAS PRESCHOOL COMPENSATORY EDUCATION FAILED? ED049834
DIRECTED RESEARCH PROGRAM IN READING, EARLY CHILDHOOD, VOCATIONAL EDUCATION, SCHOOL ORGANIZATION AND ADMINISTRATION, FY 72 - FY 76. ED051871
CHILDREN UNDER THREE - FINDING WAYS TO STIMULATE DEVELOPMENT. I. ISSUES IN RESEARCH EJ 006 980
INDIVIDUALIZING INSTRUCTION THROUGH DIAGNOSIS AND EVALUATION EJ 021 629
THE ROLE OF A LABORATORY NURSERY SCHOOL EJ 036 332
PRESCHOOL EDUCATION IN ISRAEL EJ 050 199
AREAS OF RECENT RESEARCH IN EARLY CHILDHOOD EDUCATION EJ 054 380
RESEARCH ON ASPECTS OF LEADERSHIP ROLES IN EARLY AND ELEMENTARY EDUCATION EJ 055 205
CHANGES IN SELF-PERCEPTIONS OF HEAD-START TRAINEES EJ 055 213
PARENTS AS EDUCATORS: EVIDENCE FROM CROSS-SECTIONAL, LONGITUDINAL AND INTERVENTION RESEARCH EJ 056 608

EDUCATIONAL RESEARCHERS
RESEARCH AND DEVELOPMENT REGISTER IN EARLY CHILDHOOD EDUCATION, 1970. ED049815

EDUCATIONAL RESOURCES
PROJECT HEAD START--SUMMER 1966. FINAL REPORT. SECTION TWO, FACILITIES AND RESOURCES OF HEAD START CENTERS. ED018247
HOW TO USE ERIC. REVISED EDITION. ED027059

EDUCATIONAL RESPONSIBILITY
PROCESS ACCOUNTABILITY IN CURRICULUM DEVELOPMENT. ED040757
AN ENVIRONMENT THAT SUPPORTS MAN EJ 029 389

EDUCATIONAL RETARDATION
THE EARLY TRAINING PROJECT: A SEVENTH-YEAR REPORT EJ 033 777

EDUCATIONAL SOCIOLOGY
A SOCIAL PSYCHOLOGICAL ANALYSIS OF THE TRANSITION FROM HOME TO SCHOOL. FINAL REPORT. ED015017

EDUCATIONAL SPECIFICATIONS
MEMORANDUM ON--FACILITIES FOR EARLY CHILDHOOD EDUCATION. ED015023

EDUCATIONAL STATUS COMPARISON
AN ASSESSMENT AND COMPARISON OF SELECTED CHARACTERISTICS AMONG CULTURALLY DISADVANTAGED HEADSTART CHILDREN (SUMMER PROGRAM 1965), CULTURALLY DISADVANTAGED NON-HEADSTART CHILDREN, AND NON-CULTURALLY DISADVANTAGED CHILDREN. (TITLE SUPPLIED). ED014330
THE EFFECTS OF JUNIOR KINDERGARTEN ON ACHIEVEMENT--THE FIRST FIVE YEARS. ED016526

EDUCATIONAL STRATEGIES
OPTIMIZING EDUCATIONAL INVESTMENT STRATEGIES. ED015780
EARLY LEARNING IN THE HOME. ED019127
THE DEUTSCH MODEL--INSTITUTE FOR DEVELOPMENTAL STUDIES. ED020009
COMMUNICATIVE COMPETENCE OF LOW-INCOME CHILDREN--ASSUMPTIONS AND PROGRAMS. ED020775
THE TEACHING OF INQUIRY SKILLS TO ELEMENTARY SCHOOL CHILDREN. FINAL REPORT. ED020805
PROBLEMS AND PROSPECTS OF EDUCATION IN THE BIG CITIES AS EXEMPLIFIED BY PITTSBURGH, PENNSYLVANIA. ED022542
CHILD DEVELOPMENT AND SOCIAL SCIENCE EDUCATION. PART IV: A TEACHING STRATEGY DERIVED FROM SOME PIAGETIAN CONCEPTS. ED023467
THE CONCEPT OF DEVELOPMENTAL LEARNING. ED023484
CONCEPT LEARNING IN EARLY CHILDHOOD. ED024454
PRODUCTIVE THINKING IN EDUCATION. ED024459
THE PREPARED ENVIRONMENT AND ITS RELATIONSHIP TO LEARNING. ED025302
TECHNOLOGY AND THE EDUCATION OF THE DISADVANTAGED. ED031293
IMPLICATIONS OF STUDIES ON SELF-ESTEEM FOR EDUCATIONAL RESEARCH AND PRACTICE. ED033742
IMPLEMENTING DIFFERENT AND BETTER SCHOOLS. ED039926
ENRICHMENT APPROACH VERSUS DIRECT INSTRUCTIONAL APPROACH AND THEIR EFFECTS ON DIFFERENTIAL PRESCHOOL EXPERIENCES. ED043369
CHALLENGES AHEAD FOR EARLY CHILDHOOD EDUCATION EJ 006 983
PEER TUTORING AS A TECHNIQUE FOR TEACHING THE UNMOTIVATED EJ 045 393
A CHANGE AGENT STRATEGY: PRELIMINARY REPORT EJ 054 727

EDUCATIONAL TECHNOLOGY
TECHNOLOGY AND THE EDUCATION OF THE DISADVANTAGED. ED031293
EDUCATIONAL TECHNOLOGY: A CRITIQUE EJ 029 343

EDUCATIONAL TELEVISION
A NATIONAL DEMONSTRATION PROJECT UTILIZING TELEVISED MATERIALS FOR THE FORMAL EDUCATION OF CULTURALLY DISADVANTAGED PRESCHOOL CHILDREN. FINAL REPORT. ED015788
A COMPARATIVE STUDY OF CURRENT EDUCATIONAL TELEVISION PROGRAMS FOR PRESCHOOL CHILDREN. FINAL REPORT. ED032123
DESIGNING A PROGRAM FOR BROADCAST TELEVISION. ED033768
TELEVISION GUIDELINES FOR EARLY CHILDHOOD EDUCATION. ED040739
THE FIRST YEAR OF SESAME STREET: A HISTORY AND OVERVIEW. FINAL REPORT, VOLUME I OF V VOLUMES. ED047821
THE FIRST YEAR OF SESAME STREET: THE FORMATIVE RESEARCH. FINAL REPORT, VOLUME II OF V VOLUMES. ED047822
THE FIRST YEAR OF SESAME STREET: AN EVALUATION. FINAL REPORT, VOLUME III OF V VOLUMES. ED047823
THE FIRST YEAR OF SESAME STREET: A SUMMARY OF AUDIENCE SURVEYS. FINAL REPORT, VOLUME IV OF V VOLUMES. ED047824
PRE-READING ON SESAME STREET. FINAL REPORT, VOLUME V OF V VOLUMES. ED047825
GUIDE FOR RIPPLES. ED051872
TO LAUGH IS TO KNOW: A DISCUSSION OF THE COGNITIVE ELEMENT IN CHILDREN'S HUMOR. ED051879
THE EVALUATION OF "SESAME STREET'S" SOCIAL GOALS: THE INTERPERSONAL STRATEGIES OF COOPERATION, CONFLICT RESOLUTION, AND DIFFERING PERSPECTIVES. ED052824
ANALYSIS OF CHILDREN'S REACTIONS TO AEL'S PRESCHOOL TELEVISION PROGRAM. ED052841
A COMPARISON OF PARENTS' ATTITUDES TOWARD AEL'S "AROUND THE BEND" AND OTHER CHILDREN'S TELEVISION PROGRAMS. ED052842
CAN POVERTY CHILDREN LIVE ON "SESAME STREET?" EJ 034 509
IS SESAME STREET EXPORTABLE? EJ 061 442
TELEVISION INSTRUCTION AND THE PRESCHOOL CHILD EJ 062 592

EDUCATIONAL TESTING
AN EVALUATION OF THE EFFECTS OF A SUMMER HEAD START PROGRAM. ED014327
SUMMARY REPORT OF A STUDY OF THE FULL-YEAR 1966 HEAD START PROGRAMS. ED014328

EDUCATIONAL THEORIES
THE INTERNATIONAL WALDORF SCHOOL MOVEMENT. ED015019
ON RESPONSIVE ENVIRONMENTS. ED018278
EARLY CHILDHOOD EDUCATION AND THE WALDORF SCHOOL PLAN. ED019114
THE SPIRIT OF THE TIMES IN CHILDHOOD EDUCATION. THE FIRST EVANGELINE BURGESS MEMORIAL LECTURE. ED027081
TRAINING THE INTELLECT VERSUS DEVELOPMENT OF THE CHILD. ED034573
MONTESSORI INDEX. THIRD EDITION. ED035435
A STUDY OF THE INFLUENCE OF CERTAIN PRESCHOOL EDUCATIONAL MOVEMENTS ON CONTEMPORARY PRESCHOOL PRACTICES. ED035450
AN ANALYSIS AND EVALUATION OF THE MONTESSORI THEORY OF INNER DISCIPLINE. ED040746
RADICAL SCHOOL REFORM. ED048934
A GUIDE TO READING PIAGET. ED053819
AN ESSAY FOR TEACHERS EJ 006 981
WHAT ARE THE SOURCES OF EARLY CHILDHOOD CURRICULUM? EJ 027 943
ON PLAY EJ 051 471
LEARNING FROM OUR CRITICS EJ 054 289
CONFRONTING PERSISTENT CONCERNS EJ 054 382
DEVELOPMENTAL THEORY: ITS PLACE AND RELEVANCE IN EARLY INTERVENTION PROGRAMS EJ 060 013

EDUCATIONAL THERAPY
STRUCTURED FAMILY-ORIENTED THERAPY FOR SCHOOL BEHAVIOR AND LEARNING DISORDERS EJ 019 022
TERMINATION OF RESIDENTIAL TREATMENT OF CHILDREN EJ 029 102

EDUCATIONAL TRENDS
INDEPENDENT AND GROUP LEARNING. ED017332
THE NEW ELEMENTARY SCHOOL. ED017341
SOCIAL STUDIES IN ELEMENTARY SCHOOLS (THIRTY-SECOND YEARBOOK). ED018275
ELEMENTARY EDUCATION RESPONDS TO A CHANGING SOCIETY ED024448
THE SCHOOL SOCIAL WORKER'S ROLE IN OVERCOMING LEARNING HANDICAPS EJ 046 401

EDUCATIONALLY DISADVANTAGED
LANGUAGE DEVELOPMENT EXPERIENCES FOR YOUNG CHILDREN. ED019125

CRITICAL OVERVIEW OF EARLY CHILDHOOD EDUCATION PROGRAMS. ED019142
A STUDY OF COGNITIVE AND SOCIAL FUNCTIONING. PROJECT II ED025310
THE FIRST YEAR OF SESAME STREET: AN EVALUATION. FINAL REPORT, VOLUME III OF V VOLUMES. ED047823
MODIFICATION OF BEHAVIOR PATTERNS OF INDIAN CHILDREN EJ 051 472

EFFECTIVE TEACHING
FACTORS ASSOCIATED WITH A PROGRAM FOR ENCOURAGING SELF-INITIATED ACTIVITIES BY FIFTH AND SIXTH GRADE STUDENTS IN A SELECTED ELEMENTARY SCHOOL EMPHASIZING INDIVIDUALIZED INSTRUCTION. ED015785
THE NATIONAL TEACHER CORPS PROGRAM, 1966-67 EVALUATION REPORT. ED019110
ACHIEVEMENT, CREATIVITY, AND SELF-CONCEPT CORRELATES OF TEACHER-PUPIL TRANSACTIONS IN ELEMENTARY SCHOOL CLASSROOMS. ED024463
AN INTEGRATIVE APPROACH TO CLASSROOM LEARNING. ED033749
TEACHER EFFECTIVENESS: A POSITION. ED039928
THE INFLUENCE OF SET INDUCTION UPON STUDENT ACHIEVEMENT AND ASSESSMENT OF EFFECTIVE TEACHING EJ 027 031

EIDETIC IMAGES
EIDETIC IMAGERY IN CHILDREN. FINAL REPORT. ED029707
IMAGERY AND MULTIPLE-LIST PAIRED ASSOCIATE LEARNING IN YOUNG CHILDREN EJ 057 904

ELECTRICAL STIMULI
AN APPLIANCE FOR AUTOINDUCED ADVERSE CONTROL OF SELF-INJURIOUS BEHAVIOR EJ 029 916
EGO IDENTITY STATUS AND MORALITY: THE RELATIONSHIP BETWEEN TWO DEVELOPMENTAL CONSTRUCTS EJ 058 141

ELECTROMECHANICAL AIDS
THE EFFECTS OF IMMEDIATE FEEDBACK ON THE BEHAVIOR OF TEACHERS-IN-TRAINING EJ 059 672

ELECTRONIC DATA PROCESSING
FOLLOW-UP OF OPERATION HEAD START PARTICIPANTS IN THE STATE OF IOWA. FINAL REPORT. ED015771

ELECTRONIC EQUIPMENT
A TECHNIQUE FOR GATHERING CHILDREN'S LANGUAGE SAMPLES FROM NATURALISTIC SETTINGS. ED016532

ELEMENTARY EDUCATION
THE STUDY OF MUSIC IN THE ELEMENTARY SCHOOL--A CONCEPTUAL APPROACH. ED017328
HOW TO HELP YOUR CHILD LEARN, A HANDBOOK FOR PARENTS OF CHILDREN IN KINDERGARTEN THROUGH GRADE 6. ED017342
ART EDUCATION IN THE ELEMENTARY SCHOOL. ED018274
GUIDELINES FOR ELEMENTARY SOCIAL STUDIES. ED019998
THE USE OF CONTEMPORARY MATERIALS IN THE CLASSROOM. ED020013
TEACHING MUSIC IN THE ELEMENTARY SCHOOL, OPINION AND COMMENT. ED020014
EDUCATIONAL SPECIFICATIONS FOR PIEDMONT ELEMENTARY SCHOOL. ED022547
SOCIAL STUDIES EDUCATION: THE ELEMENTARY SCHOOL. ED027061
INDEPENDENT LEARNING IN THE ELEMENTARY SCHOOL CLASSROOM. ED036326
FOLLOW THROUGH: PROGRAM APPROACHES, SCHOOL YEAR 1970-71. ED047787
CURRENT EXPENDITURES BY LOCAL EDUCATION AGENCIES FOR FREE PUBLIC ELEMENTARY AND SECONDARY EDUCATION, 1968-69. ED052826
EDUCATIONAL TECHNOLOGY: A CRITIQUE EJ 029 343
IS IT TIME TO BREAK THE SILENCE ON VIOLENCE? EJ 032 564
ALTERNATIVE LEARNING ENVIRONMENTS: A PHILADELPHIA STORY EJ 033 156
NEW DAY IN NORTH DAKOTA: CHANGING TEACHERS AND CHANGING SCHOOLS EJ 033 157
DESIGNING TOMORROW'S SCHOOL TODAY: THE MULTI-SENSORY EXPERIENCE CENTER EJ 033 784
WIDER WINDOWS FOR ELEMENTARY SCHOOLS EJ 034 133
TOP PRIORITY: UNDERSTANDING SELF AND OTHERS EJ 050 072
INSTRUCTIONAL PROGRAMMING FOR THE INDIVIDUAL PUPIL IN THE MULTIUNIT ELEMENTARY SCHOOL EJ 050 591
DIRECTION SPORTS: A TUTORIAL PROGRAM FOR ELEMENTARY-SCHOOL PUPILS EJ 050 982
LEARNING FROM LOOKING WITHIN: A DIFFERENT FOCUS, RELATING AND RESPONDING THROUGH THE ARTS EJ 057 326

ELEMENTARY GRADES
GUIDE FOR TEACHING PHYSICAL EDUCATION, GRADES 1-6. ED019126
PHYSICAL EDUCATION ACTIVITIES FOR THE ELEMENTARY SCHOOL. ED019995
PRELIMINARY FINDINGS FROM A LONGITUDINAL EDUCATIONAL IMPROVEMENT PROJECT BEING CONDUCTED FOR INSTRUCTIONALLY IMPOVERISHED PUPILS IN INTACT SCHOOLS IN THE URBAN SOUTH. ED020021
SCIENCE ADVENTURES IN CHILDREN'S PLAY. ED026146
TEACHING SAFETY IN THE ELEMENTARY SCHOOL. ED026147
ECONOMICS IN THE ELEMENTARY SCHOOL ED028839
ELEMENTARY PHYSICAL EDUCATION: TOPEKA PUBLIC SCHOOLS. ED035445
ANCONA MONTESSORI RESEARCH PROJECT FOR CULTURALLY DISADVANTAGED CHILDREN. SEPTEMBER 1, 1968 TO AUGUST 31, 1969. FINAL REPORT. ED044166
PROCEEDINGS OF FOLLOW THROUGH CONFERENCE (GAINESVILLE, FLORIDA, DECEMBER 9-10, 1969). ED047773
ARE MOVERS LOSERS? EJ 018 958
ENVIRONMENTAL ECOLOGICAL EDUCATION IN CHILDREN'S BOOKS EJ 029 393
AN INTEGRATED DAY WORKSHOP EJ 033 159

ELEMENTARY SCHOOL CHILDREN
THE INFLUENCE OF INCENTIVES ON MEMORY STAGES IN CHILDREN EJ 049 428
LOCUS OF CONTROL AND ACHIEVEMENT IN MIDDLE- AND LOWER-CLASS CHILDREN EJ 052 448

ELEMENTARY SCHOOL COUNSELING
COLLABORATION IN SCHOOL GUIDANCE: TASK-ORIENTED GUIDANCE AND ITS STRUCTURE EJ 027 918
SCHOOL COUNSELING BY CONTRACT EJ 038 985

ELEMENTARY SCHOOL CURRICULUM
CHILD DEVELOPMENT AND SOCIAL SCIENCE EDUCATION. PART I: THE PROBLEM, PART II: CONFERENCE REPORT. ED023465
THE INTERGROUP RELATIONS CURRICULUM: A PROGRAM FOR ELEMENTARY SCHOOL EDUCATION. VOLUMES I AND II. ED029704
FAMILY LIFE AROUND THE WORLD, LEVEL I. ED032116
THE SOUTHSIDE EXPERIMENT IN PERSONALIZED EDUCATION. ED042505
THE WORLD OF THE CHILD. ED050826
SOME NOTES ON STRATEGY AND CONTENT FOR ELEMENTARY READING PROGRAMS IN THE '70'S EJ 035 664

ELEMENTARY SCHOOL GUIDANCE
COLLABORATION IN SCHOOL GUIDANCE: TASK-ORIENTED GUIDANCE AND ITS STRUCTURE EJ 027 918

ELEMENTARY SCHOOL LIBRARIES
WIDER WINDOWS FOR ELEMENTARY SCHOOLS EJ 034 133

ELEMENTARY SCHOOL MATHEMATICS
IN-SERVICE EDUCATION IN ELEMENTARY SCHOOL MATHEMATICS. ED018272
MATHEMATICS FOR ELEMENTARY SCHOOL TEACHERS. ED018276
THE EFFECTS OF TWO VARIABLES ON THE PROBLEM-SOLVING ABILITIES OF FIRST-GRADE CHILDREN. ED019113
MAKING PRIMARY ARITHMETIC MEANINGFUL TO CHILDREN. ED020015
BIBLIOGRAPHY OF RESEARCH STUDIES IN ELEMENTARY SCHOOL AND PRE-SCHOOL MATHEMATICS. ED023464
ELEMENTARY SCHOOL MATHEMATICS: A GUIDE TO CURRENT RESEARCH. THIRD EDITION. ED026123
ARITHMETIC AND MATHEMATICS. DIMENSIONS IN EARLY LEARNING SERIES. ED026136
THE ELEMENTARY MATHEMATICS STUDY: AN INTERIM REPORT ON KINDERGARTEN YEAR RESULTS. ED027937

ELEMENTARY SCHOOL ROLE
MEETING SOCIO-EDUCATIONAL NEEDS EJ 027 916

ELEMENTARY SCHOOL STUDENTS
DEVELOPMENT OF A TECHNIQUE FOR IDENTIFYING ELEMENTARY SCHOOL CHILDREN'S MUSICAL CONCEPTS. FINAL REPORT. ED016517
DEVELOPMENT OF AN ENLARGED MUSIC REPERTORY FOR KINDERGARTEN THROUGH GRADE SIX (JUILLIARD REPERTORY PROJECT). FINAL REPORT. ED016521
SUMMARY OF BEHAVIOR PATTERNS OF NORMAL CHILDREN. ED016531
A REPLICATIVE INVESTIGATION OF THE BUCKINGHAM-DOLCH FREE-ASSOCIATION WORD STUDY. FINAL REPORT. ED017333
GUIDE FOR TEACHING PHYSICAL EDUCATION, GRADES 1-6. ED019126
A DEVELOPMENTAL STUDY OF THE RELATIONSHIP BETWEEN REACTION-TIME AND PROBLEM-SOLVING EFFICIENCY. FINAL REPORT. ED020018
FAMILY BACKGROUND EFFECTS ON PERSONALITY DEVELOPMENT AND SOCIAL ACCEPTANCE. ED020020
AN ANALYSIS OF A CLASS OF PROBLEM SOLVING BEHAVIOR. FINAL REPORT. ED020776
COGNITIVE PROCESSES IN THE DEVELOPMENT OF CHILDREN'S APPRECIATION OF HUMOR. ED020784
STUDY TO DETERMINE THE FEASIBILITY OF ADAPTING THE CARL ORFF APPROACH TO ELEMENTARY SCHOOLS IN AMERICA. FINAL REPORT. ED020804
THE TEACHING OF INQUIRY SKILLS TO ELEMENTARY SCHOOL CHILDREN. FINAL REPORT. ED020805
THE DEVELOPMENT OF A BEHAVIOR CHECKLIST FOR BOYS. ED023468
LEARNING OF INCENTIVE-VALUE BY CHILDREN. ED023473
SOCIO-CULTURAL INFLUENCES ON ATTENTION IN ELEMENTARY SCHOOL CHILDREN. FINAL REPORT. ED024456
MOTHER-CHILD RELATIONS AND CHILDREN'S ACHIEVEMENT. TERMINAL REPORT. ED024465
THE POLITICAL SOCIALIZATION OF CHILDREN AND THE STRUCTURE OF THE ELEMENTARY SCHOOL. ED024468

A PRELIMINARY SEARCH FOR FORMAL OPERATIONS STRUCTURES. ED024471
INVESTMENTS IN PREVENTION, AN ACTIVITY GROUP PROGRAM FOR YOUNG CHILDREN, SUMMER - 1967. ED025311
THE EFFECTIVENESS OF THE PEABODY LANGUAGE DEVELOPMENT KITS AND THE INITIAL TEACHING ALPHABET WITH DISADVANTAGED CHILDREN IN THE PRIMARY GRADES: AFTER TWO YEARS. ED026125
A LONGITUDINAL INVESTIGATION OF CHANGE IN THE FACTORIAL COMPOSITION OF INTELLIGENCE WITH AGE IN YOUNG SCHOOL CHILDREN. ED026149
THE EFFECTS OF TEACHER IN-SERVICE EDUCATION ON THE DEVELOPMENT OF ART IDEAS WITH SIX-YEAR OLD CULTURALLY DEPRIVED CHILDREN. FINAL REPORT. ED027066
DESIRABLE ATHLETIC COMPETITION FOR CHILDREN OF ELEMENTARY SCHOOL AGE. ED027086
MENTAL HEALTH. WHAT RESEARCH SAYS TO THE TEACHER SERIES NUMBER 24. ED027087
A PILOT STUDY INTEGRATING VISUAL FORM AND ANTHROPOLOGICAL CONTENT FOR TEACHING CHILDREN AGES 6 TO 11 ABOUT CULTURES AND PEOPLES OF THE WORLD ED027095
A COMPARATIVE STUDY OF THE SELF-IMAGES OF DISADVANTAGED CHILDREN. ED028821
A STUDY OF PUBLIC AND PRIVATE KINDERGARTEN AND NON-KINDERGARTEN CHILDREN IN THE PRIMARY GRADES. ED028837
AGE OF ENTRANCE INTO THE FIRST GRADE AS RELATED TO RATE OF SCHOLASTIC ACHIEVEMENT. ED028843
IMPLICIT VERBAL BEHAVIOR IN ELEMENTARY SCHOOL CHILDREN, (INTERNAL VERBAL RESPONSES OF ELEMENTARY SCHOOL CHILDREN ELICITED BY THE ASSOCIATION OF WORDS). FINAL REPORT. ED028848
A STUDY OF COMPOSITION ABILITY AS ASSESSED WITH A STANDARDIZED INSTRUMENT FOR SECOND AND THIRD GRADE CHILDREN. ED029696
A STUDY COMPARING GLOBAL QUALITY AND SYNTACTIC MATURITY IN THE WRITING COMPOSITION OF SECOND AND THIRD GRADE STUDENTS. ED029697
THE ACQUISITION OF SELF-REWARD PATTERNS BY CHILDREN. FINAL REPORT. ED032137
FIGURAL CREATIVITY, INTELLIGENCE, AND PERSONALITY IN CHILDREN: A FACTOR ANALYTIC STUDY. ED032931
LOGICAL THINKING IN SECOND GRADE. FINAL REPORT. ED033747
QUASI-DISGUISED AND STRUCTURED MEASURE OF SCHOOLCHILDREN'S RACIAL PREFERENCES. ED035440
DETERMINANTS OF CHILDREN'S ATTEMPTS TO HELP ANOTHER CHILD IN DISTRESS. ED039023
THE EFFECTS OF DIFFERENT TYPES OF REINFORCEMENT ON YOUNG CHILDREN'S INCIDENTAL LEARNING. ED044184
RULE STRUCTURE AND PROPORTION OF POSITIVE INSTANCES AS DETERMINANTS OF CONCEPT ATTAINMENT IN CHILDREN. ED046500
ATTITUDES OF PRESCHOOL AND ELEMENTARY SCHOOL CHILDREN TO AUTHORITY FIGURES. ED046506
FACTORS? IN CHILD DEVELOPMENT: PEER RELATIONS. ED047796
GUIDE FOR RIPPLES. ED051872
A PRELIMINARY SEARCH FOR FORMAL OPERATIONS STRUCTURES EJ 023 192
AGE DIFFERENCES IN JUDGMENTS OF RECENCY FOR SHORT SEQUENCES OF PICTURES EJ 026 375
PROBABILITY LEARNING AS A FUNCTION OF SEX OF THE SUBJECT, TEST ANXIETY, AND PERCENTAGE OF REINFORCEMENT EJ 027 181
THE OTHER MOUTH: WRITING IN THE SCHOOLS EJ 027 881
ORGANIZING FOR READING INSTRUCTION EJ 028 960
A THIRD STUDY OF THE EFFECTS OF A LEARNING EXPERIENCE UPON PREFERENCE FOR COMPLEXITY-ASYMMETRY IN FOURTH, FIFTH, AND SIXTH GRADE CHILDREN EJ 029 281
DEVELOPMENTAL ASPECTS OF REACTION TO POSITIVE INDUCEMENTS EJ 029 359
SEQUENCE EFFECTS IN THE ABSTRACTION OF THE CONCEPT OF PROGRESSIVE CHANGE EJ 029 532
EFFECT OF SUCCESS AND FAILURE ON THE REFLECTIVE AND IMPULSIVE CHILD EJ 029 768
LETTER TO THE TEACHER OF A HARD-OF-HEARING CHILD EJ 029 917
SOME DETERMINANTS OF CHILDREN'S SELF-REWARD BEHAVIOR AFTER EXPOSURE TO DISCREPANT REWARD CRITERIA EJ 030 511
THE WORLD TEST: DEVELOPMENTAL ASPECTS OF A PLAY TECHNIQUE EJ 031 629
CHILDREN'S USE OF CONTEXT IN JUDGMENT OF WEIGHT EJ 033 053
FUNCTIONS OF VISUAL IMAGERY IN THE LEARNING AND CONCEPT FORMATION OF CHILDREN EJ 033 779
LEARNING OF MEDIA CONTENT: A DEVELOPMENTAL STUDY EJ 033 782
TRANSFER OF VERBAL PAIRED ASSOCIATES IN MENTALLY RETARDED INDIVIDUALS AND NORMAL CHILDREN AS A FUNCTION OF INTERLIST SIMILARITY EJ 033 785
ARE THESE TWO STIMULI FROM THE SAME SET? RESPONSE TIMES OF CHILDREN AND ADULTS WITH FAMILIAR AND ARBITRARY SETS EJ 033 788
THE ABILITY OF PERSONALITY VARIABLES IN DISCRIMINATING AMONG THREE INTELLECTUAL GROUPS OF PREADOLESCENT BOYS AND GIRLS EJ 034 044
INDIVIDUALLY GUIDED MOTIVATION: DEVELOPING SELF-DIRECTION AND PROSOCIAL BEHAVIORS EJ 034 159
ATTITUDES OF PRESCHOOL AND ELEMENTARY SCHOOL CHILDREN TO AUTHORITY FIGURES EJ 034 452
OCCUPATIONAL PRESTIGE AS SEEN BY DISADVANTAGED BLACK CHILDREN EJ 034 453
MEASURES OF FORM CONSTANCY: DEVELOPMENTAL TRENDS EJ 034 611
THE RELATIONSHIP BETWEEN TIME OF MEASUREMENT AND AGE IN COGNITIVE DEVELOPMENT OF CHILDREN: AN APPLICATION OF CROSS-SECTIONAL SEQUENCES EJ 034 714
DISADVANTAGED AND NONDISADVANTAGED CHILDREN'S EXPECTANCY IN SKILL AND CHANCE OUTCOMES EJ 034 903
THE "MENTAL STEP" HYPOTHESIS IN SOLVING VERBAL PROBLEMS: EFFECTS OF VARIATIONS IN QUESTION-PHRASING ON A GRADE SCHOOL POPULATION EJ 035 372
DEVELOPMENTAL TRENDS IN THE INTENTIONAL AND INCIDENTAL LEARNING COMPONENTS OF A VERBAL DISCRIMINATION TASK EJ 035 375
THE EFFECTS OF CONNOTATIVE SIMILARITY IN CHILDREN'S LEARNING OF A PAIRED-ASSOCIATE TASK EJ 035 376
SOME RELATIONSHIPS BETWEEN VERBAL AND PERCEPTUAL CAPABILITIES AND THE DEVELOPMENT OF RELATIVE THINKING EJ 035 383
AN EXAMINATION OF FRUSTRATION AGGRESSION RELATIONS IN BOYS DURING MIDDLE CHILDHOOD EJ 035 628
RACE AND CONFORMITY AMONG CHILDREN EJ 038 937
ANTICIPATORY IMAGERY AND MODIFIED ANAGRAM SOLUTIONS: A DEVELOPMENTAL STUDY EJ 041 141
COGNITIVE STYLE AND READING ABILITY EJ 043 239
SEX DIFFERENCES IN THE EXPRESSION OF VOCATIONAL ASPIRATIONS BY ELEMENTARY SCHOOL CHILDREN EJ 043 481
CHILDREN AND THE POLITICS OF TRUST EJ 045 394
EYE MOVEMENTS, PERCEPTUAL ACTIVITY, AND CONSERVATION DEVELOPMENT EJ 046 249
WHAT'S A SCHOOL FOR? EJ 046 788
THE ACQUISITION AND PERFORMANCE OF A SOCIALLY NEUTRAL RESPONSE AS A FUNCTION OF VICARIOUS REWARD EJ 046 889
DEVELOPMENT OF MEMORIZATION STRATEGIES EJ 047 679
EARLY ADMISSION: OPINION VERSUS EVIDENCE EJ 048 045
BEHAVIOUR PROBLEMS IN THE INFANT SCHOOL EJ 048 306
MEANING CONDITIONING AND AWARENESS AMONG CHILDREN EJ 049 426
MATCHING AUDITORY AND VISUAL SERIES: MODALITY PROBLEM OR TRANSLATION PROBLEM? EJ 051 569
A REEXAMINATION OF THE DEVELOPMENT OF MORAL JUDGMENTS IN CHILDREN EJ 052 456
CONCEPTUAL STYLE AND CONCEPTUAL ABILITY IN KINDERGARTEN THROUGH THE EIGHTH GRADE EJ 053 484
TITLE I AND REMEDIAL READING COMPONENTS FOR DISADVANTAGED STUDENTS EJ 053 676
INCONSISTENT VERBAL INSTRUCTIONS AND CHILDREN'S RESISTANCE-TO-TEMPTATION BEHAVIOR EJ 053 741
THE EFFECTS OF DIFFERENT TYPES OF REINFORCEMENT ON YOUNG CHILDREN'S INCIDENTAL LEARNING EJ 053 752
CROSS-MODAL MATCHING AMONG NORMAL AND RETARDED CHILDREN EJ 053 755
HAPTIC RECOGNITION OF OBJECTS IN CHILDREN EJ 055 099
DEVELOPMENT OF HIERARCHIES OF DIMENSIONAL SALIENCE EJ 055 102
SOME SOCIAL EFFECTS OF CROSS-GRADE GROUPING EJ 055 107
SELECTIVE STRATEGIES IN CHILDREN'S ATTENTION TO TASK-RELEVANT INFORMATION EJ 055 537
MOTIVATIONAL AND ACHIEVEMENT DIFFERENCES AMONG CHILDREN OF VARIOUS ORDINAL BIRTH POSITIONS EJ 055 547
LITERATURE, CREATIVITY AND IMAGINATION EJ 056 090
VARIABLES AFFECTING ASSOCIATIVE RECALL IN CHILDREN EJ 056 400
EFFECTS OF SYNTACTICAL MEDIATION, AGE, AND MODES OF REPRESENTATION ON PAIRED-ASSOCIATE LEARNING EJ 056 615
GENERALITY OF PERCEPTUAL BIASES IN INFERENCE AND CONCEPT USAGE EJ 056 618
SEMANTIC INTEGRATION, AGE, AND THE RECALL OF SENTENCES EJ 056 620
CONCEPTUAL ENCODING AND CONCEPT RECALL-RECOVERY IN CHILDREN EJ 056 628
A DEVELOPMENTAL STUDY OF THE EFFECTS OF PRETRAINING ON A PERCEPTUAL RECOGNITION TASK EJ 056 630
THE EFFECT OF SYSTEMATIC STORY CHANGES ON INTENTIONALITY IN CHILDREN'S MORAL JUDGMENTS EJ 056 636
RELATIONSHIP BETWEEN LATERAL PREFERENCE AND SELECTED BEHAVIORAL VARIABLES FOR CHILDREN FAILING ACADEMICALLY EJ 056 718
CIVIC BOOKS AND CIVIC CULTURE EJ 057 017
REPORT CARDS FOR TEACHERS EJ 057 441
REINSTATEMENT EFFECTS IN CHILDREN EJ 057 899
PERSEVERATION AND ALTERNATION PRETRAINING AND BINARY PREDICTION EJ 057 902
INITIAL PROBABILITY REHEARSAL, AND CONSTRAINT IN ASSOCIATIVE CLASS SELECTION EJ 057 903
THE EFFECTS OF THE DUSO GUIDANCE PROGRAM ON THE SELF-CONCEPTS OF PRIMARY SCHOOL CHILDREN EJ 058 132
STOP, LOOK, LISTEN -- AND KEEP ON!! EJ 058 133
ACHIEVEMENT MOTIVATION AND FEAR OF FAILURE IN FAMILY AND SCHOOL EJ 058 143

EFFECTS OF PROVISION FOR INDIVIDUAL DIFFERENCES AND TEACHER ATTENTION UPON STUDY BEHAVIOR AND ASSIGNMENTS COMPLETED EJ 058 353
A PERCEPTUAL TEST BATTERY: DEVELOPMENT AND STANDARDIZATION EJ 058 395
LEARNING DISABILITY: A NEW LOOK AT UNDERACHIEVING EJ 058 411
TASK ORIENTATION VERSUS SOCIAL ORIENTATION IN YOUNG CHILDREN AND THEIR ATTENTION TO RELEVANT SOCIAL CUES EJ 058 413
THE RELATIONSHIP BETWEEN CHILDREN'S ACADEMIC PERFORMANCE AND ACHIEVEMENT ACCOUNTABILITY EJ 058 414
THE DEVELOPMENT OF DEMOCRATIC VALUES AND BEHAVIOR AMONG MEXICAN-AMERICAN CHILDREN EJ 058 509
THE RELATIONSHIP BETWEEN LIQUID CONSERVATION AND COMPENSATION EJ 059 313
THE EFFECTS OF GROUPING ON SHORT-TERM SERIAL RECALL OF DIGITS BY CHILDREN: DEVELOPMENTAL TRENDS EJ 059 320
SELF CONCEPT AND SOCIO-ECONOMIC STATUS EJ 059 509
EXPECTANCY TO PERFORM AND VICARIOUS REWARD: THEIR EFFECTS UPON IMITATION EJ 059 513
CHILDREN'S REPORTS OF PARENTAL CHILD-REARING BEHAVIOR AT FIVE GRADE LEVELS EJ 060 385
THE DEVELOPMENT OF THE LANGUAGE OF EMOTIONS: I. THEORETICAL AND METHODOLOGICAL INTRODUCTION EJ 061 059
THE DEVELOPMENT OF THE LANGUAGE OF EMOTIONS: II. INTENTIONALITY IN THE EXPERIENCE OF AFFECT EJ 061 064
THE DEVELOPMENT OF THE LANGUAGE OF EMOTIONS: III. TYPE OF ANXIETY IN THE EXPERIENCE OF AFFECT EJ 061 065
IMITATION OF TEACHER PREFERENCES IN A FIELD SETTING EJ 061 070
SIMPLE REACTION TIME IN CHILDREN: EFFECTS OF INCENTIVE, INCENTIVE-SHIFT AND OTHER TRAINING VARIABLES EJ 061 075
RACE OF EXPERIMENTER AS A VARIABLE IN RESEARCH WITH CHILDREN EJ 061 085
GIVEN NAMES AND STEREOTYPING EJ 061 234

ELEMENTARY SCHOOL TEACHERS

ACHIEVEMENT, CREATIVITY, AND SELF-CONCEPT CORRELATES OF TEACHER-PUPIL TRANSACTIONS IN ELEMENTARY SCHOOL CLASSROOMS. ED024463
LEARNING AND TEACHING, GRADES N-9 (EMPHASIS ON MIDDLE GRADES). ED024467
THE ROLE OF THE TEACHER IN THE INFANT AND NURSERY SCHOOL. ED029703
A STUDY OF EARLY ELEMENTARY TEACHER EVALUATION OF SELECTED EYE-HAND COORDINATION SKILLS OF KINDERGARTEN CHILDREN. INGHAM INTERMEDIATE COOPERATIVE RESEARCH PROJECT, 1967-68: SUMMARY REPORT. ED030488
WHAT INFLUENCES THE MATHEMATICAL UNDERSTANDING OF ELEMENTARY-SCHOOL TEACHERS? EJ 018 422
LOOKING BACK WITH APPRECIATION EJ 058 054
LOOKING IN -- TO SELF DISCOVERY EJ 058 134

ELEMENTARY SCHOOLS

DEPARTMENTALIZATION IN ELEMENTARY SCHOOLS. ED017329
THE NEW ELEMENTARY SCHOOL. ED017341
SOCIAL STUDIES IN ELEMENTARY SCHOOLS (THIRTY-SECOND YEARBOOK). ED018275
SKILL DEVELOPMENT THROUGH GAMES AND RHYTHMIC ACTIVITIES. ED019996
TEAM TEACHING IN ELEMENTARY GRADES. ED020800
SKILL GAMES FOR MATHEMATICS. ED022548
ELEMENTARY EDUCATION RESPONDS TO A CHANGING SOCIETY ED024448
AN EVALUATION OF THE LANGUAGE ARTS PROGRAM OF THE DISTRICT OF COLUMBIA. FINAL REPORT. ED024449
GROUPING. ED026135
THE PRINCIPAL AND THE KINDERGARTEN EJ 016 716
THE ADMINISTRATION OF "SELECTIVITY" IN THE BREAKFAST PROGRAM OF A PUBLIC ELEMENTARY SCHOOL EJ 036 580

EMERGENCY PROGRAMS

A CHILD PROTECTION SERVICE ON A 24-HOUR, 365-DAY BASIS EJ 017 445

EMOTIONAL ADJUSTMENT

WHEN THE CHILD IS ANGRY. ED017331
VERBAL REINFORCEMENT AS AN ADJUSTMENT PREDICTOR WITH KINDERGARTEN CHILDREN. FINAL REPORT. ED031313
THE EFFECTS OF MOTHERS' PRESENCE AND PREVISITS ON CHILDREN'S EMOTIONAL REACTIONS TO STARTING NURSERY SCHOOL. ED034596
THE INFLUENCE OF TWO COUNSELING METHODS ON THE PHYSICAL AND VERBAL AGGRESSION OF PRESCHOOL INDIAN CHILDREN. PART OF THE FINAL REPORT ON HEAD START EVALUATION AND RESEARCH: 1968-69 TO THE OFFICE OF ECONOMIC OPPORTUNITY. ED037243
ANGER IN CHILDREN: CAUSES, CHARACTERISTICS, AND CONSIDERATIONS. ED039917
STARTING NURSERY SCHOOL, II: PREDICTION OF CHILDREN'S INITIAL EMOTIONAL REACTIONS FROM BACKGROUND INFORMATION. FINAL REPORT. ED047814
THE ABILITY OF PERSONALITY VARIABLES IN DISCRIMINATING AMONG THREE INTELLECTUAL GROUPS OF PREADOLESCENT BOYS AND GIRLS EJ 034 044
ADJUSTMENT DIFFERENCES OF SELECTED FOREIGN-BORN PUPILS EJ 041 962
THE EFFECTS OF MOTHERS' PRESENCE AND PREVISITS ON CHILDREN'S EMOTIONAL REACTION TO STARTING NURSERY SCHOOL EJ 046 469
RELATIONSHIP OF PRESCHOOL SOCIAL-EMOTIONAL FUNCTIONING TO LATER INTELLECTUAL ACHIEVEMENT EJ 058 138
FOUR CHILDREN EJ 061 073

EMOTIONAL DEVELOPMENT

THE INTERPLAY OF SOME EGO FUNCTIONS IN SIX YEAR OLD CHILDREN. ED020005
PROCEEDINGS OF THE ANNUAL CONVENTION OF THE CHRISTIAN ASSOCIATION FOR PSYCHOLOGICAL STUDIES ON THE DYNAMICS OF LEARNING CHRISTIAN CONCEPTS (12TH, GRAND RAPIDS, MICHIGAN, MARCH 31-APRIL 1, 1965). ED023476
INTERRELATIONS BETWEEN SOCIAL-EMOTIONAL BEHAVIOR AND INFORMATION ACHIEVEMENT OF HEAD START CHILDREN. REPORT NUMBER 5. ED030479
SOCIAL-EMOTIONAL TASK FORCE. FINAL REPORT. ED033744
ANGER IN CHILDREN: CAUSES, CHARACTERISTICS, AND CONSIDERATIONS. ED039917
EMOTIONAL DEVELOPMENT IN THE FIRST TWO YEARS. ED039936
EMOTIONAL CHARACTERISTICS OF DISADVANTAGED CHILDREN OF APPALACHIA. ED043383
THE UNIT-BASED CURRICULUM. YPSILANTI PRESCHOOL CURRICULUM DEMONSTRATION PROJECT. ED049831
INDIVIDUAL DIFFERENCES IN THE DEVELOPMENT OF SOME ATTACHMENT BEHAVIORS. ED050827
A STUDY IN CHILD CARE (CASE STUDY FROM VOLUME II-A): "TACOS AND TULIPS." DAY CARE PROGRAMS REPRINT SERIES. ED051893
CONCERNED CITIZENS IN THE MAKING EJ 000 192
HELPING CHILDREN COPE WITH FEELINGS. EJ 002 018
THE FEELINGS OF LEARNING EJ 003 082
CLARIFYING FEELINGS THROUGH PEER INTERACTION EJ 003 083
A PARENT'S GIFT EJ 016 773
IT MAKES ME FEEL BAD WHEN YOU CALL ME "STINKY" EJ 029 358
THE CAPACITY TO LOVE: A POSSIBLE REFORMULATION EJ 034 709
WHY NOT FEELINGS AND VALUES IN INSTRUCTIONAL TELEVISION? EJ 038 906
INTERPERSONAL PERCEPTION OF YOUNG CHILDREN: EGOCENTRISM OR EMPATHY? EJ 043 606
EMOTIONAL SENSITIVITY AND INTELLIGENCE IN CHILDREN FROM ORPHANAGES AND NORMAL HOMES EJ 043 859
DEVELOPMENTAL CHARACTERISTICS OF EMOTIONAL EXPERIENCE EJ 043 860
CORRELATES OF CURIOSITY AND EXPLORATORY BEHAVIOR IN PRESCHOOL DISADVANTAGED CHILDREN EJ 045 456
144 FOSTER CHILDREN EJ 046 787
THE DEVELOPMENT OF THE LANGUAGE OF EMOTIONS: CONDITIONS OF EMOTIONAL AROUSAL EJ 052 391

EMOTIONAL EXPERIENCE

HEAD START EVALUATION AND RESEARCH CENTER, BOSTON UNIVERSITY. REPORT C-I, PERCEPTION OF EMOTION AMONG CHILDREN: RACE AND SEX DIFFERENCES. ED022561
ON SEPARATION AND SCHOOL ENTRANCE EJ 017 902
WHEN WORDS FAIL...DANCE EJ 019 507
DEVELOPMENTAL CHARACTERISTICS OF EMOTIONAL EXPERIENCE EJ 043 860
AN EXPERIENCE WITH FEAR IN THE LIVES OF CHILDREN EJ 045 389
THE DEVELOPMENT OF THE LANGUAGE OF EMOTIONS: I. THEORETICAL AND METHODOLOGICAL INTRODUCTION EJ 061 059
THE DEVELOPMENT OF THE LANGUAGE OF EMOTIONS: II. INTENTIONALITY IN THE EXPERIENCE OF AFFECT EJ 061 064
THE DEVELOPMENT OF THE LANGUAGE OF EMOTIONS: III. TYPE OF ANXIETY IN THE EXPERIENCE OF AFFECT EJ 061 065

EMOTIONAL MALADJUSTMENT

THE IMPACT OF OBJECT LOSS ON A SIX-YEAR-OLD EJ 030 514

EMOTIONAL PROBLEMS

DIFFERENTIATION BETWEEN NORMAL AND DISORDERED CHILDREN BY A COMPUTER ANALYSIS OF EMOTIONAL AND VERBAL BEHAVIOR. ED019138
CONDITION WITH CAUTION: THINK THRICE BEFORE CONDITIONING. (ROUGH DRAFT). ED046539
A THERAPEUTIC APPROACH TO SPEECH PHOBIA: ELECTIVE MUTISM REEXAMINED EJ 035 625
THE EFFECT OF EMOTION ON GROWTH EJ 053 653

EMOTIONAL RESPONSE

THE VICARIOUS CONDITIONING OF EMOTIONAL RESPONSES IN NURSERY SCHOOL CHILDREN. FINAL REPORT. ED046540
STARTING NURSERY SCHOOL, II: PREDICTION OF CHILDREN'S INITIAL EMOTIONAL REACTIONS FROM BACKGROUND INFORMATION. FINAL REPORT. ED047814
EMOTIONAL CONCOMITANTS OF VISUAL MASTERY IN INFANTS: THE EFFECTS OF STIMULUS MOVEMENT ON SMILING AND VOCALIZING EJ 033 794
SMILING TO SOCIAL STIMULI: ELICITING AND CONDITIONING EFFECTS EJ 034 536

EMOTIONAL REACTIONS OF YOUNG CHILDREN TO TV VIOLENCE EJ 036 082
EMOTIONAL SENSITIVITY AND INTELLIGENCE IN CHILDREN FROM ORPHANAGES AND NORMAL HOMES EJ 043 859
CONTRIBUTIONS OF CRITICISM TO PARENT, FAMILY-LIFE AND SEX EDUCATION EJ 054 381

EMOTIONALLY DISTURBED CHILDREN

DESIGN FOR A PLAYROOM. ED019133
COVERT PROJECT, YEAR 1. ED019137
HEAD START EVALUATION AND RESEARCH CENTER, BOSTON UNIVERSITY. REPORT B-I, PRIMARY AND SECONDARY PREVENTION STUDYING CLINICAL PROCESS AND DISTURBANCE WITH PRESCHOOL CHILDREN. ED022560
BEHAVIOR MODIFICATION OF AN ADJUSTMENT CLASS: A TOKEN REINFORCEMENT PROGRAM. ED023462
INVESTMENTS IN PREVENTION, AN ACTIVITY GROUP PROGRAM FOR YOUNG CHILDREN, SUMMER - 1967. ED025311
PSYCHOLOBIOLOGICAL REFERENTS FOR THE TREATMENT OF AUTISM. ED028814
DISTURBANCE AND DISSONANCE - COMMUNITY UNIVERSITY COLLABORATION IN DIAGNOSIS AND TREATMENT OF DISTURBANCES. ED030485
VERBAL REINFORCEMENT AS AN ADJUSTMENT PREDICTOR WITH KINDERGARTEN CHILDREN. FINAL REPORT. ED031313
A SCHOOL GUIDANCE CLASS FOR EMOTIONALLY DISTURBED CHILDREN EJ 007 875
A PRESCHOOL WORKSHOP FOR EMOTIONALLY DISTURBED CHILDREN EJ 013 234
THE USE OF PLAY TECHNIQUES IN THE TREATMENT OF CHILDREN EJ 016 380
RELATIONSHIP OF SOCIOECONOMIC STATUS, SEX, AND AGE TO AGGRESSION OF EMOTIONALLY DISTURBED CHILDREN IN MOTHERS' PRESENCE EJ 017 424
FROM THE TEACHER'S NOTEBOOK EJ 020 103
SECOND STAGE TEACHING PROBLEMS IN A PUBLIC SCHOOL CLASS FOR EMOTIONALLY DISTURBED CHILDREN EJ 020 104
PEER- OBSERVER CONSULTATION EJ 022 532
HELPING CHILDREN WITH EMOTIONAL PROBLEMS AT SCHOOL EJ 022 975
WHO ARE THEY? IDENTIFYING DISTURBED CHILDREN IN THE CLASSROOM EJ 022 976
IF SCHOOLS ARE TO MEET THEIR RESPONSIBILITIES TO ALL CHILDREN EJ 022 977
ECOLOGICAL PLANNING FOR DISTURBED CHILDREN EJ 022 978
RESIDENTIAL TREATMENT OF CHILDREN; A SURVEY OF INSTITUTIONAL CHARACTERISTICS EJ 022 980
DIAGNOSING MINIMAL BRAIN DAMAGE IN CHILDREN: A COMPARISON OF TWO BENDER SCORING SYSTEMS EJ 027 585
A GROUP METHOD FOR FINDING AND DEVELOPING FOSTER HOMES EJ 027 920
AN INTERDISCIPLINARY APPROACH IN DAY TREATMENT OF EMOTIONALLY DISTURBED CHILDREN EJ 029 167
THE IMPACT OF OBJECT LOSS ON A SIX-YEAR-OLD EJ 030 514
PREVENTIVE THERAPY WITH SIBLINGS OF A DYING CHILD EJ 030 515
SCHOOL PHOBIA AND SELF-EVALUATION EJ 031 445
AN ATTEMPT TO COMBINE CLINICAL AND EDUCATIONAL RESOURCES: A REPORT ON THE FIRST YEAR'S EXPERIENCE OF A THERAPEUTIC SCHOOL EJ 035 539
INTERPERSONAL RELATIONSHIPS IN RESIDENTIAL TREATMENT CENTERS FOR DISTURBED CHILDREN EJ 037 183
FAMILY TREATMENT WITHIN THE MILIEU OF A RESIDENTIAL TREATMENT CENTER EJ 037 236
HELPING FOSTER PARENTS UNDERSTAND DISTURBED CHILDREN EJ 037 238
AN ACTIVITY GROUP APPROACH TO SERIOUSLY DISTURBED LATENCY BOYS EJ 043 194
EARLY INTERVENTION AND SOCIAL CLASS: DIAGNOSIS AND TREATMENT OF PRESCHOOL CHILDREN IN A DAY CARE CENTER EJ 050 497
PSYCHIATRIC DISORDER IN THE CHILDREN OF CARIBBEAN IMMIGRANTS EJ 051 152
THE RELIABILITY OF RATING SCALES FOR ASSESSING THE BEHAVIOUR OF DISTURBED CHILDREN IN A RESIDENTIAL UNIT EJ 051 153
VIOLENCE AS A SYMPTOM OF CHILDHOOD EMOTIONAL ILLNESS EJ 055 536
HELPING PARENTS TO HELP THEIR CHILDREN IN PLACEMENT EJ 058 055
RESIDENTIAL TREATMENT OF EMOTIONALLY DISTURBED CHILDREN IN NORWAY EJ 058 135
PROJECT TREAT: A NEW APPROACH TO THE SEVERELY DISTURBED CHILD EJ 061 000

EMPATHY

EFFECT ON RESISTANCE TO DEVIATION OF OBSERVING A MODEL'S AFFECTIVE REACTION TO RESPONSE CONSEQUENCES EJ 043 283
INTERPERSONAL PERCEPTION OF YOUNG CHILDREN: EGOCENTRISM OR EMPATHY? EJ 043 606
THE USE OF ROLE PLAYING AND INDUCTION IN CHILDREN'S LEARNING OF HELPING AND SHARING BEHAVIOR EJ 046 467

ENGLISH (SECOND LANGUAGE)

ESOL-SESD GUIDE: KINDERGARTEN. ED033748
UNIVERSITY OF HAWAII PRESCHOOL LANGUAGE CURRICULUM, HONOLULU, HAWAII: A PROGRAM OF ENGLISH CONVERSATION FOR PRESCHOOL CHILDREN OF MULTIETHNIC BACKGROUNDS. MODEL PROGRAMS--CHILDHOOD EDUCATION. ED045220
CHILDREN WHO SPEAK NAVAJO EJ 014 918
A COMPARATIVE STUDY OF ENGLISH PLURALIZATION BY NATIVE AND NON-NATIVE ENGLISH SPEAKERS EJ 052 465

ENGLISH INSTRUCTION

A PROCESS FOR POETRY-WRITING EJ 055 364

ENRICHMENT ACTIVITIES

HANDBOOK FOR PROJECT HEAD START. ED015018
KICKAPOO - NORTH CANADIAN PROJECT, 1966-67. FINAL REPORT. ED015781
LET'S TRY THIS IN NURSERY SCHOOL AND KINDERGARTEN. ED022556
EARLY CHILDHOOD EDUCATION PROGRAM FOR NURSERY, KINDERGARTEN CHILDREN. ED052846

ENRICHMENT EXPERIENCE

SIX MONTHS LATER--A COMPARISON OF CHILDREN WHO HAD HEAD START, SUMMER, 1965, WITH THEIR CLASSMATES IN KINDERGARTEN, A CASE STUDY OF THE KINDERGARTENS IN FOUR PUBLIC ELEMENTARY SCHOOLS, NEW YORK CITY. STUDY I. ED015025

ENRICHMENT PROGRAMS

THE CHILDREN'S CENTER--A MICROCOSMIC HEALTH, EDUCATION, AND WELFARE UNIT. PROGRESS REPORT. ED013116
AN EVALUATION OF HEAD START PRESCHOOL ENRICHMENT PROGRAMS AS THEY AFFECT THE INTELLECTUAL ABILITY, THE SOCIAL ADJUSTMENT, AND THE ACHIEVEMENT LEVEL OF FIVE-YEAR-OLD CHILDREN ENROLLED IN LINCOLN, NEBRASKA. ED015011
FACTORS INFLUENCING THE RECRUITMENT OF CHILDREN INTO THE HEAD START PROGRAM, SUMMER 1965--A CASE STUDY OF SIX CENTERS IN NEW YORK CITY. STUDY II. ED015026
FACTORS AFFECTING COGNITIVE GROWTH IN PROJECT HEAD START CHILDREN--WHAT KINDS OF CHANGES OCCUR IN WHAT KINDS OF CHILDREN UNDER WHAT KINDS OF PROGRAMS. ED015794
THE EARLY TRAINING PROJECT FOR DISADVANTAGED CHILDREN--A REPORT AFTER FIVE YEARS. ED016514
PROJECT HEAD START--SUMMER 1966. FINAL REPORT. SECTION ONE, SOME CHARACTERISTICS OF CHILDREN IN THE HEAD START PROGRAM. ED018246
PROJECT HEAD START--SUMMER 1966. FINAL REPORT. SECTION TWO, FACILITIES AND RESOURCES OF HEAD START CENTERS. ED018247
GUIDEBOOK FOR TEACHERS. ED020001
MAKING WAVES, DENVER HEAD START. ED020802
CULTURAL ENVIRONMENTAL ACHIEVEMENT PROJECT, A SUMMARIZATION AND EVALUATION OF AN EXPERIMENTAL PRE-SCHOOL PROGRAM. ED021610
RESEARCH ON THE NEW NURSERY SCHOOL. PART I, A SUMMARY OF THE EVALUATION OF THE EXPERIMENTAL PROGRAM FOR DEPRIVED CHILDREN AT THE NEW NURSERY SCHOOL USING SOME EXPERIMENTAL MEASURES. INTERIM REPORT. ED027076
EVALUATION OF INKSTER PRESCHOOL PROJECT. FINAL REPORT. ED027093
THE NEW NURSERY SCHOOL RESEARCH PROJECT ED042518
THE EFFECT OF THREE HOME VISITING STRATEGIES UPON MEASURES OF CHILDREN'S ACADEMIC APTITUDE AND MATERNAL TEACHING BEHAVIORS. FINAL REPORT. ED044175
ENVIRONMENTALLY ENRICHED CLASSROOMS AND THE DEVELOPMENT OF DISADVANTAGED PRESCHOOL CHILDREN. ED045192
A COMPARATIVE ANALYSIS OF THE PIAGETIAN DEVELOPMENT OF TWELVE MONTH OLD DISADVANTAGED INFANTS IN AN ENRICHMENT CENTER WITH OTHERS NOT IN SUCH A CENTER. ED047778
SYMPOSIUM ON PARENT-CENTERED EDUCATION: 2. LEARNING THROUGH (AND FROM) MOTHERS EJ 054 378

ENROLLMENT

PREPRIMARY ENROLLMENT OF CHILDREN UNDER SIX: OCTOBER 1967. ED027094
AGE OF ENTRANCE INTO THE FIRST GRADE AS RELATED TO RATE OF SCHOLASTIC ACHIEVEMENT. ED028843
PREPRIMARY ENROLLMENT OF CHILDREN UNDER SIX: OCTOBER 1968. ED032118

ENROLLMENT INFLUENCES

FACTORS INFLUENCING THE RECRUITMENT OF CHILDREN INTO THE HEAD START PROGRAM, SUMMER 1965--A CASE STUDY OF SIX CENTERS IN NEW YORK CITY. STUDY II. ED015026
STUDY OF ACHIEVEMENT--JUNIOR KINDERGARTEN, WHO IS SERVED AND WHO GOES. ED017322
PREPRIMARY ENROLLMENT, OCTOBER 1969. ED049816

ENROLLMENT RATE

PREPRIMARY ENROLLMENT, OCTOBER 1969. ED049816

ENROLLMENT TRENDS

STUDY OF ACHIEVEMENT--JUNIOR KINDERGARTEN, WHO IS SERVED AND WHO GOES. ED017322
PREPRIMARY ENROLLMENT TRENDS OF CHILDREN UNDER SIX: 1964-1968. ED042502

ENUNCIATION IMPROVEMENT
HEAD START EVALUATION AND RESEARCH CENTER, UNIVERSITY OF KANSAS. REPORT NO. VIIA, A CASE STUDY IN ESTABLISHING A DIFFERENTIATED SPEECH RESPONSE THROUGH GENERALIZATION PROCEDURES. ED021640

ENVIRONMENT
CHILDREN'S ENVIRONMENTS AND CHILD WELFARE EJ 037 184
THE WORLD HOUSE: BUILDING A QUALITATIVE ENVIRONMENT FOR ALL THE WORLD'S CHILDREN EJ 037 736

ENVIRONMENTAL EDUCATION
EDUCATION FOR SURVIVAL. ED039021
MAKING TOMORROW NOW: BUILDING A QUALITATIVE ENVIRONMENT FOR ALL CHILDREN EJ 026 771
ENVIRONMENTAL EDUCATION: THE STATE OF THE ART EJ 026 772
TURNBOW CABIN EJ 029 043
THE LIVING WORLD: THE PHYSICAL ENVIRONEMNT EJ 029 388
AN ENVIRONMENT THAT SUPPORTS MAN EJ 029 389
ROCKS, RIVERS AND CITY CHILDREN EJ 029 390
OCEANS AND CHILDREN: MARINE SCIENCE AND ECOLOGICAL UNDERSTANDING EJ 029 391
RESOURCES FOR ENVIRONMENTAL EDUCATORS: ECOLOGY AND TEACHERS EJ 029 392
ENVIRONMENTAL ECOLOGICAL EDUCATION IN CHILDREN'S BOOKS EJ 029 393
"ENVIRONMENT," AN OLD CONCEPT IN EDUCATION: A CHILDHOOD EDUCATION SPECIAL (SECOND IN A SERIES), CLASSICAL STATEMENTS FROM THE EDUCATOR'S ARCHIVES EJ 029 623
TOUCH-FEEL LEARNING AT THE TALLAHASSEE JUNIOR MUSEUM EJ 033 158
WHAT THE WORLD NEEDS NOW: ENVIRONMENTAL EDUCATION FOR YOUNG CHILDREN EJ 039 637

ENVIRONMENTAL INFLUENCES
A SOCIAL PSYCHOLOGICAL ANALYSIS OF THE TRANSITION FROM HOME TO SCHOOL. FINAL REPORT. ED015017
COGNITIVE DEVELOPMENT IN INFANTS OF DIFFERENT AGE LEVELS AND FROM DIFFERENT ENVIRONMENTAL BACKGROUNDS. ED015786
STUDY OF ACHIEVEMENT--REPORT POPULATION STUDY OF JUNIOR AND SENIOR KINDERGARTEN PUPILS, 1960-61 AND 1961-62. ED017321
THE DEUTSCH MODEL--INSTITUTE FOR DEVELOPMENTAL STUDIES. ED020009
PRE-SCHOOL EDUCATION. ED020785
THE EFFECT OF EARLY STIMULATION: THE PROBLEM OF FOCUS IN DEVELOPMENTAL STIMULATION. ED022535
THE IDENTIFICATION AND ASSESSMENT OF THINKING ABILITY IN YOUNG CHILDREN. FINAL REPORT. ED025316
HELPING THE CHILD DEVELOP HIS CREATIVE POTENTIAL. ED026113
SEX DIFFERENCES IN MENTAL AND BEHAVIORAL TRAITS. ED026117
FURTHER EVIDENCE ON THE RELATION BETWEEN AGE OF SEPARATION AND SIMILARITY IN IQ AMONG PAIRS OF SEPARATED IDENTICAL TWINS. ED027058
LANGUAGE AND ENVIRONMENT: AN INTERIM REPORT ON A LONGITUDINAL STUDY. ED032136
RESEARCH AND CONSULTATION IN THE NATURAL ENVIRONMENT. ED037240
THE RELATION OF CERTAIN HOME ENVIRONMENT FACTORS TO THE THINKING ABILITIES OF THREE-YEAR-OLD CHILDREN. FINAL REPORT. ED039041
NEED FOR EARLY AND CONTINUING EDUCATION. ED040750
AN EXPERIMENTAL ANALYSIS OF PROCEDURES FOR INCREASING SPECIFIC VOCALIZATIONS OF CHILDREN WHO DO NOT DEVELOP FUNCTIONAL SPEECH. PROGRESS REPORT. ED042495
EMOTIONAL CHARACTERISTICS OF DISADVANTAGED CHILDREN OF APPALACHIA. ED043383
THE EFFECT ON AGGRESSION OF VARIATION IN AMOUNT OF OPPORTUNITY FOR PLAY. (INTERNAL REPORT). ED043384
SENSORHESIS AS A MOTIVE FOR PLAY AND STEREOTYPED BEHAVIOR. ED044176
KEY ISSUES IN INFANT MORTALITY. ED045208
CHILDREN WHO ARE INJURED. 1970 WHITE HOUSE CONFERENCE ON CHILDREN, REPORT OF FORUM 13. (WORKING COPY). ED046529
IMPLICATIONS OF POST-NATAL CORTICAL DEVELOPMENT FOR CREATIVITY RESEARCH. ED047802
EFFECTS OF DURATION OF A NURSERY SCHOOL SETTING ON ENVIRONMENTAL CONSTRAINTS AND CHILDREN'S MODES OF ADAPTATION. ED047812
A LONGITUDINAL ASSESSMENT OF THINKING ABILITY OF PRELITERATE CHILDREN DURING A TWO-YEAR PERIOD. FINAL REPORT. ED048946
ENVIRONMENTAL FORCES IN THE HOME LIVES OF THREE-YEAR-OLD CHILDREN IN THREE POPULATION SUBGROUPS. ED050802
PERSPECTIVE ON THE JENSEN AFFAIR EJ 020 519
AN EXAMINATION OF CHILDREN'S DAILY SCHEDULES IN THREE SOCIAL CLASSES AND THEIR RELATION TO FIRST-GRADE READING ACHIEVEMENT EJ 021 079
THE ENVIRONMENTAL MYSTIQUE: TRAINING THE INTELLECT VERSUS DEVELOPMENT OF THE CHILD EJ 022 138
EFFECT OF FAMILIAR AND UNFAMILIAR ENVIRONMENTS ON PROXIMITY BEHAVIOR OF YOUNG CHILDREN EJ 024 935
SOCIOECONOMIC STATUS AND INTELLECTIVE PERFORMANCE AMONG NEGRO PRESCHOOL BOYS EJ 024 938
EFFECTS OF SOCIAL CLASS ON CHILDREN'S MOTORIC EXPRESSION EJ 025 149
A CHILD'S FIRST STEPS: SOME SPECULATIONS EJ 033 057
EXPERIMENTAL PRESCHOOL INTERVENTION IN THE APPALACHIAN HOME EJ 036 395
DEVELOPMENTAL GENETICS OF BEHAVIORAL CAPACITIES: THE NATURE-NURTURE PROBLEM RE-EVALUATED EJ 037 516
THE EFFECTS OF THE ENVIRONMENT UPON STATE CYCLES IN THE HUMAN NEWBORN EJ 044 119
COGNITIVE DEVELOPMENT IN INFANTS OF DIFFERENT AGE LEVELS AND FROM DIFFERENT ENVIRONMENTAL BACKGROUNDS: AN EXPLANATORY INVESTIGATION EJ 046 244
LE MONDE DES TOUT PETITS EST-IL INFLUENCE PAR NOTRE MONDE MODERNE? (IS THE WORLD OF CHILDREN INFLUENCED BY OUR MODERN WORLD?) EJ 049 895
RELATIONSHIPS BETWEEN ATTRIBUTES OF MOTHERS AND THEIR INFANTS' IQ SCORES EJ 051 568
AGE, STATE, AND MATERNAL BEHAVIOR ASSOCIATED WITH INFANT VOCALIZATIONS EJ 052 444
CHILDREN OF TECHNOLOGY: IMAGES OR THE REAL THING EJ 054 472
A TRANSFORMATIONAL ANALYSIS OF ORAL SYNTACTIC STRUCTURES OF CHILDREN REPRESENTING VARYING ETHNOLINGUISTIC COMMUNITIES EJ 056 713
INFANTS' RESPONSES TO NOVELTY IN FAMILIAR AND UNFAMILIAR SETTINGS EJ 056 731
STATE AS AN INFANT-ENVIRONMENT INTERACTION: AN ANALYSIS OF MOTHER-INFANT INTERACTIONS AS A FUNCTION OF SEX EJ 058 221
ENVIRONMENTAL EFFECTS ON LANGUAGE DEVELOPMENT: A STUDY OF YOUNG CHILDREN IN LONG-STAY RESIDENTIAL NURSERIES EJ 058 859
DIMENSIONS OF EARLY STIMULATION AND THEIR DIFFERENTIAL EFFECTS ON INFANT DEVELOPMENT EJ 059 873
PRINCIPLES OF INTERACTION IN LANGUAGE LEARNING EJ 059 875
PHENOMENAL ENVIRONMENTAL OPPRESSIVENESS IN SUICIDAL ADOLESCENTS EJ 061 063

ENVIRONMENTAL RESEARCH
HEAD START EVALUATION AND RESEARCH CENTER. PROGRESS REPORT OF RESEARCH STUDIES 1966 TO 1967. DOCUMENT 4, DEVELOPMENT OF OBSERVATION PROCEDURES FOR ASSESSING PRESCHOOL CLASSROOM ENVIRONMENT. ED021626
AN ECOLOGICAL STUDY OF THREE-YEAR-OLDS AT HOME. FINAL REPORT. ED037238
RESEARCH, CHANGE, AND SOCIAL RESPONSIBILITY: STUDIES OF THE IMPRINT OF THE LOW-INCOME HOME ON YOUNG CHILDREN. ED039935
EMOTIONAL CHARACTERISTICS OF DISADVANTAGED CHILDREN OF APPALACHIA. ED043383
APPLICATION OF MARKOV PROCESSES TO THE CONCEPT OF STATE. ED053813

EQUIPMENT
PROGRAMS FOR INFANTS AND YOUNG CHILDREN. PART IV: FACILITIES AND EQUIPMENT. ED047810
AN INEXPENSIVE AND PORTABLE MEANS FOR ONE-WAY OBSERVATION EJ 045 797

EQUIPMENT EVALUATION
HYPERACTIVITY AND THE MACHINE: THE ACTOMETER EJ 055 876

EQUIPMENT MANUFACTURERS
CHILD DEVELOPMENT AND MATERIAL SURVEY. PART II, MATERIAL SURVEY. FINAL REPORT. ED027085

EQUIPMENT UTILIZATION
POSITION EFFECTS IN PLAY EQUIPMENT PREFERENCES OF NURSERY SCHOOL CHILDREN. ED045185

ERROR PATTERNS
MODIFYING RESPONSE LATENCY AND ERROR RATE OF IMPULSIVE CHILDREN. ED050819
CONCEPTUAL TEMPO IN YOUNG GRADE-SCHOOL CHILDREN EJ 041 450
THE STAGE IV ERROR IN PIAGET'S THEORY OF OBJECT CONCEPT DEVELOPMENT: DIFFICULTIES IN OBJECT CONCEPTUALIZATION OR SPATIAL LOCALIZATION? EJ 059 318

ESSAYS
ESSAYS ON EQUILIBRIUM EJ 008 171

ESTIMATED COSTS
KINDERGARTEN OVERSEAS, A STUDY OF THE REQUIREMENTS FOR ESTABLISHING KINDERGARTEN AS PART OF THE DEPARTMENT OF DEFENSE OVERSEAS DEPENDENTS SCHOOLS. FINAL REPORT. ED017340

ETHIC STUDIES
TEACHERS' RATINGS OF URBAN CHILDREN'S READING PERFORMANCE EJ 035 662

ETHICAL INSTRUCTION
THE EFFECT OF TRAINING CHILDREN TO MAKE MORAL JUDGMENTS THAT ARE INDEPENDENT OF SANCTIONS EJ 044 507

ETHICS
SEX DIFFERENCES IN YIELDING TO TEMPTATION: A FUNCTION OF THE SITUATION EJ 035 711
ETHICAL ISSUES IN RESEARCH IN EARLY CHILDHOOD INTERVENTION EJ 037 578
INCENTIVE PREFERENCE AND RESISTANCE TO TEMPTATION EJ 041 631
SOCIAL PARTICIPATION AS A FACTOR IN THE MORAL DEVELOPMENT OF PREADOLESCENTS EJ 043 605
CORRESPONDENCE BETWEEN BEHAVIORAL AND DOLL-PLAY MEASURES OF CONSCIENCE EJ 045 190
THE YOUNG CHILD'S UNDERSTANDING OF SOCIAL JUSTICE EJ 046 887
MORALS, MORALS EVERYWHERE: VALUES IN CHILDREN'S FICTION EJ 051 270

ETHNIC DIFFERENCES
DIFFERENTIAL COGNITIVE DEVELOPMENT WITHIN AND BETWEEN RACIAL AND ETHNIC GROUPS OF DISADVANTAGED PRESCHOOL AND KINDERGARTEN CHILDREN EJ 049 172

ETHNIC GROUPS
FINAL REPORT ON HEAD START EVALUATION AND RESEARCH--1966-67 TO THE INSTITUTE FOR EDUCATIONAL DEVELOPMENT. SECTION VII, SENSORY AND PERCEPTUAL STUDIES. ED019123
COOPERATIVE, TRUSTING BEHAVIOR AS A FUNCTION OF ETHNIC GROUP SIMILARITY-DISSIMILARITY AND OF IMMEDIATE AND DELAYED REWARD IN A TWO-PERSON GAME. PART OF THE FINAL REPORT. ED025322
DEPENDENCY AND SOCIAL PERFORMANCE: THE DEVELOPMENT OF A SCALE TO MEASURE LEVEL OF INDEPENDENCE IN SMALL CHILDREN. PART OF THE FINAL REPORT. ED026129
MULTI-ETHNIC BOOKS FOR YOUNG CHILDREN: ANNOTATED BIBLIOGRAPHY FOR PARENTS AND TEACHERS. ED046519
FIELD TEST OF THE UNIVERSITY OF HAWAII PRESCHOOL LANGUAGE CURRICULUM. FINAL REPORT. ED048924
CHILD NEGLECT AMONG THE POOR: A STUDY OF PARENTAL ADEQUACY IN FAMILIES OF THREE ETHNIC GROUPS EJ 018 326
COOPERATIVE AND COMPETITIVE BEHAVIOR OF URBAN AFRO-AMERICAN, ANGLO-AMERICAN, MEXICAN-AMERICAN, AND MEXICAN VILLAGE CHILDREN EJ 024 033
THE CULTURE OF THE CULTURALLY DEPRIVED EJ 035 537
CLASSIFICATION PATTERNS OF UNDERPRIVILEGED CHILDREN IN ISRAEL EJ 041 140

ETHNIC RELATIONS
ANALYSIS OF STORY RETELLING AS A MEASURE OF THE EFFECTS OF ETHNIC CONTENT IN STORIES. FINAL REPORT. ED014326

ETHNIC STEREOTYPES
PERCEPTIONS OF NEGRO BOYS REGARDING COLOR AND OCCUPATIONAL STATUS EJ 045 392

ETHNIC STUDIES
A COMPARISON OF THE ORAL LANGUAGE PATTERNS OF THREE LOW SOCIOECONOMIC GROUPS OF PUPILS ENTERING FIRST GRADE. ED032943
RACIAL AWARENESS IN YOUNG MEXICAN-AMERICAN, NEGRO AND ANGLO CHILDREN EJ 028 926

ETHNICS
CALIFORNIA ADVISORY COUNCIL ON EDUCATIONAL RESEARCH SUGGESTED POLICY ON EDUCATIONAL RESEARCH FOR CALIFORNIA SCHOOL DISTRICTS EJ 018 016

ETIOLOGY
FAMILY HARMONY: AN ETIOLOGIC FACTOR IN ALIENATION EJ 058 508

EVALUATION
MEMO--COMMENTS ON THE WOLFF AND STEIN STUDY. ED015029
TECHNIQUES FOR ASSESSING COGNITIVE AND SOCIAL ABILITIES OF CHILDREN AND PARENTS IN PROJECT HEAD START. ED015772
HEAD START EVALUATION AND RESEARCH CENTER, THE UNIVERSITY OF CHICAGO. REPORT E, COMPARATIVE USE OF ALTERNATIVE MODES FOR ASSESSING COGNITIVE DEVELOPMENT IN BILINGUAL OR NON-ENGLISH SPEAKING CHILDREN. ED022554
HEAD START EVALUATION AND RESEARCH CENTER, BOSTON UNIVERSITY. REPORT A-I, TEACHING STYLE: THE DEVELOPMENT OF TEACHING TASKS. ED022557
HEAD START EVALUATION AND RESEARCH CENTER, BOSTON UNIVERSITY. REPORT A-II, OBSERVATION OF TEACHERS AND TEACHING: STRATEGIES AND APPLICATIONS. ED022558
HEAD START EVALUATION AND RESEARCH CENTER, BOSTON UNIVERSITY. REPORT D-I, LANGUAGE PROJECT: THE EFFECTS OF A TEACHER DEVELOPED PRE-SCHOOL LANGUAGE TRAINING PROGRAM ON FIRST GRADE READING ACHIEVEMENT. ED022563
FURTHER EVIDENCE ON THE STABILITY OF THE FACTOR STRUCTURE OF THE TEST ANXIETY SCALE FOR SCHILDREN. ED023485
PARENTS AS TEACHERS, HOW LOWER-CLASS AND MIDDLE-CLASS MOTHERS TEACH. ED025301
THE ASSESSMENT OF ACHIEVEMENT ANXIETIES IN CHILDREN: HOW IMPORTANT IS RESPONSE SET AND MULTIDIMENSIONALITY IN THE TEST ANXIETY SCALE FOR CHILDREN? ED025313
AN EVALUATION OF A SIX-WEEK HEADSTART PROGRAM USING AN ACADEMICALLY ORIENTED CURRICULUM: CANTON, 1967. ED026114
CHILD DEVELOPMENT AND MATERIAL SURVEY. PART II, MATERIAL SURVEY. FINAL REPORT. ED027085
A STUDY OF EARLY ELEMENTARY TEACHER EVALUATION OF SELECTED EYE-HAND COORDINATION SKILLS OF KINDERGARTEN CHILDREN. INGHAM INTERMEDIATE COOPERATIVE RESEARCH PROJECT, 1967-68: SUMMARY REPORT. ED030488
A COMPARATIVE STUDY OF THREE FORMS OF THE METROPOLITAN READINESS TEST AT TWO SOCIO-ECONOMIC LEVELS. ED035448
PROCESS ACCOUNTABILITY IN CURRICULUM DEVELOPMENT. ED040757
UNDERSTANDING OF QUANTITATIVE CONCEPTS IN 3 1/2-4 1/2 YEAR-OLD CHILDREN. ED046491
CHOOSING CHILDREN'S BOOKS ABOUT OTHER COUNTRIES EJ 000 393
CHILD DEVELOPMENT RESEARCH: AN EDIFICE WITHOUT A FOUNDATION EJ 004 045
THE CASE FOR THE ACADEMIC PRESCHOOL: FACT OR FICTION? EJ 015 059
NATURAL ASSESSMENT OF EDUCATIONAL PROGRESS EJ 021 411
RESEARCH FOR UNDERSTANDING EJ 051 150

EVALUATION CRITERIA
GUIDELINES FOR ELEMENTARY SOCIAL STUDIES. ED019998
HEAD START EVALUATION AND RESEARCH CENTER. PROGRESS REPORT OF RESEARCH STUDIES 1966 TO 1967. DOCUMENT 4, DEVELOPMENT OF OBSERVATION PROCEDURES FOR ASSESSING PRESCHOOL CLASSROOM ENVIRONMENT. ED021626
THE IMPLICATIONS OF DESIGN AND MODEL SELECTION FOR THE EVALUATION OF PROGRAMS FOR THE DISADVANTAGED CHILD. ED047792
EVALUATION GUIDE FOR EARLY CHILDHOOD EDUCATION PROGRAMS. ED048938
EVALUATING SETTINGS FOR LEARNING EJ 019 966
A GUIDE FOR COLLECTING AND ORGANIZING INFORMATION ON EARLY CHILDHOOD PROGRAMS EJ 058 463

EVALUATION METHODS
HEADSTART OPERATIONAL FIELD ANALYSIS. PROGRESS REPORT I. ED015774
EXPANDED PREKINDERGARTEN PROGRAM, EVALUATION OF NEW YORK CITY TITLE I EDUCATIONAL PROJECTS 1966-67. ED019115
EVALUATION OF EDUCATIONAL PROGRAMS AS RESEARCH ON EDUCATIONAL PROCESS. ED038165
A REVIEW OF THE EVALUATION OF THE FOLLOW THROUGH PROGRAM. ED041642
EVALUATION OF FOLLOW THROUGH, 1968 - 1969. ED044172
EVALUATION AND RESEARCH CENTER FOR PROJECT HEAD START, UNIVERSITY OF SOUTH CAROLINA. INTERIM EVALUATION REPORT. ED045197
AN EVALUATION OF NINE TOYS AND ACCOMPANYING LEARNING EPISODES IN THE RESPONSIVE MODEL PARENT/CHILD COMPONENT. ED045205
THE IMPLICATIONS OF DESIGN AND MODEL SELECTION FOR THE EVALUATION OF PROGRAMS FOR THE DISADVANTAGED CHILD. ED047792
ANALYSIS OF VISUAL PERCEPTION OF CHILDREN IN THE EARLY CHILDHOOD EDUCATION PROGRAM (RESULTS OF THE MARIANNE FROSTIG DEVELOPMENTAL TEST OF VISUAL PERCEPTION). ED052839
A REPORT ON EVALUATION STUDIES OF PROJECT HEAD START EJ 049 896
CONSIDERATIONS FOR THE STUDY OF LANGUAGE IN YOUNG LOW-INCOME MINORITY GROUP CHILDREN EJ 052 440
FREEDOM FROM EXTERNAL EVALUATION EJ 055 897

EVALUATION NEEDS
FROM THEORY TO THE CLASSROOM, BACKGROUND INFORMATION ON THE FIRST GRADE PROJECT IN NEW YORK CITY SCHOOLS. ED015770

EVALUATION TECHNIQUES
DEVELOPMENT OF APPROPRIATE EVALUATION TECHNIQUES FOR SCREENING CHILDREN IN A HEAD START PROGRAM. A PILOT PROJECT. ED015006
COMPARATIVE STUDIES OF A GROUP OF HEAD START AND A GROUP OF NON-HEAD START PRESCHOOL CHILDREN. FINAL REPORT. ED015013
PROBLEMS OF EDUCATIONAL EVALUATION IN PROJECT HEAD START--SAMPLING, DESIGN, AND CONTROL GROUPS. ED015793
IDENTIFICATION AND EVALUATION OF CHARACTERISTICS OF KINDERGARTEN CHILDREN THAT FORETELL EARLY LEARNING PROBLEMS. FINAL REPORT. ED020006
IDENTIFICATION AND EVALUATION OF CHARACTERISTICS OF KINDERGARTEN CHILDREN THAT FORETELL EARLY LEARNING PROBLEMS. SUMMARY REPORT. ED020007
METHODOLIGICAL CONSIDERATIONS IN DEVISING HEAD START PROGRAM EVALUATIONS. ED025319
A PIAGETIAN METHOD OF EVALUATING PRESCHOOL CHILDREN'S DEVELOPMENT IN CLASSIFICATION. ED039013
MAXIMIZING THE VALUE OF EVALUATION FOR THE HEAD START TEACHER. FINAL REPORT. ED041631
EVALUATION OF FOLLOW THROUGH, 1968 - 1969. ED044172
AN INVESTIGATION OF THE RELATIVE EFFECTIVENESS OF SELECTED CURRICULUM VARIABLES IN THE LANGUAGE DEVELOPMENT OF HEAD START CHILDREN. ED046497

PRE-KINDERGARTEN PROGRAM, 1968-69. EVALUATION REPORT FOR THE PROJECT. ED046511
THE ASSESSMENT OF "SELF-CONCEPT" IN EARLY CHILDHOOD EDUCATION. ED050822
LANGUAGE TRAINING IN EARLY CHILDHOOD EDUCATION. ED051881
EVALUATION OF CLASSROOM CLIMATE EJ 002 421
A PARENTING SCALE AND SEPARATION DECISIONS EJ 039 286
METODO DE ARCHIVAR LAS OBSERVACIONES DEL COMPORTAMIENTO DEL NINO, COMO GUIA PARA ENTENDERLO MEJOR (METHODS OF RECORDING OBSERVATIONS OF CHILDREN'S BEHAVIOR, A GUIDE FOR BETTER UNDERSTANDING) EJ 049 938
SYMPOSIUM ON CHILD-OBSERVATION: 2. THE TWO-A-DAY OBSERVATION PLAN EJ 056 862

EVALUATIVE THINKING
EVALUATION DIMENSION OF THE AFFECTIVE MEANING SYSTEM OF THE PRESCHOOL CHILD EJ 054 049

EVOLUTION
PERSONALITY DEVELOPMENT IN INFANCY ED024439

EXAMINERS
PRIOR REINFORCEMENT HISTORY AS AN EXPLANATION FOR THE EFFECTS OF SEX OF SUBJECT AND EXPERIMENTER IN SOCIAL REINFORCEMENT PARADIGMS EJ 030 297
RACIAL FACTORS IN TEST PERFORMANCE EJ 053 887
SEX DIFFERENCES IN PERFORMANCE AS A FUNCTION OF PRAISE AND BLAME EJ 055 098
RACE OF EXPERIMENTER AS A VARIABLE IN RESEARCH WITH CHILDREN EJ 061 085

EXCEPTIONAL (ATYPICAL)
THE USE OF CREATIVITY TRAINING MATERIALS WITH SPECIAL CHILDREN: A REPORT OF A FEASIBILITY EXPERIENCE EJ 046 058
PLANNING TRIPS FOR VULNERABLE CHILDREN EJ 048 998

EXCEPTIONAL CHILD EDUCATION
HEAD START EVALUATION AND RESEARCH CENTER, UNIVERSITY OF KANSAS. REPORT NO. VIID, A CASE STUDY ILLUSTRATING AN EXPERIMENTAL DESIGN FOR EVALUATING THE EFFECTS OF SHAPING GROSS MOTOR COORDINATION IN A 31 MONTH OLD CHILD. ED021643
ECOLOGICAL PLANNING FOR DISTURBED CHILDREN EJ 022 978
A CLINIC FOR CHILDREN WITH LEARNING DISABILITIES EJ 024 471

EXCEPTIONAL CHILD RESEARCH
HEAD START EVALUATION AND RESEARCH CENTER, UNIVERSITY OF KANSAS. REPORT NO. VIID, A CASE STUDY ILLUSTRATING AN EXPERIMENTAL DESIGN FOR EVALUATING THE EFFECTS OF SHAPING GROSS MOTOR COORDINATION IN A 31 MONTH OLD CHILD. ED021643
AN ARTICULATION STUDY OF 15,255 SEATTLE FIRST GRADE CHILDREN WITH AND WITHOUT KINDERGARTEN. ED024438
SEASON OF BIRTH AND INTELLIGENCE EJ 025 268
EFFECTS OF CONCURRENT AND SERIAL TRAINING ON GENERALIZED VOCAL IMITATION IN RETARDED CHILDREN EJ 055 210

EXCEPTIONAL CHILDREN
HEAD START EVALUATION AND RESEARCH CENTER, UNIVERSITY OF KANSAS. REPORT NO. VIID, A CASE STUDY ILLUSTRATING AN EXPERIMENTAL DESIGN FOR EVALUATING THE EFFECTS OF SHAPING GROSS MOTOR COORDINATION IN A 31 MONTH OLD CHILD. ED021643
DIFFERENCES IN VOCABULARY INPUT-OUTPUT IN PSYCHODIAGNOSIS OF CHILDREN. ED024450
MBD - AN EDUCATIONAL PUZZLEMENT. ED032130
EFFECT OF SENSORIMOTOR ACTIVITY ON PERCEPTION AND LEARNING IN THE NEUROLOGICALLY HANDICAPPED CHILD. FINAL PROGRESS REPORT. ED033757
WILLINGNESS TO ADOPT ATYPICAL CHILDREN EJ 020 860
AUDIO-VISUAL MATERIALS IN EARLY CHILDHOOD EDUCATION EJ 038 907

EXERCISE (PHYSIOLOGY)
COMPLEX MOTOR LEARNING IN FOUR-YEAR-OLDS EJ 046 236

EXPECTANCY TABLES
CURRICULUM GUIDE FOR EARLY CHILDHOOD EDUCATION. BEHAVIORAL GOALS - PRE-K THROUGH ONE. ED027940

EXPECTATION
TEACHER-PUPIL INTERACTION AS IT RELATES TO ATTEMPTED CHANGES IN TEACHER EXPECTANCY OF ACADEMIC ABILITY AND ACHIEVEMENT. ED041630
DELAY OF GRATIFICATION AND INTERNAL VERSUS EXTERNAL CONTROL AMONG ADOLESCENTS OF LOW SOCIOECONOMIC STATUS EJ 034 539
DISADVANTAGED AND NONDISADVANTAGED CHILDREN'S EXPECTANCY IN SKILL AND CHANCE OUTCOMES EJ 034 903
SPATIAL ABILITIES AND SPATIAL EGOCENTRISM IN THE YOUNG CHILD EJ 037 066
NORMAL AND RETARDED CHILDREN'S EXPECTANCY FOR FAILURE EJ 039 266
TEACHER EXPECTANCY AS RELATED TO THE ACADEMIC AND PERSONAL GROWTH OF PRIMARY-AGE CHILDREN EJ 057 018
EXPECTANCY TO PERFORM AND VICARIOUS REWARD: THEIR EFFECTS UPON IMITATION EJ 059 513

EXPENDITURES
CURRENT EXPENDITURES BY LOCAL EDUCATION AGENCIES FOR FREE PUBLIC ELEMENTARY AND SECONDARY EDUCATION, 1968-69. ED052826

EXPERIENCE
EXPERIENCES AND LANGUAGE DEVELOPMENT EJ 011 842

EXPERIMENTAL CURRICULUM
PILOT STUDY OF FIVE METHODS OF PRESENTING THE SUMMER HEAD START CURRICULAR PROGRAM. ED021622
A PILOT EXPERIMENT IN EARLY CHILDHOOD POLITICAL LEARNING. REPORT FROM THE PROJECT ON CONCEPTS IN POLITICAL SCIENCE. ED043368
PLANNED VARIATION IN HEAD START PROGRAMS EJ 031 848

EXPERIMENTAL GROUPS
WHAT'S THROWN OUT WITH THE BATH WATER: A BABY? ED053801
AN ONTOGENY OF MEDIATIONAL DEFICIENCY EJ 056 631

EXPERIMENTAL PROGRAMS
CONCEPT FORMATION AS A FUNCTION OF METHOD OF PRESENTATION AND RATIO OF POSITIVE TO NEGATIVE INSTANCES. ED015779
EFFECTS OF A STRUCTURED PROGRAM OF PRESCHOOL MATHEMATICS ON COGNITIVE BEHAVIOR. ED015791
THE CREATIVE-AESTHETIC APPROACH TO SCHOOL READINESS AND MEASURED CREATIVE GROWTH. ED017344
EDUCATION FOR INITIATIVE AND RESPONSIBILITY, COMMENTS ON A VISIT TO THE SCHOOLS OF LEICESTERSHIRE COUNTY, APRIL 1967. SECOND EDITION. ED020795
THE YPSILANTI EARLY EDUCATION PROGRAM. ED022531
FINAL REPORT ON HEAD START EVALUATION AND RESEARCH: 1967-68 TO THE OFFICE OF ECONOMIC OPPORTUNITY. SECTION I: PARTS A AND B. ED023457
THE PRESCHOOL LANGUAGE PROJECT. A REPORT OF THE FIRST YEAR'S WORK. ED023482
THE EFFECT OF A STRUCTURED TUTORIAL PROGRAM ON THE COGNITIVE AND LANGUAGE DEVELOPMENT OF CULTURALLY DISADVANTAGED INFANTS. ED026110
KINDERGARTEN RESEARCH STUDY: LEVEL OF SKILLS DEVELOPMENT RELATED TO GROWTH IN SKILLS AND TO READINESS FOR THE FIRST PRIMARY YEAR. ED026111
AN EVALUATION OF A SIX-WEEK HEADSTART PROGRAM USING AN ACADEMICALLY ORIENTED CURRICULUM: CANTON, 1967. ED026114
DIFFUSION OF INTERVENTION EFFECTS IN DISADVANTAGED FAMILIES. ED026127
THE EFFECTS OF TEACHER IN-SERVICE EDUCATION ON THE DEVELOPMENT OF ART IDEAS WITH SIX-YEAR OLD CULTURALLY DEPRIVED CHILDREN. FINAL REPORT. ED027066
RESEARCH ON THE NEW NURSERY SCHOOL. PART II: A REPORT ON THE USE OF TYPEWRITERS AND RELATED EQUIPMENT WITH THREE- AND FOUR-YEAR-OLD CHILDREN AT THE NEW NURSERY SCHOOL. INTERIM REPORT. ED027077
A STUDY OF THE EFFECTS OF TEACHER ATTITUDE AND CURRICULUM STRUCTURE ON PRESCHOOL DISADVANTAGED CHILDREN. ANNUAL PROGRESS REPORT I. ED027079
FUN WHILE LEARNING AND EARNING. A LOOK INTO CHATTANOOGA PUBLIC SCHOOLS' TOKEN REINFORCEMENT PROGRAM. ED027952
INDUCING CONSERVATION OF NUMBER, WEIGHT, VOLUME, AREA, AND MASS IN PRE-SCHOOL CHILDREN. ED028822
AN EXPERIMENTAL PROGRAM DESIGNED TO INCREASE AUDITORY DISCRIMINATION WITH HEAD START CHILDREN. ED029680
LEICESTERSHIRE REVISITED. ED029683
A TWO-YEAR LANGUAGE ARTS PROGRAM FOR PRE-FIRST GRADE CHILDREN: FIRST YEAR REPORT. ED029686
COMPETENCE VS. PERFORMANCE IN YOUNG CHILDREN'S USE OF COMPLEX LINGUISTIC STRUCTURES. ED029687
YOUNG CHILDREN'S USE OF LANGUAGE IN INFERENTIAL BEHAVIOR. ED029691
THE COMPARATIVE EFFICACIES OF SPANISH, ENGLISH AND BILINGUAL COGNITIVE VERBAL INSTRUCTION WITH MEXICAN-AMERICAN HEAD START CHILDREN. FINAL REPORT. ED030473
THE EFFECTS OF A LEARNING PROGRAM IN PERCEPTUAL-MOTOR ACTIVITY UPON THE VISUAL PERCEPTION OF SHAPE. FINAL REPORT. ED030494
A PREVENTIVE SUMMER PROGRAM FOR KINDERGARTEN CHILDREN LIKELY TO FAIL IN FIRST GRADE READING. FINAL REPORT. ED030495
DEVELOPMENTAL LEARNING AS A CONCEPT IN EARLY READING. ED031289
A STUDY IN VISUAL-MOTOR-PERCEPTUAL TRAINING IN FIRST GRADE. ED031292
A STUDY OF THE EFFECTS OF A GROUP LANGUAGE DEVELOPMENT PROGRAM UPON THE PSYCHOLINGUISTIC ABILITIES AND LATER BEGINNING READING SUCCESS OF KINDERGARTEN CHILDREN. ED031315
PEDAGOGICAL ATTITUDES OF CONVENTIONAL AND SPECIALLY-TRAINED TEACHERS. ED034587

AN EVALUATION OF A PILOT PROJECT TO ASSESS THE INTRODUCTION OF THE MODERN ENGLISH INFANT SCHOOL APPROACH TO LEARNING WITH SECOND AND THIRD YEAR DISADVANTAGED CHILDREN. ED034595
THE EFFECTS OF MOTHERS' PRESENCE AND PREVISITS ON CHILDREN'S EMOTIONAL REACTIONS TO STARTING NURSERY SCHOOL. ED034596
A PILOT STUDY TO ASSESS THE ACADEMIC PROGRESS OF DISADVANTAGED FIRST GRADERS ASSIGNED TO CLASS BY SEX AND TAUGHT BY A TEACHER OF THE SAME SEX. ED035462
CHILDREN AND TEACHERS IN TWO TYPES OF HEAD START CLASSES. ED036324
THE INFLUENCE OF TWO COUNSELING METHODS ON THE PHYSICAL AND VERBAL AGGRESSION OF PRESCHOOL INDIAN CHILDREN. PART OF THE FINAL REPORT ON HEAD START EVALUATION AND RESEARCH: 1968-69 TO THE OFFICE OF ECONOMIC OPPORTUNITY. ED037243
A PILOT PROJECT USING A LANGUAGE DEVELOPMENT PROGRAM WITH PRESCHOOL DISADVANTAGED CHILDREN. PART OF THE FINAL REPORT ON HEAD START EVALUATION AND RESEARCH: 1968-69 TO THE OFFICE OF ECONOMIC OPPORTUNITY. ED037245
CHILD STUDY-KINDERGARTEN, 1968-69: AN INFORMATION REPORT. ED039015
EDUCATIONAL DAY CARE: AN INSTALLATION MANUAL. ED039918
AN EXPERIMENTAL PROGRAM IN CLASSIFICATION AND ATTENTIONAL TRAINING WITH HEAD START CHILDREN. ED044171
AN EXPERIMENTAL SUMMER KINDERGARTEN FOR CULTURALLY DEPRIVED CHILDREN. ED044174
REVIEW OF SELECTED EARLY EDUCATION RESEARCH IN THE SCHOOL DISTRICT OF UNIVERSITY CITY, MISSOURI, JUNE, 1970. ED044182
CHANGING THE LEARNING PATTERNS OF THE CULTURALLY DIFFERENT. ED045184
PRELIMINARY ANALYSIS OF 1968-69 HEAD START DATA. ED045203
HEAD START PLANNED VARIATION STUDY. ED047782
CHILDREN UNDER THREE - FINDING WAYS TO STIMULATE DEVELOPMENT. II. SOME CURRENT EXPERIMENTS: LEARNING AT TWO EJ 007 409
CHILDREN UNDER THREE - FINDING WAYS TO STIMULATE DEVELOPMENT. II. SOME CURRENT EXPERIMENTS: STIMULATION VIA PARENT EDUCATION EJ 007 410
CHILDREN UNDER THREE - FINDING WAYS TO STIMULATE DEVELOPMENT. II. SOME CURRENT EXPERIMENTS: A HOME TUTORING PROGRAM EJ 007 411
THE GHETTO AS A SOURCE OF FOSTER HOMES EJ 020 858
THE EFFECT OF BLACK HISTORY ON AN INTERRACIAL GROUP OF CHILDREN EJ 026 735
DEVELOPING A LEARNING ENVIRONMENT OF QUALITY EJ 027 028
PRIORITIES FOR CHANGE--SOME PRELIMINARY PROPOSALS FROM THE WHITE HOUSE CONFERENCE ON CHILDREN EJ 032 611
AN EXPERIMENTAL STUDY OF TWO METHODS OF PRESENTING THE INVERSION ALGORITHM IN DIVISION OF FRACTIONS EJ 033 863
EXPERIMENTAL PRESCHOOL INTERVENTION IN THE APPALACHIAN HOME EJ 036 395
THE DEVELOPMENT OF PRE-READING SKILLS IN AN EXPERIMENTAL KINDERGARTEN PROGRAM EJ 037 099
AN ISRAELI EXPERIMENTAL GROUP WITH PRIMARY SCHOOL DROPOUTS OUTSIDE THE SCHOOL SETTING EJ 041 630
LEARNING FROM CHILDREN: THE ROLE OF OCD EJ 044 285
A PROGRAM FOR HOSPITALIZED PSYCHOTIC CHILDREN: REGULAR ATTENDANCE, AWAY FROM THE HOSPITAL, AT A COMMUNITY NURSERY SCHOOL EJ 050 938
LONGITUDINAL DEVELOPMENT OF VERY YOUNG CHILDREN IN A COMPREHENSIVE DAY CARE PROGRAM: THE FIRST TWO YEARS EJ 056 707
IS SESAME STREET EXPORTABLE? EJ 061 442

EXPERIMENTAL PSYCHOLOGY
CATEGORIES AND UNDERLYING PROCESSES, OR REPRESENTATIVE BEHAVIOR SAMPLES AND S-R ANALYSIS: OPPOSING STRATEGIES. ED032120
SOME PARAMETERS OF PUNISHMENT AFFECTING RESISTANCE TO DEVIATION AND GENERALIZATION OF A PROHIBITION EJ 052 457
SOCIAL REINFORCEMENT SATIATION: AN OUTCOME OF FREQUENCY OR AMBIGUITY? EJ 058 144

EXPERIMENTAL SCHOOLS
MYTHOLOGY IN AMERICAN EDUCATION: A GUIDE TO CONSTRUCTIVE CONFRONTATION. 1970 WHITE HOUSE CONFERENCE ON CHILDREN, REPORT OF FORUM 8. (WORKING COPY). ED046526
THE WORLD OF THE CHILD. ED050826
A.S. NEILL: LATTER-DAY DEWEY? EJ 020 839
WIDER WINDOWS FOR ELEMENTARY SCHOOLS EJ 034 133

EXPERIMENTAL TEACHING
A COMPARISON STUDY OF THE COGNITIVE DEVELOPMENT OF DISADVANTAGED FIRST GRADE PUPILS (AS MEASURED BY SELECTED PIAGETIAN TASKS). ED051874

EXPERIMENTS
POSITION STRATEGIES IN AN OBJECT DISCRIMINATION TASK EJ 052 458

EXPRESSIVE LANGUAGE
SCHOOL AND HOME: NOT EITHER-OR EJ 046 246
THE DEVELOPMENT OF THE LANGUAGE OF EMOTIONS: I. THEORETICAL AND METHODOLOGICAL INTRODUCTION EJ 061 059

EXTINCTION (PSYCHOLOGY)
MODIFICATION OF THE CLASSROOM BEHAVIOR OF A "DISADVANTAGED" KINDERGARTEN BOY BY SOCIAL REINFORCEMENT AND ISOLATION. ED045181
VICARIOUS REINFORCEMENT EFFECTS ON EXTINCTION EJ 018 325
GENERALIZED IMITATION AS A FUNCTION OF DISCRIMINATION DIFFICULTY AND CHOICE EJ 038 455
EXTINCTION OF CONSERVATION: A METHODOLOGICAL AND THEORETICAL ANALYSIS EJ 046 245
AVOIDANCE CONDITIONING IN YOUNG CHILDREN WITH INTERRUPTION OF A POSITIVE STIMULUS AS THE AVERSIVE EVENT EJ 053 719
INTERACTIONS BETWEEN THE FACILITATIVE AND INHIBITORY EFFECTS OF A PUNISHING STIMULUS IN THE CONTROL OF CHILDREN'S HITTING BEHAVIOR EJ 053 734
ATTENTION SPAN AND GENERALIZATION OF TASK-RELATED STIMULUS CONTROL: EFFECTS OF REINFORCEMENT CONTINGENCIES EJ 059 878

EYE FIXATIONS
A TEST OF HABITUATION IN HUMAN INFANTS AS AN ACQUISITION PROCESS IN A RETROACTIVE INHIBITION PARADIGM. ED046490
INDIVIDUAL DIFFERENCES IN THE VISUAL PURSUIT BEHAVIOR OF NEONATES EJ 036 092
EYE CONTACT IN CHILDREN AS A FUNCTION OF AGE, SEX, SOCIAL AND INTELLECTIVE VARIABLES EJ 038 943
ORIENTATION DISCRIMINATION IN INFANTS: A COMPARISON OF VISUAL FIXATION AND OPERANT TRAINING METHODS EJ 041 981
A MICRO-ANALYSIS OF MOTHER-INFANT INTERACTION. BEHAVIOR REGULATING SOCIAL CONTACT BETWEEN A MOTHER AND HER 3 1/2 MONTH-OLD TWINS EJ 048 300
VISUAL RESPONSE DECREMENT AS A FUNCTION OF AGE OF HUMAN NEWBORNS EJ 056 716
HABITUATION AND RECOVERY OF VISUAL RESPONSE IN THE ALERT HUMAN NEWBORN EJ 057 116
DEVELOPMENTAL CHANGE IN INFANT VISUAL FIXATION TO DIFFERING COMPLEXITY LEVELS AMONG CROSS-SECTIONALLY AND LONGITUDINALLY STUDIED INFANTS EJ 061 141
AN INFANT CONTROL PROCEDURE FOR STUDYING INFANT VISUAL FIXATIONS EJ 061 142

EYE HAND COORDINATION
A STUDY OF EARLY ELEMENTARY TEACHER EVALUATION OF SELECTED EYE-HAND COORDINATION SKILLS OF KINDERGARTEN CHILDREN. INGHAM INTERMEDIATE COOPERATIVE RESEARCH PROJECT, 1967-68: SUMMARY REPORT. ED030488
MOTOR COORDINATION AND YOUNG CHILDREN'S DRAWING ABILITIES EJ 046 257

EYE MOVEMENTS
A CHANGE OF POSSIBLE NEUROLOGICAL AND PSYCHOLOGICAL SIGNIFICANCE WITHIN THE FIRST WEEK OF NEONATE LIFE: SLEEPING REM RATE. ED034580
THE OCULAR RESPONSE OF HUMAN NEWBORNS TO INTERMITTANT VISUAL MOVEMENT EJ 015 394
INDIVIDUAL DIFFERENCES IN THE VISUAL PURSUIT BEHAVIOR OF NEONATES EJ 036 092
EYE CONTACT IN CHILDREN AS A FUNCTION OF AGE, SEX, SOCIAL AND INTELLECTIVE VARIABLES EJ 038 943
INFANT-CARETAKER INTERACTIONS EJ 043 670
DEVELOPMENT OF VISUAL SCANNING STRATEGIES FOR DIFFERENTIATING WORDS EJ 043 703
EYE MOVEMENTS, PERCEPTUAL ACTIVITY, AND CONSERVATION DEVELOPMENT EJ 046 249
ACCOMMODATION OF VISUAL TRACKING PATTERNS IN HUMAN INFANTS TO OBJECT MOVEMENT PATTERNS EJ 046 250
NEONATAL SMILING IN REM STATES, IV: PREMATURE STUDY EJ 053 758

FACILITIES
NIGHT CARE CENTER EJ 050 379
ONE MORNING A WEEK EJ 051 238

FACILITY GUIDELINES
PLANNING ENVIRONMENTS FOR YOUNG CHILDREN: PHYSICAL SPACE. ED038162
THE KINDERGARTEN, A PLACE FOR LEARNING. BULLETIN ONE: MATERIALS AND EQUIPMENT FOR THE FOURS AND FIVES. ED039026

FACILITY UTILIZATION RESEARCH
REALISTIC PLANNING FOR THE DAY CARE CONSUMER. ED043374

FACTOR ANALYSIS
STUDY OF ACHIEVEMENT--REPORT POPULATION STUDY OF JUNIOR AND SENIOR KINDERGARTEN PUPILS, 1960-61 AND 1961-62. ED017321
A LONGITUDINAL INVESTIGATION OF CHANGE IN THE FACTORIAL COMPOSITION OF INTELLIGENCE WITH AGE IN YOUNG SCHOOL CHILDREN. ED026149
THE FACTORIAL STRUCTURE OF REASONING, MORAL JUDGMENT, AND MORAL CONDUCT. ED031302

FIGURAL CREATIVITY, INTELLIGENCE, AND PERSONALITY IN CHILDREN: A FACTOR ANALYTIC STUDY. ED032931
A FACTOR ANALYSIS OF A THREE-YEAR LONGITUDINAL STUDY OF CONSERVATION OF NUMBER AND RELATED MATHEMATICAL CONCEPTS. ED039934
FACTOR ANALYSIS OF THE EARLY CHILDHOOD EDUCATION TEST DATA. ED052840
SYMPTOM PATTERNS IN HYPERKINETIC, NEUROTIC, AND NORMAL CHILDREN EJ 025 360
A CHECK ON THE STRUCTURE OF PARENTAL REPORTS OF CHILD-REARING PRACTICES EJ 045 388
A FACTOR-ANALYTIC STUDY OF THE RELATIONSHIP OF MOTOR FACTORS TO ACADEMIC CRITERIA FOR FIRST- AND THIRD-GRADE BOYS EJ 052 451
PIAGET AND GESELL: A PSYCHOMETRIC ANALYSIS OF TESTS BUILT FROM THEIR TASKS EJ 053 927
HYPOTHESIS OF ORIGIN AND NATURE FOR THE "SOMINDENCE-DISSOFRUSTANCE" PERSONALITY FACTOR, U.I. 30 EJ 061 061

FACTOR STRUCTURE

SIX STRUCTURE-OF-INTELLECT HYPOTHESES IN SIX-YEAR-OLD CHILDREN. ED023469
FURTHER EVIDENCE ON THE STABILITY OF THE FACTOR STRUCTURE OF THE TEST ANXIETY SCALE FOR SCHILDREN. ED023485
A LONGITUDINAL INVESTIGATION OF CHANGE IN THE FACTORIAL COMPOSITION OF INTELLIGENCE WITH AGE IN YOUNG SCHOOL CHILDREN. ED026149
FACTOR ANALYSIS OF THE EARLY CHILDHOOD EDUCATION TEST DATA. ED052840
A FACTOR-ANALYTIC STUDY OF THE RELATIONSHIP OF MOTOR FACTORS TO ACADEMIC CRITERIA FOR FIRST- AND THIRD-GRADE BOYS EJ 052 451
FACTOR STRUCTURE OF CHILDREN'S PERSONAL SPACE SCHEMATA EJ 052 466
PIAGET AND GESELL: A PSYCHOMETRIC ANALYSIS OF TESTS BUILT FROM THEIR TASKS EJ 053 927
FACTORIAL STRUCTURE OF SELECTED PSYCHO-EDUCATIONAL MEASURES AND PIAGETIAN REASONING ASSESSMENTS EJ 055 112
A SOCIAL COMPETENCE SCALE AND SYMPTOM CHECKIST FOR THE PRESCHOOL CHILD: FACTOR DIMENSIONS, THEIR CROSS-INSTRUMENT GENERALITY, AND LONGITUDINAL PERSISTENCE EJ 057 476
HYPOTHESIS OF ORIGIN AND NATURE FOR THE "SOMINDENCE-DISSOFRUSTANCE" PERSONALITY FACTOR, U.I. 30 EJ 061 061

FAILURE FACTORS

THE EFFECTS OF NEUROLOGICAL AND ENVIRONMENTAL FACTORS ON THE LANGUAGE DEVELOPMENT OF HEAD START CHILDREN--A EVALUATION OF THE HEAD START PROGRAM. ED017317
PREVENTION OF FAILURE. ED020777
A COMPARATIVE STUDY OF FAILURE AVOIDANCE IN CULTURALLY DISADVANTAGED AND NON-CULTURALLY DISADVANTAGED FIRST GRADE CHILDREN. ED044170
CHILDREN'S REACTIONS TO FAILURE AS A FUNCTION OF INSTRUCTIONS AND GOAL DISTANCE EJ 019 415
EFFECT OF SUCCESS AND FAILURE ON THE REFLECTIVE AND IMPULSIVE CHILD EJ 029 768
SELF-ESTEEM, SUCCESS-FAILURE, AND LOCUS OF CONTROL IN NEGRO CHILDREN EJ 035 621
NORMAL AND RETARDED CHILDREN'S EXPECTANCY FOR FAILURE EJ 039 266
CHILDREN'S REACTIONS TO FAILURE AS A FUNCTION OF INTERRESPONSE INTERVAL EJ 045 043
LEARNING DISORDERS IN CHILDREN: SIBLING STUDIES EJ 057 584

FAMILY (SOCIOLOGICAL UNIT)

FAMILY SOCIOLOGY OR WIVES' FAMILY SOCIOLOGY? A COMPARISON OF HUSBANDS' AND WIVES' ANSWERS ABOUT DECISION MAKING IN THE GREEK AND AMERICAN CULTURE. REPORT NUMBER 4. ED030478
CHANGING FAMILIES IN A CHANGING SOCIETY. 1970 WHITE HOUSE CONFERENCE ON CHILDREN, REPORT OF FORUM 14. (WORKING COPY). ED046530
CHILDREN AND PARENTS: TOGETHER IN THE WORLD. 1970 WHITE HOUSE CONFERENCE ON CHILDREN, REPORT OF FORUM 15. (WORKING COPY). ED046531
KINSHIP INTERACTION AND MARITAL SOLIDARITY EJ 007 449
PATTERNS OF FAMILY ORGANIZATION: AN APPROACH TO CHILD STUDY EJ 030 714
SELECTING PRIORITIES AT THE WHITE HOUSE CONFERENCE ON CHILDREN EJ 035 619
PARENTHOOD: SOME ANTECEDENTS AND CONSEQUENCES: A PRELIMINARY SURVEY OF THE MENTAL HEALTH LITERATURE EJ 041 342
CHANGES IN PARENTAL BEHAVIOR REPORTED BY CHILDREN IN WEST GERMANY AND THE UNITED STATES EJ 048 397
SYMPOSIUM ON ALTERNATIVE COMMUNITIES: CHILDREN OF THE GROUP FAMILY EJ 049 657

FAMILY ATTITUDES

WILLINGNESS TO ADOPT ATYPICAL CHILDREN EJ 020 860
THE OBJECTIVE MEASUREMENT OF CHILDREN'S INTRAFAMILIAL ATTITUDE AND SENTIMENT STRUCTURE AND THE INVESTMENT-SUBSIDIATION MODEL EJ 034 542
A DISCONTINUITY IN THE SOCIALIZATION OF MALES IN THE UNITED STATES EJ 040 799

FAMILY BACKGROUND

FAMILY BACKGROUND EFFECTS ON PERSONALITY DEVELOPMENT AND SOCIAL ACCEPTANCE. ED020020

FAMILY CHARACTERISTICS

A FOLLOWUP STUDY OF ADOPTIONS: POST-PLACEMENT FUNCTIONING OF ADOPTION FAMILIES. ED039018
PRESCHOOLER STUDY: THE MEDICAL, SOCIAL AND ECONOMIC CORRELATES OF POVERTY IN PRESCHOOL CHILDREN OF BRITISH COLUMBIA. A PILOT STUDY. ED046518
EDUCATIONAL INTERVENTION IN EARLY CHILDHOOD: A REPORT OF A FIVE-YEAR LONGITUDINAL STUDY OF THE EFFECTS OF EARLY EDUCATIONAL INTERVENTION IN THE LIVES OF DISADVANTAGED CHILDREN IN DURHAM, NORTH CAROLINA. FINAL REPORT, VOLUME I. ED050814
EDUCATIONAL INTERVENTION IN EARLY CHILDHOOD: APPENDIXES. FINAL REPORT, VOLUME II. ED050815
THE PARENTAL ROLE, A FUNCTIONAL-COGNITIVE APPROACH EJ 013 946
INTRAFAMILY COMPARISON OF LOVING-REJECTING CHILD-REARING PRACTICES EJ 021 081
SOME RELATIONSHIPS AMONG CHILDREN'S PERCEPTIONS OF PARENTAL CHARACTERISTICS EJ 025 318
PATTERNS OF FAMILY ORGANIZATION: AN APPROACH TO CHILD STUDY EJ 030 714
HARMONIOUS PARENTS AND THEIR PRESCHOOL CHILDREN EJ 034 708
SEX-ROLE IDENTITY AND SIBLING COMPOSITION EJ 035 626

FAMILY COUNSELING

STRUCTURED FAMILY-ORIENTED THERAPY FOR SCHOOL BEHAVIOR AND LEARNING DISORDERS EJ 019 022
A PLAN FOR PROTECTION: THE CHILD-ABUSE CENTER EJ 027 917
THE CHILD WELFARE AGENCY AS THE EXTENDED FAMILY EJ 052 493

FAMILY ENVIRONMENT

HOW TO HELP YOUR CHILD LEARN, A HANDBOOK FOR PARENTS OF CHILDREN IN KINDERGARTEN THROUGH GRADE 6. ED017342
NORTHFIELD, VERMONT--A COMMUNITY DEPTH STUDY. ED018245
TEACHERS' BELIEFS, CLASSROOM ATMOSPHERE AND STUDENT BEHAVIOR. FINAL REPORT. ED018249
MATERNAL BEHAVIOR AND THE DEVELOPMENT OF READING READINESS IN URBAN NEGRO CHILDREN. ED031309
CHILDREN LEARNING: SAMPLES OF EVERYDAY LIFE OF CHILDREN AT HOME. ED033763
ANALYSIS OF HOME ENVIRONMENT AND DEVELOPMENT OF PARENT INTERVENTION. ED035458
RESEARCH, CHANGE, AND SOCIAL RESPONSIBILITY: STUDIES OF THE IMPRINT OF THE LOW-INCOME HOME ON YOUNG CHILDREN. ED039935
ENVIRONMENTALLY DEPRIVED CHILDREN. ED039937
A STUDY OF HOME ENVIRONMENT AND READINESS FOR ACHIEVEMENT AT SCHOOL. FINAL REPORT. ED041637
ETHNIC AND SOCIOECONOMIC INFLUENCES ON THE HOME LANGUAGE EXPERIENCES OF CHILDREN. ED043377
PARENTAL CONCEPTUAL SYSTEMS, HOME PLAY ENVIRONMENT, AND POTENTIAL CREATIVITY IN CHILDREN. ED043386
THE PHYSICAL ENVIRONMENT AS A MEDIATING FACTOR IN SCHOOL ACHIEVEMENT. ED046496
RELATIONSHIPS BETWEEN SELECTED FAMILY VARIABLES AND MATERNAL AND INFANT BEHAVIOR IN A DISADVANTAGED POPULATION. A SUPPLEMENTARY REPORT. ED047784
THE DAY CARE NEIGHBOR SERVICE: A HANDBOOK FOR THE ORGANIZATION AND OPERATION OF A NEW APPROACH TO FAMILY DAY CARE. ED049810
PARENT-CHILD VERBAL INTERACTION: A STUDY OF DIALOGUE STRATEGIES AND VERBAL ABILITY. ED049824
AN EXAMINATION OF CHILDREN'S DAILY SCHEDULES IN THREE SOCIAL CLASSES AND THEIR RELATION TO FIRST-GRADE READING ACHIEVEMENT EJ 021 079
THE ROLE OF GEOGRAPHIC MOBILITY IN SOME ADJUSTMENT PROBLEMS OF CHILDREN AND FAMILIES EJ 023 430
HOME LANGUAGE AND PERFORMANCE ON STANDARDIZED TESTS EJ 032 678
COGNITIVE DEVELOPMENT IN INFANTS OF DIFFERENT AGE LEVELS AND FROM DIFFERENT ENVIRONMENTAL BACKGROUNDS: AN EXPLANATORY INVESTIGATION EJ 046 244
THE EFFECTS OF OWN-HOME AND INSTITUTION-REARING ON THE BEHAVIOURAL DEVELOPMENT OF NORMAL AND MONGOL CHILDREN EJ 048 905
CONDITIONING OF INFANT VOCALIZATIONS IN THE HOME ENVIRONMENT EJ 055 214
FAMILY HARMONY: AN ETIOLOGIC FACTOR IN ALIENATION EJ 058 508

FAMILY INCOME

FAMILY PLANNING AND FAMILY ECONOMICS. 1970 WHITE HOUSE CONFERENCE ON CHILDREN, REPORT OF FORUM 16. (WORKING COPY). ED046532

FAMILY INFLUENCE
A STUDY OF SOME ECOLOGICAL, ECONOMIC AND SOCIAL FACTORS INFLUENCING PARENTAL PARTICIPATION IN PROJECT HEAD START. ED014331
FAMILY BACKGROUND EFFECTS ON PERSONALITY DEVELOPMENT AND SOCIAL ACCEPTANCE. ED020020
THE INTERACTION OF FATHER-ABSENCE AND SIBLING-PRESENCE ON COGNITIVE ABILITIES. ED020024
A STUDY OF FAMILY INFLUENCES ON THE EDUCATION OF NEGRO LOWER-CLASS CHILDREN. PROJECT I. ED025309
FAMILY FACTORS RELATED TO COMPETENCE IN YOUNG, DISADVANTAGED MEXICAN-AMERICAN CHILDREN. PART OF THE FINAL REPORT ON HEAD START EVALUATION AND RESEARCH: 1968-69 TO THE OFFICE OF ECONOMIC OPPORTUNITY. ED037248
PROCEEDINGS: EARLY CHILDHOOD INTERVENTION RESEARCH CONFERENCE (UNIVERSITY OF SOUTH FLORIDA, TAMPA, MARCH 5 AND 6, 1970). ED045194
CRISIS IN VALUES. 1970 WHITE HOUSE CONFERENCE ON CHILDREN, REPORT OF FORUM 4. (WORKING COPY). ED046523
SCHOOL ACHIEVEMENT: A PRELIMINARY LOOK AT THE EFFECTS OF THE HOME. ED047777
PATTERNS OF FAMILY ORGANIZATION: AN APPROACH TO CHILD STUDY EJ 030 714
PARENT-CHILD SEPARATION: PSYCHOLOGICAL EFFECTS ON THE CHILDREN EJ 051 019
DEVELOPMENTAL FACTORS IN ADOLESCENT DRUG USE: A STUDY OF PSYCHEDELIC DRUG USERS EJ 051 020
SIBLING RESEMBLANCES IN DIVERGENT THINKING EJ 055 106
LEARNING DISORDERS IN CHILDREN: SIBLING STUDIES EJ 057 584
FAMILY CORRELATES OF VERBAL REASONING ABILITY EJ 061 069

FAMILY INVOLVEMENT
A REPORT FROM ABROAD...FAMILY PARTICIPATION IN HOSPITAL CARE FOR CHILDREN EJ 024 497
FAMILY TREATMENT WITHIN THE MILIEU OF A RESIDENTIAL TREATMENT CENTER EJ 037 236
LEARNING FROM EACH OTHER EJ 044 008
FAMILY INTERACTION VARIABLES AND ADJUSTMENT OF NONCLINIC BOYS EJ 053 737

FAMILY LIFE
FAMILY LIFE AROUND THE WORLD, LEVEL I. ED032116
PARENTAL BEHAVIOR AND CHILDREN'S SCHOOL ACHIEVEMENT: IMPLICATIONS FOR HEAD START. PROCEEDINGS OF THE HEAD START RESEARCH SEMINARS: SEMINAR NO. 5, INTERVENTION IN FAMILY LIFE (1ST, WASHINGTON, D.C., JANUARY 13, 1969). ED036332
PROFILES OF CHILDREN: 1970 WHITE HOUSE CONFERENCE ON CHILDREN. ED046520
THE POVERTY CULTURE EJ 011 823
PSYCHOSOCIAL DEVELOPMENT IN CROSS-CULTURAL PERSPECTIVE: A NEW LOOK AT AN OLD ISSUE EJ 046 888

FAMILY LIFE EDUCATION
FAMILY PLANNING AND FAMILY ECONOMICS. 1970 WHITE HOUSE CONFERENCE ON CHILDREN, REPORT OF FORUM 16. (WORKING COPY). ED046532
STUDENT EVALUATION OF A HIGH SCHOOL SEX EDUCATION PROGRAM EJ 045 390
PROJECT TREAT: A NEW APPROACH TO THE SEVERELY DISTURBED CHILD EJ 061 000
GROUP HOME CARE AS AN ADJUNCT TO RESIDENTIAL TREATMENT EJ 061 233

FAMILY PLANNING
FAMILY PLANNING AND FAMILY ECONOMICS. 1970 WHITE HOUSE CONFERENCE ON CHILDREN, REPORT OF FORUM 16. (WORKING COPY). ED046532
CHILD HEALTH AND HUMAN DEVELOPMENT: PROGRESS 1963-1970. A REPORT OF THE NATIONAL INSTITUTE OF CHILD HEALTH AND HUMAN DEVELOPMENT. ED053799
PSYCHOLOGICAL SOURCES OF "RESISTANCE" TO FAMILY PLANNING EJ 027 502
PARENTHOOD: SOME ANTECEDENTS AND CONSEQUENCES: A PRELIMINARY SURVEY OF THE MENTAL HEALTH LITERATURE EJ 041 342

FAMILY PROBLEMS
THE IMPLICATIONS OF PARENT EFFECTIVENESS TRAINING FOR FOSTER PARENTS. ED052821
FAMILIES OF CHILDREN IN FOSTER CARE EJ 007 452
FAMILY PROBLEMS CONCERNING THE MENTALLY RETARDED CHILD EJ 010 859
THE EFFECTS OF FATHER ABSENCE ON CHILD DEVELOPMENT EJ 035 800
A DEMONSTRATION SUMMER PRESCHOOL PROGRAM EJ 060 999
FOUR CHILDREN EJ 061 073

FAMILY PROGRAMS
DIFFUSION OF INTERVENTION EFFECTS IN DISADVANTAGED FAMILIES. ED026127
WORKING WITH FAMILIES OF DELINQUENT BOYS EJ 007 727
WHO CARES FOR AMERICA'S CHILDREN? EJ 032 565

FAMILY RELATIONSHIP
PATTERNS OF FAMILY ORGANIZATION: AN APPROACH TO CHILD STUDY EJ 030 714
THE OBJECTIVE MEASUREMENT OF CHILDREN'S INTRAFAMILIAL ATTITUDE AND SENTIMENT STRUCTURE AND THE INVESTMENT-SUBSIDIATION MODEL EJ 034 542
SHARING PARENTS WITH STRANGERS: THE ROLE OF THE GROUP HOME FOSTER FAMILY'S OWN CHILDREN EJ 053 600
FAMILY INTERACTION VARIABLES AND ADJUSTMENT OF NONCLINIC BOYS EJ 053 737

FAMILY RESOURCES
THE COGNITIVE ENVIRONMENTS OF URBAN PRE-SCHOOL CHILDREN. MANUAL OF INSTRUCTIONS FOR ADMINISTERING AND SCORING HOME RESOURCES PATTERNS. ED018260

FAMILY ROLE
FAMILY FACTORS RELATED TO COMPETENCE IN YOUNG DISADVANTAGED MEXICAN-AMERICAN CHILDREN EJ 053 753

FAMILY SCHOOL RELATIONSHIP
PARENTS: ACTIVE PARTNERS IN EDUCATION. A STUDY/ACTION PUBLICATION. ED050823
A STUDY IN CHILD CARE (CASE STUDY FROM VOLUME II-A): "THEY UNDERSTAND." DAY CARE PROGRAMS REPRINT SERIES. ED051892
PARENTS TEACH KINDERGARTEN READING AT HOME EJ 020 774
SCHOOL AND HOME: NOT EITHER-OR EJ 046 246

FAMILY STRUCTURE
CHANGING FAMILIES IN A CHANGING SOCIETY. 1970 WHITE HOUSE CONFERENCE ON CHILDREN, REPORT OF FORUM 14. (WORKING COPY). ED046530

FANTASY
PLAY AS A FUNCTION OF TOY STRUCTURE AND FANTASY PREDISPOSITION EJ 021 083
INVISIBLE FACTORS IN A CHILD'S REACTION TO TELEVISION EJ 032 934

FATHERLESS FAMILY
THE INTERACTION OF FATHER-ABSENCE AND SIBLING-PRESENCE ON COGNITIVE ABILITIES. ED020024
RESISTANCE TO TEMPTATION IN YOUNG NEGRO CHILDREN IN RELATION TO SEX OF THE SUBJECT, SEX OF THE EXPERIMENTER AND FATHER ABSENCE OR PRESENCE. ED032138
FATHER ABSENCE AND THE PERSONALITY DEVELOPMENT OF THE MALE CHILD EJ 019 018
PATERNAL ABSENCE, SEX TYPING, AND IDENTIFICATION EJ 019 020
WISC SUBTEST AND IQ SCORE CORRELATES OF FATHER ABSENCE EJ 029 219
RESISTANCE TO TEMPTATION IN YOUNG NEGRO CHILDREN EJ 032 894
OLDER BROTHERS' INFLUENCE ON SEX-TYPED, AGGRESSIVE, AND DEPENDENT BEHAVIOR IN FATHER-ABSENT CHILDREN EJ 034 901
THE EFFECTS OF FATHER ABSENCE ON CHILD DEVELOPMENT EJ 035 800
FATHER ABSENCE, PERCEIVED MATERNAL BEHAVIOR, AND MASCULINITY OF SELF-CONCEPT AMONG JUNIOR HIGH SCHOOL BOYS EJ 035 804
FATHER AVAILABILITY AND ACADEMIC PERFORMANCE AMONG THIRD-GRADE BOYS EJ 038 730
FATHER ABSENCE AND CONSCIENCE DEVELOPMENT EJ 038 854
THE MOTHER-CHILD RELATIONSHIP AND THE FATHER-ABSENT BOY'S PERSONALITY DEVELOPMENT 27-241 EJ 040 456
FAMILIES WITHOUT FATHERS EJ 049 656
RELATION OF TYPE AND ONSET OF FATHER ABSENCE TO COGNITIVE DEVELOPMENT EJ 058 695

FATHERS
FATHERS' VERBAL INTERACTION WITH INFANTS IN THE FIRST THREE MONTHS OF LIFE EJ 036 126
FATHER AVAILABILITY AND ACADEMIC PERFORMANCE AMONG THIRD-GRADE BOYS EJ 038 730
FATHER-CHILD INTERACTION AND THE INTELLECTUAL FUNCTIONING OF FOUR-YEAR-OLD BOYS EJ 054 290

FEAR
FEAR AND ATTACHMENT IN YOUNG CHILDREN. RESEARCH PROJECT NUMBER 4 OF PROJECT HEAD START RESEARCH AND EVALUATION CENTER, SYRACUSE UNIVERSITY RESEARCH INSTITUTE. FINAL REPORT, NOVEMBER 1, 1967. ED026141
THE VICARIOUS CONDITIONING OF EMOTIONAL RESPONSES IN NURSERY SCHOOL CHILDREN. FINAL REPORT. ED046540
CHILDREN'S FEAR IN A DENTAL SITUATION AS A FUNCTION OF BIRTH ORDER EJ 015 099
PATTERNS OF FEAR DEVELOPMENT DURING INFANCY EJ 020 718
A THERAPEUTIC APPROACH TO SPEECH PHOBIA: ELECTIVE MUTISM REEXAMINED EJ 035 625
ANXIETY IN YOUNG CHILDREN EJ 045 049
AN EXPERIENCE WITH FEAR IN THE LIVES OF CHILDREN EJ 045 389
HOW TO TEACH FEAR EJ 061 058

FEASIBILITY STUDIES
KINDERGARTEN OVERSEAS, A STUDY OF THE REQUIREMENTS FOR ESTABLISHING KINDERGARTEN AS PART OF THE DEPARTMENT OF DEFENSE OVERSEAS DEPENDENTS SCHOOLS. FINAL REPORT. ED017340

STUDY TO DETERMINE THE FEASIBILITY OF ADAPTING THE CARL ORFF APPROACH TO ELEMENTARY SCHOOLS IN AMERICA. FINAL REPORT. ED020804
CONDITIONING TASKS PERFORMANCE IN INFANCY AND EARLY CHILDHOOD AS A STABLE AND MEASURABLE ASPECT OF BEHAVIOR. FINAL REPORT. ED051890
THE TRAINING OF FAMILY DAY-CARE WORKERS: A FEASIBILITY STUDY AND INITIAL PILOT EFFORTS. FINAL REPORT. ED053787
THE USE OF CREATIVITY TRAINING MATERIALS WITH SPECIAL CHILDREN: A REPORT OF A FEASIBILITY EXPERIENCE EJ 046 058

FEDERAL AID

FEDERAL INTERAGENCY DAY CARE REQUIREMENTS, PURSUANT TO SEC. 522 (D) OF THE ECONOMIC OPPORTUNITY ACT. ED026145
FEDERAL PROGRAMS ASSISTING CHILDREN AND YOUTH. ED028840
FEDERAL FUNDS FOR DAY CARE PROJECTS. (REVISED EDITION). ED033741
FEDERAL PROGRAMS ASSISTING CHILDREN AND YOUTH. REVISED EDITION. ED038161
FEDERAL INVOLVEMENT IN DAY CARE. ED048931

FEDERAL GOVERNMENT

STATEMENT BY THE PRESIDENT ON THE ESTABLISHMENT OF AN OFFICE OF CHILD DEVELOPMENT EJ 007 091

FEDERAL LAWS

FUNDING CHILD CARE PROGRAMS UNDER TITLE IV-A EJ 060 452

FEDERAL LEGISLATION

STATEMENT BY MARSDEN G. WAGNER, M. D. REPRESENTING THE AMERICAN PUBLIC HEALTH ASSOCIATION BEFORE THE SELECT SUBCOMMITTEE ON EDUCATION, MARCH 3, 1970. ED039940
STATEMENT ON COMPREHENSIVE PRESCHOOL EDUCATION AND CHILD DAY CARE ACT OF 1969 BEFORE THE SELECT SUBCOMMITTEE ON EDUCATION, FEBRUARY 27, 1970. ED039941
A STATEMENT ON THE COMPREHENSIVE PRESCHOOL EDUCATION AND CHILD DAY-CARE ACT OF 1969 BEFORE THE SELECT SUBCOMMITTEE ON EDUCATION OF THE HOUSE COMMITTEE ON EDUCATION AND LABOR, MARCH 3, 1970. ED040752
[A STATEMENT REGARDING THE COMPREHENSIVE PRESCHOOL EDUCATION AND CHILD DAY CARE ACT OF 1969, AND OTHER RELATED BILLS.] ED040761
[A STATEMENT REGARDING THE COMPREHENSIVE PRESCHOOL EDUCATION AND CHILD DAY CARE ACT OF 1969, AND OTHER RELATED BILLS.] ED040762
[A STATEMENT REGARDING THE COMPREHENSIVE PRESCHOOL EDUCATION AND CHILD DAY CARE ACT OF 1969, AND OTHER RELATED BILLS.] ED041624
DAY CARE: CRISIS AND CHALLENGE EJ 046 455
DAY CARE CHALLENGE: THE UNMET NEEDS OF MOTHERS AND CHILDREN EJ 046 456
CHILDREN: OUR CHALLENGE EJ 050 423

FEDERAL PROGRAMS

FEDERAL PROGRAMS ASSISTING CHILDREN AND YOUTH. ED028840
FEDERAL FUNDS FOR DAY CARE PROJECTS. (REVISED EDITION). ED033741
HEAD START PROGRAMS AND PARTICIPANTS 1965-1967. ED034569
A REPORT ON EVALUATION STUDIES OF PROJECT HEAD START. ED037239
FEDERAL PROGRAMS ASSISTING CHILDREN AND YOUTH. REVISED EDITION. ED038161
HEAD START PLANNED VARIATION PROGRAM. ED038170
A NATIONAL SURVEY OF THE IMPACTS OF HEAD START CENTERS ON COMMUNITY INSTITUTIONS. ED045195
A NATIONAL SURVEY OF THE IMPACTS OF HEAD START CENTERS ON COMMUNITY INSTITUTIONS. SUMMARY REPORT. ED046516
DELIVERY OF CHILD HEALTH SERVICES. 1970 WHITE HOUSE CONFERENCE ON CHILDREN, REPORT OF FORUM 11. (WORKING PAPER). ED046528
FAMILY PLANNING AND FAMILY ECONOMICS. 1970 WHITE HOUSE CONFERENCE ON CHILDREN, REPORT OF FORUM 16. (WORKING COPY). ED046532
THE CHILD ADVOCATE. 1970 WHITE HOUSE CONFERENCE ON CHILDREN, REPORT OF FORUM 24. (WORKING COPY). ED046538
FEDERAL PROGRAMS FOR YOUNG CHILDREN. ED047811
COMMUNITY COORDINATED CHILD CARE: A FEDERAL PARTNERSHIP IN BEHALF OF CHILDREN. FINAL REPORT. ED048925
FEDERAL INVOLVEMENT IN DAY CARE. ED048931
COMMUNITY COORDINATED CHILD CARE: A FEDERAL PARTNERSHIP IN BEHALF OF CHILDREN. SUMMARY. ED048944
PARENT AND CHILD CENTERS--WHAT THEY ARE, WHERE THEY ARE GOING EJ 007 089
THE 4-C PROGRAM EJ 007 090
STATEMENT BY THE PRESIDENT ON THE ESTABLISHMENT OF AN OFFICE OF CHILD DEVELOPMENT EJ 007 091
TWO CONGRESSMEN LOOK AT AMERICAN EDUCATION EJ 009 032
A NATIONAL PRIORITY: RAISING THE QUALITY OF CHILDREN'S LIVES EJ 027 501
PARENT AND CHILD CENTERS--IMPETUS, IMPLEMENTATION, IN-DEPTH VIEW EJ 030 469
CONTEMPORARY CONCERNS IN EARLY CHILDHOOD EDUCATION EJ 032 059
PRIORITIES FOR CHANGE--SOME PRELIMINARY PROPOSALS FROM THE WHITE HOUSE CONFERENCE ON CHILDREN EJ 032 611
SOME THOUGHTS ON PLANNING HEALTH CARE FOR CHILDREN AND YOUTH EJ 038 021
LEARNING FROM CHILDREN: THE ROLE OF OCD EJ 044 285
CHILDREN: OUR CHALLENGE EJ 050 423
CHILD ADVOCACY -- REFLECTIONS EJ 051 241
PRACTICAL APPROACHES FOR RESOLVING THE PROBLEM OF NUTRITION AMONG LOW-INCOME FAMILIES EJ 052 065

FEEDBACK

HEAD START EVALUATION AND RESEARCH CENTER, UNIVERSITY OF KANSAS. REPORT NO. I, THE OBSERVATION OF REINFORCEMENT BEHAVIOR OF TEACHERS IN HEAD START CLASSROOMS AND THE MODIFICATION OF A TEACHER'S ATTENDING BEHAVIOR. ED021633
CONDITIONS FOSTERING THE USE OF INFORMATIVE FEEDBACK BY YOUNG CHILDREN. ED029688
INFORMATION VALUE OF FEEDBACK WITH PRESCHOOL CHILDREN. ED031311
CONDITIONS FOSTERING THE USE OF INFORMATION FEEDBACK BY YOUNG CHILDREN. (REVISED REPORT). ED039950
MAXIMIZING THE VALUE OF EVALUATION FOR THE HEAD START TEACHER. FINAL REPORT. ED041631
THE EFFECTS OF ADULT VERBAL MODELING AND FEEDBACK ON THE ORAL LANGUAGE OF HEAD START CHILDREN. ED047793
PUPILS' PERCEPTION OF TEACHERS' VERBAL FEEDBACK EJ 027 880
REACTION TO SUCESS AND FAILURE IN COMPLEX LEARNING: A POSTFEEDBACK EFFECT EJ 029 413
PERSISTENCE AS A FUNCTION OF CONCEPTUAL STRUCTURE AND QUALITY OF FEEDBACK EJ 032 932
TIME ESTIMATION BY YOUNG CHILDREN WITH AND WITHOUT INFORMATIONAL FEEDBACK EJ 033 787
EFFECT OF CORRELATED VISUAL AND TACTUAL FEEDBACK ON AUDITORY PATTERN LEARNING AT DIFFERENT AGE LEVELS EJ 037 517
THE EFFECTS OF FEEDBACK VARIATIONS ON REFERENTIAL COMMUNICATION OF CHILDREN EJ 040 360
VERBAL PARTICIPATION AS A FUNCTION OF THE PRESENCE OF PRIOR INFORMATION CONCERNING APTITUDE EJ 042 348
TRAINING AND GENERALIZATION OF DENSITY CONSERVATION: EFFECTS OF FEEDBACK AND CONSECUTIVE SIMILAR STIMULI EJ 046 231
A REEXAMINATION OF THE ROLE OF INCENTIVE IN CHILDREN'S DISCRIMINATION LEARNING EJ 046 237
EFFECTS OF IMITATION OF DIFFERENT REINFORCEMENT COMBINATIONS TO A MODEL EJ 046 255
DELAY OF FEEDBACK INTERVAL, POSTFEEDBACK INTERVAL, DISTRACTION, AND TASK DIFFICULTY AS FACTORS IN A MODIFIED CONCEPT-IDENTIFICATION TASK WITH JUNIOR HIGH SCHOOL SUBJECTS EJ 047 677
DISCRIMINATION LEARNING BY REFLECTIVE AND IMPULSIVE CHILDREN AS A FUNCTION OF REINFORCEMENT SCHEDULE EJ 053 717
THE EFFECTS OF IMMEDIATE FEEDBACK ON THE BEHAVIOR OF TEACHERS-IN-TRAINING EJ 059 672

FELLOWSHIPS

ENCOURAGING STUDENTS' RESEARCH ON COGNITIVE DEVELOPMENT. ED031301

FEMALES

THE FATHER-DAUGHTER RELATIONSHIP AND THE PERSONALITY DEVELOPMENT OF THE FEMALE EJ 017 904
COMPLEXITY, CONTOUR, AND AREA AS DETERMINANTS OF ATTENTION IN INFANTS EJ 029 361
TIMING AND SOURCES OF INFORMATION ABOUT, AND ATTITUDES TOWARD, MENSTRUATION AMONG COLLEGE FEMALES EJ 029 533
CHANGING PROSPECTS FOR CHILDREN WITH HEMOPHILIA EJ 029 952
RELIABILITY ASSESSMENT OF OBSERVATION DATA: A POSSIBLE METHODOLOGICAL PROBLEM EJ 033 313
GIRLS' ATTITUDES TOWARD MODELED BEHAVIORS AND THE CONTENT OF IMITATIVE PRIVATE PLAY EJ 036 079
ROLE MODEL INFLUENCES ON COLLEGE WOMEN'S CAREER ASPIRATIONS EJ 041 632
THE USE OF BEHAVIOR-MODIFICATION TECHNIQUES WITH FEMALE DELINQUENTS EJ 051 473
FORMAL OPERATIONS IN FEMALES FROM ELEVEN TO FIFTY-FOUR YEARS OF AGE EJ 055 215
PARENTAL ATTITUDES AND INTERACTIONS IN DELINQUENCY EJ 056 611
THE EFFECT OF A TELEVISION MODEL UPON RULE ADOPTION BEHAVIOR OF CHILDREN EJ 056 733
SEX ROLE IDENTITY OF ADOLESCENT GIRLS IN FOSTER HOMES AND INSTITUTIONS EJ 059 644

FICTION

THE BEAUTIFUL PEOPLE IN CHILDREN'S BOOKS EJ 020 541

FIELD INTERVIEWS
HEAD START EVALUATION AND RESEARCH CENTER, BOSTON UNIVERSITY. REPORT E-I, THE UTILIZATION OF NON-PROFESSIONAL INTERVIEWERS IN THE NEW ENGLAND AND MISSISSIPPI SAMPLES BY THE BOSTON UNIVERSITY HEAD START EVALUATION AND RESEARCH PROGRAM, 1966-1967. ED022566

FIELD STUDIES
DEMOGRAPHIC AND SOCIO-ECONOMIC DATA OF THE BECKLEY, WEST VIRGINIA AREA AND 1968-1970 DEVELOPMENTAL COSTS OF THE EARLY CHILDHOOD EDUCATION FIELD STUDY. TECHNICAL REPORT NO. 1. ED052832

FIELD TRIPS
SOCIAL STUDIES UNIT: FIRST GRADE. BOSTON-NORTHAMPTON LANGUAGE ARTS PROGRAM, ESEA - 1965, PROJECTS TO ADVANCE CREATIVITY IN EDUCATION. ED027945
ROCKS, RIVERS AND CITY CHILDREN EJ 029 390
OCEANS AND CHILDREN: MARINE SCIENCE AND ECOLOGICAL UNDERSTANDING EJ 029 391
GOING ON A TRIP EJ 035 842
PLANNING TRIPS FOR VULNERABLE CHILDREN EJ 048 998

FIGURAL AFTEREFFECTS
PARAMETERS OF THE SPIRAL AFTER-EFFECT IN ORGANICS, SCHIZOPHRENICS, AND NORMALS EJ 061 060

FILM LIBRARIES
FILMS SUITABLE FOR HEAD START CHILD DEVELOPMENT PROGRAMS. ED047818

FILM STUDY
SYMPOSIUM ON CHILD-OBSERVATION: 1. FILM-MAKING AS AN OBSERVATION TECHNIQUE EJ 056 861

FILMS
HEAD START EVALUATION AND RESEARCH CENTER, BOSTON UNIVERSITY. REPORT A-I, TEACHING STYLE: THE DEVELOPMENT OF TEACHING TASKS. ED022557
A SHOE IS TO TIE: A FILM DEMONSTRATION OF PROGRAMMING SELF-HELP SKILLS FOR PRESCHOOL CHILDREN. PROGRESS REPORT. ED042500
FILMS SUITABLE FOR HEAD START CHILD DEVELOPMENT PROGRAMS. ED047818
EMOTIONAL REACTIONS OF YOUNG CHILDREN TO TV VIOLENCE EJ 036 082
THEY BECAME WHAT THEY BEHELD EJ 045 423

FINANCIAL SUPPORT
ISSUES AND REALITIES IN EARLY CHILDHOOD EDUCATION. ED041621
A STUDY IN CHILD CARE (CASE STUDY FROM VOLUME II-A): "CHILDREN AS 'KIDS'." DAY CARE PROGRAMS REPRINT SERIES. ED051900
A STUDY IN CHILD CARE (CASE STUDY FROM VOLUME II-A): "HEY, GEORGIE GET YOURSELF TOGETHER." DAY CARE PROGRAMS REPRINT SERIES. ED051902
FUNDING CHILD CARE PROGRAMS UNDER TITLE IV-A EJ 060 452

FINE ARTS
ARTS AND HUMANITIES FOR YOUNG SCHOOL CHILDREN. ED032945
CHILDREN AND THEIR EXPANDING WORLD OF KNOWLEDGE EJ 026 734

FIRE SCIENCE EDUCATION
A STUDY OF THE EFFECTIVENESS OF SPECIFIC TEACHING OF CONSERVATION TO CHILDREN IN SELECTED ELEMENTARY SCHOOLS OF BUTTE COUNTY, CALIFORNIA EJ 027 029

FLEXIBLE PROGRESSION
SEQUENCE IN LEARNING--FACT OR FICTION. ED017330

FOLLOWUP STUDIES
SIX MONTHS LATER--A COMPARISON OF CHILDREN WHO HAD HEAD START, SUMMER, 1965, WITH THEIR CLASSMATES IN KINDERGARTEN, A CASE STUDY OF THE KINDERGARTENS IN FOUR PUBLIC ELEMENTARY SCHOOLS, NEW YORK CITY. STUDY I. ED015025
MEMO--COMMENTS ON THE WOLFF AND STEIN STUDY. ED015029
REMARKS ON THE MAX WOLFF REPORT. ED015030
THE IMPACT OF HEAD START: AN EVALUATION OF THE EFFECTS OF HEAD START ON CHILDREN'S COGNITIVE AND AFFECTIVE DEVELOPMENT. (EXECUTIVE SUMMARY). ED036321
A COMPARISON OF HEAD START CHILDREN WITH A GROUP OF HEAD START ELIGIBLES AFTER ONE YEAR IN ELEMENTARY SCHOOL. PART OF THE FINAL REPORT ON HEAD START EVALUATION AND RESEARCH: 1968-69 TO THE OFFICE OF ECONOMIC OPPORTUNITY. ED037247
THE COGNITIVE ENVIRONMENTS OF URBAN PRESCHOOL CHILDREN: FOLLOW-UP PHASE. FINAL REPORT. ED045180
INTELLECTUAL DEVELOPMENT OF CULTURALLY DEPRIVED CHILDREN IN A DAY CARE PROGRAM: A FOLLOW-UP STUDY. ED045186
A FOLLOW-UP NORMATIVE STUDY OF NEGRO INTELLIGENCE AND ACHIEVEMENT EJ 003 658
A FOLLOW-UP STUDY OF SCHOOL PHOBIC ADOLESCENTS ADMITTED TO AN IN-PATIENT UNIT EJ 026 157

FOOD
PROGRAMS FOR INFANTS AND YOUNG CHILDREN. PART II: NUTRITION. ED047808

FOODS INSTRUCTION
PRACTICAL APPROACHES FOR RESOLVING THE PROBLEM OF NUTRITION AMONG LOW-INCOME FAMILIES EJ 052 065

FOREIGN COUNTRIES
KINDERGARTEN OVERSEAS, A STUDY OF THE REQUIREMENTS FOR ESTABLISHING KINDERGARTEN AS PART OF THE DEPARTMENT OF DEFENSE OVERSEAS DEPENDENTS SCHOOLS. FINAL REPORT. ED017340
LEICESTERSHIRE REVISITED. ED029683
EARLY CHILDHOOD EDUCATION IN AMERICAN SAMOA, 1968. ED032114
FOUR YEARS ON. A FOLLOW-UP STUDY AT SCHOOL LEAVING AGE OF CHILDREN FORMERLY ATTENDING A TRADITIONAL AND A PROGRESSIVE JUNIOR SCHOOL. ED035434
KINDERGARTEN HANDBOOK: A GUIDE TO THOSE ACTIVELY INTERESTED IN KINDERGARTENS AND IN ESTABLISHING NEW CENTRES. THIRD EDITION. ED039925
LANGUAGE PROGRAMS FOR YOUNG CHILDREN: NOTES FROM ENGLAND AND WALES. ED040763
PRE-SCHOOL EDUCATION IN EUROPE. ED047779
SOME EUROPEAN NURSERY SCHOOLS AND PLAYGROUNDS. ED048928
LENIN'S GRANDCHILDREN: PRESCHOOL EDUCATION IN THE SOVIET UNION. ED049830
THE SWEDISH CHILD: A SURVEY OF THE LEGAL, ECONOMIC, EDUCATIONAL, MEDICAL AND SOCIAL SITUATION OF CHILDREN AND YOUNG PEOPLE IN SWEDEN. ED050811
OF DREAMS AND REALITY: KIBBUTZ CHILDREN EJ 006 922
UPBRINGING OF CHILDREN IN KIBBUTZIM OF ISRAEL EJ 007 447
THE DAYS THAT MAKE US HAPPY: GAMES AROUND THE WORLD EJ 038 407
LE NOUVEAU PROGRAMME D'ACTIVITES EDUCATRICES DANS LES ESTABLISSEMENTS PRESCOLAIRES EN YOUGOSLAVIE EJ 045 011
SOS CHILDREN'S VILLAGES THROUGHOUT THE WORLD: SUBSTITUTE OR SUPERIOR SERVICE? EJ 058 964
AESTHETIC EDUCATION IN SOVIET SCHOOLS EJ 060 105
IS SESAME STREET EXPORTABLE? EJ 061 442
EARLY CHILDHOOD EDUCATION IN JAPAN EJ 061 692
INVESTIGACIONES EN EL CAMPO EDUCATIVE (INVESTIGATIONS IN EDUCATION FIELD) EJ 062 593

FOREIGN CULTURE
REPORT ON ACTIVITIES, 1964-1966. ED020016
THE DEVELOPMENT OF CHILDREN'S VIEWS OF FOREIGN PEOPLES EJ 000 392
CHOOSING CHILDREN'S BOOKS ABOUT OTHER COUNTRIES EJ 000 393
THE CARE AND EDUCATION OF PRESCHOOL NONWHITES IN THE REPUBLIC OF SOUTH AFRICA EJ 010 125

FOREIGN NATIONALS
HUMAN RESOURCES FOR INTERNATIONAL STUDIES EJ 038 393

FOREIGN STUDENTS
A BIBLIOGRAPHY OF RESEARCH ON FOREIGN STUDENT AFFAIRS. ED021629

FORM CLASSES (LANGUAGES)
ANALYSES OF STORIES DICTATED IN CLASSES OF THE COOPERATIVE PROJECT. ED019993
THE EFFECTS OF DIFFERENTIATED INSTRUCTION IN VISUO-MOTOR SKILLS ON DEVELOPMENTAL GROWTH AND READING READINESS AT KINDERGARTEN LEVEL. FINAL REPORT. ED053821
THE LEARNING OF VERBAL STRINGS AS A FUNCTION OF CONNECTIVE FORM CLASS EJ 018 817
WORD ASSOCIATION AND DEFINITION IN MIDDLE CHILDHOOD EJ 030 294

FOSTER CHILDREN
THE IMPLICATIONS OF PARENT EFFECTIVENESS TRAINING FOR FOSTER PARENTS. ED052821
FAMILY TIES AND THE INSTITUTIONAL CHILD EJ 012 579
REUNITING CHILDREN AND PARENTS THROUGH CASEWORK AND GROUP WORK EJ 027 342
FOSTER FAMILY SERVICES FOR MENTALLY RETARDED CHILDREN EJ 030 653
WHEN IS SUBSIDIZED ADOPTION PREFERABLE TO LONG-TERM FOSTER CARE? EJ 035 949
SEX EDUCATION FOR THE CHILD IN FOSTER CARE EJ 036 328
THE EXIT OF CHILDREN FROM FOSTER CARE: AN INTERIM RESEARCH REPORT EJ 039 798
144 FOSTER CHILDREN EJ 046 787
WORKING WITH SEPARATION EJ 046 893
THE BOY WHO DID NOT CRY EJ 052 310
SHARING PARENTS WITH STRANGERS: THE ROLE OF THE GROUP HOME FOSTER FAMILY'S OWN CHILDREN EJ 053 600
ADOPTION: IDENTIFICATION AND SERVICE EJ 058 307
SOS CHILDREN'S VILLAGES THROUGHOUT THE WORLD: SUBSTITUTE OR SUPERIOR SERVICE? EJ 058 964
JOINING TOGETHER TO HELP FOSTER CHILDREN EJ 060 900

FOSTER FAMILY
A FOLLOWUP STUDY OF ADOPTIONS: POST-PLACEMENT FUNCTIONING OF ADOPTION FAMILIES. ED039018
CHILD WELFARE SERVICES: A SOURCEBOOK. ED047813

THE IMPLICATIONS OF PARENT EFFECTIVENESS TRAINING FOR FOSTER PARENTS. ED052821
SERVICES TO CHILDREN LIVING WITH RELATIVES OR GUARDIANS EJ 007 445
FAMILY TIES AND THE INSTITUTIONAL CHILD EJ 012 579
THE GHETTO AS A SOURCE OF FOSTER HOMES EJ 020 858
THE RIGHTS OF FOSTER PARENTS EJ 022 182
A GROUP METHOD FOR FINDING AND DEVELOPING FOSTER HOMES EJ 027 920
FOSTER FAMILY SERVICES FOR MENTALLY RETARDED CHILDREN EJ 030 653
THE USE OF DEVELOPMENTAL PLANS FOR MENTALLY RETARDED CHILDREN IN FOSTER FAMILY CARE EJ 035 803
SEX EDUCATION FOR THE CHILD IN FOSTER CARE EJ 036 328
HELPING FOSTER PARENTS UNDERSTAND DISTURBED CHILDREN EJ 037 238
THIRTY YEARS OF INNOVATION IN FOSTER CARE EJ 044 230
CLARIFYING THE ROLE OF FOSTER PARENTS EJ 061 235

FOSTER HOMES
THE GHETTO AS A SOURCE OF FOSTER HOMES EJ 020 858
FOSTER CARE FOR MENTALLY RETARDED CHILDREN: HOW DOES CHILD WELFARE MEET THIS CHALLENGE? EJ 020 859
A DIFFERENTIAL USE OF GROUP HOMES FOR DELINQUENT BOYS EJ 024 028
A GROUP METHOD FOR FINDING AND DEVELOPING FOSTER HOMES EJ 027 920
THE USE OF DEVELOPMENTAL PLANS FOR MENTALLY RETARDED CHILDREN IN FOSTER FAMILY CARE EJ 035 803
THIRTY YEARS OF INNOVATION IN FOSTER CARE EJ 044 230
SHARING PARENTS WITH STRANGERS: THE ROLE OF THE GROUP HOME FOSTER FAMILY'S OWN CHILDREN EJ 053 600
THE TEAM APPROACH IN HOME CARE OF MENTALLY RETARDED CHILDREN EJ 053 601

FRACTIONS
AN EXPERIMENTAL STUDY OF TWO METHODS OF PRESENTING THE INVERSION ALGORITHM IN DIVISION OF FRACTIONS EJ 033 863

FREEHAND DRAWING
THE RELATION OF CONCEPTUAL STYLES AND MODE OF PERCEPTION TO GRAPHIC EXPRESSION. ED040743
BODY PROPORTIONS IN CHILDREN'S DRAWINGS OF A MAN EJ 025 305
IDEATIONAL CREATIVITY AND EXPRESSIVE ASPECTS OF HUMAN FIGURE DRAWING IN KINDERGARTEN-AGE CHILDREN EJ 039 629
ORIENTATION IN CHILDREN'S HUMAN FIGURE DRAWINGS: AN ASPECT OF GRAPHIC LANGUAGE EJ 061 067

FRIENDSHIP
FACTORS? IN CHILD DEVELOPMENT: PEER RELATIONS. ED047796
NEIGHBORHOOD FAMILY DAY CARE AS A CHILD-REARING ENVIRONMENT. ED049840

FUNCTION WORDS
LANGUAGE TEACHING: PREPOSITIONS AND CONJUNCTIVES. ED034597
SURFACE STRUCTURE AND THE TOPIC-COMMENT DISTINCTION: A DEVELOPMENTAL STUDY EJ 056 717

FUNDAMENTAL CONCEPTS
DEVELOPMENT OF A TECHNIQUE FOR IDENTIFYING ELEMENTARY SCHOOL CHILDREN'S MUSICAL CONCEPTS. FINAL REPORT. ED016517

FURNITURE DESIGN
WORKTABLE ON WHEELS. ED035451

GAME THEORY
DEVELOPMENTAL ASPECTS OF REACTION TO POSITIVE INDUCEMENTS EJ 029 359

GAMES
PHYSICAL EDUCATION ACTIVITIES FOR THE ELEMENTARY SCHOOL. ED019995
SKILL DEVELOPMENT THROUGH GAMES AND RHYTHMIC ACTIVITIES. ED019996
THE PLAYFUL MODES OF KNOWING. ED050806
CHILDREN AND WAR GAMES EJ 034 533
EFFECTS OF COMPETITION-INDUCED FRUSTRATION ON TWO CLASSES OF MODELED BEHAVIOR EJ 043 284

GENERALIZATION
A STUDY OF ONE LEARNER COGNITIVE STYLE AND THE ABILITY TO GENERALIZE BEHAVIORAL COMPETENCIES. ED040758
LEARNING: THE ROLE OF FACTS AND GENERALIZATIONS EJ 028 638
DECISION PROCESSES IN MULTIDIMENSIONAL GENERALIZATION EJ 038 265
GENERALIZED IMITATION AS A FUNCTION OF DISCRIMINATION DIFFICULTY AND CHOICE EJ 038 455
EFFECTS OF CONTINGENT AND NONCONTINGENT REINFORCEMENT UPON GENERALIZED IMITATION EJ 041 448
EFFECTS OF EXPOSURE TO MODELS ON CONCEPT IDENTIFICATION IN KINDERGARTEN AND SECOND-GRADE CHILDREN EJ 046 240
MEANING CONDITIONING AND AWARENESS AMONG CHILDREN EJ 049 426
CONCEPT ATTAINMENT, GENERALIZATION, AND RETENTION THROUGH OBSERVATION AND VERBAL CODING EJ 053 726
OBSERVATION, REPETITION, AND ETHNIC BACKGROUND IN CONCEPT ATTAINMENT AND GENERALIZATION EJ 059 316

GENETICS
BIOGENETICS OF RACE AND CLASS. ED036317
HUMAN BEHAVIOR GENETICS: PRESENT STATUS AND SUGGESTIONS FOR FUTURE RESEARCH EJ 004 046
CHANGING PROSPECTS FOR CHILDREN WITH HEMOPHILIA EJ 029 952
CHILDHOOD PSYCHOSIS COMBINED WITH XYZ ABNORMALITIES EJ 035 078
DEVELOPMENTAL GENETICS OF BEHAVIORAL CAPACITIES: THE NATURE-NURTURE PROBLEM RE-EVALUATED EJ 037 516
MEDICAL GENETICS AND ADOPTION EJ 037 577
GENETIC FACTORS IN TESTS OF PERCEPTION AND THE RORSCHACH EJ 045 045

GEOGRAPHIC CONCEPTS
DEVELOPMENT OF CHILDREN'S ABILITY TO COORDINATE PERSPECTIVES. ED016516

GEOGRAPHY
INDEPENDENT AND SMALL GROUP ACTIVITIES FOR SOCIAL STUDIES IN THE PRIMARY GRADES. ED031305
LEARNING FROM GEOGRAPHERS EJ 051 206

GEOGRAPHY INSTRUCTION
A STUDY IN THE USE OF A PROGRAMMED GEOGRAPHY UNIT EJ 016 930
LEARNING FROM GEOGRAPHERS EJ 051 206

GEOMETRIC CONCEPTS
MEASURES OF FORM CONSTANCY: DEVELOPMENTAL TRENDS EJ 034 611
A DEVELOPMENTAL STUDY OF SIZE CONSTANCY FOR TWO-VERSUS THREE-DIMENSIONAL STIMULI EJ 040 454

GIFTED
THE RELATIONSHIPS BETWEEN CERTAIN TEACHER CHARACTERISTICS AND ACHIEVEMENT AND CREATIVITY OF GIFTED ELEMENTARY SCHOOL STUDENTS. FINAL REPORT SUMMARY. ED015787
THE CONCEPT OF DEVELOPMENTAL LEARNING. ED023484
EARLY ADMISSION: OPINION VERSUS EVIDENCE EJ 048 045

GOAL ORIENTATION
WHERE IS DAY CARE HEADING. ED016530
THE USE OF INDIVIDUAL GOAL-SETTING CONFERENCES AS A MOTIVATIONAL TECHNIQUE. ED053816
THE PARENTAL ROLE, A FUNCTIONAL-COGNITIVE APPROACH EJ 013 946
TERMINATION OF RESIDENTIAL TREATMENT OF CHILDREN EJ 029 102

GOODNESS OF FIT
THE EFFECTS OF VERBAL PRETRAINING ON THE MULTIDIMENSIONAL GENERALIZATION BEHAVIOR OF CHILDREN EJ 060 784
THREE-CUE SELECTION MODELS APPLIED TO MULTIDIMENSIONAL STIMULUS CLASSIFICATION: ALTERNATIVES TO THE SPIKER, CROLL, AND MILLER ANALYSIS EJ 060 785
ON THE COMPARISON OF PSYCHOLOGICAL THEORIES: A REPLY TO PROFESSOR BOGARTZ EJ 060 786

GOVERNMENT ROLE
CRISIS IN VALUES. 1970 WHITE HOUSE CONFERENCE ON CHILDREN, REPORT OF FORUM 4. (WORKING COPY). ED046523
CHANGING FAMILIES IN A CHANGING SOCIETY. 1970 WHITE HOUSE CONFERENCE ON CHILDREN, REPORT OF FORUM 14. (WORKING COPY). ED046530
CHILDREN AND PARENTS: TOGETHER IN THE WORLD. 1970 WHITE HOUSE CONFERENCE ON CHILDREN, REPORT OF FORUM 15. (WORKING COPY). ED046531
THE SWEDISH CHILD: A SURVEY OF THE LEGAL, ECONOMIC, EDUCATIONAL, MEDICAL AND SOCIAL SITUATION OF CHILDREN AND YOUNG PEOPLE IN SWEDEN. ED050811
RECENT DEVELOPMENTS IN KOREAN SERVICES FOR CHILDREN EJ 032 563
TRENDS AND DILEMMAS IN CHILD WELFARE RESEARCH EJ 038 571

GRADE REPETITION
SUFFER THE LITTLE KENTUCKY FIRST-GRADERS EJ 037 283

GRADE 1
THE PERFORMANCE OF FIRST GRADE CHILDREN IN FOUR LEVELS OF CONSERVATION OF NUMEROUSNESS AND THREE IQ GROUPS WHEN SOLVING ARITHMETIC ADDITION PROBLEMS. ED016535
THE EFFECTS OF TWO VARIABLES ON THE PROBLEM-SOLVING ABILITIES OF FIRST-GRADE CHILDREN. ED019113
A COMPARISON BETWEEN THE ORAL AND WRITTEN RESPONSES OF FIRST-GRADE CHILDREN IN I.T.A. AND T.O. CLASSES. ED019144
ANALYSES OF STORIES DICTATED IN CLASSES OF THE COOPERATIVE PROJECT. ED019993
THE INTERPLAY OF SOME EGO FUNCTIONS IN SIX YEAR OLD CHILDREN. ED020005

SOCIAL STUDIES UNIT: FIRST GRADE. BOSTON-NORTHAMPTON LANGUAGE ARTS PROGRAM, ESEA - 1965, PROJECTS TO ADVANCE CREATIVITY IN EDUCATION. ED027945
GRADE 1: LIVING AND WORKING TOGETHER IN THE COMMUNITY. COURSE OF STUDY AND RELATED LEARNING ACTIVITIES. (CURRICULUM BULLETIN, 1967-68 SERIES, NO. 2B.) ED029682
MATCHED-PAIR SCORING TECHNIQUE USED ON A FIRST-GRADE YES-NO TYPE ECONOMICS ACHIEVEMENT TEST. ED029699
SRA ECONOMICS MATERIALS IN GRADES ONE AND TWO. EVALUATION REPORTS. ED029700
A STUDY IN VISUAL-MOTOR-PERCEPTUAL TRAINING IN FIRST GRADE. ED031292
FAMILY LIFE AROUND THE WORLD, LEVEL I. ED032116
A PILOT STUDY TO ASSESS THE ACADEMIC PROGRESS OF DISADVANTAGED FIRST GRADERS ASSIGNED TO CLASS BY SEX AND TAUGHT BY A TEACHER OF THE SAME SEX. ED035462
PREDICTION OF READINESS IN KINDERGARTEN AND ACHIEVEMENT IN THE FIRST PRIMARY YEAR. STUDY NUMBER TWO. ED043393
A COMPARATIVE STUDY OF FAILURE AVOIDANCE IN CULTURALLY DISADVANTAGED AND NON-CULTURALLY DISADVANTAGED FIRST GRADE CHILDREN. ED044170
EVALUATION OF FOLLOW THROUGH, 1968 - 1969. ED044172
PREDICTION OF ACHIEVEMENT IN THE FIRST PRIMARY YEAR. STUDY NUMBER ONE. ED044180
THE DEVELOPMENT OF TEMPORAL DISCRIMINATION IN YOUNG CHILDREN. ED045187
PRELIMINARY ANALYSIS ON KINDERGARTEN AND FIRST GRADE FOLLOW THROUGH TEST RESULTS FOR 1968-69. ED045202
HARTFORD EARLY CHILDHOOD PROGRAM, HARTFORD, CONNECTICUT: AN URBAN PUBLIC SCHOOL SYSTEM'S LARGE-SCALE APPROACH TOWARD RESTRUCTURING EARLY CHILDHOOD EDUCATION. MODEL PROGRAMS--CHILDHOOD EDUCATION. ED045211
MODEL OBSERVATION KINDERGARTEN AND FIRST GRADE, AMHERST, MASSACHUSETTS: MODEL CLASSROOMS WHICH OFFER COMPLETELY INDIVIDUALIZED SCHEDULING FOR MIXED AGE GROUPS OF KINDERGARTEN AND FIRST-GRADE STUDENTS. MODEL PROGRAMS--CHILDHOOD EDUCATION. ED045219
THE ABILITY OF KINDERGARTEN AND FIRST GRADE CHILDREN TO USE THE TRANSITIVE PROPERTY OF THREE LENGTH RELATIONS IN THREE PERCEPTUAL SITUATIONS. ED048936
HOME LANGUAGE AND PERFORMANCE ON STANDARDIZED TESTS EJ 032 678
INTELLECTUAL OPERATIONS IN TEACHER QUESTION-ASKING BEHAVIOR EJ 032 895
A METHOD OF INCREASING THE ABILITY OF FIRST GRADE PUPILS TO USE PHONETIC GENERALIZATIONS EJ 033 279
TIME ESTIMATION BY YOUNG CHILDREN WITH AND WITHOUT INFORMATIONAL FEEDBACK EJ 033 787
PAIRED-ASSOCIATE LEARNING OF CHILDREN WITH MIXED LIST DESIGNS EJ 035 369
CHAOTIC REINFORCEMENT: A SOCIOECONOMIC LEVELER EJ 035 371
TRAINING CREATIVITY IN YOUNG CHILDREN EJ 035 373
MOTIVATIONAL AND ATTITUDINAL CONTENT OF FIRST GRADE READING TEXTBOOKS EJ 045 084
MOTOR COORDINATION AND YOUNG CHILDREN'S DRAWING ABILITIES EJ 046 257
CHILDREN'S ACQUISITION OF VISUO-SPATIAL DIMENSIONALITY: A CONSERVATION STUDY EJ 047 681
A BASIC VOCABULARY FOR BEGINNING READING EJ 047 894
EFFECT OF REINFORCEMENT CONTINGENCIES IN INCREASING PROGRAMMED READING AND MATHEMATICS BEHAVIORS IN FIRST-GRADE CHILDREN EJ 049 168
EFFECTS OF SOCIOECONOMIC STATUS AND THE VALUE OF A REINFORCER UPON SELF-REINFORCEMENT BY CHILDREN EJ 056 726
DEVELOPMENTAL CHANGES IN CLUSTERING CRITERIA EJ 058 145
STABILITY OF FIRST-GRADE CHILDREN'S DIMENSIONAL PREFERENCES EJ 059 319
"RIGHT," "WRONG," AND DISCRIMINATION LEARNING IN CHILDREN EJ 060 774

GRADE 2

ANALYSES OF STORIES DICTATED IN CLASSES OF THE COOPERATIVE PROJECT. ED019993
GRADE 2: HOW PEOPLE LIVE IN CITY COMMUNITIES AROUND THE WORLD. COURSE OF STUDY AND RELATED LEARNING ACTIVITIES. (CURRICULUM BULLETIN, 1968-69 SERIES, NO. 2.) ED029694
PIAGET'S CONCEPT OF CLASSIFICATION: A COMPARATIVE STUDY OF SOCIALLY DISADVANTAGED AND MIDDLE-CLASS YOUNG CHILDREN. ED046499
INDEPENDENT STUDY AT SEVEN EJ 029 168
EFFECTS OF MEMORY AIDS ON HYPOTHESIS BEHAVIOR AND FOCUSING IN YOUNG CHILDREN AND ADULTS EJ 033 789
MOTIVATIONAL EFFECTS OF BOREDOM ON CHILDREN'S RESPONSE SPEEDS EJ 055 211
MODELING EFFECTS UPON CONCEPTUAL STYLE AND COGNITIVE TEMPO EJ 056 396

GRADE 3

THE PHYSICAL ENVIRONMENT AS A MEDIATING FACTOR IN SCHOOL ACHIEVEMENT. ED046496
PAIRED-ASSOCIATE LEARNING OF CHILDREN WITH MIXED LIST DESIGNS EJ 035 369
FATHER AVAILABILITY AND ACADEMIC PERFORMANCE AMONG THIRD-GRADE BOYS EJ 038 730
THE SUGAR-COATED WORLD OF THE THIRD-GRADE READER EJ 058 171
AGGRESSION ANXIETY, PERCEPTION OF AGGRESSIVE CUES, AND EXPECTED RETALIATION EJ 061 071

GRADE 4

RECOGNITION OF FLASHED WORDS BY CHILDREN EJ 032 676
THE EARLY TRAINING PROJECT: A SEVENTH-YEAR REPORT EJ 033 777
PERCEPTIONS OF NEGRO BOYS REGARDING COLOR AND OCCUPATIONAL STATUS EJ 045 392
MODIFICATION OF IMPULSIVE AND REFLECTIVE COGNITIVE STYLES THROUGH OBSERVATION OF FILM-MEDIATED MODELS EJ 047 676

GRADE 5

ACADEMIC CHEATING: THE CONTRIBUTION OF SEX, PERSONALITY AND SITUATIONAL VARIABLES EJ 055 104
NEGRO PARENTAL BEHAVIOR AND SOCIAL CLASS VARIABLES EJ 059 871

GRADE 6

AN EXPERIMENTAL STUDY OF TWO METHODS OF PRESENTING THE INVERSION ALGORITHM IN DIVISION OF FRACTIONS EJ 033 863
THE MANIPULATION AND MEASUREMENT OF SELF-DISCLOSURE IN PREADOLESCENTS EJ 034 298
EFFECT OF INSTRUCTIONAL SET ON TWELVE-YEAR-OLD CHILDREN'S PERCEPTION OF INTERRUPTION EJ 034 921
CHILDREN'S PERFORMANCE IN SIMPLE AND SUCCESSIVE-REVERSAL CONCEPT IDENTIFICATION PROBLEMS EJ 049 170

GRADE 7

TEACHING GENERAL MUSIC, A RESOURCE HANDBOOK FOR GRADES 7 AND 8. ED018277

GRADE 8

TEACHING GENERAL MUSIC, A RESOURCE HANDBOOK FOR GRADES 7 AND 8. ED018277
FREEDOM FROM EXTERNAL EVALUATION EJ 055 897

GRADING

EFFECTS OF INSTRUCTIONS ON THEME GRADING: GRAMMATICAL VS. HOLISTIC EJ 040 724

GRAMMAR

EXPERIMENTS IN GRAMMATICAL PROCESSING IN CHILDREN. RESEARCH PROJECT NUMBER 1 OF PROJECT HEAD START RESEARCH AND EVALUATION CENTER, SYRACUSE UNIVERSITY RESEARCH INSTITUTE. FINAL REPORT, NOVEMBER 1, 1967. ED026138
EFFECTS OF INSTRUCTIONS ON THEME GRADING: GRAMMATICAL VS. HOLISTIC EJ 040 724
THE EXPERIMENTAL FACILITATION OF CHILDREN'S COMPREHENSION AND PRODUCTION OF FOUR SYNTACTIC STRUCTURES EJ 056 723
CHILDREN'S IMITATION OF GRAMMATICAL AND UNGRAMMATICAL SENTENCES EJ 059 555

GRANDPARENTS

THE CHILDCARE ATTITUDES OF TWO GENERATIONS OF MOTHERS EJ 032 796

GRAPHIC ARTS

A NEW THEORY OF SCRIBBLING AND DRAWING IN CHILDREN. ED017324

GRIEVANCE PROCEDURES

WANTED: RX FOR THE EQUITABLE MANAGEMENT OF PARENT-SCHOOL CONFLICT EJ 014 433

GROUP ACTIVITIES

COOPERATIVE, TRUSTING BEHAVIOR AS A FUNCTION OF ETHNIC GROUP SIMILARITY-DISSIMILARITY AND OF IMMEDIATE AND DELAYED REWARD IN A TWO-PERSON GAME. PART OF THE FINAL REPORT. ED025322
COOPERATION AND COMPETITION OF MEXICAN, MEXICAN-AMERICAN, AND ANGLO-AMERICAN CHILDREN OF TWO AGES UNDER FOUR INSTRUCTIONAL SETS EJ 041 957
THE EFFECTS OF DIFFERENT COMPETITIVE CONTINGENCIES ON COOPERATIVE BEHAVIOR EJ 042 208

GROUP BEHAVIOR

SOCIAL INFLUENCES ON CHILDREN'S HUMOR RESPONSES. ED039933
THE ACQUISITION OF CONSERVATION THROUGH SOCIAL INTERACTION. ED047801
THE EFFECTS OF DIFFERENT COMPETITIVE CONTINGENCIES ON COOPERATIVE BEHAVIOR EJ 042 208
"STRUCTURE" CAN IMPROVE THE GROUP BEHAVIOR OF FIVE-YEAR-OLD CHILDREN EJ 049 937
THE DEVELOPMENT OF DEMOCRATIC VALUES AND BEHAVIOR AMONG MEXICAN-AMERICAN CHILDREN EJ 058 509

GROUP COUNSELING

GROUP WORK WITH PARENTS OF CHILDREN WITH LEARNING DISORDERS. ED019130
A STUDY OF HOME ENVIRONMENT AND READINESS FOR ACHIEVEMENT AT SCHOOL. FINAL REPORT. ED041637
A GROUP METHOD FOR FINDING AND DEVELOPING FOSTER HOMES EJ 027 920

IMPROVING THE SELF-CONCEPTS OF ACADEMIC UNDERACHIEVERS THROUGH MATERNAL GROUP COUNSELING EJ 043 200

GROUP DISCUSSION
INDEPENDENT AND GROUP LEARNING. ED017332
HEAD START EVALUATION AND RESEARCH CENTER, BOSTON UNIVERSITY. REPORT E-II, TEACHER SEMINAR. ED022567
APPLICATION OF GROUP DYNAMICS PROCEDURES TO PROMOTE COMMUNICATION AMONG PARENTS AND TEACHERS. ED042512
ATTITUDE OF BLACK NATURAL PARENTS REGARDING ADOPTION EJ 038 792
A PRESCHOOL EXCHANGE: BLACK MOTHERS SPEAK AND A WHITE TEACHER LISTENS EJ 022 137

GROUP DYNAMICS
A FEASIBILITY STUDY OF PARENT AWARENESS PROGRAMS. FINAL REPORT. ED040742
INCREASING THE EFFECTIVENESS OF PARENTS-AS-TEACHERS. ED048939
THE DEVELOPMENT OF COOPERATION IN ALTERNATIVE TASK SITUATIONS EJ 015 393
SMALL GROUPS - AN EFFECTIVE TREATMENT APPROACH IN RESIDENTIAL PROGRAMS FOR ADOLESCENTS EJ 017 900
RACE AND CONFORMITY AMONG CHILDREN EJ 038 937

GROUP EXPERIENCE
THE EFFECT OF PRESCHOOL GROUP EXPERIENCE ON VARIOUS LANGUAGE AND SOCIAL SKILLS IN DISADVANTAGED CHILDREN. FINAL REPORT. ED019989
COMBINING SOCIAL CASEWORK AND GROUP WORK METHODS IN A CHILDREN'S HOSPITAL EJ 008 319
EXPANDING THE CHILD'S WORLD THROUGH DRAMA AND MOVEMENT EJ 034 421
VALUES AND TECHNIQUES OF CREATIVE DRAMATICS EJ 034 422
DAY CARE FOR CHILDREN: ASSETS AND LIABILITIES EJ 035 802

GROUP GUIDANCE
USING SENSITIVITY TRAINING WITH JUNIOR HIGH SCHOOL STUDENTS EJ 035 169
GROUP SERVICES FOR UNMARRIED MOTHERS: AN INTERDISCIPLINARY APPROACH EJ 035 538

GROUP INTELLIGENCE TESTS
FIVE-YEAR STABILITY OF INTELLIGENCE QUOTIENTS FROM LANGUAGE AND NONLANGUAGE GROUP TESTS EJ 041 723

GROUP LIVING
ALIENATION OF YOUTH AS REFLECTED IN THE HIPPIE MOVEMENT EJ 023 427
SOS CHILDREN'S VILLAGES THROUGHOUT THE WORLD: SUBSTITUTE OR SUPERIOR SERVICE? EJ 058 964

GROUP NORMS
A COMPARISON OF THE NORMS OF THE PERSONAL SOCIAL DEVELOPMENT OF THE PRE-SCHOOL CHILDREN OF DELHI CENTRE AS OBTAINED BY THE CROSS-SECTIONAL STUDY AND THE LONGITUDINAL STUDY. ED039947
THE PROFESSIONAL SELF IMAGE AND THE ATTRIBUTES OF A PROFESSION: AN EXPLORATORY STUDY OF THE PRESCHOOL TEACHER. ED044183

GROUP READING
HAVE YOU DISABLED A POTENTIAL READ'N' DROPOUT LATELY? EJ 016 463

GROUP RELATIONS
THE ACQUISITION OF CONSERVATION THROUGH SOCIAL INTERACTION. ED047801
THE EFFECT OF INDIVIDUAL-CONTINGENT GROUP REINFORCEMENT ON POPULARITY EJ 034 158
INTERPERSONAL RELATIONSHIPS IN RESIDENTIAL TREATMENT CENTERS FOR DISTURBED CHILDREN EJ 037 183
WHAT DOES RESEARCH TEACH US ABOUT DAY CARE: FOR CHILDREN OVER THREE EJ 051 237
THE EFFECT OF SOCIAL INTERACTION ON ACTIVITY LEVELS IN SIX-TO EIGHT-YEAR-OLD BOYS EJ 052 463

GROUP TESTS
DEVELOPMENT OF A GROUP MEASURE TO ASSESS THE EXTENT OF PRE-LOGICAL AND PRE-CAUSAL THINKING IN PRIMARY SCHOOL AGE CHILDREN. ED019136
CONCEPT AND LANGUAGE DEVELOPMENT OF A GROUP OF FIVE YEAR OLDS WHO HAVE ATTENDED THE SYRACUSE UNIVERSITY CHILDREN'S CENTER INTERVENTION PROGRAM. ED046515
FAKABILITY OF SCORES ON THE GROUP PERSONALITY PROJECTIVE TEST EJ 030 792

GROUP THERAPY
COMBINING SOCIAL CASEWORK AND GROUP WORK METHODS IN A CHILDREN'S HOSPITAL EJ 008 319
TANGIBLE REINFORCERS AND CHILD GROUP THERAPY EJ 026 935
REUNITING CHILDREN AND PARENTS THROUGH CASEWORK AND GROUP WORK EJ 027 342
A SENSITIVITY-TRAINING APPROACH TO GROUP THERAPY WITH CHILDREN EJ 039 501
THE PARENTS' CENTER PROJECT: A MULTISERVICE APPROACH TO THE PREVENTION OF CHILD ABUSE EJ 040 043
AN ACTIVITY GROUP APPROACH TO SERIOUSLY DISTURBED LATENCY BOYS EJ 043 194
THE BOY WHO DID NOT CRY EJ 052 310

GROUPING
CONTINUOUS PUPIL PROGRESS IN THE NON-GRADED SCHOOL: HOPE OR HOAX? EJ 028 100

GROUPING (INSTRUCTIONAL PURPOSES)
DEPARTMENTALIZATION IN ELEMENTARY SCHOOLS. ED017329
GROUPING. ED026135
POSITIVE EFFECTS OF A BICULTURAL PRESCHOOL PROGRAM ON THE INTELLECTUAL PERFORMANCE OF MEXICAN-AMERICAN CHILDREN. ED028827
A PILOT STUDY TO ASSESS THE ACADEMIC PROGRESS OF DISADVANTAGED FIRST GRADERS ASSIGNED TO CLASS BY SEX AND TAUGHT BY A TEACHER OF THE SAME SEX. ED035462
HETEROGENEOUS VS. HOMOGENEOUS SOCIAL CLASS GROUPING OF PRESCHOOL CHILDREN IN HEAD START CLASSROOMS. ED045176
A PILOT STUDY OF A PRESCHOOL METHOD OF PREVENTIVE EDUCATION. FINAL REPORT. ED046541
RELATIONSHIP OF CLASSROOM GROUPING PRACTICES TO DIFFUSION OF STUDENTS' SOCIOMETRIC CHOICES AND DIFFUSION OF STUDENTS' PERCEPTION OF SOCIOMETRIC CHOICE EJ 042 791

GROUPING PROCEDURES
CULTURAL DIFFERENCES IN COLOR/FORM PREFERENCE AND IN CLASSIFICATORY BEHAVIOR EJ 024 034

GROUPS
OF TIME AND THE PRONOUN: A NEW METHODOLOGY FOR RESEARCH IN HIGHER EDUCATION EJ 042 881
SYMPOSIUM ON ALTERNATIVE COMMUNITIES: CHILDREN OF THE GROUP FAMILY EJ 049 657

GROWTH PATTERNS
THE ECOLOGY OF GROWTH AND DEVELOPMENT IN A MEXICAN PREINDUSTRIAL COMMUNITY. REPORT 1: METHOD AND FINDINGS FROM BIRTH TO ONE MONTH OF AGE EJ 007 791
GROWTH OF HEAD, FACE, TRUNK, AND LIMBS IN PHILADEPHIA WHITE AND NEGRO CHILDREN OF ELEMENTARY AND HIGH SCHOOL AGE EJ 022 582
MOTHER-INFANT RELATIONSHIP AND WEIGHT GAIN IN THE FIRST MONTH OF LIFE EJ 026 508
THE HOSPITAL AND THE PRESCHOOL CHILD EJ 027 341
PHYSICAL GROWTH AND BODY COMPOSITION: PAPERS FROM THE KYOTO SYMPOSIUM ON ANTHROPOLOGICAL ASPECTS OF HUMAN GROWTH EJ 029 387
THE EFFECT OF EMOTION ON GROWTH EJ 053 653
NUTRITION AND BRAIN DEVELOPMENT IN INFANTS EJ 058 223

GUIDANCE OBJECTIVES
A SCHOOL GUIDANCE CLASS FOR EMOTIONALLY DISTURBED CHILDREN EJ 007 875

GUIDANCE PROGRAMS
COLLABORATION IN SCHOOL GUIDANCE: TASK-ORIENTED GUIDANCE AND ITS STRUCTURE EJ 027 918

GUIDELINES
GUIDELINES FOR ELEMENTARY SOCIAL STUDIES. ED019998
GUIDELINES: PRE-SCHOOL PROJECTS, HEAD START: EARLY CHILDHOOD EDUCATION. REVISED EDITION. ED027948
JDC GUIDE FOR DAY CARE CENTERS, A HANDBOOK TO AID COMMUNITIES IN DEVELOPING DAY CARE CENTER PROGRAMS FOR PRE-SCHOOL CHILDREN. ED027961
COMMUNITY COORDINATED CHILD CARE: 1. INTERIM POLICY GUIDANCE FOR THE 4-C PROGRAM ED034579
AN INSTITUTIONAL ANALYSIS OF DAY CARE PROGRAM. PART I, GROUP DAY CARE: A STUDY IN DIVERSITY. FINAL REPORT. ED036319
TELEVISION GUIDELINES FOR EARLY CHILDHOOD EDUCATION. ED040739
MODELS FOR NONGRADING SCHOOLS: A REPORT OF A NATIONAL SEMINAR. ED049827
CALIFORNIA ADVISORY COUNCIL ON EDUCATIONAL RESEARCH SUGGESTED POLICY ON EDUCATIONAL RESEARCH FOR CALIFORNIA SCHOOL DISTRICTS EJ 018 016
ADOPTIVE PLACEMENT OF THE OLDER CHILD EJ 027 644
PLANNING TRIPS FOR VULNERABLE CHILDREN EJ 048 998
A GUIDE FOR COLLECTING AND ORGANIZING INFORMATION ON EARLY CHILDHOOD PROGRAMS EJ 058 463
A MATTER OF LIFE AND DEATH EJ 059 746

GUIDES
COORDINATED HELPS IN LANGUAGE DEVELOPMENT (CHILD). NORTHWEST REGIONAL EDUCATIONAL LABORATORY STUDY. SECOND EXPERIMENTAL EDITION. ED028831
PERSPECTIVES ON TEACHER-AIDES. A TEACHING TEXT. ED028836
INDIVIDUALIZED MOTOR-PERCEPTUAL STUDY. ED029692
REDUCING BEHAVIOR PROBLEMS: AN OPERANT CONDITIONING GUIDE FOR TEACHERS. ED034570

SCIENCE FOR THE PRIMARY GRADES: QUESTIONS AND ANSWERS. ED035461
PLANNING PARENT-IMPLEMENTED PROGRAMS: A GUIDE FOR PARENTS, SCHOOLS AND COMMUNITIES. ED036322
BOOKS IN PRESCHOOL: A GUIDE TO SELECTING, PURCHASING, AND USING CHILDREN'S BOOKS. ED038178
KINDERGARTEN HANDBOOK: A GUIDE TO THOSE ACTIVELY INTERESTED IN KINDERGARTENS AND IN ESTABLISHING NEW CENTRES. THIRD EDITION. ED039925

HABIT FORMATION
SLEEP PROBLEMS EJ 011 345
RHYTHMIC HABIT PATTERNS IN INFANCY: THEIR SEQUENCE, AGE OF ONSET, AND FREQUENCY EJ 040 295
INFANT HABITUATION AND GENERALIZATION TO DIFFERING DEGREES OF STIMULUS NOVELTY EJ 043 195
HABITUATION AND MEMORY: INFANT CARDIAC RESPONSES TO FAMILIAR AND DISCREPANT AUDITORY STIMULI EJ 056 633
HABITUATION AND RECOVERY OF VISUAL RESPONSE IN THE ALERT HUMAN NEWBORN EJ 057 116
VISUAL HABITUATION IN THE HUMAN INFANT EJ 059 511

HANDICAPPED CHILDREN
SENSORIMOTOR EXPERIENCE AND CONCEPT FORMATION IN EARLY CHILDHOOD. FINAL REPORT. ED019143
THE DESIGN OF A PRE-SCHOOL "LEARNING LABORATORY" IN A REHABILITATION CENTER. ED033764
[A STATEMENT REGARDING THE COMPREHENSIVE PRESCHOOL EDUCATION AND CHILD DAY CARE ACT OF 1969, AND OTHER RELATED BILLS.] ED040761
[A STATEMENT REGARDING THE COMPREHENSIVE PRESCHOOL EDUCATION AND CHILD DAY CARE ACT OF 1969, AND OTHER RELATED BILLS.] ED040762
CONTROL OF LEAD POISONING IN CHILDREN. (PRE-PUBLICATION DRAFT). ED050825
A STUDY IN CHILD CARE (CASE STUDY FROM VOLUME II-A) ED051905
"TUBE" PLAY EJ 008 263
A MULTIHANDICAPPED RUBELLA BABY: THE FIRST EIGHTEEN MONTHS EJ 022 979
BIBLIOGRAPHY ON HOSPITALIZED AND HANDICAPPED CHILDREN EJ 028 677
A PLAY CENTER FOR DEVELOPMENTALLY HANDICAPPED INFANTS EJ 045 012
AN ADVENTURE PLAYGROUND FOR HANDICAPPED CHILDREN IN LONDON EJ 050 487

HANDICRAFTS
INCREASING THE AWARENESS OF ART IDEAS OF CULTURALLY DEPRIVED KINDERGARTEN CHILDREN THROUGH EXPERIENCES WITH CERAMICS. FINAL REPORT. ED016519

HANDWRITING INSTRUCTION
HANDWRITING: THE STATE OF THE CRAFT EJ 048 999

HANDWRITING SKILLS
ILLEGIBILITIES IN THE CURSIVE HANDWRITING OF SIXTH-GRADERS EJ 019 443

HAPTIC PERCEPTION
A LONGITUDINAL ASSESSMENT OF PRESCHOOL CHILDREN IN HAPTIC LEARNING. FINAL REPORT. ED020019
A DEVELOPMENTAL INVESTIGATION OF VISUAL AND HAPTIC PREFERENCES FOR SHAPE AND TEXTURE EJ 008 780
VISUAL AND HAPTIC DIMENSIONAL PREFERENCE: A DEVELOPMENTAL STUDY EJ 026 506
A DEVELOPMENTAL INVESTIGATION OF THE EFFECT OF SENSORY MODALITY ON FORM RECOGNITION IN CHILDREN EJ 026 507
A COMPARATIVE STUDY OF PIAGET'S DEVELOPMENTAL SCHEMA OF SIGHTED CHILDREN WITH THAT OF A GROUP OF BLIND CHILDREN EJ 040 319
VISUAL AND HAPTIC CUE UTILIZATION BY PRESCHOOL CHILDREN: THE RECOGNITION OF VISUAL AND HAPTIC STIMULI PRESENTED SEPARATELY AND TOGETHER EJ 044 698
DISCRIMINATION OF STEREOMETRIC OJBECTS AND PHOTOGRAPHS OF OBJECTS BY CHILDREN EJ 053 749
CROSS-MODAL MATCHING AMONG NORMAL AND RETARDED CHILDREN EJ 053 755
HAPTIC RECOGNITION OF OBJECTS IN CHILDREN EJ 055 099
PSYCHOPHYSICALLY SCALED CUE DIFFERENCES, LEARNING RATE, AND ATTENTIONAL STRATEGIES IN A TACTILE DISCRIMINATION TASK EJ 058 146

HARD OF HEARING
LETTER TO THE TEACHER OF A HARD-OF-HEARING CHILD EJ 029 917

HEALTH
RESEARCH ISSUES IN THE HEALTH AND NUTRITION IN EARLY CHILDHOOD. ED027970
MALNUTRITION, LEARNING AND INTELLECTUAL DEVELOPMENT: RESEARCH AND REMEDIATION. ED039017
THE PREVALENCE OF ANEMIA IN HEAD START CHILDREN. NUTRITION EVALUATION, 1968-69. ED041629
PROFILES OF CHILDREN: 1970 WHITE HOUSE CONFERENCE ON CHILDREN. ED046520
NUTRITIONAL STATUS OF NEW ORLEANS, MISSISSIPPI AND ALABAMA HEAD START CHILDREN. FINAL REPORT. ED047785
THE PSYCHOLOGICAL EFFECTS OF PREGNANCY AND NEONATAL HEALTH THREATS ON CHILD DEVELOPMENT. ED048921
HEALTH AND NUTRITION IN DISADVANTAGED CHILDREN AND THEIR RELATIONSHIP WITH INTELLECTUAL DEVELOPMENT. COLLABORATIVE RESEARCH REPORT. ED052816
THE HEALTH OF CHILDREN--1970: SELECTED DATA FROM THE NATIONAL CENTER FOR HEALTH STATISTICS. ED052827
EARLY MALNUTRITION AND HUMAN DEVELOPMENT EJ 011 914

HEALTH EDUCATION
TEACHING NUTRITION IN THE ELEMENTARY SCHOOL. ED026148
HEAD START ON HEALTH. ED027972
PREVENTION OF IRON-DEFICIENCY ANEMIA IN INFANTS AND CHILDREN OF PRESCHOOL AGE. ED052830

HEALTH GUIDES
HEAD START ON HEALTH. ED027972

HEALTH NEEDS
KEEPING CHILDREN HEALTHY: HEALTH PROTECTION AND DISEASE PREVENTION. 1970 WHITE HOUSE CONFERENCE ON CHILDREN, REPORT OF FORUM 10. (WORKING PAPER). ED046527
HEALTH CARE OF CHILDREN: A CHALLENGE. ED050804
PREVENTION OF IRON-DEFICIENCY ANEMIA IN INFANTS AND CHILDREN OF PRESCHOOL AGE. ED052830
PRIORITIES FOR CHANGE--SOME PRELIMINARY PROPOSALS FROM THE WHITE HOUSE CONFERENCE ON CHILDREN EJ 032 611

HEALTH OCCUPATIONS EDUCATION
NURSES GAIN FROM FIELD WORK WITH YOUNG CHILDREN EJ 007 301

HEALTH PERSONNEL
PROGRAMS FOR INFANTS AND YOUNG CHILDREN. PART III: HEALTH. ED047809

HEALTH PROGRAMS
HEAD START EVALUATION AND RESEARCH CENTER, UNIVERSITY OF KANSAS. FINAL REPORT ON RESEARCH ACTIVITIES. ED021614
HEAD START EVALUATION AND RESEARCH CENTER, UNIVERSITY OF KANSAS. REPORT NO. VIII, PHYSICAL DEVELOPMENT OF CHILDREN IN THE HEAD START PROGRAM IN THE CENTRAL UNITED STATES. ED021644
THE RELATIONSHIP BETWEEN HEMOGLOBIN LEVEL AND INTELLECTUAL FUNCTION. ED028830
PROGRAMS FOR INFANTS AND YOUNG CHILDREN. PART III: HEALTH. ED047809
COMBATING MALNUTRITION THROUGH MATERNAL AND CHILD HEALTH PROGRAMS EJ 007 161
NEW ZEALAND'S DENTAL SERVICE FOR CHILDREN EJ 007 162
PLANNING FOR A MASS ATTACK ON RUBELLA EJ 007 164
PROMOTING CHILD HEALTH THROUGH COMPREHENSIVE CARE EJ 007 165
HEALTH CARE THROUGH HEAD START EJ 024 496
CHILD HEALTH ISSUES IN NEW YORK EJ 060 523

HEALTH SERVICES
RESEARCH ISSUES IN CHILD HEALTH, I-IV. PROCEEDINGS OF THE HEAD START RESEARCH SEMINARS: SEMINAR NO. 4, HEALTH AND NUTRITION IN EARLY CHILDHOOD (1ST, WASHINGTON, D.C., NOVEMBER 1, 1968). ED036331
KEEPING CHILDREN HEALTHY: HEALTH PROTECTION AND DISEASE PREVENTION. 1970 WHITE HOUSE CONFERENCE ON CHILDREN, REPORT OF FORUM 10. (WORKING PAPER). ED046527
DELIVERY OF CHILD HEALTH SERVICES. 1970 WHITE HOUSE CONFERENCE ON CHILDREN, REPORT OF FORUM 11. (WORKING PAPER). ED046528
A STUDY IN CHILD CARE (CASE STUDY FROM VOLUME II-A): "A SMALL U. N." DAY CARE PROGRAMS REPRINT SERIES. ED051904
PROMOTING CHILD HEALTH THROUGH COMPREHENSIVE CARE EJ 007 165
AN INTERVIEW WITH ANN DEHUFF PETERS EJ 008 043
HEAD START: A HEAD START TO HEALTH? EJ 036 581
SOME THOUGHTS ON PLANNING HEALTH CARE FOR CHILDREN AND YOUTH EJ 038 021
ADOLESCENT MATERNITY SERVICES: A TEAM APPROACH EJ 047 354
CARING FOR CHILDREN WITH SICKLE CELL ANEMIA EJ 047 355
CHILD HEALTH ISSUES IN NEW YORK EJ 060 523

HEARING LOSS
HEARING LEVELS OF CHILDREN BY AGE AND SEX: UNITED STATES. ED047799

HEART RATE
CARDIAC CLASSICAL CONDITIONING AND REVERSAL IN THE MONGOLOID, ENCEPHALOPATHIC, AND NORMAL CHILD EJ 025 375
AN EXPLORATORY STUDY OF RESTING CARDIAC RATE AND VARIABILITY FROM THE LAST TRIMESTER OF PRENATAL LIFE THROUGH THE FIRST YEAR OF POSTNATAL LIFE EJ 025 376
PATTERNS OF MOTHER-INFANT CONTACT: THE SIGNIFICANCE OF LATERAL PREFERENCE EJ 030 513
ATTENTIONAL RESPONSES OF FIVE-MONTH GIRLS TO DISCREPANT AUDITORY STIMULI EJ 032 893

TERMINOLOGY AND METHODOLOGY RELATED TO THE USE OF HEART RATE RESPONSIVITY IN INFANCY RESEARCH EJ 034 566
CAN NEWBORNS SHOW CARDIAC ORIENTING? EJ 036 078
AGE CHANGES IN CARDIAC DECELERATION WITHIN A FIXED FOREPERIOD REACTION-TIME TASK: AN INDEX OF ATTENTION EJ 043 667
AUTONOMIC RESPONSES OF MALE ADOLESCENTS EXHIBITING REFRACTORY BEHAVIOUR IN SCHOOL EJ 045 109
CARDIAC DECELERATION AND ITS STABILITY IN HUMAN NEWBORNS EJ 046 891
HABITUATION AND MEMORY: INFANT CARDIAC RESPONSES TO FAMILIAR AND DISCREPANT AUDITORY STIMULI EJ 056 633
STABILITY OF THE ORIENTING REFLEX IN INFANTS TO AUDITORY AND VISUAL STIMULI AS INDEXED BY CARDIAC DECELERATION EJ 056 720

HELPING RELATIONSHIP
A CHILD IN DISTRESS: THE INFLUENCE OF NURTURANCE AND MODELING ON CHILDREN'S ATTEMPTS TO HELP EJ 043 314
THE USE OF ROLE PLAYING AND INDUCTION IN CHILDREN'S LEARNING OF HELPING AND SHARING BEHAVIOR EJ 046 467

HEREDITY
FURTHER EVIDENCE ON THE RELATION BETWEEN AGE OF SEPARATION AND SIMILARITY IN IQ AMONG PAIRS OF SEPARATED IDENTICAL TWINS. ED027058
AN INVESTIGATION OF SIMILARITIES IN PARENT-CHILD TEST SCORES FOR EVIDENCE OF HEREDITARY COMPONENTS. ED027060
PERSPECTIVE ON THE JENSEN AFFAIR. ED040760
PERSPECTIVE ON THE JENSEN AFFAIR EJ 020 519
TWINNING: A MARKER FOR BIOLOGICAL INSULTS EJ 021 188
THE INTELLIGENCE OF CHILDREN OF SCHIZOPHRENICS EJ 021 763
DEVELOPMENTAL GENETICS OF BEHAVIORAL CAPACITIES: THE NATURE-NURTURE PROBLEM RE-EVALUATED EJ 037 516
MEDICAL GENETICS AND ADOPTION EJ 037 577

HETEROGENEOUS GROUPING
MULTI-AGE GROUPING--ENRICHING THE LEARNING ENVIRONMENT. ED017343
HETEROGENEOUS VS. HOMOGENEOUS SOCIAL CLASS GROUPING OF PRESCHOOL CHILDREN IN HEAD START CLASSROOMS. ED045176
SOCIAL INTERACTION IN HETEROGENEOUS PRE-SCHOOLS IN ISRAEL. ED049839

HIGH SCHOOL CURRICULUM
IMPROVING HIGH SCHOOL LEARNING PREDICTIONS WITH MULTIPLE JUNIOR HIGH TEST SCORES EJ 016 653

HIGH SCHOOL STUDENTS
PERSISTENCE AS A FUNCTION OF CONCEPTUAL STRUCTURE AND QUALITY OF FEEDBACK EJ 032 932
WORD FLUENCY--INTELLECT OR PERSONALITY? EJ 034 313
SIBLING RESEMBLANCES IN DIVERGENT THINKING EJ 055 106
A COMPARATIVE STUDY OF COUNSELEE PREFERENCES FOR BEHAVIORIST AND CLIENT-CENTERED COUNSELING APPROACHES EJ 058 628
A YOUNG MAN AROUND THE CLASS EJ 059 445

HIGHER EDUCATION
OF TIME AND THE PRONOUN: A NEW METHODOLOGY FOR RESEARCH IN HIGHER EDUCATION EJ 042 881

HISTORICAL REVIEWS
THE INTERNATIONAL WALDORF SCHOOL MOVEMENT. ED015019
CONCEPTUAL EMPHASIS IN THE HISTORY OF DEVELOPMENTAL PSYCHOLOGY: EVOLUTIONARY THEORY, TELEOLOGY, AND THE NATURE-NURTURE ISSUE EJ 034 043
THE HISTORY OF LONGITUDINAL RESEARCH: IMPLICATIONS FOR THE FUTURE EJ 051 779
HOMER FOLKS'S "THE CARE OF DESTITUTE, NEGLECTED AND DELINQUENT CHILDREN" EJ 059 593

HOME INSTRUCTION
PARENT HANDBOOK: DEVELOPING YOUR CHILD'S SKILLS AND ABILITIES AT HOME. ED036327
MOTHERS' TRAINING PROGRAM: EDUCATIONAL INTERVENTION BY THE MOTHERS OF DISADVANTAGED INFANTS. ED043378

HOME PROGRAMS
PRESCHOOL INTERVENTION--A PRELIMINARY REPORT OF THE PERRY PRESCHOOL PROJECT. ED018251
MODIFICATION OF A DEVIANT SIBLING INTERACTION PATTERN IN THE HOME. ED023461
TEACHING MOTHERS TO TEACH: A HOME COUNSELING PROGRAM FOR LOW-INCOME PARENTS. ED028819
ANALYSIS OF HOME ENVIRONMENT AND DEVELOPMENT OF PARENT INTERVENTION. ED035458
EDUCATIONAL INTERVENTION AT HOME BY MOTHERS OF DISADVANTAGED INFANTS. ED039944
A TUTORIAL LANGUAGE PROGRAM FOR DISADVANTAGED INFANTS. ED040766
EDUCATIONAL INTERVENTION IN THE HOME AND PARAPROFESSIONAL CAREER DEVELOPMENT: A FIRST GENERATION MOTHER STUDY. ED045190
DAME SCHOOL PROJECT (BI-LINGUAL PRE SCHOOL PROJECT), SANTA CLARA COUNTY OFFICE OF EDUCATION. FINAL REPORT, AUGUST 1, 1970. ED046514
PROGRAMS FOR INFANTS AND YOUNG CHILDREN. PART II: NUTRITION. ED047808
A STUDY IN CHILD CARE (CASE STUDY FROM VOLUME II-B): "I'M A NEW WOMAN NOW." DAY CARE PROGRAMS REPRINT SERIES. ED051897
A STUDY IN CHILD CARE (CASE STUDY FROM VOLUME II-B): "SOMEPLACE SECURE." DAY CARE PROGRAMS REPRINT SERIES. ED051908
A STUDY IN CHILD CARE (CASE STUDY FROM VOLUME II-B): "THEY BRAG ON A CHILD TO MAKE HIM FEEL GOOD." DAY CARE PROGRAMS REPRINT SERIES. ED051910
EDUCATIONAL INTERVENTION IN THE HOME AND PARAPROFESSIONAL CAREER DEVELOPMENT: A SECOND GENERATION MOTHER STUDY WITH AN EMPHASIS ON COSTS AND BENEFITS. FINAL REPORT. ED052814
THE TRAINING OF FAMILY DAY-CARE WORKERS: A FEASIBILITY STUDY AND INITIAL PILOT EFFORTS. FINAL REPORT. ED053787
CHILDREN UNDER THREE - FINDING WAYS TO STIMULATE DEVELOPMENT. II. SOME CURRENT EXPERIMENTS: STIMULATION VIA PARENT EDUCATION EJ 007 410
CHILDREN UNDER THREE - FINDING WAYS TO STIMULATE DEVELOPMENT. II. SOME CURRENT EXPERIMENTS: A HOME TUTORING PROGRAM EJ 007 411
PARENTS TEACH KINDERGARTEN READING AT HOME EJ 020 774
EDUCATIONAL INTERVENTION AT HOME BY MOTHERS OF DISADVANTAGED INFANTS EJ 034 002
EARLY CHILD STIMULATION THROUGH PARENT EDUCATION EJ 044 006

HOME VISITS
EDUCATIONAL INTERVENTION IN THE HOME AND PARAPROFESSIONAL CAREER DEVELOPMENT: A SECOND GENERATION MOTHER STUDY WITH AN EMPHASIS ON COSTS AND BENEFITS. FINAL REPORT. ED052814
ATTAINMENT OF COGNITIVE OBJECTIVES. TECHNICAL REPORT NO. 3. ED052833
RESULTS OF PARENT AND STUDENT REACTION QUESTIONNAIRE. TECHNICAL REPORT NO. 8. ED052836
REACHING THE YOUNG CHILD THROUGH PARENT EDUCATION EJ 017 852
TEACHER-PARENT WORK IN THE HOME: AN ASPECT OF CHILD GUIDANCE CLINIC SERVICES EJ 027 448
INVOLVING PARENTS IN CHILDREN'S LEARNING EJ 028 845
INTERVENTION IN INFANCY: A PROGRAM FOR BLIND INFANTS EJ 048 904
SYMPOSIUM ON PARENT-CENTERED EDUCATION: 1. THE CHILD'S FIRST TEACHER EJ 054 377

HOMEBOUND CHILDREN
RESEARCH FOR SERVICE TO SEVERELY RETARDED CHILDREN EJ 038 531

HOMOGENEOUS GROUPING
SOCIAL INTERACTION IN HETEROGENEOUS PRE-SCHOOLS IN ISRAEL. ED049839

HOSPITALIZED CHILDREN
PLAY FOR HOSPITALIZED CHILDREN EJ 007 316
COMBINING SOCIAL CASEWORK AND GROUP WORK METHODS IN A CHILDREN'S HOSPITAL EJ 008 319
THE GOAL OF LIFE ENHANCEMENT FOR A FATALLY ILL CHILD EJ 017 423
A REPORT FROM ABROAD...FAMILY PARTICIPATION IN HOSPITAL CARE FOR CHILDREN EJ 024 497
THE USE OF A PLAY PROGRAM BY HOSPITALIZED CHILDREN EJ 026 774
THE HOSPITAL AND THE PRESCHOOL CHILD EJ 027 341
BIBLIOGRAPHY ON HOSPITALIZED AND HANDICAPPED CHILDREN EJ 028 677
IQ CHANGES IN HOSPITALIZED MENTAL RETARDATES EJ 046 727
CARING FOR CHILDREN WITH SICKLE CELL ANEMIA EJ 047 355
A PROGRAM FOR HOSPITALIZED PSYCHOTIC CHILDREN: REGULAR ATTENDANCE, AWAY FROM THE HOSPITAL, AT A COMMUNITY NURSERY SCHOOL EJ 050 938

HOSPITALS
A REPORT FROM ABROAD...FAMILY PARTICIPATION IN HOSPITAL CARE FOR CHILDREN EJ 024 497

HOUSEWIVES
ROLE ORIENTATIONS, MARITAL AGE, AND LIFE PATTERNS IN ADULTHOOD EJ 052 529

HUMAN BODY
BODY SIZE OF CONTEMPORARY GROUPS OF EIGHT-YEAR-OLD CHILDREN STUDIED IN DIFFERENT PARTS OF THE WORLD EJ 003 459
PHYSICAL GROWTH AND BODY COMPOSITION: PAPERS FROM THE KYOTO SYMPOSIUM ON ANTHROPOLOGICAL ASPECTS OF HUMAN GROWTH EJ 029 387
I SEE WHAT YOU MEAN EJ 035 370
BODY BUILD, SEX-ROLE PREFERENCE, AND SEX-ROLE ADOPTION IN JUNIOR HIGH SCHOOL BOYS EJ 035 627
ARTICULATION OF THE BODY CONCEPT AMONG FIRST-GRADE ISRAELI CHILDREN EJ 053 744

EVOLUTION OF THE HUMAN FIGURE IN A THREE-DIMENSIONAL MEDIUM EJ 057 897

HUMAN DEVELOPMENT
A RATIONALE FOR DEVELOPMENTAL TESTING AND TRAINING. ED028835
THE EFFECTS OF PSYCHOSOCIAL DEPRIVATION ON HUMAN DEVELOPMENT IN INFANCY. ED034574
ISSUES IN HUMAN DEVELOPMENT: AN INVENTORY OF PROBLEMS, UNFINISHED BUSINESS AND DIRECTIONS FOR RESEARCH. ED051888
HUMAN BEHAVIOR GENETICS: PRESENT STATUS AND SUGGESTIONS FOR FUTURE RESEARCH EJ 004 046
NEW LIGHT ON THE HUMAN POTENTIAL EJ 026 373
THE EFFECTS OF PSYCHOSOCIAL DEPRIVATION ON HUMAN DEVELOPMENT IN INFANCY EJ 026 815
PHYSICAL GROWTH AND BODY COMPOSITION: PAPERS FROM THE KYOTO SYMPOSIUM ON ANTHROPOLOGICAL ASPECTS OF HUMAN GROWTH EJ 029 387
EXPLORATION OF DEVELOPMENTAL VARIABLES BY MANIPULATION AND SIMULATION OF AGE DIFFERENCES IN BEHAVIOR EJ 048 472
DESIRABILITY JUDGMENTS AS A FUNCTION OF ITEM CONTENT, INSTRUCTIONAL SET, AND SET: A LIFE-SPAN DEVELOPMENTAL STUDY EJ 048 473
LEARNING FROM LOOKING WITHIN: A DIFFERENT FOCUS, RELATING AND RESPONDING THROUGH THE ARTS EJ 057 326
STOP, LOOK, LISTEN -- AND KEEP ON!! EJ 058 133
LOOKING IN -- TO SELF DISCOVERY EJ 058 134
SEX DIFFERENCES IN HUMAN DEVELOPMENT EJ 060 015

HUMAN POSTURE
LEARNING TO OBSERVE--OBSERVING TO LEARN. ED047815

HUMAN RELATIONS
RELATING AND RESPONDING: THE ADULT EJ 050 936

HUMAN RESOURCES
HUMAN RESOURCES FOR INTERNATIONAL STUDIES EJ 038 393

HUMAN SERVICES
KEEPING CHILDREN HEALTHY: HEALTH PROTECTION AND DISEASE PREVENTION. 1970 WHITE HOUSE CONFERENCE ON CHILDREN, REPORT OF FORUM 10. (WORKING PAPER). ED046527
BLACK IDENTITY AND THE HELPING PERSON EJ 008 461
A PLAY PROGRAM IN A PEDIATRIC CLINIC EJ 029 951

HUMANISM
VALUES OF MEXICAN-AMERICAN, NEGRO, AND ANGLO BLUE-COLLAR AND WHITE-COLLAR CHILDREN EJ 052 653

HUMANITIES
ARTS AND HUMANITIES FOR YOUNG SCHOOL CHILDREN. ED032945

HUMOR
SOCIAL INFLUENCES ON CHILDREN'S HUMOR RESPONSES. ED039933
TO LAUGH IS TO KNOW: A DISCUSSION OF THE COGNITIVE ELEMENT IN CHILDREN'S HUMOR. ED051879
DEPENDENCE OF LAUGHTER ON COGNITIVE STRATEGIES EJ 023 964
COGNITIVE DEVELOPMENT AND CHILDREN'S COMPREHENSION OF HUMOR EJ 036 820
THE ROLE OF OPERATIONAL THINKING IN CHILDREN'S COMPREHENSION AND APPRECIATION OF HUMOR EJ 046 233
THE ROLE OF INCONGRUITY AND RESOLUTION IN CHILDREN'S APPRECIATION OF CARTOON HUMOR EJ 060 781

HUNGER
SOME HIGHLIGHTS FROM THE NUTRITION CONFERENCE EJ 017 447
NUTRITION REHABILITATION CENTRES EJ 029 953
HUNGER AND MOTOR RESTRAINT ON AROUSAL AND VISUAL ATTENTION IN THE INFANT EJ 040 298

HYPERACTIVITY
THE USE OF STIMULANT DRUGS IN TREATING HYPERACTIVE CHILDREN EJ 038 022
COGNITIVE STYLES IN HYPERACTIVE CHILDREN AND THE EFFECT OF METHYLPHENIDATE EJ 041 963
ATTENTION IN HYPERACTIVE CHILDREN AND THE EFFECT OF METHYLPHENIDATE (RITALIN) EJ 043 669
PLAYROOM OBSERVATIONS OF HYPERACTIVE CHILDREN ON MEDICATION EJ 048 301
HYPERACTIVITY AND THE MACHINE: THE ACTOMETER EJ 055 876

HYPNOSIS
THE DEVELOPMENT OF HYPNOTIC SUSCEPTIBILITY: A LONGITUDINAL (CONVERGENCE) STUDY EJ 041 449

HYPOTHESIS TESTING
FACTORS ASSOCIATED WITH A PROGRAM FOR ENCOURAGING SELF-INITIATED ACTIVITIES BY FIFTH AND SIXTH GRADE STUDENTS IN A SELECTED ELEMENTARY SCHOOL EMPHASIZING INDIVIDUALIZED INSTRUCTION. ED015785
A COMPARATIVE STUDY OF TWO PRESCHOOL PROGRAMS FOR CULTURALLY DISADVANTAGED CHILDREN--A HIGHLY STRUCTURED AND A TRADITIONAL PROGRAM. ED016524
A REPLICATIVE INVESTIGATION OF THE BUCKINGHAM-DOLCH FREE-ASSOCIATION WORD STUDY. FINAL REPORT. ED017333
SIX STRUCTURE-OF-INTELLECT HYPOTHESES IN SIX-YEAR-OLD CHILDREN. ED023469
GROSS ACTIVITY OF CHILDREN AT PLAY. (INTERNAL REPORT). ED043385
RELATIONSHIPS BETWEEN SELECTED FAMILY VARIABLES AND MATERNAL AND INFANT BEHAVIOR IN A DISADVANTAGED POPULATION. A SUPPLEMENTARY REPORT. ED047784
CORRELATION OF PAIRED-ASSOCIATE PERFORMANCE WITH SCHOOL ACHIEVEMENT AS A FUNCTION OF TASK AND SAMPLE VARIATION. ED049813
COGNITIVE SYNTHESIS, CONSERVATION, AND TASK ANALYSIS EJ 021 768
CONJUNCTIVE AND DISJUNCTIVE RULE LEARNING AS A FUNCTION OF AGE AND FORCED VERBALIZATION EJ 028 637
RECENCY AND SUMMATION EFFECTS OF NONREWARD IN CHILDREN EJ 028 895
ESTIMATES AND ESTIMATE-BASED INFERENCES IN YOUNG CHILDREN EJ 034 541
CHRONOLOGICAL AGE AND PERFORMANCE ON PROBLEMS WITH REPEATED PRESOLUTION SHIFTS EJ 039 628
SEX DIFFERENCES IN BEHAVIOURAL IMPULSIVITY, INTELLECTUAL IMPULSIVITY, AND ATTAINMENT IN YOUNG CHILDREN EJ 051 151
POSITION STRATEGIES IN AN OBJECT DISCRIMINATION TASK EJ 052 458
CHILDREN'S JUDGMENTS OF AGE EJ 052 461
SELF-INITIATED VERBAL REINFORCEMENT AND POSITIVE SELF-CONCEPT EJ 052 462
STIMULUS INTERACTION AND PROBLEM DIFFICULTY IN CHILDREN'S DISCRIMINATION LEARNING EJ 053 480
NONVERBAL INFORMATION STORAGE IN CHILDREN AND DEVELOPMENTAL INFORMATION PROCESSING CHANNEL CAPACITY EJ 053 720
INFANT SMILING TO NONSOCIAL STIMULI AND THE RECOGNITION HYPOTHESIS EJ 053 731
THE ROLE OF LIGHTNESS CONTRAST IN DETERMINING THE MAGNITUDE OF THE DELBOEUF ILLUSION: A REJOINDER TO WEINTRAUB AND COOPER EJ 055 101
AN EVALUATION OF A THEORY OF SPECIFIC DEVELOPMENTAL DYSLEXIA EJ 055 875
HYPOTHESES, STRATEGIES, AND STEREOTYPES IN DISCRIMINATION LEARNING EJ 060 779

IDENTIFICATION
IDENTIFICATION AND EVALUATION OF CHARACTERISTICS OF KINDERGARTEN CHILDREN THAT FORETELL EARLY LEARNING PROBLEMS. FINAL REPORT. ED020006
IDENTIFICATION AND EVALUATION OF CHARACTERISTICS OF KINDERGARTEN CHILDREN THAT FORETELL EARLY LEARNING PROBLEMS. SUMMARY REPORT. ED020007
REVIEW OF SELECTED EARLY EDUCATION RESEARCH IN THE SCHOOL DISTRICT OF UNIVERSITY CITY, MISSOURI, JUNE, 1970. ED044182
DEVELOPMENTAL GROUPINGS OF PRE-SCHOOL CHILDREN. ED046513
PROJECT GENESIS. FINAL REPORT. ED049820
ON THE CONSERVATION OF LIQUIDS EJ 039 640
DEVELOPMENTAL AND EXPERIMENTAL FACTORS ASSOCIATED WITH INFERENTIAL BEHAVIOR EJ 057 905
QUANTITATIVE AND QUALITATIVE ASPECTS OF MEMORY FOR PICTURE STIMULI EJ 057 907

IDENTIFICATION (PSYCHOLOGICAL)
FINAL REPORT ON HEAD START EVALUATION AND RESEARCH: 1967-68 TO THE OFFICE OF ECONOMIC OPPORTUNITY. SECTION I: PART B, ACCURACY OF SELF-PERCEPTION AMONG CULTURALLY DEPRIVED PRESCHOOLS. ED023455
RACE AND SEX IDENTIFICATION IN PRESCHOOL CHILDREN. ED041634
THE PROFESSIONAL SELF IMAGE AND THE ATTRIBUTES OF A PROFESSION: AN EXPLORATORY STUDY OF THE PRESCHOOL TEACHER. ED044183
WHAT DO YOUNG PEOPLE WANT? EJ 011 784
PINK IS A GOOD COLOR. ? EJ 011 785
HERO MODELS EJ 016 607
ROLE PERCEPTIONS AND JOB SATISFACTION AMONG LOWER AND MIDDLE LEVEL JUNIOR COLLEGE ADMINISTRATORS EJ 016 774
PATERNAL ABSENCE, SEX TYPING, AND IDENTIFICATION EJ 019 020
LONGITUDINAL STUDY OF DEVELOPMENT OF THE BODY CONCEPT EJ 021 993
THE IMPACT OF WORDS AND DEEDS CONCERNING ALTRUISM UPON CHILDREN EJ 026 154
PRIOR REINFORCEMENT HISTORY AS AN EXPLANATION FOR THE EFFECTS OF SEX OF SUBJECT AND EXPERIMENTER IN SOCIAL REINFORCEMENT PARADIGMS EJ 030 297
THE EFFECTS OF SEX-ROLE STANDARDS FOR ACHIEVEMENT AND SEX-ROLE PREFERENCE ON THREE DETERMINANTS OF ACHIEVEMENT MOTIVATION EJ 034 454
OLDER BROTHERS' INFLUENCE ON SEX-TYPED, AGGRESSIVE, AND DEPENDENT BEHAVIOR IN FATHER-ABSENT CHILDREN EJ 034 901
SEX-ROLE IDENTITY AND SIBLING COMPOSITION EJ 035 626
BODY BUILD, SEX-ROLE PREFERENCE, AND SEX-ROLE ADOPTION IN JUNIOR HIGH SCHOOL BOYS EJ 035 627
THE RELATION OF ROLE TAKING TO THE DEVELOPMENT OF MORAL JUDGMENT IN CHILDREN EJ 035 991
THE RELATIONSHIP OF BIRTH ORDER AND SEX OF SIBLINGS TO GENDER ROLE IDENTITY EJ 039 901
CONFORMITY IN CHILDREN AS A FUNCTION OF GRADE LEVEL, AND REAL VERSUS HYPOTHETICAL ADULT AND PEER MODELS EJ 040 294

A METHOD FOR STUDYING THE DEVELOPMENT OF GENDER IDENTITY EJ 046 784
SEX-ROLE AND NEED FOR APPROVAL IN ADOLESCENTS EJ 051 014
SELF-ESTEEM, PARENT IDENTIFICATION AND SEX ROLE DEVELOPMENT IN PRESCHOOL AGE BOYS AND GIRLS EJ 051 015
IDENTIFICATION AND CONSCIENCE DEVELOPMENT EJ 052 447
CROSS-SEX IDENTITY IN BARBADOS EJ 058 136

ILLEGITIMATE BIRTHS
MARGINAL CHILDREN OF WAR: AN EXPLORATORY STUDY OF AMERICAN-KOREAN CHILDREN. ED047781
A STUDY OF WED AND UNWED MOTHERHOOD IN ADOLESCENTS AND YOUNG ADULTS EJ 030 715
UNWED MOTHERS AND THEIR DECISIONS TO KEEP OR SURRENDER CHILDREN EJ 040 042
PREVENTING ILLEGITIMATE TEENAGE PREGNANCY THROUGH SYSTEMS INTERACTION EJ 059 671

IMAGERY
THE ROLE OF OVERT ACTIVITY IN CHILDREN'S IMAGERY PRODUCTION EJ 059 315

IMAGINATION
LITERATURE, CREATIVITY AND IMAGINATION EJ 033 510
VALUES AND TECHNIQUES OF CREATIVE DRAMATICS EJ 034 422
A CREATIVE PLAYGROUND EJ 042 406
LITERATURE, CREATIVITY AND IMAGINATION EJ 056 090

IMITATION
HEAD START EVALUATION AND RESEARCH CENTER, UNIVERSITY OF KANSAS. REPORT NO. IIB, AN EXPERIMENTAL ANALYSIS OF VERBAL IMITATION IN PRESCHOOL CHILDREN. ED021635
PUPIL IMITATION OF A REWARDING TEACHER'S VERBAL BEHAVIOR. ED038185
WORDS AND DEEDS ABOUT ALTRUISM AND THE SUBSEQUENT REINFORCEMENT POWER OF THE MODEL. ED043390
ACQUISITION OF COGNITIVE RESPONSES UNDER DIFFERENT PATTERNS OF VERBAL REWARDS EJ 017 712
IMITATION AS A FUNCTION OF VICARIOUS AND DIRECT REWARD EJ 018 323
A PARTIAL TEST OF A SOCIAL LEARNING THEORY OF CHILDREN'S CONFORMITY EJ 018 890
FACTORS INFLUENCING IMITATIVE LEARNING IN PRESCHOOL CHILDREN EJ 018 892
EFFECTS OF REINFORCEMENT BASE-LINE-INPUT DISCREPANCY UPON IMITATION IN CHILDREN EJ 019 009
IMITATION OF AN ANIMATED PUPPET AS A FUNCTION OF MODELING, PRAISE, AND DIRECTIONS EJ 024 693
TRANSFER OF MATCHING AND MISMATCHING BEHAVIOR IN PRESCHOOL CHILDREN EJ 024 701
LONG-TERM RETENTION OF VERBAL IMITATION EJ 024 941
EFFECTS OF VICARIOUS CONSEQUENCES ON IMITATIVE PERFORMANCE EJ 025 635
GENERALIZED IMITATION AND THE DISCRIMINATION HYPOTHESIS EJ 028 636
THE MODELING OF SHARING: EFFECTS ASSOCIATED WITH VICARIOUS REINFORCEMENT, SYMBOLIZATION, AGE, AND GENERALIZATION EJ 028 894
SUBJECT-MODEL SEXUAL STATUS AND VERBAL IMITATIVE PERFORMANCE IN KINDERGARTEN CHILDREN EJ 030 178
A NOTE ON SELECTIVE IMITATION BY A SIX-WEEK-OLD INFANT EJ 034 045
ASSOCIATION AND ABSTRACTION AS MECHANISMS OF IMITATIVE LEARNING EJ 035 367
POWER AND THE INTERNALIZATION OF SELF-DENIAL EJ 036 077
GIRLS' ATTITUDES TOWARD MODELED BEHAVIORS AND THE CONTENT OF IMITATIVE PRIVATE PLAY EJ 036 079
CHILDREN'S "IMITATION" AS A FUNCTION OF THE PRESENCE OR ABSENCE OF A MODEL AND THE DESCRIPTION OF HIS INSTRUMENTAL BEHAVIORS EJ 036 080
THE EFFECTS OF SOCIAL ISOLATION AND CHARACTERISTICS OF THE MODEL ON ACCENT IMITATION IN FOURTH-GRADE CHILDREN EJ 038 171
GENERALIZED IMITATION AS A FUNCTION OF DISCRIMINATION DIFFICULTY AND CHOICE EJ 038 455
EFFECT OF THE PRESENCE OF A HUMAN MODEL ON IMITATIVE BEHAVIOR IN CHILDREN EJ 039 904
IMITATIVE AGGRESSION IN CHILDREN AS A FUNCTION OF OBSERVING A HUMAN MODEL EJ 039 907
ACOUSTIC ANALYSIS OF THE ACQUISITION OF ACCEPTABLE "R" IN AMERICAN ENGLISH EJ 041 056
EFFECTS OF CONTINGENT AND NONCONTINGENT REINFORCEMENT UPON GENERALIZED IMITATION EJ 041 448
THE CONTROL OF IMITATIVE AND NONIMITATIVE BEHAVIORS IN SEVERELY RETARDED CHILDREN THROUGH "GENERALIZED-INSTRUCTION FOLLOWING" EJ 043 196
LEARNING OF AGGRESSION AS A FUNCTION OF PRESENCE OF A HUMAN MODEL, RESPONSE INTENSITY, AND TARGET OF THE RESPONSE EJ 043 198
DISCRIMINATION AND INSTRUCTIONS AS FACTORS IN THE CONTROL OF NONREINFORCED IMITATION EJ 044 157
CONDITIONS GOVERNING NONREINFORCED IMITATION EJ 045 042
GENERALIZED IMITATION: THE EFFECTS OF EXPERIMENTER ABSENCE, DIFFERENTIAL REINFORCEMENT, AND STIMULUS COMPLEXITY EJ 045 044
THE EFFECT OF SUBJECT RACE, MODEL RACE, AND VICARIOUS PRAISE ON VICARIOUS LEARNING EJ 045 458
IMITATION LEARNING OF INFORMATION-PROCESSING EJ 046 252
EFFECTS OF IMITATION OF DIFFERENT REINFORCEMENT COMBINATIONS TO A MODEL EJ 046 255
THE ACQUISITION AND PERFORMANCE OF A SOCIALLY NEUTRAL RESPONSE AS A FUNCTION OF VICARIOUS REWARD EJ 046 889
ABSTRACTION, INFERENCE, AND THE PROCESS OF IMITATIVE LEARNING EJ 047 685
LEARNING TO BE GENEROUS OR STINGY: IMITATION OF SHARING BEHAVIOR AS A FUNCTION OF MODEL GENEROSITY AND VICARIOUS REINFORCEMENT EJ 052 443
DEVELOPMENTAL ASPECTS OF VARIABLES RELEVANT TO OBSERVATIONAL LEARNING EJ 053 740
EFFECTS OF CONCURRENT AND SERIAL TRAINING ON GENERALIZED VOCAL IMITATION IN RETARDED CHILDREN EJ 055 210
COMPARISON OF IMITATION AND COMPREHENSION SCORES BETWEEN TWO LOWER-CLASS GROUPS AND THE EFFECTS OF TWO WARM-UP CONDITIONS ON IMITATION OF THE SAME GROUPS EJ 056 709
MODEL AFFECT AND CHILDREN'S IMITATIVE ALTRUISM EJ 056 719
EFFECTS OF SOCIAL COMPARISON UPON THE IMITATION OF NEUTRAL AND ALTRUISTIC BEHAVIORS BY YOUNG CHILDREN EJ 056 728
EFFECTS OF VICARIOUS CONSEQUENCES AND RACE OF MODEL UPON IMITATIVE PERFORMANCE BY BLACK CHILDREN EJ 058 139
SOME IMMEDIATE EFFECTS OF TELEVISED VIOLENCE ON CHILDREN'S BEHAVIOR EJ 058 216
OUTERDIRECTEDNESS AND IMITATIVE BEHAVIOR OF INSTITUTIONALIZED AND NONINSTITUTIONALIZED YOUNGER AND OLDER CHILDREN EJ 058 694
EXPECTANCY TO PERFORM AND VICARIOUS REWARD: THEIR EFFECTS UPON IMITATION EJ 059 513
CHILDREN'S IMITATION OF GRAMMATICAL AND UNGRAMMATICAL SENTENCES EJ 059 555
SOME FACTORS AFFECTING THE COMPLEXITY OF CHILDREN'S SENTENCES: THE EFFECTS OF MODELING, AGE, SEX, AND BILINGUALISM EJ 060 780
PRODUCTION OF NOVEL AND GRAMMATICAL UTTERANCES BY YOUNG CHILDREN EJ 060 783
IMITATION OF TEACHER PREFERENCES IN A FIELD SETTING EJ 061 070

IMMIGRANTS
AN ISRAELI EXPERIMENTAL GROUP WITH PRIMARY SCHOOL DROPOUTS OUTSIDE THE SCHOOL SETTING EJ 041 630
ADJUSTMENT DIFFERENCES OF SELECTED FOREIGN-BORN PUPILS EJ 041 962
PSYCHIATRIC DISORDER IN THE CHILDREN OF CARIBBEAN IMMIGRANTS EJ 051 152

IMPROVEMENT PROGRAMS
PRELIMINARY FINDINGS FROM A LONGITUDINAL EDUCATIONAL IMPROVEMENT PROJECT BEING CONDUCTED FOR INSTRUCTIONALLY IMPOVERISHED PUPILS IN INTACT SCHOOLS IN THE URBAN SOUTH. ED020021

INCIDENTAL LEARNING
THE EFFECTS OF DIFFERENT TYPES OF REINFORCEMENT ON YOUNG CHILDREN'S INCIDENTAL LEARNING. ED044184
LEARNING OF MEDIA CONTENT: A DEVELOPMENTAL STUDY EJ 033 782
THE RELATIONSHIP BETWEEN INTENTIONAL LEARNING, INCIDENTAL LEARNING, AND TYPE OF REWARD IN PRESCHOOL, EDUCABLE, MENTAL RETARDATES EJ 033 783
DEVELOPMENTAL TRENDS IN THE INTENTIONAL AND INCIDENTAL LEARNING COMPONENTS OF A VERBAL DISCRIMINATION TASK EJ 035 375
THE EFFECTS OF DIFFERENT TYPES OF REINFORCEMENT ON YOUNG CHILDREN'S INCIDENTAL LEARNING EJ 053 752

INCOME
SOCIAL CLASS AND PARENT'S ASPIRATIONS FOR THEIR CHILDREN. REPORT NUMBER 8. ED030482

INDEPENDENT STUDY
EDUCATION FOR INITIATIVE AND RESPONSIBILITY, COMMENTS ON A VISIT TO THE SCHOOLS OF LEICESTERSHIRE COUNTY, APRIL 1967. SECOND EDITION. ED020795
INDEPENDENT LEARNING IN THE ELEMENTARY SCHOOL CLASSROOM. ED036326
HARTFORD EARLY CHILDHOOD PROGRAM, HARTFORD, CONNECTICUT: AN URBAN PUBLIC SCHOOL SYSTEM'S LARGE-SCALE APPROACH TOWARD RESTRUCTURING EARLY CHILDHOOD EDUCATION. MODEL PROGRAMS--CHILDHOOD EDUCATION. ED045211
MORE ON LEARNING-RESOURCE CENTERS EJ 016 819
INDEPENDENT STUDY AT SEVEN EJ 029 168

INDEXES (LOCATERS)
INDEX AND DESCRIPTION OF TESTS. ED025304
MONTESSORI INDEX. THIRD EDITION. ED035435

INDIGENOUS PERSONNEL
CHILD DEVELOPMENT RESEARCH UNIT PROGRESS REPORT, FEBRUARY, 1970. ED049819

INDIVIDUAL ACTIVITIES

THE TEACHING OF INQUIRY SKILLS TO ELEMENTARY SCHOOL CHILDREN. FINAL REPORT. ED020805
INTEGRATED, INDEPENDENT AND INDIVIDUAL LEARNING ACTIVITIES, FIRST AND SECOND GRADES. SUMMER LEARNING ACTIVITIES, SECOND AND THIRD GRADES. BOSTON-NORTHAMPTON LANGUAGE ARTS PROGRAM, ESEA - 1965, PROJECTS TO ADVANCE CREATIVITY IN EDUCATION. ED027946

INDIVIDUAL CHARACTERISTICS

SEX AND RACE DIFFERENCES IN THE DEVELOPMENT OF UNDERPRIVILEGED PRESCHOOL CHILDREN. ED019992
HELPING THE CHILD DEVELOP HIS CREATIVE POTENTIAL. ED026113
IDENTIFICATION AND DEVELOPMENT OF CREATIVE ABILITIES. ED027965
A THEORETICAL APPROACH FOR SELECTING ELEMENTARY SCHOOL ENVIRONMENTAL VARIABLES. ED028834
A DESCRIPTIVE STUDY OF COGNITIVE AND AFFECTIVE TRENDS DIFFERENTIATING SELECTED GROUPS OF PRE-SCHOOL CHILDREN. ED031314
IMPULSIVITY & REFLECTIVITY AS REFLECTED BY THE VARIABLES OF TIME AND ERROR. ED047820
CHILD CARE PARAPROFESSIONALS: CHARACTERISTICS FOR SELECTION. ED053800
SIMILARITIES IN VALUES AND OTHER PERSONALITY CHARACTERISTICS IN COLLEGE STUDENTS AND THEIR PARENTS EJ 012 718
YOUNG CHILDREN IN INSTITUTIONS: SOME ADDITIONAL EVIDENCE EJ 019 359
TWO MODES OF MATERNAL IMMATURITY AND THEIR CONSEQUENCES EJ 023 424
SOME PSYCHIATRIC OBSERVATIONS ON A GROUP OF MALADJUSTED DEAF CHILDREN EJ 026 155
A COMPARISON OF THE CHARACTERISTICS OF JUNIOR HIGH SCHOOL STUDENTS EJ 026 325
EFFECT OF SUCCESS AND FAILURE ON THE REFLECTIVE AND IMPULSIVE CHILD EJ 029 768
EYE CONTACT IN CHILDREN AS A FUNCTION OF AGE, SEX, SOCIAL AND INTELLECTIVE VARIABLES EJ 038 943
EXPRESSIONS OF PERSONALITY IN CREATIONS OF LATENCY AGE CHILDREN EJ 041 446
SOME DEVELOPMENTAL CHANGES IN THE ORGANIZATION OF SELF-EVALUATIONS EJ 044 186
SEX DIFFERENCES IN ADAPTIVE STYLES EJ 045 046
THE INFLUENCE OF NEGRO AND WHITE TEACHERS RATED AS EFFECTIVE OR NONEFFECTIVE ON THE PERFORMANCE OF NEGRO AND WHITE LOWER-CLASS CHILDREN EJ 045 068
CHILD EFFECTS ON ADULT BEHAVIOR EJ 045 107
SOME ANGLES ON PARENT-TEACHER LEARNING EJ 054 162
THE DEVELOPMENT OF THE LANGUAGE OF EMOTIONS: II. INTENTIONALITY IN THE EXPERIENCE OF AFFECT EJ 061 064
PERSONALITY, COGNITIVE, AND DEMOGRAPHIC CHARACTERISTICS OF STUDENT ACTIVISTS AND ACTIVE STUDENTS EJ 061 194

INDIVIDUAL COUNSELING

STRUCTURED FAMILY-ORIENTED THERAPY FOR SCHOOL BEHAVIOR AND LEARNING DISORDERS EJ 019 022

INDIVIDUAL DEVELOPMENT

SEQUENCE IN LEARNING--FACT OR FICTION. ED017330
INDEPENDENT AND GROUP LEARNING. ED017332
THE EFFECT OF EARLY STIMULATION: THE PROBLEM OF FOCUS IN DEVELOPMENTAL STIMULATION. ED022535
SCHOOL READINESS, BEHAVIOR TESTS USED AT THE GESELL INSTITUTE. ED023449
A COMPARISON OF THE NORMS OF THE PERSONAL SOCIAL DEVELOPMENT OF THE PRE-SCHOOL CHILDREN OF DELHI CENTRE AS OBTAINED BY THE CROSS-SECTIONAL STUDY AND THE LONGITUDINAL STUDY. ED039947
DEPENDENCE AND COMPETENCE IN FOUR-YEAR-OLD BOYS AS RELATED TO PARENTAL TREATMENT OF THE CHILD. ED039952
MODEL OBSERVATION KINDERGARTEN AND FIRST GRADE, AMHERST, MASSACHUSETTS: MODEL CLASSROOMS WHICH OFFER COMPLETELY INDIVIDUALIZED SCHEDULING FOR MIXED AGE GROUPS OF KINDERGARTEN AND FIRST-GRADE STUDENTS. MODEL PROGRAMS--CHILDHOOD EDUCATION. ED045219
EMERGENCE OF IDENTITY: THE FIRST YEARS. 1970 WHITE HOUSE CONFERENCE ON CHILDREN, REPORT OF FORUM 2. (WORKING COPY). ED046521
A LONGITUDINAL ASSESSMENT OF THINKING ABILITY OF PRELITERATE CHILDREN DURING A TWO-YEAR PERIOD. FINAL REPORT. ED048946
ISSUES IN HUMAN DEVELOPMENT: AN INVENTORY OF PROBLEMS, UNFINISHED BUSINESS AND DIRECTIONS FOR RESEARCH. ED051888
OR PSYCHOANALYTIC THEORY OF ADOLESCENCE? EJ 007 790
ON SEPARATION AND SCHOOL ENTRANCE EJ 017 902
PRECURSORS OF INTELLIGENCE AND CREATIVITY: A LONGITUDINAL STUDY OF ONE CHILD'S DEVELOPMENT EJ 020 521
ALIENATION: AN ESSENTIAL PROCESS OF THE PSYCHOLOGY OF ADOLESCENCE EJ 023 426
LET DO IT MY WAY EJ 028 846
BRIDGING THE CONCEPT GAP IN WORK WITH YOUTH EJ 031 644
THEORETICAL NOTES ON POWER MOTIVATION EJ 032 677
LITERATURE, CREATIVITY AND IMAGINATION EJ 033 510
CONCEPTUAL EMPHASIS IN THE HISTORY OF DEVELOPMENTAL PSYCHOLOGY: EVOLUTIONARY THEORY, TELEOLOGY, AND THE NATURE-NURTURE ISSUE EJ 034 043
CHILDREN: THEIR POTENTIALS EJ 034 312
INCREASING AND RELEASING HUMAN POTENTIALS EJ 034 710
NEW CONCEPTS OF HUMAN POTENTIALS: NEW CHALLENGE FOR TEACHERS EJ 034 711
A TEST OF ERIKSON'S THEORY OF EGO EPIGENESIS EJ 039 898
INTELLECTUAL EVOLUTION FROM ADOLESCENCE TO ADULTHOOD EJ 050 073
SELF-GUIDANCE AS AN EDUCATIONAL GOAL AND THE SELECTION OF OBJECTIVES EJ 052 878
CONFRONTING PERSISTENT CONCERNS EJ 054 382

INDIVIDUAL DIFFERENCES

HEAD START EVALUATION AND RESEARCH CENTER, THE UNIVERSITY OF CHICAGO. REPORT A, MATERNAL INFLUENCES UPON DEVELOPMENT OF COGNITION. ED022550
AN EXPLORATORY INVESTIGATION OF THE CARROLL LEARNING MODEL AND THE BLOOM STRATEGY FOR MASTERY LEARNING. ED028841
THE RELATIONSHIP OF INDIVIDUAL DIFFERENCES IN THE ORIENTING RESPONSE TO COMPLEX LEARNING IN KINDERGARTNERS. ED031299
PERSONALITY DEVELOPMENT IN DISADVANTAGED FOUR-YEAR-OLD BOYS: OBSERVATIONS WITH PLAY TECHNIQUES. ED031310
THE RELATION OF CONCEPTUAL STYLES AND MODE OF PERCEPTION TO GRAPHIC EXPRESSION. ED040743
THE RELATIONSHIP OF INDIVIDUAL DIFFERENCES IN THE ORIENTING RESPONSE TO COMPLEX LEARNING IN KINDERGARTNERS. REPORT FROM THE MOTIVATION AND INDIVIDUAL DIFFERENCES IN LEARNING AND RETENTION PROJECT. ED046544
INDIVIDUAL DIFFERENCES IN THE DEVELOPMENT OF SOME ATTACHMENT BEHAVIORS. ED050827
ALL ABOUT ME. UNIT 1 CURRICULUM GUIDE. ED053789
MOVEMENT AND MOVEMENT PATTERNS OF EARLY CHILDHOOD. ED053796
DESIGNS AND PROPOSAL FOR EARLY CHILDHOOD RESEARCH: A NEW LOOK: ON ATTAINING THE GOALS OF EARLY CHILDHOOD EDUCATION. (ONE IN A SERIES OF SIX PAPERS). ED053807
I WAS A SLOW-LEARNER EJ 017 422
THE BEHAVIORAL AROUSAL THRESHOLD IN INFANT SLEEP AS A FUNCTION OF TIME AND SLEEP STATE EJ 036 091
INDIVIDUAL DIFFERENCES IN THE VISUAL PURSUIT BEHAVIOR OF NEONATES EJ 036 092
EVALUATION UNDER INDIVIDUALIZED INSTRUCTION EJ 036 826
A LONGITUDINAL STUDY OF CHANGES IN EGO IDENTITY STATUS DURING THE FRESHMAN YEAR AT COLLEGE EJ 043 193
LE NOUVEAU PROGRAMME D'ACTIVITES EDUCATRICES DANS LES ESTABLISSEMENTS PRESCOLAIRES EN YOUGOSLAVIE EJ 045 011
INDIVIDUAL DIFFERENCES IN CHILDREN'S REACTIONS TO REWARD AND NONREWARD EJ 045 459
EMERGENCE AND PERSISTENCE OF BEHAVIORAL DIFFERENCES IN TWINS EJ 053 732
THE SORE-FOOTED DUCK EJ 053 929
STATE AS VARIABLE, AS OBSTACLE, AND AS MEDIATOR OF STIMULATION IN INFANT RESEARCH EJ 058 220
INDIVIDUAL DIFFERENCES IN THE DEVELOPMENT OF SOME ATTACHMENT BEHAVIORS EJ 058 222
INCENTIVE EFFECTS IN CHILDREN'S CREATIVITY EJ 059 317
RELATIONSHIPS OF PARENTAL BEHAVIOR TO "DISADVANTAGED" CHILDREN'S INTRINSIC-EXTRINSIC MOTIVATION FOR TASK STRIVING EJ 059 870

INDIVIDUAL INSTRUCTION

THE DEVELOPMENT OF AN ELEMENTARY SCHOOL MATHEMATICS CURRICULUM FOR INDIVIDUALIZED INSTRUCTION. ED013120
AN INDIVIDUALIZED SCIENCE LABORATORY. ED013664
FACTORS ASSOCIATED WITH A PROGRAM FOR ENCOURAGING SELF-INITIATED ACTIVITIES BY FIFTH AND SIXTH GRADE STUDENTS IN A SELECTED ELEMENTARY SCHOOL EMPHASIZING INDIVIDUALIZED INSTRUCTION. ED015785
EARLY INTELLECTIVE TRAINING AND SCHOOL PERFORMANCE. SUMMARY OF NIH GRANT NUMBER HD-02253. ED025324
EVERY CHILD A TEACHER EJ 044 508

INDIVIDUAL NEEDS

A PLAN FOR CONTINUING GROWTH. ED046493
THE RIGHTS OF CHILDREN. 1970 WHITE HOUSE CONFERENCE ON CHILDREN, REPORT OF FORUM 22. (WORKING COPY). ED046537
ENCOURAGEMENT FOR THE YOUNG WRITER EJ 029 414
LETTER TO THE TEACHER OF A HARD-OF-HEARING CHILD EJ 029 917
NEW CONCEPTS OF HUMAN POTENTIALS: NEW CHALLENGE FOR TEACHERS EJ 034 711
WHAT IS A GOOD KINDERGARTEN? EJ 035 243
THE NEW SCHOOL EJ 036 327
EVALUATION UNDER INDIVIDUALIZED INSTRUCTION EJ 036 826
WHAT DOES RESEARCH TEACH US ABOUT DAY CARE: FOR CHILDREN OVER THREE EJ 051 237
THE SORE-FOOTED DUCK EJ 053 929
LEARNING FROM LOOKING WITHIN: A DIFFERENT FOCUS, RELATING AND RESPONDING THROUGH THE ARTS EJ 057 326

INDIVIDUAL POWER
THEORETICAL NOTES ON POWER MOTIVATION EJ 032 677
POWER AND THE INTERNALIZATION OF SELF-DENIAL EJ 036 077
SELF-GUIDANCE AS AN EDUCATIONAL GOAL AND THE SELECTION OF OBJECTIVES EJ 052 878

INDIVIDUAL TESTS
THE WORLD TEST: DEVELOPMENTAL ASPECTS OF A PLAY TECHNIQUE EJ 031 629
A SHORT, RELIABLE, EASY TO ADMINISTER INDIVIDUAL INTELLIGENCE TEST FOR SPECIAL CLASS PLACEMENT EJ 041 724

INDIVIDUALIZED CURRICULUM
WHAT'S AHEAD FOR PREADOLESCENCE? EJ 009 034
HOW ELSE? EJ 015 060
INDIVIDUALIZING INSTRUCTION THROUGH DIAGNOSIS AND EVALUATION EJ 021 629

INDIVIDUALIZED DIFFERENCES
A TEACHER DISCOVERS INDIVIDUALIZED INSTRUCTION EJ 035 171

INDIVIDUALIZED INSTRUCTION
THE MISPLACED ADAPTATION TO INDIVIDUAL DIFFERENCES. ED040754
THE SOUTHSIDE EXPERIMENT IN PERSONALIZED EDUCATION. ED042505
3 ON 2 PROGRAM: ADMINISTRATIVE GUIDE AND IMPLEMENTATION HANDBOOK. (REVISED EDITION). ED050812
PERSONALIZED EDUCATION IN SOUTHSIDE SCHOOL EJ 013 561
THE COMPUTER CAN HELP INDIVIDUALIZE INSTRUCTION EJ 018 306
TEACHING THE UNTEACHABLES EJ 021 514
THE STUDENT IN PROJECT PLAN: A FUNCTIONING PROGRAM OF INDIVIDUALIZED EDUCATION EJ 028 501
EDUCATIONAL TECHNOLOGY: A CRITIQUE EJ 029 343
A TEACHER DISCOVERS INDIVIDUALIZED INSTRUCTION EJ 035 171
EVALUATION UNDER INDIVIDUALIZED INSTRUCTION EJ 036 826
EVALUATIVE USES OF UNCONVENTIONAL MEASUREMENT TECHNIQUES IN AN EDUCATIONAL SYSTEM EJ 042 347
CREATING A CLIMATE FOR INDIVIDUALIZING INSTRUCTION EJ 044 511
INSTRUCTIONAL PROGRAMMING FOR THE INDIVIDUAL PUPIL IN THE MULTIUNIT ELEMENTARY SCHOOL EJ 050 591
INDIVIDUALIZATION - TEACHERS' VIEWS EJ 052 067

INDIVIDUALIZED PROGRAMS
THE EFFECTS OF ASSESSMENT AND PERSONALIZED PROGRAMMING ON SUBSEQUENT INTELLECTUAL DEVELOPMENT OF PREKINDERGARTEN AND KINDERGARTEN CHILDREN. ED013663
KINDERGARTEN RESEARCH STUDY: LEVEL OF SKILLS DEVELOPMENT RELATED TO GROWTH IN SKILLS AND TO READINESS FOR THE FIRST PRIMARY YEAR. ED026111
AN EXPLORATORY INVESTIGATION OF THE CARROLL LEARNING MODEL AND THE BLOOM STRATEGY FOR MASTERY LEARNING. ED028841
THE EFFECTS OF ASSESSMENT AND PERSONALIZED PROGRAMMING ON SUBSEQUENT INTELLECTUAL DEVELOPMENT OF PREKINDERGARTEN AND KINDERGARTEN CHILDREN. FINAL REPORT. ED045198
PROJECT GENESIS. FINAL REPORT. ED049820
IF SCHOOLS ARE TO MEET THEIR RESPONSIBILITIES TO ALL CHILDREN EJ 022 977

INDUSTRIAL ARTS
INDUSTRIAL ARTS FOR THE PRIMARY GRADES. ED035459

INDUSTRIALIZATION
INDUSTRIALIZATION, CHILD-REARING PRACTICES, AND CHILDREN'S PERSONALITY EJ 015 199

INDUSTRY
PROCEEDINGS OF THE CONFERENCE ON INDUSTRY AND DAY CARE (URBAN RESEARCH CORPORATION, CHICAGO, 1970). ED047780
A STUDY IN CHILD CARE (CASE STUDY FROM VOLUME II-A): "HEY, GEORGIE GET YOURSELF TOGETHER." DAY CARE PROGRAMS REPRINT SERIES. ED051902
INDUSTRY AND DAY CARE EJ 050 380

INFANCY
COGNITIVE DEVELOPMENT IN INFANTS OF DIFFERENT AGE LEVELS AND FROM DIFFERENT ENVIRONMENTAL BACKGROUNDS. ED015786
SOCIAL CLASS AND COGNITIVE DEVELOPMENT IN INFANCY. ED019111
PLAY BEHAVIOR IN THE YEAR-OLD INFANT: EARLY SEX DIFFERENCES. ED022545
PERSONALITY DEVELOPMENT IN INFANCY ED024439
INFORMAL EDUCATION DURING THE FIRST MONTHS OF LIFE. ED024452
INFANCY IN HOLLAND: THE FIRST THREE MONTHS. ED031296
INFANT DAY CARE AND ATTACHMENT. ED033755
AN EDUCATION SYSTEM FOR HIGH-RISK INFANTS: A PREVENTIVE APPROACH TO DEVELOPMENTAL AND LEARNING DISABILITIES. ED043379
INTRODUCTION TO THE 1968 INFANT CONFERENCE PAPERS EJ 003 552
PERCEPTUAL-COGNITIVE DEVELOPMENT IN INFANCY: A GENERALIZED EXPECTANCY MODEL AS A FUNCTION OF THE MOTHER-INFANT INTERACTION EJ 003 553
CONTINUNITY IN COGNITIVE DEVELOPMENT DURING THE FIRST YEAR EJ 003 554
RECEPTIVE LANGUAGE DEVELOPMENT IN INFANCY: ISSUES AND PROBLEMS EJ 020 396
ATTENTIONAL PREFERENCE AND EXPERIENCE: II. AN EXPLORATORY LONGITUDINAL STUDY OF THE EFFECT OF VISUAL FAMILIARITY AND RESPONSIVENESS EJ 025 363
ATTENTIONAL PREFERENCE AND EXPERIENCE: III. VISUAL FAMILIARITY AND LOOKING TIME EJ 025 364
AN EXPLORATORY STUDY OF RESTING CARDIAC RATE AND VARIABILITY FROM THE LAST TRIMESTER OF PRENATAL LIFE THROUGH THE FIRST YEAR OF POSTNATAL LIFE EJ 025 376
PSYCHOLOGICAL DEVELOPMENT--PREDICTIONS FROM INFANCY EJ 025 626
THE EFFECTS OF PSYCHOSOCIAL DEPRIVATION ON HUMAN DEVELOPMENT IN INFANCY EJ 026 815
COGNITIVE DEVELOPMENT IN INFANCY: ASSESSMENT, ACCELERATION, AND ACTUALIZATION EJ 037 493
COGNITIVE-PERCEPTUAL DEVELOPMENT IN INFANCY: SETTING FOR THE SEVENTIES EJ 038 262
ORIGINS OF SOCIAL DEVELOPMENT IN INFANCY EJ 038 570
MOTHER-INFANT INTERACTION AND INFANT DEVELOPMENT AMONG THE WOLOF OF SENEGAL EJ 051 017
INFANCY AND THE OPTIMAL LEVEL OF STIMULATION EJ 058 697
PIAGET'S CONSTRUCTIONIST THEORY EJ 059 876

INFANT BEHAVIOR
SOCIAL AND EMOTIONAL BEHAVIOR IN INFANCY--SOME DEVELOPMENTAL ISSUES AND PROBLEMS. ED015789
THE INITIAL COORDINATION OF SENSORIMOTOR SCHEMAS IN HUMAN INFANTS - PIAGET'S IDEAS AND THE ROLE OF EXPERIENCE. ED016511
AN INFANT RATING SCALE, ITS VALIDATION AND USEFULNESS. ED016513
A NEW THEORY OF SCRIBBLING AND DRAWING IN CHILDREN. ED017324
NOVELTY AND FAMILIARITY AS DETERMINANTS OF INFANT ATTENTION WITHIN THE FIRST YEAR. ED023483
MEMORY AND "CONTINGENCY ANALYSIS" IN INFANT LEARNING. ED024437
DETERMINANTS OF INFANT BEHAVIOUR IV. ED032947
AN ANALYSIS OF BEHAVIORAL MECHANISMS INVOLVED IN CONTROL OVER INFANT FEEDING BEHAVIOR ED037236
STUDIES OF SUCKING BEHAVIOR IN THE HUMAN NEWBORN: THE DIAGNOSTIC AND PREDICTIVE VALUE OF MEASURES OF EARLIEST ORAL BEHAVIOR. ED039014
AN APPROACH TO THE STUDY OF INFANT BEHAVIOR. ED039031
EMOTIONAL DEVELOPMENT IN THE FIRST TWO YEARS. ED039936
ATTENTIONAL PREFERENCE AND EXPERIENCE: II. AN EXPLORATORY LONGITUDINAL STUDY OF THE EFFECTS OF VISUAL FAMILIARITY AND RESPONSIVENESS. ED039938
ATTENTIONAL PREFERENCE AND EXPERIENCE: III. VISUAL FAMILIARITY AND LOOKING TIME. ED039939
ATTENTIONAL PREFERENCE AND EXPERIENCE: I. INTRODUCTION. ED040751
RELATIVE SOOTHING EFFECTS OF VERTICAL AND HORIZONTAL ROCKING. ED046504
THE ROLE OF EXPERIENCE IN THE BEHAVIORAL DEVELOPMENT OF HUMAN INFANTS: CURRENT STATUS AND RECOMMENDATIONS. ED048917
STATE AS VARIABLE, AS OBSTACLE AND AS MEDIATOR OF STIMULATION IN INFANT RESEARCH. ED049825
INFANT DEVELOPMENT IN LOWER CLASS AMERICAN FAMILIES. ED049836
INDIVIDUAL DIFFERENCES IN THE DEVELOPMENT OF SOME ATTACHMENT BEHAVIORS. ED050827
MOTHER-INFANT INTERACTION AND INFANT DEVELOPMENT AMONG THE WOLOF OF SENEGAL. ED051885
CONDITIONING TASKS PERFORMANCE IN INFANCY AND EARLY CHILDHOOD AS A STABLE AND MEASURABLE ASPECT OF BEHAVIOR. FINAL REPORT. ED051890
INFANT REACTIVITY TO REDUNDANT PROPRIOCEPTIVE AND AUDITORY STIMULATION: A TWIN STUDY. ED052825
STATE AS AN INFANT-ENVIRONMENT INTERACTION: AN ANALYSIS OF MOTHER-INFANT BEHAVIOR AS A FUNCTION OF SEX. ED052829
WHAT'S THROWN OUT WITH THE BATH WATER: A BABY? ED053801
THE EFFECTS OF EXPERIENCE ON INFANTS' REACTIONS TO SEPARATION FROM THEIR MOTHERS. ED053802
APPLICATION OF MARKOV PROCESSES TO THE CONCEPT OF STATE. ED053813
A DEVELOPMENTAL STUDY OF INFORMATION PROCESSING WITHIN THE FIRST THREE YEARS OF LIFE: RESPONSE DECREMENT TO A REDUNDANT SIGNAL EJ 013 947
THE OCULAR RESPONSE OF HUMAN NEWBORNS TO INTERMITTANT VISUAL MOVEMENT EJ 015 394
THE EFFECTS OF TEMPERATURE AND POSITION ON THE SUCKING PRESSURE OF NEWBORN INFANTS EJ 018 260
INDIVIDUAL DIFFERENCES IN THE INFANT'S DISTRIBUTION OF ATTENTION TO STIMULUS DISCREPANCY EJ 019 014
ON RELATING AN INFANT'S OBSERVATION TIME OF VISUAL STIMULI WITH CHOICE-THEORY ANALYSIS EJ 019 016
ATTACHMENT BEHAVIORS IN HUMAN INFANTS: DISCRIMINATIVE VOCALIZATION ON MATERNAL SEPARATION EJ 019 019
EARLY MOTHER-INFANT INTERACTION AND 24-HOUR PATTERNS OF ACTIVITY AND SLEEP EJ 019 594

DIFFERENTIAL VISUAL BEHAVIOR TO HUMAN AND HUMANOID FACES IN EARLY INFANCY EJ 019 595
PATTERNS OF FEAR DEVELOPMENT DURING INFANCY EJ 020 718
EASE OF HABITUATION TO REPEATED AUDITORY AND SOMESTHETIC STIMULATION IN THE HUMAN NEWBORN EJ 021 077
RECOVERY OF HABITUATION IN INFANTS EJ 021 078
THE RELATION BETWEEN THE AMOUNT OF TIME INFANTS SPEND AT VARIOUS STATES AND THE DEVELOPMENT OF VISUAL BEHAVIOR EJ 021 082
MEMORY IN THE INFANT EJ 021 760
THE DEVELOPMENT OF THE CONCEPT OF OBJECT AS RELATED TO INFANT-MOTHER ATTACHMENT EJ 021 998
THE ROLE OF OBJECT ORIENTATION IN INFANT PERCEPTION EJ 024 695
EFFECT OF FAMILIAR AND UNFAMILIAR ENVIRONMENTS ON PROXIMITY BEHAVIOR OF YOUNG CHILDREN EJ 024 935
VISUAL ALERTNESS IN NEONATES AS EVOKED BY MATERNAL CARE EJ 027 847
CHANGES IN THE NONNUTRITIVE SUCKING RESPONSE TO STIMULATION DURING INFANCY EJ 027 848
COMPLEXITY, CONTOUR, AND AREA AS DETERMINANTS OF ATTENTION IN INFANTS EJ 029 361
FIXATION TIME AND TEMPO OF PLAY IN INFANTS EJ 029 363
ON THE RELIABILITY OF THE GRAHAM/ROSENBLITH BEHAVIOUR TEST FOR NEONATES EJ 031 630
NEONATE-MOTHER INTERACTION: EFFECTS OF PARITY ON FEEDING BEHAVIOR EJ 032 892
A NOTE ON SELECTIVE IMITATION BY A SIX-WEEK-OLD INFANT EJ 034 045
SMILING TO SOCIAL STIMULI: ELICITING AND CONDITIONING EFFECTS EJ 034 536
STIMULUS CONTROL OF PARENT OR CARETAKER BEHAVIOR BY OFFSPRING EJ 034 538
IRRELEVANCE OF NEWBORN WAKING STATES TO SOME MOTOR AND APPETITIVE RESPONSES EJ 036 076
THE BEHAVIORAL AROUSAL THRESHOLD IN INFANT SLEEP AS A FUNCTION OF TIME AND SLEEP STATE EJ 036 091
DELAYED REINFORCEMENT AND VOCALIZATION RATES OF INFANTS EJ 036 127
INFANTS' RECOGNITION MEMORY FOR A SERIES OF VISUAL STIMULI EJ 037 342
THE MEASUREMENT OF VISUAL ATTENTION IN INFANTS: A COMPARISON OF TWO METHODOLOGIES EJ 037 494
DEVELOPMENT OF THE OBJECT CONCEPT AS MANIFESTED IN CHANGES IN THE TRACKING BEHAVIOR OF INFANTS BETWEEN 7 AND 20 WEEKS OF AGE EJ 038 264
A DECADE OF INFANT CONDITIONING AND LEARNING RESEARCH EJ 038 454
COGNITIVE COMPONENTS OF SEPARATION ANXIETY EJ 039 900
THE IMPACT OF MOTHER'S PRESENCE UPON BEHAVIOR: THE FIRST YEAR EJ 039 908
RHYTHMIC HABIT PATTERNS IN INFANCY: THEIR SEQUENCE, AGE OF ONSET, AND FREQUENCY EJ 040 295
ATTENTION DISTRIBUTION IN THE 24-MONTH-OLD CHILD: VARIATIONS IN COMPLEXITY AND INCONGRUITY OF THE HUMAN FORM EJ 040 296
PRESTIMULUS ACTIVITY LEVEL AND RESPONSIVITY IN THE NEONATE EJ 040 297
HUNGER AND MOTOR RESTRAINT ON AROUSAL AND VISUAL ATTENTION IN THE INFANT EJ 040 298
NEWBORN'S RESPONSE TO THE CRY OF ANOTHER INFANT EJ 041 959
EFFECTS OF DIFFERENTIAL EXPERIENCE ON INFANTS' PERFORMANCE IN A PIAGETIAN STAGE IV OBJECT-CONCEPT TASK EJ 042 956
SATIATION OF VISUAL REINFORCEMENT IN YOUNG INFANTS EJ 043 666
INFANT-CARETAKER INTERACTIONS EJ 043 670
NEWBORN AND PRESCHOOLER: ORGANIZATION OF BEHAVIOR AND RELATIONS BETWEEN PERIODS EJ 045 110
A MICRO-ANALYSIS OF MOTHER-INFANT INTERACTION. BEHAVIOR REGULATING SOCIAL CONTACT BETWEEN A MOTHER AND HER 3 1/2 MONTH-OLD TWINS EJ 048 300
MOTHER-INFANT INTERACTION AND INFANT DEVELOPMENT AMONG THE WOLOF OF SENEGAL EJ 051 017
EXPLORATORY AND PLAY BEHAVIORS OF INFANTS REARED IN AN INSTITUTION AND IN LOWER- AND MIDDLE-CLASS HOMES EJ 052 441
AGE, STATE, AND MATERNAL BEHAVIOR ASSOCIATED WITH INFANT VOCALIZATIONS EJ 052 444
INFANT OBEDIENCE AND MATERNAL BEHAVIOR: THE ORIGINS OF SOCALIZATION RECONSIDERED EJ 052 446
TOYS DELAY THE INFANT'S FOLLOWING OF HIS MOTHER EJ 053 713
INFANT SMILING TO NONSOCIAL STIMULI AND THE RECOGNITION HYPOTHESIS EJ 053 731
FEEDING BEHAVIORS OF NEWBORN INFANTS AS A FUNCTION OF PARITY OF THE MOTHER EJ 053 736
CONTINUITY IN THE DEVELOPMENT OF VISUAL BEHAVIOR IN YOUNG INFANTS EJ 053 746
NEONATAL SMILING IN REM STATES, IV: PREMATURE STUDY EJ 053 758
COMPARISONS OF VOCAL IMITATION, TACTILE STIMULATION, AND FOOD AS REINFORCERS FOR INFANT VOCALIZATIONS EJ 055 206
INTERRELATIONS IN THE ATTACHMENT BEHAVIOR OF HUMAN INFANTS EJ 055 208
THE STABILITY OF ATTACHMENT BEHAVIORS IN THE HUMAN INFANT EJ 055 209
CONDITIONING OF INFANT VOCALIZATIONS IN THE HOME ENVIRONMENT EJ 055 214
STABILITY OF THE ORIENTING REFLEX IN INFANTS TO AUDITORY AND VISUAL STIMULI AS INDEXED BY CARDIAC DECELERATION EJ 056 720
BEHAVIORAL SLEEP CYCLES IN THE HUMAN NEWBORN EJ 056 722
INFANTS' RESPONSES TO NOVELTY IN FAMILIAR AND UNFAMILIAR SETTINGS EJ 056 731
HABITUATION AND RECOVERY OF VISUAL RESPONSE IN THE ALERT HUMAN NEWBORN EJ 057 116
STATE AS VARIABLE, AS OBSTACLE, AND AS MEDIATOR OF STIMULATION IN INFANT RESEARCH EJ 058 220
STATE AS AN INFANT-ENVIRONMENT INTERACTION: AN ANALYSIS OF MOTHER-INFANT INTERACTIONS AS A FUNCTION OF SEX EJ 058 221
INDIVIDUAL DIFFERENCES IN THE DEVELOPMENT OF SOME ATTACHMENT BEHAVIORS EJ 058 222
ATTACHMENT: ITS ORIGINS AND COURSE EJ 058 586
RELATIONSHIPS BETWEEN INFANTS' SOCIAL BEHAVIOR AND THEIR MOTHERS' BEHAVIOR EJ 058 587
THE RELATIVE EFFICACY OF CONTACT AND VESTIBULAR-PROPRIOCEPTIVE STIMULATION IN SOOTHING NEONATES EJ 058 588
EVIDENCE FOR THE UNCONDITIONABILITY OF THE BABKIN REFLEX IN NEWBORNS EJ 058 589
DIMENSIONS OF EARLY STIMULATION AND THEIR DIFFERENTIAL EFFECTS ON INFANT DEVELOPMENT EJ 059 873
REACTIONS TO RESPONSE-CONTINGENT STIMULATION IN EARLY INFANCY EJ 059 874
EFFECTS OF SOCIAL AND VOCAL STIMULATION ON INFANT BABBLING EJ 061 140

INFANT MORTALITY

THE HEALTH OF CHILDREN--1970: SELECTED DATA FROM THE NATIONAL CENTER FOR HEALTH STATISTICS. ED052827

INFANTS

SOCIAL AND EMOTIONAL BEHAVIOR IN INFANCY--SOME DEVELOPMENTAL ISSUES AND PROBLEMS. ED015789
A PARENT EDUCATION APPROACH TO PROVISION OF EARLY STIMULATION FOR THE CULTURALLY DISADVANTAGED. FINAL REPORT. ED017339
THE EXTENSION OF CONTROL IN VERBAL BEHAVIOR. FINAL REPORT. ED021619
METHODOLOGICAL ISSUES IN THE STUDY OF AGE DIFFERENCES IN INFANTS' ATTENTION TO STIMULI VARYING IN MOVEMENT AND COMPLEXITY. ED023477
NOVELTY AND FAMILIARITY AS DETERMINANTS OF INFANT ATTENTION WITHIN THE FIRST YEAR. ED023483
MEMORY AND "CONTINGENCY ANALYSIS" IN INFANT LEARNING. ED024437
LEARNING IN INFANTS. ED024446
INFANTS' RESPONSES TO FACIAL STIMULI DURING THE FIRST YEAR OF LIFE: EXPLORATORY STUDIES IN THE DEVELOPMENT OF A FACE SCHEMA. ED024455
PERCEPTUAL-COGNITIVE DEVELOPMENT IN INFANCY: A GENERALIZED EXPECTANCY MODEL AS A FUNCTION OF THE MOTHER-INFANT INTERACTION. ED024470
A DISTINCTIVE FEATURES ANALYSIS OF PRE-LINGUISTIC INFANT VOCALIZATIONS. ED025330
DEVELOPMENT OF THE PROSODIC FEATURES OF INFANTS' VOCALIZING. ED025331
AUDITORY COMPONENTS OF NEONATAL EXPERIENCE: A PRELIMINARY REPORT. ED025336
INFANT AND PRESCHOOL MENTAL TESTS: REVIEW AND EVALUATION. ED026109
THE EFFECT OF A STRUCTURED TUTORIAL PROGRAM ON THE COGNITIVE AND LANGUAGE DEVELOPMENT OF CULTURALLY DISADVANTAGED INFANTS. ED026110
A RATIONALE FOR A STRUCTURED EDUCATIONAL PROGRAM AND SUGGESTED ACTIVITIES FOR CULTURALLY DISADVANTAGED INFANTS. ED026112
INFANT EDUCATION RESEARCH PROJECT, WASHINGTON, D.C. ED027976
INFANT MORTALITY: A CHALLENGE TO THE NATION. ED032122
INFANT EDUCATION. ED033760
VISUAL SCANNING BY HUMAN NEWBORNS: RESPONSES TO COMPLETE TRIANGLE, TO SIDES ONLY, AND TO CORNERS ONLY. ED035439
EARLY INFANT STIMULATION AND MOTOR DEVELOPMENT. ED038179
AN EDUCATIONAL SYSTEM FOR DEVELOPMENTALLY DISABLED INFANTS. ED040749
A TUTORIAL LANGUAGE PROGRAM FOR DISADVANTAGED INFANTS. ED040766
DEMONSTRATION INFANT DAY CARE AND EDUCATION PROGRAM. INTERIM REPORT, 1969-1970. ED041632
MOTHERS' TRAINING PROGRAM: EDUCATIONAL INTERVENTION BY THE MOTHERS OF DISADVANTAGED INFANTS. ED043378
ISSUES AND IMPLICATIONS OF THE DISTRIBUTION OF ATTENTION IN THE HUMAN INFANT. ED043387
DEVELOPMENTAL-BEHAVIORAL PATTERNS IN TWENTY-SIX CULTURALLY DISADVANTAGED INFANTS. ED044173
MOTHER-CHILD INTERACTION: SOCIAL CLASS DIFFERENCES IN THE FIRST YEAR OF LIFE. ED044177

INFANT STIMULATION AND THE ETIOLOGY OF COGNITIVE PROCESSES. ED045174
KEY ISSUES IN INFANT MORTALITY. ED045208
A TEST OF HABITUATION IN HUMAN INFANTS AS AN ACQUISITION PROCESS IN A RETROACTIVE INHIBITION PARADIGM. ED046490
ACTIVITIES FOR INFANT STIMULATION OR MOTHER-INFANT GAMES. ED046510
A COMPARATIVE ANALYSIS OF THE PIAGETIAN DEVELOPMENT OF TWELVE MONTH OLD DISADVANTAGED INFANTS IN AN ENRICHMENT CENTER WITH OTHERS NOT IN SUCH A CENTER. ED047778
RELATIONSHIPS BETWEEN SELECTED FAMILY VARIABLES AND MATERNAL AND INFANT BEHAVIOR IN A DISADVANTAGED POPULATION. A SUPPLEMENTARY REPORT. ED047784
EDUCATION OF THE INFANT AND YOUNG CHILD. ED048930
AN INTEGRATED PROGRAM OF GROUP CARE AND EDUCATION FOR SOCIOECONOMICALLY ADVANTAGED AND DISADVANTAGED INFANTS. ED048937
A REVIEW OF EXPERIENCE: ESTABLISHING, OPERATING, EVALUATING A DEMONSTRATION NURSERY CENTER FOR THE DAYTIME CARE OF INFANTS AND TODDLERS, 1967-1970. FINAL REPORT. ED050810
CURRICULUM FOR THE INFANT AND TODDLER. A COLOR SLIDE SERIES WITH SCRIPT. (SCRIPT ONLY). ED050817
MOTHER-INFANT INTERACTION AND INFANT DEVELOPMENT AMONG THE WOLOF OF SENEGAL. ED051885
STANDARDS FOR DAY CARE CENTERS FOR INFANTS AND CHILDREN UNDER 3 YEARS OF AGE. ED053794
WHAT'S THROWN OUT WITH THE BATH WATER: A BABY? ED053801
NEW HOPE FOR BABIES OF RH NEGATIVE MOTHERS EJ 003 743
THE EFFECT OF A STRUCTURED TUTORIAL PROGRAM ON THE COGNITIVE AND LANGUAGE DEVELOPMENT OF CULTURALLY DISADVANTAGED INFANTS EJ 008 272
INFANT EDUCATION: A COMMUNITY PROJECT EJ 008 462
TRANSITIONAL OBJECTS AND THE PROCESS OF INDIVIDUATION: A STUDY IN THREE DIFFERENT SOCIAL GROUPS EJ 022 476
PSYCHOLOGICAL ASSESSMENT INSTRUMENTS FOR USE WITH HUMAN INFANTS EJ 025 231
BODY SIZE OF CONTEMPORARY GROUPS OF ONE-YEAR-OLD INFANTS STUDIED IN DIFFERENT PARTS OF THE WORLD EJ 025 469
MOTHER-INFANT RELATIONSHIP AND WEIGHT GAIN IN THE FIRST MONTH OF LIFE EJ 026 508
NEWBORN ATTENTION: DIFFERENTIAL RESPONSE DECREMENT TO VISUAL STIMULI EJ 027 846
COMPLEXITY, CONTOUR, AND AREA AS DETERMINANTS OF ATTENTION IN INFANTS EJ 029 361
BIOLOGICAL AND ECOLOGICAL INFLUENCES ON DEVELOPMENT AT 12 MONTHS OF AGE EJ 029 385
VISUAL ABILITIES AND PATTERN PREFERENCES OF PREMATURE INFANTS AND FULL-TERM NEONATES EJ 029 531
PATTERNS OF MOTHER-INFANT CONTACT: THE SIGNIFICANCE OF LATERAL PREFERENCE EJ 030 513
ON THE RELIABILITY OF THE GRAHAM/ROSENBLITH BEHAVIOUR TEST FOR NEONATES EJ 031 630
ATTENTIONAL RESPONSES OF FIVE-MONTH GIRLS TO DISCREPANT AUDITORY STIMULI EJ 032 893
A CHILD'S FIRST STEPS: SOME SPECULATIONS EJ 033 057
EMOTIONAL CONCOMITANTS OF VISUAL MASTERY IN INFANTS: THE EFFECTS OF STIMULUS MOVEMENT ON SMILING AND VOCALIZING EJ 033 794
EDUCATIONAL INTERVENTION AT HOME BY MOTHERS OF DISADVANTAGED INFANTS EJ 034 002
NOVELTY, FAMILIARITY, AND THE DEVELOPMENT OF INFANT ATTENTION EJ 034 529
A STIMULUS SIMILARITY SCALE FOR TEMPORAL MEASURES OF ATTENTION IN INFANTS AND CHILDREN EJ 034 530
SMILING TO SOCIAL STIMULI: ELICITING AND CONDITIONING EFFECTS EJ 034 536
TERMINOLOGY AND METHODOLOGY RELATED TO THE USE OF HEART RATE RESPONSIVITY IN INFANCY RESEARCH EJ 034 566
RESPONSE TO VOICE OF MOTHER AND STRANGER BY BABIES IN THE FIRST YEAR EJ 035 269
OPERANT LEARNING OF VISUAL PATTERN DISCRIMINATION IN YOUNG INFANTS EJ 035 623
CUMULATIVE EFFECTS OF CONTINUOUS STIMULATION ON AROUSAL LEVEL IN INFANTS EJ 036 075
IRRELEVANCE OF NEWBORN WAKING STATES TO SOME MOTOR AND APPETITIVE RESPONSES EJ 036 076
CAN NEWBORNS SHOW CARDIAC ORIENTING? EJ 036 078
THE BEHAVIORAL AROUSAL THRESHOLD IN INFANT SLEEP AS A FUNCTION OF TIME AND SLEEP STATE EJ 036 091
INDIVIDUAL DIFFERENCES IN THE VISUAL PURSUIT BEHAVIOR OF NEONATES EJ 036 092
FATHERS' VERBAL INTERACTION WITH INFANTS IN THE FIRST THREE MONTHS OF LIFE EJ 036 126
DELAYED REINFORCEMENT AND VOCALIZATION RATES OF INFANTS EJ 036 127
AUDIO-VISUAL MATERIALS IN EARLY CHILDHOOD EDUCATION EJ 038 907
RELATIONSHIPS BETWEEN INFANTS' VOCALIZATIONS AND THEIR MOTHERS' BEHAVIORS EJ 040 455
STATE IV OF PIAGET'S THEORY OF INFANT'S OBJECT CONCEPTS: A LONGITUDINAL STUDY EJ 041 134
CAN CONDITIONED RESPONSES BE ESTABLISHED IN THE NEWBORN INFANT: 1971? EJ 041 956
NEWBORN'S RESPONSE TO THE CRY OF ANOTHER INFANT EJ 041 959
ORIENTATION DISCRIMINATION IN INFANTS: A COMPARISON OF VISUAL FIXATION AND OPERANT TRAINING METHODS EJ 041 981
INFANT HABITUATION AND GENERALIZATION TO DIFFERING DEGREES OF STIMULUS NOVELTY EJ 043 195
INFANT-CARETAKER INTERACTIONS EJ 043 670
THE EFFECTS OF THE ENVIRONMENT UPON STATE CYCLES IN THE HUMAN NEWBORN EJ 044 119
A PLAY CENTER FOR DEVELOPMENTALLY HANDICAPPED INFANTS EJ 045 012
CONSONANT CUE PERCEPTION BY TWENTY- TO TWENTY-FOUR-WEEK-OLD INFANTS EJ 045 597
ACCELERATING VISUAL COMPLEXITY LEVELS IN THE HUMAN INFANT EJ 045 598
COGNITIVE DEVELOPMENT IN INFANTS OF DIFFERENT AGE LEVELS AND FROM DIFFERENT ENVIRONMENTAL BACKGROUNDS: AN EXPLANATORY INVESTIGATION EJ 046 244
ACCOMMODATION OF VISUAL TRACKING PATTERNS IN HUMAN INFANTS TO OBJECT MOVEMENT PATTERNS EJ 046 250
CARDIAC DECELERATION AND ITS STABILITY IN HUMAN NEWBORNS EJ 046 891
THE EFFECTS OF ENRICHED NEONATAL EXPERIENCES UPON LATER COGNITIVE FUNCTIONING EJ 047 689
OBJECT CONSTRUCTION AND IMITATION UNDER DIFFERING CONDITIONS OF REARING EJ 048 305
INTERVENTION IN INFANCY: A PROGRAM FOR BLIND INFANTS EJ 048 904
RELATIONSHIPS BETWEEN ATTRIBUTES OF MOTHERS AND THEIR INFANTS' IQ SCORES EJ 051 568
EXPLORATORY AND PLAY BEHAVIORS OF INFANTS REARED IN AN INSTITUTION AND IN LOWER- AND MIDDLE-CLASS HOMES EJ 052 441
WHAT'S THROWN OUT WITH THE BATH WATER: A BABY? EJ 052 445
AUDITORY-LINGUISTIC SENSITIVITY IN EARLY INFANCY EJ 053 479
FEEDING BEHAVIORS OF NEWBORN INFANTS AS A FUNCTION OF PARITY OF THE MOTHER EJ 053 736
NEONATAL SMILING IN REM STATES, IV: PREMATURE STUDY EJ 053 758
MOTHER-CHILD INTERACTION IN THE FIRST YEAR OF LIFE EJ 056 632
HABITUATION AND MEMORY: INFANT CARDIAC RESPONSES TO FAMILIAR AND DISCREPANT AUDITORY STIMULI EJ 056 633
THE ONSET OF WARINESS EJ 056 635
VISUAL RESPONSE DECREMENT AS A FUNCTION OF AGE OF HUMAN NEWBORNS EJ 056 716
BEHAVIORAL SLEEP CYCLES IN THE HUMAN NEWBORN EJ 056 722
SOCIAL CLASS INTELLIGENCE, AND COGNITIVE STYLE IN INFANCY EJ 056 725
EXECUTIVE COMPETENCE AND SPONTANEOUS SOCIAL BEHAVIOR IN ONE-YEAR-OLDS EJ 056 732
HABITUATION AND RECOVERY OF VISUAL RESPONSE IN THE ALERT HUMAN NEWBORN EJ 057 116
A DEVELOPMENTAL LEARNING APPROACH TO INFANT CARE IN A GROUP SETTING EJ 057 442
MALE AND FEMALE AUDITORY REINFORCEMENT OF INFANT VOCALIZATIONS EJ 058 217
NONSOCIAL REINFORCEMENT OF INFANTS' VOCALIZATIONS EJ 058 219
INDIVIDUAL DIFFERENCES IN THE DEVELOPMENT OF SOME ATTACHMENT BEHAVIORS EJ 058 222
NUTRITION AND BRAIN DEVELOPMENT IN INFANTS EJ 058 223
THE RELATIVE EFFICACY OF CONTACT AND VESTIBULAR-PROPRIOCEPTIVE STIMULATION IN SOOTHING NEONATES EJ 058 588
EVIDENCE FOR THE UNCONDITIONABILITY OF THE BABKIN REFLEX IN NEWBORNS EJ 058 589
A STUDY OF THE RELATIVE DOMINANCE OF VISION AND TOUCH IN SIX-MONTH-OLD INFANTS EJ 058 594
VIOLATION OF A RULE AS A METHOD OF DIAGNOSING INFANTS' LEVELS OF OBJECT CONCEPT EJ 059 314
THE STAGE IV ERROR IN PIAGET'S THEORY OF OBJECT CONCEPT DEVELOPMENT: DIFFICULTIES IN OBJECT CONCEPTUALIZATION OR SPATIAL LOCALIZATION? EJ 059 318
VISUAL HABITUATION IN THE HUMAN INFANT EJ 059 511
REACTIONS TO RESPONSE-CONTINGENT STIMULATION IN EARLY INFANCY EJ 059 874
INFANT DEVELOPMENT IN LOWER-CLASS AMERICAN FAMILIES EJ 060 012
CHANGES IN INFANTS' VOCALIZATIONS AS A FUNCTION OF DIFFERENTIAL ACOUSTIC STIMULATION EJ 061 139
EFFECTS OF SOCIAL AND VOCAL STIMULATION ON INFANT BABBLING EJ 061 140
DEVELOPMENTAL CHANGE IN INFANT VISUAL FIXATION TO DIFFERING COMPLEXITY LEVELS AMONG CROSS-SECTIONALLY AND LONGITUDINALLY STUDIED INFANTS EJ 061 141
AN INFANT CONTROL PROCEDURE FOR STUDYING INFANT VISUAL FIXATIONS EJ 061 142
INFANT CARE AND GROWTH IN URBAN ZAMBIA EJ 061 231

IMPLICATIONS OF INFANT DEVELOPMENT AMONG THE MAYAN INDIANS OF MEXICO EJ 061 232

INFORMATION CENTERS
HOW TO USE ERIC. REVISED EDITION. ED027059
THE DEVELOPMENT OF AN INFORMATION UNIT REVIEWING SELECTED WELL-DEVELOPED MODELS OF EARLY CHILDHOOD EDUCATION PROGRAMS. FINAL REPORT. ED045223

INFORMATION DISSEMINATION
PROJECT HEAD START, REPORT ON THE PREKINDERGARTEN PROGRAM, 1965. ED021611
DISSEMINATION AND UTILIZATION OF KNOWLEDGE IN THE AREA OF EARLY CHILDHOOD EDUCATION: A DESCRIPTION OF SOME OF THE PROBLEMS. ED044185
EDUCATIONAL INTERVENTION IN EARLY CHILDHOOD: APPENDIXES. FINAL REPORT, VOLUME II. ED050815

INFORMATION NEEDS
THE DEVELOPMENT OF AN INFORMATION UNIT REVIEWING SELECTED WELL-DEVELOPED MODELS OF EARLY CHILDHOOD EDUCATION PROGRAMS. FINAL REPORT. ED045223

INFORMATION PROCESSING
INTELLECTUAL DEVELOPMENT AND THE ABILITY TO PROCESS VISUAL AND VERBAL INFORMATION. ED043373
IMITATION LEARNING OF INFORMATION-PROCESSING EJ 046 252
AGE, ICONIC STORAGE, AND VISUAL INFORMATION PROCESSING EJ 053 725
DEVELOPMENT OF THE ABILITY TO ENCODE WITHIN EVALUATIVE DIMENSIONS EJ 053 728
MEMORY FOR RHYTHMIC SERIES: AGE CHANGES IN ACCURACY AND NUMBER CODING EJ 054 805
SELECTIVE STRATEGIES IN CHILDREN'S ATTENTION TO TASK-RELEVANT INFORMATION EJ 055 537
VISUAL MASKING AND DEVELOPMENTAL DIFFERENCES IN INFORMATION PROCESSING EJ 059 514

INFORMATION RETRIEVAL
FOLLOW-UP OF OPERATION HEAD START PARTICIPANTS IN THE STATE OF IOWA. FINAL REPORT. ED015771
EFFECTS OF AGE UPON RETRIEVAL FROM SHORT-TERM MEMORY EJ 055 109
NOUN-PAIR LEARNING IN CHILDREN AND ADULTS: UNDERLYING STRINGS AND RETRIEVAL TIME EJ 056 402

INFORMATION SEEKING
INFORMATION SEEKING ABOUT UNCERTAIN BUT UNAVOIDABLE OUTCOMES: EFFECTS OF PROBABILITY, VALENCE, AND INTERVENING ACTIVITY EJ 042 962

INFORMATION SERVICES
HOW TO USE ERIC. REVISED EDITION. ED027059
THE DEVELOPMENT OF AN INFORMATION UNIT REVIEWING SELECTED WELL-DEVELOPED MODELS OF EARLY CHILDHOOD EDUCATION PROGRAMS. FINAL REPORT. ED045223

INFORMATION SOURCES
FEDERAL PROGRAMS FOR YOUNG CHILDREN. ED047811

INFORMATION SYSTEMS
FOLLOW-UP OF OPERATION HEAD START PARTICIPANTS IN THE STATE OF IOWA. FINAL REPORT. ED015771

INFORMATION UTILIZATION
DISSEMINATION AND UTILIZATION OF KNOWLEDGE IN THE AREA OF EARLY CHILDHOOD EDUCATION: A DESCRIPTION OF SOME OF THE PROBLEMS. ED044185
THE DEVELOPMENT OF AN INFORMATION UNIT REVIEWING SELECTED WELL-DEVELOPED MODELS OF EARLY CHILDHOOD EDUCATION PROGRAMS. FINAL REPORT. ED045223

INHIBITION
A TEST OF HABITUATION IN HUMAN INFANTS AS AN ACQUISITION PROCESS IN A RETROACTIVE INHIBITION PARADIGM. ED046490
AGGRESSION AS A FUNCTION OF EXPECTED RETALIATION AND AGGRESSION LEVEL OF TARGET AND AGGRESSOR EJ 043 192
SOME PARAMETERS OF PUNISHMENT AFFECTING RESISTANCE TO DEVIATION AND GENERALIZATION OF A PROHIBITION EJ 052 457
RETROACTIVE AND PROACTIVE MULTIPLE LIST INTERFERENCE WITH DISADVANTAGED CHILDREN EJ 057 895
CONCEPTUAL TEMPO AND INHIBITION OF MOVEMENT IN BLACK PRESCHOOL CHILDREN EJ 059 512

INITIAL TEACHING ALPHABET
THE INITIAL TEACHING ALPHABET AND THE WORLD OF ENGLISH. (PROCEEDINGS OF THE SECOND ANNUAL INTERNATIONAL CONFERENCE ON THE INITIAL TEACHING ALPHABET, AUGUST 18-20, 1965). ED019108
A COMPARISON BETWEEN THE ORAL AND WRITTEN RESPONSES OF FIRST-GRADE CHILDREN IN I.T.A. AND T.O. CLASSES. ED019144
THE I.T.A. READING EXPERIMENT IN BRITAIN. ED032133

INJURIES
CHILDREN WHO ARE INJURED. 1970 WHITE HOUSE CONFERENCE ON CHILDREN, REPORT OF FORUM 13. (WORKING COPY). ED046529
AN APPLIANCE FOR AUTOINDUCED ADVERSE CONTROL OF SELF-INJURIOUS BEHAVIOR EJ 029 916

INNER CITY
SESAME STREET. A SURVEY OF TWO CITIES: VIEWING PATTERNS IN INNER CITY LOS ANGELES AND CHICAGO. ED047788
NURSERIES IN CROSS-CULTURAL EDUCATION. FINAL REPORT. ED053815
AN ATTEMPT TO COMBINE CLINICAL AND EDUCATIONAL RESOURCES: A REPORT ON THE FIRST YEAR'S EXPERIENCE OF A THERAPEUTIC SCHOOL EJ 035 539
EARLY GRADE SCHOOL PERFORMANCE OF INNER CITY NEGRO HIGH SCHOOL HIGH ACHIEVERS, LOW ACHIEVERS, AND DROPOUTS EJ 039 572

INNER SPEECH (SUBVOCAL)
THE CHRONOLOGY OF THE DEVELOPMENT OF COVERT SPEECH IN CHILDREN EJ 047 594

INNOVATION
CHILD ABUSE LEGISLATION IN THE 1970'S. ED049826

INQUIRY TRAINING
THE TEACHING OF INQUIRY SKILLS TO ELEMENTARY SCHOOL CHILDREN. FINAL REPORT. ED020805
INSTRUCTIONAL SPECIFICITY AND OUTCOME-EXPECTATION IN OBSERVATIONALLY-INDUCED QUESTION FORMULATION. ED047789

INSERVICE EDUCATION
PERSPECTIVES ON TEACHER-AIDES. A TEACHING TEXT. ED028836
USING A STEP TOWARD PROFESSIONALISM IN TRAINING OF CHILD CARE STAFF EJ 017 850

INSERVICE PROGRAMS
CURRICULUM DEVELOPMENT PROGRAM FOR PRESCHOOL TEACHER AIDES. FINAL REPORT. ED013122
KICKAPOO - NORTH CANADIAN PROJECT, 1966-67. FINAL REPORT. ED015781
EVALUATION OF THE PRESCHOOL CHILD AND PARENT EDUCATION PROJECT AS EXPANDED THROUGH THE USE OF ELEMENTARY AND SECONDARY EDUCATION ACT, TITLE I, FUNDS. ED021621
NEW DIMENSIONS IN STAFF DEVELOPMENT IN A JUVENILE CORRECTIONAL SYSTEM EJ 043 858

INSERVICE TEACHER EDUCATION
INTERIM PROGRESS REPORT OF A REMOTE TEACHER TRAINING INSTITUTE FOR EARLY CHILDHOOD EDUCATORS (FUNDED BY NDEA TITLE XI). ED017326
IN-SERVICE EDUCATION IN ELEMENTARY SCHOOL MATHEMATICS. ED018272
THE EFFECTS OF TEACHER IN-SERVICE EDUCATION ON THE DEVELOPMENT OF ART IDEAS WITH SIX-YEAR OLD CULTURALLY DEPRIVED CHILDREN. FINAL REPORT. ED027066
PRESCHOOL AND PRIMARY EDUCATION PROJECT. 1967-68 ANNUAL PROGRESS REPORT TO THE FORD FOUNDATION. ED027936
HELP FOR TEACHERS IN PRESCHOOLS: A PROPOSAL. ED031308

INSTITUTES (TRAINING PROGRAMS)
INTERIM PROGRESS REPORT OF A REMOTE TEACHER TRAINING INSTITUTE FOR EARLY CHILDHOOD EDUCATORS (FUNDED BY NDEA TITLE XI). ED017326

INSTITUTIONAL ENVIRONMENT
YOUNG CHILDREN IN INSTITUTIONS: SOME ADDITIONAL EVIDENCE EJ 019 359
THE EFFECTS OF OWN-HOME AND INSTITUTION-REARING ON THE BEHAVIOURAL DEVELOPMENT OF NORMAL AND MONGOL CHILDREN EJ 048 905
EXPLORATORY AND PLAY BEHAVIORS OF INFANTS REARED IN AN INSTITUTION AND IN LOWER- AND MIDDLE-CLASS HOMES EJ 052 441

INSTITUTIONAL FACILITIES
RESIDENTIAL TREATMENT OF CHILDREN; A SURVEY OF INSTITUTIONAL CHARACTERISTICS EJ 022 980

INSTITUTIONAL PERSONNEL
HELPING HOUSEPARENTS FIND AND USE THEIR CREATIVITY EJ 022 215

INSTITUTIONAL RESEARCH
REPORT ON ACTIVITIES, 1964-1966. ED020016
A PERSPECTIVE ON RESIDENTIAL CHILD CARE PROGRAMS EJ 051 234

INSTITUTIONAL ROLE
CRISIS IN VALUES. 1970 WHITE HOUSE CONFERENCE ON CHILDREN, REPORT OF FORUM 4. (WORKING COPY). ED046523
INSTITUTIONALIZATION AND THE EFFECTIVENESS OF SOCIAL REINFORCEMENT: A FIVE- AND EIGHT-YEAR FOLLOW-UP STUDY EJ 027 185
A PERSPECTIVE ON RESIDENTIAL CHILD CARE PROGRAMS EJ 051 234

INSTITUTIONALIZED (PERSONS)
YOUNG CHILDREN IN INSTITUTIONS: SOME ADDITIONAL EVIDENCE EJ 019 359
INSTITUTIONALIZATION AND THE EFFECTIVENESS OF SOCIAL REINFORCEMENT: A FIVE- AND EIGHT-YEAR FOLLOW-UP STUDY EJ 027 185
THE CHILD CARE COUNSELOR: NEW THERAPIST IN CHILDREN'S INSTITUTIONS EJ 027 919

A PRELIMINARY VIEW OF TRENDS IN AGE, EDUCATION, AND INTELLIGENCE OF PROBLEM YOUTH EJ 030 431
OUTERDIRECTEDNESS IN THE PROBLEM-SOLVING OF INSTITUTIONALIZED AND NONINSTITUTIONALIZED NORMAL AND RETARDED CHILDREN EJ 035 366
GROUP CARE AND INTELLECTUAL DEVELOPMENT EJ 040 041
AN ACTIVITY GROUP APPROACH TO SERIOUSLY DISTURBED LATENCY BOYS EJ 043 194
COLONIAL CHILD CARE INSTITUTIONS: OUR HERITAGE OF CARE EJ 043 315
EMOTIONAL SENSITIVITY AND INTELLIGENCE IN CHILDREN FROM ORPHANAGES AND NORMAL HOMES EJ 043 859
PSYCHOSOCIAL DEVELOPMENT IN CROSS-CULTURAL PERSPECTIVE: A NEW LOOK AT AN OLD ISSUE EJ 046 888
LONGITUDINAL ASSESSMENT OF THE RELATION BETWEEN MEASURED INTELLIGENCE OF INSTITUTIONALIZED RETARDATES AND HOSPITAL AGE EJ 047 340
OBJECT CONSTRUCTION AND IMITATION UNDER DIFFERING CONDITIONS OF REARING EJ 048 305
DEVELOPMENTAL COURSE OF RESPONSIVENESS TO SOCIAL REINFORCEMENT IN NORMAL CHILDREN AND INSTITUTIONALIZED RETARDED CHILDREN EJ 053 648
INSTITUTIONALIZED RETARDATES' ANIMAL DRAWINGS; THEIR MEANINGS AND SIGNIFICANCE EJ 055 108
ENVIRONMENTAL EFFECTS ON LANGUAGE DEVELOPMENT: A STUDY OF YOUNG CHILDREN IN LONG-STAY RESIDENTIAL NURSERIES EJ 058 859
SEX ROLE IDENTITY OF ADOLESCENT GIRLS IN FOSTER HOMES AND INSTITUTIONS EJ 059 644

WHY CHILDREN ARE IN JAIL AND HOW TO KEEP THEM OUT EJ 013 329

INSTRUCTIONAL AIDS

THE USE OF CONTEMPORARY MATERIALS IN THE CLASSROOM. ED020013
THE USE OF COLOURED RODS IN TEACHING PRIMARY NUMBERWORK. ED028823
DOES THE USE OF CUISENAIRE RODS IN KINDERGARTEN, FIRST AND SECOND GRADES UPGRADE ARITHMETIC ACHIEVEMENT? ED032128
THE EFFECTS OF CARTOON CHARACTERS AS MOTIVATORS OF PRESCHOOL DISADVANTAGED CHILDREN. FINAL REPORT. ED045210
THE CAMERA FOCUSES ON READING EJ 032 192

INSTRUCTIONAL DESIGN

PSYCHOLOGICAL BASES FOR INSTRUCTIONAL DESIGN. ED013121
THE USE OF HIERARCHIES IN CURRICULUM ANALYSIS AND INSTRUCTIONAL PLANNING EJ 033 574
DESIGNING INSTRUCTIONAL SETTINGS FOR CHILDREN LABELED "RETARDED": SOME REFLECTIONS EJ 057 733

INSTRUCTIONAL IMPROVEMENT

CHILDREN LEARN AND GROW THROUGH ART EXPERIENCES. ILLINOIS CURRICULUM PROGRAM, THE SUBJECT FIELD SERIES. ED019132
DEVELOPING A LEARNING ENVIRONMENT OF QUALITY EJ 027 028

INSTRUCTIONAL INNOVATION

RADICAL SCHOOL REFORM. ED048934
INFLUENCES OF A PIAGET-ORIENTED CURRICULUM ON INTELLECTUAL FUNCTIONING OF LOWER-CLASS KINDERGARTEN CHILDREN. ED049823
AN ACADEMIC PRESCHOOL FOR DISADVANTAGED CHILDREN: REVIEW OF FINDINGS. PRELIMINARY DRAFT. ED051878
BRITISH PRIMARY EDUCATION: AN ANNOTATED BIBLIOGRAPHY. ED052843
THE TEACHER'S VIEW OF THE PRINCIPAL'S ROLE IN INNOVATION EJ 018 957
LET DO IT MY WAY EJ 028 846
DEVELOPING NEW TEACHING TEAMS EJ 029 169
IT MAKES ME FEEL BAD WHEN YOU CALL ME "STINKY" EJ 029 358
DO YOU REALLY WANT TO IMPROVE THE CURRICULUM? EJ 031 850
A CHANGE AGENT STRATEGY: PRELIMINARY REPORT EJ 054 727

INSTRUCTIONAL MATERIALS

A NATIONAL DEMONSTRATION PROJECT UTILIZING TELEVISED MATERIALS FOR THE FORMAL EDUCATION OF CULTURALLY DISADVANTAGED PRESCHOOL CHILDREN. FINAL REPORT. ED015788
DEVELOPMENT OF AN ENLARGED MUSIC REPERTORY FOR KINDERGARTEN THROUGH GRADE SIX (JUILLIARD REPERTORY PROJECT). FINAL REPORT. ED016521
SUPPLEMENTARY MATERIALS FOR TEACHER AIDE TRAINING PROGRAMS, TO SUPPLEMENT THE PUBLICATION "TEACHER AIDES: HANDBOOK FOR INSTRUCTORS AND ADMINISTRATORS." ED024462
CHILD DEVELOPMENT AND MATERIAL SURVEY. PART II, MATERIAL SURVEY. FINAL REPORT. ED027085
SOCIAL STUDIES UNIT: FIRST GRADE. BOSTON-NORTHAMPTON LANGUAGE ARTS PROGRAM, ESEA - 1965, PROJECTS TO ADVANCE CREATIVITY IN EDUCATION. ED027945
A STUDY OF THE EFFECTS OF A GROUP LANGUAGE DEVELOPMENT PROGRAM UPON THE PSYCHOLINGUISTIC ABILITIES AND LATER BEGINNING READING SUCCESS OF KINDERGARTEN CHILDREN. ED031315
SOURCE BOOK OF SELECTED MATERIALS FOR EARLY CHILDHOOD EDUCATION IN THE ARTS. ED033746
THE KINDERGARTEN, A PLACE FOR LEARNING. BULLETIN ONE: MATERIALS AND EQUIPMENT FOR THE FOURS AND FIVES. ED039026
ADDRESS AT COMBINED MEETING OF N.Y.C. EARLY CHILDHOOD COUNCIL AND THE METROPOLITAN ASSOCIATION FOR CHILDHOOD EDUCATION ON "LANGUAGE ARTS MATERIALS IN EARLY CHILDHOOD" (TEACHERS COLLEGE, COLUMBIA UNIVERSITY, APRIL 6, 1968): ED039951
THE EFFECTS OF EXTRANEOUS MATERIAL AND NEGATIVE EXEMPLARS ON A SOCIAL SCIENCE CONCEPT-LEARNING TASK FOR PRE-SCHOOL CHILDREN. ED047819
A DOLL CORNER UPSTAIRS EJ 013 296
EFFECT OF VISUAL STIMULI IN COMPLEMENTING TELEVISED INSTRUCTION EJ 015 382
MORE ON LEARNING-RESOURCE CENTERS EJ 016 819
RESOURCES FOR ENVIRONMENTAL EDUCATORS: ECOLOGY AND TEACHERS EJ 029 392
ON SELECTING MATERIALS FOR THE CLASSROOM EJ 032 865
FOSTERING A NEED TO READ EJ 052 420
CURRICULUM BOON OR BANE? EJ 052 766

INSTRUCTIONAL PROGRAM DIVISIONS

DEPARTMENTALIZATION IN ELEMENTARY SCHOOLS. ED017329
THE MYTH BEHIND GRADED CONTENT EJ 052 126

INSTRUCTIONAL PROGRAMS

A CURRICULUM OF TRAINING FOR PARENT PARTICIPATION IN PROJECT HEAD START. ED026144
THE EFFECT OF DIRECT INSTRUCTION IN LISTENING ON THE LISTENING AND READING COMPREHENSION OF FIRST GRADE CHILDREN. DISSERTATION ABSTRACT. ED029693
FOUR YEARS ON. A FOLLOW-UP STUDY AT SCHOOL LEAVING AGE OF CHILDREN FORMERLY ATTENDING A TRADITIONAL AND A PROGRESSIVE JUNIOR SCHOOL. ED035434
A STUDY OF THE EFFECTIVENESS OF SPECIFIC TEACHING OF CONSERVATION TO CHILDREN IN SELECTED ELEMENTARY SCHOOLS OF BUTTE COUNTY, CALIFORNIA EJ 027 029

INSTRUCTIONAL STAFF

A STUDY IN CHILD CARE (CASE STUDY FROM VOLUME II-A): "HEY, GEORGIE GET YOURSELF TOGETHER." DAY CARE PROGRAMS REPRINT SERIES. ED051902

INSTRUCTIONAL TECHNOLOGY

ON RESPONSIVE ENVIRONMENTS. ED018278

INSTRUCTIONAL TELEVISION

DISCRIMINATING CHARACTERISTICS OF FAMILIES WATCHING SESAME STREET. EARLY DEVELOPMENTAL ADVERSITY PROGRAM: PHASE III, EDAP TECHNICAL NOTE 15.1. ED039943
TELEVISION GUIDELINES FOR EARLY CHILDHOOD EDUCATION. ED040739
STATEMENT OF THE INSTRUCTIONAL GOALS FOR CHILDREN'S TELEVISION WORKSHOP. ED041627
WHY NOT FEELINGS AND VALUES IN INSTRUCTIONAL TELEVISION? EJ 038 906

INTEGRATED ACTIVITIES

EDUCATION FOR INITIATIVE AND RESPONSIBILITY, COMMENTS ON A VISIT TO THE SCHOOLS OF LEICESTERSHIRE COUNTY, APRIL 1967. SECOND EDITION. ED020795
INTEGRATED, INDEPENDENT AND INDIVIDUAL LEARNING ACTIVITIES, FIRST AND SECOND GRADES. SUMMER LEARNING ACTIVITIES, SECOND AND THIRD GRADES. BOSTON-NORTHAMPTON LANGUAGE ARTS PROGRAM, ESEA - 1965, PROJECTS TO ADVANCE CREATIVITY IN EDUCATION. ED027946

INTEGRATED CURRICULUM

GROWTH IN READING IN AN INTEGRATED DAY CLASSROOM EJ 055 154

INTEGRATION EFFECTS

A DISTANCE MEASURE OF RACIAL ATTITUDES IN PRIMARY GRADE CHILDREN: AN EXPLORATORY STUDY. ED026133
PUERTO RICAN CHILDREN IN MAINLAND SCHOOLS. A SOURCE BOOK FOR TEACHERS. ED027953
POSITIVE EFFECTS OF A BICULTURAL PRESCHOOL PROGRAM ON THE INTELLECTUAL PERFORMANCE OF MEXICAN-AMERICAN CHILDREN. ED028827

INTELLECTUAL DEVELOPMENT

ACCELERATION OF INTELLECTUAL DEVELOPMENT IN EARLY CHILDHOOD. FINAL REPORT. ED014332
SIX MONTHS LATER--A COMPARISON OF CHILDREN WHO HAD HEAD START, SUMMER, 1965, WITH THEIR CLASSMATES IN KINDERGARTEN, A CASE STUDY OF THE KINDERGARTENS IN FOUR PUBLIC ELEMENTARY SCHOOLS, NEW YORK CITY. STUDY I. ED015025
FROM THEORY TO THE CLASSROOM, BACKGROUND INFORMATION ON THE FIRST GRADE PROJECT IN NEW YORK CITY SCHOOLS. ED015770
THE EFFECTS OF NEUROLOGICAL AND ENVIRONMENTAL FACTORS ON THE LANGUAGE DEVELOPMENT OF HEAD START CHILDREN--A EVALUATION OF THE HEAD START PROGRAM. ED017317
SOCIAL CLASS AND COGNITIVE DEVELOPMENT IN INFANCY. ED019111

HEAD START EVALUATION AND RESEARCH CENTER, THE UNIVERSITY OF CHICAGO. REPORT B, MATERNAL ANTECEDENTS OF INTELLECTUAL ACHIEVEMENT BEHAVIORS IN LOWER CLASS PRESCHOOL CHILDREN. ED022551
PRESCHOOL PROGRAMS AND THE INTELLECTUAL DEVELOPMENT OF DISADVANTAGED CHILDREN. ED024473
CHANGING PARENT ATTITUDES AND IMPROVING LANGUAGE AND INTELLECTUAL ABILITIES OF CULTURALLY DISADVANTAGED FOUR-YEAR-OLD CHILDREN THROUGH PARENT INVOLVEMENT. ED027942
INTELLECTUAL OPERATIONS IN TEACHER-CHILD INTERACTION. ED039011
AN ANALYSIS OF MOTHERS' SPEECH AS A FACTOR IN THE DEVELOPMENT OF CHILDREN'S INTELLIGENCE. ED042504
INTELLECTUAL DEVELOPMENT AND THE ABILITY TO PROCESS VISUAL AND VERBAL INFORMATION. ED043373
EFFECTS OF AGE OF ENTRY AND DURATION OF PARTICIPATION IN A COMPENSATORY EDUCATION PROGRAM. ED043380
INTELLECTUAL DEVELOPMENT OF CULTURALLY DEPRIVED CHILDREN IN A DAY CARE PROGRAM: A FOLLOW-UP STUDY. ED045186
THE EFFECTS OF ASSESSMENT AND PERSONALIZED PROGRAMMING ON SUBSEQUENT INTELLECTUAL DEVELOPMENT OF PREKINDERGARTEN AND KINDERGARTEN CHILDREN. FINAL REPORT. ED045198
PRELIMINARY ANALYSIS ON KINDERGARTEN AND FIRST GRADE FOLLOW THROUGH TEST RESULTS FOR 1968-69. ED045202
AN ASSESSMENT OF COGNITIVE GROWTH IN CHILDREN WHO HAVE PARTICIPATED IN THE TOY-LENDING COMPONENT OF THE PARENT-CHILD PROGRAM. ED045204
A PROGRESS REPORT ON THE PARENT/CHILD COURSE AND TOY LIBRARY. ED045206
OVERVIEW OF RESPONSIVE MODEL PROGRAM. ED045207
A REVISION OF THE BASIC PROGRAM PLAN OF EDUCATION AT AGE THREE. ED047774
A STUDY IN TRAINING NURSERY CHILDREN ON LOGICAL OPERATIONAL SKILLS. ED047803
DECENTRATION IN CHILDREN: ITS GENERALITY AND CORRELATES. ED048926
HEAD START GRADUATES: ONE YEAR LATER. ED048929
A LONGITUDINAL ASSESSMENT OF THINKING ABILITY OF PRELITERATE CHILDREN DURING A TWO-YEAR PERIOD. FINAL REPORT. ED048946
MEASURING DIFFERENTIAL DEVELOPMENT IN YOUNG CHILDREN. ED050818
ON EARLY LEARNING: THE MODIFIABILITY OF HUMAN POTENTIAL. ED051876
A STUDY IN CHILD CARE (CASE STUDY FROM VOLUME II-A): "A ROLLS-ROYCE OF DAY CARE." DAY CARE PROGRAMS REPRINT SERIES. ED051895
HEALTH AND NUTRITION IN DISADVANTAGED CHILDREN AND THEIR RELATIONSHIP WITH INTELLECTUAL DEVELOPMENT. COLLABORATIVE RESEARCH REPORT. ED052816
A GUIDE TO READING PIAGET. ED053819
ESSAYS ON EQUILIBRIUM EJ 008 171
INFANT DEVELOPMENT, PRESCHOOL IQ, AND SOCIAL CLASS EJ 018 465
PATTERNS OF WISC SCORES FOR CHILDREN OF TWO SOCIOECONOMIC CLASSES AND RACES EJ 021 775
RELATIONSHIP OF CONSERVATION EXPLANATIONS TO ITEM DIFFICULTY EJ 030 295
CONSEQUENCES OF LOW BIRTH WEIGHT EJ 030 430
ESTIMATION OF LINE LENGTH AND NUMBER: A DEVELOPMENTAL STUDY EJ 030 590
THE USEFULNESS OF CUMULATIVE DEPRIVATION AS AN EXPLANATION OF EDUCATIONAL DEFICIENCIES EJ 033 056
SOCIAL-CLASS DIFFERENTIATION IN COGNITIVE DEVELOPMENT AMONG BLACK PRESCHOOL CHILDREN EJ 036 819
DEVELOPMENTAL SHIFTS IN VERBAL RECALL BETWEEN MENTAL AGES TWO AND FIVE EJ 036 825
GROUP CARE AND INTELLECTUAL DEVELOPMENT EJ 040 041
EFFECTS OF HEMOPHILIA UPON INTELLECTUAL GROWTH AND ACADEMIC ACHIEVEMENT EJ 044 009
DIFFERENTIAL COGNITIVE DEVELOPMENT WITHIN AND BETWEEN RACIAL AND ETHNIC GROUPS OF DISADVANTAGED PRESCHOOL AND KINDERGARTEN CHILDREN EJ 049 172
INTELLECTUAL EVOLUTION FROM ADOLESCENCE TO ADULTHOOD EJ 050 073
RELATIONSHIPS BETWEEN ATTRIBUTES OF MOTHERS AND THEIR INFANTS' IQ SCORES EJ 051 568
PREDICTION OF INTELLECTUAL PERFORMANCE AT 3 YEARS FROM INFANT TESTS AND PERSONALITY MEASURES EJ 052 237
THE MODIFICATION OF INTELLIGENCE BY TRAINING IN THE VERBALIZATION OF WORD DEFINITIONS AND SIMPLE CONCEPTS EJ 052 594
EFFECTS OF AGE, SEX, SYSTEMATIC CONCEPTUAL LEARNING, ACQUISITION OF LEARNING SETS, AND PROGRAMMED SOCIAL INTERACTION ON THE INTELLECTUAL AND CONCEPTUAL DEVELOPMENT OF PRESCHOOL CHILDREN FROM POVERTY BACKGROUNDS EJ 053 733
A PIAGETIAN QUESTIONNAIRE APPLIED TO PUPILS IN A SECONDARY SCHOOL EJ 053 907
FATHER-CHILD INTERACTION AND THE INTELLECTUAL FUNCTIONING OF FOUR-YEAR-OLD BOYS EJ 054 290
FACTORIAL STRUCTURE OF SELECTED PSYCHO-EDUCATIONAL MEASURES AND PIAGETIAN REASONING ASSESSMENTS EJ 055 112
NUTRITION AND EDUCATIONAL EXPERIENCE: INTERRELATED VARIABLES IN CHILDREN'S LEARNING EJ 059 643
LIMITATIONS ON THE GENERALIZABILITY OF GROWTH CURVES OF INTELLIGENCE: A REANALYSIS OF SOME DATA FROM THE HARVARD GROWTH STUDY EJ 060 014

INTELLECTUALIZATION

THE RELATIONSHIP BETWEEN PRIMARY STUDENTS' RATIONALIZATION OF CONSERVATION AND THEIR MATHEMATICAL ACHIEVEMENT EJ 046 672

INTELLIGENCE

HEAD START EVALUATION AND RESEARCH CENTER, THE UNIVERSITY OF CHICAGO. REPORT D, THE INTERACTION OF INTELLIGENCE AND BEHAVIOR AS ONE PREDICTOR OF EARLY SCHOOL ACHIEVEMENT IN WORKING CLASS AND CULTURALLY DISADVANTAGED HEAD START CHILDREN. ED022553
THE SOCIAL DEVELOPMENT OF HUMAN INTELLIGENCE. ED028817
A THEORETICAL APPROACH FOR SELECTING ELEMENTARY SCHOOL ENVIRONMENTAL VARIABLES. ED028834
A FOLLOW-UP NORMATIVE STUDY OF NEGRO INTELLIGENCE AND ACHIEVEMENT EJ 003 658
SOCIOECONOMIC STATUS AND INTELLECTIVE PERFORMANCE AMONG NEGRO PRESCHOOL BOYS EJ 024 938
WORD FLUENCY--INTELLECT OR PERSONALITY? EJ 034 313
CREATIVITY AS RELATED TO FIELD INDEPENDENCE AND MOBILITY EJ 035 380
THE RELATIONSHIP BETWEEN INTELLIGENCE AND PERFORMANCE ON THE STROOP COLOR-WORD TEST IN SECOND- AND FIFTH-GRADE CHILDREN EJ 035 887
STORY RECALL IN KINDERGARTEN CHILDREN: EFFECT OF METHOD OF PRESENTATION ON PSYCHOLINGUISTIC PERFORMANCE EJ 036 748
AN EXPERIMENTAL STUDY OF BASIC LEARNING ABILITY AND INTELLIGENCE IN LOW-SOCIOECONOMIC-STATUS CHILDREN EJ 036 818
CHILDREN'S RECALL STRATEGIES IN DICHOTIC LISTENING EJ 044 700
THE MODIFICATION OF INTELLIGENCE BY TRAINING IN THE VERBALIZATION OF WORD DEFINITIONS AND SIMPLE CONCEPTS EJ 052 594
PARENTS AS EDUCATORS: EVIDENCE FROM CROSS-SECTIONAL, LONGITUDINAL AND INTERVENTION RESEARCH EJ 056 608
EFFECTS OF SEX AND BIRTH ORDER ON SEX-ROLE DEVELOPMENT AND INTELLIGENCE AMONG KINDERGARTEN CHILDREN EJ 057 133
LIMITATIONS ON THE GENERALIZABILITY OF GROWTH CURVES OF INTELLIGENCE: A REANALYSIS OF SOME DATA FROM THE HARVARD GROWTH STUDY EJ 060 014

INTELLIGENCE DIFFERENCES

EVALUATION OF CHANGES OCCURRING IN CHILDREN WHO PARTICIPATED IN PROJECT HEAD START. ED017316
FURTHER EVIDENCE ON THE RELATION BETWEEN AGE OF SEPARATION AND SIMILARITY IN IQ AMONG PAIRS OF SEPARATED IDENTICAL TWINS. ED027058
SOCIAL CLASS DIFFERENTIATION IN COGNITIVE DEVELOPMENT: A LONGITUDINAL STUDY. ED033754
PRESCHOOL INTELLIGENCE OF OVERSIZED NEWBORNS. ED034582
DIFFERENTIAL FACTOR STRUCTURE OF SEVENTH GRADE STUDENTS EJ 030 298
THE ABILITY OF PERSONALITY VARIABLES IN DISCRIMINATING AMONG THREE INTELLECTUAL GROUPS OF PREADOLESCENT BOYS AND GIRLS EJ 034 044
MOTIVATIONAL AND ACHIEVEMENT DIFFERENCES AMONG CHILDREN OF VARIOUS ORDINAL BIRTH POSITIONS EJ 055 547
RELATIONS OF AGE AND INTELLIGENCE TO SHORT-TERM COLOR MEMORY EJ 056 392

INTELLIGENCE FACTORS

COGNITIVE DEVELOPMENT IN INFANTS OF DIFFERENT AGE LEVELS AND FROM DIFFERENT ENVIRONMENTAL BACKGROUNDS. ED015786
PRODUCTIVE THINKING IN EDUCATION. ED024459
A LONGITUDINAL INVESTIGATION OF CHANGE IN THE FACTORIAL COMPOSITION OF INTELLIGENCE WITH AGE IN YOUNG SCHOOL CHILDREN. ED026149
SELF-CONCEPTS OF HIGH- AND LOW-CURIOSITY BOYS EJ 019 005
DIFFERENTIAL FACTOR STRUCTURE OF SEVENTH GRADE STUDENTS EJ 030 298
APPARENT VISUAL SIZE AS A FUNCTION OF AGE, INTELLIGENCE, AND A SURROUNDING FRAME OF REFERENCE FOR NORMAL AND MENTALLY RETARDED SUBJECTS EJ 043 704
DEVELOPMENTAL FACTORS IN ADOLESCENT DRUG USE: A STUDY OF PSYCHEDELIC DRUG USERS EJ 051 020
CONCEPTUAL TEMPO AND INHIBITION OF MOVEMENT IN BLACK PRESCHOOL CHILDREN EJ 059 512
CHILDREN'S ABILITY TO ORDER FACIAL AND NONFACIAL CONTINUA AS A FUNCTION OF MA, CA, AND IQ EJ 059 699
PERSONALITY, COGNITIVE, AND DEMOGRAPHIC CHARACTERISTICS OF STUDENT ACTIVISTS AND ACTIVE STUDENTS EJ 061 194

INTELLIGENCE LEVEL

THE IMPACT OF COGNITIVE MATURITY ON THE DEVELOPMENT OF SEX-ROLE ATTITUDES IN THE YEARS 4 TO 8. ED019109
INTERACTION PATTERNS AS A SOURCE OF ERROR IN TEACHERS' EVALUATIONS OF HEAD START CHILDREN. FINAL REPORT. ED023453

EFFECTIVENESS OF DIRECT VERBAL INSTRUCTION ON IQ PERFORMANCE AND ACHIEVEMENT IN READING AND ARITHMETIC. ED030496
A PRELIMINARY VIEW OF TRENDS IN AGE, EDUCATION, AND INTELLIGENCE OF PROBLEM YOUTH EJ 030 431
IQ CHANGES IN HOSPITALIZED MENTAL RETARDATES EJ 046 727

INTELLIGENCE QUOTIENT

THE PERFORMANCE OF FIRST GRADE CHILDREN IN FOUR LEVELS OF CONSERVATION OF NUMEROUSNESS AND THREE IQ GROUPS WHEN SOLVING ARITHMETIC ADDITION PROBLEMS. ED016535
PRELIMINARY FINDINGS FROM A LONGITUDINAL EDUCATIONAL IMPROVEMENT PROJECT BEING CONDUCTED FOR INSTRUCTIONALLY IMPOVERISHED PUPILS IN INTACT SCHOOLS IN THE URBAN SOUTH. ED020021
HEAD START EVALUATION AND RESEARCH CENTER, UNIVERSITY OF KANSAS. REPORT NO. VI, A FAILURE TO SHOW AND INVOLVEMENT OF CURRENT MOTIVATIONAL VARIABLES IN THE RESPONSE OF HEAD START CHILDREN IN THE ASSESSMENT OF INTELLIGENCE BY MEANS OF THE STANFORD BINET TEST. ED021639
ERROR, RESPONSE TIME AND IQ: SEX DIFFERENCES IN COGNITIVE STYLE OF PRESCHOOL CHILDREN. ED026122
EVALUATING BEHAVIORAL CHANGE DURING A SIX-WEEK PRE-KINDERGARTEN INTERVENTION EXPERIENCE. RESEARCH PROJECT NUMBER 5 OF PROJECT HEAD START RESEARCH AND EVALUATION CENTER, SYRACUSE UNIVERSITY RESEARCH INSTITUTE. FINAL REPORT, NOVEMBER 1, 1967. ED026142
SOCIAL CLASS DIFFERENTIATION IN COGNITIVE DEVELOPMENT: A LONGITUDINAL STUDY. ED033754
HAWAII HEAD START EVALUATION FOLLOW-UP--1968-69. FINA L REPORT. ED042515
EFFECTS OF AGE OF ENTRY AND DURATION OF PARTICIPATION IN A COMPENSATORY EDUCATION PROGRAM. ED043380
"NEED ACHIEVEMENT" TRAINING FOR HEAD START CHILDREN AND THEIR MOTHERS. ED048943
ANALYSIS OF INTELLIGENCE SCORES. ED052838
SEASON OF BIRTH AND INTELLIGENCE EJ 025 268
INFANT MENTAL DEVELOPMENT AND NEUROLOGICAL STATUS, FAMILY SOCIOECONOMIC STATUS, AND INTELLIGENCE AT AGE FOUR EJ 032 675
CONCEPTUAL TEMPO IN YOUNG GRADE-SCHOOL CHILDREN EJ 041 450
FIVE-YEAR STABILITY OF INTELLIGENCE QUOTIENTS FROM LANGUAGE AND NONLANGUAGE GROUP TESTS EJ 041 723
ACTIVITY LEVEL AND MOTOR INHIBITION: THEIR RELATIONSHIP TO INTELLIGENCE-TEST PERFORMANCE IN NORMAL CHILDREN EJ 046 242
LONGITUDINAL ASSESSMENT OF THE RELATION BETWEEN MEASURED INTELLIGENCE OF INSTITUTIONALIZED RETARDATES AND HOSPITAL AGE EJ 047 340
RELATIONSHIPS BETWEEN ATTRIBUTES OF MOTHERS AND THEIR INFANTS' IQ SCORES EJ 051 568
FATHER-CHILD INTERACTION AND THE INTELLECTUAL FUNCTIONING OF FOUR-YEAR-OLD BOYS EJ 054 290
AREAS OF RECENT RESEARCH IN EARLY CHILDHOOD EDUCATION EJ 054 380
OVERLAP: HYPOTHESIS OR TAUTOLOGY? EJ 054 508

INTELLIGENCE TESTS

THE 1965 HEAD START PSYCHOLOGICAL SCREENING PROGRAM. FINAL REPORT ON THE DATA ANALYSIS. ED014333
MOTIVATIONAL FACTORS AND IQ-CHANGES IN CULTURALLY DEPRIVED CHILDREN ATTENDING NURSERY SCHOOL. ED020017
THE LIMITATIONS OF BRIEF INTELLIGENCE TESTING WITH YOUNG CHILDREN. ED020774
THE JOHNS HOPKINS PERCEPTUAL TEST, THE DEVELOPMENT OF A RAPID INTELLIGENCE TEST FOR THE PRE-SCHOOL CHILD. ED020787
HEAD START EVALUATION AND RESEARCH CENTER, UNIVERSITY OF KANSAS. REPORT NO. VI, A FAILURE TO SHOW AND INVOLVEMENT OF CURRENT MOTIVATIONAL VARIABLES IN THE RESPONSE OF HEAD START CHILDREN IN THE ASSESSMENT OF INTELLIGENCE BY MEANS OF THE STANFORD BINET TEST. ED021639
A COMPARISON OF WISC AND OSA IN ASSESSING THE INTELLIGENCE OF IMMIGRANT CHILDREN OF NON-ENGLISH SPEAKING BACKGROUND. A PILOT PROJECT. ED022526
DIFFERENCES IN VOCABULARY INPUT-OUTPUT IN PSYCHODIAGNOSIS OF CHILDREN. ED024450
INFANT AND PRESCHOOL MENTAL TESTS: REVIEW AND EVALUATION. ED026109
THE USE OF THE GOODENOUGH DRAW-A-MAN TEST AS A PREDICTOR OF ACADEMIC ACHIEVEMENT. ED029695
THE RELATIONSHIP BETWEEN INSTRUMENTAL ASSERTION AND THE STANFORD-BINET. ED030474
PROJECT HEAD START RESEARCH AND EVALUATION CENTER, SYRACUSE UNIVERSITY, RESEARCH INSTITUTE. FINAL REPORT. ED030486
MODIFICATION OF THE PEABODY PICTURE VOCABULARY TEST. ED033752
STANDARDIZED TESTS AND THE DISADVANTAGED. ED034594
TEACHER EXPECTANCY OR MY FAIR LADY. ED038183
REPORT ON THE UTILITY OF A PIAGET-BASED INFANT SCALE WITH OLDER RETARDED CHILDREN EJ 022 247
WISC SUBTEST AND IQ SCORE CORRELATES OF FATHER ABSENCE EJ 029 219
LANGUAGE DIALECT, REINFORCEMENT, AND THE INTELLIGENCE-TEST PERFORMANCE OF NEGRO CHILDREN EJ 035 912
FIVE-YEAR STABILITY OF INTELLIGENCE QUOTIENTS FROM LANGUAGE AND NONLANGUAGE GROUP TESTS EJ 041 723
A SHORT, RELIABLE, EASY TO ADMINISTER INDIVIDUAL INTELLIGENCE TEST FOR SPECIAL CLASS PLACEMENT EJ 041 724
THE RELATIONSHIP BETWEEN THE WECHSLER INTELLIGENCE SCALE FOR CHILDREN AND THE SLOSSON INTELLIGENCE TEST EJ 041 725
SOME EFFECTS OF TESTING PROCEDURE ON DIVERGENT THINKING EJ 052 992
FACTORIAL STRUCTURE OF SELECTED PSYCHO-EDUCATIONAL MEASURES AND PIAGETIAN REASONING ASSESSMENTS EJ 055 112
THE INFLUENCE OF NONINTELLECTIVE FACTORS ON THE IQ SCORES OF MIDDLE- AND LOWER-CLASS CHILDREN EJ 056 621
SOCIAL CLASS INTELLIGENCE, AND COGNITIVE STYLE IN INFANCY EJ 056 725
DIFFERENTIAL OUTCOMES OF A MONTESSORI CURRICULUM EJ 060 330

INTENTIONAL LEARNING

DEVELOPMENTAL TRENDS IN THE INTENTIONAL AND INCIDENTAL LEARNING COMPONENTS OF A VERBAL DISCRIMINATION TASK EJ 035 375

INTERACTION

THE RELATION BETWEEN TEST ANXIETY AND NEED FOR MEMORY SUPPORT IN PROBLEM SOLVING. REVISED RESEARCH MEMORANDUM NO. 11. ED021616
HEAD START EVALUATION AND RESEARCH CENTER, THE UNIVERSITY OF CHICAGO. REPORT D, THE INTERACTION OF INTELLIGENCE AND BEHAVIOR AS ONE PREDICTOR OF EARLY SCHOOL ACHIEVEMENT IN WORKING CLASS AND CULTURALLY DISADVANTAGED HEAD START CHILDREN. ED022553
CONCEPT IDENTIFICATION STRATEGIES. RESEARCH PROJECT NUMBER 3 OF PROJECT HEAD START RESEARCH AND EVALUATION CENTER, SYRACUSE UNIVERSITY RESEARCH INSTITUTE, NOVEMBER 1, 1967. ED026140
INFORMATION EXCHANGE IN MOTHER-CHILD INTERACTIONS. ED034599
A STUDY OF COMMUNICATION PATTERNS IN DISADVANTAGED CHILDREN. ED037250
CLARIFYING FEELINGS THROUGH PEER INTERACTION EJ 003 083
LOCATION AS A FEATURE OF INSTRUCTIONAL INTERACTION EJ 012 717
WHAT THE WORLD NEEDS NOW: ENVIRONMENTAL EDUCATION FOR YOUNG CHILDREN EJ 039 637
CORRELATES OF LOCUS OF CONTROL IN A SECONDARY SCHOOL POPULATION EJ 039 905
A DEVELOPMENTAL INVESTIGATION OF TELEVISED MODELED VERBALIZATIONS ON RESISTANCE TO DEVIATION EJ 058 218

INTERACTION PROCESS ANALYSIS

NORTHFIELD, VERMONT--A COMMUNITY DEPTH STUDY. ED018245
TEACHERS' BELIEFS, CLASSROOM ATMOSPHERE AND STUDENT BEHAVIOR. FINAL REPORT. ED018249
THE COGNITIVE ENVIRONMENTS OF URBAN PRE-SCHOOL CHILDREN. MANUAL OF INSTRUCTIONS FOR ADMINISTERING AND SCORING THE EIGHT-BLOCK SORTING TASK. ED018265
THE COGNITIVE ENVIRONMENTS OF URBAN PRE-SCHOOL CHILDREN. MANUAL FOR CODING MOTHER-CHILD INTERACTION ON THE EIGHT-BLOCK SORTING TASK. ED018266
THE COGNITIVE ENVIRONMENTS OF URBAN PRE-SCHOOL CHILDREN. MANUAL OF INSTRUCTIONS FOR ADMINISTERING AND SCORING "ETCH-A-SKETCH" TASK. ED018267
THE COGNITIVE ENVIRONMENTS OF URBAN PRE-SCHOOL CHILDREN. MANUAL OF RECORDING AND OBSERVATION TECHNIQUES FOR MOTHER-CHILD INTERACTION. ED018269
OBSERVED COGNITIVE COMMUNICATION PATTERNS OF ADULTS AND CHILDREN IN FOUR PRE-SCHOOL AGE GROUPS. ED036325
INFLUENCE TECHNIQUES IN DYADS COMPOSED OF INTERDEPENDENT MIDDLE AND LOWER CLASS PRESCHOOL CHILDREN. FINAL REPORT ED042489
ETHNIC AND SOCIOECONOMIC INFLUENCES ON THE HOME LANGUAGE EXPERIENCES OF CHILDREN. ED043377
THE EFFECT ON AGGRESSION OF VARIATION IN AMOUNT OF OPPORTUNITY FOR PLAY. (INTERNAL REPORT). ED043384
THE SAMPLE: OPERATIONS IN THE HEAD START YEAR. ED043391
STATE AS AN INFANT-ENVIRONMENT INTERACTION: AN ANALYSIS OF MOTHER-INFANT BEHAVIOR AS A FUNCTION OF SEX. ED052829
MATERNAL BEHAVIOR TOWARD OWN AND OTHER PRESCHOOL CHILDREN: THE PROBLEM OF "OWNNESS" EJ 026 324
THE EFFECT OF SOCIAL INTERACTION ON ACTIVITY LEVELS IN SIX-TO EIGHT-YEAR-OLD BOYS EJ 052 463
ACQUISITION OF CONSERVATION THROUGH SOCIAL INTERACTION EJ 053 708
RESPONSE TO SOCIAL REINFORCEMENT RATES AS A FUNCTION OF REINFORCEMENT HISTORY EJ 053 715
WORDS AND DEEDS ABOUT ALTRUISM AND THE SUBSEQUENT REINFORCEMENT POWER OF THE MODEL EJ 053 739
INCONSISTENT VERBAL INSTRUCTIONS AND CHILDREN'S RESISTANCE-TO-TEMPTATION BEHAVIOR EJ 053 741
AGE OF SUBJECT, TYPE OF SOCIAL CONTACT, AND RESPONSIVENESS TO SOCIAL REINFORCEMENT EJ 055 093
THE EFFECT OF SIBLING RELATIONSHIP ON CONCEPT LEARNING OF YOUNG CHILDREN TAUGHT BY CHILD-TEACHERS EJ 056 399

MOTHER-CHILD INTERACTION IN THE FIRST YEAR OF LIFE EJ 056 632
GRADE INTERACTION WITH WORDS AND PICTURES IN A PAIRED-ASSOCIATE TASK: A PROPOSED EXPLANATION EJ 057 910
EYE CONTACT, ATTITUDES, AND ATTITUDE CHANGE AMONG MALES EJ 059 813
PRINCIPLES OF INTERACTION IN LANGUAGE LEARNING EJ 059 875

INTERAGENCY COOPERATION
ADOPTION: IDENTIFICATION AND SERVICE EJ 058 307

INTERCULTURAL PROGRAMS
A PILOT STUDY INTEGRATING VISUAL FORM AND ANTHROPOLOGICAL CONTENT FOR TEACHING CHILDREN AGES 6 TO 11 ABOUT CULTURES AND PEOPLES OF THE WORLD ED027095
CROSS-CULTURAL FAMILY CENTER, SAN FRANCISCO, CALIFORNIA: A NURSERY SCHOOL PROVIDING A MULTICULTURAL CURRICULUM TO PROMOTE RACIAL UNDERSTANDING AND ACCEPTANCE. MODEL PROGRAMS--CHILDHOOD EDUCATION. ED045214
NURSERIES IN CROSS-CULTURAL EDUCATION. FINAL REPORT. ED053815
UNDERSTANDING ONE ANOTHER: UNESCO'S ASSOCIATED SCHOOLS PROJECT EJ 037 426
HUMAN RESOURCES FOR INTERNATIONAL STUDIES EJ 038 393

INTERDIMENSIONAL SHIFT
CONCEPTUAL BEHAVIOR IN YOUNG CHILDREN: LEARNING TO SHIFT DIMENSIONAL ATTENTION EJ 044 697

INTERDISCIPLINARY APPROACH
A PRELIMINARY INVESTIGATION TO ESTABLISH A REGIONAL CENTER FOR EDUCATIONAL DEVELOPMENTAL STUDIES OF DISADVANTAGED PRESCHOOL CHILDREN. FINAL REPORT. ED017318
HEAD START EVALUATION AND RESEARCH CENTER, BOSTON UNIVERSITY. REPORT B-I, PRIMARY AND SECONDARY PREVENTION STUDYING CLINICAL PROCESS AND DISTURBANCE WITH PRESCHOOL CHILDREN. ED022560
CHILD DEVELOPMENT AND SOCIAL SCIENCE EDUCATION. PART I: THE PROBLEM, PART II: CONFERENCE REPORT. ED023465
THE NEED FOR A MULTI-DIMENSIONAL APPROACH TO LEARNING DISABILITIES. A MULTI-DISCIPLINARY SYMPOSIUM ON DYSLEXIS AND ASSOCIATED LEARNING DISABILITIES. ED027956
EVALUATION OF AN INTERDISCIPLINARY APPROACH TO PREVENTION OF EARLY SCHOOL FAILURE. FOLLOW-UP STUDY, FINAL REPORT. ED031295
SOCIAL STUDIES IN THE PRIMARY GRADES. ED035460
ISSUES IN HUMAN DEVELOPMENT: AN INVENTORY OF PROBLEMS, UNFINISHED BUSINESS AND DIRECTIONS FOR RESEARCH. ED051888
AN INTERDISCIPLINARY APPROACH IN DAY TREATMENT OF EMOTIONALLY DISTURBED CHILDREN EJ 029 167
OCEANS AND CHILDREN: MARINE SCIENCE AND ECOLOGICAL UNDERSTANDING EJ 029 391
OCCUPATIONAL THERAPY AND SPECIAL EDUCATION EJ 045 234

INTEREST RESEARCH
SOCIOECONOMIC STATUS AND CHILDREN'S INTERESTS EJ 016 775
THE RELATIONSHIP OF ORDINAL POSITION AND SEX TO INTEREST PATTERNS EJ 045 111

INTEREST TESTS
THE COGNITIVE ENVIRONMENTS OF URBAN PRE-SCHOOL CHILDREN. MANUAL OF INSTRUCTIONS FOR ADMINISTERING AND SCORING PLUTCHIK EXPLORATORY-INTEREST QUESTIONNAIRE. ED018262

INTERFERENCE (LANGUAGE LEARNING)
THE EFFECTS OF STANDARD DIALECT TRAINING ON NEGRO FIRST-GRADERS LEARNING TO READ. FINAL REPORT. ED029717
VERBAL MEDIATION AND SATIATION IN YOUNG CHILDREN EJ 056 613

INTERGROUP RELATIONS
THE INTERGROUP RELATIONS CURRICULUM: A PROGRAM FOR ELEMENTARY SCHOOL EDUCATION. VOLUMES I AND II. ED029704
VALUES AND TECHNIQUES OF CREATIVE DRAMATICS EJ 034 422

INTERIOR DESIGN
PROGRAMS FOR INFANTS AND YOUNG CHILDREN. PART IV: FACILITIES AND EQUIPMENT. ED047810

INTERIOR SPACE
A DOLL CORNER UPSTAIRS EJ 013 296

INTERMEDIATE GRADES
LEARNING AND TEACHING, GRADES N-9 (EMPHASIS ON EARLY CHILDHOOD). ED023459

INTERMODE DIFFERENCES
SENSORY-MODALITY EFFECTS ON SHAPE PERCEPTION IN PRESCHOOL CHILDREN EJ 029 383

INTERNAL SCALING
THE RELATIONSHIP BETWEEN CHILDREN'S ACADEMIC PERFORMANCE AND ACHIEVEMENT ACCOUNTABILITY EJ 058 414

INTERNATIONAL EDUCATION
A DAY CARE PROGRAM IN THE MIDDLE EAST EJ 009 815
VISIT TO A MISSION SCHOOL FOR ABORIGINAL CHILDREN EJ 014 292

INTERNATIONAL ORGANIZATIONS
ENRICHING CHILDREN'S LIVES: INTERNATIONAL CO-OPERATION THROUGH UNICEF AND OMEP EJ 062 417

INTERNATIONAL PROGRAMS
NUTRITION REHABILITATION CENTRES EJ 029 953
A FRESH LOOK AT INTERCOUNTRY ADOPTIONS EJ 047 968

INTERNSHIP PROGRAMS
STUDYING HUMAN ECOLOGY: TEACHER EDUCATION AND THE CULTURALLY DIVERSE EJ 048 395

INTERPERSONAL COMPETENCE
COMPETENCE AND DEPENDENCE IN CHILDREN. PARENTAL TREATMENT OF FOUR-YEAR-OLD GIRLS. FINAL REPORT. ED030497
MODELS, NORMS AND SHARING. ED046512
SOCIAL SKILLS DEVELOPMENT IN THE EARLY CHILDHOOD EDUCATION PROJECT. TECHNICAL REPORT NO. 7. ED052835
EARLY ANTECEDENTS OF ROLE-TAKING AND ROLE-PLAYING ABILITY EJ 008 318
CHILDREN'S SOCIAL SENSITIVITY AND THE RELATIONSHIP TO INTERPERSONAL COMPETENCE, INTRAPERSONAL COMFORT, AND INTELLECTUAL LEVEL EJ 022 136
SOCIAL PARTICIPATION AS A FACTOR IN THE MORAL DEVELOPMENT OF PREADOLESCENTS EJ 043 605
A SOCIAL COMPETENCE SCALE AND SYMPTOM CHECKIST FOR THE PRESCHOOL CHILD: FACTOR DIMENSIONS, THEIR CROSS-INSTRUMENT GENERALITY, AND LONGITUDINAL PERSISTENCE EJ 057 476

INTERPERSONAL PROBLEMS
HEAD START EVALUATION AND RESEARCH CENTER. PROGRESS REPORT OF RESEARCH STUDIES 1966 TO 1967. DOCUMENT 2, STUDIES OF THE SOCIAL ORGANIZATION OF HEAD START CENTERS. ED021624

INTERPERSONAL RELATIONSHIP
THE DEVELOPMENT OF SELF-OTHER RELATIONSHIPS DURING PROJECT HEAD START. ED015008
SELF-SOCIAL CONSTRUCTS OF CHILDREN. ED021615
MODELS, NORMS AND SHARING. ED046512
IMPLICATIONS OF POST-NATAL CORTICAL DEVELOPMENT FOR CREATIVITY RESEARCH. ED047802
SELF-DISCLOSURE AND RELATIONSHIP TO THE TARGET PERSON EJ 007 431
SHARING IN CHILDREN AS A FUNCTION OF THE NUMBER OF SHAREES AND RECIPROCITY EJ 016 840
CHILDREN'S JUDGMENTS OF KINDNESS EJ 018 259
ROLE MODELSHIP AND INTERACTION IN ADOLESCENCE AND YOUNG ADULTHOOD EJ 019 386
EVALUATING SETTINGS FOR LEARNING EJ 019 966
AN EXPERIMENTAL STUDY OF THE SOCIAL RESPONSIVENESS OF CHILDREN WITH AUTISTIC BEHAVIORS EJ 024 470
NON-SOCIAL SPEECH IN FOUR-YEAR-OLD CHILDREN AS A FUNCTION OF BIRTH ORDER AND INTERPERSONAL SITUATION EJ 033 702
THE OBJECTIVE MEASUREMENT OF CHILDREN'S INTRAFAMILIAL ATTITUDE AND SENTIMENT STRUCTURE AND THE INVESTMENT-SUBSIDIATION MODEL EJ 034 542
THE CAPACITY TO LOVE: A POSSIBLE REFORMULATION EJ 034 709
I SEE WHAT YOU MEAN EJ 035 370
THE RELATION OF ROLE TAKING TO THE DEVELOPMENT OF MORAL JUDGMENT IN CHILDREN EJ 035 991
INTERPERSONAL RELATIONSHIPS IN RESIDENTIAL TREATMENT CENTERS FOR DISTURBED CHILDREN EJ 037 183
WHITE STAFF, BLACK CHILDREN: IS THERE A PROBLEM? EJ 039 799
CHILDREN'S DESCRIPTIONS OF PEERS: A WERNERIAN DEVELOPMENTAL ANALYSIS EJ 041 591
TELEVISED AGGRESSION AND THE INTERPERSONAL AGGRESSION OF PRESCHOOL CHILDREN EJ 043 197
A CHILD IN DISTRESS: THE INFLUENCE OF NURTURANCE AND MODELING ON CHILDREN'S ATTEMPTS TO HELP EJ 043 314
"THIS YEAR I GOT MY BUDDY TO LAUGH" EJ 044 509
CHILD-PARENT SPATIAL PATTERNS UNDER PRAISE AND REPROOF EJ 045 159
FACTOR STRUCTURE OF CHILDREN'S PERSONAL SPACE SCHEMATA EJ 052 466
THE EFFECT OF AGGRESSIVE CARTOONS ON CHILDREN'S INTERPERSONAL PLAY EJ 053 750
SOME ANGLES ON PARENT-TEACHER LEARNING EJ 054 162
PERSON SPECIFICITY OF THE "SOCIAL DEPRIVATION-SATIATION EFFECT" EJ 055 207
LEARNING FROM LOOKING WITHIN: A DIFFERENT FOCUS, RELATING AND RESPONDING THROUGH THE ARTS EJ 057 326
EYE CONTACT, ATTITUDES, AND ATTITUDE CHANGE AMONG MALES EJ 059 813

INTERPRETIVE SKILLS
THE PRESCHOOL CHILD'S ABILITY TO FOLLOW DIRECTIONS. ED043395
CHILD VERSUS ADULT PERCEPTION OF EVALUATIVE MESSAGES IN VERBAL, VOCAL, AND VISUAL CHANNELS EJ 021 765
EFFECTS OF PROBING CHILDREN'S PHENOMENISTIC EXPLANATIONS OF CAUSE AND EFFECT EJ 030 292

INTERPROFESSIONAL RELATIONSHIP
COMPREHENSIVE CHILD PSYCHIATRY THROUGH A TEAM APPROACH EJ 008 042

INTERVAL PACING
STEADY-STATE BEHAVIOR IN CHILDREN: A METHOD AND SOME DATA EJ 053 730
NOUN-PAIR LEARNING IN CHILDREN AND ADULTS: UNDERLYING STRINGS AND RETRIEVAL TIME EJ 056 402

INTERVENTION
COMMUNICATIVE COMPETENCE OF LOW-INCOME CHILDREN--ASSUMPTIONS AND PROGRAMS. ED020775
HEAD START EVALUATION AND RESEARCH CENTER, TEACHERS COLLEGE, COLUMBIA UNIVERSITY. ANNUAL REPORT (1ST), SEPTEMBER 1966-AUGUST 1967. (TITLE SUPPLIED). ED020781
HEAD START EVALUATION AND RESEARCH CENTER. PROGRESS REPORT OF RESEARCH STUDIES 1966 TO 1967. DOCUMENT 6, INDIVIDUAL INSTRUCTION PROJECT I. ED021628
INVESTMENTS IN PREVENTION, AN ACTIVITY GROUP PROGRAM FOR YOUNG CHILDREN, SUMMER - 1967. ED025311
DIFFUSION OF INTERVENTION EFFECTS IN DISADVANTAGED FAMILIES. ED026127
REVIEW OF SELECTED INTERVENTION RESEARCH WITH YOUNG CHILDREN. ED027091
TOWARD THE PREVENTION OF INCOMPETENCE. ED028812
EVALUATION OF AN INTERDISCIPLINARY APPROACH TO PREVENTION OF EARLY SCHOOL FAILURE. FOLLOW-UP STUDY, FINAL REPORT. ED031295
THE EARLY TRAINING PROJECT: A SEVENTH YEAR REPORT. ED032934
PRESCHOOL INTERVENTION THROUGH SOCIAL LEARNING. ED036316
PARENTAL BEHAVIOR AND CHILDREN'S SCHOOL ACHIEVEMENT: IMPLICATIONS FOR HEAD START. PROCEEDINGS OF THE HEAD START RESEARCH SEMINARS: SEMINAR NO. 5, INTERVENTION IN FAMILY LIFE (1ST, WASHINGTON, D.C., JANUARY 13, 1969). ED036332
INTRA-FAMILY DIFFUSION OF SELECTED COGNITIVE SKILLS AS A FUNCTION OF EDUCATIONAL STIMULATION. ED037233
RESEARCH AND CONSULTATION IN THE NATURAL ENVIRONMENT. ED037240
RESEARCH IN A BLACK COMMUNITY: FOUR YEARS IN REVIEW. ED039035
AN EDUCATIONAL SYSTEM FOR DEVELOPMENTALLY DISABLED INFANTS. ED040749
A TUTORIAL LANGUAGE PROGRAM FOR DISADVANTAGED INFANTS. ED040766
AN EDUCATION SYSTEM FOR HIGH-RISK INFANTS: A PREVENTIVE APPROACH TO DEVELOPMENTAL AND LEARNING DISABILITIES. ED043379
PARENTS AS PRIMARY CHANGE AGENTS IN AN EXPERIMENTAL HEAD START PROGRAM OF LANGUAGE INTERVENTION. EXPERIMENTAL PROGRAM REPORT. ED044168
PROCEEDINGS: EARLY CHILDHOOD INTERVENTION RESEARCH CONFERENCE (UNIVERSITY OF SOUTH FLORIDA, TAMPA, MARCH 5 AND 6, 1970). ED045194
INFORMATION ON INTERVENTION PROGRAMS OF THE DEMONSTRATION AND RESEARCH CENTER FOR EARLY EDUCATION. ED046492
NEGRO CULTURE AND EARLY CHILDHOOD EDUCATION. ED046495
PRESCHOOL EDUCATION AND POVERTY: THE DISTANCE IN BETWEEN. FINAL REPORT OF 1968-69 INTERVENTIONAL PROGRAM. ED046501
HEAD START PLANNED VARIATION STUDY. ED047782
"NEED ACHIEVEMENT" TRAINING FOR HEAD START CHILDREN AND THEIR MOTHERS. ED048943
THE INFLUENCE OF SELECTED VARIABLES ON THE EFFECTIVENESS OF PRESCHOOL PROGRAMS FOR DISADVANTAGED CHILDREN. ED049835
INTERVENTION WITH MOTHERS AND YOUNG CHILDREN: A STUDY OF INTRAFAMILY EFFECTS. ED050809
EDUCATIONAL INTERVENTION IN EARLY CHILDHOOD: A REPORT OF A FIVE-YEAR LONGITUDINAL STUDY OF THE EFFECTS OF EARLY EDUCATIONAL INTERVENTION IN THE LIVES OF DISADVANTAGED CHILDREN IN DURHAM, NORTH CAROLINA. FINAL REPORT, VOLUME I. ED050814
EDUCATIONAL INTERVENTION IN EARLY CHILDHOOD: APPENDIXES. FINAL REPORT, VOLUME II. ED050815
EDUCATIONAL INTERVENTION IN EARLY CHILDHOOD: ABSTRACTS OF THE 1965-1970 SPECIAL STUDIES RESEARCH AND EVALUATION REPORT. FINAL REPORT, VOLUME III. ED050816
THE EFFECT OF EARLY STIMULATION: THE PROBLEM OF FOCUS IN DEVELOPMENTAL STIMULATION EJ 006 921
A METHODOLOGICAL AND PHILOSOPHICAL CRITIQUE OF INTERVENTION-ORIENTED RESEARCH EJ 019 323
DEFICITS AND VALUE JUDGMENTS: A COMMENT ON SROUFE'S CRITIQUE EJ 019 324
EDUCATIONAL INTERVENTION AT HOME BY MOTHERS OF DISADVANTAGED INFANTS EJ 034 002
EXPERIMENTAL PRESCHOOL INTERVENTION IN THE APPALACHIAN HOME EJ 036 395
COGNITIVE DEVELOPMENT IN INFANCY: ASSESSMENT, ACCELERATION, AND ACTUALIZATION EJ 037 493
ETHICAL ISSUES IN RESEARCH IN EARLY CHILDHOOD INTERVENTION EJ 037 578
VIOLENCE BEGINS AT HOME. THE PARENTS' CENTER PROJECT FOR THE STUDY AND PREVENTION OF CHILD ABUSE EJ 043 671
INTERVENTION IN INFANCY: A PROGRAM FOR BLIND INFANTS EJ 048 904
THE RELATIVE EFFICACY OF CONTACT AND VESTIBULAR-PROPRIOCEPTIVE STIMULATION IN SOOTHING NEONATES EJ 058 588
DEVELOPMENTAL THEORY: ITS PLACE AND RELEVANCE IN EARLY INTERVENTION PROGRAMS EJ 060 013

INTERVIEWS
FACTORS INFLUENCING THE RECRUITMENT OF CHILDREN INTO THE HEAD START PROGRAM, SUMMER 1965--A CASE STUDY OF SIX CENTERS IN NEW YORK CITY. STUDY II. ED015026
THE MANIPULATION AND MEASUREMENT OF SELF-DISCLOSURE IN PREADOLESCENTS EJ 034 298
AN INTERVIEW WITH GEORGIA MCMURRAY, NEW YORK CITY'S COMMISSIONER FOR CHILD DEVELOPMENT EJ 050 274
A PARENT SPEAKS EJ 051 240
EMERGENCE AND PERSISTENCE OF BEHAVIORAL DIFFERENCES IN TWINS EJ 053 732

INTONATION
LANGUAGE STRUCTURE AND THE FREE RECALL OF VERBAL MESSAGES BY CHILDREN EJ 044 693

INVESTIGATIONS
NOUN PLURAL DEVELOPMENT IN PRIMARY GRADE CHILDREN EJ 052 179
OVERLAP: HYPOTHESIS OR TAUTOLOGY? EJ 054 508
A DEVELOPMENTAL LEARNING APPROACH TO INFANT CARE IN A GROUP SETTING EJ 057 442

INVESTMENT
OPTIMIZING EDUCATIONAL INVESTMENT STRATEGIES. ED015780

ITEM ANALYSIS
HEAD START EVALUATION AND RESEARCH CENTER, TEACHERS COLLEGE, COLUMBIA UNIVERSITY. ANNUAL REPORT (1ST), SEPTEMBER 1966-AUGUST 1967. (TITLE SUPPLIED). ED020781
HEAD START EVALUATION AND RESEARCH CENTER. PROGRESS REPORT OF RESEARCH STUDIES 1966 TO 1967. DOCUMENT 5, COMPARATIVE ITEM-CONTENT ANALYSIS OF ACHIEVEMENT TEST PERFORMANCE IN YOUNG CHILDREN. ED021627
THE EFFECT OF SYSTEMATIC STORY CHANGES ON INTENTIONALITY IN CHILDREN'S MORAL JUDGMENTS EJ 056 636

ITINERANT TEACHERS
THE ITINERANT TEACHER. ED045191
THE ITINERANT TEACHER EJ 060 930

JAPANESE
THE ACQUISITION OF DIRECT AND INDIRECT OBJECTS IN JAPANESE EJ 036 745

JEWS
INFLUENCES OF CULTURAL PATTERNS ON THE THINKING OF CHILDREN IN CERTAIN ETHNIC GROUPS, A STUDY OF THE EFFECT OF JEWISH SUBCULTURE ON THE FIELD-DEPENDENCE-INDEPENDENCE DIMENSION OF COGNITION. ED020796
LEARNING READINESS IN TWO JEWISH GROUPS: A STUDY IN "CULTURAL DEPRIVATION." AN OCCASIONAL PAPER. ED026126

JOB TRAINING
[A STATEMENT REGARDING THE COMPREHENSIVE PRESCHOOL EDUCATION AND CHILD DAY CARE ACT OF 1969, AND OTHER RELATED BILLS.] ED041624
THE FAMILY DAY CARE PROGRAM IN MILWAUKEE: A 3-FACETED APPROACH TO COMMUNITY ENRICHMENT EJ 023 391
HEALTH CARE THROUGH HEAD START EJ 024 496

JUNIOR COLLEGES
ROLE PERCEPTIONS AND JOB SATISFACTION AMONG LOWER AND MIDDLE LEVEL JUNIOR COLLEGE ADMINISTRATORS EJ 016 774

JUNIOR HIGH SCHOOL STUDENTS
A COMPARISON OF THE CHARACTERISTICS OF JUNIOR HIGH SCHOOL STUDENTS EJ 026 325
THE EFFECT OF INDIVIDUAL-CONTINGENT GROUP REINFORCEMENT ON POPULARITY EJ 034 158
USING SENSITIVITY TRAINING WITH JUNIOR HIGH SCHOOL STUDENTS EJ 035 169
DELAY OF FEEDBACK INTERVAL, POSTFEEDBACK INTERVAL, DISTRACTION, AND TASK DIFFICULTY AS FACTORS IN A MODIFIED CONCEPT-IDENTIFICATION TASK WITH JUNIOR HIGH SCHOOL SUBJECTS EJ 047 677

JUNIOR HIGH SCHOOLS
THE MIDDLE SCHOOL: A SELECTED BIBLIOGRAPHY WITH INTRODUCTION. ED029714
ALTERNATIVE LEARNING ENVIRONMENTS: A PHILADELPHIA STORY EJ 033 156

KINDERGARTEN
IMPACT OF SUMMER 1965 HEAD START ON CHILDREN'S CONCEPT ATTAINMENT DURING KINDERGARTEN. FINAL REPORT. ED015773

HEADSTART OPERATIONAL FIELD ANALYSIS. PROGRESS REPORT III. ED015776
A STUDY OF THE KINDERGARTEN PROGRAM, FULL-DAY OR HALF-DAY. ED017327
KINDERGARTEN OVERSEAS, A STUDY OF THE REQUIREMENTS FOR ESTABLISHING KINDERGARTEN AS PART OF THE DEPARTMENT OF DEFENSE OVERSEAS DEPENDENTS SCHOOLS. FINAL REPORT. ED017340
KINDERGARTEN GUIDEBOOK. ED020008
BLOCKBUILDING. ED020011
LET'S TRY THIS IN NURSERY SCHOOL AND KINDERGARTEN. ED022556
THE EFFECTS OF ASSESSMENT AND PERSONALIZED PROGRAMMING ON SUBSEQUENT INTELLECTUAL DEVELOPMENT OF PREKINDERGARTEN AND KINDERGARTEN CHILDREN. FINAL REPORT OF PHASE II. ED023487
AN ARTICULATION STUDY OF 15,255 SEATTLE FIRST GRADE CHILDREN WITH AND WITHOUT KINDERGARTEN. ED024438
AN EVALUATION OF THE LANGUAGE ARTS PROGRAM OF THE DISTRICT OF COLUMBIA. FINAL REPORT. ED024449
KINDERGARTEN, 1967-68. AN EVALUATION REPORT. ED025315
DEVELOPMENT AND IMPLEMENTATION OF A COMPREHENSIVE EVALUATION AND REPORTING SYSTEM FOR KINDERGARTEN AND PRIMARY GRADE SCHOOLS. FINAL REPORT. ED026116
A GUIDE FOR PERCEPTUAL-MOTOR TRAINING ACTIVITIES. ED027075
THE CHANGE PROCESS IN ACTION: KINDERGARTEN ED027949
CONCEPT AND LANGUAGE DEVELOPMENT IN A KINDERGARTEN OF DISADVANTAGED CHILDREN. ED027967
COORDINATED HELPS IN LANGUAGE DEVELOPMENT (CHILD). NORTHWEST REGIONAL EDUCATIONAL LABORATORY STUDY. SECOND EXPERIMENTAL EDITION. ED028831
A STUDY OF PUBLIC AND PRIVATE KINDERGARTEN AND NON-KINDERGARTEN CHILDREN IN THE PRIMARY GRADES. ED028837
KINDERGARTEN: THE CHILD IN HIS HOME AND SCHOOL ENVIRONMENTS. COURSE OF STUDY AND RELATED LEARNING ACTIVITIES. (CURRICULUM BULLETIN, 1967-68 SERIES, NO. 2A.) ED029681
EFFECTS OF KINDERGARTEN ATTENDANCE ON DEVELOPMENT OF SCHOOL READINESS AND LANGUAGE SKILLS. INTERIM REPORT. ED029706
CONCEPT AND LANGUAGE DEVELOPMENT. A RESOURCE GUIDE FOR TEACHING YOUNG CHILDREN. ED030472
EFFECT OF A KINDERGARTEN PROGRAM OF PERCEPTUAL TRAINING UPON THE LATER DEVELOPMENT OF READING SKILLS. FINAL REPORT. ED030491
A PREVENTIVE SUMMER PROGRAM FOR KINDERGARTEN CHILDREN LIKELY TO FAIL IN FIRST GRADE READING. FINAL REPORT. ED030495
A COMPARISON OF READING READINESS ACHIEVEMENT OF KINDERGARTEN CHILDREN OF DISPARATE ENTRANCE AGES. ED033745
ESOL-SESD GUIDE: KINDERGARTEN. ED033748
KINDERGARTEN CURRICULUM GUIDE: EARLY CHILDHOOD EDUCATION. ED034575
A SOCIALLY INTEGRATED KINDERGARTEN. ED034578
MATERIALS FOR KINDERGARTEN. ED037237
CHILD STUDY-KINDERGARTEN, 1968-69: AN INFORMATION REPORT. ED039015
THE KINDERGARTEN, A PLACE FOR LEARNING. BULLETIN TWO: OPERATIONAL GUIDELINES FOR ADMINISTRATORS. ED039024
THE KINDERGARTEN, A PLACE FOR LEARNING. BULLETIN ONE: MATERIALS AND EQUIPMENT FOR THE FOURS AND FIVES. ED039026
KINDERGARTEN HANDBOOK: A GUIDE TO THOSE ACTIVELY INTERESTED IN KINDERGARTENS AND IN ESTABLISHING NEW CENTRES. THIRD EDITION. ED039925
KINDERGARTEN CURRICULUM GUIDE. ED039929
THE EFFECT OF SUPPLEMENTARY SMALL GROUP EXPERIENCE ON TASK ORIENTATION AND COGNITIVE PERFORMANCE IN KINDERGARTEN CHILDREN. A FINAL REPORT OF THE KINDERGARTEN 'LEARNING TO LEARN' PROGRAM EVALUATION PROJECT. ED039948
EXPERIMENTS IN HEAD START AND EARLY EDUCATION: THE EFFECTS OF TEACHER ATTITUDE AND CURRICULUM STRUCTURE ON PRESCHOOL DISADVANTAGED CHILDREN. FINAL REPORT. ED041615
ENRICHMENT APPROACH VERSUS DIRECT INSTRUCTIONAL APPROACH AND THEIR EFFECTS ON DIFFERENTIAL PRESCHOOL EXPERIENCES. ED043369
AN EXPERIMENTAL SUMMER KINDERGARTEN FOR CULTURALLY DEPRIVED CHILDREN. ED044174
MODIFICATION OF THE CLASSROOM BEHAVIOR OF A "DISADVANTAGED" KINDERGARTEN BOY BY SOCIAL REINFORCEMENT AND ISOLATION. ED045181
PRELIMINARY ANALYSIS ON KINDERGARTEN AND FIRST GRADE FOLLOW THROUGH TEST RESULTS FOR 1968-69. ED045202
MODEL OBSERVATION KINDERGARTEN AND FIRST GRADE, AMHERST, MASSACHUSETTS: MODEL CLASSROOMS WHICH OFFER COMPLETELY INDIVIDUALIZED SCHEDULING FOR MIXED AGE GROUPS OF KINDERGARTEN AND FIRST-GRADE STUDENTS. MODEL PROGRAMS--CHILDHOOD EDUCATION. ED045219
PRESCHOOL EDUCATION AND SCHOOL ADMISSION PRACTICES IN NEW ZEALAND. ED046487
A COMPARISON OF CONTRASTING PROGRAMS IN EARLY CHILDHOOD EDUCATION. ED046509
A PILOT STUDY OF A PRESCHOOL METHOD OF PREVENTIVE EDUCATION. FINAL REPORT. ED046541
PROCEEDINGS OF FOLLOW THROUGH CONFERENCE (GAINESVILLE, FLORIDA, DECEMBER 9-10, 1969). ED047773
EFFECTS OF VIEWING VIDEOTAPED SAME AND OPPOSITE COLOR CHILD-TEACHERS ON INTEGRATED AND ALL-WHITE KINDERGARTNERS. ED047805
KINDERGARTEN: WHO? WHAT? WHERE? ED049829
EXPERIMENTAL VARIATION OF HEAD START CURRICULA: A COMPARISON OF CURRENT APPROACHES. PROGRESS REPORT NO. 9, MARCH 1, 1971 - MAY 31, 1971. ED053814
CLASSROOM LANGUAGE OF TEACHERS OF YOUNG CHILDREN. ED053820
FIRST STEPS IN SCHOOL EJ 007 205
DISTORTIONS IN THE KINDERGARTEN EJ 007 214
HIS OWN HELLO EJ 013 230
CONCEPT LEARNING THROUGH MOVEMENT IMPROVISATION: THE TEACHER'S ROLE AS CATALYST EJ 014 945
AWARENESS--ONE KEY TO READING READINESS EJ 027 551
EARLY AGE EDUCATION EJ 029 620
LA EDUCACION PRE-ESCOLAR EN LAS ESCUELAS PUBLICAS DE PUERTO RICO EJ 029 622
SHOWING AND SHARING IN THE KINDERGARTEN EJ 032 933
WHAT IS A GOOD KINDERGARTEN? EJ 035 243
THE KINDERGARTEN AGAINST APPALACHIAN POVERTY EJ 037 021
CONTINUITY FROM PREKINDERGARTEN TO KINDERGARTEN EJ 039 058
THE DECLINE OF PLAY IN URBAN KINDERGARTENS EJ 041 961
A BASIC VOCABULARY FOR BEGINNING READING EJ 047 894
TEACHING READING IN THE KINDERGARTEN: A REVIEW OF RECENT STUDIES EJ 055 153
HOW FREE IS FREE PLAY? EJ 055 535
A YOUNG MAN AROUND THE CLASS EJ 059 445
REFLECTIONS ON REVISITING VIENNA'S YOUNG CITIZENS EJ 060 107
EARLY CHILDHOOD EDUCATION IN JAPAN EJ 061 692

KINDERGARTEN CHILDREN

CONCEPT FORMATION BY KINDERGARTEN CHILDREN IN A CARD-SORTING TASK. PSYCHOLOGY SERIES. ED013665
AN ASSESSMENT AND COMPARISON OF SELECTED CHARACTERISTICS AMONG CULTURALLY DISADVANTAGED HEADSTART CHILDREN (SUMMER PROGRAM 1965), CULTURALLY DISADVANTAGED NON-HEADSTART CHILDREN, AND NON-CULTURALLY DISADVANTAGED CHILDREN. (TITLE SUPPLIED). ED014330
SIX MONTHS LATER--A COMPARISON OF CHILDREN WHO HAD HEAD START, SUMMER, 1965, WITH THEIR CLASSMATES IN KINDERGARTEN, A CASE STUDY OF THE KINDERGARTENS IN FOUR PUBLIC ELEMENTARY SCHOOLS, NEW YORK CITY. STUDY I. ED015025
APPENDIX, STUDIES I, II AND III. ORIGINAL INSTRUMENTS USED AND BIBLIOGRAPHY. ED015028
REMARKS ON THE MAX WOLFF REPORT. ED015030
HEADSTART OPERATIONAL FIELD ANALYSIS. PROGRESS REPORT IV. ED015777
INCREASING THE AWARENESS OF ART IDEAS OF CULTURALLY DEPRIVED KINDERGARTEN CHILDREN THROUGH EXPERIENCES WITH CERAMICS. FINAL REPORT. ED016519
EVALUATION OF CHANGES OCCURRING IN CHILDREN WHO PARTICIPATED IN PROJECT HEAD START. ED017316
STUDY OF ACHIEVEMENT--REPORT POPULATION STUDY OF JUNIOR AND SENIOR KINDERGARTEN PUPILS, 1960-61 AND 1961-62. ED017321
STUDY OF ACHIEVEMENT--JUNIOR KINDERGARTEN, WHO IS SERVED AND WHO GOES. ED017322
STUDY OF ACHIEVEMENT, TORONTO INFORMATION BULLETIN NO. 1. ED017323
EFFECTS OF DIFFERENTIAL PRIOR EXPOSURE ON YOUNG CHILDREN'S SUBSEQUENT OBSERVING AND CHOICE OF NOVEL STIMULI. ED017336
THE CREATIVE-AESTHETIC APPROACH TO SCHOOL READINESS AND MEASURED CREATIVE GROWTH. ED017344
EXTINCTION IN DISCRIMINATION LEARNING--PRESENTATION AND CONTINGENCY VARIABLES AND ASSOCIATED SIDE EFFECTS. ED019139
SEX AND RACE DIFFERENCES IN THE DEVELOPMENT OF UNDERPRIVILEGED PRESCHOOL CHILDREN. ED019992
THE INTERPLAY OF SOME EGO FUNCTIONS IN SIX YEAR OLD CHILDREN. ED020005
IDENTIFICATION AND EVALUATION OF CHARACTERISTICS OF KINDERGARTEN CHILDREN THAT FORETELL EARLY LEARNING PROBLEMS. FINAL REPORT. ED020006
IDENTIFICATION AND EVALUATION OF CHARACTERISTICS OF KINDERGARTEN CHILDREN THAT FORETELL EARLY LEARNING PROBLEMS. SUMMARY REPORT. ED020007
THE DEUTSCH MODEL--INSTITUTE FOR DEVELOPMENTAL STUDIES. ED020009
LOGICAL OPERATIONS AND CONCEPTS OF CONSERVATION IN CHILDREN, A TRAINING STUDY. FINAL REPORT. ED020010
AN EVALUATION AND FOLLOW-UP STUDY OF SUMMER 1966 HEAD START CHILDREN IN WASHINGTON, D.C. ED020794
VARIABLES AFFECTING THE PERFORMANCE OF YOUNG CHILDREN ON A LETTER DISCRIMINATION TASK. ED020797
RESPONSE TO VARYING LEVELS OF CONDITIONING REWARDS. FINAL REPORT. ED020803
EARLY CHILDHOOD EDUCATION TODAY. ED021631

AN EXPERIMENTAL STUDY OF FORMAL READING INSTRUCTION AT THE KINDERGARTEN LEVEL. ED022533
SIX STRUCTURE-OF-INTELLECT HYPOTHESES IN SIX-YEAR-OLD CHILDREN. ED023469
A COMPARISON OF PRE-KINDERGARTEN AND PRE-1ST GRADE BOYS AND GIRLS ON MEASURES OF SCHOOL READINESS AND LANGUAGE DEVELOPMENT. INTERIM REPORT. ED023474
THE SHIFT FROM COLOR TO FORM PREFERENCE IN YOUNG CHILDRE N OF DIFFERENT ETHNIC BACKGROUNDS. PART OF THE FINAL REPORT. ED025321
KINDERGARTEN RESEARCH STUDY: LEVEL OF SKILLS DEVELOPMENT RELATED TO GROWTH IN SKILLS AND TO READINESS FOR THE FIRST PRIMARY YEAR. ED026111
THE ELEMENTARY MATHEMATICS STUDY: AN INTERIM REPORT ON KINDERGARTEN YEAR RESULTS. ED027937
THE VALUE OF THE SPOKEN RESPONSE IN TEACHING LISTENING SKILLS TO YOUNG CHILDREN THROUGH PROGRAMMED INSTRUCTION. FINAL REPORT. ED027973
TEACHING MOTHERS TO TEACH: A HOME COUNSELING PROGRAM FOR LOW-INCOME PARENTS. ED028819
PERFORMANCE OF KINDERGARTEN CHILDREN FROM LOW INCOME FAMILIES ON SELECTED CONCEPT CATEGORIES. ED028847
YOUNG CHILDREN'S USE OF LANGUAGE IN INFERENTIAL BEHAVIOR. ED029691
A COMPARISON OF THE READING READINESS OF KINDERGARTEN PUPILS EXPOSED TO CONCEPTUAL-LANGUAGE AND BASAL READER PREREADING PROGRAMS. A PILOT STUDY. FINAL REPORT. ED029709
EVALUATION OF AN INTERDISCIPLINARY APPROACH TO PREVENTION OF EARLY SCHOOL FAILURE. FOLLOW-UP STUDY, FINAL REPORT. ED031295
A STUDY OF THE EFFECTS OF A GROUP LANGUAGE DEVELOPMENT PROGRAM UPON THE PSYCHOLINGUISTIC ABILITIES AND LATER BEGINNING READING SUCCESS OF KINDERGARTEN CHILDREN. ED031315
PREPRIMARY ENROLLMENT OF CHILDREN UNDER SIX: OCTOBER 1968. ED032118
TEACHING KINDERGARTEN CHILDREN TO APPLY CONCEPT-DEFINING RULES. ED037231
PREPRIMARY ENROLLMENT TRENDS OF CHILDREN UNDER SIX: 1964-1968. ED042502
THE SOCIAL MATURITY OF DISADVANTAGED CHILDREN. SPECIAL STUDIES PROJECT #2: ED042507
PSYCHOLINGUISTIC BEHAVIORS OF ISOLATED, RURAL CHILDREN WITH AND WITHOUT KINDERGARTEN. ED042510
EVALUATION OF FOLLOW THROUGH, 1968 - 1969. ED044172
PREDICTION OF ACHIEVEMENT IN THE FIRST PRIMARY YEAR. STUDY NUMBER ONE. ED044180
THE EFFECTS OF DIFFERENT TYPES OF REINFORCEMENT ON YOUNG CHILDREN'S INCIDENTAL LEARNING. ED044184
PIAGET'S CONCEPT OF CLASSIFICATION: A COMPARATIVE STUDY OF SOCIALLY DISADVANTAGED AND MIDDLE-CLASS YOUNG CHILDREN. ED046499
PRESCHOOLER STUDY: THE MEDICAL, SOCIAL AND ECONOMIC CORRELATES OF POVERTY IN PRESCHOOL CHILDREN OF BRITISH COLUMBIA. A PILOT STUDY. ED046518
SCHOOL ACHIEVEMENT: A PRELIMINARY LOOK AT THE EFFECTS OF THE HOME. ED047777
NUTRITIONAL STATUS OF NEW ORLEANS, MISSISSIPPI AND ALABAMA HEAD START CHILDREN. FINAL REPORT. ED047785
THE ABILITY OF KINDERGARTEN AND FIRST GRADE CHILDREN TO USE THE TRANSITIVE PROPERTY OF THREE LENGTH RELATIONS IN THREE PERCEPTUAL SITUATIONS. ED048936
DIFFERENTIAL PERFORMANCE OF KINDERGARTEN CHILDREN ON TRANSITIVITY OF THREE MATCHING RELATIONS. ED048942
THE EFFECTS OF INSTRUCTION ON THE DEVELOPMENT OF THE CONCEPT OF CONSERVATION OF NUMEROUSNESS BY KINDERGARTEN CHILDREN. REPORT FROM THE PROJECT ON INDIVIDUALLY GUIDED ELEMENTARY MATHEMATICS ED049821
KINDERGARTEN: WHO? WHAT? WHERE? ED049829
RACIAL ATTITUDES AMONG WHITE KINDERGARTEN CHILDREN FROM THREE DIFFERENT ENVIRONMENTS. ED051882
EARLY CHILDHOOD EDUCATION PROGRAM FOR NURSERY, KINDERGARTEN CHILDREN. ED052846
THE EFFECTS OF DIFFERENTIATED INSTRUCTION IN VISUO-MOTOR SKILLS ON DEVELOPMENTAL GROWTH AND READING READINESS AT KINDERGARTEN LEVEL. FINAL REPORT. ED053821
ON SEPARATION AND SCHOOL ENTRANCE EJ 017 902
AN EXAMINATION OF CHILDREN'S DAILY SCHEDULES IN THREE SOCIAL CLASSES AND THEIR RELATION TO FIRST-GRADE READING ACHIEVEMENT EJ 021 079
VERBAL MEDIATORS AND CUE DISCRIMINATION IN THE TRANSITION FROM NONCONSERVATION TO CONSERVATION OF NUMBER EJ 025 958
MODIFYING BEHAVIOR OF KINDERGARTEN CHILDREN EJ 026 493
DISCRIMINATION SHIFT PERFORMANCE OF KINDERGARTEN CHILDREN AS A FUNCTION OF VARIATION OF THE IRRELEVANT SHIFT DIMENSION EJ 027 183
FREEDOM TO MANIPULATE OBJECTS AND QUESTION-ASKING PERFORMANCE OF SIX-YEAR-OLDS EJ 029 217
SUBJECT-MODEL SEXUAL STATUS AND VERBAL IMITATIVE PERFORMANCE IN KINDERGARTEN CHILDREN EJ 030 178
PARENTS: SUMMER READING TEACHERS EJ 032 510
WHAT GENERATION GAP? EJ 032 763
YOUNG CHILDREN'S ORIENTATION OF LETTERS AS A FUNCTION OF AXIS OF SYMMETRY AND STIMULUS ALIGNMENT EJ 032 909
THE GENERALITY OF COLOR-FORM PREFERENCE AS A FUNCTION OF MATERIALS AND TASK REQUIREMENTS AMONG LOWER-CLASS NEGRO CHILDREN EJ 033 052
TRANSFER AND SEQUENCE IN LEARNING DOUBLE CLASSIFICATION SKILLS EJ 035 379
SEQUENTIAL LEARNING BY CHILDREN EJ 035 381
IDEATIONAL CREATIVITY AND EXPRESSIVE ASPECTS OF HUMAN FIGURE DRAWING IN KINDERGARTEN-AGE CHILDREN EJ 039 629
ART - FOR THE CHILD'S SAKE EJ 041 829
KINDERGARTEN CHILDREN'S ACTIVE VOCABULARY ABOUT BODY BUILD EJ 041 857
VARIETY OF EXEMPLARS VERSUS LINGUISTIC CONTEXTS IN CONCEPT ATTAINMENT IN YOUNG CHILDREN EJ 042 955
AN EXPERIENCE WITH FEAR IN THE LIVES OF CHILDREN EJ 045 389
THE INFLUENCE OF COGNITIVE STYLE ON PERCEPTUAL LEARNING EJ 046 238
INTERACTION EFFECTS OF SOCIAL AND TANGIBLE REINFORCEMENT EJ 048 296
YOUNG CHILDREN'S COMPREHENSION OF LOGICAL CONNECTIVES EJ 049 117
EFFECTS OF PERCEPTUAL TRAINING ON CHILDREN'S HUMAN FIGURE DRAWINGS EJ 049 173
SEX DIFFERENCES IN EFFECTS OF KINDERGARTEN ATTENDANCE ON DEVELOPMENT OF SCHOOL READINESS AND LANGUAGE SKILLS EJ 052 723
INSTANT LAW AND ORDER EJ 055 534
HOW FREE IS FREE PLAY? EJ 055 535
THE SPANISH-SPEAKING FIVE-YEAR-OLD EJ 056 391
LOGICAL CAPACITY OF VERY YOUNG CHILDREN: NUMBER INVARIANCE RULES EJ 056 394
THE SEQUENCE OF DEVELOPMENT OF SOME EARLY MATHEMATICS BEHAVIORS EJ 056 710
COGNITIVE AND AFFECTIVE REACTIONS OF KINDERGARTNERS TO VIDEO DISPLAYS EJ 057 016
EFFECTS OF SEX AND BIRTH ORDER ON SEX-ROLE DEVELOPMENT AND INTELLIGENCE AMONG KINDERGARTEN CHILDREN EJ 057 133
WINDOW BEGINS WITH AN "L" EJ 058 507

KINESTHETIC METHODS
AN EXPLORATION OF THE USES OF RHYTHMIC MOVEMENT TO DEVELOP AESTHETIC CONCEPTS IN THE PRIMARY GRADES. ED020770

KINESTHETIC PERCEPTION
THE EFFECT OF SUBJECT-DETERMINED VERBALIZATION ON DISCRIMINATION LEARNING IN PRESCHOOLERS. ED021620
DEVELOPMENT OF CUTANEOUS AND KINESTHETIC LOCALIZATION BY BLIND AND SIGHTED CHILDREN EJ 055 113
DEVELOPMENT OF DIRECTIONALITY IN CHILDREN: AGES SIX THROUGH TWELVE EJ 058 137

KNOWLEDGE LEVEL
ANALYSE DE L'ADOPTION DE LA NOTION DE "FLEUR" CHEZ LES ENFANTS DE 6 ANS EJ 044 703

KOREAN CULTURE
MARGINAL CHILDREN OF WAR: AN EXPLORATORY STUDY OF AMERICAN-KOREAN CHILDREN. ED047781

LABOR UNIONS
A STUDY IN CHILD CARE (CASE STUDY FROM VOLUME II-A): "A ROLLS-ROYCE OF DAY CARE." DAY CARE PROGRAMS REPRINT SERIES. ED051895
STRIKES, SANCTIONS, OR SURRENDER? EJ 003 417
LABOR'S VIEWS ON TEACHER STRIKES EJ 003 418
UNIONS AND DAY CARE CENTERS FOR THE CHILDREN OF WORKING MOTHERS EJ 038 643

LABORATORY EQUIPMENT
A MULTIPLE-CHOICE AUDIO-VISUAL DISCRIMINATION APPARATUS WITH QUICK INTER-CHANGE DISPLAY AND RESPONSE PANELS EJ 018 307

LABORATORY SCHOOLS
THE ROLE OF A LABORATORY NURSERY SCHOOL EJ 036 332
MICRO-TEACHING FOR PREPARING TEACHERS OF CULTURALLY DIVERSE CHILDREN EJ 052 068

LABORATORY TRAINING
HUMAN RELATIONS TRAINING FOR TEACHERS: THE EFFECTIVENESS OF SENSITIVITY TRAINING EJ 015 979

LANGUAGE
THE HUMAN CONNECTION--LANGUAGE AND LITERATURE. ED018271
EARLY CHILDHOOD SELECTED BIBLIOGRAPHIES SERIES. NUMBER 2, LANGUAGE. ED022538

LANGUAGE ABILITY
THE COGNITIVE ENVIRONMENTS OF URBAN PRE-SCHOOL CHILDREN. MANUAL OF INSTRUCTIONS FOR ADMINISTERING AND SCORING MATERNAL LANGUAGE STYLES. ED018270
EVALUATING THE CHILD'S LANGUAGE COMPETENCE. ED019141

SOCIOECONOMIC STATUS AND LEARNING PROFICIENCY IN YOUNG CHILDREN. ED020023
LANGUAGE CONTROL IN A GROUP OF HEAD START CHILDREN. ED020789
PRELIMINARY EVALUATION OF A LANGUAGE CURRICULUM FOR PRESCHOOL CHILDREN. FINAL REPORT. ED021618
A COMPARISON OF THE PSYCHOLINGUISTIC FUNCTIONING OF "EDUCATIONALLY-DEPRIVED" AND "EDUCATIONALLY-ADVANTAGED" CHILDREN. ED022537
LANGUAGE ABILITY AND READINESS FOR SCHOOL OF CHILDREN WHO PARTICIPATED IN HEAD START PROGRAMS. A DISSERTATION ABSTRACT. ED025299
FAMILY FACTORS RELATED TO COMPETENCE IN YOUNG, DISADVANTAGED MEXICAN-AMERICAN CHILDREN. PART OF THE FINAL REPORT ON HEAD START EVALUATION AND RESEARCH: 1968-69 TO THE OFFICE OF ECONOMIC OPPORTUNITY. ED037248
PSYCHOLINGUISTIC BEHAVIORS OF BLACK, DISADVANTAGED RURAL CHILDREN. ED039037
SOME LANGUAGE COMPREHENSION TESTS. ED040765
CHILDREN'S ACQUISITION OF VISUO-SPATIAL DIMENSIONALITY: A CONSERVATION STUDY. ED041636
ETHNIC AND SOCIOECONOMIC INFLUENCES ON THE HOME LANGUAGE EXPERIENCES OF CHILDREN. ED043377
SOME LANGUAGE-RELATED COGNITIVE ADVANTAGES OF BILINGUAL FIVE-YEAR-OLDS EJ 041 343

LANGUAGE ARTS

AN EVALUATION OF THE LANGUAGE ARTS PROGRAM OF THE DISTRICT OF COLUMBIA. FINAL REPORT. ED024449
CONCEPT AND LANGUAGE DEVELOPMENT. A RESOURCE GUIDE FOR TEACHING YOUNG CHILDREN. ED030472
CURRICULAR INTERVENTION IN LANGUAGE ARTS READINESS FOR HEAD START CHILDREN. TULANE UNIVERSITY, HEAD START EVALUATION AND RESEARCH CENTER ANNUAL REPORT TO THE OFFICE OF ECONOMIC OPPORTUNITY. ED038175
LANGUAGE FOR LEARNING: ORAL LANGUAGE AND COGNITIVE DEVELOPMENT, PRE-K, K, GRADE 1. SECTION 1, TEACHER'S GUIDE. ED039921
ADDRESS AT COMBINED MEETING OF N.Y.C. EARLY CHILDHOOD COUNCIL AND THE METROPOLITAN ASSOCIATION FOR CHILDHOOD EDUCATION ON "LANGUAGE ARTS MATERIALS IN EARLY CHILDHOOD" (TEACHERS COLLEGE, COLUMBIA UNIVERSITY, APRIL 6, 1968): ED039951
CURRICULAR INTERVENTION IN LANGUAGE ARTS READINESS FOR HEAD START CHILDREN. TULANE UNIVERSITY, HEAD START EVALUATION AND RESEARCH CENTER, 1968-1969 INTERVENTION REPORT. SUPPLEMENT TO THE ANNUAL REPORT TO THE OFFICE OF ECONOMIC OPPORTUNITY. ED047795
GROWTH IN READING IN AN INTEGRATED DAY CLASSROOM EJ 055 154

LANGUAGE DEVELOPMENT

AN OBJECTIVE MEASURE OF STRUCTURAL COMPLEXITY IN CHILDREN'S WRITING. ED016534
FINAL REPORT ON HEAD START EVALUATION AND RESEARCH--1966-67 TO THE INSTITUTE FOR EDUCATIONAL DEVELOPMENT. SECTION IV, AN EXPLORATORY STUDY OF ORAL LANGUAGE DEVELOPMENT AMONG CULTURALLY DIFFERENT CHILDREN. ED019120
LANGUAGE DEVELOPMENT EXPERIENCES FOR YOUNG CHILDREN. ED019125
HEAD START EVALUATION AND RESEARCH CENTER, TULANE UNIVERSITY. FINAL REPORT. (TITLE SUPPLIED). ED020782
THE SYNTACTIC STRUCTURES OF 5-YEAR-OLD CULTURALLY DEPRIVED CHILDREN. ED020788
HEAD START EVALUATION AND RESEARCH CENTER, UNIVERSITY OF KANSAS. REPORT NO. IIB, AN EXPERIMENTAL ANALYSIS OF VERBAL IMITATION IN PRESCHOOL CHILDREN. ED021635
HEAD START EVALUATION AND RESEARCH CENTER, UNIVERSITY OF KANSAS. REPORT NO. III, EFFECTS OF A LANGUAGE PROGRAM ON CHILDREN IN A HEAD START NURSERY. ED021636
HEAD START EVALUATION AND RESEARCH CENTER, UNIVERSITY OF KANSAS. REPORT NO. XI, VERBAL RECALL RESEARCH. ED021647
A STUDY OF LANGUAGE DEVELOPMENT FROM INFANCY TO AGE 5. ED022539
THE DEVELOPMENT OF FORMS OF THE NEGATIVE. ED022549
GAMES AND OTHER ACTIVITIES FOR DEVELOPING LANGUAGE SKILLS. ED022555
ON LEARNING TO TALK: ARE PRINCIPLES DERIVED FROM THE LEARNING LABORATORY APPLICABLE? ED023481
THE PRESCHOOL LANGUAGE PROJECT. A REPORT OF THE FIRST YEAR'S WORK. ED023482
TWO STUDIES OF THE SYNTACTIC KNOWLEDGE OF YOUNG CHILDREN. A PRELIMINARY REPORT. ED024451
THE MARIE HUGHES LANGUAGE TRAINING MODEL. ED025305
A STUDY OF COGNITIVE AND SOCIAL FUNCTIONING. PROJECT II ED025310
THE DEVELOPMENT OF LANGUAGE FUNCTIONS. REPORT NUMBER 8, DEVELOPMENT OF LANGUAGE FUNCTIONS: A RESEARCH PROGRAM PROJECT. ED025325
GRAMMATICAL DEVELOPMENT IN RUSSIAN-SPEAKING CHILDREN. ED025332
THE DEVELOPMENT OF INTERROGATIVE STRUCTURES IN CHILDREN'S SPEECH. ED025333
A RATIONALE FOR A STRUCTURED EDUCATIONAL PROGRAM AND SUGGESTED ACTIVITIES FOR CULTURALLY DISADVANTAGED INFANTS. ED026112
A STUDY OF LANGUAGE DEVIATIONS AND COGNITIVE PROCESSES. PROGRESS REPORT NO. 3. ED027958
CONCEPT AND LANGUAGE DEVELOPMENT IN A KINDERGARTEN OF DISADVANTAGED CHILDREN. ED027967
PRESCHOOL PROGRAM, FRESNO, CALIFORNIA ED027977
COORDINATED HELPS IN LANGUAGE DEVELOPMENT (CHILD). NORTHWEST REGIONAL EDUCATIONAL LABORATORY STUDY. SECOND EXPERIMENTAL EDITION. ED028831
SOME LANGUAGE-RELATED COGNITIVE ADVANTAGES OF BILINGUAL FIVE YEAR OLDS. ED031307
A STUDY OF THE EFFECTS OF A GROUP LANGUAGE DEVELOPMENT PROGRAM UPON THE PSYCHOLINGUISTIC ABILITIES AND LATER BEGINNING READING SUCCESS OF KINDERGARTEN CHILDREN. ED031315
LANGUAGE AND ENVIRONMENT: AN INTERIM REPORT ON A LONGITUDINAL STUDY. ED032136
A COMPARISON OF THE ORAL LANGUAGE PATTERNS OF THREE LOW SOCIOECONOMIC GROUPS OF PUPILS ENTERING FIRST GRADE. ED032943
A TRANSFORMATIONAL ANALYSIS OF THE LANGUAGE OF KINDERGARTEN AND ELEMENTARY SCHOOL CHILDREN. ED034592
SYNTACTIC COMPLEXITY IN MOTHER-CHILD INTERACTIONS. ED035454
A PILOT PROJECT USING A LANGUAGE DEVELOPMENT PROGRAM WITH PRESCHOOL DISADVANTAGED CHILDREN. PART OF THE FINAL REPORT ON HEAD START EVALUATION AND RESEARCH: 1968-69 TO THE OFFICE OF ECONOMIC OPPORTUNITY. ED037245
EFFECTS OF TRAINING YOUNG BLACK CHILDREN IN VOCABULARY VS. SENTENCE CONSTRUCTION. ED038176
LANGUAGE PROGRAMS FOR YOUNG CHILDREN: NOTES FROM ENGLAND AND WALES. ED040763
ON THE HETEROGENEITY OF PSYCHOLOGICAL PROCESSES IN SYNTACTIC DEVELOPMENT. ED040764
LANGUAGE RESEARCH AND PRESCHOOL LANGUAGE TRAINING. ED040767
THE DEVELOPMENT OF THE CONTROL OF ADULT INSTRUCTIONS OVER NON-VERBAL BEHAVIOR. ED041620
EARLY CHILDHOOD EDUCATION LEARNING SYSTEM ED041625
DEVELOPMENT OF GRAMMATICAL STRUCTURES AND ATTRIBUTES IN PRE-SCHOOL AGE CHILDREN. FINAL REPORT. ED041639
LANGUAGE DEVELOPMENT OF SOCIALLY DISADVANTAGED PRESCHOOL CHILDREN. FINAL REPORT. ED041641
DEVELOPMENT OF GRAMMATICAL STRUCTURES IN PRE-SCHOOL AGE CHILDREN. ED042485
AN EXPERIMENTAL ANALYSIS OF PROCEDURES FOR INCREASING SPECIFIC VOCALIZATIONS OF CHILDREN WHO DO NOT DEVELOP FUNCTIONAL SPEECH. PROGRESS REPORT. ED042495
A PARENT-CHILD CENTER, NOVEMBER-DECEMBER 1968. ED042506
HAWAII HEAD START EVALUATION--1968-69. FINAL REPORT. ED042511
THE "TELL-AND-FIND PICTURE GAME" FOR YOUNG CHILDREN. ED042513
THE EFFECT OF FOUR COMMUNICATION PATTERNS AND SEX ON LENGTH OF VERBALIZATION IN SPEECH OF FOUR YEAR OLD CHILDREN. FINAL REPORT. ED042514
THE EFFECTS OF A PRESCHOOL LANGUAGE PROGRAM ON TWO-YEAR-OLD CHILDREN AND THEIR MOTHERS. FINAL REPORT. ED045224
DAME SCHOOL PROJECT (BI-LINGUAL PRE SCHOOL PROJECT), SANTA CLARA COUNTY OFFICE OF EDUCATION. FINAL REPORT, AUGUST 1, 1970. ED046514
CONCEPT AND LANGUAGE DEVELOPMENT OF A GROUP OF FIVE YEAR OLDS WHO HAVE ATTENDED THE SYRACUSE UNIVERSITY CHILDREN'S CENTER INTERVENTION PROGRAM. ED046515
THE NEW NURSERY SCHOOL RESEARCH PROJECT ED048940
LANGUAGE ACQUISITION AND COGNITIVE DEVELOPMENT. ED049811
LANGUAGE TRAINING IN EARLY CHILDHOOD EDUCATION. ED051881
A STUDY IN CHILD CARE (CASE STUDY FROM VOLUME II-A): "A ROLLS-ROYCE OF DAY CARE." DAY CARE PROGRAMS REPRINT SERIES. ED051895
A STUDY IN CHILD CARE (CASE STUDY FROM VOLUME II-B): "...WHILE [THEY TOOK] CARE OF OUR CHILDREN, THEIRS WEREN'T BEING CARED FOR." DAY CARE PROGRAMS REPRINT SERIES. ED051909
DETAILED ANALYSIS OF LANGUAGE DEVELOPMENT OF PRESCHOOL CHILDREN IN ECE PROGRAM. TECHNICAL REPORT NO. 4. ED052834
AN APPROACH TO LANGUAGE LEARNING EJ 008 119
INFANT EDUCATION: A COMMUNITY PROJECT EJ 008 462
ON VALUING DIVERSITY IN LANGUAGE EJ 011 840
TOO MUCH SHUSHING - LET CHILDREN TALK EJ 011 841
EXPERIENCES AND LANGUAGE DEVELOPMENT EJ 011 842
BRINGING THEIR OWN: LANGUAGE DEVELOPMENT IN THE MIDDLE GRADES EJ 011 844
SUGGESTIONS FROM STUDIES OF EARLY LANGUAGE ACQUISITION EJ 012 396
THE EFFECTS OF INSTRUCTION ON LANGUAGE DEVELOPMENT EJ 013 625
CHILDREN'S QUESTIONS: THEIR FORMS, FUNCTIONS AND ROLES IN EDUCATION EJ 017 608
SYNTACTIC MATURITY IN SCHOOL CHILDREN AND ADULTS EJ 018 818

RECEPTIVE LANGUAGE DEVELOPMENT IN INFANCY: ISSUES AND PROBLEMS EJ 020 396
CHILDREN'S SPATIAL REPRESENTATIONS AND HORIZONTAL DIRECTIONALITY EJ 023 190
IMITATION AND ECHOING IN YOUNG SCHIZOPHRENIC CHILDREN EJ 026 494
CANDIDATE FOR INTEGRATION: A HEARING-IMPAIRED CHILD IN A REGULAR NURSERY SCHOOL EJ 026 915
THE ROLE OF SYNTAX IN CHILDREN'S COMPREHENSION FROM AGES SIX TO TWELVE EJ 028 578
AGE-DEVELOPMENT IN THE LINEAR REPRESENTATION OF WORDS AND OBJECTS EJ 030 296
A REEXAMINATION OF SOME ASSUMPTIONS ABOUT THE LANGUAGE OF THE DISADVANTAGED CHILD EJ 033 700
FUNCTIONS OF VISUAL IMAGERY IN THE LEARNING AND CONCEPT FORMATION OF CHILDREN EJ 033 779
LANGUAGE DEVELOPMENT OF DISADVANTAGED CHILDREN EJ 036 211
THE ACQUISITION OF DIRECT AND INDIRECT OBJECTS IN JAPANESE EJ 036 745
PROCESSING OF PHONOLOGICAL SEQUENCES BY YOUNG CHILDREN AND ADULTS EJ 036 747
"FOCAL" COLOR AREAS AND THE DEVELOPMENT OF COLOR NAMES EJ 039 057
SOME LANGUAGE-RELATED COGNITIVE ADVANTAGES OF BILINGUAL FIVE-YEAR-OLDS EJ 041 343
LANGUAGE LEARNING--FRESH VIVID AND THEIR OWN EJ 044 613
YOUNG CHILDREN'S COMPREHENSION OF LOGICAL CONNECTIVES EJ 049 117
DIFFERENTIAL COGNITIVE DEVELOPMENT WITHIN AND BETWEEN RACIAL AND ETHNIC GROUPS OF DISADVANTAGED PRESCHOOL AND KINDERGARTEN CHILDREN EJ 049 172
THINKING BEFORE LANGUAGE? A SYMPOSIUM: 1. RELATIONSHIPS BETWEEN LANGUAGE AND THOUGHT EJ 050 075
MOTHER'S MODE OF DISCIPLINE AND CHILD'S VERBAL ABILITY EJ 050 794
THE TEACHER'S ROLE IN HELPING YOUNG CHILDREN DEVELOP LANGUAGE COMPETENCE EJ 051 566
SENTENCE REPETITION: ELICITED IMITATION OF A CONTROLLED SET OF SYNTACTIC STRUCTURES BY FOUR LANGUAGE GROUPS EJ 052 175
CREATIVE DRAMA AND LANGUAGE GROWTH EJ 052 176
SPEECH REGISTERS IN YOUNG CHILDREN EJ 052 450
SOME COGNITIVE AND AFFECTIVE ASPECTS OF EARLY LANGUAGE DEVELOPMENT EJ 055 655
CHILDREN'S COMPREHENSION OF RELATIVIZED ENGLISH SENTENCES EJ 056 715
SURFACE STRUCTURE AND THE TOPIC-COMMENT DISTINCTION: A DEVELOPMENTAL STUDY EJ 056 717
THE DEVELOPMENT OF COMPETENCE IN AN EXCEPTIONAL LANGUAGE STRUCTURE IN OLDER CHILDREN AND YOUNG ADULTS EJ 056 727
MOTHERS' SPEECH TO CHILDREN LEARNING LANGUAGE EJ 058 696
ENVIRONMENTAL EFFECTS ON LANGUAGE DEVELOPMENT: A STUDY OF YOUNG CHILDREN IN LONG-STAY RESIDENTIAL NURSERIES EJ 058 859
CHILDREN'S IMITATION OF GRAMMATICAL AND UNGRAMMATICAL SENTENCES EJ 059 555
PRINCIPLES OF INTERACTION IN LANGUAGE LEARNING EJ 059 875
INFANT DEVELOPMENT IN LOWER-CLASS AMERICAN FAMILIES EJ 060 012
CHANGES IN INFANTS' VOCALIZATIONS AS A FUNCTION OF DIFFERENTIAL ACOUSTIC STIMULATION EJ 061 139

LANGUAGE ENRICHMENT
LANGUAGE DEVELOPMENT EXPERIENCES FOR YOUNG CHILDREN. ED019125
HEAD START EVALUATION AND RESEARCH CENTER, UNIVERSITY OF KANSAS. REPORT NO. III, EFFECTS OF A LANGUAGE PROGRAM ON CHILDREN IN A HEAD START NURSERY. ED021636
LANGUAGE. ED029718
A COMPARATIVE ANALYSIS OF THE PIAGETIAN DEVELOPMENT OF TWELVE MONTH OLD DISADVANTAGED INFANTS IN AN ENRICHMENT CENTER WITH OTHERS NOT IN SUCH A CENTER. ED047778
CREATIVE DRAMA AND LANGUAGE GROWTH EJ 052 176
REGISTER: SOCIAL VARIATION IN LANGUAGE USE EJ 052 177

LANGUAGE EXPERIENCE APPROACH
GRADE EQUIVALENT COMPARISONS BETWEEN DISADVANTAGED NEGRO URBAN CHILDREN WITH AND WITHOUT KINDERGARTEN EXPERIENCE WHEN TAUGHT TO READ BY SEVERAL METHODS. ED020798
THE MARIE HUGHES LANGUAGE TRAINING MODEL. ED025305
LEARNING TO READ THROUGH EXPERIENCE. SECOND EDITION. ED027067
LANGUAGE EXPERIENCES WHICH PROMOTE READING. ED034571

LANGUAGE HANDICAPS
PROBLEMS OF DIALECT. ED025300
EVALUATION OF INKSTER PRESCHOOL PROJECT. FINAL REPORT. ED027093
COMPETENCE VS. PERFORMANCE IN YOUNG CHILDREN'S USE OF COMPLEX LINGUISTIC STRUCTURES. ED029687
A PRESCHOOL ARTICULATION AND LANGUAGE SCREENING FOR THE IDENTIFICATION OF SPEECH DISORDERS. FINAL REPORT. ED051889
CHILDREN WHO SPEAK NAVAJO EJ 014 918

LANGUAGE INSTRUCTION
TEACHING A TEACHING LANGUAGE TO DISADVANTAGED CHILDREN. ED015021
THE EFFECTS OF DIFFERENT LANGUAGE INSTRUCTION ON THE USE OF ATTRIBUTES OF PRE-KINDERGARTEN DISADVANTAGED CHILDREN. ED016522
THE HUMAN CONNECTION--LANGUAGE AND LITERATURE. ED018271
PRELIMINARY EVALUATION OF A LANGUAGE CURRICULUM FOR PRESCHOOL CHILDREN. FINAL REPORT. ED021618
COMPARATIVE EFFECTIVENESS OF ECHOIC AND MODELING PROCEDURES IN LANGUAGE INSTRUCTION WITH CULTURALLY DISADVANTAGED CHILDREN. ED025314
A BILINGUAL ORAL LANGUAGE AND CONCEPTUAL DEVELOPMENT PROGRAM FOR SPANISH-SPEAKING PRE-SCHOOL CHILDREN. ED034568
LANGUAGE TEACHING: PREPOSITIONS AND CONJUNCTIVES. ED034597
LANGUAGE TRAINING FOR TEACHERS OF DEPRIVED CHILDREN. ED040744
UNIVERSITY OF HAWAII PRESCHOOL LANGUAGE CURRICULUM, HONOLULU, HAWAII: A PROGRAM OF ENGLISH CONVERSATION FOR PRESCHOOL CHILDREN OF MULTIETHNIC BACKGROUNDS. MODEL PROGRAMS--CHILDHOOD EDUCATION. ED045220
ON VALUING DIVERSITY IN LANGUAGE EJ 011 840

LANGUAGE LEARNING LEVELS
HEAD START EVALUATION AND RESEARCH CENTER, UNIVERSITY OF KANSAS. REPORT NO. XI, VERBAL RECALL RESEARCH. ED021647
A COMPARISON OF THE PSYCHOLINGUISTIC FUNCTIONING OF "EDUCATIONALLY-DEPRIVED" AND "EDUCATIONALLY-ADVANTAGED" CHILDREN. ED022537
THE ACQUISITION OF LINGUISTIC STRUCTURE. TECHNICAL REPORT VIII, A STUDY IN THE ACQUISITION OF LANGUAGE: FREE RESPONSES TO COMMANDS. ED023486
GRAMMATICAL DEVELOPMENT IN RUSSIAN-SPEAKING CHILDREN. ED025332
AN APPROACH TO LANGUAGE LEARNING EJ 008 119
ON LANGUAGE AND KNOWING IN PIAGET'S DEVELOPMENTAL THEORY EJ 034 713
A COMPARATIVE STUDY OF ENGLISH PLURALIZATION BY NATIVE AND NON-NATIVE ENGLISH SPEAKERS EJ 052 465

LANGUAGE PATTERNS
LANGUAGE RESEARCH STUDY--PROJECT HEAD START. DEVELOPMENT OF METHODOLOGY FOR OBTAINING AND ANALYZING SPONTANEOUS VERBALIZATIONS USED BY PRE-KINDERGARTEN CHILDREN IN SELECTED HEAD START PROGRAMS--A PILOT STUDY. ED015007
TEACHING A TEACHING LANGUAGE TO DISADVANTAGED CHILDREN. ED015021
THE DEVELOPMENT OF A TEST TO ASSESS THE OCCURRENCE OF SELECTED FEATURES OF NON-STANDARD ENGLISH IN THE SPEECH OF DISADVANTAGED PRIMARY CHILDREN. ED015790
ORAL OR WRITTEN LANGUAGE--THE CONSEQUENCES FOR COGNITIVE DEVELOPMENT IN AFRICA AND THE UNITED STATES. ED018279
THE ACQUISITION OF LINGUISTIC STRUCTURE. TECHNICAL REPORT VIII, A STUDY IN THE ACQUISITION OF LANGUAGE: FREE RESPONSES TO COMMANDS. ED023486
THE DEVELOPMENT OF A COMPUTER TECHNIQUE FOR THE CONTENT ANALYSIS OF PSYCHO-SOCIAL FACTORS IN THE ORAL LANGUAGE OF KINDERGARTEN CHILDREN. ED038184
AN ANALYSIS OF MOTHERS' SPEECH AS A FACTOR IN THE DEVELOPMENT OF CHILDREN'S INTELLIGENCE. ED042504
THE ELEMENTS OF EFFECTIVE COMMUNICATION EJ 011 845
IMITATION AND ECHOING IN YOUNG SCHIZOPHRENIC CHILDREN EJ 026 494
THE PSYCHOLOGICAL CORRELATES OF SPEECH CHARACTERISTICS OF SOUNDING "DISADVANTAGED": A SOUTHERN REPLICATION EJ 040 685
LANGUAGE PATTERNS WITHIN THE YOUTH SUBCULTURE: DEVELOPMENT OF SLANG VOCABULARIES EJ 060 720

LANGUAGE PROFICIENCY
ADMINISTRATION MANUAL FOR TESTS OF BASIC LANGUAGE COMPETENCE IN ENGLISH AND SPANISH. LEVEL I (PRESCHOOL) ED027063
ADMINISTRATION MANUAL FOR TESTS OF BASIC LANGUAGE COMPETENCE IN ENGLISH AND SPANISH. LEVEL II (PRIMARY GRADES): CHILDREN AGES SIX TO TEN, ENGLISH AND SPANISH VERSIONS, FORMS A AND B. PART OF THE FINAL REPORT. ED027064
COMPARATIVE EFFECTIVENESS OF SPEAKING VERSUS LISTENING IN IMPROVING THE SPOKEN LANGUAGE OF DISADVANTAGED YOUNG CHILDREN. ED029689
AN EXPERIMENTAL STUDY OF SYNTACTICAL FACTORS INFLUENCING CHILDREN'S COMPREHENSION OF CERTAIN COMPLEX RELATIONSHIPS. FINAL REPORT. ED030492
LANGUAGE TEACHING: PREPOSITIONS AND CONJUNCTIVES. ED034597
INCREASING THE EFFECTIVENESS OF PARENTS-AS-TEACHERS. ED048939

LANGUAGE PROGRAMS
TEACHING A TEACHING LANGUAGE TO DISADVANTAGED CHILDREN. ED015021

COMMUNICATIVE COMPETENCE OF LOW-INCOME CHILDREN--ASSUMPTIONS AND PROGRAMS. ED020775
PRELIMINARY EVALUATION OF A LANGUAGE CURRICULUM FOR PRESCHOOL CHILDREN. FINAL REPORT. ED021618
HEAD START EVALUATION AND RESEARCH CENTER, UNIVERSITY OF KANSAS. REPORT NO. III, EFFECTS OF A LANGUAGE PROGRAM ON CHILDREN IN A HEAD START NURSERY. ED021636
HEAD START EVALUATION AND RESEARCH CENTER, BOSTON UNIVERSITY. REPORT D-I, LANGUAGE PROJECT: THE EFFECTS OF A TEACHER DEVELOPED PRE-SCHOOL LANGUAGE TRAINING PROGRAM ON FIRST GRADE READING ACHIEVEMENT. ED022563
AN EVALUATION OF A SIX-WEEK HEADSTART PROGRAM USING AN ACADEMICALLY ORIENTED CURRICULUM: CANTON, 1967. ED026114
THE EFFECTIVENESS OF THE PEABODY LANGUAGE DEVELOPMENT KITS AND THE INITIAL TEACHING ALPHABET WITH DISADVANTAGED CHILDREN IN THE PRIMARY GRADES: AFTER TWO YEARS. ED026125
COORDINATED HELPS IN LANGUAGE DEVELOPMENT (CHILD). NORTHWEST REGIONAL EDUCATIONAL LABORATORY STUDY. SECOND EXPERIMENTAL EDITION. ED028831
DEVELOPMENT OF A PRESCHOOL LANGUAGE-ORIENTED CURRICULUM WITH A STRUCTURED PARENT EDUCATION PROGRAM. FINAL REPORT. ED028845
THE EFFECT OF THE REINSTEIN REINFORCEMENT SCHEDULE ON LEARNING OF SPECIFIC CONCEPTS CONTAINED IN THE BUCHANAN LANGUAGE PROGRAM. PART OF THE FINAL REPORT ON HEAD START EVALUATION AND RESEARCH: 1968-69 TO THE OFFICE OF ECONOMIC OPPORTUNITY. ED037242
AN EARLY CHILDHOOD EDUCATION MODEL: A BILINGUAL APPROACH. ED038167
CURRICULAR INTERVENTION TO ENHANCE THE ENGLISH LANGUAGE COMPETENCE OF HEAD START CHILDREN. PART OF THE FINAL REPORT ON HEAD START EVALUATION AND RESEARCH: 1968-69 TO THE OFFICE OF ECONOMIC OPPORTUNITY. ED039032
THE EFFECTIVENESS OF A STANDARD LANGUAGE READINESS PROGRAM AS A FUNCTION OF TEACHER DIFFERENCES. ED039932
LANGUAGE PROGRAMS FOR YOUNG CHILDREN: NOTES FROM ENGLAND AND WALES. ED040763
A TUTORIAL LANGUAGE PROGRAM FOR DISADVANTAGED INFANTS. ED040766
LANGUAGE RESEARCH AND PRESCHOOL LANGUAGE TRAINING. ED040767
A COMPARISON OF THREE INTERVENTION PROGRAMS WITH DISADVANTAGED PRESCHOOL CHILDREN. UNIVERSITY OF CALIFORNIA HEAD START RESEARCH AND EVALUATION CENTER. FINAL REPORT 1968-1969. ED041616
DIRECT VERBAL INSTRUCTION CONTRASTED WITH MONTESSORI METHODS IN THE TEACHING OF NORMAL FOUR-YEAR-OLD CHILDREN. ED041619
PARENTS AS PRIMARY CHANGE AGENTS IN AN EXPERIMENTAL HEAD START PROGRAM OF LANGUAGE INTERVENTION. EXPERIMENTAL PROGRAM REPORT. ED044168
AN OVERVIEW OF COGNITIVE AND LANGUAGE PROGRAMS FOR 3, 4, & 5 YEAR OLD CHILDREN. ED045209
THE EFFECTS OF A PRESCHOOL LANGUAGE PROGRAM ON TWO-YEAR-OLD CHILDREN AND THEIR MOTHERS. FINAL REPORT. ED045224
AN INVESTIGATION OF THE RELATIVE EFFECTIVENESS OF SELECTED CURRICULUM VARIABLES IN THE LANGUAGE DEVELOPMENT OF HEAD START CHILDREN. ED046497
AN ANALYSIS OF PUBLISHED PRESCHOOL LANGUAGE PROGRAMS. ED047786
FIELD TEST OF THE UNIVERSITY OF HAWAII PRESCHOOL LANGUAGE CURRICULUM. FINAL REPORT. ED048924
PROGRAMS OF HEAD START PARENT INVOLVEMENT IN HAWAII. A SECTION OF THE FINAL REPORT FOR 1969-70. ED048935

LANGUAGE RESEARCH

LANGUAGE RESEARCH STUDY--PROJECT HEAD START. DEVELOPMENT OF METHODOLOGY FOR OBTAINING AND ANALYZING SPONTANEOUS VERBALIZATIONS USED BY PRE-KINDERGARTEN CHILDREN IN SELECTED HEAD START PROGRAMS--A PILOT STUDY. ED015007
A TECHNIQUE FOR GATHERING CHILDREN'S LANGUAGE SAMPLES FROM NATURALISTIC SETTINGS. ED016532
THE INITIAL TEACHING ALPHABET AND THE WORLD OF ENGLISH. (PROCEEDINGS OF THE SECOND ANNUAL INTERNATIONAL CONFERENCE ON THE INITIAL TEACHING ALPHABET, AUGUST 18-20, 1965). ED019108
THE SYNTACTIC STRUCTURES OF 5-YEAR-OLD CULTURALLY DEPRIVED CHILDREN. ED020788
HEAD START RESEARCH AND EVALUATION OFFICE, UNIVERSITY OF CALIFORNIA AT LOS ANGELES. APPENDIX I TO THE ANNUAL REPORT, NOVEMBER 1967. ED020793
HEAD START EVALUATION AND RESEARCH CENTER, UNIVERSITY OF KANSAS. FINAL REPORT ON RESEARCH ACTIVITIES. ED021614
THE DEVELOPMENT OF FORMS OF THE NEGATIVE. ED022549
ON LEARNING TO TALK: ARE PRINCIPLES DERIVED FROM THE LEARNING LABORATORY APPLICABLE? ED023481
THE ACQUISITION OF LINGUISTIC STRUCTURE. TECHNICAL REPORT VIII, A STUDY IN THE ACQUISITION OF LANGUAGE: FREE RESPONSES TO COMMANDS. ED023486
LINGUISTIC AND PSYCHOLOGICAL FACTORS IN THE SPEECH REGULATION OF BEHAVIOR IN VERY YOUNG CHILDREN. ED024442
TWO STUDIES OF THE SYNTACTIC KNOWLEDGE OF YOUNG CHILDREN. A PRELIMINARY REPORT. ED024451
PROBLEMS OF DIALECT. ED025300
THE DEVELOPMENT OF LANGUAGE FUNCTIONS. REPORT NUMBER 8, DEVELOPMENT OF LANGUAGE FUNCTIONS: A RESEARCH PROGRAM PROJECT. ED025325
WORD ASSOCIATIONS AS RELATED TO CHILDREN'S VERBAL HABITS. ED025329
AN INVESTIGATION OF THE STANDARD-NONSTANDARD DIMENSION OF CENTRAL TEXAN ENGLISH. PART OF THE FINAL REPORT. ED026130
A STUDY OF LANGUAGE DEVIATIONS AND COGNITIVE PROCESSES. PROGRESS REPORT NO. 3. ED027958
THE EFFECTS OF STANDARD DIALECT TRAINING ON NEGRO FIRST-GRADERS LEARNING TO READ. FINAL REPORT. ED029717
AN EXPERIMENTAL STUDY OF SYNTACTICAL FACTORS INFLUENCING CHILDREN'S COMPREHENSION OF CERTAIN COMPLEX RELATIONSHIPS. FINAL REPORT. ED030492
SOME LANGUAGE-RELATED COGNITIVE ADVANTAGES OF BILINGUAL FIVE YEAR OLDS. ED031307
A TRANSFORMATIONAL ANALYSIS OF THE LANGUAGE OF KINDERGARTEN AND ELEMENTARY SCHOOL CHILDREN. ED034592
MEXICAN-AMERICANS AND LANGUAGE LEARNING EJ 012 397
CONSIDERATIONS FOR THE STUDY OF LANGUAGE IN YOUNG LOW-INCOME MINORITY GROUP CHILDREN EJ 052 440
SPEECH REGISTERS IN YOUNG CHILDREN EJ 052 450
A COMPARATIVE STUDY OF ENGLISH PLURALIZATION BY NATIVE AND NON-NATIVE ENGLISH SPEAKERS EJ 052 465
DIALECT, RACE, AND LANGUAGE PROFICIENCY: ANOTHER DEAD HEAT ON THE MERRY-GO-ROUND EJ 053 747
A TRANSFORMATIONAL ANALYSIS OF ORAL SYNTACTIC STRUCTURES OF CHILDREN REPRESENTING VARYING ETHNOLINGUISTIC COMMUNITIES EJ 056 713
CHILDREN'S COMPREHENSION OF RELATIVIZED ENGLISH SENTENCES EJ 056 715
SURFACE STRUCTURE AND THE TOPIC-COMMENT DISTINCTION: A DEVELOPMENTAL STUDY EJ 056 717
THE EXPERIMENTAL FACILITATION OF CHILDREN'S COMPREHENSION AND PRODUCTION OF FOUR SYNTACTIC STRUCTURES EJ 056 723
THE DEVELOPMENT OF COMPETENCE IN AN EXCEPTIONAL LANGUAGE STRUCTURE IN OLDER CHILDREN AND YOUNG ADULTS EJ 056 727
MOTHERS' SPEECH TO CHILDREN LEARNING LANGUAGE EJ 058 696
LINGUISTIC FACTORS IN READING EJ 059 537
CHILDREN'S IMITATION OF GRAMMATICAL AND UNGRAMMATICAL SENTENCES EJ 059 555
CHANGES IN INFANTS' VOCALIZATIONS AS A FUNCTION OF DIFFERENTIAL ACOUSTIC STIMULATION EJ 061 139

LANGUAGE RHYTHM

TEACHING NUMBER SENSE THROUGH RHYTHMICAL COUNTING EJ 028 717

LANGUAGE ROLE

THE HUMAN CONNECTION--LANGUAGE AND LITERATURE. ED018271
LINGUISTIC AND PSYCHOLOGICAL FACTORS IN THE SPEECH REGULATION OF BEHAVIOR IN VERY YOUNG CHILDREN. ED024442
LURIA'S MODEL OF THE VERBAL CONTROL OF BEHAVIOR. STUDY F: MOTIVATIONAL AND CONTROL IN THE DEVELOPMENT OF LANGUAGE FUNCTIONS, D. BIRCH. ED024443
THE DEVELOPMENT OF LANGUAGE FUNCTIONS. REPORT NUMBER 8, DEVELOPMENT OF LANGUAGE FUNCTIONS: A RESEARCH PROGRAM PROJECT. ED025325
SUBJECTS' HYPOTHESES, EXPERIMENTAL INSTRUCTIONS AND AUTONOMIC "CONDITIONING". ED025335
STRONG WORDS EJ 001 116
ESTIMATES AND ESTIMATE-BASED INFERENCES IN YOUNG CHILDREN EJ 034 541
OF TIME AND THE PRONOUN: A NEW METHODOLOGY FOR RESEARCH IN HIGHER EDUCATION EJ 042 881
THE MODIFICATION OF INTELLIGENCE BY TRAINING IN THE VERBALIZATION OF WORD DEFINITIONS AND SIMPLE CONCEPTS EJ 052 594
PERCEPTION AND LANGUAGE: A GERMAN REPLICATION OF THE PIAGET-INHELDER POSITION EJ 060 773
THE DEVELOPMENT OF THE LANGUAGE OF EMOTIONS: II. INTENTIONALITY IN THE EXPERIENCE OF AFFECT EJ 061 064
THE DEVELOPMENT OF THE LANGUAGE OF EMOTIONS: III. TYPE OF ANXIETY IN THE EXPERIENCE OF AFFECT EJ 061 065

LANGUAGE SKILLS

ANALYSIS OF STORY RETELLING AS A MEASURE OF THE EFFECTS OF ETHNIC CONTENT IN STORIES. FINAL REPORT. ED014326
THE EFFECTS OF DIFFERENT LANGUAGE INSTRUCTION ON THE USE OF ATTRIBUTES OF PRE-KINDERGARTEN DISADVANTAGED CHILDREN. ED016522
THE EFFECT OF PRESCHOOL GROUP EXPERIENCE ON VARIOUS LANGUAGE AND SOCIAL SKILLS IN DISADVANTAGED CHILDREN. FINAL REPORT. ED019989
LANGUAGE LEARNING ACTIVITIES FOR THE DISADVANTAGED CHILD. ED020002

LANGUAGE CONTROL IN A GROUP OF HEAD START CHILDREN. ED020789
HEAD START EVALUATION AND RESEARCH CENTER, BOSTON UNIVERSITY. REPORT D-I, LANGUAGE PROJECT: THE EFFECTS OF A TEACHER DEVELOPED PRE-SCHOOL LANGUAGE TRAINING PROGRAM ON FIRST GRADE READING ACHIEVEMENT. ED022563
COGNITIVE AND LINGUISTIC DEFICITS IN PSYCHOTIC CHILDREN. STUDY M: DEVELOPMENT OF SELECTIVE ATTENTION ABILITIES. ED024440
CHANGING PARENT ATTITUDES AND IMPROVING LANGUAGE AND INTELLECTUAL ABILITIES OF CULTURALLY DISADVANTAGED FOUR-YEAR-OLD CHILDREN THROUGH PARENT INVOLVEMENT. ED027942
EVALUATION OF THE EFFECTS OF HEAD START EXPERIENCE IN THE AREA OF SELF-CONCEPT, SOCIAL SKILLS, AND LANGUAGE SKILLS. PRE-PUBLICATION DRAFT. ED028832
EFFECTS OF KINDERGARTEN ATTENDANCE ON DEVELOPMENT OF SCHOOL READINESS AND LANGUAGE SKILLS. INTERIM REPORT. ED029706
AN EXPERIMENTAL GAME IN ORAL LANGUAGE COMPREHENSION. ED038171
PSYCHOLINGUISTIC BEHAVIORS OF BLACK, DISADVANTAGED RURAL CHILDREN. ED039037
ECHOIC RESPONSE INVENTORY FOR CHILDREN (ERIC). ED039931
PSYCHOLINGUISTIC BEHAVIORS OF ISOLATED, RURAL CHILDREN WITH AND WITHOUT KINDERGARTEN. ED042510
INCREASING VERBAL COMMUNICATION SKILLS IN CULTURALLY DISADVANTAGED PRE-SCHOOL CHILDREN. FINAL REPORT. ED044186
DETAILED ANALYSIS OF LANGUAGE DEVELOPMENT OF PRESCHOOL CHILDREN IN ECE PROGRAM. TECHNICAL REPORT NO. 4. ED052834
AUDITORY DISCRIMINATION ABILITIES OF DISADVANTAGED ANGLO- AND MEXICAN-AMERICAN CHILDREN EJ 015 258
INTERVENTION STRATEGIES FOR SPANISH-SPEAKING PRESCHOOL CHILDREN EJ 036 746
DIALECT, RACE, AND LANGUAGE PROFICIENCY: ANOTHER DEAD HEAT ON THE MERRY-GO-ROUND EJ 053 747
PATTERNS OF RESPONDING IN THE WORD ASSOCIATIONS OF WEST AFRICAN CHILDREN EJ 056 634
COMPARISON OF IMITATION AND COMPREHENSION SCORES BETWEEN TWO LOWER-CLASS GROUPS AND THE EFFECTS OF TWO WARM-UP CONDITIONS ON IMITATION OF THE SAME GROUPS EJ 056 709

LANGUAGE STYLES
THE COGNITIVE ENVIRONMENTS OF URBAN PRE-SCHOOL CHILDREN. MANUAL OF INSTRUCTIONS FOR ADMINISTERING AND SCORING MOTHER-TEACHER PICTURE. ED018259
ROLE OF MOTHERS' LANGUAGE STYLES IN MEDIATING THEIR PRESCHOOL CHILDREN'S COGNITIVE DEVELOPMENT. ED025298
LANGUAGE STYLE OF THE LOWER CLASS MOTHER: A PRELIMINARY STUDY OF A THERAPEUTIC TECHNIQUE. ED027943
LANGUAGE, SOCIALIZATION, AND DELINQUENCY EJ 039 587
REGISTER: SOCIAL VARIATION IN LANGUAGE USE EJ 052 177

LANGUAGE TESTS
EVALUATING THE CHILD'S LANGUAGE COMPETENCE. ED019141
LANGUAGE CONTROL IN A GROUP OF HEAD START CHILDREN. ED020789
ECHOIC RESPONSE INVENTORY FOR CHILDREN (ERIC). ED039931
SOME LANGUAGE COMPREHENSION TESTS. ED040765
DETAILED ANALYSIS OF LANGUAGE DEVELOPMENT OF PRESCHOOL CHILDREN IN ECE PROGRAM. TECHNICAL REPORT NO. 4. ED052834

LANGUAGE UNIVERSALS
"FOCAL" COLOR AREAS AND THE DEVELOPMENT OF COLOR NAMES EJ 039 057

LANGUAGE USAGE
ORAL OR WRITTEN LANGUAGE--THE CONSEQUENCES FOR COGNITIVE DEVELOPMENT IN AFRICA AND THE UNITED STATES. ED018279
HEAD START EVALUATION AND RESEARCH CENTER, TULANE UNIVERSITY. FINAL REPORT. (TITLE SUPPLIED). ED020782
A COMPARISON OF THE PSYCHOLINGUISTIC FUNCTIONING OF "EDUCATIONALLY-DEPRIVED" AND "EDUCATIONALLY-ADVANTAGED" CHILDREN. ED022537
A STUDY OF LANGUAGE DEVIATIONS AND COGNITIVE PROCESSES. PROGRESS REPORT NO. 3. ED027958

LARGE GROUP INSTRUCTION
ON TEAM TEACHING EJ 046 057

LATE SCHOOL ENTRANCE
AGE OF ENTRANCE INTO THE FIRST GRADE AS RELATED TO ARITHMETIC ACHIEVEMENT. ED020801

LATERAL DOMINANCE
CHILDREN'S ACQUISITION OF VISUO-SPATIAL DIMENSIONALITY: A CONSERVATION STUDY. ED041636
FACTORS AFFECTING LATERAL DIFFERENTIATION IN THE HUMAN NEWBORN EJ 015 395
CHILDREN'S ACQUISITION OF VISUO-SPATIAL DIMENSIONALITY: A CONSERVATION STUDY EJ 047 681
RELATIONSHIP BETWEEN LATERAL PREFERENCE AND SELECTED BEHAVIORAL VARIABLES FOR CHILDREN FAILING ACADEMICALLY EJ 056 718

LAWS
THE RIGHTS OF CHILDREN EJ 060 473

LAY TEACHERS
FINAL REPORT ON HEAD START EVALUATION AND RESEARCH: 1967-68 TO THE OFFICE OF ECONOMIC OPPORTUNITY. SECTION I: PART A, MIDDLE CLASS MOTHER-TEACHERS IN AN EXPERIMENTAL PRESCHOOL PROGRAM FOR SOCIALLY DISADVANTAGED CHILDREN. ED023454
FINAL REPORT ON HEAD START EVALUATION AND RESEARCH: 1967-68 TO THE OFFICE OF ECONOMIC OPPORTUNITY. SECTION I: PART B, ACCURACY OF SELF-PERCEPTION AMONG CULTURALLY DEPRIVED PRESCHOOLS. ED023455
FINAL REPORT ON HEAD START EVALUATION AND RESEARCH: 1967-68 TO THE OFFICE OF ECONOMIC OPPORTUNITY. SECTION I: PARTS A AND B. ED023457

LEADERSHIP QUALITIES
RESEARCH ON ASPECTS OF LEADERSHIP ROLES IN EARLY AND ELEMENTARY EDUCATION EJ 055 205

LEADERSHIP RESPONSIBILITY
AN INSTITUTIONAL ANALYSIS OF DAY CARE PROGRAM. PART II, GROUP DAY CARE: THE GROWTH OF AN INSTITUTION. FINAL REPORT. ED043394

LEARNING
AN INTEGRATIVE APPROACH TO CLASSROOM LEARNING. ED033749
LEARNING INTO THE TWENTY-FIRST CENTURY. 1970 WHITE HOUSE CONFERENCE ON CHILDREN, REPORT OF FORUM 5. (WORKING COPY). ED046524
A REVISION OF THE BASIC PROGRAM PLAN OF EDUCATION AT AGE THREE. ED047774
THE EFFECTS OF EXTRANEOUS MATERIAL AND NEGATIVE EXEMPLARS ON A SOCIAL SCIENCE CONCEPT-LEARNING TASK FOR PRE-SCHOOL CHILDREN. ED047819
THE FIRST YEAR OF SESAME STREET: AN EVALUATION. FINAL REPORT, VOLUME III OF V VOLUMES. ED047823
LIVING WITH CHILDREN: NEW METHODS FOR PARENTS AND TEACHERS. ED051887
A COMPARISON OF THE EFFECT OF VERBAL AND MATERIAL REWARD ON THE LEARNING OF LOWER CLASS PRESCHOOL CHILDREN. ED052817
LEARNING BY DISCOVERY: A REVIEW OF THE RESEARCH METHODOLOGY. REPORT FROM THE PROJECT ON VARIABLES AND PROCESSES IN COGNITIVE LEARNING. ED053793
DESIGNS AND PROPOSAL FOR EARLY CHILDHOOD RESEARCH: A NEW LOOK: MALNUTRITION, LEARNING AND INTELLIGENCE. (ONE IN A SERIES OF SIX PAPERS). ED053811
WHAT IS LEARNED AND WHAT IS TAUGHT EJ 010 443
EXPERIENCES AND LANGUAGE DEVELOPMENT EJ 011 842
A DEVELOPMENTAL STUDY OF INFORMATION PROCESSING WITHIN THE FIRST THREE YEARS OF LIFE: RESPONSE DECREMENT TO A REDUNDANT SIGNAL EJ 013 947
CHILDREN'S PERFORMANCE ON AN ODDITY PROBLEM AS A FUNCTION OF THE NUMBER OF VALUES ON THE RELEVANT DIMENSION EJ 024 694
DIMENSIONAL PREFERENCE AND DISCRIMINATION SHIFT LEARNING IN CHILDREN EJ 025 959
THE FUNDAMENTAL LEARNING NEEDS OF TODAY'S YOUNG CHILDREN EJ 027 531
LEARNING: THE ROLE OF FACTS AND GENERALIZATIONS EJ 028 638
ANXIETY - A CLASSROOM CLOSE-UP EJ 028 896
LEARNING AND PROBLEM SOLVING BY THE MENTALLY RETARDED UNDER THREE TESTING CONDITIONS EJ 030 290
THE USEFULNESS OF CUMULATIVE DEPRIVATION AS AN EXPLANATION OF EDUCATIONAL DEFICIENCIES EJ 033 056
CONTROL OF ORIENTING BEHAVIOR IN CHILDREN UNDER FIVE YEARS OF AGE EJ 034 535
LEARNING, CURIOSITY, AND SOCIAL GROUP MEMBERSHIP EJ 035 378
A CASE AGAINST A CASE AGAINST BEHAVIORAL OBJECTIVES EJ 036 083
DELAYED REINFORCEMENT AND VOCALIZATION RATES OF INFANTS EJ 036 127
AN EXPERIMENTAL STUDY OF BASIC LEARNING ABILITY AND INTELLIGENCE IN LOW-SOCIOECONOMIC-STATUS CHILDREN EJ 036 818
THE LEARNING AND TRANSFER OF DOUBLE-CLASSIFICATION SKILLS BY FIRST GRADERS EJ 036 821
EVALUATION UNDER INDIVIDUALIZED INSTRUCTION EJ 036 826
CHILDREN'S ACQUISITION AND REVERSAL BEHAVIOR IN A PROBABILITY LEARNING SITUATION AS A FUNCTION OF PROGRAMMED INSTRUCTION, INTERNAL-EXTERNAL CONTROL, AND SCHEDULES OF REINFORCEMENT EJ 037 495
CONTINUITY FROM PREKINDERGARTEN TO KINDERGARTEN EJ 039 058
YOUNG CHILDREN'S PERFORMANCE ON A TWO-CHOICE TASK AS A FUNCTION OF SOCIAL REINFORCEMENT, BASE-LINE PREFERENCE, AND RESPONSE STRATEGY EJ 039 635
EFFECT OF THE PRESENCE OF A HUMAN MODEL ON IMITATIVE BEHAVIOR IN CHILDREN EJ 039 904
VARIETY OF EXEMPLARS VERSUS LINGUISTIC CONTEXTS IN CONCEPT ATTAINMENT IN YOUNG CHILDREN EJ 042 955
EFFECTS OF SOCIAL REINFORCEMENT ON LEARNING AND RETENTION IN CHILDREN EJ 042 957
VERBAL PAIRED-ASSOCIATE LEARNING IN CHILDREN AND ADULTS WITH ANTICIPATION, RECOGNITION, AND RECALL METHODS EJ 042 959

THE "FEATURE POSITIVE EFFECT" AND SIMULTANEOUS DISCRIMINATION LEARNING EJ 042 963
LEARNING OF AGGRESSION AS A FUNCTION OF PRESENCE OF A HUMAN MODEL, RESPONSE INTENSITY, AND TARGET OF THE RESPONSE EJ 043 198
THE EFFECTS OF VISUALLY REPRESENTED CUES ON LEARNING OF LINEAR FUNCTION RULES EJ 044 701
OBSERVATIONAL LEARNING: THE EFFECTS OF AGE, TASK DIFFICULTY, AND OBSERVERS' MOTORIC REHEARSAL EJ 044 702
IMITATION LEARNING OF INFORMATION-PROCESSING EJ 046 252
THE ROLE OF REINFORCEMENT PROCEDURE IN CHILDREN'S PROBABILITY LEARNING AS A FUNCTION OF AGE AND NUMBER OF RESPONSE ALTERNATIVES EJ 046 253
THE LEARNING AND TRANSFER OF DOUBLE-CLASSIFICATION SKILLS: A REPLICATION AND EXTENSION EJ 046 254
ABSTRACTION, INFERENCE, AND THE PROCESS OF IMITATIVE LEARNING EJ 047 685
PERSEVERATION AND ALTERNATION PRETRAINING AND BINARY PREDICTION EJ 057 902
AN APPLICATION OF BRUNSWIK'S LENS MODEL TO DEVELOPMENTAL CHANGES IN PROBABILITY LEARNING EJ 058 142
EXPECTANCY TO PERFORM AND VICARIOUS REWARD: THEIR EFFECTS UPON IMITATION EJ 059 513

LEARNING ACTIVITIES

LANGUAGE LEARNING ACTIVITIES FOR THE DISADVANTAGED CHILD. ED020002
BLOCKBUILDING. ED020011
LEARNING TO READ THROUGH EXPERIENCE. SECOND EDITION. ED027067
INTEGRATED, INDEPENDENT AND INDIVIDUAL LEARNING ACTIVITIES, FIRST AND SECOND GRADES. SUMMER LEARNING ACTIVITIES, SECOND AND THIRD GRADES. BOSTON-NORTHAMPTON LANGUAGE ARTS PROGRAM, ESEA - 1965, PROJECTS TO ADVANCE CREATIVITY IN EDUCATION. ED027946
CAN I LOVE THIS PLACE? A STAFF GUIDE TO OPERATING CHILD CARE CENTERS FOR THE DISADVANTAGED. ED049809
THE UNIT-BASED CURRICULUM. YPSILANTI PRESCHOOL CURRICULUM DEMONSTRATION PROJECT. ED049831
TOO MUCH SHUSHING - LET CHILDREN TALK EJ 011 841
ENVIRONMENTAL EDUCATION: THE STATE OF THE ART EJ 026 772
LABELING AND IMAGING AS AIDS TO MEMORY EJ 041 143

LEARNING BEHAVIOR

A CASE AGAINST BEHAVIORAL OBJECTIVES EJ 027 826

LEARNING CHARACTERISTICS

SOCIOECONOMIC STATUS AND LEARNING PROFICIENCY IN YOUNG CHILDREN. ED020023
VISUAL AND AUDITORY MEMORY IN CHILDREN. PART OF THE FINAL REPORT ON HEAD START EVALUATION AND RESEARCH: 1968-69 TO THE OFFICE OF ECONOMIC OPPORTUNITY. ED037246
HAVE YOU DISABLED A POTENTIAL READ'N' DROPOUT LATELY? EJ 016 463
WHAT IS LEARNED IN PROBABILITY LEARNING EJ 018 879
EFFECTS OF ENFORCED ATTENTION AND STIMULUS PHASING UPON RULE LEARNING IN CHILDREN EJ 024 697
THE INFLUENCE OF SET INDUCTION UPON STUDENT ACHIEVEMENT AND ASSESSMENT OF EFFECTIVE TEACHING EJ 027 031
THE EFFECTS OF CHRONOLOGICAL AGE, TRIALS, AND LIST CHARACTERISTICS UPON CHILDREN'S CATEGORY CLUSTERING EJ 052 454

LEARNING DIFFICULTIES

PRESCHOOL PREDICTION AND PREVENTION OF LEARNING DISABILITIES. ED013118
IDENTIFICATION AND EVALUATION OF CHARACTERISTICS OF KINDERGARTEN CHILDREN THAT FORETELL EARLY LEARNING PROBLEMS. FINAL REPORT. ED020006
IDENTIFICATION AND EVALUATION OF CHARACTERISTICS OF KINDERGARTEN CHILDREN THAT FORETELL EARLY LEARNING PROBLEMS. SUMMARY REPORT. ED020007
INTELLIGENCE QUOTIENT VERSUS LEARNING QUOTIENT: IMPLICATIONS FOR ELEMENTARY CURRICULA. ED031304
GROUP SCREENING OF AUDITORY AND VISUAL PERCEPTUAL ABILITIES: AN APPROACH TO PERCEPTUAL ASPECTS OF BEGINNING READING. ED033751
REVIEW OF SELECTED EARLY EDUCATION RESEARCH IN THE SCHOOL DISTRICT OF UNIVERSITY CITY, MISSOURI, JUNE, 1970. ED044182
DIAGNOSTIC TEACHING: A MODEST PROPOSAL EJ 014 522
CERTAIN ANTENATAL, PERINATAL, AND DEVELOPMENTAL VARIABLES AND READING RETAR RETARDATION IN MIDDLE-CLASS BOYS EJ 022 057
RECIPROCAL CONTRIBUTIONS BETWEEN PSYCHOANALYSIS AND PSYCHOEDUCATION EJ 045 048

LEARNING DISABILITIES

COGNITIVE AND LINGUISTIC DEFICITS IN PSYCHOTIC CHILDREN. STUDY M: DEVELOPMENT OF SELECTIVE ATTENTION ABILITIES. ED024440
THE PSYCHOEDUCATIONAL APPROACH TO LEARNING DISABILITIES. ED027950
THE NEED FOR A MULTI-DIMENSIONAL APPROACH TO LEARNING DISABILITIES. A MULTI-DISCIPLINARY SYMPOSIUM ON DYSLEXIS AND ASSOCIATED LEARNING DISABILITIES. ED027956
THE CONCEPT, "PERCEPTUALLY HANDICAPPED," ITS ASSETS AND LIMITATIONS. ED027960
EFFECT OF SENSORIMOTOR ACTIVITY ON PERCEPTION AND LEARNING IN THE NEUROLOGICALLY HANDICAPPED CHILD. FINAL PROGRESS REPORT. ED033757
LONG DISTANCE INTERDISCIPLINARY EVALUATION OF DEVELOPMENTAL DISABILITIES. ED040748
AN EDUCATION SYSTEM FOR HIGH-RISK INFANTS: A PREVENTIVE APPROACH TO DEVELOPMENTAL AND LEARNING DISABILITIES. ED043379
A PILOT STUDY OF A PRESCHOOL METHOD OF PREVENTIVE EDUCATION. FINAL REPORT. ED046541
PROJECT GENESIS. FINAL REPORT. ED049820
LEARNING DISABILITIES: A TEAM APPROACH EJ 014 521
A CLINIC FOR CHILDREN WITH LEARNING DISABILITIES EJ 024 471
THE OFF-KILTERED KIDS EJ 028 383
SCHOOL AND HOME: NOT EITHER-OR EJ 046 246
THE SCHOOL SOCIAL WORKER'S ROLE IN OVERCOMING LEARNING HANDICAPS EJ 046 401
THE DIAGNOSTIC EVALUATION OF CHILDREN WITH LEARNING PROBLEMS: A COMMUNICATION PROCESS EJ 050 321
LEARNING DISORDERS IN CHILDREN: SIBLING STUDIES EJ 057 584
LEARNING DISABILITY: A NEW LOOK AT UNDERACHIEVING EJ 058 411
TREATMENT OF PROBLEMS ASSOCIATED WITH COGNITIVE AND PERCEPTUAL-MOTOR DEFICITS EJ 060 501

LEARNING EXPERIENCE

"PRE-SCHOOL" EDUCATION, PROS AND CONS. A SURVEY OF "PRE-SCHOOL" EDUCATION WITH EMPHASIS ON RESEARCH PAST, PRESENT, AND FUTURE. ED016525
EDUCATION OF THE INFANT AND YOUNG CHILD. ED048930
EXPERIMENTAL LEARNING REEVALUATED EJ 026 814
AN INTEGRATED DAY WORKSHOP EJ 033 159
GOING ON A TRIP EJ 035 842
WHAT THE WORLD NEEDS NOW: ENVIRONMENTAL EDUCATION FOR YOUNG CHILDREN EJ 039 637
LEARNING FROM PLAY IN OTHER CULTURES EJ 045 532
A DEVELOPMENTAL LEARNING APPROACH TO INFANT CARE IN A GROUP SETTING EJ 057 442

LEARNING LABORATORIES

INDIVIDUALIZING INSTRUCTION THROUGH DIAGNOSIS AND EVALUATION EJ 021 629

LEARNING MODALITIES

PSYCHOPHYSICALLY SCALED CUE DIFFERENCES, LEARNING RATE, AND ATTENTIONAL STRATEGIES IN A TACTILE DISCRIMINATION TASK EJ 058 146

LEARNING MOTIVATION

A FRESH APPROACH TO EARLY CHILDHOOD EDUCATION AND A STUDY OF ITS EFFECTIVENESS. LEARNING TO LEARN PROGRAM. ED019117
AN OVERVIEW OF RESEARCH IN LEARNING, MOTIVATION, AND PERCEPTION. ED020799
THE EFFECTS OF CARTOON CHARACTERS AS MOTIVATORS OF PRESCHOOL DISADVANTAGED CHILDREN. FINAL REPORT. ED045210
THE BEHAVIOR ANALYSIS CLASSROOM. ED047775
A TOKEN MANUAL FOR BEHAVIOR ANALYSIS CLASSROOMS. ED047776
CHILDREN COME FIRST: THE INSPIRED WORK OF ENGLISH PRIMARY SCHOOLS. ED050820
A COMPARISON OF THE EFFECT OF VERBAL AND MATERIAL REWARD ON THE LEARNING OF LOWER CLASS PRESCHOOL CHILDREN. ED052817
ALTERNATIVE LEARNING ENVIRONMENTS: A PHILADELPHIA STORY EJ 033 156
DIRECTION SPORTS: A TUTORIAL PROGRAM FOR ELEMENTARY-SCHOOL PUPILS EJ 050 982

LEARNING PROCESSES

THE EFFECTS OF SEVERAL VERBAL PRETRAINING CONDITIONS ON PRESCHOOL CHILDREN'S TRANSFER IN PROBLEM SOLVING. FINAL REPORT. ED015778
LOGICAL OPERATIONS AND CONCEPTS OF CONSERVATION IN CHILDREN, A TRAINING STUDY. FINAL REPORT. ED020010
LEARNING IN INFANTS. ED024446
SUBJECTS' HYPOTHESES, EXPERIMENTAL INSTRUCTIONS AND AUTONOMIC "CONDITIONING". ED025335
A RATIONALE FOR DEVELOPMENTAL TESTING AND TRAINING. ED028835
EFFECT OF VARIETY ON THE LEARNING OF A SOCIAL STUDIES CONCEPT BY PRESCHOOL CHILDREN. ED029690
INVESTIGATION OF CONCEPT LEARNING IN YOUNG CHILDREN. FINAL REPORT. ED030498
THE RELATIONSHIP OF INDIVIDUAL DIFFERENCES IN THE ORIENTING RESPONSE TO COMPLEX LEARNING IN KINDERGARTNERS. ED031299
INFORMATION VALUE OF FEEDBACK WITH PRESCHOOL CHILDREN. ED031311
UNDERSTANDING READINESS: AN OCCASIONAL PAPER. ED032117
THE ROLE OF UNDERDETERMINACY AND REFERENCE IN THE SENTENCE RECALL OF YOUNG CHILDREN. ED035449
INVESTIGATIONS OF THE ROLE OF SELECTED CUES IN CHILDREN'S PAIRED-ASSOCIATE LEARNING. REPORT FROM THE READING PROJECT. ED036315

A STUDY OF THE ABILITY OF PRIMARY SCHOOL CHILDREN TO GENERALIZE BEHAVIORAL COMPETENCIES SPECIFIED FOR "SCIENCE--A PROCESS APPROACH" TO OTHER CONTENT SETTINGS. ED039038
RULE AND ATTRIBUTE LEARNING IN THE USE AND IDENTIFICATION OF CONCEPTS WITH YOUNG DISADVANTAGED CHILDREN. ED040747
AN EXPERIMENTAL ANALYSIS OF ERROR INTERACTION ON "ERRORLESS" AND TRIAL-AND-ERROR PROGRAMS. PROGRESS REPORT. ED042491
A FOLLOW-UP EVALUATION OF THE EFFECTS OF A UNIQUE SEQUENTIAL LEARNING PROGRAM, A TRADITIONAL PRESCHOOL PROGRAM AND A NO TREATMENT PROGRAM ON CULTURALLY DEPRIVED CHILDREN. FINAL REPORT. ED042516
CREATIVITY AND THE LEARNING PROCESS. 1970 WHITE HOUSE CONFERENCE ON CHILDREN, REPORT OF FORUM 6. (WORKING PAPER). ED046525
THE RELATIONSHIP OF INDIVIDUAL DIFFERENCES IN THE ORIENTING RESPONSE TO COMPLEX LEARNING IN KINDERGARTNERS. REPORT FROM THE MOTIVATION AND INDIVIDUAL DIFFERENCES IN LEARNING AND RETENTION PROJECT. ED046544
MODELING BY EXEMPLIFICATION AND INSTRUCTION IN TRAINING CONSERVATION. ED047790
THE FIRST YEAR OF SESAME STREET: A HISTORY AND OVERVIEW. FINAL REPORT, VOLUME I OF V VOLUMES. ED047821
THE EFFICACY OF A MATHEMATICS READINESS PROGRAM FOR INDUCING CONSERVATION OF NUMBER, WEIGHT, AREA, MASS, AND VOLUME IN DISADVANTAGED PRESCHOOL CHILDREN IN THE SOUTHERN UNITED STATES. ED048923
VISUAL IMAGERY INSTRUCTION AND NON-ACTION VERSUS ACTION SITUATIONS RELATIVE TO RECALL BY CHILDREN. FINAL REPORT. ED050828
SOCIAL SKILLS DEVELOPMENT IN THE EARLY CHILDHOOD EDUCATION PROJECT. TECHNICAL REPORT NO. 7. ED052835
LEARNING BY DISCOVERY: A REVIEW OF THE RESEARCH METHODOLOGY. REPORT FROM THE PROJECT ON VARIABLES AND PROCESSES IN COGNITIVE LEARNING. ED053793
VISIT TO A MISSION SCHOOL FOR ABORIGINAL CHILDREN EJ 014 292
A STUDY IN THE USE OF A PROGRAMMED GEOGRAPHY UNIT EJ 016 930
CHILDREN'S REACTIONS TO DISTRACTORS IN A LEARNING SITUATION EJ 018 881
TRANSFER EFFECTS IN CHILDREN'S ODDITY LEARNING EJ 018 887
EFFECT OF VERBALIZATION ON YOUNG CHILDREN'S LEARNING OF A MANIPULATIVE SKILL EJ 020 520
PROBLEMS OF DEPRIVATION AND DEVELOPMENTAL LEARNING EJ 024 691
VERBAL AND IMAGERY PROCESSES IN CHILDREN'S PAIRED-ASSOCIATE LEARNING EJ 024 699
CONJUNCTIVE AND DISJUNCTIVE RULE LEARNING AS A FUNCTION OF AGE AND FORCED VERBALIZATION EJ 028 637
DEVELOPMENT OF FREE RECALL LEARNING IN CHILDREN EJ 035 359
INTERRELATIONS AMONG LEARNING AND PERFORMANCE TASKS AT THE PRESCHOOL LEVEL EJ 035 361
PAIRED-ASSOCIATE LEARNING OF CHILDREN WITH MIXED LIST DESIGNS EJ 035 369
THE EFFECTS OF REHEARSAL AND CHUNKING INSTRUCTIONS ON CHILDREN'S MULTITRIAL FREE RECALL EJ 035 377
TRANSFER AND SEQUENCE IN LEARNING DOUBLE CLASSIFICATION SKILLS EJ 035 379
EFFECTS OF STIMULUS AVAILABILITY ON CHILDREN'S INFERENCES EJ 036 822
RETENTION FOLLOWING A CHANGE IN AMBIENT CONTEXTUAL STIMULI FOR SIX AGE GROUPS EJ 039 631
FREE RECALL AND CLUSTERING AT FOUR AGE LEVELS: EFFECTS OF LEARNING TO LEARN AND PRESENTATION METHOD EJ 039 636
MEMORY AND ATTENTION IN CHILDREN'S DOUBLE-ALTERNATION LEARNING EJ 042 966
THE USE OF VERBAL MEDIATION IN THE RETARDED AS A FUNCTION OF DEVELOPMENTAL LEVEL AND RESPONSE AVAILABILITY EJ 044 699
THE INFLUENCE OF COGNITIVE STYLE ON PERCEPTUAL LEARNING EJ 046 238
THE STABILITY AND TRANSFERABILITY OF CONCEPTUAL CODING IN CHILDREN EJ 046 251
CONCEPTUAL RULE LEARNING AND CHRONOLOGICAL AGE EJ 047 687
MEMORY FOR RHYTHMIC SERIES: AGE CHANGES IN ACCURACY AND NUMBER CODING EJ 054 805
LOOKING IN -- TO SELF DISCOVERY EJ 058 134

LEARNING READINESS

OPERATION HEAD START--AN EVALUATION. FINAL REPORT. ED013117
PSYCHOLOGICAL BASES FOR INSTRUCTIONAL DESIGN. ED013121
THE EFFECTS OF ASSESSMENT AND PERSONALIZED PROGRAMMING ON SUBSEQUENT INTELLECTUAL DEVELOPMENT OF PREKINDERGARTEN AND KINDERGARTEN CHILDREN. ED013663
PROJECT TOBI, THE DEVELOPMENT OF A PRE-SCHOOL ACHIEVEMENT TEST. FINAL REPORT. ED016520
EFFECTIVENESS OF THE HEAD START PROGRAM IN ENHANCING SCHOOL READINESS OF CULTURALLY DEPRIVED CHILDREN. ED020771
EFFECTS OF KINDERGARTEN ATTENDANCE ON DEVELOPMENT OF SCHOOL READINESS AND LANGUAGE SKILLS. INTERIM REPORT. ED029706
SEX DIFFERENCES IN EFFECTS OF KINDERGARTEN ATTENDANCE ON DEVELOPMENT OF SCHOOL READINESS AND LANGUAGE SKILLS EJ 052 723
RELATIONSHIP OF PRESCHOOL SOCIAL-EMOTIONAL FUNCTIONING TO LATER INTELLECTUAL ACHIEVEMENT EJ 058 138

LEARNING THEORIES

THE HIERARCHICAL ORGANIZATION OF INTELLECTUAL STRUCTURES. ED022534
A STUDY OF LANGUAGE DEVELOPMENT FROM INFANCY TO AGE 5. ED022539
LEARNING AND TEACHING, GRADES N-9 (EMPHASIS ON EARLY CHILDHOOD). ED023459
LEARNING IN INFANTS. ED024446
LEARNING AND TEACHING, GRADES N-9 (EMPHASIS ON MIDDLE GRADES). ED024467
DEVELOPMENTAL LEARNING AS A CONCEPT IN EARLY READING. ED031289
FUNCTIONAL PRINCIPLES OF LEARNING. ED032946
A STUDY OF NON-VERBAL REPRESENTATION IN YOUNG CHILDREN. ED036336
PIAGET'S THEORY AND SPECIFIC INSTRUCTION: A RESPONSE TO BEREITER AND KOHLBERG. ED038164
THE EFFECT OF MEDIATIONAL INSTRUCTIONS ON ASSOCIATIVE SKILLS OF FIRST GRADE INNERCITY CHILDREN. ED038177
APPROACHES TO THE VALIDATION OF LEARNING HIERARCHIES. ED043376
LEARNING TO LEARN ON A CONCEPT ATTAINMENT TASK AS A FUNCTION OF AGE AND SOCIOECONOMIC LEVEL. REPORT FROM THE PROJECT ON SITUATIONAL VARIABLES AND EFFICIENCY OF CONCEPT LEARNING. ED046505
CORRELATION OF PAIRED-ASSOCIATE PERFORMANCE WITH SCHOOL ACHIEVEMENT AS A FUNCTION OF TASK AND SAMPLE VARIATION. ED049813
ESSAYS ON EQUILIBRIUM EJ 008 171
CHILDREN AND TEACHERS IN TWO TYPES OF HEAD START CLASSES EJ 008 172
RESPONSE STRATEGIES IN THE ODDITY DISCRIMINATION OF PRESCHOOL CHILDREN EJ 021 759
IMITATION OF AN ANIMATED PUPPET AS A FUNCTION OF MODELING, PRAISE, AND DIRECTIONS EJ 024 693
DEVELOPMENTAL PROCESSES IN DISCRIMINATION LEARNING EJ 024 705
AN AGE-IRRELEVANT CONCEPT OF DEVELOPMENT EJ 027 437
AN ORGANISM ORIENTED CONCEPT OF DEVELOPMENT EJ 027 438
TRANSFER OF VERBAL PAIRED ASSOCIATES IN MENTALLY RETARDED INDIVIDUALS AND NORMAL CHILDREN AS A FUNCTION OF INTERLIST SIMILARITY EJ 033 785
TRANSFER AND SEQUENCE IN LEARNING DOUBLE CLASSIFICATION SKILLS EJ 035 379
BEHAVIORAL COMPLIANCE AND DEVALUATION OF THE FORBIDDEN OBJECT AS A FUNCTION OF PROBABILITY OF DETECTION AND SEVERITY OF THREAT EJ 038 935
EXTINCTION OF CONSERVATION: A METHODOLOGICAL AND THEORETICAL ANALYSIS EJ 046 245
PAIRED-ASSOCIATE LEARNING AND BIDIRECTIONAL ASSOCIATIVE RECALL IN FIRST, THIRD, FIFTH AND SEVENTH GRADERS EJ 053 481
NOUN-PAIR LEARNING IN CHILDREN AND ADULTS: UNDERLYING STRINGS AND RETRIEVAL TIME EJ 056 402
AN ONTOGENY OF MEDIATIONAL DEFICIENCY EJ 056 631
REINSTATEMENT EFFECTS IN CHILDREN EJ 057 899
TRANSFER BETWEEN THE ODDITY AND RELATIVE SIZE CONCEPTS: REVERSAL AND EXTRADIMENSIONAL SHIFTS EJ 057 906
THE STAGE IV ERROR IN PIAGET'S THEORY OF OBJECT CONCEPT DEVELOPMENT: DIFFICULTIES IN OBJECT CONCEPTUALIZATION OR SPATIAL LOCALIZATION? EJ 059 318
THE EFFECTS OF VERBAL PRETRAINING ON THE MULTIDIMENSIONAL GENERALIZATION BEHAVIOR OF CHILDREN EJ 060 784
THREE-CUE SELECTION MODELS APPLIED TO MULTIDIMENSIONAL STIMULUS CLASSIFICATION: ALTERNATIVES TO THE SPIKER, CROLL, AND MILLER ANALYSIS EJ 060 785
ON THE COMPARISON OF PSYCHOLOGICAL THEORIES: A REPLY TO PROFESSOR BOGARTZ EJ 060 786

LEGAL PROBLEMS

THE RIGHTS OF FOSTER PARENTS EJ 022 182
EARLY LEGAL ADOPTION EJ 022 533

LEGAL RESPONSIBILITY

THE RIGHTS OF CHILDREN. 1970 WHITE HOUSE CONFERENCE ON CHILDREN, REPORT OF FORUM 22. (WORKING COPY). ED046537
THE RIGHTS OF CHILDREN EJ 060 473

LEGISLATION

THE EXECUTIVE DIRECTOR'S TESTIMONY BEFORE THE HOUSE EDUCATION AND LABOR COMMITTEE EJ 017 848
SELECTING PRIORITIES AT THE WHITE HOUSE CONFERENCE ON CHILDREN EJ 035 619

LEISURE TIME

THE CHILD AND LEISURE TIME. 1970 WHITE HOUSE CONFERENCE ON CHILDREN, REPORT OF FORUM 21. (WORKING COPY). ED046536

LESSON OBSERVATION CRITERIA
THE TEACHER STRUCTURE CHECKLIST: A POSSIBLE TOOL FOR COMMUNICATION EJ 051 352

LESSON PLANS
A GUIDE FOR PERCEPTUAL-MOTOR TRAINING ACTIVITIES. ED027075
LANGUAGE FOR LEARNING: ORAL LANGUAGE AND COGNITIVE DEVELOPMENT, PRE-K, K, GRADE 1. SECTION 1, TEACHER'S GUIDE. ED039921
THE COGNITIVE CURRICULUM. YPSILANTI PRESCHOOL CURRICULUM DEMONSTRATION PROJECT. ED049832
THE EFFECT OF PLANNING ON TEACHING EJ 028 503
THE USE OF HIERARCHIES IN CURRICULUM ANALYSIS AND INSTRUCTIONAL PLANNING EJ 033 574
A PROCESS FOR POETRY-WRITING EJ 055 364

LETTERS (ALPHABET)
RECOGNITION OF ENGLISH AND HEBREW LETTERS AS A FUNCTION OF AGE AND DISPLAY PREDICTABILITY EJ 047 893
EFFECTS OF HEBREW AND ENGLISH LETTERS ON CHILDREN'S PERCEPTUAL SET EJ 053 721

LIMITED EXPERIENCE
THE RELATIONSHIP BETWEEN SPECIFIC AND GENERAL TEACHING EXPERIENCE AND TEACHER ATTITUDES TOWARD PROJECT HEAD START. PART OF THE FINAL REPORT. ED025323

LINGUISTIC COMPETENCE
LANGUAGE TEACHING: PREPOSITIONS AND CONJUNCTIVES. ED034597
LANGUAGE TRAINING FOR TEACHERS OF DEPRIVED CHILDREN. ED040744
COMMUNICATIVE COMPETENCE AND THE DISADVANTAGED CHILD: A STUDY OF THE RELATIONSHIP BETWEEN LANGUAGE MODELS AND THE DEVELOPMENT OF COMMUNICATION SKILLS IN DISADVANTAGED PRESCHOOLERS. FINAL REPORT. ED047806
THE ROLE OF SYNTAX IN CHILDREN'S COMPREHENSION FROM AGES SIX TO TWELVE EJ 028 578
COMPETENCE VERSUS PERFORMANCE IN YOUNG CHILDREN'S USE OF ADJECTIVAL COMPARATIVES EJ 033 701
WRITE FIRST, READ LATER EJ 034 069
THE GROWTH OF CHILDREN'S SEMANTIC MEMORY: SEMANTIC ELEMENTS EJ 038 170
DEVELOPMENT OF SYNTACTIC COMPREHENSION IN PRESCHOOL CHILDREN AS A FUNCTION OF SOCIOECONOMIC LEVEL EJ 043 480
CONSONANT CUE PERCEPTION BY TWENTY- TO TWENTY-FOUR-WEEK-OLD INFANTS EJ 045 597
FAMILY FACTORS RELATED TO COMPETENCE IN YOUNG DISADVANTAGED MEXICAN-AMERICAN CHILDREN EJ 053 753

LINGUISTIC PATTERNS
PROCESSING OF PHONOLOGICAL SEQUENCES BY YOUNG CHILDREN AND ADULTS EJ 036 747
LINGUISTIC AND THEMATIC VARIABLES IN RECALL OF A STORY BY DISADVANTAGED CHILDREN EJ 041 142

LINGUISTIC PERFORMANCE
PROCESSING OF PHONOLOGICAL SEQUENCES BY YOUNG CHILDREN AND ADULTS EJ 036 747
STORY RECALL IN KINDERGARTEN CHILDREN: EFFECT OF METHOD OF PRESENTATION ON PSYCHOLINGUISTIC PERFORMANCE EJ 036 748
PRODUCTION OF NOVEL AND GRAMMATICAL UTTERANCES BY YOUNG CHILDREN EJ 060 783

LINGUISTIC THEORY
THE SYNTACTIC STRUCTURES OF 5-YEAR-OLD CULTURALLY DEPRIVED CHILDREN. ED020788
ON LEARNING TO TALK: ARE PRINCIPLES DERIVED FROM THE LEARNING LABORATORY APPLICABLE? ED023481
ON THE PSYCHOLINGUISTIC METHOD OF TEACHING READING EJ 030 547
ON LANGUAGE AND KNOWING IN PIAGET'S DEVELOPMENTAL THEORY EJ 034 713
DICTIONARY SYLLABICATION - HOW USEFUL EJ 052 180

LINGUISTICS
LINGUISTICS IN THE ELEMENTARY SCHOOL. ED019134
A STUDY OF LANGUAGE DEVELOPMENT FROM INFANCY TO AGE 5. ED022539
A REEXAMINATION OF SOME ASSUMPTIONS ABOUT THE LANGUAGE OF THE DISADVANTAGED CHILD EJ 033 700
VARIETY OF EXEMPLARS VERSUS LINGUISTIC CONTEXTS IN CONCEPT ATTAINMENT IN YOUNG CHILDREN EJ 042 955
LINGUISTIC FACTORS IN READING EJ 059 537

LISTENING
THE EFFECT OF DIRECT INSTRUCTION IN LISTENING ON THE LISTENING AND READING COMPREHENSION OF FIRST GRADE CHILDREN. DISSERTATION ABSTRACT. ED029693
SHOWING AND SHARING IN THE KINDERGARTEN EJ 032 933
A NONVERBAL TECHNIQUE FOR STUDYING MUSIC PREFERENCE EJ 043 285
CHILDREN'S RECALL STRATEGIES IN DICHOTIC LISTENING EJ 044 700
STOP, LOOK, LISTEN -- AND KEEP ON!! EJ 058 133
WINDOW BEGINS WITH AN "L" EJ 058 507

LISTENING COMPREHENSION
TWO STUDIES OF THE SYNTACTIC KNOWLEDGE OF YOUNG CHILDREN. A PRELIMINARY REPORT. ED024451
THE VALUE OF THE SPOKEN RESPONSE IN TEACHING LISTENING SKILLS TO YOUNG CHILDREN THROUGH PROGRAMMED INSTRUCTION. FINAL REPORT. ED027973
THE EFFECT OF DIRECT INSTRUCTION IN LISTENING ON THE LISTENING AND READING COMPREHENSION OF FIRST GRADE CHILDREN. DISSERTATION ABSTRACT. ED029693
SOME LANGUAGE COMPREHENSION TESTS. ED040765
THE "TELL-AND-FIND PICTURE GAME" FOR YOUNG CHILDREN. ED042513
YOUNG CHILDREN'S COMPREHENSION OF LOGICAL CONNECTIVES EJ 049 117
THE TEACHER'S ROLE IN HELPING YOUNG CHILDREN DEVELOP LANGUAGE COMPETENCE EJ 051 566
LEARNING TO LISTEN: A STUDY IN AUDITORY PERCEPTION EJ 053 485

LISTENING HABITS
THE TEACHER'S ROLE IN HELPING YOUNG CHILDREN DEVELOP LANGUAGE COMPETENCE EJ 051 566

LISTENING SKILLS
LISTENING. WHAT RESEARCH SAYS TO THE TEACHER, NO. 29. ED026120
THE VALUE OF THE SPOKEN RESPONSE IN TEACHING LISTENING SKILLS TO YOUNG CHILDREN THROUGH PROGRAMMED INSTRUCTION. FINAL REPORT. ED027973
YOUNG BLACK AND WHITE LISTENERS. ED038180
LEARNING TO LISTEN: A STUDY IN AUDITORY PERCEPTION EJ 053 485

LITERATURE
LITERATURE AND THE YOUNG CHILD. ED028828
DEVELOPMENT OF A LITERATURE CURRICULUM FOR YOUNG CHILDREN. CAREL ARTS AND HUMANITIES CURRICULUM DEVELOPMENT PROGRAM FOR YOUNG CHILDREN. ED032940
LITERATURE FOR YOUNG CHILDREN EJ 002 654
IS THERE A LITERATURE FOR THE DISADVANTAGED CHILD? EJ 007 178
THE NON-STRUCTURED APPROACH TO CHILDREN'S LITERATURE EJ 015 980

LITERATURE APPRECIATION
BUILDING ON EXPERIENCES IN LITERATURE EJ 013 022
LITERATURE, CREATIVITY AND IMAGINATION EJ 033 510
LITERATURE, CREATIVITY AND IMAGINATION EJ 056 090

LITERATURE GUIDES
LITERATURE AND THE YOUNG CHILD. ED028828

LITERATURE REVIEWS
THE STATUS OF BEHAVIORAL MEASUREMENT AND ASSESSMENT IN CHILDREN. ED018252
EFFECTIVENESS OF THE HEAD START PROGRAM IN ENHANCING SCHOOL READINESS OF CULTURALLY DEPRIVED CHILDREN. ED020771
A BIBLIOGRAPHY OF RESEARCH ON FOREIGN STUDENT AFFAIRS. ED021629
TANGENT TO EXPERIMENTAL TECHNIQUES OF VERBAL CONTROL. ED025334
A PREKINDERGARTEN PROGRAM FOR FOUR-YEAR-OLDS, WITH A REVIEW OF THE LITERATURE ON PRESCHOOL EDUCATION. AN OCCASIONAL PAPER. ED026124
PSYCHOMOTOR EDUCATION - THEORY AND PRACTICE. ED029684
SELECTED LONGITUDINAL STUDIES OF COMPENSATORY EDUCATION--A LOOK FROM THE INSIDE. ED033762
LANGUAGE RESEARCH AND PRESCHOOL LANGUAGE TRAINING. ED040767
A COMPARISON OF THE EFFECT OF VERBAL AND MATERIAL REWARD ON THE LEARNING OF LOWER CLASS PRESCHOOL CHILDREN. ED052817
AN EVALUATION OF LOGICAL OPERATIONS INSTRUCTION IN THE PRESCHOOL. ED053791
ATTENTIONAL PREFERENCE AND EXPERIENCE: I. INTRODUCTION EJ 025 988
RESEARCH IN READING RETARDATION: TWO CRITICAL PROBLEMS EJ 045 108
SOME THOUGHTS ON HOW CHILDREN LEARN TO REMEMBER EJ 049 432
AN ANALYSIS OF THE CONCEPT OF CULTURAL DEPRIVATION EJ 055 111
TEACHING READING IN THE KINDERGARTEN: A REVIEW OF RECENT STUDIES EJ 055 153
RESEARCH ON ASPECTS OF LEADERSHIP ROLES IN EARLY AND ELEMENTARY EDUCATION EJ 055 205

LOGIC
YOUNG CHILDREN'S COMPREHENSION OF LOGICAL CONNECTIVES. ED033756
CHILDREN'S UTILIZATION OF LOGICAL SYMBOLS: AN INTERPRETATION OF CONCEPTUAL BEHAVIOR BASED ON PIAGETIAN THEORY EJ 024 942

LOGICAL THINKING
AN ANALYSIS OF A CLASS OF PROBLEM SOLVING BEHAVIOR. FINAL REPORT. ED020776

MODIFICATION OF CLASSIFICATORY COMPETENCE AND LEVEL OF REPRESENTATION AMONG LOWER-CLASS NEGRO KINDERGARTEN CHILDREN. ED021608
YOUNG CHILDREN'S USE OF LANGUAGE IN INFERENTIAL BEHAVIOR. ED029691
MODIFICATION OF COGNITIVE SKILLS AMONG LOWER-CLASS NEGRO CHILDREN: A FOLLOW-UP TRAINING STUDY. REPORT NUMBER 6. ED030480
DEVELOPMENT OF THE UNDERSTANDING OF LOGICAL CONNECTIVES. ED032125
LOGICAL THINKING IN SECOND GRADE. FINAL REPORT. ED033747
ON COGNIZING COGNITIVE PROCESSES. ED035437
AN INVESTIGATION OF THE MANNER IN WHICH YOUNG CHILDREN PROCESS INTELLECTUAL INFORMATION. FINAL REPORT. ED036313
LOGICAL INFERENCE IN DISCRIMINATION LEARNING OF YOUNG CHILDREN. REPORT FROM THE RULE LEARNING PROJECT. ED036314
TEACHING KINDERGARTEN CHILDREN TO APPLY CONCEPT-DEFINING RULES. ED037231
CONDITIONAL LOGIC AND PRIMARY CHILDREN. ED038186
A PIAGETIAN METHOD OF EVALUATING PRESCHOOL CHILDREN'S DEVELOPMENT IN CLASSIFICATION. ED039013
A FACTOR ANALYTIC STUDY OF CHILDREN'S CAUSAL REASONING. ED040759
A STUDY IN TRAINING NURSERY CHILDREN ON LOGICAL OPERATIONAL SKILLS. ED047803
THE INTERSITUATIONAL GENERALITY OF FORMAL THOUGHT EJ 015 097
TRANSITIVE INFERENCE WITH NONTRANSITIVE SOLUTIONS CONTROLLED EJ 018 882
LOGICAL THINKING IN CHILDREN AGES SIX THROUGH THIRTEEN EJ 025 960
THE UTILIZATION BY CHILDREN AND ADULTS OF BINARY PROPOSITIONAL THINKING IN CONCEPT LEARNING EJ 030 285
THE ROLE OF MEMORY IN MAKING TRANSITIVE JUDGMENTS EJ 030 288
EFFECTS OF PROBING CHILDREN'S PHENOMENISTIC EXPLANATIONS OF CAUSE AND EFFECT EJ 030 292
DEVELOPMENTAL PATTERNS FOR CHILDREN'S CLASS AND CONDITIONAL REASONING ABILITIES EJ 035 362
CHILDREN'S ABILITY TO OPERATE WITHIN A MATRIX: A DEVELOPMENTAL STUDY EJ 035 363
SOME RELATIONSHIPS BETWEEN VERBAL AND PERCEPTUAL CAPABILITIES AND THE DEVELOPMENT OF RELATIVE THINKING EJ 035 383
THE LEARNING AND TRANSFER OF DOUBLE-CLASSIFICATION SKILLS BY FIRST GRADERS EJ 036 821
INTERDEPENDENCE OF INHELDER AND PIAGET'S MODEL OF LOGICAL THINKING EJ 039 633
THE ROLE OF FAMILIARITY IN CHILDREN'S EXPLANATIONS OF PHYSICAL CAUSALITY EJ 046 232
LOGICAL SYMBOL USE IN DEAF AND HEARING CHILDREN AND ADOLESCENTS EJ 047 339
CLASSIFICATORY SCHEMES IN RELATION TO CLASS INCLUSION BEFORE AND AFTER TRAINING EJ 049 171
FIGURATIVE AND OPERATIVE ASPECTS OF CHILDREN'S INFERENCE EJ 056 616
SOCIAL-CLASS DIFFERENCES AND TASK VARIABLES IN THE DEVELOPMENT OF MULTIPLICATIVE CLASSIFICATION EJ 056 619

LONGITUDINAL STUDIES

BEHAVIOR PATTERNS OF NORMAL CHILDREN. ED015016
LONG-RANGE EFFECT OF PRE-SCHOOLING ON READING ACHIEVEMENT. STUDY III. ED015027
THE EARLY TRAINING PROJECT FOR DISADVANTAGED CHILDREN--A REPORT AFTER FIVE YEARS. ED016514
SUMMARY OF BEHAVIOR PATTERNS OF NORMAL CHILDREN. ED016531
A REPLICATIVE INVESTIGATION OF THE BUCKINGHAM-DOLCH FREE-ASSOCIATION WORD STUDY. FINAL REPORT. ED017333
CHILDREN WHO READ EARLY, TWO LONGITUDINAL STUDIES. ED019107
A COMPARATIVE STUDY OF VARIOUS PROJECT HEAD START PROGRAMS. ED019987
EVALUATION OF THE CLEVELAND CHILD DEVELOPMENT PROGRAM. A LONGITUDINAL STUDY (FIRST YEAR REPORT). ED020000
A LONGITUDINAL ASSESSMENT OF PRESCHOOL CHILDREN IN HAPTIC LEARNING. FINAL REPORT. ED020019
A FOLLOW-UP STUDY OF INTELLIGENCE CHANGES IN CHILDREN WHO PARTICIPATED IN PROJECT HEADSTART. ED020786
THE TWO YEAR OLD. ED022536
A STUDY OF COGNITIVE AND SOCIAL FUNCTIONING. PROJECT II ED025310
EARLY INTELLECTIVE TRAINING AND SCHOOL PERFORMANCE. SUMMARY OF NIH GRANT NUMBER HD-02253. ED025324
A LONGITUDINAL INVESTIGATION OF CHANGE IN THE FACTORIAL COMPOSITION OF INTELLIGENCE WITH AGE IN YOUNG SCHOOL CHILDREN. ED026149
THE ELEMENTARY MATHEMATICS STUDY: AN INTERIM REPORT ON KINDERGARTEN YEAR RESULTS. ED027937
AN APPRAISAL OF HEAD START PARTICIPANTS AND NON-PARTICIPANTS: EXPANDED CONSIDERATIONS ON LEARNING DISABILITIES AMONG DISADVANTAGED CHILDREN. ED027939
EARLY CHILDHOOD PROJECT, NEW YORK CITY ED027974
DIAGNOSTICALLY BASED CURRICULUM, BLOOMINGTON, INDIANA ED027978
AGE OF ENTRANCE INTO THE FIRST GRADE AS RELATED TO RATE OF SCHOLASTIC ACHIEVEMENT. ED028843
EIDETIC IMAGERY IN CHILDREN. FINAL REPORT. ED029707
IDENTIFICATION IN THE KINDERGARTEN OF FACTORS THAT MAKE FOR FUTURE SUCCESS IN READING AND IDENTIFICATION AND DIAGNOSIS IN THE KINDERGARTEN OF POTENTIAL READING DISABILITY CASES. FINAL REPORT. ED029710
PRELIMINARY RESULTS FROM A LONGITUDINAL STUDY OF DISADVANTAGED PRESCHOOL CHILDREN. ED030490
THE I.T.A. READING EXPERIMENT IN BRITAIN. ED032133
LANGUAGE AND ENVIRONMENT: AN INTERIM REPORT ON A LONGITUDINAL STUDY. ED032136
THE EARLY TRAINING PROJECT: A SEVENTH YEAR REPORT. ED032934
SOCIAL CLASS DIFFERENTIATION IN COGNITIVE DEVELOPMENT: A LONGITUDINAL STUDY. ED033754
INFANT DAY CARE AND ATTACHMENT. ED033755
INFANT EDUCATION. ED033760
SELECTED LONGITUDINAL STUDIES OF COMPENSATORY EDUCATION--A LOOK FROM THE INSIDE. ED033762
A LONGITUDINAL INVESTIGATION OF MONTESSORI AND TRADITIONAL PREKINDERGARTEN TRAINING WITH INNER CITY CHILDREN: A COMPARATIVE ASSESSMENT OF LEARNING OUTCOMES. THREE PART STUDY. ED034588
A LONGITUDINAL STUDY OF DISADVANTAGED CHILDREN WHO PARTICIPATED IN THREE DIFFERENT PRESCHOOL PROGRAMS. ED036338
THE EFFECT OF A PRESCHOOL EXPERIENCE UPON INTELLECTUAL FUNCTIONING AMONG FOUR-YEAR-OLD, WHITE CHILDREN IN RURAL MINNESOTA. ED039030
SOCIAL CLASS DIFFERENTIATION IN COGNITIVE DEVELOPMENT AMONG BLACK PRESCHOOL CHILDREN. ED039039
THE ETS-OEO LONGITUDINAL STUDY OF DISADVANTAGED CHILDREN. ED039927
A FACTOR ANALYSIS OF A THREE-YEAR LONGITUDINAL STUDY OF CONSERVATION OF NUMBER AND RELATED MATHEMATICAL CONCEPTS. ED039934
A LONGITUDINAL STUDY OF PIAGET'S DEVELOPMENTAL STAGES AND OF THE CONCEPT OF REGRESSION. ED043372
FROM THEORY TO OPERATIONS. DISADVANTAGED CHILDREN AND THEIR FIRST SCHOOL EXPERIENCES, ETS-HEAD START LONGITUDINAL STUDY. ED043397
IMPACT OF THE HEAD START PROGRAM. PHASE I OF A PROJECTED LONGITUDINAL STUDY TO THE U. S. OFFICE OF ECONOMIC OPPORTUNITY. FINAL REPORT. ED045193
DEVELOPMENTAL GROUPINGS OF PRE-SCHOOL CHILDREN. ED046513
EFFECTS OF PRESCHOOL STIMULATION UPON SUBSEQUENT SCHOOL PERFORMANCE AMONG THE CULTURALLY DISADVANTAGED. ED046545
SCHOOL ACHIEVEMENT: A PRELIMINARY LOOK AT THE EFFECTS OF THE HOME. ED047777
DISADVANTAGED CHILDREN AND THEIR FIRST SCHOOL EXPERIENCES. ETS-HEAD START LONGITUDINAL STUDY: PRELIMINARY DESCRIPTION OF THE INITIAL SAMPLE PRIOR TO SCHOOL ENROLLMENT. A REPORT IN TWO VOLUMES: VOLUME 1. ED047797
DISADVANTAGED CHILDREN AND THEIR FIRST SCHOOL EXPERIENCES. ETS-HEAD START LONGITUDINAL STUDY: PRELIMINARY DESCRIPTION OF THE INITIAL SAMPLE PRIOR TO SCHOOL ENROLLMENT. A REPORT IN TWO VOLUMES: VOLUME 2--TABLES. ED047798
THE ECOLOGY OF GROWTH AND DEVELOPMENT IN A MEXICAN PREINDUSTRIAL COMMUNITY. REPORT 1: METHOD AND FINDINGS FROM BIRTH TO ONE MONTH OF AGE EJ 007 791
INFANT DEVELOPMENT, PRESCHOOL IQ, AND SOCIAL CLASS EJ 018 465
FEAR OF VISUAL NOVELTY: DEVELOPMENTAL PATTERNS IN MALES AND FEMALES EJ 019 011
PRECURSORS OF INTELLIGENCE AND CREATIVITY: A LONGITUDINAL STUDY OF ONE CHILD'S DEVELOPMENT EJ 020 521
GROWTH OF HEAD, FACE, TRUNK, AND LIMBS IN PHILADEPHIA WHITE AND NEGRO CHILDREN OF ELEMENTARY AND HIGH SCHOOL AGE EJ 022 582
THE DEVELOPMENT OF CLASSIFICATORY SKILLS IN YOUNG CHILDREN: A TRAINING PROGRAM EJ 031 872
THE EXIT OF CHILDREN FROM FOSTER CARE: AN INTERIM RESEARCH REPORT EJ 039 798
THE DEVELOPMENT OF HYPNOTIC SUSCEPTIBILITY: A LONGITUDINAL (CONVERGENCE) STUDY EJ 041 449
A LONGITUDINAL STUDY OF CHANGES IN EGO IDENTITY STATUS DURING THE FRESHMAN YEAR AT COLLEGE EJ 043 193
NEWBORN AND PRESCHOOLER: ORGANIZATION OF BEHAVIOR AND RELATIONS BETWEEN PERIODS EJ 045 110
ANXIETY IN THE EVALUATIVE CONTEXT EJ 051 018
THE HISTORY OF LONGITUDINAL RESEARCH: IMPLICATIONS FOR THE FUTURE EJ 051 779
CONTINUITY IN THE DEVELOPMENT OF VISUAL BEHAVIOR IN YOUNG INFANTS EJ 053 746
THE ONSET OF WARINESS EJ 056 635
LONGITUDINAL DEVELOPMENT OF VERY YOUNG CHILDREN IN A COMPREHENSIVE DAY CARE PROGRAM: THE FIRST TWO YEARS EJ 056 707
CREATIVE ABILITY OVER A FIVE-YEAR SPAN EJ 058 412

LOW ABILITY STUDENTS
A PREVENTIVE SUMMER PROGRAM FOR KINDERGARTEN CHILDREN LIKELY TO FAIL IN FIRST GRADE READING. FINAL REPORT. ED030495

LOW ACHIEVEMENT FACTORS
THE CHILD WHO DISLIKES GOING TO SCHOOL. ED019999
LONG TERM STUDY OF PREMATURES: SUMMARY OF PUBLISHED FINDINGS. ED043389
TO KEEP AN INNER BALANCE EJ 002 313
COMBATTING RETARDATION IN INFANTS WITH DOWN'S SYNDROME EJ 026 640
FACTORS RELATED TO SCHOOL ACHIEVEMENT IN AN ECONOMICALLY DISADVANTAGED GROUP EJ 056 614

LOW ACHIEVERS
TEACHING READING TO CHILDREN WITH LOW MA'S. ED015020
THE EFFECTS OF DIFFERENTIAL REINFORCEMENT ON THE DISCRIMINATION LEARNING OF NORMAL AND LOW-ACHIEVING MIDDLE-CLASS BOYS EJ 056 398
RELATIONSHIP BETWEEN LATERAL PREFERENCE AND SELECTED BEHAVIORAL VARIABLES FOR CHILDREN FAILING ACADEMICALLY EJ 056 718

LOW INCOME COUNTIES
THE ITINERANT TEACHER EJ 060 930

LOW INCOME GROUPS
FACTORS INFLUENCING THE RECRUITMENT OF CHILDREN INTO THE HEAD START PROGRAM, SUMMER 1965--A CASE STUDY OF SIX CENTERS IN NEW YORK CITY. STUDY II. ED015026
FINAL REPORT ON HEAD START EVALUATION AND RESEARCH--1966-67 TO THE INSTITUTE FOR EDUCATIONAL DEVELOPMENT. SECTION VIII, RELATIONSHIPS BETWEEN SELF-CONCEPT AND SPECIFIC VARIABLES IN A LOW-INCOME CULTURALLY DIFFERENT POPULATION. ED019124
GUIDEBOOK FOR TEACHERS. ED020001
PERFORMANCE OF KINDERGARTEN CHILDREN FROM LOW INCOME FAMILIES ON SELECTED CONCEPT CATEGORIES. ED028847
NEIGHBORHOOD HOUSE CHILD CARE SERVICES, SEATTLE, WASHINGTON: SEATTLE'S ANSWER TO CHILD CARE PROBLEMS OF LOW-INCOME FAMILIES. MODEL PROGRAMS--CHILDHOOD EDUCATION. ED045213
INFORMATION ON INTERVENTION PROGRAMS OF THE DEMONSTRATION AND RESEARCH CENTER FOR EARLY EDUCATION. ED046492
NUTRITION SURVEY OF WHITE MOUNTAIN APACHE PRESCHOOL CHILDREN. ED046508
FOLLOW THROUGH: PROGRAM APPROACHES, SCHOOL YEAR 1970-71. ED047787
SESAME STREET. A SURVEY OF TWO CITIES: VIEWING PATTERNS IN INNER CITY LOS ANGELES AND CHICAGO. ED047788
A STUDY IN CHILD CARE (CASE STUDY FROM VOLUME II-B): "SOMEPLACE SECURE." DAY CARE PROGRAMS REPRINT SERIES. ED051908
DESIGNS AND PROPOSAL FOR EARLY CHILDHOOD RESEARCH: A NEW LOOK: A MULTIPLE SYSTEMS-SERVICE APPROACH TO PROGRAMS AND RESEARCH FOR HELPING POOR CHILDREN. (ONE IN A SERIES OF SIX PAPERS). ED053806
THE EARLY TRAINING PROJECT: A SEVENTH-YEAR REPORT EJ 033 777

LOW MOTIVATION
PEER TUTORING AS A TECHNIQUE FOR TEACHING THE UNMOTIVATED EJ 045 393

LOWER CLASS
DEVELOPING COGNITIVE LEARNINGS WITH YOUNG CHILDREN. ED041614
INFLUENCES OF A PIAGET-ORIENTED CURRICULUM ON INTELLECTUAL FUNCTIONING OF LOWER-CLASS KINDERGARTEN CHILDREN. ED049823
MEXICAN-AMERICAN CULTURAL MEMBERSHIP AND ADJUSTMENT TO SCHOOL EJ 035 620
MATERNAL WARMTH, ACHIEVEMENT MOTIVATION, AND COGNITIVE FUNCTIONING IN LOWER-CLASS PRESCHOOL CHILDREN EJ 053 745
COMPARISON OF IMITATION AND COMPREHENSION SCORES BETWEEN TWO LOWER-CLASS GROUPS AND THE EFFECTS OF TWO WARM-UP CONDITIONS ON IMITATION OF THE SAME GROUPS EJ 056 709

LOWER CLASS PARENTS
A NOTE ON PUNISHMENT PATTERNS IN PARENTS OF PRESCHOOL CHILDREN. REPORT NUMBER 3. ED030477

LOWER CLASS STUDENTS
DELAY OF GRATIFICATION AND INTERNAL VERSUS EXTERNAL CONTROL AMONG ADOLESCENTS OF LOW SOCIOECONOMIC STATUS EJ 034 539
THE INFLUENCE OF NEGRO AND WHITE TEACHERS RATED AS EFFECTIVE OR NONEFFECTIVE ON THE PERFORMANCE OF NEGRO AND WHITE LOWER-CLASS CHILDREN EJ 045 068
SELF CONCEPT AND SOCIO-ECONOMIC STATUS EJ 059 509

LUNCH PROGRAMS
KICKAPOO - NORTH CANADIAN PROJECT, 1966-67. FINAL REPORT. ED015781

MAGNETIC TAPE CASSETTE RECORDERS
A TEAM APPROACH USING CASSETTE TAPES EJ 061 001

MAJORITY ATTITUDES
WHAT'S DEPRIVED ABOUT BEING DIFFERENT? EJ 046 968

MALADJUSTMENT
SOME PSYCHIATRIC OBSERVATIONS ON A GROUP OF MALADJUSTED DEAF CHILDREN EJ 026 155

MALES
"OF HAIRY ARMS AND A DEEP BARITONE VOICE": A SYMPOSIUM MEN IN YOUNG CHILDREN'S LIVES EJ 028 795
REACTION TIME AND REMOTE ASSOCIATION IN TALENTED MALE ADOLESCENTS EJ 029 360
EFFECT OF SUCCESS AND FAILURE ON THE REFLECTIVE AND IMPULSIVE CHILD EJ 029 768
CHANGING PROSPECTS FOR CHILDREN WITH HEMOPHILIA EJ 029 952
THE RELATIONSHIP BETWEEN CONTROLLED PROJECTION RESPONSES AND SOCIOMETRIC STATUS EJ 031 541
MODIFYING RISK-TAKING BEHAVIOR EJ 032 891
YOUNG CHILDREN'S ORIENTATION OF LETTERS AS A FUNCTION OF AXIS OF SYMMETRY AND STIMULUS ALIGNMENT EJ 032 909
OLDER BROTHERS' INFLUENCE ON SEX-TYPED, AGGRESSIVE, AND DEPENDENT BEHAVIOR IN FATHER-ABSENT CHILDREN EJ 034 901
CHILDHOOD PSYCHOSIS COMBINED WITH XYZ ABNORMALITIES EJ 035 078
BODY BUILD, SEX-ROLE PREFERENCE, AND SEX-ROLE ADOPTION IN JUNIOR HIGH SCHOOL BOYS EJ 035 627
AN EXAMINATION OF FRUSTRATION AGGRESSION RELATIONS IN BOYS DURING MIDDLE CHILDHOOD EJ 035 628
FATHER AVAILABILITY AND ACADEMIC PERFORMANCE AMONG THIRD-GRADE BOYS EJ 038 730
CHRONOLOGICAL AGE AND PERFORMANCE ON PROBLEMS WITH REPEATED PRESOLUTION SHIFTS EJ 039 628
A TEST OF ERIKSON'S THEORY OF EGO EPIGENESIS EJ 039 898
INCORPORATION OF VALUES BY LOWER AND MIDDLE SOCIOECONOMIC CLASS PRESCHOOL BOYS EJ 040 210
A DISCONTINUITY IN THE SOCIALIZATION OF MALES IN THE UNITED STATES EJ 040 799
AUTONOMIC RESPONSES OF MALE ADOLESCENTS EXHIBITING REFRACTORY BEHAVIOUR IN SCHOOL EJ 045 109
WHAT TO DO TILL THE MALE MAN COMES EJ 048 697
SOURCES OF MANPOWER FOR THE PRESCHOOL CLASSROOM EJ 049 526
FAMILY INTERACTION VARIABLES AND ADJUSTMENT OF NONCLINIC BOYS EJ 053 737
FATHER-CHILD INTERACTION AND THE INTELLECTUAL FUNCTIONING OF FOUR-YEAR-OLD BOYS EJ 054 290
STYLE OF ADAPTATION TO AVERSIVE MATERNAL CONTROL AND PARANOID BEHAVIOR EJ 055 105
CHILDREN'S OBSERVATION AND INTEGRATION OF AGGRESSIVE EXPERIENCES EJ 055 212
SITUATIONAL EFFECTS ON JUSTIFIABLENESS OF AGGRESSION AT THREE AGE LEVELS EJ 056 734
EYE CONTACT, ATTITUDES, AND ATTITUDE CHANGE AMONG MALES EJ 059 813
WE HAVE MEN ON THE STAFF EJ 060 929

MANAGEMENT DEVELOPMENT
NEW DIMENSIONS IN STAFF DEVELOPMENT IN A JUVENILE CORRECTIONAL SYSTEM EJ 043 858

MANIPULATIVE MATERIALS
BLOCKBUILDING. ED020011
GAMES AND OTHER ACTIVITIES FOR DEVELOPING LANGUAGE SKILLS. ED022555
THE USE OF COLOURED RODS IN TEACHING PRIMARY NUMBERWORK. ED028823
HAVE YOU EVER THOUGHT OF A PROP BOX? EJ 031 781

MANPOWER DEVELOPMENT
A REPORT ON A CWLA PILOT PROJECT TO TRAIN NEW CHILD CARE WORKERS EJ 017 849

MANPOWER NEEDS
DEVELOPING MANPOWER FOR THE WORLD'S SOCIAL WELFARE NEEDS. SOME OBSERVATIONS FROM THE CONFERENCE OF MINISTERS RESPONSIBLE FOR SOCIAL WELFARE.. EJ 004 093

MANUALS
PHYSICAL EDUCATION ACTIVITIES FOR THE ELEMENTARY SCHOOL. ED019995
ADMINISTRATION MANUAL FOR THE INVENTORY OF SOCIALIZATION OF BILINGUAL CHILDREN AGES THREE TO TEN. PART OF THE FINAL REPORT. ED027062
ADMINISTRATION MANUAL FOR TESTS OF BASIC LANGUAGE COMPETENCE IN ENGLISH AND SPANISH. LEVEL I (PRESCHOOL) ED027063
ADMINISTRATION MANUAL FOR TESTS OF BASIC LANGUAGE COMPETENCE IN ENGLISH AND SPANISH. LEVEL II (PRIMARY GRADES): CHILDREN AGES SIX TO TEN, ENGLISH AND SPANISH VERSIONS, FORMS A AND B. PART OF THE FINAL REPORT. ED027064
CONCEPT AND LANGUAGE DEVELOPMENT. A RESOURCE GUIDE FOR TEACHING YOUNG CHILDREN. ED030472
RECORDING INDIVIDUAL PUPIL EXPERIENCES IN THE CLASSROOM: A MANUAL FOR PROSE RECORDERS. ED038163
COMMUNITY COORDINATED CHILD CARE (4-C) MANUAL. ED039016

THE EVOLUTION OF DEVELOPMENTAL PSYCHOLOGY: A COMPARISON OF HANDBOOKS EJ 061 074

MAP SKILLS

ROCKS, RIVERS AND CITY CHILDREN EJ 029 390

MARINE BIOLOGY

OCEANS AND CHILDREN: MARINE SCIENCE AND ECOLOGICAL UNDERSTANDING EJ 029 391

MARRIAGE

KINSHIP INTERACTION AND MARITAL SOLIDARITY EJ 007 449
ROLE ORIENTATIONS, MARITAL AGE, AND LIFE PATTERNS IN ADULTHOOD EJ 052 529

MASS MEDIA

CHILDREN AND THE MASS MEDIA EJ 029 341
THEY BECAME WHAT THEY BEHELD EJ 045 423

MASTER PLANS

A PLAN OF ACTION FOR PARENT-CHILD EDUCATIONAL CENTERS. ED027959

MATCHED GROUPS

THE KINDERGARTEN AGAINST APPALACHIAN POVERTY EJ 037 021

MATHEMATICAL CONCEPTS

THE FORMATION OF ADDITION AND SUBTRACTION CONCEPTS BY PUPILS IN GRADES ONE AND TWO. FINAL REPORT. ED015015
TRAINING EFFECTS AND CONCEPT DEVELOPMENT--A STUDY OF THE CONSERVATION OF CONTINUOUS QUANTITY IN CHILDREN. ED016533
MATHEMATICS FOR ELEMENTARY SCHOOL TEACHERS. ED018276
SKILL GAMES FOR MATHEMATICS. ED022548
AN INVESTIGATION IN THE LEARNING OF EQUIVALENCE AND ORDER RELATIONS BY FOUR- AND FIVE-YEAR-OLD CHILDREN. ED045178
UNDERSTANDING OF QUANTITATIVE CONCEPTS IN 3 1/2-4 1/2 YEAR-OLD CHILDREN. ED046491
THE ABILITY OF KINDERGARTEN AND FIRST GRADE CHILDREN TO USE THE TRANSITIVE PROPERTY OF THREE LENGTH RELATIONS IN THREE PERCEPTUAL SITUATIONS. ED048936
DIFFERENTIAL PERFORMANCE OF KINDERGARTEN CHILDREN ON TRANSITIVITY OF THREE MATCHING RELATIONS. ED048942
THE EFFECTS OF INSTRUCTION ON THE DEVELOPMENT OF THE CONCEPT OF CONSERVATION OF NUMEROUSNESS BY KINDERGARTEN CHILDREN. REPORT FROM THE PROJECT ON INDIVIDUALLY GUIDED ELEMENTARY MATHEMATICS ED049821
BOOKS WHICH GIVE MATHEMATICAL CONCEPTS TO YOUNG CHILDREN: AN ANNOTATED BIBLIOGRAPHY EJ 007 274
ESTIMATION OF LINE LENGTH AND NUMBER: A DEVELOPMENTAL STUDY EJ 030 590
BEFORE CHILDREN CAN MEASURE EJ 032 359
WHAT PUPILS KNOW ABOUT VOCABULARY IN MATHEMATICS--1930 AND 1968 EJ 035 466
THE SEQUENCE OF DEVELOPMENT OF SOME EARLY MATHEMATICS BEHAVIORS EJ 056 710

MATHEMATICAL MODELS

FINAL REPORT ON HEAD START EVALUATION AND RESEARCH--1966-67 TO THE INSTITUTE FOR EDUCATIONAL DEVELOPMENT. SECTION II, ON THE INTERPRETATION OF MULTIVARIATE SYSTEMS. ED019118
EXTENSION OF A THEORY OF PREDICTIVE BEHAVIOR TO IMMEDIATE RECALL BY PRESCHOOL CHILDREN. ED025326
FREE-ASSOCIATION NORMS AND ASSOCIATIVE STRUCTURE. ED025328
YOUNG CHILDREN'S COMPREHENSION OF LOGICAL CONNECTIVES. ED033756
SEPARATING ENDOGENOUS, EXOGENOUS, ECOGENIC, AND EPOGENIC COMPONENT CURVES IN DEVELOPMENTAL DATA EJ 027 552

MATHEMATICAL VOCABULARY

WHAT PUPILS KNOW ABOUT VOCABULARY IN MATHEMATICS--1930 AND 1968 EJ 035 466

MATHEMATICS

BIBLIOGRAPHY OF RESEARCH STUDIES IN ELEMENTARY SCHOOL AND PRESCHOOL MATHEMATICS. ED023464
THE RELATIONSHIP BETWEEN PRIMARY STUDENTS' RATIONALIZATION OF CONSERVATION AND THEIR MATHEMATICAL ACHIEVEMENT EJ 046 672

MATHEMATICS CURRICULUM

THE DEVELOPMENT OF AN ELEMENTARY SCHOOL MATHEMATICS CURRICULUM FOR INDIVIDUALIZED INSTRUCTION. ED013120
BEYOND NUFFIELD EJ 028 718
THE NUFFIELD MATHEMATICS PROJECT EJ 033 864

MATHEMATICS EDUCATION

IN-SERVICE EDUCATION IN ELEMENTARY SCHOOL MATHEMATICS. ED018272
MAKING PRIMARY ARITHMETIC MEANINGFUL TO CHILDREN. ED020015
PROBLEM SOLVING AND CONCEPT FORMATION: ANNOTATED LISTING OF NATIONAL AND INTERNATIONAL CURRICULAR PROJECTS AT THE EARLY CHILDHOOD LEVEL. ED029685
DOES THE USE OF CUISENAIRE RODS IN KINDERGARTEN, FIRST AND SECOND GRADES UPGRADE ARITHMETIC ACHIEVEMENT? ED032128
PRESCHOOL MATHEMATICS CURRICULUM PROJECT. FINAL REPORT. ED038168
AN INVESTIGATION IN THE LEARNING OF EQUIVALENCE AND ORDER RELATIONS BY FOUR- AND FIVE-YEAR-OLD CHILDREN. ED045178

MATHEMATICS INSTRUCTION

EFFECTS OF A STRUCTURED PROGRAM OF PRESCHOOL MATHEMATICS ON COGNITIVE BEHAVIOR. ED015791
MATHEMATICS FOR ELEMENTARY SCHOOL TEACHERS. ED018276
THE EFFECTS OF TWO VARIABLES ON THE PROBLEM-SOLVING ABILITIES OF FIRST-GRADE CHILDREN. ED019113
MAKING PRIMARY ARITHMETIC MEANINGFUL TO CHILDREN. ED020015
ARITHMETIC AND MATHEMATICS. DIMENSIONS IN EARLY LEARNING SERIES. ED026136
THE USE OF COLOURED RODS IN TEACHING PRIMARY NUMBERWORK. ED028823
THE EFFECTS OF INSTRUCTION ON THE DEVELOPMENT OF THE CONCEPT OF CONSERVATION OF NUMEROUSNESS BY KINDERGARTEN CHILDREN. REPORT FROM THE PROJECT ON INDIVIDUALLY GUIDED ELEMENTARY MATHEMATICS ED049821
AN EXPERIMENTAL STUDY OF TWO METHODS OF PRESENTING THE INVERSION ALGORITHM IN DIVISION OF FRACTIONS EJ 033 863
THE NUFFIELD MATHEMATICS PROJECT EJ 033 864
EFFECT OF REINFORCEMENT CONTINGENCIES IN INCREASING PROGRAMMED READING AND MATHEMATICS BEHAVIORS IN FIRST-GRADE CHILDREN EJ 049 168

MATHEMATICS TEACHERS

WHAT INFLUENCES THE MATHEMATICAL UNDERSTANDING OF ELEMENTARY-SCHOOL TEACHERS? EJ 018 422

MATURATION

AN EVALUATION OF LOGICAL OPERATIONS INSTRUCTION IN THE PRESCHOOL. ED053791
CHILD HEALTH AND HUMAN DEVELOPMENT: PROGRESS 1963-1970. A REPORT OF THE NATIONAL INSTITUTE OF CHILD HEALTH AND HUMAN DEVELOPMENT. ED053799
ENJOYING PREADOLESCENCE: THE FORGOTTEN YEARS EJ 016 966
TIMING AND SOURCES OF INFORMATION ABOUT, AND ATTITUDES TOWARD, MENSTRUATION AMONG COLLEGE FEMALES EJ 029 533
CONCEPTUAL EMPHASIS IN THE HISTORY OF DEVELOPMENTAL PSYCHOLOGY: EVOLUTIONARY THEORY, TELEOLOGY, AND THE NATURE-NURTURE ISSUE EJ 034 043
NORMAL PSYCHOSEXUAL DEVELOPMENT EJ 038 944
DEVELOPMENTAL CHANGES IN IDIODYNAMIC SET RESPONSES OF CHILDREN'S WORD ASSOCIATIONS EJ 042 880
AN EVALUATION OF A THEORY OF SPECIFIC DEVELOPMENTAL DYSLEXIA EJ 055 875
LIMITATIONS ON THE GENERALIZABILITY OF GROWTH CURVES OF INTELLIGENCE: A REANALYSIS OF SOME DATA FROM THE HARVARD GROWTH STUDY EJ 060 014
SEX DIFFERENCES IN HUMAN DEVELOPMENT EJ 060 015

MATURITY TESTS

AN OBJECTIVE MEASURE OF STRUCTURAL COMPLEXITY IN CHILDREN'S WRITING. ED016534
A STUDY COMPARING GLOBAL QUALITY AND SYNTACTIC MATURITY IN THE WRITING COMPOSITION OF SECOND AND THIRD GRADE STUDENTS. ED029697
PSYCHOSOCIAL DEVELOPMENT IN CROSS-CULTURAL PERSPECTIVE: A NEW LOOK AT AN OLD ISSUE EJ 046 888

MEASUREMENT

BODY SIZE OF CONTEMPORARY GROUPS OF EIGHT-YEAR-OLD CHILDREN STUDIED IN DIFFERENT PARTS OF THE WORLD EJ 003 459

MEASUREMENT GOALS

THE SAMPLE: OPERATIONS IN THE HEAD START YEAR. ED043391
EVALUATION OF EDUCATIONAL PROGRAMS EJ 007 047

MEASUREMENT INSTRUMENTS

A QUANTITATIVE MEASURE FOR PROGRAMMED INSTRUCTION. ED014317
THE PRESCHOOL INVENTORY. ED014334
APPENDIX, STUDIES I, II AND III. ORIGINAL INSTRUMENTS USED AND BIBLIOGRAPHY. ED015028
TECHNIQUES FOR ASSESSING COGNITIVE AND SOCIAL ABILITIES OF CHILDREN AND PARENTS IN PROJECT HEAD START. ED015772
DEVELOPMENT OF CHILDREN'S ABILITY TO COORDINATE PERSPECTIVES. ED016516
DEVELOPMENT OF A TECHNIQUE FOR IDENTIFYING ELEMENTARY SCHOOL CHILDREN'S MUSICAL CONCEPTS. FINAL REPORT. ED016517
AN OBJECTIVE MEASURE OF STRUCTURAL COMPLEXITY IN CHILDREN'S WRITING. ED016534
THE COGNITIVE ENVIRONMENTS OF URBAN PRE-SCHOOL CHILDREN. MANUAL OF INSTRUCTIONS FOR ADMINISTERING AND SCORING THE HOME INTERVIEW. ED018253
THE COGNITIVE ENVIRONMENTS OF URBAN PRE-SCHOOL CHILDREN. MANUAL OF INSTRUCTIONS FOR ADMINISTERING AND SCORING MOTHER'S ATTITUDES TOWARD CHILD'S BEHAVIOR LEADING TO MASTERY. ED018256

THE COGNITIVE ENVIRONMENTS OF URBAN PRE-SCHOOL CHILDREN. MANUAL OF INSTRUCTIONS FOR ADMINISTERING AND SCORING THE TWENTY QUESTIONS TASK. ED018261
THE COGNITIVE ENVIRONMENTS OF URBAN PRE-SCHOOL CHILDREN. MANUAL OF INSTRUCTIONS FOR ADMINISTERING AND SCORING PLUTCHIK EXPLORATORY-INTEREST QUESTIONNAIRE. ED018262
THE COGNITIVE ENVIRONMENTS OF URBAN PRE-SCHOOL CHILDREN. MANUAL OF INSTRUCTIONS FOR ADMINISTERING AND SCORING SIGEL CONCEPTUAL STYLE SORTING TASKS. ED018263
THE COGNITIVE ENVIRONMENTS OF URBAN PRE-SCHOOL CHILDREN. MANUAL OF INSTRUCTIONS FOR ADMINISTERING AND SCORING THE EIGHT-BLOCK SORTING TASK. ED018265
THE COGNITIVE ENVIRONMENTS OF URBAN PRE-SCHOOL CHILDREN. MANUAL OF INSTRUCTIONS FOR ADMINISTERING AND SCORING THE CURIOSITY TASK. ED018268
THE COGNITIVE ENVIRONMENTS OF URBAN PRE-SCHOOL CHILDREN. MANUAL OF INSTRUCTIONS FOR ADMINISTERING AND SCORING MATERNAL LANGUAGE STYLES. ED018270
FINAL REPORT ON HEAD START EVALUATION AND RESEARCH--1966-67 TO THE INSTITUTE FOR EDUCATIONAL DEVELOPMENT. SECTION VI, THE MEASUREMENT OF BILINGUALISM AND BICULTURAL SOCIALIZATION OF THE CHILD IN THE SCHOOL SETTING--THE DEVELOPMENT OF INSTRUMENTS. ED019122
A STUDY OF A MEASUREMENT RESOURCE IN CHILD RESEARCH, PROJECT HEAD START. ED020790
MEASUREMENT OF MOTIVATION TO ACHIEVE IN PRESCHOOL CHILDREN. FINAL REPORT. ED021617
INDEX AND DESCRIPTION OF TESTS. ED025304
ADMINISTRATION MANUAL FOR THE INVENTORY OF SOCIALIZATION OF BILINGUAL CHILDREN AGES THREE TO TEN. PART OF THE FINAL REPORT. ED027062
THE THOMAS SELF-CONCEPT VALUES TEST. ED027068
RECORDING INDIVIDUAL PUPIL EXPERIENCES IN THE CLASSROOM: A MANUAL FOR PROSE RECORDERS. ED038163
YOUNG BLACK AND WHITE LISTENERS. ED038180
THE DEVELOPMENT OF A COMPUTER TECHNIQUE FOR THE CONTENT ANALYSIS OF PSYCHO-SOCIAL FACTORS IN THE ORAL LANGUAGE OF KINDERGARTEN CHILDREN. ED038184
OSCAR GOES TO NURSERY SCHOOL: A NEW TECHNIQUE FOR RECORDING PUPIL BEHAVIOR. ED039923
DEVELOPMENTAL NORMS OF CHILDREN AGED 2 1/2-5 YEARS: A PILOT STUDY. ED039949
EXPERIMENTAL VARIATION OF HEAD START CURRICULA: A COMPARISON OF CURRENT APPROACHES. ANNUAL REPORT, JUNE 12, 1968-JUNE 11, 1969. ED041618
GROSS ACTIVITY OF CHILDREN AT PLAY. (INTERNAL REPORT). ED043385
ENVIRONMENTALLY ENRICHED CLASSROOMS AND THE DEVELOPMENT OF DISADVANTAGED PRESCHOOL CHILDREN. ED045192
UNDERSTANDING OF QUANTITATIVE CONCEPTS IN 3 1/2-4 1/2 YEAR-OLD CHILDREN. ED046491
RELATIVE SOOTHING EFFECTS OF VERTICAL AND HORIZONTAL ROCKING. ED046504
MEASURING DIFFERENTIAL DEVELOPMENT IN YOUNG CHILDREN. ED050818
THE ASSESSMENT OF "SELF-CONCEPT" IN EARLY CHILDHOOD EDUCATION. ED050822
MEASURES OF VOCABULARY AND GRAMMATICAL SKILLS FOR CHILDREN UP TO AGE SIX EJ 021 683
CHILDREN'S DEPENDENCY SCALE EJ 025 232
THE ORGANIZATIONAL CLIMATE OF SCHOOLS IN FIVE URBAN AREAS EJ 027 704
CHILDREN'S PERCEPTIONS OF A TEACHING TEAM EJ 051 772
HYPERACTIVITY AND THE MACHINE: THE ACTOMETER EJ 055 876
REPORT CARDS FOR TEACHERS EJ 057 441
DELINQUENCY PREDICTION SCALES AND PERSONALITY INVENTORIES EJ 057 475
A SOCIAL COMPETENCE SCALE AND SYMPTOM CHECKIST FOR THE PRESCHOOL CHILD: FACTOR DIMENSIONS, THEIR CROSS-INSTRUMENT GENERALITY, AND LONGITUDINAL PERSISTENCE EJ 057 476

MEASUREMENT TECHNIQUES

AN ASSESSMENT OF INTELLIGENCE, PSYCHOLINGUISTIC ABILITIES AND LEARNING APTITUDES AMONG PRESCHOOL CHILDREN. ED014323
AN EVALUATION OF THE EFFECTS OF A SUMMER HEAD START PROGRAM. ED014327
THE EFFECTS OF NEUROLOGICAL AND ENVIRONMENTAL FACTORS ON THE LANGUAGE DEVELOPMENT OF HEAD START CHILDREN--A EVALUATION OF THE HEAD START PROGRAM. ED017317
THE STATUS OF BEHAVIORAL MEASUREMENT AND ASSESSMENT IN CHILDREN. ED018252
THE COGNITIVE ENVIRONMENTS OF URBAN PRE-SCHOOL CHILDREN. MANUAL OF INSTRUCTIONS FOR ADMINISTERING AND SCORING THE HOME INTERVIEW. ED018253
THE COGNITIVE ENVIRONMENTS OF URBAN PRE-SCHOOL CHILDREN. MANUAL OF INSTRUCTIONS FOR ADMINISTERING AND SCORING TOY SORTING TASK. ED018264
THE COGNITIVE ENVIRONMENTS OF URBAN PRE-SCHOOL CHILDREN. MANUAL OF INSTRUCTIONS FOR ADMINISTERING AND SCORING "ETCH-A-SKETCH" TASK. ED018267
THE COGNITIVE ENVIRONMENTS OF URBAN PRE-SCHOOL CHILDREN. MANUAL OF INSTRUCTIONS FOR ADMINISTERING AND SCORING THE CURIOSITY TASK. ED018268
FINAL REPORT ON HEAD START EVALUATION AND RESEARCH--1966-67 TO THE INSTITUTE FOR EDUCATIONAL DEVELOPMENT. SECTION VI, THE MEASUREMENT OF BILINGUALISM AND BICULTURAL SOCIALIZATION OF THE CHILD IN THE SCHOOL SETTING--THE DEVELOPMENT OF INSTRUMENTS. ED019122
HEAD START EVALUATION AND RESEARCH CENTER, BOSTON UNIVERSITY. REPORT C-II, THE EXPRESSION OF AGGRESSION IN PRE-SCHOOL CHILDREN. ED022562
A DISTANCE MEASURE OF RACIAL ATTITUDES IN PRIMARY GRADE CHILDREN: AN EXPLORATORY STUDY. ED026133
A THEORETICAL APPROACH FOR SELECTING ELEMENTARY SCHOOL ENVIRONMENTAL VARIABLES. ED028834
A COMPARATIVE STUDY OF CURRENT EDUCATIONAL TELEVISION PROGRAMS FOR PRESCHOOL CHILDREN. FINAL REPORT. ED032123
MEASURING PERCEPTUAL MOTOR ABILITY IN PRESCHOOL CHILDREN. ED032932
CHILD REARING. AN INQUIRY INTO RESEARCH AND METHODS. ED036344
CHILD BEHAVIOR SURVEY INSTRUMENT: MANUAL OF INSTRUCTIONS AND DEFINITIONS. ED037230
ANALYSIS OF THE OBJECT CATEGORIZATION TEST AND THE PICTURE CATEGORIZATION TEST FOR PRESCHOOL CHILDREN. ED038174
THE DEVELOPMENT OF A COMPUTER TECHNIQUE FOR THE CONTENT ANALYSIS OF PSYCHO-SOCIAL FACTORS IN THE ORAL LANGUAGE OF KINDERGARTEN CHILDREN. ED038184
STUDIES OF SUCKING BEHAVIOR IN THE HUMAN NEWBORN: THE DIAGNOSTIC AND PREDICTIVE VALUE OF MEASURES OF EARLIEST ORAL BEHAVIOR. ED039014
EXPERIMENTAL VARIATION OF HEAD START CURRICULA: A COMPARISON OF CURRENT APPROACHES. ANNUAL REPORT, JUNE 12, 1968-JUNE 11, 1969. ED041618
TERMINOLOGY AND METHODOLOGY RELATED TO THE USE OF HEART RATE RESPONSIVITY IN INFANCY RESEARCH EJ 034 566
EVALUATIVE USES OF UNCONVENTIONAL MEASUREMENT TECHNIQUES IN AN EDUCATIONAL SYSTEM EJ 042 347
SOME EFFECTS OF TESTING PROCEDURE ON DIVERGENT THINKING EJ 052 992
OVERLAP: HYPOTHESIS OR TAUTOLOGY? EJ 054 508
THE STRUCTURING OF SOCIAL ATTITUDES IN CHILDREN EJ 055 489

MECHANICAL TEACHING AIDS

GAMES AND OTHER ACTIVITIES FOR DEVELOPING LANGUAGE SKILLS. ED022555

MEDIATION THEORY

MEDIATIONAL STYLES: AN INDIVIDUAL DIFFERENCE VARIABLE IN CHILDREN'S VERBAL LEARNING ABILITY. ED027955
THE EFFECT OF VERBALIZATION OF RELEVANT AND IRRELEVANT DIMENSIONS ON CONCEPT FORMATION. ED030484
EFFECT OF VERBALIZATION ON YOUNG CHILDREN'S LEARNING OF A MANIPULATIVE SKILL. ED035447
THE EFFECT OF MEDIATIONAL INSTRUCTIONS ON ASSOCIATIVE SKILLS OF FIRST GRADE INNERCITY CHILDREN. ED038177
STATE AS VARIABLE, AS OBSTACLE AND AS MEDIATOR OF STIMULATION IN INFANT RESEARCH. ED049825
EFFECT OF VERBALIZATION ON YOUNG CHILDREN'S LEARNING OF A MANIPULATIVE SKILL EJ 020 520
DIMENSIONAL LEARNING ACROSS SENSORY MODALITIES IN NURSERY SCHOOL CHILDREN EJ 021 756
NONVERBAL MNEMONIC MEDIATION IN PRESCHOOL CHILDREN EJ 021 777
CHILDREN'S SHIFT PERFORMANCE IN THE ABSENCE OF DIMENSIONALITY AND A LEARNED REPRESENTATIONAL RESPONSE EJ 033 786
YOUNG CHILDREN'S USE OF THE SPEECH CODE IN A RECALL TASK EJ 033 792
FACILITATING AND INTERFERING EFFECTS OF STIMULUS NAMING ON CHILDREN'S MOTOR PAIRED-ASSOCIATE LEARNING EJ 033 793
MEDIATION AND PERCEPTUAL TRANSFER IN CHILDREN EJ 035 365
ASSOCIATION AND ABSTRACTION AS MECHANISMS OF IMITATIVE LEARNING EJ 035 367
THE ROLE OF VERBAL MEDIATION IN MENTAL DEVELOPMENT EJ 035 382
THE EFFECTS OF ATTENTION AND MEDIATION ON CHILDREN'S MEMORY EJ 039 638
THE PART PLAYED BY MEDIATION PROCESSES IN THE RETENTION OF TEMPORAL SEQUENCES BY TWO READING GROUPS EJ 039 909
THE USE OF VERBAL MEDIATION IN THE RETARDED AS A FUNCTION OF DEVELOPMENTAL LEVEL AND RESPONSE AVAILABILITY EJ 044 699
SINGLE VERSUS CUMULATIVE PRESENTATION OF STIMULI TO KINDERGARTNERS IN REVERSAL SHIFT BEHAVIOR EJ 047 678
COGNITIVE MEDIATION OF DEVELOPMENTAL TRENDS IN EXTREME RESPONSE CHOICE EJ 047 688
SOME THOUGHTS ON HOW CHILDREN LEARN TO REMEMBER EJ 049 432
VERBAL MEDIATION AND SATIATION IN YOUNG CHILDREN EJ 056 613
EFFECTS OF SYNTACTICAL MEDIATION, AGE, AND MODES OF REPRESENTATION ON PAIRED-ASSOCIATE LEARNING EJ 056 615
AN ONTOGENY OF MEDIATIONAL DEFICIENCY EJ 056 631

TRANSFER BETWEEN THE ODDITY AND RELATIVE SIZE CONCEPTS: REVERSAL AND EXTRADIMENSIONAL SHIFTS EJ 057 906

MEDICAL EVALUATION

USE OF NON-PROFESSIONAL PERSONNEL FOR HEALTH SCREENING OF HEAD START CHILDREN. FINAL REPORT. ED029702
LEARNING FROM EACH OTHER: PREDIATRICIANS AND TEACHERS EJ 050 320
THE DIAGNOSTIC EVALUATION OF CHILDREN WITH LEARNING PROBLEMS: A COMMUNICATION PROCESS EJ 050 321

MEDICAL RESEARCH

NEW HOPE FOR BABIES OF RH NEGATIVE MOTHERS EJ 003 743
INFORMED CONSENT IN PEDIATRIC RESEARCH EJ 007 413

MEDICAL SERVICES

DELIVERY OF CHILD HEALTH SERVICES. 1970 WHITE HOUSE CONFERENCE ON CHILDREN, REPORT OF FORUM 11. (WORKING PAPER). ED046528
PROGRAMS FOR INFANTS AND YOUNG CHILDREN. PART III: HEALTH. ED047809
LEARNING FROM EACH OTHER: PREDIATRICIANS AND TEACHERS EJ 050 320

MEDICAL TREATMENT

1. OBSTETRICAL MEDICATION AND INFANT OUTCOME: A REVIEW OF THE LITERATURE EJ 023 013
II. DELIVERY MEDICATION AND INFANT OUTCOME: AN EMPIRICAL STUDY EJ 023 014
III. OBSTETRICAL MEDICATION AND INFANT OUTCOME: SOME SUMMARY CONSIDERATIONS EJ 023 015
THE USE OF STIMULANT DRUGS IN TREATING HYPERACTIVE CHILDREN EJ 038 022

MEMORIZING

EFFECT OF LABELS ON MEMORY IN THE ABSENCE OF REHEARSAL. ED051883
THE CHRONOLOGY OF THE DEVELOPMENT OF COVERT SPEECH IN CHILDREN EJ 047 594
DEVELOPMENT OF MEMORIZATION STRATEGIES EJ 047 679

MEMORY

THE RELATION BETWEEN TEST ANXIETY AND NEED FOR MEMORY SUPPORT IN PROBLEM SOLVING. REVISED RESEARCH MEMORANDUM NO. 11. ED021616
MEMORY AND "CONTINGENCY ANALYSIS" IN INFANT LEARNING. ED024437
INDUCED VERSUS SPONTANEOUS REHEARSAL IN SHORT-TERM MEMORY IN NURSERY SCHOOL CHILDREN. STUDY M: DEVELOPMENT OF SELECTIVE ATTENTION ABILITIES. ED024444
AGE AND MEMORY AS FACTORS IN PROBLEM SOLVING. ED025327
CONCEPT IDENTIFICATION STRATEGIES. RESEARCH PROJECT NUMBER 3 OF PROJECT HEAD START RESEARCH AND EVALUATION CENTER, SYRACUSE UNIVERSITY RESEARCH INSTITUTE, NOVEMBER 1, 1967. ED026140
DISCRIMINATION OF RECENCY IN CHILDREN. FINAL REPORT. ED030493
EFFECT OF LABELS ON MEMORY IN THE ABSENCE OF REHEARSAL. ED051883
SHORT-TERM RECOGNITION MEMORY IN CHILDREN EJ 018 873
MOTOR ACTIVITY: EFFECTS ON MEMORY EJ 021 769
NONVERBAL MNEMONIC MEDIATION IN PRESCHOOL CHILDREN EJ 021 777
SHORT-TERM MEMORY FOR VISUAL INFORMATION IN CHILDREN AND ADULTS EJ 024 700
AGE DIFFERENCES IN JUDGMENTS OF RECENCY FOR SHORT SEQUENCES OF PICTURES EJ 026 375
SHORT-TERM MEMORY IN CHILDREN: KEEPING TRACK OF VARIABLES WITH FEW OR MANY STATES EJ 029 444
THE ROLE OF MEMORY IN MAKING TRANSITIVE JUDGMENTS EJ 030 288
THE RELATIONSHIP BETWEEN AUDITORY AND VISUAL SHORT-TERM MEMORY AND READING ACHIEVEMENT EJ 033 780
ARE THESE TWO STIMULI FROM THE SAME SET? RESPONSE TIMES OF CHILDREN AND ADULTS WITH FAMILIAR AND ARBITRARY SETS EJ 033 788
EFFECTS OF MEMORY AIDS ON HYPOTHESIS BEHAVIOR AND FOCUSING IN YOUNG CHILDREN AND ADULTS EJ 033 789
SEQUENTIAL CONTIGUITY AND SHORT-TERM MEMORY IN CHILDREN'S DISCRIMINATION LEARNING EJ 033 790
A DECREMENTAL EFFECT OF REDUNDANCY IN DISCRIMINATION LEARNING EJ 033 795
DEVELOPMENT OF FREE RECALL LEARNING IN CHILDREN EJ 035 359
THE EFFECTS OF REHEARSAL AND CHUNKING INSTRUCTIONS ON CHILDREN'S MULTITRIAL FREE RECALL EJ 035 377
EFFECTS OF STIMULUS AVAILABILITY ON CHILDREN'S INFERENCES EJ 036 822
INFANTS' RECOGNITION MEMORY FOR A SERIES OF VISUAL STIMULI EJ 037 342
THE GROWTH OF CHILDREN'S SEMANTIC MEMORY: SEMANTIC ELEMENTS EJ 038 170
FREE RECALL OF WORDS AND OBJECTS EJ 039 634
THE EFFECTS OF ATTENTION AND MEDIATION ON CHILDREN'S MEMORY EJ 039 638
LABELING AND IMAGING AS AIDS TO MEMORY EJ 041 143
NAMING AND MEMORY IN NURSERY SCHOOL CHILDREN IN THE ABSENCE OF REHEARSAL EJ 042 961
RECOGNITION MEMORY FOR PICTURES IN PRESCHOOL CHILDREN EJ 042 964
MEMORY AND ATTENTION IN CHILDREN'S DOUBLE-ALTERNATION LEARNING EJ 042 966
RECOGNITION MEMORY: THE RELATIONSHIP OF ACCURACY AND LATENCY OF RESPONSE UNDER DIFFERENT MEMORY LOADS IN RETARDATES EJ 046 256
MEMORY: INTERACTION OF STIMULUS AND ORGANISMIC FACTORS EJ 049 429
WHAT THE DEVELOPMENT OF SHORT-TERM MEMORY IS EJ 049 430
DEVELOPMENTAL CHANGES IN VISUAL INFORMATION PROCESSING AND SHORT-TERM VISUAL MEMORY EJ 049 431
SOME THOUGHTS ON HOW CHILDREN LEARN TO REMEMBER EJ 049 432
FIRST DISCUSSANT'S COMMENTS: WHAT IS MEMORY DEVELOPMENT THE DEVELOPMENT OF? EJ 049 433
SECOND DISCUSSANT'S COMMENTS: WHAT'S LEFT TO SAY? EJ 049 434
EFFECT OF OVERT VERBAL LABELING ON SHORT-TERM MEMORY IN CULTURALLY DEPRIVED AND NONDEPRIVED CHILDREN EJ 053 710
THE DEVELOPMENT OF MEMORY-ENCODING PROCESSES IN YOUNG CHILDREN EJ 053 716
MEANINGFULNESS, SERIAL POSITION AND RETENTION INTERVAL IN RECOGNITION SHORT-TERM MEMORY EJ 053 724
AGE, ICONIC STORAGE, AND VISUAL INFORMATION PROCESSING EJ 053 725
PRIMACY IN PRESCHOOLERS' SHORT-TERM MEMORY: THE EFFECTS OF REPEATED TESTS AND SHIFT TRIALS EJ 053 729
MEMORY FOR RHYTHMIC SERIES: AGE CHANGES IN ACCURACY AND NUMBER CODING EJ 054 805
EFFECTS OF AGE UPON RETRIEVAL FROM SHORT-TERM MEMORY EJ 055 109
RELATIONS OF AGE AND INTELLIGENCE TO SHORT-TERM COLOR MEMORY EJ 056 392
INFORMATION AND STRATEGY IN THE YOUNG CHILD'S SEARCH FOR HIDDEN OBJECTS EJ 056 395
HABITUATION AND MEMORY: INFANT CARDIAC RESPONSES TO FAMILIAR AND DISCREPANT AUDITORY STIMULI EJ 056 633
REINSTATEMENT EFFECTS IN CHILDREN EJ 057 899
QUANTITATIVE AND QUALITATIVE ASPECTS OF MEMORY FOR PICTURE STIMULI EJ 057 907
A PERCEPTUAL TEST BATTERY: DEVELOPMENT AND STANDARDIZATION EJ 058 395

MENTAL DEVELOPMENT

A SOCIAL PSYCHOLOGICAL ANALYSIS OF THE TRANSITION FROM HOME TO SCHOOL. FINAL REPORT. ED015017
LOGICAL THINKING IN SECOND GRADE. FINAL REPORT. ED033747
ISSUES AND IMPLICATIONS OF THE DISTRIBUTION OF ATTENTION IN THE HUMAN INFANT. ED043387
LONG TERM STUDY OF PREMATURES: SUMMARY OF PUBLISHED FINDINGS. ED043389
DEVELOPMENTAL-BEHAVIORAL PATTERNS IN TWENTY-SIX CULTURALLY DISADVANTAGED INFANTS. ED044173
A STUDY OF CAUSAL THINKING IN ELEMENTARY SCHOOL CHILDREN. FINAL REPORT. ED050830
DESIGNS AND PROPOSAL FOR EARLY CHILDHOOD RESEARCH: A NEW LOOK: MALNUTRITION, LEARNING AND INTELLIGENCE. (ONE IN A SERIES OF SIX PAPERS). ED053811
INFANT MENTAL DEVELOPMENT AND NEUROLOGICAL STATUS, FAMILY SOCIOECONOMIC STATUS, AND INTELLIGENCE AT AGE FOUR EJ 032 675
THE ROLE OF VERBAL MEDIATION IN MENTAL DEVELOPMENT EJ 035 382
VALIDITY OF THE DENVER DEVELOPMENTAL SCREENING TEST EJ 041 722
AN EXAMINATION OF THE DEVELOPMENTAL RELATIONS BETWEEN CERTAIN SPATIAL TASKS EJ 051 563
PREDICTION OF INTELLECTUAL PERFORMANCE AT 3 YEARS FROM INFANT TESTS AND PERSONALITY MEASURES EJ 052 237

MENTAL HEALTH

MENTAL HEALTH. WHAT RESEARCH SAYS TO THE TEACHER SERIES NUMBER 24. ED027087
DEVELOPMENTAL GROUPINGS OF PRE-SCHOOL CHILDREN. ED046513
MEETING SOCIO-EDUCATIONAL NEEDS EJ 027 916
ISSUES IN ASSESSING DEVELOPMENT EJ 030 516
ADVOCACY FOR CHILDREN: CHALLENGE FOR THE 1970'S EJ 032 108
VIEWPOINT: GAP AND THE JOINT COMMISSION ON MENTAL HEALTH OF CHILDREN EJ 060 203

MENTAL HEALTH CLINICS

DISTURBANCE AND DISSONANCE - COMMUNITY UNIVERSITY COLLABORATION IN DIAGNOSIS AND TREATMENT OF DISTURBANCES. ED030485

MENTAL HEALTH PROGRAMS

NURSERIES IN CROSS-CULTURAL EDUCATION. FINAL REPORT. ED053815
BEHAVIORAL SCIENCE FOR ELEMENTARY-SCHOOL PUPILS EJ 014 306
A SUMMARY OF THE REPORT OF THE JOINT COMMISSION ON MENTAL HEALTH OF CHILDREN EJ 023 678

MENTAL ILLNESS
CONCRETE OPERATIONAL THINKING IN MENTALLY ILL ADOLESCENTS EJ 060 778

MENTAL RETARDATION
AN OVERVIEW OF RESEARCH IN LEARNING, MOTIVATION, AND PERCEPTION. ED020799
CONTROL OF LEAD POISONING IN CHILDREN. (PRE-PUBLICATION DRAFT). ED050825
THE USE OF DEVELOPMENTAL PLANS FOR MENTALLY RETARDED CHILDREN IN FOSTER FAMILY CARE EJ 035 803
IQ CHANGES IN HOSPITALIZED MENTAL RETARDATES EJ 046 727
LONGITUDINAL ASSESSMENT OF THE RELATION BETWEEN MEASURED INTELLIGENCE OF INSTITUTIONALIZED RETARDATES AND HOSPITAL AGE EJ 047 340
AN ESSAY REVIEW: MENTAL RETARDATION AS A SOCIAL PROBLEM EJ 047 341
PHYSIOLOGICAL INDICATIONS OF ORGANIC INVOLVEMENT EJ 051 016
INSTITUTIONALIZED RETARDATES' ANIMAL DRAWINGS; THEIR MEANINGS AND SIGNIFICANCE EJ 055 108
PARENTS OF CHILDREN WITH PKU EJ 060 522

MENTAL TESTS
INFANT AND PRESCHOOL MENTAL TESTS: REVIEW AND EVALUATION. ED026109

MENTALLY HANDICAPPED
LANGUAGE DEVELOPMENT EXPERIENCES FOR YOUNG CHILDREN. ED019125
RETARDED CHILDREN AT CAMP WITH NORMAL CHILDREN EJ 012 199
BEHAVIOR DEVIATIONS IN MENTALLY RETARDED CHILDREN EJ 022 475
CARDIAC CLASSICAL CONDITIONING AND REVERSAL IN THE MONGOLOID, ENCEPHALOPATHIC, AND NORMAL CHILD EJ 025 375
ODDITY PREFERENCE BY MENTAL RETARDATES EJ 027 825
FOSTER FAMILY SERVICES FOR MENTALLY RETARDED CHILDREN EJ 030 653
APPARENT VISUAL SIZE AS A FUNCTION OF AGE, INTELLIGENCE, AND A SURROUNDING FRAME OF REFERENCE FOR NORMAL AND MENTALLY RETARDED SUBJECTS EJ 043 704
THE USE OF VERBAL MEDIATION IN THE RETARDED AS A FUNCTION OF DEVELOPMENTAL LEVEL AND RESPONSE AVAILABILITY EJ 044 699
THE EFFECTS OF OWN-HOME AND INSTITUTION-REARING ON THE BEHAVIOURAL DEVELOPMENT OF NORMAL AND MONGOL CHILDREN EJ 048 905
TRANSFERENCE TOWARD THE CHILD THERAPIST AND OTHER PARENT SURROGATES EJ 049 427

METHODS RESEARCH
LANGUAGE RESEARCH STUDY--PROJECT HEAD START. DEVELOPMENT OF METHODOLOGY FOR OBTAINING AND ANALYZING SPONTANEOUS VERBALIZATIONS USED BY PRE-KINDERGARTEN CHILDREN IN SELECTED HEAD START PROGRAMS--A PILOT STUDY. ED015007
THE FORMATION OF ADDITION AND SUBTRACTION CONCEPTS BY PUPILS IN GRADES ONE AND TWO. FINAL REPORT. ED015015
RECOLLECTIONS OF CHILDHOOD: A STUDY OF THE RETROSPECTIVE METHOD EJ 025 047
TEACHING MULTIPLE CLASSIFICATION TO YOUNG CHILDREN EJ 056 711

MEXICAN AMERICANS
AN EVALUATION OF OPERATION HEAD START BILINGUAL CHILDREN, SUMMER, 1965. ED013667
THE COMPARATIVE EFFICACIES OF SPANISH, ENGLISH AND BILINGUAL COGNITIVE VERBAL INSTRUCTION WITH MEXICAN-AMERICAN HEAD START CHILDREN. FINAL REPORT. ED030473
EFFECTS OF SOCIAL REINFORCEMENT ON SELF-ESTEEM OF MEXICAN-AMERICAN CHILDREN. LONG ABSTRACT. ED033767
FAMILY FACTORS RELATED TO COMPETENCE IN YOUNG, DISADVANTAGED MEXICAN-AMERICAN CHILDREN. PART OF THE FINAL REPORT ON HEAD START EVALUATION AND RESEARCH: 1968-69 TO THE OFFICE OF ECONOMIC OPPORTUNITY. ED037248
RISK-TAKING BEHAVIOR IN PRESCHOOL CHILDREN FROM THREE ETHNIC BACKGROUNDS. ED042486
EARLY CHILDHOOD EDUCATION LEARNING SYSTEM FOR THREE-AND FOUR-YEAR-OLD MIGRANT CHILDREN, MCALLEN, TEXAS. EVALUATION REPORT, 1968-1969. ED043370
DAME SCHOOL PROJECT (BI-LINGUAL PRE SCHOOL PROJECT), SANTA CLARA COUNTY OFFICE OF EDUCATION. FINAL REPORT, AUGUST 1, 1970. ED046514
EFFECTS OF PRESCHOOL STIMULATION UPON SUBSEQUENT SCHOOL PERFORMANCE AMONG THE CULTURALLY DISADVANTAGED. ED046545
DEMONSTRATION AND TRAINING PROJECT FOR MIGRANT CHILDREN, MCALLEN, TEXAS. EARLY CHILDHOOD LEARNING SYSTEM. FINAL EVALUATION REPORT, 1970-71. ED053812
MEXICAN-AMERICANS AND LANGUAGE LEARNING EJ 012 397
CHILDREARING PRACTICES AMONG SELECTED CULTURALLY DEPRIVED MINORITIES EJ 023 613
A TRAINING PROGRAM FOR VOLUNTEERS EJ 028 502
SELF CONCEPTS OF DISADVANTAGED AND ADVANTAGED STUDENTS EJ 035 618
MEXICAN-AMERICAN CULTURAL MEMBERSHIP AND ADJUSTMENT TO SCHOOL EJ 035 620
INTERVENTION STRATEGIES FOR SPANISH-SPEAKING PRESCHOOL CHILDREN EJ 036 746
COOPERATION AND COMPETITION OF MEXICAN, MEXICAN-AMERICAN, AND ANGLO-AMERICAN CHILDREN OF TWO AGES UNDER FOUR INSTRUCTIONAL SETS EJ 041 957
VALUES OF MEXICAN-AMERICAN, NEGRO, AND ANGLO BLUE-COLLAR AND WHITE-COLLAR CHILDREN EJ 052 653
FAMILY FACTORS RELATED TO COMPETENCE IN YOUNG DISADVANTAGED MEXICAN-AMERICAN CHILDREN EJ 053 753
THE DEVELOPMENT OF DEMOCRATIC VALUES AND BEHAVIOR AMONG MEXICAN-AMERICAN CHILDREN EJ 058 509

MICROTEACHING
INTERIM PROGRESS REPORT OF A REMOTE TEACHER TRAINING INSTITUTE FOR EARLY CHILDHOOD EDUCATORS (FUNDED BY NDEA TITLE XI). ED017326
MICRO-TEACHING FOR PREPARING TEACHERS OF CULTURALLY DIVERSE CHILDREN EJ 052 068

MIDDLE CLASS
HEAD START EVALUATION AND RESEARCH CENTER. PROGRESS REPORT OF RESEARCH STUDIES 1966 TO 1967. DOCUMENT 5, COMPARATIVE ITEM-CONTENT ANALYSIS OF ACHIEVEMENT TEST PERFORMANCE IN YOUNG CHILDREN. ED021627
DEVELOPING COGNITIVE LEARNINGS WITH YOUNG CHILDREN. ED041614
CONSCIENCE, PERSONALITY, AND SOCIALIZATION TECHNIQUES EJ 023 858

MIDDLE CLASS MOTHERS
FINAL REPORT ON HEAD START EVALUATION AND RESEARCH: 1967-68 TO THE OFFICE OF ECONOMIC OPPORTUNITY. SECTION I: PART A, MIDDLE CLASS MOTHER-TEACHERS IN AN EXPERIMENTAL PRESCHOOL PROGRAM FOR SOCIALLY DISADVANTAGED CHILDREN. ED023454
FINAL REPORT ON HEAD START EVALUATION AND RESEARCH: 1967-68 TO THE OFFICE OF ECONOMIC OPPORTUNITY. SECTION I: PARTS A AND B. ED023457

MIDDLE SCHOOLS
THE MIDDLE SCHOOL: A SELECTED BIBLIOGRAPHY WITH INTRODUCTION. ED029714
WHAT'S AHEAD FOR PREADOLESCENCE? EJ 009 034

MIGRANT CHILD CARE CENTERS
A GUIDE FOR MANAGERS OF CHILD DAY CARE AGENCIES. ED046486
A GUIDE TO THE PLANNING AND OPERATION OF A CHILD DEVELOPMENT CENTER FOR MIGRANT CHILDREN AND A REPORT OF THE HOOPESTON CHILD DEVELOPMENT CENTER ED049838

MIGRANT CHILD EDUCATION
EARLY CHILDHOOD EDUCATION LEARNING SYSTEM FOR THREE-AND FOUR-YEAR-OLD MIGRANT CHILDREN, MCALLEN, TEXAS. EVALUATION REPORT, 1968-1969. ED043370

MIGRANT CHILDREN
A STUDY IN CHILD CARE (CASE STUDY FROM VOLUME II-B): "WE COME WITH THE DUST AND WE GO WITH THE WIND." DAY CARE PROGRAMS REPRINT SERIES. ED051907
DEMONSTRATION AND TRAINING PROJECT FOR MIGRANT CHILDREN, MCALLEN, TEXAS. EARLY CHILDHOOD LEARNING SYSTEM. FINAL EVALUATION REPORT, 1970-71. ED053812
FLORIDA'S EARLY CHILDHOOD LEARNING PROGRAM FOR MIGRANT CHILDREN EJ 043 089

MIGRANT WORKERS
A STUDY IN CHILD CARE (CASE STUDY FROM VOLUME II-A): "TACOS AND TULIPS." DAY CARE PROGRAMS REPRINT SERIES. ED051893

MIGRATION
THE ROLE OF GEOGRAPHIC MOBILITY IN SOME ADJUSTMENT PROBLEMS OF CHILDREN AND FAMILIES EJ 023 430

MILIEU THERAPY
RESIDENTIAL TREATMENT OF EMOTIONALLY DISTURBED CHILDREN IN NORWAY EJ 058 135

MINIMALLY BRAIN INJURED
THE OFF-KILTERED KIDS EJ 028 383
AGE DIFFERENCES IN VISUAL REACTION TIME OF "BRAIN DAMAGED" AND NORMAL CHILDREN UNDER IRREGULAR PREPARATORY INTERVAL CONDITIONS EJ 060 109
TREATMENT OF PROBLEMS ASSOCIATED WITH COGNITIVE AND PERCEPTUAL-MOTOR DEFICITS EJ 060 501

MINORITY GROUP CHILDREN
ONE-PARENT ADOPTIONS EJ 022 180
KEYS TO STANDARD ENGLISH EJ 028 577

MNEMONICS
IMPLICATIONS OF MNEMONICS RESEARCH FOR COGNITIVE THEORY. ED045199
MEMORY AND ATTENTION IN CHILDREN'S DOUBLE-ALTERNATION LEARNING EJ 042 966

MEMORY FOR RHYTHMIC SERIES: AGE CHANGES IN ACCURACY AND NUMBER CODING EJ 054 805
IMAGERY AND MULTIPLE-LIST PAIRED ASSOCIATE LEARNING IN YOUNG CHILDREN EJ 057 904

MOBILE CLASSROOMS
WAKULLA COUNTY PRESCHOOL. FINAL REPORT. ED039022
THE EFFECTIVENESS OF SPECIAL PROGRAMS FOR RURAL ISOLATED FOUR-YEAR-OLD CHILDREN. FINAL REPORT. ED041638
APPALACHIA PRESCHOOL EDUCATION PROGRAM, CHARLESTON, WEST VIRGINIA: A THREE-PART PRESCHOOL PROGRAM COMBINING A TELEVISION PROGRAM, PARAPROFESSIONAL HOME VISITORS, AND A MOBILE CLASSROOM. MODEL PROGRAMS--CHILDHOOD EDUCATION. ED045216
PRESCHOOL INSTRUCTION MOBILE FACILITIES: DESCRIPTION AND ANALYSIS. SCHOOL PRACTICES REPORT NO. 3. ED050803
A STUDY IN CHILD CARE (CASE STUDY FROM VOLUME II-B): "WE COME WITH THE DUST AND WE GO WITH THE WIND." DAY CARE PROGRAMS REPRINT SERIES. ED051907

MOBILE EDUCATIONAL SERVICES
PRESCHOOL INSTRUCTION MOBILE FACILITIES: DESCRIPTION AND ANALYSIS. SCHOOL PRACTICES REPORT NO. 3. ED050803
A MOBILE PRESCHOOL EJ 006 982

MOBILE LABORATORIES
AN INEXPENSIVE AND PORTABLE MEANS FOR ONE-WAY OBSERVATION EJ 045 797

MOBILITY
THE ROLE OF GEOGRAPHIC MOBILITY IN SOME ADJUSTMENT PROBLEMS OF CHILDREN AND FAMILIES EJ 023 430

MODELS
SIX STRUCTURE-OF-INTELLECT HYPOTHESES IN SIX-YEAR-OLD CHILDREN. ED023469
A STRUCTURE-PROCESS APPROACH TO COGNITIVE DEVELOPMENT OF PRESCHOOL NEGRO CHILDREN: RATIONALE AND EFFECTS. ED033743
THE TUCSON EARLY EDUCATION MODEL. ED033753
AN ATTRIBUTIONAL (COGNITIVE) MODEL OF MOTIVATION. ED038173
AN APPROACH TO THE STUDY OF INFANT BEHAVIOR. ED039031
WORDS AND DEEDS ABOUT ALTRUISM AND THE SUBSEQUENT REINFORCEMENT POWER OF THE MODEL. ED043390
FOLLOW THROUGH: PROGRAM APPROACHES, SCHOOL YEAR 1970-71. ED047787
MODELING BY EXEMPLIFICATION AND INSTRUCTION IN TRAINING CONSERVATION. ED047790
THE IMPLICATIONS OF DESIGN AND MODEL SELECTION FOR THE EVALUATION OF PROGRAMS FOR THE DISADVANTAGED CHILD. ED047792
MODELS FOR NONGRADING SCHOOLS: A REPORT OF A NATIONAL SEMINAR. ED049827
DEVELOPMENTAL PROCESSES IN DISCRIMINATION LEARNING EJ 024 705
THE MODELING OF SHARING: EFFECTS ASSOCIATED WITH VICARIOUS REINFORCEMENT, SYMBOLIZATION, AGE, AND GENERALIZATION EJ 028 894
PLANNED VARIATION IN HEAD START PROGRAMS EJ 031 848
A TEST OF THE GENERALITY OF THE EFFECTS OF DEVIANT PRESCHOOL MODELS EJ 034 531
THE OBJECTIVE MEASUREMENT OF CHILDREN'S INTRAFAMILIAL ATTITUDE AND SENTIMENT STRUCTURE AND THE INVESTMENT-SUBSIDIATION MODEL EJ 034 542
POWER AND THE INTERNALIZATION OF SELF-DENIAL EJ 036 077
CHILDREN'S "IMITATION" AS A FUNCTION OF THE PRESENCE OR ABSENCE OF A MODEL AND THE DESCRIPTION OF HIS INSTRUMENTAL BEHAVIORS EJ 036 080
THE EFFECTS OF SOCIAL ISOLATION AND CHARACTERISTICS OF THE MODEL ON ACCENT IMITATION IN FOURTH-GRADE CHILDREN EJ 038 171
EFFECT OF THE PRESENCE OF A HUMAN MODEL ON IMITATIVE BEHAVIOR IN CHILDREN EJ 039 904
IMITATIVE AGGRESSION IN CHILDREN AS A FUNCTION OF OBSERVING A HUMAN MODEL EJ 039 907
ROLE MODEL INFLUENCES ON COLLEGE WOMEN'S CAREER ASPIRATIONS EJ 041 632
LEARNING OF AGGRESSION AS A FUNCTION OF PRESENCE OF A HUMAN MODEL, RESPONSE INTENSITY, AND TARGET OF THE RESPONSE EJ 043 198
EFFECT ON RESISTANCE TO DEVIATION OF OBSERVING A MODEL'S AFFECTIVE REACTION TO RESPONSE CONSEQUENCES EJ 043 283
EFFECTS OF COMPETITION-INDUCED FRUSTRATION ON TWO CLASSES OF MODELED BEHAVIOR EJ 043 284
THE EFFECT OF SUBJECT RACE, MODEL RACE, AND VICARIOUS PRAISE ON VICARIOUS LEARNING EJ 045 458
EFFECTS OF IMITATION OF DIFFERENT REINFORCEMENT COMBINATIONS TO A MODEL EJ 046 255
MODIFICATION OF IMPULSIVE AND REFLECTIVE COGNITIVE STYLES THROUGH OBSERVATION OF FILM-MEDIATED MODELS EJ 047 676
ABSTRACTION, INFERENCE, AND THE PROCESS OF IMITATIVE LEARNING EJ 047 685
LEARNING TO BE GENEROUS OR STINGY: IMITATION OF SHARING BEHAVIOR AS A FUNCTION OF MODEL GENEROSITY AND VICARIOUS REINFORCEMENT EJ 052 443
EFFECTS OF ADULT AND PEER OBSERVERS ON BOYS' AND GIRLS' RESPONSES TO AN AGGRESSIVE MODEL EJ 052 459
WORDS AND DEEDS ABOUT ALTRUISM AND THE SUBSEQUENT REINFORCEMENT POWER OF THE MODEL EJ 053 739
DEVELOPMENTAL ASPECTS OF VARIABLES RELEVANT TO OBSERVATIONAL LEARNING EJ 053 740
MODELING EFFECTS UPON CONCEPTUAL STYLE AND COGNITIVE TEMPO EJ 056 396
THE EFFECT OF A TELEVISION MODEL UPON RULE ADOPTION BEHAVIOR OF CHILDREN EJ 056 733
MODELING BY EXEMPLIFICATION AND INSTRUCTION IN TRAINING CONSERVATION EJ 057 898
EFFECTS OF VICARIOUS CONSEQUENCES AND RACE OF MODEL UPON IMITATIVE PERFORMANCE BY BLACK CHILDREN EJ 058 139
INFLUENCE OF MODELING, EXHORTATIVE VERBALIZATION, AND SURVEILLANCE ON CHILDREN'S SHARING EJ 058 214
A DEVELOPMENTAL INVESTIGATION OF TELEVISED MODELED VERBALIZATIONS ON RESISTANCE TO DEVIATION EJ 058 218
MODELING AND THE FEARFUL CHILD PATIENT EJ 058 354
OBSERVATION, REPETITION, AND ETHNIC BACKGROUND IN CONCEPT ATTAINMENT AND GENERALIZATION EJ 059 316

MONGOLISM
COMBATTING RETARDATION IN INFANTS WITH DOWN'S SYNDROME EJ 026 640

MORAL ISSUES
TEACHING AND THE NEW MORALITY EJ 016 776
THE RIGHTS OF FOSTER PARENTS EJ 022 182

MORAL VALUES
SOME STUDIES OF THE MORAL DEVELOPMENT OF CHILDREN. ED024445
THE FACTORIAL STRUCTURE OF REASONING, MORAL JUDGMENT, AND MORAL CONDUCT. ED031302
PIAGET MISUNDERSTOOD: A CRITIQUE OF THE CRITICISMS OF HIS THEORY OF MORAL DEVELOPMENT EJ 011 915
THE IMPACT OF CHANGE EJ 011 982
DEVELOPMENT OF MORAL ATTITUDES IN WHITE AND NEGRO BOYS EJ 021 027
CONSCIENCE, PERSONALITY, AND SOCIALIZATION TECHNIQUES EJ 023 858
HONESTY AND ALTRUISM AMONG PREADOLESCENTS EJ 026 450
DEVELOPMENTAL ASPECTS OF REACTION TO POSITIVE INDUCEMENTS EJ 029 359
THE RELATION OF ROLE TAKING TO THE DEVELOPMENT OF MORAL JUDGMENT IN CHILDREN EJ 035 991
FATHER ABSENCE AND CONSCIENCE DEVELOPMENT EJ 038 854
INCORPORATION OF VALUES BY LOWER AND MIDDLE SOCIOECONOMIC CLASS PRESCHOOL BOYS EJ 040 210
SOCIAL PARTICIPATION AS A FACTOR IN THE MORAL DEVELOPMENT OF PREADOLESCENTS EJ 043 605
THE EFFECT OF TRAINING CHILDREN TO MAKE MORAL JUDGMENTS THAT ARE INDEPENDENT OF SANCTIONS EJ 044 507
THE YOUNG CHILD'S UNDERSTANDING OF SOCIAL JUSTICE EJ 046 887
MORALS, MORALS EVERYWHERE: VALUES IN CHILDREN'S FICTION EJ 051 270
IDENTIFICATION AND CONSCIENCE DEVELOPMENT EJ 052 447
THE DEVELOPMENT OF ELEMENTARY SCHOOL CHILDREN'S JUDGMENT OF INTENT EJ 052 581
ANXIETY AND MORAL JUDGMENT IN EARLY ADOLESCENCE EJ 055 094
CHILDREN'S MORAL REASONING EJ 055 097
THE RELATIONSHIP BETWEEN VALUES AND BEHAVIOR: A DEVELOPMENTAL HYPOTHESIS EJ 056 622
THE EFFECT OF SYSTEMATIC STORY CHANGES ON INTENTIONALITY IN CHILDREN'S MORAL JUDGMENTS EJ 056 636
EGO IDENTITY STATUS AND MORALITY: THE RELATIONSHIP BETWEEN TWO DEVELOPMENTAL CONSTRUCTS EJ 058 141

MOTHER ATTITUDES
THE COGNITIVE ENVIRONMENTS OF URBAN PRE-SCHOOL CHILDREN. MANUAL OF INSTRUCTIONS FOR ADMINISTERING AND SCORING MOTHER'S ATTITUDES TOWARD CHILD'S BEHAVIOR LEADING TO MASTERY. ED018256
THE COGNITIVE ENVIRONMENTS OF URBAN PRE-SCHOOL CHILDREN. MANUAL OF INSTRUCTIONS FOR ADMINISTERING AND SCORING MOTHER-TEACHER PICTURE. ED018259
THE COGNITIVE ENVIRONMENTS OF URBAN PRE-SCHOOL CHILDREN. MANUAL OF INSTRUCTIONS FOR ADMINISTERING AND SCORING HOME RESOURCES PATTERNS. ED018260
FINAL REPORT ON HEAD START EVALUATION AND RESEARCH--1966-67 TO THE INSTITUTE FOR EDUCATIONAL DEVELOPMENT. SECTION III, INFLUENCING ATTITUDES OF PARENTS AND TEACHERS THROUGH REWARDING CHILDREN. ED019119
HEAD START EVALUATION AND RESEARCH CENTER, THE UNIVERSITY OF CHICAGO. REPORT F, SOCIALIZATION INTO THE ROLE OF PUPIL. ED023456
MOTHER-CHILD RELATIONS AND CHILDREN'S ACHIEVEMENT. TERMINAL REPORT. ED024465

ROLE OF MOTHERS' LANGUAGE STYLES IN MEDIATING THEIR PRESCHOOL CHILDREN'S COGNITIVE DEVELOPMENT. ED025298
A STUDY OF FAMILY INFLUENCES ON THE EDUCATION OF NEGRO LOWER-CLASS CHILDREN. PROJECT I. ED025309
EFFECTS OF PARENTAL EXPECTATIONS OF EDUCATIONAL PLANS OF WHITE AND NONWHITE ADOLESCENTS. FINAL REPORT. ED027096
EFFECT OF MATERNAL ATTITUDES, TEACHER ATTITUDES, AND TYPE OF NURSERY SCHOOL TRAINING ON THE ABILITIES OF PRESCHOOL CHILDREN. FINAL REPORT. ED028844
ENVIRONMENT INFLUENCES ON THE DEVELOPMENT OF ABILITIES. ED032126
LANGUAGE DEVELOPMENT OF SOCIALLY DISADVANTAGED PRESCHOOL CHILDREN. FINAL REPORT. ED041641
DIFFERENTIAL RESPONSE PATTERNS AS THEY AFFECT THE SELF ESTEEM OF THE CHILD. ED046542
THE PSYCHOLOGICAL EFFECTS OF PREGNANCY AND NEONATAL HEALTH THREATS ON CHILD DEVELOPMENT. ED048921
CONSISTENCY OF MATERNAL ATTITUDES AND PERSONALITY FROM PREGNANCY TO EIGHT MONTHS FOLLOWING CHILDBIRTH EJ 021 026
MATERNAL BEHAVIOR TOWARD OWN AND OTHER PRESCHOOL CHILDREN: THE PROBLEM OF "OWNNESS" EJ 026 324
MOTHER-INFANT RELATIONSHIP AND WEIGHT GAIN IN THE FIRST MONTH OF LIFE EJ 026 508
THE HOSPITAL AND THE PRESCHOOL CHILD EJ 027 341
THE CHILDCARE ATTITUDES OF TWO GENERATIONS OF MOTHERS EJ 032 796
CHILD-REARING PRACTICES IN MOUNTAIN COUNTY, KENTUCKY EJ 036 210
THE MOTHER-CHILD RELATIONSHIP AND THE FATHER-ABSENT BOY'S PERSONALITY DEVELOPMENT 27-241 EJ 040 456
CURIOSITY AND THE PARENT-CHILD RELATIONSHIP EJ 041 447
IMPROVING THE SELF-CONCEPTS OF ACADEMIC UNDERACHIEVERS THROUGH MATERNAL GROUP COUNSELING EJ 043 200
THE ROLE OF RETROSPECTIVE ACCOUNTS IN THE STUDY OF INTERGENERATIONAL ATTITUDES EJ 051 564
THE INTERPRETATION OF INTERGENERATIONAL ATTITUDES EJ 051 565
MATERNAL CONTROL AND OBEDIENCE IN THE TWO-YEAR-OLD EJ 056 714
RELATIONSHIPS BETWEEN INFANTS' SOCIAL BEHAVIOR AND THEIR MOTHERS' BEHAVIOR EJ 058 587

MOTHERS

A TRAINING PROGRAM FOR MOTHERS. ED017334
AN APPROACH FOR WORKING WITH MOTHERS OF DISADVANTAGED PRESCHOOL CHILDREN. ED017335
CHILD REARING IN CALIFORNIA, A STUDY OF MOTHERS WITH YOUNG CHILDREN. ED020783
PARENTS AS TEACHERS, HOW LOWER-CLASS AND MIDDLE-CLASS MOTHERS TEACH. ED025301
LANGUAGE STYLE OF THE LOWER CLASS MOTHER: A PRELIMINARY STUDY OF A THERAPEUTIC TECHNIQUE. ED027943
MOTHERS AS TEACHERS OF THEIR OWN PRESCHOOL CHILDREN: THE INFLUENCE OF SOCIO-ECONOMIC STATUS AND TASK STRUCTURE ON TEACHING SPECIFICITY. ED031294
PRIMARY INFLUENCES ON THE DEVELOPMENT OF COMPETENCE: THE DEVELOPMENT OF A MATERNAL BEHAVIOR SCALE. PROGRESS REPORT. ED032127
MOTHERS' TRAINING PROGRAM: THE GROUP PROCESS. ED032926
CHILDREN LEARNING: SAMPLES OF EVERYDAY LIFE OF CHILDREN AT HOME. ED033763
CHILD CARE ARRANGEMENTS OF WORKING MOTHERS IN THE UNITED STATES. ED040738
MOTHERS' TRAINING PROGRAM: EDUCATIONAL INTERVENTION BY THE MOTHERS OF DISADVANTAGED INFANTS. ED043378
THE EFFECT OF THREE HOME VISITING STRATEGIES UPON MEASURES OF CHILDREN'S ACADEMIC APTITUDE AND MATERNAL TEACHING BEHAVIORS. FINAL REPORT. ED044175
CHILD CARE AND WORKING MOTHERS: A STUDY OF ARRANGEMENTS MADE FOR DAYTIME CARE OF CHILDREN. ED045175
THE COGNITIVE ENVIRONMENTS OF URBAN PRESCHOOL CHILDREN. FINAL REPORT. ED045179
THE EFFECTS OF A PRESCHOOL LANGUAGE PROGRAM ON TWO-YEAR-OLD CHILDREN AND THEIR MOTHERS. FINAL REPORT. ED045224
DELIVERY OF CHILD HEALTH SERVICES. 1970 WHITE HOUSE CONFERENCE ON CHILDREN, REPORT OF FORUM 11. (WORKING PAPER). ED046528
INFANT DEVELOPMENT IN LOWER CLASS AMERICAN FAMILIES. ED049836
A STUDY IN CHILD CARE (CASE STUDY FROM VOLUME II-B): "I'M A NEW WOMAN NOW." DAY CARE PROGRAMS REPRINT SERIES. ED051897
EDUCATIONAL INTERVENTION IN THE HOME AND PARAPROFESSIONAL CAREER DEVELOPMENT: A SECOND GENERATION MOTHER STUDY WITH AN EMPHASIS ON COSTS AND BENEFITS. FINAL REPORT. ED052814
STATE AS AN INFANT-ENVIRONMENT INTERACTION: AN ANALYSIS OF MOTHER-INFANT BEHAVIOR AS A FUNCTION OF SEX. ED052829
THE EFFECTS OF EXPERIENCE ON INFANTS' REACTIONS TO SEPARATION FROM THEIR MOTHERS. ED053802
TRANSITIONAL OBJECTS AND THE PROCESS OF INDIVIDUATION: A STUDY IN THREE DIFFERENT SOCIAL GROUPS EJ 022 476
TWO MODES OF MATERNAL IMMATURITY AND THEIR CONSEQUENCES EJ 023 424
EXPERIMENTAL ANALYSIS OF THE FACTORS DETERMINING OBEDIENCE OF FOUR-YEAR-OLD CHILDREN TO ADULT FEMALES EJ 026 152
A TRAINING PROGRAM FOR VOLUNTEERS EJ 028 502
PATTERNS OF MOTHER-INFANT CONTACT: THE SIGNIFICANCE OF LATERAL PREFERENCE EJ 030 513
NEONATE-MOTHER INTERACTION: EFFECTS OF PARITY ON FEEDING BEHAVIOR EJ 032 892
EDUCATIONAL INTERVENTION AT HOME BY MOTHERS OF DISADVANTAGED INFANTS EJ 034 002
RESPONSE TO VOICE OF MOTHER AND STRANGER BY BABIES IN THE FIRST YEAR EJ 035 269
THE IMPACT OF MOTHER'S PRESENCE UPON BEHAVIOR: THE FIRST YEAR EJ 039 908
RELATIONSHIPS BETWEEN INFANTS' VOCALIZATIONS AND THEIR MOTHERS' BEHAVIORS EJ 040 455
IMPROVING THE SELF-CONCEPTS OF ACADEMIC UNDERACHIEVERS THROUGH MATERNAL GROUP COUNSELING EJ 043 200
EARLY CHILD STIMULATION THROUGH PARENT EDUCATION EJ 044 006
ADOLESCENT MATERNITY SERVICES: A TEAM APPROACH EJ 047 354
MOTHER-CHILD INTERACTIONS AND COGNITIVE DEVELOPMENT IN CHILDREN EJ 051 567
AGE, STATE, AND MATERNAL BEHAVIOR ASSOCIATED WITH INFANT VOCALIZATIONS EJ 052 444
THE UNSUPERVISED CHILD OF THE WORKING MOTHER EJ 053 709
TOYS DELAY THE INFANT'S FOLLOWING OF HIS MOTHER EJ 053 713
FEEDING BEHAVIORS OF NEWBORN INFANTS AS A FUNCTION OF PARITY OF THE MOTHER EJ 053 736
THE EFFECTS OF A FAMILIAR TOY AND MOTHER'S PRESENCE ON EXPLORATORY AND ATTACHMENT BEHAVIORS IN YOUNG CHILDREN EJ 053 759
SYMPOSIUM ON PARENT-CENTERED EDUCATION: 1. THE CHILD'S FIRST TEACHER EJ 054 377
SYMPOSIUM ON PARENT-CENTERED EDUCATION: 2. LEARNING THROUGH (AND FROM) MOTHERS EJ 054 378
SYMPOSIUM ON PARENT-CENTERED EDUCATION: 3. LEARNING THROUGH PARENTS: LESSONS FOR TEACHERS EJ 054 379
MOTHER-CHILD INTERACTION IN THE FIRST YEAR OF LIFE EJ 056 632
BEHAVIOR MODIFICATION IN THE HOME WITH THE MOTHER AS THE EXPERIMENTER: THE EFFECT OF DIFFERENTIAL REINFORCEMENT ON SIBLING NEGATIVE RESPONSE RATES EJ 056 721
MOTHERS' SPEECH TO CHILDREN LEARNING LANGUAGE EJ 058 696

MOTION

A METHOD TO INVESTIGATE THE MOVEMENT PATTERNS OF CHILDREN. ED027938
LEARNING TO OBSERVE--OBSERVING TO LEARN. ED047815
MOVEMENT AND MOVEMENT PATTERNS OF EARLY CHILDHOOD. ED053796
CHILDREN DANCE IN THE CLASSROOM. ED053804
DEVELOPMENT OF THE OBJECT CONCEPT AS MANIFESTED IN CHANGES IN THE TRACKING BEHAVIOR OF INFANTS BETWEEN 7 AND 20 WEEKS OF AGE EJ 038 264

MOTIVATION

THE COGNITIVE ENVIRONMENTS OF URBAN PRE-SCHOOL CHILDREN. MANUAL OF INSTRUCTIONS FOR ADMINISTERING AND SCORING PLUTCHIK EXPLORATORY-INTEREST QUESTIONNAIRE. ED018262
SOCIAL CLASS AND COGNITIVE DEVELOPMENT IN INFANCY. ED019111
MEASUREMENT OF MOTIVATION TO ACHIEVE IN PRESCHOOL CHILDREN. FINAL REPORT. ED021617
FINAL REPORT ON HEAD START EVALUATION AND RESEARCH: 1967-68 TO THE OFFICE OF ECONOMIC OPPORTUNITY. SECTION II: ACHIEVEMENT MOTIVATION AND PATTERNS OF REINFORCEMENT IN HEAD START CHILDREN. ED023458
THE ROLE OF INCENTIVES IN DISCRIMINATION LEARNING OF CHILDREN WITH VARYING PRE-SCHOOL EXPERIENCE. ED031290
AN ATTRIBUTIONAL (COGNITIVE) MODEL OF MOTIVATION. ED038173
A REPORT ON THE RESULTS OF THE ADMINISTRATION OF THE GUMPGOOKIES TEST TO THE TEXAS EVALUATION SAMPLE. PART OF THE FINAL REPORT ON HEAD START EVALUATION AND RESEARCH: 1968-69 TO THE OFFICE OF ECONOMIC OPPORTUNITY. ED039033
SOCIAL FACILITATION OF HEAD START PERFORMANCE. PROGRESS REPORT. ED042493
A COMPARATIVE STUDY OF FAILURE AVOIDANCE IN CULTURALLY DISADVANTAGED AND NON-CULTURALLY DISADVANTAGED FIRST GRADE CHILDREN. ED044170
THE DEFINITION, MEASUREMENT AND DEVELOPMENT OF SOCIAL MOTIVES UNDERLYING COOPERATIVE AND COMPETITIVE BEHAVIOR. ED045188
PROGRAMS OF HEAD START PARENT INVOLVEMENT IN HAWAII. A SECTION OF THE FINAL REPORT FOR 1969-70. ED048935
"NEED ACHIEVEMENT" TRAINING FOR HEAD START CHILDREN AND THEIR MOTHERS. ED048943
INFLUENCE OF SUBJECT AND SITUATIONAL VARIABLES ON THE PERSISTENCE OF FIRST GRADE CHILDREN IN A TEST-LIKE SITUATION. ED052819

THE USE OF INDIVIDUAL GOAL-SETTING CONFERENCES AS A MOTIVATIONAL TECHNIQUE. ED053816
MOTIVATIONAL EFFECTS OF PRAISE AND CRITICISM ON CHILDREN'S LEARNING EJ 024 702
MATERNAL CHILD-REARING EXPERIENCE AND SELF- REINFORCEMENT EFFECTIVENESS EJ 024 944
SELF-REINFORCEMENT VERSUS EXTERNAL REINFORCEMENT IN BEHAVIOR MODIFICATION WITH CHILDREN EJ 024 947
RECENCY AND SUMMATION EFFECTS OF NONREWARD IN CHILDREN EJ 028 895
REACTION TO SUCESS AND FAILURE IN COMPLEX LEARNING: A POSTFEEDBACK EFFECT EJ 029 413
INDIVIDUAL DIFFERENCES IN CHILDREN'S REACTIONS TO FRUSTRATIVE NONREWARD EJ 030 591
THEORETICAL NOTES ON POWER MOTIVATION EJ 032 677
PERSISTENCE AS A FUNCTION OF CONCEPTUAL STRUCTURE AND QUALITY OF FEEDBACK EJ 032 932
THE RELATIONSHIP BETWEEN INTENTIONAL LEARNING, INCIDENTAL LEARNING, AND TYPE OF REWARD IN PRESCHOOL, EDUCABLE, MENTAL RETARDATES EJ 033 783
INDIVIDUALLY GUIDED MOTIVATION: DEVELOPING SELF-DIRECTION AND PROSOCIAL BEHAVIORS EJ 034 159
THE EFFECTS OF SEX-ROLE STANDARDS FOR ACHIEVEMENT AND SEX-ROLE PREFERENCE ON THREE DETERMINANTS OF ACHIEVEMENT MOTIVATION EJ 034 454
THE INFLUENCE OF MASCULINE, FEMININE, AND NEUTRAL TASKS ON CHILDREN'S ACHIEVEMENT BEHAVIOR, EXPECTANCIES OF SUCCESS, AND ATTAINMENT VALUES EJ 037 318
EFFECT OF INCENTIVES AND AGE ON THE VISUAL RECOGNITION OF RETARDED READERS EJ 037 535
THE EFFECTS OF SOCIAL ISOLATION AND CHARACTERISTICS OF THE MODEL ON ACCENT IMITATION IN FOURTH-GRADE CHILDREN EJ 038 171
EFFECT OF INCENTIVES UPON RETARDED AND NORMAL READERS ON A VISUAL-ASSOCIATE LEARNING TASK EJ 038 266
YOUNG CHILDREN'S PERFORMANCE ON A TWO-CHOICE TASK AS A FUNCTION OF SOCIAL REINFORCEMENT, BASE-LINE PREFERENCE, AND RESPONSE STRATEGY EJ 039 635
THE DISCRIMINATION LEARNING OF NORMAL AND RETARDED CHILDREN AS A FUNCTION OF PENALTY CONDITIONS AND ETIOLOGY OF THE RETARDED EJ 041 136
THE EFFECTS OF REWARD AND PUNISHMENT UPON CHILDREN'S ATTENTION, MOTIVATION, AND DISCRIMINATION LEARNING EJ 041 137
INCENTIVE PREFERENCE AND RESISTANCE TO TEMPTATION EJ 041 631
THE INCENTIVE VALUE OF UNCERTAINTY REDUCTION FOR CHILDREN EJ 045 454
INDIVIDUAL DIFFERENCES IN CHILDREN'S REACTIONS TO REWARD AND NONREWARD EJ 045 459
A REEXAMINATION OF THE ROLE OF INCENTIVE IN CHILDREN'S DISCRIMINATION LEARNING EJ 046 237
THE RATIONAL ZERO POINT ON INCENTIVE-OBJECT PREFERENCE SCALES: A DEVELOPMENTAL STUDY EJ 048 099
DEVELOPMENTAL ASPECTS OF VARIABLES RELEVANT TO OBSERVATIONAL LEARNING EJ 053 740
MOTIVATIONAL AND ACHIEVEMENT DIFFERENCES AMONG CHILDREN OF VARIOUS ORDINAL BIRTH POSITIONS EJ 055 547
FREEDOM FROM EXTERNAL EVALUATION EJ 055 897
ACHIEVEMENT MOTIVATION AND FEAR OF FAILURE IN FAMILY AND SCHOOL EJ 058 143
INCENTIVE EFFECTS IN CHILDREN'S CREATIVITY EJ 059 317
RELATIONSHIPS OF PARENTAL BEHAVIOR TO "DISADVANTAGED" CHILDREN'S INTRINSIC-EXTRINSIC MOTIVATION FOR TASK STRIVING EJ 059 870

MOTIVATION TECHNIQUES

DISCRIMINATION LEARNING, PROBLEM SOLVING, AND CHOICE PATTERNING BY CHILDREN AS A FUNCTION OF INCENTIVE VALUE, MOTIVATION, AND SEQUENTIAL DEPENDENCIES. FINAL REPORT. ED016518
HEAD START EVALUATION AND RESEARCH CENTER, BOSTON UNIVERSITY. REPORT D-III, A STUDY OF PREFERENCES AMONG QUALITATIVELY DIFFERING UNCERTAINTIES. ED022565
LONG TERM EFFECT OF STRUCTURED TRAINING ON 3 YOUNG CHILDREN. ED023480
MOTIVATIONAL AND SOCIAL COMPONENTS IN COMPENSATORY EDUCATION PROGRAMS: SUGGESTED PRINCIPLES, PRACTICES, AND RESEARCH DESIGNS. ED024464
REPLICATION OF THE "MOTIVATED LEARNING" COGNITIVE TRAINING PROCEDURES WITH CULTURALLY DEPRIVED PRESCHOOLERS. REPORT FROM PROJECT MOTIVATED LEARNING. ED029708
MOTIVATIONAL EFFECTS OF INDIVIDUAL CONFERENCES AND GOAL SETTING ON PERFORMANCE AND ATTITUDES IN ARITHMETIC. REPORT FROM THE PROJECT ON SITUATIONAL VARIABLES AND EFFICIENCY OF CONCEPT LEARNING. ED032113
PEER TUTORING AS A TECHNIQUE FOR TEACHING THE UNMOTIVATED EJ 045 393
EFFECTS OF PROVISION FOR INDIVIDUAL DIFFERENCES AND TEACHER ATTENTION UPON STUDY BEHAVIOR AND ASSIGNMENTS COMPLETED EJ 058 353

MOTOR DEVELOPMENT

HEAD START EVALUATION AND RESEARCH CENTER, UNIVERSITY OF KANSAS. REPORT NO. VIID, A CASE STUDY ILLUSTRATING AN EXPERIMENTAL DESIGN FOR EVALUATING THE EFFECTS OF SHAPING GROSS MOTOR COORDINATION IN A 31 MONTH OLD CHILD. ED021643
INDIVIDUALIZED MOTOR-PERCEPTUAL STUDY. ED029692
EARLY INFANT STIMULATION AND MOTOR DEVELOPMENT. ED038179
THE EFFECT OF A PERCEPTUAL-MOTOR TRAINING PROGRAM UPON THE READINESS AND PERCEPTUAL DEVELOPMENT OF CULTURALLY DISADVANTAGED KINDERGARTEN CHILDREN. ED041633
DEVELOPMENTAL-BEHAVIORAL PATTERNS IN TWENTY-SIX CULTURALLY DISADVANTAGED INFANTS. ED044173
MOVEMENT AND MOVEMENT PATTERNS OF EARLY CHILDHOOD. ED053796
A CHILD'S FIRST STEPS: SOME SPECULATIONS EJ 033 057
ACTIVITY LEVEL AND MOTOR INHIBITION: THEIR RELATIONSHIP TO INTELLIGENCE-TEST PERFORMANCE IN NORMAL CHILDREN EJ 046 242

MOTOR REACTIONS

GROSS ACTIVITY OF CHILDREN AT PLAY. (INTERNAL REPORT). ED043385
IRRELEVANCE OF NEWBORN WAKING STATES TO SOME MOTOR AND APPETITIVE RESPONSES EJ 036 076
RHYTHMIC HABIT PATTERNS IN INFANCY: THEIR SEQUENCE, AGE OF ONSET, AND FREQUENCY EJ 040 295
PRESTIMULUS ACTIVITY LEVEL AND RESPONSIVITY IN THE NEONATE EJ 040 297
HUNGER AND MOTOR RESTRAINT ON AROUSAL AND VISUAL ATTENTION IN THE INFANT EJ 040 298
OBSERVATIONAL LEARNING: THE EFFECTS OF AGE, TASK DIFFICULTY, AND OBSERVERS' MOTORIC REHEARSAL EJ 044 702
ACTIVITY LEVEL AND MOTOR INHIBITION: THEIR RELATIONSHIP TO INTELLIGENCE-TEST PERFORMANCE IN NORMAL CHILDREN EJ 046 242
CONCEPTUAL TEMPO AND INHIBITION OF MOVEMENT IN BLACK PRESCHOOL CHILDREN EJ 059 512

MULTIGRADED CLASSES

MULTI-AGE GROUPING--ENRICHING THE LEARNING ENVIRONMENT. ED017343

MULTIMEDIA INSTRUCTION

KINDERGARTEN: THE CHILD IN HIS HOME AND SCHOOL ENVIRONMENTS. COURSE OF STUDY AND RELATED LEARNING ACTIVITIES. (CURRICULUM BULLETIN, 1967-68 SERIES, NO. 2A.) ED029681
GRADE 1: LIVING AND WORKING TOGETHER IN THE COMMUNITY. COURSE OF STUDY AND RELATED LEARNING ACTIVITIES. (CURRICULUM BULLETIN, 1967-68 SERIES, NO. 2B.) ED029682
GRADE 2: HOW PEOPLE LIVE IN CITY COMMUNITIES AROUND THE WORLD. COURSE OF STUDY AND RELATED LEARNING ACTIVITIES. (CURRICULUM BULLETIN, 1968-69 SERIES, NO. 2.) ED029694

MULTISENSORY LEARNING

DESIGNING TOMORROW'S SCHOOL TODAY: THE MULTI-SENSORY EXPERIENCE CENTER EJ 033 784

MUSEUMS

EARLY CHILDHOOD EDUCATION PROGRAM, ESEA TITLE I, FY 1970. PROJECT REPORTS, VOLUME 5, BOOK 2, 1970. ED052820
TOUCH-FEEL LEARNING AT THE TALLAHASSEE JUNIOR MUSEUM EJ 033 158

MUSIC

DEVELOPMENT OF A TECHNIQUE FOR IDENTIFYING ELEMENTARY SCHOOL CHILDREN'S MUSICAL CONCEPTS. FINAL REPORT. ED016517
A PILOT STUDY INTEGRATING VISUAL FORM AND ANTHROPOLOGICAL CONTENT FOR TEACHING CHILDREN AGES 6 TO 11 ABOUT CULTURES AND PEOPLES OF THE WORLD ED027095
CONCEPT LEARNING THROUGH MOVEMENT IMPROVISATION: THE TEACHER'S ROLE AS CATALYST EJ 014 945
A NONVERBAL TECHNIQUE FOR STUDYING MUSIC PREFERENCE EJ 043 285
AESTHETIC EDUCATION IN SOVIET SCHOOLS EJ 060 105

MUSIC ACTIVITIES

TEACHING MUSIC IN THE ELEMENTARY SCHOOL, OPINION AND COMMENT. ED020014
USING MUSIC WITH HEAD START CHILDREN. ED022543
MUSIC IN THE BEGINNING READING PROGRAM EJ 006 811
LISTEN TO WHAT I MADE. FROM MUSICAL THEORY TO USABLE INSTRUMENT EJ 029 280
COMPLEX MOTOR LEARNING IN FOUR-YEAR-OLDS EJ 046 236

MUSIC APPRECIATION

WRITE YOUR OWN SONGS EJ 027 673

MUSIC EDUCATION

DEVELOPMENT OF A TECHNIQUE FOR IDENTIFYING ELEMENTARY SCHOOL CHILDREN'S MUSICAL CONCEPTS. FINAL REPORT. ED016517
DEVELOPMENT OF AN ENLARGED MUSIC REPERTORY FOR KINDERGARTEN THROUGH GRADE SIX (JUILLIARD REPERTORY PROJECT). FINAL REPORT. ED016521

THE STUDY OF MUSIC IN THE ELEMENTARY SCHOOL--A CONCEPTUAL APPROACH. ED017328
TEACHING GENERAL MUSIC, A RESOURCE HANDBOOK FOR GRADES 7 AND 8. ED018277
TEACHING MUSICAL CONCEPTS RELATED TO MELODY, RHYTHM, FORM, AND HARMONY, TEACHER RESOURCE MATERIAL KINDERGARTEN, GRADES 1 AND 2. ED019991
TEACHING MUSIC IN THE ELEMENTARY SCHOOL, OPINION AND COMMENT. ED020014
STUDY TO DETERMINE THE FEASIBILITY OF ADAPTING THE CARL ORFF APPROACH TO ELEMENTARY SCHOOLS IN AMERICA. FINAL REPORT. ED020804
DEVELOPMENT OF A MUSIC CURRICULUM FOR YOUNG CHILDREN. CAREL ARTS AND HUMANITIES CURRICULUM DEVELOPMENT PROGRAM FOR YOUNG CHILDREN. ED032938
WRITE YOUR OWN SONGS EJ 027 673
LISTEN TO WHAT I MADE. FROM MUSICAL THEORY TO USABLE INSTRUMENT EJ 029 280

MUSIC TECHNIQUES
STUDY TO DETERMINE THE FEASIBILITY OF ADAPTING THE CARL ORFF APPROACH TO ELEMENTARY SCHOOLS IN AMERICA. FINAL REPORT. ED020804

MUSICAL COMPOSITION
WRITE YOUR OWN SONGS EJ 027 673

MUSICAL INSTRUMENTS
LISTEN TO WHAT I MADE. FROM MUSICAL THEORY TO USABLE INSTRUMENT EJ 029 280

NATIONAL DEMOGRAPHY
PREPRIMARY ENROLLMENT OF CHILDREN UNDER SIX: OCTOBER 1967. ED027094
PREPRIMARY ENROLLMENT, OCTOBER 1969. ED049816
THE HEALTH OF CHILDREN--1970: SELECTED DATA FROM THE NATIONAL CENTER FOR HEALTH STATISTICS. ED052827

NATIONAL ORGANIZATIONS
JOINING TOGETHER TO HELP FOSTER CHILDREN EJ 060 900

NATIONAL PROGRAMS
FACTORS AFFECTING COGNITIVE GROWTH IN PROJECT HEAD START CHILDREN--WHAT KINDS OF CHANGES OCCUR IN WHAT KINDS OF CHILDREN UNDER WHAT KINDS OF PROGRAMS. ED015794
PROJECT HEAD START: EVALUATION AND RESEARCH SUMMARY 1965-1967. ED028826
CHILDREN AND THEIR PHYSICAL AND SOCIAL ENVIRONMENT. 1970 WHITE HOUSE CONFERENCE ON CHILDREN, REPORT OF FORUM 19. (WORKING COPY). ED046535
A NATIONAL SURVEY OF THE PARENT-CHILD CENTER PROGRAM. ED048933
REVIEW AND SUMMARY OF A NATIONAL SURVEY OF THE PARENT-CHILD CENTER PROGRAM. ED048941

NATIONAL SURVEYS
TEAM TEACHING IN ELEMENTARY GRADES. ED020800
HEAD START PROGRAMS OPERATED BY PUBLIC SCHOOL SYSTEMS, 1966-67. ED026115
DESIRABLE ATHLETIC COMPETITION FOR CHILDREN OF ELEMENTARY SCHOOL AGE. ED027086
PREPRIMARY ENROLLMENT OF CHILDREN UNDER SIX: OCTOBER 1968. ED032118
INFANT MORTALITY: A CHALLENGE TO THE NATION. ED032122
HEAD START PROGRAMS AND PARTICIPANTS 1965-1967. ED034569
PROJECT HEAD START AT WORK. REPORT OF A SURVEY STUDY OF 335 PROJECT HEAD START CENTERS, SUMMER, 1965. ED036311
AN ANALYSIS OF EARLY CHILDHOOD EDUCATION RESEARCH AND DEVELOPMENT. ED039028
CHILD CARE ARRANGEMENTS OF WORKING MOTHERS IN THE UNITED STATES. ED040738
HEARING LEVELS OF CHILDREN BY AGE AND SEX: UNITED STATES. ED047799
PROJECT HEAD START 1968: A DESCRIPTIVE REPORT OF PROGRAMS AND PARTICIPANTS. ED047816
HEIGHT AND WEIGHT OF CHILDREN: UNITED STATES. ED050808
DAY CARE SURVEY-1970. SUMMARY REPORT AND BASIC ANALYSIS. ED051880
NATURAL ASSESSMENT OF EDUCATIONAL PROGRESS EJ 021 411

NATURAL RESOURCES
OPENING UP THE CLASSROOM: A WALK AROUND THE SCHOOL. ED053817

NATURE CENTERS
TOUCH-FEEL LEARNING AT THE TALLAHASSEE JUNIOR MUSEUM EJ 033 158

NEEDS
THE DAY CARE CHALLENGE: THE UNMET NEEDS OF MOTHERS AND CHILDREN. ED050821
DAY CARE SURVEY-1970. SUMMARY REPORT AND BASIC ANALYSIS. ED051880

NEGATIVE FORMS (LANGUAGE)
THE DEVELOPMENT OF FORMS OF THE NEGATIVE. ED022549

NEGATIVE REINFORCEMENT
THE EFFECTS OF DIFFERENT TYPES OF REINFORCEMENT ON YOUNG CHILDREN'S INCIDENTAL LEARNING. ED044184
THE INFLUENCE OF DIFFERENT RESPONSE CONSEQUENCES ON CHILDREN'S PREFERENCE FOR TIME-OUT EJ 022 213
"RIGHT," "WRONG," AND DISCRIMINATION LEARNING IN CHILDREN EJ 060 774

NEGRO ACHIEVEMENT
A FOLLOW-UP NORMATIVE STUDY OF NEGRO INTELLIGENCE AND ACHIEVEMENT EJ 003 658

NEGRO ATTITUDES
ON BEING A WHITEY IN THE MIDST OF A RACIAL CRISIS EJ 007 362
BLACK IDENTITY AND THE HELPING PERSON EJ 008 461
PERCEPTIONS OF NEGRO BOYS REGARDING COLOR AND OCCUPATIONAL STATUS EJ 045 392
BLACK CLIENTS AND WHITE WORKERS; A REPORT FROM THE FIELD EJ 051 062

NEGRO CULTURE
SELECTED BOOKS ABOUT THE AFRO-AMERICAN FOR VERY YOUNG CHILDREN K-2. ED039029
NEGRO CULTURE AND EARLY CHILDHOOD EDUCATION. ED046495
VALUING THE DIGNITY OF BLACK CHILDREN: A BLACK TEACHER SPEAKS EJ 019 506
THE BEAUTIFUL PEOPLE IN CHILDREN'S BOOKS EJ 020 541

NEGRO DIALECTS
ORAL OR WRITTEN LANGUAGE--THE CONSEQUENCES FOR COGNITIVE DEVELOPMENT IN AFRICA AND THE UNITED STATES. ED018279
NEGRO CULTURE AND EARLY CHILDHOOD EDUCATION. ED046495
READING, WRITING, AND BLACK ENGLISH EJ 052 178
DIALECT, RACE, AND LANGUAGE PROFICIENCY: ANOTHER DEAD HEAT ON THE MERRY-GO-ROUND EJ 053 747
NEGRO DIALECT AND BINET PERFORMANCE IN SEVERELY DISADVANTAGED BLACK FOUR-YEAR-OLDS EJ 056 914

NEGRO EDUCATION
DESIGNS AND PROPOSAL FOR EARLY CHILDHOOD RESEARCH: A NEW LOOK: THE UNACKNOWLEDGED ROLE OF CULTURE CONFLICT IN NEGRO EDUCATION. (ONE IN A SERIES OF SIX PAPERS). ED053810

NEGRO HOUSING
THE HOUSING ENVIRONMENT AS A FACTOR IN CHILD DEVELOPMENT. FINAL REPORT. ED014322

NEGRO LITERATURE
MULTI-ETHNIC BOOKS FOR HEAD START CHILDREN. PART I: BLACK AND INTEGRATED LITERATURE. ED031312
NEGRO HERITAGE: A SELECTED BOOK LIST FOR ALL AGES. ED036341

NEGRO MOTHERS
THE COGNITIVE ENVIRONMENTS OF URBAN PRE-SCHOOL CHILDREN. MANUAL OF INSTRUCTIONS FOR ADMINISTERING AND SCORING THE HOME INTERVIEW. ED018253
THE COGNITIVE ENVIRONMENTS OF URBAN PRE-SCHOOL CHILDREN. MANUAL OF INSTRUCTIONS FOR ADMINISTERING AND SCORING "SCHOOLS" QUESTION. ED018254
THE COGNITIVE ENVIRONMENTS OF URBAN PRE-SCHOOL CHILDREN. MANUAL OF INSTRUCTIONS FOR ADMINISTERING AND SCORING EDUCATIONAL ATTITUDE SURVEY. ED018255
THE COGNITIVE ENVIRONMENTS OF URBAN PRE-SCHOOL CHILDREN. MANUAL OF INSTRUCTIONS FOR ADMINISTERING AND SCORING MOTHER'S ATTITUDES TOWARD CHILD'S BEHAVIOR LEADING TO MASTERY. ED018256
THE COGNITIVE ENVIRONMENTS OF URBAN PRE-SCHOOL CHILDREN. MANUAL OF INSTRUCTIONS FOR ADMINISTERING AND SCORING MOTHER'S ROLE IN TEACHER/CHILD AND CHILD/PEER SCHOOL SITUATIONS. ED018257
THE COGNITIVE ENVIRONMENTS OF URBAN PRE-SCHOOL CHILDREN. MANUAL OF INSTRUCTIONS FOR ADMINISTERING AND SCORING FIRST DAY. ED018258
THE COGNITIVE ENVIRONMENTS OF URBAN PRE-SCHOOL CHILDREN. MANUAL OF INSTRUCTIONS FOR ADMINISTERING AND SCORING MOTHER-TEACHER PICTURE. ED018259
THE COGNITIVE ENVIRONMENTS OF URBAN PRE-SCHOOL CHILDREN. MANUAL OF INSTRUCTIONS FOR ADMINISTERING AND SCORING THE TWENTY QUESTIONS TASK. ED018261
THE COGNITIVE ENVIRONMENTS OF URBAN PRE-SCHOOL CHILDREN. MANUAL OF INSTRUCTIONS FOR ADMINISTERING AND SCORING PLUTCHIK EXPLORATORY-INTEREST QUESTIONNAIRE. ED018262
THE COGNITIVE ENVIRONMENTS OF URBAN PRE-SCHOOL CHILDREN. MANUAL OF INSTRUCTIONS FOR ADMINISTERING AND SCORING SIGEL CONCEPTUAL STYLE SORTING TASKS. ED018263
THE COGNITIVE ENVIRONMENTS OF URBAN PRE-SCHOOL CHILDREN. MANUAL OF INSTRUCTIONS FOR ADMINISTERING AND SCORING TOY SORTING TASK. ED018264
THE COGNITIVE ENVIRONMENTS OF URBAN PRE-SCHOOL CHILDREN. MANUAL OF INSTRUCTIONS FOR ADMINISTERING AND SCORING THE EIGHT-BLOCK SORTING TASK. ED018265

THE COGNITIVE ENVIRONMENTS OF URBAN PRE-SCHOOL CHILDREN. MANUAL FOR CODING MOTHER-CHILD INTERACTION ON THE EIGHT-BLOCK SORTING TASK. ED018266
THE COGNITIVE ENVIRONMENTS OF URBAN PRE-SCHOOL CHILDREN. MANUAL OF INSTRUCTIONS FOR ADMINISTERING AND SCORING "ETCH-A-SKETCH" TASK. ED018267
THE COGNITIVE ENVIRONMENTS OF URBAN PRE-SCHOOL CHILDREN. MANUAL OF RECORDING AND OBSERVATION TECHNIQUES FOR MOTHER-CHILD INTERACTION. ED018269
THE COGNITIVE ENVIRONMENTS OF URBAN PRE-SCHOOL CHILDREN. MANUAL OF INSTRUCTIONS FOR ADMINISTERING AND SCORING MATERNAL LANGUAGE STYLES. ED018270
A STUDY OF FAMILY INFLUENCES ON THE EDUCATION OF NEGRO LOWER-CLASS CHILDREN. PROJECT I. ED025309
MATERNAL BEHAVIOR AND THE DEVELOPMENT OF READING READINESS IN URBAN NEGRO CHILDREN. ED031309

NEGRO STUDENTS
THE EFFECTS OF STANDARD DIALECT TRAINING ON NEGRO FIRST-GRADERS LEARNING TO READ. FINAL REPORT. ED029717

NEGRO YOUTH
EVALUATION OF PROJECT HEAD START READING READINESS IN ISSAQUENA AND SHARKEY COUNTIES, MISSISSIPPI, SUMMER, 1965. FINAL REPORT. ED014319
PRESCHOOL INTERVENTION--A PRELIMINARY REPORT OF THE PERRY PRESCHOOL PROJECT. ED018251
THE COGNITIVE ENVIRONMENTS OF URBAN PRESCHOOL CHILDREN: FOLLOW-UP PHASE. FINAL REPORT. ED045180
EFFECTS OF SOCIAL CLASS INTEGRATION OF PRESCHOOL NEGRO CHILDREN ON TEST PERFORMANCE AND SELF-CONCEPT. FINAL REPORT. ED050831
DESIGNS AND PROPOSAL FOR EARLY CHILDHOOD RESEARCH: A NEW LOOK: THE UNACKNOWLEDGED ROLE OF CULTURE CONFLICT IN NEGRO EDUCATION. (ONE IN A SERIES OF SIX PAPERS). ED053810
WHEN WORDS FAIL...DANCE EJ 019 507
UNDERSTANDING THE BLACK CHILD EJ 020 717
SCHOOL ACHIEVERS AND UNDERACHIEVERS IN AN URBAN GHETTO EJ 027 614
THE GENERALITY OF COLOR-FORM PREFERENCE AS A FUNCTION OF MATERIALS AND TASK REQUIREMENTS AMONG LOWER-CLASS NEGRO CHILDREN EJ 033 052
OCCUPATIONAL PRESTIGE AS SEEN BY DISADVANTAGED BLACK CHILDREN EJ 034 453
THE CULTURE OF THE CULTURALLY DEPRIVED EJ 035 537
SOCIAL-CLASS DIFFERENTIATION IN COGNITIVE DEVELOPMENT AMONG BLACK PRESCHOOL CHILDREN EJ 036 819
WHITE STAFF, BLACK CHILDREN: IS THERE A PROBLEM? EJ 039 799
KNOWLEDGE OF ACTION AND OBJECT WORDS: A COMPARISON OF LOWER- AND MIDDLE-CLASS NEGRO PRESCHOOLERS EJ 040 453
RACIAL ATTITUDES OF NEGRO PRESCHOOLERS EJ 041 858
ON TRANSRACIAL ADOPTION OF BLACK CHILDREN EJ 053 853
AN EXPLORATORY STUDY OF SOCIALIZATION EFFECTS ON BLACK CHILDREN: SOME BLACK-WHITE COMPARISONS EJ 055 656
THE EFFECTS OF TRAINING AND SOCIOECONOMIC CLASS UPON THE ACQUISITION OF CONSERVATION CONCEPTS EJ 056 401
FACTORS RELATED TO SCHOOL ACHIEVEMENT IN AN ECONOMICALLY DISADVANTAGED GROUP EJ 056 614
WHITE ADULT BEHAVIOR TOWARD BLACK AND WHITE CHILDREN EJ 056 729
NEGRO DIALECT AND BINET PERFORMANCE IN SEVERELY DISADVANTAGED BLACK FOUR-YEAR-OLDS EJ 056 914
EFFECTS OF VICARIOUS CONSEQUENCES AND RACE OF MODEL UPON IMITATIVE PERFORMANCE BY BLACK CHILDREN EJ 058 139
SOME DISCRIMINATIVE PROPERTIES OF RACE AND SEX FOR CHILDREN FROM AN ALL-NEGRO NEIGHBORHOOD EJ 058 510
PERSONAL ORIENTATION TO SUCCESS AND FAILURE IN URBAN BLACK CHILDREN EJ 061 072

NEGROES
A FOLLOW-UP NORMATIVE STUDY OF NEGRO INTELLIGENCE AND ACHIEVEMENT EJ 003 658
RESISTANCE TO TEMPTATION IN YOUNG NEGRO CHILDREN EJ 032 894
A CHILD'S FIRST STEPS: SOME SPECULATIONS EJ 033 057
EARLY GRADE SCHOOL PERFORMANCE OF INNER CITY NEGRO HIGH SCHOOL HIGH ACHIEVERS, LOW ACHIEVERS, AND DROPOUTS EJ 039 572
THE EFFECT OF SUBJECT RACE, MODEL RACE, AND VICARIOUS PRAISE ON VICARIOUS LEARNING EJ 045 458
CARING FOR CHILDREN WITH SICKLE CELL ANEMIA EJ 047 355
VALUES OF MEXICAN-AMERICAN, NEGRO, AND ANGLO BLUE-COLLAR AND WHITE-COLLAR CHILDREN EJ 052 653
NEGRO PARENTAL BEHAVIOR AND SOCIAL CLASS VARIABLES EJ 059 871

NEIGHBORHOOD
THE DAY CARE NEIGHBOR SERVICE: A HANDBOOK FOR THE ORGANIZATION AND OPERATION OF A NEW APPROACH TO FAMILY DAY CARE. ED049810

NEIGHBORHOOD CENTERS
REALISTIC PLANNING FOR THE DAY CARE CONSUMER. ED043374

CHILD HEALTH ISSUES IN NEW YORK EJ 060 523

NEUROLOGICAL DEFECTS
A STANDARDIZED NEUROLOGICAL EXAMINATION: ITS VALIDITY IN PREDICTING SCHOOL ACHIEVEMENT IN HEAD START AND OTHER POPULATIONS. FINAL REPORT. ED023475
EFFECT OF SENSORIMOTOR ACTIVITY ON PERCEPTION AND LEARNING IN THE NEUROLOGICALLY HANDICAPPED CHILD. FINAL PROGRESS REPORT. ED033757
CONSEQUENCES OF LOW BIRTH WEIGHT EJ 030 430

NEUROLOGICAL ORGANIZATION
IMPLICATIONS OF POST-NATAL CORTICAL DEVELOPMENT FOR CREATIVITY RESEARCH. ED047802
EARLY MALNUTRITION AND CENTRAL NERVOUS SYSTEM FUNCTION EJ 012 207
INFANT MENTAL DEVELOPMENT AND NEUROLOGICAL STATUS, FAMILY SOCIOECONOMIC STATUS, AND INTELLIGENCE AT AGE FOUR EJ 032 675
UNILATERAL DOMINANCE IS NOT RELATED TO NEUROPSYCHOLOGICAL INTEGRITY EJ 056 624

NEUROLOGICALLY HANDICAPPED
MINIMAL BRAIN DAMAGE: A MEANINGFUL DIAGNOSIS OR AN IRRELEVANT LABEL? EJ 018 707
DIAGNOSING MINIMAL BRAIN DAMAGE IN CHILDREN: A COMPARISON OF TWO BENDER SCORING SYSTEMS EJ 027 585
UNILATERAL DOMINANCE IS NOT RELATED TO NEUROPSYCHOLOGICAL INTEGRITY EJ 056 624
PARAMETERS OF THE SPIRAL AFTER-EFFECT IN ORGANICS, SCHIZOPHRENICS, AND NORMALS EJ 061 060

NEUROLOGY
A CHANGE OF POSSIBLE NEUROLOGICAL AND PSYCHOLOGICAL SIGNIFICANCE WITHIN THE FIRST WEEK OF NEONATE LIFE: SLEEPING REM RATE. ED034580
SOME CHARACTERISTICS OF NEURAL PROCESSING IN THE CHILD. ED040740

NEUROTIC CHILDREN
MODIFYING RISK-TAKING BEHAVIOR EJ 032 891

NEWSLETTERS
TEAM TEACHING IN ELEMENTARY GRADES. ED020800
A BRIEF GUIDE TO NEWSLETTERS IN EARLY CHILDHOOD EDUCATION. ED048932

NEWSPAPERS
TELL IT LIKE IT IS EJ 014 139

NOMINALS
NOUN PLURAL DEVELOPMENT IN PRIMARY GRADE CHILDREN EJ 052 179
A COMPARATIVE STUDY OF ENGLISH PLURALIZATION BY NATIVE AND NON-NATIVE ENGLISH SPEAKERS EJ 052 465

NON ENGLISH SPEAKING
A COMPARISON OF WISC AND OSA IN ASSESSING THE INTELLIGENCE OF IMMIGRANT CHILDREN OF NON-ENGLISH SPEAKING BACKGROUND. A PILOT PROJECT. ED022526
HEAD START EVALUATION AND RESEARCH CENTER, THE UNIVERSITY OF CHICAGO. REPORT E, COMPARATIVE USE OF ALTERNATIVE MODES FOR ASSESSING COGNITIVE DEVELOPMENT IN BILINGUAL OR NON-ENGLISH SPEAKING CHILDREN. ED022554
UNIVERSITY OF HAWAII PRESCHOOL LANGUAGE CURRICULUM, HONOLULU, HAWAII: A PROGRAM OF ENGLISH CONVERSATION FOR PRESCHOOL CHILDREN OF MULTIETHNIC BACKGROUNDS. MODEL PROGRAMS--CHILDHOOD EDUCATION. ED045220

NONDIRECTIVE COUNSELING
A COMPARATIVE STUDY OF COUNSELEE PREFERENCES FOR BEHAVIORIST AND CLIENT-CENTERED COUNSELING APPROACHES EJ 058 628

NONGRADED CLASSES
MODELS FOR NONGRADING SCHOOLS: A REPORT OF A NATIONAL SEMINAR. ED049827

NONGRADED PRIMARY SYSTEM
3 ON 2 PROGRAM: ADMINISTRATIVE GUIDE AND IMPLEMENTATION HANDBOOK. (REVISED EDITION). ED050812
CONTINUOUS PUPIL PROGRESS IN THE NON-GRADED SCHOOL: HOPE OR HOAX? EJ 028 100

NONGRADED SYSTEM
A BIBLIOGRAPHY (WITH SELECTED ANNOTATIONS) ON NONGRADED ELEMENTARY SCHOOLS. ED015024
EVALUATION OF SELECTED COMPONENTS OF: A SUPPLEMENTARY CENTER FOR EARLY CHILDHOOD EDUCATION. TITLE III. ED032927
IMPLEMENTING DIFFERENT AND BETTER SCHOOLS. ED039926
MODELS FOR NONGRADING SCHOOLS: A REPORT OF A NATIONAL SEMINAR. ED049827
3 ON 2 PROGRAM: ADMINISTRATIVE GUIDE AND IMPLEMENTATION HANDBOOK. (REVISED EDITION). ED050812
ACHIEVEMENT OF FIRST- AND SECOND-YEAR PUPILS IN GRADED AND NONGRADED CLASSROOMS EJ 018 969

THE STUDENT IN PROJECT PLAN: A FUNCTIONING PROGRAM OF INDIVIDUALIZED EDUCATION EJ 028 501

NONPROFESSIONAL PERSONNEL

HEADSTART OPERATIONAL FIELD ANALYSIS. PROGRESS REPORT II. ED015775
HEAD START EVALUATION AND RESEARCH CENTER, BOSTON UNIVERSITY. REPORT E-I, THE UTILIZATION OF NON-PROFESSIONAL INTERVIEWERS IN THE NEW ENGLAND AND MISSISSIPPI SAMPLES BY THE BOSTON UNIVERSITY HEAD START EVALUATION AND RESEARCH PROGRAM, 1966-1967. ED022566
USE OF NON-PROFESSIONAL PERSONNEL FOR HEALTH SCREENING OF HEAD START CHILDREN. FINAL REPORT. ED029702
EARLY CHILD STIMULATION THROUGH PARENT EDUCATION. ED038166
CASE CONFERENCE: A PSYCHOTHERAPEUTIC AIDE IN A HEADSTART PROGRAM. I. THEORY AND PRACTICE EJ 003 955
CASE CONFERENCE: A PSYCHOTHERAPEUTIC AIDE IN A HEADSTART PROGRAM. II. COMMENTARY EJ 003 956
EARLY CHILD STIMULATION THROUGH PARENT EDUCATION EJ 044 006

NONSTANDARD DIALECTS

FINAL REPORT ON HEAD START EVALUATION AND RESEARCH--1966-67 TO THE INSTITUTE FOR EDUCATIONAL DEVELOPMENT. SECTION V, THE ROLE OF DIALECT IN THE SCHOOL-SOCIALIZATION OF LOWER CLASS CHILDREN. ED019121
KEYS TO STANDARD ENGLISH EJ 028 577
LANGUAGE DIALECT, REINFORCEMENT, AND THE INTELLIGENCE-TEST PERFORMANCE OF NEGRO CHILDREN EJ 035 912
READING, WRITING, AND BLACK ENGLISH EJ 052 178

NONVERBAL ABILITY

HEAD START EVALUATION AND RESEARCH CENTER. PROGRESS REPORT OF RESEARCH STUDIES 1966 TO 1967. DOCUMENT 3, AN EXPERIMENTAL APPROACH TO STUDYING NON-VERBAL REPRESENTATION IN YOUNG CHILDREN. ED021625
HEAD START EVALUATION AND RESEARCH CENTER, UNIVERSITY OF KANSAS. REPORT NO. VIIB, ESTABLISHMENT OF NONVERBAL COLOR DISCRIMINATION RESPONSES TO AUDITORY COLOR-LABELING STIMULI AND SUBSEQUENT EFFECTS ON COLOR-LABELING RESPONSES. ED021641
A THIRD STUDY OF SOME RELATIONSHIPS BETWEEN CREATIVITY AND PERCEPTION IN 6TH GRADE CHILDREN EJ 016 166

NONVERBAL COMMUNICATION

SOME NONVERBAL ASPECTS OF COMMUNICATION BETWEEN MOTHER AND PRESCHOOL CHILD EJ 025 386
I SEE WHAT YOU MEAN EJ 035 370
EYE CONTACT IN CHILDREN AS A FUNCTION OF AGE, SEX, SOCIAL AND INTELLECTIVE VARIABLES EJ 038 943
NONVERBAL INFORMATION STORAGE IN CHILDREN AND DEVELOPMENTAL INFORMATION PROCESSING CHANNEL CAPACITY EJ 053 720
ORIENTATION IN CHILDREN'S HUMAN FIGURE DRAWINGS: AN ASPECT OF GRAPHIC LANGUAGE EJ 061 067

NONVERBAL LEARNING

FREE RECALL OF WORDS AND OBJECTS EJ 039 634
THE DEVELOPMENT OF THE CONTROL OF ADULT INSTRUCTIONS OVER NONVERBAL BEHAVIOR EJ 061 138

NONVERBAL TESTS

THE DEVELOPMENT OF PROBABILISTIC THINKING IN CHILDREN: A COMPARISON OF TWO METHODS OF ASSESSMENT EJ 023 193

NORMS

MODELS, NORMS AND SHARING. ED046512
PRESCHOOL PLAY NORMS: A REPLICATION EJ 041 958

NORWEGIAN

COMPARISON OF AMERICAN AND NORWEGIAN NURSERY SCHOOL CHILDREN ON INDEPENDENCE BEHAVIOR AND TRAINING. ED024457

NUMBER CONCEPTS

THE PERFORMANCE OF FIRST GRADE CHILDREN IN FOUR LEVELS OF CONSERVATION OF NUMEROUSNESS AND THREE IQ GROUPS WHEN SOLVING ARITHMETIC ADDITION PROBLEMS. ED016535
NUMBER TRAINING TECHNIQUES AND THEIR EFFECTS ON DIFFERENT POPULATIONS. FINAL REPORT. ED019988
HEAD START EVALUATION AND RESEARCH CENTER, BOSTON UNIVERSITY. REPORT D-II, TRAINING FOR NUMBER CONCEPT. ED022564
SUCCESSFUL NUMBER CONSERVATION TRAINING. ED031297
THE EFFECT OF SELECTED TRAINING EXPERIENCES ON PERFORMANCE ON A TEST OF CONSERVATION OF NUMEROUSNESS. REPORT FROM PHASE 2 OF THE PROTOTYPIC INSTRUCTIONAL SYSTEMS IN ELEMENTARY MATHEMATICS PROJECT. ED036334
NUMBER GAMES WITH YOUNG CHILDREN EJ 007 273
TEACHING NUMBER SENSE THROUGH RHYTHMICAL COUNTING EJ 028 717
THE SEQUENCE OF DEVELOPMENT OF CERTAIN NUMBER CONCEPTS IN PRESCHOOL CHILDREN EJ 044 694
THE DEVELOPMENT OF THE UNDERSTANDING OF CERTAIN NUMBER CONCEPTS EJ 044 695
THE ROLE OF BODY PARTS AND READINESS IN ACQUISITION OF NUMBER CONSERVATION EJ 053 757
LOGICAL CAPACITY OF VERY YOUNG CHILDREN: NUMBER INVARIANCE RULES EJ 056 394
PRECOCIOUS THOUGHTS ON NUMBER: THE LONG AND THE SHORT OF IT EJ 060 776

NURSERY SCHOOLS

MOTIVATIONAL FACTORS AND IQ-CHANGES IN CULTURALLY DEPRIVED CHILDREN ATTENDING NURSERY SCHOOL. ED020017
CO-OPERATIVE NURSERY SCHOOLS--A HANDBOOK FOR PARENTS. A GUIDE FOR ORGANIZATION AND ADMINISTRATION. REVISED EDITION. ED020022
EARLY CHILDHOOD EDUCATION TODAY. ED021631
LET'S TRY THIS IN NURSERY SCHOOL AND KINDERGARTEN. ED022556
SPONTANEOUS PLAY: AN AVENUE FOR INTELLECTUAL DEVELOPMENT. ED023444
A PREKINDERGARTEN PROGRAM FOR FOUR-YEAR-OLDS, WITH A REVIEW OF THE LITERATURE ON PRESCHOOL EDUCATION. AN OCCASIONAL PAPER. ED026124
RESEARCH ON THE NEW NURSERY SCHOOL. PART II: A REPORT ON THE USE OF TYPEWRITERS AND RELATED EQUIPMENT WITH THREE- AND FOUR-YEAR-OLD CHILDREN AT THE NEW NURSERY SCHOOL. INTERIM REPORT. ED027077
POINTERS FOR PARTICIPATING PARENTS. ED028825
PROGRESS REPORT ON RESEARCH AT THE NEW NURSERY SCHOOL: GENERAL BACKGROUND AND PROGRAM RATIONALE. ED032930
PRELUDE TO SCHOOL: AN EVALUATION OF AN INNER-CITY PRESCHOOL PROGRAM. ED033750
THE EFFECTS OF MOTHERS' PRESENCE AND PREVISITS ON CHILDREN'S EMOTIONAL REACTIONS TO STARTING NURSERY SCHOOL. ED034596
THE EFFECTS OF MANIPULATION OF TEACHER COMMUNICATION STYLE IN THE PRESCHOOL. ED034598
NEW NURSERY SCHOOL RESEARCH PROJECT, OCTOBER 1, 1968 TO SEPTEMBER 30, 1969. ANNUAL PROGRESS REPORT. ED036320
ANCONA MONTESSORI RESEARCH PROJECT FOR CULTURALLY DISADVANTAGED CHILDREN. SEPTEMBER 1, 1968 TO AUGUST 31, 1969. FINAL REPORT. ED044166
POSITION EFFECTS IN PLAY EQUIPMENT PREFERENCES OF NURSERY SCHOOL CHILDREN. ED045185
CROSS-CULTURAL FAMILY CENTER, SAN FRANCISCO, CALIFORNIA: A NURSERY SCHOOL PROVIDING A MULTICULTURAL CURRICULUM TO PROMOTE RACIAL UNDERSTANDING AND ACCEPTANCE. MODEL PROGRAMS--CHILDHOOD EDUCATION. ED045214
DEMONSTRATION NURSERY CENTER FOR INFANTS AND TODDLERS, GREENSBORO, NORTH CAROLINA: A MODEL DAY CARE CENTER FOR CHILDREN UNDER 3 YEARS OLD. MODEL PROGRAMS--CHILDHOOD EDUCATION. ED045215
THE DAY NURSERY ASSOCIATION OF CLEVELAND, CLEVELAND, OHIO: A LONG HISTORY OF CARE FOR CHILDREN, INVOLVEMENT OF PARENTS, AND SERVICE TO THE COMMUNITY. MODEL PROGRAMS--CHILDHOOD EDUCATION. ED045218
COMMUNITY COOPERATIVE NURSERY SCHOOL, MENLO PARK, CALIFORNIA: A PRESCHOOL PROGRAM INVOLVING MOTHERS AS ORGANIZERS, HELPERS, AND DECISION-MAKERS. MODEL PROGRAMS--CHILDHOOD EDUCATION. ED045222
THE VICARIOUS CONDITIONING OF EMOTIONAL RESPONSES IN NURSERY SCHOOL CHILDREN. FINAL REPORT. ED046540
A STUDY IN TRAINING NURSERY CHILDREN ON LOGICAL OPERATIONAL SKILLS. ED047803
EFFECTS OF DURATION OF A NURSERY SCHOOL SETTING ON ENVIRONMENTAL CONSTRAINTS AND CHILDREN'S MODES OF ADAPTATION. ED047812
STARTING NURSERY SCHOOL, II: PREDICTION OF CHILDREN'S INITIAL EMOTIONAL REACTIONS FROM BACKGROUND INFORMATION. FINAL REPORT. ED047814
SOME EUROPEAN NURSERY SCHOOLS AND PLAYGROUNDS. ED048928
THE NEW NURSERY SCHOOL RESEARCH PROJECT ED048940
A REVIEW OF EXPERIENCE: ESTABLISHING, OPERATING, EVALUATING A DEMONSTRATION NURSERY CENTER FOR THE DAYTIME CARE OF INFANTS AND TODDLERS, 1967-1970. FINAL REPORT. ED050810
BEFORE SCHOOL STARTS. FOR CHILDREN'S MINDS--NOT JUST TO MIND THE CHILDREN. THE CHILD CENTRE--AS SEEN BY A PARENT. ED051873
NURSERIES IN THE CZECHOSLOVAK SOCIALIST REPUBLIC EJ 001 672
SEPARATION REACTIONS IN YOUNG, MILDLY RETARDED CHILDREN. EJ 003 972
BING NURSERY SCHOOL EJ 007 425
A ROOM PLANNED BY CHILDREN EJ 007 876
A DOLL CORNER UPSTAIRS EJ 013 296
CANDIDATE FOR INTEGRATION: A HEARING-IMPAIRED CHILD IN A REGULAR NURSERY SCHOOL EJ 026 915
PATTERNS OF INFORMATION PROCESSING USED BY AND WITH YOUNG CHILDREN IN A NURSERY SCHOOL SETTING EJ 032 890
UN EXEMPLE D'OBSERVATION INTENSIVE DU COMPORTEMENT DE JEUNES ENFANTS DANS LE CADRE D'UNE GARDERIE EJ 034 534
THE ROLE OF A LABORATORY NURSERY SCHOOL EJ 036 332
EDUCATION OF TEACHERS FOR NURSERY SCHOOLS: A CREATIVE APPROACH EJ 036 336
EFFECTS OF VARIATIONS IN THE NURSERY SCHOOL SETTING ON ENVIRONMENTAL CONSTRAINTS AND CHILDREN'S MODES OF ADAPTATION EJ 045 455

THE EFFECTS OF MOTHERS' PRESENCE AND PREVISITS ON CHILDREN'S EMOTIONAL REACTION TO STARTING NURSERY SCHOOL EJ 046 469
A PROGRAM FOR HOSPITALIZED PSYCHOTIC CHILDREN: REGULAR ATTENDANCE, AWAY FROM THE HOSPITAL, AT A COMMUNITY NURSERY SCHOOL EJ 050 938
A PARENT SPEAKS EJ 051 240
NURSERY SCHOOLS FIFTY YEARS AGO EJ 055 736
TEACHING RACE RELATIONS IN THE NURSERY SCHOOL EJ 056 864

NURSES
NURSES GAIN FROM FIELD WORK WITH YOUNG CHILDREN EJ 007 301
CREATIVITY CHANGE IN STUDENT NURSES: A CROSS-SECTIONAL AND LONGITUDINAL STUDY EJ 030 291
GROUP SERVICES FOR UNMARRIED MOTHERS: AN INTERDISCIPLINARY APPROACH EJ 035 538

NUTRITION
HEAD START EVALUATION AND RESEARCH CENTER, UNIVERSITY OF KANSAS. REPORT NO. VIII, PHYSICAL DEVELOPMENT OF CHILDREN IN THE HEAD START PROGRAM IN THE CENTRAL UNITED STATES. ED021644
TEACHING NUTRITION IN THE ELEMENTARY SCHOOL. ED026148
RESEARCH ISSUES IN THE HEALTH AND NUTRITION IN EARLY CHILDHOOD. ED027970
A STUDY OF FOOD AND POVERTY AMONG 113 HEAD START CHILDREN IN MISSOULA, MONTANA. ED028829
THE RELATIONSHIP BETWEEN HEMOGLOBIN LEVEL AND INTELLECTUAL FUNCTION. ED028830
RESEARCH ISSUES IN CHILD HEALTH, I-IV. PROCEEDINGS OF THE HEAD START RESEARCH SEMINARS: SEMINAR NO. 4, HEALTH AND NUTRITION IN EARLY CHILDHOOD (1ST, WASHINGTON, D.C., NOVEMBER 1, 1968). ED036331
NUTRITION AND MENTAL DEVELOPMENT. RESEARCH REPORT NO. 5. ED037252
MALNUTRITION, LEARNING AND INTELLECTUAL DEVELOPMENT: RESEARCH AND REMEDIATION. ED039017
THE PREVALENCE OF ANEMIA IN HEAD START CHILDREN. NUTRITION EVALUATION, 1968-69. ED041629
A NUTRITIONAL SURVEY OF CHILDREN IN HEAD START CENTERS IN CENTRAL UNITED STATES. ED042487
BEHAVIORAL DATA FROM THE TULANE NUTRITION STUDY. ED043375
NUTRITION SURVEY OF WHITE MOUNTAIN APACHE PRESCHOOL CHILDREN. ED046508
NUTRITIONAL STATUS OF NEW ORLEANS, MISSISSIPPI AND ALABAMA HEAD START CHILDREN. FINAL REPORT. ED047785
PROGRAMS FOR INFANTS AND YOUNG CHILDREN. PART II: NUTRITION. ED047808
A STUDY IN CHILD CARE (CASE STUDY FROM VOLUME II-B): "...WHILE [THEY TOOK] CARE OF OUR CHILDREN, THEIRS WEREN'T BEING CARED FOR." DAY CARE PROGRAMS REPRINT SERIES. ED051909
HEALTH AND NUTRITION IN DISADVANTAGED CHILDREN AND THEIR RELATIONSHIP WITH INTELLECTUAL DEVELOPMENT. COLLABORATIVE RESEARCH REPORT. ED052816
PREVENTION OF IRON-DEFICIENCY ANEMIA IN INFANTS AND CHILDREN OF PRESCHOOL AGE. ED052830
DESIGNS AND PROPOSAL FOR EARLY CHILDHOOD RESEARCH: A NEW LOOK: MALNUTRITION, LEARNING AND INTELLIGENCE. (ONE IN A SERIES OF SIX PAPERS). ED053811
NUTRITION IN DAY CARE CENTERS EJ 011 595
EARLY MALNUTRITION AND HUMAN DEVELOPMENT EJ 011 914
EARLY MALNUTRITION AND CENTRAL NERVOUS SYSTEM FUNCTION EJ 012 207
SOME HIGHLIGHTS FROM THE NUTRITION CONFERENCE EJ 017 447
MATERNAL FOOD RESTRICTION: EFFECTS ON OFFSPRING DEVELOPMENT, LEARNING, AND A PROGRAM OF THERAPY EJ 029 218
SEVERE PROTEIN-CALORIE MALNUTRITION AND COGNITIVE DEVELOPMENT IN INFANCY AND EARLY CHILDHOOD EJ 039 627
NUTRITION AND BRAIN DEVELOPMENT IN INFANTS EJ 058 223
NUTRITION AND EDUCATIONAL EXPERIENCE: INTERRELATED VARIABLES IN CHILDREN'S LEARNING EJ 059 643

NUTRITION EDUCATION
COMBATING MALNUTRITION THROUGH MATERNAL AND CHILD HEALTH PROGRAMS EJ 007 161

NUTRITION INSTRUCTION
PREVENTION OF IRON-DEFICIENCY ANEMIA IN INFANTS AND CHILDREN OF PRESCHOOL AGE. ED052830
PRACTICAL APPROACHES FOR RESOLVING THE PROBLEM OF NUTRITION AMONG LOW-INCOME FAMILIES EJ 052 065

OBERVATION
THE USE OF A PLAY PROGRAM BY HOSPITALIZED CHILDREN EJ 026 774

OBJECT MANIPULATION
FREEDOM TO MANIPULATE OBJECTS AND QUESTION-ASKING PERFORMANCE OF SIX-YEAR-OLDS EJ 029 217

OBJECTIVES
TEACHING THE YOUNG CHILD: GOALS FOR ILLINOIS. ED053805
WHAT DO YOUNG PEOPLE WANT? EJ 011 784
WHO SELECTS THE OBJECTIVES FOR LEARNING--AND WHY? EJ 031 849
HANDWRITING: THE STATE OF THE CRAFT EJ 048 999

OBSERVATION
HEADSTART OPERATIONAL FIELD ANALYSIS. PROGRESS REPORT I. ED015774
POSITIVE SOCIAL REINFORCEMENT IN THE NURSERY SCHOOL PEER GROUP. ED016515
THE COGNITIVE ENVIRONMENTS OF URBAN PRE-SCHOOL CHILDREN. MANUAL OF RECORDING AND OBSERVATION TECHNIQUES FOR MOTHER-CHILD INTERACTION. ED018269
HEAD START EVALUATION AND RESEARCH CENTER, BOSTON UNIVERSITY. REPORT A-II, OBSERVATION OF TEACHERS AND TEACHING: STRATEGIES AND APPLICATIONS. ED022558
HEAD START EVALUATION AND RESEARCH CENTER, BOSTON UNIVERSITY. REPORT A-III, OBSERVATIONAL STRATEGIES FOR OBTAINING DATA ON CHILDREN AND TEACHERS IN HEAD START CLASSES. (OSOD). ED022559
NATURALISTIC OBSERVATION IN THE STUDY OF PARENT-CHILD INTERACTION. ED027073
A DISCUSSION OF RESEARCH AIMS AND STRATEGIES FOR STUDYING EDUCATION IN THE INNER-CITY (A CRITIQUE OF NON-PARTICIPANT OBSERVATIONS). PRELIMINARY DRAFT. ED038187
LONG DISTANCE INTERDISCIPLINARY EVALUATION OF DEVELOPMENTAL DISABILITIES. ED040748
LEARNING TO OBSERVE--OBSERVING TO LEARN. ED047815
A DESCRIPTIVE ACCOUNT OF FOUR MODES OF CHILDREN'S PLAY BETWEEN ONE AND FIVE YEARS. ED049833
CUES FOR OBSERVING CHILDREN'S BEHAVIOR EJ 007 062
RELIABILITY ASSESSMENT OF OBSERVATION DATA: A POSSIBLE METHODOLOGICAL PROBLEM EJ 033 313
A NOTE ON SELECTIVE IMITATION BY A SIX-WEEK-OLD INFANT EJ 034 045
ASSOCIATION AND ABSTRACTION AS MECHANISMS OF IMITATIVE LEARNING EJ 035 367
STATE IV OF PIAGET'S THEORY OF INFANT'S OBJECT CONCEPTS: A LONGITUDINAL STUDY EJ 041 134
AN AUDITORY PROMPTING DEVICE FOR BEHAVIOR OBSERVATION EJ 043 316
AN INEXPENSIVE AND PORTABLE MEANS FOR ONE-WAY OBSERVATION EJ 045 797
OBSERVATION STUDIES OF PARENT-CHILD INTERACTION: A METHODOLOGICAL REVIEW EJ 046 466
PLAYROOM OBSERVATIONS OF HYPERACTIVE CHILDREN ON MEDICATION EJ 048 301
EFFECTS OF ADULT AND PEER OBSERVERS ON BOYS' AND GIRLS' RESPONSES TO AN AGGRESSIVE MODEL EJ 052 459
OBSERVING BEHAVIOR AND CHILDREN'S DISCRIMINATION LEARNING EJ 053 754
INFLUENCE OF MODELING, EXHORTATIVE VERBALIZATION, AND SURVEILLANCE ON CHILDREN'S SHARING EJ 058 214

OCCUPATIONAL ASPIRATION
SOCIAL CLASS AND PARENT'S ASPIRATIONS FOR THEIR CHILDREN. REPORT NUMBER 8. ED030482
SEX DIFFERENCES IN THE EXPRESSION OF VOCATIONAL ASPIRATIONS BY ELEMENTARY SCHOOL CHILDREN EJ 043 481

OCCUPATIONAL CHOICE
OCCUPATIONAL PRESTIGE AS SEEN BY DISADVANTAGED BLACK CHILDREN EJ 034 453

OCCUPATIONAL THERAPY
OCCUPATIONAL THERAPY AND SPECIAL EDUCATION EJ 045 234

OCCUPATIONS
COGNITIVE ASPECTS OF CHILDREN'S OCCUPATIONAL PRESTIGE RANKINGS. ED039924
SHIFTS IN CHILD-REARING ATTITUDES LINKED WITH PARENTHOOD AND OCCUPATION EJ 038 853

OLDER ADULTS
SENSORY-SET FACTORS IN AGE DIFFERENCES IN REACTION TIME EJ 048 304
DISCRIMINATION LEARNING AND TRANSFER OF TRAINING IN THE AGED EJ 055 204

ONE PARENT FAMILY
THE EFFECTS OF FATHER ABSENCE ON CHILD DEVELOPMENT EJ 035 800
FAMILIES WITHOUT FATHERS EJ 049 656

OPEN PLAN SCHOOLS
A STUDY IN CHILD CARE (CASE STUDY FROM VOLUME II-A): "IT'S A WELL-RUN BUSINESS, TOO." DAY CARE PROGRAMS REPRINT SERIES. ED051896
AN OVERVIEW OF BRITISH INFANT SCHOOLS EJ 026 835
SWEDISH PRESCHOOLS: ENVIRONMENTS OF SENSITIVITY EJ 037 737
LEARNING FROM THE BRITISH PRIMARY SCHOOLS EJ 057 327

OPERANT CONDITIONING
MODIFICATION OF A DEVIANT SIBLING INTERACTION PATTERN IN THE HOME. ED023461
REINFORCEMENT GROWS UP: THE EXPERIMENTAL ANALYSIS OF BEHAVIOR AS A SYSTEMATIC APPROACH TO THE TEACHING OF DEVELOPMENTAL PSYCHOLOGY. ED023479

REDUCING BEHAVIOR PROBLEMS: AN OPERANT CONDITIONING GUIDE FOR TEACHERS. ED034570
TRAINING ELEMENTARY READING SKILLS THROUGH REINFORCEMENT AND FADING TECHNIQUES. ED034583
MODIFICATION OF THE CLASSROOM BEHAVIOR OF A "DISADVANTAGED" KINDERGARTEN BOY BY SOCIAL REINFORCEMENT AND ISOLATION. ED045181
CONDITION WITH CAUTION: THINK THRICE BEFORE CONDITIONING. (ROUGH DRAFT). ED046539
INSTRUMENTAL PERFORMANCE AS A FUNCTION OF REINFORCEMENT SCHEDULE, LUCK VERSUS SKILL INSTRUCTIONS, AND SEX OF CHILD EJ 024 934
SELF-REINFORCEMENT ESTABLISHED FOR A DISCRIMINATION TASK EJ 025 964
TANGIBLE REINFORCERS AND CHILD GROUP THERAPY EJ 026 935
ABOUT RESEARCH: PART II. IS A BEHAVIORAL APPROACH SUPERFICIAL? IS OPERANT CONDITIONING FAIR? WHY DO RESEARCH? EJ 029 015
EXAMINATION AND REEVALUATION OF PROSTHETIC LENSES EMPLOYING AN OPERANT PROCEDURE FOR MEASURING SUBJECTIVE VISUAL ACUITY IN A RETARDED CHILD EJ 029 382
OPERANT LEARNING OF VISUAL PATTERN DISCRIMINATION IN YOUNG INFANTS EJ 035 623
A DECADE OF INFANT CONDITIONING AND LEARNING RESEARCH EJ 038 454
ORIENTATION DISCRIMINATION IN INFANTS: A COMPARISON OF VISUAL FIXATION AND OPERANT TRAINING METHODS EJ 041 981
NIGHT TRAINING THROUGH PARENTS' IMPLICIT USE OF OPERANT CONDITIONING EJ 045 457
CONDITIONING INDEPENDENT WORK BEHAVIOR IN READING WITH SEVEN YEAR OLD CHILDREN IN A REGULAR EARLY CHILDHOOD CLASSROOM EJ 050 795
AVOIDANCE CONDITIONING IN YOUNG CHILDREN WITH INTERRUPTION OF A POSITIVE STIMULUS AS THE AVERSIVE EVENT EJ 053 719
CONDITIONING OF INFANT VOCALIZATIONS IN THE HOME ENVIRONMENT EJ 055 214
CONDITION WITH CAUTION EJ 058 585

OPINIONS

SYMPOSIUM: FOR AND AGAINST STRIKES EJ 003 416
CHILDREN'S DESCRIPTIONS OF PEERS: A WERNERIAN DEVELOPMENTAL ANALYSIS EJ 041 591
DESIRABILITY JUDGMENTS AS A FUNCTION OF ITEM CONTENT, INSTRUCTIONAL SET, AND SET: A LIFE-SPAN DEVELOPMENTAL STUDY EJ 048 473

ORAL COMMUNICATION

SAN ANTONIO LANGUAGE RESEARCH PROJECT, 1965-66 (YEAR TWO) FINDINGS. ED022528
AN ANALYSIS OF MOTHERS' SPEECH AS A FACTOR IN THE DEVELOPMENT OF CHILDREN'S INTELLIGENCE. ED042504
INCREASING VERBAL COMMUNICATION SKILLS IN CULTURALLY DISADVANTAGED PRE-SCHOOL CHILDREN. FINAL REPORT. ED044186
FIELD TEST OF THE UNIVERSITY OF HAWAII PRESCHOOL LANGUAGE CURRICULUM. FINAL REPORT. ED048924
CHILDREN'S JUDGMENTS OF PERSONALITY ON THE BASIS OF VOICE QUALITY EJ 030 512
SHOWING AND SHARING IN THE KINDERGARTEN EJ 032 933
DELAYED REINFORCEMENT AND VOCALIZATION RATES OF INFANTS EJ 036 127
CHILDREN'S COMMUNICATION ACCURACY RELATED TO RACE AND SOCIOECONOMIC STATUS EJ 040 359
CHANGES IN INFANTS' VOCALIZATIONS AS A FUNCTION OF DIFFERENTIAL ACOUSTIC STIMULATION EJ 061 139
EFFECTS OF SOCIAL AND VOCAL STIMULATION ON INFANT BABBLING EJ 061 140

ORAL EXPRESSION

DIFFERENTIATION BETWEEN NORMAL AND DISORDERED CHILDREN BY A COMPUTER ANALYSIS OF EMOTIONAL AND VERBAL BEHAVIOR. ED019138
HEAD START EVALUATION AND RESEARCH CENTER, UNIVERSITY OF KANSAS. REPORT NO. IV, A COMPARISON OF FOUR MODES OF ELICITING BRIEF ORAL RESPONSES FROM CHILDREN. ED021637
A DISTINCTIVE FEATURES ANALYSIS OF PRE-LINGUISTIC INFANT VOCALIZATIONS. ED025330
DEVELOPMENT OF THE PROSODIC FEATURES OF INFANTS' VOCALIZING. ED025331
THE VALUE OF THE SPOKEN RESPONSE IN TEACHING LISTENING SKILLS TO YOUNG CHILDREN THROUGH PROGRAMMED INSTRUCTION. FINAL REPORT. ED027973
THE EFFECTS OF ADULT VERBAL MODELING AND FEEDBACK ON THE ORAL LANGUAGE OF HEAD START CHILDREN. ED047793
EXPERIMENTAL LEARNING REEVALUATED EJ 026 814
CREATIVE DRAMA AND LANGUAGE GROWTH EJ 052 176

ORAL READING

ORAL READING ACHIEVEMENT OF SCOTTISH AND AMERICAN CHILDREN EJ 030 548
TEACHERS' RATINGS OF URBAN CHILDREN'S READING PERFORMANCE EJ 035 662

ORGANIZATION

THE HIERARCHICAL ORGANIZATION OF INTELLECTUAL STRUCTURES. ED022534
A PRELIMINARY SEARCH FOR FORMAL OPERATIONS STRUCTURES. ED024471
A STUDY IN CHILD CARE. VOLUME III: COST AND QUALITY ISSUES FOR OPERATORS. DAY CARE PROGRAMS REPRINT SERIES. ED051912

ORGANIZATIONAL CLIMATE

HEAD START EVALUATION AND RESEARCH CENTER. PROGRESS REPORT OF RESEARCH STUDIES 1966 TO 1967. DOCUMENT 2, STUDIES OF THE SOCIAL ORGANIZATION OF HEAD START CENTERS. ED021624
THE ORGANIZATIONAL CLIMATE OF SCHOOLS IN FIVE URBAN AREAS EJ 027 704

ORGANIZATIONS (GROUPS)

TEACHING THE YOUNG CHILD: GOALS FOR ILLINOIS. ED053805

ORIENTATION

ORIENTATION DISCRIMINATION IN INFANTS: A COMPARISON OF VISUAL FIXATION AND OPERANT TRAINING METHODS EJ 041 981

ORIGINALITY

RATE AND UNIQUENESS IN CHILDREN'S CREATIVE RESPONDING. ED034581

ORTHOGONAL ROTATION

FACTOR ANALYSIS OF THE EARLY CHILDHOOD EDUCATION TEST DATA. ED052840

OUTDOOR EDUCATION

ROCKS, RIVERS AND CITY CHILDREN EJ 029 390
OCEANS AND CHILDREN: MARINE SCIENCE AND ECOLOGICAL UNDERSTANDING EJ 029 391

PAIRED ASSOCIATE LEARNING

SOCIOECONOMIC STATUS AND LEARNING PROFICIENCY IN YOUNG CHILDREN. ED020023
ON LEARNING TO TALK: ARE PRINCIPLES DERIVED FROM THE LEARNING LABORATORY APPLICABLE? ED023481
MEMORY AND "CONTINGENCY ANALYSIS" IN INFANT LEARNING. ED024437
ACQUISTION AND TRANSFER DIFFERENCES BETWEEN KINDERGARTENERS AND SECOND-GRADERS ON AURALLY AND VISUALLY PRESENTED PAIRED-ASSOCIATES USING AN A-B, A-C DESIGN RESEARCH PROJECT NUMBER 2 OF PROJECT HEAD START RESEARCH AND EVALUATION CENTER, SYRACUSE UNIVERSITY RESEARCH INSTITUTE. FINAL REPORT, NOVEMBER 1, 1967. ED026139
MEDIATIONAL STYLES: AN INDIVIDUAL DIFFERENCE VARIABLE IN CHILDREN'S VERBAL LEARNING ABILITY. ED027955
CONDITIONS FOSTERING THE USE OF INFORMATIVE FEEDBACK BY YOUNG CHILDREN. ED029688
THE RELATIONSHIP OF INDIVIDUAL DIFFERENCES IN THE ORIENTING RESPONSE TO COMPLEX LEARNING IN KINDERGARTNERS. ED031299
INVESTIGATIONS OF THE ROLE OF SELECTED CUES IN CHILDREN'S PAIRED-ASSOCIATE LEARNING. REPORT FROM THE READING PROJECT. ED036315
CONDITIONS FOSTERING THE USE OF INFORMATION FEEDBACK BY YOUNG CHILDREN. (REVISED REPORT). ED039950
IMPLICATIONS OF MNEMONICS RESEARCH FOR COGNITIVE THEORY. ED045199
THE RELATIONSHIP OF INDIVIDUAL DIFFERENCES IN THE ORIENTING RESPONSE TO COMPLEX LEARNING IN KINDERGARTNERS. REPORT FROM THE MOTIVATION AND INDIVIDUAL DIFFERENCES IN LEARNING AND RETENTION PROJECT. ED046544
CORRELATION OF PAIRED-ASSOCIATE PERFORMANCE WITH SCHOOL ACHIEVEMENT AS A FUNCTION OF TASK AND SAMPLE VARIATION. ED049813
INTERRELATIONS IN CHILDREN'S LEARNING OF VERBAL AND PICTORIAL PAIRED ASSOCIATES. ED051886
THE LEARNING OF VERBAL STRINGS AS A FUNCTION OF CONNECTIVE FORM CLASS EJ 018 817
IMAGERY IN CHILDREN'S PAIRED-ASSOCIATE LEARNING EJ 021 757
THE INTERACTION OF PRONUNCIABILITY AND RESPONSE PRETRAINING ON THE PAIRED-ASSOCIATE PERFORMANCE OF THIRD-GRADE CHILDREN EJ 021 762
BACKWARD ASSOCIATIONS IN PAIRED-ASSOCIATE LEARNING OF RETARDATES AND NORMAL CHILDREN EJ 021 770
SINGLE-LETTER CUE SELECTION IN THE PAIRED-ASSOCIATE LEARNING OF NORMAL CHILDREN AND RETARDATES EJ 024 698
VERBAL AND IMAGERY PROCESSES IN CHILDREN'S PAIRED-ASSOCIATE LEARNING EJ 024 699
SYNTACTICAL MEDIATION OF PAIRED-ASSOCIATE LEARNING AS A FUNCTION OF AGE EJ 030 286
AGE-DEVELOPMENT IN THE LINEAR REPRESENTATION OF WORDS AND OBJECTS EJ 030 296
FUNCTIONS OF VISUAL IMAGERY IN THE LEARNING AND CONCEPT FORMATION OF CHILDREN EJ 033 779
TRANSFER OF VERBAL PAIRED ASSOCIATES IN MENTALLY RETARDED INDIVIDUALS AND NORMAL CHILDREN AS A FUNCTION OF INTERLIST SIMILARITY EJ 033 785
CHILDREN'S SHIFT PERFORMANCE IN THE ABSENCE OF DIMENSIONALITY AND A LEARNED REPRESENTATIONAL RESPONSE EJ 033 786

FACILITATING AND INTERFERING EFFECTS OF STIMULUS NAMING ON CHILDREN'S MOTOR PAIRED-ASSOCIATE LEARNING EJ 033 793
PAIRED-ASSOCIATE LEARNING OF CHILDREN WITH MIXED LIST DESIGNS EJ 035 369
THE EFFECTS OF CONNOTATIVE SIMILARITY IN CHILDREN'S LEARNING OF A PAIRED-ASSOCIATE TASK EJ 035 376
EFFECT OF INCENTIVES UPON RETARDED AND NORMAL READERS ON A VISUAL-ASSOCIATE LEARNING TASK EJ 038 266
PHONETIC COMPATIBILITY IN PAIRED-ASSOCIATE LEARNING OF FIRST- AND THIRD-GRADE CHILDREN EJ 044 692
OBSERVATIONAL LEARNING: THE EFFECTS OF AGE, TASK DIFFICULTY, AND OBSERVERS' MOTORIC REHEARSAL EJ 044 702
PAIRED-ASSOCIATE LEARNING AND BIDIRECTIONAL ASSOCIATIVE RECALL IN FIRST, THIRD, FIFTH AND SEVENTH GRADERS EJ 053 481
EFFECTS OF SYNTACTICAL MEDIATION, AGE, AND MODES OF REPRESENTATION ON PAIRED-ASSOCIATE LEARNING EJ 056 615
RETROACTIVE AND PROACTIVE MULTIPLE LIST INTERFERENCE WITH DISADVANTAGED CHILDREN EJ 057 895
IMAGERY AND MULTIPLE-LIST PAIRED ASSOCIATE LEARNING IN YOUNG CHILDREN EJ 057 904
GRADE INTERACTION WITH WORDS AND PICTURES IN A PAIRED-ASSOCIATE TASK: A PROPOSED EXPLANATION EJ 057 910
DEVELOPMENTAL CHANGES IN CLUSTERING CRITERIA EJ 058 145
THE ROLE OF OVERT ACTIVITY IN CHILDREN'S IMAGERY PRODUCTION EJ 059 315

THE EFFECTS OF FEEDBACK VARIATIONS ON REFERENTIAL COMMUNICATION OF CHILDREN EJ 040 360

VERBAL PAIRED-ASSOCIATE LEARNING IN CHILDREN AND ADULTS WITH ANTICIPATION, RECOGNITION, AND RECALL METHODS EJ 042 959

PAPAGO

CHILDREARING PRACTICES AMONG SELECTED CULTURALLY DEPRIVED MINORITIES EJ 023 613

PARALINGUISTICS

SPEECH REGISTERS IN YOUNG CHILDREN EJ 052 450

PARAPROFESSIONAL SCHOOL PERSONNEL

AIDES TO TEACHERS AND CHILDREN. ED027090
PRELIMINARY REPORT OF THE AD HOC JOINT COMMITTEE ON THE PREPARATION OF NURSERY AND KINDERGARTEN TEACHERS. ED032924
[A STATEMENT REGARDING THE COMPREHENSIVE PRESCHOOL EDUCATION AND CHILD DAY CARE ACT OF 1969, AND OTHER RELATED BILLS.] ED041624
EDUCATIONAL INTERVENTION IN THE HOME AND PARAPROFESSIONAL CAREER DEVELOPMENT: A SECOND GENERATION MOTHER STUDY WITH AN EMPHASIS ON COSTS AND BENEFITS. FINAL REPORT. ED052814
CHILD CARE PARAPROFESSIONALS: CHARACTERISTICS FOR SELECTION. ED053800

PARENT ASSOCIATIONS

HELPS FOR PARENTS IN HOUSING ED025312
JOINING TOGETHER TO HELP FOSTER CHILDREN EJ 060 900

PARENT ATTITUDES

AN EVALUATION OF DIFFERENCES AMONG DIFFERENT CLASSES OF HEAD START PARTICIPANTS. FINAL REPORT. ED015012
CHILDREARING ANTECEDENTS OF FLEXIBLE THINKING. ED022530
PARENTAL BEHAVIOR TOWARD BOYS AND GIRLS OF PRESCHOOL AGE. ED026119
CHANGING PARENT ATTITUDES AND IMPROVING LANGUAGE AND INTELLECTUAL ABILITIES OF CULTURALLY DISADVANTAGED FOUR-YEAR-OLD CHILDREN THROUGH PARENT INVOLVEMENT. ED027942
ATTITUDES, EXPECTATIONS, AND BEHAVIOR OF PARENTS OF HEAD START AND NON-HEAD START CHILDREN. REPORT NUMBER 1. ED030475
A NOTE ON PUNISHMENT PATTERNS IN PARENTS OF PRESCHOOL CHILDREN. REPORT NUMBER 3. ED030477
PARENT INVOLVEMENT IN PROJECT HEAD START. PART OF THE FINAL REPORT ON HEAD START EVALUATION AND RESEARCH: 1968-1969 TO THE OFFICE OF ECONOMIC OPPORTUNITY. ED037244
A FOLLOWUP STUDY OF ADOPTIONS: POST-PLACEMENT FUNCTIONING OF ADOPTION FAMILIES. ED039018
PARENTAL CONCEPTUAL SYSTEMS, HOME PLAY ENVIRONMENT, AND POTENTIAL CREATIVITY IN CHILDREN. ED043386
ATTITUDINAL STUDY OF ROMAN CATHOLIC PARENTS OF PRE-SCHOOL CHILDREN REGARDING THE OPTION OF "CATHOLIC" OR PUBLIC SCHOOL EDUCATION FOR THEIR CHILDREN. ED046488
INCREASING THE EFFECTIVENESS OF PARENTS-AS-TEACHERS. ED048939
PARENTS: ACTIVE PARTNERS IN EDUCATION. A STUDY/ACTION PUBLICATION. ED050823
THREE DEGREES OF PARENT INVOLVEMENT IN A PRESCHOOL PROGRAM: IMPACT ON MOTHERS AND CHILDREN. ED052831
RESULTS OF PARENT AND STUDENT REACTION QUESTIONNAIRE. TECHNICAL REPORT NO. 8. ED052836
A COMPARISON OF PARENTS' ATTITUDES TOWARD AEL'S "AROUND THE BEND" AND OTHER CHILDREN'S TELEVISION PROGRAMS. ED052842
THE GENERATION GAP IN THE EYES OF YOUTH EJ 018 067
CHILD NEGLECT AMONG THE POOR: A STUDY OF PARENTAL ADEQUACY IN FAMILIES OF THREE ETHNIC GROUPS EJ 018 326
POSTADOPTION COUNSELING: A PROFESSIONAL OBLIGATION EJ 028 792
TERMINATION OF RESIDENTIAL TREATMENT OF CHILDREN EJ 029 102
HARMONIOUS PARENTS AND THEIR PRESCHOOL CHILDREN EJ 034 708
SHIFTS IN CHILD-REARING ATTITUDES LINKED WITH PARENTHOOD AND OCCUPATION EJ 038 853
PARENTHOOD: SOME ANTECEDENTS AND CONSEQUENCES: A PRELIMINARY SURVEY OF THE MENTAL HEALTH LITERATURE EJ 041 342
A CHECK ON THE STRUCTURE OF PARENTAL REPORTS OF CHILD-REARING PRACTICES EJ 045 388
PARENTAL CONCEPTUAL SYSTEMS, HOME PLAY ENVIRONMENT, AND POTENTIAL CREATIVITY IN CHILDREN EJ 048 234
PARENTAL ATTITUDES AND INTERACTIONS IN DELINQUENCY EJ 056 611
FAMILY HARMONY: AN ETIOLOGIC FACTOR IN ALIENATION EJ 058 508
THE IMPORTANCE OF SECURITY IN THE EDUCATION OF YOUNG CHILDREN EJ 062 549

PARENT CHILD RELATIONSHIP

THE COGNITIVE ENVIRONMENTS OF URBAN PRE-SCHOOL CHILDREN. MANUAL OF INSTRUCTIONS FOR ADMINISTERING AND SCORING TOY SORTING TASK. ED018264
THE COGNITIVE ENVIRONMENTS OF URBAN PRE-SCHOOL CHILDREN. MANUAL OF INSTRUCTIONS FOR ADMINISTERING AND SCORING THE EIGHT-BLOCK SORTING TASK. ED018265
THE COGNITIVE ENVIRONMENTS OF URBAN PRE-SCHOOL CHILDREN. MANUAL FOR CODING MOTHER-CHILD INTERACTION ON THE EIGHT-BLOCK SORTING TASK. ED018266
THE COGNITIVE ENVIRONMENTS OF URBAN PRE-SCHOOL CHILDREN. MANUAL OF INSTRUCTIONS FOR ADMINISTERING AND SCORING "ETCH-A-SKETCH" TASK. ED018267
CHILDREARING ANTECEDENTS OF FLEXIBLE THINKING. ED022530
PERCEPTUAL-COGNITIVE DEVELOPMENT IN INFANCY: A GENERALIZED EXPECTANCY MODEL AS A FUNCTION OF THE MOTHER-INFANT INTERACTION. ED024470
PARENTS AS TEACHERS, HOW LOWER-CLASS AND MIDDLE-CLASS MOTHERS TEACH. ED025301
PARENT-CHILD INTERACTION AND THE CHILD'S APPROACH TO TASK SITUATIONS. ED025307
PARENTAL BEHAVIOR TOWARD BOYS AND GIRLS OF PRESCHOOL AGE. ED026119
AN INVESTIGATION OF SIMILARITIES IN PARENT-CHILD TEST SCORES FOR EVIDENCE OF HEREDITARY COMPONENTS. ED027060
NATURALISTIC OBSERVATION IN THE STUDY OF PARENT-CHILD INTERACTION. ED027073
A THEORY OF PARENT EFFECTIVENESS. ED028815
COMPETENCE AND DEPENDENCE IN CHILDREN: PARENTAL TREATMENT OF FOUR-YEAR-OLD GIRLS. FINAL REPORT. ED030497
MOTHERS AS TEACHERS OF THEIR OWN PRESCHOOL CHILDREN: THE INFLUENCE OF SOCIO-ECONOMIC STATUS AND TASK STRUCTURE ON TEACHING SPECIFICITY. ED031294
ENVIRONMENT INFLUENCES ON THE DEVELOPMENT OF ABILITIES. ED032126
DETERMINANTS OF INFANT BEHAVIOUR IV. ED032947
INFANT DAY CARE AND ATTACHMENT. ED033755
CHILDREN LEARNING: SAMPLES OF EVERYDAY LIFE OF CHILDREN AT HOME. ED033763
INFORMATION EXCHANGE IN MOTHER-CHILD INTERACTIONS. ED034599
A STUDY OF COMMUNICATION PATTERNS IN DISADVANTAGED CHILDREN. ED037250
ATTACHMENT AND RECIPROCITY IN THE TWO-YEAR-OLD CHILD. ED039946
DEPENDENCE AND COMPETENCE IN FOUR-YEAR-OLD BOYS AS RELATED TO PARENTAL TREATMENT OF THE CHILD. ED039952
PARENT PREFERENCE OF PRESCHOOL CHILDREN. ED041628
LANGUAGE DEVELOPMENT OF SOCIALLY DISADVANTAGED PRESCHOOL CHILDREN. FINAL REPORT. ED041641
AN ANALYSIS OF MOTHERS' SPEECH AS A FACTOR IN THE DEVELOPMENT OF CHILDREN'S INTELLIGENCE. ED042504
A PARENT-CHILD CENTER, NOVEMBER-DECEMBER 1968. ED042506
ETHNIC AND SOCIOECONOMIC INFLUENCES ON THE HOME LANGUAGE EXPERIENCES OF CHILDREN. ED043377
78 BATTERED CHILDREN: A RETROSPECTIVE STUDY. ED043382
MOTHER-CHILD INTERACTION: SOCIAL CLASS DIFFERENCES IN THE FIRST YEAR OF LIFE. ED044177
THE COGNITIVE ENVIRONMENTS OF URBAN PRESCHOOL CHILDREN. FINAL REPORT. ED045179
EVALUATION OF A PARENT AND CHILD CENTER PROGRAM. ED045189
DIFFERENTIAL RESPONSE PATTERNS AS THEY AFFECT THE SELF ESTEEM OF THE CHILD. ED046542
COMMUNICATIVE COMPETENCE AND THE DISADVANTAGED CHILD: A STUDY OF THE RELATIONSHIP BETWEEN LANGUAGE MODELS AND THE DEVELOPMENT OF COMMUNICATION SKILLS IN DISADVANTAGED PRESCHOOLERS. FINAL REPORT. ED047806
PARENTS ARE TEACHERS: A CHILD MANAGEMENT PROGRAM. ED047826
THE PSYCHOLOGICAL EFFECTS OF PREGNANCY AND NEONATAL HEALTH THREATS ON CHILD DEVELOPMENT. ED048921

TINY DRAMAS: VOCAL COMMUNICATION BETWEEN MOTHER AND INFANT IN JAPANESE AND AMERICAN FAMILIES. ED048927
PARENT-CHILD VERBAL INTERACTION: A STUDY OF DIALOGUE STRATEGIES AND VERBAL ABILITY. ED049824
INFANT DEVELOPMENT IN LOWER CLASS AMERICAN FAMILIES. ED049836
AN ANALYSIS OF EXCELLENT EARLY EDUCATIONAL PRACTICES: PRELIMINARY REPORT. ED050805
INDIVIDUAL DIFFERENCES IN THE DEVELOPMENT OF SOME ATTACHMENT BEHAVIORS. ED050827
MOTHER-INFANT INTERACTION AND INFANT DEVELOPMENT AMONG THE WOLOF OF SENEGAL. ED051885
THE IMPLICATIONS OF PARENT EFFECTIVENESS TRAINING FOR FOSTER PARENTS. ED052821
THE EFFECTS OF EXPERIENCE ON INFANTS' REACTIONS TO SEPARATION FROM THEIR MOTHERS. ED053802
APPLICATION OF MARKOV PROCESSES TO THE CONCEPT OF STATE. ED053813
PERCEPTUAL-COGNITIVE DEVELOPMENT IN INFANCY: A GENERALIZED EXPECTANCY MODEL AS A FUNCTION OF THE MOTHER-INFANT INTERACTION EJ 003 553
EARLY ANTECEDENTS OF ROLE-TAKING AND ROLE-PLAYING ABILITY EJ 008 318
FAMILY TIES AND THE INSTITUTIONAL CHILD EJ 012 579
THE PARENTAL ROLE, A FUNCTIONAL-COGNITIVE APPROACH EJ 013 946
PREADOLESCENTS - WHAT MAKES THEM TICK? A CHILDHOOD EDUCATION SPECIAL (FIRST IN A SERIES): CLASSIC STATEMENTS FROM THE EDUCATOR'S ARCHIVES EJ 016 839
THE GOAL OF LIFE ENHANCEMENT FOR A FATALLY ILL CHILD EJ 017 423
REACHING THE YOUNG CHILD THROUGH PARENT EDUCATION EJ 017 852
THE FATHER-DAUGHTER RELATIONSHIP AND THE PERSONALITY DEVELOPMENT OF THE FEMALE EJ 017 904
THE GENERATION GAP IN THE EYES OF YOUTH EJ 018 067
PARENTAL DETERMINANTS OF PEER-ORIENTATION AND SELF-ORIENTATION AMONG PREADOLESCENTS EJ 019 387
SEX EDUCATION OF THE YOUNG CHILD EJ 019 862
CONSISTENCY OF MATERNAL ATTITUDES AND PERSONALITY FROM PREGNANCY TO EIGHT MONTHS FOLLOWING CHILDBIRTH EJ 021 026
INTRAFAMILY COMPARISON OF LOVING-REJECTING CHILD-REARING PRACTICES EJ 021 081
THE FAMILY ROMANCE FANTASY IN CHILDREN ADOPTED IN INFANCY EJ 022 478
CERTAIN CULTURAL AND FAMILIAL FACTORS CONTRIBUTING TO ADOLESCENT ALIENATION EJ 022 536
THE RELATION OF PARENTAL TRAINING TO CONCEPTUAL STRUCTURE IN PREADOLESCENTS EJ 023 191
TWO MODES OF MATERNAL IMMATURITY AND THEIR CONSEQUENCES EJ 023 424
ALIENATION OF PRESENT-DAY ADOLESCENTS EJ 023 428
CHILDREARING PRACTICES AMONG SELECTED CULTURALLY DEPRIVED MINORITIES EJ 023 613
MATERNAL CHILD-REARING EXPERIENCE AND SELF- REINFORCEMENT EFFECTIVENESS EJ 024 944
AWARENESS, AFFECTION, AND PERCEIVED SIMILARITY IN THE PARENT-CHILD RELATIONSHIP EJ 025 377
SOME NONVERBAL ASPECTS OF COMMUNICATION BETWEEN MOTHER AND PRESCHOOL CHILD EJ 025 386
EXPERIMENTAL ANALYSIS OF THE FACTORS DETERMINING OBEDIENCE OF FOUR-YEAR-OLD CHILDREN TO ADULT FEMALES EJ 026 152
MATERNAL BEHAVIOR TOWARD OWN AND OTHER PRESCHOOL CHILDREN: THE PROBLEM OF "OWNNESS" EJ 026 324
MOTHER-INFANT RELATIONSHIP AND WEIGHT GAIN IN THE FIRST MONTH OF LIFE EJ 026 508
THE FUNCTION OF AMBIGUITY IN CHILD CRISES EJ 027 344
TEACHER-PARENT WORK IN THE HOME: AN ASPECT OF CHILD GUIDANCE CLINIC SERVICES EJ 027 448
WISC SUBTEST AND IQ SCORE CORRELATES OF FATHER ABSENCE EJ 029 219
CLINICAL IMPLICATIONS OF MATERNAL EMPLOYMENT: A REVIEW OF RESEARCH EJ 030 432
PARENT AND CHILD CENTERS--IMPETUS, IMPLEMENTATION, IN-DEPTH VIEW EJ 030 469
SOCIALIZATION AND INSTRUMENTAL COMPETENCE IN YOUNG CHILDREN EJ 030 510
PATTERNS OF MOTHER-INFANT CONTACT: THE SIGNIFICANCE OF LATERAL PREFERENCE EJ 030 513
THE IMPACT OF OBJECT LOSS ON A SIX-YEAR-OLD EJ 030 514
PATTERNS OF FAMILY ORGANIZATION: AN APPROACH TO CHILD STUDY EJ 030 714
THE CHILDCARE ATTITUDES OF TWO GENERATIONS OF MOTHERS EJ 032 796
NEONATE-MOTHER INTERACTION: EFFECTS OF PARITY ON FEEDING BEHAVIOR EJ 032 892
INVISIBLE FACTORS IN A CHILD'S REACTION TO TELEVISION EJ 032 934
A NOTE ON SELECTIVE IMITATION BY A SIX-WEEK-OLD INFANT EJ 034 045
STIMULUS CONTROL OF PARENT OR CARETAKER BEHAVIOR BY OFFSPRING EJ 034 538
THE CAPACITY TO LOVE: A POSSIBLE REFORMULATION EJ 034 709
FATHER ABSENCE, PERCEIVED MATERNAL BEHAVIOR, AND MASCULINITY OF SELF-CONCEPT AMONG JUNIOR HIGH SCHOOL BOYS EJ 035 804
FATHER ABSENCE AND CONSCIENCE DEVELOPMENT EJ 038 854
A FACTOR ANALYSIS OF FIFTH AND SIXTH GRADERS' REPORTS OF PARENTAL CHILD-REARING BEHAVIOR EJ 038 855
A PARENTING SCALE AND SEPARATION DECISIONS EJ 039 286
COGNITIVE COMPONENTS OF SEPARATION ANXIETY EJ 039 900
THE IMPACT OF MOTHER'S PRESENCE UPON BEHAVIOR: THE FIRST YEAR EJ 039 908
RELATIONSHIPS BETWEEN INFANTS' VOCALIZATIONS AND THEIR MOTHERS' BEHAVIORS EJ 040 455
THE MOTHER-CHILD RELATIONSHIP AND THE FATHER-ABSENT BOY'S PERSONALITY DEVELOPMENT 27-241 EJ 040 456
CURIOSITY AND THE PARENT-CHILD RELATIONSHIP EJ 041 447
SELF-PARENTAL DISTANCE, CONTROL OF REINFORCEMENT, AND PERSONAL FUTURE TIME PERSPECTIVE EJ 045 047
NIGHT TRAINING THROUGH PARENTS' IMPLICIT USE OF OPERANT CONDITIONING EJ 045 457
A CROSS-CULTURAL COMPARISON OF MATERNAL COMMUNICATION EJ 045 505
OBSERVATION STUDIES OF PARENT-CHILD INTERACTION: A METHODOLOGICAL REVIEW EJ 046 466
A CROSS-CULTURAL STUDY OF THE CHILD'S COMMUNICATION WITH HIS MOTHER EJ 046 890
HELPING PARENTS IN A PEDIATRIC CLINIC EJ 046 963
A MICRO-ANALYSIS OF MOTHER-INFANT INTERACTION. BEHAVIOR REGULATING SOCIAL CONTACT BETWEEN A MOTHER AND HER 3 1/2 MONTH-OLD TWINS EJ 048 300
MATERNAL CHILD REARING AND CREATIVITY IN SONS EJ 048 302
INTERVENTION IN INFANCY: A PROGRAM FOR BLIND INFANTS EJ 048 904
MOTHER-INFANT INTERACTION AND INFANT DEVELOPMENT AMONG THE WOLOF OF SENEGAL EJ 051 017
PARENT-CHILD SEPARATION: PSYCHOLOGICAL EFFECTS ON THE CHILDREN EJ 051 019
MOTHER-CHILD INTERACTIONS AND COGNITIVE DEVELOPMENT IN CHILDREN EJ 051 567
AGE, STATE, AND MATERNAL BEHAVIOR ASSOCIATED WITH INFANT VOCALIZATIONS EJ 052 444
INFANT OBEDIENCE AND MATERNAL BEHAVIOR: THE ORIGINS OF SOCIALIZATION RECONSIDERED EJ 052 446
IDENTIFICATION AND CONSCIENCE DEVELOPMENT EJ 052 447
MOTHERS' TEST OF ANXIETY AND TASK SELECTION AND CHILDREN'S PERFORMANCE WITH MOTHER OR A STRANGER EJ 052 449
THE EFFECT OF EMOTION ON GROWTH EJ 053 653
TOYS DELAY THE INFANT'S FOLLOWING OF HIS MOTHER EJ 053 713
MATERNAL WARMTH, ACHIEVEMENT MOTIVATION, AND COGNITIVE FUNCTIONING IN LOWER-CLASS PRESCHOOL CHILDREN EJ 053 745
PROXIMITY AND INTERACTIONAL BEHAVIOR OF YOUNG CHILDREN TO THEIR "SECURITY" BLANKETS EJ 053 748
THE EFFECTS OF A FAMILIAR TOY AND MOTHER'S PRESENCE ON EXPLORATORY AND ATTACHMENT BEHAVIORS IN YOUNG CHILDREN EJ 053 759
FATHER-CHILD INTERACTION AND THE INTELLECTUAL FUNCTIONING OF FOUR-YEAR-OLD BOYS EJ 054 290
SYMPOSIUM ON PARENT-CENTERED EDUCATION: 1. THE CHILD'S FIRST TEACHER EJ 054 377
SYMPOSIUM ON PARENT-CENTERED EDUCATION: 2. LEARNING THROUGH (AND FROM) MOTHERS EJ 054 378
SYMPOSIUM ON PARENT-CENTERED EDUCATION: 3. LEARNING THROUGH PARENTS: LESSONS FOR TEACHERS EJ 054 379
STYLE OF ADAPTATION TO AVERSIVE MATERNAL CONTROL AND PARANOID BEHAVIOR EJ 055 105
INTERRELATIONS IN THE ATTACHMENT BEHAVIOR OF HUMAN INFANTS EJ 055 208
THE STABILITY OF ATTACHMENT BEHAVIORS IN THE HUMAN INFANT EJ 055 209
SOME COGNITIVE AND AFFECTIVE ASPECTS OF EARLY LANGUAGE DEVELOPMENT EJ 055 655
AN EXPLORATORY STUDY OF SOCIALIZATION EFFECTS ON BLACK CHILDREN: SOME BLACK-WHITE COMPARISONS EJ 055 656
PARENTS AS EDUCATORS: EVIDENCE FROM CROSS-SECTIONAL, LONGITUDINAL AND INTERVENTION RESEARCH EJ 056 608
PARENTAL ATTITUDES AND INTERACTIONS IN DELINQUENCY EJ 056 611
MOTHER-CHILD INTERACTION IN THE FIRST YEAR OF LIFE EJ 056 632
MATERNAL CONTROL AND OBEDIENCE IN THE TWO-YEAR-OLD EJ 056 714
EXECUTIVE COMPETENCE AND SPONTANEOUS SOCIAL BEHAVIOR IN ONE-YEAR-OLDS EJ 056 732
HELPING PARENTS TO HELP THEIR CHILDREN IN PLACEMENT EJ 058 055
ACHIEVEMENT MOTIVATION AND FEAR OF FAILURE IN FAMILY AND SCHOOL EJ 058 143
STATE AS AN INFANT-ENVIRONMENT INTERACTION: AN ANALYSIS OF MOTHER-INFANT INTERACTIONS AS A FUNCTION OF SEX EJ 058 221
FAMILY HARMONY: AN ETIOLOGIC FACTOR IN ALIENATION EJ 058 508

ATTACHMENT: ITS ORIGINS AND COURSE EJ 058 586
RELATIONSHIPS BETWEEN INFANTS' SOCIAL BEHAVIOR AND THEIR MOTHERS' BEHAVIOR EJ 058 587
MOTHERS' SPEECH TO CHILDREN LEARNING LANGUAGE EJ 058 696
NEGRO PARENTAL BEHAVIOR AND SOCIAL CLASS VARIABLES EJ 059 871
PRINCIPLES OF INTERACTION IN LANGUAGE LEARNING EJ 059 875
INFANT DEVELOPMENT IN LOWER-CLASS AMERICAN FAMILIES EJ 060 012
CHILDREN'S REPORTS OF PARENTAL CHILD-REARING BEHAVIOR AT FIVE GRADE LEVELS EJ 060 385
INFANT CARE AND GROWTH IN URBAN ZAMBIA EJ 061 231
IMPLICATIONS OF INFANT DEVELOPMENT AMONG THE MAYAN INDIANS OF MEXICO EJ 061 232
MOTHER-ATTACHMENT AND STRANGER-REACTIONS IN THE THIRD YEAR OF LIFE EJ 062 594

PARENT CONFERENCES

A PRESCHOOL EXCHANGE: BLACK MOTHERS SPEAK AND A WHITE TEACHER LISTENS EJ 022 137
LISTENING BEYOND WORDS: LEARNING FROM PARENTS IN CONFERENCES EJ 055 363

PARENT COUNSELING

GROUP WORK WITH PARENTS OF CHILDREN WITH LEARNING DISORDERS. ED019130
STRUCTURED FAMILY-ORIENTED THERAPY FOR SCHOOL BEHAVIOR AND LEARNING DISORDERS EJ 019 022
THE PARENTS' CENTER PROJECT: A MULTISERVICE APPROACH TO THE PREVENTION OF CHILD ABUSE EJ 040 043
VIOLENCE BEGINS AT HOME. THE PARENTS' CENTER PROJECT FOR THE STUDY AND PREVENTION OF CHILD ABUSE EJ 043 671
SCHOOL AND HOME: NOT EITHER-OR EJ 046 246
HELPING PARENTS IN A PEDIATRIC CLINIC EJ 046 963

PARENT EDUCATION

A PARENT EDUCATION APPROACH TO PROVISION OF EARLY STIMULATION FOR THE CULTURALLY DISADVANTAGED. FINAL REPORT. ED017339
EVALUATION OF THE PRESCHOOL CHILD AND PARENT EDUCATION PROJECT AS EXPANDED THROUGH THE USE OF ELEMENTARY AND SECONDARY EDUCATION ACT, TITLE I, FUNDS. ED021621
REACHING THE HARD-TO-REACH: THE USE OF PARTICIPANT GROUP METHODS WITH MOTHERS OF CULTURALLY DISADVANTAGED PRESCHOOL CHILDREN. ED024469
THE IDENTIFICATION AND ASSESSMENT OF THINKING ABILITY IN YOUNG CHILDREN. FINAL REPORT. ED025316
PRESCHOOL PARENT EDUCATION PROGRAM: A CURRICULUM GUIDE FOR USE BY TEACHERS CONDUCTING PARENT EDUCATION PROGRAMS AS A PART OF OVER-ALL COMPENSATORY PRESCHOOL PROJECTS. EXPERIMENTAL EDITION. ED026118
PRESCHOOL AND PRIMARY EDUCATION PROJECT. 1967-68 ANNUAL PROGRESS REPORT TO THE FORD FOUNDATION. ED027936
PIAGET, SKINNER, AND AN INTENSIVE PRESCHOOL PROGRAM FOR LOWER CLASS CHILDREN AND THEIR MOTHERS. ED027966
TOWARD THE PREVENTION OF INCOMPETENCE. ED028812
TEACHING MOTHERS TO TEACH: A HOME COUNSELING PROGRAM FOR LOW-INCOME PARENTS. ED028819
DEVELOPMENT OF A PRESCHOOL LANGUAGE-ORIENTED CURRICULUM WITH A STRUCTURED PARENT EDUCATION PROGRAM. FINAL REPORT. ED028845
A REPORT ON THE 1967-68 PROGRAM FOR PRESCHOOL CHILDREN AND THEIR PARENTS. RESEARCH REPORT SERIES 1968-69, NO. 4. ED029713
MOTHERS' TRAINING PROGRAM: THE GROUP PROCESS. ED032926
FOCUS ON PARENT EDUCATION AS A MEANS OF ALTERING THE CHILD'S ENVIRONMENT. ED033758
EARLY CHILD STIMULATION THROUGH PARENT EDUCATION. ED038166
AN ASSESSMENT OF COGNITIVE GROWTH IN CHILDREN WHO HAVE PARTICIPATED IN THE TOY-LENDING COMPONENT OF THE PARENT-CHILD PROGRAM. ED045204
A PROGRESS REPORT ON THE PARENT/CHILD COURSE AND TOY LIBRARY. ED045206
UNIVERSITY OF HAWAII PRESCHOOL LANGUAGE CURRICULUM, HONOLULU, HAWAII: A PROGRAM OF ENGLISH CONVERSATION FOR PRESCHOOL CHILDREN OF MULTIETHNIC BACKGROUNDS. MODEL PROGRAMS--CHILDHOOD EDUCATION. ED045220
THE EFFECTS OF A PRESCHOOL LANGUAGE PROGRAM ON TWO-YEAR-OLD CHILDREN AND THEIR MOTHERS. FINAL REPORT. ED045224
PROGRAMS OF HEAD START PARENT INVOLVEMENT IN HAWAII. A SECTION OF THE FINAL REPORT FOR 1969-70. ED048935
SIMULATION ACTIVITIES FOR TRAINING PARENTS AND TEACHERS AS EDUCATIONAL PARTNERS: A REPORT AND EVALUATION. ED048945
CHILDREN UNDER THREE - FINDING WAYS TO STIMULATE DEVELOPMENT. II. SOME CURRENT EXPERIMENTS: STIMULATION VIA PARENT EDUCATION EJ 007 410
REACHING THE YOUNG CHILD THROUGH PARENT EDUCATION EJ 017 852
PARENTAL EDUCATION, SEX DIFFERENCES, AND PERFORMANCE ON COGNITIVE TASKS AMONG TWO-YEAR-OLD CHILDREN EJ 035 364
EARLY CHILD STIMULATION THROUGH PARENT EDUCATION EJ 044 006
A MOTHERS' TRAINING PROGRAM--THE ROAD TO A PURPOSEFUL EXISTENCE EJ 044 007
INVOLVING PARENTS IN RESIDENTIAL TREATMENT OF CHILDREN EJ 045 233
CHILDREN AND ROAD ACCIDENTS EJ 050 496
SYMPOSIUM ON PARENT-CENTERED EDUCATION: 1. THE CHILD'S FIRST TEACHER EJ 054 377
SYMPOSIUM ON PARENT-CENTERED EDUCATION: 2. LEARNING THROUGH (AND FROM) MOTHERS EJ 054 378
SYMPOSIUM ON PARENT-CENTERED EDUCATION: 3. LEARNING THROUGH PARENTS: LESSONS FOR TEACHERS EJ 054 379
NUTRITION AND EDUCATIONAL EXPERIENCE: INTERRELATED VARIABLES IN CHILDREN'S LEARNING EJ 059 643
CLARIFYING THE ROLE OF FOSTER PARENTS EJ 061 235

PARENT INFLUENCE

THE EFFECTS OF JUNIOR KINDERGARTEN ON ACHIEVEMENT--THE FIRST FIVE YEARS. ED016526
STUDY OF ACHIEVEMENT--JUNIOR KINDERGARTEN, WHO IS SERVED AND WHO GOES. ED017322
CHILDREARING ANTECEDENTS OF FLEXIBLE THINKING. ED022530
PLAY BEHAVIOR IN THE YEAR-OLD INFANT: EARLY SEX DIFFERENCES. ED022545
HEAD START EVALUATION AND RESEARCH CENTER, THE UNIVERSITY OF CHICAGO. REPORT B, MATERNAL ANTECEDENTS OF INTELLECTUAL ACHIEVEMENT BEHAVIORS IN LOWER CLASS PRESCHOOL CHILDREN. ED022551
HEAD START EVALUATION AND RESEARCH CENTER, THE UNIVERSITY OF CHICAGO. ANNUAL REPORT, 1966-1967. ED023445
EXTRA-CURRICULAR PARENT-CHILD CONTACT AND CHILDREN'S SOCIALLY REINFORCED TASK BEHAVIOR. ED023447
HEAD START EVALUATION AND RESEARCH CENTER, THE UNIVERSITY OF CHICAGO. REPORT F, SOCIALIZATION INTO THE ROLE OF PUPIL. ED023456
PARENTAL ANTECEDENTS OF CHILDREN'S BELIEFS IN INTERNAL-EXTERNAL CONTROL OF REINFORCEMENTS IN INTELLECTUAL ACHIEVEMENT SITUATIONS. ED024447
MOTHER-CHILD RELATIONS AND CHILDREN'S ACHIEVEMENT. TERMINAL REPORT. ED024465
PERCEPTUAL-COGNITIVE DEVELOPMENT IN INFANCY: A GENERALIZED EXPECTANCY MODEL AS A FUNCTION OF THE MOTHER-INFANT INTERACTION. ED024470
HELPING THE CHILD DEVELOP HIS CREATIVE POTENTIAL. ED026113
FEAR AND ATTACHMENT IN YOUNG CHILDREN. RESEARCH PROJECT NUMBER 4 OF PROJECT HEAD START RESEARCH AND EVALUATION CENTER, SYRACUSE UNIVERSITY RESEARCH INSTITUTE. FINAL REPORT, NOVEMBER 1, 1967. ED026141
COMPETENCE AND DEPENDENCE IN CHILDREN: PARENTAL TREATMENT OF FOUR-YEAR-OLD GIRLS. FINAL REPORT. ED030497
MATERNAL BEHAVIOR AND THE DEVELOPMENT OF READING READINESS IN URBAN NEGRO CHILDREN. ED031309
THE RELATION OF CERTAIN HOME ENVIRONMENT FACTORS TO THE THINKING ABILITIES OF THREE-YEAR-OLD CHILDREN. FINAL REPORT. ED039041
THREE DEGREES OF PARENT INVOLVEMENT IN A PRESCHOOL PROGRAM: IMPACT ON MOTHERS AND CHILDREN. ED052831
MOTHERS AS TEACHERS OF THEIR OWN PRESCHOOL CHILDREN: THE INFLUENCE OF SOCIOECONOMIC STATUS AND TASK STRUCTURE ON TEACHING SPECIFICITY EJ 019 414
TWO MODES OF MATERNAL IMMATURITY AND THEIR CONSEQUENCES EJ 023 424
HARMONIOUS PARENTS AND THEIR PRESCHOOL CHILDREN EJ 034 708
FATHER ABSENCE, PERCEIVED MATERNAL BEHAVIOR, AND MASCULINITY OF SELF-CONCEPT AMONG JUNIOR HIGH SCHOOL BOYS EJ 035 804
SELF-ESTEEM, PARENT IDENTIFICATION AND SEX ROLE DEVELOPMENT IN PRESCHOOL AGE BOYS AND GIRLS EJ 051 015
PARENTS AS EDUCATORS: EVIDENCE FROM CROSS-SECTIONAL, LONGITUDINAL AND INTERVENTION RESEARCH EJ 056 608
RELATIONSHIPS BETWEEN INFANTS' SOCIAL BEHAVIOR AND THEIR MOTHERS' BEHAVIOR EJ 058 587
MOTHERS' SPEECH TO CHILDREN LEARNING LANGUAGE EJ 058 696
NEGRO PARENTAL BEHAVIOR AND SOCIAL CLASS VARIABLES EJ 059 871

PARENT PARTICIPATION

HEADSTART OPERATIONAL FIELD ANALYSIS. PROGRESS REPORT I. ED015774
HEADSTART OPERATIONAL FIELD ANALYSIS. PROGRESS REPORT II. ED015775
CO-OPERATIVE NURSERY SCHOOLS--A HANDBOOK FOR PARENTS. A GUIDE FOR ORGANIZATION AND ADMINISTRATION. REVISED EDITION. ED020022
MAKING WAVES, DENVER HEAD START. ED020802
THE YPSILANTI EARLY EDUCATION PROGRAM. ED022531
HEAD START EVALUATION AND RESEARCH CENTER, BOSTON UNIVERSITY. REPORT E-I, THE UTILIZATION OF NON-PROFESSIONAL INTERVIEWERS IN THE NEW ENGLAND AND MISSISSIPPI SAMPLES BY THE BOSTON UNIVERSITY HEAD START EVALUATION AND RESEARCH PROGRAM, 1966-1967. ED022566

PRESCHOOL PARENT EDUCATION PROGRAM: A CURRICULUM GUIDE FOR USE BY TEACHERS CONDUCTING PARENT EDUCATION PROGRAMS AS A PART OF OVER-ALL COMPENSATORY PRESCHOOL PROJECTS. EXPERIMENTAL EDITION. ED026118
A CURRICULUM OF TRAINING FOR PARENT PARTICIPATION IN PROJECT HEAD START. ED026144
CURRICULUM GUIDE FOR CHILDREN'S ACTIVITIES, PARENT PRESCHOOL PROGRAM. ED027078
CHANGING PARENT ATTITUDES AND IMPROVING LANGUAGE AND INTELLECTUAL ABILITIES OF CULTURALLY DISADVANTAGED FOUR-YEAR-OLD CHILDREN THROUGH PARENT INVOLVEMENT. ED027942
LANGUAGE STYLE OF THE LOWER CLASS MOTHER: A PRELIMINARY STUDY OF A THERAPEUTIC TECHNIQUE. ED027943
A SOURCE REPORT FOR DEVELOPING PARENT-CHILD EDUCATIONAL CENTERS. ED027944
A PLAN OF ACTION FOR PARENT-CHILD EDUCATIONAL CENTERS. ED027959
POINTERS FOR PARTICIPATING PARENTS. ED028825
ATTITUDES, EXPECTATIONS, AND BEHAVIOR OF PARENTS OF HEAD START AND NON-HEAD START CHILDREN. REPORT NUMBER 1. ED030475
[THE JUNIPER GARDENS PARENT COOPERATIVE NURSERY.] FINAL PROGRESS REPORT FOR OEO CAP GRANT CG-8474 A/O. ED032920
PRELUDE TO SCHOOL: AN EVALUATION OF AN INNER-CITY PRESCHOOL PROGRAM. ED033750
FOCUS ON PARENT EDUCATION AS A MEANS OF ALTERING THE CHILD'S ENVIRONMENT. ED033758
PLANNING PARENT-IMPLEMENTED PROGRAMS: A GUIDE FOR PARENTS, SCHOOLS AND COMMUNITIES. ED036322
RESEARCH AND CONSULTATION IN THE NATURAL ENVIRONMENT. ED037240
THE INFLUENCE OF TWO COUNSELING METHODS ON THE PHYSICAL AND VERBAL AGGRESSION OF PRESCHOOL INDIAN CHILDREN. PART OF THE FINAL REPORT ON HEAD START EVALUATION AND RESEARCH: 1968-69 TO THE OFFICE OF ECONOMIC OPPORTUNITY. ED037243
PARENT INVOLVEMENT IN PROJECT HEAD START. PART OF THE FINAL REPORT ON HEAD START EVALUATION AND RESEARCH: 1968-1969 TO THE OFFICE OF ECONOMIC OPPORTUNITY. ED037244
EARLY CHILD STIMULATION THROUGH PARENT EDUCATION. ED038166
EDUCATIONAL INTERVENTION AT HOME BY MOTHERS OF DISADVANTAGED INFANTS. ED039944
PARENT INVOLVEMENT IN COMPENSATORY EDUCATION. ED039954
A FEASIBILITY STUDY OF PARENT AWARENESS PROGRAMS. FINAL REPORT. ED040742
[A STATEMENT REGARDING THE COMPREHENSIVE PRESCHOOL EDUCATION AND CHILD DAY CARE ACT OF 1969, AND OTHER RELATED BILLS.] ED041624
HAWAII HEAD START EVALUATION--1968-69. FINAL REPORT. ED042511
EARLY CHILDHOOD EDUCATION LEARNING SYSTEM FOR THREE-AND FOUR-YEAR-OLD MIGRANT CHILDREN, MCALLEN, TEXAS. EVALUATION REPORT, 1968-1969. ED043370
PARENTS AS PRIMARY CHANGE AGENTS IN AN EXPERIMENTAL HEAD START PROGRAM OF LANGUAGE INTERVENTION. EXPERIMENTAL PROGRAM REPORT. ED044168
EVALUATION OF A PARENT AND CHILD CENTER PROGRAM. ED045189
EDUCATIONAL INTERVENTION IN THE HOME AND PARAPROFESSIONAL CAREER DEVELOPMENT: A FIRST GENERATION MOTHER STUDY. ED045190
AN ASSESSMENT OF COGNITIVE GROWTH IN CHILDREN WHO HAVE PARTICIPATED IN THE TOY-LENDING COMPONENT OF THE PARENT-CHILD PROGRAM. ED045204
AN EVALUATION OF NINE TOYS AND ACCOMPANYING LEARNING EPISODES IN THE RESPONSIVE MODEL PARENT/CHILD COMPONENT. ED045205
OVERVIEW OF RESPONSIVE MODEL PROGRAM. ED045207
CROSS-CULTURAL FAMILY CENTER, SAN FRANCISCO, CALIFORNIA: A NURSERY SCHOOL PROVIDING A MULTICULTURAL CURRICULUM TO PROMOTE RACIAL UNDERSTANDING AND ACCEPTANCE. MODEL PROGRAMS--CHILDHOOD EDUCATION. ED045214
COMMUNITY COOPERATIVE NURSERY SCHOOL, MENLO PARK, CALIFORNIA: A PRESCHOOL PROGRAM INVOLVING MOTHERS AS ORGANIZERS, HELPERS, AND DECISION-MAKERS. MODEL PROGRAMS--CHILDHOOD EDUCATION. ED045222
A GUIDE FOR MANAGERS OF CHILD DAY CARE AGENCIES. ED046486
PRESCHOOL EDUCATION AND POVERTY: THE DISTANCE IN BETWEEN. FINAL REPORT OF 1968-69 INTERVENTIONAL PROGRAM. ED046501
PROGRAMS OF HEAD START PARENT INVOLVEMENT IN HAWAII. A SECTION OF THE FINAL REPORT FOR 1969-70. ED048935
INCREASING THE EFFECTIVENESS OF PARENTS-AS-TEACHERS. ED048939
THE NEW YORK STATE EXPERIMENTAL PREKINDERGARTEN PROGRAM. SUMMARY REPORT, 1969-70. ED049814
PARENTS: ACTIVE PARTNERS IN EDUCATION. A STUDY/ACTION PUBLICATION. ED050823
A STUDY IN CHILD CARE (CASE STUDY FROM VOLUME II-A): "GOOD VIBES." DAY CARE PROGRAMS REPRINT SERIES. ED051894
A STUDY IN CHILD CARE (CASE STUDY FROM VOLUME II-A): "LIKE BEING AT HOME." DAY CARE PROGRAMS REPRINT SERIES. ED051899
A STUDY IN CHILD CARE (CASE STUDY FROM VOLUME II-A): "A SMALL U. N." DAY CARE PROGRAMS REPRINT SERIES. ED051904
THREE DEGREES OF PARENT INVOLVEMENT IN A PRESCHOOL PROGRAM: IMPACT ON MOTHERS AND CHILDREN. ED052831
A STUDY IN THE UTILIZATION OF TECHNOLOGICALLY ADVANCED TECHNIQUES FOR TEACHER-PARENT-CHILD ASSESSMENT. FINAL REPORT. ED053818
INVOLVING PARENTS IN THEIR CHILDREN'S DAY-CARE EXPERIENCES EJ 007 451
HEAD START IN ALASKA EJ 008 273
LANGUAGE LEARNING AT ROUGH ROCK EJ 011 874
PARENTS TEACH KINDERGARTEN READING AT HOME EJ 020 774
A PRESCHOOL EXCHANGE: BLACK MOTHERS SPEAK AND A WHITE TEACHER LISTENS EJ 022 137
HEAD START'S INFLUENCE ON COMMUNITY CHANGE EJ 026 773
REUNITING CHILDREN AND PARENTS THROUGH CASEWORK AND GROUP WORK EJ 027 342
A PLAN FOR PROTECTION: THE CHILD-ABUSE CENTER EJ 027 917
INVOLVING PARENTS IN CHILDREN'S LEARNING EJ 028 845
TERMINATION OF RESIDENTIAL TREATMENT OF CHILDREN EJ 029 102
PARENT AND CHILD CENTERS--IMPETUS, IMPLEMENTATION, IN-DEPTH VIEW EJ 030 469
PARENTS: SUMMER READING TEACHERS EJ 032 510
SUB-PROFESSIONAL BEHAVIOR MODIFICATION AND THE DEVELOPMENT OF TOKEN-REINFORCEMENT SYSTEMS IN INCREASING ACADEMIC MOTIVATION AND ACHIEVEMENT EJ 034 527
FAMILY TREATMENT WITHIN THE MILIEU OF A RESIDENTIAL TREATMENT CENTER EJ 037 236
ETHICAL ISSUES IN RESEARCH IN EARLY CHILDHOOD INTERVENTION EJ 037 578
PSYCHOLOGICAL CONSULTATION IN A PRESCHOOL EJ 038 394
A MOTHERS' TRAINING PROGRAM--THE ROAD TO A PURPOSEFUL EXISTENCE EJ 044 007
INVOLVING PARENTS IN RESIDENTIAL TREATMENT OF CHILDREN EJ 045 233
INVOLVING PARENTS IN A CHILDREN'S CLINIC EJ 047 353
TEACHERS AND PARENTS: CHANGING ROLES AND GOALS EJ 055 362
EVALUATION OF A PARENT AND CHILD CENTER PROGRAM EJ 056 569

PARENT REACTION

A THEORY OF PARENT EFFECTIVENESS. ED028815
BEFORE SCHOOL STARTS. FOR CHILDREN'S MINDS--NOT JUST TO MIND THE CHILDREN. THE CHILD CENTRE--AS SEEN BY A PARENT. ED051873
RECIPES FOR MOM EJ 018 131
PARENTS OF CHILDREN WITH PKU EJ 060 522

PARENT RESPONSIBILITY

THE NURSERY YEARS: THE MIND OF THE CHILD FROM BIRTH TO SIX YEARS. ED029711
COMMUNITY COOPERATIVE NURSERY SCHOOL, MENLO PARK, CALIFORNIA: A PRESCHOOL PROGRAM INVOLVING MOTHERS AS ORGANIZERS, HELPERS, AND DECISION-MAKERS. MODEL PROGRAMS--CHILDHOOD EDUCATION. ED045222

PARENT ROLE

A PARENT EDUCATION APPROACH TO PROVISION OF EARLY STIMULATION FOR THE CULTURALLY DISADVANTAGED. FINAL REPORT. ED017339
HOW TO HELP YOUR CHILD LEARN, A HANDBOOK FOR PARENTS OF CHILDREN IN KINDERGARTEN THROUGH GRADE 6. ED017342
THE COGNITIVE ENVIRONMENTS OF URBAN PRE-SCHOOL CHILDREN. MANUAL OF INSTRUCTIONS FOR ADMINISTERING AND SCORING MOTHER'S ROLE IN TEACHER/CHILD AND CHILD/PEER SCHOOL SITUATIONS. ED018257
REACHING THE HARD-TO-REACH: THE USE OF PARTICIPANT GROUP METHODS WITH MOTHERS OF CULTURALLY DISADVANTAGED PRESCHOOL CHILDREN. ED024469
THE MAGIC YEARS: UNDERSTANDING AND HANDLING THE PROBLEMS OF EARLY CHILDHOOD. ED029712
ON CLASS DIFFERENCES AND EARLY DEVELOPMENT. ED044167
AN EVALUATION OF NINE TOYS AND ACCOMPANYING LEARNING EPISODES IN THE RESPONSIVE MODEL PARENT/CHILD COMPONENT. ED045205
COMO CONTESTAN LOS PADRES LAS PREGUNTAS DE SUS NINOS? (HOW DO PARENTS RESPOND TO CHILDREN'S QUESTIONS?) EJ 011 843
THE PARENTAL ROLE, A FUNCTIONAL-COGNITIVE APPROACH EJ 013 946
A PARENT'S GIFT EJ 016 773
CONSCIENCE, PERSONALITY, AND SOCIALIZATION TECHNIQUES EJ 023 858
COMBATTING RETARDATION IN INFANTS WITH DOWN'S SYNDROME EJ 026 640
TERMINATION OF RESIDENTIAL TREATMENT OF CHILDREN EJ 029 102
INVISIBLE FACTORS IN A CHILD'S REACTION TO TELEVISION EJ 032 934
ATTITUDES OF PRESCHOOL AND ELEMENTARY SCHOOL CHILDREN TO AUTHORITY FIGURES EJ 034 452
THE USE OF DEVELOPMENTAL PLANS FOR MENTALLY RETARDED CHILDREN IN FOSTER FAMILY CARE EJ 035 803
CHANGES IN PARENTAL BEHAVIOR REPORTED BY CHILDREN IN WEST GERMANY AND THE UNITED STATES EJ 048 397
FAMILIES WITHOUT FATHERS EJ 049 656
SOME THOUGHTS ON COMMUNAL CHILDREARING EJ 049 658

SYMPOSIUM ON PARENT-CENTERED EDUCATION: 1. THE CHILD'S FIRST TEACHER EJ 054 377
CLARIFYING THE ROLE OF FOSTER PARENTS EJ 061 235

PARENT SCHOOL RELATIONSHIP
A TRAINING PROGRAM FOR MOTHERS. ED017334
PARENTS: ACTIVE PARTNERS IN EDUCATION. A STUDY/ACTION PUBLICATION. ED050823
SPECIAL CONSIDERATIONS IN THE OPERATION OF A HEAD START PROGRAM BY A COMMUNITY CHILD GUIDANCE CLINIC EJ 023 704
INVOLVING PARENTS IN CHILDREN'S LEARNING EJ 028 845
SOME ANGLES ON PARENT-TEACHER LEARNING EJ 054 162
TEACHERS AND PARENTS: CHANGING ROLES AND GOALS EJ 055 362
LISTENING BEYOND WORDS: LEARNING FROM PARENTS IN CONFERENCES EJ 055 363

PARENT STUDENT RELATIONSHIP
EXTRA-CURRICULAR PARENT-CHILD CONTACT AND CHILDREN'S SOCIALLY REINFORCED TASK BEHAVIOR. ED023447

PARENT TEACHER CONFERENCES
THE COGNITIVE ENVIRONMENTS OF URBAN PRE-SCHOOL CHILDREN. MANUAL OF INSTRUCTIONS FOR ADMINISTERING AND SCORING MOTHER-TEACHER PICTURE. ED018259
A STUDY IN THE UTILIZATION OF TECHNOLOGICALLY ADVANCED TECHNIQUES FOR TEACHER-PARENT-CHILD ASSESSMENT. FINAL REPORT. ED053818

PARENT TEACHER COOPERATION
PRESCHOOL INTERVENTION--A PRELIMINARY REPORT OF THE PERRY PRESCHOOL PROJECT. ED018251
APPLICATION OF GROUP DYNAMICS PROCEDURES TO PROMOTE COMMUNICATION AMONG PARENTS AND TEACHERS. ED042512
PARENTS: ACTIVE PARTNERS IN EDUCATION. A STUDY/ACTION PUBLICATION. ED050823
WHAT MOTHERS NEED EJ 013 233
TEACHER-PARENT WORK IN THE HOME: AN ASPECT OF CHILD GUIDANCE CLINIC SERVICES EJ 027 448
INVOLVING PARENTS IN CHILDREN'S LEARNING EJ 028 845
SYMPOSIUM ON PARENT-CENTERED EDUCATION: 3. LEARNING THROUGH PARENTS: LESSONS FOR TEACHERS EJ 054 379
TEACHERS AND PARENTS: CHANGING ROLES AND GOALS EJ 055 362

PARENT WORKSHOPS
EVALUATION OF THE PRESCHOOL CHILD AND PARENT EDUCATION PROJECT AS EXPANDED THROUGH THE USE OF ELEMENTARY AND SECONDARY EDUCATION ACT, TITLE I, FUNDS. ED021621
REACHING THE HARD-TO-REACH: THE USE OF PARTICIPANT GROUP METHODS WITH MOTHERS OF CULTURALLY DISADVANTAGED PRESCHOOL CHILDREN. ED024469

PARENTAL ASPIRATION
A STUDY OF FAMILY INFLUENCES ON THE EDUCATION OF NEGRO LOWER-CLASS CHILDREN. PROJECT I. ED025309
SOCIAL CLASS AND PARENT'S ASPIRATIONS FOR THEIR CHILDREN. REPORT NUMBER 8. ED030482
SOCIAL CLASS AND PARENTS' ASPIRATIONS FOR THEIR CHILDREN. RESEARCH REPORT NO. 3 (REVISED). ED043371

PARENTAL BACKGROUND
THE EFFECTS OF JUNIOR KINDERGARTEN ON ACHIEVEMENT--THE FIRST FIVE YEARS. APPENDIX. ED016527
THE CHILDCARE ATTITUDES OF TWO GENERATIONS OF MOTHERS EJ 032 796
PARENTAL EDUCATION, SEX DIFFERENCES, AND PERFORMANCE ON COGNITIVE TASKS AMONG TWO-YEAR-OLD CHILDREN EJ 035 364

PARENTS
APPENDIX, STUDIES I, II AND III. ORIGINAL INSTRUMENTS USED AND BIBLIOGRAPHY. ED015028
A DIGEST OF THE RESEARCH ACTIVITIES OF REGIONAL EVALUATION AND RESEARCH CENTERS FOR PROJECT HEAD START (SEPTEMBER 1, 1966 TO NOVEMBER 30, 1967). ED023446
FAMILIES OF CHILDREN IN FOSTER CARE EJ 007 452
ATTITUDE OF BLACK NATURAL PARENTS REGARDING ADOPTION EJ 038 792
PARENTHOOD: SOME ANTECEDENTS AND CONSEQUENCES: A PRELIMINARY SURVEY OF THE MENTAL HEALTH LITERATURE EJ 041 342

PAROCHIAL SCHOOLS
ATTITUDINAL STUDY OF ROMAN CATHOLIC PARENTS OF PRE-SCHOOL CHILDREN REGARDING THE OPTION OF "CATHOLIC" OR PUBLIC SCHOOL EDUCATION FOR THEIR CHILDREN. ED046488

PARTICIPANT CHARACTERISTICS
A STUDY OF SOME ECOLOGICAL, ECONOMIC AND SOCIAL FACTORS INFLUENCING PARENTAL PARTICIPATION IN PROJECT HEAD START. ED014331
PROJECT HEAD START--SUMMER 1966. FINAL REPORT. SECTION ONE, SOME CHARACTERISTICS OF CHILDREN IN THE HEAD START PROGRAM. ED018246
RESULTS OF THE SUMMER 1965 PROJECT HEAD START. VOLUMES I AND II. ED018250
HEAD START PROGRAMS AND PARTICIPANTS 1965-1967. ED034569
DISCRIMINATING CHARACTERISTICS OF FAMILIES WATCHING SESAME STREET. EARLY DEVELOPMENTAL ADVERSITY PROGRAM: PHASE III, EDAP TECHNICAL NOTE 15.1. ED039943
PROJECT HEAD START 1968: A DESCRIPTIVE REPORT OF PROGRAMS AND PARTICIPANTS. ED047816

PARTICIPANT INVOLVEMENT
COMMENTS ON SOCIAL DESIRABILITY AND PERSUASION EJ 025 803

PATIENTS (PERSONS)
THE RELIABILITY OF RATING SCALES FOR ASSESSING THE BEHAVIOUR OF DISTURBED CHILDREN IN A RESIDENTIAL UNIT EJ 051 153

PATTERN DRILLS (LANGUAGE)
ESOL-SESD GUIDE: KINDERGARTEN. ED033748

PATTERN RECOGNITION
SENSORY-MODALITY EFFECTS ON SHAPE PERCEPTION IN PRESCHOOL CHILDREN EJ 029 383
HOW ADULTS AND CHILDREN SEARCH AND RECOGNIZE PICTURES EJ 029 384
TACTILE IDENTIFICATION OF LETTERS: A COMPARISON OF DEAF AND HEARING CHILDRENS' PERFORMANCES EJ 034 567
MEASURES OF FORM CONSTANCY: DEVELOPMENTAL TRENDS EJ 034 611
OPERANT LEARNING OF VISUAL PATTERN DISCRIMINATION IN YOUNG INFANTS EJ 035 623
DEVELOPMENTAL GENERALITY OF A FORM RECOGNITION STRATEGY EJ 037 534
EFFECT OF INCENTIVES AND AGE ON THE VISUAL RECOGNITION OF RETARDED READERS EJ 037 535
LABELING AND IMAGING AS AIDS TO MEMORY EJ 041 143
JUDGING OUTLINE FACES: A DEVELOPMENTAL STUDY EJ 045 599
MATCHING AUDITORY AND VISUAL SERIES: MODALITY PROBLEM OR TRANSLATION PROBLEM? EJ 051 569
THE DEVELOPMENT OF MEMORY-ENCODING PROCESSES IN YOUNG CHILDREN EJ 053 716
EFFECTS OF HEBREW AND ENGLISH LETTERS ON CHILDREN'S PERCEPTUAL SET EJ 053 721
PERCEPTION OF RHYTHM BY SUBJECTS WITH NORMAL AND DEFICIENT HEARING EJ 060 502

PATTERNED RESPONSES
FAKABILITY OF SCORES ON THE GROUP PERSONALITY PROJECTIVE TEST EJ 030 792

PECEPTION
EFFECTS OF HEBREW AND ENGLISH LETTERS ON CHILDREN'S PERCEPTUAL SET EJ 053 721

PEER ACCEPTANCE
FAMILY BACKGROUND EFFECTS ON PERSONALITY DEVELOPMENT AND SOCIAL ACCEPTANCE. ED020020
CONFORMITY IN EARLY AND LATE ADOLESCENCE EJ 038 936
MODIFICATION OF PEER PREFERENCE OF FIRST-GRADE CHILDREN EJ 039 987
SOME SOCIAL EFFECTS OF CROSS-GRADE GROUPING EJ 055 107

PEER GROUP DENTIFICATION (PSYCHOLOGICAL)
CONFORMITY IN CHILDREN AS A FUNCTION OF GRADE LEVEL, AND REAL VERSUS HYPOTHETICAL ADULT AND PEER MODELS EJ 040 294

PEER GROUPS
COOPERATIVE, TRUSTING BEHAVIOR AS A FUNCTION OF ETHNIC GROUP SIMILARITY-DISSIMILARITY AND OF IMMEDIATE AND DELAYED REWARD IN A TWO-PERSON GAME. PART OF THE FINAL REPORT. ED025322
THE EFFECT OF FOUR COMMUNICATION PATTERNS AND SEX ON LENGTH OF VERBALIZATION IN SPEECH OF FOUR YEAR OLD CHILDREN. FINAL REPORT. ED042514
SOCIOECONOMIC STATUS AND SEX DIFFERENCES IN ADOLESCENT REFERENCE-GROUP ORIENTATION EJ 023 614
MASCULINITY AND FEMININITY IN THE ELEMENTARY AND JUNIOR HIGH SCHOOL YEARS EJ 034 902
CONFORMITY IN CHILDREN AS A FUNCTION OF GRADE LEVEL, AND REAL VERSUS HYPOTHETICAL ADULT AND PEER MODELS EJ 040 294
THE EFFECTS OF DIFFERENT COMPETITIVE CONTINGENCIES ON COOPERATIVE BEHAVIOR EJ 042 208

PEER RELATIONSHIP
POSITIVE SOCIAL REINFORCEMENT IN THE NURSERY SCHOOL PEER GROUP. ED016515
HEAD START EVALUATION AND RESEARCH CENTER, UNIVERSITY OF KANSAS. REPORT NO. V, A COMPARATIVE BEHAVIORAL ANALYSIS OF PEER-GROUP INFLUENCE TECHNIQUES IN HEAD START AND MIDDLE CLASS POPULATIONS. ED021638
PROJECT HEAD START RESEARCH AND EVALUATION CENTER, SYRACUSE UNIVERSITY, RESEARCH INSTITUTE. FINAL REPORT. ED030486
THE DEVELOPMENT OF EARLY SOCIAL INTERACTION--AN ETHOLOGICAL APPROACH. ED031291
PUPIL IMITATION OF A REWARDING TEACHER'S VERBAL BEHAVIOR. ED038185
BEHAVIOR MODIFICATION PROCEDURES APPLIED TO THE ISOLATE BEHAVIOR OF A NURSERY SCHOOL CHILD. ED041635
SOCIAL FACILITATION OF HEAD START PERFORMANCE. PROGRESS REPORT. ED042493

FACTORS? IN CHILD DEVELOPMENT: PEER RELATIONS. ED047796
CLARIFYING FEELINGS THROUGH PEER INTERACTION EJ 003 083
NEED FOR APPROVAL, CHILDREN'S SHARING BEHAVIOR, AND RECIPROCITY IN SHARING EJ 018 321
CHANGES IN FRIENDSHIP STATUS AS A FUNCTION OF REINFORCEMENT EJ 019 004
PARENTAL DETERMINANTS OF PEER-ORIENTATION AND SELF-ORIENTATION AMONG PREADOLESCENTS EJ 019 387
THE RELATIONSHIP BETWEEN CONTROLLED PROJECTION RESPONSES AND SOCIOMETRIC STATUS EJ 031 541
CLASSROOM BEHAVIOR: MESSAGES FROM CHILDREN EJ 031 780
UN EXEMPLE D'OBSERVATION INTENSIVE DU COMPORTEMENT DE JEUNES ENFANTS DANS LE CADRE D'UNE GARDERIE EJ 034 534
SEX DIFFERENCES IN ADOLESCENT REACTIONS TOWARD NEWCOMERS EJ 039 899
MODIFICATION OF PEER PREFERENCE OF FIRST-GRADE CHILDREN EJ 039 987
CHILDREN'S DESCRIPTIONS OF PEERS: A WERNERIAN DEVELOPMENTAL ANALYSIS EJ 041 591
SOCIAL COMPARISON BY YOUNG CHILDREN EJ 043 672
TAKING ANOTHER'S PERSPECTIVE: ROLE-TAKING DEVELOPMENT IN EARLY CHILDHOOD EJ 056 610
PEER INTERACTION AND COGNITIVE DEVELOPMENT EJ 056 708

PEER TEACHING

TEACHING STYLES IN FOUR-YEAR-OLDS. ED036340
FOR BETTER READING - A MORE POSITIVE SELF-IMAGE EJ 013 562
PEER TUTORING AS A TECHNIQUE FOR TEACHING THE UNMOTIVATED EJ 045 393

PERCEPTION

VARIABLES AFFECTING THE PERFORMANCE OF YOUNG CHILDREN ON A LETTER DISCRIMINATION TASK. ED020797
AN OVERVIEW OF RESEARCH IN LEARNING, MOTIVATION, AND PERCEPTION. ED020799
HEAD START EVALUATION AND RESEARCH CENTER, BOSTON UNIVERSITY. REPORT D-II, TRAINING FOR NUMBER CONCEPT. ED022564
CHILDREN'S CONSERVATION OF MULTIPLE SPACE RELATIONS: EFFECTS OF PERCEPTION AND REPRESENTATION. ED044179
A STUDY OF THE DEVELOPMENT OF EGOCENTRISM AND THE COORDINATION OF SPATIAL PERCEPTIONS IN ELEMENTARY SCHOOL CHILDREN. FINAL REPORT. ED050829
SOME BASIC PERCEPTUAL PROCESSES IN READING EJ 015 126
EARLY RECOLLECTIONS AND THE PERCEPTION OF OTHERS: A STUDY OF DELINQUENT ADOLESCENTS EJ 022 477
ONTOGENY OF THE LOCUS AND ORIENTATION OF THE PERCEIVER: A CONFIRMATION AND AN ADDITION EJ 023 433
SHORT-TERM MEMORY FOR VISUAL INFORMATION IN CHILDREN AND ADULTS EJ 024 700
CHILDREN'S SENSITIVITY TO PAINTING STYLES EJ 025 304
SOME RELATIONSHIPS AMONG CHILDREN'S PERCEPTIONS OF PARENTAL CHARACTERISTICS EJ 025 318
MEASURES OF FORM CONSTANCY: DEVELOPMENTAL TRENDS EJ 034 611
DISADVANTAGED AND NONDISADVANTAGED CHILDREN'S EXPECTANCY IN SKILL AND CHANCE OUTCOMES EJ 034 903
EFFECT OF INSTRUCTIONAL SET ON TWELVE-YEAR-OLD CHILDREN'S PERCEPTION OF INTERRUPTION EJ 034 921
MEDIATION AND PERCEPTUAL TRANSFER IN CHILDREN EJ 035 365
A THIRD STUDY OF PERCEPTUAL BEHAVIOR IN SIXTH GRADE CHILDREN IN RELATION TO THEIR BEHAVIOR IN ART EJ 041 830
INTERPERSONAL PERCEPTION OF YOUNG CHILDREN: EGOCENTRISM OR EMPATHY? EJ 043 606
AGE, SEX, RACE, AND THE PERCEPTION OF FACIAL BEAUTY EJ 046 783
STIMULUS PREFERENCE AND MULTIPLICATIVE CLASSIFICATION IN CHILDREN EJ 047 686
MEANING CONDITIONING AND AWARENESS AMONG CHILDREN EJ 049 426
AN EXAMINATION OF THE DEVELOPMENTAL RELATIONS BETWEEN CERTAIN SPATIAL TASKS EJ 051 563
EFFECTS OF TYPE AND SOURCE OF LABELS ON CHILDREN'S PERCEPTUAL JUDGMENTS AND DISCRIMINATION LEARNING EJ 053 756
PERCEPTUAL INADEQUACY AND COMMUNICATIVE INEFFECTIVENESS IN INTERPERSONAL COMMUNICATION EJ 056 627
A DEVELOPMENTAL STUDY OF THE EFFECTS OF PRETRAINING ON A PERCEPTUAL RECOGNITION TASK EJ 056 630
WINDOW BEGINS WITH AN "L" EJ 058 507
PERCEPTION AND LANGUAGE: A GERMAN REPLICATION OF THE PIAGET-INHELDER POSITION EJ 060 773
THE DEVELOPMENT OF THE LANGUAGE OF EMOTIONS: I. THEORETICAL AND METHODOLOGICAL INTRODUCTION EJ 061 059
PHENOMENAL ENVIRONMENTAL OPPRESSIVENESS IN SUICIDAL ADOLESCENTS EJ 061 063

PERCEPTION TESTS

THE JOHNS HOPKINS PERCEPTUAL TEST, THE DEVELOPMENT OF A RAPID INTELLIGENCE TEST FOR THE PRE-SCHOOL CHILD. ED020787
PERCEPTUAL TESTING AND TRAINING METHODS USED IN THE PRIMARY GRADES. ED027971
SOME DIMENSIONS OF CREATIVE THINKING ABILITY ACHIEVEMENT, AND INTELLIGENCE IN FIRST GRADE. ED028818
GROUP SCREENING OF AUDITORY AND VISUAL PERCEPTUAL ABILITIES: AN APPROACH TO PERCEPTUAL ASPECTS OF BEGINNING READING. ED033751
GENETIC FACTORS IN TESTS OF PERCEPTION AND THE RORSCHACH EJ 045 045
A PERCEPTUAL TEST BATTERY: DEVELOPMENT AND STANDARDIZATION EJ 058 395

PERCEPTUAL DEVELOPMENT

METHODOLOGICAL ISSUES IN THE STUDY OF AGE DIFFERENCES IN INFANTS' ATTENTION TO STIMULI VARYING IN MOVEMENT AND COMPLEXITY. ED023477
INFORMAL EDUCATION DURING THE FIRST MONTHS OF LIFE. ED024452
PERCEPTUAL-COGNITIVE DEVELOPMENT IN INFANCY: A GENERALIZED EXPECTANCY MODEL AS A FUNCTION OF THE MOTHER-INFANT INTERACTION. ED024470
VISUAL LEARNING. DIMENSIONS IN EARLY LEARNING SERIES. ED027089
PERCEPTUAL TESTING AND TRAINING METHODS USED IN THE PRIMARY GRADES. ED027971
VISION TRAINING - A NEW DEVELOPMENTAL CONCEPT IN CHILD VISION. ED028842
INDIVIDUALIZED MOTOR-PERCEPTUAL STUDY. ED029692
RELATION OF SPATIAL EGOCENTRISM AND SPATIAL ABILITIES OF THE YOUNG CHILD. REPORT NUMBER 7. ED030481
OPTOMETRIC CHILD VISION CARE AND GUIDANCE. A SERIES OF PAPERS RELEASED BY THE OPTOMETRIC EXTENSION PROGRAM TO ITS MEMBERSHIP 1966-1967. ED032111
VISUAL SCANNING BY HUMAN NEWBORNS: RESPONSES TO COMPLETE TRIANGLE, TO SIDES ONLY, AND TO CORNERS ONLY. ED035439
THE RELATION OF CONCEPTUAL STYLES AND MODE OF PERCEPTION TO GRAPHIC EXPRESSION. ED040743
THE EFFECT OF A PERCEPTUAL-MOTOR TRAINING PROGRAM UPON THE READINESS AND PERCEPTUAL DEVELOPMENT OF CULTURALLY DISADVANTAGED KINDERGARTEN CHILDREN. ED041633
CHILDREN'S ACQUISITION OF VISUO-SPATIAL DIMENSIONALITY: A CONSERVATION STUDY. ED041636
CHILDREN'S JUDGMENTS OF AGE. ED043392
A SUCCESSFUL ATTEMPT TO TRAIN CHILDREN IN COORDINATION OF PROJECTIVE SPACE. ED048916
LANGUAGE ACQUISITION AND COGNITIVE DEVELOPMENT. ED049811
PERCEPTUAL-COGNITIVE DEVELOPMENT IN INFANCY: A GENERALIZED EXPECTANCY MODEL AS A FUNCTION OF THE MOTHER-INFANT INTERACTION EJ 003 553
THE DISCRIMINABILITY OF FORM AMONG YOUNG CHILDREN EJ 016 164
A THIRD STUDY OF SOME RELATIONSHIPS BETWEEN CREATIVITY AND PERCEPTION IN 6TH GRADE CHILDREN EJ 016 166
PROJECTIVE VISUAL IMAGERY AS A FUNCTION OF AGE AND DEAFNESS EJ 018 877
EFFECT OF VERBAL RESPONSE CLASS ON SHIFT IN THE PRESCHOOL CHILD'S JUDGMENT OF LENGTH IN RESPONSE TO AN ANCHOR STIMULUS EJ 019 012
SENSORY ORGANIZATION IN RETARDATES AND NORMALS EJ 019 013
INDIVIDUAL DIFFERENCES IN THE INFANT'S DISTRIBUTION OF ATTENTION TO STIMULUS DISCREPANCY EJ 019 014
PROBLEM SOLVING AND THE PERCEPTUAL SALIENCE OF VARIABILITY AND CONSTANCY: A DEVELOPMENTAL STUDY EJ 021 755
A COMPARISON OF RETARDATES AND NORMALS ON THE POGGENDORFF AND OPPEL-KUNDT ILLUSIONS EJ 024 943
AWARENESS--ONE KEY TO READING READINESS EJ 027 551
DEVELOPMENTAL DIFFERENCES IN THE INTEGRATION OF PICTURE SERIES: EFFECTS OF VARIATIONS IN OBJECT-ATTRIBUTE RELATIONSHIPS EJ 029 386
SEQUENCE EFFECTS IN THE ABSTRACTION OF THE CONCEPT OF PROGRESSIVE CHANGE EJ 029 532
PERCEPTUAL EXPLORATION IN ISRAELI CHILDREN EJ 033 054
STIMULUS CORRELATES OF AREA JUDGMENTS: A PSYCHOPHYSICAL DEVELOPMENTAL STUDY EJ 034 707
SOME RELATIONSHIPS BETWEEN VERBAL AND PERCEPTUAL CAPABILITIES AND THE DEVELOPMENT OF RELATIVE THINKING EJ 035 383
COGNITIVE-PERCEPTUAL DEVELOPMENT IN INFANCY: SETTING FOR THE SEVENTIES EJ 038 262
SOME RELATIONSHIPS BETWEEN CLASS INCLUSION, PERCEPTUAL CAPABILITIES, VERBAL CAPABILITIES AND RACE EJ 039 639
A DEVELOPMENTAL STUDY OF SIZE CONSTANCY FOR TWO-VERSUS THREE-DIMENSIONAL STIMULI EJ 040 454
METHODOLOGICAL STUDY OF FORM CONSTANCY DEVELOPMENT EJ 043 706
CONSONANT CUE PERCEPTION BY TWENTY- TO TWENTY-FOUR-WEEK-OLD INFANTS EJ 045 597
ARTISTIC STYLE AS CONCEPT FORMATION FOR CHILDREN AND ADULTS EJ 046 247
EYE MOVEMENTS, PERCEPTUAL ACTIVITY, AND CONSERVATION DEVELOPMENT EJ 046 249
RECOGNITION OF ENGLISH AND HEBREW LETTERS AS A FUNCTION OF AGE AND DISPLAY PREDICTABILITY EJ 047 893
PERCEPTUAL AND LOGICAL FACTORS IN THE DEVELOPMENT OF MULTIPLICATIVE CLASSIFICATION EJ 053 649
DEVELOPMENTAL DIFFERENCES IN THE FIELD OF VIEW DURING TACHISTOSCOPIC PRESENTATION EJ 053 743

COMING OF AGE WITH THE DELBOEUF ILLUSION: BRIGHTNESS CONTRAST, COGNITION AND PERCEPTUAL DEVELOPMENT EJ 055 100
DEVELOPMENT OF HIERARCHIES OF DIMENSIONAL SALIENCE EJ 055 102
A PERCEPTUAL TEST BATTERY: DEVELOPMENT AND STANDARDIZATION EJ 058 395
DEVELOPMENTAL DIFFERENCES IN THE PERCEPTION AND PRODUCTION OF FACIAL EXPRESSIONS EJ 058 693
INFANCY AND THE OPTIMAL LEVEL OF STIMULATION EJ 058 697
VISUAL HABITUATION IN THE HUMAN INFANT EJ 059 511
PERCEPTION OF RHYTHM BY SUBJECTS WITH NORMAL AND DEFICIENT HEARING EJ 060 502
AGE- AND SEX-RELATED VARIATION IN PERFORMANCE ON A FIGURAL-CONCEPTUAL TASK EJ 061 066

PERCEPTUAL MOTOR COORDINATION

THE INITIAL COORDINATION OF SENSORIMOTOR SCHEMAS IN HUMAN INFANTS - PIAGET'S IDEAS AND THE ROLE OF EXPERIENCE. ED016511
INDIVIDUALIZED MOTOR-PERCEPTUAL STUDY. ED029692
MEASURING PERCEPTUAL MOTOR ABILITY IN PRESCHOOL CHILDREN. ED032932
ANALYSIS OF VISUAL PERCEPTION OF CHILDREN IN THE EARLY CHILDHOOD EDUCATION PROGRAM (RESULTS OF THE MARIANNE FROSTIG DEVELOPMENTAL TEST OF VISUAL PERCEPTION). ED052839
COMPARATIVE PERCEPTUAL MOTOR PERFORMANCE OF NEGRO AND WHITE YOUNG MENTAL RETARDATES EJ 019 015
THE OFF-KILTERED KIDS EJ 028 383
PATTERN COPYING UNDER THREE CONDITIONS OF AN EXPANDED SPATIAL FIELD EJ 035 622
COGNITIVE-PERCEPTUAL DEVELOPMENT IN INFANCY: SETTING FOR THE SEVENTIES EJ 038 262

PERCEPTUAL MOTOR LEARNING

A GUIDE FOR PERCEPTUAL-MOTOR TRAINING ACTIVITIES. ED027075
A RATIONALE FOR DEVELOPMENTAL TESTING AND TRAINING. ED028835
A STUDY IN VISUAL-MOTOR-PERCEPTUAL TRAINING IN FIRST GRADE. ED031292
STAGES OF SENSORIMOTOR DEVELOPMENT: A REPLICATION STUDY EJ 011 916
SENSORY ORGANIZATION AND INTELLIGENCE: A MODIFICATION AND REPLICATION EJ 024 946
A TEST OF LURIA'S HYPOTHESES CONCERNING THE DEVELOPMENT OF VERBAL SELF-REGULATION EJ 025 956

PERCEPTUALLY HANDICAPPED

A READING READINESS TRAINING PROGRAM FOR PERCEPTUALLY HANDICAPPED KINDERGARTEN PUPILS OF NORMAL VISION. FINAL REPORT. ED013119
GROUP WORK WITH PARENTS OF CHILDREN WITH LEARNING DISORDERS. ED019130
THE CONCEPT, "PERCEPTUALLY HANDICAPPED," ITS ASSETS AND LIMITATIONS. ED027960
THE OFF-KILTERED KIDS EJ 028 383
TREATMENT OF PROBLEMS ASSOCIATED WITH COGNITIVE AND PERCEPTUAL-MOTOR DEFICITS EJ 060 501

PERFORMANCE

THE PERFORMANCE OF FIRST GRADE CHILDREN IN FOUR LEVELS OF CONSERVATION OF NUMEROUSNESS AND THREE IQ GROUPS WHEN SOLVING ARITHMETIC ADDITION PROBLEMS. ED016535
COMPETENCE VERSUS PERFORMANCE IN YOUNG CHILDREN'S USE OF ADJECTIVAL COMPARATIVES EJ 033 701
LANGUAGE DIALECT, REINFORCEMENT, AND THE INTELLIGENCE-TEST PERFORMANCE OF NEGRO CHILDREN EJ 035 912
NOUN PLURAL DEVELOPMENT IN PRIMARY GRADE CHILDREN EJ 052 179

PERFORMANCE CRITERIA

HEAD START EVALUATION AND RESEARCH CENTER, TEACHERS COLLEGE, COLUMBIA UNIVERSITY. ANNUAL REPORT (1ST), SEPTEMBER 1966-AUGUST 1967. (TITLE SUPPLIED). ED020781
RELIABILITY ASSESSMENT OF OBSERVATION DATA: A POSSIBLE METHODOLOGICAL PROBLEM EJ 033 313

PERFORMANCE FACTORS

LONG-RANGE EFFECT OF PRE-SCHOOLING ON READING ACHIEVEMENT. STUDY III. ED015027
AN EVALUATION AND FOLLOW-UP STUDY OF SUMMER 1966 HEAD START CHILDREN IN WASHINGTON, D.C. ED020794
AGE OF ENTRANCE INTO THE FIRST GRADE AS RELATED TO ARITHMETIC ACHIEVEMENT. ED020801
MEASUREMENT OF MOTIVATION TO ACHIEVE IN PRESCHOOL CHILDREN. FINAL REPORT. ED021617
A COMPARISON OF PRE-KINDERGARTEN AND PRE-1ST GRADE BOYS AND GIRLS ON MEASURES OF SCHOOL READINESS AND LANGUAGE DEVELOPMENT. INTERIM REPORT. ED023474
PROBLEM SOLVING PERFORMANCES OF FIRST GRADE CHILDREN. ED041623
BEHAVIORAL DATA FROM THE TULANE NUTRITION STUDY. ED043375
THE DISTRACTING EFFECTS OF MATERIAL REINFORCERS IN THE DISCRIMINATION LEARNING OF LOWER- AND MIDDLE-CLASS CHILDREN EJ 018 871
THE EFFECT OF ANXIETY OVER INTELLECTUAL PERFORMANCE ON REFLECTION-IMPULSIVITY IN CHILDREN EJ 026 153
DISCRIMINATION SHIFT PERFORMANCE OF KINDERGARTEN CHILDREN AS A FUNCTION OF VARIATION OF THE IRRELEVANT SHIFT DIMENSION EJ 027 183
CHAOTIC REINFORCEMENT: A SOCIOECONOMIC LEVELER EJ 035 371
CUE AND INCENTIVE MOTIVATIONAL PROPERTIES OF REINFORCERS IN CHILDREN'S DISCRIMINATION LEARNING EJ 035 374
VERBAL PARTICIPATION AS A FUNCTION OF THE PRESENCE OF PRIOR INFORMATION CONCERNING APTITUDE EJ 042 348
DISCRIMINATION AND INSTRUCTIONS AS FACTORS IN THE CONTROL OF NONREINFORCED IMITATION EJ 044 157
THE INFLUENCE OF NEGRO AND WHITE TEACHERS RATED AS EFFECTIVE OR NONEFFECTIVE ON THE PERFORMANCE OF NEGRO AND WHITE LOWER-CLASS CHILDREN EJ 045 068
EFFECT OF CLASSROOM NOISE ON NUMBER IDENTIFICATION BY RETARDED CHILDREN EJ 045 793
MOTHERS' TEST OF ANXIETY AND TASK SELECTION AND CHILDREN'S PERFORMANCE WITH MOTHER OR A STRANGER EJ 052 449
TRANSFER OF TRAINING: SOME BOUNDARY CONDITIONS AND INITIAL THEORY EJ 053 722
THE INFLUENCE OF NONINTELLECTIVE FACTORS ON THE IQ SCORES OF MIDDLE- AND LOWER-CLASS CHILDREN EJ 056 621
SOCIAL REINFORCEMENT SATIATION: AN OUTCOME OF FREQUENCY OR AMBIGUITY? EJ 058 144
THE RELATIONSHIP BETWEEN CHILDREN'S ACADEMIC PERFORMANCE AND ACHIEVEMENT ACCOUNTABILITY EJ 058 414
TRAINING COMMUNICATION SKILLS IN YOUNG CHILDREN EJ 058 606
RELATIONSHIPS OF PARENTAL BEHAVIOR TO "DISADVANTAGED" CHILDREN'S INTRINSIC-EXTRINSIC MOTIVATION FOR TASK STRIVING EJ 059 870
PERSONAL ORIENTATION TO SUCCESS AND FAILURE IN URBAN BLACK CHILDREN EJ 061 072
SIMPLE REACTION TIME IN CHILDREN: EFFECTS OF INCENTIVE, INCENTIVE-SHIFT AND OTHER TRAINING VARIABLES EJ 061 075
RACE OF EXPERIMENTER AS A VARIABLE IN RESEARCH WITH CHILDREN EJ 061 085
THE DEVELOPMENT OF THE CONTROL OF ADULT INSTRUCTIONS OVER NONVERBAL BEHAVIOR EJ 061 138

PERFORMANCE TESTS

A STUDY OF THE FULL-YEAR 1966 HEAD START PROGRAMS. ED015010
EFFECT OF VERBALIZATION ON YOUNG CHILDREN'S LEARNING OF A MANIPULATIVE SKILL. ED035447
RACIAL FACTORS IN TEST PERFORMANCE EJ 053 887
SEX DIFFERENCES IN PERFORMANCE AS A FUNCTION OF PRAISE AND BLAME EJ 055 098

PERMISSIVE ENVIRONMENT

IMITATIVE AGGRESSION IN CHILDREN AS A FUNCTION OF OBSERVING A HUMAN MODEL EJ 039 907
SAY YOU COME FROM MISSOURI EJ 047 103

PERSISTENCE

INFLUENCE OF SUBJECT AND SITUATIONAL VARIABLES ON THE PERSISTENCE OF FIRST GRADE CHILDREN IN A TEST-LIKE SITUATION. ED052819

PERSONAL ADJUSTMENT

LONG TERM EFFECT OF STRUCTURED TRAINING ON 3 YOUNG CHILDREN. ED023480

PERSONAL GROWTH

LITERATURE, CREATIVITY AND IMAGINATION EJ 033 510

PERSONAL VALUES

AGE, SEX, RACE, AND THE PERCEPTION OF FACIAL BEAUTY EJ 046 783

PERSONALITY

EARLY CHILDHOOD SELECTED BIBLIOGRAPHIES SERIES. NUMBER 6, PERSONALITY. ED024475
CONDITIONING TASKS PERFORMANCE IN INFANCY AND EARLY CHILDHOOD AS A STABLE AND MEASURABLE ASPECT OF BEHAVIOR. FINAL REPORT. ED051890
SCHOOL ACHIEVERS AND UNDERACHIEVERS IN AN URBAN GHETTO EJ 027 614
PERSONALITY, COGNITIVE, AND ACADEMIC CORRELATES OF PROBLEM-SOLVING FLEXIBILITY EJ 039 632
CORRELATES OF LOCUS OF CONTROL IN A SECONDARY SCHOOL POPULATION EJ 039 905
LEVEL OF "N" ACHIEVEMENT AND PROBABILITY IN CHILDREN EJ 039 906
EXPRESSIONS OF PERSONALITY IN CREATIONS OF LATENCY AGE CHILDREN EJ 041 446
DIVERGENT THINKING AND PERSONALITY MEASURES OF ENGLISH AND AMERICAN EDUCATION MAJORS EJ 044 707
VERBAL RECALL AS A FUNCTION OF PERSONALITY CHARACTERISTICS EJ 054 806
ACADEMIC CHEATING: THE CONTRIBUTION OF SEX, PERSONALITY AND SITUATIONAL VARIABLES EJ 055 104

PERSONALITY ASSESSMENT
THE 1965 HEAD START PSYCHOLOGICAL SCREENING PROGRAM. FINAL REPORT ON THE DATA ANALYSIS. ED014333
IDENTIFICATION AND DEVELOPMENT OF CREATIVE ABILITIES. ED027965
INTERRELATIONS BETWEEN SOCIAL-EMOTIONAL BEHAVIOR AND INFORMATION ACHIEVEMENT OF HEAD START CHILDREN. REPORT NUMBER 5. ED030479
INVESTIGATION OF METHODS TO ASSESS THE EFFECTS OF CULTURAL DEPRIVATION. FINAL REPORT. ED032121
INDIVIDUAL DIFFERENCES IN GHETTO FOUR-YEAR-OLDS. ED034572
CHILD DEVELOPMENT RESEARCH AND EVALUATION CENTER FOR HEAD START, TEMPLE UNIVERSITY, 1968 - 1969. ANNUAL REPORT. ED043388
NEED FOR APPROVAL, CHILDREN'S SHARING BEHAVIOR, AND RECIPROCITY IN SHARING EJ 018 321
HONESTY AND ALTRUISM AMONG PREADOLESCENTS EJ 026 450
CHILDREN'S JUDGMENTS OF PERSONALITY ON THE BASIS OF VOICE QUALITY EJ 030 512
MASCULINITY AND FEMININITY IN THE ELEMENTARY AND JUNIOR HIGH SCHOOL YEARS EJ 034 902
JUDGING OUTLINE FACES: A DEVELOPMENTAL STUDY EJ 045 599
THE CURIOSITY DIMENSION OF FIFTH-GRADE CHILDREN: A FACTORIAL DISCRIMINANT ANALYSIS EJ 056 623
DELINQUENCY PREDICTION SCALES AND PERSONALITY INVENTORIES EJ 057 475
THE EFFECTS OF THE DUSO GUIDANCE PROGRAM ON THE SELF-CONCEPTS OF PRIMARY SCHOOL CHILDREN EJ 058 132

PERSONALITY DEVELOPMENT
THINKING, FEELING, EXPERIENCING--TOWARD REALIZATION OF FULL POTENTIAL. ED020012
FAMILY BACKGROUND EFFECTS ON PERSONALITY DEVELOPMENT AND SOCIAL ACCEPTANCE. ED020020
FINAL REPORT ON HEAD START EVALUATION AND RESEARCH: 1967-68 TO THE OFFICE OF ECONOMIC OPPORTUNITY. SECTION I: PART B, ACCURACY OF SELF-PERCEPTION AMONG CULTURALLY DEPRIVED PRESCHOOLS. ED023455
FINAL REPORT ON HEAD START EVALUATION AND RESEARCH: 1967-68 TO THE OFFICE OF ECONOMIC OPPORTUNITY. SECTION I: PARTS A AND B. ED023457
FINAL REPORT ON HEAD START EVALUATION AND RESEARCH: 1967-68 TO THE OFFICE OF ECONOMIC OPPORTUNITY. SECTION II: ACHIEVEMENT MOTIVATION AND PATTERNS OF REINFORCEMENT IN HEAD START CHILDREN. ED023458
PERSONALITY DEVELOPMENT IN INFANCY ED024439
A STUDY OF COGNITIVE AND SOCIAL FUNCTIONING. PROJECT II ED025310
THE MAGIC YEARS: UNDERSTANDING AND HANDLING THE PROBLEMS OF EARLY CHILDHOOD. ED029712
PERSONALITY DEVELOPMENT IN DISADVANTAGED FOUR-YEAR-OLD BOYS: OBSERVATIONS WITH PLAY TECHNIQUES. ED031310
FROM LEARNING FOR LOVE TO LOVE OF LEARNING: ESSAYS ON PSYCHOANALYSIS AND EDUCATION. ED032925
DEPENDENCE AND COMPETENCE IN FOUR-YEAR-OLD BOYS AS RELATED TO PARENTAL TREATMENT OF THE CHILD. ED039952
ON EARLY LEARNING: THE MODIFIABILITY OF HUMAN POTENTIAL. ED051876
ADOLESCENT NORMS AND BEHAVIOR: ORGANIZATION AND CONFORMITY EJ 007 450
THE FATHER-DAUGHTER RELATIONSHIP AND THE PERSONALITY DEVELOPMENT OF THE FEMALE EJ 017 904
FATHER ABSENCE AND THE PERSONALITY DEVELOPMENT OF THE MALE CHILD EJ 019 018
PATERNAL ABSENCE, SEX TYPING, AND IDENTIFICATION EJ 019 020
A DEVELOPMENTAL STUDY OF THE RELATIONSHIP BETWEEN CONCEPTUAL, EGO, AND MORAL DEVELOPMENT EJ 021 999
L'EDUCATEUR ET L'EPANOUISSEMENT DE LA PERSONNALITE DE L'ENFANT EJ 028 102
SOME DETERMINANTS OF CHILDREN'S SELF-REWARD BEHAVIOR AFTER EXPOSURE TO DISCREPANT REWARD CRITERIA EJ 030 511
ADOLESCENCE, IDENTITY, AND FOSTER FAMILY CARE EJ 030 652
LA FORMATION THEATRALE DANS L'EDUCATION PRESCOLAIRE EJ 034 420
LA FORMATION THEATRALE DANS L'EDUCATION PRESCOLAIRE EJ 034 420
FATHER ABSENCE AND CONSCIENCE DEVELOPMENT EJ 038 854
THE MOTHER-CHILD RELATIONSHIP AND THE FATHER-ABSENT BOY'S PERSONALITY DEVELOPMENT 27-241 EJ 040 456
INFANT-CARETAKER INTERACTIONS EJ 043 670

PERSONALITY STUDIES
TEACHERS BELIEF SYSTEMS AND PRESCHOOL ATMOSPHERES. ED014320
THE CHILD WHO DISLIKES GOING TO SCHOOL. ED019999
THE ABILITY OF PERSONALITY VARIABLES IN DISCRIMINATING AMONG THREE INTELLECTUAL GROUPS OF PREADOLESCENT BOYS AND GIRLS EJ 034 044
WORD FLUENCY--INTELLECT OR PERSONALITY? EJ 034 313
A LONGITUDINAL STUDY OF CHANGES IN EGO IDENTITY STATUS DURING THE FRESHMAN YEAR AT COLLEGE EJ 043 193
STEREOTYPIC AFFECTIVE PROPERTIES OF PERSONAL NAMES AND SOMATOTYPES IN CHILDREN EJ 043 352
AGE CHANGES AND COHORT DIFFERENCES IN PERSONALITY EJ 055 110
EXTENSION OF PERSONAL FUTURE TIME PERSPECTIVE, AGE, AND LIFE-SATISFACTION OF CHILDREN AND ADOLESCENTS EJ 058 140
HYPOTHESIS OF ORIGIN AND NATURE FOR THE "SOMINDENCE-DISSOFRUSTANCE" PERSONALITY FACTOR, U.I. 30 EJ 061 061

PERSONALITY TESTS
SELF-SOCIAL CONSTRUCTS OF CHILDREN. ED021615
INDIVIDUAL DIFFERENCES IN GHETTO FOUR-YEAR-OLDS. ED034572
FAKABILITY OF SCORES ON THE GROUP PERSONALITY PROJECTIVE TEST EJ 030 792
THE WORLD TEST: DEVELOPMENTAL ASPECTS OF A PLAY TECHNIQUE EJ 031 629
AGE CHANGES AND COHORT DIFFERENCES IN PERSONALITY EJ 055 110

PERSONALITY THEORIES
SELF-SOCIAL CONSTRUCTS OF CHILDREN. ED021615
FACTORS? IN CHILD DEVELOPMENT: PEER RELATIONS. ED047796
IMPULSIVITY & REFLECTIVITY AS REFLECTED BY THE VARIABLES OF TIME AND ERROR. ED047820
THE EFFECT OF ANXIETY OVER INTELLECTUAL PERFORMANCE ON REFLECTION-IMPULSIVITY IN CHILDREN EJ 026 153
OLDER BROTHERS' INFLUENCE ON SEX-TYPED, AGGRESSIVE, AND DEPENDENT BEHAVIOR IN FATHER-ABSENT CHILDREN EJ 034 901
AGE CHANGES AND COHORT DIFFERENCES IN PERSONALITY EJ 055 110

PERSONALITY TRAITS
EFFECTS OF BRIEF OBSERVATION OF MODEL BEHAVIOR ON CONCEPTUAL TEMPO OF IMPULSIVE CHILDREN EJ 019 010

PERSONNEL MANAGEMENT
PSYCHOLOGICAL CONSULTATION IN A PRESCHOOL EJ 038 394

PERSONNEL SELECTION
CHILD CARE PARAPROFESSIONALS: CHARACTERISTICS FOR SELECTION. ED053800

PHILOSOPHY
A CITY FOR CHILDREN: THE YEAR 2005 EJ 049 562

PHONEMES
PROCESSING OF PHONOLOGICAL SEQUENCES BY YOUNG CHILDREN AND ADULTS EJ 036 747

PHONETIC ANALYSIS
ACOUSTIC ANALYSIS OF THE ACQUISITION OF ACCEPTABLE "R" IN AMERICAN ENGLISH EJ 041 056

PHONETICS
PHONETIC COMPATIBILITY IN PAIRED-ASSOCIATE LEARNING OF FIRST- AND THIRD-GRADE CHILDREN EJ 044 692
DICTIONARY SYLLABICATION - HOW USEFUL EJ 052 180

PHONICS
WHAT DO YOU MEAN, "AUDITORY PERCEPTION"? EJ 013 560

PHONOLOGY
DICTIONARY SYLLABICATION - HOW USEFUL EJ 052 180

PHOTOGRAPHY
A METHOD TO INVESTIGATE THE MOVEMENT PATTERNS OF CHILDREN. ED027938
THE CHILD'S EYE VIEW: EXPERIMENTAL PHOTOGRAPHY WITH PRESCHOOL CHILDREN EJ 029 342
THE CAMERA FOCUSES ON READING EJ 032 192

PHYSICAL ACTIVITIES
PHYSICAL EDUCATION ACTIVITIES FOR THE ELEMENTARY SCHOOL. ED019995
SKILL DEVELOPMENT THROUGH GAMES AND RHYTHMIC ACTIVITIES. ED019996
FREEDOM TO MOVE. ED020778
THE EFFECT OF SOCIAL INTERACTION ON ACTIVITY LEVELS IN SIX-TO EIGHT-YEAR-OLD BOYS EJ 052 463

PHYSICAL CHARACTERISTICS
HEAD START EVALUATION AND RESEARCH CENTER, UNIVERSITY OF KANSAS. REPORT NO. VIII, PHYSICAL DEVELOPMENT OF CHILDREN IN THE HEAD START PROGRAM IN THE CENTRAL UNITED STATES. ED021644
EARLY CHILDHOOD SELECTED BIBLIOGRAPHIES SERIES. NUMBER 1, PHYSICAL. ED022532
ANTHROPOMETRIC MEASUREMENTS OF CHILDREN IN THE HEAD START PROGRAM. ED042488
BODY SIZE OF CONTEMPORARY YOUTH IN DIFFERENT PARTS OF THE WORLD EJ 010 312
GROWTH OF HEAD, FACE, TRUNK, AND LIMBS IN PHILADEPHIA WHITE AND NEGRO CHILDREN OF ELEMENTARY AND HIGH SCHOOL AGE EJ 022 582
BODY BUILD, SEX-ROLE PREFERENCE, AND SEX-ROLE ADOPTION IN JUNIOR HIGH SCHOOL BOYS EJ 035 627
AGE, SEX, RACE, AND THE PERCEPTION OF FACIAL BEAUTY EJ 046 783

PHYSIQUE IDENTIFICATION, PREFERENCE, AND AVERSION IN KINDERGARTEN CHILDREN EJ 046 785

PHYSICAL DESIGN NEEDS
DESIGN FOR A PLAYROOM. ED019133

PHYSICAL DEVELOPMENT
FREEDOM TO MOVE. ED020778
EARLY CHILDHOOD SELECTED BIBLIOGRAPHIES SERIES. NUMBER 1, PHYSICAL. ED022532
ANTHROPOMETRIC MEASUREMENTS OF CHILDREN IN THE HEAD START PROGRAM. ED042488
HEIGHT AND WEIGHT OF CHILDREN: UNITED STATES. ED050808
FACTORS AFFECTING LATERAL DIFFERENTIATION IN THE HUMAN NEWBORN EJ 015 395
A MULTIHANDICAPPED RUBELLA BABY: THE FIRST EIGHTEEN MONTHS EJ 022 979
BODY SIZE OF CONTEMPORARY GROUPS OF ONE-YEAR-OLD INFANTS STUDIED IN DIFFERENT PARTS OF THE WORLD EJ 025 469
PHYSICAL GROWTH AND BODY COMPOSITION: PAPERS FROM THE KYOTO SYMPOSIUM ON ANTHROPOLOGICAL ASPECTS OF HUMAN GROWTH EJ 029 387
CONSEQUENCES OF LOW BIRTH WEIGHT EJ 030 430
BODY BUILD, SEX-ROLE PREFERENCE, AND SEX-ROLE ADOPTION IN JUNIOR HIGH SCHOOL BOYS EJ 035 627
DIFFERENTIAL ADJUSTMENT TO PUBESCENCE AND COGNITIVE STYLE PATTERNS EJ 039 903
VERBAL REGULATION OF MOTOR BEHAVIOR-SOVIET RESEARCH AND NON-SOVIET REPLICATIONS EJ 050 074

PHYSICAL EDUCATION
GUIDE FOR TEACHING PHYSICAL EDUCATION, GRADES 1-6. ED019126
PHYSICAL EDUCATION ACTIVITIES FOR THE ELEMENTARY SCHOOL. ED019995
SKILL DEVELOPMENT THROUGH GAMES AND RHYTHMIC ACTIVITIES. ED019996
ELEMENTARY PHYSICAL EDUCATION: TOPEKA PUBLIC SCHOOLS. ED035445
CURRICULUM GUIDE FOR PHYSICAL EDUCATION: KINDERGARTEN AND UNGRADED PRIMARY. ED038169

PHYSICAL ENVIRONMENT
THE EFFECT ON AGGRESSION OF VARIATION IN AMOUNT OF OPPORTUNITY FOR PLAY. (INTERNAL REPORT). ED043384
GROSS ACTIVITY OF CHILDREN AT PLAY. (INTERNAL REPORT). ED043385
THE PHYSICAL ENVIRONMENT AS A MEDIATING FACTOR IN SCHOOL ACHIEVEMENT. ED046496
CHILDREN AND THEIR PHYSICAL AND SOCIAL ENVIRONMENT. 1970 WHITE HOUSE CONFERENCE ON CHILDREN, REPORT OF FORUM 19. (WORKING COPY). ED046535
CONTROL OF LEAD POISONING IN CHILDREN. (PRE-PUBLICATION DRAFT). ED050825
EVALUATING SETTINGS FOR LEARNING EJ 019 966
THE LIVING WORLD: THE PHYSICAL ENVIRONEMNT EJ 029 388

PHYSICAL FACILITIES
THE DESIGN OF A PRE-SCHOOL "LEARNING LABORATORY" IN A REHABILITATION CENTER. ED033764
PROGRAMS FOR INFANTS AND YOUNG CHILDREN. PART IV: FACILITIES AND EQUIPMENT. ED047810

PHYSICAL HEALTH
NUTRITION SURVEY OF WHITE MOUNTAIN APACHE PRESCHOOL CHILDREN. ED046508
LEAD POISONING IN CHILDREN. ED048919
HEALTH CARE OF CHILDREN: A CHALLENGE. ED050804
HEALTH AND NUTRITION IN DISADVANTAGED CHILDREN AND THEIR RELATIONSHIP WITH INTELLECTUAL DEVELOPMENT. COLLABORATIVE RESEARCH REPORT. ED052816

PHYSICAL RECREATION PROGRAMS
GUIDE FOR TEACHING PHYSICAL EDUCATION, GRADES 1-6. ED019126

PHYSIOLOGY
THE RELATIONSHIP OF INDIVIDUAL DIFFERENCES IN THE ORIENTING RESPONSE TO COMPLEX LEARNING IN KINDERGARTNERS. ED031299
THE RELATIONSHIP OF INDIVIDUAL DIFFERENCES IN THE ORIENTING RESPONSE TO COMPLEX LEARNING IN KINDERGARTNERS. REPORT FROM THE MOTIVATION AND INDIVIDUAL DIFFERENCES IN LEARNING AND RETENTION PROJECT. ED046544
BIRTH ORDER AND PHYSIOLOGICAL STRESS RESPONSE EJ 022 000
PREDICTION OF DEVELOPMENTAL OUTCOME AT SEVEN YEARS FROM PRENATAL, PERINATAL, AND POSTNATAL EVENTS EJ 058 927

PICTORIAL STIMULI
COGNITIVE PROCESSES IN THE DEVELOPMENT OF CHILDREN'S APPRECIATION OF HUMOR. ED020784
HEAD START EVALUATION AND RESEARCH CENTER, BOSTON UNIVERSITY. REPORT C-I, PERCEPTION OF EMOTION AMONG CHILDREN: RACE AND SEX DIFFERENCES. ED022561
INDUCED VERSUS SPONTANEOUS REHEARSAL IN SHORT-TERM MEMORY IN NURSERY SCHOOL CHILDREN. STUDY M: DEVELOPMENT OF SELECTIVE ATTENTION ABILITIES. ED024444
INFANTS' RESPONSES TO FACIAL STIMULI DURING THE FIRST YEAR OF LIFE: EXPLORATORY STUDIES IN THE DEVELOPMENT OF A FACE SCHEMA. ED024455
SOME DIMENSIONS OF CREATIVE THINKING ABILITY ACHIEVEMENT, AND INTELLIGENCE IN FIRST GRADE. ED028818
DEVELOPMENTAL TRENDS IN THE SELECTIVE PERCEPTION OF RACE AND AFFECT BY YOUNG NEGRO AND CAUCASIAN CHILDREN. ED046498
INSTRUCTIONAL SPECIFICITY AND OUTCOME-EXPECTATION IN OBSERVATIONALLY-INDUCED QUESTION FORMULATION. ED047789
INTERRELATIONS IN CHILDREN'S LEARNING OF VERBAL AND PICTORIAL PAIRED ASSOCIATES. ED051886
AGE DIFFERENCES IN JUDGMENTS OF RECENCY FOR SHORT SEQUENCES OF PICTURES EJ 026 375
DEVELOPMENTAL CHANGES IN THE USE OF EMOTION CUES IN A CONCEPT-FORMATION TASK EJ 029 362
DEVELOPMENTAL DIFFERENCES IN THE INTEGRATION OF PICTURE SERIES: EFFECTS OF VARIATIONS IN OBJECT-ATTRIBUTE RELATIONSHIPS EJ 029 386
SHORT-TERM MEMORY IN CHILDREN: KEEPING TRACK OF VARIABLES WITH FEW OR MANY STATES EJ 029 444
COMPARISON OF PICTORIAL AND VERBAL SEMANTIC SCALES AS USED BY CHILDREN EJ 029 769
THE GENERALITY OF COLOR-FORM PREFERENCE AS A FUNCTION OF MATERIALS AND TASK REQUIREMENTS AMONG LOWER-CLASS NEGRO CHILDREN EJ 033 052
DIMENSIONAL SALIENCE AND IDENTIFICATION OF THE RELEVANT DIMENSION IN PROBLEM SOLVING: A DEVELOPMENTAL STUDY EJ 035 360
EFFECT OF INCENTIVES UPON RETARDED AND NORMAL READERS ON A VISUAL-ASSOCIATE LEARNING TASK EJ 038 266
ATTENTION DISTRIBUTION IN THE 24-MONTH-OLD CHILD: VARIATIONS IN COMPLEXITY AND INCONGRUITY OF THE HUMAN FORM EJ 040 296
THE INFLUENCE OF STIMULUS EXPOSURE ON RATED PREFERENCE: EFFECTS OF AGE, PATTERN OF EXPOSURE, AND STIMULUS MEANINGFULNESS EJ 041 960
EFFECTS OF CONTEXT ON PRESCHOOL CHILDREN'S JUDGMENTS EJ 042 968
VISUAL LEARNING: AN ANALYSIS BY SEX AND GRADE LEVEL EJ 045 424
QUANTITATIVE AND QUALITATIVE ASPECTS OF MEMORY FOR PICTURE STIMULI EJ 057 907

PILOT PROJECTS
PROCESSES OF CURIOSITY AND EXPLORATION IN PRESCHOOL DISADVANTAGED CHILDREN. ED023470
THE INITIAL PHASE OF A PRESCHOOL CURRICULUM DEVELOPMENT PROJECT. FINAL REPORT. ED027071
A PILOT STUDY INTEGRATING VISUAL FORM AND ANTHROPOLOGICAL CONTENT FOR TEACHING CHILDREN AGES 6 TO 11 ABOUT CULTURES AND PEOPLES OF THE WORLD ED027095
SUPERMARKET DISCOVERY CENTER, PILOT STUDY, MAY - SEPTEMBER, 1968. INITIAL REPORT. ED027941
THE CHANGE PROCESS IN ACTION: KINDERGARTEN ED027949
A COMPARISON OF THE READING READINESS OF KINDERGARTEN PUPILS EXPOSED TO CONCEPTUAL-LANGUAGE AND BASAL READER PREREADING PROGRAMS. A PILOT STUDY. FINAL REPORT. ED029709
EARLY CHILDHOOD EDUCATION IN AMERICAN SAMOA, 1968. ED032114
AN EVALUATION OF A PILOT PROJECT TO ASSESS THE INTRODUCTION OF THE MODERN ENGLISH INFANT SCHOOL APPROACH TO LEARNING WITH SECOND AND THIRD YEAR DISADVANTAGED CHILDREN. ED034595
AN EXPERIMENTAL GAME IN ORAL LANGUAGE COMPREHENSION. ED038171
EVALUATION REPORT: EARLY CHILDHOOD EDUCATION PROGRAM, 1969 FIELD TEST. ED041626
THE ARTS ARE ALIVE AND THRIVING IN ST. LOUIS EJ 022 334
A PILOT STUDY OF COMPUTER-ASSISTED DRILL AND PRACTICE IN SEVENTH GRADE REMEDIAL MATHEMATICS EJ 027 030
UNIONS AND DAY CARE CENTERS FOR THE CHILDREN OF WORKING MOTHERS EJ 038 643
PROJECT PLAYPEN -- PRIMARY PREVENTION EJ 058 213

PLACEMENT
ADOPTIVE PLACEMENT OF THE OLDER CHILD EJ 027 644
A SHORT, RELIABLE, EASY TO ADMINISTER INDIVIDUAL INTELLIGENCE TEST FOR SPECIAL CLASS PLACEMENT EJ 041 724
THE RELATIONSHIP BETWEEN THE WECHSLER INTELLIGENCE SCALE FOR CHILDREN AND THE SLOSSON INTELLIGENCE TEST EJ 041 725

PLANNING
SOME THOUGHTS ON PLANNING HEALTH CARE FOR CHILDREN AND YOUTH EJ 038 021

PLANNING COMMISSIONS
CHILDREN AND THEIR PHYSICAL AND SOCIAL ENVIRONMENT. 1970 WHITE HOUSE CONFERENCE ON CHILDREN, REPORT OF FORUM 19. (WORKING COPY). ED046535

PLAY
POSITION EFFECTS IN PLAY EQUIPMENT PREFERENCES OF NURSERY SCHOOL CHILDREN. ED045185
THE EFFECT OF AGGRESSIVE CARTOONS: CHILDREN'S INTERPERSONAL PLAY. ED046543

PLAY BEHAVIOR AND EFFICACY IN GHETTO FOUR-YEAR-OLDS: ORGANIZATION AND PSYCHOSEXUAL CONTENT OF PLAY. ED048920
A DESCRIPTIVE ACCOUNT OF FOUR MODES OF CHILDREN'S PLAY BETWEEN ONE AND FIVE YEARS. ED049833
THE PLAYFUL MODES OF KNOWING. ED050806
HAVE YOU EVER THOUGHT OF A PROP BOX? EJ 031 781
PLAY PERSISTENCE: SOME EFFECTS OF INTERRUPTION, SOCIAL REINFORCEMENT, AND DEFECTIVE TOYS EJ 034 532
CHILDREN AND WAR GAMES EJ 034 533
PRESCHOOL PLAY NORMS: A REPLICATION EJ 041 958
THE DECLINE OF PLAY IN URBAN KINDERGARTENS EJ 041 961
ON THE VALUE OF BOTH PLAY AND STRUCTURE IN EARLY EDUCATION EJ 044 010
A PLAY CENTER FOR DEVELOPMENTALLY HANDICAPPED INFANTS EJ 045 012
LEARNING FROM PLAY IN OTHER CULTURES EJ 045 532
PLAY, THE ESSENTIAL INGREDIENT EJ 046 248
PARENTAL CONCEPTUAL SYSTEMS, HOME PLAY ENVIRONMENT, AND POTENTIAL CREATIVITY IN CHILDREN EJ 048 234
EFFECTS OF COOPERATIVE RESPONSE ACQUISITION ON SOCIAL BEHAVIOR DURING FREE-PLAY EJ 048 297
PLAYROOM OBSERVATIONS OF HYPERACTIVE CHILDREN ON MEDICATION EJ 048 301
PLAY BEHAVIOR IN YOUNG CHILDREN: A CROSS-CULTURAL STUDY EJ 048 303
ON PLAY EJ 051 471
HOW FREE IS FREE PLAY? EJ 055 535
LE PROBLEME DE LA LIBERTE ET DE LA DISCIPLINE DANS LE JEU (PROBLEMS OF FREEDOM AND DISCIPLINE IN PLAY) EJ 061 465

PLAY THERAPY
DESIGN FOR A PLAYROOM. ED019133
THE EFFECTS OF SOCIODRAMATIC PLAY ON DISADVANTAGED PRESCHOOL CHILDREN. ED033761
PLAY FOR HOSPITALIZED CHILDREN EJ 007 316
"TUBE" PLAY EJ 008 263
THE USE OF PLAY TECHNIQUES IN THE TREATMENT OF CHILDREN EJ 016 380
A PLAY PROGRAM IN A PEDIATRIC CLINIC EJ 029 951

PLAYGROUNDS
CHILD'S PLAY, A CREATIVE APPROACH TO PLAYSPACES FOR TODAY'S CHILDREN. ED021630
SOME EUROPEAN NURSERY SCHOOLS AND PLAYGROUNDS. ED048928
CREATIVE LEARNING IN CHILDREN'S PLAYGROUNDS EJ 007 071
AUDIO-VISUAL MATERIALS IN EARLY CHILDHOOD EDUCATION EJ 038 907
A CREATIVE PLAYGROUND EJ 042 406
AN ADVENTURE PLAYGROUND FOR HANDICAPPED CHILDREN IN LONDON EJ 050 487

PLURALS
NOUN PLURAL DEVELOPMENT IN PRIMARY GRADE CHILDREN EJ 052 179
A COMPARATIVE STUDY OF ENGLISH PLURALIZATION BY NATIVE AND NON-NATIVE ENGLISH SPEAKERS EJ 052 465

POETRY
FANTASIZING AND POETRY CONSTRUCTION IN PRESCHOOLERS EJ 018 132
A PROCESS FOR POETRY-WRITING EJ 055 364

POLICY
NEA VIEWS ON TEACHER STRIKES EJ 003 629
EDUCATIONAL RESEARCH POLICIES OF SCHOOL DISTRICTS NATIONWIDE EJ 012 677

POLICY FORMATION
DESIRABLE ATHLETIC COMPETITION FOR CHILDREN OF ELEMENTARY SCHOOL AGE. ED027086

POLITICAL ATTITUDES
THE POLITICAL SOCIALIZATION OF CHILDREN AND THE STRUCTURE OF THE ELEMENTARY SCHOOL. ED024468
CHILDREN AND THE POLITICS OF TRUST EJ 045 394

POLITICAL POWER
LOOKING BEYOND THE STRIKES EJ 003 630

POLITICAL SCIENCE
A PILOT EXPERIMENT IN EARLY CHILDHOOD POLITICAL LEARNING. REPORT FROM THE PROJECT ON CONCEPTS IN POLITICAL SCIENCE. ED043368

POLITICAL SOCIALIZATION
THE POLITICAL SOCIALIZATION OF CHILDREN AND THE STRUCTURE OF THE ELEMENTARY SCHOOL. ED024468
CHILDREN AND THE POLITICS OF TRUST EJ 045 394
CIVIC BOOKS AND CIVIC CULTURE EJ 057 017
THE DEVELOPMENT OF DEMOCRATIC VALUES AND BEHAVIOR AMONG MEXICAN-AMERICAN CHILDREN EJ 058 509

POLLUTION
AN ENVIRONMENT THAT SUPPORTS MAN EJ 029 389

POPULATION GROWTH
FAMILY PLANNING AND FAMILY ECONOMICS. 1970 WHITE HOUSE CONFERENCE ON CHILDREN, REPORT OF FORUM 16. (WORKING COPY). ED046532

POSITIVE REINFORCEMENT
POSITIVE SOCIAL REINFORCEMENT IN THE NURSERY SCHOOL PEER GROUP. ED016515
EFFECTS OF ADULT SOCIAL REINFORCEMENT ON CHILD BEHAVIOR. ED019997
HEAD START EVALUATION AND RESEARCH CENTER, UNIVERSITY OF KANSAS. REPORT NO. VI, A FAILURE TO SHOW AND INVOLVEMENT OF CURRENT MOTIVATIONAL VARIABLES IN THE RESPONSE OF HEAD START CHILDREN IN THE ASSESSMENT OF INTELLIGENCE BY MEANS OF THE STANFORD BINET TEST. ED021639
HEAD START EVALUATION AND RESEARCH CENTER, UNIVERSITY OF KANSAS. REPORT NO. VIIC, ERRORLESS DISCRIMINATION IN PRESCHOOL CHILDREN: A PROGRAM FOR ESTABLISHING A ONE-MINUTE DELAY OF REINFORCEMENT. ED021642
HEAD START EVALUATION AND RESEARCH CENTER, UNIVERSITY OF KANSAS. REPORT NO. X, ENHANCEMENT OF THE SOCIAL REINFORCING VALUE OF A PRESCHOOL TEACHER. ED021646
BEHAVIOR MODIFICATION OF AN ADJUSTMENT CLASS: A TOKEN REINFORCEMENT PROGRAM. ED023462
FUN WHILE LEARNING AND EARNING. A LOOK INTO CHATTANOOGA PUBLIC SCHOOLS' TOKEN REINFORCEMENT PROGRAM. ED027952
CONDITIONS FOSTERING THE USE OF INFORMATIVE FEEDBACK BY YOUNG CHILDREN. ED029688
REPLICATION OF THE "MOTIVATED LEARNING" COGNITIVE TRAINING PROCEDURES WITH CULTURALLY DEPRIVED PRESCHOOLERS. REPORT FROM PROJECT MOTIVATED LEARNING. ED029708
ESTABLISHING TOKEN PROGRAMS IN SCHOOLS: ISSUES AND PROBLEMS. ED039020
AN INVESTIGATION OF THE EFFECTS OF TEACHER VERBAL REINFORCEMENT AS IT RELATES TO SCHOLASTIC APTITUDE AND ACHIEVEMENT WITH ELEMENTARY SCHOOL CHILDREN. PROGRESS REPORT. ED042494
THE EFFECTS OF DIFFERENT TYPES OF REINFORCEMENT ON YOUNG CHILDREN'S INCIDENTAL LEARNING. ED044184
THE BEHAVIOR ANALYSIS CLASSROOM. ED047775
A TOKEN MANUAL FOR BEHAVIOR ANALYSIS CLASSROOMS. ED047776
SIMULATION ACTIVITIES FOR TRAINING PARENTS AND TEACHERS AS EDUCATIONAL PARTNERS: A REPORT AND EVALUATION. ED048945
MATERIAL REINFORCEMENT AND SUCCESS IN SPELLING EJ 018 423
MODIFYING BEHAVIOR OF KINDERGARTEN CHILDREN EJ 026 493
THE EFFECT OF INDIVIDUAL-CONTINGENT GROUP REINFORCEMENT ON POPULARITY EJ 034 158
THE SYSTEMATIC USE OF THE PEMACK PRINCIPLE IN MODIFYING CLASSROOM BEHAVIORS EJ 034 528
EFFECTS OF SOCIAL COMPARISON UPON CHILDREN'S SELF-REINFORCEMENT AND ALTRUISM TOWARD COMPETITORS AND FRIENDS EJ 041 856
NIGHT TRAINING THROUGH PARENTS' IMPLICIT USE OF OPERANT CONDITIONING EJ 045 457
INTERACTION EFFECTS OF SOCIAL AND TANGIBLE REINFORCEMENT EJ 048 296
EFFECTS OF COOPERATIVE RESPONSE ACQUISITION ON SOCIAL BEHAVIOR DURING FREE-PLAY EJ 048 297
EFFECT OF REINFORCEMENT CONTINGENCIES IN INCREASING PROGRAMMED READING AND MATHEMATICS BEHAVIORS IN FIRST-GRADE CHILDREN EJ 049 168
EFFECTS OF PROVISION FOR INDIVIDUAL DIFFERENCES AND TEACHER ATTENTION UPON STUDY BEHAVIOR AND ASSIGNMENTS COMPLETED EJ 058 353

POST DOCTORAL EDUCATION
POSTDOCTORAL RESEARCH TRAINING PROGRAM IN EDUCATIONAL STIMULATION. FINAL REPORT. ED035455

POST TESTING
EVALUATION OF HEADSTART EDUCATIONAL PROGRAM IN CAMBRIDGE, MASSACHUSETTS. FINAL REPORT. ED013668
A HEAD START CONTROL GROUP. PART OF THE FINAL REPORT. ED026128
REEXAMINING VARIABLES AFFECTING COGNITIVE FUNCTIONING IN PRESCHOOL CHILDREN: A FOLLOW-UP. ED052818

POVERTY PROGRAMS
PROJECT HEAD START AND THE CULTURALLY DEPRIVED IN ROCHESTER, NEW YORK, A STUDY OF PARTICIPATING AND NON-PARTICIPATING FAMILIES IN AREAS SERVED BY PROJECT HEAD START IN ROCHESTER, FINAL REPORT. ED013669
SUMMARY AND OBSERVATIONS IN THE DAKOTAS AND MINNESOTA. INDIAN COMMUNITIES AND PROJECT HEAD START. ED013670
AN APPRAISAL OF POSSIBILITIES FOR A HEAD START PROGRAM AMONG THE POTAWATOMI INDIANS OF KANSAS. INDIAN COMMUNITIES AND PROJECT HEAD START. ED013671
IMPACT OF SUMMER 1965 HEAD START ON CHILDREN'S CONCEPT ATTAINMENT DURING KINDERGARTEN. FINAL REPORT. ED015773

INDIAN COMMUNITIES AND PROJECT HEAD START. SUMMARY AND OBSERVATIONS IN THE DAKOTAS AND MINNESOTA, TOGETHER WITH AN APPRAISAL OF POSSIBILITIES FOR A HEAD START PROGRAM AMONG THE POTAWATOMI INDIANS OF KANSAS. ED016510
DAY CARE AS A SOCIAL INSTRUMENT: A POLICY PAPER. ED027065
A REPORT ON A CWLA PILOT PROJECT TO TRAIN NEW CHILD CARE WORKERS EJ 017 849

POVERTY RESEARCH
PRESCHOOLER STUDY: THE MEDICAL, SOCIAL AND ECONOMIC CORRELATES OF POVERTY IN PRESCHOOL CHILDREN OF BRITISH COLUMBIA. A PILOT STUDY. ED046518
DESIGNS AND PROPOSAL FOR EARLY CHILDHOOD RESEARCH: A NEW LOOK: A MULTIPLE SYSTEMS-SERVICE APPROACH TO PROGRAMS AND RESEARCH FOR HELPING POOR CHILDREN. (ONE IN A SERIES OF SIX PAPERS). ED053806

POWER STRUCTURE
ATTITUDES OF PRESCHOOL AND ELEMENTARY SCHOOL CHILDREN TO AUTHORITY FIGURES. ED046506

PREDICTION
EXTENSION OF A THEORY OF PREDICTIVE BEHAVIOR TO IMMEDIATE RECALL BY PRESCHOOL CHILDREN. ED025326
SPATIAL ABILITIES AND SPATIAL EGOCENTRISM IN THE YOUNG CHILD EJ 037 066
EARLY GRADE SCHOOL PERFORMANCE OF INNER CITY NEGRO HIGH SCHOOL HIGH ACHIEVERS, LOW ACHIEVERS, AND DROPOUTS EJ 039 572
LEVEL OF "N" ACHIEVEMENT AND PROBABILITY IN CHILDREN EJ 039 906
UNWED MOTHERS AND THEIR DECISIONS TO KEEP OR SURRENDER CHILDREN EJ 040 042
POSITION STRATEGIES IN AN OBJECT DISCRIMINATION TASK EJ 052 458
PERSEVERATION AND ALTERNATION PRETRAINING AND BINARY PREDICTION EJ 057 902

PREDICTIVE ABILITY (TESTING)
PERCEPTUAL MODE DOMINANCE: AN APPROACH TO ASSESSMENT OF FIRST GRADE READING AND SPELLING. ED026132
IDENTIFICATION IN THE KINDERGARTEN OF FACTORS THAT MAKE FOR FUTURE SUCCESS IN READING AND IDENTIFICATION AND DIAGNOSIS IN THE KINDERGARTEN OF POTENTIAL READING DISABILITY CASES. FINAL REPORT. ED029710
VERBAL REINFORCEMENT AS AN ADJUSTMENT PREDICTOR WITH KINDERGARTEN CHILDREN. FINAL REPORT. ED031313
ISSUES AND IMPLICATIONS OF THE DISTRIBUTION OF ATTENTION IN THE HUMAN INFANT. ED043387
PREDICTION OF READINESS IN KINDERGARTEN AND ACHIEVEMENT IN THE FIRST PRIMARY YEAR. STUDY NUMBER TWO. ED043393
PREDICTION OF ACHIEVEMENT IN THE FIRST PRIMARY YEAR. STUDY NUMBER ONE. ED044180
IMPROVING HIGH SCHOOL LEARNING PREDICTIONS WITH MULTIPLE JUNIOR HIGH TEST SCORES EJ 016 653
PSYCHOLOGICAL DEVELOPMENT--PREDICTIONS FROM INFANCY EJ 025 626
THE USE OF METROPOLITCAN READINESS TESTS WITH MEXICAN-AMERICAN CHILDREN EJ 026 810
NEGRO-WHITE, MALE-FEMALE EIGHT-MONTH DEVELOPMENTAL SCORES COMPARED WITH SEVEN-YEAR WISC AND BENDER TEST SCORES EJ 040 723

PREDICTIVE MEASUREMENT
TECHNIQUES FOR ASSESSING COGNITIVE AND SOCIAL ABILITIES OF CHILDREN AND PARENTS IN PROJECT HEAD START. ED015772
A STANDARDIZED NEUROLOGICAL EXAMINATION: ITS VALIDITY IN PREDICTING SCHOOL ACHIEVEMENT IN HEAD START AND OTHER POPULATIONS. FINAL REPORT. ED023475
PREDICTION OF READINESS IN KINDERGARTEN AND ACHIEVEMENT IN THE FIRST PRIMARY YEAR. STUDY NUMBER TWO. ED043393
BIOLOGICAL AND ECOLOGICAL INFLUENCES ON DEVELOPMENT AT 12 MONTHS OF AGE EJ 029 385
DELINQUENCY PREDICTION SCALES AND PERSONALITY INVENTORIES EJ 057 475
PREDICTION OF DEVELOPMENTAL OUTCOME AT SEVEN YEARS FROM PRENATAL, PERINATAL, AND POSTNATAL EVENTS EJ 058 927
TESTS BUILT FROM PIAGET'S AND GESELL'S TASKS AS PREDICTORS OF FIRST-GRADE ACHIEVEMENT EJ 058 928

PREDICTIVE VALIDITY
CREATIVE ABILITY OVER A FIVE-YEAR SPAN EJ 058 412
TESTS BUILT FROM PIAGET'S AND GESELL'S TASKS AS PREDICTORS OF FIRST-GRADE ACHIEVEMENT EJ 058 928

PREDICTOR VARIABLES
STARTING NURSERY SCHOOL, II: PREDICTION OF CHILDREN'S INITIAL EMOTIONAL REACTIONS FROM BACKGROUND INFORMATION. FINAL REPORT. ED047814

GENERALIZED IMITATION AND THE DISCRIMINATION HYPOTHESIS EJ 028 636
PREDICTION OF DEVELOPMENTAL OUTCOME AT SEVEN YEARS FROM PRENATAL, PERINATAL, AND POSTNATAL EVENTS EJ 058 927

PREGNANCY
KEY ISSUES IN INFANT MORTALITY. ED045208
1. OBSTETRICAL MEDICATION AND INFANT OUTCOME: A REVIEW OF THE LITERATURE EJ 023 013
II. DELIVERY MEDICATION AND INFANT OUTCOME: AN EMPIRICAL STUDY EJ 023 014
III. OBSTETRICAL MEDICATION AND INFANT OUTCOME: SOME SUMMARY CONSIDERATIONS EJ 023 015
COMMUNITY ACTION ON BEHALF OF PREGNANT SCHOOL-AGE GIRLS: EDUCATIONAL POLICIES AND BEYOND EJ 023 392
A STUDY OF WED AND UNWED MOTHERHOOD IN ADOLESCENTS AND YOUNG ADULTS EJ 030 715

PREMATURE INFANTS
LONG TERM STUDY OF PREMATURES: SUMMARY OF PUBLISHED FINDINGS. ED043389
VISUAL ABILITIES AND PATTERN PREFERENCES OF PREMATURE INFANTS AND FULL-TERM NEONATES EJ 029 531
CONSEQUENCES OF LOW BIRTH WEIGHT EJ 030 430

PRENATAL INFLUENCES
PRESCHOOL INTELLIGENCE OF OVERSIZED NEWBORNS. ED034582
THE PSYCHOLOGICAL EFFECTS OF PREGNANCY AND NEONATAL HEALTH THREATS ON CHILD DEVELOPMENT. ED048921
CHILD HEALTH AND HUMAN DEVELOPMENT: PROGRESS 1963-1970. A REPORT OF THE NATIONAL INSTITUTE OF CHILD HEALTH AND HUMAN DEVELOPMENT. ED053799
RUBELLA AND ITS AFTERMATH EJ 007 163
1. OBSTETRICAL MEDICATION AND INFANT OUTCOME: A REVIEW OF THE LITERATURE EJ 023 013
III. OBSTETRICAL MEDICATION AND INFANT OUTCOME: SOME SUMMARY CONSIDERATIONS EJ 023 015
MATERNAL FOOD RESTRICTION: EFFECTS ON OFFSPRING DEVELOPMENT, LEARNING, AND A PROGRAM OF THERAPY EJ 029 218
DEVELOPMENTAL GENETICS OF BEHAVIORAL CAPACITIES: THE NATURE-NURTURE PROBLEM RE-EVALUATED EJ 037 516
PREDICTION OF DEVELOPMENTAL OUTCOME AT SEVEN YEARS FROM PRENATAL, PERINATAL, AND POSTNATAL EVENTS EJ 058 927

PREREADING EXPERIENCE
ANALYSIS OF STORY RETELLING AS A MEASURE OF THE EFFECTS OF ETHNIC CONTENT IN STORIES. FINAL REPORT. ED014326
A COMPARISON OF THE READING READINESS OF KINDERGARTEN PUPILS EXPOSED TO CONCEPTUAL-LANGUAGE AND BASAL READER PREREADING PROGRAMS. A PILOT STUDY. FINAL REPORT. ED029709
PRE-READING ON SESAME STREET. FINAL REPORT, VOLUME V OF V VOLUMES. ED047825
THE DEVELOPMENT OF PRE-READING SKILLS IN AN EXPERIMENTAL KINDERGARTEN PROGRAM EJ 037 099

PRESCHOOL CHILDREN
THE CHILDREN'S CENTER--A MICROCOSMIC HEALTH, EDUCATION, AND WELFARE UNIT. PROGRESS REPORT. ED013116
CURRICULUM DEVELOPMENT PROGRAM FOR PRESCHOOL TEACHER AIDES. FINAL REPORT. ED013122
REPORT ON THE ARTICULATORY AND INTELLIGIBILITY STATUS OF SOCIALLY DISADVANTAGED PRE-SCHOOL CHILDREN. ED014321
AN ASSESSMENT OF INTELLIGENCE, PSYCHOLINGUISTIC ABILITIES AND LEARNING APTITUDES AMONG PRESCHOOL CHILDREN. ED014323
ANALYSIS OF STORY RETELLING AS A MEASURE OF THE EFFECTS OF ETHNIC CONTENT IN STORIES. FINAL REPORT. ED014326
ACCELERATION OF INTELLECTUAL DEVELOPMENT IN EARLY CHILDHOOD. FINAL REPORT. ED014332
LANGUAGE RESEARCH STUDY--PROJECT HEAD START. DEVELOPMENT OF METHODOLOGY FOR OBTAINING AND ANALYZING SPONTANEOUS VERBALIZATIONS USED BY PRE-KINDERGARTEN CHILDREN IN SELECTED HEAD START PROGRAMS--A PILOT STUDY. ED015007
AN EVALUATION OF HEAD START PRESCHOOL ENRICHMENT PROGRAMS AS THEY AFFECT THE INTELLECTUAL ABILITY, THE SOCIAL ADJUSTMENT, AND THE ACHIEVEMENT LEVEL OF FIVE-YEAR-OLD CHILDREN ENROLLED IN LINCOLN, NEBRASKA. ED015011
COMPARATIVE STUDIES OF A GROUP OF HEAD START AND A GROUP OF NON-HEAD START PRESCHOOL CHILDREN. FINAL REPORT. ED015013
BEHAVIOR PATTERNS OF NORMAL CHILDREN. ED015016
TEACHING READING TO CHILDREN WITH LOW MA'S. ED015020
THE DIRECT INSTRUCTION PROGRAM FOR TEACHING READING. ED015022
TECHNIQUES FOR ASSESSING COGNITIVE AND SOCIAL ABILITIES OF CHILDREN AND PARENTS IN PROJECT HEAD START. ED015772
A NATIONAL DEMONSTRATION PROJECT UTILIZING TELEVISED MATERIALS FOR THE FORMAL EDUCATION OF CULTURALLY DISADVANTAGED PRESCHOOL CHILDREN. FINAL REPORT. ED015788
EFFECTS OF A STRUCTURED PROGRAM OF PRESCHOOL MATHEMATICS ON COGNITIVE BEHAVIOR. ED015791
FACTORS AFFECTING COGNITIVE GROWTH IN PROJECT HEAD START CHILDREN--WHAT KINDS OF CHANGES OCCUR IN WHAT KINDS OF CHILDREN UNDER WHAT KINDS OF PROGRAMS. ED015794

POSITIVE SOCIAL REINFORCEMENT IN THE NURSERY SCHOOL PEER GROUP. ED016515
PROJECT TOBI, THE DEVELOPMENT OF A PRE-SCHOOL ACHIEVEMENT TEST. FINAL REPORT. ED016520
THE EFFECTS OF JUNIOR KINDERGARTEN ON ACHIEVEMENT--THE FIRST FIVE YEARS. ED016526
SUMMARY OF BEHAVIOR PATTERNS OF NORMAL CHILDREN. ED016531
A TECHNIQUE FOR GATHERING CHILDREN'S LANGUAGE SAMPLES FROM NATURALISTIC SETTINGS. ED016532
THE EFFECTS OF NEUROLOGICAL AND ENVIRONMENTAL FACTORS ON THE LANGUAGE DEVELOPMENT OF HEAD START CHILDREN--A EVALUATION OF THE HEAD START PROGRAM. ED017317
A PRELIMINARY INVESTIGATION TO ESTABLISH A REGIONAL CENTER FOR EDUCATIONAL DEVELOPMENTAL STUDIES OF DISADVANTAGED PRESCHOOL CHILDREN. FINAL REPORT. ED017318
MONTESSORI PRE-SCHOOL EDUCATION. FINAL REPORT. ED017320
A NEW THEORY OF SCRIBBLING AND DRAWING IN CHILDREN. ED017324
AN APPROACH FOR WORKING WITH MOTHERS OF DISADVANTAGED PRESCHOOL CHILDREN. ED017335
EFFECTS OF DIFFERENTIAL PRIOR EXPOSURE ON YOUNG CHILDREN'S SUBSEQUENT OBSERVING AND CHOICE OF NOVEL STIMULI. ED017336
RESULTS OF THE SUMMER 1965 PROJECT HEAD START. VOLUMES I AND II. ED018250
THE STATUS OF BEHAVIORAL MEASUREMENT AND ASSESSMENT IN CHILDREN. ED018252
THE COGNITIVE ENVIRONMENTS OF URBAN PRE-SCHOOL CHILDREN. MANUAL OF INSTRUCTIONS FOR ADMINISTERING AND SCORING THE HOME INTERVIEW. ED018253
THE COGNITIVE ENVIRONMENTS OF URBAN PRE-SCHOOL CHILDREN. MANUAL OF INSTRUCTIONS FOR ADMINISTERING AND SCORING "SCHOOLS" QUESTION. ED018254
THE COGNITIVE ENVIRONMENTS OF URBAN PRE-SCHOOL CHILDREN. MANUAL OF INSTRUCTIONS FOR ADMINISTERING AND SCORING EDUCATIONAL ATTITUDE SURVEY. ED018255
THE COGNITIVE ENVIRONMENTS OF URBAN PRE-SCHOOL CHILDREN. MANUAL OF INSTRUCTIONS FOR ADMINISTERING AND SCORING MOTHER'S ATTITUDES TOWARD CHILD'S BEHAVIOR LEADING TO MASTERY. ED018256
THE COGNITIVE ENVIRONMENTS OF URBAN PRE-SCHOOL CHILDREN. MANUAL OF INSTRUCTIONS FOR ADMINISTERING AND SCORING MOTHER'S ROLE IN TEACHER/CHILD AND CHILD/PEER SCHOOL SITUATIONS. ED018257
THE COGNITIVE ENVIRONMENTS OF URBAN PRE-SCHOOL CHILDREN. MANUAL OF INSTRUCTIONS FOR ADMINISTERING AND SCORING FIRST DAY. ED018258
THE COGNITIVE ENVIRONMENTS OF URBAN PRE-SCHOOL CHILDREN. MANUAL OF INSTRUCTIONS FOR ADMINISTERING AND SCORING MOTHER-TEACHER PICTURE. ED018259
THE COGNITIVE ENVIRONMENTS OF URBAN PRE-SCHOOL CHILDREN. MANUAL OF INSTRUCTIONS FOR ADMINISTERING AND SCORING HOME RESOURCES PATTERNS. ED018260
THE COGNITIVE ENVIRONMENTS OF URBAN PRE-SCHOOL CHILDREN. MANUAL OF INSTRUCTIONS FOR ADMINISTERING AND SCORING SIGEL CONCEPTUAL STYLE SORTING TASKS. ED018263
THE COGNITIVE ENVIRONMENTS OF URBAN PRE-SCHOOL CHILDREN. MANUAL OF INSTRUCTIONS FOR ADMINISTERING AND SCORING TOY SORTING TASK. ED018264
THE COGNITIVE ENVIRONMENTS OF URBAN PRE-SCHOOL CHILDREN. MANUAL OF INSTRUCTIONS FOR ADMINISTERING AND SCORING THE EIGHT-BLOCK SORTING TASK. ED018265
THE COGNITIVE ENVIRONMENTS OF URBAN PRE-SCHOOL CHILDREN. MANUAL FOR CODING MOTHER-CHILD INTERACTION ON THE EIGHT-BLOCK SORTING TASK. ED018266
THE COGNITIVE ENVIRONMENTS OF URBAN PRE-SCHOOL CHILDREN. MANUAL OF INSTRUCTIONS FOR ADMINISTERING AND SCORING "ETCH-A-SKETCH" TASK. ED018267
THE COGNITIVE ENVIRONMENTS OF URBAN PRE-SCHOOL CHILDREN. MANUAL OF INSTRUCTIONS FOR ADMINISTERING AND SCORING THE CURIOSITY TASK. ED018268
THE COGNITIVE ENVIRONMENTS OF URBAN PRE-SCHOOL CHILDREN. MANUAL OF RECORDING AND OBSERVATION TECHNIQUES FOR MOTHER-CHILD INTERACTION. ED018269
THE COGNITIVE ENVIRONMENTS OF URBAN PRE-SCHOOL CHILDREN. MANUAL OF INSTRUCTIONS FOR ADMINISTERING AND SCORING MATERNAL LANGUAGE STYLES. ED018270
A REPORT OF THE SOUTHERN REGIONAL CONFERENCE ON EARLY CHILDHOOD EDUCATION. ED019112
FINAL REPORT ON HEAD START EVALUATION AND RESEARCH--1966-67 TO THE INSTITUTE FOR EDUCATIONAL DEVELOPMENT. SECTION VII, SENSORY AND PERCEPTUAL STUDIES. ED019123
LANGUAGE DEVELOPMENT EXPERIENCES FOR YOUNG CHILDREN. ED019125
SENSORIMOTOR EXPERIENCE AND CONCEPT FORMATION IN EARLY CHILDHOOD. FINAL REPORT. ED019143
A COMPARATIVE STUDY OF VARIOUS PROJECT HEAD START PROGRAMS. ED019987
TEACHING FORMAL OPERATIONS TO PRESCHOOL ADVANTAGED AND DISADVANTAGED CHILDREN. ED019990
EFFECTS OF ADULT SOCIAL REINFORCEMENT ON CHILD BEHAVIOR. ED019997
EVALUATION OF THE CLEVELAND CHILD DEVELOPMENT PROGRAM. A LONGITUDINAL STUDY (FIRST YEAR REPORT). ED020000
THE DEUTSCH MODEL--INSTITUTE FOR DEVELOPMENTAL STUDIES. ED020009
MOTIVATIONAL FACTORS AND IQ-CHANGES IN CULTURALLY DEPRIVED CHILDREN ATTENDING NURSERY SCHOOL. ED020017
A LONGITUDINAL ASSESSMENT OF PRESCHOOL CHILDREN IN HAPTIC LEARNING. FINAL REPORT. ED020019
THE EFFECT OF HEADSTART ON DEVELOPMENTAL PROCESSES. ED020026
THE LIMITATIONS OF BRIEF INTELLIGENCE TESTING WITH YOUNG CHILDREN. ED020774
SEMO PROJECT HEAD START, PSYCHOLOGICAL SERVICES REPORT, 1966-67 YEAR PROGRAM. ED020780
THE SYNTACTIC STRUCTURES OF 5-YEAR-OLD CULTURALLY DEPRIVED CHILDREN. ED020788
LANGUAGE CONTROL IN A GROUP OF HEAD START CHILDREN. ED020789
REGIONAL EVALUATION AND RESEARCH CENTER FOR HEAD START, SOUTHERN UNIVERSITY. ANNUAL REPORT. ED020792
CULTURAL ENVIRONMENTAL ACHIEVEMENT PROJECT, A SUMMARIZATION AND EVALUATION OF AN EXPERIMENTAL PRE-SCHOOL PROGRAM. ED021610
HEAD START RESEARCH AND EVALUATION OFFICE, UNIVERSITY OF CALIFORNIA AT LOS ANGELES. ANNUAL REPORT, NOVEMBER 1967. SECTION II. ED021613
HEAD START EVALUATION AND RESEARCH CENTER, UNIVERSITY OF KANSAS. FINAL REPORT ON RESEARCH ACTIVITIES. ED021614
MEASUREMENT OF MOTIVATION TO ACHIEVE IN PRESCHOOL CHILDREN. FINAL REPORT. ED021617
PRELIMINARY EVALUATION OF A LANGUAGE CURRICULUM FOR PRESCHOOL CHILDREN. FINAL REPORT. ED021618
THE EFFECT OF SUBJECT-DETERMINED VERBALIZATION ON DISCRIMINATION LEARNING IN PRESCHOOLERS. ED021620
HEAD START EVALUATION AND RESEARCH CENTER. PROGRESS REPORT OF RESEARCH STUDIES 1966 TO 1967. DOCUMENT 6, INDIVIDUAL INSTRUCTION PROJECT I. ED021628
EARLY CHILDHOOD EDUCATION TODAY. ED021631
HEAD START EVALUATION AND RESEARCH CENTER, UNIVERSITY OF KANSAS. REPORT NO. IIB, AN EXPERIMENTAL ANALYSIS OF VERBAL IMITATION IN PRESCHOOL CHILDREN. ED021635
HEAD START EVALUATION AND RESEARCH CENTER, UNIVERSITY OF KANSAS. REPORT NO. IV, A COMPARISON OF FOUR MODES OF ELICITING BRIEF ORAL RESPONSES FROM CHILDREN. ED021637
HEAD START EVALUATION AND RESEARCH CENTER, UNIVERSITY OF KANSAS. REPORT NO. V, A COMPARATIVE BEHAVIORAL ANALYSIS OF PEER-GROUP INFLUENCE TECHNIQUES IN HEAD START AND MIDDLE CLASS POPULATIONS. ED021638
HEAD START EVALUATION AND RESEARCH CENTER, UNIVERSITY OF KANSAS. REPORT NO. VI, A FAILURE TO SHOW AND INVOLVEMENT OF CURRENT MOTIVATIONAL VARIABLES IN THE RESPONSE OF HEAD START CHILDREN IN THE ASSESSMENT OF INTELLIGENCE BY MEANS OF THE STANFORD BINET TEST. ED021639
HEAD START EVALUATION AND RESEARCH CENTER, UNIVERSITY OF KANSAS. REPORT NO. VIIA, A CASE STUDY IN ESTABLISHING A DIFFERENTIATED SPEECH RESPONSE THROUGH GENERALIZATION PROCEDURES. ED021640
HEAD START EVALUATION AND RESEARCH CENTER, UNIVERSITY OF KANSAS. REPORT NO. VIIB, ESTABLISHMENT OF NONVERBAL COLOR DISCRIMINATION RESPONSES TO AUDITORY COLOR-LABELING STIMULI AND SUBSEQUENT EFFECTS ON COLOR-LABELING RESPONSES. ED021641
HEAD START EVALUATION AND RESEARCH CENTER, UNIVERSITY OF KANSAS. REPORT NO. VIIC, ERRORLESS DISCRIMINATION IN PRESCHOOL CHILDREN: A PROGRAM FOR ESTABLISHING A ONE-MINUTE DELAY OF REINFORCEMENT. ED021642
HEAD START EVALUATION AND RESEARCH CENTER, UNIVERSITY OF KANSAS. REPORT NO. VIII, PHYSICAL DEVELOPMENT OF CHILDREN IN THE HEAD START PROGRAM IN THE CENTRAL UNITED STATES. ED021644
HEAD START EVALUATION AND RESEARCH CENTER, UNIVERSITY OF KANSAS. REPORT NO. X, ENHANCEMENT OF THE SOCIAL REINFORCING VALUE OF A PRESCHOOL TEACHER. ED021646
HEAD START EVALUATION AND RESEARCH CENTER, UNIVERSITY OF KANSAS. REPORT NO. XI, VERBAL RECALL RESEARCH. ED021647
THE DEVELOPMENT OF FORMS OF THE NEGATIVE. ED022549
HEAD START EVALUATION AND RESEARCH CENTER, THE UNIVERSITY OF CHICAGO. REPORT E, COMPARATIVE USE OF ALTERNATIVE MODES FOR ASSESSING COGNITIVE DEVELOPMENT IN BILINGUAL OR NON-ENGLISH SPEAKING CHILDREN. ED022554
GAMES AND OTHER ACTIVITIES FOR DEVELOPING LANGUAGE SKILLS. ED022555
HEAD START EVALUATION AND RESEARCH CENTER, BOSTON UNIVERSITY. REPORT C-II, THE EXPRESSION OF AGGRESSION IN PRE-SCHOOL CHILDREN. ED022562
HEAD START EVALUATION AND RESEARCH CENTER, BOSTON UNIVERSITY. REPORT D-III, A STUDY OF PREFERENCES AMONG QUALITATIVELY DIFFERING UNCERTAINTIES. ED022565

HEAD START EVALUATION AND RESEARCH CENTER, THE UNIVERSITY OF CHICAGO. ANNUAL REPORT, 1966-1967. ED023445
STIMULUS DIMENSIONALITY AND MANIPULABILITY IN VISUAL PERCEPTUAL LEARNING. ED023452
INTERACTION PATTERNS AS A SOURCE OF ERROR IN TEACHERS' EVALUATIONS OF HEAD START CHILDREN. FINAL REPORT. ED023453
FINAL REPORT ON HEAD START EVALUATION AND RESEARCH: 1967-68 TO THE OFFICE OF ECONOMIC OPPORTUNITY. SECTION I: PART A, MIDDLE CLASS MOTHER-TEACHERS IN AN EXPERIMENTAL PRESCHOOL PROGRAM FOR SOCIALLY DISADVANTAGED CHILDREN. ED023454
FINAL REPORT ON HEAD START EVALUATION AND RESEARCH: 1967-68 TO THE OFFICE OF ECONOMIC OPPORTUNITY. SECTION II: ACHIEVEMENT MOTIVATION AND PATTERNS OF REINFORCEMENT IN HEAD START CHILDREN. ED023458
PROCESSES OF CURIOSITY AND EXPLORATION IN PRESCHOOL DISADVANTAGED CHILDREN. ED023470
A COMPARISON OF PRE-KINDERGARTEN AND PRE-1ST GRADE BOYS AND GIRLS ON MEASURES OF SCHOOL READINESS AND LANGUAGE DEVELOPMENT. INTERIM REPORT. ED023474
LONG TERM EFFECT OF STRUCTURED TRAINING ON 3 YOUNG CHILDREN. ED023480
LINGUISTIC AND PSYCHOLOGICAL FACTORS IN THE SPEECH REGULATION OF BEHAVIOR IN VERY YOUNG CHILDREN. ED024442
LURIA'S MODEL OF THE VERBAL CONTROL OF BEHAVIOR. STUDY F: MOTIVATIONAL AND CONTROL IN THE DEVELOPMENT OF LANGUAGE FUNCTIONS, D. BIRCH. ED024443
INDUCED VERSUS SPONTANEOUS REHEARSAL IN SHORT-TERM MEMORY IN NURSERY SCHOOL CHILDREN. STUDY M: DEVELOPMENT OF SELECTIVE ATTENTION ABILITIES. ED024444
TWO STUDIES OF THE SYNTACTIC KNOWLEDGE OF YOUNG CHILDREN. A PRELIMINARY REPORT. ED024451
COMPARISON OF AMERICAN AND NORWEGIAN NURSERY SCHOOL CHILDREN ON INDEPENDENCE BEHAVIOR AND TRAINING. ED024457
BIG QUESTIONS AND LITTLE CHILDREN: SCIENCE AND HEAD START. ED024458
REACHING THE HARD-TO-REACH: THE USE OF PARTICIPANT GROUP METHODS WITH MOTHERS OF CULTURALLY DISADVANTAGED PRESCHOOL CHILDREN. ED024469
PRESCHOOL PROGRAMS AND THE INTELLECTUAL DEVELOPMENT OF DISADVANTAGED CHILDREN. ED024473
COMPARISON OF AMERICAN AND NORWEGIAN NURSERY SCHOOL CHILDREN OF INDEPENDENCE BEHAVIOR AND TRAINING. SUMMARY REPORT. ED024476
ROLE OF MOTHERS' LANGUAGE STYLES IN MEDIATING THEIR PRESCHOOL CHILDREN'S COGNITIVE DEVELOPMENT. ED025298
PARENT-CHILD INTERACTION AND THE CHILD'S APPROACH TO TASK SITUATIONS. ED025307
COMPARATIVE EFFECTIVENESS OF ECHOIC AND MODELING PROCEDURES IN LANGUAGE INSTRUCTION WITH CULTURALLY DISADVANTAGED CHILDREN. ED025314
THE IDENTIFICATION AND ASSESSMENT OF THINKING ABILITY IN YOUNG CHILDREN. FINAL REPORT. ED025316
HEAD START CRIB. CHILDHOOD RESEARCH INFORMATION BULLETIN: SELECTED RESUMES OF EARLY CHILDHOOD RESEARCH REPORTS. BULLETIN NO. 1. ED025318
EARLY INTELLECTIVE TRAINING AND SCHOOL PERFORMANCE. SUMMARY OF NIH GRANT NUMBER HD-02253. ED025324
EXTENSION OF A THEORY OF PREDICTIVE BEHAVIOR TO IMMEDIATE RECALL BY PRESCHOOL CHILDREN. ED025326
THE DEVELOPMENT OF INTERROGATIVE STRUCTURES IN CHILDREN'S SPEECH. ED025333
INFANT AND PRESCHOOL MENTAL TESTS: REVIEW AND EVALUATION. ED026109
THE EFFECT OF A STRUCTURED TUTORIAL PROGRAM ON THE COGNITIVE AND LANGUAGE DEVELOPMENT OF CULTURALLY DISADVANTAGED INFANTS. ED026110
PRESCHOOL PARENT EDUCATION PROGRAM: A CURRICULUM GUIDE FOR USE BY TEACHERS CONDUCTING PARENT EDUCATION PROGRAMS AS A PART OF OVER-ALL COMPENSATORY PRESCHOOL PROJECTS. EXPERIMENTAL EDITION. ED026118
ERROR, RESPONSE TIME AND IQ: SEX DIFFERENCES IN COGNITIVE STYLE OF PRESCHOOL CHILDREN. ED026122
LEARNING READINESS IN TWO JEWISH GROUPS: A STUDY IN "CULTURAL DEPRIVATION." AN OCCASIONAL PAPER. ED026126
DEPENDENCY AND SOCIAL PERFORMANCE: THE DEVELOPMENT OF A SCALE TO MEASURE LEVEL OF INDEPENDENCE IN SMALL CHILDREN. PART OF THE FINAL REPORT. ED026129
A METHODOLOGY FOR FOSTERING ABSTRACT THINKING IN DEPRIVED CHILDREN. ED026131
SEX ROLE TYPING IN THE PRESCHOOL YEARS: AN OVERVIEW. ED026134
FEAR AND ATTACHMENT IN YOUNG CHILDREN. RESEARCH PROJECT NUMBER 4 OF PROJECT HEAD START RESEARCH AND EVALUATION CENTER, SYRACUSE UNIVERSITY RESEARCH INSTITUTE. FINAL REPORT, NOVEMBER 1, 1967. ED026141
COGNITIVE GROWTH IN PRESCHOOL CHILDREN. ED027057
ADMINISTRATION MANUAL FOR TESTS OF BASIC LANGUAGE COMPETENCE IN ENGLISH AND SPANISH. LEVEL I (PRESCHOOL) ED027063
NATURALISTIC OBSERVATION IN THE STUDY OF PARENT-CHILD INTERACTION. ED027073
RESEARCH ON THE NEW NURSERY SCHOOL. PART I, A SUMMARY OF THE EVALUATION OF THE EXPERIMENTAL PROGRAM FOR DEPRIVED CHILDREN AT THE NEW NURSERY SCHOOL USING SOME EXPERIMENTAL MEASURES. INTERIM REPORT. ED027076
THE PROGRAM OF RESEARCH OF THE MERRILL-PALMER INSTITUTE IN CONJUNCTION WITH THE HEAD START EVALUATION AND RESEARCH CENTER, MICHIGAN STATE UNIVERSITY. ANNUAL REPORT. VOLUME II: RESEARCH. ED027088
EVALUATION OF INKSTER PRESCHOOL PROJECT. FINAL REPORT. ED027093
PREPRIMARY ENROLLMENT OF CHILDREN UNDER SIX: OCTOBER 1967. ED027094
CHANGING PARENT ATTITUDES AND IMPROVING LANGUAGE AND INTELLECTUAL ABILITIES OF CULTURALLY DISADVANTAGED FOUR-YEAR-OLD CHILDREN THROUGH PARENT INVOLVEMENT. ED027942
LANGUAGE STYLE OF THE LOWER CLASS MOTHER: A PRELIMINARY STUDY OF A THERAPEUTIC TECHNIQUE. ED027943
HEAD START ON HEALTH. ED027972
A STUDY OF FOOD AND POVERTY AMONG 113 HEAD START CHILDREN IN MISSOULA, MONTANA. ED028829
AN EXPERIMENTAL PROGRAM DESIGNED TO INCREASE AUDITORY DISCRIMINATION WITH HEAD START CHILDREN. ED029680
A TWO-YEAR LANGUAGE ARTS PROGRAM FOR PRE-FIRST GRADE CHILDREN: FIRST YEAR REPORT. ED029686
COMPETENCE VS. PERFORMANCE IN YOUNG CHILDREN'S USE OF COMPLEX LINGUISTIC STRUCTURES. ED029687
EFFECT OF VARIETY ON THE LEARNING OF A SOCIAL STUDIES CONCEPT BY PRESCHOOL CHILDREN. ED029690
USE OF NON-PROFESSIONAL PERSONNEL FOR HEALTH SCREENING OF HEAD START CHILDREN. FINAL REPORT. ED029702
HEAD START EVALUATION AND RESEARCH CENTER, TULANE UNIVERSITY. ANNUAL REPORT. ED029705
REPLICATION OF THE "MOTIVATED LEARNING" COGNITIVE TRAINING PROCEDURES WITH CULTURALLY DEPRIVED PRESCHOOLERS. REPORT FROM PROJECT MOTIVATED LEARNING. ED029708
THE RELATIONSHIP BETWEEN INSTRUMENTAL ASSERTION AND THE STANFORD-BINET. ED030474
SOCIAL ANTECEDENTS OF PRESCHOOL CHILDREN'S BEHAVIORS. REPORT NUMBER 2. ED030476
THE RELATIONSHIP BETWEEN RACE AND PERCEPTION OF RACIALLY-RELATED STIMULI IN PRESCHOOL CHILDREN. ED030483
THE EFFECTS OF A LEARNING PROGRAM IN PERCEPTUAL-MOTOR ACTIVITY UPON THE VISUAL PERCEPTION OF SHAPE. FINAL REPORT. ED030494
THE ROLE OF INCENTIVES IN DISCRIMINATION LEARNING OF CHILDREN WITH VARYING PRE-SCHOOL EXPERIENCE. ED031290
A STUDY OF THE INTERRELATIONSHIPS OF CONSERVATION OF LENGTH RELATIONS, CONSERVATIONS OF LENGTH, AND TRANSITIVITY OF LENGTH RELATIONS OF THE AGE OF FOUR AND FIVE YEARS. ED031303
MATERNAL BEHAVIOR AND THE DEVELOPMENT OF READING READINESS IN URBAN NEGRO CHILDREN. ED031309
PERSONALITY DEVELOPMENT IN DISADVANTAGED FOUR-YEAR-OLD BOYS: OBSERVATIONS WITH PLAY TECHNIQUES. ED031310
INFORMATION VALUE OF FEEDBACK WITH PRESCHOOL CHILDREN. ED031311
A DESCRIPTIVE STUDY OF COGNITIVE AND AFFECTIVE TRENDS DIFFERENTIATING SELECTED GROUPS OF PRE-SCHOOL CHILDREN. ED031314
PREPRIMARY ENROLLMENT OF CHILDREN UNDER SIX: OCTOBER 1968. ED032118
THE EFFECTS OF MODE OF PRESENTATION AND NUMBER OF CATEGORIES ON 4-YEAR-OLDS' PROPORTION ESTIMATES. ED032132
CHILDREN'S PERCEPTIONS OF ADULT ROLES AS AFFECTED BY CLASS, FATHER-ABSENCE AND RACE. ED032134
RESISTANCE TO TEMPTATION IN YOUNG NEGRO CHILDREN IN RELATION TO SEX OF THE SUBJECT, SEX OF THE EXPERIMENTER AND FATHER ABSENCE OR PRESENCE. ED032138
SOCIOECONOMIC BACKGROUND AND COGNITIVE FUNCTIONING IN PRESCHOOL CHILDREN. ED032929
MEASURING PERCEPTUAL MOTOR ABILITY IN PRESCHOOL CHILDREN. ED032932
MODIFICATION OF THE PEABODY PICTURE VOCABULARY TEST. ED033752
YOUNG CHILDREN'S COMPREHENSION OF LOGICAL CONNECTIVES. ED033756
CHILDREN LEARNING: SAMPLES OF EVERYDAY LIFE OF CHILDREN AT HOME. ED033763
A BILINGUAL ORAL LANGUAGE AND CONCEPTUAL DEVELOPMENT PROGRAM FOR SPANISH-SPEAKING PRE-SCHOOL CHILDREN. ED034568
COLOR AND PHYSIOGNOMY AS VARIABLES IN RACIAL MISIDENTIFICATION AMONG CHILDREN. ED034584
INSTITUTE FOR DEVELOPMENTAL STUDIES INTERIM PROGRESS REPORT. PART II: RESEARCH AND EVALUATION. ED036312
OBSERVED COGNITIVE COMMUNICATION PATTERNS OF ADULTS AND CHILDREN IN FOUR PRE-SCHOOL AGE GROUPS. ED036325
PARENT HANDBOOK: DEVELOPING YOUR CHILD'S SKILLS AND ABILITIES AT HOME. ED036327

POPULATION CHARACTERISTICS OF DISADVANTAGED PRESCHOOL CHILDREN. PROCEEDINGS OF THE HEAD START RESEARCH SEMINARS: SEMINAR NO. 3, HEAD START POPULATIONS (1ST, WASHINGTON, D.C., OCTOBER 9, 1968). ED036330
A STUDY OF NON-VERBAL REPRESENTATION IN YOUNG CHILDREN. ED036336
TEACHING STYLES IN FOUR-YEAR-OLDS. ED036340
TEACHING MATHEMATICAL CONCEPTS TO TWO- AND THREE-YEAR-OLDS: SOME EXPERIMENTAL STUDIES. ED037234
FAMILY FACTORS RELATED TO COMPETENCE IN YOUNG, DISADVANTAGED MEXICAN-AMERICAN CHILDREN. PART OF THE FINAL REPORT ON HEAD START EVALUATION AND RESEARCH: 1968-69 TO THE OFFICE OF ECONOMIC OPPORTUNITY. ED037248
A REPLICATION AND EXTENSION STUDY ON N-LENGTH, INHIBITION AND COOPERATIVE BEHAVIOR WITH A MEXICAN-AMERICAN POPULATION. PART OF THE FINAL REPORT ON HEAD START EVALUATION AND RESEARCH: 1968-69 TO THE OFFICE OF ECONOMIC OPPORTUNITY. ED037249
CHARACTERIZATION OF THE EFFECT OF SPACE, MATERIALS, AND TEACHER BEHAVIOR ON PRESCHOOL CHILDREN'S FREE PLAY ACTIVITY PATTERNS. RESEARCH REPORT NO. 1. ED037251
DEVELOPMENT OF A READINESS TEST FOR DISADVANTAGED PRE-SCHOOL CHILDREN IN THE UNITED STATES. FINAL REPORT. ED037253
THE RELATION OF CERTAIN HOME ENVIRONMENT FACTORS TO THE THINKING ABILITIES OF THREE-YEAR-OLD CHILDREN. FINAL REPORT. ED039041
A COMPARISON OF PARENT AND TEACHER RATINGS ON THE PRESCHOOL ATTAINMENT RECORD OF SEVENTEEN FIVE-YEAR-OLD DISADVANTAGED CHILDREN. ED039922
A COMPARISON OF THREE INTERVENTION PROGRAMS WITH DISADVANTAGED PRESCHOOL CHILDREN. UNIVERSITY OF CALIFORNIA HEAD START RESEARCH AND EVALUATION CENTER. FINAL REPORT 1968-1969. ED041616
EXPERIMENTAL VARIATION OF HEAD START CURRICULA: A COMPARISON OF CURRENT APPROACHES. (NOVEMBER 1, 1969-JANUARY 31, 1970). ED041617
THE PREVALENCE OF ANEMIA IN HEAD START CHILDREN. NUTRITION EVALUATION, 1968-69. ED041629
DEVELOPMENT OF GRAMMATICAL STRUCTURES AND ATTRIBUTES IN PRE-SCHOOL AGE CHILDREN. FINAL REPORT. ED041639
LANGUAGE DEVELOPMENT OF SOCIALLY DISADVANTAGED PRESCHOOL CHILDREN. FINAL REPORT. ED041641
INFLUENCE TECHNIQUES IN DYADS COMPOSED OF INTERDEPENDENT MIDDLE AND LOWER CLASS PRESCHOOL CHILDREN. FINAL REPORT ED042489
A SHOE IS TO TIE: A FILM DEMONSTRATION OF PROGRAMMING SELF-HELP SKILLS FOR PRESCHOOL CHILDREN. PROGRESS REPORT. ED042500
PREPRIMARY ENROLLMENT TRENDS OF CHILDREN UNDER SIX: 1964-1968. ED042502
PROGRAM-PROJECT RESUMES, 1969-1970. ED042503
CLASSIFICATION AND ATTENTION TRAINING CURRICULA FOR HEAD START CHILDREN. ED042508
THE "TELL-AND-FIND PICTURE GAME" FOR YOUNG CHILDREN. ED042513
THE NEW NURSERY SCHOOL RESEARCH PROJECT ED042518
THE EFFECT ON AGGRESSION OF VARIATION IN AMOUNT OF OPPORTUNITY FOR PLAY. (INTERNAL REPORT). ED043384
GROSS ACTIVITY OF CHILDREN AT PLAY. (INTERNAL REPORT). ED043385
PARENTAL CONCEPTUAL SYSTEMS, HOME PLAY ENVIRONMENT, AND POTENTIAL CREATIVITY IN CHILDREN. ED043386
THE PRESCHOOL CHILD'S ABILITY TO FOLLOW DIRECTIONS. ED043395
FROM THEORY TO OPERATIONS. DISADVANTAGED CHILDREN AND THEIR FIRST SCHOOL EXPERIENCES, ETS-HEAD START LONGITUDINAL STUDY. ED043397
PARENTS AS PRIMARY CHANGE AGENTS IN AN EXPERIMENTAL HEAD START PROGRAM OF LANGUAGE INTERVENTION. EXPERIMENTAL PROGRAM REPORT. ED044168
AN EXPERIMENTAL PROGRAM IN CLASSIFICATION AND ATTENTIONAL TRAINING WITH HEAD START CHILDREN. ED044171
PREDICTION OF ACHIEVEMENT IN THE FIRST PRIMARY YEAR. STUDY NUMBER ONE. ED044180
HETEROGENEOUS VS. HOMOGENEOUS SOCIAL CLASS GROUPING OF PRESCHOOL CHILDREN IN HEAD START CLASSROOMS. ED045176
SUBPOPULATIONAL PROFILING OF THE PSYCHOEDUCATIONAL DIMENSIONS OF DISADVANTAGED PRESCHOOL CHILDREN: A CONCEPTUAL PROSPECTUS FOR AN INTERDISCIPLINARY RESEARCH. ED045177
AN INVESTIGATION IN THE LEARNING OF EQUIVALENCE AND ORDER RELATIONS BY FOUR- AND FIVE-YEAR-OLD CHILDREN. ED045178
THE COGNITIVE ENVIRONMENTS OF URBAN PRESCHOOL CHILDREN. FINAL REPORT. ED045179
RESULTS AND IMPLICATIONS OF A HEAD START CLASSIFICATION AND ATTENTION TRAINING PROGRAM. ED045182
POSITION EFFECTS IN PLAY EQUIPMENT PREFERENCES OF NURSERY SCHOOL CHILDREN. ED045185
EVALUATION OF A PARENT AND CHILD CENTER PROGRAM. ED045189
EDUCATIONAL INTERVENTION IN THE HOME AND PARAPROFESSIONAL CAREER DEVELOPMENT: A FIRST GENERATION MOTHER STUDY. ED045190
PRELIMINARY ANALYSIS OF 1968-69 HEAD START DATA. ED045203
A PROGRESS REPORT ON THE PARENT/CHILD COURSE AND TOY LIBRARY. ED045206
THE EFFECTS OF A PRESCHOOL LANGUAGE PROGRAM ON TWO-YEAR-OLD CHILDREN AND THEIR MOTHERS. FINAL REPORT. ED045224
UNDERSTANDING OF QUANTITATIVE CONCEPTS IN 3 1/2-4 1/2 YEAR-OLD CHILDREN. ED046491
AN APPLICATION OF PIAGET'S THEORY TO THE CONCEPTUALIZATION OF A PRESCHOOL CURRICULUM. ED046502
ATTITUDES OF PRESCHOOL AND ELEMENTARY SCHOOL CHILDREN TO AUTHORITY FIGURES. ED046506
RELATIONSHIPS BETWEEN CHILDREN'S QUESTIONS AND NURSERY SCHOOL TEACHERS' RESPONSES. ED046507
NUTRITION SURVEY OF WHITE MOUNTAIN APACHE PRESCHOOL CHILDREN. ED046508
DEVELOPMENTAL GROUPINGS OF PRE-SCHOOL CHILDREN. ED046513
MICHIGAN STATE UNIVERSITY, HEAD START EVALUATION AND RESEARCH, 1967-68 RESEARCH ABSTRACTS AND PROGRESS REPORTS. ED047771
SCHOOL ACHIEVEMENT: A PRELIMINARY LOOK AT THE EFFECTS OF THE HOME. ED047777
NUTRITIONAL STATUS OF NEW ORLEANS, MISSISSIPPI AND ALABAMA HEAD START CHILDREN. FINAL REPORT. ED047785
THE EFFECTS OF ADULT VERBAL MODELING AND FEEDBACK ON THE ORAL LANGUAGE OF HEAD START CHILDREN. ED047793
THE MEANING OF AN ORIENTING RESPONSE: A STUDY IN THE HIERARCHICAL ORDER OF ATTENDING. ED047794
DISADVANTAGED CHILDREN AND THEIR FIRST SCHOOL EXPERIENCES. ETS-HEAD START LONGITUDINAL STUDY: PRELIMINARY DESCRIPTION OF THE INITIAL SAMPLE PRIOR TO SCHOOL ENROLLMENT. A REPORT IN TWO VOLUMES: VOLUME 1. ED047797
PROGRAMS FOR INFANTS AND YOUNG CHILDREN. PART III: HEALTH. ED047809
THE FIRST YEAR OF SESAME STREET: A HISTORY AND OVERVIEW. FINAL REPORT, VOLUME I OF V VOLUMES. ED047821
THE FIRST YEAR OF SESAME STREET: THE FORMATIVE RESEARCH. FINAL REPORT, VOLUME II OF V VOLUMES. ED047822
LEAD POISONING IN CHILDREN. ED048919
PLAY BEHAVIOR AND EFFICACY IN GHETTO FOUR-YEAR-OLDS: ORGANIZATION AND PSYCHOSEXUAL CONTENT OF PLAY. ED048920
THE EFFICACY OF A MATHEMATICS READINESS PROGRAM FOR INDUCING CONSERVATION OF NUMBER, WEIGHT, AREA, MASS, AND VOLUME IN DISADVANTAGED PRESCHOOL CHILDREN IN THE SOUTHERN UNITED STATES. ED048923
A LONGITUDINAL ASSESSMENT OF THINKING ABILITY OF PRELITERATE CHILDREN DURING A TWO-YEAR PERIOD. FINAL REPORT. ED048946
PREPRIMARY ENROLLMENT, OCTOBER 1969. ED049816
THE UNIT-BASED CURRICULUM. YPSILANTI PRESCHOOL CURRICULUM DEMONSTRATION PROJECT. ED049831
A DESCRIPTIVE ACCOUNT OF FOUR MODES OF CHILDREN'S PLAY BETWEEN ONE AND FIVE YEARS. ED049833
SOCIAL INTERACTION IN HETEROGENEOUS PRE-SCHOOLS IN ISRAEL. ED049839
ENVIRONMENTAL FORCES IN THE HOME LIVES OF THREE-YEAR-OLD CHILDREN IN THREE POPULATION SUBGROUPS. ED050802
HEALTH CARE OF CHILDREN: A CHALLENGE. ED050804
MEASURING DIFFERENTIAL DEVELOPMENT IN YOUNG CHILDREN. ED050818
EFFECTS OF SOCIAL CLASS INTEGRATION OF PRESCHOOL NEGRO CHILDREN ON TEST PERFORMANCE AND SELF-CONCEPT. FINAL REPORT. ED050831
EFFECT OF LABELS ON MEMORY IN THE ABSENCE OF REHEARSAL. ED051883
A PRESCHOOL ARTICULATION AND LANGUAGE SCREENING FOR THE IDENTIFICATION OF SPEECH DISORDERS. FINAL REPORT. ED051889
A COMPARISON OF THE EFFECT OF VERBAL AND MATERIAL REWARD ON THE LEARNING OF LOWER CLASS PRESCHOOL CHILDREN. ED052817
EVALUATION REPORT: EARLY CHILDHOOD EDUCATION PROGRAM, 1969-1970 FIELD TEST. SUMMARY REPORT. ED052837
ANALYSIS OF CHILDREN'S REACTIONS TO AEL'S PRESCHOOL TELEVISION PROGRAM. ED052841
EARLY CHILDHOOD EDUCATION PROGRAM FOR NURSERY, KINDERGARTEN CHILDREN. ED052846
STUDY OF SELECTED CHILDREN IN HEAD START PLANNED VARIATION, 1969-1970. FIRST YEAR REPORT: 3 - CASE STUDIES OF CHILDREN. ED052847
AN EVALUATION OF LOGICAL OPERATIONS INSTRUCTION IN THE PRESCHOOL. ED053791
STANDARDS FOR DAY CARE CENTERS FOR INFANTS AND CHILDREN UNDER 3 YEARS OF AGE. ED053794
MOVEMENT AND MOVEMENT PATTERNS OF EARLY CHILDHOOD. ED053796
LITERATURE FOR YOUNG CHILDREN EJ 002 654
SUGGESTIONS FROM STUDIES OF EARLY LANGUAGE ACQUISITION EJ 012 396
PRESCHOOL CHILDREN'S UNDERSTANDING OF THE COORDINATED CONCEPTS OF DISTANCE, MOVEMENT, NUMBER, AND TIME EJ 015 100
INSTRUMENTAL AND AFFECTIONAL DEPENDENCY AND NURTURANCE IN PRESCHOOL CHILDREN EJ 015 101
A PARENT'S GIFT EJ 016 773

FANTASIZING AND POETRY CONSTRUCTION IN PRESCHOOLERS EJ 018 132
AGE DIFFERENCES IN THE DISCRIMINATION SHIFT LEARNING OF YOUNG CHILDREN EJ 025 963
IMITATION AND ECHOING IN YOUNG SCHIZOPHRENIC CHILDREN EJ 026 494
EXPERIMENTAL LEARNING REEVALUATED EJ 026 814
DISCRIMINATION SHIFTS IN THREE-YEAR-OLDS AS A FUNCTION OF SHIFT PROCEDURE EJ 027 184
THE CHILD'S EYE VIEW: EXPERIMENTAL PHOTOGRAPHY WITH PRESCHOOL CHILDREN EJ 029 342
SENSORY-MODALITY EFFECTS ON SHAPE PERCEPTION IN PRESCHOOL CHILDREN EJ 029 383
SHORT-TERM MEMORY IN CHILDREN: KEEPING TRACK OF VARIABLES WITH FEW OR MANY STATES EJ 029 444
NUTRITION REHABILITATION CENTRES EJ 029 953
PARENT AND CHILD CENTERS--IMPETUS, IMPLEMENTATION, IN-DEPTH VIEW EJ 030 469
SOCIALIZATION AND INSTRUMENTAL COMPETENCE IN YOUNG CHILDREN EJ 030 510
ISSUES IN ASSESSING DEVELOPMENT EJ 030 516
LEARNING AND COGNITIVE DEVELOPMENT: REPRESENTATIVE SAMPLES, CUMULATIVE-HIERARCHICAL LEARNING, AND EXPERIMENTAL-LONGITUDINAL METHODS EJ 032 509
RESISTANCE TO TEMPTATION IN YOUNG NEGRO CHILDREN EJ 032 894
YOUNG CHILDREN'S ORIENTATION OF LETTERS AS A FUNCTION OF AXIS OF SYMMETRY AND STIMULUS ALIGNMENT EJ 032 909
CHILDREN'S USE OF CONTEXT IN JUDGMENT OF WEIGHT EJ 033 053
CHILDREN'S SELECTIVE ATTENTION TO STIMULI: STAGE OR SET? EJ 033 573
COMPETENCE VERSUS PERFORMANCE IN YOUNG CHILDREN'S USE OF ADJECTIVAL COMPARATIVES EJ 033 701
NON-SOCIAL SPEECH IN FOUR-YEAR-OLD CHILDREN AS A FUNCTION OF BIRTH ORDER AND INTERPERSONAL SITUATION EJ 033 702
THE RELATIONSHIP BETWEEN INTENTIONAL LEARNING, INCIDENTAL LEARNING, AND TYPE OF REWARD IN PRESCHOOL, EDUCABLE, MENTAL RETARDATES EJ 033 783
TIME ESTIMATION BY YOUNG CHILDREN WITH AND WITHOUT INFORMATIONAL FEEDBACK EJ 033 787
SEQUENTIAL CONTIGUITY AND SHORT-TERM MEMORY IN CHILDREN'S DISCRIMINATION LEARNING EJ 033 790
YOUNG CHILDREN'S USE OF THE SPEECH CODE IN A RECALL TASK EJ 033 792
ATTITUDES OF PRESCHOOL AND ELEMENTARY SCHOOL CHILDREN TO AUTHORITY FIGURES EJ 034 452
A TEST OF THE GENERALITY OF THE EFFECTS OF DEVIANT PRESCHOOL MODELS EJ 034 531
PLAY PERSISTENCE: SOME EFFECTS OF INTERRUPTION, SOCIAL REINFORCEMENT, AND DEFECTIVE TOYS EJ 034 532
UN EXEMPLE D'OBSERVATION INTENSIVE DU COMPORTEMENT DE JEUNES ENFANTS DANS LE CADRE D'UNE GARDERIE EJ 034 534
CONTROL OF ORIENTING BEHAVIOR IN CHILDREN UNDER FIVE YEARS OF AGE EJ 034 535
LINGUISTIC AND PSYCHOLOGICAL FACTORS IN THE SPEECH REGULATION OF BEHAVIOR IN YOUNG CHILDREN EJ 034 540
DISCRIMINATION OF SPATIALLY CONFUSABLE LETTERS BY YOUNG CHILDREN EJ 034 565
PARENTAL EDUCATION, SEX DIFFERENCES, AND PERFORMANCE ON COGNITIVE TASKS AMONG TWO-YEAR-OLD CHILDREN EJ 035 364
FREE RECALL OF OBJECT NAMES IN PRESCHOOL CHILDREN AS A FUNCTION OF INTRACATEGORY VARIATION EJ 035 368
I SEE WHAT YOU MEAN EJ 035 370
EFFECT OF PRETRAINING AND INSTRUCTIONS ON AVOIDANCE CONDITIONING IN PRESCHOOL CHILDREN EJ 035 624
GOING ON A TRIP EJ 035 842
A DEVELOPMENTAL STUDY OF PRESCHOOL CHILDREN'S PREFERENCE FOR RANDOM FORMS EJ 035 990
CHILDREN'S "IMITATION" AS A FUNCTION OF THE PRESENCE OR ABSENCE OF A MODEL AND THE DESCRIPTION OF HIS INSTRUMENTAL BEHAVIORS EJ 036 080
EXPERIMENTAL PRESCHOOL INTERVENTION IN THE APPALACHIAN HOME EJ 036 395
SOCIAL-CLASS DIFFERENTIATION IN COGNITIVE DEVELOPMENT AMONG BLACK PRESCHOOL CHILDREN EJ 036 819
A PERSPECTIVE ON COGNITIVE DEVELOPMENT: THE PRESCHOOL CHILD'S PERFORMANCE IN CLASSIFICATION TASKS EJ 036 827
DEVELOPMENTAL GENERALITY OF A FORM RECOGNITION STRATEGY EJ 037 534
A NONARBITRARY BEHAVIORAL CRITERION FOR CONSERVATION OF ILLUSION-DISTORTED LENGTH IN FIVE-YEAR-OLDS EJ 038 263
DECISION PROCESSES IN MULTIDIMENSIONAL GENERALIZATION EJ 038 265
THE INFLUENCE OF AGE AND STIMULUS DIMENSIONALITY ON FORM PERCEPTION BY PRESCHOOL CHILDREN EJ 039 630
YOUNG CHILDREN'S PERFORMANCE ON A TWO-CHOICE TASK AS A FUNCTION OF SOCIAL REINFORCEMENT, BASE-LINE PREFERENCE, AND RESPONSE STRATEGY EJ 039 635
IMITATIVE AGGRESSION IN CHILDREN AS A FUNCTION OF OBSERVING A HUMAN MODEL EJ 039 907
AN EXPERIMENT ON EYEBROW-RAISING AND VISUAL SEARCHING IN CHILDREN EJ 039 947
INCORPORATION OF VALUES BY LOWER AND MIDDLE SOCIOECONOMIC CLASS PRESCHOOL BOYS EJ 040 210
KNOWLEDGE OF ACTION AND OBJECT WORDS: A COMPARISON OF LOWER- AND MIDDLE-CLASS NEGRO PRESCHOOLERS EJ 040 453
A DEVELOPMENTAL STUDY OF SIZE CONSTANCY FOR TWO-VERSUS THREE-DIMENSIONAL STIMULI EJ 040 454
THE EFFECTS OF STIMULUS REDUNDANCY ON TRANSFER OF STIMULUS PRETRAINING EJ 041 138
NUMBER CONSERVATION IN VERY YOUNG CHILDREN: THE EFFECT OF AGE AND MODE OF RESPONDING EJ 041 139
CONSERVATION OF NUMBER IN VERY YOUNG CHILDREN: A FAILURE TO REPLICATE MEHLER AND BEVER EJ 041 144
SOME LANGUAGE-RELATED COGNITIVE ADVANTAGES OF BILINGUAL FIVE-YEAR-OLDS EJ 041 343
EFFECTS OF CONTINGENT AND NONCONTINGENT REINFORCEMENT UPON GENERALIZED IMITATION EJ 041 448
VERBAL OPERANT CONDITIONING OF AN ACTIVE-NON-ACTIVE VERBAL DIFFERENTIAL IN EARLY SCHOOL CHILDREN EJ 041 451
VALIDITY OF THE DENVER DEVELOPMENTAL SCREENING TEST EJ 041 722
EFFECTS OF SOCIAL COMPARISON UPON CHILDREN'S SELF-REINFORCEMENT AND ALTRUISM TOWARD COMPETITORS AND FRIENDS EJ 041 856
RACIAL ATTITUDES OF NEGRO PRESCHOOLERS EJ 041 858
PRESCHOOL PLAY NORMS: A REPLICATION EJ 041 958
A BEHAVIOURAL SCREENING QUESTIONNAIRE FOR USE WITH THREE-YEAR-OLD CHILDREN. PRELIMINARY FINDINGS EJ 042 349
IDENTIFICATION OF VERBAL CONCEPTS BY PRESCHOOL CHILDREN EJ 042 958
NAMING AND MEMORY IN NURSERY SCHOOL CHILDREN IN THE ABSENCE OF REHEARSAL EJ 042 961
THE "FEATURE POSITIVE EFFECT" AND SIMULTANEOUS DISCRIMINATION LEARNING EJ 042 963
RECOGNITION MEMORY FOR PICTURES IN PRESCHOOL CHILDREN EJ 042 964
THE PERFORMANCE OF PRESCHOOL CHILDREN ON REVERSAL AND TWO TYPES OF EXTRADIMENSIONAL SHIFTS EJ 042 967
EFFECTS OF CONTEXT ON PRESCHOOL CHILDREN'S JUDGMENTS EJ 042 968
BOOKS FOR YOUNG CHILDREN EJ 043 020
TELEVISED AGGRESSION AND THE INTERPERSONAL AGGRESSION OF PRESCHOOL CHILDREN EJ 043 197
DEVELOPMENT OF SYNTACTIC COMPREHENSION IN PRESCHOOL CHILDREN AS A FUNCTION OF SOCIOECONOMIC LEVEL EJ 043 480
LEVELS OF ASPIRATION, ACHIEVEMENT, AND SOCIOCULTURAL DIFFERENCES IN PRESCHOOL CHILDREN EJ 043 482
EVIDENCE FOR COMPETITION AND COORDINATION BETWEEN VOCAL AND MANUAL RESPONSES IN PRESCHOOL CHILDREN EJ 043 668
A MOTHERS' TRAINING PROGRAM--THE ROAD TO A PURPOSEFUL EXISTENCE EJ 044 007
THE EFFECT OF TRAINING CHILDREN TO MAKE MORAL JUDGMENTS THAT ARE INDEPENDENT OF SANCTIONS EJ 044 507
CARPENTRY FOR YOUNG CHILDREN EJ 044 512
THE SEQUENCE OF DEVELOPMENT OF CERTAIN NUMBER CONCEPTS IN PRESCHOOL CHILDREN EJ 044 694
GENERALIZED LABELING ON THE BASIS OF STRUCTURAL RESPONSE CLASSES BY TWO YOUNG CHILDREN EJ 044 696
CONCEPTUAL BEHAVIOR IN YOUNG CHILDREN: LEARNING TO SHIFT DIMENSIONAL ATTENTION EJ 044 697
VISUAL AND HAPTIC CUE UTILIZATION BY PRESCHOOL CHILDREN: THE RECOGNITION OF VISUAL AND HAPTIC STIMULI PRESENTED SEPARATELY AND TOGETHER EJ 044 698
GENERALIZED IMITATION: THE EFFECTS OF EXPERIMENTER ABSENCE, DIFFERENTIAL REINFORCEMENT, AND STIMULUS COMPLEXITY EJ 045 044
NEWBORN AND PRESCHOOLER: ORGANIZATION OF BEHAVIOR AND RELATIONS BETWEEN PERIODS EJ 045 110
CORRESPONDENCE BETWEEN BEHAVIORAL AND DOLL-PLAY MEASURES OF CONSCIENCE EJ 045 190
COOPERATION AND COMPETITION IN FOUR-YEAR-OLDS AS A FUNCTION OF REWARD CONTINGENCY AND SUBCULTURE EJ 045 453
CORRELATES OF CURIOSITY AND EXPLORATORY BEHAVIOR IN PRESCHOOL DISADVANTAGED CHILDREN EJ 045 456
EFFECTS OF AN ADULT'S PRESENCE AND PRAISE ON YOUNG CHILDREN'S PERFORMANCE EJ 045 460
REFLECTION-IMPULSIVITY AND COLOR-FORM SORTING EJ 046 234
COMPLEX MOTOR LEARNING IN FOUR-YEAR-OLDS EJ 046 236
THE EFFECTS OF MOTHERS' PRESENCE AND PREVISITS ON CHILDREN'S EMOTIONAL REACTION TO STARTING NURSERY SCHOOL EJ 046 469
THE YOUNG CHILD'S UNDERSTANDING OF SOCIAL JUSTICE EJ 046 887
PARENTAL CONCEPTUAL SYSTEMS, HOME PLAY ENVIRONMENT, AND POTENTIAL CREATIVITY IN CHILDREN EJ 048 234
PLAY BEHAVIOR IN YOUNG CHILDREN: A CROSS-CULTURAL STUDY EJ 048 303
STRENGTH OF DIMENSIONAL PREFERENCES AS A PREDICTOR OF NURSERY-SCHOOL CHILDREN'S PERFORMANCE ON A CONCEPT-SHIFT TASK EJ 049 169

DIFFERENTIAL COGNITIVE DEVELOPMENT WITHIN AND BETWEEN RACIAL AND ETHNIC GROUPS OF DISADVANTAGED PRESCHOOL AND KINDERGARTEN CHILDREN EJ 049 172
CHILDREN AND ROAD ACCIDENTS EJ 050 496
EARLY INTERVENTION AND SOCIAL CLASS: DIAGNOSIS AND TREATMENT OF PRESCHOOL CHILDREN IN A DAY CARE CENTER EJ 050 497
WHAT DOES RESEARCH TEACH US ABOUT DAY CARE: FOR CHILDREN UNDER THREE EJ 051 236
ONE MORNING A WEEK EJ 051 238
THE EFFECTS OF MANIPULATION OF TEACHER COMMUNICATION STYLE IN THE PRESCHOOL EJ 052 455
PRIMACY IN PRESCHOOLERS' SHORT-TERM MEMORY: THE EFFECTS OF REPEATED TESTS AND SHIFT TRIALS EJ 053 729
EFFECTS OF AGE, SEX, SYSTEMATIC CONCEPTUAL LEARNING, ACQUISITION OF LEARNING SETS, AND PROGRAMMED SOCIAL INTERACTION ON THE INTELLECTUAL AND CONCEPTUAL DEVELOPMENT OF PRESCHOOL CHILDREN FROM POVERTY BACKGROUNDS EJ 053 733
DO MATERIAL REWARDS ENHANCE THE PERFORMANCE OF LOWER-CLASS CHILDREN? EJ 053 735
COLOR DOMINANCE IN PRESCHOOL CHILDREN AS A FUNCTION OF SPECIFIC CUE PREFERENCES EJ 053 738
MATERNAL WARMTH, ACHIEVEMENT MOTIVATION, AND COGNITIVE FUNCTIONING IN LOWER-CLASS PRESCHOOL CHILDREN EJ 053 745
THE EFFECTS OF A FAMILIAR TOY AND MOTHER'S PRESENCE ON EXPLORATORY AND ATTACHMENT BEHAVIORS IN YOUNG CHILDREN EJ 053 759
RELIABILITY AND STABILITY OF THE DENVER DEVELOPMENTAL SCREENING TEST EJ 053 905
EVALUATION DIMENSION OF THE AFFECTIVE MEANING SYSTEM OF THE PRESCHOOL CHILD EJ 054 049
DEVELOPMENT OF YOUNG CHILDREN'S ATTENTION TO NORMAL AND DISTORTED STIMULI: A CROSS CULTURAL STUDY EJ 055 103
AN EXPLORATORY STUDY OF SOCIALIZATION EFFECTS ON BLACK CHILDREN: SOME BLACK-WHITE COMPARISONS EJ 055 656
THE RELATION OF FORM RECOGNITION TO CONCEPT DEVELOPMENT EJ 056 393
LOGICAL CAPACITY OF VERY YOUNG CHILDREN: NUMBER INVARIANCE RULES EJ 056 394
SESAME STREET: MAGIC OR MALEVOLENCE? EJ 056 607
PROBLEM-SOLVING THINKING AND ADJUSTMENT AMONG DISADVANTAGED PRESCHOOL CHILDREN EJ 056 612
VERBAL MEDIATION AND SATIATION IN YOUNG CHILDREN EJ 056 613
THE INFLUENCE OF NONINTELLECTIVE FACTORS ON THE IQ SCORES OF MIDDLE- AND LOWER-CLASS CHILDREN EJ 056 621
RACE AND SEX DIFFERENCES IN THE CHILD'S PERCEPTION OF EMOTION EJ 056 625
RACIAL PREFERENCES IN YOUNG CHILDREN EJ 056 626
PERCEPTUAL INADEQUACY AND COMMUNICATIVE INEFFECTIVENESS IN INTERPERSONAL COMMUNICATION EJ 056 627
THE MEASUREMENT OF CHILDREN'S SELF-CONCEPT AS RELATED TO RACIAL MEMBERSHIP EJ 056 629
CHILDREN'S COMPREHENSION OF RELATIVIZED ENGLISH SENTENCES EJ 056 715
THE EXPERIMENTAL FACILITATION OF CHILDREN'S COMPREHENSION AND PRODUCTION OF FOUR SYNTACTIC STRUCTURES EJ 056 723
EFFECTS OF SOCIAL COMPARISON UPON THE IMITATION OF NEUTRAL AND ALTRUISTIC BEHAVIORS BY YOUNG CHILDREN EJ 056 728
TEACHING RACE RELATIONS IN THE NURSERY SCHOOL EJ 056 864
A SOCIAL COMPETENCE SCALE AND SYMPTOM CHECKIST FOR THE PRESCHOOL CHILD: FACTOR DIMENSIONS, THEIR CROSS-INSTRUMENT GENERALITY, AND LONGITUDINAL PERSISTENCE EJ 057 476
RETROACTIVE AND PROACTIVE MULTIPLE LIST INTERFERENCE WITH DISADVANTAGED CHILDREN EJ 057 895
VERBAL AND NONVERBAL REWARDS AND PUNISHMENT IN THE DISCRIMINATION LEARNING OF CHILDREN OF VARYING SOCIOECONOMIC STATUS EJ 057 896
EVOLUTION OF THE HUMAN FIGURE IN A THREE-DIMENSIONAL MEDIUM EJ 057 897
INTERMODAL AND INTRAMODAL RETENTION OF VISUAL AND TACTUAL INFORMATION IN YOUNG CHILDREN EJ 057 900
IMAGERY AND MULTIPLE-LIST PAIRED ASSOCIATE LEARNING IN YOUNG CHILDREN EJ 057 904
TRANSFER BETWEEN THE ODDITY AND RELATIVE SIZE CONCEPTS: REVERSAL AND EXTRADIMENSIONAL SHIFTS EJ 057 906
GENERALIZATION AS A FUNCTION OF THE RANGE OF TEST STIMULI: THE ROLES OF DISCRIMINABILITY AND RESPONSE BIAS EJ 057 909
PSYCHOPHYSICALLY SCALED CUE DIFFERENCES, LEARNING RATE, AND ATTENTIONAL STRATEGIES IN A TACTILE DISCRIMINATION TASK EJ 058 146
ENVIRONMENTAL EFFECTS ON LANGUAGE DEVELOPMENT: A STUDY OF YOUNG CHILDREN IN LONG-STAY RESIDENTIAL NURSERIES EJ 058 859
CONCEPTUAL TEMPO AND INHIBITION OF MOVEMENT IN BLACK PRESCHOOL CHILDREN EJ 059 512
CHILDREN'S IMITATION OF GRAMMATICAL AND UNGRAMMATICAL SENTENCES EJ 059 555
A MATTER OF LIFE AND DEATH EJ 059 746
FEMINIZATION IN PRESCHOOL EJ 059 872
HEAD START IN MICRONESIA EJ 060 108
PRODUCTION OF NOVEL AND GRAMMATICAL UTTERANCES BY YOUNG CHILDREN EJ 060 783
A DEMONSTRATION SUMMER PRESCHOOL PROGRAM EJ 060 999
THE DEVELOPMENT OF THE CONTROL OF ADULT INSTRUCTIONS OVER NONVERBAL BEHAVIOR EJ 061 138
LE PROBLEME DE LA LIBERTE ET DE LA DISCIPLINE DANS LE JEU (PROBLEMS OF FREEDOM AND DISCIPLINE IN PLAY) EJ 061 465
ENRICHING CHILDREN'S LIVES: INTERNATIONAL CO-OPERATION THROUGH UNICEF AND OMEP EJ 062 417
TELEVISION INSTRUCTION AND THE PRESCHOOL CHILD EJ 062 592
INVESTIGACIONES EN EL CAMPO EDUCATIVE (INVESTIGATIONS IN EDUCATION FIELD) EJ 062 593
MOTHER-ATTACHMENT AND STRANGER-REACTIONS IN THE THIRD YEAR OF LIFE EJ 062 594

PRESCHOOL CURRICULUM

PRESCHOOL INTERVENTION--A PRELIMINARY REPORT OF THE PERRY PRESCHOOL PROJECT. ED018251
AN EVALUATION OF THE EFFECTS OF A UNIQUE SEQUENTIAL LEARNING PROGRAM ON CULTURALLY DEPRIVED PRESCHOOL CHILDREN. FINAL REPORT. ED019994
THE PRESCHOOL LANGUAGE PROJECT. A REPORT OF THE FIRST YEAR'S WORK. ED023482
THE INITIAL PHASE OF A PRESCHOOL CURRICULUM DEVELOPMENT PROJECT. FINAL REPORT. ED027071
CURRICULUM GUIDE FOR CHILDREN'S ACTIVITIES, PARENT PRESCHOOL PROGRAM. ED027078
PIAGET, SKINNER, AND AN INTENSIVE PRESCHOOL PROGRAM FOR LOWER CLASS CHILDREN AND THEIR MOTHERS. ED027966
DIAGNOSTICALLY BASED CURRICULUM, BLOOMINGTON, INDIANA ED027978
PROGRESS REPORT ON RESEARCH AT THE NEW NURSERY SCHOOL: GENERAL BACKGROUND AND PROGRAM RATIONALE. ED032930
PRESCHOOL CURRICULUM GUIDE FOR CHILDREN'S CENTERS IN CALIFORNIA. ED037241
PIAGET'S THEORY AND SPECIFIC INSTRUCTION: A RESPONSE TO BEREITER AND KOHLBERG. ED038164
A PIAGETIAN METHOD OF EVALUATING PRESCHOOL CHILDREN'S DEVELOPMENT IN CLASSIFICATION. ED039013
THE EFFECT OF SUPPLEMENTARY SMALL GROUP EXPERIENCE ON TASK ORIENTATION AND COGNITIVE PERFORMANCE IN KINDERGARTEN CHILDREN. A FINAL REPORT OF THE KINDERGARTEN 'LEARNING TO LEARN' PROGRAM EVALUATION PROJECT. ED039948
A SKILL DEVELOPMENT CURRICULUM FOR 3, 4, AND 5 YEAR OLD DISADVANTAGED CHILDREN. ED040755
LANGUAGE PROGRAMS FOR YOUNG CHILDREN: NOTES FROM ENGLAND AND WALES. ED040763
EXPERIMENTAL VARIATION OF HEAD START CURRICULA: A COMPARISON OF CURRENT APPROACHES. ANNUAL REPORT, JUNE 12, 1968-JUNE 11, 1969. ED041618
EARLY CHILDHOOD EDUCATION PROGRAM AND ITS COMPONENTS: PSYCHOLOGICAL EVALUATION, SENSORIMOTOR SKILLS PROGRAM, NEW VISIONS - A CHILDREN'S MUSEUM. PROJECT REPORTS, VOLUME 4, BOOK 1, 1969. ED045183
HEAD START CURRICULUM MODELS: A REFERENCE LIST. ED046517
FIELD TEST OF THE UNIVERSITY OF HAWAII PRESCHOOL LANGUAGE CURRICULUM. FINAL REPORT. ED048924
HEAD START CURRICULUM MODELS: A REFERENCE LIST. (REVISED EDITION). ED048947
THE COGNITIVE CURRICULUM. YPSILANTI PRESCHOOL CURRICULUM DEMONSTRATION PROJECT. ED049832
RELATIONSHIP OF CURRICULUM, TEACHING, AND LEARNING IN PRESCHOOL EDUCATION. ED049837
CURRICULUM FOR THE INFANT AND TODDLER. A COLOR SLIDE SERIES WITH SCRIPT. (SCRIPT ONLY). ED050817
A STUDY IN CHILD CARE (CASE STUDY FROM VOLUME II-A): "THEY UNDERSTAND." DAY CARE PROGRAMS REPRINT SERIES. ED051892
PRESCHOOL PROGRAMS. IJR PRESCHOOL PROJECT REPORT, VOLUME I. ED052815
EARLY CHILDHOOD EDUCATION PROGRAM, ESEA TITLE I, FY 1970. PROJECT REPORTS, VOLUME 5, BOOK 2, 1970. ED052820
AN EVALUATION OF LOGICAL OPERATIONS INSTRUCTION IN THE PRESCHOOL. ED053791
WHAT ARE THE SOURCES OF EARLY CHILDHOOD CURRICULUM? EJ 027 943
RESISTING PRESSURES IN THE PRE-SCHOOL CENTRE P 15-27 EJ 029 621
PLANNED VARIATION IN HEAD START PROGRAMS EJ 031 848
PRESCHOOL EDUCATION IN ISRAEL EJ 050 199
TEACHING RACE RELATIONS IN THE NURSERY SCHOOL EJ 056 864

PRESCHOOL EDUCATION

EVALUATION OF HEADSTART EDUCATIONAL PROGRAM IN CAMBRIDGE, MASSACHUSETTS. FINAL REPORT. ED013668
EVALUATION OF PROJECT HEAD START READING READINESS IN ISSAQUENA AND SHARKEY COUNTIES, MISSISSIPPI, SUMMER, 1965. FINAL REPORT. ED014319
THE HOUSING ENVIRONMENT AS A FACTOR IN CHILD DEVELOPMENT. FINAL REPORT. ED014322

A STUDY OF SOME ECOLOGICAL, ECONOMIC AND SOCIAL FACTORS INFLUENCING PARENTAL PARTICIPATION IN PROJECT HEAD START. ED014331
ACCELERATION OF INTELLECTUAL DEVELOPMENT IN EARLY CHILDHOOD. FINAL REPORT. ED014332
THE EFFECTS OF MONTESSORI EDUCATIONAL TECHNIQUES ON CULTURALLY DISADVANTAGED HEAD START CHILDREN. ED015009
AN EVALUATION OF DIFFERENCES AMONG DIFFERENT CLASSES OF HEAD START PARTICIPANTS. FINAL REPORT. ED015012
LONG-RANGE EFFECT OF PRE-SCHOOLING ON READING ACHIEVEMENT. STUDY III. ED015027
A CREATIVE GUIDE FOR PRESCHOOL TEACHERS. GOALS, ACTIVITIES, AND SUGGESTED MATERIALS FOR AN ORGANIZED PROGRAM. ED016512
"PRE-SCHOOL" EDUCATION, PROS AND CONS. A SURVEY OF "PRE-SCHOOL" EDUCATION WITH EMPHASIS ON RESEARCH PAST, PRESENT, AND FUTURE. ED016525
A TRAINING PROGRAM FOR MOTHERS. ED017334
RESULTS OF THE SUMMER 1965 PROJECT HEAD START. VOLUMES I AND II. ED018250
PRE-SCHOOL EDUCATION. ED020785
PROBLEMS AND PROSPECTS OF EDUCATION IN THE BIG CITIES AS EXEMPLIFIED BY PITTSBURGH, PENNSYLVANIA. ED022542
BIBLIOGRAPHY OF RESEARCH STUDIES IN ELEMENTARY SCHOOL AND PRE-SCHOOL MATHEMATICS. ED023464
THE EFFECTS OF ASSESSMENT AND PERSONALIZED PROGRAMMING ON SUBSEQUENT INTELLECTUAL DEVELOPMENT OF PREKINDERGARTEN AND KINDERGARTEN CHILDREN. FINAL REPORT OF PHASE II. ED023487
EVALUATION OF THE PRESCHOOL PROGRAM, 1966-67, FUNDED UNDER ESEA TITLE I, P.L. 89-10. ED026143
THE MONTESSORI RESEARCH PROJECT. FOUR PROGRESS REPORTS. ED030489
THE SCHOOL SOCIAL WORKER IN THE NEW YORK STATE EXPERIMENTAL PREKINDERGARTEN PROGRAM. ED036337
A NEW ROLE FOR TEACHERS: INVOLVING THE ENTIRE FAMILY IN THE EDUCATION OF PRESCHOOL DISADVANTAGED CHILDREN. ED036339
VIEWS ON PRE-SCHOOL EDUCATION AND DAY CARE. ED040753
STATEMENT OF THE INSTRUCTIONAL GOALS FOR CHILDREN'S TELEVISION WORKSHOP. ED041627
THE EFFECTIVENESS OF SPECIAL PROGRAMS FOR RURAL ISOLATED FOUR-YEAR-OLD CHILDREN. FINAL REPORT. ED041638
FINAL REPORT ON PRESCHOOL EDUCATION TO OHIO DEPARTMENT OF EDUCATION. ED045200
APPALACHIA PRESCHOOL EDUCATION PROGRAM, CHARLESTON, WEST VIRGINIA: A THREE-PART PRESCHOOL PROGRAM COMBINING A TELEVISION PROGRAM, PARAPROFESSIONAL HOME VISITORS, AND A MOBILE CLASSROOM. MODEL PROGRAMS--CHILDHOOD EDUCATION. ED045216
PRESCHOOL EDUCATION AND SCHOOL ADMISSION PRACTICES IN NEW ZEALAND. ED046487
PRESCHOOL EDUCATION AND POVERTY: THE DISTANCE IN BETWEEN. FINAL REPORT OF 1968-69 INTERVENTIONAL PROGRAM. ED046501
HEAD START CURRICULUM MODELS: A REFERENCE LIST. ED046517
PRE-SCHOOL EDUCATION IN EUROPE. ED047779
HEAD START CURRICULUM MODELS: A REFERENCE LIST. (REVISED EDITION). ED048947
LENIN'S GRANDCHILDREN: PRESCHOOL EDUCATION IN THE SOVIET UNION. ED049830
RELATIONSHIP OF CURRICULUM, TEACHING, AND LEARNING IN PRESCHOOL EDUCATION. ED049837
AN ACADEMIC PRESCHOOL FOR DISADVANTAGED CHILDREN: REVIEW OF FINDINGS. PRELIMINARY DRAFT. ED051878
PRESCHOOL PROGRAMS: AN ANNOTATED BIBLIOGRAPHY. ED052822
IMPLEMENTATION OF PLANNED VARIATION IN HEAD START. I. REVIEW AND SUMMARY OF THE STANFORD RESEARCH INSTITUTE INTERIM REPORT: FIRST YEAR OF EVALUATION. ED052845
CONTEMPORARY INFLUENCES IN EARLY CHILDHOOD EDUCATION. ED053797
DESIGNS AND PROPOSAL FOR EARLY CHILDHOOD RESEARCH: A NEW LOOK: PRESCHOOL RESEARCH AND PRESCHOOL EDUCATIONAL OBJECTIVES ED053808
DESIGNS AND PROPOSAL FOR EARLY CHILDHOOD RESEARCH: A NEW LOOK: A SYSTEMS APPROACH TO PRE-SCHOOL EDUCATION. (ONE IN A SERIES OF SIX PAPERS). ED053809
CHILDREN AND TEACHERS IN TWO TYPES OF HEAD START CLASSES EJ 008 172
TELL IT LIKE IT IS EJ 014 139
TEACHING IN PRESCHOOLS: ROLES AND GOALS EJ 018 133
PRE-SCHOOL EDUCATION IN THE WORK OF J.A. COMENIUS (KOMENSKY) EJ 029 619
RESISTING PRESSURES IN THE PRE-SCHOOL CENTRE P 15-27 EJ 029 621
LA EDUCACION PRE-ESCOLAR EN LAS ESCUELAS PUBLICAS DE PUERTO RICO EJ 029 622
"THERE WAS A CHILD WENT FORTH"--A PHILOSOPHY OF EARLY EDUCATION EJ 031 049
CONTEMPORARY CONCERNS IN EARLY CHILDHOOD EDUCATION EJ 032 059
LA FORMATION DU PERSONNEL NON MEDICAL S'OCCUPANT DU PETIT ENFANT DE 1 A 6 ANS EJ 035 170
THE PLACE OF PRESCHOOL EDUCATION IN THE EDUCATIONAL SYSTEM EJ 036 329
DEVELOPMENT OF THE MONTESSORI METHOD EJ 036 330
COMMUNITY PARTICIPATION IN PRESCHOOL EDUCATION--WHY AND HOW EJ 036 331
THE ROLE OF A LABORATORY NURSERY SCHOOL EJ 036 332
PRESCHOOL EDUCATION, PARENTS AND THE COMMUNITY IN A DEVELOPING SOCIETY EJ 036 333
THE PRESCHOOL IN RURAL INDIA EJ 036 334
SWEDISH PRESCHOOLS: ENVIRONMENTS OF SENSITIVITY EJ 037 737
CONTINUITY FROM PREKINDERGARTEN TO KINDERGARTEN EJ 039 058
EARLY COGNITIVE DEVELOPMENT AND PRESCHOOL EDUCATION EJ 043 857
LE NOUVEAU PROGRAMME D'ACTIVITES EDUCATRICES DANS LES ESTABLISSEMENTS PRESCOLAIRES EN YOUGOSLAVIE EJ 045 011
SOURCES OF MANPOWER FOR THE PRESCHOOL CLASSROOM EJ 049 526
PRESCHOOL EDUCATION IN ISRAEL EJ 050 199
DIFFERENTIAL OUTCOMES OF A MONTESSORI CURRICULUM EJ 060 330

PRESCHOOL EVALUATION

PRESCHOOL PREDICTION AND PREVENTION OF LEARNING DISABILITIES. ED013118
EVALUATION OF TWO ASSOCIATED YM-YWHA HEADSTART PROGRAMS. FINAL REPORT. ED014318
THE HOUSING ENVIRONMENT AS A FACTOR IN CHILD DEVELOPMENT. FINAL REPORT. ED014322
THE 1965 HEAD START PSYCHOLOGICAL SCREENING PROGRAM. FINAL REPORT ON THE DATA ANALYSIS. ED014333
THE PRESCHOOL INVENTORY. ED014334
THE EFFECTS OF MONTESSORI EDUCATIONAL TECHNIQUES ON CULTURALLY DISADVANTAGED HEAD START CHILDREN. ED015009
A STUDY OF THE FULL-YEAR 1966 HEAD START PROGRAMS. ED015010
SECOND-YEAR REPORT ON AN EVALUATIVE STUDY OF PREKINDERGARTEN PROGRAMS FOR EDUCATIONALLY DISADVANTAGED CHILDREN. ED016523
"PRE-SCHOOL" EDUCATION, PROS AND CONS. A SURVEY OF "PRE-SCHOOL" EDUCATION WITH EMPHASIS ON RESEARCH PAST, PRESENT, AND FUTURE. ED016525
AN EVALUATION OF A PRESCHOOL TRAINING PROGRAM FOR CULTURALLY DEPRIVED CHILDREN. FINAL REPORT. ED019135
DEVELOPMENT OF A SOCIAL COMPETENCY SCALE FOR PRESCHOOL CHILDREN. FINAL REPORT. ED020004
A STANDARDIZED NEUROLOGICAL EXAMINATION: ITS VALIDITY IN PREDICTING SCHOOL ACHIEVEMENT IN HEAD START AND OTHER POPULATIONS. FINAL REPORT. ED023475
PROJECT HEAD START RESEARCH AND EVALUATION CENTER, SYRACUSE UNIVERSITY RESEARCH INSTITUTE. FINAL REPORT, NOVEMBER 1, 1967. ED026137
EVALUATING BEHAVIORAL CHANGE DURING A SIX-WEEK PRE-KINDERGARTEN INTERVENTION EXPERIENCE. RESEARCH PROJECT NUMBER 5 OF PROJECT HEAD START RESEARCH AND EVALUATION CENTER, SYRACUSE UNIVERSITY RESEARCH INSTITUTE. FINAL REPORT, NOVEMBER 1, 1967. ED026142
RESEARCH ON THE NEW NURSERY SCHOOL. PART I, A SUMMARY OF THE EVALUATION OF THE EXPERIMENTAL PROGRAM FOR DEPRIVED CHILDREN AT THE NEW NURSERY SCHOOL USING SOME EXPERIMENTAL MEASURES. INTERIM REPORT. ED027076
A DIAGNOSTIC-PRESCRIPTIVE APPROACH TO PRESCHOOL EDUCATION. ED041622
THE NEW NURSERY SCHOOL RESEARCH PROJECT ED042518
HAS PRESCHOOL COMPENSATORY EDUCATION FAILED? ED049834
ANALYSIS OF EARLY CHILDHOOD PROGRAMS: A SEARCH FOR COMPARATIVE DIMENSIONS. ED051877

PRESCHOOL LEARNING

OPERATION HEAD START--AN EVALUATION. FINAL REPORT. ED013117
A STUDY OF THE FULL-YEAR 1966 HEAD START PROGRAMS. ED015010
THE EFFECTS OF SEVERAL VERBAL PRETRAINING CONDITIONS ON PRESCHOOL CHILDREN'S TRANSFER IN PROBLEM SOLVING. FINAL REPORT. ED015778
EFFECTS OF A STRUCTURED PROGRAM OF PRESCHOOL MATHEMATICS ON COGNITIVE BEHAVIOR. ED015791
CHILDREN WHO READ EARLY, TWO LONGITUDINAL STUDIES. ED019107
THE EFFECTS OF A HIGHLY STRUCTURED PRESCHOOL PROGRAM ON THE MEASURED INTELLIGENCE OF CULTURALLY DISADVANTAGED FOUR-YEAR-OLD CHILDREN. INTERIM REPORT. ED019116
TEACHING FORMAL OPERATIONS TO PRESCHOOL ADVANTAGED AND DISADVANTAGED CHILDREN. ED019990
REGIONAL EVALUATION AND RESEARCH CENTER FOR PROJECT HEAD START, SUPPLEMENTARY RESEARCH REPORT, SEPTEMBER 1, 1967-DECEMBER 31, 1967. ED020791
THE PREPARED ENVIRONMENT AND ITS RELATIONSHIP TO LEARNING. ED025302
EARLY INTELLECTIVE TRAINING AND SCHOOL PERFORMANCE. SUMMARY OF NIH GRANT NUMBER HD-02253. ED025324
READING. DIMENSIONS IN EARLY LEARNING SERIES. ED027070
LANGUAGE. ED029718
INVESTIGATION OF CONCEPT LEARNING IN YOUNG CHILDREN. FINAL REPORT. ED030498

CHILDREN UNDER THREE - FINDING WAYS TO STIMULATE DEVELOPMENT. II. SOME CURRENT EXPERIMENTS: LEARNING AT TWO EJ 007 409
RESISTING PRESSURES IN THE PRE-SCHOOL CENTRE P 15-27 EJ 029 621

PRESCHOOL PROGRAMS

THE EFFECTS OF ASSESSMENT AND PERSONALIZED PROGRAMMING ON SUBSEQUENT INTELLECTUAL DEVELOPMENT OF PREKINDERGARTEN AND KINDERGARTEN CHILDREN. ED013663
AN EVALUATION OF THE EFFECTS OF A SUMMER HEAD START PROGRAM. ED014327
REPORT OF A RESEARCH AND DEMONSTRATION PROJECT FOR CULTURALLY DISADVANTAGED CHILDREN IN THE ANCONA MONTESSORI SCHOOL. ED015014
KICKAPOO - NORTH CANADIAN PROJECT, 1966-67. FINAL REPORT. ED015781
THE EVALUATION OF PROJECT HEAD START--A CONCEPTUAL STATEMENT. ED015792
A COMPARATIVE STUDY OF TWO PRESCHOOL PROGRAMS FOR CULTURALLY DISADVANTAGED CHILDREN--A HIGHLY STRUCTURED AND A TRADITIONAL PROGRAM. ED016524
A RESEARCH PROGRAM TO DETERMINE THE EFFECTS OF VARIOUS PRESCHOOL INTERVENTION PROGRAMS ON THE DEVELOPMENT OF DISADVANTAGED CHILDREN AND THE STRATEGIC AGE FOR SUCH INTERVENTION. ED017319
MONTESSORI PRE-SCHOOL EDUCATION. FINAL REPORT. ED017320
HEAD START, WEST VIRGINIA, SUMMER 1966--A SEVEN-COUNTY OVERVIEW, A SPECIAL ASSIGNMENT OF THE WEST VIRGINIA DEPARTMENT OF MENTAL HEALTH. ED017338
EARLY CHILDHOOD EDUCATION AND THE WALDORF SCHOOL PLAN. ED019114
EXPANDED PREKINDERGARTEN PROGRAM, EVALUATION OF NEW YORK CITY TITLE I EDUCATIONAL PROJECTS 1966-67. ED019115
THE EFFECTS OF A HIGHLY STRUCTURED PRESCHOOL PROGRAM ON THE MEASURED INTELLIGENCE OF CULTURALLY DISADVANTAGED FOUR-YEAR-OLD CHILDREN. INTERIM REPORT. ED019116
A FRESH APPROACH TO EARLY CHILDHOOD EDUCATION AND A STUDY OF ITS EFFECTIVENESS. LEARNING TO LEARN PROGRAM. ED019117
EARLY LEARNING IN THE HOME. ED019127
CRITICAL OVERVIEW OF EARLY CHILDHOOD EDUCATION PROGRAMS. ED019142
A COMPARATIVE STUDY OF VARIOUS PROJECT HEAD START PROGRAMS. ED019987
THE EFFECT OF PRESCHOOL GROUP EXPERIENCE ON VARIOUS LANGUAGE AND SOCIAL SKILLS IN DISADVANTAGED CHILDREN. FINAL REPORT. ED019989
AN EVALUATION OF THE EFFECTS OF A UNIQUE SEQUENTIAL LEARNING PROGRAM ON CULTURALLY DEPRIVED PRESCHOOL CHILDREN. FINAL REPORT. ED019994
GUIDEBOOK FOR TEACHERS. ED020001
CO-OPERATIVE NURSERY SCHOOLS--A HANDBOOK FOR PARENTS. A GUIDE FOR ORGANIZATION AND ADMINISTRATION. REVISED EDITION. ED020022
THE EFFECT OF HEADSTART ON DEVELOPMENTAL PROCESSES. ED020026
EFFECTIVENESS OF THE HEAD START PROGRAM IN ENHANCING SCHOOL READINESS OF CULTURALLY DEPRIVED CHILDREN. ED020771
THE IMPACT OF OPERATION HEAD START ON GREENE COUNTY, OHIO, AN EVALUATION REPORT. ED020772
SEMO PROJECT HEAD START, PSYCHOLOGICAL SERVICES REPORT, SUMMER 1967. PHASE THREE FINAL REPORT. ED020779
MAKING WAVES, DENVER HEAD START. ED020802
CULTURAL ENVIRONMENTAL ACHIEVEMENT PROJECT, A SUMMARIZATION AND EVALUATION OF AN EXPERIMENTAL PRE-SCHOOL PROGRAM. ED021610
PROJECT HEAD START, REPORT ON THE PREKINDERGARTEN PROGRAM, 1965. ED021611
HEAD START EVALUATION AND RESEARCH CENTER. PROGRESS REPORT OF RESEARCH STUDIES, 1966-1967. ED021612
EVALUATION OF THE PRESCHOOL CHILD AND PARENT EDUCATION PROJECT AS EXPANDED THROUGH THE USE OF ELEMENTARY AND SECONDARY EDUCATION ACT, TITLE I, FUNDS. ED021621
PILOT STUDY OF FIVE METHODS OF PRESENTING THE SUMMER HEAD START CURRICULAR PROGRAM. ED021622
HEAD START EVALUATION AND RESEARCH CENTER. PROGRESS REPORT OF RESEARCH STUDIES 1966 TO 1967. DOCUMENT 4, DEVELOPMENT OF OBSERVATION PROCEDURES FOR ASSESSING PRESCHOOL CLASSROOM ENVIRONMENT. ED021626
PROJECT HEAD START, THE URBAN AND RURAL CHALLENGE. FINAL REPORT. ED022527
HEAD START EVALUATION AND RESEARCH CENTER, BOSTON UNIVERSITY. REPORT OF RESEARCH, SEPTEMBER, 1966-AUGUST, 1967. ED022529
THE YPSILANTI EARLY EDUCATION PROGRAM. ED022531
PRE-SCHOOL RESEARCH AND EVALUATION PROJECT. ED022541
USING MUSIC WITH HEAD START CHILDREN. ED022543
HEAD START EVALUATION AND RESEARCH CENTER, BOSTON UNIVERSITY. REPORT B-I, PRIMARY AND SECONDARY PREVENTION STUDYING CLINICAL PROCESS AND DISTURBANCE WITH PRESCHOOL CHILDREN. ED022560
HEAD START EVALUATION AND RESEARCH CENTER, BOSTON UNIVERSITY. REPORT D-I, LANGUAGE PROJECT: THE EFFECTS OF A TEACHER DEVELOPED PRE-SCHOOL LANGUAGE TRAINING PROGRAM ON FIRST GRADE READING ACHIEVEMENT. ED022563
HEAD START EVALUATION AND RESEARCH CENTER, BOSTON UNIVERSITY. REPORT E-II, TEACHER SEMINAR. ED022567
A STUDY OF VISUAL PERCEPTIONS IN EARLY CHILDHOOD. ED023451
FINAL REPORT ON HEAD START EVALUATION AND RESEARCH: 1967-68 TO THE OFFICE OF ECONOMIC OPPORTUNITY. SECTION I: PART B, ACCURACY OF SELF-PERCEPTION AMONG CULTURALLY DEPRIVED PRESCHOOLS. ED023455
GUIDELINES FOR PLANNING PRESCHOOL PROGRAMS FOR EDUCATIONALLY DEPRIVED CHILDREN UNDER TITLE I OF THE ELEMENTARY AND SECONDARY EDUCATION ACT OF 1965. ED023463
AN EVALUATION OF THE PRESCHOOL READINESS CENTERS PROGRAM IN EAST ST. LOUIS, ILLINOIS, JULY 1, 1967-JUNE 30, 1968. FINAL REPORT. ED023472
THE PRESCHOOL LANGUAGE PROJECT. A REPORT OF THE FIRST YEAR'S WORK. ED023482
CONCEPT LEARNING IN EARLY CHILDHOOD. ED024454
PROJECT HEAD START, PSYCHOLOGICAL SERVICES REPORT, RESEARCH, SUMMER 1968. ED024460
PRESCHOOL PROGRAMS AND THE INTELLECTUAL DEVELOPMENT OF DISADVANTAGED CHILDREN. ED024473
INKSTER PUBLIC SCHOOLS IMPLEMENT CHILD DEVELOPMENT CENTER. ED025303
METHODOLIGICAL CONSIDERATIONS IN DEVISING HEAD START PROGRAM EVALUATIONS. ED025319
ANNUAL RESEARCH REPORT OF COMPLETED AND INCOMPLETE INVESTIGATIONS FOR NATIONAL HEAD START EVALUATION. ED025320
A RATIONALE FOR A STRUCTURED EDUCATIONAL PROGRAM AND SUGGESTED ACTIVITIES FOR CULTURALLY DISADVANTAGED INFANTS. ED026112
AN EVALUATION OF A SIX-WEEK HEADSTART PROGRAM USING AN ACADEMICALLY ORIENTED CURRICULUM: CANTON, 1967. ED026114
A PREKINDERGARTEN PROGRAM FOR FOUR-YEAR-OLDS, WITH A REVIEW OF THE LITERATURE ON PRESCHOOL EDUCATION. AN OCCASIONAL PAPER. ED026124
DIFFUSION OF INTERVENTION EFFECTS IN DISADVANTAGED FAMILIES. ED026127
EVALUATION OF THE PRESCHOOL PROGRAM, 1966-67, FUNDED UNDER ESEA TITLE I, P.L. 89-10. ED026143
PREPRIMARY PROGRAM. 1968 REPORT. ED027072
A STUDY OF THE EFFECTS OF TEACHER ATTITUDE AND CURRICULUM STRUCTURE ON PRESCHOOL DISADVANTAGED CHILDREN. ANNUAL PROGRESS REPORT I. ED027079
EVALUATION OF THE PRESCHOOL PROGRAM, 1967-68, FUNDED UNDER ESEA TITLE I, P.L. 89-10. ED027080
PREPRIMARY ENROLLMENT OF CHILDREN UNDER SIX: OCTOBER 1967. ED027094
SUPERMARKET DISCOVERY CENTER, PILOT STUDY, MAY - SEPTEMBER, 1968. INITIAL REPORT. ED027941
A SOURCE REPORT FOR DEVELOPING PARENT-CHILD EDUCATIONAL CENTERS. ED027944
GUIDELINES: PRE-SCHOOL PROJECTS, HEAD START: EARLY CHILDHOOD EDUCATION. REVISED EDITION. ED027948
PROGRAM FOR EARLY CHILDHOOD EDUCATION. ED027957
A PLAN OF ACTION FOR PARENT-CHILD EDUCATIONAL CENTERS. ED027959
EARLY CHILDHOOD PROJECT, NEW YORK CITY ED027974
PERRY PRESCHOOL PROJECT, YPSILANTI, MICHIGAN ED027975
PRESCHOOL PROGRAM, FRESNO, CALIFORNIA ED027977
ACADEMIC PRESCHOOL, CHAMPAIGN, ILLINOIS ED027979
INDUCING CONSERVATION OF NUMBER, WEIGHT, VOLUME, AREA, AND MASS IN PRE-SCHOOL CHILDREN. ED028822
PROJECT HEAD START: EVALUATION AND RESEARCH SUMMARY 1965-1967. ED028826
POSITIVE EFFECTS OF A BICULTURAL PRESCHOOL PROGRAM ON THE INTELLECTUAL PERFORMANCE OF MEXICAN-AMERICAN CHILDREN. ED028827
THE RELATIONSHIP BETWEEN HEMOGLOBIN LEVEL AND INTELLECTUAL FUNCTION. ED028830
EFFECT OF MATERNAL ATTITUDES, TEACHER ATTITUDES, AND TYPE OF NURSERY SCHOOL TRAINING ON THE ABILITIES OF PRESCHOOL CHILDREN. FINAL REPORT. ED028844
DEVELOPMENT OF A PRESCHOOL LANGUAGE-ORIENTED CURRICULUM WITH A STRUCTURED PARENT EDUCATION PROGRAM. FINAL REPORT. ED028845
A REPORT ON THE 1967-68 PROGRAM FOR PRESCHOOL CHILDREN AND THEIR PARENTS. RESEARCH REPORT SERIES 1968-69, NO. 4. ED029713
HEAD START IN ACTION. ED030471
THE COMPARATIVE EFFICACIES OF SPANISH, ENGLISH AND BILINGUAL COGNITIVE VERBAL INSTRUCTION WITH MEXICAN-AMERICAN HEAD START CHILDREN. FINAL REPORT. ED030473
CHILD DEVELOPMENT RESEARCH AND EVALUATION CENTER FOR HEAD START, TEMPLE UNIVERSITY. ANNUAL REPORT. ED030487
PRELIMINARY RESULTS FROM A LONGITUDINAL STUDY OF DISADVANTAGED PRESCHOOL CHILDREN. ED030490

EFFECTIVENESS OF DIRECT VERBAL INSTRUCTION ON IQ PERFORMANCE AND ACHIEVEMENT IN READING AND ARITHMETIC. ED030496
A GUIDE FOR PRESCHOOLS: A HANDBOOK ABOUT THE OPERATION AND FUNCTION OF PRESCHOOLS IN THE FRESNO CITY UNIFIED SCHOOL DISTRICT. ED030499
EARLY CHILDHOOD EDUCATION IN AMERICAN SAMOA, 1968. ED032114
PHILOSOPHY: A CRUCIAL DISTINCTION. ED032129
[THE JUNIPER GARDENS PARENT COOPERATIVE NURSERY.] FINAL PROGRESS REPORT FOR OEO CAP GRANT CG-8474 A/O. ED032920
RESEARCH, CHANGE, AND SOCIAL RESPONSIBILITY: AN ILLUSTRATIVE MODEL FROM EARLY EDUCATION. ED032922
EVALUATION OF SELECTED COMPONENTS OF: A SUPPLEMENTARY CENTER FOR EARLY CHILDHOOD EDUCATION. TITLE III. ED032927
PROGRESS REPORT ON RESEARCH AT THE NEW NURSERY SCHOOL: GENERAL BACKGROUND AND PROGRAM RATIONALE. ED032930
CHILDHOOD RESOURCES INFORMATION BULLETIN. VOLUME 1, NUMBER 2, FALL 1969. ED032948
PRELUDE TO SCHOOL: AN EVALUATION OF AN INNER-CITY PRESCHOOL PROGRAM. ED033750
THE DESIGN OF A PRE-SCHOOL "LEARNING LABORATORY" IN A REHABILITATION CENTER. ED033764
THE SATURDAY SCHOOL: AN INSTALLATION MANUAL. ED033765
HEAD START PROGRAMS AND PARTICIPANTS 1965-1967. ED034569
DAY CARE AND CHILD DEVELOPMENT IN YOUR COMMUNITY. ED034576
COMMUNITY COORDINATED CHILD CARE: 1. INTERIM POLICY GUIDANCE FOR THE 4-C PROGRAM ED034579
AN EVALUATION OF THE PRESCHOOL READINESS CENTERS PROGRAM IN EAST ST. LOUIS, ILLINOIS, JULY 1, 1968 - JUNE 30, 1969. FINAL REPORT. ED034585
A LONGITUDINAL INVESTIGATION OF MONTESSORI AND TRADITIONAL PREKINDERGARTEN TRAINING WITH INNER CITY CHILDREN: A COMPARATIVE ASSESSMENT OF LEARNING OUTCOMES. THREE PART STUDY. ED034588
STAFFING PRESCHOOLS: BACKGROUND INFORMATION. ED034589
AN EDUCATIONAL IMPERATIVE AND ITS FALLOUT IMPLICATIONS. ED034590
THE ADVANTAGED: A PRESCHOOL PROGRAM FOR THE DISADVANTAGED. ED035436
A STUDY OF THE INFLUENCE OF CERTAIN PRESCHOOL EDUCATIONAL MOVEMENTS ON CONTEMPORARY PRESCHOOL PRACTICES. ED035450
MAKING A CHILD'S OWN BOOK. ED035452
ASSESSING PROCESS AND PRODUCT WITH YOUNG CHILDREN IN SCHOOL SETTINGS. ED035453
EXEMPLARY AND INNOVATIVE PRESCHOOL CHILD DEVELOPMENT DEMONSTRATION CENTERS, 1966-1969. THREE YEAR EVALUATION AND NARRATIVE REPORT. ED035456
PROJECT HEAD START AT WORK. REPORT OF A SURVEY STUDY OF 335 PROJECT HEAD START CENTERS, SUMMER, 1965. ED036311
THE IMPACT OF HEAD START: AN EVALUATION OF THE EFFECTS OF HEAD START ON CHILDREN'S COGNITIVE AND AFFECTIVE DEVELOPMENT. (EXECUTIVE SUMMARY). ED036321
CHILDREN AND TEACHERS IN TWO TYPES OF HEAD START CLASSES. ED036324
THE SCHOOL SOCIAL WORKER IN THE NEW YORK STATE EXPERIMENTAL PREKINDERGARTEN PROGRAM. ED036337
A LONGITUDINAL STUDY OF DISADVANTAGED CHILDREN WHO PARTICIPATED IN THREE DIFFERENT PRESCHOOL PROGRAMS. ED036338
A NEW ROLE FOR TEACHERS: INVOLVING THE ENTIRE FAMILY IN THE EDUCATION OF PRESCHOOL DISADVANTAGED CHILDREN. ED036339
THE ANALYSIS OF DATA GENERATED IN A RESEARCH DESIGNED TO SECURE BASELINE INFORMATION ON A HEAD START PROGRAM. A REPORT TO THE U.S. OFFICE OF ECONOMIC OPPORTUNITY FROM THE DEPARTMENT OF RESEARCH, MONTGOMERY COUNTY, MARYLAND PUBLIC SCHOOLS. ED037232
A REPORT ON EVALUATION STUDIES OF PROJECT HEAD START. ED037239
THE EFFECT OF THE REINSTEIN REINFORCEMENT SCHEDULE ON LEARNING OF SPECIFIC CONCEPTS CONTAINED IN THE BUCHANAN LANGUAGE PROGRAM. PART OF THE FINAL REPORT ON HEAD START EVALUATION AND RESEARCH: 1968-69 TO THE OFFICE OF ECONOMIC OPPORTUNITY. ED037242
THE INFLUENCE OF TWO COUNSELING METHODS ON THE PHYSICAL AND VERBAL AGGRESSION OF PRESCHOOL INDIAN CHILDREN. PART OF THE FINAL REPORT ON HEAD START EVALUATION AND RESEARCH: 1968-69 TO THE OFFICE OF ECONOMIC OPPORTUNITY. ED037243
A PILOT PROJECT USING A LANGUAGE DEVELOPMENT PROGRAM WITH PRESCHOOL DISADVANTAGED CHILDREN. PART OF THE FINAL REPORT ON HEAD START EVALUATION AND RESEARCH: 1968-69 TO THE OFFICE OF ECONOMIC OPPORTUNITY. ED037245
EARLY CHILD STIMULATION THROUGH PARENT EDUCATION. ED038166
AN EARLY CHILDHOOD EDUCATION MODEL: A BILINGUAL APPROACH. ED038167
PRESCHOOL MATHEMATICS CURRICULUM PROJECT. FINAL REPORT. ED038168
HEAD START PLANNED VARIATION PROGRAM. ED038170
CURRICULAR INTERVENTION IN LANGUAGE ARTS READINESS FOR HEAD START CHILDREN. TULANE UNIVERSITY, HEAD START EVALUATION AND RESEARCH CENTER ANNUAL REPORT TO THE OFFICE OF ECONOMIC OPPORTUNITY. ED038175
DEVELOPMENT OF THE EARLY CHILDHOOD EDUCATION PROGRAM. BASIC PLAN. ED038181
WAKULLA COUNTY PRESCHOOL. FINAL REPORT. ED039022
A SUPPLEMENTARY REPORT ON EVALUATION OF THE NEW NURSERY SCHOOL PROGRAM AT COLORADO STATE COLLEGE. ED039919
STATEMENT BY MARSDEN G. WAGNER, M. D. REPRESENTING THE AMERICAN PUBLIC HEALTH ASSOCIATION BEFORE THE SELECT SUBCOMMITTEE ON EDUCATION, MARCH 3, 1970. ED039940
STATEMENT ON COMPREHENSIVE PRESCHOOL EDUCATION AND CHILD DAY CARE ACT OF 1969 BEFORE THE SELECT SUBCOMMITTEE ON EDUCATION, FEBRUARY 27, 1970. ED039941
PARENT INVOLVEMENT IN COMPENSATORY EDUCATION. ED039954
DESIGN AND MEASURES OF 1967-68 AND 1968-69 HEAD START E&R EVALUATION STUDIES. ED040745
A STATEMENT ON THE COMPREHENSIVE PRESCHOOL EDUCATION AND CHILD DAY-CARE ACT OF 1969 BEFORE THE SELECT SUBCOMMITTEE ON EDUCATION OF THE HOUSE COMMITTEE ON EDUCATION AND LABOR, MARCH 3, 1970. ED040752
A SKILL DEVELOPMENT CURRICULUM FOR 3, 4, AND 5 YEAR OLD DISADVANTAGED CHILDREN. ED040755
[A STATEMENT REGARDING THE COMPREHENSIVE PRESCHOOL EDUCATION AND CHILD DAY CARE ACT OF 1969, AND OTHER RELATED BILLS.] ED040762
EXPERIMENTS IN HEAD START AND EARLY EDUCATION: THE EFFECTS OF TEACHER ATTITUDE AND CURRICULUM STRUCTURE ON PRESCHOOL DISADVANTAGED CHILDREN. FINAL REPORT. ED041615
DIRECT VERBAL INSTRUCTION CONTRASTED WITH MONTESSORI METHODS IN THE TEACHING OF NORMAL FOUR-YEAR-OLD CHILDREN. ED041619
[A STATEMENT REGARDING THE COMPREHENSIVE PRESCHOOL EDUCATION AND CHILD DAY CARE ACT OF 1969, AND OTHER RELATED BILLS.] ED041624
EARLY CHILDHOOD EDUCATION LEARNING SYSTEM ED041625
EVALUATION REPORT: EARLY CHILDHOOD EDUCATION PROGRAM, 1969 FIELD TEST. ED041626
DEMONSTRATION INFANT DAY CARE AND EDUCATION PROGRAM. INTERIM REPORT, 1969-1970. ED041632
THE EFFECT OF A PERCEPTUAL-MOTOR TRAINING PROGRAM UPON THE READINESS AND PERCEPTUAL DEVELOPMENT OF CULTURALLY DISADVANTAGED KINDERGARTEN CHILDREN. ED041633
THE EFFECTS OF SCHOOL ENVIRONMENT ON DISADVANTAGED KINDERGARTEN CHILDREN, WITH AND WITHOUT A HEAD START BACKGROUND. FINAL REPORT. ED041640
A COMPARATIVE STUDY OF THE IMPACT OF TWO CONTRASTING EDUCATIONAL APPROACHES IN HEAD START, 1968-69. ED041643
PRESCHOOLS AND THEIR GRADUATES. ED041644
COMPARATIVE STUDY OF THREE PRESCHOOL CURRICULA. ED042484
DEVELOPMENT OF GRAMMATICAL STRUCTURES IN PRE-SCHOOL AGE CHILDREN. ED042485
PROGRAM-PROJECT RESUMES, 1969-1970. ED042503
A PARENT-CHILD CENTER, NOVEMBER-DECEMBER 1968. ED042506
HAWAII HEAD START EVALUATION--1968-69. FINAL REPORT. ED042511
HAWAII HEAD START EVALUATION FOLLOW-UP--1968-69. FINA L REPORT. ED042515
A FOLLOW-UP EVALUATION OF THE EFFECTS OF A UNIQUE SEQUENTIAL LEARNING PROGRAM, A TRADITIONAL PRESCHOOL PROGRAM AND A NO TREATMENT PROGRAM ON CULTURALLY DEPRIVED CHILDREN. FINAL REPORT. ED042516
A SEQUENTIAL APPROACH TO EARLY CHILDHOOD AND ELEMENTARY EDUCATION, PHASE I. GRANT REPORT. ED042517
ENRICHMENT APPROACH VERSUS DIRECT INSTRUCTIONAL APPROACH AND THEIR EFFECTS ON DIFFERENTIAL PRESCHOOL EXPERIENCES. ED043369
EARLY CHILDHOOD EDUCATION LEARNING SYSTEM FOR THREE-AND FOUR-YEAR-OLD MIGRANT CHILDREN, MCALLEN, TEXAS. EVALUATION REPORT, 1968-1969. ED043370
CHILD DEVELOPMENT RESEARCH AND EVALUATION CENTER FOR HEAD START, TEMPLE UNIVERSITY, 1968 - 1969. ANNUAL REPORT. ED043388
ENVIRONMENTALLY ENRICHED CLASSROOMS AND THE DEVELOPMENT OF DISADVANTAGED PRESCHOOL CHILDREN. ED045192
IMPACT OF THE HEAD START PROGRAM. PHASE I OF A PROJECTED LONGITUDINAL STUDY TO THE U. S. OFFICE OF ECONOMIC OPPORTUNITY. FINAL REPORT. ED045193
A NATIONAL SURVEY OF THE IMPACTS OF HEAD START CENTERS ON COMMUNITY INSTITUTIONS. ED045195
EXPERIMENTAL VARIATION OF HEAD START CURRICULA: A COMPARISON OF CURRENT APPROACHES. ANNUAL PROGRESS REPORT, JUNE 1, 1969 - MAY 31, 1970. ED045196
EVALUATION AND RESEARCH CENTER FOR PROJECT HEAD START, UNIVERSITY OF SOUTH CAROLINA. INTERIM EVALUATION REPORT. ED045197
FINAL REPORT ON PRESCHOOL EDUCATION TO OHIO DEPARTMENT OF EDUCATION. ED045200
AN ASSESSMENT OF COGNITIVE GROWTH IN CHILDREN WHO HAVE PARTICIPATED IN THE TOY-LENDING COMPONENT OF THE PARENT-CHILD PROGRAM. ED045204
AN OVERVIEW OF COGNITIVE AND LANGUAGE PROGRAMS FOR 3, 4, & 5 YEAR OLD CHILDREN. ED045209

THE EFFECTS OF CARTOON CHARACTERS AS MOTIVATORS OF PRESCHOOL DISADVANTAGED CHILDREN. FINAL REPORT. ED045210
HARTFORD EARLY CHILDHOOD PROGRAM, HARTFORD, CONNECTICUT: AN URBAN PUBLIC SCHOOL SYSTEM'S LARGE-SCALE APPROACH TOWARD RESTRUCTURING EARLY CHILDHOOD EDUCATION. MODEL PROGRAMS--CHILDHOOD EDUCATION. ED045211
SANTA MONICA CHILDREN'S CENTERS, SANTA MONICA, CALIFORNIA: LOW-COST DAY CARE FACILITIES FOR CHILDREN OF WORKING MOTHERS MADE AVAILABLE THROUGH THE COOPERATION OF THE CALIFORNIA STATE GOVERNMENT AND LOCAL SCHOOL DISTRICT. MODEL PROGRAMS--CHILDHOOD EDUCATION. ED045212
NEIGHBORHOOD HOUSE CHILD CARE SERVICES, SEATTLE, WASHINGTON: SEATTLE'S ANSWER TO CHILD CARE PROBLEMS OF LOW-INCOME FAMILIES. MODEL PROGRAMS--CHILDHOOD EDUCATION. ED045213
CROSS-CULTURAL FAMILY CENTER, SAN FRANCISCO, CALIFORNIA: A NURSERY SCHOOL PROVIDING A MULTICULTURAL CURRICULUM TO PROMOTE RACIAL UNDERSTANDING AND ACCEPTANCE. MODEL PROGRAMS--CHILDHOOD EDUCATION. ED045214
DEMONSTRATION NURSERY CENTER FOR INFANTS AND TODDLERS, GREENSBORO, NORTH CAROLINA: A MODEL DAY CARE CENTER FOR CHILDREN UNDER 3 YEARS OLD. MODEL PROGRAMS--CHILDHOOD EDUCATION. ED045215
APPALACHIA PRESCHOOL EDUCATION PROGRAM, CHARLESTON, WEST VIRGINIA: A THREE-PART PRESCHOOL PROGRAM COMBINING A TELEVISION PROGRAM, PARAPROFESSIONAL HOME VISITORS, AND A MOBILE CLASSROOM. MODEL PROGRAMS--CHILDHOOD EDUCATION. ED045216
COGNITIVELY ORIENTED CURRICULUM, YPSILANTI, MICHIGAN: A PROGRAM THAT EXPOSES PRESCHOOL CHILDREN TO A VARIETY OF MATERIALS AND EQUIPMENT TO TEACH CONCEPTS THROUGH PHYSICAL AND VERBAL EXPERIENCES. MODEL PROGRAMS--CHILDHOOD EDUCATION. ED045217
THE DAY NURSERY ASSOCIATION OF CLEVELAND, CLEVELAND, OHIO: A LONG HISTORY OF CARE FOR CHILDREN, INVOLVEMENT OF PARENTS, AND SERVICE TO THE COMMUNITY. MODEL PROGRAMS--CHILDHOOD EDUCATION. ED045218
UNIVERSITY OF HAWAII PRESCHOOL LANGUAGE CURRICULUM, HONOLULU, HAWAII: A PROGRAM OF ENGLISH CONVERSATION FOR PRESCHOOL CHILDREN OF MULTIETHNIC BACKGROUNDS. MODEL PROGRAMS--CHILDHOOD EDUCATION. ED045220
TACOMA PUBLIC SCHOOLS EARLY CHILDHOOD PROGRAM, TACOMA, WASHINGTON: COMBINED LOCAL, STATE, AND FEDERAL FUNDS SUPPORT A LARGE-SCALE EARLY CHILDHOOD PROGRAM IN THE PUBLIC SCHOOLS. MODEL PROGRAMS--CHILDHOOD EDUCATION. ED045221
COMMUNITY COOPERATIVE NURSERY SCHOOL, MENLO PARK, CALIFORNIA: A PRESCHOOL PROGRAM INVOLVING MOTHERS AS ORGANIZERS, HELPERS, AND DECISION-MAKERS. MODEL PROGRAMS--CHILDHOOD EDUCATION. ED045222
INFORMATION ON INTERVENTION PROGRAMS OF THE DEMONSTRATION AND RESEARCH CENTER FOR EARLY EDUCATION. ED046492
AN INVESTIGATION OF THE RELATIVE EFFECTIVENESS OF SELECTED CURRICULUM VARIABLES IN THE LANGUAGE DEVELOPMENT OF HEAD START CHILDREN. ED046497
YPSILANTI PRESCHOOL CURRICULUM DEMONSTRATION PROJECT, 1968-1971. ED046503
PRE-KINDERGARTEN PROGRAM, 1968-69. EVALUATION REPORT FOR THE PROJECT. ED046511
DAME SCHOOL PROJECT (BI-LINGUAL PRE SCHOOL PROJECT), SANTA CLARA COUNTY OFFICE OF EDUCATION. FINAL REPORT, AUGUST 1, 1970. ED046514
A NATIONAL SURVEY OF THE IMPACTS OF HEAD START CENTERS ON COMMUNITY INSTITUTIONS. SUMMARY REPORT. ED046516
HEAD START CURRICULUM MODELS: A REFERENCE LIST. ED046517
EFFECTS OF PRESCHOOL STIMULATION UPON SUBSEQUENT SCHOOL PERFORMANCE AMONG THE CULTURALLY DISADVANTAGED. ED046545
HEAD START PLANNED VARIATION STUDY. ED047782
AN ANALYSIS OF PUBLISHED PRESCHOOL LANGUAGE PROGRAMS. ED047786
A SEQUENTIAL APPROACH TO EARLY CHILDHOOD AND ELEMENTARY EDUCATION, PHASE II. GRANT REPORT. ED047791
PROJECT HEAD START 1968: A DESCRIPTIVE REPORT OF PROGRAMS AND PARTICIPANTS. ED047816
FILMS SUITABLE FOR HEAD START CHILD DEVELOPMENT PROGRAMS. ED047818
COMMUNITY COORDINATED CHILD CARE: A FEDERAL PARTNERSHIP IN BEHALF OF CHILDREN. FINAL REPORT. ED048925
A NATIONAL SURVEY OF THE PARENT-CHILD CENTER PROGRAM. ED048933
AN INTEGRATED PROGRAM OF GROUP CARE AND EDUCATION FOR SOCIOECONOMICALLY ADVANTAGED AND DISADVANTAGED INFANTS. ED048937
REVIEW AND SUMMARY OF A NATIONAL SURVEY OF THE PARENT-CHILD CENTER PROGRAM. ED048941
COMMUNITY COORDINATED CHILD CARE: A FEDERAL PARTNERSHIP IN BEHALF OF CHILDREN. SUMMARY. ED048944
HEAD START CURRICULUM MODELS: A REFERENCE LIST. (REVISED EDITION). ED048947
THE NEW YORK STATE EXPERIMENTAL PREKINDERGARTEN PROGRAM. SUMMARY REPORT, 1969-70. ED049814
HAS PRESCHOOL COMPENSATORY EDUCATION FAILED? ED049834
THE INFLUENCE OF SELECTED VARIABLES ON THE EFFECTIVENESS OF PRESCHOOL PROGRAMS FOR DISADVANTAGED CHILDREN. ED049835
PRESCHOOL INSTRUCTION MOBILE FACILITIES: DESCRIPTION AND ANALYSIS. SCHOOL PRACTICES REPORT NO. 3. ED050803
AN ANALYSIS OF EXCELLENT EARLY EDUCATIONAL PRACTICES: PRELIMINARY REPORT. ED050805
INTERVENTION WITH MOTHERS AND YOUNG CHILDREN: A STUDY OF INTRAFAMILY EFFECTS. ED050809
NON-PUBLIC PRESCHOOL PROGRAMS IN INDIANA. ED050813
TWO KINDS OF KINDERGARTEN AFTER FOUR TYPES OF HEAD START. ED050824
BEFORE SCHOOL STARTS. FOR CHILDREN'S MINDS--NOT JUST TO MIND THE CHILDREN. THE CHILD CENTRE--AS SEEN BY A PARENT. ED051873
ANALYSIS OF EARLY CHILDHOOD PROGRAMS: A SEARCH FOR COMPARATIVE DIMENSIONS. ED051877
AN ACADEMIC PRESCHOOL FOR DISADVANTAGED CHILDREN: REVIEW OF FINDINGS. PRELIMINARY DRAFT. ED051878
A STUDY IN CHILD CARE. VOLUME I: FINDINGS. DAY CARE PROGRAMS REPRINT SERIES. ED051911
PRESCHOOL PROGRAMS. IJR PRESCHOOL PROJECT REPORT, VOLUME I. ED052815
EARLY CHILDHOOD EDUCATION PROGRAM, ESEA TITLE I, FY 1970. PROJECT REPORTS, VOLUME 5, BOOK 2, 1970. ED052820
PRESCHOOL PROGRAMS: AN ANNOTATED BIBLIOGRAPHY. ED052822
DAY CARE: AN ANNOTATED BIBLIOGRAPHY. ED052823
THREE DEGREES OF PARENT INVOLVEMENT IN A PRESCHOOL PROGRAM: IMPACT ON MOTHERS AND CHILDREN. ED052831
DEMOGRAPHIC AND SOCIO-ECONOMIC DATA OF THE BECKLEY, WEST VIRGINIA AREA AND 1968-1970 DEVELOPMENTAL COSTS OF THE EARLY CHILDHOOD EDUCATION FIELD STUDY. TECHNICAL REPORT NO. 1. ED052832
ATTAINMENT OF COGNITIVE OBJECTIVES. TECHNICAL REPORT NO. 3. ED052833
DETAILED ANALYSIS OF LANGUAGE DEVELOPMENT OF PRESCHOOL CHILDREN IN ECE PROGRAM. TECHNICAL REPORT NO. 4. ED052834
SOCIAL SKILLS DEVELOPMENT IN THE EARLY CHILDHOOD EDUCATION PROJECT. TECHNICAL REPORT NO. 7. ED052835
RESULTS OF PARENT AND STUDENT REACTION QUESTIONNAIRE. TECHNICAL REPORT NO. 8. ED052836
EVALUATION REPORT: EARLY CHILDHOOD EDUCATION PROGRAM, 1969-1970 FIELD TEST. SUMMARY REPORT. ED052837
ANALYSIS OF INTELLIGENCE SCORES. ED052838
ANALYSIS OF VISUAL PERCEPTION OF CHILDREN IN THE EARLY CHILDHOOD EDUCATION PROGRAM (RESULTS OF THE MARIANNE FROSTIG DEVELOPMENTAL TEST OF VISUAL PERCEPTION). ED052839
FACTOR ANALYSIS OF THE EARLY CHILDHOOD EDUCATION TEST DATA. ED052840
ANALYSIS OF CHILDREN'S REACTIONS TO AEL'S PRESCHOOL TELEVISION PROGRAM. ED052841
A COMPARISON OF PARENTS' ATTITUDES TOWARD AEL'S "AROUND THE BEND" AND OTHER CHILDREN'S TELEVISION PROGRAMS. ED052842
IMPLEMENTATION OF PLANNED VARIATION IN HEAD START: PRELIMINARY EVALUATIONS OF PLANNED VARIATION IN HEAD START ACCORDING TO FOLLOW THROUGH APPROACHES (1969-1970). INTERIM REPORT: FIRST YEAR OF EVALUATION, PART II. ED052844
IMPLEMENTATION OF PLANNED VARIATION IN HEAD START. I. REVIEW AND SUMMARY OF THE STANFORD RESEARCH INSTITUTE INTERIM REPORT: FIRST YEAR OF EVALUATION. ED052845
STUDY OF SELECTED CHILDREN IN HEAD START PLANNED VARIATION, 1969-1970. FIRST YEAR REPORT: 3 - CASE STUDIES OF CHILDREN. ED052847
CONTEMPORARY INFLUENCES IN EARLY CHILDHOOD EDUCATION. ED053797
EXPERIMENTAL VARIATION OF HEAD START CURRICULA: A COMPARISON OF CURRENT APPROACHES. PROGRESS REPORT NO. 9, MARCH 1, 1971 - MAY 31, 1971. ED053814
NURSERIES IN CROSS-CULTURAL EDUCATION. FINAL REPORT. ED053815
"THIS IS ME!" EJ 003 029
CASE CONFERENCE: A PSYCHOTHERAPEUTIC AIDE IN A HEADSTART PROGRAM. I. THEORY AND PRACTICE EJ 003 955
CASE CONFERENCE: A PSYCHOTHERAPEUTIC AIDE IN A HEADSTART PROGRAM. II. COMMENTARY EJ 003 956
A MOBILE PRESCHOOL EJ 006 982
HEAD START IN ALASKA EJ 008 273
COMPARISON OF VERBAL INTERACTION IN TWO PRESCHOOL PROGRAMS EJ 008 274
GOALS AND METHODS IN A PRESCHOOL PROGRAM FOR DISADVANTAGED CHILDREN EJ 013 800
THE CASE FOR THE ACADEMIC PRESCHOOL: FACT OR FICTION? EJ 015 059
EDUCATIONAL AND GROWTH NEEDS OF CHILDREN IN DAY CARE EJ 016 351
PRESCHOOL PROGRAMS OF THE U.S.S.R EJ 016 352
THE PRESCHOOL COOPERATIVE AS A THERAPY FOR MOTHERS EJ 016 381

CONTRASTING VIEWS OF EARLY CHILDHOOD EDUCATION EJ 017 851
SOVIET PRESCHOOL EDUCATION EJ 020 840
SPECIAL CONSIDERATIONS IN THE OPERATION OF A HEAD START PROGRAM BY A COMMUNITY CHILD GUIDANCE CLINIC EJ 023 704
THE CHILD'S RIGHT TO QUALITY DAY CARE: AN ACEI POSITION PAPER EJ 029 103
THE EARLY TRAINING PROJECT: A SEVENTH-YEAR REPORT EJ 033 777
EDUCATIONAL INTERVENTION AT HOME BY MOTHERS OF DISADVANTAGED INFANTS EJ 034 002
CAN POVERTY CHILDREN LIVE ON "SESAME STREET?" EJ 034 509
THE KINDERGARTEN AGAINST APPALACHIAN POVERTY EJ 037 021
COGNITIVE DEVELOPMENT IN INFANCY: ASSESSMENT, ACCELERATION, AND ACTUALIZATION EJ 037 493
PSYCHOLOGICAL CONSULTATION IN A PRESCHOOL EJ 038 394
ON THE VALUE OF BOTH PLAY AND STRUCTURE IN EARLY EDUCATION EJ 044 010
A PLAY CENTER FOR DEVELOPMENTALLY HANDICAPPED INFANTS EJ 045 012
CHILDREN: OUR CHALLENGE EJ 050 423
EVALUATION OF A PARENT AND CHILD CENTER PROGRAM EJ 056 569

PRESCHOOL TEACHERS
INTERIM PROGRESS REPORT OF A REMOTE TEACHER TRAINING INSTITUTE FOR EARLY CHILDHOOD EDUCATORS (FUNDED BY NDEA TITLE XI). ED017326
EXPANDED PREKINDERGARTEN PROGRAM, EVALUATION OF NEW YORK CITY TITLE I EDUCATIONAL PROJECTS 1966-67. ED019115
HEAD START EVALUATION AND RESEARCH CENTER, THE UNIVERSITY OF CHICAGO. REPORT C, COGNITIVE INTERACTION BETWEEN TEACHER AND PUPIL IN A PRESCHOOL SETTING. ED022552
HEAD START EVALUATION AND RESEARCH CENTER, BOSTON UNIVERSITY. REPORT A-I, TEACHING STYLE: THE DEVELOPMENT OF TEACHING TASKS. ED022557
HEAD START EVALUATION AND RESEARCH CENTER, BOSTON UNIVERSITY. REPORT E-II, TEACHER SEMINAR. ED022567
THE ROLE OF THE TEACHER IN THE INFANT AND NURSERY SCHOOL. ED029703
HELP FOR TEACHERS IN PRESCHOOLS: A PROPOSAL. ED031308
SOME PARAMETERS OF TEACHER EFFECTIVENESS AS ASSESSED BY AN ECOLOGICAL APPROACH. ED032928
TEACHING IN PRESCHOOLS: ROLES AND GOALS. ED032942
STAFFING PRESCHOOLS: BACKGROUND INFORMATION. ED034589
THE TEACHER, TEACHER STYLE, AND CLASSROOM MANAGEMENT. PROCEEDINGS OF THE HEAD START RESEARCH SEMINARS: SEMINAR NO. 2, THE TEACHER AND CLASSROOM MANAGEMENT (1ST, WASHINGTON, D.C., JULY 22, 1968). ED035463
THE MODIFICATION OF TEACHER BEHAVIORS WHICH MODIFY CHILD BEHAVIORS. PROGRESS REPORT. ED042499
THE DISTRIBUTION OF TEACHER APPROVAL AND DISAPPROVAL OF HEAD START CHILDREN. FINAL REPORT. ED042509
THE PROFESSIONAL SELF IMAGE AND THE ATTRIBUTES OF A PROFESSION: AN EXPLORATORY STUDY OF THE PRESCHOOL TEACHER. ED044183
THE ITINERANT TEACHER. ED045191
TEACHER-CHILD RELATIONSHIPS IN DAY CARE CENTERS. WORKING PAPER. ED046494
AND A FRIENDLY GOODBYE EJ 028 310
"OF HAIRY ARMS AND A DEEP BARITONE VOICE": A SYMPOSIUM MEN IN YOUNG CHILDREN'S LIVES EJ 028 795
LA FORMATION DU PERSONNEL NON MEDICAL S'OCCUPANT DU PETIT ENFANT DE 1 A 6 ANS EJ 035 170
EDUCATION OF TEACHERS FOR NURSERY SCHOOLS: A CREATIVE APPROACH EJ 036 336
NURSERY SCHOOLS FIFTY YEARS AGO EJ 055 736

PRESCHOOL TESTS
EVALUATION OF HEADSTART EDUCATIONAL PROGRAM IN CAMBRIDGE, MASSACHUSETTS. FINAL REPORT. ED013668
THE PRESCHOOL INVENTORY. ED014334
DEVELOPMENT OF A SOCIAL COMPETENCY SCALE FOR PRESCHOOL CHILDREN. FINAL REPORT. ED020004
THE JOHNS HOPKINS PERCEPTUAL TEST, THE DEVELOPMENT OF A RAPID INTELLIGENCE TEST FOR THE PRE-SCHOOL CHILD. ED020787
HEAD START EVALUATION AND RESEARCH CENTER. PROGRESS REPORT OF RESEARCH STUDIES 1966 TO 1967. DOCUMENT 3, AN EXPERIMENTAL APPROACH TO STUDYING NON-VERBAL REPRESENTATION IN YOUNG CHILDREN. ED021625
INDEX AND DESCRIPTION OF TESTS. ED025304
PERFORMANCE OF KINDERGARTEN CHILDREN FROM LOW INCOME FAMILIES ON SELECTED CONCEPT CATEGORIES. ED028847
IDENTIFICATION IN THE KINDERGARTEN OF FACTORS THAT MAKE FOR FUTURE SUCCESS IN READING AND IDENTIFICATION AND DIAGNOSIS IN THE KINDERGARTEN OF POTENTIAL READING DISABILITY CASES. FINAL REPORT. ED029710
SIX SCHOOL READINESS SCREENING DEVICES USED IN PEDIATRIC OFFICES: CONCURRENT VALIDITY. FINAL REPORT. ED029719
SOCIAL-EMOTIONAL TASK FORCE. FINAL REPORT. ED033744

PRESCHOOL WORKSHOPS
A PRESCHOOL WORKSHOP FOR EMOTIONALLY DISTURBED CHILDREN EJ 013 234

PRESERVICE EDUCATION
EDUCATIONAL INTERVENTION IN THE HOME AND PARAPROFESSIONAL CAREER DEVELOPMENT: A FIRST GENERATION MOTHER STUDY. ED045190

PRETESTING
AN EXPLORATORY STUDY OF THE RELATIONSHIP BETWEEN COGNITIVE PRETESTING AND COURSE ACHIEVEMENT EJ 041 758

PREVENTION
PREVENTION OF FAILURE. ED020777
CHILDREN WHO ARE INJURED. 1970 WHITE HOUSE CONFERENCE ON CHILDREN, REPORT OF FORUM 13. (WORKING COPY). ED046529
A PILOT STUDY OF A PRESCHOOL METHOD OF PREVENTIVE EDUCATION. FINAL REPORT. ED0465[illegible]1
LEAD POISONING IN CHILDREN. ED048919
PREVENTION OF IRON-DEFICIENCY ANEMIA IN INFANTS AND CHILDREN OF PRESCHOOL AGE. ED052830
BEHAVIORAL SCIENCE FOR ELEMENTARY-SCHOOL PUPILS EJ 014 306
MEETING SOCIO-EDUCATIONAL NEEDS EJ 027 916
ADVOCACY FOR CHILDREN: CHALLENGE FOR THE 1970'S EJ 032 108
A SOCIOCULTURAL PERSPECTIVE ON PHYSICAL CHILD ABUSE EJ 043 353
PREVENTING ILLEGITIMATE TEENAGE PREGNANCY THROUGH SYSTEMS INTERACTION EJ 059 671
PARENTS OF CHILDREN WITH PKU EJ 060 522

PREVENTIVE MEDICINE
KEEPING CHILDREN HEALTHY: HEALTH PROTECTION AND DISEASE PREVENTION. 1970 WHITE HOUSE CONFERENCE ON CHILDREN, REPORT OF FORUM 10. (WORKING PAPER). ED046527
PLANNING FOR A MASS ATTACK ON RUBELLA EJ 007 164

PRIMACY EFFECT
PRIMACY IN PRESCHOOLERS' SHORT-TERM MEMORY: THE EFFECTS OF REPEATED TESTS AND SHIFT TRIALS EJ 053 729

PRIMARY EDUCATION
LANGUAGE LEARNING ACTIVITIES FOR THE DISADVANTAGED CHILD. ED020002
TACOMA PUBLIC SCHOOLS EARLY CHILDHOOD PROGRAM, TACOMA, WASHINGTON: COMBINED LOCAL, STATE, AND FEDERAL FUNDS SUPPORT A LARGE-SCALE EARLY CHILDHOOD PROGRAM IN THE PUBLIC SCHOOLS. MODEL PROGRAMS--CHILDHOOD EDUCATION. ED045221
TOWARDS AN INDIAN PHILOSOPHY OF PRIMARY EDUCATION EJ 036 337
LEARNING FROM THE BRITISH PRIMARY SCHOOLS EJ 057 327

PRIMARY GRADES
AN INDIVIDUALIZED SCIENCE LABORATORY. ED013664
LINGUISTICS IN THE ELEMENTARY SCHOOL. ED019134
DEVELOPMENT OF A GROUP MEASURE TO ASSESS THE EXTENT OF PRE-LOGICAL AND PRE-CAUSAL THINKING IN PRIMARY SCHOOL AGE CHILDREN. ED019136
TEACHING MUSICAL CONCEPTS RELATED TO MELODY, RHYTHM, FORM, AND HARMONY, TEACHER RESOURCE MATERIAL KINDERGARTEN, GRADES 1 AND 2. ED019991
EFFECT OF TRIMESTER SCHOOL OPERATION ON THE ACHIEVEMENT AND ADJUSTMENT OF KINDERGARTEN AND FIRST THROUGH THIRD GRADE CHILDREN. FINAL REPORT. ED020003
BLOCKBUILDING. ED020011
AN EXPLORATION OF THE USES OF RHYTHMIC MOVEMENT TO DEVELOP AESTHETIC CONCEPTS IN THE PRIMARY GRADES. ED020770
THERE IS A BETTER WAY. A PREMISE POINTS THE WAY, A PROFILE WITH PROMISE, A COMPOSITE OF THE SURVEY. ED023471
DEVELOPMENT AND IMPLEMENTATION OF A COMPREHENSIVE EVALUATION AND REPORTING SYSTEM FOR KINDERGARTEN AND PRIMARY GRADE SCHOOLS. FINAL REPORT. ED026116
A DISTANCE MEASURE OF RACIAL ATTITUDES IN PRIMARY GRADE CHILDREN: AN EXPLORATORY STUDY. ED026133
ADMINISTRATION MANUAL FOR TESTS OF BASIC LANGUAGE COMPETENCE IN ENGLISH AND SPANISH. LEVEL II (PRIMARY GRADES): CHILDREN AGES SIX TO TEN, ENGLISH AND SPANISH VERSIONS, FORMS A AND B. PART OF THE FINAL REPORT. ED027064
TEAM TEACHING. A DESCRIPTIVE AND EVALUATIVE STUDY OF A PROGRAM FOR THE PRIMARY GRADES. ED027083
INTEGRATED, INDEPENDENT AND INDIVIDUAL LEARNING ACTIVITIES, FIRST AND SECOND GRADES. SUMMER LEARNING ACTIVITIES, SECOND AND THIRD GRADES. BOSTON-NORTHAMPTON LANGUAGE ARTS PROGRAM, ESEA - 1965, PROJECTS TO ADVANCE CREATIVITY IN EDUCATION. ED027946
THE USE OF COLOURED RODS IN TEACHING PRIMARY NUMBERWORK. ED028823
A STUDY OF PUBLIC AND PRIVATE KINDERGARTEN AND NON-KINDERGARTEN CHILDREN IN THE PRIMARY GRADES. ED028837
[REGIONAL RESEARCH AND RESOURCE CENTER IN EARLY CHILDHOOD.] FINAL REPORT. ED028846
COMPARISON OF YES-NO, MATCHED-PAIRS, AND ALL-NO SCORING OF A FIRST-GRADE ECONOMICS ACHIEVEMENT TEST. ED029701
SPOTLIGHT ON FOLLOW THROUGH. ED029720

INDEPENDENT AND SMALL GROUP ACTIVITIES FOR SOCIAL STUDIES IN THE PRIMARY GRADES. ED031305
ARTS AND HUMANITIES FOR YOUNG SCHOOL CHILDREN. ED032945
INDUSTRIAL ARTS FOR THE PRIMARY GRADES. ED035459
SOCIAL STUDIES IN THE PRIMARY GRADES. ED035460
SCIENCE FOR THE PRIMARY GRADES: QUESTIONS AND ANSWERS. ED035461
CHARACTERISTICS OF PRIMARY LEVEL CHILDREN. ED036343
A PILOT EXPERIMENT IN EARLY CHILDHOOD POLITICAL LEARNING. REPORT FROM THE PROJECT ON CONCEPTS IN POLITICAL SCIENCE. ED043368
INTELLECTUAL DEVELOPMENT AND THE ABILITY TO PROCESS VISUAL AND VERBAL INFORMATION. ED043373
WORDS AND DEEDS ABOUT ALTRUISM AND THE SUBSEQUENT REINFORCEMENT POWER OF THE MODEL. ED043390
THE COGNITIVE ENVIRONMENTS OF URBAN PRESCHOOL CHILDREN: FOLLOW-UP PHASE. FINAL REPORT. ED045180
PRESCHOOL EDUCATION AND SCHOOL ADMISSION PRACTICES IN NEW ZEALAND. ED046487
NON-VERBAL INFORMATION STORAGE IN HUMANS AND DEVELOPMENTAL INFORMATION PROCESSING CHANNEL CAPACITY. ED047800
LOOK--I SEE ME EJ 028 897
IT MAKES ME FEEL BAD WHEN YOU CALL ME "STINKY" EJ 029 358
ENCOURAGEMENT FOR THE YOUNG WRITER EJ 029 414
RELATIONSHIP OF CONSERVATION EXPLANATIONS TO ITEM DIFFICULTY EJ 030 295
PIAGETIAN TASKS AS CLASSROOM EVALUATIVE TOOLS EJ 032 679
SHOWING AND SHARING IN THE KINDERGARTEN EJ 032 933
CHILDREN'S SELECTIVE ATTENTION TO STIMULI: STAGE OR SET? EJ 033 573
MEANING AND ATTENTION AS DETERMINANTS OF SOCIAL REINFORCER EFFECTIVENESS EJ 033 781
CHILDREN'S SHIFT PERFORMANCE IN THE ABSENCE OF DIMENSIONALITY AND A LEARNED REPRESENTATIONAL RESPONSE EJ 033 786
BOOKS FOR YOUNG CHILDREN EJ 043 020
THE EFFECTS OF THE DUSO GUIDANCE PROGRAM ON THE SELF-CONCEPTS OF PRIMARY SCHOOL CHILDREN EJ 058 132

PRINCIPALS

THE TEACHER'S VIEW OF THE PRINCIPAL'S ROLE IN INNOVATION EJ 018 957
RESEARCH ON ASPECTS OF LEADERSHIP ROLES IN EARLY AND ELEMENTARY EDUCATION EJ 055 205

PRIVATE AGENCIES

REALISTIC PLANNING FOR THE DAY CARE CONSUMER. ED043374
NON-PUBLIC PRESCHOOL PROGRAMS IN INDIANA. ED050813
A STUDY IN CHILD CARE (CASE STUDY FROM VOLUME II-A): "IT'S A WELL-RUN BUSINESS, TOO." DAY CARE PROGRAMS REPRINT SERIES. ED051896
OPTIMAL OPERATION OF PUBLIC/PRIVATE CHILD WELFARE DELIVERY SYSTEMS EJ 031 540

PRIVATE SCHOOLS

STEPS PURSUANT TO SECURING ACCREDITATION BY PRIVATE SECONDARY SCHOOLS EJ 016 606

PROBABILITY

HEAD START EVALUATION AND RESEARCH CENTER, BOSTON UNIVERSITY. REPORT D-III, A STUDY OF PREFERENCES AMONG QUALITATIVELY DIFFERING UNCERTAINTIES. ED022565
EXTENSION OF A THEORY OF PREDICTIVE BEHAVIOR TO IMMEDIATE RECALL BY PRESCHOOL CHILDREN. ED025326
FREE-ASSOCIATION NORMS AND ASSOCIATIVE STRUCTURE. ED025328
WHAT IS LEARNED IN PROBABILITY LEARNING EJ 018 879
MAGNITUDE-PROBABILITY PREFERENCES OF PRESCHOOL CHILDREN FROM TWO SOCIOECONOMIC LEVELS EJ 019 017
PROBABILITY LEARNING AS A FUNCTION OF AGE, SEX, AND TYPE OF CONSTRAINT EJ 021 766
CHILDREN'S UNDERSTANDING OF PROBABILITY CONCEPTS EJ 036 824
CHILDREN'S ACQUISITION AND REVERSAL BEHAVIOR IN A PROBABILITY LEARNING SITUATION AS A FUNCTION OF PROGRAMMED INSTRUCTION, INTERNAL-EXTERNAL CONTROL, AND SCHEDULES OF REINFORCEMENT EJ 037 495
INFORMATION SEEKING ABOUT UNCERTAIN BUT UNAVOIDABLE OUTCOMES: EFFECTS OF PROBABILITY, VALENCE, AND INTERVENING ACTIVITY EJ 042 962
THE ROLE OF REINFORCEMENT PROCEDURE IN CHILDREN'S PROBABILITY LEARNING AS A FUNCTION OF AGE AND NUMBER OF RESPONSE ALTERNATIVES EJ 046 253
PERSEVERATION AND ALTERNATION PRETRAINING AND BINARY PREDICTION EJ 057 902
AN APPLICATION OF BRUNSWIK'S LENS MODEL TO DEVELOPMENTAL CHANGES IN PROBABILITY LEARNING EJ 058 142

PROBLEM CHILDREN

THE IMPACT OF OBJECT LOSS ON A SIX-YEAR-OLD EJ 030 514
A SENSITIVITY-TRAINING APPROACH TO GROUP THERAPY WITH CHILDREN EJ 039 501
THE BOY WHO DID NOT CRY EJ 052 310
THE SORE-FOOTED DUCK EJ 053 929

PROBLEM SOLVING

THE EFFECTS OF SEVERAL VERBAL PRETRAINING CONDITIONS ON PRESCHOOL CHILDREN'S TRANSFER IN PROBLEM SOLVING. FINAL REPORT. ED015778
DISCRIMINATION LEARNING, PROBLEM SOLVING, AND CHOICE PATTERNING BY CHILDREN AS A FUNCTION OF INCENTIVE VALUE, MOTIVATION, AND SEQUENTIAL DEPENDENCIES. FINAL REPORT. ED016518
THE PERFORMANCE OF FIRST GRADE CHILDREN IN FOUR LEVELS OF CONSERVATION OF NUMEROUSNESS AND THREE IQ GROUPS WHEN SOLVING ARITHMETIC ADDITION PROBLEMS. ED016535
THE EFFECTS OF TWO VARIABLES ON THE PROBLEM-SOLVING ABILITIES OF FIRST-GRADE CHILDREN. ED019113
REGIONAL EVALUATION AND RESEARCH CENTER FOR PROJECT HEAD START, SUPPLEMENTARY RESEARCH REPORT, SEPTEMBER 1, 1967-DECEMBER 31, 1967. ED020791
THE RELATION BETWEEN TEST ANXIETY AND NEED FOR MEMORY SUPPORT IN PROBLEM SOLVING. REVISED RESEARCH MEMORANDUM NO. 11. ED021616
AGE AND MEMORY AS FACTORS IN PROBLEM SOLVING. ED025327
THE MONTESSORI RESEARCH PROJECT. FOUR PROGRESS REPORTS. ED030489
ON COGNIZING COGNITIVE PROCESSES. ED035437
AN INVESTIGATION OF THE MANNER IN WHICH YOUNG CHILDREN PROCESS INTELLECTUAL INFORMATION. FINAL REPORT. ED036313
PROBLEM SOLVING PERFORMANCES OF FIRST GRADE CHILDREN. ED041623
RULE STRUCTURE AND PROPORTION OF POSITIVE INSTANCES AS DETERMINANTS OF CONCEPT ATTAINMENT IN CHILDREN. ED046500
THE ACQUISITION OF CONSERVATION THROUGH SOCIAL INTERACTION. ED047801
THE NEW NURSERY SCHOOL RESEARCH PROJECT ED048940
A NOTE ON TEACHING FOR CREATIVITY EJ 018 130
INFORMATION PROCESSING IN PROBLEM SOLVING AS A FUNCTION OF DEVELOPMENTAL LEVEL AND STIMULUS SALIENCY EJ 018 884
THE ROLE OF COMPREHENSION IN CHILDREN'S PROBLEM SOLVING EJ 021 764
DEVELOPMENT CHANGES IN PROBLEM-SOLVING STRATEGIES: PERMUTATION EJ 021 767
A PRELIMINARY SEARCH FOR FORMAL OPERATIONS STRUCTURES EJ 023 192
TRANSFER IN NURSERY SCHOOL CHILDREN BETWEEN TWO RELATIONAL TASKS EJ 024 704
THE EFFECT OF INFORMATIVE FEEDBACK ON PROBLEM SOLVING EJ 025 961
A SEX DIFFERENCE IN THE WECHSLER IQ VOCABULARY SCORE AS A PREDICTOR OF STRATEGY IN A PROBABILITY-LEARNING TASK PERFORMED BY ADOLESCENTS EJ 026 376
MATERNAL FOOD RESTRICTION: EFFECTS ON OFFSPRING DEVELOPMENT, LEARNING, AND A PROGRAM OF THERAPY EJ 029 218
LEARNING AND PROBLEM SOLVING BY THE MENTALLY RETARDED UNDER THREE TESTING CONDITIONS EJ 030 290
DIMENSIONAL SALIENCE AND IDENTIFICATION OF THE RELEVANT DIMENSION IN PROBLEM SOLVING: A DEVELOPMENTAL STUDY EJ 035 360
INTERRELATIONS AMONG LEARNING AND PERFORMANCE TASKS AT THE PRESCHOOL LEVEL EJ 035 361
OUTERDIRECTEDNESS IN THE PROBLEM-SOLVING OF INSTITUTIONALIZED AND NONINSTITUTIONALIZED NORMAL AND RETARDED CHILDREN EJ 035 366
THE "MENTAL STEP" HYPOTHESIS IN SOLVING VERBAL PROBLEMS: EFFECTS OF VARIATIONS IN QUESTION-PHRASING ON A GRADE SCHOOL POPULATION EJ 035 372
THE LEARNING AND TRANSFER OF DOUBLE-CLASSIFICATION SKILLS BY FIRST GRADERS EJ 036 821
CONDITIONAL DISCRIMINATION LEARNING IN CHILDREN: TWO RELEVANT FACTORS EJ 036 823
THE GROWTH OF CHILDREN'S SEMANTIC MEMORY: SEMANTIC ELEMENTS EJ 038 170
A NONARBITRARY BEHAVIORAL CRITERION FOR CONSERVATION OF ILLUSION-DISTORTED LENGTH IN FIVE-YEAR-OLDS EJ 038 263
CHRONOLOGICAL AGE AND PERFORMANCE ON PROBLEMS WITH REPEATED PRESOLUTION SHIFTS EJ 039 628
PERSONALITY, COGNITIVE, AND ACADEMIC CORRELATES OF PROBLEM-SOLVING FLEXIBILITY EJ 039 632
INTERDEPENDENCE OF INHELDER AND PIAGET'S MODEL OF LOGICAL THINKING EJ 039 633
SOME RELATIONSHIPS BETWEEN CLASS INCLUSION, PERCEPTUAL CAPABILITIES, VERBAL CAPABILITIES AND RACE EJ 039 639
COGNITIVE STYLES IN HYPERACTIVE CHILDREN AND THE EFFECT OF METHYLPHENIDATE EJ 041 963
FACTORS INFLUENCING CHILDREN'S CONCEPT IDENTIFICATION PERFORMANCE WITH NONPREFERRED RELEVANT ATTRIBUTES EJ 042 965
EFFECTS OF TUTORIAL EXPERIENCES ON THE PROBLEM-SOLVING BEHAVIOR OF SIXTH-GRADERS EJ 043 415
EFFECTS OF EXPOSURE TO MODELS ON CONCEPT IDENTIFICATION IN KINDERGARTEN AND SECOND-GRADE CHILDREN EJ 046 240
PROBLEM-SOLVING THINKING AND ADJUSTMENT AMONG DISADVANTAGED PRESCHOOL CHILDREN EJ 056 612

OUTERDIRECTEDNESS AND IMITATIVE BEHAVIOR OF INSTITUTIONALIZED AND NONINSTITUTIONALIZED YOUNGER AND OLDER CHILDREN EJ 058 694

PROBLEMS

PROBLEMS OF EDUCATIONAL EVALUATION IN PROJECT HEAD START--SAMPLING, DESIGN, AND CONTROL GROUPS. ED015793

A HOTLINE TELEPHONE SERVICE FOR YOUNG PEOPLE IN CRISIS EJ 007 713

ILLEGIBILITIES IN THE CURSIVE HANDWRITING OF SIXTH-GRADERS EJ 019 443

PRODUCTIVE THINKING

PRODUCTIVE THINKING IN EDUCATION. ED024459

PRODUCTIVITY

NEW LIGHT ON THE HUMAN POTENTIAL EJ 026 373

PROFESSIONAL ASSOCIATIONS

EPILOGUE AND A NEW BEGINNING EJ 022 371

PROFESSIONAL PERSONNEL

PRELIMINARY REPORT OF THE AD HOC JOINT COMMITTEE ON THE PREPARATION OF NURSERY AND KINDERGARTEN TEACHERS. ED032924

CONSULTATION IN DAY CARE. ED051884

A NEW CHILD CARE PROFESSION: THE CHILD DEVELOPMENT ASSOCIATE EJ 050 937

PROFESSIONAL RECOGNITION

THE PROFESSIONAL SELF IMAGE AND THE ATTRIBUTES OF A PROFESSION: AN EXPLORATORY STUDY OF THE PRESCHOOL TEACHER. ED044183

PROFESSIONAL TRAINING

LA FORMATION DU PERSONNEL NON MEDICAL S'OCCUPANT DU PETIT ENFANT DE 1 A 6 ANS EJ 035 170

PROFESSORS

THE EFFECT OF STUDENT EVALUATIONS OF COLLEGE INSTRUCTION UPON SUBSEQUENT EVALUATIONS EJ 017 245

PROFILE EVALUATION

[ACHIEVEMENT TEST CORRELATION STUDY: SURVEY OF 40 CHILDREN.] ED027954

PROGNOSTIC TESTS

TECHNIQUES FOR ASSESSING COGNITIVE AND SOCIAL ABILITIES OF CHILDREN AND PARENTS IN PROJECT HEAD START. ED015772

GROUP SCREENING OF AUDITORY AND VISUAL PERCEPTUAL ABILITIES: AN APPROACH TO PERCEPTUAL ASPECTS OF BEGINNING READING. ED033751

A COMPARATIVE STUDY OF THREE FORMS OF THE METROPOLITAN READINESS TEST AT TWO SOCIO-ECONOMIC LEVELS. ED035448

PROGRAM ADMINISTRATION

PROJECT HEAD START, THE URBAN AND RURAL CHALLENGE. FINAL REPORT. ED022527

PLANNING A DAY CARE CENTER. ED053795

CONTEMPORARY CONCERNS IN EARLY CHILDHOOD EDUCATION EJ 032 059

PROGRAM CONTENT

PROJECT HEAD START--SUMMER 1966. FINAL REPORT. SECTION THREE, PUPILS AND PROGRAMS. ED018248

TEACHING GENERAL MUSIC, A RESOURCE HANDBOOK FOR GRADES 7 AND 8. ED018277

AN INTERDISCIPLINARY APPROACH IN DAY TREATMENT OF EMOTIONALLY DISTURBED CHILDREN EJ 029 167

PROGRAM COORDINATION

COVERT PROJECT, YEAR 1. ED019137

PROGRAM COSTS

CLASSIFYING DAY CARE CENTERS FOR COST ANALYSIS. ED047783

EVALUATION REPORT: EARLY CHILDHOOD EDUCATION PROGRAM, 1969-1970 FIELD TEST. SUMMARY REPORT. ED052837

PLANNING A DAY CARE CENTER. ED053795

CONSIDERATIONS IN DAY CARE COST ANALYSIS EJ 040 722

PROGRAM DESCRIPTIONS

COVERT PROJECT, YEAR 1. ED019137

KINDERGARTEN GUIDEBOOK. ED020008

EDUCATION FOR INITIATIVE AND RESPONSIBILITY, COMMENTS ON A VISIT TO THE SCHOOLS OF LEICESTERSHIRE COUNTY, APRIL 1967. SECOND EDITION. ED020795

MAKING WAVES, DENVER HEAD START. ED020802

PROJECT HEAD START, REPORT ON THE PREKINDERGARTEN PROGRAM, 1965. ED021611

THE YPSILANTI EARLY EDUCATION PROGRAM. ED022531

PROBLEMS AND PROSPECTS OF EDUCATION IN THE BIG CITIES AS EXEMPLIFIED BY PITTSBURGH, PENNSYLVANIA. ED022542

NURSERIES IN CROSS-CULTURAL EDUCATION. PROGRESS REPORT. ED023460

SAN MATEO COUNTY HUMAN RESOURCES COMMISSION PROJECT HEAD START - SUMMER 1966. AN EVALUATIONAL REPORT. ED023478

INKSTER PUBLIC SCHOOLS IMPLEMENT CHILD DEVELOPMENT CENTER. ED025303

THE MARIE HUGHES LANGUAGE TRAINING MODEL. ED025305

ENGINEERING VERBAL BEHAVIOR. ED025308

INVESTMENTS IN PREVENTION, AN ACTIVITY GROUP PROGRAM FOR YOUNG CHILDREN, SUMMER - 1967. ED025311

KINDERGARTEN, 1967-68. AN EVALUATION REPORT. ED025315

TEAM TEACHING. A DESCRIPTIVE AND EVALUATIVE STUDY OF A PROGRAM FOR THE PRIMARY GRADES. ED027083

INTEGRATED, INDEPENDENT AND INDIVIDUAL LEARNING ACTIVITIES, FIRST AND SECOND GRADES. SUMMER LEARNING ACTIVITIES, SECOND AND THIRD GRADES. BOSTON-NORTHAMPTON LANGUAGE ARTS PROGRAM, ESEA - 1965, PROJECTS TO ADVANCE CREATIVITY IN EDUCATION. ED027946

GUIDELINES: PRE-SCHOOL PROJECTS, HEAD START: EARLY CHILDHOOD EDUCATION. REVISED EDITION. ED027948

PROGRAM FOR EARLY CHILDHOOD EDUCATION. ED027957

A PLAN OF ACTION FOR PARENT-CHILD EDUCATIONAL CENTERS. ED027959

EARLY CHILDHOOD PROJECT, NEW YORK CITY ED027974

PERRY PRESCHOOL PROJECT, YPSILANTI, MICHIGAN ED027975

INFANT EDUCATION RESEARCH PROJECT, WASHINGTON, D.C. ED027976

A REPORT ON THE 1967-68 PROGRAM FOR PRESCHOOL CHILDREN AND THEIR PARENTS. RESEARCH REPORT SERIES 1968-69, NO. 4. ED029713

SPOTLIGHT ON FOLLOW THROUGH. ED029720

HEAD START IN ACTION. ED030471

DISTURBANCE AND DISSONANCE - COMMUNITY UNIVERSITY COLLABORATION IN DIAGNOSIS AND TREATMENT OF DISTURBANCES. ED030485

EVAULATION OF THE DEMONSTRATION PHASE OF THE TEEN TUTORIAL PROGRAM: A MODEL OF INTERRELATIONSHIP OF SEVENTH GRADERS, KINDERGARTEN PUPILS AND PARENTS TO MEET THE DEVELOPMENTAL NEEDS OF DISADVANTAGED CHILDREN. ED032115

PHILOSOPHY: A CRUCIAL DISTINCTION. ED032129

[THE JUNIPER GARDENS PARENT COOPERATIVE NURSERY.] FINAL PROGRESS REPORT FOR OEO CAP GRANT CG-8474 A/O. ED032920

RESEARCH, CHANGE, AND SOCIAL RESPONSIBILITY: AN ILLUSTRATIVE MODEL FROM EARLY EDUCATION. ED032922

MOTHERS' TRAINING PROGRAM: THE GROUP PROCESS. ED032926

DEVELOPMENT OF A DANCE CURRICULUM FOR YOUNG CHILDREN. CAREL ARTS AND HUMANITIES CURRICULUM DEVELOPMENT PROGRAM FOR YOUNG CHILDREN. ED032936

DEVELOPMENT OF A THEATRE ARTS CURRICULUM FOR YOUNG CHILDREN. CAREL ARTS AND HUMANITIES CURRICULUM DEVELOPMENT PROGRAM FOR YOUNG CHILDREN. ED032937

DEVELOPMENT OF A MUSIC CURRICULUM FOR YOUNG CHILDREN. CAREL ARTS AND HUMANITIES CURRICULUM DEVELOPMENT PROGRAM FOR YOUNG CHILDREN. ED032938

DEVELOPMENT OF A VISUAL ARTS CURRICULUM FOR YOUNG CHILDREN. CAREL ARTS AND HUMANITIES CURRICULUM DEVELOPMENT PROGRAM FOR YOUNG CHILDREN. ED032939

DEVELOPMENT OF A LITERATURE CURRICULUM FOR YOUNG CHILDREN. CAREL ARTS AND HUMANITIES CURRICULUM DEVELOPMENT PROGRAM FOR YOUNG CHILDREN. ED032940

ARTS AND HUMANITIES FOR YOUNG SCHOOL CHILDREN. ED032945

A STRUCTURE-PROCESS APPROACH TO COGNITIVE DEVELOPMENT OF PRESCHOOL NEGRO CHILDREN: RATIONALE AND EFFECTS. ED033743

PRELUDE TO SCHOOL: AN EVALUATION OF AN INNER-CITY PRESCHOOL PROGRAM. ED033750

THE TUCSON EARLY EDUCATION MODEL. ED033753

FOCUS ON PARENT EDUCATION AS A MEANS OF ALTERING THE CHILD'S ENVIRONMENT. ED033758

PENNSYLVANIA PRESCHOOL AND PRIMARY EDUCATION PROJECT: 1968-1969 FINAL REPORT TO THE FORD FOUNDATION. ED033759

THE DESIGN OF A PRE-SCHOOL "LEARNING LABORATORY" IN A REHABILITATION CENTER. ED033764

THE SATURDAY SCHOOL: AN INSTALLATION MANUAL. ED033765

EFFECTS OF SOCIAL REINFORCEMENT ON SELF-ESTEEM OF MEXICAN-AMERICAN CHILDREN. LONG ABSTRACT. ED033767

ARIZONA CENTER FOR EARLY CHILDHOOD EDUCATION ANNUAL REPORT, JUNE 1968 - JUNE 1969. ED034586

THE ADVANTAGED: A PRESCHOOL PROGRAM FOR THE DISADVANTAGED. ED035436

EXEMPLARY AND INNOVATIVE PRESCHOOL CHILD DEVELOPMENT DEMONSTRATION CENTERS, 1966-1969. THREE YEAR EVALUATION AND NARRATIVE REPORT. ED035456

THE STORY OF AN AFTER - SCHOOL PROGRAM. ED035464

NEW NURSERY SCHOOL RESEARCH PROJECT, OCTOBER 1, 1968 TO SEPTEMBER 30, 1969. ANNUAL PROGRESS REPORT. ED036320

THE ANALYSIS OF DATA GENERATED IN A RESEARCH DESIGNED TO SECURE BASELINE INFORMATION ON A HEAD START PROGRAM. A REPORT TO THE U.S. OFFICE OF ECONOMIC OPPORTUNITY FROM THE DEPARTMENT OF RESEARCH, MONTGOMERY COUNTY, MARYLAND PUBLIC SCHOOLS. ED037232

DEVELOPMENT OF THE EARLY CHILDHOOD EDUCATION PROGRAM. BASIC PLAN. ED038181

[NATIONAL LABORATORY ON EARLY CHILDHOOD EDUCATION PROGRAM ED039012

CHILD STUDY-KINDERGARTEN, 1968-69: AN INFORMATION REPORT. ED039015

COMMUNITY COORDINATED CHILD CARE (4-C) MANUAL. ED039016

A SOCIAL LEARNING APPROACH TO EARLY CHILDHOOD EDUCATION. ED039025
AN ANALYSIS OF EARLY CHILDHOOD EDUCATION RESEARCH AND DEVELOPMENT. ED039028
EXPERIMENTAL VARIATION OF HEAD START CURRICULA: A COMPARISON OF CURRENT APPROACHES. ANNUAL REPORT, JUNE 12, 1968-JUNE 11, 1969. ED041618
PROGRAM-PROJECT RESUMES, 1969-1970. ED042503
EARLY CHILDHOOD EDUCATION PROGRAM AND ITS COMPONENTS: PSYCHOLOGICAL EVALUATION, SENSORIMOTOR SKILLS PROGRAM, NEW VISIONS - A CHILDREN'S MUSEUM. PROJECT REPORTS, VOLUME 4, BOOK 1, 1969. ED045183
CHANGING THE LEARNING PATTERNS OF THE CULTURALLY DIFFERENT. ED045184
EXPERIMENTAL VARIATION OF HEAD START CURRICULA: A COMPARISON OF CURRENT APPROACHES. ANNUAL PROGRESS REPORT, JUNE 1, 1969 - MAY 31, 1970. ED045196
A PROGRESS REPORT ON THE PARENT/CHILD COURSE AND TOY LIBRARY. ED045206
OVERVIEW OF RESPONSIVE MODEL PROGRAM. ED045207
AN OVERVIEW OF COGNITIVE AND LANGUAGE PROGRAMS FOR 3, 4, & 5 YEAR OLD CHILDREN. ED045209
NEIGHBORHOOD HOUSE CHILD CARE SERVICES, SEATTLE, WASHINGTON: SEATTLE'S ANSWER TO CHILD CARE PROBLEMS OF LOW-INCOME FAMILIES. MODEL PROGRAMS--CHILDHOOD EDUCATION. ED045213
COGNITIVELY ORIENTED CURRICULUM, YPSILANTI, MICHIGAN: A PROGRAM THAT EXPOSES PRESCHOOL CHILDREN TO A VARIETY OF MATERIALS AND EQUIPMENT TO TEACH CONCEPTS THROUGH PHYSICAL AND VERBAL EXPERIENCES. MODEL PROGRAMS--CHILDHOOD EDUCATION. ED045217
THE DAY NURSERY ASSOCIATION OF CLEVELAND, CLEVELAND, OHIO: A LONG HISTORY OF CARE FOR CHILDREN, INVOLVEMENT OF PARENTS, AND SERVICE TO THE COMMUNITY. MODEL PROGRAMS--CHILDHOOD EDUCATION. ED045218
MODEL OBSERVATION KINDERGARTEN AND FIRST GRADE, AMHERST, MASSACHUSETTS: MODEL CLASSROOMS WHICH OFFER COMPLETELY INDIVIDUALIZED SCHEDULING FOR MIXED AGE GROUPS OF KINDERGARTEN AND FIRST-GRADE STUDENTS. MODEL PROGRAMS--CHILDHOOD EDUCATION. ED045219
TACOMA PUBLIC SCHOOLS EARLY CHILDHOOD PROGRAM, TACOMA, WASHINGTON: COMBINED LOCAL, STATE, AND FEDERAL FUNDS SUPPORT A LARGE-SCALE EARLY CHILDHOOD PROGRAM IN THE PUBLIC SCHOOLS. MODEL PROGRAMS--CHILDHOOD EDUCATION. ED045221
INFORMATION ON INTERVENTION PROGRAMS OF THE DEMONSTRATION AND RESEARCH CENTER FOR EARLY EDUCATION. ED046492
PRE-KINDERGARTEN PROGRAM, 1968-69. EVALUATION REPORT FOR THE PROJECT. ED046511
PROCEEDINGS OF FOLLOW THROUGH CONFERENCE (GAINESVILLE, FLORIDA, DECEMBER 9-10, 1969). ED047773
A REVISION OF THE BASIC PROGRAM PLAN OF EDUCATION AT AGE THREE. ED047774
THE BEHAVIOR ANALYSIS CLASSROOM. ED047775
AN ANALYSIS OF PUBLISHED PRESCHOOL LANGUAGE PROGRAMS. ED047786
PROGRAMS FOR INFANTS AND YOUNG CHILDREN. PART I: EDUCATION AND DAY CARE. ED047807
PROGRAMS FOR INFANTS AND YOUNG CHILDREN. PART II: NUTRITION. ED047808
PROGRAMS FOR INFANTS AND YOUNG CHILDREN. PART III: HEALTH. ED047809
FEDERAL PROGRAMS FOR YOUNG CHILDREN. ED047811
PROJECT HEAD START 1968: A DESCRIPTIVE REPORT OF PROGRAMS AND PARTICIPANTS. ED047816
A NATIONAL SURVEY OF THE PARENT-CHILD CENTER PROGRAM. ED048933
REVIEW AND SUMMARY OF A NATIONAL SURVEY OF THE PARENT-CHILD CENTER PROGRAM. ED048941
A DEVELOPMENTAL LEARNING APPROACH TO INFANT CARE IN A GROUP SETTING. ED049818
PRESCHOOL INSTRUCTION MOBILE FACILITIES: DESCRIPTION AND ANALYSIS. SCHOOL PRACTICES REPORT NO. 3. ED050803
3 ON 2 PROGRAM: ADMINISTRATIVE GUIDE AND IMPLEMENTATION HANDBOOK. (REVISED EDITION). ED050812
A STUDY IN CHILD CARE. VOLUME I: FINDINGS. DAY CARE PROGRAMS REPRINT SERIES. ED051911
PRESCHOOL PROGRAMS. IJR PRESCHOOL PROJECT REPORT, VOLUME I. ED052815
EARLY CHILDHOOD EDUCATION PROGRAM, ESEA TITLE I, FY 1970. PROJECT REPORTS, VOLUME 5, BOOK 2, 1970. ED052820
CHILD CARE WORKER TRAINING PROJECT. OPERATIONAL PHASE AND EMPLOYMENT. FINAL REPORT. ED053788
NURSERIES IN THE CZECHOSLOVAK SOCIALIST REPUBLIC EJ 001 672
PARENT AND CHILD CENTERS--WHAT THEY ARE, WHERE THEY ARE GOING EJ 007 089
PROMOTING CHILD HEALTH THROUGH COMPREHENSIVE CARE EJ 007 165
CHILDREN UNDER THREE - FINDING WAYS TO STIMULATE DEVELOPMENT. II. SOME CURRENT EXPERIMENTS: FROM INFANCY THROUGH SCHOOL EJ 007 412
INVOLVING PARENTS IN THEIR CHILDREN'S DAY-CARE EXPERIENCES EJ 007 451
THE CARE AND EDUCATION OF PRESCHOOL NONWHITES IN THE REPUBLIC OF SOUTH AFRICA EJ 010 125
ASK ME SOMETHING I KNOW EJ 012 580
PERSONALIZED EDUCATION IN SOUTHSIDE SCHOOL EJ 013 561
A BACKWARD GLANCE--A FORWARD STEP? EJ 020 295
THE STUDENT IN PROJECT PLAN: A FUNCTIONING PROGRAM OF INDIVIDUALIZED EDUCATION EJ 028 501
NEW DAY IN NORTH DAKOTA: CHANGING TEACHERS AND CHANGING SCHOOLS EJ 033 157
GROUP SERVICES FOR UNMARRIED MOTHERS: AN INTERDISCIPLINARY APPROACH EJ 035 538
A CAREER DEVELOPMENT PROGRAM IN THE CHICAGO PUBLIC SCHOOLS EJ 035 579
THE PRESCHOOL IN RURAL INDIA EJ 036 334
CLASSROOM PRACTICES IN PRE-BASIC SCHOOLS EJ 036 335
HELPING PARENTS TO HELP THEIR CHILDREN IN PLACEMENT EJ 058 055

PROGRAM DESIGN

A QUANTITATIVE MEASURE FOR PROGRAMMED INSTRUCTION. ED014317
CANDIDATE FOR INTEGRATION: A HEARING-IMPAIRED CHILD IN A REGULAR NURSERY SCHOOL EJ 026 915

PROGRAM DEVELOPMENT

ACCELERATION OF INTELLECTUAL DEVELOPMENT IN EARLY CHILDHOOD. FINAL REPORT. ED014332
DISTURBANCE AND DISSONANCE - COMMUNITY UNIVERSITY COLLABORATION IN DIAGNOSIS AND TREATMENT OF DISTURBANCES. ED030485
INSTRUCTIONAL PROGRAMMING FOR THE INDIVIDUAL PUPIL IN THE MULTIUNIT ELEMENTARY SCHOOL EJ 050 591

PROGRAM EFFECTIVENESS

SUMMARY REPORT OF A STUDY OF THE FULL-YEAR 1966 HEAD START PROGRAMS. ED014328
A STUDY OF THE FULL-YEAR 1966 HEAD START PROGRAMS. ED015010
THE EVALUATION OF PROJECT HEAD START--A CONCEPTUAL STATEMENT. ED015792
THE EFFECTS OF DIFFERENT LANGUAGE INSTRUCTION ON THE USE OF ATTRIBUTES OF PRE-KINDERGARTEN DISADVANTAGED CHILDREN. ED016522
"PRE-SCHOOL" EDUCATION, PROS AND CONS. A SURVEY OF "PRE-SCHOOL" EDUCATION WITH EMPHASIS ON RESEARCH PAST, PRESENT, AND FUTURE. ED016525
THE EFFECTS OF JUNIOR KINDERGARTEN ON ACHIEVEMENT--THE FIRST FIVE YEARS. ED016526
A RESEARCH PROGRAM TO DETERMINE THE EFFECTS OF VARIOUS PRESCHOOL INTERVENTION PROGRAMS ON THE DEVELOPMENT OF DISADVANTAGED CHILDREN AND THE STRATEGIC AGE FOR SUCH INTERVENTION. ED017319
REPORT OF THE EFFECTIVENESS OF PROJECT HEAD START, LUBBOCK, TEXAS. PARTS I, II, AND APPENDICES. ED019131
AN EVALUATION OF A PRESCHOOL TRAINING PROGRAM FOR CULTURALLY DEPRIVED CHILDREN. FINAL REPORT. ED019135
EFFECTIVENESS OF THE HEAD START PROGRAM IN ENHANCING SCHOOL READINESS OF CULTURALLY DEPRIVED CHILDREN. ED020771
A FOLLOW-UP STUDY OF INTELLIGENCE CHANGES IN CHILDREN WHO PARTICIPATED IN PROJECT HEADSTART. ED020786
FINAL REPORT ON HEAD START EVALUATION AND RESEARCH: 1967-68 TO THE OFFICE OF ECONOMIC OPPORTUNITY. SECTION II: ACHIEVEMENT MOTIVATION AND PATTERNS OF REINFORCEMENT IN HEAD START CHILDREN. ED023458
GROUP DAY CARE AS A CHILD-REARING ENVIRONMENT. AN OBSERVATIONAL STUDY OF DAY CARE PROGRAM. ED024453
LANGUAGE ABILITY AND READINESS FOR SCHOOL OF CHILDREN WHO PARTICIPATED IN HEAD START PROGRAMS. A DISSERTATION ABSTRACT. ED025299
A PREKINDERGARTEN PROGRAM FOR FOUR-YEAR-OLDS, WITH A REVIEW OF THE LITERATURE ON PRESCHOOL EDUCATION. AN OCCASIONAL PAPER. ED026124
THE EFFECTIVENESS OF THE PEABODY LANGUAGE DEVELOPMENT KITS AND THE INITIAL TEACHING ALPHABET WITH DISADVANTAGED CHILDREN IN THE PRIMARY GRADES: AFTER TWO YEARS. ED026125
PREPRIMARY PROGRAM. 1968 REPORT. ED027072
EVALUATION OF INKSTER PRESCHOOL PROJECT. FINAL REPORT. ED027093
AN APPRAISAL OF HEAD START PARTICIPANTS AND NON-PARTICIPANTS: EXPANDED CONSIDERATIONS ON LEARNING DISABILITIES AMONG DISADVANTAGED CHILDREN. ED027939
AN EXPERIMENTAL PROGRAM DESIGNED TO INCREASE AUDITORY DISCRIMINATION WITH HEAD START CHILDREN. ED029680
COMPARATIVE EFFECTIVENESS OF SPEAKING VERSUS LISTENING IN IMPROVING THE SPOKEN LANGUAGE OF DISADVANTAGED YOUNG CHILDREN. ED029689
THE COMPARATIVE EFFICACIES OF SPANISH, ENGLISH AND BILINGUAL COGNITIVE VERBAL INSTRUCTION WITH MEXICAN-AMERICAN HEAD START CHILDREN. FINAL REPORT. ED030473
ATTITUDES, EXPECTATIONS, AND BEHAVIOR OF PARENTS OF HEAD START AND NON-HEAD START CHILDREN. REPORT NUMBER 1. ED030475

MODIFICATION OF COGNITIVE SKILLS AMONG LOWER-CLASS NEGRO CHILDREN: A FOLLOW-UP TRAINING STUDY. REPORT NUMBER 6. ED030480
PRELIMINARY RESULTS FROM A LONGITUDINAL STUDY OF DISADVANTAGED PRESCHOOL CHILDREN. ED030490
A PREVENTIVE SUMMER PROGRAM FOR KINDERGARTEN CHILDREN LIKELY TO FAIL IN FIRST GRADE READING. FINAL REPORT. ED030495
EFFECTIVENESS OF DIRECT VERBAL INSTRUCTION ON IQ PERFORMANCE AND ACHIEVEMENT IN READING AND ARITHMETIC. ED030496
THE ROLE OF INCENTIVES IN DISCRIMINATION LEARNING OF CHILDREN WITH VARYING PRE-SCHOOL EXPERIENCE. ED031290
A STUDY OF THE EFFECTS OF A GROUP LANGUAGE DEVELOPMENT PROGRAM UPON THE PSYCHOLINGUISTIC ABILITIES AND LATER BEGINNING READING SUCCESS OF KINDERGARTEN CHILDREN. ED031315
THE IMPACT OF HEAD START: AN EVALUATION OF THE EFFECTS OF HEAD START ON CHILDREN'S COGNITIVE AND AFFECTIVE DEVELOPMENT. (EXECUTIVE SUMMARY). ED036321
CHILDREN AND TEACHERS IN TWO TYPES OF HEAD START CLASSES. ED036324
PARENT INVOLVEMENT IN PROJECT HEAD START. PART OF THE FINAL REPORT ON HEAD START EVALUATION AND RESEARCH: 1968-1969 TO THE OFFICE OF ECONOMIC OPPORTUNITY. ED037244
A PILOT PROJECT USING A LANGUAGE DEVELOPMENT PROGRAM WITH PRESCHOOL DISADVANTAGED CHILDREN. PART OF THE FINAL REPORT ON HEAD START EVALUATION AND RESEARCH: 1968-69 TO THE OFFICE OF ECONOMIC OPPORTUNITY. ED037245
A COMPARISON OF HEAD START CHILDREN WITH A GROUP OF HEAD START ELIGIBLES AFTER ONE YEAR IN ELEMENTARY SCHOOL. PART OF THE FINAL REPORT ON HEAD START EVALUATION AND RESEARCH: 1968-69 TO THE OFFICE OF ECONOMIC OPPORTUNITY. ED037247
THE EFFECT OF SUPPLEMENTARY SMALL GROUP EXPERIENCE ON TASK ORIENTATION AND COGNITIVE PERFORMANCE IN KINDERGARTEN CHILDREN. A FINAL REPORT OF THE KINDERGARTEN 'LEARNING TO LEARN' PROGRAM EVALUATION PROJECT. ED039948
DIRECT VERBAL INSTRUCTION CONTRASTED WITH MONTESSORI METHODS IN THE TEACHING OF NORMAL FOUR-YEAR-OLD CHILDREN. ED041619
THE EFFECTIVENESS OF SPECIAL PROGRAMS FOR RURAL ISOLATED FOUR-YEAR-OLD CHILDREN. FINAL REPORT. ED041638
ENRICHMENT APPROACH VERSUS DIRECT INSTRUCTIONAL APPROACH AND THEIR EFFECTS ON DIFFERENTIAL PRESCHOOL EXPERIENCES. ED043369
ANCONA MONTESSORI RESEARCH PROJECT FOR CULTURALLY DISADVANTAGED CHILDREN. SEPTEMBER 1, 1968 TO AUGUST 31, 1969. FINAL REPORT. ED044166
EARLY CHILDHOOD EDUCATION PROGRAM AND ITS COMPONENTS: PSYCHOLOGICAL EVALUATION, SENSORIMOTOR SKILLS PROGRAM, NEW VISIONS - A CHILDREN'S MUSEUM. PROJECT REPORTS, VOLUME 4, BOOK 1, 1969. ED045183
IMPACT OF THE HEAD START PROGRAM. PHASE I OF A PROJECTED LONGITUDINAL STUDY TO THE U. S. OFFICE OF ECONOMIC OPPORTUNITY. FINAL REPORT. ED045193
EXPERIMENTAL VARIATION OF HEAD START CURRICULA: A COMPARISON OF CURRENT APPROACHES. ANNUAL PROGRESS REPORT, JUNE 1, 1969 - MAY 31, 1970. ED045196
AN ASSESSMENT OF COGNITIVE GROWTH IN CHILDREN WHO HAVE PARTICIPATED IN THE TOY-LENDING COMPONENT OF THE PARENT-CHILD PROGRAM. ED045204
CONCEPT AND LANGUAGE DEVELOPMENT OF A GROUP OF FIVE YEAR OLDS WHO HAVE ATTENDED THE SYRACUSE UNIVERSITY CHILDREN'S CENTER INTERVENTION PROGRAM. ED046515
PROGRAMS FOR INFANTS AND YOUNG CHILDREN. PART I: EDUCATION AND DAY CARE. ED047807
AN INTEGRATED PROGRAM OF GROUP CARE AND EDUCATION FOR SOCIOECONOMICALLY ADVANTAGED AND DISADVANTAGED INFANTS. ED048937
THE NEW NURSERY SCHOOL RESEARCH PROJECT ED048940
THE EFFECTS OF INSTRUCTION ON THE DEVELOPMENT OF THE CONCEPT OF CONSERVATION OF NUMEROUSNESS BY KINDERGARTEN CHILDREN. REPORT FROM THE PROJECT ON INDIVIDUALLY GUIDED ELEMENTARY MATHEMATICS ED049821
INFLUENCES OF A PIAGET-ORIENTED CURRICULUM ON INTELLECTUAL FUNCTIONING OF LOWER-CLASS KINDERGARTEN CHILDREN. ED049823
THE INFLUENCE OF SELECTED VARIABLES ON THE EFFECTIVENESS OF PRESCHOOL PROGRAMS FOR DISADVANTAGED CHILDREN. ED049835
INTERVENTION WITH MOTHERS AND YOUNG CHILDREN: A STUDY OF INTRAFAMILY EFFECTS. ED050809
TWO KINDS OF KINDERGARTEN AFTER FOUR TYPES OF HEAD START. ED050824
THREE DEGREES OF PARENT INVOLVEMENT IN A PRESCHOOL PROGRAM: IMPACT ON MOTHERS AND CHILDREN. ED052831
ATTAINMENT OF COGNITIVE OBJECTIVES. TECHNICAL REPORT NO. 3. ED052833
DETAILED ANALYSIS OF LANGUAGE DEVELOPMENT OF PRESCHOOL CHILDREN IN ECE PROGRAM. TECHNICAL REPORT NO. 4. ED052834
EVALUATION REPORT: EARLY CHILDHOOD EDUCATION PROGRAM, 1969-1970 FIELD TEST. SUMMARY REPORT. ED052837
FACTOR ANALYSIS OF THE EARLY CHILDHOOD EDUCATION TEST DATA. ED052840
IMPLEMENTATION OF PLANNED VARIATION IN HEAD START: PRELIMINARY EVALUATIONS OF PLANNED VARIATION IN HEAD START ACCORDING TO FOLLOW THROUGH APPROACHES (1969-1970). INTERIM REPORT: FIRST YEAR OF EVALUATION, PART II. ED052844
IMPLEMENTATION OF PLANNED VARIATION IN HEAD START. I. REVIEW AND SUMMARY OF THE STANFORD RESEARCH INSTITUTE INTERIM REPORT: FIRST YEAR OF EVALUATION. ED052845
THE EFFECT OF A STRUCTURED TUTORIAL PROGRAM ON THE COGNITIVE AND LANGUAGE DEVELOPMENT OF CULTURALLY DISADVANTAGED INFANTS EJ 008 272
REUNITING CHILDREN AND PARENTS THROUGH CASEWORK AND GROUP WORK EJ 027 342
CAN POVERTY CHILDREN LIVE ON "SESAME STREET?" EJ 034 509
INTERVENTION STRATEGIES FOR SPANISH-SPEAKING PRESCHOOL CHILDREN EJ 036 746

PROGRAM EVALUATION

A SURVEY AND EVALUATION OF PROJECT HEAD START AS ESTABLISHED AND OPERATED IN COMMUNITIES OF THE COMMONWEALTH OF MASSACHUSETTS DURING THE SUMMER OF 1965. ED014324
AN EVALUATION OF HEAD START PRESCHOOL ENRICHMENT PROGRAMS AS THEY AFFECT THE INTELLECTUAL ABILITY, THE SOCIAL ADJUSTMENT, AND THE ACHIEVEMENT LEVEL OF FIVE-YEAR-OLD CHILDREN ENROLLED IN LINCOLN, NEBRASKA. ED015011
AN EVALUATION OF DIFFERENCES AMONG DIFFERENT CLASSES OF HEAD START PARTICIPANTS. FINAL REPORT. ED015012
REMARKS ON THE MAX WOLFF REPORT. ED015030
IMPACT OF SUMMER 1965 HEAD START ON CHILDREN'S CONCEPT ATTAINMENT DURING KINDERGARTEN. FINAL REPORT. ED015773
FACTORS AFFECTING COGNITIVE GROWTH IN PROJECT HEAD START CHILDREN--WHAT KINDS OF CHANGES OCCUR IN WHAT KINDS OF CHILDREN UNDER WHAT KINDS OF PROGRAMS. ED015794
A COMPARATIVE STUDY OF TWO PRESCHOOL PROGRAMS FOR CULTURALLY DISADVANTAGED CHILDREN--A HIGHLY STRUCTURED AND A TRADITIONAL PROGRAM. ED016524
A STUDY OF THE KINDERGARTEN PROGRAM, FULL-DAY OR HALF-DAY. ED017327
HEAD START, WEST VIRGINIA, SUMMER 1966--A SEVEN-COUNTY OVERVIEW, A SPECIAL ASSIGNMENT OF THE WEST VIRGINIA DEPARTMENT OF MENTAL HEALTH. ED017338
RESULTS OF THE SUMMER 1965 PROJECT HEAD START. VOLUMES I AND II. ED018250
A FRESH APPROACH TO EARLY CHILDHOOD EDUCATION AND A STUDY OF ITS EFFECTIVENESS. LEARNING TO LEARN PROGRAM. ED019117
A COMPARATIVE STUDY OF VARIOUS PROJECT HEAD START PROGRAMS. ED019987
EFFECT OF TRIMESTER SCHOOL OPERATION ON THE ACHIEVEMENT AND ADJUSTMENT OF KINDERGARTEN AND FIRST THROUGH THIRD GRADE CHILDREN. FINAL REPORT. ED020003
THE EFFECT OF HEADSTART ON DEVELOPMENTAL PROCESSES. ED020026
THE IMPACT OF OPERATION HEAD START ON GREENE COUNTY, OHIO, AN EVALUATION REPORT. ED020772
HEAD START EVALUATION AND RESEARCH CENTER, TEACHERS COLLEGE, COLUMBIA UNIVERSITY. ANNUAL REPORT (1ST), SEPTEMBER 1966-AUGUST 1967. (TITLE SUPPLIED). ED020781
HEAD START RESEARCH AND EVALUATION OFFICE, UNIVERSITY OF CALIFORNIA AT LOS ANGELES. APPENDIX I TO THE ANNUAL REPORT, NOVEMBER 1967. ED020793
STUDY TO DETERMINE THE FEASIBILITY OF ADAPTING THE CARL ORFF APPROACH TO ELEMENTARY SCHOOLS IN AMERICA. FINAL REPORT. ED020804
PARENTS' EVALUATION OF THE HEAD START PROGRAM IN THE MILWAUKEE PUBLIC SCHOOLS. ED020806
PROJECT HEAD START, REPORT ON THE PREKINDERGARTEN PROGRAM, 1965. ED021611
EVALUATION OF THE PRESCHOOL CHILD AND PARENT EDUCATION PROJECT AS EXPANDED THROUGH THE USE OF ELEMENTARY AND SECONDARY EDUCATION ACT, TITLE I, FUNDS. ED021621
HEAD START EVALUATION AND RESEARCH CENTER. PROGRESS REPORT OF RESEARCH STUDIES 1966 TO 1967. DOCUMENT 2, STUDIES OF THE SOCIAL ORGANIZATION OF HEAD START CENTERS. ED021624
HEAD START EVALUATION AND RESEARCH CENTER. PROGRESS REPORT OF RESEARCH STUDIES 1966 TO 1967. DOCUMENT 6, INDIVIDUAL INSTRUCTION PROJECT I. ED021628
PRE-SCHOOL RESEARCH AND EVALUATION PROJECT. ED022541
HEAD START EVALUATION AND RESEARCH CENTER, BOSTON UNIVERSITY. REPORT E-II, TEACHER SEMINAR. ED022567
A DIGEST OF THE RESEARCH ACTIVITIES OF REGIONAL EVALUATION AND RESEARCH CENTERS FOR PROJECT HEAD START (SEPTEMBER 1, 1966 TO NOVEMBER 30, 1967). ED023446
FINAL REPORT ON HEAD START EVALUATION AND RESEARCH: 1967-68 TO THE OFFICE OF ECONOMIC OPPORTUNITY. SECTION I: PART A, MIDDLE CLASS MOTHER-TEACHERS IN AN EXPERIMENTAL PRESCHOOL PROGRAM FOR SOCIALLY DISADVANTAGED CHILDREN. ED023454
AN EVALUATION OF THE PRESCHOOL READINESS CENTERS PROGRAM IN EAST ST. LOUIS, ILLINOIS, JULY 1, 1967-JUNE 30, 1968. FINAL REPORT. ED023472

SAN MATEO COUNTY HUMAN RESOURCES COMMISSION PROJECT HEAD START - SUMMER 1966. AN EVALUATIONAL REPORT. ED023478
AN EVALUATION OF THE LANGUAGE ARTS PROGRAM OF THE DISTRICT OF COLUMBIA. FINAL REPORT. ED024449
GROUP DAY CARE AS A CHILD-REARING ENVIRONMENT. AN OBSERVATIONAL STUDY OF DAY CARE PROGRAM. ED024453
PROJECT HEAD START, PSYCHOLOGICAL SERVICES REPORT, RESEARCH, SUMMER 1968. ED024460
KINDERGARTEN, 1967-68. AN EVALUATION REPORT. ED025315
METHODOLIGICAL CONSIDERATIONS IN DEVISING HEAD START PROGRAM EVALUATIONS. ED025319
ANNUAL RESEARCH REPORT OF COMPLETED AND INCOMPLETE INVESTIGATIONS FOR NATIONAL HEAD START EVALUATION. ED025320
A PREKINDERGARTEN PROGRAM FOR FOUR-YEAR-OLDS, WITH A REVIEW OF THE LITERATURE ON PRESCHOOL EDUCATION. AN OCCASIONAL PAPER. ED026124
THE EFFECTIVENESS OF THE PEABODY LANGUAGE DEVELOPMENT KITS AND THE INITIAL TEACHING ALPHABET WITH DISADVANTAGED CHILDREN IN THE PRIMARY GRADES: AFTER TWO YEARS. ED026125
EVALUATION OF THE PRESCHOOL PROGRAM, 1966-67, FUNDED UNDER ESEA TITLE I, P.L. 89-10. ED026143
PREPRIMARY PROGRAM. 1968 REPORT. ED027072
RESEARCH ON THE NEW NURSERY SCHOOL. PART II: A REPORT ON THE USE OF TYPEWRITERS AND RELATED EQUIPMENT WITH THREE- AND FOUR-YEAR-OLD CHILDREN AT THE NEW NURSERY SCHOOL. INTERIM REPORT. ED027077
EVALUATION OF THE PRESCHOOL PROGRAM, 1967-68, FUNDED UNDER ESEA TITLE I, P.L. 89-10. ED027080
TEAM TEACHING. A DESCRIPTIVE AND EVALUATIVE STUDY OF A PROGRAM FOR THE PRIMARY GRADES. ED027083
EVALUATION OF INKSTER PRESCHOOL PROJECT. FINAL REPORT. ED027093
PRESCHOOL AND PRIMARY EDUCATION PROJECT. 1967-68 ANNUAL PROGRESS REPORT TO THE FORD FOUNDATION. ED027936
THE CHANGE PROCESS IN ACTION: KINDERGARTEN ED027949
LEICESTERSHIRE REPORT: THE CLASSROOM ENVIRONMENT. ED027964
EARLY CHILDHOOD PROJECT, NEW YORK CITY ED027974
PERRY PRESCHOOL PROJECT, YPSILANTI, MICHIGAN ED027975
INFANT EDUCATION RESEARCH PROJECT, WASHINGTON, D.C. ED027976
PRESCHOOL PROGRAM, FRESNO, CALIFORNIA ED027977
ACADEMIC PRESCHOOL, CHAMPAIGN, ILLINOIS ED027979
PROJECT HEAD START: EVALUATION AND RESEARCH SUMMARY 1965-1967. ED028826
EVALUATION OF THE EFFECTS OF HEAD START EXPERIENCE IN THE AREA OF SELF-CONCEPT, SOCIAL SKILLS, AND LANGUAGE SKILLS. PRE-PUBLICATION DRAFT. ED028832
EFFECT OF MATERNAL ATTITUDES, TEACHER ATTITUDES, AND TYPE OF NURSERY SCHOOL TRAINING ON THE ABILITIES OF PRESCHOOL CHILDREN. FINAL REPORT. ED028844
[REGIONAL RESEARCH AND RESOURCE CENTER IN EARLY CHILDHOOD.] FINAL REPORT. ED028846
LEICESTERSHIRE REVISITED. ED029683
HEAD START EVALUATION AND RESEARCH CENTER, TULANE UNIVERSITY. ANNUAL REPORT. ED029705
HEAD START IN ACTION. ED030471
INTERRELATIONS BETWEEN SOCIAL-EMOTIONAL BEHAVIOR AND INFORMATION ACHIEVEMENT OF HEAD START CHILDREN. REPORT NUMBER 5. ED030479
A DESCRIPTIVE STUDY OF COGNITIVE AND AFFECTIVE TRENDS DIFFERENTIATING SELECTED GROUPS OF PRE-SCHOOL CHILDREN. ED031314
EVAULATION OF THE DEMONSTRATION PHASE OF THE TEEN TUTORIAL PROGRAM: A MODEL OF INTERRELATIONSHIP OF SEVENTH GRADERS, KINDERGARTEN PUPILS AND PARENTS TO MEET THE DEVELOPMENTAL NEEDS OF DISADVANTAGED CHILDREN. ED032115
[THE JUNIPER GARDENS PARENT COOPERATIVE NURSERY.] FINAL PROGRESS REPORT FOR OEO CAP GRANT CG-8474 A/O. ED032920
AN EXPERIMENTAL STUDY OF VISUAL PERCEPTUAL TRAINING AND READINESS SCORES WITH CERTAIN FIRST-GRADE CHILDREN. ED032921
RESEARCH, CHANGE, AND SOCIAL RESPONSIBILITY: AN ILLUSTRATIVE MODEL FROM EARLY EDUCATION. ED032922
EVALUATION OF SELECTED COMPONENTS OF: A SUPPLEMENTARY CENTER FOR EARLY CHILDHOOD EDUCATION. TITLE III. ED032927
PROGRESS REPORT ON RESEARCH AT THE NEW NURSERY SCHOOL: GENERAL BACKGROUND AND PROGRAM RATIONALE. ED032930
THE EARLY TRAINING PROJECT: A SEVENTH YEAR REPORT. ED032934
DEVELOPMENT OF A DANCE CURRICULUM FOR YOUNG CHILDREN. CAREL ARTS AND HUMANITIES CURRICULUM DEVELOPMENT PROGRAM FOR YOUNG CHILDREN. ED032936
A STRUCTURE-PROCESS APPROACH TO COGNITIVE DEVELOPMENT OF PRESCHOOL NEGRO CHILDREN: RATIONALE AND EFFECTS. ED033743
SOCIAL-EMOTIONAL TASK FORCE. FINAL REPORT. ED033744
PRELUDE TO SCHOOL: AN EVALUATION OF AN INNER-CITY PRESCHOOL PROGRAM. ED033750
PENNSYLVANIA PRESCHOOL AND PRIMARY EDUCATION PROJECT: 1968-1969 FINAL REPORT TO THE FORD FOUNDATION. ED033759
A SOCIALLY INTEGRATED KINDERGARTEN. ED034578
AN EVALUATION OF THE PRESCHOOL READINESS CENTERS PROGRAM IN EAST ST. LOUIS, ILLINOIS, JULY 1, 1968 - JUNE 30, 1969. FINAL REPORT. ED034585
A LONGITUDINAL INVESTIGATION OF MONTESSORI AND TRADITIONAL PREKINDERGARTEN TRAINING WITH INNER CITY CHILDREN: A COMPARATIVE ASSESSMENT OF LEARNING OUTCOMES. THREE PART STUDY. ED034588
AN EVALUATION OF A PILOT PROJECT TO ASSESS THE INTRODUCTION OF THE MODERN ENGLISH INFANT SCHOOL APPROACH TO LEARNING WITH SECOND AND THIRD YEAR DISADVANTAGED CHILDREN. ED034595
ASSESSING PROCESS AND PRODUCT WITH YOUNG CHILDREN IN SCHOOL SETTINGS. ED035453
EXEMPLARY AND INNOVATIVE PRESCHOOL CHILD DEVELOPMENT DEMONSTRATION CENTERS, 1966-1969. THREE YEAR EVALUATION AND NARRATIVE REPORT. ED035456
PROJECT HEAD START AT WORK. REPORT OF A SURVEY STUDY OF 335 PROJECT HEAD START CENTERS, SUMMER, 1965. ED036311
THE IMPACT OF HEAD START: AN EVALUATION OF THE EFFECTS OF HEAD START ON CHILDREN'S COGNITIVE AND AFFECTIVE DEVELOPMENT. (EXECUTIVE SUMMARY). ED036321
A LONGITUDINAL STUDY OF DISADVANTAGED CHILDREN WHO PARTICIPATED IN THREE DIFFERENT PRESCHOOL PROGRAMS. ED036338
A NEW ROLE FOR TEACHERS: INVOLVING THE ENTIRE FAMILY IN THE EDUCATION OF PRESCHOOL DISADVANTAGED CHILDREN. ED036339
A REPORT ON EVALUATION STUDIES OF PROJECT HEAD START. ED037239
PARENT INVOLVEMENT IN PROJECT HEAD START. PART OF THE FINAL REPORT ON HEAD START EVALUATION AND RESEARCH: 1968-1969 TO THE OFFICE OF ECONOMIC OPPORTUNITY. ED037244
A COMPARISON OF HEAD START CHILDREN WITH A GROUP OF HEAD START ELIGIBLES AFTER ONE YEAR IN ELEMENTARY SCHOOL. PART OF THE FINAL REPORT ON HEAD START EVALUATION AND RESEARCH: 1968-69 TO THE OFFICE OF ECONOMIC OPPORTUNITY. ED037247
EVALUATION OF EDUCATIONAL PROGRAMS AS RESEARCH ON EDUCATIONAL PROCESS. ED038165
HEAD START PLANNED VARIATION PROGRAM. ED038170
CURRICULAR INTERVENTION IN LANGUAGE ARTS READINESS FOR HEAD START CHILDREN. TULANE UNIVERSITY, HEAD START EVALUATION AND RESEARCH CENTER ANNUAL REPORT TO THE OFFICE OF ECONOMIC OPPORTUNITY. ED038175
CHILD STUDY-KINDERGARTEN, 1968-69: AN INFORMATION REPORT. ED039015
WAKULLA COUNTY PRESCHOOL. FINAL REPORT. ED039022
A SOCIAL LEARNING APPROACH TO EARLY CHILDHOOD EDUCATION. ED039025
FOLLOW THROUGH PROJECT, WICHITA UNIFIED SCHOOL DISTRICT 259: INITIAL YEAR, SEPTEMBER 1968 - MAY 1969 EVALUATION REPORT. ED039027
THE EFFECT OF A PRESCHOOL EXPERIENCE UPON INTELLECTUAL FUNCTIONING AMONG FOUR-YEAR-OLD, WHITE CHILDREN IN RURAL MINNESOTA. ED039030
A SUPPLEMENTARY REPORT ON EVALUATION OF THE NEW NURSERY SCHOOL PROGRAM AT COLORADO STATE COLLEGE. ED039919
A REPORT ON THE EVALUATION OF THE STATE PRESCHOOL PROGRAM CONTRASTED WITH THE WESTINGHOUSE REPORT ON HEAD START. ED039920
THE EFFECTIVENESS OF A STANDARD LANGUAGE READINESS PROGRAM AS A FUNCTION OF TEACHER DIFFERENCES. ED039932
THE EFFECT OF SUPPLEMENTARY SMALL GROUP EXPERIENCE ON TASK ORIENTATION AND COGNITIVE PERFORMANCE IN KINDERGARTEN CHILDREN. A FINAL REPORT OF THE KINDERGARTEN 'LEARNING TO LEARN' PROGRAM EVALUATION PROJECT. ED039948
DESIGN AND MEASURES OF 1967-68 AND 1968-69 HEAD START E&R EVALUATION STUDIES. ED040745
THE MISPLACED ADAPTATION TO INDIVIDUAL DIFFERENCES. ED040754
EXPERIMENTS IN HEAD START AND EARLY EDUCATION: THE EFFECTS OF TEACHER ATTITUDE AND CURRICULUM STRUCTURE ON PRESCHOOL DISADVANTAGED CHILDREN. FINAL REPORT. ED041615
A COMPARISON OF THREE INTERVENTION PROGRAMS WITH DISADVANTAGED PRESCHOOL CHILDREN. UNIVERSITY OF CALIFORNIA HEAD START RESEARCH AND EVALUATION CENTER. FINAL REPORT 1968-1969. ED041616
EXPERIMENTAL VARIATION OF HEAD START CURRICULA: A COMPARISON OF CURRENT APPROACHES. (NOVEMBER 1, 1969-JANUARY 31, 1970). ED041617
EXPERIMENTAL VARIATION OF HEAD START CURRICULA: A COMPARISON OF CURRENT APPROACHES. ANNUAL REPORT, JUNE 12, 1968-JUNE 11, 1969. ED041618
EARLY CHILDHOOD EDUCATION LEARNING SYSTEM ED041625
EVALUATION REPORT: EARLY CHILDHOOD EDUCATION PROGRAM, 1969 FIELD TEST. ED041626
STATEMENT OF THE INSTRUCTIONAL GOALS FOR CHILDREN'S TELEVISION WORKSHOP. ED041627
A REVIEW OF THE EVALUATION OF THE FOLLOW THROUGH PROGRAM. ED041642
COMPARATIVE STUDY OF THREE PRESCHOOL CURRICULA. ED042484
DEVELOPMENT OF GRAMMATICAL STRUCTURES IN PRE-SCHOOL AGE CHILDREN. ED042485
HAWAII HEAD START EVALUATION--1968-69. FINAL REPORT. ED042511

HAWAII HEAD START EVALUATION FOLLOW-UP--1968-69. FINA L REPORT. ED042515
A FOLLOW-UP EVALUATION OF THE EFFECTS OF A UNIQUE SEQUENTIAL LEARNING PROGRAM, A TRADITIONAL PRESCHOOL PROGRAM AND A NO TREATMENT PROGRAM ON CULTURALLY DEPRIVED CHILDREN. FINAL REPORT. ED042516
A SEQUENTIAL APPROACH TO EARLY CHILDHOOD AND ELEMENTARY EDUCATION, PHASE I. GRANT REPORT. ED042517
EFFECTS OF AGE OF ENTRY AND DURATION OF PARTICIPATION IN A COMPENSATORY EDUCATION PROGRAM. ED043380
CHILD DEVELOPMENT RESEARCH AND EVALUATION CENTER FOR HEAD START, TEMPLE UNIVERSITY, 1968 - 1969. ANNUAL REPORT. ED043388
FROM THEORY TO OPERATIONS. DISADVANTAGED CHILDREN AND THEIR FIRST SCHOOL EXPERIENCES, ETS-HEAD START LONGITUDINAL STUDY. ED043397
REPORT OF CHILD PLACEMENT STUDY COMMITTEE, JANUARY, 1969. ED044169
EVALUATION OF FOLLOW THROUGH, 1968 - 1969. ED044172
THE EFFECT OF THREE HOME VISITING STRATEGIES UPON MEASURES OF CHILDREN'S ACADEMIC APTITUDE AND MATERNAL TEACHING BEHAVIORS. FINAL REPORT. ED044175
EVALUATION AND RESEARCH CENTER FOR PROJECT HEAD START, UNIVERSITY OF SOUTH CAROLINA. INTERIM EVALUATION REPORT. ED045197
THE EFFECTS OF ASSESSMENT AND PERSONALIZED PROGRAMMING ON SUBSEQUENT INTELLECTUAL DEVELOPMENT OF PREKINDERGARTEN AND KINDERGARTEN CHILDREN. FINAL REPORT. ED045198
OVERVIEW OF RESPONSIVE MODEL PROGRAM. ED045207
AN INVESTIGATION OF THE RELATIVE EFFECTIVENESS OF SELECTED CURRICULUM VARIABLES IN THE LANGUAGE DEVELOPMENT OF HEAD START CHILDREN. ED046497
A COMPARISON OF CONTRASTING PROGRAMS IN EARLY CHILDHOOD EDUCATION. ED046509
PRE-KINDERGARTEN PROGRAM, 1968-69. EVALUATION REPORT FOR THE PROJECT. ED046511
THE FIRST YEAR OF SESAME STREET: AN EVALUATION. FINAL REPORT, VOLUME III OF V VOLUMES. ED047823
THE FIRST YEAR OF SESAME STREET: A SUMMARY OF AUDIENCE SURVEYS. FINAL REPORT, VOLUME IV OF V VOLUMES. ED047824
HEAD START GRADUATES: ONE YEAR LATER. ED048929
THE NEW YORK STATE EXPERIMENTAL PREKINDERGARTEN PROGRAM. SUMMARY REPORT, 1969-70. ED049814
A DEVELOPMENTAL LEARNING APPROACH TO INFANT CARE IN A GROUP SETTING. ED049818
THE INFLUENCE OF SELECTED VARIABLES ON THE EFFECTIVENESS OF PRESCHOOL PROGRAMS FOR DISADVANTAGED CHILDREN. ED049835
PRESCHOOL INSTRUCTION MOBILE FACILITIES: DESCRIPTION AND ANALYSIS. SCHOOL PRACTICES REPORT NO. 3. ED050803
EDUCATIONAL INTERVENTION IN EARLY CHILDHOOD: A REPORT OF A FIVE-YEAR LONGITUDINAL STUDY OF THE EFFECTS OF EARLY EDUCATIONAL INTERVENTION IN THE LIVES OF DISADVANTAGED CHILDREN IN DURHAM, NORTH CAROLINA. FINAL REPORT, VOLUME I. ED050814
EDUCATIONAL INTERVENTION IN EARLY CHILDHOOD: APPENDIXES. FINAL REPORT, VOLUME II. ED050815
ANALYSIS OF EARLY CHILDHOOD PROGRAMS: A SEARCH FOR COMPARATIVE DIMENSIONS. ED051877
EARLY CHILDHOOD EDUCATION PROGRAM, ESEA TITLE I, FY 1970. PROJECT REPORTS, VOLUME 5, BOOK 2, 1970. ED052820
THE EVALUATION OF "SESAME STREET'S" SOCIAL GOALS: THE INTERPERSONAL STRATEGIES OF COOPERATION, CONFLICT RESOLUTION, AND DIFFERING PERSPECTIVES. ED052824
EVALUATION REPORT: EARLY CHILDHOOD EDUCATION PROGRAM, 1969-1970 FIELD TEST. SUMMARY REPORT. ED052837
ANALYSIS OF INTELLIGENCE SCORES. ED052838
IMPLEMENTATION OF PLANNED VARIATION IN HEAD START: PRELIMINARY EVALUATIONS OF PLANNED VARIATION IN HEAD START ACCORDING TO FOLLOW THROUGH APPROACHES (1969-1970). INTERIM REPORT: FIRST YEAR OF EVALUATION, PART II. ED052844
STUDY OF SELECTED CHILDREN IN HEAD START PLANNED VARIATION, 1969-1970. FIRST YEAR REPORT: 3 - CASE STUDIES OF CHILDREN. ED052847
DEMONSTRATION AND TRAINING PROJECT FOR MIGRANT CHILDREN, MCALLEN, TEXAS. EARLY CHILDHOOD LEARNING SYSTEM. FINAL EVALUATION REPORT, 1970-71. ED053812
EXPERIMENTAL VARIATION OF HEAD START CURRICULA: A COMPARISON OF CURRENT APPROACHES. PROGRESS REPORT NO. 9, MARCH 1, 1971 - MAY 31, 1971. ED053814
CASE CONFERENCE: A PSYCHOTHERAPEUTIC AIDE IN A HEADSTART PROGRAM. II. COMMENTARY EJ 003 956
EVALUATION OF EDUCATIONAL PROGRAMS EJ 007 047
DISTORTIONS IN THE KINDERGARTEN EJ 007 214
THE EFFECTS OF INSTRUCTION ON LANGUAGE DEVELOPMENT EJ 013 625
EDUCATIONAL EVALUATION AS RESEARCH FOR PROGRAM IMPROVEMENT EJ 021 380
THE IMPACT OF HEAD START: AN EVALUATION OF THE EFFECTS OF HEAD START ON CHILDREN'S COGNITIVE AND AFFECTIVE DEVELOPMENT BY VICTOR G. CICIRELLI EJ 021 965
A STUDY OF THE EFFECTIVENESS OF SPECIFIC TEACHING OF CONSERVATION TO CHILDREN IN SELECTED ELEMENTARY SCHOOLS OF BUTTE COUNTY, CALIFORNIA EJ 027 029
A METHOD OF INCREASING THE ABILITY OF FIRST GRADE PUPILS TO USE PHONETIC GENERALIZATIONS EJ 033 279
THE NUFFIELD MATHEMATICS PROJECT EJ 033 864
HEAD START: A HEAD START TO HEALTH? EJ 036 581
EVALUATIVE USES OF UNCONVENTIONAL MEASUREMENT TECHNIQUES IN AN EDUCATIONAL SYSTEM EJ 042 347
A REPORT ON EVALUATION STUDIES OF PROJECT HEAD START EJ 049 896
LONGITUDINAL DEVELOPMENT OF VERY YOUNG CHILDREN IN A COMPREHENSIVE DAY CARE PROGRAM: THE FIRST TWO YEARS EJ 056 707

PROGRAM GUIDES

THE CHILDREN'S CENTER--A MICROCOSMIC HEALTH, EDUCATION, AND WELFARE UNIT. PROGRESS REPORT. ED013116
A CREATIVE GUIDE FOR PRESCHOOL TEACHERS. GOALS, ACTIVITIES, AND SUGGESTED MATERIALS FOR AN ORGANIZED PROGRAM. ED016512
GUIDE FOR TEACHING PHYSICAL EDUCATION, GRADES 1-6. ED019126
KINDERGARTEN GUIDEBOOK. ED020008
TEACHING MUSIC IN THE ELEMENTARY SCHOOL, OPINION AND COMMENT. ED020014
GUIDELINES FOR PLANNING PRESCHOOL PROGRAMS FOR EDUCATIONALLY DEPRIVED CHILDREN UNDER TITLE I OF THE ELEMENTARY AND SECONDARY EDUCATION ACT OF 1965. ED023463
SAN MATEO COUNTY HUMAN RESOURCES COMMISSION PROJECT HEAD START - SUMMER 1966. AN EVALUATIONAL REPORT. ED023478
HELPS FOR PARENTS IN HOUSING ED025312
FEDERAL INTERAGENCY DAY CARE REQUIREMENTS, PURSUANT TO SEC. 522 (D) OF THE ECONOMIC OPPORTUNITY ACT. ED026145
GUIDELINES: PRE-SCHOOL PROJECTS, HEAD START: EARLY CHILDHOOD EDUCATION. REVISED EDITION. ED027948
PROGRAM FOR EARLY CHILDHOOD EDUCATION. ED027957
POINTERS FOR PARTICIPATING PARENTS. ED028825
A GUIDE FOR PRESCHOOLS: A HANDBOOK ABOUT THE OPERATION AND FUNCTION OF PRESCHOOLS IN THE FRESNO CITY UNIFIED SCHOOL DISTRICT. ED030499
A BILINGUAL ORAL LANGUAGE AND CONCEPTUAL DEVELOPMENT PROGRAM FOR SPANISH-SPEAKING PRE-SCHOOL CHILDREN. ED034568
CAN I LOVE THIS PLACE? A STAFF GUIDE TO OPERATING CHILD CARE CENTERS FOR THE DISADVANTAGED. ED049809
CURRICULUM FOR THE INFANT AND TODDLER. A COLOR SLIDE SERIES WITH SCRIPT. (SCRIPT ONLY). ED050817
GUIDE FOR RIPPLES. ED051872

PROGRAM IMPROVEMENT

DEVELOPMENT OF AN ENLARGED MUSIC REPERTORY FOR KINDERGARTEN THROUGH GRADE SIX (JUILLIARD REPERTORY PROJECT). FINAL REPORT. ED016521
PROJECT HEAD START, PSYCHOLOGICAL SERVICES REPORT, RESEARCH, SUMMER 1968. ED024460
EDUCATIONAL EVALUATION AS RESEARCH FOR PROGRAM IMPROVEMENT EJ 021 380
RESEARCH FOR SERVICE TO SEVERELY RETARDED CHILDREN EJ 038 531

PROGRAM LENGTH

A STUDY OF THE KINDERGARTEN PROGRAM, FULL-DAY OR HALF-DAY. ED017327
PRESCHOOLS AND THEIR GRADUATES. ED041644
EFFECTS OF DURATION OF A NURSERY SCHOOL SETTING ON ENVIRONMENTAL CONSTRAINTS AND CHILDREN'S MODES OF ADAPTATION. ED047812

PROGRAM PLANNING

ART EDUCATION IN THE ELEMENTARY SCHOOL. ED018274
SKILL DEVELOPMENT THROUGH GAMES AND RHYTHMIC ACTIVITIES. ED019996
GUIDELINES FOR PLANNING PRESCHOOL PROGRAMS FOR EDUCATIONALLY DEPRIVED CHILDREN UNDER TITLE I OF THE ELEMENTARY AND SECONDARY EDUCATION ACT OF 1965. ED023463
SAN MATEO COUNTY HUMAN RESOURCES COMMISSION PROJECT HEAD START - SUMMER 1966. AN EVALUATIONAL REPORT. ED023478
HELPS FOR PARENTS IN HOUSING ED025312
THE CHANGE PROCESS IN ACTION: KINDERGARTEN ED027949
JDC GUIDE FOR DAY CARE CENTERS, A HANDBOOK TO AID COMMUNITIES IN DEVELOPING DAY CARE CENTER PROGRAMS FOR PRE-SCHOOL CHILDREN. ED027961
A GUIDE TO THE PLANNING AND OPERATION OF A CHILD DEVELOPMENT CENTER FOR MIGRANT CHILDREN AND A REPORT OF THE HOOPESTON CHILD DEVELOPMENT CENTER ED049838
A STUDY IN CHILD CARE. VOLUME III: COST AND QUALITY ISSUES FOR OPERATORS. DAY CARE PROGRAMS REPRINT SERIES. ED051912
PLANNING A DAY CARE CENTER. ED053795
THE FUNDAMENTAL LEARNING NEEDS OF TODAY'S YOUNG CHILDREN EJ 027 531
DAY CARE IN THE 1970S: PLANNING FOR EXPANSION EJ 037 237

PROGRAM PROPOSALS
KINDERGARTEN OVERSEAS, A STUDY OF THE REQUIREMENTS FOR ESTABLISHING KINDERGARTEN AS PART OF THE DEPARTMENT OF DEFENSE OVERSEAS DEPENDENTS SCHOOLS. FINAL REPORT. ED017340
A POSITION PAPER ON EARLY CHILDHOOD EDUCATION. ED019128
GUIDEBOOK FOR TEACHERS. ED020001
CHILD'S PLAY, A CREATIVE APPROACH TO PLAYSPACES FOR TODAY'S CHILDREN. ED021630
DAY CARE AS A SOCIAL INSTRUMENT: A POLICY PAPER. ED027065
A SOURCE REPORT FOR DEVELOPING PARENT-CHILD EDUCATIONAL CENTERS. ED027944
TOWARD THE PREVENTION OF INCOMPETENCE. ED028812
AN EVALUATION OF THE INTERIM CLASS: AN EXTENDED READINESS PROGRAM. ED028820
THE CHILD ADVOCATE. 1970 WHITE HOUSE CONFERENCE ON CHILDREN, REPORT OF FORUM 24. (WORKING COPY). ED046538

PROGRAMED INSTRUCTION
PSYCHOLOGICAL BASES FOR INSTRUCTIONAL DESIGN. ED013121
A QUANTITATIVE MEASURE FOR PROGRAMMED INSTRUCTION. ED014317
PROGRAMED INSTRUCTION AS A STRATEGY FOR DEVELOPING CURRICULA FOR CHILDREN FROM DISADVANTAGED BACKGROUNDS. ED015782
THERE IS A BETTER WAY. A PREMISE POINTS THE WAY, A PROFILE WITH PROMISE, A COMPOSITE OF THE SURVEY. ED023471
THE VALUE OF THE SPOKEN RESPONSE IN TEACHING LISTENING SKILLS TO YOUNG CHILDREN THROUGH PROGRAMMED INSTRUCTION. FINAL REPORT. ED027973
PROGRAMMED INSTRUCTION AS A MEANS OF ESTABLISHING "ERRORLESS" LEARNING WITH KINDERGARTEN LEVEL CHILDREN. FINAL REPORT. ED039955
THE SOUTHSIDE EXPERIMENT IN PERSONALIZED EDUCATION. ED042505
A NOTE ON TEACHING FOR CREATIVITY EJ 018 130
THE COMPUTER CAN HELP INDIVIDUALIZE INSTRUCTION EJ 018 306
CHILDREN'S ACQUISITION AND REVERSAL BEHAVIOR IN A PROBABILITY LEARNING SITUATION AS A FUNCTION OF PROGRAMMED INSTRUCTION, INTERNAL-EXTERNAL CONTROL, AND SCHEDULES OF REINFORCEMENT EJ 037 495
INSTRUCTIONAL PROGRAMMING FOR THE INDIVIDUAL PUPIL IN THE MULTIUNIT ELEMENTARY SCHOOL EJ 050 591

PROGRAMED MATERIALS
PROGRAMMING CREATIVE BEHAVIOR EJ 021 080

PROGRAMED TUTORING
MY MON CAN TEACH READING TOO! EJ 051 082

PROGRAMED UNITS
A STUDY IN THE USE OF A PROGRAMMED GEOGRAPHY UNIT EJ 016 930

PROGRESSIVE EDUCATION
RADICAL SCHOOL REFORM. ED048934
A.S. NEILL: LATTER-DAY DEWEY? EJ 020 839

PROGRESSIVE RETARDATION
THE EARLY TRAINING PROJECT: A SEVENTH-YEAR REPORT EJ 033 777

PROJECTIVE TESTS
FOUR YEARS ON. A FOLLOW-UP STUDY AT SCHOOL LEAVING AGE OF CHILDREN FORMERLY ATTENDING A TRADITIONAL AND A PROGRESSIVE JUNIOR SCHOOL. ED035434
USE OF THE IT SCALE FOR CHILDREN IN ASSESSING SEX-ROLE PREFERENCE IN PRESCHOOL NEGRO CHILDREN EJ 021 991
THE RELATIONSHIP BETWEEN CONTROLLED PROJECTION RESPONSES AND SOCIOMETRIC STATUS EJ 031 541
STUDYING AGGRESSIVE CHILDREN THROUGH RESPONSE TO FRUSTRATING SITUATIONS EJ 051 013

PROMPTING
AN AUDITORY PROMPTING DEVICE FOR BEHAVIOR OBSERVATION EJ 043 316

PRONOUNS
OF TIME AND THE PRONOUN: A NEW METHODOLOGY FOR RESEARCH IN HIGHER EDUCATION EJ 042 881

PRONUNCIATION
HEAD START EVALUATION AND RESEARCH CENTER, UNIVERSITY OF KANSAS. REPORT NO. IIA, A STUDY OF AUDITORY DISCRIMINATION AND VERBAL RESPONDING. ED021634
ACOUSTIC ANALYSIS OF THE ACQUISITION OF ACCEPTABLE "R" IN AMERICAN ENGLISH EJ 041 056

PSYCHIATRIC SERVICES
COMPREHENSIVE CHILD PSYCHIATRY THROUGH A TEAM APPROACH EJ 008 042

PSYCHIATRISTS
VIEWPOINT: GAP AND THE JOINT COMMISSION ON MENTAL HEALTH OF CHILDREN EJ 060 203

PSYCHIATRY
CHILD PSYCHIATRY: THE PAST QUARTER CENTURY. ED027951
FROM LEARNING FOR LOVE TO LOVE OF LEARNING: ESSAYS ON PSYCHOANALYSIS AND EDUCATION. ED032925
ANNUAL PROGRESS IN CHILD PSYCHIATRY AND CHILD DEVELOPMENT 1969. ED032941
SEX EDUCATION OF THE YOUNG CHILD EJ 019 862
"YOUTH UNREST": REFLECTIONS OF A PSYCHOANALYST EJ 023 425
THE LIFE AND WORKS OF ERIK ERIKSON EJ 044 757
RECIPROCAL CONTRIBUTIONS BETWEEN PSYCHOANALYSIS AND PSYCHOEDUCATION EJ 045 048

PSYCHOEDUCATIONAL CLINICS
THE NEED FOR A MULTI-DIMENSIONAL APPROACH TO LEARNING DISABILITIES. A MULTI-DISCIPLINARY SYMPOSIUM ON DYSLEXIS AND ASSOCIATED LEARNING DISABILITIES. ED027956

PSYCHOEDUCATIONAL PROCESSES
LONG TERM EFFECT OF STRUCTURED TRAINING ON 3 YOUNG CHILDREN. ED023480
THE PSYCHOEDUCATIONAL APPROACH TO LEARNING DISABILITIES. ED027950
RECIPROCAL CONTRIBUTIONS BETWEEN PSYCHOANALYSIS AND PSYCHOEDUCATION EJ 045 048
FACTORIAL STRUCTURE OF SELECTED PSYCHO-EDUCATIONAL MEASURES AND PIAGETIAN REASONING ASSESSMENTS EJ 055 112

PSYCHOLINGUISTICS
LURIA'S MODEL OF THE VERBAL CONTROL OF BEHAVIOR. STUDY F: MOTIVATIONAL AND CONTROL IN THE DEVELOPMENT OF LANGUAGE FUNCTIONS, D. BIRCH. ED024443
GRAMMATICAL DEVELOPMENT IN RUSSIAN-SPEAKING CHILDREN. ED025332
TANGENT TO EXPERIMENTAL TECHNIQUES OF VERBAL CONTROL. ED025334
ON THE HETEROGENEITY OF PSYCHOLOGICAL PROCESSES IN SYNTACTIC DEVELOPMENT. ED040764
INTELLECTUAL DEVELOPMENT AND THE ABILITY TO PROCESS VISUAL AND VERBAL INFORMATION. ED043373
COMMUNICATIVE COMPETENCE AND THE DISADVANTAGED CHILD: A STUDY OF THE RELATIONSHIP BETWEEN LANGUAGE MODELS AND THE DEVELOPMENT OF COMMUNICATION SKILLS IN DISADVANTAGED PRESCHOOLERS. FINAL REPORT. ED047806
LANGUAGE TRAINING IN EARLY CHILDHOOD EDUCATION. ED051881
PSYCHOLINGUISTIC ABILITIES OF GOOD AND POOR READING DISADVANTAGED FIRST-GRADERS EJ 018 198
ON THE PSYCHOLINGUISTIC METHOD OF TEACHING READING EJ 030 547
SELF-DESCRIPTION AS A FUNCTION OF EVALUATIVE AND ACTIVITY RATINGS AMONG AMERICAN AND INDIAN ADOLESCENTS EJ 034 042
STORY RECALL IN KINDERGARTEN CHILDREN: EFFECT OF METHOD OF PRESENTATION ON PSYCHOLINGUISTIC PERFORMANCE EJ 036 748
CUE SYSTEMS AVAILABLE DURING THE READING PROCESS: A PSYCHOLINGUISTIC VIEWPOINT EJ 053 399

PSYCHOLOGICAL CHARACTERISTICS
THE INTERPLAY OF SOME EGO FUNCTIONS IN SIX YEAR OLD CHILDREN. ED020005
AN INVESTIGATION OF SIMILARITIES IN PARENT-CHILD TEST SCORES FOR EVIDENCE OF HEREDITARY COMPONENTS. ED027060
CHILDREN'S FEAR IN A DENTAL SITUATION AS A FUNCTION OF BIRTH ORDER EJ 015 099
INSTRUMENTAL AND AFFECTIONAL DEPENDENCY AND NURTURANCE IN PRESCHOOL CHILDREN EJ 015 101
PERCEPTUAL CORRELATES OF IMPULSIVE AND REFLECTIVE BEHAVIOR EJ 018 322
INDIVIDUAL DIFFERENCES IN THE CONSIDERATION OF INFORMATION AMONG TWO-YEAR-OLD CHILDREN EJ 018 324
RELATION OF EARLY SOCIALIZATION EXPERIENCES TO SELF-CONCEPTS AND GENDER ROLE IN MIDDLE CHILDHOOD EJ 021 997
PSYCHOLOGICAL DEVELOPMENT--PREDICTIONS FROM INFANCY EJ 025 626
DEVELOPMENTAL FACTORS IN ADOLESCENT DRUG USE: A STUDY OF PSYCHEDELIC DRUG USERS EJ 051 020
AN ANALYSIS OF THE CONCEPT OF CULTURAL DEPRIVATION EJ 055 111
ANALYSIS AND MODIFICATION OF SEARCH STRATEGIES OF IMPULSIVE AND REFLECTIVE CHILDREN ON THE MATCHING FAMILIAR FIGURES TEST EJ 059 510

PSYCHOLOGICAL EVALUATION
HEADSTART OPERATIONAL FIELD ANALYSIS. PROGRESS REPORT I. ED015774
SEMO PROJECT HEAD START, PSYCHOLOGICAL SERVICES REPORT, SUMMER 1967. PHASE THREE FINAL REPORT. ED020779
SEMO PROJECT HEAD START, PSYCHOLOGICAL SERVICES REPORT, 1966-67 YEAR PROGRAM. ED020780
THE THOMAS SELF-CONCEPT VALUES TEST. ED027068
THE DEVELOPMENT OF A COMPUTER TECHNIQUE FOR THE CONTENT ANALYSIS OF PSYCHO-SOCIAL FACTORS IN THE ORAL LANGUAGE OF KINDERGARTEN CHILDREN. ED038184
OR PSYCHOANALYTIC THEORY OF ADOLESCENCE? EJ 007 790
THE WORLD TEST: DEVELOPMENTAL ASPECTS OF A PLAY TECHNIQUE EJ 031 629

PSYCHOLOGICAL NEEDS
SEPARATION REACTIONS IN YOUNG, MILDLY RETARDED CHILDREN. EJ 003 972
THE HOSPITAL AND THE PRESCHOOL CHILD EJ 027 341
FOUR CHILDREN EJ 061 073
THE IMPORTANCE OF SECURITY IN THE EDUCATION OF YOUNG CHILDREN EJ 062 549

PSYCHOLOGICAL PATTERNS
WHEN THE CHILD IS ANGRY. ED017331
ANGER IN CHILDREN: CAUSES, CHARACTERISTICS, AND CONSIDERATIONS. ED039917
EMOTIONAL DEVELOPMENT IN THE FIRST TWO YEARS. ED039936
SOME CORRELATES OF AVERAGE LEVEL OF HAPPINESS AMONG COLLEGE STUDENTS EJ 021 994
PSYCHOLOGICAL SOURCES OF "RESISTANCE" TO FAMILY PLANNING EJ 027 502
A FACTOR ANALYSIS OF FIFTH AND SIXTH GRADERS' REPORTS OF PARENTAL CHILD-REARING BEHAVIOR EJ 038 855
A STUDY OF SLEEP BEHAVIOR IN TWO-YEAR-OLD CHILDREN EJ 048 299
THE DEVELOPMENT OF THE LANGUAGE OF EMOTIONS: CONDITIONS OF EMOTIONAL AROUSAL EJ 052 391
CONDITION WITH CAUTION EJ 058 585
HYPOTHESIS OF ORIGIN AND NATURE FOR THE "SOMINDENCE-DISSOFRUSTANCE" PERSONALITY FACTOR, U.I. 30 EJ 061 061
PERSONALITY, COGNITIVE, AND DEMOGRAPHIC CHARACTERISTICS OF STUDENT ACTIVISTS AND ACTIVE STUDENTS EJ 061 194

PSYCHOLOGICAL SERVICES
SEMO PROJECT HEAD START, PSYCHOLOGICAL SERVICES REPORT, SUMMER 1967. PHASE THREE FINAL REPORT. ED020779
SEMO PROJECT HEAD START, PSYCHOLOGICAL SERVICES REPORT, 1966-67 YEAR PROGRAM. ED020780
A DAY IN THE LIFE OF A SCHOOL PSYCHOLOGIST EJ 018 956

PSYCHOLOGICAL STUDIES
THE INTERPLAY OF SOME EGO FUNCTIONS IN SIX YEAR OLD CHILDREN. ED020005
ADAPTATIONAL TASKS IN CHILDHOOD IN OUR CULTURE. ED021632
COMPETENCE AND DEPENDENCE IN CHILDREN: PARENTAL TREATMENT OF FOUR-YEAR-OLD GIRLS. FINAL REPORT. ED030497
IMPLICATIONS OF STUDIES ON SELF-ESTEEM FOR EDUCATIONAL RESEARCH AND PRACTICE. ED033742
A REPLICATION AND EXTENSION STUDY ON N-LENGTH, INHIBITION AND COOPERATIVE BEHAVIOR WITH A MEXICAN-AMERICAN POPULATION. PART OF THE FINAL REPORT ON HEAD START EVALUATION AND RESEARCH: 1968-69 TO THE OFFICE OF ECONOMIC OPPORTUNITY. ED037249
STIMULUS GENERALIZATION ACROSS INDIVIDUALS ALONG DIMENSIONS OF SEX AND RACE: SOME FINDINGS WITH CHILDREN FROM AN ALL-NEGRO NEIGHBORHOOD. PROGRESS REPORT. ED042497
SELF-DISCLOSURE AND RELATIONSHIP TO THE TARGET PERSON EJ 007 431
PARENT-CHILD SEPARATION: PSYCHOLOGICAL EFFECTS ON THE CHILDREN EJ 051 019
THE DEVELOPMENT OF THE LANGUAGE OF EMOTIONS: CONDITIONS OF EMOTIONAL AROUSAL EJ 052 391
EXPERIMENTAL ANALYSES OF COOPERATION AND COMPETITION OF ANGLO-AMERICAN AND MEXICAN CHILDREN EJ 053 647
PERCEPTUAL AND LOGICAL FACTORS IN THE DEVELOPMENT OF MULTIPLICATIVE CLASSIFICATION EJ 053 649
DEVELOPMENT OF THE CONCEPT OF SERIATION EJ 053 650
DEVELOPMENT OF CONSERVATION IN NORMAL AND RETARDED CHILDREN EJ 053 651
THE THREE WISHES OF LATENCY AGE CHILDREN EJ 053 652
VERBAL RECALL AS A FUNCTION OF PERSONALITY CHARACTERISTICS EJ 054 806
AGE OF SUBJECT, TYPE OF SOCIAL CONTACT, AND RESPONSIVENESS TO SOCIAL REINFORCEMENT EJ 055 093
ANXIETY AND MORAL JUDGMENT IN EARLY ADOLESCENCE EJ 055 094
SPONTANEOUS MEASUREMENT IN YOUNG CHILDREN: A RE-EXAMINATION EJ 055 095
WORD-ASSOCIATION RESPONSES OF CHILDREN AS A FUNCTION OF AGE, SEX AND INSTRUCTIONS EJ 055 096
SEX DIFFERENCES IN PERFORMANCE AS A FUNCTION OF PRAISE AND BLAME EJ 055 098
HAPTIC RECOGNITION OF OBJECTS IN CHILDREN EJ 055 099
COMING OF AGE WITH THE DELBOEUF ILLUSION: BRIGHTNESS CONTRAST, COGNITION AND PERCEPTUAL DEVELOPMENT EJ 055 100
THE ROLE OF LIGHTNESS CONTRAST IN DETERMINING THE MAGNITUDE OF THE DELBOEUF ILLUSION: A REJOINDER TO WEINTRAUB AND COOPER EJ 055 101
DEVELOPMENT OF HIERARCHIES OF DIMENSIONAL SALIENCE EJ 055 102
DEVELOPMENT OF YOUNG CHILDREN'S ATTENTION TO NORMAL AND DISTORTED STIMULI: A CROSS CULTURAL STUDY EJ 055 103
ACADEMIC CHEATING: THE CONTRIBUTION OF SEX, PERSONALITY AND SITUATIONAL VARIABLES EJ 055 104
STYLE OF ADAPTATION TO AVERSIVE MATERNAL CONTROL AND PARANOID BEHAVIOR EJ 055 105
SIBLING RESEMBLANCES IN DIVERGENT THINKING EJ 055 106
INSTITUTIONALIZED RETARDATES' ANIMAL DRAWINGS; THEIR MEANINGS AND SIGNIFICANCE EJ 055 108
EFFECTS OF AGE UPON RETRIEVAL FROM SHORT-TERM MEMORY EJ 055 109
DEVELOPMENT OF CUTANEOUS AND KINESTHETIC LOCALIZATION BY BLIND AND SIGHTED CHILDREN EJ 055 113
MULTIDIMENSIONAL SCALING OF DIMENSIONAL PREFERENCES: A METHODOLOGICAL STUDY EJ 056 609
TAKING ANOTHER'S PERSPECTIVE: ROLE-TAKING DEVELOPMENT IN EARLY CHILDHOOD EJ 056 610
PARENTAL ATTITUDES AND INTERACTIONS IN DELINQUENCY EJ 056 611
PROBLEM-SOLVING THINKING AND ADJUSTMENT AMONG DISADVANTAGED PRESCHOOL CHILDREN EJ 056 612
VERBAL MEDIATION AND SATIATION IN YOUNG CHILDREN EJ 056 613
FACTORS RELATED TO SCHOOL ACHIEVEMENT IN AN ECONOMICALLY DISADVANTAGED GROUP EJ 056 614
FIGURATIVE AND OPERATIVE ASPECTS OF CHILDREN'S INFERENCE EJ 056 616
DEVELOPMENT OF A SENSE OF SELF-IDENTITY IN CHILDREN EJ 056 617
GENERALITY OF PERCEPTUAL BIASES IN INFERENCE AND CONCEPT USAGE EJ 056 618
SOCIAL-CLASS DIFFERENCES AND TASK VARIABLES IN THE DEVELOPMENT OF MULTIPLICATIVE CLASSIFICATION EJ 056 619
SEMANTIC INTEGRATION, AGE, AND THE RECALL OF SENTENCES EJ 056 620
THE INFLUENCE OF NONINTELLECTIVE FACTORS ON THE IQ SCORES OF MIDDLE- AND LOWER-CLASS CHILDREN EJ 056 621
THE CURIOSITY DIMENSION OF FIFTH-GRADE CHILDREN: A FACTORIAL DISCRIMINANT ANALYSIS EJ 056 623
UNILATERAL DOMINANCE IS NOT RELATED TO NEUROPSYCHOLOGICAL INTEGRITY EJ 056 624
RACE AND SEX DIFFERENCES IN THE CHILD'S PERCEPTION OF EMOTION EJ 056 625
RACIAL PREFERENCES IN YOUNG CHILDREN EJ 056 626
PERCEPTUAL INADEQUACY AND COMMUNICATIVE INEFFECTIVENESS IN INTERPERSONAL COMMUNICATION EJ 056 627
CONCEPTUAL ENCODING AND CONCEPT RECALL-RECOVERY IN CHILDREN EJ 056 628
THE MEASUREMENT OF CHILDREN'S SELF-CONCEPT AS RELATED TO RACIAL MEMBERSHIP EJ 056 629
THE EFFECT OF SYSTEMATIC STORY CHANGES ON INTENTIONALITY IN CHILDREN'S MORAL JUDGMENTS EJ 056 636
INITIAL PROBABILITY REHEARSAL, AND CONSTRAINT IN ASSOCIATIVE CLASS SELECTION EJ 057 903
ACHIEVEMENT MOTIVATION AND FEAR OF FAILURE IN FAMILY AND SCHOOL EJ 058 143
PARAMETERS OF THE SPIRAL AFTER-EFFECT IN ORGANICS, SCHIZOPHRENICS, AND NORMALS EJ 061 060
ORIENTATION IN CHILDREN'S HUMAN FIGURE DRAWINGS: AN ASPECT OF GRAPHIC LANGUAGE EJ 061 067

PSYCHOLOGICAL TESTING
HEADSTART OPERATIONAL FIELD ANALYSIS. PROGRESS REPORT II. ED015775
A TEST OF ERIKSON'S THEORY OF EGO EPIGENESIS EJ 039 898

PSYCHOLOGICAL TESTS
FURTHER EVIDENCE ON THE STABILITY OF THE FACTOR STRUCTURE OF THE TEST ANXIETY SCALE FOR SCHILDREN. ED023485
IT SCORE VARIATIONS BY INSTRUCTIONAL STYLE EJ 022 142
INK-BLOT RESPONSES OF IDENTICAL AND FRATERNAL TWINS EJ 044 946
GENETIC FACTORS IN TESTS OF PERCEPTION AND THE RORSCHACH EJ 045 045

PSYCHOLOGISTS
PSYCHOLOGICAL CONSULTATION IN A PRESCHOOL EJ 038 394

PSYCHOLOGY
MOTHER'S MODE OF DISCIPLINE AND CHILD'S VERBAL ABILITY EJ 050 794
SEX-ROLE AND NEED FOR APPROVAL IN ADOLESCENTS EJ 051 014

PSYCHOMETRICS
ADMINISTRATION MANUAL FOR THE INVENTORY OF SOCIALIZATION OF BILINGUAL CHILDREN AGES THREE TO TEN. PART OF THE FINAL REPORT. ED027062
ANALYSIS OF THE OBJECT CATEGORIZATION TEST AND THE PICTURE CATEGORIZATION TEST FOR PRESCHOOL CHILDREN. ED038174
PIAGET AND GESELL: A PSYCHOMETRIC ANALYSIS OF TESTS BUILT FROM THEIR TASKS EJ 053 927

PSYCHOMOTOR SKILLS
PSYCHOMOTOR EDUCATION - THEORY AND PRACTICE. ED029684
A COMPARATIVE ANALYSIS OF THE PIAGETIAN DEVELOPMENT OF TWELVE MONTH OLD DISADVANTAGED INFANTS IN AN ENRICHMENT CENTER WITH OTHERS NOT IN SUCH A CENTER. ED047778
CLASSROOM LANGUAGE OF TEACHERS OF YOUNG CHILDREN. ED053820
"TUBE" PLAY EJ 008 263
EFFECT OF VERBALIZATION ON YOUNG CHILDREN'S LEARNING OF A MANIPULATIVE SKILL EJ 020 520

CHILDREN'S SPATIAL REPRESENTATIONS AND HORIZONTAL DIRECTIONALITY EJ 023 190
COMPLEX MOTOR LEARNING IN FOUR-YEAR-OLDS EJ 046 236
MOTOR COORDINATION AND YOUNG CHILDREN'S DRAWING ABILITIES EJ 046 257
BLOCK MANIPULATION BY CHILDREN AS A FUNCTION OF SOCIAL REINFORCEMENT, ANXIETY, AROUSAL, AND ABILITY PATTERN EJ 046 468
A FACTOR-ANALYTIC STUDY OF THE RELATIONSHIP OF MOTOR FACTORS TO ACADEMIC CRITERIA FOR FIRST- AND THIRD-GRADE BOYS EJ 052 451
THE ROLE OF OVERT ACTIVITY IN CHILDREN'S IMAGERY PRODUCTION EJ 059 315

PSYCHOPATHOLOGY
THE PREVALENCE OF BEHAVIOR SYMPTOMS IN YOUNGER ELEMENTARY SCHOOL CHILDREN. ED039040
SYMPTOM PATTERNS IN HYPERKINETIC, NEUROTIC, AND NORMAL CHILDREN EJ 025 360
AGE PATTERNS IN CHILDREN'S PSYCHIATRIC SYMPTOMS EJ 025 374

PSYCHOPHYSIOLOGY
SOME CHARACTERISTICS OF NEURAL PROCESSING IN THE CHILD. ED040740
PSYCHOPHYSIOLOGIC AND CONVERSION REACTIONS IN CHILDREN: SELECTIVE INCIDENCE IN VERBAL AND NONVERBAL FAMILIES EJ 023 429
PHYSIOLOGICAL INDICATIONS OF ORGANIC INVOLVEMENT EJ 051 016
THE EFFECT OF EMOTION ON GROWTH EJ 053 653
PSYCHOPHYSICALLY SCALED CUE DIFFERENCES, LEARNING RATE, AND ATTENTIONAL STRATEGIES IN A TACTILE DISCRIMINATION TASK EJ 058 146

PSYCHOSIS
CHILDHOOD PSYCHOSIS COMBINED WITH XYZ ABNORMALITIES EJ 035 078

PSYCHOSOMATIC DISEASES
PSYCHOPHYSIOLOGIC AND CONVERSION REACTIONS IN CHILDREN: SELECTIVE INCIDENCE IN VERBAL AND NONVERBAL FAMILIES EJ 023 429

PSYCHOTHERAPY
PSYCHOLOBIOLOGICAL REFERENTS FOR THE TREATMENT OF AUTISM. ED028814
CASE CONFERENCE: A PSYCHOTHERAPEUTIC AIDE IN A HEADSTART PROGRAM. I. THEORY AND PRACTICE EJ 003 955
CASE CONFERENCE: A PSYCHOTHERAPEUTIC AIDE IN A HEADSTART PROGRAM. II. COMMENTARY EJ 003 956
FROM THE TEACHER'S NOTEBOOK EJ 020 103
EARLY INTERVENTION AND SOCIAL CLASS. DIAGNOSIS AND TREATMENT OF PRESCHOOL CHILDREN IN A DAY CARE CENTER EJ 050 497

PSYCHOTIC CHILDREN
CHILDHOOD PSYCHOSIS COMBINED WITH XYZ ABNORMALITIES EJ 035 078
A PROGRAM FOR HOSPITALIZED PSYCHOTIC CHILDREN: REGULAR ATTENDANCE, AWAY FROM THE HOSPITAL, AT A COMMUNITY NURSERY SCHOOL EJ 050 938

PUBLIC HEALTH
CONTROL OF LEAD POISONING IN CHILDREN. (PRE-PUBLICATION DRAFT). ED050825

PUBLIC POLICY
RESEARCH, EVALUATION, AND PUBLIC POLICY: AN INVITED EDITORIAL EJ 021 381

PUBLIC SCHOOL SYSTEMS
HEAD START PROGRAMS OPERATED BY PUBLIC SCHOOL SYSTEMS, 1966-67. ED026115
EVALUATION OF THE PRESCHOOL PROGRAM, 1967-68, FUNDED UNDER ESEA TITLE I, P.L. 89-10. ED027080
A GUIDE FOR PRESCHOOLS: A HANDBOOK ABOUT THE OPERATION AND FUNCTION OF PRESCHOOLS IN THE FRESNO CITY UNIFIED SCHOOL DISTRICT. ED030499
EVALUATION OF SELECTED COMPONENTS OF: A SUPPLEMENTARY CENTER FOR EARLY CHILDHOOD EDUCATION. TITLE III. ED032927
HARTFORD EARLY CHILDHOOD PROGRAM, HARTFORD, CONNECTICUT: AN URBAN PUBLIC SCHOOL SYSTEM'S LARGE-SCALE APPROACH TOWARD RESTRUCTURING EARLY CHILDHOOD EDUCATION. MODEL PROGRAMS--CHILDHOOD EDUCATION. ED045211
MYTHOLOGY IN AMERICAN EDUCATION: A GUIDE TO CONSTRUCTIVE CONFRONTATION. 1970 WHITE HOUSE CONFERENCE ON CHILDREN, REPORT OF FORUM 8. (WORKING COPY). ED046526
CALIFORNIA ADVISORY COUNCIL ON EDUCATIONAL RESEARCH SUGGESTED POLICY ON EDUCATIONAL RESEARCH FOR CALIFORNIA SCHOOL DISTRICTS EJ 018 016
DO YOU REALLY WANT TO IMPROVE THE CURRICULUM? EJ 031 850
AN ATTEMPT TO COMBINE CLINICAL AND EDUCATIONAL RESOURCES: A REPORT ON THE FIRST YEAR'S EXPERIENCE OF A THERAPEUTIC SCHOOL EJ 035 539
TOWARD A DEMOCRATIC ELEMENTARY-SCHOOL CLASSROOM EJ 058 308

PUBLIC SCHOOLS
HEALTH, EDUCATION, AND WELFARE: THE PROGRESSIVE IMPULSE IN THE NEW YORK CITY PUBLIC SCHOOLS EJ 029 104
LA EDUCACION PRE-ESCOLAR EN LAS ESCUELAS PUBLICAS DE PUERTO RICO EJ 029 622
THE ADMINISTRATION OF "SELECTIVITY" IN THE BREAKFAST PROGRAM OF A PUBLIC ELEMENTARY SCHOOL EJ 036 580
SUPERINTENDENT JULIA RICHMAN: A SOCIAL PROGRESSIVE IN THE PUBLIC SCHOOLS EJ 060 106

PUBLICATIONS
CHILD DEVELOPMENT AND SOCIAL SCIENCE EDUCATION. PART III: ABSTRACTS OF RELEVANT LITERATURE. ED023466
VIEWPOINT: GAP AND THE JOINT COMMISSION ON MENTAL HEALTH OF CHILDREN EJ 060 203

PUBLISHING INDUSTRY
CHILDREN AND THE MASS MEDIA EJ 029 341

PUERTO RICAN CULTURE
PUERTO RICAN CHILDREN IN MAINLAND SCHOOLS. A SOURCE BOOK FOR TEACHERS. ED027953

PUERTO RICANS
PUERTO RICAN CHILDREN IN MAINLAND SCHOOLS. A SOURCE BOOK FOR TEACHERS. ED027953
LA EDUCACION PRE-ESCOLAR EN LAS ESCUELAS PUBLICAS DE PUERTO RICO EJ 029 622

PUNISHMENT
EFFECTS OF INCONSISTENT PUNISHMENT ON AGGRESSION IN CHILDREN EJ 021 992

PUPILLARY DILATION
EFFECTS OF ARITHMETIC PROBLEM DIFFICULTY ON PUPILLARY DILATION IN NORMALS AND EDUCABLE RETARDATES EJ 021 986

QUESTION ANSWER INTERVIEWS
THE COGNITIVE ENVIRONMENTS OF URBAN PRE-SCHOOL CHILDREN. MANUAL OF INSTRUCTIONS FOR ADMINISTERING AND SCORING "SCHOOLS" QUESTION. ED018254
THE COGNITIVE ENVIRONMENTS OF URBAN PRE-SCHOOL CHILDREN. MANUAL OF INSTRUCTIONS FOR ADMINISTERING AND SCORING EDUCATIONAL ATTITUDE SURVEY. ED018255
THE COGNITIVE ENVIRONMENTS OF URBAN PRE-SCHOOL CHILDREN. MANUAL OF INSTRUCTIONS FOR ADMINISTERING AND SCORING FIRST DAY. ED018258
THE COGNITIVE ENVIRONMENTS OF URBAN PRE-SCHOOL CHILDREN. MANUAL OF INSTRUCTIONS FOR ADMINISTERING AND SCORING HOME RESOURCES PATTERNS. ED018260

QUESTIONING TECHNIQUES
THE COGNITIVE ENVIRONMENTS OF URBAN PRE-SCHOOL CHILDREN. MANUAL OF INSTRUCTIONS FOR ADMINISTERING AND SCORING THE TWENTY QUESTIONS TASK. ED018261
INTELLECTUAL OPERATIONS IN TEACHER-CHILD INTERACTION. ED039011
RELATIONSHIPS BETWEEN CHILDREN'S QUESTIONS AND NURSERY SCHOOL TEACHERS' RESPONSES. ED046507
INSTRUCTIONAL SPECIFICITY AND OUTCOME-EXPECTATION IN OBSERVATIONALLY-INDUCED QUESTION FORMULATION. ED047789
FREEDOM TO MANIPULATE OBJECTS AND QUESTION-ASKING PERFORMANCE OF SIX-YEAR-OLDS EJ 029 217
INTELLECTUAL OPERATIONS IN TEACHER QUESTION-ASKING BEHAVIOR EJ 032 895
THE "MENTAL STEP" HYPOTHESIS IN SOLVING VERBAL PROBLEMS: EFFECTS OF VARIATIONS IN QUESTION-PHRASING ON A GRADE SCHOOL POPULATION EJ 035 372
LEARNING, CURIOSITY, AND SOCIAL GROUP MEMBERSHIP EJ 035 378
METODO DE ARCHIVAR LAS OBSERVACIONES DEL COMPORTAMIENTO DEL NINO, COMO GUIA PARA ENTENDERLO MEJOR (METHODS OF RECORDING OBSERVATIONS OF CHILDREN'S BEHAVIOR, A GUIDE FOR BETTER UNDERSTANDING) EJ 049 938
READING INSTRUCTION AND COGNITIVE DEVELOPMENT EJ 052 066

QUESTIONNAIRES
APPENDIX, STUDIES I, II AND III. ORIGINAL INSTRUMENTS USED AND BIBLIOGRAPHY. ED015028
PARENTS' EVALUATION OF THE HEAD START PROGRAM IN THE MILWAUKEE PUBLIC SCHOOLS. ED020806
THERE IS A BETTER WAY. A PREMISE POINTS THE WAY, A PROFILE WITH PROMISE, A COMPOSITE OF THE SURVEY. ED023471
A NUTRITIONAL SURVEY OF CHILDREN IN HEAD START CENTERS IN CENTRAL UNITED STATES. ED042487
ATTITUDINAL STUDY OF ROMAN CATHOLIC PARENTS OF PRE-SCHOOL CHILDREN REGARDING THE OPTION OF "CATHOLIC" OR PUBLIC SCHOOL EDUCATION FOR THEIR CHILDREN. ED046488
RESULTS OF PARENT AND STUDENT REACTION QUESTIONNAIRE. TECHNICAL REPORT NO. 8. ED052836
A BEHAVIOURAL SCREENING QUESTIONNAIRE FOR USE WITH THREE-YEAR-OLD CHILDREN. PRELIMINARY FINDINGS EJ 042 349

METODO DE ARCHIVAR LAS OBSERVACIONES DEL COMPORTAMIENTO DEL NINO, COMO GUIA PARA ENTENDERLO MEJOR EJ 045 232
FRIENDSHIPS AMONG STUDENTS IN DESEGREGATED SCHOOLS EJ 053 668
A PIAGETIAN QUESTIONNAIRE APPLIED TO PUPILS IN A SECONDARY SCHOOL EJ 053 907

RACE

RACE AND SEX IDENTIFICATION IN PRESCHOOL CHILDREN. ED041634

RACE RELATIONS

PREJUDICE IN THE SCHOOLS EJ 001 498
ON BEING A WHITEY IN THE MIDST OF A RACIAL CRISIS EJ 007 362
BLACK IDENTITY AND THE HELPING PERSON EJ 008 461
THE EFFECT OF BLACK HISTORY ON AN INTERRACIAL GROUP OF CHILDREN EJ 026 735
FRIENDSHIPS AMONG STUDENTS IN DESEGREGATED SCHOOLS EJ 053 668

RACIAL ATTITUDES

THE RELATIONSHIP BETWEEN RACE AND PERCEPTION OF RACIALLY-RELATED STIMULI IN PRESCHOOL CHILDREN. ED030483
QUASI-DISGUISED AND STRUCTURED MEASURE OF SCHOOLCHILDREN'S RACIAL PREFERENCES. ED035440
THE DISTRIBUTION OF TEACHER APPROVAL AND DISAPPROVAL OF HEAD START CHILDREN. FINAL REPORT. ED042509
DEVELOPMENTAL TRENDS IN THE SELECTIVE PERCEPTION OF RACE AND AFFECT BY YOUNG NEGRO AND CAUCASIAN CHILDREN. ED046498
RACIAL ATTITUDES AMONG WHITE KINDERGARTEN CHILDREN FROM THREE DIFFERENT ENVIRONMENTS. ED051882
RACIAL AWARENESS IN YOUNG MEXICAN-AMERICAN, NEGRO AND ANGLO CHILDREN EJ 028 926
RACIAL ATTITUDES OF NEGRO PRESCHOOLERS EJ 041 858
THE FORMATION AND REVERSAL OF AN ATTITUDE AS FUNCTIONS OF ASSUMED SELF-CONCEPT, RACE, AND SOCIOECONOMIC CLASS EJ 052 652
EVALUATION DIMENSION OF THE AFFECTIVE MEANING SYSTEM OF THE PRESCHOOL CHILD EJ 054 049
THE MEASUREMENT OF CHILDREN'S SELF-CONCEPT AS RELATED TO RACIAL MEMBERSHIP EJ 056 629
WHITE ADULT BEHAVIOR TOWARD BLACK AND WHITE CHILDREN EJ 056 729
TEACHING RACE RELATIONS IN THE NURSERY SCHOOL EJ 056 864
RACE OF EXPERIMENTER AS A VARIABLE IN RESEARCH WITH CHILDREN EJ 061 085

RACIAL CHARACTERISTICS

COMPARATIVE PERCEPTUAL MOTOR PERFORMANCE OF NEGRO AND WHITE YOUNG MENTAL RETARDATES EJ 019 015
THE INFLUENCE OF NEGRO AND WHITE TEACHERS RATED AS EFFECTIVE OR NONEFFECTIVE ON THE PERFORMANCE OF NEGRO AND WHITE LOWER-CLASS CHILDREN EJ 045 068
RACIAL PREFERENCES IN YOUNG CHILDREN EJ 056 626

RACIAL DIFFERENCES

SEX AND RACE DIFFERENCES IN THE DEVELOPMENT OF UNDERPRIVILEGED PRESCHOOL CHILDREN. ED019992
HEAD START EVALUATION AND RESEARCH CENTER, BOSTON UNIVERSITY. REPORT C-I, PERCEPTION OF EMOTION AMONG CHILDREN: RACE AND SEX DIFFERENCES. ED022561
INTELLIGENCE QUOTIENT VERSUS LEARNING QUOTIENT: IMPLICATIONS FOR ELEMENTARY CURRICULA. ED031304
BIOGENETICS OF RACE AND CLASS. ED036317
DO NEGRO CHILDREN PROJECT A SELF-IMAGE OF HELPLESSNESS AND INADEQUACY IN DRAWING A PERSON? ED036329
PERSPECTIVE ON THE JENSEN AFFAIR. ED040760
DEVELOPING COGNITIVE LEARNINGS WITH YOUNG CHILDREN. ED041614
DEVELOPMENT OF GRAMMATICAL STRUCTURES AND ATTRIBUTES IN PRESCHOOL AGE CHILDREN. FINAL REPORT. ED041639
RACIAL DIFFERENCES IN INDICES OF EGO FUNCTIONING RELEVANT TO ACADEMIC ACHIEVEMENT EJ 015 096
DELAY OF GRATIFICATION AND INTERNAL VERSUS EXTERNAL CONTROL AMONG ADOLESCENTS OF LOW SOCIOECONOMIC STATUS EJ 034 539
ADOPTION RESOURCES FOR BLACK CHILDREN EJ 035 801
AN EXPERIMENTAL STUDY OF BASIC LEARNING ABILITY AND INTELLIGENCE IN LOW-SOCIOECONOMIC-STATUS CHILDREN EJ 036 818
RACE AND CONFORMITY AMONG CHILDREN EJ 038 937
CHILDREN'S COMMUNICATION ACCURACY RELATED TO RACE AND SOCIOECONOMIC STATUS EJ 040 359
NEGRO-WHITE, MALE-FEMALE EIGHT-MONTH DEVELOPMENTAL SCORES COMPARED WITH SEVEN-YEAR WISC AND BENDER TEST SCORES EJ 040 723
ON TRANSRACIAL ADOPTION OF BLACK CHILDREN EJ 053 853
RACE AND SEX DIFFERENCES IN THE CHILD'S PERCEPTION OF EMOTION EJ 056 625

RACIAL DISCRIMINATION

CHILDREN WITHOUT PREJUDICE. 1970 WHITE HOUSE CONFERENCE ON CHILDREN, REPORT OF FORUM 18. (WORKING PAPER). ED046534
MARGINAL CHILDREN OF WAR: AN EXPLORATORY STUDY OF AMERICAN-KOREAN CHILDREN. ED047781
RACIAL ATTITUDES AMONG WHITE KINDERGARTEN CHILDREN FROM THREE DIFFERENT ENVIRONMENTS. ED051882
AN ATTACK ON IMPEDIMENTS TO EFFECTIVE CROSS-CULTURAL TEACHING EJ 032 553
WHITE STAFF, BLACK CHILDREN: IS THERE A PROBLEM? EJ 039 799

RACIAL FACTORS

COLOR AND PHYSIOGNOMY AS VARIABLES IN RACIAL MISIDENTIFICATION AMONG CHILDREN. ED034584
EFFECTS OF VIEWING VIDEOTAPED SAME AND OPPOSITE COLOR CHILD-TEACHERS ON INTEGRATED AND ALL-WHITE KINDERGARTNERS. ED047805
PATTERNS OF WISC SCORES FOR CHILDREN OF TWO SOCIOECONOMIC CLASSES AND RACES EJ 021 775
THE INFLUENCE OF TEACHER-CHILD INTERACTION ON THE LEARNING PROCESS EJ 048 235
BLACK CLIENTS AND WHITE WORKERS; A REPORT FROM THE FIELD EJ 051 062
RACIAL FACTORS IN TEST PERFORMANCE EJ 053 887
EFFECTS OF VICARIOUS CONSEQUENCES AND RACE OF MODEL UPON IMITATIVE PERFORMANCE BY BLACK CHILDREN EJ 058 139
SOME DISCRIMINATIVE PROPERTIES OF RACE AND SEX FOR CHILDREN FROM AN ALL-NEGRO NEIGHBORHOOD EJ 058 510
IMITATION OF TEACHER PREFERENCES IN A FIELD SETTING EJ 061 070
RACE OF EXPERIMENTER AS A VARIABLE IN RESEARCH WITH CHILDREN EJ 061 085

RACIAL INTEGRATION

A DISTANCE MEASURE OF RACIAL ATTITUDES IN PRIMARY GRADE CHILDREN: AN EXPLORATORY STUDY. ED026133
REACHING FOR THE DREAM: AN EXPERIMENT IN TWO-WAY BUSING EJ 025 078

RACIAL RECOGNITION

COLOR AND PHYSIOGNOMY AS VARIABLES IN RACIAL MISIDENTIFICATION AMONG CHILDREN. ED034584
RACIAL AWARENESS IN YOUNG MEXICAN-AMERICAN, NEGRO AND ANGLO CHILDREN EJ 028 926

RACIAL SEGREGATION

A DISTANCE MEASURE OF RACIAL ATTITUDES IN PRIMARY GRADE CHILDREN: AN EXPLORATORY STUDY. ED026133

RACISM

ISSUES AND REALITIES IN EARLY CHILDHOOD EDUCATION. ED041621

RATING SCALES

SUMMARY REPORT OF A STUDY OF THE FULL-YEAR 1966 HEAD START PROGRAMS. ED014328
AN INFANT RATING SCALE, ITS VALIDATION AND USEFULNESS. ED016513
A STUDY OF COMPOSITION ABILITY AS ASSESSED WITH A STANDARDIZED INSTRUMENT FOR SECOND AND THIRD GRADE CHILDREN. ED029696
SOUTHWESTERN COOPERATIVE EDUCATIONAL LABORATORY INTERACTION OBSERVATION SCHEDULE (SCIOS): A SYSTEM FOR ANALYZING TEACHER-PUPIL INTERACTION IN THE AFFECTIVE DOMAIN. ED038188
COGNITIVE ASPECTS OF CHILDREN'S OCCUPATIONAL PRESTIGE RANKINGS. ED039924
CHILD CARE PARAPROFESSIONALS: CHARACTERISTICS FOR SELECTION. ED053800
COMPARISON OF PICTORIAL AND VERBAL SEMANTIC SCALES AS USED BY CHILDREN EJ 029 769
SELF-DESCRIPTION AS A FUNCTION OF EVALUATIVE AND ACTIVITY RATINGS AMONG AMERICAN AND INDIAN ADOLESCENTS EJ 034 042
THE MANIPULATION AND MEASUREMENT OF SELF-DISCLOSURE IN PREADOLESCENTS EJ 034 298
OCCUPATIONAL PRESTIGE AS SEEN BY DISADVANTAGED BLACK CHILDREN EJ 034 453
A STIMULUS SIMILARITY SCALE FOR TEMPORAL MEASURES OF ATTENTION IN INFANTS AND CHILDREN EJ 034 530
THE DEVELOPMENT OF ELEMENTARY SCHOOL CHILDREN'S JUDGMENT OF INTENT EJ 052 581
THE STRUCTURING OF SOCIAL ATTITUDES IN CHILDREN EJ 055 489
DELINQUENCY PREDICTION SCALES AND PERSONALITY INVENTORIES EJ 057 475
LOCUS OF CONTROL: AN EXAMPLE OF DANGERS IN USING CHILDREN'S SCALES WITH CHILDREN EJ 058 929

RATIOS (MATHEMATICS)

THE EFFECTS OF MODE OF PRESENTATION AND NUMBER OF CATEGORIES ON 4-YEAR-OLDS' PROPORTION ESTIMATES. ED032132

REACTION TIME

SOME CHARACTERISTICS OF NEURAL PROCESSING IN THE CHILD. ED040740
IMPULSIVITY & REFLECTIVITY AS REFLECTED BY THE VARIABLES OF TIME AND ERROR. ED047820
MODIFYING RESPONSE LATENCY AND ERROR RATE OF IMPULSIVE CHILDREN. ED050819
THE EFFECT OF ANXIETY OVER INTELLECTUAL PERFORMANCE ON REFLECTION-IMPULSIVITY IN CHILDREN EJ 026 153
REACTION TIME AND REMOTE ASSOCIATION IN TALENTED MALE ADOLESCENTS EJ 029 360

INDIVIDUAL DIFFERENCES IN CHILDREN'S REACTIONS TO FRUSTRATIVE NONREWARD EJ 030 591
RECOGNITION OF FLASHED WORDS BY CHILDREN EJ 032 676
EMOTIONAL CONCOMITANTS OF VISUAL MASTERY IN INFANTS: THE EFFECTS OF STIMULUS MOVEMENT ON SMILING AND VOCALIZING EJ 033 794
DEVELOPMENTAL GENERALITY OF A FORM RECOGNITION STRATEGY EJ 037 534
CONCEPTUAL TEMPO IN YOUNG GRADE-SCHOOL CHILDREN EJ 041 450
INFORMATION SEEKING ABOUT UNCERTAIN BUT UNAVOIDABLE OUTCOMES: EFFECTS OF PROBABILITY, VALENCE, AND INTERVENING ACTIVITY EJ 042 962
AGE CHANGES IN CARDIAC DECELERATION WITHIN A FIXED FOREPERIOD REACTION-TIME TASK: AN INDEX OF ATTENTION EJ 043 667
CHILDREN'S REACTIONS TO FAILURE AS A FUNCTION OF INTERRESPONSE INTERVAL EJ 045 043
MODIFICATION OF IMPULSIVE AND REFLECTIVE COGNITIVE STYLES THROUGH OBSERVATION OF FILM-MEDIATED MODELS EJ 047 676
SENSORY-SET FACTORS IN AGE DIFFERENCES IN REACTION TIME EJ 048 304
INFORMATION PROCESSING AND THE MODIFICATION OF AN "IMPULSIVE CONCEPTUAL TEMPO" EJ 052 460
MOTIVATIONAL EFFECTS OF BOREDOM ON CHILDREN'S RESPONSE SPEEDS EJ 055 211
INFANTS' RESPONSES TO NOVELTY IN FAMILIAR AND UNFAMILIAR SETTINGS EJ 056 731
ANALYSIS AND MODIFICATION OF SEARCH STRATEGIES OF IMPULSIVE AND REFLECTIVE CHILDREN ON THE MATCHING FAMILIAR FIGURES TEST EJ 059 510
VISUAL MASKING AND DEVELOPMENTAL DIFFERENCES IN INFORMATION PROCESSING EJ 059 514
RESPONSE DEPRESSION AND FACILITATION COMPONENTS OF THE FRUSTRATION EFFECT IN CHILDREN'S BEHAVIOR EJ 059 877
AGE DIFFERENCES IN VISUAL REACTION TIME OF "BRAIN DAMAGED" AND NORMAL CHILDREN UNDER IRREGULAR PREPARATORY INTERVAL CONDITIONS EJ 060 109
SIMPLE REACTION TIME IN CHILDREN: EFFECTS OF INCENTIVE, INCENTIVE-SHIFT AND OTHER TRAINING VARIABLES EJ 061 075

REACTIVE BEHAVIOR

HEAD START EVALUATION AND RESEARCH CENTER, UNIVERSITY OF KANSAS. REPORT NO. IV, A COMPARISON OF FOUR MODES OF ELICITING BRIEF ORAL RESPONSES FROM CHILDREN. ED021637
FEAR AND ATTACHMENT IN YOUNG CHILDREN. RESEARCH PROJECT NUMBER 4 OF PROJECT HEAD START RESEARCH AND EVALUATION CENTER, SYRACUSE UNIVERSITY RESEARCH INSTITUTE. FINAL REPORT, NOVEMBER 1, 1967. ED026141
RATE AND UNIQUENESS IN CHILDREN'S CREATIVE RESPONDING. ED034581
DETERMINANTS OF CHILDREN'S ATTEMPTS TO HELP ANOTHER CHILD IN DISTRESS. ED039023
RELATIVE SOOTHING EFFECTS OF VERTICAL AND HORIZONTAL ROCKING. ED046504
FEAR OF VISUAL NOVELTY: DEVELOPMENTAL PATTERNS IN MALES AND FEMALES EJ 019 011
CLASSROOM BEHAVIOR: MESSAGES FROM CHILDREN EJ 031 780
A NOTE ON SELECTIVE IMITATION BY A SIX-WEEK-OLD INFANT EJ 034 045
REACTIONS TO RESPONSE-CONTINGENT STIMULATION IN EARLY INFANCY EJ 059 874
PERSONAL ORIENTATION TO SUCCESS AND FAILURE IN URBAN BLACK CHILDREN EJ 061 072

READABILITY

THE READABILITY OF SELECTED SECOND GRADE SOCIAL STUDIES TEXTBOOKS. ED027968

READINESS

SECOND-YEAR REPORT ON AN EVALUATIVE STUDY OF PREKINDERGARTEN PROGRAMS FOR EDUCATIONALLY DISADVANTAGED CHILDREN. ED016523
THE COGNITIVE ENVIRONMENTS OF URBAN PRE-SCHOOL CHILDREN. MANUAL OF INSTRUCTIONS FOR ADMINISTERING AND SCORING FIRST DAY. ED018258
SCHOOL READINESS, BEHAVIOR TESTS USED AT THE GESELL INSTITUTE. ED023449
AN EVALUATION OF THE PRESCHOOL READINESS CENTERS PROGRAM IN EAST ST. LOUIS, ILLINOIS, JULY 1, 1967-JUNE 30, 1968. FINAL REPORT. ED023472
LANGUAGE ABILITY AND READINESS FOR SCHOOL OF CHILDREN WHO PARTICIPATED IN HEAD START PROGRAMS. A DISSERTATION ABSTRACT. ED025299
LEARNING READINESS IN TWO JEWISH GROUPS: A STUDY IN "CULTURAL DEPRIVATION." AN OCCASIONAL PAPER. ED026126
AN EVALUATION OF THE INTERIM CLASS: AN EXTENDED READINESS PROGRAM. ED028820
AN EXPERIMENTAL STUDY OF VISUAL PERCEPTUAL TRAINING AND READINESS SCORES WITH CERTAIN FIRST-GRADE CHILDREN. ED032921
THE MAKING OF A PUPIL: CHANGING CHILDREN INTO SCHOOL CHILDREN. ED037235
DEVELOPMENT OF A READINESS TEST FOR DISADVANTAGED PRE-SCHOOL CHILDREN IN THE UNITED STATES. FINAL REPORT. ED037253
PIAGETIAN TASKS AS CLASSROOM EVALUATIVE TOOLS EJ 032 679

READINESS (MENTAL)

YOUNG CHILDREN'S THINKING, STUDIES OF SOME ASPECTS OF PIAGET'S THEORY. ED013662
UNDERSTANDING READINESS: AN OCCASIONAL PAPER. ED032117
PREDICTION OF READINESS IN KINDERGARTEN AND ACHIEVEMENT IN THE FIRST PRIMARY YEAR. STUDY NUMBER TWO. ED043393
COMMUNITY COOPERATIVE NURSERY SCHOOL, MENLO PARK, CALIFORNIA: A PRESCHOOL PROGRAM INVOLVING MOTHERS AS ORGANIZERS, HELPERS, AND DECISION-MAKERS. MODEL PROGRAMS--CHILDHOOD EDUCATION. ED045222
PRESCHOOLER STUDY: THE MEDICAL, SOCIAL AND ECONOMIC CORRELATES OF POVERTY IN PRESCHOOL CHILDREN OF BRITISH COLUMBIA. A PILOT STUDY. ED046518
CURRICULAR INTERVENTION IN LANGUAGE ARTS READINESS FOR HEAD START CHILDREN. TULANE UNIVERSITY, HEAD START EVALUATION AND RESEARCH CENTER, 1968-1969 INTERVENTION REPORT. SUPPLEMENT TO THE ANNUAL REPORT TO THE OFFICE OF ECONOMIC OPPORTUNITY. ED047795
EFFECTS OF PERCEPTUAL TRAINING ON CHILDREN'S HUMAN FIGURE DRAWINGS EJ 049 173

READING

READING. DIMENSIONS IN EARLY LEARNING SERIES. ED027070
DEVELOPMENTAL SKILL AND ACHIEVEMENT DIFFERENCES OF CHILDREN IDENTIFIED AS EXCELLENT, GOOD, AND AVERAGE IN READING AND ARITHMETIC ACHIEVEMENT. STUDY NUMBER THREE. ED044181
DIRECTED RESEARCH PROGRAM IN READING, EARLY CHILDHOOD, VOCATIONAL EDUCATION, SCHOOL ORGANIZATION AND ADMINISTRATION, FY 72 - FY 76. ED051871
CONFERENCE ON READING AND EARLY CHILDHOOD. ED051875
AN INCREASING EFFECT OF DISORIENTATION ON THE DISCRIMINATION OF PRINT: A DEVELOPMENTAL STUDY EJ 024 982

READING ABILITY

INVESTIGATIONS OF THE ROLE OF SELECTED CUES IN CHILDREN'S PAIRED-ASSOCIATE LEARNING. REPORT FROM THE READING PROJECT. ED036315
PSYCHOLINGUISTIC ABILITIES OF GOOD AND POOR READING DISADVANTAGED FIRST-GRADERS EJ 018 198
REPRESENTATIONAL AND SYNTACTIC COMPETENCE OF PROBLEM READERS EJ 026 208
ORGANIZING FOR READING INSTRUCTION EJ 028 960
TEACHERS' RATINGS OF URBAN CHILDREN'S READING PERFORMANCE EJ 035 662
COGNITIVE STYLE AND READING ABILITY EJ 043 239

READING ACHIEVEMENT

LONG-RANGE EFFECT OF PRE-SCHOOLING ON READING ACHIEVEMENT. STUDY III. ED015027
CHILDREN WHO READ EARLY, TWO LONGITUDINAL STUDIES. ED019107
HEAD START EVALUATION AND RESEARCH CENTER, TULANE UNIVERSITY. FINAL REPORT. (TITLE SUPPLIED). ED020782
SAN ANTONIO LANGUAGE RESEARCH PROJECT, 1965-66 (YEAR TWO) FINDINGS. ED022528
PERCEPTUAL MODE DOMINANCE: AN APPROACH TO ASSESSMENT OF FIRST GRADE READING AND SPELLING. ED026132
THE EFFECT OF DIRECT INSTRUCTION IN LISTENING ON THE LISTENING AND READING COMPREHENSION OF FIRST GRADE CHILDREN. DISSERTATION ABSTRACT. ED029693
IDENTIFICATION IN THE KINDERGARTEN OF FACTORS THAT MAKE FOR FUTURE SUCCESS IN READING AND IDENTIFICATION AND DIAGNOSIS IN THE KINDERGARTEN OF POTENTIAL READING DISABILITY CASES. FINAL REPORT. ED029710
GROUP SCREENING OF AUDITORY AND VISUAL PERCEPTUAL ABILITIES: AN APPROACH TO PERCEPTUAL ASPECTS OF BEGINNING READING. ED033751
READING - DIRECTED OR NOT? EJ 015 125
ARE MOVERS LOSERS? EJ 018 958
ORAL READING ACHIEVEMENT OF SCOTTISH AND AMERICAN CHILDREN EJ 030 548
THE RELATIONSHIP BETWEEN AUDITORY AND VISUAL SHORT-TERM MEMORY AND READING ACHIEVEMENT EJ 033 780
SIX SUCCESSFUL READING PROGRAMS FOR INNER-CITY SCHOOLS EJ 035 663
ANTICIPATORY IMAGERY AND MODIFIED ANAGRAM SOLUTIONS: A DEVELOPMENTAL STUDY EJ 041 141
THE INFLUENCE OF TEACHER-CHILD INTERACTION ON THE LEARNING PROCESS EJ 048 235

READING COMPREHENSION

READING - DIRECTED OR NOT? EJ 015 125

READING DEVELOPMENT

LEARNING TO READ THROUGH EXPERIENCE. SECOND EDITION. ED027067
THE I.T.A. READING EXPERIMENT IN BRITAIN. ED032133
CERTAIN ANTENATAL, PERINATAL, AND DEVELOPMENTAL VARIABLES AND READING RETAR RETARDATION IN MIDDLE-CLASS BOYS EJ 022 057
READING: AN ETERNAL DYNAMIC EJ 028 959

LEARNING AND COGNITIVE DEVELOPMENT: REPRESENTATIVE SAMPLES, CUMULATIVE-HIERARCHICAL LEARNING, AND EXPERIMENTAL-LONGITUDINAL METHODS EJ 032 509
GROWTH IN READING IN AN INTEGRATED DAY CLASSROOM EJ 055 154

READING DIAGNOSIS
TITLE I AND REMEDIAL READING COMPONENTS FOR DISADVANTAGED STUDENTS EJ 053 676

READING DIFFICULTY
SOME BASIC PERCEPTUAL PROCESSES IN READING EJ 015 126
AUDITORY DISCRIMINATION ABILITIES OF DISADVANTAGED ANGLO- AND MEXICAN-AMERICAN CHILDREN EJ 015 258
READING DISABILITY AND DIFFICULTIES IN FINGER LOCALIZATION AND RIGHT-LEFT DISCRIMINATION EJ 045 083
RESEARCH IN READING RETARDATION: TWO CRITICAL PROBLEMS EJ 045 108

READING HABITS
RECOGNITION OF ENGLISH AND HEBREW LETTERS AS A FUNCTION OF AGE AND DISPLAY PREDICTABILITY EJ 047 893

READING IMPROVEMENT
AN EARLY INTERVENTION PROGRAM THAT FAILED. ED021609

READING INSTRUCTION
TEACHING READING TO CHILDREN WITH LOW MA'S. ED015020
THE INITIAL TEACHING ALPHABET AND THE WORLD OF ENGLISH. (PROCEEDINGS OF THE SECOND ANNUAL INTERNATIONAL CONFERENCE ON THE INITIAL TEACHING ALPHABET, AUGUST 18-20, 1965). ED019108
GRADE EQUIVALENT COMPARISONS BETWEEN DISADVANTAGED NEGRO URBAN CHILDREN WITH AND WITHOUT KINDERGARTEN EXPERIENCE WHEN TAUGHT TO READ BY SEVERAL METHODS. ED020798
AN EARLY INTERVENTION PROGRAM THAT FAILED. ED021609
AN EXPERIMENTAL STUDY OF FORMAL READING INSTRUCTION AT THE KINDERGARTEN LEVEL. ED022533
A TWO-YEAR LANGUAGE ARTS PROGRAM FOR PRE-FIRST GRADE CHILDREN: FIRST YEAR REPORT. ED029686
LANGUAGE EXPERIENCES WHICH PROMOTE READING. ED034571
CONFERENCE ON READING AND EARLY CHILDHOOD. ED051875
READING: AN ETERNAL DYNAMIC EJ 028 959
ORGANIZING FOR READING INSTRUCTION EJ 028 960
ON THE PSYCHOLINGUISTIC METHOD OF TEACHING READING EJ 030 547
THE CAMERA FOCUSES ON READING EJ 032 192
WRITE FIRST, READ LATER EJ 034 069
REMEDIAL READING INSTRUCTION BY TRAINED PUPIL TUTORS EJ 035 172
SOME NOTES ON STRATEGY AND CONTENT FOR ELEMENTARY READING PROGRAMS IN THE '70'S EJ 035 664
WORKING TOGETHER WORKS EJ 044 510
AUTOMATED READING INSTRUCTION IN THE GHETTO EJ 045 798
EFFECT OF REINFORCEMENT CONTINGENCIES IN INCREASING PROGRAMMED READING AND MATHEMATICS BEHAVIORS IN FIRST-GRADE CHILDREN EJ 049 168
MY MON CAN TEACH READING TOO! EJ 051 082
READING INSTRUCTION AND COGNITIVE DEVELOPMENT EJ 052 066
FOSTERING A NEED TO READ EJ 052 420
CUE SYSTEMS AVAILABLE DURING THE READING PROCESS: A PSYCHOLINGUISTIC VIEWPOINT EJ 053 399
TEACHING READING IN THE KINDERGARTEN: A REVIEW OF RECENT STUDIES EJ 055 153

READING LEVEL
ORGANIZING FOR READING INSTRUCTION EJ 028 960

READING MATERIALS
MORALS, MORALS EVERYWHERE: VALUES IN CHILDREN'S FICTION EJ 051 270
THE SUGAR-COATED WORLD OF THE THIRD-GRADE READER EJ 058 171

READING PROGRAMS
TEACHING READING TO CHILDREN WITH LOW MA'S. ED015020
GRADE EQUIVALENT COMPARISONS BETWEEN DISADVANTAGED NEGRO URBAN CHILDREN WITH AND WITHOUT KINDERGARTEN EXPERIENCE WHEN TAUGHT TO READ BY SEVERAL METHODS. ED020798
LEARNING TO READ THROUGH EXPERIENCE. SECOND EDITION. ED027067
INITIAL TEACHING ALPHABET AND TRADITIONAL ORTHOGRAPHY--THEIR IMPACT ON SPELLING AND WRITINGS EJ 016 464
PARENTS: SUMMER READING TEACHERS EJ 032 510
A METHOD OF INCREASING THE ABILITY OF FIRST GRADE PUPILS TO USE PHONETIC GENERALIZATIONS EJ 033 279
SIX SUCCESSFUL READING PROGRAMS FOR INNER-CITY SCHOOLS EJ 035 663
SOME NOTES ON STRATEGY AND CONTENT FOR ELEMENTARY READING PROGRAMS IN THE '70'S EJ 035 664
FOSTERING A NEED TO READ EJ 052 420

READING READINESS
CHILDREN WHO READ EARLY, TWO LONGITUDINAL STUDIES. ED019107
AN EXPERIMENTAL STUDY OF FORMAL READING INSTRUCTION AT THE KINDERGARTEN LEVEL. ED022533
HEAD START EVALUATION AND RESEARCH CENTER, BOSTON UNIVERSITY. REPORT D-I, LANGUAGE PROJECT: THE EFFECTS OF A TEACHER DEVELOPED PRE-SCHOOL LANGUAGE TRAINING PROGRAM ON FIRST GRADE READING ACHIEVEMENT. ED022563
AN EVALUATION OF THE INTERIM CLASS: AN EXTENDED READINESS PROGRAM. ED028820
A COMPARISON OF THE READING READINESS OF KINDERGARTEN PUPILS EXPOSED TO CONCEPTUAL-LANGUAGE AND BASAL READER PREREADING PROGRAMS. A PILOT STUDY. FINAL REPORT. ED029709
EFFECT OF A KINDERGARTEN PROGRAM OF PERCEPTUAL TRAINING UPON THE LATER DEVELOPMENT OF READING SKILLS. FINAL REPORT. ED030491
MATERNAL BEHAVIOR AND THE DEVELOPMENT OF READING READINESS IN URBAN NEGRO CHILDREN. ED031309
A COMPARISON OF READING READINESS ACHIEVEMENT OF KINDERGARTEN CHILDREN OF DISPARATE ENTRANCE AGES. ED033745
PRE-READING ON SESAME STREET. FINAL REPORT, VOLUME V OF V VOLUMES. ED047825
CLASSROOM LANGUAGE OF TEACHERS OF YOUNG CHILDREN. ED053820
L'EDUCATION PRESCOLAIRE ET L'APPRENTISSAGE DE LA LECTURE (PRE SCHOOL EDUCATION AND INTRODUCTION TO READING) EJ 010 653
AWARENESS--ONE KEY TO READING READINESS EJ 027 551
THE DEVELOPMENT OF PRE-READING SKILLS IN AN EXPERIMENTAL KINDERGARTEN PROGRAM EJ 037 099

READING READINESS TESTS
A READING READINESS TRAINING PROGRAM FOR PERCEPTUALLY HANDICAPPED KINDERGARTEN PUPILS OF NORMAL VISION. FINAL REPORT. ED013119

READING RESEARCH
THE INTERPLAY OF SOME EGO FUNCTIONS IN SIX YEAR OLD CHILDREN. ED020005
TRAINING ELEMENTARY READING SKILLS THROUGH REINFORCEMENT AND FADING TECHNIQUES. ED034583
SOME BASIC PERCEPTUAL PROCESSES IN READING EJ 015 126
THE DEVELOPMENT OF PRE-READING SKILLS IN AN EXPERIMENTAL KINDERGARTEN PROGRAM EJ 037 099
COGNITIVE STYLE AND READING ABILITY EJ 043 239
DEVELOPMENT OF VISUAL SCANNING STRATEGIES FOR DIFFERENTIATING WORDS EJ 043 703
RESEARCH IN READING RETARDATION: TWO CRITICAL PROBLEMS EJ 045 108
TEACHING READING IN THE KINDERGARTEN: A REVIEW OF RECENT STUDIES EJ 055 153
LINGUISTIC FACTORS IN READING EJ 059 537

READING SKILLS
HEAD START RESEARCH AND EVALUATION OFFICE, UNIVERSITY OF CALIFORNIA AT LOS ANGELES. APPENDIX I TO THE ANNUAL REPORT, NOVEMBER 1967. ED020793
AN EARLY INTERVENTION PROGRAM THAT FAILED. ED021609
THE EFFECTS OF STANDARD DIALECT TRAINING ON NEGRO FIRST-GRADERS LEARNING TO READ. FINAL REPORT. ED029717
SURVIVAL SKILLS AND FIRST GRADE ACADEMIC ACHIEVEMENT. REPORT #1. ED050807
PARENTS: SUMMER READING TEACHERS EJ 032 510
READING DISABILITY AND DIFFICULTIES IN FINGER LOCALIZATION AND RIGHT-LEFT DISCRIMINATION EJ 045 083
READING, WRITING, AND BLACK ENGLISH EJ 052 178

RECALL (PSYCHOLOGICAL)
DEVELOPMENTAL LEVEL AND CONCEPT-LEARNING--A REPLICATION AND EXTENSION. ED016528
CENTRAL AND INCIDENTAL LEARNING IN CHILDREN. ED023450
INDUCED VERSUS SPONTANEOUS REHEARSAL IN SHORT-TERM MEMORY IN NURSERY SCHOOL CHILDREN. STUDY M: DEVELOPMENT OF SELECTIVE ATTENTION ABILITIES. ED024444
AUDITORY COMPONENTS OF NEONATAL EXPERIENCE: A PRELIMINARY REPORT. ED025336
DISCRIMINATION OF RECENCY IN CHILDREN. FINAL REPORT. ED030493
LANGUAGE STRUCTURE AND THE FREE RECALL OF VERBAL MESSAGES BY CHILDREN. ED032933
THE ROLE OF UNDERDETERMINACY AND REFERENCE IN THE SENTENCE RECALL OF YOUNG CHILDREN. ED035449
VISUAL AND AUDITORY MEMORY IN CHILDREN. PART OF THE FINAL REPORT ON HEAD START EVALUATION AND RESEARCH: 1968-69 TO THE OFFICE OF ECONOMIC OPPORTUNITY. ED037246
VISUAL IMAGERY INSTRUCTION AND NON-ACTION VERSUS ACTION SITUATIONS RELATIVE TO RECALL BY CHILDREN. FINAL REPORT. ED050828
EFFECT OF LABELS ON MEMORY IN THE ABSENCE OF REHEARSAL. ED051883
SHORT-TERM RECOGNITION MEMORY IN CHILDREN EJ 018 873
SEMANTICS, PHRASE STRUCTURE, AND AGE AS VARIABLES IN SENTENCE RECALL EJ 025 962

THE DEVELOPMENT OF FREE CLASSIFICATION AND FREE RECALL IN CHILDREN EJ 030 293
THE RELATIONSHIP BETWEEN AUDITORY AND VISUAL SHORT-TERM MEMORY AND READING ACHIEVEMENT EJ 033 780
YOUNG CHILDREN'S USE OF THE SPEECH CODE IN A RECALL TASK EJ 033 792
DEVELOPMENT OF FREE RECALL LEARNING IN CHILDREN EJ 035 359
ASSOCIATION AND ABSTRACTION AS MECHANISMS OF IMITATIVE LEARNING EJ 035 367
FREE RECALL OF OBJECT NAMES IN PRESCHOOL CHILDREN AS A FUNCTION OF INTRACATEGORY VARIATION EJ 035 368
THE EFFECTS OF REHEARSAL AND CHUNKING INSTRUCTIONS ON CHILDREN'S MULTITRIAL FREE RECALL EJ 035 377
LEARNING, CURIOSITY, AND SOCIAL GROUP MEMBERSHIP EJ 035 378
STORY RECALL IN KINDERGARTEN CHILDREN: EFFECT OF METHOD OF PRESENTATION ON PSYCHOLINGUISTIC PERFORMANCE EJ 036 748
DEVELOPMENTAL SHIFTS IN VERBAL RECALL BETWEEN MENTAL AGES TWO AND FIVE EJ 036 825
RETENTION FOLLOWING A CHANGE IN AMBIENT CONTEXTUAL STIMULI FOR SIX AGE GROUPS EJ 039 631
FREE RECALL OF WORDS AND OBJECTS EJ 039 634
FREE RECALL AND CLUSTERING AT FOUR AGE LEVELS: EFFECTS OF LEARNING TO LEARN AND PRESENTATION METHOD EJ 039 636
DEVELOPMENT OF RETENTION AND ORGANIZATION OCCURRING IN FREE RECALL IN TURKISH CHILDREN EJ 041 133
LINGUISTIC AND THEMATIC VARIABLES IN RECALL OF A STORY BY DISADVANTAGED CHILDREN EJ 041 142
VERBAL PAIRED-ASSOCIATE LEARNING IN CHILDREN AND ADULTS WITH ANTICIPATION, RECOGNITION, AND RECALL METHODS EJ 042 959
NAMING AND MEMORY IN NURSERY SCHOOL CHILDREN IN THE ABSENCE OF REHEARSAL EJ 042 961
RECOGNITION MEMORY FOR PICTURES IN PRESCHOOL CHILDREN EJ 042 964
SELECTIVE ATTENTION IN MENTAL RETARDATES EJ 043 058
LANGUAGE STRUCTURE AND THE FREE RECALL OF VERBAL MESSAGES BY CHILDREN EJ 044 693
CHILDREN'S RECALL STRATEGIES IN DICHOTIC LISTENING EJ 044 700
ABSTRACTION, INFERENCE, AND THE PROCESS OF IMITATIVE LEARNING EJ 047 685
THE INFLUENCE OF INCENTIVES ON MEMORY STAGES IN CHILDREN EJ 049 428
WHAT THE DEVELOPMENT OF SHORT-TERM MEMORY IS EJ 049 430
THE EFFECTS OF CHRONOLOGICAL AGE, TRIALS, AND LIST CHARACTERISTICS UPON CHILDREN'S CATEGORY CLUSTERING EJ 052 454
PAIRED-ASSOCIATE LEARNING AND BIDIRECTIONAL ASSOCIATIVE RECALL IN FIRST, THIRD, FIFTH AND SEVENTH GRADERS EJ 053 481
DEVELOPMENT OF THE ABILITY TO ENCODE WITHIN EVALUATIVE DIMENSIONS EJ 053 728
THE EFFECTS OF DIFFERENT TYPES OF REINFORCEMENT ON YOUNG CHILDREN'S INCIDENTAL LEARNING EJ 053 752
MEMORY FOR RHYTHMIC SERIES: AGE CHANGES IN ACCURACY AND NUMBER CODING EJ 054 805
VARIABLES AFFECTING ASSOCIATIVE RECALL IN CHILDREN EJ 056 400
SEMANTIC INTEGRATION, AGE, AND THE RECALL OF SENTENCES EJ 056 620
CONCEPTUAL ENCODING AND CONCEPT RECALL-RECOVERY IN CHILDREN EJ 056 628
QUANTITATIVE AND QUALITATIVE ASPECTS OF MEMORY FOR PICTURE STIMULI EJ 057 907
DEVELOPMENTAL CHANGES IN CLUSTERING CRITERIA EJ 058 145
THE EFFECTS OF GROUPING ON SHORT-TERM SERIAL RECALL OF DIGITS BY CHILDREN: DEVELOPMENTAL TRENDS EJ 059 320

RECEPTIVE LANGUAGE

RECEPTIVE LANGUAGE DEVELOPMENT IN INFANCY: ISSUES AND PROBLEMS EJ 020 396

RECOGNITION

DEVELOPMENTAL LEVEL AND CONCEPT-LEARNING--A REPLICATION AND EXTENSION. ED016528
MEMORY IN THE INFANT EJ 021 760
A DEVELOPMENTAL INVESTIGATION OF THE EFFECT OF SENSORY MODALITY ON FORM RECOGNITION IN CHILDREN EJ 026 507
DEVELOPMENTAL CHANGES IN THE USE OF EMOTION CUES IN A CONCEPT-FORMATION TASK EJ 029 362
SMILING TO SOCIAL STIMULI: ELICITING AND CONDITIONING EFFECTS EJ 034 536
DISCRIMINATION OF SPATIALLY CONFUSABLE LETTERS BY YOUNG CHILDREN EJ 034 565
INFANTS' RECOGNITION MEMORY FOR A SERIES OF VISUAL STIMULI EJ 037 342
ON THE CONSERVATION OF LIQUIDS EJ 039 640
RECOGNITION MEMORY FOR PICTURES IN PRESCHOOL CHILDREN EJ 042 964
A STUDY OF RECOGNITION AND REPRODUCTION OF BENDER GESTALT FIGURES BY CHILDREN OF AVERAGE AND BELOW INTELLIGENCE EJ 043 707
EMOTIONAL SENSITIVITY AND INTELLIGENCE IN CHILDREN FROM ORPHANAGES AND NORMAL HOMES EJ 043 859
RECOGNITION MEMORY: THE RELATIONSHIP OF ACCURACY AND LATENCY OF RESPONSE UNDER DIFFERENT MEMORY LOADS IN RETARDATES EJ 046 256
RECOGNITION OF ENGLISH AND HEBREW LETTERS AS A FUNCTION OF AGE AND DISPLAY PREDICTABILITY EJ 047 893
THE RELATION OF FORM RECOGNITION TO CONCEPT DEVELOPMENT EJ 056 393
A DEVELOPMENTAL STUDY OF THE EFFECTS OF PRETRAINING ON A PERCEPTUAL RECOGNITION TASK EJ 056 630

RECREATIONAL ACTIVITIES

CHARACTERIZATION OF THE EFFECT OF SPACE, MATERIALS, AND TEACHER BEHAVIOR ON PRESCHOOL CHILDREN'S FREE PLAY ACTIVITY PATTERNS. RESEARCH REPORT NO. 1. ED037251
THE CHILD AND LEISURE TIME. 1970 WHITE HOUSE CONFERENCE ON CHILDREN, REPORT OF FORUM 21. (WORKING COPY). ED046536
A PLAY PROGRAM IN A PEDIATRIC CLINIC EJ 029 951

RECREATIONAL FACILITIES

DANISH RECREATION HOMES FOR YOUNG CHILDREN EJ 003 946
AN ADVENTURE PLAYGROUND FOR HANDICAPPED CHILDREN IN LONDON EJ 050 487

RECREATIONAL PROGRAMS

DANISH RECREATION HOMES FOR YOUNG CHILDREN EJ 003 946
RETARDED CHILDREN AT CAMP WITH NORMAL CHILDREN EJ 012 199

RECREATIONAL READING

MORALS, MORALS EVERYWHERE: VALUES IN CHILDREN'S FICTION EJ 051 270

RECRUITMENT

FACTORS INFLUENCING THE RECRUITMENT OF CHILDREN INTO THE HEAD START PROGRAM, SUMMER 1965--A CASE STUDY OF SIX CENTERS IN NEW YORK CITY. STUDY II. ED015026
STAFFING PRESCHOOLS: BACKGROUND INFORMATION. ED034589

REDUNDANCY

INFANT REACTIVITY TO REDUNDANT PROPRIOCEPTIVE AND AUDITORY STIMULATION: A TWIN STUDY. ED052825
A DECREMENTAL EFFECT OF REDUNDANCY IN DISCRIMINATION LEARNING EJ 033 795
THE EFFECTS OF STIMULUS REDUNDANCY ON TRANSFER OF STIMULUS PRETRAINING EJ 041 138

REFERENCE MATERIALS

BRINGING THEIR OWN: LANGUAGE DEVELOPMENT IN THE MIDDLE GRADES EJ 011 844

REFERRAL

REPORT OF CHILD PLACEMENT STUDY COMMITTEE, JANUARY, 1969. ED044169
HEAD START: A HEAD START TO HEALTH? EJ 036 581

REGIONAL DIALECTS

AN INVESTIGATION OF THE STANDARD-NONSTANDARD DIMENSION OF CENTRAL TEXAN ENGLISH. PART OF THE FINAL REPORT. ED026130

REHABILITATION

PROJECT TREAT: A NEW APPROACH TO THE SEVERELY DISTURBED CHILD EJ 061 000
GROUP HOME CARE AS AN ADJUNCT TO RESIDENTIAL TREATMENT EJ 061 233

REHABILITATION CENTERS

A STUDY IN CHILD CARE (CASE STUDY FROM VOLUME II-A): "CHILDREN AS 'KIDS'." DAY CARE PROGRAMS REPRINT SERIES. ED051900
NUTRITION REHABILITATION CENTRES EJ 029 953

REHABILITATION PROGRAMS

A DIFFERENTIAL USE OF GROUP HOMES FOR DELINQUENT BOYS EJ 024 028

REINFORCEMENT

AN ANNOTATED BIBLIOGRAPHY OF BEHAVIOR MODIFICATION WITH CHILDREN AND RETARDATES. ED020025
REGIONAL EVALUATION AND RESEARCH CENTER FOR HEAD START, SOUTHERN UNIVERSITY. ANNUAL REPORT. ED020792
HEAD START EVALUATION AND RESEARCH CENTER, UNIVERSITY OF KANSAS. REPORT NO. I, THE OBSERVATION OF REINFORCEMENT BEHAVIOR OF TEACHERS IN HEAD START CLASSROOMS AND THE MODIFICATION OF A TEACHER'S ATTENDING BEHAVIOR. ED021633
HEAD START EVALUATION AND RESEARCH CENTER, UNIVERSITY OF KANSAS. REPORT NO. IIB, AN EXPERIMENTAL ANALYSIS OF VERBAL IMITATION IN PRESCHOOL CHILDREN. ED021635
EXTRA-CURRICULAR PARENT-CHILD CONTACT AND CHILDREN'S SOCIALLY REINFORCED TASK BEHAVIOR. ED023447
ACADEMIC PRESCHOOL, CHAMPAIGN, ILLINOIS ED027979
INFORMATION VALUE OF FEEDBACK WITH PRESCHOOL CHILDREN. ED031311
A TOKEN REINFORCEMENT SYSTEM IN THE PUBLIC SCHOOLS. ED036323
TEACHING STYLES IN FOUR-YEAR-OLDS. ED036340

THE EFFECT OF THE REINSTEIN REINFORCEMENT SCHEDULE ON LEARNING OF SPECIFIC CONCEPTS CONTAINED IN THE BUCHANAN LANGUAGE PROGRAM. PART OF THE FINAL REPORT ON HEAD START EVALUATION AND RESEARCH: 1968-69 TO THE OFFICE OF ECONOMIC OPPORTUNITY. ED037242
THE EFFECT OF N-LENGTH ON THE DEVELOPMENT OF COOPERATIVE AND NON-COOPERATIVE BEHAVIOR IN A TWO-PERSON GAME. PART OF THE FINAL REPORT ON HEAD START EVALUATION AND RESEARCH: 1968-69 TO THE OFFICE OF ECONOMIC OPPORTUNITY. ED038172
BEHAVIORAL RESEARCH RELEVANT TO THE CLASSROOM. ED039036
CONDITIONS FOSTERING THE USE OF INFORMATION FEEDBACK BY YOUNG CHILDREN. (REVISED REPORT). ED039950
BEHAVIOR MODIFICATION PROCEDURES APPLIED TO THE ISOLATE BEHAVIOR OF A NURSERY SCHOOL CHILD. ED041635
A STUDY OF HOME ENVIRONMENT AND READINESS FOR ACHIEVEMENT AT SCHOOL. FINAL REPORT. ED041637
RISK-TAKING BEHAVIOR IN PRESCHOOL CHILDREN FROM THREE ETHNIC BACKGROUNDS. ED042486
A PROGRAM OF STIMULUS CONTROL FOR ESTABLISHING A ONE-MINUTE WAIT FOR REINFORCEMENT IN PRESCHOOL CHILDREN. PROGRESS REPORT. ED042492
EXPERIMENTAL ANALYSIS OF EFFECTS OF TEACHER ATTENTION OF PRESCHOOL CHILDREN'S BLOCK BUILDING BEHAVIOR. PROGRESS REPORT. ED042498
FIELD STUDIES OF SOCIAL REINFORCEMENT IN A PRESCHOOL. ED047772
PARENTS ARE TEACHERS: A CHILD MANAGEMENT PROGRAM. ED047826
THE VALUE OF CLASSROOM REWARDS IN EARLY EDUCATION. ED049828
LIVING WITH CHILDREN: NEW METHODS FOR PARENTS AND TEACHERS. ED051887
INTERACTION OF SEX OF SUBJECT AND DEPENDENCY-TRAINING PROCEDURES IN A SOCIAL-REINFORCEMENT STUDY EJ 006 877
ACQUISITION OF COGNITIVE RESPONSES UNDER DIFFERENT PATTERNS OF VERBAL REWARDS EJ 017 712
VICARIOUS REINFORCEMENT EFFECTS ON EXTINCTION EJ 018 325
THE DISTRACTING EFFECTS OF MATERIAL REINFORCERS IN THE DISCRIMINATION LEARNING OF LOWER- AND MIDDLE-CLASS CHILDREN EJ 018 871
WHAT IS LEARNED IN PROBABILITY LEARNING EJ 018 879
CHANGES IN FRIENDSHIP STATUS AS A FUNCTION OF REINFORCEMENT EJ 019 004
MAGNITUDE-PROBABILITY PREFERENCES OF PRESCHOOL CHILDREN FROM TWO SOCIOECONOMIC LEVELS EJ 019 017
BEHAVIORAL COUNSELING FOR ELEMENTARY-SCHOOL CHILDREN EJ 019 669
INTERACTIVE EFFECTS OF INFORMATIONAL AND AFFECTIVE COMPONENTS OF SOCIAL AND NONSOCIAL REINFORCERS ON INDEPENDENT AND DEPENDENT CHILDREN EJ 022 141
THE INFLUENCE OF DIFFERENT RESPONSE CONSEQUENCES ON CHILDREN'S PREFERENCE FOR TIME-OUT EJ 022 213
GENERALIZATION OF ADULT'S STIMULUS CONTROL OF CHILDREN'S BEHAVIOR EJ 022 214
IMITATION OF AN ANIMATED PUPPET AS A FUNCTION OF MODELING, PRAISE, AND DIRECTIONS EJ 024 693
VISUAL ORIENTATION IN CHILDREN'S DISCRIMINATION LEARNING UNDER CONSTANT, VARIABLE, AND COVARIABLE DELAY OF REINFORCEMENT EJ 024 696
TRANSFER OF MATCHING AND MISMATCHING BEHAVIOR IN PRESCHOOL CHILDREN EJ 024 701
MOTIVATIONAL EFFECTS OF PRAISE AND CRITICISM ON CHILDREN'S LEARNING EJ 024 702
INSTRUMENTAL PERFORMANCE AS A FUNCTION OF REINFORCEMENT SCHEDULE, LUCK VERSUS SKILL INSTRUCTIONS, AND SEX OF CHILD EJ 024 934
EFFECTS OF REINFORCEMENT HISTORY ON TIMING (DRL) PERFORMANCE IN YOUNG CHILDREN EJ 024 936
SELF-REINFORCEMENT VERSUS EXTERNAL REINFORCEMENT IN BEHAVIOR MODIFICATION WITH CHILDREN EJ 024 947
INTERACTION OF REWARD, PUNISHMENT, AND SEX IN A TWO-CHOICE DISCRIMINATION TASK WITH CHILDREN EJ 024 948
THE EFFECT OF INFORMATIVE FEEDBACK ON PROBLEM SOLVING EJ 025 961
PROBABILITY LEARNING AS A FUNCTION OF SEX OF THE SUBJECT, TEST ANXIETY, AND PERCENTAGE OF REINFORCEMENT EJ 027 181
THE APPLICATION OF PREMACK'S GENERALIZATION ON REINFORCEMENT TO THE MANAGEMENT OF CLASSROOM BEHAVIOR EJ 028 634
RECENCY AND SUMMATION EFFECTS OF NONREWARD IN CHILDREN EJ 028 895
SUB-PROFESSIONAL BEHAVIOR MODIFICATION AND THE DEVELOPMENT OF TOKEN-REINFORCEMENT SYSTEMS IN INCREASING ACADEMIC MOTIVATION AND ACHIEVEMENT EJ 034 527
DELAY OF GRATIFICATION AND INTERNAL VERSUS EXTERNAL CONTROL AMONG ADOLESCENTS OF LOW SOCIOECONOMIC STATUS EJ 034 539
CHAOTIC REINFORCEMENT: A SOCIOECONOMIC LEVELER EJ 035 371
CUE AND INCENTIVE MOTIVATIONAL PROPERTIES OF REINFORCERS IN CHILDREN'S DISCRIMINATION LEARNING EJ 035 374
LANGUAGE DIALECT, REINFORCEMENT, AND THE INTELLIGENCE-TEST PERFORMANCE OF NEGRO CHILDREN EJ 035 912
DELAYED REINFORCEMENT AND VOCALIZATION RATES OF INFANTS EJ 036 127
CHILDREN'S ACQUISITION AND REVERSAL BEHAVIOR IN A PROBABILITY LEARNING SITUATION AS A FUNCTION OF PROGRAMMED INSTRUCTION, INTERNAL-EXTERNAL CONTROL, AND SCHEDULES OF REINFORCEMENT EJ 037 495
GENERALIZED IMITATION AS A FUNCTION OF DISCRIMINATION DIFFICULTY AND CHOICE EJ 038 455
THE DISCRIMINATION LEARNING OF NORMAL AND RETARDED CHILDREN AS A FUNCTION OF PENALTY CONDITIONS AND ETIOLOGY OF THE RETARDED EJ 041 136
THE EFFECTS OF REWARD AND PUNISHMENT UPON CHILDREN'S ATTENTION, MOTIVATION, AND DISCRIMINATION LEARNING EJ 041 137
EFFECTS OF CONTINGENT AND NONCONTINGENT REINFORCEMENT UPON GENERALIZED IMITATION EJ 041 448
VERBAL OPERANT CONDITIONING OF AN ACTIVE-NON-ACTIVE VERBAL DIFFERENTIAL IN EARLY SCHOOL CHILDREN EJ 041 451
FACTORS INFLUENCING CHILDREN'S CONCEPT IDENTIFICATION PERFORMANCE WITH NONPREFERRED RELEVANT ATTRIBUTES EJ 042 965
THE CONTROL OF IMITATIVE AND NONIMITATIVE BEHAVIORS IN SEVERELY RETARDED CHILDREN THROUGH "GENERALIZED-INSTRUCTION FOLLOWING" EJ 043 196
SATIATION OF VISUAL REINFORCEMENT IN YOUNG INFANTS EJ 043 666
DISCRIMINATION AND INSTRUCTIONS AS FACTORS IN THE CONTROL OF NONREINFORCED IMITATION EJ 044 157
CONDITIONS GOVERNING NONREINFORCED IMITATION EJ 045 042
GENERALIZED IMITATION: THE EFFECTS OF EXPERIMENTER ABSENCE, DIFFERENTIAL REINFORCEMENT, AND STIMULUS COMPLEXITY EJ 045 044
SELF-PARENTAL DISTANCE, CONTROL OF REINFORCEMENT, AND PERSONAL FUTURE TIME PERSPECTIVE EJ 045 047
CHILD EFFECTS ON ADULT BEHAVIOR EJ 045 107
THE INCENTIVE VALUE OF UNCERTAINTY REDUCTION FOR CHILDREN EJ 045 454
EFFECTS OF SPATIAL SEPARATION OF STIMULUS, RESPONSE, AND REWARD IN DISCRIMINATION LEARNING BY CHILDREN EJ 046 243
THE ROLE OF REINFORCEMENT PROCEDURE IN CHILDREN'S PROBABILITY LEARNING AS A FUNCTION OF AGE AND NUMBER OF RESPONSE ALTERNATIVES EJ 046 253
EFFECTS OF IMITATION OF DIFFERENT REINFORCEMENT COMBINATIONS TO A MODEL EJ 046 255
SELF-INITIATED VERBAL REINFORCEMENT AND POSITIVE SELF-CONCEPT EJ 052 462
DISCRIMINATION LEARNING BY REFLECTIVE AND IMPULSIVE CHILDREN AS A FUNCTION OF REINFORCEMENT SCHEDULE EJ 053 717
MODIFICATION OF FORM AND COLOR RESPONDING IN YOUNG CHILDREN AS A FUNCTION OF DIFFERENTIAL REINFORCEMENT EJ 053 723
DO MATERIAL REWARDS ENHANCE THE PERFORMANCE OF LOWER-CLASS CHILDREN? EJ 053 735
THE EFFECTS OF DIFFERENT TYPES OF REINFORCEMENT ON YOUNG CHILDREN'S INCIDENTAL LEARNING EJ 053 752
EVALUATION DIMENSION OF THE AFFECTIVE MEANING SYSTEM OF THE PRESCHOOL CHILD EJ 054 049
SEX DIFFERENCES IN PERFORMANCE AS A FUNCTION OF PRAISE AND BLAME EJ 055 098
THE EFFECTS OF DIFFERENTIAL REINFORCEMENT ON THE DISCRIMINATION LEARNING OF NORMAL AND LOW-ACHIEVING MIDDLE-CLASS BOYS EJ 056 398
MODEL AFFECT AND CHILDREN'S IMITATIVE ALTRUISM EJ 056 719
EFFECTS OF SOCIOECONOMIC STATUS AND THE VALUE OF A REINFORCER UPON SELF-REINFORCEMENT BY CHILDREN EJ 056 726
VERBAL AND NONVERBAL REWARDS AND PUNISHMENT IN THE DISCRIMINATION LEARNING OF CHILDREN OF VARYING SOCIOECONOMIC STATUS EJ 057 896
PERSEVERATION AND ALTERNATION PRETRAINING AND BINARY PREDICTION EJ 057 902
EFFECTS OF VICARIOUS CONSEQUENCES AND RACE OF MODEL UPON IMITATIVE PERFORMANCE BY BLACK CHILDREN EJ 058 139
MALE AND FEMALE AUDITORY REINFORCEMENT OF INFANT VOCALIZATIONS EJ 058 217
NONSOCIAL REINFORCEMENT OF INFANTS' VOCALIZATIONS EJ 058 219
FEMINIZATION IN PRESCHOOL EJ 059 872
ATTENTION SPAN AND GENERALIZATION OF TASK-RELATED STIMULUS CONTROL: EFFECTS OF REINFORCEMENT CONTINGENCIES EJ 059 878

REINFORCERS

BEHAVIOR MODIFICATION OF AN ADJUSTMENT CLASS: A TOKEN REINFORCEMENT PROGRAM. ED023462
PARENTS ARE TEACHERS: A CHILD MANAGEMENT PROGRAM. ED047826
SELF-REINFORCEMENT ESTABLISHED FOR A DISCRIMINATION TASK EJ 025 964
MEANING AND ATTENTION AS DETERMINANTS OF SOCIAL REINFORCER EFFECTIVENESS EJ 033 781
THE SYSTEMATIC USE OF THE PEMACK PRINCIPLE IN MODIFYING CLASSROOM BEHAVIORS EJ 034 528
COMPARISONS OF VOCAL IMITATION, TACTILE STIMULATION, AND FOOD AS REINFORCERS FOR INFANT VOCALIZATIONS EJ 055 206

RELATIONSHIP
THE RELATIONSHIPS BETWEEN CERTAIN TEACHER CHARACTERISTICS AND ACHIEVEMENT AND CREATIVITY OF GIFTED ELEMENTARY SCHOOL STUDENTS. FINAL REPORT SUMMARY. ED015787
PERCEPTUAL MODE DOMINANCE: AN APPROACH TO ASSESSMENT OF FIRST GRADE READING AND SPELLING. ED026132
BEHAVIORAL DATA FROM THE TULANE NUTRITION STUDY. ED043375
RELATION OF TYPE AND ONSET OF FATHER ABSENCE TO COGNITIVE DEVELOPMENT EJ 058 695

RELEVANCE (EDUCATION)
THE EFFECTS OF PSYCHOSOCIAL DEPRIVATION ON HUMAN DEVELOPMENT IN INFANCY EJ 026 815
TOWARDS AN INDIAN PHILOSOPHY OF PRIMARY EDUCATION EJ 036 337
THE WORLD HOUSE: BUILDING A QUALITATIVE ENVIRONMENT FOR ALL THE WORLD'S CHILDREN EJ 037 736
A GEOMETRIC REPRESENTATION OF THE NOTIONS OF RELIABILITY, RELEVANCE, AND VALIDITY EJ 043 456
CONTRIBUTIONS OF CRITICISM TO PARENT, FAMILY-LIFE AND SEX EDUCATION EJ 054 381
CHILD WELFARE: SEARCHING FOR RELEVANT LEARNING ON THE UNDERGRADUATE LEVEL EJ 056 762

RELEVANCE (INFORMATION RETRIEVAL)
SELECTIVE STRATEGIES IN CHILDREN'S ATTENTION TO TASK-RELEVANT INFORMATION EJ 055 537

RELIABILITY
RELIABILITY ASSESSMENT OF OBSERVATION DATA: A POSSIBLE METHODOLOGICAL PROBLEM EJ 033 313
A BEHAVIOURAL SCREENING QUESTIONNAIRE FOR USE WITH THREE-YEAR-OLD CHILDREN. PRELIMINARY FINDINGS EJ 042 349
WHAT'S THROWN OUT WITH THE BATH WATER: A BABY? EJ 052 445
LOCUS OF CONTROL: AN EXAMPLE OF DANGERS IN USING CHILDREN'S SCALES WITH CHILDREN EJ 058 929

RELIGIOUS EDUCATION
PROCEEDINGS OF THE ANNUAL CONVENTION OF THE CHRISTIAN ASSOCIATION FOR PSYCHOLOGICAL STUDIES ON THE DYNAMICS OF LEARNING CHRISTIAN CONCEPTS (12TH, GRAND RAPIDS, MICHIGAN, MARCH 31-APRIL 1, 1965). ED023476

REMEDIAL MATHEMATICS
A PILOT STUDY OF COMPUTER-ASSISTED DRILL AND PRACTICE IN SEVENTH GRADE REMEDIAL MATHEMATICS EJ 027 030

REMEDIAL PROGRAMS
COVERT PROJECT, YEAR 1. ED019137
[THE JUNIPER GARDENS CHILDREN'S PROJECT.] FINAL PROGRESS REPORT FOR OEO GRANT CG-8180. ED027947
MINIMAL BRAIN DAMAGE: A MEANINGFUL DIAGNOSIS OR AN IRRELEVANT LABEL? EJ 018 707

REMEDIAL READING
FOR BETTER READING - A MORE POSITIVE SELF-IMAGE EJ 013 562
REMEDIAL READING INSTRUCTION BY TRAINED PUPIL TUTORS EJ 035 172

REMEDIAL READING PROGRAMS
TAKE A GIANT STEP --A REMEDIAL PROGRAM IN A CAMP SETTING EJ 020 773
MY MON CAN TEACH READING TOO! EJ 051 082
TITLE I AND REMEDIAL READING COMPONENTS FOR DISADVANTAGED STUDENTS EJ 053 676

RESEARCH
A DIGEST OF THE RESEARCH ACTIVITIES OF REGIONAL EVALUATION AND RESEARCH CENTERS FOR PROJECT HEAD START (SEPTEMBER 1, 1966 TO NOVEMBER 30, 1967). ED023446
PROMISING DIRECTIONS FOR RESEARCH AND DEVELOPMENT IN EARLY CHILDHOOD EDUCATION. ED023448
BIBLIOGRAPHY OF RESEARCH STUDIES IN ELEMENTARY SCHOOL AND PRE-SCHOOL MATHEMATICS. ED023464
HEAD START CRIB. CHILDHOOD RESEARCH INFORMATION BULLETIN: SELECTED RESUMES OF EARLY CHILDHOOD RESEARCH REPORTS. BULLETIN NO. 1. ED025318
THE PROGRAM OF RESEARCH OF THE MERRILL-PALMER INSTITUTE IN CONJUNCTION WITH THE HEAD START EVALUATION AND RESEARCH CENTER, MICHIGAN STATE UNIVERSITY. ANNUAL REPORT. VOLUME II: RESEARCH. ED027088
THE EFFECTS OF MODE OF PRESENTATION AND NUMBER OF CATEGORIES ON 4-YEAR-OLDS' PROPORTION ESTIMATES. ED032132
RESEARCH FOR SERVICE TO SEVERELY RETARDED CHILDREN EJ 038 531
HANDWRITING: THE STATE OF THE CRAFT EJ 048 999
A REPORT ON EVALUATION STUDIES OF PROJECT HEAD START EJ 049 896
WHAT DOES RESEARCH TEACH US ABOUT DAY CARE: FOR CHILDREN UNDER THREE EJ 051 236
WHAT DOES RESEARCH TEACH US ABOUT DAY CARE: FOR CHILDREN OVER THREE EJ 051 237
EXPLORATORY AND PLAY BEHAVIORS OF INFANTS REARED IN AN INSTITUTION AND IN LOWER- AND MIDDLE-CLASS HOMES EJ 052 441
WHAT'S THROWN OUT WITH THE BATH WATER: A BABY? EJ 052 445
THE DEVELOPMENT OF SOME INTENTION CONCEPTS IN YOUNG CHILDREN EJ 052 452
THE CONCEPT OF DEATH IN EARLY CHILDHOOD EJ 052 464
"OPENNESS" OF SCHOOL CLIMATE AND ALIENATION OF HIGH SCHOOL STUDENTS EJ 052 654
PAIRED-ASSOCIATE LEARNING AND BIDIRECTIONAL ASSOCIATIVE RECALL IN FIRST, THIRD, FIFTH AND SEVENTH GRADERS EJ 053 481
COGNITIVE STYLE: METHODOLOGICAL AND DEVELOPMENTAL CONSIDERATIONS EJ 053 482
ACQUIRED DISTINCTIVENESS AND EQUIVALENCE OF CUES IN YOUNG CHILDREN EJ 053 654
ACQUISITION OF CONSERVATION THROUGH SOCIAL INTERACTION EJ 053 708
THE UNSUPERVISED CHILD OF THE WORKING MOTHER EJ 053 709
EFFECT OF OVERT VERBAL LABELING ON SHORT-TERM MEMORY IN CULTURALLY DEPRIVED AND NONDEPRIVED CHILDREN EJ 053 710
EFFECT OF A CHILD'S SEX ON ADULT INTERPRETATIONS OF ITS BEHAVIOR EJ 053 711
EFFECTS OF RATE OF STIMULUS PRESENTATION AND PENALTY CONDITIONS ON THE DISCRIMINATION LEARNING OF NORMAL AND RETARDED CHILDREN EJ 053 712
RACE, SOCIAL CLASS, AND AGE OF ACHIEVEMENT OF CONSERVATION ON PIAGET'S TASKS EJ 053 714
THE DEVELOPMENT OF MEMORY-ENCODING PROCESSES IN YOUNG CHILDREN EJ 053 716
DISCRIMINATION LEARNING BY REFLECTIVE AND IMPULSIVE CHILDREN AS A FUNCTION OF REINFORCEMENT SCHEDULE EJ 053 717
AVOIDANCE CONDITIONING IN YOUNG CHILDREN WITH INTERRUPTION OF A POSITIVE STIMULUS AS THE AVERSIVE EVENT EJ 053 719
NONVERBAL INFORMATION STORAGE IN CHILDREN AND DEVELOPMENTAL INFORMATION PROCESSING CHANNEL CAPACITY EJ 053 720
EFFECTS OF HEBREW AND ENGLISH LETTERS ON CHILDREN'S PERCEPTUAL SET EJ 053 721
TRANSFER OF TRAINING: SOME BOUNDARY CONDITIONS AND INITIAL THEORY EJ 053 722
MODIFICATION OF FORM AND COLOR RESPONDING IN YOUNG CHILDREN AS A FUNCTION OF DIFFERENTIAL REINFORCEMENT EJ 053 723
MEANINGFULNESS, SERIAL POSITION AND RETENTION INTERVAL IN RECOGNITION SHORT-TERM MEMORY EJ 053 724
AGE, ICONIC STORAGE, AND VISUAL INFORMATION PROCESSING EJ 053 725
CONCEPT ATTAINMENT, GENERALIZATION, AND RETENTION THROUGH OBSERVATION AND VERBAL CODING EJ 053 726
DEVELOPMENT OF THE ABILITY TO ENCODE WITHIN EVALUATIVE DIMENSIONS EJ 053 728
PRIMACY IN PRESCHOOLERS' SHORT-TERM MEMORY: THE EFFECTS OF REPEATED TESTS AND SHIFT TRIALS EJ 053 729
EFFECTS OF AGE, SEX, SYSTEMATIC CONCEPTUAL LEARNING, ACQUISITION OF LEARNING SETS, AND PROGRAMMED SOCIAL INTERACTION ON THE INTELLECTUAL AND CONCEPTUAL DEVELOPMENT OF PRESCHOOL CHILDREN FROM POVERTY BACKGROUNDS EJ 053 733
FAMILY INTERACTION VARIABLES AND ADJUSTMENT OF NONCLINIC BOYS EJ 053 737
DEVELOPMENTAL DIFFERENCES IN THE FIELD OF VIEW DURING TACHISTOSCOPIC PRESENTATION EJ 053 743
THE EFFECTS OF DIFFERENT TYPES OF REINFORCEMENT ON YOUNG CHILDREN'S INCIDENTAL LEARNING EJ 053 752
FAMILY FACTORS RELATED TO COMPETENCE IN YOUNG DISADVANTAGED MEXICAN-AMERICAN CHILDREN EJ 053 753
OBSERVING BEHAVIOR AND CHILDREN'S DISCRIMINATION LEARNING EJ 053 754
CROSS-MODAL MATCHING AMONG NORMAL AND RETARDED CHILDREN EJ 053 755
EFFECTS OF TYPE AND SOURCE OF LABELS ON CHILDREN'S PERCEPTUAL JUDGMENTS AND DISCRIMINATION LEARNING EJ 053 756
THE ROLE OF BODY PARTS AND READINESS IN ACQUISITION OF NUMBER CONSERVATION EJ 053 757
RACIAL FACTORS IN TEST PERFORMANCE EJ 053 887
RELATION BETWEEN IDENTITY CONSERVATION AND EQUIVALENCE CONSERVATION WITHIN FOUR CONCEPTUAL DOMAINS EJ 054 804
DISCRIMINATION LEARNING AND TRANSFER OF TRAINING IN THE AGED EJ 055 204
PEER INTERACTION AND COGNITIVE DEVELOPMENT EJ 056 708
COMPARISON OF IMITATION AND COMPREHENSION SCORES BETWEEN TWO LOWER-CLASS GROUPS AND THE EFFECTS OF TWO WARM-UP CONDITIONS ON IMITATION OF THE SAME GROUPS EJ 056 709
USE OF LABELS AND CUES IN CHILDREN'S CONCEPT IDENTIFICATION EJ 056 712
THE YOUNG CHILD'S COMPREHENSION OF TIME CONNECTIVES EJ 056 724

RESEARCH AND DEVELOPMENT CENTERS
A PRELIMINARY INVESTIGATION TO ESTABLISH A REGIONAL CENTER FOR EDUCATIONAL DEVELOPMENTAL STUDIES OF DISADVANTAGED PRESCHOOL CHILDREN. FINAL REPORT. ED017318

RESEARCH APPRENTICESHIPS
CHILD DEVELOPMENT RESEARCH UNIT PROGRESS REPORT, FEBRUARY, 1970. ED049819

RESEARCH COMMITTEES
VIEWPOINT: GAP AND THE JOINT COMMISSION ON MENTAL HEALTH OF CHILDREN EJ 060 203

RESEARCH CRITERIA
ABOUT RESEARCH: PART I, THE NATURE OF RESEARCH... CHANGING EMPHASES EJ 027 435
CONSIDERATIONS FOR THE STUDY OF LANGUAGE IN YOUNG LOW-INCOME MINORITY GROUP CHILDREN EJ 052 440

RESEARCH DESIGN
PROBLEMS OF EDUCATIONAL EVALUATION IN PROJECT HEAD START--SAMPLING, DESIGN, AND CONTROL GROUPS. ED015793
DESIGN FOR A PLAYROOM. ED019133
CHILD REARING. AN INQUIRY INTO RESEARCH AND METHODS. ED036344
THE DEVELOPMENT OF TEMPORAL DISCRIMINATION IN YOUNG CHILDREN. ED045187
DESIGNS AND PROPOSAL FOR EARLY CHILDHOOD RESEARCH: A NEW LOOK: A MULTIPLE SYSTEMS-SERVICE APPROACH TO PROGRAMS AND RESEARCH FOR HELPING POOR CHILDREN. (ONE IN A SERIES OF SIX PAPERS). ED053806
DESIGNS AND PROPOSAL FOR EARLY CHILDHOOD RESEARCH: A NEW LOOK: ON ATTAINING THE GOALS OF EARLY CHILDHOOD EDUCATION. (ONE IN A SERIES OF SIX PAPERS). ED053807
DESIGNS AND PROPOSAL FOR EARLY CHILDHOOD RESEARCH: A NEW LOOK: PRESCHOOL RESEARCH AND PRESCHOOL EDUCATIONAL OBJECTIVES ED053808
DESIGNS AND PROPOSAL FOR EARLY CHILDHOOD RESEARCH: A NEW LOOK: A SYSTEMS APPROACH TO PRE-SCHOOL EDUCATION. (ONE IN A SERIES OF SIX PAPERS). ED053809
DESIGNS AND PROPOSAL FOR EARLY CHILDHOOD RESEARCH: A NEW LOOK: THE UNACKNOWLEDGED ROLE OF CULTURE CONFLICT IN NEGRO EDUCATION. (ONE IN A SERIES OF SIX PAPERS). ED053810
DESIGNS AND PROPOSAL FOR EARLY CHILDHOOD RESEARCH: A NEW LOOK: MALNUTRITION, LEARNING AND INTELLIGENCE. (ONE IN A SERIES OF SIX PAPERS). ED053811
CLASSROOM LANGUAGE OF TEACHERS OF YOUNG CHILDREN. ED053820
AN AGE-IRRELEVANT CONCEPT OF DEVELOPMENT EJ 027 437
AN ORGANISM ORIENTED CONCEPT OF DEVELOPMENT EJ 027 438

RESEARCH METHODOLOGY
MEMO--COMMENTS ON THE WOLFF AND STEIN STUDY. ED015029
REMARKS ON THE MAX WOLFF REPORT. ED015030
PROBLEMS OF EDUCATIONAL EVALUATION IN PROJECT HEAD START--SAMPLING, DESIGN, AND CONTROL GROUPS. ED015793
FINAL REPORT ON HEAD START EVALUATION AND RESEARCH--1966-67 TO THE INSTITUTE FOR EDUCATIONAL DEVELOPMENT. SECTION II, ON THE INTERPRETATION OF MULTIVARIATE SYSTEMS. ED019118
METHODOLIGICAL CONSIDERATIONS IN DEVISING HEAD START PROGRAM EVALUATIONS. ED025319
CATEGORIES AND UNDERLYING PROCESSES, OR REPRESENTATIVE BEHAVIOR SAMPLES AND S-R ANALYSIS: OPPOSING STRATEGIES. ED032120
CHILD REARING. AN INQUIRY INTO RESEARCH AND METHODS. ED036344
A DISCUSSION OF RESEARCH AIMS AND STRATEGIES FOR STUDYING EDUCATION IN THE INNER-CITY (A CRITIQUE OF NON-PARTICIPANT OBSERVATIONS). PRELIMINARY DRAFT. ED038187
RESEARCH, CHANGE, AND SOCIAL RESPONSIBILITY: STUDIES OF THE IMPRINT OF THE LOW-INCOME HOME ON YOUNG CHILDREN. ED039935
THE SAMPLE: OPERATIONS IN THE HEAD START YEAR. ED043391
FROM THEORY TO OPERATIONS. DISADVANTAGED CHILDREN AND THEIR FIRST SCHOOL EXPERIENCES, ETS-HEAD START LONGITUDINAL STUDY. ED043397
MODELS, NORMS AND SHARING. ED046512
LEARNING BY DISCOVERY: A REVIEW OF THE RESEARCH METHODOLOGY. REPORT FROM THE PROJECT ON VARIABLES AND PROCESSES IN COGNITIVE LEARNING. ED053793
APPLICATION OF MARKOV PROCESSES TO THE CONCEPT OF STATE. ED053813
LEVELS OF CONCEPTUAL ANALYSIS IN ENVIRONMENT-INFANT INTERACTION RESEARCH EJ 004 044
CALIFORNIA ADVISORY COUNCIL ON EDUCATIONAL RESEARCH SUGGESTED POLICY ON EDUCATIONAL RESEARCH FOR CALIFORNIA SCHOOL DISTRICTS EJ 018 016
CONCEPT LEARNING IN DISCRIMINATION TASKS EJ 018 878
ON RELATING AN INFANT'S OBSERVATION TIME OF VISUAL STIMULI WITH CHOICE-THEORY ANALYSIS EJ 019 016
PERSPECTIVE ON THE JENSEN AFFAIR EJ 020 519
RESEARCH STRATEGIES AND CONCEPTS OF DEVELOPMENT AND LEARNING. INTRODUCTION EJ 027 436
A METHODOLOGY FOR CONDUCTING AN EXPERIMENTAL ANALYSIS OF CHEATING BEHAVIOR EJ 030 589
ESTIMATION OF LINE LENGTH AND NUMBER: A DEVELOPMENTAL STUDY EJ 030 590
YOUNG CHILDREN'S USE OF THE SPEECH CODE IN A RECALL TASK EJ 033 792
THE ABILITY OF PERSONALITY VARIABLES IN DISCRIMINATING AMONG THREE INTELLECTUAL GROUPS OF PREADOLESCENT BOYS AND GIRLS EJ 034 044
THE MEASUREMENT OF VISUAL ATTENTION IN INFANTS: A COMPARISON OF TWO METHODOLOGIES EJ 037 494
A NONVERBAL TECHNIQUE FOR STUDYING MUSIC PREFERENCE EJ 043 285
AN AUDITORY PROMPTING DEVICE FOR BEHAVIOR OBSERVATION EJ 043 316
AGE CHANGES IN CARDIAC DECELERATION WITHIN A FIXED FOREPERIOD REACTION-TIME TASK: AN INDEX OF ATTENTION EJ 043 667
METHODOLOGICAL STUDY OF FORM CONSTANCY DEVELOPMENT EJ 043 706
A CHECK ON THE STRUCTURE OF PARENTAL REPORTS OF CHILD-REARING PRACTICES EJ 045 388
EXPLORATION OF DEVELOPMENTAL VARIABLES BY MANIPULATION AND SIMULATION OF AGE DIFFERENCES IN BEHAVIOR EJ 048 472
SEX DIFFERENCES IN BEHAVIOURAL IMPULSIVITY, INTELLECTUAL IMPULSIVITY, AND ATTAINMENT IN YOUNG CHILDREN EJ 051 151
PSYCHIATRIC DISORDER IN THE CHILDREN OF CARIBBEAN IMMIGRANTS EJ 051 152
THE HISTORY OF LONGITUDINAL RESEARCH: IMPLICATIONS FOR THE FUTURE EJ 051 779
HELPING BEHAVIOR AMONG NORMAL AND RETARDED CHILDREN EJ 052 442
LEARNING TO BE GENEROUS OR STINGY: IMITATION OF SHARING BEHAVIOR AS A FUNCTION OF MODEL GENEROSITY AND VICARIOUS REINFORCEMENT EJ 052 443
CHILDREN'S JUDGMENTS OF AGE EJ 052 461
STEADY-STATE BEHAVIOR IN CHILDREN: A METHOD AND SOME DATA EJ 053 730
DIALECT, RACE, AND LANGUAGE PROFICIENCY: ANOTHER DEAD HEAT ON THE MERRY-GO-ROUND EJ 053 747
THE ROLE OF LIGHTNESS CONTRAST IN DETERMINING THE MAGNITUDE OF THE DELBOEUF ILLUSION: A REJOINDER TO WEINTRAUB AND COOPER EJ 055 101
MULTIDIMENSIONAL SCALING OF DIMENSIONAL PREFERENCES: A METHODOLOGICAL STUDY EJ 056 609
A DEVELOPMENTAL STUDY OF FREE CLASSIFICATION IN CHILDREN EJ 056 730
CREATIVITY: IDEA QUANTITY AND IDEA QUALITY EJ 058 212
CHARITY IN CHILDREN: THE INFLUENCE OF "CHARITY" STIMULI AND AN AUDIENCE EJ 058 224
DEVELOPMENTAL CHANGE IN INFANT VISUAL FIXATION TO DIFFERING COMPLEXITY LEVELS AMONG CROSS-SECTIONALLY AND LONGITUDINALLY STUDIED INFANTS EJ 061 141
AN INFANT CONTROL PROCEDURE FOR STUDYING INFANT VISUAL FIXATIONS EJ 061 142

RESEARCH NEEDS
AN OVERVIEW OF RESEARCH IN LEARNING, MOTIVATION, AND PERCEPTION. ED020799
PROMISING DIRECTIONS FOR RESEARCH AND DEVELOPMENT IN EARLY CHILDHOOD EDUCATION. ED023448
SOME STUDIES OF THE MORAL DEVELOPMENT OF CHILDREN. ED024445
LEARNING IN INFANTS. ED024446
CHILD PSYCHIATRY: THE PAST QUARTER CENTURY. ED027951
RESEARCH ISSUES IN THE HEALTH AND NUTRITION IN EARLY CHILDHOOD. ED027970
THE EFFECTS OF PSYCHOSOCIAL DEPRIVATION ON HUMAN DEVELOPMENT IN INFANCY. ED034574
THE TEACHER, TEACHER STYLE, AND CLASSROOM MANAGEMENT. PROCEEDINGS OF THE HEAD START RESEARCH SEMINARS: SEMINAR NO. 2, THE TEACHER AND CLASSROOM MANAGEMENT (1ST, WASHINGTON, D.C., JULY 22, 1968). ED035463
EVALUATION OF EDUCATIONAL PROGRAMS AS RESEARCH ON EDUCATIONAL PROCESS. ED038165
EARLY CHILDHOOD EDUCATION AS A DISCIPLINE. ED043396
KEY ISSUES IN INFANT MORTALITY. ED045208
EARLY CHILDHOOD EDUCATION AS A DISCIPLINE EJ 029 617
TRENDS AND DILEMMAS IN CHILD WELFARE RESEARCH EJ 038 571

RESEARCH PROBLEMS
NATURALISTIC OBSERVATION IN THE STUDY OF PARENT-CHILD INTERACTION. ED027073
CATEGORIES AND UNDERLYING PROCESSES, OR REPRESENTATIVE BEHAVIOR SAMPLES AND S-R ANALYSIS: OPPOSING STRATEGIES. ED032120
SELECTED LONGITUDINAL STUDIES OF COMPENSATORY EDUCATION--A LOOK FROM THE INSIDE. ED033762
THE EFFECTS OF PSYCHOSOCIAL DEPRIVATION ON HUMAN DEVELOPMENT IN INFANCY. ED034574
A DISCUSSION OF RESEARCH AIMS AND STRATEGIES FOR STUDYING EDUCATION IN THE INNER-CITY (A CRITIQUE OF NON-PARTICIPANT OBSERVATIONS). PRELIMINARY DRAFT. ED038187
RESEARCH IN A BLACK COMMUNITY: FOUR YEARS IN REVIEW. ED039035

A COMPARATIVE STUDY OF THE IMPACT OF TWO CONTRASTING EDUCATIONAL APPROACHES IN HEAD START, 1968-69. ED041643
STATE AS VARIABLE, AS OBSTACLE AND AS MEDIATOR OF STIMULATION IN INFANT RESEARCH. ED049825
MEASURING DIFFERENTIAL DEVELOPMENT IN YOUNG CHILDREN. ED050818
WHAT'S THROWN OUT WITH THE BATH WATER: A BABY? ED053801
LEVELS OF CONCEPTUAL ANALYSIS IN ENVIRONMENT-INFANT INTERACTION RESEARCH EJ 004 044
CHILD DEVELOPMENT RESEARCH: AN EDIFICE WITHOUT A FOUNDATION EJ 004 045
INFORMED CONSENT IN PEDIATRIC RESEARCH EJ 007 413
A METHODOLOGICAL AND PHILOSOPHICAL CRITIQUE OF INTERVENTION-ORIENTED RESEARCH EJ 019 323
DEFICITS AND VALUE JUDGMENTS: A COMMENT ON SROUFE'S CRITIQUE EJ 019 324
EDUCATIONAL EVALUATION AS RESEARCH FOR PROGRAM IMPROVEMENT EJ 021 380
COGNITIVE SYNTHESIS, CONSERVATION, AND TASK ANALYSIS EJ 021 768
TERMINOLOGY AND METHODOLOGY RELATED TO THE USE OF HEART RATE RESPONSIVITY IN INFANCY RESEARCH EJ 034 566
TRENDS AND DILEMMAS IN CHILD WELFARE RESEARCH EJ 038 571
INCENTIVE PREFERENCE AND RESISTANCE TO TEMPTATION EJ 041 631
RESEARCH IN READING RETARDATION: TWO CRITICAL PROBLEMS EJ 045 108
LOCUS OF CONTROL: AN EXAMPLE OF DANGERS IN USING CHILDREN'S SCALES WITH CHILDREN EJ 058 929

RESEARCH PROJECTS
SOCIAL AND EMOTIONAL BEHAVIOR IN INFANCY--SOME DEVELOPMENTAL ISSUES AND PROBLEMS. ED015789
FINAL REPORT ON HEAD START EVALUATION AND RESEARCH--1966-67 TO THE INSTITUTE FOR EDUCATIONAL DEVELOPMENT. SECTION V, THE ROLE OF DIALECT IN THE SCHOOL-SOCIALIZATION OF LOWER CLASS CHILDREN. ED019121
BIBLIOGRAPHY OF PAPERS COVERING WORK UNDER OEO CONTRACT NUMBER 510. FINAL REPORT. (TITLE SUPPLIED). ED020773
HEAD START EVALUATION AND RESEARCH CENTER, TEACHERS COLLEGE, COLUMBIA UNIVERSITY. ANNUAL REPORT (1ST), SEPTEMBER 1966-AUGUST 1967. (TITLE SUPPLIED). ED020781
REGIONAL EVALUATION AND RESEARCH CENTER FOR PROJECT HEAD START, SUPPLEMENTARY RESEARCH REPORT, SEPTEMBER 1, 1967-DECEMBER 31, 1967. ED020791
RESPONSE TO VARYING LEVELS OF CONDITIONING REWARDS. FINAL REPORT. ED020803
HEAD START EVALUATION AND RESEARCH CENTER. PROGRESS REPORT OF RESEARCH STUDIES, 1966-1967. ED021612
HEAD START EVALUATION AND RESEARCH CENTER, BOSTON UNIVERSITY. REPORT OF RESEARCH, SEPTEMBER, 1966-AUGUST, 1967. ED022529
HEAD START EVALUATION AND RESEARCH CENTER, BOSTON UNIVERSITY. REPORT A-III, OBSERVATIONAL STRATEGIES FOR OBTAINING DATA ON CHILDREN AND TEACHERS IN HEAD START CLASSES. (OSOD). ED022559
PROJECT HEAD START RESEARCH AND EVALUATION CENTER, SYRACUSE UNIVERSITY RESEARCH INSTITUTE. FINAL REPORT, NOVEMBER 1, 1967. ED026137
THE INITIAL PHASE OF A PRESCHOOL CURRICULUM DEVELOPMENT PROJECT. FINAL REPORT. ED027071
[THE JUNIPER GARDENS CHILDREN'S PROJECT.] FINAL PROGRESS REPORT FOR OEO GRANT CG-8180. ED027947
PROBLEM SOLVING AND CONCEPT FORMATION: ANNOTATED LISTING OF NATIONAL AND INTERNATIONAL CURRICULAR PROJECTS AT THE EARLY CHILDHOOD LEVEL. ED029685
THE MONTESSORI RESEARCH PROJECT. FOUR PROGRESS REPORTS. ED030489
[COMPETENCE IN YOUNG CHILDREN.] ED032124
INSTITUTE FOR DEVELOPMENTAL STUDIES INTERIM PROGRESS REPORT. PART II: RESEARCH AND EVALUATION. ED036312
[NATIONAL LABORATORY ON EARLY CHILDHOOD EDUCATION PROGRAM ED039012
THE NATIONAL LABORATORY ON EARLY CHILDHOOD EDUCATION: TOWARD CONSTRUCTIVE CHANGE. ED039953
DESIGN AND MEASURES OF 1967-68 AND 1968-69 HEAD START E&R EVALUATION STUDIES. ED040745
MICHIGAN STATE UNIVERSITY, HEAD START EVALUATION AND RESEARCH, 1967-68 RESEARCH ABSTRACTS AND PROGRESS REPORTS. ED047771
RESEARCH AND DEVELOPMENT REGISTER IN EARLY CHILDHOOD EDUCATION, 1970. ED049815
CHILD DEVELOPMENT RESEARCH UNIT PROGRESS REPORT, FEBRUARY, 1970. ED049819
EDUCATIONAL RESEARCH POLICIES OF SCHOOL DISTRICTS NATIONWIDE EJ 012 677
ANXIETY IN THE EVALUATIVE CONTEXT EJ 051 018
RESEARCH FOR UNDERSTANDING EJ 051 150
A PARENT SPEAKS EJ 051 240

RESEARCH PROPOSALS
REGIONAL EVALUATION AND RESEARCH CENTER FOR HEAD START, SOUTHERN UNIVERSITY. ANNUAL REPORT. ED020792
ON LEARNING TO TALK: ARE PRINCIPLES DERIVED FROM THE LEARNING LABORATORY APPLICABLE? ED023481
THE CONCEPT OF DEVELOPMENTAL LEARNING. ED023484
VERBAL BEHAVIOR OF PRESCHOOL TEACHERS. A VERY PRELIMINARY REPORT. ED034577
THE DEFINITION, MEASUREMENT AND DEVELOPMENT OF SOCIAL MOTIVES UNDERLYING COOPERATIVE AND COMPETITIVE BEHAVIOR. ED045188
EDUCATIONAL INTERVENTION IN EARLY CHILDHOOD: A REPORT OF A FIVE-YEAR LONGITUDINAL STUDY OF THE EFFECTS OF EARLY EDUCATIONAL INTERVENTION IN THE LIVES OF DISADVANTAGED CHILDREN IN DURHAM, NORTH CAROLINA. FINAL REPORT, VOLUME I. ED050814
CHILDREN UNDER THREE - FINDING WAYS TO STIMULATE DEVELOPMENT. II. SOME CURRENT EXPERIMENTS: A THREE PRONGED PROJECT EJ 007 408

RESEARCH REVIEWS (PUBLICATIONS)
ABSTRACTS OF RESEARCH PERTAINING TO--UNGRADED VS SELF-CONTAINED CLASSROOM ORGANIZATION IN THE ELEMENTARY SCHOOL (GRADES 1-7). ED019129
THE TWO YEAR OLD. ED022536
A DIGEST OF THE RESEARCH ACTIVITIES OF REGIONAL EVALUATION AND RESEARCH CENTERS FOR PROJECT HEAD START (SEPTEMBER 1, 1966 TO NOVEMBER 30, 1967). ED023446
SOME STUDIES OF THE MORAL DEVELOPMENT OF CHILDREN. ED024445
PROBLEMS OF DIALECT. ED025300
INFANT AND PRESCHOOL MENTAL TESTS: REVIEW AND EVALUATION. ED026109
SEX DIFFERENCES IN MENTAL AND BEHAVIORAL TRAITS. ED026117
CONCEPT GROWTH AND THE EDUCATION OF THE CHILD: A SURVEY OF RESEARCH ON CONCEPTUALIZATION. NATIONAL FOUNDATION FOR EDUCATIONAL RESEARCH IN ENGLAND AND WALES OCCASIONAL PUBLICATION SERIES NO. 12. ED026121
ELEMENTARY SCHOOL MATHEMATICS: A GUIDE TO CURRENT RESEARCH. THIRD EDITION. ED026123
SEX ROLE TYPING IN THE PRESCHOOL YEARS: AN OVERVIEW. ED026134
GROUPING. ED026135
MENTAL HEALTH. WHAT RESEARCH SAYS TO THE TEACHER SERIES NUMBER 24. ED027087
REVIEW OF SELECTED INTERVENTION RESEARCH WITH YOUNG CHILDREN. ED027091
CHILD PSYCHIATRY: THE PAST QUARTER CENTURY. ED027951
THE SOCIOLOGY OF EARLY CHILDHOOD EDUCATION: A REVIEW OF LITERATURE. TECHNICAL REPORT NO. 1. ED032944
A REPORT ON EVALUATION STUDIES OF PROJECT HEAD START. ED037239
MALNUTRITION, LEARNING AND INTELLECTUAL DEVELOPMENT: RESEARCH AND REMEDIATION. ED039017
AN ANALYSIS OF EARLY CHILDHOOD EDUCATION RESEARCH AND DEVELOPMENT. ED039028
BEHAVIORAL RESEARCH RELEVANT TO THE CLASSROOM. ED039036
PARENT INVOLVEMENT IN COMPENSATORY EDUCATION. ED039954
TEACHER-CHILD RELATIONSHIPS IN DAY CARE CENTERS. WORKING PAPER. ED046494
HUMAN BEHAVIOR GENETICS: PRESENT STATUS AND SUGGESTIONS FOR FUTURE RESEARCH EJ 004 046
PSYCHOLOGICAL DEPRIVATION: WHAT WE DO, DON'T, AND SHOULD KNOW ABOUT IT EJ 012 676
DEVELOPMENTAL PROCESSES IN DISCRIMINATION LEARNING EJ 024 705
THE EFFECTS OF PSYCHOSOCIAL DEPRIVATION ON HUMAN DEVELOPMENT IN INFANCY EJ 026 815
AN ORGANISM ORIENTED CONCEPT OF DEVELOPMENT EJ 027 438
CHILDREN'S REACTIONS TO TV VIOLENCE: A REVIEW OF RESEARCH EJ 028 676

RESEARCH TOOLS
FROM THEORY TO OPERATIONS. DISADVANTAGED CHILDREN AND THEIR FIRST SCHOOL EXPERIENCES, ETS-HEAD START LONGITUDINAL STUDY. ED043397

RESEARCH UTILIZATION
RESEARCH, EVALUATION, AND PUBLIC POLICY: AN INVITED EDITORIAL EJ 021 381
ABOUT RESEARCH: PART II. IS A BEHAVIORAL APPROACH SUPERFICIAL? IS OPERANT CONDITIONING FAIR? WHY DO RESEARCH? EJ 029 015
LINGUISTIC FACTORS IN READING EJ 059 537

RESEARCHERS
RESEARCH AND DEVELOPMENT REGISTER IN EARLY CHILDHOOD EDUCATION, 1970. ED049815
EXPERIMENTER BIAS IN PERFORMANCE OF CHILDREN AT A SIMPLE MOTOR TASK EJ 035 710

RESIDENT CAMP PROGRAMS
THE DAY NURSERY ASSOCIATION OF CLEVELAND, CLEVELAND, OHIO: A LONG HISTORY OF CARE FOR CHILDREN, INVOLVEMENT OF PARENTS, AND SERVICE TO THE COMMUNITY. MODEL PROGRAMS--CHILDHOOD EDUCATION. ED045218
TAKE A GIANT STEP --A REMEDIAL PROGRAM IN A CAMP SETTING EJ 020 773

RESIDENTIAL CARE
NEIGHBORHOOD FAMILY DAY CARE AS A CHILD-REARING ENVIRONMENT. ED049840
A PERSPECTIVE ON RESIDENTIAL CHILD CARE PROGRAMS EJ 051 234
HELPING PARENTS TO HELP THEIR CHILDREN IN PLACEMENT EJ 058 055
RESIDENTIAL TREATMENT OF EMOTIONALLY DISTURBED CHILDREN IN NORWAY EJ 058 135
A TEAM APPROACH USING CASSETTE TAPES EJ 061 001
GROUP HOME CARE AS AN ADJUNCT TO RESIDENTIAL TREATMENT EJ 061 233

RESIDENTIAL CENTERS
RESIDENTIAL TREATMENT OF CHILDREN; A SURVEY OF INSTITUTIONAL CHARACTERISTICS EJ 022 980
INTERPERSONAL RELATIONSHIPS IN RESIDENTIAL TREATMENT CENTERS FOR DISTURBED CHILDREN EJ 037 183
FAMILY TREATMENT WITHIN THE MILIEU OF A RESIDENTIAL TREATMENT CENTER EJ 037 236
INVOLVING PARENTS IN RESIDENTIAL TREATMENT OF CHILDREN EJ 045 233

RESIDENTIAL PROGRAMS
INVOLVING PARENTS IN RESIDENTIAL TREATMENT OF CHILDREN EJ 045 233
A PERSPECTIVE ON RESIDENTIAL CHILD CARE PROGRAMS EJ 051 234
HELPING PARENTS TO HELP THEIR CHILDREN IN PLACEMENT EJ 058 055

RESOURCE ALLOCATIONS
OPTIMIZING EDUCATIONAL INVESTMENT STRATEGIES. ED015780

RESOURCE GUIDES
TEACHING MUSICAL CONCEPTS RELATED TO MELODY, RHYTHM, FORM, AND HARMONY, TEACHER RESOURCE MATERIAL KINDERGARTEN, GRADES 1 AND 2. ED019991
HOW TO USE ERIC. REVISED EDITION. ED027059
A SOURCE REPORT FOR DEVELOPING PARENT-CHILD EDUCATIONAL CENTERS. ED027944
JDC HANDBOOK FOR TEACHERS IN DAY CARE CENTERS. ED027962
RESOURCES FOR ENVIRONMENTAL EDUCATORS: ECOLOGY AND TEACHERS EJ 029 392

RESOURCE MATERIALS
TEACHING MUSICAL CONCEPTS RELATED TO MELODY, RHYTHM, FORM, AND HARMONY, TEACHER RESOURCE MATERIAL KINDERGARTEN, GRADES 1 AND 2. ED019991
THE USE OF CONTEMPORARY MATERIALS IN THE CLASSROOM. ED020013
SUPPLEMENTARY MATERIALS FOR TEACHER AIDE TRAINING PROGRAMS, TO SUPPLEMENT THE PUBLICATION "TEACHER AIDES: HANDBOOK FOR INSTRUCTORS AND ADMINISTRATORS." ED024462
SOURCE BOOK OF SELECTED MATERIALS FOR EARLY CHILDHOOD EDUCATION IN THE ARTS. ED033746

RESOURCE STAFF ROLE
INKSTER PUBLIC SCHOOLS IMPLEMENT CHILD DEVELOPMENT CENTER. ED025303

RESOURCE UNITS
SEX EDUCATION: RESOURCE UNIT ED035457

RESPONSE MODE
DIFFERENTIATION BETWEEN NORMAL AND DISORDERED CHILDREN BY A COMPUTER ANALYSIS OF EMOTIONAL AND VERBAL BEHAVIOR. ED019138
A DEVELOPMENTAL STUDY OF THE RELATIONSHIP BETWEEN REACTION-TIME AND PROBLEM-SOLVING EFFICIENCY. FINAL REPORT. ED020018
HEAD START EVALUATION AND RESEARCH CENTER, BOSTON UNIVERSITY. REPORT D-III, A STUDY OF PREFERENCES AMONG QUALITATIVELY DIFFERING UNCERTAINTIES. ED022565
INFANTS' RESPONSES TO FACIAL STIMULI DURING THE FIRST YEAR OF LIFE: EXPLORATORY STUDIES IN THE DEVELOPMENT OF A FACE SCHEMA. ED024455
THE SHIFT FROM COLOR TO FORM PREFERENCE IN YOUNG CHILDRE N OF DIFFERENT ETHNIC BACKGROUNDS. PART OF THE FINAL REPORT. ED025321
THE EFFECT OF AGGRESSIVE CARTOONS: CHILDREN'S INTERPERSONAL PLAY. ED046543
THE MEANING OF AN ORIENTING RESPONSE: A STUDY IN THE HIERARCHICAL ORDER OF ATTENDING. ED047794
NON-VERBAL INFORMATION STORAGE IN HUMANS AND DEVELOPMENTAL INFORMATION PROCESSING CHANNEL CAPACITY. ED047800
INFANT REACTIVITY TO REDUNDANT PROPRIOCEPTIVE AND AUDITORY STIMULATION: A TWIN STUDY. ED052825
SEX DIFFERENCES IN CHILDREN'S MODES OF AGGRESSIVE RESPONSES TOWARD OUTSIDERS EJ 007 690
SOCIAL REINFORCEMENT FOR EXPRESSION VS. SUPPRESSION OF AGGRESSION EJ 007 691
SEMANTIC AND PHONETIC RELATIONS IN THE FALSE RECOGNITION OF WORDS BY THIRD- AND SIXTH-GRADE CHILDREN EJ 026 374
ODDITY PREFERENCE BY MENTAL RETARDATES EJ 027 825
REACTION TO SUCESS AND FAILURE IN COMPLEX LEARNING: A POSTFEEDBACK EFFECT EJ 029 413
RELATIONSHIP OF CONSERVATION EXPLANATIONS TO ITEM DIFFICULTY EJ 030 295
PRIOR REINFORCEMENT HISTORY AS AN EXPLANATION FOR THE EFFECTS OF SEX OF SUBJECT AND EXPERIMENTER IN SOCIAL REINFORCEMENT PARADIGMS EJ 030 297
ESTIMATION OF LINE LENGTH AND NUMBER: A DEVELOPMENTAL STUDY EJ 030 590
CHILDREN'S TWO-CHOICE LEARNING OF PREDOMINANTLY ALTERNATING AND REPEATING SEQUENCES EJ 033 791
FACILITATING AND INTERFERING EFFECTS OF STIMULUS NAMING ON CHILDREN'S MOTOR PAIRED-ASSOCIATE LEARNING EJ 033 793
STIMULUS AND RESPONSE ALTERNATION IN YOUNG CHILDREN EJ 034 537
CAN NEWBORNS SHOW CARDIAC ORIENTING? EJ 036 078
YOUNG CHILDREN'S PERFORMANCE ON A TWO-CHOICE TASK AS A FUNCTION OF SOCIAL REINFORCEMENT, BASE-LINE PREFERENCE, AND RESPONSE STRATEGY EJ 039 635
PRESTIMULUS ACTIVITY LEVEL AND RESPONSIVITY IN THE NEONATE EJ 040 297
NUMBER CONSERVATION IN VERY YOUNG CHILDREN: THE EFFECT OF AGE AND MODE OF RESPONDING EJ 041 139
CHARACTERISTICS OF WORD ASSOCIATION RESPONSES OBTAINED FROM CHILDREN IN GRADES ONE THROUGH FOUR EJ 042 960
LEARNING OF AGGRESSION AS A FUNCTION OF PRESENCE OF A HUMAN MODEL, RESPONSE INTENSITY, AND TARGET OF THE RESPONSE EJ 043 198
SATIATION OF VISUAL REINFORCEMENT IN YOUNG INFANTS EJ 043 666
EVIDENCE FOR COMPETITION AND COORDINATION BETWEEN VOCAL AND MANUAL RESPONSES IN PRESCHOOL CHILDREN EJ 043 668
DEVELOPMENTAL CHARACTERISTICS OF EMOTIONAL EXPERIENCE EJ 043 860
DISCRIMINATION AND INSTRUCTIONS AS FACTORS IN THE CONTROL OF NONREINFORCED IMITATION EJ 044 157
GENERALIZED LABELING ON THE BASIS OF STRUCTURAL RESPONSE CLASSES BY TWO YOUNG CHILDREN EJ 044 696
EFFECTS OF VARIATIONS IN THE NURSERY SCHOOL SETTING ON ENVIRONMENTAL CONSTRAINTS AND CHILDREN'S MODES OF ADAPTATION EJ 045 455
INDIVIDUAL DIFFERENCES IN CHILDREN'S REACTIONS TO REWARD AND NONREWARD EJ 045 459
EFFECTS OF SPATIAL SEPARATION OF STIMULUS, RESPONSE, AND REWARD IN DISCRIMINATION LEARNING BY CHILDREN EJ 046 243
NONVERBAL INFORMATION STORAGE IN CHILDREN AND DEVELOPMENTAL INFORMATION PROCESSING CHANNEL CAPACITY EJ 053 720
PATTERNS OF RESPONDING IN THE WORD ASSOCIATIONS OF WEST AFRICAN CHILDREN EJ 056 634
VISUAL RESPONSE DECREMENT AS A FUNCTION OF AGE OF HUMAN NEWBORNS EJ 056 716
PROBLEMS OF CONTROL IN SIMULTANEOUS DISCRIMINATION TASKS EJ 058 215
WINDOW BEGINS WITH AN "L" EJ 058 507
VIOLATION OF A RULE AS A METHOD OF DIAGNOSING INFANTS' LEVELS OF OBJECT CONCEPT EJ 059 314
RESPONSE DEPRESSION AND FACILITATION COMPONENTS OF THE FRUSTRATION EFFECT IN CHILDREN'S BEHAVIOR EJ 059 877
AGGRESSION ANXIETY, PERCEPTION OF AGGRESSIVE CUES, AND EXPECTED RETALIATION EJ 061 071

RESPONSE STYLE (TESTS)
DEVELOPMENTAL CHANGES IN IDIODYNAMIC SET RESPONSES OF CHILDREN'S WORD ASSOCIATIONS EJ 042 880
GENERALIZATION AS A FUNCTION OF THE RANGE OF TEST STIMULI: THE ROLES OF DISCRIMINABILITY AND RESPONSE BIAS EJ 057 909

RESPONSIBILITY
PARENTAL ANTECEDENTS OF CHILDREN'S BELIEFS IN INTERNAL-EXTERNAL CONTROL OF REINFORCEMENTS IN INTELLECTUAL ACHIEVEMENT SITUATIONS. ED024447

RETARDATION
SENSORY ORGANIZATION IN RETARDATES AND NORMALS EJ 019 013
SEVERE PROTEIN-CALORIE MALNUTRITION AND COGNITIVE DEVELOPMENT IN INFANCY AND EARLY CHILDHOOD EJ 039 627

RETARDED CHILDREN
AN ANNOTATED BIBLIOGRAPHY OF BEHAVIOR MODIFICATION WITH CHILDREN AND RETARDATES. ED020025
AN OVERVIEW OF RESEARCH IN LEARNING, MOTIVATION, AND PERCEPTION. ED020799
THE FACTORIAL STRUCTURE OF REASONING, MORAL JUDGMENT, AND MORAL CONDUCT. ED031302
EARLY INFANT STIMULATION AND MOTOR DEVELOPMENT. ED038179

SEPARATION REACTIONS IN YOUNG, MILDLY RETARDED CHILDREN. EJ 003 972
FAMILY PROBLEMS CONCERNING THE MENTALLY RETARDED CHILD EJ 010 859
COMPARISON OF GROSS, INTENSIVE, AND EXTENSIVE QUANTITIES BY RETARDATES EJ 015 098
FOSTER CARE FOR MENTALLY RETARDED CHILDREN: HOW DOES CHILD WELFARE MEET THIS CHALLENGE? EJ 020 859
BACKWARD ASSOCIATIONS IN PAIRED-ASSOCIATE LEARNING OF RETARDATES AND NORMAL CHILDREN EJ 021 770
GENERALIZATION OF ADULT'S STIMULUS CONTROL OF CHILDREN'S BEHAVIOR EJ 022 214
REPORT ON THE UTILITY OF A PIAGET-BASED INFANT SCALE WITH OLDER RETARDED CHILDREN EJ 022 247
BEHAVIOR DEVIATIONS IN MENTALLY RETARDED CHILDREN EJ 022 475
THE EFFECTS OF A PAY-OFF MATRIX ON SELECTIVE ATTENTION EJ 023 436
A LEARNING EXPERIENCE IN HELPING PARENTS GET WHAT THEY WANT EJ 024 027
AN EXPERIMENTAL STUDY OF THE SOCIAL RESPONSIVENESS OF CHILDREN WITH AUTISTIC BEHAVIORS EJ 024 470
SINGLE-LETTER CUE SELECTION IN THE PAIRED-ASSOCIATE LEARNING OF NORMAL CHILDREN AND RETARDATES EJ 024 698
A COMPARISON OF RETARDATES AND NORMALS ON THE POGGENDORFF AND OPPEL-KUNDT ILLUSIONS EJ 024 943
SENSORY ORGANIZATION AND INTELLIGENCE: A MODIFICATION AND REPLICATION EJ 024 946
EXAMINATION AND REEVALUATION OF PROSTHETIC LENSES EMPLOYING AN OPERANT PROCEDURE FOR MEASURING SUBJECTIVE VISUAL ACUITY IN A RETARDED CHILD EJ 029 382
FOSTER FAMILY SERVICES FOR MENTALLY RETARDED CHILDREN EJ 030 653
TRANSFER OF VERBAL PAIRED ASSOCIATES IN MENTALLY RETARDED INDIVIDUALS AND NORMAL CHILDREN AS A FUNCTION OF INTERLIST SIMILARITY EJ 033 785
OUTERDIRECTEDNESS IN THE PROBLEM-SOLVING OF INSTITUTIONALIZED AND NONINSTITUTIONALIZED NORMAL AND RETARDED CHILDREN EJ 035 366
RESEARCH FOR SERVICE TO SEVERELY RETARDED CHILDREN EJ 038 531
RHYTHMIC HABIT PATTERNS IN INFANCY: THEIR SEQUENCE, AGE OF ONSET, AND FREQUENCY EJ 040 295
THE DISCRIMINATION LEARNING OF NORMAL AND RETARDED CHILDREN AS A FUNCTION OF PENALTY CONDITIONS AND ETIOLOGY OF THE RETARDED EJ 041 136
SELECTIVE ATTENTION IN MENTAL RETARDATES EJ 043 058
THE CONTROL OF IMITATIVE AND NONIMITATIVE BEHAVIORS IN SEVERELY RETARDED CHILDREN THROUGH "GENERALIZED-INSTRUCTION FOLLOWING" EJ 043 196
A NONVERBAL TECHNIQUE FOR STUDYING MUSIC PREFERENCE EJ 043 285
EFFECT OF CLASSROOM NOISE ON NUMBER IDENTIFICATION BY RETARDED CHILDREN EJ 045 793
RECOGNITION MEMORY: THE RELATIONSHIP OF ACCURACY AND LATENCY OF RESPONSE UNDER DIFFERENT MEMORY LOADS IN RETARDATES EJ 046 256
ESTABLISHMENT OF DAY CARE PROGRAMS FOR THE MENTALLY RETARDED EJ 047 342
HELPING BEHAVIOR AMONG NORMAL AND RETARDED CHILDREN EJ 052 442
THE TEAM APPROACH IN HOME CARE OF MENTALLY RETARDED CHILDREN EJ 053 601
DEVELOPMENTAL COURSE OF RESPONSIVENESS TO SOCIAL REINFORCEMENT IN NORMAL CHILDREN AND INSTITUTIONALIZED RETARDED CHILDREN EJ 053 648
DEVELOPMENT OF CONSERVATION IN NORMAL AND RETARDED CHILDREN EJ 053 651
EFFECTS OF RATE OF STIMULUS PRESENTATION AND PENALTY CONDITIONS ON THE DISCRIMINATION LEARNING OF NORMAL AND RETARDED CHILDREN EJ 053 712
CROSS-MODAL MATCHING AMONG NORMAL AND RETARDED CHILDREN EJ 053 755
EFFECTS OF CONCURRENT AND SERIAL TRAINING ON GENERALIZED VOCAL IMITATION IN RETARDED CHILDREN EJ 055 210
DESIGNING INSTRUCTIONAL SETTINGS FOR CHILDREN LABELED "RETARDED": SOME REFLECTIONS EJ 057 733
ATTENTION SPAN AND GENERALIZATION OF TASK-RELATED STIMULUS CONTROL: EFFECTS OF REINFORCEMENT CONTINGENCIES EJ 059 878
A TEAM APPROACH USING CASSETTE TAPES EJ 061 001

RETARDED READERS
EFFECT OF INCENTIVES AND AGE ON THE VISUAL RECOGNITION OF RETARDED READERS EJ 037 535
EFFECT OF INCENTIVES UPON RETARDED AND NORMAL READERS ON A VISUAL-ASSOCIATE LEARNING TASK EJ 038 266
READING DISABILITY AND DIFFICULTIES IN FINGER LOCALIZATION AND RIGHT-LEFT DISCRIMINATION EJ 045 083

RETARDED SPEECH DEVELOPMENT
BETTER FEEDING CAN MEAN BETTER SPEAKING. ED025306

RETENTION
CONCEPT FORMATION BY KINDERGARTEN CHILDREN IN A CARD-SORTING TASK. PSYCHOLOGY SERIES. ED013665
EXTENSION OF A THEORY OF PREDICTIVE BEHAVIOR TO IMMEDIATE RECALL BY PRESCHOOL CHILDREN. ED025326
THE AUDITORY MEMORY OF CHILDREN FROM DIFFERENT SOCIO-ECONOMIC BACKGROUNDS. ED027092
THE EFFICACY OF A MATHEMATICS READINESS PROGRAM FOR INDUCING CONSERVATION OF NUMBER, WEIGHT, AREA, MASS, AND VOLUME IN DISADVANTAGED PRESCHOOL CHILDREN IN THE SOUTHERN UNITED STATES. ED048923
THE EFFECTS OF OVERLEARNING ON CHILDREN'S NONREVERSAL AND REVERSAL LEARNING USING UNRELATED STIMULI EJ 028 633
RETENTION FOLLOWING A CHANGE IN AMBIENT CONTEXTUAL STIMULI FOR SIX AGE GROUPS EJ 039 631
WHAT THE WORLD NEEDS NOW: ENVIRONMENTAL EDUCATION FOR YOUNG CHILDREN EJ 039 637
THE PART PLAYED BY MEDIATION PROCESSES IN THE RETENTION OF TEMPORAL SEQUENCES BY TWO READING GROUPS EJ 039 909
DEVELOPMENT OF RETENTION AND ORGANIZATION OCCURRING IN FREE RECALL IN TURKISH CHILDREN EJ 041 133
EFFECTS OF SOCIAL REINFORCEMENT ON LEARNING AND RETENTION IN CHILDREN EJ 042 957
RECOGNITION MEMORY FOR PICTURES IN PRESCHOOL CHILDREN EJ 042 964
MEANINGFULNESS, SERIAL POSITION AND RETENTION INTERVAL IN RECOGNITION SHORT-TERM MEMORY EJ 053 724
CONCEPT ATTAINMENT, GENERALIZATION, AND RETENTION THROUGH OBSERVATION AND VERBAL CODING EJ 053 726
RELATIONS OF AGE AND INTELLIGENCE TO SHORT-TERM COLOR MEMORY EJ 056 392
CONCEPTUAL ENCODING AND CONCEPT RECALL-RECOVERY IN CHILDREN EJ 056 628
IMAGERY AND MULTIPLE-LIST PAIRED ASSOCIATE LEARNING IN YOUNG CHILDREN EJ 057 904

RETENTION STUDIES
YOUNG CHILDREN'S THINKING, STUDIES OF SOME ASPECTS OF PIAGET'S THEORY. ED013662
A LONGITUDINAL ASSESSMENT OF PRESCHOOL CHILDREN IN HAPTIC LEARNING. FINAL REPORT. ED020019
HEAD START EVALUATION AND RESEARCH CENTER, UNIVERSITY OF KANSAS. REPORT NO. XI, VERBAL RECALL RESEARCH. ED021647
MEDIATIONAL STYLES: AN INDIVIDUAL DIFFERENCE VARIABLE IN CHILDREN'S VERBAL LEARNING ABILITY. ED027955
DIGIT SPAN, PRACTICE AND DICHOTIC LISTENING PERFORMANCE IN THE MENTALLY RETARDED EJ 015 850
RETENTION FOLLOWING A CHANGE IN AMBIENT CONTEXTUAL STIMULI FOR SIX AGE GROUPS EJ 039 631
DEVELOPMENT OF RETENTION AND ORGANIZATION OCCURRING IN FREE RECALL IN TURKISH CHILDREN EJ 041 133
EFFECTS OF SOCIAL REINFORCEMENT ON LEARNING AND RETENTION IN CHILDREN EJ 042 957
VERBAL RECALL AS A FUNCTION OF PERSONALITY CHARACTERISTICS EJ 054 806
RETROACTIVE AND PROACTIVE MULTIPLE LIST INTERFERENCE WITH DISADVANTAGED CHILDREN EJ 057 895
REINSTATEMENT EFFECTS IN CHILDREN EJ 057 899
INTERMODAL AND INTRAMODAL RETENTION OF VISUAL AND TACTUAL INFORMATION IN YOUNG CHILDREN EJ 057 900
QUANTITATIVE AND QUALITATIVE ASPECTS OF MEMORY FOR PICTURE STIMULI EJ 057 907

REVIEW (REEXAMINATION)
CURRENT ISSUES IN RESEARCH ON EARLY DEVELOPMENT. ED028813
INSTRUCTIONAL AND EXPRESSIVE EDUCATIONAL OBJECTIVES: THEIR FORMULATION AND USE IN CURRICULUM. ED028838

REWARDS
DISCRIMINATION LEARNING, PROBLEM SOLVING, AND CHOICE PATTERNING BY CHILDREN AS A FUNCTION OF INCENTIVE VALUE, MOTIVATION, AND SEQUENTIAL DEPENDENCIES. FINAL REPORT. ED016518
FINAL REPORT ON HEAD START EVALUATION AND RESEARCH--1966-67 TO THE INSTITUTE FOR EDUCATIONAL DEVELOPMENT. SECTION III, INFLUENCING ATTITUDES OF PARENTS AND TEACHERS THROUGH REWARDING CHILDREN. ED019119
REGIONAL EVALUATION AND RESEARCH CENTER FOR HEAD START, SOUTHERN UNIVERSITY. ANNUAL REPORT. ED020792
RESPONSE TO VARYING LEVELS OF CONDITIONING REWARDS. FINAL REPORT. ED020803
HEAD START EVALUATION AND RESEARCH CENTER, BOSTON UNIVERSITY. REPORT D-III, A STUDY OF PREFERENCES AMONG QUALITATIVELY DIFFERING UNCERTAINTIES. ED022565
LEARNING OF INCENTIVE-VALUE BY CHILDREN. ED023473
CONDITIONS FOSTERING THE USE OF INFORMATIVE FEEDBACK BY YOUNG CHILDREN. ED029688
A TOKEN REINFORCEMENT SYSTEM IN THE PUBLIC SCHOOLS. ED036323
RISK-TAKING BEHAVIOR IN PRESCHOOL CHILDREN FROM THREE ETHNIC BACKGROUNDS. ED042486
THE BEHAVIOR ANALYSIS CLASSROOM. ED047775

A TOKEN MANUAL FOR BEHAVIOR ANALYSIS CLASSROOMS. ED047776
A COMPARISON OF THE EFFECT OF VERBAL AND MATERIAL REWARD ON THE LEARNING OF LOWER CLASS PRESCHOOL CHILDREN. ED052817
IMITATION AS A FUNCTION OF VICARIOUS AND DIRECT REWARD EJ 018 323
RECENCY AND SUMMATION EFFECTS OF NONREWARD IN CHILDREN EJ 028 895
DEVELOPMENTAL ASPECTS OF REACTION TO POSITIVE INDUCEMENTS EJ 029 359
INDIVIDUAL DIFFERENCES IN CHILDREN'S REACTIONS TO FRUSTRATIVE NONREWARD EJ 030 591
THE RELATIONSHIP BETWEEN INTENTIONAL LEARNING, INCIDENTAL LEARNING, AND TYPE OF REWARD IN PRESCHOOL, EDUCABLE, MENTAL RETARDATES EJ 033 783
SUB-PROFESSIONAL BEHAVIOR MODIFICATION AND THE DEVELOPMENT OF TOKEN-REINFORCEMENT SYSTEMS IN INCREASING ACADEMIC MOTIVATION AND ACHIEVEMENT EJ 034 527
CUE AND INCENTIVE MOTIVATIONAL PROPERTIES OF REINFORCERS IN CHILDREN'S DISCRIMINATION LEARNING EJ 035 374
LEARNING, CURIOSITY, AND SOCIAL GROUP MEMBERSHIP EJ 035 378
BEHAVIORAL COMPLIANCE AND DEVALUATION OF THE FORBIDDEN OBJECT AS A FUNCTION OF PROBABILITY OF DETECTION AND SEVERITY OF THREAT EJ 038 935
THE EFFECTS OF REWARD AND PUNISHMENT UPON CHILDREN'S ATTENTION, MOTIVATION, AND DISCRIMINATION LEARNING EJ 041 137
SOCIAL COMPARISON BY YOUNG CHILDREN EJ 043 672
CHILDREN'S REACTIONS TO FAILURE AS A FUNCTION OF INTERRESPONSE INTERVAL EJ 045 043
COOPERATION AND COMPETITION IN FOUR-YEAR-OLDS AS A FUNCTION OF REWARD CONTINGENCY AND SUBCULTURE EJ 045 453
THE INCENTIVE VALUE OF UNCERTAINTY REDUCTION FOR CHILDREN EJ 045 454
INDIVIDUAL DIFFERENCES IN CHILDREN'S REACTIONS TO REWARD AND NONREWARD EJ 045 459
A REEXAMINATION OF THE ROLE OF INCENTIVE IN CHILDREN'S DISCRIMINATION LEARNING EJ 046 237
THE ACQUISITION AND PERFORMANCE OF A SOCIALLY NEUTRAL RESPONSE AS A FUNCTION OF VICARIOUS REWARD EJ 046 889
THE RATIONAL ZERO POINT ON INCENTIVE-OBJECT PREFERENCE SCALES: A DEVELOPMENTAL STUDY EJ 048 099
DO MATERIAL REWARDS ENHANCE THE PERFORMANCE OF LOWER-CLASS CHILDREN? EJ 053 735
WORDS AND DEEDS ABOUT ALTRUISM AND THE SUBSEQUENT REINFORCEMENT POWER OF THE MODEL EJ 053 739
STIMULUS NOVELTY AS A VARIABLE IN CHILDREN'S WIN-STAY, LOSE-SHIFT DISCRIMINATION LEARNING SET EJ 053 751
EFFECTS OF SOCIAL COMPARISON UPON THE IMITATION OF NEUTRAL AND ALTRUISTIC BEHAVIORS BY YOUNG CHILDREN EJ 056 728
SOCIAL REINFORCEMENT SATIATION: AN OUTCOME OF FREQUENCY OR AMBIGUITY? EJ 058 144
INCENTIVE EFFECTS IN CHILDREN'S CREATIVITY EJ 059 317
EXPECTANCY TO PERFORM AND VICARIOUS REWARD: THEIR EFFECTS UPON IMITATION EJ 059 513
RESPONSE DEPRESSION AND FACILITATION COMPONENTS OF THE FRUSTRATION EFFECT IN CHILDREN'S BEHAVIOR EJ 059 877
"RIGHT," "WRONG," AND DISCRIMINATION LEARNING IN CHILDREN EJ 060 774
SIMPLE REACTION TIME IN CHILDREN: EFFECTS OF INCENTIVE, INCENTIVE-SHIFT AND OTHER TRAINING VARIABLES EJ 061 075

RISK

RISK-TAKING BEHAVIOR IN PRESCHOOL CHILDREN FROM THREE ETHNIC BACKGROUNDS. ED042486

ROLE CONFLICT

THE ROLE OF WOMEN IN THE DEVELOPMENT OF THEIR COUNTRIES: COMMENTS FROM OMEP ON A QUESTIONNAIRE FROM U.N EJ 011 346

ROLE PERCEPTION

THE IMPACT OF COGNITIVE MATURITY ON THE DEVELOPMENT OF SEX-ROLE ATTITUDES IN THE YEARS 4 TO 8. ED019109
SEX ROLE TYPING IN THE PRESCHOOL YEARS: AN OVERVIEW. ED026134
THE DEVELOPMENT OF ROLE-TAKING AND COMMUNICATION SKILLS IN CHILDREN. ED027082
CHILDREN'S PERCEPTIONS OF ADULT ROLES AS AFFECTED BY CLASS, FATHER-ABSENCE AND RACE. ED032134
ADOLESCENT NORMS AND BEHAVIOR: ORGANIZATION AND CONFORMITY EJ 007 450
THE DEVELOPMENT OF ROLE-TAKING AS REFLECTED BY BEHAVIOR OF BRIGHT, AVERAGE, AND RETARDED CHILDREN IN A SOCIAL GUESSING GAME EJ 025 361
POSTADOPTION COUNSELING: A PROFESSIONAL OBLIGATION EJ 028 792
SOCIAL SCHEMATA OF SCHOOL BEGINNERS: SOME DEMOGRAPHIC CORRELATES EJ 030 713
THE RELATIONSHIP OF BIRTH ORDER AND SEX OF SIBLINGS TO GENDER ROLE IDENTITY EJ 039 901
THE MOTHER-CHILD RELATIONSHIP AND THE FATHER-ABSENT BOY'S PERSONALITY DEVELOPMENT 27-241 EJ 040 456
A DISCONTINUITY IN THE SOCIALIZATION OF MALES IN THE UNITED STATES EJ 040 799
ROLE MODEL INFLUENCES ON COLLEGE WOMEN'S CAREER ASPIRATIONS EJ 041 632
EFFECTS OF SEX-TYPED INFORMATION ON CHILDREN'S TOY PREFERENCES EJ 045 191
A METHOD FOR STUDYING THE DEVELOPMENT OF GENDER IDENTITY EJ 046 784
CONCEPTS OF SOCIAL SEX ROLES AMONG CHILEAN ADOLESCENTS EJ 048 396
WHAT TO DO TILL THE MALE MAN COMES EJ 048 697
SEX-ROLE AND NEED FOR APPROVAL IN ADOLESCENTS EJ 051 014
EFFECT OF A CHILD'S SEX ON ADULT INTERPRETATIONS OF ITS BEHAVIOR EJ 053 711
EFFECTS OF SEX AND BIRTH ORDER ON SEX-ROLE DEVELOPMENT AND INTELLIGENCE AMONG KINDERGARTEN CHILDREN EJ 057 133
SEX ROLE IDENTITY OF ADOLESCENT GIRLS IN FOSTER HOMES AND INSTITUTIONS EJ 059 644

ROLE PLAYING

A PILOT INVESTIGATION OF THE EFFECTS OF TRAINING TECHNIQUES DESIGNED TO ACCELERATE CHILDRENS' ACQUISITION OF CONSERVATION OF DISCONTINUOUS QUANTITY. FINAL REPORT. ED044178
SIMULATION ACTIVITIES FOR TRAINING PARENTS AND TEACHERS AS EDUCATIONAL PARTNERS: A REPORT AND EVALUATION. ED048945
EARLY ANTECEDENTS OF ROLE-TAKING AND ROLE-PLAYING ABILITY EJ 008 318
LOOK--I SEE ME EJ 028 897
FAKABILITY OF SCORES ON THE GROUP PERSONALITY PROJECTIVE TEST EJ 030 792
HAVE YOU EVER THOUGHT OF A PROP BOX? EJ 031 781
A PILOT INVESTIGATION OF THE EFFECTS OF TRAINING TECHNIQUES DESIGNED TO ACCELERATE CHILDREN'S ACQUISITION OF CONSERVATION OF DISCONTINOUS QUANTITY EJ 044 705
THE USE OF ROLE PLAYING AND INDUCTION IN CHILDREN'S LEARNING OF HELPING AND SHARING BEHAVIOR EJ 046 467

ROLE THEORY

INSTRUMENTAL AND AFFECTIONAL DEPENDENCY AND NURTURANCE IN PRESCHOOL CHILDREN EJ 015 101
SEX-ROLE IDENTITY AND SIBLING COMPOSITION EJ 035 626
THE RELATION OF ROLE TAKING TO THE DEVELOPMENT OF MORAL JUDGMENT IN CHILDREN EJ 035 991
THE EFFECT OF SIBLING RELATIONSHIP ON CONCEPT LEARNING OF YOUNG CHILDREN TAUGHT BY CHILD-TEACHERS EJ 056 399
CROSS-SEX IDENTITY IN BARBADOS EJ 058 136

ROTE LEARNING

LEARNING BY DISCOVERY: A REVIEW OF THE RESEARCH METHODOLOGY. REPORT FROM THE PROJECT ON VARIABLES AND PROCESSES IN COGNITIVE LEARNING. ED053793

RUBELLA

RUBELLA AND ITS AFTERMATH EJ 007 163
PLANNING FOR A MASS ATTACK ON RUBELLA EJ 007 164
A MULTIHANDICAPPED RUBELLA BABY: THE FIRST EIGHTEEN MONTHS EJ 022 979

RURAL AREAS

THE EFFECTIVENESS OF SPECIAL PROGRAMS FOR RURAL ISOLATED FOUR-YEAR-OLD CHILDREN. FINAL REPORT. ED041638
APPALACHIA PRESCHOOL EDUCATION PROGRAM, CHARLESTON, WEST VIRGINIA: A THREE-PART PRESCHOOL PROGRAM COMBINING A TELEVISION PROGRAM, PARAPROFESSIONAL HOME VISITORS, AND A MOBILE CLASSROOM. MODEL PROGRAMS--CHILDHOOD EDUCATION. ED045216
DEMOGRAPHIC AND SOCIO-ECONOMIC DATA OF THE BECKLEY, WEST VIRGINIA AREA AND 1968-1970 DEVELOPMENTAL COSTS OF THE EARLY CHILDHOOD EDUCATION FIELD STUDY. TECHNICAL REPORT NO. 1. ED052832
CHILD-REARING PRACTICES IN MOUNTAIN COUNTY, KENTUCKY EJ 036 210
THE PRESCHOOL IN RURAL INDIA EJ 036 334
CLASSROOM PRACTICES IN PRE-BASIC SCHOOLS EJ 036 335
THE ITINERANT TEACHER EJ 060 930

RURAL EDUCATION

PSYCHOLINGUISTIC BEHAVIORS OF ISOLATED, RURAL CHILDREN WITH AND WITHOUT KINDERGARTEN. ED042510

RURAL FAMILY

A STUDY OF WED AND UNWED MOTHERHOOD IN ADOLESCENTS AND YOUNG ADULTS EJ 030 715

RURAL POPULATION

THE EFFECT OF A PRESCHOOL EXPERIENCE UPON INTELLECTUAL FUNCTIONING AMONG FOUR-YEAR-OLD, WHITE CHILDREN IN RURAL MINNESOTA. ED039030

RURAL URBAN DIFFERENCES

PROJECT HEAD START, THE URBAN AND RURAL CHALLENGE. FINAL REPORT. ED022527

RURAL YOUTH

A STUDY OF VISUAL PERCEPTIONS IN EARLY CHILDHOOD. ED023451

RUSSIAN
GRAMMATICAL DEVELOPMENT IN RUSSIAN-SPEAKING CHILDREN. ED025332

SAFETY EDUCATION
TEACHING SAFETY IN THE ELEMENTARY SCHOOL. ED026147
CHILDREN AND ROAD ACCIDENTS EJ 050 496

SCHEDULE MODULES
THE STUDENT IN PROJECT PLAN: A FUNCTIONING PROGRAM OF INDIVIDUALIZED EDUCATION EJ 028 501

SCHEDULING
A PROGRAM OF STIMULUS CONTROL FOR ESTABLISHING A ONE-MINUTE WAIT FOR REINFORCEMENT IN PRESCHOOL CHILDREN. PROGRESS REPORT. ED042492
EFFECTS OF REINFORCEMENT HISTORY ON TIMING (DRL) PERFORMANCE IN YOUNG CHILDREN EJ 024 936

SCHEMATIC STUDIES
THE INITIAL COORDINATION OF SENSORIMOTOR SCHEMAS IN HUMAN INFANTS - PIAGET'S IDEAS AND THE ROLE OF EXPERIENCE. ED016511
FACTOR STRUCTURE OF CHILDREN'S PERSONAL SPACE SCHEMATA EJ 052 466

SCHIZOPHRENIA
THE INTELLIGENCE OF CHILDREN OF SCHIZOPHRENICS EJ 021 763
IMITATION AND ECHOING IN YOUNG SCHIZOPHRENIC CHILDREN EJ 026 494
THE EFFECTS OF OBJECT LOSS ON THE BODY IMAGE OF SCHIZOPHRENIC GIRLS EJ 027 345
PARAMETERS OF THE SPIRAL AFTER-EFFECT IN ORGANICS, SCHIZOPHRENICS, AND NORMALS EJ 061 060

SCHOOL ADMINISTRATION
DIRECTED RESEARCH PROGRAM IN READING, EARLY CHILDHOOD, VOCATIONAL EDUCATION, SCHOOL ORGANIZATION AND ADMINISTRATION, FY 72 - FY 76. ED051871

SCHOOL ARCHITECTURE
THE PREPARED ENVIRONMENT AND ITS RELATIONSHIP TO LEARNING. ED025302

SCHOOL ATTITUDES
AN EXPERIMENTAL STUDY OF FORMAL READING INSTRUCTION AT THE KINDERGARTEN LEVEL. ED022533

SCHOOL BUSES
WHAT ABOUT THE SCHOOL BUS? EJ 020 294

SCHOOL COMMUNITY RELATIONSHIP
A CAREER DEVELOPMENT PROGRAM IN THE CHICAGO PUBLIC SCHOOLS EJ 035 579
THE NEW SCHOOL EJ 036 327

SCHOOL DESIGN
EDUCATIONAL SPECIFICATIONS FOR PIEDMONT ELEMENTARY SCHOOL. ED022547
THE PREPARED ENVIRONMENT AND ITS RELATIONSHIP TO LEARNING. ED025302
DESIGNING TOMORROW'S SCHOOL TODAY: THE MULTI-SENSORY EXPERIENCE CENTER EJ 033 784

SCHOOL DISTRICTS
A STUDY IN CHILD CARE (CASE STUDY FROM VOLUME II-B): "A SENSE OF BELONGING." DAY CARE PROGRAMS REPRINT SERIES. ED051898
EDUCATIONAL RESEARCH POLICIES OF SCHOOL DISTRICTS NATIONWIDE EJ 012 677

SCHOOL ENVIRONMENT
HEAD START EVALUATION AND RESEARCH CENTER. PROGRESS REPORT OF RESEARCH STUDIES 1966 TO 1967. DOCUMENT 4, DEVELOPMENT OF OBSERVATION PROCEDURES FOR ASSESSING PRESCHOOL CLASSROOM ENVIRONMENT. ED021626
CULTURE OF THE SCHOOL: A CONSTRUCT FOR RESEARCH AND EXPLANATION IN EDUCATION. ED039945
EVALUATING SETTINGS FOR LEARNING EJ 019 966
EFFECTS OF VARIATIONS IN THE NURSERY SCHOOL SETTING ON ENVIRONMENTAL CONSTRAINTS AND CHILDREN'S MODES OF ADAPTATION EJ 045 455
"OPENNESS" OF SCHOOL CLIMATE AND ALIENATION OF HIGH SCHOOL STUDENTS EJ 052 654
HOW TO TEACH FEAR EJ 061 058

SCHOOL HOLDING POWER
THE WARRIOR DROPOUTS. ED016529

SCHOOL IMPROVEMENT
THE COGNITIVE ENVIRONMENTS OF URBAN PRE-SCHOOL CHILDREN. MANUAL OF INSTRUCTIONS FOR ADMINISTERING AND SCORING "SCHOOLS" QUESTION. ED018254

SCHOOL INTEGRATION
EFFECTS OF SOCIAL CLASS INTEGRATION OF PRESCHOOL NEGRO CHILDREN ON TEST PERFORMANCE AND SELF-CONCEPT. FINAL REPORT. ED050831
REACHING FOR THE DREAM: AN EXPERIMENT IN TWO-WAY BUSING EJ 025 078
DEMOCRATIZATION OF EDUCATIONAL OPPORTUNITY. AN ESSAY REVIEW EJ 038 471
FRIENDSHIPS AMONG STUDENTS IN DESEGREGATED SCHOOLS EJ 053 668

SCHOOL ORGANIZATION
DEPARTMENTALIZATION IN ELEMENTARY SCHOOLS. ED017329
THE NEW ELEMENTARY SCHOOL. ED017341
THE POLITICAL SOCIALIZATION OF CHILDREN AND THE STRUCTURE OF THE ELEMENTARY SCHOOL. ED024468
LEICESTERSHIRE REPORT: THE CLASSROOM ENVIRONMENT. ED027964
ASSESSING THE ALTERNATIVES EJ 033 055

SCHOOL PERSONNEL
WHAT'S AHEAD IN TEACHER EDUCATION? EJ 009 031

SCHOOL PHOBIA
A FOLLOW-UP STUDY OF SCHOOL PHOBIC ADOLESCENTS ADMITTED TO AN IN-PATIENT UNIT EJ 026 157
SCHOOL PHOBIA AND SELF-EVALUATION EJ 031 445

SCHOOL PLANNING
EDUCATIONAL SPECIFICATIONS FOR PIEDMONT ELEMENTARY SCHOOL. ED022547
A SOURCE REPORT FOR DEVELOPING PARENT-CHILD EDUCATIONAL CENTERS. ED027944

SCHOOL POLICY
HOW DO INNER-CITY TEACHERS USE A SYSTEM-WIDE CURRICULUM? EJ 015 487

SCHOOL PSYCHOLOGISTS
A DAY IN THE LIFE OF A SCHOOL PSYCHOLOGIST EJ 018 956

SCHOOL READINESS TESTS
PIAGET AND GESELL: A PSYCHOMETRIC ANALYSIS OF TESTS BUILT FROM THEIR TASKS EJ 053 927
TESTS BUILT FROM PIAGET'S AND GESELL'S TASKS AS PREDICTORS OF FIRST-GRADE ACHIEVEMENT EJ 058 928

SCHOOL ROLE
CRISIS IN VALUES. 1970 WHITE HOUSE CONFERENCE ON CHILDREN, REPORT OF FORUM 4. (WORKING COPY). ED046523
CHILDREN AND PARENTS: TOGETHER IN THE WORLD. 1970 WHITE HOUSE CONFERENCE ON CHILDREN, REPORT OF FORUM 15. (WORKING COPY). ED046531
VALUING THE DIGNITY OF BLACK CHILDREN: A BLACK TEACHER SPEAKS EJ 019 506
IF SCHOOLS ARE TO MEET THEIR RESPONSIBILITIES TO ALL CHILDREN EJ 022 977
HEALTH, EDUCATION, AND WELFARE: THE PROGRESSIVE IMPULSE IN THE NEW YORK CITY PUBLIC SCHOOLS EJ 029 104
THE WORLD HOUSE: BUILDING A QUALITATIVE ENVIRONMENT FOR ALL THE WORLD'S CHILDREN EJ 037 736

SCHOOL SOCIAL WORKERS
THE SCHOOL SOCIAL WORKER'S ROLE IN OVERCOMING LEARNING HANDICAPS EJ 046 401

SCHOOL SUPERINTENDENTS
SUPERINTENDENT JULIA RICHMAN: A SOCIAL PROGRESSIVE IN THE PUBLIC SCHOOLS EJ 060 106

SCHOOL SURVEYS
DEPARTMENTALIZATION IN ELEMENTARY SCHOOLS. ED017329
TEAM TEACHING IN ELEMENTARY GRADES. ED020800
HEAD START PROGRAMS OPERATED BY PUBLIC SCHOOL SYSTEMS, 1966-67. ED026115

SCHOOL VISITATION
LEICESTERSHIRE REPORT: THE CLASSROOM ENVIRONMENT. ED027964

SCIENCE ACTIVITIES
BIG QUESTIONS AND LITTLE CHILDREN: SCIENCE AND HEAD START. ED024458
SCIENCE ADVENTURES IN CHILDREN'S PLAY. ED026146
SCIENCING FOR YOUNG CHILDREN EJ 056 863

SCIENCE CURRICULUM
AN INDIVIDUALIZED SCIENCE LABORATORY. ED013664
LOGICAL THINKING IN SECOND GRADE. FINAL REPORT. ED033747

SCIENCE EDUCATION
BIG QUESTIONS AND LITTLE CHILDREN: SCIENCE AND HEAD START. ED024458
SCIENCE ADVENTURES IN CHILDREN'S PLAY. ED026146
PROBLEM SOLVING AND CONCEPT FORMATION: ANNOTATED LISTING OF NATIONAL AND INTERNATIONAL CURRICULAR PROJECTS AT THE EARLY CHILDHOOD LEVEL. ED029685
SCIENCE FOR THE PRIMARY GRADES: QUESTIONS AND ANSWERS. ED035461

SCIENCE LABORATORIES
AN INDIVIDUALIZED SCIENCE LABORATORY. ED013664

SCIENCE MATERIALS
SCIENCING FOR YOUNG CHILDREN EJ 056 863

SCIENCE PROGRAMS
BIG QUESTIONS AND LITTLE CHILDREN: SCIENCE AND HEAD START. ED024458
INDEPENDENT STUDY AT SEVEN EJ 029 168

SCIENCE UNITS
AUTUMN. UNIT 3 CURRICULUM GUIDE. ED053790

SCIENTIFIC RESEARCH
THE SEVENTIES: A TIME FOR GIANT STEPS EJ 009 030
NUTRITION AND BRAIN DEVELOPMENT IN INFANTS EJ 058 223

SCORES
CURRICULAR INTERVENTION IN LANGUAGE ARTS READINESS FOR HEAD START CHILDREN. TULANE UNIVERSITY, HEAD START EVALUATION AND RESEARCH CENTER, 1968-1969 INTERVENTION REPORT. SUPPLEMENT TO THE ANNUAL REPORT TO THE OFFICE OF ECONOMIC OPPORTUNITY. ED047795

SCORING
RECORDING INDIVIDUAL PUPIL EXPERIENCES IN THE CLASSROOM: A MANUAL FOR PROSE RECORDERS. ED038163

SCREENING TESTS
PRESCHOOL PREDICTION AND PREVENTION OF LEARNING DISABILITIES. ED013118
THE 1965 HEAD START PSYCHOLOGICAL SCREENING PROGRAM. FINAL REPORT ON THE DATA ANALYSIS. ED014333
DEVELOPMENT OF APPROPRIATE EVALUATION TECHNIQUES FOR SCREENING CHILDREN IN A HEAD START PROGRAM. A PILOT PROJECT. ED015006
AN INFANT RATING SCALE, ITS VALIDATION AND USEFULNESS. ED016513
USE OF NON-PROFESSIONAL PERSONNEL FOR HEALTH SCREENING OF HEAD START CHILDREN. FINAL REPORT. ED029702
SIX SCHOOL READINESS SCREENING DEVICES USED IN PEDIATRIC OFFICES: CONCURRENT VALIDITY. FINAL REPORT. ED029719
VERBAL REINFORCEMENT AS AN ADJUSTMENT PREDICTOR WITH KINDERGARTEN CHILDREN. FINAL REPORT. ED031313
A PRESCHOOL ARTICULATION AND LANGUAGE SCREENING FOR THE IDENTIFICATION OF SPEECH DISORDERS. FINAL REPORT. ED051889
STANDARDIZATION OF A RESEARCH INSTRUMENT FOR IDENTIFYING ASSOCIATIVE RESPONDING IN CHILDREN EJ 019 021
VALIDITY OF THE DENVER DEVELOPMENTAL SCREENING TEST EJ 041 722
THE RELATIONSHIP BETWEEN THE WECHSLER INTELLIGENCE SCALE FOR CHILDREN AND THE SLOSSON INTELLIGENCE TEST EJ 041 725
RELIABILITY AND STABILITY OF THE DENVER DEVELOPMENTAL SCREENING TEST EJ 053 905

SEARCH STRATEGIES
INFORMATION AND STRATEGY IN THE YOUNG CHILD'S SEARCH FOR HIDDEN OBJECTS EJ 056 395
ANALYSIS AND MODIFICATION OF SEARCH STRATEGIES OF IMPULSIVE AND REFLECTIVE CHILDREN ON THE MATCHING FAMILIAR FIGURES TEST EJ 059 510

SECOND LANGUAGE LEARNING
FINAL REPORT ON HEAD START EVALUATION AND RESEARCH--1966-67 TO THE INSTITUTE FOR EDUCATIONAL DEVELOPMENT. SECTION VI, THE MEASUREMENT OF BILINGUALISM AND BICULTURAL SOCIALIZATION OF THE CHILD IN THE SCHOOL SETTING--THE DEVELOPMENT OF INSTRUMENTS. ED019122
MEXICAN-AMERICANS AND LANGUAGE LEARNING EJ 012 397
CHILDREN WHO SPEAK NAVAJO EJ 014 918

SECONDARY EDUCATION
CURRENT EXPENDITURES BY LOCAL EDUCATION AGENCIES FOR FREE PUBLIC ELEMENTARY AND SECONDARY EDUCATION, 1968-69. ED052826

SECONDARY GRADES
ENVIRONMENTAL ECOLOGICAL EDUCATION IN CHILDREN'S BOOKS EJ 029 393

SECONDARY SCHOOL STUDENTS
"OPENNESS" OF SCHOOL CLIMATE AND ALIENATION OF HIGH SCHOOL STUDENTS EJ 052 654
A PIAGETIAN QUESTIONNAIRE APPLIED TO PUPILS IN A SECONDARY SCHOOL EJ 053 907

SECONDARY SCHOOL TEACHERS
A COMPARISON OF CHARACTERISTICS OF PROSPECTIVE SECONDARY SCHOOL TEACHERS ENROLLED IN TWO DIFFERENT DEGREE PROGRAMS EJ 029 618

SECURITY
PROXIMITY AND INTERACTIONAL BEHAVIOR OF YOUNG CHILDREN TO THEIR "SECURITY" BLANKETS EJ 053 748
THE IMPORTANCE OF SECURITY IN THE EDUCATION OF YOUNG CHILDREN EJ 062 549

SELECTION
EFFECTS OF DIFFERENTIAL PRIOR EXPOSURE ON YOUNG CHILDREN'S SUBSEQUENT OBSERVING AND CHOICE OF NOVEL STIMULI. ED017336
LITERATURE AND THE YOUNG CHILD. ED028828

SELF ACTUALIZATION
FACTORS ASSOCIATED WITH A PROGRAM FOR ENCOURAGING SELF-INITIATED ACTIVITIES BY FIFTH AND SIXTH GRADE STUDENTS IN A SELECTED ELEMENTARY SCHOOL EMPHASIZING INDIVIDUALIZED INSTRUCTION. ED015785
FINAL REPORT ON HEAD START EVALUATION AND RESEARCH: 1967-68 TO THE OFFICE OF ECONOMIC OPPORTUNITY. SECTION I: PART B, ACCURACY OF SELF-PERCEPTION AMONG CULTURALLY DEPRIVED PRESCHOOLS. ED023455
EMERGENCE OF IDENTITY: THE FIRST YEARS. 1970 WHITE HOUSE CONFERENCE ON CHILDREN, REPORT OF FORUM 2. (WORKING COPY). ED046521
NEW LIGHT ON THE HUMAN POTENTIAL EJ 026 373
THE EFFECTS OF OBJECT LOSS ON THE BODY IMAGE OF SCHIZOPHRENIC GIRLS EJ 027 345
A NATIONAL PRIORITY: RAISING THE QUALITY OF CHILDREN'S LIVES EJ 027 501
TOP PRIORITY: UNDERSTANDING SELF AND OTHERS EJ 050 072
LOOKING IN -- TO SELF DISCOVERY EJ 058 134

SELF CARE SKILLS
COMPARISON OF AMERICAN AND NORWEGIAN NURSERY SCHOOL CHILDREN ON INDEPENDENCE BEHAVIOR AND TRAINING. ED024457
COMPARISON OF AMERICAN AND NORWEGIAN NURSERY SCHOOL CHILDREN OF INDEPENDENCE BEHAVIOR AND TRAINING. SUMMARY REPORT. ED024476

SELF CONCEPT
THE DEVELOPMENT OF SELF-OTHER RELATIONSHIPS DURING PROJECT HEAD START. ED015008
FINAL REPORT ON HEAD START EVALUATION AND RESEARCH--1966-67 TO THE INSTITUTE FOR EDUCATIONAL DEVELOPMENT. SECTION VIII, RELATIONSHIPS BETWEEN SELF-CONCEPT AND SPECIFIC VARIABLES IN A LOW-INCOME CULTURALLY DIFFERENT POPULATION. ED019124
PREVENTION OF FAILURE. ED020777
SELF-SOCIAL CONSTRUCTS OF CHILDREN. ED021615
THE THOMAS SELF-CONCEPT VALUES TEST. ED027068
A COMPARATIVE STUDY OF THE SELF-IMAGES OF DISADVANTAGED CHILDREN. ED028821
EVALUATION OF THE EFFECTS OF HEAD START EXPERIENCE IN THE AREA OF SELF-CONCEPT, SOCIAL SKILLS, AND LANGUAGE SKILLS. PRE-PUBLICATION DRAFT. ED028832
THE EFFECT OF TEACHERS' INFERRED SELF CONCEPT UPON STUDENT ACHIEVEMENT. ED031300
DO NEGRO CHILDREN PROJECT A SELF-IMAGE OF HELPLESSNESS AND INADEQUACY IN DRAWING A PERSON? ED036329
THE EFFECT OF THE MALE ELEMENTARY TEACHER ON CHILDREN'S SELF-CONCEPTS. ED039034
RACE AND SEX IDENTIFICATION IN PRESCHOOL CHILDREN. ED041634
A STUDY OF HOME ENVIRONMENT AND READINESS FOR ACHIEVEMENT AT SCHOOL. FINAL REPORT. ED041637
THE PROFESSIONAL SELF IMAGE AND THE ATTRIBUTES OF A PROFESSION: AN EXPLORATORY STUDY OF THE PRESCHOOL TEACHER. ED044183
EMERGENCE OF IDENTITY: THE FIRST YEARS. 1970 WHITE HOUSE CONFERENCE ON CHILDREN, REPORT OF FORUM 2. (WORKING COPY). ED046521
EXPRESSIONS OF IDENTITY: THE SCHOOL-AGE CHILD. 1970 WHITE HOUSE CONFERENCE ON CHILDREN, REPORT OF FORUM 3. (WORKING COPY). ED046522
A REVISION OF THE BASIC PROGRAM PLAN OF EDUCATION AT AGE THREE. ED047774
DECENTRATION IN CHILDREN: ITS GENERALITY AND CORRELATES. ED048926
THE ASSESSMENT OF "SELF-CONCEPT" IN EARLY CHILDHOOD EDUCATION. ED050822
A STUDY OF THE DEVELOPMENT OF EGOCENTRISM AND THE COORDINATION OF SPATIAL PERCEPTIONS IN ELEMENTARY SCHOOL CHILDREN. FINAL REPORT. ED050829
ON EARLY LEARNING: THE MODIFIABILITY OF HUMAN POTENTIAL. ED051876
A STUDY IN CHILD CARE (CASE STUDY FROM VOLUME II-A): "A HOUSE FULL OF CHILDREN." DAY CARE PROGRAMS REPRINT SERIES. ED051891
ALL ABOUT ME. UNIT 1 CURRICULUM GUIDE. ED053789
"THIS IS ME!" EJ 003 029
FOR BETTER READING - A MORE POSITIVE SELF-IMAGE EJ 013 562
ESTEEM AND ACHIEVEMENT IN ARITHMETIC EJ 015 160
SELF-CONCEPTS OF HIGH- AND LOW-CURIOSITY BOYS EJ 019 005
RELATION OF EARLY SOCIALIZATION EXPERIENCES TO SELF-CONCEPTS AND GENDER ROLE IN MIDDLE CHILDHOOD EJ 021 997
A DEVELOPMENTAL STUDY OF THE RELATIONSHIP BETWEEN CONCEPTUAL, EGO, AND MORAL DEVELOPMENT EJ 021 999
SCHOOL ACHIEVERS AND UNDERACHIEVERS IN AN URBAN GHETTO EJ 027 614

SELF-PERCEPTIONS OF PUPILS IN AN EXPERIMENTAL ELEMENTARY SCHOOL EJ 028 239
LET DO IT MY WAY EJ 028 846
ANXIETY - A CLASSROOM CLOSE-UP EJ 028 896
RACIAL AWARENESS IN YOUNG MEXICAN-AMERICAN, NEGRO AND ANGLO CHILDREN EJ 028 926
ADOLESCENCE, IDENTITY, AND FOSTER FAMILY CARE EJ 030 652
SOCIAL SCHEMATA OF SCHOOL BEGINNERS: SOME DEMOGRAPHIC CORRELATES EJ 030 713
SELF-DESCRIPTION AS A FUNCTION OF EVALUATIVE AND ACTIVITY RATINGS AMONG AMERICAN AND INDIAN ADOLESCENTS EJ 034 042
THE MANIPULATION AND MEASUREMENT OF SELF-DISCLOSURE IN PREADOLESCENTS EJ 034 298
NEW CONCEPTS OF HUMAN POTENTIALS: NEW CHALLENGE FOR TEACHERS EJ 034 711
SELF CONCEPTS OF DISADVANTAGED AND ADVANTAGED STUDENTS EJ 035 618
SELF-ESTEEM, SUCCESS-FAILURE, AND LOCUS OF CONTROL IN NEGRO CHILDREN EJ 035 621
A THERAPEUTIC APPROACH TO SPEECH PHOBIA: ELECTIVE MUTISM REEXAMINED EJ 035 625
SEX-ROLE IDENTITY AND SIBLING COMPOSITION EJ 035 626
FATHER ABSENCE, PERCEIVED MATERNAL BEHAVIOR, AND MASCULINITY OF SELF-CONCEPT AMONG JUNIOR HIGH SCHOOL BOYS EJ 035 804
A TEST OF ERIKSON'S THEORY OF EGO EPIGENESIS EJ 039 898
CHANGE IN EFFICIENCY OF EGO FUNCTIONING AND COMPLEXITY FROM ADOLESCENCE TO YOUNG ADULTHOOD EJ 039 902
DIFFERENTIAL ADJUSTMENT TO PUBESCENCE AND COGNITIVE STYLE PATTERNS EJ 039 903
LEVEL OF "N" ACHIEVEMENT AND PROBABILITY IN CHILDREN EJ 039 906
A LONGITUDINAL STUDY OF CHANGES IN EGO IDENTITY STATUS DURING THE FRESHMAN YEAR AT COLLEGE EJ 043 193
IMPROVING THE SELF-CONCEPTS OF ACADEMIC UNDERACHIEVERS THROUGH MATERNAL GROUP COUNSELING EJ 043 200
INTERPERSONAL PERCEPTION OF YOUNG CHILDREN: EGOCENTRISM OR EMPATHY? EJ 043 606
SOME DEVELOPMENTAL CHANGES IN THE ORGANIZATION OF SELF-EVALUATIONS EJ 044 186
RECIPROCAL CONTRIBUTIONS BETWEEN PSYCHOANALYSIS AND PSYCHOEDUCATION EJ 045 048
PERCEPTIONS OF NEGRO BOYS REGARDING COLOR AND OCCUPATIONAL STATUS EJ 045 392
A METHOD FOR STUDYING THE DEVELOPMENT OF GENDER IDENTITY EJ 046 784
SELF-ESTEEM, PARENT IDENTIFICATION AND SEX ROLE DEVELOPMENT IN PRESCHOOL AGE BOYS AND GIRLS EJ 051 015
SELF-INITIATED VERBAL REINFORCEMENT AND POSITIVE SELF-CONCEPT EJ 052 462
THE FORMATION AND REVERSAL OF AN ATTITUDE AS FUNCTIONS OF ASSUMED SELF-CONCEPT, RACE, AND SOCIOECONOMIC CLASS EJ 052 652
SOME SOCIAL EFFECTS OF CROSS-GRADE GROUPING EJ 055 107
CHANGES IN SELF-PERCEPTIONS OF HEAD-START TRAINEES EJ 055 213
SUCCESS AND ACCOUNTABILITY EJ 055 533
DEVELOPMENT OF A SENSE OF SELF-IDENTITY IN CHILDREN EJ 056 617
THE MEASUREMENT OF CHILDREN'S SELF-CONCEPT AS RELATED TO RACIAL MEMBERSHIP EJ 056 629
TEACHER EXPECTANCY AS RELATED TO THE ACADEMIC AND PERSONAL GROWTH OF PRIMARY-AGE CHILDREN EJ 057 018
THE EFFECTS OF THE DUSO GUIDANCE PROGRAM ON THE SELF-CONCEPTS OF PRIMARY SCHOOL CHILDREN EJ 058 132
STOP, LOOK, LISTEN -- AND KEEP ON!! EJ 058 133
LOOKING IN -- TO SELF DISCOVERY EJ 058 134
CROSS-SEX IDENTITY IN BARBADOS EJ 058 136
EXTENSION OF PERSONAL FUTURE TIME PERSPECTIVE, AGE, AND LIFE-SATISFACTION OF CHILDREN AND ADOLESCENTS EJ 058 140
EGO IDENTITY STATUS AND MORALITY: THE RELATIONSHIP BETWEEN TWO DEVELOPMENTAL CONSTRUCTS EJ 058 141
THE RELATIONSHIP BETWEEN CHILDREN'S ACADEMIC PERFORMANCE AND ACHIEVEMENT ACCOUNTABILITY EJ 058 414
EGOCENTRISM AND SOCIAL INFLUENCE IN CHILDREN EJ 058 590
SEX ROLE IDENTITY OF ADOLESCENT GIRLS IN FOSTER HOMES AND INSTITUTIONS EJ 059 644
HOW TO TEACH FEAR EJ 061 058
PERSONAL ORIENTATION TO SUCCESS AND FAILURE IN URBAN BLACK CHILDREN EJ 061 072

SELF CONCEPT PSYCHOLOGICAL PATTERNS
THE FEELINGS OF LEARNING EJ 003 082

SELF CONCEPT TESTS
SELF CONCEPT AND SOCIO-ECONOMIC STATUS EJ 059 509

SELF CONTAINED CLASSROOMS
ABSTRACTS OF RESEARCH PERTAINING TO--UNGRADED VS SELF-CONTAINED CLASSROOM ORGANIZATION IN THE ELEMENTARY SCHOOL (GRADES 1-7). ED019129
EFFECT OF CLASSROOM NOISE ON NUMBER IDENTIFICATION BY RETARDED CHILDREN EJ 045 391

SELF CONTROL
PARENTAL ANTECEDENTS OF CHILDREN'S BELIEFS IN INTERNAL-EXTERNAL CONTROL OF REINFORCEMENTS IN INTELLECTUAL ACHIEVEMENT SITUATIONS. ED024447
THE ACQUISITION OF SELF-REWARD PATTERNS BY CHILDREN. FINAL REPORT. ED032137
RESISTANCE TO TEMPTATION IN YOUNG NEGRO CHILDREN IN RELATION TO SEX OF THE SUBJECT, SEX OF THE EXPERIMENTER AND FATHER ABSENCE OR PRESENCE. ED032138
AN ANALYSIS AND EVALUATION OF THE MONTESSORI THEORY OF INNER DISCIPLINE. ED040746
MODIFYING RESPONSE LATENCY AND ERROR RATE OF IMPULSIVE CHILDREN. ED050819
SOCIAL REINFORCEMENT FOR EXPRESSION VS. SUPPRESSION OF AGGRESSION EJ 007 691
A TEST OF THE GENERALITY OF THE EFFECTS OF DEVIANT PRESCHOOL MODELS EJ 034 531
SEX DIFFERENCES IN ADAPTIVE STYLES EJ 045 046
SELF-PARENTAL DISTANCE, CONTROL OF REINFORCEMENT, AND PERSONAL FUTURE TIME PERSPECTIVE EJ 045 047

SELF DIRECTED CLASSROOMS
WHEN CHILDREN ENJOY SCHOOL: SOME LESSONS FROM BRITAIN EJ 018 047

SELF DIRECTED GROUPS
THE TEACHING OF INQUIRY SKILLS TO ELEMENTARY SCHOOL CHILDREN. FINAL REPORT. ED020805

SELF ESTEEM
IMPLICATIONS OF STUDIES ON SELF-ESTEEM FOR EDUCATIONAL RESEARCH AND PRACTICE. ED033742
EXPRESSIONS OF IDENTITY: THE SCHOOL-AGE CHILD. 1970 WHITE HOUSE CONFERENCE ON CHILDREN, REPORT OF FORUM 3. (WORKING COPY). ED046522
DIFFERENTIAL RESPONSE PATTERNS AS THEY AFFECT THE SELF ESTEEM OF THE CHILD. ED046542
IMAGES OF THE IDEAL PUPIL HELD BY TEACHERS IN PREPARATION EJ 012 679
PSYCHIATRIC DISORDER AND ADULT AND PEER GROUP REJECTION OF THE CHILD'S NAME EJ 026 156
SELF-ESTEEM, SUCCESS-FAILURE, AND LOCUS OF CONTROL IN NEGRO CHILDREN EJ 035 621
NORMAL AND RETARDED CHILDREN'S EXPECTANCY FOR FAILURE EJ 039 266
PERCEPTIONS OF NEGRO BOYS REGARDING COLOR AND OCCUPATIONAL STATUS EJ 045 392
SELF-ESTEEM, PARENT IDENTIFICATION AND SEX ROLE DEVELOPMENT IN PRESCHOOL AGE BOYS AND GIRLS EJ 051 015
SELF CONCEPT AND SOCIO-ECONOMIC STATUS EJ 059 509

SELF EVALUATION
EVALUATION OF CLASSROOM CLIMATE EJ 002 421
LONG-TERM RETENTION OF VERBAL IMITATION EJ 024 941
SCHOOL PHOBIA AND SELF-EVALUATION EJ 031 445
EFFECT OF INSTRUCTIONAL SET ON TWELVE-YEAR-OLD CHILDREN'S PERCEPTION OF INTERRUPTION EJ 034 921
CONFORMITY IN EARLY AND LATE ADOLESCENCE EJ 038 936
SOME DEVELOPMENTAL CHANGES IN THE ORGANIZATION OF SELF-EVALUATIONS EJ 044 186

SELF EXPRESSION
WHEN THE CHILD IS ANGRY. ED017331
CLASSROOM OPPORTUNITIES TO EXPRESS FEELINGS EJ 001 912
EFFECTS OF SOCIAL CLASS ON CHILDREN'S MOTORIC EXPRESSION EJ 025 149
THE CHILD'S EYE VIEW: EXPERIMENTAL PHOTOGRAPHY WITH PRESCHOOL CHILDREN EJ 029 342
EXPANDING THE CHILD'S WORLD THROUGH DRAMA AND MOVEMENT EJ 034 421
CHILDREN AND WAR GAMES EJ 034 533
EXPRESSIONS OF PERSONALITY IN CREATIONS OF LATENCY AGE CHILDREN EJ 041 446

SELF PACING MACHINES
ON RESPONSIVE ENVIRONMENTS. ED018278

SELF REWARD
RESEARCH ON THE NEW NURSERY SCHOOL. PART II: A REPORT ON THE USE OF TYPEWRITERS AND RELATED EQUIPMENT WITH THREE- AND FOUR-YEAR-OLD CHILDREN AT THE NEW NURSERY SCHOOL. INTERIM REPORT. ED027077
THE ACQUISITION OF SELF-REWARD PATTERNS BY CHILDREN. FINAL REPORT. ED032137
SELF-REINFORCEMENT ESTABLISHED FOR A DISCRIMINATION TASK EJ 025 964
SOME DETERMINANTS OF CHILDREN'S SELF-REWARD BEHAVIOR AFTER EXPOSURE TO DISCREPANT REWARD CRITERIA EJ 030 511
POWER AND THE INTERNALIZATION OF SELF-DENIAL EJ 036 077
EFFECTS OF SOCIAL COMPARISON UPON CHILDREN'S SELF-REINFORCEMENT AND ALTRUISM TOWARD COMPETITORS AND FRIENDS EJ 041 856
SOCIAL COMPARISON BY YOUNG CHILDREN EJ 043 672

EFFECTS OF SOCIOECONOMIC STATUS AND THE VALUE OF A REINFORCER UPON SELF-REINFORCEMENT BY CHILDREN EJ 056 726

SEMANTICS

SEMANTIC RELATIONSHIP AND THE LEARNING OF SYNTACTIC WORD PAIRS IN CHILDREN EJ 016 163
COMPARISON OF PICTORIAL AND VERBAL SEMANTIC SCALES AS USED BY CHILDREN EJ 029 769
THE EFFECTS OF CONNOTATIVE SIMILARITY IN CHILDREN'S LEARNING OF A PAIRED-ASSOCIATE TASK EJ 035 376
THE GROWTH OF CHILDREN'S SEMANTIC MEMORY: SEMANTIC ELEMENTS EJ 038 170
IDENTIFICATION OF VERBAL CONCEPTS BY PRESCHOOL CHILDREN EJ 042 958
CONCEPT CONSERVATION IN CHILDREN: THE DEPENDENCE OF BELIEF SYSTEMS ON SEMANTIC REPRESENTATION EJ 053 742
DEVELOPMENT OF RELATIONAL CONCEPTS AND WORD DEFINITION IN CHILDREN FIVE THROUGH ELEVEN EJ 056 397

SEMINARS

THE TEACHER, TEACHER STYLE, AND CLASSROOM MANAGEMENT. PROCEEDINGS OF THE HEAD START RESEARCH SEMINARS: SEMINAR NO. 2, THE TEACHER AND CLASSROOM MANAGEMENT (1ST, WASHINGTON, D.C., JULY 22, 1968). ED035463

SENIOR CITIZENS

WHAT GENERATION GAP? EJ 032 763

SENSITIVITY TRAINING

SENSITIVITY TRAINING: WHAT IS IT? HOW CAN IT HELP STUDENTS, TEACHERS, ADMINISTRATORS? EJ 023 702
IT MAKES ME FEEL BAD WHEN YOU CALL ME "STINKY" EJ 029 358
USING SENSITIVITY TRAINING WITH JUNIOR HIGH SCHOOL STUDENTS EJ 035 169
A SENSITIVITY-TRAINING APPROACH TO GROUP THERAPY WITH CHILDREN EJ 039 501

SENSORY DEPRIVATION

THE USEFULNESS OF CUMULATIVE DEPRIVATION AS AN EXPLANATION OF EDUCATIONAL DEFICIENCIES EJ 033 056
EARLY AUDITORY DEPRIVATION AND SENSORY COMPENSATION EJ 044 118

SENSORY EXPERIENCE

SENSORIMOTOR EXPERIENCE AND CONCEPT FORMATION IN EARLY CHILDHOOD. FINAL REPORT. ED019143
A LONGITUDINAL ASSESSMENT OF PRESCHOOL CHILDREN IN HAPTIC LEARNING. FINAL REPORT. ED020019
INFORMAL EDUCATION DURING THE FIRST MONTHS OF LIFE. ED024452
DESIGNING TOMORROW'S SCHOOL TODAY: THE MULTI-SENSORY EXPERIENCE CENTER EJ 033 784
GOING ON A TRIP EJ 035 842
CAN NEWBORNS SHOW CARDIAC ORIENTING? EJ 036 078
THE EFFECTS OF THE ENVIRONMENT UPON STATE CYCLES IN THE HUMAN NEWBORN EJ 044 119
CARDIAC DECELERATION AND ITS STABILITY IN HUMAN NEWBORNS EJ 046 891
COMPARISONS OF VOCAL IMITATION, TACTILE STIMULATION, AND FOOD AS REINFORCERS FOR INFANT VOCALIZATIONS EJ 055 206

SENSORY INTEGRATION

INFORMAL EDUCATION DURING THE FIRST MONTHS OF LIFE. ED024452
DEVELOPMENTAL DIFFERENCES IN THE INTEGRATION OF PICTURE SERIES: EFFECTS OF VARIATIONS IN OBJECT-ATTRIBUTE RELATIONSHIPS EJ 029 386
SEQUENCE EFFECTS IN THE ABSTRACTION OF THE CONCEPT OF PROGRESSIVE CHANGE EJ 029 532
DEVELOPMENT OF CUTANEOUS AND KINESTHETIC LOCALIZATION BY BLIND AND SIGHTED CHILDREN EJ 055 113
INTERMODAL AND INTRAMODAL RETENTION OF VISUAL AND TACTUAL INFORMATION IN YOUNG CHILDREN EJ 057 900

SENSORY TRAINING

A GUIDE FOR PERCEPTUAL-MOTOR TRAINING ACTIVITIES. ED027075
VISION TRAINING - A NEW DEVELOPMENTAL CONCEPT IN CHILD VISION. ED028842
EFFECT OF A KINDERGARTEN PROGRAM OF PERCEPTUAL TRAINING UPON THE LATER DEVELOPMENT OF READING SKILLS. FINAL REPORT. ED030491
THE EFFECTS OF A LEARNING PROGRAM IN PERCEPTUAL-MOTOR ACTIVITY UPON THE VISUAL PERCEPTION OF SHAPE. FINAL REPORT. ED030494
A STUDY IN VISUAL-MOTOR-PERCEPTUAL TRAINING IN FIRST GRADE. ED031292
AN EXPERIMENTAL STUDY OF VISUAL PERCEPTUAL TRAINING AND READINESS SCORES WITH CERTAIN FIRST-GRADE CHILDREN. ED032921
EFFECT OF SENSORIMOTOR ACTIVITY ON PERCEPTION AND LEARNING IN THE NEUROLOGICALLY HANDICAPPED CHILD. FINAL PROGRESS REPORT. ED033757
CHILDREN'S SELECTIVE ATTENTION TO STIMULI: STAGE OR SET? EJ 033 573

SENTENCE STRUCTURE

EXPERIMENTS IN GRAMMATICAL PROCESSING IN CHILDREN. RESEARCH PROJECT NUMBER 1 OF PROJECT HEAD START RESEARCH AND EVALUATION CENTER, SYRACUSE UNIVERSITY RESEARCH INSTITUTE. FINAL REPORT, NOVEMBER 1, 1967. ED026138
THE ACQUISITION OF DIRECT AND INDIRECT OBJECTS IN JAPANESE EJ 036 745
NOUN-PAIR LEARNING IN CHILDREN AND ADULTS: UNDERLYING STRINGS AND RETRIEVAL TIME EJ 056 402
CHILDREN'S COMPREHENSION OF RELATIVIZED ENGLISH SENTENCES EJ 056 715
SURFACE STRUCTURE AND THE TOPIC-COMMENT DISTINCTION: A DEVELOPMENTAL STUDY EJ 056 717
THE DEVELOPMENT OF COMPETENCE IN AN EXCEPTIONAL LANGUAGE STRUCTURE IN OLDER CHILDREN AND YOUNG ADULTS EJ 056 727

SENTENCES

EFFECTS OF TRAINING YOUNG BLACK CHILDREN IN VOCABULARY VS. SENTENCE CONSTRUCTION. ED038176
SEMANTICS, PHRASE STRUCTURE, AND AGE AS VARIABLES IN SENTENCE RECALL EJ 025 962
SEMANTIC INTEGRATION, AGE, AND THE RECALL OF SENTENCES EJ 056 620
THE YOUNG CHILD'S COMPREHENSION OF TIME CONNECTIVES EJ 056 724
SOME FACTORS AFFECTING THE COMPLEXITY OF CHILDREN'S SENTENCES: THE EFFECTS OF MODELING, AGE, SEX, AND BILINGUALISM EJ 060 780

SEQUENTIAL APPROACH

CHILD DEVELOPMENT AND MATERIAL SURVEY. PART I, TECHNICAL REPORT. FINAL REPORT. ED027084
A SEQUENTIAL APPROACH TO EARLY CHILDHOOD AND ELEMENTARY EDUCATION, PHASE II. GRANT REPORT. ED047791
THE MYTH BEHIND GRADED CONTENT EJ 052 126

SEQUENTIAL LEARNING

SEQUENCE IN LEARNING--FACT OR FICTION. ED017330
A FRESH APPROACH TO EARLY CHILDHOOD EDUCATION AND A STUDY OF ITS EFFECTIVENESS. LEARNING TO LEARN PROGRAM. ED019117
AN EVALUATION OF THE EFFECTS OF A UNIQUE SEQUENTIAL LEARNING PROGRAM ON CULTURALLY DEPRIVED PRESCHOOL CHILDREN. FINAL REPORT. ED019994
A SEQUENTIAL APPROACH TO EARLY CHILDHOOD AND ELEMENTARY EDUCATION, PHASE I. GRANT REPORT. ED042517
A SEQUENTIAL APPROACH TO EARLY CHILDHOOD AND ELEMENTARY EDUCATION, PHASE II. GRANT REPORT. ED047791
THINKING ABOUT PEOPLE THINKING ABOUT PEOPLE THINKING ABOUT...: A STUDY OF SOCIAL COGNITIVE DEVELOPMENT EJ 025 953
TRANSFER AND SEQUENCE IN LEARNING DOUBLE CLASSIFICATION SKILLS EJ 035 379
SEQUENTIAL LEARNING BY CHILDREN EJ 035 381
THE SEQUENCE OF DEVELOPMENT OF CERTAIN NUMBER CONCEPTS IN PRESCHOOL CHILDREN EJ 044 694

SEQUENTIAL PROGRAMS

A SEQUENTIAL APPROACH TO EARLY CHILDHOOD AND ELEMENTARY EDUCATION, PHASE II. GRANT REPORT. ED047791

SEQUENTIAL READING PROGRAMS

THE DEVELOPMENT OF PRE-READING SKILLS IN AN EXPERIMENTAL KINDERGARTEN PROGRAM EJ 037 099

SERIAL LEARNING

VISUAL AND AUDITORY MEMORY IN CHILDREN. PART OF THE FINAL REPORT ON HEAD START EVALUATION AND RESEARCH: 1968-69 TO THE OFFICE OF ECONOMIC OPPORTUNITY. ED037246
IMPLICATIONS OF MNEMONICS RESEARCH FOR COGNITIVE THEORY. ED045199
SPATIO-TEMPORAL SERIAL PERFORMANCE IN CHILDREN AND ADULTS EJ 021 758
EFFECTS OF CONCURRENT AND SERIAL TRAINING ON GENERALIZED VOCAL IMITATION IN RETARDED CHILDREN EJ 055 210

SERIAL ORDERING

MATCHING AUDITORY AND VISUAL SERIES: MODALITY PROBLEM OR TRANSLATION PROBLEM? EJ 051 569
DEVELOPMENT OF THE CONCEPT OF SERIATION EJ 053 650
EFFECTS OF HEBREW AND ENGLISH LETTERS ON CHILDREN'S PERCEPTUAL SET EJ 053 721
MEANINGFULNESS, SERIAL POSITION AND RETENTION INTERVAL IN RECOGNITION SHORT-TERM MEMORY EJ 053 724
FIGURATIVE AND OPERATIVE ASPECTS OF CHILDREN'S INFERENCE EJ 056 616
SOCIAL-CLASS DIFFERENCES AND TASK VARIABLES IN THE DEVELOPMENT OF MULTIPLICATIVE CLASSIFICATION EJ 056 619
THE EFFECTS OF GROUPING ON SHORT-TERM SERIAL RECALL OF DIGITS BY CHILDREN: DEVELOPMENTAL TRENDS EJ 059 320
VISUAL HABITUATION IN THE HUMAN INFANT EJ 059 511
CHILDREN'S ABILITY TO ORDER FACIAL AND NONFACIAL CONTINUA AS A FUNCTION OF MA, CA, AND IQ EJ 059 699
PERCEPTION AND LANGUAGE: A GERMAN REPLICATION OF THE PIAGET-INHELDER POSITION EJ 060 773

SET THEORY

MATHEMATICS FOR ELEMENTARY SCHOOL TEACHERS. ED018276

SEX (CHARACTERISTICS)

THE IMPACT OF COGNITIVE MATURITY ON THE DEVELOPMENT OF SEX-ROLE ATTITUDES IN THE YEARS 4 TO 8. ED019109
SEX ROLE TYPING IN THE PRESCHOOL YEARS: AN OVERVIEW. ED026134
RACE AND SEX IDENTIFICATION IN PRESCHOOL CHILDREN. ED041634
TIMING AND SOURCES OF INFORMATION ABOUT, AND ATTITUDES TOWARD, MENSTRUATION AMONG COLLEGE FEMALES EJ 029 533
MASCULINITY AND FEMININITY IN THE ELEMENTARY AND JUNIOR HIGH SCHOOL YEARS EJ 034 902
THE INFLUENCE OF MASCULINE, FEMININE, AND NEUTRAL TASKS ON CHILDREN'S ACHIEVEMENT BEHAVIOR, EXPECTANCIES OF SUCCESS, AND ATTAINMENT VALUES EJ 037 318
NORMAL PSYCHOSEXUAL DEVELOPMENT EJ 038 944
THE PRIORITY OF CUES IN SEX DISCRIMINATION BY CHILDREN AND ADULTS EJ 044 691
ACADEMIC CHEATING: THE CONTRIBUTION OF SEX, PERSONALITY AND SITUATIONAL VARIABLES EJ 055 104
EFFECTS OF SEX AND BIRTH ORDER ON SEX-ROLE DEVELOPMENT AND INTELLIGENCE AMONG KINDERGARTEN CHILDREN EJ 057 133
CROSS-SEX IDENTITY IN BARBADOS EJ 058 136
SEX DIFFERENCES IN HUMAN DEVELOPMENT EJ 060 015

SEX DIFFERENCES

HEADSTART OPERATIONAL FIELD ANALYSIS. PROGRESS REPORT III. ED015776
SEX AND RACE DIFFERENCES IN THE DEVELOPMENT OF UNDERPRIVILEGED PRESCHOOL CHILDREN. ED019992
PLAY BEHAVIOR IN THE YEAR-OLD INFANT: EARLY SEX DIFFERENCES. ED022545
HEAD START EVALUATION AND RESEARCH CENTER, BOSTON UNIVERSITY. REPORT C-I, PERCEPTION OF EMOTION AMONG CHILDREN: RACE AND SEX DIFFERENCES. ED022561
A COMPARISON OF PRE-KINDERGARTEN AND PRE-1ST GRADE BOYS AND GIRLS ON MEASURES OF SCHOOL READINESS AND LANGUAGE DEVELOPMENT. INTERIM REPORT. ED023474
SEX DIFFERENCES IN MENTAL AND BEHAVIORAL TRAITS. ED026117
PARENTAL BEHAVIOR TOWARD BOYS AND GIRLS OF PRESCHOOL AGE. ED026119
ERROR, RESPONSE TIME AND IQ: SEX DIFFERENCES IN COGNITIVE STYLE OF PRESCHOOL CHILDREN. ED026122
SEX ROLE TYPING IN THE PRESCHOOL YEARS: AN OVERVIEW. ED026134
THE RELATIONSHIP OF INDIVIDUAL DIFFERENCES IN THE ORIENTING RESPONSE TO COMPLEX LEARNING IN KINDERGARTNERS. ED031299
CHILDREN'S PERCEPTIONS OF ADULT ROLES AS AFFECTED BY CLASS, FATHER-ABSENCE AND RACE. ED032134
A PILOT STUDY TO ASSESS THE ACADEMIC PROGRESS OF DISADVANTAGED FIRST GRADERS ASSIGNED TO CLASS BY SEX AND TAUGHT BY A TEACHER OF THE SAME SEX. ED035462
THE DEVELOPMENT OF A COMPUTER TECHNIQUE FOR THE CONTENT ANALYSIS OF PSYCHO-SOCIAL FACTORS IN THE ORAL LANGUAGE OF KINDERGARTEN CHILDREN. ED038184
THE EFFECT OF THE MALE ELEMENTARY TEACHER ON CHILDREN'S SELF-CONCEPTS. ED039034
DEVELOPING COGNITIVE LEARNINGS WITH YOUNG CHILDREN. ED041614
PARENT PREFERENCE OF PRESCHOOL CHILDREN. ED041628
A STUDY OF HOME ENVIRONMENT AND READINESS FOR ACHIEVEMENT AT SCHOOL. FINAL REPORT. ED041637
RISK-TAKING BEHAVIOR IN PRESCHOOL CHILDREN FROM THREE ETHNIC BACKGROUNDS. ED042486
THE EFFECT OF FOUR COMMUNICATION PATTERNS AND SEX ON LENGTH OF VERBALIZATION IN SPEECH OF FOUR YEAR OLD CHILDREN. FINAL REPORT. ED042514
THE EFFECT OF AGGRESSIVE CARTOONS: CHILDREN'S INTERPERSONAL PLAY. ED046543
THE RELATIONSHIP OF INDIVIDUAL DIFFERENCES IN THE ORIENTING RESPONSE TO COMPLEX LEARNING IN KINDERGARTNERS. REPORT FROM THE MOTIVATION AND INDIVIDUAL DIFFERENCES IN LEARNING AND RETENTION PROJECT. ED046544
TWO KINDS OF KINDERGARTEN AFTER FOUR TYPES OF HEAD START. ED050824
STATE AS AN INFANT-ENVIRONMENT INTERACTION: AN ANALYSIS OF MOTHER-INFANT BEHAVIOR AS A FUNCTION OF SEX. ED052829
INTERACTION OF SEX OF SUBJECT AND DEPENDENCY-TRAINING PROCEDURES IN A SOCIAL-REINFORCEMENT STUDY EJ 006 877
SEX DIFFERENCES IN CHILDREN'S MODES OF AGGRESSIVE RESPONSES TOWARD OUTSIDERS EJ 007 690
FEAR OF VISUAL NOVELTY: DEVELOPMENTAL PATTERNS IN MALES AND FEMALES EJ 019 011
PROBABILITY LEARNING AS A FUNCTION OF AGE, SEX, AND TYPE OF CONSTRAINT EJ 021 766
IT SCORE VARIATIONS BY INSTRUCTIONAL STYLE EJ 022 142
SEX IDENTITY IN LONDON CHILDREN: MEMORY, KNOWLEDGE AND PREFERENCE TESTS EJ 023 435
SOCIOECONOMIC STATUS AND SEX DIFFERENCES IN ADOLESCENT REFERENCE-GROUP ORIENTATION EJ 023 614
SEX DIFFERENCES IN PRESCHOOL CHILDREN WITHOUT HISTORIES OF COMPLICATIONS OF PREGNANCY AND DELIVERY EJ 024 939
AGGRESSION IN CHILDREN AS A FUNCTION OF SEX OF SUBJECT AND SEX OF OPPONENT EJ 024 945
INTERACTION OF REWARD, PUNISHMENT, AND SEX IN A TWO-CHOICE DISCRIMINATION TASK WITH CHILDREN EJ 024 948
SOME RELATIONSHIPS AMONG CHILDREN'S PERCEPTIONS OF PARENTAL CHARACTERISTICS EJ 025 318
HONESTY AND ALTRUISM AMONG PREADOLESCENTS EJ 026 450
PROBABILITY LEARNING AS A FUNCTION OF SEX OF THE SUBJECT, TEST ANXIETY, AND PERCENTAGE OF REINFORCEMENT EJ 027 181
NEWBORN ATTENTION: DIFFERENTIAL RESPONSE DECREMENT TO VISUAL STIMULI EJ 027 846
DIFFERENTIAL FACTOR STRUCTURE OF SEVENTH GRADE STUDENTS EJ 030 298
CHILDREN'S TWO-CHOICE LEARNING OF PREDOMINANTLY ALTERNATING AND REPEATING SEQUENCES EJ 033 791
THE EFFECTS OF SEX-ROLE STANDARDS FOR ACHIEVEMENT AND SEX-ROLE PREFERENCE ON THREE DETERMINANTS OF ACHIEVEMENT MOTIVATION EJ 034 454
CHILDREN AND WAR GAMES EJ 034 533
STIMULUS AND RESPONSE ALTERNATION IN YOUNG CHILDREN EJ 034 537
HARMONIOUS PARENTS AND THEIR PRESCHOOL CHILDREN EJ 034 708
MASCULINITY AND FEMININITY IN THE ELEMENTARY AND JUNIOR HIGH SCHOOL YEARS EJ 034 902
DISADVANTAGED AND NONDISADVANTAGED CHILDREN'S EXPECTANCY IN SKILL AND CHANCE OUTCOMES EJ 034 903
TRAINING CREATIVITY IN YOUNG CHILDREN EJ 035 373
PATTERN COPYING UNDER THREE CONDITIONS OF AN EXPANDED SPATIAL FIELD EJ 035 622
EXPERIMENTER BIAS IN PERFORMANCE OF CHILDREN AT A SIMPLE MOTOR TASK EJ 035 710
SEX DIFFERENCES IN YIELDING TO TEMPTATION: A FUNCTION OF THE SITUATION EJ 035 711
THE EFFECTS OF FATHER ABSENCE ON CHILD DEVELOPMENT EJ 035 800
FATHERS' VERBAL INTERACTION WITH INFANTS IN THE FIRST THREE MONTHS OF LIFE EJ 036 126
ORIGINS OF SOCIAL DEVELOPMENT IN INFANCY EJ 038 570
FATHER ABSENCE AND CONSCIENCE DEVELOPMENT EJ 038 854
RACE AND CONFORMITY AMONG CHILDREN EJ 038 937
SEX DIFFERENCES IN ADOLESCENT REACTIONS TOWARD NEWCOMERS EJ 039 899
THE RELATIONSHIP OF BIRTH ORDER AND SEX OF SIBLINGS TO GENDER ROLE IDENTITY EJ 039 901
CHANGE IN EFFICIENCY OF EGO FUNCTIONING AND COMPLEXITY FROM ADOLESCENCE TO YOUNG ADULTHOOD EJ 039 902
EFFECT OF THE PRESENCE OF A HUMAN MODEL ON IMITATIVE BEHAVIOR IN CHILDREN EJ 039 904
CORRELATES OF LOCUS OF CONTROL IN A SECONDARY SCHOOL POPULATION EJ 039 905
MODIFICATION OF PEER PREFERENCE OF FIRST-GRADE CHILDREN EJ 039 987
NEGRO-WHITE, MALE-FEMALE EIGHT-MONTH DEVELOPMENTAL SCORES COMPARED WITH SEVEN-YEAR WISC AND BENDER TEST SCORES EJ 040 723
DEVELOPMENT OF RETENTION AND ORGANIZATION OCCURRING IN FREE RECALL IN TURKISH CHILDREN EJ 041 133
CLASSIFICATION PATTERNS OF UNDERPRIVILEGED CHILDREN IN ISRAEL EJ 041 140
DEVELOPMENTAL CHANGES IN IDIODYNAMIC SET RESPONSES OF CHILDREN'S WORD ASSOCIATIONS EJ 042 880
IDENTIFICATION OF VERBAL CONCEPTS BY PRESCHOOL CHILDREN EJ 042 958
SEX DIFFERENCES IN THE EXPRESSION OF VOCATIONAL ASPIRATIONS BY ELEMENTARY SCHOOL CHILDREN EJ 043 481
THE PRIORITY OF CUES IN SEX DISCRIMINATION BY CHILDREN AND ADULTS EJ 044 691
THE FRANCK DRAWING COMPLETION TEST AS A MEASURE OF CREATIVITY EJ 044 704
SEX DIFFERENCES IN ADAPTIVE STYLES EJ 045 046
THE RELATIONSHIP OF ORDINAL POSITION AND SEX TO INTEREST PATTERNS EJ 045 111
EFFECTS OF SEX-TYPED INFORMATION ON CHILDREN'S TOY PREFERENCES EJ 045 191
VISUAL LEARNING: AN ANALYSIS BY SEX AND GRADE LEVEL EJ 045 424
A METHOD FOR STUDYING THE DEVELOPMENT OF GENDER IDENTITY EJ 046 784
SEX AND AGE DIFFERENCES IN PATTERN ORGANIZATION IN A FIGURAL-CONCEPTUAL TASK EJ 047 680
SEX DIFFERENCES IN BEHAVIOURAL IMPULSIVITY, INTELLECTUAL IMPULSIVITY, AND ATTAINMENT IN YOUNG CHILDREN EJ 051 151
PSYCHIATRIC DISORDER IN THE CHILDREN OF CARIBBEAN IMMIGRANTS EJ 051 152
SEX DIFFERENCES IN EFFECTS OF KINDERGARTEN ATTENDANCE ON DEVELOPMENT OF SCHOOL READINESS AND LANGUAGE SKILLS EJ 052 723
THE NAMING OF PRIMARY COLORS BY CHILDREN EJ 053 483
THE THREE WISHES OF LATENCY AGE CHILDREN EJ 053 652

EFFECT OF A CHILD'S SEX ON ADULT INTERPRETATIONS OF ITS BEHAVIOR EJ 053 711
SEX DIFFERENCES IN PERFORMANCE AS A FUNCTION OF PRAISE AND BLAME EJ 055 098
RACE AND SEX DIFFERENCES IN THE CHILD'S PERCEPTION OF EMOTION EJ 056 625
NONSOCIAL REINFORCEMENT OF INFANTS' VOCALIZATIONS EJ 058 219
CREATIVE ABILITY OVER A FIVE-YEAR SPAN EJ 058 412
SOME DISCRIMINATIVE PROPERTIES OF RACE AND SEX FOR CHILDREN FROM AN ALL-NEGRO NEIGHBORHOOD EJ 058 510
LIMITATIONS ON THE GENERALIZABILITY OF GROWTH CURVES OF INTELLIGENCE: A REANALYSIS OF SOME DATA FROM THE HARVARD GROWTH STUDY EJ 060 014
SEX DIFFERENCES IN HUMAN DEVELOPMENT EJ 060 015
WE HAVE MEN ON THE STAFF EJ 060 929
DEVELOPMENTAL TRENDS IN GENERAL AND TEST ANXIETY AMONG JUNIOR AND SENIOR HIGH SCHOOL STUDENTS EJ 061 062
AGE- AND SEX-RELATED VARIATION IN PERFORMANCE ON A FIGURAL-CONCEPTUAL TASK EJ 061 066

SEX EDUCATION
SEX EDUCATION: RESOURCE UNIT ED035457
SEX EDUCATION OF THE YOUNG CHILD EJ 019 862
TIMING AND SOURCES OF INFORMATION ABOUT, AND ATTITUDES TOWARD, MENSTRUATION AMONG COLLEGE FEMALES EJ 029 533
SEX EDUCATION FOR THE CHILD IN FOSTER CARE EJ 036 328
STUDENT EVALUATION OF A HIGH SCHOOL SEX EDUCATION PROGRAM EJ 045 390
CONTRIBUTIONS OF CRITICISM TO PARENT, FAMILY-LIFE AND SEX EDUCATION EJ 054 381

SEX ROLES
CONCEPTS OF SOCIAL SEX ROLES AMONG CHILEAN ADOLESCENTS EJ 048 396

SEXUALITY
ALIENATION: AN ESSENTIAL PROCESS OF THE PSYCHOLOGY OF ADOLESCENCE EJ 023 426
NORMAL PSYCHOSEXUAL DEVELOPMENT EJ 038 944
CONTRIBUTIONS OF CRITICISM TO PARENT, FAMILY-LIFE AND SEX EDUCATION EJ 054 381

SHARED SERVICES
OPTIMAL OPERATION OF PUBLIC/PRIVATE CHILD WELFARE DELIVERY SYSTEMS EJ 031 540

SHIFT STUDIES
DISCRIMINATION SHIFT PERFORMANCE OF KINDERGARTEN CHILDREN AS A FUNCTION OF VARIATION OF THE IRRELEVANT SHIFT DIMENSION EJ 027 183
DISCRIMINATION SHIFTS IN THREE-YEAR-OLDS AS A FUNCTION OF SHIFT PROCEDURE EJ 027 184
THE EFFECTS OF OVERLEARNING ON CHILDREN'S NONREVERSAL AND REVERSAL LEARNING USING UNRELATED STIMULI EJ 028 633
CHILDREN'S SHIFT PERFORMANCE IN THE ABSENCE OF DIMENSIONALITY AND A LEARNED REPRESENTATIONAL RESPONSE EJ 033 786
THE PART PLAYED BY MEDIATION PROCESSES IN THE RETENTION OF TEMPORAL SEQUENCES BY TWO READING GROUPS EJ 039 909
THE PERFORMANCE OF PRESCHOOL CHILDREN ON REVERSAL AND TWO TYPES OF EXTRADIMENSIONAL SHIFTS EJ 042 967
CONCEPTUAL BEHAVIOR IN YOUNG CHILDREN: LEARNING TO SHIFT DIMENSIONAL ATTENTION EJ 044 697
SINGLE VERSUS CUMULATIVE PRESENTATION OF STIMULI TO KINDERGARTNERS IN REVERSAL SHIFT BEHAVIOR EJ 047 678
VERBAL-LABELING AND CUE-TRAINING IN REVERSAL-SHIFT BEHAVIOR EJ 053 727
PRIMACY IN PRESCHOOLERS' SHORT-TERM MEMORY: THE EFFECTS OF REPEATED TESTS AND SHIFT TRIALS EJ 053 729
DISCRIMINATION LEARNING AND TRANSFER OF TRAINING IN THE AGED EJ 055 204
CONCEPTUAL ENCODING AND CONCEPT RECALL-RECOVERY IN CHILDREN EJ 056 628
TRANSFER BETWEEN THE ODDITY AND RELATIVE SIZE CONCEPTS: REVERSAL AND EXTRADIMENSIONAL SHIFTS EJ 057 906
STABILITY OF FIRST-GRADE CHILDREN'S DIMENSIONAL PREFERENCES EJ 059 319
REVERSALS PRIOR TO SOLUTION OF CONCEPT IDENTIFICATION IN CHILDREN EJ 060 782

SIBLINGS
THE INTERACTION OF FATHER-ABSENCE AND SIBLING-PRESENCE ON COGNITIVE ABILITIES. ED020024
MODIFICATION OF A DEVIANT SIBLING INTERACTION PATTERN IN THE HOME. ED023461
INTRA-FAMILY DIFFUSION OF SELECTED COGNITIVE SKILLS AS A FUNCTION OF EDUCATIONAL STIMULATION. ED037233
PREVENTIVE THERAPY WITH SIBLINGS OF A DYING CHILD EJ 030 515
OLDER BROTHERS' INFLUENCE ON SEX-TYPED, AGGRESSIVE, AND DEPENDENT BEHAVIOR IN FATHER-ABSENT CHILDREN EJ 034 901
SEX-ROLE IDENTITY AND SIBLING COMPOSITION EJ 035 626
THE RELATIONSHIP OF BIRTH ORDER AND SEX OF SIBLINGS TO GENDER ROLE IDENTITY EJ 039 901
BIRTH ORDER, NUMBER OF SIBLINGS AND SOCIAL REINFORCER EFFECTIVENESS IN CHILDREN EJ 052 453
SIBLING RESEMBLANCES IN DIVERGENT THINKING EJ 055 106
THE EFFECT OF SIBLING RELATIONSHIP ON CONCEPT LEARNING OF YOUNG CHILDREN TAUGHT BY CHILD-TEACHERS EJ 056 399
BEHAVIOR MODIFICATION IN THE HOME WITH THE MOTHER AS THE EXPERIMENTER: THE EFFECT OF DIFFERENTIAL REINFORCEMENT ON SIBLING NEGATIVÈ RESPONSE RATES EJ 056 721
LEARNING DISORDERS IN CHILDREN: SIBLING STUDIES EJ 057 584

SIMULATION
SIMULATION ACTIVITIES FOR TRAINING PARENTS AND TEACHERS AS EDUCATIONAL PARTNERS: A REPORT AND EVALUATION. ED048945
FAKABILITY OF SCORES ON THE GROUP PERSONALITY PROJECTIVE TEST EJ 030 792
PROBLEMS OF CONTROL IN SIMULTANEOUS DISCRIMINATION TASKS EJ 058 215

SINGING
THE CULTURE OF THE CULTURALLY DEPRIVED EJ 035 537

SITUATIONAL TESTS
SEX DIFFERENCES IN YIELDING TO TEMPTATION: A FUNCTION OF THE SITUATION EJ 035 711
SITUATIONAL EFFECTS ON JUSTIFIABLENESS OF AGGRESSION AT THREE AGE LEVELS EJ 056 734

SKILL DEVELOPMENT
THE DIRECT INSTRUCTION PROGRAM FOR TEACHING READING. ED015022
KINDERGARTEN RESEARCH STUDY: LEVEL OF SKILLS DEVELOPMENT RELATED TO GROWTH IN SKILLS AND TO READINESS FOR THE FIRST PRIMARY YEAR. ED026111
LISTENING. WHAT RESEARCH SAYS TO THE TEACHER, NO. 29. ED026120
THE CONCEPT, "PERCEPTUALLY HANDICAPPED," ITS ASSETS AND LIMITATIONS. ED027960
UNDERSTANDING READINESS: AN OCCASIONAL PAPER. ED032117
EFFECT OF VERBALIZATION ON YOUNG CHILDREN'S LEARNING OF A MANIPULATIVE SKILL. ED035447
A SKILL DEVELOPMENT CURRICULUM FOR 3, 4, AND 5 YEAR OLD DISADVANTAGED CHILDREN. ED040755
EXPERIMENTAL ANALYSIS OF EFFECTS OF TEACHER ATTENTION OF PRESCHOOL CHILDREN'S BLOCK BUILDING BEHAVIOR. PROGRESS REPORT. ED042498
A SHOE IS TO TIE: A FILM DEMONSTRATION OF PROGRAMMING SELF-HELP SKILLS FOR PRESCHOOL CHILDREN. PROGRESS REPORT. ED042500
REVIEW OF SELECTED EARLY EDUCATION RESEARCH IN THE SCHOOL DISTRICT OF UNIVERSITY CITY, MISSOURI, JUNE, 1970. ED044182
ACTIVITIES FOR INFANT STIMULATION OR MOTHER-INFANT GAMES. ED046510
ALL ABOUT ME. UNIT 1 CURRICULUM GUIDE. ED053789
AUTUMN. UNIT 3 CURRICULUM GUIDE. ED053790
DESIGNS AND PROPOSAL FOR EARLY CHILDHOOD RESEARCH: A NEW LOOK: ON ATTAINING THE GOALS OF EARLY CHILDHOOD EDUCATION. (ONE IN A SERIES OF SIX PAPERS). ED053807
THE DEVELOPMENT OF CLASSIFICATORY SKILLS IN YOUNG CHILDREN: A TRAINING PROGRAM EJ 031 872
CARPENTRY FOR YOUNG CHILDREN EJ 044 512
THE NAMING OF PRIMARY COLORS BY CHILDREN EJ 053 483
LEARNING TO LISTEN: A STUDY IN AUDITORY PERCEPTION EJ 053 485
TEACHING MULTIPLE CLASSIFICATION TO YOUNG CHILDREN EJ 056 711
TRAINING COMMUNICATION SKILLS IN YOUNG CHILDREN EJ 058 606

SKILLS
DEVELOPMENTAL SKILL AND ACHIEVEMENT DIFFERENCES OF CHILDREN IDENTIFIED AS EXCELLENT, GOOD, AND AVERAGE IN READING AND ARITHMETIC ACHIEVEMENT. STUDY NUMBER THREE. ED044181

SLEEP
A CHANGE OF POSSIBLE NEUROLOGICAL AND PSYCHOLOGICAL SIGNIFICANCE WITHIN THE FIRST WEEK OF NEONATE LIFE: SLEEPING REM RATE. ED034580
SLEEP PROBLEMS EJ 011 345
THE BEHAVIORAL AROUSAL THRESHOLD IN INFANT SLEEP AS A FUNCTION OF TIME AND SLEEP STATE EJ 036 091
A STUDY OF SLEEP BEHAVIOR IN TWO-YEAR-OLD CHILDREN EJ 048 299
BEHAVIORAL SLEEP CYCLES IN THE HUMAN NEWBORN EJ 056 722

SLIDES
CURRICULUM FOR THE INFANT AND TODDLER. A COLOR SLIDE SERIES WITH SCRIPT. (SCRIPT ONLY). ED050817

SLOW LEARNERS
THE DIRECT INSTRUCTION PROGRAM FOR TEACHING READING. ED015022
I WAS A SLOW-LEARNER EJ 017 422

SLUM ENVIRONMENT
THE HOUSING ENVIRONMENT AS A FACTOR IN CHILD DEVELOPMENT. FINAL REPORT. ED014322

SOCIAL ACTION
COMMUNITY PARTICIPATION IN PRESCHOOL EDUCATION--WHY AND HOW EJ 036 331
SOCIAL ISSUES, SOCIAL ACTION, AND THE SOCIAL STUDIES EJ 052 767

SOCIAL ADJUSTMENT
FINAL REPORT ON HEAD START EVALUATION AND RESEARCH--1966-67 TO THE INSTITUTE FOR EDUCATIONAL DEVELOPMENT. SECTION VI, THE MEASUREMENT OF BILINGUALISM AND BICULTURAL SOCIALIZATION OF THE CHILD IN THE SCHOOL SETTING--THE DEVELOPMENT OF INSTRUMENTS. ED019122
ADAPTATIONAL TASKS IN CHILDHOOD IN OUR CULTURE. ED021632
DEPENDENCY AND SOCIAL PERFORMANCE: THE DEVELOPMENT OF A SCALE TO MEASURE LEVEL OF INDEPENDENCE IN SMALL CHILDREN. PART OF THE FINAL REPORT. ED026129
EVALUATION OF THE EFFECTS OF HEAD START EXPERIENCE IN THE AREA OF SELF-CONCEPT, SOCIAL SKILLS, AND LANGUAGE SKILLS. PRE-PUBLICATION DRAFT. ED028832
SOCIAL FACILITATION OF HEAD START PERFORMANCE. PROGRESS REPORT. ED042493
CHILDREN'S SOCIAL SENSITIVITY AND THE RELATIONSHIP TO INTERPERSONAL COMPETENCE, INTRAPERSONAL COMFORT, AND INTELLECTUAL LEVEL EJ 022 136
SELF-ESTEEM, SUCCESS-FAILURE, AND LOCUS OF CONTROL IN NEGRO CHILDREN EJ 035 621
THE KINDERGARTEN AGAINST APPALACHIAN POVERTY EJ 037 021
ADJUSTMENT DIFFERENCES OF SELECTED FOREIGN-BORN PUPILS EJ 041 962
WORKING WITH SEPARATION EJ 046 893

SOCIAL AGENCIES
BRIDGING THE CONCEPT GAP IN WORK WITH YOUTH EJ 031 644
THE PARENTS' CENTER PROJECT: A MULTISERVICE APPROACH TO THE PREVENTION OF CHILD ABUSE EJ 040 043
ADOPTION: IDENTIFICATION AND SERVICE EJ 058 307

SOCIAL ATTITUDES
EFFECTS OF VIEWING VIDEOTAPED SAME AND OPPOSITE COLOR CHILD-TEACHERS ON INTEGRATED AND ALL-WHITE KINDERGARTNERS. ED047805
ADOPTION RESOURCES FOR BLACK CHILDREN EJ 035 801
MOTIVATIONAL AND ATTITUDINAL CONTENT OF FIRST GRADE READING TEXTBOOKS EJ 045 084
PHYSIQUE IDENTIFICATION, PREFERENCE, AND AVERSION IN KINDERGARTEN CHILDREN EJ 046 785
THE STRUCTURING OF SOCIAL ATTITUDES IN CHILDREN EJ 055 489

SOCIAL BEHAVIOR
MODELS, NORMS AND SHARING. ED046512
THE EVALUATION OF "SESAME STREET'S" SOCIAL GOALS: THE INTERPERSONAL STRATEGIES OF COOPERATION, CONFLICT RESOLUTION, AND DIFFERING PERSPECTIVES. ED052824
UN EXEMPLE D'OBSERVATION INTENSIVE DU COMPORTEMENT DE JEUNES ENFANTS DANS LE CADRE D'UNE GARDERIE EJ 034 534
ORIGINS OF SOCIAL DEVELOPMENT IN INFANCY EJ 038 570
CONFORMITY IN EARLY AND LATE ADOLESCENCE EJ 038 936
SEX DIFFERENCES IN ADOLESCENT REACTIONS TOWARD NEWCOMERS EJ 039 899
AN EXPERIMENT ON EYEBROW-RAISING AND VISUAL SEARCHING IN CHILDREN EJ 039 947
CONFORMITY IN CHILDREN AS A FUNCTION OF GRADE LEVEL, AND REAL VERSUS HYPOTHETICAL ADULT AND PEER MODELS EJ 040 294
EFFECTS OF SOCIAL COMPARISON UPON CHILDREN'S SELF-REINFORCEMENT AND ALTRUISM TOWARD COMPETITORS AND FRIENDS EJ 041 856
A CHILD IN DISTRESS: THE INFLUENCE OF NURTURANCE AND MODELING ON CHILDREN'S ATTEMPTS TO HELP EJ 043 314
SOCIAL COMPARISON BY YOUNG CHILDREN EJ 043 672
EFFECTS OF VARIATIONS IN THE NURSERY SCHOOL SETTING ON ENVIRONMENTAL CONSTRAINTS AND CHILDREN'S MODES OF ADAPTATION EJ 045 455
THE USE OF ROLE PLAYING AND INDUCTION IN CHILDREN'S LEARNING OF HELPING AND SHARING BEHAVIOR EJ 046 467
DEVELOPMENTAL CONFORMITY EJ 046 892
EFFECTS OF COOPERATIVE RESPONSE ACQUISITION ON SOCIAL BEHAVIOR DURING FREE-PLAY EJ 048 297
INSTANT LAW AND ORDER EJ 055 534
THE CURIOSITY DIMENSION OF FIFTH-GRADE CHILDREN: A FACTORIAL DISCRIMINANT ANALYSIS EJ 056 623
EXECUTIVE COMPETENCE AND SPONTANEOUS SOCIAL BEHAVIOR IN ONE-YEAR-OLDS EJ 056 732
RELATIONSHIP OF PRESCHOOL SOCIAL-EMOTIONAL FUNCTIONING TO LATER INTELLECTUAL ACHIEVEMENT EJ 058 138
RELATIONSHIPS BETWEEN INFANTS' SOCIAL BEHAVIOR AND THEIR MOTHERS' BEHAVIOR EJ 058 587
LE PROBLEME DE LA LIBERTE ET DE LA DISCIPLINE, DANS LE JEU (PROBLEMS OF FREEDOM AND DISCIPLINE IN PLAY) EJ 061 465

SOCIAL CHANGE
MYTHOLOGY IN AMERICAN EDUCATION: A GUIDE TO CONSTRUCTIVE CONFRONTATION. 1970 WHITE HOUSE CONFERENCE ON CHILDREN, REPORT OF FORUM 8. (WORKING COPY). ED046526
CHILD PSYCHOLOGY IN FUTURE SOCIETY EJ 011 344
THE IMPACT OF CHANGE EJ 011 982
THE IMPACT OF CHANGE. A REBUTTAL EJ 011 983
ADOLESCENCE AND SOCIAL CHANGE EJ 023 611
CHILDREN: THEIR POTENTIALS EJ 034 312
INCREASING AND RELEASING HUMAN POTENTIALS EJ 034 710
PRESCHOOL EDUCATION, PARENTS AND THE COMMUNITY IN A DEVELOPING SOCIETY EJ 036 333
PRESCHOOL PLAY NORMS: A REPLICATION EJ 041 958

SOCIAL CHARACTERISTICS
SOCIAL ANTECEDENTS OF PRESCHOOL CHILDREN'S BEHAVIORS. REPORT NUMBER 2. ED030476
THE SOCIAL MATURITY OF DISADVANTAGED CHILDREN. SPECIAL STUDIES PROJECT #2: ED042507
CONSCIENCE, PERSONALITY, AND SOCIALIZATION TECHNIQUES EJ 023 858
A COMPARISON OF THE CHARACTERISTICS OF JUNIOR HIGH SCHOOL STUDENTS EJ 026 325

SOCIAL CLASS
SOCIAL CLASS AND PARENT'S ASPIRATIONS FOR THEIR CHILDREN. REPORT NUMBER 8. ED030482
TEACHING STYLES IN FOUR-YEAR-OLDS. ED036340
SOCIAL CLASS AND PARENTS' ASPIRATIONS FOR THEIR CHILDREN. RESEARCH REPORT NO. 3 (REVISED). ED043371
EFFECTS OF SOCIAL CLASS INTEGRATION OF PRESCHOOL NEGRO CHILDREN ON TEST PERFORMANCE AND SELF-CONCEPT. FINAL REPORT. ED050831
KNOWLEDGE OF ACTION AND OBJECT WORDS: A COMPARISON OF LOWER- AND MIDDLE-CLASS NEGRO PRESCHOOLERS EJ 040 453
PARENTHOOD: SOME ANTECEDENTS AND CONSEQUENCES: A PRELIMINARY SURVEY OF THE MENTAL HEALTH LITERATURE EJ 041 342
SOCIAL CLASS INTELLIGENCE, AND COGNITIVE STYLE IN INFANCY EJ 056 725

SOCIAL DEVELOPMENT
SIX MONTHS LATER--A COMPARISON OF CHILDREN WHO HAD HEAD START, SUMMER, 1965, WITH THEIR CLASSMATES IN KINDERGARTEN, A CASE STUDY OF THE KINDERGARTENS IN FOUR PUBLIC ELEMENTARY SCHOOLS, NEW YORK CITY. STUDY I. ED015025
THE EFFECT OF PRESCHOOL GROUP EXPERIENCE ON VARIOUS LANGUAGE AND SOCIAL SKILLS IN DISADVANTAGED CHILDREN. FINAL REPORT. ED019989
PROCEEDINGS OF THE ANNUAL CONVENTION OF THE CHRISTIAN ASSOCIATION FOR PSYCHOLOGICAL STUDIES ON THE DYNAMICS OF LEARNING CHRISTIAN CONCEPTS (12TH, GRAND RAPIDS, MICHIGAN, MARCH 31-APRIL 1, 1965). ED023476
EARLY CHILDHOOD SELECTED BIBLIOGRAPHIES SERIES. NUMBER 5, SOCIAL. ED024472
PREPRIMARY PROGRAM. 1968 REPORT. ED027072
NATURALISTIC OBSERVATION IN THE STUDY OF PARENT-CHILD INTERACTION. ED027073
THE SOCIAL DEVELOPMENT OF HUMAN INTELLIGENCE. ED028817
THE DEVELOPMENT OF EARLY SOCIAL INTERACTION--AN ETHOLOGICAL APPROACH. ED031291
CHILDREN'S UNDERSTANDING OF SOCIAL INTERACTION. ED031298
THE ACQUISITION OF SELF-REWARD PATTERNS BY CHILDREN. FINAL REPORT. ED032137
SOCIAL-EMOTIONAL TASK FORCE. FINAL REPORT. ED033744
DETERMINANTS OF CHILDREN'S ATTEMPTS TO HELP ANOTHER CHILD IN DISTRESS. ED039023
ATTACHMENT AND RECIPROCITY IN THE TWO-YEAR-OLD CHILD. ED039946
A COMPARISON OF THE NORMS OF THE PERSONAL SOCIAL DEVELOPMENT OF THE PRE-SCHOOL CHILDREN OF DELHI CENTRE AS OBTAINED BY THE CROSS-SECTIONAL STUDY AND THE LONGITUDINAL STUDY. ED039947
PREACHING AND PRACTICING SELF-SACRIFICE: THEIR LOCUS OF EFFECT UPON CHILDREN'S BEHAVIOR AND COGNITION. ED040741
DEMONSTRATION INFANT DAY CARE AND EDUCATION PROGRAM. INTERIM REPORT, 1969-1970. ED041632
FACTORS? IN CHILD DEVELOPMENT: PEER RELATIONS. ED047796
THE UNIT-BASED CURRICULUM. YPSILANTI PRESCHOOL CURRICULUM DEMONSTRATION PROJECT. ED049831
A STUDY IN CHILD CARE (CASE STUDY FROM VOLUME II-A): "TACOS AND TULIPS." DAY CARE PROGRAMS REPRINT SERIES. ED051893
CONCERNED CITIZENS IN THE MAKING EJ 000 192
RECIPROCITY AND GENEROSITY: SOME DETERMINANTS OF SHARING IN CHILDREN EJ 022 139
COMMENTS ON SOCIAL DESIRABILITY AND PERSUASION EJ 025 803
LOOK--I SEE ME EJ 028 897
ORIGINS OF SOCIAL DEVELOPMENT IN INFANCY EJ 038 570
A DISCONTINUITY IN THE SOCIALIZATION OF MALES IN THE UNITED STATES EJ 040 799
INTERPERSONAL PERCEPTION OF YOUNG CHILDREN: EGOCENTRISM OR EMPATHY? EJ 043 606
PSYCHOSOCIAL DEVELOPMENT IN CROSS-CULTURAL PERSPECTIVE: A NEW LOOK AT AN OLD ISSUE EJ 046 888
ROLE ORIENTATIONS, MARITAL AGE, AND LIFE PATTERNS IN ADULTHOOD EJ 052 529

TAKING ANOTHER'S PERSPECTIVE: ROLE-TAKING DEVELOPMENT IN EARLY CHILDHOOD EJ 056 610
PEER INTERACTION AND COGNITIVE DEVELOPMENT EJ 056 708
ATTACHMENT: ITS ORIGINS AND COURSE EJ 058 586

SOCIAL DIALECTS
REGISTER: SOCIAL VARIATION IN LANGUAGE USE EJ 052 177

SOCIAL DIFFERENCES
THE ROLE OF SOCIALIZATION AND SOCIAL INFLUENCE IN A COMPENSATORY PRESCHOOL PROGRAM. ED017337
SOCIAL CLASS AND COGNITIVE DEVELOPMENT IN INFANCY. ED019111
BIOGENETICS OF RACE AND CLASS. ED036317
A STUDY OF COMMUNICATION PATTERNS IN DISADVANTAGED CHILDREN. ED037250
SOCIAL CLASS DIFFERENTIATION IN COGNITIVE DEVELOPMENT AMONG BLACK PRESCHOOL CHILDREN. ED039039
CROSS-CULTURAL VERBAL COOPERATION. PROGRESS REPORT. ED042496
ON CLASS DIFFERENCES AND EARLY DEVELOPMENT. ED044167
MOTHER-CHILD INTERACTION: SOCIAL CLASS DIFFERENCES IN THE FIRST YEAR OF LIFE. ED044177
DIFFERENTIAL RESPONSE PATTERNS AS THEY AFFECT THE SELF ESTEEM OF THE CHILD. ED046542
INFANT DEVELOPMENT IN LOWER CLASS AMERICAN FAMILIES. ED049836
THE EFFECTS OF EXPERIENCE ON INFANTS' REACTIONS TO SEPARATION FROM THEIR MOTHERS. ED053802
AN APPROACH TO LANGUAGE LEARNING EJ 008 119
SOCIOECONOMIC STATUS AND CHILDREN'S INTERESTS EJ 016 775
THE DISTRACTING EFFECTS OF MATERIAL REINFORCERS IN THE DISCRIMINATION LEARNING OF LOWER- AND MIDDLE-CLASS CHILDREN EJ 018 871
MAGNITUDE-PROBABILITY PREFERENCES OF PRESCHOOL CHILDREN FROM TWO SOCIOECONOMIC LEVELS EJ 019 017
MOTHERS AS TEACHERS OF THEIR OWN PRESCHOOL CHILDREN: THE INFLUENCE OF SOCIOECONOMIC STATUS AND TASK STRUCTURE ON TEACHING SPECIFICITY EJ 019 414
SOCIOECONOMIC STATUS AND INTELLECTIVE PERFORMANCE AMONG NEGRO PRESCHOOL BOYS EJ 024 938
WISC SUBTEST AND IQ SCORE CORRELATES OF FATHER ABSENCE EJ 029 219
PERSISTENCE AS A FUNCTION OF CONCEPTUAL STRUCTURE AND QUALITY OF FEEDBACK EJ 032 932
SOCIAL-CLASS DIFFERENTIATION IN COGNITIVE DEVELOPMENT AMONG BLACK PRESCHOOL CHILDREN EJ 036 819
CLASSIFICATION PATTERNS OF UNDERPRIVILEGED CHILDREN IN ISRAEL EJ 041 140
SOCIAL CLASS DIFFERENCES IN TEACHER ATTITUDES TOWARD CHILDREN EJ 053 908
SOCIAL-CLASS DIFFERENCES AND TASK VARIABLES IN THE DEVELOPMENT OF MULTIPLICATIVE CLASSIFICATION EJ 056 619
THE INFLUENCE OF NONINTELLECTIVE FACTORS ON THE IQ SCORES OF MIDDLE- AND LOWER-CLASS CHILDREN EJ 056 621
MOTHER-CHILD INTERACTION IN THE FIRST YEAR OF LIFE EJ 056 632
INFANT DEVELOPMENT IN LOWER-CLASS AMERICAN FAMILIES EJ 060 012

SOCIAL DISADVANTAGEMENT
AN EVALUATION OF OPERATION HEAD START BILINGUAL CHILDREN, SUMMER, 1965. ED013667
REPORT ON THE ARTICULATORY AND INTELLIGIBILITY STATUS OF SOCIALLY DISADVANTAGED PRE-SCHOOL CHILDREN. ED014321
THE DEVELOPMENT OF SELF-OTHER RELATIONSHIPS DURING PROJECT HEAD START. ED015008

SOCIAL DISCRIMINATION
THE DISTRIBUTION OF TEACHER APPROVAL AND DISAPPROVAL OF HEAD START CHILDREN. FINAL REPORT. ED042509
CHILDREN WITHOUT PREJUDICE. 1970 WHITE HOUSE CONFERENCE ON CHILDREN, REPORT OF FORUM 18. (WORKING PAPER). ED046534
THE NATURE AND NURTURE OF PREJUDICE EJ 000 191
STRONG WORDS EJ 001 116
PREJUDICE IN THE SCHOOLS EJ 001 498
PINK IS A GOOD COLOR. ? EJ 011 785
VALUING THE DIGNITY OF BLACK CHILDREN: A BLACK TEACHER SPEAKS EJ 019 506

SOCIAL ENVIRONMENT
A SURVEY AND EVALUATION OF PROJECT HEAD START AS ESTABLISHED AND OPERATED IN COMMUNITIES OF THE COMMONWEALTH OF MASSACHUSETTS DURING THE SUMMER OF 1965. ED014324
CHILDREN AND THEIR PHYSICAL AND SOCIAL ENVIRONMENT. 1970 WHITE HOUSE CONFERENCE ON CHILDREN, REPORT OF FORUM 19. (WORKING COPY). ED046535
INSTITUTIONALIZATION AND THE EFFECTIVENESS OF SOCIAL REINFORCEMENT: A FIVE- AND EIGHT-YEAR FOLLOW-UP STUDY EJ 027 185
PATTERNS OF INFORMATION PROCESSING USED BY AND WITH YOUNG CHILDREN IN A NURSERY SCHOOL SETTING EJ 032 890
SOME DISCRIMINATIVE PROPERTIES OF RACE AND SEX FOR CHILDREN FROM AN ALL-NEGRO NEIGHBORHOOD EJ 058 510

SOCIAL EXPERIENCE
STARTING NURSERY SCHOOL, II: PREDICTION OF CHILDREN'S INITIAL EMOTIONAL REACTIONS FROM BACKGROUND INFORMATION. FINAL REPORT. ED047814

SOCIAL FACTORS
IMPULSIVITY & REFLECTIVITY AS REFLECTED BY THE VARIABLES OF TIME AND ERROR. ED047820
UNWED MOTHERS AND THEIR DECISIONS TO KEEP OR SURRENDER CHILDREN EJ 040 042
A SOCIOCULTURAL PERSPECTIVE ON PHYSICAL CHILD ABUSE EJ 043 353
SOCIAL COMPARISON BY YOUNG CHILDREN EJ 043 672

SOCIAL IMMATURITY
CONDITION WITH CAUTION: THINK THRICE BEFORE CONDITIONING. (ROUGH DRAFT). ED046539

SOCIAL INFLUENCES
THE ROLE OF SOCIALIZATION AND SOCIAL INFLUENCE IN A COMPENSATORY PRESCHOOL PROGRAM. ED017337
INFLUENCES OF CULTURAL PATTERNS ON THE THINKING OF CHILDREN IN CERTAIN ETHNIC GROUPS, A STUDY OF THE EFFECT OF JEWISH SUBCULTURE ON THE FIELD-DEPENDENCE-INDEPENDENCE DIMENSION OF COGNITION. ED020796
SOCIO-CULTURAL INFLUENCES ON ATTENTION IN ELEMENTARY SCHOOL CHILDREN. FINAL REPORT. ED024456
THE POLITICAL SOCIALIZATION OF CHILDREN AND THE STRUCTURE OF THE ELEMENTARY SCHOOL. ED024468
ANXIETY AS A FACTOR IN THE CHILD'S RESPONSIVENESS TO SOCIAL REINFORCEMENT. ED027074
SOCIAL CLASS DIFFERENTIATION IN COGNITIVE DEVELOPMENT AMONG BLACK PRESCHOOL CHILDREN. ED039039
THE RIGHTS OF CHILDREN. 1970 WHITE HOUSE CONFERENCE ON CHILDREN, REPORT OF FORUM 22. (WORKING COPY). ED046537
BIOLOGICAL AND ECOLOGICAL INFLUENCES ON DEVELOPMENT AT 12 MONTHS OF AGE EJ 029 385
GENERALIZED IMITATION AS A FUNCTION OF DISCRIMINATION DIFFICULTY AND CHOICE EJ 038 455
SOCIAL REINFORCEMENT SATIATION: AN OUTCOME OF FREQUENCY OR AMBIGUITY? EJ 058 144
CHARITY IN CHILDREN: THE INFLUENCE OF "CHARITY" STIMULI AND AN AUDIENCE EJ 058 224
TASK ORIENTATION VERSUS SOCIAL ORIENTATION IN YOUNG CHILDREN AND THEIR ATTENTION TO RELEVANT SOCIAL CUES EJ 058 413
EGOCENTRISM AND SOCIAL INFLUENCE IN CHILDREN EJ 058 590
LANGUAGE PATTERNS WITHIN THE YOUTH SUBCULTURE: DEVELOPMENT OF SLANG VOCABULARIES EJ 060 720
FAMILY CORRELATES OF VERBAL REASONING ABILITY EJ 061 069

SOCIAL INTEGRATION
A SOCIALLY INTEGRATED KINDERGARTEN. ED034578
HETEROGENEOUS VS. HOMOGENEOUS SOCIAL CLASS GROUPING OF PRESCHOOL CHILDREN IN HEAD START CLASSROOMS. ED045176
EFFECTS OF SOCIAL CLASS INTEGRATION OF PRESCHOOL NEGRO CHILDREN ON TEST PERFORMANCE AND SELF-CONCEPT. FINAL REPORT. ED050831
A NONSEGREGATED APPROACH TO HEAD START EJ 007 363

SOCIAL ISOLATION
THE EFFECTS OF SOCIAL ISOLATION AND CHARACTERISTICS OF THE MODEL ON ACCENT IMITATION IN FOURTH-GRADE CHILDREN EJ 038 171

SOCIAL MATURITY
SOCIALIZATION AND INSTRUMENTAL COMPETENCE IN YOUNG CHILDREN EJ 030 510
THEORETICAL NOTES ON POWER MOTIVATION EJ 032 677

SOCIAL PLANNING
CHANGING FAMILIES IN A CHANGING SOCIETY. 1970 WHITE HOUSE CONFERENCE ON CHILDREN, REPORT OF FORUM 14. (WORKING COPY). ED046530
THE ADMINISTRATION OF "SELECTIVITY" IN THE BREAKFAST PROGRAM OF A PUBLIC ELEMENTARY SCHOOL EJ 036 580

SOCIAL PROBLEMS
THE SOCIAL DEVELOPMENT OF HUMAN INTELLIGENCE. ED028817
BIBLIOGRAPHY ON THE BATTERED CHILD. (REVISED EDITION). ED039942
KEEPING CHILDREN HEALTHY: HEALTH PROTECTION AND DISEASE PREVENTION. 1970 WHITE HOUSE CONFERENCE ON CHILDREN, REPORT OF FORUM 10. (WORKING PAPER). ED046527
INFORMED CONSENT IN PEDIATRIC RESEARCH EJ 007 413
THE IMPACT OF CHANGE. A REBUTTAL EJ 011 983

SOCIAL PSYCHOLOGY
THE DEFINITION, MEASUREMENT AND DEVELOPMENT OF SOCIAL MOTIVES UNDERLYING COOPERATIVE AND COMPETITIVE BEHAVIOR. ED045188
SUGGESTIBILITY IN RELATION TO SCHOOL GRADE, SEX, AND SOURCE OF INFLUENCE EJ 023 431
ENVIRONMENTAL DISCONTINUITY, STRESS, AND SEX EFFECTS UPON SUSCEPTIBILITY TO SOCIAL INFLUENCE EJ 023 432

AN ACTIVITY GROUP APPROACH TO SERIOUSLY DISTURBED LATENCY BOYS EJ 043 194

SOCIAL REINFORCEMENT

MODIFICATION BY SOCIAL REINFORCEMENT OF DEFICIENT SOCIAL BEHAVIOR OF DISADVANTAGED KINDERGARTEN CHILDREN. ED043381
FIELD STUDIES OF SOCIAL REINFORCEMENT IN A PRESCHOOL. ED047772
THE VALUE OF CLASSROOM REWARDS IN EARLY EDUCATION. ED049828
PERCEIVED MATERNAL CHILD-REARING EXPERIENCE AND THE EFFECTS OF VICARIOUS AND DIRECT REINFORCEMENT ON MALES EJ 019 008
EFFECTS OF REINFORCEMENT BASE-LINE-INPUT DISCREPANCY UPON IMITATION IN CHILDREN EJ 019 009
INTERACTIVE EFFECTS OF INFORMATIONAL AND AFFECTIVE COMPONENTS OF SOCIAL AND NONSOCIAL REINFORCERS ON INDEPENDENT AND DEPENDENT CHILDREN EJ 022 141
AN EXPERIMENTAL STUDY OF THE SOCIAL RESPONSIVENESS OF CHILDREN WITH AUTISTIC BEHAVIORS EJ 024 470
MODIFYING BEHAVIOR OF KINDERGARTEN CHILDREN EJ 026 493
INSTITUTIONALIZATION AND THE EFFECTIVENESS OF SOCIAL REINFORCEMENT: A FIVE- AND EIGHT-YEAR FOLLOW-UP STUDY EJ 027 185
PRIOR REINFORCEMENT HISTORY AS AN EXPLANATION FOR THE EFFECTS OF SEX OF SUBJECT AND EXPERIMENTER IN SOCIAL REINFORCEMENT PARADIGMS EJ 030 297
MEANING AND ATTENTION AS DETERMINANTS OF SOCIAL REINFORCER EFFECTIVENESS EJ 033 781
PLAY PERSISTENCE: SOME EFFECTS OF INTERRUPTION, SOCIAL REINFORCEMENT, AND DEFECTIVE TOYS EJ 034 532
OPERANT LEARNING OF VISUAL PATTERN DISCRIMINATION IN YOUNG INFANTS EJ 035 623
EXPERIMENTER BIAS IN PERFORMANCE OF CHILDREN AT A SIMPLE MOTOR TASK EJ 035 710
YOUNG CHILDREN'S PERFORMANCE ON A TWO-CHOICE TASK AS A FUNCTION OF SOCIAL REINFORCEMENT, BASE-LINE PREFERENCE, AND RESPONSE STRATEGY EJ 039 635
EFFECTS OF SOCIAL REINFORCEMENT ON LEARNING AND RETENTION IN CHILDREN EJ 042 957
EFFECTS OF AN ADULT'S PRESENCE AND PRAISE ON YOUNG CHILDREN'S PERFORMANCE EJ 045 460
BLOCK MANIPULATION BY CHILDREN AS A FUNCTION OF SOCIAL REINFORCEMENT, ANXIETY, AROUSAL, AND ABILITY PATTERN EJ 046 468
INTERACTION EFFECTS OF SOCIAL AND TANGIBLE REINFORCEMENT EJ 048 296
MATERNAL CHILD REARING AND CREATIVITY IN SONS EJ 048 302
BIRTH ORDER, NUMBER OF SIBLINGS AND SOCIAL REINFORCER EFFECTIVENESS IN CHILDREN EJ 052 453
DEVELOPMENTAL COURSE OF RESPONSIVENESS TO SOCIAL REINFORCEMENT IN NORMAL CHILDREN AND INSTITUTIONALIZED RETARDED CHILDREN EJ 053 648
RESPONSE TO SOCIAL REINFORCEMENT RATES AS A FUNCTION OF REINFORCEMENT HISTORY EJ 053 715
WORDS AND DEEDS ABOUT ALTRUISM AND THE SUBSEQUENT REINFORCEMENT POWER OF THE MODEL EJ 053 739
AGE OF SUBJECT, TYPE OF SOCIAL CONTACT, AND RESPONSIVENESS TO SOCIAL REINFORCEMENT EJ 055 093
PERSON SPECIFICITY OF THE "SOCIAL DEPRIVATION-SATIATION EFFECT" EJ 055 207
SOCIAL REINFORCEMENT SATIATION: AN OUTCOME OF FREQUENCY OR AMBIGUITY? EJ 058 144

SOCIAL RELATIONS

COMPARATIVE STUDIES OF A GROUP OF HEAD START AND A GROUP OF NON-HEAD START PRESCHOOL CHILDREN. FINAL REPORT. ED015013
CROSS-CULTURAL VERBAL COOPERATION. PROGRESS REPORT. ED042496
THE DEFINITION, MEASUREMENT AND DEVELOPMENT OF SOCIAL MOTIVES UNDERLYING COOPERATIVE AND COMPETITIVE BEHAVIOR. ED045188
THE ACQUISITION OF CONSERVATION THROUGH SOCIAL INTERACTION. ED047801
SOCIAL INTERACTION IN HETEROGENEOUS PRE-SCHOOLS IN ISRAEL. ED049839
EDUCATIONAL INTERVENTION IN EARLY CHILDHOOD: ABSTRACTS OF THE 1965-1970 SPECIAL STUDIES RESEARCH AND EVALUATION REPORT. FINAL REPORT, VOLUME III. ED050816
ALL ABOUT ME. UNIT 1 CURRICULUM GUIDE. ED053789
ALIENATION OF YOUTH AS REFLECTED IN THE HIPPIE MOVEMENT EJ 023 427
AN EXPLORATORY STUDY OF THE 3-, 5-, AND 7-YEAR OLD FEMALE'S COMPREHENSION OF COOPERATIVE AND UNCOOPERATIVE SOCIAL INTERACTION EJ 023 612
SOCIAL SCHEMATA OF SCHOOL BEGINNERS: SOME DEMOGRAPHIC CORRELATES EJ 030 713
THE RELATIONSHIP BETWEEN CONTROLLED PROJECTION RESPONSES AND SOCIOMETRIC STATUS EJ 031 541
WHO CARES FOR AMERICA'S CHILDREN? EJ 032 565
STIMULUS CONTROL OF PARENT OR CARETAKER BEHAVIOR BY OFFSPRING EJ 034 538
EYE CONTACT IN CHILDREN AS A FUNCTION OF AGE, SEX, SOCIAL AND INTELLECTIVE VARIABLES EJ 038 943
MODIFICATION OF PEER PREFERENCE OF FIRST-GRADE CHILDREN EJ 039 987
INFANT-CARETAKER INTERACTIONS EJ 043 670
COOPERATION AND COMPETITION IN FOUR-YEAR-OLDS AS A FUNCTION OF REWARD CONTINGENCY AND SUBCULTURE EJ 045 453
A MICRO-ANALYSIS OF MOTHER-INFANT INTERACTION. BEHAVIOR REGULATING SOCIAL CONTACT BETWEEN A MOTHER AND HER 3 1/2 MONTH-OLD TWINS EJ 048 300

SOCIAL RESPONSIBILITY

AN ESSAY REVIEW: MENTAL RETARDATION AS A SOCIAL PROBLEM EJ 047 341
TOWARD A DEMOCRATIC ELEMENTARY-SCHOOL CLASSROOM EJ 058 308

SOCIAL SCIENCES

CHILD DEVELOPMENT AND SOCIAL SCIENCE EDUCATION. PART I: THE PROBLEM, PART II: CONFERENCE REPORT. ED023465
CHILD DEVELOPMENT AND SOCIAL SCIENCE EDUCATION. PART III: ABSTRACTS OF RELEVANT LITERATURE. ED023466
CHILD DEVELOPMENT AND SOCIAL SCIENCE EDUCATION. PART IV: A TEACHING STRATEGY DERIVED FROM SOME PIAGETIAN CONCEPTS. ED023467
THE EFFECTS OF EXTRANEOUS MATERIAL AND NEGATIVE EXEMPLARS ON A SOCIAL SCIENCE CONCEPT-LEARNING TASK FOR PRE-SCHOOL CHILDREN. ED047819

SOCIAL SERVICES

A STUDY IN CHILD CARE (CASE STUDY FROM VOLUME II-B): "SOMEPLACE SECURE." DAY CARE PROGRAMS REPRINT SERIES. ED051908
A STUDY IN CHILD CARE (CASE STUDY FROM VOLUME II-B): "THEY BRAG ON A CHILD TO MAKE HIM FEEL GOOD." DAY CARE PROGRAMS REPRINT SERIES. ED051910
A SOCIAL WORK MISSION TO HIPPIELAND EJ 004 092
SERVICES TO CHILDREN LIVING WITH RELATIVES OR GUARDIANS EJ 007 445
THE RIGHTS OF CHILDREN EMERGE: HISTORICAL NOTES ON THE FIRST WHITE HOUSE CONFERENCE ON CHILDREN EJ 023 283
THE ADMINISTRATION OF "SELECTIVITY" IN THE BREAKFAST PROGRAM OF A PUBLIC ELEMENTARY SCHOOL EJ 036 580
AN INTERVIEW WITH GEORGIA MCMURRAY, NEW YORK CITY'S COMMISSIONER FOR CHILD DEVELOPMENT EJ 050 274

SOCIAL STRUCTURE

RELATIONSHIP OF CLASSROOM GROUPING PRACTICES TO DIFFUSION OF STUDENTS' SOCIOMETRIC CHOICES AND DIFFUSION OF STUDENTS' PERCEPTION OF SOCIOMETRIC CHOICE EJ 042 791

SOCIAL STUDIES

SOCIAL STUDIES IN ELEMENTARY SCHOOLS (THIRTY-SECOND YEARBOOK). ED018275
GUIDELINES FOR ELEMENTARY SOCIAL STUDIES. ED019998
SOCIAL STUDIES EDUCATION: THE ELEMENTARY SCHOOL. ED027061
ECONOMICS IN THE ELEMENTARY SCHOOL ED028839
KINDERGARTEN: THE CHILD IN HIS HOME AND SCHOOL ENVIRONMENTS. COURSE OF STUDY AND RELATED LEARNING ACTIVITIES. (CURRICULUM BULLETIN, 1967-68 SERIES, NO. 2A.) ED029681
GRADE 1: LIVING AND WORKING TOGETHER IN THE COMMUNITY. COURSE OF STUDY AND RELATED LEARNING ACTIVITIES. (CURRICULUM BULLETIN, 1967-68 SERIES, NO. 2B.) ED029682
GRADE 2: HOW PEOPLE LIVE IN CITY COMMUNITIES AROUND THE WORLD. COURSE OF STUDY AND RELATED LEARNING ACTIVITIES. (CURRICULUM BULLETIN, 1968-69 SERIES, NO. 2.) ED029694
INDEPENDENT AND SMALL GROUP ACTIVITIES FOR SOCIAL STUDIES IN THE PRIMARY GRADES. ED031305
FAMILY LIFE AROUND THE WORLD, LEVEL I. ED032116
SOCIAL STUDIES IN THE PRIMARY GRADES. ED035460
A SOCIAL WORK MISSION TO HIPPIELAND EJ 004 092
BLACK HISTORY EJ 015 184
TURNBOW CABIN EJ 029 043
TOUCH-FEEL LEARNING AT THE TALLAHASSEE JUNIOR MUSEUM EJ 033 158
SOCIAL ISSUES, SOCIAL ACTION, AND THE SOCIAL STUDIES EJ 052 767
A CHANGE AGENT STRATEGY: PRELIMINARY REPORT EJ 054 727

SOCIAL STUDIES UNITS

SOCIAL STUDIES UNIT: FIRST GRADE. BOSTON-NORTHAMPTON LANGUAGE ARTS PROGRAM, ESEA - 1965, PROJECTS TO ADVANCE CREATIVITY IN EDUCATION. ED027945

SOCIAL VALUES

FINAL REPORT ON HEAD START EVALUATION AND RESEARCH--1966-67 TO THE INSTITUTE FOR EDUCATIONAL DEVELOPMENT. SECTION VIII, RELATIONSHIPS BETWEEN SELF-CONCEPT AND SPECIFIC VARIABLES IN A LOW-INCOME CULTURALLY DIFFERENT POPULATION. ED019124
THE NATURE AND NURTURE OF PREJUDICE EJ 000 191
A SOCIAL WORK MISSION TO HIPPIELAND EJ 004 092
SOCIAL ACTION FOR THE PRIMARY SCHOOLS EJ 018 066
INCORPORATION OF VALUES BY LOWER AND MIDDLE SOCIOECONOMIC CLASS PRESCHOOL BOYS EJ 040 210
PLAY, THE ESSENTIAL INGREDIENT EJ 046 248

VALUES OF MEXICAN-AMERICAN, NEGRO, AND ANGLO BLUE-COLLAR AND WHITE-COLLAR CHILDREN EJ 052 653

SOCIAL WELFARE

CHILD WELFARE SERVICES: A SOURCEBOOK. ED047813
DEVELOPING MANPOWER FOR THE WORLD'S SOCIAL WELFARE NEEDS. SOME OBSERVATIONS FROM THE CONFERENCE OF MINISTERS RESPONSIBLE FOR SOCIAL WELFARE.. EJ 004 093

SOCIAL WORK

THE DAY CARE NEIGHBOR SERVICE: A HANDBOOK FOR THE ORGANIZATION AND OPERATION OF A NEW APPROACH TO FAMILY DAY CARE. ED049810

SOCIAL WORKERS

THE SCHOOL SOCIAL WORKER IN THE NEW YORK STATE EXPERIMENTAL PREKINDERGARTEN PROGRAM. ED036337
PEER- OBSERVER CONSULTATION EJ 022 532
VOLUNTEERING TO HELP INDIANS HELP THEMSELVES EJ 032 412
GROUP SERVICES FOR UNMARRIED MOTHERS: AN INTERDISCIPLINARY APPROACH EJ 035 538
SCHOOL COUNSELING BY CONTRACT EJ 038 985
WHITE STAFF, BLACK CHILDREN: IS THERE A PROBLEM? EJ 039 799
BLACK CLIENTS AND WHITE WORKERS; A REPORT FROM THE FIELD EJ 051 062
THE TEAM APPROACH IN HOME CARE OF MENTALLY RETARDED CHILDREN EJ 053 601

SOCIALIZATION

OPERATION HEAD START--AN EVALUATION. FINAL REPORT. ED013117
THE ROLE OF SOCIALIZATION AND SOCIAL INFLUENCE IN A COMPENSATORY PRESCHOOL PROGRAM. ED017337
FINAL REPORT ON HEAD START EVALUATION AND RESEARCH--1966-67 TO THE INSTITUTE FOR EDUCATIONAL DEVELOPMENT. SECTION V, THE ROLE OF DIALECT IN THE SCHOOL-SOCIALIZATION OF LOWER CLASS CHILDREN. ED019121
THE DEVELOPMENT OF A BEHAVIOR CHECKLIST FOR BOYS. ED023468
ADMINISTRATION MANUAL FOR THE INVENTORY OF SOCIALIZATION OF BILINGUAL CHILDREN AGES THREE TO TEN. PART OF THE FINAL REPORT. ED027062
NURTURANCE, DEPENDENCE, AND EXPLORATORY BEHAVIOR IN PREKINDERGARTENERS. ED035443
PRESCHOOL INTERVENTION THROUGH SOCIAL LEARNING. ED036316
SOCIAL INFLUENCES ON CHILDREN'S HUMOR RESPONSES. ED039933
PRESCHOOLS AND THEIR GRADUATES. ED041644
MARGINAL CHILDREN OF WAR: AN EXPLORATORY STUDY OF AMERICAN-KOREAN CHILDREN. ED047781
THE PLAYFUL MODES OF KNOWING. ED050806
SETTING AND THE EMERGENCE OF COMPETENCE DURING ADULT SOCIALIZATION: WORKING AT HOME VS. WORKING "OUT THERE" EJ 012 719
IMITATION AS A FUNCTION OF VICARIOUS AND DIRECT REWARD EJ 018 323
A PARTIAL TEST OF A SOCIAL LEARNING THEORY OF CHILDREN'S CONFORMITY EJ 018 890
MOTHERS AS TEACHERS OF THEIR OWN PRESCHOOL CHILDREN: THE INFLUENCE OF SOCIOECONOMIC STATUS AND TASK STRUCTURE ON TEACHING SPECIFICITY EJ 019 414
RELATION OF EARLY SOCIALIZATION EXPERIENCES TO SELF-CONCEPTS AND GENDER ROLE IN MIDDLE CHILDHOOD EJ 021 997
PREACHING AND PRACTICING GENEROSITY: CHILDREN'S ACTIONS AND REACTIONS EJ 022 140
CHILDREN AND THEIR EXPANDING WORLD OF KNOWLEDGE EJ 026 734
THE MODELING OF SHARING: EFFECTS ASSOCIATED WITH VICARIOUS REINFORCEMENT, SYMBOLIZATION, AGE, AND GENERALIZATION EJ 028 894
LANGUAGE, SOCIALIZATION, AND DELINQUENCY EJ 039 587
A DISCONTINUITY IN THE SOCIALIZATION OF MALES IN THE UNITED STATES EJ 040 799
ON TEAM TEACHING EJ 046 057
OBSERVATION STUDIES OF PARENT-CHILD INTERACTION: A METHODOLOGICAL REVIEW EJ 046 466
THE YOUNG CHILD'S UNDERSTANDING OF SOCIAL JUSTICE EJ 046 887
DESIRABILITY JUDGMENTS AS A FUNCTION OF ITEM CONTENT, INSTRUCTIONAL SET, AND SET: A LIFE-SPAN DEVELOPMENTAL STUDY EJ 048 473
INFANT OBEDIENCE AND MATERNAL BEHAVIOR: THE ORIGINS OF SOCALIZATION RECONSIDERED EJ 052 446
VALUES OF MEXICAN-AMERICAN, NEGRO, AND ANGLO BLUE-COLLAR AND WHITE-COLLAR CHILDREN EJ 052 653
CHILDREN'S OBSERVATION AND INTEGRATION OF AGGRESSIVE EXPERIENCES EJ 055 212
COGNITIVE AND AFFECTIVE REACTIONS OF KINDERGARTNERS TO VIDEO DISPLAYS EJ 057 016

SOCIALLY DEVIANT BEHAVIOR

THE COGNITIVE ENVIRONMENTS OF URBAN PRE-SCHOOL CHILDREN. MANUAL OF INSTRUCTIONS FOR ADMINISTERING AND SCORING MOTHER'S ATTITUDES TOWARD CHILD'S BEHAVIOR LEADING TO MASTERY. ED018256
MODIFICATION OF A DEVIANT SIBLING INTERACTION PATTERN IN THE HOME. ED023461
BEHAVIOR MODIFICATION OF AN ADJUSTMENT CLASS: A TOKEN REINFORCEMENT PROGRAM. ED023462
FUN WHILE LEARNING AND EARNING. A LOOK INTO CHATTANOOGA PUBLIC SCHOOLS' TOKEN REINFORCEMENT PROGRAM. ED027952
A TEST OF THE GENERALITY OF THE EFFECTS OF DEVIANT PRESCHOOL MODELS EJ 034 531
EFFECT ON RESISTANCE TO DEVIATION OF OBSERVING A MODEL'S AFFECTIVE REACTION TO RESPONSE CONSEQUENCES EJ 043 283
DEVELOPMENTAL FACTORS IN ADOLESCENT DRUG USE: A STUDY OF PSYCHEDELIC DRUG USERS EJ 051 020

SOCIALLY DISADVANTAGED

PROJECT TOBI, THE DEVELOPMENT OF A PRE-SCHOOL ACHIEVEMENT TEST. FINAL REPORT. ED016520
LANGUAGE DEVELOPMENT OF DISADVANTAGED CHILDREN EJ 036 211
OUTERDIRECTEDNESS AND IMITATIVE BEHAVIOR OF INSTITUTIONALIZED AND NONINSTITUTIONALIZED YOUNGER AND OLDER CHILDREN EJ 058 694

SOCIALLY MALADJUSTED

BEHAVIOR MODIFICATION PROCEDURES APPLIED TO THE ISOLATE BEHAVIOR OF A NURSERY SCHOOL CHILD. ED041635
MODIFICATION BY SOCIAL REINFORCEMENT OF DEFICIENT SOCIAL BEHAVIOR OF DISADVANTAGED KINDERGARTEN CHILDREN. ED043381

SOCIOCEONOMIC STATUS

SOCIOECONOMIC STATUS AND INTELLECTIVE PERFORMANCE AMONG NEGRO PRESCHOOL BOYS EJ 024 938

SOCIOCULTURAL PATTERNS

SOCIO-CULTURAL INFLUENCES ON ATTENTION IN ELEMENTARY SCHOOL CHILDREN. FINAL REPORT. ED024456
FAMILY SOCIOLOGY OR WIVES' FAMILY SOCIOLOGY? A COMPARISON OF HUSBANDS' AND WIVES' ANSWERS ABOUT DECISION MAKING IN THE GREEK AND AMERICAN CULTURE. REPORT NUMBER 4. ED030478
INFANCY IN HOLLAND: THE FIRST THREE MONTHS. ED031296
AN ANALYSIS OF MOTHERS' SPEECH AS A FACTOR IN THE DEVELOPMENT OF CHILDREN'S INTELLIGENCE. ED042504
THE TEMPER OF THE TIMES EJ 000 391
TRENDS AND DILEMMAS IN CHILD WELFARE RESEARCH EJ 038 571

SOCIODRAMA

THE EFFECTS OF SOCIODRAMATIC PLAY ON DISADVANTAGED PRESCHOOL CHILDREN. ED033761

SOCIOECONOMIC BACKGROUND

INFLUENCE OF SUBJECT AND SITUATIONAL VARIABLES ON THE PERSISTENCE OF FIRST GRADE CHILDREN IN A TEST-LIKE SITUATION. ED052819
DEMOGRAPHIC AND SOCIO-ECONOMIC DATA OF THE BECKLEY, WEST VIRGINIA AREA AND 1968-1970 DEVELOPMENTAL COSTS OF THE EARLY CHILDHOOD EDUCATION FIELD STUDY. TECHNICAL REPORT NO. 1. ED052832

SOCIOECONOMIC INFLUENCES

A SOCIAL PSYCHOLOGICAL ANALYSIS OF THE TRANSITION FROM HOME TO SCHOOL. FINAL REPORT. ED015017
SOCIOECONOMIC STATUS AND LEARNING PROFICIENCY IN YOUNG CHILDREN. ED020023
HEAD START EVALUATION AND RESEARCH CENTER, UNIVERSITY OF KANSAS. REPORT NO. V, A COMPARATIVE BEHAVIORAL ANALYSIS OF PEER-GROUP INFLUENCE TECHNIQUES IN HEAD START AND MIDDLE CLASS POPULATIONS. ED021638
HEAD START EVALUATION AND RESEARCH CENTER, THE UNIVERSITY OF CHICAGO. ANNUAL REPORT, 1966-1967. ED023445
SOCIO-CULTURAL INFLUENCES ON ATTENTION IN ELEMENTARY SCHOOL CHILDREN. FINAL REPORT. ED024456
THE AUDITORY MEMORY OF CHILDREN FROM DIFFERENT SOCIO-ECONOMIC BACKGROUNDS. ED027092
SOCIAL ANTECEDENTS OF PRESCHOOL CHILDREN'S BEHAVIORS. REPORT NUMBER 2. ED030476
A COMPARISON OF THE ORAL LANGUAGE PATTERNS OF THREE LOW SOCIOECONOMIC GROUPS OF PUPILS ENTERING FIRST GRADE. ED032943
SOCIAL CLASS DIFFERENTIATION IN COGNITIVE DEVELOPMENT: A LONGITUDINAL STUDY. ED033754
AN ECOLOGICAL STUDY OF THREE-YEAR-OLDS AT HOME. FINAL REPORT. ED037238
THE SOCIAL MATURITY OF DISADVANTAGED CHILDREN. SPECIAL STUDIES PROJECT #2: ED042507
THE COGNITIVE ENVIRONMENTS OF URBAN PRESCHOOL CHILDREN. FINAL REPORT. ED045179
EARLY ANTECEDENTS OF ROLE-TAKING AND ROLE-PLAYING ABILITY EJ 008 318
LANGUAGE, SOCIALIZATION, AND DELINQUENCY EJ 039 587
WHAT DOES RESEARCH TEACH US ABOUT DAY CARE: FOR CHILDREN OVER THREE EJ 051 237
THE FORMATION AND REVERSAL OF AN ATTITUDE AS FUNCTIONS OF ASSUMED SELF-CONCEPT, RACE, AND SOCIOECONOMIC CLASS EJ 052 652
LISTENING BEYOND WORDS: LEARNING FROM PARENTS IN CONFERENCES EJ 055 363

SOCIOECONOMIC STATUS

MOTHERS AS TEACHERS OF THEIR OWN PRESCHOOL CHILDREN: THE INFLUENCE OF SOCIO-ECONOMIC STATUS AND TASK STRUCTURE ON TEACHING SPECIFICITY. ED031294
CLASSIFICATION AND INFERENTIAL THINKING IN CHILDREN OF VARYING AGE AND SOCIAL CLASS. ED035446
A COMPARATIVE STUDY OF THREE FORMS OF THE METROPOLITAN READINESS TEST AT TWO SOCIO-ECONOMIC LEVELS. ED035448
SOCIAL CLASS DIFFERENTIATION IN COGNITIVE DEVELOPMENT AMONG BLACK PRESCHOOL CHILDREN. ED039039
PRESCHOOLS AND THEIR GRADUATES. ED041644
LEARNING TO LEARN ON A CONCEPT ATTAINMENT TASK AS A FUNCTION OF AGE AND SOCIOECONOMIC LEVEL. REPORT FROM THE PROJECT ON SITUATIONAL VARIABLES AND EFFICIENCY OF CONCEPT LEARNING. ED046505
ENVIRONMENTAL FORCES IN THE HOME LIVES OF THREE-YEAR-OLD CHILDREN IN THREE POPULATION SUBGROUPS. ED050802
SURVIVAL SKILLS AND FIRST GRADE ACADEMIC ACHIEVEMENT. REPORT #1. ED050807
INFANT DEVELOPMENT, PRESCHOOL IQ, AND SOCIAL CLASS EJ 018 465
SOCIOECONOMIC BACKGROUND AND COGNITIVE FUNCTIONING IN PRESCHOOL CHILDREN EJ 021 774
PATTERNS OF WISC SCORES FOR CHILDREN OF TWO SOCIOECONOMIC CLASSES AND RACES EJ 021 775
SEX IDENTITY IN LONDON CHILDREN: MEMORY, KNOWLEDGE AND PREFERENCE TESTS EJ 023 435
SOCIOECONOMIC STATUS AND SEX DIFFERENCES IN ADOLESCENT REFERENCE-GROUP ORIENTATION EJ 023 614
LEVEL OF ASPIRATION AND THE PROBABILITY LEARNING OF MIDDLE- AND LOWER-CLASS CHILDREN EJ 024 703
EFFECTS OF SOCIAL CLASS ON CHILDREN'S MOTORIC EXPRESSION EJ 025 149
SOME NONVERBAL ASPECTS OF COMMUNICATION BETWEEN MOTHER AND PRESCHOOL CHILD EJ 025 386
INFANT MENTAL DEVELOPMENT AND NEUROLOGICAL STATUS, FAMILY SOCIOECONOMIC STATUS, AND INTELLIGENCE AT AGE FOUR EJ 032 675
CHAOTIC REINFORCEMENT: A SOCIOECONOMIC LEVELER EJ 035 371
AN EXPERIMENTAL STUDY OF BASIC LEARNING ABILITY AND INTELLIGENCE IN LOW-SOCIOECONOMIC-STATUS CHILDREN EJ 036 818
CHILDREN'S COMMUNICATION ACCURACY RELATED TO RACE AND SOCIOECONOMIC STATUS EJ 040 359
LINGUISTIC AND THEMATIC VARIABLES IN RECALL OF A STORY BY DISADVANTAGED CHILDREN EJ 041 142
DEVELOPMENT OF SYNTACTIC COMPREHENSION IN PRESCHOOL CHILDREN AS A FUNCTION OF SOCIOECONOMIC LEVEL EJ 043 480
THE EFFECTS OF TRAINING AND SOCIOECONOMIC CLASS UPON THE ACQUISITION OF CONSERVATION CONCEPTS EJ 056 401
EFFECTS OF SOCIOECONOMIC STATUS AND THE VALUE OF A REINFORCER UPON SELF-REINFORCEMENT BY CHILDREN EJ 056 726
VERBAL AND NONVERBAL REWARDS AND PUNISHMENT IN THE DISCRIMINATION LEARNING OF CHILDREN OF VARYING SOCIOECONOMIC STATUS EJ 057 896
OBSERVATION, REPETITION, AND ETHNIC BACKGROUND IN CONCEPT ATTAINMENT AND GENERALIZATION EJ 059 316
INFANT DEVELOPMENT IN LOWER-CLASS AMERICAN FAMILIES EJ 060 012

SOCIOLINGUISTICS

FINAL REPORT ON HEAD START EVALUATION AND RESEARCH--1966-67 TO THE INSTITUTE FOR EDUCATIONAL DEVELOPMENT. SECTION V, THE ROLE OF DIALECT IN THE SCHOOL-SOCIALIZATION OF LOWER CLASS CHILDREN. ED019121
HEAD START RESEARCH AND EVALUATION OFFICE, UNIVERSITY OF CALIFORNIA AT LOS ANGELES. ANNUAL REPORT, NOVEMBER 1967. SECTION II. ED021613
AN INVESTIGATION OF THE STANDARD-NONSTANDARD DIMENSION OF CENTRAL TEXAN ENGLISH. PART OF THE FINAL REPORT. ED026130
DEVELOPMENT OF GRAMMATICAL STRUCTURES AND ATTRIBUTES IN PRESCHOOL AGE CHILDREN. FINAL REPORT. ED041639
THE EFFECTS OF SOCIAL ISOLATION AND CHARACTERISTICS OF THE MODEL ON ACCENT IMITATION IN FOURTH-GRADE CHILDREN EJ 038 171
OF TIME AND THE PRONOUN: A NEW METHODOLOGY FOR RESEARCH IN HIGHER EDUCATION EJ 042 881
REGISTER: SOCIAL VARIATION IN LANGUAGE USE EJ 052 177

SOCIOLOGY

FAMILY SOCIOLOGY OR WIVES' FAMILY SOCIOLOGY? A COMPARISON OF HUSBANDS' AND WIVES' ANSWERS ABOUT DECISION MAKING IN THE GREEK AND AMERICAN CULTURE. REPORT NUMBER 4. ED030478
THE SOCIOLOGY OF EARLY CHILDHOOD EDUCATION: A REVIEW OF LITERATURE. TECHNICAL REPORT NO. 1. ED032944
KINSHIP INTERACTION AND MARITAL SOLIDARITY EJ 007 449

SOCIOMETRIC TECHNIQUES

THE RELATIONSHIP BETWEEN CONTROLLED PROJECTION RESPONSES AND SOCIOMETRIC STATUS EJ 031 541
RELATIONSHIP OF CLASSROOM GROUPING PRACTICES TO DIFFUSION OF STUDENTS' SOCIOMETRIC CHOICES AND DIFFUSION OF STUDENTS' PERCEPTION OF SOCIOMETRIC CHOICE EJ 042 791

SOCIOPSYCHOLOGICAL SERVICES

BRIDGING THE CONCEPT GAP IN WORK WITH YOUTH EJ 031 644

SORTING PROCEDURES

THE COGNITIVE ENVIRONMENTS OF URBAN PRE-SCHOOL CHILDREN. MANUAL OF INSTRUCTIONS FOR ADMINISTERING AND SCORING SIGEL CONCEPTUAL STYLE SORTING TASKS. ED018263
CONCEPT FORMATION IN CHILDREN: A STUDY USING NONSENSE STIMULI AND A FREE-SORT TASK. ED031306

SOUTHERN STATES

A REPORT OF THE SOUTHERN REGIONAL CONFERENCE ON EARLY CHILDHOOD EDUCATION. ED019112

SPACE

THE "TELL-AND-FIND PICTURE GAME" FOR YOUNG CHILDREN. ED042513

SPACE ORIENTATION

RELATION OF SPATIAL EGOCENTRISM AND SPATIAL ABILITIES OF THE YOUNG CHILD. REPORT NUMBER 7. ED030481
CHILDREN'S ACQUISITION OF VISUO-SPATIAL DIMENSIONALITY: A CONSERVATION STUDY. ED041636
CHILDREN'S CONSERVATION OF MULTIPLE SPACE RELATIONS: EFFECTS OF PERCEPTION AND REPRESENTATION. ED044179
A SUCCESSFUL ATTEMPT TO TRAIN CHILDREN IN COORDINATION OF PROJECTIVE SPACE. ED048916
A STUDY OF THE DEVELOPMENT OF EGOCENTRISM AND THE COORDINATION OF SPATIAL PERCEPTIONS IN ELEMENTARY SCHOOL CHILDREN. FINAL REPORT. ED050829
PREDICTIVE VERSUS PERCEPTUAL RESPONSES TO PIAGET'S WATER-LINE TASK AND THEIR RELATION TO DISTANCE CONSERVATION EJ 018 875
CHILDREN'S SPATIAL REPRESENTATIONS AND HORIZONTAL DIRECTIONALITY EJ 023 190
THE ROLE OF OBJECT ORIENTATION IN INFANT PERCEPTION EJ 024 695
VISUAL ORIENTATION IN CHILDREN'S DISCRIMINATION LEARNING UNDER CONSTANT, VARIABLE, AND COVARIABLE DELAY OF REINFORCEMENT EJ 024 696
AN INCREASING EFFECT OF DISORIENTATION ON THE DISCRIMINATION OF PRINT: A DEVELOPMENTAL STUDY EJ 024 982
PATTERN COPYING UNDER THREE CONDITIONS OF AN EXPANDED SPATIAL FIELD EJ 035 622
SPATIAL ABILITIES AND SPATIAL EGOCENTRISM IN THE YOUNG CHILD EJ 037 066
FACTOR STRUCTURE OF CHILDREN'S PERSONAL SPACE SCHEMATA EJ 052 466
THE ROLE OF FRONT-BACK FEATURES IN CHILDREN'S "FRONT," "BACK," AND "BESIDE" PLACEMENTS OF OBJECTS EJ 060 777

SPACE UTILIZATION

PLANNING ENVIRONMENTS FOR YOUNG CHILDREN: PHYSICAL SPACE. ED038162
PROGRAMS FOR INFANTS AND YOUNG CHILDREN. PART IV: FACILITIES AND EQUIPMENT. ED047810
AND A FRIENDLY GOODBYE EJ 028 310

SPANISH AMERICAN LITERATURE

HISPANIC HERITAGE: A SELECTED BOOK LIST FOR ALL AGES. ED036342

SPANISH AMERICANS

RESEARCH ON THE NEW NURSERY SCHOOL. PART I, A SUMMARY OF THE EVALUATION OF THE EXPERIMENTAL PROGRAM FOR DEPRIVED CHILDREN AT THE NEW NURSERY SCHOOL USING SOME EXPERIMENTAL MEASURES. INTERIM REPORT. ED027076
THE NEW NURSERY SCHOOL RESEARCH PROJECT ED042518

SPANISH SPEAKING

LANGUAGE. ED029718
FILMS SUITABLE FOR HEAD START CHILD DEVELOPMENT PROGRAMS. ED047818
A STUDY IN CHILD CARE (CASE STUDY FROM VOLUME II-B): "WILL YOU MARRY ME?" DAY CARE PROGRAM REPRINT SERIES. ED051906
HOME LANGUAGE AND PERFORMANCE ON STANDARDIZED TESTS EJ 032 678
INTERVENTION STRATEGIES FOR SPANISH-SPEAKING PRESCHOOL CHILDREN EJ 036 746
THE SPANISH-SPEAKING FIVE-YEAR-OLD EJ 056 391

SPATIAL RELATIONSHIP

HEAD START EVALUATION AND RESEARCH CENTER, BOSTON UNIVERSITY. REPORT D-II, TRAINING FOR NUMBER CONCEPT. ED022564
POSITION EFFECTS IN PLAY EQUIPMENT PREFERENCES OF NURSERY SCHOOL CHILDREN. ED045185
CHILDREN'S ACQUISITION OF VISUO-SPATIAL DIMENSIONALITY: A CONSERVATION STUDY EJ 047 681
CHILDREN'S UNDERSTANDING OF SPATIAL RELATIONS: COORDINATION OF PERSPECTIVES EJ 061 068

SPECIAL CLASSES

A SHORT, RELIABLE, EASY TO ADMINISTER INDIVIDUAL INTELLIGENCE TEST FOR SPECIAL CLASS PLACEMENT EJ 041 724

SPECIAL EDUCATION
EDUCATIONAL APPLICATION OF BEHAVIOR MODIFICATION TECHNIQUES WITH SEVERELY RETARDED CHILDREN IN A CHILD DEVELOPMENT CENTER EJ 017 421
SECOND STAGE TEACHING PROBLEMS IN A PUBLIC SCHOOL CLASS FOR EMOTIONALLY DISTURBED CHILDREN EJ 020 104
TEACHING THE UNTEACHABLES EJ 021 514
OCCUPATIONAL THERAPY AND SPECIAL EDUCATION EJ 045 234
THE SORE-FOOTED DUCK EJ 053 929
DESIGNING INSTRUCTIONAL SETTINGS FOR CHILDREN LABELED "RETARDED": SOME REFLECTIONS EJ 057 733

SPECIAL HEALTH PROBLEMS
RESEARCH ISSUES IN THE HEALTH AND NUTRITION IN EARLY CHILDHOOD. ED027970
RESEARCH ISSUES IN CHILD HEALTH, I-IV. PROCEEDINGS OF THE HEAD START RESEARCH SEMINARS: SEMINAR NO. 4, HEALTH AND NUTRITION IN EARLY CHILDHOOD (1ST, WASHINGTON, D.C., NOVEMBER 1, 1968). ED036331
LEAD POISONING IN CHILDREN. ED048919
NEW HOPE FOR BABIES OF RH NEGATIVE MOTHERS EJ 003 743
RUBELLA AND ITS AFTERMATH EJ 007 163
CHILDHOOD LEAD POISONING...AN ERADICABLE DISEASE EJ 013 482
INFANT MORTALITY: AN URGENT NATIONAL PROBLEM EJ 021 523
CHANGING PROSPECTS FOR CHILDREN WITH HEMOPHILIA EJ 029 952
CARING FOR CHILDREN WITH SICKLE CELL ANEMIA EJ 047 355

SPECIAL PROGRAMS
THE DESIGN OF A PRE-SCHOOL "LEARNING LABORATORY" IN A REHABILITATION CENTER. ED033764
ESTABLISHING TOKEN PROGRAMS IN SCHOOLS: ISSUES AND PROBLEMS. ED039020

SPECIAL SCHOOLS
A LEARNING EXPERIENCE IN HELPING PARENTS GET WHAT THEY WANT EJ 024 027

SPECTROGRAMS
DEVELOPMENT OF THE PROSODIC FEATURES OF INFANTS' VOCALIZING. ED025331

SPEECH
DEVELOPMENT OF THE PROSODIC FEATURES OF INFANTS' VOCALIZING. ED025331
NON-SOCIAL SPEECH IN FOUR-YEAR-OLD CHILDREN AS A FUNCTION OF BIRTH ORDER AND INTERPERSONAL SITUATION EJ 033 702
YOUNG CHILDREN'S USE OF THE SPEECH CODE IN A RECALL TASK EJ 033 792
TEACHERS' RATINGS OF URBAN CHILDREN'S READING PERFORMANCE EJ 035 662
ACOUSTIC ANALYSIS OF THE ACQUISITION OF ACCEPTABLE "R" IN AMERICAN ENGLISH EJ 041 056
SPEECH REGISTERS IN YOUNG CHILDREN EJ 052 450

SPEECH EVALUATION
THE DEVELOPMENT OF A TEST TO ASSESS THE OCCURRENCE OF SELECTED FEATURES OF NON-STANDARD ENGLISH IN THE SPEECH OF DISADVANTAGED PRIMARY CHILDREN. ED015790
THE PSYCHOLOGICAL CORRELATES OF SPEECH CHARACTERISTICS OF SOUNDING "DISADVANTAGED": A SOUTHERN REPLICATION EJ 040 685

SPEECH HABITS
REPORT ON THE ARTICULATORY AND INTELLIGIBILITY STATUS OF SOCIALLY DISADVANTAGED PRE-SCHOOL CHILDREN. ED014321

SPEECH HANDICAPS
HEAD START EVALUATION AND RESEARCH CENTER, UNIVERSITY OF KANSAS. REPORT NO. IIA, A STUDY OF AUDITORY DISCRIMINATION AND VERBAL RESPONDING. ED021634
HEAD START EVALUATION AND RESEARCH CENTER, UNIVERSITY OF KANSAS. REPORT NO. VIIA, A CASE STUDY IN ESTABLISHING A DIFFERENTIATED SPEECH RESPONSE THROUGH GENERALIZATION PROCEDURES. ED021640
AN ARTICULATION STUDY OF 15,255 SEATTLE FIRST GRADE CHILDREN WITH AND WITHOUT KINDERGARTEN. ED024438
THE CHILD WHO STUTTERS EJ 007 220

SPEECH IMPROVEMENT
HEAD START EVALUATION AND RESEARCH CENTER, UNIVERSITY OF KANSAS. REPORT NO. IIA, A STUDY OF AUDITORY DISCRIMINATION AND VERBAL RESPONDING. ED021634
BETTER FEEDING CAN MEAN BETTER SPEAKING. ED025306

SPEECH PATHOLOGY
A THERAPEUTIC APPROACH TO SPEECH PHOBIA: ELECTIVE MUTISM REEXAMINED EJ 035 625

SPEECH SKILLS
REPORT ON THE ARTICULATORY AND INTELLIGIBILITY STATUS OF SOCIALLY DISADVANTAGED PRE-SCHOOL CHILDREN. ED014321
A COMPARISON BETWEEN THE ORAL AND WRITTEN RESPONSES OF FIRST-GRADE CHILDREN IN I.T.A. AND T.O. CLASSES. ED019144
LANGUAGE CONTROL IN A GROUP OF HEAD START CHILDREN. ED020789
SHOWING AND SHARING IN THE KINDERGARTEN EJ 032 933

SPEECH THERAPY
HEAD START EVALUATION AND RESEARCH CENTER, UNIVERSITY OF KANSAS. FINAL REPORT ON RESEARCH ACTIVITIES. ED021614
HEAD START EVALUATION AND RESEARCH CENTER, UNIVERSITY OF KANSAS. REPORT NO. IIA, A STUDY OF AUDITORY DISCRIMINATION AND VERBAL RESPONDING. ED021634
HEAD START EVALUATION AND RESEARCH CENTER, UNIVERSITY OF KANSAS. REPORT NO. VIIA, A CASE STUDY IN ESTABLISHING A DIFFERENTIATED SPEECH RESPONSE THROUGH GENERALIZATION PROCEDURES. ED021640
BETTER FEEDING CAN MEAN BETTER SPEAKING. ED025306
THE CHILD WHO STUTTERS EJ 007 220
DEVELOPMENTAL SPEECH INACCURACY AND SPEECH THERAPY IN THE EARLY SCHOOL YEARS EJ 013 624

SPELLING
WRITE FIRST, READ LATER EJ 034 069

SPELLING INSTRUCTION
MATERIAL REINFORCEMENT AND SUCCESS IN SPELLING EJ 018 423

SPONTANEOUS BEHAVIOR
PLAY BEHAVIOR IN THE YEAR-OLD INFANT: EARLY SEX DIFFERENCES. ED022545
SPONTANEOUS PLAY: AN AVENUE FOR INTELLECTUAL DEVELOPMENT. ED023444
NURTURANCE, DEPENDENCE, AND EXPLORATORY BEHAVIOR IN PREKINDERGARTENERS. ED035443
SEX DIFFERENCES IN GENERALITY AND CONTINUITY OF VERBAL RESPONSIVITY. ED035444
THE EFFECTS OF OWN-HOME AND INSTITUTION-REARING ON THE BEHAVIOURAL DEVELOPMENT OF NORMAL AND MONGOL CHILDREN EJ 048 905
EXECUTIVE COMPETENCE AND SPONTANEOUS SOCIAL BEHAVIOR IN ONE-YEAR-OLDS EJ 056 732

STAFF IMPROVEMENT
LA FORMATION DU PERSONNEL NON MEDICAL S'OCCUPANT DU PETIT ENFANT DE 1 A 6 ANS EJ 035 170
NEW DIMENSIONS IN STAFF DEVELOPMENT IN A JUVENILE CORRECTIONAL SYSTEM EJ 043 858

STAFF ROLE
PRESCHOOL PROGRAMS OF THE U.S.S.R EJ 016 352

STANDARD SPOKEN USAGE
KEYS TO STANDARD ENGLISH EJ 028 577

STANDARDIZED TESTS
PROJECT TOBI, THE DEVELOPMENT OF A PRE-SCHOOL ACHIEVEMENT TEST. FINAL REPORT. ED016520
DEVELOPMENT OF A SOCIAL COMPETENCY SCALE FOR PRESCHOOL CHILDREN. FINAL REPORT. ED020004
A COMPARISON OF PRE-KINDERGARTEN AND PRE-1ST GRADE BOYS AND GIRLS ON MEASURES OF SCHOOL READINESS AND LANGUAGE DEVELOPMENT. INTERIM REPORT. ED023474
A HEAD START CONTROL GROUP. PART OF THE FINAL REPORT. ED026128

STANDARDS
FREE-ASSOCIATION NORMS AND ASSOCIATIVE STRUCTURE. ED025328
FEDERAL INTERAGENCY DAY CARE REQUIREMENTS, PURSUANT TO SEC. 522 (D) OF THE ECONOMIC OPPORTUNITY ACT. ED026145
CHILD WELFARE LEAGUE OF AMERICA STANDARDS FOR DAY CARE SERVICE. REVISED EDITION. ED039019
STANDARDS AND COSTS FOR DAY CARE. ED042501
AN INSTITUTIONAL ANALYSIS OF DAY CARE PROGRAM. PART II, GROUP DAY CARE: THE GROWTH OF AN INSTITUTION. FINAL REPORT. ED043394
LICENSING OF CHILD CARE FACILITIES BY STATE WELFARE DEPARTMENTS: A CONCEPTUAL STATEMENT. ED046489
STANDARDS FOR DAY CARE CENTERS FOR INFANTS AND CHILDREN UNDER 3 YEARS OF AGE. ED053794
DESIGNS AND PROPOSAL FOR EARLY CHILDHOOD RESEARCH: A NEW LOOK: PRESCHOOL RESEARCH AND PRESCHOOL EDUCATIONAL OBJECTIVES ED053808
TURNING THE TIDE IN TEACHER QUALITY EJ 034 231
DAY CARE LICENSING EJ 051 271

STATE AID
DEVELOPING PUBLIC DAY CARE FACILITIES IN MARYLAND EJ 018 970

STATE FEDERAL AID
TACOMA PUBLIC SCHOOLS EARLY CHILDHOOD PROGRAM, TACOMA, WASHINGTON: COMBINED LOCAL, STATE, AND FEDERAL FUNDS SUPPORT A LARGE-SCALE EARLY CHILDHOOD PROGRAM IN THE PUBLIC SCHOOLS. MODEL PROGRAMS--CHILDHOOD EDUCATION. ED045221

STATE LAWS
CHILD ABUSE LEGISLATION IN THE 1970'S. ED049826

STATE LEGISLATION
BASIC FACTS ABOUT LICENSING OF DAY CARE. ED047817

CHILD ABUSE LEGISLATION IN THE 1970'S. ED049826

STATE LICENSING BOARDS

LICENSING OF CHILD CARE FACILITIES BY STATE WELFARE DEPARTMENTS: A CONCEPTUAL STATEMENT. ED046489

BASIC FACTS ABOUT LICENSING OF DAY CARE. ED047817

DAY CARE LICENSING EJ 051 271

STATE PROGRAMS

A REPORT OF THE SOUTHERN REGIONAL CONFERENCE ON EARLY CHILDHOOD EDUCATION. ED019112

CREATING CHILD CARE COMMUNITIES THROUGH 4-C PROGRAMS EJ 051 239

STATE STANDARDS

MINIMUM STANDARDS FOR LICENSED DAY CARE CENTERS AND NIGHT-TIME CENTERS. REVISED EDITION. ED048918

EVALUATION GUIDE FOR EARLY CHILDHOOD EDUCATION PROGRAMS. ED048938

STEPS PURSUANT TO SECURING ACCREDITATION BY PRIVATE SECONDARY SCHOOLS EJ 016 606

STATE SURVEYS

CHILD REARING IN CALIFORNIA, A STUDY OF MOTHERS WITH YOUNG CHILDREN. ED020783

REPORT OF CHILD PLACEMENT STUDY COMMITTEE, JANUARY, 1969. ED044169

STATISTICAL ANALYSIS

FINAL REPORT ON HEAD START EVALUATION AND RESEARCH--1966-67 TO THE INSTITUTE FOR EDUCATIONAL DEVELOPMENT. SECTION II, ON THE INTERPRETATION OF MULTIVARIATE SYSTEMS. ED019118

DEVELOPMENT OF THE PROSODIC FEATURES OF INFANTS' VOCALIZING. ED025331

A LONGITUDINAL STUDY OF PIAGET'S DEVELOPMENTAL STAGES AND OF THE CONCEPT OF REGRESSION. ED043372

BIOLOGICAL AND ECOLOGICAL INFLUENCES ON DEVELOPMENT AT 12 MONTHS OF AGE EJ 029 385

THE EXIT OF CHILDREN FROM FOSTER CARE: AN INTERIM RESEARCH REPORT EJ 039 798

STATISTICAL DATA

PREPRIMARY ENROLLMENT TRENDS OF CHILDREN UNDER SIX: 1964-1968. ED042502

DISADVANTAGED CHILDREN AND THEIR FIRST SCHOOL EXPERIENCES. ETS-HEAD START LONGITUDINAL STUDY: PRELIMINARY DESCRIPTION OF THE INITIAL SAMPLE PRIOR TO SCHOOL ENROLLMENT. A REPORT IN TWO VOLUMES: VOLUME 2--TABLES. ED047798

CURRENT EXPENDITURES BY LOCAL EDUCATION AGENCIES FOR FREE PUBLIC ELEMENTARY AND SECONDARY EDUCATION, 1968-69. ED052826

THE HEALTH OF CHILDREN--1970: SELECTED DATA FROM THE NATIONAL CENTER FOR HEALTH STATISTICS. ED052827

STATISTICAL STUDIES

PROJECT HEAD START--SUMMER 1966. FINAL REPORT. SECTION ONE, SOME CHARACTERISTICS OF CHILDREN IN THE HEAD START PROGRAM. ED018246

STATISTICAL SURVEYS

PROJECT HEAD START--SUMMER 1966. FINAL REPORT. SECTION TWO, FACILITIES AND RESOURCES OF HEAD START CENTERS. ED018247

ADOPTION TRENDS: JANUARY-JUNE 1971 EJ 047 001

A FRESH LOOK AT INTERCOUNTRY ADOPTIONS EJ 047 968

STATISTICS

PROFILES OF CHILDREN: 1970 WHITE HOUSE CONFERENCE ON CHILDREN. ED046520

DAY CARE IN THE 1970S: PLANNING FOR EXPANSION EJ 037 237

STATUS NEED

SOME SOCIAL EFFECTS OF CROSS-GRADE GROUPING EJ 055 107

STEREOPSIS

THE CONTROL OF RELATIVE SIZE BY PICTORIAL DEPTH CUES IN CHILDREN AND ADULTS EJ 042 506

DISCRIMINATION OF STEREOMETRIC OJBECTS AND PHOTOGRAPHS OF OBJECTS BY CHILDREN EJ 053 749

STEREOTYPES

THE RELATIONSHIP BETWEEN RACE AND PERCEPTION OF RACIALLY-RELATED STIMULI IN PRESCHOOL CHILDREN. ED030483

STEREOTYPIC AFFECTIVE PROPERTIES OF PERSONAL NAMES AND SOMATOTYPES IN CHILDREN EJ 043 352

JUDGING OUTLINE FACES: A DEVELOPMENTAL STUDY EJ 045 599

GIVEN NAMES AND STEREOTYPING EJ 061 234

STIMULANTS

THE USE OF STIMULANT DRUGS IN TREATING HYPERACTIVE CHILDREN EJ 038 022

STIMULATION

INFANT STIMULATION AND THE ETIOLOGY OF COGNITIVE PROCESSES. ED045174

EVALUATION OF A PARENT AND CHILD CENTER PROGRAM. ED045189

ACTIVITIES FOR INFANT STIMULATION OR MOTHER-INFANT GAMES. ED046510

RELATIONSHIPS BETWEEN SELECTED FAMILY VARIABLES AND MATERNAL AND INFANT BEHAVIOR IN A DISADVANTAGED POPULATION. A SUPPLEMENTARY REPORT. ED047784

COMMUNICATIVE COMPETENCE AND THE DISADVANTAGED CHILD: A STUDY OF THE RELATIONSHIP BETWEEN LANGUAGE MODELS AND THE DEVELOPMENT OF COMMUNICATION SKILLS IN DISADVANTAGED PRESCHOOLERS. FINAL REPORT. ED047806

AN INTEGRATED PROGRAM OF GROUP CARE AND EDUCATION FOR SOCIOECONOMICALLY ADVANTAGED AND DISADVANTAGED INFANTS. ED048937

STATE AS VARIABLE, AS OBSTACLE AND AS MEDIATOR OF STIMULATION IN INFANT RESEARCH. ED049825

ON EARLY LEARNING: THE MODIFIABILITY OF HUMAN POTENTIAL. ED051876

NEW CONCEPTS OF HUMAN POTENTIALS: NEW CHALLENGE FOR TEACHERS EJ 034 711

CUMULATIVE EFFECTS OF CONTINUOUS STIMULATION ON AROUSAL LEVEL IN INFANTS EJ 036 075

CAN NEWBORNS SHOW CARDIAC ORIENTING? EJ 036 078

THE BEHAVIORAL AROUSAL THRESHOLD IN INFANT SLEEP AS A FUNCTION OF TIME AND SLEEP STATE EJ 036 091

COGNITIVE-PERCEPTUAL DEVELOPMENT IN INFANCY: SETTING FOR THE SEVENTIES EJ 038 262

ORIGINS OF SOCIAL DEVELOPMENT IN INFANCY EJ 038 570

A CREATIVE PLAYGROUND EJ 042 406

EARLY CHILD STIMULATION THROUGH PARENT EDUCATION EJ 044 006

THE EFFECTS OF THE ENVIRONMENT UPON STATE CYCLES IN THE HUMAN NEWBORN EJ 044 119

THE EFFECTS OF ENRICHED NEONATAL EXPERIENCES UPON LATER COGNITIVE FUNCTIONING EJ 047 689

STABILITY OF THE ORIENTING REFLEX IN INFANTS TO AUDITORY AND VISUAL STIMULI AS INDEXED BY CARDIAC DECELERATION EJ 056 720

STATE AS VARIABLE, AS OBSTACLE, AND AS MEDIATOR OF STIMULATION IN INFANT RESEARCH EJ 058 220

THE RELATIVE EFFICACY OF CONTACT AND VESTIBULAR-PROPRIOCEPTIVE STIMULATION IN SOOTHING NEONATES EJ 058 588

INFANCY AND THE OPTIMAL LEVEL OF STIMULATION EJ 058 697

DIMENSIONS OF EARLY STIMULATION AND THEIR DIFFERENTIAL EFFECTS ON INFANT DEVELOPMENT EJ 059 873

REACTIONS TO RESPONSE-CONTINGENT STIMULATION IN EARLY INFANCY EJ 059 874

EFFECTS OF SOCIAL AND VOCAL STIMULATION ON INFANT BABBLING EJ 061 140

STIMULI

STIMULUS ABSTRACTNESS AND THE CONSERVATION OF WEIGHT. ED035441

ROLE OF DISCRIMINATIVE STIMULI IN THE FORMATION OF FUNCTIONAL RESPONSE CLASSES EJ 024 937

VISUAL ALERTNESS IN NEONATES AS EVOKED BY MATERNAL CARE EJ 027 847

NOVELTY, FAMILIARITY, AND THE DEVELOPMENT OF INFANT ATTENTION EJ 034 529

A STIMULUS SIMILARITY SCALE FOR TEMPORAL MEASURES OF ATTENTION IN INFANTS AND CHILDREN EJ 034 530

STIMULUS AND RESPONSE ALTERNATION IN YOUNG CHILDREN EJ 034 537

THE INFLUENCE OF STIMULUS EXPOSURE ON RATED PREFERENCE: EFFECTS OF AGE, PATTERN OF EXPOSURE, AND STIMULUS MEANINGFULNESS EJ 041 960

DEVELOPMENTAL CHANGES IN IDIODYNAMIC SET RESPONSES OF CHILDREN'S WORD ASSOCIATIONS EJ 042 880

ACQUIRED DISTINCTIVENESS AND EQUIVALENCE OF CUES IN YOUNG CHILDREN EJ 053 654

MODIFICATION OF FORM AND COLOR RESPONDING IN YOUNG CHILDREN AS A FUNCTION OF DIFFERENTIAL REINFORCEMENT EJ 053 723

STIMULUS BEHAVIOR

EFFECTS OF DIFFERENTIAL PRIOR EXPOSURE ON YOUNG CHILDREN'S SUBSEQUENT OBSERVING AND CHOICE OF NOVEL STIMULI. ED017336

FINAL REPORT ON HEAD START EVALUATION AND RESEARCH--1966-67 TO THE INSTITUTE FOR EDUCATIONAL DEVELOPMENT. SECTION VII, SENSORY AND PERCEPTUAL STUDIES. ED019123

NOVELTY AND FAMILIARITY AS DETERMINANTS OF INFANT ATTENTION WITHIN THE FIRST YEAR. ED023483

ISSUES AND IMPLICATIONS OF THE DISTRIBUTION OF ATTENTION IN THE HUMAN INFANT. ED043387

CHILDREN'S JUDGMENTS OF AGE. ED043392

SENSORHESIS AS A MOTIVE FOR PLAY AND STEREOTYPED BEHAVIOR. ED044176

THE MEANING OF AN ORIENTING RESPONSE: A STUDY IN THE HIERARCHICAL ORDER OF ATTENDING. ED047794

A DEVELOPMENTAL INVESTIGATION OF VISUAL AND HAPTIC PREFERENCES FOR SHAPE AND TEXTURE EJ 008 780

EFFECTS OF STIMULUS-RESPONSE SIMILARITY AND DISSIMILARITY ON CHILDREN'S MATCHING PERFORMANCE EJ 016 350

THE EFFECTS OF TEMPERATURE AND POSITION ON THE SUCKING PRESSURE OF NEWBORN INFANTS EJ 018 260

CHILDREN'S PERFORMANCE ON AN ODDITY PROBLEM AS A FUNCTION OF THE NUMBER OF VALUES ON THE RELEVANT DIMENSION EJ 024 694
EFFECTS OF ENFORCED ATTENTION AND STIMULUS PHASING UPON RULE LEARNING IN CHILDREN EJ 024 697
SINGLE-LETTER CUE SELECTION IN THE PAIRED-ASSOCIATE LEARNING OF NORMAL CHILDREN AND RETARDATES EJ 024 698
AMOUNT OF SHORT-TERM FAMILIARIZATION AND THE RESPONSE TO AUDITORY DISCREPANCIES EJ 025 362
CARDIAC CLASSICAL CONDITIONING AND REVERSAL IN THE MONGOLOID, ENCEPHALOPATHIC, AND NORMAL CHILD EJ 025 375
VISUAL AND HAPTIC DIMENSIONAL PREFERENCE: A DEVELOPMENTAL STUDY EJ 026 506
ODDITY PREFERENCE BY MENTAL RETARDATES EJ 027 825
NEWBORN ATTENTION: DIFFERENTIAL RESPONSE DECREMENT TO VISUAL STIMULI EJ 027 846
CHANGES IN THE NONNUTRITIVE SUCKING RESPONSE TO STIMULATION DURING INFANCY EJ 027 848
NOVELTY, FAMILIARITY, AND THE DEVELOPMENT OF INFANT ATTENTION EJ 034 529
A STIMULUS SIMILARITY SCALE FOR TEMPORAL MEASURES OF ATTENTION IN INFANTS AND CHILDREN EJ 034 530
STIMULUS AND RESPONSE ALTERNATION IN YOUNG CHILDREN EJ 034 537
STIMULUS CONTROL OF PARENT OR CARETAKER BEHAVIOR BY OFFSPRING EJ 034 538
LINGUISTIC AND PSYCHOLOGICAL FACTORS IN THE SPEECH REGULATION OF BEHAVIOR IN YOUNG CHILDREN EJ 034 540
RESPONSE TO VOICE OF MOTHER AND STRANGER BY BABIES IN THE FIRST YEAR EJ 035 269
CUMULATIVE EFFECTS OF CONTINUOUS STIMULATION ON AROUSAL LEVEL IN INFANTS EJ 036 075
PRESTIMULUS ACTIVITY LEVEL AND RESPONSIVITY IN THE NEONATE EJ 040 297
NEWBORN'S RESPONSE TO THE CRY OF ANOTHER INFANT EJ 041 959
THE INFLUENCE OF STIMULUS EXPOSURE ON RATED PREFERENCE: EFFECTS OF AGE, PATTERN OF EXPOSURE, AND STIMULUS MEANINGFULNESS EJ 041 960
EFFECTS OF COMPETITION-INDUCED FRUSTRATION ON TWO CLASSES OF MODELED BEHAVIOR EJ 043 284
STIMULUS PREFERENCE AND MULTIPLICATIVE CLASSIFICATION IN CHILDREN EJ 047 686
STIMULUS INTERACTION AND PROBLEM DIFFICULTY IN CHILDREN'S DISCRIMINATION LEARNING EJ 053 480
EFFECTS OF RATE OF STIMULUS PRESENTATION AND PENALTY CONDITIONS ON THE DISCRIMINATION LEARNING OF NORMAL AND RETARDED CHILDREN EJ 053 712
DEVELOPMENTAL DETERMINANTS OF ATTENTION: A CROSS-CULTURAL REPLICATION EJ 053 718
AVOIDANCE CONDITIONING IN YOUNG CHILDREN WITH INTERRUPTION OF A POSITIVE STIMULUS AS THE AVERSIVE EVENT EJ 053 719
NONVERBAL INFORMATION STORAGE IN CHILDREN AND DEVELOPMENTAL INFORMATION PROCESSING CHANNEL CAPACITY EJ 053 720
INFANT SMILING TO NONSOCIAL STIMULI AND THE RECOGNITION HYPOTHESIS EJ 053 731
STIMULUS NOVELTY AS A VARIABLE IN CHILDREN'S WIN-STAY, LOSE-SHIFT DISCRIMINATION LEARNING SET EJ 053 751
OBSERVING BEHAVIOR AND CHILDREN'S DISCRIMINATION LEARNING EJ 053 754
DEVELOPMENT OF YOUNG CHILDREN'S ATTENTION TO NORMAL AND DISTORTED STIMULI: A CROSS CULTURAL STUDY EJ 055 103
PERSON SPECIFICITY OF THE "SOCIAL DEPRIVATION-SATIATION EFFECT" EJ 055 207
MOTIVATIONAL EFFECTS OF BOREDOM ON CHILDREN'S RESPONSE SPEEDS EJ 055 211
GENERALITY OF PERCEPTUAL BIASES IN INFERENCE AND CONCEPT USAGE EJ 056 618
THE ONSET OF WARINESS EJ 056 635
INFANTS' RESPONSES TO NOVELTY IN FAMILIAR AND UNFAMILIAR SETTINGS EJ 056 731
INITIAL PROBABILITY REHEARSAL, AND CONSTRAINT IN ASSOCIATIVE CLASS SELECTION EJ 057 903
INSTABILITY OF DIMENSIONAL PREFERENCE FOLLOWING CHANGES IN RELATIVE CUE SIMILARITY EJ 057 908
CHARITY IN CHILDREN: THE INFLUENCE OF "CHARITY" STIMULI AND AN AUDIENCE EJ 058 224
REACTIONS TO RESPONSE-CONTINGENT STIMULATION IN EARLY INFANCY EJ 059 874
RESPONSE DEPRESSION AND FACILITATION COMPONENTS OF THE FRUSTRATION EFFECT IN CHILDREN'S BEHAVIOR EJ 059 877
HYPOTHESES, STRATEGIES, AND STEREOTYPES IN DISCRIMINATION LEARNING EJ 060 779
PRODUCTION OF NOVEL AND GRAMMATICAL UTTERANCES BY YOUNG CHILDREN EJ 060 783
AN INFANT CONTROL PROCEDURE FOR STUDYING INFANT VISUAL FIXATIONS EJ 061 142

STIMULUS DEVICES
THE DEVELOPMENT OF TEMPORAL DISCRIMINATION IN YOUNG CHILDREN. ED045187

STIMULUS GENERALIZATION
A STUDY OF THE ABILITY OF PRIMARY SCHOOL CHILDREN TO GENERALIZE BEHAVIORAL COMPETENCIES SPECIFIED FOR "SCIENCE--A PROCESS APPROACH" TO OTHER CONTENT SETTINGS. ED039038
STIMULUS GENERALIZATION ACROSS INDIVIDUALS ALONG DIMENSIONS OF SEX AND RACE: SOME FINDINGS WITH CHILDREN FROM AN ALL-NEGRO NEIGHBORHOOD. PROGRESS REPORT. ED042497
INSTRUCTIONAL SPECIFICITY AND OUTCOME-EXPECTATION IN OBSERVATIONALLY-INDUCED QUESTION FORMULATION. ED047789
MODELING BY EXEMPLIFICATION AND INSTRUCTION IN TRAINING CONSERVATION. ED047790
GENERALIZATION IN A STIMULUS CLASSIFICATION TASK: STIMULUS SELECTION WITHIN AND AMONG DIMENSIONS EJ 021 987
GENERALIZATION OF ADULT'S STIMULUS CONTROL OF CHILDREN'S BEHAVIOR EJ 022 214
INFANT HABITUATION AND GENERALIZATION TO DIFFERING DEGREES OF STIMULUS NOVELTY EJ 043 195
GENERALIZATION AS A FUNCTION OF THE RANGE OF TEST STIMULI: THE ROLES OF DISCRIMINABILITY AND RESPONSE BIAS EJ 057 909
ATTENTION SPAN AND GENERALIZATION OF TASK-RELATED STIMULUS CONTROL: EFFECTS OF REINFORCEMENT CONTINGENCIES EJ 059 878
THE EFFECTS OF VERBAL PRETRAINING ON THE MULTIDIMENSIONAL GENERALIZATION BEHAVIOR OF CHILDREN EJ 060 784
THREE-CUE SELECTION MODELS APPLIED TO MULTIDIMENSIONAL STIMULUS CLASSIFICATION: ALTERNATIVES TO THE SPIKER, CROLL, AND MILLER ANALYSIS EJ 060 785
ON THE COMPARISON OF PSYCHOLOGICAL THEORIES: A REPLY TO PROFESSOR BOGARTZ EJ 060 786

STORY READING
LANGUAGE STYLE OF THE LOWER CLASS MOTHER: A PRELIMINARY STUDY OF A THERAPEUTIC TECHNIQUE. ED027943

STORY TELLING
ANALYSIS OF STORY RETELLING AS A MEASURE OF THE EFFECTS OF ETHNIC CONTENT IN STORIES. FINAL REPORT. ED014326

STRESS VARIABLES
ENVIRONMENTAL DISCONTINUITY, STRESS, AND SEX EFFECTS UPON SUSCEPTIBILITY TO SOCIAL INFLUENCE EJ 023 432
SHIFTS IN CHILD-REARING ATTITUDES LINKED WITH PARENTHOOD AND OCCUPATION EJ 038 853

STRUCTURAL ANALYSIS
THE COGNITIVE ENVIRONMENTS OF URBAN PRE-SCHOOL CHILDREN. MANUAL OF INSTRUCTIONS FOR ADMINISTERING AND SCORING MATERNAL LANGUAGE STYLES. ED018270
ANALYSES OF STORIES DICTATED IN CLASSES OF THE COOPERATIVE PROJECT. ED019993
GENERALIZED LABELING ON THE BASIS OF STRUCTURAL RESPONSE CLASSES BY TWO YOUNG CHILDREN EJ 044 696
A TRANSFORMATIONAL ANALYSIS OF ORAL SYNTACTIC STRUCTURES OF CHILDREN REPRESENTING VARYING ETHNOLINGUISTIC COMMUNITIES EJ 056 713

STRUCTURAL GRAMMAR
THE DEVELOPMENT OF COMPETENCE IN AN EXCEPTIONAL LANGUAGE STRUCTURE IN OLDER CHILDREN AND YOUNG ADULTS EJ 056 727

STRUCTURAL LINGUISTICS
A STUDY OF THE COMMUNICATIVE ABILITIES OF DISADVANTAGED CHILDREN. FINAL REPORT. ED032119

STUDENT ADJUSTMENT
EFFECT OF TRIMESTER SCHOOL OPERATION ON THE ACHIEVEMENT AND ADJUSTMENT OF KINDERGARTEN AND FIRST THROUGH THIRD GRADE CHILDREN. FINAL REPORT. ED020003
INVESTIGATION OF METHODS TO ASSESS THE EFFECTS OF CULTURAL DEPRIVATION. FINAL REPORT. ED032121
FAMILY FACTORS RELATED TO COMPETENCE IN YOUNG, DISADVANTAGED MEXICAN-AMERICAN CHILDREN. PART OF THE FINAL REPORT ON HEAD START EVALUATION AND RESEARCH: 1968-69 TO THE OFFICE OF ECONOMIC OPPORTUNITY. ED037248
EFFECTS OF DURATION OF A NURSERY SCHOOL SETTING ON ENVIRONMENTAL CONSTRAINTS AND CHILDREN'S MODES OF ADAPTATION. ED047812
A FOLLOW-UP STUDY OF SCHOOL PHOBIC ADOLESCENTS ADMITTED TO AN IN-PATIENT UNIT EJ 026 157
MEXICAN-AMERICAN CULTURAL MEMBERSHIP AND ADJUSTMENT TO SCHOOL EJ 035 620
BEHAVIOUR PROBLEMS IN THE INFANT SCHOOL EJ 048 306

STUDENT ALIENATION
THE EDUCATION OF YOUNG CHILDREN: AT THE CROSSROADS? EJ 013 229
I WAS A SLOW-LEARNER EJ 017 422
"OPENNESS" OF SCHOOL CLIMATE AND ALIENATION OF HIGH SCHOOL STUDENTS EJ 052 654

STUDENT ATTITUDES
THE FORMATION OF ADDITION AND SUBTRACTION CONCEPTS BY PUPILS IN GRADES ONE AND TWO. FINAL REPORT. ED015015
THE CHILD WHO DISLIKES GOING TO SCHOOL. ED019999

EFFECTS OF PARENTAL EXPECTATIONS OF EDUCATIONAL PLANS OF WHITE AND NONWHITE ADOLESCENTS. FINAL REPORT. ED027096
COGNITIVE ASPECTS OF CHILDREN'S OCCUPATIONAL PRESTIGE RANKINGS. ED039924
AN EXAMINATION OF CHANGES IN ATTITUDES TO VISUAL COMPLEXITY WITH INCREASING AGE. ED039930
RESULTS OF PARENT AND STUDENT REACTION QUESTIONNAIRE. TECHNICAL REPORT NO. 8. ED052836
SOME CORRELATES OF AVERAGE LEVEL OF HAPPINESS AMONG COLLEGE STUDENTS EJ 021 994
CREATIVITY AND ALIENATION: AN EXPLORATION OF THEIR RELATIONSHIP IN ADOLESCENCE EJ 021 996
MEXICAN-AMERICAN CULTURAL MEMBERSHIP AND ADJUSTMENT TO SCHOOL EJ 035 620
CHILDREN AND THE POLITICS OF TRUST EJ 045 394
CHILDREN'S PERCEPTIONS OF A TEACHING TEAM EJ 051 772
FRIENDSHIPS AMONG STUDENTS IN DESEGREGATED SCHOOLS EJ 053 668
CHILDREN OF TECHNOLOGY: IMAGES OR THE REAL THING EJ 054 472
REPORT CARDS FOR TEACHERS EJ 057 441
A COMPARATIVE STUDY OF COUNSELEE PREFERENCES FOR BEHAVIORIST AND CLIENT-CENTERED COUNSELING APPROACHES EJ 058 628

STUDENT BEHAVIOR
HEAD START EVALUATION AND RESEARCH CENTER, UNIVERSITY OF KANSAS. REPORT NO. X, ENHANCEMENT OF THE SOCIAL REINFORCING VALUE OF A PRESCHOOL TEACHER. ED021646
ASSESSING PROCESS AND PRODUCT WITH YOUNG CHILDREN IN SCHOOL SETTINGS. ED035453
A TOKEN REINFORCEMENT SYSTEM IN THE PUBLIC SCHOOLS. ED036323
PUPIL IMITATION OF A REWARDING TEACHER'S VERBAL BEHAVIOR. ED038185
RELATIONSHIPS BETWEEN TEACHER BEHAVIOR, PUPIL BEHAVIOR, AND PUPIL ACHIEVEMENT. ED038189
LEARNING TO OBSERVE--OBSERVING TO LEARN. ED047815
CONSCIENCE, PERSONALITY, AND SOCIALIZATION TECHNIQUES EJ 023 858
CLASSROOM MANAGEMENT--MORE THAN CONDITIONING EJ 027 827
BEHAVIOUR PROBLEMS IN THE INFANT SCHOOL EJ 048 306
STUDYING AGGRESSIVE CHILDREN THROUGH RESPONSE TO FRUSTRATING SITUATIONS EJ 051 013

STUDENT CENTERED CURRICULUM
ASPEN MORNINGS WITH SYLVIA ASHTON-WARNER EJ 056 860

STUDENT CHARACTERISTICS
HEAD START EVALUATION AND RESEARCH CENTER, TULANE UNIVERSITY. FINAL REPORT. (TITLE SUPPLIED). ED020782
[ACHIEVEMENT TEST CORRELATION STUDY: SURVEY OF 40 CHILDREN.] ED027954
INSTITUTE FOR DEVELOPMENTAL STUDIES INTERIM PROGRESS REPORT. PART II: RESEARCH AND EVALUATION. ED036312
POPULATION CHARACTERISTICS OF DISADVANTAGED PRESCHOOL CHILDREN. PROCEEDINGS OF THE HEAD START RESEARCH SEMINARS: SEMINAR NO. 3, HEAD START POPULATIONS (1ST, WASHINGTON, D.C., OCTOBER 9, 1968). ED036330
IMAGES OF THE IDEAL PUPIL HELD BY TEACHERS IN PREPARATION EJ 012 679
I AM--I WANT--I NEED: PREADOLESCENTS LOOK AT THEMSELVES AND THEIR VALUES EJ 017 446
THE CHANGING CHILDREN OF PREADOLESCENCE (OR THE QUESTIONABLE JOY OF BEING PRE-ANYTHING) EJ 017 901
WHEN CHILDREN ENJOY SCHOOL: SOME LESSONS FROM BRITAIN EJ 018 047
PERSONALITY, COGNITIVE, AND DEMOGRAPHIC CHARACTERISTICS OF STUDENT ACTIVISTS AND ACTIVE STUDENTS EJ 061 194

STUDENT DEVELOPMENT
HOW TO HELP YOUR CHILD LEARN, A HANDBOOK FOR PARENTS OF CHILDREN IN KINDERGARTEN THROUGH GRADE 6. ED017342

STUDENT DISTRIBUTION
PROJECT HEAD START--SUMMER 1966. FINAL REPORT. SECTION ONE, SOME CHARACTERISTICS OF CHILDREN IN THE HEAD START PROGRAM. ED018246

STUDENT EVALUATION
STUDY OF ACHIEVEMENT--REPORT POPULATION STUDY OF JUNIOR AND SENIOR KINDERGARTEN PUPILS, 1960-61 AND 1961-62. ED017321
STUDY OF ACHIEVEMENT, TORONTO INFORMATION BULLETIN NO. 1. ED017323
DEVELOPMENT AND IMPLEMENTATION OF A COMPREHENSIVE EVALUATION AND REPORTING SYSTEM FOR KINDERGARTEN AND PRIMARY GRADE SCHOOLS. FINAL REPORT. ED026116
EVALUATION UNDER INDIVIDUALIZED INSTRUCTION EJ 036 826
THE PSYCHOLOGICAL CORRELATES OF SPEECH CHARACTERISTICS OF SOUNDING "DISADVANTAGED": A SOUTHERN REPLICATION EJ 040 685
STUDENT EVALUATION OF A HIGH SCHOOL SEX EDUCATION PROGRAM EJ 045 390
LEARNING FROM EACH OTHER: PREDIATRICIANS AND TEACHERS EJ 050 320

STUDENT EXPERIENCE
EXPERIENCES AND LANGUAGE DEVELOPMENT EJ 011 842

STUDENT GROUPING
RELATIONSHIP OF CLASSROOM GROUPING PRACTICES TO DIFFUSION OF STUDENTS' SOCIOMETRIC CHOICES AND DIFFUSION OF STUDENTS' PERCEPTION OF SOCIOMETRIC CHOICE EJ 042 791

STUDENT IMPROVEMENT
FINAL REPORT ON HEAD START EVALUATION AND RESEARCH--1966-67 TO THE INSTITUTE FOR EDUCATIONAL DEVELOPMENT. SECTION IV, AN EXPLORATORY STUDY OF ORAL LANGUAGE DEVELOPMENT AMONG CULTURALLY DIFFERENT CHILDREN. ED019120
LANGUAGE ABILITY AND READINESS FOR SCHOOL OF CHILDREN WHO PARTICIPATED IN HEAD START PROGRAMS. A DISSERTATION ABSTRACT. ED025299
THE EFFECT OF TEACHERS' INFERRED SELF CONCEPT UPON STUDENT ACHIEVEMENT. ED031300

STUDENT INTERESTS
THE WORLD OF THE CHILD. ED050826

STUDENT MOBILITY
ARE MOVERS LOSERS? EJ 018 958

STUDENT MOTIVATION
CHILDREN LEARN AND GROW THROUGH ART EXPERIENCES. ILLINOIS CURRICULUM PROGRAM, THE SUBJECT FIELD SERIES. ED019132
MOTIVATIONAL FACTORS AND IQ-CHANGES IN CULTURALLY DEPRIVED CHILDREN ATTENDING NURSERY SCHOOL. ED020017
OPENING UP THE CLASSROOM: A WALK AROUND THE SCHOOL. ED053817
MOTIVATIONAL AND ATTITUDINAL CONTENT OF FIRST GRADE READING TEXTBOOKS EJ 045 084
EFFECTS OF PROVISION FOR INDIVIDUAL DIFFERENCES AND TEACHER ATTENTION UPON STUDY BEHAVIOR AND ASSIGNMENTS COMPLETED EJ 058 353

STUDENT NEEDS
THE PROFESSIONAL RESPONSE. ED048922
HIS OWN HELLO EJ 013 230
UNDERSTANDING THE BLACK CHILD EJ 020 717

STUDENT OPINION
THE EFFECT OF STUDENT EVALUATIONS OF COLLEGE INSTRUCTION UPON SUBSEQUENT EVALUATIONS EJ 017 245
STUDENT EVALUATION OF A HIGH SCHOOL SEX EDUCATION PROGRAM EJ 045 390
EFFECT OF CLASSROOM NOISE ON NUMBER IDENTIFICATION BY RETARDED CHILDREN EJ 045 391
WHAT'S A SCHOOL FOR? EJ 046 788
REPORT CARDS FOR TEACHERS EJ 057 441

STUDENT PARTICIPATION
A ROOM PLANNED BY CHILDREN EJ 007 876
WHO SELECTS THE OBJECTIVES FOR LEARNING--AND WHY? EJ 031 849
TOWARD A DEMOCRATIC ELEMENTARY-SCHOOL CLASSROOM EJ 058 308

STUDENT PLACEMENT
SCHOOL READINESS, BEHAVIOR TESTS USED AT THE GESELL INSTITUTE. ED023449

STUDENT PROMOTION
SUFFER THE LITTLE KENTUCKY FIRST-GRADERS EJ 037 283

STUDENT REACTION
CHILDREN AND THE SCHOOL STRIKE EJ 003 419
SEPARATION REACTIONS IN YOUNG, MILDLY RETARDED CHILDREN. EJ 003 972
EXPERIMENTAL LEARNING REEVALUATED EJ 026 814
FRIENDSHIPS AMONG STUDENTS IN DESEGREGATED SCHOOLS EJ 053 668

STUDENT RECORDS
FOLLOW-UP OF OPERATION HEAD START PARTICIPANTS IN THE STATE OF IOWA. FINAL REPORT. ED015771
DEVELOPMENT AND IMPLEMENTATION OF A COMPREHENSIVE EVALUATION AND REPORTING SYSTEM FOR KINDERGARTEN AND PRIMARY GRADE SCHOOLS. FINAL REPORT. ED026116

STUDENT RESEARCH
ENCOURAGING STUDENTS' RESEARCH ON COGNITIVE DEVELOPMENT. ED031301

STUDENT TEACHER RATIO
THE EFFECT OF FOUR COMMUNICATION PATTERNS AND SEX ON LENGTH OF VERBALIZATION IN SPEECH OF FOUR YEAR OLD CHILDREN. FINAL REPORT. ED042514

STUDENT TEACHER RELATIONSHIP
TEACHERS BELIEF SYSTEMS AND PRESCHOOL ATMOSPHERES. ED014320
OUTCOMES OF INDIVIDUAL AND PROGRAMMATIC VARIATIONS AMONG PROJECT HEAD START CENTERS, SUMMER, 1965. FINAL REPORT. ED014325

THE DEVELOPMENT OF SELF-OTHER RELATIONSHIPS DURING PROJECT HEAD START. ED015008
WHEN THE CHILD IS ANGRY. ED017331
HEAD START EVALUATION AND RESEARCH CENTER, BOSTON UNIVERSITY. REPORT A-III, OBSERVATIONAL STRATEGIES FOR OBTAINING DATA ON CHILDREN AND TEACHERS IN HEAD START CLASSES. (OSOD). ED022559
ACHIEVEMENT, CREATIVITY, AND SELF-CONCEPT CORRELATES OF TEACHER-PUPIL TRANSACTIONS IN ELEMENTARY SCHOOL CLASSROOMS. ED024463
SOUTHWESTERN COOPERATIVE EDUCATIONAL LABORATORY INTERACTION OBSERVATION SCHEDULE (SCIOS): A SYSTEM FOR ANALYZING TEACHER-PUPIL INTERACTION IN THE AFFECTIVE DOMAIN. ED038188
RELATIONSHIPS BETWEEN TEACHER BEHAVIOR, PUPIL BEHAVIOR, AND PUPIL ACHIEVEMENT. ED038189
THE EFFECT OF THE MALE ELEMENTARY TEACHER ON CHILDREN'S SELF-CONCEPTS. ED039034
TEACHER-PUPIL INTERACTION AS IT RELATES TO ATTEMPTED CHANGES IN TEACHER EXPECTANCY OF ACADEMIC ABILITY AND ACHIEVEMENT. ED041630
THE DISTRIBUTION OF TEACHER APPROVAL AND DISAPPROVAL OF HEAD START CHILDREN. FINAL REPORT. ED042509
MODIFICATION BY SOCIAL REINFORCEMENT OF DEFICIENT SOCIAL BEHAVIOR OF DISADVANTAGED KINDERGARTEN CHILDREN. ED043381
TEACHER-CHILD RELATIONSHIPS IN DAY CARE CENTERS. WORKING PAPER. ED046494
RELATIONSHIPS BETWEEN CHILDREN'S QUESTIONS AND NURSERY SCHOOL TEACHERS' RESPONSES. ED046507
AN ANALYSIS OF PUBLISHED PRESCHOOL LANGUAGE PROGRAMS. ED047786
THE PROFESSIONAL RESPONSE. ED048922
THE VALUE OF CLASSROOM REWARDS IN EARLY EDUCATION. ED049828
HAS PRESCHOOL COMPENSATORY EDUCATION FAILED? ED049834
LANGUAGE TRAINING IN EARLY CHILDHOOD EDUCATION. ED051881
HELPING CHILDREN COPE WITH FEELINGS. EJ 002 018
TO KEEP AN INNER BALANCE EJ 002 313
THE ELEMENTS OF EFFECTIVE COMMUNICATION EJ 011 845
AN EXPERIMENTAL APPROACH TO THE EFFECT OF GROUP ANIMADVERSION EJ 012 678
IMAGES OF THE IDEAL PUPIL HELD BY TEACHERS IN PREPARATION EJ 012 679
WHICH PUPILS DO TEACHERS CALL ON? EJ 012 871
HIS OWN HELLO EJ 013 230
TEACHING AND THE NEW MORALITY EJ 016 776
PRAISE, CRITICISM, AND RACE EJ 019 388
PUPILS' PERCEPTION OF TEACHERS' VERBAL FEEDBACK EJ 027 880
THE EFFECT OF PLANNING ON TEACHING EJ 028 503
ANXIETY - A CLASSROOM CLOSE-UP EJ 028 896
CLASSROOM BEHAVIOR: MESSAGES FROM CHILDREN EJ 031 780
THE SYSTEMATIC USE OF THE PEMACK PRINCIPLE IN MODIFYING CLASSROOM BEHAVIORS EJ 034 528
EFFECT OF CLASSROOM NOISE ON NUMBER IDENTIFICATION BY RETARDED CHILDREN EJ 045 391
THE INFLUENCE OF TEACHER-CHILD INTERACTION ON THE LEARNING PROCESS EJ 048 235
WHAT CAN TEACHERS LEARN FROM DIRECTORS IN THE PERFORMING ARTS? EJ 051 410
LOOKING BACK WITH APPRECIATION EJ 058 054
A GLANCE AT A HEAD START PROGRAM IN AN ALASKAN CITY EJ 058 768
FEMINIZATION IN PRESCHOOL EJ 059 872

STUDENT TEACHERS
SUPERMARKET DISCOVERY CENTER, PILOT STUDY, MAY - SEPTEMBER, 1968. INITIAL REPORT. ED027941
THE EFFICACY OF A MATHEMATICS READINESS PROGRAM FOR INDUCING CONSERVATION OF NUMBER, WEIGHT, AREA, MASS, AND VOLUME IN DISADVANTAGED PRESCHOOL CHILDREN IN THE SOUTHERN UNITED STATES. ED048923

STUDENT TEACHING
DO STUDENTS' IDEAS AND ATTITUDES SURVIVE PRACTICE TEACHING? EJ 013 228
SYMPOSIUM ON CHILD-OBSERVATION: 1. FILM-MAKING AS AN OBSERVATION TECHNIQUE EJ 056 861

STUDENT TESTING
OUTCOMES OF INDIVIDUAL AND PROGRAMMATIC VARIATIONS AMONG PROJECT HEAD START CENTERS, SUMMER, 1965. FINAL REPORT. ED014325
TESTING IN THE SCHOOLS: A RESPONSE TO JOHN HOLT EJ 013 227
DEVELOPMENTAL TRENDS IN GENERAL AND TEST ANXIETY AMONG JUNIOR AND SENIOR HIGH SCHOOL STUDENTS EJ 061 062

STUDENT VOLUNTEERS
SANTA MONICA CHILDREN'S CENTERS, SANTA MONICA, CALIFORNIA: LOW-COST DAY CARE FACILITIES FOR CHILDREN OF WORKING MOTHERS MADE AVAILABLE THROUGH THE COOPERATION OF THE CALIFORNIA STATE GOVERNMENT AND LOCAL SCHOOL DISTRICT. MODEL PROGRAMS--CHILDHOOD EDUCATION. ED045212

STUDY GUIDES
CHARACTERISTICS OF PRIMARY LEVEL CHILDREN. ED036343

STUTTERING
THE CHILD WHO STUTTERS EJ 007 220
THE MODIFICATION OF CHILDHOOD STUTTERING: SOME RESPONSE-RESPONSE RELATIONSHIPS EJ 023 965

SUBCULTURE
INFLUENCES OF CULTURAL PATTERNS ON THE THINKING OF CHILDREN IN CERTAIN ETHNIC GROUPS, A STUDY OF THE EFFECT OF JEWISH SUBCULTURE ON THE FIELD-DEPENDENCE-INDEPENDENCE DIMENSION OF COGNITION. ED020796
A STUDY OF LANGUAGE DEVIATIONS AND COGNITIVE PROCESSES. PROGRESS REPORT NO. 3. ED027958
ALIENATION OF YOUTH AS REFLECTED IN THE HIPPIE MOVEMENT EJ 023 427
COOPERATIVE AND COMPETITIVE BEHAVIOR OF URBAN AFRO-AMERICAN, ANGLO-AMERICAN, MEXICAN-AMERICAN, AND MEXICAN VILLAGE CHILDREN EJ 024 033
LANGUAGE PATTERNS WITHIN THE YOUTH SUBCULTURE: DEVELOPMENT OF SLANG VOCABULARIES EJ 060 720

SUBPROFESSIONALS
SUB-PROFESSIONAL BEHAVIOR MODIFICATION AND THE DEVELOPMENT OF TOKEN-REINFORCEMENT SYSTEMS IN INCREASING ACADEMIC MOTIVATION AND ACHIEVEMENT EJ 034 527

SUCCESS FACTORS
MOTHER-CHILD RELATIONS AND CHILDREN'S ACHIEVEMENT. TERMINAL REPORT. ED024465
DEVELOPMENTAL SKILL AND ACHIEVEMENT DIFFERENCES OF CHILDREN IDENTIFIED AS EXCELLENT, GOOD, AND AVERAGE IN READING AND ARITHMETIC ACHIEVEMENT. STUDY NUMBER THREE. ED044181
MATERIAL REINFORCEMENT AND SUCCESS IN SPELLING EJ 018 423
EFFECT OF SUCCESS AND FAILURE ON THE REFLECTIVE AND IMPULSIVE CHILD EJ 029 768
SELF-ESTEEM, SUCCESS-FAILURE, AND LOCUS OF CONTROL IN NEGRO CHILDREN EJ 035 621
THE INFLUENCE OF MASCULINE, FEMININE, AND NEUTRAL TASKS ON CHILDREN'S ACHIEVEMENT BEHAVIOR, EXPECTANCIES OF SUCCESS, AND ATTAINMENT VALUES EJ 037 318
NORMAL AND RETARDED CHILDREN'S EXPECTANCY FOR FAILURE EJ 039 266
SUCCESS AND ACCOUNTABILITY EJ 055 533

SUICIDE
PHENOMENAL ENVIRONMENTAL OPPRESSIVENESS IN SUICIDAL ADOLESCENTS EJ 061 063

SUMMER INSTITUTES
AFFECTIVE DIMENSIONS OF TEACHERS OF DISADVANTAGED CHILDREN IN SIX MAJORITY NEGRO SCHOOL DISTRICTS. ED028833

SUMMER PROGRAMS
PROJECT HEAD START, PSYCHOLOGICAL SERVICES REPORT, RESEARCH, SUMMER 1968. ED024460
INVESTMENTS IN PREVENTION, AN ACTIVITY GROUP PROGRAM FOR YOUNG CHILDREN, SUMMER - 1967. ED025311
TEAM TEACHING. A DESCRIPTIVE AND EVALUATIVE STUDY OF A PROGRAM FOR THE PRIMARY GRADES. ED027083
HEAD START IN ACTION. ED030471
A PREVENTIVE SUMMER PROGRAM FOR KINDERGARTEN CHILDREN LIKELY TO FAIL IN FIRST GRADE READING. FINAL REPORT. ED030495
AN EXPERIMENTAL SUMMER KINDERGARTEN FOR CULTURALLY DEPRIVED CHILDREN. ED044174
EARLY CHILDHOOD EDUCATION PROGRAM FOR NURSERY, KINDERGARTEN CHILDREN. ED052846
RETARDED CHILDREN AT CAMP WITH NORMAL CHILDREN EJ 012 199
TAKE A GIANT STEP --A REMEDIAL PROGRAM IN A CAMP SETTING EJ 020 773
PARENTS: SUMMER READING TEACHERS EJ 032 510
A DEMONSTRATION SUMMER PRESCHOOL PROGRAM EJ 060 999

SUMMER WORKSHOPS
CHILDREN AND THE ARTS. PRESENTATIONS FROM A WRITING CONFERENCE. ED025317

SUPERVISORS
CREATIVE SUPERVISION OF HEAD START CENTERS EJ 013 231
ROLE PERCEPTIONS AND JOB SATISFACTION AMONG LOWER AND MIDDLE LEVEL JUNIOR COLLEGE ADMINISTRATORS EJ 016 774

SUPERVISORY TRAINING
TEACHER AIDES: HANDBOOK FOR INSTRUCTORS AND ADMINISTRATORS. ED024461

SUPPLEMENTARY EDUCATION
THE ITINERANT TEACHER. ED045191

SUPPLEMENTARY READING MATERIALS
SUPPLEMENTARY MATERIALS FOR TEACHER AIDE TRAINING PROGRAMS, TO SUPPLEMENT THE PUBLICATION "TEACHER AIDES: HANDBOOK FOR INSTRUCTORS AND ADMINISTRATORS." ED024462

SURVEYS
SOCIAL STUDIES IN ELEMENTARY SCHOOLS (THIRTY-SECOND YEARBOOK). ED018275
A STUDY OF A MEASUREMENT RESOURCE IN CHILD RESEARCH, PROJECT HEAD START. ED020790
PARENTS' EVALUATION OF THE HEAD START PROGRAM IN THE MILWAUKEE PUBLIC SCHOOLS. ED020806
EARLY CHILDHOOD EDUCATION TODAY. ED021631
CHILD DEVELOPMENT AND MATERIAL SURVEY. PART II, MATERIAL SURVEY. FINAL REPORT. ED027085
[ACHIEVEMENT TEST CORRELATION STUDY: SURVEY OF 40 CHILDREN.] ED027954
TEENAGERS DISCUSS AGE RESTRICTIONS EJ 046 786
INDUSTRY AND DAY CARE EJ 050 380
INVESTIGACIONES EN EL CAMPO EDUCATIVE (INVESTIGATIONS IN EDUCATION FIELD) EJ 062 593

SYLLABLES
DICTIONARY SYLLABICATION - HOW USEFUL EJ 052 180

SYMBOLIC LEARNING
THE FORMATION OF ADDITION AND SUBTRACTION CONCEPTS BY PUPILS IN GRADES ONE AND TWO. FINAL REPORT. ED015015
THE DISTANCING HYPOTHESIS: A HYPOTHESIS CRUCIAL TO THE DEVELOPMENT OF REPRESENTATIONAL COMPETENCE. ED024466
COGNITIVE SYNTHESIS IN NEGRO AND WHITE CHILDREN EJ 020 522
CHILDREN'S UTILIZATION OF LOGICAL SYMBOLS: AN INTERPRETATION OF CONCEPTUAL BEHAVIOR BASED ON PIAGETIAN THEORY EJ 024 942
AGE-DEVELOPMENT IN THE LINEAR REPRESENTATION OF WORDS AND OBJECTS EJ 030 296
LOGICAL SYMBOL USE IN DEAF AND HEARING CHILDREN AND ADOLESCENTS EJ 047 339

SYMPOSIA
ISSUES IN HUMAN DEVELOPMENT: AN INVENTORY OF PROBLEMS, UNFINISHED BUSINESS AND DIRECTIONS FOR RESEARCH. ED051888
SYMPOSIUM: FOR AND AGAINST STRIKES EJ 003 416

SYNTAX
AN OBJECTIVE MEASURE OF STRUCTURAL COMPLEXITY IN CHILDREN'S WRITING. ED016534
EVALUATING THE CHILD'S LANGUAGE COMPETENCE. ED019141
A COMPARISON OF THE PSYCHOLINGUISTIC FUNCTIONING OF "EDUCATIONALLY-DEPRIVED" AND "EDUCATIONALLY-ADVANTAGED" CHILDREN. ED022537
THE DEVELOPMENT OF FORMS OF THE NEGATIVE. ED022549
TWO STUDIES OF THE SYNTACTIC KNOWLEDGE OF YOUNG CHILDREN. A PRELIMINARY REPORT. ED024451
THE DEVELOPMENT OF INTERROGATIVE STRUCTURES IN CHILDREN'S SPEECH. ED025333
AN EXPERIMENTAL STUDY OF SYNTACTICAL FACTORS INFLUENCING CHILDREN'S COMPREHENSION OF CERTAIN COMPLEX RELATIONSHIPS. FINAL REPORT. ED030492
LANGUAGE STRUCTURE AND THE FREE RECALL OF VERBAL MESSAGES BY CHILDREN. ED032933
A TRANSFORMATIONAL ANALYSIS OF THE LANGUAGE OF KINDERGARTEN AND ELEMENTARY SCHOOL CHILDREN. ED034592
SYNTACTIC COMPLEXITY IN MOTHER-CHILD INTERACTIONS. ED035454
THE EFFECTS OF ADULT VERBAL MODELING AND FEEDBACK ON THE ORAL LANGUAGE OF HEAD START CHILDREN. ED047793
SYNTACTIC MATURITY IN SCHOOL CHILDREN AND ADULTS EJ 018 818
LANGUAGE STRUCTURE AND THE FREE RECALL OF VERBAL MESSAGES BY CHILDREN EJ 044 693
READING, WRITING, AND BLACK ENGLISH EJ 052 178
CHILDREN'S COMPREHENSION OF RELATIVIZED ENGLISH SENTENCES EJ 056 715
THE EXPERIMENTAL FACILITATION OF CHILDREN'S COMPREHENSION AND PRODUCTION OF FOUR SYNTACTIC STRUCTURES EJ 056 723

SYSTEMS ANALYSIS
DESIGNS AND PROPOSAL FOR EARLY CHILDHOOD RESEARCH: A NEW LOOK: A SYSTEMS APPROACH TO PRE-SCHOOL EDUCATION. (ONE IN A SERIES OF SIX PAPERS). ED053809

SYSTEMS APPROACH
THE NEED FOR A MULTI-DIMENSIONAL APPROACH TO LEARNING DISABILITIES. A MULTI-DISCIPLINARY SYMPOSIUM ON DYSLEXIS AND ASSOCIATED LEARNING DISABILITIES. ED027956
A STUDY IN CHILD CARE (CASE STUDY FROM VOLUME II-B): "A SENSE OF BELONGING." DAY CARE PROGRAMS REPRINT SERIES. ED051898
DESIGNS AND PROPOSAL FOR EARLY CHILDHOOD RESEARCH: A NEW LOOK: A SYSTEMS APPROACH TO PRE-SCHOOL EDUCATION. (ONE IN A SERIES OF SIX PAPERS). ED053809
EVALUATION OF EDUCATIONAL PROGRAMS EJ 007 047
PROBLEMS OF CONTROL IN SIMULTANEOUS DISCRIMINATION TASKS EJ 058 215

SYSTEMS DEVELOPMENT
DEVELOPMENT AND IMPLEMENTATION OF A COMPREHENSIVE EVALUATION AND REPORTING SYSTEM FOR KINDERGARTEN AND PRIMARY GRADE SCHOOLS. FINAL REPORT. ED026116

T GROUPS
SENSITIVITY TRAINING: WHAT IS IT? HOW CAN IT HELP STUDENTS, TEACHERS, ADMINISTRATORS? EJ 023 702
A SENSITIVITY-TRAINING APPROACH TO GROUP THERAPY WITH CHILDREN EJ 039 501

TABLES (DATA)
A RESEARCH PROGRAM TO DETERMINE THE EFFECTS OF VARIOUS PRESCHOOL INTERVENTION PROGRAMS ON THE DEVELOPMENT OF DISADVANTAGED CHILDREN AND THE STRATEGIC AGE FOR SUCH INTERVENTION. ED017319
PROJECT HEAD START--SUMMER 1966. FINAL REPORT. SECTION TWO, FACILITIES AND RESOURCES OF HEAD START CENTERS. ED018247
PREPRIMARY ENROLLMENT, OCTOBER 1969. ED049816
NON-PUBLIC PRESCHOOL PROGRAMS IN INDIANA. ED050813
DAY CARE SURVEY-1970. SUMMARY REPORT AND BASIC ANALYSIS. ED051880

TACHISTOSCOPES
DEVELOPMENTAL DIFFERENCES IN THE FIELD OF VIEW DURING TACHISTOSCOPIC PRESENTATION EJ 053 743
VISUAL MASKING AND DEVELOPMENTAL DIFFERENCES IN INFORMATION PROCESSING EJ 059 514

TACTUAL PERCEPTION
FREEDOM TO MANIPULATE OBJECTS AND QUESTION-ASKING PERFORMANCE OF SIX-YEAR-OLDS EJ 029 217
SENSORY-MODALITY EFFECTS ON SHAPE PERCEPTION IN PRESCHOOL CHILDREN EJ 029 383
TACTILE IDENTIFICATION OF LETTERS: A COMPARISON OF DEAF AND HEARING CHILDRENS' PERFORMANCES EJ 034 567
EFFECT OF CORRELATED VISUAL AND TACTUAL FEEDBACK ON AUDITORY PATTERN LEARNING AT DIFFERENT AGE LEVELS EJ 037 517
A COMPARATIVE STUDY OF PIAGET'S DEVELOPMENTAL SCHEMA OF SIGHTED CHILDREN WITH THAT OF A GROUP OF BLIND CHILDREN EJ 040 319
INTERMODAL AND INTRAMODAL RETENTION OF VISUAL AND TACTUAL INFORMATION IN YOUNG CHILDREN EJ 057 900
A STUDY OF THE RELATIVE DOMINANCE OF VISION AND TOUCH IN SIX-MONTH-OLD INFANTS EJ 058 594

TALENT
CHILDREN: THEIR POTENTIALS EJ 034 312

TALENT DEVELOPMENT
INCREASING AND RELEASING HUMAN POTENTIALS EJ 034 710

TAPE RECORDINGS
THE COGNITIVE ENVIRONMENTS OF URBAN PRE-SCHOOL CHILDREN. MANUAL OF RECORDING AND OBSERVATION TECHNIQUES FOR MOTHER-CHILD INTERACTION. ED018269

TASK PERFORMANCE
TEACHING FORMAL OPERATIONS TO PRESCHOOL ADVANTAGED AND DISADVANTAGED CHILDREN. ED019990
EXTRA-CURRICULAR PARENT-CHILD CONTACT AND CHILDREN'S SOCIALLY REINFORCED TASK BEHAVIOR. ED023447
A PRELIMINARY SEARCH FOR FORMAL OPERATIONS STRUCTURES. ED024471
PARENT-CHILD INTERACTION AND THE CHILD'S APPROACH TO TASK SITUATIONS. ED025307
AGE AND MEMORY AS FACTORS IN PROBLEM SOLVING. ED025327
ERROR, RESPONSE TIME AND IQ: SEX DIFFERENCES IN COGNITIVE STYLE OF PRESCHOOL CHILDREN. ED026122
ANXIETY AS A FACTOR IN THE CHILD'S RESPONSIVENESS TO SOCIAL REINFORCEMENT. ED027074
CHILDREN'S ABILITY TO OPERATE WITHIN A MATRIX: A DEVELOPMENTAL STUDY. ED029715
THE UTILIZATIONS OF CONCRETE, FUNCTIONAL, AND DESIGNATIVE CONCEPTS IN MULTIPLE CLASSIFICATION. ED032112
A COMPARISON OF RELATIVE STRUCTURAL LEVELS ON A VARIETY OF COGNITIVE TASKS. ED032923
EFFECT OF VERBALIZATION ON YOUNG CHILDREN'S LEARNING OF A MANIPULATIVE SKILL. ED035447
CONDITIONS FOSTERING THE USE OF INFORMATION FEEDBACK BY YOUNG CHILDREN. (REVISED REPORT). ED039950
BEHAVIORAL DATA FROM THE TULANE NUTRITION STUDY. ED043375
THE PRESCHOOL CHILD'S ABILITY TO FOLLOW DIRECTIONS. ED043395
UNDERSTANDING OF QUANTITATIVE CONCEPTS IN 3 1/2-4 1/2 YEAR-OLD CHILDREN. ED046491
DEVELOPMENTAL TRENDS IN THE SELECTIVE PERCEPTION OF RACE AND AFFECT BY YOUNG NEGRO AND CAUCASIAN CHILDREN. ED046498
LEARNING TO LEARN ON A CONCEPT ATTAINMENT TASK AS A FUNCTION OF AGE AND SOCIOECONOMIC LEVEL. REPORT FROM THE PROJECT ON SITUATIONAL VARIABLES AND EFFICIENCY OF CONCEPT LEARNING. ED046505
THE EFFECT OF VARYING OBJECT NUMBER AND TYPE OF ARRANGEMENT ON CHILDREN'S ABILITY TO COORDINATE PERSPECTIVES. ED047804
SOCIAL SKILLS DEVELOPMENT IN THE EARLY CHILDHOOD EDUCATION PROJECT. TECHNICAL REPORT NO. 7. ED052835
TRANSFER FROM PERCEPTUAL PRETRAINING AS A FUNCTION OF NUMBER OF TASK DIMENSIONS EJ 016 165

EFFECTS OF STIMULUS-RESPONSE SIMILARITY AND DISSIMILARITY ON CHILDREN'S MATCHING PERFORMANCE EJ 016 350
THE EFFECTS OF A PAY-OFF MATRIX ON SELECTIVE ATTENTION EJ 023 436
CHILDREN'S PERFORMANCE ON AN ODDITY PROBLEM AS A FUNCTION OF THE NUMBER OF VALUES ON THE RELEVANT DIMENSION EJ 024 694
EFFECTS OF ENFORCED ATTENTION AND STIMULUS PHASING UPON RULE LEARNING IN CHILDREN EJ 024 697
INTERACTION OF REWARD, PUNISHMENT, AND SEX IN A TWO-CHOICE DISCRIMINATION TASK WITH CHILDREN EJ 024 948
INTERRELATIONS AND CORRELATES OVER TIME IN CHILDREN'S LEARNING EJ 025 954
STUDIES IN PATTERN DETECTION IN NORMAL AND AUTISTIC CHILDREN. II. REPRODUCTION AND PRODUCTION OF COLOR SEQUENCES EJ 027 613
PERSISTENCE AS A FUNCTION OF CONCEPTUAL STRUCTURE AND QUALITY OF FEEDBACK EJ 032 932
THE GENERALITY OF COLOR-FORM PREFERENCE AS A FUNCTION OF MATERIALS AND TASK REQUIREMENTS AMONG LOWER-CLASS NEGRO CHILDREN EJ 033 052
VERBAL FACTORS IN COMPENSATION PERFORMANCE AND THE RELATION BETWEEN CONSERVATION AND COMPENSATION EJ 033 778
MEANING AND ATTENTION AS DETERMINANTS OF SOCIAL REINFORCER EFFECTIVENESS EJ 033 781
ESTIMATES AND ESTIMATE-BASED INFERENCES IN YOUNG CHILDREN EJ 034 541
EFFECT OF INSTRUCTIONAL SET ON TWELVE-YEAR-OLD CHILDREN'S PERCEPTION OF INTERRUPTION EJ 034 921
INTERRELATIONS AMONG LEARNING AND PERFORMANCE TASKS AT THE PRESCHOOL LEVEL EJ 035 361
CHILDREN'S ABILITY TO OPERATE WITHIN A MATRIX: A DEVELOPMENTAL STUDY EJ 035 363
PARENTAL EDUCATION, SEX DIFFERENCES, AND PERFORMANCE ON COGNITIVE TASKS AMONG TWO-YEAR-OLD CHILDREN EJ 035 364
EXPERIMENTER BIAS IN PERFORMANCE OF CHILDREN AT A SIMPLE MOTOR TASK EJ 035 710
CHILDREN'S UNDERSTANDING OF PROBABILITY CONCEPTS EJ 036 824
A PERSPECTIVE ON COGNITIVE DEVELOPMENT: THE PRESCHOOL CHILD'S PERFORMANCE IN CLASSIFICATION TASKS EJ 036 827
SPATIAL ABILITIES AND SPATIAL EGOCENTRISM IN THE YOUNG CHILD EJ 037 066
EFFECT OF INCENTIVES AND AGE ON THE VISUAL RECOGNITION OF RETARDED READERS EJ 037 535
CHRONOLOGICAL AGE AND PERFORMANCE ON PROBLEMS WITH REPEATED PRESOLUTION SHIFTS EJ 039 628
THE ASSESSMENT OF DIFFERENCES IN CONCEPTUAL STYLE EJ 041 146
INCENTIVE PREFERENCE AND RESISTANCE TO TEMPTATION EJ 041 631
COGNITIVE STYLE AND CLASSIFICATION EJ 044 706
CHILDREN'S REACTIONS TO FAILURE AS A FUNCTION OF INTERRESPONSE INTERVAL EJ 045 043
EFFECTS OF AN ADULT'S PRESENCE AND PRAISE ON YOUNG CHILDREN'S PERFORMANCE EJ 045 460
EFFECTS OF STIMULUS ABSTRACTNESS AND FAMILIARITY ON LISTENER'S PERFORMANCE IN A COMMUNICATION TASK EJ 046 241
BLOCK MANIPULATION BY CHILDREN AS A FUNCTION OF SOCIAL REINFORCEMENT, ANXIETY, AROUSAL, AND ABILITY PATTERN EJ 046 468
MOTHERS' TEST OF ANXIETY AND TASK SELECTION AND CHILDREN'S PERFORMANCE WITH MOTHER OR A STRANGER EJ 052 449
POSITION STRATEGIES IN AN OBJECT DISCRIMINATION TASK EJ 052 458
INFORMATION PROCESSING AND THE MODIFICATION OF AN "IMPULSIVE CONCEPTUAL TEMPO" EJ 052 460
EFFECT OF OVERT VERBAL LABELING ON SHORT-TERM MEMORY IN CULTURALLY DEPRIVED AND NONDEPRIVED CHILDREN EJ 053 710
FREEDOM FROM EXTERNAL EVALUATION EJ 055 897
MODELING EFFECTS UPON CONCEPTUAL STYLE AND COGNITIVE TEMPO EJ 056 396
TASK ORIENTATION VERSUS SOCIAL ORIENTATION IN YOUNG CHILDREN AND THEIR ATTENTION TO RELEVANT SOCIAL CUES EJ 058 413
RELATIONSHIPS OF PARENTAL BEHAVIOR TO "DISADVANTAGED" CHILDREN'S INTRINSIC-EXTRINSIC MOTIVATION FOR TASK STRIVING EJ 059 870
DIFFERENTIAL OUTCOMES OF A MONTESSORI CURRICULUM EJ 060 330
AGE- AND SEX-RELATED VARIATION IN PERFORMANCE ON A FIGURAL-CONCEPTUAL TASK EJ 061 066
SIMPLE REACTION TIME IN CHILDREN: EFFECTS OF INCENTIVE, INCENTIVE-SHIFT AND OTHER TRAINING VARIABLES EJ 061 075

TAXONOMY

A DISTINCTIVE FEATURES ANALYSIS OF PRE-LINGUISTIC INFANT VOCALIZATIONS. ED025330
CHILD DEVELOPMENT AND MATERIAL SURVEY. PART I, TECHNICAL REPORT. FINAL REPORT. ED027084

TEACHER AIDES

CURRICULUM DEVELOPMENT PROGRAM FOR PRESCHOOL TEACHER AIDES. FINAL REPORT. ED013122
KICKAPOO - NORTH CANADIAN PROJECT, 1966-67. FINAL REPORT. ED015781
A TRAINING PROGRAM FOR MOTHERS. ED017334
TEACHER AIDES: HANDBOOK FOR INSTRUCTORS AND ADMINISTRATORS. ED024461
SUPPLEMENTARY MATERIALS FOR TEACHER AIDE TRAINING PROGRAMS, TO SUPPLEMENT THE PUBLICATION "TEACHER AIDES: HANDBOOK FOR INSTRUCTORS AND ADMINISTRATORS." ED024462
AIDES TO TEACHERS AND CHILDREN. ED027090
PERSPECTIVES ON TEACHER-AIDES. A TEACHING TEXT. ED028836
CHARACTERISTICS OF PRIMARY LEVEL CHILDREN. ED036343
A YOUNG MAN AROUND THE CLASS EJ 059 445

TEACHER ATTITUDES

TEACHERS BELIEF SYSTEMS AND PRESCHOOL ATMOSPHERES. ED014320
THE NATIONAL TEACHER CORPS PROGRAM, 1966-67 EVALUATION REPORT. ED019110
FINAL REPORT ON HEAD START EVALUATION AND RESEARCH--1966-67 TO THE INSTITUTE FOR EDUCATIONAL DEVELOPMENT. SECTION III, INFLUENCING ATTITUDES OF PARENTS AND TEACHERS THROUGH REWARDING CHILDREN. ED019119
THE RELATIONSHIP BETWEEN SPECIFIC AND GENERAL TEACHING EXPERIENCE AND TEACHER ATTITUDES TOWARD PROJECT HEAD START. PART OF THE FINAL REPORT. ED025323
A STUDY OF THE EFFECTS OF TEACHER ATTITUDE AND CURRICULUM STRUCTURE ON PRESCHOOL DISADVANTAGED CHILDREN. ANNUAL PROGRESS REPORT I. ED027079
AFFECTIVE DIMENSIONS OF TEACHERS OF DISADVANTAGED CHILDREN IN SIX MAJORITY NEGRO SCHOOL DISTRICTS. ED028833
EFFECT OF MATERNAL ATTITUDES, TEACHER ATTITUDES, AND TYPE OF NURSERY SCHOOL TRAINING ON THE ABILITIES OF PRESCHOOL CHILDREN. FINAL REPORT. ED028844
PEDAGOGICAL ATTITUDES OF CONVENTIONAL AND SPECIALLY-TRAINED TEACHERS. ED034587
EXTENDING OPEN EDUCATION IN THE UNITED STATES. ED038182
TEACHER EXPECTANCY OR MY FAIR LADY. ED038183
TEACHER-PUPIL INTERACTION AS IT RELATES TO ATTEMPTED CHANGES IN TEACHER EXPECTANCY OF ACADEMIC ABILITY AND ACHIEVEMENT. ED041630
THE DISTRIBUTION OF TEACHER APPROVAL AND DISAPPROVAL OF HEAD START CHILDREN. FINAL REPORT. ED042509
IMAGES OF THE IDEAL PUPIL HELD BY TEACHERS IN PREPARATION EJ 012 679
WHICH PUPILS DO TEACHERS CALL ON? EJ 012 871
DO STUDENTS' IDEAS AND ATTITUDES SURVIVE PRACTICE TEACHING? EJ 013 228
UNDERSTANDING THE BLACK CHILD EJ 020 717
THE INFLUENCE OF SET INDUCTION UPON STUDENT ACHIEVEMENT AND ASSESSMENT OF EFFECTIVE TEACHING EJ 027 031
THE ORGANIZATIONAL CLIMATE OF SCHOOLS IN FIVE URBAN AREAS EJ 027 704
AND A FRIENDLY GOODBYE EJ 028 310
KEYS TO STANDARD ENGLISH EJ 028 577
"OF HAIRY ARMS AND A DEEP BARITONE VOICE": A SYMPOSIUM MEN IN YOUNG CHILDREN'S LIVES EJ 028 795
A COMPARISON OF CHARACTERISTICS OF PROSPECTIVE SECONDARY SCHOOL TEACHERS ENROLLED IN TWO DIFFERENT DEGREE PROGRAMS EJ 029 618
CLASSROOM DISCIPLINE: A NEW APPROACH EJ 032 896
MASCULINITY AND FEMININITY IN THE ELEMENTARY AND JUNIOR HIGH SCHOOL YEARS EJ 034 902
TEACHERS' RATINGS OF URBAN CHILDREN'S READING PERFORMANCE EJ 035 662
BEHAVIOUR PROBLEMS IN THE INFANT SCHOOL EJ 048 306
INDIVIDUALIZATION - TEACHERS' VIEWS EJ 052 067
SOCIAL CLASS DIFFERENCES IN TEACHER ATTITUDES TOWARD CHILDREN EJ 053 908
CHANGES IN SELF-PERCEPTIONS OF HEAD-START TRAINEES EJ 055 213
TEACHER EXPECTANCY AS RELATED TO THE ACADEMIC AND PERSONAL GROWTH OF PRIMARY-AGE CHILDREN EJ 057 018

TEACHER BEHAVIOR

HEAD START EVALUATION AND RESEARCH CENTER, UNIVERSITY OF KANSAS. REPORT NO. I, THE OBSERVATION OF REINFORCEMENT BEHAVIOR OF TEACHERS IN HEAD START CLASSROOMS AND THE MODIFICATION OF A TEACHER'S ATTENDING BEHAVIOR. ED021633
HEAD START EVALUATION AND RESEARCH CENTER, BOSTON UNIVERSITY. REPORT A-II, OBSERVATION OF TEACHERS AND TEACHING: STRATEGIES AND APPLICATIONS. ED022558
THE ROLE OF THE TEACHER IN THE INFANT AND NURSERY SCHOOL. ED029703
RELATIONSHIPS BETWEEN TEACHER BEHAVIOR, PUPIL BEHAVIOR, AND PUPIL ACHIEVEMENT. ED038189
INTELLECTUAL OPERATIONS IN TEACHER-CHILD INTERACTION. ED039011
THE MODIFICATION OF TEACHER BEHAVIORS WHICH MODIFY CHILD BEHAVIORS. PROGRESS REPORT. ED042499
THE PROFESSIONAL RESPONSE. ED048922
EVALUATION OF CLASSROOM CLIMATE EJ 002 421
PRAISE, CRITICISM, AND RACE EJ 019 388
INTELLECTUAL OPERATIONS IN TEACHER QUESTION-ASKING BEHAVIOR EJ 032 895

WINDOW BEGINS WITH AN "L" EJ 058 507
THE EFFECTS OF IMMEDIATE FEEDBACK ON THE BEHAVIOR OF TEACHERS-IN-TRAINING EJ 059 672
FEMINIZATION IN PRESCHOOL EJ 059 872

TEACHER CHARACTERISTICS
TEACHERS BELIEF SYSTEMS AND PRESCHOOL ATMOSPHERES. ED014320
THE DEVELOPMENT OF SELF-OTHER RELATIONSHIPS DURING PROJECT HEAD START. ED015008
THE RELATIONSHIPS BETWEEN CERTAIN TEACHER CHARACTERISTICS AND ACHIEVEMENT AND CREATIVITY OF GIFTED ELEMENTARY SCHOOL STUDENTS. FINAL REPORT SUMMARY. ED015787
THE NEW ELEMENTARY SCHOOL. ED017341
GROUP DAY CARE AS A CHILD-REARING ENVIRONMENT. AN OBSERVATIONAL STUDY OF DAY CARE PROGRAM. ED024453
ACHIEVEMENT, CREATIVITY, AND SELF-CONCEPT CORRELATES OF TEACHER-PUPIL TRANSACTIONS IN ELEMENTARY SCHOOL CLASSROOMS. ED024463
THE RELATIONSHIP BETWEEN SPECIFIC AND GENERAL TEACHING EXPERIENCE AND TEACHER ATTITUDES TOWARD PROJECT HEAD START. PART OF THE FINAL REPORT. ED025323
BIBLIOGRAPHY: TEACHER CHARACTERISTICS. ED029716
THE EFFECT OF TEACHERS' INFERRED SELF CONCEPT UPON STUDENT ACHIEVEMENT. ED031300
TEACHER EXPECTANCY OR MY FAIR LADY. ED038183
TEACHER EFFECTIVENESS: A POSITION. ED039928
THE EFFECTIVENESS OF A STANDARD LANGUAGE READINESS PROGRAM AS A FUNCTION OF TEACHER DIFFERENCES. ED039932
VISIT TO A MISSION SCHOOL FOR ABORIGINAL CHILDREN EJ 014 292
A COMPARISON OF CHARACTERISTICS OF PROSPECTIVE SECONDARY SCHOOL TEACHERS ENROLLED IN TWO DIFFERENT DEGREE PROGRAMS EJ 029 618
FOUR QUESTIONS ON EARLY CHILDHOOD EDUCATION EJ 034 784
WHAT IS A GOOD KINDERGARTEN? EJ 035 243
THE INFLUENCE OF NEGRO AND WHITE TEACHERS RATED AS EFFECTIVE OR NONEFFECTIVE ON THE PERFORMANCE OF NEGRO AND WHITE LOWER-CLASS CHILDREN EJ 045 068
STOP, LOOK, LISTEN -- AND KEEP ON!! EJ 058 133

TEACHER DEVELOPED MATERIALS
LET DO IT MY WAY EJ 028 846

TEACHER EDUCATION
"PRE-SCHOOL" EDUCATION, PROS AND CONS. A SURVEY OF "PRE-SCHOOL" EDUCATION WITH EMPHASIS ON RESEARCH PAST, PRESENT, AND FUTURE. ED016525
THE MODIFICATION OF TEACHER BEHAVIORS WHICH MODIFY CHILD BEHAVIORS. PROGRESS REPORT. ED042499
LEARNING INTO THE TWENTY-FIRST CENTURY. 1970 WHITE HOUSE CONFERENCE ON CHILDREN, REPORT OF FORUM 5. (WORKING COPY). ED046524
FIELD TEST OF THE UNIVERSITY OF HAWAII PRESCHOOL LANGUAGE CURRICULUM. FINAL REPORT. ED048924
EVALUATION GUIDE FOR EARLY CHILDHOOD EDUCATION PROGRAMS. ED048938
SIMULATION ACTIVITIES FOR TRAINING PARENTS AND TEACHERS AS EDUCATIONAL PARTNERS: A REPORT AND EVALUATION. ED048945
A TEACHING LEARNING SCHEMA FOR TEACHER TRAINING AND CURRICULUM DEVELOPMENT IN EARLY EDUCATION. ED049812
A DAY CARE PROGRAM IN THE MIDDLE EAST EJ 009 815
DIAGNOSTIC TEACHING: A MODEST PROPOSAL EJ 014 522
HUMAN RELATIONS TRAINING FOR TEACHERS: THE EFFECTIVENESS OF SENSITIVITY TRAINING EJ 015 979
THE SCHOOL AND THE UNIVERSITY: CO-OPERATIVE ROLES IN STUDENT TEACHING EJ 015 981
COLLEGE TRAINING FOR HEAD START WORKERS: A BOOST TOWARD CAREER ADVANCEMENT EJ 017 097
A COMPARISON OF CHARACTERISTICS OF PROSPECTIVE SECONDARY SCHOOL TEACHERS ENROLLED IN TWO DIFFERENT DEGREE PROGRAMS EJ 029 618
ALTERNATIVE LEARNING ENVIRONMENTS: A PHILADELPHIA STORY EJ 033 156
NEW DAY IN NORTH DAKOTA: CHANGING TEACHERS AND CHANGING SCHOOLS EJ 033 157
THE USE OF HIERARCHIES IN CURRICULUM ANALYSIS AND INSTRUCTIONAL PLANNING EJ 033 574
TURNING THE TIDE IN TEACHER QUALITY EJ 034 231
THE NEW SCHOOL EJ 036 327
EDUCATION OF TEACHERS FOR NURSERY SCHOOLS: A CREATIVE APPROACH EJ 036 336
CREATING A CLIMATE FOR INDIVIDUALIZING INSTRUCTION EJ 044 511
STUDYING HUMAN ECOLOGY: TEACHER EDUCATION AND THE CULTURALLY DIVERSE EJ 048 395
MICRO-TEACHING FOR PREPARING TEACHERS OF CULTURALLY DIVERSE CHILDREN EJ 052 068
SYMPOSIUM ON CHILD-OBSERVATION: 1. FILM-MAKING AS AN OBSERVATION TECHNIQUE EJ 056 861

TEACHER EDUCATION CURRICULUM
LEARNING AND TEACHING, GRADES N-9 (EMPHASIS ON EARLY CHILDHOOD). ED023459
EVALUATION GUIDE FOR EARLY CHILDHOOD EDUCATION PROGRAMS. ED048938

TEACHER EDUCATORS
EDUCATION OF TEACHERS FOR NURSERY SCHOOLS: A CREATIVE APPROACH EJ 036 336
THE ITINERANT TEACHER EJ 060 930

TEACHER EVALUATION
REMARKS ON THE MAX WOLFF REPORT. ED015030
ACHIEVEMENT, CREATIVITY, AND SELF-CONCEPT CORRELATES OF TEACHER-PUPIL TRANSACTIONS IN ELEMENTARY SCHOOL CLASSROOMS. ED024463
SOME PARAMETERS OF TEACHER EFFECTIVENESS AS ASSESSED BY AN ECOLOGICAL APPROACH. ED032928
MAXIMIZING THE VALUE OF EVALUATION FOR THE HEAD START TEACHER. FINAL REPORT. ED041631
PRELIMINARY ANALYSIS OF 1968-69 HEAD START DATA. ED045203
CHILDREN'S PERCEPTIONS OF A TEACHING TEAM EJ 051 772
REPORT CARDS FOR TEACHERS EJ 057 441

TEACHER EXPERIENCE
THE RELATIONSHIP BETWEEN SPECIFIC AND GENERAL TEACHING EXPERIENCE AND TEACHER ATTITUDES TOWARD PROJECT HEAD START. PART OF THE FINAL REPORT. ED025323

TEACHER GUIDANCE
JDC HANDBOOK FOR TEACHERS IN DAY CARE CENTERS. ED027962

TEACHER INFLUENCE
THE NATIONAL TEACHER CORPS PROGRAM, 1966-67 EVALUATION REPORT. ED019110
THE EFFECTS OF A HIGHLY STRUCTURED PRESCHOOL PROGRAM ON THE MEASURED INTELLIGENCE OF CULTURALLY DISADVANTAGED FOUR-YEAR-OLD CHILDREN. INTERIM REPORT. ED019116
EFFECTS OF ADULT SOCIAL REINFORCEMENT ON CHILD BEHAVIOR. ED019997
THE EFFECT OF TEACHERS' INFERRED SELF CONCEPT UPON STUDENT ACHIEVEMENT. ED031300
MODIFICATION BY SOCIAL REINFORCEMENT OF DEFICIENT SOCIAL BEHAVIOR OF DISADVANTAGED KINDERGARTEN CHILDREN. ED043381
IMITATION OF TEACHER PREFERENCES IN A FIELD SETTING EJ 061 070

TEACHER INTERNS
THE NATIONAL TEACHER CORPS PROGRAM, 1966-67 EVALUATION REPORT. ED019110
MICRO-TEACHING FOR PREPARING TEACHERS OF CULTURALLY DIVERSE CHILDREN EJ 052 068
THE EFFECTS OF IMMEDIATE FEEDBACK ON THE BEHAVIOR OF TEACHERS-IN-TRAINING EJ 059 672

TEACHER ORIENTATION
FIRST STEPS IN SCHOOL EJ 007 205

TEACHER PROGRAMS
ENCOURAGING STUDENTS' RESEARCH ON COGNITIVE DEVELOPMENT. ED031301

TEACHER RATING
OUTCOMES OF INDIVIDUAL AND PROGRAMMATIC VARIATIONS AMONG PROJECT HEAD START CENTERS, SUMMER, 1965. FINAL REPORT. ED014325
STUDY OF ACHIEVEMENT, TORONTO INFORMATION BULLETIN NO. 1. ED017323
INTERACTION PATTERNS AS A SOURCE OF ERROR IN TEACHERS' EVALUATIONS OF HEAD START CHILDREN. FINAL REPORT. ED023453

TEACHER RESPONSE
HEAD START EVALUATION AND RESEARCH CENTER, BOSTON UNIVERSITY. REPORT A-I, TEACHING STYLE: THE DEVELOPMENT OF TEACHING TASKS. ED022557
THERE IS A BETTER WAY. A PREMISE POINTS THE WAY, A PROFILE WITH PROMISE, A COMPOSITE OF THE SURVEY. ED023471
RELATIONSHIPS BETWEEN CHILDREN'S QUESTIONS AND NURSERY SCHOOL TEACHERS' RESPONSES. ED046507
THE PROFESSIONAL RESPONSE. ED048922

TEACHER RESPONSIBILITY
THE ROLE OF THE PRIMARY TEACHER IN CHARACTER EDUCATION EJ 013 232

TEACHER RETIREMENT
LOOKING BACK WITH APPRECIATION EJ 058 054

TEACHER ROLE
TEACHERS' BELIEFS, CLASSROOM ATMOSPHERE AND STUDENT BEHAVIOR. FINAL REPORT. ED018249
THINKING, FEELING, EXPERIENCING--TOWARD REALIZATION OF FULL POTENTIAL. ED020012
THE ROLE OF THE TEACHER IN THE INFANT AND NURSERY SCHOOL. ED029703
TEACHING IN PRESCHOOLS: ROLES AND GOALS. ED032942

THE ROLE OF THE TEACHER IN INTERVENTION PROGRAMS. PROCEEDINGS OF THE HEAD START RESEARCH SEMINARS: SEMINAR NO. 6, THE TEACHER IN INTERVENTION PROGRAMS (1ST, WASHINGTON, D.C., APRIL 18, 1969). ED036333
A PLAN FOR CONTINUING GROWTH. ED046493
TEACHER-CHILD RELATIONSHIPS IN DAY CARE CENTERS. WORKING PAPER. ED046494
LEARNING TO OBSERVE--OBSERVING TO LEARN. ED047815
GUIDE FOR RIPPLES. ED051872
OPENING UP THE CLASSROOM: A WALK AROUND THE SCHOOL. ED053817
TO KEEP AN INNER BALANCE EJ 002 313
CHILDREN AND TEACHERS IN TWO TYPES OF HEAD START CLASSES EJ 008 172
THE ROLE OF THE PRIMARY TEACHER IN CHARACTER EDUCATION EJ 013 232
TEACHING IN PRESCHOOLS: ROLES AND GOALS EJ 018 133
HELPING CHILDREN WITH EMOTIONAL PROBLEMS AT SCHOOL EJ 022 975
WHO ARE THEY? IDENTIFYING DISTURBED CHILDREN IN THE CLASSROOM EJ 022 976
THE TEACHER AS COUNSELOR: THERAPEUTIC APPROACHES TO UNDERSTANDING SELF AND OTHERS EJ 023 703
AN OVERVIEW OF BRITISH INFANT SCHOOLS EJ 026 835
MAKING TOMORROW NOW: THE PEOPLE ENVIRONMENT EJ 028 200
ANXIETY - A CLASSROOM CLOSE-UP EJ 028 896
EDUCATIONAL TECHNOLOGY: A CRITIQUE EJ 029 343
NEW DAY IN NORTH DAKOTA: CHANGING TEACHERS AND CHANGING SCHOOLS EJ 033 157
NEW CONCEPTS OF HUMAN POTENTIALS: NEW CHALLENGE FOR TEACHERS EJ 034 711
A TEACHER DISCOVERS INDIVIDUALIZED INSTRUCTION EJ 035 171
GOING ON A TRIP EJ 035 842
PRESCHOOL EDUCATION, PARENTS AND THE COMMUNITY IN A DEVELOPING SOCIETY EJ 036 333
TEACHERS IN CHILDREN'S ROLES? EJ 037 235
THE DECLINE OF PLAY IN URBAN KINDERGARTENS EJ 041 961
CREATING A CLIMATE FOR INDIVIDUALIZING INSTRUCTION EJ 044 511
AN EXPERIENCE WITH FEAR IN THE LIVES OF CHILDREN EJ 045 389
THE INFLUENCE OF TEACHER-CHILD INTERACTION ON THE LEARNING PROCESS EJ 048 235
SYMPOSIUM ON PARENT-CENTERED EDUCATION: 3. LEARNING THROUGH PARENTS: LESSONS FOR TEACHERS EJ 054 379
TEACHERS AND PARENTS: CHANGING ROLES AND GOALS EJ 055 362
SCIENCING FOR YOUNG CHILDREN EJ 056 863
A MATTER OF LIFE AND DEATH EJ 059 746
LE PROBLEME DE LA LIBERTE ET DE LA DISCIPLINE DANS LE JEU (PROBLEMS OF FREEDOM AND DISCIPLINE IN PLAY) EJ 061 465

TEACHER SELECTION

L'EDUCATEUR ET L'EPANOUISSEMENT DE LA PERSONNALITE DE L'ENFANT EJ 028 102

TEACHER SEMINARS

HEAD START EVALUATION AND RESEARCH CENTER, BOSTON UNIVERSITY. REPORT E-II, TEACHER SEMINAR. ED022567

TEACHER STRIKES

SYMPOSIUM: FOR AND AGAINST STRIKES EJ 003 416
STRIKES, SANCTIONS, OR SURRENDER? EJ 003 417
LABOR'S VIEWS ON TEACHER STRIKES EJ 003 418
CHILDREN AND THE SCHOOL STRIKE EJ 003 419
NEA VIEWS ON TEACHER STRIKES EJ 003 629
LOOKING BEYOND THE STRIKES EJ 003 630

TEACHER TRAINING

DO STUDENTS' IDEAS AND ATTITUDES SURVIVE PRACTICE TEACHING? EJ 013 228

TEACHER WORKSHOPS

TEACHER AIDES: HANDBOOK FOR INSTRUCTORS AND ADMINISTRATORS. ED024461
AN INTEGRATED DAY WORKSHOP EJ 033 159
THE CREATIVE ENVIRONMENT WORKSHOP EJ 035 168
ASPEN MORNINGS WITH SYLVIA ASHTON-WARNER EJ 056 860

TEACHERS

PRELIMINARY RESULTS FROM RELATIONSHIP BETWEEN TEACHERS' VOCABULARY USAGE AND THE VOCABULARY OF KINDERGARTEN AND FIRST GRADE STUDENTS. ED032135
LEARNING FROM EACH OTHER: PREDIATRICIANS AND TEACHERS EJ 050 320
WE HAVE MEN ON THE STAFF EJ 060 929

TEACHING GUIDES

A CREATIVE GUIDE FOR PRESCHOOL TEACHERS. GOALS, ACTIVITIES, AND SUGGESTED MATERIALS FOR AN ORGANIZED PROGRAM. ED016512
MATHEMATICS FOR ELEMENTARY SCHOOL TEACHERS. ED018276
LINGUISTICS IN THE ELEMENTARY SCHOOL. ED019134
SKILL GAMES FOR MATHEMATICS. ED022548
LET'S TRY THIS IN NURSERY SCHOOL AND KINDERGARTEN. ED022556
LISTENING. WHAT RESEARCH SAYS TO THE TEACHER, NO. 29. ED026120
TEACHING SAFETY IN THE ELEMENTARY SCHOOL. ED026147
TEACHING NUTRITION IN THE ELEMENTARY SCHOOL. ED026148
HEAD START ON HEALTH. ED027972
EXEL ED029698
INDEPENDENT AND SMALL GROUP ACTIVITIES FOR SOCIAL STUDIES IN THE PRIMARY GRADES. ED031305
CHILDHOOD RESOURCES INFORMATION BULLETIN. VOLUME 1, NUMBER 2, FALL 1969. ED032948
ESOL-SESD GUIDE: KINDERGARTEN. ED033748
ELEMENTARY PHYSICAL EDUCATION: TOPEKA PUBLIC SCHOOLS. ED035445
THE TEACHER STRUCTURE CHECKLIST: A POSSIBLE TOOL FOR COMMUNICATION EJ 051 352
FOSTERING A NEED TO READ EJ 052 420

TEACHING MACHINES

EDUCATIONAL TECHNOLOGY: A CRITIQUE EJ 029 343

TEACHING METHODS

PROGRAMED INSTRUCTION AS A STRATEGY FOR DEVELOPING CURRICULA FOR CHILDREN FROM DISADVANTAGED BACKGROUNDS. ED015782
INCREASING THE AWARENESS OF ART IDEAS OF CULTURALLY DEPRIVED KINDERGARTEN CHILDREN THROUGH EXPERIENCES WITH CERAMICS. FINAL REPORT. ED016519
INDEPENDENT AND GROUP LEARNING. ED017332
TEACHING MUSIC IN THE ELEMENTARY SCHOOL, OPINION AND COMMENT. ED020014
LEARNING AND TEACHING, GRADES N-9 (EMPHASIS ON EARLY CHILDHOOD). ED023459
CHILD DEVELOPMENT AND SOCIAL SCIENCE EDUCATION. PART IV: A TEACHING STRATEGY DERIVED FROM SOME PIAGETIAN CONCEPTS. ED023467
LEARNING AND TEACHING, GRADES N-9 (EMPHASIS ON MIDDLE GRADES). ED024467
COMPARATIVE EFFECTIVENESS OF ECHOIC AND MODELING PROCEDURES IN LANGUAGE INSTRUCTION WITH CULTURALLY DISADVANTAGED CHILDREN. ED025314
ELEMENTARY SCHOOL MATHEMATICS: A GUIDE TO CURRENT RESEARCH. THIRD EDITION. ED026123
READING. DIMENSIONS IN EARLY LEARNING SERIES. ED027070
A LONDON INFANT SCHOOL. AN INTERVIEW. ED027963
YOUNG CHILDREN'S USE OF LANGUAGE IN INFERENTIAL BEHAVIOR. ED029691
A COMPARISON OF THE READING READINESS OF KINDERGARTEN PUPILS EXPOSED TO CONCEPTUAL-LANGUAGE AND BASAL READER PREREADING PROGRAMS. A PILOT STUDY. FINAL REPORT. ED029709
ORCHESTRATED INSTRUCTION: A COOKING EXPERIENCE. ED034593
TRANSPLANTING ENGLISH INFANT SCHOOL IDEAS TO AMERICAN CLASSROOMS AND SOME EFFECTS ON LANGUAGE USE. ED040756
AN ANALYSIS OF PUBLISHED PRESCHOOL LANGUAGE PROGRAMS. ED047786
BRITISH PRIMARY EDUCATION: AN ANNOTATED BIBLIOGRAPHY. ED052843
CHILDREN DANCE IN THE CLASSROOM. ED053804
CONCEPT LEARNING THROUGH MOVEMENT IMPROVISATION: THE TEACHER'S ROLE AS CATALYST EJ 014 945
CHILDREN'S QUESTIONS: THEIR FORMS, FUNCTIONS AND ROLES IN EDUCATION EJ 017 608
COMBATTING RETARDATION IN INFANTS WITH DOWN'S SYNDROME EJ 026 640
THE EFFECT OF BLACK HISTORY ON AN INTERRACIAL GROUP OF CHILDREN EJ 026 735
AWARENESS--ONE KEY TO READING READINESS EJ 027 551
THE OTHER MOUTH: WRITING IN THE SCHOOLS EJ 027 881
BEYOND NUFFIELD EJ 028 718
AN EXPERIMENTAL STUDY OF TWO METHODS OF PRESENTING THE INVERSION ALGORITHM IN DIVISION OF FRACTIONS EJ 033 863
DEVELOPMENT OF THE MONTESSORI METHOD EJ 036 330
FREE RECALL AND CLUSTERING AT FOUR AGE LEVELS: EFFECTS OF LEARNING TO LEARN AND PRESENTATION METHOD EJ 039 636
THE DECLINE OF PLAY IN URBAN KINDERGARTENS EJ 041 961
ON TEAM TEACHING EJ 046 057
TEACHING MULTIPLE CLASSIFICATION TO YOUNG CHILDREN EJ 056 711
ASPEN MORNINGS WITH SYLVIA ASHTON-WARNER EJ 056 860

TEACHING MODELS

CURRICULUM DEVELOPMENT PROGRAM FOR PRESCHOOL TEACHER AIDES. FINAL REPORT. ED013122
INTERIM PROGRESS REPORT OF A REMOTE TEACHER TRAINING INSTITUTE FOR EARLY CHILDHOOD EDUCATORS (FUNDED BY NDEA TITLE XI). ED017326
ETHNIC AND SOCIOECONOMIC INFLUENCES ON THE HOME LANGUAGE EXPERIENCES OF CHILDREN. ED043377
IMPLEMENTATION OF PLANNED VARIATION IN HEAD START. I. REVIEW AND SUMMARY OF THE STANFORD RESEARCH INSTITUTE INTERIM REPORT: FIRST YEAR OF EVALUATION. ED052845

TEACHING PROCEDURES

TEACHING READING TO CHILDREN WITH LOW MA'S. ED015020
THE DIRECT INSTRUCTION PROGRAM FOR TEACHING READING. ED015022

THE EFFECTS OF DIFFERENT LANGUAGE INSTRUCTION ON THE USE OF ATTRIBUTES OF PRE-KINDERGARTEN DISADVANTAGED CHILDREN. ED016522
AN APPROACH TO LANGUAGE LEARNING EJ 008 119
TEACHING NUMBER SENSE THROUGH RHYTHMICAL COUNTING EJ 028 717

TEACHING PROGRAMS
NUMBER TRAINING TECHNIQUES AND THEIR EFFECTS ON DIFFERENT POPULATIONS. FINAL REPORT. ED019988
SUPPLEMENTARY MATERIALS FOR TEACHER AIDE TRAINING PROGRAMS, TO SUPPLEMENT THE PUBLICATION "TEACHER AIDES: HANDBOOK FOR INSTRUCTORS AND ADMINISTRATORS." ED024462

TEACHING QUALITY
TURNING THE TIDE IN TEACHER QUALITY EJ 034 231

TEACHING SKILLS
SOME PARAMETERS OF TEACHER EFFECTIVENESS AS ASSESSED BY AN ECOLOGICAL APPROACH. ED032928

TEACHING STYLES
HEADSTART OPERATIONAL FIELD ANALYSIS. PROGRESS REPORT III. ED015776
HEAD START EVALUATION AND RESEARCH CENTER, BOSTON UNIVERSITY. REPORT A-I, TEACHING STYLE: THE DEVELOPMENT OF TEACHING TASKS. ED022557
HEAD START EVALUATION AND RESEARCH CENTER, BOSTON UNIVERSITY. REPORT A-II, OBSERVATION OF TEACHERS AND TEACHING: STRATEGIES AND APPLICATIONS. ED022558
PARENTS AS TEACHERS, HOW LOWER-CLASS AND MIDDLE-CLASS MOTHERS TEACH. ED025301
MOTHERS AS TEACHERS OF THEIR OWN PRESCHOOL CHILDREN: THE INFLUENCE OF SOCIO-ECONOMIC STATUS AND TASK STRUCTURE ON TEACHING SPECIFICITY. ED031294
TEACHING IN PRESCHOOLS: ROLES AND GOALS. ED032942
THE EFFECTS OF MANIPULATION OF TEACHER COMMUNICATION STYLE IN THE PRESCHOOL. ED034598
THE TEACHER, TEACHER STYLE, AND CLASSROOM MANAGEMENT. PROCEEDINGS OF THE HEAD START RESEARCH SEMINARS: SEMINAR NO. 2, THE TEACHER AND CLASSROOM MANAGEMENT (1ST, WASHINGTON, D.C., JULY 22, 1968). ED035463
THE EFFECT OF THREE HOME VISITING STRATEGIES UPON MEASURES OF CHILDREN'S ACADEMIC APTITUDE AND MATERNAL TEACHING BEHAVIORS. FINAL REPORT. ED044175
AN EXPERIMENTAL APPROACH TO THE EFFECT OF GROUP ANIMADVERSION EJ 012 678
TEACHING IN PRESCHOOLS: ROLES AND GOALS EJ 018 133
MOTHERS AS TEACHERS OF THEIR OWN PRESCHOOL CHILDREN: THE INFLUENCE OF SOCIOECONOMIC STATUS AND TASK STRUCTURE ON TEACHING SPECIFICITY EJ 019 414
TEACHERS IN CHILDREN'S ROLES? EJ 037 235
THE INFLUENCE OF TEACHER-CHILD INTERACTION ON THE LEARNING PROCESS EJ 048 235
WHAT CAN TEACHERS LEARN FROM DIRECTORS IN THE PERFORMING ARTS? EJ 051 410
THE EFFECTS OF MANIPULATION OF TEACHER COMMUNICATION STYLE IN THE PRESCHOOL EJ 052 455

TEACHING TECHNIQUES
THE EFFECTS OF MONTESSORI EDUCATIONAL TECHNIQUES ON CULTURALLY DISADVANTAGED HEAD START CHILDREN. ED015009
REPORT OF A RESEARCH AND DEMONSTRATION PROJECT FOR CULTURALLY DISADVANTAGED CHILDREN IN THE ANCONA MONTESSORI SCHOOL. ED015014
TEACHING A TEACHING LANGUAGE TO DISADVANTAGED CHILDREN. ED015021
CONCEPT FORMATION AS A FUNCTION OF METHOD OF PRESENTATION AND RATIO OF POSITIVE TO NEGATIVE INSTANCES. ED015779
LINGUISTICS IN THE ELEMENTARY SCHOOL. ED019134
HEAD START EVALUATION AND RESEARCH CENTER, UNIVERSITY OF KANSAS. REPORT NO. X, ENHANCEMENT OF THE SOCIAL REINFORCING VALUE OF A PRESCHOOL TEACHER. ED021646
SAN ANTONIO LANGUAGE RESEARCH PROJECT, 1965-66 (YEAR TWO) FINDINGS. ED022528
CONCEPT LEARNING IN EARLY CHILDHOOD. ED024454
A METHODOLOGY FOR FOSTERING ABSTRACT THINKING IN DEPRIVED CHILDREN. ED026131
SUCCESSFUL NUMBER CONSERVATION TRAINING. ED031297
INDUSTRIAL ARTS FOR THE PRIMARY GRADES. ED035459
DIRECT VERBAL INSTRUCTION CONTRASTED WITH MONTESSORI METHODS IN THE TEACHING OF NORMAL FOUR-YEAR-OLD CHILDREN. ED041619
ERRORLESS ESTABLISHMENT OF A MATCH-TO-SAMPLE FORM DISCRIMINATION IN PRESCHOOL CHILDREN. I. A MODIFICATION OF ANIMAL LABORATORY PROCEDURES FOR CHILDREN, II. A COMPARISON OF ERRORLESS AND TRIAL-AND-ERROR DISCRIMINATION. PROGRESS REPORT. ED042490
AN INVESTIGATION OF THE EFFECTS OF TEACHER VERBAL REINFORCEMENT AS IT RELATES TO SCHOLASTIC APTITUDE AND ACHIEVEMENT WITH ELEMENTARY SCHOOL CHILDREN. PROGRESS REPORT. ED042494
EXPERIMENTAL ANALYSIS OF EFFECTS OF TEACHER ATTENTION OF PRESCHOOL CHILDREN'S BLOCK BUILDING BEHAVIOR. PROGRESS REPORT. ED042498
A SHOE IS TO TIE: A FILM DEMONSTRATION OF PROGRAMMING SELF-HELP SKILLS FOR PRESCHOOL CHILDREN. PROGRESS REPORT. ED042500
ENRICHMENT APPROACH VERSUS DIRECT INSTRUCTIONAL APPROACH AND THEIR EFFECTS ON DIFFERENTIAL PRESCHOOL EXPERIENCES. ED043369
PRE-READING ON SESAME STREET. FINAL REPORT, VOLUME V OF V VOLUMES. ED047825
THE PROFESSIONAL RESPONSE. ED048922
THE WORLD OF THE CHILD. ED050826
VISUAL IMAGERY INSTRUCTION AND NON-ACTION VERSUS ACTION SITUATIONS RELATIVE TO RECALL BY CHILDREN. FINAL REPORT. ED050828
TO LAUGH IS TO KNOW: A DISCUSSION OF THE COGNITIVE ELEMENT IN CHILDREN'S HUMOR. ED051879
OPENING UP THE CLASSROOM: A WALK AROUND THE SCHOOL. ED053817
CLASSROOM LANGUAGE OF TEACHERS OF YOUNG CHILDREN. ED053820
NUMBER GAMES WITH YOUNG CHILDREN EJ 007 273
TOO MUCH SHUSHING - LET CHILDREN TALK EJ 011 841
MEXICAN-AMERICANS AND LANGUAGE LEARNING EJ 012 397
TOY TALK: THE NEW CONVERSATION BETWEEN GENERATIONS EJ 020 395
WRITE YOUR OWN SONGS EJ 027 673
LETTER TO THE TEACHER OF A HARD-OF-HEARING CHILD EJ 029 917
AN ATTACK ON IMPEDIMENTS TO EFFECTIVE CROSS-CULTURAL TEACHING EJ 032 553
EXPANDING THE CHILD'S WORLD THROUGH DRAMA AND MOVEMENT EJ 034 421
VALUES AND TECHNIQUES OF CREATIVE DRAMATICS EJ 034 422
ANALYSE DE L'ADOPTION DE LA NOTION DE "FLEUR" CHEZ LES ENFANTS DE 6 ANS EJ 044 703
THE TEACHER STRUCTURE CHECKLIST: A POSSIBLE TOOL FOR COMMUNICATION EJ 051 352
READING INSTRUCTION AND COGNITIVE DEVELOPMENT EJ 052 066
CREATIVE DRAMA AND LANGUAGE GROWTH EJ 052 176
A PROCESS FOR POETRY-WRITING EJ 055 364
INSTANT LAW AND ORDER EJ 055 534
CHILD WELFARE: SEARCHING FOR RELEVANT LEARNING ON THE UNDERGRADUATE LEVEL EJ 056 762
TEACHING RACE RELATIONS IN THE NURSERY SCHOOL EJ 056 864

TEAM TEACHING
TEAM TEACHING IN ELEMENTARY GRADES. ED020800
TEAM TEACHING. A DESCRIPTIVE AND EVALUATIVE STUDY OF A PROGRAM FOR THE PRIMARY GRADES. ED027083
3 ON 2 PROGRAM: ADMINISTRATIVE GUIDE AND IMPLEMENTATION HANDBOOK. (REVISED EDITION). ED050812
DEVELOPING NEW TEACHING TEAMS EJ 029 169
EFFECT OF CLASSROOM NOISE ON NUMBER IDENTIFICATION BY RETARDED CHILDREN EJ 045 391
ON TEAM TEACHING EJ 046 057
CHILDREN'S PERCEPTIONS OF A TEACHING TEAM EJ 051 772

TEAMWORK
PEER- OBSERVER CONSULTATION EJ 022 532
HELPING CHILDREN WITH EMOTIONAL PROBLEMS AT SCHOOL EJ 022 975

TECHNICAL ASSISTANCE
CONSULTATION IN DAY CARE. ED051884

TECHNICAL REPORTS
HEAD START CRIB. CHILDHOOD RESEARCH INFORMATION BULLETIN: SELECTED RESUMES OF EARLY CHILDHOOD RESEARCH REPORTS. BULLETIN NO. 1. ED025318
PROJECT HEAD START RESEARCH AND EVALUATION CENTER, SYRACUSE UNIVERSITY RESEARCH INSTITUTE. FINAL REPORT, NOVEMBER 1, 1967. ED026137
THE PROGRAM OF RESEARCH OF THE MERRILL-PALMER INSTITUTE IN CONJUNCTION WITH THE HEAD START EVALUATION AND RESEARCH CENTER, MICHIGAN STATE UNIVERSITY. ANNUAL REPORT. VOLUME II: RESEARCH. ED027088

TECHNIQUES
SOME HELPFUL TECHNIQUES WHEN PLACING OLDER CHILDREN FOR ADOPTION EJ 029 166

TECHNOLOGICAL ADVANCEMENT
ON RESPONSIVE ENVIRONMENTS. ED018278

TECHNOLOGY
CHILDREN OF TECHNOLOGY: IMAGES OR THE REAL THING EJ 054 472

TEENAGE GIRLS
A SERVICE PATTERN FOR HELPING UNMARRIED PREGNANT TEENAGERS EJ 022 181

TEENAGERS
EVAULATION OF THE DEMONSTRATION PHASE OF THE TEEN TUTORIAL PROGRAM: A MODEL OF INTERRELATIONSHIP OF SEVENTH GRADERS, KINDERGARTEN PUPILS AND PARENTS TO MEET THE DEVELOPMENTAL NEEDS OF DISADVANTAGED CHILDREN. ED032115
AGGRESSIVE GROUP WORK WITH TEENAGE DELINQUENT BOYS EJ 007 444
THE GENERATION GAP IN THE EYES OF YOUTH EJ 018 067
YOUTH AS ADVISERS TO ADULTS AND VICE VERSA EJ 018 068
TEENAGERS DISCUSS AGE RESTRICTIONS EJ 046 786
PREVENTING ILLEGITIMATE TEENAGE PREGNANCY THROUGH SYSTEMS INTERACTION EJ 059 671

TELEPHONE COMMUNICATION SYSTEMS
A HOTLINE TELEPHONE SERVICE FOR YOUNG PEOPLE IN CRISIS EJ 007 713

TELEVISED INSTRUCTION
CHILDREN AND TV, TELEVISION'S IMPACT ON THE CHILD. ED013666
COGNITIVE AND AFFECTIVE REACTIONS OF KINDERGARTNERS TO VIDEO DISPLAYS EJ 057 016

TELEVISION
CHILDREN AND TV, TELEVISION'S IMPACT ON THE CHILD. ED013666
EFFECTS OF VIEWING VIDEOTAPED SAME AND OPPOSITE COLOR CHILD-TEACHERS ON INTEGRATED AND ALL-WHITE KINDERGARTNERS. ED047805
THE EVALUATION OF "SESAME STREET'S" SOCIAL GOALS: THE INTERPERSONAL STRATEGIES OF COOPERATION, CONFLICT RESOLUTION, AND DIFFERING PERSPECTIVES. ED052824
TELEVISION VIOLENCE EJ 006 855
CHILDREN AND THE MASS MEDIA EJ 029 341
EMOTIONAL REACTIONS OF YOUNG CHILDREN TO TV VIOLENCE EJ 036 082
TELEVISED AGGRESSION AND THE INTERPERSONAL AGGRESSION OF PRESCHOOL CHILDREN EJ 043 197
THEY BECAME WHAT THEY BEHELD EJ 045 423

TELEVISION CURRICULUM
GUIDE FOR RIPPLES. ED051872
ANALYSIS OF CHILDREN'S REACTIONS TO AEL'S PRESCHOOL TELEVISION PROGRAM. ED052841

TELEVISION RESEARCH
CHILDREN AND TV, TELEVISION'S IMPACT ON THE CHILD. ED013666
A COMPARATIVE STUDY OF CURRENT EDUCATIONAL TELEVISION PROGRAMS FOR PRESCHOOL CHILDREN. FINAL REPORT. ED032123
THE FIRST YEAR OF SESAME STREET: THE FORMATIVE RESEARCH. FINAL REPORT, VOLUME II OF V VOLUMES. ED047822
THE FIRST YEAR OF SESAME STREET: AN EVALUATION. FINAL REPORT, VOLUME III OF V VOLUMES. ED047823
CHILDREN'S REACTIONS TO TV VIOLENCE: A REVIEW OF RESEARCH EJ 028 676
TELEVISION INSTRUCTION AND THE PRESCHOOL CHILD EJ 062 592

TELEVISION SURVEYS
SESAME STREET. A SURVEY OF TWO CITIES: VIEWING PATTERNS IN INNER CITY LOS ANGELES AND CHICAGO. ED047788
THE FIRST YEAR OF SESAME STREET: A SUMMARY OF AUDIENCE SURVEYS. FINAL REPORT, VOLUME IV OF V VOLUMES. ED047824
A COMPARISON OF PARENTS' ATTITUDES TOWARD AEL'S "AROUND THE BEND" AND OTHER CHILDREN'S TELEVISION PROGRAMS. ED052842
TELEVISION VIOLENCE EJ 006 855

TELEVISION VIEWING
CHILDREN AND TV, TELEVISION'S IMPACT ON THE CHILD. ED013666
DISCRIMINATING CHARACTERISTICS OF FAMILIES WATCHING SESAME STREET. EARLY DEVELOPMENTAL ADVERSITY PROGRAM: PHASE III, EDAP TECHNICAL NOTE 15.1. ED039943
SESAME STREET. A SURVEY OF TWO CITIES: VIEWING PATTERNS IN INNER CITY LOS ANGELES AND CHICAGO. ED047788
THE FIRST YEAR OF SESAME STREET: A HISTORY AND OVERVIEW. FINAL REPORT, VOLUME I OF V VOLUMES. ED047821
THE FIRST YEAR OF SESAME STREET: THE FORMATIVE RESEARCH. FINAL REPORT, VOLUME II OF V VOLUMES. ED047822
THE FIRST YEAR OF SESAME STREET: A SUMMARY OF AUDIENCE SURVEYS. FINAL REPORT, VOLUME IV OF V VOLUMES. ED047824
ANALYSIS OF CHILDREN'S REACTIONS TO AEL'S PRESCHOOL TELEVISION PROGRAM. ED052841
A COMPARISON OF PARENTS' ATTITUDES TOWARD AEL'S "AROUND THE BEND" AND OTHER CHILDREN'S TELEVISION PROGRAMS. ED052842
CHILDREN'S REACTIONS TO TV VIOLENCE: A REVIEW OF RESEARCH EJ 028 676
INVISIBLE FACTORS IN A CHILD'S REACTION TO TELEVISION EJ 032 934
EMOTIONAL REACTIONS OF YOUNG CHILDREN TO TV VIOLENCE EJ 036 082
CHILDREN OF TECHNOLOGY: IMAGES OR THE REAL THING EJ 054 472
SESAME STREET: MAGIC OR MALEVOLENCE? EJ 056 607
SOME IMMEDIATE EFFECTS OF TELEVISED VIOLENCE ON CHILDREN'S BEHAVIOR EJ 058 216
A DEVELOPMENTAL INVESTIGATION OF TELEVISED MODELED VERBALIZATIONS ON RESISTANCE TO DEVIATION EJ 058 218

TEST CONSTRUCTION
FROM THEORY TO THE CLASSROOM, BACKGROUND INFORMATION ON THE FIRST GRADE PROJECT IN NEW YORK CITY SCHOOLS. ED015770
THE DEVELOPMENT OF A TEST TO ASSESS THE OCCURRENCE OF SELECTED FEATURES OF NON-STANDARD ENGLISH IN THE SPEECH OF DISADVANTAGED PRIMARY CHILDREN. ED015790
DEVELOPMENT OF A SOCIAL COMPETENCY SCALE FOR PRESCHOOL CHILDREN. FINAL REPORT. ED020004
THE JOHNS HOPKINS PERCEPTUAL TEST, THE DEVELOPMENT OF A RAPID INTELLIGENCE TEST FOR THE PRE-SCHOOL CHILD. ED020787
HEAD START EVALUATION AND RESEARCH CENTER. PROGRESS REPORT OF RESEARCH STUDIES, 1966-1967. ED021612
HEAD START EVALUATION AND RESEARCH CENTER. PROGRESS REPORT OF RESEARCH STUDIES 1966 TO 1967. DOCUMENT 1, DEVELOPMENT OF THE MATRIX TEST. ED021623
HEAD START EVALUATION AND RESEARCH CENTER. PROGRESS REPORT OF RESEARCH STUDIES 1966 TO 1967. DOCUMENT 3, AN EXPERIMENTAL APPROACH TO STUDYING NON-VERBAL REPRESENTATION IN YOUNG CHILDREN. ED021625
THE DEVELOPMENT OF A BEHAVIOR CHECKLIST FOR BOYS. ED023468
THE ASSESSMENT OF ACHIEVEMENT ANXIETIES IN CHILDREN: HOW IMPORTANT IS RESPONSE SET AND MULTIDIMENSIONALITY IN THE TEST ANXIETY SCALE FOR CHILDREN? ED025313
DEPENDENCY AND SOCIAL PERFORMANCE: THE DEVELOPMENT OF A SCALE TO MEASURE LEVEL OF INDEPENDENCE IN SMALL CHILDREN. PART OF THE FINAL REPORT. ED026129
PERFORMANCE OF KINDERGARTEN CHILDREN FROM LOW INCOME FAMILIES ON SELECTED CONCEPT CATEGORIES. ED028847
MATCHED-PAIR SCORING TECHNIQUE USED ON A FIRST-GRADE YES-NO TYPE ECONOMICS ACHIEVEMENT TEST. ED029699
SRA ECONOMICS MATERIALS IN GRADES ONE AND TWO. EVALUATION REPORTS. ED029700
COMPARISON OF YES-NO, MATCHED-PAIRS, AND ALL-NO SCORING OF A FIRST-GRADE ECONOMICS ACHIEVEMENT TEST. ED029701
THE MONTESSORI RESEARCH PROJECT. FOUR PROGRESS REPORTS. ED030489
INVESTIGATION OF METHODS TO ASSESS THE EFFECTS OF CULTURAL DEPRIVATION. FINAL REPORT. ED032121
PRIMARY INFLUENCES ON THE DEVELOPMENT OF COMPETENCE: THE DEVELOPMENT OF A MATERNAL BEHAVIOR SCALE. PROGRESS REPORT. ED032127
GROUP SCREENING OF AUDITORY AND VISUAL PERCEPTUAL ABILITIES: AN APPROACH TO PERCEPTUAL ASPECTS OF BEGINNING READING. ED033751
PAPER-AND-PENCIL VERSUS CONCRETE PERFORMANCE OF NORMALS AND RETARDATES ON THE ETS WRITTEN EXERCISES. ED035442
POSTDOCTORAL RESEARCH TRAINING PROGRAM IN EDUCATIONAL STIMULATION. FINAL REPORT. ED035455
DEVELOPMENT OF A READINESS TEST FOR DISADVANTAGED PRE-SCHOOL CHILDREN IN THE UNITED STATES. FINAL REPORT. ED037253
YOUNG BLACK AND WHITE LISTENERS. ED038180
A REPORT ON THE RESULTS OF THE ADMINISTRATION OF THE GUMPGOOKIES TEST TO THE TEXAS EVALUATION SAMPLE. PART OF THE FINAL REPORT ON HEAD START EVALUATION AND RESEARCH: 1968-69 TO THE OFFICE OF ECONOMIC OPPORTUNITY. ED039033
ECHOIC RESPONSE INVENTORY FOR CHILDREN (ERIC). ED039931
DEVELOPMENTAL NORMS OF CHILDREN AGED 2 1/2-5 YEARS: A PILOT STUDY. ED039949
INCREASING VERBAL COMMUNICATION SKILLS IN CULTURALLY DISADVANTAGED PRE-SCHOOL CHILDREN. FINAL REPORT. ED044186
DIFFERENTIAL PERFORMANCE OF KINDERGARTEN CHILDREN ON TRANSITIVITY OF THREE MATCHING RELATIONS. ED048942
ATTAINMENT OF COGNITIVE OBJECTIVES. TECHNICAL REPORT NO. 3. ED052833
STANDARDIZATION OF A RESEARCH INSTRUMENT FOR IDENTIFYING ASSOCIATIVE RESPONDING IN CHILDREN EJ 019 021
AN INSTRUMENT FOR MEASURING CREATIVITY IN YOUNG CHILDREN: THE GROSS GEOMETRIC FORMS EJ 027 586
A METHOD OF INCREASING THE ABILITY OF FIRST GRADE PUPILS TO USE PHONETIC GENERALIZATIONS EJ 033 279
THE MANIPULATION AND MEASUREMENT OF SELF-DISCLOSURE IN PREADOLESCENTS EJ 034 298
THE ASSESSMENT OF DIFFERENCES IN CONCEPTUAL STYLE EJ 041 146
PERFORMANCE OF CULTURALLY DEPRIVED CHILDREN ON THE CONCEPT ASSESSMENT KIT--CONSERVATION EJ 053 906
A PIAGETIAN QUESTIONNAIRE APPLIED TO PUPILS IN A SECONDARY SCHOOL EJ 053 907
A PERCEPTUAL TEST BATTERY: DEVELOPMENT AND STANDARDIZATION EJ 058 395

TEST INTERPRETATION
THE EFFECTS OF JUNIOR KINDERGARTEN ON ACHIEVEMENT--THE FIRST FIVE YEARS. APPENDIX. ED016527
DIFFERENCES IN VOCABULARY INPUT-OUTPUT IN PSYCHODIAGNOSIS OF CHILDREN. ED024450
A HEAD START CONTROL GROUP. PART OF THE FINAL REPORT. ED026128

EVALUATING BEHAVIORAL CHANGE DURING A SIX-WEEK PRE-KINDERGARTEN INTERVENTION EXPERIENCE. RESEARCH PROJECT NUMBER 5 OF PROJECT HEAD START RESEARCH AND EVALUATION CENTER, SYRACUSE UNIVERSITY RESEARCH INSTITUTE. FINAL REPORT, NOVEMBER 1, 1967. ED026142
SOME DIMENSIONS OF CREATIVE THINKING ABILITY ACHIEVEMENT, AND INTELLIGENCE IN FIRST GRADE. ED028818
INITIAL AND FINAL CONSONANT RELATIONSHIPS IN SPEECH-SOUND TESTS: A DISCRIMINATION OR RESPONSE SET PROBLEM? ED032131
THE WORLD TEST: DEVELOPMENTAL ASPECTS OF A PLAY TECHNIQUE EJ 031 629
THE RELATIONSHIP BETWEEN INTELLIGENCE AND PERFORMANCE ON THE STROOP COLOR-WORD TEST IN SECOND- AND FIFTH-GRADE CHILDREN EJ 035 887
RELIABILITY AND STABILITY OF THE DENVER DEVELOPMENTAL SCREENING TEST EJ 053 905

TEST RELIABILITY

A STUDY OF A MEASUREMENT RESOURCE IN CHILD RESEARCH, PROJECT HEAD START. ED020790
USE OF NON-PROFESSIONAL PERSONNEL FOR HEALTH SCREENING OF HEAD START CHILDREN. FINAL REPORT. ED029702
STANDARDIZED TESTS AND THE DISADVANTAGED. ED034594
A COMPARISON OF PARENT AND TEACHER RATINGS ON THE PRESCHOOL ATTAINMENT RECORD OF SEVENTEEN FIVE-YEAR-OLD DISADVANTAGED CHILDREN. ED039922
PRELIMINARY ANALYSIS ON KINDERGARTEN AND FIRST GRADE FOLLOW THROUGH TEST RESULTS FOR 1968-69. ED045202
A PRESCHOOL ARTICULATION AND LANGUAGE SCREENING FOR THE IDENTIFICATION OF SPEECH DISORDERS. FINAL REPORT. ED051889
ON THE RELIABILITY OF THE GRAHAM/ROSENBLITH BEHAVIOUR TEST FOR NEONATES EJ 031 630
THE RELATIONSHIP BETWEEN INTELLIGENCE AND PERFORMANCE ON THE STROOP COLOR-WORD TEST IN SECOND- AND FIFTH-GRADE CHILDREN EJ 035 887
THE ASSESSMENT OF DIFFERENCES IN CONCEPTUAL STYLE EJ 041 146
VALIDITY OF THE DENVER DEVELOPMENTAL SCREENING TEST EJ 041 722
THE RELATIONSHIP BETWEEN THE WECHSLER INTELLIGENCE SCALE FOR CHILDREN AND THE SLOSSON INTELLIGENCE TEST EJ 041 725
A GEOMETRIC REPRESENTATION OF THE NOTIONS OF RELIABILITY, RELEVANCE, AND VALIDITY EJ 043 456
COGNITIVE STYLE: METHODOLOGICAL AND DEVELOPMENTAL CONSIDERATIONS EJ 053 482
RACIAL FACTORS IN TEST PERFORMANCE EJ 053 887
RELIABILITY AND STABILITY OF THE DENVER DEVELOPMENTAL SCREENING TEST EJ 053 905

TEST RESULTS

SUMMARY REPORT OF A STUDY OF THE FULL-YEAR 1966 HEAD START PROGRAMS. ED014328
HEAD START EVALUATION AND RESEARCH CENTER. PROGRESS REPORT OF RESEARCH STUDIES 1966 TO 1967. DOCUMENT 5, COMPARATIVE ITEM-CONTENT ANALYSIS OF ACHIEVEMENT TEST PERFORMANCE IN YOUNG CHILDREN. ED021627
A COMPARATIVE STUDY OF THE IMPACT OF TWO CONTRASTING EDUCATIONAL APPROACHES IN HEAD START, 1968-69. ED041643
THE SOCIAL MATURITY OF DISADVANTAGED CHILDREN. SPECIAL STUDIES PROJECT #2: ED042507
PRELIMINARY ANALYSIS ON KINDERGARTEN AND FIRST GRADE FOLLOW THROUGH TEST RESULTS FOR 1968-69. ED045202
CURRICULAR INTERVENTION IN LANGUAGE ARTS READINESS FOR HEAD START CHILDREN. TULANE UNIVERSITY, HEAD START EVALUATION AND RESEARCH CENTER, 1968-1969 INTERVENTION REPORT. SUPPLEMENT TO THE ANNUAL REPORT TO THE OFFICE OF ECONOMIC OPPORTUNITY. ED047795
DISADVANTAGED CHILDREN AND THEIR FIRST SCHOOL EXPERIENCES. ETS-HEAD START LONGITUDINAL STUDY: PRELIMINARY DESCRIPTION OF THE INITIAL SAMPLE PRIOR TO SCHOOL ENROLLMENT. A REPORT IN TWO VOLUMES: VOLUME 2--TABLES. ED047798
WHAT PUPILS KNOW ABOUT VOCABULARY IN MATHEMATICS--1930 AND 1968 EJ 035 466
NEGRO-WHITE, MALE-FEMALE EIGHT-MONTH DEVELOPMENTAL SCORES COMPARED WITH SEVEN-YEAR WISC AND BENDER TEST SCORES EJ 040 723
FIVE-YEAR STABILITY OF INTELLIGENCE QUOTIENTS FROM LANGUAGE AND NONLANGUAGE GROUP TESTS EJ 041 723

TEST SELECTION

AN EVALUATIVE STUDY OF COLOR-VISION TESTS FOR KINDERGARTEN AND FIRST GRADE PUPILS. ED028816
THE USE OF THE GOODENOUGH DRAW-A-MAN TEST AS A PREDICTOR OF ACADEMIC ACHIEVEMENT. ED029695
SIX SCHOOL READINESS SCREENING DEVICES USED IN PEDIATRIC OFFICES: CONCURRENT VALIDITY. FINAL REPORT. ED029719
SOCIAL-EMOTIONAL TASK FORCE. FINAL REPORT. ED033744

TEST VALIDITY

DEVELOPMENT OF APPROPRIATE EVALUATION TECHNIQUES FOR SCREENING CHILDREN IN A HEAD START PROGRAM. A PILOT PROJECT. ED015006
THE LIMITATIONS OF BRIEF INTELLIGENCE TESTING WITH YOUNG CHILDREN. ED020774
HEAD START EVALUATION AND RESEARCH CENTER. PROGRESS REPORT OF RESEARCH STUDIES 1966 TO 1967. DOCUMENT 1, DEVELOPMENT OF THE MATRIX TEST. ED021623
FURTHER EVIDENCE ON THE STABILITY OF THE FACTOR STRUCTURE OF THE TEST ANXIETY SCALE FOR SCHILDREN. ED023485
DIFFERENCES IN VOCABULARY INPUT-OUTPUT IN PSYCHODIAGNOSIS OF CHILDREN. ED024450
A STUDY OF COMPOSITION ABILITY AS ASSESSED WITH A STANDARDIZED INSTRUMENT FOR SECOND AND THIRD GRADE CHILDREN. ED029696
MEASURES OF VOCABULARY AND GRAMMATICAL SKILLS FOR CHILDREN UP TO AGE SIX EJ 021 683
USE OF THE IT SCALE FOR CHILDREN IN ASSESSING SEX-ROLE PREFERENCE IN PRESCHOOL NEGRO CHILDREN EJ 021 991
COMPARING VALIDITY OF CHANCE LEVEL AND HIGHER TEST SCORES EJ 022 248
VALIDITY OF THE DENVER DEVELOPMENTAL SCREENING TEST EJ 041 722
A SHORT, RELIABLE, EASY TO ADMINISTER INDIVIDUAL INTELLIGENCE TEST FOR SPECIAL CLASS PLACEMENT EJ 041 724
A GEOMETRIC REPRESENTATION OF THE NOTIONS OF RELIABILITY, RELEVANCE, AND VALIDITY EJ 043 456
SOME EFFECTS OF TESTING PROCEDURE ON DIVERGENT THINKING EJ 052 992
PIAGET AND GESELL: A PSYCHOMETRIC ANALYSIS OF TESTS BUILT FROM THEIR TASKS EJ 053 927
FACTORIAL STRUCTURE OF SELECTED PSYCHO-EDUCATIONAL MEASURES AND PIAGETIAN REASONING ASSESSMENTS EJ 055 112
NEGRO DIALECT AND BINET PERFORMANCE IN SEVERELY DISADVANTAGED BLACK FOUR-YEAR-OLDS EJ 056 914

TESTING

EVALUATION OF TWO ASSOCIATED YM-YWHA HEADSTART PROGRAMS. FINAL REPORT. ED014318
EVALUATION OF CHANGES OCCURRING IN CHILDREN WHO PARTICIPATED IN PROJECT HEAD START. ED017316
ADMINISTRATION MANUAL FOR TESTS OF BASIC LANGUAGE COMPETENCE IN ENGLISH AND SPANISH. LEVEL I (PRESCHOOL) ED027063
ADMINISTRATION MANUAL FOR TESTS OF BASIC LANGUAGE COMPETENCE IN ENGLISH AND SPANISH. LEVEL II (PRIMARY GRADES): CHILDREN AGES SIX TO TEN, ENGLISH AND SPANISH VERSIONS, FORMS A AND B. PART OF THE FINAL REPORT. ED027064
A COMPARATIVE STUDY OF THREE FORMS OF THE METROPOLITAN READINESS TEST AT TWO SOCIO-ECONOMIC LEVELS. ED035448
A COMPARISON OF PARENT AND TEACHER RATINGS ON THE PRESCHOOL ATTAINMENT RECORD OF SEVENTEEN FIVE-YEAR-OLD DISADVANTAGED CHILDREN. ED039922
A PILOT INVESTIGATION OF THE EFFECTS OF TRAINING TECHNIQUES DESIGNED TO ACCELERATE CHILDRENS' ACQUISITION OF CONSERVATION OF DISCONTINUOUS QUANTITY. FINAL REPORT. ED044178
RESULTS AND IMPLICATIONS OF A HEAD START CLASSIFICATION AND ATTENTION TRAINING PROGRAM. ED045182
EXPERIMENTAL VARIATION OF HEAD START CURRICULA: A COMPARISON OF CURRENT APPROACHES. ANNUAL PROGRESS REPORT, JUNE 1, 1969 - MAY 31, 1970. ED045196
REASONS FOR FAILURE ON THE CLASS INCLUSION PROBLEM EJ 018 872
LEARNING AND PROBLEM SOLVING BY THE MENTALLY RETARDED UNDER THREE TESTING CONDITIONS EJ 030 290
EFFECTS OF PROBING CHILDREN'S PHENOMENISTIC EXPLANATIONS OF CAUSE AND EFFECT EJ 030 292
CHILDREN'S SELECTIVE ATTENTION TO STIMULI: STAGE OR SET? EJ 033 573
VERBAL FACTORS IN COMPENSATION PERFORMANCE AND THE RELATION BETWEEN CONSERVATION AND COMPENSATION EJ 033 778
DISCRIMINATION OF SPATIALLY CONFUSABLE LETTERS BY YOUNG CHILDREN EJ 034 565
SELF CONCEPTS OF DISADVANTAGED AND ADVANTAGED STUDENTS EJ 035 618
THE INFLUENCE OF MASCULINE, FEMININE, AND NEUTRAL TASKS ON CHILDREN'S ACHIEVEMENT BEHAVIOR, EXPECTANCIES OF SUCCESS, AND ATTAINMENT VALUES EJ 037 318
CHARACTERISTICS OF WORD ASSOCIATION RESPONSES OBTAINED FROM CHILDREN IN GRADES ONE THROUGH FOUR EJ 042 960
A PILOT INVESTIGATION OF THE EFFECTS OF TRAINING TECHNIQUES DESIGNED TO ACCELERATE CHILDREN'S ACQUISITION OF CONSERVATION OF DISCONTINOUS QUANTITY EJ 044 705
AN INEXPENSIVE AND PORTABLE MEANS FOR ONE-WAY OBSERVATION EJ 045 797
THE RATIONAL ZERO POINT ON INCENTIVE-OBJECT PREFERENCE SCALES: A DEVELOPMENTAL STUDY EJ 048 099
SOME EFFECTS OF TESTING PROCEDURE ON DIVERGENT THINKING EJ 052 992
PERFORMANCE OF CULTURALLY DEPRIVED CHILDREN ON THE CONCEPT ASSESSMENT KIT--CONSERVATION EJ 053 906

TESTING PROBLEMS

A HEAD START CONTROL GROUP. PART OF THE FINAL REPORT. ED026128

MATCHED-PAIR SCORING TECHNIQUE USED ON A FIRST-GRADE YES-NO TYPE ECONOMICS ACHIEVEMENT TEST. ED029699
COMPARISON OF YES-NO, MATCHED-PAIRS, AND ALL-NO SCORING OF A FIRST-GRADE ECONOMICS ACHIEVEMENT TEST. ED029701
THE MISPLACED ADAPTATION TO INDIVIDUAL DIFFERENCES. ED040754
IT SCORE VARIATIONS BY INSTRUCTIONAL STYLE EJ 022 142
THE USE OF METROPOLITCAN READINESS TESTS WITH MEXICAN-AMERICAN CHILDREN EJ 026 810

TESTING PROGRAMS
SCHOOL READINESS, BEHAVIOR TESTS USED AT THE GESELL INSTITUTE. ED023449
EVALUATING BEHAVIORAL CHANGE DURING A SIX-WEEK PRE-KINDERGARTEN INTERVENTION EXPERIENCE. RESEARCH PROJECT NUMBER 5 OF PROJECT HEAD START RESEARCH AND EVALUATION CENTER, SYRACUSE UNIVERSITY RESEARCH INSTITUTE. FINAL REPORT, NOVEMBER 1, 1967. ED026142
A DESCRIPTIVE STUDY OF COGNITIVE AND AFFECTIVE TRENDS DIFFERENTIATING SELECTED GROUPS OF PRE-SCHOOL CHILDREN. ED031314

TESTS
THRESHOLD BY IDENTIFICATION OF PICTURES (TIP) TEST AND DISCRIMINATION BY IDENTIFICATION OF PICTURES (DIP) TEST. ED015784
A STUDY OF A MEASUREMENT RESOURCE IN CHILD RESEARCH, PROJECT HEAD START. ED020790
INDEX AND DESCRIPTION OF TESTS. ED025304
THE ASSESSMENT OF "SELF-CONCEPT" IN EARLY CHILDHOOD EDUCATION. ED050822
PSYCHOLOGICAL ASSESSMENT INSTRUMENTS FOR USE WITH HUMAN INFANTS EJ 025 231
NEGRO-WHITE, MALE-FEMALE EIGHT-MONTH DEVELOPMENTAL SCORES COMPARED WITH SEVEN-YEAR WISC AND BENDER TEST SCORES EJ 040 723
A GEOMETRIC REPRESENTATION OF THE NOTIONS OF RELIABILITY, RELEVANCE, AND VALIDITY EJ 043 456
ANXIETY IN THE EVALUATIVE CONTEXT EJ 051 018

TESTS OF SIGNIFICANCE
THE EFFECTS OF JUNIOR KINDERGARTEN ON ACHIEVEMENT--THE FIRST FIVE YEARS. APPENDIX. ED016527

TEXT BOOKS
PERSPECTIVES ON TEACHER-AIDES. A TEACHING TEXT. ED028836

TEXTBOOK CONTENT
MOTIVATIONAL AND ATTITUDINAL CONTENT OF FIRST GRADE READING TEXTBOOKS EJ 045 084
CIVIC BOOKS AND CIVIC CULTURE EJ 057 017
THE SUGAR-COATED WORLD OF THE THIRD-GRADE READER EJ 058 171

TEXTBOOK EVALUATION
THE READABILITY OF SELECTED SECOND GRADE SOCIAL STUDIES TEXTBOOKS. ED027968
CIVIC BOOKS AND CIVIC CULTURE EJ 057 017

TEXTBOOK SELECTION
DIACRITICAL MARKS IN TEXTBOOK ADOPTION EJ 012 815

THEATER ARTS
DEVELOPMENT OF A THEATRE ARTS CURRICULUM FOR YOUNG CHILDREN. CAREL ARTS AND HUMANITIES CURRICULUM DEVELOPMENT PROGRAM FOR YOUNG CHILDREN. ED032937
LA FORMATION THEATRALE DANS L'EDUCATION PRESCOLAIRE EJ 034 420
WHAT CAN TEACHERS LEARN FROM DIRECTORS IN THE PERFORMING ARTS? EJ 051 410

THEORIES
FROM THEORY TO THE CLASSROOM, BACKGROUND INFORMATION ON THE FIRST GRADE PROJECT IN NEW YORK CITY SCHOOLS. ED015770
PERSONALITY DEVELOPMENT IN INFANCY ED024439
IMPLICATIONS OF MNEMONICS RESEARCH FOR COGNITIVE THEORY. ED045199
PIAGET MISUNDERSTOOD: A CRITIQUE OF THE CRITICISMS OF HIS THEORY OF MORAL DEVELOPMENT EJ 011 915
ATTACHMENT, EXPLORATION, AND SEPARATION: ILLUSTRATED BY THE BEHAVIOR OF ONE-YEAR-OLDS IN A STRANGE SITUATION EJ 018 320
A TEST OF PIAGET'S THEORY OF "NOMINAL REALISM" EJ 023 189
ONTOGENY OF THE LOCUS AND ORIENTATION OF THE PERCEIVER: A CONFIRMATION AND AN ADDITION EJ 023 433
CONCEPTUAL EMPHASIS IN THE HISTORY OF DEVELOPMENTAL PSYCHOLOGY: EVOLUTIONARY THEORY, TELEOLOGY, AND THE NATURE-NURTURE ISSUE EJ 034 043
UNILATERAL DOMINANCE IS NOT RELATED TO NEUROPSYCHOLOGICAL INTEGRITY EJ 056 624
CHILDREN'S UNDERSTANDING OF SPATIAL RELATIONS: COORDINATION OF PERSPECTIVES EJ 061 068

THERAPEUTIC ENVIRONMENT
A SCHOOL GUIDANCE CLASS FOR EMOTIONALLY DISTURBED CHILDREN EJ 007 875
A PROGRAM FOR HOSPITALIZED PSYCHOTIC CHILDREN: REGULAR ATTENDANCE, AWAY FROM THE HOSPITAL, AT A COMMUNITY NURSERY SCHOOL EJ 050 938
RESIDENTIAL TREATMENT OF EMOTIONALLY DISTURBED CHILDREN IN NORWAY EJ 058 135

THERAPISTS
TRANSFERENCE TOWARD THE CHILD THERAPIST AND OTHER PARENT SURROGATES EJ 049 427

THERAPY
OPTOMETRIC CHILD VISION CARE AND GUIDANCE. A SERIES OF PAPERS RELEASED BY THE OPTOMETRIC EXTENSION PROGRAM TO ITS MEMBERSHIP 1966-1967. ED032111
THE PRESCHOOL COOPERATIVE AS A THERAPY FOR MOTHERS EJ 016 381
PEER- OBSERVER CONSULTATION EJ 022 532
MODIFYING RISK-TAKING BEHAVIOR EJ 032 891
A THERAPEUTIC APPROACH TO SPEECH PHOBIA: ELECTIVE MUTISM REEXAMINED EJ 035 625

THOUGHT PROCESSES
YOUNG CHILDREN'S THINKING, STUDIES OF SOME ASPECTS OF PIAGET'S THEORY. ED013662
CHILDREARING ANTECEDENTS OF FLEXIBLE THINKING. ED022530
CLASSIFICATION AND INFERENTIAL THINKING IN CHILDREN OF VARYING AGE AND SOCIAL CLASS. ED035446
THE ROLE OF UNDERDETERMINACY AND REFERENCE IN THE SENTENCE RECALL OF YOUNG CHILDREN. ED035449
THE RELATION OF CERTAIN HOME ENVIRONMENT FACTORS TO THE THINKING ABILITIES OF THREE-YEAR-OLD CHILDREN. FINAL REPORT. ED039041
PARENTAL CONCEPTUAL SYSTEMS, HOME PLAY ENVIRONMENT, AND POTENTIAL CREATIVITY IN CHILDREN. ED043386
NON-VERBAL INFORMATION STORAGE IN HUMANS AND DEVELOPMENTAL INFORMATION PROCESSING CHANNEL CAPACITY. ED047800
LANGUAGE ACQUISITION AND COGNITIVE DEVELOPMENT. ED049811
VISUAL IMAGERY INSTRUCTION AND NON-ACTION VERSUS ACTION SITUATIONS RELATIVE TO RECALL BY CHILDREN. FINAL REPORT. ED050828
A STUDY OF CAUSAL THINKING IN ELEMENTARY SCHOOL CHILDREN. FINAL REPORT. ED050830
THINKING ABOUT PEOPLE THINKING ABOUT PEOPLE THINKING ABOUT...: A STUDY OF SOCIAL COGNITIVE DEVELOPMENT EJ 025 953
EFFECTS OF PROBING CHILDREN'S PHENOMENISTIC EXPLANATIONS OF CAUSE AND EFFECT EJ 030 292
DEVELOPMENTAL PATTERNS FOR CHILDREN'S CLASS AND CONDITIONAL REASONING ABILITIES EJ 035 362
THE "MENTAL STEP" HYPOTHESIS IN SOLVING VERBAL PROBLEMS: EFFECTS OF VARIATIONS IN QUESTION-PHRASING ON A GRADE SCHOOL POPULATION EJ 035 372
SOME RELATIONSHIPS BETWEEN VERBAL AND PERCEPTUAL CAPABILITIES AND THE DEVELOPMENT OF RELATIVE THINKING EJ 035 383
INTERDEPENDENCE OF INHELDER AND PIAGET'S MODEL OF LOGICAL THINKING EJ 039 633
THE DEVELOPMENT OF COGNITIVE BALANCE AND THE TRANSITION FROM CONCRETE TO FORMAL OPERATIONAL THOUGHT EJ 041 145
THE ROLE OF FAMILIARITY IN CHILDREN'S EXPLANATIONS OF PHYSICAL CAUSALITY EJ 046 232
THE ROLE OF OPERATIONAL THINKING IN CHILDREN'S COMPREHENSION AND APPRECIATION OF HUMOR EJ 046 233
THE CHILDREN'S ASSOCIATIVE RESPONDING TEST: A TWO-YEAR FOLLOW-UP EJ 047 683
CHILDREN'S PERFORMANCE IN SIMPLE AND SUCCESSIVE-REVERSAL CONCEPT IDENTIFICATION PROBLEMS EJ 049 170
THINKING BEFORE LANGUAGE? A SYMPOSIUM: 1. RELATIONSHIPS BETWEEN LANGUAGE AND THOUGHT EJ 050 075
WORD-ASSOCIATION RESPONSES OF CHILDREN AS A FUNCTION OF AGE, SEX AND INSTRUCTIONS EJ 055 096
DEVELOPMENT OF RELATIONAL CONCEPTS AND WORD DEFINITION IN CHILDREN FIVE THROUGH ELEVEN EJ 056 397
MODEL FOR A THINKING MCHINE: AN INFORMATION-PROCESSING FRAMEWORK FOR THE STUDY OF COGNITIVE DEVELOPMENT EJ 030 289

TIME
TIME ESTIMATION BY YOUNG CHILDREN WITH AND WITHOUT INFORMATIONAL FEEDBACK EJ 033 787

TIME FACTORS (LEARNING)
A FOLLOW-UP STUDY OF INTELLIGENCE CHANGES IN CHILDREN WHO PARTICIPATED IN PROJECT HEADSTART. ED020786
HEAD START EVALUATION AND RESEARCH CENTER, UNIVERSITY OF KANSAS. REPORT NO. VIIC, ERRORLESS DISCRIMINATION IN PRESCHOOL CHILDREN: A PROGRAM FOR ESTABLISHING A ONE-MINUTE DELAY OF REINFORCEMENT. ED021642
MEMORY AND "CONTINGENCY ANALYSIS" IN INFANT LEARNING. ED024437
THE DEVELOPMENT OF TEMPORAL DISCRIMINATION IN YOUNG CHILDREN. ED045187
MODIFYING RESPONSE LATENCY AND ERROR RATE OF IMPULSIVE CHILDREN. ED050819
SPATIO-TEMPORAL SERIAL PERFORMANCE IN CHILDREN AND ADULTS EJ 021 758

AN AGE-IRRELEVANT CONCEPT OF DEVELOPMENT EJ 027 437
EFFECTS OF AGE UPON RETRIEVAL FROM SHORT-TERM MEMORY EJ 055 109
THE YOUNG CHILD'S COMPREHENSION OF TIME CONNECTIVES EJ 056 724

TIME PERSPECTIVE

A METHOD TO INVESTIGATE THE MOVEMENT PATTERNS OF CHILDREN. ED027938
THE DEVELOPMENT OF TEMPORAL DISCRIMINATION IN YOUNG CHILDREN. ED045187
TIME ESTIMATION BY YOUNG CHILDREN WITH AND WITHOUT INFORMATIONAL FEEDBACK EJ 033 787
SEX DIFFERENCES IN ADAPTIVE STYLES EJ 045 046
EXTENSION OF PERSONAL FUTURE TIME PERSPECTIVE, AGE, AND LIFE-SATISFACTION OF CHILDREN AND ADOLESCENTS EJ 058 140
PERCEPTION OF RHYTHM BY SUBJECTS WITH NORMAL AND DEFICIENT HEARING EJ 060 502

TOYS

AN EVALUATION OF NINE TOYS AND ACCOMPANYING LEARNING EPISODES IN THE RESPONSIVE MODEL PARENT/CHILD COMPONENT. ED045205
A PROGRESS REPORT ON THE PARENT/CHILD COURSE AND TOY LIBRARY. ED045206
SELF-MADE TOYS IN CHILDREN'S GAMES EJ 011 253
PLAY PERSISTENCE: SOME EFFECTS OF INTERRUPTION, SOCIAL REINFORCEMENT, AND DEFECTIVE TOYS EJ 034 532
EFFECTS OF SEX-TYPED INFORMATION ON CHILDREN'S TOY PREFERENCES EJ 045 191
TOYS DELAY THE INFANT'S FOLLOWING OF HIS MOTHER EJ 053 713
SON OF ROBOT COMMANDO EJ 055 488

TRACKING

DEVELOPMENT OF THE OBJECT CONCEPT AS MANIFESTED IN CHANGES IN THE TRACKING BEHAVIOR OF INFANTS BETWEEN 7 AND 20 WEEKS OF AGE EJ 038 264

TRADITIONAL SCHOOLS

SELF-PERCEPTIONS OF PUPILS IN AN EXPERIMENTAL ELEMENTARY SCHOOL EJ 028 239

TRAFFIC ACCIDENTS

CHILDREN AND ROAD ACCIDENTS EJ 050 496

TRAINING

AN APPROACH FOR WORKING WITH MOTHERS OF DISADVANTAGED PRESCHOOL CHILDREN. ED017335
HEAD START EVALUATION AND RESEARCH CENTER, BOSTON UNIVERSITY. REPORT D-II, TRAINING FOR NUMBER CONCEPT. ED022564
A CURRICULUM OF TRAINING FOR PARENT PARTICIPATION IN PROJECT HEAD START. ED026144
A PILOT INVESTIGATION OF THE EFFECTS OF TRAINING TECHNIQUES DESIGNED TO ACCELERATE CHILDRENS' ACQUISITION OF CONSERVATION OF DISCONTINUOUS QUANTITY. FINAL REPORT. ED044178
"NEED ACHIEVEMENT" TRAINING FOR HEAD START CHILDREN AND THEIR MOTHERS. ED048943
CASE CONFERENCE: A PSYCHOTHERAPEUTIC AIDE IN A HEADSTART PROGRAM. I. THEORY AND PRACTICE EJ 003 955
WHAT'S AHEAD IN TEACHER EDUCATION? EJ 009 031
CREATIVITY CHANGE IN STUDENT NURSES: A CROSS-SECTIONAL AND LONGITUDINAL STUDY EJ 030 291
TRAINING CREATIVITY IN YOUNG CHILDREN EJ 035 373
THE LEARNING AND TRANSFER OF DOUBLE-CLASSIFICATION SKILLS BY FIRST GRADERS EJ 036 821
THE EFFECTS OF STIMULUS REDUNDANCY ON TRANSFER OF STIMULUS PRETRAINING EJ 041 138
THE "FEATURE POSITIVE EFFECT" AND SIMULTANEOUS DISCRIMINATION LEARNING EJ 042 963
THE PERFORMANCE OF PRESCHOOL CHILDREN ON REVERSAL AND TWO TYPES OF EXTRADIMENSIONAL SHIFTS EJ 042 967
THE EFFECT OF TRAINING CHILDREN TO MAKE MORAL JUDGMENTS THAT ARE INDEPENDENT OF SANCTIONS EJ 044 507
A PILOT INVESTIGATION OF THE EFFECTS OF TRAINING TECHNIQUES DESIGNED TO ACCELERATE CHILDREN'S ACQUISITION OF CONSERVATION OF DISCONTINOUS QUANTITY EJ 044 705
TRAINING AND GENERALIZATION OF DENSITY CONSERVATION: EFFECTS OF FEEDBACK AND CONSECUTIVE SIMILAR STIMULI EJ 046 231
CLASSIFICATORY SCHEMES IN RELATION TO CLASS INCLUSION BEFORE AND AFTER TRAINING EJ 049 171
TRAINING WORKERS FOR CHILD CARE CENTERS EJ 050 935
EFFECTS OF CONCURRENT AND SERIAL TRAINING ON GENERALIZED VOCAL IMITATION IN RETARDED CHILDREN EJ 055 210
MODELING BY EXEMPLIFICATION AND INSTRUCTION IN TRAINING CONSERVATION EJ 057 898

TRAINING OBJECTIVES

A TRAINING PROGRAM FOR MOTHERS. ED017334
HELP FOR TEACHERS IN PRESCHOOLS: A PROPOSAL. ED031308
INCREASING VERBAL COMMUNICATION SKILLS IN CULTURALLY DISADVANTAGED PRE-SCHOOL CHILDREN. FINAL REPORT. ED044186

TRAINING PROGRAMS

EFFECTS OF PERCEPTUAL TRAINING ON CHILDREN'S HUMAN FIGURE DRAWINGS EJ 049 173

TRAINING TECHNIQUES

EFFECTS OF A STRUCTURED PROGRAM OF PRESCHOOL MATHEMATICS ON COGNITIVE BEHAVIOR. ED015791
AN APPROACH FOR WORKING WITH MOTHERS OF DISADVANTAGED PRESCHOOL CHILDREN. ED017335
LOGICAL OPERATIONS AND CONCEPTS OF CONSERVATION IN CHILDREN, A TRAINING STUDY. FINAL REPORT. ED020010
THE MARIE HUGHES LANGUAGE TRAINING MODEL. ED025305
EARLY INFANT STIMULATION AND MOTOR DEVELOPMENT. ED038179
CLASSIFICATION AND ATTENTION TRAINING CURRICULA FOR HEAD START CHILDREN. ED042508
INSTRUCTIONAL SPECIFICITY AND OUTCOME-EXPECTATION IN OBSERVATIONALLY-INDUCED QUESTION FORMULATION. ED047789
MODELING BY EXEMPLIFICATION AND INSTRUCTION IN TRAINING CONSERVATION. ED047790
MODIFYING RESPONSE LATENCY AND ERROR RATE OF IMPULSIVE CHILDREN. ED050819
TRAINING IN CONSERVATION OF WEIGHT EJ 021 761
GENERALIZATION OF ADULT'S STIMULUS CONTROL OF CHILDREN'S BEHAVIOR EJ 022 214
VERBAL MEDIATORS AND CUE DISCRIMINATION IN THE TRANSITION FROM NONCONSERVATION TO CONSERVATION OF NUMBER EJ 025 958
A TRAINING PROGRAM FOR VOLUNTEERS EJ 028 502

TRANSFER OF TRAINING

CONCEPT FORMATION BY KINDERGARTEN CHILDREN IN A CARD-SORTING TASK. PSYCHOLOGY SERIES. ED013665
TRAINING EFFECTS AND CONCEPT DEVELOPMENT--A STUDY OF THE CONSERVATION OF CONTINUOUS QUANTITY IN CHILDREN. ED016533
COMPARATIVE EFFECTIVENESS OF SPEAKING VERSUS LISTENING IN IMPROVING THE SPOKEN LANGUAGE OF DISADVANTAGED YOUNG CHILDREN. ED029689
EFFECT OF VARIETY ON THE LEARNING OF A SOCIAL STUDIES CONCEPT BY PRESCHOOL CHILDREN. ED029690
EFFECTS OF TRAINING YOUNG BLACK CHILDREN IN VOCABULARY VS. SENTENCE CONSTRUCTION. ED038176
A STUDY OF THE ABILITY OF PRIMARY SCHOOL CHILDREN TO GENERALIZE BEHAVIORAL COMPETENCIES SPECIFIED FOR "SCIENCE--A PROCESS APPROACH" TO OTHER CONTENT SETTINGS. ED039038
TRANSFER FROM PERCEPTUAL PRETRAINING AS A FUNCTION OF NUMBER OF TASK DIMENSIONS EJ 016 165
THE STABILITY OF DIMENSIONAL PREFERENCE FOLLOWING ODDITY TRAINING EJ 021 988
TRANSFER PERFORMANCE IN CHILDREN'S ODDITY LEARNING AS A FUNCTION OF DIMENSIONAL PREFERENCE, SHIFT PARADIGM AND OVERTRAINING EJ 024 692
TRANSFER OF MATCHING AND MISMATCHING BEHAVIOR IN PRESCHOOL CHILDREN EJ 024 701
TRANSFER IN NURSERY SCHOOL CHILDREN BETWEEN TWO RELATIONAL TASKS EJ 024 704
ROLE OF DISCRIMINATIVE STIMULI IN THE FORMATION OF FUNCTIONAL RESPONSE CLASSES EJ 024 937
EFFECTS OF NAMING RELEVANT AND IRRELEVANT STIMULI ON THE DISCRIMINATION LEARNING OF CHILDREN EJ 025 955
TRANSPOSITION AND TRANSFER OF ABSOLUTE RESPONDING AS FUNCTIONS OF LEARNING-SET TRAINING AND STIMULUS SIMILARITY EJ 028 635
VERBAL-DISCRIMINATION LEARNING AND TRANSFER WITH VERBAL AND PICTORIAL MATERIALS EJ 030 287
TRANSFER OF VERBAL PAIRED ASSOCIATES IN MENTALLY RETARDED INDIVIDUALS AND NORMAL CHILDREN AS A FUNCTION OF INTERLIST SIMILARITY EJ 033 785
CHILDREN'S SHIFT PERFORMANCE IN THE ABSENCE OF DIMENSIONALITY AND A LEARNED REPRESENTATIONAL RESPONSE EJ 033 786
TRAINING, TRANSFER, AND THE DEVELOPMENT OF COMPLEX BEHAVIOR EJ 034 712
SEQUENTIAL LEARNING BY CHILDREN EJ 035 381
THE LEARNING AND TRANSFER OF DOUBLE-CLASSIFICATION SKILLS BY FIRST GRADERS EJ 036 821
THE EFFECTS OF STIMULUS REDUNDANCY ON TRANSFER OF STIMULUS PRETRAINING EJ 041 138
THE INFLUENCE OF COGNITIVE STYLE ON PERCEPTUAL LEARNING EJ 046 238
THE LEARNING AND TRANSFER OF DOUBLE-CLASSIFICATION SKILLS: A REPLICATION AND EXTENSION EJ 046 254
ACQUIRED DISTINCTIVENESS AND EQUIVALENCE OF CUES IN YOUNG CHILDREN EJ 053 654
TRANSFER OF TRAINING: SOME BOUNDARY CONDITIONS AND INITIAL THEORY EJ 053 722
DISCRIMINATION LEARNING AND TRANSFER OF TRAINING IN THE AGED EJ 055 204
THE EFFECTS OF TRAINING AND SOCIOECONOMIC CLASS UPON THE ACQUISITION OF CONSERVATION CONCEPTS EJ 056 401
TRAINING COMMUNICATION SKILLS IN YOUNG CHILDREN EJ 058 606

GROUP HOME CARE AS AN ADJUNCT TO RESIDENTIAL TREATMENT EJ 061 233

TRANSFORMATIONS (LANGUAGE)
A TRANSFORMATIONAL ANALYSIS OF ORAL SYNTACTIC STRUCTURES OF CHILDREN REPRESENTING VARYING ETHNOLINGUISTIC COMMUNITIES EJ 056 713

TRANSFORMATIONS (MATHEMATICS)
BEFORE CHILDREN CAN MEASURE EJ 032 359

TREND ANALYSIS
DEVELOPMENTAL TRENDS IN GENERAL AND TEST ANXIETY AMONG JUNIOR AND SENIOR HIGH SCHOOL STUDENTS EJ 061 062

TRIMESTER SCHEDULES
EFFECT OF TRIMESTER SCHOOL OPERATION ON THE ACHIEVEMENT AND ADJUSTMENT OF KINDERGARTEN AND FIRST THROUGH THIRD GRADE CHILDREN. FINAL REPORT. ED020003

TUTORIAL PROGRAMS
HEAD START EVALUATION AND RESEARCH CENTER. PROGRESS REPORT OF RESEARCH STUDIES 1966 TO 1967. DOCUMENT 6, INDIVIDUAL INSTRUCTION PROJECT I. ED021628
THE EFFECT OF A STRUCTURED TUTORIAL PROGRAM ON THE COGNITIVE AND LANGUAGE DEVELOPMENT OF CULTURALLY DISADVANTAGED INFANTS. ED026110
A METHODOLOGY FOR FOSTERING ABSTRACT THINKING IN DEPRIVED CHILDREN. ED026131
SUPERMARKET DISCOVERY CENTER, PILOT STUDY, MAY - SEPTEMBER, 1968. INITIAL REPORT. ED027941
PIAGET, SKINNER, AND AN INTENSIVE PRESCHOOL PROGRAM FOR LOWER CLASS CHILDREN AND THEIR MOTHERS. ED027966
INFANT EDUCATION RESEARCH PROJECT, WASHINGTON, D.C. ED027976
EVALUATION OF AN INTERDISCIPLINARY APPROACH TO PREVENTION OF EARLY SCHOOL FAILURE. FOLLOW-UP STUDY, FINAL REPORT. ED031295
EVAULATION OF THE DEMONSTRATION PHASE OF THE TEEN TUTORIAL PROGRAM: A MODEL OF INTERRELATIONSHIP OF SEVENTH GRADERS, KINDERGARTEN PUPILS AND PARENTS TO MEET THE DEVELOPMENTAL NEEDS OF DISADVANTAGED CHILDREN. ED032115
INFANT EDUCATION. ED033760
CONDITIONAL LOGIC AND PRIMARY CHILDREN. ED038186
A TUTORIAL LANGUAGE PROGRAM FOR DISADVANTAGED INFANTS. ED040766
THE EFFECT OF A STRUCTURED TUTORIAL PROGRAM ON THE COGNITIVE AND LANGUAGE DEVELOPMENT OF CULTURALLY DISADVANTAGED INFANTS EJ 008 272
INFANT EDUCATION: A COMMUNITY PROJECT EJ 008 462
REMEDIAL READING INSTRUCTION BY TRAINED PUPIL TUTORS EJ 035 172
EVERY CHILD A TEACHER EJ 044 508
WORKING TOGETHER WORKS EJ 044 510
MY MON CAN TEACH READING TOO! EJ 051 082

TUTORING
CHILDREN UNDER THREE - FINDING WAYS TO STIMULATE DEVELOPMENT. II. SOME CURRENT EXPERIMENTS: A HOME TUTORING PROGRAM EJ 007 411
EFFECTS OF TUTORIAL EXPERIENCES ON THE PROBLEM-SOLVING BEHAVIOR OF SIXTH-GRADERS EJ 043 415
EVERY CHILD A TEACHER EJ 044 508

TWINS
FURTHER EVIDENCE ON THE RELATION BETWEEN AGE OF SEPARATION AND SIMILARITY IN IQ AMONG PAIRS OF SEPARATED IDENTICAL TWINS. ED027058
INFANT REACTIVITY TO REDUNDANT PROPRIOCEPTIVE AND AUDITORY STIMULATION: A TWIN STUDY. ED052825
TWINNING: A MARKER FOR BIOLOGICAL INSULTS EJ 021 188
THE BEHAVIOR OF TWINS: EFFECTS OF BIRTH WEIGHT AND BIRTH SEQUENCE EJ 036 081
INK-BLOT RESPONSES OF IDENTICAL AND FRATERNAL TWINS EJ 044 946
GENETIC FACTORS IN TESTS OF PERCEPTION AND THE RORSCHACH EJ 045 045
EMERGENCE AND PERSISTENCE OF BEHAVIORAL DIFFERENCES IN TWINS EJ 053 732

TYPEWRITING
PRELIMINARY ANALYSIS OF 1968-69 BOOTH ACHIEVEMENT. ED045201

UNDERACHIEVERS
SCHOOL ACHIEVERS AND UNDERACHIEVERS IN AN URBAN GHETTO EJ 027 614
IMPROVING THE SELF-CONCEPTS OF ACADEMIC UNDERACHIEVERS THROUGH MATERNAL GROUP COUNSELING EJ 043 200
LEARNING DISABILITY: A NEW LOOK AT UNDERACHIEVING EJ 058 411

UNGRADED CURRICULUM
THE MYTH BEHIND GRADED CONTENT EJ 052 126

UNGRADED ELEMENTARY PROGRAMS
A BIBLIOGRAPHY (WITH SELECTED ANNOTATIONS) ON NONGRADED ELEMENTARY SCHOOLS. ED015024
ABSTRACTS OF RESEARCH PERTAINING TO--UNGRADED VS SELF-CONTAINED CLASSROOM ORGANIZATION IN THE ELEMENTARY SCHOOL (GRADES 1-7). ED019129
SELF-PERCEPTIONS OF PUPILS IN AN EXPERIMENTAL ELEMENTARY SCHOOL EJ 028 239

UNIFIED STUDIES PROGRAMS
THE INTERNATIONAL WALDORF SCHOOL MOVEMENT. ED015019

UNIVERSAL EDUCATION
PRE-SCHOOL EDUCATION IN THE WORK OF J.A. COMENIUS (KOMENSKY) EJ 029 619

UNWED MOTHERS
A SERVICE PATTERN FOR HELPING UNMARRIED PREGNANT TEENAGERS EJ 022 181
COMMUNITY ACTION ON BEHALF OF PREGNANT SCHOOL-AGE GIRLS: EDUCATIONAL POLICIES AND BEYOND EJ 023 392
A STUDY OF WED AND UNWED MOTHERHOOD IN ADOLESCENTS AND YOUNG ADULTS EJ 030 715
GROUP SERVICES FOR UNMARRIED MOTHERS: AN INTERDISCIPLINARY APPROACH EJ 035 538
ATTITUDE OF BLACK NATURAL PARENTS REGARDING ADOPTION EJ 038 792
UNWED MOTHERS AND THEIR DECISIONS TO KEEP OR SURRENDER CHILDREN EJ 040 042
ADOLESCENT MATERNITY SERVICES: A TEAM APPROACH EJ 047 354

URBAN EDUCATION
NURSERIES IN CROSS-CULTURAL EDUCATION. PROGRESS REPORT. ED023460
URBAN EDUCATION BIBLIOGRAPHY: AN ANNOTATED LISTING. ED024474
SIX SUCCESSFUL READING PROGRAMS FOR INNER-CITY SCHOOLS EJ 035 663
THE DECLINE OF PLAY IN URBAN KINDERGARTENS EJ 041 961

URBAN SCHOOLS
WIDER WINDOWS FOR ELEMENTARY SCHOOLS EJ 034 133

URBAN YOUTH
ROCKS, RIVERS AND CITY CHILDREN EJ 029 390

VALIDITY
A NUTRITIONAL SURVEY OF CHILDREN IN HEAD START CENTERS IN CENTRAL UNITED STATES. ED042487
THE RELIABILITY OF RATING SCALES FOR ASSESSING THE BEHAVIOUR OF DISTURBED CHILDREN IN A RESIDENTIAL UNIT EJ 051 153
WHAT'S THROWN OUT WITH THE BATH WATER: A BABY? EJ 052 445
A SOCIAL COMPETENCE SCALE AND SYMPTOM CHECKIST FOR THE PRESCHOOL CHILD: FACTOR DIMENSIONS, THEIR CROSS-INSTRUMENT GENERALITY, AND LONGITUDINAL PERSISTENCE EJ 057 476

VALUES
THE THOMAS SELF-CONCEPT VALUES TEST. ED027068
CRISIS IN VALUES. 1970 WHITE HOUSE CONFERENCE ON CHILDREN, REPORT OF FORUM 4. (WORKING COPY). ED046523
DIFFERENTIAL RESPONSE PATTERNS AS THEY AFFECT THE SELF ESTEEM OF THE CHILD. ED046542
SIMILARITIES IN VALUES AND OTHER PERSONALITY CHARACTERISTICS IN COLLEGE STUDENTS AND THEIR PARENTS EJ 012 718
I AM--I WANT--I NEED: PREADOLESCENTS LOOK AT THEMSELVES AND THEIR VALUES EJ 017 446
THE RIGHTS OF THE CHILD - THE REALIZATION OF HIS POTENTIAL EJ 028 101
INCORPORATION OF VALUES BY LOWER AND MIDDLE SOCIOECONOMIC CLASS PRESCHOOL BOYS EJ 040 210
CONFRONTING PERSISTENT CONCERNS EJ 054 382

VERBAL ABILITY
THE EFFECTS OF SEVERAL VERBAL PRETRAINING CONDITIONS ON PRESCHOOL CHILDREN'S TRANSFER IN PROBLEM SOLVING. FINAL REPORT. ED015778
FINAL REPORT ON HEAD START EVALUATION AND RESEARCH--1966-67 TO THE INSTITUTE FOR EDUCATIONAL DEVELOPMENT. SECTION IV, AN EXPLORATORY STUDY OF ORAL LANGUAGE DEVELOPMENT AMONG CULTURALLY DIFFERENT CHILDREN. ED019120
THE EXTENSION OF CONTROL IN VERBAL BEHAVIOR. FINAL REPORT. ED021619
HEAD START EVALUATION AND RESEARCH CENTER, UNIVERSITY OF KANSAS. REPORT NO. IV, A COMPARISON OF FOUR MODES OF ELICITING BRIEF ORAL RESPONSES FROM CHILDREN. ED021637
SOME EFFECTS OF SOCIAL CLASS AND RACE ON CHILDREN'S LANGUAGE AND INTELLECTUAL ABILITIES. ED022540
THE EFFECTS OF SCHOOL ENVIRONMENT ON DISADVANTAGED KINDERGARTEN CHILDREN, WITH AND WITHOUT A HEAD START BACKGROUND. FINAL REPORT. ED041640
PARENT-CHILD VERBAL INTERACTION: A STUDY OF DIALOGUE STRATEGIES AND VERBAL ABILITY. ED049824
ANALYSIS OF INTELLIGENCE SCORES. ED052838
MEASURES OF VOCABULARY AND GRAMMATICAL SKILLS FOR CHILDREN UP TO AGE SIX EJ 021 683
WORD FLUENCY--INTELLECT OR PERSONALITY? EJ 034 313
SOME RELATIONSHIPS BETWEEN VERBAL AND PERCEPTUAL CAPABILITIES AND THE DEVELOPMENT OF RELATIVE THINKING EJ 035 383

SOME RELATIONSHIPS BETWEEN CLASS INCLUSION, PERCEPTUAL CAPABILITIES, VERBAL CAPABILITIES AND RACE EJ 039 639
THE MODIFICATION OF INTELLIGENCE BY TRAINING IN THE VERBALIZATION OF WORD DEFINITIONS AND SIMPLE CONCEPTS EJ 052 594
LOCUS OF CONTROL: AN EXAMPLE OF DANGERS IN USING CHILDREN'S SCALES WITH CHILDREN EJ 058 929
FAMILY CORRELATES OF VERBAL REASONING ABILITY EJ 061 069

VERBAL COMMUNICATION

LANGUAGE RESEARCH STUDY--PROJECT HEAD START. DEVELOPMENT OF METHODOLOGY FOR OBTAINING AND ANALYZING SPONTANEOUS VERBALIZATIONS USED BY PRE-KINDERGARTEN CHILDREN IN SELECTED HEAD START PROGRAMS--A PILOT STUDY. ED015007
A TECHNIQUE FOR GATHERING CHILDREN'S LANGUAGE SAMPLES FROM NATURALISTIC SETTINGS. ED016532
HEAD START EVALUATION AND RESEARCH CENTER, THE UNIVERSITY OF CHICAGO. REPORT C, COGNITIVE INTERACTION BETWEEN TEACHER AND PUPIL IN A PRESCHOOL SETTING. ED022552
VERBAL BEHAVIOR OF PRESCHOOL TEACHERS. A VERY PRELIMINARY REPORT. ED034577
INFORMATION EXCHANGE IN MOTHER-CHILD INTERACTIONS. ED034599
PUPIL IMITATION OF A REWARDING TEACHER'S VERBAL BEHAVIOR. ED038185
THE DEVELOPMENT OF THE CONTROL OF ADULT INSTRUCTIONS OVER NON-VERBAL BEHAVIOR. ED041620
CROSS-CULTURAL VERBAL COOPERATION. PROGRESS REPORT. ED042496
THE EFFECT OF FOUR COMMUNICATION PATTERNS AND SEX ON LENGTH OF VERBALIZATION IN SPEECH OF FOUR YEAR OLD CHILDREN. FINAL REPORT. ED042514
MOTHER-CHILD INTERACTION: SOCIAL CLASS DIFFERENCES IN THE FIRST YEAR OF LIFE. ED044177
RELATIONSHIPS BETWEEN CHILDREN'S QUESTIONS AND NURSERY SCHOOL TEACHERS' RESPONSES. ED046507
COMMUNICATIVE COMPETENCE AND THE DISADVANTAGED CHILD: A STUDY OF THE RELATIONSHIP BETWEEN LANGUAGE MODELS AND THE DEVELOPMENT OF COMMUNICATION SKILLS IN DISADVANTAGED PRESCHOOLERS. FINAL REPORT. ED047806
TINY DRAMAS: VOCAL COMMUNICATION BETWEEN MOTHER AND INFANT IN JAPANESE AND AMERICAN FAMILIES. ED048927
PARENT-CHILD VERBAL INTERACTION: A STUDY OF DIALOGUE STRATEGIES AND VERBAL ABILITY. ED049824
APPLICATION OF MARKOV PROCESSES TO THE CONCEPT OF STATE. ED053813
EVALUATION OF CLASSROOM CLIMATE EJ 002 421
COMPARISON OF VERBAL INTERACTION IN TWO PRESCHOOL PROGRAMS EJ 008 274
PUPILS' PERCEPTION OF TEACHERS' VERBAL FEEDBACK EJ 027 880
FATHERS' VERBAL INTERACTION WITH INFANTS IN THE FIRST THREE MONTHS OF LIFE EJ 036 126
CHILDREN'S COMMUNICATION ACCURACY RELATED TO RACE AND SOCIOECONOMIC STATUS EJ 040 359
THE EFFECTS OF FEEDBACK VARIATIONS ON REFERENTIAL COMMUNICATION OF CHILDREN EJ 040 360
VERBAL PARTICIPATION AS A FUNCTION OF THE PRESENCE OF PRIOR INFORMATION CONCERNING APTITUDE EJ 042 348
LANGUAGE STRUCTURE AND THE FREE RECALL OF VERBAL MESSAGES BY CHILDREN EJ 044 693
EFFECTS OF STIMULUS ABSTRACTNESS AND FAMILIARITY ON LISTENER'S PERFORMANCE IN A COMMUNICATION TASK EJ 046 241
A CROSS-CULTURAL STUDY OF THE CHILD'S COMMUNICATION WITH HIS MOTHER EJ 046 890
THE EFFECT OF A TELEVISION MODEL UPON RULE ADOPTION BEHAVIOR OF CHILDREN EJ 056 733
VERBAL AND NONVERBAL REWARDS AND PUNISHMENT IN THE DISCRIMINATION LEARNING OF CHILDREN OF VARYING SOCIOECONOMIC STATUS EJ 057 896
INFLUENCE OF MODELING, EXHORTATIVE VERBALIZATION, AND SURVEILLANCE ON CHILDREN'S SHARING EJ 058 214
A DEVELOPMENTAL INVESTIGATION OF TELEVISED MODELED VERBALIZATIONS ON RESISTANCE TO DEVIATION EJ 058 218
PRINCIPLES OF INTERACTION IN LANGUAGE LEARNING EJ 059 875
THE DEVELOPMENT OF THE LANGUAGE OF EMOTIONS: I. THEORETICAL AND METHODOLOGICAL INTRODUCTION EJ 061 059
THE DEVELOPMENT OF THE LANGUAGE OF EMOTIONS: II. INTENTIONALITY IN THE EXPERIENCE OF AFFECT EJ 061 064
THE DEVELOPMENT OF THE LANGUAGE OF EMOTIONS: III. TYPE OF ANXIETY IN THE EXPERIENCE OF AFFECT EJ 061 065
THE DEVELOPMENT OF THE CONTROL OF ADULT INSTRUCTIONS OVER NONVERBAL BEHAVIOR EJ 061 138

VERBAL DEVELOPMENT

THE EXTENSION OF CONTROL IN VERBAL BEHAVIOR. FINAL REPORT. ED021619
LURIA'S MODEL OF THE VERBAL CONTROL OF BEHAVIOR. STUDY F: MOTIVATIONAL AND CONTROL IN THE DEVELOPMENT OF LANGUAGE FUNCTIONS, D. BIRCH. ED024443
A DISTINCTIVE FEATURES ANALYSIS OF PRE-LINGUISTIC INFANT VOCALIZATIONS. ED025330
SEX DIFFERENCES IN GENERALITY AND CONTINUITY OF VERBAL RESPONSIVITY. ED035444
LANGUAGE TRAINING FOR TEACHERS OF DEPRIVED CHILDREN. ED040744
AN EXPERIMENTAL ANALYSIS OF PROCEDURES FOR INCREASING SPECIFIC VOCALIZATIONS OF CHILDREN WHO DO NOT DEVELOP FUNCTIONAL SPEECH. PROGRESS REPORT. ED042495
INCREASING VERBAL COMMUNICATION SKILLS IN CULTURALLY DISADVANTAGED PRE-SCHOOL CHILDREN. FINAL REPORT. ED044186
DEVELOPMENTAL SPEECH INACCURACY AND SPEECH THERAPY IN THE EARLY SCHOOL YEARS EJ 013 624
THE ROLE OF VERBAL MEDIATION IN MENTAL DEVELOPMENT EJ 035 382
KNOWLEDGE OF ACTION AND OBJECT WORDS: A COMPARISON OF LOWER- AND MIDDLE-CLASS NEGRO PRESCHOOLERS EJ 040 453
RELATIONSHIPS BETWEEN INFANTS' VOCALIZATIONS AND THEIR MOTHERS' BEHAVIORS EJ 040 455
IDENTIFICATION OF VERBAL CONCEPTS BY PRESCHOOL CHILDREN EJ 042 958
LANGUAGE LEARNING--FRESH VIVID AND THEIR OWN EJ 044 613
VERBAL REGULATION OF MOTOR BEHAVIOR-SOVIET RESEARCH AND NON-SOVIET REPLICATIONS EJ 050 074
SOME COGNITIVE AND AFFECTIVE ASPECTS OF EARLY LANGUAGE DEVELOPMENT EJ 055 655

VERBAL LEARNING

THE EFFECTS OF SEVERAL VERBAL PRETRAINING CONDITIONS ON PRESCHOOL CHILDREN'S TRANSFER IN PROBLEM SOLVING. FINAL REPORT. ED015778
ENGINEERING VERBAL BEHAVIOR. ED025308
MEDIATIONAL STYLES: AN INDIVIDUAL DIFFERENCE VARIABLE IN CHILDREN'S VERBAL LEARNING ABILITY. ED027955
IMPLICIT VERBAL BEHAVIOR IN ELEMENTARY SCHOOL CHILDREN, (INTERNAL VERBAL RESPONSES OF ELEMENTARY SCHOOL CHILDREN ELICITED BY THE ASSOCIATION OF WORDS). FINAL REPORT. ED028848
COMPARATIVE EFFECTIVENESS OF SPEAKING VERSUS LISTENING IN IMPROVING THE SPOKEN LANGUAGE OF DISADVANTAGED YOUNG CHILDREN. ED029689
THE EFFECT OF VERBALIZATION OF RELEVANT AND IRRELEVANT DIMENSIONS ON CONCEPT FORMATION. ED030484
LANGUAGE STRUCTURE AND THE FREE RECALL OF VERBAL MESSAGES BY CHILDREN. ED032933
PARENT-CHILD VERBAL INTERACTION: A STUDY OF DIALOGUE STRATEGIES AND VERBAL ABILITY. ED049824
EFFECT OF LABELS ON MEMORY IN THE ABSENCE OF REHEARSAL. ED051883
SEMANTIC RELATIONSHIP AND THE LEARNING OF SYNTACTIC WORD PAIRS IN CHILDREN EJ 016 163
EFFECT OF VERBAL PRETRAINING AND SINGLE-PROBLEM MASTERY ON WEIGL LEARNING-SET FORMATION IN CHILDREN EJ 018 883
EFFECT OF VERBAL RESPONSE CLASS ON SHIFT IN THE PRESCHOOL CHILD'S JUDGMENT OF LENGTH IN RESPONSE TO AN ANCHOR STIMULUS EJ 019 012
A TEST OF LURIA'S HYPOTHESES CONCERNING THE DEVELOPMENT OF VERBAL SELF-REGULATION EJ 025 956
SUBJECT-MODEL SEXUAL STATUS AND VERBAL IMITATIVE PERFORMANCE IN KINDERGARTEN CHILDREN EJ 030 178
DEVELOPMENT OF FREE RECALL LEARNING IN CHILDREN EJ 035 359
MEDIATION AND PERCEPTUAL TRANSFER IN CHILDREN EJ 035 365
DEVELOPMENTAL TRENDS IN THE INTENTIONAL AND INCIDENTAL LEARNING COMPONENTS OF A VERBAL DISCRIMINATION TASK EJ 035 375
DEVELOPMENTAL SHIFTS IN VERBAL RECALL BETWEEN MENTAL AGES TWO AND FIVE EJ 036 825
FREE RECALL OF WORDS AND OBJECTS EJ 039 634
PHONETIC COMPATIBILITY IN PAIRED-ASSOCIATE LEARNING OF FIRST- AND THIRD-GRADE CHILDREN EJ 044 692
GENERALIZED LABELING ON THE BASIS OF STRUCTURAL RESPONSE CLASSES BY TWO YOUNG CHILDREN EJ 044 696
THE CHRONOLOGY OF THE DEVELOPMENT OF COVERT SPEECH IN CHILDREN EJ 047 594
SOME THOUGHTS ON HOW CHILDREN LEARN TO REMEMBER EJ 049 432
MOTHER'S MODE OF DISCIPLINE AND CHILD'S VERBAL ABILITY EJ 050 794
THE SPANISH-SPEAKING FIVE-YEAR-OLD EJ 056 391
EFFECTS OF SYNTACTICAL MEDIATION, AGE, AND MODES OF REPRESENTATION ON PAIRED-ASSOCIATE LEARNING EJ 056 615

VERBAL OPERANT CONDITIONING

THE EXTENSION OF CONTROL IN VERBAL BEHAVIOR. FINAL REPORT. ED021619
ENGINEERING VERBAL BEHAVIOR. ED025308
SUBJECTS' HYPOTHESES, EXPERIMENTAL INSTRUCTIONS AND AUTONOMIC "CONDITIONING". ED025335
COGNITIVE FACTORS IN SEMANTIC CONDITIONING. A THESIS IN EDUCATIONAL PSYCHOLOGY. ED027069
VERBAL REINFORCEMENT AS AN ADJUSTMENT PREDICTOR WITH KINDERGARTEN CHILDREN. FINAL REPORT. ED031313
WORDS AND DEEDS ABOUT ALTRUISM AND THE SUBSEQUENT REINFORCEMENT POWER OF THE MODEL. ED043390
VERBAL OPERANT CONDITIONING OF AN ACTIVE-NON-ACTIVE VERBAL DIFFERENTIAL IN EARLY SCHOOL CHILDREN EJ 041 451

VERBAL STIMULI
HEAD START EVALUATION AND RESEARCH CENTER, UNIVERSITY OF KANSAS. REPORT NO. VIIB, ESTABLISHMENT OF NONVERBAL COLOR DISCRIMINATION RESPONSES TO AUDITORY COLOR-LABELING STIMULI AND SUBSEQUENT EFFECTS ON COLOR-LABELING RESPONSES. ED021641
THE AUDITORY MEMORY OF CHILDREN FROM DIFFERENT SOCIO-ECONOMIC BACKGROUNDS. ED027092
INTERRELATIONS IN CHILDREN'S LEARNING OF VERBAL AND PICTORIAL PAIRED ASSOCIATES. ED051886
SUGGESTIBILITY IN RELATION TO SCHOOL GRADE, SEX, AND SOURCE OF INFLUENCE EJ 023 431
SELF-REINFORCEMENT ESTABLISHED FOR A DISCRIMINATION TASK EJ 025 964
THE MODELING OF SHARING: EFFECTS ASSOCIATED WITH VICARIOUS REINFORCEMENT, SYMBOLIZATION, AGE, AND GENERALIZATION EJ 028 894
VERBAL FACTORS IN COMPENSATION PERFORMANCE AND THE RELATION BETWEEN CONSERVATION AND COMPENSATION EJ 033 778
MEANING AND ATTENTION AS DETERMINANTS OF SOCIAL REINFORCER EFFECTIVENESS EJ 033 781
THE EFFECT OF INDIVIDUAL-CONTINGENT GROUP REINFORCEMENT ON POPULARITY EJ 034 158
LINGUISTIC AND PSYCHOLOGICAL FACTORS IN THE SPEECH REGULATION OF BEHAVIOR IN YOUNG CHILDREN EJ 034 540
THE EFFECTS OF CONNOTATIVE SIMILARITY IN CHILDREN'S LEARNING OF A PAIRED-ASSOCIATE TASK EJ 035 376
PROCESSING OF PHONOLOGICAL SEQUENCES BY YOUNG CHILDREN AND ADULTS EJ 036 747
CHARACTERISTICS OF WORD ASSOCIATION RESPONSES OBTAINED FROM CHILDREN IN GRADES ONE THROUGH FOUR EJ 042 960
THE USE OF VERBAL MEDIATION IN THE RETARDED AS A FUNCTION OF DEVELOPMENTAL LEVEL AND RESPONSE AVAILABILITY EJ 044 699
MALE AND FEMALE AUDITORY REINFORCEMENT OF INFANT VOCALIZATIONS EJ 058 217
THE EFFECTS OF VERBAL PRETRAINING ON THE MULTIDIMENSIONAL GENERALIZATION BEHAVIOR OF CHILDREN EJ 060 784

VERBAL TESTS
THE DEVELOPMENT OF PROBABILISTIC THINKING IN CHILDREN: A COMPARISON OF TWO METHODS OF ASSESSMENT EJ 023 193

VIDEO TAPE RECORDINGS
A STUDY IN THE UTILIZATION OF TECHNOLOGICALLY ADVANCED TECHNIQUES FOR TEACHER-PARENT-CHILD ASSESSMENT. FINAL REPORT. ED053818

VIOLENCE
TELEVISION VIOLENCE EJ 006 855
CHILDREN'S REACTIONS TO TV VIOLENCE: A REVIEW OF RESEARCH EJ 028 676
IS IT TIME TO BREAK THE SILENCE ON VIOLENCE? EJ 032 564
INVISIBLE FACTORS IN A CHILD'S REACTION TO TELEVISION EJ 032 934
EMOTIONAL REACTIONS OF YOUNG CHILDREN TO TV VIOLENCE EJ 036 082
VIOLENCE BEGINS AT HOME. THE PARENTS' CENTER PROJECT FOR THE STUDY AND PREVENTION OF CHILD ABUSE EJ 043 671
SON OF ROBOT COMMANDO EJ 055 488
VIOLENCE AS A SYMPTOM OF CHILDHOOD EMOTIONAL ILLNESS EJ 055 536

VISION TESTS
AN EVALUATIVE STUDY OF COLOR-VISION TESTS FOR KINDERGARTEN AND FIRST GRADE PUPILS. ED028816

VISUAL ACUITY
EXAMINATION AND REEVALUATION OF PROSTHETIC LENSES EMPLOYING AN OPERANT PROCEDURE FOR MEASURING SUBJECTIVE VISUAL ACUITY IN A RETARDED CHILD EJ 029 382

VISUAL ARTS
DEVELOPMENT OF A VISUAL ARTS CURRICULUM FOR YOUNG CHILDREN. CAREL ARTS AND HUMANITIES CURRICULUM DEVELOPMENT PROGRAM FOR YOUNG CHILDREN. ED032939
CHILDREN'S SENSITIVITY TO PAINTING STYLES EJ 025 304

VISUAL DISCRIMINATION
HEAD START RESEARCH AND EVALUATION OFFICE, UNIVERSITY OF CALIFORNIA AT LOS ANGELES. APPENDIX I TO THE ANNUAL REPORT, NOVEMBER 1967. ED020793
VARIABLES AFFECTING THE PERFORMANCE OF YOUNG CHILDREN ON A LETTER DISCRIMINATION TASK. ED020797
HEAD START EVALUATION AND RESEARCH CENTER, UNIVERSITY OF KANSAS. REPORT NO. VIIB, ESTABLISHMENT OF NONVERBAL COLOR DISCRIMINATION RESPONSES TO AUDITORY COLOR-LABELING STIMULI AND SUBSEQUENT EFFECTS ON COLOR-LABELING RESPONSES. ED021641
STIMULUS DIMENSIONALITY AND MANIPULABILITY IN VISUAL PERCEPTUAL LEARNING. ED023452
METHODOLOGICAL ISSUES IN THE STUDY OF AGE DIFFERENCES IN INFANTS' ATTENTION TO STIMULI VARYING IN MOVEMENT AND COMPLEXITY. ED023477
AN EVALUATIVE STUDY OF COLOR-VISION TESTS FOR KINDERGARTEN AND FIRST GRADE PUPILS. ED028816
DIFFERENTIAL VISUAL BEHAVIOR TO HUMAN AND HUMANOID FACES IN EARLY INFANCY EJ 019 595
CHILDREN'S SENSITIVITY TO PAINTING STYLES EJ 025 304
SENSORY-MODALITY EFFECTS ON SHAPE PERCEPTION IN PRESCHOOL CHILDREN EJ 029 383
YOUNG CHILDREN'S ORIENTATION OF LETTERS AS A FUNCTION OF AXIS OF SYMMETRY AND STIMULUS ALIGNMENT EJ 032 909
DISCRIMINATION OF SPATIALLY CONFUSABLE LETTERS BY YOUNG CHILDREN EJ 034 565
OPERANT LEARNING OF VISUAL PATTERN DISCRIMINATION IN YOUNG INFANTS EJ 035 623
ORIENTATION DISCRIMINATION IN INFANTS: A COMPARISON OF VISUAL FIXATION AND OPERANT TRAINING METHODS EJ 041 981
DEVELOPMENT OF VISUAL SCANNING STRATEGIES FOR DIFFERENTIATING WORDS EJ 043 703
EFFECTS OF SPATIAL SEPARATION OF STIMULUS, RESPONSE, AND REWARD IN DISCRIMINATION LEARNING BY CHILDREN EJ 046 243
PERCEPTUAL INADEQUACY AND COMMUNICATIVE INEFFECTIVENESS IN INTERPERSONAL COMMUNICATION EJ 056 627
DEVELOPMENTAL DIFFERENCES IN THE PERCEPTION AND PRODUCTION OF FACIAL EXPRESSIONS EJ 058 693

VISUAL ENVIRONMENT
ACCELERATING VISUAL COMPLEXITY LEVELS IN THE HUMAN INFANT EJ 045 598

VISUAL LEARNING
VISUAL LEARNING. DIMENSIONS IN EARLY LEARNING SERIES. ED027089
EFFECT OF VISUAL STIMULI IN COMPLEMENTING TELEVISED INSTRUCTION EJ 015 382
IMAGERY IN CHILDREN'S PAIRED-ASSOCIATE LEARNING EJ 021 757
ATTENTIONAL PREFERENCE AND EXPERIENCE: I. INTRODUCTION EJ 025 988
VISUAL LEARNING: AN ANALYSIS BY SEX AND GRADE LEVEL EJ 045 424

VISUAL MEASURES
A REPORT ON THE RESULTS OF THE ADMINISTRATION OF THE GUMPGOOKIES TEST TO THE TEXAS EVALUATION SAMPLE. PART OF THE FINAL REPORT ON HEAD START EVALUATION AND RESEARCH: 1968-69 TO THE OFFICE OF ECONOMIC OPPORTUNITY. ED039033
ANALYSIS OF VISUAL PERCEPTION OF CHILDREN IN THE EARLY CHILDHOOD EDUCATION PROGRAM (RESULTS OF THE MARIANNE FROSTIG DEVELOPMENTAL TEST OF VISUAL PERCEPTION). ED052839
COMPARISON OF PICTORIAL AND VERBAL SEMANTIC SCALES AS USED BY CHILDREN EJ 029 769
CONTINUITY IN THE DEVELOPMENT OF VISUAL BEHAVIOR IN YOUNG INFANTS EJ 053 746
THE RELATION OF FORM RECOGNITION TO CONCEPT DEVELOPMENT EJ 056 393
VARIABLES AFFECTING ASSOCIATIVE RECALL IN CHILDREN EJ 056 400
MULTIDIMENSIONAL SCALING OF DIMENSIONAL PREFERENCES: A METHODOLOGICAL STUDY EJ 056 609

VISUAL PERCEPTION
A READING READINESS TRAINING PROGRAM FOR PERCEPTUALLY HANDICAPPED KINDERGARTEN PUPILS OF NORMAL VISION. FINAL REPORT. ED013119
THE INITIAL COORDINATION OF SENSORIMOTOR SCHEMAS IN HUMAN INFANTS - PIAGET'S IDEAS AND THE ROLE OF EXPERIENCE. ED016511
A NEW THEORY OF SCRIBBLING AND DRAWING IN CHILDREN. ED017324
FINAL REPORT ON HEAD START EVALUATION AND RESEARCH--1966-67 TO THE INSTITUTE FOR EDUCATIONAL DEVELOPMENT. SECTION VII, SENSORY AND PERCEPTUAL STUDIES. ED019123
SEMO PROJECT HEAD START, PSYCHOLOGICAL SERVICES REPORT, 1966-67 YEAR PROGRAM. ED020780
A STUDY OF VISUAL PERCEPTIONS IN EARLY CHILDHOOD. ED023451
PERCEPTUAL MODE DOMINANCE: AN APPROACH TO ASSESSMENT OF FIRST GRADE READING AND SPELLING. ED026132
PERCEPTUAL TESTING AND TRAINING METHODS USED IN THE PRIMARY GRADES. ED027971
VISION TRAINING - A NEW DEVELOPMENTAL CONCEPT IN CHILD VISION. ED028842
EIDETIC IMAGERY IN CHILDREN. FINAL REPORT. ED029707
AN EXPERIMENTAL STUDY OF VISUAL PERCEPTUAL TRAINING AND READINESS SCORES WITH CERTAIN FIRST-GRADE CHILDREN. ED032921
ANALYSIS OF VISUAL PERCEPTION OF CHILDREN IN THE EARLY CHILDHOOD EDUCATION PROGRAM (RESULTS OF THE MARIANNE FROSTIG DEVELOPMENTAL TEST OF VISUAL PERCEPTION). ED052839
A DEVELOPMENTAL INVESTIGATION OF VISUAL AND HAPTIC PREFERENCES FOR SHAPE AND TEXTURE EJ 008 780
SUGGESTIBILITY IN RELATION TO SCHOOL GRADE, SEX, AND SOURCE OF INFLUENCE EJ 023 431
ENVIRONMENTAL DISCONTINUITY, STRESS, AND SEX - EFFECTS UPON SUSCEPTIBILITY TO SOCIAL INFLUENCE EJ 023 432
THE EFFECTS OF PERSONALITY VARIABLES ON DISTORTION THRESHOLDS IN THE AMES ROOM EJ 023 434

THE ROLE OF OBJECT ORIENTATION IN INFANT PERCEPTION EJ 024 695
BODY PROPORTIONS IN CHILDREN'S DRAWINGS OF A MAN EJ 025 305
VISUAL AND HAPTIC DIMENSIONAL PREFERENCE: A DEVELOPMENTAL STUDY EJ 026 506
A DEVELOPMENTAL INVESTIGATION OF THE EFFECT OF SENSORY MODALITY ON FORM RECOGNITION IN CHILDREN EJ 026 507
VISUAL ALERTNESS IN NEONATES AS EVOKED BY MATERNAL CARE EJ 027 847
A THIRD STUDY OF THE EFFECTS OF A LEARNING EXPERIENCE UPON PREFERENCE FOR COMPLEXITY-ASYMMETRY IN FOURTH, FIFTH, AND SIXTH GRADE CHILDREN EJ 029 281
HOW ADULTS AND CHILDREN SEARCH AND RECOGNIZE PICTURES EJ 029 384
DEVELOPMENTAL DIFFERENCES IN THE INTEGRATION OF PICTURE SERIES: EFFECTS OF VARIATIONS IN OBJECT-ATTRIBUTE RELATIONSHIPS EJ 029 386
SEQUENCE EFFECTS IN THE ABSTRACTION OF THE CONCEPT OF PROGRESSIVE CHANGE EJ 029 532
EFFECT OF CORRELATED VISUAL AND TACTUAL FEEDBACK ON AUDITORY PATTERN LEARNING AT DIFFERENT AGE LEVELS EJ 037 517
A NONARBITRARY BEHAVIORAL CRITERION FOR CONSERVATION OF ILLUSION-DISTORTED LENGTH IN FIVE-YEAR-OLDS EJ 038 263
"FOCAL" COLOR AREAS AND THE DEVELOPMENT OF COLOR NAMES EJ 039 057
THE INFLUENCE OF AGE AND STIMULUS DIMENSIONALITY ON FORM PERCEPTION BY PRESCHOOL CHILDREN EJ 039 630
THE CONTROL OF RELATIVE SIZE BY PICTORIAL DEPTH CUES IN CHILDREN AND ADULTS EJ 042 506
APPARENT VISUAL SIZE AS A FUNCTION OF AGE, INTELLIGENCE, AND A SURROUNDING FRAME OF REFERENCE FOR NORMAL AND MENTALLY RETARDED SUBJECTS EJ 043 704
METHODOLOGICAL STUDY OF FORM CONSTANCY DEVELOPMENT EJ 043 706
A STUDY OF RECOGNITION AND REPRODUCTION OF BENDER GESTALT FIGURES BY CHILDREN OF AVERAGE AND BELOW INTELLIGENCE EJ 043 707
ACCELERATING VISUAL COMPLEXITY LEVELS IN THE HUMAN INFANT EJ 045 598
ACCOMMODATION OF VISUAL TRACKING PATTERNS IN HUMAN INFANTS TO OBJECT MOVEMENT PATTERNS EJ 046 250
JUDGMENTS OF PATTERN GOODNESS AND PATTERN PREFERENCE AS FUNCTIONS OF AGE AND PATTERN UNCERTAINTY EJ 046 782
A MICRO-ANALYSIS OF MOTHER-INFANT INTERACTION. BEHAVIOR REGULATING SOCIAL CONTACT BETWEEN A MOTHER AND HER 3 1/2 MONTH-OLD TWINS EJ 048 300
EFFECTS OF PERCEPTUAL TRAINING ON CHILDREN'S HUMAN FIGURE DRAWINGS EJ 049 173
DEVELOPMENTAL DIFFERENCES IN THE FIELD OF VIEW DURING TACHISTOSCOPIC PRESENTATION EJ 053 743
CONTINUITY IN THE DEVELOPMENT OF VISUAL BEHAVIOR IN YOUNG INFANTS EJ 053 746
CROSS-MODAL MATCHING AMONG NORMAL AND RETARDED CHILDREN EJ 053 755
THE ROLE OF LIGHTNESS CONTRAST IN DETERMINING THE MAGNITUDE OF THE DELBOEUF ILLUSION: A REJOINDER TO WEINTRAUB AND COOPER EJ 055 101
INTERMODAL AND INTRAMODAL RETENTION OF VISUAL AND TACTUAL INFORMATION IN YOUNG CHILDREN EJ 057 900
A STUDY OF THE RELATIVE DOMINANCE OF VISION AND TOUCH IN SIX-MONTH-OLD INFANTS EJ 058 594
AGE DIFFERENCES IN VISUAL REACTION TIME OF "BRAIN DAMAGED" AND NORMAL CHILDREN UNDER IRREGULAR PREPARATORY INTERVAL CONDITIONS EJ 060 109

VISUAL STIMULI

A NEW THEORY OF SCRIBBLING AND DRAWING IN CHILDREN. ED017324
HEAD START EVALUATION AND RESEARCH CENTER, UNIVERSITY OF KANSAS. REPORT NO. IV, A COMPARISON OF FOUR MODES OF ELICITING BRIEF ORAL RESPONSES FROM CHILDREN. ED021637
STIMULUS DIMENSIONALITY AND MANIPULABILITY IN VISUAL PERCEPTUAL LEARNING. ED023452
NOVELTY AND FAMILIARITY AS DETERMINANTS OF INFANT ATTENTION WITHIN THE FIRST YEAR. ED023483
THE SHIFT FROM COLOR TO FORM PREFERENCE IN YOUNG CHILDRE N OF DIFFERENT ETHNIC BACKGROUNDS. PART OF THE FINAL REPORT. ED025321
ACQUISTION AND TRANSFER DIFFERENCES BETWEEN KINDERGARTENERS AND SECOND-GRADERS ON AURALLY AND VISUALLY PRESENTED PAIRED-ASSOCIATES USING AN A-B, A-C DESIGN RESEARCH PROJECT NUMBER 2 OF PROJECT HEAD START RESEARCH AND EVALUATION CENTER, SYRACUSE UNIVERSITY RESEARCH INSTITUTE. FINAL REPORT, NOVEMBER 1, 1967. ED026139
AN EXAMINATION OF CHANGES IN ATTITUDES TO VISUAL COMPLEXITY WITH INCREASING AGE. ED039930
ATTENTIONAL PREFERENCE AND EXPERIENCE: II. AN EXPLORATORY LONGITUDINAL STUDY OF THE EFFECTS OF VISUAL FAMILIARITY AND RESPONSIVENESS. ED039938
ATTENTIONAL PREFERENCE AND EXPERIENCE: III. VISUAL FAMILIARITY AND LOOKING TIME. ED039939
THE MEANING OF AN ORIENTING RESPONSE: A STUDY IN THE HIERARCHICAL ORDER OF ATTENDING. ED047794
NON-VERBAL INFORMATION STORAGE IN HUMANS AND DEVELOPMENTAL INFORMATION PROCESSING CHANNEL CAPACITY. ED047800
THE EFFECT OF VARYING OBJECT NUMBER AND TYPE OF ARRANGEMENT ON CHILDREN'S ABILITY TO COORDINATE PERSPECTIVES. ED047804
A DEVELOPMENTAL STUDY OF INFORMATION PROCESSING WITHIN THE FIRST THREE YEARS OF LIFE: RESPONSE DECREMENT TO A REDUNDANT SIGNAL EJ 013 947
ON RELATING AN INFANT'S OBSERVATION TIME OF VISUAL STIMULI WITH CHOICE-THEORY ANALYSIS EJ 019 016
THE EFFECTS OF A PAY-OFF MATRIX ON SELECTIVE ATTENTION EJ 023 436
SHORT-TERM MEMORY FOR VISUAL INFORMATION IN CHILDREN AND ADULTS EJ 024 700
ATTENTIONAL PREFERENCE AND EXPERIENCE: II. AN EXPLORATORY LONGITUDINAL STUDY OF THE EFFECT OF VISUAL FAMILIARITY AND RESPONSIVENESS EJ 025 363
ATTENTIONAL PREFERENCE AND EXPERIENCE: III. VISUAL FAMILIARITY AND LOOKING TIME EJ 025 364
NEWBORN ATTENTION: DIFFERENTIAL RESPONSE DECREMENT TO VISUAL STIMULI EJ 027 846
COMPLEXITY, CONTOUR, AND AREA AS DETERMINANTS OF ATTENTION IN INFANTS EJ 029 361
FIXATION TIME AND TEMPO OF PLAY IN INFANTS EJ 029 363
VISUAL ABILITIES AND PATTERN PREFERENCES OF PREMATURE INFANTS AND FULL-TERM NEONATES EJ 029 531
AGE-DEVELOPMENT IN THE LINEAR REPRESENTATION OF WORDS AND OBJECTS EJ 030 296
THE RELATIONSHIP BETWEEN AUDITORY AND VISUAL SHORT-TERM MEMORY AND READING ACHIEVEMENT EJ 033 780
SEQUENTIAL CONTIGUITY AND SHORT-TERM MEMORY IN CHILDREN'S DISCRIMINATION LEARNING EJ 033 790
A DECREMENTAL EFFECT OF REDUNDANCY IN DISCRIMINATION LEARNING EJ 033 795
ESTIMATES AND ESTIMATE-BASED INFERENCES IN YOUNG CHILDREN EJ 034 541
STIMULUS CORRELATES OF AREA JUDGMENTS: A PSYCHOPHYSICAL DEVELOPMENTAL STUDY EJ 034 707
DIMENSIONAL SALIENCE AND IDENTIFICATION OF THE RELEVANT DIMENSION IN PROBLEM SOLVING: A DEVELOPMENTAL STUDY EJ 035 360
FREE RECALL OF OBJECT NAMES IN PRESCHOOL CHILDREN AS A FUNCTION OF INTRACATEGORY VARIATION EJ 035 368
PATTERN COPYING UNDER THREE CONDITIONS OF AN EXPANDED SPATIAL FIELD EJ 035 622
AGE DIFFERENCES IN PLEASANTNESS OF VISUAL PATTERNS OF DIFFERENT VARIABILITY IN LATE CHILDHOOD AND ADOLESCENCE EJ 035 989
A DEVELOPMENTAL STUDY OF PRESCHOOL CHILDREN'S PREFERENCE FOR RANDOM FORMS EJ 035 990
INDIVIDUAL DIFFERENCES IN THE VISUAL PURSUIT BEHAVIOR OF NEONATES EJ 036 092
EFFECTS OF STIMULUS AVAILABILITY ON CHILDREN'S INFERENCES EJ 036 822
CONDITIONAL DISCRIMINATION LEARNING IN CHILDREN: TWO RELEVANT FACTORS EJ 036 823
INFANTS' RECOGNITION MEMORY FOR A SERIES OF VISUAL STIMULI EJ 037 342
DEVELOPMENTAL GENERALITY OF A FORM RECOGNITION STRATEGY EJ 037 534
DEVELOPMENT OF THE OBJECT CONCEPT AS MANIFESTED IN CHANGES IN THE TRACKING BEHAVIOR OF INFANTS BETWEEN 7 AND 20 WEEKS OF AGE EJ 038 264
DECISION PROCESSES IN MULTIDIMENSIONAL GENERALIZATION EJ 038 265
THE DEVELOPMENT OF COGNITIVE BALANCE AND THE TRANSITION FROM CONCRETE TO FORMAL OPERATIONAL THOUGHT EJ 041 145
INFANT HABITUATION AND GENERALIZATION TO DIFFERING DEGREES OF STIMULUS NOVELTY EJ 043 195
SATIATION OF VISUAL REINFORCEMENT IN YOUNG INFANTS EJ 043 666
EVIDENCE FOR COMPETITION AND COORDINATION BETWEEN VOCAL AND MANUAL RESPONSES IN PRESCHOOL CHILDREN EJ 043 668
DEVELOPMENT OF VISUAL SCANNING STRATEGIES FOR DIFFERENTIATING WORDS EJ 043 703
STIMULUS SELECTION AS A FUNCTION OF LETTER COLOR AND AGE IN PAIRED-ASSOCIATE LEARNING EJ 043 705
METHODOLOGICAL STUDY OF FORM CONSTANCY DEVELOPMENT EJ 043 706
VISUAL AND HAPTIC CUE UTILIZATION BY PRESCHOOL CHILDREN: THE RECOGNITION OF VISUAL AND HAPTIC STIMULI PRESENTED SEPARATELY AND TOGETHER EJ 044 698
THE EFFECTS OF VISUALLY REPRESENTED CUES ON LEARNING OF LINEAR FUNCTION RULES EJ 044 701
OBSERVATIONAL LEARNING: THE EFFECTS OF AGE, TASK DIFFICULTY, AND OBSERVERS' MOTORIC REHEARSAL EJ 044 702
ACCELERATING VISUAL COMPLEXITY LEVELS IN THE HUMAN INFANT EJ 045 598
JUDGING OUTLINE FACES: A DEVELOPMENTAL STUDY EJ 045 599
TRAINING AND GENERALIZATION OF DENSITY CONSERVATION: EFFECTS OF FEEDBACK AND CONSECUTIVE SIMILAR STIMULI EJ 046 231
REFLECTION-IMPULSIVITY AND COLOR-FORM SORTING EJ 046 234

DEVELOPMENTAL CHANGES IN VISUAL INFORMATION PROCESSING AND SHORT-TERM VISUAL MEMORY EJ 049 431
AGE, ICONIC STORAGE, AND VISUAL INFORMATION PROCESSING EJ 053 725
VISUAL RESPONSE DECREMENT AS A FUNCTION OF AGE OF HUMAN NEWBORNS EJ 056 716
HABITUATION AND RECOVERY OF VISUAL RESPONSE IN THE ALERT HUMAN NEWBORN EJ 057 116
VISUAL HABITUATION IN THE HUMAN INFANT EJ 059 511

FACILITATING AND INTERFERING EFFECTS OF STIMULUS NAMING ON CHILDREN'S MOTOR PAIRED-ASSOCIATE LEARNING EJ 033 793

VISUALIZATION
VISUAL IMAGERY INSTRUCTION AND NON-ACTION VERSUS ACTION SITUATIONS RELATIVE TO RECALL BY CHILDREN. FINAL REPORT. ED050828
FUNCTIONS OF VISUAL IMAGERY IN THE LEARNING AND CONCEPT FORMATION OF CHILDREN EJ 033 779
LABELING AND IMAGING AS AIDS TO MEMORY EJ 041 143
THE ROLE OF OVERT ACTIVITY IN CHILDREN'S IMAGERY PRODUCTION EJ 059 315

VISUALLY HANDICAPPED
A STUDY OF VISUAL PERCEPTIONS IN EARLY CHILDHOOD. ED023451
OPTOMETRIC CHILD VISION CARE AND GUIDANCE. A SERIES OF PAPERS RELEASED BY THE OPTOMETRIC EXTENSION PROGRAM TO ITS MEMBERSHIP 1966-1967. ED032111

VOCABULARY
PRELIMINARY RESULTS FROM RELATIONSHIP BETWEEN TEACHERS' VOCABULARY USAGE AND THE VOCABULARY OF KINDERGARTEN AND FIRST GRADE STUDENTS. ED032135
EFFECTS OF TRAINING YOUNG BLACK CHILDREN IN VOCABULARY VS. SENTENCE CONSTRUCTION. ED038176
WHAT DO YOU MEAN, "AUDITORY PERCEPTION"? EJ 013 560
TERMINOLOGY AND METHODOLOGY RELATED TO THE USE OF HEART RATE RESPONSIVITY IN INFANCY RESEARCH EJ 034 566
KINDERGARTEN CHILDREN'S ACTIVE VOCABULARY ABOUT BODY BUILD EJ 041 857
A BASIC VOCABULARY FOR BEGINNING READING EJ 047 894
A CHILD-CENTERED DICTIONARY EJ 053 506

VOCABULARY DEVELOPMENT
A REPLICATIVE INVESTIGATION OF THE BUCKINGHAM-DOLCH FREE-ASSOCIATION WORD STUDY. FINAL REPORT. ED017333
PRE-READING ON SESAME STREET. FINAL REPORT, VOLUME V OF V VOLUMES. ED047825
ANALYSIS OF INTELLIGENCE SCORES. ED052838
THE EFFECTS OF DIFFERENTIATED INSTRUCTION IN VISUO-MOTOR SKILLS ON DEVELOPMENTAL GROWTH AND READING READINESS AT KINDERGARTEN LEVEL. FINAL REPORT. ED053821
LONGITUDINAL STUDY OF COGNITIVE DICTIONARIES FROM AGES NINE TO SEVENTEEN EJ 024 940
THE CAMERA FOCUSES ON READING EJ 032 192

VOCABULARY SKILLS
DIFFERENCES IN VOCABULARY INPUT-OUTPUT IN PSYCHODIAGNOSIS OF CHILDREN. ED024450

VOCATIONAL EDUCATION
DIRECTED RESEARCH PROGRAM IN READING, EARLY CHILDHOOD, VOCATIONAL EDUCATION, SCHOOL ORGANIZATION AND ADMINISTRATION, FY 72 - FY 76. ED051871
TRAINING WORKERS FOR CHILD CARE CENTERS EJ 050 935

VOLUNTEER TRAINING
A TRAINING PROGRAM FOR VOLUNTEERS EJ 028 502

VOLUNTEERS
A STUDY IN CHILD CARE (CASE STUDY FROM VOLUME II-A) ED051905
A STUDY IN CHILD CARE (CASE STUDY FROM VOLUME II-B): "THEY BRAG ON A CHILD TO MAKE HIM FEEL GOOD." DAY CARE PROGRAMS REPRINT SERIES. ED051910
VOLUNTEERING TO HELP INDIANS HELP THEMSELVES EJ 032 412
COMMUNITY PARTICIPATION IN PRESCHOOL EDUCATION--WHY AND HOW EJ 036 331
SOURCES OF MANPOWER FOR THE PRESCHOOL CLASSROOM EJ 049 526
PROJECT PLAYPEN -- PRIMARY PREVENTION EJ 058 213
A YOUNG MAN AROUND THE CLASS EJ 059 445

WELFARE AGENCIES
SCHOOL COUNSELING BY CONTRACT EJ 038 985
A PARENTING SCALE AND SEPARATION DECISIONS EJ 039 286
THE CHILD WELFARE AGENCY AS THE EXTENDED FAMILY EJ 052 493

WELFARE SERVICES
PROJECT TREAT: A NEW APPROACH TO THE SEVERELY DISTURBED CHILD EJ 061 000

WOLOF
ORAL OR WRITTEN LANGUAGE--THE CONSEQUENCES FOR COGNITIVE DEVELOPMENT IN AFRICA AND THE UNITED STATES. ED018279

WOMENS EDUCATION
CHANGE IN EFFICIENCY OF EGO FUNCTIONING AND COMPLEXITY FROM ADOLESCENCE TO YOUNG ADULTHOOD EJ 039 902

WOODWORKING
CARPENTRY FOR YOUNG CHILDREN EJ 044 512

WORD RECOGNITION
IMPLICIT VERBAL BEHAVIOR IN ELEMENTARY SCHOOL CHILDREN, (INTERNAL VERBAL RESPONSES OF ELEMENTARY SCHOOL CHILDREN ELICITED BY THE ASSOCIATION OF WORDS). FINAL REPORT. ED028848
PRELIMINARY RESULTS FROM RELATIONSHIP BETWEEN TEACHERS' VOCABULARY USAGE AND THE VOCABULARY OF KINDERGARTEN AND FIRST GRADE STUDENTS. ED032135
TRAINING ELEMENTARY READING SKILLS THROUGH REINFORCEMENT AND FADING TECHNIQUES. ED034583
SEMANTIC AND PHONETIC RELATIONS IN THE FALSE RECOGNITION OF WORDS BY THIRD- AND SIXTH-GRADE CHILDREN EJ 026 374
WORD ASSOCIATION AND DEFINITION IN MIDDLE CHILDHOOD EJ 030 294
RECOGNITION OF FLASHED WORDS BY CHILDREN EJ 032 676
KNOWLEDGE OF ACTION AND OBJECT WORDS: A COMPARISON OF LOWER-AND MIDDLE-CLASS NEGRO PRESCHOOLERS EJ 040 453
ANTICIPATORY IMAGERY AND MODIFIED ANAGRAM SOLUTIONS: A DEVELOPMENTAL STUDY EJ 041 141
VERBAL PAIRED-ASSOCIATE LEARNING IN CHILDREN AND ADULTS WITH ANTICIPATION, RECOGNITION, AND RECALL METHODS EJ 042 959
THE DEVELOPMENT OF MEMORY-ENCODING PROCESSES IN YOUNG CHILDREN EJ 053 716

WORK ATTITUDES
ROLE PERCEPTIONS AND JOB SATISFACTION AMONG LOWER AND MIDDLE LEVEL JUNIOR COLLEGE ADMINISTRATORS EJ 016 774

WORK EXPERIENCE
THE RELATIONSHIP BETWEEN SPECIFIC AND GENERAL TEACHING EXPERIENCE AND TEACHER ATTITUDES TOWARD PROJECT HEAD START. PART OF THE FINAL REPORT. ED025323

WORKING PARENTS
THE UNSUPERVISED CHILD OF THE WORKING MOTHER EJ 053 709
PROJECT PLAYPEN -- PRIMARY PREVENTION EJ 058 213

WORKING WOMEN
CHILD CARE ARRANGEMENTS OF WORKING MOTHERS IN THE UNITED STATES. ED040738
CHILD CARE AND WORKING MOTHERS: A STUDY OF ARRANGEMENTS MADE FOR DAYTIME CARE OF CHILDREN. ED045175
SANTA MONICA CHILDREN'S CENTERS, SANTA MONICA, CALIFORNIA: LOW-COST DAY CARE FACILITIES FOR CHILDREN OF WORKING MOTHERS MADE AVAILABLE THROUGH THE COOPERATION OF THE CALIFORNIA STATE GOVERNMENT AND LOCAL SCHOOL DISTRICT. MODEL PROGRAMS--CHILDHOOD EDUCATION. ED045212
NEIGHBORHOOD HOUSE CHILD CARE SERVICES, SEATTLE, WASHINGTON: SEATTLE'S ANSWER TO CHILD CARE PROBLEMS OF LOW-INCOME FAMILIES. MODEL PROGRAMS--CHILDHOOD EDUCATION. ED045213
FEDERAL INVOLVEMENT IN DAY CARE. ED048931
NEIGHBORHOOD FAMILY DAY CARE AS A CHILD-REARING ENVIRONMENT. ED049840
THE DAY CARE CHALLENGE: THE UNMET NEEDS OF MOTHERS AND CHILDREN. ED050821
WORKING MOTHERS AND THEIR CHILDREN EJ 028 793
THE CHILD'S RIGHT TO QUALITY DAY CARE: AN ACEI POSITION PAPER EJ 029 103
CLINICAL IMPLICATIONS OF MATERNAL EMPLOYMENT: A REVIEW OF RESEARCH EJ 030 432
UNIONS AND DAY CARE CENTERS FOR THE CHILDREN OF WORKING MOTHERS EJ 038 643

WORKSHOPS
THE CREATIVE ENVIRONMENT WORKSHOP EJ 035 168

WORLD PROBLEMS
DEVELOPING MANPOWER FOR THE WORLD'S SOCIAL WELFARE NEEDS. SOME OBSERVATIONS FROM THE CONFERENCE OF MINISTERS RESPONSIBLE FOR SOCIAL WELFARE.. EJ 004 093

WRITING SKILLS
ENCOURAGEMENT FOR THE YOUNG WRITER EJ 029 414
READING, WRITING, AND BLACK ENGLISH EJ 052 178

WRITTEN LANGUAGE
AN OBJECTIVE MEASURE OF STRUCTURAL COMPLEXITY IN CHILDREN'S WRITING. ED016534

YOUNG ADULTS
VERBAL RECALL AS A FUNCTION OF PERSONALITY CHARACTERISTICS EJ 054 806

YOUTH
FEDERAL PROGRAMS ASSISTING CHILDREN AND YOUTH. ED028840
FEDERAL PROGRAMS ASSISTING CHILDREN AND YOUTH. REVISED EDITION. ED038161
WHAT DO YOUNG PEOPLE WANT? EJ 011 784

YOUTH PROBLEMS
THE EDUCATION OF YOUNG CHILDREN: AT THE CROSSROADS? EJ 013 229
CERTAIN CULTURAL AND FAMILIAL FACTORS CONTRIBUTING TO ADOLESCENT ALIENATION EJ 022 536
"YOUTH UNREST": REFLECTIONS OF A PSYCHOANALYST EJ 023 425
ALIENATION OF PRESENT-DAY ADOLESCENTS EJ 023 428
DRUG USE AMONG THE YOUNG: AS TEENAGERS SEE IT EJ 029 950
BRIDGING THE CONCEPT GAP IN WORK WITH YOUTH EJ 031 644
TEENAGERS DISCUSS AGE RESTRICTIONS EJ 046 786

YOUTH PROGRAMS
A SOCIAL WORK MISSION TO HIPPIELAND EJ 004 092

AUTHOR INDEX

AARON, DAVID
CHILD'S PLAY, A CREATIVE APPROACH TO PLAYSPACES FOR TODAY'S CHILDREN. ED021630

ABBOTT, MARGARET, COMP.
RESOURCES FOR ENVIRONMENTAL EDUCATORS: ECOLOGY AND TEACHERS EJ 029 392

ABELES, GINA
INFANCY IN HOLLAND: THE FIRST THREE MONTHS. ED031296

ABLES, BILLIE
THE THREE WISHES OF LATENCY AGE CHILDREN EJ 053 652

ABRAMS, NAOMI
CHILDHOOD PSYCHOSIS COMBINED WITH XYZ ABNORMALITIES EJ 035 078

ABRAVANEL, EUGENE
AN EXAMINATION OF THE DEVELOPMENTAL RELATIONS BETWEEN CERTAIN SPATIAL TASKS EJ 051 563

ACHENBACH, THOMAS M.
"CONSERVATION" BELOW AGE THREE: FACT OR ARTIFACT? ED035438
STANDARDIZATION OF A RESEARCH INSTRUMENT FOR IDENTIFYING ASSOCIATIVE RESPONDING IN CHILDREN EJ 019 021
THE CHILDREN'S ASSOCIATIVE RESPONDING TEST: A TWO-YEAR FOLLOW-UP EJ 047 683

ACKERMAN, SATOKO I.
LIVING AND LEARNING: AN ANNOTATED BIBLIOGRAPHY FOR THOSE WHO LIVE AND LEARN WITH YOUNG CHILDREN. ED032935

ADAIR, THELMA
CHOICES, CHOICES, CHOICES! PEAK EXPERIENCES FROM THE AFRO-AMERICAN HERITAGE EJ 020 857

ADAMS, JANICE FREEMAN
LEARNING TO LEARN ON A CONCEPT ATTAINMENT TASK AS A FUNCTION OF AGE AND SOCIOECONOMIC LEVEL. REPORT FROM THE PROJECT ON SITUATIONAL VARIABLES AND EFFICIENCY OF CONCEPT LEARNING. ED046505
VERBAL AND IMAGERY PROCESSES IN CHILDREN'S PAIRED-ASSOCIATE LEARNING EJ 024 699

ADAMS, JOHN E.
A FRESH LOOK AT INTERCOUNTRY ADOPTIONS EJ 047 968

ADAMS, MARGARET E.
FOSTER CARE FOR MENTALLY RETARDED CHILDREN: HOW DOES CHILD WELFARE MEET THIS CHALLENGE? EJ 020 859

ADAMS, PAUL L.
THE IMPACT OF CHANGE. A REBUTTAL EJ 011 983

ADAMS, RAYMOND S.
LOCATION AS A FEATURE OF INSTRUCTIONAL INTERACTION EJ 012 717

ADAMS, RUSSEL L.
MOTIVATIONAL AND ACHIEVEMENT DIFFERENCES AMONG CHILDREN OF VARIOUS ORDINAL BIRTH POSITIONS EJ 055 547

ADCOCK, CAROLYN
SUCCESSFUL NUMBER CONSERVATION TRAINING. ED031297

ADELSON, RICHARD
MODELING AND THE FEARFUL CHILD PATIENT EJ 058 354

ADKINS, DOROTHY
MEASUREMENT OF MOTIVATION TO ACHIEVE IN PRESCHOOL CHILDREN. FINAL REPORT. ED021617

ADKINS, DOROTHY C.
PRELIMINARY EVALUATION OF A LANGUAGE CURRICULUM FOR PRESCHOOL CHILDREN. FINAL REPORT. ED021618
DEVELOPMENT OF A PRESCHOOL LANGUAGE-ORIENTED CURRICULUM WITH A STRUCTURED PARENT EDUCATION PROGRAM. FINAL REPORT. ED028845
PRESCHOOL MATHEMATICS CURRICULUM PROJECT. FINAL REPORT. ED038168
HAWAII HEAD START EVALUATION--1968-69. FINAL REPORT. ED042511
HAWAII HEAD START EVALUATION FOLLOW-UP--1968-69. FINA L REPORT. ED042515
FIELD TEST OF THE UNIVERSITY OF HAWAII PRESCHOOL LANGUAGE CURRICULUM. FINAL REPORT. ED048924
PROGRAMS OF HEAD START PARENT INVOLVEMENT IN HAWAII. A SECTION OF THE FINAL REPORT FOR 1969-70. ED048935

ADLER, JACK
INTERPERSONAL RELATIONSHIPS IN RESIDENTIAL TREATMENT CENTERS FOR DISTURBED CHILDREN EJ 037 183

AHAMMER, INGE M.
DESIRABILITY JUDGMENTS AS A FUNCTION OF ITEM CONTENT, INSTRUCTIONAL SET, AND SET: A LIFE-SPAN DEVELOPMENTAL STUDY EJ 048 473

AHLBRAND, WILLIAM P., JR.
SOME SOCIAL EFFECTS OF CROSS-GRADE GROUPING EJ 055 107

AHR, A. EDWARD
PARENT HANDBOOK: DEVELOPING YOUR CHILD'S SKILLS AND ABILITIES AT HOME. ED036327

AHR, PAUL R.
REASONS FOR FAILURE ON THE CLASS INCLUSION PROBLEM EJ 018 872

AINSWORTH, MARY D. SALTER
INDIVIDUAL DIFFERENCES IN THE DEVELOPMENT OF SOME ATTACHMENT BEHAVIORS. ED050827
ATTACHMENT, EXPLORATION, AND SEPARATION: ILLUSTRATED BY THE BEHAVIOR OF ONE-YEAR-OLDS IN A STRANGE SITUATION EJ 018 320
INDIVIDUAL DIFFERENCES IN THE DEVELOPMENT OF SOME ATTACHMENT BEHAVIORS EJ 058 222

AIRASIAN, PETER W.
THE USE OF HIERARCHIES IN CURRICULUM ANALYSIS AND INSTRUCTIONAL PLANNING EJ 033 574

AKAMATSU, T. JOHN
THE ACQUISITION AND PERFORMANCE OF A SOCIALLY NEUTRAL RESPONSE AS A FUNCTION OF VICARIOUS REWARD EJ 046 889

AKERS, MILTON E.
THE EXECUTIVE DIRECTOR'S TESTIMONY BEFORE THE HOUSE EDUCATION AND LABOR COMMITTEE EJ 017 848

ALDEN, STEVEN E.
THE EFFECT OF INDIVIDUAL-CONTINGENT GROUP REINFORCEMENT ON POPULARITY EJ 034 158

ALDOUS, JOAN
CHILDREN'S PERCEPTIONS OF ADULT ROLES AS AFFECTED BY CLASS, FATHER-ABSENCE AND RACE. ED032134

ALEXANDER, LLOYD
LITERATURE, CREATIVITY AND IMAGINATION EJ 033 510

ALEXANDER, ROBERT
DEVELOPMENT OF A THEATRE ARTS CURRICULUM FOR YOUNG CHILDREN. CAREL ARTS AND HUMANITIES CURRICULUM DEVELOPMENT PROGRAM FOR YOUNG CHILDREN. ED032937

ALEXANDER, THERON
DIFFERENTIATION BETWEEN NORMAL AND DISORDERED CHILDREN BY A COMPUTER ANALYSIS OF EMOTIONAL AND VERBAL BEHAVIOR. ED019138
EMOTIONAL CHARACTERISTICS OF DISADVANTAGED CHILDREN OF APPALACHIA. ED043383
CHILD DEVELOPMENT RESEARCH AND EVALUATION CENTER FOR HEAD START, TEMPLE UNIVERSITY, 1968 - 1969. ANNUAL REPORT. ED043388
DEVELOPMENTAL CHARACTERISTICS OF EMOTIONAL EXPERIENCE EJ 043 860

ALEXANIAN, SANDRA
HEAD START EVALUATION AND RESEARCH CENTER, BOSTON UNIVERSITY. REPORT D-I, LANGUAGE PROJECT: THE EFFECTS OF A TEACHER DEVELOPED PRE-SCHOOL LANGUAGE TRAINING PROGRAM ON FIRST GRADE READING ACHIEVEMENT. ED022563
HEAD START EVALUATION AND RESEARCH CENTER, BOSTON UNIVERSITY. REPORT E-II, TEACHER SEMINAR. ED022567

ALIOTTI, NICHOLAS C.
SOME DIMENSIONS OF CREATIVE THINKING ABILITY ACHIEVEMENT, AND INTELLIGENCE IN FIRST GRADE. ED028818

ALISSI, ALBERT S.
BRIDGING THE CONCEPT GAP IN WORK WITH YOUTH EJ 031 644

ALKIN, MARVIN C.
A REVIEW OF THE EVALUATION OF THE FOLLOW THROUGH PROGRAM. ED041642

ALLEN, AUDRIANNA
CONFRONTING PERSISTENT CONCERNS EJ 054 382

ALLEN, JAMES E., JR.
EDUCATION FOR SURVIVAL. ED039021
LOOKING FORWARD TO THE SEVENTIES EJ 009 029

ALLEN, P. DAVID
CUE SYSTEMS AVAILABLE DURING THE READING PROCESS: A PSYCHOLINGUISTIC VIEWPOINT EJ 053 399

ALLEN, R. V.
LEARNING TO READ THROUGH EXPERIENCE. SECOND EDITION. ED027067

ALLEN, ROBERT M.
A STUDY OF RECOGNITION AND REPRODUCTION OF BENDER GESTALT FIGURES BY CHILDREN OF AVERAGE AND BELOW INTELLIGENCE EJ 043 707

ALLEN, SARA A.
EFFECTS OF SOCIAL REINFORCEMENT ON LEARNING AND RETENTION IN CHILDREN EJ 042 957

ALLEN, TERRY WALTER
TRAINING AND GENERALIZATION OF DENSITY CONSERVATION: EFFECTS OF FEEDBACK AND CONSECUTIVE SIMILAR STIMULI EJ 046 231

ALLENDER, JEROME S.
THE TEACHING OF INQUIRY SKILLS TO ELEMENTARY SCHOOL CHILDREN. FINAL REPORT. ED020805

ALLERHAND, MELVIN E.
IMPACT OF SUMMER 1965 HEAD START ON CHILDREN'S CONCEPT ATTAINMENT DURING KINDERGARTEN. FINAL REPORT. ED015773
HEADSTART OPERATIONAL FIELD ANALYSIS. PROGRESS REPORT I. ED015774
HEADSTART OPERATIONAL FIELD ANALYSIS. PROGRESS REPORT II. ED015775
HEADSTART OPERATIONAL FIELD ANALYSIS. PROGRESS REPORT III. ED015776
HEADSTART OPERATIONAL FIELD ANALYSIS. PROGRESS REPORT IV. ED015777

ALLEY, GORDON R.
COMPARATIVE PERCEPTUAL MOTOR PERFORMANCE OF NEGRO AND WHITE YOUNG MENTAL RETARDATES EJ 019 015

ALLGAIER, JANET FAGAN, COMP.
A BRIEF GUIDE TO NEWSLETTERS IN EARLY CHILDHOOD EDUCATION. ED048932

ALMQUIST, ELIZABETH M.
ROLE MODEL INFLUENCES ON COLLEGE WOMEN'S CAREER ASPIRATIONS EJ 041 632

ALMY, MILLIE
YOUNG CHILDREN'S THINKING, STUDIES OF SOME ASPECTS OF PIAGET'S THEORY. ED013662
SPONTANEOUS PLAY: AN AVENUE FOR INTELLECTUAL DEVELOPMENT. ED023444
LOGICAL THINKING IN SECOND GRADE. FINAL REPORT. ED033747

ALPERN, GERALD D.
METHODOLIGICAL CONSIDERATIONS IN DEVISING HEAD START PROGRAM EVALUATIONS. ED025319

ALTMAN, KARL
EFFECTS OF COOPERATIVE RESPONSE ACQUISITION ON SOCIAL BEHAVIOR DURING FREE-PLAY EJ 048 297

AMBRON, SUEANN R.
SUBPOPULATIONAL PROFILING OF THE PSYCHOEDUCATIONAL DIMENSIONS OF DISADVANTAGED PRESCHOOL CHILDREN: A CONCEPTUAL PROSPECTUS FOR AN INTERDISCIPLINARY RESEARCH. ED045177

AMENT, AARON
THE BOY WHO DID NOT CRY EJ 052 310

AMES, ELINOR W.
METHODOLOGICAL ISSUES IN THE STUDY OF AGE DIFFERENCES IN INFANTS' ATTENTION TO STIMULI VARYING IN MOVEMENT AND COMPLEXITY. ED023477

AMES, LOUISE BATES
SCHOOL READINESS, BEHAVIOR TESTS USED AT THE GESELL INSTITUTE. ED023449

AMIDON, JEANETTE
DEVELOPMENT OF A LITERATURE CURRICULUM FOR YOUNG CHILDREN. CAREL ARTS AND HUMANITIES CURRICULUM DEVELOPMENT PROGRAM FOR YOUNG CHILDREN. ED032940

AMMON, MARY SUE
EFFECTS OF TRAINING YOUNG BLACK CHILDREN IN VOCABULARY VS. SENTENCE CONSTRUCTION. ED038176

AMMON, PAUL R.
EFFECTS OF TRAINING YOUNG BLACK CHILDREN IN VOCABULARY VS. SENTENCE CONSTRUCTION. ED038176

ANANDALAKSHMY, S.
CONCEPTUAL EMPHASIS IN THE HISTORY OF DEVELOPMENTAL PSYCHOLOGY: EVOLUTIONARY THEORY, TELEOLOGY, AND THE NATURE-NURTURE ISSUE EJ 034 043
A PERSPECTIVE ON COGNITIVE DEVELOPMENT: THE PRESCHOOL CHILD'S PERFORMANCE IN CLASSIFICATION TASKS EJ 036 827

ANASTASI, ANNE
THE FRANCK DRAWING COMPLETION TEST AS A MEASURE OF CREATIVITY EJ 044 704

ANDERS, TERRY R.
EFFECTS OF AGE UPON RETRIEVAL FROM SHORT-TERM MEMORY EJ 055 109

ANDERSEN, DAN W.
MICRO-TEACHING FOR PREPARING TEACHERS OF CULTURALLY DIVERSE CHILDREN EJ 052 068

ANDERSON, JESSIE T.
GUIDE FOR TEACHING PHYSICAL EDUCATION, GRADES 1-6. ED019126

ANDERSON, RICHARD C.
AN ANALYSIS OF A CLASS OF PROBLEM SOLVING BEHAVIOR. FINAL REPORT. ED020776

ANDERSON, SCARVIA B.
PROJECT HEAD START--SUMMER 1966. FINAL REPORT. SECTION THREE, PUPILS AND PROGRAMS. ED018248
THE MAKING OF A PUPIL: CHANGING CHILDREN INTO SCHOOL CHILDREN. ED037235

ANDREWS, FRANCES M.
DEVELOPMENT OF A TECHNIQUE FOR IDENTIFYING ELEMENTARY SCHOOL CHILDREN'S MUSICAL CONCEPTS. FINAL REPORT. ED016517

ANDREWS, HENRY B., JR.
THE SYSTEMATIC USE OF THE PEMACK PRINCIPLE IN MODIFYING CLASSROOM BEHAVIORS EJ 034 528

ANDREWS, J. EDWARD, JR.
LOOKING BEYOND THE STRIKES EJ 003 630

ANDREWS, ROBERTA G.
WHEN IS SUBSIDIZED ADOPTION PREFERABLE TO LONG-TERM FOSTER CARE? EJ 035 949

ANDRONICO, MICHAEL P.
CASE CONFERENCE: A PSYCHOTHERAPEUTIC AIDE IN A HEADSTART PROGRAM. I. THEORY AND PRACTICE EJ 003 955

ANGRIST, SHIRLEY S.
ROLE MODEL INFLUENCES ON COLLEGE WOMEN'S CAREER ASPIRATIONS EJ 041 632

ANISFELD, MOSHE
SEMANTIC AND PHONETIC RELATIONS IN THE FALSE RECOGNITION OF WORDS BY THIRD- AND SIXTH-GRADE CHILDREN EJ 026 374

ANTES, JOHN M.
STUDYING HUMAN ECOLOGY: TEACHER EDUCATION AND THE CULTURALLY DIVERSE EJ 048 395
MICRO-TEACHING FOR PREPARING TEACHERS OF CULTURALLY DIVERSE CHILDREN EJ 052 068

ANTTONEN, RALPH C.
TEACHER EXPECTANCY OR MY FAIR LADY. ED038183

ANTTONEN, RALPH G.
TEACHER EXPECTANCY AS RELATED TO THE ACADEMIC AND PERSONAL GROWTH OF PRIMARY-AGE CHILDREN EJ 057 018

ANYAN, WALTER R., JR.
THE NAMING OF PRIMARY COLORS BY CHILDREN EJ 053 483

APLEY, JOHN
SLEEP PROBLEMS EJ 011 345

APPLEBEE, ARTHUR N.
RESEARCH IN READING RETARDATION: TWO CRITICAL PROBLEMS EJ 045 108

ARASTEH, JOSEPHINE D.
PARENTHOOD: SOME ANTECEDENTS AND CONSEQUENCES: A PRELIMINARY SURVEY OF THE MENTAL HEALTH LITERATURE EJ 041 342

ARMENTROUT, JAMES A.
A FACTOR ANALYSIS OF FIFTH AND SIXTH GRADERS' REPORTS OF PARENTAL CHILD-REARING BEHAVIOR EJ 038 855
EFFECTS OF PERCEPTUAL TRAINING ON CHILDREN'S HUMAN FIGURE DRAWINGS EJ 049 173
CHILDREN'S REPORTS OF PARENTAL CHILD-REARING BEHAVIOR AT FIVE GRADE LEVELS EJ 060 385

ARMINGTON, DAVID
LEICESTERSHIRE REVISITED. ED029683

ARMINGTON, DAVID E.
A PLAN FOR CONTINUING GROWTH. ED046493

ARMSBY, RICHARD E.
A REEXAMINATION OF THE DEVELOPMENT OF MORAL JUDGMENTS IN CHILDREN EJ 052 456

ARMSTRONG, ROBERT J.
A SHORT, RELIABLE, EASY TO ADMINISTER INDIVIDUAL INTELLIGENCE TEST FOR SPECIAL CLASS PLACEMENT EJ 041 724

ARNER, ROBERT S.
A RATIONALE FOR DEVELOPMENTAL TESTING AND TRAINING. ED028835

ARNOLD, CAROLE REVELLE
ROLE OF DISCRIMINATIVE STIMULI IN THE FORMATION OF FUNCTIONAL RESPONSE CLASSES EJ 024 937

ARNOLD, IRENE L.
RESEARCH FOR SERVICE TO SEVERELY RETARDED CHILDREN EJ 038 531

ARNOLD, RICHARD D.
SAN ANTONIO LANGUAGE RESEARCH PROJECT, 1965-66 (YEAR TWO) FINDINGS. ED022528
MEXICAN-AMERICANS AND LANGUAGE LEARNING EJ 012 397
AUDITORY DISCRIMINATION ABILITIES OF DISADVANTAGED ANGLO- AND MEXICAN-AMERICAN CHILDREN EJ 015 258

ARTLEY, A. STERL
READING INSTRUCTION AND COGNITIVE DEVELOPMENT EJ 052 066

ASCH, HARVEY
HEAD START EVALUATION AND RESEARCH CENTER. PROGRESS REPORT OF RESEARCH STUDIES 1966 TO 1967. DOCUMENT 1, DEVELOPMENT OF THE MATRIX TEST. ED021623

ASCHER, MICHELLE
THE RELATIONSHIP BETWEEN THE TEACHER AND THE TAUGHT. FIRST IMPRESSIONS OF A STUDENT TEACHER EJ 011 839

ASCHNER, MARY JANE, ED.
PRODUCTIVE THINKING IN EDUCATION. ED024459

ASHEAR, VICTOR
EYE CONTACT IN CHILDREN AS A FUNCTION OF AGE, SEX, SOCIAL AND INTELLECTIVE VARIABLES EJ 038 943

ASHTON, R.
THE EFFECTS OF THE ENVIRONMENT UPON STATE CYCLES IN THE HUMAN NEWBORN EJ 044 119
BEHAVIORAL SLEEP CYCLES IN THE HUMAN NEWBORN EJ 056 722

ASPY, DAVID N.
THE EFFECT OF TEACHERS' INFERRED SELF CONCEPT UPON STUDENT ACHIEVEMENT. ED031300

ASSO, DOREEN
DISCRIMINATION OF SPATIALLY CONFUSABLE LETTERS BY YOUNG CHILDREN EJ 034 565

ATEMA, JAN M.
AGE OF SUBJECT, TYPE OF SOCIAL CONTACT, AND RESPONSIVENESS TO SOCIAL REINFORCEMENT EJ 055 093

ATHEY, IRENE
THE CHILD'S EYE VIEW: EXPERIMENTAL PHOTOGRAPHY WITH PRESCHOOL CHILDREN EJ 029 342

AUG, ROBERT G.
A STUDY OF WED AND UNWED MOTHERHOOD IN ADOLESCENTS AND YOUNG ADULTS EJ 030 715

AURBACH, HERBERT A.
THE USEFULNESS OF CUMULATIVE DEPRIVATION AS AN EXPLANATION OF EDUCATIONAL DEFICIENCIES EJ 033 056

AUSTRIN, HARVEY R.
FACTORS RELATED TO SCHOOL ACHIEVEMENT IN AN ECONOMICALLY DISADVANTAGED GROUP EJ 056 614

AUSUBEL, DAVID P.
THE INTERSITUATIONAL GENERALITY OF FORMAL THOUGHT EJ 015 097

AVEN, SAMUEL D.
A STUDY IN THE USE OF A PROGRAMMED GEOGRAPHY UNIT EJ 016 930

AVERILL, BONNIE E.
EFFECTS OF TYPE AND SOURCE OF LABELS ON CHILDREN'S PERCEPTUAL JUDGMENTS AND DISCRIMINATION LEARNING EJ 053 756

AVILA, DON
CLASSROOM DISCIPLINE: A NEW APPROACH EJ 032 896

AWE, RUTH
A BIBLIOGRAPHY OF RESEARCH ON FOREIGN STUDENT AFFAIRS. ED021629

AYRES, A. JEAN
EFFECT OF SENSORIMOTOR ACTIVITY ON PERCEPTION AND LEARNING IN THE NEUROLOGICALLY HANDICAPPED CHILD. FINAL PROGRESS REPORT. ED033757

AZARNOFF, PAT
A PLAY PROGRAM IN A PEDIATRIC CLINIC EJ 029 951

BABAD, ELISHA Y.
PERSON SPECIFICITY OF THE "SOCIAL DEPRIVATION-SATIATION EFFECT" EJ 055 207

BABSON, S. GORHAM
PRESCHOOL INTELLIGENCE OF OVERSIZED NEWBORNS. ED034582

BADGER, EARLADEEN
MOTHERS' TRAINING PROGRAM: EDUCATIONAL INTERVENTION BY THE MOTHERS OF DISADVANTAGED INFANTS. ED043378
ACTIVITIES FOR INFANT STIMULATION OR MOTHER-INFANT GAMES. ED046510

BADGER, EARLADEEN D.
MOTHERS' TRAINING PROGRAM: THE GROUP PROCESS. ED032926
A MOTHERS' TRAINING PROGRAM--THE ROAD TO A PURPOSEFUL EXISTENCE EJ 044 007

BAER, DONALD M.
HEAD START EVALUATION AND RESEARCH CENTER, UNIVERSITY OF KANSAS. REPORT NO. VI, A FAILURE TO SHOW AND INVOLVEMENT OF CURRENT MOTIVATIONAL VARIABLES IN THE RESPONSE OF HEAD START CHILDREN IN THE ASSESSMENT OF INTELLIGENCE BY MEANS OF THE STANFORD BINET TEST. ED021639
REINFORCEMENT GROWS UP: THE EXPERIMENTAL ANALYSIS OF BEHAVIOR AS A SYSTEMATIC APPROACH TO THE TEACHING OF DEVELOPMENTAL PSYCHOLOGY. ED023479
AN AGE-IRRELEVANT CONCEPT OF DEVELOPMENT EJ 027 437
EFFECTS OF CONCURRENT AND SERIAL TRAINING ON GENERALIZED VOCAL IMITATION IN RETARDED CHILDREN EJ 055 210

BAGLEY, CHRISTOPHER
PSYCHIATRIC DISORDER AND ADULT AND PEER GROUP REJECTION OF THE CHILD'S NAME EJ 026 156

BAGUR, J. SUSANA
CONSIDERATIONS FOR THE STUDY OF LANGUAGE IN YOUNG LOW-INCOME MINORITY GROUP CHILDREN EJ 052 440

BAHM, ROBERT M.
FATHER ABSENCE, PERCEIVED MATERNAL BEHAVIOR, AND MASCULINITY OF SELF-CONCEPT AMONG JUNIOR HIGH SCHOOL BOYS EJ 035 804

BAKER, NANCY E.
THE INFUENCE OF SOME TASK VARIABLES AND OF SOCIOECONOMIC CLASS ON THE MANIFESTATION OF CONSERVATION OF NUMBER EJ 017 711

BAKER, WILLIAM E.
THE CREATIVE ENVIRONMENT WORKSHOP EJ 035 168

BAKKER, D. J.
THE PART PLAYED BY MEDIATION PROCESSES IN THE RETENTION OF TEMPORAL SEQUENCES BY TWO READING GROUPS EJ 039 909

BALDWIN, A. L.
SYNTACTIC COMPLEXITY IN MOTHER-CHILD INTERACTIONS. ED035454

BALDWIN, ALFRED L.
CHILDREN'S JUDGMENTS OF KINDNESS EJ 018 259

BALDWIN, CLARA P.
INFORMATION EXCHANGE IN MOTHER-CHILD INTERACTIONS. ED034599
CHILDREN'S JUDGMENTS OF KINDNESS EJ 018 259

BALDWIN, THELMA L.
CHILDREN'S COMMUNICATION ACCURACY RELATED TO RACE AND SOCIOECONOMIC STATUS EJ 040 359

BALDWIN, VIRGINIA
INTEGRATED, INDEPENDENT AND INDIVIDUAL LEARNING ACTIVITIES, FIRST AND SECOND GRADES. SUMMER LEARNING ACTIVITIES, SECOND AND THIRD GRADES. BOSTON-NORTHAMPTON LANGUAGE ARTS PROGRAM, ESEA - 1965, PROJECTS TO ADVANCE CREATIVITY IN EDUCATION. ED027946

BALDWIN, WILLIAM O.
CURRICULUM GUIDE FOR PHYSICAL EDUCATION: KINDERGARTEN AND UNGRADED PRIMARY. ED038169

BALL, BARBARA
INDEPENDENT AND SMALL GROUP ACTIVITIES FOR SOCIAL STUDIES IN THE PRIMARY GRADES. ED031305

BALL, RACHEL S.
THE IDENTIFICATION AND ASSESSMENT OF THINKING ABILITY IN YOUNG CHILDREN. FINAL REPORT. ED025316
THE RELATION OF CERTAIN HOME ENVIRONMENT FACTORS TO THE THINKING ABILITIES OF THREE-YEAR-OLD CHILDREN. FINAL REPORT. ED039041
A LONGITUDINAL ASSESSMENT OF THINKING ABILITY OF PRELITERATE CHILDREN DURING A TWO-YEAR PERIOD. FINAL REPORT. ED048946

BALL, RACHELL S.
INFANT AND PRESCHOOL MENTAL TESTS: REVIEW AND EVALUATION. ED026109

BALL, SAMUEL
THE FIRST YEAR OF SESAME STREET: AN EVALUATION. FINAL REPORT, VOLUME III OF V VOLUMES. ED047823

BALLA, DAVID
DEVELOPMENTAL COURSE OF RESPONSIVENESS TO SOCIAL REINFORCEMENT IN NORMAL CHILDREN AND INSTITUTIONALIZED RETARDED CHILDREN EJ 053 648

BALLING, JOHN D.
MEMORY AND ATTENTION IN CHILDREN'S DOUBLE-ALTERNATION LEARNING EJ 042 966

BALOW, BRUCE
A COMPARISON OF PRE-KINDERGARTEN AND PRE-1ST GRADE BOYS AND GIRLS ON MEASURES OF SCHOOL READINESS AND LANGUAGE DEVELOPMENT. INTERIM REPORT. ED023474

BALTER, LAWRENCE
PSYCHOLOGICAL CONSULTATION IN A PRESCHOOL EJ 038 394

BALTES, P. B.
THE RELATIONSHIP BETWEEN TIME OF MEASUREMENT AND AGE IN COGNITIVE DEVELOPMENT OF CHILDREN: AN APPLICATION OF CROSS-SECTIONAL SEQUENCES EJ 034 714

BALTES, PAUL B.
AGE DIFFERENCES IN PLEASANTNESS OF VISUAL PATTERNS OF DIFFERENT VARIABILITY IN LATE CHILDHOOD AND ADOLESCENCE EJ 035 989
EXPLORATION OF DEVELOPMENTAL VARIABLES BY MANIPULATION AND SIMULATION OF AGE DIFFERENCES IN BEHAVIOR EJ 048 472

BANDURA, ALBERT
CONDITIONS GOVERNING NONREINFORCED IMITATION EJ 045 042

BANIKIOTES, FLORENCE G.
MALE AND FEMALE AUDITORY REINFORCEMENT OF INFANT VOCALIZATIONS EJ 058 217

BANKS, MARY ALICE
TEACHING NUTRITION IN THE ELEMENTARY SCHOOL. ED026148

BANTA, THOMAS J.
THE MONTESSORI RESEARCH PROJECT. FOUR PROGRESS REPORTS. ED030489
RACIAL FACTORS IN TEST PERFORMANCE EJ 053 887

BARAB, PETER G.
CONDITIONS GOVERNING NONREINFORCED IMITATION EJ 045 042

BARABASZ, ARREED F.
A COMPARATIVE STUDY OF COUNSELEE PREFERENCES FOR BEHAVIORIST AND CLIENT-CENTERED COUNSELING APPROACHES EJ 058 628

BARATZ, STEPHEN S.
NEGRO CULTURE AND EARLY CHILDHOOD EDUCATION. ED046495

BARBRACK, CHRISTOPHER R.
THE EFFECT OF THREE HOME VISITING STRATEGIES UPON MEASURES OF CHILDREN'S ACADEMIC APTITUDE AND MATERNAL TEACHING BEHAVIORS. FINAL REPORT. ED044175
EDUCATIONAL INTERVENTION IN THE HOME AND PARAPROFESSIONAL CAREER DEVELOPMENT: A FIRST GENERATION MOTHER STUDY. ED045190
INFORMATION ON INTERVENTION PROGRAMS OF THE DEMONSTRATION AND RESEARCH CENTER FOR EARLY EDUCATION. ED046492
EDUCATIONAL INTERVENTION IN THE HOME AND PARAPROFESSIONAL CAREER DEVELOPMENT: A SECOND GENERATION MOTHER STUDY WITH AN EMPHASIS ON COSTS AND BENEFITS. FINAL REPORT. ED052814

BARCLAY, LISA FRANCES KURCZ
THE COMPARATIVE EFFICACIES OF SPANISH, ENGLISH AND BILINGUAL COGNITIVE VERBAL INSTRUCTION WITH MEXICAN-AMERICAN HEAD START CHILDREN. FINAL REPORT. ED030473

BARMAN, ALICEROSE S.
GROUP WORK WITH PARENTS OF CHILDREN WITH LEARNING DISORDERS. ED019130

BARNES, KEITH E.
PRESCHOOL PLAY NORMS: A REPLICATION EJ 041 958

BARON, ROBERT A.
SOME IMMEDIATE EFFECTS OF TELEVISED VIOLENCE ON CHILDREN'S BEHAVIOR EJ 058 216

BARR, RICHARD H.
CURRENT EXPENDITURES BY LOCAL EDUCATION AGENCIES FOR FREE PUBLIC ELEMENTARY AND SECONDARY EDUCATION, 1968-69. ED052826

BARRAGY, SISTER MICHELEEN
THE EFFECT OF VARYING OBJECT NUMBER AND TYPE OF ARRANGEMENT ON CHILDREN'S ABILITY TO COORDINATE PERSPECTIVES. ED047804

BARRETT, FRANKLIN T.
BLACK CLIENTS AND WHITE WORKERS; A REPORT FROM THE FIELD EJ 051 062

BARRITT, LOREN S.
A COMPARISON OF THE PSYCHOLINGUISTIC FUNCTIONING OF "EDUCATIONALLY-DEPRIVED" AND "EDUCATIONALLY-ADVANTAGED" CHILDREN. ED022537
THE AUDITORY MEMORY OF CHILDREN FROM DIFFERENT SOCIO-ECONOMIC BACKGROUNDS. ED027092

BARTEL, NETTIE R.
LOCUS OF CONTROL AND ACHIEVEMENT IN MIDDLE- AND LOWER-CLASS CHILDREN EJ 052 448

BARTEN, SYBIL
INDIVIDUAL DIFFERENCES IN THE VISUAL PURSUIT BEHAVIOR OF NEONATES EJ 036 092
CONTINUITY IN THE DEVELOPMENT OF VISUAL BEHAVIOR IN YOUNG INFANTS EJ 053 746

BARTH, ROLAND S.
WHEN CHILDREN ENJOY SCHOOL: SOME LESSONS FROM BRITAIN EJ 018 047
ON SELECTING MATERIALS FOR THE CLASSROOM EJ 032 865

BARTLETT, ELSA JAFFE
AN ANALYSIS OF PUBLISHED PRESCHOOL LANGUAGE PROGRAMS. ED047786

BARTON, KEITH
BLOCK MANIPULATION BY CHILDREN AS A FUNCTION OF SOCIAL REINFORCEMENT, ANXIETY, AROUSAL, AND ABILITY PATTERN EJ 046 468

BARTUSKOVA, MARIA
NURSERIES IN THE CZECHOSLOVAK SOCIALIST REPUBLIC EJ 001 672

BASOW, SUSAN
THE RELATIONSHIP BETWEEN AUDITORY AND VISUAL SHORT-TERM MEMORY AND READING ACHIEVEMENT EJ 033 780

BASS, WILLIAM
HEAD START EVALUATION AND RESEARCH CENTER, UNIVERSITY OF KANSAS. REPORT NO. VIII, PHYSICAL DEVELOPMENT OF CHILDREN IN THE HEAD START PROGRAM IN THE CENTRAL UNITED STATES. ED021644

BASS, WILLIAM M.
ANTHROPOMETRIC MEASUREMENTS OF CHILDREN IN THE HEAD START PROGRAM. ED042488

BATCHELDER, MILDRED L.
CHOOSING CHILDREN'S BOOKS ABOUT OTHER COUNTRIES EJ 000 393

BATH, JOHN
A PRELIMINARY VIEW OF TRENDS IN AGE, EDUCATION, AND INTELLIGENCE OF PROBLEM YOUTH EJ 030 431

BAUER, DAVID H.
DESIGNING INSTRUCTIONAL SETTINGS FOR CHILDREN LABELED "RETARDED": SOME REFLECTIONS EJ 057 733

BAUMEISTER, ALFRED A.
BACKWARD ASSOCIATIONS IN PAIRED-ASSOCIATE LEARNING OF RETARDATES AND NORMAL CHILDREN EJ 021 770
SINGLE-LETTER CUE SELECTION IN THE PAIRED-ASSOCIATE LEARNING OF NORMAL CHILDREN AND RETARDATES EJ 024 698
TRANSFER OF VERBAL PAIRED ASSOCIATES IN MENTALLY RETARDED INDIVIDUALS AND NORMAL CHILDREN AS A FUNCTION OF INTERLIST SIMILARITY EJ 033 785
THE USE OF VERBAL MEDIATION IN THE RETARDED AS A FUNCTION OF DEVELOPMENTAL LEVEL AND RESPONSE AVAILABILITY EJ 044 699

BAUMRIND, DIANA
NATURALISTIC OBSERVATION IN THE STUDY OF PARENT-CHILD INTERACTION. ED027073
SOCIALIZATION AND INSTRUMENTAL COMPETENCE IN YOUNG CHILDREN EJ 030 510
HARMONIOUS PARENTS AND THEIR PRESCHOOL CHILDREN EJ 034 708
AN EXPLORATORY STUDY OF SOCIALIZATION EFFECTS ON BLACK CHILDREN: SOME BLACK-WHITE COMPARISONS EJ 055 656

BAYER, HELEN
ANALYSIS OF HOME ENVIRONMENT AND DEVELOPMENT OF PARENT INTERVENTION. ED035458

BAYLEY, NANCY
THE TWO YEAR OLD. ED022536

BEAN, SHIRLEY L.
THE PARENTS' CENTER PROJECT: A MULTISERVICE APPROACH TO THE PREVENTION OF CHILD ABUSE EJ 040 043

BEAR, NANCY R.
PRELIMINARY RESULTS FROM RELATIONSHIP BETWEEN TEACHERS' VOCABULARY USAGE AND THE VOCABULARY OF KINDERGARTEN AND FIRST GRADE STUDENTS. ED032135

BEATON, VIRGINIA L.
DELAY OF FEEDBACK INTERVAL, POSTFEEDBACK INTERVAL, DISTRACTION, AND TASK DIFFICULTY AS FACTORS IN A MODIFIED CONCEPT-IDENTIFICATION TASK WITH JUNIOR HIGH SCHOOL SUBJECTS EJ 047 677
TRANSFER OF TRAINING: SOME BOUNDARY CONDITIONS AND INITIAL THEORY EJ 053 722

BEATTIE, IAN
TEACHING READING IN THE KINDERGARTEN: A REVIEW OF RECENT STUDIES EJ 055 153

BEATTY, WALCOTT H.
THE FEELINGS OF LEARNING EJ 003 082

BEAUCHAMP, GEORGE A.
HOW DO INNER-CITY TEACHERS USE A SYSTEM-WIDE CURRICULUM? EJ 015 487

BECENTI, MAEBAH
CHILDREN WHO SPEAK NAVAJO EJ 014 918

BECKER, JOHN TO.
RELATIONSHIP BETWEEN LATERAL PREFERENCE AND SELECTED BEHAVIORAL VARIABLES FOR CHILDREN FAILING ACADEMICALLY EJ 056 718

BECKER, WESLEY C.
BEHAVIOR MODIFICATION OF AN ADJUSTMENT CLASS: A TOKEN REINFORCEMENT PROGRAM. ED023462
REDUCING BEHAVIOR PROBLEMS: AN OPERANT CONDITIONING GUIDE FOR TEACHERS. ED034570
PARENTS ARE TEACHERS: A CHILD MANAGEMENT PROGRAM. ED047826

BECKMAN, LINDA
DEVELOPMENTAL CONFORMITY EJ 046 892

BECKWITH, LEILA
RELATIONSHIPS BETWEEN INFANTS' VOCALIZATIONS AND THEIR MOTHERS' BEHAVIORS EJ 040 455
RELATIONSHIPS BETWEEN ATTRIBUTES OF MOTHERS AND THEIR INFANTS' IQ SCORES EJ 051 568
RELATIONSHIPS BETWEEN INFANTS' SOCIAL BEHAVIOR AND THEIR MOTHERS' BEHAVIOR EJ 058 587

BEE, HELEN L.
DEFICITS AND VALUE JUDGMENTS: A COMMENT ON SROUFE'S CRITIQUE EJ 019 324
MOTHER-CHILD INTERACTIONS AND COGNITIVE DEVELOPMENT IN CHILDREN EJ 051 567

BEE, ROBERT L.
AN APPRAISAL OF POSSIBILITIES FOR A HEAD START PROGRAM AMONG THE POTAWATOMI INDIANS OF KANSAS. INDIAN COMMUNITIES AND PROJECT HEAD START. ED013671

BEERG, IAN
SCHOOL PHOBIA AND SELF-EVALUATION EJ 031 445

BEERY, KEITH E.
PRESCHOOL PREDICTION AND PREVENTION OF LEARNING DISABILITIES. ED013118
SIX SCHOOL READINESS SCREENING DEVICES USED IN PEDIATRIC OFFICES: CONCURRENT VALIDITY. FINAL REPORT. ED029719

BEHRMANN, POLLY
EXEL ED029698

BEISWENGER, HUGO
LURIA'S MODEL OF THE VERBAL CONTROL OF BEHAVIOR. STUDY F: MOTIVATIONAL AND CONTROL IN THE DEVELOPMENT OF LANGUAGE FUNCTIONS, D. BIRCH. ED024443
LINGUISTIC AND PSYCHOLOGICAL FACTORS IN THE SPEECH REGULATION OF BEHAVIOR IN YOUNG CHILDREN EJ 034 540

BEISWENGER, HUGO A.
LINGUISTIC AND PSYCHOLOGICAL FACTORS IN THE SPEECH REGULATION OF BEHAVIOR IN VERY YOUNG CHILDREN. ED024442

BELL, ALAN P.
ROLE MODELSHIP AND INTERACTION IN ADOLESCENCE AND YOUNG ADULTHOOD EJ 019 386

BELL, ELISABETH A.
A REPORT FROM ABROAD...FAMILY PARTICIPATION IN HOSPITAL CARE FOR CHILDREN EJ 024 497

BELL, JOHN E.
A REPORT FROM ABROAD...FAMILY PARTICIPATION IN HOSPITAL CARE FOR CHILDREN EJ 024 497

BELL, RICHARD Q.
SEX DIFFERENCES IN PRESCHOOL CHILDREN WITHOUT HISTORIES OF COMPLICATIONS OF PREGNANCY AND DELIVERY EJ 024 939
STIMULUS CONTROL OF PARENT OR CARETAKER BEHAVIOR BY OFFSPRING EJ 034 538
IRRELEVANCE OF NEWBORN WAKING STATES TO SOME MOTOR AND APPETITIVE RESPONSES EJ 036 076
NEWBORN AND PRESCHOOLER: ORGANIZATION OF BEHAVIOR AND RELATIONS BETWEEN PERIODS EJ 045 110

BELL, ROBERT R.
A STUDY OF FAMILY INFLUENCES ON THE EDUCATION OF NEGRO LOWER-CLASS CHILDREN. PROJECT I. ED025309

BELL, SILVIA M.
ATTACHMENT, EXPLORATION, AND SEPARATION: ILLUSTRATED BY THE BEHAVIOR OF ONE-YEAR-OLDS IN A STRANGE SITUATION EJ 018 320
THE DEVELOPMENT OF THE CONCEPT OF OBJECT AS RELATED TO INFANT-MOTHER ATTACHMENT EJ 021 998

BELLER, E. KUNO
A STUDY OF COGNITIVE AND SOCIAL FUNCTIONING. PROJECT II ED025310

BELLUGI-KLIMA, URSULA
SOME LANGUAGE COMPREHENSION TESTS. ED040765

BELLUGI, URSULA
THE DEVELOPMENT OF INTERROGATIVE STRUCTURES IN CHILDREN'S SPEECH. ED025333

BELMONT, J. M.
WHAT THE DEVELOPMENT OF SHORT-TERM MEMORY IS EJ 049 430

BELMONT, JOHN M.
RELATIONS OF AGE AND INTELLIGENCE TO SHORT-TERM COLOR MEMORY EJ 056 392

BELTON, JOHN
PARENTS' EVALUATION OF THE HEAD START PROGRAM IN THE MILWAUKEE PUBLIC SCHOOLS. ED020806

BEM, SANDRA L.
THE ROLE OF COMPREHENSION IN CHILDREN'S PROBLEM SOLVING EJ 021 764

BEMIS, KATHERINE A.
THE USE OF THE GOODENOUGH DRAW-A-MAN TEST AS A PREDICTOR OF ACADEMIC ACHIEVEMENT. ED029695
SOUTHWESTERN COOPERATIVE EDUCATIONAL LABORATORY INTERACTION OBSERVATION SCHEDULE (SCIOS): A SYSTEM FOR ANALYZING TEACHER-PUPIL INTERACTION IN THE AFFECTIVE DOMAIN. ED038188
RELATIONSHIPS BETWEEN TEACHER BEHAVIOR, PUPIL BEHAVIOR, AND PUPIL ACHIEVEMENT. ED038189

BENCH, JOHN
ON THE RELIABILITY OF THE GRAHAM/ROSENBLITH BEHAVIOUR TEST FOR NEONATES EJ 031 630

BENDER, JUDITH
HAVE YOU EVER THOUGHT OF A PROP BOX? EJ 031 781

BENGOA, JOSE M.
NUTRITION REHABILITATION CENTRES EJ 029 953

BENJAMIN, LORNA S.
NIGHT TRAINING THROUGH PARENTS' IMPLICIT USE OF OPERANT CONDITIONING EJ 045 457

BENNETT, ROGER W.
BEHAVIORAL COUNSELING FOR ELEMENTARY-SCHOOL CHILDREN EJ 019 669

BENNETT, STEPHEN
INFANT-CARETAKER INTERACTIONS EJ 043 670

BENTLER, P. M.
THE PRIORITY OF CUES IN SEX DISCRIMINATION BY CHILDREN AND ADULTS EJ 044 691

BENZINGER, THOMAS L.
THE EFFECTS OF INSTRUCTION ON THE DEVELOPMENT OF THE CONCEPT OF CONSERVATION OF NUMEROUSNESS BY KINDERGARTEN CHILDREN. REPORT FROM THE PROJECT ON INDIVIDUALLY GUIDED ELEMENTARY MATHEMATICS ED049821

BERCH, DANIEL B.
VISUAL ORIENTATION IN CHILDREN'S DISCRIMINATION LEARNING UNDER CONSTANT, VARIABLE, AND COVARIABLE DELAY OF REINFORCEMENT EJ 024 696
STIMULUS INTERACTION AND PROBLEM DIFFICULTY IN CHILDREN'S DISCRIMINATION LEARNING EJ 053 480

BEREITER, CARL
ACCELERATION OF INTELLECTUAL DEVELOPMENT IN EARLY CHILDHOOD. FINAL REPORT. ED014332
LANGUAGE LEARNING ACTIVITIES FOR THE DISADVANTAGED CHILD. ED020002
ARITHMETIC AND MATHEMATICS. DIMENSIONS IN EARLY LEARNING SERIES. ED026136
EFFECTIVENESS OF DIRECT VERBAL INSTRUCTION ON IQ PERFORMANCE AND ACHIEVEMENT IN READING AND ARITHMETIC. ED030496
AN ACADEMIC PRESCHOOL FOR DISADVANTAGED CHILDREN: REVIEW OF FINDINGS. PRELIMINARY DRAFT. ED051878

BERG, JAN
A FOLLOW-UP STUDY OF SCHOOL PHOBIC ADOLESCENTS ADMITTED TO AN IN-PATIENT UNIT EJ 026 157

BERGAN, JOHN R.
INTELLECTUAL OPERATIONS IN TEACHER-CHILD INTERACTION. ED039011
INTELLECTUAL OPERATIONS IN TEACHER QUESTION-ASKING BEHAVIOR EJ 032 895

BERGER, ALLAN S.
SEX EDUCATION OF THE YOUNG CHILD EJ 019 862
ANXIETY IN YOUNG CHILDREN EJ 045 049

BERGER, BARBARA
A LONGITUDINAL INVESTIGATION OF MONTESSORI AND TRADITIONAL PREKINDERGARTEN TRAINING WITH INNER CITY CHILDREN: A COMPARATIVE ASSESSMENT OF LEARNING OUTCOMES. THREE PART STUDY. ED034588

BERGER, STANLEY I.
DEVELOPMENT OF APPROPRIATE EVALUATION TECHNIQUES FOR SCREENING CHILDREN IN A HEAD START PROGRAM. A PILOT PROJECT. ED015006

BERGSTEIN, PATRICIA
A STUDY IN CHILD CARE (CASE STUDY FROM VOLUME II-A): "HEY, GEORGIE GET YOURSELF TOGETHER." DAY CARE PROGRAMS REPRINT SERIES. ED051902

BERK, LAURA E.
EFFECTS OF DURATION OF A NURSERY SCHOOL SETTING ON ENVIRONMENTAL CONSTRAINTS AND CHILDREN'S MODES OF ADAPTATION. ED047812
EFFECTS OF VARIATIONS IN THE NURSERY SCHOOL SETTING ON ENVIRONMENTAL CONSTRAINTS AND CHILDREN'S MODES OF ADAPTATION EJ 045 455

BERKE, MELVYN
THE ROLE OF INCENTIVES IN DISCRIMINATION LEARNING OF CHILDREN WITH VARYING PRE-SCHOOL EXPERIENCE. ED031290

BERMAN, PHYLLIS W.
AGE CHANGES IN CHILDREN'S LEARNING SET WITH WIN-STAY, LOSE-SHIFT PROBLEMS EJ 018 885
STIMULUS NOVELTY AS A VARIABLE IN CHILDREN'S WIN-STAY, LOSE-SHIFT DISCRIMINATION LEARNING SET EJ 053 751

BERMAN, SAMUEL P.
A REPORT ON A CWLA PILOT PROJECT TO TRAIN NEW CHILD CARE WORKERS EJ 017 849

BERMAN, SIDNEY
ALIENATION: AN ESSENTIAL PROCESS OF THE PSYCHOLOGY OF ADOLESCENCE EJ 023 426

BERMAN, STIDNEY
EPILOGUE AND A NEW BEGINNING EJ 022 371

BERMAN, YITZCHAK
AN ISRAELI EXPERIMENTAL GROUP WITH PRIMARY SCHOOL DROPOUTS OUTSIDE THE SCHOOL SETTING EJ 041 630

BERNABEI, RAYMOND
AN EVALUATION OF THE INTERIM CLASS: AN EXTENDED READINESS PROGRAM. ED028820

BERNEY, TOMI D.
ANALYSIS OF STORY RETELLING AS A MEASURE OF THE EFFECTS OF ETHNIC CONTENT IN STORIES. FINAL REPORT. ED014326

BERNHEIM, GLORIA D.
THE EFFECTS OF SEVERAL VERBAL PRETRAINING CONDITIONS ON PRESCHOOL CHILDREN'S TRANSFER IN PROBLEM SOLVING. FINAL REPORT. ED015778

BERNSTEIN, ALAN
VARIABLES AFFECTING ASSOCIATIVE RECALL IN CHILDREN EJ 056 400

BERNSTEIN, MARTIN E.
THE FORMATION AND REVERSAL OF AN ATTITUDE AS FUNCTIONS OF ASSUMED SELF-CONCEPT, RACE, AND SOCIOECONOMIC CLASS EJ 052 652

BERROL, SELMA C.
HEALTH, EDUCATION, AND WELFARE: THE PROGRESSIVE IMPULSE IN THE NEW YORK CITY PUBLIC SCHOOLS EJ 029 104
SUPERINTENDENT JULIA RICHMAN: A SOCIAL PROGRESSIVE IN THE PUBLIC SCHOOLS EJ 060 106

BERRY, FRANKLIN M.
SINGLE-LETTER CUE SELECTION IN THE PAIRED-ASSOCIATE LEARNING OF NORMAL CHILDREN AND RETARDATES EJ 024 698

BERSON, DEBBIE
SYMPOSIUM ON ALTERNATIVE COMMUNITIES: CHILDREN OF THE GROUP FAMILY EJ 049 657

BERTRAM, CHARLES L.
DEMOGRAPHIC AND SOCIO-ECONOMIC DATA OF THE BECKLEY, WEST VIRGINIA AREA AND 1968-1970 DEVELOPMENTAL COSTS OF THE EARLY CHILDHOOD EDUCATION FIELD STUDY. TECHNICAL REPORT NO. 1. ED052832
EVALUATION REPORT: EARLY CHILDHOOD EDUCATION PROGRAM, 1969-1970 FIELD TEST. SUMMARY REPORT. ED052837
A COMPARISON OF PARENTS' ATTITUDES TOWARD AEL'S "AROUND THE BEND" AND OTHER CHILDREN'S TELEVISION PROGRAMS. ED052842

BERZONSKY, MICHAEL D.
A FACTOR ANALYTIC STUDY OF CHILDREN'S CAUSAL REASONING. ED040759
EFFECTS OF PROBING CHILDREN'S PHENOMENISTIC EXPLANATIONS OF CAUSE AND EFFECT EJ 030 292
INTERDEPENDENCE OF INHELDER AND PIAGET'S MODEL OF LOGICAL THINKING EJ 039 633
THE ROLE OF FAMILIARITY IN CHILDREN'S EXPLANATIONS OF PHYSICAL CAUSALITY EJ 046 232

BEYER, EVELYN
LANGUAGE LEARNING--FRESH VIVID AND THEIR OWN EJ 044 613

BEYTAGH, LUZ A. MALDONADO
INDUSTRIALIZATION, CHILD-REARING PRACTICES, AND CHILDREN'S PERSONALITY EJ 015 199

BIAGGIO, ANGELA
BEHAVIORAL COMPLIANCE AND DEVALUATION OF THE FORBIDDEN OBJECT AS A FUNCTION OF PROBABILITY OF DETECTION AND SEVERITY OF THREAT EJ 038 935

BIASINI, AMERICOLE
DEVELOPMENT OF A MUSIC CURRICULUM FOR YOUNG CHILDREN. CAREL ARTS AND HUMANITIES CURRICULUM DEVELOPMENT PROGRAM FOR YOUNG CHILDREN. ED032938

BIBELHEIMER, MILO
FIVE-YEAR STABILITY OF INTELLIGENCE QUOTIENTS FROM LANGUAGE AND NONLANGUAGE GROUP TESTS EJ 041 723

BIBER, BARBARA
CHALLENGES AHEAD FOR EARLY CHILDHOOD EDUCATION EJ 006 983
GOALS AND METHODS IN A PRESCHOOL PROGRAM FOR DISADVANTAGED CHILDREN EJ 013 800

BIBER, HENRY
FEMINIZATION IN PRESCHOOL EJ 059 872

BIERI, JAMES
INTELLECTUAL DEVELOPMENT OF CULTURALLY DEPRIVED CHILDREN IN A DAY CARE PROGRAM: A FOLLOW-UP STUDY. ED045186

BIESBROCK, EDIEANN
A STUDY OF COMPOSITION ABILITY AS ASSESSED WITH A STANDARDIZED INSTRUMENT FOR SECOND AND THIRD GRADE CHILDREN. ED029696

BIESBROCK, EDIEANN F.
A STUDY COMPARING GLOBAL QUALITY AND SYNTACTIC MATURITY IN THE WRITING COMPOSITION OF SECOND AND THIRD GRADE STUDENTS. ED029697

BIJKERK, ROEL
PROCEEDINGS OF THE ANNUAL CONVENTION OF THE CHRISTIAN ASSOCIATION FOR PSYCHOLOGICAL STUDIES ON THE DYNAMICS OF LEARNING CHRISTIAN CONCEPTS (12TH, GRAND RAPIDS, MICHIGAN, MARCH 31-APRIL 1, 1965). ED023476

BILLER, HENRY B.
THE FATHER-DAUGHTER RELATIONSHIP AND THE PERSONALITY DEVELOPMENT OF THE FEMALE EJ 017 904
FATHER ABSENCE AND THE PERSONALITY DEVELOPMENT OF THE MALE CHILD EJ 019 018
AGGRESSION IN CHILDREN AS A FUNCTION OF SEX OF SUBJECT AND SEX OF OPPONENT EJ 024 945
BODY BUILD, SEX-ROLE PREFERENCE, AND SEX-ROLE ADOPTION IN JUNIOR HIGH SCHOOL BOYS EJ 035 627
FATHER ABSENCE, PERCEIVED MATERNAL BEHAVIOR, AND MASCULINITY OF SELF-CONCEPT AMONG JUNIOR HIGH SCHOOL BOYS EJ 035 804
FATHER AVAILABILITY AND ACADEMIC PERFORMANCE AMONG THIRD-GRADE BOYS EJ 038 730
THE MOTHER-CHILD RELATIONSHIP AND THE FATHER-ABSENT BOY'S PERSONALITY DEVELOPMENT 27-241 EJ 040 456

BILLINGSLEY, ANDREW
CHILD NEGLECT AMONG THE POOR: A STUDY OF PARENTAL ADEQUACY IN FAMILIES OF THREE ETHNIC GROUPS EJ 018 326

BILLS, GARLAND
AN INVESTIGATION OF THE STANDARD-NONSTANDARD DIMENSION OF CENTRAL TEXAN ENGLISH. PART OF THE FINAL REPORT. ED026130

BILODEAU, EDWARD A.
FREE-ASSOCIATION NORMS AND ASSOCIATIVE STRUCTURE. ED025328

BILODEAU, INA MCD.
TANGENT TO EXPERIMENTAL TECHNIQUES OF VERBAL CONTROL. ED025334

BILSKY, LINDA
CUE NOVELTY AND TRAINING LEVEL IN THE DISCRIMINATION SHIFT PERFORMANCE OF RETARDATES EJ 015 851

BINDSEIL, BEVERLY D.
THE DEVELOPMENT OF COGNITIVE BALANCE AND THE TRANSITION FROM CONCRETE TO FORMAL OPERATIONAL THOUGHT EJ 041 145

BINSTOCK, ELEANOR
REVIEW AND SUMMARY OF A NATIONAL SURVEY OF THE PARENT-CHILD CENTER PROGRAM. ED048941

BIRCH, DAVID
EVIDENCE FOR COMPETITION AND COORDINATION BETWEEN VOCAL AND MANUAL RESPONSES IN PRESCHOOL CHILDREN EJ 043 668

BIRCH, HERBERT G.
DESIGNS AND PROPOSAL FOR EARLY CHILDHOOD RESEARCH: A NEW LOOK: MALNUTRITION, LEARNING AND INTELLIGENCE. (ONE IN A SERIES OF SIX PAPERS). ED053811

BIRCH, JACK W.
PRESCHOOL EDUCATION AND SCHOOL ADMISSION PRACTICES IN NEW ZEALAND. ED046487

BIRCH, JANE R.
PRESCHOOL EDUCATION AND SCHOOL ADMISSION PRACTICES IN NEW ZEALAND. ED046487

BIRNBAUM, MORTON P.
ANXIETY AND MORAL JUDGMENT IN EARLY ADOLESCENCE EJ 055 094

BIRNS, BEVERLY
SOCIAL CLASS AND COGNITIVE DEVELOPMENT IN INFANCY. ED019111
THE BEHAVIORAL AROUSAL THRESHOLD IN INFANT SLEEP AS A FUNCTION OF TIME AND SLEEP STATE EJ 036 091
PREDICTION OF INTELLECTUAL PERFORMANCE AT 3 YEARS FROM INFANT TESTS AND PERSONALITY MEASURES EJ 052 237
SOCIAL CLASS INTELLIGENCE, AND COGNITIVE STYLE IN INFANCY EJ 056 725

BIRREN, JAMES E.
AGE CHANGES AND COHORT DIFFERENCES IN PERSONALITY EJ 055 110

BISH, CHARLES E., ED.
PRODUCTIVE THINKING IN EDUCATION. ED024459

BISHOP, BARBARA R.
DEVELOPMENTAL CONFORMITY EJ 046 892

BISHOP, DOYLE W.
PARENTAL CONCEPTUAL SYSTEMS, HOME PLAY ENVIRONMENT, AND POTENTIAL CREATIVITY IN CHILDREN. ED043386
PARENTAL CONCEPTUAL SYSTEMS, HOME PLAY ENVIRONMENT, AND POTENTIAL CREATIVITY IN CHILDREN EJ 048 234

BISSELL, JOAN S.
IMPLEMENTATION OF PLANNED VARIATION IN HEAD START. I. REVIEW AND SUMMARY OF THE STANFORD RESEARCH INSTITUTE INTERIM REPORT: FIRST YEAR OF EVALUATION. ED052845

BITTNER, MARGUERITE L.
AN EVALUATION OF THE PRESCHOOL READINESS CENTERS PROGRAM IN EAST ST. LOUIS, ILLINOIS, JULY 1, 1967-JUNE 30, 1968. FINAL REPORT. ED023472
AN EVALUATION OF THE PRESCHOOL READINESS CENTERS PROGRAM IN EAST ST. LOUIS, ILLINOIS, JULY 1, 1968 - JUNE 30, 1969. FINAL REPORT. ED034585

BIZOT, JUDITHE
UNDERSTANDING ONE ANOTHER: UNESCO'S ASSOCIATED SCHOOLS PROJECT EJ 037 426

BLACK, F. WILLIAM
SEASON OF BIRTH AND INTELLIGENCE EJ 025 268

BLACK, KATHRYN NORCROSS
A DEVELOPMENTAL STUDY OF PRESCHOOL CHILDREN'S PREFERENCE FOR RANDOM FORMS EJ 035 990
CONCEPTUAL TEMPO IN YOUNG GRADE-SCHOOL CHILDREN EJ 041 450

BLACKSTONE, TESSA
PRE-SCHOOL EDUCATION IN EUROPE. ED047779

BLAIR, JOHN RAYMOND
THE EFFECTS OF DIFFERENTIAL REINFORCEMENT ON THE DISCRIMINATION LEARNING OF NORMAL AND LOW-ACHIEVING MIDDLE-CLASS BOYS EJ 056 398

BLAKER, KENNETH E.
BEHAVIORAL COUNSELING FOR ELEMENTARY-SCHOOL CHILDREN EJ 019 669

BLANCHARD, EDWARD B.
THE DEVELOPMENT OF COGNITIVE BALANCE AND THE TRANSITION FROM CONCRETE TO FORMAL OPERATIONAL THOUGHT EJ 041 145
A DEVELOPMENTAL STUDY OF COGNITIVE BALANCE EJ 043 856

BLANCHARD, IRENE
BETTER FEEDING CAN MEAN BETTER SPEAKING. ED025306

BLANCHARD, ROBERT W.
FATHER AVAILABILITY AND ACADEMIC PERFORMANCE AMONG THIRD-GRADE BOYS EJ 038 730

BLANK, MARION
A METHODOLOGY FOR FOSTERING ABSTRACT THINKING IN DEPRIVED CHILDREN. ED026131
DIMENSIONAL LEARNING ACROSS SENSORY MODALITIES IN NURSERY SCHOOL CHILDREN EJ 021 756
STORY RECALL IN KINDERGARTEN CHILDREN: EFFECT OF METHOD OF PRESENTATION ON PSYCHOLINGUISTIC PERFORMANCE EJ 036 748

BLANTON, WILLIAM E.
SOME DIMENSIONS OF CREATIVE THINKING ABILITY ACHIEVEMENT, AND INTELLIGENCE IN FIRST GRADE. ED028818

BLASDEL, JOAN
BEHAVIOR MODIFICATION PROCEDURES APPLIED TO THE ISOLATE BEHAVIOR OF A NURSERY SCHOOL CHILD. ED041635

BLAU, BURTON
CHANGES IN FRIENDSHIP STATUS AS A FUNCTION OF REINFORCEMENT EJ 019 004

BLECHMAN, ELAINE A.
MOTHERS' TEST OF ANXIETY AND TASK SELECTION AND CHILDREN'S PERFORMANCE WITH MOTHER OR A STRANGER EJ 052 449

BLOCH, JUDITH
A PRESCHOOL WORKSHOP FOR EMOTIONALLY DISTURBED CHILDREN EJ 013 234

BLOCK, JAMES D.
CARDIAC CLASSICAL CONDITIONING AND REVERSAL IN THE MONGOLOID, ENCEPHALOPATHIC, AND NORMAL CHILD EJ 025 375

BLOM, GASTON E.
THE PSYCHOEDUCATIONAL APPROACH TO LEARNING DISABILITIES. ED027950
THE NEED FOR A MULTI-DIMENSIONAL APPROACH TO LEARNING DISABILITIES. A MULTI-DISCIPLINARY SYMPOSIUM ON DYSLEXIS AND ASSOCIATED LEARNING DISABILITIES. ED027956
THE CONCEPT, "PERCEPTUALLY HANDICAPPED," ITS ASSETS AND LIMITATIONS. ED027960
PSYCHOMOTOR EDUCATION - THEORY AND PRACTICE. ED029684
MOTIVATIONAL AND ATTITUDINAL CONTENT OF FIRST GRADE READING TEXTBOOKS EJ 045 084

BLOOD, ROBERT O.
KINSHIP INTERACTION AND MARITAL SOLIDARITY EJ 007 449

BLOOM, BENJAMIN S.
EARLY LEARNING IN THE HOME. ED019127

BLOOMBERG, MORTON
CREATIVITY AS RELATED TO FIELD INDEPENDENCE AND MOBILITY EJ 035 380

BLOOMBERG, WARNER, JR.
A CITY FOR CHILDREN: THE YEAR 2005 EJ 049 562

BLUM, A. H.
HEAD START EVALUATION AND RESEARCH CENTER, BOSTON UNIVERSITY. REPORT D-II, TRAINING FOR NUMBER CONCEPT. ED022564

BLUM, ABRAHAM H.
SUCCESSFUL NUMBER CONSERVATION TRAINING. ED031297

BLUM, WILLIAM L.
CHAOTIC REINFORCEMENT: A SOCIOECONOMIC LEVELER EJ 035 371

BLUMENFELD, PHYLLIS
THE "TELL-AND-FIND PICTURE GAME" FOR YOUNG CHILDREN. ED042513

BOEHM, JOHN J.
RHYTHMIC HABIT PATTERNS IN INFANCY: THEIR SEQUENCE, AGE OF ONSET, AND FREQUENCY EJ 040 295

BOERSMA, FREDERIC
EFFECTS OF ARITHMETIC PROBLEM DIFFICULTY ON PUPILLARY DILATION IN NORMALS AND EDUCABLE RETARDATES EJ 021 986

BOERSMA, FREDERIC J.
EYE MOVEMENTS, PERCEPTUAL ACTIVITY, AND CONSERVATION DEVELOPMENT EJ 046 249

BOGARTZ, RICHARD S.
EXTENSION OF A THEORY OF PREDICTIVE BEHAVIOR TO IMMEDIATE RECALL BY PRESCHOOL CHILDREN. ED025326
THREE-CUE SELECTION MODELS APPLIED TO MULTIDIMENSIONAL STIMULUS CLASSIFICATION: ALTERNATIVES TO THE SPIKER, CROLL, AND MILLER ANALYSIS EJ 060 785

BOGER, ROBERT P.
SOCIAL-EMOTIONAL TASK FORCE. FINAL REPORT. ED033744
CHARACTERIZATION OF THE EFFECT OF SPACE, MATERIALS, AND TEACHER BEHAVIOR ON PRESCHOOL CHILDREN'S FREE PLAY ACTIVITY PATTERNS. RESEARCH REPORT NO. 1. ED037251
PARENTS AS PRIMARY CHANGE AGENTS IN AN EXPERIMENTAL HEAD START PROGRAM OF LANGUAGE INTERVENTION. EXPERIMENTAL PROGRAM REPORT. ED044168
AN EXPERIMENTAL PROGRAM IN CLASSIFICATION AND ATTENTIONAL TRAINING WITH HEAD START CHILDREN. ED044171
HETEROGENEOUS VS. HOMOGENEOUS SOCIAL CLASS GROUPING OF PRESCHOOL CHILDREN IN HEAD START CLASSROOMS. ED045176
SUBPOPULATIONAL PROFILING OF THE PSYCHOEDUCATIONAL DIMENSIONS OF DISADVANTAGED PRESCHOOL CHILDREN: A CONCEPTUAL PROSPECTUS FOR AN INTERDISCIPLINARY RESEARCH. ED045177

BOGGAN, LUCILLE B.
LIVING AND LEARNING: AN ANNOTATED BIBLIOGRAPHY FOR THOSE WHO LIVE AND LEARN WITH YOUNG CHILDREN. ED032935

BOHAN, JANIS BEEBE
DEVELOPMENT OF A SENSE OF SELF-IDENTITY IN CHILDREN EJ 056 617

BOHN, MARTIN J., JR.
OCCUPATIONAL PRESTIGE AS SEEN BY DISADVANTAGED BLACK CHILDREN EJ 034 453

BOMMARITO, JAMES
A STUDY OF A MEASUREMENT RESOURCE IN CHILD RESEARCH, PROJECT HEAD START. ED020790

BOMMARITO, JAMES W.
VERBAL REINFORCEMENT AS AN ADJUSTMENT PREDICTOR WITH KINDERGARTEN CHILDREN. FINAL REPORT. ED031313

BORKE, HELENE
INTERPERSONAL PERCEPTION OF YOUNG CHILDREN: EGOCENTRISM OR EMPATHY? EJ 043 606

BOROWITZ, GENE H.
PERSONALITY DEVELOPMENT IN DISADVANTAGED FOUR-YEAR-OLD BOYS: OBSERVATIONS WITH PLAY TECHNIQUES. ED031310
PLAY BEHAVIOR AND EFFICACY IN GHETTO FOUR-YEAR-OLDS: ORGANIZATION AND PSYCHOSEXUAL CONTENT OF PLAY. ED048920

BOSCO, JAMES
INDIVIDUALIZATION - TEACHERS' VIEWS EJ 052 067

BOTWINICK, JACK
SENSORY-SET FACTORS IN AGE DIFFERENCES IN REACTION TIME EJ 048 304

BOUCHARD, RUTH A.
A PREKINDERGARTEN PROGRAM FOR FOUR-YEAR-OLDS, WITH A REVIEW OF THE LITERATURE ON PRESCHOOL EDUCATION. AN OCCASIONAL PAPER. ED026124

BOURNE, L. E., JR.
CHRONOLOGICAL AGE AND PERFORMANCE ON PROBLEMS WITH REPEATED PRESOLUTION SHIFTS EJ 039 628
CONCEPTUAL RULE LEARNING AND CHRONOLOGICAL AGE EJ 047 687

BOWER, T. G. R.
DEVELOPMENT OF THE OBJECT CONCEPT AS MANIFESTED IN CHANGES IN THE TRACKING BEHAVIOR OF INFANTS BETWEEN 7 AND 20 WEEKS OF AGE EJ 038 264

BOWERS, NORMAN D.
PUPIL IMITATION OF A REWARDING TEACHER'S VERBAL BEHAVIOR. ED038185

BOWES, WATSON A., JR.
1. OBSTETRICAL MEDICATION AND INFANT OUTCOME: A REVIEW OF THE LITERATURE EJ 023 013

BOYCE, KATHLEEN D.
GENERALIZED IMITATION AS A FUNCTION OF DISCRIMINATION DIFFICULTY AND CHOICE EJ 038 455

BOYD, JOSEPH L.
PROJECT HEAD START--SUMMER 1966. FINAL REPORT. SECTION TWO, FACILITIES AND RESOURCES OF HEAD START CENTERS. ED018247

BOYLE, JOHN
A LEARNING EXPERIENCE IN HELPING PARENTS GET WHAT THEY WANT EJ 024 027

BRACKBILL, YVONNE
II. DELIVERY MEDICATION AND INFANT OUTCOME: AN EMPIRICAL STUDY EJ 023 014
CUMULATIVE EFFECTS OF CONTINUOUS STIMULATION ON AROUSAL LEVEL IN INFANTS EJ 036 075

BRADSHAW, CAROL E.
THE POVERTY CULTURE EJ 011 823

BRADSHAW, J. L.
JUDGING OUTLINE FACES: A DEVELOPMENTAL STUDY EJ 045 599

BRAGA, JOSEPH L.
EARLY ADMISSION: OPINION VERSUS EVIDENCE EJ 048 045

BRAINERD, CHARLES J.
CONTINUITY AND DISCONTINUITY HYPOTHESES IN STUDIES OF CONSERVATION EJ 027 182
TRAINING AND GENERALIZATION OF DENSITY CONSERVATION: EFFECTS OF FEEDBACK AND CONSECUTIVE SIMILAR STIMULI EJ 046 231
THE DEVELOPMENT OF THE PROPORTIONALITY SCHEME IN CHILDREN AND ADOLESCENTS EJ 047 682

BRANDHOFER, MARIJANE
CARPENTRY FOR YOUNG CHILDREN EJ 044 512

BRANDWINE, ALIZA
UPBRINGING OF CHILDREN IN KIBBUTZIM OF ISRAEL EJ 007 447

BRANHAM, ETHEL
ONE-PARENT ADOPTIONS EJ 022 180

BRANNIGAN, CHRISTOPHER
I SEE WHAT YOU MEAN EJ 035 370

BRANNIGAN, GARY G.
SEX DIFFERENCES IN ADAPTIVE STYLES EJ 045 046
SELF-PARENTAL DISTANCE, CONTROL OF REINFORCEMENT, AND PERSONAL FUTURE TIME PERSPECTIVE EJ 045 047

BRANTLEY, MABEL
RECIPES FOR MOM EJ 018 131

BRAUN, CARL
FOSTERING A NEED TO READ EJ 052 420
A TRANSFORMATIONAL ANALYSIS OF ORAL SYNTACTIC STRUCTURES OF CHILDREN REPRESENTING VARYING ETHNOLINGUISTIC COMMUNITIES EJ 056 713

BRAUN, SAMUEL J.
TEACHER-PARENT WORK IN THE HOME: AN ASPECT OF CHILD GUIDANCE CLINIC SERVICES EJ 027 448

BRAZELTON, T. B.
IMPLICATIONS OF INFANT DEVELOPMENT AMONG THE MAYAN INDIANS OF MEXICO EJ 061 232

BRAZZIEL, WILLIAM F.
PERSPECTIVE ON THE JENSEN AFFAIR. ED040760
PERSPECTIVE ON THE JENSEN AFFAIR EJ 020 519

BREARLEY, MOLLY
A GUIDE TO READING PIAGET. ED053819

BREED, GEORGE
EYE CONTACT, ATTITUDES, AND ATTITUDE CHANGE AMONG MALES EJ 059 813

BREIVOGEL, WILLIAM F., ED.
PROCEEDINGS OF FOLLOW THROUGH CONFERENCE (GAINESVILLE, FLORIDA, DECEMBER 9-10, 1969). ED047773

BRENNAN, MATTHEW J.
MAKING TOMORROW NOW: BUILDING A QUALITATIVE ENVIRONMENT FOR ALL CHILDREN EJ 026 771

BRENT, SANDOR B.
A STUDY OF LANGUAGE DEVIATIONS AND COGNITIVE PROCESSES. PROGRESS REPORT NO. 3. ED027958

BRESNAHAN, JEAN L.
CHAOTIC REINFORCEMENT: A SOCIOECONOMIC LEVELER EJ 035 371

BRICKNER, C. ANN
AN EXPERIMENTAL PROGRAM DESIGNED TO INCREASE AUDITORY DISCRIMINATION WITH HEAD START CHILDREN. ED029680

BRIELAND, DONALD
BLACK IDENTITY AND THE HELPING PERSON EJ 008 461

BRIGHAM, THOMAS A.
HEAD START EVALUATION AND RESEARCH CENTER, UNIVERSITY OF KANSAS. REPORT NO. IIA, A STUDY OF AUDITORY DISCRIMINATION AND VERBAL RESPONDING. ED021634
HEAD START EVALUATION AND RESEARCH CENTER, UNIVERSITY OF KANSAS. REPORT NO. IIB, AN EXPERIMENTAL ANALYSIS OF VERBAL IMITATION IN PRESCHOOL CHILDREN. ED021635

BRIGHT, THOMAS P.
A STUDY OF WED AND UNWED MOTHERHOOD IN ADOLESCENTS AND YOUNG ADULTS EJ 030 715

BRILL, SHEILA
A COMPARATIVE ANALYSIS OF THE PIAGETIAN DEVELOPMENT OF TWELVE MONTH OLD DISADVANTAGED INFANTS IN AN ENRICHMENT CENTER WITH OTHERS NOT IN SUCH A CENTER. ED047778

BRINKHOUS, KENNETH M.
CHANGING PROSPECTS FOR CHILDREN WITH HEMOPHILIA EJ 029 952

BRITTON, JEAN E.
SELECTED BOOKS ABOUT THE AFRO-AMERICAN FOR VERY YOUNG CHILDREN K-2. ED039029

BROCKMAN, LOIS M.
SEVERE PROTEIN-CALORIE MALNUTRITION AND COGNITIVE DEVELOPMENT IN INFANCY AND EARLY CHILDHOOD EJ 039 627

BRODY, ERNESS BRIGHT
ACHIEVEMENT OF FIRST- AND SECOND-YEAR PUPILS IN GRADED AND NONGRADED CLASSROOMS EJ 018 969

BRODZINSKY, DAVID
PERCEPTUAL AND LOGICAL FACTORS IN THE DEVELOPMENT OF MULTIPLICATIVE CLASSIFICATION EJ 053 649

BROMAN, BETTY L.
TOO MUCH SHUSHING - LET CHILDREN TALK EJ 011 841
THE SHORT ATTENTION SPAN: FACT AND MYTH EJ 028 898
THE SPANISH-SPEAKING FIVE-YEAR-OLD EJ 056 391

BRONFENBRENNER, URIE
MEMO--COMMENTS ON THE WOLFF AND STEIN STUDY. ED015029
MOTIVATIONAL AND SOCIAL COMPONENTS IN COMPENSATORY EDUCATION PROGRAMS: SUGGESTED PRINCIPLES, PRACTICES, AND RESEARCH DESIGNS. ED024464
WHO CARES FOR AMERICA'S CHILDREN? EJ 032 565

BRONSON, GORDON W.
FEAR OF VISUAL NOVELTY: DEVELOPMENTAL PATTERNS IN MALES AND FEMALES EJ 019 011

BROOK, JUDITH S.
A TEST OF PIAGET'S THEORY OF "NOMINAL REALISM" EJ 023 189

BROOKS, IRA MAE
A COMPARISON OF RELATIVE STRUCTURAL LEVELS ON A VARIETY OF COGNITIVE TASKS. ED032923

BROOKS, MARY M.
PLAY FOR HOSPITALIZED CHILDREN EJ 007 316

BROPHY, JERE E.
EFFECTS OF SEX AND BIRTH ORDER ON SEX-ROLE DEVELOPMENT AND INTELLIGENCE AMONG KINDERGARTEN CHILDREN EJ 057 133

BROPHY, JERE EDWARD
MOTHERS AS TEACHERS OF THEIR OWN PRESCHOOL CHILDREN: THE INFLUENCE OF SOCIO-ECONOMIC STATUS AND TASK STRUCTURE ON TEACHING SPECIFICITY. ED031294
MOTHERS AS TEACHERS OF THEIR OWN PRESCHOOL CHILDREN: THE INFLUENCE OF SOCIOECONOMIC STATUS AND TASK STRUCTURE ON TEACHING SPECIFICITY EJ 019 414

BROTSKY, S. JOYCE
STABILITY OF THE ORIENTING REFLEX IN INFANTS TO AUDITORY AND VISUAL STIMULI AS INDEXED BY CARDIAC DECELERATION EJ 056 720

BROWN, ANN L.
THE STABILITY OF DIMENSIONAL PREFERENCE FOLLOWING ODDITY TRAINING EJ 021 988
TRANSFER PERFORMANCE IN CHILDREN'S ODDITY LEARNING AS A FUNCTION OF DIMENSIONAL PREFERENCE, SHIFT PARADIGM AND OVERTRAINING EJ 024 692
RECOGNITION MEMORY FOR PICTURES IN PRESCHOOL CHILDREN EJ 042 964
COLOR DOMINANCE IN PRESCHOOL CHILDREN AS A FUNCTION OF SPECIFIC CUE PREFERENCES EJ 053 738
TRANSFER BETWEEN THE ODDITY AND RELATIVE SIZE CONCEPTS: REVERSAL AND EXTRADIMENSIONAL SHIFTS EJ 057 906
PSYCHOPHYSICALLY SCALED CUE DIFFERENCES, LEARNING RATE, AND ATTENTIONAL STRATEGIES IN A TACTILE DISCRIMINATION TASK EJ 058 146

BROWN, ANNE M.
TWINNING: A MARKER FOR BIOLOGICAL INSULTS EJ 021 188
THE BEHAVIOR OF TWINS: EFFECTS OF BIRTH WEIGHT AND BIRTH SEQUENCE EJ 036 081

BROWN, H, DOUGLAS
CHILDREN'S COMPREHENSION OF RELATIVIZED ENGLISH SENTENCES EJ 056 715

BROWN, JANET L.
PRECURSORS OF INTELLIGENCE AND CREATIVITY: A LONGITUDINAL STUDY OF ONE CHILD'S DEVELOPMENT EJ 020 521

BROWN, L. BARBARA
LOOK--I SEE ME EJ 028 897

BROWN, RICHARD A.
INTERACTION EFFECTS OF SOCIAL AND TANGIBLE REINFORCEMENT EJ 048 296

BROWN, STANLEY B.
LOOK--I SEE ME EJ 028 897

BROWN, WILLIAM E.
PRAISE, CRITICISM, AND RACE EJ 019 388

BROZEK, JOSEF, E.
PHYSICAL GROWTH AND BODY COMPOSITION: PAPERS FROM THE KYOTO SYMPOSIUM ON ANTHROPOLOGICAL ASPECTS OF HUMAN GROWTH EJ 029 387

BROZOVICH, RICHARD
FAKABILITY OF SCORES ON THE GROUP PERSONALITY PROJECTIVE TEST EJ 030 792

BRUCE, TERRI
THE EFFECTS OF ADULT VERBAL MODELING AND FEEDBACK ON THE ORAL LANGUAGE OF HEAD START CHILDREN. ED047793

BRUDENELL, GERALD A.
INTERIM PROGRESS REPORT OF A REMOTE TEACHER TRAINING INSTITUTE FOR EARLY CHILDHOOD EDUCATORS (FUNDED BY NDEA TITLE XI). ED017326

BRUININKS, ROBERT H.
PSYCHOLINGUISTIC ABILITIES OF GOOD AND POOR READING DISADVANTAGED FIRST-GRADERS EJ 018 198

BRUNER, ELAINE C.
THE DIRECT INSTRUCTION PROGRAM FOR TEACHING READING. ED015022

BRUNING, JAMES L.
GIVEN NAMES AND STEREOTYPING EJ 061 234

BRUNNER, J. S.
HOW ADULTS AND CHILDREN SEARCH AND RECOGNIZE PICTURES EJ 029 384

BRYAN, JAMES H.
PREACHING AND PRACTICING SELF-SACRIFICE: THEIR LOCUS OF EFFECT UPON CHILDREN'S BEHAVIOR AND COGNITION. ED040741
WORDS AND DEEDS ABOUT ALTRUISM AND THE SUBSEQUENT REINFORCEMENT POWER OF THE MODEL. ED043390
PREACHING AND PRACTICING GENEROSITY: CHILDREN'S ACTIONS AND REACTIONS EJ 022 140
THE IMPACT OF WORDS AND DEEDS CONCERNING ALTRUISM UPON CHILDREN EJ 026 154
WORDS AND DEEDS ABOUT ALTRUISM AND THE SUBSEQUENT REINFORCEMENT POWER OF THE MODEL EJ 053 739
MODEL AFFECT AND CHILDREN'S IMITATIVE ALTRUISM EJ 056 719
THE EFFECT OF A TELEVISION MODEL UPON RULE ADOPTION BEHAVIOR OF CHILDREN EJ 056 733

BRYCE, MARVIN E.
144 FOSTER CHILDREN EJ 046 787

BRYSON, JUANITA
COMPETENCE VS. PERFORMANCE IN YOUNG CHILDREN'S USE OF COMPLEX LINGUISTIC STRUCTURES. ED029687
COMPETENCE VERSUS PERFORMANCE IN YOUNG CHILDREN'S USE OF ADJECTIVAL COMPARATIVES EJ 033 701

BUCCHIONI, EUGENE, ED.
PUERTO RICAN CHILDREN IN MAINLAND SCHOOLS. A SOURCE BOOK FOR TEACHERS. ED027953

BUCK, MILDREN R.
FACTORS RELATED TO SCHOOL ACHIEVEMENT IN AN ECONOMICALLY DISADVANTAGED GROUP EJ 056 614

BUCKY, STEVEN F.
RACIAL FACTORS IN TEST PERFORMANCE EJ 053 887

BUDNER, STANLEY
RESEARCH FOR SERVICE TO SEVERELY RETARDED CHILDREN EJ 038 531

BUFFORD, RODGER K.
DISCRIMINATION AND INSTRUCTIONS AS FACTORS IN THE CONTROL OF NONREINFORCED IMITATION EJ 044 157

BUGENTAL, DAPHNE E.
CHILD VERSUS ADULT PERCEPTION OF EVALUATIVE MESSAGES IN VERBAL, VOCAL, AND VISUAL CHANNELS EJ 021 765

BUKTENICA, NORMAN A.
PERCEPTUAL MODE DOMINANCE: AN APPROACH TO ASSESSMENT OF FIRST GRADE READING AND SPELLING. ED026132
VISUAL LEARNING. DIMENSIONS IN EARLY LEARNING SERIES. ED027089
GROUP SCREENING OF AUDITORY AND VISUAL PERCEPTUAL ABILITIES: AN APPROACH TO PERCEPTUAL ASPECTS OF BEGINNING READING. ED033751

BURCHARD, JOHN D.
A METHODOLOGY FOR CONDUCTING AN EXPERIMENTAL ANALYSIS OF CHEATING BEHAVIOR EJ 030 589

BURGER, GARY K.
A FACTOR ANALYSIS OF FIFTH AND SIXTH GRADERS' REPORTS OF PARENTAL CHILD-REARING BEHAVIOR EJ 038 855
CHILDREN'S REPORTS OF PARENTAL CHILD-REARING BEHAVIOR AT FIVE GRADE LEVELS EJ 060 385

BURKE, DEBORAH
APPARENT VISUAL SIZE AS A FUNCTION OF AGE, INTELLIGENCE, AND A SURROUNDING FRAME OF REFERENCE FOR NORMAL AND MENTALLY RETARDED SUBJECTS EJ 043 704
THE EFFECTS OF GROUPING ON SHORT-TERM SERIAL RECALL OF DIGITS BY CHILDREN: DEVELOPMENTAL TRENDS EJ 059 320

BURNES, KAY
PATTERNS OF WISC SCORES FOR CHILDREN OF TWO SOCIOECONOMIC CLASSES AND RACES EJ 021 775

BURNETT, ALICE
PREJUDICE IN THE SCHOOLS EJ 001 498

BURNETT, JACQUETTA H.
CULTURE OF THE SCHOOL: A CONSTRUCT FOR RESEARCH AND EXPLANATION IN EDUCATION. ED039945

BURNS, BRENDA S.
THE USE OF PLAY TECHNIQUES IN THE TREATMENT OF CHILDREN EJ 016 380

BURNS, CRAWFORD E.
WHITE STAFF, BLACK CHILDREN: IS THERE A PROBLEM? EJ 039 799

BURNS, SISTER ALICIA
AN ANALYSIS AND EVALUATION OF THE MONTESSORI THEORY OF INNER DISCIPLINE. ED040746

BURROWS, ROY E.
PHYSIOLOGICAL INDICATIONS OF ORGANIC INVOLVEMENT EJ 051 016

BURTON, ROGER V.
CORRESPONDENCE BETWEEN BEHAVIORAL AND DOLL-PLAY MEASURES OF CONSCIENCE EJ 045 190
AN INEXPENSIVE AND PORTABLE MEANS FOR ONE-WAY OBSERVATION EJ 045 797
THE INTERPRETATION OF INTERGENERATIONAL ATTITUDES EJ 051 565
CROSS-SEX IDENTITY IN BARBADOS EJ 058 136

BUSCHHOFF, LOTTE K.
GOING ON A TRIP EJ 035 842

BUSER, ROBERT L.
LEARNING: THE ROLE OF FACTS AND GENERALIZATIONS EJ 028 638

BUSHELL, DON, JR.
THE SIMULTANEOUS REHABILITATION OF MOTHERS AND THEIR CHILDREN. ED034591
THE BEHAVIOR ANALYSIS CLASSROOM. ED047775
A TOKEN MANUAL FOR BEHAVIOR ANALYSIS CLASSROOMS. ED047776

BUSSARD, FRAN
A GROUP METHOD FOR FINDING AND DEVELOPING FOSTER HOMES EJ 027 920

BUSSE, PAULINE
NEGRO PARENTAL BEHAVIOR AND SOCIAL CLASS VARIABLES EJ 059 871

BUSSE, THOMAS V.
CHILDREARING ANTECEDENTS OF FLEXIBLE THINKING. ED022530
ENVIRONMENTALLY ENRICHED CLASSROOMS AND THE DEVELOPMENT OF DISADVANTAGED PRESCHOOL CHILDREN. ED045192
ONTOGENY OF THE LOCUS AND ORIENTATION OF THE PERCEIVER: A CONFIRMATION AND AN ADDITION EJ 023 433
NEGRO PARENTAL BEHAVIOR AND SOCIAL CLASS VARIABLES EJ 059 871

BUSSIS, ANNE M.
FROM THEORY TO THE CLASSROOM, BACKGROUND INFORMATION ON THE FIRST GRADE PROJECT IN NEW YORK CITY SCHOOLS. ED015770

BUTLER, ANNIE L.
THE CHILD'S RIGHT TO QUALITY DAY CARE: AN ACEI POSITION PAPER EJ 029 103
AREAS OF RECENT RESEARCH IN EARLY CHILDHOOD EDUCATION EJ 054 380

BUTTER, ELIOT J.
A DEVELOPMENTAL INVESTIGATION OF THE EFFECT OF SENSORY MODALITY ON FORM RECOGNITION IN CHILDREN EJ 026 507

BUTTERFIELD, E. C.
WHAT THE DEVELOPMENT OF SHORT-TERM MEMORY IS EJ 049 430

BUTTERFIELD, EARL C.
MOTIVATIONAL FACTORS AND IQ-CHANGES IN CULTURALLY DEPRIVED CHILDREN ATTENDING NURSERY SCHOOL. ED020017
THE INTERACTION OF PRONUNCIABILITY AND RESPONSE PRETRAINING ON THE PAIRED-ASSOCIATE PERFORMANCE OF THIRD-GRADE CHILDREN EJ 021 762

BUZMAN, RICHARD D.
DEVELOPMENT OF HIERARCHIES OF DIMENSIONAL SALIENCE EJ 055 102

BYERS, LIBBY
TO LAUGH IS TO KNOW: A DISCUSSION OF THE COGNITIVE ELEMENT IN CHILDREN'S HUMOR. ED051879

BYRNE, MARGARET C.
HEAD START EVALUATION AND RESEARCH CENTER, UNIVERSITY OF KANSAS. REPORT NO. III, EFFECTS OF A LANGUAGE PROGRAM ON CHILDREN IN A HEAD START NURSERY. ED021636

CAIRNS, NANCY U.
YOUNG CHILDREN'S ORIENTATION OF LETTERS AS A FUNCTION OF AXIS OF SYMMETRY AND STIMULUS ALIGNMENT EJ 032 909

CAIRNS, ROBERT B.
ATTACHMENT BEHAVIORS IN HUMAN INFANTS: DISCRIMINATIVE VOCALIZATION ON MATERNAL SEPARATION EJ 019 019
MEANING AND ATTENTION AS DETERMINANTS OF SOCIAL REINFORCER EFFECTIVENESS EJ 033 781
SOCIAL REINFORCEMENT SATIATION: AN OUTCOME OF FREQUENCY OR AMBIGUITY? EJ 058 144

CALDWELL, BETTYE
CODING MANUAL FOR APPROACH (A PROCEDURE FOR PATTERNING RESPONSES OF ADULTS AND CHILDREN). ED015005

CALDWELL, BETTYE M.
THE CHILDREN'S CENTER--A MICROCOSMIC HEALTH, EDUCATION, AND WELFARE UNIT. PROGRESS REPORT. ED013116
THE PRESCHOOL INVENTORY. ED014334
INFANT DAY CARE AND ATTACHMENT. ED033755
THE EFFECTS OF PSYCHOSOCIAL DEPRIVATION ON HUMAN DEVELOPMENT IN INFANCY. ED034574
THE EFFECTS OF PSYCHOSOCIAL DEPRIVATION ON HUMAN DEVELOPMENT IN INFANCY EJ 026 815
WHAT DOES RESEARCH TEACH US ABOUT DAY CARE: FOR CHILDREN UNDER THREE EJ 051 236

CALDWELL, EDWARD C.
CONCEPT LEARNING IN DISCRIMINATION TASKS EJ 018 878

CALDWELL, WILLARD E.
THE EFFECTS OF PERSONALITY VARIABLES ON DISTORTION THRESHOLDS IN THE AMES ROOM EJ 023 434

CALFEE, ROBERT C.
SHORT-TERM RECOGNITION MEMORY IN CHILDREN EJ 018 873

CALHOUN, L. G.
NUMBER CONSERVATION IN VERY YOUNG CHILDREN: THE EFFECT OF AGE AND MODE OF RESPONDING EJ 041 139

CALHOUN, LAWRENCE G.
SEX-ROLE AND NEED FOR APPROVAL IN ADOLESCENTS EJ 051 014

CALLAHAN, LEROY G.
ELEMENTARY SCHOOL MATHEMATICS: A GUIDE TO CURRENT RESEARCH. THIRD EDITION. ED026123

CAMBIER, ANNE
UN EXEMPLE D'OBSERVATION INTENSIVE DU COMPORTEMENT DE JEUNES ENFANTS DANS LE CADRE D'UNE GARDERIE EJ 034 534

CAMP, JANET
ALL ABOUT ME. UNIT 1 CURRICULUM GUIDE. ED053789
AUTUMN. UNIT 3 CURRICULUM GUIDE. ED053790

CAMP, JANET C.
A SKILL DEVELOPMENT CURRICULUM FOR 3, 4, AND 5 YEAR OLD DISADVANTAGED CHILDREN. ED040755

CAMPBELL, SUSAN B.
COGNITIVE STYLES IN HYPERACTIVE CHILDREN AND THE EFFECT OF METHYLPHENIDATE EJ 041 963

CAMPIONE, JOSEPH C.
THE EFFECTS OF STIMULUS REDUNDANCY ON TRANSFER OF STIMULUS PRETRAINING EJ 041 138
THE PERFORMANCE OF PRESCHOOL CHILDREN ON REVERSAL AND TWO TYPES OF EXTRADIMENSIONAL SHIFTS EJ 042 967
TRANSFER OF TRAINING: SOME BOUNDARY CONDITIONS AND INITIAL THEORY EJ 053 722
COLOR DOMINANCE IN PRESCHOOL CHILDREN AS A FUNCTION OF SPECIFIC CUE PREFERENCES EJ 053 738

CANTOR, GORDON N.
EFFECTS OF CONTEXT ON PRESCHOOL CHILDREN'S JUDGMENTS EJ 042 968

CANTOR, JOAN H.
FACILITATING AND INTERFERING EFFECTS OF STIMULUS NAMING ON CHILDREN'S MOTOR PAIRED-ASSOCIATE LEARNING EJ 033 793

CAPKOVA, DAGMAR
PRE-SCHOOL EDUCATION IN THE WORK OF J.A. COMENIUS (KOMENSKY) EJ 029 619

CAPUTO, DANIEL V.
CONSEQUENCES OF LOW BIRTH WEIGHT EJ 030 430

CAREY, RUSSEL L.
A STUDY OF THE INTERRELATIONSHIPS OF CONSERVATION OF LENGTH RELATIONS, CONSERVATIONS OF LENGTH, AND TRANSITIVITY OF LENGTH RELATIONS OF THE AGE OF FOUR AND FIVE YEARS. ED031303

CAREY, RUSSELL L.
AN INVESTIGATION IN THE LEARNING OF EQUIVALENCE AND ORDER RELATIONS BY FOUR- AND FIVE-YEAR-OLD CHILDREN. ED045178
BEFORE CHILDREN CAN MEASURE EJ 032 359

CARKIN, HELEN S.
A STUDY OF THE EFFECTIVENESS OF SPECIFIC TEACHING OF CONSERVATION TO CHILDREN IN SELECTED ELEMENTARY SCHOOLS OF BUTTE COUNTY, CALIFORNIA EJ 027 029

CARLSON, J. S.
SOME RELATIONSHIPS BETWEEN CLASS INCLUSION, PERCEPTUAL CAPABILITIES, VERBAL CAPABILITIES AND RACE EJ 039 639

CARLSON, JERRY S.
THE DEVELOPMENT OF PROBABILISTIC THINKING IN CHILDREN: A COMPARISON OF TWO METHODS OF ASSESSMENT EJ 023 193
SOME RELATIONSHIPS BETWEEN VERBAL AND PERCEPTUAL CAPABILITIES AND THE DEVELOPMENT OF RELATIVE THINKING EJ 035 383

CARMEAN, C. JEAN
POSITION STRATEGIES IN AN OBJECT DISCRIMINATION TASK EJ 052 458

CARMEAN, STEPHEN L.
POSITION STRATEGIES IN AN OBJECT DISCRIMINATION TASK EJ 052 458

CARMICHAEL, LARAINE MORES
EXPRESSIONS OF PERSONALITY IN CREATIONS OF LATENCY AGE CHILDREN EJ 041 446

CARMON, HANNA
AN ANALYSIS OF MOTHERS' SPEECH AS A FACTOR IN THE DEVELOPMENT OF CHILDREN'S INTELLIGENCE. ED042504

CARON, ALBERT J.
DISCRIMINATION SHIFTS IN THREE-YEAR-OLDS AS A FUNCTION OF SHIFT PROCEDURE EJ 027 184

CARON, ROSE F.
SATIATION OF VISUAL REINFORCEMENT IN YOUNG INFANTS EJ 043 666

CARPENTER, ETHELOUISE
FREEDOM TO MOVE. ED020778

CARPENTER, GENEVIEVE C.
DIFFERENTIAL VISUAL BEHAVIOR TO HUMAN AND HUMANOID FACES IN EARLY INFANCY EJ 019 595
VISUAL RESPONSE DECREMENT AS A FUNCTION OF AGE OF HUMAN NEWBORNS EJ 056 716

CARTER, BARBARA
A REPORT OF THE SOUTHERN REGIONAL CONFERENCE ON EARLY CHILDHOOD EDUCATION. ED019112

CARTER, HAROLD D.
A GEOMETRIC REPRESENTATION OF THE NOTIONS OF RELIABILITY, RELEVANCE, AND VALIDITY EJ 043 456

CARTER, HEATHER L.
A STUDY OF THE ABILITY OF PRIMARY SCHOOL CHILDREN TO GENERALIZE BEHAVIORAL COMPETENCIES SPECIFIED FOR "SCIENCE--A PROCESS APPROACH" TO OTHER CONTENT SETTINGS. ED039038
A STUDY OF ONE LEARNER COGNITIVE STYLE AND THE ABILITY TO GENERALIZE BEHAVIORAL COMPETENCIES. ED040758

CARTER, JAMES
HEALTH AND NUTRITION IN DISADVANTAGED CHILDREN AND THEIR RELATIONSHIP WITH INTELLECTUAL DEVELOPMENT. COLLABORATIVE RESEARCH REPORT. ED052816

CARTER, LAMORE J.
AN ATTACK ON IMPEDIMENTS TO EFFECTIVE CROSS-CULTURAL TEACHING EJ 032 553

CARTWRIGHT, WALTER J.
REPORT OF THE EFFECTIVENESS OF PROJECT HEAD START, LUBBOCK, TEXAS. PARTS I, II, AND APPENDICES. ED019131

CASELLI, RON
KEYS TO STANDARD ENGLISH EJ 028 577

CASS, JOAN E.
THE ROLE OF THE TEACHER IN THE INFANT AND NURSERY SCHOOL. ED029703

CASSEL, RUSSELL N.
IMPROVING HIGH SCHOOL LEARNING PREDICTIONS WITH MULTIPLE JUNIOR HIGH TEST SCORES EJ 016 653

CASTELL, ROLF
EFFECT OF FAMILIAR AND UNFAMILIAR ENVIRONMENTS ON PROXIMITY BEHAVIOR OF YOUNG CHILDREN EJ 024 935

CASTLE, RAYMOND L.
78 BATTERED CHILDREN: A RETROSPECTIVE STUDY. ED043382

CATHCART, W. GEORGE
THE RELATIONSHIP BETWEEN PRIMARY STUDENTS' RATIONALIZATION OF CONSERVATION AND THEIR MATHEMATICAL ACHIEVEMENT EJ 046 672

CATTELL, RAYMOND B.
SEPARATING ENDOGENOUS, EXOGENOUS, ECOGENIC, AND EPOGENIC COMPONENT CURVES IN DEVELOPMENTAL DATA EJ 027 552

CAUDILL, WILLIAM
TINY DRAMAS: VOCAL COMMUNICATION BETWEEN MOTHER AND INFANT IN JAPANESE AND AMERICAN FAMILIES. ED048927

CAUSEY, J. P.
SYMPOSIUM: FOR AND AGAINST STRIKES EJ 003 416

CAWLEY, JOHN F.
AN ASSESSMENT OF INTELLIGENCE, PSYCHOLINGUISTIC ABILITIES AND LEARNING APTITUDES AMONG PRESCHOOL CHILDREN. ED014323
AN APPRAISAL OF HEAD START PARTICIPANTS AND NON-PARTICIPANTS: EXPANDED CONSIDERATIONS ON LEARNING DISABILITIES AMONG DISADVANTAGED CHILDREN. ED027939

CAZDEN, COURTNEY B.
ELEMENTARY EDUCATION RESPONDS TO A CHANGING SOCIETY ED024448
A LONDON INFANT SCHOOL. AN INTERVIEW. ED027963
TRANSPLANTING ENGLISH INFANT SCHOOL IDEAS TO AMERICAN CLASSROOMS AND SOME EFFECTS ON LANGUAGE USE. ED040756
LANGUAGE PROGRAMS FOR YOUNG CHILDREN: NOTES FROM ENGLAND AND WALES. ED040763
SUGGESTIONS FROM STUDIES OF EARLY LANGUAGE ACQUISITION EJ 012 396
CHILDREN'S QUESTIONS: THEIR FORMS, FUNCTIONS AND ROLES IN EDUCATION EJ 017 608

CECIL, HENRY S.
THE PSYCHOLOGICAL EFFECTS OF PREGNANCY AND NEONATAL HEALTH THREATS ON CHILD DEVELOPMENT. ED048921

CERMAK, LAIRD S.
DEVELOPMENT OF THE ABILITY TO ENCODE WITHIN EVALUATIVE DIMENSIONS EJ 053 728

CERVENKA, EDWARD J.
FINAL REPORT ON HEAD START EVALUATION AND RESEARCH--1966-67 TO THE INSTITUTE FOR EDUCATIONAL DEVELOPMENT. SECTION VI, THE MEASUREMENT OF BILINGUALISM AND BICULTURAL SOCIALIZATION OF THE CHILD IN THE SCHOOL SETTING--THE DEVELOPMENT OF INSTRUMENTS. ED019122

CERVENKA, EDWARD JOHN
ADMINISTRATION MANUAL FOR THE INVENTORY OF SOCIALIZATION OF BILINGUAL CHILDREN AGES THREE TO TEN. PART OF THE FINAL REPORT. ED027062
ADMINISTRATION MANUAL FOR TESTS OF BASIC LANGUAGE COMPETENCE IN ENGLISH AND SPANISH. LEVEL I (PRESCHOOL) ED027063
ADMINISTRATION MANUAL FOR TESTS OF BASIC LANGUAGE COMPETENCE IN ENGLISH AND SPANISH. LEVEL II (PRIMARY GRADES): CHILDREN AGES SIX TO TEN, ENGLISH AND SPANISH VERSIONS, FORMS A AND B. PART OF THE FINAL REPORT. ED027064

CHACE, CHARLES A.
PARENTAL CONCEPTUAL SYSTEMS, HOME PLAY ENVIRONMENT, AND POTENTIAL CREATIVITY IN CHILDREN. ED043386
PARENTAL CONCEPTUAL SYSTEMS, HOME PLAY ENVIRONMENT, AND POTENTIAL CREATIVITY IN CHILDREN EJ 048 234

CHAFFEE, EVERETT
TEACHING MUSICAL CONCEPTS RELATED TO MELODY, RHYTHM, FORM, AND HARMONY, TEACHER RESOURCE MATERIAL KINDERGARTEN, GRADES 1 AND 2. ED019991

CHAMBERS, DONALD E.
WILLINGNESS TO ADOPT ATYPICAL CHILDREN EJ 020 860

CHAMPAGNE, DAVID W.
SIMULATION ACTIVITIES FOR TRAINING PARENTS AND TEACHERS AS EDUCATIONAL PARTNERS: A REPORT AND EVALUATION. ED048945

CHANCE, JUNE ELIZABETH
MOTHER-CHILD RELATIONS AND CHILDREN'S ACHIEVEMENT. TERMINAL REPORT. ED024465

CHANDLER, MARVIN
PROJECT HEAD START AND THE CULTURALLY DEPRIVED IN ROCHESTER, NEW YORK, A STUDY OF PARTICIPATING AND NON-PARTICIPATING FAMILIES IN AREAS SERVED BY PROJECT HEAD START IN ROCHESTER, FINAL REPORT. ED013669

CHANSKY, NORMAN M.
ESTEEM AND ACHIEVEMENT IN ARITHMETIC EJ 015 160

CHARLESWORTH, ROSALIND
POSITIVE SOCIAL REINFORCEMENT IN THE NURSERY SCHOOL PEER GROUP. ED016515

CHAZAN, MAURICE
BEHAVIOUR PROBLEMS IN THE INFANT SCHOOL EJ 048 306

CHEMA, REGINA
ADOPTIVE PLACEMENT OF THE OLDER CHILD EJ 027 644

CHEN, MARTIN K.
AN EXPERIMENTAL STUDY OF FORMAL READING INSTRUCTION AT THE KINDERGARTEN LEVEL. ED022533

CHENOWETH, ALICE D.
PLANNING FOR A MASS ATTACK ON RUBELLA EJ 007 164

CHERTOW, DORIS S.
PROJECT HEAD START, THE URBAN AND RURAL CHALLENGE. FINAL REPORT. ED022527

CHESS, STELLA
BEHAVIOR DEVIATIONS IN MENTALLY RETARDED CHILDREN EJ 022 475

CHESS, STELLA, ED.
ANNUAL PROGRESS IN CHILD PSYCHIATRY AND CHILD DEVELOPMENT 1969. ED032941

CHESTEEN, HILLIARD E., JR.
EFFECTIVENESS OF THE HEAD START PROGRAM IN ENHANCING SCHOOL READINESS OF CULTURALLY DEPRIVED CHILDREN. ED020771

CHETHIK, MORTON
THE IMPACT OF OBJECT LOSS ON A SIX-YEAR-OLD EJ 030 514

CHEYNE, J. A.
EFFECTS OF IMITATION OF DIFFERENT REINFORCEMENT COMBINATIONS TO A MODEL EJ 046 255
SOME PARAMETERS OF PUNISHMENT AFFECTING RESISTANCE TO DEVIATION AND GENERALIZATION OF A PROHIBITION EJ 052 457

CHEYNE, WILLIAM M.
EMOTIONAL SENSITIVITY AND INTELLIGENCE IN CHILDREN FROM ORPHANAGES AND NORMAL HOMES EJ 043 859

CHILDERS, PERRY
THE CONCEPT OF DEATH IN EARLY CHILDHOOD EJ 052 464

CHILMAN, CATHERINE
DESIGNS AND PROPOSAL FOR EARLY CHILDHOOD RESEARCH: A NEW LOOK: A MULTIPLE SYSTEMS-SERVICE APPROACH TO PROGRAMS AND RESEARCH FOR HELPING POOR CHILDREN. (ONE IN A SERIES OF SIX PAPERS). ED053806

CHILMAN, CATHERINE S.
SOME ANGLES ON PARENT-TEACHER LEARNING EJ 054 162

CHISSOM, BRAD S.
A FACTOR-ANALYTIC STUDY OF THE RELATIONSHIP OF MOTOR FACTORS TO ACADEMIC CRITERIA FOR FIRST- AND THIRD-GRADE BOYS EJ 052 451

CHITTENDEN, EDWARD A.
UNDERSTANDING OF QUANTITATIVE CONCEPTS IN 3 1/2-4 1/2 YEAR-OLD CHILDREN. ED046491
WHAT IS LEARNED AND WHAT IS TAUGHT EJ 010 443

CHOMSKY, CAROL
WRITE FIRST, READ LATER EJ 034 069

CHOROST, SHERWOOD B.
AN EVALUATION OF THE EFFECTS OF A SUMMER HEAD START PROGRAM. ED014327

CHOW, STANLEY H. L.
THE DEVELOPMENT OF AN INFORMATION UNIT REVIEWING SELECTED WELL-DEVELOPED MODELS OF EARLY CHILDHOOD EDUCATION PROGRAMS. FINAL REPORT. ED045223

CHRISTOPHERSON, JOAN
A BACKWARD GLANCE--A FORWARD STEP? EJ 020 295

CHRISTY, PAULINE R.
EFFECTS OF COMPETITION-INDUCED FRUSTRATION ON TWO CLASSES OF MODELED BEHAVIOR EJ 043 284

CIACCIO, N. V.
A TEST OF ERIKSON'S THEORY OF EGO EPIGENESIS EJ 039 898

CICIRELLI, VICTOR G.
THE EFFECT OF SIBLING RELATIONSHIP ON CONCEPT LEARNING OF YOUNG CHILDREN TAUGHT BY CHILD-TEACHERS EJ 056 399

CLAMAN, LAWRENCE
SECOND STAGE TEACHING PROBLEMS IN A PUBLIC SCHOOL CLASS FOR EMOTIONALLY DISTURBED CHILDREN EJ 020 104

CLAPP, WILLIAM F.
DEPENDENCE AND COMPETENCE IN FOUR-YEAR-OLD BOYS AS RELATED TO PARENTAL TREATMENT OF THE CHILD. ED039952

CLAPP, WILLIAM FORD
COMPETENCE AND DEPENDENCE IN CHILDREN: PARENTAL TREATMENT OF FOUR-YEAR-OLD GIRLS. FINAL REPORT. ED030497

CLARK, NORMA
SELF-REINFORCEMENT ESTABLISHED FOR A DISCRIMINATION TASK EJ 025 964

CLARK, PHILIP M.
PERSONALITY, COGNITIVE, AND DEMOGRAPHIC CHARACTERISTICS OF STUDENT ACTIVISTS AND ACTIVE STUDENTS EJ 061 194

CLASS, NORRIS E.
LICENSING OF CHILD CARE FACILITIES BY STATE WELFARE DEPARTMENTS: A CONCEPTUAL STATEMENT. ED046489

CLAY, MARIE M.
AN INCREASING EFFECT OF DISORIENTATION ON THE DISCRIMINATION OF PRINT: A DEVELOPMENTAL STUDY EJ 024 982
SENTENCE REPETITION: ELICITED IMITATION OF A CONTROLLED SET OF SYNTACTIC STRUCTURES BY FOUR LANGUAGE GROUPS EJ 052 175

CLAY, SUZANNE
HEAD START EVALUATION AND RESEARCH CENTER, BOSTON UNIVERSITY. REPORT E-I, THE UTILIZATION OF NON-PROFESSIONAL INTERVIEWERS IN THE NEW ENGLAND AND MISSISSIPPI SAMPLES BY THE BOSTON UNIVERSITY HEAD START EVALUATION AND RESEARCH PROGRAM, 1966-1967. ED022566

CLEARY, T. ANNE
THE RELATIONSHIP BETWEEN CHILDREN'S ACADEMIC PERFORMANCE AND ACHIEVEMENT ACCOUNTABILITY EJ 058 414

CLEMENT, DAVID E.
JUDGMENTS OF PATTERN GOODNESS AND PATTERN PREFERENCE AS FUNCTIONS OF AGE AND PATTERN UNCERTAINTY EJ 046 782

CLEMENT, PAUL W.
TANGIBLE REINFORCERS AND CHILD GROUP THERAPY EJ 026 935

CLIFFORD, MARGARET M.
THE RELATIONSHIP BETWEEN CHILDREN'S ACADEMIC PERFORMANCE AND ACHIEVEMENT ACCOUNTABILITY EJ 058 414

CLINE, MARVIN
AN EVALUATION AND FOLLOW-UP STUDY OF SUMMER 1966 HEAD START CHILDREN IN WASHINGTON, D.C. ED020794

CLOSE, KATHRYN
PROMOTING CHILD HEALTH THROUGH COMPREHENSIVE CARE EJ 007 165
SELECTING PRIORITIES AT THE WHITE HOUSE CONFERENCE ON CHILDREN EJ 035 619

COATES, BRIAN
INTERRELATIONS IN THE ATTACHMENT BEHAVIOR OF HUMAN INFANTS EJ 055 208
THE STABILITY OF ATTACHMENT BEHAVIORS IN THE HUMAN INFANT EJ 055 209
WHITE ADULT BEHAVIOR TOWARD BLACK AND WHITE CHILDREN EJ 056 729

COBB, JOSEPH A.
SURVIVAL SKILLS AND FIRST GRADE ACADEMIC ACHIEVEMENT. REPORT #1. ED050807

COBB, JUDITH
HEAD START EVALUATION AND RESEARCH CENTER. PROGRESS REPORT OF RESEARCH STUDIES 1966 TO 1967. DOCUMENT 3, AN EXPERIMENTAL APPROACH TO STUDYING NON-VERBAL REPRESENTATION IN YOUNG CHILDREN. ED021625

COCHRANE, HORTENCE S.
HEALTH CARE OF CHILDREN: A CHALLENGE. ED050804

COFFMAN, ALICE O.
THE EFFECTS OF ASSESSMENT AND PERSONALIZED PROGRAMMING ON SUBSEQUENT INTELLECTUAL DEVELOPMENT OF PREKINDERGARTEN AND KINDERGARTEN CHILDREN. ED013663
THE EFFECTS OF ASSESSMENT AND PERSONALIZED PROGRAMMING ON SUBSEQUENT INTELLECTUAL DEVELOPMENT OF PREKINDERGARTEN AND KINDERGARTEN CHILDREN. FINAL REPORT OF PHASE II. ED023487
THE EFFECTS OF ASSESSMENT AND PERSONALIZED PROGRAMMING ON SUBSEQUENT INTELLECTUAL DEVELOPMENT OF PREKINDERGARTEN AND KINDERGARTEN CHILDREN. FINAL REPORT. ED045198

COHEN, DONALD J.
VIEWPOINT: GAP AND THE JOINT COMMISSION ON MENTAL HEALTH OF CHILDREN EJ 060 203

COHEN, DOROTHY H.
ADDRESS AT COMBINED MEETING OF N.Y.C. EARLY CHILDHOOD COUNCIL AND THE METROPOLITAN ASSOCIATION FOR CHILDHOOD EDUCATION ON "LANGUAGE ARTS MATERIALS IN EARLY CHILDHOOD" (TEACHERS COLLEGE, COLUMBIA UNIVERSITY, APRIL 6, 1968): ED039951
LEARNING TO OBSERVE--OBSERVING TO LEARN. ED047815
CONTINUITY FROM PREKINDERGARTEN TO KINDERGARTEN EJ 039 058
CHILDREN OF TECHNOLOGY: IMAGES OR THE REAL THING EJ 054 472

COHEN, LESLIE B.
RECOVERY OF HABITUATION IN INFANTS EJ 021 078
INFANT HABITUATION AND GENERALIZATION TO DIFFERING DEGREES OF STIMULUS NOVELTY EJ 043 195

COHEN, MIRIAM
EXTINCTION IN DISCRIMINATION LEARNING--PRESENTATION AND CONTINGENCY VARIABLES AND ASSOCIATED SIDE EFFECTS. ED019139

COHEN, SHIRLEY
PLANNING TRIPS FOR VULNERABLE CHILDREN EJ 048 998

COHEN, STEWART
AN EXAMINATION OF FRUSTRATION AGGRESSION RELATIONS IN BOYS DURING MIDDLE CHILDHOOD EJ 035 628
CHILDREN'S OBSERVATION AND INTEGRATION OF AGGRESSIVE EXPERIENCES EJ 055 212

COHEN, STUART J.
A CASE AGAINST A CASE AGAINST BEHAVIORAL OBJECTIVES EJ 036 083

COHLER, BERTRAM J.
THE CHILDCARE ATTITUDES OF TWO GENERATIONS OF MOTHERS EJ 032 796
THE ROLE OF RETROSPECTIVE ACCOUNTS IN THE STUDY OF INTERGENERATIONAL ATTITUDES EJ 051 564

COHN, MAXINE
FOR BETTER READING - A MORE POSITIVE SELF-IMAGE EJ 013 562

COHNSTAEDT, MARTIN L.
THE IMPACT OF OPERATION HEAD START ON GREENE COUNTY, OHIO, AN EVALUATION REPORT. ED020772

COITEUX, PAUL F.
LEARNING TO BE GENEROUS OR STINGY: IMITATION OF SHARING BEHAVIOR AS A FUNCTION OF MODEL GENEROSITY AND VICARIOUS REINFORCEMENT EJ 052 443

COKIN, MOLLY
HELPING PARENTS IN A PEDIATRIC CLINIC EJ 046 963

COLE, LAWRENCE E.
PAIRED-ASSOCIATE LEARNING AND BIDIRECTIONAL ASSOCIATIVE RECALL IN FIRST, THIRD, FIFTH AND SEVENTH GRADERS EJ 053 481

COLE, MICHAEL
DEVELOPMENT OF FREE RECALL LEARNING IN CHILDREN EJ 035 359
PATTERNS OF RESPONDING IN THE WORD ASSOCIATIONS OF WEST AFRICAN CHILDREN EJ 056 634

COLLARD, ROBERTA R.
EXPLORATORY AND PLAY BEHAVIORS OF INFANTS REARED IN AN INSTITUTION AND IN LOWER- AND MIDDLE-CLASS HOMES EJ 052 441

COLLER, ALAN R.
INITIAL AND FINAL CONSONANT RELATIONSHIPS IN SPEECH-SOUND TESTS: A DISCRIMINATION OR RESPONSE SET PROBLEM? ED032131
THE ASSESSMENT OF "SELF-CONCEPT" IN EARLY CHILDHOOD EDUCATION. ED050822

COLLINS, ALICE H.
THE DAY CARE NEIGHBOR SERVICE: A HANDBOOK FOR THE ORGANIZATION AND OPERATION OF A NEW APPROACH TO FAMILY DAY CARE. ED049810

COLLINS, CAMILLA
THE ITINERANT TEACHER. ED045191
THE ITINERANT TEACHER EJ 060 930

COLLINS, W. ANDREW
LEARNING OF MEDIA CONTENT: A DEVELOPMENTAL STUDY EJ 033 782

COLTON, FRANK V.
EFFECTS OF VIEWING VIDEOTAPED SAME AND OPPOSITE COLOR CHILD-TEACHERS ON INTEGRATED AND ALL-WHITE KINDERGARTNERS. ED047805
COGNITIVE AND AFFECTIVE REACTIONS OF KINDERGARTNERS TO VIDEO DISPLAYS EJ 057 016

COMBS, ARTHUR W.
NEW CONCEPTS OF HUMAN POTENTIALS: NEW CHALLENGE FOR TEACHERS EJ 034 711

COMBS, ELOYCE F.
FLORIDA'S EARLY CHILDHOOD LEARNING PROGRAM FOR MIGRANT CHILDREN EJ 043 089

CONANT, MARGARET M.
TEACHERS AND PARENTS: CHANGING ROLES AND GOALS EJ 055 362

CONCANNON, SISTER JOSEPHINA
A LONGITUDINAL ASSESSMENT OF PRESCHOOL CHILDREN IN HAPTIC LEARNING. FINAL REPORT. ED020019

CONNERS, C. KEITH
THE EFFECT OF HEADSTART ON DEVELOPMENTAL PROCESSES. ED020026
A FOLLOW-UP STUDY OF INTELLIGENCE CHANGES IN CHILDREN WHO PARTICIPATED IN PROJECT HEADSTART. ED020786
SYMPTOM PATTERNS IN HYPERKINETIC, NEUROTIC, AND NORMAL CHILDREN EJ 025 360

CONNET, MARGARET
A GLANCE AT A HEAD START PROGRAM IN AN ALASKAN CITY EJ 058 768

CONNOR, ANGIE
USE OF NON-PROFESSIONAL PERSONNEL FOR HEALTH SCREENING OF HEAD START CHILDREN. FINAL REPORT. ED029702

CONRAD, R.
THE CHRONOLOGY OF THE DEVELOPMENT OF COVERT SPEECH IN CHILDREN EJ 047 594

CONSTANTINOPLE, ANNE
SOME CORRELATES OF AVERAGE LEVEL OF HAPPINESS AMONG COLLEGE STUDENTS EJ 021 994

CONWAY, C. B.
A STUDY OF PUBLIC AND PRIVATE KINDERGARTEN AND NON-KINDERGARTEN CHILDREN IN THE PRIMARY GRADES. ED028837

CONWAY, ESTHER
II. DELIVERY MEDICATION AND INFANT OUTCOME: AN EMPIRICAL STUDY EJ 023 014

COOK, DORIS M., ED.
TEACHER AIDES: HANDBOOK FOR INSTRUCTORS AND ADMINISTRATORS. ED024461
SUPPLEMENTARY MATERIALS FOR TEACHER AIDE TRAINING PROGRAMS, TO SUPPLEMENT THE PUBLICATION "TEACHER AIDES: HANDBOOK FOR INSTRUCTORS AND ADMINISTRATORS." ED024462

COOK, HAROLD
VERBAL MEDIATION AND SATIATION IN YOUNG CHILDREN EJ 056 613

COOK, PATRICIA
A STUDY IN CHILD CARE (CASE STUDY FROM VOLUME II-B): "WILL YOU MARRY ME?" DAY CARE PROGRAM REPRINT SERIES. ED051906

COONEY, JOAN GANZ
THE FIRST YEAR OF SESAME STREET: A HISTORY AND OVERVIEW. FINAL REPORT, VOLUME I OF V VOLUMES. ED047821

COOPER, CARIN
INVESTIGATIONS OF THE ROLE OF SELECTED CUES IN CHILDREN'S PAIRED-ASSOCIATE LEARNING. REPORT FROM THE READING PROJECT. ED036315

COOPER, DEBORAH L.
CONDITIONAL DISCRIMINATION LEARNING IN CHILDREN: TWO RELEVANT FACTORS EJ 036 823

COOPER, LESLIE M.
THE DEVELOPMENT OF HYPNOTIC SUSCEPTIBILITY: A LONGITUDINAL (CONVERGENCE) STUDY EJ 041 449

COOPER, LYNN A.
COMING OF AGE WITH THE DELBOEUF ILLUSION: BRIGHTNESS CONTRAST, COGNITION AND PERCEPTUAL DEVELOPMENT EJ 055 100

COOPER, MARGARET
HEAD START EVALUATION AND RESEARCH CENTER, UNIVERSITY OF KANSAS. REPORT NO. I, THE OBSERVATION OF REINFORCEMENT BEHAVIOR OF TEACHERS IN HEAD START CLASSROOMS AND THE MODIFICATION OF A TEACHER'S ATTENDING BEHAVIOR. ED021633

COOPER, MARGARET L.
EXPERIMENTAL ANALYSIS OF EFFECTS OF TEACHER ATTENTION OF PRESCHOOL CHILDREN'S BLOCK BUILDING BEHAVIOR. PROGRESS REPORT. ED042498
THE MODIFICATION OF TEACHER BEHAVIORS WHICH MODIFY CHILD BEHAVIORS. PROGRESS REPORT. ED042499
A SHOE IS TO TIE: A FILM DEMONSTRATION OF PROGRAMMING SELF-HELP SKILLS FOR PRESCHOOL CHILDREN. PROGRESS REPORT. ED042500

COOPERSMITH, STANLEY
IMPLICATIONS OF STUDIES ON SELF-ESTEEM FOR EDUCATIONAL RESEARCH AND PRACTICE. ED033742

COOPERSMITH, STANLEY, COMP.
A RESOURCE AND REFERENCE BIBLIOGRAPHY IN EARLY CHILDHOOD EDUCATION AND DEVELOPMENTAL PSYCHOLOGY: THE AFFECTIVE DOMAIN. ED049817

COPPINGER, N. W.
DISCRIMINATION LEARNING AND TRANSFER OF TRAINING IN THE AGED EJ 055 204

CORDASCO, FRANCESCO, ED.
PUERTO RICAN CHILDREN IN MAINLAND SCHOOLS. A SOURCE BOOK FOR TEACHERS. ED027953

CORLE, CLYDE G.
SKILL GAMES FOR MATHEMATICS. ED022548

CORMAN, H. H.
THE IMPACT OF MOTHER'S PRESENCE UPON BEHAVIOR: THE FIRST YEAR EJ 039 908

CORMAN, HARVEY H.
STAGES OF SENSORIMOTOR DEVELOPMENT: A REPLICATION STUDY EJ 011 916

CORNELIUS, RUTH
STOP, LOOK, LISTEN -- AND KEEP ON!! EJ 058 133

CORSINI, D. A.
MEMORY: INTERACTION OF STIMULUS AND ORGANISMIC FACTORS EJ 049 429

CORT, H. RUSSELL, JR.
A STUDY OF THE FULL-YEAR 1966 HEAD START PROGRAMS. ED015010
RESULTS OF THE SUMMER 1965 PROJECT HEAD START. VOLUMES I AND II. ED018250

CORTER, CARL M.
TOYS DELAY THE INFANT'S FOLLOWING OF HIS MOTHER EJ 053 713

CORTES, CARLOS F.
EVALUATION OF THE CLEVELAND CHILD DEVELOPMENT PROGRAM. A LONGITUDINAL STUDY (FIRST YEAR REPORT). ED020000

COSTELLO, JOAN
MODIFICATION OF THE PEABODY PICTURE VOCABULARY TEST. ED033752
RESEARCH IN A BLACK COMMUNITY: FOUR YEARS IN REVIEW. ED039035
REVIEW AND SUMMARY OF A NATIONAL SURVEY OF THE PARENT-CHILD CENTER PROGRAM. ED048941
PRESCHOOL PROGRAMS. IJR PRESCHOOL PROJECT REPORT, VOLUME I. ED052815
SCHOOL ACHIEVERS AND UNDERACHIEVERS IN AN URBAN GHETTO EJ 027 614

COSTIN, LELA B.
NEW DIRECTIONS IN THE LICENSING OF CHILD CARE FACILITIES EJ 016 608

COTTER, VANCE W.
A NONVERBAL TECHNIQUE FOR STUDYING MUSIC PREFERENCE EJ 043 285

COURSIN, DAVID BAIRD
NUTRITION AND BRAIN DEVELOPMENT IN INFANTS EJ 058 223

COURSON, CLIFFORD C.
FREEDOM OF CHOICE- WHO'S KIDDING WHOM?; FREEDOM- CHOICE AND RESPONSIBILITY. A SYMPOSIUM EJ 011 984

COURTNEY, ROSALEA G.
A DEVELOPMENTAL STUDY OF NONCONSERVATION CHOICES IN YOUNG CHILDREN EJ 011 917

COWE, EILEEN
SHOWING AND SHARING IN THE KINDERGARTEN EJ 032 933

COWLES, JAMES D.
AN EXPERIMENTAL STUDY OF VISUAL PERCEPTUAL TRAINING AND READINESS SCORES WITH CERTAIN FIRST-GRADE CHILDREN. ED032921

COWLES, MILLY
PSYCHOLINGUISTIC BEHAVIORS OF BLACK, DISADVANTAGED RURAL CHILDREN. ED039037
PSYCHOLINGUISTIC BEHAVIORS OF ISOLATED, RURAL CHILDREN WITH AND WITHOUT KINDERGARTEN. ED042510

COWLING, DOROTHY N. C.
LANGUAGE ABILITY AND READINESS FOR SCHOOL OF CHILDREN WHO PARTICIPATED IN HEAD START PROGRAMS. A DISSERTATION ABSTRACT. ED025299

COX, FRANCES M.
EVALUATION OF THE PRESCHOOL PROGRAM, 1966-67, FUNDED UNDER ESEA TITLE I, P.L. 89-10. ED026143

COX, HELEN R.
EFFECT OF MATERNAL ATTITUDES, TEACHER ATTITUDES, AND TYPE OF NURSERY SCHOOL TRAINING ON THE ABILITIES OF PRESCHOOL CHILDREN. FINAL REPORT. ED028844

COX, JANET
DISADVANTAGED AND NONDISADVANTAGED CHILDREN'S EXPECTANCY IN SKILL AND CHANCE OUTCOMES EJ 034 903

COX, SAMUEL H.
FAMILY BACKGROUND EFFECTS ON PERSONALITY DEVELOPMENT AND SOCIAL ACCEPTANCE. ED020020
INTRAFAMILY COMPARISON OF LOVING-REJECTING CHILD-REARING PRACTICES EJ 021 081

COYLE, SISTER JOHN VIANNEY
A LONGITUDINAL ASSESSMENT OF PRESCHOOL CHILDREN IN HAPTIC LEARNING. FINAL REPORT. ED020019

CRABB, PAULINE
A PARENT'S GIFT EJ 016 773

CRAIG, MARJORIE L.
ENRICHING CHILDREN'S LIVES: INTERNATIONAL CO-OPERATION THROUGH UNICEF AND OMEP EJ 062 417

CRAMER, WARD
ARE MOVERS LOSERS? EJ 018 958
MY MON CAN TEACH READING TOO! EJ 051 082

CRAVIOTO, J.
THE ECOLOGY OF GROWTH AND DEVELOPMENT IN A MEXICAN PREINDUSTRIAL COMMUNITY. REPORT 1: METHOD AND FINDINGS FROM BIRTH TO ONE MONTH OF AGE EJ 007 791

CRAWFORD, ALAN N.
A PILOT STUDY OF COMPUTER-ASSISTED DRILL AND PRACTICE IN SEVENTH GRADE REMEDIAL MATHEMATICS EJ 027 030

CRAWFORD, GAIL
AN EXAMINATION OF CHANGES IN ATTITUDES TO VISUAL COMPLEXITY WITH INCREASING AGE. ED039930

CRAWFORD, PATRICIA
SCHOOL ACHIEVEMENT: A PRELIMINARY LOOK AT THE EFFECTS OF THE HOME. ED047777

CREEK, LEON VANDE
A PRELIMINARY VIEW OF TRENDS IN AGE, EDUCATION, AND INTELLIGENCE OF PROBLEM YOUTH EJ 030 431

CRINELLA, FRANCIS M.
UNILATERAL DOMINANCE IS NOT RELATED TO NEUROPSYCHOLOGICAL INTEGRITY EJ 056 624

CRISCUOLO, NICHOLAS P.
SIX SUCCESSFUL READING PROGRAMS FOR INNER-CITY SCHOOLS EJ 035 663

CRIST, ROBERT L.
PROGRAMMED INSTRUCTION AS A MEANS OF ESTABLISHING "ERRORLESS" LEARNING WITH KINDERGARTEN LEVEL CHILDREN. FINAL REPORT. ED039955

CROLL, WILLIAM L.
RESPONSE STRATEGIES IN THE ODDITY DISCRIMINATION OF PRESCHOOL CHILDREN EJ 021 759
GENERALIZATION IN A STIMULUS CLASSIFICATION TASK: STIMULUS SELECTION WITHIN AND AMONG DIMENSIONS EJ 021 987
SEQUENTIAL CONTIGUITY AND SHORT-TERM MEMORY IN CHILDREN'S DISCRIMINATION LEARNING EJ 033 790
DECISION PROCESSES IN MULTIDIMENSIONAL GENERALIZATION EJ 038 265
GENERALIZATION AS A FUNCTION OF THE RANGE OF TEST STIMULI: THE ROLES OF DISCRIMINABILITY AND RESPONSE BIAS EJ 057 909

CROPLEY, A. J.
TRAINING CREATIVITY IN YOUNG CHILDREN EJ 035 373

CROSS, AMY R.
PARENT PREFERENCE OF PRESCHOOL CHILDREN. ED041628

CROSS, HERBERT J.
THE RELATION OF PARENTAL TRAINING TO CONCEPTUAL STRUCTURE IN PREADOLESCENTS EJ 023 191

CROSS, JANE
AGE, SEX, RACE, AND THE PERCEPTION OF FACIAL BEAUTY EJ 046 783

CROSS, JOHN F.
AGE, SEX, RACE, AND THE PERCEPTION OF FACIAL BEAUTY EJ 046 783

CROSS, MARIE Z.
A NUTRITIONAL SURVEY OF CHILDREN IN HEAD START CENTERS IN CENTRAL UNITED STATES. ED042487

CROWDER, ALETHA M. H.
TIME ESTIMATION BY YOUNG CHILDREN WITH AND WITHOUT INFORMATIONAL FEEDBACK EJ 033 787

CROWELL, DORIS C.
FIELD TEST OF THE UNIVERSITY OF HAWAII PRESCHOOL LANGUAGE CURRICULUM. FINAL REPORT. ED048924

CROWLEY, FRANCIS J.
THE DEVELOPMENT OF A COMPUTER TECHNIQUE FOR THE CONTENT ANALYSIS OF PSYCHO-SOCIAL FACTORS IN THE ORAL LANGUAGE OF KINDERGARTEN CHILDREN. ED038184

CROXEN, MARY E.
READING DISABILITY AND DIFFICULTIES IN FINGER LOCALIZATION AND RIGHT-LEFT DISCRIMINATION EJ 045 083

CRYSTAL, DAVID
A SOCIAL WORK MISSION TO HIPPIELAND EJ 004 092

CUCINOTTA, PATTIANN
THE EFFECTS OF ENRICHED NEONATAL EXPERIENCES UPON LATER COGNITIVE FUNCTIONING EJ 047 689

CUNNINGHAM, GROVER
A HEAD START CONTROL GROUP. PART OF THE FINAL REPORT. ED026128
A PILOT PROJECT USING A LANGUAGE DEVELOPMENT PROGRAM WITH PRESCHOOL DISADVANTAGED CHILDREN. PART OF THE FINAL REPORT ON HEAD START EVALUATION AND RESEARCH: 1968-69 TO THE OFFICE OF ECONOMIC OPPORTUNITY. ED037245
A COMPARISON OF HEAD START CHILDREN WITH A GROUP OF HEAD START ELIGIBLES AFTER ONE YEAR IN ELEMENTARY SCHOOL. PART OF THE FINAL REPORT ON HEAD START EVALUATION AND RESEARCH: 1968-69 TO THE OFFICE OF ECONOMIC OPPORTUNITY. ED037247
CURRICULAR INTERVENTION TO ENHANCE THE ENGLISH LANGUAGE COMPETENCE OF HEAD START CHILDREN. PART OF THE FINAL REPORT ON HEAD START EVALUATION AND RESEARCH: 1968-69 TO THE OFFICE OF ECONOMIC OPPORTUNITY. ED039032

CUNNINGHAM, JANE
AND A FRIENDLY GOODBYE EJ 028 310

CUNNINGHAM, MORRIS A.
THE RELIABILITY OF RATING SCALES FOR ASSESSING THE BEHAVIOUR OF DISTURBED CHILDREN IN A RESIDENTIAL UNIT EJ 051 153

CURCIO, FRANK
THE ROLE OF BODY PARTS AND READINESS IN ACQUISITION OF NUMBER CONSERVATION EJ 053 757

CURWOOD, SARAH T.
A SURVEY AND EVALUATION OF PROJECT HEAD START AS ESTABLISHED AND OPERATED IN COMMUNITIES OF THE COMMONWEALTH OF MASSACHUSETTS DURING THE SUMMER OF 1965. ED014324

CUVO, ANTHONY J.
THE INFLUENCE OF INCENTIVES ON MEMORY STAGES IN CHILDREN EJ 049 428

CZUDNER, G.
AGE DIFFERENCES IN VISUAL REACTION TIME OF "BRAIN DAMAGED" AND NORMAL CHILDREN UNDER IRREGULAR PREPARATORY INTERVAL CONDITIONS EJ 060 109

D'HEURLE, ADMA
ON PLAY EJ 051 471
THE SUGAR-COATED WORLD OF THE THIRD-GRADE READER EJ 058 171

DACEY, JOHN
IMPLICATIONS OF POST-NATAL CORTICAL DEVELOPMENT FOR CREATIVITY RESEARCH. ED047802

DAEHLER, MARVIN W.
CHILDREN'S MANIPULATION OF ILLUSORY AND AMBIGUOUS STIMULI, DISCRIMINATIVE PERFORMANCE, AN IMPLICATIONS FOR CONCEPTUAL DEVELOPMENT EJ 019 007
SPONTANEOUS MEASUREMENT IN YOUNG CHILDREN: A RE-EXAMINATION EJ 055 095
DEVELOPMENTAL AND EXPERIMENTAL FACTORS ASSOCIATED WITH INFERENTIAL BEHAVIOR EJ 057 905

DAHL, ERNEST W.
ROLE PERCEPTIONS AND JOB SATISFACTION AMONG LOWER AND MIDDLE LEVEL JUNIOR COLLEGE ADMINISTRATORS EJ 016 774

DAILEY, JOHN T.
AN EVALUATION OF THE LANGUAGE ARTS PROGRAM OF THE DISTRICT OF COLUMBIA. FINAL REPORT. ED024449

DAIRY, LORNA
DOES THE USE OF CUISENAIRE RODS IN KINDERGARTEN, FIRST AND SECOND GRADES UPGRADE ARITHMETIC ACHIEVEMENT? ED032128

DANFORTH, JOYCE
GROUP SERVICES FOR UNMARRIED MOTHERS: AN INTERDISCIPLINARY APPROACH EJ 035 538

DANIEL, KATHRYN BARCHARD
PSYCHOLINGUISTIC BEHAVIORS OF BLACK, DISADVANTAGED RURAL CHILDREN. ED039037

DATTA, LOIS-ELLIN
A REPORT ON EVALUATION STUDIES OF PROJECT HEAD START. ED037239
HEAD START'S INFLUENCE ON COMMUNITY CHANGE EJ 026 773
A REPORT ON EVALUATION STUDIES OF PROJECT HEAD START EJ 049 896

DAVES, WALTER F.
FREE RECALL OF OBJECT NAMES IN PRESCHOOL CHILDREN AS A FUNCTION OF INTRACATEGORY VARIATION EJ 035 368
RECOGNITION OF ENGLISH AND HEBREW LETTERS AS A FUNCTION OF AGE AND DISPLAY PREDICTABILITY EJ 047 893

DAVIDS, ANTHONY
CONSISTENCY OF MATERNAL ATTITUDES AND PERSONALITY FROM PREGNANCY TO EIGHT MONTHS FOLLOWING CHILDBIRTH EJ 021 026

DAVIDSON, NANCY HENDERSHOTT
RECENCY AND SUMMATION EFFECTS OF NONREWARD IN CHILDREN EJ 028 895

DAVIDSON, ROBERT E.
VERBAL AND IMAGERY PROCESSES IN CHILDREN'S PAIRED-ASSOCIATE LEARNING EJ 024 699

DAVIES, DON
WHAT'S AHEAD IN TEACHER EDUCATION? EJ 009 031

DAVIES, GRAHAM M.
QUANTITATIVE AND QUALITATIVE ASPECTS OF MEMORY FOR PICTURE STIMULI EJ 057 907

DAVIES, JOHN G. V.
AUTONOMIC RESPONSES OF MALE ADOLESCENTS EXHIBITING REFRACTORY BEHAVIOUR IN SCHOOL EJ 045 109

DAVIS, ALBERT J.
COGNITIVE STYLE: METHODOLOGICAL AND DEVELOPMENTAL CONSIDERATIONS EJ 053 482

DAVIS, KEITH E.
HELPING BEHAVIOR AMONG NORMAL AND RETARDED CHILDREN EJ 052 442

DAVY, ACHSAH J.
RACIAL AWARENESS IN YOUNG MEXICAN-AMERICAN, NEGRO AND ANGLO CHILDREN EJ 028 926

DAY, DAVID E.
THE EFFECTS OF DIFFERENT LANGUAGE INSTRUCTION ON THE USE OF ATTRIBUTES OF PRE-KINDERGARTEN DISADVANTAGED CHILDREN. ED016522
DEVELOPMENT OF GRAMMATICAL STRUCTURES AND ATTRIBUTES IN PRESCHOOL AGE CHILDREN. FINAL REPORT. ED041639
DEVELOPMENT OF GRAMMATICAL STRUCTURES IN PRE-SCHOOL AGE CHILDREN. ED042485
THE EFFECTS OF INSTRUCTION ON LANGUAGE DEVELOPMENT EJ 013 625

DAY, H. I.
AN EXAMINATION OF CHANGES IN ATTITUDES TO VISUAL COMPLEXITY WITH INCREASING AGE. ED039930

DAY, MARY C.
THE USE OF PERCEPTUAL, FUNCTIONAL, AND ABSTRACT ATTRIBUTES IN MULTIPLE CLASSIFICATION EJ 044 825

DAY, R. H.
OPERANT LEARNING OF VISUAL PATTERN DISCRIMINATION IN YOUNG INFANTS EJ 035 623
ORIENTATION DISCRIMINATION IN INFANTS: A COMPARISON OF VISUAL FIXATION AND OPERANT TRAINING METHODS EJ 041 981

DAYTON, DELBERT H.
EARLY MALNUTRITION AND HUMAN DEVELOPMENT EJ 011 914

DE AVILA, EDWARD
DEVELOPMENT OF A GROUP MEASURE TO ASSESS THE EXTENT OF PRE-LOGICAL AND PRE-CAUSAL THINKING IN PRIMARY SCHOOL AGE CHILDREN. ED019136

DE FRANCIS, VINCENT
CHILD ABUSE LEGISLATION IN THE 1970'S. ED049826

DEAL, THERRY N.
EFFECTS OF A STRUCTURED PROGRAM OF PRESCHOOL MATHEMATICS ON COGNITIVE BEHAVIOR. ED015791
A FACTOR ANALYSIS OF A THREE-YEAR LONGITUDINAL STUDY OF CONSERVATION OF NUMBER AND RELATED MATHEMATICAL CONCEPTS. ED039934

DEARDEN, RONALD A.
KINDERGARTEN, 1967-68. AN EVALUATION REPORT. ED025315
THE CHANGE PROCESS IN ACTION: KINDERGARTEN ED027949

DEBUS, RAY L.
EFFECTS OF BRIEF OBSERVATION OF MODEL BEHAVIOR ON CONCEPTUAL TEMPO OF IMPULSIVE CHILDREN EJ 019 010

DECASPER, ANTHONY J.
STEADY-STATE BEHAVIOR IN CHILDREN: A METHOD AND SOME DATA EJ 053 730

DEEM, MICHAEL A.
A STANDARDIZED NEUROLOGICAL EXAMINATION: ITS VALIDITY IN PREDICTING SCHOOL ACHIEVEMENT IN HEAD START AND OTHER POPULATIONS. FINAL REPORT. ED023475

DEEP, DONALD
THE COMPUTER CAN HELP INDIVIDUALIZE INSTRUCTION EJ 018 306

DEFEE, JR., JOHN F.
CHILDREN'S FEAR IN A DENTAL SITUATION AS A FUNCTION OF BIRTH ORDER EJ 015 099

DEFFENBACHER, KENNETH
AN APPLICATION OF BRUNSWIK'S LENS MODEL TO DEVELOPMENTAL CHANGES IN PROBABILITY LEARNING EJ 058 142

DEFRANCO, ELLEN
CURRICULUM GUIDE FOR CHILDREN'S ACTIVITIES, PARENT PRESCHOOL PROGRAM. ED027078

DEICHMANN, JOHN W.
DEVELOPMENTAL TRENDS IN THE INTENTIONAL AND INCIDENTAL LEARNING COMPONENTS OF A VERBAL DISCRIMINATION TASK EJ 035 375

DEIHL, NED C.
DEVELOPMENT OF A TECHNIQUE FOR IDENTIFYING ELEMENTARY SCHOOL CHILDREN'S MUSICAL CONCEPTS. FINAL REPORT. ED016517

DELEON, J. L.
SENSORY-MODALITY EFFECTS ON SHAPE PERCEPTION IN PRESCHOOL CHILDREN EJ 029 383

DELHEES, KARL H.
THE OBJECTIVE MEASUREMENT OF CHILDREN'S INTRAFAMILIAL ATTITUDE AND SENTIMENT STRUCTURE AND THE INVESTMENT-SUBSIDIATION MODEL EJ 034 542
HYPOTHESIS OF ORIGIN AND NATURE FOR THE "SOMINDENCE-DISSOFRUSTANCE" PERSONALITY FACTOR, U.I. 30 EJ 061 061

DELLIQUADRI, P. FREDERICK
DEVELOPING MANPOWER FOR THE WORLD'S SOCIAL WELFARE NEEDS. SOME OBSERVATIONS FROM THE CONFERENCE OF MINISTERS RESPONSIBLE FOR SOCIAL WELFARE.. EJ 004 093

DEMBO, MYRON H.
THE EFFECT OF VERBALIZATION OF RELEVANT AND IRRELEVANT DIMENSIONS ON CONCEPT FORMATION. ED030484
A DIAGNOSTIC-PRESCRIPTIVE APPROACH TO PRESCHOOL EDUCATION. ED041622

DEMYER, SANDRA
STIMULUS AND RESPONSE ALTERNATION IN YOUNG CHILDREN EJ 034 537

DENENBERG, VICTOR H.
PROGRAMMING LIFE HISTORIES: EFFECTS OF STRESS IN ONTOGENY UPON EMOTIONAL REACTIVITY EJ 020 719

DENENBERG, VICTOR H., ED.
EDUCATION OF THE INFANT AND YOUNG CHILD. ED048930

DENNER, BRUCE
REPRESENTATIONAL AND SYNTACTIC COMPETENCE OF PROBLEM READERS EJ 026 208

DENNEY, DOUGLAS
THE ASSESSMENT OF DIFFERENCES IN CONCEPTUAL STYLE EJ 041 146

DENNEY, DOUGLAS R.
MODELING EFFECTS UPON CONCEPTUAL STYLE AND COGNITIVE TEMPO EJ 056 396

DENNEY, NANCY WADSWORTH
A DEVELOPMENTAL STUDY OF FREE CLASSIFICATION IN CHILDREN EJ 056 730
DEVELOPMENTAL CHANGES IN CLUSTERING CRITERIA EJ 058 145

DENNIS, JACK
A PILOT EXPERIMENT IN EARLY CHILDHOOD POLITICAL LEARNING. REPORT FROM THE PROJECT ON CONCEPTS IN POLITICAL SCIENCE. ED043368

DENNIS, LAWRENCE
PLAY IN DEWEY'S THEORY OF EDUCATION EJ 017 710

DENNISON, ANN
FIGURATIVE AND OPERATIVE ASPECTS OF CHILDREN'S INFERENCE EJ 056 616

DERSHOWITZ, ZACHARY
INFLUENCES OF CULTURAL PATTERNS ON THE THINKING OF CHILDREN IN CERTAIN ETHNIC GROUPS, A STUDY OF THE EFFECT OF JEWISH SUBCULTURE ON THE FIELD-DEPENDENCE-INDEPENDENCE DIMENSION OF COGNITION. ED020796

DESTEFANO, JOHANNA S.
REGISTER: SOCIAL VARIATION IN LANGUAGE USE EJ 052 177

DEUR, JAN L.
EFFECTS OF INCONSISTENT PUNISHMENT ON AGGRESSION IN CHILDREN EJ 021 992
THE EFFECTS OF FATHER ABSENCE ON CHILD DEVELOPMENT EJ 035 800

DEUTSCH, KARL W.
RELATING AND RESPONDING: THE ADULT EJ 050 936

DEUTSCH, MARTIN
MEMORANDUM ON--FACILITIES FOR EARLY CHILDHOOD EDUCATION. ED015023
INSTITUTE FOR DEVELOPMENTAL STUDIES INTERIM PROGRESS REPORT. PART II: RESEARCH AND EVALUATION. ED036312

DEVERS, DIANA DEE, ED.
CHILDREN AND THE ARTS. PRESENTATIONS FROM A WRITING CONFERENCE. ED025317

DEVINE, HOWARD F.
PERSONALITY, COGNITIVE, AND DEMOGRAPHIC CHARACTERISTICS OF STUDENT ACTIVISTS AND ACTIVE STUDENTS EJ 061 194

DEVOR, GERALDINE
TEACHING STYLES IN FOUR-YEAR-OLDS. ED036340

DEVRIES, RHETA
THE DEVELOPMENT OF ROLE-TAKING AS REFLECTED BY BEHAVIOR OF BRIGHT, AVERAGE, AND RETARDED CHILDREN IN A SOCIAL GUESSING GAME EJ 025 361

DI LORENZO, LOUIS T.
SECOND-YEAR REPORT ON AN EVALUATIVE STUDY OF PREKINDERGARTEN PROGRAMS FOR EDUCATIONALLY DISADVANTAGED CHILDREN. ED016523

DI SCIPIO, WILLIAM J.
DIVERGENT THINKING AND PERSONALITY MEASURES OF ENGLISH AND AMERICAN EDUCATION MAJORS EJ 044 707

DI VESTA, FRANCIS J.
THE EFFECTS OF CONNOTATIVE SIMILARITY IN CHILDREN'S LEARNING OF A PAIRED-ASSOCIATE TASK EJ 035 376
IDENTIFICATION OF VERBAL CONCEPTS BY PRESCHOOL CHILDREN EJ 042 958
THE FORMATION AND REVERSAL OF AN ATTITUDE AS FUNCTIONS OF ASSUMED SELF-CONCEPT, RACE, AND SOCIOECONOMIC CLASS EJ 052 652

DIAMOND, FLORENCE
A PLAY CENTER FOR DEVELOPMENTALLY HANDICAPPED INFANTS EJ 045 012

DIBUONO, THEODORE
HEALTH CARE OF CHILDREN: A CHALLENGE. ED050804

DICKERSON, DONALD J.
EFFECTS OF NAMING RELEVANT AND IRRELEVANT STIMULI ON THE DISCRIMINATION LEARNING OF CHILDREN EJ 025 955
DISCRIMINATION SHIFT PERFORMANCE OF KINDERGARTEN CHILDREN AS A FUNCTION OF VARIATION OF THE IRRELEVANT SHIFT DIMENSION EJ 027 183
ODDITY PREFERENCE BY MENTAL RETARDATES EJ 027 825

DICKEY, GEORGE
DEVELOPMENT OF AN ENLARGED MUSIC REPERTORY FOR KINDERGARTEN THROUGH GRADE SIX (JUILLIARD REPERTORY PROJECT). FINAL REPORT. ED016521

DICKEY, MARGUERITE
AN EVALUATION AND FOLLOW-UP STUDY OF SUMMER 1966 HEAD START CHILDREN IN WASHINGTON, D.C. ED020794

DICKIE, JOYCE
CONSIDERATIONS FOR THE STUDY OF LANGUAGE IN YOUNG LOW-INCOME MINORITY GROUP CHILDREN EJ 052 440

DICKINSON, MARIE B.
INDEPENDENT AND GROUP LEARNING. ED017332

DIELMAN, T. E.
A CHECK ON THE STRUCTURE OF PARENTAL REPORTS OF CHILD-REARING PRACTICES EJ 045 388

DIGGLES, MARY W.
THE CHILD CARE COUNSELOR: NEW THERAPIST IN CHILDREN'S INSTITUTIONS EJ 027 919

DIMOCK, EDMUND
VOLUNTEERING TO HELP INDIANS HELP THEMSELVES EJ 032 412

DIMONDSTEIN, GERALDINE
DEVELOPMENT OF A DANCE CURRICULUM FOR YOUNG CHILDREN. CAREL ARTS AND HUMANITIES CURRICULUM DEVELOPMENT PROGRAM FOR YOUNG CHILDREN. ED032936
CHILDREN DANCE IN THE CLASSROOM. ED053804

DINKMEYER, DON
THE TEACHER AS COUNSELOR: THERAPEUTIC APPROACHES TO UNDERSTANDING SELF AND OTHERS EJ 023 703
TOP PRIORITY: UNDERSTANDING SELF AND OTHERS EJ 050 072

DISHART, MARTIN
ARTS AND HUMANITIES FOR YOUNG SCHOOL CHILDREN. ED032945

DISTEFANO, M. K., JR.
CHANGES IN SUCCESS-FAILURE ATTITUDES DURING ADOLESCENCE EJ 016 777

DITTMANN, LAURA L.
STUDY OF SELECTED CHILDREN IN HEAD START PLANNED VARIATION, 1969-1970. FIRST YEAR REPORT: 3 - CASE STUDIES OF CHILDREN. ED052847

DIVERS, BENJAMIN P., JR.
THE ABILITY OF KINDERGARTEN AND FIRST GRADE CHILDREN TO USE THE TRANSITIVE PROPERTY OF THREE LENGTH RELATIONS IN THREE PERCEPTUAL SITUATIONS. ED048936

DIVESTA, FRANCIS J.
COGNITIVE FACTORS IN THE CONDITIONING OF CHILDREN'S PREFERENCES EJ 021 989

DIXON, NATHANIEL R.
WIDER WINDOWS FOR ELEMENTARY SCHOOLS EJ 034 133

DMITRUK, VICTOR M.
INCENTIVE PREFERENCE AND RESISTANCE TO TEMPTATION EJ 041 631

DOAN, HELEN MCK.
CONDITIONAL DISCRIMINATION LEARNING IN CHILDREN: TWO RELEVANT FACTORS EJ 036 823

DODD, BARBARA J.
EFFECTS OF SOCIAL AND VOCAL STIMULATION ON INFANT BABBLING EJ 061 140

DODGE, JAMES
SOS CHILDREN'S VILLAGES THROUGHOUT THE WORLD: SUBSTITUTE OR SUPERIOR SERVICE? EJ 058 964

DOKE, LARRY A.
STIMULUS GENERALIZATION ACROSS INDIVIDUALS ALONG DIMENSIONS OF SEX AND RACE: SOME FINDINGS WITH CHILDREN FROM AN ALL-NEGRO NEIGHBORHOOD. PROGRESS REPORT. ED042497
SOME DISCRIMINATIVE PROPERTIES OF RACE AND SEX FOR CHILDREN FROM AN ALL-NEGRO NEIGHBORHOOD EJ 058 510

DOKECKI, PAUL R.
THE TRAINING OF FAMILY DAY-CARE WORKERS: A FEASIBILITY STUDY AND INITIAL PILOT EFFORTS. FINAL REPORT. ED053787

DOLIVE, EARLINE
LINGUISTICS IN THE ELEMENTARY SCHOOL. ED019134

DONALDSON, PATRICIA L.
DIALECT, RACE, AND LANGUAGE PROFICIENCY: ANOTHER DEAD HEAT ON THE MERRY-GO-ROUND EJ 053 747

DONDERO, ANNE E.
NURSES GAIN FROM FIELD WORK WITH YOUNG CHILDREN EJ 007 301

DONOHUE, DANIEL T.
ESTABLISHMENT OF DAY CARE PROGRAMS FOR THE MENTALLY RETARDED EJ 047 342

DOPYERA, JOHN
ANALYSIS OF EARLY CHILDHOOD PROGRAMS: A SEARCH FOR COMPARATIVE DIMENSIONS. ED051877

DORMAN, LYNN
THE RELATIONSHIP BETWEEN INSTRUMENTAL ASSERTION AND THE STANFORD-BINET. ED030474

DORMAN, LYNN M.
HEAD START EVALUATION AND RESEARCH CENTER, BOSTON UNIVERSITY. REPORT C-II, THE EXPRESSION OF AGGRESSION IN PRE-SCHOOL CHILDREN. ED022562

DORNBUSH, RHEA L.
THE RELATIONSHIP BETWEEN AUDITORY AND VISUAL SHORT-TERM MEMORY AND READING ACHIEVEMENT EJ 033 780

DORSEY, SUZANNE
ARE MOVERS LOSERS? EJ 018 958

DOUGLAS, NANCY J.
INCREASING THE AWARENESS OF ART IDEAS OF CULTURALLY DEPRIVED KINDERGARTEN CHILDREN THROUGH EXPERIENCES WITH CERAMICS. FINAL REPORT. ED016519
THE EFFECTS OF TEACHER IN-SERVICE EDUCATION ON THE DEVELOPMENT OF ART IDEAS WITH SIX-YEAR OLD CULTURALLY DEPRIVED CHILDREN. FINAL REPORT. ED027066

DOUGLASS, H. JEFF
CHRONOLOGICAL AGE AND PERFORMANCE ON PROBLEMS WITH REPEATED PRESOLUTION SHIFTS EJ 039 628

DOWLEY, EDITH
CUES FOR OBSERVING CHILDREN'S BEHAVIOR EJ 007 062

DOWNEY, JOHN J.
WHY CHILDREN ARE IN JAIL AND HOW TO KEEP THEM OUT EJ 013 329

DOWNING, JOHN
THE I.T.A. READING EXPERIMENT IN BRITAIN. ED032133
A CHILD-CENTERED DICTIONARY EJ 053 506

DRAKE, DIANA MACK
PERCEPTUAL CORRELATES OF IMPULSIVE AND REFLECTIVE BEHAVIOR EJ 018 322

DREYER, ALBERT S.
DIFFERENTIAL ADJUSTMENT TO PUBESCENCE AND COGNITIVE STYLE PATTERNS EJ 039 903

DRISCOLL, SALLY A.
CHILDREN'S "IMITATION" AS A FUNCTION OF THE PRESENCE OR ABSENCE OF A MODEL AND THE DESCRIPTION OF HIS INSTRUMENTAL BEHAVIORS EJ 036 080

DUBANOSKI, RICHARD A.
EFFECT OF THE PRESENCE OF A HUMAN MODEL ON IMITATIVE BEHAVIOR IN CHILDREN EJ 039 904
IMITATIVE AGGRESSION IN CHILDREN AS A FUNCTION OF OBSERVING A HUMAN MODEL EJ 039 907

DUBNER, EDITH SCHELL
WRITE YOUR OWN SONGS EJ 027 673

DUBOIS, ELIOSE BARCLAY
VALUES AND TECHNIQUES OF CREATIVE DRAMATICS EJ 034 422

DUCKETT, CAMILLE L.
CARING FOR CHILDREN WITH SICKLE CELL ANEMIA EJ 047 355

DUDEK, S. Z.
A LONGITUDINAL STUDY OF PIAGET'S DEVELOPMENTAL STAGES AND OF THE CONCEPT OF REGRESSION. ED043372

DUGGER, CHESTER W.
A TEACHER DISCOVERS INDIVIDUALIZED INSTRUCTION EJ 035 171

DUNBAR, PHILIP W.
VISUAL AND AUDITORY MEMORY IN CHILDREN. PART OF THE FINAL REPORT ON HEAD START EVALUATION AND RESEARCH: 1968-69 TO THE OFFICE OF ECONOMIC OPPORTUNITY. ED037246

DUNCAN, PAM
PARENTAL ATTITUDES AND INTERACTIONS IN DELINQUENCY EJ 056 611

DUNHAM, FRANCES Y.
TIMING AND SOURCES OF INFORMATION ABOUT, AND ATTITUDES TOWARD, MENSTRUATION AMONG COLLEGE FEMALES EJ 029 533

DUNHAM, MARGARET A.
TEACHING NUTRITION IN THE ELEMENTARY SCHOOL. ED026148

DUNLAP, JAMES M.
THE EFFECTS OF ASSESSMENT AND PERSONALIZED PROGRAMMING ON SUBSEQUENT INTELLECTUAL DEVELOPMENT OF PREKINDERGARTEN AND KINDERGARTEN CHILDREN. ED013663
THE EFFECTS OF ASSESSMENT AND PERSONALIZED PROGRAMMING ON SUBSEQUENT INTELLECTUAL DEVELOPMENT OF PREKINDERGARTEN AND KINDERGARTEN CHILDREN. FINAL REPORT OF PHASE II. ED023487
THE EFFECTS OF ASSESSMENT AND PERSONALIZED PROGRAMMING ON SUBSEQUENT INTELLECTUAL DEVELOPMENT OF PREKINDERGARTEN AND KINDERGARTEN CHILDREN. FINAL REPORT. ED045198

DUNN, LLOYD M.
THE EFFECTIVENESS OF THE PEABODY LANGUAGE DEVELOPMENT KITS AND THE INITIAL TEACHING ALPHABET WITH DISADVANTAGED CHILDREN IN THE PRIMARY GRADES: AFTER TWO YEARS. ED026125

DUNWORTH, JOHN
KINDERGARTEN OVERSEAS, A STUDY OF THE REQUIREMENTS FOR ESTABLISHING KINDERGARTEN AS PART OF THE DEPARTMENT OF DEFENSE OVERSEAS DEPENDENTS SCHOOLS. FINAL REPORT. ED017340

DUPARC, GERMAINE
LE MONDE DES TOUT PETITS EST-IL INFLUENCE PAR NOTRE MONDE MODERNE? (IS THE WORLD OF CHILDREN INFLUENCED BY OUR MODERN WORLD?) EJ 049 895

DURKIN, DOLORES
CHILDREN WHO READ EARLY, TWO LONGITUDINAL STUDIES. ED019107
A TWO-YEAR LANGUAGE ARTS PROGRAM FOR PRE-FIRST GRADE CHILDREN: FIRST YEAR REPORT. ED029686

DUROJAIYE, M. O. A.
THE RELATIONSHIP BETWEEN CONTROLLED PROJECTION RESPONSES AND SOCIOMETRIC STATUS EJ 031 541

DURRETT, MARY ELLEN
RACIAL AWARENESS IN YOUNG MEXICAN-AMERICAN, NEGRO AND ANGLO CHILDREN EJ 028 926
CHANGES IN SELF-PERCEPTIONS OF HEAD-START TRAINEES EJ 055 213

DUSEK, JEROME B.
PROBABILITY LEARNING AS A FUNCTION OF SEX OF THE SUBJECT, TEST ANXIETY, AND PERCENTAGE OF REINFORCEMENT EJ 027 181
EXPERIMENTER BIAS IN PERFORMANCE OF CHILDREN AT A SIMPLE MOTOR TASK EJ 035 710

DWYER, FRANCIS M., JR.
VISUAL LEARNING: AN ANALYSIS BY SEX AND GRADE LEVEL EJ 045 424

DWYER, JR., FRANCIS M.
EFFECT OF VISUAL STIMULI IN COMPLEMENTING TELEVISED INSTRUCTION EJ 015 382

DYER, G. B.
A LONGITUDINAL STUDY OF PIAGET'S DEVELOPMENTAL STAGES AND OF THE CONCEPT OF REGRESSION. ED043372

DYER, JEAN L.
EXPERIMENTAL VARIATION OF HEAD START CURRICULA: A COMPARISON OF CURRENT APPROACHES. ANNUAL PROGRESS REPORT, JUNE 1, 1969 - MAY 31, 1970. ED045196
TWO KINDS OF KINDERGARTEN AFTER FOUR TYPES OF HEAD START. ED050824

DYTELL, RITA SCHER
TACTILE IDENTIFICATION OF LETTERS: A COMPARISON OF DEAF AND HEARING CHILDRENS' PERFORMANCES EJ 034 567

DZIUBAN, CHARLES
THE NATIONAL TEACHER CORPS PROGRAM, 1966-67 EVALUATION REPORT. ED019110

EAGLE, CAROL J.
SPECIAL CONSIDERATIONS IN THE OPERATION OF A HEAD START PROGRAM BY A COMMUNITY CHILD GUIDANCE CLINIC EJ 023 704

EARHART, EILEEN M.
CLASSIFICATION AND ATTENTION TRAINING CURRICULA FOR HEAD START CHILDREN. ED042508

EASON, GARY
SCHOOL ACHIEVEMENT: A PRELIMINARY LOOK AT THE EFFECTS OF THE HOME. ED047777

EBBECK, FREDERICK N.
LEARNING FROM PLAY IN OTHER CULTURES EJ 045 532

ECKHOFF, EVA
PARENTAL BEHAVIOR TOWARD BOYS AND GIRLS OF PRESCHOOL AGE. ED026119

EDELMAN, MURRAY S.
THE DEVELOPMENT OF EARLY SOCIAL INTERACTION--AN ETHOLOGICAL APPROACH. ED031291

EDGAR, IRVIN T.
SCIENCE FOR THE PRIMARY GRADES: QUESTIONS AND ANSWERS. ED035461

EDINGER, HANNI B.
REUNITING CHILDREN AND PARENTS THROUGH CASEWORK AND GROUP WORK EJ 027 342

EDMAN, MARION
CHOOSING CHILDREN'S BOOKS ABOUT OTHER COUNTRIES EJ 000 393

EDWARDS, J.B.
SOME STUDIES OF THE MORAL DEVELOPMENT OF CHILDREN. ED024445

EDWARDS, JOSEPH
A COMPARISON OF THREE INTERVENTION PROGRAMS WITH DISADVANTAGED PRESCHOOL CHILDREN. UNIVERSITY OF CALIFORNIA HEAD START RESEARCH AND EVALUATION CENTER. FINAL REPORT 1968-1969. ED041616

EGAN, MARY C.
COMBATING MALNUTRITION THROUGH MATERNAL AND CHILD HEALTH PROGRAMS EJ 007 161

EGELAND, BYRON
MODIFYING RESPONSE LATENCY AND ERROR RATE OF IMPULSIVE CHILDREN. ED050819

EHLERT, ROGER C.
144 FOSTER CHILDREN EJ 046 787

EHMER, CHARLES L.
WHAT PUPILS KNOW ABOUT VOCABULARY IN MATHEMATICS--1930 AND 1968 EJ 035 466

EIMAS, PETER D.
INFORMATION PROCESSING IN PROBLEM SOLVING AS A FUNCTION OF DEVELOPMENTAL LEVEL AND STIMULUS SALIENCY EJ 018 884
EFFECTS OF MEMORY AIDS ON HYPOTHESIS BEHAVIOR AND FOCUSING IN YOUNG CHILDREN AND ADULTS EJ 033 789

EININGER, MARY ANN
INSTRUMENTAL AND AFFECTIONAL DEPENDENCY AND NURTURANCE IN PRESCHOOL CHILDREN EJ 015 101

EISDORFER, CARL
PRESTIMULUS ACTIVITY LEVEL AND RESPONSIVITY IN THE NEONATE EJ 040 297

EISENBERG, LEON
THE EFFECT OF HEADSTART ON DEVELOPMENTAL PROCESSES. ED020026
BIBLIOGRAPHY OF PAPERS COVERING WORK UNDER OEO CONTRACT NUMBER 510. FINAL REPORT. (TITLE SUPPLIED). ED020773
CHILD PSYCHIATRY: THE PAST QUARTER CENTURY. ED027951
THE SOCIAL DEVELOPMENT OF HUMAN INTELLIGENCE. ED028817

EISENBERG, WILLIAM D.
MORALS, MORALS EVERYWHERE: VALUES IN CHILDREN'S FICTION EJ 051 270

EISENMAN, RUSSELL
CREATIVITY CHANGE IN STUDENT NURSES: A CROSS-SECTIONAL AND LONGITUDINAL STUDY EJ 030 291

EISNER, ELLIOT W.
INSTRUCTIONAL AND EXPRESSIVE EDUCATIONAL OBJECTIVES: THEIR FORMULATION AND USE IN CURRICULUM. ED028838

EISNER, ELLIOTT W.
A COMPARISON OF THE DEVELOPMENTAL DRAWING CHARACTERISTICS OF CULTURALLY ADVANTAGED AND CULTURALLY DISADVANTAGED CHILDREN. FINAL REPORT. ED015783

EKSTEIN, RUDOLF
FROM LEARNING FOR LOVE TO LOVE OF LEARNING: ESSAYS ON PSYCHOANALYSIS AND EDUCATION. ED032925

ELARDO, RICHARD
THE EXPERIMENTAL FACILITATION OF CHILDREN'S COMPREHENSION AND PRODUCTION OF FOUR SYNTACTIC STRUCTURES EJ 056 723

ELBOW, LINDA
A STUDY IN CHILD CARE (CASE STUDY FROM VOLUME II-A): "GOOD VIBES." DAY CARE PROGRAMS REPRINT SERIES. ED051894
A STUDY IN CHILD CARE (CASE STUDY FROM VOLUME II-B): "A SENSE OF BELONGING." DAY CARE PROGRAMS REPRINT SERIES. ED051898
A STUDY IN CHILD CARE (CASE STUDY FROM VOLUME II-B): "WE COME WITH THE DUST AND WE GO WITH THE WIND." DAY CARE PROGRAMS REPRINT SERIES. ED051907

ELDER, GLEN H., JR.
ROLE ORIENTATIONS, MARITAL AGE, AND LIFE PATTERNS IN ADULTHOOD EJ 052 529

ELDER, MARY SCOVILL
THE EFFECTS OF TEMPERATURE AND POSITION ON THE SUCKING PRESSURE OF NEWBORN INFANTS EJ 018 260

ELDER, RICHARD D.
ORAL READING ACHIEVEMENT OF SCOTTISH AND AMERICAN CHILDREN EJ 030 548

ELIOT, ABIGAIL ADAMS
NURSERY SCHOOLS FIFTY YEARS AGO EJ 055 736

ELKIND, DAVID
THE CASE FOR THE ACADEMIC PRESCHOOL: FACT OR FICTION? EJ 015 059
REPRESENTATIONAL LEVEL AND CONCEPT PRODUCTION IN CHILDREN AND ADOLESCENTS EJ 018 880
DETERMINANTS OF PART-WHOLE PERCEPTION IN CHILDREN EJ 021 772
INCREASING AND RELEASING HUMAN POTENTIALS EJ 034 710
IDENTITY AND EQUIVALENCE CONSERVATION AT TWO AGE LEVELS EJ 057 901

ELLIOTT, DAVID L.
PROMISING DIRECTIONS FOR RESEARCH AND DEVELOPMENT IN EARLY CHILDHOOD EDUCATION. ED023448

ELLIOTT, JR., RAYMOND N.
BLACK HISTORY EJ 015 184

ELLIOTT, ROGERS
THE MODELING OF SHARING: EFFECTS ASSOCIATED WITH VICARIOUS REINFORCEMENT, SYMBOLIZATION, AGE, AND GENERALIZATION EJ 028 894
SIMPLE REACTION TIME IN CHILDREN: EFFECTS OF INCENTIVE, INCENTIVE-SHIFT AND OTHER TRAINING VARIABLES EJ 061 075

ELLIS, LILLIAN
SHARING PARENTS WITH STRANGERS: THE ROLE OF THE GROUP HOME FOSTER FAMILY'S OWN CHILDREN EJ 053 600

ELLIS, M. J.
SENSORHESIS AS A MOTIVE FOR PLAY AND STEREOTYPED BEHAVIOR. ED044176

ELLIS, NORMAN R.
EFFECT OF OVERT VERBAL LABELING ON SHORT-TERM MEMORY IN CULTURALLY DEPRIVED AND NONDEPRIVED CHILDREN EJ 053 710

ELLIS, PATRICIA
REMEDIAL READING INSTRUCTION BY TRAINED PUPIL TUTORS EJ 035 172

ELLIS, STEPHEN
THE EFFECTS OF OVERLEARNING ON CHILDREN'S NONREVERSAL AND REVERSAL LEARNING USING UNRELATED STIMULI EJ 028 633

ELLISON, ALFRED
THE MYTH BEHIND GRADED CONTENT EJ 052 126

ELLISOR, MILDRED
CLASSROOM OPPORTUNITIES TO EXPRESS FEELINGS EJ 001 912

ELSTER, RUTH
LOOKING BACK WITH APPRECIATION EJ 058 054

ELWELL, RICHARD R.
ONE MORNING A WEEK EJ 051 238

ELZEY, FREEMAN F.
DEVELOPMENT OF A SOCIAL COMPETENCY SCALE FOR PRESCHOOL CHILDREN. FINAL REPORT. ED020004

EMDE, ROBERT N.
NEONATAL SMILING IN REM STATES, IV: PREMATURE STUDY EJ 053 758

EMLEN, ARTHUR C.
REALISTIC PLANNING FOR THE DAY CARE CONSUMER. ED043374
NEIGHBORHOOD FAMILY DAY CARE AS A CHILD-REARING ENVIRONMENT. ED049840

EMMERICH, WALTER
THE PARENTAL ROLE, A FUNCTIONAL-COGNITIVE APPROACH EJ 013 946
COGNITIVE MEDIATION OF DEVELOPMENTAL TRENDS IN EXTREME RESPONSE CHOICE EJ 047 688

ENDRES, JEANNETTE
NUTRITION IN DAY CARE CENTERS EJ 011 595

ENDSLEY, R. C.
EMOTIONAL REACTIONS OF YOUNG CHILDREN TO TV VIOLENCE EJ 036 082

ENDSLEY, RICHARD C.
EFFECTS OF DIFFERENTIAL PRIOR EXPOSURE ON YOUNG CHILDREN'S SUBSEQUENT OBSERVING AND CHOICE OF NOVEL STIMULI. ED017336
CHILDREN'S REACTIONS TO TV VIOLENCE: A REVIEW OF RESEARCH EJ 028 676

ENGEL, ROSE C.
LANGUAGE DEVELOPMENT EXPERIENCES FOR YOUNG CHILDREN. ED019125

ENGELMANN, SIEGFRIED
TEACHING READING TO CHILDREN WITH LOW MA'S. ED015020
TEACHING FORMAL OPERATIONS TO PRESCHOOL ADVANTAGED AND DISADVANTAGED CHILDREN. ED019990
LANGUAGE LEARNING ACTIVITIES FOR THE DISADVANTAGED CHILD. ED020002
EFFECTIVENESS OF DIRECT VERBAL INSTRUCTION ON IQ PERFORMANCE AND ACHIEVEMENT IN READING AND ARITHMETIC. ED030496

ENNIS, ROBERT H.
CONDITIONAL LOGIC AND PRIMARY CHILDREN. ED038186

ENZMANN, ARTHUR M.
DEVELOPING NEW TEACHING TEAMS EJ 029 169

EPPS, EDGAR G.
EFFECTS OF SOCIAL CLASS INTEGRATION OF PRESCHOOL NEGRO CHILDREN ON TEST PERFORMANCE AND SELF-CONCEPT. FINAL REPORT. ED050831

EPPS, FRANCES M. J.
HEAD START IN ACTION. ED030471

EPSTEIN, NOEL
PRIORITIES FOR CHANGE--SOME PRELIMINARY PROPOSALS FROM THE WHITE HOUSE CONFERENCE ON CHILDREN EJ 032 611

EPSTEIN, RALPH
EFFECTS OF REINFORCEMENT BASE-LINE-INPUT DISCREPANCY UPON IMITATION IN CHILDREN EJ 019 009
SELF-ESTEEM, SUCCESS-FAILURE, AND LOCUS OF CONTROL IN NEGRO CHILDREN EJ 035 621

ERICKSON, EDSEL L.
A STUDY OF THE EFFECTS OF TEACHER ATTITUDE AND CURRICULUM STRUCTURE ON PRESCHOOL DISADVANTAGED CHILDREN. ANNUAL PROGRESS REPORT I. ED027079
EXPERIMENTS IN HEAD START AND EARLY EDUCATION: THE EFFECTS OF TEACHER ATTITUDE AND CURRICULUM STRUCTURE ON PRESCHOOL DISADVANTAGED CHILDREN. FINAL REPORT. ED041615

ERIKSEN, CHARLES W.
SUBJECTS' HYPOTHESES, EXPERIMENTAL INSTRUCTIONS AND AUTONOMIC "CONDITIONING". ED025335

ERMALINSKI, RICHARD
INCORPORATION OF VALUES BY LOWER AND MIDDLE SOCIOECONOMIC CLASS PRESCHOOL BOYS EJ 040 210

ESCALONA, S. K.
THE IMPACT OF MOTHER'S PRESENCE UPON BEHAVIOR: THE FIRST YEAR EJ 039 908

ESCALONA, SIBYLLE K.
STAGES OF SENSORIMOTOR DEVELOPMENT: A REPLICATION STUDY EJ 011 916

ESKA, BRUNHILDE
CONCEPTUAL TEMPO IN YOUNG GRADE-SCHOOL CHILDREN EJ 041 450

ESPIE, J. G.
NEW ZEALAND'S DENTAL SERVICE FOR CHILDREN EJ 007 162

ESPINOSA, RENATO
FINAL REPORT ON HEAD START EVALUATION AND RESEARCH: 1967-68 TO THE OFFICE OF ECONOMIC OPPORTUNITY. SECTION II: ACHIEVEMENT MOTIVATION AND PATTERNS OF REINFORCEMENT IN HEAD START CHILDREN. ED023458
THE EFFECT OF THE REINSTEIN REINFORCEMENT SCHEDULE ON LEARNING OF SPECIFIC CONCEPTS CONTAINED IN THE BUCHANAN LANGUAGE PROGRAM. PART OF THE FINAL REPORT ON HEAD START EVALUATION AND RESEARCH: 1968-69 TO THE OFFICE OF ECONOMIC OPPORTUNITY. ED037242
A REPORT ON THE RESULTS OF THE ADMINISTRATION OF THE GUMPGOOKIES TEST TO THE TEXAS EVALUATION SAMPLE. PART OF THE FINAL REPORT ON HEAD START EVALUATION AND RESEARCH: 1968-69 TO THE OFFICE OF ECONOMIC OPPORTUNITY. ED039033

ESSEX, MARY LANGMUIR
THE RIGHTS OF THE CHILD - THE REALIZATION OF HIS POTENTIAL EJ 028 101

ETAUGH, ALFRED F.
OVERLAP: HYPOTHESIS OR TAUTOLOGY? EJ 054 508

ETAUGH, CLAIRE F.
EFFECTS OF TYPE AND SOURCE OF LABELS ON CHILDREN'S PERCEPTUAL JUDGMENTS AND DISCRIMINATION LEARNING EJ 053 756

ETAUGH, CLAIRE FALK
DISCRIMINATION OF STEREOMETRIC OJBECTS AND PHOTOGRAPHS OF OBJECTS BY CHILDREN EJ 053 749
OVERLAP: HYPOTHESIS OR TAUTOLOGY? EJ 054 508

ETZEL, BARBARA C.
HEAD START EVALUATION AND RESEARCH CENTER, UNIVERSITY OF KANSAS. FINAL REPORT ON RESEARCH ACTIVITIES. ED021614
HEAD START EVALUATION AND RESEARCH CENTER, UNIVERSITY OF KANSAS. REPORT NO. VIIA, A CASE STUDY IN ESTABLISHING A DIFFERENTIATED SPEECH RESPONSE THROUGH GENERALIZATION PROCEDURES. ED021640
HEAD START EVALUATION AND RESEARCH CENTER, UNIVERSITY OF KANSAS. REPORT NO. VIIC, ERRORLESS DISCRIMINATION IN PRESCHOOL CHILDREN: A PROGRAM FOR ESTABLISHING A ONE-MINUTE DELAY OF REINFORCEMENT. ED021642
HEAD START EVALUATION AND RESEARCH CENTER, UNIVERSITY OF KANSAS. REPORT NO. VIID, A CASE STUDY ILLUSTRATING AN EXPERIMENTAL DESIGN FOR EVALUATING THE EFFECTS OF SHAPING GROSS MOTOR COORDINATION IN A 31 MONTH OLD CHILD. ED021643
A PROGRAM OF STIMULUS CONTROL FOR ESTABLISHING A ONE-MINUTE WAIT FOR REINFORCEMENT IN PRESCHOOL CHILDREN. PROGRESS REPORT. ED042492

EVAN-WONG, LOUISE
PSYCHIATRIC DISORDER AND ADULT AND PEER GROUP REJECTION OF THE CHILD'S NAME EJ 026 156

EVANS, ELLIS D.
CONTEMPORARY INFLUENCES IN EARLY CHILDHOOD EDUCATION. ED053797

EVANS, WILSON
THE STAGE IV ERROR IN PIAGET'S THEORY OF OBJECT CONCEPT DEVELOPMENT: DIFFICULTIES IN OBJECT CONCEPTUALIZATION OR SPATIAL LOCALIZATION? EJ 059 318

EVELOFF, HERBERT H.
SOME COGNITIVE AND AFFECTIVE ASPECTS OF EARLY LANGUAGE DEVELOPMENT EJ 055 655

EZEKIEL, RAPHAEL S.
SETTING AND THE EMERGENCE OF COMPETENCE DURING ADULT SOCIALIZATION: WORKING AT HOME VS. WORKING "OUT THERE" EJ 012 719

FAGAN, JOSEPH F., III
MEMORY IN THE INFANT EJ 021 760
INFANTS' RECOGNITION MEMORY FOR A SERIES OF VISUAL STIMULI EJ 037 342

FAIZUNISA, ALI
MODIFICATION OF THE PEABODY PICTURE VOCABULARY TEST. ED033752

FALKNER, FRANK
INFANT MORTALITY: AN URGENT NATIONAL PROBLEM EJ 021 523

FALKNER, FRANK, ED.
KEY ISSUES IN INFANT MORTALITY. ED045208

CHILD HEALTH AND HUMAN DEVELOPMENT: PROGRESS 1963-1970. A REPORT OF THE NATIONAL INSTITUTE OF CHILD HEALTH AND HUMAN DEVELOPMENT. ED053799

FANSHEL, DAVID
THE EXIT OF CHILDREN FROM FOSTER CARE: AN INTERIM RESEARCH REPORT EJ 039 798

FARBER, ANNE E.
A COMPARISON OF THE EFFECT OF VERBAL AND MATERIAL REWARD ON THE LEARNING OF LOWER CLASS PRESCHOOL CHILDREN. ED052817

FARGO, GEORGE A.
EVALUATION OF AN INTERDISCIPLINARY APPROACH TO PREVENTION OF EARLY SCHOOL FAILURE. FOLLOW-UP STUDY, FINAL REPORT. ED031295

FARLEY, FRANK H.
THE RELATIONSHIP OF INDIVIDUAL DIFFERENCES IN THE ORIENTING RESPONSE TO COMPLEX LEARNING IN KINDERGARTNERS. ED031299
THE RELATIONSHIP OF INDIVIDUAL DIFFERENCES IN THE ORIENTING RESPONSE TO COMPLEX LEARNING IN KINDERGARTNERS. REPORT FROM THE MOTIVATION AND INDIVIDUAL DIFFERENCES IN LEARNING AND RETENTION PROJECT. ED046544

FARNHAM-DIGGORY, S.
PLAY PERSISTENCE: SOME EFFECTS OF INTERRUPTION, SOCIAL REINFORCEMENT, AND DEFECTIVE TOYS EJ 034 532

FARNHAM-DIGGORY, SYLVIA
COGNITIVE SYNTHESIS IN NEGRO AND WHITE CHILDREN EJ 020 522

FATERSON, HANNA F.
LONGITUDINAL STUDY OF DEVELOPMENT OF THE BODY CONCEPT EJ 021 993

FAULK, CHARLES J.
WHO ARE THEY? IDENTIFYING DISTURBED CHILDREN IN THE CLASSROOM EJ 022 976

FAVELL, JUDITH ELBERT
AN EXPERIMENTAL ANALYSIS OF ERROR INTERACTION ON "ERRORLESS" AND TRIAL-AND-ERROR PROGRAMS. PROGRESS REPORT. ED042491

FAW, TERRY T.
THE INFLUENCE OF STIMULUS EXPOSURE ON RATED PREFERENCE: EFFECTS OF AGE, PATTERN OF EXPOSURE, AND STIMULUS MEANINGFULNESS EJ 041 960

FEATHERSTONE, JOSEPH
SCHOOLS WHERE CHILDREN LEARN. ED053803

FEHR, FRED S.
YOUNG CHILDREN'S USE OF THE SPEECH CODE IN A RECALL TASK EJ 033 792

FEIGENBAUM, KENNETH
ACTIVITIES TO TEACH THE CONCEPT OF CONSERVATION EJ 007 311

FEIGENBAUM, KENNETH D.
A PILOT INVESTIGATION OF THE EFFECTS OF TRAINING TECHNIQUES DESIGNED TO ACCELERATE CHILDRENS' ACQUISITION OF CONSERVATION OF DISCONTINUOUS QUANTITY. FINAL REPORT. ED044178
AN EXPLORATORY STUDY OF THE 3-, 5-, AND 7-YEAR OLD FEMALE'S COMPREHENSION OF COOPERATIVE AND UNCOOPERATIVE SOCIAL INTERACTION EJ 023 612
A PILOT INVESTIGATION OF THE EFFECTS OF TRAINING TECHNIQUES DESIGNED TO ACCELERATE CHILDREN'S ACQUISITION OF CONSERVATION OF DISCONTINOUS QUANTITY EJ 044 705

FEIMER, JOEL N.
ON PLAY EJ 051 471

FEINBERG, DANIEL
PREVENTIVE THERAPY WITH SIBLINGS OF A DYING CHILD EJ 030 515

FEITELSON, DINA
SOCIAL INTERACTION IN HETEROGENEOUS PRE-SCHOOLS IN ISRAEL. ED049839

FELD, SHEILA
FURTHER EVIDENCE ON THE STABILITY OF THE FACTOR STRUCTURE OF THE TEST ANXIETY SCALE FOR SCHILDREN. ED023485
THE ASSESSMENT OF ACHIEVEMENT ANXIETIES IN CHILDREN: HOW IMPORTANT IS RESPONSE SET AND MULTIDIMENSIONALITY IN THE TEST ANXIETY SCALE FOR CHILDREN? ED025313

FELDHUSEN, JOHN F.
STUDYING AGGRESSIVE CHILDREN THROUGH RESPONSE TO FRUSTRATING SITUATIONS EJ 051 013

FELDMAN, CAROL
SOME LANGUAGE-RELATED COGNITIVE ADVANTAGES OF BILINGUAL FIVE YEAR OLDS. ED031307
SOME LANGUAGE-RELATED COGNITIVE ADVANTAGES OF BILINGUAL FIVE-YEAR-OLDS EJ 041 343

FELDMAN, CAROL FLEISHER
CONCEPT FORMATION IN CHILDREN: A STUDY USING NONSENSE STIMULI AND A FREE-SORT TASK. ED031306
THE ROLE OF UNDERDETERMINACY AND REFERENCE IN THE SENTENCE RECALL OF YOUNG CHILDREN. ED035449

FELDMAN, DAVID H.
CORRELATION OF PAIRED-ASSOCIATE PERFORMANCE WITH SCHOOL ACHIEVEMENT AS A FUNCTION OF TASK AND SAMPLE VARIATION. ED049813

FELDMAN, RONALD, COMP.
A RESOURCE AND REFERENCE BIBLIOGRAPHY IN EARLY CHILDHOOD EDUCATION AND DEVELOPMENTAL PSYCHOLOGY: THE AFFECTIVE DOMAIN. ED049817

FELDMAN, S. SHIRLEY
MOTHER-ATTACHMENT AND STRANGER-REACTIONS IN THE THIRD YEAR OF LIFE EJ 062 594

FELDMAN, SHIRLEY
YOUNG CHILDREN'S COMPREHENSION OF LOGICAL CONNECTIVES. ED033756
YOUNG CHILDREN'S COMPREHENSION OF LOGICAL CONNECTIVES EJ 049 117

FELDSTEIN, JEROME H.
THE INCENTIVE VALUE OF UNCERTAINTY REDUCTION FOR CHILDREN EJ 045 454

FELKER, DONALD W.
ACQUISITION OF COGNITIVE RESPONSES UNDER DIFFERENT PATTERNS OF VERBAL REWARDS EJ 017 712
USE OF THE IT SCALE FOR CHILDREN IN ASSESSING SEX-ROLE PREFERENCE IN PRESCHOOL NEGRO CHILDREN EJ 021 991
SELF-INITIATED VERBAL REINFORCEMENT AND POSITIVE SELF-CONCEPT EJ 052 462

FELZEN, ENID
SEMANTIC AND PHONETIC RELATIONS IN THE FALSE RECOGNITION OF WORDS BY THIRD- AND SIXTH-GRADE CHILDREN EJ 026 374

FENBY, BARBARA LOU
THE PRESCHOOL COOPERATIVE AS A THERAPY FOR MOTHERS EJ 016 381

FERGUSON, BESS
TELL IT LIKE IT IS EJ 014 139

FERGUSON, LUCY RAU
ORIGINS OF SOCIAL DEVELOPMENT IN INFANCY EJ 038 570

FERNANDEZ, LUIS E.
IMITATION AS A FUNCTION OF VICARIOUS AND DIRECT REWARD EJ 018 323
EFFECTS OF VICARIOUS CONSEQUENCES ON IMITATIVE PERFORMANCE EJ 025 635

FERRARO, DOUGLAS P.
TITRATING DELAYED MATCHING TO SAMPLE IN CHILDREN EJ 047 684

FERRER, LEONA
BLACK HISTORY EJ 015 184

FERRIS, M. SCOTT
ANTHROPOMETRIC MEASUREMENTS OF CHILDREN IN THE HEAD START PROGRAM. ED042488

FERVER, JACK C., ED.
SUPPLEMENTARY MATERIALS FOR TEACHER AIDE TRAINING PROGRAMS, TO SUPPLEMENT THE PUBLICATION "TEACHER AIDES: HANDBOOK FOR INSTRUCTORS AND ADMINISTRATORS." ED024462

FERVER, JACK, ED.
TEACHER AIDES: HANDBOOK FOR INSTRUCTORS AND ADMINISTRATORS. ED024461

FESHBACH, NORMA
SEX DIFFERENCES IN ADOLESCENT REACTIONS TOWARD NEWCOMERS EJ 039 899
CHILDREN'S AGGRESSION EJ 043 199

FESHBACH, NORMA D.
TEACHING STYLES IN FOUR-YEAR-OLDS. ED036340
SEX DIFFERENCES IN CHILDREN'S MODES OF AGGRESSIVE RESPONSES TOWARD OUTSIDERS EJ 007 690
IMITATION OF TEACHER PREFERENCES IN A FIELD SETTING EJ 061 070

FESHBACH, SEYMOUR
CHILDREN'S AGGRESSION EJ 043 199
IMITATION OF TEACHER PREFERENCES IN A FIELD SETTING EJ 061 070

FESTINGER, TRUDY BRADLEY
UNWED MOTHERS AND THEIR DECISIONS TO KEEP OR SURRENDER CHILDREN EJ 040 042

FEURING, ELSIE
TRAINING CREATIVITY IN YOUNG CHILDREN EJ 035 373

FIGURELLI, JENNIFER C.
THE EFFECTS OF TRAINING AND SOCIOECONOMIC CLASS UPON THE ACQUISITION OF CONSERVATION CONCEPTS EJ 056 401

FILEP, ROBERT
SESAME STREET. A SURVEY OF TWO CITIES: VIEWING PATTERNS IN INNER CITY LOS ANGELES AND CHICAGO. ED047788

FILEP, ROBERT T.
SUPERMARKET DISCOVERY CENTER, PILOT STUDY, MAY - SEPTEMBER, 1968. INITIAL REPORT. ED027941

FILHO, M. B. LOURENCO
L'EDUCATION PRESCOLAIRE ET L'APPRENTISSAGE DE LA LECTURE (PRE SCHOOL EDUCATION AND INTRODUCTION TO READING) EJ 010 653

FILLERUP, JOSEPH M.
THE PROFESSIONAL RESPONSE. ED048922

FINCK, GEORGE H.
PROJECT PLAYPEN -- PRIMARY PREVENTION EJ 058 213

FINDLEY, WARREN G.
POSTDOCTORAL RESEARCH TRAINING PROGRAM IN EDUCATIONAL STIMULATION. FINAL REPORT. ED035455

FINKELSTEIN, ELSIE L.
A COMPARISON OF THE CHARACTERISTICS OF JUNIOR HIGH SCHOOL STUDENTS EJ 026 325

FINLEY, GORDON E.
PLAY BEHAVIOR IN YOUNG CHILDREN: A CROSS-CULTURAL STUDY EJ 048 303
DEVELOPMENT OF YOUNG CHILDREN'S ATTENTION TO NORMAL AND DISTORTED STIMULI: A CROSS CULTURAL STUDY EJ 055 103

FIRESTER, JOAN
WANTED: RX FOR THE EQUITABLE MANAGEMENT OF PARENT-SCHOOL CONFLICT EJ 014 433

FIRESTER, LEE
WANTED: RX FOR THE EQUITABLE MANAGEMENT OF PARENT-SCHOOL CONFLICT EJ 014 433

FIRMA, THEREZA PENNA
EFFECTS OF SOCIAL REINFORCEMENT ON SELF-ESTEEM OF MEXICAN-AMERICAN CHILDREN. LONG ABSTRACT. ED033767

FISCHBEIN, EFRAIM
COMPARISON OF RATIOS AND THE CHANCE CONCEPT IN CHILDREN EJ 021 771

FISCHER, GEORGE D.
STATEMENT ON COMPREHENSIVE PRESCHOOL EDUCATION AND CHILD DAY CARE ACT OF 1969 BEFORE THE SELECT SUBCOMMITTEE ON EDUCATION, FEBRUARY 27, 1970. ED039941

FISCHER, ROBERT J.
DISTORTIONS IN THE KINDERGARTEN EJ 007 214

FISH, CAROLINE
HEAD START EVALUATION AND RESEARCH CENTER, BOSTON UNIVERSITY. REPORT B-I, PRIMARY AND SECONDARY PREVENTION STUDYING CLINICAL PROCESS AND DISTURBANCE WITH PRESCHOOL CHILDREN. ED022560

FISH, CAROLINE C.
DISTURBANCE AND DISSONANCE - COMMUNITY UNIVERSITY COLLABORATION IN DIAGNOSIS AND TREATMENT OF DISTURBANCES. ED030485

FISHBEIN, HAROLD D.
THE EFFECTS OF FEEDBACK VARIATIONS ON REFERENTIAL COMMUNICATION OF CHILDREN EJ 040 360
CHILDREN'S UNDERSTANDING OF SPATIAL RELATIONS: COORDINATION OF PERSPECTIVES EJ 061 068

FISHER, DENNIS F.
VERBAL RECALL AS A FUNCTION OF PERSONALITY CHARACTERISTICS EJ 054 806

FISHER, MAURICE D.
THE EFFECT OF A PERCEPTUAL-MOTOR TRAINING PROGRAM UPON THE READINESS AND PERCEPTUAL DEVELOPMENT OF CULTURALLY DISADVANTAGED KINDERGARTEN CHILDREN. ED041633

FISHER, VIRGINIA LEE
COGNITIVE ASPECTS OF CHILDREN'S OCCUPATIONAL PRESTIGE RANKINGS. ED039924

FITZGERALD, HIRAM E.
RECENCY AND SUMMATION EFFECTS OF NONREWARD IN CHILDREN EJ 028 895
A DECADE OF INFANT CONDITIONING AND LEARNING RESEARCH EJ 038 454

FITZSIMMONS, STEPHEN J.
A STUDY IN CHILD CARE. VOLUME I: FINDINGS. DAY CARE PROGRAMS REPRINT SERIES. ED051911

FLAMMER, DONALD P.
SELF-ESTEEM, PARENT IDENTIFICATION AND SEX ROLE DEVELOPMENT IN PRESCHOOL AGE BOYS AND GIRLS EJ 051 015

FLAPAN, DOROTHY
CHILDREN'S UNDERSTANDING OF SOCIAL INTERACTION. ED031298
DEVELOPMENTAL GROUPINGS OF PRE-SCHOOL CHILDREN. ED046513
ISSUES IN ASSESSING DEVELOPMENT EJ 030 516

FLAVELL, H. H.
FIRST DISCUSSANT'S COMMENTS: WHAT IS MEMORY DEVELOPMENT THE DEVELOPMENT OF? EJ 049 433

FLAVELL, JOHN H.
THE DEVELOPMENT OF ROLE-TAKING AND COMMUNICATION SKILLS IN CHILDREN. ED027082
VERBAL FACTORS IN COMPENSATION PERFORMANCE AND THE RELATION BETWEEN CONSERVATION AND COMPENSATION EJ 033 778

FLAX, NORMAN
RETARDED CHILDREN AT CAMP WITH NORMAL CHILDREN EJ 012 199

FLEEGE, URBAN H.
MONTESSORI PRE-SCHOOL EDUCATION. FINAL REPORT. ED017320

FLEEGE, VIRGINIA B.
MONTESSORI INDEX. THIRD EDITION. ED035435

FLEENER, DON E.
ATTACHMENT BEHAVIORS IN HUMAN INFANTS: DISCRIMINATIVE VOCALIZATION ON MATERNAL SEPARATION EJ 019 019

FLEMING, ELYSE S.
TEACHER EXPECTANCY OR MY FAIR LADY. ED038183
TEACHER EXPECTANCY AS RELATED TO THE ACADEMIC AND PERSONAL GROWTH OF PRIMARY-AGE CHILDREN EJ 057 018

FLEMING, JAMES T.
TEACHERS' RATINGS OF URBAN CHILDREN'S READING PERFORMANCE EJ 035 662

FLEMING, ROBERT S.
LEARNING FROM LOOKING WITHIN: A DIFFERENT FOCUS, RELATING AND RESPONDING THROUGH THE ARTS EJ 057 326

FLETCHER, HAROLD J.
LOGICAL INFERENCE IN DISCRIMINATION LEARNING OF YOUNG CHILDREN. REPORT FROM THE RULE LEARNING PROJECT. ED036314

FLINTON, DORIS HOLT
LANGUAGE FOR LEARNING: ORAL LANGUAGE AND COGNITIVE DEVELOPMENT, PRE-K, K, GRADE 1. SECTION 1, TEACHER'S GUIDE. ED039921

FLURRY, RUTH
HOW ELSE? EJ 015 060

FLYNN, JOHN
COLLEGE TRAINING FOR HEAD START WORKERS: A BOOST TOWARD CAREER ADVANCEMENT EJ 017 097

FODOR, IRIS E.
THE USE OF BEHAVIOR-MODIFICATION TECHNIQUES WITH FEMALE DELINQUENTS EJ 051 473

FOLEY, WALTER J.
FOLLOW-UP OF OPERATION HEAD START PARTICIPANTS IN THE STATE OF IOWA. FINAL REPORT. ED015771

FOLEY, WAYNE EDWARD
SPATIO-TEMPORAL SERIAL PERFORMANCE IN CHILDREN AND ADULTS EJ 021 758

FOLLMAN, JOHN
EFFECTS OF INSTRUCTIONS ON THEME GRADING: GRAMMATICAL VS. HOLISTIC EJ 040 724
DELINQUENCY PREDICTION SCALES AND PERSONALITY INVENTORIES EJ 057 475

FOMON, SAMUEL J.
PREVENTION OF IRON-DEFICIENCY ANEMIA IN INFANTS AND CHILDREN OF PRESCHOOL AGE. ED052830

FORBES, WILLIAM H.
RULE STRUCTURE AND PROPORTION OF POSITIVE INSTANCES AS DETERMINANTS OF CONCEPT ATTAINMENT IN CHILDREN. ED046500

FORD, LEROY H., JR.
PREDICTIVE VERSUS PERCEPTUAL RESPONSES TO PIAGET'S WATER-LINE TASK AND THEIR RELATION TO DISTANCE CONSERVATION EJ 018 875

FOREIT, KAREN G.
DIALECT, RACE, AND LANGUAGE PROFICIENCY: ANOTHER DEAD HEAT ON THE MERRY-GO-ROUND EJ 053 747

FORER, LOIS G.
THE RIGHTS OF CHILDREN EJ 060 473

FORMANEK, RUTH
ENCOURAGING STUDENTS' RESEARCH ON COGNITIVE DEVELOPMENT. ED031301
ATTITUDES OF PRESCHOOL AND ELEMENTARY SCHOOL CHILDREN TO AUTHORITY FIGURES. ED046506
ATTITUDES OF PRESCHOOL AND ELEMENTARY SCHOOL CHILDREN TO AUTHORITY FIGURES EJ 034 452

FORTHMAN, ROBERT C.
CHILD WELFARE: SEARCHING FOR RELEVANT LEARNING ON THE UNDERGRADUATE LEVEL EJ 056 762

FOSS, B. M., ED.
DETERMINANTS OF INFANT BEHAVIOUR IV. ED032947

FOSTER, BETTY J.
CURRENT EXPENDITURES BY LOCAL EDUCATION AGENCIES FOR FREE PUBLIC ELEMENTARY AND SECONDARY EDUCATION, 1968-69. ED052826

FOSTER, FLORENCE P.
LITERATURE AND THE YOUNG CHILD. ED028828
PLANNING PARENT-IMPLEMENTED PROGRAMS: A GUIDE FOR PARENTS, SCHOOLS AND COMMUNITIES. ED036322
NUTRITION AND EDUCATIONAL EXPERIENCE: INTERRELATED VARIABLES IN CHILDREN'S LEARNING EJ 059 643

FOSTERLING, CHARLES
PEER- OBSERVER CONSULTATION EJ 022 532

FOUTS, GREGORY
CHARITY IN CHILDREN: THE INFLUENCE OF "CHARITY" STIMULI AND AN AUDIENCE EJ 058 224

FOUTS, GREGORY T.
EFFECTS OF STIMULUS-RESPONSE SIMILARITY AND DISSIMILARITY ON CHILDREN'S MATCHING PERFORMANCE EJ 016 350

FOWLER, W.
COMPLEX MOTOR LEARNING IN FOUR-YEAR-OLDS EJ 046 236

FOWLER, WILLIAM
THE EFFECT OF EARLY STIMULATION: THE PROBLEM OF FOCUS IN DEVELOPMENTAL STIMULATION. ED022535
THE CONCEPT OF DEVELOPMENTAL LEARNING. ED023484
CONCEPT LEARNING IN EARLY CHILDHOOD. ED024454
DEVELOPMENTAL LEARNING AS A CONCEPT IN EARLY READING. ED031289
INFANT STIMULATION AND THE ETIOLOGY OF COGNITIVE PROCESSES. ED045174
AN INTEGRATED PROGRAM OF GROUP CARE AND EDUCATION FOR SOCIOECONOMICALLY ADVANTAGED AND DISADVANTAGED INFANTS. ED048937
A DEVELOPMENTAL LEARNING APPROACH TO INFANT CARE IN A GROUP SETTING. ED049818
THE EFFECT OF EARLY STIMULATION: THE PROBLEM OF FOCUS IN DEVELOPMENTAL STIMULATION EJ 006 921
PROBLEMS OF DEPRIVATION AND DEVELOPMENTAL LEARNING EJ 024 691
ON THE VALUE OF BOTH PLAY AND STRUCTURE IN EARLY EDUCATION EJ 044 010
A DEVELOPMENTAL LEARNING APPROACH TO INFANT CARE IN A GROUP SETTING EJ 057 442

FOZARD, JAMES L.
AGE DIFFERENCES IN JUDGMENTS OF RECENCY FOR SHORT SEQUENCES OF PICTURES EJ 026 375

FRAIBERG, SELMA
INTERVENTION IN INFANCY: A PROGRAM FOR BLIND INFANTS EJ 048 904

FRAIBERG, SELMA H.
THE MAGIC YEARS: UNDERSTANDING AND HANDLING THE PROBLEMS OF EARLY CHILDHOOD. ED029712

FRANCIS, SARAH H.
THE EFFECTS OF OWN-HOME AND INSTITUTION-REARING ON THE BEHAVIOURAL DEVELOPMENT OF NORMAL AND MONGOL CHILDREN EJ 048 905

FRANK, LAWRENCE K.
EVALUATION OF EDUCATIONAL PROGRAMS EJ 007 047

FRANK, S. M.
SYNTACTIC COMPLEXITY IN MOTHER-CHILD INTERACTIONS. ED035454

FRANK, SHELDON M.
STORY RECALL IN KINDERGARTEN CHILDREN: EFFECT OF METHOD OF PRESENTATION ON PSYCHOLINGUISTIC PERFORMANCE EJ 036 748

FRANKENBURG, WILLIAM K.
VALIDITY OF THE DENVER DEVELOPMENTAL SCREENING TEST EJ 041 722
RELIABILITY AND STABILITY OF THE DENVER DEVELOPMENTAL SCREENING TEST EJ 053 905

FRANKLIN, MARGERY
HEAD START EVALUATION AND RESEARCH CENTER. PROGRESS REPORT OF RESEARCH STUDIES 1966 TO 1967. DOCUMENT 3, AN EXPERIMENTAL APPROACH TO STUDYING NON-VERBAL REPRESENTATION IN YOUNG CHILDREN. ED021625

FRANKLIN, MARGERY B.
A STUDY OF NON-VERBAL REPRESENTATION IN YOUNG CHILDREN. ED036336

FRASER, DAVID W.
WHAT'S AHEAD FOR PREADOLESCENCE? EJ 009 034

FRAUNFELKER, BARBARA S.
PHONETIC COMPATIBILITY IN PAIRED-ASSOCIATE LEARNING OF FIRST- AND THIRD-GRADE CHILDREN EJ 044 692

FRAYER, DOROTHY A.
LEARNING BY DISCOVERY: A REVIEW OF THE RESEARCH METHODOLOGY. REPORT FROM THE PROJECT ON VARIABLES AND PROCESSES IN COGNITIVE LEARNING. ED053793

FRAZIER, ALEXANDER
CHILDREN AND THEIR EXPANDING WORLD OF KNOWLEDGE EJ 026 734

FRAZIER, ALEXANDER, ED.
THE NEW ELEMENTARY SCHOOL. ED017341
EARLY CHILDHOOD EDUCATION TODAY. ED021631

FREEDLE, ROY
APPLICATION OF MARKOV PROCESSES TO THE CONCEPT OF STATE. ED053813
ON RELATING AN INFANT'S OBSERVATION TIME OF VISUAL STIMULI WITH CHOICE-THEORY ANALYSIS EJ 019 016
A STIMULUS SIMILARITY SCALE FOR TEMPORAL MEASURES OF ATTENTION IN INFANTS AND CHILDREN EJ 034 530

FREEDMAN, D. G.
PERSONALITY DEVELOPMENT IN INFANCY ED024439

FREEDMAN, DAVID A.
A MULTIHANDICAPPED RUBELLA BABY: THE FIRST EIGHTEEN MONTHS EJ 022 979

FREIS, RUTH
A NONSEGREGATED APPROACH TO HEAD START EJ 007 363

FREITAG, GILBERT
AN EXPERIMENTAL STUDY OF THE SOCIAL RESPONSIVENESS OF CHILDREN WITH AUTISTIC BEHAVIORS EJ 024 470

FRICHTL, CHRIS
EARLY INFANT STIMULATION AND MOTOR DEVELOPMENT. ED038179

FRIEDLANDER, BERNARD Z.
RECEPTIVE LANGUAGE DEVELOPMENT IN INFANCY: ISSUES AND PROBLEMS EJ 020 396

FRIEDLANDER, GEORGE H.
REPORT ON THE ARTICULATORY AND INTELLIGIBILITY STATUS OF SOCIALLY DISADVANTAGED PRE-SCHOOL CHILDREN. ED014321

FRIEDMAN, FAY T.
MBD - AN EDUCATIONAL PUZZLEMENT. ED032130

FRIEDMAN, MYLES I.
REGIONAL EVALUATION AND RESEARCH CENTER FOR PROJECT HEAD START, SUPPLEMENTARY RESEARCH REPORT, SEPTEMBER 1, 1967-DECEMBER 31, 1967. ED020791
EVALUATION AND RESEARCH CENTER FOR PROJECT HEAD START, UNIVERSITY OF SOUTH CAROLINA. INTERIM EVALUATION REPORT. ED045197
AN INVESTIGATION OF THE RELATIVE EFFECTIVENESS OF SELECTED CURRICULUM VARIABLES IN THE LANGUAGE DEVELOPMENT OF HEAD START CHILDREN. ED046497

FRIEDMAN, MYLES I., ED.
POPULATION CHARACTERISTICS OF DISADVANTAGED PRESCHOOL CHILDREN. PROCEEDINGS OF THE HEAD START RESEARCH SEMINARS: SEMINAR NO. 3, HEAD START POPULATIONS (1ST, WASHINGTON, D.C., OCTOBER 9, 1968). ED036330

FRIEDMAN, PHILIP
PUPIL IMITATION OF A REWARDING TEACHER'S VERBAL BEHAVIOR. ED038185

FRIEDMAN, ROBERT
STRUCTURED FAMILY-ORIENTED THERAPY FOR SCHOOL BEHAVIOR AND LEARNING DISORDERS EJ 019 022

FRIEDMAN, RONALD
THE RELATIONSHIP BETWEEN INTELLIGENCE AND PERFORMANCE ON THE STROOP COLOR-WORD TEST IN SECOND- AND FIFTH-GRADE CHILDREN EJ 035 887

FRIEDMAN, SARAH
ORIENTATION IN CHILDREN'S HUMAN FIGURE DRAWINGS: AN ASPECT OF GRAPHIC LANGUAGE EJ 061 067

FRIEDMAN, STANLEY R.
DEVELOPMENTAL LEVEL AND CONCEPT-LEARNING--A REPLICATION AND EXTENSION. ED016528
A DEVELOPMENTAL STUDY OF THE RELATIONSHIP BETWEEN REACTION-TIME AND PROBLEM-SOLVING EFFICIENCY. FINAL REPORT. ED020018

FRIEDMAN, STEVEN
NEWBORN ATTENTION: DIFFERENTIAL RESPONSE DECREMENT TO VISUAL STIMULI EJ 027 846
VISUAL RESPONSE DECREMENT AS A FUNCTION OF AGE OF HUMAN NEWBORNS EJ 056 716

HABITUATION AND RECOVERY OF VISUAL RESPONSE IN THE ALERT HUMAN NEWBORN EJ 057 116

FRIEDRICHS, ANN G.
INTERRELATIONS AMONG LEARNING AND PERFORMANCE TASKS AT THE PRESCHOOL LEVEL EJ 035 361

FRIEND, MAURICE R.
"YOUTH UNREST": REFLECTIONS OF A PSYCHOANALYST EJ 023 425

FRISK, GUY C.
LONGITUDINAL ASSESSMENT OF THE RELATION BETWEEN MEASURED INTELLIGENCE OF INSTITUTIONALIZED RETARDATES AND HOSPITAL AGE EJ 047 340

FRITH, SANDRA
CLASSROOM LANGUAGE OF TEACHERS OF YOUNG CHILDREN. ED053820

FRITH, UTA
STUDIES IN PATTERN DETECTION IN NORMAL AND AUTISTIC CHILDREN. II. REPRODUCTION AND PRODUCTION OF COLOR SEQUENCES EJ 027 613

FROIMSON, MARCIA
REPORT ON ACTIVITIES, 1964-1966. ED020016

FROST, JOE L.
A STRUCTURE-PROCESS APPROACH TO COGNITIVE DEVELOPMENT OF PRESCHOOL NEGRO CHILDREN: RATIONALE AND EFFECTS. ED033743
THE SEVENTIES: A TIME FOR GIANT STEPS EJ 009 030

FRYE, KENNETH
GUIDEBOOK FOR TEACHERS. ED020001

FULD, PAULA ALTMAN
SYNTACTICAL MEDIATION OF PAIRED-ASSOCIATE LEARNING AS A FUNCTION OF AGE EJ 030 286

FULLERTON, T. J.
A DISCRIMINATION TASK WHICH INDUCES CONSERVATION OF NUMBER EJ 018 876

FURBY, LITA
RACIAL PREFERENCES IN YOUNG CHILDREN EJ 056 626

FURTH, H. G.
ON LANGUAGE AND KNOWING IN PIAGET'S DEVELOPMENTAL THEORY EJ 034 713

FURTH, HANS G.
CHILDREN'S UTILIZATION OF LOGICAL SYMBOLS: AN INTERPRETATION OF CONCEPTUAL BEHAVIOR BASED ON PIAGETIAN THEORY EJ 024 942
THINKING BEFORE LANGUAGE? A SYMPOSIUM: 2. A SCHOOL FOR THINKING EJ 050 200

GAA, JOHN P.
THE USE OF INDIVIDUAL GOAL-SETTING CONFERENCES AS A MOTIVATIONAL TECHNIQUE. ED053816

GADDINI, EUGENIO
TRANSITIONAL OBJECTS AND THE PROCESS OF INDIVIDUATION: A STUDY IN THREE DIFFERENT SOCIAL GROUPS EJ 022 476

GADDINI, RENATA
TRANSITIONAL OBJECTS AND THE PROCESS OF INDIVIDUATION: A STUDY IN THREE DIFFERENT SOCIAL GROUPS EJ 022 476

GAINES, ROSSLYN
THE DISCRIMINABILITY OF FORM AMONG YOUNG CHILDREN EJ 016 164
CHILDREN'S SELECTIVE ATTENTION TO STIMULI: STAGE OR SET? EJ 033 573

GALAWAY, BURT
CLARIFYING THE ROLE OF FOSTER PARENTS EJ 061 235

GALDSTON, RICHARD
VIOLENCE BEGINS AT HOME. THE PARENTS' CENTER PROJECT FOR THE STUDY AND PREVENTION OF CHILD ABUSE EJ 043 671

GALEN, HARLENE
A MATTER OF LIFE AND DEATH EJ 059 746

GALLAGHER, JAMES J.
THE SOCIAL MATURITY OF DISADVANTAGED CHILDREN. SPECIAL STUDIES PROJECT #2: ED042507

GALLAGHER, JOSEPH W.
SEMANTIC RELATIONSHIP AND THE LEARNING OF SYNTACTIC WORD PAIRS IN CHILDREN EJ 016 163
PAIRED-ASSOCIATE LEARNING OF CHILDREN WITH MIXED LIST DESIGNS EJ 035 369

GALLAGHER, URSULA M.
ADOPTION RESOURCES FOR BLACK CHILDREN EJ 035 801

GALLOWAY, CHARLES G.
MATERIAL REINFORCEMENT AND SUCCESS IN SPELLING EJ 018 423
MODIFICATION OF BEHAVIOR PATTERNS OF INDIAN CHILDREN EJ 051 472

GANTER, ROBERT L.
A CLINIC FOR CHILDREN WITH LEARNING DISABILITIES EJ 024 471

GARAI, JOSEF E.
SEX DIFFERENCES IN MENTAL AND BEHAVIORAL TRAITS. ED026117

GARBER, HOWARD L.
MEASURING DIFFERENTIAL DEVELOPMENT IN YOUNG CHILDREN. ED050818

GARBER, MICHAEL
THE GHETTO AS A SOURCE OF FOSTER HOMES EJ 020 858

GARDNER, D. BRUCE
THE INFLUENCE OF THEORETICAL CONCEPTIONS OF HUMAN DEVELOPMENT ON THE PRACTICE OF EARLY CHILDHOOD EDUCATION. ED033766

GARDNER, DOROTHY E.M.
THE ROLE OF THE TEACHER IN THE INFANT AND NURSERY SCHOOL. ED029703

GARDNER, HOWARD
CHILDREN'S SENSITIVITY TO PAINTING STYLES EJ 025 304
A NOTE ON SELECTIVE IMITATION BY A SIX-WEEK-OLD INFANT EJ 034 045

GARDNER, JUDITH
A NOTE ON SELECTIVE IMITATION BY A SIX-WEEK-OLD INFANT EJ 034 045

GARELL, DALE C.
A HOTLINE TELEPHONE SERVICE FOR YOUNG PEOPLE IN CRISIS EJ 007 713

GARFUNKEL, FRANK
HEAD START EVALUATION AND RESEARCH CENTER, BOSTON UNIVERSITY. REPORT OF RESEARCH, SEPTEMBER, 1966-AUGUST, 1967. ED022529
HEAD START EVALUATION AND RESEARCH CENTER, BOSTON UNIVERSITY. REPORT A-I, TEACHING STYLE: THE DEVELOPMENT OF TEACHING TASKS. ED022557
HEAD START EVALUATION AND RESEARCH CENTER, BOSTON UNIVERSITY. REPORT A-II, OBSERVATION OF TEACHERS AND TEACHING: STRATEGIES AND APPLICATIONS. ED022558
HEAD START EVALUATION AND RESEARCH CENTER, BOSTON UNIVERSITY. REPORT A-III, OBSERVATIONAL STRATEGIES FOR OBTAINING DATA ON CHILDREN AND TEACHERS IN HEAD START CLASSES. (OSOD). ED022559
PRESCHOOL EDUCATION AND POVERTY: THE DISTANCE IN BETWEEN. FINAL REPORT OF 1968-69 INTERVENTIONAL PROGRAM. ED046501

GARNER, JOHN
AGE DIFFERENCES IN THE DISCRIMINATION SHIFT LEARNING OF YOUNG CHILDREN EJ 025 963
SEX DIFFERENCES IN BEHAVIOURAL IMPULSIVITY, INTELLECTUAL IMPULSIVITY, AND ATTAINMENT IN YOUNG CHILDREN EJ 051 151

GARRETT, ALICE M.
PERSONAL ORIENTATION TO SUCCESS AND FAILURE IN URBAN BLACK CHILDREN EJ 061 072

GARRETT, BEATRICE L.
THE RIGHTS OF FOSTER PARENTS EJ 022 182
FOSTER FAMILY SERVICES FOR MENTALLY RETARDED CHILDREN EJ 030 653

GARRETTSON, JUDY
COGNITIVE STYLE AND CLASSIFICATION EJ 044 706

GARSKE, JOHN P.
LOGICAL INFERENCE IN DISCRIMINATION LEARNING OF YOUNG CHILDREN. REPORT FROM THE RULE LEARNING PROJECT. ED036314

GARTNER, ALAN
EVERY CHILD A TEACHER EJ 044 508

GARY, CHARLES L., ED.
THE STUDY OF MUSIC IN THE ELEMENTARY SCHOOL--A CONCEPTUAL APPROACH. ED017328

GAUDIA, GIL
RACE, SOCIAL CLASS, AND AGE OF ACHIEVEMENT OF CONSERVATION ON PIAGET'S TASKS EJ 053 714

GAUTHIER, JOAN PRESTON
EFFECTS OF STIMULUS ABSTRACTNESS AND FAMILIARITY ON LISTENER'S PERFORMANCE IN A COMMUNICATION TASK EJ 046 241

GEIGER, EDWIN L.
EFFECTS OF SOCIAL CLASS INTEGRATION OF PRESCHOOL NEGRO CHILDREN ON TEST PERFORMANCE AND SELF-CONCEPT. FINAL REPORT. ED050831

GEIS, ROBLEY
A PREVENTIVE SUMMER PROGRAM FOR KINDERGARTEN CHILDREN LIKELY TO FAIL IN FIRST GRADE READING. FINAL REPORT. ED030495

GELMAN, ROCHEL
LOGICAL CAPACITY OF VERY YOUNG CHILDREN: NUMBER INVARIANCE RULES EJ 056 394
THE RELATIONSHIP BETWEEN LIQUID CONSERVATION AND COMPENSATION EJ 059 313

GERHARDT, FRANK
HUMAN RESOURCES FOR INTERNATIONAL STUDIES EJ 038 393

GERSHAW, N. JAME
THE EFFECTS OF A FAMILIAR TOY AND MOTHER'S PRESENCE ON EXPLORATORY AND ATTACHMENT BEHAVIORS IN YOUNG CHILDREN EJ 053 759

GERTLER, DIANE B.
PREPRIMARY ENROLLMENT OF CHILDREN UNDER SIX: OCTOBER 1967. ED027094

GESHURI, YOSSEF
LEARNING OF AGGRESSION AS A FUNCTION OF PRESENCE OF A HUMAN MODEL, RESPONSE INTENSITY, AND TARGET OF THE RESPONSE EJ 043 198

GETZELS, J.W.
PRE-SCHOOL EDUCATION. ED020785

GEWIRTZ, JACOB L.
LEVELS OF CONCEPTUAL ANALYSIS IN ENVIRONMENT-INFANT INTERACTION RESEARCH EJ 004 044

GHOLSON, BARRY
HYPOTHESES, STRATEGIES, AND STEREOTYPES IN DISCRIMINATION LEARNING EJ 060 779

GIACOMAN, SHARON L.
HUNGER AND MOTOR RESTRAINT ON AROUSAL AND VISUAL ATTENTION IN THE INFANT EJ 040 298

GIBBON, SAMUEL Y., JR.
PRE-READING ON SESAME STREET. FINAL REPORT, VOLUME V OF V VOLUMES. ED047825

GIBBS, VANITA
NON-PUBLIC PRESCHOOL PROGRAMS IN INDIANA. ED050813

GIBNEY, THOMAS C.
WHAT INFLUENCES THE MATHEMATICAL UNDERSTANDING OF ELEMENTARY-SCHOOL TEACHERS? EJ 018 422

GIBSON, JAMES J.
A NEW THEORY OF SCRIBBLING AND DRAWING IN CHILDREN. ED017324

GIBSON, JOHN S.
THE INTERGROUP RELATIONS CURRICULUM: A PROGRAM FOR ELEMENTARY SCHOOL EDUCATION. VOLUMES I AND II. ED029704

GIESY, ROSEMARY
A GUIDE FOR COLLECTING AND ORGANIZING INFORMATION ON EARLY CHILDHOOD PROGRAMS EJ 058 463

GIL, DAVID G.
A SOCIOCULTURAL PERSPECTIVE ON PHYSICAL CHILD ABUSE EJ 043 353

GILBERT, DOROTHEA
EDUCATIONAL AND GROWTH NEEDS OF CHILDREN IN DAY CARE EJ 016 351

GILBERT, JOHN H.
THE LEARNING OF SPEECHLIKE STIMULI BY CHILDREN EJ 018 815
VOWEL PRODUCTIONS AND IDENTIFICATION BY NORMAL AND LANGUAGE DELAYED CHILDREN EJ 018 816

GILBERT, LYNN ELLEN
AN INTRODUCTION OF LENGTH CONCEPTS TO KINDERGARTEN CHILDREN. REPORT FROM THE PROJECT ON ANALYSIS OF MATHEMATICS INSTRUCTION. ED036335

GILL, ROBERT
THE EFFECTS OF CARTOON CHARACTERS AS MOTIVATORS OF PRESCHOOL DISADVANTAGED CHILDREN. FINAL REPORT. ED045210

GILLEN, WILLIAM
A GUIDE FOR PRESCHOOLS: A HANDBOOK ABOUT THE OPERATION AND FUNCTION OF PRESCHOOLS IN THE FRESNO CITY UNIFIED SCHOOL DISTRICT. ED030499

GILLIES, EMILY
BILLY MEARNS: FRIEND AND TEACHER. HUGHES MEARNS, 1875-1965 EJ 002 655

GILMER, BARBARA R.
INTRA-FAMILY DIFFUSION OF SELECTED COGNITIVE SKILLS AS A FUNCTION OF EDUCATIONAL STIMULATION. ED037233
INTERVENTION WITH MOTHERS AND YOUNG CHILDREN: A STUDY OF INTRAFAMILY EFFECTS. ED050809

GINSBERG, ROSE
INVESTIGATION OF CONCEPT LEARNING IN YOUNG CHILDREN. FINAL REPORT. ED030498

GINSBURG, BENSON E.
DEVELOPMENTAL GENETICS OF BEHAVIORAL CAPACITIES: THE NATURE-NURTURE PROBLEM RE-EVALUATED EJ 037 516

GINSBURG, HERBERT
THE EFFECTS OF MODE OF PRESENTATION AND NUMBER OF CATEGORIES ON 4-YEAR-OLDS' PROPORTION ESTIMATES. ED032132

GIOVANNONI, JEANNE M.
CHILD NEGLECT AMONG THE POOR: A STUDY OF PARENTAL ADEQUACY IN FAMILIES OF THREE ETHNIC GROUPS EJ 018 326

GITTER, A. G.
COLOR AND PHYSIOGNOMY AS VARIABLES IN RACIAL MISIDENTIFICATION AMONG CHILDREN. ED034584

GITTER, A. GEORGE
HEAD START EVALUATION AND RESEARCH CENTER, BOSTON UNIVERSITY. REPORT C-I, PERCEPTION OF EMOTION AMONG CHILDREN: RACE AND SEX DIFFERENCES. ED022561
RACE AND SEX DIFFERENCES IN THE CHILD'S PERCEPTION OF EMOTION EJ 056 625

GITTER, LENA L.
REFLECTIONS ON REVISITING VIENNA'S YOUNG CITIZENS EJ 060 107

GLADEN, FRANK H.
A STUDY OF THE EFFECTIVENESS OF SPECIFIC TEACHING OF CONSERVATION TO CHILDREN IN SELECTED ELEMENTARY SCHOOLS OF BUTTE COUNTY, CALIFORNIA EJ 027 029

GLANCY, BARBARA
THE BEAUTIFUL PEOPLE IN CHILDREN'S BOOKS EJ 020 541

GLASER, ROBERT
PSYCHOLOGICAL BASES FOR INSTRUCTIONAL DESIGN. ED013121

GLASGOW, ROBERT B.
STUDY TO DETERMINE THE FEASIBILITY OF ADAPTING THE CARL ORFF APPROACH TO ELEMENTARY SCHOOLS IN AMERICA. FINAL REPORT. ED020804

GLASNAPP, DOUGLAS R.
A COMPARATIVE STUDY OF THREE FORMS OF THE METROPOLITAN READINESS TEST AT TWO SOCIO-ECONOMIC LEVELS. ED035448

GLAVACH, MATHEW
TEACHING THE UNTEACHABLES EJ 021 514

GLENNON, VINCENT J.
ELEMENTARY SCHOOL MATHEMATICS: A GUIDE TO CURRENT RESEARCH. THIRD EDITION. ED026123

GLICK, JOSEPH
RELATION BETWEEN IDENTITY CONSERVATION AND EQUIVALENCE CONSERVATION WITHIN FOUR CONCEPTUAL DOMAINS EJ 054 804

GLIDDEN, LARAINE MASTERS
MEANINGFULNESS, SERIAL POSITION AND RETENTION INTERVAL IN RECOGNITION SHORT-TERM MEMORY EJ 053 724

GLINER, CYNTHIA R.
A DEVELOPMENTAL INVESTIGATION OF VISUAL AND HAPTIC PREFERENCES FOR SHAPE AND TEXTURE EJ 008 780

GLINES, DON E.
IMPLEMENTING DIFFERENT AND BETTER SCHOOLS. ED039926

GLOCKNER, MARY
WORKTABLE ON WHEELS. ED035451

GODGART, MARTIN, ED.
PERSPECTIVES ON TEACHER-AIDES. A TEACHING TEXT. ED028836

GOFFENEY, BARBARA
NEGRO-WHITE, MALE-FEMALE EIGHT-MONTH DEVELOPMENTAL SCORES COMPARED WITH SEVEN-YEAR WISC AND BENDER TEST SCORES EJ 040 723

GOLD, IRWIN H.
A SOCIAL WORK MISSION TO HIPPIELAND EJ 004 092

GOLDBERG, SIDNEY
PARENTS' EVALUATION OF THE HEAD START PROGRAM IN THE MILWAUKEE PUBLIC SCHOOLS. ED020806

GOLDBERG, SUSAN
PLAY BEHAVIOR IN THE YEAR-OLD INFANT: EARLY SEX DIFFERENCES. ED022545
PERCEPTUAL-COGNITIVE DEVELOPMENT IN INFANCY: A GENERALIZED EXPECTANCY MODEL AS A FUNCTION OF THE MOTHER-INFANT INTERACTION. ED024470
PERCEPTUAL-COGNITIVE DEVELOPMENT IN INFANCY: A GENERALIZED EXPECTANCY MODEL AS A FUNCTION OF THE MOTHER-INFANT INTERACTION EJ 003 553
INFANT CARE AND GROWTH IN URBAN ZAMBIA EJ 061 231

GOLDEN, MARK
SOCIAL CLASS AND COGNITIVE DEVELOPMENT IN INFANCY. ED019111
SOCIAL CLASS DIFFERENTIATION IN COGNITIVE DEVELOPMENT: A LONGITUDINAL STUDY. ED033754

SOCIAL CLASS DIFFERENTIATION IN COGNITIVE DEVELOPMENT AMONG BLACK PRESCHOOL CHILDREN. ED039039
SOCIAL-CLASS DIFFERENTIATION IN COGNITIVE DEVELOPMENT AMONG BLACK PRESCHOOL CHILDREN EJ 036 819
PREDICTION OF INTELLECTUAL PERFORMANCE AT 3 YEARS FROM INFANT TESTS AND PERSONALITY MEASURES EJ 052 237
SOCIAL CLASS INTELLIGENCE, AND COGNITIVE STYLE IN INFANCY EJ 056 725

GOLDENBERG, IRENE
SOCIAL CLASS DIFFERENCES IN TEACHER ATTITUDES TOWARD CHILDREN EJ 053 908

GOLDFRIED, MARVIN R.
MODELING AND THE FEARFUL CHILD PATIENT EJ 058 354

GOLDMAN, RICHARD M.
SIMULATION ACTIVITIES FOR TRAINING PARENTS AND TEACHERS AS EDUCATIONAL PARTNERS: A REPORT AND EVALUATION. ED048945

GOLDMAN, RUTH K.
PSYCHOSOCIAL DEVELOPMENT IN CROSS-CULTURAL PERSPECTIVE: A NEW LOOK AT AN OLD ISSUE EJ 046 888

GOLDSCHMID, MARCEL L.
EARLY COGNITIVE DEVELOPMENT AND PRESCHOOL EDUCATION EJ 043 857

GOLDSMITH, VIRGINIA G.
HAVE YOU DISABLED A POTENTIAL READ'N' DROPOUT LATELY? EJ 016 463

GOLDSTEIN, HARRIET
A PARENTING SCALE AND SEPARATION DECISIONS EJ 039 286

GOLDSTEIN, SONDRA BLEVINS
OBSERVING BEHAVIOR AND CHILDREN'S DISCRIMINATION LEARNING EJ 053 754

GOLIGHTLY, CAROLE
CHILDREN'S DEPENDENCY SCALE EJ 025 232

GOLLIN, EUGENE S.
AN ORGANISM ORIENTED CONCEPT OF DEVELOPMENT EJ 027 438
PROBLEMS OF CONTROL IN SIMULTANEOUS DISCRIMINATION TASKS EJ 058 215

GOLOMB, CLAIRE
EVOLUTION OF THE HUMAN FIGURE IN A THREE-DIMENSIONAL MEDIUM EJ 057 897

GOLUB, LESTER S.
READING, WRITING, AND BLACK ENGLISH EJ 052 178

GOOCH, S.
FOUR YEARS ON. A FOLLOW-UP STUDY AT SCHOOL LEAVING AGE OF CHILDREN FORMERLY ATTENDING A TRADITIONAL AND A PROGRESSIVE JUNIOR SCHOOL. ED035434

GOOD, THOMAS L.
WHICH PUPILS DO TEACHERS CALL ON? EJ 012 871

GOODMAN, KENNETH S.
ON VALUING DIVERSITY IN LANGUAGE EJ 011 840
ON THE PSYCHOLINGUISTIC METHOD OF TEACHING READING EJ 030 547

GOODMAN, MARY ELLEN
THE IMPACT OF CHANGE EJ 011 982

GOODMAN, NORMAN
ADOLESCENT NORMS AND BEHAVIOR: ORGANIZATION AND CONFORMITY EJ 007 450

GOODMAN, YETTA M.
THE CULTURE OF THE CULTURALLY DEPRIVED EJ 035 537

GOODNOW, JACQUELINE
MEMORY FOR RHYTHMIC SERIES: AGE CHANGES IN ACCURACY AND NUMBER CODING EJ 054 805

GOODNOW, JACQUELINE J.
MOTOR ACTIVITY: EFFECTS ON MEMORY EJ 021 769
MATCHING AUDITORY AND VISUAL SERIES: MODALITY PROBLEM OR TRANSLATION PROBLEM? EJ 051 569
ORIENTATION IN CHILDREN'S HUMAN FIGURE DRAWINGS: AN ASPECT OF GRAPHIC LANGUAGE EJ 061 067

GOOLER, DENNIS D.
PROCESS ACCOUNTABILITY IN CURRICULUM DEVELOPMENT. ED040757

GORDON, ANNE
HEAD START EVALUATION AND RESEARCH CENTER. PROGRESS REPORT OF RESEARCH STUDIES 1966 TO 1967. DOCUMENT 4, DEVELOPMENT OF OBSERVATION PROCEDURES FOR ASSESSING PRESCHOOL CLASSROOM ENVIRONMENT. ED021626

GORDON, DONALD A.
THE USE OF VERBAL MEDIATION IN THE RETARDED AS A FUNCTION OF DEVELOPMENTAL LEVEL AND RESPONSE AVAILABILITY EJ 044 699

GORDON, EDMUND W.
REMARKS ON THE MAX WOLFF REPORT. ED015030
DEMOCRATIZATION OF EDUCATIONAL OPPORTUNITY. AN ESSAY REVIEW EJ 038 471

GORDON, IRA J.
A PARENT EDUCATION APPROACH TO PROVISION OF EARLY STIMULATION FOR THE CULTURALLY DISADVANTAGED. FINAL REPORT. ED017339
EARLY CHILD STIMULATION THROUGH PARENT EDUCATION. ED038166
PARENT INVOLVEMENT IN COMPENSATORY EDUCATION. ED039954
RELATIONSHIPS BETWEEN SELECTED FAMILY VARIABLES AND MATERNAL AND INFANT BEHAVIOR IN A DISADVANTAGED POPULATION. A SUPPLEMENTARY REPORT. ED047784
ON EARLY LEARNING: THE MODIFIABILITY OF HUMAN POTENTIAL. ED051876
CHILDREN UNDER THREE - FINDING WAYS TO STIMULATE DEVELOPMENT. II. SOME CURRENT EXPERIMENTS: STIMULATION VIA PARENT EDUCATION EJ 007 410
REACHING THE YOUNG CHILD THROUGH PARENT EDUCATION EJ 017 852
EARLY CHILD STIMULATION THROUGH PARENT EDUCATION EJ 044 006
SUCCESS AND ACCOUNTABILITY EJ 055 533

GORDON, JACK
EFFECTS OF VIEWING VIDEOTAPED SAME AND OPPOSITE COLOR CHILD-TEACHERS ON INTEGRATED AND ALL-WHITE KINDERGARTNERS. ED047805

GORDON, MARJORY
IMPLICATIONS OF POST-NATAL CORTICAL DEVELOPMENT FOR CREATIVITY RESEARCH. ED047802

GORDON, RONNIE
THE DESIGN OF A PRE-SCHOOL "LEARNING LABORATORY" IN A REHABILITATION CENTER. ED033764

GORDON, SOL
EVALUATION OF PROJECT HEAD START READING READINESS IN ISSAQUENA AND SHARKEY COUNTIES, MISSISSIPPI, SUMMER, 1965. FINAL REPORT. ED014319

GORDON, SUSAN B.
ETHNIC AND SOCIOECONOMIC INFLUENCES ON THE HOME LANGUAGE EXPERIENCES OF CHILDREN. ED043377

GORDON, THOMAS
A THEORY OF PARENT EFFECTIVENESS. ED028815

GORMLY, JOHN
ACADEMIC CHEATING: THE CONTRIBUTION OF SEX, PERSONALITY AND SITUATIONAL VARIABLES EJ 055 104

GORSUCH, RICHARD L.
LOCUS OF CONTROL: AN EXAMPLE OF DANGERS IN USING CHILDREN'S SCALES WITH CHILDREN EJ 058 929

GORTON, HARRY B.
A STUDY OF THE KINDERGARTEN PROGRAM, FULL-DAY OR HALF-DAY. ED017327

GOTKIN, LASSAR G.
PROGRAMED INSTRUCTION AS A STRATEGY FOR DEVELOPING CURRICULA FOR CHILDREN FROM DISADVANTAGED BACKGROUNDS. ED015782
GAMES AND OTHER ACTIVITIES FOR DEVELOPING LANGUAGE SKILLS. ED022555

GOTTESMAN, I. I.
BIOGENETICS OF RACE AND CLASS. ED036317

GOTTESMAN, MILTON
A COMPARATIVE STUDY OF PIAGET'S DEVELOPMENTAL SCHEMA OF SIGHTED CHILDREN WITH THAT OF A GROUP OF BLIND CHILDREN EJ 040 319

GOUDEY, CHARLES E.
READING - DIRECTED OR NOT? EJ 015 125

GOULET, L. R.
VERBAL-DISCRIMINATION LEARNING AND TRANSFER WITH VERBAL AND PICTORIAL MATERIALS EJ 030 287
CHILDREN'S SHIFT PERFORMANCE IN THE ABSENCE OF DIMENSIONALITY AND A LEARNED REPRESENTATIONAL RESPONSE EJ 033 786
TRAINING, TRANSFER, AND THE DEVELOPMENT OF COMPLEX BEHAVIOR EJ 034 712
EFFECTS OF SPATIAL SEPARATION OF STIMULUS, RESPONSE, AND REWARD IN DISCRIMINATION LEARNING BY CHILDREN EJ 046 243
EXPLORATION OF DEVELOPMENTAL VARIABLES BY MANIPULATION AND SIMULATION OF AGE DIFFERENCES IN BEHAVIOR EJ 048 472

GOWAN, JOHN C.
EDUCATIONAL RESEARCH POLICIES OF SCHOOL DISTRICTS NATIONWIDE EJ 012 677

GOYEN, JUDITH D.
EFFECT OF INCENTIVES AND AGE ON THE VISUAL RECOGNITION OF RETARDED READERS EJ 037 535
EFFECT OF INCENTIVES UPON RETARDED AND NORMAL READERS ON A VISUAL-ASSOCIATE LEARNING TASK EJ 038 266

GOZALI, JOAV
COMMENTS ON SOCIAL DESIRABILITY AND PERSUASION EJ 025 803

GRAHAM, JORY
HANDBOOK FOR PROJECT HEAD START. ED015018

GRAHAM, P. J.
A BEHAVIOURAL SCREENING QUESTIONNAIRE FOR USE WITH THREE-YEAR-OLD CHILDREN. PRELIMINARY FINDINGS EJ 042 349

GRAMS, ARMIN
CONTRIBUTIONS OF CRITICISM TO PARENT, FAMILY-LIFE AND SEX EDUCATION EJ 054 381

GRAMZA, ANTHONY F.
POSITION EFFECTS IN PLAY EQUIPMENT PREFERENCES OF NURSERY SCHOOL CHILDREN. ED045185

GRANATO, SAM J.
DAY CARE LICENSING EJ 051 271

GRATCH, GERALD
A STUDY OF THE RELATIVE DOMINANCE OF VISION AND TOUCH IN SIX-MONTH-OLD INFANTS EJ 058 594
VIOLATION OF A RULE AS A METHOD OF DIAGNOSING INFANTS' LEVELS OF OBJECT CONCEPT EJ 059 314
THE STAGE IV ERROR IN PIAGET'S THEORY OF OBJECT CONCEPT DEVELOPMENT: DIFFICULTIES IN OBJECT CONCEPTUALIZATION OR SPATIAL LOCALIZATION? EJ 059 318

GRATH, GERALD
STATE IV OF PIAGET'S THEORY OF INFANT'S OBJECT CONCEPTS: A LONGITUDINAL STUDY EJ 041 134

GRATZ, PAULINE
AN ENVIRONMENT THAT SUPPORTS MAN EJ 029 389

GRAVES, MICHAEL F.
NOUN PLURAL DEVELOPMENT IN PRIMARY GRADE CHILDREN EJ 052 179

GRAY, CYNTHIA ROBERTS
AGE, ICONIC STORAGE, AND VISUAL INFORMATION PROCESSING EJ 053 725

GRAY, NAN
CHILDREN AND TV, TELEVISION'S IMPACT ON THE CHILD. ED013666

GRAY, SUSAN W.
THE EARLY TRAINING PROJECT FOR DISADVANTAGED CHILDREN--A REPORT AFTER FIVE YEARS. ED016514
RESISTANCE TO TEMPTATION IN YOUNG NEGRO CHILDREN IN RELATION TO SEX OF THE SUBJECT, SEX OF THE EXPERIMENTER AND FATHER ABSENCE OR PRESENCE. ED032138
RESEARCH, CHANGE, AND SOCIAL RESPONSIBILITY: AN ILLUSTRATIVE MODEL FROM EARLY EDUCATION. ED032922
THE EARLY TRAINING PROJECT: A SEVENTH YEAR REPORT. ED032934
SELECTED LONGITUDINAL STUDIES OF COMPENSATORY EDUCATION--A LOOK FROM THE INSIDE. ED033762
RESISTANCE TO TEMPTATION IN YOUNG NEGRO CHILDREN EJ 032 894
THE EARLY TRAINING PROJECT: A SEVENTH-YEAR REPORT EJ 033 777
ETHICAL ISSUES IN RESEARCH IN EARLY CHILDHOOD INTERVENTION EJ 037 578
SYMPOSIUM ON PARENT-CENTERED EDUCATION: 1. THE CHILD'S FIRST TEACHER EJ 054 377

GRAYSON, MARY
DEVELOPMENT OF A VISUAL ARTS CURRICULUM FOR YOUNG CHILDREN. CAREL ARTS AND HUMANITIES CURRICULUM DEVELOPMENT PROGRAM FOR YOUNG CHILDREN. ED032939

GREEN, ARTHUR H.
THE EFFECTS OF OBJECT LOSS ON THE BODY IMAGE OF SCHIZOPHRENIC GIRLS EJ 027 345

GREEN, FREDERICK C.
CHILD ADVOCACY -- REFLECTIONS EJ 051 241

GREEN, MELVENA
THE TEAM APPROACH IN HOME CARE OF MENTALLY RETARDED CHILDREN EJ 053 601

GREEN, MORRIS
KEEPING CHILDREN HEALTHY: HEALTH PROTECTION AND DISEASE PREVENTION. 1970 WHITE HOUSE CONFERENCE ON CHILDREN, REPORT OF FORUM 10. (WORKING PAPER). ED046527

GREENBERG, ARTHUR
GROUP HOME CARE AS AN ADJUNCT TO RESIDENTIAL TREATMENT EJ 061 233

GREENBERG, DAVID
ATTENTIONAL PREFERENCE AND EXPERIENCE: III. VISUAL FAMILIARITY AND LOOKING TIME. ED039939
ATTENTIONAL PREFERENCE AND EXPERIENCE: III. VISUAL FAMILIARITY AND LOOKING TIME EJ 025 364

GREENBERG, DAVID J.
THE MEASUREMENT OF VISUAL ATTENTION IN INFANTS: A COMPARISON OF TWO METHODOLOGIES EJ 037 494
ACCELERATING VISUAL COMPLEXITY LEVELS IN THE HUMAN INFANT EJ 045 598
INFANCY AND THE OPTIMAL LEVEL OF STIMULATION EJ 058 697

GREENBERGER, ELLEN
PERSONALITY, COGNITIVE, AND ACADEMIC CORRELATES OF PROBLEM-SOLVING FLEXIBILITY EJ 039 632

GREENFELD, NORMAN
A COMPARISON OF THE CHARACTERISTICS OF JUNIOR HIGH SCHOOL STUDENTS EJ 026 325

GREENFIELD, PATRICIA M.
ORAL OR WRITTEN LANGUAGE--THE CONSEQUENCES FOR COGNITIVE DEVELOPMENT IN AFRICA AND THE UNITED STATES. ED018279
TEACHING MATHEMATICAL CONCEPTS TO TWO- AND THREE-YEAR-OLDS: SOME EXPERIMENTAL STUDIES. ED037234

GREENGLASS, ESTHER R.
A CROSS-CULTURAL COMPARISON OF MATERNAL COMMUNICATION EJ 045 505
A CROSS-CULTURAL STUDY OF THE CHILD'S COMMUNICATION WITH HIS MOTHER EJ 046 890

GREER, WILLIAM C.
[A STATEMENT REGARDING THE COMPREHENSIVE PRESCHOOL EDUCATION AND CHILD DAY CARE ACT OF 1969, AND OTHER RELATED BILLS.] ED040761

GRENIER, WALTER J.
NEW DIMENSIONS IN STAFF DEVELOPMENT IN A JUVENILE CORRECTIONAL SYSTEM EJ 043 858

GREY, ALEXANDER
CREATIVE LEARNING IN CHILDREN'S PLAYGROUNDS EJ 007 071

GREY, CATHERINE
FOUR CHILDREN EJ 061 073

GRIFFIN, LOUISE
USING MUSIC WITH HEAD START CHILDREN. ED022543
BIG QUESTIONS AND LITTLE CHILDREN: SCIENCE AND HEAD START. ED024458
HOW TO USE ERIC. REVISED EDITION. ED027059
BOOKS IN PRESCHOOL: A GUIDE TO SELECTING, PURCHASING, AND USING CHILDREN'S BOOKS. ED038178

GRIFFIN, LOUISE, COMP.
MULTI-ETHNIC BOOKS FOR YOUNG CHILDREN: ANNOTATED BIBLIOGRAPHY FOR PARENTS AND TEACHERS. ED046519

GRIFFIN, WILLIAM J.
A TRANSFORMATIONAL ANALYSIS OF THE LANGUAGE OF KINDERGARTEN AND ELEMENTARY SCHOOL CHILDREN. ED034592

GRINDER, ROBERT E.
CONCEPTUAL EMPHASIS IN THE HISTORY OF DEVELOPMENTAL PSYCHOLOGY: EVOLUTIONARY THEORY, TELEOLOGY, AND THE NATURE-NURTURE ISSUE EJ 034 043

GRISSETT, HELEN T.
TOUCH-FEEL LEARNING AT THE TALLAHASSEE JUNIOR MUSEUM EJ 033 158

GRISSOM, CATHERINE E.
LISTENING BEYOND WORDS: LEARNING FROM PARENTS IN CONFERENCES EJ 055 363

GRITZKA, KAREN
AN INTERDISCIPLINARY APPROACH IN DAY TREATMENT OF EMOTIONALLY DISTURBED CHILDREN EJ 029 167

GROB, HARRY E., JR.
AGGRESSIVE GROUP WORK WITH TEENAGE DELINQUENT BOYS EJ 007 444
HELPING HOUSEPARENTS FIND AND USE THEIR CREATIVITY EJ 022 215

GROENENDAAL, H. A.
THE PART PLAYED BY MEDIATION PROCESSES IN THE RETENTION OF TEMPORAL SEQUENCES BY TWO READING GROUPS EJ 039 909

GROFF, PATRICK
THE NON-STRUCTURED APPROACH TO CHILDREN'S LITERATURE EJ 015 980
DICTIONARY SYLLABICATION - HOW USEFUL EJ 052 180

GROSS, BEATRICE
LEARNING FROM OUR CRITICS EJ 054 289

GROSS, BEATRICE, ED.
RADICAL SCHOOL REFORM. ED048934

GROSS, DOROTHY W.
ON SEPARATION AND SCHOOL ENTRANCE EJ 017 902

GROSS, LOUISE
SOME THOUGHTS ON COMMUNAL CHILDREARING EJ 049 658

GROSS, MORRIS
LEARNING READINESS IN TWO JEWISH GROUPS: A STUDY IN "CULTURAL DEPRIVATION." AN OCCASIONAL PAPER. ED026126

GROSS, NORMAN M.
REACHING FOR THE DREAM: AN EXPERIMENT IN TWO-WAY BUSING EJ 025 078

GROSS, PAULA KUHN
A GROUP METHOD FOR FINDING AND DEVELOPING FOSTER HOMES EJ 027 920

GROSS, RONALD
LEARNING FROM OUR CRITICS EJ 054 289

GROSS, RONALD, ED.
RADICAL SCHOOL REFORM. ED048934

GROSS, RUTH B.
AN INSTRUMENT FOR MEASURING CREATIVITY IN YOUNG CHILDREN: THE GROSS GEOMETRIC FORMS EJ 027 586

GROSSMAN, BRUCE D.
EXTRA-CURRICULAR PARENT-CHILD CONTACT AND CHILDREN'S SOCIALLY REINFORCED TASK BEHAVIOR. ED023447
ANXIETY AS A FACTOR IN THE CHILD'S RESPONSIVENESS TO SOCIAL REINFORCEMENT. ED027074

GROSSMAN, EUGENE E.
THE EFFECTS OF REWARD AND PUNISHMENT UPON CHILDREN'S ATTENTION, MOTIVATION, AND DISCRIMINATION LEARNING EJ 041 137

GROSSMAN, MARVIN
MOTOR COORDINATION AND YOUNG CHILDREN'S DRAWING ABILITIES EJ 046 257

GROTBERG, EDITH H.
WHAT DOES RESEARCH TEACH US ABOUT DAY CARE: FOR CHILDREN OVER THREE EJ 051 237

GROTBERG, EDITH H., ED.
DESIGNS AND PROPOSAL FOR EARLY CHILDHOOD RESEARCH: A NEW LOOK: A MULTIPLE SYSTEMS-SERVICE APPROACH TO PROGRAMS AND RESEARCH FOR HELPING POOR CHILDREN. (ONE IN A SERIES OF SIX PAPERS). ED053806
DESIGNS AND PROPOSAL FOR EARLY CHILDHOOD RESEARCH: A NEW LOOK: ON ATTAINING THE GOALS OF EARLY CHILDHOOD EDUCATION. (ONE IN A SERIES OF SIX PAPERS). ED053807
DESIGNS AND PROPOSAL FOR EARLY CHILDHOOD RESEARCH: A NEW LOOK: PRESCHOOL RESEARCH AND PRESCHOOL EDUCATIONAL OBJECTIVES ED053808
DESIGNS AND PROPOSAL FOR EARLY CHILDHOOD RESEARCH: A NEW LOOK: A SYSTEMS APPROACH TO PRE-SCHOOL EDUCATION. (ONE IN A SERIES OF SIX PAPERS). ED053809
DESIGNS AND PROPOSAL FOR EARLY CHILDHOOD RESEARCH: A NEW LOOK: THE UNACKNOWLEDGED ROLE OF CULTURE CONFLICT IN NEGRO EDUCATION. (ONE IN A SERIES OF SIX PAPERS). ED053810
DESIGNS AND PROPOSAL FOR EARLY CHILDHOOD RESEARCH: A NEW LOOK: MALNUTRITION, LEARNING AND INTELLIGENCE. (ONE IN A SERIES OF SIX PAPERS). ED053811

GROTELUESCHEN, ARDEN
PROCESS ACCOUNTABILITY IN CURRICULUM DEVELOPMENT. ED040757

GRUEN, GERALD
LEVEL OF ASPIRATION AND THE PROBABILITY LEARNING OF MIDDLE- AND LOWER-CLASS CHILDREN EJ 024 703

GRUEN, GERALD E.
THE ROLE OF MEMORY IN MAKING TRANSITIVE JUDGMENTS EJ 030 288
LEVEL OF "N" ACHIEVEMENT AND PROBABILITY IN CHILDREN EJ 039 906
THE EFFECTS OF CHRONOLOGICAL AGE, TRIALS, AND LIST CHARACTERISTICS UPON CHILDREN'S CATEGORY CLUSTERING EJ 052 454
DEVELOPMENT OF CONSERVATION IN NORMAL AND RETARDED CHILDREN EJ 053 651

GRUNELIUS, ELIZABETH M.
EARLY CHILDHOOD EDUCATION AND THE WALDORF SCHOOL PLAN. ED019114

GRUSEC, JOAN E.
POWER AND THE INTERNALIZATION OF SELF-DENIAL EJ 036 077
INFORMATION SEEKING ABOUT UNCERTAIN BUT UNAVOIDABLE OUTCOMES: EFFECTS OF PROBABILITY, VALENCE, AND INTERVENING ACTIVITY EJ 042 962

GRUSEC, THEODORE
INFORMATION SEEKING ABOUT UNCERTAIN BUT UNAVOIDABLE OUTCOMES: EFFECTS OF PROBABILITY, VALENCE, AND INTERVENING ACTIVITY EJ 042 962

GRUSHCOW, ROCHELLE
EFFECTS OF STIMULUS ABSTRACTNESS AND FAMILIARITY ON LISTENER'S PERFORMANCE IN A COMMUNICATION TASK EJ 046 241

GUARDO, CAROL J.
CHILD-PARENT SPATIAL PATTERNS UNDER PRAISE AND REPROOF EJ 045 159
FACTOR STRUCTURE OF CHILDREN'S PERSONAL SPACE SCHEMATA EJ 052 466
DEVELOPMENT OF A SENSE OF SELF-IDENTITY IN CHILDREN EJ 056 617

GUERNEY, BERNARD G.
TOWARD A DEMOCRATIC ELEMENTARY-SCHOOL CLASSROOM EJ 058 308

GUERNEY, BERNARD G., JR.
CASE CONFERENCE: A PSYCHOTHERAPEUTIC AIDE IN A HEADSTART PROGRAM. I. THEORY AND PRACTICE EJ 003 955

GUINAGH, BARRY J.
AN EXPERIMENTAL STUDY OF BASIC LEARNING ABILITY AND INTELLIGENCE IN LOW-SOCIOECONOMIC-STATUS CHILDREN EJ 036 818

GULLION, M. ELIZABETH
LIVING WITH CHILDREN: NEW METHODS FOR PARENTS AND TEACHERS. ED051887

GUMMERMAN, KENT
AGE, ICONIC STORAGE, AND VISUAL INFORMATION PROCESSING EJ 053 725

GUPTA, WILLA
COMPARATIVE EFFECTIVENESS OF SPEAKING VERSUS LISTENING IN IMPROVING THE SPOKEN LANGUAGE OF DISADVANTAGED YOUNG CHILDREN. ED029689

GUSINOW, JOAN F.
MODIFICATION OF FORM AND COLOR RESPONDING IN YOUNG CHILDREN AS A FUNCTION OF DIFFERENTIAL REINFORCEMENT EJ 053 723

GUTKIN, DANIEL C.
THE EFFECT OF SYSTEMATIC STORY CHANGES ON INTENTIONALITY IN CHILDREN'S MORAL JUDGMENTS EJ 056 636

GUTTMAN, RUTH
SEX AND AGE DIFFERENCES IN PATTERN ORGANIZATION IN A FIGURAL-CONCEPTUAL TASK EJ 047 680
AGE- AND SEX-RELATED VARIATION IN PERFORMANCE ON A FIGURAL-CONCEPTUAL TASK EJ 061 066

GUZMAN, RICHARD D.
PROBLEM SOLVING AND THE PERCEPTUAL SALIENCE OF VARIABILITY AND CONSTANCY: A DEVELOPMENTAL STUDY EJ 021 755

HAAF, ROBERT A.
CUE AND INCENTIVE MOTIVATIONAL PROPERTIES OF REINFORCERS IN CHILDREN'S DISCRIMINATION LEARNING EJ 035 374
IRRELEVANCE OF NEWBORN WAKING STATES TO SOME MOTOR AND APPETITIVE RESPONSES EJ 036 076
THE RATIONAL ZERO POINT ON INCENTIVE-OBJECT PREFERENCE SCALES: A DEVELOPMENTAL STUDY EJ 048 099

HABER, RALPH NORMAN
EIDETIC IMAGERY IN CHILDREN. FINAL REPORT. ED029707

HABERMAN, MARTIN, ED.
PRELIMINARY REPORT OF THE AD HOC JOINT COMMITTEE ON THE PREPARATION OF NURSERY AND KINDERGARTEN TEACHERS. ED032924

HAGBERG, KATHERINE L.
COMBINING SOCIAL CASEWORK AND GROUP WORK METHODS IN A CHILDREN'S HOSPITAL EJ 008 319

HAGEN, J. W.
THE EFFECTS OF A PAY-OFF MATRIX ON SELECTIVE ATTENTION EJ 023 436
SOME THOUGHTS ON HOW CHILDREN LEARN TO REMEMBER EJ 049 432

HAGEN, JOHN W.
CENTRAL AND INCIDENTAL LEARNING IN CHILDREN. ED023450
COGNITIVE AND LINGUISTIC DEFICITS IN PSYCHOTIC CHILDREN. STUDY M: DEVELOPMENT OF SELECTIVE ATTENTION ABILITIES. ED024440
INDUCED VERSUS SPONTANEOUS REHEARSAL IN SHORT-TERM MEMORY IN NURSERY SCHOOL CHILDREN. STUDY M: DEVELOPMENT OF SELECTIVE ATTENTION ABILITIES. ED024444
ESTIMATES AND ESTIMATE-BASED INFERENCES IN YOUNG CHILDREN EJ 034 541
SELECTIVE ATTENTION IN MENTAL RETARDATES EJ 043 058

HAGEN, JOHN WILLIAM
THE EFFECTS OF ATTENTION AND MEDIATION ON CHILDREN'S MEMORY EJ 039 638

HAITH, M. M.
DEVELOPMENTAL CHANGES IN VISUAL INFORMATION PROCESSING AND SHORT-TERM VISUAL MEMORY EJ 049 431

HAITH, MARSHALL M.
SHORT-TERM MEMORY FOR VISUAL INFORMATION IN CHILDREN AND ADULTS EJ 024 700

HALASA, OFELIA
ENRICHMENT APPROACH VERSUS DIRECT INSTRUCTIONAL APPROACH AND THEIR EFFECTS ON DIFFERENTIAL PRESCHOOL EXPERIENCES. ED043369

HALBROOK, MARY CAROL
THE UTILIZATIONS OF CONCRETE, FUNCTIONAL, AND DESIGNATIVE CONCEPTS IN MULTIPLE CLASSIFICATION. ED032112

HALE, GORDON A.
INTERRELATIONS IN CHILDREN'S LEARNING OF VERBAL AND PICTORIAL PAIRED ASSOCIATES. ED051886

HALE, WILLIAM
TELEVISION VIOLENCE EJ 006 855

HALES, LOYDE W.
THE EFFECTS OF THE DUSO GUIDANCE PROGRAM ON THE SELF-CONCEPTS OF PRIMARY SCHOOL CHILDREN EJ 058 132

HALFORD, G. S.
A DISCRIMINATION TASK WHICH INDUCES CONSERVATION OF NUMBER EJ 018 876

HALL, ALFRED E.
DEVELOPMENT OF RELATIONAL CONCEPTS AND WORD DEFINITION IN CHILDREN FIVE THROUGH ELEVEN EJ 056 397

HALL, JAMES W.
IMPLICIT VERBAL BEHAVIOR IN ELEMENTARY SCHOOL CHILDREN, (INTERNAL VERBAL RESPONSES OF ELEMENTARY SCHOOL CHILDREN ELICITED BY THE ASSOCIATION OF WORDS). FINAL REPORT. ED028848
THE DEVELOPMENT OF MEMORY-ENCODING PROCESSES IN YOUNG CHILDREN EJ 053 716

HALL, LINCOLN H.
PERFORMANCES OF AVERAGE ABILITY STUDENTS IN A JUNIOR COLLEGE AND IN FOUR-YEAR INSTITUTIONS, 1953 TO 1968 EJ 017 244

HALL, ROBERT
LEVELS OF ASPIRATION, ACHIEVEMENT, AND SOCIOCULTURAL DIFFERENCES IN PRESCHOOL CHILDREN EJ 043 482

HALL, RONALD B.
INDUSTRIAL ARTS FOR THE PRIMARY GRADES. ED035459

HALL, VERNON
PROJECT HEAD START RESEARCH AND EVALUATION CENTER, SYRACUSE UNIVERSITY RESEARCH INSTITUTE. FINAL REPORT, NOVEMBER 1, 1967. ED026137
EFFECT OF SUCCESS AND FAILURE ON THE REFLECTIVE AND IMPULSIVE CHILD EJ 029 768

HALL, VERNON C.
VARIABLES AFFECTING THE PERFORMANCE OF YOUNG CHILDREN ON A LETTER DISCRIMINATION TASK. ED020797
ACQUISTION AND TRANSFER DIFFERENCES BETWEEN KINDERGARTENERS AND SECOND-GRADERS ON AURALLY AND VISUALLY PRESENTED PAIRED-ASSOCIATES USING AN A-B, A-C DESIGN RESEARCH PROJECT NUMBER 2 OF PROJECT HEAD START RESEARCH AND EVALUATION CENTER, SYRACUSE UNIVERSITY RESEARCH INSTITUTE. FINAL REPORT, NOVEMBER 1, 1967. ED026139
CONCEPT LEARNING IN DISCRIMINATION TASKS EJ 018 878
COGNITIVE SYNTHESIS, CONSERVATION, AND TASK ANALYSIS EJ 021 768
COMPARISON OF IMITATION AND COMPREHENSION SCORES BETWEEN TWO LOWER-CLASS GROUPS AND THE EFFECTS OF TWO WARM-UP CONDITIONS ON IMITATION OF THE SAME GROUPS EJ 056 709

HALLER, EMIL J.
THE POLITICAL SOCIALIZATION OF CHILDREN AND THE STRUCTURE OF THE ELEMENTARY SCHOOL. ED024468

HALLIWELL, STANLEY
THE I.T.A. READING EXPERIMENT IN BRITAIN. ED032133

HALPERIN, MARCIA S.
THE DEVELOPMENT OF MEMORY-ENCODING PROCESSES IN YOUNG CHILDREN EJ 053 716

HALPERN, WERNER I.
A THERAPEUTIC APPROACH TO SPEECH PHOBIA: ELECTIVE MUTISM REEXAMINED EJ 035 625

HALVERSON, CHARLES F., JR.
MATERNAL BEHAVIOR TOWARD OWN AND OTHER PRESCHOOL CHILDREN: THE PROBLEM OF "OWNNESS" EJ 026 324

HAMEL, B. REMMO
ON THE CONSERVATION OF LIQUIDS EJ 039 640

HAMILL, PETER V. V.
HEIGHT AND WEIGHT OF CHILDREN: UNITED STATES. ED050808

HAMILTON, J.
INK-BLOT RESPONSES OF IDENTICAL AND FRATERNAL TWINS EJ 044 946

HAMILTON, MARSHALL L.
EVALUATION OF A PARENT AND CHILD CENTER PROGRAM. ED045189
VICARIOUS REINFORCEMENT EFFECTS ON EXTINCTION EJ 018 325
RESPONSE TO SOCIAL REINFORCEMENT RATES AS A FUNCTION OF REINFORCEMENT HISTORY EJ 053 715
EVALUATION OF A PARENT AND CHILD CENTER PROGRAM EJ 056 569

HAMM, NORMAN H.
A PARTIAL TEST OF A SOCIAL LEARNING THEORY OF CHILDREN'S CONFORMITY EJ 018 890
CONFORMITY IN CHILDREN AS A FUNCTION OF GRADE LEVEL, AND REAL VERSUS HYPOTHETICAL ADULT AND PEER MODELS EJ 040 294
AN APPLICATION OF BRUNSWIK'S LENS MODEL TO DEVELOPMENTAL CHANGES IN PROBABILITY LEARNING EJ 058 142

HAMMAR, STINA
CHILDREN AND WAR GAMES EJ 034 533

HAMMES, RICHARD
THE EFFECTS OF SCHOOL ENVIRONMENT ON DISADVANTAGED KINDERGARTEN CHILDREN, WITH AND WITHOUT A HEAD START BACKGROUND. FINAL REPORT. ED041640

HAMREUS, DALE G.
STUDY TO DETERMINE THE FEASIBILITY OF ADAPTING THE CARL ORFF APPROACH TO ELEMENTARY SCHOOLS IN AMERICA. FINAL REPORT. ED020804

HANDLER, ELLEN O.
THE PROFESSIONAL SELF IMAGE AND THE ATTRIBUTES OF A PROFESSION: AN EXPLORATORY STUDY OF THE PRESCHOOL TEACHER. ED044183

HANDLER, ELLEN OPPENHEIMER
PRESCHOOLS AND THEIR GRADUATES. ED041644

HANDLER, JUNE MOSS
PINK IS A GOOD COLOR. ? EJ 011 785

HANDRICH, MILLICENT
SEX ROLE TYPING IN THE PRESCHOOL YEARS: AN OVERVIEW. ED026134

HANKS, CHERYL
FATHERS' VERBAL INTERACTION WITH INFANTS IN THE FIRST THREE MONTHS OF LIFE EJ 036 126

HANLON, CAMILLE C.
THE EFFECTS OF SOCIAL ISOLATION AND CHARACTERISTICS OF THE MODEL ON ACCENT IMITATION IN FOURTH-GRADE CHILDREN EJ 038 171

HANNA, GERALD S.
COMPARING VALIDITY OF CHANCE LEVEL AND HIGHER TEST SCORES EJ 022 248

HANSEN, HALVOR P.
LANGUAGE TRAINING FOR TEACHERS OF DEPRIVED CHILDREN. ED040744

HAPGOOD, MARILYN
LETTERS FROM ENGLAND EJ 037 738

HAPKIEWICZ, WALTER G.
THE EFFECT OF AGGRESSIVE CARTOONS: CHILDREN'S INTERPERSONAL PLAY. ED046543
THE EFFECT OF AGGRESSIVE CARTOONS ON CHILDREN'S INTERPERSONAL PLAY EJ 053 750

HARASYM, CAROLYN R.
SEMANTIC DIFFERENTIAL ANALYSIS OF RELATIONAL TERMS USED IN CONSERVATION EJ 046 235

HARDEMAN, MILDRED
CHILDREN'S MORAL REASONING EJ 055 097

HARDING, JOHN
A COMPARATIVE STUDY OF VARIOUS PROJECT HEAD START PROGRAMS. ED019987

HARDY, JANET B.
RUBELLA AND ITS AFTERMATH EJ 007 163

HARMS, THELMA
EVALUATING SETTINGS FOR LEARNING EJ 019 966

HARRIS, ALBERT J.
GRADE EQUIVALENT COMPARISONS BETWEEN DISADVANTAGED NEGRO URBAN CHILDREN WITH AND WITHOUT KINDERGARTEN EXPERIENCE WHEN TAUGHT TO READ BY SEVERAL METHODS. ED020798

HARRIS, BEECHER H.
DISTORTIONS IN THE KINDERGARTEN EJ 007 214

HARRIS, CORNELIA C.
HIS OWN HELLO EJ 013 230

HARRIS, DALE B.
BODY PROPORTIONS IN CHILDREN'S DRAWINGS OF A MAN EJ 025 305

HARRIS, FLORENCE R.
EFFECTS OF ADULT SOCIAL REINFORCEMENT ON CHILD BEHAVIOR. ED019997

FIELD STUDIES OF SOCIAL REINFORCEMENT IN A PRESCHOOL. ED047772

HARRIS, GILBERT J.
THE EFFECTS OF GROUPING ON SHORT-TERM SERIAL RECALL OF DIGITS BY CHILDREN: DEVELOPMENTAL TRENDS EJ 059 320

HARRIS, HELENA
DEVELOPMENT OF MORAL ATTITUDES IN WHITE AND NEGRO BOYS EJ 021 027

HARRIS, LAUREN
THE EFFECTS OF STIMULUS TYPE ON PERFORMANCE IN A COLOR-FORM SORTING TASK WITH PRESCHOOL, KINDERGARTEN, FIRST-GRADE, AND THIRD-GRADE CHILDREN EJ 019 006

HARRIS, LAUREN JAY
THE ROLE OF FRONT-BACK FEATURES IN CHILDREN'S "FRONT," "BACK," AND "BESIDE" PLACEMENTS OF OBJECTS EJ 060 777

HARRIS, MARY B.
MODELS, NORMS AND SHARING. ED046512
RECIPROCITY AND GENEROSITY: SOME DETERMINANTS OF SHARING IN CHILDREN EJ 022 139
"RIGHT," "WRONG," AND DISCRIMINATION LEARNING IN CHILDREN EJ 060 774
SOME FACTORS AFFECTING THE COMPLEXITY OF CHILDREN'S SENTENCES: THE EFFECTS OF MODELING, AGE, SEX, AND BILINGUALISM EJ 060 780

HARRISON, ALGEA
CONCEPTUAL TEMPO AND INHIBITION OF MOVEMENT IN BLACK PRESCHOOL CHILDREN EJ 059 512

HARRISON, FREDERICA
A PARENT-CHILD CENTER, NOVEMBER-DECEMBER 1968. ED042506

HARTER, SUSAN
THE DISCRIMINATION LEARNING OF NORMAL AND RETARDED CHILDREN AS A FUNCTION OF PENALTY CONDITIONS AND ETIOLOGY OF THE RETARDED EJ 041 136
SMILING IN CHILDREN AS A FUNCTION OF THEIR SENSE OF MASTERY EJ 048 298
EFFECTS OF RATE OF STIMULUS PRESENTATION AND PENALTY CONDITIONS ON THE DISCRIMINATION LEARNING OF NORMAL AND RETARDED CHILDREN EJ 053 712
CHILDREN'S ABILITY TO ORDER FACIAL AND NONFACIAL CONTINUA AS A FUNCTION OF MA, CA, AND IQ EJ 059 699

HARTLAGE, LAWRENCE C.
LEARNING DISABILITY: A NEW LOOK AT UNDERACHIEVING EJ 058 411

HARTLEY, MARVIN C.
"OPENNESS" OF SCHOOL CLIMATE AND ALIENATION OF HIGH SCHOOL STUDENTS EJ 052 654

HARTLEY, RUTH E.
PLAY, THE ESSENTIAL INGREDIENT EJ 046 248

HARTLEY, RUTH N.
A METHOD OF INCREASING THE ABILITY OF FIRST GRADE PUPILS TO USE PHONETIC GENERALIZATIONS EJ 033 279

HARTSELL, O.M.
TEACHING MUSIC IN THE ELEMENTARY SCHOOL, OPINION AND COMMENT. ED020014

HARTUP, WILLARD W.
POSITIVE SOCIAL REINFORCEMENT IN THE NURSERY SCHOOL PEER GROUP. ED016515

HARVEY, O.J.
TEACHERS BELIEF SYSTEMS AND PRESCHOOL ATMOSPHERES. ED014320
TEACHERS' BELIEFS, CLASSROOM ATMOSPHERE AND STUDENT BEHAVIOR. FINAL REPORT. ED018249

HARWITZ, MARCIA
THE MEANING OF AN ORIENTING RESPONSE: A STUDY IN THE HIERARCHICAL ORDER OF ATTENDING. ED047794

HASKELL, LUCY A., COMP.
BRITISH PRIMARY EDUCATION: AN ANNOTATED BIBLIOGRAPHY. ED052843

HASKETT, GARY JOSH
MODIFICATION OF PEER PREFERENCE OF FIRST-GRADE CHILDREN EJ 039 987

HASPIEL, GEORGE S.
THRESHOLD BY IDENTIFICATION OF PICTURES (TIP) TEST AND DISCRIMINATION BY IDENTIFICATION OF PICTURES (DIP) TEST. ED015784

HASS, WILBUR A.
ON THE HETEROGENEITY OF PSYCHOLOGICAL PROCESSES IN SYNTACTIC DEVELOPMENT. ED040764
AGE-DEVELOPMENT IN THE LINEAR REPRESENTATION OF WORDS AND OBJECTS EJ 030 296

HASSEMER, WENDY G.
SOME FACTORS AFFECTING THE COMPLEXITY OF CHILDREN'S SENTENCES: THE EFFECTS OF MODELING, AGE, SEX, AND BILINGUALISM EJ 060 780

HASSIBI, MAHIN
BEHAVIOR DEVIATIONS IN MENTALLY RETARDED CHILDREN EJ 022 475

HATCH, EVELYN
THE YOUNG CHILD'S COMPREHENSION OF TIME CONNECTIVES EJ 056 724

HATCH, VIRGINIA B.
CREATIVE SUPERVISION OF HEAD START CENTERS EJ 013 231

HAUGAN, GERTRUDE M.
COMPARISONS OF VOCAL IMITATION, TACTILE STIMULATION, AND FOOD AS REINFORCERS FOR INFANT VOCALIZATIONS EJ 055 206

HAUPT, CHARLOTTE
TO KEEP AN INNER BALANCE EJ 002 313

HAUPT, DOROTHY
DEVELOPING COGNITIVE LEARNINGS WITH YOUNG CHILDREN. ED041614
RELATIONSHIPS BETWEEN CHILDREN'S QUESTIONS AND NURSERY SCHOOL TEACHERS' RESPONSES. ED046507

HAUSERMAN, NORMA
TRAINING ELEMENTARY READING SKILLS THROUGH REINFORCEMENT AND FADING TECHNIQUES. ED034583

HAYDEN, BENJAMIN S.
DIAGNOSING MINIMAL BRAIN DAMAGE IN CHILDREN: A COMPARISON OF TWO BENDER SCORING SYSTEMS EJ 027 585

HAYES, ELOISE
EXPANDING THE CHILD'S WORLD THROUGH DRAMA AND MOVEMENT EJ 034 421

HAYES, MABEL E.
A DIAGNOSTIC-PRESCRIPTIVE APPROACH TO PRESCHOOL EDUCATION. ED041622

HAYWARD, RUTH
RECIPROCAL CONTRIBUTIONS BETWEEN PSYCHOANALYSIS AND PSYCHOEDUCATION EJ 045 048

HAYWEISER, LOIS
EVALUATING BEHAVIORAL CHANGE DURING A SIX-WEEK PRE-KINDERGARTEN INTERVENTION EXPERIENCE. RESEARCH PROJECT NUMBER 5 OF PROJECT HEAD START RESEARCH AND EVALUATION CENTER, SYRACUSE UNIVERSITY RESEARCH INSTITUTE. FINAL REPORT, NOVEMBER 1, 1967. ED026142

HEAL, LAIRD W.
CUE NOVELTY AND TRAINING LEVEL IN THE DISCRIMINATION SHIFT PERFORMANCE OF RETARDATES EJ 015 851

HEAPS, RICHARD A.
SOME RELATIONSHIPS AMONG CHILDREN'S PERCEPTIONS OF PARENTAL CHARACTERISTICS EJ 025 318

HEARD, IDA MAE
NUMBER GAMES WITH YOUNG CHILDREN EJ 007 273

HEATH, DOUGLAS H.
THE EDUCATION OF YOUNG CHILDREN: AT THE CROSSROADS? EJ 013 229

HEATHERS, GLEN
GROUPING. ED026135

HEBBLE, PETER W.
THE DEVELOPMENT OF ELEMENTARY SCHOOL CHILDREN'S JUDGMENT OF INTENT EJ 052 581

HEBDA, MARY ELLEN
AGGRESSION ANXIETY, PERCEPTION OF AGGRESSIVE CUES, AND EXPECTED RETALIATION EJ 061 071

HEDGES, WILLIAM D.
DEVELOPMENT AND IMPLEMENTATION OF A COMPREHENSIVE EVALUATION AND REPORTING SYSTEM FOR KINDERGARTEN AND PRIMARY GRADE SCHOOLS. FINAL REPORT. ED026116

HEFFERNAN, HELEN
"THERE WAS A CHILD WENT FORTH"--A PHILOSOPHY OF EARLY EDUCATION EJ 031 049

HEIDER, ELEANOR ROSCH
"FOCAL" COLOR AREAS AND THE DEVELOPMENT OF COLOR NAMES EJ 039 057
INFORMATION PROCESSING AND THE MODIFICATION OF AN "IMPULSIVE CONCEPTUAL TEMPO" EJ 052 460

HEILBRUN, ALFRED B., JR.
PERCEIVED MATERNAL CHILD-REARING EXPERIENCE AND THE EFFECTS OF VICARIOUS AND DIRECT REINFORCEMENT ON MALES EJ 019 008
MATERNAL CHILD-REARING EXPERIENCE AND SELF- REINFORCEMENT EFFECTIVENESS EJ 024 944

MATERNAL CHILD REARING AND CREATIVITY IN SONS EJ 048 302
STYLE OF ADAPTATION TO AVERSIVE MATERNAL CONTROL AND PARANOID BEHAVIOR EJ 055 105

HEINICKE, CHRISTOPH M.
PARENT-CHILD INTERACTION AND THE CHILD'S APPROACH TO TASK SITUATIONS. ED025307

HEINSTEIN, MARTIN
CHILD REARING IN CALIFORNIA, A STUDY OF MOTHERS WITH YOUNG CHILDREN. ED020783

HEITING, KENNETH H.
INVOLVING PARENTS IN RESIDENTIAL TREATMENT OF CHILDREN EJ 045 233

HELFER, RAY E.
A PLAN FOR PROTECTION: THE CHILD-ABUSE CENTER EJ 027 917

HELGE, SWEN
THE RELATIONSHIP BETWEEN SPECIFIC AND GENERAL TEACHING EXPERIENCE AND TEACHER ATTITUDES TOWARD PROJECT HEAD START. PART OF THE FINAL REPORT. ED025323

HELLMUTH, JEROME, ED.
COGNITIVE STUDIES VOLUME 2: DEFICITS IN COGNITION. ED053792

HELPER, MALCOLM M.
COMPARISON OF PICTORIAL AND VERBAL SEMANTIC SCALES AS USED BY CHILDREN EJ 029 769

HENDERSON, EDMUND H.
SOCIAL SCHEMATA OF SCHOOL BEGINNERS: SOME DEMOGRAPHIC CORRELATES EJ 030 713

HENDERSON, KENT
REACTION TO SUCESS AND FAILURE IN COMPLEX LEARNING: A POSTFEEDBACK EFFECT EJ 029 413

HENDERSON, NORMAN B.
DO NEGRO CHILDREN PROJECT A SELF-IMAGE OF HELPLESSNESS AND INADEQUACY IN DRAWING A PERSON? ED036329

HENDERSON, RONALD W.
POSITIVE EFFECTS OF A BICULTURAL PRESCHOOL PROGRAM ON THE INTELLECTUAL PERFORMANCE OF MEXICAN-AMERICAN CHILDREN. ED028827
STANDARDIZED TESTS AND THE DISADVANTAGED. ED034594
RESEARCH AND CONSULTATION IN THE NATURAL ENVIRONMENT. ED037240

HENDRICK, JOANNE
WHAT MOTHERS NEED EJ 013 233

HENDRICKSON, NOREJANE
AUDIO-VISUAL MATERIALS IN EARLY CHILDHOOD EDUCATION EJ 006 854
AUDIO-VISUAL MATERIALS IN EARLY CHILDHOOD EDUCATION EJ 038 907

HENKER, BARBARA A.
SOCIAL INFLUENCES ON CHILDREN'S HUMOR RESPONSES. ED039933

HENNING, C. WALLIS
AN INVESTIGATION OF THE EFFECTS OF TEACHER VERBAL REINFORCEMENT AS IT RELATES TO SCHOLASTIC APTITUDE AND ACHIEVEMENT WITH ELEMENTARY SCHOOL CHILDREN. PROGRESS REPORT. ED042494

HENNINGS, JAMES S., S. J.
A DEVELOPMENTAL STUDY OF THE EFFECTS OF PRETRAINING ON A PERCEPTUAL RECOGNITION TASK EJ 056 630

HENRIKSEN, GRETHE
DANISH RECREATION HOMES FOR YOUNG CHILDREN EJ 003 946

HENRY, JIM G.
CHILD-REARING PRACTICES IN MOUNTAIN COUNTY, KENTUCKY EJ 036 210

HENSHEL, ANNE-MARIE
THE RELATIONSHIP BETWEEN VALUES AND BEHAVIOR: A DEVELOPMENTAL HYPOTHESIS EJ 056 622

HENSLEY, OLIVER D.
AN ATTACK ON IMPEDIMENTS TO EFFECTIVE CROSS-CULTURAL TEACHING EJ 032 553

HERMAN, HANNAH
HAWAII HEAD START EVALUATION--1968-69. FINAL REPORT. ED042511
HAWAII HEAD START EVALUATION FOLLOW-UP--1968-69. FINA L REPORT. ED042515

HERMANS, HUBERT J. M.
ACHIEVEMENT MOTIVATION AND FEAR OF FAILURE IN FAMILY AND SCHOOL EJ 058 143

HERR, BLODWEN
SOCIAL STUDIES UNIT: FIRST GRADE. BOSTON-NORTHAMPTON LANGUAGE ARTS PROGRAM, ESEA - 1965, PROJECTS TO ADVANCE CREATIVITY IN EDUCATION. ED027945

HERSEN, MICHEL
PARAMETERS OF THE SPIRAL AFTER-EFFECT IN ORGANICS, SCHIZOPHRENICS, AND NORMALS EJ 061 060

HERSH, RICHARD H.
A CASE AGAINST A CASE AGAINST BEHAVIORAL OBJECTIVES EJ 036 083

HERVEY, SARAH D.
ATTITUDES, EXPECTATIONS, AND BEHAVIOR OF PARENTS OF HEAD START AND NON-HEAD START CHILDREN. REPORT NUMBER 1. ED030475
A NOTE ON PUNISHMENT PATTERNS IN PARENTS OF PRESCHOOL CHILDREN. REPORT NUMBER 3. ED030477
INTERRELATIONS BETWEEN SOCIAL-EMOTIONAL BEHAVIOR AND INFORMATION ACHIEVEMENT OF HEAD START CHILDREN. REPORT NUMBER 5. ED030479

HERZOG, ELIZABETH
PSYCHOLOGICAL DEPRIVATION: WHAT WE DO, DON'T, AND SHOULD KNOW ABOUT IT EJ 012 676
THE GENERATION GAP IN THE EYES OF YOUTH EJ 018 067
DRUG USE AMONG THE YOUNG: AS TEENAGERS SEE IT EJ 029 950
FAMILIES WITHOUT FATHERS EJ 049 656

HESS, ROBERT
PARENTS AS TEACHERS, HOW LOWER-CLASS AND MIDDLE-CLASS MOTHERS TEACH. ED025301

HESS, ROBERT D.
TECHNIQUES FOR ASSESSING COGNITIVE AND SOCIAL ABILITIES OF CHILDREN AND PARENTS IN PROJECT HEAD START. ED015772
THE COGNITIVE ENVIRONMENTS OF URBAN PRE-SCHOOL CHILDREN. MANUAL OF INSTRUCTIONS FOR ADMINISTERING AND SCORING THE HOME INTERVIEW. ED018253
THE COGNITIVE ENVIRONMENTS OF URBAN PRE-SCHOOL CHILDREN. MANUAL OF INSTRUCTIONS FOR ADMINISTERING AND SCORING "SCHOOLS" QUESTION. ED018254
THE COGNITIVE ENVIRONMENTS OF URBAN PRE-SCHOOL CHILDREN. MANUAL OF INSTRUCTIONS FOR ADMINISTERING AND SCORING EDUCATIONAL ATTITUDE SURVEY. ED018255
THE COGNITIVE ENVIRONMENTS OF URBAN PRE-SCHOOL CHILDREN. MANUAL OF INSTRUCTIONS FOR ADMINISTERING AND SCORING MOTHER'S ATTITUDES TOWARD CHILD'S BEHAVIOR LEADING TO MASTERY. ED018256
THE COGNITIVE ENVIRONMENTS OF URBAN PRE-SCHOOL CHILDREN. MANUAL OF INSTRUCTIONS FOR ADMINISTERING AND SCORING MOTHER'S ROLE IN TEACHER/CHILD AND CHILD/PEER SCHOOL SITUATIONS. ED018257
THE COGNITIVE ENVIRONMENTS OF URBAN PRE-SCHOOL CHILDREN. MANUAL OF INSTRUCTIONS FOR ADMINISTERING AND SCORING FIRST DAY. ED018258
THE COGNITIVE ENVIRONMENTS OF URBAN PRE-SCHOOL CHILDREN. MANUAL OF INSTRUCTIONS FOR ADMINISTERING AND SCORING MOTHER-TEACHER PICTURE. ED018259
THE COGNITIVE ENVIRONMENTS OF URBAN PRE-SCHOOL CHILDREN. MANUAL OF INSTRUCTIONS FOR ADMINISTERING AND SCORING HOME RESOURCES PATTERNS. ED018260
THE COGNITIVE ENVIRONMENTS OF URBAN PRE-SCHOOL CHILDREN. MANUAL OF INSTRUCTIONS FOR ADMINISTERING AND SCORING THE TWENTY QUESTIONS TASK. ED018261
THE COGNITIVE ENVIRONMENTS OF URBAN PRE-SCHOOL CHILDREN. MANUAL OF INSTRUCTIONS FOR ADMINISTERING AND SCORING PLUTCHIK EXPLORATORY-INTEREST QUESTIONNAIRE. ED018262
THE COGNITIVE ENVIRONMENTS OF URBAN PRE-SCHOOL CHILDREN. MANUAL OF INSTRUCTIONS FOR ADMINISTERING AND SCORING SIGEL CONCEPTUAL STYLE SORTING TASKS. ED018263
THE COGNITIVE ENVIRONMENTS OF URBAN PRE-SCHOOL CHILDREN. MANUAL OF INSTRUCTIONS FOR ADMINISTERING AND SCORING TOY SORTING TASK. ED018264
THE COGNITIVE ENVIRONMENTS OF URBAN PRE-SCHOOL CHILDREN. MANUAL OF INSTRUCTIONS FOR ADMINISTERING AND SCORING THE EIGHT-BLOCK SORTING TASK. ED018265
THE COGNITIVE ENVIRONMENTS OF URBAN PRE-SCHOOL CHILDREN. MANUAL FOR CODING MOTHER-CHILD INTERACTION ON THE EIGHT-BLOCK SORTING TASK. ED018266
THE COGNITIVE ENVIRONMENTS OF URBAN PRE-SCHOOL CHILDREN. MANUAL OF INSTRUCTIONS FOR ADMINISTERING AND SCORING "ETCH-A-SKETCH" TASK. ED018267
THE COGNITIVE ENVIRONMENTS OF URBAN PRE-SCHOOL CHILDREN. MANUAL OF INSTRUCTIONS FOR ADMINISTERING AND SCORING THE CURIOSITY TASK. ED018268
THE COGNITIVE ENVIRONMENTS OF URBAN PRE-SCHOOL CHILDREN. MANUAL OF RECORDING AND OBSERVATION TECHNIQUES FOR MOTHER-CHILD INTERACTION. ED018269
THE COGNITIVE ENVIRONMENTS OF URBAN PRE-SCHOOL CHILDREN. MANUAL OF INSTRUCTIONS FOR ADMINISTERING AND SCORING MATERNAL LANGUAGE STYLES. ED018270
HEAD START EVALUATION AND RESEARCH CENTER, THE UNIVERSITY OF CHICAGO. REPORT A, MATERNAL INFLUENCES UPON DEVELOPMENT OF COGNITION. ED022550

HEAD START EVALUATION AND RESEARCH CENTER, THE UNIVERSITY OF CHICAGO. REPORT B, MATERNAL ANTECEDENTS OF INTELLECTUAL ACHIEVEMENT BEHAVIORS IN LOWER CLASS PRESCHOOL CHILDREN. ED022551
HEAD START EVALUATION AND RESEARCH CENTER, THE UNIVERSITY OF CHICAGO. REPORT C, COGNITIVE INTERACTION BETWEEN TEACHER AND PUPIL IN A PRESCHOOL SETTING. ED022552
HEAD START EVALUATION AND RESEARCH CENTER, THE UNIVERSITY OF CHICAGO. REPORT D, THE INTERACTION OF INTELLIGENCE AND BEHAVIOR AS ONE PREDICTOR OF EARLY SCHOOL ACHIEVEMENT IN WORKING CLASS AND CULTURALLY DISADVANTAGED HEAD START CHILDREN. ED022553
HEAD START EVALUATION AND RESEARCH CENTER, THE UNIVERSITY OF CHICAGO. REPORT F, SOCIALIZATION INTO THE ROLE OF PUPIL. ED023456
MATERNAL BEHAVIOR AND THE DEVELOPMENT OF READING READINESS IN URBAN NEGRO CHILDREN. ED031309
PARENTAL BEHAVIOR AND CHILDREN'S SCHOOL ACHIEVEMENT: IMPLICATIONS FOR HEAD START. PROCEEDINGS OF THE HEAD START RESEARCH SEMINARS: SEMINAR NO. 5, INTERVENTION IN FAMILY LIFE (1ST, WASHINGTON, D.C., JANUARY 13, 1969). ED036332
THE COGNITIVE ENVIRONMENTS OF URBAN PRESCHOOL CHILDREN. FINAL REPORT. ED045179
THE COGNITIVE ENVIRONMENTS OF URBAN PRESCHOOL CHILDREN: FOLLOW-UP PHASE. FINAL REPORT. ED045180

HETHERINGTON, E. MAVIS
THE EFFECTS OF FATHER ABSENCE ON CHILD DEVELOPMENT EJ 035 800

HETRICK, SUZANNE H.
FIGURAL CREATIVITY, INTELLIGENCE, AND PERSONALITY IN CHILDREN: A FACTOR ANALYTIC STUDY. ED032931

HETZEL, DONNA C.
AN OVERVIEW OF BRITISH INFANT SCHOOLS EJ 026 835

HEUSSENSTAMM, FRANCES K.
CREATIVITY AND ALIENATION: AN EXPLORATION OF THEIR RELATIONSHIP IN ADOLESCENCE EJ 021 996

HEXCOX, KURT E.
ESTIMATES AND ESTIMATE-BASED INFERENCES IN YOUNG CHILDREN EJ 034 541

HEYMAN, MARK
LEARNING FROM THE BRITISH PRIMARY SCHOOLS EJ 057 327

HICKS, DAVID
A NOTE ON TEACHING FOR CREATIVITY EJ 018 130

HICKS, DAVID J.
GIRLS' ATTITUDES TOWARD MODELED BEHAVIORS AND THE CONTENT OF IMITATIVE PRIVATE PLAY EJ 036 079

HICKS, RUTH
FIRST STEPS IN SCHOOL EJ 007 205

HIGBEE, KENNETH L.
SELF-DISCLOSURE AND RELATIONSHIP TO THE TARGET PERSON EJ 007 431

HILL, A. LEWIS
APPARENT VISUAL SIZE AS A FUNCTION OF AGE, INTELLIGENCE, AND A SURROUNDING FRAME OF REFERENCE FOR NORMAL AND MENTALLY RETARDED SUBJECTS EJ 043 704

HILL, DOROTHY L.
INTERACTION OF SEX OF SUBJECT AND DEPENDENCY-TRAINING PROCEDURES IN A SOCIAL-REINFORCEMENT STUDY EJ 006 877

HILL, IONE A.
KINDERGARTEN GUIDEBOOK. ED020008

HILL, JOHN P.
INSTRUMENTAL AND AFFECTIONAL DEPENDENCY AND NURTURANCE IN PRESCHOOL CHILDREN EJ 015 101

HILL, KENNEDY T.
PROBABILITY LEARNING AS A FUNCTION OF SEX OF THE SUBJECT, TEST ANXIETY, AND PERCENTAGE OF REINFORCEMENT EJ 027 181
YOUNG CHILDREN'S PERFORMANCE ON A TWO-CHOICE TASK AS A FUNCTION OF SOCIAL REINFORCEMENT, BASE-LINE PREFERENCE, AND RESPONSE STRATEGY EJ 039 635
ANXIETY IN THE EVALUATIVE CONTEXT EJ 051 018

HILL, WILHELMINA
ENVIRONMENTAL EDUCATION: THE STATE OF THE ART EJ 026 772

HILLERY, MILTON C.
A DESCRIPTIVE STUDY OF COGNITIVE AND AFFECTIVE TRENDS DIFFERENTIATING SELECTED GROUPS OF PRE-SCHOOL CHILDREN. ED031314

HILLIARD, EVERETT
A COMPARISON STUDY OF THE COGNITIVE DEVELOPMENT OF DISADVANTAGED FIRST GRADE PUPILS (AS MEASURED BY SELECTED PIAGETIAN TASKS). ED051874

HILTON, ERNEST
SOME NOTES ON STRATEGY AND CONTENT FOR ELEMENTARY READING PROGRAMS IN THE '70'S EJ 035 664

HIMELSTEIN, PHILIP
CHILDREN'S FEAR IN A DENTAL SITUATION AS A FUNCTION OF BIRTH ORDER EJ 015 099

HINES, BRAINARD
ATTAINMENT OF COGNITIVE OBJECTIVES. TECHNICAL REPORT NO. 3. ED052833
RESULTS OF PARENT AND STUDENT REACTION QUESTIONNAIRE. TECHNICAL REPORT NO. 8. ED052836

HINES, BRAINARD W.
DETAILED ANALYSIS OF LANGUAGE DEVELOPMENT OF PRESCHOOL CHILDREN IN ECE PROGRAM. TECHNICAL REPORT NO. 4. ED052834
ANALYSIS OF INTELLIGENCE SCORES. ED052838
ANALYSIS OF VISUAL PERCEPTION OF CHILDREN IN THE EARLY CHILDHOOD EDUCATION PROGRAM (RESULTS OF THE MARIANNE FROSTIG DEVELOPMENTAL TEST OF VISUAL PERCEPTION). ED052839

HIRSCH, JAY G.
PERSONALITY DEVELOPMENT IN DISADVANTAGED FOUR-YEAR-OLD BOYS: OBSERVATIONS WITH PLAY TECHNIQUES. ED031310
INDIVIDUAL DIFFERENCES IN GHETTO FOUR-YEAR-OLDS. ED034572
SCHOOL ACHIEVERS AND UNDERACHIEVERS IN AN URBAN GHETTO EJ 027 614

HIRSCHBERG, J. COTTER
TERMINATION OF RESIDENTIAL TREATMENT OF CHILDREN EJ 029 102

HIRST, WILMA E.
IDENTIFICATION IN THE KINDERGARTEN OF FACTORS THAT MAKE FOR FUTURE SUCCESS IN READING AND IDENTIFICATION AND DIAGNOSIS IN THE KINDERGARTEN OF POTENTIAL READING DISABILITY CASES. FINAL REPORT. ED029710

HITCHFIELD, ELIZABETH
A GUIDE TO READING PIAGET. ED053819

HJERTHOLM, ELSE WERNO
COMPARISON OF AMERICAN AND NORWEGIAN NURSERY SCHOOL CHILDREN ON INDEPENDENCE BEHAVIOR AND TRAINING. ED024457
COMPARISON OF AMERICAN AND NORWEGIAN NURSERY SCHOOL CHILDREN OF INDEPENDENCE BEHAVIOR AND TRAINING. SUMMARY REPORT. ED024476

HOBSON, ARLINE
THE MARIE HUGHES LANGUAGE TRAINING MODEL. ED025305

HOBSON, ARLINE B.
LANGUAGE TEACHING: PREPOSITIONS AND CONJUNCTIVES. ED034597

HODES, MARION R.
AN ASSESSMENT AND COMPARISON OF SELECTED CHARACTERISTICS AMONG CULTURALLY DISADVANTAGED HEADSTART CHILDREN (SUMMER PROGRAM 1965), CULTURALLY DISADVANTAGED NON-HEADSTART CHILDREN, AND NON-CULTURALLY DISADVANTAGED CHILDREN. (TITLE SUPPLIED). ED014330

HODGES, WALTER L.
THE IMPLICATIONS OF DESIGN AND MODEL SELECTION FOR THE EVALUATION OF PROGRAMS FOR THE DISADVANTAGED CHILD. ED047792
A TEACHING LEARNING SCHEMA FOR TEACHER TRAINING AND CURRICULUM DEVELOPMENT IN EARLY EDUCATION. ED049812
THE VALUE OF CLASSROOM REWARDS IN EARLY EDUCATION. ED049828

HODGINS, AUDREY
THE EFFECTS OF A HIGHLY STRUCTURED PRESCHOOL PROGRAM ON THE MEASURED INTELLIGENCE OF CULTURALLY DISADVANTAGED FOUR-YEAR-OLD CHILDREN. INTERIM REPORT. ED019116

HOEMANN, HARRY W.
CHILDREN'S UNDERSTANDING OF PROBABILITY CONCEPTS EJ 036 824

HOFFMAN, MARTIN L.
CONSCIENCE, PERSONALITY, AND SOCIALIZATION TECHNIQUES EJ 023 858
FATHER ABSENCE AND CONSCIENCE DEVELOPMENT EJ 038 854
IDENTIFICATION AND CONSCIENCE DEVELOPMENT EJ 052 447

HOFFMAN, MARVIN
THE OTHER MOUTH: WRITING IN THE SCHOOLS EJ 027 881

HOFFMAN, VIRGINIA
LANGUAGE LEARNING AT ROUGH ROCK EJ 011 874

HOFFMANN, ERIKA
EARLY AGE EDUCATION EJ 029 620

HOHLE, RAYMOND H.
TIME ESTIMATION BY YOUNG CHILDREN WITH AND WITHOUT INFORMATIONAL FEEDBACK EJ 033 787

HOHN, ROBERT L.
MEDIATIONAL STYLES: AN INDIVIDUAL DIFFERENCE VARIABLE IN CHILDREN'S VERBAL LEARNING ABILITY. ED027955
SHIFTS IN CHILD-REARING ATTITUDES LINKED WITH PARENTHOOD AND OCCUPATION EJ 038 853

HOLDEN, RAYMOND H.
CONSISTENCY OF MATERNAL ATTITUDES AND PERSONALITY FROM PREGNANCY TO EIGHT MONTHS FOLLOWING CHILDBIRTH EJ 021 026

HOLLAND, JAMES G.
A QUANTITATIVE MEASURE FOR PROGRAMMED INSTRUCTION. ED014317
THE MISPLACED ADAPTATION TO INDIVIDUAL DIFFERENCES. ED040754

HOLLAND, R. FOUNT
SCHOOL IN CHEROKEE AND ENGLISH EJ 061 184

HOLLANDER, EDWIN P.
PARENTAL DETERMINANTS OF PEER-ORIENTATION AND SELF-ORIENTATION AMONG PREADOLESCENTS EJ 019 387

HOLLENBERG, CLEMENTINA KUHLMAN
FUNCTIONS OF VISUAL IMAGERY IN THE LEARNING AND CONCEPT FORMATION OF CHILDREN EJ 033 779

HOLMAN, GERALD H.
LEARNING FROM EACH OTHER: PREDIATRICIANS AND TEACHERS EJ 050 320

HOLMES, DAVID S.
FINAL REPORT ON HEAD START EVALUATION AND RESEARCH--1966-67 TO THE INSTITUTE FOR EDUCATIONAL DEVELOPMENT. SECTION VII, SENSORY AND PERCEPTUAL STUDIES. ED019123

HOLMES, DOUGLAS
EVALUATION OF TWO ASSOCIATED YM-YWHA HEADSTART PROGRAMS. FINAL REPORT. ED014318
AN EVALUATION OF DIFFERENCES AMONG DIFFERENT CLASSES OF HEAD START PARTICIPANTS. FINAL REPORT. ED015012

HOLMES, MONICA B.
EVALUATION OF TWO ASSOCIATED YM-YWHA HEADSTART PROGRAMS. FINAL REPORT. ED014318

HOLMES, MONICA BYCHOWSKI
AN EVALUATION OF DIFFERENCES AMONG DIFFERENT CLASSES OF HEAD START PARTICIPANTS. FINAL REPORT. ED015012
INTERACTION PATTERNS AS A SOURCE OF ERROR IN TEACHERS' EVALUATIONS OF HEAD START CHILDREN. FINAL REPORT. ED023453

HOLT, CAROL
CHARACTERIZATION OF THE EFFECT OF SPACE, MATERIALS, AND TEACHER BEHAVIOR ON PRESCHOOL CHILDREN'S FREE PLAY ACTIVITY PATTERNS. RESEARCH REPORT NO. 1. ED037251

HOLT, GARY L.
EFFECT OF REINFORCEMENT CONTINGENCIES IN INCREASING PROGRAMMED READING AND MATHEMATICS BEHAVIORS IN FIRST-GRADE CHILDREN EJ 049 168

HOLT, JULIA RAE
CONJUNCTIVE AND DISJUNCTIVE RULE LEARNING AS A FUNCTION OF AGE AND FORCED VERBALIZATION EJ 028 637

HONIG, ALICE S.
OBSERVED COGNITIVE COMMUNICATION PATTERNS OF ADULTS AND CHILDREN IN FOUR PRE-SCHOOL AGE GROUPS. ED036325
A COMPARATIVE ANALYSIS OF THE PIAGETIAN DEVELOPMENT OF TWELVE MONTH OLD DISADVANTAGED INFANTS IN AN ENRICHMENT CENTER WITH OTHERS NOT IN SUCH A CENTER. ED047778
PATTERNS OF INFORMATION PROCESSING USED BY AND WITH YOUNG CHILDREN IN A NURSERY SCHOOL SETTING EJ 032 890

HOOPER, FRANK H.
THE INITIAL PHASE OF A PRESCHOOL CURRICULUM DEVELOPMENT PROJECT. FINAL REPORT. ED027071
AN EVALUATION OF LOGICAL OPERATIONS INSTRUCTION IN THE PRESCHOOL. ED053791
A DEVELOPMENTAL COMPARISON OF IDENTITY AND EQUIVALENCE CONSERVATIONS EJ 049 167

HOOPES, JANET L.
AN INFANT RATING SCALE, ITS VALIDATION AND USEFULNESS. ED016513

HOPKINS, KENNETH D.
FIVE-YEAR STABILITY OF INTELLIGENCE QUOTIENTS FROM LANGUAGE AND NONLANGUAGE GROUP TESTS EJ 041 723

HORE, TERENCE
SOME NONVERBAL ASPECTS OF COMMUNICATION BETWEEN MOTHER AND PRESCHOOL CHILD EJ 025 386

HORNBURGER, JANE M.
BRINGING THEIR OWN: LANGUAGE DEVELOPMENT IN THE MIDDLE GRADES EJ 011 844

HORNBY, PETER A.
SURFACE STRUCTURE AND THE TOPIC-COMMENT DISTINCTION: A DEVELOPMENTAL STUDY EJ 056 717

HORNER, VIVIAN M.
A TECHNIQUE FOR GATHERING CHILDREN'S LANGUAGE SAMPLES FROM NATURALISTIC SETTINGS. ED016532

HOROWITZ, ALAN B.
HABITUATION AND MEMORY: INFANT CARDIAC RESPONSES TO FAMILIAR AND DISCREPANT AUDITORY STIMULI EJ 056 633

HOROWITZ, FLOYD R.
HEAD START EVALUATION AND RESEARCH CENTER, UNIVERSITY OF KANSAS. REPORT NO. XI, VERBAL RECALL RESEARCH. ED021647

HOROWITZ, FRANCES DEGEN
COMPARATIVE STUDIES OF A GROUP OF HEAD START AND A GROUP OF NON-HEAD START PRESCHOOL CHILDREN. FINAL REPORT. ED015013
HEAD START EVALUATION AND RESEARCH CENTER, UNIVERSITY OF KANSAS. REPORT NO. XI, VERBAL RECALL RESEARCH. ED021647
RESEARCH STRATEGIES AND CONCEPTS OF DEVELOPMENT AND LEARNING. INTRODUCTION EJ 027 436
DEVELOPMENTAL CHANGE IN INFANT VISUAL FIXATION TO DIFFERING COMPLEXITY LEVELS AMONG CROSS-SECTIONALLY AND LONGITUDINALLY STUDIED INFANTS EJ 061 141
AN INFANT CONTROL PROCEDURE FOR STUDYING INFANT VISUAL FIXATIONS EJ 061 142

HORTON, DELLA M.
A TRAINING PROGRAM FOR MOTHERS. ED017334
EDUCATIONAL INTERVENTION IN THE HOME AND PARAPROFESSIONAL CAREER DEVELOPMENT: A FIRST GENERATION MOTHER STUDY. ED045190
EDUCATIONAL INTERVENTION IN THE HOME AND PARAPROFESSIONAL CAREER DEVELOPMENT: A SECOND GENERATION MOTHER STUDY WITH AN EMPHASIS ON COSTS AND BENEFITS. FINAL REPORT. ED052814

HORTON, DONALD
HEAD START EVALUATION AND RESEARCH CENTER. PROGRESS REPORT OF RESEARCH STUDIES, 1966-1967. ED021612
HEAD START EVALUATION AND RESEARCH CENTER. PROGRESS REPORT OF RESEARCH STUDIES 1966 TO 1967. DOCUMENT 2, STUDIES OF THE SOCIAL ORGANIZATION OF HEAD START CENTERS. ED021624

HORTON, LOWELL W.
ILLEGIBILITIES IN THE CURSIVE HANDWRITING OF SIXTH-GRADERS EJ 019 443

HOSHINO, GEORGE
THE ADMINISTRATION OF "SELECTIVITY" IN THE BREAKFAST PROGRAM OF A PUBLIC ELEMENTARY SCHOOL EJ 036 580

HOULIHAN, KEVIN A.
RELATIONSHIPS OF PARENTAL BEHAVIOR TO "DISADVANTAGED" CHILDREN'S INTRINSIC-EXTRINSIC MOTIVATION FOR TASK STRIVING EJ 059 870

HOUSE, BETTY J.
A DECREMENTAL EFFECT OF REDUNDANCY IN DISCRIMINATION LEARNING EJ 033 795

HOUSTON, SUSAN H.
A REEXAMINATION OF SOME ASSUMPTIONS ABOUT THE LANGUAGE OF THE DISADVANTAGED CHILD EJ 033 700

HOVING, KENNETH L.
CONFORMITY IN CHILDREN AS A FUNCTION OF GRADE LEVEL, AND REAL VERSUS HYPOTHETICAL ADULT AND PEER MODELS EJ 040 294
REINSTATEMENT EFFECTS IN CHILDREN EJ 057 899

HOWARD, NORMA KEMEN, COMP.
DAY CARE: AN ANNOTATED BIBLIOGRAPHY. ED052823

HOWARD, ROBERT G.
TWINNING: A MARKER FOR BIOLOGICAL INSULTS EJ 021 188

HOWSE, JENNIFER
PRESCHOOL INSTRUCTION MOBILE FACILITIES: DESCRIPTION AND ANALYSIS. SCHOOL PRACTICES REPORT NO. 3. ED050803

HOY, WAYNE K.
"OPENNESS" OF SCHOOL CLIMATE AND ALIENATION OF HIGH SCHOOL STUDENTS EJ 052 654

HUBBARD, JAMES L.
FINAL REPORT ON HEAD START EVALUATION AND RESEARCH--1966-67 TO THE INSTITUTE FOR EDUCATIONAL DEVELOPMENT. SECTION IV, AN EXPLORATORY STUDY OF ORAL LANGUAGE DEVELOPMENT AMONG CULTURALLY DIFFERENT CHILDREN. ED019120

HUBER, PAUL
HEARING LEVELS OF CHILDREN BY AGE AND SEX: UNITED STATES. ED047799

HUCKLESBY, SYLVIA
OPENING UP THE CLASSROOM: A WALK AROUND THE SCHOOL. ED053817

HUGHES, MARIE M.
ANALYSES OF STORIES DICTATED IN CLASSES OF THE COOPERATIVE PROJECT. ED019993
THE TUCSON EARLY EDUCATION MODEL. ED033753

HUGHES, S. EILEEN DOLORES
EFFECTS OF SYNTACTICAL MEDIATION, AGE, AND MODES OF REPRESENTATION ON PAIRED-ASSOCIATE LEARNING EJ 056 615

HUGHES, SHIRLEY L.
SERVICES TO CHILDREN LIVING WITH RELATIVES OR GUARDIANS EJ 007 445

HUGHSTON, KAREN
THE EFFECT OF TRAINING CHILDREN TO MAKE MORAL JUDGMENTS THAT ARE INDEPENDENT OF SANCTIONS EJ 044 507

HUITT, RAY
HANDWRITING: THE STATE OF THE CRAFT EJ 048 999

HULL, WILLIAM P.
LEICESTERSHIRE REVISITED. ED029683

HULTSCH, DAVID
CONCEPT IDENTIFICATION STRATEGIES. RESEARCH PROJECT NUMBER 3 OF PROJECT HEAD START RESEARCH AND EVALUATION CENTER, SYRACUSE UNIVERSITY RESEARCH INSTITUTE, NOVEMBER 1, 1967. ED026140

HULTSCH, DAVID F.
THE DEVELOPMENT OF FREE CLASSIFICATION AND FREE RECALL IN CHILDREN EJ 030 293

HUMPHREYS, LLOYD G.
FUNCTIONAL PRINCIPLES OF LEARNING. ED032946

HUMPHRIES, DAVID
I SEE WHAT YOU MEAN EJ 035 370

HUNT, ELEANOR
INFANT MORTALITY TRENDS AND MATERNAL AND INFANT CARE EJ 021 524

HUNT, GRACE B.
DEVELOPING PUBLIC DAY CARE FACILITIES IN MARYLAND EJ 018 970

HUNT, J. MCV.
ATTENTIONAL PREFERENCE AND EXPERIENCE: II. AN EXPLORATORY LONGITUDINAL STUDY OF THE EFFECTS OF VISUAL FAMILIARITY AND RESPONSIVENESS. ED039938
ATTENTIONAL PREFERENCE AND EXPERIENCE: I. INTRODUCTION. ED040751
ATTENTIONAL PREFERENCE AND EXPERIENCE: II. AN EXPLORATORY LONGITUDINAL STUDY OF THE EFFECT OF VISUAL FAMILIARITY AND RESPONSIVENESS EJ 025 363
ATTENTIONAL PREFERENCE AND EXPERIENCE: I. INTRODUCTION EJ 025 988
OBJECT CONSTRUCTION AND IMITATION UNDER DIFFERING CONDITIONS OF REARING EJ 048 305

HUNT, J. MCVICKER
TOWARD THE PREVENTION OF INCOMPETENCE. ED028812

HUNT, KELLOGG W.
SYNTACTIC MATURITY IN SCHOOL CHILDREN AND ADULTS EJ 018 818

HUNTER, ELIZABETH
REPORT CARDS FOR TEACHERS EJ 057 441

HUNTER, GERTRUDE T.
HEALTH CARE THROUGH HEAD START EJ 024 496

HUNTER, MADELINE
THE ELEMENTS OF EFFECTIVE COMMUNICATION EJ 011 845

HUNTSMAN, NANCY J.
SELECTIVE ATTENTION IN MENTAL RETARDATES EJ 043 058

HURD, GORDON E.
PREPRIMARY ENROLLMENT OF CHILDREN UNDER SIX: OCTOBER 1968. ED032118
PREPRIMARY ENROLLMENT TRENDS OF CHILDREN UNDER SIX: 1964-1968. ED042502
PREPRIMARY ENROLLMENT, OCTOBER 1969. ED049816

HURH, WON MOO
MARGINAL CHILDREN OF WAR: AN EXPLORATORY STUDY OF AMERICAN-KOREAN CHILDREN. ED047781

HURLEY, JOHN R.
SHIFTS IN CHILD-REARING ATTITUDES LINKED WITH PARENTHOOD AND OCCUPATION EJ 038 853

HURT, MAURE, JR.
THE USE OF METROPOLITCAN READINESS TESTS WITH MEXICAN-AMERICAN CHILDREN EJ 026 810

HUSA, FREDERICK T.
GIVEN NAMES AND STEREOTYPING EJ 061 234

HUTINGER, PATRICIA
THE EFFECTS OF ADULT VERBAL MODELING AND FEEDBACK ON THE ORAL LANGUAGE OF HEAD START CHILDREN. ED047793

HUTT, CORINNE
SEX DIFFERENCES IN HUMAN DEVELOPMENT EJ 060 015

HYMES, JAMES L., JR.
EARLY CHILDHOOD EDUCATION: AN INTRODUCTION TO THE PROFESSION. ED036328
MAKING TOMORROW NOW: THE PEOPLE ENVIRONMENT EJ 028 200

IACONO, CARMINE H.
DIFFERENTIAL FACTOR STRUCTURE OF SEVENTH GRADE STUDENTS EJ 030 298

ILG, FRANCES L.
SCHOOL READINESS, BEHAVIOR TESTS USED AT THE GESELL INSTITUTE. ED023449

ILIKA, JOSEPH
AGE OF ENTRANCE INTO THE FIRST GRADE AS RELATED TO ARITHMETIC ACHIEVEMENT. ED020801
AGE OF ENTRANCE INTO THE FIRST GRADE AS RELATED TO RATE OF SCHOLASTIC ACHIEVEMENT. ED028843

ILLENBERG, GREGORY J.
RELATIONSHIP OF CLASSROOM GROUPING PRACTICES TO DIFFUSION OF STUDENTS' SOCIOMETRIC CHOICES AND DIFFUSION OF STUDENTS' PERCEPTION OF SOCIOMETRIC CHOICE EJ 042 791

INGERSOLL, GARY M.
AN EXPERIMENTAL STUDY OF TWO METHODS OF PRESENTING THE INVERSION ALGORITHM IN DIVISION OF FRACTIONS EJ 033 863

IRELAND, RALPH R.
THE CARE AND EDUCATION OF PRESCHOOL NONWHITES IN THE REPUBLIC OF SOUTH AFRICA EJ 010 125

IRELAND, VERA M.
EVALUATION OF THE PRESCHOOL PROGRAM, 1966-67, FUNDED UNDER ESEA TITLE I, P.L. 89-10. ED026143
EVALUATION OF THE PRESCHOOL PROGRAM, 1967-68, FUNDED UNDER ESEA TITLE I, P.L. 89-10. ED027080

IRETON, HAROLD
INFANT MENTAL DEVELOPMENT AND NEUROLOGICAL STATUS, FAMILY SOCIOECONOMIC STATUS, AND INTELLIGENCE AT AGE FOUR EJ 032 675

IRONS, PETER H.
THE IMPACT OF OPERATION HEAD START ON GREENE COUNTY, OHIO, AN EVALUATION REPORT. ED020772

IRWIN, D. MICHELLE
THE YOUNG CHILD'S UNDERSTANDING OF SOCIAL JUSTICE EJ 046 887

IRWIN, JOHN V.
HEAD START EVALUATION AND RESEARCH CENTER, UNIVERSITY OF KANSAS. REPORT NO. IV, A COMPARISON OF FOUR MODES OF ELICITING BRIEF ORAL RESPONSES FROM CHILDREN. ED021637

ISAACS, SUSAN
THE NURSERY YEARS: THE MIND OF THE CHILD FROM BIRTH TO SIX YEARS. ED029711

ISMAIL, A. H.
THE ABILITY OF PERSONALITY VARIABLES IN DISCRIMINATING AMONG THREE INTELLECTUAL GROUPS OF PREADOLESCENT BOYS AND GIRLS EJ 034 044

IZARD, CARROLL E.
DEVELOPMENTAL CHANGES IN THE USE OF EMOTION CUES IN A CONCEPT-FORMATION TASK EJ 029 362

JACKLIN, CAROL N.
CARDIAC DECELERATION AND ITS STABILITY IN HUMAN NEWBORNS EJ 046 891

JACKSON, JAN C.
CAN NEWBORNS SHOW CARDIAC ORIENTING? EJ 036 078

JACKSON, MARTHA E.
EDUCATIONAL APPLICATION OF BEHAVIOR MODIFICATION TECHNIQUES WITH SEVERELY RETARDED CHILDREN IN A CHILD DEVELOPMENT CENTER EJ 017 421

JACKSON, NEWTON L. P., JR.
EDUCATIONAL APPLICATION OF BEHAVIOR MODIFICATION TECHNIQUES WITH SEVERELY RETARDED CHILDREN IN A CHILD DEVELOPMENT CENTER EJ 017 421

JACKSON, SUSAN
BEHAVIOUR PROBLEMS IN THE INFANT SCHOOL EJ 048 306

JACOBS, HUGH DONALD
A REPLICATIVE INVESTIGATION OF THE BUCKINGHAM-DOLCH FREE-ASSOCIATION WORD STUDY. FINAL REPORT. ED017333

JACOBS, PAUL I.
THE LEARNING AND TRANSFER OF DOUBLE-CLASSIFICATION SKILLS BY FIRST GRADERS EJ 036 821
THE LEARNING AND TRANSFER OF DOUBLE-CLASSIFICATION SKILLS: A REPLICATION AND EXTENSION EJ 046 254

JACOBS, SYLVIA H.
PARENT INVOLVEMENT IN PROJECT HEAD START. PART OF THE FINAL REPORT ON HEAD START EVALUATION AND RESEARCH: 1968-1969 TO THE OFFICE OF ECONOMIC OPPORTUNITY. ED037244

JACOBSON, JOAN M.
HEAD START EVALUATION AND RESEARCH CENTER, UNIVERSITY OF KANSAS. REPORT NO. VIIA, A CASE STUDY IN ESTABLISHING A DIFFERENTIATED SPEECH RESPONSE THROUGH GENERALIZATION PROCEDURES. ED021640
THE SIMULTANEOUS REHABILITATION OF MOTHERS AND THEIR CHILDREN. ED034591

JACOBSON, LEONARD I.
EFFECTS OF AGE, SEX, SYSTEMATIC CONCEPTUAL LEARNING, ACQUISITION OF LEARNING SETS, AND PROGRAMMED SOCIAL INTERACTION ON THE INTELLECTUAL AND CONCEPTUAL DEVELOPMENT OF PRESCHOOL CHILDREN FROM POVERTY BACKGROUNDS EJ 053 733

JACQUOT, WILLARD S.
LEARNING DISABILITIES: A TEAM APPROACH EJ 014 521

JAHODA, GUSTAV
EMOTIONAL SENSITIVITY AND INTELLIGENCE IN CHILDREN FROM ORPHANAGES AND NORMAL HOMES EJ 043 859

JAROLIMEK, JOHN
GUIDELINES FOR ELEMENTARY SOCIAL STUDIES. ED019998

JAROLIMEK, JOHN, ED.
SOCIAL STUDIES EDUCATION: THE ELEMENTARY SCHOOL. ED027061

JARVIS, D. L.
PREVENTING ILLEGITIMATE TEENAGE PREGNANCY THROUGH SYSTEMS INTERACTION EJ 059 671

JENKINS, J. J.
SECOND DISCUSSANT'S COMMENTS: WHAT'S LEFT TO SAY? EJ 049 434

JENKINS, SHIRLEY
FAMILIES OF CHILDREN IN FOSTER CARE EJ 007 452

JENKINS, W.O.
THE STATUS OF BEHAVIORAL MEASUREMENT AND ASSESSMENT IN CHILDREN. ED018252

JENKINSON, MARION D.
READING: AN ETERNAL DYNAMIC EJ 028 959

JENS, DOROTHY
PROJECT GENESIS. FINAL REPORT. ED049820

JENSEN, ARTHUR R.
UNDERSTANDING READINESS: AN OCCASIONAL PAPER. ED032117
THE ROLE OF VERBAL MEDIATION IN MENTAL DEVELOPMENT EJ 035 382

JENSEN, JUDITH
REPORT OF A RESEARCH AND DEMONSTRATION PROJECT FOR CULTURALLY DISADVANTAGED CHILDREN IN THE ANCONA MONTESSORI SCHOOL. ED015014
ANCONA MONTESSORI RESEARCH PROJECT FOR CULTURALLY DISADVANTAGED CHILDREN. SEPTEMBER 1, 1968 TO AUGUST 31, 1969. FINAL REPORT. ED044166

JENSEN, LARRY
THE EFFECT OF TRAINING CHILDREN TO MAKE MORAL JUDGMENTS THAT ARE INDEPENDENT OF SANCTIONS EJ 044 507

JENSEN, LARRY C.
RETENTION FOLLOWING A CHANGE IN AMBIENT CONTEXTUAL STIMULI FOR SIX AGE GROUPS EJ 039 631

JEROME, ALICE
FROM THE TEACHER'S NOTEBOOK EJ 020 103

JERUCHIMOWICZ, RITA
KNOWLEDGE OF ACTION AND OBJECT WORDS: A COMPARISON OF LOWER- AND MIDDLE-CLASS NEGRO PRESCHOOLERS EJ 040 453

JESTER, R. EMILE
PRELIMINARY RESULTS FROM RELATIONSHIP BETWEEN TEACHERS' VOCABULARY USAGE AND THE VOCABULARY OF KINDERGARTEN AND FIRST GRADE STUDENTS. ED032135
FOCUS ON PARENT EDUCATION AS A MEANS OF ALTERING THE CHILD'S ENVIRONMENT. ED033758

JOHN, VERA
COMMUNICATIVE COMPETENCE OF LOW-INCOME CHILDREN--ASSUMPTIONS AND PROGRAMS. ED020775

JOHN, VERA P.
ANALYSIS OF STORY RETELLING AS A MEASURE OF THE EFFECTS OF ETHNIC CONTENT IN STORIES. FINAL REPORT. ED014326

JOHNSON, ADELE M., COMP.
PRESCHOOL PROGRAMS: AN ANNOTATED BIBLIOGRAPHY. ED052822

JOHNSON, CHARLES D.
ACADEMIC CHEATING: THE CONTRIBUTION OF SEX, PERSONALITY AND SITUATIONAL VARIABLES EJ 055 104

JOHNSON, CHARLES F.
HYPERACTIVITY AND THE MACHINE: THE ACTOMETER EJ 055 876

JOHNSON, DALE D.
A BASIC VOCABULARY FOR BEGINNING READING EJ 047 894

JOHNSON, DAVID C.
PROBLEM SOLVING PERFORMANCES OF FIRST GRADE CHILDREN. ED041623

JOHNSON, DONNA JEAN
DIACRITICAL MARKS IN TEXTBOOK ADOPTION EJ 012 815

JOHNSON, EDWARD E.
REGIONAL EVALUATION AND RESEARCH CENTER FOR HEAD START, SOUTHERN UNIVERSITY. ANNUAL REPORT. ED020792
THE ROLE OF INCENTIVES IN DISCRIMINATION LEARNING OF CHILDREN WITH VARYING PRE-SCHOOL EXPERIENCE. ED031290
INSTRUMENTAL PERFORMANCE AS A FUNCTION OF REINFORCEMENT SCHEDULE, LUCK VERSUS SKILL INSTRUCTIONS, AND SEX OF CHILD EJ 024 934

JOHNSON, HENRY S.
A STUDY OF SOME ECOLOGICAL, ECONOMIC AND SOCIAL FACTORS INFLUENCING PARENTAL PARTICIPATION IN PROJECT HEAD START. ED014331

JOHNSON, HENRY SIOUX
THE EFFECTS OF MONTESSORI EDUCATIONAL TECHNIQUES ON CULTURALLY DISADVANTAGED HEAD START CHILDREN. ED015009

JOHNSON, LEE ELLEN
CORRELATION OF PAIRED-ASSOCIATE PERFORMANCE WITH SCHOOL ACHIEVEMENT AS A FUNCTION OF TASK AND SAMPLE VARIATION. ED049813

JOHNSON, NORMA
WHAT'S THROWN OUT WITH THE BATH WATER: A BABY? ED053801
WHAT'S THROWN OUT WITH THE BATH WATER: A BABY? EJ 052 445

JOHNSON, ORVAL G.
A STUDY OF A MEASUREMENT RESOURCE IN CHILD RESEARCH, PROJECT HEAD START. ED020790

JOHNSON, PEDER J.
EFFECTS OF ENFORCED ATTENTION AND STIMULUS PHASING UPON RULE LEARNING IN CHILDREN EJ 024 697
FACTORS INFLUENCING CHILDREN'S CONCEPT IDENTIFICATION PERFORMANCE WITH NONPREFERRED RELEVANT ATTRIBUTES EJ 042 965
THE STABILITY AND TRANSFERABILITY OF CONCEPTUAL CODING IN CHILDREN EJ 046 251

JOHNSON, PETER A.
STEREOTYPIC AFFECTIVE PROPERTIES OF PERSONAL NAMES AND SOMATOTYPES IN CHILDREN EJ 043 352

JOHNSON, RONALD C.
FURTHER EVIDENCE ON THE RELATION BETWEEN AGE OF SEPARATION AND SIMILARITY IN IQ AMONG PAIRS OF SEPARATED IDENTICAL TWINS. ED027058

JOHNSON, STEPHEN M.
SELF-REINFORCEMENT VERSUS EXTERNAL REINFORCEMENT IN BEHAVIOR MODIFICATION WITH CHILDREN EJ 024 947

JOHNSON, VIRGINIA
AUDITORY COMPONENTS OF NEONATAL EXPERIENCE: A PRELIMINARY REPORT. ED025336

JOHNSTON, BETTY.
EARLY CHILDHOOD EDUCATION IN AMERICAN SAMOA, 1968. ED032114

JOHNSTON, JOHN M.
"OF HAIRY ARMS AND A DEEP BARITONE VOICE": A SYMPOSIUM MEN IN YOUNG CHILDREN'S LIVES EJ 028 795

JOINER, LEE M.
EFFECT OF CLASSROOM NOISE ON NUMBER IDENTIFICATION BY RETARDED CHILDREN EJ 045 793

JONES, BILL
DEVELOPMENT OF CUTANEOUS AND KINESTHETIC LOCALIZATION BY BLIND AND SIGHTED CHILDREN EJ 055 113

JONES, EDMOND D.
ON TRANSRACIAL ADOPTION OF BLACK CHILDREN EJ 053 853

JONES, ELIZABETH
INVOLVING PARENTS IN CHILDREN'S LEARNING EJ 028 845
DAY CARE FOR CHILDREN: ASSETS AND LIABILITIES EJ 035 802

JONES, JOANNA
FINAL REPORT ON HEAD START EVALUATION AND RESEARCH: 1967-68 TO THE OFFICE OF ECONOMIC OPPORTUNITY. SECTION I: PART B, ACCURACY OF SELF-PERCEPTION AMONG CULTURALLY DEPRIVED PRESCHOOLS. ED023455

JONES, N. G. BLURTON
AN EXPERIMENT ON EYEBROW-RAISING AND VISUAL SEARCHING IN CHILDREN EJ 039 947

JONES, SANDRA J.
CHILDREN'S TWO-CHOICE LEARNING OF PREDOMINANTLY ALTERNATING AND REPEATING SEQUENCES EJ 033 791
AGE, STATE, AND MATERNAL BEHAVIOR ASSOCIATED WITH INFANT VOCALIZATIONS EJ 052 444

JONES, SHUELL H.
HEAD START EVALUATION AND RESEARCH CENTER, TULANE UNIVERSITY. FINAL REPORT. (TITLE SUPPLIED). ED020782
CURRICULAR INTERVENTION IN LANGUAGE ARTS READINESS FOR HEAD START CHILDREN. TULANE UNIVERSITY, HEAD START EVALUATION AND RESEARCH CENTER ANNUAL REPORT TO THE OFFICE OF ECONOMIC OPPORTUNITY. ED038175
CURRICULAR INTERVENTION IN LANGUAGE ARTS READINESS FOR HEAD START CHILDREN. TULANE UNIVERSITY, HEAD START EVALUATION AND RESEARCH CENTER, 1968-1969 INTERVENTION REPORT. SUPPLEMENT TO THE ANNUAL REPORT TO THE OFFICE OF ECONOMIC OPPORTUNITY. ED047795

JOOSTEN, A. M.
DEVELOPMENT OF THE MONTESSORI METHOD EJ 036 330

JORDAN, ROSALIE
STIMULUS PREFERENCE AND MULTIPLICATIVE CLASSIFICATION IN CHILDREN EJ 047 686

JORDAN, T. E.
BIOLOGICAL AND ECOLOGICAL INFLUENCES ON DEVELOPMENT AT 12 MONTHS OF AGE EJ 029 385

JORDAN, THOMAS E.
DISCRIMINATING CHARACTERISTICS OF FAMILIES WATCHING SESAME STREET. EARLY DEVELOPMENTAL ADVERSITY PROGRAM: PHASE III, EDAP TECHNICAL NOTE 15.1. ED039943

JOSE, JEAN
TEACHER-PUPIL INTERACTION AS IT RELATES TO ATTEMPTED CHANGES IN TEACHER EXPECTANCY OF ACADEMIC ABILITY AND ACHIEVEMENT. ED041630

JOSSELYN, IRENE M.
THE CAPACITY TO LOVE: A POSSIBLE REFORMULATION EJ 034 709

JOYCE, BRUCE R.
SOCIAL ACTION FOR THE PRIMARY SCHOOLS EJ 018 066

JUHASZ, ANNE MCCREARY
STUDENT EVALUATION OF A HIGH SCHOOL SEX EDUCATION PROGRAM EJ 045 390

JUNG, STEVEN M.
EVALUATIVE USES OF UNCONVENTIONAL MEASUREMENT TECHNIQUES IN AN EDUCATIONAL SYSTEM EJ 042 347

KADUSHIN, ALFRED
CHILD WELFARE SERVICES: A SOURCEBOOK. ED047813

KAESS, DALE W.
MEASURES OF FORM CONSTANCY: DEVELOPMENTAL TRENDS EJ 034 611
METHODOLOGICAL STUDY OF FORM CONSTANCY DEVELOPMENT EJ 043 706

KAGAN, JEROME
ON CLASS DIFFERENCES AND EARLY DEVELOPMENT. ED044167
MOTHER-CHILD INTERACTION: SOCIAL CLASS DIFFERENCES IN THE FIRST YEAR OF LIFE. ED044177
CONTINUNITY IN COGNITIVE DEVELOPMENT DURING THE FIRST YEAR EJ 003 554
AN ESSAY FOR TEACHERS EJ 006 981
INDIVIDUAL DIFFERENCES IN THE INFANT'S DISTRIBUTION OF ATTENTION TO STIMULUS DISCREPANCY EJ 019 014
MOTHER-CHILD INTERACTION IN THE FIRST YEAR OF LIFE EJ 056 632
STABILITY OF THE ORIENTING REFLEX IN INFANTS TO AUDITORY AND VISUAL STIMULI AS INDEXED BY CARDIAC DECELERATION EJ 056 720

KAGAN, SPENCER
COOPERATION AND COMPETITION OF MEXICAN, MEXICAN-AMERICAN, AND ANGLO-AMERICAN CHILDREN OF TWO AGES UNDER FOUR INSTRUCTIONAL SETS EJ 041 957
EXPERIMENTAL ANALYSES OF COOPERATION AND COMPETITION OF ANGLO-AMERICAN AND MEXICAN CHILDREN EJ 053 647

KAHANA, BOAZ
STAGES OF THE DREAM CONCEPT AMONG HASIDIC CHILDREN EJ 017 903
WORD-ASSOCIATION RESPONSES OF CHILDREN AS A FUNCTION OF AGE, SEX AND INSTRUCTIONS EJ 055 096

KAHNEMAN, IRAH
SEX AND AGE DIFFERENCES IN PATTERN ORGANIZATION IN A FIGURAL-CONCEPTUAL TASK EJ 047 680
AGE- AND SEX-RELATED VARIATION IN PERFORMANCE ON A FIGURAL-CONCEPTUAL TASK EJ 061 066

KAISER, HENRY F.
A GEOMETRIC REPRESENTATION OF THE NOTIONS OF RELIABILITY, RELEVANCE, AND VALIDITY EJ 043 456

KALBAUGH, JANET COX
RETROACTIVE AND PROACTIVE MULTIPLE LIST INTERFERENCE WITH DISADVANTAGED CHILDREN EJ 057 895

KAMEYA, LAWRENCE I.
THE RELATION BETWEEN TEST ANXIETY AND NEED FOR MEMORY SUPPORT IN PROBLEM SOLVING. REVISED RESEARCH MEMORANDUM NO. 11. ED021616

KAMII, CONSTANCE
THE YPSILANTI EARLY EDUCATION PROGRAM. ED022531
PIAGET'S THEORY AND SPECIFIC INSTRUCTION: A RESPONSE TO BEREITER AND KOHLBERG. ED038164
A PIAGETIAN METHOD OF EVALUATING PRESCHOOL CHILDREN'S DEVELOPMENT IN CLASSIFICATION. ED039013
AN APPLICATION OF PIAGET'S THEORY TO THE CONCEPTUALIZATION OF A PRESCHOOL CURRICULUM. ED046502

KAMP, L. N. J.
THE WORLD TEST: DEVELOPMENTAL ASPECTS OF A PLAY TECHNIQUE EJ 031 629

KANAK, N. JACK
PAIRED-ASSOCIATE LEARNING AND BIDIRECTIONAL ASSOCIATIVE RECALL IN FIRST, THIRD, FIFTH AND SEVENTH GRADERS EJ 053 481

KANAREFF, VERA T.
SHARING IN CHILDREN AS A FUNCTION OF THE NUMBER OF SHAREES AND RECIPROCITY EJ 016 840

KANE, ELMER R.
DEVELOPMENT AND IMPLEMENTATION OF A COMPREHENSIVE EVALUATION AND REPORTING SYSTEM FOR KINDERGARTEN AND PRIMARY GRADE SCHOOLS. FINAL REPORT. ED026116

KANNEGIETER, RUTHAN BRINKERHOFF
THE EFFECTS OF A LEARNING PROGRAM IN PERCEPTUAL-MOTOR ACTIVITY UPON THE VISUAL PERCEPTION OF SHAPE. FINAL REPORT. ED030494

KAPLAN, BERT L.
ANXIETY - A CLASSROOM CLOSE-UP EJ 028 896

KAPPELMAN, MURRAY M.
A CLINIC FOR CHILDREN WITH LEARNING DISABILITIES EJ 024 471

KARLSON, ALFRED L.
DIFFERENTIAL OUTCOMES OF A MONTESSORI CURRICULUM EJ 060 330

KARNES, MERLE B.
A COMPARATIVE STUDY OF TWO PRESCHOOL PROGRAMS FOR CULTURALLY DISADVANTAGED CHILDREN--A HIGHLY STRUCTURED AND A TRADITIONAL PROGRAM. ED016524
A RESEARCH PROGRAM TO DETERMINE THE EFFECTS OF VARIOUS PRESCHOOL INTERVENTION PROGRAMS ON THE DEVELOPMENT OF DISADVANTAGED CHILDREN AND THE STRATEGIC AGE FOR SUCH INTERVENTION. ED017319
AN APPROACH FOR WORKING WITH MOTHERS OF DISADVANTAGED PRESCHOOL CHILDREN. ED017335
THE EFFECTS OF A HIGHLY STRUCTURED PRESCHOOL PROGRAM ON THE MEASURED INTELLIGENCE OF CULTURALLY DISADVANTAGED FOUR-YEAR-OLD CHILDREN. INTERIM REPORT. ED019116
A LONGITUDINAL STUDY OF DISADVANTAGED CHILDREN WHO PARTICIPATED IN THREE DIFFERENT PRESCHOOL PROGRAMS. ED036338
A NEW ROLE FOR TEACHERS: INVOLVING THE ENTIRE FAMILY IN THE EDUCATION OF PRESCHOOL DISADVANTAGED CHILDREN. ED036339
EDUCATIONAL INTERVENTION AT HOME BY MOTHERS OF DISADVANTAGED INFANTS. ED039944
EDUCATIONAL INTERVENTION AT HOME BY MOTHERS OF DISADVANTAGED INFANTS EJ 034 002

KARRE, MARIANNE
BEFORE SCHOOL STARTS. FOR CHILDREN'S MINDS--NOT JUST TO MIND THE CHILDREN. THE CHILD CENTRE--AS SEEN BY A PARENT. ED051873

KASDORF, C. A., III
DEVELOPMENTAL DIFFERENCES IN THE INTEGRATION OF PICTURE SERIES: EFFECTS OF VARIATIONS IN OBJECT-ATTRIBUTE RELATIONSHIPS EJ 029 386

KASPAR, J. C.
THE EFFECT OF SOCIAL INTERACTION ON ACTIVITY LEVELS IN SIX-TO EIGHT-YEAR-OLD BOYS EJ 052 463

KATKOVSKY, WALTER
PARENTAL ANTECEDENTS OF CHILDREN'S BELIEFS IN INTERNAL-EXTERNAL CONTROL OF REINFORCEMENTS IN INTELLECTUAL ACHIEVEMENT SITUATIONS. ED024447

KATZ, EVELYN W.
A STUDY OF LANGUAGE DEVIATIONS AND COGNITIVE PROCESSES. PROGRESS REPORT NO. 3. ED027958

KATZ, JUDITH MILSTEIN
REFLECTION-IMPULSIVITY AND COLOR-FORM SORTING EJ 046 234

KATZ, LILIAN G.
HELP FOR TEACHERS IN PRESCHOOLS: A PROPOSAL. ED031308
TEACHING IN PRESCHOOLS: ROLES AND GOALS. ED032942
VERBAL BEHAVIOR OF PRESCHOOL TEACHERS. A VERY PRELIMINARY REPORT. ED034577
STAFFING PRESCHOOLS: BACKGROUND INFORMATION. ED034589
CHILDREN AND TEACHERS IN TWO TYPES OF HEAD START CLASSES. ED036324
CHILD BEHAVIOR SURVEY INSTRUMENT: MANUAL OF INSTRUCTIONS AND DEFINITIONS. ED037230
EARLY CHILDHOOD EDUCATION AS A DISCIPLINE. ED043396
TEACHER-CHILD RELATIONSHIPS IN DAY CARE CENTERS. WORKING PAPER. ED046494
CONDITION WITH CAUTION: THINK THRICE BEFORE CONDITIONING. (ROUGH DRAFT). ED046539
TEACHING THE YOUNG CHILD: GOALS FOR ILLINOIS. ED053805
CHILDREN AND TEACHERS IN TWO TYPES OF HEAD START CLASSES EJ 008 172
TEACHING IN PRESCHOOLS: ROLES AND GOALS EJ 018 133
EARLY CHILDHOOD EDUCATION AS A DISCIPLINE EJ 029 617
FOUR QUESTIONS ON EARLY CHILDHOOD EDUCATION EJ 034 784
CONDITION WITH CAUTION EJ 058 585

KATZ, PHYLLIS A.
MEDIATION AND PERCEPTUAL TRANSFER IN CHILDREN EJ 035 365

KATZ, ROGER C.
INTERACTIONS BETWEEN THE FACILITATIVE AND INHIBITORY EFFECTS OF A PUNISHING STIMULUS IN THE CONTROL OF CHILDREN'S HITTING BEHAVIOR EJ 053 734

KATZENMEYER, WILLIAM G.
EFFECTS OF AGE OF ENTRY AND DURATION OF PARTICIPATION IN A COMPENSATORY EDUCATION PROGRAM. ED043380

KAUFMAN, ALAN S.
PIAGET AND GESELL: A PSYCHOMETRIC ANALYSIS OF TESTS BUILT FROM THEIR TASKS EJ 053 927
TESTS BUILT FROM PIAGET'S AND GESELL'S TASKS AS PREDICTORS OF FIRST-GRADE ACHIEVEMENT EJ 058 928

KAUFMAN, NADEEN L.
TESTS BUILT FROM PIAGET'S AND GESELL'S TASKS AS PREDICTORS OF FIRST-GRADE ACHIEVEMENT EJ 058 928

KEAN, JOHN M.
THE IMPACT OF HEAD START: AN EVALUATION OF THE EFFECTS OF HEAD START ON CHILDREN'S COGNITIVE AND AFFECTIVE DEVELOPMENT BY VICTOR G. CICIRELLI EJ 021 965

KEARNS, BESSIE JEAN RULEY
CHILDREARING PRACTICES AMONG SELECTED CULTURALLY DEPRIVED MINORITIES EJ 023 613

KEASEY, CHARLES BLAKE
SEX DIFFERENCES IN YIELDING TO TEMPTATION: A FUNCTION OF THE SITUATION EJ 035 711
SOCIAL PARTICIPATION AS A FACTOR IN THE MORAL DEVELOPMENT OF PREADOLESCENTS EJ 043 605

KEELY, SUZANN
KICKAPOO - NORTH CANADIAN PROJECT, 1966-67. FINAL REPORT. ED015781

KEEN, SUSAN P.
VERBAL RECALL AS A FUNCTION OF PERSONALITY CHARACTERISTICS EJ 054 806

KEENAN, VERNE
EFFECTS OF HEBREW AND ENGLISH LETTERS ON CHILDREN'S PERCEPTUAL SET EJ 053 721

KEISLAR, EVAN
COMPARATIVE EFFECTIVENESS OF ECHOIC AND MODELING PROCEDURES IN LANGUAGE INSTRUCTION WITH CULTURALLY DISADVANTAGED CHILDREN. ED025314

KEISLAR, EVAN R.
THE VALUE OF THE SPOKEN RESPONSE IN TEACHING LISTENING SKILLS TO YOUNG CHILDREN THROUGH PROGRAMMED INSTRUCTION. FINAL REPORT. ED027973
YOUNG CHILDREN'S USE OF LANGUAGE IN INFERENTIAL BEHAVIOR. ED029691
TEACHING KINDERGARTEN CHILDREN TO APPLY CONCEPT-DEFINING RULES. ED037231
AN EXPERIMENTAL GAME IN ORAL LANGUAGE COMPREHENSION. ED038171
THE "TELL-AND-FIND PICTURE GAME" FOR YOUNG CHILDREN. ED042513

KEISTER, MARY ELIZABETH
A REVIEW OF EXPERIENCE: ESTABLISHING, OPERATING, EVALUATING A DEMONSTRATION NURSERY CENTER FOR THE DAYTIME CARE OF INFANTS AND TODDLERS, 1967-1970. FINAL REPORT. ED050810
CURRICULUM FOR THE INFANT AND TODDLER. A COLOR SLIDE SERIES WITH SCRIPT. (SCRIPT ONLY). ED050817

KELIHER, ALICE V.
PARENT AND CHILD CENTERS--WHAT THEY ARE, WHERE THEY ARE GOING EJ 007 089

KELLAGHAN, THOMAS
FAMILY CORRELATES OF VERBAL REASONING ABILITY EJ 061 069

KELLAS, GEORGE
THE INTERACTION OF PRONUNCIABILITY AND RESPONSE PRETRAINING ON THE PAIRED-ASSOCIATE PERFORMANCE OF THIRD-GRADE CHILDREN EJ 021 762

KELLER, ALAN B.
PSYCHOLOGICAL SOURCES OF "RESISTANCE" TO FAMILY PLANNING EJ 027 502

KELLER, HAROLD R.
CHILDREN'S ACQUISITION AND REVERSAL BEHAVIOR IN A PROBABILITY LEARNING SITUATION AS A FUNCTION OF PROGRAMMED INSTRUCTION, INTERNAL-EXTERNAL CONTROL, AND SCHEDULES OF REINFORCEMENT EJ 037 495
THE EFFECTS OF TRAINING AND SOCIOECONOMIC CLASS UPON THE ACQUISITION OF CONSERVATION CONCEPTS EJ 056 401

KELLEY, MARJORIE L.
AN EXPERIMENTAL STUDY OF FORMAL READING INSTRUCTION AT THE KINDERGARTEN LEVEL. ED022533

KELLY, INGA K.
THE EFFECTS OF DIFFERENTIATED INSTRUCTION IN VISUO-MOTOR SKILLS ON DEVELOPMENTAL GROWTH AND READING READINESS AT KINDERGARTEN LEVEL. FINAL REPORT. ED053821

KEMBLE, VIRGINIA
A FEASIBILITY STUDY OF PARENT AWARENESS PROGRAMS. FINAL REPORT. ED040742

KEMP, CLAIRE JACKSON
FAMILY TREATMENT WITHIN THE MILIEU OF A RESIDENTIAL TREATMENT CENTER EJ 037 236

KEMPLER, BERNHARD
STIMULUS CORRELATES OF AREA JUDGMENTS: A PSYCHOPHYSICAL DEVELOPMENTAL STUDY EJ 034 707

KENDALL, EARLINE
WE HAVE MEN ON THE STAFF EJ 060 929

KENDLER, H. H.
DEVELOPMENTAL PROCESSES IN DISCRIMINATION LEARNING EJ 024 705

KENDLER, HOWARD H.
AN ONTOGENY OF OPTIONAL SHIFT BEHAVIOR EJ 019 003
SINGLE VERSUS CUMULATIVE PRESENTATION OF STIMULI TO KINDERGARTNERS IN REVERSAL SHIFT BEHAVIOR EJ 047 678
VERBAL-LABELING AND CUE-TRAINING IN REVERSAL-SHIFT BEHAVIOR EJ 053 727

KENDLER, T. S.
DEVELOPMENTAL PROCESSES IN DISCRIMINATION LEARNING EJ 024 705

KENDLER, TRACY S.
AN ONTOGENY OF OPTIONAL SHIFT BEHAVIOR EJ 019 003
AN ONTOGENY OF MEDIATIONAL DEFICIENCY EJ 056 631

KENNEDY, BARBARA J.
MOTIVATIONAL EFFECTS OF INDIVIDUAL CONFERENCES AND GOAL SETTING ON PERFORMANCE AND ATTITUDES IN ARITHMETIC. REPORT FROM THE PROJECT ON SITUATIONAL VARIABLES AND EFFICIENCY OF CONCEPT LEARNING. ED032113

KENNEDY, WALLACE A.
A FOLLOW-UP NORMATIVE STUDY OF NEGRO INTELLIGENCE AND ACHIEVEMENT EJ 003 658

KENNEY, JAMES B.
THE ORGANIZATIONAL CLIMATE OF SCHOOLS IN FIVE URBAN AREAS EJ 027 704

KEOGH, BARBARA K.
EFFECT OF INSTRUCTIONAL SET ON TWELVE-YEAR-OLD CHILDREN'S PERCEPTION OF INTERRUPTION EJ 034 921
PATTERN COPYING UNDER THREE CONDITIONS OF AN EXPANDED SPATIAL FIELD EJ 035 622
NORMAL AND RETARDED CHILDREN'S EXPECTANCY FOR FAILURE EJ 039 266

KEOHANE, MARY
A.S. NEILL: LATTER-DAY DEWEY? EJ 020 839

KERCKHOFF, ALAN C.
EARLY ANTECEDENTS OF ROLE-TAKING AND ROLE-PLAYING ABILITY EJ 008 318

KERCKHOFF, RICHARD K.
TEACHING RACE RELATIONS IN THE NURSERY SCHOOL EJ 056 864

KERLIN, SARAH M.
ROCKS, RIVERS AND CITY CHILDREN EJ 029 390

KERPELMAN, LARRY C.
STIMULUS DIMENSIONALITY AND MANIPULABILITY IN VISUAL PERCEPTUAL LEARNING. ED023452

KERSHNER, JOHN R.
CHILDREN'S ACQUISITION OF VISUO-SPATIAL DIMENSIONALITY: A CONSERVATION STUDY. ED041636
CHILDREN'S CONSERVATION OF MULTIPLE SPACE RELATIONS: EFFECTS OF PERCEPTION AND REPRESENTATION. ED044179
CHILDREN'S SPATIAL REPRESENTATIONS AND HORIZONTAL DIRECTIONALITY EJ 023 190
CHILDREN'S ACQUISITION OF VISUO-SPATIAL DIMENSIONALITY: A CONSERVATION STUDY EJ 047 681

KERSHNER, KEITH M.
PENNSYLVANIA PRESCHOOL AND PRIMARY EDUCATION PROJECT: 1968-1969 FINAL REPORT TO THE FORD FOUNDATION. ED033759

KESSEL, FRANK S.
THE ROLE OF SYNTAX IN CHILDREN'S COMPREHENSION FROM AGES SIX TO TWELVE EJ 028 578

KESSEL, LESLEY D.
EFFECTS OF DIFFERENTIAL PRIOR EXPOSURE ON YOUNG CHILDREN'S SUBSEQUENT OBSERVING AND CHOICE OF NOVEL STIMULI. ED017336

KESSEN, WILLIAM
VISUAL SCANNING BY HUMAN NEWBORNS: RESPONSES TO COMPLETE TRIANGLE, TO SIDES ONLY, AND TO CORNERS ONLY. ED035439
EARLY LEARNING AND COMPENSATORY EDUCATION: CONTRIBUTION OF BASIC RESEARCH. ED036318

KESSLER, E. S.
THE WORLD TEST: DEVELOPMENTAL ASPECTS OF A PLAY TECHNIQUE EJ 031 629

KESSLER, JANES W.
SEPARATION REACTIONS IN YOUNG, MILDLY RETARDED CHILDREN. EJ 003 972

KEYSERLING, MARY DUBLIN
THE DAY CARE CHALLENGE: THE UNMET NEEDS OF MOTHERS AND CHILDREN. ED050821
DAY CARE: CRISIS AND CHALLENGE EJ 046 455
DAY CARE CHALLENGE: THE UNMET NEEDS OF MOTHERS AND CHILDREN EJ 046 456

KHALAKDINA, MARGARET
THE PRESCHOOL IN RURAL INDIA EJ 036 334

KIER, RAE JEANNE
CHILDREN'S ABILITY TO ORDER FACIAL AND NONFACIAL CONTINUA AS A FUNCTION OF MA, CA, AND IQ EJ 059 699

KIES, KATHLEEN M.
ALTERNATIVE LEARNING ENVIRONMENTS: A PHILADELPHIA STORY EJ 033 156

KIESTER, DOROTHY J.
CONSULTATION IN DAY CARE. ED051884

KIM, HYUNG BOK
A FRESH LOOK AT INTERCOUNTRY ADOPTIONS EJ 047 968

KIMMEL, ELLEN
THE EFFECTS OF IMMEDIATE FEEDBACK ON THE BEHAVIOR OF TEACHERS-IN-TRAINING EJ 059 672

KINCAID, CAROLYN
A STUDY IN TRAINING NURSERY CHILDREN ON LOGICAL OPERATIONAL SKILLS. ED047803

KING, MICHAEL
THE DEVELOPMENT OF SOME INTENTION CONCEPTS IN YOUNG CHILDREN EJ 052 452

KING, WILLIAM L.
CONJUNCTIVE AND DISJUNCTIVE RULE LEARNING AS A FUNCTION OF AGE AND FORCED VERBALIZATION EJ 028 637
A NONARBITRARY BEHAVIORAL CRITERION FOR CONSERVATION OF ILLUSION-DISTORTED LENGTH IN FIVE-YEAR-OLDS EJ 038 263

KINGSLEY, PHILLIP R.
INDUCED VERSUS SPONTANEOUS REHEARSAL IN SHORT-TERM MEMORY IN NURSERY SCHOOL CHILDREN. STUDY M: DEVELOPMENT OF SELECTIVE ATTENTION ABILITIES. ED024444

KINNIE, ERNEST J.
THE INFLUENCE OF NONINTELLECTIVE FACTORS ON THE IQ SCORES OF MIDDLE- AND LOWER-CLASS CHILDREN EJ 056 621

KIRCHER, MARY
RACIAL PREFERENCES IN YOUNG CHILDREN EJ 056 626

KIRKENDALL, DON R.
THE ABILITY OF PERSONALITY VARIABLES IN DISCRIMINATING AMONG THREE INTELLECTUAL GROUPS OF PREADOLESCENT BOYS AND GIRLS EJ 034 044

KLACKENBERG, GUNNAR
FAMILY PROBLEMS CONCERNING THE MENTALLY RETARDED CHILD EJ 010 859

KLASSEN, BERNARD
A TRANSFORMATIONAL ANALYSIS OF ORAL SYNTACTIC STRUCTURES OF CHILDREN REPRESENTING VARYING ETHNOLINGUISTIC COMMUNITIES EJ 056 713

KLAUS, RUPERT A.
THE EARLY TRAINING PROJECT FOR DISADVANTAGED CHILDREN--A REPORT AFTER FIVE YEARS. ED016514
THE EARLY TRAINING PROJECT: A SEVENTH YEAR REPORT. ED032934
THE EARLY TRAINING PROJECT: A SEVENTH-YEAR REPORT EJ 033 777

KLAUSMEIER, HERBERT J.
INDIVIDUALLY GUIDED MOTIVATION: DEVELOPING SELF-DIRECTION AND PROSOCIAL BEHAVIORS EJ 034 159
INSTRUCTIONAL PROGRAMMING FOR THE INDIVIDUAL PUPIL IN THE MULTIUNIT ELEMENTARY SCHOOL EJ 050 591

KLEIN, GENEVIEVE
COVERT PROJECT, YEAR 1. ED019137

KLEIN, JENNY
HEAD START PLANNED VARIATION PROGRAM. ED038170

KLEIN, JENNY W.
PLANNED VARIATION IN HEAD START PROGRAMS EJ 031 848
EDUCATIONAL COMPONENT OF DAY CARE EJ 051 235

KLEIN, M. FRANCES
CURRICULUM BOON OR BANE? EJ 052 766

KLEIN, ROBERT P.
ACOUSTIC ANALYSIS OF THE ACQUISITION OF ACCEPTABLE "R" IN AMERICAN ENGLISH EJ 041 056

KLEIN, STEPHEN P.
DIRECTION SPORTS: A TUTORIAL PROGRAM FOR ELEMENTARY-SCHOOL PUPILS EJ 050 982

KLIG, SALLY
DIMENSIONAL LEARNING ACROSS SENSORY MODALITIES IN NURSERY SCHOOL CHILDREN EJ 021 756

KLIMA, URSULA BELLUGI
EVALUATING THE CHILD'S LANGUAGE COMPETENCE. ED019141

KLINEBERG, OTTO
THE DEVELOPMENT OF CHILDREN'S VIEWS OF FOREIGN PEOPLES EJ 000 392

KLUGE, JEAN
WHAT THE WORLD NEEDS NOW: ENVIRONMENTAL EDUCATION FOR YOUNG CHILDREN EJ 039 637

KNIGHT, DON A.
THE SCHOOL AND THE UNIVERSITY: CO-OPERATIVE ROLES IN STUDENT TEACHING EJ 015 981

KNIGHT, SARAH S.
SOCIAL-EMOTIONAL TASK FORCE. FINAL REPORT. ED033744

KNOLL, CHERYL
MEANING CONDITIONING AND AWARENESS AMONG CHILDREN EJ 049 426

KNOPF, IRWIN J.
SOCIO-CULTURAL INFLUENCES ON ATTENTION IN ELEMENTARY SCHOOL CHILDREN. FINAL REPORT. ED024456

KNOX, LOIS
THE USE OF CONTEMPORARY MATERIALS IN THE CLASSROOM. ED020013

KNOX, PATRICIA
IMPROVING HIGH SCHOOL LEARNING PREDICTIONS WITH MULTIPLE JUNIOR HIGH TEST SCORES EJ 016 653

KNOX, WILLIAM E.
A DISCONTINUITY IN THE SOCIALIZATION OF MALES IN THE UNITED STATES EJ 040 799

KOBASIGAWA, AKIRA
EFFECTS OF EXPOSURE TO MODELS ON CONCEPT IDENTIFICATION IN KINDERGARTEN AND SECOND-GRADE CHILDREN EJ 046 240

KODMAN, FRANK, JR.
LANGUAGE DEVELOPMENT OF DISADVANTAGED CHILDREN EJ 036 211

KOENIG, FREDRICK
MOTHER'S MODE OF DISCIPLINE AND CHILD'S VERBAL ABILITY EJ 050 794

KOGAN, KATE L.
A STUDY OF COMMUNICATION PATTERNS IN DISADVANTAGED CHILDREN. ED037250

KOGAN, NATHAN
CREATIVE ABILITY OVER A FIVE-YEAR SPAN EJ 058 412

KOHLBERG, LAWRENCE
REPORT OF A RESEARCH AND DEMONSTRATION PROJECT FOR CULTURALLY DISADVANTAGED CHILDREN IN THE ANCONA MONTESSORI SCHOOL. ED015014
THE IMPACT OF COGNITIVE MATURITY ON THE DEVELOPMENT OF SEX-ROLE ATTITUDES IN THE YEARS 4 TO 8. ED019109

KOHLWES, GARY F.
SEX AND RACE DIFFERENCES IN THE DEVELOPMENT OF UNDERPRIVILEGED PRESCHOOL CHILDREN. ED019992

KOHN, MARTIN
A SOCIAL COMPETENCE SCALE AND SYMPTOM CHECKIST FOR THE PRESCHOOL CHILD: FACTOR DIMENSIONS, THEIR CROSS-INSTRUMENT GENERALITY, AND LONGITUDINAL PERSISTENCE EJ 057 476
RELATIONSHIP OF PRESCHOOL SOCIAL-EMOTIONAL FUNCTIONING TO LATER INTELLECTUAL ACHIEVEMENT EJ 058 138

KOLB, DORIS H.
HEAD START EVALUATION AND RESEARCH CENTER, UNIVERSITY OF KANSAS. REPORT NO. VIIC, ERRORLESS DISCRIMINATION IN PRESCHOOL CHILDREN: A PROGRAM FOR ESTABLISHING A ONE-MINUTE DELAY OF REINFORCEMENT. ED021642
A PROGRAM OF STIMULUS CONTROL FOR ESTABLISHING A ONE-MINUTE WAIT FOR REINFORCEMENT IN PRESCHOOL CHILDREN. PROGRESS REPORT. ED042492

KOMER, M. JOAN
INFANT SMILING TO NONSOCIAL STIMULI AND THE RECOGNITION HYPOTHESIS EJ 053 731

KOMORITA, S. S.
SELF-ESTEEM, SUCCESS-FAILURE, AND LOCUS OF CONTROL IN NEGRO CHILDREN EJ 035 621

KONNER, M. J.
AN EXPERIMENT ON EYEBROW-RAISING AND VISUAL SEARCHING IN CHILDREN EJ 039 947

KOONTZ, ELIZABETH D.
NEA VIEWS ON TEACHER STRIKES EJ 003 629

KORNELLY, DONALD
FOR BETTER READING - A MORE POSITIVE SELF-IMAGE EJ 013 562

KORNER, ANNELIESE F.
STATE AS VARIABLE, AS OBSTACLE AND AS MEDIATOR OF STIMULATION IN INFANT RESEARCH. ED049825
VISUAL ALERTNESS IN NEONATES AS EVOKED BY MATERNAL CARE EJ 027 847
STATE AS VARIABLE, AS OBSTACLE, AND AS MEDIATOR OF STIMULATION IN INFANT RESEARCH EJ 058 220
THE RELATIVE EFFICACY OF CONTACT AND VESTIBULAR-PROPRIOCEPTIVE STIMULATION IN SOOTHING NEONATES EJ 058 588

KORNREICH, L. BERELL
A DEVELOPMENTAL STUDY OF THE EFFECTS OF PRETRAINING ON A PERCEPTUAL RECOGNITION TASK EJ 056 630

KOSLIN, SANDRA COHEN
A DISTANCE MEASURE OF RACIAL ATTITUDES IN PRIMARY GRADE CHILDREN: AN EXPLORATORY STUDY. ED026133
QUASI-DISGUISED AND STRUCTURED MEASURE OF SCHOOLCHILDREN'S RACIAL PREFERENCES. ED035440

KOSSLYN, STEPHEN M.
SOCIAL INFLUENCES ON CHILDREN'S HUMOR RESPONSES. ED039933

KOSSUTH, GINA L.
FREE RECALL OF WORDS AND OBJECTS EJ 039 634

KOTTMEYER, WAYNE A.
EFFECT OF CLASSROOM NOISE ON NUMBER IDENTIFICATION BY RETARDED CHILDREN EJ 045 793

KOVAL, CALISTA B.
THE EFFECTS OF THE DUSO GUIDANCE PROGRAM ON THE SELF-CONCEPTS OF PRIMARY SCHOOL CHILDREN EJ 058 132

KOWATRAKUL, SURANG
PAPER-AND-PENCIL VERSUS CONCRETE PERFORMANCE OF NORMALS AND RETARDATES ON THE ETS WRITTEN EXERCISES. ED035442
"NEED ACHIEVEMENT" TRAINING FOR HEAD START CHILDREN AND THEIR MOTHERS. ED048943

KOZIOL, STEPHEN
NOUN PLURAL DEVELOPMENT IN PRIMARY GRADE CHILDREN EJ 052 179

KRAFT, IVOR
PRELUDE TO SCHOOL: AN EVALUATION OF AN INNER-CITY PRESCHOOL PROGRAM. ED033750

KRAMER, PAMELA E.
THE DEVELOPMENT OF COMPETENCE IN AN EXCEPTIONAL LANGUAGE STRUCTURE IN OLDER CHILDREN AND YOUNG ADULTS EJ 056 727

KRANTZ, MURRAY
HAPTIC RECOGNITION OF OBJECTS IN CHILDREN EJ 055 099

KRAVITZ, HARVEY
RHYTHMIC HABIT PATTERNS IN INFANCY: THEIR SEQUENCE, AGE OF ONSET, AND FREQUENCY EJ 040 295

KRAYNAK, AUDREY R.
THE INFLUENCE OF AGE AND STIMULUS DIMENSIONALITY ON FORM PERCEPTION BY PRESCHOOL CHILDREN EJ 039 630

KREITLER, HANS
DEPENDENCE OF LAUGHTER ON COGNITIVE STRATEGIES EJ 023 964

KREITLER, SHULAMITH
DEPENDENCE OF LAUGHTER ON COGNITIVE STRATEGIES EJ 023 964

KRESH, ESTHER
CHILDREN'S ABILITY TO OPERATE WITHIN A MATRIX: A DEVELOPMENTAL STUDY. ED029715
CHILDREN'S ABILITY TO OPERATE WITHIN A MATRIX: A DEVELOPMENTAL STUDY EJ 035 363

KREUSLER, ABRAHAM
SOVIET PRESCHOOL EDUCATION EJ 020 840

KRIDER, MARY A.
AN EVALUATION OF HEAD START PRESCHOOL ENRICHMENT PROGRAMS AS THEY AFFECT THE INTELLECTUAL ABILITY, THE SOCIAL ADJUSTMENT, AND THE ACHIEVEMENT LEVEL OF FIVE-YEAR-OLD CHILDREN ENROLLED IN LINCOLN, NEBRASKA. ED015011

KRITCHEVSKY, SYBIL
PLANNING ENVIRONMENTS FOR YOUNG CHILDREN: PHYSICAL SPACE. ED038162

KROES, WILLIAM H.
CONCEPTUAL ENCODING AND CONCEPT RECALL-RECOVERY IN CHILDREN EJ 056 628

KROGMAN, WILTON MARION
GROWTH OF HEAD, FACE, TRUNK, AND LIMBS IN PHILADEPHIA WHITE AND NEGRO CHILDREN OF ELEMENTARY AND HIGH SCHOOL AGE EJ 022 582

KRON, REUBEN E.
AN ANALYSIS OF BEHAVIORAL MECHANISMS INVOLVED IN CONTROL OVER INFANT FEEDING BEHAVIOR ED037236
STUDIES OF SUCKING BEHAVIOR IN THE HUMAN NEWBORN: THE DIAGNOSTIC AND PREDICTIVE VALUE OF MEASURES OF EARLIEST ORAL BEHAVIOR. ED039014

KRUGMAN, DOROTHY C.
WORKING WITH SEPARATION EJ 046 893

KUBOSE, SUNNAN K.
MOTIVATIONAL EFFECTS OF BOREDOM ON CHILDREN'S RESPONSE SPEEDS EJ 055 211

KUBZANSKY, PHILIP E.
A DEVELOPMENTAL STUDY OF SIZE CONSTANCY FOR TWO-VERSUS THREE-DIMENSIONAL STIMULI EJ 040 454

KUGEL, ROBERT B.
COMBATTING RETARDATION IN INFANTS WITH DOWN'S SYNDROME EJ 026 640

KUGELMASS, SOL
PERCEPTUAL EXPLORATION IN ISRAELI CHILDREN EJ 033 054

KUHMERKER, LISA
MUSIC IN THE BEGINNING READING PROGRAM EJ 006 811

KULIK, JAMES A.
LANGUAGE, SOCIALIZATION, AND DELINQUENCY EJ 039 587

KUNREUTHER, SYLVIA CLIFFORD
A PRESCHOOL EXCHANGE: BLACK MOTHERS SPEAK AND A WHITE TEACHER LISTENS EJ 022 137

KUPFERER, HARRIET J.
A DISCONTINUITY IN THE SOCIALIZATION OF MALES IN THE UNITED STATES EJ 040 799

L'ABATE, LUCIANO
DESIGN FOR A PLAYROOM. ED019133
AN ANNOTATED BIBLIOGRAPHY OF BEHAVIOR MODIFICATION WITH CHILDREN AND RETARDATES. ED020025
DIFFERENCES IN VOCABULARY INPUT-OUTPUT IN PSYCHODIAGNOSIS OF CHILDREN. ED024450

LA BELLE, THOMAS J.
WHAT'S DEPRIVED ABOUT BEING DIFFERENT? EJ 046 968

LABEAUNE, CAROL
PARENTS: SUMMER READING TEACHERS EJ 032 510

LACEY, HARVEY M.
MINIMAL BRAIN DAMAGE: A MEANINGFUL DIAGNOSIS OR AN IRRELEVANT LABEL? EJ 018 707

LACROSSE, E. ROBERT, JR.
PRIMARY INFLUENCES ON THE DEVELOPMENT OF COMPETENCE: THE DEVELOPMENT OF A MATERNAL BEHAVIOR SCALE. PROGRESS REPORT. ED032127
PSYCHOLOGIST AND TEACHER: COOPERATION OR CONFLICT? EJ 017 709

LADY ALLEN OF HURTWOOD
AN ADVENTURE PLAYGROUND FOR HANDICAPPED CHILDREN IN LONDON EJ 050 487

LAIRD, JAMES D.
SOME DEVELOPMENTAL CHANGES IN THE ORGANIZATION OF SELF-EVALUATIONS EJ 044 186

LAMAL, PETER A.
IMITATION LEARNING OF INFORMATION-PROCESSING EJ 046 252

LAMB, HOWARD E.
THE DEVELOPMENT OF SELF-OTHER RELATIONSHIPS DURING PROJECT HEAD START. ED015008

LAMBERT, CARROLL
"THIS IS ME!" EJ 003 029

LAMBERT, WALLACE E.
THE DEVELOPMENT OF CHILDREN'S VIEWS OF FOREIGN PEOPLES EJ 000 392

LAMBERT, WILLIAM W.
IS SESAME STREET EXPORTABLE? EJ 061 442

LAMPE, JOHN M.
AN EVALUATIVE STUDY OF COLOR-VISION TESTS FOR KINDERGARTEN AND FIRST GRADE PUPILS. ED028816

LAMPER, CELIA
PRESTIMULUS ACTIVITY LEVEL AND RESPONSIVITY IN THE NEONATE EJ 040 297

LAND, KENNETH C.
FINAL REPORT ON HEAD START EVALUATION AND RESEARCH--1966-67 TO THE INSTITUTE FOR EDUCATIONAL DEVELOPMENT. SECTION II, ON THE INTERPRETATION OF MULTIVARIATE SYSTEMS. ED019118

LANDAUER, T. K.
EXPERIMENTAL ANALYSIS OF THE FACTORS DETERMINING OBEDIENCE OF FOUR-YEAR-OLD CHILDREN TO ADULT FEMALES EJ 026 152

LANDERS, WILLIAM F.
STATE IV OF PIAGET'S THEORY OF INFANT'S OBJECT CONCEPTS: A LONGITUDINAL STUDY EJ 041 134
EFFECTS OF DIFFERENTIAL EXPERIENCE ON INFANTS' PERFORMANCE IN A PIAGETIAN STAGE IV OBJECT-CONCEPT TASK EJ 042 956

LANDMAN, GEORGE
THE CHILD'S EYE VIEW: EXPERIMENTAL PHOTOGRAPHY WITH PRESCHOOL CHILDREN EJ 029 342

LANDSBAUM, JANE B.
CONFORMITY IN EARLY AND LATE ADOLESCENCE EJ 038 936

LANE, ELIZABETH M., ED.
EARLY CHILDHOOD EDUCATION PROGRAM AND ITS COMPONENTS: PSYCHOLOGICAL EVALUATION, SENSORIMOTOR SKILLS PROGRAM, NEW VISIONS - A CHILDREN'S MUSEUM. PROJECT REPORTS, VOLUME 4, BOOK 1, 1969. ED045183
EARLY CHILDHOOD EDUCATION PROGRAM, ESEA TITLE I, FY 1970. PROJECT REPORTS, VOLUME 5, BOOK 2, 1970. ED052820

LANE, ELLEN A.
THE INTELLIGENCE OF CHILDREN OF SCHIZOPHRENICS EJ 021 763

LANE, HARLAN
DEVELOPMENT OF THE PROSODIC FEATURES OF INFANTS' VOCALIZING. ED025331

LANE, MARY B.
NURSERIES IN CROSS-CULTURAL EDUCATION. FINAL REPORT. ED053815

LANG, NORMA J.
DEVELOPMENT OF VISUAL SCANNING STRATEGIES FOR DIFFERENTIATING WORDS EJ 043 703

LANGE, GARRETT W.
THE DEVELOPMENT OF FREE CLASSIFICATION AND FREE RECALL IN CHILDREN EJ 030 293

LANGELLOTTO, EUGENE
INVOLVING PARENTS IN A CHILDREN'S CLINIC EJ 047 353

LANGER, JONAS
OPERATIONAL THOUGHT INDUCEMENT EJ 018 874

LAOSA, LUIS M.
EFFECTS OF SEX AND BIRTH ORDER ON SEX-ROLE DEVELOPMENT AND INTELLIGENCE AMONG KINDERGARTEN CHILDREN EJ 057 133

LAPOINTE, ROGER E.
L'EDUCATEUR ET L'EPANOUISSEMENT DE LA PERSONNALITE DE L'ENFANT EJ 028 102

LARKINS, A. GUY
MATCHED-PAIR SCORING TECHNIQUE USED ON A FIRST-GRADE YES-NO TYPE ECONOMICS ACHIEVEMENT TEST. ED029699
SRA ECONOMICS MATERIALS IN GRADES ONE AND TWO. EVALUATION REPORTS. ED029700
COMPARISON OF YES-NO, MATCHED-PAIRS, AND ALL-NO SCORING OF A FIRST-GRADE ECONOMICS ACHIEVEMENT TEST. ED029701

LARRABEE, MARGERY M.
INVOLVING PARENTS IN THEIR CHILDREN'S DAY-CARE EXPERIENCES EJ 007 451

LARSEN, GARY Y.
VERBAL FACTORS IN COMPENSATION PERFORMANCE AND THE RELATION BETWEEN CONSERVATION AND COMPENSATION EJ 033 778
AN EXAMINATION OF THE DEVELOPMENTAL RELATIONS BETWEEN CERTAIN SPATIAL TASKS EJ 051 563

LARSEN, MARIE
WHAT GENERATION GAP? EJ 032 763

LARSON, DARO E.
THE EFFECT OF A PRESCHOOL EXPERIENCE UPON INTELLECTUAL FUNCTIONING AMONG FOUR-YEAR-OLD, WHITE CHILDREN IN RURAL MINNESOTA. ED039030

LARSON, RICHARD G.
HOW DO INNER-CITY TEACHERS USE A SYSTEM-WIDE CURRICULUM? EJ 015 487

LASSEGARD, DICK
A DAY IN THE LIFE OF A SCHOOL PSYCHOLOGIST EJ 018 956

LAUGHLIN, PATRICK R.
AN INVESTIGATION OF THE MANNER IN WHICH YOUNG CHILDREN PROCESS INTELLECTUAL INFORMATION. FINAL REPORT. ED036313

LAVATELLI, C.B.
CRITICAL OVERVIEW OF EARLY CHILDHOOD EDUCATION PROGRAMS. ED019142

LAVATELLI, CELIA B., ED.
THE DEVELOPMENT OF FORMS OF THE NEGATIVE. ED022549
PROBLEMS OF DIALECT. ED025300

LAVATELLI, CELIA STENDLER, ED.
LANGUAGE TRAINING IN EARLY CHILDHOOD EDUCATION. ED051881
AN APPROACH TO LANGUAGE LEARNING EJ 008 119
CONTRASTING VIEWS OF EARLY CHILDHOOD EDUCATION EJ 017 851

LAWDER, ELIZABETH A.
A FOLLOWUP STUDY OF ADOPTIONS: POST-PLACEMENT FUNCTIONING OF ADOPTION FAMILIES. ED039018
POSTADOPTION COUNSELING: A PROFESSIONAL OBLIGATION EJ 028 792

LAWLER, PATRICIA R.
CHILDREN'S PERCEPTIONS OF A TEACHING TEAM EJ 051 772

LAY, MARGARET
THE EFFECT OF SUPPLEMENTARY SMALL GROUP EXPERIENCE ON TASK ORIENTATION AND COGNITIVE PERFORMANCE IN KINDERGARTEN CHILDREN. A FINAL REPORT OF THE KINDERGARTEN 'LEARNING TO LEARN' PROGRAM EVALUATION PROJECT. ED039948
ANALYSIS OF EARLY CHILDHOOD PROGRAMS: A SEARCH FOR COMPARATIVE DIMENSIONS. ED051877

LAYNE, OTTIS, JR.
PLAY BEHAVIOR IN YOUNG CHILDREN: A CROSS-CULTURAL STUDY EJ 048 303

LAZAR, IRVING
A NATIONAL SURVEY OF THE PARENT-CHILD CENTER PROGRAM. ED048933

LEAVERTON, PAUL
DIFFERENTIATION BETWEEN NORMAL AND DISORDERED CHILDREN BY A COMPUTER ANALYSIS OF EMOTIONAL AND VERBAL BEHAVIOR. ED019138

LEBLANC, JUDITH M.
ERRORLESS ESTABLISHMENT OF A MATCH-TO-SAMPLE FORM DISCRIMINATION IN PRESCHOOL CHILDREN. I. A MODIFICATION OF ANIMAL LABORATORY PROCEDURES FOR CHILDREN, II. A COMPARISON OF ERRORLESS AND TRIAL-AND-ERROR DISCRIMINATION. PROGRESS REPORT. ED042490
AN EXPERIMENTAL ANALYSIS OF PROCEDURES FOR INCREASING SPECIFIC VOCALIZATIONS OF CHILDREN WHO DO NOT DEVELOP FUNCTIONAL SPEECH. PROGRESS REPORT. ED042495

LECOMPTE, GUNEY K.
VIOLATION OF A RULE AS A METHOD OF DIAGNOSING INFANTS' LEVELS OF OBJECT CONCEPT EJ 059 314

LEE, DORRIS M.
LEARNING TO READ THROUGH EXPERIENCE. SECOND EDITION. ED027067

LEE, SEONG-SOO
THE EFFECTS OF VISUALLY REPRESENTED CUES ON LEARNING OF LINEAR FUNCTION RULES EJ 044 701

LEE, WALTER S.
HUMAN RELATIONS TRAINING FOR TEACHERS: THE EFFECTIVENESS OF SENSITIVITY TRAINING EJ 015 979

LEFEBVRE, ANDRE
OCCUPATIONAL PRESTIGE AS SEEN BY DISADVANTAGED BLACK CHILDREN EJ 034 453

LEGANT, PATRICIA
EFFECT OF LABELS ON MEMORY IN THE ABSENCE OF REHEARSAL. ED051883
NAMING AND MEMORY IN NURSERY SCHOOL CHILDREN IN THE ABSENCE OF REHEARSAL EJ 042 961

LEHMAN, ELYSE BRAUCH
MEMORY FOR RHYTHMIC SERIES: AGE CHANGES IN ACCURACY AND NUMBER CODING EJ 054 805
SELECTIVE STRATEGIES IN CHILDREN'S ATTENTION TO TASK-RELEVANT INFORMATION EJ 055 537

LEHRMAN, WENDY
A SCHOOL GUIDANCE CLASS FOR EMOTIONALLY DISTURBED CHILDREN EJ 007 875

LEIDERMAN, GLORIA F.
THE ELEMENTARY MATHEMATICS STUDY: AN INTERIM REPORT ON KINDERGARTEN YEAR RESULTS. ED027937

LEIFER, A. D.
AN AUDITORY PROMPTING DEVICE FOR BEHAVIOR OBSERVATION EJ 043 316

LEIFER, AIMEE DORR
DEVELOPMENTAL ASPECTS OF VARIABLES RELEVANT TO OBSERVATIONAL LEARNING EJ 053 740

LEIFER, L. J.
AN AUDITORY PROMPTING DEVICE FOR BEHAVIOR OBSERVATION EJ 043 316

LEIGH, TERRENCE M.
HEAD START: A HEAD START TO HEALTH? EJ 036 581
SUFFER THE LITTLE KENTUCKY FIRST-GRADERS EJ 037 283

LEITHWOOD, K. A.
COMPLEX MOTOR LEARNING IN FOUR-YEAR-OLDS EJ 046 236

LELER, HAZEL
LANGUAGE DEVELOPMENT OF SOCIALLY DISADVANTAGED PRESCHOOL CHILDREN. FINAL REPORT. ED041641

LEMOND, CAROLYN M.
DEVELOPMENTAL DIFFERENCES IN THE PERCEPTION AND PRODUCTION OF FACIAL EXPRESSIONS EJ 058 693

LERNER, RICHARD M.
KINDERGARTEN CHILDREN'S ACTIVE VOCABULARY ABOUT BODY BUILD EJ 041 857
PHYSIQUE IDENTIFICATION, PREFERENCE, AND AVERSION IN KINDERGARTEN CHILDREN EJ 046 785

LERNER, SANDRA
CONCRETE OPERATIONAL THINKING IN MENTALLY ILL ADOLESCENTS EJ 060 778

LESHAN, EDA J.
COMO CONTESTAN LOS PADRES LAS PREGUNTAS DE SUS NINOS? (HOW DO PARENTS RESPOND TO CHILDREN'S QUESTIONS?) EJ 011 843

LESKOW, SONIA
DEVELOPMENT CHANGES IN PROBLEM-SOLVING STRATEGIES: PERMUTATION EJ 021 767

LESSER, GERALD S.
DESIGNING A PROGRAM FOR BROADCAST TELEVISION. ED033768

LESSING, ELISE E.
RACIAL DIFFERENCES IN INDICES OF EGO FUNCTIONING RELEVANT TO ACADEMIC ACHIEVEMENT EJ 015 096
WISC SUBTEST AND IQ SCORE CORRELATES OF FATHER ABSENCE EJ 029 219
EXTENSION OF PERSONAL FUTURE TIME PERSPECTIVE, AGE, AND LIFE-SATISFACTION OF CHILDREN AND ADOLESCENTS EJ 058 140

LESTER, SEELIG
CHILDREN AND THE SCHOOL STRIKE EJ 003 419

LEVE, ROBERT M.
AN ATTEMPT TO COMBINE CLINICAL AND EDUCATIONAL RESOURCES: A REPORT ON THE FIRST YEAR'S EXPERIENCE OF A THERAPEUTIC SCHOOL EJ 035 539

LEVENSON, MARVIN
PHENOMENAL ENVIRONMENTAL OPPRESSIVENESS IN SUICIDAL ADOLESCENTS EJ 061 063

LEVENSTEIN, PHYLLIS
SYMPOSIUM ON PARENT-CENTERED EDUCATION: 2. LEARNING THROUGH (AND FROM) MOTHERS EJ 054 378

LEVIN, BARBARA
A PRESCHOOL ARTICULATION AND LANGUAGE SCREENING FOR THE IDENTIFICATION OF SPEECH DISORDERS. FINAL REPORT. ED051889

LEVIN, JOEL R.
THE ROLE OF OVERT ACTIVITY IN CHILDREN'S IMAGERY PRODUCTION EJ 059 315

LEVINE, LOUIS S.
A PRELIMINARY INVESTIGATION TO ESTABLISH A REGIONAL CENTER FOR EDUCATIONAL DEVELOPMENTAL STUDIES OF DISADVANTAGED PRESCHOOL CHILDREN. FINAL REPORT. ED017318

LEVINE, SAMUEL
DEVELOPMENT OF A SOCIAL COMPETENCY SCALE FOR PRESCHOOL CHILDREN. FINAL REPORT. ED020004

LEVINSON, ELIZABETH J.
THE MODIFICATION OF INTELLIGENCE BY TRAINING IN THE VERBALIZATION OF WORD DEFINITIONS AND SIMPLE CONCEPTS EJ 052 594

LEVITT, EUGENE E.
METHODOLIGICAL CONSIDERATIONS IN DEVISING HEAD START PROGRAM EVALUATIONS. ED025319

LEWIS, CLAUDIA
LITERATURE FOR YOUNG CHILDREN EJ 002 654
BOOKS FOR YOUNG CHILDREN EJ 043 020

LEWIS, GERTRUDE M.
I AM--I WANT--I NEED: PREADOLESCENTS LOOK AT THEMSELVES AND THEIR VALUES EJ 017 446

LEWIS, HAROLD
PARENTAL AND COMMUNITY NEGLECT--TWIN RESPONSIBILITIES OF PROTECTIVE SERVICES EJ 007 446

LEWIS, JUDITH
FURTHER EVIDENCE ON THE STABILITY OF THE FACTOR STRUCTURE OF THE TEST ANXIETY SCALE FOR SCHILDREN. ED023485
THE ASSESSMENT OF ACHIEVEMENT ANXIETIES IN CHILDREN: HOW IMPORTANT IS RESPONSE SET AND MULTIDIMENSIONALITY IN THE TEST ANXIETY SCALE FOR CHILDREN? ED025313

LEWIS, M.
MOTHER-INFANT INTERACTION AND INFANT DEVELOPMENT AMONG THE WOLOF OF SENEGAL EJ 051 017
INFANT DEVELOPMENT IN LOWER-CLASS AMERICAN FAMILIES EJ 060 012

LEWIS, MELVIN
INFORMED CONSENT IN PEDIATRIC RESEARCH EJ 007 413

LEWIS, MICHAEL
NOVELTY AND FAMILIARITY AS DETERMINANTS OF INFANT ATTENTION WITHIN THE FIRST YEAR. ED023483
INFANTS' RESPONSES TO FACIAL STIMULI DURING THE FIRST YEAR OF LIFE: EXPLORATORY STUDIES IN THE DEVELOPMENT OF A FACE SCHEMA. ED024455
PERCEPTUAL-COGNITIVE DEVELOPMENT IN INFANCY: A GENERALIZED EXPECTANCY MODEL AS A FUNCTION OF THE MOTHER-INFANT INTERACTION. ED024470
ERROR, RESPONSE TIME AND IQ: SEX DIFFERENCES IN COGNITIVE STYLE OF PRESCHOOL CHILDREN. ED026122
THE MEANING OF AN ORIENTING RESPONSE: A STUDY IN THE HIERARCHICAL ORDER OF ATTENDING. ED047794
INFANT DEVELOPMENT IN LOWER CLASS AMERICAN FAMILIES. ED049836
MOTHER-INFANT INTERACTION AND INFANT DEVELOPMENT AMONG THE WOLOF OF SENEGAL. ED051885
STATE AS AN INFANT-ENVIRONMENT INTERACTION: AN ANALYSIS OF MOTHER-INFANT BEHAVIOR AS A FUNCTION OF SEX. ED052829
WHAT'S THROWN OUT WITH THE BATH WATER: A BABY? ED053801
APPLICATION OF MARKOV PROCESSES TO THE CONCEPT OF STATE. ED053813
PERCEPTUAL-COGNITIVE DEVELOPMENT IN INFANCY: A GENERALIZED EXPECTANCY MODEL AS A FUNCTION OF THE MOTHER-INFANT INTERACTION EJ 003 553
A DEVELOPMENTAL STUDY OF INFORMATION PROCESSING WITHIN THE FIRST THREE YEARS OF LIFE: RESPONSE DECREMENT TO A REDUNDANT SIGNAL EJ 013 947
ON RELATING AN INFANT'S OBSERVATION TIME OF VISUAL STIMULI WITH CHOICE-THEORY ANALYSIS EJ 019 016

AN EXPLORATORY STUDY OF RESTING CARDIAC RATE AND VARIABILITY FROM THE LAST TRIMESTER OF PRENATAL LIFE THROUGH THE FIRST YEAR OF POSTNATAL LIFE EJ 025 376
ATTENTION DISTRIBUTION IN THE 24-MONTH-OLD CHILD: VARIATIONS IN COMPLEXITY AND INCONGRUITY OF THE HUMAN FORM EJ 040 296
WHAT'S THROWN OUT WITH THE BATH WATER: A BABY? EJ 052 445
STATE AS AN INFANT-ENVIRONMENT INTERACTION: AN ANALYSIS OF MOTHER-INFANT INTERACTIONS AS A FUNCTION OF SEX EJ 058 221

LEWIS, WILBERT W.
ECOLOGICAL PLANNING FOR DISTURBED CHILDREN EJ 022 978

LEWIS, WILLIAM C.
THE DEVELOPMENT OF THE LANGUAGE OF EMOTIONS: II. INTENTIONALITY IN THE EXPERIENCE OF AFFECT EJ 061 064
THE DEVELOPMENT OF THE LANGUAGE OF EMOTIONS: III. TYPE OF ANXIETY IN THE EXPERIENCE OF AFFECT EJ 061 065

LIBBY, WILLIAM L., JR.
CONCEPTUAL ENCODING AND CONCEPT RECALL-RECOVERY IN CHILDREN EJ 056 628

LIBERTY, PAUL G.
SOUTHWESTERN COOPERATIVE EDUCATIONAL LABORATORY INTERACTION OBSERVATION SCHEDULE (SCIOS): A SYSTEM FOR ANALYZING TEACHER-PUPIL INTERACTION IN THE AFFECTIVE DOMAIN. ED038188

LIBLEY, WILLIAM L., JR.
REACTION TIME AND REMOTE ASSOCIATION IN TALENTED MALE ADOLESCENTS EJ 029 360

LICKONA, THOMAS
PIAGET MISUNDERSTOOD: A CRITIQUE OF THE CRITICISMS OF HIS THEORY OF MORAL DEVELOPMENT EJ 011 915

LIEBERMAN, JANET E.
THE CAMERA FOCUSES ON READING EJ 032 192

LIEBERT, ROBERT M.
THE ACQUISITION OF SELF-REWARD PATTERNS BY CHILDREN. FINAL REPORT. ED032137
IMITATION AS A FUNCTION OF VICARIOUS AND DIRECT REWARD EJ 018 323
EFFECTS OF VICARIOUS CONSEQUENCES ON IMITATIVE PERFORMANCE EJ 025 635
ASSOCIATION AND ABSTRACTION AS MECHANISMS OF IMITATIVE LEARNING EJ 035 367
EFFECTS OF SEX-TYPED INFORMATION ON CHILDREN'S TOY PREFERENCES EJ 045 191
ABSTRACTION, INFERENCE, AND THE PROCESS OF IMITATIVE LEARNING EJ 047 685
EFFECTS OF VICARIOUS CONSEQUENCES AND RACE OF MODEL UPON IMITATIVE PERFORMANCE BY BLACK CHILDREN EJ 058 139
INFLUENCE OF MODELING, EXHORTATIVE VERBALIZATION, AND SURVEILLANCE ON CHILDREN'S SHARING EJ 058 214
SOME IMMEDIATE EFFECTS OF TELEVISED VIOLENCE ON CHILDREN'S BEHAVIOR EJ 058 216

LIEBLICH, AMIA
PERCEPTUAL EXPLORATION IN ISRAELI CHILDREN EJ 033 054

LIEBMAN, DONALD A.
BODY BUILD, SEX-ROLE PREFERENCE, AND SEX-ROLE ADOPTION IN JUNIOR HIGH SCHOOL BOYS EJ 035 627

LIKE, DORIS W.
MORE ON LEARNING-RESOURCE CENTERS EJ 016 819

LIKOVER, BELLE
THE EFFECT OF BLACK HISTORY ON AN INTERRACIAL GROUP OF CHILDREN EJ 026 735

LIN-FU, JANE S.
LEAD POISONING IN CHILDREN. ED048919
NEW HOPE FOR BABIES OF RH NEGATIVE MOTHERS EJ 003 743
CHILDHOOD LEAD POISONING...AN ERADICABLE DISEASE EJ 013 482

LINDSEY, JAMES F.
A NOTE ON TEACHING FOR CREATIVITY EJ 018 130

LINDSEY, JAMES M.
A LONGITUDINAL INVESTIGATION OF CHANGE IN THE FACTORIAL COMPOSITION OF INTELLIGENCE WITH AGE IN YOUNG SCHOOL CHILDREN. ED026149

LINDSKOLD, SVENN
DEVELOPMENTAL ASPECTS OF REACTION TO POSITIVE INDUCEMENTS EJ 029 359

LINDSTROM, DAVID
THE DISTRIBUTION OF TEACHER APPROVAL AND DISAPPROVAL OF HEAD START CHILDREN. FINAL REPORT. ED042509
CONCEPT AND LANGUAGE DEVELOPMENT OF A GROUP OF FIVE YEAR OLDS WHO HAVE ATTENDED THE SYRACUSE UNIVERSITY CHILDREN'S CENTER INTERVENTION PROGRAM. ED046515

LINDVALL, C. M.
AN EXPLORATORY INVESTIGATION OF THE CARROLL LEARNING MODEL AND THE BLOOM STRATEGY FOR MASTERY LEARNING. ED028841

LINSKY, RONALD B.
OCEANS AND CHILDREN: MARINE SCIENCE AND ECOLOGICAL UNDERSTANDING EJ 029 391

LIPPITT, RONALD
SENSITIVITY TRAINING: WHAT IS IT? HOW CAN IT HELP STUDENTS, TEACHERS, ADMINISTRATORS? EJ 023 702

LIPPMAN, LOUIS G.
SPATIO-TEMPORAL SERIAL PERFORMANCE IN CHILDREN AND ADULTS EJ 021 758

LIPSITT, LEWIS P.
CARDIAC DECELERATION AND ITS STABILITY IN HUMAN NEWBORNS EJ 046 891

LIPSON, JOSEPH I.
THE DEVELOPMENT OF AN ELEMENTARY SCHOOL MATHEMATICS CURRICULUM FOR INDIVIDUALIZED INSTRUCTION. ED013120
AN INDIVIDUALIZED SCIENCE LABORATORY. ED013664

LIPSON, ROSELLA
A MOBILE PRESCHOOL EJ 006 982

LIPTON, AARON
CLASSROOM BEHAVIOR: MESSAGES FROM CHILDREN EJ 031 780

LIPTON, CHERYL
ANTICIPATORY IMAGERY AND MODIFIED ANAGRAM SOLUTIONS: A DEVELOPMENTAL STUDY EJ 041 141

LITMAN, FRANCES
ENVIRONMENT INFLUENCES ON THE DEVELOPMENT OF ABILITIES. ED032126

LITTENBERG, RONNIE
COGNITIVE COMPONENTS OF SEPARATION ANXIETY EJ 039 900

LITTLE, AUDREY
SEQUENTIAL LEARNING BY CHILDREN EJ 035 381

LITTNER, NER
VIOLENCE AS A SYMPTOM OF CHILDHOOD EMOTIONAL ILLNESS EJ 055 536

LIVESEY, P. J.
SEQUENTIAL LEARNING BY CHILDREN EJ 035 381

LIVINGSTON, MYRA COHN
LITERATURE, CREATIVITY AND IMAGINATION EJ 056 090

LIVINGSTONE, JOHN B.
COMPREHENSIVE CHILD PSYCHIATRY THROUGH A TEAM APPROACH EJ 008 042

LLOYD, BARBARA B.
STUDIES OF CONSERVATION WITH YORUBA CHILDREN OF DIFFERING AGES AND EXPERIENCE EJ 041 135

LOCATIS, CRAIG
PERFORMANCE OF KINDERGARTEN CHILDREN FROM LOW INCOME FAMILIES ON SELECTED CONCEPT CATEGORIES. ED028847

LOCKE, JOHN L.
YOUNG CHILDREN'S USE OF THE SPEECH CODE IN A RECALL TASK EJ 033 792

LOEFFLER, MARGARET HOWARD
THE PREPARED ENVIRONMENT AND ITS RELATIONSHIP TO LEARNING. ED025302

LOMBARD, AVIMA
HEAD START RESEARCH AND EVALUATION OFFICE, UNIVERSITY OF CALIFORNIA AT LOS ANGELES. APPENDIX I TO THE ANNUAL REPORT, NOVEMBER 1967. ED020793
EFFECT OF VERBALIZATION ON YOUNG CHILDREN'S LEARNING OF A MANIPULATIVE SKILL. ED035447
EFFECT OF VERBALIZATION ON YOUNG CHILDREN'S LEARNING OF A MANIPULATIVE SKILL EJ 020 520

LOMBARD, AVIMA D.
PRESCHOOL EDUCATION IN ISRAEL EJ 050 199

LONDON, PERRY
LABELING AND IMAGING AS AIDS TO MEMORY EJ 041 143
THE DEVELOPMENT OF HYPNOTIC SUSCEPTIBILITY: A LONGITUDINAL (CONVERGENCE) STUDY EJ 041 449

LONG, ATAN B.
DEVELOPMENT OF DIRECTIONALITY IN CHILDREN: AGES SIX THROUGH TWELVE EJ 058 137

LONG, BARBARA ELLIS
BEHAVIORAL SCIENCE FOR ELEMENTARY-SCHOOL PUPILS EJ 014 306

LONG, BARBARA H.
SOCIAL SCHEMATA OF SCHOOL BEGINNERS: SOME DEMOGRAPHIC CORRELATES EJ 030 713

SELF-DESCRIPTION AS A FUNCTION OF EVALUATIVE AND ACTIVITY RATINGS AMONG AMERICAN AND INDIAN ADOLESCENTS EJ 034 042

LONG, BARBARA H., ED.
SELF-SOCIAL CONSTRUCTS OF CHILDREN. ED021615

LONG, NICHOLAS
HELPING CHILDREN COPE WITH FEELINGS. EJ 002 018

LONGHURST, THOMAS M.
PERCEPTUAL INADEQUACY AND COMMUNICATIVE INEFFECTIVENESS IN INTERPERSONAL COMMUNICATION EJ 056 627

LOO, CHALSA
ACTIVITY LEVEL AND MOTOR INHIBITION: THEIR RELATIONSHIP TO INTELLIGENCE-TEST PERFORMANCE IN NORMAL CHILDREN EJ 046 242

LOOFF, DAVID H.
PSYCHOPHYSIOLOGIC AND CONVERSION REACTIONS IN CHILDREN: SELECTIVE INCIDENCE IN VERBAL AND NONVERBAL FAMILIES EJ 023 429

LOOFT, W. R.
THE EVOLUTION OF DEVELOPMENTAL PSYCHOLOGY: A COMPARISON OF HANDBOOKS EJ 061 074

LOOFT, WILLIAM R.
CHILDREN'S JUDGMENTS OF AGE. ED043392
SEX DIFFERENCES IN THE EXPRESSION OF VOCATIONAL ASPIRATIONS BY ELEMENTARY SCHOOL CHILDREN EJ 043 481
CHILDREN'S JUDGMENTS OF AGE EJ 052 461
DEVELOPMENT OF DIRECTIONALITY IN CHILDREN: AGES SIX THROUGH TWELVE EJ 058 137

LOPATE, PHILLIP
PRESCHOOL PROGRAMS AND THE INTELLECTUAL DEVELOPMENT OF DISADVANTAGED CHILDREN. ED024473

LOUGHERY, DONALD L., JR.
OPTIMAL OPERATION OF PUBLIC/PRIVATE CHILD WELFARE DELIVERY SYSTEMS EJ 031 540

LOURIE, NORMAN V.
FUNDING CHILD CARE PROGRAMS UNDER TITLE IV-A EJ 060 452

LOVANO, JESSIE J.
THE RELATION OF CONCEPTUAL STYLES AND MODE OF PERCEPTION TO GRAPHIC EXPRESSION. ED040743

LOVE, JOHN M.
CHILDREN'S IMITATION OF GRAMMATICAL AND UNGRAMMATICAL SENTENCES EJ 059 555

LOVINGER, SOPHIE L.
THE INTERPLAY OF SOME EGO FUNCTIONS IN SIX YEAR OLD CHILDREN. ED020005

LOVRIC, MILENA
LE NOUVEAU PROGRAMME D'ACTIVITES EDUCATRICES DANS LES ESTABLISSEMENTS PRESCOLAIRES EN YOUGOSLAVIE EJ 045 011

LOW, SETH
CHILD CARE ARRANGEMENTS OF WORKING MOTHERS IN THE UNITED STATES. ED040738

LOWENSTEIN, R.
THE EFFECT OF SOCIAL INTERACTION ON ACTIVITY LEVELS IN SIX-TO EIGHT-YEAR-OLD BOYS EJ 052 463

LUCAS, MARK
CHILDREN'S PERFORMANCE IN SIMPLE AND SUCCESSIVE-REVERSAL CONCEPT IDENTIFICATION PROBLEMS EJ 049 170

LUFT, MAX
RELATIONSHIPS BETWEEN TEACHER BEHAVIOR, PUPIL BEHAVIOR, AND PUPIL ACHIEVEMENT. ED038189

LURIA, ZELLA
VARIABLES AFFECTING ASSOCIATIVE RECALL IN CHILDREN EJ 056 400

LUSK, DIANE
MOTHER-INFANT INTERACTION AND INFANT DEVELOPMENT AMONG THE WOLOF OF SENEGAL. ED051885
MOTHER-INFANT INTERACTION AND INFANT DEVELOPMENT AMONG THE WOLOF OF SENEGAL EJ 051 017

LYLE, J. G.
CERTAIN ANTENATAL, PERINATAL, AND DEVELOPMENTAL VARIABLES AND READING RETAR RETARDATION IN MIDDLE-CLASS BOYS EJ 022 057
EFFECT OF INCENTIVES AND AGE ON THE VISUAL RECOGNITION OF RETARDED READERS EJ 037 535
EFFECT OF INCENTIVES UPON RETARDED AND NORMAL READERS ON A VISUAL-ASSOCIATE LEARNING TASK EJ 038 266

LYNCH, DANIEL O.
THE EFFECTS OF SCHOOL ENVIRONMENT ON DISADVANTAGED KINDERGARTEN CHILDREN, WITH AND WITHOUT A HEAD START BACKGROUND. FINAL REPORT. ED041640

LYNCH, E. DOLLIE
DAY CARE LICENSING EJ 051 271

LYNCH, STEVE
GRADE INTERACTION WITH WORDS AND PICTURES IN A PAIRED-ASSOCIATE TASK: A PROPOSED EXPLANATION EJ 057 910

LYNN, DAVID B.
PARENT PREFERENCE OF PRESCHOOL CHILDREN. ED041628

LYTTON, HUGH
READING DISABILITY AND DIFFICULTIES IN FINGER LOCALIZATION AND RIGHT-LEFT DISCRIMINATION EJ 045 083
OBSERVATION STUDIES OF PARENT-CHILD INTERACTION: A METHODOLOGICAL REVIEW EJ 046 466

MAAS, HENRY S.
CHILDREN'S ENVIRONMENTS AND CHILD WELFARE EJ 037 184

MACCOBY, ELEANOR E.
MOTHER-ATTACHMENT AND STRANGER-REACTIONS IN THE THIRD YEAR OF LIFE EJ 062 594

MACDONALD, A. P., JR.
ANXIETY, AFFILIATION, AND SOCIAL ISOLATION EJ 027 343

MACDONALD, JAMES B.
A CASE AGAINST BEHAVIORAL OBJECTIVES EJ 027 826

MACDOUGALL, JAMES C.
EARLY AUDITORY DEPRIVATION AND SENSORY COMPENSATION EJ 044 118

MACHT, JOEL
EXAMINATION AND REEVALUATION OF PROSTHETIC LENSES EMPLOYING AN OPERANT PROCEDURE FOR MEASURING SUBJECTIVE VISUAL ACUITY IN A RETARDED CHILD EJ 029 382

MACINTYRE, J. MCEWAN
ADOLESCENCE, IDENTITY, AND FOSTER FAMILY CARE EJ 030 652

MACKAY, C. K.
MATRICES, THREE BY THREE: CLASSIFICATION AND SERIATION EJ 025 470

MACKEITH, RONALD
SLEEP PROBLEMS EJ 011 345

MACKINNON, DONALD W.
IDENTIFICATION AND DEVELOPMENT OF CREATIVE ABILITIES. ED027965

MACKLER, BERNARD
A PREKINDERGARTEN PROGRAM FOR FOUR-YEAR-OLDS, WITH A REVIEW OF THE LITERATURE ON PRESCHOOL EDUCATION. AN OCCASIONAL PAPER. ED026124

MACKWORTH, N. H.
HOW ADULTS AND CHILDREN SEARCH AND RECOGNIZE PICTURES EJ 029 384

MACMILLAN, DONALD L.
EFFECT OF INSTRUCTIONAL SET ON TWELVE-YEAR-OLD CHILDREN'S PERCEPTION OF INTERRUPTION EJ 034 921
NORMAL AND RETARDED CHILDREN'S EXPECTANCY FOR FAILURE EJ 039 266

MACNAMARA, JOHN
FAMILY CORRELATES OF VERBAL REASONING ABILITY EJ 061 069

MADDOX, G. A.
STRONG WORDS EJ 001 116

MADSEN, MILLARD C.
COOPERATION AND COMPETITION OF MEXICAN, MEXICAN-AMERICAN, AND ANGLO-AMERICAN CHILDREN OF TWO AGES UNDER FOUR INSTRUCTIONAL SETS EJ 041 957
COOPERATION AND COMPETITION IN FOUR-YEAR-OLDS AS A FUNCTION OF REWARD CONTINGENCY AND SUBCULTURE EJ 045 453
EXPERIMENTAL ANALYSES OF COOPERATION AND COMPETITION OF ANGLO-AMERICAN AND MEXICAN CHILDREN EJ 053 647

MADSEN, MILLARD, C.
COOPERATIVE AND COMPETITIVE BEHAVIOR OF URBAN AFRO-AMERICAN, ANGLO-AMERICAN, MEXICAN-AMERICAN, AND MEXICAN VILLAGE CHILDREN EJ 024 033

MAEHR, MARTIN L.
PERSISTENCE AS A FUNCTION OF CONCEPTUAL STRUCTURE AND QUALITY OF FEEDBACK EJ 032 932
FREEDOM FROM EXTERNAL EVALUATION EJ 055 897

MAGARO, PETER A.
THE CONNOTATIVE MEANING OF PARENT-CHILD RELATIONSHIPS AS RELATED TO PERCEIVED MATERNAL WARMTH AND CONTROL EJ 025 471

MAGOON, A. JON
THE CURIOSITY DIMENSION OF FIFTH-GRADE CHILDREN: A FACTORIAL DISCRIMINANT ANALYSIS EJ 056 623

MAHAN, JAMES M.
THE TEACHER'S VIEW OF THE PRINCIPAL'S ROLE IN INNOVATION EJ 018 957

MAJORS, HUGHIE LEE
WORKING TOGETHER WORKS EJ 044 510

MALIPHANT, RODNEY
AUTONOMIC RESPONSES OF MALE ADOLESCENTS EXHIBITING REFRACTORY BEHAVIOUR IN SCHOOL EJ 045 109

MALONE, MARGARET
FEDERAL INVOLVEMENT IN DAY CARE. ED048931

MALUCCIO, ANTHONY N.
USING A STEP TOWARD PROFESSIONALISM IN TRAINING OF CHILD CARE STAFF EJ 017 850

MAMULA, RICHARD A.
THE USE OF DEVELOPMENTAL PLANS FOR MENTALLY RETARDED CHILDREN IN FOSTER FAMILY CARE EJ 035 803

MANDEL, DAVID MARC
FINAL REPORT ON HEAD START EVALUATION AND RESEARCH--1966-67 TO THE INSTITUTE FOR EDUCATIONAL DEVELOPMENT. SECTION III, INFLUENCING ATTITUDES OF PARENTS AND TEACHERS THROUGH REWARDING CHILDREN. ED019119

MANDELL, WALLACE
CONSEQUENCES OF LOW BIRTH WEIGHT EJ 030 430

MANLEY, MERLIN J.
DEVELOPMENTAL TRENDS IN GENERAL AND TEST ANXIETY AMONG JUNIOR AND SENIOR HIGH SCHOOL STUDENTS EJ 061 062

MANN, MARLIS
THE EFFECTS OF A PRESCHOOL LANGUAGE PROGRAM ON TWO-YEAR-OLD CHILDREN AND THEIR MOTHERS. FINAL REPORT. ED045224

MANNING, BRAD A.
COOPERATIVE, TRUSTING BEHAVIOR AS A FUNCTION OF ETHNIC GROUP SIMILARITY-DISSIMILARITY AND OF IMMEDIATE AND DELAYED REWARD IN A TWO-PERSON GAME. PART OF THE FINAL REPORT. ED025322
A REPLICATION AND EXTENSION STUDY ON N-LENGTH, INHIBITION AND COOPERATIVE BEHAVIOR WITH A MEXICAN-AMERICAN POPULATION. PART OF THE FINAL REPORT ON HEAD START EVALUATION AND RESEARCH: 1968-69 TO THE OFFICE OF ECONOMIC OPPORTUNITY. ED037249
THE EFFECT OF N-LENGTH ON THE DEVELOPMENT OF COOPERATIVE AND NON-COOPERATIVE BEHAVIOR IN A TWO-PERSON GAME. PART OF THE FINAL REPORT ON HEAD START EVALUATION AND RESEARCH: 1968-69 TO THE OFFICE OF ECONOMIC OPPORTUNITY. ED038172

MANSKE, MARY E.
THE RELATIONSHIP OF INDIVIDUAL DIFFERENCES IN THE ORIENTING RESPONSE TO COMPLEX LEARNING IN KINDERGARTNERS. ED031299
THE RELATIONSHIP OF INDIVIDUAL DIFFERENCES IN THE ORIENTING RESPONSE TO COMPLEX LEARNING IN KINDERGARTNERS. REPORT FROM THE MOTIVATION AND INDIVIDUAL DIFFERENCES IN LEARNING AND RETENTION PROJECT. ED046544

MANSON, GARY
SOCIAL ISSUES, SOCIAL ACTION, AND THE SOCIAL STUDIES EJ 052 767

MARASCUILO, LEONARD A.
LEARNING TO LISTEN: A STUDY IN AUDITORY PERCEPTION EJ 053 485

MARCIA, JAMES E.
PARENTAL DETERMINANTS OF PEER-ORIENTATION AND SELF-ORIENTATION AMONG PREADOLESCENTS EJ 019 387

MARCUS, IRWIN M.
THE INFLUENCE OF TEACHER-CHILD INTERACTION ON THE LEARNING PROCESS EJ 048 235

MARGOLIN, EDYTHE
CRUCIAL ISSUES IN CONTEMPORARY EARLY CHILDHOOD EDUCATION EJ 006 984

MARLAND, SIDNEY P.
PROBLEMS AND PROSPECTS OF EDUCATION IN THE BIG CITIES AS EXEMPLIFIED BY PITTSBURGH, PENNSYLVANIA. ED022542

MARSDEN, GERALD
RESIDENTIAL TREATMENT OF CHILDREN; A SURVEY OF INSTITUTIONAL CHARACTERISTICS EJ 022 980

MARSH, MARION
AN INSTRUMENT FOR MEASURING CREATIVITY IN YOUNG CHILDREN: THE GROSS GEOMETRIC FORMS EJ 027 586

MARSHALL, WILLIAM H.
THE INITIAL PHASE OF A PRESCHOOL CURRICULUM DEVELOPMENT PROJECT. FINAL REPORT. ED027071

MARTIN, BILL, JR.
THE HUMAN CONNECTION--LANGUAGE AND LITERATURE. ED018271

MARTIN, CLAUDE
VARIETY OF EXEMPLARS VERSUS LINGUISTIC CONTEXTS IN CONCEPT ATTAINMENT IN YOUNG CHILDREN EJ 042 955

MARTIN, CLESSEN J.
MEDIATIONAL STYLES: AN INDIVIDUAL DIFFERENCE VARIABLE IN CHILDREN'S VERBAL LEARNING ABILITY. ED027955

MARTIN, JERRY A.
THE CONTROL OF IMITATIVE AND NONIMITATIVE BEHAVIORS IN SEVERELY RETARDED CHILDREN THROUGH "GENERALIZED-INSTRUCTION FOLLOWING" EJ 043 196

MARTIN, JOHN HENRY
TECHNOLOGY AND THE EDUCATION OF THE DISADVANTAGED. ED031293

MARTIN, JUDITH A. GARDNER
A REEXAMINATION OF THE ROLE OF INCENTIVE IN CHILDREN'S DISCRIMINATION LEARNING EJ 046 237

MARTIN, MARIAN
BEHAVIORAL RESEARCH RELEVANT TO THE CLASSROOM. ED039036

MARTIN, MARIAN F.
EFFECTS OF ADULT AND PEER OBSERVERS ON BOYS' AND GIRLS' RESPONSES TO AN AGGRESSIVE MODEL EJ 052 459

MARTIN, MARILYN L.
EFFECTS OF SOCIAL CLASS ON CHILDREN'S MOTORIC EXPRESSION EJ 025 149

MARTIN, WILLIAM A.
WORD FLUENCY--INTELLECT OR PERSONALITY? EJ 034 313

MARTINDALE, COLIN
SEASON OF BIRTH AND INTELLIGENCE EJ 025 268

MARTORELLA, PETER H.
THE EFFECTS OF EXTRANEOUS MATERIAL AND NEGATIVE EXEMPLARS ON A SOCIAL SCIENCE CONCEPT-LEARNING TASK FOR PRE-SCHOOL CHILDREN. ED047819

MARVIN, ROBERT S., II
ATTACHMENT AND RECIPROCITY IN THE TWO-YEAR-OLD CHILD. ED039946

MASSARI, DAVID J.
REINFORCER EFFECTI EJ 038 267
DISCRIMINATION LEARNING BY REFLECTIVE AND IMPULSIVE CHILDREN AS A FUNCTION OF REINFORCEMENT SCHEDULE EJ 053 717

MASTERS, JOHN C.
CHILDREN'S "IMITATION" AS A FUNCTION OF THE PRESENCE OR ABSENCE OF A MODEL AND THE DESCRIPTION OF HIS INSTRUMENTAL BEHAVIORS EJ 036 080
EFFECTS OF CONTINGENT AND NONCONTINGENT REINFORCEMENT UPON GENERALIZED IMITATION EJ 041 448
EFFECTS OF SOCIAL COMPARISON UPON CHILDREN'S SELF-REINFORCEMENT AND ALTRUISM TOWARD COMPETITORS AND FRIENDS EJ 041 856
SOCIAL COMPARISON BY YOUNG CHILDREN EJ 043 672
EFFECTS OF SOCIOECONOMIC STATUS AND THE VALUE OF A REINFORCER UPON SELF-REINFORCEMENT BY CHILDREN EJ 056 726
EFFECTS OF SOCIAL COMPARISON UPON THE IMITATION OF NEUTRAL AND ALTRUISTIC BEHAVIORS BY YOUNG CHILDREN EJ 056 728

MATHENY, ADAM P., JR.
THE BEHAVIOR OF TWINS: EFFECTS OF BIRTH WEIGHT AND BIRTH SEQUENCE EJ 036 081

MATHEWS, MARY ELIZABETH
DISCRIMINATION OF RECENCY IN CHILDREN. FINAL REPORT. ED030493
AGE DIFFERENCES IN JUDGMENTS OF RECENCY FOR SHORT SEQUENCES OF PICTURES EJ 026 375

MATTICK, ELSE
THE TEACHER'S ROLE IN HELPING YOUNG CHILDREN DEVELOP LANGUAGE COMPETENCE EJ 051 566

MAW, ETHEL W.
SELF-CONCEPTS OF HIGH- AND LOW-CURIOSITY BOYS EJ 019 005
NATURE OF CREATIVITY IN HIGH- AND LOW-CURIOSITY BOYS EJ 021 990

MAW, WALLACE H.
SELF-CONCEPTS OF HIGH- AND LOW-CURIOSITY BOYS EJ 019 005
NATURE OF CREATIVITY IN HIGH- AND LOW-CURIOSITY BOYS EJ 021 990
THE CURIOSITY DIMENSION OF FIFTH-GRADE CHILDREN: A FACTORIAL DISCRIMINANT ANALYSIS EJ 056 623

MAX, DAVID
REPORT ON ACTIVITIES, 1964-1966. ED020016

MAXWELL, MICHAEL T.
THE RELATIONSHIP BETWEEN THE WECHSLER INTELLIGENCE SCALE FOR CHILDREN AND THE SLOSSON INTELLIGENCE TEST EJ 041 725

MAY, ROBERT R.
A METHOD FOR STUDYING THE DEVELOPMENT OF GENDER IDENTITY EJ 046 784

MAYER, ANNA B.
DAY CARE AS A SOCIAL INSTRUMENT: A POLICY PAPER. ED027065

MAYER, MORRIS F.
GROUP HOME CARE AS AN ADJUNCT TO RESIDENTIAL TREATMENT EJ 061 233

MAYER, SHIRLEY
CHILD HEALTH ISSUES IN NEW YORK EJ 060 523

MAYNARD, MARJORIE
NURSES GAIN FROM FIELD WORK WITH YOUNG CHILDREN EJ 007 301

MAZURKIEWICZ, ALBERT J.
THE INITIAL TEACHING ALPHABET AND THE WORLD OF ENGLISH. (PROCEEDINGS OF THE SECOND ANNUAL INTERNATIONAL CONFERENCE ON THE INITIAL TEACHING ALPHABET, AUGUST 18-20, 1965). ED019108

MAZYCK, HAROLD EUGENE, JR.
CHILD CARE PARAPROFESSIONALS: CHARACTERISTICS FOR SELECTION. ED053800

MAZZELLA DE BEVILACQUA, ANUNCIACION
INVESTIGACIONES EN EL CAMPO EDUCATIVE (INVESTIGATIONS IN EDUCATION FIELD) EJ 062 593

MC CULLERS, JOHN C.
VERBAL PAIRED-ASSOCIATE LEARNING IN CHILDREN AND ADULTS WITH ANTICIPATION, RECOGNITION, AND RECALL METHODS EJ 042 959

MCBURNEY, DONALD H.
ESTIMATION OF LINE LENGTH AND NUMBER: A DEVELOPMENTAL STUDY EJ 030 590

MCCAFFREY, ARTHUR
COMMUNICATIVE COMPETENCE AND THE DISADVANTAGED CHILD: A STUDY OF THE RELATIONSHIP BETWEEN LANGUAGE MODELS AND THE DEVELOPMENT OF COMMUNICATION SKILLS IN DISADVANTAGED PRESCHOOLERS. FINAL REPORT. ED047806

MCCALL, ROBERT B.
ISSUES AND IMPLICATIONS OF THE DISTRIBUTION OF ATTENTION IN THE HUMAN INFANT. ED043387
INDIVIDUAL DIFFERENCES IN THE INFANT'S DISTRIBUTION OF ATTENTION TO STIMULUS DISCREPANCY EJ 019 014
AMOUNT OF SHORT-TERM FAMILIARIZATION AND THE RESPONSE TO AUDITORY DISCREPANCIES EJ 025 362
COMPLEXITY, CONTOUR, AND AREA AS DETERMINANTS OF ATTENTION IN INFANTS EJ 029 361
ATTENTIONAL RESPONSES OF FIVE-MONTH GIRLS TO DISCREPANT AUDITORY STIMULI EJ 032 893

MCCANDLESS, BOYD R.
IT SCORE VARIATIONS BY INSTRUCTIONAL STYLE EJ 022 142

MCCARSON, CAROLE
FREE RECALL OF OBJECT NAMES IN PRESCHOOL CHILDREN AS A FUNCTION OF INTRACATEGORY VARIATION EJ 035 368

MCCARTHY, JAN
NON-PUBLIC PRESCHOOL PROGRAMS IN INDIANA. ED050813

MCCARTHY, JANET LEE GORRELL
CHANGING PARENT ATTITUDES AND IMPROVING LANGUAGE AND INTELLECTUAL ABILITIES OF CULTURALLY DISADVANTAGED FOUR-YEAR-OLD CHILDREN THROUGH PARENT INVOLVEMENT. ED027942

MCCARVER, RONALD B.
EFFECT OF OVERT VERBAL LABELING ON SHORT-TERM MEMORY IN CULTURALLY DEPRIVED AND NONDEPRIVED CHILDREN EJ 053 710

MCCLELLAN, KEITH
CLASSIFYING DAY CARE CENTERS FOR COST ANALYSIS. ED047783
CONSIDERATIONS IN DAY CARE COST ANALYSIS EJ 040 722

MCCLELLAND, DONNA
THE UNIT-BASED CURRICULUM. YPSILANTI PRESCHOOL CURRICULUM DEMONSTRATION PROJECT. ED049831
THE COGNITIVE CURRICULUM. YPSILANTI PRESCHOOL CURRICULUM DEMONSTRATION PROJECT. ED049832

MCCLELLAND, JAMES N.
THE EFFECT OF STUDENT EVALUATIONS OF COLLEGE INSTRUCTION UPON SUBSEQUENT EVALUATIONS EJ 017 245

MCCLINTOCK, CHARLES G.
THE DEFINITION, MEASUREMENT AND DEVELOPMENT OF SOCIAL MOTIVES UNDERLYING COOPERATIVE AND COMPETITIVE BEHAVIOR. ED045188

MCCLINTON, SANDRA
STIMULUS SELECTION AS A FUNCTION OF LETTER COLOR AND AGE IN PAIRED-ASSOCIATE LEARNING EJ 043 705

MCCONNELL, FREEMAN
[A STATEMENT REGARDING THE COMPREHENSIVE PRESCHOOL EDUCATION AND CHILD DAY CARE ACT OF 1969, AND OTHER RELATED BILLS.] ED040762

MCCORD, IVALEE H.
A CREATIVE PLAYGROUND EJ 042 406

MCCULLERS, JOHN C.
A REEXAMINATION OF THE ROLE OF INCENTIVE IN CHILDREN'S DISCRIMINATION LEARNING EJ 046 237

MCDANIEL, ELIZABETH LOGAN
FINAL REPORT ON HEAD START EVALUATION AND RESEARCH--1966-67 TO THE INSTITUTE FOR EDUCATIONAL DEVELOPMENT. SECTION VIII, RELATIONSHIPS BETWEEN SELF-CONCEPT AND SPECIFIC VARIABLES IN A LOW-INCOME CULTURALLY DIFFERENT POPULATION. ED019124

MCDAVID, JOHN W.
THE EVALUATION OF PROJECT HEAD START--A CONCEPTUAL STATEMENT. ED015792
PROBLEMS OF EDUCATIONAL EVALUATION IN PROJECT HEAD START--SAMPLING, DESIGN, AND CONTROL GROUPS. ED015793
FACTORS AFFECTING COGNITIVE GROWTH IN PROJECT HEAD START CHILDREN--WHAT KINDS OF CHANGES OCCUR IN WHAT KINDS OF CHILDREN UNDER WHAT KINDS OF PROGRAMS. ED015794

MCDONALD, D. LYNN
THE EVALUATION OF "SESAME STREET'S" SOCIAL GOALS: THE INTERPERSONAL STRATEGIES OF COOPERATION, CONFLICT RESOLUTION, AND DIFFERING PERSPECTIVES. ED052824

MCEWAN, ROBERT C.
CHILDREN'S REACTIONS TO FAILURE AS A FUNCTION OF INSTRUCTIONS AND GOAL DISTANCE EJ 019 415

MCFADDEN, DENNIS N.
FINAL REPORT ON PRESCHOOL EDUCATION TO OHIO DEPARTMENT OF EDUCATION. ED045200

MCFARLAND, MARGARET B.
EXPRESSIONS OF PERSONALITY IN CREATIONS OF LATENCY AGE CHILDREN EJ 041 446

MCGAUGHRAN, LAURENCE S.
CONTINUITY IN THE DEVELOPMENT OF CONCEPTUAL BEHAVIOR IN PRESCHOOL CHILDREN: RESPONSE TO A REJOINDER EJ 018 889

MCGEE, DONALD
A STUDY OF LANGUAGE DEVELOPMENT FROM INFANCY TO AGE 5. ED022539

MCGHEE, PAUL E.
COGNITIVE DEVELOPMENT AND CHILDREN'S COMPREHENSION OF HUMOR EJ 036 820
THE ROLE OF OPERATIONAL THINKING IN CHILDREN'S COMPREHENSION AND APPRECIATION OF HUMOR EJ 046 233

MCGILLIGAN, ROBERT P.
A PILOT STUDY OF A PRESCHOOL METHOD OF PREVENTIVE EDUCATION. FINAL REPORT. ED046541

MCGLATHERY, GLENN
WINDOW BEGINS WITH AN "L" EJ 058 507

MCGRATH, FRANCIS JOSEPH
ATTITUDINAL STUDY OF ROMAN CATHOLIC PARENTS OF PRE-SCHOOL CHILDREN REGARDING THE OPTION OF "CATHOLIC" OR PUBLIC SCHOOL EDUCATION FOR THEIR CHILDREN. ED046488

MCGURK, HARRY
THE ROLE OF OBJECT ORIENTATION IN INFANT PERCEPTION EJ 024 695

MCINERNEY, BEATRICE L.
PRESCHOOL AND PRIMARY EDUCATION PROJECT. 1967-68 ANNUAL PROGRESS REPORT TO THE FORD FOUNDATION. ED027936

MCINTIRE, ROGER
TRAINING ELEMENTARY READING SKILLS THROUGH REINFORCEMENT AND FADING TECHNIQUES. ED034583

MCINTYRE, BARBARA M.
SOURCE BOOK OF SELECTED MATERIALS FOR EARLY CHILDHOOD EDUCATION IN THE ARTS. ED033746

MCINTYRE, MARGARET
BOOKS WHICH GIVE MATHEMATICAL CONCEPTS TO YOUNG CHILDREN: AN ANNOTATED BIBLIOGRAPHY EJ 007 274

MCINTYRE, ROGER W.
COMPARISONS OF VOCAL IMITATION, TACTILE STIMULATION, AND FOOD AS REINFORCERS FOR INFANT VOCALIZATIONS EJ 055 206

MCKEE, CHARLES J. L., ED.
CAN I LOVE THIS PLACE? A STAFF GUIDE TO OPERATING CHILD CARE CENTERS FOR THE DISADVANTAGED. ED049809

MCKENZIE, B. E.
JUDGING OUTLINE FACES: A DEVELOPMENTAL STUDY EJ 045 599

MCKENZIE, BERYL
OPERANT LEARNING OF VISUAL PATTERN DISCRIMINATION IN YOUNG INFANTS EJ 035 623
ORIENTATION DISCRIMINATION IN INFANTS: A COMPARISON OF VISUAL FIXATION AND OPERANT TRAINING METHODS EJ 041 981

MCKENZIE, RICHARD B.
THE ECONOMIC LITERACY OF ELEMENTARY-SCHOOL PUPILS EJ 029 042

MCKENZIE, RICHARD E.
FAMILY FACTORS RELATED TO COMPETENCE IN YOUNG, DISADVANTAGED MEXICAN-AMERICAN CHILDREN. PART OF THE FINAL REPORT ON HEAD START EVALUATION AND RESEARCH: 1968-69 TO THE OFFICE OF ECONOMIC OPPORTUNITY. ED037248
FAMILY FACTORS RELATED TO COMPETENCE IN YOUNG DISADVANTAGED MEXICAN-AMERICAN CHILDREN EJ 053 753

MCLOUGHLIN, WILLIAM P.
CONTINUOUS PUPIL PROGRESS IN THE NON-GRADED SCHOOL: HOPE OR HOAX? EJ 028 100

MCMANIS, DONALD L.
COMPARISON OF GROSS, INTENSIVE, AND EXTENSIVE QUANTITIES BY RETARDATES EJ 015 098

MCMURRAY, GEORGIA L.
COMMUNITY ACTION ON BEHALF OF PREGNANT SCHOOL-AGE GIRLS: EDUCATIONAL POLICIES AND BEYOND EJ 023 392

MCMURTRY, C. ALLEN
EVALUATION DIMENSION OF THE AFFECTIVE MEANING SYSTEM OF THE PRESCHOOL CHILD EJ 054 049

MCNAMARA, FRANK P.
PEER- OBSERVER CONSULTATION EJ 022 532

MCNAMARA, J. REGIS
EVALUATION OF THE EFFECTS OF HEAD START EXPERIENCE IN THE AREA OF SELF-CONCEPT, SOCIAL SKILLS, AND LANGUAGE SKILLS. PRE-PUBLICATION DRAFT. ED028832

MCNARY, SHIRLEY R.
THE RELATIONSHIPS BETWEEN CERTAIN TEACHER CHARACTERISTICS AND ACHIEVEMENT AND CREATIVITY OF GIFTED ELEMENTARY SCHOOL STUDENTS. FINAL REPORT SUMMARY. ED015787

MCNEIL, ELTON B.
THE CHANGING CHILDREN OF PREADOLESCENCE (OR THE QUESTIONABLE JOY OF BEING PRE-ANYTHING) EJ 017 901

MCNEILL, DAVID
THE ACQUISITION OF DIRECT AND INDIRECT OBJECTS IN JAPANESE EJ 036 745

MCPHEE, MIRIAM
BOOKS FOR YOUNG CHILDREN EJ 043 020

MCWHINNIE, HAROLD J.
A THIRD STUDY OF SOME RELATIONSHIPS BETWEEN CREATIVITY AND PERCEPTION IN 6TH GRADE CHILDREN EJ 016 166
A THIRD STUDY OF THE EFFECTS OF A LEARNING EXPERIENCE UPON PREFERENCE FOR COMPLEXITY-ASYMMETRY IN FOURTH, FIFTH, AND SIXTH GRADE CHILDREN EJ 029 281
A THIRD STUDY OF PERCEPTUAL BEHAVIOR IN SIXTH GRADE CHILDREN IN RELATION TO THEIR BEHAVIOR IN ART EJ 041 830

MCWHIRTER, MARY ESTHER
THE DAYS THAT MAKE US HAPPY: GAMES AROUND THE WORLD EJ 038 407

MEAD, MARGARET
WORKING MOTHERS AND THEIR CHILDREN EJ 028 793

MEANS, GLADYS H.
VERBAL PARTICIPATION AS A FUNCTION OF THE PRESENCE OF PRIOR INFORMATION CONCERNING APTITUDE EJ 042 348

MEATHENIA, PEGGY SUE
AN EXPERIENCE WITH FEAR IN THE LIVES OF CHILDREN EJ 045 389

MEDDOCK, TERRY D.
EFFECTS OF AN ADULT'S PRESENCE AND PRAISE ON YOUNG CHILDREN'S PERFORMANCE EJ 045 460

MEDLEY, DONALD M.
RECORDING INDIVIDUAL PUPIL EXPERIENCES IN THE CLASSROOM: A MANUAL FOR PROSE RECORDERS. ED038163
OSCAR GOES TO NURSERY SCHOOL: A NEW TECHNIQUE FOR RECORDING PUPIL BEHAVIOR. ED039923

MEDNICK, MIRIAM F.
AN ESSAY REVIEW: MENTAL RETARDATION AS A SOCIAL PROBLEM EJ 047 341

MEDOW, MIRIAM LUCAS
CONCEPT CONSERVATION IN CHILDREN: THE DEPENDENCE OF BELIEF SYSTEMS ON SEMANTIC REPRESENTATION EJ 053 742

MEHRABIAN, ALBERT
MEASURES OF VOCABULARY AND GRAMMATICAL SKILLS FOR CHILDREN UP TO AGE SIX EJ 021 683

MEHRENS, WILLIAM A.
NATURAL ASSESSMENT OF EDUCATIONAL PROGRESS EJ 021 411

MEIER, JOHN
LONG DISTANCE INTERDISCIPLINARY EVALUATION OF DEVELOPMENTAL DISABILITIES. ED040748
AN EDUCATIONAL SYSTEM FOR DEVELOPMENTALLY DISABLED INFANTS. ED040749

MEIER, JOHN H.
INTERIM PROGRESS REPORT OF A REMOTE TEACHER TRAINING INSTITUTE FOR EARLY CHILDHOOD EDUCATORS (FUNDED BY NDEA TITLE XI). ED017326
AN EDUCATION SYSTEM FOR HIGH-RISK INFANTS: A PREVENTIVE APPROACH TO DEVELOPMENTAL AND LEARNING DISABILITIES. ED043379

MEISELS, MURRAY
CHILD-PARENT SPATIAL PATTERNS UNDER PRAISE AND REPROOF EJ 045 159
FACTOR STRUCTURE OF CHILDREN'S PERSONAL SPACE SCHEMATA EJ 052 466

MELCER, DONALD
SENSORIMOTOR EXPERIENCE AND CONCEPT FORMATION IN EARLY CHILDHOOD. FINAL REPORT. ED019143
RESULTS AND IMPLICATIONS OF A HEAD START CLASSIFICATION AND ATTENTION TRAINING PROGRAM. ED045182

MELSON, WILLIAM H.
AMOUNT OF SHORT-TERM FAMILIARIZATION AND THE RESPONSE TO AUDITORY DISCREPANCIES EJ 025 362
COMPLEXITY, CONTOUR, AND AREA AS DETERMINANTS OF ATTENTION IN INFANTS EJ 029 361
ATTENTIONAL RESPONSES OF FIVE-MONTH GIRLS TO DISCREPANT AUDITORY STIMULI EJ 032 893

MELTON, RICHARD S.
COGNITIVE GROWTH IN PRESCHOOL CHILDREN. ED027057

MENDELSON, ANNA
A YOUNG MAN AROUND THE CLASS EJ 059 445

MEREDITH, HOWARD V.
BODY SIZE OF CONTEMPORARY GROUPS OF EIGHT-YEAR-OLD CHILDREN STUDIED IN DIFFERENT PARTS OF THE WORLD EJ 003 459
BODY SIZE OF CONTEMPORARY YOUTH IN DIFFERENT PARTS OF THE WORLD EJ 010 312
BODY SIZE OF CONTEMPORARY GROUPS OF ONE-YEAR-OLD INFANTS STUDIED IN DIFFERENT PARTS OF THE WORLD EJ 025 469

MERMELSTEIN, EGON
NUMBER TRAINING TECHNIQUES AND THEIR EFFECTS ON DIFFERENT POPULATIONS. FINAL REPORT. ED019988

MERRIAM, MARY-LINDA
TOWARD A DEMOCRATIC ELEMENTARY-SCHOOL CLASSROOM EJ 058 308

MESSER, STANLEY
THE EFFECT OF ANXIETY OVER INTELLECTUAL PERFORMANCE ON REFLECTION-IMPULSIVITY IN CHILDREN EJ 026 153

MESSER, STANLEY B.
FIXATION TIME AND TEMPO OF PLAY IN INFANTS EJ 029 363

MESSICK, DAVID M.
THE DEFINITION, MEASUREMENT AND DEVELOPMENT OF SOCIAL MOTIVES UNDERLYING COOPERATIVE AND COMPETITIVE BEHAVIOR. ED045188

MESSICK, SAMUEL
EVALUATION OF EDUCATIONAL PROGRAMS AS RESEARCH ON EDUCATIONAL PROCESS. ED038165
A STATEMENT ON THE COMPREHENSIVE PRESCHOOL EDUCATION AND CHILD DAY-CARE ACT OF 1969 BEFORE THE SELECT SUBCOMMITTEE ON EDUCATION OF THE HOUSE COMMITTEE ON EDUCATION AND LABOR, MARCH 3, 1970. ED040752
EDUCATIONAL EVALUATION AS RESEARCH FOR PROGRAM IMPROVEMENT EJ 021 380

METALITZ, BEATRICE R.
INSTANT LAW AND ORDER EJ 055 534

METZNER, SEYMOUR
TURNING THE TIDE IN TEACHER QUALITY EJ 034 231

MEYER, DOLORES A.
CREATING CHILD CARE COMMUNITIES THROUGH 4-C PROGRAMS EJ 051 239

MEYER, EDWINA
NUMBER TRAINING TECHNIQUES AND THEIR EFFECTS ON DIFFERENT POPULATIONS. FINAL REPORT. ED019988

MEYER, JOHN W.
EFFECT OF A CHILD'S SEX ON ADULT INTERPRETATIONS OF ITS BEHAVIOR EJ 053 711

MEYER, MARGRIT
FAMILY TIES AND THE INSTITUTIONAL CHILD EJ 012 579

MEYER, WILLIAM J.
CONCEPT IDENTIFICATION STRATEGIES. RESEARCH PROJECT NUMBER 3 OF PROJECT HEAD START RESEARCH AND EVALUATION CENTER, SYRACUSE UNIVERSITY RESEARCH INSTITUTE, NOVEMBER 1, 1967. ED026140
PROJECT HEAD START RESEARCH AND EVALUATION CENTER, SYRACUSE UNIVERSITY, RESEARCH INSTITUTE. FINAL REPORT. ED030486
MEASURING PERCEPTUAL MOTOR ABILITY IN PRESCHOOL CHILDREN. ED032932
THE DISTRIBUTION OF TEACHER APPROVAL AND DISAPPROVAL OF HEAD START CHILDREN. FINAL REPORT. ED042509

MEYERS, C.E.
SIX STRUCTURE-OF-INTELLECT HYPOTHESES IN SIX-YEAR-OLD CHILDREN. ED023469

MEYERSON, DANIEL W.
A READING READINESS TRAINING PROGRAM FOR PERCEPTUALLY HANDICAPPED KINDERGARTEN PUPILS OF NORMAL VISION. FINAL REPORT. ED013119

MEYERSON, MARION D.
THE BILINGUAL CHILD EJ 007 221

MIALARET, GASTON
LA FORMATION DU PERSONNEL NON MEDICAL S'OCCUPANT DU PETIT ENFANT DE 1 A 6 ANS EJ 035 170

MICHAELIS, JOHN U., ED.
SOCIAL STUDIES IN ELEMENTARY SCHOOLS (THIRTY-SECOND YEARBOOK). ED018275

MICHEALIS, MARY LOU
HEAD START EVALUATION AND RESEARCH CENTER, UNIVERSITY OF KANSAS. REPORT NO. VIID, A CASE STUDY ILLUSTRATING AN EXPERIMENTAL DESIGN FOR EVALUATING THE EFFECTS OF SHAPING GROSS MOTOR COORDINATION IN A 31 MONTH OLD CHILD. ED021643

MICHELSON, WILLIAM
THE PHYSICAL ENVIRONMENT AS A MEDIATING FACTOR IN SCHOOL ACHIEVEMENT. ED046496

MICKELSEN, OLAF
THE PREVALENCE OF ANEMIA IN HEAD START CHILDREN. NUTRITION EVALUATION, 1968-69. ED041629

MICKELSON, NORMA I.
MODIFICATION OF BEHAVIOR PATTERNS OF INDIAN CHILDREN EJ 051 472

MICOTTI, ANTONIA R.
DAME SCHOOL PROJECT (BI-LINGUAL PRE SCHOOL PROJECT), SANTA CLARA COUNTY OFFICE OF EDUCATION. FINAL REPORT, AUGUST 1, 1970. ED046514

MIDDLEMAN, RUTH R.
ON BEING A WHITEY IN THE MIDST OF A RACIAL CRISIS EJ 007 362
A SERVICE PATTERN FOR HELPING UNMARRIED PREGNANT TEENAGERS EJ 022 181

MIEL, ALICE
SEQUENCE IN LEARNING--FACT OR FICTION. ED017330
THE WORLD HOUSE: BUILDING A QUALITATIVE ENVIRONMENT FOR ALL THE WORLD'S CHILDREN EJ 037 736

MIKESELL, RICHARD H.
SEX-ROLE AND NEED FOR APPROVAL IN ADOLESCENTS EJ 051 014

MILGRAM, JOEL I.
SOURCES OF MANPOWER FOR THE PRESCHOOL CLASSROOM EJ 049 526

MILGRAM, NORMAN A.
THE EFFECTS OF NEUROLOGICAL AND ENVIRONMENTAL FACTORS ON THE LANGUAGE DEVELOPMENT OF HEAD START CHILDREN--A EVALUATION OF THE HEAD START PROGRAM. ED017317
LINGUISTIC AND THEMATIC VARIABLES IN RECALL OF A STORY BY DISADVANTAGED CHILDREN EJ 041 142

MILHOLLAN, FRANK
ACQUISITION OF COGNITIVE RESPONSES UNDER DIFFERENT PATTERNS OF VERBAL REWARDS EJ 017 712

MILICH, CYNTHIA
AN INSTITUTIONAL ANALYSIS OF DAY CARE PROGRAM. PART I, GROUP DAY CARE: A STUDY IN DIVERSITY. FINAL REPORT. ED036319

MILLAR, SUSANNA
VISUAL AND HAPTIC CUE UTILIZATION BY PRESCHOOL CHILDREN: THE RECOGNITION OF VISUAL AND HAPTIC STIMULI PRESENTED SEPARATELY AND TOGETHER EJ 044 698

MILLAR, T. P.
THE HOSPITAL AND THE PRESCHOOL CHILD EJ 027 341

MILLER, ADAM
MEANING CONDITIONING AND AWARENESS AMONG CHILDREN EJ 049 426

MILLER, ADAM W., JR.
SELF-REINFORCEMENT ESTABLISHED FOR A DISCRIMINATION TASK EJ 025 964

MILLER, DELORES J.
A METHODOLOGICAL INVESTIGATION OF PIAGET'S THEORY OF OBJECT CONCEPT DEVELOPMENT IN THE SENSORY-MOTOR PERIOD EJ 018 891

MILLER, DOLORES J.
A TEST OF HABITUATION IN HUMAN INFANTS AS AN ACQUISITION PROCESS IN A RETROACTIVE INHIBITION PARADIGM. ED046490
VISUAL HABITUATION IN THE HUMAN INFANT EJ 059 511

MILLER, FRANK D.
EFFECT OF PRETRAINING AND INSTRUCTIONS ON AVOIDANCE CONDITIONING IN PRESCHOOL CHILDREN EJ 035 624

MILLER, GEORGE
SOCIAL SKILLS DEVELOPMENT IN THE EARLY CHILDHOOD EDUCATION PROJECT. TECHNICAL REPORT NO. 7. ED052835

MILLER, GEORGE L.
ANALYSIS OF CHILDREN'S REACTIONS TO AEL'S PRESCHOOL TELEVISION PROGRAM. ED052841

MILLER, HAROLDINE G.
A SUCCESSFUL ATTEMPT TO TRAIN CHILDREN IN COORDINATION OF PROJECTIVE SPACE. ED048916
INDIVIDUALIZING INSTRUCTION THROUGH DIAGNOSIS AND EVALUATION EJ 021 629

MILLER, HELEN
RECENT DEVELOPMENTS IN KOREAN SERVICES FOR CHILDREN EJ 032 563

MILLER, J. O.
SOCIOECONOMIC BACKGROUND AND COGNITIVE FUNCTIONING IN PRESCHOOL CHILDREN EJ 021 774

MILLER, JACK W.
DEVELOPMENT OF CHILDREN'S ABILITY TO COORDINATE PERSPECTIVES. ED016516
A SUCCESSFUL ATTEMPT TO TRAIN CHILDREN IN COORDINATION OF PROJECTIVE SPACE. ED048916
INDIVIDUALIZING INSTRUCTION THROUGH DIAGNOSIS AND EVALUATION EJ 021 629

MILLER, JAMES O.
DIFFUSION OF INTERVENTION EFFECTS IN DISADVANTAGED FAMILIES. ED026127
REVIEW OF SELECTED INTERVENTION RESEARCH WITH YOUNG CHILDREN. ED027091
SOCIOECONOMIC BACKGROUND AND COGNITIVE FUNCTIONING IN PRESCHOOL CHILDREN. ED032929
AN EDUCATIONAL IMPERATIVE AND ITS FALLOUT IMPLICATIONS. ED034590

MILLER, JOYCE D.
UNIONS AND DAY CARE CENTERS FOR THE CHILDREN OF WORKING MOTHERS EJ 038 643

MILLER, LEON K.
DEVELOPMENTAL DIFFERENCES IN THE FIELD OF VIEW DURING TACHISTOSCOPIC PRESENTATION EJ 053 743
VISUAL MASKING AND DEVELOPMENTAL DIFFERENCES IN INFORMATION PROCESSING EJ 059 514

MILLER, LOUISE B.
EXPERIMENTAL VARIATION OF HEAD START CURRICULA: A COMPARISON OF CURRENT APPROACHES. (NOVEMBER 1, 1969-JANUARY 31, 1970). ED041617
EXPERIMENTAL VARIATION OF HEAD START CURRICULA: A COMPARISON OF CURRENT APPROACHES. ANNUAL REPORT, JUNE 12, 1968-JUNE 11, 1969. ED041618
EXPERIMENTAL VARIATION OF HEAD START CURRICULA: A COMPARISON OF CURRENT APPROACHES. ANNUAL PROGRESS REPORT, JUNE 1, 1969 - MAY 31, 1970. ED045196
TWO KINDS OF KINDERGARTEN AFTER FOUR TYPES OF HEAD START. ED050824
EXPERIMENTAL VARIATION OF HEAD START CURRICULA: A COMPARISON OF CURRENT APPROACHES. PROGRESS REPORT NO. 9, MARCH 1, 1971 - MAY 31, 1971. ED053814

MILLER, PATRICIA H.
THINKING ABOUT PEOPLE THINKING ABOUT PEOPLE THINKING ABOUT...: A STUDY OF SOCIAL COGNITIVE DEVELOPMENT EJ 025 953

MILLER, ROMANA
LA FORMATION THEATRALE DANS L'EDUCATION PRESCOLAIRE EJ 034 420

MILLER, SCOTT A.
A TEST OF LURIA'S HYPOTHESES CONCERNING THE DEVELOPMENT OF VERBAL SELF-REGULATION EJ 025 956
EXTINCTION OF CONSERVATION: A METHODOLOGICAL AND THEORETICAL ANALYSIS EJ 046 245

MILLER, THOMAS W.
DIFFERENTIAL RESPONSE PATTERNS AS THEY AFFECT THE SELF ESTEEM OF THE CHILD. ED046542

MILLER, WILMA H.
AN EXAMINATION OF CHILDREN'S DAILY SCHEDULES IN THREE SOCIAL CLASSES AND THEIR RELATION TO FIRST-GRADE READING ACHIEVEMENT EJ 021 079

MILLIGAN, JERRY L.
A STUDY OF THE EFFECTS OF A GROUP LANGUAGE DEVELOPMENT PROGRAM UPON THE PSYCHOLINGUISTIC ABILITIES AND LATER BEGINNING READING SUCCESS OF KINDERGARTEN CHILDREN. ED031315

MILLMAN, HOWARD L.
TREATMENT OF PROBLEMS ASSOCIATED WITH COGNITIVE AND PERCEPTUAL-MOTOR DEFICITS EJ 060 501

MILLMAN, JOAN
EXEL ED029698

MINARD, JAMES
A CHANGE OF POSSIBLE NEUROLOGICAL AND PSYCHOLOGICAL SIGNIFICANCE WITHIN THE FIRST WEEK OF NEONATE LIFE: SLEEPING REM RATE. ED034580

MINTON, CHERYL
SEX DIFFERENCES IN GENERALITY AND CONTINUITY OF VERBAL RESPONSIVITY. ED035444
MATERNAL CONTROL AND OBEDIENCE IN THE TWO-YEAR-OLD EJ 056 714

MINUCHIN, PATRICIA
PROCESSES OF CURIOSITY AND EXPLORATION IN PRESCHOOL DISADVANTAGED CHILDREN. ED023470
CORRELATES OF CURIOSITY AND EXPLORATORY BEHAVIOR IN PRESCHOOL DISADVANTAGED CHILDREN EJ 045 456

MIRANDA, CONSUELO
A BILINGUAL ORAL LANGUAGE AND CONCEPTUAL DEVELOPMENT PROGRAM FOR SPANISH-SPEAKING PRE-SCHOOL CHILDREN. ED034568

MIRANDA, SIMON B.
VISUAL ABILITIES AND PATTERN PREFERENCES OF PREMATURE INFANTS AND FULL-TERM NEONATES EJ 029 531

MIRON, MURRAY S.
EXPERIMENTS IN GRAMMATICAL PROCESSING IN CHILDREN. RESEARCH PROJECT NUMBER 1 OF PROJECT HEAD START RESEARCH AND EVALUATION CENTER, SYRACUSE UNIVERSITY RESEARCH INSTITUTE. FINAL REPORT, NOVEMBER 1, 1967. ED026138

MISHRA, SHITALA P.
THE USE OF METROPOLITCAN READINESS TESTS WITH MEXICAN-AMERICAN CHILDREN EJ 026 810

MITCHELL-BATEMAN, M.
HEAD START, WEST VIRGINIA, SUMMER 1966--A SEVEN-COUNTY OVERVIEW, A SPECIAL ASSIGNMENT OF THE WEST VIRGINIA DEPARTMENT OF MENTAL HEALTH. ED017338

MITCHELL, JAMES V., JR.
MENTAL HEALTH. WHAT RESEARCH SAYS TO THE TEACHER SERIES NUMBER 24. ED027087

MITCHELL, MARLYS MARIE
OCCUPATIONAL THERAPY AND SPECIAL EDUCATION EJ 045 234

MITCHELL, SHEILA
THE CHILD WHO DISLIKES GOING TO SCHOOL. ED019999

MITHAUG, DENNIS E.
THE DEVELOPMENT OF COOPERATION IN ALTERNATIVE TASK SITUATIONS EJ 015 393

MOAN, CHARLES E.
PEER INTERACTION AND COGNITIVE DEVELOPMENT EJ 056 708

MOCK, RONALD L.
RACE AND CONFORMITY AMONG CHILDREN EJ 038 937

MOELLENBERG, WAYNE P.
INVESTIGATION OF METHODS TO ASSESS THE EFFECTS OF CULTURAL DEPRIVATION. FINAL REPORT. ED032121

MOELY, BARBARA E.
FREE RECALL AND CLUSTERING AT FOUR AGE LEVELS: EFFECTS OF LEARNING TO LEARN AND PRESENTATION METHOD EJ 039 636

MOERK, ERNST
PRINCIPLES OF INTERACTION IN LANGUAGE LEARNING EJ 059 875

MOFFAT, GENE H.
EFFECT OF PRETRAINING AND INSTRUCTIONS ON AVOIDANCE CONDITIONING IN PRESCHOOL CHILDREN EJ 035 624
AVOIDANCE CONDITIONING IN YOUNG CHILDREN WITH INTERRUPTION OF A POSITIVE STIMULUS AS THE AVERSIVE EVENT EJ 053 719

MOFFITT, ALAN R.
CONSONANT CUE PERCEPTION BY TWENTY- TO TWENTY-FOUR-WEEK-OLD INFANTS EJ 045 597

MOHAN, MADAN
PEER TUTORING AS A TECHNIQUE FOR TEACHING THE UNMOTIVATED EJ 045 393

MONATOVA, LILY
ANALYSE DE L'ADOPTION DE LA NOTION DE "FLEUR" CHEZ LES ENFANTS DE 6 ANS EJ 044 703

MONDALE, WALTER F.
CHILDREN: OUR CHALLENGE EJ 050 423

MONROE, CHARLES E.
STEPS PURSUANT TO SECURING ACCREDITATION BY PRIVATE SECONDARY SCHOOLS EJ 016 606

MONTAGUE, RUTH B.
THE EFFECT OF MEDIATIONAL INSTRUCTIONS ON ASSOCIATIVE SKILLS OF FIRST GRADE INNERCITY CHILDREN. ED038177

MONTEZ, PHILIP
AN EVALUATION OF OPERATION HEAD START BILINGUAL CHILDREN, SUMMER, 1965. ED013667

MOODY, MARK
PROBLEMS OF CONTROL IN SIMULTANEOUS DISCRIMINATION TASKS EJ 058 215

MOORE, DONALD R.
LANGUAGE RESEARCH AND PRESCHOOL LANGUAGE TRAINING. ED040767

MOORE, FREDRICKA
SKILL DEVELOPMENT THROUGH GAMES AND RHYTHMIC ACTIVITIES. ED019996

MOORE, HAROLD E.
A SOURCE REPORT FOR DEVELOPING PARENT-CHILD EDUCATIONAL CENTERS. ED027944
A PLAN OF ACTION FOR PARENT-CHILD EDUCATIONAL CENTERS. ED027959

MOORE, OMAR KHAYYAM
ON RESPONSIVE ENVIRONMENTS. ED018278

MOORE, SHIRLEY G.
THE YOUNG CHILD'S UNDERSTANDING OF SOCIAL JUSTICE EJ 046 887

MOORE, WINIFRED A.
ENRICHING CHILDREN'S LIVES: INTERNATIONAL CO-OPERATION THROUGH UNICEF AND OMEP EJ 062 417

MORAN, LOUIS J.
LONGITUDINAL STUDY OF COGNITIVE DICTIONARIES FROM AGES NINE TO SEVENTEEN EJ 024 940

MOREAU, TINA
EASE OF HABITUATION TO REPEATED AUDITORY AND SOMESTHETIC STIMULATION IN THE HUMAN NEWBORN EJ 021 077

MOREHEAD, DONALD M.
PROCESSING OF PHONOLOGICAL SEQUENCES BY YOUNG CHILDREN AND ADULTS EJ 036 747

MORENCY, ANNE S.
DEVELOPMENTAL SPEECH INACCURACY AND SPEECH THERAPY IN THE EARLY SCHOOL YEARS EJ 013 624

MORIN, ROBERT E.
SHORT-TERM MEMORY IN CHILDREN: KEEPING TRACK OF VARIABLES WITH FEW OR MANY STATES EJ 029 444
ARE THESE TWO STIMULI FROM THE SAME SET? RESPONSE TIMES OF CHILDREN AND ADULTS WITH FAMILIAR AND ARBITRARY SETS EJ 033 788

MORRIS, BERNIECE E.
EVALUATION OF CHANGES OCCURRING IN CHILDREN WHO PARTICIPATED IN PROJECT HEAD START. ED017316

MORRIS, GEORGE L.
EVALUATION OF CHANGES OCCURRING IN CHILDREN WHO PARTICIPATED IN PROJECT HEAD START. ED017316

MORRIS, MARJORIE SIMPSON
THE CALIFORNIA CREDENTIAL STORY: A NEW SPECIALIZATION FOR TEACHERS OF YOUNG CHILDREN EJ 020 892

MORRIS, RICHARD J.
EFFECTS OF CONTINGENT AND NONCONTINGENT REINFORCEMENT UPON GENERALIZED IMITATION EJ 041 448

MORRIS, RUBY
THE ROLE OF THE PRIMARY TEACHER IN CHARACTER EDUCATION EJ 013 232

MORRISON, COLEMAN
GRADE EQUIVALENT COMPARISONS BETWEEN DISADVANTAGED NEGRO URBAN CHILDREN WITH AND WITHOUT KINDERGARTEN EXPERIENCE WHEN TAUGHT TO READ BY SEVERAL METHODS. ED020798

MORSE, JOAN
THE GOAL OF LIFE ENHANCEMENT FOR A FATALLY ILL CHILD EJ 017 423

MORSE, WILLIAM C.
IF SCHOOLS ARE TO MEET THEIR RESPONSIBILITIES TO ALL CHILDREN EJ 022 977

MOSELEY, DOLLY
A SOCIALLY INTEGRATED KINDERGARTEN. ED034578

MOSS, HOWARD A.
THE RELATION BETWEEN THE AMOUNT OF TIME INFANTS SPEND AT VARIOUS STATES AND THE DEVELOPMENT OF VISUAL BEHAVIOR EJ 021 082
AGE, STATE, AND MATERNAL BEHAVIOR ASSOCIATED WITH INFANT VOCALIZATIONS EJ 052 444

MOSS, JOY
AN INTEGRATED DAY WORKSHOP EJ 033 159

MOSS, JOY F.
GROWTH IN READING IN AN INTEGRATED DAY CLASSROOM EJ 055 154

MOSS, MARGARET H.
PROJECT TOBI, THE DEVELOPMENT OF A PRE-SCHOOL ACHIEVEMENT TEST. FINAL REPORT. ED016520

MOSTOFSKY, DAVID
HEAD START EVALUATION AND RESEARCH CENTER, BOSTON UNIVERSITY. REPORT D-III, A STUDY OF PREFERENCES AMONG QUALITATIVELY DIFFERING UNCERTAINTIES. ED022565

MOTTO, ROCCO L.
FROM LEARNING FOR LOVE TO LOVE OF LEARNING: ESSAYS ON PSYCHOANALYSIS AND EDUCATION. ED032925

MOTULSKY, ARNO G.
MEDICAL GENETICS AND ADOPTION EJ 037 577

MOYLES, E. WILLIAM
GROUP CARE AND INTELLECTUAL DEVELOPMENT EJ 040 041

MOYNAHAN, ELLEN
RELATION BETWEEN IDENTITY CONSERVATION AND EQUIVALENCE CONSERVATION WITHIN FOUR CONCEPTUAL DOMAINS EJ 054 804

MUKERJI, ROSE
A NATIONAL DEMONSTRATION PROJECT UTILIZING TELEVISED MATERIALS FOR THE FORMAL EDUCATION OF CULTURALLY DISADVANTAGED PRESCHOOL CHILDREN. FINAL REPORT. ED015788
CONCEPT AND LANGUAGE DEVELOPMENT IN A KINDERGARTEN OF DISADVANTAGED CHILDREN. ED027967
TELEVISION GUIDELINES FOR EARLY CHILDHOOD EDUCATION. ED040739
WHEN WORDS FAIL...DANCE EJ 019 507
WHY NOT FEELINGS AND VALUES IN INSTRUCTIONAL TELEVISION? EJ 038 906

MULLENER, NATHANAEL
SOME DEVELOPMENTAL CHANGES IN THE ORGANIZATION OF SELF-EVALUATIONS EJ 044 186

MULRY, RAY C.
VISUAL AND AUDITORY MEMORY IN CHILDREN. PART OF THE FINAL REPORT ON HEAD START EVALUATION AND RESEARCH: 1968-69 TO THE OFFICE OF ECONOMIC OPPORTUNITY. ED037246

MUMBAUER, CORINNE C.
RESISTANCE TO TEMPTATION IN YOUNG NEGRO CHILDREN IN RELATION TO SEX OF THE SUBJECT, SEX OF THE EXPERIMENTER AND FATHER ABSENCE OR PRESENCE. ED032138
SOCIOECONOMIC BACKGROUND AND COGNITIVE FUNCTIONING IN PRESCHOOL CHILDREN. ED032929
REEXAMINING VARIABLES AFFECTING COGNITIVE FUNCTIONING IN PRESCHOOL CHILDREN: A FOLLOW-UP. ED052818
INFLUENCE OF SUBJECT AND SITUATIONAL VARIABLES ON THE PERSISTENCE OF FIRST GRADE CHILDREN IN A TEST-LIKE SITUATION. ED052819
SOCIOECONOMIC BACKGROUND AND COGNITIVE FUNCTIONING IN PRESCHOOL CHILDREN EJ 021 774
RESISTANCE TO TEMPTATION IN YOUNG NEGRO CHILDREN EJ 032 894
DIMENSIONAL SALIENCE AND IDENTIFICATION OF THE RELEVANT DIMENSION IN PROBLEM SOLVING: A DEVELOPMENTAL STUDY EJ 035 360

MUNNELLY, ROBERT J.
IS IT TIME TO BREAK THE SILENCE ON VIOLENCE? EJ 032 564

MUNRO, NANCY
A STUDY OF FOOD AND POVERTY AMONG 113 HEAD START CHILDREN IN MISSOULA, MONTANA. ED028829
THE RELATIONSHIP BETWEEN HEMOGLOBIN LEVEL AND INTELLECTUAL FUNCTION. ED028830

MURALIDHARAN, RAJALAKSHMI
A COMPARISON OF THE NORMS OF THE PERSONAL SOCIAL DEVELOPMENT OF THE PRE-SCHOOL CHILDREN OF DELHI CENTRE AS OBTAINED BY THE CROSS-SECTIONAL STUDY AND THE LONGITUDINAL STUDY. ED039947
DEVELOPMENTAL NORMS OF CHILDREN AGED 2 1/2-5 YEARS: A PILOT STUDY. ED039949

MURAWSKI, BENJAMIN J.
GENETIC FACTORS IN TESTS OF PERCEPTION AND THE RORSCHACH EJ 045 045

MURFIN, MARK
I WAS A SLOW-LEARNER EJ 017 422

MURPHY, GARDNER
CHILDREN: THEIR POTENTIALS EJ 034 312

MURPHY, LOIS B.
ADAPTATIONAL TASKS IN CHILDHOOD IN OUR CULTURE. ED021632

MURPHY, LOIS BARCLAY
CASE CONFERENCE: A PSYCHOTHERAPEUTIC AIDE IN A HEADSTART PROGRAM. II. COMMENTARY EJ 003 956
CHILDREN UNDER THREE - FINDING WAYS TO STIMULATE DEVELOPMENT. I. ISSUES IN RESEARCH EJ 006 980
FOUNDATIONS FOR GOOD BEGINNINGS EJ 010 588
ENJOYING PREADOLESCENCE: THE FORGOTTEN YEARS EJ 016 966
CHILDREN: THEIR POTENTIALS EJ 034 312

MURRAY, FRANK B.
STIMULUS ABSTRACTNESS AND THE CONSERVATION OF WEIGHT. ED035441
THE ACQUISITION OF CONSERVATION THROUGH SOCIAL INTERACTION. ED047801
ACQUISITION OF CONSERVATION THROUGH SOCIAL INTERACTION EJ 053 708

MURRAY, JOHN P.
TRANSITIVE INFERENCE WITH NONTRANSITIVE SOLUTIONS CONTROLLED EJ 018 882

MURRELL, STANLEY A.
FAMILY INTERACTION VARIABLES AND ADJUSTMENT OF NONCLINIC BOYS EJ 053 737

MURROW, CASEY
CHILDREN COME FIRST: THE INSPIRED WORK OF ENGLISH PRIMARY SCHOOLS. ED050820

MURROW, LIZA
CHILDREN COME FIRST: THE INSPIRED WORK OF ENGLISH PRIMARY SCHOOLS. ED050820

MUSKOPF, ALLAN
AN INTEGRATED DAY WORKSHOP EJ 033 159

MUSSEN, PAUL
INDUSTRIALIZATION, CHILD-REARING PRACTICES, AND CHILDREN'S PERSONALITY EJ 015 199
HONESTY AND ALTRUISM AMONG PREADOLESCENTS EJ 026 450

MYERS, NANCY A.
MEMORY AND ATTENTION IN CHILDREN'S DOUBLE-ALTERNATION LEARNING EJ 042 966

MYERS, NANCY ANGRIST
PERSEVERATION AND ALTERNATION PRETRAINING AND BINARY PREDICTION EJ 057 902

MYERS, ROBERT M.
SCHOOL COUNSELING BY CONTRACT EJ 038 985

MYERSON, EDITH S.
LISTEN TO WHAT I MADE. FROM MUSICAL THEORY TO USABLE INSTRUMENT EJ 029 280

NADELMAN, LORRAINE
SEX IDENTITY IN LONDON CHILDREN: MEMORY, KNOWLEDGE AND PREFERENCE TESTS EJ 023 435
CONCEPTUAL TEMPO AND INHIBITION OF MOVEMENT IN BLACK PRESCHOOL CHILDREN EJ 059 512

NAGEL, CHARLES
SKILL DEVELOPMENT THROUGH GAMES AND RHYTHMIC ACTIVITIES. ED019996

NAKAMURA, CHARLES Y.
INTERACTIVE EFFECTS OF INFORMATIONAL AND AFFECTIVE COMPONENTS OF SOCIAL AND NONSOCIAL REINFORCERS ON INDEPENDENT AND DEPENDENT CHILDREN EJ 022 141
MOTHERS' TEST OF ANXIETY AND TASK SELECTION AND CHILDREN'S PERFORMANCE WITH MOTHER OR A STRANGER EJ 052 449

TASK ORIENTATION VERSUS SOCIAL ORIENTATION IN YOUNG CHILDREN AND THEIR ATTENTION TO RELEVANT SOCIAL CUES EJ 058 413

NASH, HARRIETT
BIG STEPS ON BEHALF OF LITTLE PEOPLE EJ 058 769

NASH, HARVEY
BODY PROPORTIONS IN CHILDREN'S DRAWINGS OF A MAN EJ 025 305

NATALICIO, DIANA S.
A COMPARATIVE STUDY OF ENGLISH PLURALIZATION BY NATIVE AND NON-NATIVE ENGLISH SPEAKERS EJ 052 465

NATALICIO, LUIZ F. S.
A COMPARATIVE STUDY OF ENGLISH PLURALIZATION BY NATIVE AND NON-NATIVE ENGLISH SPEAKERS EJ 052 465

NATHAN, SUSAN W.
AGE-DEVELOPMENT IN THE LINEAR REPRESENTATION OF WORDS AND OBJECTS EJ 030 296

NAVILLE, SUZANNE
PSYCHOMOTOR EDUCATION - THEORY AND PRACTICE. ED029684

NAWAS, M. MIKE
CHANGE IN EFFICIENCY OF EGO FUNCTIONING AND COMPLEXITY FROM ADOLESCENCE TO YOUNG ADULTHOOD EJ 039 902

NAYLOR, NAOMI L.
CURRICULUM DEVELOPMENT PROGRAM FOR PRESCHOOL TEACHER AIDES. FINAL REPORT. ED013122

NEDLER, SHARI
AN EARLY CHILDHOOD EDUCATION MODEL: A BILINGUAL APPROACH. ED038167
INTERVENTION STRATEGIES FOR SPANISH-SPEAKING PRESCHOOL CHILDREN EJ 036 746

NEEL, ANN F.
TRENDS AND DILEMMAS IN CHILD WELFARE RESEARCH EJ 038 571

NEFF, LEONARD
RECIPROCAL CONTRIBUTIONS BETWEEN PSYCHOANALYSIS AND PSYCHOEDUCATION EJ 045 048

NEHRKE, MILTON F.
DISCRIMINATION LEARNING AND TRANSFER OF TRAINING IN THE AGED EJ 055 204

NEHRT, ROY C.
PREPRIMARY ENROLLMENT OF CHILDREN UNDER SIX: OCTOBER 1968. ED032118

NEIMARK, EDITH
DEVELOPMENT OF MEMORIZATION STRATEGIES EJ 047 679

NEIMARK, EDITH D.
A PRELIMINARY SEARCH FOR FORMAL OPERATIONS STRUCTURES. ED024471
DEVELOPMENT OF THE UNDERSTANDING OF LOGICAL CONNECTIVES. ED032125
A PRELIMINARY SEARCH FOR FORMAL OPERATIONS STRUCTURES EJ 023 192
MODEL FOR A THINKING MCHINE: AN INFORMATION-PROCESSING FRAMEWORK FOR THE STUDY OF COGNITIVE DEVELOPMENT EJ 030 289

NELSEN, EDWARD A.
SOCIAL REINFORCEMENT FOR EXPRESSION VS. SUPPRESSION OF AGGRESSION EJ 007 691

NELSON, EDWARD A.
LANGUAGE PATTERNS WITHIN THE YOUTH SUBCULTURE: DEVELOPMENT OF SLANG VOCABULARIES EJ 060 720

NELSON, KATHERINE
THE RELATION OF FORM RECOGNITION TO CONCEPT DEVELOPMENT EJ 056 393

NELSON, KEITH
VISUAL SCANNING BY HUMAN NEWBORNS: RESPONSES TO COMPLETE TRIANGLE, TO SIDES ONLY, AND TO CORNERS ONLY. ED035439

NELSON, KEITH E.
ACCOMMODATION OF VISUAL TRACKING PATTERNS IN HUMAN INFANTS TO OBJECT MOVEMENT PATTERNS EJ 046 250

NELSON, LINDEN
COOPERATION AND COMPETITION IN FOUR-YEAR-OLDS AS A FUNCTION OF REWARD CONTINGENCY AND SUBCULTURE EJ 045 453

NELSON, THOMAS M.
AN EXPERIMENTAL STUDY OF THE SELECTIVE ATTENTION OF CHILDREN OF 1896 AND 1966 EJ 060 775

NELSON, VIOLET
ORCHESTRATED INSTRUCTION: A COOKING EXPERIENCE. ED034593

NEUBAUER, PETER B.
DEVELOPMENTAL GROUPINGS OF PRE-SCHOOL CHILDREN. ED046513
ISSUES IN ASSESSING DEVELOPMENT EJ 030 516

NEUMAN, DONALD
SCIENCING FOR YOUNG CHILDREN EJ 056 863

NEURINGER, CHARLES
PHENOMENAL ENVIRONMENTAL OPPRESSIVENESS IN SUICIDAL ADOLESCENTS EJ 061 063

NEYMAN, CLINTON A., JR.
AN EVALUATION OF THE LANGUAGE ARTS PROGRAM OF THE DISTRICT OF COLUMBIA. FINAL REPORT. ED024449

NIAS, D. K. B.
THE STRUCTURING OF SOCIAL ATTITUDES IN CHILDREN EJ 055 489

NICHOLLS, JOHN G.
SOME EFFECTS OF TESTING PROCEDURE ON DIVERGENT THINKING EJ 052 992

NICHOLS, KEITH A.
SCHOOL PHOBIA AND SELF-EVALUATION EJ 031 445

NICKI, R. M.
LEARNING, CURIOSITY, AND SOCIAL GROUP MEMBERSHIP EJ 035 378

NICKSE, RUTH S.
THE USE OF CREATIVITY TRAINING MATERIALS WITH SPECIAL CHILDREN: A REPORT OF A FEASIBILITY EXPERIENCE EJ 046 058

NICOL, A. R.
PSYCHIATRIC DISORDER IN THE CHILDREN OF CARIBBEAN IMMIGRANTS EJ 051 152

NIEDERER, MARGARET
ENCOURAGEMENT FOR THE YOUNG WRITER EJ 029 414

NIEDERMEYER, FRED C.
PARENTS TEACH KINDERGARTEN READING AT HOME EJ 020 774
REMEDIAL READING INSTRUCTION BY TRAINED PUPIL TUTORS EJ 035 172
DIRECTION SPORTS: A TUTORIAL PROGRAM FOR ELEMENTARY-SCHOOL PUPILS EJ 050 982

NIELSEN, WILHELMINE R.
EXPERIENCES AND LANGUAGE DEVELOPMENT EJ 011 842

NIKAS, GEORGE B.
INITIAL TEACHING ALPHABET AND TRADITIONAL ORTHOGRAPHY--THEIR IMPACT ON SPELLING AND WRITINGS EJ 016 464

NIMNICHT, GLEN
RESEARCH ON THE NEW NURSERY SCHOOL. PART I, A SUMMARY OF THE EVALUATION OF THE EXPERIMENTAL PROGRAM FOR DEPRIVED CHILDREN AT THE NEW NURSERY SCHOOL USING SOME EXPERIMENTAL MEASURES. INTERIM REPORT. ED027076
RESEARCH ON THE NEW NURSERY SCHOOL. PART II: A REPORT ON THE USE OF TYPEWRITERS AND RELATED EQUIPMENT WITH THREE- AND FOUR-YEAR-OLD CHILDREN AT THE NEW NURSERY SCHOOL. INTERIM REPORT. ED027077
PROGRESS REPORT ON RESEARCH AT THE NEW NURSERY SCHOOL: GENERAL BACKGROUND AND PROGRAM RATIONALE. ED032930
A SUPPLEMENTARY REPORT ON EVALUATION OF THE NEW NURSERY SCHOOL PROGRAM AT COLORADO STATE COLLEGE. ED039919
ENVIRONMENTALLY DEPRIVED CHILDREN. ED039937

NIMNICHT, GLEN P.
PRELIMINARY ANALYSIS OF 1968-69 BOOTH ACHIEVEMENT. ED045201
PRELIMINARY ANALYSIS OF 1968-69 HEAD START DATA. ED045203
AN EVALUATION OF NINE TOYS AND ACCOMPANYING LEARNING EPISODES IN THE RESPONSIVE MODEL PARENT/CHILD COMPONENT. ED045205
A PROGRESS REPORT ON THE PARENT/CHILD COURSE AND TOY LIBRARY. ED045206
OVERVIEW OF RESPONSIVE MODEL PROGRAM. ED045207
A REVISION OF THE BASIC PROGRAM PLAN OF EDUCATION AT AGE THREE. ED047774

NIR, YEHUDA
SPECIAL CONSIDERATIONS IN THE OPERATION OF A HEAD START PROGRAM BY A COMMUNITY CHILD GUIDANCE CLINIC EJ 023 704

NIXON, RICHARD M.
STATEMENT BY THE PRESIDENT ON THE ESTABLISHMENT OF AN OFFICE OF CHILD DEVELOPMENT EJ 007 091

NOBLE, MARJORIE
INTERRELATIONS BETWEEN SOCIAL-EMOTIONAL BEHAVIOR AND INFORMATION ACHIEVEMENT OF HEAD START CHILDREN. REPORT NUMBER 5. ED030479

NODINE, CALVIN F.
DEVELOPMENT OF VISUAL SCANNING STRATEGIES FOR DIFFERENTIATING WORDS EJ 043 703

NOECKER, ALBERTINE
A DOLL CORNER UPSTAIRS EJ 013 296

NOLAN, JEANEDA H.
A REPORT ON THE EVALUATION OF THE STATE PRESCHOOL PROGRAM CONTRASTED WITH THE WESTINGHOUSE REPORT ON HEAD START. ED039920

NORBERT, NANCYANN
MATERNAL CHILD-REARING EXPERIENCE AND SELF- REINFORCEMENT EFFECTIVENESS EJ 024 944
STYLE OF ADAPTATION TO AVERSIVE MATERNAL CONTROL AND PARANOID BEHAVIOR EJ 055 105

NORMAN, ELAINE
FAMILIES OF CHILDREN IN FOSTER CARE EJ 007 452

NORTH, A. FREDERICK, JR.
RESEARCH ISSUES IN THE HEALTH AND NUTRITION IN EARLY CHILDHOOD. ED027970
RESEARCH ISSUES IN CHILD HEALTH, I-IV. PROCEEDINGS OF THE HEAD START RESEARCH SEMINARS: SEMINAR NO. 4, HEALTH AND NUTRITION IN EARLY CHILDHOOD (1ST, WASHINGTON, D.C., NOVEMBER 1, 1968). ED036331

NORTH, ROBERT D.
PRE-KINDERGARTEN PROGRAM, 1968-69. EVALUATION REPORT FOR THE PROJECT. ED046511

NORTHCOTT, WINIFRED H.
CANDIDATE FOR INTEGRATION: A HEARING-IMPAIRED CHILD IN A REGULAR NURSERY SCHOOL EJ 026 915

NORWICH, ANTHONY L.
A CAREER DEVELOPMENT PROGRAM IN THE CHICAGO PUBLIC SCHOOLS EJ 035 579

NOSHPITZ, JOSEPH D.
CERTAIN CULTURAL AND FAMILIAL FACTORS CONTRIBUTING TO ADOLESCENT ALIENATION EJ 022 536

NOWICKI, STEPHEN, JR.
CORRELATES OF LOCUS OF CONTROL IN A SECONDARY SCHOOL POPULATION EJ 039 905

NUMMEDAL, SUSAN G.
HEAD START GRADUATES: ONE YEAR LATER. ED048929

NUNNALLY, JUM C.
LEARNING OF INCENTIVE-VALUE BY CHILDREN. ED023473

NURSS, JOANNE R.
DEVELOPMENT OF GRAMMATICAL STRUCTURES AND ATTRIBUTES IN PRE-SCHOOL AGE CHILDREN. FINAL REPORT. ED041639
DEVELOPMENT OF GRAMMATICAL STRUCTURES IN PRE-SCHOOL AGE CHILDREN. ED042485
THE EFFECTS OF INSTRUCTION ON LANGUAGE DEVELOPMENT EJ 013 625

NZIMANDE, A.
CULTURAL DIFFERENCES IN COLOR/FORM PREFERENCE AND IN CLASSIFICATORY BEHAVIOR EJ 024 034

O'BANION, KATY
CONCEPTUAL RULE LEARNING AND CHRONOLOGICAL AGE EJ 047 687

O'BRIEN, ROSLYN A.
PRESCHOOL PROGRAMS AND THE INTELLECTUAL DEVELOPMENT OF DISADVANTAGED CHILDREN. ED024473

O'BRIEN, THOMAS C.
LOGICAL THINKING IN CHILDREN AGES SIX THROUGH THIRTEEN EJ 025 960

O'BRYAN, KENNETH G.
EYE MOVEMENTS, PERCEPTUAL ACTIVITY, AND CONSERVATION DEVELOPMENT EJ 046 249

O'BRYAN, SHARLEEN
EVAULATION OF THE DEMONSTRATION PHASE OF THE TEEN TUTORIAL PROGRAM: A MODEL OF INTERRELATIONSHIP OF SEVENTH GRADERS, KINDERGARTEN PUPILS AND PARENTS TO MEET THE DEVELOPMENTAL NEEDS OF DISADVANTAGED CHILDREN. ED032115

O'DONNELL, C. MICHAEL P.
A COMPARISON OF THE READING READINESS OF KINDERGARTEN PUPILS EXPOSED TO CONCEPTUAL-LANGUAGE AND BASAL READER PREREADING PROGRAMS. A PILOT STUDY. FINAL REPORT. ED029709

O'DONNELL, CAROLYN, COMP.
HEAD START CRIB. CHILDHOOD RESEARCH INFORMATION BULLETIN: SELECTED RESUMES OF EARLY CHILDHOOD RESEARCH REPORTS. BULLETIN NO. 1. ED025318

O'DONNELL, ROY C.
AN OBJECTIVE MEASURE OF STRUCTURAL COMPLEXITY IN CHILDREN'S WRITING. ED016534

O'DONNELL, WILLIAM J.
INFANCY AND THE OPTIMAL LEVEL OF STIMULATION EJ 058 697

O'FARRELL, BRIGID
A STUDY IN CHILD CARE (CASE STUDY FROM VOLUME II-A): "THEY UNDERSTAND." DAY CARE PROGRAMS REPRINT SERIES. ED051892
A STUDY IN CHILD CARE (CASE STUDY FROM VOLUME II-A): "TACOS AND TULIPS." DAY CARE PROGRAMS REPRINT SERIES. ED051893
A STUDY IN CHILD CARE (CASE STUDY FROM VOLUME II-A): "A ROLLS-ROYCE OF DAY CARE." DAY CARE PROGRAMS REPRINT SERIES. ED051895
A STUDY IN CHILD CARE (CASE STUDY FROM VOLUME II-A): "CHILDREN AS 'KIDS'." DAY CARE PROGRAMS REPRINT SERIES. ED051900
A STUDY IN CHILD CARE (CASE STUDY FROM VOLUME II-A): "LIFE IS GOOD, RIGHT? RIGHT!" DAY CARE PROGRAMS REPRINT SERIES. ED051901
A STUDY IN CHILD CARE (CASE STUDY FROM VOLUME II-A) ED051905

O'LEARY, K. DANIEL
MODIFICATION OF A DEVIANT SIBLING INTERACTION PATTERN IN THE HOME. ED023461
BEHAVIOR MODIFICATION OF AN ADJUSTMENT CLASS: A TOKEN REINFORCEMENT PROGRAM. ED023462
A TOKEN REINFORCEMENT SYSTEM IN THE PUBLIC SCHOOLS. ED036323
ESTABLISHING TOKEN PROGRAMS IN SCHOOLS: ISSUES AND PROBLEMS. ED039020

O'NEIL, BARBARA B.
DISSEMINATION AND UTILIZATION OF KNOWLEDGE IN THE AREA OF EARLY CHILDHOOD EDUCATION: A DESCRIPTION OF SOME OF THE PROBLEMS. ED044185

O'NEIL, CARLE F.
WORKING WITH FAMILIES OF DELINQUENT BOYS EJ 007 727

O'NEILL, MARY M.
ADOPTION: IDENTIFICATION AND SERVICE EJ 058 307

O'PIELA, JOAN
EVALUATION OF THE PRESCHOOL CHILD AND PARENT EDUCATION PROJECT AS EXPANDED THROUGH THE USE OF ELEMENTARY AND SECONDARY EDUCATION ACT, TITLE I, FUNDS. ED021621

O'PIELA, JOAN M.
PILOT STUDY OF FIVE METHODS OF PRESENTING THE SUMMER HEAD START CURRICULAR PROGRAM. ED021622

O'REILLY, ALORA
RACIAL ATTITUDES OF NEGRO PRESCHOOLERS EJ 041 858

O'REILLY, EDMOND
CHILDREN'S USE OF CONTEXT IN JUDGMENT OF WEIGHT EJ 033 053

O'REILLY, ROBERT P.
RELATIONSHIP OF CLASSROOM GROUPING PRACTICES TO DIFFUSION OF STUDENTS' SOCIOMETRIC CHOICES AND DIFFUSION OF STUDENTS' PERCEPTION OF SOCIOMETRIC CHOICE EJ 042 791

OBERLANDER, MARK I.
THE RELATIONSHIP OF ORDINAL POSITION AND SEX TO INTEREST PATTERNS EJ 045 111

OCHOA, ANNA
SOCIAL ISSUES, SOCIAL ACTION, AND THE SOCIAL STUDIES EJ 052 767

ODOM, PENELOPE B.
PERCEPTION OF RHYTHM BY SUBJECTS WITH NORMAL AND DEFICIENT HEARING EJ 060 502

ODOM, RICHARD
DEVELOPMENT OF HIERARCHIES OF DIMENSIONAL SALIENCE EJ 055 102

ODOM, RICHARD D.
PROBLEM SOLVING AND THE PERCEPTUAL SALIENCE OF VARIABILITY AND CONSTANCY: A DEVELOPMENTAL STUDY EJ 021 755
DIMENSIONAL SALIENCE AND IDENTIFICATION OF THE RELEVANT DIMENSION IN PROBLEM SOLVING: A DEVELOPMENTAL STUDY EJ 035 360
THE INFLUENCE OF COGNITIVE STYLE ON PERCEPTUAL LEARNING EJ 046 238
DEVELOPMENTAL DIFFERENCES IN THE PERCEPTION AND PRODUCTION OF FACIAL EXPRESSIONS EJ 058 693

OFFENBACH, STUART I.
STABILITY OF FIRST-GRADE CHILDREN'S DIMENSIONAL PREFERENCES EJ 059 319

OGLETREE, EARL J.
TEACHING NUMBER SENSE THROUGH RHYTHMICAL COUNTING EJ 028 717

OHANIAN, VERA
EDUCATIONAL TECHNOLOGY: A CRITIQUE EJ 029 343

OJEMANN, RALPH H.
SHOULD EDUCATIONAL OBJECTIVES BE STATED IN BEHAVIORAL TERMS? - PART III EJ 014 228
WHO SELECTS THE OBJECTIVES FOR LEARNING--AND WHY? EJ 031 849
SELF-GUIDANCE AS AN EDUCATIONAL GOAL AND THE SELECTION OF OBJECTIVES EJ 052 878

OLANDER, HERBERT T.
WHAT PUPILS KNOW ABOUT VOCABULARY IN MATHEMATICS--1930 AND 1968 EJ 035 466

OLCH, DORIS
EFFECTS OF HEMOPHILIA UPON INTELLECTUAL GROWTH AND ACADEMIC ACHIEVEMENT EJ 044 009

OLDS, CHARLES B.
EARLY LEGAL ADOPTION EJ 022 533

OLDS, HENRY F., JR.
AN EXPERIMENTAL STUDY OF SYNTACTICAL FACTORS INFLUENCING CHILDREN'S COMPREHENSION OF CERTAIN COMPLEX RELATIONSHIPS. FINAL REPORT. ED030492

OLIM, ELLIS G.
ROLE OF MOTHERS' LANGUAGE STYLES IN MEDIATING THEIR PRESCHOOL CHILDREN'S COGNITIVE DEVELOPMENT. ED025298

OLIVE, HELEN
SIBLING RESEMBLANCES IN DIVERGENT THINKING EJ 055 106

OLIVER, MARVIN E.
ORGANIZING FOR READING INSTRUCTION EJ 028 960

OLLENDICK, RHOMAS H.
LEVEL OF "N" ACHIEVEMENT AND PROBABILITY IN CHILDREN EJ 039 906

OLMSTED, PATRICIA
MODIFICATION OF CLASSIFICATORY COMPETENCE AND LEVEL OF REPRESENTATION AMONG LOWER-CLASS NEGRO KINDERGARTEN CHILDREN. ED021608
MODIFICATION OF COGNITIVE SKILLS AMONG LOWER-CLASS NEGRO CHILDREN: A FOLLOW-UP TRAINING STUDY. REPORT NUMBER 6. ED030480

OLMSTED, PATRICIA P.
ANALYSIS OF THE OBJECT CATEGORIZATION TEST AND THE PICTURE CATEGORIZATION TEST FOR PRESCHOOL CHILDREN. ED038174
THE GENERALITY OF COLOR-FORM PREFERENCE AS A FUNCTION OF MATERIALS AND TASK REQUIREMENTS AMONG LOWER-CLASS NEGRO CHILDREN EJ 033 052

OLSEN, MARY
IT MAKES ME FEEL BAD WHEN YOU CALL ME "STINKY" EJ 029 358

OLSON, DAVID
VARIETY OF EXEMPLARS VERSUS LINGUISTIC CONTEXTS IN CONCEPT ATTAINMENT IN YOUNG CHILDREN EJ 042 955

OLSON, DAVID R.
LANGUAGE ACQUISITION AND COGNITIVE DEVELOPMENT. ED049811

OMARK, DONALD R.
THE DEVELOPMENT OF EARLY SOCIAL INTERACTION--AN ETHOLOGICAL APPROACH. ED031291

ORHAN, SHIJE
TEACHING MOTHERS TO TEACH: A HOME COUNSELING PROGRAM FOR LOW-INCOME PARENTS. ED028819

ORLICH, DONALD C.
A CHANGE AGENT STRATEGY: PRELIMINARY REPORT EJ 054 727

ORNSTEIN, ALLAN C.
WHO ARE THE DISADVANTAGED? EJ 039 800

OROST, JEAN H.
RACIAL ATTITUDES AMONG WHITE KINDERGARTEN CHILDREN FROM THREE DIFFERENT ENVIRONMENTS. ED051882

ORPET, R.E.
SIX STRUCTURE-OF-INTELLECT HYPOTHESES IN SIX-YEAR-OLD CHILDREN. ED023469

ORTAR, GINA
AN ANALYSIS OF MOTHERS' SPEECH AS A FACTOR IN THE DEVELOPMENT OF CHILDREN'S INTELLIGENCE. ED042504

ORTIZ, ALFONSO
PROJECT HEAD START IN AN INDIAN COMMUNITY. ED014329

OSBORN, D. K.
EMOTIONAL REACTIONS OF YOUNG CHILDREN TO TV VIOLENCE EJ 036 082

OSBORN, D. KEITH
TELEVISION VIOLENCE EJ 006 855
CHILDREN'S REACTIONS TO TV VIOLENCE: A REVIEW OF RESEARCH EJ 028 676
SON OF ROBOT COMMANDO EJ 055 488

OSBORN, D. KEITH, ED.
KINDERGARTEN: WHO? WHAT? WHERE? ED049829

OSBORN, JEAN
TEACHING A TEACHING LANGUAGE TO DISADVANTAGED CHILDREN. ED015021

OSBORN, WILLIAM P.
ADJUSTMENT DIFFERENCES OF SELECTED FOREIGN-BORN PUPILS EJ 041 962

OSBORNE, MARTA
THE EFFECTS OF FEEDBACK VARIATIONS ON REFERENTIAL COMMUNICATION OF CHILDREN EJ 040 360

OSBORNE, R. TRAVIS
A LONGITUDINAL INVESTIGATION OF CHANGE IN THE FACTORIAL COMPOSITION OF INTELLIGENCE WITH AGE IN YOUNG SCHOOL CHILDREN. ED026149

OSSER, HARRY
THE SYNTACTIC STRUCTURES OF 5-YEAR-OLD CULTURALLY DEPRIVED CHILDREN. ED020788
LANGUAGE CONTROL IN A GROUP OF HEAD START CHILDREN. ED020789
A STUDY OF THE COMMUNICATIVE ABILITIES OF DISADVANTAGED CHILDREN. FINAL REPORT. ED032119

OTTINGER, DONALD R.
MATERNAL FOOD RESTRICTION: EFFECTS ON OFFSPRING DEVELOPMENT, LEARNING, AND A PROGRAM OF THERAPY EJ 029 218

OTTO, HERBERT A.
NEW LIGHT ON THE HUMAN POTENTIAL EJ 026 373

OTTO, WAYNE
INVESTIGATIONS OF THE ROLE OF SELECTED CUES IN CHILDREN'S PAIRED-ASSOCIATE LEARNING. REPORT FROM THE READING PROJECT. ED036315

OURTH, L. LYNN
DELAYED REINFORCEMENT AND VOCALIZATION RATES OF INFANTS EJ 036 127

OVERBECK, CARLA
TRAINING IN CONSERVATION OF WEIGHT EJ 021 761

OVERTON, WILLIS F.
ANTICIPATORY IMAGERY AND MODIFIED ANAGRAM SOLUTIONS: A DEVELOPMENTAL STUDY EJ 041 141
STIMULUS PREFERENCE AND MULTIPLICATIVE CLASSIFICATION IN CHILDREN EJ 047 686
PERCEPTUAL AND LOGICAL FACTORS IN THE DEVELOPMENT OF MULTIPLICATIVE CLASSIFICATION EJ 053 649
SOCIAL-CLASS DIFFERENCES AND TASK VARIABLES IN THE DEVELOPMENT OF MULTIPLICATIVE CLASSIFICATION EJ 056 619

OVITT, JEAN M.
WHAT ABOUT THE SCHOOL BUS? EJ 020 294

OWEN, DEAN H.
DEVELOPMENTAL GENERALITY OF A FORM RECOGNITION STRATEGY EJ 037 534

OWEN, FREYA WEAVER
LEARNING DISORDERS IN CHILDREN: SIBLING STUDIES EJ 057 584

OWEN, GEORGE M.
NUTRITION SURVEY OF WHITE MOUNTAIN APACHE PRESCHOOL CHILDREN. ED046508

OWEN, NEVILLE
RESPONSE DEPRESSION AND FACILITATION COMPONENTS OF THE FRUSTRATION EFFECT IN CHILDREN'S BEHAVIOR EJ 059 877

OWENS, DOUGLAS T.
DIFFERENTIAL PERFORMANCE OF KINDERGARTEN CHILDREN ON TRANSITIVITY OF THREE MATCHING RELATIONS. ED048942

OZER, MARK N.
THE EFFECTS OF NEUROLOGICAL AND ENVIRONMENTAL FACTORS ON THE LANGUAGE DEVELOPMENT OF HEAD START CHILDREN--A EVALUATION OF THE HEAD START PROGRAM. ED017317
A STANDARDIZED NEUROLOGICAL EXAMINATION: ITS VALIDITY IN PREDICTING SCHOOL ACHIEVEMENT IN HEAD START AND OTHER POPULATIONS. FINAL REPORT. ED023475
THE DIAGNOSTIC EVALUATION OF CHILDREN WITH LEARNING PROBLEMS: A COMMUNICATION PROCESS EJ 050 321

PACKWOOD, MARY M., ED.
ART EDUCATION IN THE ELEMENTARY SCHOOL. ED018274

PADEN, LUCILE Y.
HEAD START EVALUATION AND RESEARCH CENTER, UNIVERSITY OF KANSAS. REPORT NO. X, ENHANCEMENT OF THE SOCIAL REINFORCING VALUE OF A PRESCHOOL TEACHER. ED021646

PAGE, RAY
CHILDREN LEARN AND GROW THROUGH ART EXPERIENCES. ILLINOIS CURRICULUM PROGRAM, THE SUBJECT FIELD SERIES. ED019132

PAIGE, MARJORIE L.
BUILDING ON EXPERIENCES IN LITERATURE EJ 013 022

PAINTER, GENEVIEVE
THE EFFECT OF A STRUCTURED TUTORIAL PROGRAM ON THE COGNITIVE AND LANGUAGE DEVELOPMENT OF CULTURALLY DISADVANTAGED INFANTS. ED026110
A RATIONALE FOR A STRUCTURED EDUCATIONAL PROGRAM AND SUGGESTED ACTIVITIES FOR CULTURALLY DISADVANTAGED INFANTS. ED026112
INFANT EDUCATION. ED033760
A TUTORIAL LANGUAGE PROGRAM FOR DISADVANTAGED INFANTS. ED040766
THE EFFECT OF A STRUCTURED TUTORIAL PROGRAM ON THE COGNITIVE AND LANGUAGE DEVELOPMENT OF CULTURALLY DISADVANTAGED INFANTS EJ 008 272

PALARDY, J. MICHAEL
CLASSROOM MANAGEMENT--MORE THAN CONDITIONING EJ 027 827

PALERMO, DAVID S.
ON LEARNING TO TALK: ARE PRINCIPLES DERIVED FROM THE LEARNING LABORATORY APPLICABLE? ED023481
WORD ASSOCIATIONS AS RELATED TO CHILDREN'S VERBAL HABITS. ED025329
CHARACTERISTICS OF WORD ASSOCIATION RESPONSES OBTAINED FROM CHILDREN IN GRADES ONE THROUGH FOUR EJ 042 960

PALETZ, MERRILL, D.
PRIOR REINFORCEMENT HISTORY AS AN EXPLANATION FOR THE EFFECTS OF SEX OF SUBJECT AND EXPERIMENTER IN SOCIAL REINFORCEMENT PARADIGMS EJ 030 297

PALMER, EDWARD L.
A COMPARATIVE STUDY OF CURRENT EDUCATIONAL TELEVISION PROGRAMS FOR PRESCHOOL CHILDREN. FINAL REPORT. ED032123
PRE-READING ON SESAME STREET. FINAL REPORT, VOLUME V OF V VOLUMES. ED047825
TELEVISION INSTRUCTION AND THE PRESCHOOL CHILD EJ 062 592

PALMER, FRANCIS H.
EARLY INTELLECTIVE TRAINING AND SCHOOL PERFORMANCE. SUMMARY OF NIH GRANT NUMBER HD-02253. ED025324
CHILDREN UNDER THREE - FINDING WAYS TO STIMULATE DEVELOPMENT. II. SOME CURRENT EXPERIMENTS: LEARNING AT TWO EJ 007 409
SOCIOECONOMIC STATUS AND INTELLECTIVE PERFORMANCE AMONG NEGRO PRESCHOOL BOYS EJ 024 938

PALMER, JUDITH A.
"PRE-SCHOOL" EDUCATION, PROS AND CONS. A SURVEY OF "PRE-SCHOOL" EDUCATION WITH EMPHASIS ON RESEARCH PAST, PRESENT, AND FUTURE. ED016525
THE EFFECTS OF JUNIOR KINDERGARTEN ON ACHIEVEMENT--THE FIRST FIVE YEARS. ED016526
THE EFFECTS OF JUNIOR KINDERGARTEN ON ACHIEVEMENT--THE FIRST FIVE YEARS. APPENDIX. ED016527

PALMER, LEE, ED.
THE WORLD OF THE CHILD. ED050826

PALOMARES, UVALDO H.
A STUDY OF SOME ECOLOGICAL, ECONOMIC AND SOCIAL FACTORS INFLUENCING PARENTAL PARTICIPATION IN PROJECT HEAD START. ED014331

PANANDIKAR, S.
THE PLACE OF PRESCHOOL EDUCATION IN THE EDUCATIONAL SYSTEM EJ 036 329

PANCRATZ, CHARITY N.
RECOVERY OF HABITUATION IN INFANTS EJ 021 078

PANKAJAM, G.
CLASSROOM PRACTICES IN PRE-BASIC SCHOOLS EJ 036 335

PANKOVE, ETHEL
CREATIVE ABILITY OVER A FIVE-YEAR SPAN EJ 058 412

PANSINO, LOUIS P., COMP.
THE MIDDLE SCHOOL: A SELECTED BIBLIOGRAPHY WITH INTRODUCTION. ED029714

PAPALIA, DIANE E.
A DEVELOPMENTAL COMPARISON OF IDENTITY AND EQUIVALENCE CONSERVATIONS EJ 049 167

PAPOUSEK, HANUS
LEARNING IN INFANTS. ED024446

PARASKEVOPOULOS, JOHN
OBJECT CONSTRUCTION AND IMITATION UNDER DIFFERING CONDITIONS OF REARING EJ 048 305

PARISI, DOMENICO
DEVELOPMENT OF SYNTACTIC COMPREHENSION IN PRESCHOOL CHILDREN AS A FUNCTION OF SOCIOECONOMIC LEVEL EJ 043 480

PARKE, ROSS D.
SOME EFFECTS OF PUNISHMENT ON CHILDREN'S BEHAVIOR EJ 006 876
EFFECTS OF INCONSISTENT PUNISHMENT ON AGGRESSION IN CHILDREN EJ 021 992
EFFECT ON RESISTANCE TO DEVIATION OF OBSERVING A MODEL'S AFFECTIVE REACTION TO RESPONSE CONSEQUENCES EJ 043 283

PARKER-ROBINSON, CLEO
CHILDREN'S IMITATION OF GRAMMATICAL AND UNGRAMMATICAL SENTENCES EJ 059 555

PARKER, ANNE
ON THE RELIABILITY OF THE GRAHAM/ROSENBLITH BEHAVIOUR TEST FOR NEONATES EJ 031 630

PARKER, RONALD K.
THE UTILIZATIONS OF CONCRETE, FUNCTIONAL, AND DESIGNATIVE CONCEPTS IN MULTIPLE CLASSIFICATION. ED032112
WAKULLA COUNTY PRESCHOOL. FINAL REPORT. ED039022
THE EFFECTIVENESS OF SPECIAL PROGRAMS FOR RURAL ISOLATED FOUR-YEAR-OLD CHILDREN. FINAL REPORT. ED041638
THE USE OF PERCEPTUAL, FUNCTIONAL, AND ABSTRACT ATTRIBUTES IN MULTIPLE CLASSIFICATION EJ 044 825
TEACHING MULTIPLE CLASSIFICATION TO YOUNG CHILDREN EJ 056 711

PARKER, RONALD K., COMP.
AN OVERVIEW OF COGNITIVE AND LANGUAGE PROGRAMS FOR 3, 4, & 5 YEAR OLD CHILDREN. ED045209

PARNES, SIDNEY J.
PROGRAMMING CREATIVE BEHAVIOR EJ 021 080

PARRISH, VALINDA E.
THE SATURDAY SCHOOL: AN INSTALLATION MANUAL. ED033765

PARRY, MEYER H.
INFANTS' RESPONSES TO NOVELTY IN FAMILIAR AND UNFAMILIAR SETTINGS EJ 056 731

PARTEN, CARROLL B.
A TRAINING PROGRAM FOR VOLUNTEERS EJ 028 502

PARTON, DAVID A.
IMITATION OF AN ANIMATED PUPPET AS A FUNCTION OF MODELING, PRAISE, AND DIRECTIONS EJ 024 693
EFFECT OF THE PRESENCE OF A HUMAN MODEL ON IMITATIVE BEHAVIOR IN CHILDREN EJ 039 904
IMITATIVE AGGRESSION IN CHILDREN AS A FUNCTION OF OBSERVING A HUMAN MODEL EJ 039 907
LEARNING OF AGGRESSION AS A FUNCTION OF PRESENCE OF A HUMAN MODEL, RESPONSE INTENSITY, AND TARGET OF THE RESPONSE EJ 043 198

PARTONG, DAVID A.
EFFECTS OF STIMULUS-RESPONSE SIMILARITY AND DISSIMILARITY ON CHILDREN'S MATCHING PERFORMANCE EJ 016 350

PASSANTINO, RICHARD J.
SWEDISH PRESCHOOLS: ENVIRONMENTS OF SENSITIVITY EJ 037 737

PATON, CORA L.
PATTERNS OF FAMILY ORGANIZATION: AN APPROACH TO CHILD STUDY EJ 030 714

PATRICK, RAYMOND
THE IMPLICATIONS OF PARENT EFFECTIVENESS TRAINING FOR FOSTER PARENTS. ED052821

PATTERSON, GERALD R.
LIVING WITH CHILDREN: NEW METHODS FOR PARENTS AND TEACHERS. ED051887

PAUL, NORMAN L.
INVISIBLE FACTORS IN A CHILD'S REACTION TO TELEVISION EJ 032 934

PAULSON, F. LEON
THE EVALUATION OF "SESAME STREET'S" SOCIAL GOALS: THE INTERPERSONAL STRATEGIES OF COOPERATION, CONFLICT RESOLUTION, AND DIFFERING PERSPECTIVES. ED052824

PAULSON, MORRIS J.
FAMILY HARMONY: AN ETIOLOGIC FACTOR IN ALIENATION EJ 058 508

PAULUS, DIETER H.
DEVELOPMENTAL PATTERNS FOR CHILDREN'S CLASS AND CONDITIONAL REASONING ABILITIES EJ 035 362

PAYNE, JOSEPH N.
THE FORMATION OF ADDITION AND SUBTRACTION CONCEPTS BY PUPILS IN GRADES ONE AND TWO. FINAL REPORT. ED015015

PEARSON, JOHN W.
A DIFFERENTIAL USE OF GROUP HOMES FOR DELINQUENT BOYS EJ 024 028

PECAN, ERENE V.
PROBABILITY LEARNING AS A FUNCTION OF AGE, SEX, AND TYPE OF CONSTRAINT EJ 021 766

PECCOLO, CHARLES M.
DO STUDENTS' IDEAS AND ATTITUDES SURVIVE PRACTICE TEACHING? EJ 013 228

PECK, DONNA
CHARACTERISTICS OF PRIMARY LEVEL CHILDREN. ED036343

PECK, ROBERT F.
SENSORIMOTOR EXPERIENCE AND CONCEPT FORMATION IN EARLY CHILDHOOD. FINAL REPORT. ED019143
MENTAL HEALTH. WHAT RESEARCH SAYS TO THE TEACHER SERIES NUMBER 24. ED027087

PEDERSEN, DARHL M.
SELF-DISCLOSURE AND RELATIONSHIP TO THE TARGET PERSON EJ 007 431

PEDERSEN, FRANK A.
SEX DIFFERENCES IN PRESCHOOL CHILDREN WITHOUT HISTORIES OF COMPLICATIONS OF PREGNANCY AND DELIVERY EJ 024 939

PEDERSON, CLARA A.
NEW DAY IN NORTH DAKOTA: CHANGING TEACHERS AND CHANGING SCHOOLS EJ 033 157

PEDERSON, DAVID R.
RELATIVE SOOTHING EFFECTS OF VERTICAL AND HORIZONTAL ROCKING. ED046504
CHILDREN'S REACTIONS TO FAILURE AS A FUNCTION OF INSTRUCTIONS AND GOAL DISTANCE EJ 019 415
CHILDREN'S REACTIONS TO FAILURE AS A FUNCTION OF INTERRESPONSE INTERVAL EJ 045 043

PEDERSON, FRANK A.
ATTACHMENT: ITS ORIGINS AND COURSE EJ 058 586

PEDROW, DONALD P.
ONTOGENY OF THE LOCUS AND ORIENTATION OF THE PERCEIVER: A CONFIRMATION AND AN ADDITION EJ 023 433

PEET, ANNE
HELPS FOR PARENTS IN HOUSING ED025312

PEISACH, ESTELLE
PERCEPTUAL AND SENSORIMOTOR SUPPORTS FOR CONSERVATION TASKS EJ 018 886
RELATIONSHIP OF CONSERVATION EXPLANATIONS TO ITEM DIFFICULTY EJ 030 295

PELL, CLAIBORNE
TWO CONGRESSMEN LOOK AT AMERICAN EDUCATION EJ 009 032

PENA, DEAGELIA
SOCIAL SKILLS DEVELOPMENT IN THE EARLY CHILDHOOD EDUCATION PROJECT. TECHNICAL REPORT NO. 7. ED052835
FACTOR ANALYSIS OF THE EARLY CHILDHOOD EDUCATION TEST DATA. ED052840

PENDERGAST, KATHLEEN
AN ARTICULATION STUDY OF 15,255 SEATTLE FIRST GRADE CHILDREN WITH AND WITHOUT KINDERGARTEN. ED024438

PENFIELD, DOUGLAS A.
LEARNING TO LISTEN: A STUDY IN AUDITORY PERCEPTION EJ 053 485

PENK, WALTER
DEVELOPMENTAL CHANGES IN IDIODYNAMIC SET RESPONSES OF CHILDREN'S WORD ASSOCIATIONS EJ 042 880

PENNEKAMP, MARIANNE
COLLABORATION IN SCHOOL GUIDANCE: TASK-ORIENTED GUIDANCE AND ITS STRUCTURE EJ 027 918

PENTZ, THOMAS
SITUATIONAL EFFECTS ON JUSTIFIABLENESS OF AGGRESSION AT THREE AGE LEVELS EJ 056 734

PEPER, JOHN B.
ESTEEM AND ACHIEVEMENT IN ARITHMETIC EJ 015 160

PEPER, ROBERT
A PIAGETIAN METHOD OF EVALUATING PRESCHOOL CHILDREN'S DEVELOPMENT IN CLASSIFICATION. ED039013

PERGAMENT, EUGENE
CHILDHOOD PSYCHOSIS COMBINED WITH XYZ ABNORMALITIES EJ 035 078

PERKINS, HUGH V.
CLARIFYING FEELINGS THROUGH PEER INTERACTION EJ 003 083

PERLMUTTER, FELICE
BLACK CLIENTS AND WHITE WORKERS; A REPORT FROM THE FIELD EJ 051 062

PERRONE, VITO
THE NEW SCHOOL EJ 036 327

PERRY, MARY H.
HELPING CHILDREN WITH EMOTIONAL PROBLEMS AT SCHOOL EJ 022 975

PERSKY, BLANCHE, ED.
PRELIMINARY REPORT OF THE AD HOC JOINT COMMITTEE ON THE PREPARATION OF NURSERY AND KINDERGARTEN TEACHERS. ED032924

PESKAY, JOEL
EFFECTS OF SOCIOECONOMIC STATUS AND THE VALUE OF A REINFORCER UPON SELF-REINFORCEMENT BY CHILDREN EJ 056 726

PETERS, DIANNE S.
OF TIME AND THE PRONOUN: A NEW METHODOLOGY FOR RESEARCH IN HIGHER EDUCATION EJ 042 881

PETERS, DONALD L.
SAN MATEO COUNTY HUMAN RESOURCES COMMISSION PROJECT HEAD START - SUMMER 1966. AN EVALUATIONAL REPORT. ED023478
VERBAL MEDIATORS AND CUE DISCRIMINATION IN THE TRANSITION FROM NONCONSERVATION TO CONSERVATION OF NUMBER EJ 025 958

PETERS, EDWARD N.
RETARDED CHILDREN AT CAMP WITH NORMAL CHILDREN EJ 012 199

PETERS, EVELYN
A DAY CARE PROGRAM IN THE MIDDLE EAST EJ 009 815
INTRODUCTION OF NEW CHILDREN INTO A DAY CARE CENTER EJ 011 302

PETERSON, ESTHER
LABOR AND EDUCATION EJ 009 033

PETERSON, LINDA WHITNEY
EARLY INFANT STIMULATION AND MOTOR DEVELOPMENT. ED038179

PETERSON, ROBERT F.
GENERALIZED IMITATION: THE EFFECTS OF EXPERIMENTER ABSENCE, DIFFERENTIAL REINFORCEMENT, AND STIMULUS COMPLEXITY EJ 045 044

PETERSON, ROLF A.
AGGRESSION AS A FUNCTION OF EXPECTED RETALIATION AND AGGRESSION LEVEL OF TARGET AND AGGRESSOR EJ 043 192

PETRINI, ALMA MARIA
ESOL-SESD GUIDE: KINDERGARTEN. ED033748

PETSCHE, MARY
AN EVALUATION OF HEAD START PRESCHOOL ENRICHMENT PROGRAMS AS THEY AFFECT THE INTELLECTUAL ABILITY, THE SOCIAL ADJUSTMENT, AND THE ACHIEVEMENT LEVEL OF FIVE-YEAR-OLD CHILDREN ENROLLED IN LINCOLN, NEBRASKA. ED015011

PFAU, DONALD W.
SYMPOSIUM: FOR AND AGAINST STRIKES EJ 003 416

PFLUGER, LUTHER W.
A ROOM PLANNED BY CHILDREN EJ 007 876

PHILLIPS, BEEMAN N.
MOTIVATIONAL AND ACHIEVEMENT DIFFERENCES AMONG CHILDREN OF VARIOUS ORDINAL BIRTH POSITIONS EJ 055 547

PHILLIS, JUDITH A.
FACTORS? IN CHILD DEVELOPMENT: PEER RELATIONS. ED047796
CHILDREN'S JUDGMENTS OF PERSONALITY ON THE BASIS OF VOICE QUALITY EJ 030 512

PHINNEY, JEAN
AN EXPERIMENTAL GAME IN ORAL LANGUAGE COMPREHENSION. ED038171

PIAGET, J.
INTELLECTUAL EVOLUTION FROM ADOLESCENCE TO ADULTHOOD EJ 050 073

PICK, ANNE D.
SOME BASIC PERCEPTUAL PROCESSES IN READING EJ 015 126

PIEN, DIANA
THE INFLUENCE OF STIMULUS EXPOSURE ON RATED PREFERENCE: EFFECTS OF AGE, PATTERN OF EXPOSURE, AND STIMULUS MEANINGFULNESS EJ 041 960

PIEPER, ALICE M.
PARENT AND CHILD CENTERS--IMPETUS, IMPLEMENTATION, IN-DEPTH VIEW EJ 030 469

PIERCE-JONES, JOHN
OUTCOMES OF INDIVIDUAL AND PROGRAMMATIC VARIATIONS AMONG PROJECT HEAD START CENTERS, SUMMER, 1965. FINAL REPORT. ED014325
FINAL REPORT ON HEAD START EVALUATION AND RESEARCH: 1967-68 TO THE OFFICE OF ECONOMIC OPPORTUNITY. SECTION I: PART A, MIDDLE CLASS MOTHER-TEACHERS IN AN EXPERIMENTAL PRESCHOOL PROGRAM FOR SOCIALLY DISADVANTAGED CHILDREN. ED023454
FINAL REPORT ON HEAD START EVALUATION AND RESEARCH: 1967-68 TO THE OFFICE OF ECONOMIC OPPORTUNITY. SECTION I: PART B, ACCURACY OF SELF-PERCEPTION AMONG CULTURALLY DEPRIVED PRESCHOOLS. ED023455

FINAL REPORT ON HEAD START EVALUATION AND RESEARCH: 1967-68 TO THE OFFICE OF ECONOMIC OPPORTUNITY. SECTION I: PARTS A AND B. ED023457
ANNUAL RESEARCH REPORT OF COMPLETED AND INCOMPLETE INVESTIGATIONS FOR NATIONAL HEAD START EVALUATION. ED025320
THE RELATIONSHIP BETWEEN SPECIFIC AND GENERAL TEACHING EXPERIENCE AND TEACHER ATTITUDES TOWARD PROJECT HEAD START. PART OF THE FINAL REPORT. ED025323
PARENT INVOLVEMENT IN PROJECT HEAD START. PART OF THE FINAL REPORT ON HEAD START EVALUATION AND RESEARCH: 1968-1969 TO THE OFFICE OF ECONOMIC OPPORTUNITY. ED037244
A PILOT PROJECT USING A LANGUAGE DEVELOPMENT PROGRAM WITH PRESCHOOL DISADVANTAGED CHILDREN. PART OF THE FINAL REPORT ON HEAD START EVALUATION AND RESEARCH: 1968-69 TO THE OFFICE OF ECONOMIC OPPORTUNITY. ED037245
A COMPARISON OF HEAD START CHILDREN WITH A GROUP OF HEAD START ELIGIBLES AFTER ONE YEAR IN ELEMENTARY SCHOOL. PART OF THE FINAL REPORT ON HEAD START EVALUATION AND RESEARCH: 1968-69 TO THE OFFICE OF ECONOMIC OPPORTUNITY. ED037247
THE EFFECT OF N-LENGTH ON THE DEVELOPMENT OF COOPERATIVE AND NON-COOPERATIVE BEHAVIOR IN A TWO-PERSON GAME. PART OF THE FINAL REPORT ON HEAD START EVALUATION AND RESEARCH: 1968-69 TO THE OFFICE OF ECONOMIC OPPORTUNITY. ED038172
CURRICULAR INTERVENTION TO ENHANCE THE ENGLISH LANGUAGE COMPETENCE OF HEAD START CHILDREN. PART OF THE FINAL REPORT ON HEAD START EVALUATION AND RESEARCH: 1968-69 TO THE OFFICE OF ECONOMIC OPPORTUNITY. ED039032
A REPORT ON THE RESULTS OF THE ADMINISTRATION OF THE GUMPGOOKIES TEST TO THE TEXAS EVALUATION SAMPLE. PART OF THE FINAL REPORT ON HEAD START EVALUATION AND RESEARCH: 1968-69 TO THE OFFICE OF ECONOMIC OPPORTUNITY. ED039033

PIERCE, WILLIAM L.
DAY CARE IN THE 1970S: PLANNING FOR EXPANSION EJ 037 237

PIERSON, JEANNE
EFFECT OF CLASSROOM NOISE ON NUMBER IDENTIFICATION BY RETARDED CHILDREN EJ 045 391

PIKAART, LEN
BIBLIOGRAPHY OF RESEARCH STUDIES IN ELEMENTARY SCHOOL AND PRESCHOOL MATHEMATICS. ED023464

PINNEAU, SAMUEL R.
BEHAVIOR PATTERNS OF NORMAL CHILDREN. ED015016
SUMMARY OF BEHAVIOR PATTERNS OF NORMAL CHILDREN. ED016531

PITTEL, STEPHEN M.
DEVELOPMENTAL FACTORS IN ADOLESCENT DRUG USE: A STUDY OF PSYCHEDELIC DRUG USERS EJ 051 020

PLANT, WALTER T.
EFFECTS OF PRESCHOOL STIMULATION UPON SUBSEQUENT SCHOOL PERFORMANCE AMONG THE CULTURALLY DISADVANTAGED. ED046545
DIFFERENTIAL COGNITIVE DEVELOPMENT WITHIN AND BETWEEN RACIAL AND ETHNIC GROUPS OF DISADVANTAGED PRESCHOOL AND KINDERGARTEN CHILDREN EJ 049 172

PLATTOR, STANTON D.
PRELIMINARY FINDINGS FROM A LONGITUDINAL EDUCATIONAL IMPROVEMENT PROJECT BEING CONDUCTED FOR INSTRUCTIONALLY IMPOVERISHED PUPILS IN INTACT SCHOOLS IN THE URBAN SOUTH. ED020021

PLATTS, HAL K.
FACTS AGAINST IMPRESSIONS: MOTHERS SEEKING TO RELINQUISH CHILDREN FOR ADOPTION EJ 013 330

PLOGHOFT, MILTON E.
HUMAN RESOURCES FOR INTERNATIONAL STUDIES EJ 038 393

PLUMER, DAVENPORT
PARENT-CHILD VERBAL INTERACTION: A STUDY OF DIALOGUE STRATEGIES AND VERBAL ABILITY. ED049824

PLUNKETT, VIRGINIA R. L.
SPOTLIGHT ON FOLLOW THROUGH. ED029720

PODD, MARVIN H.
EGO IDENTITY STATUS AND MORALITY: THE RELATIONSHIP BETWEEN TWO DEVELOPMENTAL CONSTRUCTS EJ 058 141

POGONOWSKI, LEE
DEVELOPMENT OF A MUSIC CURRICULUM FOR YOUNG CHILDREN. CAREL ARTS AND HUMANITIES CURRICULUM DEVELOPMENT PROGRAM FOR YOUNG CHILDREN. ED032938

POLLACK, DONALD
A SENSITIVITY-TRAINING APPROACH TO GROUP THERAPY WITH CHILDREN EJ 039 501

POLLACK, ROBERT H.
THE ROLE OF LIGHTNESS CONTRAST IN DETERMINING THE MAGNITUDE OF THE DELBOEUF ILLUSION: A REJOINDER TO WEINTRAUB AND COOPER EJ 055 101

POLLAK, RUTH S.
GUIDE FOR RIPPLES. ED051872

POLLOCK, KENNETH C.
LETTER TO THE TEACHER OF A HARD-OF-HEARING CHILD EJ 029 917

POLLOCK, MARGARET B.
LETTER TO THE TEACHER OF A HARD-OF-HEARING CHILD EJ 029 917

POPE, JANE F.
GUIDELINES: PRE-SCHOOL PROJECTS, HEAD START: EARLY CHILDHOOD EDUCATION. REVISED EDITION. ED027948

PORGES, STEPHEN W.
A DECADE OF INFANT CONDITIONING AND LEARNING RESEARCH EJ 038 454

PORTER, MAYNARD
EYE CONTACT, ATTITUDES, AND ATTITUDE CHANGE AMONG MALES EJ 059 813

PORTER, PHILIP J.
EVALUATION OF HEADSTART EDUCATIONAL PROGRAM IN CAMBRIDGE, MASSACHUSETTS. FINAL REPORT. ED013668

POTTER, ROBERT E.
THE CHILD WHO STUTTERS EJ 007 220

POULOS, RITA W.
INFLUENCE OF MODELING, EXHORTATIVE VERBALIZATION, AND SURVEILLANCE ON CHILDREN'S SHARING EJ 058 214

POZNANSKI, ELVA
CLINICAL IMPLICATIONS OF MATERNAL EMPLOYMENT: A REVIEW OF RESEARCH EJ 030 432

PRENTICE, NORMAN M.
INTELLECTUAL DEVELOPMENT OF CULTURALLY DEPRIVED CHILDREN IN A DAY CARE PROGRAM: A FOLLOW-UP STUDY. ED045186

PRESBIE, ROBERT J.
SHARING IN CHILDREN AS A FUNCTION OF THE NUMBER OF SHAREES AND RECIPROCITY EJ 016 840
LEARNING TO BE GENEROUS OR STINGY: IMITATION OF SHARING BEHAVIOR AS A FUNCTION OF MODEL GENEROSITY AND VICARIOUS REINFORCEMENT EJ 052 443

PRESCOTT, ELIZABETH
GROUP DAY CARE AS A CHILD-REARING ENVIRONMENT. AN OBSERVATIONAL STUDY OF DAY CARE PROGRAM. ED024453
AN INSTITUTIONAL ANALYSIS OF DAY CARE PROGRAM. PART II, GROUP DAY CARE: THE GROWTH OF AN INSTITUTION. FINAL REPORT. ED043394
DAY CARE FOR CHILDREN: ASSETS AND LIABILITIES EJ 035 802

PRESTWICH, SHELDON
THE INFLUENCE OF TWO COUNSELING METHODS ON THE PHYSICAL AND VERBAL AGGRESSION OF PRESCHOOL INDIAN CHILDREN. PART OF THE FINAL REPORT ON HEAD START EVALUATION AND RESEARCH: 1968-69 TO THE OFFICE OF ECONOMIC OPPORTUNITY. ED037243

PREVOTS, NAIMA
DEVELOPMENT OF A DANCE CURRICULUM FOR YOUNG CHILDREN. CAREL ARTS AND HUMANITIES CURRICULUM DEVELOPMENT PROGRAM FOR YOUNG CHILDREN. ED032936

PRICE, FRANK
EFFECTS OF REINFORCEMENT BASE-LINE-INPUT DISCREPANCY UPON IMITATION IN CHILDREN EJ 019 009

PRICE, KATINA C.
A DEVELOPMENTAL STUDY OF COGNITIVE BALANCE EJ 043 856

PRICE, LOUIS E.
MODIFICATION OF FORM AND COLOR RESPONDING IN YOUNG CHILDREN AS A FUNCTION OF DIFFERENTIAL REINFORCEMENT EJ 053 723

PRILLAMAN, DOUGLAS
DIAGNOSTIC TEACHING: A MODEST PROPOSAL EJ 014 522

PRIMUS, PEARL E.
A PILOT STUDY INTEGRATING VISUAL FORM AND ANTHROPOLOGICAL CONTENT FOR TEACHING CHILDREN AGES 6 TO 11 ABOUT CULTURES AND PEOPLES OF THE WORLD ED027095

PRINGLE, M. L. KELLMER
FOUR YEARS ON. A FOLLOW-UP STUDY AT SCHOOL LEAVING AGE OF CHILDREN FORMERLY ATTENDING A TRADITIONAL AND A PROGRESSIVE JUNIOR SCHOOL. ED035434

PROUTY, ROBERT W.
DIAGNOSTIC TEACHING: A MODEST PROPOSAL EJ 014 522

PROVENCE, SALLY
CHILDREN UNDER THREE - FINDING WAYS TO STIMULATE DEVELOPMENT. II. SOME CURRENT EXPERIMENTS: A THREE PRONGED PROJECT EJ 007 408
THE COMPLEXITY OF INFANT DEVELOPMENT. AN ESSAY REVIEW EJ 013 062

PRUNTY, ODESSA
THE SCHOOL SOCIAL WORKER'S ROLE IN OVERCOMING LEARNING HANDICAPS EJ 046 401

PRYKE, DAVID
THEY BECAME WHAT THEY BEHELD EJ 045 423
ON TEAM TEACHING EJ 046 057

PUFALL, PETER B.
PRECOCIOUS THOUGHTS ON NUMBER: THE LONG AND THE SHORT OF IT EJ 060 776

PULASKI, MARY ANN SPENCER
PLAY AS A FUNCTION OF TOY STRUCTURE AND FANTASY PREDISPOSITION EJ 021 083

PUNKE, HAROLD H.
HERO MODELS EJ 016 607

PURDY, ROBERT J.
TEACHING MUSICAL CONCEPTS RELATED TO MELODY, RHYTHM, FORM, AND HARMONY, TEACHER RESOURCE MATERIAL KINDERGARTEN, GRADES 1 AND 2. ED019991

PURKEY, WILLIAM W.
SELF-PERCEPTIONS OF PUPILS IN AN EXPERIMENTAL ELEMENTARY SCHOOL EJ 028 239
CLASSROOM DISCIPLINE: A NEW APPROACH EJ 032 896

PURNELL, JOHN C.
A DEMONSTRATION SUMMER PRESCHOOL PROGRAM EJ 060 999

PURNELL, RICHARD F.
SOCIOECONOMIC STATUS AND SEX DIFFERENCES IN ADOLESCENT REFERENCE-GROUP ORIENTATION EJ 023 614

PUSTEL, GABRIEL
INSTITUTIONALIZED RETARDATES' ANIMAL DRAWINGS; THEIR MEANINGS AND SIGNIFICANCE EJ 055 108

PUTKO, ALEXANDER
AESTHETIC EDUCATION IN SOVIET SCHOOLS EJ 060 105

QUARTERMAN, CAROLE J.
AGE DIFFERENCES IN THE IDENTIFICATION OF CONCEPTS OF THE NATURAL LANGUAGE. STUDY B: DEVELOPMENTAL STUDIES IN SEMANTICS. ED024441

QUAY, HERBERT C.
THE PREVALENCE OF BEHAVIOR SYMPTOMS IN YOUNGER ELEMENTARY SCHOOL CHILDREN. ED039040

QUAY, LORENE C.
LANGUAGE DIALECT, REINFORCEMENT, AND THE INTELLIGENCE-TEST PERFORMANCE OF NEGRO CHILDREN EJ 035 912
NEGRO DIALECT AND BINET PERFORMANCE IN SEVERELY DISADVANTAGED BLACK FOUR-YEAR-OLDS EJ 056 914

QUIE, ALBERT H.
TWO CONGRESSMEN LOOK AT AMERICAN EDUCATION EJ 009 032

QUILLIAN, WARREN W., II
THE NAMING OF PRIMARY COLORS BY CHILDREN EJ 053 483

QUIRK, THOMAS J.
THE STUDENT IN PROJECT PLAN: A FUNCTIONING PROGRAM OF INDIVIDUALIZED EDUCATION EJ 028 501

RABIN, ALBERT I.
OF DREAMS AND REALITY: KIBBUTZ CHILDREN EJ 006 922

RABINOVITCH, M. SAM
EARLY AUDITORY DEPRIVATION AND SENSORY COMPENSATION EJ 044 118
CHILDREN'S RECALL STRATEGIES IN DICHOTIC LISTENING EJ 044 700
AUDITORY-LINGUISTIC SENSITIVITY IN EARLY INFANCY EJ 053 479

RABINOWITZ, F. MICHAEL
STIMULUS SELECTION AS A FUNCTION OF LETTER COLOR AND AGE IN PAIRED-ASSOCIATE LEARNING EJ 043 705
DELAY OF FEEDBACK INTERVAL, POSTFEEDBACK INTERVAL, DISTRACTION, AND TASK DIFFICULTY AS FACTORS IN A MODIFIED CONCEPT-IDENTIFICATION TASK WITH JUNIOR HIGH SCHOOL SUBJECTS EJ 047 677

RABINOWITZ, JOSHUA
A SEX DIFFERENCE IN THE WECHSLER IQ VOCABULARY SCORE AS A PREDICTOR OF STRATEGY IN A PROBABILITY-LEARNING TASK PERFORMED BY ADOLESCENTS EJ 026 376

RABINWITZ, F. MICHAEL
STIMULUS AND RESPONSE ALTERNATION IN YOUNG CHILDREN EJ 034 537

RADIN, NORMA
THE ROLE OF SOCIALIZATION AND SOCIAL INFLUENCE IN A COMPENSATORY PRESCHOOL PROGRAM. ED017337
THE YPSILANTI EARLY EDUCATION PROGRAM. ED022531
PIAGET, SKINNER, AND AN INTENSIVE PRESCHOOL PROGRAM FOR LOWER CLASS CHILDREN AND THEIR MOTHERS. ED027966
TEACHING MOTHERS TO TEACH: A HOME COUNSELING PROGRAM FOR LOW-INCOME PARENTS. ED028819
THREE DEGREES OF PARENT INVOLVEMENT IN A PRESCHOOL PROGRAM: IMPACT ON MOTHERS AND CHILDREN. ED052831
PRESCHOOL PROGRAMS OF THE U.S.S.R EJ 016 352
MATERNAL WARMTH, ACHIEVEMENT MOTIVATION, AND COGNITIVE FUNCTIONING IN LOWER-CLASS PRESCHOOL CHILDREN EJ 053 745
FATHER-CHILD INTERACTION AND THE INTELLECTUAL FUNCTIONING OF FOUR-YEAR-OLD BOYS EJ 054 290

RADOV, ANEITA SHARPLES
CHANGES IN SELF-PERCEPTIONS OF HEAD-START TRAINEES EJ 055 213

RAFFERTY, JANET
CHANGES IN FRIENDSHIP STATUS AS A FUNCTION OF REINFORCEMENT EJ 019 004

RAGINS, NAOMI
A STUDY OF SLEEP BEHAVIOR IN TWO-YEAR-OLD CHILDREN EJ 048 299

RAIM, JOAN
ENCOURAGEMENT FOR THE YOUNG WRITER EJ 029 414

RAINS, SYLVESTER
THE ROLE OF THE PRIMARY TEACHER IN CHARACTER EDUCATION EJ 013 232

RAMBUSCH, NANCY MCCORMICK
VIEWS ON PRE-SCHOOL EDUCATION AND DAY CARE. ED040753

RAMEY, CRAIG T.
DELAYED REINFORCEMENT AND VOCALIZATION RATES OF INFANTS EJ 036 127
EFFECTS OF SPATIAL SEPARATION OF STIMULUS, RESPONSE, AND REWARD IN DISCRIMINATION LEARNING BY CHILDREN EJ 046 243
REACTIONS TO RESPONSE-CONTINGENT STIMULATION IN EARLY INFANCY EJ 059 874

RAMEY, CRAIN T.
NONSOCIAL REINFORCEMENT OF INFANTS' VOCALIZATIONS EJ 058 219

RAMIREZ, JUDITH VALLA
EFFECTS OF TUTORIAL EXPERIENCES ON THE PROBLEM-SOLVING BEHAVIOR OF SIXTH-GRADERS EJ 043 415

RAMIREZ, MANUEL, III.
MEXICAN-AMERICAN CULTURAL MEMBERSHIP AND ADJUSTMENT TO SCHOOL EJ 035 620

RAMSEY, BARBARA
PLAY PERSISTENCE: SOME EFFECTS OF INTERRUPTION, SOCIAL REINFORCEMENT, AND DEFECTIVE TOYS EJ 034 532

RAND, HELENE
EXPERIMENTAL LEARNING REEVALUATED EJ 026 814

RANDHAWA, B. (RANDY)
INTELLECTUAL DEVELOPMENT AND THE ABILITY TO PROCESS VISUAL AND VERBAL INFORMATION. ED043373

RANDHAWA, BIKKAR S.
NON-VERBAL INFORMATION STORAGE IN HUMANS AND DEVELOPMENTAL INFORMATION PROCESSING CHANNEL CAPACITY. ED047800
NONVERBAL INFORMATION STORAGE IN CHILDREN AND DEVELOPMENTAL INFORMATION PROCESSING CHANNEL CAPACITY EJ 053 720

RANDOLPH, H. HELEN
URBAN EDUCATION BIBLIOGRAPHY: AN ANNOTATED LISTING. ED024474

RANDS, RALPH C.
DO YOU REALLY WANT TO IMPROVE THE CURRICULUM? EJ 031 850

RANKIN, RICHARD J.
STANDARDIZED TESTS AND THE DISADVANTAGED. ED034594

RAPH, JANE
INFLUENCES OF A PIAGET-ORIENTED CURRICULUM ON INTELLECTUAL FUNCTIONING OF LOWER-CLASS KINDERGARTEN CHILDREN. ED049823

RAPH, JANE BEASLEY
LANGUAGE RESEARCH STUDY--PROJECT HEAD START. DEVELOPMENT OF METHODOLOGY FOR OBTAINING AND ANALYZING SPONTANEOUS VERBALIZATIONS USED BY PRE-KINDERGARTEN CHILDREN IN SELECTED HEAD START PROGRAMS--A PILOT STUDY. ED015007

RAPOPORT, JUDITH
PLAYROOM OBSERVATIONS OF HYPERACTIVE CHILDREN ON MEDICATION EJ 048 301

RAPPAPORT, DAVID
BEYOND NUFFIELD EJ 028 718
THE NUFFIELD MATHEMATICS PROJECT EJ 033 864

RARDIN, DONALD R.
PEER INTERACTION AND COGNITIVE DEVELOPMENT EJ 056 708

RASHID, MARTHA
THE TEACHER, TEACHER STYLE, AND CLASSROOM MANAGEMENT. PROCEEDINGS OF THE HEAD START RESEARCH SEMINARS: SEMINAR NO. 2, THE TEACHER AND CLASSROOM MANAGEMENT (1ST, WASHINGTON, D.C., JULY 22, 1968). ED035463

RASKIN, LARRY M.
THE INFLUENCE OF AGE AND STIMULUS DIMENSIONALITY ON FORM PERCEPTION BY PRESCHOOL CHILDREN EJ 039 630

RATHBONE, CHARLES H.
ASSESSING THE ALTERNATIVES EJ 033 055

RATLIFF, ANNE R.
SESAME STREET: MAGIC OR MALEVOLENCE? EJ 056 607

RATLIFF, RICHARD G.
INTERACTION OF REWARD, PUNISHMENT, AND SEX IN A TWO-CHOICE DISCRIMINATION TASK WITH CHILDREN EJ 024 948
SESAME STREET: MAGIC OR MALEVOLENCE? EJ 056 607

RAU, MARGOT
RELATIONSHIP OF SOCIOECONOMIC STATUS, SEX, AND AGE TO AGGRESSION OF EMOTIONALLY DISTURBED CHILDREN IN MOTHERS' PRESENCE EJ 017 424

RAVEY, PHYLLIS
A STUDY IN THE UTILIZATION OF TECHNOLOGICALLY ADVANCED TECHNIQUES FOR TEACHER-PARENT-CHILD ASSESSMENT. FINAL REPORT. ED053818

RAY, HENRY W.
DESIGNING TOMORROW'S SCHOOL TODAY: THE MULTI-SENSORY EXPERIENCE CENTER EJ 033 784

RAY, MARGARET
ANALYSIS OF HOME ENVIRONMENT AND DEVELOPMENT OF PARENT INTERVENTION. ED035458

RAYDER, NICHOLAS F.
PRELIMINARY ANALYSIS ON KINDERGARTEN AND FIRST GRADE FOLLOW THROUGH TEST RESULTS FOR 1968-69. ED045202
AN ASSESSMENT OF COGNITIVE GROWTH IN CHILDREN WHO HAVE PARTICIPATED IN THE TOY-LENDING COMPONENT OF THE PARENT-CHILD PROGRAM. ED045204

RAYMER, ELIZABETH
RACE AND SEX IDENTIFICATION IN PRESCHOOL CHILDREN. ED041634

REA, JANE HARWOOD
TEENAGERS DISCUSS AGE RESTRICTIONS EJ 046 786

REALI, NORMA
EFFECT OF SUCCESS AND FAILURE ON THE REFLECTIVE AND IMPULSIVE CHILD EJ 029 768

REASER, GEORGIA PERKINS, ED.
CHILD HEALTH AND HUMAN DEVELOPMENT: PROGRESS 1963-1970. A REPORT OF THE NATIONAL INSTITUTE OF CHILD HEALTH AND HUMAN DEVELOPMENT. ED053799

REASONER, ROBERT W.
TEAM TEACHING. A DESCRIPTIVE AND EVALUATIVE STUDY OF A PROGRAM FOR THE PRIMARY GRADES. ED027083

REBELSKY, FREDA
THE RELATIONSHIP BETWEEN INSTRUMENTAL ASSERTION AND THE STANFORD-BINET. ED030474
INFANCY IN HOLLAND: THE FIRST THREE MONTHS. ED031296
FATHERS' VERBAL INTERACTION WITH INFANTS IN THE FIRST THREE MONTHS OF LIFE EJ 036 126

REDD, WILLIAM H.
GENERALIZATION OF ADULT'S STIMULUS CONTROL OF CHILDREN'S BEHAVIOR EJ 022 214
ATTENTION SPAN AND GENERALIZATION OF TASK-RELATED STIMULUS CONTROL: EFFECTS OF REINFORCEMENT CONTINGENCIES EJ 059 878

REDL, FRITZ
THE NATURE AND NURTURE OF PREJUDICE EJ 000 191
PREADOLESCENTS - WHAT MAKES THEM TICK? A CHILDHOOD EDUCATION SPECIAL (FIRST IN A SERIES): CLASSIC STATEMENTS FROM THE EDUCATOR'S ARCHIVES EJ 016 839

REEBACK, ROBERT T.
THE EXTENSION OF CONTROL IN VERBAL BEHAVIOR. FINAL REPORT. ED021619

REECE, WILLIAM K.
IDENTIFICATION AND EVALUATION OF CHARACTERISTICS OF KINDERGARTEN CHILDREN THAT FORETELL EARLY LEARNING PROBLEMS. FINAL REPORT. ED020006
IDENTIFICATION AND EVALUATION OF CHARACTERISTICS OF KINDERGARTEN CHILDREN THAT FORETELL EARLY LEARNING PROBLEMS. SUMMARY REPORT. ED020007

REED, MILDRED A.
WHERE IS DAY CARE HEADING. ED016530

REENS, RENEE
HEAD START EVALUATION AND RESEARCH CENTER. PROGRESS REPORT OF RESEARCH STUDIES 1966 TO 1967. DOCUMENT 6, INDIVIDUAL INSTRUCTION PROJECT I. ED021628

REESE, HAYNE W.
IMPLICATIONS OF MNEMONICS RESEARCH FOR COGNITIVE THEORY. ED045199
PROGRAMMING CREATIVE BEHAVIOR EJ 021 080
IMAGERY IN CHILDREN'S PAIRED-ASSOCIATE LEARNING EJ 021 757
ACQUIRED DISTINCTIVENESS AND EQUIVALENCE OF CUES IN YOUNG CHILDREN EJ 053 654
IMAGERY AND MULTIPLE-LIST PAIRED ASSOCIATE LEARNING IN YOUNG CHILDREN EJ 057 904

REESE, NANCY MANN
CROSS-CULTURAL VERBAL COOPERATION. PROGRESS REPORT. ED042496

REEVES, BARBARA FRENGEL
THE FIRST YEAR OF SESAME STREET: THE FORMATIVE RESEARCH. FINAL REPORT, VOLUME II OF V VOLUMES. ED047822

REICHLER, ROBERT J.
PSYCHOLOBIOLOGICAL REFERENTS FOR THE TREATMENT OF AUTISM. ED028814

REID, DONALD R.
PAIRED-ASSOCIATE LEARNING OF CHILDREN WITH MIXED LIST DESIGNS EJ 035 369

REID, JOHN B.
RELIABILITY ASSESSMENT OF OBSERVATION DATA: A POSSIBLE METHODOLOGICAL PROBLEM EJ 033 313

REIMANIS, GUNARS
A STUDY OF HOME ENVIRONMENT AND READINESS FOR ACHIEVEMENT AT SCHOOL. FINAL REPORT. ED041637

REISER, NANCY R.
TEACHER-PARENT WORK IN THE HOME: AN ASPECT OF CHILD GUIDANCE CLINIC SERVICES EJ 027 448

REMER, VICTOR
TAKE A GIANT STEP --A REMEDIAL PROGRAM IN A CAMP SETTING EJ 020 773

RENTZ, R. ROBERT
THE ORGANIZATIONAL CLIMATE OF SCHOOLS IN FIVE URBAN AREAS EJ 027 704

REPPUCCI, N. DICKON
INDIVIDUAL DIFFERENCES IN THE CONSIDERATION OF INFORMATION AMONG TWO-YEAR-OLD CHILDREN EJ 018 324
PARENTAL EDUCATION, SEX DIFFERENCES, AND PERFORMANCE ON COGNITIVE TASKS AMONG TWO-YEAR-OLD CHILDREN EJ 035 364

RESENFELD, HOWARD M.
COMPARATIVE STUDIES OF A GROUP OF HEAD START AND A GROUP OF NON-HEAD START PRESCHOOL CHILDREN. FINAL REPORT. ED015013

RESNICK, LAUREN B.
APPROACHES TO THE VALIDATION OF LEARNING HIERARCHIES. ED043376
FOLLOW THROUGH: PROGRAM APPROACHES, SCHOOL YEAR 1970-71. ED047787
TRANSFER AND SEQUENCE IN LEARNING DOUBLE CLASSIFICATION SKILLS EJ 035 379

REYNOLDS, JAMES A.
SOME SOCIAL EFFECTS OF CROSS-GRADE GROUPING EJ 055 107

RHODES, ALBERT LEWIS
EFFECTS OF PARENTAL EXPECTATIONS OF EDUCATIONAL PLANS OF WHITE AND NONWHITE ADOLESCENTS. FINAL REPORT. ED027096

RICCARDS, MICHAEL P.
CHILDREN AND THE POLITICS OF TRUST EJ 045 394
CIVIC BOOKS AND CIVIC CULTURE EJ 057 017

RICCIUTI, HENRY N.
SOCIAL AND EMOTIONAL BEHAVIOR IN INFANCY--SOME DEVELOPMENTAL ISSUES AND PROBLEMS. ED015789
MALNUTRITION, LEARNING AND INTELLECTUAL DEVELOPMENT: RESEARCH AND REMEDIATION. ED039017
EMOTIONAL DEVELOPMENT IN THE FIRST TWO YEARS. ED039936
SEVERE PROTEIN-CALORIE MALNUTRITION AND COGNITIVE DEVELOPMENT IN INFANCY AND EARLY CHILDHOOD EJ 039 627

RICE, ROBERT R.
THE HOUSING ENVIRONMENT AS A FACTOR IN CHILD DEVELOPMENT. FINAL REPORT. ED014322

RICH, IRENE S.
LET DO IT MY WAY EJ 028 846

RICHARDS, CATHERINE V.
WHAT DO YOUNG PEOPLE WANT? EJ 011 784

RICHARDSON, H. BURTT, JR.
THE DIAGNOSTIC EVALUATION OF CHILDREN WITH LEARNING PROBLEMS: A COMMUNICATION PROCESS EJ 050 321

RICHEK, HERBERT G.
A COMPARISON OF CHARACTERISTICS OF PROSPECTIVE SECONDARY SCHOOL TEACHERS ENROLLED IN TWO DIFFERENT DEGREE PROGRAMS EJ 029 618

RICHMAN, N.
A BEHAVIOURAL SCREENING QUESTIONNAIRE FOR USE WITH THREE-YEAR-OLD CHILDREN. PRELIMINARY FINDINGS EJ 042 349

RICHMOND, JULIUS B.
THE CHILDREN'S CENTER--A MICROCOSMIC HEALTH, EDUCATION, AND WELFARE UNIT. PROGRESS REPORT. ED013116

RICKARD, HENRY C.
SUBJECT-MODEL SEXUAL STATUS AND VERBAL IMITATIVE PERFORMANCE IN KINDERGARTEN CHILDREN EJ 030 178

RIDBERG, EUGENE H.
MODIFICATION OF IMPULSIVE AND REFLECTIVE COGNITIVE STYLES THROUGH OBSERVATION OF FILM-MEDIATED MODELS EJ 047 676

RIDER, GERALD S.
TITLE I AND REMEDIAL READING COMPONENTS FOR DISADVANTAGED STUDENTS EJ 053 676

RIEGEL, BARBARA
VOLUNTEERING TO HELP INDIANS HELP THEMSELVES EJ 032 412

RIEGEL, KLAUS F.
AGE DIFFERENCES IN THE IDENTIFICATION OF CONCEPTS OF THE NATURAL LANGUAGE. STUDY B: DEVELOPMENTAL STUDIES IN SEMANTICS. ED024441

RIEGEL, KLAUS F., ED.
THE DEVELOPMENT OF LANGUAGE FUNCTIONS. REPORT NUMBER 8, DEVELOPMENT OF LANGUAGE FUNCTIONS: A RESEARCH PROGRAM PROJECT. ED025325

RIEGER, EDYTHE
SCIENCE ADVENTURES IN CHILDREN'S PLAY. ED026146

RIESSMAN, FRANK
[A STATEMENT REGARDING THE COMPREHENSIVE PRESCHOOL EDUCATION AND CHILD DAY CARE ACT OF 1969, AND OTHER RELATED BILLS.] ED041624

RILEIGH, KATHRYN K.
PERCEPTION OF RHYTHM BY SUBJECTS WITH NORMAL AND DEFICIENT HEARING EJ 060 502

RILEY, CLARA M. D.
HEAD START IN ACTION. ED030471

RIMOLDI, H. J. A.
ON COGNIZING COGNITIVE PROCESSES. ED035437

RINGWALL, EGAN A.
A DISTINCTIVE FEATURES ANALYSIS OF PRE-LINGUISTIC INFANT VOCALIZATIONS. ED025330

RIPPLE, RICHARD E.
THE USE OF CREATIVITY TRAINING MATERIALS WITH SPECIAL CHILDREN: A REPORT OF A FEASIBILITY EXPERIENCE EJ 046 058

RISIKOFF, ROSE
CHILDREN AND THE SCHOOL STRIKE EJ 003 419

RISLEY, TODD R.
SOME DISCRIMINATIVE PROPERTIES OF RACE AND SEX FOR CHILDREN FROM AN ALL-NEGRO NEIGHBORHOOD EJ 058 510

ROACH, JAMES L.
TURNBOW CABIN EJ 029 043

ROBERGE, JAMES J.
DEVELOPMENTAL PATTERNS FOR CHILDREN'S CLASS AND CONDITIONAL REASONING ABILITIES EJ 035 362

ROBERTS, JEAN
HEARING LEVELS OF CHILDREN BY AGE AND SEX: UNITED STATES. ED047799

ROBERTSON, ANNE DE SHAZO
PROJECTIVE VISUAL IMAGERY AS A FUNCTION OF AGE AND DEAFNESS EJ 018 877

ROBINSON, DANIEL N.
SOME CHARACTERISTICS OF NEURAL PROCESSING IN THE CHILD. ED040740

ROBINSON, HALBERT B.
CHILDREN UNDER THREE - FINDING WAYS TO STIMULATE DEVELOPMENT. II. SOME CURRENT EXPERIMENTS: FROM INFANCY THROUGH SCHOOL EJ 007 412
LONGITUDINAL DEVELOPMENT OF VERY YOUNG CHILDREN IN A COMPREHENSIVE DAY CARE PROGRAM: THE FIRST TWO YEARS EJ 056 707

ROBINSON, JAMES P.
LABELING AND IMAGING AS AIDS TO MEMORY EJ 041 143

ROBINSON, NANCY M.
LONGITUDINAL DEVELOPMENT OF VERY YOUNG CHILDREN IN A COMPREHENSIVE DAY CARE PROGRAM: THE FIRST TWO YEARS EJ 056 707

ROBINSON, RICHARD L.
A STUDY OF THE KINDERGARTEN PROGRAM, FULL-DAY OR HALF-DAY. ED017327

ROBISON, HELEN F.
CONCEPT AND LANGUAGE DEVELOPMENT IN A KINDERGARTEN OF DISADVANTAGED CHILDREN. ED027967
THE DECLINE OF PLAY IN URBAN KINDERGARTENS EJ 041 961

ROBSON, KENNETH S.
THE RELATION BETWEEN THE AMOUNT OF TIME INFANTS SPEND AT VARIOUS STATES AND THE DEVELOPMENT OF VISUAL BEHAVIOR EJ 021 082

ROCKWELL, ROBERT E.
NUTRITION IN DAY CARE CENTERS EJ 011 595

RODEN, AUBREY H.
THE EFFECT OF AGGRESSIVE CARTOONS: CHILDREN'S INTERPERSONAL PLAY. ED046543
THE EFFECT OF AGGRESSIVE CARTOONS ON CHILDREN'S INTERPERSONAL PLAY EJ 053 750

RODGERS, DENIS
A PROCESS FOR POETRY-WRITING EJ 055 364

RODGERS, R. R.
CHANGES IN PARENTAL BEHAVIOR REPORTED BY CHILDREN IN WEST GERMANY AND THE UNITED STATES EJ 048 397

RODMAN, HYMAN
SOCIAL CLASS AND PARENT'S ASPIRATIONS FOR THEIR CHILDREN. REPORT NUMBER 8. ED030482
SOCIAL CLASS AND PARENTS' ASPIRATIONS FOR THEIR CHILDREN. RESEARCH REPORT NO. 3 (REVISED). ED043371

RODRIGUES, AROLDO
BEHAVIORAL COMPLIANCE AND DEVALUATION OF THE FORBIDDEN OBJECT AS A FUNCTION OF PROBABILITY OF DETECTION AND SEVERITY OF THREAT EJ 038 935

ROGERS, DONALD J.
HOW TO TEACH FEAR EJ 061 058

ROHWER, WILLIAM D., JR.
SOCIOECONOMIC STATUS AND LEARNING PROFICIENCY IN YOUNG CHILDREN. ED020023
INTELLIGENCE QUOTIENT VERSUS LEARNING QUOTIENT: IMPLICATIONS FOR ELEMENTARY CURRICULA. ED031304
DESIGNS AND PROPOSAL FOR EARLY CHILDHOOD RESEARCH: A NEW LOOK: ON ATTAINING THE GOALS OF EARLY CHILDHOOD EDUCATION. (ONE IN A SERIES OF SIX PAPERS). ED053807
THE LEARNING OF VERBAL STRINGS AS A FUNCTION OF CONNECTIVE FORM CLASS EJ 018 817
GRADE INTERACTION WITH WORDS AND PICTURES IN A PAIRED-ASSOCIATE TASK: A PROPOSED EXPLANATION EJ 057 910

ROLL, SAMUEL
REVERSIBILITY TRAINING AND STIMULUS DESIRABILITY AS FACTORS IN CONSERVATION OF NUMBER EJ 021 776

RONCH, JUDAH
CONTINUITY IN THE DEVELOPMENT OF VISUAL BEHAVIOR IN YOUNG INFANTS EJ 053 746

ROODIN, MARLENE L.
THE ROLE OF MEMORY IN MAKING TRANSITIVE JUDGMENTS EJ 030 288

ROOZE, GENE E.
LEARNING: THE ROLE OF FACTS AND GENERALIZATIONS EJ 028 638

ROSCOE, JOHN T.
COMPARING VALIDITY OF CHANCE LEVEL AND HIGHER TEST SCORES EJ 022 248

ROSE, SUSAN A.
INTERMODAL AND INTRAMODAL RETENTION OF VISUAL AND TACTUAL INFORMATION IN YOUNG CHILDREN EJ 057 900

ROSEMEIR, ROBERT A.
DEVELOPMENTAL TRENDS IN GENERAL AND TEST ANXIETY AMONG JUNIOR AND SENIOR HIGH SCHOOL STUDENTS EJ 061 062

ROSENBAUM, EDWARD
LANGUAGE PATTERNS WITHIN THE YOUTH SUBCULTURE: DEVELOPMENT OF SLANG VOCABULARIES EJ 060 720

ROSENBERG, B. G.
SEX-ROLE IDENTITY AND SIBLING COMPOSITION EJ 035 626

ROSENBERG, BEATRICE
FEDERAL FUNDS FOR DAY CARE PROJECTS. (REVISED EDITION). ED033741

ROSENBERG, LEON A.
THE LIMITATIONS OF BRIEF INTELLIGENCE TESTING WITH YOUNG CHILDREN. ED020774
THE JOHNS HOPKINS PERCEPTUAL TEST, THE DEVELOPMENT OF A RAPID INTELLIGENCE TEST FOR THE PRE-SCHOOL CHILD. ED020787

ROSENBERG, SHELDON
SEMANTICS, PHRASE STRUCTURE, AND AGE AS VARIABLES IN SENTENCE RECALL EJ 025 962
SEMANTIC INTEGRATION, AGE, AND THE RECALL OF SENTENCES EJ 056 620

ROSENDORF, SIDNEY
JOINING TOGETHER TO HELP FOSTER CHILDREN EJ 060 900

ROSENFELD, HOWARD M.
HEAD START EVALUATION AND RESEARCH CENTER, UNIVERSITY OF KANSAS. REPORT NO. V, A COMPARATIVE BEHAVIORAL ANALYSIS OF PEER-GROUP INFLUENCE TECHNIQUES IN HEAD START AND MIDDLE CLASS POPULATIONS. ED021638
INFLUENCE TECHNIQUES IN DYADS COMPOSED OF INTERDEPENDENT MIDDLE AND LOWER CLASS PRESCHOOL CHILDREN. FINAL REPORT ED042489
SOCIAL FACILITATION OF HEAD START PERFORMANCE. PROGRESS REPORT. ED042493

ROSENHAN, DAVID
THE KINDNESSES OF CHILDREN EJ 010 444

ROSENTHAL-HILL, IRENE
CONCEPT FORMATION BY KINDERGARTEN CHILDREN IN A CARD-SORTING TASK. PSYCHOLOGY SERIES. ED013665
THE ELEMENTARY MATHEMATICS STUDY: AN INTERIM REPORT ON KINDERGARTEN YEAR RESULTS. ED027937

ROSENTHAL, KRISTINE
A STUDY IN CHILD CARE (CASE STUDY FROM VOLUME II-A): "IT'S A WELL-RUN BUSINESS, TOO." DAY CARE PROGRAMS REPRINT SERIES. ED051896
A STUDY IN CHILD CARE (CASE STUDY FROM VOLUME II-B): "SOMEPLACE SECURE." DAY CARE PROGRAMS REPRINT SERIES. ED051908
A STUDY IN CHILD CARE (CASE STUDY FROM VOLUME II-B): "...WHILE [THEY TOOK] CARE OF OUR CHILDREN, THEIRS WEREN'T BEING CARED FOR." DAY CARE PROGRAMS REPRINT SERIES. ED051909
A STUDY IN CHILD CARE (CASE STUDY FROM VOLUME II-B): "THEY BRAG ON A CHILD TO MAKE HIM FEEL GOOD." DAY CARE PROGRAMS REPRINT SERIES. ED051910

ROSENTHAL, MURIEL
A COMPARISON OF READING READINESS ACHIEVEMENT OF KINDERGARTEN CHILDREN OF DISPARATE ENTRANCE AGES. ED033745

ROSENTHAL, TED L.
PEDAGOGICAL ATTITUDES OF CONVENTIONAL AND SPECIALLY-TRAINED TEACHERS. ED034587
INSTRUCTIONAL SPECIFICITY AND OUTCOME-EXPECTATION IN OBSERVATIONALLY-INDUCED QUESTION FORMULATION. ED047789
MODELING BY EXEMPLIFICATION AND INSTRUCTION IN TRAINING CONSERVATION. ED047790
CONCEPT ATTAINMENT, GENERALIZATION, AND RETENTION THROUGH OBSERVATION AND VERBAL CODING EJ 053 726
MODELING BY EXEMPLIFICATION AND INSTRUCTION IN TRAINING CONSERVATION EJ 057 898
INITIAL PROBABILITY REHEARSAL, AND CONSTRAINT IN ASSOCIATIVE CLASS SELECTION EJ 057 903
OBSERVATION, REPETITION, AND ETHNIC BACKGROUND IN CONCEPT ATTAINMENT AND GENERALIZATION EJ 059 316

ROSMAN, BERNICE
RELATIONSHIP OF PRESCHOOL SOCIAL-EMOTIONAL FUNCTIONING TO LATER INTELLECTUAL ACHIEVEMENT EJ 058 138

ROSMAN, BERNICE L.
A SOCIAL COMPETENCE SCALE AND SYMPTOM CHECKIST FOR THE PRESCHOOL CHILD: FACTOR DIMENSIONS, THEIR CROSS-INSTRUMENT GENERALITY, AND LONGITUDINAL PERSISTENCE EJ 057 476

ROSNER, SUE R.
THE EFFECTS OF REHEARSAL AND CHUNKING INSTRUCTIONS ON CHILDREN'S MULTITRIAL FREE RECALL EJ 035 377
PRIMACY IN PRESCHOOLERS' SHORT-TERM MEMORY: THE EFFECTS OF REPEATED TESTS AND SHIFT TRIALS EJ 053 729

ROSS, ALAN O.
THE DEVELOPMENT OF A BEHAVIOR CHECKLIST FOR BOYS. ED023468
INCREASING VERBAL COMMUNICATION SKILLS IN CULTURALLY DISADVANTAGED PRE-SCHOOL CHILDREN. FINAL REPORT. ED044186

ROSS, BRUCE M.
WHAT IS LEARNED IN PROBABILITY LEARNING EJ 018 879
CHILDREN'S UNDERSTANDING OF PROBABILITY CONCEPTS EJ 036 824

ROSS, DOROTHEA
THE RELATIONSHIP BETWEEN INTENTIONAL LEARNING, INCIDENTAL LEARNING, AND TYPE OF REWARD IN PRESCHOOL, EDUCABLE, MENTAL RETARDATES EJ 033 783

ROSS, R. S.
STRONG WORDS EJ 001 116

ROSS, ROBERT T.
IQ CHANGES IN HOSPITALIZED MENTAL RETARDATES EJ 046 727

ROSS, SHEILA A.
A TEST OF THE GENERALITY OF THE EFFECTS OF DEVIANT PRESCHOOL MODELS EJ 034 531

ROSSI, SHEILA
DEVELOPMENTAL SHIFTS IN VERBAL RECALL BETWEEN MENTAL AGES TWO AND FIVE EJ 036 825

ROTH, HERRICK S.
LABOR'S VIEWS ON TEACHER STRIKES EJ 003 418

ROTHBERG, CAROLE
"RIGHT," "WRONG," AND DISCRIMINATION LEARNING IN CHILDREN EJ 060 774

ROTHENBERG, BARBARA B.
A DEVELOPMENTAL STUDY OF NONCONSERVATION CHOICES IN YOUNG CHILDREN EJ 011 917
PRESCHOOL CHILDREN'S UNDERSTANDING OF THE COORDINATED CONCEPTS OF DISTANCE, MOVEMENT, NUMBER, AND TIME EJ 015 100
CHILDREN'S SOCIAL SENSITIVITY AND THE RELATIONSHIP TO INTERPERSONAL COMPETENCE, INTRAPERSONAL COMFORT, AND INTELLECTUAL LEVEL EJ 022 136

ROUNDTREE, JULIA
CORRELATES OF LOCUS OF CONTROL IN A SECONDARY SCHOOL POPULATION EJ 039 905

ROURKE, B. P.
AGE DIFFERENCES IN VISUAL REACTION TIME OF "BRAIN DAMAGED" AND NORMAL CHILDREN UNDER IRREGULAR PREPARATORY INTERVAL CONDITIONS EJ 060 109

ROUTH, DONALD K.
EFFECT OF VERBAL PRETRAINING AND SINGLE-PROBLEM MASTERY ON WEIGL LEARNING-SET FORMATION IN CHILDREN EJ 018 883

ROWE, MARY
A STUDY IN CHILD CARE (CASE STUDY FROM VOLUME II-A): "ALL KINDS OF LOVE--IN A CHINESE RESTAURANT." DAY CARE PROGRAMS REPRINT SERIES. ED051903

ROWE, MARY P.
A STUDY IN CHILD CARE. VOLUME I: FINDINGS. DAY CARE PROGRAMS REPRINT SERIES. ED051911

ROWEN, BETTY J.R.
AN EXPLORATION OF THE USES OF RHYTHMIC MOVEMENT TO DEVELOP AESTHETIC CONCEPTS IN THE PRIMARY GRADES. ED020770

ROWETON, WILLIAM E.
CREATIVITY: IDEA QUANTITY AND IDEA QUALITY EJ 058 212

ROWLAND, G. THOMAS
THE SEVENTIES: A TIME FOR GIANT STEPS EJ 009 030

ROY, IRVING
EFFECT OF A KINDERGARTEN PROGRAM OF PERCEPTUAL TRAINING UPON THE LATER DEVELOPMENT OF READING SKILLS. FINAL REPORT. ED030491

ROY, MURIEL L.
EFFECT OF A KINDERGARTEN PROGRAM OF PERCEPTUAL TRAINING UPON THE LATER DEVELOPMENT OF READING SKILLS. FINAL REPORT. ED030491

RUBIN, KENNETH H.
NON-SOCIAL SPEECH IN FOUR-YEAR-OLD CHILDREN AS A FUNCTION OF BIRTH ORDER AND INTERPERSONAL SITUATION EJ 033 702

RUBIN, ROSALYN
A COMPARISON OF PRE-KINDERGARTEN AND PRE-1ST GRADE BOYS AND GIRLS ON MEASURES OF SCHOOL READINESS AND LANGUAGE DEVELOPMENT. INTERIM REPORT. ED023474
EFFECTS OF KINDERGARTEN ATTENDANCE ON DEVELOPMENT OF SCHOOL READINESS AND LANGUAGE SKILLS. INTERIM REPORT. ED029706
SEX DIFFERENCES IN EFFECTS OF KINDERGARTEN ATTENDANCE ON DEVELOPMENT OF SCHOOL READINESS AND LANGUAGE SKILLS EJ 052 723

RUBIN, SOL
CHILDREN AS VICTIMS OF INSTITUTIONALIZATION EJ 051 205

RUBLE, DIANE N.
TASK ORIENTATION VERSUS SOCIAL ORIENTATION IN YOUNG CHILDREN AND THEIR ATTENTION TO RELEVANT SOCIAL CUES EJ 058 413

RUBOW, CAROL L.
THE PROFESSIONAL RESPONSE. ED048922

RUDERMAN, FLORENCE A.
CHILD CARE AND WORKING MOTHERS: A STUDY OF ARRANGEMENTS MADE FOR DAYTIME CARE OF CHILDREN. ED045175

RUEVENI, URI
USING SENSITIVITY TRAINING WITH JUNIOR HIGH SCHOOL STUDENTS EJ 035 169

RUOPP, RICHARD R.
A STUDY IN CHILD CARE (CASE STUDY FROM VOLUME II-A): "A HOUSE FULL OF CHILDREN." DAY CARE PROGRAMS REPRINT SERIES. ED051891
A STUDY IN CHILD CARE (CASE STUDY FROM VOLUME II-A): "LIKE BEING AT HOME." DAY CARE PROGRAMS REPRINT SERIES. ED051899
A STUDY IN CHILD CARE (CASE STUDY FROM VOLUME II-A): "A SMALL U. N." DAY CARE PROGRAMS REPRINT SERIES. ED051904
A STUDY IN CHILD CARE (CASE STUDY FROM VOLUME II-A) ED051905

RUSCELLI, VINCENT
INCORPORATION OF VALUES BY LOWER AND MIDDLE SOCIOECONOMIC CLASS PRESCHOOL BOYS EJ 040 210

RUSK, BRUCE A.
AN EVALUATION OF A SIX-WEEK HEADSTART PROGRAM USING AN ACADEMICALLY ORIENTED CURRICULUM: CANTON, 1967. ED026114

RUSSELL, JAMES E.
PROXIMITY AND INTERACTIONAL BEHAVIOR OF YOUNG CHILDREN TO THEIR "SECURITY" BLANKETS EJ 053 748

RUSSELL, RICHARD L.
HEAD START EVALUATION AND RESEARCH CENTER, UNIVERSITY OF KANSAS. REPORT NO. V, A COMPARATIVE BEHAVIORAL ANALYSIS OF PEER-GROUP INFLUENCE TECHNIQUES IN HEAD START AND MIDDLE CLASS POPULATIONS. ED021638
INFLUENCE TECHNIQUES IN DYADS COMPOSED OF INTERDEPENDENT MIDDLE AND LOWER CLASS PRESCHOOL CHILDREN. FINAL REPORT ED042489

RUST, VAL
TEACHERS IN CHILDREN'S ROLES? EJ 037 235

RUTH, MARY K.
THE ADMINISTRATION OF "SELECTIVITY" IN THE BREAKFAST PROGRAM OF A PUBLIC ELEMENTARY SCHOOL EJ 036 580

RUTHERFORD, RICHARD
FREEDOM OF CHOICE- WHO'S KIDDING WHOM?; FREEDOM- CHOICE AND RESPONSIBILITY. A SYMPOSIUM EJ 011 984

RUTNER, MURRAY
MODIFYING RESPONSE LATENCY AND ERROR RATE OF IMPULSIVE CHILDREN. ED050819

RUTTER, MICHAEL
PSYCHOLOGICAL DEVELOPMENT--PREDICTIONS FROM INFANCY EJ 025 626
NORMAL PSYCHOSEXUAL DEVELOPMENT EJ 038 944
PARENT-CHILD SEPARATION: PSYCHOLOGICAL EFFECTS ON THE CHILDREN EJ 051 019

RYAN, DAVID
EFFECTS OF EXPOSURE TO MODELS ON CONCEPT IDENTIFICATION IN KINDERGARTEN AND SECOND-GRADE CHILDREN EJ 046 240

RYAN, SARAH M.
NONVERBAL MNEMONIC MEDIATION IN PRESCHOOL CHILDREN EJ 021 777

RYBACK, DAVID
SUB-PROFESSIONAL BEHAVIOR MODIFICATION AND THE DEVELOPMENT OF TOKEN-REINFORCEMENT SYSTEMS IN INCREASING ACADEMIC MOTIVATION AND ACHIEVEMENT EJ 034 527
VERBAL OPERANT CONDITIONING OF AN ACTIVE-NON-ACTIVE VERBAL DIFFERENTIAL IN EARLY SCHOOL CHILDREN EJ 041 451

RYCKMAN, DAVID B.
EVALUATION OF INKSTER PRESCHOOL PROJECT. FINAL REPORT. ED027093

RYSTROM, RICHARD
THE EFFECTS OF STANDARD DIALECT TRAINING ON NEGRO FIRST-GRADERS LEARNING TO READ. FINAL REPORT. ED029717
LINGUISTIC FACTORS IN READING EJ 059 537

SAADATMAND, BIJAN
NURTURANCE, NURTURANCE WITHDRAWAL, AND RESISTANCE TO TEMPTATION AMONG THREE AGE GROUPS EJ 021 995

SABATINO, DAVID A.
RELATIONSHIP BETWEEN LATERAL PREFERENCE AND SELECTED BEHAVIORAL VARIABLES FOR CHILDREN FAILING ACADEMICALLY EJ 056 718

SABO, RUTH
CENTRAL AND INCIDENTAL LEARNING IN CHILDREN. ED023450

SACHDEVA, DARSHAN
FRIENDSHIPS AMONG STUDENTS IN DESEGREGATED SCHOOLS EJ 053 668

SACHS, LEWIS B.
LONGITUDINAL ASSESSMENT OF THE RELATION BETWEEN MEASURED INTELLIGENCE OF INSTITUTIONALIZED RETARDATES AND HOSPITAL AGE EJ 047 340

SADOW, SUE
PRACTICAL APPROACHES FOR RESOLVING THE PROBLEM OF NUTRITION AMONG LOW-INCOME FAMILIES EJ 052 065

SAETVEIT, JOSEPH G.
TEACHING GENERAL MUSIC, A RESOURCE HANDBOOK FOR GRADES 7 AND 8. ED018277

SAFFORD, PHILIP L.
PIAGETIAN TASKS AS CLASSROOM EVALUATIVE TOOLS EJ 032 679

SAFILIOS-ROTHSCHILD, CONSTANTINA
FAMILY SOCIOLOGY OR WIVES' FAMILY SOCIOLOGY? A COMPARISON OF HUSBANDS' AND WIVES' ANSWERS ABOUT DECISION MAKING IN THE GREEK AND AMERICAN CULTURE. REPORT NUMBER 4. ED030478

SAHGAL, S. P.
EDUCATION OF TEACHERS FOR NURSERY SCHOOLS: A CREATIVE APPROACH EJ 036 336

SAINSBURY, ROBERT
THE "FEATURE POSITIVE EFFECT" AND SIMULTANEOUS DISCRIMINATION LEARNING EJ 042 963

SALAPATEK, PHILIP
PATTERNS OF FEAR DEVELOPMENT DURING INFANCY EJ 020 718

SALE, JUNE
PROGRAMS FOR INFANTS AND YOUNG CHILDREN. PART IV: FACILITIES AND EQUIPMENT. ED047810

SALTER, RUTH
SECOND-YEAR REPORT ON AN EVALUATIVE STUDY OF PREKINDERGARTEN PROGRAMS FOR EDUCATIONALLY DISADVANTAGED CHILDREN. ED016523

SALTZ, ELI
CONCEPT CONSERVATION IN CHILDREN: THE DEPENDENCE OF BELIEF SYSTEMS ON SEMANTIC REPRESENTATION EJ 053 742

SALZINGER, SUZANNE
EFFECT OF VERBAL RESPONSE CLASS ON SHIFT IN THE PRESCHOOL CHILD'S JUDGMENT OF LENGTH IN RESPONSE TO AN ANCHOR STIMULUS EJ 019 012

SAMEROFF, ARNOLD J.
CHANGES IN THE NONNUTRITIVE SUCKING RESPONSE TO STIMULATION DURING INFANCY EJ 027 848
CAN CONDITIONED RESPONSES BE ESTABLISHED IN THE NEWBORN INFANT: 1971? EJ 041 956

SAMUELS, BRUCE, COMP.
THE FIRST YEAR OF SESAME STREET: A SUMMARY OF AUDIENCE SURVEYS. FINAL REPORT, VOLUME IV OF V VOLUMES. ED047824

SAMUELS, S. JAY
RECOGNITION OF FLASHED WORDS BY CHILDREN EJ 032 676

SANCTUARY, GERALD P.
SEX EDUCATION FOR THE CHILD IN FOSTER CARE EJ 036 328

SANDEL, LENORE
A COMPARISON BETWEEN THE ORAL AND WRITTEN RESPONSES OF FIRST-GRADE CHILDREN IN I.T.A. AND T.O. CLASSES. ED019144

SANDER, LOUIS W.
EARLY MOTHER-INFANT INTERACTION AND 24-HOUR PATTERNS OF ACTIVITY AND SLEEP EJ 019 594

SANDERS, FRANK J.
FUN WHILE LEARNING AND EARNING. A LOOK INTO CHATTANOOGA PUBLIC SCHOOLS' TOKEN REINFORCEMENT PROGRAM. ED027952

SANTROCK, JOHN W.
PATERNAL ABSENCE, SEX TYPING, AND IDENTIFICATION EJ 019 020
RELATION OF TYPE AND ONSET OF FATHER ABSENCE TO COGNITIVE DEVELOPMENT EJ 058 695

SAPON, STANLEY M.
ENGINEERING VERBAL BEHAVIOR. ED025308

SARAVO, ANNE
TRANSFER EFFECTS IN CHILDREN'S ODDITY LEARNING EJ 018 887

SARVIS, MARY A.
COLLABORATION IN SCHOOL GUIDANCE: TASK-ORIENTED GUIDANCE AND ITS STRUCTURE EJ 027 918

SATOW, YOICHI
COLOR AND PHYSIOGNOMY AS VARIABLES IN RACIAL MISIDENTIFICATION AMONG CHILDREN. ED034584

SATTEL, LUDWIG
SCHOOL AND HOME: NOT EITHER-OR EJ 046 246
PERCEPTION AND LANGUAGE: A GERMAN REPLICATION OF THE PIAGET-INHELDER POSITION EJ 060 773

SATZ, PAUL
AN EVALUATION OF A THEORY OF SPECIFIC DEVELOPMENTAL DYSLEXIA EJ 055 875

SAUNDERS, MINTA M.
CURRICULUM FOR THE INFANT AND TODDLER. A COLOR SLIDE SERIES WITH SCRIPT. (SCRIPT ONLY). ED050817

SAUSE, EDWIN F.
THE DEVELOPMENT OF A COMPUTER TECHNIQUE FOR THE CONTENT ANALYSIS OF PSYCHO-SOCIAL FACTORS IN THE ORAL LANGUAGE OF KINDERGARTEN CHILDREN. ED038184

SAVITSKY, JEFFREY C.
DEVELOPMENTAL CHANGES IN THE USE OF EMOTION CUES IN A CONCEPT-FORMATION TASK EJ 029 362

SAXE, RICHARD W.
WHAT'S A SCHOOL FOR? EJ 046 788

SAXE, ROBERT M.
CURIOSITY AND THE PARENT-CHILD RELATIONSHIP EJ 041 447

SAYLER, MARY LOU
PARENTS: ACTIVE PARTNERS IN EDUCATION. A STUDY/ACTION PUBLICATION. ED050823

SCANLON, ROBERT G.
FACTORS ASSOCIATED WITH A PROGRAM FOR ENCOURAGING SELF-INITIATED ACTIVITIES BY FIFTH AND SIXTH GRADE STUDENTS IN A SELECTED ELEMENTARY SCHOOL EMPHASIZING INDIVIDUALIZED INSTRUCTION. ED015785

SCARFE, N. V.
THE IMPORTANCE OF SECURITY IN THE EDUCATION OF YOUNG CHILDREN EJ 062 549

SCARFE, NEVILLE V.
LEARNING FROM GEOGRAPHERS EJ 051 206

SCARLETT, HELAINE H.
CHILDREN'S DESCRIPTIONS OF PEERS: A WERNERIAN DEVELOPMENTAL ANALYSIS EJ 041 591

SCARR, SANDRA
PATTERNS OF FEAR DEVELOPMENT DURING INFANCY EJ 020 718

SCHACHTER, JOSEPH
A STUDY OF SLEEP BEHAVIOR IN TWO-YEAR-OLD CHILDREN EJ 048 299

SCHACK, MARY LOU
DISCRIMINATION LEARNING BY REFLECTIVE AND IMPULSIVE CHILDREN AS A FUNCTION OF REINFORCEMENT SCHEDULE EJ 053 717

SCHAEFER, CHARLES E.
THE FRANCK DRAWING COMPLETION TEST AS A MEASURE OF CREATIVITY EJ 044 704

SCHAEFER, EARL S.
NEED FOR EARLY AND CONTINUING EDUCATION. ED040750
CHILDREN UNDER THREE - FINDING WAYS TO STIMULATE DEVELOPMENT. II. SOME CURRENT EXPERIMENTS: A HOME TUTORING PROGRAM EJ 007 411
LEARNING FROM EACH OTHER EJ 044 008
PARENTS AS EDUCATORS: EVIDENCE FROM CROSS-SECTIONAL, LONGITUDINAL AND INTERVENTION RESEARCH EJ 056 608

SCHAEFFER, BENSON
THE EFFECTS OF OVERLEARNING ON CHILDREN'S NONREVERSAL AND REVERSAL LEARNING USING UNRELATED STIMULI EJ 028 633
THE GROWTH OF CHILDREN'S SEMANTIC MEMORY: SEMANTIC ELEMENTS EJ 038 170

SCHAFFEL, ADRIENNE
VISION TRAINING - A NEW DEVELOPMENTAL CONCEPT IN CHILD VISION. ED028842

SCHAFFER, H. RUDOLPH
THE ONSET OF WARINESS EJ 056 635

SCHAIE, K. W.
LIMITATIONS ON THE GENERALIZABILITY OF GROWTH CURVES OF INTELLIGENCE: A REANALYSIS OF SOME DATA FROM THE HARVARD GROWTH STUDY EJ 060 014

SCHAIE, K. WARNER
THE 1965 HEAD START PSYCHOLOGICAL SCREENING PROGRAM. FINAL REPORT ON THE DATA ANALYSIS. ED014333

SCHECHTER, MARSHALL D.
THE OFF-KILTERED KIDS EJ 028 383

SCHEINER, LOUIS
AN EVALUATION OF A PILOT PROJECT TO ASSESS THE INTRODUCTION OF THE MODERN ENGLISH INFANT SCHOOL APPROACH TO LEARNING WITH SECOND AND THIRD YEAR DISADVANTAGED CHILDREN. ED034595
A PILOT STUDY TO ASSESS THE ACADEMIC PROGRESS OF DISADVANTAGED FIRST GRADERS ASSIGNED TO CLASS BY SEX AND TAUGHT BY A TEACHER OF THE SAME SEX. ED035462

SCHEINFELD, AMRAM
SEX DIFFERENCES IN MENTAL AND BEHAVIORAL TRAITS. ED026117

SCHELL, DONNA J.
CONCEPTUAL BEHAVIOR IN YOUNG CHILDREN: LEARNING TO SHIFT DIMENSIONAL ATTENTION EJ 044 697

SCHERMOLY, GERALDINE
TRAINING WORKERS FOR CHILD CARE CENTERS EJ 050 935

SCHIFF, WILLIAM
TACTILE IDENTIFICATION OF LETTERS: A COMPARISON OF DEAF AND HEARING CHILDRENS' PERFORMANCES EJ 034 567

SCHILD, SYLVIA
PARENTS OF CHILDREN WITH PKU EJ 060 522

SCHINDLER-RAINMAN, EVA
COMMUNICATING WITH TODAY'S TEENAGERS; AN EXERCISE BETWEEN GENERATIONS EJ 011 838

SCHLAPPICH, LEON
SOCIAL STUDIES IN THE PRIMARY GRADES. ED035460

SCHLESINGER, JOY
LEICESTERSHIRE REPORT: THE CLASSROOM ENVIRONMENT. ED027964

SCHMIDT, KATALIN
THE BEHAVIORAL AROUSAL THRESHOLD IN INFANT SLEEP AS A FUNCTION OF TIME AND SLEEP STATE EJ 036 091

SCHMIDT, VELMA E.
A STUDY OF THE INFLUENCE OF CERTAIN PRESCHOOL EDUCATIONAL MOVEMENTS ON CONTEMPORARY PRESCHOOL PRACTICES. ED035450

SCHMIDT, W. H. O.
CULTURAL DIFFERENCES IN COLOR/FORM PREFERENCE AND IN CLASSIFICATORY BEHAVIOR EJ 024 034

SCHMIDT, WILFRED H. O.
SOME NONVERBAL ASPECTS OF COMMUNICATION BETWEEN MOTHER AND PRESCHOOL CHILD EJ 025 386

SCHNALL, M.
DEVELOPMENTAL DIFFERENCES IN THE INTEGRATION OF PICTURE SERIES: EFFECTS OF VARIATIONS IN OBJECT-ATTRIBUTE RELATIONSHIPS EJ 029 386
SEQUENCE EFFECTS IN THE ABSTRACTION OF THE CONCEPT OF PROGRESSIVE CHANGE EJ 029 532

SCHOENFELD, EVA
IDENTITY AND EQUIVALENCE CONSERVATION AT TWO AGE LEVELS EJ 057 901

SCHOGGEN, MAXINE
CHILDREN LEARNING: SAMPLES OF EVERYDAY LIFE OF CHILDREN AT HOME. ED033763
AN ECOLOGICAL STUDY OF THREE-YEAR-OLDS AT HOME. FINAL REPORT. ED037238
RESEARCH, CHANGE, AND SOCIAL RESPONSIBILITY: STUDIES OF THE IMPRINT OF THE LOW-INCOME HOME ON YOUNG CHILDREN. ED039935
ENVIRONMENTAL FORCES IN THE HOME LIVES OF THREE-YEAR-OLD CHILDREN IN THREE POPULATION SUBGROUPS. ED050802

SCHOGGEN, PHIL
ENVIRONMENTAL FORCES IN THE HOME LIVES OF THREE-YEAR-OLD CHILDREN IN THREE POPULATION SUBGROUPS. ED050802

SCHOLINICK, ELLIN KOFSKY
SCALOGRAM ANALYSIS OF LOGICAL AND PERCEPTUAL COMPONENTS OF CONSERVATION OF DISCONTINUOUS QUANTITY EJ 025 957

SCHOLNICK, ELLIN KOBSKY
GENERALITY OF PERCEPTUAL BIASES IN INFERENCE AND CONCEPT USAGE EJ 056 618

SCHOLNICK, ELLIN KOFSKY
INFERENCE AND PREFERENCE IN CHILDREN'S CONCEPTUAL PERFORMANCE EJ 021 773
EFFECTS OF STIMULUS AVAILABILITY ON CHILDREN'S INFERENCES EJ 036 822
USE OF LABELS AND CUES IN CHILDREN'S CONCEPT IDENTIFICATION EJ 056 712

SCHOPLER, ERIC
PSYCHOLOBIOLOGICAL REFERENTS FOR THE TREATMENT OF AUTISM. ED028814

SCHROEDER, CHRISTINE
KINDERGARTEN CHILDREN'S ACTIVE VOCABULARY ABOUT BODY BUILD EJ 041 857
PHYSIQUE IDENTIFICATION, PREFERENCE, AND AVERSION IN KINDERGARTEN CHILDREN EJ 046 785

SCHROEDER, GERALD L.
EFFECTS OF CONCURRENT AND SERIAL TRAINING ON GENERALIZED VOCAL IMITATION IN RETARDED CHILDREN EJ 055 210

SCHROEDER, GLENN B.
THE USE OF THE GOODENOUGH DRAW-A-MAN TEST AS A PREDICTOR OF ACADEMIC ACHIEVEMENT. ED029695

SCHROTH, MARVIN L.
THE EFFECT OF INFORMATIVE FEEDBACK ON PROBLEM SOLVING EJ 025 961

SCHUCK, ROBERT F.
THE INFLUENCE OF SET INDUCTION UPON STUDENT ACHIEVEMENT AND ASSESSMENT OF EFFECTIVE TEACHING EJ 027 031

SCHULTZ, AMELIA L.
MEDICAL GENETICS AND ADOPTION EJ 037 577

SCHULTZ, CHARLES B.
THE USEFULNESS OF CUMULATIVE DEPRIVATION AS AN EXPLANATION OF EDUCATIONAL DEFICIENCIES EJ 033 056

SCHULTZ, THOMAS R.
THE ROLE OF INCONGRUITY AND RESOLUTION IN CHILDREN'S APPRECIATION OF CARTOON HUMOR EJ 060 781

SCHUTZ, SAMUEL
RULE AND ATTRIBUTE LEARNING IN THE USE AND IDENTIFICATION OF CONCEPTS WITH YOUNG DISADVANTAGED CHILDREN. ED040747

SCHUTZ, SAMUEL R.
TEACHING KINDERGARTEN CHILDREN TO APPLY CONCEPT-DEFINING RULES. ED037231

SCHVANEVELDT, ROGER W.
PROBABILITY LEARNING AS A FUNCTION OF AGE, SEX, AND TYPE OF CONSTRAINT EJ 021 766

SCHWAB, LYNNE
EFFECT OF VARIETY ON THE LEARNING OF A SOCIAL STUDIES CONCEPT BY PRESCHOOL CHILDREN. ED029690

SCHWARTZ, CONRAD
THE EFFECTS OF MOTHERS' PRESENCE AND PREVISITS ON CHILDREN'S EMOTIONAL REACTIONS TO STARTING NURSERY SCHOOL. ED034596

SCHWARTZ, EDWARD M.
THE FAMILY ROMANCE FANTASY IN CHILDREN ADOPTED IN INFANCY EJ 022 478

SCHWARTZ, JULIA B.
INCREASING THE AWARENESS OF ART IDEAS OF CULTURALLY DEPRIVED KINDERGARTEN CHILDREN THROUGH EXPERIENCES WITH CERAMICS. FINAL REPORT. ED016519
THE EFFECTS OF TEACHER IN-SERVICE EDUCATION ON THE DEVELOPMENT OF ART IDEAS WITH SIX-YEAR OLD CULTURALLY DEPRIVED CHILDREN. FINAL REPORT. ED027066

SCHWARTZ, MARIAN
TRAINING IN CONSERVATION OF WEIGHT EJ 021 761

SCHWARTZ, MARILYN MILLER
SCALOGRAM ANALYSIS OF LOGICAL AND PERCEPTUAL COMPONENTS OF CONSERVATION OF DISCONTINUOUS QUANTITY EJ 025 957

SCHWARTZ, SYDNEY L.
EXPANDED PREKINDERGARTEN PROGRAM, EVALUATION OF NEW YORK CITY TITLE I EDUCATIONAL PROJECTS 1966-67. ED019115

SCHWARZ, J. CONRAD
FEAR AND ATTACHMENT IN YOUNG CHILDREN. RESEARCH PROJECT NUMBER 4 OF PROJECT HEAD START RESEARCH AND EVALUATION CENTER, SYRACUSE UNIVERSITY RESEARCH INSTITUTE. FINAL REPORT, NOVEMBER 1, 1967. ED026141
STARTING NURSERY SCHOOL, II: PREDICTION OF CHILDREN'S INITIAL EMOTIONAL REACTIONS FROM BACKGROUND INFORMATION. FINAL REPORT. ED047814
THE EFFECTS OF MOTHERS' PRESENCE AND PREVISITS ON CHILDREN'S EMOTIONAL REACTION TO STARTING NURSERY SCHOOL EJ 046 469
THE EFFECTS OF A FAMILIAR TOY AND MOTHER'S PRESENCE ON EXPLORATORY AND ATTACHMENT BEHAVIORS IN YOUNG CHILDREN EJ 053 759

SCHWEITZER, THOMAS M.
SEQUENCE EFFECTS IN THE ABSTRACTION OF THE CONCEPT OF PROGRESSIVE CHANGE EJ 029 532

SCIARA, FRANK J.
PERCEPTIONS OF NEGRO BOYS REGARDING COLOR AND OCCUPATIONAL STATUS EJ 045 392

SCIARRA, DOROTHY JUNE
WHAT TO DO TILL THE MALE MAN COMES EJ 048 697

SCOGGINS, ROY T., JR.
A TEAM APPROACH USING CASSETTE TAPES EJ 061 001

SCOTT, GAIL S.
DECENTRATION IN CHILDREN: ITS GENERALITY AND CORRELATES. ED048926

SCOTT, JOSEPH A.
THE EFFECT OF SELECTED TRAINING EXPERIENCES ON PERFORMANCE ON A TEST OF CONSERVATION OF NUMEROUSNESS. REPORT FROM PHASE 2 OF THE PROTOTYPIC INSTRUCTIONAL SYSTEMS IN ELEMENTARY MATHEMATICS PROJECT. ED036334
LEARNING BY DISCOVERY: A REVIEW OF THE RESEARCH METHODOLOGY. REPORT FROM THE PROJECT ON VARIABLES AND PROCESSES IN COGNITIVE LEARNING. ED053793

SCOTT, KEITH G.
DIGIT SPAN, PRACTICE AND DICHOTIC LISTENING PERFORMANCE IN THE MENTALLY RETARDED EJ 015 850
A MULTIPLE-CHOICE AUDIO-VISUAL DISCRIMINATION APPARATUS WITH QUICK INTER-CHANGE DISPLAY AND RESPONSE PANELS EJ 018 307

SCOTT, MARCIA S.
TRANSFER IN NURSERY SCHOOL CHILDREN BETWEEN TWO RELATIONAL TASKS EJ 024 704
RECOGNITION MEMORY FOR PICTURES IN PRESCHOOL CHILDREN EJ 042 964
TRANSFER BETWEEN THE ODDITY AND RELATIVE SIZE CONCEPTS: REVERSAL AND EXTRADIMENSIONAL SHIFTS EJ 057 906

SCOTT, MAX L.
SMALL GROUPS - AN EFFECTIVE TREATMENT APPROACH IN RESIDENTIAL PROGRAMS FOR ADOLESCENTS EJ 017 900

SCOTT, MYRTLE
SOME PARAMETERS OF TEACHER EFFECTIVENESS AS ASSESSED BY AN ECOLOGICAL APPROACH. ED032928
AN ANALYSIS OF EARLY CHILDHOOD EDUCATION RESEARCH AND DEVELOPMENT. ED039028
TEACHER EFFECTIVENESS: A POSITION. ED039928

SCOTT, PHYLLIS M.
ABOUT RESEARCH: PART I, THE NATURE OF RESEARCH... CHANGING EMPHASES EJ 027 435
ABOUT RESEARCH: PART II. IS A BEHAVIORAL APPROACH SUPERFICIAL? IS OPERANT CONDITIONING FAIR? WHY DO RESEARCH? EJ 029 015

SCOTT, RALPH
SCHOOL AND HOME: NOT EITHER-OR EJ 046 246
PERCEPTION AND LANGUAGE: A GERMAN REPLICATION OF THE PIAGET-INHELDER POSITION EJ 060 773

SCOY, HOLLY VAN
AN ACTIVITY GROUP APPROACH TO SERIOUSLY DISTURBED LATENCY BOYS EJ 043 194

SCRIMSHAW, NEVIN S.
EARLY MALNUTRITION AND CENTRAL NERVOUS SYSTEM FUNCTION EJ 012 207

SEABERG, DOROTHY I.
IS THERE A LITERATURE FOR THE DISADVANTAGED CHILD? EJ 007 178
WHAT CAN TEACHERS LEARN FROM DIRECTORS IN THE PERFORMING ARTS? EJ 051 410

SEARS, ROBERT R.
RELATION OF EARLY SOCIALIZATION EXPERIENCES TO SELF-CONCEPTS AND GENDER ROLE IN MIDDLE CHILDHOOD EJ 021 997

SEBERA, PEGGY
INTERVENTION STRATEGIES FOR SPANISH-SPEAKING PRESCHOOL CHILDREN EJ 036 746

SECORD, PAUL F.
A SOCIAL PSYCHOLOGICAL ANALYSIS OF THE TRANSITION FROM HOME TO SCHOOL. FINAL REPORT. ED015017

SEGGIE, J. L.
THE UTILIZATION BY CHILDREN AND ADULTS OF BINARY PROPOSITIONAL THINKING IN CONCEPT LEARNING EJ 030 285

SEGNER, LESLIE
AN EDUCATIONAL SYSTEM FOR DEVELOPMENTALLY DISABLED INFANTS. ED040749

SEIFERT, KELVIN
COMPARISON OF VERBAL INTERACTION IN TWO PRESCHOOL PROGRAMS EJ 008 274

SEITZ, VICTORIA
STRENGTH OF DIMENSIONAL PREFERENCES AS A PREDICTOR OF NURSERY-SCHOOL CHILDREN'S PERFORMANCE ON A CONCEPT-SHIFT TASK EJ 049 169

SEITZ, VICTORIA R.
MULTIDIMENSIONAL SCALING OF DIMENSIONAL PREFERENCES: A METHODOLOGICAL STUDY EJ 056 609

SELDEN, DAVID
STRIKES, SANCTIONS, OR SURRENDER? EJ 003 417

SELIG, HANNAH
SOCIOECONOMIC STATUS AND CHILDREN'S INTERESTS EJ 016 775

SELLARS, SOPHIA N.
ASK ME SOMETHING I KNOW EJ 012 580

SELLERS, MARTHA JULIA
DEVELOPMENTAL DETERMINANTS OF ATTENTION: A CROSS-CULTURAL REPLICATION EJ 053 718

SELMAN, ROBERT L.
THE RELATION OF ROLE TAKING TO THE DEVELOPMENT OF MORAL JUDGMENT IN CHILDREN EJ 035 991
TAKING ANOTHER'S PERSPECTIVE: ROLE-TAKING DEVELOPMENT IN EARLY CHILDHOOD EJ 056 610

SENN, MILTON J. E.
THE SPIRIT OF THE TIMES IN CHILDHOOD EDUCATION. THE FIRST EVANGELINE BURGESS MEMORIAL LECTURE. ED027081
EARLY CHILDHOOD EDUCATION - FOR WHAT GOALS? EJ 003 595

SETTLAGE, CALVIN F.
ADOLESCENCE AND SOCIAL CHANGE EJ 023 611

SEVERY, LAWRENCE J.
HELPING BEHAVIOR AMONG NORMAL AND RETARDED CHILDREN EJ 052 442

SEWARD, GEORGENE H.
CONCEPTS OF SOCIAL SEX ROLES AMONG CHILEAN ADOLESCENTS EJ 048 396

SEYMOUR, DOROTHY
WHAT DO YOU MEAN, "AUDITORY PERCEPTION"? EJ 013 560

SHAMO, G. WAYNE
THE PSYCHOLOGICAL CORRELATES OF SPEECH CHARACTERISTICS OF SOUNDING "DISADVANTAGED": A SOUTHERN REPLICATION EJ 040 685

SHANTZ, CAROLYN A.
RELATION OF SPATIAL EGOCENTRISM AND SPATIAL ABILITIES OF THE YOUNG CHILD. REPORT NUMBER 7. ED030481

SHANTZ, CAROLYN U.
SPATIAL ABILITIES AND SPATIAL EGOCENTRISM IN THE YOUNG CHILD EJ 037 066

SHANTZ, CAROLYN UHLINGER
LOGICAL OPERATIONS AND CONCEPTS OF CONSERVATION IN CHILDREN, A TRAINING STUDY. FINAL REPORT. ED020010
ESSAYS ON EQUILIBRIUM EJ 008 171
TRAINING COMMUNICATION SKILLS IN YOUNG CHILDREN EJ 058 606

SHANTZ, DAVID W.
SITUATIONAL EFFECTS ON JUSTIFIABLENESS OF AGGRESSION AT THREE AGE LEVELS EJ 056 734

SHAPIRA, ARIELLA
COOPERATIVE AND COMPETITIVE BEHAVIOR OF URBAN AFRO-AMERICAN, ANGLO-AMERICAN, MEXICAN-AMERICAN, AND MEXICAN VILLAGE CHILDREN EJ 024 033

SHAPIRO, BERNARD J.
TESTING IN THE SCHOOLS: A RESPONSE TO JOHN HOLT EJ 013 227
LOGICAL THINKING IN CHILDREN AGES SIX THROUGH THIRTEEN EJ 025 960

SHAPIRO, MARTIN M.
MAGNITUDE-PROBABILITY PREFERENCES OF PRESCHOOL CHILDREN FROM TWO SOCIOECONOMIC LEVELS EJ 019 017

SHAPIRO, PHYLLIS P.
TESTING IN THE SCHOOLS: A RESPONSE TO JOHN HOLT EJ 013 227

SHAPIRO, S. I.
FREE RECALL AND CLUSTERING AT FOUR AGE LEVELS: EFFECTS OF LEARNING TO LEARN AND PRESENTATION METHOD EJ 039 636

SHAPIRO, THEODORE
IMITATION AND ECHOING IN YOUNG SCHIZOPHRENIC CHILDREN EJ 026 494

SHARAN, SHLOMO
CLASSIFICATION PATTERNS OF UNDERPRIVILEGED CHILDREN IN ISRAEL EJ 041 140

SHARP, DONALD
PATTERNS OF RESPONDING IN THE WORD ASSOCIATIONS OF WEST AFRICAN CHILDREN EJ 056 634

SHARP, RICHARD M.
TURNING THE TIDE IN TEACHER QUALITY EJ 034 231

SHARRAR, MARY LOU
SOME HELPFUL TECHNIQUES WHEN PLACING OLDER CHILDREN FOR ADOPTION EJ 029 166
ATTITUDE OF BLACK NATURAL PARENTS REGARDING ADOPTION EJ 038 792

SHAVER, JAMES P.
MATCHED-PAIR SCORING TECHNIQUE USED ON A FIRST-GRADE YES-NO TYPE ECONOMICS ACHIEVEMENT TEST. ED029699
SRA ECONOMICS MATERIALS IN GRADES ONE AND TWO. EVALUATION REPORTS. ED029700
COMPARISON OF YES-NO, MATCHED-PAIRS, AND ALL-NO SCORING OF A FIRST-GRADE ECONOMICS ACHIEVEMENT TEST. ED029701

SHAW, JEAN W.
CHILDREN LEARNING: SAMPLES OF EVERYDAY LIFE OF CHILDREN AT HOME. ED033763

SHAW, JON A.
MOTHER-INFANT RELATIONSHIP AND WEIGHT GAIN IN THE FIRST MONTH OF LIFE EJ 026 508

SHAW, ROBERT E.
PRECOCIOUS THOUGHTS ON NUMBER: THE LONG AND THE SHORT OF IT EJ 060 776

SHEA, J. F.
LEARNING, CURIOSITY, AND SOCIAL GROUP MEMBERSHIP EJ 035 378

SHECHTMAN, AUDREY
AGE PATTERNS IN CHILDREN'S PSYCHIATRIC SYMPTOMS EJ 025 374

SHELDON, BERNICE S.
HEAD START IN ALASKA EJ 008 273

SHEN, MICHAEL
SOME LANGUAGE-RELATED COGNITIVE ADVANTAGES OF BILINGUAL FIVE YEAR OLDS. ED031307
SOME LANGUAGE-RELATED COGNITIVE ADVANTAGES OF BILINGUAL FIVE-YEAR-OLDS EJ 041 343

SHEPARD, WINIFRED O.
WORD ASSOCIATION AND DEFINITION IN MIDDLE CHILDHOOD EJ 030 294

SHEPHERD, MICHAEL
THE CHILD WHO DISLIKES GOING TO SCHOOL. ED019999

SHEPPARD, JEAN B.
IMPULSIVITY & REFLECTIVITY AS REFLECTED BY THE VARIABLES OF TIME AND ERROR. ED047820

SHEPPARD, WILLIAM
DEVELOPMENT OF THE PROSODIC FEATURES OF INFANTS' VOCALIZING. ED025331

SHER, ABIGAIL B.
A TECHNIQUE FOR GATHERING CHILDREN'S LANGUAGE SAMPLES FROM NATURALISTIC SETTINGS. ED016532

SHERK, LINDA
NEED FOR APPROVAL, CHILDREN'S SHARING BEHAVIOR, AND RECIPROCITY IN SHARING EJ 018 321

SHERMAN, JAMES A.
HEAD START EVALUATION AND RESEARCH CENTER, UNIVERSITY OF KANSAS. REPORT NO. IX, DEVELOPMENT OF "MATCHING" ABSTRACTIONS IN YOUNG CHILDREN. ED021645
TRANSFER OF MATCHING AND MISMATCHING BEHAVIOR IN PRESCHOOL CHILDREN EJ 024 701

SHEVIAKOV, GEORGE
ANGER IN CHILDREN: CAUSES, CHARACTERISTICS, AND CONSIDERATIONS. ED039917

SHINN, BYRON M., JR.
A BIBLIOGRAPHY (WITH SELECTED ANNOTATIONS) ON NONGRADED ELEMENTARY SCHOOLS. ED015024

SHIPLEY, ELIZABETH F.
THE ACQUISITION OF LINGUISTIC STRUCTURE. TECHNICAL REPORT VIII, A STUDY IN THE ACQUISITION OF LANGUAGE: FREE RESPONSES TO COMMANDS. ED023486

SHIPLEY, FERNE
FREEDOM TO MOVE. ED020778

SHIPMAN, VIRGINIA
PARENTS AS TEACHERS, HOW LOWER-CLASS AND MIDDLE-CLASS MOTHERS TEACH. ED025301

SHIPMAN, VIRGINIA C.
HEAD START EVALUATION AND RESEARCH CENTER, THE UNIVERSITY OF CHICAGO. REPORT A, MATERNAL INFLUENCES UPON DEVELOPMENT OF COGNITION. ED022550
HEAD START EVALUATION AND RESEARCH CENTER, THE UNIVERSITY OF CHICAGO. REPORT B, MATERNAL ANTECEDENTS OF INTELLECTUAL ACHIEVEMENT BEHAVIORS IN LOWER CLASS PRESCHOOL CHILDREN. ED022551
HEAD START EVALUATION AND RESEARCH CENTER, THE UNIVERSITY OF CHICAGO. REPORT C, COGNITIVE INTERACTION BETWEEN TEACHER AND PUPIL IN A PRESCHOOL SETTING. ED022552
HEAD START EVALUATION AND RESEARCH CENTER, THE UNIVERSITY OF CHICAGO. REPORT D, THE INTERACTION OF INTELLIGENCE AND BEHAVIOR AS ONE PREDICTOR OF EARLY SCHOOL ACHIEVEMENT IN WORKING CLASS AND CULTURALLY DISADVANTAGED HEAD START CHILDREN. ED022553
HEAD START EVALUATION AND RESEARCH CENTER, THE UNIVERSITY OF CHICAGO. REPORT E, COMPARATIVE USE OF ALTERNATIVE MODES FOR ASSESSING COGNITIVE DEVELOPMENT IN BILINGUAL OR NON-ENGLISH SPEAKING CHILDREN. ED022554

HEAD START EVALUATION AND RESEARCH CENTER, THE UNIVERSITY OF CHICAGO. ANNUAL REPORT, 1966-1967. ED023445
HEAD START EVALUATION AND RESEARCH CENTER, THE UNIVERSITY OF CHICAGO. REPORT F, SOCIALIZATION INTO THE ROLE OF PUPIL. ED023456

SHLOMO, SHARAN (SINGER)
ARTICULATION OF THE BODY CONCEPT AMONG FIRST-GRADE ISRAELI CHILDREN EJ 053 744

SHORTELL, JAMES R.
AGGRESSION IN CHILDREN AS A FUNCTION OF SEX OF SUBJECT AND SEX OF OPPONENT EJ 024 945

SHULTZ, THOMAS R.
EMOTIONAL CONCOMITANTS OF VISUAL MASTERY IN INFANTS: THE EFFECTS OF STIMULUS MOVEMENT ON SMILING AND VOCALIZING EJ 033 794

SHURE, MYRNA B.
PROBLEM-SOLVING THINKING AND ADJUSTMENT AMONG DISADVANTAGED PRESCHOOL CHILDREN EJ 056 612

SIBLEY, SALLY A.
MODIFICATION BY SOCIAL REINFORCEMENT OF DEFICIENT SOCIAL BEHAVIOR OF DISADVANTAGED KINDERGARTEN CHILDREN. ED043381
AN EXPERIMENTAL SUMMER KINDERGARTEN FOR CULTURALLY DEPRIVED CHILDREN. ED044174
MODIFICATION OF THE CLASSROOM BEHAVIOR OF A "DISADVANTAGED" KINDERGARTEN BOY BY SOCIAL REINFORCEMENT AND ISOLATION. ED045181
MODIFYING BEHAVIOR OF KINDERGARTEN CHILDREN EJ 026 493

SIEBER, JOAN E.
THE RELATION BETWEEN TEST ANXIETY AND NEED FOR MEMORY SUPPORT IN PROBLEM SOLVING. REVISED RESEARCH MEMORANDUM NO. 11. ED021616

SIEGEL, ALBERTA E.
CURRENT ISSUES IN RESEARCH ON EARLY DEVELOPMENT. ED028813

SIEGEL, ALENXANDER W.,
VISUAL AND HAPTIC DIMENSIONAL PREFERENCE: A DEVELOPMENTAL STUDY EJ 026 506

SIEGEL, ALEXANDER W.
CHILDREN'S ABILITY TO OPERATE WITHIN A MATRIX: A DEVELOPMENTAL STUDY. ED029715
THE EFFECTS OF DIFFERENT TYPES OF REINFORCEMENT ON YOUNG CHILDREN'S INCIDENTAL LEARNING. ED044184
ESTIMATION OF LINE LENGTH AND NUMBER: A DEVELOPMENTAL STUDY EJ 030 590
CHILDREN'S ABILITY TO OPERATE WITHIN A MATRIX: A DEVELOPMENTAL STUDY EJ 035 363
THE EFFECTS OF DIFFERENT TYPES OF REINFORCEMENT ON YOUNG CHILDREN'S INCIDENTAL LEARNING EJ 053 752
OBSERVING BEHAVIOR AND CHILDREN'S DISCRIMINATION LEARNING EJ 053 754

SIEGEL, LINDA S.
RULE STRUCTURE AND PROPORTION OF POSITIVE INSTANCES AS DETERMINANTS OF CONCEPT ATTAINMENT IN CHILDREN. ED046500
THE SEQUENCE OF DEVELOPMENT OF CERTAIN NUMBER CONCEPTS IN PRESCHOOL CHILDREN EJ 044 694
THE DEVELOPMENT OF THE UNDERSTANDING OF CERTAIN NUMBER CONCEPTS EJ 044 695
DEVELOPMENT OF THE CONCEPT OF SERIATION EJ 053 650

SIEGENTHALER, BRUCE M.
THRESHOLD BY IDENTIFICATION OF PICTURES (TIP) TEST AND DISCRIMINATION BY IDENTIFICATION OF PICTURES (DIP) TEST. ED015784

SIGEL, IRVING
CHILD DEVELOPMENT AND SOCIAL SCIENCE EDUCATION. PART I: THE PROBLEM, PART II: CONFERENCE REPORT. ED023465
CHILD DEVELOPMENT AND SOCIAL SCIENCE EDUCATION. PART III: ABSTRACTS OF RELEVANT LITERATURE. ED023466
CHILD DEVELOPMENT AND SOCIAL SCIENCE EDUCATION. PART IV: A TEACHING STRATEGY DERIVED FROM SOME PIAGETIAN CONCEPTS. ED023467
THE DISTANCING HYPOTHESIS: A HYPOTHESIS CRUCIAL TO THE DEVELOPMENT OF REPRESENTATIONAL COMPETENCE. ED024466

SIGEL, IRVING E.
LOGICAL OPERATIONS AND CONCEPTS OF CONSERVATION IN CHILDREN, A TRAINING STUDY. FINAL REPORT. ED020010
MODIFICATION OF CLASSIFICATORY COMPETENCE AND LEVEL OF REPRESENTATION AMONG LOWER-CLASS NEGRO KINDERGARTEN CHILDREN. ED021608
THE PROGRAM OF RESEARCH OF THE MERRILL-PALMER INSTITUTE IN CONJUNCTION WITH THE HEAD START EVALUATION AND RESEARCH CENTER, MICHIGAN STATE UNIVERSITY. ANNUAL REPORT. VOLUME II: RESEARCH. ED027088
MODIFICATION OF COGNITIVE SKILLS AMONG LOWER-CLASS NEGRO CHILDREN: A FOLLOW-UP TRAINING STUDY. REPORT NUMBER 6. ED030480
THE ROLE OF THE TEACHER IN INTERVENTION PROGRAMS. PROCEEDINGS OF THE HEAD START RESEARCH SEMINARS: SEMINAR NO. 6, THE TEACHER IN INTERVENTION PROGRAMS (1ST, WASHINGTON, D.C., APRIL 18, 1969). ED036333
ANALYSIS OF THE OBJECT CATEGORIZATION TEST AND THE PICTURE CATEGORIZATION TEST FOR PRESCHOOL CHILDREN. ED038174
INTRODUCTION TO THE 1968 INFANT CONFERENCE PAPERS EJ 003 552
THE DEVELOPMENT OF CLASSIFICATORY SKILLS IN YOUNG CHILDREN: A TRAINING PROGRAM EJ 031 872
THE GENERALITY OF COLOR-FORM PREFERENCE AS A FUNCTION OF MATERIALS AND TASK REQUIREMENTS AMONG LOWER-CLASS NEGRO CHILDREN EJ 033 052
DEVELOPMENTAL THEORY: ITS PLACE AND RELEVANCE IN EARLY INTERVENTION PROGRAMS EJ 060 013

SIKORSKI, LINDA A.
THE DEVELOPMENT OF AN INFORMATION UNIT REVIEWING SELECTED WELL-DEVELOPED MODELS OF EARLY CHILDHOOD EDUCATION PROGRAMS. FINAL REPORT. ED045223

SILBERFARB, ROBERT M.
THE EFFECTS OF PERSONALITY VARIABLES ON DISTORTION THRESHOLDS IN THE AMES ROOM EJ 023 434

SILBERSTEIN, RUTH
RISK-TAKING BEHAVIOR IN PRESCHOOL CHILDREN FROM THREE ETHNIC BACKGROUNDS. ED042486

SILFEN, CAROLE K.
METHODOLOGICAL ISSUES IN THE STUDY OF AGE DIFFERENCES IN INFANTS' ATTENTION TO STIMULI VARYING IN MOVEMENT AND COMPLEXITY. ED023477

SILK, STEPHEN
HEAD START EVALUATION AND RESEARCH CENTER. PROGRESS REPORT OF RESEARCH STUDIES 1966 TO 1967. DOCUMENT 5, COMPARATIVE ITEM-CONTENT ANALYSIS OF ACHIEVEMENT TEST PERFORMANCE IN YOUNG CHILDREN. ED021627

SILVAROLI, NICHOLAS J.
A COMPARISON OF THE ORAL LANGUAGE PATTERNS OF THREE LOW SOCIOECONOMIC GROUPS OF PUPILS ENTERING FIRST GRADE. ED032943

SILVERMAN, MARTIN A.
EARLY INTERVENTION AND SOCIAL CLASS: DIAGNOSIS AND TREATMENT OF PRESCHOOL CHILDREN IN A DAY CARE CENTER EJ 050 497

SILVERMAN, ROBERT E.
RESPONSE TO VARYING LEVELS OF CONDITIONING REWARDS. FINAL REPORT. ED020803

SILVERMAN, STEPHAN M.
MAGNITUDE-PROBABILITY PREFERENCES OF PRESCHOOL CHILDREN FROM TWO SOCIOECONOMIC LEVELS EJ 019 017

SILVERMAN, STUART
THE EFFECTS OF IMMEDIATE FEEDBACK ON THE BEHAVIOR OF TEACHERS-IN-TRAINING EJ 059 672

SILVERSTONE, NAOMI, ED.
PROGRAMS FOR INFANTS AND YOUNG CHILDREN. PART I: EDUCATION AND DAY CARE. ED047807

SIMMS, MIMI
SOME HIGHLIGHTS FROM THE NUTRITION CONFERENCE EJ 017 447
INDUSTRY AND DAY CARE EJ 050 380

SIMNER, MARVIN L.
NEWBORN'S RESPONSE TO THE CRY OF ANOTHER INFANT EJ 041 959

SIMONS, BENITA
PARENT HANDBOOK: DEVELOPING YOUR CHILD'S SKILLS AND ABILITIES AT HOME. ED036327

SINCLAIR, CAROLINE B.
MOVEMENT AND MOVEMENT PATTERNS OF EARLY CHILDHOOD. ED053796

SINCLAIR, ROBERT L.
A THEORETICAL APPROACH FOR SELECTING ELEMENTARY SCHOOL ENVIRONMENTAL VARIABLES. ED028834

SINCLAIR, WARD
FIRST STEPS IN SCHOOL EJ 007 205

SINGER, DAVID L.
IDEATIONAL CREATIVITY AND EXPRESSIVE ASPECTS OF HUMAN FIGURE DRAWING IN KINDERGARTEN-AGE CHILDREN EJ 039 629

SINGH, R. P.
TOWARDS AN INDIAN PHILOSOPHY OF PRIMARY EDUCATION EJ 036 337

SISTRUNK, FRANK
JUDGMENTS OF PATTERN GOODNESS AND PATTERN PREFERENCE AS FUNCTIONS OF AGE AND PATTERN UNCERTAINTY EJ 046 782
DEVELOPMENTAL COMPARISONS OF CONFORMITY ACROSS TWO CULTURES EJ 051 470

SJOSTROM, KRISTEN
THE ROLE OF LIGHTNESS CONTRAST IN DETERMINING THE MAGNITUDE OF THE DELBOEUF ILLUSION: A REJOINDER TO WEINTRAUB AND COOPER EJ 055 101

SKARD, AASE GRUDA
CHILD PSYCHOLOGY IN FUTURE SOCIETY EJ 011 344
THE ROLE OF WOMEN IN THE DEVELOPMENT OF THEIR COUNTRIES: COMMENTS FROM OMEP ON A QUESTIONNAIRE FROM U.N EJ 011 346

SKINNER, ANGELA E.
78 BATTERED CHILDREN: A RETROSPECTIVE STUDY. ED043382

SLABY, RONALD G.
EFFECT ON RESISTANCE TO DEVIATION OF OBSERVING A MODEL'S AFFECTIVE REACTION TO RESPONSE CONSEQUENCES EJ 043 283

SLOBIN, DAN I.
GRAMMATICAL DEVELOPMENT IN RUSSIAN-SPEAKING CHILDREN. ED025332

SLOTNICK, NAN S.
DEVELOPMENT OF THE UNDERSTANDING OF LOGICAL CONNECTIVES. ED032125

SMALL, MELINDA Y.
CHILDREN'S PERFORMANCE ON AN ODDITY PROBLEM AS A FUNCTION OF THE NUMBER OF VALUES ON THE RELEVANT DIMENSION EJ 024 694
CHILDREN'S PERFORMANCE IN SIMPLE AND SUCCESSIVE-REVERSAL CONCEPT IDENTIFICATION PROBLEMS EJ 049 170

SMALLEY, JEANNETTE
PHYSICAL EDUCATION ACTIVITIES FOR THE ELEMENTARY SCHOOL. ED019995

SMILANSKY, SARA
THE EFFECTS OF SOCIODRAMATIC PLAY ON DISADVANTAGED PRESCHOOL CHILDREN. ED033761

SMILEY, SANDRA S.
INSTABILITY OF DIMENSIONAL PREFERENCE FOLLOWING CHANGES IN RELATIVE CUE SIMILARITY EJ 057 908

SMILLIE, D.
PIAGET'S CONSTRUCTIONIST THEORY EJ 059 876

SMITH, A. C.
PREDICTION OF DEVELOPMENTAL OUTCOME AT SEVEN YEARS FROM PRENATAL, PERINATAL, AND POSTNATAL EVENTS EJ 058 927

SMITH, CARLOTA S.
TWO STUDIES OF THE SYNTACTIC KNOWLEDGE OF YOUNG CHILDREN. A PRELIMINARY REPORT. ED024451

SMITH, DENNIS R.
THE EFFECT OF FOUR COMMUNICATION PATTERNS AND SEX ON LENGTH OF VERBALIZATION IN SPEECH OF FOUR YEAR OLD CHILDREN. FINAL REPORT. ED042514

SMITH, ELEANOR W.
ADOLESCENT MATERNITY SERVICES: A TEAM APPROACH EJ 047 354

SMITH, FRANK
ON THE PSYCHOLINGUISTIC METHOD OF TEACHING READING EJ 030 547

SMITH, FRANK A.
PERFORMANCE OF KINDERGARTEN CHILDREN FROM LOW INCOME FAMILIES ON SELECTED CONCEPT CATEGORIES. ED028847

SMITH, JACK L.
NUTRITIONAL STATUS OF NEW ORLEANS, MISSISSIPPI AND ALABAMA HEAD START CHILDREN. FINAL REPORT. ED047785

SMITH, MARILYN
A GUIDE FOR COLLECTING AND ORGANIZING INFORMATION ON EARLY CHILDHOOD PROGRAMS EJ 058 463

SMITH, MICHAEL J.
ADOPTION TRENDS: JANUARY-JUNE 1971 EJ 047 001

SMITH, WILLIAM F.
FUN WHILE LEARNING AND EARNING. A LOOK INTO CHATTANOOGA PUBLIC SCHOOLS' TOKEN REINFORCEMENT PROGRAM. ED027952
[ACHIEVEMENT TEST CORRELATION STUDY: SURVEY OF 40 CHILDREN.] ED027954

SMOCK, CHARLES D.
DEVELOPMENT CHANGES IN PROBLEM-SOLVING STRATEGIES: PERMUTATION EJ 021 767

SMOTHERGILL, DANIEL
VERBAL MEDIATION AND SATIATION IN YOUNG CHILDREN EJ 056 613

SMOTHERGILL, NANCY L.
THE EFFECTS OF MANIPULATION OF TEACHER COMMUNICATION STYLE IN THE PRESCHOOL. ED034598
THE PRESCHOOL CHILD'S ABILITY TO FOLLOW DIRECTIONS. ED043395
THE EFFECTS OF MANIPULATION OF TEACHER COMMUNICATION STYLE IN THE PRESCHOOL EJ 052 455

SMUCKLER, NANCY SIDON
CONCEPT FORMATION AS A FUNCTION OF METHOD OF PRESENTATION AND RATIO OF POSITIVE TO NEGATIVE INSTANCES. ED015779

SNIDER, BILL
COMPARATIVE PERCEPTUAL MOTOR PERFORMANCE OF NEGRO AND WHITE YOUNG MENTAL RETARDATES EJ 019 015

SNORTUM, JOHN R.
EYE CONTACT IN CHILDREN AS A FUNCTION OF AGE, SEX, SOCIAL AND INTELLECTIVE VARIABLES EJ 038 943

SNOW, CATHERINE E.
MOTHERS' SPEECH TO CHILDREN LEARNING LANGUAGE EJ 058 696

SNUPPES, PATRICK
YOUNG CHILDREN'S COMPREHENSION OF LOGICAL CONNECTIVES EJ 049 117

SNYDER, AGNES, COMP.
"ENVIRONMENT," AN OLD CONCEPT IN EDUCATION: A CHILDHOOD EDUCATION SPECIAL (SECOND IN A SERIES), CLASSICAL STATEMENTS FROM THE EDUCATOR'S ARCHIVES EJ 029 623

SOAR, ROBERT S.
AN INTEGRATIVE APPROACH TO CLASSROOM LEARNING. ED033749

SOARES, ANTHONY T.
A COMPARATIVE STUDY OF THE SELF-IMAGES OF DISADVANTAGED CHILDREN. ED028821
SELF CONCEPTS OF DISADVANTAGED AND ADVANTAGED STUDENTS EJ 035 618

SOARES, LOUISE M.
A COMPARATIVE STUDY OF THE SELF-IMAGES OF DISADVANTAGED CHILDREN. ED028821
SELF CONCEPTS OF DISADVANTAGED AND ADVANTAGED STUDENTS EJ 035 618

SOBIESZEK, BARBARA I.
EFFECT OF A CHILD'S SEX ON ADULT INTERPRETATIONS OF ITS BEHAVIOR EJ 053 711

SODERBERG, LANNY O.
AN EXPLORATORY STUDY OF THE RELATIONSHIP BETWEEN COGNITIVE PRETESTING AND COURSE ACHIEVEMENT EJ 041 758

SOLAN, HAROLD A.
PERCEPTUAL TESTING AND TRAINING METHODS USED IN THE PRIMARY GRADES. ED027971

SOLKOFF, NORMAN
RACE OF EXPERIMENTER AS A VARIABLE IN RESEARCH WITH CHILDREN EJ 061 085

SOLNIT, ALBERT J.
THE LIFE AND WORKS OF ERIK ERIKSON EJ 044 757

SOLOMON, DANIEL
EARLY GRADE SCHOOL PERFORMANCE OF INNER CITY NEGRO HIGH SCHOOL HIGH ACHIEVERS, LOW ACHIEVERS, AND DROPOUTS EJ 039 572
THE DEVELOPMENT OF DEMOCRATIC VALUES AND BEHAVIOR AMONG MEXICAN-AMERICAN CHILDREN EJ 058 509
RELATIONSHIPS OF PARENTAL BEHAVIOR TO "DISADVANTAGED" CHILDREN'S INTRINSIC-EXTRINSIC MOTIVATION FOR TASK STRIVING EJ 059 870

SOLTYS, JOHN J., JR.
WHEN THE CHILD IS ANGRY. ED017331

SONES, GITTELLE
SEX DIFFERENCES IN ADOLESCENT REACTIONS TOWARD NEWCOMERS EJ 039 899

SONTAG, LESTER
THE HISTORY OF LONGITUDINAL RESEARCH: IMPLICATIONS FOR THE FUTURE EJ 051 779

SOSTEK, ANITA M.
EVIDENCE FOR THE UNCONDITIONABILITY OF THE BABKIN REFLEX IN NEWBORNS EJ 058 589

SOTO-PADIN, JOSE L.
DEPENDENCY AND SOCIAL PERFORMANCE: THE DEVELOPMENT OF A SCALE TO MEASURE LEVEL OF INDEPENDENCE IN SMALL CHILDREN. PART OF THE FINAL REPORT. ED026129

SOULE, ALLEN
NORTHFIELD, VERMONT--A COMMUNITY DEPTH STUDY. ED018245

SOULE, DONALD
THE PRESCHOOL INVENTORY. ED014334

SOUTHERN, MARA L.
EFFECTS OF PRESCHOOL STIMULATION UPON SUBSEQUENT SCHOOL PERFORMANCE AMONG THE CULTURALLY DISADVANTAGED. ED046545
DIFFERENTIAL COGNITIVE DEVELOPMENT WITHIN AND BETWEEN RACIAL AND ETHNIC GROUPS OF DISADVANTAGED PRESCHOOL AND KINDERGARTEN CHILDREN EJ 049 172

SPANER, S. D.
BIOLOGICAL AND ECOLOGICAL INFLUENCES ON DEVELOPMENT AT 12 MONTHS OF AGE EJ 029 385

SPAULDING, ROBERT L.
ACHIEVEMENT, CREATIVITY, AND SELF-CONCEPT CORRELATES OF TEACHER-PUPIL TRANSACTIONS IN ELEMENTARY SCHOOL CLASSROOMS. ED024463
A SOCIAL LEARNING APPROACH TO EARLY CHILDHOOD EDUCATION. ED039025
THE SOUTHSIDE EXPERIMENT IN PERSONALIZED EDUCATION. ED042505
EFFECTS OF AGE OF ENTRY AND DURATION OF PARTICIPATION IN A COMPENSATORY EDUCATION PROGRAM. ED043380
CHANGING THE LEARNING PATTERNS OF THE CULTURALLY DIFFERENT. ED045184
EDUCATIONAL INTERVENTION IN EARLY CHILDHOOD: A REPORT OF A FIVE-YEAR LONGITUDINAL STUDY OF THE EFFECTS OF EARLY EDUCATIONAL INTERVENTION IN THE LIVES OF DISADVANTAGED CHILDREN IN DURHAM, NORTH CAROLINA. FINAL REPORT, VOLUME I. ED050814
EDUCATIONAL INTERVENTION IN EARLY CHILDHOOD: APPENDIXES. FINAL REPORT, VOLUME II. ED050815
EDUCATIONAL INTERVENTION IN EARLY CHILDHOOD: ABSTRACTS OF THE 1965-1970 SPECIAL STUDIES RESEARCH AND EVALUATION REPORT. FINAL REPORT, VOLUME III. ED050816
PERSONALIZED EDUCATION IN SOUTHSIDE SCHOOL EJ 013 561

SPEAR, PAUL S.
MOTIVATIONAL EFFECTS OF PRAISE AND CRITICISM ON CHILDREN'S LEARNING EJ 024 702

SPELLMANN, CHARLES MAC
THE SHIFT FROM COLOR TO FORM PREFERENCE IN YOUNG CHILDRE N OF DIFFERENT ETHNIC BACKGROUNDS. PART OF THE FINAL REPORT. ED025321

SPENCE, ALLYN G.
HOME LANGUAGE AND PERFORMANCE ON STANDARDIZED TESTS EJ 032 678

SPENCE, JANET T.
DO MATERIAL REWARDS ENHANCE THE PERFORMANCE OF LOWER-CLASS CHILDREN? EJ 053 735

SPENCE, JANET TAYLOR
THE DISTRACTING EFFECTS OF MATERIAL REINFORCERS IN THE DISCRIMINATION LEARNING OF LOWER- AND MIDDLE-CLASS CHILDREN EJ 018 871
VERBAL AND NONVERBAL REWARDS AND PUNISHMENT IN THE DISCRIMINATION LEARNING OF CHILDREN OF VARYING SOCIOECONOMIC STATUS EJ 057 896

SPENCER, MIMA, COMP.
BIBLIOGRAPHY: TEACHER CHARACTERISTICS. ED029716

SPENCER, RICHARD E.
A BIBLIOGRAPHY OF RESEARCH ON FOREIGN STUDENT AFFAIRS. ED021629

SPERBER, ZANWIL
PATTERNS OF MOTHER-INFANT CONTACT: THE SIGNIFICANCE OF LATERAL PREFERENCE EJ 030 513

SPICKER, HOWARD H.
THE INFLUENCE OF SELECTED VARIABLES ON THE EFFECTIVENESS OF PRESCHOOL PROGRAMS FOR DISADVANTAGED CHILDREN. ED049835

SPIKER, CHARLES C.
THE EFFECTS OF VERBAL PRETRAINING ON THE MULTIDIMENSIONAL GENERALIZATION BEHAVIOR OF CHILDREN EJ 060 784
ON THE COMPARISON OF PSYCHOLOGICAL THEORIES: A REPLY TO PROFESSOR BOGARTZ EJ 060 786

SPINDLER, PEARL G.
CHILD CARE ARRANGEMENTS OF WORKING MOTHERS IN THE UNITED STATES. ED040738

SPITZ, HERMAN H.
A COMPARISON OF RETARDATES AND NORMALS ON THE POGGENDORFF AND OPPEL-KUNDT ILLUSIONS EJ 024 943

SPITZE, GLENNYS S.
FANTASIZING AND POETRY CONSTRUCTION IN PRESCHOOLERS EJ 018 132

SPODEK, BERNARD
EXTENDING OPEN EDUCATION IN THE UNITED STATES. ED038182
ISSUES AND REALITIES IN EARLY CHILDHOOD EDUCATION. ED041621
WHAT ARE THE SOURCES OF EARLY CHILDHOOD CURRICULUM? EJ 027 943

SPRADLIN, JOSEPH E.
A NONVERBAL TECHNIQUE FOR STUDYING MUSIC PREFERENCE EJ 043 285

SPRIGLE, HERBERT
A FRESH APPROACH TO EARLY CHILDHOOD EDUCATION AND A STUDY OF ITS EFFECTIVENESS. LEARNING TO LEARN PROGRAM. ED019117

SPRIGLE, HERBERT A.
CAN POVERTY CHILDREN LIVE ON "SESAME STREET?" EJ 034 509

SROUFE, L. ALAN
A METHODOLOGICAL AND PHILOSOPHICAL CRITIQUE OF INTERVENTION-ORIENTED RESEARCH EJ 019 323
AGE CHANGES IN CARDIAC DECELERATION WITHIN A FIXED FOREPERIOD REACTION-TIME TASK: AN INDEX OF ATTENTION EJ 043 667

STAATS, ARTHUR W.
REPLICATION OF THE "MOTIVATED LEARNING" COGNITIVE TRAINING PROCEDURES WITH CULTURALLY DEPRIVED PRESCHOOLERS. REPORT FROM PROJECT MOTIVATED LEARNING. ED029708
CATEGORIES AND UNDERLYING PROCESSES, OR REPRESENTATIVE BEHAVIOR SAMPLES AND S-R ANALYSIS: OPPOSING STRATEGIES. ED032120
LEARNING AND COGNITIVE DEVELOPMENT: REPRESENTATIVE SAMPLES, CUMULATIVE-HIERARCHICAL LEARNING, AND EXPERIMENTAL-LONGITUDINAL METHODS EJ 032 509

STABENAU, JOAN C.
INFANT EDUCATION: A COMMUNITY PROJECT EJ 008 462

STABLER, JOHN R.
THE RELATIONSHIP BETWEEN RACE AND PERCEPTION OF RACIALLY-RELATED STIMULI IN PRESCHOOL CHILDREN. ED030483
INSTRUMENTAL PERFORMANCE AS A FUNCTION OF REINFORCEMENT SCHEDULE, LUCK VERSUS SKILL INSTRUCTIONS, AND SEX OF CHILD EJ 024 934
THE MEASUREMENT OF CHILDREN'S SELF-CONCEPT AS RELATED TO RACIAL MEMBERSHIP EJ 056 629

STAFFIERI, J. ROBERT
STEREOTYPIC AFFECTIVE PROPERTIES OF PERSONAL NAMES AND SOMATOTYPES IN CHILDREN EJ 043 352

STAFFORD, RICHARD E.
AN INVESTIGATION OF SIMILARITIES IN PARENT-CHILD TEST SCORES FOR EVIDENCE OF HEREDITARY COMPONENTS. ED027060

STALLINGS, WILLIAM M.
FREEDOM FROM EXTERNAL EVALUATION EJ 055 897

STAMP, ISLA M.
METODO DE ARCHIVAR LAS OBSERVACIONES DEL COMPORTAMIENTO DEL NINO, COMO GUIA PARA ENTENDERLO MEJOR EJ 045 232
METODO DE ARCHIVAR LAS OBSERVACIONES DEL COMPORTAMIENTO DEL NINO, COMO GUIA PARA ENTENDERLO MEJOR (METHODS OF RECORDING OBSERVATIONS OF CHILDREN'S BEHAVIOR, A GUIDE FOR BETTER UNDERSTANDING) EJ 049 938

STANCHFIELD, JO M.
THE DEVELOPMENT OF PRE-READING SKILLS IN AN EXPERIMENTAL KINDERGARTEN PROGRAM EJ 037 099

STANT, MARGARET ADAMS
LET'S TRY THIS IN NURSERY SCHOOL AND KINDERGARTEN. ED022556

STAPP, WILLIAM B.
THE LIVING WORLD: THE PHYSICAL ENVIRONEMNT EJ 029 388

STARKS, ESTHER B.
BLOCKBUILDING. ED020011

STARKWEATHER, ELIZABETH KEZIA
PRE-SCHOOL RESEARCH AND EVALUATION PROJECT. ED022541

STARR, R. H., JR.
NURTURANCE, DEPENDENCE, AND EXPLORATORY BEHAVIOR IN PREKINDERGARTENERS. ED035443

STARR, RAYMOND H., JR.
COGNITIVE DEVELOPMENT IN INFANCY: ASSESSMENT, ACCELERATION, AND ACTUALIZATION EJ 037 493

STAUB, ERVIN
DETERMINANTS OF CHILDREN'S ATTEMPTS TO HELP ANOTHER CHILD IN DISTRESS. ED039023
NEED FOR APPROVAL, CHILDREN'S SHARING BEHAVIOR, AND RECIPROCITY IN SHARING EJ 018 321
A CHILD IN DISTRESS: THE INFLUENCE OF NURTURANCE AND MODELING ON CHILDREN'S ATTEMPTS TO HELP EJ 043 314
THE USE OF ROLE PLAYING AND INDUCTION IN CHILDREN'S LEARNING OF HELPING AND SHARING BEHAVIOR EJ 046 467

STAUBER, KATHLEEN A.
IDENTIFICATION OF VERBAL CONCEPTS BY PRESCHOOL CHILDREN EJ 042 958

STAYTON, DONELDA J.
INFANT OBEDIENCE AND MATERNAL BEHAVIOR: THE ORIGINS OF SOCIALIZATION RECONSIDERED EJ 052 446

STAYTON, SAMUEL E.
SENSORY ORGANIZATION IN RETARDATES AND NORMALS EJ 019 013
SENSORY ORGANIZATION AND INTELLIGENCE: A MODIFICATION AND REPLICATION EJ 024 946

STECHER, MIRIAM B.
CONCEPT LEARNING THROUGH MOVEMENT IMPROVISATION: THE TEACHER'S ROLE AS CATALYST EJ 014 945

STEDMAN, DONALD J.
AN APPROACH TO THE STUDY OF INFANT BEHAVIOR. ED039031
A COMPARISON OF PARENT AND TEACHER RATINGS ON THE PRESCHOOL ATTAINMENT RECORD OF SEVENTEEN FIVE-YEAR-OLD DISADVANTAGED CHILDREN. ED039922
A COMPARATIVE STUDY OF FAILURE AVOIDANCE IN CULTURALLY DISADVANTAGED AND NON-CULTURALLY DISADVANTAGED FIRST GRADE CHILDREN. ED044170
DEVELOPMENTAL-BEHAVIORAL PATTERNS IN TWENTY-SIX CULTURALLY DISADVANTAGED INFANTS. ED044173

STEDMAN, JAMES M.
FAMILY FACTORS RELATED TO COMPETENCE IN YOUNG, DISADVANTAGED MEXICAN-AMERICAN CHILDREN. PART OF THE FINAL REPORT ON HEAD START EVALUATION AND RESEARCH: 1968-69 TO THE OFFICE OF ECONOMIC OPPORTUNITY. ED037248
FAMILY FACTORS RELATED TO COMPETENCE IN YOUNG DISADVANTAGED MEXICAN-AMERICAN CHILDREN EJ 053 753

STEELE, CAROLYN I.
SEX ROLE IDENTITY OF ADOLESCENT GIRLS IN FOSTER HOMES AND INSTITUTIONS EJ 059 644

STEFFE, LESLIE P.
THE PERFORMANCE OF FIRST GRADE CHILDREN IN FOUR LEVELS OF CONSERVATION OF NUMEROUSNESS AND THREE IQ GROUPS WHEN SOLVING ARITHMETIC ADDITION PROBLEMS. ED016535
THE EFFECTS OF TWO VARIABLES ON THE PROBLEM-SOLVING ABILITIES OF FIRST-GRADE CHILDREN. ED019113
A STUDY OF THE INTERRELATIONSHIPS OF CONSERVATION OF LENGTH RELATIONS, CONSERVATIONS OF LENGTH, AND TRANSITIVITY OF LENGTH RELATIONS OF THE AGE OF FOUR AND FIVE YEARS. ED031303
PROBLEM SOLVING PERFORMANCES OF FIRST GRADE CHILDREN. ED041623
AN INVESTIGATION IN THE LEARNING OF EQUIVALENCE AND ORDER RELATIONS BY FOUR- AND FIVE-YEAR-OLD CHILDREN. ED045178
THE ABILITY OF KINDERGARTEN AND FIRST GRADE CHILDREN TO USE THE TRANSITIVE PROPERTY OF THREE LENGTH RELATIONS IN THREE PERCEPTUAL SITUATIONS. ED048936
DIFFERENTIAL PERFORMANCE OF KINDERGARTEN CHILDREN ON TRANSITIVITY OF THREE MATCHING RELATIONS. ED048942
BEFORE CHILDREN CAN MEASURE EJ 032 359

STEGER, JOSEPH A.
CHILDREN'S USE OF CONTEXT IN JUDGMENT OF WEIGHT EJ 033 053

STEGLICH, W.G.
REPORT OF THE EFFECTIVENESS OF PROJECT HEAD START, LUBBOCK, TEXAS. PARTS I, II, AND APPENDICES. ED019131

STEIN, ALETHA HUSTON
THE EFFECTS OF SEX-ROLE STANDARDS FOR ACHIEVEMENT AND SEX-ROLE PREFERENCE ON THREE DETERMINANTS OF ACHIEVEMENT MOTIVATION EJ 034 454
THE INFLUENCE OF MASCULINE, FEMININE, AND NEUTRAL TASKS ON CHILDREN'S ACHIEVEMENT BEHAVIOR, EXPECTANCIES OF SUCCESS, AND ATTAINMENT VALUES EJ 037 318

STEIN, ANNIE
SIX MONTHS LATER--A COMPARISON OF CHILDREN WHO HAD HEAD START, SUMMER, 1965, WITH THEIR CLASSMATES IN KINDERGARTEN, A CASE STUDY OF THE KINDERGARTENS IN FOUR PUBLIC ELEMENTARY SCHOOLS, NEW YORK CITY. STUDY I. ED015025
FACTORS INFLUENCING THE RECRUITMENT OF CHILDREN INTO THE HEAD START PROGRAM, SUMMER 1965--A CASE STUDY OF SIX CENTERS IN NEW YORK CITY. STUDY II. ED015026
LONG-RANGE EFFECT OF PRE-SCHOOLING ON READING ACHIEVEMENT. STUDY III. ED015027

STEIN, GERALD M.
THE EFFECT OF A TELEVISION MODEL UPON RULE ADOPTION BEHAVIOR OF CHILDREN EJ 056 733

STEIN, MYRON
THE FUNCTION OF AMBIGUITY IN CHILD CRISES EJ 027 344

STEIN, NANCY L.
SAN MATEO COUNTY HUMAN RESOURCES COMMISSION PROJECT HEAD START - SUMMER 1966. AN EVALUATIONAL REPORT. ED023478

STEINMAN, WARREN M.
GENERALIZED IMITATION AND THE DISCRIMINATION HYPOTHESIS EJ 028 636
GENERALIZED IMITATION AS A FUNCTION OF DISCRIMINATION DIFFICULTY AND CHOICE EJ 038 455

STEINSCHNEIDER, ALFRED
III. OBSTETRICAL MEDICATION AND INFANT OUTCOME: SOME SUMMARY CONSIDERATIONS EJ 023 015

STEPHENS, BETH
THE FACTORIAL STRUCTURE OF REASONING, MORAL JUDGMENT, AND MORAL CONDUCT. ED031302
FACTORIAL STRUCTURE OF SELECTED PSYCHO-EDUCATIONAL MEASURES AND PIAGETIAN REASONING ASSESSMENTS EJ 055 112

STEPHENS, WILL BETH
PAPER-AND-PENCIL VERSUS CONCRETE PERFORMANCE OF NORMALS AND RETARDATES ON THE ETS WRITTEN EXERCISES. ED035442

STERN, CAROLYN
HEAD START RESEARCH AND EVALUATION OFFICE, UNIVERSITY OF CALIFORNIA AT LOS ANGELES. APPENDIX I TO THE ANNUAL REPORT, NOVEMBER 1967. ED020793
HEAD START RESEARCH AND EVALUATION OFFICE, UNIVERSITY OF CALIFORNIA AT LOS ANGELES. ANNUAL REPORT, NOVEMBER 1967. SECTION II. ED021613
THE PRESCHOOL LANGUAGE PROJECT. A REPORT OF THE FIRST YEAR'S WORK. ED023482
COMPARATIVE EFFECTIVENESS OF ECHOIC AND MODELING PROCEDURES IN LANGUAGE INSTRUCTION WITH CULTURALLY DISADVANTAGED CHILDREN. ED025314
THE VALUE OF THE SPOKEN RESPONSE IN TEACHING LISTENING SKILLS TO YOUNG CHILDREN THROUGH PROGRAMMED INSTRUCTION. FINAL REPORT. ED027973
COMPETENCE VS. PERFORMANCE IN YOUNG CHILDREN'S USE OF COMPLEX LINGUISTIC STRUCTURES. ED029687
CONDITIONS FOSTERING THE USE OF INFORMATIVE FEEDBACK BY YOUNG CHILDREN. ED029688
COMPARATIVE EFFECTIVENESS OF SPEAKING VERSUS LISTENING IN IMPROVING THE SPOKEN LANGUAGE OF DISADVANTAGED YOUNG CHILDREN. ED029689
EFFECT OF VARIETY ON THE LEARNING OF A SOCIAL STUDIES CONCEPT BY PRESCHOOL CHILDREN. ED029690
YOUNG CHILDREN'S USE OF LANGUAGE IN INFERENTIAL BEHAVIOR. ED029691
INFORMATION VALUE OF FEEDBACK WITH PRESCHOOL CHILDREN. ED031311
EFFECT OF VERBALIZATION ON YOUNG CHILDREN'S LEARNING OF A MANIPULATIVE SKILL. ED035447
ASSESSING PROCESS AND PRODUCT WITH YOUNG CHILDREN IN SCHOOL SETTINGS. ED035453
ECHOIC RESPONSE INVENTORY FOR CHILDREN (ERIC). ED039931
THE EFFECTIVENESS OF A STANDARD LANGUAGE READINESS PROGRAM AS A FUNCTION OF TEACHER DIFFERENCES. ED039932
A COMPARISON OF THREE INTERVENTION PROGRAMS WITH DISADVANTAGED PRESCHOOL CHILDREN. UNIVERSITY OF CALIFORNIA HEAD START RESEARCH AND EVALUATION CENTER. FINAL REPORT 1968-1969. ED041616
MAXIMIZING THE VALUE OF EVALUATION FOR THE HEAD START TEACHER. FINAL REPORT. ED041631
APPLICATION OF GROUP DYNAMICS PROCEDURES TO PROMOTE COMMUNICATION AMONG PARENTS AND TEACHERS. ED042512
HEAD START GRADUATES: ONE YEAR LATER. ED048929
INCREASING THE EFFECTIVENESS OF PARENTS-AS-TEACHERS. ED048939
CLASSROOM LANGUAGE OF TEACHERS OF YOUNG CHILDREN. ED053820
EFFECT OF VERBALIZATION ON YOUNG CHILDREN'S LEARNING OF A MANIPULATIVE SKILL EJ 020 520
COMPETENCE VERSUS PERFORMANCE IN YOUNG CHILDREN'S USE OF ADJECTIVAL COMPARATIVES EJ 033 701

STERN, DANIEL N.
A MICRO-ANALYSIS OF MOTHER-INFANT INTERACTION. BEHAVIOR REGULATING SOCIAL CONTACT BETWEEN A MOTHER AND HER 3 1/2 MONTH-OLD TWINS EJ 048 300

STERN, HARRIS W.
REACHING THE HARD-TO-REACH: THE USE OF PARTICIPANT GROUP METHODS WITH MOTHERS OF CULTURALLY DISADVANTAGED PRESCHOOL CHILDREN. ED024469

STERN, VIRGINIA
HEAD START EVALUATION AND RESEARCH CENTER. PROGRESS REPORT OF RESEARCH STUDIES 1966 TO 1967. DOCUMENT 4, DEVELOPMENT OF OBSERVATION PROCEDURES FOR ASSESSING PRESCHOOL CLASSROOM ENVIRONMENT. ED021626

STERNECK, ROSALIE
WORD-ASSOCIATION RESPONSES OF CHILDREN AS A FUNCTION OF AGE, SEX AND INSTRUCTIONS EJ 055 096

STERNLOF, RICHARD E.
THE INFLUENCE OF NONINTELLECTIVE FACTORS ON THE IQ SCORES OF MIDDLE- AND LOWER-CLASS CHILDREN EJ 056 621

STERNS, HARVEY L.
VERBAL-DISCRIMINATION LEARNING AND TRANSFER WITH VERBAL AND PICTORIAL MATERIALS EJ 030 287

STEUER, FAYE B.
TELEVISED AGGRESSION AND THE INTERPERSONAL AGGRESSION OF PRESCHOOL CHILDREN EJ 043 197

STEVENSON, HAROLD W.
INTERRELATIONS AND CORRELATES OVER TIME IN CHILDREN'S LEARNING EJ 025 954
LEARNING AND PROBLEM SOLVING BY THE MENTALLY RETARDED UNDER THREE TESTING CONDITIONS EJ 030 290

STEWARD, MARGARET S.
YOUNG CHILDREN'S ORIENTATION OF LETTERS AS A FUNCTION OF AXIS OF SYMMETRY AND STIMULUS ALIGNMENT EJ 032 909

STEWART, ANN H.
THE EFFECT OF EMOTION ON GROWTH EJ 053 653

STEWART, E. ELIZABETH
PROJECT HEAD START--SUMMER 1966. FINAL REPORT. SECTION ONE, SOME CHARACTERISTICS OF CHILDREN IN THE HEAD START PROGRAM. ED018246

STEWART, JEFFREY E.
THE EFFECTS OF DIFFERENT COMPETITIVE CONTINGENCIES ON COOPERATIVE BEHAVIOR EJ 042 208

STEWART, MARY LOU
A CHILD'S FIRST STEPS: SOME SPECULATIONS EJ 033 057

STEWART, WILLIAM A.
DESIGNS AND PROPOSAL FOR EARLY CHILDHOOD RESEARCH: A NEW LOOK: THE UNACKNOWLEDGED ROLE OF CULTURE CONFLICT IN NEGRO EDUCATION. (ONE IN A SERIES OF SIX PAPERS). ED053810

STEWIG, JOHN WARREN
CREATIVE DRAMA AND LANGUAGE GROWTH EJ 052 176

STILLWELL, CONNIE
EFFECTS OF PROVISION FOR INDIVIDUAL DIFFERENCES AND TEACHER ATTENTION UPON STUDY BEHAVIOR AND ASSIGNMENTS COMPLETED EJ 058 353

STODOLSKY, SUSAN S.
ANCONA MONTESSORI RESEARCH PROJECT FOR CULTURALLY DISADVANTAGED CHILDREN. SEPTEMBER 1, 1968 TO AUGUST 31, 1969. FINAL REPORT. ED044166
DIFFERENTIAL OUTCOMES OF A MONTESSORI CURRICULUM EJ 060 330

STOLLAK, GARY E.
CURIOSITY AND THE PARENT-CHILD RELATIONSHIP EJ 041 447

STOLZ, WALTER
AN INVESTIGATION OF THE STANDARD-NONSTANDARD DIMENSION OF CENTRAL TEXAN ENGLISH. PART OF THE FINAL REPORT. ED026130

STOLZ, WALTER S.
FINAL REPORT ON HEAD START EVALUATION AND RESEARCH--1966-67 TO THE INSTITUTE FOR EDUCATIONAL DEVELOPMENT. SECTION V, THE ROLE OF DIALECT IN THE SCHOOL-SOCIALIZATION OF LOWER CLASS CHILDREN. ED019121

STONE, MARY ANN
THE INTERSITUATIONAL GENERALITY OF FORMAL THOUGHT EJ 015 097

STONER, DONOVAN
TEACHING THE UNTEACHABLES EJ 021 514

STOTT, LELAND H.
THE IDENTIFICATION AND ASSESSMENT OF THINKING ABILITY IN YOUNG CHILDREN. FINAL REPORT. ED025316
INFANT AND PRESCHOOL MENTAL TESTS: REVIEW AND EVALUATION. ED026109

STOUT, IRVING W.
A SOURCE REPORT FOR DEVELOPING PARENT-CHILD EDUCATIONAL CENTERS. ED027944
A PLAN OF ACTION FOR PARENT-CHILD EDUCATIONAL CENTERS. ED027959

STOUWIE, ROGER J.
SOME DETERMINANTS OF CHILDREN'S SELF-REWARD BEHAVIOR AFTER EXPOSURE TO DISCREPANT REWARD CRITERIA EJ 030 511
INCONSISTENT VERBAL INSTRUCTIONS AND CHILDREN'S RESISTANCE-TO-TEMPTATION BEHAVIOR EJ 053 741

STRAIN, BARBARA
DEVELOPMENTAL TRENDS IN THE SELECTIVE PERCEPTION OF RACE AND AFFECT BY YOUNG NEGRO AND CAUCASIAN CHILDREN. ED046498

STRANDBERG, WARREN
THE NEW SCHOOL EJ 036 327

STRANG, HAROLD R.
AUTOMATED READING INSTRUCTION IN THE GHETTO EJ 045 798

STRANG, RUTH
READING. DIMENSIONS IN EARLY LEARNING SERIES. ED027070

STRAUSS, SIDNEY
OPERATIONAL THOUGHT INDUCEMENT EJ 018 874

STREAN, HERBERT S.
YOUTH AS ADVISERS TO ADULTS AND VICE VERSA EJ 018 068

STREET, PAUL
THE KINDERGARTEN AGAINST APPALACHIAN POVERTY EJ 037 021
SUFFER THE LITTLE KENTUCKY FIRST-GRADERS EJ 037 283

STREET, VIRGINIA
THE STORY OF AN AFTER - SCHOOL PROGRAM. ED035464

STREISSGUTH, ANN PYTKOWICS
MOTHER-CHILD INTERACTIONS AND COGNITIVE DEVELOPMENT IN CHILDREN EJ 051 567

STRETCH, JOHN J.
THE RIGHTS OF CHILDREN EMERGE: HISTORICAL NOTES ON THE FIRST WHITE HOUSE CONFERENCE ON CHILDREN EJ 023 283

STROM, ROBERT D.
TOY TALK: THE NEW CONVERSATION BETWEEN GENERATIONS EJ 020 395

STROMMEN, ELLEN A.
THE ROLE OF FRONT-BACK FEATURES IN CHILDREN'S "FRONT," "BACK," AND "BESIDE" PLACEMENTS OF OBJECTS EJ 060 777

STRONG, EMILY
CONDITIONING TASKS PERFORMANCE IN INFANCY AND EARLY CHILDHOOD AS A STABLE AND MEASURABLE ASPECT OF BEHAVIOR. FINAL REPORT. ED051890

STROUD, MICHAEL
THE LIMITATIONS OF BRIEF INTELLIGENCE TESTING WITH YOUNG CHILDREN. ED020774

STRUTHERS, JOSEPH A.
DEVELOPMENT OF A GROUP MEASURE TO ASSESS THE EXTENT OF PRE-LOGICAL AND PRE-CAUSAL THINKING IN PRIMARY SCHOOL AGE CHILDREN. ED019136

STUBBS, BETH
RESISTING PRESSURES IN THE PRE-SCHOOL CENTRE P 15-27 EJ 029 621

STUEMPFIG, DANIEL W.
PERSISTENCE AS A FUNCTION OF CONCEPTUAL STRUCTURE AND QUALITY OF FEEDBACK EJ 032 932

SUBOTNIK, LEO
TRANSFERENCE TOWARD THE CHILD THERAPIST AND OTHER PARENT SURROGATES EJ 049 427

SUDIA, CECELIA
TEENAGERS DISCUSS AGE RESTRICTIONS EJ 046 786

SUDIA, CECELIA E.
THE GENERATION GAP IN THE EYES OF YOUTH EJ 018 067
FAMILIES WITHOUT FATHERS EJ 049 656

SUGARMAN, JULE M.
THE 4-C PROGRAM EJ 007 090
RESEARCH, EVALUATION, AND PUBLIC POLICY: AN INVITED EDITORIAL EJ 021 381

SULLIVAN, EDMUND V.
A COMPARISON OF RELATIVE STRUCTURAL LEVELS ON A VARIETY OF COGNITIVE TASKS. ED032923
THE INFUENCE OF SOME TASK VARIABLES AND OF SOCIOECONOMIC CLASS ON THE MANIFESTATION OF CONSERVATION OF NUMBER EJ 017 711
A DEVELOPMENTAL STUDY OF THE RELATIONSHIP BETWEEN CONCEPTUAL, EGO, AND MORAL DEVELOPMENT EJ 021 999

SULLIVAN, FRANK J.
WHAT IS LEARNED IN PROBABILITY LEARNING EJ 018 879

SULLIVAN, HOWARD J.
PARENTS: SUMMER READING TEACHERS EJ 032 510

SULZER, JEFFERSON L.
BEHAVIORAL DATA FROM THE TULANE NUTRITION STUDY. ED043375

SUMMERS, DARRYL L.
USE OF THE IT SCALE FOR CHILDREN IN ASSESSING SEX-ROLE PREFERENCE IN PRESCHOOL NEGRO CHILDREN EJ 021 991

SUNDERLIN, SYLVIA
CHILDREN AND TV, TELEVISION'S IMPACT ON THE CHILD. ED013666

SUNDERLIN, SYLVIA, ED.
BIBLIOGRAPHY OF BOOKS FOR CHILDREN. 1971 EDITION. ED053798

SUNLEY, ROBERT
THINKING SKILLS AS A GOAL IN AN AFTER-SCHOOL PROGRAM EJ 037 635

SUPPES, PATRICK
CONCEPT FORMATION BY KINDERGARTEN CHILDREN IN A CARD-SORTING TASK. PSYCHOLOGY SERIES. ED013665
YOUNG CHILDREN'S COMPREHENSION OF LOGICAL CONNECTIVES. ED033756

SUTTON-SMITH, B.
THE INTERACTION OF FATHER-ABSENCE AND SIBLING-PRESENCE ON COGNITIVE ABILITIES. ED020024
SEX-ROLE IDENTITY AND SIBLING COMPOSITION EJ 035 626

SUTTON-SMITH, BRIAN
A DESCRIPTIVE ACCOUNT OF FOUR MODES OF CHILDREN'S PLAY BETWEEN ONE AND FIVE YEARS. ED049833
THE PLAYFUL MODES OF KNOWING. ED050806
DEVELOPMENTAL LAWS AND THE EXPERIMENTALIST'S ONTOLOGY EJ 027 439

SUZUKI, NANCY
THE LEARNING OF VERBAL STRINGS AS A FUNCTION OF CONNECTIVE FORM CLASS EJ 018 817

SUZUKI, NANCY S.
NOUN-PAIR LEARNING IN CHILDREN AND ADULTS: UNDERLYING STRINGS AND RETRIEVAL TIME EJ 056 402

SWAMINATHAN, INDIRA
PRESCHOOL EDUCATION, PARENTS AND THE COMMUNITY IN A DEVELOPING SOCIETY EJ 036 333

SWAMINATHAN, MINA
COMMUNITY PARTICIPATION IN PRESCHOOL EDUCATION--WHY AND HOW EJ 036 331

SWARTZ, JON D.
LONGITUDINAL STUDY OF COGNITIVE DICTIONARIES FROM AGES NINE TO SEVENTEEN EJ 024 940

SWARTZ, KARYL
DEVELOPMENT OF RELATIONAL CONCEPTS AND WORD DEFINITION IN CHILDREN FIVE THROUGH ELEVEN EJ 056 397

SWEELY, H. D.
THE EFFECT OF THE MALE ELEMENTARY TEACHER ON CHILDREN'S SELF-CONCEPTS. ED039034

SWENSON, ESTHER J.
MAKING PRIMARY ARITHMETIC MEANINGFUL TO CHILDREN. ED020015

SWENSON, SHARON A.
ASSOCIATION AND ABSTRACTION AS MECHANISMS OF IMITATIVE LEARNING EJ 035 367
ABSTRACTION, INFERENCE, AND THE PROCESS OF IMITATIVE LEARNING EJ 047 685

SWETT, MANETTE
"THIS YEAR I GOT MY BUDDY TO LAUGH" EJ 044 509

SWIFT, MARSHALL
LANGUAGE STYLE OF THE LOWER CLASS MOTHER: A PRELIMINARY STUDY OF A THERAPEUTIC TECHNIQUE. ED027943

SYKES, DONALD H.
ATTENTION IN HYPERACTIVE CHILDREN AND THE EFFECT OF METHYLPHENIDATE (RITALIN) EJ 043 669

TAFT, JEROME
THE DEVELOPMENT OF A TEST TO ASSESS THE OCCURRENCE OF SELECTED FEATURES OF NON-STANDARD ENGLISH IN THE SPEECH OF DISADVANTAGED PRIMARY CHILDREN. ED015790

TALBERT, CAROL
A DISCUSSION OF RESEARCH AIMS AND STRATEGIES FOR STUDYING EDUCATION IN THE INNER-CITY (A CRITIQUE OF NON-PARTICIPANT OBSERVATIONS). PRELIMINARY DRAFT. ED038187

TAMMINEN, ARMAS W.
AN EVALUATION OF A PRESCHOOL TRAINING PROGRAM FOR CULTURALLY DEPRIVED CHILDREN. FINAL REPORT. ED019135

TANAKA, MASAKO N.
UNDERSTANDING OF QUANTITATIVE CONCEPTS IN 3 1/2-4 1/2 YEAR-OLD CHILDREN. ED046491

TANGUAY, PETER E.
A PROGRAM FOR HOSPITALIZED PSYCHOTIC CHILDREN: REGULAR ATTENDANCE, AWAY FROM THE HOSPITAL, AT A COMMUNITY NURSERY SCHOOL EJ 050 938

TANNENBAUM, ABRAHAM J.
AN EARLY INTERVENTION PROGRAM THAT FAILED. ED021609

TANNENBAUM, JORDAN
CONCEPT AND LANGUAGE DEVELOPMENT OF A GROUP OF FIVE YEAR OLDS WHO HAVE ATTENDED THE SYRACUSE UNIVERSITY CHILDREN'S CENTER INTERVENTION PROGRAM. ED046515

TAYLOR, ARTHUR M.
VISUAL IMAGERY INSTRUCTION AND NON-ACTION VERSUS ACTION SITUATIONS RELATIVE TO RECALL BY CHILDREN. FINAL REPORT. ED050828

TAYLOR, JEWELL C.
ANALYSES OF STORIES DICTATED IN CLASSES OF THE COOPERATIVE PROJECT. ED019993

TAYLOR, JOSEPH L.
THE CHILD WELFARE AGENCY AS THE EXTENDED FAMILY EJ 052 493

TAYLOR, STANFORD E.
LISTENING. WHAT RESEARCH SAYS TO THE TEACHER, NO. 29. ED026120

TAYLOR, T. WILLIAM
"TUBE" PLAY EJ 008 263

TAYLOR, THOMASINE H
MEXICAN-AMERICANS AND LANGUAGE LEARNING EJ 012 397

TEAGER, JOYCE
CONDITIONS FOSTERING THE USE OF INFORMATIVE FEEDBACK BY YOUNG CHILDREN. ED029688
INFORMATION VALUE OF FEEDBACK WITH PRESCHOOL CHILDREN. ED031311
CONDITIONS FOSTERING THE USE OF INFORMATION FEEDBACK BY YOUNG CHILDREN. (REVISED REPORT). ED039950

TEGHTSOONIAN, MARTHA
THE CONTROL OF RELATIVE SIZE BY PICTORIAL DEPTH CUES IN CHILDREN AND ADULTS EJ 042 506

TEMKIN, POLLY B.
THE OFF-KILTERED KIDS EJ 028 383

TEMP, GEORGE
PROJECT HEAD START--SUMMER 1966. FINAL REPORT. SECTION THREE, PUPILS AND PROGRAMS. ED018248

TENNIS, MELVIN
THE DEVELOPMENT OF A TEST TO ASSESS THE OCCURRENCE OF SELECTED FEATURES OF NON-STANDARD ENGLISH IN THE SPEECH OF DISADVANTAGED PRIMARY CHILDREN. ED015790

THELEN, MARK H.
LONG-TERM RETENTION OF VERBAL IMITATION EJ 024 941
THE EFFECT OF SUBJECT RACE, MODEL RACE, AND VICARIOUS PRAISE ON VICARIOUS LEARNING EJ 045 458
THE ACQUISITION AND PERFORMANCE OF A SOCIALLY NEUTRAL RESPONSE AS A FUNCTION OF VICARIOUS REWARD EJ 046 889
EXPECTANCY TO PERFORM AND VICARIOUS REWARD: THEIR EFFECTS UPON IMITATION EJ 059 513

THOGERSON, ANN
A PARENT-CHILD CENTER, NOVEMBER-DECEMBER 1968. ED042506

THOMAN, EVELYN B.
VISUAL ALERTNESS IN NEONATES AS EVOKED BY MATERNAL CARE EJ 027 847
NEONATE-MOTHER INTERACTION: EFFECTS OF PARITY ON FEEDING BEHAVIOR EJ 032 892
THE RELATIVE EFFICACY OF CONTACT AND VESTIBULAR-PROPRIOCEPTIVE STIMULATION IN SOOTHING NEONATES EJ 058 588

THOMAS, ALEXANDER, ED.
ANNUAL PROGRESS IN CHILD PSYCHIATRY AND CHILD DEVELOPMENT 1969. ED032941

THOMAS, CAROLYN B.
HELPING FOSTER PARENTS UNDERSTAND DISTURBED CHILDREN EJ 037 238

THOMAS, EVELYN B.
FEEDING BEHAVIORS OF NEWBORN INFANTS AS A FUNCTION OF PARITY OF THE MOTHER EJ 053 736

THOMAS, HOBEN
PSYCHOLOGICAL ASSESSMENT INSTRUMENTS FOR USE WITH HUMAN INFANTS EJ 025 231

THOMAS, JOHN I.
STRUCTURE OF-OR FOR-KNOWLEDGE? EJ 050 038

THOMAS, SUSAN BAHLKE
SELF-INITIATED VERBAL REINFORCEMENT AND POSITIVE SELF-CONCEPT EJ 052 462

THOMAS, WALTER L.
THE THOMAS SELF-CONCEPT VALUES TEST. ED027068

THOMPSON, ALICE C.
THE SORE-FOOTED DUCK EJ 053 929

THOMPSON, JACK M.
THE IMPLICATIONS OF PARENT EFFECTIVENESS TRAINING FOR FOSTER PARENTS. ED052821

THOMPSON, LYNN C.
A STUDY IN CHILD CARE. VOLUME III: COST AND QUALITY ISSUES FOR OPERATORS. DAY CARE PROGRAMS REPRINT SERIES. ED051912

THOMPSON, NANCY
HEAD START ON HEALTH. ED027972

THOMPSON, NORMAN L., JR.
IT SCORE VARIATIONS BY INSTRUCTIONAL STYLE EJ 022 142

THOMPSON, SPENCER K.
THE PRIORITY OF CUES IN SEX DISCRIMINATION BY CHILDREN AND ADULTS EJ 044 691

THOMSON, CAROLYN
HEAD START EVALUATION AND RESEARCH CENTER, UNIVERSITY OF KANSAS. REPORT NO. I, THE OBSERVATION OF REINFORCEMENT BEHAVIOR OF TEACHERS IN HEAD START CLASSROOMS AND THE MODIFICATION OF A TEACHER'S ATTENDING BEHAVIOR. ED021633

THOMSON, CAROLYN L.
THE MODIFICATION OF TEACHER BEHAVIORS WHICH MODIFY CHILD BEHAVIORS. PROGRESS REPORT. ED042499

THOMSON, ERIC W.
MATERIAL REINFORCEMENT AND SUCCESS IN SPELLING EJ 018 423

THORN, ELIZABETH A.
THE EFFECT OF DIRECT INSTRUCTION IN LISTENING ON THE LISTENING AND READING COMPREHENSION OF FIRST GRADE CHILDREN. DISSERTATION ABSTRACT. ED029693

THORNDIKE, ROBERT L.
HEAD START EVALUATION AND RESEARCH CENTER, TEACHERS COLLEGE, COLUMBIA UNIVERSITY. ANNUAL REPORT (1ST), SEPTEMBER 1966-AUGUST 1967. (TITLE SUPPLIED). ED020781

THORNTON, SAM
PROJECT HEAD START, PSYCHOLOGICAL SERVICES REPORT, RESEARCH, SUMMER 1968. ED024460

THORNTON, SAM M.
SEMO PROJECT HEAD START, PSYCHOLOGICAL SERVICES REPORT, SUMMER 1967. PHASE THREE FINAL REPORT. ED020779
SEMO PROJECT HEAD START, PSYCHOLOGICAL SERVICES REPORT, 1966-67 YEAR PROGRAM. ED020780

THORSELL, SIV
BEFORE SCHOOL STARTS. FOR CHILDREN'S MINDS--NOT JUST TO MIND THE CHILDREN. THE CHILD CENTRE--AS SEEN BY A PARENT. ED051873

THORSON, SONDRA J.
THE POLITICAL SOCIALIZATION OF CHILDREN AND THE STRUCTURE OF THE ELEMENTARY SCHOOL. ED024468

THURMAN, ROBERT S.
THE PRINCIPAL AND THE KINDERGARTEN EJ 016 716

TIEDER, MYRA
THIRTY YEARS OF INNOVATION IN FOSTER CARE EJ 044 230

TIGHE, LOUISE S.
TRANSFER FROM PERCEPTUAL PRETRAINING AS A FUNCTION OF NUMBER OF TASK DIMENSIONS EJ 016 165
OPTIONAL SHIFT BEHAVIOR OF CHILDREN AS A FUNCTION OF AGE, TYPE OF PRETRAINING AND STIMULUS SALIENCE EJ 021 849
DIMENSIONAL PREFERENCE AND DISCRIMINATION SHIFT LEARNING IN CHILDREN EJ 025 959
REVERSALS PRIOR TO SOLUTION OF CONCEPT IDENTIFICATION IN CHILDREN EJ 060 782

TIGHE, THOMAS J
TRANSFER FROM PERCEPTUAL PRETRAINING AS A FUNCTION OF NUMBER OF TASK DIMENSIONS EJ 016 165

TIGHE, THOMAS J.
OPTIONAL SHIFT BEHAVIOR OF CHILDREN AS A FUNCTION OF AGE, TYPE OF PRETRAINING AND STIMULUS SALIENCE EJ 021 849
REVERSALS PRIOR TO SOLUTION OF CONCEPT IDENTIFICATION IN CHILDREN EJ 060 782

TILLMAN, RODNEY
DEVELOPING A LEARNING ENVIRONMENT OF QUALITY EJ 027 028

TIMBERLAKE, PATRICIA
ART - FOR THE CHILD'S SAKE EJ 041 829

TINDALL, ROBERT C.
INTERACTION OF REWARD, PUNISHMENT, AND SEX IN A TWO-CHOICE DISCRIMINATION TASK WITH CHILDREN EJ 024 948

TISHER, R. P.
A PIAGETIAN QUESTIONNAIRE APPLIED TO PUPILS IN A SECONDARY SCHOOL EJ 053 907

TISZA, VERONICA B.
THE USE OF A PLAY PROGRAM BY HOSPITALIZED CHILDREN EJ 026 774

TIZARD, BARBARA
ENVIRONMENTAL EFFECTS ON LANGUAGE DEVELOPMENT: A STUDY OF YOUNG CHILDREN IN LONG-STAY RESIDENTIAL NURSERIES EJ 058 859

TOBIN, MICHAEL F.
BIG STEPS ON BEHALF OF LITTLE PEOPLE EJ 058 769

TODD, JUDY
INTERACTIVE EFFECTS OF INFORMATIONAL AND AFFECTIVE COMPONENTS OF SOCIAL AND NONSOCIAL REINFORCERS ON INDEPENDENT AND DEPENDENT CHILDREN EJ 022 141

TOLOR, ALEXANDER
SEX DIFFERENCES IN ADAPTIVE STYLES EJ 045 046
SELF-PARENTAL DISTANCE, CONTROL OF REINFORCEMENT, AND PERSONAL FUTURE TIME PERSPECTIVE EJ 045 047

TOMLINSON-KEASEY, C.
CONDITIONING OF INFANT VOCALIZATIONS IN THE HOME ENVIRONMENT EJ 055 214
FORMAL OPERATIONS IN FEMALES FROM ELEVEN TO FIFTY-FOUR YEARS OF AGE EJ 055 215

TONKIN, ROGER S.
PRESCHOOLER STUDY: THE MEDICAL, SOCIAL AND ECONOMIC CORRELATES OF POVERTY IN PRESCHOOL CHILDREN OF BRITISH COLUMBIA. A PILOT STUDY. ED046518

TOOLEY, KAY
OR PSYCHOANALYTIC THEORY OF ADOLESCENCE? EJ 007 790
THE ROLE OF GEOGRAPHIC MOBILITY IN SOME ADJUSTMENT PROBLEMS OF CHILDREN AND FAMILIES EJ 023 430

TOPINSKA, ZOFIA
LE PROBLEME DE LA LIBERTE ET DE LA DISCIPLINE DANS LE JEU (PROBLEMS OF FREEDOM AND DISCIPLINE IN PLAY) EJ 061 465

TORRANCE, E. PAUL
THE CREATIVE-AESTHETIC APPROACH TO SCHOOL READINESS AND MEASURED CREATIVE GROWTH. ED017344
UNDERSTANDING THE FOURTH GRADE SLUMP IN CREATIVE THINKING. FINAL REPORT. ED018273
FREEDOM TO MANIPULATE OBJECTS AND QUESTION-ASKING PERFORMANCE OF SIX-YEAR-OLDS EJ 029 217
"STRUCTURE" CAN IMPROVE THE GROUP BEHAVIOR OF FIVE-YEAR-OLD CHILDREN EJ 049 937

TOUGH, JOAN
LANGUAGE AND ENVIRONMENT: AN INTERIM REPORT ON A LONGITUDINAL STUDY. ED032136

TOWLER, J.O.
TRAINING EFFECTS AND CONCEPT DEVELOPMENT--A STUDY OF THE CONSERVATION OF CONTINUOUS QUANTITY IN CHILDREN. ED016533

TOWLER, JOHN O.
A STUDY OF THE DEVELOPMENT OF EGOCENTRISM AND THE COORDINATION OF SPATIAL PERCEPTIONS IN ELEMENTARY SCHOOL CHILDREN. FINAL REPORT. ED050829

TRACHY, SHARON
CONSERVATION OF NUMBER IN VERY YOUNG CHILDREN: A FAILURE TO REPLICATE MEHLER AND BEVER EJ 041 144

TRATTNER, WALTER I.
HOMER FOLKS'S "THE CARE OF DESTITUTE, NEGLECTED AND DELINQUENT CHILDREN" EJ 059 593

TREHUB, SANDRA E.
AUDITORY-LINGUISTIC SENSITIVITY IN EARLY INFANCY EJ 053 479

TRELLA, SHERRY CRANE
TEACHING RACE RELATIONS IN THE NURSERY SCHOOL EJ 056 864

TROLL, LILLIAN E.
SIMILARITIES IN VALUES AND OTHER PERSONALITY CHARACTERISTICS IN COLLEGE STUDENTS AND THEIR PARENTS EJ 012 718

TROWBRIDGE, NORMA
SELF CONCEPT AND SOCIO-ECONOMIC STATUS EJ 059 509

TUDDENHAM, READ D.
RACE AND CONFORMITY AMONG CHILDREN EJ 038 937

TULKIN, STEVEN R.
MOTHER-CHILD INTERACTION: SOCIAL CLASS DIFFERENCES IN THE FIRST YEAR OF LIFE. ED044177
THE EFFECTS OF EXPERIENCE ON INFANTS' REACTIONS TO SEPARATION FROM THEIR MOTHERS. ED053802
AN ANALYSIS OF THE CONCEPT OF CULTURAL DEPRIVATION EJ 055 111
MOTHER-CHILD INTERACTION IN THE FIRST YEAR OF LIFE EJ 056 632

TUMIN, MELVIN
EARLY EDUCATION: THE CREATION OF CAPACITY. ED028824

TURAIDS, DAINIS
A PERCEPTUAL TEST BATTERY: DEVELOPMENT AND STANDARDIZATION EJ 058 395

TURKEWITZ, GERALD
FACTORS AFFECTING LATERAL DIFFERENTIATION IN THE HUMAN NEW-BORN EJ 015 395

TURKNETT, CAROLYN NORRIS
THE SOCIOLOGY OF EARLY CHILDHOOD EDUCATION: A REVIEW OF LITERATURE. TECHNICAL REPORT NO. 1. ED032944

TURNER, DEVONNE GAE
THE READABILITY OF SELECTED SECOND GRADE SOCIAL STUDIES TEXTBOOKS. ED027968

TURNER, RALPH R.
COMPARISON OF IMITATION AND COMPREHENSION SCORES BETWEEN TWO LOWER-CLASS GROUPS AND THE EFFECTS OF TWO WARM-UP CONDITIONS ON IMITATION OF THE SAME GROUPS EJ 056 709

TURNER, ROBERT V.
THE EFFECT OF A PERCEPTUAL-MOTOR TRAINING PROGRAM UPON THE READINESS AND PERCEPTUAL DEVELOPMENT OF CULTURALLY DISADVANTAGED KINDERGARTEN CHILDREN. ED041633

TURNER, RUTH M.
SECOND STAGE TEACHING PROBLEMS IN A PUBLIC SCHOOL CLASS FOR EMOTIONALLY DISTURBED CHILDREN EJ 020 104

TURNURE, CYNTHIA
RESPONSE TO VOICE OF MOTHER AND STRANGER BY BABIES IN THE FIRST YEAR EJ 035 269

TURNURE, JAMES E.
CHILDREN'S REACTIONS TO DISTRACTORS IN A LEARNING SITUATION EJ 018 881
CONTROL OF ORIENTING BEHAVIOR IN CHILDREN UNDER FIVE YEARS OF AGE EJ 034 535
PERCEPTUAL INADEQUACY AND COMMUNICATIVE INEFFECTIVENESS IN INTERPERSONAL COMMUNICATION EJ 056 627

TWINING, GERALDINE
LOOKING IN -- TO SELF DISCOVERY EJ 058 134

TYLER, LOUIS L.
CURRICULUM BOON OR BANE? EJ 052 766

UNDERWOOD, ANA R.
LA EDUCACION PRE-ESCOLAR EN LAS ESCUELAS PUBLICAS DE PUERTO RICO EJ 029 622

UNRUH, SUSAN GULICK
BIRTH ORDER, NUMBER OF SIBLINGS AND SOCIAL REINFORCER EFFECTIVENESS IN CHILDREN EJ 052 453

URBANO, RICHARD C.
DIGIT SPAN, PRACTICE AND DICHOTIC LISTENING PERFORMANCE IN THE MENTALLY RETARDED EJ 015 850
RECOGNITION MEMORY: THE RELATIONSHIP OF ACCURACY AND LATENCY OF RESPONSE UNDER DIFFERENT MEMORY LOADS IN RETARDATES EJ 046 256

UTZINGER, ROBERT C.
SOME EUROPEAN NURSERY SCHOOLS AND PLAYGROUNDS. ED048928

UZGIRIS, INA C.
ATTENTIONAL PREFERENCE AND EXPERIENCE: II. AN EXPLORATORY LONGITUDINAL STUDY OF THE EFFECTS OF VISUAL FAMILIARITY AND RESPONSIVENESS. ED039938
ATTENTIONAL PREFERENCE AND EXPERIENCE: II. AN EXPLORATORY LONGITUDINAL STUDY OF THE EFFECT OF VISUAL FAMILIARITY AND RESPONSIVENESS EJ 025 363

VALLERY, ARLEE
CONDITIONING TASKS PERFORMANCE IN INFANCY AND EARLY CHILDHOOD AS A STABLE AND MEASURABLE ASPECT OF BEHAVIOR. FINAL REPORT. ED051890

VALOTTO, EVELYN
KINDERGARTEN, 1967-68. AN EVALUATION REPORT. ED025315
THE CHANGE PROCESS IN ACTION: KINDERGARTEN ED027949
CHILD STUDY-KINDERGARTEN, 1968-69: AN INFORMATION REPORT. ED039015

VAN ALLEN, ROACH
LANGUAGE EXPERIENCES WHICH PROMOTE READING. ED034571

VAN CAMP, SARAH S.
HOW FREE IS FREE PLAY? EJ 055 535

VAN CARA, FLO
THE EFFECTS OF DIFFERENT TYPES OF REINFORCEMENT ON YOUNG CHILDREN'S INCIDENTAL LEARNING. ED044184
THE EFFECTS OF DIFFERENT TYPES OF REINFORCEMENT ON YOUNG CHILDREN'S INCIDENTAL LEARNING EJ 053 752

VAN DE RIET, HANI
AN EVALUATION OF THE EFFECTS OF A UNIQUE SEQUENTIAL LEARNING PROGRAM ON CULTURALLY DEPRIVED PRESCHOOL CHILDREN. FINAL REPORT. ED019994
A FOLLOW-UP EVALUATION OF THE EFFECTS OF A UNIQUE SEQUENTIAL LEARNING PROGRAM, A TRADITIONAL PRESCHOOL PROGRAM AND A NO TREATMENT PROGRAM ON CULTURALLY DEPRIVED CHILDREN. FINAL REPORT. ED042516
A SEQUENTIAL APPROACH TO EARLY CHILDHOOD AND ELEMENTARY EDUCATION, PHASE I. GRANT REPORT. ED042517

VAN DE RIET, VERNON
AN EVALUATION OF THE EFFECTS OF A UNIQUE SEQUENTIAL LEARNING PROGRAM ON CULTURALLY DEPRIVED PRESCHOOL CHILDREN. FINAL REPORT. ED019994
A FOLLOW-UP EVALUATION OF THE EFFECTS OF A UNIQUE SEQUENTIAL LEARNING PROGRAM, A TRADITIONAL PRESCHOOL PROGRAM AND A NO TREATMENT PROGRAM ON CULTURALLY DEPRIVED CHILDREN. FINAL REPORT. ED042516
A SEQUENTIAL APPROACH TO EARLY CHILDHOOD AND ELEMENTARY EDUCATION, PHASE I. GRANT REPORT. ED042517
A SEQUENTIAL APPROACH TO EARLY CHILDHOOD AND ELEMENTARY EDUCATION, PHASE II. GRANT REPORT. ED047791

VAN DEN DAELE, LELAND D.
PRESCHOOL INTERVENTION THROUGH SOCIAL LEARNING. ED036316
INFANT REACTIVITY TO REDUNDANT PROPRIOCEPTIVE AND AUDITORY STIMULATION: A TWIN STUDY. ED052825
CONTINUITY IN THE DEVELOPMENT OF CONCEPTUAL BEHAVIOR IN PRESCHOOL CHILDREN: A REJOINDER EJ 018 888

VAN DER DOES, V. I.
CHILDREN AND ROAD ACCIDENTS EJ 050 496

VAN DOREN, ERIC E.
AGGRESSIVE GROUP WORK WITH TEENAGE DELINQUENT BOYS EJ 007 444
HELPING HOUSEPARENTS FIND AND USE THEIR CREATIVITY EJ 022 215

VAN DUYNE, H. JOHN
THE DEVELOPMENT OF THE CONTROL OF ADULT INSTRUCTIONS OVER NON-VERBAL BEHAVIOR. ED041620
THE DEVELOPMENT OF THE CONTROL OF ADULT INSTRUCTIONS OVER NONVERBAL BEHAVIOR EJ 061 138

VAN EGMOND, ELMER
OPERATION HEAD START--AN EVALUATION. FINAL REPORT. ED013117

VAN EVERY, PHILLIP
EVALUATION OF INKSTER PRESCHOOL PROJECT. FINAL REPORT. ED027093

VAN SICKLE, DOUGLAS
DISCRIMINATION OF STEREOMETRIC OJBECTS AND PHOTOGRAPHS OF OBJECTS BY CHILDREN EJ 053 749

VAN TIL, WILLIAM
THE TEMPER OF THE TIMES EJ 000 391

VAN WYCK, BETTY
RESEARCH FOR UNDERSTANDING EJ 051 150

VANCE, BARBARA J.
THE EFFECT OF PRESCHOOL GROUP EXPERIENCE ON VARIOUS LANGUAGE AND SOCIAL SKILLS IN DISADVANTAGED CHILDREN. FINAL REPORT. ED019989

VANCE, BILLIE J.
VISUAL AND HAPTIC DIMENSIONAL PREFERENCE: A DEVELOPMENTAL STUDY EJ 026 506

VANDENBERG, STEVEN G.
FURTHER EVIDENCE ON THE RELATION BETWEEN AGE OF SEPARATION AND SIMILARITY IN IQ AMONG PAIRS OF SEPARATED IDENTICAL TWINS. ED027058
HUMAN BEHAVIOR GENETICS: PRESENT STATUS AND SUGGESTIONS FOR FUTURE RESEARCH EJ 004 046

VANDEVENTER, MARY
THE LEARNING AND TRANSFER OF DOUBLE-CLASSIFICATION SKILLS BY FIRST GRADERS EJ 036 821
THE LEARNING AND TRANSFER OF DOUBLE-CLASSIFICATION SKILLS: A REPLICATION AND EXTENSION EJ 046 254

VANEVERY, HARDYN
SEMANTICS, PHRASE STRUCTURE, AND AGE AS VARIABLES IN SENTENCE RECALL EJ 025 962

VASTA, ROSS
THE MODELING OF SHARING: EFFECTS ASSOCIATED WITH VICARIOUS REINFORCEMENT, SYMBOLIZATION, AGE, AND GENERALIZATION EJ 028 894

VAUGHAN, VICTOR C., III, ED.
ISSUES IN HUMAN DEVELOPMENT: AN INVENTORY OF PROBLEMS, UNFINISHED BUSINESS AND DIRECTIONS FOR RESEARCH. ED051888

VAUGHN, JOHN W.
DO YOU REALLY WANT TO IMPROVE THE CURRICULUM? EJ 031 850

VEAL, L. RAMON
A STUDY COMPARING GLOBAL QUALITY AND SYNTACTIC MATURITY IN THE WRITING COMPOSITION OF SECOND AND THIRD GRADE STUDENTS. ED029697

VEDEL-PETERSEN, JACOB
WHAT IS A GOOD KINDERGARTEN? EJ 035 243

VEENSTRA, MARJORIE SHAFER
BEHAVIOR MODIFICATION IN THE HOME WITH THE MOTHER AS THE EXPERIMENTER: THE EFFECT OF DIFFERENTIAL REINFORCEMENT ON SIBLING NEGATIVE RESPONSE RATES EJ 056 721

VENN, JERRY R.
THE VICARIOUS CONDITIONING OF EMOTIONAL RESPONSES IN NURSERY SCHOOL CHILDREN. FINAL REPORT. ED046540

VERMA, AMITA
THE ROLE OF A LABORATORY NURSERY SCHOOL EJ 036 332

VEROFF, JOANNE B.
THEORETICAL NOTES ON POWER MOTIVATION EJ 032 677

VEROFF, JOSEPH
THEORETICAL NOTES ON POWER MOTIVATION EJ 032 677

VERSELE, BERNARD-ALEXANDER
UN EXEMPLE D'OBSERVATION INTENSIVE DU COMPORTEMENT DE JEUNES ENFANTS DANS LE CADRE D'UNE GARDERIE EJ 034 534

VERSTEEG, ARLEN
LEVELS OF ASPIRATION, ACHIEVEMENT, AND SOCIOCULTURAL DIFFERENCES IN PRESCHOOL CHILDREN EJ 043 482

VERY, PHILIP S.
DIFFERENTIAL FACTOR STRUCTURE OF SEVENTH GRADE STUDENTS EJ 030 298

VINCE-BAKONYI, AGNES
SELF-MADE TOYS IN CHILDREN'S GAMES EJ 011 253

VOLKERS, JANICE J.
CONCERNED CITIZENS IN THE MAKING EJ 000 192

VON BARAVALLE, HERMANN
THE INTERNATIONAL WALDORF SCHOOL MOVEMENT. ED015019

VONDRACEK, FRED W.
THE MANIPULATION AND MEASUREMENT OF SELF-DISCLOSURE IN PREADOLESCENTS EJ 034 298

VONDRACEK, SARAH I.
THE MANIPULATION AND MEASUREMENT OF SELF-DISCLOSURE IN PREADOLESCENTS EJ 034 298

VORE, DAVID A.
MATERNAL FOOD RESTRICTION: EFFECTS ON OFFSPRING DEVELOPMENT, LEARNING, AND A PROGRAM OF THERAPY EJ 029 218
DEVELOPMENT OF CONSERVATION IN NORMAL AND RETARDED CHILDREN EJ 053 651

VOYAT, GILBERT
THINKING BEFORE LANGUAGE? A SYMPOSIUM: 1. RELATIONSHIPS BETWEEN LANGUAGE AND THOUGHT EJ 050 075

VOYDANOFF, PATRICIA
SOCIAL CLASS AND PARENT'S ASPIRATIONS FOR THEIR CHILDREN. REPORT NUMBER 8. ED030482
SOCIAL CLASS AND PARENTS' ASPIRATIONS FOR THEIR CHILDREN. RESEARCH REPORT NO. 3 (REVISED). ED043371

VROEGH, KAREN
SEX ROLE TYPING IN THE PRESCHOOL YEARS: AN OVERVIEW. ED026134
MASCULINITY AND FEMININITY IN THE ELEMENTARY AND JUNIOR HIGH SCHOOL YEARS EJ 034 902
THE RELATIONSHIP OF BIRTH ORDER AND SEX OF SIBLINGS TO GENDER ROLE IDENTITY EJ 039 901

VUKILICH, CAROL
TEACHING READING IN THE KINDERGARTEN: A REVIEW OF RECENT STUDIES EJ 055 153

WACHS, HARRY
THINKING BEFORE LANGUAGE? A SYMPOSIUM: 2. A SCHOOL FOR THINKING EJ 050 200

WACHS, THEODORE D.
COGNITIVE DEVELOPMENT IN INFANTS OF DIFFERENT AGE LEVELS AND FROM DIFFERENT ENVIRONMENTAL BACKGROUNDS. ED015786
REPORT ON THE UTILITY OF A PIAGET-BASED INFANT SCALE WITH OLDER RETARDED CHILDREN EJ 022 247
COGNITIVE DEVELOPMENT IN INFANTS OF DIFFERENT AGE LEVELS AND FROM DIFFERENT ENVIRONMENTAL BACKGROUNDS: AN EXPLANATORY INVESTIGATION EJ 046 244
THE EFFECTS OF ENRICHED NEONATAL EXPERIENCES UPON LATER COGNITIVE FUNCTIONING EJ 047 689
THE EFFECTS OF CHRONOLOGICAL AGE, TRIALS, AND LIST CHARACTERISTICS UPON CHILDREN'S CATEGORY CLUSTERING EJ 052 454

WADE, CAMILLE
THE FAMILY DAY CARE PROGRAM IN MILWAUKEE: A 3-FACETED APPROACH TO COMMUNITY ENRICHMENT EJ 023 391

WADLINGTON, WALTER
A NEW LOOK AT THE COURTS AND CHILDREN'S RIGHTS EJ 007 092

WADSWORTH, H. G.
MEETING SOCIO-EDUCATIONAL NEEDS EJ 027 916

WAGNER, MARSDEN G.
STATEMENT BY MARSDEN G. WAGNER, M. D. REPRESENTING THE AMERICAN PUBLIC HEALTH ASSOCIATION BEFORE THE SELECT SUBCOMMITTEE ON EDUCATION, MARCH 3, 1970. ED039940

WAGNER, MURIEL G.
NUTRITION AND MENTAL DEVELOPMENT. RESEARCH REPORT NO. 5. ED037252

WAHLER, R. G.
THE MODIFICATION OF CHILDHOOD STUTTERING: SOME RESPONSE-RESPONSE RELATIONSHIPS EJ 023 965

WAKEFIELD, WILLIAM M.
AWARENESS, AFFECTION, AND PERCEIVED SIMILARITY IN THE PARENT-CHILD RELATIONSHIP EJ 025 377

WALBEK, NANCY H.
THE IMPACT OF WORDS AND DEEDS CONCERNING ALTRUISM UPON CHILDREN EJ 026 154

WALBEK, NANCY HODGES
PREACHING AND PRACTICING GENEROSITY: CHILDREN'S ACTIONS AND REACTIONS EJ 022 140

WALDROP, MARY F.
MATERNAL BEHAVIOR TOWARD OWN AND OTHER PRESCHOOL CHILDREN: THE PROBLEM OF "OWNNESS" EJ 026 324

WALK, RICHARD D.
ARTISTIC STYLE AS CONCEPT FORMATION FOR CHILDREN AND ADULTS EJ 046 247

WALKER, JOHN
THE DEVELOPMENT OF TEMPORAL DISCRIMINATION IN YOUNG CHILDREN. ED045187

WALKER, WANDA
DEVELOPMENT OF A READINESS TEST FOR DISADVANTAGED PRE-SCHOOL CHILDREN IN THE UNITED STATES. FINAL REPORT. ED037253

WALL, HARVEY R.
TEAM TEACHING. A DESCRIPTIVE AND EVALUATIVE STUDY OF A PROGRAM FOR THE PRIMARY GRADES. ED027083

WALLACE, HELEN M.
SOME THOUGHTS ON PLANNING HEALTH CARE FOR CHILDREN AND YOUTH EJ 038 021

WALLACE, J. G.
CONCEPT GROWTH AND THE EDUCATION OF THE CHILD: A SURVEY OF RESEARCH ON CONCEPTUALIZATION. NATIONAL FOUNDATION FOR EDUCATIONAL RESEARCH IN ENGLAND AND WALES OCCASIONAL PUBLICATION SERIES NO. 12. ED026121

WALLACH, MICHAEL A.
EFFECTS OF SOCIAL CLASS ON CHILDREN'S MOTORIC EXPRESSION EJ 025 149

WALLER, DAVID A.
A FOLLOW-UP STUDY OF INTELLIGENCE CHANGES IN CHILDREN WHO PARTICIPATED IN PROJECT HEADSTART. ED020786

WALLS, RICHARD T.
COGNITIVE FACTORS IN SEMANTIC CONDITIONING. A THESIS IN EDUCATIONAL PSYCHOLOGY. ED027069
COGNITIVE FACTORS IN THE CONDITIONING OF CHILDREN'S PREFERENCES EJ 021 989
DISADVANTAGED AND NONDISADVANTAGED CHILDREN'S EXPECTANCY IN SKILL AND CHANCE OUTCOMES EJ 034 903
RETROACTIVE AND PROACTIVE MULTIPLE LIST INTERFERENCE WITH DISADVANTAGED CHILDREN EJ 057 895

WALSH, JOHN F.
EFFECTS OF SYNTACTICAL MEDIATION, AGE, AND MODES OF REPRESENTATION ON PAIRED-ASSOCIATE LEARNING EJ 056 615

WALTERS, ELIZABETH
YOUNG BLACK AND WHITE LISTENERS. ED038180

WALTERS, RICHARD H.
INTERACTION OF SEX OF SUBJECT AND DEPENDENCY-TRAINING PROCEDURES IN A SOCIAL-REINFORCEMENT STUDY EJ 006 877

WANG, MARGARET
AN EXPLORATORY INVESTIGATION OF THE CARROLL LEARNING MODEL AND THE BLOOM STRATEGY FOR MASTERY LEARNING. ED028841

WANG, MARGARET C.
APPROACHES TO THE VALIDATION OF LEARNING HIERARCHIES. ED043376
EVALUATION UNDER INDIVIDUALIZED INSTRUCTION EJ 036 826
THE SEQUENCE OF DEVELOPMENT OF SOME EARLY MATHEMATICS BEHAVIORS EJ 056 710

WARD, EDNA M.
A STUDY OF CAUSAL THINKING IN ELEMENTARY SCHOOL CHILDREN. FINAL REPORT. ED050830

WARD, JAMES W.
SINGLE VERSUS CUMULATIVE PRESENTATION OF STIMULI TO KINDERGARTNERS IN REVERSAL SHIFT BEHAVIOR EJ 047 678

WARD, WILLIAM C.
RATE AND UNIQUENESS IN CHILDREN'S CREATIVE RESPONDING. ED034581
EFFECT OF LABELS ON MEMORY IN THE ABSENCE OF REHEARSAL. ED051883
NAMING AND MEMORY IN NURSERY SCHOOL CHILDREN IN THE ABSENCE OF REHEARSAL EJ 042 961
INCENTIVE EFFECTS IN CHILDREN'S CREATIVITY EJ 059 317

WARREN, VERA L.
SOCIAL REINFORCEMENT SATIATION: AN OUTCOME OF FREQUENCY OR AMBIGUITY? EJ 058 144

WARREN, VIRGINIA LEE
AN INTERVIEW WITH GEORGIA MCMURRAY, NEW YORK CITY'S COMMISSIONER FOR CHILD DEVELOPMENT EJ 050 274
NIGHT CARE CENTER EJ 050 379

WASIK, BARBARA H.
AN EXPERIMENTAL SUMMER KINDERGARTEN FOR CULTURALLY DEPRIVED CHILDREN. ED044174
THE APPLICATION OF PREMACK'S GENERALIZATION ON REINFORCEMENT TO THE MANAGEMENT OF CLASSROOM BEHAVIOR EJ 028 634
PERFORMANCE OF CULTURALLY DEPRIVED CHILDREN ON THE CONCEPT ASSESSMENT KIT--CONSERVATION EJ 053 906

WASIK, JOHN L.
PERFORMANCE OF CULTURALLY DEPRIVED CHILDREN ON THE CONCEPT ASSESSMENT KIT--CONSERVATION EJ 053 906

WASSERMAN, SUSAN A.
VALUES OF MEXICAN-AMERICAN, NEGRO, AND ANGLO BLUE-COLLAR AND WHITE-COLLAR CHILDREN EJ 052 653

WASSERMANN, SELMA
ASPEN MORNINGS WITH SYLVIA ASHTON-WARNER EJ 056 860

WATERMAN, ALAN S.
A LONGITUDINAL STUDY OF CHANGES IN EGO IDENTITY STATUS DURING THE FRESHMAN YEAR AT COLLEGE EJ 043 193

WATERMAN, CAROLINE K.
A LONGITUDINAL STUDY OF CHANGES IN EGO IDENTITY STATUS DURING THE FRESHMAN YEAR AT COLLEGE EJ 043 193

WATERS, ELINOR
CHILD DEVELOPMENT AND SOCIAL SCIENCE EDUCATION. PART III: ABSTRACTS OF RELEVANT LITERATURE. ED023466

WATSON, EUNICE L.
THE DAY CARE NEIGHBOR SERVICE: A HANDBOOK FOR THE ORGANIZATION AND OPERATION OF A NEW APPROACH TO FAMILY DAY CARE. ED049810

WATSON, JOHN S.
MEMORY AND "CONTINGENCY ANALYSIS" IN INFANT LEARNING. ED024437
RELATION OF SPATIAL EGOCENTRISM AND SPATIAL ABILITIES OF THE YOUNG CHILD. REPORT NUMBER 7. ED030481
SPATIAL ABILITIES AND SPATIAL EGOCENTRISM IN THE YOUNG CHILD EJ 037 066
COGNITIVE-PERCEPTUAL DEVELOPMENT IN INFANCY: SETTING FOR THE SEVENTIES EJ 038 262
NONSOCIAL REINFORCEMENT OF INFANTS' VOCALIZATIONS EJ 058 219
REACTIONS TO RESPONSE-CONTINGENT STIMULATION IN EARLY INFANCY EJ 059 874

WATSON, PETER
INDIVIDUAL DIFFERENCES IN CHILDREN'S REACTIONS TO FRUSTRATIVE NONREWARD EJ 030 591
INDIVIDUAL DIFFERENCES IN CHILDREN'S REACTIONS TO REWARD AND NONREWARD EJ 045 459

WATT, LOIS B., COMP.
ENVIRONMENTAL ECOLOGICAL EDUCATION IN CHILDREN'S BOOKS EJ 029 393

WATTS, GRAEME H.
YOUNG CHILDREN'S PERFORMANCE ON A TWO-CHOICE TASK AS A FUNCTION OF SOCIAL REINFORCEMENT, BASE-LINE PREFERENCE, AND RESPONSE STRATEGY EJ 039 635

WAX, MURRAY L.
SUMMARY AND OBSERVATIONS IN THE DAKOTAS AND MINNESOTA. INDIAN COMMUNITIES AND PROJECT HEAD START. ED013670
INDIAN COMMUNITIES AND PROJECT HEAD START. SUMMARY AND OBSERVATIONS IN THE DAKOTAS AND MINNESOTA, TOGETHER WITH AN APPRAISAL OF POSSIBILITIES FOR A HEAD START PROGRAM AMONG THE POTAWATOMI INDIANS OF KANSAS. ED016510

WAX, ROSALIE H.
SUMMARY AND OBSERVATIONS IN THE DAKOTAS AND MINNESOTA. INDIAN COMMUNITIES AND PROJECT HEAD START. ED013670
THE WARRIOR DROPOUTS. ED016529

WAXLER, CAROLYN ZAHN
FACTORS INFLUENCING IMITATIVE LEARNING IN PRESCHOOL CHILDREN EJ 018 892

WAYNE, JACK I.
THE SCHOOL AND THE UNIVERSITY: CO-OPERATIVE ROLES IN STUDENT TEACHING EJ 015 981

WEAVER, KITTY D.
LENIN'S GRANDCHILDREN: PRESCHOOL EDUCATION IN THE SOVIET UNION. ED049830

WEBB, ROGER A.
INFORMATION AND STRATEGY IN THE YOUNG CHILD'S SEARCH FOR HIDDEN OBJECTS EJ 056 395

WEBBINK, PATRICIA G.
A COMPARATIVE STUDY OF FAILURE AVOIDANCE IN CULTURALLY DISADVANTAGED AND NON-CULTURALLY DISADVANTAGED FIRST GRADE CHILDREN. ED044170

WEBER, JAMES
SOCIAL ANTECEDENTS OF PRESCHOOL CHILDREN'S BEHAVIORS. REPORT NUMBER 2. ED030476

WEBER, ROBERT E.
OPTIMIZING EDUCATIONAL INVESTMENT STRATEGIES. ED015780

WEBSTER, PATRICIA ROWE
THE TEACHER STRUCTURE CHECKLIST: A POSSIBLE TOOL FOR COMMUNICATION EJ 051 352

WEBSTER, R. L.
CHANGES IN INFANTS' VOCALIZATIONS AS A FUNCTION OF DIFFERENTIAL ACOUSTIC STIMULATION EJ 061 139

WECHSLER, JILL D.
IMPROVING THE SELF-CONCEPTS OF ACADEMIC UNDERACHIEVERS THROUGH MATERNAL GROUP COUNSELING EJ 043 200

WEEKS, THELMA E.
SPEECH REGISTERS IN YOUNG CHILDREN EJ 052 450

WEENER, PAUL
LANGUAGE STRUCTURE AND THE FREE RECALL OF VERBAL MESSAGES BY CHILDREN. ED032933
LANGUAGE STRUCTURE AND THE FREE RECALL OF VERBAL MESSAGES BY CHILDREN EJ 044 693

WEI, TAM T. D.
PIAGET'S CONCEPT OF CLASSIFICATION: A COMPARATIVE STUDY OF SOCIALLY DISADVANTAGED AND MIDDLE-CLASS YOUNG CHILDREN EJ 046 239

WEI, TAM THI DANG
PIAGET'S CONCEPT OF CLASSIFICATION: A COMPARATIVE STUDY OF SOCIALLY DISADVANTAGED AND MIDDLE-CLASS YOUNG CHILDREN. ED046499

WEIKART, DAVID P.
PRELIMINARY RESULTS FROM A LONGITUDINAL STUDY OF DISADVANTAGED PRESCHOOL CHILDREN. ED030490
COMPARATIVE STUDY OF THREE PRESCHOOL CURRICULA. ED042484
YPSILANTI PRESCHOOL CURRICULUM DEMONSTRATION PROJECT, 1968-1971. ED046503
HAS PRESCHOOL COMPENSATORY EDUCATION FAILED? ED049834
RELATIONSHIP OF CURRICULUM, TEACHING, AND LEARNING IN PRESCHOOL EDUCATION. ED049837
SYMPOSIUM ON PARENT-CENTERED EDUCATION: 3. LEARNING THROUGH PARENTS: LESSONS FOR TEACHERS EJ 054 379

WEIKART, DAVID P., ED.
PRESCHOOL INTERVENTION--A PRELIMINARY REPORT OF THE PERRY PRESCHOOL PROJECT. ED018251

WEIL, LINN B., ED.
CAN I LOVE THIS PLACE? A STAFF GUIDE TO OPERATING CHILD CARE CENTERS FOR THE DISADVANTAGED. ED049809

WEILAND, I. HYMAN
PATTERNS OF MOTHER-INFANT CONTACT: THE SIGNIFICANCE OF LATERAL PREFERENCE EJ 030 513

WEIN, NORMAN
RELATIONSHIP OF CONSERVATION EXPLANATIONS TO ITEM DIFFICULTY EJ 030 295

WEINBERG, DENISE HOOTSTEIN
THE RELATIONSHIP BETWEEN LIQUID CONSERVATION AND COMPENSATION EJ 059 313

WEINBERG, SHEILA
A SEX DIFFERENCE IN THE WECHSLER IQ VOCABULARY SCORE AS A PREDICTOR OF STRATEGY IN A PROBABILITY-LEARNING TASK PERFORMED BY ADOLESCENTS EJ 026 376

WEINER, BARBARA
MOTOR ACTIVITY: EFFECTS ON MEMORY EJ 021 769

WEINER, BERNARD
AN ATTRIBUTIONAL (COGNITIVE) MODEL OF MOTIVATION. ED038173

WEINHEIMER, SIDNEY
EGOCENTRISM AND SOCIAL INFLUENCE IN CHILDREN EJ 058 590

WEINSTOCK, HENRY R.
DO STUDENTS' IDEAS AND ATTITUDES SURVIVE PRACTICE TEACHING? EJ 013 228

WEINTRAUB, DANIEL J.
COMING OF AGE WITH THE DELBOEUF ILLUSION: BRIGHTNESS CONTRAST, COGNITION AND PERCEPTUAL DEVELOPMENT EJ 055 100

WEIR, MARY K.
HELP FOR TEACHERS IN PRESCHOOLS: A PROPOSAL. ED031308
STAFFING PRESCHOOLS: BACKGROUND INFORMATION. ED034589

WEIR, MORTON W.
AGE AND MEMORY AS FACTORS IN PROBLEM SOLVING. ED025327
THE ROLE OF REINFORCEMENT PROCEDURE IN CHILDREN'S PROBABILITY LEARNING AS A FUNCTION OF AGE AND NUMBER OF RESPONSE ALTERNATIVES EJ 046 253
STRENGTH OF DIMENSIONAL PREFERENCES AS A PREDICTOR OF NURSERY-SCHOOL CHILDREN'S PERFORMANCE ON A CONCEPT-SHIFT TASK EJ 049 169

WEISBERG, PAUL
EFFECTS OF REINFORCEMENT HISTORY ON TIMING (DRL) PERFORMANCE IN YOUNG CHILDREN EJ 024 936

WEISER, MARGARET
AWARENESS--ONE KEY TO READING READINESS EJ 027 551

WEISER, MARGARET G.
TEACHING AND THE NEW MORALITY EJ 016 776

WEISMAN, LORRAINE I.
PIAGETIAN TASKS AS CLASSROOM EVALUATIVE TOOLS EJ 032 679

WEISS, JONATHAN H.
BIRTH ORDER AND PHYSIOLOGICAL STRESS RESPONSE EJ 022 000

WEISS, STEPHAN D.
THE FATHER-DAUGHTER RELATIONSHIP AND THE PERSONALITY DEVELOPMENT OF THE FEMALE EJ 017 904

WEISSBERG, PAUL
PROXIMITY AND INTERACTIONAL BEHAVIOR OF YOUNG CHILDREN TO THEIR "SECURITY" BLANKETS EJ 053 748

WEIZMANN, FREDRIC
NOVELTY, FAMILIARITY, AND THE DEVELOPMENT OF INFANT ATTENTION EJ 034 529
THE MEASUREMENT OF VISUAL ATTENTION IN INFANTS: A COMPARISON OF TWO METHODOLOGIES EJ 037 494

WELLER, LEONARD
CLASSIFICATION PATTERNS OF UNDERPRIVILEGED CHILDREN IN ISRAEL EJ 041 140
ARTICULATION OF THE BODY CONCEPT AMONG FIRST-GRADE ISRAELI CHILDREN EJ 053 744

WENAR, CHARLES
ACTIVITY LEVEL AND MOTOR INHIBITION: THEIR RELATIONSHIP TO INTELLIGENCE-TEST PERFORMANCE IN NORMAL CHILDREN EJ 046 242
EXECUTIVE COMPETENCE AND SPONTANEOUS SOCIAL BEHAVIOR IN ONE-YEAR-OLDS EJ 056 732

WENDER, KARL
AGE DIFFERENCES IN PLEASANTNESS OF VISUAL PATTERNS OF DIFFERENT VARIABILITY IN LATE CHILDHOOD AND ADOLESCENCE EJ 035 989

WENZEL, LAWRENCE A.
AN EXPERIMENTAL APPROACH TO THE EFFECT OF GROUP ANIMADVERSION EJ 012 678

WERRY, JOHN S.
THE PREVALENCE OF BEHAVIOR SYMPTOMS IN YOUNGER ELEMENTARY SCHOOL CHILDREN. ED039040

WERZBERGER, JONAS B.
RECOGNITION OF ENGLISH AND HEBREW LETTERS AS A FUNCTION OF AGE AND DISPLAY PREDICTABILITY EJ 047 893

WEST, JOEL D.
MODIFYING RISK-TAKING BEHAVIOR EJ 032 891

WEST, R. F.
THE EFFECTS OF A PAY-OFF MATRIX ON SELECTIVE ATTENTION EJ 023 436

WESTER, ASTRID
THE SWEDISH CHILD: A SURVEY OF THE LEGAL, ECONOMIC, EDUCATIONAL, MEDICAL AND SOCIAL SITUATION OF CHILDREN AND YOUNG PEOPLE IN SWEDEN. ED050811

WHEELER, ALAN H.
CREATING A CLIMATE FOR INDIVIDUALIZING INSTRUCTION EJ 044 511

WHITAKER, DANIEL L.
AN ANNOTATED BIBLIOGRAPHY OF BEHAVIOR MODIFICATION WITH CHILDREN AND RETARDATES. ED020025

WHITCOMB, MARY WAKEFIELD
A COMPARISON OF THE ORAL LANGUAGE PATTERNS OF THREE LOW SOCIOECONOMIC GROUPS OF PUPILS ENTERING FIRST GRADE. ED032943

WHITE, BURTON L.
THE INITIAL COORDINATION OF SENSORIMOTOR SCHEMAS IN HUMAN INFANTS - PIAGET'S IDEAS AND THE ROLE OF EXPERIENCE. ED016514
INFORMAL EDUCATION DURING THE FIRST MONTHS OF LIFE. ED024452
[COMPETENCE IN YOUNG CHILDREN.] ED032124
THE ROLE OF EXPERIENCE IN THE BEHAVIORAL DEVELOPMENT OF HUMAN INFANTS: CURRENT STATUS AND RECOMMENDATIONS. ED048917
AN ANALYSIS OF EXCELLENT EARLY EDUCATIONAL PRACTICES: PRELIMINARY REPORT. ED050805
CHILD DEVELOPMENT RESEARCH: AN EDIFICE WITHOUT A FOUNDATION EJ 004 045

WHITE, DORIS, COMP.
MULTI-ETHNIC BOOKS FOR HEAD START CHILDREN. PART I: BLACK AND INTEGRATED LITERATURE. ED031312

WHITE, GLENN M.
INITIAL PROBABILITY REHEARSAL, AND CONSTRAINT IN ASSOCIATIVE CLASS SELECTION EJ 057 903

WHITE, KATHLEEN M.
CONCEPTUAL STYLE AND CONCEPTUAL ABILITY IN KINDERGARTEN THROUGH THE EIGHTH GRADE EJ 053 484

WHITE, SHELDON H.
THE HIERARCHICAL ORGANIZATION OF INTELLECTUAL STRUCTURES. ED022534

WHITE, WILLIAM F.
AFFECTIVE DIMENSIONS OF TEACHERS OF DISADVANTAGED CHILDREN IN SIX MAJORITY NEGRO SCHOOL DISTRICTS. ED028833

WHITEHURST, GROVER J.
GENERALIZED LABELING ON THE BASIS OF STRUCTURAL RESPONSE CLASSES BY TWO YOUNG CHILDREN EJ 044 696
PRODUCTION OF NOVEL AND GRAMMATICAL UTTERANCES BY YOUNG CHILDREN EJ 060 783

WHITELEY, JACK
SAY YOU COME FROM MISSOURI EJ 047 103

WHITEMAN, MARTIN
SOME EFFECTS OF SOCIAL CLASS AND RACE ON CHILDREN'S LANGUAGE AND INTELLECTUAL ABILITIES. ED022540
PERCEPTUAL AND SENSORIMOTOR SUPPORTS FOR CONSERVATION TASKS EJ 018 886

WHITON, MARY BETH
IDEATIONAL CREATIVITY AND EXPRESSIVE ASPECTS OF HUMAN FIGURE DRAWING IN KINDERGARTEN-AGE CHILDREN EJ 039 629

WHITTAKER, JAMES K.
COLONIAL CHILD CARE INSTITUTIONS: OUR HERITAGE OF CARE EJ 043 315

WHITTINGTON, KATHRYN D.
CHILDREN'S PERCEPTIONS OF A TEACHING TEAM EJ 051 772

WICKELGREN, LYN W.
THE OCULAR RESPONSE OF HUMAN NEWBORNS TO INTERMITTANT VISUAL MOVEMENT EJ 015 394

WIDOM, CATHY SPATZ
THE EFFECTS OF MODE OF PRESENTATION AND NUMBER OF CATEGORIES ON 4-YEAR-OLDS' PROPORTION ESTIMATES. ED032132

WIENER, GERALD
LONG TERM STUDY OF PREMATURES: SUMMARY OF PUBLISHED FINDINGS. ED043389

WILCOX, BARBARA LEE
THE CONTROL OF RELATIVE SIZE BY PICTORIAL DEPTH CUES IN CHILDREN AND ADULTS EJ 042 506

WILCOX, STEPHEN J.
TRANSFER OF VERBAL PAIRED ASSOCIATES IN MENTALLY RETARDED INDIVIDUALS AND NORMAL CHILDREN AS A FUNCTION OF INTERLIST SIMILARITY EJ 033 785

WILKERSON, DOXEY A.
UNDERSTANDING THE BLACK CHILD EJ 020 717
WILKERSON, PEGGY
ALL ABOUT ME. UNIT 1 CURRICULUM GUIDE. ED053789
WILLERMAN, EMILY G.
A DIGEST OF THE RESEARCH ACTIVITIES OF REGIONAL EVALUATION AND RESEARCH CENTERS FOR PROJECT HEAD START (SEPTEMBER 1, 1966 TO NOVEMBER 30, 1967). ED023446
WILLERMAN, LEE
INFANT DEVELOPMENT, PRESCHOOL IQ, AND SOCIAL CLASS EJ 018 465
WILLIAMS, A. KENTON
UNIVERSAL CHILD CARE EJ 043 354
WILLIAMS, BRUCE M.
AUDIO-VISUAL MATERIALS IN EARLY CHILDHOOD EDUCATION EJ 006 854
AUDIO-VISUAL MATERIALS IN EARLY CHILDHOOD EDUCATION EJ 038 907
WILLIAMS, BRUCE W.
"OF HAIRY ARMS AND A DEEP BARITONE VOICE": A SYMPOSIUM MEN IN YOUNG CHILDREN'S LIVES EJ 028 795
WILLIAMS, CAROL J.
HELPING PARENTS TO HELP THEIR CHILDREN IN PLACEMENT EJ 058 055
WILLIAMS, CHARLES RAY
A COMPARISON OF CONTRASTING PROGRAMS IN EARLY CHILDHOOD EDUCATION. ED046509
WILLIAMS, CYRIL E.
SOME PSYCHIATRIC OBSERVATIONS ON A GROUP OF MALADJUSTED DEAF CHILDREN EJ 026 155
WILLIAMS, F. NEIL
TRAINING WORKERS FOR CHILD CARE CENTERS EJ 050 935
WILLIAMS, FRANK E.
HELPING THE CHILD DEVELOP HIS CREATIVE POTENTIAL. ED026113
WILLIAMS, FRANK S.
ALIENATION OF YOUTH AS REFLECTED IN THE HIPPIE MOVEMENT EJ 023 427
WILLIAMS, JOHN E.
EVALUATION DIMENSION OF THE AFFECTIVE MEANING SYSTEM OF THE PRESCHOOL CHILD EJ 054 049
WILLIAMS, KERRY G.
CHILDREN'S SHIFT PERFORMANCE IN THE ABSENCE OF DIMENSIONALITY AND A LEARNED REPRESENTATIONAL RESPONSE EJ 033 786
WILLIAMS, LOIS E.
INDEPENDENT LEARNING IN THE ELEMENTARY SCHOOL CLASSROOM. ED036326
WILLIAMS, MELANIE L.
OBSERVATIONAL LEARNING: THE EFFECTS OF AGE, TASK DIFFICULTY, AND OBSERVERS' MOTORIC REHEARSAL EJ 044 702
WILLIAMS, RICHARD H.
PROJECT HEAD START--SUMMER 1966. FINAL REPORT. SECTION ONE, SOME CHARACTERISTICS OF CHILDREN IN THE HEAD START PROGRAM. ED018246
WILLIAMSON, JACK
EXPERIMENTAL PRESCHOOL INTERVENTION IN THE APPALACHIAN HOME EJ 036 395
WILLIAMSON, R. C.
CONCEPTS OF SOCIAL SEX ROLES AMONG CHILEAN ADOLESCENTS EJ 048 396
WILLIS, ERLINE
A STUDY IN CHILD CARE (CASE STUDY FROM VOLUME II-B): "I'M A NEW WOMAN NOW." DAY CARE PROGRAMS REPRINT SERIES. ED051897
WILLIS, RICHARD H.
CONFORMITY IN EARLY AND LATE ADOLESCENCE EJ 038 936
WILLNER, MILTON
PROJECT TREAT: A NEW APPROACH TO THE SEVERELY DISTURBED CHILD EJ 061 000
WILLOUGHBY, R. H.
THE INFLUENCE OF DIFFERENT RESPONSE CONSEQUENCES ON CHILDREN'S PREFERENCE FOR TIME-OUT EJ 022 213
OBSERVATIONAL LEARNING: THE EFFECTS OF AGE, TASK DIFFICULTY, AND OBSERVERS' MOTORIC REHEARSAL EJ 044 702
PERSONAL ORIENTATION TO SUCCESS AND FAILURE IN URBAN BLACK CHILDREN EJ 061 072
WILLOUGHBY, ROBERT H.
CONSERVATION OF NUMBER IN VERY YOUNG CHILDREN: A FAILURE TO REPLICATE MEHLER AND BEVER EJ 041 144
WILLS, CLARICE
SYMPOSIUM ON CHILD-OBSERVATION: 2. THE TWO-A-DAY OBSERVATION PLAN EJ 056 862
WILSON, CORNELIA D.
INFANT DEVELOPMENT IN LOWER CLASS AMERICAN FAMILIES. ED049836
WILSON, CORNIELIA
INFANT DEVELOPMENT IN LOWER-CLASS AMERICAN FAMILIES EJ 060 012
WILSON, JOHN A.R.
LONG TERM EFFECT OF STRUCTURED TRAINING ON 3 YOUNG CHILDREN. ED023480
WILSON, KARL E.
TRAINING COMMUNICATION SKILLS IN YOUNG CHILDREN EJ 058 606
WILSON, RONALD S.
EMERGENCE AND PERSISTENCE OF BEHAVIORAL DIFFERENCES IN TWINS EJ 053 732
WILSON, WINSTON T.
THE SATURDAY SCHOOL: AN INSTALLATION MANUAL. ED033765
WIMBERGER, HERBERT C.
A STUDY OF COMMUNICATION PATTERNS IN DISADVANTAGED CHILDREN. ED037250
WIMMER, MARY
THE CONCEPT OF DEATH IN EARLY CHILDHOOD EJ 052 464
WINAWER, BONNIE P.
CHILD'S PLAY, A CREATIVE APPROACH TO PLAYSPACES FOR TODAY'S CHILDREN. ED021630
WINEMAN, JOHN
COGNITIVE STYLE AND READING ABILITY EJ 043 239
WINICK, MARIANN PEZZELLA
SYMPOSIUM ON CHILD-OBSERVATION: 1. FILM-MAKING AS AN OBSERVATION TECHNIQUE EJ 056 861
WINN, MILDRED
INDEPENDENT STUDY AT SEVEN EJ 029 168
WINSTON, SHIRLEY
CHILDREN AND THE MASS MEDIA EJ 029 341
WISCHNER, GEORGE J.
EFFECT OF VERBAL PRETRAINING AND SINGLE-PROBLEM MASTERY ON WEIGL LEARNING-SET FORMATION IN CHILDREN EJ 018 883
WISE, LOUIS J.
ALIENATION OF PRESENT-DAY ADOLESCENTS EJ 023 428
WIST, ANNE H.
AUDITORY DISCRIMINATION ABILITIES OF DISADVANTAGED ANGLO- AND MEXICAN-AMERICAN CHILDREN EJ 015 258
WITELSON, SANDRA F.
CHILDREN'S RECALL STRATEGIES IN DICHOTIC LISTENING EJ 044 700
WITHALL, JOHN
EVALUATION OF CLASSROOM CLIMATE EJ 002 421
WITHERSPOON, RALPH L.
EFFECT OF TRIMESTER SCHOOL OPERATION ON THE ACHIEVEMENT AND ADJUSTMENT OF KINDERGARTEN AND FIRST THROUGH THIRD GRADE CHILDREN. FINAL REPORT. ED020003
WITHYCOMBE, JERALDINE S.
HEAD START IN MICRONESIA EJ 060 108
WITKIN, HERMAN A.
LONGITUDINAL STUDY OF DEVELOPMENT OF THE BODY CONCEPT EJ 021 993
WITRYOL, SAM L.
DISCRIMINATION LEARNING, PROBLEM SOLVING, AND CHOICE PATTERNING BY CHILDREN AS A FUNCTION OF INCENTIVE VALUE, MOTIVATION, AND SEQUENTIAL DEPENDENCIES. FINAL REPORT. ED016518
THE INCENTIVE VALUE OF UNCERTAINTY REDUCTION FOR CHILDREN EJ 045 454
THE INFLUENCE OF INCENTIVES ON MEMORY STAGES IN CHILDREN EJ 049 428
WITT, PETER A.
POSITION EFFECTS IN PLAY EQUIPMENT PREFERENCES OF NURSERY SCHOOL CHILDREN. ED045185
WITTE, KENNETH L.
THE EFFECTS OF REWARD AND PUNISHMENT UPON CHILDREN'S ATTENTION, MOTIVATION, AND DISCRIMINATION LEARNING EJ 041 137
WITTIG, MICHELE ANDRISIN
THE ROLE OF REINFORCEMENT PROCEDURE IN CHILDREN'S PROBABILITY LEARNING AS A FUNCTION OF AGE AND NUMBER OF RESPONSE ALTERNATIVES EJ 046 253

WITTROCK, M. C.
DEVELOPMENTAL SHIFTS IN VERBAL RECALL BETWEEN MENTAL AGES TWO AND FIVE EJ 036 825

WOHLFORD, PAUL
REACHING THE HARD-TO-REACH: THE USE OF PARTICIPANT GROUP METHODS WITH MOTHERS OF CULTURALLY DISADVANTAGED PRESCHOOL CHILDREN. ED024469
OLDER BROTHERS' INFLUENCE ON SEX-TYPED, AGGRESSIVE, AND DEPENDENT BEHAVIOR IN FATHER-ABSENT CHILDREN EJ 034 901

WOHLWILL, JOACHIM F.
EFFECT OF CORRELATED VISUAL AND TACTUAL FEEDBACK ON AUDITORY PATTERN LEARNING AT DIFFERENT AGE LEVELS EJ 037 517

WOLF, MONTROSE M.
AUTOMATED READING INSTRUCTION IN THE GHETTO EJ 045 798

WOLF, THOMAS M.
A DEVELOPMENTAL INVESTIGATION OF TELEVISED MODELED VERBALIZATIONS ON RESISTANCE TO DEVIATION EJ 058 218

WOLFE, DEBORAH PARTRIDGE
VALUING THE DIGNITY OF BLACK CHILDREN: A BLACK TEACHER SPEAKS EJ 019 506

WOLFF, JOSEPH L.
THE EFFECT OF SUBJECT-DETERMINED VERBALIZATION ON DISCRIMINATION LEARNING IN PRESCHOOLERS. ED021620

WOLFF, MAX
SIX MONTHS LATER--A COMPARISON OF CHILDREN WHO HAD HEAD START, SUMMER, 1965, WITH THEIR CLASSMATES IN KINDERGARTEN, A CASE STUDY OF THE KINDERGARTENS IN FOUR PUBLIC ELEMENTARY SCHOOLS, NEW YORK CITY. STUDY I. ED015025
FACTORS INFLUENCING THE RECRUITMENT OF CHILDREN INTO THE HEAD START PROGRAM, SUMMER 1965--A CASE STUDY OF SIX CENTERS IN NEW YORK CITY. STUDY II. ED015026
LONG-RANGE EFFECT OF PRE-SCHOOLING ON READING ACHIEVEMENT. STUDY III. ED015027
APPENDIX, STUDIES I, II AND III. ORIGINAL INSTRUMENTS USED AND BIBLIOGRAPHY. ED015028

WOLFF, PETER
THE ROLE OF OVERT ACTIVITY IN CHILDREN'S IMAGERY PRODUCTION EJ 059 315

WOLFSON, BERNICE J.
A CASE AGAINST BEHAVIORAL OBJECTIVES EJ 027 826

WOLFSON, EVA
EARLY INTERVENTION AND SOCIAL CLASS: DIAGNOSIS AND TREATMENT OF PRESCHOOL CHILDREN IN A DAY CARE CENTER EJ 050 497

WOLINS, MARTIN
YOUNG CHILDREN IN INSTITUTIONS: SOME ADDITIONAL EVIDENCE EJ 019 359
GROUP CARE AND INTELLECTUAL DEVELOPMENT EJ 040 041

WOLMAN, MARIANNE
VISIT TO A MISSION SCHOOL FOR ABORIGINAL CHILDREN EJ 014 292

WOLMAN, RICHARD N.
EARLY RECOLLECTIONS AND THE PERCEPTION OF OTHERS: A STUDY OF DELINQUENT ADOLESCENTS EJ 022 477
THE DEVELOPMENT OF THE LANGUAGE OF EMOTIONS: CONDITIONS OF EMOTIONAL AROUSAL EJ 052 391
THE DEVELOPMENT OF THE LANGUAGE OF EMOTIONS: I. THEORETICAL AND METHODOLOGICAL INTRODUCTION EJ 061 059

WOOD, ROGER
THE EFFECTS OF EXTRANEOUS MATERIAL AND NEGATIVE EXEMPLARS ON A SOCIAL SCIENCE CONCEPT-LEARNING TASK FOR PRE-SCHOOL CHILDREN. ED047819

WOODCOCK, JAMES M.
TERMINOLOGY AND METHODOLOGY RELATED TO THE USE OF HEART RATE RESPONSIVITY IN INFANCY RESEARCH EJ 034 566

WOODRUFF, DIANA S.
AGE CHANGES AND COHORT DIFFERENCES IN PERSONALITY EJ 055 110

WOODS, MARGARET S.
THINKING, FEELING, EXPERIENCING--TOWARD REALIZATION OF FULL POTENTIAL. ED020012

WOODS, MERILYN B.
THE UNSUPERVISED CHILD OF THE WORKING MOTHER EJ 053 709

WOOG, PIERRE
ATTITUDES OF PRESCHOOL AND ELEMENTARY SCHOOL CHILDREN TO AUTHORITY FIGURES. ED046506
ATTITUDES OF PRESCHOOL AND ELEMENTARY SCHOOL CHILDREN TO AUTHORITY FIGURES EJ 034 452

WOOLMAN, MYRON
DESIGNS AND PROPOSAL FOR EARLY CHILDHOOD RESEARCH: A NEW LOOK: A SYSTEMS APPROACH TO PRE-SCHOOL EDUCATION. (ONE IN A SERIES OF SIX PAPERS). ED053809

WORK, HENRY
ADVOCACY FOR CHILDREN: CHALLENGE FOR THE 1970'S EJ 032 108

WOZNIAK, R. H.
VERBAL REGULATION OF MOTOR BEHAVIOR-SOVIET RESEARCH AND NON-SOVIET REPLICATIONS EJ 050 074

WRIGHT, REVILLA
A PRESCHOOL ARTICULATION AND LANGUAGE SCREENING FOR THE IDENTIFICATION OF SPEECH DISORDERS. FINAL REPORT. ED051889

WROBEL, PATRICIA A.
HEAD START EVALUATION AND RESEARCH CENTER, UNIVERSITY OF KANSAS. REPORT NO. VIIB, ESTABLISHMENT OF NONVERBAL COLOR DISCRIMINATION RESPONSES TO AUDITORY COLOR-LABELING STIMULI AND SUBSEQUENT EFFECTS ON COLOR-LABELING RESPONSES. ED021641

WUELLNER, LANCE
THE EFFECT ON AGGRESSION OF VARIATION IN AMOUNT OF OPPORTUNITY FOR PLAY. (INTERNAL REPORT). ED043384
GROSS ACTIVITY OF CHILDREN AT PLAY. (INTERNAL REPORT). ED043385

WUELLNER, LANCE H.
A METHOD TO INVESTIGATE THE MOVEMENT PATTERNS OF CHILDREN. ED027938

WYETH, EZRA
EDUCATIONAL RESEARCH POLICIES OF SCHOOL DISTRICTS NATIONWIDE EJ 012 677

WYKE, MARIA
DISCRIMINATION OF SPATIALLY CONFUSABLE LETTERS BY YOUNG CHILDREN EJ 034 565

WYLIE, ALEXANDER A.
CONTINUITY IN THE DEVELOPMENT OF CONCEPTUAL BEHAVIOR IN PRESCHOOL CHILDREN: RESPONSE TO A REJOINDER EJ 018 889

WYLIE, JOANNE, ED.
A CREATIVE GUIDE FOR PRESCHOOL TEACHERS. GOALS, ACTIVITIES, AND SUGGESTED MATERIALS FOR AN ORGANIZED PROGRAM. ED016512

WYNN, RUTH
STARTING NURSERY SCHOOL, II: PREDICTION OF CHILDREN'S INITIAL EMOTIONAL REACTIONS FROM BACKGROUND INFORMATION. FINAL REPORT. ED047814
THE EFFECTS OF MOTHERS' PRESENCE AND PREVISITS ON CHILDREN'S EMOTIONAL REACTION TO STARTING NURSERY SCHOOL EJ 046 469

YAMAMOTO, KAORU
IMAGES OF THE IDEAL PUPIL HELD BY TEACHERS IN PREPARATION EJ 012 679
DESIGNING INSTRUCTIONAL SETTINGS FOR CHILDREN LABELED "RETARDED": SOME REFLECTIONS EJ 057 733

YAMASHITA, T.
EARLY CHILDHOOD EDUCATION IN JAPAN EJ 061 692

YANDO, REGINA
OUTERDIRECTEDNESS IN THE PROBLEM-SOLVING OF INSTITUTIONALIZED AND NONINSTITUTIONALIZED NORMAL AND RETARDED CHILDREN EJ 035 366
THE INFLUENCE OF NEGRO AND WHITE TEACHERS RATED AS EFFECTIVE OR NONEFFECTIVE ON THE PERFORMANCE OF NEGRO AND WHITE LOWER-CLASS CHILDREN EJ 045 068
OUTERDIRECTEDNESS AND IMITATIVE BEHAVIOR OF INSTITUTIONALIZED AND NONINSTITUTIONALIZED YOUNGER AND OLDER CHILDREN EJ 058 694

YARROW, LEON J.
ATTACHMENT: ITS ORIGINS AND COURSE EJ 058 586
DIMENSIONS OF EARLY STIMULATION AND THEIR DIFFERENTIAL EFFECTS ON INFANT DEVELOPMENT EJ 059 873

YARROW, MARIAN R.
CHILD EFFECTS ON ADULT BEHAVIOR EJ 045 107

YARROW, MARIAN RADKE
CHILD REARING. AN INQUIRY INTO RESEARCH AND METHODS. ED036344
FACTORS INFLUENCING IMITATIVE LEARNING IN PRESCHOOL CHILDREN EJ 018 892
RECOLLECTIONS OF CHILDHOOD: A STUDY OF THE RETROSPECTIVE METHOD EJ 025 047

YAVUZ, HALIDE S.
DEVELOPMENT OF RETENTION AND ORGANIZATION OCCURRING IN FREE RECALL IN TURKISH CHILDREN EJ 041 133

YAWKEY, THOMAS D.
CONDITIONING INDEPENDENT WORK BEHAVIOR IN READING WITH SEVEN YEAR OLD CHILDREN IN A REGULAR EARLY CHILDHOOD CLASSROOM EJ 050 795

YEAGER, JOHN L.
EVALUATION UNDER INDIVIDUALIZED INSTRUCTION EJ 036 826

YEAKEL, MARY H.
AN APPLIANCE FOR AUTOINDUCED ADVERSE CONTROL OF SELF-INJURIOUS BEHAVIOR EJ 029 916

YEH, JOYCE CHING-YI WU
TRANSPOSITION AND TRANSFER OF ABSOLUTE RESPONDING AS FUNCTIONS OF LEARNING-SET TRAINING AND STIMULUS SIMILARITY EJ 028 635

YEOMANS, EDWARD
EDUCATION FOR INITIATIVE AND RESPONSIBILITY, COMMENTS ON A VISIT TO THE SCHOOLS OF LEICESTERSHIRE COUNTY, APRIL 1967. SECOND EDITION. ED020795

YONAS, PATRICIA M.
A NEW THEORY OF SCRIBBLING AND DRAWING IN CHILDREN. ED017324

YONEMURA, MARGARET
RESEARCH ON ASPECTS OF LEADERSHIP ROLES IN EARLY AND ELEMENTARY EDUCATION EJ 055 205

YORK, MARY ELIZABETH
A GUIDE TO THE PLANNING AND OPERATION OF A CHILD DEVELOPMENT CENTER FOR MIGRANT CHILDREN AND A REPORT OF THE HOOPESTON CHILD DEVELOPMENT CENTER ED049838

YOST, CHARLES PETER
TEACHING SAFETY IN THE ELEMENTARY SCHOOL. ED026147

YOUNG, BEVERLY S.
INDUCING CONSERVATION OF NUMBER, WEIGHT, VOLUME, AREA, AND MASS IN PRE-SCHOOL CHILDREN. ED028822
THE EFFICACY OF A MATHEMATICS READINESS PROGRAM FOR INDUCING CONSERVATION OF NUMBER, WEIGHT, AREA, MASS, AND VOLUME IN DISADVANTAGED PRESCHOOL CHILDREN IN THE SOUTHERN UNITED STATES. ED048923

YOUNISS, J.
CLASSIFICATORY SCHEMES IN RELATION TO CLASS INCLUSION BEFORE AND AFTER TRAINING EJ 049 171

YOUNISS, JAMES
REASONS FOR FAILURE ON THE CLASS INCLUSION PROBLEM EJ 018 872
PROJECTIVE VISUAL IMAGERY AS A FUNCTION OF AGE AND DEAFNESS EJ 018 877
TRANSITIVE INFERENCE WITH NONTRANSITIVE SOLUTIONS CONTROLLED EJ 018 882
LOGICAL SYMBOL USE IN DEAF AND HEARING CHILDREN AND ADOLESCENTS EJ 047 339
FIGURATIVE AND OPERATIVE ASPECTS OF CHILDREN'S INFERENCE EJ 056 616

ZAHORIK, JOHN A.
PUPILS' PERCEPTION OF TEACHERS' VERBAL FEEDBACK EJ 027 880
THE EFFECT OF PLANNING ON TEACHING EJ 028 503

ZARATE, LEONORE T.
FINAL REPORT ON HEAD START EVALUATION AND RESEARCH--1966-67 TO THE INSTITUTE FOR EDUCATIONAL DEVELOPMENT. SECTION IV, AN EXPLORATORY STUDY OF ORAL LANGUAGE DEVELOPMENT AMONG CULTURALLY DIFFERENT CHILDREN. ED019120

ZECKHAUSER, SALLY
A STUDY IN CHILD CARE (CASE STUDY FROM VOLUME II-A): "A HOUSE FULL OF CHILDREN." DAY CARE PROGRAMS REPRINT SERIES. ED051891

ZEILER, MICHAEL D.
STEADY-STATE BEHAVIOR IN CHILDREN: A METHOD AND SOME DATA EJ 053 730

ZELAZO, PHILIP R.
SMILING TO SOCIAL STIMULI: ELICITING AND CONDITIONING EFFECTS EJ 034 536
INFANT SMILING TO NONSOCIAL STIMULI AND THE RECOGNITION HYPOTHESIS EJ 053 731

ZELNIKER, TAMAR
ANALYSIS AND MODIFICATION OF SEARCH STRATEGIES OF IMPULSIVE AND REFLECTIVE CHILDREN ON THE MATCHING FAMILIAR FIGURES TEST EJ 059 510

ZERN, DAVID
THE "MENTAL STEP" HYPOTHESIS IN SOLVING VERBAL PROBLEMS: EFFECTS OF VARIATIONS IN QUESTION-PHRASING ON A GRADE SCHOOL POPULATION EJ 035 372

ZIEGLER, STAN
RESIDENTIAL TREATMENT OF EMOTIONALLY DISTURBED CHILDREN IN NORWAY EJ 058 135

ZIGLER, EDWARD
THE IMPACT OF COGNITIVE MATURITY ON THE DEVELOPMENT OF SEX-ROLE ATTITUDES IN THE YEARS 4 TO 8. ED019109
MOTIVATIONAL FACTORS AND IQ-CHANGES IN CULTURALLY DEPRIVED CHILDREN ATTENDING NURSERY SCHOOL. ED020017
COGNITIVE PROCESSES IN THE DEVELOPMENT OF CHILDREN'S APPRECIATION OF HUMOR. ED020784
AN OVERVIEW OF RESEARCH IN LEARNING, MOTIVATION, AND PERCEPTION. ED020799
TRAINING THE INTELLECT VERSUS DEVELOPMENT OF THE CHILD. ED034573
THE ENVIRONMENTAL MYSTIQUE: TRAINING THE INTELLECT VERSUS DEVELOPMENT OF THE CHILD EJ 022 138
INSTITUTIONALIZATION AND THE EFFECTIVENESS OF SOCIAL REINFORCEMENT: A FIVE- AND EIGHT-YEAR FOLLOW-UP STUDY EJ 027 185
CONTEMPORARY CONCERNS IN EARLY CHILDHOOD EDUCATION EJ 032 059
EMOTIONAL CONCOMITANTS OF VISUAL MASTERY IN INFANTS: THE EFFECTS OF STIMULUS MOVEMENT ON SMILING AND VOCALIZING EJ 033 794
OUTERDIRECTEDNESS IN THE PROBLEM-SOLVING OF INSTITUTIONALIZED AND NONINSTITUTIONALIZED NORMAL AND RETARDED CHILDREN EJ 035 366
LEARNING FROM CHILDREN: THE ROLE OF OCD EJ 044 285
A NEW CHILD CARE PROFESSION: THE CHILD DEVELOPMENT ASSOCIATE EJ 050 937
DEVELOPMENTAL COURSE OF RESPONSIVENESS TO SOCIAL REINFORCEMENT IN NORMAL CHILDREN AND INSTITUTIONALIZED RETARDED CHILDREN EJ 053 648
EFFECTS OF RATE OF STIMULUS PRESENTATION AND PENALTY CONDITIONS ON THE DISCRIMINATION LEARNING OF NORMAL AND RETARDED CHILDREN EJ 053 712
OUTERDIRECTEDNESS AND IMITATIVE BEHAVIOR OF INSTITUTIONALIZED AND NONINSTITUTIONALIZED YOUNGER AND OLDER CHILDREN EJ 058 694

ZIGLER, EDWARD F.
A NATIONAL PRIORITY: RAISING THE QUALITY OF CHILDREN'S LIVES EJ 027 501

ZILLER, ROBERT C., ED.
SELF-SOCIAL CONSTRUCTS OF CHILDREN. ED021615

ZIMILES, HERBERT
HEAD START EVALUATION AND RESEARCH CENTER. PROGRESS REPORT OF RESEARCH STUDIES, 1966-1967. ED021612
HEAD START EVALUATION AND RESEARCH CENTER. PROGRESS REPORT OF RESEARCH STUDIES 1966 TO 1967. DOCUMENT 1, DEVELOPMENT OF THE MATRIX TEST. ED021623
HEAD START EVALUATION AND RESEARCH CENTER. PROGRESS REPORT OF RESEARCH STUDIES 1966 TO 1967. DOCUMENT 5, COMPARATIVE ITEM-CONTENT ANALYSIS OF ACHIEVEMENT TEST PERFORMANCE IN YOUNG CHILDREN. ED021627
CLASSIFICATION AND INFERENTIAL THINKING IN CHILDREN OF VARYING AGE AND SOCIAL CLASS. ED035446

ZIMMERMAN, BARRY J.
INTELLECTUAL OPERATIONS IN TEACHER-CHILD INTERACTION. ED039011
INSTRUCTIONAL SPECIFICITY AND OUTCOME-EXPECTATION IN OBSERVATIONALLY-INDUCED QUESTION FORMULATION. ED047789
MODELING BY EXEMPLIFICATION AND INSTRUCTION IN TRAINING CONSERVATION. ED047790
INTELLECTUAL OPERATIONS IN TEACHER QUESTION-ASKING BEHAVIOR EJ 032 895
MODELING BY EXEMPLIFICATION AND INSTRUCTION IN TRAINING CONSERVATION EJ 057 898
OBSERVATION, REPETITION, AND ETHNIC BACKGROUND IN CONCEPT ATTAINMENT AND GENERALIZATION EJ 059 316

ZINSMASTER, WANNA M.
WHAT CAN TEACHERS LEARN FROM DIRECTORS IN THE PERFORMING ARTS? EJ 051 410

ZIOBROWSKI, MARTIN
DEVELOPMENTAL CHANGES IN CLUSTERING CRITERIA EJ 058 145

ZIV, ABNER
SEX DIFFERENCES IN PERFORMANCE AS A FUNCTION OF PRAISE AND BLAME EJ 055 098

ZIV, AVNER
CHILDREN'S BEHAVIOR PROBLEMS AS VIEWED BY TEACHERS, PSYCHOLOGISTS, AND CHILDREN EJ 026 313

ZOHNER, DORIN
SUGGESTIBILITY IN RELATION TO SCHOOL GRADE, SEX, AND SOURCE OF INFLUENCE EJ 023 431
ENVIRONMENTAL DISCONTINUITY, STRESS, AND SEX EFFECTS UPON SUSCEPTIBILITY TO SOCIAL INFLUENCE EJ 023 432

ZOLA, JESSIE M.
A ROOM PLANNED BY CHILDREN EJ 007 876

ZUNG, BURTON J.
A DEVELOPMENTAL INVESTIGATION OF THE EFFECT OF SENSORY MODALITY ON FORM RECOGNITION IN CHILDREN EJ 026 507
CROSS-MODAL MATCHING AMONG NORMAL AND RETARDED CHILDREN EJ 053 755

ZYTKOSKEE, ADRIAN
DELAY OF GRATIFICATION AND INTERNAL VERSUS EXTERNAL CONTROL AMONG ADOLESCENTS OF LOW SOCIOECONOMIC STATUS EJ 034 539